D1514771

The Great Rock Discography

"Illustrated with some humour and considerable expertise by Harry Horse, it's a killer tome well worth the money that Canongate are asking … as far as discographical books are concerned, this one can safely be filed under 'unbelievable' " – **Fred Dellar, N.M.E.**

"Exhaustive and refreshingly opinionated" – **The Guardian**

"Strong is rock's Leslie Halliwell" – **Scotland on Sunday**

"The book, which took ten years to compile, is a worthy rival to the Music Master catalogue" – **The Times**

"A labour of love which has produced a monumental chronicle of rock music … mighty" **– The Herald**

"Far more accurate and comprehensive than many other similar books" **– Time Out**

"Extremely well-presented and more readable than a reference book has any right to be" – **Mojo**

"If you really want to know EVERYTHING, you need The Great Rock Discography" – **The Sun**

"This is THE rock reference bible" – **What's On**

"A Herculean labour of love … Strong should provide hours of useful diversions for record collectors" – **Q**

"The last word in rock 'n' roll trainspotting" – **The Guardian**

"An essential tome for music obsessives" – **The Face**

The Great Rock Discography

The Great Rock Discography

M. C. Strong

Illustrations by Harry Horse

CANONGATE

Third edition published in 1996 in Great Britain
by Canongate Books Ltd, 14 High St, Edinburgh EH1 1TE

ISBN 0 86241 604 3

British Library Cataloguing in Publication Data
A catalogue for this book is available on request from the British Library

Typeset by Æsthetex Ltd, Edinburgh

Printed and bound in Great Britain
by Unwins Ltd, Woking

The book is dedicated to…
my mother JEAN FOTHERINGHAM
(born: 6th January 1929,
died: 31st August 1985)

Thank you mum up there for
pulling my strings, and
guiding me through all
the hard times.

* * *

Acknowledgements

I wish to thank the following GREAT people who've encouraged and helped me throughout the history of the ROCK DISCOGRAPHY.

My daughters SHIRLEY and SUZANNE, my dad GERRY (GEOFF) STRONG, EILEEN SCOTT-MONCRIEFF, VIC ZDZIEBLO, ALLAN BREWSTER, SANDY McCRAE, MICHAEL FLETCHER, all the regulars at The Commercial Bar, Falkirk (including boss JIMMY LAING), The Pop Quiz Team: TED MOCHAR, DAVIE SEATH and FRANNIE FITZPATRICK (who died 23rd May 1996); HAMISH McLEOD-PRENTICE, STEPHEN McELROY, BRIAN McELROY, PAUL McELROY, DOUGIE NIVEN, DEREK IRVINE, BRIAN and MARGARET HUNTER, TAM MORRISON, The SCOTT-MONCRIEFFs; SIMON, COLIN, ALAN, JAS and SUZANNAH (plus AUDREY, EMILY and MAUREEN); LINDA TONER, LES O'CONNOR (deceased), GEORGE BROWN, COLIN TAYLOR, DAVIE BLAIR, PETER WAUGH, PAUL KLEMM, IAIN McLEAN, IAIN SUTHERLAND, PETER GRAHAM (at the BBC), CHRIS LORIMER, MALCOLM STEWART (Jimpress, Hendrix fanzine), FORREST DUNCAN, CHRIS HILL and LEE HARVEY (National Sound Archive), DEREK KILLAH and staff at Falkirk library, ALAN LAWSON (Aesthetex typesetters), and Canongate Books staff (JAMIE BYNG, NEVILLE MOIR, JAMES CLARK, SHEILA McAINSH, FIONA MURRAY, HUGH ANDREW and STEPHANIE WOLFE-MURRAY).

Thanks to all those around the world who wrote me letters of congratulation and encouragement on the second edition, alongside lists of useful information. Some also sent me their ROCK SURVEYS (see my back pages):

JULIA ARMSTRONG, RUSSELL BAILLIE, STEPHEN BAIRD, DIETER BANSCH, STEFFEN BAUER, JURGEN BELING, MARTIN BERTSCH, ULRICH BEUTEFUHR, MARGARET BLACK, STEVE BOISMAISON, ROB BOLTON (U. S. A.), BERNDT BUCH, CHARLES BUTLER, DAVE CHAMBERS, MICHAEL CHANDLER, PAUL COPE, GUY DEEMING, LESLIE FAIR, SIMON "Fish" FISHER, TIM FOOTMAN, JORG FOTH (also wanted to know the piano lady of the early 70s whose lyrics "And When The War Is Over And The Soldiers Come Home, We'll Be Sitting By The Fireside And Leave The World Alone": fax 030/44 27 263), DALE GARDNER, HARTWIG GIERKE, JURGEN GOLDNER, PETER GOLDSMITH, JAMIE GOODMAN, ALICE GRANDISON, TRISTAN GUY-DEMEN, THOMAS HAMILL, Mr. S. HARKER, JIM HENDERSON, FRANK HERGER, ANDREAS HERGER, SIMON HESS, KARSTEN HOEFT, KELVIN HOLMES, SOREN JAKOBS, IAN JONES, HAROLD KAYSER, LARS KIESEL, RAINER KRAKER, MICHAEL KURENKO (Siberia), HUGH "Shug" MACKIE, JOE MACKLE, ADE MACROW, GRAHAM MILNES, ANDREAS MOLLER, PHIL NEWTON (Australia), MARTIN NISBET, DOUGLAS NOBLE, CHRIS OWEN, NEIL PARRY, BRIAN PATTON, PIPPO PIARULLI (Italy), B.C. PIRES (West Indies), ANA POPVIC and VLADIMIR JOVANDIC (Yugoslavia), SANDY PRENTICE, SIEGFRIED RIEDEL, LIAM RIGBY, IAN ROBERTSON, NEIL ROBINSON, ALEXEI ROUDITCHEV, ARTHUR ROUSSELLE (German *Rolling Stone* reviewer who gave it 5 stars), KEVIN SALT, ULI SCHMIDT, STEFANIE SCHMITT, MATTHIAS SCHOLTEN, STEPHEN SCOTT, RAY SHEPPARD, HARTMUT SIEGEL, JOE SIMPSON, NEIL SPORGO, ALLAN STREETER, GUY SUTTON, DAVID SWIFT, ECKEHARD TEBBE, ANNE-KATRIN TURN, DAVID WARNOCK, PAUL WHITTINGHAM and DON WYNNE.

Preface

This third edition contains nearly 1000 pages covering over 1000 major rock artists and groups (including 250 fringe rock/pop entries in grey). As the title suggests, it is a book of discographies (i.e. record releases in an easy-to-read chronological fashion). I could have made this simple enough, listing singles or albums and left it at that, but I include all UK and US releases (all formats: vinyl, cassette and cd), the B-sides, the album track listings (now in correct order I hope) and who played what on each disc. I also include the record labels, the UK and US Top 100 chart numbers, the alternative US release dates, compilations, etc. Each discography comes with a biography (some large, some small) and this EXTRA info states their places of origin, birthdays, band members, style of music, songwriters, cover versions, and trivia, as well as unbiased recommendations for album listening. Whew! Not a lot missing eh!? Probably just thousands of artists and groups I didn't have space for. These will be catered for in further specialist editions. Can't give too much away on that subject as I hear there are 300-odd journalists working for someone to produce all music on the internet. You better hurry folks because this one-man research unit has all discographies at hand and is setting up his own somewhat smaller team to produce the 1996 updates.

If you bought the first two editions of the book, I would like to say thanks, although you can safely put them in your bookcase as this one takes over. If you see any errors or omissions (however minor) don't hesitate to contact me (c/o CANONGATE).It will be much appreciated, as the acknowledgement page shows. Nothing released in 1996 will be in this edition, as the deadline for releases was 31st December 1995. That's the reason why SUPERGRASS, SALAD, ALANIS MORISSETTE and WEEZER are new entries, while OCEAN COLOUR SCENE, BIS and SUPER FURRY ANIMALS are not. I've tried to select a wide range of ROCK music from around the globe. not necessarily the biggest sellers. What is ROCK and what is POP? Probably the hardest question one could ask anybody. My definition is simply this. I see ROCK music as written by the artist(s) for his or herself not with the initial intention of making money, but to make individual music and to possibly stretch its limits and boundaries a little further. Hence the term "a classic of its time or generation". This is the music that normally stands the test of time and is loved decades after its inception. Take for example:– EDDIE COCHRAN, The BEATLES, JIMI HENDRIX, SEX PISTOLS or R.E.M. These ROCK artists, I agree, have also become great POP icons, although they will never lose their ROCK credibility. However, POP music is written with the sole intention (normally) of making money either for themselves or more so their record label. This mainly appeals to the younger generation, who like its easy-listening aspect. Most of them later in life find they like more demanding material. If The BEATLES adapted from the screaming mania brigade of teeny-boppers to a more sophisticated popular ROCK/POP, why can't others? I think the difference was that they were also accomplished musicians as well as singers. Don't look for TAKE THAT, EAST 17 and California girl SHEENA EASTON in this book and don't write to me to tell me they should be in. They might get into THE GREAT POP DISCOGRAPHY – only if I get someone to help me write it. Crap is not my middle name. Charles is! Another book, the 'wee' *Rock Discography*, will be available just before Christmas priced £12.99 and this paperback version will include around 500 artists. Its main added feature will be vinyl catalogue numbers and estimates of how much they're currently worth. THERE WILL BE NO *Great Rock Discography* FOR ANOTHER 2 YEARS NOW. If you think anything should go into further editions and off-shoots, please send me info, tapings, etc., as these will help me in deciding quickly if you're right or not. It's not a request book though, and I might still think them unworthy. I would like to buy lots of albums, etc, but can't yet. Maybe record labels might take the opportunity to send me their stuff to assess. Can't send anything back however except a thank-you letter or maybe a phone-call and a drink if we're in the same area at the same time.

Signing off, no did that last year ... MARTIN. Now go to the back of the book to find out about THE GREAT ROCK SURVEY.

Introduction

I'm now in my fourteenth year writing *The Great Rock Discography,* currently in its third edition. I still stay in the same flat in the large town of Falkirk in Scotland, although recently it underwent a complete renovation. After five long years, I actually have a bathroom, a fitted kitchen and gas central heating; all yer mod cons! Paid fór from my second edition royalties. Success hasn't gone to my head yet and neither has any new hair. Last year I probably had one of the greatest days of my life so far, when on 31st August my second edition was launched in Edinburgh. Although I was apprehensive about my speech and keeping sober enough to remember the experience, I thought I came through it okay. Anyway with the help from all my friends, my daughters, my dad, my publishers and over a hundred well-behaved guests, it was a day I'll always remember. The crush of "heavy" punk guitarist BIG JOHN DUNCAN's handshake just before I stepped up to the mic, made me somewhat feel at home. Thankyou for giving me my two minutes JOHN. His guitar playing somewhat ruffled my dad though, and I pray for a less noisy occasion next time. However it did drown out the thumping from the lesbian trapeze act upstairs at the festival.

Sales of the second edition were in excess of 15,000, even reaching the shores of Germany (5,000 in a month), America, Australia, etc. Over 200 people wrote to me about my GREAT achievement (see acknowledgements). I would have loved to have heard from some of the stars in the book, but maybe if you're reading this you'll give my publishers a phone-call.

At the beginning of the year, my publishers rewarded me with a new computer to write the third edition more easily … and more. I can access the whole book and make the necessary changes to small or large errors. I'll be the first to admit, the second edition had mistakes, some deliberate I might add (plagiarists beware). I worked on the third edition, morning, day and night from 3rd January to 10th of June and I thought this one-man research unit might crack under the strain. My simple (to me) formula for getting information has been eased somewhat by having a wee bit of money to buy food, clothes, music papers and to pay my many bills. I had days off during this five months, which I spent with the "love of my life" Eileen. I'm not always trainspotting, Mr Journalist!

I make a good living now from my royalties, but to many it seems to have made me a millionaire. They think I get most or even all of the sale price and forget there are other people who receive much more than I do. Depending on how many copies are sold, I get around 10 per cent of the price you buy it for, while my publishers get about double that, having gambled thousands initially on its creation (i.e. typesetters, illustrations, printers, binders, shipping costs, etc.). Where does the rest go? Well around half of the sale price goes to the bookshops (the larger the better) who, if they don't sell them, can give them back on the "sale or return" principle. Kind of like going around to a betting shop, sticking it on a horse (each-way!) and when it's last, asking the nice wee bookie for your money back. Do you think this is fair Mr and Mrs Bookseller? Surely not (and don't tell me about overheads, you've thousands of books to sell not just mine). Surely the most important person of the three is actually the writer, as there simply would be no book without him or her. Of course, you need a good publisher (i.e. CANONGATE) to do the rest of the work and get it to the shops. One needs the other and we need the bookseller to sell it to the public, but what we do need to re-address is a fair balance of payment, although this obviously won't happen overnight.

How To Read The Book

GROUP / ARTIST(s)

If lettering is grey, it is one of the non-rock artists which a book of this kind could not do without.

Formed/Born: where . . . when . . . birthplace . . . brief history . . . other info.
Style: music type/sound . . . influences . . . fashion.
Songwriters: the pensmiths . . . covers (originals or hitmakers in brackets).
Trivia/Miscellaneous: virtually anything else (i.e. producers, marriages, colour of underpants, etc.).
Recommended: Top selective recommendation (* 5–10). Amalgamation of music press reviews + myself.

Group:
SINGER (born, when, where) – **vocals** (ex-GROUP)
MUSICIANS (born, when, where) – **instrument(s)** (ex-GROUPS)

Discography listed in chronological order (chart positions shown in **bold)**

		UK-label (a)	US-label (a)	
UK-release date.	(format) **ALBUM or EP name** – (album or EP tracks) *(UK re-issue + if on different label)*	**1**	**99**	US-date
UK-date.	(format) **'A' SINGLE./ 'B'SIDE**	**75**	**10**	

If group leaves label (a), the new record company label (b) appears above the subsequent chart position boxes.

— **NEW SINGER/MUSICIAN** (b. 1 Jan '50) – vocals/ instrument(s) (ex-GROUP?) repl.(aced) out-going member who might have joined another group.

Below single didn't hit UK chart and wasn't issued in US

		UK-label (b)	US-label
UK-date.	(7")(c-s) **'A' SINGLE ./'B-SIDE**		-

(other format +=) Extra track(s) of above single.
(other format ++=) Extra track(s) of above extra.
(other format +=) Extra tracks(s) to the above single
(other format) ('A' side above)/ any other track(s)/ (no 'B' side).

ARTIST(s)

If they've changed group name more permanently, or if a sub-group is formed.

		UK-label	US-label	
Dec 95.	(cd)(c)(lp) **ALBUM** – Album tracks/ etc. (now in correct sequence, I hope).	1	1	Oct 95

– compilations, others, etc. –

For the most part the Group/Artist(s) compilation and other releases are shown separately after the main discography.

		Virgin	not issued	
date.	(format) **ALBUM/ EP (or) SINGLE**		-	blank

RECORD-LABEL ABBREVIATIONS

Amphetamine Reptile – A. Reptile
Beachheads in Space – Beachheads
Blanco y Negro – Blanco Y N.
Coast to Coast – CoastCoast
Factory Benelux – Factory Ben.
Hypertension – Hypertens
Magnum Force – Magnum F.
Music Of Life – M.O.L.
One Little Indian – O L Indian
Paisley Park – Paisley P.
Regal Starline – Regal Star
Road Goes on Forever – Road Goes
Silva Screen – SilvaScreen

Thunderbolt – Thunderb.
Vinyl Solution – Vinyl Sol.
Worker's Playtime – Worker's P.
4th & Broadway – 4th & Broad.

ABC Paramount – ABC Para
Beat Goes On – B.G.O.
Castle Communications – Castle
Def American – Def Amer.
FanClub – Fan Club
Les Tempes Modern – Les Temps
Marble Arch – Marble A.
Music for Nations – M. F. N.
Pacific Jazz – Pacific J.
RCA Victor – RCA Victor
Regal Zonophone – Regal Zono.
Sacred Heart – Sacred H.
Special Delivery – Special D.

Transatlantic – Transatla.
Vinyl Japan – Vinyl Jap
World Pacific – World Pac.
20th Century – 20th Cent

Alternative Tentacles – Alt.Tent.
Beggar's Banquet – Beggar's B.
Cooking Vinyl – Cooking V.
Emergency Broadcast – Emergency
Food For Thought – Food for Tht.
Les Disques Du Crepescule – Crepescule
MintyFresh – MintyFresh
Music for Midgets – M. F. Midgets
Pye International – Pye Inter
Red Rhino Europe – R.R.E.
Return to Sender – R. T. S.
Seminal Tway – Seminal Tw
Sympathy for the Record Industry – SympathyF.
United Artists – United Art
Warner Brothers – Warners
Workers PlaytimeWorkers Pl
92 Happy Customers – 92 Happy C.

Formats & Abbreviations

VINYL (black coloured unless stated)

(lp) = The (LONG PLAYER) record . . . circular 12" plays at 33⅓ r.p.m., and has photo or artwork sleeve. Approximate playing time . . . 30–50 minutes with average 10 tracks. Introduced in the mid-50's on mono until stereo took over in the mid-60's. Quadrophonic had a spell in the 70's, but only on mainly best selling lp's, that had been previously released. Because of higher costs to the manufacturer and buyer, the quad sunk around 1978. Also note that around the mid-50's, some albums were released on 10 inch.
Note:- Average cost to the customer as of January 1996 = £8.50 (new). Budget re-issues are around £5 or under. Collectors can pay anything from £1 to £500, depending on the quality of the recording. Very scratched records can be worthless, but unplayed mint deletions are worth a small fortune to the right person. Auctions and record fairs can be the place to find that long lost recording that's eluded you. This applies to all other vinyl below.

(d-lp) = The (DOUBLE–LONG PLAYER) record . . . as before. Playing time 50–90 minutes on 4 sides, with average 17 tracks. Introduced to rock/pop world in the late 60's, to compliement compilations, concept & concert (aka live) albums.[1]
Compilations:- are a selection of greatest hits or rare tracks, demos, etc.
Concepts:- are near uninterrupted pieces of music, based around a theme.
Note that normal lp's could also be compilations, live or concept. Some record companies through the wishes of their artists, released double lp's at the price of one lp. If not, price new would be around £15.

(t-lp) = The (TRIPLE–LONG PLAYER) record . . . as before. Playing time over 100 minutes with normally over 20 tracks. Because of the cost to the consumer, most artists steered clear of this format. Depending on the artwork on the sleeve, these cost over £17.50. (See its replacement, the CD.)

(4-lp-box) = The (BOXED–LONG PLAYER) record (could be between 4 and 10 in each boxed-set). As the triple album would deal with live, concept or compilation side, the boxed-set would be mostly re-issues of all the artist's album material, with probably a bonus lp thrown in, to make it collectable. Could be very pricey, due to lavish outlay in packaging. They cost over £25 new.

(m-lp) = The (MINI–LONG PLAYER) record . . . playing time between 20–30 minutes and containing on average 7 tracks. Introduced for early 80's independent market, and cost around £4.
Note:- This could be confused at times with the extended-play 12" single.

(pic-lp) = The (PICTURE DISC–LONG PLAYER) record . . . as before but with album artwork/ design on the vinyl grooves. Mainly for the collector because of the slightly inferior sound quality. If unplayed, these can fetch between £10 and £250.

(coloured-lp) = The (COLOURED–LONG PLAYER) record; can be in a variety of colours including . . . white/ blue/ red/ clear/ purple/ green/ pink/ gold/ silver.

(red-lp) = The (RED VINYL–LONG PLAYER) record would be an example of this.

(7") = The (7 INCH SINGLE). Arrived in the late 50's, and plays at 45 r.p.m. Before this its equivalent was the 10" on 78 r.p.m. Playing time now averages 4 minutes per side, but during the late 50's up to mid-60's, each side averaged 2 and half minutes. Punk rock/new wave in 1977/78, resurrected this idea. In the 80's, some disco releases increased playing time. Another idea that was resurrected in 1977 was the picture sleeve. This had been introduced in the 60's, but mostly only in the States.
Note:- Cost at the start of 1996, was just under £2. Second-hand rarities can cost between 25p to £200, depending again on its condition. These also might contain limited freebies/gifts (i.e. posters, patches, stickers, badges, etc.). Due to the confusion this would cause, I have omitted this information, and kept to the vinyl aspect in this book. Another omission has been DJ promos, demos, acetates, magazine freebies, various artists' compilations, etc. Only official shop releases get a mention.

(7" m) = The (7 INCH MAXI-SINGLE). Named so because of the extra track, mostly on the B-side. Introduced widely during the early 70's; one being ROCKET MAN by ELTON JOHN.

(7" ep) = The (7 INCH EXTENDED PLAY SINGLE). Plays mostly at 33⅓ r.p.m., with average playing time 10–15 minutes and 4 tracks. Introduced in the late 50's as compilations for people to sample their albums. These had a *title* and were also re-introduced in 1977 onwards, but this time for punk groups' new songs.

(d7") = The (DOUBLE 7 INCH SINGLE). Basically just two singles combined . . . 4 tracks. Introduced in the late 70's for the "new wave/romantics", and would cost slightly more than normal equivalent.

(7" pic-d) = The (7 INCH PICTURE-DISC SINGLE). This was vinyl that had a picture on the grooves, which could be viewed through a see-through plastic cover.

(7" sha-pic-d) = The (7 INCH SHAPED-PICTURE-DISC SINGLE). Vinyl as above but with shape (i.e. gun, mask, group) around the edge of the groove. Awkward because it would not fit into the collectors' singles box. Initially limited and this can still be obtained at record fairs for over £3. Note:- However, in the book the type of shape has not been mentioned, due to the lack of space.

1: **Note:** – Interview long players mainly released on 'Babatak' label, have not been included due to the fact this book only gives artists' music discography.

(7" coloured) = The (7 INCH COLOURED SINGLE). Vinyl that is not black (i.e. any other colour; red, yellow, etc.). Note:- (7" multi) would be a combination of two or more colours (i.e. pink/purple).

(7" flexi) = The (7 INCH FLEXIBLE SINGLE). One-sided freebies, mostly given away by magazines, at concerts or as mentioned here; free with single or lp. Worth keeping in mint condition and well protected.

(12") = The (12 INCH SINGLE). plays at 45 r.p.m., and can have extended or extra tracks to its 7" counterpart (+=) or (++=). B-sides playing speed could be at 33 r.p.m. Playing time could be between 8 and 15 minutes. Introduced in 1977 with the advent of new wave and punk. They were again a must for collectors, for the new wave of British heavy metal scene.

(12" ep) = The (12 INCH EXTENDED PLAY SINGLE). Virtually same as above but *titled* like the 7" ep. Playing time over 12 minutes, and could have between 3 and 5 tracks.

(d12") = The (DOUBLE 12 INCH SINGLE). See double 7" . Can become very collectable and would cost new as normal 12", £3.50.

(12" pic-d) = The (12 INCH PICTURE-DISC SINGLE). As with 7" equivalent . . . see above.

(12" sha-pic-d) = The (12 INCH SHAPED-PICTURE-DISC SINGLE). See above 7" equivalent.

(12" colrd) = The (12 INCH COLOURED SINGLE). Not black vinyl . . . see above 7" equivalent.

(10") = The (10 INCH SINGLE). Plays at 45 r.p.m., and like the 12" can have extra tracks (+=). Very collectable, it surfaced in its newer form around the early 80's, and can be obtained in shops at £4. Note:- also (10" ep)/ (d10")/ (10" coloured)/ (10" pic-d)/ (10" sha-pic-d).

CASSETTES

(c) = The (CASSETTE) album . . . size in case 4 and a half inches high. Playing-time same as lp album, although after the mid-80's cd revolution, released some with extra tracks. Introduced in the late 60's, to compete with the much bulkier lp. Until the 80's, most cassettes were lacking in group info, lyric sheets, and freebies. Note:- Cost to the consumer as of January 1996 = £9 new. But for a few exceptions, most do not increase in price, and can be bought second-hand or budget-priced for around £6.

(d-c) = The (DOUBLE-CASSETTE) album . . . as above, and would hold same tracks as d-lp or even t-lp. Price between £15–£20.

(c-s) = The (CASSETTE-SINGLE). Now released mostly with same two tracks as 7" equivalent. The other side played the same 2 or 3 tracks. Introduced unsuccessfully in the US around the late 60's. Re-introduced there and in Britain in the mid-80's. In the States, it and its cd counterpart has replaced the charting 7" single for the 90's. Cost new is around £1–£2.50, and might well become quite collectable.

(c-ep) = The (CASSETTE-EXTENDED PLAY SINGLE). Same as above but *titled* as 12" .

COMPACT DISCS

(cd) = The (COMPACT DISC) album. All 5" circular and mostly silver on its groove side. Perspex casing also includes lyrics & info, etc. Introduced late in 1982, and widely the following year (even earlier for classical music). Initially for top recording artists, but now in 1996 nearly every release is in cd format. Playing time normally over 50 minutes and containing extra tracks or mixes. Possible playing time is just under 80 minutes. Marketed as unscratchable, although if they go uncleaned, they will stick just as vinyl. Average price as early 1996 is £15, and will become collectable, possibly early in the next century if, like most predictions, they do not deteriorate with time.

(d-cd) = The (DOUBLE-COMPACT DISC) album . . . same as above although very pricey, between £16 and £25..

(cd-s) = The (COMPACT DISC-SINGLE). Mainly all 5" (but some 3" cd-s could only be played with a compatible gadget inside the normal cd player). Playing time over 15 minutes to average 25 minutes, containing 4 or 5 tracks. Introduced in 1986 to compete with the 12" ep or cassette. 99% contained extra tracks to normal formats. Cost new around over £5.00, which soon rise to over double that, after a couple years of release.

(pic-cd-s) = The (PICTURE-COMPACT DISC-SINGLE). Has picture on disc, which gives it its collectability. Also on (pic-cd-ep).

(vid-pic-s) = The (VIDEO-COMPACT DISC-SINGLE). A video cd, which can be played through stereo onto normal compatible TV screen. Very costly procedure, but still might be the format of the future. Promo videos can be seen on pub juke-boxes, which has made redundant the returning Wurlitzer style. Note:- The is the only mention of videos in the book, although a selective videography might be introduced for a mid-90's update.

DIGITAL AUDIO TAPE

(dat) = The (DIGITAL AUDIO TAPE) album. Introduced in the mid-80's, and except for Japan and the rich yuppie, are not widely issued. It is a smaller version of the cassette, with the quality of the cd.

Another format (which I have not included) is the CARTRIDGE, which was available at the same time as the cassette. When the cassette finally won the battle in the early 80's, the cartridge became redundant. All car-owners over the world were happy when thieves made them replace the stolen cartridge player with the resurrected cassette. You can still buy these second-hand, but remember you'll have to obtain a second-hand 20-year-old player, with parts possibly not available.

Other abbreviations: repl. = replaced / comp = compilation / re-iss. = re-issued / re-dist. = re-distributed

ABBA

Formed: Stockholm, Sweden . . . 1971 by BJORN and BENNY with partners AGNETHA and ANNI-FRID. They were already established in their own right previous to this inevitable formation (see further solo). In 1973 they entered for The Eurovision Song Contest with track 'RING RING'. It didn't win, but the following years' 'WATERLOO' did, and soon went to No.1 in the UK. The name ABBA was soon on the lips of everyone worldwide, as from late 1975 they scored a run of 15 UK Top 5's (including 8 chart-toppers), until mid-'81. They had become the biggest pop group of the 70's. But for their matrimonial splits in 1979 & 1981, they certainly would have been a force in the 80's too. However, in the 90's, their songs and image were recreated by an Australian parody group BJORN AGAIN, who fortunately gave life and interest back into ABBA material, which re-released hit the charts again. • **Style:** English-singing visually stunning pop group, who were loved by everyone from teenyboppers to grandparents. • **Songwriters:** BENNY & BJORN. • **Trivia:** (For more info: see end of discog. & read the book 'ABBA' written 1976 by Harry Edgington and Peter Himmelstrand.)

Recommended: ABBA – GOLD GREATEST HITS (*6)

AGNETHA FALTSKOG (-ULVAEUS) (b. 5 Apr'50, Jonkopping, Sweden) – vocals / **BJORN ULVAEUS** (b.25 Apr'45, Gothenburg, Sweden) – guitar, vocals / **BENNY ANDERSSON** (b.16 Dec'46, Stockholm, Sweden) – keyboards, synth, vocals (both ex-HEP STARS, ex-HOOTENANNY SINGERS) / **ANNI-FRID LYNGSTAD-FREDRIKSSON** (b.15 Nov'45, Norway) – vocals

In May 72, a single by **BJORN, BENNY, AGNETHA + FRIDA** hit Swedish No. 2

ABBA

(Debut single below released in Sweden Feb73, hit No.1)

		Epic	Atlantic	
Oct 73.	(7") **RING RING. / ROCK'N'ROLL BAND**		-	
Apr 74.	(7") **WATERLOO. / WATCH OUT**	1	6	Jun 74

(re-iss.Feb78 & Nov86)

May 74. (lp)(c) **WATERLOO** — 28 —
– Waterloo / Watch out / King Kong song / Hasta manana / My mama said / Dance (while the music still goes on) / Honey, honey / What about Livingstone / Gonna sing you my love song / Suzy hang around / Ring ring. *(re-iss.Mar81) (cd-iss.Aug90 on 'Polydor' & re-iss.Sep92)(re-iss.cd+c on 'Spectrum')*

Jul 74. (7") **RING RING (2nd version). / HASTA MANANA** — 32 —
Sep 74. (7") **HONEY, HONEY. / DANCE (WHILE THE MUSIC STILL GOES ON)** — - — 27
Nov 74. (7") **SO LONG. / I'VE BEEN WAITING FOR YOU** — —
Apr 75. (7") **I DO, I DO, I DO, I DO, I DO. / ROCK ME** — 38 — 15 Mar 76
Aug 75. (7") **S.O.S. / MAN IN THE MIDDLE** — 6 — 15
Dec 75. (7") **MAMMA MIA. / INTERMEZZO No.1** — 1 — -
Jun 75. (lp)(c) **ABBA** — 13 —
– Mamma mia / Hey, hey Helen / Tropical loveland / S.O.S. / Man in the middle / Bang-a-boomerang / I do, I do, I do, I do, I do / Rock me / Intermezzo No.1 / I've been waiting for you / So long. *(re-iss.Nov81) (cd-iss.Mar90 on 'Polydor' += Waterloo / Hasta manana / Honey honey / Ring ring / Nina, pretty ballerina) (re-iss.cd+c.Sep92)*

Feb 76. (7") **BANG-A-BOOMERANG. / I DO I DO I DO I DO I DO** — - —
Mar 76. (7") **FERNANDO. / HEY HEY HELEN** — 1 — 13 Sep 76
(re-iss.Feb78 & Mar82)

Apr 76. (lp)(c) **GREATEST HITS** (compilation) — 1 — 48 Sep 76
– Fernando / S.O.S. / He is your brother / Hasta manana / Dance (while the music still goes on) / Another town, another train / Mamma mia / Waterloo / I do, I do, I do, I do, I do / Honey honey / People need love / Ring ring / Bang-a-boomerang / Nina, pretty ballerina / So long. *(re-iss.Apr85, and cd+c-iss.Sep92 on 'Polydor')*

Jun 76. (7") **MAMMA MIA./ TROPICAL LOVELAND** — - — 32
Aug 76. (7") **DANCING QUEEN. / THAT'S ME** — 1 — 1 Jan 77
Nov 76. (7") **MONEY, MONEY, MONEY. / CRAZY WORLD** — 3 — 56 Oct77

Nov 76. (lp)(c) **ARRIVAL** — 1 — 20 Feb 77
– My love my life / When I kissed the teacher / Dancing queen / Dum dum diddle / Knowing me knowing you / Money, money, money / That's me / Why did it have to be me / Tiger / Arrival. *(re-iss.Jul83) (cd-iss.Nov84, re-iss.Sep92 on 'Polydor')*

Feb 77. (7") **KNOWING ME, KNOWING YOU. / HAPPY HAWAII** — 1 — 14 May 77
Oct 77. (7") **THE NAME OF THE GAME. / I WONDER (DEPARTURE)** — 1 — 12 Dec77
Jan 78. (7") **TAKE A CHANCE ON ME. / I'M A MARIONETTE** — 1 — 3 Mar 78
(re-iss.May82)

Jan 78. (lp)(c) **THE ALBUM** — 1 — 14 Mar 78
– Eagle / Take a chance on me / One man, one woman / The name of the game / Move on / Hole in your soul / The girl with the golden hair (three scenes from a mini musical): Thank you for the music – I wonder (departure) – I'm a marionette. *(re-iss.+cd.Nov84 & Mar90 +cd, re-iss.Sep92)*

Sep 78. (7") **SUMMER NIGHT CITY. / MEDLEY (PICK A PALE OF COTTON – OLD SMOKEY – MAKING IT SPECIAL)** — 5 —
Jan 79. (7") **CHIQUITITA. / LOVELIGHT** — 2 — 29 Nov 79
(re-iss.May82)

Apr 79. (7") **DOES YOUR MOTHER KNOW. / KISSES OF FIRE** — 4 — 19 May 79
May 79. (lp)(c)(pic-lp) **VOULEZ-VOUS** — 1 — 19 Jul 79
– As good as new / Voulez-vous / I have a dream / Angel eyes / The king has lost his crown / Does your mother know / If it wasn't for the night / Chiquitita / Lovers (like a little longer) / Kisses of fire. *(re-iss.Jul86) (re-iss.+cd.Mar90 on 'Polydor', re-iss.Sep92)*

Jul 79. (7") **ANGEL EYES. / VOULEZ-VOUS** — 3 — 64
— — 80
(re-iss.Feb89 on 'Old Gold')

Oct 79. (7") **GIMME GIMME GIMME (A MAN AFTER MIDNIGHT). / THE KING HAS LOST HIS CROWN** — 3 —
Nov 79. (lp)(c) **GREATEST HITS VOL.2** (compilation 1976-1979) — 1 — 46
– Take a chance on me / Gimme gimme gimme (a man after midnight) / Money money money / Rock me / Eagle / Angel eyes / Dancing queen / Does your mother know / Chiquitita / Summer night city / I wonder / Name of the game / Thank you for the music / Knowing me, knowing you. *(re-iss.+cd.May87) (re-iss.+cd.Mar90 on 'Polydor', re-iss.Sep92)*

Dec 79. (7")(12") **I HAVE A DREAM. / TAKE A CHANCE ON ME (live)** — 2 —
Jul 80. (7")(12") **THE WINNER TAKES IT ALL. / ELAINE** — 1 — 8 Nov 80
Nov 80. (7") **SUPER TROUPER. / THE PIPER** — 1 — 45
(c-s+=) – The winner takes it all / One of us / Lay all your love on me *(7".re-iss.1983)*

Nov 80. (lp)(c)(lp-box) **SUPER TROUPER** — 1 — 17 Dec 80
– Super trouper / The winner takes it all / On and on and on / Andante andante / He and I / Happy New Year / Our last summer / The piper / Lay all your love on me / The way old friends do. *(cd-iss.May83) (re-iss.+cd.Mar90 on 'Polydor', re-iss.Sep92 & Feb95)*

Jul 81. (7")(12") **LAY ALL YOUR LOVE ON ME. / ON AND ON AND ON** — 7 — 90 B-side
Dec 81. (7")(7"pic-d) **ONE OF US. / SHOULD I LAUGH OR CRY** — 3 —
Dec 81. (lp)(c) **THE VISITORS** — 1 — 29 Jan 82
– The visitors / Head over heels / When all is said and done / Soldiers / I let the music speak / One of us / Two for the price of one / Slipping through my fingers / Like an angel / Passing through my room / Eagle. *(cd-iss.May83) (re-iss.Mar90 on 'Polydor', re-iss.Sep92)*

Jan 82. (7") **WHEN ALL IS SAID AND DONE. / SHOULD I LAUGH OR CRY** — - — 27
Feb 82. (7") **HEAD OVER HEELS. / THE VISITORS** — 25 — 63 B-side
Oct 82. (7") **THE DAY BEFORE YOU CAME. / CASSANDRA** — 32 —

—— Broke up as a group late 1982. All had semi-successful solo careers. (see further below)

– compilations, others, etc. –

Nov 82. Epic/ US= Atlantic; (d-lp)(c)(cd) **THE SINGLES – THE FIRST TEN YEARS** — 1 — 62
(also iss.d-pic-lp) (cd-iss.Sep83) (re-iss.+cd.Mar90 on 'Polydor')

Aug 82. Epic; (c-ep) **SUPER TROUPER / THE WINNER TAKES IT ALL / LAY ALL YOUR LOVE ON ME** — — -
Dec 82. Epic; (7")(7"pic-d) **UNDER ATTACK. / YOU OWE ME ONE** — 26 —
Nov 83. Epic; (7")(7"sha-pic-d) **THANK YOU FOR THE MUSIC (live). / OUR LAST SUMMER (live)** — 33 —
Nov 83. Epic/ US= Atlantic; (lp)(c) **THANK YOU FOR THE MUSIC (live)** — 17 —
– My love, my life / I wonder / Happy New Year / Slipping through my fingers / Fernando / One man, one woman / Eagle / I have a dream / Our last summer / The day before you came / Chiquitita / Should I laugh or cry / The old way friends do / Thank you for the music. *(originally rel.Mar81 as 'GRACIAS POR LA MUSICA')*

Apr 84. Epic; (26x7"box) **ANNIVERSARY BOX SET** — —
Aug 86. Polydor; (lp)(c)(cd) **ABBA LIVE (live)** — —
(cd-iss.Apr91)

Sep 92. Polydor; (7")(c-s) **DANCING QUEEN. / LAY YOUR LOVE ON ME** — 16 —
(12"+=)(cd-s+=) – The day before you came / Eagle.

Sep 92. Polydor; (cd)(c)(d-lp) **ABBA – GOLD GREATEST HITS** — 1 — 63
Nov 92. Polydor; (7")(c-s) **THANK YOU FOR THE MUSIC. / HAPPY NEW YEAR** — —
(cd-s+=) – The way old friends do.

Dec 92. Polydor; (cd-s) **VOULEZ VOUS. / ?** — —
Jan 93. Polydor; (c) **MAMMA MIA** — — -
May 93. Polydor; (cd)(c)(lp) **MORE ABBA GOLD** — 14 —
Nov 94. Polydor; (4xcd-box) **THANK YOU FOR THE MUSIC** — —
Jan 87. Old Gold; (7") **TAKE A CHANCE ON ME. / CHIQUITITA** — — -
Nov 87. Old Gold; (7") **DANCING QUEEN. / FERNANDO** — — -
Jan 88. Old Gold; (7") **WATERLOO. / MAMMA MIA** — — -
Feb 89. Old Gold; (7") **KNOWING ME KNOWING YOU. / THE WINNER TAKES IT ALL** — — -

Feb 89. Old Gold; (7") **GIMME GIMME GIMME (A MAN AFTER MIDNIGHT). / DOES YOUR MOTHER KNOW** | | -
Jan 90. Old Gold; (12") **LAY ALL YOUR LOVE ON ME. / SUMMER NIGHT CITY** | | -
Sep 87. Hallmark; (lp)(c)(cd) **THE HITS** | | -
Feb 88. Hallmark; (lp)(c)(cd) **THE HITS 2** | | -
Sep 88. Hallmark; (lp)(c)(cd) **THE HITS 3** | | -
(re-iss.as box set of above 3, 1991 on 'Pickwick')
1987. Castle; (d-lp)(c)(cd) **ABBA – THE COLLECTION** | | -
Nov 88. Castle; (d-lp)(c)(cd) **ABBA – THE COLLECTION 2** | | -
Nov 88. Telstar; (lp)(c)(cd) **ABSOLUTE ABBA** | 70 | -
Dec 89. Pickwick; (lp)(c)(cd) **THE LOVE SONGS** | | -
Nov 95. Polydor; (3xcd-box) **VOULEZ VOUS / SUPER TROUPER / ARRIVAL** | | -

FRIDA

Her solo (pre-ABBA days), from 1967-1972, had 'Columbia' of Sweden, release numerous 45's, and 2 albums; **'NIN EGAN STAD'** (1971) + **'ANNI-FRIDLYNSTAD'** (1972 compilation). In 1973-74, she moved to 'Polar' records in Sweden, and although she issued more singles/albums there, she now totally concentrated on ABBA.
(her post-ABBA days)

Epic | Atlantic

Aug 82. (7") **I KNOW THERE'S SOMETHING GOING ON. / THRENODY** | 43 | 13 Oct 82
Sep 82. (lp)(c) **SOMETHING'S GOING ON** | 18 | 41 Nov 82
– Tell me it's over / I see red / I got something / Strangers / To turn the stone / I know there's something's going on / Threnody / Baby don't you cry no more / Way you do / You know what I mean / Here we'll stay. *(cd-iss.1988 on 'Polydor')(cd-iss.Mar93)*
Sep 82. (7") **TO TURN TO STONE. / I GOT SOMETHING** | |
Jun 83. (7") **HERE WE'LL STAY. / STRANGERS** | |
Dec 83. (7") **TIME. (with "B.A. ROBERTSON") / ('B'side B.A.ROBERTSON)** | 45 |
Sep 84. (7") **SHINE. / THAT'S TOUGH** | |
(12") – ('A'extended).
Oct 84. (lp)(c) **SHINE** | 67 |
– Shine / One little lie / Face / Twist in the dark / Slowly / Heart of the country / Come to me / Chemistry tonight / Don't do it / Comfort me. *(cd-iss.1988 on 'Polydor')(cd-iss.Mar93)*
Nov 84. (7") **HEART OF THE COUNTRY. / SLOWLY** | |
(12"+=) – I know there's something going on (extended).

AGNETHA FALTSKOG

solo (pre-ABBA days). Alongside many singles, her Swedish albums were; AGNETHA FALTSKOG (Cupol – 1968), **AGNETHA VOL.2** (Cupol – 1969), **SOM JAG AR** (Cupol – 1970), **NAR EN VACKER TAKE BLIR ENSANG** (Cupol – 1971), **AGNETHA FALTSKOG'S BASTA** (Cupol – 1972 comp.). She released another album in 1975 'ELVA KNIVVOR I ETT HUS' while ABBA were high in European chart euphoria.
(her post-ABBA days)

Epic | Polydor

Oct 82. (7") **NEVER AGAIN. / JUST FOR THE FUN (with "TOMAS LEDIN")** | | -
May 83. (7")(7"pic-d) **THE HEAT IS ON. / MAN** | 35 |
Jun 83. (lp)(c) **WRAP YOUR ARMS AROUND ME** | 18 |
– The heat is on / Can't shake loose / Shame / Stay / Once burned, twice shy / Mr.Persuasion / Wrap your arms around me / To love / I wish tonight could last forever / Man / Take good care of your children / Stand by my side. *(cd-iss Jan90 on 'Polydor')*
Aug 83. (7") **WRAP YOUR ARMS AROUND ME. / TAKE GOOD CARE OF YOUR CHILDREN** | 44 |
('B'extended-12"+=) – The heat is on.
Oct 83. (7")(7"pic-d) **CAN'T SHAKE LOOSE. / TO LOVE** | 63 | 29
Apr 85. (7") **I WON'T LET YOU GO. / YOU'RE THERE** | |
(12"extended) – (same tracks)
Apr 85. (lp)(c)(cd) **EYES OF A WOMAN** | 38 |
– One way love / Just one heart / I won't let you go / Angels cry / Click track / We should be together / I won't be leaving you / Save me / I keep turning off lights / We move as one. *(cd-iss.Jun87 on 'Polydor')*
Jun 85. (7")(12") **ONE WAY LOVE. / TURN THE WORLD AROUND** | |

WEA | Atlantic

Jan 88. (7") **THE LAST TIME./ARE YOU GONNA THROW IT ALL AWAY** | |
(12"+=) – ('A'extended).
Feb 88. (lp)(c)(cd) **I STAND ALONE** | 72 |
– The last time / Little white secrets / I wasn't the one (who said goodbye) / Love in a world gone mad / Maybe it was magic / Let it shine / We got a way / I stand alone / Are you gonna throw it all away / If you need somebody tonight.
Apr 88. (7") **I WASN'T THE ONE (WHO SAID GOODBYE). ("AGNETHA FALTSKOG & PETER CETERA") / IF YOU NEED SOMEBODY TONIGHT** | | 93
(12") – ('A'extended) / Yo no fui quien dijo adios ('A'Spanish)
Sep 88. (7") **LET IT SHINE. / MAYBE IT WAS MAGIC** | |
(12") – ('A'extended) / ('A' bright mix).

BENNY & BJORN in 1984 collaborated with TIM RICE on 'CHESS' stage show. Released as d-lp,d-c,d-cd on 'RCA' Oct84; it hit UK No.10. It featured many singers, including MURRAY HEAD who scored UK No.12 / US No.3 hit with ONE NIGHT IN BANGKOK. To end the year '84, ELAINE PAIGE & BARBARA DICKSON hit UK No.1 duetting on I KNOW HIM SO WELL. ELAINE was to release more solo flops from the musical between late 1984-Spring 1986. In Oct85 'Telstar' issued lp,c,cd. 'CHESS PIECES – THE BEST OF CHESS' to attemt to cash in musicals' success. In 1986, both wrote and backed brother/sister duo GEMINI. An eponymous album was issued on 'Polydor', as were 2 singles 'JUST LIKE THAT' & 'ANOTHER YOU, ANOTHER ME'. The following year, another album GEMINISM was released on 'Polar' in Sweden only. Later in '87, BENNY released debut solo album 'KLINGA MINA KLOCKOR' on own label 'Mono Music' in Sweden. BENNY and BJORN went on to work with and produce most artists on that label.
Please note:- BENNY and BJORN had been a duo in the early 70's, releasing many singles for the Swedish label 'Polar'. Will mention or give info in further editions.

ABC

Formed: Sheffield, England. 1979 as VICE VERSA by Singleton and White. Late 1980 they found 'Modern Drugs' fanzine editor Martin Fry and became ABC. They started own 'Neutron' label which was soon (early 1982) distributed by major Phonogram. Their fist 45 'TEARS ARE NOT ENOUGH', broke through into the UK Top 20 and they soon became leading contenders to attempt to dethrone DURAN DURAN and SPANDAU BALLET. • **Style:** Soulful "New Romantics" with slick well-dressed image. Moved into "Electro-soul" by the mid 80's. • **Songwriters:** Fry / White. Nearest to a cover, was a tribute to WHEN SMOKEY (Robinson) SINGS. • **Miscellaneous:** In 1986, Fry contracted "Hodgkin's Disease" (a form of cancer) but he steadily recovered.

Recommended: ABSOLUTELY ABC (*7) / THE LEXICON OF LOVE (*9)

VICE VERSA

MARK WHITE (b. 1 Apr'61) – guitar, synthesizers / **STEPHEN SINGLETON** (b.17 Apr'59) – saxophone, synthesizers

Neutron | not issued

1979. (7"ep) **MUSIC 4** | | -
– New girls / Neutrons / Science-fact / Riot squad / Camille.
— added **MARTIN FRY** (b. 9 Mar'58, Manchester) – vocals

Dutch

Jun 81. (7") **STILYAGI. / EYES OF CHRIST . . .** | - |

ABC

— added **MARK LICKLEY** – bass / **DAVID ROBINSON** – drums

Neutron | Mercury

Oct 81. (7") **TEARS ARE NOT ENOUGH. / ALPHABET SOUP** | 19 |
(12"+=) – ('A'+'B'extended).
Jan 82. (7") **POISON ARROW. / THEME FROM MANTRAP** | 6 | 25 Jan 83
(12"+=) – Mantrap (The Lounge Sequence).
— **DAVID PALMER**(b.29 May'61, Chesterfield) – drums repl. ROBINSON
May 82. (7") **THE LOOK OF LOVE. / (Part 2)** | 4 | 18 Aug 82
(12"+=) – (Part 3 & 4) *(re-iss.Oct83)*
Jun 82. (lp)(c) **THE LEXICON OF LOVE** | 1 | 24 Sep 82
– Show me / Poison arrow / Many happy returns / Tears are not enough / Valentine's day / The look of love / Date stamp / All of my heart / 4 ever 2 gether / The look of love. *(cd-iss.Feb83)*
Aug 82. (7")(12") **ALL OF MY HEART. / OVERTURE** | 5 |
— guest session man **ANDY NEWMARK** – drums repl. PALMER
Oct 83. (7")(12") **THAT WAS THEN BUT THIS IS NOW. / VERTIGO** | 18 | 89 Jan 84
Nov 83. (lp)(c)(cd) **BEAUTY STAB** | 12 | 69
– That was then but this is now / Love's a dangerous language / If I ever thought you'd be lonely / The power of persuasion / Beauty stab / By default by design / Hey citizen / King money / Bite the hand / Unzip / S.O.S. / United Kingdom.
Jan 84. (7")(12")(7"pic-d) **S.O.S. / UNITED KINGDOM** | 39 |
— **FRY** and **WHITE** recruited new members (alongside other sessioners) **DAVID YARRITH** – keyboards repl. SINGLETON / **EDEN** (b.FIONA RUSSELL-POWELL) – keyboards repl. LICKLEY
Oct 84. (7") **HOW TO BE A MILLIONAIRE. / HOW TO BE A BILLIONAIRE** | 49 | 20 Jan 86
(12") – ('A'extended) / ('A' acappella version) / How to be a zillionaire (mix).
(extra-12") – (above 'A' acappella & Zillionaire mixes only).
Mar 85. (7") **BE NEAR ME. / A TO Z** | 26 | 9 Aug 85
(d7"+=) – Poison arrow / The look of love (U.S.mix).
(12") – ('A'disco mix) / WHAT'S YOUR DESTINATION (2 tracks only).
Jun 85. (7")(7"sha-pic-d) **VANITY KILLS. / JUDY'S JEWELS** | 70 | 91 May 86
(d7"+=) – S.O.S. / United Kingdom.
(12"+=) – You love you (instrumental). (diff.'B'versions)
(12"+=) – Be near me (ecstacy mix).
Oct 85. (lp)(c)(cd) **HOW TO BE A . . . ZILLIONAIRE!** | 28 | 30
– Tower of London / How to be a millionaire / Ocean blue / Fear of the world* / Vanity kills* / Be near me* / A to Z / So hip it hurts / Between you and me / 15 storey halo. (c+cd+=diff.track mixes*)
Jan 86. (7") **OCEAN BLUE. / TOWER OF LONDON (instrumental)** | 51 |
(d7"+=) – All of my heart / The look of love.
(12"+=) – ('A'mix) / Be near me (mix).
(12"+=) – ABC Megamix.
— Now trimmed to **FRY** and **WHITE** duo plus sessioners (unknown)
May 87. (7") **WHEN SMOKEY SINGS. / CHICAGO (Pt 1)** (12"+=) – Chicago (Pt 2). | 11 | 5
(cd-s+=) – All of my heart (live).
Aug 87. (7") **THE NIGHT YOU MURDERED LOVE. / MINNEAPOLIS** | 31 |
(12"+=)(c-s+=) – ('A'version).
Oct 87. (lp)(c)(cd) **ALPHABET CITY** | 7 | 48 Aug87
– Avenue A / When Smokey sings / The night you murdered love / Think again / rage and then regret / Arkangel / King without a crown / Bad blood / Jealous lover / One day / Avenue Z. (cd.+=4 versions of last 2 singles 7")
Nov 87. (7") **KING WITHOUT A CROWN. / THE LOOK OF LOVE (live)** | 44 |
(c-s+=)(12"pic-d+=) – Poison arrow (live).
(12"++=) – All of my heart (live).
May 89. (7") **ONE BETTER WORLD. / ('A' percappella mix).** | 32 |

(cd-s+=) – ('A'club mix) / ('A'garage mix).
(12"+=) – (above 3 extra mixes only; not 7" version)
Aug 89. (lp)(c)(cd) **UP** [58] [ ]
– Never more than now / The real thing / One better world / Where is the Heaven? / The greatest love of all / I'm in love with you / Paper thin. *(re-iss. cd Aug 94)*
Sep 89. (7") **THE REAL THING. / THE GREATEST LOVE OF ALL** [68] [ ]
(cd-s+=) – North
(cd-s++=) – The look of love (pt.5).
(12"+=) – When Smokey sings / Be near me.
Mar 90. (7") **THE LOOK OF LOVE (1990 remix). / OCEAN BLUE** [68] [ ]
(12"+=)(cd-s+=) – Vanity kills.
Apr 90. (cd)(c)(lp) **ABSOLUTELY ABC** (compilation) [7] [ ]
– Poison arrow / The look of love / All of my heart / Tears are not enough / That was then but this is now / S.O.S. / How to be a millionaire / Be near me / When Smokey sings / The night you murdered love / King without a crown / One better world. (c+cd+=) – Look of love (1990 remix) / When Smokey sings (12"remix) / Be near me (12"remix) / One better world (12"remix) / Ocean blue.

Parlophone Capitol?

Jun 91. (7")(c-s) **LOVE CONQUERS ALL. / WHAT'S GOOD ABOUT GOODBYE** [47] [ ]
(cd-s+=) – ('A'extended) / ('A' percappella).
Jun 91. (cd)(c)(lp) **ABRACADABRA** [50] [ ]
– Love conquers all / Unhook the secrets of your heart / Answered prayer / Spell-bound / Say it / Welcome to the real world / Satori / All that matters / This must be magic.
Aug 91. (7")(c-s) **SAY IT (black box mix). / ('A'abracadabra mix)** [ ] [ ]
(12"+=) – Satori.
(cd-s+=) – ('A'piano mix / ('A'instrumental).
(re-iss.Jan92, hit UK NO.42)

– compilations, etc. –

Mar 93. Connoisseur; (cd)(c) **THE REMIX COLLECTION** [ ] [-]
May 93. Spectrum; (cd)(c) **TEARS ARE NOT ENOUGH** [ ] [-]

AC/DC

Formed: Sydney, Australia . . . 1973, by brothers MALCOLM and ANGUS YOUNG. By 1974 they had moved to Melbourne, where among other new men, they found petty criminal BON SCOTT. Older brother GEORGE YOUNG and HARRY VANDA (ex-EASYBEATS) set-up contract on their 'Albert' records, and also guided them with production. Early 1976 they signed to 'Atlantic' UK, and moved base to London. With constant touring they were soon to become one of the largest worldwide attractions. In 1980, they even overcame sudden death of BON, by replacing him with soundalike Englishman BRIAN JOHNSON. After the release of No.1 album 'BACK IN BLACK', they grew into top international group in the 80's. • **Style:** Initially branded as punks, probably due to schoolboy uniformed ANGUS. Metal fans started to appreciate his boogie style guitar picking, and also BON's bare-chested high screech vocals. With typical though tongue-in-cheek / double-entendre sexist lyrics, their blend of hard rock heavy metal has and will last for years. • **Songwriters:** Most by YOUNG brothers, some with SCOTT or JOHNSON. Covered; BABY PLEASE DON'T GO (Muddy Waters) / BONNY (trad). • **Miscellaneous:** At two seperate US concerts Nov'90 / Jan'91, three youths were killed.

Recommended: HIGH VOLTAGE (UK *8) / DIRTY DEEDS DONE DIRT CHEAP (*7) / LET THERE BE ROCK (*7) / HIGHWAY TO HELL (*7) / BACK IN BLACK (*7) / IF YOU WANT BLOOD . . . (*8) / BALLBREAKER (*7)

ANGUS YOUNG (b.31 Mar'59, Glasgow, Scotland) – guitar / **MALCOLM YOUNG** (b. 6 Jan'53, Glasgow) – guitar / **DAVE EVANS** – vocals / **ROB BAILEY** – bass / **PETER CLACK** – drums

not iss. Albert AUSTRALIA

Jul 74. (7") **CAN I SIT NEXT TO YOU. / ROCKIN' IN THE PARLOUR** [-] [-]

—— When all but the brothers departed, they recruited (i.e.DAVE joined RABBIT) **BON SCOTT** (b.RONALD SCOTT, 9 Jul'46, Kirriemuir, Scotland) – vocals (ex-VALENTINES, ex-FRATERNITY, ex-SPECTORS, ex-MOUNT LOFTY RANGERS) / **MARK EVANS** – (b. 2 Mar'56, Melbourne) – bass (ex-BUSTER BROWN) / **PHIL RUDD** (b.19 May'54, Melbourne) – drums

Albert AUSTRALIA

Jan 75. (lp) **HIGH VOLTAGE** [-] [-]
– Baby please don't go / You ain't got a hold of me / Soul stripper / Show business / Love song / Stick around / Little lover / She's got balls.
1975. (7") **DOG EAT DOG. / CARRY ME HOME** [-] [-]
Dec 75. (lp) **T.N.T.** [-] [-]
– It's a long way to the top (if you wanna rock'n'roll) / Rock'n'roll singer / Can I sit next to you, girl? / T.N.T. / Live wire / High voltage / The jack / School days / Rocker.

Atlantic Atco

Apr 76. (7") **IT'S A LONG WAY TO THE TOP (IF YOU WANNA ROCK'N'ROLL). / CAN I SIT NEXT TO YOU, GIRL?** [ ] [-]
(re-iss.Jun80 on 'Heavy Metal-Atlantic', hit UK 55)
May 76. (lp)(c) **HIGH VOLTAGE** (comp.from 2 above) [ ] [-]
– It's a long way to the top (if you wanna rock'n'roll) / Rock'n'roll singer / She's got the jack / T.N.T. / Can I sit next to you girl? / Little lover / She's got balls / High voltage / Live wire. *(US-iss.Apr81) (re-iss.+cd.Oct87) (re-iss.cd+c Jul94)*
Aug 76. (7") **JAILBREAK. / FLING THING** [ ] [-]
Oct 76. (7") **HIGH VOLTAGE. / LIVE WIRE** [ ] [-]
(re-iss.Jun80 on 'Heavy Metal-Atlantic', hit UK 48)
1976. (7") **HIGH VOLTAGE. / IT'S A LONG WAY TO THE TOP** [-] [ ]
Dec 76. (lp)(c) **DIRTY DEEDS DONE DIRT CHEAP** [ ] [-]
– Dirty deeds done dirt cheap / Love at first feel / Big balls / Rocker / Problem child / There's gonna be some rockin' / Ain't no fun (waiting round to be a millionaire) / Ride on / Squealer. *(US-iss.Apr81 hit No.3 (UK-re-iss.+cd.Aug87) (re-iss.cd+c Jul94)*
Jan 77. (7"m) **DIRTY DEEDS DONE DIRT CHEAP. / BIG BALLS / THE JACK** [ ] [-]
(re-iss.Jun80 on 'Heavy Metal-Atlantic', hit UK 47)

—— **CLIFF WILLIAMS** (b.14 Dec'49, Romford, England) – bass (ex-HOME, ex-BANDIT) repl. MARK

Sep 77. (7") **LET THERE BE ROCK. / PROBLEM CHILD** [ ] [ ]
Oct 77. (lp)(c) **LET THERE BE ROCK** [17] [ ]
– Go down / Dog eat dog / Let there be rock / Bad boy boogie / Overdose / Crapsody in blue / Hell ain't a bad place to be / Whole lotta Rosie. *(cd Jun89) (re-iss.cd,c,lp Oct94)*

Atlantic Atlantic

May 78. (lp)(c) **POWERAGE** [26] [ ]
– Gimme a bullet / Down payment blues / Up to my neck in you / Sin city / Gone shooting / What's next to the Moon / Riff raff / Cold hearted man / Kicked in the teeth. *(cd-iss.Jun89) (re-iss.cd,c Oct94)*
May 78. (7")(12") **ROCK'N'ROLL DAMNATION. / SIN CITY** [24] [ ]
Jun 78. (7") **ROCK'N'ROLL DAMNATION. / KICKED IN THE TEETH** [-] [ ]
Oct 78. (lp)(c) **IF YOU WANT BLOOD, YOU'VE GOT IT (live)** [13] [ ]
– Riff raff / Hell ain't a bad place to be / Bad boy boogie / The jack / Problem child / Whole lotta Rosie / Rock'n'roll damnation / High voltage / Let there be rock / Rocker. *(cd-iss.Jun89) (re-iss.cd,c Oct94)*
Oct 78. (7")(12") **WHOLE LOTTA ROSIE (live). / HELL AIN'T A BAD PLACE TO BE (live)** [ ] [ ]
(re-iss.Jun80 on 'Heavy Metal-Atlantic', hit UK 36)
Aug 79. (lp)(c) **HIGHWAY TO HELL** [8] [17]
– Highway to Hell / Girl's got rhythm / Touch too much / Beating around the bush / Shot down in flames / Get it hot / If you want blood (you've got it) / Love hungry / Night prowler. *(re-iss.+cd.Jul87) (re-cd. 1989)*
Aug 79. (7") **HIGHWAY TO HELL. / IF YOU WANT BLOOD (YOU'VE GOT IT)** [56] [-]
Aug 79. (7") **HIGHWAY TO HELL. / NIGHT PROWLER** [-] [47]
Oct 79. (7") **GIRL'S GOT RHYTHM. / GET IT HOT** [ ] [-]
(7"ep) – ('A'side) / If you want blood (you've got it) / Hell ain't a bad place to be (live) / Rock'n'roll damnation.
Jan 80. (7"m) **TOUCH TOO MUCH (live). / LIVE WIRE (live) / SHOT DOWN IN FLAMES (live)** [29] [ ]

—— **BRIAN JOHNSON** (b.5 Oct'47, Newcastle, England) – vocals (ex-GEORDIE) repl. BON SCOTT who died 20 Feb'80, after drunken binge.

Jul 80. (lp)(c) **BACK IN BLACK** [1] [4]
– Back in black / Hell's bells / Shoot to thrill / Give the dog a bone / What do you do for money, honey? / Rock'n'roll ain't noise pollution / Let me put my love into you / You shook me all night long / Shake a leg / Have a drink on me. *(re-iss.+cd.Feb87)*
Sep 80. (7") **YOU SHOOK ME ALL NIGHT LONG. / HAVE A DRINK ON ME** [38] [35]
Nov 80. (7")(12") **ROCK'N'ROLL AIN'T NOISE POLLUTION. / HELL'S BELLS** [15] [ ]
Feb 81. (7") **BACK IN BLACK. /WHAT DO YOU DO FOR MONEY HONEY** [-] [37]
Nov 81. (lp)(c) **FOR THOSE ABOUT TO ROCK (WE SALUTE YOU)** [3] [1]
– For those about to rock (we salute you) / Put the finger on you / Let's get it up / Inject the venom / Snowballed / Evil walk / C.O.D. / Breaking the laws / Night of the long knives / Spellbound. *(re-iss.+cd Jul87) (re-iss.cd+c Jul94)*
Jan 82. (7") **LET'S GET IT UP. / BACK IN BLACK (live)** [13] [-]
(12"+=) – T.N.T.(live).
Jan 82 (7") **LET'S GET IT UP. / SNOWBALLED** [-] [44]
Jun 82 (7") **FOR THOSE ABOUT TO ROCK (WE SALUTE YOU). / T.N.T.** [-] [ ]
Jun 82. (7")(12") **FOR THOSE ABOUT TO ROCK (WE SALUTE YOU). / LET THERE BE ROCK (live)** [15] [ ]
Aug 83. (lp)(c) **FLICK OF THE SWITCH** [4] [15]
– Rising power / This house is on fire / Flick of the switch / Nervous shakedown / Landslide / Guns for fire / Deep in the hole / Bedlam in Belguim / Badlands / Brain shake. *(re-iss.+cd.Jul87) (re-iss.cd,c Oct94)*
Sep 83. (7")(7"sha-pic-d) **GUNS FOR HIRE. / LANDSLIDE** [37] [84]
Jan 84. (7") **JAILBREAK. / SHOW BUSINESS** [-] [ ]
Mar 84. (7") **FLICK OF THE SWITCH. / BADLANDS** [-] [ ]

—— **SIMON WRIGHT** (b.19 Jun'63) – drums (ex-A II Z, ex-TYTAN) repl. RUDD

Jul 84. (7")(7"sha-pic-d) **NERVOUS SHAKEDOWN. / ROCK'N'ROLL AIN'T NOISE POLLUTION (live)** [35] [ ]
(12"+=)(c-s+=) – Sin city (live) / This house is on fire (live).
Jun 85. (7")(12")(7"sha-pic-d) **DANGER. / BACK IN BUSINESS** [48] [ ]
Jul 85. (lp)(c)(cd) **FLY ON THE WALL** [7] [32]
– Fly on the wall / Shake your foundations / First blood / Danger / Sink the pink / Playing with the girls / Stand up / Hell or high water / Back in business / Send for the man.
Jan 86. (7")(7"sha-pic-d) **SHAKE YOUR FOUNDATIONS. / STAND UP** [24] [ ]
Nov 85. (7") **SHAKE YOUR FOUNDATIONS. / SEND FOR THE MAN** [-] [ ]
(12"+=) – Jailbreak.
May 86. (7")(7"sha-pic-d) **WHO MADE WHO. / GUNS FOR HIRE (live)** [16] [ ]
(12") – ('A'collectors mix).
May 86. (lp)(c) **WHO MADE WHO (Soundtrack; Maximum Overdrive)**(part compilation) [11] [33]
– Who made who / You shook me all night long / D.T. / Sink the pink / Ride on / Hells bells / Shake your foundations / Chase the ace / For those about to rock (we salute you). *(cd-iss. 1988)*
Jan 88. (7") **HEATSEEKER. / GO ZONE** [12] [ ]
(12"+=)(12"pic-d+=) – Snake high.
Feb 88. (lp)(c)(cd) **BLOW UP YOUR VIDEO** [2] [12]
– Heatseeker / That's the way I wanna rock'n'roll / Meanstreak / Go zone / Kissin' dynamite / Nick of time / Some sin for nuthin' / Ruff stuff / Two's up / Some sin

for nuthin' / This means war.

Mar 88. (7") **THAT'S THE WAY I WANNA ROCK'N'ROLL. / KISSIN' DYNAMITE** [22] [ ]
(12"+=)(12"pic-d+=) – Borrowed time.
(cd-s+=) – Shoot to thrill (live) / Whole lotta Rosie (live).

— (Apr88) cousin **STEVE YOUNG** – guitar briefly replaces MALCOLM on tour

— (1989) (ANGUS, MALCOLM, BRIAN & CLIFF) bring in **CHRIS SLADE** (b.30 Oct'46) – drums (ex-GARY MOORE, ex-MANFRED MANN EARTHBAND, ex-FIRM) repl. WRIGHT who had joined DIO.

Atco / Atco

Sep 90. (7")(c-s)(10"pic-d) **THUNDERSTRUCK. / FIRE YOUR GUNS** [13] [ ]
(12"+=)(cd-s+=) – D.T. / Chase the ace.

Oct 90. (cd)(c)(lp) **THE RAZOR'S EDGE** [4] [2]
– Thunderstruck / Fire your guns / Moneytalks / The razor's edge / Mistress for Christmas / Rock your heart out / Are you ready / Got you by the balls / Shot of love / Let's make it / Goodbye & good riddance to bad luck / If you dare.

Nov 90. (7")(c-s) **MONEYTALKS. / MISTRESS FOR CHRISTMAS** [36] [23]
(12"+=)(cd-s+=)(12"sha-pic-d+=) – Borrowed time.

Apr 91. (7")(c-s)(7"pic-d) **ARE YOU READY. / GOT YOU BY THE BALLS** [34] [ ]
(12"+=)(cd-s+=) – The razor's edge.

Oct 92. (7") **HIGHWAY TO HELL (live) / HELL'S BELLS (live)** [14] [ ]
(12"pic-d) – ('A'side)/ High voltage (live).
(cd-s+= of above; 2 diff.) – The jack (live)/ or / Hell ain't a bad place to be (live).

Oct 92. (cd)(pic-d-cd)(c)(d-lp) **LIVE (live)** [5] [15]
– Thunderstruck / Shoot to thrill / Back in black / Sin city / Who made who / Fire your guns / Jailbreak / The jack / The razor's edge / Dirty deeds done dirt cheap / Hells bells / Heatseeker / That's the way I wanna rock'n'roll / High voltage / You shook me all night long / Whole lotta Rosie / Let there be rock / Medley:- Bonny – Highway to Hell / T.N.T. / For those about to rock (we salute you). *(In the US, a SPECIAL COLLECTOR'S EDITION hit No.26)*

Feb 93. (12")(cd-s) **DIRTY DEEDS DONE DIRT CHEAP (live). / SHOOT TO THRILL (live)/ DIRTY DEEDS DONE DIRT CHEAP** [68] [ ]

Jun 93. (7")(c-s) **BIG GUN. / BACK IN BLACK (live)** [23] [65]
(12"+=)(cd-s+=) – For those about to rock (live).
(cd-s) – (excludes B-side).

Sep 95. (7"yellow)(cd-s)(cd-s) **HARD AS A ROCK. / CAUGHT WITH YOUR PANTS DOWN** [33] [ ]

Sep 95. (cd)(c)(lp) **BALLBREAKER** [6] [4]
– Whisky on the rocks / The honey roll / The furor / Love bomb / Hard as a rock / Hail Caesar / Cover you in oil / Caught with your pants down / Burnin' alive / Boogie man / Ballbreaker.

– compilations, others, etc. –

Aug 86. Atlantic; (7")(7"sha-pic-d) **YOU SHOOK ME ALL NIGHT LONG. / SHE'S GOT BALLS (live)** [46] [ ]
(12")(12"sha-pic-d) – ('B'extended) / ('A'live).

Aug 84. US= Atco; (m-lp) **JAILBREAK '74** (early demos..) [-] [76]
(re-iss.cd Oct94)

1991. Atco; (3xcd-box) **BOX SET** [ ] [-]
– HIGHWAY TO HELL / BACK IN BLACK / FOR THOSE ABOUT TO ROCK.

– Australian compilations (selective) – (on 'E.M.I.')

Sep 87. (6xbox-lp) **BOX SET** [-] [-]
– (lp's) – TNT / HIGH VOLTAGE / DIRTY DEEDS.. / LET THERE.. / POWERAGE / HIGHWAY. (12"free w/above) **COLD HEARTED MAN. /**

Dec 87. (5xbox-lp) **BOX SET 2** [-] [-]
– (lp's) – BACK IN.. / FOR THOSE.. / FLICK OF.. / FLY ON THE WALL / WHO MADE WHO

A CERTAIN RATIO

Formed: Manchester, England ... 1977. By late 70's they had signed to Tony Wilson's 'Factory' indie label. They released a number of deserved indie hit albums, before progressing to 'A&M' in 1988. Never shone through commercially, and they set up own 'Rob's' label in the 90's to guarantee sparse recordings. • **Style:** Moody bassy punk-funk, incorporating avant-garde jazz to later Latin-American salsa, dance, etc. • **Songwriters:** Group compositions, except SHACK UP (Banbarra) / DON'T YOU WORRY 'BOUT A THING (Stevie Wonder). • **Trivia:** DONALD JOHNSON'S brother BARRY was a member of soul/pop outfit SWEET SENSATION. SHAUN RYDER of HAPPY MONDAYS and BARNEY SUMNER of NEW ORDER guested vocals on 1990 ep '4 FOR THE FLOOR'. At various times in the 80's, MOSCROP + KERR were part of KALIMA, with TONY QUIGLEY.

Recommended: THE OLD AND THE NEW (*9) / FORCE (*7).

JEREMY KERR – bass, vocals / **SIMON TOPPING** – vocals, trumpet / **MARTIN MOSCROP** – guitar, vocals / **PETER TERREL** – guitar

Factory / not issued

Sep 79. (7" ltd.) **ALL NIGHT PARTY. / THE THIN BOYS** [ ] [-]

Added **DONALD JOHNSON – percussion, drums**

Dec 79. (c) **THE GRAVEYARD AND THE BALLROOM** (some live) [ ] [-]
– Flight / Faceless / Crippled child / Strain / Do the du (casse) / I feel / The choir / Flight / All night party / The fox / Genotype-phenotype / Oceans / The choir / Suspect. *(re-iss.Nov85) (cd-iss.Nov94 on 'Creation Rev-Ola')*

Jul 80. Factory Benelux; (7")(12") **SHACK UP. / AND THE AGAIN (live)** [-] [-] Belg.

Nov 80. (12") **FLIGHT. / BLOWN AWAY / AND THEN AGAIN** [ ] [-]

Jan 81. (12"ep) **SHACK UP / SON AND HEIR. / DO THE DU (casse) / THE FOX** [ ] [-]

added **MARTHA TILSON – vocals (ex-OCCULT CHEMISTRY)**

May 81. (lp) **TO EACH . . .** [ ] [-]
– Felch / My spirit / Forced laugh / Choir / Back to the start / The fox / Loss / Oceans / Winter hill. *(cd-iss.Nov94 on 'Creation Rev-Ola')*

Sep 81. (d-12") **THE DOUBLE 12":- (singles Nov 80+ Jan 81)** [-] [-] Italy

Dec 81. (12") **WATERLINE. / FUNAEZEKEA** [ ] [-]

Jan 82. (lp)(c) **SEXTET** [53] [-]
– Lucinda / Crystal / Gum / Knife slits water / Skipscada / Day one / Rub down / Rialto / Below the canal. *(cd-iss.Nov94 on 'Creation Rev-Ola')*

Jul 82. Factory Benelux; (12") **GUESS WHO. / (part 2)** [-] [-]

Sep 82. (7") **KNIFE SLITS WATER. / TUMBA RUMBA** [ ] [-]
(12") – ('A'side) / KETHER-HOT KNIVES MIX-IN SPECIAL

Reverted to quintet when **MARTHA** departed.

Nov 82. (lp)(c) **I'D LIKE TO SEE YOU AGAIN** [ ] [-]
– I'd like to see you again / Axis / Saturn / Touch / Showcase / Guess who / Hot knights / Sesano apriti-cordo vada. *(cd-iss.Nov94 on 'Creation Rev-Ola')*

— **ANDY CONNELL** – keyboards, vocals repl. TERREL / **CAROL McKENZIE** – (guest) vocals repl. TOPPING who formed T-COY

Sep 83. (12") **I NEED SOMEONE TONIGHT. / DON'T YOU WORRY 'BOUT A THING** [ ] [-]

TONY QUIGLEY – sax (also of KALIMA) repl. McKENZIE

Nov 84. (12") **LIFE'S A SCREAM. / THERE'S ONLY THIS** [ ] [-]

Feb 85. Factory Benelux; (12") **BRAZILIA. / BRAZILIA (extended)** [-] [-]

Jun 85. (12") **WILD PARTY. / SOUNDS LIKE SOMETHING DIRTY** [ ] [-]
(c-s+=) – Life's a scream (live) / Force (live) / Wild party (live).

Dec 85. (lp)(c) **THE OLD AND THE NEW** (best of; remixed) [ ] [ ]
– Flight / Do the du / And then again / The fox / Blown away / Sounds like something dirty / Life's a scream / There's only this / Wild party. (w/ free 7") – SHACK UP. / THE THIN BOYS *(cd-iss.Nov94 on 'Creation Rev-Ola')*

added guests **CORRINE DREWERY** – vocals / **TOM BARRISH** – trombone / **PAUL HARRISON** – bass programme.

Factory / Qwest

Sep 86. (12") **MICKEY WAY (THE CANDY BAR). / INSIDE / SI FERMO O GRIDO** [ ] [-]

Nov 86. (lp)(c)(cd) **FORCE** [ ] [ ]
– Only together / Bootsy / Fever / Naked and white / Mickey Way (the candy bar) / And then she smiles / Take me down / Anthem. (cd+=) – Nostrama a go-go / Inside / Si fermi o grido. *(cd-iss.Nov94 on 'Creation Rev-Ola')*

Dojo / not issued

Feb 87. (lp)(cd) **LIVE IN AMERICA (live)** [ ] [-]
– Sounds like something dirty / The fox / Shack up / Life's a scream / Wild party / Flight / And then again / Touch / Knife slits water / Si fermi o grido.

Materili Sonori / not issued

Jul 87. (12"ep) **GREETINGS FOUR** [-] [-] Italy
– The runner / Inside / Bootsy.

— Now line-up **KERR, MOSCROP, JOHNSON** and **QUIGLEY** (1987) when CONNELL took guest DREWERY to form SWING OUT SISTER

A & M / A & M

Jun 89. (7") **THE BIG E (I WON'T STOP LOVING YOU). / LOVE IS THE WAY** (instrumental) [ ] [-]
(12"+=)(cd-s+=) – Day 2.

Aug 89. (7") **BACKS TO THE WALL. / BE WHAT YOU WANT TO BE** [ ] [-]
(12"+=)(cd-s+=) – ('A' instrumental).

Sep 89. (lp)(c)(cd) **GOOD TOGETHER** [ ] [ ]
– Your blue eyes / Your little world / The big E / God's own girl / Love is the way / Backs to the wall / River's edge / Every pleasure / Coldest days / Good together / Repercussions / 2000 a.d.

Oct 89. (7") **YOUR BLUE EYES. / THIN GREY LINE** [ ] [-]
(12"+=)(cd-s+=) – Coldest days.

Feb 90. (7") **GOOD TOGETHER (live). / BE WHAT YOU WANNA BE (live)** [ ] [-]
(12"ep)(cd-s) – '4 FOR THE FLOOR'EP (+=) – Spirit dance / Tribeca

Jun 90. (7") **WON'T STOP LOVING YOU. / THE BIG E** [55] [-]
(c-s) ('A'-Bernard Sumner mix) / ('A'-Norman Cook mix)
(12") – ('A'side) / Love is the way / Repercussions (live).
(cd-s++=) – ('A'version).

Jul 90. (cd)(c)(lp) **M.C.R.(live)** (as **"A.C.R."**) [ ] [ ]
– Spirit dance / Won't stop loving you / B.T.T.W.90 / Be what you wanna be / Good together / Funky Heaven / Tribeca / Repercussions.

— added guest vocals **DENISE JOHNSON**

Rob's / not issued

Jul 91. (7")(ext.12") **THE PLANET. / LOOSEN UP YOUR MIND** [ ] [-]
(cd-s+=) – ('A'+'B' versions)

Nov 91. (7") **27 FOREVER. / ('A'loose mix)** [ ] [-]
(12"+=) – ('A'vocal remix).
(cd-s+=) – ('A'higher plane edit).
(12") ('A' Da Silver 2 mixes)

Oct 92. (12"ep) **MELLO** [ ] [-]
– Mello'd up / Mello dub / 27 forever (testimonial mix) / Mello (303 dub).(12")(cd-s) – Mello (pt.1 & 2) / Mello (Fon mix) / Mello (soundstation).

Oct 92. (cd)(c)(lp) **UP IN DOWNSVILLE** [ ] [-]
– Manik / Turn me on / Mello / Wonder Y / Up in Downsville (pt.1) / 27 forever / Tekno 4 an answer / Salvador's (fish) / Up in Downsville (pt.2).

ACR

Feb 93. (12"ep)(cd-ep) **TURN ME ON** [ ] [ ]
– Turn Me On ("O" Mix) / Turn Me On (Tackle Mix) / Turn Me On (Primetime Mix) / Turn Me On (M21 Mix)

Dec 93. (12")(cd-s) **TEKNO (way out west mix). / TEKNO (lip mix)** [ ] [ ]

Creation

May 94. (12"ep)(cd-ep) **SHACK UP (3 mixes). / LIFE'S A SCREAM (mix)** [ ] [ ]

Jul 94. (cd)(c)(d-lp) **LOOKING FOR A CERTAIN RATIO** (remixes) [ ] [-]

– compilations, others, etc. –

Dec 94. Creation Rev-OLa; (lp) **SAMPLER** [ ] [-]

SIR HORATIO

a pseudonym for A CERTAIN RATIO

Jan 82. Rock Steady; (12") **ABRACADUBRA. / SOMMADUB** [ ] [-]

ADAM & THE ANTS

Formed: London, England . . . April'77 by STUART GODDARD (aka ADAM ANT), LESTER SQUARE – guitar / ANDY WARREN – bass / PAUL FLANAGAN – drums. ADAM acted! in Derek Jarman's controversial punk movie JUBILEE (Released Feb'78). By then DAVE BARBE was on drums / JORDAN extra vocals and MARK GAUMONT – guitar. Recorded 'Plastic Surgery' and 'Deutcher Girls' for film. On latter JOHNNY BIVOUAC had replaced GAUMONT (Oct'77). In mid '78 and with another change of line-up (see below) they signed one-off deal with 'Decca'. The following year indie 'Do-It' label gave them another break. 1980 saw them/him on 'CBS' and taking UK charts by storm. After two 1981 chart-toppers 'STAND AND DELIVER' & 'PRINCE CHARMING', ADAM went solo, immediately striking the top again with 'GOODY TWO SHOES'. Things slowed down and finally ground to a halt by 1985, although a 1990 comeback saw 'ROOM AT THE TOP' hit UK & US Top 20. • **Style:** Punk "indie" pop which in the mid 80's; guided by manager/svengali MALCOLM McLAREN, saw them incorporating old Borundi-style dual drummers. Fashion too had moved ADAM into teeny-bop market as his stage attire moved into and from pirate to highwayman. • **Songwriters:** GODDARD / ASHMAN in the 70's, to GODDARD / PIRRONI in the 80's. • **Trivia:** He acted in stage production of 'Entertaining Mr.Sloane'. After retiring to the States in 1986 he took parts in 'Slam Dance' film, and 'Equalizer' TV serial.

Recommended: DIRK WEAR WHITE SOX (*6) / HITS (1980-1985) (*5)

ADAM ANT (b. STUART GODDARD, 3 Nov'54) – vocals, guitar / **MATTHEW ASHMAN** (b.'62) – guitar, vocals (ex-KAMERAS) / **ANDY WARREN** (b.'61) – bass, vocals / **DAVE BARBE** (b.'61) – drums (ex-DESOLATION ANGELS)

Decca — not issued

Oct 78. (7") **YOUNG PARISIANS. / LADY** [ ] [-]
(re-iss.Dec80 hit 9) (re-iss.Oct89 on 'Damaged Goods')

Do-It — not issued

Jun 79. (7") **ZEROX. / PHYSICAL (YOU'RE SO) (ltd.3,000)** [ ] [-]
(later Jun79 copies had B-side **WHIP IN MY VALISE**) (This version also re-iss.Jan81 hit 45)

Nov 79. (lp) **DIRK WEARS WHITE SOX** [ ] [-]
– Cartrouble (part 1 & 2) / Digital tenderness / Nine plan failed / Day I met God * / Tabletalk / Cleopatra / Catholic day / Never trust a man (with egg on his face) / Animals and men / Family of noise / The idea. *(re-iss.Jan81 hit 16) (remixed re-iss.Apr83 on 'CBS', track* replaced by; Zerox / Kick! / Whip in my valise). (cd-iss.Jul95 on 'Columbia')*

— **LEIGH GORMAN** – bass (on B-side) repl. WARREN who joined MONOCHROME SET

Feb 80. (7") **CARTROUBLE. / KICK!** [ ] [-]
(re-iss.Jan81 hit 33)

— (Jan80) until (Mar80 when ADAM brought in entire new group) **MARCO PIRRONI** – guitar, vocals (ex-MODELS) repl. ASHMAN / **MERRICK** (b.CHRIS HUGHES) – drums repl. BARBE / **KEVIN MOONEY** – bass, vocals repl. GORMAN (who with above 2 formed BOW WOW WOW) / added **TERRY LEE MIALL** – 2nd drummer (ex-MODELS)

C.B.S. — Epic

Jul 80. (7") **KINGS OF THE WILD FRONTIER. / PRESS DARLINGS** [48] [ ]

Sep 80. (7") **DOG EAT DOG. / PHYSICAL (YOU'RE SO)** [4] [ ]

Nov 80. (lp)(c) **KINGS OF THE WILD FRONTIER** [1] [44] Feb81
– Dog eat dog / Ant music / Feed me to the lions / Los Rancheros / Ants invasion / Killer in the home / Kings of the wild frontier / The magnificent five / Don't be square (be there) / Jolly Roger / Making history / The human beings. *(re-iss.cd Oct93 on 'Sony Europe')*

Nov 80. (7") **ANT MUSIC. / FALL IN** [2] [-]

Jan 81. (7")(12") **ANT MUSIC. / DON'T BE SQUARE (BE THERE)** [-] [ ]

Feb 81. (7") **KINGS OF THE WILD FRONTIER. / PRESS DARLING** [2] [ ]
(re-issue)

— **GARY TIBBS** – bass (ex-ROXY MUSIC, ex-VIBRATORS) repl. MOONEY

May 81. (7")(US-12") **STAND AND DELIVER. / BEAT MY GUEST** [1] [ ]

Sep 81. (7") **PRINCE CHARMING. / CHRISTIAN D'OR** [1] [ ]

Nov 81. (lp)(c) **PRINCE CHARMING** [2] [94]
– Prince Charming / The Scorpios / Picasso visita el Planeta de los Simios / 5 guns west / That voodoo / Stand and deliver / Mile high club / Ant rap / Mowhok / S.E.X. *(re-iss.cd Oct93 on 'Sony Europe')*

Dec 81. (7")(7"pic-d) **ANT RAP. / FRIENDS** [3] [ ]

— (ADAM & THE ANTS broke up Jan82)

Adam ANT

continued solo augmented by **PIRRONI** and sessioners.

May 82. (7")(7"pic-d) **GOODY TWO SHOES. / RED SCAB** [1] [-]

Sep 82. (7")(7"pic-d) **FRIEND OR FOE. / JUANITO THE BANDITO** [9] [ ]

Oct 82. (lp)(c) **FRIEND OR FOE** [5] [16]
– Friend or foe / Something girls / Place in the country / Desperate but not serious / Here comes the grump / Hello I love you / Goody two shoes / Crackpot history and the right to lie / Made of money / Cajun twisters / Try this for sighs / A man called Marco.

Nov 82. (7")(7"pic-d) **DESPERATE BUT NOT SERIOUS. / WHY DO GIRLS LOVE HORSES?** [33] [ ] Mar 83

Jan 83. (7") **GOODY TWO SHOES. / CRACKPOT HISTORY** [-] [12]

Mar 83. (7") **DESPERATE BUT NOT SERIOUS. / PLACE IN THE COUNTRY** [-] [66]

Oct 83. (7")(7"pic-d) **PUSS'N'BOOTS. / KISS THE DRUMMER** [5] [ ] May 84
(12"+=) – ('A'+'B'extended).

Nov 83. (lp)(c) **STRIP** [20] [65]
– Baby let me scream at you / Libertine / Spanish games / Vanity / Puss'n'boots / Playboy / Strip / Montreal / Navel to neck / Amazon. *(cd-iss.Jul84)*

Dec 83. (7")(7"pic-d) **STRIP. / YOURS, YOURS, YOURS** [41] [42]
(12"+=) – ('A'&'B'extended).

Sep 84. (7")(12") **APOLLO 9. / B SIDE BABY** [13] [ ]
(extra 12") – ('A'side) / ('A'instrumental).

Jul 85. (7") **VIVE LE ROCK. / GRETA X** [50] [ ]
(12"+=) – ('A'instrumental).

Sep 85. (lp)(c)(cd) **VIVE LE ROCK** [42] [ ]
– Vive le rock / Miss Thing / Razor keen / Rip down / Scorpio rising / Apollo 9 / Hell's eight acres / Mohair lockeroom pin-up boys / No zap / P.O.E. (c+=) – Human bondage den. (cd+=) – Apollo 9 (acappella). *(re-iss.cd Mar95 on 'Rewind')*

— ADAM retired for 4 years. MARCO joined SPEAR OF DESTINY

ADAM ANT

brought back MARCO to resurrect career.

M.C.A. — M.C.A.

Feb 90. (7")(c-s) **ROOM AT THE TOP. / BRUCE LEE** [13] [17]
(12"+=)(cd-s+=) – ('A'house vocals).

Mar 90. (cd)(c)(lp) **MANNERS & PHYSICIQUE** [19] [57]
– Room at the top / If you keep on / Can't set rules about love / Bright lights black leather / Young dumb and full of it / Rough stuff / Manners & physicique / U.S.S.A. / Piccadilly / Anger Inc.

Apr 90. (7")(c-s) **CAN'T SET RULES ABOUT LOVE. / HOW TO STEAL THE WORLD** [47] [ ]
(12"+=) – Brand new torso.
(cd-s++=) – ('A'-lp version).

Jun 90. (7") **BRIGHT LIGHTS BLACK LEATHER. / ROUGH STUFF** [-] [ ]

— w/ **PIRRONI** / **BOZ BOORER** – guitars / **BRUCE WITKIN** – bass / **DAVE RUFFY** – drums

E.M.I. — Capitol

Jan 95. (7")(c-s) **WONDERFUL. / GOES AROUND** [32] [ ]
(cd-s+=) – Norman / Woman love run through me.
(cd-s) – ('A'side) / If / Phoenix.

Mar 95. (7")(c-s) **BEAUTIFUL DREAM. / LET'S HAVE A FIGHT** [ ] [ ]
(cd-s+=) – Billy boy / Wonderful (acoustic).
(cd-s) – ('A'side) / Shake your hips / Ant music (acoustic) / ('A'-Lucas master mix).

Apr 95. (cd)(c) **WONDERFUL** [24] [39]
– Won't take that talk / Beautiful dream / Wonderful / 1969 again / Yin & Yang / Image of yourself / Alien / Gotta be a sin / Vampires / Angel / Very long ride.

May 95. (c-s) **GOTTA BE A SIN / DOG EAT DOG (live)** [48] [ ]
(cd-s) – ('A'side) / Cleopatra (live) / Beat my guest (live) / Red scab (live).
(cd-s) – ('A'side) / Desperate but not serious (live) / Car trouble (live) / Physical (you're so) (live).

– compilations, others, etc. –

Feb 82. E.G.; (7") **DEUTCHER GIRLS. / PLASTIC SURGERY** [13] [-]

Mar 82. Do-It; (7"ep)(7"pic-d) **THE B-SIDES** [46] [-]
– Friends / Kick! / Physical (you're so).
(12"ep) – ANTMUSIC (+=) – Cartrouble (part 1 & 2).

Jan 88. Old Gold; (7") **ANT MUSIC. / STAND AND DELIVER** [ ] [-]

Nov 90. Old Gold; (7") **PRINCE CHARMING. / GOODY TWO SHOES** [ ] [-]

Sep 86. C.B.S./ US= Epic; (lp)(c)(cd) **HITS** (1980-85) [ ] [ ]
– Kings of the wild frontier / Dog eat dog / Ant music / Stand and deliver / Prince Charming / Ant rap / Goody two shoes / Friend or foe / Desperate but not serious / Puss'n'boots / Strip / Apollo 9 / Vive le rock.

Feb 91. Strange Fruit; (cd)(lp) **THE PEEL SESSIONS** (early 1979 material) [ ] [-]

Jun 91. Columbia; (cd)(c) **ANTICS IN THE FORBIDDEN ZONE** (solo) [ ] [-]
(re-iss.cd Oct94 on 'Rewind')

Oct 94. Columbia; (cd) **THE BEST (ADAM ANT)** [ ] [ ]

Aug 93. Arcade; (cd)(c) **ANTMUSIC – THE VERY BEST OF ADAM ANT ("ADAM ANT / ADAM & THE ANTS")** [6] [-]

Mar 94. Arcade; (cd) **ANTMUSIC – THE VERY BEST OF ADAM ANT** [30] [-]
– (w /free cd) **LIVE (live)**

May 95. Columbia; (cd) **BSIDES BABIES** [ ] [-]

Bryan ADAMS

Born:5 Nov'59, Vancouver, Canada. In 1977 he set up writing partnership with JIM VALLANCE, drummer with techo-rock band PRISM. Numerous groups including LOVERBOY / KISS / BACHMAN-TURNER OVERDRIVE / etc. used their songs before BRYAN ADAMS solo signed contract with 'A&M' early 1979. After 4 years wait, he finally broke into US Top 10 with 'STRAIGHT FROM THE HEART'. He was soon Canada's biggest export, becoming an international star, after the release of 'RUN TO YOU' single in 1984. • **Style:** Hard-edged rock/pop merging at times with 'AOR'. • **Songwriters:** ADAMS continued to write with VALLANCE until 1988, when he added producer MUTT LANGE. Covered: WALKING AFTER MIDNIGHT (D.Hecht /A.Block) / I FOUGHT THE LAW (Sonny Curtis). • **Trivia:** In '91, he stayed a record 16 consecutive weeks at UK No.1 with 'EVERYTHING I DO' from the film 'Robin Hood (Prince Of Thieves)'.

Recommended: SO FAR SO GOOD (*6)

BRYAN ADAMS – vocals, guitar with **JIM VALLANCE** – drums, keyboards, guitar, bass

A & M A & M

Jul 79. (7")(12") **LET ME TAKE YOU DANCIN'. / DON'T TURN ME AWAY** [ ] [ ]

Apr 80. (7") **HIDIN' FROM LOVE. / WAIT AND SEE** [ ] [ ]

Mar 81. (lp)(c) **BRYAN ADAMS** [ ] [ ]
– Hidin' from love / Win some, lose some / Wait and see / Give me your love / Wastin' time / Don't ya say it / Remember / State of mind / Try to see it my way. *(cd-iss.Jan87 + 1988)*

Apr 81. (7") **GIVE ME YOUR LOVE. / WAIT AND SEE** [-] [ ]

now with **TOMMY HANDEL** – keyboards / **BRIAN STANLEY** – bass + **MICKEY CURRY** – drums repl. VALLANCE (he continued to co-write + play piano + percussion for ADAMS until '88).

Mar 82. (7") **LONELY NIGHTS. / DON'T LOOK NOW** [ ] [84]

Apr 82. (lp)(c) **YOU WANT IT, YOU GOT IT** [78] [ ]
– Lonely nights / One good reason / Don't look now / Jealousy / Coming home / Fits ya good / Tonight / You want it, you got it / Last chance / No one makes it right. *(cd-iss.Aug88 + 1988)*

1982. (7") **COMING HOME. / FITS YA GOOD** [-] [ ]

— **DAVE TAYLOR** – bass repl STANLEY / added **KEITH SCOTT** – guitar, vocals

Feb 83. (7") **CUTS LIKE A KNIFE. / ONE GOOD REASON** [-] [ ]

Apr 83. (7")(12") **STRAIGHT FROM THE HEART. / LONELY NIGHTS** [ ] [-]

Apr 83. (7") **STRAIGHT FROM THE HEART. / ONE GOOD REASON** [-] [10]

May 83. (lp)(c) **CUTS LIKE A KNIFE** [ ] [8]
– The only one / Take me back / This time / Straight from the heart / Cuts like a knife / I'm ready / What's it gonna be / Don't leave me lonely / The best has yet to come. *(re-iss.+cd.Mar86 hit UK 21) (cd re-iss.'88)*

Jun 83. (7") **CUTS LIKE A KNIFE. / LONELY NIGHTS** [-] [15]

Jul 83. (7") **CUTS LIKE A KNIFE. / FITS YA GOOD** [ ] [-]
(12"+=) – Hidin' from love.

Aug 83. (7") **THIS TIME. / FITS YA GOOD** [-] [24]

Nov 83. (7") **THE BEST HAS YET TO COME. / I'M READY** [-] [ ]

Dec 84. (7")(12") **RUN TO YOU. / I'M READY** [11] [6] Oct 84
(12"+=) – Cuts like a knife.
(d7"++=) – Lonely nights.

Feb 85. (lp)(c)(cd) **RECKLESS** [7] [1] Nov 84
– One night love affair / She's only happy when she's dancin' / Run to you / Heaven / Somebody / Summer of '69 / It's only love / Kids wanna rock / Long gone / Ain't gonna cry. *(re-iss.Jul91 hit UK No.29, Apr92 hit No.36)*

Mar 85. (7")(12")(7"pic-d) **SOMEBODY. / LONG GONE** [35] [11] Jan 85

May 85. (7")(12") **HEAVEN. / DIANA** (US B-side='A' live) [38] [1] Apr 85
(12"+=) – Fits ya good / ('A'version)
(d7"+=) – Straight from the heart / You want it, you got it.

Jun 85. (7") **SUMMER OF '69. / THE BEST HAS YET TO COME** [-] [5]

Jul 85. (7") **SUMMER OF '69. / KIDS WANNA ROCK (live)** [42] [-]
(12"+=) – The Bryan Adams mix.

Sep 85. (7") **ONE NIGHT LOVE AFFAIR. / LONELY NIGHTS** [-] [13]

Oct 85. (7")(12") **IT'S ONLY LOVE. (as "Bryan ADAMS & Tina TURNER") / THE BEST WAS YET TO COME** [29] [-]
(d7"+=) – Somebody. / Long gone.

Nov 85. (7") **IT'S ONLY LOVE (w/ TINA TURNER). / THE ONLY ONE** [-] [15]

Dec 85. (7")(12") **CHRISTMAS TIME. / REGGAE CHRISTMAS** [55] [ ]

Mar 87. (7")(12") **HEAT OF THE NIGHT. / ANOTHER DAY** [50] [6]

Mar 87. (lp)(c)(cd) **INTO THE FIRE** [10] [7]
– Heat of the night / Into the fire / Victim of love / Another day / Native son / Only the strong survive / Remembrance day / Rebel rebel / Hearts on fire / Home again. *(re-iss.cd+c Mar93)*

May 87. (7") **HEARTS ON FIRE. / THE BEST HAS YET TO COME** [-] [26]

May 87. (7")(c-s) **HEARTS ON FIRE. / RUN TO YOU** [57] [-]
(12"+=) – Native Sun.

Aug 87. (7") **VICTIM OF LOVE. / INTO THE FIRE** [-] [32]

Oct 87. (7")(c-s) **VICTIM OF LOVE. / HEAT OF THE NIGHT (live)** [68] [-]
(12"+=) – ('A'-live version).

— BRYAN now used session people?

Jun 91. (7")(c-s) **(EVERYTHING I DO) I DO IT FOR YOU. / SHE'S ONLY HAPPY WHEN SHE'S DANCING (live)** [1] [1]
(12"+=)(cd-s+=) – ('A'extended) / Cuts like a knife.

Aug 91. (7")(c-s) **CAN'T STOP THIS THING WE STARTED. / IT'S ONLY LOVE (live)** [12] [2]
(12"+=)(cd-s+=) – Hearts on fire.

Sep 91. (cd)(c)(lp) **WAKING UP THE NEIGHBOURS** [1] [6]
– Is your mama gonna miss ya? / Hey honey – I'm rockin' you in! / Can't stop this thing we started / Thought I'd died and gone to Heaven / Not guilty / House arrest / Vanishing / Do I have to say the words? / There will never be another tonight / All I want is you / Depend on me / (Everything I do) I do it for you / If you wanna leave me (can I come too?) / Touch the hand / Don't drop that bomb on me.

Nov 91. (7")(c-s) **THERE WILL NEVER BE ANOTHER TONIGHT. / INTO THE FIRE (live)** [32] [31]
(12"+=)(cd-s+=) – One night love affair (live).

Feb 92. (7")(c-s) **I THOUGHT I'D DIED AND GONE TO HEAVEN. / SOMEBODY (live)** [8] [13]
(12"+=) – (Everything I do) I do it for you.
(cd-s+=) – Heart of the night (live).

Jul 92. (7")(c-s) **ALL I WANT IS YOU. / RUN TO YOU** [22] [-]
(12"+=)(cd-s+=) – Long gone.

Sep 92. (7")(c-s) **DO I HAVE TO SAY THE WORDS?. / SUMMER OF '69** [30] [11] Jul 92
(12"+=)(cd-s+=) – Kids wanna rock / Can't stop this thing we started.

Oct 93. (7")(c-s) **PLEASE FORGIVE ME. / C'MON EVERYBODY** [2] [7]
(cd-s+=) – Can't stop this thing we started / There will never be another tonight.

Nov 93. (cd)(c)(lp) **SO FAR SO GOOD** (compilation) [2] [7]
– Summer of '69 / Straight from the heart / It's only love / Can't stop this thing we started / Do I have to say the words? / This time / Run to you / Heaven / Cuts like a knife / (Everything I do) I do it for you / Somebody / Kids wanna rock / Heat of the night / Please forgive me

Jan 94. (7")(c-s) **ALL FOR LOVE. ("BRYAN ADAMS / ROD STEWART / STING") / ('A'instrumental)** [2] [1] Nov 93
(cd-s) – ('A'side) / Straight from the heart (live) (BRYAN ADAMS) / If only (ROD STEWART) / Love is stronger than justice (live) (STING).

— Above hit from the film 'The Three Musketeers'.

Jul 94. (cd)(c) **LIVE! LIVE! LIVE!** (rec.live Belguim 1988) [17] [ ]
– She's only happy when she's dancin' / It's only love / Cuts like a knife / Kids wanna rock / Hearts on fire / Take me back / The best was yet to come / Heaven / Heat of the night / Run to you / One night love affair / Long gone / Summer of '69 / Somebody / Walking after midnight / I fought the law / Into the fire.

Apr 95. (7")(c-s)(cd-s) **HAVE YOU EVER REALLY LOVED A WOMAN?. / LOW LIFE** [4] [1]

– compilations, others, etc. –

Feb 86. A&M; (7") **THIS TIME. / I'M READY** [41] [-]
(12"+=) – Lonely nights.

Jul 86. A&M; (7") **STRAIGHT FROM THE HEART. / FITS YA GOOD** [51] [-]
(12"+=) – ('A'-live version).

Jun 89. A&M; (c) **CUTS LIKE A KNIFE / RECKLESS** [ ] [-]

SWEENY TODD

On the 2nd lp below he had replaced NICK GILDER.

1992. Receiver; (cd)(lp) **IF WISHES WERE HORSES** (re-issue) [ ] [-]

ADVERTS

Formed: London, England . . . late 1976 by TV SMITH and GAYE. Gigged constantly at The Roxy where they made first recording BORED TEENAGERS (later mid'77 released on Various Artists lp 'Live At The Roxy'). DAVE VANIAN of the DAMNED recommended them to indie 'Stiff' records, who gave them one-off deal. Pulled off a UK hit with 'Anchor' records in 1977, when 'GARY GILMORE'S EYES' made Top 20. • **Style:** Punk-rock outfit featuring sultry punkette GAYE ADVERT. By 1979, their attitute and sound had turned more mainstream, although Smith's vocals still portrayed angst. **Songwriters:** TV SMITH nearly all. • **Trivia:** 'GARY GILMORE'S EYES' was inspired by the mass killer who donated his eyes to science after he was finally executed.

Recommended: CROSSING THE RED SEA WITH THE ADVERTS (*6).

TV SMITH – vocals (b.Cornwall) / **GAYE ADVERT** – bass (b.29 Aug'56) / **HOWARD PICKUP** – guitar / **LAURIE DRIVER** – drums

Stiff not issued

Apr 77. (7") **ONE CHORD WONDERS. / QUICKSTEP** [ ] [-]

Anchor not issued

Aug 77. (7") **GARY GILMORE'S EYES. / BORED TEENAGERS** [18] [-]

Oct 77. (7") **SAFETY IN NUMBERS. / WE WHO WAIT** [ ] [-]

Bright-CBS not issued

Jan 78. (7") **NO TIME TO BE 21. / NEW DAY DAWNING** [38] [-]

Feb 78. (red-lp)(lp)(c) **CROSSING THE RED SEA WITH THE ADVERTS** [38] [-]
– One chord wonders / Bored teenagers / New church / On the roof / New boys / Bomb site boy / Mo time to be 21 / Safety in numbers / Drowning men / On wheels / Great British mistake / Gary Gilmore's eyes. *(re-iss.+cd.Dec88) (re-iss.Oct81 +Sep83; red-lp on 'Butt') (re-iss.Mar90 on 'Link')*

— **JOHN TOWE** – drums (ex-ALTERNATIVE TV, ex-GENERATION X) repl. DRIVER (Spring'78) **ROD LATTER** – drums (ex-MANIACS, ex-RINGS) repl. TOWE

R.C.A. not issued

Nov 78. (7") **TELEVISION'S OVER. / BACK FROM THE DEAD** [ ] [-]

Jun 79. (7") **MY PLACE. / NEW CHURCH (live)** [ ] [-]

Sep 79. (7") **CAST OF THOUSANDS. / I WILL WALK YOU HOME** [ ] [-]

added **TIM CROSS** – keyboards, synthesizers (of MIKE OLDFIELD BAND)

Oct 79. (lp)(c) **CAST OF THOUSANDS** [ ] [-]
– Cast of thousands / The adverts / My place / Male assault / Television's over / Fate of criminals / I looked at the Sun / Love songs / I surrender / I will walk you home.

— **PAUL MARTINEZ** repl. HOWARD with his brother **RICK** repl. ROD. After manager MICHAEL DEMPSEY was electrocuted to death, TV, GAYE and TIM decided to split late 1979.

– compilations, others, etc. –

May 83. Bright-CBS; (7"m) **GARY GILMORE'S EYES / WE WHO WAIT / NEW DAY DAWNING** [ ] [-]

Oct 87. Strange Fruit; (12"ep) **THE PEEL SESSIONS (25.4.77)** [ ] [-]
– Quickstep / Gary Gilmore's eyes / Bored teenagers / New boys / One chord wonders.

TV SMITH'S EXPLORERS

were formed late 79 by **TV** and **TIM CROSS TOWE**, plus **ERIC RUSSELL** – guitar / **COLIN STONER** – bass (ex-DOCTORS OF MADNESS)

— (Mar'80) **MEL WESSON** repl. CROSS who rejoined MIKE OLDFIELD / **DAVE SINCLAIR** (of LONDON ZOO) repl. TOWE, who later joined UK SUBS

Big Beat / not issued

Nov 80. (7") **TOMAHAWK CRUISE. / SEE EUROPE** [ ] [-]
(re-iss.Jan81 on 'Chiswick')

Kalei-doscope / Epic

Apr 81. (7") **THE SERVANT. / LOOKING DOWN ON LONDON** [ ] [-]
(c-s+=) (ltd.500 copies) – Walk in a straight line.

Jun 81. (7") **HAVE FUN. / IMAGINATION** [ ] [-]

Jul 81. (lp)(c) **THE LAST WORDS OF THE GREAT EXPLORER** [ ] [ ]
– I live for everything / The servant / Have fun / Walk away / The last words of the great explorer / Imagination / The easy way / The unwelcome guest / The perfect life. (c+=) (free 7"w/above) **WALK IN A STRAIGHT LINE. / WORLD OF MY OWN**

Oct 81. (7") **THE PERFECT LIFE. / IMAGINATION** [ ] [-]

—— (Oct'81) disbanded

TV SMITH

went solo, recruiting yet again **TIM CROSS** plus **TIM RENWICK** – guitar (ex-MIKE OLDFIELD, ex-SUTHERLAND BROTHERS)

Expulsion / not issued

May 83. (7") **WAR FEVER. / LIES** [ ] [-]

Jun 83. (lp) **CHANNEL 5** [ ] [-]

PRODUCTION HOUSE

were group formed by same line-up above.

Produc-tion House / not issued

May 85. (7") **COMING ROUND. / WOODPECKER** [ ] [-]

CHEAP

were formed late'86 by **TV** plus **SIMON BUDD** – drums / **ANDY BENNY** – bass (ex-SLEAZE) / **MIK HESLIN** – guitar (ex-CHAOTIC DISCHORD)
Donated a few songs to Various Artists albums before releasing 7" in '89.
MARTIN DENTZ – drums repl. BUDD (in 1988)

Deltic / not issued

Mar 90. (7") **THIRD TERM. / BURIED BY THE MACHINE** [ ] [-]

TV SMITH

(solo again)

Cooking V. / not issued

Jul 92. (cd)(c)(lp) **MARCH OF THE GIANTS** [ ] [-]
– Lion and the lamb / March of the giants / Can't pay won't pay / Atlantic tunnel / Haves and have-nots / Straight and narrow / Free world / Ship in a bottle / Empty wallet / Useless / Runaway train driver / Borderline. *(re-iss.cd+c Mar94)*

T.V. SMITH'S CHEAP

Humbug / not issued

Jun 93. (cd) **RIP . . . EVERYTHING MUST GO!** [ ] [-]
– Leisure time / My string will snap / New ways are best / Free world / Silicon Valley holiday / Luxury in exile / Buried by the machine / Ghosts / Ready for the axe to drop / The newshound / Beauty treatment / The Lords Prayer.

1995. (cd) **THE IMMORTAL RICH** [ ] [-]
– The immortal rich / Living world / Walk the plank / We want the road / High society / Head on! dear! / The day we caught the big fish / Thin green line / Let 'em go / In there / Earth 2.

AEROSMITH

Formed: Sunapee, New Hampshire, USA . . . Summer 1970, by PERRY and TYLER, who with others moved to Boston, Massachusetts. By 1972, through a Max's Kansas City gig, they were signed to 'Columbia' by Clive Davis for a six figure sum. Soon became one of America's top live attractions earning platinum record sales in the process. Still going strong in the 90's and unleashed another great slice of rock'n'roll in 1993 'GET A GRIP'. • **Style:** Heavyweight hard glam-rock outfit, fronted by JAGGER lookalike STEVE TYLER. Cited by many new breed heavy bands as major influence. • **Songwriters:** PERRY / TYLER (aka TOXIC TWINS) except; COME TOGETHER (Beatles) / WALKIN' THE DOG (Rufus Thomas) / REMEMBER WALKIN' IN THE SAND (Shangri-la's) / TRAIN KEPT A-ROLLIN' (Johnny Burnette Trio) / MILK COW BLUES (Kokomo Arnold) / CRY ME A RIVER (Julie London) / MY ADIDAS (Run DMC). THE JOE PERRY PROJECT:- GET IT ON (BANG A GONG) (T.Rex) /BIG TEN-INCH RECORD (F.Weismantel; blues artist?) / ALL YOUR LOVE (Otis Rush) / HELTER SKELTER (Beatles) / CHIP AWAY THE STONE (Richie Supa) / . • **Miscellaneous:** In 1978 group appeared in the 'SGT. PEPPER' Beatles film. Early 1981 TYLER was nearly killed in a motorcycle accident, thus delaying 8th lp release.

Recommended: GREATEST HITS (*9) / PUMP (*8) / GET A GRIP (*7).

STEVE TYLER (b.STEVEN TALARICO, 26 Mar'48, New York) – vocals / **JOE PERRY** (b.10 Sep'50) – guitar (ex-JAM BAND) / **BRAD WHITFORD** (b.23 Feb'52, Winchester, Mass.) – guitar repl. RAY TABANO / **TOM HAMILTON** (b.31 Dec'51, Colorado Springs) – bass (ex-JAM BAND) / **JOEY KRAMER** (b.21 Jun'50, New York) – drums

C.B.S. / Columbia

Jun 73. (lp)(c) **AEROSMITH** [-] [ ]
– Make it / Somebody / Dream on / One way street / Mama kin / Write me (a letter) / Movin' out / Walkin' the dog. *(UK-iss.Sep74) (US re-iss.Mar76 hit No.21) (US re-iss.Sep87, cd-May88) (UK cd Mar92) (re-iss.cd Dec93 on 'Columbia')*

Nov 73. (7") **DREAM ON. / SOMEBODY** [ ] [59] Oct 73
(UK re-iss.Apr76, didn't chart) (US re-iss.Jan76, reached no.6)

Mar 74. (7") **SPACED. / TRAIN KEPT A-ROLLIN'** [-] [ ]

Jun 74. (7") **S.O.S. (TOO BAD). / LORD OF THE THIGHS** [-] [ ]

Nov 74. (lp)(c) **GET YOUR WINGS** [ ] [74] Mar 74
– Same old song and dance / Lord of the thighs / Spaced / Woman of the world / S.O.S. (too bad) / The train kept a-rollin' / Season's of winter / Pandora's box. *(US re-iss.Sep87, cd-May88) (UK-cd Mar92) (re-iss.cd Dec93 on 'Columbia')*

Nov 74. (7") **SAME OLD SONG AND DANCE. / PANDORA'S BOX** [-] [ ]

Jul 75. (lp)(c) **TOYS IN THE ATTIC** [ ] [11] Apr 75
– Toys in the attic / Uncle Salty / Adam's apple / Walk this way / Big ten inch record / Sweet emotion / No more, no more / Round and round / You see me crying. *(re-iss.1987 on 'Castle') (US re-iss.Sep87, cd-May88) (UK re-iss.+cd.Apr91 & Nov93 on 'Columbia')*

Jun 75. (7") **SWEET EMOTION. / UNCLE SALTY** [-] [36]

Sep 75. (7") **WALK THIS WAY. / ROUND AND ROUND** [-] [ ]

Nov 75. (7") **TOYS IN THE ATTIC. / YOU SEE ME CRYING** [-] [ ]

Jun 76. (lp)(c) **ROCKS** [ ] [3] May 76
– Back in the saddle / Last child / Rats in the cellar / Combination / Sick as a dog / Nobody's fault / Get the lead out / Lick and a promise / Home tonight. *(re-iss.+cd.Nov89) (US re-iss.+cd.Sep87) (re-iss.cd Dec93 on 'Columbia')*

Aug 76. (7") **LAST CHILD. / COMBINATION** [ ] [21] Jun 76

Sep 76. (7") **HOME TONIGHT. / PANDORA'S BOX** [-] [71]

Feb 77. (7") **WALK THIS WAY. / UNCLE SALTY** [-] [10] Nov 76

Apr 77. (7") **BACK IN THE SADDLE. / NOBODY'S FAULT** [-] [38]

Oct 77. (7") **DRAW THE LINE. / BRIGHT LIGHT FRIGHT** [-] [42]

Jan 78. (lp)(c) **DRAW THE LINE** [ ] [11] Dec 77
– Draw the line / I wanna know why / Critical mass / Get it up / Bright light fright / Kings and queens / The hand that feeds / Sight for sore eyes / Milk cow blues. *(US re-iss.Sep87, cd-May88) (re-iss.cd Dec93 on 'Columbia')*

Mar 78. (7") **KINGS AND QUEENS. / CRITICAL MASS** [-] [70]

Aug 78. (7") **COME TOGETHER. / KINGS AND QUEENS** [ ] [23]

Nov 78. (7") **GET IT UP. / MILK COW BLUES** [-] [ ]

Jan 79. (d-lp)(d-c) **LIVE! BOOTLEG (live)** [ ] [13] Nov 78
– Back in the saddle / Sweet emotion / Lord of the thighs / Toys in the attic / Last child / Come together / Walk this way / Sick as a dog / Dream on / Mama kin / S.O.S. (too bad) / Train kept a-rollin' / Sight for sore eyes / Chip away the stone / I ain't got you / Mother popcorn. *(US re-iss.Dec87) (re-iss.cd Dec93 on 'Columbia')*

Jan 79. (7") **CHIP AWAY THE STONE (live). / ('A' studio)** [-] [77]

Jan 80. (lp)(c) **NIGHT IN THE RUTS** [ ] [14] Nov 79
– No surprize / Chiquita / Remember (walkin' in the sand) / Cheesecake / Three mile smile / Reefer head woman / Bone to bone (Coney Island white fish boy) / Think about it / Mia. *(US re-iss.Sep87) (UK cd-iss.Mar92) (re-iss.cd Dec93 on 'Columbia')*

Feb 80. (7") **REMEMBER (WALKIN' IN THE SAND). / BONE TO BONE (CONEY ISLAND WHITE FISH BOY)** [ ] [67] Jan 80

—— (Dec79) **JIMMY CREPSO** – guitar (ex-FLAME) repl. JOE PERRY who went solo.

—— (Feb80) **RICK DUFAY** – guitar repl. WHITFORD who teamed up with ST. HOLMES

Oct 82. (lp)(c) **ROCK IN A HARD PLACE** [ ] [32] Sep 82
– Jailbait / Lightning strikes / Bitch's brew / Bolivian ragamuffin / Cry me a river / Prelude to Joanie / Joanie's butterfly / Rock in a hard place (Cheshire cat) / Jig it up / Push comes to shove. *(US re-iss.Sep87) (re-iss.cd Dec93 on 'Columbia')*

—— (Mar84) original 1970's line-up reform (see above)

Nov 85. (7") **SHEILA. / GYPSY BOOTS** [-] [ ]

Geffen / Geffen

Dec 85. (lp)(c) **DONE WITH MIRRORS** [ ] [36] Nov 85
– Let the music do the talking / My fist your face / Shame on you / The reason a dog / Shela / Gypsy boots / She's on fire / The hop. (c+=) – Darkness. *(US cd-Oct87) (UK re-iss.+cd.Jun89 on 'WEA') (re-iss.cd+c Jun94)*

Aug86 AEROSMITH were credited on 45 version of **WALK THIS WAY** by **RUN DMC**

Aug 87. (lp)(c)(cd) **PERMANENT VACATION** [37] [11]
– Heart's done time / Magic touch / Rag doll / Simoriah / Dude (looks like a lady) / St.John / Hangman jury / Girls keep coming apart / Angel / Permanent vacation / I'm down / The movie. *(re-iss.cd+c Jun94)*

Oct 87. (7") **DUDE (LOOKS LIKE A LADY). / SIMORIAH** [45] [14]
(12"+=)(12"pic-d+=) – Once is enough.

Apr 88. (7") **ANGEL. / GIRL KEEPS COMING APART** [69] [3] Jan 88
(12"+=)(12"pic-d+=) – ('A'-AOR remix).

Jun 88. (12") **RAG DOLL. / ST.JOHN** [-] [17]

Aug 89. (7")(c-s) **LOVE IN AN ELEVATOR. / YOUNG LUST** [13] [5]
(3"cd-s+=)(12"+=)(10"pic-d+=) – Ain't enough.

Sep 89. (lp)(c)(cd) **PUMP** [3] [5]
– Young lust / F.I.N.E. / Going down / Love in an elevator / Monkey on my back / Water song / Janie's got a gun / Dulcimer stomp / The other side / My girl / Don't get mad, get even / Voodoo medicine man / What it takes. *(re-iss.cd+c Jun94)*

Nov 89. (7")(12")(c-s)(7"sha-pic-d) **JANIE'S GOT A GUN. / VOODOO MEDICINE MAN** [ ] [4]
(12"+=)(cd-s+=) – Rag doll (live).

Feb 90. (7")(7"pic-d)(7"sha-pic-d) **DUDE (LOOKS LIKE A LADY) (remix). / MONKEY ON MY BACK** [20] [-]
(12")(cd-s) – ('A'side) / Love in an elevator (live) / Walk this way (live).

Apr 90. (7") **RAG DOLL. / SIMORIAH** [42] [-]
(12")(cd-s) – ('A'side) / Mama kin (live) / Let it rain (live).

Mar 90. (7")(c-s) **WHAT IT TAKES. / MONKEY ON MY BACK** [-] [9]

Jul 90. (7")(c-s) **THE OTHER SIDE. / MY GIRL** [46] [22] Jun 90
(12"+=) – Theme from 'Wayne's World' / ('A' honky tonk version)
(12") – ('A'side) / Love in an elevator / Dude (looks like a lady) / Walk this way.

Mar 93. (cd-s)(12"pic-d) **LIVIN' ON THE EDGE. / DON'T STOP / FLESH** [19] [18]
(cd-s) – ('A'side) / ('A'acoustic) / Can't stop messin'.

Apr 93. (cd)(c)(lp) **GET A GRIP** [2] [1]
– Intro / Eat the rich / Get a grip / Fever / Livin' on the edge / Flesh / Walk on down / Shut up and dance / Cryin' / Gotta love it / Crazy / Line up / Can't stop messin' / Amazing / Boogie man.

Jun 93. (10"colrd) **EAT THE RICH. / FEVER / HEAD FIRST** [34] [ ] Apr 93
(cd-s+=) – Livin' on the edge (demo).

Oct 93. (12"m) **CRYIN'. / WALK ON DOWN / I'M DOWN** [17] [12] Jul 93

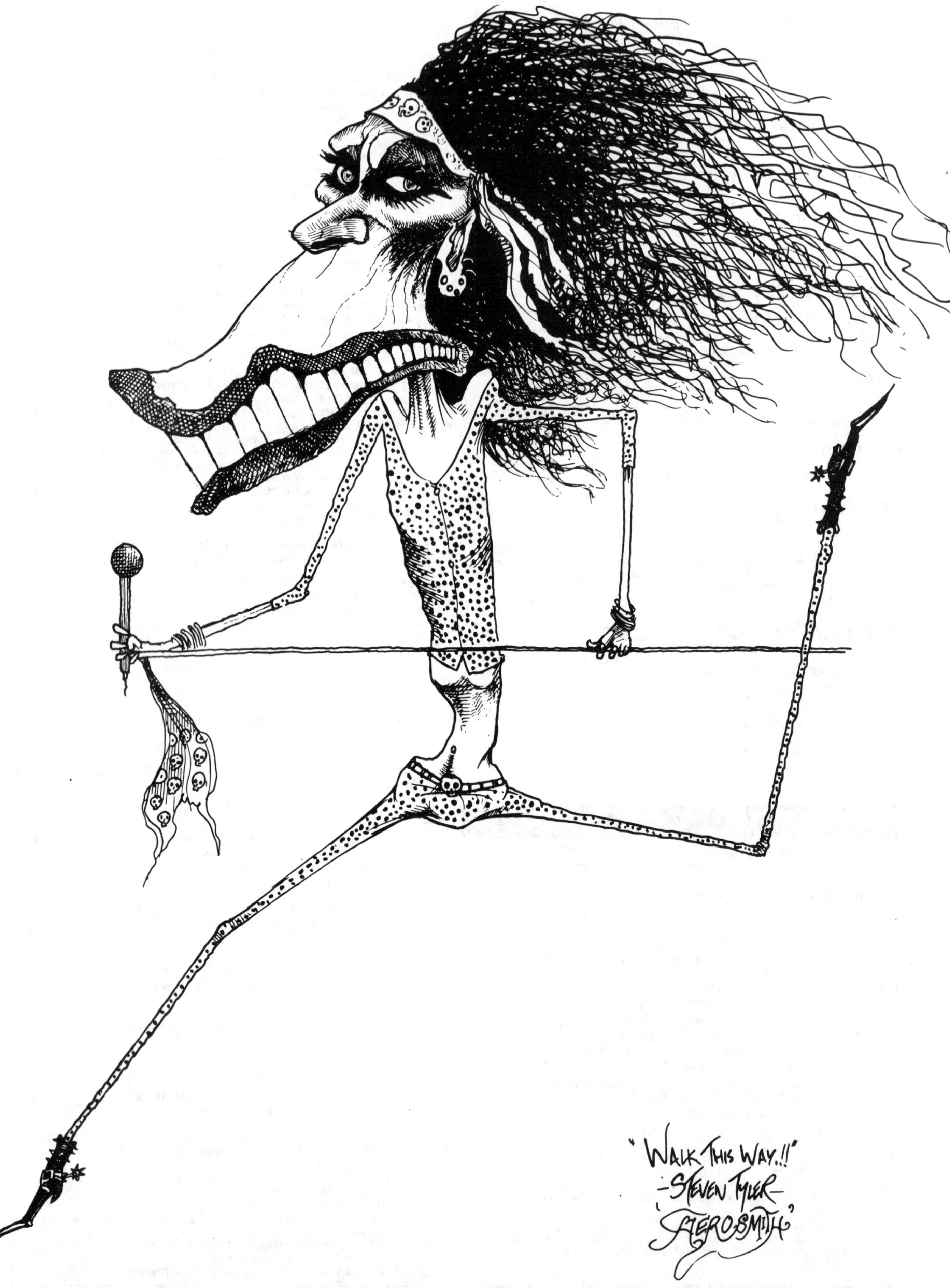
"WALK THIS WAY!!"
-STEVEN TYLER-
'AEROSMITH'

(cd-s+=) – My fist your face
(cd-s) – (first 2 tracks) / Love in an elevator / Janie's got a gun.
Dec 93. (12"m) **AMAZING. / GOTTA LOVE IT / AMAZING (acoustic)** [57] [24] Nov 93
(cd-s+=) – ('A'orchestral).
Jun 94. (7")(c-s) **SHUT UP AND DANCE. / DEUCES ARE WILD** [24] [ ]
(cd-s+=) – Crazy (orchestral) / Line up.
Oct 94. (c-s) **CRAZY. / BLIND MAN** [23] [17] Jun94
(cd-s+=) – Shut up and dance (live) / Blind man (mix).
Nov 94. (cd)(c)(d-lp) **BIG ONES** (compilation) [7] [6]
– Walk on water / Love in an elevator / Rag doll / What it takes / Dude (looks like a lady) / Janie's got a gun / Cryin' / Amazing / Blind man / Deuces are wild / The other side / Crazy / Eat the rich / Angel / Livin' on the edge / Dude (looks like a lady) (live).
Dec 94. (c-s)(cd-s) **BLIND MAN. / ?** [-] [49]

– compilations, others, etc. –

Jan 81. C.B.S./ US= Columbia; (lp)(c) **AEROSMITH'S GREATEST HITS** [ ] [53] Nov80
– Dream on / Same old song and dance / Sweet emotion / Walk this way / Remember (walking in the sand) / Back in the saddle / Draw the line / Kings and queens / Come together / Last child. *(US re-iss.Sep87, cd-Feb88 + UK pic-lp) (UK re-iss.+cd.Nov89) (re-iss.cd Dec93 on 'Columbia')*
Sep 86. C.B.S./ US= Columbia; (lp)(c) **CLASSICS LIVE!** (live 1977-1983) [ ] [84] Apr 86
– Train kept a-rollin' / Kings and queens / Sweet emotion / Dream on / Mama kin / Three mile smile / Reefer head woman / Lord of the thighs / Major Barbra. *(US cd-Nov87) (re-iss.cd Dec93 on 'Columbia')*
Aug 87. C.B.S./ Columbia; (lp)(c) **CLASSICS LIVE II (live)** [-] [ ]
– Back in the saddle / Walk this way / Movin' out / Draw the line / Same old song and dance / Last child / Let the music do the talking / Toys in the attic. *(UK-iss.+cd.Nov89 & Dec92 on 'Columbia')*
Aug 88. Columbia; (3"cd-s) **WALK THIS WAY / DREAM ON** [-] [ ]
Nov 89. C.B.S./ US= Columbia; (lp)(c)(cd) **GEMS** [ ] [ ] Dec 88
– Rats in the cellar / Lick and a promise / Chip away the stone / No surprize / Mama kin / Adam's apple / Nobody's fault / Round and round / Critical mass / Lord of the thighs / Jailbait / Train kept a rollin'.
(UK re-iss.Apr91 & Dec93 on 'Columbia')
Jun 88. Raw Power; (d-lp)(cd) **ANTHOLOGY** [ ] [-]
Dec 91. Columbia; (t-cd)(t-c) **PANDORA'S BOX** [ ] [45]
– When I needed you / Make it / Movin' out / One way street / On the road again / Mama kin / Same old song and dance / Train kept a-rollin' / Seasons of wither / Write me a letter / Dream on / Pandora's Box / Rattlesnake shake / Walkin' the dog / Lord of the thighs // Toys in the attic / Round and round / Krawhitham / You see me crying / Sweet emotion / No More no more / Walk this way / I wanna know why / Big ten inch record / Rats in the cellar / Last child / All your love / Soul saver / Nobody's fault / Lick and a promise / Adam's apple / Draw the line / Critical mass // Kings and queens / Milk cow blues / I live in Connecticut / Three mile smile / Let it slide / Cheese cake / Bone to bone (Coney Island white fish boy) / No surprize / Come together / Downtown Charlie / Sharpshooter / Shit house shuffle / South station blues / Riff & roll / Jailbait / Major Barbara / Chip away the stone / Helter skelter / Back in the saddle / Circle jerk.
Jun 94. Columbia; (cd) **PANDORA'S TOYS (BEST)** (compilation of '. . .BOX') [ ] [ ]
– Sweet emotion / Draw the line / Walk this way / Dream on / Train kept a rollin' / Mama kin / Nobody's fault / Seasons of wither / Big ten-inch record / All your love / Helter skelter / Chip away the stone.
Aug 94. Columbia; (c-s) **SWEET EMOTION / SUBWAY** [74] [ ] Dec 91
(cd-s+=) – Circle jerk.

JOE PERRY PROJECT

(while not an AEROSMITH member) with **RALPH NORMAN** – vocals / **DAVID HULL** – bass / **RONNIE STEWART** – drums

C.B.S. Columbia
Mar 80. (lp) **LET THE MUSIC DO THE TALKING** [ ] [47]
– Let the music do the talking / Conflict of interest / Discount dogs / Shooting star / Break song / Rockin' train / The mist is rising / Ready on the firing line / Life at a glance.
Aug 80. (7") **LET THE MUSIC DO THE TALKING. / BONE TO BONE** [ ] [ ]
— **CHARLIE FARREN** – vocals repl. NORMAN
Jun 81. (lp) **I'VE GOT THE ROCK'N'ROLLS AGAIN** [-] [ ]
– East Coast, West Coast / No substitute for arrogance / I've got the rock'n'rolls again / Buzz buzz / Soldier of fortune / T.V. police / Listen to the rock / Dirty little things / Play the game / South station blues.
1981. (7") **BUZZ BUZZ. / EAST COAST, WEST COAST** [-] [ ]
— **PERRY** new line-up **MARK BELL** – vocals / **DANNY HARGROVE** – bass / **JOE PET** – drums

M.C.A. M.C.A.
Jan 84. (lp)(c) **ONCE A ROCKER, ALWAYS A ROCKER** [ ] [ ]
– Once a rocker, always a rocker / Black velvet pants / Woman in chains / Guns west / Crossfire / King of the kings / Never wanna stop / Adrianna / Get it on (bang-a-gong) / Walk with me Sally.

WHITFORD / ST.HOLMES

BRAD WHITFORD – guitar, vocals / **ST.HOLMES** – guitar (ex-TED NUGENT) also **DAVID HEWITT** – bass / **STEVE PACE** – drums

not issued Columbia
1981. (7") **SHY AWAY. / MYSTERY GIRL** [-] [ ]
1981. (lp) **WHITFORD / ST.HOLMES** [-] [ ]
– I need love / Whiskey woman / Hold on / Sharp shouter / Every morning / Action / Shy away / Does it really matter / Spanish box / Mystery girl.

AFGHAN WHIGS

Formed: Denver, Colorado, USA . . .Oct'86, by DULLI and McCOLLUM who met in a prison. They moved to Cincinatti, Ohio, after signing for Seattle based indie label 'Sub Pop' in 1989. Now live in California after signing for 'Elektra' in the US and releasing minor 1993 hit album 'GENTLEMEN'. • **Style:** Soulful grunge rock similar to DINOSAUR JR. • **Songwriters:** DULLI, some McCOLLUM except; covers by Diana Ross / Al Green / BAND OF GOLD (Freda Payne) / I KEEP COMING BACK (Austell-Graham).

Recommended: CONGREGATION (*6) / GENTLEMEN (*7)

GREG DULLI – vocals, guitar / **RICK McCOLLUM** – guitar / **JOHN CURREY** – bass / **STEVE EARLE** – drums

not issued Ultrasuede
Oct 88. (lp) **BIG TOP HALLOWEEN** [-] [ ]
– Here comes Jesus / In my town / Priscilla's wedding day / Push / Scream / But listen / Big top Halloween / Life in a day / Sammy / Doughball / Back o' the line / Greek is extra.

Sub Pop Sub Pop
Aug 89. (7") **I AM THE STICKS. / WHITE TRASH PARTY** [ ] [ ]
Apr 90. (cd)(c)(lp)(orange-lp) **UP IN IT** [ ] [ ]
– Retarded / White trash party / Hated / Southpaw / Amphetamines and coffee / Now can we begin / You my flower / Son of the south / I know your secret. (cd/c+=) I am the sticks. *(re-iss.Aug90 on 'Glitterhouse')*
Oct 90. (7")(7"red) **SISTER BROTHER. / HEY CUZ** [ ] [ ]
Dec 90. (12"ep) **THE RETARD EP** [ ] [ ]
– Retarded / Sister brother / Hey cuz / Turning in two. *(re-iss.+cd-ep May93;)*
Jan 92. (cd)(c)(lp) **CONGREGATION** [ ] [ ]
– Her against me / I'm her slave / Turn on the water / Conjure me / Kiss the floor / Congregation / This is my confession / Dedicate it / The temple / Let me lie to you / Tonight.
Jan 92. (12"ep) **TURN ON THE WATER. / MILES IZ DEAD / DELTA KONG** [ ] [ ]
(cd-ep+=) – Chalk outline.
May 92. (7"white)(7"lavender) **CONJURE ME. / MY WORLD IS EMPTY WITHOUT YOU** [ ] [ ]
(12"+=)(cd-s+=) – My flower.
Oct 92. (7"ep) **UPTOWN AVONDALE EP: BAND OF GOLD. / COME SEE ABOUT ME** [ ] [ ]
(12"+=) – True love travels on a gravel road / Beware.
(cd-s++=) – Rebirth of the cool.
(above release could have been issued earlier in US, early 1990)

Blast First Elektra
Sep 93. (7") **GENTLEMEN. / MR.SUPERLOVE** [ ] [ ]
(12"+=)(cd-s+=) – The dark end of the street.
Oct 93. (cd)(c)(lp) **GENTLEMEN** [58] [ ]
– If I were going / Gentlemen / Be sweet / Debonair / When we two parted / Fountain and fairfax / What jail is like / My curse / Now you know / I keep coming back / Brother Woodrow – Closing prayer. (lp w /free 7"ep) – ROT. / TONIGHT
— guests on the album: **HAROLD CHICHESTER** – keyboards / **BARB HUNTER** – cello / **JODY STEPHENS** – b. vocals / **MARCY MAYS** – vocals
Feb 94. (7"ep)(12"ep)(cd-ep) **BROKEN PROMISES EP** [ ] [ ]
– Debonair / My curse / Little girl blue / Ready.
(cd-s) – ('A'side) / Rot / I keep coming back / Tonight.
— Mar'94, 'MR.SUPERLOVE' was iss. on B-side of ASS PONY's single on 'Monocat'.

A FLOCK OF SEAGULLS

Formed: Liverpool, England ... 1980 by hairdresser MIKE and brother ALI SCORE. Recorded one-off 45 for Bill Nelson's 'Cocteau' label, before moving to London and signing to CBS subsidiary 'Jive'. Found initial success in America where their videos were played on newly formed MTV. • **Style:** New-age/futurist techno rock-pop which featured the cockatoo hair-do style of MIKE. **Songwriters:** MIKE wrote most of material.

Recommended: THE BEST OF A FLOCK OF SEAGULLS (*6)

MIKE SCORE (b. 5 Nov'57) – vocals, keyboards / **PAUL REYNOLDS** (b. 4 Aug'62) – guitar / **FRANK MAUDSLEY** (b.10 Nov'59) – bass / **ALI SCORE** – drums

Cocteau not issued
Jul 81. (7") **IT'S NOT ME TALKING. / FACTORY MUSIC** [ ] [-]
(re-iss.Mar83)

Jive Jive
Sep 81. (7")(12") **TELECOMMUNICATION. / INTRO** [ ] [ ]
Nov 81. (7") **MODERN LOVE IS AUTOMATIC. / WINDOWS** [ ] [ ]
(d7"+=) – You can run / D.N.A.
Jan 82. (7")(12") **TELECOMMUNICATION. / MODERN LOVE IS AUTOMATIC** [ ] [ ]
Mar 82. (7")(7"pic-d) **I RAN. / PICK ME UP** [43] [9] Jun 82
(12"+=) – Messages.
Apr 82. (lp)(c) **A FLOCK OF SEAGULLS** [32] [10]
– Modern love is automatic / Messages / I ran / Space age love song / You can run / Telecommunication / Standing in the doorway / Don't ask me / D.N.A. / Tokyo / Man made. *(re-iss.Jun86) (pic-lp.'83)*
May 82. (7")(12")(7"pic-d) **SPACE AGE LOVE SONG. / WINDOWS** [34] [30] Nov 82
Oct 82. (7")(12") **WISHING (I HAD A PHOTOGRAPH OF YOU). / COMMITTED** [10] [26] Apr 83
Apr 83. (7")(12")(7"pic-d) **NIGHTMARES. / ROSEN MONTAG** [53] [ ]
(12"+=) – Last flight.
May 83. (lp)(pic-lp)(c) **LISTEN** [16] [16]
– Nightmares / Wishing (I had a photograph of you) / The fall / Tanglimara / Transfer affection / (It's not me) Talking / What am I supposed to do / Electrics / The traveller /

Over the border / 2:30.

Jun 83. (7")(12")(7"pic-d) **TRANSFER AFFECTION. / I RAN (live)** 38

Aug 83. (7")(12") **(IT'S NOT ME) TALKING. / TANGLIMARA**

Jun 84. (7")(12")(7"pic-d) **THE MORE YOU LIVE, THE MORE YOU LOVE. / LOST CONTROL** 26 56

Aug 84. (lp)(c)(cd) **THE STORY OF A YOUNG HEART** 30 66
– The story of a young heart / Never again (the dancer) / The more you live, the more you love / European (I wish I was) / Remember David / Over my head / Heart of steel / The end / Suicide day.

Sep 84. (7") **NEVER AGAIN (THE DANCER). / LIVING IN HEAVEN**
(12"+=) – The more you live, the more you love.

—— Now basically a trio plus **GARY STEADMAN** – guitar (ex-CLASSIX NOUVEAUX) repl. REYNOLDS

Oct 85. (7") **WHO'S THAT GIRL (SHE'S GOT IT). / WISHING (I HAD A PHOTOGRAPH OF YOU** 66
(12"+=) – (Hits medley).

Feb 86. (7") **HEARTBEAT LIKE A DRUM. / ('A'instrumental)**
(12"+=) – ('A'version).

Apr 86. (lp)(c) **DREAM COME TRUE**
– Better & better / Heartbeat like a drum / Who's that girl (she's got it) / Hot tonight / Cry like a baby / Say so much / Love on your knees / How could you ever leave me / Whole lot of loving.

—— (late 1986) **MIKE SCORE** brought in Philadelphian musicians to replace others. **STEADMAN** joined The ROYTERS.

– compilations, others, etc. –

Jul 85. Jive; (10x7"box)(10x12"box) **COLLECTION OF TEN SINGLES**

Oct 86. Jive; (lp)(c) **THE BEST OF A FLOCK OF SEAGULLS**
– I ran / Space age love song / Telecommunication / The more you live, the more you love / Nightmares / Wishing (I had a photograph of you) / It's not me talking / Transfer affection / Who's that girl (she's got it) / D.N.A. *(re-iss.Mar88 /Nov89 +cd /Jun91 +cd)* (+=) – Wishing (extended) / +1.

Apr 89. Old Gold; (7") **WISHING (IF I HAD A PHOTOGRAPH OF YOU) / THE MORE YOU LIVE, THE MORE YOU LOVE** -

Sep 93. Elite; (cd)(c) **TELECOMMUNICATIONS** -
(re-iss.May95)

Mar 95. Emporio; (cd)(c) **20 CLASSICS OF THE 80'S** -

A-HA

Formed: Manglerud, Oslo, Norway. In 1979 PAL and MAGS had been BRIDGES which evolved out of (Doors influenced) SPIDER EMPIRE. They met MORTEN in 1981, changed name to A-HA and moved to London early '83. The trio found manager Terry Slater and signed to 'Warners' end of '83. Failure of debut 'TAKE ON ME' in 1984 nearly split them up, until a Steve Barron $100,000 animated video received exposure on MTV and the rest is history. (see below) • **Style:** Highly talented pin-ups who can range between pop/rock to AOR electronic. • **Songwriters:** PAL and MAGS pen most, except CRYING IN THE RAIN (Everly Brothers) / • **Trivia:** THE LIVING DAYLIGHTS was co-written by PAL and John Barry for the "Bond" 1987 film.

Recommended: HEADLINES & DEADLINES / THE HITS OF A-HA (*6)

BRIDGES

PAL WAAKTAAR (b. 6 Sep'61, Oslo) – guitar, vocals / **MAGNE "MAGS" FURUHOLMEN** (b. 1 Nov'62, Oslo) – keyboards plus / **VIGGO BONDI** – bass / **OYSTEIN JEVANORD** – drums

Vakenatt / not issued

Oct 80. (lp) **FAKKELTOG** (means TORCHLIGHT PROCESSION) - - Norway

A-HA

PAL and **MAGS** (let go **OYSTEIN and VIGGO;** former still on session) introduced **MORTEN HARKET** (b.14 Sep'59, Kongsberg, Norway) – vocals

Warners / Warners

Oct 84. (7") **TAKE ON ME. / AND YOU TELL ME**
(12"+=) – Stop and make your mind up.

May 85. (7")(12") **TAKE ON ME. / LOVE IS REASON**
(12"+=) – ('A'extended).

Sep 85. *(re-iss. of above 7"+12")* 2 1 Jul 85

Oct 85. (lp)(c)(cd) **HUNTING HIGH AND LOW** 2 15
– Take on me / Train of thought / Hunting high and low / The blue sky / Living a boy's adventure tale / The Sun always shines on TV / And you tell me / Love is reason / Dream myself alive / Here I stand and face the rain.

Nov 85. (7")(7"sha-pic-d) **THE SUN ALWAYS SHINES ON TV. / DRIFTWOOD** 1 20
(12"+=) – ('A'instrumental).

Mar 86. (7")(12")(7"sha-pic-d) **TRAIN OF THOUGHT (remix). / AND YOU TELL ME** 8

May 86. (7")(12")(7"pic-d) **HUNTING HIGH AND LOW (remix). / THE BLUE SKY (demo)** 5

Sep 86. (7")(12") **I'VE BEEN LOSING YOU. / THIS ALONE IS LOVE** 8

Oct 86. (lp)(c)(cd) **SCOUNDREL DAYS** 2 74
– Scoundrel days / THe swing of things / I've been losing you / October / Manhattan skyline / Cry wolf / Looking for the whales / The weight of the wind / Maybe maybe / Soft rains of April. *(re-iss.cd Feb95)*

Nov 86. (7") **CRY WOLF. / MAYBE MAYBE** 7 50 Jan 87
(12"+=)(12"pic-d+=) – ('A'extended).

Feb 87. (7") **MANHATTAN SKYLINE. / WE'RE LOOKING FOR THE WHALES (live)** 13
(12"+=)(12"pic-d+=) – ('A'extended remix).

Jul 87. (7") **THE LIVING DAYLIGHTS. / ('A'instrumental)** 5
(12"+=)(12"pic-d+=) – ('A'extended).

Apr 88. (7") **STAY ON THESE ROADS. / SOFT RAINS OF APRIL (mix)** 5
(12"+=)(12"pic-d) – ('A'extended).
(3"cd-s++=) – Cry wolf / Take on me.

Apr 88. (lp)(c)(cd)(pic-lp) **STAY ON THESE ROADS** 2
– The blood that moves the body / Touchy! / This alone is love / Hurry home / The living daylights / There's never a forever thing / Out of blue comes green / You are the one / You'll end up crying / Stay on these roads. *(re-iss.cd Feb95)*

May 88. (7") **THE BLOOD THAT MOVES THE BODY. / THERE'S NEVER A FOREVER THING** 25
(12"+=)(12"pic-d+=) – ('A'extended).
(3"cd-s++=) – The living daylights.

Aug 88. (7") **TOUCHY!. / HURRY HOME** 11
(12"+=) – Touchy! (go-go mix).
(3"cd-s++=) – Hunting high and low.

Nov 88. (7") **YOU ARE THE ONE (remix). / OUT OF BLUE COMES GREEN** 13
(12"+=)(cd-s+=)(12"pic-d+=) – ('A'instrumental).

Oct 90. (7")(c-s) **CRYING IN THE RAIN. / (SEEMINGLY) NON-STOP JULY** 13
(12"+=)(cd-s+=) – Cry wolf.

Oct 90. (cd)(c)(lp) **EAST OF THE SUN, WEST OF THE MOON** 12
– Crying in the rain / Early morning / I call your name / Slender frame / East of the sun / Sycamore leaves / Waiting for her / Cold river / The way we talk / Rolling thunder / (Seemingly) Non-stop July.

Dec 90. (7") **I CALL YOUR NAME. / THE WAY WE TALK** 44
(12"+=)(cd-s+=) – The blood that moves the body.
(d7"+=) – Hunting high and low / The Sun always shines on TV.

Feb 91. (7")(c-s) **EARLY MORNING. / EAST OF THE SUN**
(12"+=)(cd-s+=) – Train of thought.

Oct 91. (7")(c-s) **MOVE TO MEMPHIS. / CRYING IN THE RAIN (live)** 47
(cd-s+=) – Early morning (live) / Manhattan skyline (live).
(12") – ('A'side) / I've been losing you (live) / East of the sun (live) / (Seemingly) Non-stop July (live).

Nov 91. (cd)(c)(lp) **HEADLINES & DEADLINES, THE HITS OF A-HA** (compilation) 12
– Take on me / Cry wolf / Touchy / You are the one / Manhattan skyline / The blood that moves the body / Hunting high and low / Move to Memphis / I've been losing you / The living daylights / Crying in the rain / I call your name / Stay on these roads / The Sun always shines on TV. (cd/c+=) – Early morning / Train of thought.

Mar 92. (7") **THE BLOOD THAT MOVES THE BODY (The Gun mix). / ('A' Two-Time Gun Mix)**
(12"+=)(cd-s+=) – ('A' mixes).

—— added **J.B. BOGEBERG** – bass / **PER HILLESTAD** – drums

May 93. (7")(c-s) **DARK IS THE NIGHT. / ANGEL IN THE SNOW** 19
(cd-s+=) – I've been losing you (live) / Cry wolf (live).
(cd-s) – ('A'side) / The Sun always shines on T.V. / Hunting high and low / Crying in the rain.

Jun 93. (cd)(c)(lp) **MEMORIAL BEACH** 17
– Dark Is The Night / Move To Memphis / Cold As Stone / Angel In The Snow / Locust / Lie Down In Darkness / How Sweet It Was / Lamb To The Slaughter / Between Your Mama And Yourself / Memorial Beach

Sep 93. (7") **ANGEL. / I CALL YOUR NAME (live)** 41
(cd-s+=) – The Sun always shines on TV (live) / Early morning (live).

Mar 94. (7")(c-s)(cd-s) **SHAPES THAT GO TOGETHER. / COLD AS STONE (remix)** 27
(cd-s) – ('A'side) / Touchy / Slender frame / Rolling thunder (all live).

MORTEN HARKET

WEA / WEA

Aug 95. (c-s)(cd-s) **A KIND OF CHRISTMAS CARD / A CHANGE IS GONNA COME / LAY ME DOWN TONIGHT** 53
(re-iss.Dec95)

Sep 95. (cd)(c) **WILD SEED**
– A kind of Christmas card / Spanish steps / Half in love half in hate / Brodsky tune / Wild seed / Los Angeles / East Tinor / Lay me down tonight / Tell me what you see / Stay / Lord / Ready to go home.

A HOUSE

Formed: Dublin, Ireland ... 1985 by DAVE COUSE, etc (see below). They soon flitted across the border to Belfast, having just supported The WATERBOYS. After releases on 'RIP', they signed in '87 to WEA subsidiary 'Blanco Y Negro'. • **Style:** Alternative rock act with pop sensibility and using many directions. Hard to pigeonhole. • **Songwriters:** Group or COUSE, except CHILDREN OF THE REVOLUTION (T.Rex) / I FEEL LOVE (Donna Summer) / LOVE SONG (Damned).

Recommended: I AM THE GREATEST (*8)

DAVE COUSE – vocals, acoustic guitar / **FEARGAL BUNBURY** – guitar / **MARTIN HEALY** – bass / **DERMOT WYLIE** – drums

R.I.P. / not issued

Mar 87. (7") **KICK ME AGAIN JESUS. / WHEN I CHANGE** -
(12"+=) – I want you.

Jun 87. (7")(12") **SNOWBALL DOWN. / Y.O.U.** -

Aug 87. (12"ep) **KISS ME AGAIN JESUS / I WANT YOU / WHEN I CHANGE. / SNOWBALL DOWN / Y.O.U.** -

Blanco Y Negro / Warners

Nov 87. (7") **HEART HAPPY. / PRETTY SOMETHING**

(12"+=) – Oh God I hurt inside.
Jun 88. (7") **CALL ME BLUE. / FREAK OUT** [ ] [ ]
(12"+=) – Michael / Plane or pearl. *(re-iss.Mar89)*
Sep 88. (7") **I'LL ALWAYS BE GRATEFUL. / FUNNY MAN** [ ] [ ]
(12"+=) – This child is yours not mine / There's only one thing wrong with the perfect.
Oct 88. (lp)(c)(cd) **ON OUR BIG FAT MERRY-GO-ROUND** [ ] [ ]
– Call me blue / I'll always be grateful / Don't ever think you're different / Love of the eighties / Love quarry / Stone the crows / I want to kill something / My little greenhouse / That's not the truth / Violent love / Clump of trees. (cd+=) – Make hay when the sun shines.
Apr 90. (7") **I THINK I'M GOING MAD. / I WANT TOO MUCH** [ ] [ ]
(12"+=)(cd-s+=) – Why must we argue.
May 90. (cd)(c)(lp) **I WANT TOO MUCH** [ ] [ ]
– I want too much / Talking / The patron saint of mediocrity / Shivers up my spine / Marry me / I give you now / Now that I'm sick / I think I'm going mad / Bring down the beast / Manstrong / Keep the homefires burning / You'll cry when I die / Small talk.

Setanta Capitol?

Nov 90. (12"ep)(cd-ep) **DOODLE EP** [ ] [ ]
– The last to know / Bugaboo / A minute of your time / Sometimes I feel.
Sep 91. (12"ep) **BINGO SPINSTER EP** [ ] [ ]
– Spinster / Easy way out / Senses / There is no time.
(c-ep)(cd-ep) – (1st track) / Angeline / I want to be allowed to love you / I'll make it up to you.
Oct 91. (cd)(c)(lp) **I AM THE GREATEST** [ ] [ ]
– I don't care / You're too young / Endless art / Blind faith / Cotton pickers / How strong is love / When I first saw you / I am afraid / Victor / Take it easy on me / Creatures of craze / Slipping away / I wanted to die / I lied / Live life dead die / I am the greatest. *(re-iss.cd Aug92)*
Jan 92. (7") **YOU'RE TOO YOUNG. / TAKE IT EASY ON ME** [ ] [ ]
(12"ep+=) ZOP EP – Serious lovin' / When I first saw you (long).
(cd-ep+=) ZOP EP – Baby, you're too much / Our love is good enough.
Jun 92. (7") **ENDLESS ART. / MORE ENDLESS ART** [46] [ ]
(12"+=)(cd-s+=) – Freak show / Charity. *(re-iss.from Nov91)*
Aug 92. (7")(c-s) **TAKE IT EASY ON ME. / I LOVE YOU** [55] [ ]
(12"+=)(cd-s+=) – Everything's wrong. (w /free flexi) **Force fed.**
Sep 92. (7"mail-order) **WHEN I FIRST SAW YOU (live). / I WANT TO KILL SOMETHING / SECOND WIND** [-] [-]
Jun 94. (7")(c-s) **WHY ME. / I HOPE I'M WRONG / MY HEART BLEEDS FOR YOU** [52] [ ]
(10") – (first 2 tracks) / Angeline / You think you know.
(cd-s) – (first & third tracks) / I will never forget you / This hurts me.
Jul 94. (cd)(c)(lp) **WIDE EYED AND IGNORANT** [ ] [ ]
– Intro / Here comes the good times / She keeps me humble / Why me / Make me proud / Everything I am / Curious / These things / The comedy is over / The strong & the silent / Big talk / Deadhead / I want to be allowed to love you.
Sep 94. (7")(c-s) **HERE COME THE GOOD TIMES. / CHILDREN OF THE REVOLUTION / I FEEL LOVE** [37] [ ]
(cd-s+=) – Love song.
(10")(cd-s) – ('A'side) / Everybody needs something / Soon / All I need.

AIRFORCE (see under ⇒ BAKER, Ginger)

Jan AKKERMAN (see under ⇒ FOCUS)

ALARM

Formed: Rhyl, Wales . . . 1977 as punk band The TOILETS. They became "mod" outfit "17" before the same quartet changed again to The ALARM in 1981. After one indie 45 on 'White Cross' label, they signed to Miles Copeland's US based 'I.R.S.' in summer '82. Just over a year later, they entered the UK Top 20, not for the last time, with '68 GUNS'. • **Style:** Inspired by a mixture of The CLASH and U2, although politics differ. Their anthem style basic rock hds its raw and smooth edges plastered into folk and war lyrics. • **Songwriters:** McDONALD / PETERS or SHARP / TWIST, except; THE BELLS OF RHYMNEY (Pete Seeger) / KNOCKIN' ON HEAVEN'S DOOR (Bob Dylan) / WORKING CLASS HERO + HAPPY XMAS (WAR IS OVER) (John Lennon) / ROCKIN' IN THE FREE WORLD (Neil Young). • **Trivia:** Sang in Welsh on single 'A NEW SOUTH WALES (HWYLIO DROS Y MOR)'.

Recommended: STANDARDS (*7).

MIKE PETERS (b.25 Jan'59) – vocals, guitar / **DAVE SHARP** (b.28 Jan'59) – guitar / **EDDIE McDONALD** (b. 1 Nov'59) – bass / **NIGEL TWIST** (b. 18 Jul'58) – drums

17

Vendetta not issued

Mar 80. (7") **DON'T LET GO. / BANK HOLIDAY WEEKEND** [ ] [-]

The ALARM

White Cross not issued

Sep 81. (7") **UNSAFE BUILDINGS. / UP FOR MURDER** [ ] [-]

I.R.S. I.R.S.

Oct 82. (7"m) **MARCHING ON. / ACROSS THE BORDER / LIE OF THE LAND** [ ] [-]
Apr 83. (7") **THE STAND. / THIRD LIGHT** [ ] [-]
(12"+=) – ('A'side) / For freedom / Reason 41.
Jun 83. (7") **THE STAND. / REASON 41** [-] [ ]
Jul 83. (m-lp) **THE ALARM** [-] [ ]
– Across the border / For freedom / Marching on / Lie of the land / The stand
Sep 83. (7")(12") **68 GUNS. / (part 2)** [17] [-]
(12"+=) – Thoughts of a young man.
Nov 83. (7") **68 GUNS. / PAVILLION STEPS** [-] [ ]
Jan 84. (7") **WHERE WERE YOU HIDING WHEN THE STORM BROKE?. / PAVILLION STEPS** [22] [ ]
(12"+=) – What kind of Hell.
Feb 84. (lp)(c) **DECLARATION** [6] [50]
– Declaration / Marching on / Where were you hiding when the storm broke? / Third light / 68 guns / We are the light / Shout to the Devil / Blaze of glory / Tell me / The deceiver / The stand (prophecy) / Howling wind. *(cd-iss.Oct88)*
Mar 84. (7")(7"clear) **THE DECEIVER. / REASON 41** [51] [ ]
(12"+=) – Second generation. (US; b-side)
(ltd.d7"+=) – Lie of the land / Legal matter.
Oct 84. (7") **THE CHANT HAS JUST BEGUN. / THE BELLS OF RHYMNEY** [48] [ ]
(12"+=) – The stand (extended).
Feb 85. (7")(12") **ABSOLUTE REALITY. / BLAZE OF GLORY** [35] [ ]
(ltd.d7"+=) – Room at the top / Reason 36.
Sep 85. (7") **STRENGTH. / MAJORITY** [40] [61]
(12"+=) – ('A'side) / Absolute reality (acoustic).
Oct 85. (lp)(c)(cd) **STRENGTH** [18] [39]
– Knife edge / Strength / awn chorus / Spirit of '76 / The day the ravens left the tower / Deeside / Father to son / Only the thunder / Walk forever by my side. *(also pic-lp) (cd-iss.Apr87) (re-cd.Jan90 on 'M.C.A.')*
Jan 86. (7")(12") **SPIRIT OF '76. / WHERE WERE YOU HIDING WHEN THE STORM BROKE? (live)** [22] [ ]
(12"+=) – Deeside (live).
(d12"++=) – Knockin' on Heaven's door (live) / 68 guns (live).
Apr 86. (7")(7"sha-pic-d) **KNIFE EDGE (edit). / CAROLINE ISENBERG** [43] [ ]
(d7"+=)(12"+=) – Howling wind / Unbreak the promise.
Sep 87. (7") **RAIN IN THE SUMMERTIME. / ROSE BEYOND THE WALL** [18] [71]
(12"+=) – The bells of Rhymney / Time to believe.
(extra 12") – ('A'-Through the haze mix) / ('A'-Lightning mix)
Nov 87. (lp)(c)(cd) **EYE OF THE HURRICANE** [23] [77]
– Rain in the summertime / Newtown Jericho / Hallowed ground / One step closer to home / Shelter / Rescue me / Permanence in change / Presence of love / Only love can set me free / Eye of the hurricane. *(re-cd.May90 on 'M.C.A.')*
Nov 87. (7")(7"blue) **RESCUE ME. / MY LAND YOUR LAND** [48] [ ]
(12"+=) – The Hurricane sessions.
Feb 88. (7")(7"pic-d) **PRESENCE OF LOVE. / KNIFE EDGE (live)** [44] [77]
(12"+=) – This train is bound for glory (live) / Dawn chorus (live).
(cd-s++=) – Rain in the summertime (live).
Oct 88. (m-lp)(c)(cd) **ELECTRIC FOLKLORE LIVE (live)** [62] [ ]
– Rescue me / Rain in the summertime / Permanence in change / Strength / Spirit pf '76 / Blaze of glory.
Sep 89. (7") **SOLD ME DOWN THE RIVER. / GWETHOCH FI I YR AFON** [43] [50]
(10"+=) – Firing line.
(12"+=)(cd-s+=) – Corridors of power.
Sep 89. (lp)(c)(cd) **CHANGE** [13] [75]
– Rivers to cross / A new South Wales / Sold me down the river / The rock / Devolution / Workin' man blues / Love don't come easy / Hard land / Change II / No frontiers / Scarlet / Where a town once stood / Prison without prison bars.
Oct 89. (7")(12") **A NEW SOUTH WALES. / THE ROCK (long version)** [31] [ ]
(cd-s+=) – Working class hero.
(10"white++=) – Rivers to cross (new version).
(7" also in Welsh) – HWYLIO DROS Y MOR. / Y GRAIG
Jan 90. (7") **LOVE DON'T COME EASY. / CROESI'R AFON** [48] [ ]
(12"+=)(cd-s+=) – No frontiers.
(10"pic-d+=) – Change II.
Oct 90. (7")(12") **UNSAFE BUILDINGS (1990). / UP FOR MURDER (1990)** [54] [ ]
(c-s+=)(cd-s+=) – Unsafe Buildings (original mix).
Nov 90. I.R.S.; (cd)(c)(lp) **STANDARDS** [47] [ ]
– The road / Unsafe buildings / The stand / 68 guns / Where were you hiding when the storm broke? / Absolute reality / Strength / Spirit of '76 / Rain in the summertime / Rescue me / Sold me down the river / A new south Wales / Happy Xmas (war is over). (cd/c+=) – Marching on / Blaze of glory.
Apr 91. (7") **RAW. / CHANGE 1** [51] [ ]
(12"+=)(cd-s+=) – Devolution / Workin' man's blues.
Apr 91. (cd)(c)(lp) **RAW** [33] [ ]
– Raw / Rockin' in the free world / God save somebody / Moments in time / Hell or high water / Lead me through the darkness / The wind blows away my words / Let the river run its course / Save your crying / Wonderful world.

—— (Jul '91) MIKE PETERS went solo

– compilations, others, etc. –

Apr 88. I.R.S.; (cd-ep) **COMPACT HITS** [ ] [-]
– 68 guns / Blaze of glory / Shout to the Devil / Where were you hiding when the storm broke?.

MIKE PETERS

Crai not issued

Jan 94. (12"ep)(c-ep)(cd-ep) **BACK INTO THE SYSTEM. / 21st CENTURY (demo) / A NEW CHAPTER** [ ] [-]
(cd-s+=) – (Welsh language version).
Apr 94. (12"ep)(cd-ep) **IT JUST DON'T GET ANY BETTER THAN THIS. / DEVIL'S WORLD / WHITE NOISE** [ ] [-]
Oct 94. (cd)(c)(d-lp) **BREATHE** [ ] [-]
– Poetic justice / All I wanted / If I can't have you / Breathe / Love is a revolution / Who's gonna make the piece / Spiritual / What the world can't give me / Levis & bibles / Beautiful thing / Into the 21st century / This is war / The message / Back into the system / It just don't get any better than this / Train a comin' / A new chapter

(reprise). *(re-iss.Jan95 as Welsh language 'AER')*

ALICE COOPER (see under ⇒ COOPER, Alice)

ALICE IN CHAINS

Formed: Seattle, Washington, USA . . . 1990 by (see below). Crashed into US chart that year, when debut 'FACELIFT' made Top 50. • **Style:** Heavy grunge merchants, similar to NIRVANA or SOUNDGARDEN. • **Songwriters:** CANTRELL or STALEY or both.

Recommended: DIRT (*5)

LAYNE STALEY – vocals / **JERRY CANTRELL** – guitar, vocals / **MICHAEL STARR** – bass (ex-SADO) / **SEAN KINNEY** – drums, percussion, megaphone

Columbia Columbia

Sep 91. (cd)(c)(lp) **FACELIFT** [ ] [42] Mar 91
– We die young / Man in the box / Love, hate, love / It ain't like that / I can't remember / Confusion / Son of sorrow / Bleed the freak / I know somethin' ('bout you) / Put you down / Sunshine / Real thing.

1991. (c-ep)(cd-ep) **MAN IN THE BOX / SEA OF SORROW / BLEED THE FREAK / SUNSHINE** [-] [ ]

Feb 92. (12"ep)(cd-ep) **SAP** [ ] [ ]
– Brother / Got me wrong / Right turn / Am I inside / Love song.

— Splintered after above, a few became MY SISTER'S MACHINE, and released album in May'92 'DIVA' on 'Caroline'.

Oct 92. (cd)(c)(lp) **DIRT** [42] [6]
– Them bones / Dam that river / Rain when I die / Down in a hole / Sickman / Rooster / Junkhead / Dirt / God smack / Hate to feel / Angry chair / Would?

Jan 93. (7") **WOULD?. / MAN IN THE BOX** [19] [ ]
(12"green+=)(pic-cd-s+=) – Brother / Right Turn

Mar 93. (7") **THEM BONES. / WE DIE YOUNG** [26] [ ]
(cd-s+=) – Got me wrong / Am I inside

May 93. (7") **ANGRY CHAIR. / I KNOW SOMETHIN' ('BOUT YOU)** [33] [ ]
(12"+=) – Bleed the freak / It ain't like that
(cd-s+=) – It ain't like that / Hate to feel

Oct 93. (7")(7"pic-d) **DOWN IN A HOLE. / ROOSTER** [36] [ ]
(12"+=) – A little bitter. / Love hate love.
(cd-s+=) – What the hell I have I. ('A' radio edit)

Jan 94. (cd)(c)(lp) **JAR OF FLIES / SAP** [4] [1]
– Rotten apple / Nutshell / I stay away / No excuses / Whale & wasp / Don't follow / Swing on this. (US-version w /out 'SAP')

Oct 95. (7")(c-s) **GRIND. / NUTSHELL** [23] [ ]
(cd-s+=) – So close / Love, hate, love.

Nov 95. (cd)(c)(d-lp) **ALICE IN CHAINS** [37] [1]
– Grind / Brush away / Sludge factory / Heaven beside you / Head creeps / Again / Shame in you / God a.m. / So close / Nothin' song / Frogs / Good night (by TED LEWIS & HIS ORCHESTRA).

MAD SEASON

— were originally called GACY BUNCH with **LAYNE STALEY** – vocals / **MIKE McCREADY** – guitar (of PEARL JAM) / **BARRETT MARTIN** – drums (of SCREAMING TREES)

Columbia Columbia

Mar 95. (cd)(c) **ABOVE** [41] [24]
– Wake up / X-ray mind / River of deceit / I'm above / Artificial red / Lifeless dead / I don't know anything / Long gone day / November hotel / All alone.

ALL ABOUT EVE

Formed: London, England . . . 1985 by music journalist JULIANNE REGAN and ex-AEMOTTI CRII member TIM BRICHENO. Named after a 1950 Bette Davis film, they released 4 indie hits on own 'Eden' records, before landing contract with 'Mercury' mid'87. Their debut for the label (a re-mix of 'IN THE CLOUDS') hit the UK Top 50, and paved the way for late 80's chart status. • **Style:** Progressive "acid-folk" to "hippy-goth" influenced by early 70's acoustic LED ZEPPELIN or even CURVED AIR for imagary & mysticism. • **Songwriters:** REGAN – lyrics / BRICHENO – music, until his departure, then group compositions. Covered; THE WITCHES' PROMISE (Jethro Tull)? • **Trivia:** '87 single OUR SUMMER was produced by WAYNE HUSSEY and SIMON HINKLER (of The MISSION). Friendship abound, JULIANNE returned favour by guesting on their GOD'S OWN MEDICINE (lp). BRICHENO also joined The MISSION after his relationship with REGAN floundered.

Recommended: ALL ABOUT EVE (*8)

JULIANNE REGAN – vocals, (some) keyboards / **TIMOTHY BRICHENO** (b. 6 Jul'63, Huddersfield, England) – guitar / **ANDY COUSIN** – bass (group augmented by a drum machine)

Eden not issued

Jul 85. (12") **D FOR DESIRE. / DON'T FOLLOW ME (MARCH HARE)** [ ] [-]

May 86. (7") **IN THE CLOUDS. / END OF THE DAY** [ ] [-]
(12"+=) – Love leads nowhere.

Apr 87. (7") **OUR SUMMER. / LADY MIDNIGHT** [ ] [-]
(12"+=) – Shelter from the rain.

Jul 87. (7") **FLOWERS IN OUR HAIR. / PARADISE** [ ] [-]
(12"+=) – Devil woman.

— added **MARK PRICE** – drums

Mercury Mercury

Oct 87. (7") **IN THE CLOUDS. / SHE MOVES THROUGH THE FAIR** [47] [ ]

Oct 87. (7") **WILD HEARTED WOMAN. / APPLE TREE MAN** [33] [ ]
(12"+=)(c-s+=) – Like Emily.
(12"++=) – What kind of fool (live).
(cd-s++=) – In the clouds.

Feb 88. (lp)(c)(cd) **ALL ABOUT EVE** [7] [ ]
– Flowers in our hair / Gypsy dance / In the clouds / Martha's harbour / Every angel / Like Emily / Shelter from the storm / She moves through the fair / Wild hearted woman / Never promise (anyone forever) / What kind of fool. (c+=)(cd+=) – Apple tree man / In the meadow / Lady Midnight.

Mar 88. (7") **EVERY ANGEL. / WILD FLOWERS** [30] [ ]
(12"+=) – Candy tree.
(10"++=)(cd-s++=) – More than this hour.

Jul 88. (7") **MARTHA'S HARBOUR. / ANOTHER DOOR** [10] [ ]
(12"+=) – In the meadow (live).
(c-s++=) – Never promise (anyone forever) (live).
(cd-s+=) – She moves through the fair (live) / Wild flowers (live).
(extra-12"+=) – In the clouds (live) / Shelter from the rain (live).

Oct 88. (7") **WHAT KIND OF FOOL. / GOLD AND SILVER** [29] [ ]
(12"+=) – The garden of Jane Delawney.
(extra-12"++=)(cd-s++=) – ('A'-Autumn rhapsody mix).
(10"+=) – Every angel (live).

Sep 89. (7")(c-s) **ROAD TO YOUR SOUL. / PIECES OF OUR HEART** [37] [ ]
(12"+=)(pic-cd-s+=) – Hard Spaniard.

Oct 89. (lp)(c)(cd) **SCARLET AND OTHER STORIES** [9] [ ]
– Road to your soul / Dream now / Gold and silver / Scarlet / December / Blind lemon Sam / More than the blues / Tuesday's child / Pieces of our heart (++=) / Hard Spaniard (+=) / The empty dancehall / Only one reason / The pearl fisherman. – (c+)(c/cd++)

Dec 89. (7") **DECEMBER. / DROWNING** [34] [ ]
(7"pic-d+=)(10"+=) – Paradise ('89 remix).
(12"+=)(c-s+=)(cd-s+=) – The witches' promise.

Apr 90. (7")(c-s) **SCARLET. / OUR SUMMER (live)** [34] [ ]
(7"ep+=)(12"+=)(cd-s+=) – Candy tree (live) / Tuesday's child (live).

(Aug90) When BRICHENO went off to join SISTERS OF MERCY.
MARTY WILLSON-PIPER (of The CHURCH) came in temp. at first, then full-time.

May 91. (7") **FAREWELL MR.SORROW. / ELIZABETH OF GLASS** [36] [ ]
(12"+=)(cd-s+=) – All the rings round Saturn.

Vertigo Mercury

Jul 91. (7")(c-s)(7"pic-d) **STRANGE WAY. / DRAWN TO EARTH** [50] [ ]
(10"+=)(pic-cd-s+=) – Share it with me.
(12"+=) – Nothing without you / Light as a feather.

Aug 91. (cd)(c)(lp) **TOUCHED BY JESUS** [17] [ ]
– Strange way / Farewell Mr.Sorrow / Wishing the hours away / Touched by Jesus / The dreamer / Share it with me (+=) / Rhythm of life / The mystery we are / Hide child / Ravens / Are you lonely. – (c/cd+=) *(re-iss.cd+c Feb93)*

Oct 91. (7") **THE DREAMER (remix). / FRIDA OF BLOOD AND GOLD** [41] [ ]
(12"+=) – Road to Damascus / Strange way (demo).
(cd-s+=) – Road to Damascus / ('A'nightmare mix).

M.C.A. M.C.A.

Sep 92. (7"ep)(c-ep)(cd-ep)(blue-10"ep) **PHASED EP** [38] [ ]
– Phased / Mine / Infrared / Ascent-descent.

Oct 92. (cd)(c)(lp) **ULTRAVIOLET** [46] [ ]
– Phased / Yesterday goodbye / Mine / Freeze / Things he told her / Infrared / I don't know / Dream butcher / Some finer day / Blindfolded visionary / Outside the Sun.

Nov 92. (7")(c-s) **SOME FINER DAY. / MOODSWING** [57] [ ]
(10"+=)(cd-s+=) – Dive in.

— Disbanded early 1993, **JULIANNE** formed HARMONY AMBULANCE, and released one-off 45 for 'Rough Trade'. In 1994, she began working with **BERNARD BUTLER** (ex-SUEDE), and signed solo to 'Permanent' for forthcoming releases '95.

– compilations, others, etc. –

Feb 91 Mercury; (12"ep)(cd-ep) **THIRTEEN (live)** [ ] [-]
– In the clouds / Never promise (anyone forever) / Scarlet / More than the blues / Road to your soul.

Nov 92. Vertigo; (cd)(c)(lp) **WINTER WORDS – HITS AND RARITIES** [ ] [-]
(re-iss.cd/c Apr95)

Nov 93. Windsong; (cd) **BBC RADIO 1 LIVE IN CONCERT – GLASTONBURY FESTIVAL (live)** [ ] [-]

Chad ALLAN (see under ⇒ GUESS WHO)

Daevid ALLEN (some of – see under ⇒ GONG)

ALLMAN BROTHERS BAND

Formed: Jacksonville, Florida, USA . . . 1967 by brothers DUANE and GREGG. Became The HOURGLASS after previously gigging under the ALLMAN JOYS banner with others:- BOB KELLER – bass, BILLY CANELL or MANARD PORTWOOD – drums. HOURGLASS released 2 albums and nearly a third for 'Liberty' before disbanding in 1968. Returned to homeland to augment BUTCH TRUCKS in his outfit 31st OF FEBRUARY, with DUANE also relying on session work for 'Atlantic'. In 1969 all three formed The ALLMAN BROTHERS BAND and moved to Macon, Georgia. They had already signed to the 'Atlantic' distributed label 'Capricorn' run by Phil Walden. The band became one of America's greats of the early 70's, although hindered by the untimely deaths of DUANE and BERRY in 71/72 (see below). Who knows of their real potential?. GREGG carried on regardless, gaining commercial success throughout the 70's and early 80's. • **Style:** Hard Southern-country rock that featured two brilliant guitarists DUANE and BETTS. • **Songwriters:** The ALLMANS and BETTS. In the 90's most were written by BETTS, HAYNES and NEEL. Covered; STATESBORO BLUES (Will McTell) / ONE WAY OUT (Elmore James) / I'M YOUR HOOCHIE COOCHIE MAN (Muddy Waters) / SLIP AWAY (Clarence Carter). • **Trivia:** DUANE ALLMAN played guitar alongside ERIC CLAPTON on his DEREK & THE DOMINOES single 'Layla'. That year (1970) also saw him sessioning for WILSON PICKETT, BOZ SCAGGS, ARETHA FRANKLIN, KING CURTIS, etc, etc . . .

Recommended: A DECADE OF HITS 1969-1979 (*8)

HOURGLASS

GREGG ALLMAN (b. 8 Dec'48, Nashville, USA) – vocals, keyboards, guitar / **DUANE ALLMAN** (b.20 Nov'46) – guitars / **PAUL HORNSBY** – keyboards, guitar, vocals / **MABRON McKINNEY** – bass / **JOHN SANDLIN** – drums

1968. (7") **POWER OF LOVE. / I STILL WANT YOUR LOVE** [-] [ ]
1968. (7") **HEARTBEAT. / NOTHING BUT TEARS** [-] [ ]

Liberty Liberty

Aug 68. (lp) **THE HOUR GLASS** [ ] [ ] Feb 68
– Out of the night / Nothing but tears / Love makes the world 'round / Cast off all my fears / I've been trying / No easy way down / Heartbeat / So much love / Got to get away / Silently / Bells.

— **JESSE WILLARD CARR** – bass, vocals repl. MABRON McKINNEY

1968. (7") **SHE'S MY WOMAN. / GOING NOWHERE** [-] [ ]
1968. (7") **NOW IS THE TIME. / SHE'S MY WOMAN** [-] [ ]
1968. (7") **CHANGING OF THE GUARD. / D-I-V-O-R-C-E** [-] [ ]
Aug 68. (lp) **POWER OF LOVE** [-] [ ]
– Power of love / Changing of the guard / To things before / I'm not afraid / I can stand alone / Down in Texas / I still want your love / Home for the summer / I'm hangin' up my heart for you / Going nowhere / Norwegian wood / Now is the time. *(re-iss. 2 1968 lp's; Mar74 on 'United Art')*
Dec 68. (7") **I'VE BEEN TRYING / SILENTLY** [-] [ ]

3rd album was withdrawn

31st FEBRUARY

DUANE and **GREGG** with **BUTCH TRUCKS** – drums / **SCOTT BOYER** – guitar, vocals / **DAVID BROWN** – bass

Mar 69. (7") **IN TEH MORNING WHEN I'M REAL. / PORCELAIN MIRRORS** [-] [ ]

An album DUANE AND GREGG was released 1973 on 'Polydor UK'/'Bold' US cont. these demos.

The ALLMAN BROTHERS BAND

(**GREGG** and **DUANE**) plus **DICKEY BETTS** (b.RICHARD, 12 Dec'43, W.Palm Beach, Florida) – guitar, vocals / **BERRY OAKLEY** (b. 4 Apr'48, Chicago, Illinois) – bass / **BUTCH TRUCKS** (b.Jacksonville, Florida) – drums, timpani / **JAIMO JOHANSON** (b.JOHN LEE JOHNSON, 8 Jul'44, Ocean Springs) – percussion.

Capricorn Atco

Nov 69. (lp) **THE ALLMAN BROTHERS BAND** [ ] [ ]
– Don't want you no more / It's my cross to bear / Black hearted woman / Trouble no more / Every hungry woman / Dreams / Whipping post.
Mar 70. (7") **BLACK HEARTED WOMAN. / EVERY HUNGRY WOMAN** [ ] [ ]

Capricorn Atlantic

Nov 70. (lp) **IDLEWIND SOUTH** [ ] [38]
– Revival (love is everywhere) / Don't keep me wonderin' / Midnight rider / In memory of Elizabeth Reed / I'm your hoochie coochie man / Please call home / Leave my blues at home. *(cd-iss.Mar89 on 'Polydor')*
Nov 70. (7") **REVIVAL (LOVE IS EVERYWHERE). / LEAVE MY BLUES AT HOME** [ ] [92]
Mar 71. (7") **MIDNIGHT RIDER. / WHIPPING POST** [ ] [ ]

Capricorn Capricorn

Jul 71. (d-lp) **AT FILLMORE EAST (live)** [ ] [13]
– Statesboro blues / Done somebody wrong / Stormy Monday / You don't love me / Hot 'Lanta / In memory of Elizabeth Reed / Whipping post. *(re-iss.Nov74) (d-cd-iss.1986 & Sep95 on 'Polydor')*

— On 29 Oct'71, DUANE was killed in a motorcycle accident in Macon. He had already contributed to 3 tracks on below album.

Feb 72. (d-lp)(d-c) **EAT A PEACH** [ ] [4]
– Ain't wastin' time no more / Les brers in A minor / Melissa / Mountain jam / One way out / Trouble no more / Stand back / Blue sky / Little Martha / Mountain jam (reprise). *(re-iss.Nov74) (cd-iss. 1986 on 'Polydor')*
Apr 72. (7") **AIN'T WASTIN' TIME NO MORE. / MELISSA** [-] [77]
Jul 72. (7") **BLUE SKY. / MELISSA** [-] [86] B-side
Oct 72. (7") **STAND BACK. / ONE WAY OUT** [-] [86] B-side

— (Jan73) **LAMAR WILLIAMS** (b.1947) – bass repl. BERRY OAKLEY who also died in a motorcyle accident, again in Macon, 11 Nov'72.

Sep 73. (lp)(c) **BROTHERS AND SISTERS** [42] [1] Aug 73
– Wasted words / Ramblin' man / Come and go blues / Jelly jelly / Southbound / Jessica / Pony boy. *(re-iss.Jun81) (cd-iss.1986 + Jun87 on 'Polydor')*
Oct 73. (7") **RAMBLIN' MAN. / PONY BOY** [ ] [2] Aug 73
Jan 74. (7") **JESSICA. / WASTED WORDS** [-] [65]
Oct 74. (7") **JESSICA. / COME AND GO BLUES** [ ] [-]
Sep 75. (lp)(c) **WIN, LOSE OR DRAW** [ ] [5]
– Can't lose what you never had / Just another love song / Nevertheless / Win, lose or draw / Louisiana Lou And Three Card Monty John / High falls / Sweet mama.
Sep 75. (7") **NEVERTHELESS. / LOUISIANA LOU AND THREE CARD MONTY JOHN** [-] [67]
[78]

— Jul 76 when GREGG was ostracized by others for giving evidence against convicted drug trafficker and road manager Scooter Herring. GREGG formed his own band. BETTS formed GREAT SOUTHERN and others formed SEA LEVEL who hit US No. 31 Mar 78 with lp 'CATS ON THE COAST'. When rifts were settled **The ALLMAN BROTHERS BAND** re-united early '79. GREGG, DICKEY, BUTCH, JAIMO plus newcomers **DAN TOLFER** – guitar / **DAVID GOLDFLIES** – bass (both ex-GREAT SOUTHERN).

Mar 79. (lp)(c) **ENLIGHTENED ROGUES** [ ] [9]
– Need your love so bad / Pegasus / Just ain't easy / Sail away / Crazy love / Try it one more time / Blind love / Can't take it with you. *(cd-iss.1987 on 'Polydor')*
Apr 79. (7") **CRAZY LOVE. / IT JUST AIN'T EASY** [ ] [29] Mar 79
Jun 79. (7") **CAN'T TAKE IT WITH YOU. / SAIL AWAY** [-] [ ]

Arista Arista

Sep 80. (lp)(c) **REACH FOR THE SKY** [ ] [27] Aug 80
– Hell & high water / Mystery woman / From the madness of the west / I gotta right to be wrong / Angeline / Famous last words / Keep on keepin' on / So long.
Sep 80. (7") **ANGELINE. / SO LONG** [-] [58]
Jan 81. (7") **MYSTERY WOMAN. / HELL OR HIGH WATER** [-] [ ]
Sep 81. (lp)(c) **BROTHERS OF THE ROAD** [ ] [44] Aug 81
– Brothers of the road / Leavin' / Straight from the road / The heat is on / Maybe we can go back to yesterday / The judgement / Two rights / Never knew how much (I needed you) / Things you used to do / I beg of you.
Sep 81. (7") **STRAIGHT FROM THE HEART. / LEAVING** [ ] [39] Aug 81
Nov 81. (7") **TWO RIGHTS. / NEVER KNEW HOW MUCH** [-] [ ]

— **CHUCK LEAVELL** rejoined but they soon disbanded once again. Past member **LAMAR** died of cancer on 25 Jan'83.

GREGG ALLMAN BAND

went solo again in 1987 with **DAN TOLER** – guitar / **DAVID 'FRANKIE' TOLER** – drums / **TIM HEDING** – keyboards / **BRUCE WAIBEL** – bass, vocals / **CHAZ TRIPPY** – percussion

Epic Epic

Jan 87. (7") **CAN'T KEEP RUNNING. / ANYTHING GOES** [-] [ ]
May 87. (lp)(c)(cd) **I'M NO ANGEL** [ ] [30] Feb87
– I'm no angel / Anything goes / Evidence of love / Yours for the asking / Things that might have been / Can't keep running / Faces without names / Lead me on / Don't want you no more / It's not my cross to bear.
May 87. (7") **I'M NO ANGEL. / LEAD ME ON** [ ] [49] Mar 87
Apr 89. (lp)(c)(cd) **JUST BEFORE THE BULLETS FLY** [ ] [ ] Aug 88
– Demons / Before the bullets fly / Slip away / Thorn and a wild rose / Ocean awash the gunwale / Can't get over you / Island / Fear of falling / Night games / Every hungry woman.
Apr 89. (7") **SLIP AWAY. / EVERY HUNGRY WOMAN** [-] [ ]

– other GREGG ALLMAN releases, etc. –

— with **SCOTT BOYER** – guitar, vocals / **TOMMY TALTON** – slide guitar / **CHUCK LEAVELL** – keyboards / **DAVID BROWN** – bass / **BILL STEWART** – drums / etc.

Capricorn Capricorn

Nov 73. (lp)(c) **LAID BACK** [ ] [13]
– Will the circle be unbroken / Don't mess up a good thing / Multi-colored lady / Please call home / Queen of hearts / Midnight rider / Don't mess up a good thing / All my friends / These days. *(cd-iss.Aug87 on 'Polydor')*
Jan 74. (7") **MIDNIGHT RIDER. / MULTI-COLORED LADY** [ ] [19] Dec 73

— (above releases were issued approx.half a year later in UK).

Mar 74. (7") **PLEASE CALL HOME. / DON'T MESS UP A GOOD THING** [-] [ ]
Oct 74. (7") **DON'T MESS WITH A GOOD THING. / MIDNIGHT RIDER** [-] [ ]
Nov 74. (d-lp)(c) **GREGG ALLMAN TOUR (live)** [ ] [50]
– Don't mess up a good thing / Queen of hearts / Feel so bad / Stand back / Time will take us / Where can you go / Double cross / Dreams / Are you lonely for me / Turn on your love light / Oncoming traffic / Will the circle be unbroken?. *(cd-iss.Oct87 on 'Polydor')*

— retained **BILL STEWART** and brought in **STEVE BECKMEIER + JOHN HUG** – guitar / **RICKY HIRSCH** – slide guitar / **NEIL LARSEN** – piano / **WILLIE WEEKS** – bass

Jun 77. (lp)(c) **PLAYIN' UP A STORM** [ ] [42]
– Come and go blues / Let this be a lesson to ya / The brightest smile in town / Bring it on back / Cryin' shame / Sweet feelin' / It ain't no use / Matthew's arrival / One more try.
Aug 77. (7") **CRYIN' SHAME. / ONE MORE TRY** [-] [ ]

ALLMAN AND WOMAN

the (Woman being GREGG's wife and singer CHER) (same line-up)

Warners Warners

Nov 77. (lp)(c) **TWO THE HARD WAY** [ ] [ ]
– Move me / I found you love / Can you fool / You've really got a hold on me / We're gonna make it / Do what you gotta do / In for the night / Shadow dream song / Island / I love makin' love to you / Love me.
Dec 77. (7") **LOVE ME. / MOVE ME** [ ] [ ]

— They soon split and were divorced 16 Jan'79.

The ALLMAN BROTHERS BAND

reformed 1989, **GREGG, DICKEY, JAIMO, BUTCH** and newcomers **ALLEN WOODY** – bass / **WARREN HAYES** – guitar / **JOHNNY NEEL** – keyboards

Epic Epic

Jul 90. (7") **GOOD CLEAN FUN. / SEVEN TURNS** [-] [ ]
Jul 90. (cd)(c)(lp) **SEVEN TURNS** [ ] [53]
– Good clean fun / Let me ride / Low down dirty mean / Shine it on / Loaded dice / Seven turns / Gambler's roll / True gravity / It ain't over yet.
Sep 90. (7") **SEVEN TURNS. / LET ME RIDE** [-] [ ]
Jul 91. (cd)(c)(lp) **SHADES OF TWO WORLDS** [ ] [85]
– End of the line / Bad rain / Nobody knows / Desert blues / Get on with your life /

Midnight man / Kind of bird / Come on in the kitchen.
Jun 92. (cd)(c)(lp) **AN EVENING WITH THE ALLMAN BROTHERS BAND**
– Southbound / Nobody knows / Revival (love is everywhere) / Midnight blues / Get on with your life / Dreams / End of the line / Blue sky.
May 95. (cd)(c) **2ND SET** - 88

– DUANE & GREGG ALLMAN compilations, etc. –

1972. Polydor/ US= Bold; (7") **MORNING DEW. / (pt. 2)** -
1973. Polydor/ US= Bold; (lp) **DUANE & GREGG ALLMAN** (rec. '68)
– Morning dew / God rest his soul / Nobody knows you when you're down and out / Come down and get me / Melissa / I'll change for you / Back down here with you / Well I know you too well / In the morning when I'm real.

– ALLMAN BROTHERS compilations, etc. –

Oct 73. Mercury/ US= Dial; (lp)(c) **EARLY ALLMANS** (as "ALLMAN JOYS")
Nov 74. Capricorn/ US= Atco; (d-lp) **BEGINNINGS** 25 Mar 73
– (first 2 ALLMAN BROTHERS BAND lp's)
1974. Capricorn; (7") **AIN'T WASTIN' TIME NO MORE. / BLUE SKY** -
1974. Capricorn; (7") **MELISSA. / RAMBLING MAN** -
Feb 76. Capricorn; (d-lp) **THE ROAD GOES ON FOREVER** 54 43 Dec75
– Black hearted woman / Dreams / Whipping post / Midnight rider / Statesboro blues / Stormy Monday / Hoochie coochie man / Stand back / One way out / Blue sky / Hot 'Lanta / Ain't wastin' time no more / Melissa / Wasted words / Jessica / Ramblin' man / Little Martha.
Dec 76. Capricorn; (d-lp) **WIPE THE WINDOWS, CHECK THE OIL, DOLLAR GAS** (demos, rarities recorded live before 1972) 75
– Wasted words / Southbound / Ramblin' man / In memory of Elizabeth Reed / Ain't wastin' time no more / Come and go blues / Can't lose what you never had / Don't want you no more / It's not my cross to bear / Jessica.
Aug 80. Capricorn; (lp)(c) **THE BEST OF THE ALLMAN BROTHERS BAND**
Jun 81. Capricorn; (d-lp)(d-c) **THE STORY OF THE ALLMAN BROTHERS BAND**
Sep 83. Polydor; (12"ep) **JESSICA / SOUTHBOUND. / WHIPPIN' POST / RAMBLIN' MAN** -
Apr 89. Polydor; (6xlp)(4xc)(4xcd) **DREAMS**
May 92. Polydor; (cd)(c)(lp) **A DECADE OF HITS 1969-1979** Nov 91
– Statesboro blues / Ramblin' man / Midnight rider / Southbound / Melissa / Jessica / Ain't wastin' time no more / Little Martha / Crazy love / Revival / Wasted words / Blue sky / One way out / In memory of Elizabeth Reed / Dreams / Whipping post.
Jul 84. Old Gold; (7") **JESSICA. / RAMBLIN' MAN** -
Feb 88. Old Gold; (7") **JESSICA. / ('b'-Derek & The Dominoes')** -
Jul 88. Knight; (lp)(c) **NIGHTRIDING** *(cd-iss.Sep89)* -
May 92. Castle; (cd) **THE COLLECTION** -
Sep 85. See For Miles; (lp) **THE SOUL OF TIME (as "Hourglass")** -

DUANE ALLMAN

exploitation compilations featuring all his guitar/sessions
Oct 74. Capricorn; (d-lp) **AN ANTHOLOGY** 28 Dec 72
– B.B.King medley / Hey Jude / The road of love / Goin' down slow / The weight / Games people play / Shake for me / Loan me a dime / Rollin' stone / Livin' on the open road / Down along the cove / lease be with me / Mean old world / Layla / Statesboro blues / Don't keep me wondering / Stand back / Dreams / Little Martha. *(d-cd.iss.Oct87 on 'Polydor')*
Jan 75. Capricorn; (d-lp) **AN ANTHOLOGY VOL.2** 49 Jul 74
– Happily married man / It ain't fair / The weight / You reap what you sow / Matchbox / Born to be wild / No money down / Been gone too long / Stuff you gotta watch / Push push / Walk on gilded splinters / Waiting for a train / Don't tell me your troubles / Goin' upstairs / Come on in my kitchen / Dimples / Goin' up the country / Done somebody wrong / Leave my blues at home / Midnight rider. *(d-cd.iss.Oct87 on 'Polydor')*
Sep 79. Capricorn; (lp)(c) **THE BEST OF DUANE ALLMAN**

RICHARD BETTS

with **CHUCK LEAVELL** – piano / **JOHNNY SANDLIN** – bass, guitar, percussion / **JOHN HUGHEY** – steel guitar / **DAVID WALSHAW** – drums, percussion / etc.
Capricorn Capricorn
Aug 74. (lp)(c) **HIGHWAY CALL** 19
– Long time gone / Rain / Highway call / Let nature sing / Hand picked / Kissimmee kid.
Sep 74. (7") **KISSIMMEE KID. / LONG TIME GONE** -
Nov 74. (7") **HIGHWAY CALL. / RAIN** -

DICKEY BETTS & GREAT SOUTHERN

with (ex-MELTING POT members) **DAN TOLER** – guitar / **KEN TIBBETS** – bass / **DONNIE SHARBONO** – drums / **TOM BROOME** – keyboards, vocals / **TOPPER PRICE** – harmonica
Arista Arista
May 77. (lp)(c) **DICKEY BETTS & GREAT SOUTHERN** 31 Apr 77
– Out to get me / Run gypsy run / Sweet Virginia / The way love goes / Nothing you can do / California blues / Bougainvilla.
1977. (7") **NOTHING YOU CAN DO. /** -
1977. (7") **SWEET VIRGINIA. / BOUGAINVILLA** -
— **MICHAEL WORKMAN** – keyboards repl. BROOME / **DAVID GOLDFLIES** – bass repl. TIBBETS / added **DAVID TOLER** – percussion, drums
Apr 78. (lp)(c) **ATLANTA'S BURNING DOWN**
– Good time feeling / Atlanta's burning down / Leaving me again / Back on the road again / Dealing with the Devil / Shady streets / You can have her / Mr. Blues man.
1978. (7") **ATLANTA'S BURNING DOWN. / MR. BLUES MAN** -

DICKEY BETTS BAND

had sort of comeback album
C.B.S. Epic
Nov 88. (lp)(c)(cd) **PATTERN DISRUPTIVE**
– Rock bottom / Stone cold heart / Time to roll / The blues ain't nothin' / Heartbreak line / Duane's tune / Under the guns of love / C'est la vie / Far cry / Loverman.

ALMIGHTY

Formed: Glasgow, Scotland . . . 1988 by WARWICK and STUMPY who had evolved from 'FM Revolver' signed band ROUGH CHARM. Broke through in 1990 when a series of heavy 45's slid into the charts 1990. • **Style:** Blistering US-influenced heavy grunge'n'roll, similar to a hard-metal ALICE COOPER. **Songwriters:** Most penned by WARWICK, with some co-written with others. Covered BODIES (Sex Pistols) / YOU AIN'T SEEN NOTHIN' YET (Bachman-Turner Overdrive) / IN A RUT (RUTS) / etc. • **Trivia:** They had meeting with Hell's Angels to discuss!? their similar group emblem/motif. ANDY CAIRNS of THERAPY? provided backing vox on 'CRANK' album.

Recommended: BLOOD, FIRE & LOVE (*7)

RICKY WARWICK – vocals, rhythm & acoustic guitars / **TANTRUM** – lead & rhythm guitars, b.vocals / **FLOYD LONDON** – bass, acoustic guitar, b.vocals / **STUMP MUNROE** – drums, percussion, b.vocals (real surnames of last 3; **JAMES, McAVOY, JULIANS**)
Polydor M.C.A.
Jul 89. (7") **DESTROYED. / LOVE ME TO DEATH** -
(12"+=)(cd-s+=) – Blood, fire & love (metal version).
Oct 89. (lp)(c)(cd) **BLOOD, FIRE & LOVE**
– Resurrection mutha / Destroyed / Wild & wonderful / Blood, fire & love / Lay down the law / Gift horse / You've gone wild / Power / Full force lovin' machine / Detroit. (c/cd+=) – New love sensation.
Jan 90. (7"ep)(c-ep) **THE POWER EP**
– Power / Detroit / Wild and wonderful (live).
(12"ep+=)(12"pic-d-ep+=)(12"clear-ep+=) – ('A'-killerwatt mix).
(cd-ep+=) – Lay down the law (live).
Jun 90. (7")(c-s)(7"pic-d) **WILD & WONDERFUL. / THUNDERBIRD / GOOD GOD ALMIGHTY** 50
(12"+=)(cd-s+=)(12"pic-d+=) – ('A'extended).
Oct 90. (cd)(c)(10"m-lp) **BLOOD, FIRE & LIVE (live)** 62
– Full force lovin' machine / You've gone wild / Lay down the love / Blood, fire & love / Destroyed / Wild and wonderful / Resurrection mutha / You ain't seen nothin' yet.
Feb 91. (7")(c-s) **FREE'N'EASY. / HELL TO PAY** 35
(12"+=)(cd-s+=) – Bodies.
Mar 91. (cd)(c)(lp) **SOUL DESTRUCTION** 22
– Crucify / Free'n'easy / Joy bang one time / Love religion / Bandaged knees / Praying to the red light / Sin against the light / Little lost sometimes / Devil's toy / What more do you want / Hell to pay / Loaded.
Apr 91. (7")(7"pic-d) **DEVIL'S TOY. / BAD TEMPTATION** 36
(12"+=)(cd-s+=) – ('A'extended).
Jun 91. (7") **LITTLE LOST SOMETIMES. / WILD ROAD TO SATISFACTION** 42
(12"+=) – Curiosity (live).
(pic-cd-s+=) – Detroit (live).
— (Apr92) **PETE FRIESEN** – lead guitar (ex-ALICE COOPER) repl. TANTRAM
Mar 93. (12"ep)(cd-ep) **ADDICTION. / ADDICTION (live) / SOUL DESTRUCTION (demo)** 38
Apr 93. (cd)(c)(lp) **POWERTRIPPIN'** 5
– Addiction / Possession / Over the edge / Jesus loves you . . . but I don't / Sick and wired / Powertrippin' / Taking hold / Out of season / Life blood / Instinct / Meathook / Eye to eye. *(re-iss.cd Apr95)*
May 93. (7")(c-s) **OUT OF SEASON. / IN A RUT** 41
(12"+=) – Insomnia / Wild & wonderful (demo).
(cd-s+=) – Free'n'easy / Keep on rockin' in the free world.
(cd-s) – ('A'side) / Fuckin' up / Out of season (demo) / Bodies.
Oct 93. (7")(c-s) **OVER THE EDGE. / TAKING HOLD (live)** 38
(cd-s) – ('A'side) / Jesus loves you (but I don't) / Powertrippin' (live) / Blind.
(7"colrd) – ('A'side) / Lifeblood.
Chrysalis Chrysalis
Sep 94. (7"clear) **WRENCH. / SHITZOPHRENIC** 26
(12"pic-d) – ('A'side) / State of emergency / Hellelujah.
(cd-s) – ('A'side) / Do anything you wanna do / Give me fire.
(cd-s) – ('A'side) / Thanks again, again / Knocking on Joe.
Oct 94. (cd)(c)(lp) **CRANK** 15
– Ultraviolent / Wrench / The unreal thing / Jonestown mind / Move right in / Crank and deceit / United state of apathy / Welcome to defiance / Way beyond belief / Crackdown / Sorry for nothing / Cheat. (cd+=) – Shitzophrenic.
Jan 95. (7"pic-d) **JONESTOWN MIND. / ADDICTION (live) / CRANK (live) / DECEIT (live)** 26
(12") – ('A'side) / Jonestown dub / The unreal thing (live) / United state of apathy (live).
(cd-s) – ('A'side) / Wrench (live) / Move right in (live).
(cd-s) – ('A'side) / Welcome to defiance (live) / Sorry for nothing (live).

Marc ALMOND (see under ⇒ SOFT CELL)

ALONE AGAIN OR (see under ⇒ SHAMEN)

ALT (see under ⇒ CROWDED HOUSE)

ALTERED IMAGES

Formed: Glasgow, Scotland ... 1979 by McELHONE, McDAID and ANDERSON. Recruited 'Gregory's Girl' bit actress CLARE GROGAN and others. By mid'80, they gained support slot to SIOUXSIE & THE BANSHEES and were soon signed to 'Epic'. In 1981, after earlier 45's had received airplay from John Peel, their 'HAPPY BIRTHDAY' 45 shot up to UK No.2. For the next couple of years, they enjoyed a healthy string of hits, which ended when now full-time actress CLARE left. • **Style:** Bright kaleidoscope alternative pop, featuring the child-like Shirley Temple vox of CLARE. By 1983, they had moved into dance style pop/rock. • **Songwriters:** McELHONE and group compositions / GROGAN lyrics. Also covered JEEPSTER (T.Rex) / SONG SUNG BLUE (Neil Diamond) / LITTLE TOWN FLIRT (Del Shannon). • **Trivia:** STEVE SEVERIN (Siouxsie & The Banshees) produced debut 45, and MARTIN RUSHENT the debut album.

Recommended: COLLECTED IMAGES (*6).

CLARE GROGAN (b.Mar'62) – vocals / **JOHNNY McELHONE** – guitar / **TONY McDAID** – bass / **MICHAEL 'Tich' ANDERSON** – drums / **CAESAR** – guitar

Epic / Portrait

Feb 81. (7") **DEAD POP STARS. / SENTIMENTAL.** 67
(c-s+=) – Leave me alone

— **JIM McIVEN** – guitar (ex-BERLIN BLONDES) repl. CAESAR who joined The WAKE

May 81. (7") **A DAY'S WAIT. / WHO CARES?**
Aug 81. (7") **HAPPY BIRTHDAY. / SO WE GO WHISPERING** 2
(12") – ('A'dance mix) / Jeepster.
Sep 81. (lp)(c) **HAPPY BIRTHDAY** 26
– (intro – Happy birthday) / Love and insects / Real toys / Idols / Legionaire / Faithless / Beckoning strings / Happy birthday / Midnight / A day's wait / Leave me alone / Insects / (utro – Happy birthday). *(re-iss.Sep83) (cd-iss.Sep91 & Jun95 on 'Columbia') (re-iss.cd+c May93 on 'Sony Collectors')*
Nov 81. (7")(7"pic-d) **I COULD BE HAPPY. / INSECTS** 7
(12") – ('A'dance mix) / Disco pop stars.
Mar 82. (7")(7"pic-d) **SEE THOSE EYES. / HOW ABOUT THAT THEN (I MISSED MY TRAIN)** 11
(12"+=) – ('A'extended).
Apr 82. (lp)(c) **PINKY BLUE** 12
– Pinky blue / See those eyes / Forgotten / Little brown head / See you later / Song sung blue / Funny funny me / Think that It might / I could be happy (version) / Jump jump / I could be happy (version) / Goodnight and I wish. *(cd-iss.Mar94 on 'Sony Collectors')*
May 82. (7")(7"pink) **PINKY BLUE. / THINK THAT IT MIGHT (dance mix)** 35
(12") – ('A'dance mix) / Jump jump.

— **STEPHEN LIRONI** – guitar, drums (ex-RESTRICTED CODE) repl. ANDERSON and McKIVEN The latter reappeared in the early 90s in ONE DOVE. Also used session people including **ANDY HAMILTON** – saxophone

Mar 83. (7")(7"pic-d) **DON'T TALK TO ME ABOUT LOVE. / LAST GOODBYE** 7
(12"+=) – ('A'extended).
May 83. (7")(7"pic-d) **BRING ME CLOSER. / SURPRISE ME** 29
(12"+=)(12"pic-d+=) – ('A'extended).
Jun 83. (lp)(c) **BITE** 16
– Bring me closer / Another lost look / Love to stay / Now that you're here / Don't talk to me about love / Stand so quiet / Change of heart / Thinking about you. (c+=) – (5 extra mixes).
Jul 83. (7") **LOVE TO STAY. / ANOTHER LOST LOOK (live)** 46
(12"+=) – ('A'extended).
Sep 83. (7") **CHANGE OF HEART. / ANOTHER LOST LOOK**
(12"+=) – Happy birthday / I could be happy.

— Had added on summer tour **DAVID WILD** – drums / **JIM PRIME** – keyboards But the inevitable split came late '83. LIRONI formed FLESH. McELHONE formed HIPSWAY and, later in 1989, formed TEXAS.

– compilations, others, etc. –

Aug 82. Epic; (7"ep)(c-ep) **GREATEST ORIGINAL HITS** –
– Happy birthday / I could be happy / Dead pop stars / A day's wait.
May 84. Epic; (lp)(c) **COLLECTED IMAGES**
Jan 87. Old Gold; (7") **HAPPY BIRTHDAY. / I COULD BE HAPPY** –
Nov 92. Receiver; (cd) **THE BEST OF ALTERED IMAGES** –

CLARE GROGAN

revived acting career, noteably in another Bill Forsyth movie 'Comfort And Joy', plus TV parts in 'Red Dwarf' & 'Blott On The Landscape'. Around this period (1986), she also went solo. Now with songwriters **DAVEY HENDERSON** (of WIN) and **HILARY MORRISON** (ex-FLOWERS)

London / not issued

May 87. (7")(12") **LOVE BOMB. / I LOVE THE WAY YOU BEG** –

— in 1989 she teamed up with **LIRONI** again, forming **UNIVERSAL LOVE SCHOOL**

ALTERNATIVE TV

Group: London, England . . . 1976 by "Sniffin' Glue" fanzine editor MARK PERRY. Free with this pamphlet was a flex-disc of LOVE LIES LIMP; their first recording for indie 'Deptford Fun City' label. 1978 was a curious year for them, as they issued 2 albums, one a commercially abandoned classic 'THE IMAGE HAS CRACKED', and the other 'VIBING UP THE SENILE MAN', a venture into synth-laden experimentation. • **Style:** Powerhouse, but raw punk-rock, with splices of reggae. However PERRY's move into avant-garde type experimentals proved to be wrong decision. • **Songwriters:** PERRY. Later on, co-wrote most with FERGUSSON. In 1990 PERRY struck up writing partnership with KYLIO. Also covered WHY DON'T YOU DO ME RIGHT (Frank Zappa). • **Trivia:** ATV made near commercial come-back in 1981 when he/ATV signed for Miles Copeland's 'IRS' label. But for PERRY's anti-establishment attitude he could have made top league.

Recommended: THE IMAGE HAS CRACKED (*9) / SPLITTING IN 2 (*9)

MARK PERRY – vocals, guitar / **ALEX FERGUSSON** (b.16 Dec'52, Glasgow) – guitar / **DENNIS BURNS** – bass / **TYRONE THOMAS** – drums.

Deptford Fun City / not issued

Dec 77. (7") **HOW MUCH LONGER. / YOU BASTARD** –
May 78. (7") **LIFE AFTER LIFE. / LIFE AFTER DUB** –
Nov 78. (7") **LIFE. / LOVE LIES LIMP** –

— **JOHN TOWE** – drums (ex-CHELSEA, ex-GENERATION X) repl. THOMAS

May 78. (7") **ACTION TIME VISION. / ANOTHER COKE** –

— Trimmed to a trio, when FERGUSSON formed CASH PUSSIES. **CHRIS BENNETT** – drums repl. TOWE who joined The ADVERTS. Added guests **KIM TURNER** – rhythm guitar / **JOOLS HOLLAND** – piano (on 2)

Jun 78. (lp) **THE IMAGE HAS CRACKED** –
– Alternatives / Action time vision / Why don't you do me right / Good times / Still life / Viva la rock'n'roll / Nasty little lonely / Red / Splitting in 2.

— Trim to duo of **PERRY & BURNS** with **GENESIS P.ORRIDGE / MICK LINEHAN**

Dec 78. (lp) **VIBING UP THE SENILE MAN (PART 1)** –
– Release the natives / Serpentine gallery / Poor association / The radio story / Facing up to the facts / The good missionary / Graves of deluxe green / Smile in the day.
May 79. (7") **FORCE IS BLIND. / LOST IN ROOM** –

GOOD MISSIONARIES

PERRY and BURNS. MARK's girlfriend **GILLIAN HANNA** – recorder / plus **DAVE GEORGE** – guitar / **HENRY BADOWSKI** – drums.

Aug 79. (lp) **FIRE FROM HEAVEN** –
– Another coke / The boby / The force is blind / Thief of fire / The radio story / Strange loons / Fire from Heaven / Release the natives / Fellow sufferer in dub / Bugger the cat.

Released more singles in 1980/81 on 'Unformality' UK indie label. **THE GOOD MISSIONARY (live). / KIFKIF'S FREAK OUT VIBING UP THE SENILE MAN EP (PART 2) DERANGED HASTINGS. / KEEP GOING BACKWARDS / ATTITUDE**

MARK PERRY

brief solo outing.

Deptford Fun City

Mar 80. (7") **THE WHOLE WORLD'S DOWN ON ME. / I LIVE – HE DIES** –
Jun 80. (lp) **SNAPPY TURNS** –
– Snappy turns / The object is to love / You know / Inside / At war / Death looks down / The game is over / Quagga's last stand.

DOOR AND THE WINDOW

off-shoot band feat. **PERRY, BENDLE and NAG.**

1980. (c) **C.C.H.(MUSIC AND MOVEMENT)** –

N.B. / not issued

1979. (lp) **PERMANENT TRANSCIENCE** –
1980. (lp) **DETAILED TWANG** –
– Dads / Habits / We do scare each other / Order and obey / He feels like a Doris / Part time punks / In the car / Subculture fashion slaves / Sticks and stones / Positive / Why must you build walls around us / Detailed twang.
1981. (7"ep) **FIRST** –
– Subculture / Fashion slaves / Nostradamus / Don't kill Colin / Worst band.
1981. (7"ep) **SECOND** –
– Production line / He feels like a Doris / Innocent / Dig / I like sound.

MARK PERRY & DENNIS BURNS (one-off)

N.B. / not issued

Mar 81. (7") **YOU CRY YOUR TEARS. / MUSIC DEATH?** –

ALTERNATIVE TV

reformed with **PERRY, BURNS** and **FERGUSSON** plus (ex-CASH PUSSIES) / **ALAN GRUNER** – keyboards / **RAY WESTON** – drums

I.R.S. / I.R.S.

Jun 81. (7") **THE ANCIENT REBELS. / SLEEP IN DUB** –
Jul 81. (lp) **STRANGE KICKS**
– The ancient rebels / Strange kicks / Communicate / Mirror boy / Anye is back / My hand is still wet / Fun city / TV operator / There goes my date with Doug / Cold rain / Who are they / Sleep in dub.
Oct 81. (7") **COMMUNICATE. / OBSESSION** –

— PERRY went into production, and FERGUSSON joined PSYCHIC TV. ATV reformed in 1984 with **PERRY, DAVE GEORGE, PROTAG + NAG.**

— By 1985 **MARK and DAVE** were joined by **STEVEN CANDEL** – bass / **ALISON PHILIPS** – drums

Noiseville / not issued

Feb 86. (12"m) **WELCOME TO THE END OF FUN. / ANTI / DEATH TIME** –
Jul 86. (12") **LOVE & SEX. / ?** –

Anagram — not issued

Aug 87. (12"m) **MY BABY'S LAUGHING. / I LOOK AT HER EYES / I HAD LOVE IN MY HANDS** [ ] [-]

Nov 87. (lp) **PEEP SHOW** [ ] [-]
– Chrissie's dream / Let's sleep now / The river / Tumbletime / My baby's laughing / Scandal / White walls / Animal.

— (were now **PERRY** and **KYLIO**)

Chapter 22 — not issued

Apr 90. (12"ep) **THE SOL EP** [ ] [-]
– Everyday / +3.

Nov 90. (lp) **DRAGON LOVE** [ ] [-]
– Coming of age / Something happened / Last rites / You pushed it a little too far / Captured fantasy / Never gonna give it up / Dragon love / Few feathers fall / (Do you believe) The time / We're through / Don't you leave me.

Over-ground — not issued

Nov 94. (cd) **MY LIFE AS A CHILD STAR** [ ] [-]

– compilations, others, etc. –

Dec 78. Deptford Fun City; (lp) **WHAT YOU SEE IS WHAT YOU ARE (live)** [ ] [-]
(1 side by **HERE & NOW**)
– Action time lemon / Circles / Fellow sufferer / Splitting in 2.

May 80. eptford Fun City; (lp) **ACTION TIME VISION** [ ] [-]

1980. Crystal; (lp) **LIVE AT THE RAT CLUB (live '77)** [ ] [-]

Feb 89. Anagram; (lp)(c)(cd) **SPLITTING IN 2 – SELECTED VIEWING** [ ] [-]
– Action time vision / Love lies limp / Life / How much longer / Another coke / Still life / You bastard / Nasty little lonely / Why don't you do me right / Facing up to the facts / Lost in room / Force in blind / Splitting in two.

Jul 93. Overground; (cd) **LIVE 1978 (live)** [ ] [-]

Feb 94. Anagram; (cd) **THE IMAGE HAS CRACKED – THE ALTERNATIVE TV COLLECTION** [ ] [-]

Oct 95. Overground; (cd) **THE RADIO SESSIONS** [ ] [-]

AMBOY DUKES (see under ⇒ NUGENT, Ted)

AMBROSE SLADE (see under ⇒ SLADE)

AMERICA

Formed: By sons of American servicemen based in London, England . . . 1969. Signed to 'Warner Bros' and their debut release A HORSE WITH NO NAME became a massive hit on both sides of the Atlantic. They returned to the USA to stay in 1972, where they secured several more big hits. • **Style:** Very much in the mould of CROSBY, STILLS & NASH, with near-like vocals of NEIL YOUNG. • **Songwriters:** Most written by trio, except YOU CAN DO MAGIC (Russ Ballard). • **Trivia:** GEORGE MARTIN produced albums from 1974 onwards.

Recommended: HISTORY (*5)

DAN PEEK (b. 1950, Florida, USA) – vocals, guitar / **GERRY BECKLEY** (b.12 Sep'52, Texas, USA) – vocals, guitar / **DEWEY BUNNELL** (b.19 Jan'52, Yorkshire, England) – vocals, guitar with guest drummer and bassmen.

Warners — Warners

Nov 71. (7") **A HORSE WITH NO NAME. / EVERYONE: MEET IS FROM CALIFORNIA** [3] [1]

Jan 72. (lp)(c) **AMERICA – A HORSE WITH NO NAME** [14] [1]
– Riverside / Sandman / Three roses / Children / I need you / Rainy day / Never found the time / Clarice / Donkey jaw / Pigeon song. *(re-iss.Sep87)*

Aug 72. (7") **I NEED YOU. / RIVERSIDE** [ ] [9] May 72

Nov 72. (7") **VENTURA HIGHWAY. / SATURN NIGHTS** [43] [8] Oct 72

Dec 72. (lp)(c) **HOMECOMING** [21] [9] Nov 72
– Ventura highway / To each his own / Don't cross the river / Moon song / Only in your heart / Till the sun comes up again / Cornwall blank / Head & heart / California revisited / Saturn nights. *(cd-iss.Mar95)*

Jan 73. (7") **DON'T CROSS THE RIVER. / TO EACH HIS OWN** [-] [35]

Apr 73. (7") **DON'T CROSS THE RIVER. / TILL THE SUN COMES UP AGAIN** [ ] [-]

Apr 73. (7") **ONLY IN YOUR HEART. / MOON SONG** [-] [62]

Aug 73. (7") **MUSKRAT LOVE. / CORNWALL BLANK** [ ] [67]

Nov 73. (lp)(c) **HAT TRICK** [41] [28]
– Muskrat love / Wind wave / She's gonna let you down / Rainbow song / Submarine ladies / It's life / Hat trick / Molten love / Green monkey / Willow tree lullaby / Goodbye. *(cd-iss.Mar95)*

Nov 73. (7") **RAINBOW SONG. / WILLOW TREE LULLABY** [-] [ ]

Apr 74. (7") **GREEN MONKEY. / SHE'S GONNA LET YOU DOWN** [-] [ ]

Feb 74. (7") **GREEN MONKEY. / RAINBOW SONG** [ ] [-]

Jul 74. (lp)(c) **HOLIDAY** [ ] [3]
– Miniature / Tin man / Another try / Lonely people / Glad to see you / Mad dog / Hollywood / Baby it's up to you / You / Old man Took / What does it matter / In the country. *(cd-iss.Mar95)*

Aug 74. (7") **TIN MAN. / IN THE COUNTRY** [-] [4]

Aug 74. (7") **TIN MAN. / MAD DOG** [ ] [ ]

Jan 75. (7") **LONELY PEOPLE. / IN THE COUNTRY** [ ] [5] Dec 74

Apr 75. (lp)(c) **HEARTS** [ ] [4]
– Daisy Jane / Half a man / Midnight / Bell tree / Old Virginia / People in the valley / Company / Woman tonight / Story of a teenager / Sister golden hair / Tomorrow / Seasons. *(cd-iss.Mar95)*

Jun 75. (7") **SISTER GOLDEN HAIR. / MIDNIGHT** [ ] [1] Apr 75

Jul 75. (7") **DAISY JANE. / TOMORROW** [-] [20]

Aug 75. (7") **DAISY JANE. / WOMAN TONIGHT** [ ] [-]

Nov 75. (7") **WOMAN TONIGHT. / BELL TREE** [-] [44]

Jan 76. (lp)(c) **HISTORY – AMERICA'S GREATEST HITS** [60] [3] Nov 75
– A horse with no name / I need you / Sandman / Ventura highway / Don't cross the river / Only in your heart / Muskrat love / Tin man / Lonely people / Sister golden hair / Daisy Jane / Woman tonight. *(cd-iss Jan 87)*

Apr 76. (lp)(c) **HIDEAWAY** [ ] [11]
– Lovely night / Amber cascades / Don't let it get you down / Watership Down / She's beside you / Hideaway (part 1) / She's a liar / Letter / Today's the day / Jet boy blue / Who loves you / Hideaway (part 2).

May 76. (7") **TODAY'S THE DAY. / HIDEAWAY (part 2)** [-] [23]

Aug 76. (7") **AMBER CASCADES. / WHO LOVES YOU** [-] [75]

Aug 76. (7") **TODAY'S THE DAY. / AMBER CASCADES** [ ] [-]

Nov 76. (7") **SHE'S A LIAR. / SHE'S BESIDE YOU** [-] [ ]

Feb 77. (7") **DOWN TO THE WATER. / GOD OF THE SUN** [-] [ ]

Mar 77. (lp)(c) **HARBOR** [ ] [21]
– God of the Sun / Sergeant Darkness / Sarah / These brown eyes / Don't cry baby / Are you there / Monster / Down to the water / Hurricane / Now she's gone / Slow down / Political poachers.

Apr 77. (7") **SLOW DOWN. / SARAH** [ ] [ ]

Jun 77. (7") **DON'T CRY BABY. / MONSTER** [-] [ ]

Jan 78. (lp)(c) **AMERICA LIVE (live at Greek Theater, LA)** [ ] [ ] Dec 77
– Tin man / Muskrat love / I need you / Old man Took / Daisy Jane / Company / Hollywood / Sergeant Darkness / Amber cascades / To each his own / Another try / Ventura highway / Sister golden hair / A horse with no name.

— Now a duo, when PEEK went solo and also a became Christian.

not issued — American Int.

Apr 79. (7") **CALIFORNIA DREAMIN'. /** [-] [56]

Capitol — Capitol

Jul 79. (lp)(c) **THE SILENT LETTER** [ ] [ ]
– Tall treasures / No fortune / 1960 / All night / Only game in town / Foolin' / And forever / One morning / All around / All my life / High in the city. *(re-iss.Nov83 on 'Fame')*

Aug 79. (7") **ONLY GAME IN TOWN. / HIGH IN THE CITY** [ ] [ ]

Oct 79. (7") **ALL MY LIFE. / ONE MORNING** [ ] [ ]

Dec 79. (7") **CATCH THAT TRAIN. / HE COULD HAVE BEEN THE ONE** [-] [ ]

Nov 80. (7") **ONE IN A MILLION. / HANGOVER** [-] [ ]

Nov 80. (lp)(c) **ALIBI** [ ] [ ] Sep 80
– Survival / Might be your love / Catch that train / You could've been the one / I don't believe in miracles / I do believe in you / Hangover / Right back to me / Coastline / Valentine / One in a million.

Oct 82. (7") **YOU CAN DO MAGIC. / EVEN THE SCORE** [59] [8] Jul 82

Nov 82. (lp)(c) **VIEW FROM THE GROUND** [ ] [41] Aug 82
– You can do magic / Never be lonely / You girl / Inspector Mills / Love on the vine / Desperate love / Right before your eyes / Jody / Sometimes lovers / Even the score. *(cd-iss.Apr95 on 'Connoisseur')*

Nov 82. (7") **RIGHT BEFORE YOUR EYES. / INSPECTOR MILLS** [-] [45]

Jan 83. (7") **JODY. / INSPECTOR MILLS** [ ] [ ]

— guest **RUSS BALLARD** – keyboards, etc. (ex-ARGENT, solo artist)

Jul 83. (7") **THE BORDER. / SOMETIMES LOVERS** [ ] [33] Jun 83

Jul 83. (lp)(c) **YOUR MOVE** [ ] [81]
– My kinda woman / She's a runaway / Cast the spirit / Love's worn out again / The border / Your move / Honey / My dear / Tonight is for dreamers / Don't let me be lonely / Someday woman.

Oct 83. (7") **CAST THE SPIRIT. / MY DEAR** [-] [ ]

Nov 84. (lp)(c) **PERSPECTIVE** [ ] [ ]
– We got all night / See how the love goes / (Can't fall asleep to a) Lullaby / Special girl / 5th Avenue / (It's like you) Never left at all / Stereo / Lady with a bluebird / Cinderela / Unconditional love / Fallin' off the world.

Nov 84. (7") **SPECIAL GIRL. / UNCONDITIONAL LOVE** [-] [ ]

Feb 85. (7") **(CAN'T FALL ASLEEP TO A) LULLABY. / FALLIN' OFF THE WORLD** [-] [ ]

— with **LEACOX / MICHAEL WOODS** – guitar, vocals / **BRAD PALMER** – bass, vocals

1985. (lp)(c) **AMERICA IN CONCERT (live)** [-] [ ]
– Tin man / I need you / The border / Sister golden hair / Company / You can do magic / Ventura highway / Daisy Jane / Horse with no name / Survival.

— Split later in 1985.

– compilations, others, etc. –

1974. Warners; (7"ep) **A HORSE WITH NO NAME / SANDMAN. / VENTURA HIGHWAY / RIVERSIDE** [ ] [-]

Jul 81. Warners; (7") **A HORSE WITH NO NAME. / VENTURA HIGHWAY** [ ] [ ]

Sep 91. Rhino; (cd)(c)(lp) **ENCORE: MORE GREATEST HITS** [ ] [ ]

AMERICAN MUSIC CLUB

Formed: Burnbank, California, USA . . .mid 80's by MARK EITZEL. Progressed steadily for the next half a decade and became Top 50 entrants in 1993 with 'Virgin' label 'MERCURY' album. • **Style:** Gloomy guitar-outfit although similar to R.E.M., GO-BETWEENS or NICK DRAKE. • **Songwriters:** EITZEL. • **Trivia:** The single 'RISE' was a tribute to MARK's friend, who died of AIDS.

Recommended: EVERCLEAR (*8) / SAN FRANCISCO (*7)

MARK EITZEL – vocals, guitar, keyboards / **VUDI** – guitar, accordion, bass / **DAN PEARSON** – bass, guitar, dulcimer, vocals, etc. / **MIKE SIMMS** – drums / **BRUCE KAPHAN** – pedal steel guitar, keyboards, bass, percussion, producer, etc.

Zippo — Zippo

Oct 87. (lp)(cd) **THE ENGINE** [ ] [ ]
– Big night / Outside this bar / At my mercy / Gary's song / Night watchman / Lloyd /

Electric light / Mom's TV / Art of love / Asleep / This year.

Demon Zippo

Oct 88. (lp)(cd) **CALIFORNIA**
– Firefly / Somewhere / Laughing stock / Lonely / Pale skinny girl / Blue and grey shirt / Bad liquor / Now you're defeated / Jenny / Western sky / Highway 5 / Last harbor.

Oct 89. (lp)(cd) **UNITED KINGDOM**
– Here they roll down / Dreamers of the dream / Never mind / United kingdom / Dream is gone / Heaven of your hands / Kathleen / The hula maiden / Animal pen. (cd+=) – California (album).

Alias Alias

Oct 91. (cd)(c)(lp) **EVERCLEAR**
– Why won't you stay / Rise / Miracle on 8th Street / Ex-girlfriend / Crabwalk / The confidential agent / Sick of food / The dead part of you / Royal cafe / What the pillar of salt held up / Jesus' hands.

Nov 91. (7") **RISE. / ?**
(12"+=)(cd-s+=) –

Virgin Int Virgin Int.

Mar 93. (cd)(c)(lp) **MERCURY** 41
– Gratitude walks / If I had a hammer / Challenger / I've been a mess / Hollywood 4-5-92 / What Godzilla said to God when his name wasn't found in the book of life / Keep me around / Dallas, airports, bodybags / Apology for an accident / Over and done / Johnny Mathis' feet / The hopes and dreams of Heaven's 10,000 whores / More hopes and dreams / Will you find me?

Apr 93. (c-s) **JOHNNY MATHIS' FEET. / THE AMILNITRATE DREAMS OF PAT ROBERTSON** 58
(cd-s+=) – What Godzilla said to God when his name wasn't found in the book of life / Dallas, airports, bodybags (demo).
(c-s)(cd-s) – ('A'side) / Will you find me / The hopes and dreams of Heaven's 10,000.

Jun 93. (c-ep)(cd-ep) **KEEP ME AROUND / CHALLENGER / IN MY ROLE AS THE MOST HATED SINGER IN THE LOCAL UNDERGROUND MUSIC SCENE / MEMO FROM AQUATIC PARK**
(cd-s) – (repl. 2nd track w /) / Walking tune / Memo from Bernal Heights.

— **TIM MOONEY** – drums repl. SIMMS (might have been earlier)

Aug 94. (7")(c-s) **WISH THE WORLD AWAY. / I JUST TOOK TWO SLEEPING PILLS AND NOW I'M LIKE A BRIDEGROOM** 46
(cd-s+=) – The revolving door (demo).
(cd-s) – ('A'side) / The President's test for physical fitness / Cape Canaveral.

Sep 94. (cd)(c)(lp) **SAN FRANCISCO** 72
– Fearless / It's your birthday / Can you help me / Love doesn't belong to anyone / Wish the world away / How many six packs to screw in a light? / Cape Canaverai / Hello Amsterdam / The revolving door / In the shadow of the valley / What holds the world together / I broke my promise / The thorn in my side is gone / I'll be gone / Fearless (reprise).

Oct 94. (7")(c-s) **CAN YOU HELP ME. / THE THORN IN MY SIDE IS GONE**
(cd-s+=) – California dreamin'.

Feb 95. (7")(c-s)(cd-s) **CAN YOU HELP ME. / THE THORN IN MY SIDE IS GONE**
(cd-s+=) – California dreamin' (alt.version).

MARK EITZEL

Demon Alias

Apr 91. (cd)(lp) **SONGS OF LOVE – LIVE AT THE BORDER-LINE (live)**
– Firefly / Chanel No.5 / Western sky / Blue and grey shirt / Gary's song / Outside this bar / Room above the club / Last harbour / Kathleen / Crabwalk / Jenny / Take courage / Nothing can bring me down.

AMON DUUL II

Formed: Munich, W.Germany . . . 1968 immediately splitting into two bands. While AMON DUUL became heavily into politics releasing German-only albums, AMON DUUL II became a little more commercial under contract with 'Liberty/UA'. Apart from homeland success, their numerous lp's, did little on sales front. • **Style:** Avant-garde space-rock in the mould of late 60's PINK FLOYD and GRATEFUL DEAD. • **Songwriters:** KARRER or WEINZIERL, with ROGNER lyrics. • **Trivia:** Note that:- There were a number of German-only singles, plus don't get mixed up with other band. AMON DUUL II members appeared on releases by POPOL VUH and EMBRYO.

Recommended: ANTHOLOGY (*7) / YETI (*7) / DANCE OF THE LEMMINGS (*6) / WOLF CITY (*6)

JOHN WEINZIERL – lead guitar, vocals / **RENATE KNAUP-KROETENSCHWANZ** – vocals / **CHRIS KARRER** – violin, guitar, vocals, sax / **FALK ROGNER** – keyboards / **DAVE ANDERSON** – bass / **SCHRAT** (b. CHRISTIAN THIELE) – bongos, vocals / **PETER LEOPOLD** – drums / **DIETER SERFAS** – drums and guests / **HOLGER TRULZSCH** – perc / **CHRISTIAN BUCHARD** – vibes

Liberty Liberty

1969. (lp) **PHALLUS DEI** –
– Kanaan / Dem guten' Schonen, wahren / Luzifers ghilom / Henriette Kroten schwantz / Phallus dei. *(re-iss.1972 on 'Sunset') (cd-iss.Apr93 on 'Repertoire')*

— now without SERFAS, but with new guests **ULRICH LEOPOLD** – bass / **RAINER BAUER** – guitar, vocals (both of other AMON DUUL)

1970. (d-lp) **YETI**
– Soda shop rock; (a) Burning sister / (b) Halluzination guillotine / (c) Gulp a sonata / (d) Flesh-coloured anti-aircraft alarm / She came through the chimney / Archangels thunderbird / Cerberus / The return of Ruebezahl / Eye-shaking king / Pale gallery / Yeti (improvisation) / Yeti talks to Yogi (improvisation) / Sandoz in the rain (improvisation). *(cd-iss.Nov92 on 'Repertoire')*

1970. (7") **SODA SHOP ROCK. / ARCHANGEL'S THUNDERBIRD** –

— **LOTHAR MEID** – bass, vocals repl. ANDERSON who joined HAWKWIND

KARL-HEINZ HAUSMANN – keyboards repl. SCHRAT who formed SAMETI + guests / **JIMMY JACKSON** – mellotron / **AL GROMER** – sitar / **HENRIETTE KROFEN SCHWANTZ** – vocals / **ROLF ZACHER** – vocals

United Art United Art

1971. (d-lp) **DANCE OF THE LEMMINGS**
– Syntelman's march of the roaring seventies; a) In the glass garden, b) Pull down your mask, c) Prayer to the silence, d) Telephone complex) / Restless skylight – transistor-child – 1) Landing in a ditch / 2) Dehypnotized toothpaste / 3) A short stop to the Transsylvanian brain-surgery / 4) Race from here to your ears; a) Little tornadoes, b) Overheated tiara, c) The flyweighted five / 5) Riding on a cloud / 6) Paralized Paradise / 7) H. G. Well's take off / Chamsin soundtrack; The Marylin Monroe memorial church / Chewing gum telegram / Stumbling over melted moon-light / Toxicological whispering. *(cd-iss.Nov92 on 'Repertoire')*

— added **DANNY SECUNDUS FICHELSCHER** – drums, congas / **RENATE KROTEN SCHWANTZ** – vox

1972. (lp) **CARNIVAL IN BABYLON**
– C.I.D. in Urik / All the years' round / Shimmering sands / Kronwinkl 12 / Tables are turned / Hawknose harlequin.

— now w/out HAUSMANN

Nov 72. (lp)(c) **WOLF CITY**
– Surrounded by the stars / Jail-house frog / Green-bubble-raincoated man / Wolf city / Wie der wind am ende einer strasse / Deutsch Nepal / Sleepwalker's time-less bridge.

— **ROBBY HEIBL** – bass repl. MEID (although he later returned)

1973. (lp) **LIVE IN LONDON (live '72)**
– Archangels thunderbird / Eye shaking king / Soap shop rock / Improvisation / Syntelman's march of the roaring seventies (Pull down your mask; Prayer to the silence; Telephone complex) / (a)Restless skylight-Transistor child-Landing in a ditch / (b)Dehypnotized toothpaste / (c)A short stop at the Transylvanian brain surgery / Race from here to your ears (a)Little tornadoes (b)Riding on a cloud (c)Paralized paradise.

1974. (lp)(c) **VIVE LA TRANCE**
– A morning excuse / Fly united / Jalousie / Im krater bluhn weider die baume / Mozambique (dedicated to Monika Ertt) / Apocalyptic bore / Dr.Trap / Pig man / Manana / Ladies mimikry.

— **ROBBY HEIBL** returned to replace MEID, KRAMPER and SECUNDUS

Atlantic Atco

1975. (lp)(c) **HI JACK**
– I can't wait (parts 1 & 2) / Mirror / Traveller / You're not alone / Explode like a star / Da Guadeloop / Lonely woman / Liquid whisper / Archy the robot.

1975. (d-lp)(c) **MADE IN GERMANY**
– Dreams / Ludwig / The king's chocolate waltz / Blue grotto / 5.5.55 / Emigrant song / La krautoma / Metropolis / Loosey girls / Gala gnome / Top of the mud / Mr.Kraut's jinx.

— **KARRER, WEINZIERL** and **LEOPOLD** were joined by **KLAUS EBART** – bass who repl. ROGNER and **STEFAN ZAUNER** – keyboards repl. KNAUP and BALDERSON

not issued Nova GER..

1976. (lp) **PYRAGONY X** –
– Flower of the Orient / Merlin / Crystal hexagram / Lost in space / Sally the seducer / Telly vision / The only thing / Capuccino.

1977. (lp) **ALMOST ALIVE** –
– One blue morning / Goodbye my love / Ain't today tomorrow's yesterday / Hallelujah / Feeling uneasy / Live in Jericho.

— now w/out WEINZIERL

Vinyl Straud GER

1978. (lp) **ONLY HUMAN**
– Another morning / Don't turn to stone / Kirk Morgan / Spaniards & spacemen / Kismet / Pharaoh / Ruby lane.

— line-up **CHRIS KARRER / RENATE ASCHAUER KNAUP / JOERG EVERS** – bass, guitar, synthesizers / **DANIEL FICHELSCHER** – drums, percussion / **FALK ROGNER** – synth / plus **JOHN WEINZIERI** – guitar / **LOTHAR MEID** – bass / **STEFAN ZAUNER** – piano, synth

not issued Lollipop G'MANY

1981. (lp) **VORTEX** – –
– Vortex / Holy west / Die 7 fetten Jahr / Wings of the wind / Mona / We are machines / Das gestern ist das heute von Morgen / Vibes in the air.

— Broke-up but reformed in the 80's with line-up below **JOHN WEINZIERL, DAVE ANDERSON, JULIE WAREING** – vocals / **ROBERT CALVERT** – vocals / **GUY EVANS** – drums (ex-VAN DER GRAAF GENERATOR)

Il-luminated not issued

Jan 83. (lp) **HAWK MEETS PENGUIN** –
– One moment of anger is two pints of blood / Meditative music from the third o before the producers pt.1 & 2. *(re-iss.as ' . . . VOL.1' 1986 on 'Demi-Monde') (cd-iss.1992 on 'Magnum')*

— disbanded again, but re-formed for gigs late 1992 with **KARRER, WEINZIERL, ROGNER, RENATE, LEOPOLD & MEID**

Schneeball not issued

Dec 95. (cd) **NADA MOONSHINE** –
–

– compilations, others, etc. –

May 75. United Artists; (lp)(c) **LEMMINGMANIA** –

Mar 87. Raw Power; (d-lp) **ANTHOLOGY** –
– Soup shock rock / Burning sister / Halluzination guillotine / Gulp a sonata / Flesh-coloured anti-aircraft alarm / Kanaan / Trap / Phallus dei / Yet (improvisation) / Wolf city / C.I.D. in Uruk / Morning excuse / Apocalyptic bone / Jailhouse frog.

Nov 92. Windsong; (cd)(lp) **LIVE IN CONCERT (live BBC '73)** –

Jun 93. Mantra; (cd) **SURROUNDED BY THE STARS/BARS** –

UTOPIA

WEINZIERI, MEID, KROTEN SCHWANTZ, FICHELSCHER, OLAF KUSLER (producer) / **ROGNER, KARRER**

United Art. United Art.

1973. (lp) **UTOPIA** [ ] [ ]
– What you gonna do / The Wolf-man Jack show / Alice / Las Vegas / Deutsch Nepal / Utopiat No. 1 / Nasi Goreng / Jazz kiste

AMORPHOUS ANDROGYNOUS (see under ⇒ FUTURE SOUND OF LONDON)

Tori AMOS

Born: MYRA ELLEN AMOS, 22 Aug '63, North Carolina, USA. Daughter of a preacher and Sioux Indian parents. In 1981, she released an independent US single BALTIMORE / WALKING WITH YOU, under her real name Ellen Amos. After signing to Atlantic in 1987 and releasing a miserable pop-metal lp 'Y TORI KANT READ', she finally became a star of 1992. • **Style:** Burnt orange-haired songstress likened to KATE BUSH or JONI MITCHELL. • **Songwriters:** All self-penned, except; SMELLS LIKE TEEN SPIRIT (Nirvana) / RING MY BELL (Anita Ward) / ANGIE (Rolling Stones) / THANK YOU (Led Zeppelin) / LITTLE DRUMMER BOY (UK-hit 1959) / HOME ON THE RANGE (trad.) / IF SIX WAS NINE (Jimi Hendrix Experience) / STRANGE FRUIT (Billie Holliday) / FAMOUS BLUE RAINCOAT (Leonard Cohen). • **Trivia:** Her 1992 album cover, also drew similarities to US version of KATE BUSH's 'THE KICK INSIDE'. TORI sang backing for AL STWEART on 'Last Days of the Century' album, plus STAN RIDGWAY's 'Mosquitos'

Recommended: LITTLE EARTHQUAKES (*8) / UNDER THE PINK (*7)

Y KANT TORI READ

TORI AMOS – vocals, piano with group: **STEVE FARRIS** – guitar (ex MR. MISTER) / **MATT SORUM** – drums /

not issued Atlantic

Jun 88. (7") **THE BIG PICTURE. / YOU GO TO MY HEAD** [-] [ ]

Jul 88. (cd)(c)(lp) **Y KANT TORI READ** [-] [ ]
– The big picture / God on your island / Fayth / Fire on the side / Pirates / Floating city / Heart attack at 23 / On the boundary / You go to my head / Etienne trilogy

Aug 88. (7") **COOL ON YOUR ISLAND. / HEART ATTACK AT 23** [-] [ ]

TORI AMOS

with **STEVE CATON** – guitar / **WILL McGREGOR** – bass / **ERIC ROSSE** – keyboards, co-producer / **JEFF SCOTT** – bass, guitar / **PAULINHO DaCOSTA** – percussion

East West Atlantic

Nov 91. (7") **SILENT ALL THESE YEARS. / ME AND A GUN** [51] [ ]
(12"ep+=)(cd-ep+=) – ME AND A GUN EP: Upside down / Thoughts.

Jan 92. (cd)(c)(lp) **LITTLE EARTHQUAKES** [14] [54] Dec 91
– Crucify / Girl / Silent all these years / Precious things / Winter / Happy phantom / China / Leather / Mother / Tear in your hand / Me and a gun / Little earthquakes.

Jan 92. (7")(c-s) **CHINA. / SUGAR** [51] [ ]
(12"+=)(cd-s+=) – Flying Dutchman / Humpty Dumpty.

Mar 92. (7")(c-s) **WINTER. / THE POOL** [25] [ ]
(cd-s+=) – Take to the sky / Sweet dreams
(cd-s) – ('A'side) / Angie / Smells like teen spirit / Thank you.

Jun 92. (7")(c-s) **CRUCIFY** (remix). / HERE, IN MY HEAD [15] [ ]
(cd-s) – ('A'side) / Little earthquakes / Precious things / Mother (all live).

Aug 92. (7")(c-s) **SILENT ALL THESE YEARS. / SMELLS LIKE TEEN SPIRIT** [26] [ ]
(cd-s) – ('A'side) / Upside down / Me and a gun / Thoughts.
(cd-s) – ('A'side) / Ode to the banana king (pt.1) / Song for Eric / Happy phantom (live).

— Now w / **GEORGE PORTER JR.** – bass / **CARLO NUCCIO** – drums / **ERIC ROSSE** – programming / **STEVE CATON** – drums / **PAULINHO DaCOSTA** – percussion

Jan 94. (7")(c-s) **CORNFLAKE GIRL. / SISTER JANET** [4] [ ]
(cd-s+=) – Piano suite: All the girls hate her – Over it.
(cd-s) – ('A'side) / A case of you / Strange fruit / If Six was nine.

Feb 94. (cd-ep) **GOD / HOME ON THE RANGE (CHEROKEE edition) / HAND SUITE: ALL THE GIRLS HATE HER – OVER IT** [-] [ ]

Feb 94. (cd)(c)(lp) **UNDER THE PINK** [1] [12]
– Pretty good year / God / Bells for her / Past the mission / Baker baker / The wrong band / The waitress / Cornflake girl / Icicle / Cloud on my tongue / Space dog / Yes, Anastasia.

Mar 94. (7")(c-s) **PRETTY GOOD YEAR. / HONEY** [7] [ ]
(cd-s+=) – The black swan.
(cd-s) – ('A'side) / Daisy dead petals / Home on the range (Cherokee version).
TRENT REZNOR of NINE INCH NAILS guested vox on 'Past The Mission'.

May 94. (7")(c-s) **PAST THE MISSION. / WINTER (live)** [31] [ ]
(cd-s+=) – The waitress (live) / Here in my head (live).
(cd-s) – ('A'side) / Upside down (live) / Icicle (live) / Flying Dutchman (live).

Oct 94. (7"pic-d)(c-s) **GOD. / ('A'mix)** [44] [72] Jan94
(12"+=)(cd-s+=) – ('A'remixes from;- The Joy / Carl Craig / CJ Bolland).

AMPS (see under ⇒ BREEDERS)

Ian ANDERSON (see under ⇒ JETHRO TULL)

Jon ANDERSON (see under ⇒ YES)

ANDERSON BRUFORD WAKEMAN HOWE (see under ⇒ YES)

Laurie ANDERSON

Born: 5 Jun'47, Chicago, Illinois, USA. She moved to New York to sculpture in the mid 70's, but soon turned to music and performance art. By 1980 she gave-up history tuition to concentrate on music. After her debut 8 minute 'O Superman' sold out on mail order, she signed surprisingly to 'Warner Bros', where it was quickly re-issued, hitting UK Top 10 for 1 week. • **Style:** Avant-garde and at times minimalist electronic rock, that thankfully holds little resemblance to her nauseating novelty hit. • **Songwriters:** All written by her. • **Trivia:** Her audio-visual concerts, complete with orchestra lasted for around 7 hours. Guests on her '84 lp, were PETER GABRIEL, NILE RODGERS and WILLIAM S. BURROUGHS.

Recommended: BIG SCIENCE (*5)

LAURIE ANDERSON – vocals, multi-instrumentalist (violin / synthesizers)

— with many on session incl. **DAVID VAN TIEGHEM** – percussion, drums / **ROMA BARAN** – accordian / **BILL OBRECHE** – sax, flute / **CHICK FISHER** – sax, clarinet / **PETER GORDON** – clarinet, sax / etc

not issued One-Ten

Sep 81. (7") **O SUPERMAN. / (Part 2)** [-] [ ]

Warners Warners

Oct 81. (7")(12") **O SUPERMAN. / WALK THE DOG** [2] [ ]
(re-iss.Jun87)

Jan 82. (7")(12") **BIG SCIENCE. / EXAMPLE 22** [ ] [ ]

Apr 82. (lp)(c) **BIG SCIENCE** [29] [ ]
– From the air / Big science / Sweaters / Walking and falling / Born, never asked / O Superman (for Massenet) / Example / Let x = x / It tango..*(cd.iss.Apr84)*

Jul 82. (7") **LET X = X. / IT TANGO** [ ] [ ]
(12"+=) – Sweaters.

Feb 84. (lp)(c) **MISTER HEARTBREAK** [93] [60]
– Sharkey's day / Language d'amour / Gravity's angel / Kokoku / Excellent birds / Blue lagoon / Sharkey's night. *(cd-iss.Jul84)*

Dec 84. (5-lp-box) **UNITED STATES LIVE (live)** [ ] [ ]
– Say hello / Walk the dog / Violin solo / Closed circuits / For a large and changing rooms / Pictures of it / The language of the future / Cartoon song / Small voice / Three walking songs / The healing horn / New Jersey turnpike / So happy birthday / English / Dance of electricity / Three songs for paper, film and video / Sax solo / Sax duet / Born, never asked / From the air / Beginning French / O Superman (for Massenet) / Talkshow / Frames for the pictures / Democratic why / Looking for you walking and falling / Private property / Neon duet / Let x = x / The Mailman's nightmare / Difficult listening hour / Language is a virus from Outer Space – (William S. Burroughs) / Reverb / If you can't talk about it, point to it / Violin walk / City song / Finnish farmers / Red map / Hey ah / Bagpipe solo / Steven Weed / Time and a half / Voices on paper / Example / Strike / False documents / New York social life / A curious phenomenon / Yankee see / I dreamed I had to take a test . . . / Running dogs / Four, three, two, one / The big top / It was up in the mountains / Odd objects / Dr. Miller / Big science / Big science (reprise) / Cello solo / It tango / Blue lagoon / Hothead (la langue d'amour) / Stiff neck / Telephone song / Sweaters / We've got four big clocks (and they're all ticking) / Song for two Jims / Over the river / Mach 20 / Rising sun / The visitors / The stranger / Classified / Going somewhere / Fireworks / Dog show / Lighting out for the territories.

Apr 86. (lp)(c)(cd) **HOME OF THE BRAVE** [ ] [ ]
– Smoke rings / White lily / Late show / Talk normal / Radar / Language is a virus from outer space / Sharkey's night / Credit racket.

May 86. (7")(12") **LANGUAGE IS A VIRUS FROM OUTER SPACE (edit). / WHITE LILY** [ ] [ ]

Nov 89. (lp)(c)(cd) **STRANGE ANGELS** [ ] [ ]
– Strange angels / Monkey's paw / Coolsville / Ramon / Babydoll / Beautiful red dress / The day the Devil / The dream before / My eyes / Hiawatha.

Oct 94. (cd)(c) **BRIGHT RED** [ ] [ ]
– Speechless / Bright red / The puppet motel / Speak my language / World without end / Freefall / Muddy river / Beautiful pea green boat / Love among the sailors / Poison / In our sleep / Night in Baghdad / Tightrope / Same time tomorrow.

Mar 95. (cd)(c) **THE UGLY ONE WITH THE JEWELS & OTHER STORIES FROM THE NERVE BIBLE** [ ] [ ]
– The end of the world / The salesman / The night flight from Houston / Word of mouth / The soul is a bird / The ouija board / The ugly one with the jewels / The geographic North Pole / John Lilly / The rotowhirl / On the way to Jerusalem / The Hollywood strangler / Maria Teresa Teresa Maria / Someone else's dream / White lily / The mysterious "J" / The cultural ambassador / Same time tomorrow.

ANGELIC UPSTARTS

Formed: Brockley Whim, South Shields, Yorkshire, England . . . 1977 by MENSI. After controversial debut "indie" 45, which questioned police brutality, they signed to 'Warner Bros' late '78. Immediately dented the UK Top 30 twice with 1979 singles 'I'M AN UPSTART' & 'TEENAGE WARNING'. • **Style:** Raw political punk rock, that kept its roots and was loved by "skins". • **Songwriters:** MENSI and MOND, except WE GOTTA GET OUT OF THIS PLACE (Animals) / GREEN FIELDS OF FRANCE (Eric Bogle) / WHITE RIOT (Clash). In 1986, MENSI, ROCKER and HAYES penned most. • **Trivia:** 1985 saw them arrested for obscenity releasing BRIGHTON BOMB (45).

Recommended: ANGEL DUST (THE COLLECTED HIGHS) (*5)

MENSI (b.THOMAS MENSFORTH) – vocals / **MOND** (b. surname COWIE ?) – guitar / **RONNIE WOODEN** (b. WARRINGTON) – bass repl. STEVE due to drug problems / **STICKS**(b. TAYLOR) – drums

Dead | not issued

Jun 78. (7") **THE MURDER OF LIDDLE TOWERS. / POLICE OPPRESSION** [ ] [-]
(re-iss.Sep78 on 'Small Wonder' / 'Rough Trade')

Warners | not issued

Apr 79. (7")(12")(7"green) **I'M AN UPSTART. / LEAVE ME ALONE** [31] [-]
Jul 79. (7")(7"red) **TEENAGE WARNING. / THE YOUNG ONES** [29] [-]
Aug 79. (lp)(c) **TEENAGE WARNING** [29] [-]
– Teenage warning / Student power / The yong ones / Never again / We are the people / Liddle Towers / I'm an upstart / Small town, small mind / Youth leader / Do anything / Let's speed / Leave me alone.
Oct 79. (7") **NEVER 'AD NOTHING. / NOWHERE TO HIDE** [52] [-]
Jan 80. (7") **OUT OF CONTROL. / SHOTGUN SOLUTION** [58] [-]
Mar 80. (7") **WE'VE GOTTA GET OUT OF THIS PLACE. / UNSUNG HEROES** [65] [-]
Apr 80. (lp)(c) **WE'VE GOTTA GET OUT OF THIS PLACE** [54] [-]
– Never 'ad nothing / Police oppression / Lonely man of Spandau / Their destiny is coming / Shotgun solution / King Coal / Out of control / Ronnie is a rocker / Listen to the steps / Can't kill a legend / Capital city / We've gotta get out of this place. *(re-iss. 1987)*

Zonophone | not issued

Jul 80. (7") **LAST NIGHT ANOTHER SOLDIER. / MAN WHO CAME IN FROM THE COLD** [51] [-]
Nov 80. (7") **ENGLAND. / STICK'S DIARY** [ ] [-]
Jan 81. (7")(12") **KIDS ON THE STREET. / THE SUN NEVER SHINES** [57] [-]
May 81. (7") **I UNDERSTAND. / NEVER COME BACK** [ ] [-]
(12"+=) – Heath's lament.
Jun 81. (lp)(c) **2,000,000 VOICES** [32] [-]
– 2,000,000 voices / Ghost town / You're nicked / England / Heath's lament / Guns for the Afghan rebels / I understand / Mensi's marauders / Mr.Politician / Kids on the street / We're gonna take the world / Last night another soldier / I wish.
Sep 81. (lp)(c) **ANGELIC UPSTARTS LIVE (live)** [27] [-]
– Teenage warning / Never 'ad nothing / Four words / Last night another soldier / Guns for the Afghan rebels / Mr.Politician / Shotgun solution / Pride without prejudice / England / Police oppression / Kids on the street / I understand / You're nicked / 2,000,000 voices / I'm an upstart. *(c+=)(free live flexi 7"with above) – THE YOUNG ONES / WHITE RIOT. / WE'RE GONNA TAKE THE WORLD / LEAVE ME ALONE*
Oct 81. (7") **DIFFERENT STROKES. / DIFFERENT DUB** [ ] [-]

— **TONY FEEDBACK** – bass repl. DECCA who went solo.

Mar 82. (7") **NEVER SAY DIE. / WE DEFY YOU** [ ] [-]
Apr 82. (lp)(c) **STILL FROM THE HEART** [ ] [-]
– Never say die / Flames of Brixton / Action man / Wasted (loved by none) / Here comes trouble / Theme for lost souls / I stand accused / Black knights of the 80's / Cry wolf / Soldier.

— (MENSI, MOND and FEEDBACK) were joined by **BRYAN HAYES** – rhythm guitar / **PAUL THOMPSON** – drums

Anagram | not issued

Nov 82. (7") **WOMAN IN DISGUISE. / LUST FOR GLORY** [ ] [-]
Mar 83. (7")(12") **SOLIDARITY. / FIVE FLEW OVER THE CUCKOO'S NEST** [ ] [-]
Jul 83. (7")(12") **THE BURGLAR. / ?** [ ] [-]

— Next 45 with guest **MAX SPLODGE** – vocals (ex-SPLODGENESSABOUNDS)

Sep 83. (7") **NOT JUST A NAME. / THE LEECH** [ ] [-]
(12"+=) – Leave me alone / White riot / Liddle Towers.
Dec 83. (lp) **REASON WHY?** [ ] [-]
– Woman in disguise / Never give up / Waiting, hating / Reason why? / Nobody was saved / Geordie's wife / Loneliness of the long distance runner / 42nd Street / The burglar / Solidarity / As the passion / A young punk / Where we started. *(cd-iss.Nov92)*

Picasso | not issued

Oct 84. (12") **MACHINE GUN KELLY. / PAINT IT IN RED / THERE'S A DRINK IN IT** [ ] [-]

Gas | not issued

Jun 85. (7") **BRIGHTON BOMB. / SOLDIER** [ ] [-]
(12"+=) – Thin red line.
Jan 86. (lp) **THE POWER OF THE PRESS** [ ] [-]
– I stand accused / Nottingham slag / Joe where are you now? / Empty street / Soldier / Brighton bomb / The power of the press / Stab in the back / Here I come / Thin red line / I'd kill her for six pence / Green fields of France.

— Disbanded 1986 and little or nothing heard of until 1992.

Road-runner | not issued

May 92. (cd)(lp) **BOMBED UP** [ ] [-]

– compilations, others, etc. –

Sep 83. Anagram; (lp)(c) **ANGEL DUST (THE COLLECTED HIGHS)** [ ] [-]
– The murder of Liddel Towers / Police oppression / I'm an upstart / Teenage warning / Never 'ad nothing / Shotgun solution / England / Last night another soldier / 2,000,000 voices / Kids on the street / Never say die / Heath's lament / I understand / Woman's disguise / Solidarity.
(cd-iss.Oct88, contains 'REASON WHY' tracks) (cd re-iss.Sep93)
Aug 85. Picasso; (lp) **LAST TANGO IN MOSCOW (live)** [ ] [-]
(re-iss.Feb88 on 'Razor') (cd-iss.Aug93 on 'Great Expectations')
Sep 85. Picasso; (lp) **LIVE IN YUGOSLAVIA (live)** [ ] [-]
(re-iss.Feb88 on 'Razor')
Mar 86. Dojo; (lp) **BOOTLEGS AND RARITIES** [ ] [-]
(cd-iss.Aug93 on 'Great Expectations')
Dec 87. Link; (lp) **BLOOD ON THE TERRACES** [ ] [-]
Jul 88. Skunx; (12"ep) **ENGLAND'S ALIVE (live)** [ ] [-]
– England / We're gonna take the world / Liddle Towers / The young ones.
Jul 92. Streetlink; (cd) **GREATEST HITS LIVE (live)** [ ] [-]
Jun 95. Anagram; (cd) **THE INDEPENDENT PUNK SINGLES COLLECTION** [ ] [-]
Nov 95. Punx; (cd) **LIVE ON TOUR IN YUGOSLAVIA (live)** [ ] [-]

ANIMAL LOGIC (see under ⇒ CLARKE, Stanley)

ANIMALS

Formed: Newcastle, England . . . 1960, as The ALAN PRICE COMBO. When ERIC BURDON joined in 1962, they became The ANIMALS, as so dubbed by their fans due to their wild stage act.. They supported the likes of SONNY BOY WILLIAMSON and JOHN LEE HOOKER, before moving to London in early '64, and signing to EMI's 'Columbia', by then unknown Mickey Most. By summer that year, they were top of the charts on both sides of the Atlantic. The song HOUSE OF THE RISING SUN (a traditional re-working) became standard rock/pop song for many future budding singers. Many top 10 hits followed but splits in ranks froze these by the late 60's, and marred any future. BURDON solo continued to sell records, especially in the States with Top 3 single 'SPILL THE WINE' with soul group WAR. • **Style:** R&B / beat group that heralded introduction of BURDON one of the all-time great and powerful vocalists. When super organ man PRICE departed, they branched out into psychedelic and heavier roots. • **Songwriters:** BURDON lyrics / PRICE arrangements songs, with covers BOOM BOOM + DIMPLES + I'M MAD AGAIN (John Lee Hooker) / I'M IN LOVE AGAIN (Fats Domino) / TALKIN' ABOUT YOU (Ray Charles) / GONNA SEND YOU BACK TO GEORGIA (Timmy Shaw) / DON'T LET ME BE MISUNDERSTOOD (Nina Simone) / PRETTY THING (Bo Diddley) / BABY LET ME TAKE YOU HOME (Russell-Farrell) / BRING IT ON HOME TO ME (Sam Cooke) / WE'VE GOTTA GET OUT OF THIS PLACE (Mann-Weil) / DON'T BRING ME DOWN (Goffin-King) / RIVER DEEP MOUNTAIN HIGH (Phil Spector) / PAINT IT BLACK (Rolling Stones) / etc. • **Trivia:** CHAS CHANDLER gave up bass to produce JIMI HENDRIX, SLADE and other 'Polydor' acts.

Recommended: SINGLES PLUS (*8) / STAR PORTRAIT (*5)

ERIC BURDON (b.11 May'41, Walker, nr.Newcastle, England) – vocals / **ALAN PRICE** (b.19 Apr'41, Fairfield, Durham, England) – keyboards, vocals / **HILTON VALENTINE** (b.21 May'43, North Shields, England) – guitar / **CHAS CHANDLER** (b.18 Dec'38, Heaton, nr.Newcastle, England) – bass / **JOHN STEEL** (b. 4 Feb'41, Gateshead, England) – drums

Columbia | M.G.M.

Apr 64. (7") **BABY LET ME TAKE YOU HOME. / GONNA SEND YOU BACK TO WALKER** (US 'A'side) [21] [57] Sep64
Jun 64. (7") **HOUSE OF THE RISING SUN. / TALKING ABOUT YOU** [1] [1] Jul 64
Sep 64. (7") **I'M CRYING. / TAKE IT EASY** [8] [19] Oct 64
Nov 64. (lp) **THE ANIMALS** [6] [7] Sep 64
– Story of Bo Diddley / Bury my body / Dimples / I've been around / I'm in love again / The girl can't help it / I'm mad again / She said yeah / The right time / Memphis / Boom boom / Around and around. *(re-iss.+c.Oct 69 on 'Starline') (US diff. tracks added 'House Of The Rising Sun')*
Nov 64. (7") **BOOM BOOM. / BLUE FEELING** [-] [43]
Jan 65. (7") **DON'T LET ME BE MISUNDERSTOOD. / CLUB A GO-GO** [3] [15] Feb 65
Apr 65. (7") **BRING IT ON HOME TO ME. / FOR MISS CAULKER** [7] [32] May 65
May 65. (lp) **ANIMAL TRACKS** [6] [57] Sep 65
– Mess around / How you've changed / Hallelujah, I love her so / I believe to my soul / Worried life blues / Roberta / I ain't got you / Bright lights, big city / Let the good times roll / For Miss Caulker / Roadrunner. *(re-iss.Sep84 +c on 'Fame')*
Jul 65. (7") **WE'VE GOTTA GET OUT OF THIS PLACE. / I CAN'T BELIEVE IT** [2] [13] Aug 65
Oct 65. (7") **IT'S MY LIFE. / I'M GONNA CHANGE THE WORLD** [7] [23] Nov 65

— **DAVE ROWBERRY** (b.27 Dec'43, Newcastle, England) – keyboards (ex-MIKE COTTON SOUND) repl. PRICE who went solo

Decca | M.G.M.

Feb 66. (7") **INSIDE – LOOKING OUT. / OUTCAST** [12] [-]
Mar 66. (7") **INSIDE – LOOKING OUT. / YOU'RE ON MY MIND** [-] [34]

— **BARRY JENKINS** (b.22 Dec'44, Leicester, England) – drums (ex-NASHVILLE TEENS) repl. STEEL

May 66. (lp) **ANIMALISM** [4] [33] Nov 66
– One monkey don't stop no show / Maudie / Outcast / Sweet little sixteen / You're on my mind / Clapping / Gin house blues / Squeeze her – Tease her / What am I living for / I put a spell on you / That's all I am to you / She'll return it.
May 66. (7") **DON'T BRING ME DOWN. / CHEATING** [6] [12]

ERIC BURDON & THE ANIMALS

Sep 66. (7") **SEE SEE RIDER. / SHE'LL RETURN IT** [-] [10]

— ERIC with session musicians incl. BENNY GOULSON

Oct 66. (7") **HELP ME GIRL. / THAT AIN'T WHERE IT'S AT** [14] [29] Dec 66
Apr 67. (lp) **ERIC IS HERE** [-] [ ]
– Help me girl / In the night / Mama told me not to come / I think it's gonna rain today / This side of goodbye / That ain't where it's at / Wait till next year / Losin' control / It's not easy / Biggest bundle of them all / It's been a long time coming / True love.

— ERIC who had earlier moved to California brought back **BARRY JENKINS** in Jan '67

— recruited **VIC BRIGGS** (b.14 Feb'45, London) – guitar (ex-STEAMPACKET) to finally repl ROWBERRY / **JOHN WIEDER** (b.21 Apr'47, London) – guitar, violin repl. VALENTINE who went solo / **DANNY McCULLOCH** (b.18 Jul'45, London) – bass repl. CHANDLER who became producer

M.G.M. M.G.M.

May 67. (7") **WHEN I WAS YOUNG. / A GIRL NAMED SANDOZ** [45] [15] Apr 67
Aug 67. (7") **GOOD TIMES. / AIN'T THAT SO** [20] [ ]
Aug 67. (7") **SAN FRANCISCAN NIGHTS. / GOOD TIMES** [-] [9]
Sep 67. (lp) **WINDS OF CHANGE** [ ] [42]
– San Franciscan nights / Good times / Winds of change / Poem by the sea / Paint it black / Black plague / Yes I am experienced / Man-woman / Hotel hell / Anything / It's all meat. *(re-iss.Apr71) (re-iss.Oct85 on 'Polydor')*
Oct 67. (7") **SAN FRANCISCAN NIGHTS. / GRATEFULLY DEAD** [7] [ ]
Dec 67. (7") **MONTEREY. / AIN'T IT SO** [-] [15]
Feb 68. (7") **SKY PILOT (pt.1). / SKY PILOT (pt.2)** [40] [14] Jun 68
Mar 68. (7") **ANYTHING. / IT'S ALL MEAT** [-] [80]
Apr 68. (lp) **THE TWAIN SHALL MEET** [ ] [79]
– Just the thought / Closer to the truth / No self pity / Orange and red beans / Sky pilot / We love you Lil / All is one.

— **ZOOT MONEY** – keyboards (ex-BIG ROLL BAND, ex-DANTALIAN'S CHARIOT) / **ANDY SOMERS** (aka SUMMERS) – guitar, bass (ex-BIG ROLL BAND, ex-DANTALIAN'S CHARIOT) repl. BRIGGS and McCULLOCH

Aug 68. (lp) **EVERY ONE OF US** [ ] [ ]
– Uppers and downers / Serenade to a sweet lady / The immigrant lad / Year of the guru / St.James infirmary / New York 1963 – America 1968 / White houses.
Nov 68. (7") **WHITE HOUSES. / RIVER DEEP MOUNTAIN HIGH** [-] [67]
Jan 69. (7") **RING OF FIRE. / I'M THE ANIMAL** [25] [ ]
Dec 68. (lp) **LOVE IS** [ ] [ ]
– River deep, mountain high / I'm the animal / I'm dying, or am I / Gemini / The madman / Ring of fire / Coloured rain / To love somebody / As tears go passing by. *(US iss.d-lp) (UK re-iss.d-lp.Apr71 + 1978 on 'ABC')*
May 69. (7") **RIVER DEEP, MOUNTAIN HIGH. / HELP ME GIRL** [ ] [ ]

— Split Feb69. WIEDER joined FAMILY, ZOOT went solo, JENKINS joined HEAVY JELLY, SOMERS became SUMMERS and joined KEVIN AYERS then KEVIN COYNE. He later helped form The POLICE

May 68. (7") **MONTEREY. / ANYTHING** [ ] [ ]

ERIC BURDON & WAR

ERIC BURDON – vocals, and WAR: – **LONNIE (LEROY) JORDAN** – keyboards, vocals / **HOWARD SCOTT** – guitar, vocals / **CHARLES MILLER** – saxophone, clarinet / **HAROLD BROWN** – drums, percussion / **B.B. DICKERSON** – bass / **THOMAS 'PAPA DEE' ALLEN** – keyboards / **LEE OSKAR** – harmonica

Polydor M.G.M.

Sep 70. (lp)(c) **ERIC BURDON DECLARES WAR** [50] [18] May 70
– Dedication / Roll on Kirk / Tobacco road / I have a dream / Spill the wine / Blues for Memphis Slim / Birth / Mother Earth / Mr.Charlie / Danish pastry / You're no stranger. *(re-iss.Oct79 on 'MCA') (cd-iss.Oct95 on 'Avenue')*
Jul 70. (7") **SPILL THE WINE. / MAGIC MOUNTAIN** [ ] [3]

Liberty M.G.M.

Dec 70. (7") **THEY CAN'T TAKE AWAY OUR MUSIC. / HOMECOOKIN'** [ ] [50]
Jan 71. (d-lp)(d-c) **BLACK MAN'S BURDON** [ ] [82] Dec 70
– Black on black in black / Paint it black / Laurel and Hardy / P.C. 3 / Black bird / Paint it black / Spirit / Beautiful new born child / Nights in white satin / Bird and the squirrel / Nuts seed and life / Out of nowhere / Sun – Moon / Pretty colours / Gun / Jimbo / Bare back ride / Home cookin' / They can't take away our music. *(re-iss.Oct79 on 'MCA') (US-cd 1993 on 'Avenue')*
Jun 71. (7") **PAINT IT BLACK. / SPIRIT** [ ] [ ]

ERIC BURDON & JIMMY WITHERSPOON

JIMMY WITHERSPOON – blues guitarist + WAR backing.

United Art. United Art.

Aug 71. (7") **SOLEDAD. / HEADIN' FOR HOME** [ ] [ ]
Dec 71. (lp)(c) **GUILTY!** [ ] [ ]
– I've been drinking / Once upon a time / Steam roller / The laws must change / Have mercy judge / Goin' down slow / Soledad / Home dream / Wicked wicked man / Headin' for home / The time has come. *(re-iss. US 1976 as 'BLACK AND WHITE BLUES')*

ERIC BURDON

performed at Reading festival (Aug73), backed by **AARON BUTLER** – guitar / **RANDY RICE** – bass / **ALVIN TAYLOR** – drums. This line-up also featured on his next long awaited album

Capitol Capitol

Feb 75. (lp)(c) **SUN SECRETS** [ ] [51] Dec 74
– It's my life / Ring of fire / Medley: When I was young – Warchild – The real me / Don't let me be misunderstood – Nina's school / Letter from the County farm / Sun secrets.
Dec 74. (7") **THE REAL ME. / LETTER FROM THE COUNTRY FARM** [-] [ ] Dec 74
Feb 75. (7") **RING OF FIRE. / THE REAL ME** [-] [ ] Dec 74

— added **JOHN STERLING** – guitar / **TERRY RYAN** – keyboards / **MOSES WHEELOCK** – percussion / **GEORGE SURANOVICH** – drums / and **KIM KESTERSON** – bass (repl. AARON BUTLER)

Aug 75. (lp)(c) **STOP** [ ] [ ]
– City boy / Gotta get it on / The man / I'm lookin' up / Rainbow / All I do / Funky fever / By mine / The way it should be / Stop.

— using different session people

Mar 78. (lp) **SURVIVOR** [ ] [ ] Mar 77
– Rocky / Woman of the rings / The kid / Tomb of the unknown singer / Famous flames / Hollywood woman / Hook of Holland / I was born to live the blues / Highway dealer / P.O. box 500.

— Early '76 the original

ORIGINAL ANIMALS

reformed to record below **BURDON, PRICE, VALENTINE, CHANDLER + STEEL**

Barn United Art.

Aug 77. (lp)(c) **BEFORE WE WERE SO RUDELY INTERRUPTED** [ ] [70]
– Brother Bill (the last clean shirt) / Many rivers to cross / Lonely avenue / Please send me someone to love / Riverside county / It's all over now, baby blue / Fire on the Sun / As the crow flies / Just a little bit / The fool.
Aug 77 (7") **PLEASE SEND ME SOMEONE TO LOVE. / RIVERSIDE COUNTY** [ ] [-]
Oct 77 (7") **MANY RIVERS TO CROSS. / BROTHER BILL (THE LAST CLEAN SHIRT)** [-] [ ]

— PRICE returned to solo work.

ERIC BURDON

solo with many session people.

Polydor not issued

1980. (lp) **DARKNESS DARKNESS** [ ] [ ]
– Darkness darkness / On the horizon / Rat race / Gospel singer / Ride on / Baby what's wrong / Cry to me / So much love / Ecstasy / Too late.

Ariola Germany not issued

1981. (lp) **THE LAST DRIVE (as "ERIC BURDON'S FIRE DEPT.")** [-] [-]
– The last drive / Power company / Bird on the beach / The rubbing out of long hair / Atom-most-fear / Dry / Female terrorist / The last poet.

ANIMALS

reformed again in 1983.

I.R.S. I.R.S.

Sep 83. (7) **THE NIGHT. / NO JOHN NO** [ ] [48]
(12"+=) – Melt down.
Sep 83. (lp)(c) **ARK** [ ] [66]
– Loose change / Love is for all time / My favourite enemy / Prisoner of the light / Being there / Hard times / The night / Trying to get to you / Just can't get enough / Melt down / Gotta get back to you / Crystal nights.
Nov 83. (7")(12") **LOVE IS FOR ALL TIME. / JUST CAN'T GET ENOUGH** [ ] [ ]
Sep 84. (lp)(c) **RIP IT TO SHREDS – THE ANIMALS GREATEST HITS LIVE (live 1983)** [ ] [ ]
– It's too late / House of the rising Sun / It's my life / Don't bring me down / Don't let me be misunderstood / I'm crying / Bring it on home to me / O lucky man / Boom boom / We've gotta get out of this place.

— (split though they did reunion gigs)

ERIC BURDON BAND

with **JOHN STERLING + SNUFFY WALDEN** – guitar / **STEVE GOLDSTEIN + LUIS CABAZA + RONNIE BARRON** – keyboards / **BILL McCUBBIN + TERRY WILSON** – bass / **TONY BRUANAGLE** – drums

Line Blackline

1982. (lp) **COMEBACK** [-] [ ]
– No more Elmore / The road / Crawling King Snake / Take it easy / Dey won't / Wall of silence / Streetwalker / It hurts me too / Lights out / Bird on the beach. *(UK-iss Jun84 as 'THE ROAD' on 'Thunderbolt')*

Bullfrog Carcre

Mar 84. (lp)(c) **POWER COMPANY** [ ] [-]
– Power company / Devil's daughter / You can't kill my spirit / Do you feel it (today) / Wicked man / Heart attack / Who gives a f*** / Sweet blood call / House of the rising Sun / Comeback. (US-iss. +cd 1988 as 'WICKED MAN on 'Big TIme')

Striped House not issued

Aug 88. (12")(cd-s) **RUN FOR YOUR LIFE. / (2 'A' versions)** [ ] [-]
Aug 88 (cd)(c) **I USED TO BE AN ANIMAL** [-] [ ]

Rhino Rhino

1990 (c-s) **SIXTEEN TONS / ('A'instrumental)** [-] [-]

ANIMALS, – compilations, US imports etc. –

1964. Columbia; (7"ep) **THE ANIMALS IS HERE** [ ] [ ]
– House of the rising sun / I'm crying / Gonna send you back to *** /Baby let me take you down.
1965. Columbia; (7"ep) **THE ANIMALS** [ ] [ ]
– Boom boom / Around and around / Dimples / I've been around.
Mar 65. US= M.G.M.; (lp) **THE ANIMALS ON TOUR (live)** [-] [99]
– Boom boom / How you've changed / I believe to my soul / Mess around bright lights / Big city / Worried life blues / Let the good times roll / Crying dimples / She said yeah.
1965. Columbia; (7"ep) **THE ANIMALS (No.2)** [ ] [ ]
– I'm in love again / Bury my body / I'm mad again / She said yeah.
1965. US= M.G.M.; (lp) **GET YOURSELF A COLLEGE GIRL** [-] [ ]
1965. Columbia; (7"ep) **THE ANIMALS ARE BACK** [ ] [ ]
1965. US= M.G.M.; (lp) **BRITISH A-GO-GO** [ ] [-]
Jan 66. Columbia; (7"ep) **ANIMAL TRACKS** [ ] [ ]
Feb 66. US= M.G.M.; (lp) **THE BEST OF THE ANIMALS** [-] [6]
(UK iss.Mar89 on 'Crusader')
Apr 66. Columbia; (lp) **MOST OF THE ANIMALS** [4] [ ]
(re-iss.Sep71 +c on 'MFP'; hit no.18)
1965. Decca; (7"ep) **IN THE BEGINNING THERE WAS EARLY ANIMALS** [ ] [ ]
– Boom boom / Pretty thing / I just wanna make love to you.
Sep 66. US= M.G.M.; (lp) **ANIMALIZATION** [-] [20]
– Don't bring me down / One monkey don't stop the show / You're on my mind / She'll return it / Cheating / Inside – looking out / See see rider / Gin house blues / Maudie / What am I living for / Sweet little sixteen / I put a spell on you.
Jun 67. Columbia/ M.G.M.; (lp) **THE BEST OF ERIC BURDON & THE ANIMALS VOL.2** [ ] [71]
Apr 69. US= M.G.M.; (lp) **THE GREATEST HITS OF ERIC BURDON & THE ANIMALS** [-] [ ]
1971. US= M.G.M.; (d-lp) **POP HISTORY** [-] [ ]
1971. US= M.G.M.; (d-lp) **STAR PORTRAIT** [-] [ ]

– Good times / Sky pilot / We love you Lil / Hey Gyp, dig the slowness / San Franciscan nights / Paint it black / When I was young / See see rider / Ring of fire / River deep, mountain high / True love (comes only once in a lifetime) / Inside – looking out / I'm an animal / Monterey / To love somebody / Anything / I'm dying, or am I?. *(cd-iss. Jul 88)*

Mar 71. M.G.M.; (7") **GOOD TIMES. / SAN FRANCISCAN NIGHTS** [ ] [-]
(re-iss.Nov82)
Oct 75. M.G.M.; (lp)(c) **ERIC BURDON & THE ANIMALS** [ ] [-]
Nov 80. M.G.M.; (d-lp)(c) **GREATEST HITS** [ ] [-]
Nov 76. A.B.C.; (lp)(c) **LOVE IS ALL AROUND (out-takes)** [ ] [ ]
Jan 77. A.B.C.; (7") **MAGIC MOUNTAIN / HOME DREAM** [-] [ ]
(above 2 by "ERIC BURDON AT WAR") *(US-cd-iss 1993 on 'Avenue') (cd-iss. Dec 88 on 'Spectrum', US-iss.Nov84 on 'Astan')*
1970. E.M.I.; (lp)(c) **HOUSE OF THE RISING SUN** [ ] [ ]
Oct 87. E.M.I.; (lp)(c)(cd) **THE SINGLES (PLUS)** [ ] [ ]
(first 10 singles 'A' & 'B')
Jul 90. E.M.I.; (d-cd)(d-c)(d-lp) **THE COMPLETE ANIMALS** [ ] [-]
Oct 90. E.M.I.; (7")(c-s) **WE GOTTA GET OUT OF THIS PLACE. / THE HOUSE OF THE RISING SUN** [ ] [ ]
(12"+=) – Baby let me follow you down.
(cd-s++=) – Blue feeling.
Sep 72. R.A.K.; (7"m) **HOUSE OF THE RISING SUN. / DON'T LET ME BE MISUNDERSTOOD / I'M CRYING** [25] [ ]
(re-iss. + pic-cd Sep'82 hit No.11)
1973. Pickwick; (lp)(c) **EARLY ANIMALS** [ ] [-]
Apr 76. D.J.M.; (lp)(c) **IN CONCERT FROM NEWCASTLE (live '63)** [ ] [-]
(re-iss Dec 76 as 'LIVE IN NEWCASTLE') (re-iss Jan 77 as 'NEWCASTLE '63 on 'Charly') (re-iss Nov 88 +cd as 'LIVE AT THE CLUB A GO GO, NEWCASTLE' on 'Decal') (cd-iss Feb 93 on 'Charly')
Jan 77. Charly; (lp) **SONNY BOY WILLIAMSON AND THE ANIMALS (live '63)** [ ] [-]
(re-iss.1982) (re-iss.Nov88 on 'Decal')
Feb 77. Charly; (lp) **ERIC BURDON & THE ANIMALS** [ ] [-]
(re-iss.Mar83)
Aug 81. Charly; (lp) **THE ANIMALS** [ ] [-]
Mar 83. Charly; (lp) **HOT ON FILE** [ ] [-]
Dec 88. See For Miles; (lp)(cd) **THE EP COLLECTION** [ ] [-]
Apr 88. Platinum (lp)(c) **GREATEST HITS : ERIC** [ ] [-]
note; next 6 releases as ERIC BURDON solo compilations.
Oct 92. Thunderbolt; (cd) **CRAWLING KING SNAKE** [ ] [-]
Apr 88. Big Time; (lp)(c) **GREATEST HITS 1970-1975** [ ] [-]
1988. Inak; (cd) **THAT'S LIVE (live by "ERIC BURDON & BAND")** [ ] [-]
Sep 92. Prestige; (cd)(c) **RARITIES** [ ] [-]
Feb 91. Raven; (cd) **ROADRUNNERS (live 66-67)** [ ] [-]
Dec 90. Decal; (cd)(c)(lp) **TRACKIN' THE HITS** [ ] [-]
Mar 91. Sequel; (cd)(c)(d-lp) **INSIDE LOOKING OUT (THE 1965-1966 SESSIONS)**(cd+= extra tracks) [ ] [-]
Sep 93. Spectrum; (cd)(c) **INSIDE OUT** [ ] [-]
Jun 90. Nightriding; (cd) **GOLDEN DECADE** [ ] [-]
1992 Blue Wax; (cd) **THE UNRELEASED** [ ] [-]
1992. Old Gold; (7") **HOUSE OF THE RISING SUN. / WE'VE GOTTA GET OUT OF THIS PLACE** [ ] [-]
1993. US= Avenue; (cd) **SUN SECRETS / STOP (ERIC BURDON)** [-] [ ]
May 94. Sixteen; (cd) **16 GREAT HITS (ANIMALS & SONNY BOY WILLIAMSON)** [ ] [-]
Jul 94. Success; (cd)(c) **I USED TO BE AN ANIMAL (ERIC BURDON)** [ ] [-]
Apr 95. Jet; (cd) **LOST WITHIN THE HALLS OF TIME (ERIC BURDON)** [ ] [-]
Oct 95. Avenue; (cd) **SINGS THE ANIMALS GREATEST HITS** [ ] [-]

ANIMALS THAT SWIM

Formed: London, England . . . 1992 by self-proclaimed genius poet HANK STARR, alongside his brothers HUGH and AL BARKER. Released 2 self-financed '45s during the next year; 'KING BEER' and 'ROY'. After another for 'Che' records in 1993, they were snapped up by 'Alternative Tentacles' subsidiary 'El-e-mental'. In the autumn of '94, they unleashed the excellent debut album 'WORKSHY', which was plauded by many including NME critics. The rest of the 90s could be theirs for the taking. • **Style:** Melancholy indie-rock outfit whose vox/snare drummer HANK STARRS lets us deja vu on a diet of CATHAL COUGHLAN (Microdisney), MARK GOLDTHORPE (Artery), JULIAN COPE or even 20s caberet star JACQUES BREL. • **Songwriters:** H. STARR'S – H.BARKER and some w/CRABTREE. • **Trivia:** DEL also moonlights for BARK PSYCHOSIS, while ANTHONY does same for MAMBO TAXI.

Recommended: WORKSHY (*10)

HANK STARRS – vocals, drums / **HUGH BARKER** – guitar / **AL BARKER** – guitar, keyboards, vocals / **DEL CRABTREE** – trumpet / **ANTHONY COOTE** – bass

Beach-heads In Space / not issued
May 92. (7") **KING BEER. /** [ ] [-]
Feb 93. (7") **ROY. /** [ ] [-]

Che / not issued
Aug 93. (10"ep) **50 DRESSES. / CHAPEL MARKET. / HOLLOWAY AVIATOR. / OREGON STATE FAIR** [ ] [-]

El-e-mental / not issued
Sep 94. (7")(cd-s) **MADAME YEVONDE. / ME AND CAPTAIN AMERICA / MAY** [ ] [-]
Sep 94. (cd)(lp) **WORKSHY** [ ] [-]
– How to make a chandelier / Smooth steps / Roy / Pink carnations / St. Francis / Action at Tescos / King Beer / Barney / Susie's friends / Madame Yevonde / Vic / Silent film / Stay with me.

— They now have a new drummer **KARL** (in Spring '95)

Mar 95. (7"ep)(cd-ep) **PINK CARNATIONS / KANDY KARS. / NEW BOOTS / HARRY DEAN / DEL FRESCO** [ ] [-]

ANNABELLA (see under ⇒ BOW WOW WOW)

ANOTHER PRETTY FACE (see under ⇒ WATERBOYS)

Adam ANT (see under ⇒ ADAM AND THE ANTS)

ANTHRAX

Formed: Queen's, New York, USA . . . mid'81, by TURBIN and LILKER. Spotted and signed mid'83 by JOHNNY Z to 'Megaforce' label which was licensed to 'Music For Nations' in Europe. In 1987, their album 'AMONG THE LIVING' was first to chart. • **Style:** Heavy "hard-core" thrash metal with punk ideals. • **Songwriters:** SCOTT IAN except; I'M EIGHTEEN (Alice Cooper) / SABBATH BLOODY SABBATH (Black Sabbath) / GOD SAVE THE QUEEN and FRIGGIN' IN THE RIGGIN' (Sex Pistols) / GOT THE TIME (Joe Jackson) / BRING THE NOISE (Public Enemy) / PROTEST AND SURVIVE (Discharge), LOOKING DOWN THE BARREL OF A GUN (Beastie Boys) / SHE (Kiss) • **Trivia:** DAN SPITZ's older brother DAVID, played bass in mid'80's with BLACK SABBATH. Made an acting/ singing appearance on a 1992 showing of US TV sit-com 'Married – With Children'. **Note:** ANTHRAX (US) not to be confused with UK "oi" band same name.

Recommended: SPREADING THE DISEASE (*7) / AMONG THE LIVING (*7) / STATE OF EUPHORIA (*7) / PERSISTENCE OF TIME (*7).

NEIL TURBIN – vocals / **DAN SPITZ** – lead guitar / **SCOTT 'Not' IAN** – rhythm guitar / **DAN LILKER** – bass / **CHARLIE BONANTE** – drums

Music For Nations / Megaforce
Nov 83. (7") **SOLDIERS OF DEATH. / HOWLING FURIES** [-] [ ]
Jan 84. (lp) **FISTFUL OF METAL** [ ] [ ]
– Deathrider / Metal thrashing mad / I'm eighteen / Panic / Subjagator / Death from above / Across the river / Anthrax. *(re-iss.c+cd+pic-lp.Apr87, cd+=)* – Soldiers of metal / Howling furies. *(re-iss.cd/c/lp Sep95)*

(Mid'84) **MATT FALLON** – vocals repl. TURBIN

— **FRANK BELLO** (b.19 Jul'65) – bass (ex-roadie) repl. LILKER

— (Aug'84) **MATT** was replaced by **JOEY BELLADONNA** (b.30 Oct', Oswego, New York) – vocals (ex-BIBLE BLACK)

Feb 85. (m-lp) **ARMED AND DANGEROUS** [-] [ ]
– Armed and dangerous / Raise Hell / God save the Queen / Metal thrashing mad / Panic. *(UK-iss.+cd Aug87 + Nov91 + Sep95)*

Island / Megaforce-Island
Feb 86. (lp)(c) **SPREADING THE DISEASE** [ ] [ ] Dec85
– A.I.R. / Lone justice / Madhouse / S.S.C – Stand or fall / The enemy / Aftershock / Armed and dangerous / Medusa / Gung ho. *(re-iss.+cd.May86 & Aug91 on 'Island')*
May 86. (7") **MADHOUSE. / A.I.R.** [ ] [ ]
(12"+=)(12"pic-d+=) – God save the Queen. *(re-iss.Sep86, some with live 'A' side)*
Feb 87. (7")(12")(7"pic-d) **I AM THE LAW. / BUD E.LUVBOMB & SATAN'S BAND** [32] [ ]
(7"red+=)(12"+=) – Madhouse (live).
(12") – I'm the man.
Apr 87. (lp)(c)(cd)(pic-lp) **AMONG THE LIVING** [18] [62]
– Among the living / Caught in the mosh / I am the law / Efilnikufesin (N.F.L.) / Among the living / Skeleton in the closet / One world / A.D.I.- horror of it all / Imitation of life.
Jun 87. (7")(12")(7"pic-d)(7"orange)(c-s) **INDIANS. / SABBATH BLOODY SABBATH: TAINT** [44] [ ]
Nov 87. (7")(7"sha-pic-d) **I'M THE MAN. / CAUGHT IN THE MOSH** [20] [-]
(12"+=) – I am the law (live).
Nov 87. (m-lp)(c)(cd) **I'M THE MAN** [-] [53]
– I'm the man (censored version) / I'm the man (Def uncensored version) / Sabbath bloody sabbath / I'm the man (live & extremely Def II uncensored version) / Caught in a mosh (live) / I am the law (live).
Sep 88. (7")(7"yellow) **MAKE ME LAUGH. / ANTI SOCIAL (live)** [26] [ ]
(12"+=) – Friggin' in the riggin'.
Sep 88. (lp)(c)(cd) **STATE OF EUPHORIA** [12] [30]
– Be all, end all / Out of sight, out of mind / Make me laugh / Antisocial / Who cares wins / Now it's dark / Schism / Misery loves company / 13 / (finale). *(re-iss.cd Apr94)*
Mar 89. (7") **ANTI-SOCIAL. / PARASITE** [44] [ ]
(12"+=)(cd-s+=) – Le-sect.

Island / Island
Aug 90. (7") **IN MY WORLD. / KEEP IT IN THE FAMILY** [29] [ ]
(10"+=)(12"+=)(cd-s+=) – ('A'&'B'extended).
Aug 90. (cd)(c)(lp) **PERSISTENCE OF TIME** [13] [24]
– Time / Blood / Keep it in the family / In my world / Gridlock / Intro to reality / Belly of the beast / Got the time / H8 red / One man stands / Discharge. *(pic-lp Jan91) (re-iss.cd+c Apr94*
Nov 90. (7")(10")(c-s) **GOT THE TIME. / WHO PUT THIS TOGETHER** [16] [ ]
(12"+=)(cd-s+=) – I'm the man (live).
Jun 91. (7")(c-s) **BRING THE NOISE. (as "ANTHRAX featuring CHUCK D.") / I AM THE LAW '91** [14] [ ]
(10"+=)(12"+=)(cd-s+=)(10"pic-d+=)(12"pic-d+=) – Keep it in the family (live).

CHUCK D. (ex-PUBLIC ENEMY)

Jun 91. (cd)(c)(lp) **ATTACK OF THE KILLER B's** (rare studio) [13] [27]
– Milk (ode to Billy) / Bring the noise / Keep it in the family (live) / Startin' up a posse / Protest and survive / Chromatic death / I'm the man '91 / Parasite / Pipeline / Sects / Belly of the beast (live) / N.F.B. (dallabnikufesin). *(re-iss.cd Apr94)*

—— (May92) **JOHN BUSH** – vocals (ex-ARMOURED SAINT) repl. MARK OSEGUEDA who had replaced BELLADONNA.

Elektra Elektra

Apr 93. (7")(c-s) **ONLY. / ONLY (mix)** [36] [ ]
(cd-s+=) – Cowboy song / Sodium pentaghol.
(cd-s) – ('A'side) / Auf wiedersehen / Noisegate.

May 93. (cd)(c)(lp) **SOUND OF WHITE NOISE** [14] [7]
– Potter's field / Only / Room for one more / Packaged rebellion / Hy pro glo / Invisible / 1000 points of hate / Black lodge / C11 H17 N2 O2 SNA / Burst / This is not an exit.

Sep 93. (7") **BLACK LODGE. / ('A'black strings mix)** [53] [ ]
(12"pic-d+=)(10"+=)(cd-s+=) – Pottersfield / Love her all I can.

Nov 93. (7") **HY PRO GLO. / LONDON** [ ] [ ]
(12"+=) – Room for one more (live).

Oct 95. (cd)(c) **STOMP 442** [ ] [47]
–

– compilations, others, etc. –

Nov 92. Island; (d-cd) **AMONG THE LIVING / PERSISTENCE OF TIME** [ ] [ ]
(re-iss.cd Apr94)

Apr 94. Island; (cd)(c)(lp) **ANTHRAX LIVE – THE ISLAND YEARS (live)** [ ] [ ]

STORMTROOPERS OF DEATH

(SOD)(off-shoot band of **SCOTT IAN & DAN LILKER** with **BILLY MILANO** – vocals

Dec 84. Roadrunner; (lp) **SPEAK ENGLISH OR DIE** [-] [-] Germ'y
– March of the S.O.D. / Sergeant "D" & the S.O.D. / Kill yourself / Milano mosh / Speak English or die / United forces / Chromatic death / Pi Alpha Nu / Anti-procrastination song / What's the noise / Freddy Kruger / Milk / Pre-menstrual princess blues / Pussy whipped / Fist banging mania.

ANTI-GROUP (see under ⇒ CLOCK DVA)

APHEX TWIN

Born: RICHARD JAMES, 1971, Cornwall, England. At a youthful 14, he recorded in his bedroom until breaking out into the dance scene. After an initial release, he put ink on paper with Belguim's 'R&S' label run by Renaat Van De Papeliere, who wanted desperately his 'DIGERIDOO' taping. • **Style:** The wonder lad was best described as an ambient TANGERINE DREAM or a techno Mozart, drawing picturesque rhythms over quite unique techniques. • **Songwriters:** Ideas JAMES; sampled various and covered FILM ME (Luxuria) / ONE DAY (Bjork). • **Trivia:** Was credited on SEEFEEL's 12"single 'Time To Find Me (remixes)'.

Recommended: SELECTED AMBIENT WORKS '85-'92 (*7)

RICHARD JAMES (aka The APHEX TWIN) – keyboards, etc.

Mighty Force / not issued

Dec 91. (12"ep) **ANALOGUE BUBBLEBATH EP** [ ] [-]

R & S Outer Rhythm / not issued

Apr 92. (12"ep) **DIGERIDOO. / FLAPHEAD / ISOPROPHLEX** [55] [ ]
(cd-ep+=) – Analogue bubblebath 1.

Jul 92. (12"ep)(cd-ep) **XYLEM TUBE EP** [ ] [-]

Nov 92. (cd)(c)(d-lp) **SELECTED AMBIENT WORKS '85-'92** [ ] [-]
– Xtal / Tha / Pulsewidth / Ageispolis / I won't let the Sun go down on me / Greencalx / Heliosphan / We are the music makers / Schotkey / Hedphelym / Delphium / Actium / Ptolemy.

Warp / not issued

Dec 93. (12"ep)(cd-ep) **ON. / 73 YIPS. / D-SCAPE / XEPHA** [32] [ ]
– (12"ep)(cd-ep) – ('A'-D-Scape mix) / ('A'reload mix) / ('A'-M-21Q) / ('A'-28 mix).

Mar 94. (d-cd)(d-c)(2xd-lp) **SELECTED AMBIENT WORKS VOLUME II** [11] [ ]
– (12 + 13 of mostly untitled tracks; 1 of them 'Blue Calx')

Feb 95. (cd)(c)(blue-d-lp) **CLASSICS** (collection) [24] [ ]
– Digeridoo / Flaphead / Phloam / Isoproplex / Polynomial-C / Tamphex / Phlange phace / Dodeccaheedron / Analogue bubblebath / En trance to exit / Afx 2 / Metapharstic/ Digeridoo (live).

Mar 95. (12"ep)(cd-ep) **VENTOLIN / ('A'-Salbutanol mix) / ('A'-Marazanovose mix) / ('A'-Plain-an-guarry mix) / ('A'-The Coppice mix) / ('A'-Crowsnegods mix)** [49] [ ]
(12"ep-remixes)(cd-ep remixes) – ('A'-Wheeze mix) / ('A'-Carnarack mix) / ('A'-Cyclob mix) / ('A'-Deep gong mix) / ('A'-Asthma beats mix).

Apr 95. (cd)(c)(d-lp) **. . .I CARE BECAUSE YOU DO** [24] [ ]
– Acrid avid Jan Shred / The waxen path / Wax the nip / Icct Hedral / Ventolin / Come on you slags / Start as you mean to go one / Wet tip hen ax / Mookid / Alberto Balsan / Cow cud is a twin / Next heap with.

Aug 95. (12"ep)(cd-ep) **DONKEY RHUBARB EP** [ ] [ ]
– Icct Hedral (credited with PHILIP GLASS) / Pancake lizard / Mass observation (the crackdown) / Film me and finish off / One day (Sabres of Paradise mix) / Vaz deferenz.

APHRODITE'S CHILD

Formed: Southern Greece . . .1963 as trio (see below). Moved to France in the late 60's and gained European smash hit with 'RAIN AND TEARS'. A couple of years passed before they released in the UK, the acclaimed double lp '666'. VANGELIS and ROUSSOS, soon concentrated on own fruitful and diverse solo careers. •**Style:** From pop/rock to near experimental in the 70's. •**Songwriters:** Group compositions. •**Trivia:** RAIN AND TEARS was inspired by 17th century song sung in English.

Recommended: 666 (*7)

VANGELIS PAPATHANASSIOU (b.EVANGELOS, 15 Jun'47, Velos) – keyboards, wind, percussion / **DEMIS ROUSSOS** (b.15 Jun'47, Alexandria, Egypt) – vocals, bass / **LUCAS SIDERAS** (b. 5 Dec'44, Athens) – drums, vocals

Mercury Mercury

Oct 68. (7") **RAIN AND TEARS. / DON'T TRY TO CATCH A RIVER** [30] [ ]

Feb 69. (7") **END OF THE WORLD. / YOU ALWAYS STAND IN THE WAY** [ ] [ ]

Feb 69. (lp) **END OF THE WORLD** [ ] [ ]
– End of the world / Don't try to catch a river / Mister Thomas / Rain and tears / The grass is not green / Valley of sadness / You always stand in my way / The shepherd and the Moon / Day of the fool.

Polydor Polydor

Jun 69. (7") **I WANT TO LIVE. / MAGIC MIRROR** [ ] [ ]

Nov 69. (7") **LET ME LOVE, LET ME LIVE. / MARIE JOLIE** [ ] [-]

Mar 70. (7") **IT'S FIVE O'CLOCK. / FUNKY MARY** [ ] [-]

1970. (lp) **IT'S FIVE O'CLOCK** [ ] [-]
– It's five o'clock / Wake up / Take your time / Annabella / Let me love, let me live / Funky Mary / Good time so fine / Marie Jolie / Such a funny night. *(re-iss.Jul78 on 'Impact'; 6886 650)*

1970. (7") **SPRING, SUMMER, WINTER AND FALL. /** [ ] [-]

Disbanded for a time, until reappeared adding **SILVER KOULOURIS** – guitar, percussion. Guests **HARRIS HALKITIS** – bass, saxophone, percussion, vocals/ **MICHEL RIPOCHE** – trombone, saxophone/ **JOHN FORST – narration/ YANNIS TSAROUCHIS** – Greek text/ **IRENE PAPAS** – vox on (1).

Vertigo Vertigo

1972. (d-lp) **666** [ ] [ ]
– The system / Babylon / Loud, loud, loud / The four horsemen / The lamb / The seventh seal / Aegian Sea / Seven bowls / The wakening beast / Lament / The marching beast / The battle of the locusts / Do it / Tribulation / The beasts / Ofis // Seven trumpets / Altamont / The wedding of the lamb / The capture of the beast / oo / Hic and nunc / All the seats were occupied / Break. *(re-iss.Feb77) (re-iss.d-lp/c May83 on 'Impact' import)*

1972. (7") **BREAK. / BABYLON** [-] [ ]
(UK-iss.Jun75)

Disbanded again in 72/73. VANGELIS went solo, as did DEMIS ROUSSOS.

compilations, others

Jun 75. Vertigo; (lp) **THE BEST OF APHRODITE'S CHILD FEATURING DEMIS ROUSSOS** [ ] [-]

Jun75. Philips; (lp) **RAIN AND TEARS** [ ] [-]
(re-iss.lp/c Aug81 as 'GREATEST HITS 1968-1970' on 'Fontana')

APOLLO XI (see under ⇒ ORB)

APRIL WINE

Formed: Nova Scotia, Canada ... 1970 by then teenager MYLES GOODWYN with his cousins DAVID and RICHIE HENMAN. Acquired large homegrown and Stateside following, where they had signed to 'Big Tree' through Canadian label 'Aquarius'. By mid 1970, their releases were now worldwide, finally hitting UK album chart in 1980. • **Style:** Hard rock outfit mixing power with melody, but falling short of major league status. • **Songwriters:** Most by GOODWYN except 21st CENTURY SCHIZOID MAN (King Crimson) / etc. • **Trivia:** Supported The ROLLING STONES at the EL MOCAMBO CLUB in Toronto, which was released as an album (see below).

Recommended: LIVE AT THE EL MOCAMBO (*5)

MYLES GOODWYN (b.23 Jun'48) – vocals, guitar / **DAVID HENMAN** – guitar / **JIM CLENCH** – bass, vocals / **RICHIE HENMAN** – drums

Pye Big Tree

Apr 72. (lp) **APRIL WINE** [-] [ ]
– Oceana / Can't find the town / Fast train / Listen mister / Page five / Song for Mary / Wench / Time.

Apr 72. (7") **YOU COULD HAVE BEEN A LADY. / TEACHER** [ ] [32] Mar 72

Dec 72. (7") **BAD SIDE OF THE MOON. / BELIEVE IN ME** [ ] [ ]

1973. (lp) **ON RECORD** [-] [ ]
– Farkus / You could have been a lady / Believe in me / Work all day / Drop your guns / Bad side of the Moon / Refugee / Flow river flow / Carry on / Didn't you. *(cd-iss.Jul93 on 'Repertoire')*

—— **GARY MOFFAT** – guitar, vocals repl. DAVID / **JERRY MERCER** – drums, vocals repl. RICHIE

1973. (7") **WEEPING WIDOW. / JUST LIKE THAT** [ ] [ ]

1973. (lp) **ELECTRIC JEWELS** [-] [ ]
– Weeping widow / Just like that / Electric jewels / You opened my eyes / Come on along / Lady run, lady hide / I can hear you callin' / Cat's claw / The band has just begun. *(cd-iss.Jul93 on 'Repertoire')*

1974. (7") **I'M ON FIRE FOR YOU BABY (live). / COME ON ALONG** [-] [ ]

1974. (lp) **LIVE (live)** [-] [ ]

– It's true / Druthers / Cat's claw / I'm on fire for you baby / The band has just begun / Good fibes / Just like that / You could have been a lady.

1975. (lp) **STAND BACK** -
– Oowantanite / Don't push me around / Cum hear the band / Slow poke / Victim of your love / Baby done got some soul / I wouldn't want to lose your love / Highway hard run / Not for you, not for rock & roll / Wouldn't want your love / Tonite is a wonderful time to fall in love. *(US re-iss.1981 on 'Capitol')*

1975. (7") **OOWATANITE. /** -

—— **STEVE LANG** – bass repl. CLENCH who joined 451 DEGREES

1976. (lp) **FOREVER, FOR NOW** -
– Forever, for now / Child's garden / Lovin' you / Holly would / You won't dance with me / Come away / Mama Laye / I'd rather be strong / Hard times / Marjorie.

London London

Sep 76. (lp)(c) **THE WHOLE WORLD'S GOIN' CRAZY**
– Gimme love / Child's garden / Rock'n'roll woman / Wings of love / Marjorie / So bad / Shotdown / Live a lover, like a song / Kick Willy Rd. / The whole world's goin' crazy.

Oct 76. (7") **CHILD'S GARDEN. / THE WHOLE WORLD'S GOIN' CRAZY**

Jul 77. (7") **YOU WON'T DANCE WITH ME. / SHOTDOWN**

Dec 77. (lp)(c) **LIVE AT THE EL MOCAMBO (live)**
– Teenage love / Tonight is a wonderful time to fall in love / Juvenile delinquent / Don't push me around / Oowatanite / Drop your guns / Slow poke / You won't dance with me / You could have been a lady.

1978. (7") **I'M ALIVE. / ROCK AND ROLL IS A VICIOUS GAME** -

—— added **BRIAN GREENWAY** – guitar

Capitol Capitol

Mar 79. (lp)(c) **FIRST GLANCE**
– Get ready for love / Hot on the wheels of love / Rock'n'roll is a vicious game / Right down to it / Roller / Comin' right down on top of me / I'm alive / Let yourself go / Silver dollar. *(US re-iss.1981)*

Apr 79. (7") **ROLLER. / RIGHT DOWN TO IT** 34

Jun 79. (7") **COMIN' RIGHT DOWN ON TOP OF ME. / GET READY FOR LOVE** -

Feb 80. (lp)(c) **HARDER . . . FASTER** 34 64 Nov 79
– Say hello / Ladies man / Babes in arms / Better do it well / Before the dawn / I like to rock / Tonite / 21st century schizoid man.

Feb 80. (7"ep) **UNRELEASED LIVE (live)** 86
– I like to rock / Rock'n'roll is a vicious game / Before the dawn / Roller.

Apr 80. (7") **BEFORE THE DAWN. / SAY HELLO** -

Jun 80. (7") **BABES IN ARMS. / I LIKE TO ROCK** -

Aug 80. (7") **LADIES MAN. / TONITE**
(12"+=) – Get ready for love / I like to rock.

Jan 81. (7") **ALL OVER TOWN. / CRASH AND BURN**

Jan 81. (lp)(c) **THE NATURE OF THE BEAST** 48 26
– All over town / Tellin' me lies / Sign of the gypsy queen / Just between you and me / Wanna rock / Caught in the crossfire / Future tense / Big city girls / Crash and burn / Bad boys / One more time.

Mar 81. (7") **JUST BETWEEN YOU AND ME. / BIG CITY GIRLS** 52 21 Feb 81

Jun 81. (7") **SIGN OF THE GYPSY QUEEN. / CRASH AND BURN** 57 May 81

Dec 81. (lp)(c) **SUMMER TOUR '81 (live)** -

Jul 82. (7") **ENOUGH IS ENOUGH. / AIN'T GOT YOUR LOVE** 50

Jul 82. (lp)(c) **POWER PLAY** 37
– Anything you want, you got it / Ain't got your love / Blood money / If you see Kay / Tell me why / Enough is enough / What if we fall in love / Doin' it right / Waiting on a miracle / Runners in the night.

Sep 82. (7") **IF YOU SEE KAY. / BLOOD MONEY** -

Feb 84. (7") **THIS COULD BE THE RIGHT ONE. / REALLY DON'T WANT YOUR LOVE** - 58

Apr 84. (lp)(c) **ANIMAL GRACE** 62 Mar 84
– This could be the right one / Sons of the pioneers / Rock tonite / Without your love / Too hot to handle / Gimme that thing called love / Hard rock kid / Money talks / Last time I'll ever sing the blues.

1985. (lp)(c) **ONE FOR THE ROAD (live)** -
– Anything you want / I like to rock / All over town / Just between you and me / Enough is enough / This could be the right one / Sign of the gypsy queen / Medley: Like a lover like a song – Comin' right down on top of me – Rock'n'roll is a vicious game / Roller.

—— **GOODWYN** and **GREENWAY** were joined by **DANIEL BARBE** – keyboards who repl. MOFFAT / **JEAN PELLERIN** – bass repl. LANG / **MARTY SIMON** – drums repl. MERCER

Sep 85. (lp)(c) **WALKING THROUGH FIRE** -
– Rock myself to sleep / Wanted dead or alive / Beg for your love / Love has remembered me / Anejo / Open soul surgery / You don't have to act that way / Hold on / All it will ever be / Wait any more.

Sep 85. (7") **ROCK MYSELF TO SLEEP. / ALL IT WILL EVER BE** -

—— Disbanded 1985, but reformed 1990. Releases USA/Canada ?

– compilations, others, etc. –

1979. US= Aquarius; (lp) **GREATEST HITS** -

Oct 93. US= F.R.E.; (cd) **ATTITUDE** -

MYLES GOODWYN

Atlantic Atlantic

Jun 88. (lp)(c)(cd) **MYLES GOODWYN** Apr 88
– Veil of tears / Do you know what I mean / Caviar / Sonja / Head on / Face the storm / Frank Sinatra can't sing / Givin' it up (for you love) / Are you still loving me / Mama won't say (it's good).

Jul 88. (7") **FRANK SINATRA CAN'T SING. / CAVIAR** -

A PRIMARY INDUSTRY (see under ⇒ ULTRAMARINE)

ARCADIA (see under ⇒ DURAN DURAN)

ARGENT

Formed: London, England . . . 1969 by ROD, who introduced BALLARD, HENRIT and cousin RODFORD. Eponymous debut released 1970, although unsuccessful, did provide a US hit (LIAR) for THREE DOG NIGHT. Two years later they had their own hit with classic 'HOLD YOUR HEAD UP', but this failed to emulate commercial appeal. • **Style:** Progressive 'flash-rock' heavies, that was typical of self-indulgent early 70's (e.g. ELP, YES, etc.). • **Songwriters:** BALLARD or ARGENT/WHITE . • **Trivia:** BALLARD went on to produce LEO SAYER and ROGER DALTREY, and write for many others.

Recommended: THE BEST OF ARGENT – AN ANTHOLOGY (*7)

ROD ARGENT (b.14 Jun'45, St.Albans) – keyboards, vocals (ex-ZOMBIES) / **RUSS BALLARD** (b.31 Oct'47, Waltham Cross) – vocals, guitar (ex-ROULETTES) / **JIM RODFORD** (b. 7 Jul'45, St.Albans, England) – bass (ex-ZOMBIES) / **BOB HENRIT** (b. 2 May'45, Broxbourne) – drums (ex-ROULETTES)

Epic Epic

Jan 70. (lp)(c) **ARGENT**
– Like honey / Liar / Be free / Schoolgirl / Dance in the smoke / Lonely hard road / The feeling's inside / Freefall / Stepping stone / Bring you joy. *(re-iss.Oct76) (re-iss.lp+cd Sep91 on 'B.G.O.')*

Jan 71. (7") **CELEBRATION. / KINGDOM**

Feb 71. (lp)(c) **RING OF HANDS**
– Celebration / Sweet Mary / Cast your spell Uranus / Lothlorien / Chained / Rejoice / Pleasure / Sleep won't help me / Where are we going wrong.

Nov 71. (7") **HOLD YOUR HEAD UP. / CLOSER TO HEAVEN**

Feb 72. (7") **HOLD YOUR HEAD UP. / KEEP ON ROLLIN'** 5 5

Apr 72. (lp)(c) **ALL TOGETHER NOW** 13 23
– Hold your head up / Keep on rollin' / Tragedy / I am the dance of ages / Be my lover, be my friend / He's a dynamo / Pure love: a) Fantasia – b) Prelude – c) Pure love – d) Finale.

Jun 72. (7") **TRAGEDY. / REJOICE** 34

Mar 73. (7") **GOD GAVE ROCK AND ROLL TO YOU. / CHRISTMAS FOR THE FREE** 18

Mar 73. (lp)(c) **IN DEEP** 49 90
– God gave rock and roll to you / It's only money (part 1 & 2) / Losing hold / Be glad / Christmas for the free / Candles on the river / Rosie. *(quad-lp also released) (cd-iss.Jun95 on 'Columbia')*

Jul 73. (7") **IT'S ONLY MONEY (part 2). / CANDLE ON THE RIVER**

Feb 74. (7") **THUNDER AND LIGHTNING. / KEEPER OF THE FLAME**

Feb 74. (lp)(c) **NEXUS**
– The comming of Kohoutek / Once around the Sun / Infinite wanderer / Love / Music from the spheres / Thunder and lightning / Keeper of the flame / Man for all reasons / Gonna meet my maker.

May 74. (7") **MAN FOR ALL REASONS. / MUSIC FROM THE SPHERES**

Nov 74. (d-lp)(d-c) **ENCORE (live)**
– The coming of Kohoutec / It's only money (part 1 & 2) / God gave rock and roll to you / Thunder and lightning / Music from the spheres / I don't believe in miracles / I am the dance of ages / Keep on rollin' / Hold your head up / Time of the season. *(cd-iss.Nov93 on 'B.G.O.')*

Nov 74. (7") **KEEP ON ROLLIN' (live). / I AM THE DANCE OF AGES (live)**

—— (May74) **JOHN GRIMALDI** (b.25 May'55) – lead guitar and **JOHN VERITY** (b. 2 May'44) – guitar (ex-Solo) repl. BALLARD who went solo, + composer

Apr 75. (lp)(c) **CIRCUS**
– Circus / Highwire / Clown / Trapeze / Shine on sunshine / The ring / The jester.

Jun 75. (7") **HIGHWIRE. / CIRCUS**

Good Earth-RCA United Art

Oct 75. (lp)(c) **COUNTERPOINT**
– On my feet again / I can't remember / But yes / Time / Waiting for the yellow one / It's off / Be strong / Rock & roll show / Butterfly / Road back home.

Oct 75. (7") **ROCK'N'ROLL SHOW. / IT'S FALLEN OFF**

—— Disbanded Jun76, when GRIMALDI quit. The rest formed PHOENIX apart from ROD ARGENT who went solo, etc.

– compilations, others, etc. –

Feb 76. Epic; (7") **HOLD YOUR HEAD UP. / GOD GAVE ROCK AND ROLL TO YOU**
(re-iss.Jul84 on 'C.B.S.)

Apr 76. Epic; (lp)(c) **AN ANTHOLOGY – THE BEST OF ARGENT**
– School girl / It's only money / Pleasure / Hold your head up / Thunder and lightning / Liar / God gave rock'n'roll to you / Keep on rollin'. *(re-iss.Sep84) (cd-iss.Apr90)*

Jun 76. Epic; (7") **HOLD YOUR HEAD UP. / IT'S ONLY MONEY**

Feb 79. Epic; (7") **HOLD YOUR HEAD UP. / TRAGEDY**

Apr 78. Hallmark; (lp)(c) **HOLD YOUR HEAD UP** -

Jul 82. Old Gold; (7") **HOLD YOUR HEAD UP. / DANCE IN THE SMOKE** -

Nov 88. Old Gold; (7") **GOD GAVE ROCK AND ROLL TO YOU. / TRAGEDY** -

May 91. Elite; (cd)(c) **MUSIC FROM THE SPHERES** -
(re-iss. Sep93)

Sep 94. Rewind; (cd) **ALL TOGETHER NOW** -

Mar 95. Windsong; (cd) **IN CONCERT (live)** -

ROD ARGENT

M.C.A. M.C.A.?

May 77. (7") **GYMNOPEDIES No.1. / LIGHT FANTASTIC** [ ] [-]

May 78. (7") **ARGENTINE MELODY (CANCION DE ARGENTINA). / ('A' version) (by SAN JOSE featuring RODRIGUEZ ARGENTINA** [14] [-]
(aka ROD ARGENT) who also composed this theme tune to for the World Cup.

Sep 78. (7") **HOME. / No.1** [ ] [-]

Oct 78. (lp)(c) **MOVING HOME** [ ] [-]
– Home / Silence / I'm in the mood / Summer / No.1 / Tenderness / Well, well, well / Pastorius mentioned / Smiling / Recollection. *(re-iss.Jul82)*

Jan 79. (7") **SILENCE. / RECOLLECTION** [ ] [-]

ROD ARGENT & BARBARA THOMPSON

M.C.A. M.C.A.

Jan 82. (7")(12") **WITH YOU. / GHOSTS** [ ] [-]

Feb 82. (lp)(c) **GHOSTS** [ ] [-]
– Poltergeist / With you / Secret soul / All alone / Ghosts / Little girl / Falling stars / Moving on / Sweet spirit.

ROD ARGENT

Vera Bra not issued

1985. (lp) **SHADOWSHOW** [-] [-] Germ'y
– Secure in you / Down on your luck / Sleepwalker / Siren / Manhattan midnite / It's over / Echoes / Moving in the morning sun / Doing what must be done / Midday riser / Times past.

M.M.C. not issued

Jun 88. (lp)(c)(cd) **RED HOUSE** [ ] [-]
– Teenage years / Salvation song / A 4th gymnopedie / Helpless / Sweet Russian / In memory / Baby don't you cry no more / First touch / Suite T / Spirits.

Sep 88. (7") **BABY DON'T YOU CRY NO MORE. / TEENAGE YEARS** [ ] [-]

ROD ARGENT & PETER VAN HOOKE featuring CLEM CLEMPSON

Weekend not issued

Mar 90. (7") **NOT WITH A BANG. / THE PIGLET FILES** [ ] [-]

Joan ARMATRADING

Born: 9 Dec'50, Basseterre, St. Kitts, West Indies. She and her family moved to Birmingham, England in '58. In 1969, she befriended PAM NESTOR (b. 28 Apr'48, Berbice, Guyana) and initiates songwriting and stage partnership. They sever this arrangement when ARMATRADING alone is credited on debut album in '73 for 'Cube'. Two years later she signed to 'A&M' for UK Top 10 eponymous 3rd album, which broke her through to wide popularity, due to it containing hit single 'LOVE AND AFFECTION'. From then on, mostly with albums, she achieved great success, culminating in 1988 when she appeared at Nelson Mandela concert at Wembley stadium. • **Style:** Black singer/songwriter guitarist, whose wide range complimented folk, jazz, rock and pop. Most too, cited JONI MITCHELL as influence, but stamped own mark on rock scene, even after TRACY CHAPMAN came about. • **Songwriters:** She writes all material, except when Nestor wrote lyrics until '75. Covered; MOONDANCE (Van Morrison). • **Trivia:** MARK KNOPFLER (Dire Straits) and MARK BRZEZICKI (Big Country) guested on her 1988 album 'THE SHOUTING STAGE'.

Recommended: THE VERY BEST OF JOAN ARMATRADING (*6)

JOAN ARMATRADING – vocals, acoustic guitar with various session people.

Cube A & M

Nov 72. (lp) **WHATEVER'S FOR US** [ ] [ ]
– My family / City girl / Spend a little time / Whatever's for us / Child star / Mean old man / Visionary mountains / It could have been better / Head of the table / Mister remember me / Give it a try / Alice / Conversation / Mean old man / All the King's garden. *(re-iss.1974, Mar78 + Oct81 +c) (re-iss.+cd.Apr89 on 'Castle')*

Jul 73. (7") **LONELY LADY. / TOGETHER IN WORDS AND MUSIC** [ ] [ ]

A&M A&M

Apr 75. (lp)(c) **BACK TO THE NIGHT** [ ] [ ]
– No love for free / Travelled so far / Steppin' out / Dry land / Cool blue / Stole my heart / Get in touch with Jesus / Body to dust / Back to the night / Let's go dancing / Come when you need me. *(re-iss.Mar82) (re-iss.Sep84 on 'Hallmark')*

Jun 75. (7") **BACK TO THE NIGHT. / SO GOOD** [ ] [ ]

Nov 75. (7") **DRY LAND. / BODY INTO DUST** [ ] [ ]

Aug 76. (lp)(c) **JOAN ARMATRADING** [12] [67]
– Down to zero / Help yourself / Water with the vine / Love and affection / Save me / Join the boys / People / Somebody who loves you / Like fire / Tall in the saddle. *(cd-iss.1988 & Aug91)*

Aug 76. (7") **LOVE AND AFFECTION. / HELP YOURSELF** [10] [ ]
(re-iss.1988)

Jan 77. (7") **DOWN TO ZERO. / LIKE FIRE** [ ] [ ]

Apr 77. (7") **WATER WITH THE WINE. / PEOPLE** [-] [ ]

Sep 77. (lp)(c) **SHOW SOME EMOTION** [6] [52]
– Woncha come on home / Show some emotion / Warm love / Never is too late / Peace in mind / Opportunity / Mama mercy / Get in the sun / Willow / Kissin' and a huggin'. *(re-iss.Apr86) (cd-iss.Aug89)*

Oct 77. (7") **WILLOW. / NO WAY OUT** [ ] [-]

Jan 78. (7") **SHOW SOME EMOTION. / PEACE IN MIND** [ ] [-]

Feb 78. (7") **SHOW SOME EMOTION. / NO WAY OUT** [-] [ ]

Mar 78. (7") **WARM LOVE. / GET IN THE SUN** [ ] [-]

May 78. (7") **WARM LOVE. / NO WAY OUT** [-] [ ]

Jun 78. (7") **FLIGHT OF THE WILD GEESE. / NO WAY OUT** [-] [ ]

Sep78. (lp)(c) **TO THE LIMIT** [13] [ ]
– Barefoot and pregnant / Your letter / Am I blue for you / You rope you tie me / Baby I / Bottom to the top / Taking my baby up town / What do you want / Wishing / Let it last. *(cd-iss.1988)*

Oct 78. (7") **BOTTOM TO THE TOP. / YOUR LETTER** [ ] [ ]

Jan 79. (7") **BAREFOOT AND PREGNANT. /YOUR LETTER** [-] [ ]

Aug 79. (lp)(c) **STEPPING OUT (live)** [ ] [ ]
– Mama mercy / Cool blue / Stole my heart / How cruel / Kissin' and a huggin' / Love song / Love and affection / Stepin' out / You rope you tie me / Kissin' and a huggin' / Tall in the saddle. *(re-iss.Sep85 +c on 'Hallmark')*

Dec 79. (m-lp) **HOW CRUEL** [-] [ ]
– How cruel / He wants her / I really must be going / Rosie.

Jan 80. (7") **ROSIE. / HOW CRUEL** [49] [ ]

Apr 80. (7") **HE WANTS HER. / SHOW SOME EMOTION** [-] [ ]

May 80. (lp)(c) **ME MYSELF I** [5] [28]
– Me myself I / Ma-me-o-beach / Friends / Is it tomorrow yet / Turn out the light / When you kisses me / All the way from America / Feeling in my heart (for you) / Simon / I need you. *(cd-iss.Sep86) (re-iss.cd+c May93 on 'Spectrum')*

Jun 80. (7") **ME MYSELF I. / WHEN YOU KISS ME** [21] [-]

Jun 80. (7") **ME MYSELF I. / FRIENDS** [-] [ ]

Aug 80. (7") **ALL THE WAY FROM AMERICA. / IS IT TOMORROW YET** [54] [ ]

Sep 80. (7") **IS IT TOMORROW YET. / MA-ME-O-BEACH** [-] [ ]

Oct 80. (7") **SIMON. / HE WANTS HER** [-] [ ]

Aug 81. (7") **I'M LUCKY. / SHINE** [46] [ ]

Sep 81. (lp)(c) **WALK UNDER LADDERS** [6] [88]
– I'm lucky / When I get it right / Romancers / I wanna hold you / The weakness in me / No love / At the hop / I can't lie to myself / Eating the bear / Only one. *(cd-iss.Nov88)*

Oct 81. (7") **WHEN I GET IT RIGHT. / CRYING** [ ] [ ]

Jan 82. (7") **NO LOVE. / DOLLARS** [50] [ ]

Jan 82. (7") **THE WEAKNESS IN ME. / CRYING** [-] [ ]

Apr 82. (7") **I WANNA HOLD YOU. / CRYING** [-] [ ]

Feb 83. (7")(12") **DROP THE PILOT. / BUSINESS IS BUSINESS** [11] [ ]

Mar 83. (lp)(c) **THE KEY** [10] [32]
– (I love it when you) Call me names / Foolish pride / Drop the pilot / The key / Everybody gotta know / Tell tale / What do boys dream / The game of love / The dealer / Bad habit / I love my baby. *(cd-iss.Jun86)*

May 83. (7") **(I LOVE IT WHEN YOU) CALL ME NAMES. / FOR THE BEST** [ ] [ ]

Nov 83. (7") **HEAVEN. / FRUSTRATION** [-] [ ]

Nov 83. (7") **HEAVEN. / BACK TO THE NIGHT** [14] [-]

Feb 85. (lp)(c)(cd) **SECRET SECRETS** [14] [73]
– Persona grata / Temptation / Moves / Talking to the wall / Love by you / Thinking man / Friends not lovers / One night / Secret secrets / Strange.

Feb 85. (7") **TEMPTATION. / TALKING TO THE WALL** [65] [ ]
(12"+=) – Spanking brand new.

May 85. (7") **THINKING MAN. / LOVE GROWS** [ ] [ ]

Aug 85. (7")(12") **LOVE BY YOU. / READ IT WRITE** [ ] [ ]

Apr 86. (7")(12") **KIND WORDS (AND A REAL GOOD HEART). / FIGURE OF SPEECH** [ ] [ ]

May 86. (lp)(c)(cd) **SLEIGHT OF HAND** [34] [68]
– Kind words (and a real good heart) / Reach out / Killing time / Angel man / Laurel and the rose / One more chance / Russian roulette / Jesse / Figure of speech / Don Juan.

Jun 86. (7") **ANGEL MAN. / RIVERS OF FIRE** [-] [ ]

Jul 86. (7") **REACH OUT. / RIVERS ON FIRE** [ ] [-]

Sep 86. (7") **JESSE. / DON JUAN** [ ] [-]
(d7"+=)(12"+=) – Love and affection / Willow.

Jul 88. (7") **LIVING FOR YOU. / INNOCENT REQUEST** [ ] [-]
(12"+=)(cd-s+=) – Cool Blue stole my heart.

Jul 88. (lp)(c)(cd) **THE SHOUTING STAGE** [28] [ ]
– The Devil I know / Living for you / Did I make you up / Stronger love / The shouting stage / Words / Straight talk / Watch you step / All a woman needs / Dark truths. (cd+=) – Innocent request.

Jul 88. (7") **LIVING FOR YOU. / I REALLY MUST BE GOING** [-] [ ]

Sep 88. (7") **THE SHOUTING STAGE. / I REALLY MUST BE GOING** [ ] [ ]
(12"+=)(cd-s+=) – He wants her.

Nov 88. (7") **STRONGER LOVE. / THE DEVIL I KNOW** [ ] [ ]

May 90. (7")(c-s) **MORE THAN ONE KIND OF LOVE. / GOOD TIMES** [75] [ ]
(12"+=)(cd-s+=) – Love and affection.

Jun 90. (lp)(c)(cd) **HEARTS AND FLOWERS** [29] [ ]
– More than one kind of love / Hearts and flowers / Promise land / Someone's in the background / Can't let go / Free / Something in the air tonight / Always / Good times / The power of dreams.

Jun 90. (7")(c-s) **PROMISE LAND. / DOWN TO ZERO (live)** [ ] [ ]
(12"+=)(cd-s+=) – Dark truths (live).

Aug 90. (7") **FREE. / THE SHOUTING STAGE (live)** [ ] [ ]
(cd-s+=) – Always.

May 92. (7") **WRAPPED AROUND HER. / PROMISE LAND (live at the BBC)** [56] [ ]
(cd-s) – ('A'side) / All the way from America / I'm lucky / Can't lie to myself (all live at the BBC).

Jun 92. (cd)(c)(lp) **SQUARE THE CIRCLE** [34] [ ]
– True love / Crazy / Wrapped around her / Sometimes I don't wanna go home / Square the circle / Weak woman / Can I get next to you / Can't get over (how I broke your heart) / If women ruled the world / Cradled in your love.

Jul 92. (7")(c-s) **TRUE LOVE. / MORE THAN ONE KIND OF LOVE (live)** [ ] [ ]
(12"+=)(cd-s+=) – Love and affection (live) / Something in the air (live).

R.C.A. R.C.A.

May 95. (cd)(c) **WHAT'S INSIDE** [48] [ ]
– In your eyes / Everyday boy / Merchant of love / Shapes and sizes / Back on the

road / Lost the love / Songs / Would you like to dance / Recommend my love / Beyond the blue / Can't stop loving you / Shape of a pony / Trouble.

– compilations, others –

Dec 76. Cube; (7") **ALICE. / ALL THE KING'S GARDEN** [ ] [-]
Jun 82. Cube; (7") **LONELY LADY. / VISIONARY MOUNTAINS** [ ] [-]
May 81. A&M; (d-c) **JOAN ARMATRADING / TO THE LIMIT** [ ] [ ]
Nov 83. A&M; (lp)(c) **TRACK RECORD** [18] [ ]
(cd-iss.Oct84)
Apr 88. A&M; (cd-ep) **COMPACT HITS** [ ] [-]
– Love and affection / All the way from America / Willow / Flight of the wild geese.
Jun 89. A&M; (c) **ME MYSELF I / TRACK RECORD** [ ] [ ]
Feb 91. A&M; (7") **LOVE AND AFFECTION (remix). / ALL THE WAY FROM AMERICA** [ ] [ ]
(12"+=)(cd-s+=) – Promise land.
Mar 91. A&M; (cd)(c)(lp) **THE VERY BEST OF JOAN ARMATRADING** [9] [ ]
– Love and affection / Down to zero / Drop the pilot / Show some emotion / The shouting stage / Willow / Rosie / I'm lucky / Me, myself, I / (I love it when you) Call me names / Bottom to the top / More than one kind of love / The weakness in me / All the way from America.
Oct 93. A&M; (cd) **ME MYSELF I / WALK UNDER LADDERS** [ ] [-]
Feb 85. Sierra; (lp)(c) **REPLAY** [ ] [-]
Jun 90. Knight; (cd)(c) **THE GOLDEN HOUR OF JOAN ARMATRADING** [ ] [-]

ARMOURY SHOW (see under ⇒ SKIDS)

ARMS AND LEGS (see under ⇒ JACKSON, Joe)

ARRESTED DEVELOPMENT

Formed: Atlanta, Georgia, USA . . . 1988 by SPEECH (ex-DISCIPLES OF LYRICAL REBELLION who evolved into SECRET SOCIETY) and HEADLINER. They signed to Chrysalis off-shoot 'Cooltempo' early 1991, and unleashed successful appropriately titled debut album '3 YEARS, 5 MONTHS AND 2 DAYS IN THE LIFE OF . . . ' in May '92. • **Style:** Influenced by The JUNGLE BROTHERS and DE LA SOUL, their Africa meeting American sound, certainly recalled the 70's moods of SLY STONE. Smooth rhythmically, their Southern hip-hop, showed an awareness for environmental values. • **Songwriters:** SPEECH. • **Trivia:** SPEECH was originally called PEACH after his complexion.

Recommended: 3 YEARS, 5 MONTHS AND 2 DAYS IN THE LIFE OF . . . (*6).

SPEECH (b. TODD THOMAS, 1968, Milwaukee) – vocals, producer, co-music director / **HEADLINER** (b. TIM BARNWELL, 1967) – turntable / **AERLE TAREE** (b. TAREE JONES, 1972) – vocals, stylist / **MONTSHO ESHE** (b. TEMELCA GARTHER, 1974) – dancer, vocals / **RASA DON** (b. DONALD JONES, 1968) – drums / **BABA OJE** (b. 1933) – spritual advisor / plus extended family **DIONNE FARRIS + SISTER PAULETTE** – vocals / **CINQUE** (TERRANCE MASON) / **BROTHER LARRY** – guitar (1) / **LARRY JACKSON** – saxophone (1)

Cooltempo Cooltempo

Apr 92. (7")(c-s) **TENNESSEE. / NATURAL** [46] [6]
(12"+=)(cd-s+=) – ('A'mix).
Oct 92. (7")(c-s) **PEOPLE EVERYDAY. / ('A'mix)** [2] [8] Jul 92
(12"+=)(cd-s+=) – Tennessee.
Oct 92. (cd)(c)(lp) **3 YEARS, 5 MONTHS AND 2 DAYS IN THE LIFE OF . . .** [3] [7] May 92
– Man's final frontier / Mama's always on stage / People everyday / Blues happy / Mr.Wendal / Children play with earth / Raining revolution / Fishin' 4 religion / Give a man a fish / U / Eve of reality / Dawn of the dreads / Tennessee / Washed away. *(re-iss.cd. Mar'94)*
Dec 92. (7")(c-s) **MR.WENDAL. / REVOLUTION** [4] [6] [90]
(12"+=)(cd-s+=) – ('A' Perfecto mix, or It ain't no baseline mix') / ('A' full mix).
Mar 93. (7")(c-s) **TENNESSEE (Edit). / FISHIN' 4 RELIGION** [18] [-]
(cd-s+=) – ('A' remix) / Mama's always on the stage

—— added **NADRIAH ALI** – vocals plus new extended family **KUNDALINI MARK BATSON** – co-music director, piano / **JU JU HOUSE** – drums / **FREDERICK CASH JR.** – bass / **BRANDON ROSS** – guitar / **ATIBA WILSON** – percussion, flute / **DAVID PLEASANT** – handmade percussion / **TERRANCE** (retained), **KELLI SAE, ARNAE, KEVIN CARNES & FULANI HART**

Chrysalis Chrysalis

Apr 93. (cd)(c)(lp) **UNPLUGGED** [40] [60] Mar 93
– Time / Give a man a fish / The gettin' / Natural / Searchin' for one soul / Raining revolution / Fishin' 4 religion / Mama's always on stage / U / Mr.Wendal / People everyday / (next 7 all instrumental-) Give a man a fish / The gettin' / Natural / Searchin' for one soul / Raining revolution / Mama's always on stage / Mr.Wendal.
May 94. (7")(c-s) **EASE MY MIND. / SHELL** [33] [45]
(12"+=)(cd-s+=) – (2 'A'versions).
Jun 94. (cd)(c)(d-lp) **ZINGALAMADUNI** [16] [55]
– WMFW (We Must Fight & Win) Fm / United minds / Ache'n for acres / United front / Africa's inside me / Pride / Shell / Mister Landlord / Warm sentiments / The drum / In the sunshine / Kneelin' at my altar / Fountain of youth / Ease my mind / Praisin' U.

ART (see under ⇒ SPOOKY TOOTH)

Neil ARTHUR (see under ⇒ BLANCMANGE)

ART OBJECTS (see under ⇒ BLUE AEROPLANES)

ART OF NOISE

Formed: London, England . . . mid'83 by DUDLEY and JECZALIK. Signed to TREVOR HORN and PAUL MORLEY's new label 'Z.T.T.' through 'Island'. Late in 1984, they secured first UK Top 10 hit with 'CLOSE TO THE EDIT'. A year later, they shifted to 'China' records, and collaborated on hit singles with DUANE EDDY ('Peter Gunn') and TOM JONES ('Kiss'). • **Style:** Mostly instrumental electronics using chants and guest vocalists. Their themes are heard on TV ads and programmes 'Krypton Factor' and 'The Return Of Sherlock Holmes'. • **Songwriters:** Group compositions except, KISS (Prince) / PETER GUNN (Duane Eddy). • **Trivia:** ANNE was pianist on children's BBC-TV programme 'Playschool' until she became part of CINDY & THE SAFFRONS with actress JOANNE WHALLEY-(KILMER). Their single 'PAST PRESENT & FUTURE' hit No.56 early 1983. She now writes / arranges / sessions for PHIL COLLINS ('Buster') / BOY GEORGE / A-HA / MOODY BLUES / PAUL McCARTNEY / LLOYD COLE / etc. Her film scores include; Disorderlines (1987), Hiding Out (1987), Dragnet (1987), Buster (1988), Silence Like Glass (1989), The Mighty Quinn (1989), Say Anything (1989), Wilt (1990), The Miracle (1991), The Pope Must Die (1991), The Crying Game (1992; nominated for an oscar) & Knight Moves (1993). JEKZALIK has produced PET SHOP BOYS / GODLEY & CREME / PAUL McCARTNEY / etc. LANGAN too has produced ABC / BILLY IDOL / SPANDAU BALLET / PUBLIC IMAGE LTD. / etc. (PAUL MORLEY as JJ quoted 'Made tea and gave titles to songs').

Recommended: (WHO'S AFRAID OF?) THE ART OF NOISE (*7).

ANNE DUDLEY – keyboards (ex-CINDY & THE SAFFRONS) / **J.J. JECZALIK** – keyboards, programmer / **GARY LANGAN** – keyboards, synthesizers / with **TREVOR HORN** – keyboards, producer (ex-YES, ex-BUGGLES)

Z.T.T.-Island Island

Aug 83. (12"ep)(c-ep) **INTO BATTLE WITH THE ART OF NOISE** [ ] [-]
– Battle / The army now / Donna / Bright noise / Flesh in armour / Come and goes / Moments in love.
Mar 84. (12") **BEATBOX (DIVERSIONS 1). / BEATBOX (DIVERSIONS 2)** [ ] [ ]
Mar 84. (7")(12") **BEATBOX. / MOMENTS IN LOVE** [ ] [ ]
Oct 84. (7")(7"pic-d) **CLOSE (TO THE EDIT). / A TIME TO HEAR (WHO'S LISTENING)** [8] [ ]
(12") – CLOSE UP. / CLOSE UP (HOP)
(12") – (above 2 plus 'A'side).
(12"pic-d) – EDITED. / A TIME TO CLEAR (IT UP)
(12") – CLOSELY CLOSELY (ENOUGH'S ENOUGH). / (7"B-side) (+=) – Close Up (Hop)/ / or / / Moments In Love.
(c-s) – ('A'side)/ (various mixes of 'A').
Oct 84. (lp)(c) **(WHO'S AFRAID OF?)** [27] [85]
– A time for fear (who's afraid?) / Beat box (diversion one) / Snapshot / Close (to the edit) / Who's afraid (of the Art Of Noise) / Moments in love / Momento / How to kill / Realisation. *(cd-iss.Dec85) (re-iss.cd+c May94)*
Mar 85. (7")(7"pic-d)(7"sha-pic-d) **MOMENTS IN LOVE. / BEATBOX** [51] [ ]
(12") – ('A'side) / Beaten / Beatbox diversion 10 / Love beat.
(c-s) – ('A'side) / (various mixes).
Jul 85. (7") **MOMENTS IN LOVE. / LOVE BEAT** [ ] [ ]
(12"+=) – (Beaten) Moments in love. *(re-iss.7"/12" Jun87)*

added guest **GEOFF DUGMORE** – drums (ex-EUROPEANS) / HORN also left

China Chrysalis

Oct 85. (7") **LEGS. / HOOPS AND MALLETS** [69] [ ]
(12"+=) – Legs (inside leg mix).
Mar 86. (7")(7"sha-pic-d) **PETER GUNN** (as "ART OF NOISE featuring DUANE EDDY" – guitar). / **SOMETHING ALWAYS HAPPENS** [8] [50]
(12"+=) – ('A'extended).
Apr 86. (lp)(c)(cd) **IN VISIBLE SILENCE** [18] [53]
– Opus 4 / Paranoimia / Eye of a needle / Legs / Peter Gunn / Slip of the tongue / Beatback / Instruments of darkness / Camilla / Chameleon's dish / Legs. (cd+=) – Peter Gunn (extended).
May 86. (7")(7"sha-pic-d) **PARANOIMIA** (as "ART OF NOISE featuring MAX HEADROOM"). / **WHY ME?** [12] [34]
(12"+=) – A nation rejects / ('A'version).
(Max= laser dummy)

—— Trimmed to duo, when LANGAN was now only part-time.

Oct 86. (7") **LEGACY. / OPUS III** [ ] [ ]
(12"+=) – Legs / ('A'version).
Jul 87. (7") **DRAGNET (ART OF NOISE '88). / ACTION ART** [60] [ ]
(12"+=)(cd-s+=) – Dragnet (Arthur Baker mix).
Aug 87. (lp)(c)(cd) **IN NO SENSE? NONSENSE!** [55] [ ]
– Galleons of stone / Dragnet / Fin du temps / How rapid? / Opus for four / Debut / E.F.L. / Ode to Don Jose / A day at the races / Counterpoint / Roundabout 727 / Random on the sand / Roller 1 / Nothing was going to stop them anyway / Crusoe / One Earth. *(re-iss.c+cd.Jul91)*
Feb 88. (7") **DRAGNET. / DRAGNET (A-O-N mix)** [ ] [ ]
(12"+=) – ('A' Arthur Baker mix).
Nov 88. (7"+cd-s) **KISS** (as "ART OF NOISE featuring TOM JONES"). / **E.F.L.** [5] [31]
(cd-s+=) – Kiss (the battery mix).
(12") – ('A'version) / Ode to Don Jose.
Mar 89. (7") **PARANOIMIA '89. / LOCUS CASSICUS** [ ] [ ]
(12"+=)(cd-s+=) – One Earth / Rounding of the sand / debut / Adananda.
Jul 89. (7") **YEBO.** (as "ART OF NOISE featuring MAHLATHINI & THE MAHOTELLA QUEENS") / **DAN DARE** [63] [ ]

(12"+=) – ('A'remix).
(12"+=)(cd-s+=) – Add to the confusion / Yebo (mbaguana mix).
(re-iss.Mar95)

Sep 89. (lp)(c)(cd) **BELOW THE WASTE** [ ] [ ]
– Yebo / Promenade 1 / Island / Chain gang / Back to back / Spit / Catwalk / Dilemma / Dan Dare / Promenade 2 / Flashback / Finale.

Jun 90. (7")(c-s) **ART OF LOVE. / HEART OF LOVE** [67] [ ]
(12"+=)(cd-s+=) – Ambience of love.

– compilations, others, etc. –

Dec 88. China; (lp)(c)(cd) **THE BEST OF ART OF NOISE** [55] [83]
– Beatbox / Moments in love / Close (to the edit) / Peter Gunn / Paranoimia / Legacy / Dragnet '88 / Kiss / Something always happens / Opus 4. (cd+=) (several extended remixes.)

Jul 90. China; (cd)(c)(lp) **THE AMBIENT COLLECTION** [ ] [ ]

Dec 91. China; (7")(c-s) **INSTRUMENTS OF DARKNESS (ALL OF US ARE ONE PEOPLE) (The Prodigy mix). / L.E.F. (Mark Brydon mix)** [45] [ ]
(12"+=)(cd-s+=) – ('A'&'B'-Prodigy remixes).

Jan 92. China; (cd)(c)(lp) **THE FON REMIXES** [ ] [ ]

Feb 92. China; (7")(c-s) **SHADES OF PARANOIMIA (Carl Cox mix). / ROLLER 20 (rhythmatic mix)** [53] [ ]
(12"+=)(cd-s+=) – Kiss / Peter Gunn / Paranoimia.

May 94. China; (cd)(c) **DAFT** [ ] [ ]

ANNE DUDLEY & JAZ COLEMAN

(JAZ – vocals, keyboards, (of KILLING JOKE)

China China

Sep 90. (7")(c-s) **MINARETS AND MEMORIES. / THE AWAKENING** [ ] [ ]
(12"+=)(cd-s+=) ('A'dance mix).

Oct 90. (cd)(c)(lp) **SONGS FROM THE VICTORIOUS CITY** [ ] [ ]
– The awakening / Endless festival / Minarets and memories / Force and fire / Mabebe / Ziggaretts of cinnamon / Hannah / The conquerer / A survivor's tale / In a timeless place.

Dec 90. (7") **MABEBE. / THE CONQUERER** [ ] [ ]
(12"+=)(cd-s+=) – In a timeless place.

ANNE DUDLEY

Echo not issued

Feb 95. (cd)(c) **ANCIENT & MODERN** [ ] [ ]
– Canticles of the Sun and the Moon / Veni sancte spiritus / Communion / Veni Emmanuel / Tallis Canon / The holly and the ivy / Coventry carol / Prelude / 3 chorals in common time.

Nov 95. (c-s) **VENI EMMANUEL / THE HOLLY AND THE IVY** [ ] [-]
(cd-s+=) – The sunset carol / The testimony of John.

ASH

Formed: Downpatrick, County Down, Ireland . . .1992 by TIM WHEELER, MARK HAMILTON and RICK McMURRAY. After a few limited indie 45's, they were signed to 'Infectious', making UK Top 20 in 1995. **•Style:** Youngsters influenced by Ramones and UNDERTONES, on the retro backlash of 90's punk America. **•Songwriters:** WHEELER or w/ HAMILTON except cover GET READY (Temptations). **•Trivia:** The cover sleeve of their single 'KUNG FU', had a photo of French Man U star footballer ERIC CANTONA, giving his famous throat and neck tackle on an abusive Crystal Palace supporter in 1995.

Recommended: TRAILER (*7)

TIM WHEELER – guitar/ **MARK HAMILTON** – bass / **RICK McMURRAY** – drums

La Land not issued

Feb 94. (7") **JACK NAMES THE PLANETS. / DON'T KNOW** [ ] [-]

Infectious Generator

Aug 94. (7"ep) **PETROL / THE LITTLE POND. / A MESSAGE FROM OSCAR WILDE AND PATRICK THE BREWER** [ ] [-]
(cd-s+=) – Things.

Oct 94. (cd)(c)(m-lp) **TRAILER** [ ] [-]
– Season / Jack names the planets / Intense thing / Uncle Pat / Get out / Petrol / Obscure thing. (lp w/free 7"yellow) SILVER SURFER. / JAZZ '59

Oct 94. (7") **UNCLE PAT. / DIFFERENT TODAY** [ ] [-]
(cd-s+=) – Hulk Hogan bubble bath.

Mar 95. (7") **KUNG FU./ DAY OF THE TRIFFIDS** [57] [-]
(7"mispressed) – ('A'side) / Luther Ingo's star cruiser.
(cd-s) – (all 3 tracks).

Jul 95. (7")(c-s) **GIRL FROM MARS. / CANTINA BAND** [11] [-]
(cd-s+=) – Astral conversations with Toulouse Lautrec.

Sep 95. (7"clear)(7"gold)("white) **PETROL. / PUNKBOY** [-] [ ]

Oct 95. (7")(c-s)(cd-s) **ANGEL INTERCEPTOR. / 5 A.M. ETERNAL / GIVE ME SOME TRUTH** [14] [-]

Dec 95. (7"red) **GET READY. / ZERO, ZERO, ZERO** [ ] [-]
(above 45 issued on 'Fantastic Plastic')

Daniel ASH (see under ⇒ BAUHAUS)

Tony ASHTON & Jon LORD (see under ⇒ DEEP PURPLE)

ASIA

Formed: London, England based . . . early 1981 by seasoned veteran rockers WETTON, HOWE, PALMER and DOWNES. These supergroup stadium fillers had no trouble finding record contract with 'Geffen'. Their eponymous debut soon climbed to No.1 in the US, and supplanted them as top group over similar challengers YES. • **Style:** AOR catering more for US audiences. • **Songwriters:** All penned by WETTON, HOWE and DOWNES. No covers. • **Trivia:** Their "Asia In Asia" concert at Budokan, Tokyo 6 Dec'83, went live to over 20 million people in US through MTV station

Recommended: THEN & NOW (*5)

JOHN WETTON (b.12 Jul'49, Derby, England) – vocals, bass (ex-URIAH HEEP, ex-ROXY MUSIC, ex-BRYAN FERRY, ex-KING CRIMSON, ex-FAMILY, ex-U.K.) / **STEVE HOWE** (b. 8 Apr'47) – guitar, vocals (ex-YES, ex-BODAST, ex-TOMORROW) / **GEOFFREY DOWNES** – keyboards, vocals (ex-YES, ex-BUGGLES, ex-ISOTOPE) / **CARL PALMER** (b.20 Mar'47, Birmingham, England) – drums, percussion (ex-EMERSON, LAKE & PALMER, ex-P.M.)

Geffen Geffen

Apr 82. (lp)(c)(pic-lp) **ASIA** [11] [1]
– Heat of the moment / Only time will tell / Sole survivor / One step closer / Time again / Wildest dream / Without you / Cutting it fine / Here comes the feeling. *(re-iss.Sep86.cd.iss.Feb87) (c+cd.re-iss.Apr91)*

Jun 82. (7") **HEAT OF THE MOMENT. / TIME AGAIN** [46] [4] Apr 82

Aug 82. (7")(7"pic-d) **ONLY TIME WILL TELL. / RIDE EASY** [54] [17] Jul 82

Oct 82. (7") **SOLE SURVIVOR. / HERE COMES THE FEELING** [ ] [ ]

Aug 83. (7")(7"sha-pic-d) **DON'T CRY. / TRUE COLOURS** [33] [10] Jul 83

Aug 83. (lp)(c) **ALPHA** [5] [6]
– Don't cry / The smile has left your eyes / Never in a million years / My own time (I'll do what I want) / The heat goes on / Eye to eye / The last to know / True colours / Midnight Sun / Open your eyes.
(c.+=) – Daylight. *(re-iss.Sep86 / cd-iss.Feb87 + Jun89) (c+cd.re-iss.Apr91)*

Oct 83. (7") **THE SMILE HAS LEFT YOUR EYES. / LYING TO YOURSELF** [ ] [34]
(12"+=)(12"red+=) – Midnight Sun.

— (Oct83) **GREG LAKE** (b.10 Nov'48, Bournemouth, England) – vocals, bass (ex-EMERSON, LAKE & PALMER, ex-Solo Artist, ex-KING CRIMSON) repl. WETTON

(Mar84). **ARMAND 'Mandy' MEYER** – guitar (ex-KROKUS) repl. HOWE who returned to YES and formed G.T.R. **JOHN WETTON** returned to replace LAKE (re-joined E.L.P.)

Nov 85. (7") **GO. / AFTER THE WAR** [ ] [46]
(12"+=) – ('A'instrumental)

Dec 85. (lp)(c)(cd) **ASTRA** [68] [67]
– Go / Voice of America / Hard on me / Wishing / Rock and roll dream / Countdown to zero / Love now till eternity / Too late / Suspicion / After the war.

Jan 86. (7") **WISHING. / TOO LATE** [-] [ ]

— (early 1986, disbanded) **WETTON** teamed up with **PHIL MANZANERA**

GEOFFREY DOWNES

released solo album.

Geffen Geffen

Sep 87. (lp)(c)(cd) **THE LIGHT PROGRAMME** [ ] [ ]
– Ethnic dance / East west / Urbanology / Symphonie electrique / Oceania electronique.

ASIA

reformed late 1989 (WETTON, DOWNES, PALMER plus **PAT THRALL** – guitar (ex-AUTOMATIC MAN). He was replaced by session men **STEVE LUKATHER, RON KOMIE, MANDY MEYER** and **SCOTT GORHAM.**

Geffen Geffen

Aug 90. (cd)(c)(lp) **THEN & NOW** [ ] [ ]
– (THEN) hits compilation / (NOW) – Days like these / Prayin' 4 a miracle / Am I in love? / Voice of America / Summer (can't last too long). *(re-iss.c+cd.Aug91)*

Sep 90. (c-s)(cd-s) **DAYS LIKE THESE. / VOICE OF AMERICA** [-] [64]

— **JOHN PAYNE** – vocals, bass repl.WETTON

— **AL PITRELLI** – guitar (ex-DANGER DANGER) repl. THRALL

— **STEVE HOWE** also made guest appearance

Re-volver FM Sony

Jun 92. (cd)(c)(lp) **AQUA** [ ] [ ] Mar 92
– Aqua (part one) / Who will stop the rain / Back in town / Love under fire / Someday / Little rich boy / The voice of reason / Lay down your arms / Crime of the heart / A far cry / Don't call me / Heaven on Earth / Aqua (part two).

Musicdisc Sony

Aug 92. (12")(10"pic-d) **WHO WILL STOP THE RAIN. / AQUA (part 1). / HEART OF GOLD** [ ] [ ]
(cd-s+=) – Obsessing.

— **MICHAEL STURGIS** – drums repl. PALMER

Bul-let Proof M.F.N.

May 94. (cd)(c)(lp) **ARIA** [ ] [ ]
– Anytime / Are you big enough? / Desire / Summer / Sad situation / Don't cut the wire (brother) / Feels like love / Remembrance day / Enough's enough / Military man / Aria.

— **VINNIE BURNS + TREVOR THORNTON** repl.PITRELLI and the injured HOWE

– compilations, etc. –

Dec 91. Cromwell; (cd) **ASIA LIVE 09-X1-90 MOCKBA (live)** [ ] [-]

ASSOCIATES

Formed: Dundee, Scotland . . . 1979 by MacKENZIE and RANKINE who had been duo in 1976 as The ABSORBIC ONES. After debut 45 on own 'Double-Hip' label, they signed to Chris Parry's 'Fiction' a subsidiary of 'Polydor' records. Their glorious debut 'THE AFFECTIONATE PUNCH' was followed by a series of 7+12" singles for independent 'Situation 2'. In 1982, they enjoyed first taste of success when 'PARTY FEARS TWO' & 'CLUB COUNTRY' both hit UK Top 20. • **Style:** Energetic alternative dance rock, featuring high passionate vocals of MacKENZIE. • **Songwriters:** Lyrics / music by duo, except BOYS KEEP SWINGING (David Bowie) / LOVE HANGOVER (Diana Ross) / HEART OF GLASS (Blondie) / KITES (Simon Dupree & The Big Sound) / GROOVIN' WITH MR.BLOE (Mr.Bloe) / GREEN TAMBOURINE (Lemon Pipers) / I'M GONNA RUN AWAY FROM YOU (Tammi Lynn). After RANKINE's departure, ASSOCIATES were virtually McKENZIE's group. • **Trivia:** McKENZIE featured on B.E.F.'s (HEAVEN 17) single IT'S OVER circa '82.

Recommended: FOURTH DRAWER DOWN (*9) / SULK (*7) / THE AFFECTIONATE PUNCH (*6) /

BILLY MacKENZIE (b.27 Mar'57) – vocals / **ALAN RANKINE** – keyboards, guitar, etc

Double Hip | not issued

Oct 79. (7") **BOYS KEEP SWINGING. / MONA PROPERTY GIRL** [ ] [-]
(re-iss.Dec79 on 'M.C.A.')

added **NIGEL GLOCKER** – drums / guest **ROBERT SMITH** – guitar (CURE)

Fiction | not issued

Aug 80. (7")(12") **THE AFFECTIONATE PUNCH. / YOU WERE YOUNG** [ ] [-]
Aug 80. (lp)(c) **THE AFFECTIONATE PUNCH** [ ] [-]
– The affectionate punch / Amused as always / Logan time / Paper house / Transport to Central / A matter of gender / Even dogs in the wild / Would I . . . bounce back / Deeply concerned / A. *(re-iss.Nov82 & Aug83)*
Oct 80. (7")(12") **WOULD I . . . BOUNCE BACK. / A** [ ] [-]
Dec 80. (7") **A MATTER OF GENDER. / EVEN DOGS IN THE WILD** [ ] [-]

— **JOHN MURPHY** (b. Australia) – drums repl. GLOCKER (to TOYAH)

Situation 2 | not issued

Apr 81. (7")(12") **TELL ME EASTER'S ON FRIDAY. / STRAW TOWELS** *(re-iss.Nov82)* [ ] [-]
Jun 81. (7") **Q: QUARTERS. / KISSED** [ ] [-]
(12"+=) – ('A'original mix). (re-iss.Nov82)
Aug 81. (7")(12") **KITCHEN PERSON. / AN EVEN WHITER CAR** [ ] [-]
(re-iss.Nov82)
Oct 81. (7")(12") **MESSAGE OBLIQUE SPEECH. / BLUE SOAP** [ ] [-]
(re-iss.Nov82)
Nov 81. (7")(12") **WHITE CAR IN GERMANY. / THE ASSOCIATE** [ ] [-]
(re-iss.Nov82)
Jan 82. (lp)(c) **FOURTH DRAWER DOWN** [ ] [-]
– White car in Germany / A girl named Property / Kitchen person / Q; quarters / Tell me Easter's on Friday / The associate / Message oblique speech / An even whiter car. *(re-iss.Nov82)*

added **MICHAEL DEMPSEY** – bass (of CURE) / **MARTHA LADLY** – backing vocals (ex-MARTHA & THE MUFFINS)

Associates-WEA | WEA

Mar 82. (7")(12") **PARTY FEARS TWO. / IT'S BETTER THIS WAY** [9] [ ]
May 82. (7")(12") **CLUB COUNTRY. / IT'S YOU AGAIN** [13] [ ]
(12"+=) – Ultragyceptemol.
Jun 82. (lp)(c) **SULK** [10] [ ]
– It's better this way / Party fears two / Club country / Love hangover / 18 carat love affair / Arrogance gave him up / No / Skipping / Nothing in something particular / Gloomy Sunday / Arrogance gave him up / White car in Germany / Gloomy Sunday / The associate. *(cd-iss.Jul88)*
Jul 82. (7") **18 CARAT LOVE AFFAIR. / LOVE HANGOVER** [21] [ ]
(12"+=) – Voluntary wishes.

Billy MacKENZIE

Oct 82. (7")(12") **ICE CREAM FACTORY. / EXCURSION ECOSSE EN ROUTE KOBLENZ** [ ] [-]

ASSOCIATES

reformed 1984 by **MacKENZIE & RANKINE,** recruiting **STEVE GOULDING** – drums / **IAN McINTOSH** – rhythm guitar / **ROBERT SUAVE** – bass / **L. HOWARD JONES** – keyboards.

May 84. (7") **THOSE FIRST IMPRESSIONS. / THIRTEEN FEELINGS** [43] [ ]
(12"+=) – Stronger in your voice.

STEPHEN REID – guitar repl. RANKINE who joined PAUL HAIG (**RANKINE** appeared on below lp.)

Aug 84. (7") **WAITING FOR THE LOVE BOAT. / SCHAMP OUT** [53] [ ]
(12") – ('A'&'B'extended) / ('A' Peel session vers.)
Jan 85. (7")(7"pic-d) **BREAKFAST. / BREAKFAST ALONE** [49] [ ]
(12"+=) – Kites.
Feb 85. (lp)(c) **PERHAPS** [23] [ ]
– Those first impressions / Waiting for the love boat / Perhaps / Schampout / Helicopter helicopter / Breakfast / Thirteen feelings / The stranger in your voice / The best of you / Don't give me that I told you so look.
Oct 85. (7") **TAKE ME TO THE GIRL. / PERHAPS** [ ] [ ]
(12"+=) – The girl that took me.
(10"+=) – God bless child / Even dogs in the wild / The boy that Santa Claus forgot.
The above 'A'side was later (in Mar88) covered by group/artist JIH.

— (early 1986) HUGHES and SUAVE joined PETE MURPHY. MacKENZIE now used different session people under **ASSOCIATES**

Sep 88. (7") **HEART OF GLASS. / HER ONLY WISH** [56] [ ]
(12"+=) – ('A'mix) / Heaven's blue.
(cd-s+=) – Breakfast / Those first impressions.
Jan 89. (7") **COUNTRY BOY. / JUST CAN'T SAY GOODBYE** [ ] [-]
(12"+=) – Heart of glass (dub). (w/ drawn)
(3"cd-s++=) – Take me to the girl. (w/drawn)

Circa | Virgin?

Mar 90. (cd)(c)(lp) **WILD AND LONELY** [71] [ ]
– Fire to ice / Fever / People we meet / Just can't say goodbye / Calling all around the world / The glamour chase / Where there's love / Something's got to give / Strasbourg Square / Ever since that day / Wild and lonely / Fever in the shadows.
Apr 90. (7")(c-s) **FEVER. / FEVER IN THE SHADOWS** [ ] [ ]
(12"+=)(cd-s+=) – Groovin' with Mr.Bloe.
Aug 90. (7") **FIRE TO ICE. / THE GLAMOUR CHASE** [ ] [ ]
(12"+=) – Green tambourine.
(10"+=)(cd-s+=) – Groovin' with Mr.Bloe.
Jan 91. (7")(12")(c-s) **JUST CAN'T SAY GOODBYE. / ONE TWO THREE** [ ] [ ]
(12"+=)(cd-s+=) – (2 other 'A'versions U.S.+piano)
(cd-s+=) – I'm gonna run away from you.

BILLY MacKENZIE

Circa | Circa

Jun 92. (7") **BABY. / SACRIFICE AND BE SACRIFICED (mix)** [ ] [-]
(cd-s+=) – Grooveature (DIDOO mix) / COLOURS WILL COME (mix)
(12") – ('A'side) / Colours will come (2 versions) / Opal Krusch.
Aug 92. (7") **COLOURS WILL COME. / OPAL KRUSCH** [ ] [-]
(12"+=)(cd-s+=) – Look what you've done / Feels like the richtergroove.
Sep 92. (cd)(c)(lp) **OUTERNATIONAL** [ ] [ ]
– Outernational / Feels like the richtergroove / Opal krusch / Colours wil come / Pastime paradise / Groovecture / Sacrifice and be sacrificed / Baby / What made me turn on the lights / Windows cell.

– (ASSOCIATES) compilations, others, etc. –

May 81. R.S.O.; (7")(12") **A GIRL NAMED POVERTY. / KITES** (by "39 LYON ST.") [ ] [-]
Oct 89. Strange Fruit; (12")(cd-s) **THE PEEL SESSIONS** ('82) [ ] [-]
– It's better this way / Nude spoons / Me myself and the tragic story / Natural gender / Ultragyceptemol.
Jan 91. East West; (cd)(c)(lp) **POPERA** [ ] [ ]
– Party fears two / Club country / 18 Carat love affair / Love hangover / Those first impressions / Waiting for the loveboat / Breakfast / Take me to the girl / Heart of glass / Country boy / The rhythm divine / Waiting for the loveboat (slight return) / Tell me Easter's on Friday / Q; quarters / Kitchen person / Message oblique speech / White car in Germany.
Jan 91. East West; (7")(c-s) **POPERETTA: WAITING FOR THE LOVEBOAT. / CLUB COUNTRY CLUB** [ ] [ ]
(12"+=)(cd-s+=) – Waiting for the loveboat (slight return) / ('B'extended).
Sep 94. Nighttracks; (cd) **THE RADIO 1 SESSIONS** [ ] [-]

ASYLUM CHOIR (see under ⇒ RUSSELL, Leon)

ATOMIC ROOSTER

Formed: London, England . . . late 1969 by VINCENT CRANE and CARL PALMER. They appeared on 'B&C' label, and soon had Top 5 UK hit with 'DEVIL'S ANSWER'. • **Style:** Initially a heavy keyboard dominated rock outfit, but on introduction of R&B veteran CHRIS FARLOWE, fell into mediocre soft blues. Although they resurrected old style when reforming in the late 70's, they did not have same early creativity. • **Songwriters:** CRANE most. • **Trivia:** One-time member JOHN CANN had a TV ad UK hit with 'DON'T BE A DUMMY'.

Recommended: HOME TO ROOST (*7)

VINCENT CRANE (b.CHEESMAN) – keyboards, vocals, bass-pedal / **CARL PALMER** – drums, percussion (both ex-CRAZY WORLD OF ARTHUR BROWN) / **NICK GRAHAM** – bass, guitar, flute, vocals

B & C | Elektra

Feb 70. (lp)(c) **ATOMIC ROOSTER** [49] [-]
– Friday the 13th / And so to bed / Broken wings / Before tomorrow / Banstead / S.L.Y. / Winter / Decline and fall. *(cd-iss.Jul93 on 'Repertoire')*
Mar 70. (7") **FRIDAY THE 13th. / BANSTEAD** [ ] [-]

— **JOHN CANN** – vocals, guitar (ex-ANDROMEDA) repl. NICK joined SKIN ALLEY **PAUL HAMMOND** – drums. percussion repl. CARL who joined EMERSON, LAKE & PALMER

Dec 70. (7") **TOMORROW NIGHT. / PLAY THE GAME** [11] [ ]
Jan 71. (lp)(c) **DEATH WALKS BEHIND YOU** [12] [90]
– Death walks behind you / Vug / Tomorrow night / Seven streets / Sleeping for years / I can't take no more / Nobody else / Gershatzer. *(cd-iss.Jul93 on 'Repertoire')*

— added **PETE FRENCH** – vocals (ex-CACTUS)

Jul 71. (7") **THE DEVIL'S ANSWER. / THE ROCK** [4] [ ]
(re-iss.Jun76)

Pegasus | Elektra

Aug 71. (7") **IN HEARING OF . . .** [18] [ ]
– Breakthrough / Break the ice / Decision – indecision / A spoonful of bromide helps the pulse rate go down / Black snake / Head in the sky / The rock / The price. *(cd-iss.Jul93 & Jul95 on 'Repertoire')*

— **CRANE** now with newcomers **CHRIS FARLOWE** (b.1940) – vocals (ex-COLOSSEUM, ex-Solo, etc.) replaced FRENCH who joined LEAFHOUND / **STEVE BOLTON** – guitar repl. CANN (to HARD STUFF) as JOHN DU CANN had 1979 hit / **RICK PARNELL** (son of composer VIC) – drums repl. HAMMOND (to HARD STUFF) added / **BILL SMITH** – bass / **LIZA STRIKE** and **DORIS TROY** – backing vocals

		Dawn	Elektra
Sep 72.	(7") **STAND BY ME. / NEVER TO LOSE**	[ ]	[ ]
Oct 72.	(lp)(c) **MADE IN ENGLAND**	[ ]	[ ]

– Time take my life / Stand by me / Little bit of inner air / Don't know what went wrong / Never to lose / Introduction / Breathless / Space cowboy / People you can't trust / All in Satan's name / Close your eyes. *(cd-iss.May91 on 'Sequel') (cd-iss.Jul93 on 'Repertoire')*

Dec 72.	(7") **SAVE ME. / CLOSE YOUR EYES**	[ ]	[-]
1973.	(7") **CAN'T FIND A REASON. ("VINCENT CRANE & CHRIS FARLOWE") / MOODS**	[ ]	[-]

—— **JOHNNY MANDELA** – guitar repl. STEVE, BILL, LIZA and DORIS

1973. (lp)(c) **NICE'N'GREASY** [ ] [-]

– All across the country / Save me / Voodoo in you / Goodbye planet Earth / Take one take / Can't find a reason / Ear in the snow / What you gonna do. *(cd-iss.Jul91 on 'Sequel') (cd-iss.Jul93 on 'Repertoire')*

		Decca	not issued
Mar 74.	(7") **TELL YOUR STORY. / O.D.**	[ ]	[-]

—— Disbanded when CHRIS FARLOWE went solo. CRANE teamed up with ARTHUR BROWN

VINCENT CRANE'S ATOMIC ROOSTER

reformed 1980, with **JOHN DU CANN** – guitar / **PRESTON HEYMAN** – drums

		E.M.I.	not issued
Jun 80.	(7")(12") **DO YOU KNOW WHO'S LOOKING FOR YOU? / THROW YOUR LOVE AWAY**	[ ]	[-]
Sep 80.	(lp)(c) **ATOMIC ROOSTER**	[ ]	[ ]

– They took control of you / She's my woman / He did it again / Where's the show? / In the shadows / Do you know who's looking for you? / Don't lose your mind / Watch out / I can't stand it / Lost in space. *(re-iss.Oct86 on 'Charisma')*

ATOMIC ROOSTER.

PAUL HAMMOND – drums repl. PRESTON

		Polydor	not issued
Sep 81.	(7")(12") **PLAY IT AGAIN. / START TO LIVE**	[ ]	[-]
Feb 82.	(7") **END OF THE DAY. / LIVING UNDERGROUND**	[ ]	[-]

(12"+=) – Devil's answer (live) / Tomorrow night (live).

—— guests **BERNIE TORME and DAVID GILMOUR** repl. HAMMOND and CANN

		Towerbell	not issued
Jun 83.	(lp)(c) **HEADLINE NEWS**	[ ]	[-]

(cd-iss.Nov94 on 'Voiceprint')

—— Finally split 1983. VINCENT CRANE joined/guested for DEXY'S MIDNIGHT RUNNERS in 1985. He committed suicide 20 Feb'89, after suffering recurring depression. In his latter days, he had also written for pop star KIM WILDE.

- compilations, others, etc. -

1974.	B&C; (lp)(c) **ASSORTMENT**	[ ]	[-]
1979.	B&C; (7"m) **DEVIL'S ANSWER. / TOMORROW NIGHT / CAN'T TAKE NO MORE**	[ ]	[-]
1977.	Mooncrest; (d-lp) **HOME TO ROOST**	[ ]	[-]

– Death walks behind you / V.U.G. / Seven sheets / Sleeping for years / Can't take no more / Nobody else / Friday the 13th / And so to bed / Broken wings / Before tomorrow / Banstead / Winter / Breakthrough / Decision-indecision / Devil's answer / Black snae / Head in the sky / A spoonful of bromide helps the pulse go down / Tomorrow night / Break the ice. *(re-iss.1983) (re-iss.+c+cd.Dec86 on 'Raw Power')*

Jun 84.	Old Gold; (7") **DEVIL'S ANSWER. / TOMORROW NIGHT**	[ ]	[-]
Apr 89.	Old Gold; (7") **DEVIL'S ANSWER. / ('B'by Humble Pie)**	[ ]	[-]
Dec 89.	Action Replay; (c)(cd) **THE BEST AND THE REST OF . . .**	[ ]	[-]
Jun 89.	Demi Monde; (lp)(c)(cd) **THE BEST OF ATOMIC ROOSTER**	[ ]	[-]
Feb 90.	Demi Monde; (cd)(lp) **THE DEVIL HIS BACK**	[ ]	[-]
Sep 89.	Receiver; (lp)(cd) **DEVIL'S ANSWER**	[ ]	[-]
Jul 94.	Success; (cd)(c) **THE BEST OF ATOMIC ROOSTER**	[ ]	[-]

A TRIBE CALLED QUEST

Formed: Queens/New York, USA . . . 1988 by (see below). Cracked the UK charts with 'BONITA APPLEBUM' and 'CAN I KICK IT?' in 1990/91. • **Style:** Afrocentric hip-hop jazz /funk rappers /samplers influenced by JUNGLE BROTHERS. • **Songwriters:** Group penned (DAVIS / TAYLOR / JONES / MUHAMMAD). Samples; SIR DUKE (Stevie Wonder) / INNER CITY BLUES (Marvin Gaye) / WALK ON THE WILD SIDE (Lou Reed) / Others:- Grace Jones + Carly Simon on 'BONITA APPLEBUM'. Q-TIP appeared on DEEE-LITE's 1990 No. 1 'Groove Is In The Heart'.

Recommended: PEOPLE'S INSTINCTIVE.. (*7) / MIDNIGHT MARAUDERS (*7)

Q-TIP (JONATHAN DAVIS, b.1970) – vocals / **ALI SHAHEED MUHAMMAD** (b. 1970) – vocals / **PHIFE** (b. MALIK TAYLOR, 1970) – / **JAROBI**

		Jive	Jive
Aug 89.	(12") **DESCRIPTION OF A FOOL (talkie). / ('A'instrumental)**	[ ]	[ ]

(12"+=) – ('A'-silent version).

Mar 90.	(12") **PUBLIC ENEMY. /**	[ ]	[ ]
May 90.	(cd)(c)(lp) **PEOPLE'S INSTINCTIVE TRAVELS AND THE PATHS OF RHYTHM**	[54]	[91] Apr90

– Push it along / Luck of Lucien / After hours / Footprints / I left my wallet in El Segundo / Bonita Applebum / Can I kick it? / Youthful expression / Rhythm (devoted to the art of moving butts) / Mr.Muhammad / Ham 'n' eggs / Go ahead in the rain / Description of a fool.

Aug 90.	(7") **BONITA APPLEBUM. / ('A'instrumental)**	[47]	[ ]

(12"+=)(cd-s+=) – Between the sheets. *(re-iss.May91)*

Jan 91.	(7") **CAN I KICK IT?. / ('A'mix)**	[15]	[ ]

(12"+=)(cd-s+=) – ('A'-Boilerhouse remix).

Mar 91.	(7") **I LEFT MY WALLET IN EL SEGUNDO (Norman Cook remix). / ('A'instrumental)**	[ ]	[ ]

(12"+=)(cd-s+=) – ('A'mixes).

—— now without JAROBI

Sep 91.	(7") **CHECK THE RHYME. / ('A'instrumental)**	[ ]	[ ]

(12"+=)(cd-s+=) – ('A'mixes).

Sep 91.	(cd)(c)(lp) **LOW END THEORY**	[58]	[45]

– Excursions / Buggin' out / Rap promoter / Butter / Verses from the abstract / Show business / Vibes and stuff / The infamous date rape / Check the rhyme / Everything is fair / Jazz (we've got) / Skypager / Scenario.

May 92.	(12"ep)(cd-ep) **SCENARIO (MC mix). / (8 mixes)**	[ ]	[57]
Oct 92.	(7") **LUCK OF LUCIEN. / BUTTER**	[ ]	[ ]

(12"+=)(cd-s+=) – ('A'mixes).

Oct 92.	(cd)(c) **REVISED QUEST FOR A SEASONED TRAVELLER** (remixes)	[ ]	[ ]
Oct 93.	(cd)(c)(d-lp) **MIDNIGHT MARAUDERS**	[70]	[8]

– Midnight marauders tour guide / Steve Biko (stir it up) / Award tour / 8 million stories / Sueka nigga / Midnight / We can get down / Electric relaxation / Interlude / Clap your hands / Oh my God / Interlude / Keep it rollin' / The chase pt.II / Lyrics to go / God lives through / Hot sex.

Nov 93.	(12"ep)(cd-ep) **AWARD TOUR. / ('A'mixes)**	[ ]	[47]
Feb 94.	(12"ep)(cd-ep) **ELECTRIC RELAXATION. / ('A'mixes)**	[ ]	[65]
May 94.	(12")(c-s) **OH MY GOD. / ('A'mixes)**	[68]	[ ]

(cd-s) – ('A'side) / Bonita Applebum / Can I kick it? / Left my wallet in El Segundo.

Nov 94.	(12"ep)(cd-ep) **A TRIBE CALLED QUEST EP**	[ ]	[ ]

– We can get down / Clap your hands / Verses from the abstract / Footprints.

ATTILA (see under ⇒ Billy JOEL)

AUDIENCE

Formed: London, England . . .1968 by HOWARD WERTH. After debut eponymous album for 'Polydor' and a support slot on LED ZEPPELIN's tour, they signed to Tony Stratton-Smith's emerging 'Charisma' label. In 1970, they contributed to the film soundtrack 'Bronco Bullfrog'. •**Style:** Intelligent progressive jazz-rock. •**Songwriters:** WERTH. •**Trivia:** GUS DUDGEON was their producer from 1971.

Recommended: AUDIENCE UNCHAINED (*6)

HOWARD WERTH – vocals, guitar / **TREVOR WILLIAMS** – bass, vocals / **TONY CONNOR** – drums, percussion, piano / **KEITH GEMMELL – saxophone**

		Polydor	not issued
1970.	(lp) **AUDIENCE**	[ ]	[-]

– Banquet / Poet / Waverley stage coach / River boat queen / Harlequin / Heaven was an island / Too late I'm gone / Maidens cry / Pleasant convalescence / Leave it unsaid / Man on the box / House on the hill. *(cd-iss.Dec95 on 'RPM')*

		Charisma	Elektra
Jun 70.	(7") **BELLADONNA MOONSHINE. / THE BIG SPELL**	[ ]	[ ]
Aug 70.	(lp) **FRIEND'S FRIEND'S FRIEND**	[ ]	[ ]

– Nothing you do / Belladonna moonshine / It brings a tear / Raid / Right on their side / Ebony variations / Priestess / Friend's friend's friend. *(re-iss.Aug76) (cd-iss.Jun92 on 'Virgin')*

Feb 71.	(7"m) **INDIAN SUMMER. / IT BRINGS A TEAR / PRINCESS**	[ ]	[-]
1971.	(7") **YOU'RE NOT SMILING. / EYE TO EYE**	[ ]	[ ]
1971.	(lp) **HOUSE ON THE HILL**	[ ]	[ ]

– Jackdaw / You're not smiling / I had a dream / Raviole / Nancy / Eye to eye / I put a spell on you / The house on the hill. *(re-iss.Aug76) (re-iss.Aug82 lp/c) (cd-iss.Oct90 on 'Virgin')*

1972.	(7") **STAND BY THE DOOR. / THUNDER AND LIGHTNIN'**	[ ]	[ ]
Jun 72.	(lp) **LUNCH**	[ ]	[ ]

– Stand by the door / Seven more bruises / Hula girl / Ain't the man you need / In accord / Barracuda Dan / Hunder and lightnin' / Party games / Trombone gulch / Buy me an island. *(re-iss.Aug76) (re-iss.Aug88 lp/c) (cd-iss.Oct90 on 'Virgin')*

PATRICK NEUBERGH – saxophone + **NICK JUDD** – keyboards repl. GEMMELL who joined STACKRIDGE. Disbanded when CONNOR joined HOT CHOCOLATE and WILLIAMS to JONATHAN KELLY.

compilations, etc

1973.	Charisma; (lp) **YOU CAN'T BEAT THEM**	[ ]	[-]

– Trombone gulch / Thunder and lightnin' / Raviole / Elixir of youth / I had a dream / You're not smiling / Ain't the man you need / It brings a tear / Indian summer / Jackdaw / Nancy.

1973.	Charisma; (7") **YOU'RE NOT SMILING. /**	[ ]	[-]
Dec 92.	Virgin; (cd) **AUDIENCE UNCHAINED**	[ ]	[-]

HOWARD WERTH & THE MOONBEAMS

with **MIKE MORAN** – keyboards / **FRED GANDY** – bass / **ROGER POPE** – drums / **BOB WESTON** – slide guitar/ + session people

		Charisma	???
Feb 74.	(7") **LUCINDA. / JOHAN**	[ ]	[-]
Jun 75.	(7") **COCKTAIL SHAKE. / SAMMY LEE LANE**	[ ]	[-]
Oct 75.	(lp) **KING BRILLIANT**	[ ]	[-]

– Cocktail shake / Got to unwind / The embezzler / A human note / Ugly water / Midnight flyer / Fading star / dear John / Roulette / The Aleph. *(cd-iss.Dec92 on 'Virgin')*

Nov 75.	(7") **DEAR JOHN. / ROULETTE**	[ ]	[-]

HOWARD WERTH

Metabop / not issued

1983. (7") **4D MAN. / WHAT'S HOPPIN'** [ ] [-]

Demon / not issued

Jan 84. (lp) **SIX OF ONE AND HALF A DOZEN OF THE OTHER** [ ] [-]
– Hovering / 4D man / Individual / Meek power / Astro logic / What's hoppin'? / Respectable / I keep forgettin' / Little bitty pretty one / Dancing little thing / Smokestack lightning / One more heartache / Show me. *(cd-iss.Jul92 on 'Mau Mau')*

Retired from music business.

Brian AUGER

Born: 18 Jul'39, Bihar, India / raised . . . London, England. Formed own trio 1964 also being part of STEAMPACKET in the mid 60's with vocalists LONG JOHN BALDRY, ROD STEWART and JULIE DRISCOLL. In 1968 his TRINITY crediting JULIE DRISCOLL, hit UK Top 5 with Bob Dylan's 'THIS WHEEL'S ON FIRE'. Personnel problems dogged set-up from then on and they never retained any more commercial success. • **Style:** Jazzy soulful R&B, which moved into folk, etc. • **Songwriters:** AUGER except INNER CITY BLUES (Marvin Gaye) / etc. STEAMPACKET supergroup were recorded with mostly covers in repertoire. • **Trivia:** BRIAN later moved to San Francisco in the 70's.

Recommended: AUGERNIZATION – THE BEST OF BRIAN AUGER (*6)

BRIAN AUGER TRINITY

BRIAN AUGER – organ / **RICK BROWN** or **ROGER SUTTON** – bass / **MICKY WALLER** or **CLIVE THACKER** or **CLEM CATTINI** – drums / **GARY BOYLE** or **VIC BRIGGS** – guitar

Columbia / not issued?

Jun 65. (7") **FOOL KILLER. / LET'S DO IT TONIGHT** [ ] [-]
Oct 65. (7") **'65 GREEN ONIONS. / KIKO** [ ] [-]
Mar 67. (7") **TIGER (solo). / OH BABY WON'T YOU COME BACK HOME TO CROYDON WHERE EVERYBODY BEEDLE'S AND BO'S** [ ] [-]

BRIAN AUGER & TRINITY

Marmalade / Atco

Oct 67. (7") **RED BEANS AND RICE. / (part 2)** [ ] [-]

JULIE DRISCOLL, BRIAN AUGER & THE TRINITY

with **JULIE** – vocals / **DAVE AMBROSE** – bass / **CLIVE THACKER** – drums

Feb 68. (7") **SAVE ME. / ('A'version)** [ ] [ ]
Apr 68. (7") **THIS WHEEL'S ON FIRE. / KIND OF LOVE-IN** [5] [ ]
May 68. (lp) **OPEN** [12] [ ]
– In and out / Isola Natale / Black cat / Lament for Miss Baker / Goodbye jungle telegraph / Tramp / Why (am I treated so bad) / Kind of love in / Break it up / Season of the witch.
Jul 68. (7") **IN AND OUT. / BLACK CAT** [-] [ ]

—— added a brass section + a string trio.

Sep 68. (7") **THE ROAD TO CAIRO. / SHADES OF YOU** [ ] [ ]

BRIAN AUGER TRINITY

1969. (7") **A DAY IN THE LIFE. / BUMPIN' ON SUNSET** [-] [ ]
Apr 69. (lp) **DEFINATELY WHAT!** [ ] [ ]
– A day in the life / George Bruno / Money / Far horizon / John Brown's body / Red beans and rice / Bumpin' on sunset / If you live / Definately what.
May 69. (7") **WHAT YOU GONNA DO? / BUMPIN' ON SUNSHINE** [ ] [ ]

JULIE DRISCOLL with THE BRIAN AUGER TRINITY

Jul 69. (d-lp) **STREETNOISE** [ ] [ ]
– Tropic of capricorn / Czechoslovakia / Medley / Take me to the water / I'm going back home / A word about colour / Light my fire / Indian rope Man / When I was a young girl / Flesh failures (Let the sunshine in) / Ellis Island / In search of the sun / Finally you found out / Looking in the eye of the world / Vauxhall to Lambeth Bridge / All blues / I've got life / Save the country.
1969. (7") **TAKE ME TO THE WATER. / INDIAN ROPE MAN** [ ] [ ]
1969. (7") **THE FLESH FAILURES (LET THE SUNSHINE IN). / SAVE THE COUNTRY** [-] [ ]
Jan 70. (lp) **STREETNOISE – Part 2 (see above)** [ ] [-]

—— added **BOYLE** + **SUTTON** / + **BARRY REEVES** + **COLIN ALLEN** – drums

R.C.A. / R.C.A.

Oct 70. (7") **LISTEN HERE. / I WANNA TAKE YOU HIGHER** [-] [100]
1970. (7") **I WANNA TAKE YOU HIGHER. / JUST ME JUST YOU** [ ] [-]
Jul 70. (lp)(c) **BE FOUR** [ ] [ ]
– I wanna take you higher / Pavane / No time to live / Maiden voyage / Listen here / Just you and me. *(cd-iss.Sep95 on 'One Way')*

BRIAN AUGER TRINITY with OBLIVION EXPRESS

with **ROBBIE McINTOSH** – drums / **BARRY DEAN** – guitar, bass / **JIM MULLEN** – guitar

R.C.A. / R.C.A.

1971. (lp)(c) **OBLIVION EXPRESS** [ ] [ ]
– Dragon song / Total eclipse / The light on the road / The sword / Oblivion express.

BRIAN AUGER'S OBLIVION EXPRESS

Polydor / R.C.A.

1971. (lp)(c) **A BETTER LAND** [ ] [ ]
– Dawn of another day / Maria's wedding / Trouble / Women of the seasons / Fill your head with laughter / On thinking it over / Tomorrow city / All the time there is / A better land.
1971. (7") **MARIA'S WEDDING. / TOMORROW CITY** [ ] [-]
1971. (7") **MARIA'S WEDDING. / TROUBLE** [-] [ ]

—— added **ALEX LIGERTWOOD** – vocals

May 72. (lp)(c) **SECOND WIND** [ ] [ ]
– Truth / Don't look away / Somebody help us / Freedom jazz dance / Just me, just you / Second wind. *(cd-iss.Nov95 on 'One Way')*
May 72. (7") **SECOND WIND. / FREEDOM JAZZ DANCE** [-] [ ]

—— **JACK MILLS** – guitar repl. MULLEN / **LENNOX LAINGTON** – bass repl. LIGERTWOOD

—— **GODFREY McLEAN** – drums repl. ROBBIE who joined AVERAGE WHITE BAND

C.B.S. / R.C.A.

Jul 73. (lp)(c) **CLOSER TO IT!** [ ] [64]
– Whenever you're ready / Happiness is just around the bend / Light on the path / Compared to what / Inner city blues / Voices of other times.
Aug 73. (7") **INNER CITY BLUES. / LIGHT ON THE PATH** [ ] [-]

—— **STEVE FERRONE** – drums (of AVERAGE WHITE BAND) repl. McLEAN

Apr 74. (7") **STRAIGHT AHEAD. / CHANGE** [ ] [-]
May 74. (lp)(c) **STRAIGHT AHEAD** [ ] [45] Apr 74
– Beginning again / Bumpin' on sunset / Straight ahead / You'll stay in my heart.

—— **LIGERTWOOD** returned to repl. LAINGTON

Dec 74. (lp)(c) **LIVE OBLIVION VOL.1 (live)** [ ] [51]
– Beginning again / Don't look away / Bumpin' on sunset / Truth // Freedom jazz dance / Happiness is just around the bend / Maiden voyage / Second wind / Whenever you're ready / Inner city blues / Straight ahead / Compared to what.
Oct 75. (lp) **REINFORCEMENTS** [-] [ ]
– Thoughts from afar / Something out of nothing / Plum / Foolish girl / Brain damage / Big yin / Future pilot.
Mar 76. (d-lp) **LIVE OBLIVION VOL.2 (live)** [-] [ ]
– Freedom jazz dance / Happiness is just around the bend / Maiden voyage / Second wind / Whenever you're ready / Inner city blues / Straight ahead / Compared to what.

BRIAN AUGER

with **LIGERTWOOD, MILLS, LAINGTON** plus **CLIVE CHAMAN** – bass / **LENNY WHITE** – drums

Warners / Warners

Feb 77. (lp)(c) **HAPPINESS HEARTACHES** [ ] [ ]
– Back street bible class / Spice island / Gimme a funky break / Never gonna come down / Happiness heartaches / Got to be born again / Paging Mr.McCoy.

BRIAN AUGER & JULIE TIPPETTS

(aka DRISCOLL, who had married KEITH TIPPETTS). **DAVID McDANIELS** – bass / **DAVE CRIGGER** – drums / **GEORGE DOERING** – guitar

Apr 78. (lp)(c) **ENCORE (live)** [ ] [ ]
– Spirit / Don't let me be misunderstood / Git up / Freedom highway / Future pilot / Rope ladder to the Moon / No time to live / Nothing will be as it was / Lock all the gates.

BRIAN AUGER

not issued / Headfirst

1981. (lp)(c) **SEARCH PARTY** [-] [ ]
– Planet Earth calling / Red alert / Sea of tranquility / Voyager 3 / I'm gone / Golden gate.

Retired until he recorded solo album in Italy 1984.

Polydor / Blue Flame

Jul 85. (lp)(c) **HERE AND NOW** [ ] [-]
– Nighttrain to nowhere / They say nothing lasts forever / Searching for your love / Heart of the hunter / The hurricane / Call me / Happiness is just around the bend / Downtown hookup.

– compilations, others, etc. –

1970. Polydor; (lp)(c) **BEST OF BRIAN AUGER TRINITY** [ ] [ ]
1971. Polydor; (7") **THIS WHEELS'S ON FIRE. / THE ROAD TO CAIRO** [ ] [-]
1972. Polydor; (lp)(c) **POP HISTORY** [ ] [-]
Mar 73. Polydor; (lp) **JULIE DRISCOLL, BRIAN AUGER TRINITY (Flasback series)** [ ] [-]
1978. Polydor; (lp) **STAR PORTRAIT** [ ] [-]
Nov 80. Polydor; (d-lp)(c) **GREATEST HITS** [ ] [-]
Dec 75. Charly; (lp) **JAM SESSION** [ ] [-]
Jan 77. Charly; (lp) **LONDON 64-67 (by "DRISCOLL & AUGER")** [ ] [-]
Jan 77. Charly; (lp) **FIRST OF THE SUPERGROUPS; EARLY DAYS ("STEAMPACKET")** [ ] [-]
Jul 84. Old Gold; (7") **THIS WHEEL'S ON FIRE. / ('B' by "Arthur Brown")** [ ] [-]
Aug 68. M.F.P.; (lp) **JULIE DRISCOLL & BRIAN AUGER : JOOLS / BRIAN** [ ] [-]
Apr 89. Decal; (lp) **THE ROAD TO VAUXHALL 1967-69** [ ] [-]
– (above by "JULIE DRISCOLL / BRIAN AUGER")
Apr 77. R.C.A.; (lp)(c) **THE BEST OF BRIAN AUGER** [-] [ ]
Jul 95. Tongue & Groove; (cd)(d-lp) **AUGERNIZATION – THE BEST OF BRIAN AUGER** [ ] [-]

AUTEURS

Formed: Southgate, London, England . . . 1992 by LUKE HAINES and girlfriend ALICE READMAN. They quickly signed to up and coming indie label 'Hut', and charted the following year, with debut album 'NEW WAVE'. • **Style:** Glossy garage indie/punk outfit, fronted by the flamboyant but cynical HAINES. • **Songwriters:** HAINES. • **Trivia:** HAINES had lived in London, then Portsmouth, before joining DAVID WESTLAKE in The SERVANTS. 'LENNY VALENTINO', was named after their 'NEW WAVE' album sleeve, depicting LENNY BRUCE dressed as RUDOLPH VALENTINO.

Recommended: NEW WAVE (*6). / NOW I'M A COWBOY (*8)

LUKE HAINES (b.Surrey) – vocals, guitar (ex-SERVANTS) / **ALICE READMAN** – bass / **GLEN COLLINS** – drums

Hut | Caroline

Dec 92. (12"ep)(cd-ep) **SHOWGIRL. / GLAD TO BE GONE / STAYING POWER** [ ] [-]

— added **JAMES BANBURY** – cello

Mar 93. (cd)(c)(lp) **NEW WAVE** [35] [ ]
– Show girl / Bailed out / American guitars / Junk shop clothes / Don't trust the stars / Starstruck / How could I be wrong / Housebreaker / Valet parking / Idiot brother / Early years / Home again. (free 7"w/lp on cd+c+=) – Untitled.

May 93. (10"ep)(12"ep)(cd-ep) **HOW COULD I BE WRONG. / HIGH DIVING HORSES / WEDDING DAY** [ ] [ ]

— **BARNEY CROCKFORD** – drums repl. COLLINS

Nov 93. (7") **LENNY VALENTINO. / DISNEY WORLD** [41] [ ]
(12") – ('A'side) / Car crazy / Vacant lot / ('A'original mix).

Apr 94. (7") **CHINESE BAKERY. / ('A'acoustic)** [42] [ ]
(cd-s+=) Government book store / Everything you say will destroy you.
(12"+=) – Modern history.

May 94. (cd)(c)(lp) **NOW I'M A COWBOY** [27] [ ]
– Lenny Valentino / Brainchild / I'm a rich man's toy / New French girlfriend / The upper classes / Chinese bakery / A sister like you / Underground movies / Life classes – Life model / Modern history / Daughter of a child. (lp w /free 1-sided 7") **MODERN HISTORY (acoustic).**

Nov 94. (m-cd)(m-lp) **THE AUTEURS VS U-ZIQ** (remixes) [ ] [ ]
– Lenny Valentino No.3 / Daughter of a child / Chinese bakery / Lenny Valentino No.1 / Lenny Valentino No.2 / Underground movies.

Dec 95. (7"ep)(c-ep)(cd-ep) **BACK WITH THE KILLER E.P.** [45] [-]
– Unsolved child murder / Back with the killer again / Former fan / Kenneth Anger's bad dream.

AVERAGE WHITE BAND

Formed: Dundee/Glasgow, Scotland . . . early 1972 by GORRIE and other noted session men. Support ERIC CLAPTON at his comeback Rainbow concert in '73, and gain enough attention to attract 'M.C.A.'. After one album, they move to Los Angeles and sign to 'Atlantic', where the US audiences relate more to their sound. Early in 1975, they had US No.1 with near instrumental 'PICK UP THE PIECES', which was lifted from self-titled top selling album. Continued to shine through until a lean period then break-up in the 80's. • **Style:** White funk/soul, with beautiful class harmonies inspired by US black groups/singers of 60's (e.g. ISLEYS, MARVIN GAYE etc.). • **Songwriters:** GORRIE and STUART, except I HEARD IT THROUGH THE GRAPEVINE (Marvin Gaye) / IMAGINE (John Lennon) / WALK ON BY (Burt Bacharach) / etc. • **Trivia:** McINTYRE and McINTOSH sessioned on CHUCK BERRY's 'My Ding-A-Ling'.

Recommended: THE BEST OF THE AVERAGE WHITE BAND (*7)

HAMISH STUART (b. 8 Oct'49, Glasgow, Scotland) – vocals, guitar / **ALAN GORRIE** (b.19 Jul'46, Perth, Scotland) – vocals, bass / **ONNIE McINTYRE** (b.25 Sep'45, Lennoxtown, Scotland) – lead guitar / **ROBBIE McINTOSH** (b. 1950, Scotland) – drums / **ROGER BALL** (b. 4 Jun'44, Dundee, Scotland) – saxophone / **MALCOLM 'MOLLY' DUNCAN** (b.24 Aug'44, Montrose, Scotland) – tenor/soprano sax

M.C.A. | M.C.A.

Jan 73. (lp)(c) **SHOW YOUR HAND** [ ] [ ]
– The jugglers / This world has music / Twilight zone / Put it where you want it / Show your hand / How can you go home / Back in '67 / Reach out / T.L.C. *(re-iss.Feb82)(re-iss.May83 on 'Fame')(US re-iss.Apr75 as 'PUT IT WHERE YOU WANT IT' hit No.39 Apr 73)*

Feb 73. (7") **PUT IT WHERE YOU WANT IT. / REACH OUT** [ ] [ ]

Jan 74. (7") **HOW CAN YOU GO HOME. / TWILIGHT ZONE** [ ] [ ]
(re-iss.Apr75)

Atlantic | Atlantic

Jul 74. (lp)(c) **AVERAGE WHITE BAND** [6] [1]
– You got it / Got the love / Pick up the pieces / Person to person / Work to do / Nothing you can do / Just wanna love you tonight / Keepin' it to myself / I just can't give you up / There's always someone waiting. *(re-iss.Oct80 on 'RCA Int.')(re-iss.Jun86 on 'Fame')*

Jul 74. (7") **PICK UP THE PIECES. / YOU GOT IT** [6] [-]
(re-iss.Dec74 when it eventually hit US, then UK chart)

Oct 74. (7") **NOTHING YOU CAN DO. / I JUST CAN'T GIVE YOU UP** [ ] [ ]

Dec 74 (7") **PICK UP THE PIECES. / WORK TO DO.** [-] [1]

— **STEVE FERRONE** – drums (ex-BRIAN AUGER) repl. ROBBIE who died of heroine overdose 23 Sep 74.

Apr 75 (7") **CUT THE CAKE. / PERSON TO PERSON** [31] [10]

Jun 75. (lp)(c) **CUT THE CAKE** [28] [4]
– Cut the cake / School boy crush / It's a mystery / Groovin' the night away / If I ever lose this Heaven / Why / High flyin' woman / Cloudy / How sweet can you get / When they bring down the curtain.

Aug 75. (7") **IF I EVER LOSE THIS HEAVEN. / HIGH FLYIN' WOMAN** [ ] [39]

Nov 75. (7") **SCHOOL BOY CRUSH. / GROOVIN' THE NIGHT AWAY** [ ] [33]

May 76. (7") **EVERYBODY'S DARLING. / WHY?** [ ] [ ]

Jul 76. (lp)(c) **SOUL SEARCHING** [60] [8]
– Overture / Love your life / I'm the one / A love of your own / Queen of my soul / Soul searching / Goin' home / Everybody's darling / Would you say / Sunny days (make me think of you) / Digging deeper. *(re-iss.Nov80 on 'RCA Int.')*

Aug 76. (7") **QUEEN OF MY SOUL. / WOULD YOU STAY** [23] [40]

Dec 76. (7") **A LOVE OF YOUR OWN. / SOUL SEARCHIN'** [ ] [ ]

Jan 77. (d-lp)(d-c) **PERSON TO PERSON (live)** [ ] [28]
– Person to person / Cut the cake / If I ever lose this Heaven / Cloudy / T.L.C. / I'm the one / Pick up the pieces / Love your life / School boy crush / I heard it through the grapevine.

Mar 77. (7") **GOIN' HOME (live). / I'M THE ONE (live)** [ ] [-]

Mar 77. (7") **CLOUDY (live). / LOVE YOUR LIFE (live)** [-] [ ]

AVERAGE WHITE BAND / BEN E. KING

Jun 77. (7") **KEEPING IT TO MYSELF. / GET IT UP** [-] [ ]

Jul 77. (lp)(c) **BENNY AND US** [ ] [33]
– Get it up for love / Fool for you anyway / A star in the ghetto / The message / What is soul / Someday we'll all be free / Imagine / Keepin' it to myself.

Jul 77. (7") **A STAR IN THE GHETTO. / KEEPIN' IT TO MYSELF** [ ] [ ]

Aug 77. (7") **A STAR IN A GHETTO. / WHAT IS SOUL** [-] [ ]

Oct 77. (7") **IMAGINE. /** [ ] [-]

Dec 77. (7") **FOOL FOR YOU ANYWAY. / THE MESSAGE** [-] [ ]

AVERAGE WHITE BAND

R.C.A. | Atlantic

Jun 78. (7") **ONE LOOK OVER MY SHOULDER. / LOVE IS A MIRACLE** [-] [ ]

Jun 78. (lp)(c) **WARMER COMMUNICATIONS** [ ] [28] Mar 78
– Your love is a miracle / Same feeling, different song / Daddy's all gone / Big city lights / She's a dream / Sweet and sour / One look over my shoulder (is this really goodbye?).

Jun 78. (7")(12") **ONE LOOK OVER MY SHOULDER (IS THIS REALLY GOODBYE?). / BIG CITY LIGHTS** [ ] [ ]

Aug 78. (7") **SHE'S A DREAM. / BIG CITY LIGHTS** [-] [ ]

Feb 79. (7") **ATLANTIC AVENUE. / SHE'S A DREAM** [ ] [ ]

Feb 79. (lp)(c) **FEEL NO FRET** [15] [32]
– When will you be mine / Please don't fall in love / Walk on by / Feel no fret / Stop the rain / Atlantic avenue / Ace of hearts / Too late to cry / Fire burning.

Apr 79. (7")(12") **WALK ON BY. / TOO LATE TO CRY** [46] [92]

May 79. (7") **FEEL NO FRET. / FIRE BURNING** [-] [ ]

Jul 79. (7")(12") **WHEN WILL YOU BE MINE. / ACE OF HEARTS** [49] [ ]

R.C.A. | Arista

Apr 80. (7")(12") **LET'S GO 'ROUND AGAIN. / (Pt.2)** [12] [-]

May 80. (7") **LET'S GO 'ROUND AGAIN. / SHINE** [-] [53]

May 80. (lp)(c) **SHINE** [14] [ ]
– Catch me / Let's go 'round again / Whatcha gonna do for me / Help is on the way / Shine / For you, for love / Into the night / Our time has come / If love only lasts for one night.

Jul 80. (7")(12") **FOR YOU, FOR LOVE. / HELP IS ON THE WAY** [46] [-]

Jul 80. (7") **FOR YOU, FOR LOVE. / WHATCHA GONNA DO FOR ME** [-] [ ]

— added guest **RITCHIE STOTTS** – guitar (ex-PLASMATICS)

Jul 82. (7")(12") **YOU'RE MY NUMBER ONE. / THEATRE OF EXCESS** [ ] [ ]

Sep 82. (lp)(c) **CUPID'S IN FASHON** [ ] [ ]
– You're my number one / Easier said than done / You wanna belong / Cupid's in fashion / Theatre of excess / I believe / Is it love that you're running from? / Reach out I'll be there / Isn't it strange / Love's a heartache.

Sep 82. (7")(12") **I BELIEVE. / REACH OUT I'LL BE THERE** [ ] [ ]

— Split 1983, reformed 1989 **GORRIE, ELLIOT LEWIS** – keyboards / **TIGER McNEIL** – drums / **McINTYRE, BALL, ALEX LIGERTWOOD** – guitar, vocals

Polydor | Track

Aug 89. (lp)(c)(cd) **AFTERSHOCK** [ ] [ ]
– The spirit of love / Aftershock / I'll get over you / Let's go all the way / Sticky situation / Love at first sight / Later we'll be greater / We're in too deep.

Oct 89. (7") **THE SPIRIT OF LOVE. / ('A'beat mix)** [ ] [ ]
(12")(cd-s) – ('A'dance) / ('A'-long beat) / ('A'-New York mix).

— HAMISH joined ERIC CLAPTON band 1990.

— In 1985, ALAN GORRIE released album **SLEEPLESS NIGHTS** for 'A&M-US', plus single; 'AGE OF STEAM / I CAN TAKE IT (after) / DIARY OF A FOOL / IN THE JUNGLE

– compilations etc. –

Jul 81. RCA-Gold; (7") **PICK UP THE PIECES. / CUT THE CAKE** [ ] [ ]

Sep 80. R.C.A.; (lp)(c) **VOLUME VIII** [-] [ ]

Sep 81. R.C.A.; (lp)(c) **THE BEST OF THE AVERAGE WHITE BAND** [ ] [-]
– Pick up the pieces / Cut the cake / Queen of my soul / A love of your own / Person to person / I heard it through the grapevine / Walk on by / You got it / Cloudy / Work to do / Atlantic avenue / When will you be mine. *(re-iss.Aug84) (re-iss.May94 on 'Repertoire')*

— Re-formed in Spring 1994, after the success of their compilation album.

Mar 94. The Hit Label; (cd)(c) **THE BEST OF THE AVERAGE WHITE BAND – LET'S GO ROUND AGAIN** [38] [ ]
–

Mar 94. The Hit Label; (7")(c-s) **LET'S GO ROUND AGAIN (the CCN mix). / ('A'mix)** [56] [ ]

(cd-s+=) – ('A'mixes).

Kevin AYERS

Born: 16 Aug'45, Herne Bay, Kent, England. Raised as a child in Malaysia, and when he left school he moved to Canterbury, where he helped form SOFT MACHINE in 1966. Late 1968 he left for Ibiza to write solo songs for new label 'Harvest'. Previous to this he had toured the States supporting JIMI HENDRIX. He was always on the verge of a breakthrough, and consistantly surfaced with some fine albums. • **Style:** Singer-songwriter whose inspirations include SYD BARRETT, NICO or even NICK DRAKE. In 1974 he moved into more commercial field, sliding well away from his early 70's creative avant-garde period. • **Songwriters:** All by him, except FALLING IN LOVE AGAIN (Marlene Dietrich), etc. • **Trivia:** In 1987, he contributed vocals to a MIKE OLDFIELD song 'FLYING START' from the album 'ISLANDS'. AYERS had also largely contributed to an album (LINGUISTIC LEPROSY) in 1974 by friend and Deya neighbour LADY JUNE.

Recommended: BANANA PRODUCTIONS – BEST OF . . . (*8)

KEVIN AYERS – vocals, guitar (ex-SOFT MACHINE, ex-WILDE FLOWERS) with **DAVID BEDFORD** – keys / **MIKE RATLEDGE** – keys / **HUGH HOPPER** – bass / **ROB TAIT** and **ROBERT WYATT** – drums / etc.

Harvest | not issued

Nov 69. (lp) **JOY OF A TOY** -
– Joy of a toy . . . / Town feeling / Clarietta rag / Girl on a swing / Song for insane times / Stop this train again doing it / Eleanor's cake which ate her / Lady Rachel / Oleh olah bandu bandong / All this crazy gift of time. *(re-iss.+cd.Jun89 on 'B.G.O.')*

Feb 70. (7") **SINGING A SONG IN THE MORNING. / ELEANOR'S CAKE WHICH ATE HER** -

— After being augmented on last single by CARAVAN members, he formed backing group "The WHOLE WIDE WORLD", which includes **DAVID BEDFORD** – keyboards / **MIKE OLDFIELD** – bass / **LOL COXHILL** – saxophone / **MICK FINCHER** – drums

Oct 70. (lp) **SHOOTING AT THE MOON** -
– May I / Rheinhardt and Geraldine / Colores para Dolores / Lunatics lament / Pisser dans un violin / The oyster and the flying fish / Underwater / Clarence in wonderland / Red, green and you, blue / Shooting at the Moon. *(re-iss.+cd.Jun89 on 'B.G.O.')*

Oct 70. (7") **BUTTERFLY DANCE. / PUIS-JE?** -

Aug 71. (7") **STRANGER IN BLUE SUEDE SHOES. / STARS** -

— The WHOLE WIDE WORLD were augmented by GONG members **DIDIER MALHERBE** – sax / **STEVE HILLAGE** – guitar / also session drummers **WYATT, DUFORT & TONY CARR**

Jan 72. (lp) **WHATEVERSHEBRINGSWESING** -
– There is loving – Among us – There is loving / Margaret / Oh my / Song from the bottom of a well / Whatevershebringswesing / Stranger in blue suede shoes / Champagne cowboy blues / Lullaby. *(re-iss.+cd.Jun89 on 'B.G.O')*

— **ARCHIE LEGGAT** – bass (ex-WONDERWHEEL) repl. OLDFIELD who went solo / **EDDIE SPARROW** – drums / etc.

Nov 72. (7") **OH! WOT A DREAM. / CONNIE ON A RUBBER BAND** -

Harvest | Sire

Apr 73. (7") **CARIBBEAN MOON. / TAKE ME TO TAHITI**
(re-iss.Jul75 & May76)

May 73. (lp)(c) **BANANAMOUR**
– Don't let it get you down / Shouting in a bucket-blues / When your parents go to sleep / Interview / International anthem / Decadence / Oh! wot a dream / Hymn / Beware of the dog. (US-iss.+=) – Caribbean Moon. *(re-iss.May86)*

— His touring '747' band incl. **HENRY CRALLAN** – keys / **FREDDIE SMITH** – drums / **CAL BATCHELOR** – guitar. In the studio he now used many session people.

Island | not issued

Apr 74. (7") **THE UP SONG. / EVERYBODY'S SOMETIMES AND SOME PEOPLE'S ALL THE TIME BLUES** -

May 74. (lp)(c) **THE CONFESSIONS OF DR.DREAM AND OTHER STORIES** -
– Day by day / See you later / Didn't feel lonely till I thought of you / Everybody's sometimes and some people's all the time blues / It begins with a blessing, but it ends with a curse / Once I awsheared / Ball bearing blues / The confessions of Dr.Dream (a) Irreversible neural damage, (b) Invitation, (c) The one chance dance, (d) Doctor Dream theme, (e) Two into 4 goes. *(re-iss.+cd.Nov90 on 'B.G.O.')*

Jul 74. (7") **AFTER THE SHOW. / THANK YOU VERY MUCH** -

— He was credited alongside ENO, NICO and JOHN CALE on 'Island' Various Artist album 'JUNE 1st, 1974', released that month. *(cd-iss.Feb90)*

— He formed backing group, which included **ZOOT MONEY** – keyboards / **RICK WILLS** – bass / **TONY NEWMAN** – drums / **OLLIE HALSALL** – guitar

Mar 75. (lp)(c) **SWEET DECEIVER** -
– Observations / Guru banana / City waltz / Toujours la voyage / Sweet deceiver / Diminished but not finished / Circular lather / Once upon an ocean / Farewell again / Another dawn.

Feb 76. (7") **FALLING IN LOVE AGAIN. / EVERYONE KNOWS THE SONG** -

— Retained ZOOT, calling in **ANDY SOMERS** – guitar / **CHARLIE McCRACKEN** – bass / **ROB TOWNSEND** – drums

Harvest | A.B.C.

Feb 76. (7") **STRANGER IN BLUE SUEDE SHOES. / FAKE MEXICAN TOURIST BLUES** -

Jun 76. (lp)(c) **YES WE HAVE NO MANANAS**
– Star / Mr.Cool / The owl / Love's gonna turn you 'round / Falling in love again (ich bin von kopf bis fuss auf liebe eingesteldt) / Help me / Ballad of Mr.Snake / Everyone knows the song / Yes I do / Blue. *(cd-iss.Apr93 on 'B.G.O.')*

Apr 77. (7") **STAR. / THE OWL** -

— **BILL LIVESY** – keyboards repl. ZOOT, etc.

Apr 78. (lp)(c) **RAINBOW TAKEAWAY** -
– Blaming it all on love / Ballad of a salesman who sold himself / A view from a mountain / Rainbow takeaway / Waltz for you / Beware of the dog 2 / Strange song / Goodnight goodnight / Hat song. *(cd-iss.May93 on 'B.G.O.')*

Feb 80. (lp)(c) **THAT'S WHAT YOU GET, BABE** -
– That's what you get, babe / Where do I go from here / You never outrun your heart / Given and taken / Idiots / Super salesman / Money, money, money / Miss Hanagal / I'm so tired / Where do the stars end. *(cd-iss.Jun93 on 'B.G.O.')*

Feb 80. (7") **MONEY, MONEY, MONEY. / STRANGER IN BLUE SUEDE SHOES** -

— Retired to Majorca in Spain. Still retained **FOLLIE** + employed new Spanish musicians.

not issued | Columbia

1982. (7") **ANIMALS. / DON'T FALL IN LOVE WITH ME** - - Spain

Charly | not issued

Jun 83. (lp) **DIAMOND JACK AND THE QUEEN OF PAIN** -
– Madame Butterfly / Lay lady lay / Who's still crazy / You keep me hangin' on / You are a big girl / Steppin' out / My speeding heart / Howling man / Give a little bit / Champagne and valium.

Jul 83. (7") **MY SPEEDIN' HEART. / CHAMPAGNE AND VALIUM** -

not issued | Blau SPAIN

1984. (lp) **DEYA VU** - -

Il-luminated | not issued

May 86. (7"promo) **STEPPING OUT. / ONLY HEAVEN KNOWS** -

Jun 86. (lp) **AS CLOSE AS YOU THINK** -
– Heaven only knows / Wish I could fall / etc.

Virgin | not issued

Feb 88. (lp)(c)(cd) **FALLING UP** -
– Saturday night (in Deya) / Flying start / The best we have / Another rolling stone / Do you believe? / That's what we did / Night fighters / Am I really Marcel?.

Permanent | not issued

Feb 92. (cd)(c)(lp) **STILL LIFE WITH GUITAR** -

– compliations, others, etc. –

Jun 75. Harvest; (d-lp) **JOY OF A TOY / SHOOTING AT THE MOON** -

Feb 76. Harvest; (lp)(c) **ODD DITTIES** -

Jun 89. Harvest; (d-lp)(c)(cd) **BANANA PRODUCTIONS – THE BEST OF KEVIN AYERS** -
– Butterfly dance / Girl on a swing / Soon soon soon / Sweet deceiver / Caribbean moon / Irreversible neural damage / Gemini child / The lady Rachel / Stranger in blue suede shoes / There is loving / Charlotte rag / Reinhardt and Geraldine / Stars / Don't let it get you down / Hat song / Singing a song in the morning / Ballad of a salesman who sold himself / Clarence in Wonderland / Diminished but not finished / Song from the bottom of a well / Among us / Colores para Dolores. (d-lp+=) – Decadence / Toujours le voyage / Blue.

Jul 83. See For Miles; (lp) **THE KEVIN AYERS COLLECTION** -
(re-iss.Jun86) (re-iss.+cd.1990)

Jul 92. Windsong; (cd) **THE BBC RADIO LIVE IN CONCERT (live)** -

1992. Connoisseur; (cd)(c) **DOCUMENT SERIES** -

AZTEC CAMERA

Formed: East Kilbride (nr.Glasgow), Scotland . . . Early 1980 by 15 year-old at the time RODDY FRAME. Released two independent 45's on ALAN HORNE's now semi-famous 'Postcard' label, before moving on to 'Rough Trade' in 1982. The following year, RODDY & group hit the top in indie charts and national Top 30 with album 'HIGH LAND, HARD RAIN'. This led to a signing to 'Warners' and another top selling album 'KNIFE', which was produced by MARK KNOPFLER (Dire Straits). • **Style:** Intelligent, and mostly acoustic, melodic rock/pop. Ballads fused with romance. • **Songwriters:** All by FRAME, except JUMP (Van Halen) / DO I LOVE YOU (Cole Porter) / I THREW IT ALL AWAY (Bob Dylan) / BAD EDUCATION (Blue Orchids) / IF PARADISE WAS HALF AS NICE (Amen Corner). • **Trivia:** In Autumn'83, while in US supporting ELVIS COSTELLO, he lied about age; 19 to get into the country.

Recommended: HIGH LAND, HARD RAIN (*8)

RODDY FRAME (b.29 Jan'64) – vocals, acoustic guitar / **DAVE MULHOLLAND** – bass / **CAMPBELL OWENS** – drums (He replaced ALAN WELSH)

Postcard | not issued

Mar 81. (7") **JUST LIKE GOLD. / WE COULD SEND LETTERS** -

Jul 81. (7") **MATTRESS OF WIRE. / LOOK OUTSIDE THE TUNNEL** -

(mid'82) added temp.member **BERNIE CLARK** – keyboards / **DAVE RUFFY** – drums (ex-RUTS) repl. MULHOLLAND

Rough Trade | Sire

Aug 82. (7")(7"pic-d) **PILLAR TO POST. / QUEEN'S TATTOO** -

Jan 83. (7") **OBLIVIOUS. / ORCHARD GIRL** 47 -
(12"+=) – Haywire.

Apr 83. (lp)(c) **HIGH LAND, HARD RAIN** 22 Aug 83
– Oblivious / The boy wonders / Walk out to winter / The bugle sounds again / We could send letters / Pillar to post / Release / Lost outside the tunnel / Back on board / Down the dip. *(re-iss.+cd.Feb87)*
(cd+=) – Haywire / Queen's tattoo / Orchard girl. *(re-iss.cd+c Sep93 on 'WEA')*

May 83. (7")(12") **WALK OUT TO WINTER. / SET THE KILLING FREE** 64

W.E.A. | W.E.A.

Oct 83. (7") **OBLIVIOUS. / ORCHARD GIRL** 18
(d7"+=)(12"+=) – We could send letters (live) / Back on board (live).

— **RODDY FRAME** retained **DUFFY** and brought into line-up. **CRAIG GANNON** – bass (ex-BLUEBELLS) repl. OWENS / added **MALCOLM ROSS** – guitar (ex-ORANGE

JUICE, ex-JOSEF K) / guest / **GUY FLETCHER** – keyboards

Aug 84. (7")(12") **ALL I NEED IS EVERYTHING. / JUMP** 34

Sep 84. (lp)(c)(cd) **KNIFE** 14
– Still on fire / Just like the U.S.A. / Head is happy (heart's insane) / The back door to Heaven / All I need is everything / Backwards and forwards / Birth of the true / Knife. *(re-iss.cd+c Sep93)*

Nov 84. (7")(7"sha-pic-d) **STILL ON FIRE. / WALK OUT TO WINTER**
(12"+=) – Mattress of wire (live) / The boy wonders (live) / The bugle sounds again (live).

Apr 85 (10"m-lp) **AZTEC CAMERA (live)** -
– Birth of the true / Mattress of wire / Jump / Bugle sounds again / Backwards and forwards.

— **FRAME & DUFFY** plus alongside other session musicians **MARCUS MILLER** – bass / **DAVID FRANK** – keyboards (ex-SYSTEM) / **STEVE JORDAN** – guitar

Sep 87. (7") **DEEP AND WIDE AND TALL. / BAD EDUCATION**
(12") – ('A'&'B'extended).

Oct 87. (lp)(c)(cd) **LOVE** 10
– Deep and wide and tall / How men are / Everybody is a number one / More than a law / Somewhere in my heart / Working in a goldmine / One and one / Paradise / Killermont Street. *(highest chart position Jun88) (re-iss.cd+c Sep93)*

Jan 88. (7") **HOW MEN ARE. / THE RED FLAG** 25
(12"+=) – Killermont Street (live) / Pillar to post (live).
(cd-s+=) – Oblivious / All I need is everything.

Apr 88. (7") **SOMEWHERE IN MY HEART. / EVERYBODY IS A NUMBER ONE '86** 3
(10+=)(12"+=) – Down the dip / Jump.
(cd-s+=) – Walk out to winter / Still on fire.

Jul 88. (7") **WORKING IN A GOLDMINE. / I THREW IT ALL AWAY** 31
(12"+=) – ('A'version).
(cd-s++=) – How men are.

Sep 88. (7") **DEEP AND WIDE AND TALL. / BAD EDUCATION** 55
(12"+=)(cd-s+=) – More than a law.

— (live band '88: augmenting **FRAME + DUFFY**) **EDDIE KULAK** – keyboards / **GARY SANFORD** – guitar / **PAUL POWELL** – bass

— (By 1990, **FRAME** had lost **DUFFY**) retained **POWELL /** and new **GARY SANCTUARY** – keyboards / **FRANK TONTOH** – drums / guests **PAUL CARRACK, EDWYN COLLINS, MICKEY GALLAGHER & STEVE SI DELYNK.**

Jun 90. (cd)(c)(lp) **STRAY** 22
– Stray / The crying scene / Get outta London / Over my head / How it is / Good morning Britain (featuring MICK JONES) / The gentle kind / Notting Hill blues / Song for a friend. *(re-iss.cd+c Sep93)*

Jun 90. (7") **THE CRYING SCENE. / TRUE COLOURS** 70
(12"+=)(cd-s+=) – Salvation. *(above re-iss.Nov90)*
(extra-10"+=) – I threw it all away (live).

— (next single featured **MICK JONES** – co/vocals (of BIG AUDIO DYNAMITE)

Sep 90. (7")(c-s) **GOOD MORNING BRITAIN. / ('A'live version)** 19
(12"+=) – ('A'remix)
(cd-s+=) – Consolation prize.

(with **EDWYN COLLINS** – co/vocals)

Jul 92. (7")(c-s) **SPANISH HORSES. / JUST LIKE THE U.S.A. (live)** 52
(cd-s) – ('A'side) / Killermont street / Birth of the true / Song for a friend.
(cd-s) – ('A'live version) / Stray (live) / The bugle sounds again (live) / Dolphins (live).

Apr 93. (7")(c-s) **DREAM SWEET DREAMS. / SISTER ANN** 67
(cd-s+=) – Good morning Britain (live) / How men are (live).
(cd-s) – ('A'side) / Mattress of wire (live) / Let your love decide (live) / Orchid girl (live).

May 93. (cd)(c)(lp) **DREAMLAND** 21
– Birds / Safe in sorrow / Black Lucia / Let your love decide / Spanish horses / Dream sweet dreams / Piano's and clocks / Sister Ann / Vertigo / Valium Summer / Belle of the ball.

Jun 93. (7")(c-s) **BIRDS. / DEEP AND WIDE AND TALL**
(cd-s) – ('A'side) / Working in a goldmine / Knife.
(cd-s) – ('A'side) / Somewhere in my heart / Oblivious / Good morning Britain.

Oct 95. (c-s) **SUN / SUNSET**
(cd-s+=) – The crying scene (live).
(cd-s) – ('A'side) / We could send letters / Black Lucia / The rainy season.

Nov 95. (cd)(c) **FRESTONIA**
– The rainy season / Sun / Crazy / On the avenue / Imperfectly / Debutante / Beautiful girl / Phenomenal world / Method of love / Sunset.

– compilations, others, etc. –

Sep 90. Old Gold; (7") **SOMEWHERE IN MY HEART. / OBLIVIOUS** -

Nov 90. Chrysalis; (7") ('A'side by "Pogues / Kirsty MacColl")
(12"+=)(cd-s+=) – DO I LOVE YOU? (from 'Red, White & Blue' Cole Porter tribute album with proceeds going to AIDS)

Oct 94. Windsong; (cd) **LIVE ON THE TEST (live)** -

BABES IN TOYLAND

Formed: Minneapolis, USA . . . late 80's by KAT BJELLAND and co. After initial releases for hometown 'Twintone' label, they transferred to 'Southern' in 1992 for UK Top 30 album 'FONTANELLE'. • **Style:** Foxy all-girl grunge trio, sounding between LYDIA LUNCH and supporters SONIC YOUTH. • **Songwriters:** Group comps except; WATCHING GIRL (Shonen Knife) / WE ARE FAMILY (hit; Sister Sledge) / DEEP SONG (Cory-Cross) / ALL BY MYSELF (Eric Carmen). • **Trivia:** Debut 1990 album, was produced by Jack Endino of 'Sub Pop'. FONTANELLE was with LEE RANALDO (Sonic Youth).

Recommended: FONTANELLE (*8) / TO MOTHER (*8)

KAT BJELLAND – vocals, guitar / **MICHELLE LEON** – bass / **LORI BARBERO** – drums, vocals

not issued / Treehouse

Jul 89. (7")(7"green) **DUST CAKE BOY. / SPIT TO SEE THE SHINE** [-] [ ]

imp / Sub Pop

Apr 90. (7")(7"gold) **HOUSE. / ARRIBA** [-] [ ]

Twin Tone / Twin Tone

Jul 90. (cd)(lp)(mauve-lp) **SPANKING MACHINE** [ ] [ ]
– Swamp pussy / He's my thing / Vomit heart / Never / Boto (w)rap / Dogg / Pain in my heart / Lashes / You're right / Dust cake boy / Fork down throat. *(re-iss.+c Dec91 on purple lp)*

Jun 91. (cd)(c)(lp) **TO MOTHER** [ ] [ ]
– Catatonic / Mad pilot / Primus / Laugh my head off / Spit to see the shine / Pipe / The quiet room.

— (Mar92) **MAUREEN HERMAN** – bass (ex-M+M STIGMATA drummer) repl. MICHELLE

Strange Fruit / not issued

Apr 92. (cd)(10"lp) **THE PEEL SESSIONS (live on John Peel show)** [ ] [-]
– Catatonic / Ripe / Primus / Spit to see the shine / Pearl / Dogg / Laugh my head off / Mad pilot.

Southern / Warners

Aug 92. (cd)(c)(red-lp) **FONTANELLE** [24] [ ]
– Bruise violet / Right now / Blue bell / Handsome & Gretel / Blood / Magick flute / Won't tell / The quiet room / Spun / Short song / Jungle train / Pearl / Real eyes / Mother / Gone.

Nov 92. (7"purple) **BRUISE VIOLET. / GONE** [ ] [ ]
(12"+=)(cd-s+=) – Magick flute.

Jun 93. (cd)(c)(lp) **PAINKILLERS (part live)** [53] [ ]
– He's my thing / Laredo / Istigkeit / Ragweed / Angel hair / Fontanellette (live at CBGB's): Bruise violet – Bluebell – Angel hair – Pearl – Blood – Magick flute – Won't tell – Real eyes – Spun – Mother – Handsome & Gretel.

— Had denied breaking-up throughout 1993, when KAT married Australian STUART GREY (of-Lubricated Goat) and sidelined with bands CRUNT and KATSTU. She had earlier splintered with husband STUART.

CRUNT

KAT BJELLAND, STUART GREY + SIMINS

Trance Syn. / Trance Syn.

Mar 94. (cd)(lp)(blue-lp) **CRUNT** [ ] [ ] Feb94
– Theme from Crunt / Swine / Black heart / Unglued / Changing my mind / Snap out of it / Sexy / Punishment / Spam / Elephant.

BABES IN TOYLAND

— re-formed (see last line-up)

Reprise / Reprise

Apr 95. (cd)(c)(lp) **NEMESISTERS** [ ] [ ]
– Hello / Oh yeah! / Drivin' / Sweet '69 / Surd / 22 / Ariel / Kiler on the road / Middle man / Memory / S.F.W. / All by myself / Deep song / We are family.

May 95. (cd-ep) **SWEET '69 / S.F.W. (live) / SWAMP PUSSY (live)** [ ] [ ]

Sep 95. (12")(cd-s) **WE ARE FAMILY (Arthur Baker remix) / ('A'-Ben Grosse remix)** [ ] [ ]
(12"+=) – (2 other Baker & Grosse mixes).

BABYS

Formed: London, England . . . 1976 and soon, due to Mike Mansfield promo video, sign to 'Chrysalis'. In 1977, they gained teen following in the States leading them to emigrate to Los Angeles. Early in 1978, they had first US hit, with 'ISN'T IT TIME'. • **Style:** Mainstream rock/pop in the mould of FOREIGNER. • **Songwriters:** WAITE and group compositions. • **Trivia:** In 1984, JOHN WAITE starred as a hairdresser in the US soap 'Paper Dolls'.

Recommended: ANTHOLOGY (*4)

JOHN WAITE (b. 4 Jul'54, Lancashire, England) – vocals, bass / **WALLY STOCKER** (b.17 Mar'54) – vocals, guitar / **MIKE CORBY** (b. 3 Jul'54) – vocals, keyboards / **TONY BROCK** (b.31 Mar'54) – drums (ex-SPONTANEOUS COMBUSTION)

Chrysalis / Chrysalis

Nov 76. (7") **IF YOU'VE GOT THE TIME. / LAURA / DYING MAN** [ ] [88]

Jan 77. (lp)(c) **THE BABYS** [ ] [ ]
– Looking for love / If you've got the time / I believe in love / Wild man / Laura / I love how you love me / Rodeo / Over and over / Read my stars / Dying man. *(re-iss.1983)*

Jan 78. (7") **ISN'T IT TIME. / GIVE ME YOUR LOVE** [45] [13] Oct 77

Jan 78. (lp)(c) **BROKEN HEART** [ ] [34] Oct 77
– Wrong or right / Give me your love / Isn't it time / And if you see me fly / The golden mile / Broken heart / I'm falling / Rescue me / Silver dreams / A piece of the action. *(re-iss.1983)*

Jan 78. (7") **SILVER DREAMS. / IF YOU SHOULD SEE ME CRY** [-] [ ]

— **JONATHAN CAIN** (b.26 Feb'50, Chicago, Illinois) – keyboards repl. CORBY. (JOHN WAITE now just vocals) added **RICKY PHILLIPS – bass**

Jan 79. (7") **EVERY TIME I THINK OF YOU. /** [-] [13]

Feb 79. (7") **EVERYTIME I THINK OF YOU. / HEAD FIRST** [ ] [-]

Feb 79. (lp)(c) **HEAD FIRST** [ ] [22] Jan 79
– Love don't prove I'm right / Every time I think of you / I was one / White lightning / Run to Mexico / Head first / You (got it) / Please don't leave me here / California. *(re-iss.1982)*

May 79. (7") **HEAD FIRST. /** [-] [ ]

Jan 80. (7") **TRUE LOVE TRUE CONFESSIONS. / BROKEN HEART / MONEY** [ ] [ ] Nov 79

Jan 80. (lp)(c) **UNION JACKS** [ ] [42]
– Back on my feet again / True love true confessions / Union Jacks / In your eyes / Anytime / Jesus are you there / Turn around in Tokyo / Love is just a mystery.

Jan 80. (7") **BACK ON MY FEET AGAIN. / TURN AROUND IN TOKYO** [-] [33]

Apr 80. (7") **MIDNIGHT RENDEZVOUS. /** [-] [ ]

— Now a quartet, when CAIN leaves to join JOURNEY

Oct 81. (7") **TURN AND WALK AWAY. / DARKER SIDE OF TOWN** [-] [42]

Nov 80. (lp)(c) **ON THE EDGE** [ ] [ ]
– Turn and walk away / Sweet 17 / She's my girl / Darker side of town / Too far gone / Rock'n'roll is (alive and well) / Downtown / Postcard / Gonna be somebody / Love don't wait.

— Disbanded late 1981. BROCK and STOCKER joined ROD STEWART tour.

– compilations, others, etc. –

Chrysalis / Chrysalis

Oct 81. (lp)(c) **THE BABYS' ANTHOLOGY** [ ] [ ]
– Head first / Isn't it time / Midnight rendezvous / Money / Back on my feet again / Give me your love / Turn and walk away / Everytime I think of you / If you've got the time / Sweet 17.

JOHN WAITE

with session people.

Chrysalis / Chrysalis

Jun 82. (lp)(c) **IGNITION** [ ] [ ]
– White heat / Change / Mr.Wonderful / Going to the top / Desperate love / Temptation / By my baby tonight / Make it happen / Still in love with you / Wild life.

EMI America / EMI America

Aug 84. (7")(12") **MISSING YOU. / FOR YOUR LOVE** [9] [1] Jun 84

Oct 84. (lp)(c) **NO BRAKES** [64] [10] Jul 84
– Saturday night / Missing you / Dark side of the Sun / Restless heart / Tears / Euroshima / Dreamtime / Shake it up / For your love / Love collision. *(cd-iss. 1987)*

Nov 84. (7") **TEARS. / DREAMTIME** [ ] [ ]
(12"+=) Shake it up.

Mar 85. (7") **RESTLESS HEART. / EUROSHIMA** [ ] [ ]
(12"+=) – Missing you (edit).

Sep 85. (7") **EVERY STEP OF THE WAY. / NO BRAKES** [ ] [26]

Oct 85. (lp)(c) **MASK OF SMILES** [ ] [36] Aug 85
– Every step of the way / Laydown / Welcome to Paradise / Lust for life / Ain't that peculiar / Just like lovers / The choice / You're the one / No brakes.

Jan 86. (7") **THE CHOICE. / NO BRAKES** [ ] [ ]

Aug 86. (7") **IF ANYBODY HAD A HEART. / JUST LIKE LOVERS** [ ] [ ]

Jul 87. (7") **THESE TIMES ARE HARD FOR LOVERS. / WILD ONE** [ ] [ ]
(12"+=) – Missing you.

Aug 87. (lp)(c)(cd) **ROVERS' RETURN** [ ] [ ] Jul 87
– These times are hard for lovers / Act of love / Encircled / Woman's touch / Wild one / Don't lose any sleep / Sometimes / She's the one / Big time for love.

		Epic	Epic
Dec 90.	(7") **DEAL FOR LIFE. / ('B'side by 'Terry Reid')** (12"+=)(cd-s+=) – (tracks by 'Chicago' & 'Maria McKee').	[ ]	[ ]
		Chrysalis	Chrysalis
Feb 92.	(cd)(c)(lp) **THE ESSENTIAL JOHN WAITE 1976-1986** (compilation)	[ ]	[ ]

– Head above the waves * / A piece of action * / Broken heart * / Love don't prove I'm right * / Love is a rose to me / White lightening / Run to Mexico / World in a bottle / Union Jacks * / Anytime / Jesus are you there? * / Darker side of town * / Rock'n'roll is (alive and well) * / Gonna be somebody * / White heat / Make it happen / Change / Mr.Wonderful / If anybody had a heart / Missing you. (tracks by BABYS *).

Feb 93. (7")(c-s) **MISSING YOU. / HEAD ABOVE THE WAVES** [ ] [ ]
(cd-s+=) – Broken heart / Love is a rose to me.

— (above re-issue)

— Virtually all The BABYS were re-united when **WAITE, CAIN & PHILLIPS** formed

BAD ENGLISH

with **NEIL SCHON** – guitar, vocals (ex-JOURNEY) / **DEAN CASTRONOVA** – drums, vocals (ex-WILD DOGS)

		Epic	Epic	
Aug 89.	(7") **FORGET ME NOT. / LAY DOWN** (12"+=)(cd-s+=) – Rockin' horse.	[ ]	[45]	Jul 89
Sep 89.	(lp)(c)(cd) **BAD ENGLISH**	[74]	[21]	Jul 89

– Best of what I got / Heaven is a 4 letter word / Possession / Forget me not / When I see you smile / Tough times don't last / Ghost in your heart / Price of love / Ready when you are / Lay down / The restless ones / Rockin horse / Don't walk away.

Oct 89.	(7")(c-s) **WHEN I SEE YOU SMILE. / ROCKIN' HORSE** (12"+=)(cd-s+=) – Tough times don't last.	[61]	[1]	Sep 89
Feb 90.	(7") **PRICE OF LOVE. / THE RESTLESS ONES** (12"+=)(cd-s+=) – Ready when you are. *(re-iss.all Apr90)*	[ ]	[5]	Dec 89
Apr 90.	(c-s+cd-s) **HEAVEN IS A 4 LETTER WORD. / LAY DOWN**	[-]	[ ]	
Jun 90.	(7")(c-s) **POSSESSION. / TOUGH TIMES DON'T LAST**	[-]	[21]	
Sep 90.	(7") **DON'T WALK AWAY. / TOUGH TIMES DON'T LAST** (12"+=)(cd-s+=) – Price of love.	[ ]	[ ]	
Aug 91.	(7")(c-s) **STRAIGHT TO YOUR HEART. / MAKE LOVE LAST** (12"+=) – Forget me not. / (cd-s++=) – When I see you smile.	[ ]	[42]	
Oct 91.	(cd)(c)(lp) **BACKLASH**	[ ]	[ ]	Sep 91

– So this is Eden / Straight to your heart / Time stood still / The time alone with you / Dancing off the edge of the world / Rebel say a prayer / Savage blue / Pray for rain / Make love last / Life at the top.

Nov 91. (7") **THE TIME ALONE WITH YOU. / MAKE LOVE LAST** [-] [ ]

— They broke-up after above release and SCHON and CASTRONOVO formed HARDLINE (see ⇒ JOURNEY)

BACHMAN-TURNER OVERDRIVE

Formed: Vancouver, Canada . . . 1972 by brothers RANDY, ROBBIE and TIM. They, with FRED TURNER signed to 'Mercury' in 1973 and began steady inroads onto US airwaves. By late '74, they had No.1 US hit with the stuttering 'YOU AIN'T SEEN NOTHIN' YET'. (In the 90's, its intro featured on Harry Enfield's UK TV show DJ creations Chas Smash and NIcey Nice). Subsequent releases provided BTO with more hits, but they couldn't reproduce any of the earlier quality. • **Style:** Heavy hard driving rock, mainly for "blue collar" brigade. • **Songwriters:** RANDY and FRED, no covers. • **Trivia:** Being of Mormon religion, the BACHMANS were not typical rock band, as their faith did not allow alcohol, drugs, tea or coffee, just women.

Recommended: THE BEST OF BTO (SO FAR) (*5)

RANDY BACHMAN

with **DAN TROIANO** – guitar / **GARRY PETERSON** – drums / **WES DAKUS** – steel guitar

		not issued	R.C.A.
1970.	(lp) **AXE**	[-]	[ ]

– Zarahemia / Not to return / Pookie's shuffle / Tally's tune / Take the long way home / La Jolla / Tin Lizzie / Suite theam / Noah.

BRAVE BELT

RANDY BACHMAN (b.27 Feb'43) – vocals, guitar (ex-GUESS WHO) / **CHAD ALLAN** – keyboards, vocals (ex-GUESS WHO) / **C.F. (FRED) TURNER** (b.16 Oct'43) – bass, vocals / **ROBBIE BACHMAN** (b.18 Feb'53) – drums, percussion

		not issued	Reprise
1971.	(lp) **BRAVE BELT**	[-]	[ ]

– Crazy arms, crazy eyes / Lifetime / Waitin' there for me / I am the man / French kin / It's over / Rock and roll band / Wandering fantasy girl / I wouldn't give up my guitar for a woman / Holy train / Anyday means tomorrow / Scarecrow.

1971.	(7") **ROCK AND ROLL BAND. / ANY DAY MEANS TOMORROW**	[-]	[ ]
1971.	(7") **CRAZY ARMS, CRAZY EYES. / HOLY TRAIN**	[-]	[ ]
1972.	(7") **NEVER COMIN' HOME. / CAN YOU FEEL IT**	[-]	[ ]
1972.	(lp) **BRAVE BELT II**	[-]	[ ]

– Too far away / Dunrobin's gone / Can you feel it / Put it in a song / Summer soldier / Never comin' home / Be a good man / Long way round / Another way out / Waterloo country.

1972. (7") **ANOTHER WAY OUT. / DUNROBIN'S GONE** [-] [ ]

BACHMAN-TURNER OVERDRIVE

TIM BACHMAN – guitar repl. CHAD

		Mercury	Mercury	
Aug 73.	(7") **GIMME YOUR MONEY PLEASE. / LITTLE GAWDY DANCER**	[-]	[ ]	
Aug 73.	(lp)(c) **BACHMAN-TURNER OVERDRIVE**	[ ]	[70]	

– Gimme your money please / Hold back the water / Blue collar / Little gandy dancer / Stayed awake all night / Down and out man / Don't get yourself in trouble / Thank you for the feelin'. *(cd-iss.Jan93)*

Sep 73.	(7") **STAYED AWAKE ALL NIGHT. / DOWN AND OUT MAN** *(re-iss.Jan77)*	[ ]	[ ]	
Nov 73.	(7") **BLUE COLLAR. / HOLD BACK THE WATER**	[-]	[68]	
Jan 74.	(7") **LET IT RIDE. / TRAMP**	[-]	[23]	
Mar 74.	(7") **LET IT RIDE. / BLUE COLLAR**	[ ]	[-]	
Mar 74.	(lp)(c) **BACHMAN-TURNER OVERDRIVE II**	[ ]	[4]	Jan 74

– Blown / Welcome home / Stonegates / Let it ride / Give it time / I don't have to / Takin' care of business / Tramp.

Aug 74. (7") **TAKIN' CARE OF BUSINESS. / STONEGATES** [ ] [12] Jun 74

— **BLAIR THORNTON** (b.23 Jul'50, Vancouver) – guitar repl. TIM who became producer

Oct 74.	(7") **YOU AIN'T SEEN NOTHIN' YET. / FREE WHEELIN'**	[2]	[1]	Sep 74
Oct 74.	(lp)(c) **NOT FRAGILE**	[12]	[1]	Aug 74

– Not fragile / Rock is my life and this is my song / Roll on down the highway / You ain't seen nothin' yet / Free wheelin' / Sledgehammer / Blue moanin' / Second hand / Givin' it all away.

Jan 75.	(7") **ROLL ON DOWN THE HIGHWAY. / SLEDGEHAMMER**	[22]	[14]	
May 75.	(7") **HEY YOU. / FLAT BROKE LOVE**	[ ]	[21]	
Jun 75.	(lp)(c) **FOUR WHEEL DRIVE**	[ ]	[5]	May 75

– Four wheel drive / She's a devil / Hey you / Flat broke love / She's keepin' time / Quick change artist / Lowland fling / Don't let the blues get you down. *(cd-iss.Jan93)*

Nov 75.	(7") **DOWN TO THE LINE. / SHE'S A DEVIL**	[-]	[43]	
Jan 76.	(7") **AWAY FROM HOME. / DOWN TO THE LINE**	[ ]	[-]	
Feb 76.	(lp)(c) **HEAD ON**	[ ]	[23]	Jan 76

– Find out about love / It's over / Average man / Woncha take me for a while / Wild spirit / Take it like a man / Lookin' out for / Away from home / Stay alive.

Feb 76.	(7") **TAKE IT LIKE A MAN. / WONCHA TAKE ME FOR A WHILE**	[-]	[33]
Apr 76.	(7") **LOOKING OUT FOR . / FIND OUT ABOUT LOVE**	[-]	[65]
May 77.	(7") **MY WHEELS WON'T TURN. / FREE WAYS**	[-]	[ ]
May 77.	(7") **MY WHEELS WON'T TURN. / LIFE STILL GOES ON**	[ ]	[-]
May 77.	(lp)(c) **FREEWAYS**	[ ]	[70] Mar 77

– Can we all come together / Life still goes on / Shotgun rider / Just for you / My wheels won't turn / Down, down / Easy groove / Freeways. *(cd-iss.Jan93)*

Sep 77.	(7") **SHOTGUN RIDER. / JUST FOR YOU**	[ ]	[-]
Sep 77.	(7") **SHOTGUN RIDER. / DOWN, DOWN**	[-]	[ ]
Dec 77.	(7") **LIFE STILL GOES ON. / JUST FOR YOU**	[-]	[ ]

B.T.O.

— **JIM CLENCH** – guitar, vocals repl. RANDY who went solo

Mar 78. (lp)(c) **STREET ACTION** [ ] [ ]

– I'm in love / Down the road / Takes a lot of people / A long time for a little while / Street action / For love / Madison Avenue / You're gonna miss me / The whole world is waiting for a love song.

Mar 78.	(7") **DOWN THE ROAD. / A LONG TIME FOR A LITTLE WHILE**	[-]	[ ]
Mar 79.	(7") **HEARTACHES. / HEAVEN TONIGHT**	[-]	[60]
Mar 79.	(7") **HEARTACHES. / ROCK'N'ROLL NIGHTS**	[ ]	[-]
Apr 79.	(lp)(c) **ROCK'N'ROLL NIGHTS (live)**	[ ]	[ ]

– Jamaica / Heartaches / Heaven tonight / Rock'n'roll nights / Wastin' time / Here she comes again / End of the line / Rock and roll hell / Amelia Earhart.

Jun 79. (7") **END OF THE LINE (live). / JAMAICA (live)** [-] [ ]

— Broke-up 1979.

BACHMAN-TURNER OVERDRIVE

Re-united mid-84 with below line-up 1984. **RANDY, TIM, FRED TURNER** and newcomer **GARRY PETERSON** – drums

		Compleat	Compleat	
Sep 84.	(7") **FOR THE WEEKEND. / JUST LOOK AT ME NOW**	[ ]	[ ]	
Nov 84.	(lp)(c) **BACHMAN-TURNER OVERDRIVE**	[ ]	[ ]	Sep 84

– For the weekend / Just look at me now / My sugaree / City's still growin' / Another fool / Lost in a fantasy / Toledo / Service with a smile.

Jan 85.	(7") **SERVICE WITH A SMILE. / MY SUGAREE**	[-]	[ ]
Mar 85.	(7") **MY SUGAREE. / (Part 2)**	[-]	[ ]
		M.C.A.	Curb
Aug 86.	(lp)(c) **LIVE! – LIVE! – LIVE!**	[ ]	[ ]

– Hey you / Mississippi queen / Sledgehammer / Fragile man / Bad news travels fast / You ain't seen nothin' yet / Roll on down the highway / Takin' care of business.

RANDY later joined with (ex-TROOPER) FRANK LUDWIG, in UNION. He also became songwriter for BEACH BOYS, etc.

– compilations, others, etc. –

Mar 75.	Reprise; (lp) **BACHMAN-TURNER OVERDRIVE AS BRAVE BELT**	[ ]	[ ]	
Sep 76.	Mercury; (7") **GIMME YOUR MONEY PLEASE. / FOUR WHEEL DRIVE**	[-]	[70]	
Sep 76.	Mercury; (7") **TAKIN' CARE OF BUSINESS. / WON'T CHA TAKE ME FOR A WHILE**	[ ]	[-]	
Nov 76.	Mercury; (lp)(c) **THE BEST OF B.T.O. (SO FAR)**	[ ]	[19]	Aug 76
1977.	Mercury; (lp) **JAPAN TOUR (live)**	[-]	[ ]	
Aug 81.	Mercury; (lp)(c) **GREATEST HITS**	[ ]	[ ]	

– Lookin' out for / Hey you / Takin' care of business / You ain't seen nothin' yet / Flat broke love / Rock'n'roll nights / Roll on down the highway / Freeways / Down, down / Let it ride / Can we all come together / Jamaica.

Oct 83.	Mercury; (lp)(c) **YOU AIN'T SEEN NOTHIN' YET**	[ ]	[ ]
Oct 84.	Mercury; (7") **YOU AIN'T SEEN NOTHIN' YET. / ROLL ON DOWN THE HIGHWAY**	[ ]	[ ]

Aug 93. Mercury; (d-cd) **ANTHOLOGY** [ ] [ ]
(re-iss.Sep95)
Mar 88. Old Gold; (7") **YOU AIN'T SEEN NOTHIN' YET. / (other artist)** [ ] [-]
Jul 88. Knight; (c) **NIGHTRIDING** [ ] [-]
Aug 94. Spectrum; (cd)(c) **ROLL ON DOWN THE HIGHWAY** [ ] [-]

RANDY BACHMAN

solo with **BURTON CUMMINGS** – keyboards / **IAN GARDINER** – bass / **JEFF PORCARO** – drums / **TOM SCOTT** – saxophone.

Polydor Polydor

Jun 78. (7") **JUST A KID. / SURVIVOR** [ ] [ ]
Jul 78. (lp)(c) **SURVIVOR** [ ] [ ]
– Just a kid / One hand clappin' / Lost in the shuffle / Is the night too cold for dancin' / You moved me / I am a star / Maybe again / Survivor.

IRONHORSE

was formed by **RANDY** with **TOM SPARKS** – guitar / **JOHN PIERCE** – bass / **MIKE BAIRD** – drums / **BARRY ALLEN** – vocals

Scotti B. Scotti B.

Mar 79. (7") **SWEET LUI-LOUISE. / WATCH ME FLY** [60] [36]
May 79. (lp)(c) **IRONHORSE** [ ] [ ]
– One and only / Sweet Lui-Louise / Jump back in the light / You gotta let go / Tumbleweed / Stateline blues / Watch me fly / Old fashioned / Dedicated to Slowhand / She's got it / There ain't no clue.
Jul 79. (7") **ONE AND ONLY. / SHE'S GOT IT** [ ] [ ]

—— **FRANK LUDWIG** – vocals, keyboards repl. BARRY / **RON FOOS** – bass / **CHRIS LEIGHTON** – drums repl. JOHN and MIKE

Nov 80. (7") **WHAT'S YOUR HURRY DARLIN'. / TRY A LITTLE HARDER** [ ] [ ]
Nov 80. (lp)(c) **EVERYTHING IS GREY** [ ] [ ]
– Everything is grey / What's your hurry darlin' / Symphony / Only way to fly / Try a little harder / I'm hurting inside / Playin' that same old song / Railroad love / Somewhere sometime / Keep your motor running.

BAD COMPANY

Formed: Based various areas of England (see below). Late summer 1973 the four got together taking name from 1972 western film starring Jeff Bridges. Peter Grant (Led Zeppelin's manager) signed them for his new 'Swan Song' label in 1974, and they soon had US No.1 debut album. For the next several years, they become one of top rock groups, hitting charts on both sides of the Atlantic. • **Style:** Classic power rock outfit, with frontman RODGERS providing heavy but soulful lyrics. By the 80's they had moved into AOR, which all but loyal fans panned. • **Songwriters:** RALPHS penned most. In the 90's RALPHS and HOWE individually co-wrote with THOMAS. • **Trivia:** MEL COLLINS (ex-King Crimson) played sax on debut.

Recommended: STRAIGHT SHOOTER (*8) / BAD CO. (*6)

PAUL RODGERS (b.12 Dec'49) – vocals, piano (ex-FREE) / **MICK RALPHS** (b.31 Mar'48) – guitar, piano (ex-MOTT THE HOOPLE) / **BOZ BURRELL** (b.RAYMOND, 1946) – bass, vocals (ex-KING CRIMSON, ex-SNAFU) / **SIMON KIRKE** (b.28 Jul'49) – drums (ex-FREE)

Island Swan Song

May 74. (7") **CAN'T GET ENOUGH. / LITTLE MISS FORTUNE** [15] [5]
Jun 74. (lp)(c) **BAD CO.** [3] [1]
– Can't get enough / Rock steady / Ready for love / Don't let me down / Bad company / The way I choose / Movin' on / Seagull. *(re-iss.Jan78 + Jun81) (cd-iss.Oct94 on 'Atlantic')*
Jan 75. (7") **MOVIN' ON. / EASY ON MY SOUL** [-] [19]
Mar 75. (7") **GOOD LOVIN' GONE BAD. / WHISKEY BOTTLE** [31] [36]
Apr 75. (lp)(c) **STRAIGHT SHOOTER** [3] [3]
– Good lovin' gone bad / Feel like makin' love / Weep no more / Shooting star / Deal with the preacher / Wild fire women / Anna / Call on me. *(re-iss.Jan78 + Jun81) (cd-iss.Oct88 on 'Swan Song') (re-iss.cd Feb93 on 'Warners') (re-iss.cd Jul94 on 'Atlantic')*
Aug 75. (7") **FEEL LIKE MAKIN' LOVE. / WILD FIRE WOMEN** [20] [10] Jul 75
Feb 76. (lp)(c) **RUN WITH THE PACK** [4] [5]
– Live for the music / Simple man / Honey child / Love me somebody / Run with the pack / Silver, blue and gold / Young blood / Do right by your woman / Sweet lil' sister / Fade away. *(re-iss.Jan78 + Jun81) (cd-iss.Oct88 on 'Swan Song') (re-iss.cd Feb93 on 'Warners') (re-iss.cd Jul94 on 'Atlantic')*
Mar 76. (7") **RUN WITH THE PACK. / DO RIGHT BY YOUR WOMAN** [ ] [-]
Mar 76. (7") **YOUNG BLOOD. / DO RIGHT BY YOUR WOMAN** [-] [20]
Jul 76. (7") **HONEY CHILD. / FADE AWAY** [-] [59]
Feb 77. (7") **EVERYTHING I NEED. / TOO BAD** [ ] [ ]
Mar 77. (lp)(c) **BURNIN' SKY** [17] [15]
– Burnin' sky / Morning Sun / Leaving you / Like water / Everything I need / Heartbeat / Peace of mind / Passing time / Too bad / Man needs woman / Master of ceremony. *(re-iss.cd Feb93 on 'Warners') (cd-iss.Oct94 on 'Atco')*
May 77. (7") **BURNIN' SKY. / EVERYTHING I NEED** [-] [78]

Swan Song Swan Song

Mar 79. (7") **ROCK'N'ROLL FANTASY. / CRAZY CIRCLES** [ ] [13]
Mar 79. (lp)(c) **DESOLATION ANGELS** [10] [3]
– Rock'n'roll fantasy / Crazy circles / Gone, gone, gone / Evil wind / Early in the morning / Lonely for your love / Oh, Atlanta / Take the time / Rhythm machine / She brings me love. *(re-iss.cd Feb93 on 'Warners')*
Jul 79. (7") **GONE, GONE, GONE. / TAKE THE TIME** [-] [56]
Aug 82. (lp)(c) **ROUGH DIAMONDS** [15] [26]
– Electricland / Untie the knot / Nuthin' on the T.V. / Painted face / Kickdown / Ballad of the band / Cross country boy / Old Mexico / Downhill ryder / Racetrack. *(cd-iss.Oct94 on 'Atlantic')*
Sep 82. (7") **ELECTRICLAND. / UNTIE THE KNOT** [-] [74]

—— (mid'83) Disbanded. RODGERS went solo before joining The FIRM. KIRKE played with WILDFIRE. BURRELL sessioned on ROGER CHAPMAN (Family) lp's.

—— **BAD COMPANY** reformed 1986. **RALPHS, KIRKE, BURRELL** and the incoming **BRIAN HOWE** – vocals (ex-TED NUGENT)

Atlantic Atlantic

Oct 86. (lp)(c)(cd) **FAME & FORTUNE** [ ] [ ]
– Burning up / This love / Fame and fortune / That girl / Tell it like it is / Long walk / Hold on my heart / Valerie / When we made love / If I'm sleeping. *(re-iss.cd Nov93)*
Nov 86. (7") **THIS LOVE. / TELL IT LIKE IT IS** [ ] [85] Oct 86
(12"+=) – Burning up / Fame & fortune.
Jan 87. (7")(12") **FAME AND FORTUNE. / WHEN WE MADE LOVE** [ ] [ ]
Aug 88. (lp)(c)(cd) **DANGEROUS AGE** [ ] [58]
– One night / Shake it up / No smoke without fire / Bad man / Dangerous age / Dirty boy / Rock of America / Something about you / The way it goes / Love attack. (cd+=) – Excited.
Apr 89. (7") **SHAKE IT UP. /** [-] [82]

—— **GEOFF WHITEHORN** – guitar (ex-BACK STREET CRAWLER) repl. RALPHS / **PAUL CULLEN** – bass repl. BURRELL / added **DAVE COLWELL** – keyboards (ex-ASAP)

Atco Atco

Jul 90. (cd)(c)(lp) **HOLY WATER** [ ] [35] Jun 90
– Holy water / Walk through fire / Stranger stranger / If you needed somebody / Fearless / Lay your love on me / Boys cry tough / With you in a heartbeat / Never too late / I don't care / Dead of the night / I can't live without you / 100 miles.
Jul 90. (7") **HOLY WATER. / I CAN'T LIVE WITHOUT YOU** [ ] [89]
(12"+=)(cd-s+=) – Love attack.
Apr 91. (7") **IF YOU NEEDED SOMEBODY. / DEAD OF NIGHT** [ ] [16] Nov 90
(12"+=)(cd-s+=) – Love attack.
Jul 91. (c-s) **WALK THROUGH FIRE. / ?** [-] [28]

—— (May91) **STEVE WALSH** – vocals (ex-KANSAS) repl. HOWE / **MICK RALPHS** also returned briefly.

Sep 92. (7")(c-s) **HOW ABOUT THAT. / HERE COMES TROUBLE** [ ] [38]
(12") – No smoke without a fire (remix) / Stranger stranger.
(cd-s+=) – No smoke without a fire (remix) / If you needed somebody.
Sep 92. (cd)(c)(lp) **HERE COMES TROUBLE** [ ] [40]
– How about that / Stranger than fiction / Here comes trouble / This could be the one / Both feet in the water / Take this town / What about you / Little angel / Hold on to my heart / Brokenhearted / My only one.
Nov 92. (c-s)(cd-s) **THIS COULD BE THE ONE. / ?** [-] [87]

—— **RALPHS / KIRKE + HART / COLWELL / LISTER**

Jul 95. (cd)(c) **COMPANY OF STRANGERS** [ ] [ ]
– Company of strangers / Clearwater highway / Judas my brother / Little Martha / Gimme gimme / Where I belong / Down down down / Abandoned and alone / Down and dirty / Pretty woman / You're the only reason / Dance with the Devil / Loving you out loud.

– compilations, others, etc. –

Jan 86. Atlantic; (lp)(c)(cd) **10 FROM 6** [ ] [ ]
– Can't get enough / Feel like makin' love / Run with the pack / Shooting star / Movin' on / Bad company / Rock'n'roll fantasy / Electricland / Ready for love / Live for the music.
Mar 90. Atlantic; (7") **CAN'T GET ENOUGH. / BAD COMPANY** [ ] [ ]
(12"+=)(cd-s+=) – No smoke without fire / Shake it up.

BAD ENGLISH (see under ⇒ BABYS)

BADFINGER

Formed: Liverpool, England, in '68 as The IVEYS, by EVANS and GIBBONS. Sign to The BEATLES' newly formed label 'Apple', and after 1 minor hit single become BADFINGER. Soon compete in the UK/US chart with the very group that gave them the break. Later in their history, they were to be virtually disregarded in the pop world, leaving them depressed, which led to the suicides of HAM and EVANS. (see below). • **Style:** Compared in sound to The BEATLES (circa 1965), and with the Fab Four breaking up, became a worthy substitute, due to • **Songwriters:** HAM and EVANS writing most of material. Covers:- COME AND GET IT (Paul McCartney). • **Trivia:** NILSSON was to hit No.1 both sides of the Atlantic in 1971 with his classic version of Ham and Evans' WITHOUT YOU.

Recommended: COME AND GET IT – THE BEST OF . . . (*7)

The IVEYS

PETE HAM (b.27 Apr'47, Swansea, Wales) – guitar, vocals / **TOMMY EVANS** (b.1947, Liverpool, England) – guitar repl. DAVID JENKINS / **RON GRIFFITHS** – bass, vocals / **MIKE GIBBONS** (b.1949, Swansea) – drums

Apple Apple

Nov 68. (7") **MAYBE TOMORROW. / AND HER DADDY'S A MILLIONAIRE** [ ] [67]

—— In Jul69, they released in JAPAN, GERMANY and ITALY an album MAYBE TOMORROW, and a single DEAR ANGIE. / NO ESCAPING YOUR LOVE for EUROPE and JAPAN. Also appeared on Various Artists 'Apple' records comp. EP for Walls ice cream, singing 'STORM IN A TEACUP'.

BADFINGER

supplied 3 tracks (*) for THE MAGIC CHRISTIAN film soundtrack released Apr70 by 'Pye' featuring other artists.

Dec 69. (7") **COME AND GET IT. / ROCK OF ALL AGES** [4] [7]

— **JOEY MOLLAND** (b.21 Jun'48, Liverpool) – lead guitar (ex-MERSEYS, etc) repl. GRIFFITHS. (EVANS switched to bass guitar)

Jan 70. (d-lp) **MAGIC CHRISTIANS MUSIC** [ ] [55]
– Come and get it / Crimson ship / Dear Angie / Fisherman / Midnight sun / Beautiful and blue / Rock of all ages / Carry on till tomorrow / Fisherman / I'm in love / Walk out in the rain / Knocking down our home / Give it a try / Maybe tomorrow. *(re-iss.d-lp/c/cd.Oct91)* (cd+=) – Storm in a teacup / Arthur.

Oct 70. (7") **NO MATTER WHAT. / CARRY ON UNTIL TOMORROW** [-] [8]

Dec 70. (7") **NO MATTER WHAT. / BETTER DAYS** [5] [-]

Dec 70. (lp) **NO DICE** [ ] [28] Nov 70
– I can't take it / I don't mind / Love me do / Midnight caller / No matter what / Without you / Blodwyn / Better days / It had to be / Watford John / Believe me / We're for the dark. *(cd-iss. Jun92+=) Get down / Friends are hard to find / Mean mean Jemima / Loving you / I'll be the one.*

Nov 71. (7") **DAY AFTER DAY. / MONEY** [-] [4] Nov 71

Dec 71. (lp) **STRAIGHT UP** [ ] [31]
– Money / Flying / Suitcase / Sweet Tuesday morning / Perfection / I'd die babe / Take it all / Baby blue / Name of the game / Day after day / Sometimes / It's over. *(cd+=)* (original sessions of songs). *(re-iss.cd+c Mar93)*

Jan 72. (7") **DAY AFTER DAY. / SWEET TUESDAY MORNING** [10] [-]

Apr 72. (7") **BABY BLUE. / FLYING** [ ] [14] Mar 72

Mar 74. (7") **APPLE OF MY EYE. / BLIND OWL** [ ] [ ]

Mar 74. (lp) **ASS** [ ] [ ] Dec 73
– Apple of my eye / Get away icicles / The winner / Blind owl / Constitution / When I say / Cowboy / Timeless / I can love you.

Warners Warners

Jun 74. (lp) **BADFINGER** [ ] [ ] Mar 74
– I miss you / Shine on / Love is easy / Song for a lost friend / Why don't we talk / Island / Matted spam / Where do we go from here? / My heart goes out / Lonely you / Give it up / Andy Norris.

Jul 74. (7") **I MISS YOU. / SHINE ON** [-] [ ]

Oct 74. (7") **LOVE IS EASY. / MY HEART GOES OUT** [ ] [ ]

Oct 74. (lp) **WISH YOU WERE HERE** [ ] [ ]
– Just a chance / You're so fine / Got to get out of here / Know one knows / Dennis / In the meantime / Love time / Some other time / King of the load (T) / Meanwhile, back at the ranch – Should I smoke.

— added **BOB JACKSON** – keyboards (MOLLAND also left to join NATURAL GAS) They split on 1 May75, PETE HAM commited suicide. EVANS joined DODGERS. Re-formed '76 by **MOLLAND** and **EVANS** who recruited new members / **KENNY HARCK** – drums / **JOE TANZIN** – guitar / session man **ANDY NEWMARK** – drums repl. HARCK on half of album

Elektra Elektra

Apr 79. (7") **LOST INSIDE YOUR LOVE. / COME DOWN HARD** [ ] [ ]

Apr 79. (lp) **AIRWAVES** [ ] [ ]
– Airwaves / Look out California / Lost inside your love / Love is gonna come at last / Sympathy / The winner / The dreamer / Come down hard / Sail away.

Jun 79. (7") **LOVE IS GONNA COME AT LAST. / SAIL AWAY** [ ] [69] Mar79

— **MOLLAND** and **EVANS** brought in **TONY KAYE** – keyboards (ex-YES) / **GLEN SHERBA** – guitar / **RICHARD BRYANS** – drums

not issued Radio

Feb 81. (7") **HOLD ON./ PASSIN' TIME** [-] [56]

Mar 81. (lp) **SAY NO MORE** [-] [ ]
– Hold on / I got you / Come on / Because I love you / Rock'n'roll contract / Passin' time / Three time loser / Too hung up on you / Crocadillo / No more.

May 81. (7") **I GOT YOU. / ROCK'N'ROLL CONTRACT** [-] [ ]

Jul 81. (7") **BECAUSE I LOVE YOU. / TOO HUNG UP ON YOU** [-] [ ]

— They split again in '83. JOEY MOLLAND released solo album AFTER THE PEARL. TOM EVANS also tragically killed himself 23 Nov'83. MOLLAND and MIKE GIBBONS still tour as BADFINGER in US 60's tour.

BADFINGER

reformed with **MOLLAND, GIBBONS** plus **RANDY ANDERSON** – guitar / **A.J. NICHOLAS** – bass

not issued Indepen-dent

1988. (lp) **TIMELESS** [-] [ ]

- compilations, others, etc. -

Apr 89. Edsel; (lp)(cd) **SHINE ON** [ ] [-]

1992. Castle; (cd) **DAY AFTER DAY (live)** [ ] [-]

Jul 92. Raven; (cd) **APPLE DAZE** (TOM EVANS interview) [ ] [-]

Jun 92. Apple; (cd) **MAYBE TOMORROW (by "IVEYS")** [ ] [-]

Sep 93. Gipsy; (cd)(c) **THE FINAL TRACKS** [ ] [-]

Apr 95. Apple; (cd)(c) **COME AND GET IT – THE BEST OF BADFINGER** [ ] [-]
– Come and get it / Maybe tomorrow / Rock of all ages / Dear Angie / Carry on till tomorrow / No matter what / Believe me / Midnight caller / Better days / Without you / Take it all / Money / Flying / The name of the game / Suitcase / Day after day / Baby blue / When I say / Icicles / I can love you / Apple of my eye.

Joan BAEZ

Born: 9 Jan'41, Staten Island, New York, USA. After successful 1959 Newport festival appearance, she signed to 'Vanguard' label in the States. • **Style:** Innovator of protest folk music, that leant on early PETE SEEGER, and was inspiration to the likes of DYLAN etc. Her defiant protest anthems made her darling of the intellectual beatniks spreading around America at the time. Until the mid 60's she was girlfriend of DYLAN, which was well interpreted in his semi-doc film 'DON'T LOOK BACK'. She later married anti draft protest leader David Harris. In the early 80's, her work campaigning for various peace causes, saw her musical output decline. • **Songwriters:** She writes her own work interspersed with covers:- (Her debut album contained some Scottish traditional ballads). IT'S ALL OVER NOW, BABY BLUE / FAREWELL ANGELINA / etc. (Bob Dylan, she also recorded whole lp ANY DAY NOW of his material) / PACK UP YOUR SORROWS (Richard Farina, her brother-in-law, who was killed in a motorcycle accident, summer '66) / THE NIGHT THEY DROVE OLD DIXIE DOWN (Band) / IN THE QUIET MORNING (Mimi Farina, her sister) / LET IT BE (Beatles) / AMSTERDAM (Janis Ian) / STONES IN THE ROAD (Mary-Chapin Carpenter) / STRANGE RIVERS (John Stewart) / STEAL ACROSS THE BORDER (Ron Davies) / THROUGH YOUR HANDS (John Hiatt) / lots more . . . • **Trivia:** In 1978 she appeared in BOB DYLAN's autobiographical film RENALDO AND CLARA. Her book 'AND A VOICE TO SING WITH' was published in 1987 and contains information that I'm unable to fit in here.

Recommended: THE BEST OF JOAN C. BAEZ (*6)

JOAN BAEZ – vocals, acoustic guitar

Fontana Vanguard

1960. (lp) **JOAN BAEZ** [ ] [ ]
– Silver dagger / East Virginia / Ten thousand miles / House of the rising sun / All my trials / Wildwood flower / Donna Donna / John Riley / Rake and rambling boy / Little Moses / Mary Hamilton / Henry Martin / El preso numero nueve (the ninth prisoner). *(re-dist.US Apr62 No.15, re-iss.UK Jun65 hit 9) (re-iss. 1973) (cd-iss.Jan94 & Oct95)*

Oct 61. (lp) **JOAN BAEZ VOL.2** [ ] [13]
– Wagoner's lad / The trees they do grow high / The lily of the west / Silkie / Engine 143 / Once I knew a pretty girl / Lonesome road / Banks of the Ohio / Pal of mine / Barbara Alen / The cherry tree carol / Old blue / Railroad boy / Plaisir d'amour. *(re-iss.Sep89) (cd-iss.Jan94 & Oct95)*

Oct 61. (7") **BANKS OF THE OHIO. / OLD BLUE** [-] [ ]

Feb 62. (7") **LONESOME ROAD. / PAL OF MINE** [-] [ ]

Oct 62. (lp) **JOAN BAEZ IN CONCERT (live)** [ ] [10]
– Babe, I'm gonna leave you / Geordie / Copper kettle / Kumbaya / What have they done to the rain / Black is the colour of my true love's hair / Danger waters / Gospel ship / The house carpenter / Pretty Boy Floyd / Lady Mary / Ate Amanha / Matty Groves. *(cd-iss.Jan94)*

Nov 62. (7") **WHAT HAVE THEY DONE TO THE RAIN. / DANGER WATERS** [-] [ ]

Oct 63. (7") **WE SHALL OVERCOME (LIVE). / WHAT HAVE THEY DONE TO THE RAIN (LIVE)** [-] [90]

May 64. (lp) **JOAN BAEZ IN CONCERT, PART 2 (live)** [8] [7] Dec 63
– Once I had a sweetheart / Jackaroe / Don't think twice it's alright / We shall overcome / Portland town / Queen of hearts / Manha de carnaval / Te ador / Long black veil / Fennario / 'Nu Bello Cardillo / With God on our side / Three fishers / Hush little baby / Battle hymn of the republic. *(cd-iss.May91) (cd-iss.Jan94)*

Jun 64. (7") **WITH GOD ON OUR SIDE. / RAILROAD BILL – DADDY YOU BEEN ON MY MIND (MEDLEY)** [-] [ ]

Nov 64. (7") **IT AIN'T ME BABE. / GO 'WAY FROM MY WINDOW** [ ] [ ]

Apr 65. (lp) **JOAN BAEZ 5** [3] [12] Nov 64
– There but for fortune / Stewball / It ain't me babe / The death of Queen Jane / Villa lobos: Bachianas Brasileias No.5 – aria / Go 'way from my window / I still miss someone / When you hear them cuckoos hollerin' / Birmingham Sunday / So we'll go no more a-rovin' / O'cangaceiro / The unquiet grave. *(cd-iss.Jan94)*

Mar 65. (7") **WE SHALL OVERCOME. / DON'T THINK TWICE** [26] [-]

Jun 65. (7") **THERE BUT FOR FORTUNE. / DADDY YOU BEEN ON MY MIND** [-] [50]

Jul 65. (7") **THERE BUT FOR FORTUNE. / PLAISIR D'AMOUR** [8] [-]

Aug 65. (7") **IT'S ALL OVER NOW, BABY BLUE. / DADDY YOU'VE BEEN ON MY MIND** [22] [-]

Nov 65. (lp) **FAREWELL ANGELINA** [5] [-]
– Farewell Angelina / Daddy, you been on my mind / It's all over now, baby blue / The ranger's command / Colours / A satisfied mind / The river in the pines / Pauvre Ruteboeuf / Sagt mir wo die blumen sind / A hard rain's a-gonna fall. *(re-iss.Aug89) (re-iss.+cd.Oct88 on 'Start') (cd-iss.Jan94 & Oct95)*

Dec 65. (7") **FAREWELL ANGELINA. / QUEEN OF HEARTS** [35] [ ]

Jun 66. (7") **PACK UP YOUR SORROWS. / SWALLOW SONG** [50] [ ]

Aug 66. (lp) **JOAN** [ ] [38]
– Be not too hard / Eleanor Rigby / Turquoise / La colombe – the dove / Dangling conversation / The lady came from Baltimore / North / Children of darkness / The greenwood side / If you were a carpenter / Annabel Lee / Saigon bride. *(cd-iss.Jan94)*

Nov 66. (7") **CANTIQUE DE NOEL. / LITTLE DRUMMER BOY** [-] [ ]

Nov 66. (lp) **NOEL (Christmas album)** [ ] [ ]
– (festive songs) *(re-iss.Aug89) (re-iss.lp/c/cd.Oct88 on 'Start') (cd-iss.Jan94)*

Jun 67. (7") **BE NOT TOO HARD. / NORTH** [ ] [ ]

Vanguard Vanguard

Aug 68. (lp) **BAPTISM – A JOURNEY THROUGH OUR TIME** [ ] [84]
– Old Welsh song / I saw the vision of armies / Minister of war / Casida of the lament / Of the dark past / London / In Guernica / Who murdered the minutes / Oh, little child / No man is an island / From portrait of the artist as a young man / All the pretty little horses / Childhood III / The magic wood / Poems from the Japanese / Colours / All in green went my love riding / Gacela of the dark death / The parable of the old man and the young / Evil / Epitaph for a poet / Old Welsh song (reprise). *(re-iss.lp,c,cd.Aug89 on 'Start')*

— added many session people **NORMAN PUTTNAM** – bass / **KEN BUTTREY** – drums / **DAVID BRIGGS** – keyboards / **GRADY MARTIN** – dobro / **PETE WADE** – guitar / etc.

Jan 69. (lp) **ANY DAY NOW** [ ] [30]
– Love minus zero – No limit / North country blues / You ain't goin' nowhere / Drifter's escape / I pity the poor immigrant / Tears of rage / Sad eyed lady of the Lowlands / Love is just a four-letter word / I dreamed I saw St. Augustine / The walls of Redwing / Dear landlord / One too many mornings / I shall be released / Boots of Spanish leather / Walkin' down the line / Restless farewell. *(re-iss.c+cd.Sep89*

on 'Start') (cd-iss.Jan94)

Apr 69. (7") **LOVE IS JUST A FOUR-LETTER WORD. / LOVE MINUS ZERO – NO LIMIT** [ ] [86]

Jun 69. (7") **IF I KNEW. / ROCK, SALT AND NAILS** [-] [ ]

Jun 69. (lp) **DAVID'S ALBUM** [ ] [36]

– If I knew / Rock / Salt and nails / Glad bluebird of happiness / Green, green grass of home / Will the circle be unbroken / Tramp on the street / I'm a poor wayfaring stranger / Just a closer walk with thee / Hickory wind / My home's across the blue ridge mountains. *(cd-iss.Jan94)*

Aug 69. (7") **HICKORY WIND. / FOUR DAYS GONE** [-] [ ]

Mar 70. (7") **NO EXPECTATIONS. / ONE DAY AT A TIME** [-] [ ]

Apr 70. (lp)(c) **ONE DAY AT A TIME** [ ] [80] Mar 70

– Seven bridges road / David's song / Sweet Sir Galahad / Long black veil / Ghetto / Carry it on / Jolie blonde / Joe Hill / No expectations / Take me back to the sweet sunny south / One day at a time. *(cd-iss.Jan94)*

Jun 70. (7") **SWEET SIR GALAHAD. / GHETTO** [-] [ ]

Jan 71. (7") **CARRY IT ON. / ROCK SALT & NAILS** [-] [ ]

Sep 71. (7") **THE NIGHT THEY DROVE OLD DIXIE DOWN. / WHEN TIME IS STOLEN** [6] [3] Aug 71

Sep 71. (d-lp)(d-c) **BLESSED ARE** [ ] [11]

– Blessed are . . . / The night they drove old Dixie down / The salt of the Earth / Three horses / Brand new Tennessee waltz / Lost lonely and wretched / Lincoln freed me today / Outside the Nashville limits / San Francisco Mabel Joy / When time is stolen / Heaven help us all / Angeline / Help me make it through the night / Let it be / Put your hand in the hand / Gabriel and me / Milanese waltz / Marie Flore / The hitch-hiker's song / The 23rd of August / Fifteen months. *(cd-iss.Jan94)*

Nov 71. (7") **LET IT BE. / POOR WAYFARING STRANGER** [-] [ ]

Nov 71. (7") **LET IT BE. / GABRIEL AND ME** [ ] [-]

Dec 71. (lp)(c) **CARRY IT ON (Soundtrack compilation)** [ ] [ ]

– Oh, happy day / Carry it on / In forty days / Hickory wind / Last thing on my mind / Life is sacred / Joe Hill / I shall be released / Do right woman, do right man / Love is just another four-letter word / Suzanne / Idols and heroes / We shall overcome.

Jan 72. (7") **WILL THE CIRCLE BE UNBROKEN. / JUST A CLOSER WALK WITH THEE** [-] [ ]

Apr 72. (7") **BLESSED ARE. / THE BRAND NEW TENNESSEE WALTZ** [-] [ ]

—— In '72, she released 2 film s-tracks 'Sacco & Vanzetti' & 'Silent Running'.

A & M / A & M

Apr 72. (7") **PRISON TRILOGY (BILLY ROSE). / SONG OF BANGLADESH** [-] [ ]

May 72. (lp)(c) **COME FROM THE SHADOWS** [ ] [48]

– Prison trilogy / Rainbow road / Love song to a stranger / Myths / In the quiet morning / Weary mothers / To Bobby / Song of Bangladesh / A stranger in my place / Tumbleweed / The partisan / Imagine.

Jul 72. (7") **IN THE QUIET MORNING. / SONG OF BANGLADESH** [ ] [-]

Jul 72. (7") **IN THE QUIET MORNING. / TO BOBBY** [-] [69]

Sep 72. (7") **LOVE SONG TO A STRANGER. / TUMBLEWEED** [-] [ ]

Mar 73. (7") **BEST OF FRIENDS. / MARY CALL** [-] [ ]

Apr 73. (lp)(c) **WHERE ARE YOU NOW, MY SON?** [ ] [ ]

– Only Heaven knows / Less than the song / A young gypsy / Mary call / Rider pass by / Best of friends / Windrose / Where are you now, my son? / *(one side was devoted to Vietnam bombing noises).*

now with complete new set of session people.

Jun 73. (7") **LESS THAN A SONG. / MARY CALL** [ ] [-]

Jun 73. (7") **LESS THAN A SONG. / WINDROSE** [-] [ ]

May 74. (lp)(c) **GRACIAS A LA VIDA (HERE'S TO LIFE)** [ ] [ ]

– Gracias a la vida / Ilego contres heridas (Come with three wounds) / La llorona (The weeping woman) / El preso numero (Prisoner number nine) / Guantanamera / Te recuerdo Amanda (I remember Amanda) / Dida / Cucurrucucu Paloma / Paso Rio (I pass a river) / El rossinyol (The nightingale) / De colores (In colours) / Las madras cansades (All the weary mothers of the Earth) / No nos moveran (We shall not be moved) / Esquinazo del guerrillo (The guerilla's serenade).

1974. (7") **GUANTANAMERA. / FOREVER YOUNG** [-] [ ]

May 75. (lp)(c) **DIAMONDS AND RUST** [ ] [11]

– Diamonds and rust / Fountain of sorrow / Never dreamed you'd leave me in summer / Children and all that jazz / Simple twist of fate / Blue sky / Hello in there / Jesse / Winds of the old days / Dida / I dream of Jeannie / Danny boy.

Jun 75. (7") **BLUE SKY. / DIDA** [-] [57]

Jul 75. (7") **NEVER DREAMED YOU'D LEAVE ME IN SUMMER. / LAST SUMMER** [ ] [-]

Oct 75. (7") **DIAMONDS AND RUST. / WINDS OF THE OLD DAYS** [ ] [35] Sep 75

1976. (7") **CHILDREN AND ALL THAT JAZZ. / NEVER DREAMED YOU'D LEAVE ME IN SUMMER** [-] [ ]

Mar 76. (d-lp) **FROM EVERY STAGE (live)** [ ] [34] Feb 76

– (Ain't gonna let nobody) Turn me around / Blessed are . . . / Suzanne / Love song to a stranger / I shall be released / Blowin' in the wind / Stewball / Natalia / The ballad of Sacco & Vanzetti / Joe Hill / Love is just a four-letter word / Forever young / Diamonds and rust / Boulder to Birmingham / Swing low sweet chariot / Oh, happy day / Please come to Boston / Lily, Rosemary and the jack of hearts / The night they drove old Dixie down / Amazing Grace.

Apr 76. (7") **PLEASE COME TO BOSTON. / LOVE SONG TO A STRANGER** [ ] [ ]

Nov 76. (lp)(c) **GULF WINDS** [ ] [62]

– Sweeter for me / Seabirds / Caruso / Still waters at night / Kingdom of childhood / O brother! / Time is passing us by / Stephanie's room / Gulf winds.

Nov 76. (7") **CARUSO. / TIME IS PASSING US BY** [-] [ ]

Feb 77. (7") **O BROTHER!. / STILL WATERS AT NIGHT** [-] [ ]

Portrait / Portrait

Jul 77. (lp)(c) **BLOWIN' AWAY** [ ] [54] Jun 77

– Sailing / Many a mile to freedom / Miracles / Yellow coat / Time rag / A heartfelt line or two / I'm blowin' away / Luba the baroness / Alter boy and the thief / Cry me a river.

Jul 77. (7") **I'M BLOWIN' AWAY. / ALTAR BOY AND THE THIEF** [-] [ ]

Jul 77. (7") **I'M BLOWIN' AWAY. / LUBA THE BARONESS** [ ] [ ]

Dec 77. (7") **TIME RAG. / MIRACLES** [ ] [ ]

Jul 79. (lp)(c) **HONEST LULLABY** [ ] [ ]

– Let your love flow / No woman, no cry / Light a light / The song at the end of the movie / Before the deluge / Honest lullaby / Michael / For Sasha / For all we know / Free at last.

Feb 81. (lp)(c) **EUROPEAN TOUR (live)** [ ] [ ]

– The boxer / Don't cry for me Argentina / Gracias a la vida / The rose / For Sasha / Diamonds and rust / Soyuz druzyei / Cambodia / Kinder (sind so kleine hande) / Here's to you / Blowin' in the wind.

—— Semi-retired for several years, although she toured Europe again in '83.

Goldcastle-Virgin / Cypress

May 88. (lp)(c)(cd) **RECENTLY** [ ] [ ] 1987

– Brothers in arms / Recently / Asimbonanga / The Moon is a harsh mistress / James and the gang / Let us break bread together (freedom) / MLK / Do right woman, do right man / Biko. *(re-iss.c+cd.Aug91) (re-iss.cd Mar94)*

Apr 89. (lp)(c)(cd) **DIAMONDS AND RUST IN THE BULLRING (live)** [ ] [ ]

– Diamonds and rust / (Ain't gotta let nobody) Turn me around / No woman, no cry / Famous blue raincoat / Swing low sweet chariot / Let it be / El preso numero nueve / Ilego contres Heridas / Txoria Txoria / Ellas danzan solas (cueca sola) / Gracias a la vida / No nos moveran. *(re-iss.c+cd.Aug91)*

Nov 89. (lp)(c)(cd) **SPEAKING OF DREAMS** [ ] [ ]

– China / Warriors of the Sun / Carrickfergus / Hand to mouth / Speaking of dreams / El Salvador / Rambler gambler – Whispering bells / Fairfax country / A mi manera. *(re-iss.c+cd.Aug91)*

—— now co-wrote with producers **WALLY WILSON** – (also) synthesizers / **KENNY GREENBERG** (also) guitars Other co-writers **KAREN O'CONNOR** or **PAT BUNCH.** Musicians:- **CHAD CROMWELL** – drums / **JERRY DOUGLAS** – various / **MARCOS SUZANO** – percussion / **EDGAR MEYER** – upright bass

Virgin / Virgin

Jan 93. (cd)(c) **DRIVING ME BACKWARDS** [ ] [ ] Nov 92

– Play me backwards / Amsterdam / Isaac & Abraham / Stones in the road / Steal across the border / I'm with you / I'm with you (reprise) / Strange rivers / Through your hands / The dream song / Edge of glory.

—— next feat. duets w/ JANIS IAN, MARY CHAPIN-CARPENTER, MARY BLACK . . .

Grapevine / Asylum

Sep 95. (cd)(c)(lp) **RING THEM BELLS (live)** [ ] [ ]

– Lily of the west / Sweet Sir Galahad / The band played Waltzing Matilda / Willie Moore / Swallow song / Don't make promises / Jesse / Ring the bells / Welcome me / Suzanne / You're ageing well / Pajarillo Barranqueno / Don't think twice it's all right / Diamonds and rust / The night they drove old Dixie down.

– compilations, others, etc. –

Nov 63. US= Squire; (lp) **THE BEST OF JOAN BAEZ** (early '59 live Newport) [-] [45]

1960s. Fontana; (7"ep) **ONCE I HAD A SWEETHEART** [ ] [-]

1960s Vanguard; (7"m) **LOVE MINUS ZERO. / NO LIMIT / LOVE IS A FOUR-LETTER WORD** [ ] [ ]

1960s Vanguard; (7") **JUST A CLOSER WALK WITH THEE. / GREEN GREEN GRASS OF HOME** [ ] [ ]

Jun 69. Vanguard; (lp) **JOAN BAEZ ON VANGUARD** [15] [ ]

Dec 70. Vanguard; (d-lp) **THE FIRST 10 YEARS** [41] [73] Nov 70

Nov 72. Vanguard; (d-lp) **THE JOAN BAEZ BALLAD BOOK** (re-iss.Aug89) [ ] [ ]

Jun 73. Vanguard; (7") **THERE BUT FOR FORTUNE. / LOVE IS JUST A FOUR-LETTER WORD** [ ] [ ]

Jun 73. Vanguard; (lp)(c) **HITS GREATEST & OTHERS** (cd-iss.May91) [ ] [ ]

Nov 74. Vanguard; (d-lp) **CONTEMPORARY BALLAD BOOK** [ ] [ ]

Oct 76. Vanguard; (lp)(c) **THE JOAN BAEZ LOVE SONG ALBUM** [ ] [ ]

Oct 79. Vanguard; (d-lp) **COUNTRY MUSIC** [ ] [ ]

Jan 83. Vanguard; (d-lp)(d-c) **VERY EARLY JOAN (live 1961-63)** *(cd-iss.Jan94)* [ ] [ ]

Aug 89. Vanguard; (lp)(c)(cd) **THE NIGHT THEY DROVE OLD DIXIE DOWN** [ ] [ ]

Jul 91. Vanguard; (cd) **THE JOAN BAEZ COUNTRY MUSIC** [ ] [ ]

Jan 94. Vanguard; (cd) **THE BEST OF . . . VOL 2.** [-] [-]

Jan 94. Vanguard; (cd) **THE WOODSTOCK YEARS** [-] [-]

Apr 94. Vanguard; (3xcd) **RARE, LIVE AND CLASSIC** [ ] [ ]

Mar 76. Golden Hour – Pye; (lp) **THE GOLDEN HOUR PRESENTS . . .** [ ] [-]

Apr 77. Golden Hour – Pye; (lp) **THE GOLDEN HOUR PRESENTS Vol.2** [ ] [-]

Dec 77. A&M; (lp)(c) **THE BEST OF JOAN C. BAEZ** [ ] [ ]
(re-iss.Mar82) (re-iss.Aug85 on 'Hallmark', cd-iss. Nov 89 on 'Pickwick')

Mar 93. A&M; (cd) **IMAGINE** [ ] [ ]

Apr 79. Flyover-A&M; (lp)(c) **SUPER DISC OF JOAN BAEZ** [ ] [-]

Oct 80. P.R.T.; (lp)(c) **SPOTLIGHT ON . . .** [ ] [-]

Jun 82. P.R.T.; (c) **100 MINUTES OF JOAN BAEZ** [ ] [-]

Jan 83. Flashback; (7") **THE NIGHT THEY DROVE OLD DIXIE DOWN. / THERE BUT FOR FORTUNE** [ ] [-]

1984. I.M.S.; (cd) **GREATEST HITS** [ ] [ ]

Dec 88. Arista; (lp)(c)(cd) **LIVE EUROPE '83 (live)** [ ] [ ]

Jan 90. Old Gold; (7") **THE NIGHT THEY DROVE OLD DIXIE DOWN. / WE SHALL OVERCOME** [ ] [-]

Jan 90. Old Gold; (7") **THERE BUT FOR FORTUNE. / IT'S ALL OVER NOW, BABY BLUE** [ ] [-]

Jun 93. Vanguard ???; (cd)(c) **IT AIN'T ME BABE** [ ] [ ]

Jun 93. Vanguard ???; (cd)(c) **QUEEN OF HEARTS** [ ] [-]

Jul 93. Laserlight; (cd)(c) **NO WOMAN NO CRY** [ ] [-]

Sep 93. Duchesse; (cd)(c) **WHERE HAVE ALL THE FLOWERS GONE** [ ] [-]

Oct 93. Spectrum; (cd)(c) **GEMS** [ ] [-]

Dec 93. Virgin; (3xcd-box) **RECENTLY / DIAMONDS AND RUST / SPEAKING OF DREAMS** [ ] [-]

Apr 94. That's Country; (cd) **JOE HILL & MORE COUNTRY SONGS** [ ] [-]

Chris BAILEY (see under ⇒ SAINTS)

Philip BAILEY (see under ⇒ EARTH, WIND & FIRE)

Dan BAIRD (see under ⇒ GEORGIA SATELLITES)

Ginger BAKER

Born: PETER BAKER, 19 Aug'39, Lewisham, London. Gained experience in the late 50's with jazz bands such as ACKER BILK, but chose new style when he joined BLUES INCORPORATED in 1962. Early in '63, he joined GRAHAM BOND ORGANISATION, but left them mid 1966 to form CREAM with ERIC CLAPTON. After their demise late '68, he and ERIC formed BLIND FAITH, but they split after only one album. Late 1969, BAKER formed AIRFORCE ensemble, which released eponymous UK Top 40 album early 1970. After a number of collaborations, he and ADRIAN GURVITZ joined forces in BAKER GURVITZ ARMY mid 70's. BAKER was to many, thee greatest drummer of all-time, his CREAM live work certainly cemented that opinion. • **Style:** His range of sounds, moved from jazz, to blues and to Nigerian/African by the early 70's. • **Songwriters:** Collaborated with many other musicians, including FELA KUTI. Covered SWEET WINE (Staple Singers) / TWELVE GATES OF THE CITY (Graham Bond) / STRAIGHT NO CHASER (Thelonius Monk) etc. • **Trivia:** As a schoolboy he also played the trumpet. He married in the mid-90's, and took surname of wife, and became GINGER LOUCKS-BAKER.

Recommended: GINGER BAKER AT HIS BEST (*6)

GINGER BAKER'S AIRFORCE

with **GRAHAM BOND** – keyboards / **DENNY LAINE** – guitar / **RICK GRECH** – bass / **HAROLD McNAIR** – saxophone / **REMI KABAKA** – percussion / plus guests **STEVE WINWOOD, CHRIS WOOD, PHIL SEAMAN & BUD BEADLE**

Polydor / Atco

Feb 70. (lp)(c) **AIRFORCE** [37] [ ]
– Da da man / Early in the morning / Don't care / Toad / Aiko biaye / Man of constant sorrow / Do what you like / Doin' it.

Mar 70. (7") **MAN OF CONSTANT SORROW. / DOIN' IT** [ ] [ ]

— guests now were mainly African percussionists, vocalists and keyboard players.

Sep 70. (lp)(c) **GINGER BAKER'S AIRFORCE II (live)** [ ] [33] May 70
– Let me ride / Sweet wine / Do u no hu yor phrenz r? / We free kings / I don't want to go on without you / Toady / Twelve gates of the city.

Oct 70. (7") **ATUNDE (WE ARE HERE). / (by "GINGER BAKER DRUM CHOIR") / (part 2)** [ ] [ ]

1972. (lp)(c) **STRATAVARIOUS** [ ] [ ]
– Ariwo / Something nice / Ju Ju / Blood brothers / 69 coda.

— In 1971, he had moved to Akeja, Nigeria to buy land to build studio. He was augmented by FELA RANSOME-KUTI and African musicians SALT.

Re-gal Zono. / Signpost

1972. (lp) **FELA RANSOME-KUTI AND THE AFRICA '70 WITH GINGER BAKER LIVE! (live)** [ ] [ ]
– Let's start / Black man's cry / Ye ye de smell / Egbe mi o.

— He retired for a while early 1973, but returned to form

BAKER GURVITZ ARMY

with **ADRIAN GURVITZ** – guitar / **PAUL GURVITZ** – bass (both ex-GUN)

Vertigo / Janus

Dec 74. (lp)(c) **BAKER GURVITZ ARMY** [22] [ ]
– Help me / Love is / Memory Lane / Inside of me / I wanna live again / Mad Jack / 4 Phil / Since beginning.
(re-iss.May77 on 'Mountain')

Mar 75. (7") **HELP ME. / I WANNA LIVE AGAIN** [ ] [ ]

— added **SNIPS** – vocals (ex-SHARKS) / **PETER LEMER** – keyboards (ex-SEVENTH WAVE)

Mountain / Atco

Aug 75. (7") **SPACE MACHINE. / THE DREAMER** [ ] [ ]

Sep 75. (lp)(c) **ELYSIAN ENCOUNTER** [ ] [ ]
– People / The key / Time / The gambler / The dreamer / Remember / The artist / The hustler. *(cd-iss.Sep93 on 'Repertoire')*

Oct 75. (7") **THE GAMBLER. / TIME** [ ] [ ]

Nov 75. (7") **NIGHT PEOPLE. / ?** [-] [ ]

— Trimmed slightly when PETER LEMER departed.

Apr 76. (7") **TRACKS OF MY LIFE. / THE ARTIST** [ ] [ ]

May 76. (lp)(c) **HEARTS ON FIRE** [ ] [ ]
– Hearts on fire / Neon lights / Smiling / Tracks of my life / Flying in and out of stardom / Dancing the night away / My mind is healing / Thirsty for the blues / Night people / Mystery.

Jun 76. (7") **DANCING THE NIGHT AWAY. / NIGHT PEOPLE** [ ] [ ]

GINGER BAKER & FRIENDS

with loads of session people.

Mountain / Sire

Jan 77. (lp)(c) **ELEVEN SIDES OF BAKER** [ ] [ ]
– Ginger man / Candlestick maker / High life / Don Dorango / Little bird / N'kon kin' n'kon n'kon / Howlin' wolf / Ice cream dragon / Winner / Pampero / Don't stop the carnival.

Jan 77. (7") **DON DORANGO. / CANDLESTICK MAKER** [ ] [-]

— Retired again to breed ponies, but formed **ENERGY** in 1980 with **JOHN MIZAROLLI** – guitar / **MIKE DAVIS** – guitar / **HENRY THOMAS** – bass. In the early 80's, he joined ATOMIC ROOSTER briefly and HAWKWIND. In 1982, he emigrated to Italy with his 2nd wife where she ran a drama school.

GINGER BAKER & BAND

recorded 1982. **DOUG BROCKIE** – vocals, guitar / **KARL HILL** – bass, vocals

C.D.G. / not issued

Jun 83. (lp)(c) **FROM HUMBLE ORANGES** [-] [-] Italy
– The eleventh hour / Too many apples / It / Under the Sun / On the road to granma's house / The land of Morder / This planet / Sore head in the morning blues / Wasting time / Lament.

In 1985, he joined PUBLIC IMAGE LTD, recording ALBUM with them. In 1986 with RAVI SHANKER and BILL LASWELL iss.HORSES AND TREES on 'Celluloid'.

Onsala Int / not issued

Apr 87. (lp) **GINGER BAKER IN CONCERT (live 1982)** [ ] [-]
– Chemical blues / Perfect nation / Everything I say / Wheelchair dance festival / Lost in space / Where are you?

GINGER BAKER & AFRICAN FORCE

with **AMPOFO** – percussion, vocals / **ANSOU MANA BANGOURA** – perc., vocals / **FRANCIS MENSAH** – percussion / **JC COMMODORE** – percussion, vocals / **KAZDA** – co writers

I.T.M. / not issued

1989. (lp)(c)(cd) **AFRICAN FORCE** (rec'86) [ ] [-]
– Brain damage / Sokoto / Ansoumania / Aboa / African force.

Apr 90. (cd)(lp) **PALANQUIN'S POLE** [ ] [-]
– Go do / Brain damage / Ansoumania / Palaquin's pole / Abyssinia-1.2.7. / Ginger's solo / Want come? go!.

Nov 92. (cd) **THE ALBUM** [ ] [-]
– Sunshine of your love / Dream battle / Black audience / Nice – jam / Brain damage.

— now with **BILL LASWELL, JAH WOBBLE + NICK SKOPELTIS**

Axiom-Mango / Axiom

Feb 92. (cd)(c)(lp) **MIDDLE PASSAGE** [ ] [ ]
– Mektoub / Under black skies / Time be time / Altamont / Basil / South to the dust.

— Having backed old friend JACK BRUCE on early 1994 live album 'CITIES', he became part of their trio BBM, alongside GARY MOORE. Their album 'AROUND THE NEXT DREAM' on 'Virgin' hit UK Top 10.

GINGER BAKER TRIO

with **CHARLIE HAYDEN** – bass (of ORNETTE COLEMAN band) / **BILL FRISWELL** – guitars (of NAKED CITY + POWER TOOLS)

Atlantic / Atlantic

Dec 94. (cd)(c) **GOING BACK HOME** [ ] [ ]

– compilations, others, etc. –

1973. Polydor/ US= R.S.O.; (d-lp)(c) **GINGER BAKER AT HIS BEST** [ ] [ ]
(re-iss.Feb76)

Jan 93. Traditional Line; (cd) **LIVE IN LONDON 1975 (BAKER GURVITZ ARMY live)** [ ] [-]

Dave BALL (see under ⇒ SOFT CELL)

Ed BALL (see under ⇒ TELEVISION PERSONALITIES)

BANCO DE GAIA

Formed: Leamington Spa, London, England . . .early 90's by TOBY MARKS. He/they issued through distribution outlet 'Club Dog' a few cassette-only long-players, before finally hitting the shops with debut EP 'DESERT WIND'. • **Style:** Techno ambient rock with soundscapes from world music (Eastern, Caribbean, etc). • **Songwriters:** MARKS some w / GUTHRIE. • **Trivia:** Have mixed SENSER (Stacked up) / LEVELLERS (This Garden).

Recommended: MAYA (*6)

TOBY MARKS – keyboards with **GUTHRIE**

Planet Dog-Ultimate / not issued

Nov 93. (12")(cd-s) **DESERT WIND (sunset mix). / GAMELAH / SHANTI (Soup Dragons mix)** [ ] [ ]

Feb 94. (cd)(c)(d-lp) **MAYA** [34] [ ]
– Heliopolis / Mafich Arabi / Sunspot / Gamelah (dub 3) / Qurna (Mister Christian on the decks) / Sheesha / Lai lah (V1.oo) / Shanti (red with white spots edit) / Maya. *(lp-iss.Jun94 w /free lp)*
(+=) – Gamelah / Shanti / Darkside / Data inadequate.

Oct 94. (12"ep)(cd-ep) **HELIOPOLIS (Michael Dog mix) / ('A'-Liquid light mix) / ('A'-Redwood mix) / ('A'original mix)** [ ] [ ]

Apr 95. (cd-s) **LAST TRAIN TO LHASA (original mix) / ('A'-extended ambient mix)** [ ] [-]
(12+=) – ('A'-radio edit).

May 95. (d-cd)(d-c)(t-lp) **LAST TRAIN TO LHASA** [31] [-]
– Last train to Lhasa / Kuos / China (clouds not mountains) / Amber / Kincajou (small and cuddly mix) / White paint / 887 (structure) / Kuos (gnomes mix) / Kincajou

(duck! asteroid) / Eagle (small steppa mix).
(cd w/free cd) – China (follow the red brick road mix) / Amber (insect intelligence) / 887 (darkside return).

BAND

Formed: 1967 after these ex-patriate Canadians had once backed RONNIE HAWKINS. That year in fact, they recorded the legendary once bootlegged THE BASEMENT TAPES, backing BOB DYLAN. Their debut album, recorded around same period at their communal home (Big Pink, Woodstock), became first-off to hit US Top 30. • **Style:** Electric folk played with effortless relaxation, mixing traditional with progressive, shifting through country, jazz and blues. • **Songwriters:** After first albums collaboration with DYLAN, ROBERTSON took over as main writer, with songs about the civil war and 30's depression. One of his songs THE NIGHT THEY DROVE OLD DIXIE DOWN was a big hit for JOAN BAEZ. They covered; TEARS OF RAGE + WHEN I PAINT MY MASTERPIECE (Bob Dylan) / DON'T DO IT (Holland-Dozier-Holland) / LONG BLACK VEIL (Wilkin-Dill) / MYSTERY TRAIN (Elvis Presley) / THE GREAT PRETENDER (Platters) / 4% PANTOMINE (co-Van Morrison / etc. • **Trivia:** In 1980, ROBERTSON went into small acting parts, noteably in THE COAL MINER'S DAUGHTER (starring Sissy Spacek) + THE RIGHT STUFF (1983). ROBBIE had earlier produced 1976 album 'Beautiful Noise' for NEIL DIAMOND. PETER GABRIEL guested on his long-awaited solo album in '87.

Recommended: TO KINGDOM COME – THE DEFINITIVE COLLECTION (*7) / THE LAST WALTZ (*8).

CANADIAN SQUIRES

ROBBIE ROBERTSON (b. 4 Jul'44, Toronto, Canada) – guitar, vocals / **RICHARD MANUEL** (b. 3 Apr'45, Stratford, Canada) – piano, vocals, drums, sax / **RICK DANKO** (b. 9 Dec'43, Simcoe, Canada) – vocals, bass, violin, trombone / **GARTH HUDSON** (b. 2 Aug'37, London, Canada) – organ, saxophone, accordion / **LEVON HELM** (b.26 May'42, Marvél, AR) – drums, vocvals, mandolin, guitar

not issued — Apex

1964. (7") **UH-UH-UH. / LEAVE ME ALONE** [-] [ ]
(re-iss. on 'Ware')

LEVON AND THE HAWKS

Atlantic — Atlantic

Mar 65. (7") **THE STONES I THROW. / HE DON'T LOVE YOU** [ ] [ ]

not issued — Atco

1968. (7") **GO GO LIZA JANE. / HE DON'T LOVE YOU** [-] [ ]

The BAND

(same line-up)

Capitol — Capitol

1968. (7") **JABBERWOCKY. / NEVER TOO MUCH LOVE** [-] [ ]
Aug 68. (lp) **MUSIC FROM BIG PINK** [ ] [30]
– Tears of rage / To kingdom come / In a station / Caledonian mission / The weight / We can talk / Long black veil / Chest fever / Lonesome Suzie / This wheel's on fire / I shall be released. *(re-iss.+c Jun81, cd-iss.May87)*
Sep 68. (7") **THE WEIGHT. / I SHALL BE RELEASED** [21] [63] Aug 68
Jan 70. (lp) **THE BAND** [25] [9] Sep 69
– Across the great divide / Rag mama rag / The night they drove old Dixie down / When you awake / Up on Cripple Creek / Whispering pines / Jemima surrender / Rockin' chair / Look out Cleveland / Jawbone / The unfaithful servant / King harvest (has surely come). *(re-iss.+c Aug86, cd-iss.Aug88 on 'EMI')*
Oct 69. (7") **UP ON CRIPPLE CREEK. / THE NIGHT THEY DROVE OLD DIXIE DOWN** [ ] [25]
Feb 70. (7") **RAG MAMA RAG. / UNFAITHFUL SERVANT** [16] [57]
Oct 70. (lp) **STAGE FRIGHT** [15] [5] Sep 70
– Strawberry wine / Sleeping / Time to kill / Just another whistle stop / All la glory / The shape I'm in / The W.S. Walcott medicine show / Daniel and the sacred harp / Stage fright / The rumor. *(re-iss.Jun81 on 'Greenlight')(cd-iss.Mar91)*
Oct 70. (7") **TIME TO KILL. / SLEEPING** [ ] [ ]
Oct 70. (7") **TIME TO KILL. / THE SHAPE I'M IN** [-] [77]
Mar 71. (7") **THE SHAPE I'M IN. / THE RUMOR** [ ] [ ]
Oct 71. (lp) **CAHOOTS** [41] [21]
– Life is a carnival / When I paint my masterpiece / Last of the blacksmiths / Where do we go from here? / 4% pantomime / Shoot out in Chinatown / The Moon struck one / Thinkin' out loud / Smoke signal / Volcano / The river hymn. *(re-iss.Jun81 on 'Greenlight') (cd-iss.May89)*
Oct 71. (7") **LIFE IS A CARNIVAL. / THE MOON STRUCK ONE** [ ] [72]
Dec 71. (7") **WHEN I PAINT MY MASTERPIECE. / WHERE DO WE GO FROM HERE?** [-] [ ]
Aug 72. (d-lp)(c) **ROCK OF AGES (live)** [ ] [6]
– Don't do it / King harvest (has surely come) / Caledonia mission / Get up Jake / The W.S. Walcott medicine show / Stage fright / The night they drove all Dixie down / Across the great divide / This wheel's on fire / Rag mama rag / The weight / The shape I'm in / The unfaithful servant / Life is a carnival / The genetic method * / Chest fever / (I don't want to) Hang up my rock and roll shoes. *(re-iss.Jul83 on 'EMI') (re-iss+cd Apr87 omitted*) (US d-cd-iss.1990 cont.track)*
Nov 72. (7") **DON'T DO IT (live). / RAG MAMA RAG (live)** [ ] [34] Sep 72
Feb 73. (7") **CALEDONIA MISSION. / (I DON'T WANT TO) HANG UP MY ROCK AND ROLL SHOES** [-] [ ]
Dec 73. (lp)(c) **MOONDOG MATINEE** [ ] [28]
– Ain'y got no home / Holy cow / Share your love / Mystery train / The Third Man theme / The promised land / The great pretender / I'm ready / Saved / A change is gonna come. *(cd-iss.Mar91)*
Nov 73. (7") **AIN'T GOT NO HOME. / GET UP JAKE** [ ] [73]

— Late '73, they renewed association with BOB DYLAN, helping out on album 'PLANET WAVES' and more so 'BEFORE THE FLOOD' a live album credited to BOB DYLAN / THE BAND. In '75 The BAND returned with brand new material.

Feb 74. (7") **THE THIRD MAN THEME. / THE W.S. WALCOTT MEDICINE SHOW** [-] [ ]
Nov 75. (7") **TWILIGHT. / ACADIAN DRIFTWOOD** [-] [ ]
Dec 75. (lp) **NORTHERN LIGHTS – SOUTHERN CROSS** [ ] [26]
– Forbidden fruit / Hobo jungle / Ophelia / Acadian driftwood / Ring your bell / It makes no difference / Jupiter hollow / Rags and bones. *(cd-iss.Mar91)*
Feb 76. (7") **OPHELIA. / HOBO JUNGLE** [-] [62]
Mar 76. (7") **RING YOUR BELL. / FORBIDDEN FRUIT** [ ] [ ]
Apr 77. (lp)(c) **ISLANDS** [ ] [64] Mar 77
– Right as rain / Street walker / Let the night fall / Ain't that a lot of love / Christmas must be tonight / Islands / The saga of Pepote Rouge / Georgia on my mind / Knockin' lost John / Livin' in a dream. *(cd-iss.Mar91)*
1977. (7") **GEORGIA ON MY MIND. / THE NIGHT THEY DROVE OLD DIXIE DOWN** [-] [ ]
Apr 77. (7") **RIGHT AS RAIN. / KNOCKIN' LOST JOHN** [ ] [ ]

— Joined by guests BOB DYLAN, NEIL YOUNG, RONNIE HAWKINS, JONI MITCHELL, ERIC CLAPTON, VAN MORRISON, NEIL DIAMOND, MUDDY WATERS, PAUL BUTTERFIELD, BOBBY CHARLES and DR. JOHN etc. Jams were from STEPHEN STILLS, RINGO STARR and RONNIE WOOD

Apr 78. (t-lp) **THE LAST WALTZ** (live 25 Nov76 – film soundtrack) [39] [16]
– Theme from the last waltz / Up on cripple creek / Who do you love / Helpless / Stage fright / Coyote / Dry your eyes / Such a night / It makes no difference / Mystery train / The shape I'm in / The night they drove old Dixie down / Mannish boy / Further on up the road / The shape I'm in / Down south in New Orleans / Ophelia / Tura lura lural (that's an Irish lullaby) / Caravan / Life is a carnival / Baby let me follow you down / I don't believe you (she acts like we never have met) / Forever young / I shall be released / The well / Evangeline / Out of the blue / The weight / The last waltz refrain / Theme from the last waltz (with orchestra). *(cd-iss Jul88)*
Jun 78. (7") **THEME FROM THE LAST WALTZ (live). / OUT OF THE BLUE (live)** [ ] [ ]
Nov 78. (7") **OUT OF THE BLUE (live). / THE WELL (live)** [-] [ ]

— After their official split in 1978, HUDSON and MANUEL went into sessions. MANUEL hung himself 6 Mar'86, after a fit of depression. RICK DANKO and LEVON HELM went solo. In 1980, ROBBIE wrote score for film CARNY, before finally getting around to recording solo album in 1987.

— Re-formed (now studio / earlier live) with **DANKO, HELM, HUDSON + JIM WEIDER** – bass / **RICHARD BELL** – piano / **RANDY CIARLANTE** – drums

Castle — Pyramid

Feb 94. (cd)(c) **JERICHO** [ ] [ ] Nov93
– Remedy / Blind Willie McTell / The caves of Jericho / Atlantic City / Too soon gone / Country boy / Move to Japan / Amazon (river of dreams) / Stuff you gotta watch / Same thing / Shine a light / Blues stay away from me.

– compilations, etc. –

Sep 76. Capitol; (d-lp)(c) **THE BEST OF THE BAND** [ ] [51]
(cd-iss.May89)
Oct 76. Capitol; (7") **THE WEIGHT. / TWILIGHT** [ ] [ ]
Jan 79. Capitol; (d-lp)(c) **ANTHOLOGY** [ ] [ ]
(cd-iss.May89, 2 Vols.)
Jul 84. E.M.I. Gold; (7") **RAG MAMA RAG. / THE WEIGHT** [ ] [-]
Oct 89. E.M.I./ US= Capitol; (t-lp)(d-cd) **TO KINGDOM COME – THE DEFINITIVE COLLECTION** [ ] [ ]
May 92. Castle; (cd) **THE COLLECTION** [ ] [-]
– Back to Memphis / Tears of rage / To kingdom come / Long black veil / Chest fever / The weight / I shall be released / Up on Cripple Creek / Loving you is sweeter than ever / Rag mama rag / The night they drove old Dixie down / Unfaithful servant / King Harvest (has surely come) / The shape I'm in / The W.S.Walcott medicine show / Daniel and the sacred harp / Stage fright / Don't do it (baby don't do it) / Life is a carnival / When I paint my masterpiece / 4% pantomine / The river hymn / Mystery train / Endless highway / Get up Jake / It makes no difference / Ophelia / Arcadian driftwood / Christmas must be tonight / The saga of Peopote rouge / Knockin' lost John.
Nov 94. Capitol; (3xcd-box) **ACROSS THE GREAT DIVIDE** [ ] [ ]
Apr 95. Capitol; (cd) **LIVE AT WATKINS GLEN (live)** [ ] [-]

BAND AID (see ⇒ BOOMTOWN RATS / Bob Geldof)

BANGLES

Formed: Los Angeles, California, USA . . . 1981 as The BANGS by sisters VICKI and DEBBI PETERSON. After a one-off US indie 45 and a change of group name, they signed to Miles Copeland's 'IRS/Faulty' records mid'82. 'CBS/Columbia' were soon at their door (1983). Struggled commercially until early 1986, when they hit US/UK Top 3 with PRINCE penned 'MANIC MONDAY'. They soon were to become top pop group for the rest of the 80's, competing with BANANARAMA, etc. • **Style:** All-girl bubblegum pop/rock, influenced by The BYRDS, The BEATLES to The GO-GO's. • **Songwriters:** Mostly HOFFS collaborations, except GOING DOWN TO LIVERPOOL (Katrina & The Waves) / HAZY SHADE OF WINTER (Simon & Garfunkel) / IF SHE KNEW WHAT SHE WANTS (Jules Shear) / WALK LIKE AN EGYPTIAN (Liam Sternberg) / SEPTEMBER GURLS (Alex Chilton). HOFFS solo; BOYS KEEP SWINGING (David Bowie) + UNCONDITIONAL LOVE (Cyndi Lauper). • **Trivia:** SUSANNA HOFFS made film acting debut in 'The Allnighter' released 1987.

Recommended: GREATEST HITS (*5).

The BANGS

SUSANNA HOFFS (b.17 Jan'57, Newport Beach, Calif.) – vocals, rhythm guitar / **VICKI PETERSON** (b.11 Jan'58) – lead guitar, vocals (ex-The FANS) / **DEBBI PETERSON** (b.22 Aug'61) – drums, vocals (ex-The FANS)

not issued – Down Kiddie

Dec 81. (7") **GETTING OUT OF HAND. / CALL ON ME** [-] [ ]

The BANGLES

added **ANNETTE ZILINSKAS** – bass

not issued – Faulty-IRS

Jun 82. (m-lp) **THE BANGLES** [-] [ ]
– How is the air up there? / Mary Street / The real world / Want you / I'm in line.

MICKI STEELE (b.MICHAEL, 2 Jun'54) – bass, vocals (ex-RUNAWAYS, ex-SLOW CHILDREN) repl. ANNETTE who joined BLOOD ON THE SADDLE

C.B.S. – Columbia.

Sep 84. (7") **HERO TAKES A FALL. / WHERE WERE YOU WHEN I NEEDED YOU** [ ] [ ]

Mar 85. (lp)(c) **ALL OVER THE PLACE** [86] [80] Jul 84
– Hero takes a fall / Live / James / All about you / Dover beach / Tell me / Restless / Going down to Liverpool / He's got a secret / Silent treatment / More than meets the eye. *(re-iss.+cd.Oct86)(re-iss.cd+c Apr93 on 'Columbia')*

Mar 85. (7") **GOING DOWN TO LIVERPOOL. / DOVER BEACH** [56] [ ]
(12"+=) – The real world / I'm in line / How is the air up there?.
(d7"+=) – Hero takes a fall / Where were you when I needed you?.

Jan 86. (7") **MANIC MONDAY. / IN A DIFFERENT LIGHT** [2] [2]
(12"+=) – Going down to Liverpool / Dover beach.

Mar 86. (lp)(c)(cd) **DIFFERENT LIGHT** [3] [2] Jan 86
– Manic Monday / In a different light / Walking down your street / Walk like an Egyptian / Standing in the hallway / Return post / If she knew what she wants / Let it go / September gurls / Angels don't fall in love / September girls / Following / Not like you. *(re-iss.lp,c,cd-Mar90)*

Apr 86. (7")(7"sha-pic-d) **IF SHE KNEW WHAT SHE WANTS. / ANGELS DON'T FALL IN LOVE** [31] [29]
(12"+=) – Manic Monday (extended).
(d7"+=) – Hero takes a fall (remix) / James.

Jul 86. (7") **GOING DOWN TO LIVERPOOL. / LET IT GO** [ ] [ ]
(12"+=) – Walking down your street – James (live medley).

Sep 86. (7") **WALK LIKE AN EGYPTIAN. / NOT LIKE YOU** [3] [1]
(12"+=) – ('A'dub version) / ('A'acapella).
(d7"+=) – Manic Monday / In a different light.

Dec 86. (7")(12") **WALKING DOWN YOUR STREET (remix). / RETURN POST** [16] [11]
(d7"+=) – Walk like an Egyptian / Not like you.

Apr 87. (7") **FOLLOWING. / DOVER BEACH** [55] [ ]
(12"+=)(d7"+=) – Bangles hit mix medley (Manic Monday – If she knew what she wants – Walking down your street – Going down to Liverpool – Walk like an Egyptian).

Next single was a one-off for movie 'Less Than Zero' on 'Def Jam/CBS' label

Jan 88. (7")(7"pic-d) **HAZY SHADE OF WINTER. / ('B'by "Joan Jett')** [11] [2]
(12") – ('A'side) / ('A'dub) / ('A'purple haze mix).
(cd-s++=) – (4 tracks above) / Walk like an Egyptian.

Oct 88. (7") **IN YOUR ROOM. / BELL JAR** [35] [5]
(12"+=)(cd-s+=)(12"pic-d+=) – Hazy shade of winter (remix).

Nov 88. (lp)(c)(cd) **EVERYTHING** [5] [15]
– In your room / Complicated girl / Bell jar / Something to believe in / Eternal flame / Be with you / Glitter years / I'll set you free / Watching the sky / Some dreams come true / Make a play for her now / Waiting for you / Crash and burn. *(re-iss.cd+c Apr93 on 'Columbia')*

Jan 89. (7") **ETERNAL FLAME. / WHAT I MEANT TO SAY** [1] [1]
(12"+=) – Bangles hitmix.
(12"+=)(cd-s+=) – Walk like an Egyptian (dance mix).

May 89. (7")(7"pic-d)(7"sha-pic-d) **BE WITH YOU. / LET IT GO** [23] [30]
(cd-s+=) – In your room (edit).

Oct 89. (7")(12") **I'LL SET YOU FREE. / WATCHING THE SKY** [74] [ ]
(cd-s+=) – Walking down your street (extended).

(Sep 90) disbanded

- compilations, others, etc. -

May 90. C.B.S./ US= Columbia; (cd)(c)(lp) **BANGLES' GREATEST HITS** [4] [97]
– Hero takes a fall / Going down to Liverpool / Manic Monday / If she knew what she wants / Walk like an Egyptian / Walking down your street / Following / Hazy shade of winter / In your room / Eternal flame / Be with you / I'll set you free / Everything I wanted / Where were you when I needed you. *(re-iss.cd/c May95 + Dec95 on 'Columbia')*

May 90. C.B.S.; (7") **WALK LIKE AN EGYPTIAN. / ('A'-Ozymandias remix)** [73] [ ]
(12"+=)(c-s+=)(cd-s+=) – ('A'extended dance) / ('A'dub) / ('A'acapella).

Susanna HOFFS (solo)

Columbia – Columbia

Feb 91. (7")(7"pic-d) **MY SIDE OF THE BED. / MADE OF STONE** [44] [30]
(12"+=)(cd-s+=) – Circus girl.

Mar 91. (cd)(c)(lp) **WHEN YOU'RE A BOY** [56] [83]
– My side of the bed / No kind of love / Wishing on Telstar / That's why girls cry / Unconditional love / Something new / So much for love / This time / Only love / It's lonely out here / Made of stone / Boys keep swinging.

Apr 91. (7")(7"pic-d) **UNCONDITIONAL LOVE. / CIRCUS GIRL** [65] [ ]
(12"+=)(cd-s+=) – It's lonely out here.

Jul 91. (c-s) **ONLY LOVE. / YOU WERE ON MY MIND** [-] [ ]

Tony BANKS (see under ⇒ GENESIS)

BARCLAY JAMES HARVEST

Formed: Oldham, Lancashire, England . . . Autumn 1966 by art school students LEES and WOLSTENHOLME. Signed to 'EMI' who soon put them on their newly formed 'Harvest' label mid '69. Eponymous debut album recorded with full orchestra conducted by ROBERT GODFREY, saw them mainly loved by college circuit. Later they became massive in Europe, especially Germany. Britain finally gave them commercial recognition in the mid-70's, when their live album dented the Top 40 in 1974. • **Style:** Stigma of always being known as 'the poor man's MOODY BLUES', probably due to their heavy use of Mellotron organ and progressive art-rock image. • **Songwriters:** Either WOOLY, LEES or HOLROYD compositions. • **Trivia:** A CONCERT FOR THE PEOPLE was recorded near the Berlin Wall and was transmitted live on German TV and radio.

Recommended: THE COMPACT BARCLAY JAMES HARVEST (*8).

STUART 'WOOLY' WOLSTENHOLME (b.15 Apr'47) – keyboards, vocals / **JOHN LEES** (b.13 Jan'48) – guitar, vocals, wind / **LES HOLROYD** (b.12 Mar'48) – bass, vocals / **MELVIN PRITCHARD** (b.20 Jan'48) – drums

Parlophone – Sire

Apr 68. (7") **EARLY MORNING. / MR. SUNSHINE** [ ] [-]

Harvest – Sire

Jun 69. (7") **BROTHER THRUSH. / POOR WAGES** [ ] [ ]

Jun 70. (lp)(c) **BARCLAY JAMES HARVEST** [ ] [ ]
– Taking some time on / Mother dear / The sun will never shine / When the world was waken / Good love child / The iron maiden / Dark now my sky.

Aug 70. (7") **TAKING SOME TIME ON. / THE IRON MAIDEN** [ ] [-]

Feb 71. (lp)(c) **ONCE AGAIN** [ ] [ ]
– She said / Happy old world / Song for dying / Galadriel / Mockingbird / Vanessa Simmons / Ball and chain / Lady loves. *(quad-lp Jul73)*

Feb 71. (7") **MOCKINGBIRD. / VANESSA SIMMONS** [ ] [-]

Nov 71. (lp)(c) **BJH AND OTHER SHORT STORIES** [ ] [ ]
– Ow / Harry's song / Ursula / Little lapwing / Song with no meaning / Blue John's blues / The poet / After the day.

Apr 72. (7") **I'M OVER YOU. / CHILD OF MAN** [ ] [-]

Sep 72. (7") **BREATHLESS. (as "BOMBADIL") / WHEN THE CITY SLEEPS** [ ] [-]
(re-iss.Mar75)

Harvest – Harvest

Oct 72. (lp)(c) **BABY JAMES HARVEST** [ ] [ ]
– Crazy (over you) / Delph town morn / Summer soldier / Thank you / One hundred thousand smiles out / Moonwater. *(re-iss.May85) (re-iss. Mar87 on 'Fame')*

Oct 72. (7") **THANK YOU. / MEDICINE MAN** [ ] [ ]

May 73. (7") **ROCK AND ROLL WOMAN. / THE JOKER** [ ] [ ]

Polydor – Capitol

May 74. (7") **POOR BOY BLUES. / CRAZY CITY** [ ] [-]

Jun 74. (lp)(c) **EVERYONE IS EVERYBODY ELSE** [ ] [ ]
– Child of the universe / Negative Earth / Paper wings / The great 1974 mining disaster / Crazy city / See me see you / Poor boy blues / Mill boys / For no one. *(re-iss.Aug83) (cd-iss.Nov87)*

Jul 74. (7") **CHILD OF THE UNIVERSE. / CRAZY CITY** [-] [ ]

Nov 74. (d-lp)(c) **BARCLAY JAMES HARVEST – LIVE (live)** [40] [ ]
– Summer soldier / Medicine man / Crazy city / After the day / The great 1974 mining disaster / Galadriel / Negative Earth / She said / Paper wings / For no one / Mockingbird.

Oct 75. (lp)(c) **TIME HONOURED GHOSTS** [32] [ ]
– In my life / Sweet Jesus / Titles / Jonathan / Beyond the grave / Song for you / Hymn for the children / Moon girl / One night. *(re-iss.Aug83) (cd-iss.Apr87)*

Nov 75. (7") **TITLES. / SONG FOR YOU** [ ] [ ]

Polydor – M.C.A.

Oct 76. (lp)(c) **OCTOBERON** [19] [ ]
– Polk street rag / Suicide? / May day / Ra / Believe in me / The world goes on / Rock'n'roll star. *(re-iss.Aug83) (cd-iss.Jun84)*

Mar 77. (7"ep) **LIVE EP (live)** [49] [ ]
– Rock'n'roll star / Medicine man (Pt.1 & 2).

Jul 77. (7") **HYMN. / OUR KID'S KID** [ ] [-]

Sep 77. (lp)(c) **GONE TO EARTH** [30] [ ]
– Hymn / Love is like a violin / Friend of mine / Poor man's Moody Blues / Hard hearted woman / Sea of tranquility / Spirit on the water / Leper's song / Taking me higher. *(cd-iss.Mar83)*

Mar 78. (7") **FRIEND OF MINE. / SUICIDE** [ ] [ ]

Apr 78. (d-lp)(c) **LIVE TAPES (live)** [ ] [-]
– Child of the universe / Rock'n'roll star / Poor man's Moody Blues / Mockingbird / Hard hearted woman / One night / Take me higher / Suicide? / Crazy city / Jonathan / For no one / Polk street rag / Hymn. *(d-cd.iss.Feb85)*

Polydor – Polydor

Sep 78. (lp)(c) **XII** [31] [ ]
– Fantasy: Loving is easy / Berlin / Classics: A tale of two sixties / Turning in circles / Fact: The closed shop / In search of England / Sip of wine / Harbour / Science fiction: Nova Lepidoptera / Giving it up / Fiction: The streets of San Francisco. *(cd-iss.Jan85)*

Nov 78. (7")(7"blue) **LOVING IS EASY. / POLK STREET RAG** [ ] [-]

Jan 79. (7") **LOVING IS EASY. / TURNING IN CIRCLES** [-] [ ]

— Trimmed to a trio plus session men when WOLSTENHOLME went solo / **KEVIN McALEA** – keyboards (ex-BEES MAKE HONEY, ex-KATE BUSH)

Nov 79. (lp)(c) **EYES OF THE UNIVERSE** [ ] [ ]
– Love on the line / Alright get down boogie (Mu ala rusic) / The song they love to sing / Skin flicks / Sperratus / Capricorn / Play to the world. *(cd-iss.Jun84)*

Dec 79. (7") **LOVE ON THE LINE. / ALRIGHT GET DOWN BOOGIE (MU ALA RUSIC)** [63] [ ]

Feb 80. (7") **CAPRICORN. / BERLIN** [ ] [ ]

Nov 80. (7") **LIFE IS FOR LIVING. / SHADES OF B. HILL** [61] [ ]

May 81. (lp)(c) **TURN OF THE TIDE** 55
– Waiting on the borderline / How do you feel now / Back to the wall / Highway for fools / Echoes and shadows / Death of the city / I'm like a train / Doctor doctor / Life is for living / In memory of the martyrs. *(cd-iss.Mar83)*
Jun 82. (lp)(c) **A CONCERT FOR THE PEOPLE (BERLIN)** 15
– Berlin / Loving is easy / Mockingbird / Sip of wine / Nova Lepidoptera / In memory of the martyrs / Life is for living / Child of the universe / Hymn. *(cd-iss.Mar83)*
May 83. (lp)(c)(cd) **RING OF CHANGES** 36
– Fifties child / Looking from the outside / Teenage heart / High wire / Midnight drug / Waiting for the right time / Just a day away / Paradiso dos cavalos / Ring of changes.
May 83. (7") **JUST A DAY AWAY. / ROCK'N'ROLL LADY (live)** 68
(7"sha-pic-d) – ('A'side) / Looking from the outside.
Oct 83. (7") **WAITING FOR THE RIGHT TIME. / BLOW ME DOWN**
(12"+=) – ('A'extended).
Mar 84. (7")(7"sha-pic-d) **VICTIMS OF CIRCUMSTANCE. / ('A'instrumental)**
(12"+=) – Love on the line (live).
Apr 84. (lp)(c)(cd) **VICTIMS OF CIRCUMSTANCE** 33
– Sideshow / Hold on / Rebel woman / Say you'll stay / For your love / Victim of circumstance / Inside my nightmare / Watching you / I've got a feeling.
Sep 84. (7") **I'VE GOT A FEELING. / REBEL WOMAN**
Nov 86. (7") **HE SAID LOVE. / ON THE WINGS OF LOVE**
Feb 87. (lp)(c)(cd) **FACE TO FACE** 65
– Prisoner of your love / He said love / Alone in the night / Turn the key / Guitar blues / African / Following me / All my life / Panic / Kiev. (cd+=) – On the wings of love.
Apr 88. (lp)(c)(cd) **GLASNOST (live)**
– Berlin / Alone in the night / Hold on / African / On the wings of love / Poor man's Moody Blues / Love on the line / Medicine man / Kiev / Hymn / Turn the key / He said love.

BJH

Feb 90. (7") **CHEAP THE BULLET. / SHADOWS ON THE SKY**
(12"+=) – Berlin.
(cd-s+=) – Alone in the night / Hold on.
Mar 90. (cd)(c)(lp) **WELCOME TO THE SHOW**
– The life you lead / Lady Macbeth / Cheap the bullet / Welcome to the show / John Lennon's guitar / African nights / Psychedelic child / Where do we go / If love is king / Halfway to freedom.

BARCLAY JAMES HARVEST

(same label)
May 92. (7")(c-s) **STAND UP. / LIFE IS FOR LIVING** -
(cd-s+=) – John Lennon's guitar / Play to the world.
(cd-s+=) – Alone in the night / Poor man's Moody Blues.
Jun 93. (cd)(c) **CAUGHT IN THE LIGHT**
– Who do we think we are? / Knoydart / Copii Romania / Back to Earth / Cold war / Forever yesterday / The great unknown / Spud-u-like / Silver wings / Once more / A matter of time / Ballad of Denshaw Mill.

– compilations etc. –

Sep 72. EMI Starline; (lp) **EARLY MORNING ONWARDS** -
– Early morning / Poor wages / Brother Thrush / Mr. Sunshine / Taking some time on / Mother dear / Mockingbird / Song with no meaning / I'm over you / Child of the man / After the day.
Mar 75. Harvest; (7") **MOCKINGBIRD. / GALADRIEL**
Jan 77. Harvest/ US= Capitol; (lp)(c) **THE BEST OF BARCLAY JAMES HARVEST**
Sep 79. Harvest/ US= Capitol; (lp)(c) **THE BEST OF BARCLAY JAMES HARVEST VOL.2**
Feb 81. Harvest/ US= Capitol; (lp)(c) **THE BEST OF BARCLAY JAMES HARVEST VOL.3**
Mar 91. Harvest; (d-cd)(d-c)(d-lp) **THE HARVEST YEARS** -
Nov 85. Polydor; (cd) **THE COMPACT STORY OF BARCLAY JAMES HARVEST**
Oct 87. E.M.I.; (cd) **ANOTHER ARABLE PARABLE** -
Dec 90. Connoisseur; (cd)(c)(lp) **ALONE WE FLY** -
– Crazy city / For no one / Mockingbird / Hymn / Our kid's kid / Berlin / Loving is easy / Love on the line / Rock'n'roll lady / Shades of B Hill / Fifties child / Waiting for the right time / Blow me down / Sideshow / He said love / Guitar blues.
May 93. Spectrum; (cd)(c) **SORCERERS KEEPERS** -
Oct 95. One Way; (cd) **BARCLAY JAMES HARVEST / ONCE AGAIN** -
Oct 95. One Way; (cd) **& OTHER SHORT STORIES / BABY JAMES HARVEST** -

JOHN LEES

Polydor Polydor
Sep 74. (7") **BEST OF MY LOVE. / YOU CAN'T GET IT**
— The next 2 releases were recorded in '73
Harvest Capitol
Jul 77. (lp)(c) **A MAJOR FANCY**
– Untitled No.1 – Heritage / Untitled No.2 / Untitled No.3 / Child of the universe / Kes (a major fancy) / Long ships / Sweet faced Jane / Witburg night.
Jul 77. (7") **CHILD OF THE UNIVERSE. / KES (A MAJOR FANCY)**

Lou BARLOW (see under ⇒ DINOSAUR JR.)

BARMY ARMY (see under ⇒ CLAIL, Gary)

Syd BARRETT

Born: ROGER KEITH BARRETT, 6 Jan'46, Cambridge, England. Founder member and songwriter for PINK FLOYD in 1967 until his acid-related L.S.D. dropout from band. His personality made him unreliable and withdrawn, leading to reclusive period in the late 60's. With help from other PINK FLOYD members, except NICK MASON, he recorded two albums released in 1970. These were not regarded highly until later, as anything but whimsical oddities, by critics and public alike. He has since been tributed and stylised by many, including TELEVISION PERSONALITIES and ROBYN HITCHCOCK (Soft Boys). • **Style:** Psychedelic eccentric/genius whose songs although brilliant, were little more than acoustic FLOYD. • **Songwriters:** All written by SYD. • **Trivia:** PINK FLOYD paid homage to SYD on their album SHINE ON YOU CRAZY DIAMOND track from album 'WISH YOU WERE HERE'. SYD attended these sessions but didn't contribute.

Recommended: THE MADCAP LAUGHS (*8) / BARRETT (*6).

SYD BARRETT – vocals, guitar (ex-PINK FLOYD) augmented by **DAVID GILMOUR** and **ROGER WATERS** (Pink Floyd) with **MIKE RATLEDGE** – keyboards / **HUGH HOPPER** – bass / **ROBERT WYATT** – drums (all of SOFT MACHINE) plus **JOHN 'WILLIE' WATSON + JERRY SHIRLEY** – rhythm

Harvest Harvest
Oct 69. (7") **OCTOPUS. / GOLDEN HAIR**
Jan 70. (lp)(c) **THE MADCAP LAUGHS** 40
– Terrapin / No good trying / Love you / No man's land / Dark globe / Here I go / Octopus / Golden Hair / Long gone / She took a long cold look / Feel / If it's in you / Late night. *(cd-iss.May87) (re-iss.cd Jun94)*
— SYD retained GILMOUR, SHIRLEY and WILSON adding **RICK WRIGHT** – keyboards (of PINK FLOYD) and guest on 1 **VIC SAYWELL** – tuba
Nov 70. (lp)(c) **BARRETT**
– Baby lemonade / Love song / Dominoes / It is obvious / Rats / Maisie / Gigolo aunt / Waving my arms in the air / Wined and dined / Wolfpack / Effervescing elephant / I never lied to you. *(cd-iss.May87) (re-iss.cd Jun94)*
— His solo career ended and he formed short-lived STARS early in '72, with **TWINK** – drums + **JACK MONK** – bass (they made no recordings)
In 1982, he was reported to be living with his mother having hung up guitar.

– compilations, others, etc. –

Sep 74. Harvest; (d-lp) **SYD BARRETT**
(re-iss. of his 2 albums from 1970)
Oct 88. Harvest; (lp)(c)(cd) **OPEL** (recorded 68-70)
– Opel / Clowns and daggers (Octopus) / Rats / Golden hair (vocal) / Dollyrocker / Word song / Wined and dined / Swan Lee (Silas Lang) / Birdie hop / Let's split / Lanky (Pt.1) / Wouldn't you miss me / Golden hair (instrumental). *(re-iss.cd Jun94)*
Oct 87. Strange Fruit; (12"ep) **THE PEEL SESSIONS (24.2.70)** -
– Terrapin / Gigolo aunt / Baby lemonade / Two of a kind / Effervescing elephant. *(cd-iss.Apr88)*
Apr 93. E.M.I.; (3xcd-box) **CRAZY DIAMOND – THE COMPLETE SYD BARRETT**
Apr 94. Cleopatra; (cd) **OCTOPUS** -
Oct 95. Strange Fruit; (cd) **THE PEEL SESSION** -

BAUHAUS

Formed: Northampton, England . . . late 1978, first calling themselves BAUHAUS 1919. Obtained one-off deal with indie 'Small Wonder' label releasing an 8 minute epic 'BELA LUGOSI'S DEAD'. By early '81, they signed to 'Beggar's B.', although throughout 1980 they had been on its subsidiary '4.a.d'. In 1982, having scored some minor hits, they smashed into UK Top 20 with a 1972 BOWIE song 'ZIGGY STARDUST'. A year later they were no more as MURPHY went solo and the others formed LOVE AND ROCKETS (who had been under the guise of splinter TONES ON TAIL, while DAVID J moonlighted solo). They had surprise US Top 3 hit in 1989 with 'SO ALIVE'. • **Style:** Combined goth, glam & punk rock, although at first accused of plagiarising BOWIE. • **Songwriters:** Group compositions, except other covers TELEGRAM SAM (T.Rex) / THIRD UNCLE (Eno) / WAITING FOR THE MAN (Velvet Underground). PETER MURPHY solo, wrote with STREATHAM and covered; FINAL SOLUTION (Pere Ubu) / THE LIGHT POURS OUT OF ME (Magazine) / FUNTIME (Iggy Pop). LOVE AND ROCKETS covered BALL OF CONFUSION (Temptations) / BODY AND SOUL (trad). DAVID J covered 4 HOURS (ClockDva) / SHIP OF FOOLS (John Cale). • **Trivia:** Late 1981 onwards, PETER MURPHY appeared in a TV ad for Maxell Tapes. In '82 group performed 'BELA LUGOSI . . . ' for the vampire film 'The Hunger', which starred Bowie and Catherine Deneuve.

Recommended: BAUHAUS 1979-1983 (*9) / NIGHT MUSIC (TONES ON TAIL *6) / LOVE AND ROCKETS (LOVE AND ROCKETS *5)

PETER MURPHY – vocals / **DANIEL ASH** – guitar, vocals / **DAVID JAY** (b.HASKINS) – bass, vocals / **KEVIN HASKINS** – drums, percussion

Small Wonder / not issued
Aug 79. (12"+12"white) **BELA LUGOSI'S DEAD. / BOYS / DARK ENTRIES** -
(12" re-dist.Mar81 & Mar82) (re-iss.Sep86 on 12"blue) (re-iss. 1987,12"pic-d) (cd-iss.May88)
Axis / not issued
Jan 80. (7") **DARK ENTRIES. / UNTITLED** -
(re-iss.Feb80 on '4.a.d.' some mispressed on 'Beggar's B.')

4.a.d. not issued

Jun 80. (7") **TERROR COUPLE KILL COLONEL. / SCOPES / TERROR COUPLE KILL COLONEL II** [ ] [-]
(7") – ('A'remix).
Oct 80. (lp) **IN A FLAT FIELD** [72] [-]
– Double dare / In a flat field / A god in an alcove / Dive / Spy in the cab / Small talk stinks / St. Vitus dance / Stigmata martyr / Nerves. *(cd-iss.Apr88)* (+=) – Untitled.
Oct 80. (7") **TELEGRAM SAM. / CROWDS** [ ] [-]
(12"+=) – Rosegarden funeral of sores.

Beggar's B. A&M (later)

Mar 81. (7")(12") **KICK IN THE EYE. / SATORI** [59] [-]
Jun 81. (7") **PASSION OF LOVERS. / 1: 2: 3: 4:** [56] [-]
Oct 81. (lp)(c) **MASK** [30] [ ]
– Hair of the dog / The passion of lovers / Of lillies and remains / Dancing / Hollow hills / Kick in the eye / Muscle in plastic / In fear of fear / Man with x-ray eyes / Mask. *(re-iss.Feb88 + cd-iss.Oct88)* (cd+=) – Satori / Harry / Earwax / In fear of dub / Kick in the eye.
Feb 82. (7"ep) **SEARCHING FOR SATORI** [45] [-]
– Kick in the eye / Harry / Earwax.
(12"ep+=) – In fear of dub.
Jun 82. (7")(7"pic-d) **SPIRIT. / TERROR COUPLE KILL COLONEL (live)** [42] [ ]
Sep 82. (7") **ZIGGY STARDUST. / THIRD UNCLE (live)** [15] [ ]
(12"+=) – Party of the first part / Waiting for the man.
Oct 82. (lp)(d-c) **THE SKY'S GONE OUT** [4] [ ]
– Third uncle / Silent hedges / In the night / Swing the heartache / Spirit / The three shadows (parts 1, 2, 3) / Silent hedges / All we ever wanted was everything / Exquisite corpse. *(cd-iss.Feb88)* (+=) – Ziggy Stardust / Watch that grandad go / Party of the first part / Spirit (extended).
Oct 82. (free lp,+ on d-c) **PRESS THE EJECT BUTTON AND GIVE ME THE TAPE (live)**
– In a flat field / Rosegarden funeral of sores / Dancing / Man with the x-ray eyes / Bela Lugosi's dead / Spy in the cab / Kick in the eye / In fear of fear / Hollow hills / Stigmata martyr / Dark entries. *(iss.lp/c/cd.Feb88)* (cd+=) – Terror couple kill colonel / Double dare / Waiting for the man / Hair of the dog / Of lillies and remains. (lp, had free 7"ep) – SATORI IN PARIS (live)
Jan 83. (7") **LAGARTIJA NICK. / PARANOIA! PARADISE** [44] [ ]
(12"+=) – Watch that grandad go / In a flat field.
Apr 83. (7")(7"pic-d) **SHE'S IN PARTIES. / DEPARTURE** [26] [ ]
(12"+=) – Here's the dub.
Jul 83. (lp)(c)(pic-lp) **BURNING FROM THE INSIDE** [13] [ ]
– She's in parties / Antonin Artaud / King Volcano / Who killed Mr. Moonlight? / Slice of life / Honeymoon croon / Kingdom's coming / Burning from the inside / Hope. *(re-iss.Feb88.=cd.Sep88)* (cd+=) – Lagartija Nick / Departure / Here's the dub / The sanity assassin.

Disbanded mid 1983. DAVID J. continued splinter solo venture, before forming LOVE AND ROCKETS with DANIEL and KEVIN, who had come from own TONES ON TAIL. MURPHY went solo (see below).

– compilations, others, etc. –

Sep 83. 4 a.d.; (12"ep) **THE 4.A.D. SINGLES** [ ] [-]
– Dark entries / Terror couple kill colonel / Telegram Sam / + 1.
Oct 83. Beggar's Banquet; (12"ep) **THE SINGLES 1981-83** [52] [-]
– The passion of lovers / Kick in the eye / Spirit / Ziggy Stardust / Lagartija Nick / She's in parties. *(re-iss.3"pic-cd.Dec88)*
Nov 85. Beggar's Banquet; (d-lp)(d-cd) **BAUHAUS 1979-1983** [36] [ ]
(re-iss.d-cd Sep95)
Jul 89. Beggar's Banquet; (d-lp)(cd) **SWING THE HEARTACHE (the BBC sessions)** [ ] [ ]
(re-iss.cd Sep95)

DALI'S CAR

were formed by **PETE MURPHY** – vocals and **MICK KARN** – bass, multi (ex-JAPAN) / **PAUL VINCENT LAWFORD** – rhythms

Paradox-B. not issued

Oct 84. (7") **THE JUDGEMENT IS THE MIRROR. / HIGH PLACES** [66] [-]
(12"+=) – Lifelong moment.
Nov 84. (lp)(c)(cd) **THE WAKING HOUR** [84] [ ]
– Dali's car / His box / Cornwall stone / Artemis / Create and melt / Moonlife / The judgement is the mirror. *(re-iss.+cdJan89 on 'Lowdown-Beggar's')*

PETER MURPHY

went solo, augmented by **JOHN McGEOGH** – guitar / **HOWARD HUGHES** – keyboards / **ROBERT SUAVE** – bass / **STEVE YOUNG** – rhythm prog. / **PLUG** – harmonica

Beggar's B. Beggar's B.

Nov 85. (7") **FINAL SOLUTION. / THE ANSWER'S CLEAR** [ ] [ ]
(12"+=) – ('A'full version).
(12"pic-d+=) – ('A'club mix).
Jun 86. (7")(12") **BLUE HEART. / CANVAS BEAUTY** [ ] [ ]
Jul 86. (lp)(c) **SHOULD THE WORLD FAIL TO FALL APART** [82] [ ]
– Canvas beauity / The light pours out of me / Confessions / Should the world fail to fall apart / Never man / God . . .sends / Blue heart / The answer is clear / Final solution / Jemal.*(re-iss.+cdJul88)*
Oct 86. (7") **TALES OF THE TONGUE. / SHOULD THE WORLD FAIL TO FALL APART** [ ] [ ]
(12"+=) – ('A'-2nd version).

— **MURPHY** brought in **PAUL STREATHAM** – co-composer, keyboards / **EDDIE BRACH** – bass / **PETER BONAS** – guitar / **TERL BRYANT** – drums

Feb 88. (7") **ALL NIGHT LONG. / I'VE GOT A SECRET CAMERA** [ ] [ ]
(12"+=) – Funtime (in cabaret).
Mar 88. (lp)(c)(cd) **LOVE HYSTERIA** [ ] [ ]
– All night long / His circle and hers meet / Dragnet drag / Socrates the python / Indigo eyes / Time has got nothing to do with it / Blind sublime / My last two weeks / Funtime. (cd+=) – I've got a miniature secret camera / Funtime (cabaret mix).

Apr 88. (7") **INDIGO EYES. / GOD SENDS (live)** [ ] [ ]
(12"+=) – Confessions (live).
Apr 90. (7") **CUTS YOU UP. / STRANGE KIND OF LOVE** [ ] [55]
(12"+=)(cd-s+=) – Roll call (reprise).
May 90. (cd)(c)(lp) **DEEP** [ ] [44]
– Deep ocean vast sea / Crystal waters / Marlene Dietrich's favourite poem / Seven veils / The line between the Devil's teeth (and that which cannot be repeated) / Cuts you up / A strange kind of love / Roll call. (cd+=) – Strange kind of love (alt.version).
Apr 92. (7") **YOU'RE SO CLOSE. / THE SWEETEST DROP** [ ] [ ]
(12"+=)(cd-s+=) – Cuts you up (live) / All night long (live).
May 92. (cd)(c)(lp) **HOLY SMOKE** [ ] [ ]
– Keep me from harm / Kill the hate / You're so close / The sweetest drop / Low room / Let me love you / Our secret garden / Dream gone by / Hit song.
Jul 92. (7") **HIT SONG. / SEVEN VEILS** [ ] [ ]
(12"+=)(cd-s+=) – The line between the Devil's teeth (and that which cannot be repeated).
Apr 95. (cd-ep) **THE SCARLET THING IN YOU / CRYSTAL WRISTS / WISH / DRAGNET DRAG (live)** [ ] [ ]
Apr 95. (cd)(c) **CASCADE** [ ] [ ]
– Mirror to my woman's mind / Subway / Gliding like a whale / Disappearing / Mercy rain / I'll fall with your knife / Scarlet thing in you / Sails wave goodbye / Wild birds flock to me / Huuvola / Cascade.

TONES ON TAILS

GLEN CAMPLING – vocals, bass, keyboards (roadie of BAUHAUS) / **DANIEL ASH** – guitar, vocals (of BAUHAUS) / **KEVIN HASKINS** – drums (of BAUHAUS)

4.a.d. not issued

Apr 82. (7"ep)(12"ep) **A BIGGER SPLASH / COPPER. / MEANS OF ESCAPE / INSTRUMENTAL** [ ] [-]

Beggar's B. not issued

Sep 82. (7")(12") **THERE'S ONLY THIS. / NOW WE LUSTRE** [ ] [-]

Situation 2 not issued

May 83 (7")**BURNING SKIES. / OK THIS IS THE POPS** [ ] [-]
(12"+=) – When you're smiling / You the night and the music.

— In 1983, they broke from BAUHAUS. ASH and HASKINS joined The JAZZ BUTCHER. **TONES ON TAILS** soon re-actified line-up.

Beggar's not issued

Mar 84. (7") **PERFORMANCE. / SHAKES** [ ] [ ]
(12"+=) – ('A'dub version).
Apr 84. (lp)(c) **POP** [ ] [ ]
– Performance / War / Lions / Happiness / The never never / Real life / Slender fungus / Movement of fear / Rain.
May 84. (7")(12")(12"red) **LIONS. / GO (LET'S GO TO YA YA'S NOW)** [ ] [ ]
Nov 84. (7")(12"blue) **CHRISTIAN SAYS. / TWIST** [ ] [ ]

— Split from this set-up.

– compilations, others, etc. –

Feb 85. Situation 2; (lp)(c) **TONES ON TAILS** (the singles) [ ] [-]
Oct 88. Beggar's Banquet; (cd) **NIGHT MUSIC** (nearly all work) [ ] [-]

LOVE AND ROCKETS

ASH + HASKINS were joined by **DAVID J.** – vocals, bass, keyboards (also ex-BAUHAUS + a solo artist)

Beggar's Big Time

May 85. (7")(12") **BALL OF CONFUSION. / INSIDE THE OUTSIDE** [ ] [ ]
Sep 85. (7")(12") **IF THERE'S A HEAVEN ABOVE. / GOD AND MR.SMITH** [ ] [ ]
Oct 85. (lp)(c) **7th DREAM OF TEENAGE HEAVEN** [ ] [ ]
– If there's a Heaven above / A private future / 7th dream of teenage Heaven / Saudade / Haunted when the minutes drag / The dog-end of a day gone by / The game. *(re-iss.+cdJan89)* (cd+=) – Ball of confusion (USA mix) / God and Mr.Smith (Mars mix) / If there's a Heaven above (Canadian mix).
Jun 86. (12"m) **KUNDALINI EXPRESS. / LUCIFER SAM / HOLIDAY ON THE MOON** [ ] [ ]
Sep 86. (7")(12") **YIN AND YANG (THE FLOWERPOT MEN). / ANGELS AND DEVILS** [ ] [ ]
Sep 86. (lp)(c) **EXPRESS** [ ] [72]
– Kundalini express / It could be sunshine / Love me / All in my mind / Life in Laralay / Yin and Yang (the flowerpot men) / An American dream / All in my mind (acoustic version). *(cd-issJan89)*
Sep 87. (lp)(c)(cd) **EARTH, SUN, MOON** [ ] [64]
– The light / Mirror people / Welcome tomorrow / Here on Earth / Lazy / Waiting for the flood / Rainbird / Telephone is empty / Everybody wants to go to Heaven / The Sun / Youth.
Oct 87. (7")(12") **THE LIGHT. / MIRROR PEOPLE (slow version)** [ ] [ ]
Mar 88. (7") **NO NEW TALE TO TELL. / EARTH, SUN, MOON** [ ] [ ]
(12"+=) – 7th dream of teenage Heaven.
May 88. (7") **MIRROR PEOPLE. / DAVID LANFAIR** [ ] [ ]
(12"+=) – ('A'live version).
Aug 88. (7") **LAZY. / THE DOG-END OF A DAY GONE BY** [ ] [ ]
(12"+=) – The purest blue.

Beggar's B. Beggar's B.

Jan 89. (12"ep) **MOTORCYCLE / I FEEL SPEED. / BIKE / BIKEDANCE** [ ] [ ]
Jul 89. (7")(12")(c-s) **SO ALIVE. / DREAMTIME** [ ] [3] May 89
(cd-s+=) – Motorcycle / Bike. *(re-issJan90)*
Sep 89. (lp)(c)(cd) **LOVE AND ROCKETS** [ ] [14]
– **** (Jungle law) / No big deal / The purest blue / Motorcycle / I feel speed / Bound for Hell / The teardrop collector / So alive / Rock and roll Babylon / No words no more.
Oct 89. (7") **NO BIG DEAL. / NO WORDS NO MORE** [ ] [82] Sep 89
(12"+=) – 100 watts of your love.
Jul 94. (12")(cd-s) **THIS HEAVEN. / (3 other 'A'mixes)** [ ] [ ]
Sep 94. (12")(cd-s) **BODY AND SOUL. / (2 extended mixes)** [ ] [ ]

Sep 94. (cd)(c)(d-lp) **HOT TRIP TO HEAVEN** [ ] [ ]
– Body and soul (parts 1 & 2) / Ugly / Trip and glide / This Heaven / No worries / Hot trip to Heaven / Eclipse / Voodoo baby / Be the revolution / Set me free. *(re-iss.cd Sep95)*

DANIEL ASH

Beggar's B. Columbia

Jun 91. (cd)(c)(lp) **COMING DOWN** [ ] [ ]
– Blue Moon / Coming down fast / Walk this way / Closer to you / Day tripper / This love / Blue angel / Me and my shadow / Candy darling / Sweet little liar / Not so fast / Coming down.

— Above features covers DAY TRIPPER (Beatles) / BLUE MOON (Rodgers / Hart) / ME AND MY SHADOW (Al Jolson/+).

Jun 91. (7") **WALK THIS WAY. / HEAVEN IS WAITING** [ ] [-]
(12") – ('A'side) / ('A'groovy vox) / ('A'groovy guitar).
(cd-s) – (all 4 tracks).

Apr 93. (12"ep)(cd-ep) **GET OUT OF CONTROL. / THE HEDONIST / GET OUT OF CONTROL (farewell mixes)** [ ] [ ]

May 93. (cd)(c)(lp) **FOOLISH THING DESIRE** [ ] [ ]
– Here she comes / Foolish thing desire / Bluebird / Dream machine / Get out of control / The void / Roll on / Here she comes again / The hedonist / Higher than this.

DAVID J.

4 a.d. not issued

Sep 81. (7") **NOTHING. / ARMOUR (by "DAVID JAY / RENE HACKETT")** [ ] [-]

Situation 2 not issued

Aug 83. (7") **JOE ORTON'S WEDDING. / THE GOSPEL ACCORDING TO FEAR** [ ] [ ]
(12"+=) – Requiem for Joe / Point of venture.

Oct 83. (lp) **ETIQUETTE OF VIOLENCE** [ ] [-]
– The gospel according to fear / I hear only silence now / No one's sending roses / The fugitive / Betrayal / Joe Orton's wedding / The promised land / With the Indians permanent / Say uncle / Disease / Roulette / Saint Jackie.

Glass not issued

Nov 83. (7") **THE PROMISED LAND. / SAINT JACKIE (by "DAVID J. & The J.WALKERS")** [ ] [-]
(12"+=) – A seducer, a doctor, a card you cannot trust.

Jun 84. (12"ep) **V FOR VENDETTA (by "DAVID J. & ALAN MOORE")** [ ] [ ]
– This vicious cabaret / V theme (intro) / V's theme (outro).

Sep 84. (7")(12") **I CAN'T SHAKE THIS SHADOW OF FEAR. / WAR GAME** [ ] [-]

Mar 85. (lp) **CROCODILE TEARS & THE VELVET COSH** [ ] [-]

Apr 85. (7") **CROCODILE TEARS & THE VELVET COSH. / ELEGY** [ ] [ ]
(12"+=) – Rene.

Jun 85. (12"ep) **BLUE MOODS TURNING TAILS** [ ] [-]
– 4 hours / The conjurors hand / Ship of fools.

Mar 86. (lp) **DAVID J. ON GLASS** (compilation) [ ] [-]

— w/ **MAX KIDER** – guitar / **ANGUS WALLACE + OWEN JONES** – drums / **DAVE ANDERSON** – steel guitar / **ALEX GREEN** – sax / **BEN HEANEY** – violin / **BEN GREENAWAY** percussion / **JANIS ZAKIS** – accordian.

Beggar's B. Beggar's..

Jun 90. (7") **I'LL BE YOUR CHAUFFEUR. / THE MOON IN THE MAN** [ ] [ ]
(12"+=) – ('A'original version).

Jul 90. (cd)(c)(lp) **SONGS FROM ANOTHER SEASON** [ ] [ ]
– Fingers in the grease / A longer look / Sad side to the sand boy / New woman is an attitude / Sweet ancenthexra / On the outskirts (of a strange dream) / I'll be your chauffeur (original) / The Moon in the man / Little star / Stranded Trans-Atlantic hotel nearly famous blues / The national anthem of nowhere / Nature boy.

BBM (see under ⇒ BRUCE, Jack)

BEACH BOYS

Formed: Hawthorne, Los Angeles, California, USA . . . 1961 by WILSON brothers BRIAN, DENNIS and KARL. They were joined by AL JARDINE and cousin MIKE LOVE. After one minor hit SURFIN' on local 'Candix' label, they signed to 'Capitol' appropriately in summer '62. Surf type hits continued with 'SURFIN' U.S.A.', etc. but surpassed this in '66 when 'GOOD VIBRATIONS' became regarded as a classic, and also UK No.1. They continued to hit both charts for the rest of the 60's, and had a major comeback in the late 70's. BRIAN WILSON became increasingly involved with 60's drug scene, and dropped out of group in 1967, although he returned to the fold full-time in 1976. • **Style:** Fun loving, girl loving, car crazy, pop combo, whose surfy FOUR FRESHMEN style close harmonies became trademark. A little more sophisticated in the 70's, but hits dried up. Nine years later (1988), the soppy 'KOKOMO' gave them return to US top spot. • **Songwriters:** Early hits were co-written by BRIAN and neighbour GARY USHER, but BRIAN soon took control, with others complimenting on some. Covered:- THE TIMES THEY ARE A-CHANGIN' (Bob Dylan) / PAPA OOM MOW MOW (Rivingtons) / I CAN HEAR MUSIC (Ronettes) / BARBARA ANN (Regents) / LOUIE LOUIE (Kingsmen) / WHY DO FOOLS FALL IN LOVE? (Frankie Lymon & the Teenagers) / MONSTER MASH (Bobby Pickett & the Crypt..) / JOHNNY B. GOODE (Chuck Berry) / DO YOU WANNA DANCE (Bobby Freeman) / YOU'VE GOT TO HIDE YOUR LOVE AWAY + I SHOULD HAVE KNOWN BETTER (Beatles) / ALLEY OOP (Hollywood Argyles) / BLUEBIRDS OVER THE MOUNTAIN (Ersel Hickey) / THEN I KISSED HER (Crystals) / COME GO WITH ME (Del-Vikings) CALIFORNIA DREAMIN' (Mamas & the Papas) / THE WANDERER (Dion) / ROCK AND ROLL MUSIC (Chuck Berry) / BLUEBERRY HILL (Fats Domino) / MONA (Bo Diddley) / PEGGY SUE (Buddy Holly) / THE AIR THAT I BREATHE (Hollies) / HOT FUN IN THE SUMMERTIME (Sly & The Family Stone) / WALKING IN THE SAND (Shangri-la's) / UNDER THE BOARDWALK (Drifters). etc. KOKOMO (co-written with John Phillips; ex-Mamas & the Papas). • **Miscellaneous:** The WILSON's father died 4 Jun'73. DENNIS was drowned at sea off Marina Del Ray on 28 Dec'83.

Recommended: THE VERY BEST OF THE BEACH BOYS (*8) / PET SOUNDS (*9)

BRIAN WILSON (b.20 Jun'42, Inglewood, California) – vocals, percussion / **CARL WILSON** (b.21 Dec'46) – guitar, vocals / **DENNIS WILSON** (b.4 Dec'44) – vocals, drums / **MIKE LOVE** (b.15 Mar'44, Baldwin Hills, California) – vocals / **AL JARDINE** (b. 3 Sep'42, Lima, Ohio) – vocals, guitar

not issued Candix

Dec 61. (7") **SURFIN'. / LUAN** [-] [75]

— **DAVID MARKS** – vocals repl. JARDINE who became dentist

Capitol Capitol

Oct 62. (7") **SURFIN' SAFARI. / 409** [ ] [14]

Nov 62. (lp) **SURFIN' SAFARI** [ ] [32]
– Surfin' safari / County fair / Ten little indians / Chug-a-lug / Little girl (you're my Miss America) / 409 / Surfin' * / Heads you win – tails I lose / Summertime blues / Cuckoo clock * / Moon dawg / The shift. *(UK-iss.Apr63) (re-iss.Jun79 omitting *)*

Jan 63. (7") **TEN LITTLE INDIANS. / COUNTY FAIR** [ ] [49]
(re-iss.Jun79)

Mar 63. (lp) **SURFIN' U.S.A.** [17] [2]
– Surfin' U.S.A. / Farmer's daughter / Misirlou / Stoked / Lonely sea / Shut down / Noble surfer / Honky tonk / Lana / Surf jam / Let's go trippin' / Finders keepers.

Jun 63. (7") **SURFIN' U.S.A.. / SHUT DOWN** [34] [3] [23]
(re-iss.Jun79)

— **AL JARDINE** – vocals returned to repl. MARKS

Aug 63. (7") **SURFER GIRL. / LITTLE DEUCE COUPE** [-] [7] [15]

Sep 63. (lp) **SURFER GIRL** [13] [7]
– Surfer girl / Catch a wave / Surfer Moon / South bay surfer / Rocking surfer / Little deuece coupe / In my room / Hawaii / Surfer's rule / Our car club / Your summer dream / Boogie woogie. *(re-iss.Aug86)*

Oct 63. (lp) **LITTLE DEUCE COUPE** [ ] [4]
– Little deuce Coupe / Ballad of ole' Betsy / Be true to your school / Car crazy cutie * / Cherry, cherry Coupe / 409 / Shut down / Spirit of America / Our car club * / No-go showboat / A young man is gone / Custom machine. *(re-iss.Jun81 omitting *) (re-iss.Aug86)*

Nov 63. (7") **BE TRUE TO YOUR SCHOOL. / IN MY ROOM** [-] [6] [23]

Dec 63. (7") **LITTLE SAINT NICK. / THE LORD'S PRAYER** [-] [ ]

Jan 64. (7") **PAMELA JEAN (as "The SURVIVORS"). / AFTER THE GAME** [-] [ ]

Mar 64. (7") **FUN, FUN, FUN. / WHY DO FOOLS FALL IN LOVE** [ ] [5]

Jul 64. (lp) **SHUT DOWN VOL.2** [ ] [13] Apr 64
– Fun, fun, fun / Don't worry baby / In the parkin' lot / "Cassius" Love vs "Sonny" Wilson / The warmth of the sun / This car of mine / Why do fools fall in love / Pom-pom play girl / Keep an eye on summer / Shut down (pt.II) / Louie louie / Denny's drum. *(re-iss.Jun89 on 'C5')*

Note:- SHUT DOWN was a various artists surf US-lp issued Jul63 reaching No.7. It contained two BEACH BOYS tracks; 409 / Shut down.

Jun 64. (7") **I GET AROUND. / DON'T WORRY BABY** [7] [1]
(re-iss.Jun79)

Jul 64. (lp) **ALL SUMMER LONG** [ ] [4]
– I get around / All summer long / Hushabye / Little Honda / We'll run away / Carl's big chance / Wendy / Do you remember? / Girls on the beach / Drive-in / Our favourite recording session / Don't back down. *(UK-iss.Jun65) (re-iss.Jul73 on 'MFP', re-iss.+c Aug86)*

Oct 64. (7") **WHEN I GROW UP (TO BE A MAN). / SHE KNOWS ME TOO WELL** [27] [9]
(re-iss.Jun79)

Oct 64. (lp) **BEACH BOYS CONCERT (live)** [ ] [1]
– Fun, fun, fun / The little old lady from Pasadena / Little deuce Coupe / Long tail Texan / In my room / Monster mash / Let's go trippin' / Papa-oom-mow-mow / The wanderer / Hawaii / / Graduation day / I get around / Johnny B. Goode. *(re-iss.Jun81 on 'Greenlight')*

Nov 64. (7"ep) **WENDY DON'T BACK DOWN / LITTLE HONDA / HUSHABYE** [-] [44]

Dec 64. (7") **THE MAN WITH ALL THE TOYS. / BLUE CHRISTMAS** [-] [ ]

Jan 65. (7") **DANCE, DANCE, DANCE. / THE WARMTH OF THE SUN** [24] [8]

— **GLEN CAMPBELL** – vocals (on tour) repl. BRIAN who suffered breakdown. However BRIAN did stay as writer/producer (6th member) (also see other US releases for further imports)

Mar 65. (7") **DO YOU WANNA DANCE?. / PLEASE LET ME WONDER** [-] [ ]

Mar 65. (7") **ALL SUMMER LONG. / DO YOU WANNA DANCE?** [ ] [ ]
(re-iss.Jun79)

Apr 65. (lp) **BEACH BOYS – TODAY!** [6] [4]
– Do you wanna dance? / Good to my baby / Don't hurt my little sister / When I grow up (to be a man) / Help me Rhonda / Dance, dance, dance / Please let me wonder / I'm so young / Kiss me baby / She knows me too well / In the back of my mind / She knew me too well. *(re-iss.UKJan72 as 'DO YOU WANNA DANCE' on 'MFP')*

— **BRUCE JOHNSTON** – vocals (ex-his combo) repl. GLEN CAMPBELL who went solo

May 65. (7") **HELP ME RHONDA. / KISS ME BABY** [27] [1]
(re-iss.Jun79)

Jul 65. (lp) **SUMMER DAYS (AND SUMMER NIGHTS!!)** [4] [2]

– The girl from New York City / Amusements parks U.S.A. / Then I kissed her / Salt Lake City / Girl don't tell me / Help me Rhonda / Let him run wild / You're so good to me / Summer means new love / I'm bugged at my ol' man / And your dream comes true. *(re-iss.+c-Jun78, re-iss.Aug86)*

Aug 65 (7") **CALIFORNIA GIRLS. / LET HIM RUN WILD** [26] [3]
(re-iss.Jun79)

Dec 65. (7") **THE LITTLE GIRL I ONCE KNEW. / THERE'S NO OTHER (LIKE MY BABY)** [ ] [20]
(re-iss.Jun79)

Feb 66. (7") **BARBARA ANN. / GIRL DON'T TELL ME** [3] [2]
(re-iss.Jun79)

Feb 66. (lp) **BEACH BOYS' PARTY!** [3] [6] Nov 65
– Hully gully / I should have known better / Tell me why / Papa-oom- mow-mow / Mountain of love / You've got to hide your love away / Devoted to you / Alley oop / There's no other (like my baby) / I get around – Little deuce Coupe / The times they are a-changin' / Barbara Ann. *(re-iss.Aug86)*

Apr 66. (7") **SLOOP JOHN B. / YOU'RE SO GOOD TO ME** [2] [3]

May 66. (lp) **PET SOUNDS** [2] [10]
– Wouldn't it be nice / You still believe in me / That's not me / Don't talk (put your head on my shoulder) / I'm waiting for the day / Let's go away for awhile / Sloop John B. / God only knows / I know there's no answer / Here today / I just wasn't made for these times / Pet sounds / Caroline, no. *(re-iss.May82 on 'Fame') (re-iss.Aug86, cd-iss.Jun90 w/+= tracks)* – Hang on to your ego / Trombone Dixie. *(re-iss.cd+c Nov93 on 'Fame')*

Jul 66. (7") **GOD ONLY KNOWS. / WOULDN'T IT BE NICE** [2] [39] [8]
(re-iss. Jun79)

Oct 66. (7") **GOOD VIBRATIONS. / LET'S GO AWAY FOR AWHILE** [-] [1]

Oct 66. (7") **GOOD VIBRATIONS. / WENDY** [1] [-]
(re-iss.Jun79)

Apr 67. (7") **THEN I KISSED HER. / MOUNTAIN OF LOVE** [4] [ ]
(re-iss.Jun79)

Capitol Brother

Aug 67. (7") **HEROES AND VILLAINS. / YOU'RE WELCOME** [8] [12]
(re-iss.Jun79)

Nov 67. (lp) **SMILEY SMILE** [9] [41] Sep 67
– Heroes and villains / Vegetables / Fall breaks and back to winter / She's goin' bald / Little pad / Good vibrations / With me tonight / Wind chimes / Gettin' hungry / Wonderful / Whistle in.

Nov 67. (7") **WILD HONEY. / WIND CHIMES** [29] [31]
(re-iss.Jun79)

Dec 67. (7") **DARLIN'. / HERE TODAY** [-] [19]

Jan 68. (7") **DARLIN'. / COUNTRY AIR** [11] [-]
(re-iss.Jun79)

Mar 68. (lp) **WILD HONEY** [7] [24] Dec 67
– Wild honey / Aren't you glad / I was made to love her / Country air / A thing or two / Darlin' / I'd love just once to see you / Here comes the night / Let the wind blow / How she boogalooed it / Mama says.

May 68. (7") **FRIENDS. / LITTLE BIRD** [25] [47]
(re-iss.Jun79)

Jul 68. (7") **DO IT AGAIN. / WAKE THE WORLD** [1] [20]

Sep 68. (lp) **FRIENDS** [13] [ ] Jun 68
– Meant for you / Friends / Wake the world / Be here in the mornin' / When a man needs a woman / Passing by / Anna Lee, the healer / Little bird / Be still / Busy doing nothin' / Diamond head / Transcendental meditation.

Dec 68. (7") **BLUEBIRDS OVER THE MOUNTAIN. / NEVER LEARN NOT TO LOVE** [33] [ ]
(re-iss.Jun79)

Feb 69. (7") **I CAN HEAR MUSIC. / ALL I WANT TO DO** [10] [24]

Feb 69. (lp) **20/20** [3] [68]
– Do it again / I can hear music / Bluebirds over the mountain / Be with me / All I want to do / The nearest faraway place / Cotton fields / I went to sleep / Time to get alone / Never learn not to love / Our prayer / Cabinessence.

Jun 69. (7") **BREAKAWAY. / CELEBRATE THE NEWS** [6] [ ]
(re-iss.Jun79)

Capitol Brother / Reprise

Feb 70. (7") **ADD SOME MUSIC TO YOUR DAY. / SUSIE CINCINATTI** [-] [ ]

May 70. (7") **COTTON FIELDS. / THE NEAREST FARAWAY PLACE** [5] [ ]
(re-iss.Jun79)

Stateside Brother / Reprise

Sep 70. (7") **SLIP ON THROUGH. / THIS WHOLE WORLD** [ ] [ ]

Nov 70. (7") **TEARS IN THE MORNING. / IT'S ABOUT ME** [ ] [ ]

Nov 70. (lp)(c) **SUNFLOWER** [29] [ ] Sep 70
– Slip on through / This whole world / Add some music to your day / Got to know the woman / Deirdre / It's about time / Tears in the morning / All I wanna do / Forever / Our sweet love / At my window / Cool, cool water. *(re-iss.Nov81. on 'Caribou'; adding 'Cotton fields') (re-iss.+cdJul91 on 'Epic')*

Feb 71. (7") **COOL, COOL WATER. / FOREVER** [-] [ ]

Jun 71. (7") **LONG PROMISED ROAD. / DEIRDRE** [-] [ ]

Oct 71. (7") **LONG PROMISED ROAD. / TILL I DIE** [-] [ ]

Nov 71. (7") **DON'T GO NEAR THE WATER. / STUDENT DEMONSTRATION TIME** [ ] [ ]

Nov 71. (lp)(c) **SURF'S UP** [15] [29] Aug 71
– Don't go near the water / Long promised road / Take a load off your feet / Disney girls (1957) / Student demonstration time / Feel flows / Lookin' at tomorrow / A day in the life of a tree / 'Til I die / Surf's up. *(re-iss.Nov81 on 'Caribou') (re-iss.+cdJul91 on 'Epic')*

Nov 71. (7") **SURF'S UP. / DON'T GO NEAR THE WATER** [-] [ ]

—— **BLONDIE CHAPLIN** – guitar repl. JOHNSTON who later went solo added **RICKY FATAAR** – drums (DENNIS now just vocals)

Reprise Reprise

May 72. (7") **YOU NEED A MESS OF HELP TO STAND ALONE. / CUDDLE UP** [ ] [ ]

Jun 72. (d-lp)(c) **CARL AND THE PASSIONS – SO TOUGH** [25] [50]
– You need a mess of help to stand alone / Here she comes / He come down / Marcella / Hold on dear brother / Make it good / All this is that / Cuddle up. (w/ 'PET SOUNDS') *(re-iss.+cdJul91 on 'Epic')*

Aug 72. (7") **MARCELLA. / HOLD ON DEAD BROTHER** [-] [ ]

Jan 73. (lp)(c) **HOLLAND** [20] [36]
– Sail on sailor / Steamboat / California saga (on my way to sunny Californ-i-a (medley):- Big sur – Beaks of eagles – California / The trader / Leaving this town / Only with you / Funky pretty.
(7"ep free-w/a) – Mount Vernon and Fairway (A fairy tale). / I'm the pied piper / Batter get back in bed / Magic transistor radio / Mount Vernon and Fairway / I'm the pied piper / Radio King Dom. *(re-iss.+cdJul91 on 'Epic')*

Feb 73. (7") **CALIFORNIA SAGA. / FUNKY PRETTY** [-] [ ]

Feb 73. (7") **CALIFORNIA SAGA: CALIFORNIA. / SAIL ON SAILOR** [37] [-]

Nov 73. (d-lp)(c) **THE BEACH BOYS IN CONCERT (live)** [ ] [25]
– Sail on sailor / Sloop John B. / The trader / You still believe me / California girls / Darlin' / Marcella / Caroline, no / Leaving this town / Heroes and villains / We got love / Don't worry baby / Surfin' U.S.A. / Good vibrations / Fun, fun, fun / Funky pretty / Let the wind blow / Help me Rhonda / Surfer girl / Wouldn't it be nice.

1974. (7") **I CAN HEAR MUSIC (live). / LET THE WIND BLOW (live)** [-] [ ]

1974. (7") **CHILD OF WINTER. / SUSIE CINCINNATI** [-] [ ]

Aug 74. (7"ep) **CALIFORNIA SAGA: CALIFORNIA. / SAIL ON SAILOR / MARCELLA / I'M THE PIED PIPER** [ ] [ ]

—— **JAMES GUERICO** – bass (on tour) repl. BLONDIE and RICKY / **DENNIS** returned to his drums

Jun 75. (7") **SAIL ON SAILOR. / ONLY WITH YOU** [ ] [49]

—— **BRIAN** returned to live work

Jul 76. (7") **ROCK AND ROLL MUSIC. / THE T.M. SONG** [36] [ ]

Jul 76. (lp)(c) **15 BIG ONES** [31] [8]
– Rock and roll music / It's O.K. / Had to phone ya / Chapel of love / Everyone's in love with you / Talk to me / That same song / The T.M. song / Palisades park / Susie Cincinatti / A casual look / Blueberry Hill / Back home / In the still of the night / Just once in my life. *(cd+c.issJul91 on 'Epic')*

Aug 76. (7") **IT'S O.K. / HAD TO PHONE YA** [ ] [ ]

Nov 76. (7") **SUSIE CINCINNATI. / EVERYONE'S IN LOVE WITH YOU** [-] [ ]

Apr 77. (7") **HONKIN' DOWN THE HIGHWAY. / SOLAR SYSTEM** [-] [ ]

Apr 77. (lp)(c) **THE BEACH BOYS LOVE YOU** [26] [53]
– Roller skating child / I'll bet he's nice / Airplane / Love is a woman / Johnny Carson / Let us go on this way / I wanna pick you up / Let's put our hearts together / Solar system / The night was so young / Ding dang / Mona / Honkin' down the highway / Good time. *(cd+c.issJun91 on 'Epic')*

Aug 77. (7"ep) **MONA. / ROCK AND ROLL MUSIC / SAIL ON SAILOR / MARCELLA** [ ] [ ]

Sep 78. (lp)(c) **M.I.U. ALBUM** [ ] [ ]
– She's got rhythm / Come go with me / Hey little tomboy / Kona coast / Peggy Sue / Wontcha come out tonight / Sweet Sunday kinda love / Belles of Paris / Pitter patter / My Diane / Match point of your love / Winds of change. *(cd+c.issJul91 on 'Epic')*

Oct 78. (7") **PEGGY SUE. / HEY LITTLE TOMBOY** [ ] [ ]

Dec 78. (7") **KONA COAST. / SWEET SUNDAY KINDA LOVE** [ ] [ ]

—— Returned **BRUCE JOHNSTON** – vocals to DENNIS, CARL, AL, MIKE and BRIAN

Caribou Caribou

Mar 79. (7") **HERE COMES THE NIGHT. / BABY BLUE** [37] [44]
(12"+=)(12"blue+=) – ('A'-disco version).

Apr 79. (lp)(c) **L.A. (LIGHT ALBUM)** [32] [100]
– Angel come home / Baby blue / Love surrounds me / Good timin' / Goin' south / Shortenin' bread / Lady Lynda / Sumahama / Full sail / Sumahama / Here comes the night. *(re-iss.Aug86) (cd-iss.Jul89 on 'Pickwick') (also on pic-lp)*

May 79. (7") **GOOD TIMIN'. / LOVE SURROUNDS ME** [-] [ ]

Jun 79. (7") **LADY LYNDA. / FULL SAIL** [6] [ ]

Aug 79. (7") **SUMAHAMA. / ANGEL COME HOME** [6] [ ]

Sep 79. (7") **SUMAHAMA. / IT'S A BEAUTIFUL DAY** [-] [ ]

Nov 79. (7") **GOOD TIMIN'. / GOIN' SOUTH** [ ] [40]

Mar 80. (7") **GOIN' ON. / ENDLESS HARMONY** [-] [ ]

Mar 80. (7") **OH DARLING. / ENDLESS HARMONY** [ ] [ ]

Mar 80. (lp)(c) **KEEPIN' THE SUMMER ALIVE** [54] [75]
– Endless harmony / When girls get together / School day (ring! ring! goes the bell) / Sunshine / Santa Ana winds / Goin' on / Some of your love / Oh darlin' / Livin' with a heartache / Keepin' the summer alive.

Jun 80. (7") **KEEPIN' THE SUMMER ALIVE. / WHEN GIRLS GET TOGETHER** [ ] [ ]

Jul 80. (7") **LIVING WITH A HEARTACHE. / SANTA ANA WINDS** [-] [ ]

Jul 80. (7") **SANTA ANA WINDS. / SUNSHINE** [ ] [ ]

—— **ADRIAN BAKER** – vocals (ex-solo) repl. CARL and BRUCE

—— **CARL WILSON** returned after short solo career

Feb 82. (7") **COME GO WITH ME. / DON'T GO NEAR THE WATER** [ ] [18]

—— Tragically on 28 Dec83, DENNIS was drowned in his swimming pool. The other original 4 (BRIAN, CARL, AL and MIKE) carried on. Next credited with **JULIO IGLESIAS** – co-vocals

1984. (7") **SHE BELIEVES IN LOVE AGAIN. / IT'S JUST A MATTER OF TIME** [-] [ ]

Mar 85. (7") **THE AIR THAT I BREATHE. / BAMBOU MEDLEY** [ ] [ ]

May 85. (7") **GETCHA BACK. / MALE EGO** [ ] [ ]
(12"+=) – Here comes the night / Lady Lynda.

Jun 85. (lp)(c) **THE BEACH BOYS** [60] [52]
– Getcha back / It's gettin' late / Crack at your love / Maybe I don't know / She believes in love again / California calling / Passing friend / I'm so lonely / Where I belong / I do love you / It's just a matter of time. (cd+=) – Male ego.

Aug 85. (7") **PASSING FRIEND. / IT'S O.K.** [ ] [ ]

Sep 86. (7") **CALIFORNIA DREAMING. / LADY LIBERTY** [ ] [ ]
(12"+=) – (Ballads medley).

—— BRIAN now departed to go solo, the rest did on-off with "FAT BOYS" ('A'side)

on their hit single WIPE OUT

Nov 88. (7")(12") **KOKOMO. / TUTTI FRUTTI (by 'Little Richard')** [25] [1]
above single was from the film 'Cocktail'

Aug 89. (7") **STILL CRUISIN'. / KOKOMO**
(cd-s+=) Rock'n'roll to the rescue (mix) / Lady Liberty.
(12"+=) – Beach Boys Medley.

Jul 90. (c-s)(cd-s) **PROBLEM CHILD /** [-]

—— **MIKE LOVE, CARL WILSON, AL JARDINE, BRUCE JOHNSTON** (now keyboards), **MELCHER** (keyboards + co-writer w/**LOVE**), **ADRIAN BAKER** (backing vocals), **KEITH WECHSLER** (keyboards / some drums), **CRAIG FALL** – guitar, keyboards / **ROD CLARK** – bass / **SAMMY MERENDINO** – drums / **VAN DYKE PARKS** – accordion, keyboards / **DANNY KORTCHMAR** – guitars / **JOEL PESKIN** – saxophone / **JOHN WESTON** – pedal steel

Brother Brother

Jun 93. (cd)(c) **SUMMER IN PARADISE**
– Hot fun in the summertime / Surfin' / Slow summer dancin' (one summer night) / Strange things happen / Remember walking in the sand / Lahaina aloha / Under the boardwalk / Summer in Paradise forever. *(re-iss.cd May95 on 'Fame')*

– compilations, exploitations, etc. –

Nov 64. Capitol; (lp) **BEACH BOYS CHRISTMAS ALBUM**
(re-iss.Dec77)

Oct 66. Capitol; (lp) **THE BEST OF THE BEACH BOYS** [2] [8]

Oct 67. Capitol; (lp) **THE BEST OF THE BEACH BOYS VOL.2** [3] [50] Aug 67

Nov 68. Capitol; (lp) **THE BEST OF THE BEACH BOYS VOL.3** [3] Sep 68
(U.S. title 'STACK O'TRACKS') *(re-iss.Dec76)*

Aug 69. Capitol; (d-lp) **CLOSE UP (SURFIN' USA / ALL SUMMER LONG)** [-]

Sep 70. Capitol; (lp)(c) **GREATEST HITS** [5]

Jan 71. Capitol; (d-lp) **THE CAPITOL YEARS**

Aug 72. Capitol; (7"ep) **WOULDN'T IT BE NICE. / FUN FUN FUN / CALIFORNIA GIRLS**

Aug 72. Capitol; (lp)(c) **LIVE IN LONDON (live 1969)** [75] Dec76
(re-iss.Sep77 on 'MfP')

Nov 72. Capitol; (7"ep) **BARBARA ANN. / DANCE DANCE DANCE / YOU'RE SO GOOD TO ME**

Nov 73. Capitol; (7") **LITTLE SAINT NICK. / THE LORD'S PRAYER**

May 74. Capitol; (7") **ALL SUMMER LONG. / SURFIN' SAFARI**

Aug 74. Capitol; (d-lp) **WILD HONEY / 20-20** [50]

Nov 74. Capitol; (d-lp)(c) **ENDLESS SUMMER** [1] Jul 74
(re-iss.Sep81 on 'MfP') (cd-iss.Feb87 on 'EMI')

Oct 74. Capitol; (d-lp) **FRIENDS / SMILEY SMILE**

Apr 75. Capitol; (d-lp) **SPIRIT OF AMERICA** [8]

Jun 75. Capitol; (7") **BREAKAWAY. / CELEBRATE THE NEWS**

Jun 76. Capitol; (7") **GOOD VIBRATIONS. / WOULDN'T IT BE NICE** [18]

Jul 76. Capitol; (lp)(c) **20 GOLDEN GREATS (on 'EMI')** [1]
(cd-iss.Nov87) (also issued 1979 on blue vinyl) (re-iss.cd+c Sep94)

Nov 77. Capitol; (7") **LITTLE SAINT NICK. / SANTA CLAUSE IS COMING TO TOWN / ('A'instrumental)**

May 78. Capitol; (7") **LITTLE DEUCE COUPE. / ('B' by 'Sunrays & Superstocks')**

Jun 78. Capitol; (7") **CALIFORNIA GIRLS. / YOU'RE SO GOOD TO ME / DO IT AGAIN**

Jun 79. Capitol; (26x7"box) **THE BEACH BOYS SINGLES COLLECTION**
(7"free-w/a) – (as "The SURVIVORS" – Pamela Jean / After the game.

Jun 80. Capitol; (7") **GOD ONLY KNOWS. / GIRLS ON THE BEACH / IN MY ROOM**

Jun 80. Capitol; (lp)(c) **GIRLS ON THE BEACH**

Aug 81. Capitol; (7") **BEACH BOYS MEDLEY. / GOD ONLY KNOWS** [47] [12]
(re-iss.Jul83)

Jul 83. Capitol; (lp)(c) **THE VERY BEST OF THE BEACH BOYS** [1]
– Surfin' safari / Surfin' U.S.A. / Shut down / Little deuce Coupe / In my room / Fun, fun, fun / I get around / Don't worry baby / When I grow up (to be a man) / Wendy / Little Honda / Dance dance dance / All summer long / Do you wanna dance / Help me Rhonda / California girls / Little girl I once knew / Barbara Ann / You're so good to me / Then I kissed her / Sloop John B. / God only knows / Wouldn't it be nice / Here today / Good vibrations / Heroes and villains / Wild honey / Darlin' / Country air / Here comes the night / Friends / Do it again / Bluebirds over the mountain / I can hear music / Breakaway / Cottonfields.

Dec 84. Capitol; (d-lp)(d-c) **TEN YEARS OF HARMONY (1970-1980)**

Jul 86. Capitol; (7")(12") **ROCK'N'ROLL TO THE RESCUE. / GOOD VIBRATIONS (live)**

Aug 86. Capitol; (d-lp)(c)(cd) **MADE IN THE U.S.A.** [96]

Jun 90. Capitol; (7") **WOULDN'T IT BE NICE. / I GET AROUND** [58]
(12"+=)(cd-s+=) – Medley of hits.

Jun 90. Capitol; (cd)(c)(d-lp) **SUMMER DREAMS** [2]

Aug 90. Capitol; (cd) **WILD HONEY / SMILEY SMILE**

Jun 91. Capitol; (7")(c-s) **DO IT AGAIN. / GOOD VIBRATIONS** [61]
(cd-s+=) – Wouldn't it be nice.

Jun 90. Capitol; (cd) **SURFIN' SAFARI / SURFIN' USA**
(contains extra tracks) (c-iss.Jul91)

Jun 90. Capitol; (cd) **SURFER GIRL / SHUTDOWN VOL.2**
(contains extra tracks) (c-iss.Jul91)

Jul 90. Capitol; (cd) **LITTLE DEUCE COUPE / ALL SUMMER LONG**
(contains extra tracks) (c-iss.Aug91)

Jul 90. Capitol; (cd) **FRIENDS / 20-20**
(contains extra tracks) (c-iss.Aug91)

Jul 90. Capitol; (cd) **PARTY / STACK O-TRACKS**
(contains extra tracks) (c-iss.Aug91)

Aug 90. Capitol; (cd) **TODAY / SUMMER DAYS (AND SUMMER NIGHTS!!)**
(contains extra tracks) (c-iss.Aug91)

Aug 90. Capitol; (cd) **BEACH BOYS' CONCERT (live) / LIVE IN LONDON (live)** *(contains extra tracks) (c-iss.Aug91)*

Jul 93. Capitol; (6xcd-box) **GOOD VIBRATIONS – THIRTY YEARS OF THE BEACH BOYS**

Also released albums with JAN & DEAN on flip side ORIGINAL HITS, etc.

May 70. Regal Starline; (lp)(c) **BUG-IN** [-]

Jul 71. Regal Starline; (lp)(c) **THE BEACH BOYS** [-]
(re-iss.Oct84 on 'Audio Fidelity')

Dec 80. Replay; (7") **SURFIN' SAFARI. / SURFIN' / SURFER GIRL** [-]

Jan 81. World Records; (7xlp-box) **THE CAPITOL YEARS** [-]

1983. Cambra; (d-c) **BEACH BOYS** [-]

Oct 83. E.M.I.; (lp)(c) **THE BEACH BOYS' RARITIES** [-]

Nov 84. Topline; (lp) **SURFER GIRL** (different) [-]

Oct 86. Meteor; (lp) **WIPE OUT** [-]

Jun 70. M.F.P.; (lp)(c) **THE BEACH BOYS** [-]

Oct 75. M.F.P./ US= Brother; (lp)(c) **GOOD VIBRATIONS – THE BEST OF BEACH BOYS** [25] Jul 75

Oct 86. M.F.P.; (lp)(c) **DO IT AGAIN** [-]

May 88. Rhino; (cd-s) **LIL' BIT OF GOLD: THE BEACH BOYS** [-]
– California girls / Help me Rhonda / Wouldn't it be nice / Good vibrations.

Jun 93. Fame; (cd)(c) **CRUISIN'** [-]

Jul 94. Success; (cd)(c) **BEACH PARTY (w / JAN & DEAN)** [-]

Nov 94. Capitol-M.F.P.; (cd)(c) **THE BEACH BOYS' CHRISTMAS ALBUM** [-]

Feb 95. B.A.M.; (cd) **PEARLS OF THE PAST** [-]

Jun 95. EMI; (cd)(c) **THE BEST OF THE BEACH BOYS** [26]

BRIAN WILSON

Capitol Capitol

Mar 66. (7") **CAROLINE NO. / SUMMER MEANS NEW LOVE** [32]

Warners Warners

May 87. (7") **LET'S GO TO HEAVEN IN MY CAR. / TOO MUCH SUGAR** [-]

Reprise Reprise

Jul 88. (lp)(c)(cd) **BRIAN WILSON** [54]
– Love and mercy / Walkin' the line / Melt away / Baby let your hair grow long / Little children / One of the boys / There's so many / Night time / Let it shine / Rio Grande / Meet me in my dreams tonight. *(re-iss.cd Dec95 as 'LOVE AND MERCY')*

Aug 88. (7") **LOVE AND MERCY. / HE COULDN'T GET HIS POOR OLD BODY TO MOVE**
(12"+=)(cd-s+=) One for the boys

Nov 88. (7") **NIGHT TIME. / ONE FOR THE BOYS**
(12"+=)(cd-s+=) Being with the one you love.

1989. (7") **MELT AWAY. / BEING WITH THE ONE YOU LOVE** [-]

—— with musicians **JIM KELTNER** – drums / **JAMES HUTCHINSON** – bass / **BENMONT TENCH** – keyboards / **MARK GOLDENBERG + WADDY WACHTEL** – guitar / **DAVID McMURRAY** – sax, flute

M.C.A. M.C.A.

Sep 95. (cd)(c) **I JUST WASN'T MADE FOR THOSE TIMES** [59]
– Meant for you / This whole world / Caroline, no / Let the wind blow / Love and mercy / Do it again / The warmth of the sun / Wonderful / Still I dream of it / Melt away / 'Til I die.

—— Late in 1995, BRIAN released 'ORANGE CRATE ART' with VAN DYKE PARKS

BRIAN WILSON and MIKE LOVE

Capitol Capitol

Sep 67. (7") **GETTIN' HUNGRY. / DEVOTED TO YOU**

MIKE LOVE

(first 3 releases as with CELEBRATION)

M.C.A. Pacific Arts

1977. (lp) **CELEBRATION**
– Gettin' hungry / Sailor / Lovestruck / She's just out to get you / I don't wanna know / Starbay / Go and get that girl / How's about a little bit / Song of creation / Country pie.

Apr 78. (7") **ALMOST SUMMER. / LOOKIN GOOD**

Jul 78. (7") **IT'S O.K. / ISLAND GIRL**

Epic Epic

Oct 81. (lp)(c) **LOOKING BACK WITH LOVE**
– Looking back with love / On and on and on / Running around the world / Over and over / Rockin' the man in the boat / Calendar girl / Be my baby / One good reason / Teach me tonight / Paradise found.

Creole not issued

Nov 83. (7")(12") **JINGLE BELL ROCK. / LET'S PARTY**

DENNIS WILSON

Stateside Brother

Dec 70. (7") **SOUND OF FREE. / RUMBO (with "RUMBO")**

Caribou Reprise

Sep 77. (lp)(c) **PACIFIC OCEAN BLUE** [96]
– Pacific Ocean blue / River song / What's wrong / Friday night / Moonshine / Dreamer / Thoughts of you / Farewell my friend / Rainbows / Time you and I / End of the show. *(re-iss.+cd Jul91 on 'Epic')*

Sep 77. (7") **RIVER SONG. / FAREWELL MY FRIEND**

Elektra Elektra

1980. (lp)(c) **ONE OF THESE PEOPLE**

CARL WILSON

Caribou Caribou

Apr 81. (lp)(c) **CARL WILSON**

– Hold me tight / Bright lights / The right lane / Seems so long ago / What you gonna do about me / Hurry love / The grammy / Heaven.

Apr 81. (7") **HEAVEN. / THE RIGHT LANE**

Feb 83. (lp)(c) **YOUNGBLOOD**
– What more can I say / She's mine / Youngblood / Given you up / One more night alone / Rockin' all over the world / One of the times / What you do to me / Too early to tell / Time / If I could talk to love.

May 83. (7") **WHAT YOU DO TO ME. / TIME**

— BRUCE JOHNSTON also had his own solo career when he wasn't with BEACH BOYS. In '77 he made an album and 3 singles all in UK/US. That year also saw BLONDIE CHAPLIN releasing a UK/US album and single.

BEASTIE BOYS

Formed: Greenwich Village, New York, USA . . . 1981 by YAUCH and DIAMOND. They recruit HOROWITZ to replace 2 others, and after two US indie releases they sign 1984 to 'Def Jam' run by DJ scratcher RICK RUBIN. Early in 1987, they took the States & Britain by storm, after unleashing the ultimate youth anthem '(YOU GOTTA) FIGHT FOR YOUR RIGHT (TO PARTY)'. Sustained commercial impact for a few years, until buying public were finally sickened from over-the-top bad boy press & media attention. • **Style:** Started off playing hardcore, but by mid 80's incorporated white rap and hard rock/punk. A fusion lying somewhere between rappers RUN DMC and the anti-social SEX PISTOLS. • **Songwriters:** Although they released little cover versions, they sampled many LED ZEPPELIN songs. In 1992 they covered JIMMY JAMES (Jimi Hendrix) + TIME FOR LIVIN' (Stewart Frontline), and collaborated with NISHITA. • **Trivia:** ADAM HOROWITZ is the son of playwrite ISRAEL. Volkswagen car owners were up in arms when fans of the group tore by the thousands, the "VW" metal emblems which they wore round necks. HOROWITZ plays cameo role in TV serial 'The Equalizer' circa '88.

Recommended: LICENSED TO 'ILL (*8) / CHECK YOUR HEAD (*7) / ILL: COMMUNICATION (*9)

'MCA' ADAM YAUCH (b.15 Aug'67, Brooklyn, New York) – vocals / **'MIKE D' MIKE DIAMOND** (b.20 Nov'65, New York) – vocals / **'KING AD-ROCK' ADAM HOROWITZ** (b.31 Oct'66, Manhattan, New York) – vocals (ex-The YOUNG & THE USELESS) repl. JOHN BERRY and KATE SCHELLENBACH.

not issued / Ratcage

Nov 82. (12"ep) **POLLY WOG STEW** [-]
– Riot fight / Transit cop / Holy snappers / Egg raid on mojo / Beastie Boys / Jimi / Ode to . . . / Michelle's farm.
(UK-iss.Apr88 +c-s)(re-iss.12"ep/c-ep/cd-ep Feb93)

Aug 83. (7") **COOKIE PUSS. / BEASTIE REVOLUTION**
(UK-iss.Jan85, re-iss.Jul87; cd-iss.Dec87)
(re-issues +=) – Bonus bater / Cookie dub / Censored. (re-iss.12"ep/c-ep/cd-ep Feb93)

added **RICK RUBIN** – scratcher DJ

Def Jam / Def Jam

Oct 85. (7") **ROCK HARD. / ?** [-]

Jan 86. (7")(12") **SHE'S ON IT. / SLOW AND LOW**

May 86. (7") **HOLD IT, NOW HIT IT. / ('A'-acappella)**
(12"+=) – ('A'instrumental).

Sep 86. (7") **SHE'S ON IT. / SLOW AND LOW**
(12"+=) – Hold it, now hit it.

Nov 86. (7") **IT'S THE NEW STYLE. / PAUL REVERE**
(12"+=) – ('A'&'B'instrumentals).
(d12"++=) – Hold it, now hit it / Hold it, now hit it (Acapulco version) / Hold it, now hit it (instrumental).

Nov 86. (lp)(c)(cd) **LICENSED TO 'ILL** [7] [1]
– Rhymin and stealin' / The new style / She's crafty / Posse in effect / Slow ride / Girls / (You gotta) Fight for your right (to party) / No sleep till Brooklyn / Paul Revere / Hold it now, hit it / Brass monkey / Slow and low / Time to get ill. *(re-iss.Nov89 on 'Capitol') (re-iss.cd+c Jun94) (cd-iss.Jul95)*

Feb 87. (7") **(YOU GOTTA) FIGHT FOR YOUR RIGHT (TO PARTY). / TIME TO GET ILL** [11] [7] Dec 86
(12"+=) – No sleep till Brooklyn.

May 87. (7")(12")(7"sha-pic-d) **NO SLEEP TILL BROOKLYN. / POSSE IN EFFECT** [14]

Jul 87. (7")(12") **SHE'S ON IT. / SLOW AND LOW** [10]

Sep 87. (7")(7"sha-pic-d) **GIRLS. / SHE'S CRAFTY** [34]
(12"+=) – Rock hard.

Mar 88. (7") **BRASS MONKEY. / POSSE IN EFFECT** [-] [48]

no more **RICK RUBIN** as DJ

Capitol / Capitol

Jul 89. (12"ep)(cd-ep) **LOVE AMERICAN STYLE** [36]
(*=+7"only) – Hey ladies *. / Shake your rump * / 33% God / Die yourself in '89 (just do it).

Jul 89. (lp)(c)(cd) **PAUL'S BOUTIQUE** [44] [14]
– To all the girls / Shake your rump / Johnny Ryall / Egg man / High plains drifter / The sound of science / 3-minute rule / Hey ladies / 5-piece chicken dinner / Looking down the barrel of a gun / Car thief / What comes around / Shadrach / Ask for Janice / B-boy bouillabaisse medley:- A year and a day – Hello Brooklyn – Dropping names – Lay it on me – Mike on the mic – A.W.O.L.

1989. (7") **SHADRACH. /** [-]

— Trio now also on instruments; MCA – bass / **AD ROCK** – keyboards / **MIKE D** – drums

Apr 92. (12"ep)(c-ep) **PASS THE MIC** [47]
– Pass the mic / Time for living / Drunken praying mantis style / Professor Booty.
(cd-ep+=) – Nethy's girl.

May 92. (cd)(c)(d-lp) **CHECK YOUR HEAD** [10]
– Jimmy James / Funky boss / Pass the mic / Gratitude / Lighten up / Finger lickin' good / So what'cha want / The biz vs. the Nuge (with TED NUGENT) / Time for livin' / Something's got to give / Blue nun / Stand together / Pow / The maestro / Groove Holmes / Live at PJ's / Mark on the bus / Professor Booty / In 3's / Mamaste. *(re-iss.Sep94)*

Jun 92. (12"white-ep) **FROZEN METAL HEAD EP** [55] [-]
– Jimmy James / The blue nun / Drinkin' wine.
(cd-ep+=) – Jimmy James (original).

Jun 92. (c-s) **SO WHAT'CHA WANT. / ?** [-] [93]

Grand Royale / Capitol

May 94. (cd)(c)(d-lp) **ILL: COMMUNICATION** [10] [1]
– Sure shot / Tough guy / Freak freak / Bobo on the corner / Root down / Sabotage / Get it together / Sabrosa / The update / Futterman's rule / Alright hear this / Eugene's lament / Flute loop / Do it / Rick's theme / Heart attack man / The scoop / Shambala / Bodhisattva vow / Transitions.

Jun 94. (7"green)(c-s) **GET IT TOGETHER. / SABOTAGE / DOPE LITTLE SONG** [19]
(10") – (1st 2 tracks) / ('A'buck wild remix) / ('A'instrumental).
(cd-s) – (1st 2 tracks) / ('A'remix) / Resolution time.

Nov 94. (7"maroon) **SURE SHOT. / MULLET HEAD** [27]
(10"+=) – ('A'mix) / The vibes.
(cd-s+=) – Son of neck bone / (2-'A'remixes).

Jun 95. (m-cd)(m-c)(m-lp) **ROOT DOWN EP** (some live) [23] [50]
– Root down (free zone mix) / Root down / Root down (PP balloon mix) / Time to get ill / Heart attack man / The maestro / Sabrosa / Flute loop / Time for livin' / Something's got to give / So what'cha want.

– compilations –

Feb 94. Honey World/ US= Capitol; (cd)(c) **SOME OLD BULLSHIT** [46]
– (compilation of 1st 2 EP's)

BEAT

Formed: Birmingham, England . . . Autumn 1978 by WAKELING, COX and STEELE. In 1979 they release hit 45 'TEARS OF A CLOWN' on JERRY DAMMER's '2-Tone' label, before moving swiftly to 'Arista' subsidiary 'Go-Feet'. There they had a string of hits including three 1980 Top 10 hits 'HANDS OFF . . . SHE'S MINE', 'MIRROR IN THE BATHROOM' & 'TOO NICE TO TALK TO'. • **Style:** Multi-racical ska revivalists, influenced from political reggae to The SPECIALS. • **Songwriters:** Group compositions, except TEARS OF A CLOWN (Smokey Robinson & The Miracles) / ROUGH RIDER (Prince Buster) / CAN'T GET USED TO LOSING YOU (Andy Williams) / • **Trivia:** In USA; to avoid confusion with another band, they were renamed The ENGLISH BEAT. 'STAND DOWN MARGARET' was a subtle hint to UK Prime Minister at the time; Margaret Thatcher.

Recommended: WHAT IS BEAT? (THE BEST OF THE BEAT) (*7)

DAVE WAKELING (b.19 Feb'56) – vocals, guitar / **ANDY COX** (b.25 Jan'56) – guitar / **DAVID STEELE** (b. 8 Sep'60, Isle Of Wight) – bass / **EVERETT MORTON** (b. 5 Apr'51, West Indies) – drums (ex-JOAN ARMATRADING BAND) / **RANKING ROGER** (b.ROGER CHARLEY, 21 Feb'61) – toaster/vocals (ex-DUM DUM BOYS / **SAXA** (b.'31, Jamaica) – saxophone (ex-PRINCE BUSTER) (temp.then permanent)

2-Tone-Chrysalis / not issued?

Dec 79. (7") **TEARS OF A CLOWN. / RANKING FULL STOP** [6]

Go Feet-Arista / Sire

Feb 80. (7") **HANDS OFF . . . SHE'S MINE. / TWIST AND CRAWL** [9]

Apr 80. (7") **MIRROR IN THE BATHROOM. / JACKPOT** [4]

May 80. (lp)(c) **I JUST CAN'T STOP IT** [3]
– Mirror in the bathroom / Hands off . . . she's mine / Two swords / Twist and crawl / Rough rider / Click click / Big shot / Whine and grine – Ranking full stop / Stand down Margaret / Noise in this world / Can't get used to losing you / Best friend / Jackpot. *(re-iss.Mar84 on 'Fame')*

Aug 80. (7") **BEST FRIEND. / STAND DOWN MARGARET** [22]

Go Feet-Arista / I.R.S.

Nov 80. (7") **TOO NICE TO TALK TO. / PSYCHEDELIC ROCKERS** [7]

Apr 81. (7")(12") **DROWNING. / ALL OUT TO GET YOU** [22]

May 81. (lp)(c) **WHA'PPEN** [3]
– Doors of your heart / All out to get you / Monkey murders / I am your flag / French toast / Drowning / Dreamhouse in N.Z. / Walk away / Over and over / Cheated / Get a job / The limits we set.

Jun 81. (7") **DOORS OF YOUR HEART. / GET A JOB** [33]
(12") – ('A'side) / Drowning.

Nov 81. (7")(12") **HIT IT. / WHICH SIDE OF THE BED** [70] [-]

Apr 82. (7")(12") **SAVE IT FOR LATER. / WHAT'S YOUR BEST THING** [47] [-]
(re-iss.Aug83)

Sep 82. (7")(12") **JEANETTE. / MARCH OF THE SWIVELHEADS** [45] [-]

Sep 82. (lp)(c) **SPECIAL BEAT SERVICE** [21] [39] Apr 83
– I confess / Jeanette / Sorry / Sole salvation / Spar with me / Rotating head / Save it for later / She's going / Pato and Roger a go talk / Sugar and stress / End of the party / Ackee 1-2-3. *(cd-iss. 1988 on 'Illegal-IRS')*

Nov 82. (7") **JEANETTE. / SAVE IT FOR LATER** [-]

(Nov82-83, below on stage only) **WESLEY** guested on last lp)

WESLEY MAGOOGAN – sax (ex-HAZEL O'CONNOR) repl. SAXA due to ill health.

DAVID 'Blockhead' WRIGHT – keyboards (guested on remainder)

Nov 82. (7") **I CONFESS. / SOLE SALVATION** [54]
(12") – ('A'&'B'remixed versions).
(d7"+=) – Spar with me (live) / Doors of your heart (live) / Mirror in the bathroom (live).

Jan 83. (7") **I CONFESS. / MARCH OF THE SWIVELHEADS** [-]

Apr 83. (7")(12") **CAN'T GET USED TO LOSING YOU (remix). / SPAR WITH ME** [3]

May 83. (lp)(c) **WHAT IS BEAT? (THE BEST OF THE BEAT)** [10] [87] Dec 83
– Tears of a clown / Hands off . . . she's mine / Mirror in the bathroom / Stand down Margaret / Twist and crawl / Doors of your heart / Save it for later / Too nice to talk to / I confess / Best friend / Drowning / Ackee 1-2-3 / Can't get used to losing you / Ranking full stop.
(free-12"of remixes) (US cd version repl. these with others 3)

Jun 83. (7") **ACKEE 1-2-3. / MONKEY MURDERS** [54] [-]
(12") – ('A'side) / I confess (U.S.remix).

(split Jul'83 when WAKELING departed. He and ROGER formed GENERAL PUBLIC in 1984. **COX** and **STEELE** formed **FINE YOUNG CANNIBALS** mid 80's.

– compilations, others, etc. –

Aug 83. Go Feet; (d-c) **I JUST CAN'T STOP IT / WHA'PPEN** [ ] [-]

BEATLES

Formed: Liverpool, England . . . by LENNON and McCARTNEY as The QUARRYMEN in 1957 at school. In 1958 HARRISON joined but they split late '59. As The SILVER BEATLES, they reformed in Spring 1960, adding PETE BEST and STU SUTCLIFFE. They soon dropped SILVER, and employed manager Alan Williams, who got them local gigs. Later that year they toured Hamburg, West Germany but had to return because GEORGE was deported for being under 18. On 21st March 1961, they debutted at Liverpool's 'Cavern Club', which was followed by a return to Hamburg for 3 months. While there, they recorded for 'Polydor' records, backing cabaret-type pop singer TONY SHERIDAN. (These recordings were later released when at the peak of their popularity). Around mid-'61, STU stayed in Hamburg to get married and study art. He was to tragically die there of a brain haemorrhage on 10th April 1962. With PAUL now on bass, and BRIAN EPSTEIN as new manager, they laid down a demo for 'Decca', but this was disregarded by DICK ROWE who instead signed BRIAN POOLE & THE TREMELOES. (Dick soon had consolation when he contracted rivals-to-be The ROLLING STONES). Summer '62 brought sunshine when George Martin brought them to EMI's 'Parlophone' label, but during rehearsals BEST was fired and replaced by RINGO. By the end of 1962 their debut single 'LOVE ME DO' was in the UK Top 20. Their follow-up 'PLEASE PLEASE ME' hit No.2 and from then on with a few exceptions, they had a continuous run of UK No.1's, until their split in 1970. In the States, where they later signed to 'Capitol' late '63, they also became greatest pop/rock group of all time. They created history there on the 4th April, 1964 when they filled the Top 5 placings in singles chart. (1. – CAN'T BUY ME LOVE, 2. – TWIST AND SHOUT, 3. – SHE LOVES YOU, 4. – I WANT TO HOLD YOUR HAND, 5. – PLEASE PLEASE ME). Later that year they starred in their own film, A HARD DAYS NIGHT. Later filmography in the 60's included 'HELP!', 'HOW I WON THE WAR' (Lennon only from 1967), 'MAGICAL MYSTERY TOUR', 'YELLOW SUBMARINE' (cartoon), 'GET BACK' and 'LET IT BE'. On the 15th August 1965, they set an audience record (56,000) when they played outdoor at Shea Stadium, New York. The end of that year saw them being awarded the M.B.E. by the Queen. • **Style:** The fab four created new melodic pop sound and image, that progressed into more cultured rock. This was due to their introduction to guru MAHARISHI and the world of pot/dope. The resulting album REVOLVER in 1966, was first to highlight sitar and other Eastern instruments. On 1st June 1967, their masterpiece 'SGT. PEPPER' was born and was soon to become regarded by pop critics as the greatest album of all time. Tragedy struck, when manager BRIAN EPSTEIN died of a drug overdose 27th August 1967. To end 1968, their largely experimental double 'WHITE ALBUM' also became regarded by many as another classic. The following year saw them announce their imminent break-up, although two albums 'ABBEY ROAD' + 'LET IT BE' were released just prior to the split. • **Songwriters:** Mostly LENNON / McCARTNEY, but HARRISON penned a few from each album. RINGO also wrote a few. Covered TWIST AND SHOUT (Isley Brothers) / A TASTE OF HONEY / THERE'S A PLACE / MONEY (Barrett Strong) / ROLL OVER BEETHOVEN + ROCK AND ROLL MUSIC (Chuck Berry) / YOU REALLY GOT A HOLD OF ME (Miracles) / PLEASE MR.POSTMAN (Marvelettes) / KANSAS CITY (Wilbert Harrison) / WORDS OF LOVE (Diamonds) / CHAINS (Cookies) / BABY IT'S YOU (Shirelles) / etc. • **Trivia:** They form own label 'Apple' in 1968. Release own records and sign others including BADFINGER, MARY HOPKINS, JAMES TAYLOR, etc.

Recommended: SGT.PEPPER'S LONELY HEARTS CLUB BAND (*10) / REVOLVER (*9) / THE BEATLES 'White Album' (*10) / THE BEATLES 1967-70 (*10) / THE BEATLES 1962-66 (*10) / LIVE AT THE BBC (*8) / RUBBER SOUL (*9) / PLEASE PLEASE ME (*6) / WITH THE BEATLES (*7) / A HARD DAY'S NIGHT (*7) / BEATLES FOR SALE (*6) / HELP (*6) / ABBEY ROAD (*8) / LET IT BE (*7).

JOHN LENNON (b. JOHN WINSTON LENNON, 9 Oct'40) – vocals, rhythm guitar
PAUL McCARTNEY (b. JAMES PAUL McCARTNEY, 18 Jun'42) – vocals, guitar
GEORGE HARRISON (b.25 Feb'43) – vocals, lead guitar
STU SUTCLIFFE (b. STUART, 23 Jun'40, Edinburgh, Scotland) – bass
PETE BEST (b.1941) – drums

TONY SHERIDAN & The BEATLES

Polydor Decca

Jan 62. (7") **MY BONNIE. / THE SAINTS** [ ] [ ] Apr 62
(UK re-iss.May63 hit 48 / UK re-Feb64 + US re-on 'MGM 26.(above 'A' was rel.Aug61 in Germany as TONY SHERIDAN & The BEAT BROTHERS)

—— Were a quartet at the time, STU stayed in Germany, died 10 Apr'62 of brain haemorrhage. McCARTNEY moved to bass and vocals.

BEATLES

(Aug62) **RINGO STARR** (b.RICHARD STARKEY, 7 Jul'40) – drums (ex-RORY STORM & THE HURRICANES)repl. BEST

Parlophone not issued

Oct 62. (7") **LOVE ME DO. / P.S. I LOVE YOU** [17] [-]
(UK re-iss.Oct82 hit 4. (UK re-iss.cd-s.1989, re-iss.Oct92, hit UK 53) (US-iss.Apr64 on 'Tollie' 1+10)

Parlophone Vee Jay

Jan 63. (7") **PLEASE PLEASE ME. / ASK ME WHY** [2] [ ]
(UK re-iss.Jan83 hit 29. (re-iss.cd-s.1989)

Mar 63. (lp) **PLEASE PLEASE ME** [1] [-]
– I saw her standing there / Misery / Anna (go to him) / Chains / Boys / Ask me why / Please please me / Love me do / P.S. I love you / Baby, it's you / Do you want to know a secret / A taste of honey / There's a place / Twist and shout. *(UK re-iss.Nov88 on 'EMI', cd-iss.Feb87 hit 32.)(c.!70's)*

Apr 63. (7") **FROM ME TO YOU. / THANK YOU GIRL** [1] [ ]
(UK re-iss.Apr83 hit 40. (re-iss.cd-s.1989)

Jul 63. (lp) **INTRODUCING . . . THE BEATLES** [-] [2] Feb 64
– (tracks nearly same as UK debut)

Aug 63. (7") **SHE LOVES YOU. / I'LL GET BY** [1] [ ]
(UK re-iss.Aug83 hit 45. (re-iss.cd-s.1989) (US-Jan64 on 'Swan' hit 1).

Nov 63. (lp) **WITH THE BEATLES** [1] [-]
– It won't be long / All I've got to do / All my loving / Don't bother me / Little child /

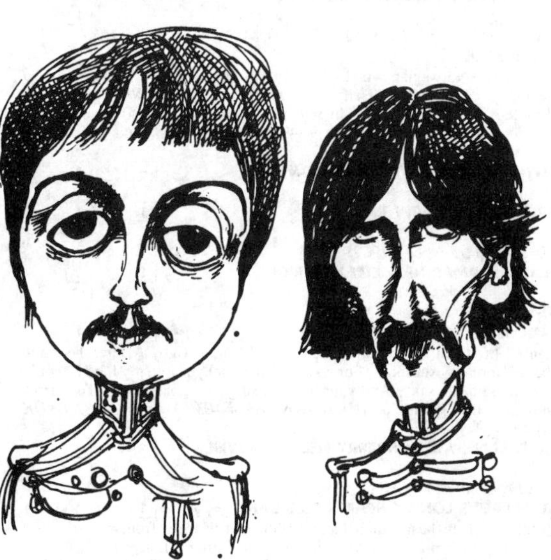

Till there was you / Please Mr.Postman / Roll over Beethoven / Hold me tight / You really got a hold of me / I wanna be your man / Don't bother me / Little child / Roll over Beethoven / Devil in her heart / Not a second time / Money. *(re-iss.Nov88 on 'EMI') (cd-iss.Feb87 hit 40. (c-iss.70's)*

Nov 63. (7") **I WANT TO HOLD YOUR HAND. / THIS BOY** 1 -
(UK re-iss.Nov83 hit 62) (re-iss.cd-s.1989)

Jan 64. (7") **PLEASE PLEASE ME. / FROM ME TO YOU** - 3

Parlophone Capitol

Jan 64. (7") **I WANT TO HOLD YOUR HAND. / I SAW HER STANDING THERE** - 1 14

Jan 64. (lp) **MEET THE BEATLES!** - 1
– I want to hold your hand / I saw her standing there / This boy / It won't be long / All I've got to do / All my loving / Don't bother me / Little child / Till there was you / Hold me tight / I wanna be your man / Not a second time.

Mar 64. (7") **CAN'T BUY ME LOVE. / YOU CAN'T DO THAT** 1 1
(UK re-iss.Mar84 hit 53) (re-iss.cd-s.1989)

Apr 64. (lp) **THE BEATLES' SECOND ALBUM** - 1
– Roll over Beethoven / Thank you girl / You really got a hold on me / Devil in her heart / Money / You can't do that / Long tall Ally / I call your name / Please Mr.Postman / I'll get you / She loves you.

Jul 64. (7") **A HARD DAY'S NIGHT. / THINGS WE SAID TODAY** 1
(UK re-iss.Jul84 hit 52) (re-iss.cd-s.1989)

Jul 64. (7") **A HARD DAY'S NIGHT. / I SHOULD HAVE KNOWN BETTER** - 1 53

Jul 64. (lp) **A HARD DAY'S NIGHT (Soundtrack)** 1 1
– A hard day's night / I should have known better / If I fell / I'm happy just to dance with you / And I love her / Tell me why / Can't buy me love / Anytime at all / I'll cry instead / Things we said today / When I get home / You can't do that / I'll be back. *(UK re-lp+c.Jan71 hit 39. re-iss.Nov88 on 'EMI') (cd-iss.Feb87 hit 30.*

Aug 64. (7") **I'LL CRY INSTEAD. / I'M HAPPY JUST TO DANCE WITH YOU** - 25 95

Aug 64. (7") **AND I LOVE HER. / IF I FELL** - 12 53

Sep 64. (7") **MATCHBOX. / SLOW DOWN** - 17 25

Nov 64. (7") **I FEEL FINE. / SHE'S A WOMAN** 1 1 4
(UK re-iss.Nov64 hit 65) (re-iss.cd-s.1989)

Dec 64. (lp) **BEATLES FOR SALE** 1 -
– No reply / I'm a loser / Baby's in black / Rock and roll music / I'll follow the sun / Mr.Moonlight / Kansas City / Eight days a week / Words of love / Honey don't / Every little thing / I don't want to spoil the party / What you're doing / Everybody's trying to be my baby. *(re-iss.Nov88 on 'EMI') (cd-iss.Feb87 hit 45. (c-iss.70's)*

Jan 65. (lp) **BEATLES '65** - 1
– (track listing near as above)

Feb 65. (7") **EIGHT DAYS A WEEK. / I DON'T WANT TO SPOIL THE PARTY** - 1 39

Apr 65. (7") **TICKET TO RIDE. / YES IT IS** 1 1
(UK re-iss.Apr85 hit 70) (re-iss.cd-s.1989)

Jul 65. (lp) **BEATLES VI** - 1
– Kansas City / Eight days a week / You like me too much / Bad boy / I don't want to spoil the party / Words of love / What you're doing / Yes it is / Dizzy Miss Lizzy / Tell me what you see / Every little thing.

Jul 65. (7") **HELP!. / I'M DOWN** 1 1
(UK re-iss.Jul85) (re-iss.cd-s.1989)

Jul 65. (lp) **HELP! (Soundtrack)** 1 1 Sep 65
– Help! / The night before / You've got to hide your love away / I need you / Another girl / You're gonna lose that girl / Ticket to ride / Act naturally / It's only love / You like me too much / Tell me what you see / I've just seen a face / Yesterday / Dizzy Miss Lizzy. *(UK re-lp+c.Jul71 33. re-iss.Nov88 on 'EMI') (cd-iss.Apr87 hit UK 61)*

Sep 65. (7") **YESTERDAY. / ACT NATURALLY** - 1

Dec 65. (7") **DAY TRIPPER. / WE CAN WORK IT OUT** 1 5 1
(UK re-iss.Dec85) (re-iss.cd-s.1989)

Dec 65. (lp) **RUBBER SOUL** 1 1
– Drive my car / Norwegian wood (this bird has flown) / You won't see me / Nowhere man / Think for yourself / The word / Michelle / What goes on? / Girl / I'm looking through you / In my life / Wait / If I needed someone / Run for your life. *(UK re-iss.Nov88 on 'EMI') (cd-iss.Apr87, hit UK 60) (c-iss.70's)*

Feb 66. (7") **NOWHERE MAN. / WHAT GOES ON** - 3 81

Jun 66. (7") **PAPERBACK WRITER. / RAIN** 1 1 23
(UK re-iss.Jun86) (re-iss.cd-s.1989)

Aug 66. (7") **YELLOW SUBMARINE. / ELEANOR RIGBY** 1 2 11
(UK re-iss.Aug86 hit 63) (re-iss.cd-s.1989)

Aug 66. (lp) **REVOLVER** 1 1
– Taxman / I love you to / I want to tell you / Eleanor Rigby / Here, there and everywhere / Good day sunshine / For no one / Got to get you into my life / I'm only sleeping / She said she said / And your bird can sing / Doctor Robert / Tomorrow never knows / Yellow submarine. *(UK re-iss.Nov88 on 'EMI') (cd-iss.Apr87, hit UK 55) (c-iss.70's)*

Feb 67. (7") **PENNY LANE. / STRAWBERRY FIELDS FOREVER** 2 1 8
(UK re-iss.Feb87 hit 65) (re-iss.cd-s.1989)

Jun 67. (lp) **SGT. PEPPER'S LONELY HEARTS CLUB BAND** 1 1
– Sgt.Pepper's lonely hearts club band / With a little help from my friends / Lucy in the sky with diamonds / Getting better / Fixing a hole / She's leaving home / Being for the benefit of Mr.Kite / Within you without you / When I'm sixty-four / Lovely Rita / Good morning, good morning / Sgt.Pepper's lonely hearts club band (reprise) / A day in the life. *(re-iss.Nov'88 on 'EMI') (cd-iss.Jun87, hit UK 3) (re-iss.Jun92 hit UK No.6) (pic-lp.1979) (c-iss.70's)*

Jul 67. (7") **ALL YOU NEED IS LOVE. / BABY YOU'RE A RICH MAN** 1 1 34
(UK re-iss.Jul87 hit 47) (re-iss.cd-s.1989)

Nov 67. (7") **HELLO GOODBYE. / I AM THE WALRUS** 1 1 56
(UK re-iss.Nov87 hit 63) (re-iss.cd-s.1989)

Dec 67. (d7"ep) **MAGICAL MYSTERY TOUR** 2 -
– Magical mystery tour / Your mother should know / Flying / Fool on the hill / Blue Jay way / I am the walrus.

Dec 67. (lp) **MAGICAL MYSTERY TOUR (Soundtrack)** 31 1
– (above UK-ep, plus 1967 singles) *(UK-iss.Oct76, cd-iss.Sep87, hit UK 52)*

Mar 68. (7") **LADY MADONNA. / THE INNER LIGHT** 1 4 96
(UK re-iss.Mar88 hit 67) (re-iss.cd-s.1989)

Apple Apple

Aug 68. (7") **HEY JUDE. / REVOLUTION** 1 1 12
(UK re-iss.Aug88 hit 52) (re-iss.cd-s.1989)

Nov 68. (d-lp) **THE BEATLES (White Album)** 1 1
– Back in the U.S.S.R / Dear Prudence / Glass onion / Ob-la-di-ob-la-da / Wild honey pie / The continuing story of Bungalow Bill / While my guitar gently weeps / Happiness is a warm gun / Martha my dear / I'm so tired / Blackbird / Piggies / Rocky raccoon / Don't pass me by / Why don't we do it in the road / I will / Julia / Birthday / Yer blues / Mother nature's son / Everybody's got something to hide except me and my monkey / Sexy Sadie / Long long long / Revolution 1 / Honey pie / Savoy truffle / Cry baby cry / Revolution 9 / Good night. *(re-white-lp.Sep78) (cd-iss.Aug87 hit 18. (re-iss.Nov88 on 'EMI')*

Jan 69. (lp) **YELLOW SUBMARINE (Soundtrack)** 4 2
– Yellow submarine / Only a northern song / All together now / Hey bulldog / It's all too much / All you need is love / Pepperland / Sea of time / Sea of holes / Sea of monsters / March of the Meanies / Pepperland laid waste / Yellow submarine in Pepperland. (with GEORGE MARTIN ORCHESTRA) *(UK re-iss.+cd.Aug87, hit UK 60) (re-iss.Nov88 on 'EMI')*

Apr 69. (7") **GET BACK. / DON'T LET ME DOWN** 1 1 35

— (above credits **BILLY PRESTON** ;on organ) (UK re-iss.Apr89 hit 74) (re-iss.cd-s.1989)

May 69. (7") **THE BALLAD OF JOHN AND YOKO. / OLD BROWN SHOE** 1 8
(UK re-iss.May89) (re-iss.cd-s.1989)

Sep 69. (lp) **ABBEY ROAD** 1 1
– Come together / Maxwell's silver hammer / Something / Oh darling / Octopus's garden / I want you (she's so heavy) / Here comes the sun / Because / You never gave me your money / Sun king / Mean Mr.Mustard / Polythene Pam / She came in through the bathroom window / Golden slumbers / Carry that weight / The end / Her majesty. *(UK re-iss.Oct87 hit 30. (re-iss.Nov88 on 'EMI')*

Oct 69. (7") **SOMETHING. / COME TOGETHER** 4 3 1
(UK re-iss.Oct89) (re-iss.cd-s.1989)

Mar 70. (7") **LET IT BE. / YOU KNOW MY NAME (LOOK UP MY NUMBER)** 2 1
(UK re-iss.Mar90) (re-iss.cd-s.1989)

May 70. (lp)(c) **LET IT BE** 1 1
– Two of us / Dig a pony / Across the universe / I me mine / Dig it / Let it be / Maggie Mae / I've got a feeling / One after 909 / The long and winding road / For you blue / Get back. *(re-iss.Nov88 on 'EMI') (cd-iss.Oct87 hit 50.)*

May 70. (7") **THE LONG AND WINDING ROAD. / FOR YOU BLUE** - 1

— Officially disbanded April 1970. All 4 had released, or were due to release, own albums. See **Paul McCARTNEY ⇒ , John LENNON ⇒ , George HARRISON ⇒ , Ringo STARR ⇒ .**

– compilations, others, etc. –

(TONY SHERIDAN & THE BEATLES)

Jan 64. Polydor; (7") **SWEET GEORGIA BROWN. / NOBODY'S CHILD** -

Mar 64. M.G.M.; (7") **WHY. / CRY FOR A SHADOW** - 88

May 64. Polydor; (7") **AIN'T SHE SWEET. / IF YOU LOVE ME BABY** 29 -

Jun 64. Polydor; (lp) **THE BEATLES FIRST** -
(re-iss.Jun71 as THE EARLY YEARS on 'Contour')(re-iss. as 'THE FIRST ALBUM' cd+c May93 on 'Spectrum', credited to TONY SHERIDAN & THE BEATLES)

Jun 64. Atco; (7") **SWEET GEORGIA BROWN. / TAKE OUT SOME INSURANCE ON ME BABY** -

Jul 64. M.G.M.; (7") **AIN'T SHE SWEET. / NOBODY'S CHILD** - 19

(BEATLES)

Mar 64. Tollie; (7") **TWIST AND SHOUT. / THERE'S A PLACE** - 2 74

Apr 64. Vee Jay; (7") **DO YOU WANT TO KNOW A SECRET. / THANK YOU GIRL** - 2 35

May 64. Swan; (7") **SIE LIEBT DICH. / I'LL GET YOU** - 97

Jul 63. Parlophone; (7"ep) **TWIST AND SHOUT** 2 -
– Twist and shout / A taste of honey / Do you want to know a secret / There's a place.

Sep 63. Parlophone; (7"ep) **THE BEATLES HITS** 14 -
– From me to you / Thank you girl / Please please me / Love me do.

Nov 63. Parlophone; (7"ep) **THE BEATLES (No.1)** 19 -
– I saw her standing there / Misery / Chains / Anna (go to him).

Feb 64. Parlophone; (7"ep) **ALL MY LOVING** 12 -
– All my loving / Ask me why / Money / P.S. I love you.

Jun 64. Parlophone; (7"ep) **LONG TALL SALLY** 14 -
– Long tall Sally / I call your name / Slow down / Matchbox.

Jun 64. Capitol; (7"ep) **FOUR BY THE BEATLES** - 92
– All my loving / This boy / Roll over Beethoven / Please Mr.Postman.

Aug 64. Capitol; (lp) **SOMETHING NEW** [-] [2]
Nov 64. Parlophone; (7"ep) **EXTRACTS FROM THE FILM 'A HARD DAY'S NIGHT'** [34] [-]
– I should have known better / If I fell / Tell me why / And I love her.
Dec 64. Parlophone; (7"ep) **EXTRACTS FROM THE FILM 'A HARD DAY'S NIGHT' 2** [ ] [-]
– Anytime at all / I'll cry instead / Things we said today / When I get home.
Dec 64. Capitol; (lp) **THE BEATLES' STORY (narrative)** [-] [7]
Feb 65. Capitol; (7"ep) **4-BY THE BEATLES** [-] [ ]
– Honey don't / I'm a loser / Mr.Moonlight / Everybody's trying to be my baby.
Apr 65. Parlophone; (7"ep) **BEATLES FOR SALE** [ ] [-]
– No reply / I'm a loser / Rock and roll music / Eight days a week.
Jun 65. Parlophone; (7"ep) **BEATLES FOR SALE No.2** [ ] [-]
– I'll follow the sun / Baby's in black / Words of love / I don't want to spoil the party.
Dec 65. Parlophone; (7"ep) **THE BEATLES MILLION SELLERS** [ ] [-]
– She loves you / Can't buy me love / I feel fine / I want to hold your hand.
Mar 66. Parlophone; (7"ep) **YESTERDAY** [ ] [-]
– Yesterday / Act naturally / You like me too much / It's only love.
Jul 66. Capitol; (lp) **YESTERDAY . . . AND TODAY** [-] [1]
Dec 66. Parlophone; (lp) **A COLLECTION OF BEATLES OLDIES** [7] [-]
(re-iss.+c.Oct83 on 'Fame')
Jul 67. Parlophone; (7"ep) **NOWHERE MAN** [ ] [-]
– Nowhere man / Drive my car / Michelle / You won't see me.
Mar 76. Parlophone; (7") **YESTERDAY. / I SHOULD HAVE KNOWN BETTER** [8] [-]
Below on 'Parlophone' UK/ 'Capitol' US unless otherwise mentioned.
Jun 76. (lp)(c) **ROCK AND ROLL MUSIC** [11] [2]
(UK re-iss.Nov80 as . . . VOL.1 / . . . VOL.2 both on 'MfP')
Jun 76. (7") **GOT TO GET YOU INTO MY LIFE. / HELTER SKELTER** [-] [7]
Jul 76. (7") **BACK IN THE U.S.S.R. / TWIST AND SHOUT** [19] [-]
Apr 77. (d-lp)(d-c) **LIVE AT THE STAR CLUB, HAMBURG, GERMANY 1962** [ ] [ ]
May 77. (lp)(c) **THE BEATLES AT THE HOLLYWOOD BOWL (live)** [1] [2]
(UK re-iss.Sep84 on 'MfP')
Dec 77. (d-lp)(d-c) **LOVE SONGS** [7] [24]
1977. (7") **OB-LA-DI, OB-LA-DA. / JULIA** [-] [ ]
Sep 78. (7") **SGT.PEPPER'S LONELY HEARTS CLUB BAND-WITH A LITTLE HELP FROM MY FRIENDS. / A DAY IN THE LIFE** [63] [71]
Nov 78. (14xlp-box) **THE BEATLES COLLECTION** [ ] [ ]
– (all original albums boxed)
Oct 79. (lp)(c) **RARITIES** [71] [21] Apr 80
Nov 80. (lp)(c) **BEATLES BALLADS** [17] [ ]
Dec 81. (14x7"ep's) **THE BEATLES EP COLLECTION** [ ] [ ]
– (all ep's above plus new SHE'S A WOMAN)
– She's a woman / Baby you're a rich man / This boy / The inner light.
Apr 82. (lp)(c) **REEL MUSIC** [ ] [19]
May 82. (7") **BEATLES MOVIE MEDLEY./ I'M HAPY UST TO DANCE WITH YOU** [10] [12]
– ('A'medley); Magical Mystery Tour – All You Need Is Love – You've Got To Hide Your Love Away – I Should Have Known Better – A Hard Day's Night – Ticket To Ride – Get Back.
Oct 82. (d-lp)(d-c) **20 GREATEST HITS** [10] [50]
Oct 88. (lp)(c)(cd-box-set) **THE ULTIMATE BOX SET** [ ] [ ]
Jun 92. (cd-ep x14-box) **COMPACT DISC EP'S** [ ] [-]
Mar 70. Apple; (lp)(c) **HEY JUDE** [-] [2]
(UK-iss.May79 on 'Parlophone')
Apr 73. Apple; (d-lp)(d-c) **THE BEATLES 1962-1966** [3] [3]
– Love me do / Please please me / She loves you / From me to you / She loves you / I want to hold your hand / All my loving / Can't buy me love / A hard day's night / And I love her / Eight days a week / I feel fine / Ticket to ride / Yesterday / Help! / You've got to hide your love away / We can work it out / Day tripper / Drive my car / Norwegian wood (this bird has flown) / Nowhere man / Michelle / In my life / Girl / Paperback writer / Eleanor Rigby / Yellow submarine. *(red-lp's iss.Sep78) (d-cd-iss.Jul91) (re-iss.d-cd Sep93 on 'Apple-Parlophone', hit UK No.3) (re-iss.red vinyl Feb94)*
Apr 73. Apple; (d-lp)(d-c) **THE BEATLES 1967-1970** [2] [1]
– Strawberry fields forever / Penny lane / Sgt. Pepper's lonely hearts club band / With a little help from my friends / Lucy in the sky with diamonds / A day in the life / All you need is love / I am the Walrus / Hello, goodbye / The fool on the hill / Magical mystery tour / Lady Madonna / Hey Jude / Revolution / Back in the U.S.S.R / While my guitar gently weeps / Ob-la-di, ob-la-da / Get back / Don't let me down / The ballad of John and Yoko / Old brown shoe / Here comes the sun / Come together / Something / Octopus's Garden / Let it be / Across the universe / The long and winding road. *(blue-lp's iss.Sep78) (d-cd-iss.Jul91) (re-iss.d-cd Sep93 on 'Apple-Parlophone', hit UK No.4) (re-iss.blue vinyl Feb94)*
Feb 88. E.M.I./ US= Capitol; (d-lp)(c)(cd) **PAST MASTERS VOL.1** [49] [ ]
Feb 88. E.M.I./ US= Capitol; (d-lp)(c)(cd) **PAST MASTERS VOL.2** [46] [ ]
Aug 91. E.M.I.; (c-s x all) **THE SINGLES** [ ] [-]
– (all 7"singles boxed)
Aug 76. Polydor; (d-lp)(c) **THE BEATLES TAPES (interviews)** [45] [-]
Jul 81. Phoenix; (lp)(c) **EARLY MUSIC VOL.1** [ ] [-]
Jul 81. Phoenix; (lp)(c) **EARLY MUSIC VOL.2** [ ] [-]
Feb 82. Phoenix; (lp)(c) **RARE BEATLES** [ ] [-]
Aug 81. A.F.E.; (d-lp)(c) **HISTORIC BEATLES** [ ] [-]
Sep 82. A.F.E.; (lp) **THE COMPLETE SILVER BEATLES** [ ] [-]
Sep 83. A.F.E.; (lp) **COMETS** [ ] [-]
Jul 82. Charly; (10"lp) **THE SAVAGE YOUNG BEATLES** [ ] [-]
(re-iss.as THE BEATLES FEATURING TONY SHERIDAN, HAMBURG on 'Topline, cd-iss. Feb 93 on 'Charly')
Nov 83. Berkeley; (lp) **AUDITION TAPES** [ ] [-]
Dec 83. Breakaway; (lp) **HAMBURG TAPES VOL.1** [ ] [-]
Dec 83. Breakaway; (lp) **HAMBURG TAPES VOL.2** [ ] [-]
Dec 83. Breakaway; (lp) **HAMBURG TAPES VOL.3** [ ] [-]
Apr 86. Showcase; (lp)(c) **LIVE BEATLES (live)** [ ] [-]
Oct 87. Topline; (lp)(c)(cd) **THE DECCA SESSIONS (1/1/62)** [ ] [-]
Jun 92. Columbia; (cd) **ROCKIN' AT THE STAR-CLUB (live)** [ ] [-]
Dec 94. Apple; (d-cd)(d-c)(d-lp) **LIVE AT THE BBC (live)** [1] [3]
– Beatle greetings / From us to you / Riding on a bus / I got a woman / Too much monkey business / Keep your hands off my baby / I'll be on my way / Young blood / A shot of rhythm and blues / Sure to fall (in love with you) / Some other guy / Thank you girl / Sha la la la la! / Baby it's you / That's all right (mama) / Carol / Soldier of love / A little rhyme / Clarabella / I'm gonna sit right down and cry (over you) / Crying, waiting, hoping / Dear Wack! / You really got a hold on me / To know her is to love her / A taste of honey / Long tall Sally / I saw her standing there / The honeymoon song / Johnny B Goode / Memphis, Tennessee / Lucille / Can't buy me love / From Fluff to you / Till there was you // Crinsk Dee night / A hard day's night / Have a banana! / I wanna be your man / Just a rumour / Roll over Beethoven / All my loving / Things we said today / She's a woman / Sweet little sixteen / 1882! / Lonesome tears in my eyes / Nothin' shakin' / The hippy hippy shake / Glad all over / I just don't understand / So how come.(no one loves me) / I feel fine / I'm a loser / Everybody's trying to be my baby / Rock and roll music / Ticket to ride / Dizzy Miss Lizzy / Medley: Kansas City – Hey! hey! hey! hey! / Set fire to that lot! / Matchbox / I forgot to remember to forget / Love these Goon shows! / I got to find my baby / Ooh! my soul / Ooh! my arms / Don't ever change / Slow down / Honey don't / Love me do.
Mar 95. Apple; (cd-ep) **BABY IT'S YOU / I'LL FOLLOW THE SUN / DEVIL IN HER HEART / BOYS** [7] [67]
Nov 95. Apple; (d-cd)(d-c)(t-lp) **ANTHOLOGY 1** [2] [1]
– Free as a bird / Speech (by JOHN LENNON) / That'll be the day / In spite of all the danger / Sometimes I'd borrow (speech by PAUL McCARTNEY) / Hallelujah I love her so / You'll be mine / Cayenne / First of all (speech by PAUL) / My Bonnie (w/ TONY SHERIDAN) / Ain't she sweet / Cry for a shadow / Brian was a beautiful guy (speech by JOHN) / Secured them an audition (speech by BRIAN EPSTEIN) / Searchin' / Three cool cats / The Sheik of Araby / Like dreamers do / Hello little girl / Well, the recording test (speech by BRIAN) / Besame mucho / Love me do / How do you do it? / Please please me / One after 909 (sequence) / One after 909 (complete) / Lend me your comb / I'll get you / We were performers (speech by JOHN) / I saw her standing there / From me to you / Money (that's what I want) / You really got a hold on me / Roll over Beethoven / She loves you / Till there was you (music man) / Twist and shout / This boy / I want to hold your hand / Boys, what I was thinking (speech by The BEATLES and MORECAMBE & WISE) / Moonlightbay (w/ MORECAMBE & WISE) / Can't buy me love / All my loving / You can't do that / And I love her / A hard day's night / I wanna be your man / Long tall Sally / Boys / Shout / I'll be back (take 2) / I'll be back (take 3) / You know what to do / No reply (demo) / Mr.Moonlight / Leave my kitten alone / No reply / Eight days a week (sequence) / Eight days a week (complete) / Kansas City – hey, hey, hey.
— (below single was recently re-recorded from JOHN LENNON's 1977 cut)
Dec 95. Apple; (7")(c-s) **FREE AS A BIRD. / CHRISTMAS TIME (IS HERE AGAIN)** [2] [ ]
(cd-s+=) – I saw her standing there (take 9) / This boy (take 13).

BEATNIGS
(see under ⇒ DISPOSABLE HEROES OF HIPHOPRISY)

BEAU BRUMMELS

Formed: Bay Area, San Francisco, USA . . . mid'64. They soon signed to Tom Donahue's 'Autumn', and with help from producer SLY STONE, had US hit with 'LAUGH LAUGH'. They scored with a few more major hits, but were soon forgotten by 1966. • **Style:** Dubbed as the American answer to the British invasion, their sound was close to The BEATLES or The SEARCHERS. With the advent The BYRDS whose 12-string guitar style was not too dissimilar, they quickly moved on to more psychedelic rock. • **Song-writers:** Group compositions, except MR.TAMBOURINE MAN + ONE TOO MANY MORNINGS (Bob Dylan) / YOU'VE GOT TO HIDE YOUR LOVE AWAY + YESTERDAY (Beatles) / LOUIE LOUIE (Kingsmen) / HOME-WARD BOUND (Simon & Garfunkel) / THESE BOOTS ARE MADE FOR WALKING (Nancy Sinatra) / PLAY WITH FIRE (Rolling Stones) / MON-DAY, MONDAY (Mamas & The Papas) / HANG ON SLOOPY (McCoys) / MRS.BROWN YOU'VE A LOVELY DAUGHTER (Herman's Hermits) / WOMAN (Peter & Gordon) / etc. • **Trivia:** ELLIOTT later sessioned for RANDY NEWMAN, EVERLY BROTHERS, etc.

Recommended: AUTUMN IN SAN FRANCISCO (*7)

RON ELLIOTT (b.21 Oct'43, Haddsberg, California) – vocals, guitar / **SAL VALENTINO** (b.SAL SPAMINATO, 8 Sep'42) – vocals / **RON MEAGHER** (b. 2 Oct'41) – bass / **JOHN PETERSON** (b. 8 Jan'42) – drums

Pye Inter. / Autumn
Feb 65. (7") **LAUGH, LAUGH. / STILL IN LOVE WITH YOU BABY** [ ] [15] Dec64
May 65. (7") **JUST A LITTLE. / THEY'LL MAKE YOU CRY** [ ] [9] Mar65
Jun 65. (lp) **INTRODUCING THE BEAU BRUMMELS** [ ] [24] May65
– Laugh, laugh / Still in love with you baby / Just a little / Just wait and see / Oh lonesome me / Ain't that loving you baby / Stick like glue / They'll make you cry / That's if you want me to / I want more loving / I would be happy / Not too long ago.
Sep 65. (7") **YOU TELL ME WHY. / I WANT YOU** [ ] [38] Jun65
Nov 65. (7") **DON'T TALK TO STRANGERS. / IN GOOD TIME** [ ] [52] Sep65
Jan 66. (7") **GOOD TIME MUSIC. / SAD LITTLE GIRL** [ ] [97] Nov65
Jan 66. (lp) **BEAU BRUMMELS VOL.2** [-] [ ]
– You tell me why / I want you / Doesn't matter / That's alright / Sometime at night / Can it be / Sad little girl / Woman / Don't talk to strangers / I've never known / When it comes to your love / In good time.
not issued / Warners
May 66. (7") **ONE TOO MANY MORNINGS. / SHE REIGNS** [-] [95]
Jul 66. (lp) **BEAU BRUMMELS '66** [-] [ ]
– You've got to hide your love away / Mr.Tambourine man / Louie Louie / Home-ward bound / These boots are made for walking / Yesterday / Bang bang / Hang on Sloopy / Play with fire / Woman / Mrs.Brown you've got a lovely daughter / Monday, Monday.
1966. (7") **FINE WITH ME. / HERE WE ARE AGAIN** [-] [ ]
— **ELLIOTT, VALENTINO + MEAGHER** were now joined by session man **VAN DYKE**

PARKS – keyboards. PETERSON later joined HARPERS BIZARRE.

Oct 67. (lp) **TRIANGLE** [-] [ ]
– Are you happy? / Only dreaming now / Painter of women / Keeper of time / It won't get better / Nine pound hammer / Magic hollow / And I've seen her / Triangle / Wolf of velvet fortune / Old Kentucky home.

1967. (7") **DON'T MAKE PROMISES. / TWO DAYS 'TIL TOMORROW** [-] [ ]

1967. (7") **MAGIC HOLLOW. / LOWER LEVEL** [-] [ ]

1968. (7") **ARE YOU HAPPY. / LIFT ME** [-] [ ]

— now duo (**ELLIOTT + VALENTIONO) + sessioners KENNY BUTTREY** – drums / **JERRY REED** – guitar / **DAVID BRIGGS** – keyboards / **NORMAN PUTTNAM** – bass

1968. (lp) **BRADLEY'S BARN** [-] [ ]
– Turn around / Added attraction / Deep water / Long walking down to misery / Little bird / Cherokee girl / I'm a sleeper / The loneliest man in town / Love can fall a long way down / Jessica / Bless you California. *(re-iss.Apr85 on 'Edsel')*

1968. (7") **I'M A SLEEPER. / LONG WALKING DOWN TO MISERY** [-] [ ]

1968. (7") **CHEROKEE GIRL. / DEEP WATER** [-] [ ]

— Disbanded Dec'68

RON ELLIOTT

not iss. | Warners

1970. (lp) **THE CANDLESTICKMAKER** [-] [ ]
– Molly in the middle / Lazy day / All time green / To the city, to the sea / Deep river runs blue / The candlestickmaker suite: Dark into down – Questions.

— He later joined PAN who released self-named album in 1973 on 'Columbia'.

— SAL VALENTINO formed STONEGROUND in 1971. They released 3 albums on 'Warners'.

BEAU BRUMMELS

originals with **DAN LEVITT** – guitar / **MARK JORDAN** – piano / etc

Warners | Warners

Apr 75. (lp)(c) **THE BEAU BRUMMELS** [ ] [ ]
– First in line / Goldrush / Today by day / Tennessee walker / Gate of hearts / Wolf / Down to the bottom / You tell me why / Singing cowboy / The lonely side.

1975. (7") **DOWN TO THE BOTTOM. / YOU TELL ME WHY** [-] [ ]

— Disbanded again mid'75.

– compilations, others, etc. –

not issued | Vault

1967. (lp) **THE BEST OF THE BEAU BRUMMELS** [-] [ ]

1968. (lp) **VOL.44** [-] [ ]

not issued | JAS

1975. (lp) **THE ORIGINAL HITS OF . . . 1964** [-] [ ]

not issued | Rhino

1981. (lp) **THE BEST OF THE BEAU BRUMMELS 1964-68** [-] [ ]

Edsel | not issued

Jul 85. (lp) **AUTUMN IN SAN FRANCISCO** [ ] [-]
– Laugh, laugh / Just a little / You tell me why / Don't talk to strangers / In good time / Sad little girl / Still in love with you baby / Stick like glue / That's if you want me to / Can it be / When it comes to your love / Gentle wanderin' ways / I grow old / Lonely man / She sends me. *(cd-iss.1990's)*

BEAUTIFUL SOUTH

Formed: Hull, England . . . early 1989 by HEATON, HEMMINGWAY and ROTHERAY. They stuck to 'Go! Discs' contract, which the former two had been with in the HOUSEMARTINS. Their debut single 'SONG FOR WHOEVER' climbed to UK No.2, and was pursued by several more hits during the next couple of years. • **Style:** Intelligent romantic ballads, that featured trade-off vocals from HEATON and CORRIGAN. • **Songwriters:** HEATON and ROTHERAY except LOVE WARS (Womack & Womack) / EVERYBODY'S TALKIN' (Fred Neil). • **Trivia:** STEED was ex-HOUSEMARTINS roadie mid-80's.

Recommended: CARRY ON UP THE CHARTS (*8).

PAUL HEATON – guitar, vocals / **DAVE HEMMINGWAY** – keyboards (both ex-HOUSEMARTINS) / **DAVID ROTHERAY** – vocals, guitar / **SEAN WELCH** – bass / **DAVID STEED** – drums

Go! Discs | Elektra

May 89. (7")(c-s) **SONG FOR WHOEVER. / STRAIGHT IN AT 37** [2] [ ]
(12"+=) – You and your big ideas.

added **BRIANNA CORRIGAN** – vocals (ex-ANTHILL RUNAWAYS) She was to join full-time in 1990.

Sep 89. (7")(c-s) **YOU KEEP IT ALL IN. / I LOVE YOU (BUT YOU'RE BORING)** [8] [ ]
(12"+=)(cd-s+=) – You can't just smile it away / ('A'version).

Oct 89. (lp)(c)(cd) **WELCOME TO THE BEAUTIFUL SOUTH** [2] [ ]
– Song for whoever / Have you ever been away? / From under the covers / I'll sail this ship alone / Girlfriend / You keep it all in / Woman in the wall / Oh Blackpool / Love is . . . / I love you (but you're boring). *(cd+=)* – Straight in at 37.

Nov 89. (7")(c-s) **I'LL SAIL THIS SHIP ALONE. / BUT TILL THEN** [31] [ ]
(12"+=)(cd-s+=) – ('A'orchestral version).

Sep 90. (7")(c-s) **A LITTLE TIME. / IN OTHER WORDS I HATE YOU** [1] [ ]
(12"+=)(cd-s+=) – What you see is what you are.

Oct 90. (cd)(c)(lp) **CHOKE** [2] [ ]
– Tonight I fancy myself / My book / Let love speak up itself / Should've kept my eyes shut / I've come for my award / Lips / I think the answer's yes / A little time / Mother's pride / I hate you (but you're interesting) / The rising of Grafton Street. *(cd+=)* – What you see is what you are. *(re-iss.cd Apr93)*

Nov 90. (7")(c-s) **MY BOOK. / BIG BEAUTIFUL SOUTH** [8] [ ]
(12"+=)(cd-s+=) – Bigger doesn't mean better / Speak to me.

Mar 91. (7")(c-s) **LET LOVE SPEAK UP ITSELF. / LOVE WARS** [51] [ ]
(12"+=)(cd-s+=) – Danielle Steele / Headbutting husband.

Go! Discs | Chameleon

Jan 92. (7")(c-s) **OLD RED EYES IS BACK. / FLEET STREET B.C.** [22] [ ]
(12"+=)(cd-s+=) – Diamonds.

Mar 92. (7")(c-s) **WE ARE EACH OTHER. / HIS TIME RAN OUT** [30] [ ]
(12"+=)(cd-s+=) – I started a joke.

Mar 92. (cd)(c)(lp) **0898** [4] [ ]
– Old red eyes is back / We are each other / The rocking chair / We'll deal with you later / Domino man / 36D / Here it is again / Something that you said / I'm your No.1 fan / Bell bottomed tear / You play glockenspiel / I'll play drums / When I'm 84.

Jun 92. (7")(c-s) **BELL BOTTOMED TEAR. / A THOUSAND LIES / THEY USED TO WEAR BLACK** [16] [ ]
(cd-s+=) – You should be dancing (live) / Woman in the wall (live).

Sep 92. (7")(c-s) **36D. / THROWING HIS SONG AWAY / TREVOR YOU'RE BIZARRE** [46] [ ]
(cd-s) – ('A'live) / From under the covers (live) / You keep it all in (live).

— **JACQUELINE ABBOTT** (b.1974) – vocals repl. CORRIGAN who went solo

Feb 94. (7")(c-s) **GOOD AS GOLD. / LOVE ADJOURNED** [23] [ ]
(cd-s+=) – Mini-correct.
(cd-s) – ('A'side) / Frank and Delores / One man's rubbish.

Mar 94. (cd)(c)(lp) **MIAOW** [6] [ ]
– Hold on to what / Good as gold (stupid as muck) / Especially for you / Everybody's talkin' / Prettiest eyes / Worthless lie / Hooligans don't fall in love / Hidden jukebox / Hole me close (underground) / Tattoo / Mini correct / Poppy.

May 94. (7")(c-s)(cd-s) **EVERYBODY'S TALKIN'. / A WAY WITH THE BLUES / LET LOVE SPEAK UP ITSELF** [12] [ ]
(cd-s) – ('A'side) / Nearer to God / A piece of sky.

Aug 94. (12")(c-s)(cd-s) **PRETTIEST EYES. / THE BEST WE CAN / SIZE** [37] [ ]
(cd-s) – ('A'side) / Why can't I / Missing her now.

Oct 94. (cd-s) **ONE LAST LOVE SONG. / RIGHT MAN FOR THE JOB** [14] [ ]
(7"+=)(cd-s+=) – Java.
(cd-s) – ('A'side) / Mr.Obsession / You're only jealous.

Nov 94. (cd)(c)(lp) **CARRY ON UP THE CHARTS – THE BEST OF THE BEAUTIFUL SOUTH** (compilation) [1] [ ]
– Song for whoever / You keep it all in / I'll sail this ship alone / A little time / My book / Let love speak up itself / Old red eyes is back / We are each other / Bell bottomed tear / 36D / Good as gold (stupid as mud) / Everybody's talkin' / Prettiest eyes / One last love song.

Nov 95. (7")(c-s)(cd-s) **PRETENDERS TO THE THRONE. / VIRGIN / A LONG DAY IN THE FIELD** [18] [ ]

BE-BOP DELUXE (see under ⇒ NELSON, Bill)

BECK

Born: 1971, Los Angeles, USA. He moved to New York in the late 80's and was initially signed to indie 'Bongload', until David 'Geffen' came along in '93. He had released an album (ONE FOOT IN THE GRAVE) in the States with CALVIN JOHNSON of The BEAT HAPPENING. Early the next year 'LOSER' cracked the US Top 20 and paved the way for debut album 'MELLOW GOLD'. • **Style:** Laid back controversial soft-grunge rock experimentalist, with one-man band explorations into other territories (samplers /synths /psychedelia). • **Songwriters:** BECK writes some with KARL STEPHENSON. 'LOSER' used a sample of DR.JOHN's 'I Walk On Guilded Splinters'. • **Trivia:** Also featured a track 'BOGUSFLOW' on 'Geffen Rarities Vol.1'.

Recommended: MELLOW GOLD (*7)

BECK – vocals, acoustic guitar with guests **RACHEL HADEN** – drums, vocals / **ANNA WARONKER** – bass, vocals / **PETRA HADEN** – violin, vocals / **MIKE BOITO** – organ / **DAVID HARTE** – drums / **ROB ZABRECKY** – bass

not issued | Bongload

1993. (12") **LOSER. /** [-] [ ]

1993. (7") **STEVE THREW UP. /** [-] [ ]
(both above UK-iss Jan95)

not issued | Fingerpaint

1993. (cd) **A WESTERN HARVEST FIELD BY MOONLIGHT** [-] [ ]

Geffen | Geffen

Feb 94. (7")(c-s) **LOSER. / ALCOHOL / FUME** [15] [10]
(cd-s) – ('A'side) / Totally confused / Corvette bumper / MTV makes me want to smoke crack.

Mar 94. (cd)(c) **MELLOW GOLD** [41] [13]
– Loser / Pay no mind (snoozer) / Fuckin with my head (mountain dew rock) / Whiskeyclone, Hotel City 1997 / Soul suckin jerk / Truckdrivin neighbors downstairs (yellow sweat) / Sweet sunshine / Beercan / Steal my body home / Nitemare hippy girl / Motherfuker / Blackhole. (hidden track cd+=) – Analog odyssey.

May 94. (7")(c-s) **PAY NO MIND (SNOOZER). / SPECIAL PEOPLE** [ ] [ ]
(12"+=)(cd-s+=) – Trouble all my days / Supergold (sunchild).

not issued | Flipside

1994. (cd) **STEREOPATHETIC SOUL MANURE** [-] [ ]
–
(UK-iss.Dec95)

K | K

Nov 95. (cd) **ONE FOOT IN THE GRAVE** [ ] [ ]
–

Jeff BECK

Born: 24 Jun'44, London, England. He began solo career early 1967 after replacing the great ERIC CLAPTON in The YARDBIRDS (Mar65). His first 3 singles all made the UK Top 30, and he soon formed own credited band. It featured ROD STEWART, and gave him and BECK first in-roads into US charts with 1968 lp 'TRUTH'. • **Style:** Mickie Most, his producer, was responsible for early use of pop material. All this was disregarded when BECK formed his own heavy rock group in the late 60's. With ROD STEWART taking most vocal chores, they were heavy fused with blues. Veered disappointingly into jazz-rock market on 1975's 'BLOW BY BLOW'. • **Songwriters:** BECK with covers being; HI HO SILVER LINING (Scott English & Larry Weiss) / TALLYMAN (Graham Gouldman) / ALL SHOOK UP + JAILHOUSE ROCK (Leiber – Stoller) / I'VE BEEN DRINKIN' (D.Tauber & J.Mercer) / SHAPES OF THINGS (Yardbirds) / I AIN'T SUPERSTITIOUS (Willie Dixon) / MORNING DEW (Tim Rose) / SUPERSTITIOUS + CAUSE WE'VE ENDED AS LOVERS (Stevie Wonder) / GREENSLEEVES (trad.) / OL' MAN RIVER ('Showboat' musical) / GOODBYE PORK PIE HAT (Charlie Mingus) / SHE'S A WOMAN (Beatles) / STAR CYCLE (Jan Hammer) / WILD THING (Troggs) / etc. • **Trivia:** Played guitar on 1990 JON BON JOVI album BLAZE OF GLORY. His song 'STAR CYCLE' (written by band members Hymas & Philips), became theme tune for 'The Tube'.

Recommended: ROUGH AND READY (*7) / THE BEST OF BECKOLOGY (*6)

JEFF BECK (solo) – vocals, lead guitar (ex-YARDBIRDS) with **JET HARRIS** – bass (ex-SHADOWS) / **VIV PRINCE** – drums (ex-PRETTY THINGS)

		Columbia	Epic
Mar 67.	(7") **HI HO SILVER LINING. / BECK'S BOLERO**	14	

— **RAY COOK** – drums repl. PRINCE

Jul 67.	(7") **TALLYMAN. / ROCK MY PLIMSOUL**	30	
Feb 68.	(7") **LOVE IS BLUE. / I'VE BEEN DRINKING**	23	

JEFF BECK GROUP

with **ROD STEWART** – vocals (also a solo artist, who sang on BECK's last 'B'side) / **RON WOOD** – bass (ex BIRDS) / **MICKY WALLER** (b. 6 Sep'44) – drums / **NICKY HOPKINS** – keyboards

Aug 68. (lp) **TRUTH** | | 15
– Shapes of things / Let me love you / Morning dew / You shook me / Ol' man river / Greensleeves / Rock my plimsoul / Beck's bolero / Blues de luxe / I ain't superstitious. *(re-iss.1985) (re-iss.Jun86 on 'Fame')*

— **TONY NEWMAN** – drums repl. WALLER

— (mid'69) The JEFF BECK GROUP teamed up with ⇒ DONOVAN, on their joint hit GOO GOO BARABAJAGAL (LOVE IS HOT). (see ⇒ DONOVAN)

Jul 69. (lp) **BECK-OLA** | 39 | 15
– All shook up / Spanish boots / Girl from Mill Valley / Jailhouse rock / Plynth (water down the drain) / Hangman's knee / Rice pudding. *(re-iss.+c Jul85)*

Sep 69. (7") **PLYNTH (WATER DOWN THE DRAIN). / HANGMAN'S KNEE** | |

— Split (Sep69) when ROD STEWART and RON WOOD joined The FACES.

JEFF BECK GROUP reformed (Apr71) with **JEFF BECK** – guitar (only) plus **BOBBY TENCH** – vocals / **MAX MIDDLETON** – keyboards / **CLIVE CHAPMAN** – bass / **COZY POWELL** – drums (ex-BIG BERTHA, ex-ACE KEFFORD STAND, ex-SORCERORS)

Epic | Epic

Oct 71. (lp)(c) **ROUGH AND READY** | | 46
– Got the feeling / Situation / Short business / Max's tune / I've been used / New ways – Train train / Jody. *(re-iss.Mar81 + Aug84) (quad-lp 1974)*

Jan 72. (7") **GOT THE FEELING. / SITUATION** | |

Jul 72. (lp)(c) **THE JEFF BECK GROUP** | | 19 May 72
– Ice cream cakes / Glad all over / I'll be staying here with you / Sugar cane / I can't give back the love I feel for you / Going down / I got to have a song / Highways / Definitely maybe. *(quad-lp 1974)*

— Broke-up when COZY POWELL went solo & joined BEDLAM. Later to RAINBOW, etc. TENCH joined STREETWALKERS then VAN MORRISON. **JEFF** formed supergroup

BECK, BOGERT & APPICE

with **TIM BOGERT** – bass, vocals / **CARMINE APPICE** – drums (both ex-VANILLA FUDGE, etc.) plus **DUANE HITCHINS** – keyboards / **JIMMY GREENSPOON** – piano / **DANNY HUTTON** – vox

Mar 73. (7") **BLACK CAT MOAN. / LIVIN' ALONE** | |

Apr 73. (lp)(c) **BECK, BOGERT & APPICE** | 28 | 12
– Black cat moan / Lady / Oh to love you / Superstition / Sweet sweet surrender / Why should I care / Love myself with you / Livin' alone / I'm so proud. *(re-iss.Sep84) (re-iss.+cd.Nov89 on 'Essential') (quad-lp 1974)*

This trio, also released widely available (JAP-import Nov74 d-lp) LIVE IN JAPAN

JEFF BECK

group reformed as instrumental line-up, **BECK + MIDDLETON / PHILIP CHEN** – bass / **RICHARD BAILEY** – drums.

Mar 75. (lp)(c) **BLOW BY BLOW** | | 4
– You know what I mean / She's a woman / Constipated duck / Air blower / Scatterbrain / Cause we've ended as lovers / Thelonius / Freeway jam / Diamond dust. *(re-iss.Sep83) (re-iss.May94) (re-iss.cd Nov95)*

May 75. (7") **SHE'S A WOMAN. / IT DOESN'T REALLY MATTER** | |

Jul 75. (7") **CONSTIPATED DUCK. / YOU KNOW WHAT I MEAN** | - |

— **JAN HAMMER** (b.1950, Prague, Czechoslavakia) – drums, synthesizer / **MICHAEL NARADA WALDEN** – keyboards, drums (both ex-MAHAVISHNU ORCHESTRA) / **WILBUR BASCOMBE** – bass (all 3 replaced CHEN)

Jul 76. (lp)(c) **WIRED** | 38 | 16 Jun 76
– Play with me / Goodbye pork pie hat / Sophie / Led boots / Head for backstage pass / Blue wind / Love is green / Come dancing. *(re-iss.Mar82) (cd-iss.1988)*

Aug 76. (7") **COME DANCING. / HEAD FOR BACKSTAGE PASS** | - |

JEFF BECK with The JAN HAMMER GROUP

(BECK, HAMMER)plus **TONY SMITH** – drums / **FERNANDO SAUNDERS** – bass / **STEVE KINDLER** – violin, synth.

Mar 77. (lp)(c) **LIVE (live)** | | 23
– Freeway jam / Earth (still our only home) / She's a woman / Full Moon boogie / Darkness / Earth in search of a sun / Scatterbrain / Blue wind. *(re-iss.Jun85)*

JEFF BECK

with **TONY HYMAS** – keys / **MO FOSTER** – bass / **SIMON PHILLIPS** – drums

Jul 80. (lp)(c) **THERE AND BACK** | 38 | 21
– Star cycle / Too much to lose / You never know / The pump / El Becko / The golden road / Space boogie / The final peace. *(re-iss.Aug84)*

Jul 80. (7") **THE FINAL PEACE. / SPACE BOOGIE** | | -

Aug 80. (7") **THE FINAL PEACE. / TOO MUCH TO LOSE** | - |

Feb 81. (d7") **THE FINAL PEACE. / SCATTERBRAIN/ / TOO MUCH TO LOSE. / LED BOOTS** | |

— Retired from studio for half a decade, before returning 1985 with **HAMMER, APPICE, HYMAS** and **JIMMY HALL** – vocals

1985. (7") **GET US ALL IN THE END. / YOU KNOW WE KNOW** | - |

Jun 85. (7") **PEOPLE GET READY** (as**"JEFF BECK with ROD STEWART) . / BACK ON THE STREET** | | 48
(12"+=) – You know we know. *(re-iss.Feb92, hit UK No.49)*

Aug 85. (lp)(c) **FLASH** | 83 | 39
– Ambitious / Gets us all in the end / Escape / People get ready / Stop, look and listen / Get workin' / Ecstasy / Night after night / You know, we know. *(re-iss.Jan89) (re-iss.cd Mar94 on 'Sony')*

Sep 85. (7") **GETS US ALL IN THE END. / YOU KNOW WE KNOW** | - |

Sep 85. (7") **STOP, LOOK AND LISTEN. / YOU KNOW WE KNOW** | | -
(12"+=) – ('A'remix).

Mar 86. (7")(12") **AMBITIOUS. / ESCAPE** | |

Jul 86. (7") **WILD THING. / GETS US ALL IN THE END** | |
(12"+=) – Nighthawk.

In 1987, JEFF BECK went to session with MICK JAGGER on his 2nd album.

JEFF BECK'S GUITAR SHOP

with TERRY BOZZIO and TONY HYMAS + still on 'Epic'.

Oct 89. (lp)(c)(cd) **JEFF BECK'S GUITAR SHOP** | | 49
– Guitar shop / Savoy / Behind the veil / Big block / Where were you / Stand on it / Day in the house / Two rivers / Sling shot.

Oct 89. (7") **GUITAR SHOP. / PEOPLE GET READY** | |
(12"+=)(cd-s+=) – Cause we've ended as lovers / Blue wind.

In 1990, sessioned for JON BON JOVI on his BLAZE OF GLORY album.

— In Sep 91 JEFF collaborated with BUDDY GUY on single 'MUSTANG SALLY' on 'Silvertone'.

JEFF BECK & THE BIG TOWN PLAYBOYS

with **MIKE SANCHEZ** – vocals, piano – / **IAN JENNINGS** – bass, vocals / **ADRIAN UTLEY** – rhythm guitar / **CLIVE DENVER** – drums, vocals / **LEO GREEN** – tenor sax / **NICK HUNT** – baritone sax.

Epic | Epic

Jun 93. (cd)(c)(lp) **CRAZY LEGS** | |
– Race with the devil / Cruisin' / Crazy legs / Double talkin' baby / Woman love / Lotta lovin' / Catman / Pink thunderbird / Baby blue / You better believe / Who slapped John? / Say mama / Red blue jeans and a pony tail / Five feet of lovin' / B-i-bickey-bi-bo-bo-go / Blues stay away from me / Pretty, pretty baby / Hold me, hug me, rock me

— Above was a tribute to GENE VINCENT & HIS BLUE CAPS.

- compilations, others, etc. -

Oct 72. R.A.K./ US= Epic; (7"m) **HI HO SILVER LINING. / BECK'S BOLERO / ROCK MY PLIMSOUL** | 14 |
(re-iss.Oct82 nearly hit UK 62)

Apr 73. R.A.K./ US= Epic; (7"m) **I'VE BEEN DRINKING. ("JEFF BECK and ROD STEWART") / MORNING DEW / GREENSLEEVES** | |

Nov 77. Embassy-CBS; (lp) **GOT THE FEELING** | |

Feb 83. Epic; (d-c) **BLOW BY BLOW / WIRED** | |

Feb 92. Epic; (3xcd-box) **BECKOLOGY** | |
(re-iss.3xcd+3xc May94)

Mar 92. Epic; (cd)(c) **THE BEST OF BECKOLOGY** | |
– Heart full of soul (YARDBIRDS) / Shapes of things (YARDBIRDS) / Over under sideways down (YARDBIRDS) / Hi ho silver lining / Tally man / Jailhouse rock / I've been drinking / I ain't superstitious / Superstition (BECK, BOGART & APPICE) / Cause we've ended as lovers / The pump / Star cycle (theme from 'The Tube') / People get ready (w / ROD STEWART) / Wild thing / Where were you (w /TERRY BOZZIO & TONY HYMAS) / Trouble in mind (TRIDENTS).

Mar 93. Epic; (3xcd-box) **FLASH / BLOW BY BLOW / THERE & BACK** | |

May 85. Fame-EMI; (lp)(c) **THE BEST OF JEFF BECK featuring ROD STEWART** | | -

Sep 88. E.M.I.; (cd) **LATE 60's WITH ROD STEWART** [ ] [-]
Feb 91. E.M.I.; (cd)(c) **TRUTH / BECK-OLA** [ ] [-]
May 89. That's Original; (d-lp)(d-cd) **JEFF BECK GROUP / ROUGH & READY** [ ] [-]
Oct 94. Charly; (cd) **SHAPES OF THINGS** [ ] [-]
Dec 95. MFP; (cd)(c) **THE BEST OF JEFF BECK** [ ] [-]

BECKIES (See under ⇒ LEFT BANKE)

BEEFEATERS (See under ⇒ BYRDS)

BEE GEES

Formed: By the GIBB brothers in Brisbane, Australia, where they had emigrated in 1958. Early in 1967 after recording some Aussie singles for 'Festival' records, they returned to Manchester, England, but learnt that their recent single SPICKS AND SPECKS had topped the chart in Australia. They stayed in UK to record for Robert Stigwood and 'Polydor'. Debut single 'NEW YORK MINING DISASTER 1941' hit UK & US Top 20 and set them on the road to stardom. They had a sticky patch throughout the early 70's, but with advent of new disco scene in 1975, had massive selling soundtrack double-lp 'SATURDAY NIGHT FEVER'. This re-established The BEE GEES as a top attraction, and they never again let go of massive appeal. • **Style:** Much parodied harmony-pop band, with initial influences The BEATLES, which was cast aside for disco mainstream pop as said. Inclusion in this book of rock was mainly due to their easy rock work in the late 60's and not so much their influence on many new disco groups of the 80's. • **Songwriters:** GIBB brothers. • **Miscellaneous:** Their younger brother ANDY was also mega-star in the US, but his addiction to cocaine probably led to his death on 10th Mar'88, aged 30. BARRY GIBB wrote and produced many songs for other artists such as DIANA ROSS, DIONNE WARWICK, BARBARA STREISAND etc. MAURICE was married to singing pop star LULU.

Recommended: THE BEST OF THE BEE GEES VOL.1 (*5)

BARRY GIBB (b. 1 Sep'47, Manchester, England) – vocals, guitar / **MAURICE GIBB** (b.22 Dec'49, Isle Of Man, nr.England) – vocals, bass / **ROBIN GIBB** (b.twin, as MAURICE) – vocals

Leedon / not issued

Mar 63. (7") **THE BATTLE OF THE BLUE AND GREY. / THE THREE KISSES OF LOVE** [-] [-] Aussie
Jun 63. (7") **TIMBER!. / TAKE HOLD OF THAT STAR** [-] [-] Aussie
Feb 64. (7") **DON'T SAY GOODBYE. / PEACE OF MIND** [-] [-] Aussie

— Jun64, they backed JOHNNY DEVLIN on 'Festival' label single 'BLUE SUEDE SHOES'. / **'WHOLE LOTTA SHAKIN' GOIN' ON'.**

Aug 64. (7") **CLAUSTROPHOBIA. / COULD IT BE** [-] [-] Aussie
Oct 64. (7") **TURN AROUND LOOK AT ME. / THEME FROM THE TRAVELS OF JAMIE McPHEETERS** [-] [-] Aussie
Dec 64. (7") **HOUSE WITHOUT WINDOWS. (w / "TREVOR GORDON") / I'LL BE HAPPY** [-] [-] Aussie
Apr 65. (7") **EVERY DAY I HAVE TO CRY. / YOU WOULDN'T KNOW IT** [-] [-] Aussie
May 65. (7") **LITTLE MISS RHYTHM AND BLUES. (w / "TREVOR GORDON") / HERE I AM** [-] [-] Aussie
Aug 65. (7") **WINE AND WOMEN. / FOLLOW THE WIND** [-] [-] Aussie
Nov 65. (7") **I WAS A LOVER AND A LEADER OF MEN. / AND THE CHILDREN LAUGHING** [-] [-] Aussie
Nov 65. (lp) **BARRY GIBB AND THE BEE GEES SING AND PLAY 14 BARRY GIBB SONGS** [-] [-] Aussie
– (AUST. re-iss.1968 as 'BARRY GIBB AND THE BEE GEES' on 'Calendar')
Mar 66. (7") **CHERRY RED. / I WANT HOME** [-] [-] Aussie

Spin / not issued

Jun 66. (7") **MONDAY'S RAIN. / ALL OF MY LIFE** [-] [-] Aussie
Sep 66. (7") **SPICKS AND SPECKS. / I AM THE WORLD** [ ] [ ]
(above was iss.UK + US Feb67 on 'Polydor')
Nov 66. (lp) **SPICKS AND SPECKS** [-] [-] Aussie
– (UK-iss.cd+c Sep93 on 'Remember')
Jan 67. (7") **BORN A MAN. / BIG CHANCE** [-] [-]
(also iss.AUST. ep's THE BEE GEES (1964) / **WINE AND WOMEN** (1966) / **SPICKS AND SPECKS** (1967).

— added **VINCE MELOUNEY** (b. Australia) – guitar / **COLIN PETERSON** (b. Australia) **-drums**

Polydor / Atco

Apr 67. (7") **NEW YORK MINING DISASTER 1941. / I CAN'T SEE NOBODY** [12] [14]
Jun 67. (7") **TO LOVE SOMEBODY. / CLOSE ANOTHER DOOR** [41] [17]
Jul 67. (lp) **FIRST** [8] [7]
– Close another door / Craise Finton Kirk Royal Academy of Arts / Cucumber castle / Every Christian lion-hearted man will show you / Holiday / I can't see nobody / I close my eyes / In my own time / New York mining disaster 1941 / One minute woman / Please read me / Red chair / Fade away / To love somebody / Turn of the century. *(re-iss.Nov83) (cd-iss.1985)*
Sep 67. (7") **MASSACHUSETTS. / SIR GEOFFREY SAVED THE WORLD** [-] [11] Nov 67
Sep 67. (7") **MASSACHUSETTS. / BARKER OF THE F.O.** [1] [-]
Oct 67. (7") **HOLIDAY. / EVERY CHRISTIAN LION-HEARTED MAN** [-] [16] Sep 67
Nov 67. (7") **WORLD. / SIR GEOFFREY SAVED THE WORLD** [9] [-]
Jan 68. (7") **WORDS. / SINKING SHIPS** [8] [15]
Feb 68. (lp) **HORIZONTAL** [16] [12]
– World / And the Sun will shine / Lemons never forget / Really and sincerely / Birdie told me / With the Sun in my eyes / Massachusetts / Harry Braff / Day time girl / The earnest of being George / Change is made / Horizontal. *(cd-iss.Feb90)*
Mar 68. (7") **JUMBO. / THE SINGER SANG HIS SONG** [25] [57]
Jul 68. (7") **I'VE GOTTA GET A MESSAGE TO YOU. / KITTY CAN** [1] [8]
Sep 68. (lp) **IDEA** [4] [17]
– Let there be love / In the summer of his years / Down to earth / I've gotta get a message to you / When the swallows fly / I started a joke / Swan song / Kitty can / Indian gin and whisky dry / Such a shame / I dea / I have decided to join the airforce / Kilburn Towers. *(cd-iss.Nov89 on 'Hanover')*
Dec 68. (7") **I STARTED A JOKE. / KILBURN TOWERS** [-] [6]
Feb 69. (7") **FIRST OF MAY. / LAMPLIGHT** [6] [37]
Mar 69. (d-lp) **ODESSA** [10] [20]
– Odessa (city on the Black Sea) / You'll never see my face again / Black diamond / Marley Purt drive / Edison / Melody fair / Give your best / Seven sea symphony with all nations (international anthem)* / Laugh in your face / Never say never again / First of May / The British opera. *(cd-iss. May 85) (*=not on cd)*

— **BARRY & MAURICE** continue, when ROBIN GIBB went solo. (VINCE and COLIN also departed)

May 69. (7") **TOMORROW TOMORROW. / SUN IN THE MORNING** [23] [54]
Aug 69. (7") **DON'T FORGET TO REMEMBER. / THE LORD** [2] [73]
Jan 70. (7") **IF ONLY I HAD MY MIND ON SOMETHING ELSE** [-] [91]
Mar 70. (7") **I.O.I.O. / SWEETHEART** [49] [-]
May 70. (7") **I.O.I.O. / THEN YOU LEFT ME** [-] [94]
May 70. (lp) **CUCUMBER CASTLE (TV film soundtrack)** [57] [94]
– If I only had my mind on something else / Then you left me / I was the child / Sweetheart / My thing / Turning tide / I.O.I.O. / I lay down and die / Bury me down the river / The chance of love / Don't forget to remember. *(cd-iss. Nov 89 on 'Hanover')*

— **ROBIN** returns to the trio

Nov 70. (7") **LONELY DAYS. / MAN FOR ALL SEASONS** [33] [3]
Dec 70. (lp)(c) **2 YEARS ON** [ ] [32]
– 2 years on / Portrait of Louise / Man for all seasons / Sincere relation / Back home / The first mistake I made / Lonely days / Alone again / Tell me why / Lay it on me / Every second, every minute / I'm weeping. *(cd-iss. Mar 90)*
Jun 71. (7") **HOW CAN YOU MEND A BROKEN HEART. / COUNTRY WOMAN** [ ] [1]
Jun 71. (lp)(c) **MELODY (TV Film Soundtrack)** [ ] [ ]
– Odessa (city on the black sea) / You'll never see my face again / Black diamond / Marley Purt drive / Edison / Melody fair / Suddenly / Whisper whisper.

— added **GEOFF BRIDGEFORD** – drums / **ALAN KENDALL** – lead guitar

Oct 71. (7") **DON'T WANNA LIVE INSIDE MYSELF. / WALKING BACK TO WATERLOO** [-] [53]
Nov 71. (lp)(c) **TRAFALGAR** [ ] [34] Sep 71
– How can you mend a broken heart / Israel / The greatest man in the world / It's just the day / Remembering / Somebody stop the music / Trafalgar / Don't wanna live inside myself / When do I / Dearest / Lion in winter / Walking back to Waterloo. *(cd-iss. Mar 90)*
Jan 72. (7") **MY WORLD. / ON TIME** [16] [16]
Jul 72. (7") **RUN TO ME. / ROAD TO ALASKA** [9] [16]
Oct 72. (lp)(c) **TO WHOM IT MAY CONCERN** [ ] [35]
– Run to me / We lost the road / Never been alone / Paper mache, cabbages & kings / I can bring love / I held a party / Please don't turn out the lights / Sea of smiling faces / Bad bad dreams / You know it's for you / Alive / Road to Alaska / Sweet song of summer. *(cd-iss.Apr93)*
Nov 72. (7") **ALIVE. / PAPERMACHE CABBAGES AND KINGS** [ ] [34]

R.S.O. / R.S.O.

Mar 73. (7") **SAW A NEW MORNING. / MY LIFE HAS BEEN A SONG** [ ] [94]

— now with **RIC GRECH** – bass / **SNEAKY PETE** – pedal steel / **JIM KELTNER** – drums / **JEROME RICHARDSON** – flute / **TOMMY MORGAN** – harmonica.

Mar 73. (lp)(c) **LIFE IN A TIN CAN** [ ] [69] Jan 73
– Saw a new morning / I don't wanna be the one / South Dakota morning / Living in Chicago / While I play / My life has been a song / Come home Johnny Bridie / Method to my madness. *(cd-iss.Apr93)*
Jun 73. (7") **WOULDN'T I BE SOMEONE. / ELISA** [ ] [ ]
Mar 74. (7") **MR. NATURAL. / IT DOESN'T MATTER MUCH TO ME** [ ] [93]
Jul 74. (lp)(c) **MR. NATURAL** [ ] [ ] Jun 74
– Charade / Throw a penny / Down the road / Voices / Give a hand take a hand / Dogs / Mr. Natural / Lost in your love / I can't let you go / Heavy breathing / Had a lot of love last night. *(cd-iss.Apr93)*
Aug 74. (7") **CHARADE. / HEAVY BREATHING** [ ] [ ]

— back-up **ALAN KENDALL** – guitar / **BLUE WEAVER** – keys / **DENNIS BYRON** – drums

May 75. (7") **JIVE TALKIN'. / WIND OF CHANGE** [5] [1]
Jun 75. (lp)(c) **MAIN COURSE** [ ] [14]
– Nights on Broadway / Jive talkin' / Winds of change / Songbird / Fanny (be tender with my love) / All this making love / Country lanes / Come on over / Edge of the universe / Baby as you turn away. *(re-iss.Aug84) (cd-iss.May88)*
Sep 75. (7") **NIGHTS ON BROADWAY. / EDGE OF THE UNIVERSE** [ ] [7]
Jan 76. (7") **FANNY (BE TENDER WITH MY LOVE). / COUNTRY LANES** [ ] [12] Dec 75
Jul 76. (7") **YOU SHOULD BE DANCING. / SUBWAY** [5] [1]
Sep 76. (7") **LOVE SO RIGHT. / YOU STEPPED INTO MY LIFE** [41] [3]
Oct 76. (lp)(c) **CHILDREN OF THE WORLD** [ ] [8] Sep 76
– You should be dancing / You stepped into my life / Love so right / Lovers / Can't keep a good man down / Boogie child / Love me / Subway / The way it was / Children of the world.
Feb 77. (7") **CHILDREN OF THE WORLD. / BOOGIE CHILD** [ ] [12] B-side
Jun 77. (d-lp)(d-c) **HERE AT LAST – BEE GEES LIVE (live)** [ ] [8]
– I've gotta get a message to you / Love so right / Edge of the universe / Come on over / Can't keep a good man down / New York mining disaster 1941 / Run to me / World / Holiday / I can't see nobody / I started a joke / Massachusetts / How can you mend a broken heart / To love somebody / You should be dancing / Boogie child / Down the road / Words / Winds of change / Nights on Broadway / Jive talkin' / Lonely days. *(re-iss.Oct84)*

Aug 77. (7") **EDGE OF THE UNIVERSE (live). / WORDS (live)** [ ] [26]
Oct 77. (7") **HOW DEEP IS YOUR LOVE. / CAN'T KEEP A GOOD MAN DOWN** [3] [1] Sep 77
Jan 78. (7") **STAYIN' ALIVE. / IF I CAN'T HAVE YOU ('B'-side "YVONNE ELLIMAN")** [4] [1] Dec 77
Mar 78. (d-lp)(d-c) **SATURDAY NIGHT FEVER (Soundtrack)** [1] [1] Nov 77
– (all tracks written by BEE GEES, contained recent singles and tracks by other artists TAVARES, YVONNE ELLIMAN, TRAMMPS, K.C. & THE SUNSHINE BAND, etc.)
Apr 78. (7") **NIGHT FEVER. / DOWN THE ROAD (live)** [1] [1] Feb 78
Nov 78. (7") **TOO MUCH HEAVEN. / REST YOUR LOVE IN ME** [3] [1]
Feb 79. (7") **TRAGEDY. / UNTIL** [1] [1]
Feb 79. (lp)(c) **SPIRITS HAVING FLOWN** [1] [1]
– Tragedy / Too much Heaven / Love you inside out / Reaching out / Search find stop (think again) / Spirits (having flown) / Living together / I'm satisfied / Until. *(re-iss.Sep83) (also iss.on US pic-lp) (cd-iss. Nov 89 on 'Hanover')*
Apr 79. (7") **LOVE YOU INSIDE OUT. / I'M SATISFIED** [13] [1]
Dec 79. (7")(12") **SPIRITS (HAVING FLOWN). / WIND OF CHANGE** [16] [ ]

— The trio now used many session people.

Sep 81. (7")(12") **HE'S A LIAR. / ('A'instrumental)** [ ] [30]
Nov 81. (lp)(c) **LIVING EYES** [73] [41]
– Living eyes / He's a liar / Paradise / Don't fall in love with me / Soldiers / I still love you / Wild flower / Nothing could be good / Cryin' every day / Be who you are. *(re-iss.Aug83) (cd-iss. Aug 84)*
Nov 81. (7") **LIVING EYES. / I STILL LOVE YOU** [ ] [45]
Jul 83. (7") **THE WOMAN IN YOU. / STAYIN' ALIVE** [ ] [24] May 83
(12") – ('A'side) / Saturday night segue.
Jul 83. (lp)(c) **STAYING ALIVE (Soundtrack)** [14] [6]
– The woman in you / Love you too much / Breakout / Someone belonging to someone / Life goes on / Stayin' alive / Far from over / Look out for number one / Finding out the hard way / Moody girl / (We dance) So close to the fire / I'm never gonna give you up.
Sep 83. (7")(12") **SOMEONE BELONGING TO SOMEONE. / I LOVE YOU TOO MUCH** [49] [49] Aug 83

Warners Warners

Sep 87. (7")(12")(c-s)(12"pic-d) **YOU WIN AGAIN. / BACKTAFUNK** [1] [75]
Sep 87. (lp)(c)(cd) **E.S.P.** [5] [96]
– E.S.P. / You win again / Live or die / Giving up the ghost / The longest night / This is your life / Angela / Overnight / Crazy for your love / Backtafunk. *(re-iss.cd Feb95)*
Dec 87. (7") **E.S.P. / OVERNIGHT** [51] [ ]
(12"+=)//(12"+=) – ('A'extended)./ / ('A'extra house vocals mix).
Feb 88. (7") **CRAZY FOR YOUR LOVE. / YOU WIN AGAIN** [ ] [ ]
(12"+=) – Giving up the ghost.
Mar 89. (7")(c-s) **ORDINARY LIVES. / WING AND A PRAYER** [54] [ ]
(12"+=)(cd-s+=) – ('A'extended).
Apr 89. (lp)(c)(cd) **ONE** [29] [68]
– Ordinary lives / Bodyguard / Tears / Flesh and blood / House of shame / One / It's my neighbourhood / Tokyo nights / Wish you were here / Will you ever let him. *(re-iss.cd Feb95)*
Jun 89. (7") **ONE. / WING AND A PRAYER** [-] [7]
Jun 89. (7")(c-s) **ONE. / FLESH AND BLOOD** [71] [-]
(12"+=)(cd-s+=) – ('A'dance mix).
Mar 91. (7")(c-s) **SECRET LOVE. / TRUE CONFESSIONS** [5] [ ]
(12"+=)(cd-s+=) – Human sacrifice.
Apr 91. (cd)(c)(lp) **HIGH CIVILIZATION** [24] [ ]
– High civilization / Secret love / When he's gone / Happy ever after / Party with no name / Ghost train / Dimensions / The only one / Human sacrifice / Evolution. *(re-iss.cd Feb95)*
May 91. (7")(c-s) **WHEN HE'S GONE. / MASSACHUSETTS (live)** [ ] [ ]
(12"+=)(cd-s+=) – You win again (live).

— with **ALAN KENDALL + TIM CANSFIELD** – guitars / **GEORGE PERRY** – bass / **TIM MOORE** – keyboards / **TREVOR MURRELL** – drums / **LUIS JARDIM** – percussion / **ED CALLE** – sax / **GUSTAVO LEZCANO** – harmonica

Polydor Polydor

Aug 93. (7") **PAYING THE PRICE OF LOVE. / MY DESTINY** [23] [74]
(cd-s+=) – (2 'A' mixes)
Sep 93. (cd)(c) **SIZE ISN'T EVERYTHING** [28] [ ]
– Paying the price of love / Kiss of life / How to fall in love, pt.1 / Omega man / Haunted house / Heart like mine / Anything for you / Blue island / Above and beyond / For whom the bell tolls / Fallen angel / Decadence.
Nov 93. (cd-s) **FOR WHOM THE BELL TOLLS. / DECADENCE (YOU SHOULD BE DANCING)** [4] [ ]
(12")(c-s) – ('A'side) / Staying alive / Too much Heaven / Massachusetts.
Apr 94. (7")(c-s) **HOW TO FALL IN LOVE PART 1. / 855 7019** [30] [ ]
(cd-s+=) – Fallen angel.
(cd-s) – ('A'side) / I've gotta get a message to you / Tragedy / New York mining disaster 1941.

– compilations, others, etc. –

Note; all below on 'Polydor' UK / 'Atco' US until stated otherwise.
Nov 68. (lp) **RARE, PRECIOUS & BEAUTIFUL** [ ] [99]
Mar 70. (lp) **RARE, PRECIOUS & BEAUTIFUL VOL.2** [ ] [100]
Oct 69. (lp)(c) **BEST OF THE BEE GEES** [7] [9] Jul 69
– Holiday / I've got to get a message to you / I can't see nobody / Words / I started a joke / Spicks and specks / First of May / World / Massachusetts / To love somebody / Every Christian lion-hearted man will show you / New York mining disaster 1941. *(cd-iss. Nov 84 on 'RSO')*
Apr 70. (lp) **RARE, PRECIOUS & BEAUTIFUL VOL.3** [ ] [ ]
Note; below on 'RSO' until . . .
Dec 76. (lp)(c) **BEE GEES GOLD, VOLUME ONE** [ ] [50] Nov 76
Jun 73. (lp)(c) **THE BEST OF THE BEE GEES, VOL.2** [ ] [98]
(re-iss.Nov77) (cd-iss. 1988 on 'RSO')
Oct 79. (d-lp)(d-c) **BEE GEES GREATEST** [6] [1]
– Children of the world / Don't throw it all away / Fanny (be tender with my love) / How deep is your love / If I can't have you / Jive talkin' / Love me / Love so right / Love you inside out / More than a woman / Night fever / Nights on Broadway / Rest of your love on me / Spirits (having flown) / Stayin' alive / Too much Heaven / Tragedy / Wind of change / You should be dancing / You stepped into my life. *(cd-iss. 1983)*
Aug 78. Pickwick; (d-lp)(d-c) **BEE GEES BONANZA – THE EARLY DAYS** [ ] [-]
Jun 79. Hallmark; (lp)(c) **THE EARLY DAYS VOL.1** [ ] [-]
Jun 79. Hallmark; (lp)(c) **THE EARLY DAYS VOL.2** [ ] [-]
Jun 79. Hallmark; (lp)(c) **THE EARLY DAYS VOL.3** [ ] [-]
Note; below on 'Old Gold' until . . .
Mar 86. (7") **I'VE GOTTA GET A MESSAGE TO YOU. / TO LOVE SOMEBODY** [ ] [-]
Mar 86. (7") **DON'T FORGET TO REMEMBER. / FIRST OF MAY** [ ] [-]
Mar 86. (7") **JIVE TALKIN'. / YOU SHOULD BE DANCING** [ ] [-]
Mar 86. (7") **MASSACHUSETTS. / NEW YORK MINING DISASTER 1941** [ ] [-]
Feb 88. (7") **SAVED BY THE BELL (Robin Gibb) / WORDS** [ ] [-]
Jun 93. (cd-s) **NIGHT FEVER / STAYIN' ALIVE / HOW DEEP IS YOUR LOVE** [ ] [-]
Jun 93. (cd-s) **TRAGEDY / TOO MUCH HEAVEN / LOVE YOU INSIDE OUT** [ ] [-]
1972. Contour; (lp) **MASSACHUSETTS** [ ] [-]
(re-iss.Aug85)
Nov 77. Contour; (lp)(c) **I'VE GOTTA GET A MESSAGE TO YOU** [ ] [-]
Oct 88. BR Music; (lp)(c) **THEIR MOST BEAUTIFUL SONGS** [ ] [ ]
Nov 90. Polydor; (cd)(c)(lp) **THE VERY BEST OF THE BEE GEES** [8] [ ]
Nov 90. Polydor; (7")(c-s) **HOW DEEP IS YOUR LOVE (1990 remix). / YOU SHOULD BE DANCING (1990 remix)** [ ] [ ]
(12"+=)(cd-s+=) – Too much Heaven / To love somebody.
Dec 90. Polydor; (4xcd) **TALES FROM THE BROTHERS GIBB: A HISTORY IN SONG 1967 – 1990** [ ] [ ]
Jan 92. Thunderbolt; (cd) **EVER INCREASING CIRCLES** (early) [ ] [-]
Apr 92. Thunderbolt; (cd) **TOMORROW THE WORLD** (1964 material onwards) [ ] [-]
Feb 94. Javelin; (cd)(c) **SPOTLIGHT ON THE BEE GEES** [ ] [-]
Dec 95. Thunderbolt; (cd) **TO BE OR NOT TO BE** [ ] [-]

BARRY GIBB

Polydor Atco

May 70. (7") **I'LL KISS YOUR MEMORY. / THIS TIME** [ ] [ ]

— In 1980, he collaborated on album GUILTY by BARBRA STREISAND.

Polydor M.C.A.

Oct 84. (7")(12")(7"mirror-pic-d) **SHINE SHINE. / SHE SAYS** [ ] [37]
Oct 84. (lp)(c) **NOW VOYAGER** [85] [72]
– I am your driver / Fine line / Face to face / Shatterproof / Shine shine / Lesson in love / One night for lovers / Stay alone / Temptation / She says / Hunter. *(cd-iss.Jun88)*
In 1986, BARRY alias The BUNBURYS iss.7".WE ARE THE BUNBURYS.
Aug 88. (7") **CHILDHOOD DAYS. / MOONLIGHT MADNESS** [ ] [ ]
(12"+=) – Cover you.
Sep 88. (lp)(c)(cd) **HAWKS (Soundtrack)** [ ] [ ]
– System of love / Childhood days / My eternal love / Moonlight madness / Where tomorrow is / Celebration de la Vic (theme) / Chain reaction / Cover you / Not in love at all / Letting go.

MAURICE GIBB

Polydor Atco

Apr 70. (7") **RAILROAD. / I'VE COME BACK** [ ] [ ]

Audiotrax not issued

Sep 84. (7")(12") **HOLD HER IN YOUR HAND. / ('A'instrumental)** [ ] [-]

ROBIN GIBB

solo (69-70 not a BEE GEE)

Polydor Atco

Jun 69. (7") **SAVED BY THE BELL. / MOTHER AND JACK** [2] [ ]
Dec 69. (7") **ONE MILLION YEARS. / WEEKEND** [ ] [ ]
Feb 70. (7") **AUGUST OCTOBER. / GIVE ME A SMILE** [45] [ ]
Apr 70. (lp)(c) **ROBIN'S REIGN** [ ] [ ]
– August October / Gone gone gone / The worst girl in town / Give me a smile / Down came the Sun / Mother and Jack / Saved by the bell / Weekend / Farmer Ferdinand Hudson / Lord bless all / Most of my life.

R.S.O. R.S.O.

Sep 78. (7") **OH DARLIN'. / SHE'S LEAVING HOME** [ ] [15]

— In Oct80, teamed up with MARCY LEVY on single HELP ME.

Polydor Mirage

Feb 83. (7") **ANOTHER LONELY NIGHT IN NEW YORK. / I BELIEVE IN MIRACLES** [ ] [ ]
(d7"+=) – ?
Feb 83. (lp)(c) **HOW OLD ARE YOU** [ ] [ ]
– Juliet / How old are you / In and out of love / Kathy's gone / Don't stop the night / Another lonely night in New York / Danger / He can't love you / Hearts on fire / I believe in miracles.
Apr 83. (7") **JULIET. / HEARTS ON FIRE** [ ] [ ]
Oct 83. (7") **HOW OLD ARE YOU. / I BELIEVE IN MIRACLES** [ ] [ ]
Jul 84. (7")(12") **BOYS (DO FALL IN LOVE). / DIAMONDS** [ ] [37]
Jul 84. (lp)(c) **SECRET AGENT** [ ] [ ]
– Boys (do fall in love) / In your diary / Rebecca / Secret agent / Living in another world / X-ray eyes / King of fools / Diamonds.
Feb 85. (lp)(c) **WALLS HAVE EYES** [ ] [ ]
– You don't say us anymore / Like a fool / Heartbeat in exile / Remedy / Toys / Someone to believe in / Gone with the wind / These walls have eyes / Possession / Do you love her.
(cd-iss.Nov85)

Apr 86. (7")(12") **LIKE A FOOL. / POSSESSION**

B.E.F. (see under ⇒ HEAVEN 17)

Maggie BELL (see under ⇒ STONE THE CROWS)

BELLY

Formed: Newport, Rhode Island, USA . . . Dec'91 by ex-THROWING MUSES and BREEDERS co-leader TANYA DONNELLY. Progressed that year and were tipped for greater things in 1993. • **Style:** Guitar-orientated indie band, not too dissimilar to THROWING MUSES. • **Songwriters:** DONNELLY except; HOT BURRITO 2 (Flying Burrito Brothers) / TRUST IN ME (Sherman Sherman; for 'Jungle Book') / ARE YOU EXPERIENCED (Jimi Hendrix). • **Trivia:** DYLAN ROY guested on late '92 single 'GEPETTO'.

Recommended: STAR (*8).

TANYA DONNELLY – vocals, guitar / **FRED ABONG** – bass / **CHRIS GORMAN** – drums / **THOMAS GORMAN** – guitar

		4 a.d.	Sire
Jun 92.	(12"ep)(cd-ep) **SLOW DUST** – Dusted / Slow dog / Dancing gold / Low red Moon.		
——	**LESLIE LANGSTON** – bass (ex-THROWING MUSES) repl. FRED ABONG		
Nov 92.	(12"ep)(cd-ep) **GEPPETO / SEXYS. / SWEET RIDER / HOT BURRITO 2**		
Jan 93.	(7")(c-s) **FEED THE TREE. / DREAM ON ME**	32	95
Jan 93.	(cd)(c)(lp) **STAR** – Someone to die for / Angel / Dusted / Every word / Gepetto / Witch / Slow dog / Low red Moon / Feed the tree / Full Moon, empty heart / White belly / Untogether / Star / Sad dress / Stay.	2	59
Mar 93.	(12"ep)(cd-ep) **GEPETTO. / HOT BURRITO 1. / SEXY S / SWEET RIDE** (c-ep)(cd-ep) – ('A'side) / It's not unusual / Star (demo) / Dusted (demo).	49	
Jan 95.	(7")(c-s) **NOW THEY'LL SLEEP. / THIEF** (12"+=)(cd-s+=) – Baby's arm / John Dark.	28	
Feb 95.	(cd)(c)(lp) **KING** – Puberty / Seal my fate / Red / Silverfish / Super-connected / The bees / King / Now they'll sleep / Untitled and unsung / Lil' Ennio / Judas my heart.	6	57
Jul 95.	(7"clear) **SEAL MY FATE. / BROKEN / JUDAS MY HEART (live)** (cd-s) – ('A'-U.S. radio mix) / Spaceman / Diamond rib cage / Think about your troubles. (cd-s) – ('A'live) / White belly (live) / Untitled and unsung (live) / The bees (live).	35	

BELOVED

Formed: Camberwell, London, England . . . 1983 as JOURNEY THROUGH, by MARSH and HARVARD. In 1984 added WADDINGTON and became The BELOVED. Through own 'Flim Flam' label, they gained success in Europe which led to major 'WEA' contract, and hits in the UK. • **Style:** Alternative jangly rock, progressing into electronic acid rock dance music. • **Songwriters:** MARSH and WADDINGTON, except GIVE IT TO ME (Bam Bam). • **Trivia:** WADDINGTON was maths graduate at Cambridge University. 'THE SUN RISING' single edit is now used on a certain UK-TV ad.

Recommended: HAPPINESS (*6)

JON MARSH – vocals, guitar / **STEVE WADDINGTON** – guitar, keyboards / **TIM HARVARD** – bass / **GUY GAUSDEN** – drums

		Flim Flam	not issued
Apr 86.	(12"m) **A HUNDRED WORDS. / SLOW DANCING / IN TROUBLE AND SHAME**		-
Sep 86.	(7") **THIS MEANS WAR. / IF ONLY** (12") – ('A'side) / Let it begin / Saints preserve us.		-
Mar 87.	(12"ep) **HAPPY NOW** – Righteous me / A kiss goodbye / If pennies came.		-
Jul 87.	(7")(12") **FOREVER DANCING. / SURPRISE ME**		-
Nov 87.	(lp) **WHERE IT IS** – A hundred words / Slow dancing / In trouble and shame / This means war / If only / Let it begin / Saints preserve us / If pennies came / Righteous me / A kiss goodbye / Surprise me / Forever dancing.		-
——	(trimmed to duo of **MARSH** and **WADDINGTON** & drum machine)	W.E.A.	Atlantic
Oct 88.	(7")(12")(cd-s) **LOVING FEELING. / ACID LOVE**		-
Jan 89.	(7") **YOUR LOVE TAKES ME HIGHER. / PARADISE (MY DARLING, MY ANGEL** (12")(cd-s) – ('A'&'B'remix).		
Oct 89.	(7")(c-s)(12"pic-d) **THE SUN RISING. / ('A'instrumental)** (12"+=)(cd-s+=) – (2 extra mixes).	26	
Jan 90.	(7")(c-s) **HELLO. / ('A' Dolly mix)** (12"+=) – ('A'mix). (cd-s++=) – ('A'extra mix).	19	
Feb 90.	(cd)(c)(lp) **HAPPINESS** – Hello / Your love takes me higher / Time after time / Don't you worry / Scarlet beautiful / The sun rising / I love you more / Wake up soon / Up, up and away / Found. *(re-iss.cd/c Feb95)*	14	
Mar 90.	(7")(c-s) **YOUR LOVE TAKES ME HIGHER. / PABLO** (12") – ('A'side) / ('A'version). (cd-s++=) – (all above tracks).	39	
May 90.	(7")(c-s) **TIME AFTER TIME. / ('A' through the round window mix)** (12"+=) – ('A' muffin mix). (cd-s+=) – ('A'extended mix).	46	
Oct 90.	(7") **IT'S ALRIGHT NOW. / ('A'instrumental)** (12"+=)(cd-s+=) – ('A'extra mix).	48	
Oct 90.	(cd)(c)(lp) **BLISSED OUT** (remixes of last album) *(re-iss.cd Feb95)*	39	-
——	**HELENA MARSH** – producer, writer (wife of JON) repl. WADDINGTON in '91.	East West	East West
Jan 93.	(7")(c-s) **SWEET HARMONY. / MOTIVATION (Empathised)** (12"+=)(cd-s+=) – (2 'A' mixes).	8	
Feb 93.	(cd)(c)(lp) **CONSCIENCE** – Spirit / Sweet harmony / Outerspace girl / Lose yourself in me / Paradise found / You've got me thinking / Celebrate your life / Rock to the rhythm of love / Let the music take you / 1000 years from today / Dream on.	2	
Mar 93.	(7")(c-s) **YOU'VE GOT ME THINKING. / CELEBRATE YOUR LIFE (Fit For Life Mix)** (12"+=)(cd-s+=) – ('B' dub mix) / Sweet harmony (club mix).	23	
Aug 93.	(7")(c-s) **OUTERSPACE GIRL. / ('A' space hopper mix)** (12") – (2 'A' mixes). (cd-s++=) – (2 'A'-space cadet + space dust mixes).	38	

Pat BENATAR

Born: PATRICIA ANDRZEJEWSKI, 10 Jan'53, Brooklyn, New York, USA. She married long-time boyfriend DENNIS BENATAR and moved to Richmond, Virginia. Retained her married name, even after their divorce in the early 80's. PAT signed to 'Chrysalis' during the late 70's, and soon became leading female artist, after 'HEARTBREAKER' reached US Top 30 in 1980. • **Style:** Although she had great beauty and an operatically trained voice, she chose soft-metal AOR. In 1991 she moved into blues rock mould. • **Songwriters:** She collaborated with others, including CHINN / CHAPMAN plus her husband/producer (from 20 Feb'82) NEIL GERALDO. She also covered YOU BETTER RUN (Young Rascals) / PAYIN' THE COST TO BE THE BOSS (B.B. King) / HELTER SKELTER (Beatles) / IF YOU THINK YOU KNOW HOW TO LOVE ME (Smokie) / INVINCIBLE (Simon Climie). • **Trivia:** Her first 7" in US 1976 as "PAT BENETAR" was DAY GIG. / LAST SATURDAY on the 'Trace' label. In 1987 she took time off to have a baby.

Recommended: BEST SHOTS (*5).

PAT BENATAR – vocals / **NEIL GERALDO** – keyboards (ex-DERRINGER) / **SCOTT ST.CLAIR SHEETS** – guitar / **ROGER CAPPS** – bass / **GLEN ALEXANDER HAMILTON** – drums

		Chrysalis	Chrysalis
Oct 79.	(7") **IF YOU THINK YOU KNOW HOW TO LOVE ME. / SO SINCERE**		
Dec 79.	(lp)(c) **IN THE HEAT OF THE NIGHT** – Heartbreaker / I need a lover / if you think you know how to love me / In the heat of the night / My clone sleeps alone / We live for love / Rated x / Don't let it show / No you don't / So sincere. *(re-iss.lp/c/cd Jun85, hit UK 98)*		12 Oct 79
Jan 80.	(7") **HEARTBREAKER. / MY CLONE SLEEPS ALONE** *(re-iss. 1983?)*		23 Dec 79
Apr 80.	(7") **WE LIVE FOR LOVE. / SO SINCERE**	-	27
Apr 80.	(7") **WE LIVE FOR LOVE. / I NEED A LOVER** (12"+=) – If you think you know how to love me.		-
——	**MYRON GROOMBACHER** – drums repl. HAMILTON		
Jul 80.	(7") **YOU BETTER RUN. / OUT-A-TOUCH**	-	42
Aug 80.	(lp)(c) **CRIMES OF PASSION** – Treat me right / You better run / Never wanna leave you / Hit me with your best shot / Hell is for children / Prisoner of love / Out-a-touch / Little Paradise / I'm gonna follow you / Wuthering heights. *(re-iss.+cd Jun85)*		2
Nov 80.	(7") **HIT ME WITH YOUR BEST SHOT. / YOU BETTER RUN** (7"red-ep+=) – Heartbreaker / We live for love.		-
Jan 81.	(7") **TREAT ME RIGHT. / NEVER WANNA LEAVE YOU**	-	18
Jan 81.	(7")(7"clear) **TREAT ME RIGHT. / HELL IS FOR CHILDREN**		-
Jul 81.	(lp)(c) **PRECIOUS TIME** – Promises in the dark / Fire and ice / Just like me / Precious time / It's a tuff life / Take it anyway you want it / Evil genius / Hard to believe / Helter skelter. *(cd-iss.Jun85)*	30	1
Jul 81.	(7")(7"clear)(7"pic-d) **FIRE AND ICE. / HARD TO BELIEVE**		17
Oct 81.	(7") **PROMISES IN THE DARK. / EVIL GENIUS**	-	38
(Feb82)	**NEIL GERALDO** now on guitar / co-production.		
Oct 82.	(7")(7"sha-pic-d)(12"blue) **SHADOWS OF THE NIGHT. / THE VICTIM** (7"ep) – ('A'side) / Treat me right / Heartbreaker / Anxiety (get nervous).		13
Nov 82.	(lp)(c)(pic-lp) **GET NERVOUS** – Shadows of the night / I want out / Looking for a stranger / Anxiety (get nervous) / Fight it out / The victim / Little too late / I'll do it / Tell it to her / Silent partner. *(cd-iss.Jun85)*	73	4
(Nov82)	**CHARLIE GIORDANO – keyboards** repl. SHEETS		
Feb 83.	(7") **LITTLE TOO LATE. / FIGHT IT OUT**	-	20
Apr 83.	(7") **LOOKING FOR A STRANGER. / ?**	-	39
Oct 83.	(7")(12")(7"pic-d) **LOVE IS A BATTLEFIELD. / HELL IS FOR CHILDREN (live)**	49	5 Sep 83
Oct 83.	(lp)(c)(pic-lp) **LIVE FROM EARTH (live)** – Fire and ice / Looking for a stranger / I want out / We live for love / Hell is for children / Hit me with your best shot / Promises in the dark / Heartbreaker / Love is a battlefield * / Lipstick lies. *(* studio track) (cd-iss.Jun85)*	60	13
Oct 84.	(7")(7"pic-d) **WE BELONG. / SUBURBAN KING** (12"+=) – We live for love '85.	22	5
Nov 84.	(lp)(c)(cd) **TROPICO**	34	14

– Diamond field / We belong / Painted desert / Temporary heroes / Love in the ice age / Ooh ooh song / Outlaw blues / Suburban king / A crazy world like this / Takin' it back.

Jan 85. (7") **OOH OOH SONG. / LA CANCION OOH OOH** [-] [36]

—— **DONNIE NOSSOV** – bass repl. CAPPS

(below is the theme from 'The Legend Of Billie Jean')

Oct 85. (7") **INVINCIBLE. / ('A'instrumental)** [53] [10] Jul 85
(12"+=) – Promises in the dark / Heartbreaker.

Dec 85. (7")(12") **SEX AS A WEAPON. / RED VISION** [67] [28] Nov 85

Dec 85. (lp)(c)(cd) **7 THE HARD WAY** [69] [26]
– Sex as a weapon / Le bel age / Walking in the underground / Big life / Red vision / 7 rooms of gloom / Run between the raindrops / Invincible / The art of letting go.

Feb 86. (7") **LE BEL AGE. / ?** [-] [54]

—— **FERNANDO SAUNDERS + FRANK LINX** – bass repl. NOSSOV

Jul 88. (7") **ALL FIRED UP. / COOL ZERO** [19] [19]
(12"+=) – Hit me with your best shot / Fire and ice / Just like me / Promises in the dark / Precious time.
(12"+=)(cd-s+=) – ('A'-US version).

Jul 88. (lp)(c)(cd) **WIDE AWAKE IN DREAMLAND** [11] [28]
– All fired up / One love / Let's stay together / Don't walk away / Too long a soldier / Cool zero / Celebral man / Lift 'em on up / Suffer the little children / Wide awake in Dreamland. *(re-iss.cd Mar94)*

Sep 88. (7") **DON'T WALK AWAY. / LIFT 'EM ON UP** [42] [ ]
(12"+=)(cd-s+=) – Hell is for children (live) / We live for love (mix).

Dec 88. (7") **ONE LOVE. / WIDE AWAKE IN DREAMLAND** [59] [ ]
(12"+=) – Sex as a weapon.
(cd-s+=) – Love is a battlefield.

Apr 91. (cd)(c)(lp) **TRUE LOVE** [40] [37]
– Bloodshot eyes / Payin' the cost to be the boss / So long / I've got papers on you / I feel lucky / True love / The good life / Evening / I get evil / Don't happen no more. *(re-iss.cd+c Mar94)*

Jun 91. (7")(c-s) **PAYIN' THE COST TO BE THE BOSS. / TRUE LOVE** [ ] [ ]
(12"+=)(cd-s+=) – Evening.

Sep 93. (c-s) **SOMEBODY'S BABY. / ('A'- A-C mix)** [48] [ ]
(cd-s+=) – Temptation / Promises in the dark (live).

Nov 93. (cd)(c) **GRAVITY'S RAINBOW** [ ] [85] Jun 93
– Pictures of a gone world / Everybody lay down / Somebody's baby / Ties that bind / You and I / Disconnected / Crazy / Everytime I fall back / Sanctuary / Rise (part 1) / Kingdom key / Tradin' down.

– compilations, others, etc. –

Dec 82. Chrysalis; (d-c) **IN THE HEAT OF THE NIGHT / CRIMES OF PASSION** [ ] [-]

Mar 85. Chrysalis; (7")(12") **LOVE IS A BATTLEFIELD. / HERE'S MY HEART** [17] [-]

Jun 85. Chrysalis; (7")(7"sha-pic-d) **SHADOWS OF THE NIGHT. / HIT ME WITH YOUR BEST SHOT** [50] [-]
(12"+=) – Fire and ice.

Nov 87. Chrysalis; (lp)(c)(cd) **BEST SHOTS** [6] [67] Nov 89
– Hit me with your best shot / Love is a battlefield / We belong / We live for love / Sex as a weapon / Invincible / Shadows of the night / Heartbreaker / Fire and ice / Treat me right / If you think you know how to love me / You better run.

Apr 94. Chrysalis; (cd)(c) **THE VERY BEST OF PAT BENATAR** [ ] [ ]

Brian BENNETT (see under ⇒ SHADOWS)

George BENSON

Born: 22 Mar'43, Pittsburgh, Pensylvania, USA. Having played guitar since the age of 8, he moved to New York in '63, joining Jack McDuff's quartet. Late in 1962, he signed a solo deal with 'Columbia', where he made a couple of albums. In 1968, he turned down an opportunity to join MILES DAVIS, and instead signed to 'A&M'. After one good selling album 'TELL IT LIKE IT IS', he moved again. This time to jazz veteran CREED TAYLOR's jazz label 'C.T.I.'. BENSON soon became noted session man for the label, and in early 1974, hit US Top 100 with album 'BAD BENSON'. The following year, he had a UK-mainstream single hit with 'SUPERSHIP'. This enabled him to get deal with major label 'Warners', where he immediately had US No.1 album 'BREEZIN''. • **Style:** His jazz/guitar WES MONTGOMERY influenced albums from the mid-60's to mid-70's, were foresaken after his 1976 mainstream success. Now more vocal in content, he crossed over to an easy-listening soulful R&B/funk. Not that that worried his growing following who grooved unanimously between home and disco. In 1987, he returned ceremoniously to his jazz roots, when an album with EARL KLUGH; 'COLLABORATION' broke into the US + UK 60. His concerts always interplayed his smooth vocals alongside brilliant guitar work. • **Songwriters:** Writes most of material collaborating with other noteably; in 1980 producer QUINCY JONES and ROD TEMPERTON. He covered; THIS MASQUERADE (Leon Russell) / ON BROADWAY (Drifters) / NATURE BOY + BEYOND THE SEA (Bobby Darin) / ALL BLUES (Miles Davis) / LOVE FOR SALE (Cole Porter) / THERE WILL NEVER BE ANOTHER YOU (Warren-Gordon) / LIL DARLIN' (Count Basie) / ABBEY ROAD album (Beatles) / LET'S DO IT AGAIN (Staple Singers) / etc. The 20/20 album featured songs specially written for him by The WOMACKS / GERRY GOFFIN / NEIL LARSON, STEVE LUKATHER, etc. • **Trivia:** He has guested on many artists albums, including STEVIE WONDER (Songs In The Key Of Life) / MINNIE RIPERTON (Love Lies Forever) / CHAKA KHAN (Chaka).

Recommended: THE GEORGE BENSON COLLECTION (*6)

GEORGE BENSON – vocals, guitar + sessions

not issued / Columbia

1962. (lp) **IT'S UPTOWN** [-] [ ]
– Clockwise / Summertime / Ain't that peculiar / Jaguar / Willow weep for me / A foggy day / Hello birdie / Bullfight / Stormy weather / Eternally / Myna bird blues. *(cd+c-iss.Jul93 as 'IT'S UPTOWN WITH THE GEORGE BENSON QUARTET' on 'Sony Collector's') (cd-iss.Dec94 on 'Columbia')*

—— next w / **JACK McDUFF** – organ / **RED HOLLOWAY** – tenor sax / **RONNIE BOYKINS** – bass / **MONTEGO JOE** – drums

May 64. (lp) **THE NEW BOSS GUITAR** [-] [ ]

1966. (lp) **GEORGE BENSON COOKBOOK** [-] [ ]
– The cooker / Benny's back / Bossa rocka / All of me / Big fat lady / Benson's river / Ready and able / The Borgia stick / Return of the prodigal son / Jumpin' with the symphony Sid. *(cd-iss.Dec94 on 'Columbia')*

1966. (d-lp) **BENSON BURNER** [-] [ ]
– *(UK-iss.Jan76 on 'CBS')*

1966. (7") **AIN'T THAT PECULIAR. / SUMMERTIME** [-] [ ]

1967. (7") **MAN FROM TOLEDO. / THE BORGIA STICK** [-] [ ]

1967. (lp) **WILLOW WEEP FOR ME** [-] [ ]
– Benson's river / Bayou / The Borgia stick / Return of the prodigal son / Bossa rocka / Farm boy / Willow weep for me / Myna bird blues / Bullfight / Hello birdie / Clockwise.

—— with loads of sessioners.

A&M / A&M

Oct 68. (lp) **SHAPE OF THINGS TO COME** [ ] [ ]
– Footin' it / Face it boy, it's over / Shapes of things to come / Chattanooga choo choo / Don't let me lose this dream / Shape of things that are and were / Last train to Clarksville. *(re-iss.1976, cd-iss.Nov88)*

Nov 68. (7") **SHAPE OF THINGS TO COME. / CHATTANOOGA CHOO CHOO** [-] [ ]

Feb 69. (7") **DON'T LET ME LOSE THIS DREAM. / (pt. 2)** [-] [ ]

1969. (7") **MY WOMAN'S GOOD TO ME. / JACKIE ALL** [-] [ ]

1969. (7") **TELL IT LIKE IT IS. / MY CHERIE AMOUR** [-] [ ]

Aug 69. (lp) **TELL IT LIKE IT IS** [-] [ ]
– Are you happy? / Water brother / Tell it like it is / Dontcha hear me callin' to ya / Jackie, all / Jama Joe / Land of a 1000 dances / My Cherie amour / My woman's good to me / Out in the cold again / Soul limbo.

1970. (7") **I GOT A WOMAN. / (pt. 2)** [-] [ ]

1970. (lp) **SOME BLUES** [-] [ ]

—— next w / **CLARENCE PALMER** – organ / **RON CARTER** – bass / **JACK DeJOHNETTE** – drums / **MICHAEL CAMERSON + ALBERT NICHOLSON** – percussion

C.T.I. / C.T.I.

Feb 71. (lp) **BEYOND THE BLUE HORIZON** [-] [ ]
– So what / The gentle rain / All clear / Ode to a Kudu / Somewhere in the east. – *(re-iss.1978)*

—— next w / **CARTER / HERBIE HANCOCK** – piano / **BILLY COBHAM** – drums / **EARL KLUGH + JAY BERLINER** – guitar / **AIRTO MOREIRA** – percussion, vocals / **PHIL KRAUS** – vibes / **JOHN FROSK + ALAN RUBIN** – trumpet, flugelhorn / **JIM BUFFINGTON** – flugelhorn / **WAYNE ANDRE** – trombone / **PHIL BODNER** – flute, oboe / **GEORGE MARGE** – flute, clarinet, etc

Nov 71. (7") **WHITE RABBIT. / ?** [ ] [ ]

Nov 71. (lp) **WHITE RABBIT** [ ] [ ]
– White rabbit / The summer of '42 theme / Little train / California dreamin' / El mar. *(re-iss.Apr77) (cd-iss.Nov95 on 'Columbia')*

—— next w / **CARTER, KLUGH, DeJOHNETTE / HAROLD MABERN** – piano / **GARY KING** – bass / **MOBLEU** – percussion +another wind section.

1973. (lp) **BODY TALK** [ ] [ ] 1970
– Dance / When love has grown / Plum / Body talk / Top of the world. *(re-iss.Feb84) (cd-iss.Dec86 on 'Musicdisc')*

—— next w / **CARTER / KENNY BARRON** – piano / **PHIL UPCHURCH** – guitar, bass / **STEVE GADD** – drums + late 1971 wind section.

Jun 74. (lp) **BAD BENSON** [ ] [78]
– Take five / Summer wishes, winter dreams / My Latin brother / No sooner said than done / Full compass / The changing world.

Sep 75. (7") **SUPERSHIP. (as "GEORGE BAD BENSON") / MY LATIN BROTHER** [30] [ ]

—— next 3 albums w / **PHIL UPCHURCH** – guitar / **RONNIE FOSTER + JORGE DALTO** – keyboards / **STANLEY BANKS** – bass / **HARVEY MASON** – drums / **RALPH McDONALD** – perc.

Warners / Warners

Aug 76. (lp)(c) **BREEZIN'** [ ] [1] Apr 76
– Breezin' / This masquerade / Six to four / Affirmation / So this is love / Lady. *(re-iss.+cd Jun89)*

Oct 76. (7") **THIS MASQUERADE. / SIX TO FOUR** [ ] [10] Jun 76

Oct 76. (7") **BREEZIN'. / LADY** [ ] [63]

Jan 77. (lp)(c) **IN FLIGHT** [19] [9]
– Nature boy / The wind and I / The world is a ghetto / Gonna love you more / Valdez in the country / Everything must change.

Apr 77. (7") **NATURE BOY. / THE WIND AND I** [26] [ ]

Jul 77. (7") **GONNA LOVE YOU MORE. / VALDEZ IN THE COUNTRY** [ ] [71]

—— In Jul 77, he released Theme from the Muhammed Ali film 'The Greatest', THE GREATEST LOVE OF ALL hit on 'Arista'. This hit UK 27 and US 24. (re-iss.Nov80)

Jan 78. (d-lp)(d-c) **WEEKEND IN L.A.(live)** [47] [5]
– The greatest love of all / Down here on the ground / Ode to a Kudu / We as love / California p.m. / Lady blue / We all remember Wes / Windsong / On Broadway / It's all in the game / Weekend in L.A.

Mar 78. (7") **ON BROADWAY (live). / WE AS LOVE (live)** [ ] [7]

May 78. (7") **LADY BLUE (live). / DOWN HERE ON THE GROUND (live)** [ ] [ ]

Feb 79. (7") **LOVE BALLAD. / YOU'RE NEVER TOO FAR FROM ME** [29] [18]

Apr 79. (d-lp)(d-c) **LIVIN' INSIDE YOUR LOVE** [24] [7] Mar 79
– Livin' inside your love / Hey girl / Nassau day / Soulful street / Prelude to fall / A change is gonna come / Love ballad / You're never too far from me / Love is a

hurtin' thing / Welcome into my world / Before you go / Unchained melody. *(cd-iss.Jun89)*

Jun 79. (7") **UNCHAINED MELODY. / BEFORE YOU GO**

Sep 79. (7") **HEY GIRL. / WELCOME INTO MY WORLD**

Aug 80. (7") **GIVE ME THE NIGHT. / BREEZIN'** 7 4 Jul 80

Sep 80. (lp)(c) **GIVE ME THE NIGHT** 3 3 Aug 80
– Love x love / Off Broadway / Moody's mood / Give me the night / What's on your mind / Dinorah, Dinorah / Love dance / Star of a story (x) / Midnight love affair / Turn out the lamplight. *(cd-iss.1983)*

Sep 80. (7")(12") **LOVE X LOVE. / OFF BROADWAY** 10 61

Jan 81. (7")(12") **WHAT'S ON YOUR MIND. / TURN OUT THE LAMPLIGHT** 45

— Aug81, duetted with ARETHA FRANKLIN on her LOVE ALL THE HURT AWAY single which scraped into both UK + US Top 50 for 'Arista'.

Oct 81. (7") **TURN YOUR LOVE AROUND. / NATURE BOY** 29 5

Jan 82. (7")(12") **NEVER GIVE UP ON A GOOD THING. / CALIFORNIA P.M.** 14 52

May 83. (7")(12") **LADY LOVE ME (ONE MORE TIME). / IN SEARCH OF A DREAM** 11 30 Jul 83

Jun 83. (lp)(c) **IN YOUR EYES** 3 27
– Feel like making love / Inside love (so personal) / Lady love me (one more time) / Love will come again / In your eyes / Never too far to fall / Being with you / Use me / Late at night / In search of a dream.

Jul 83. (7")(12") **FEEL LIKE MAKING LOVE. / USE ME** 28

Sep 83. (7") **IN YOUR EYES. / BEING WITH YOU** 7
(12"+=) – Weekend in L.A.

Dec 83. (7")(12") **INSIDE LOVE (SO PERSONAL). / ON BROAD-WAY (live)** 57 43 May 83

Mar 84. (7") **LATE AT NIGHT. / LOVE WILL COME AGAIN**
(12"+=) – Welcome into my world.

Jan 85. (7")(12") **20-20. / SHARK BITE** 29 48 Dec 84

Jan 85. (lp)(c)(cd) **20-20** 9 45
– No one emotion / Please don't walk away / I just wanna hang around you / Nothing's gonna change my love for you / Beyond the sea (la mer) / 20-20 / New day / Hold me / Stand up / You are the love of my life.

Mar 85. (7") **BEYOND THE SEA (LA MER). / BREEZIN'** 60
(12"+=) – This masquerade.

Jul 85. (7")(12") **I JUST WANNA HANG AROUND YOU. / YOU ARE THE LOVE OF MY LIFE**

Oct 85. (7")(12") **NO ONE EMOTION. ("GEORGE BENSON & ROBERTA FLACK") / YOU ARE THE LOVE OF MY LIFE**
(12"+=) – Affirmation.

Jul 86. (7")(12") **KISSES IN THE MOONLIGHT. / OPEN YOUR EYES (instrumental)** 60

Sep 86. (lp)(c)(cd) **WHILE THE CITY SLEEPS . . .** 13 77
– Shiver / Love is here tonight / Teaser / Secrets in the night / Too many times / Did you hear thunder / While the city sleeps . . . / Kisses in the moonlight. *(re-iss.cd Feb95)*

Nov 86. (7")(12") **SHIVER. / LOVE IS HERE TONIGHT** 19

Feb 87. (7")(12") **TEASER. / DID YOU HEAR THE THUNDER** 45

Jul 87. (lp)(c)(cd) **COLLABORATION (with "EARL KLUGH")** 47 59
– Mt. Airy road / Mimosa / Brazillian stomp / Dreamin' / Since you're gone / Collaboration / Jamaica. *(cd+=)* – Love theme from 'Romeo & Juliet'. *(re-iss.cd Feb95)*

1987. (7"w/EARL KLUGH) **SINCE YOU'RE GONE / LOVE THEME FROM 'ROMEO & JULIET'** -

Aug 88. (7") **LET'S DO IT AGAIN. / LET'S GO** 56
(12"+=) – ('A'extended).
(12"+=) – ('A'instrumental).
(cd-s++=) – Shiver.

Aug 88. (lp)(c)(cd) **TWICE THE LOVE** 16 76
– Twice the love / Starting all over / Good habit / Everybody does it / Living on borrowed love / Let's do it again / Stephanie / Tender love / You're still my baby / Until you believe.

Oct 88. (7") **TWICE THE LOVE. / LOVE IS HERE TONIGHT**
(12") – ('A'extended) / ('A'guitar love mix) / ('A'club).
(cd-s++=) – Breezin'.

— w / **CARTER** – bass / **McCOY TYNER** – piano / **LOUIS HAYES + AL FOSTER** – drums

Jul 89. (lp)(c)(cd) **TENDERLY** 52
– You don't know what love is / Stella by starlight / Stardust / At the Mambo Inn / Here, there and everywhere / This is all I ask / Tenderly / I could write a book.

— w / **CARTER** – bass / **BARRY EASTMOND + RICHARD TEE + LOUIS HAYES + DAVID WITHUM** – keyboards / + a host of trumpeters & saxers incl. **RANDY BRECKER**

Oct 90. (cd)(c)(lp) **BIG BOSS BAND**
– Without a song / Ready, now that you are / How do you keep the music playing / On Green Dolphin Street / Baby workout / I only have eyes for you / Portrait of Jennie / Walkin' my baby back home / Skylark / Basie's bag.

(above album features The COUNT BASIE ORCHESTRA)

1993. (cd)(c) **LOVE REMEMBERS**
– I'll be good to you / Got to be there / My heart is dancing / Love of my life / Kiss and make up / Come into my world / Love remembers / Willing to fight / Somewhere island / Lovin' on borrowed time / Lost in love / Calling you.

— released with PATTI AUSTIN:- Aug 92 (7")(c-s) **I'LL KEEP YOUR DREAMS ALIVE which hit UK 68**

– compilations, others, etc. –

Jul 76. C.T.I.; (lp)(c) **GOOD KING BAD** 51 Jun 76

Sep 76. C.T.I.; (7") **THEME FROM GOOD KING BAD. / ?**

Nov 76. C.T.I.; (lp) **BENSON & FARRELL (with "JOE FARRELL" – flute)** 100

Jan 77. C.T.I.; (lp)(c) **IN CONCERT – CARNEGIE HALL (live)** -

May 79. C.T.I.; (lp) **THE SPACE ALBUM**

1979. C.T.I.; (lp) **CAST YOUR FATE TO THE WIND** -

Jun 82. C.T.I.; (lp)(c) **THE BEST OF GEORGE BENSON – THE EARLY YEARS**
(cd-iss.Sep84)

Sep 76. A&M; (lp)(c) **THE OTHER SIDE OF ABBEY ROAD** Jul 76

1978. A&M; (lp)(c) **THE BEST OF GEORGE BENSON**
(re-iss.Mar82)

Aug 77. Embassy; (lp)(c) **SUMMERTIME**
(re-iss.Sep82 on 'Epic')

Sep 78. Embassy; (lp)(c) **STORMY WEATHER**
(re-iss.1984 on 'CBS')

Nov 81. Warners; (d-lp)(c) **THE GEORGE BENSON COLLECTION** 19 14
– Turn your love around / Love all the hurt away / Give me the night / Love ballad / Nature boy / Last train to Clarksville / Livin' inside your love / Never give up on a good thing / On Broadway / White rabbit / This masquerade / Here comes the Sun / Breezin' / Moody's mood for love (Moody's mood) / We got the love / The greatest love of all. (c+=) Cast your fate to the wind. *(re-iss.Aug86 + Nov88 on 'Deja Vu')*

Oct 82. Warners; (d-lp) **BREEZIN' / IN FLIGHT**

Nov 83. Warners; (7")(12") **ON BROADWAY. / LOVE WILL COME AGAIN**

Jun 77. Prestige; (lp) **THE NEW BOSS GUITAR OF GEORGE BENSON (w / JACK McDUFF)**
(above released 1964?) (cd-iss.Jul95 on 'Original Jazz')

Nov 83. Hallmark; (lp)(c) **THE GENIUS OF GEORGE BENSON** -

Mar 84. Proto; (lp) **THE WONDERFUL YEARS** Mar 84

Apr 84. Design; (lp)(c) **GEORGE BENSON LIVE IN CONCERT (live)** -
(re-iss.May85 on 'Premier')

May 85. Charly/ US= Affinity; (d-lp) **THE ELECTRIFYING GEORGE BENSON**
(cd-iss.Mar86)

Aug 85. Sierra; (lp)(c) **REPLAY ON . . .** -

Oct 85. K-Tel; (lp)(c) **THE LOVE SONGS** 1 -

Nov 85. Polydor; (cd) **THE SILVER COLLECTION**

Feb 88. Polydor; (c)(cd) **WALKMAN JAZZ**

May 84. Old Gold; (7") **THE GREATEST LOVE OF ALL. / (other artist)** -
(re-iss.Mar90)

Jun 85. Diamond-CBS; (d-lp)(d-c) **IT'S UPTOWN / GEORGE BENSON COOKBOOK**

Dec 92. C.B.S./ US= Columbia; (cd) **THE BEST OF GEORGE BENSON**

Nov 87. Connoisseur; (d-lp)(c) **THE EXCLUSIVE BENSON** -

Feb 88. Verve; (c)(cd) **GEORGE BENSON** -

Jul 88. Parkwood; (lp) **DETROIT'S GEORGE BENSON** -

Oct 89. Thunderbolt; (lp)(c)(cd) **MASQUERADE** -

Oct 91. Telstar; (cd)(c)(lp) **MIDNIGHT MOODS – THE LOVE COLLECTION** 25

May 93. Royal Collection; (cd)(c) **INVITATION** -

Sep 93. Magnum; (cd) **PAR EXCELLENCE** -

Sep 93. Jazz Hour; (cd) **WITCHCRAFT** -

Oct 93. Sony Europe; (cd) **ESSENTIAL TAKE FIVE** -

Feb 94. Javelin; (cd)(c) **SPOTLIGHT ON GEORGE BENSON** -

Jun 94. Verve; (cd) **VERVE JAZZ MASTERS 21** -

Aug 94. Legends In Music; (cd) **GEORGE BENSON** -

Chuck BERRY

Born: CHARLES BERRY, 18 Oct'26, San Jose, California, USA). In 1955, MUDDY WATERS helped him sign to 'Chess' records. His debut single 'MAYBELLENE' hit US Top 5, and was first of many hits, bar a few stutters. Late in 1959, he met a 14 year-old Apache Indian, who was working as a waitress, but unknown to BERRY she was a prostitute. He employed her as a hat-check girl in his night-club, but was soon arrested for violating minor control on State Line border crossing. He was convicted and sentenced to jail for 5 years, but due to the judges racist remarks, was given a retrial. Two years later, he was sentenced again, this time for 3 years, but with good behaviour he came out on Jan'64. While in jail, his work was being successfully re-issued, and many including The BEATLES and The ROLLING STONES were covering his early work for singles and album tracks. He returned to the studio in Feb'64 to record new song NADINE, which became Top 30 on both sides of The Atlantic. He also came to Britain for first time, playing many dates in a short space of time. In June '66, he signed to 'Mercury' records but this proved commercially fruitless. In 1972, after a return to the 'Chess' label three years previous, he had novelty UK No.1 hit with 'MY DING-A-LING'. Its double-entendre lyrical content, enraged morality pest Mary Whitehouse, enough for her to try and get it banned. In June 1979, he was again imprisoned (4 mths.) for tax evasion, but signed a deal with 'Atlantic', during this time. (see further on for more controversy). • **Style:** Black rebellious guitarist, whose R&B rock'n'roll was inspiration for many 60's UK beat groups. His amazing live 'duck-walk' earned him nickname of 'Crazy Legs'. • **Songwriters:** Pens own songs. • **Trivia:** Early 1988, a docu-film HAIL! HAIL! ROCK'N'ROLL was released, featuring the 1986 birthday concert. KEITH RICHARDS (of The ROLLING STONES) with others was in his backing band at the time.

Recommended: THE COLLECTION (*9)

CHUCK BERRY – vocals, guitar with **JOHNNIE JOHNSON** – piano / **JASPER THOMAS** – drums / **WILLIE DIXON** – bass / etc.

London Chess

Jul 55. (7") **MAYBELLENE. / WEE WEE HOURS** - 5

Oct 55. (7") **THIRTY DAYS. / TOGETHER WE WILL ALWAYS BE** -

(above 4 tracks were issued UK Jun56 on an EP)

May 56. (7") **THE DOWNBOUND TRAIN. / NO MONEY DOWN** Feb 56

Aug 56. (7") **TOO MUCH MONKEY BUSINESS. / BROWN EYED HANDSOME MAN** -

Feb 57. (7") **YOU CAN'T CATCH ME. / HAVANA MOON** 29 Nov 56

May 57. (7") **ROLL OVER BEETHOVEN. / DRIFTING HEART** 29 May 56

Jun 57. (7") **SCHOOL DAY. / DEEP FEELING** 24 3 Mar57

(above was issued in UK on 'Columbia')

— He retained **DIXON** and enlisted on most of 50's **FRED BELOW** – drums / **LAFAYETTE LEAKE** – piano

Jun 57. (7") **OH BABY DOLL / LA JAUNDA** - 57

1958. (lp) **AFTER SCHOOL SESSIONS** - □
– School day / Deep feeling / Too much monkey business / Wee wee hours / Roly poly / No money down / Brown-eyed handsome man / Berry pickin' / Together we will always be / Havana Moon / Downbound train / Drifting heart.

Dec 57. (7") **ROCK AND ROLL MUSIC. / BLUE FEELING** □ 8 Sep 57

Mar 58. (7") **SWEET LITTLE SIXTEEN. / REELIN' AND ROCKIN'** 16 2 Jan 58

May 58. (7") **JOHNNY B.GOODE. / AROUND AND AROUND** □ 8 Apr 58

Aug 58. (7") **BEAUTIFUL DELILAH. / VACATION TIME** □ 81 Jun 58

Oct 58. (7") **CAROL. / HEY PEDRO** □ 18 Aug 58

Nov 58. (lp) **ONE DOZEN BERRY'S** □ □
– Sweet little sixteen / Blue feeling / La juanda / Rockin' at the Philharmonic / Oh baby doll / Reelin' & rockin' / In-go / Rock and roll music / How you've changed / Low feeling / It don't take but a few minutes.

Dec 58. (7") **SWEET LITTLE ROCK AND ROLLER. / JOE JOE GUN** □ 47 / 83 Oct 58

Dec 58. (7") **RUN RUDOLPH RUN. / MERRY CHRISTMAS BABY** - 69 / 71

Jan 59. (7") **ANTHONY BOY. / THAT'S MY DESIRE** - 60

Apr 59. (7") **ALMOST GROWN. / LITTLE QUEENIE** □ 32 / 80 Mar 59

Jul 59. (7") **BACK IN THE U.S.A. / MEMPHIS, TENNESSEE** □ 37 Jun 59

1959. (lp) **CHUCK BERRY IS ON TOP** - □
– Almost grown / Carol / Maybellene / Sweet little rock and roller / Anthony boy / Johnny B.Goode / Little Queenie / Jo Jo Gunne / Roll over Beethoven / Around and around / Hey Pedro / Blues for Hawaiians. *(UK-iss.Oct87) (re-iss.cd+c Oct94)*

Oct 59. (7") **CHILDHOOD SWEETHEART. / BROKEN ARROW** - □

Mar 60. (7") **LET IT ROCK. / TOO POOPED TO POP** □ 64 / 42 Jan 60

Apr 60. (7") **BYE BYE JOHNNY. / WORRIED LIFE BLUES** - □

Jun 60. (7") **BYE BYE JOHNNY. / MAD LAD** □ -

Jun 60. (7") **MAD LAD. / I GOT TO FIND MY BABY** - □

1960. (lp) **ROCKIN' AT THE HOPS** - □
– Bye bye Johnny / Worried life blues / Down the road apiece / Confessin' the blues / Too pooped to pop ("Casey") / Mad lad / I got to find my baby / Betty Jean / Childhood sweetheart / Broken arrow / Driftin' blues / Let it rock. *(re-iss.+c.Aug87)*

Sep 60. (7") **JAGUAR AND THUNDERBIRD. / OUR LITTLE RENDEZVOUS** - □

Pye Inter... Chess

Sep 61. (7") **I'M TALKING 'BOUT YOU. / LITTLE STAR** □ □ Feb 61

— BERRY was convicted of earlier crime of transporting a minor (14 year-old) across the border. He served 2 years in prison between Feb62-Jan64.

– below are early recordings, compilations, etc released while in prison –

Jun 62. (lp) **JUKE BOX HITS** □ □ 1961
– I'm talking about you / Diploma for two / Thirteen question method / Away from you / Don't you lie to me / The way it was before / Little star / Route 66 / Sweet sixteen / Run around / Stop and listen / Rip it up. *(US-title 'NEW JUKEBOX HITS')*

May 63. (lp) **CHUCK BERRY** 12 □ 1962
– (compilation US-title 'CHUCK BERRY TWIST' diff.tracks) *(re-iss.US Dec63 as 'MORE CHUCK BERRY')(re-iss.1984 on 'Audio Fidelity') (re-iss.Dec85 on 'Astan')*

Jul 63. (7") **GO GO GO. / COME ON** 38 □ Jun 61

Aug 63. (7") **I'M TALKING 'BOUT YOU. / DIPLOMA FOR TWO** - □

Oct 63. (lp) **CHUCK BERRY ON STAGE (fake live)** 6 29 Aug 63
– Go go go / Memphis Tennessee / Maybellene / Surfin' steel (blues for Hawaiians) / Rockin' on the railroad (let it rock) / Brown eyed handsome man (new version) / I still got the blues / Surfin' USA (sweet little sixteen) / Jaguar and thunderbird / I just want to make love to you / All aboard / Trick or treat / Man and the donkey / How high the Moon.

Oct 63. (7") **MEMPHIS TENNESSEE. / SWEET LITTLE SIXTEEN** - □

Oct 63. (7") **MEMPHIS TENNESSEE. / LET IT ROCK** 6 -

Dec 63. (7") **RUN RUDOLPH RUN. / JOHNNY B.GOODE** 36 -

— Released from prison Jan64. New recordings . . .

Pye Int. Chess

Feb 64. (7") **NADINE (IS IT YOU?). / O RANGUTANG** 27 23

Apr 64. (7") **NO PARTICULAR PLACE TO GO. / LIVERPOOL DRIVE** 3 -

May 64. (7") **NO PARTICULAR PLACE TO GO. / YOU TWO** - 10

May 64. (lp) **HIS LATEST AND GREATEST** 8 -
– Nadine / Fraulein / Guitar boogie / Things I used to do / Don't you lie to me / Driftin' blues / Liverpool drive / No particular place to go / Lonely all the time (crazy arms) / Jaguar and Thunderbird / O rangutang / You two / Deep feeling / Bye bye Johnny.

Aug 64. (7") **YOU NEVER CAN TELL. / BRENDA LEE** 23 14 Jul 64

Sep 64. (lp) **YOU NEVER CAN TELL** 18 -
– You never can tell / Diploma for two / The little girl from Central / The way it was before / Around and around / Big Ben / Promised land / Back in the USA / Run around / Brenda Lee / Reeling and rockin' / Come on. *(re-iss.Dec67 on 'Marble A.')*

Oct 64. (7") **LITTLE MARIE. / GO BOBBY SOXER** □ 54 Sep64

— Late in '64, he paired up with BO DIDDLEY to record single CHUCK'S BEAT. / BO'S BEAT, and album TWO GREAT GUITARS. They had already appeared together on 1963 EP's 'CHUCK AND BO' Volumes 1,2 & 3.

Dec 64. (lp) **ST.LOUIS TO LIVERPOOL (live)** - □
– Little Marie / Our little rendezvous / No particular place to go / You two / Promised land / You never can tell / Go Bobby soxer / Things I used to do / Night beat / Liverpool drive / Merry Christmas baby / Brenda Lee. *(re-iss.+c.Aug86)*

Jan 65. (7") **THE PROMISED LAND. / THINGS I USED TO DO** 26 □

Chess Chess

Mar 65. (lp) **CHUCK BERRY IN LONDON (live)** □ □
– My little love light / She once was mine / After it's over / I got a booking / Night beat / His daughter Caroline / You came a long way from St.louis / St.Louis blues / Jamaica farewell / Dead dad / Butterscotch / The song of my love / Why should we end this way / I want to be your driver.

Mar 65. (7") **I GOT A BOOKING. / LONELY SCHOOLDAYS** - □

Mar 65. (7") **DEAR DAD./ MY LITTLE LOVELIGHT** - 95

Apr 65. (7") **DEAR DAD. / LONELY SCHOOLDAYS** - -

Oct 65. (7") **IT WASN'T ME. / WELCOME BACK PRETTY BABY** - □

Oct 65. (7") **IT WASN'T ME. / IT'S MY OWN BUSINESS** □ -

Nov 65. (lp) **FRESH BERRYS** □ □
– It wasn't me / Run Joe / Everyday we rock and roll / One for my baby / Sad day long night* / It's my own business / Right off Rampart Street / Vaya con dios / Merrily we rock and roll / My Mustang Ford / Ain't that just like a woman / Wee hours blues. *(US version omitted * for 'Welcome back pretty baby')*

Jul 66. (7") **RAMONA SAY YES. / LONELY SCHOOLDAYS** □ □ Jun 66

Aug 66. (7") **HAVANA MOON. / MEMPHIS** - □

Mercury Mercury

Dec 66. (7") **CLUB NITTY GRITTY. / LAUGH AND CRY** □ □ Nov 66

Jul 67. (7") **BACK TO MEMPHIS. / I DO REALLY LOVE YOU** □ □ Jun 67

Nov 67. (7") **FEELIN' IT. / IT HURTS ME TOO** - □

Dec 67. (lp) **IN MEMPHIS** - □
– Back to Memphis / I do really love you / My heart will always belong to you / Ramblin' Rose / Sweet little rock and roller / Oh baby doll / Check me out / It hurts me too / Bring another drink / So long / Goodnight, well it's time to go.

Apr 68. (lp) **LIVE AT THE FILLMORE AUDITORIUM** - □
– Medley: Rockin' at the Fillmore – Everyday I have the blues / C.C. rider / Driftin' blues / Feelin' it / Flying home / Hoochie coochie man / It hurts me too / Fillmore blues / Wee baby James / Johnny B.Goode.

Oct 68. (7") **ST.LOUIS TO FRISCO. / MA DEAR** □ □ Aug68

Nov 68. (lp) **FROM ST.LOUIS TO FRISCO** - □
– Louie to Frisco / Ma dear / The love I lost / I love her, I love her / Little fox / Rock cradle rock / Soul rockin' / I can't believe / Misery / My tambourine / Oh captain / Mum's the word.

May 69. (7") **ROLL OVER BEETHOVEN. / BACK TO MEMPHIS** □ -

Aug 69. (7") **GOOD LOOKING WOMAN. / IT'S TOO DARK IN THERE** - □

Nov 69. (lp) **CONCERTO IN B.GOODE** - □
– Good looking woman / My woman / It's too dark in there / Put her down / Concerto in 'B Goode'.

Chess Chess

Aug 70. (7") **TULANE. / HAVE MERCY JUDGE** - □

Jan 71. (lp)(c) **BACK HOME** □ □ 1970
– Tulane / Have mercy judge / Instrumental / Christmas / Gun / I'm a rocker / Flyin' home / Fish and chips / Some people

1971. (lp)(c) **SAN FRANCISCO DUES** □ □
– Oh Louisiana / Let's do our thing together / Your lick / Festival / Bound to lose / Bordeaux in my pirough / San Francisco dues / Viva rock and roll / My dream / Lonely school days (version 2).

Jun 72. (lp)(c) **THE LONDON SESSIONS** 8 □
– Let's boogie / Mean old world / I will not let you go / London Berry blues / I love you / Reeling and rockin'(live) / My ding-a-ling (live) / Johnny B.Goode (live).

Aug 72. (7") **DOWN THE ROAD APIECE. / JOHNNY B.GOODE** □ -

Aug 72. (7") **MY DING-A-LING. / JOHNNY B.GOODE** - 1

Oct 72. (7") **MY DING-A-LING. / LET'S BOOGIE** 1 -

Dec 72. (7") **REELIN' AND ROCKIN'(live). / LET'S BOOGIE** - 27

Jan 73. (7") **REELIN' AND ROCKIN'(live). / I WILL NOT LET YOU GO** 18 -

Sep 73. (7") **BIO. / ROLL 'EM PETE** □ □

Oct 73. (lp)(c) **BIO** □ □
– Bio / Hello little girl, goodbye / Woodpecker / Rain eyes / Aimlessly driftin' / Got it and gone / Talkin' about my buddy. *(re-iss.May88)*

Nov 73. (7") **SOUTH OF THE BORDER. / BIO** □ -

— duets with daughter INGRID GIBSON on some tracks in 1975.

Feb 75. (7") **SHAKE, RATTLE AND ROLL. / BABY WHAT YOU WANT ME TO DO** - □

Mar 75. (7") **SHAKE, RATTLE AND ROLL. / I'M JUST A NAME** □ -

Apr 75. (lp)(c) **CHUCK BERRY '75** □ □
– Swanee river / I'm just a name / I just want to make love to you / Too late / South of the border / Hi-heel sneakers / You are my sunshine / My babe / Baby what you want me to do / A deuce / Shake, rattle and roll / Sue answer / Don't you to me.

10 Jul'79, he was sentenced to 4 months jail for tax evasion.

Atlantic Atlantic

Aug 79. (7") **OH WHAT A THRILL. / CALIFORNIA** □ □

Oct 79. (lp)(c) **ROCKIT** □ □ Aug 79
– Move it / Oh what a thrill / I need you baby / If I were / House lights / I never thought / Havana moon / Pass away. *(re-iss.+cd.Nov88 on 'Magnum F.')*

— Virtually retired from the studio to live in his own amusement park in Wentzville, Missouri. In Nov'89, he played live again in a revival concert alongside BO DIDDLEY, The COASTERS, etc. The following month, more controversy surrounded him, when it was claimed he had been videoing a woman's rest-room for immoral purposes. In June 1990, his house was raided by the drugs squad, who seized marjuana, guns and homemade pornography. He was charged later with possession of drugs and child abuse. He was cleared of the abuse case, but given a fine and a 6-month prison sentence for the drugs misdemeanour.

– compilations, others, etc. –

1957. Chess; (7"ep) **AFTER SCHOOL SESSION** - □
– School day / Deep feeling / Brown eyed handsome man / Too much monkey . . .

1957. Chess; (7"ep) **ROCK AND ROLL MUSIC** - □
– Rock and roll music / Oh baby doll / La juanda / Blue feeling.

1958. Chess; (7"ep) **SWEET LITTLE SIXTEEN** - □
– Sweet little sixteen / Reelin' and rockin' / Rock at the philharmonic / Guitar boogie. *(UK-iss.Mar59 as 'REELIN' AND ROCKIN', 1 diff.track)*

1959. Chess; (7"ep) **PICKIN' BERRIES** - □
– Beautiful Delilah / Vacation time / Carol / Hey Pedro.

1959. Chess; (7"ep) **SWEET LITTLE ROCK AND ROLLERS** - □
– Johnny B.Goode / Around and around / Sweet little rock and roller / Jo Jo Gunne.

May 64. Chess; (lp) **GREATEST HITS** - 34

Oct 63. Pye International; (7"ep) **CHUCK BERRY**
– Johnny B.Goode / Oh baby doll / School day / Back in the U.S.A.
Dec 63. Pye International; (7"ep) **THIS IS CHUCK BERRY** -
– Bye bye Johnny / Rock and roll music / Childhood sweetheart / Broken arrow.
Apr 64. Pye International; (7"ep) **THE BEST OF CHUCK BERRY** -
– Memphis Tennessee / Roll over Beethoven / I'm talking 'bout you / Sweet little sixteen.
Oct 64. Pye International; (7"ep) **CHUCK BERRY HITS** -
– Johnny B.Goode / Nadine / No particular place to go / Memphis Tennessee.
Dec 64. Pye International; (7"ep) **BLUE MOOD** -
– Driftin' blues / Lonely all the time / Things I used to do / Fraulein.
Feb 67. Marble Arch; (lp) **CHUCK BERRY'S GREATEST HITS** -
Mar 65. Chess; (7"ep) **THE PROMISED LAND** -
– You never can tell / Brenda Lee / The promised land / Things I used to do.
Oct 65. Chess; (7"ep) **COME ON** -
– Reelin' and rockin' / Don't you lie to me / Around and around / Come on.
Feb 66. Chess; (7"ep) **I GOT A BOOKING** -
– I want to be your driver / St.Louis blues / Dear dad / I got a booking.
May 66. Chess; (7"ep) **YOU CAME A LONG WAY FROM ST.LOUIS** -
– You came a long way from St.Louis / His daughter Caroline / My little love-light / Jamaica farewell.
May 68. Chess; (7") **JOHNNY B.GOODE. / SWEET LITTLE SIXTEEN** -
Apr 69. Chess; (7") **NO PARTICULAR PLACE TO GO. / IT WASN'T ME** -
May 69. Chess; (lp) **GREATEST HITS** -
Mar 72. Chess; (7"m) **ROCK AND ROLL MUSIC. / JOHNNY B.GOODE / SCHOOL DAY** -
May 72. Chess; (lp)(c) **GOLDEN DECADE VOL.1** 72
VOLUME 2 / VOLUME 3 released 73 & 74 respectively.
Nov 74. Chess; (lp) **ALL-TIME GREATEST ROCK AND ROLL PARTY HITS**
May 76. Chess; (7"m) **SWEET LITTLE ROCK AND ROLLER. / BACK IN THE U.S.A. / NO PARTICULAR PLACE TO GO**
Jan 77. Chess; (lp)(c) **MOTORVATIN' (Greatest live)** 7
(re-iss.Dec87 on 'Starblend')
May 77. Chess; (7") **SWEET LITTLE SIXTEEN. / GUITAR BOOGIE**
Mar 83. Chess; (lp) **CHUCK BERRY**
Mar 83. Chess; (lp) **CHESS MASTERS**
Jul 83. Chess; (10"lp) **DUCK WALKING**
(re-iss.+cd.Jul88 on 'Entertainers')
Jul 86. Chess; (lp)(c) **NEW JUKE BOX HITS**
Jun 88. Chess; (7"ep)(12"ep) **MY DING A LING / SCHOOL DAY. / NO PARTICULAR PLACE TO GO / JOHNNY B.GOODE** -
Feb 66. Golden Guinea; (lp) **CHUCK BERRY** -
(re-iss.Sep66 on 'Marble Arch')
Mar 67. Mercury; (lp) **GOLDEN HITS**
Feb 80. Mercury; (lp) **MODS AND ROCKERS**
1981. Mercury; (lp) **ROCKIN' WITH CHUCK BERRY**
1973. Philips; (lp) **BACK IN THE U.S.A.** -
(re-iss.pic-lp Dec85 on 'Astan')
May 75. Contour; (lp) **I'M A ROCKER** -
Jul 78. Sonic; (lp) **SWEET LITTLE SIXTEEN** -
Sep 79. Hammer; (7"ep) **ROLL OVER BEETHOVEN** -
– Roll over Beethoven / Johnny B.Goode / Sweet little sixteen / Maybellene / Carol / Memphis, Tennessee.
Sep 79. Hammer; (7"ep) **SCHOOL DAY** -
– School day / Rock and roll music / Sweet little rock and roller / Reelin' and rockin' / Back in the U.S.A. / Thirty days.
Oct 79. Hammer; (lp) **20 GREATEST HITS** -
Oct 80. Spotlight; (lp)(c) **SPOTLIGHT ON . . .** -
Jul 82. Everest; (lp) **LIVE (live)** -
May 83. Stack-O-Hits; (lp) **ALIVE AND ROCKIN' (live)** -
Jan 83. Flashback-Pye; (7") **NO PARTICULAR PLACE TO GO. / SWEET LITTLE SIXTEEN** -
1983. Spot; (lp) **THE GREATEST HITS – LIVE (live)** -
Jun 83. Old Gold; (7") **MEMPHIS, TENNESSEE. / NO PARTICULAR PLACE TO GO** -
Jan 89. Old Gold; (7") **NO PARTICULAR PLACE TO GO. / MEMPHIS TENNESSEE** -
Jan 89. Old Gold; (7") **MY DING-A-LING. / REELIN' AND ROCKIN'** -
Jan 89. Old Gold; (7") **SWEET LITTLE SIXTEEN. / ROCK AND ROLL MUSIC** -
Jan 89. Old Gold; (7") **ROLL OVER BEETHOVEN. / JOHNNY B GOODE** -
(cd-s+=) – Johnny B.Goode / Rock and roll music.
Dec 85. P.R.T.; (lp)(c) **20 SUPER HITS** -
1986. Vogue (cd) **TWO DOZEN BERRY'S** -
Dec 86. Vogue; (cd) **BEST OF CHUCK BERRY** -
Oct 88. Vogue; (d-lp) **CHICAGO GOLDEN YEARS (GOLDEN DECADE VOL.1)** -
—— (also issued VOL.2 & 3).
Nov 83. Bulldog; (lp) **REELING, ROLLING & ROCKING** -
May 87. Bescoli; (cd) **21 GREATEST HITS** -
(re-iss.Jan90 on 'Zeta')
Jun 84. S.M.P.; (7") **MY DING-A-LING. / MAYBELLENE / REELIN' AND ROCKIN'** -
Jun 84. S.M.P.; (7") **SWEET LITTLE SIXTEEN. / NADINE / JOHNNY B.GOODE** -
Apr 86. Castle; (lp)(c) **GREATEST HITS** -
Jun 88. Castle; (d-lp)(c)(cd) **THE COLLECTION** -
– Sweet little sixteen / Johnny B.Goode / Back in the U.S.A. / Maybellene / Too much monkey business / Rock and roll music / Reelin' and rockin' / No particular place to go / Roll over Beethoven / You never can tell / Nadine / Carol / School days / My ding-a-ling / Almost grown / Let it rock / Little Queenie / Promised land / Memphis Tennessee / Sweet little rock'n'roller / Thirty days / Brown-eyed handsome man / Run Rudolph run / Merry Christmas baby.
Jul 86. Deja Vu; (lp) **THE COLLECTION – 20 ROCK'N'ROLL GREATS** -
Aug 87. Topline; (cd) **REELING AND ROCKING** -
1987. Checkmate; (lp) **LET IT ROCK** -
1988. Joker; (lp) **ROLL OVER BEETHOVEN VOL.1** -
Feb 88. M.C.A.; (lp)(c)(cd) **HAIL, HAIL, ROCK'N'ROLL (Soundtrack)**
(re-iss.cd.Nov93 on 'Charly')
Sep 89. M.C.A.; (lp)(c)(cd-box) **CHESS BOX**
Feb 90. M.C.A.; (cd) **ROCK'N'ROLL RARITIES**
Mar 88. Stylus; (lp)(c)(cd) **CHESS MASTERS** -
Apr 88. Platinum; (lp)(c)(cd) **DECADE 55-65** -
Jul 88. Driving Wheel; (lp) **CHUCK BERRY'S ROCK'N'ROLL PARTY** -
Dec 88. Fun; (c) **20 GREATEST HITS** -
Jun 89. Ocean; (lp)(c)(cd) **ROLL OVER BEETHOVEN** -
Jul 89. Instant; (lp)(c)(cd) **ROCK & ROLL MUSIC** -
(re-iss.cd Feb93 on 'Charly')
Nov 89. Charly; (lp)(c)(cd) **CHUCK BERRY BOX SET** -
May 94. Charly; (d-cd) **POET OF ROCK'N'ROLL** -
May 94. Charly; (cd) **TWO ON ONE** (w / BO DIDDLEY) -
Oct 94. Charly; (cd) **LET IT ROCK** -
Nov 94. Charly; (cd) **OH YEAH** -
Mar 90. Roots; (lp)(c)(cd) **ROCK & ROLL MUSIC** -
Apr 91. Vogue; (cd)(c) **THE BEST OF CHUCK BERRY VOL.1 1955-57** -
Apr 91. Vogue; (cd)(c) **THE BEST OF CHUCK BERRY VOL.2 1959-60** -
Apr 91. Vogue; (cd)(c) **THE BEST OF CHUCK BERRY VOL.3 1960-65** -
May 91. Magnum Force; (cd)(c) **THE CHESS YEARS**
Dec 91. Magnum Force; (cd) **THE CHESS MASTERS VOL.2: 1958-65**
Jun 91. See For Miles; (cd)(c)(lp) **THE EP COLLECTION** -
Aug 91. Provogue; (cd) **SWEET LITTLE SIXTEEN VOL.2** -
Apr 93. Laserlight; (cd)(c) **MR. ROCK'N'ROLL** -
Sep 93. Ace; (cd) **ON THE BLUES SIDE** -
Jan 95. Wisepack; (cd) **LEGENDS IN MUSIC** -
Apr 95. Charly; (4xcd-box+book) **THE POET OF ROCK'N'ROLL** -
Jun 95. Collection; (cd) **THE COLLECTION** -

BETTER DAYS (see under ⇒ Paul BUTTERFIELD)

Dickey BETTS (see under ⇒ ALLMAN BROTHERS BAND)

Bev BEVAN (see under ⇒ ELECTRIC LIGHT ORCHESTRA)

B-52's

Formed: Athens, Georgia, USA . . . late '76, by PIERSON, SCHNEIDER, STRICKLAND, RICKY WILSON and sister CINDY. Took name from bouffant hairdo the girls had which was named after a bomb. After one self-financed 45 sold out its 2,000 copies, they drew the attention of Island's Chris Blackwell. He signed them after a residency at Max's Kansas City late 1978, and soon re-issued debut 'ROCK LOBSTER' 45, which made UK Top 40 lists in 1979. For the next decade or so, The B-52's brightened up the rock and pop world, hitting the charts on many occasions. However life was not plain sailing, as RICKY died of AIDS on 12 Oct'85, after suffering a few years with the virus. • **Style:** Outwardly weird and visual, mixing new wave REZILLOS-type dual harmonies and danceable futuristic fun rock'n'roll. • **Songwriters:** All mainly STRICKLAND or group compositions. PLANET CLAIRE (w/ Henry Mancini) • **Trivia:** DAVID BYRNE (Talking Heads) produced their 1982 mini-lp 'MESOPOTAMIA'. In 1981, during lay-off, STRICKLAND, PIERSON and CINDY WILSON did one-off Japan venture as "MELON" with group The PLASTICS and ADRIAN BELEW. Late 1990, PIERSON contributed on singles by IGGY POP (Candy) and R.E.M. (Shiny Happy People). DON WAS and NILE RODGERS each produced half of 1992 album.

Recommended: DANCE THIS MESS AROUND THE BEST OF THE B-52's (*9)

KATE PIERSON (b.27 Apr'48, Weehawken, New Jersey) – vocals, organ, bass / **CINDY WILSON** (b.28 Feb'57) – vocals, percussion, guitar / **RICKY WILSON** (b.19 Mar'53) – guitar / **FRED SCHNEIDER** (III) (b. 1 Jul'51, Newark, Georgia) – vocals, keyboards / **KEITH 'Julian' STRICKLAND** (b.26 Oct'53) – drums

not issued Private . . .
Jul 78. (7") **ROCK LOBSTER. / 52 GIRLS** -
(re-iss.Nov78 on 'Bouffant') (some copies given free with debut lp)

Island Warners
Jul 79. (7") **ROCK LOBSTER. / 6060-842** - 56
Jul 79. (7") **ROCK LOBSTER. / RUNNING AROUND** 37 -
(re-iss.Jul81)
Jul 79. (lp)(c) **THE B-52's** 22 59
– Planet Claire / 52 girls / Dance this mess around / Rock lobster / Lava / There's a Moon in the sky (called the Moon) / Hero worship / 6060-842 / Downtown. *(re-iss.Jun86 + Oct86) (cd-iss.Jan87) (re-iss.lp Jan94 + May94)*
Sep 79. (7") **6060-842. / HERO WORSHIP**
Nov 79. (7")(7"pic-d) **PLANET CLAIRE. / THERE'S A MOON IN THE SKY (CALLED THE MOON)**
(re-iss.Jul81)
Jul 80. (7") **GIVE ME BACK MY MAN. / STROBE LIGHT** 61
Sep 80. (lp)(c) **WILD PLANET** 18 18

– Party out of bounds / Dirty back road / Runnin' around / Give me back my man / Private Idaho / Devil in my car / Quiche Lorraine / Strobe light / 53 miles west of Venus. *(cd-iss.May90)*

Oct 80. (7") **PRIVATE IDAHO. / PARTY OUT OF BOUNDS** [-] [74]

Nov 80. (7") **DIRTY BACK ROAD. / STROBE LIGHT** [ ] [ ]

Jan 81. (7") **QUICHE LORRAINE. / LAVA** [-] [ ]

Feb 82. (m-lp)(c) **MESOPOTAMIA** [18] [35]

– Loveland / Deep sleep / Mesopotamia / Cake / Throw that beat in the garbage can / Nip it in the bud. *(cd-iss.May90)*

1982. (7") **DEEP SLEEP. / NIP IT IN THE BUD** [-] [ ]

1982. (7") **MESOPOTAMIA. / THROW THAT BEAT IN THE GARBAGE CAN** [-] [ ]

Apr 83. (7") **SONG FOR A FUTURE GENERATION. / ('A'instrumental)** [63] [ ]

(12"+=) – Planet Claire.

(d7"++=) – There's a Moon in the sky (called the Moon).

May 83. (lp)(c) **WHAMMY!** [33] [29]

– Legal tender / Whammy kiss / Song for a future generation / Butterbean / Trism / Queen of Las Vegas / Don't worry / Big bird / Work that skirt. *(cd-iss.May90)*

Jul 83. (7") **LEGAL TENDER. / MOON 83** [-] [81]

Oct 83. (7") **SONG FOR A FUTURE GENERATION. / ?** [-] [ ]

RICKY suffering from full blown AIDS, finally dies 12 Oct'85. Group carry on, augmented by session man **RALPH CARNEY – guitar**

Jun 87. (7")(7"pic-d) **WIG. / SUMMER OF LOVE** [ ] [ ]

(d7"+=) – Song for a future generation / 52 girls.

(12"+=)(c-s+=) – Song for a future generation / Give me back my man.

Jul 87. (lp)(c)(cd) **BOUNCING OFF THE SATELLITES** [74] [85] Sep 86

– Summer of love / Girl from Ipanema goes to Greenland / Housework / Detour thru your mind / Wig / Theme for a nude beach / Ain't it a shame / Juicy jungle / Communicate / She brakes for rainbows. *(cd-iss.May90)*

Sep 87. (7") **SUMMER OF LOVE. / HOUSEWORK** [-] [ ]

— added on tour **PAT IRWIN – keyboards / ZACH ALFORD** – drums / **PHILIPPE SASSE** – (studio keyboards) / **SARA LEE** – bass (ex-GANG OF FOUR) (also studio)

Reprise Reprise

Jul 89. (lp)(c)(cd) **COSMIC THING** [ ] [4]

– Cosmic thing / Dry country / Deadbeat club / Love shack / Junebug / Roam / Bushfire / Channel Z / Topaz / Follow your blues. *(re-dist.Apr90, hit UK No.8)*

Aug 89. (7") **LOVE SHACK. / CHANNEL Z** [-] [3]

Sep 89. (7") **CHANNEL Z. / JUNEBUG** [61] [-]

(12")(cd-s) – ('A'side) / ('A'rock mix) / ('A'dub mix). *(re-iss.Aug90)*

Dec 89. (7") **ROAM. / BUSHFIRE** [-] [3]

Feb 90. (7") **LOVE SHACK. / PLANET CLAIRE** [2] [-]

(c-s+=)(cd-s+=)(7"pic-d+=) – Rock lobster (live).

(12") – ('A'side) / ('A'remix) / ('A'Ben Grosse mix).

Apr 90. (7") **DEADBEAT CLUB. / PLANET CLAIRE** [-] [30]

May 90. (7")(c-s)(cd-s) **ROAM. / WHAMMY KISS (live) / DANCE THIS MESS AROUND (live)** [17] [-]

(12") – ('A'side) / (2-'A'mixes).

Sep 90. (7")(c-s) **DEADBEAT CLUB. / LOVE SHACK** [ ] [-]

(12"+=)(cd-s+=) – B-52's megamix.

— now trimmed to basic trio of **PIERSON, SCHNEIDER** – vox / **& STRICKLAND** – guitar with guest musicians **IRWIN / ALFORD / LEE /** plus **JEFF PORCARO + STERLING CAMPBELL** – drums / **DAVID McMURRAY** – sax / **JAMIE MULHOBERAC + RICHARD HILTON** – keyboards / **LENNY CASTRO** – percussion / **TRACY WORMWORTH** – bass

Jun 92. (7")(c-s) **GOOD STUFF. / BAD INFLUENCE** [21] [28]

(12"+=)(cd-s+=) – Return to Dreamland.

(12") – (4 'A'mixes).

Jul 92. (cd)(c)(lp) **GOOD STUFF** [8] [16]

– Tell it like it t-i-is / Hot pants explosion / Good stuff / Revolution Earth / Dreamland / Is that you Mo-Dean? / The world's green laughter / Vision of a kiss / Breezin' / Bad influence. *(re-iss.cd/c Feb95)*

Sep 92. (7")(c-s) **TELL IT LIKE IT T-I-IS. / THE WORLD'S GREEN LAUGHTER** [61] [ ]

(12")(cd-s) – ('A' 4 other mixes).

Nov 92. (7")(c-s) **IS THAT YOU MO-DEAN?. / ('A'-Moby mix)** [ ] [ ]

(12"+=)(cd-s+=) – ('A'-2 other mixes) / Tell it like it t-i-is.

Feb 93. (7")(c-s) **HOT PANTS EXPLOSION. / LOVE SHACK** [ ] [ ]

(cd-s+=) – Channel Z / Roam.

— **SCHNEIDER, PIERSON + STRICKLAND**

next from the new film 'The Flintstones' on 'M.C.A.'.

Jun 94. (7")(c-s) **(MEET) THE FLINTSTONES. ("BC-52's") / ('A'mix)** [3] [33] May94

(cd-s+=) – (2 'A'mixes).

– compilations, others, etc. –

Jul 81. Island/ US= Warners; (m-lp)(c) **THE PARTY MIX ALBUM** [36] [55]

Aug 81. Island; (7") **GIVE ME BACK MY MAN (party mix). / PARTY OUT OF BOUNDS** [ ] [ ]

Apr 86. (7")(7"pic-d)(7"sha-pic-d) **ROCK LOBSTER. / PLANET CLAIRE** [12] [ ]

(d7"+=) – Song for a future generation / 52 girls.

(12"+=) – Song for a future generation / Give me back my man.

Jun 90. (cd)(c)(lp) **DANCE THIS MESS AROUND THE BEST OF THE B-52's** [36] [ ]

– Party out of bounds / Devil in my car / Dirty back road / 6060-842 / Wig / Dance this mess around / Private Idaho / Rock lobster / Strobe light / Give me back my man / Song for a future generation / Planet Claire / 52 girls. (cd+=) – (2 extra mixes).

Feb 91. Reprise; (cd)(c) **PARTY MIX / MESOPOTAMIA** [-] [ ]

Nov 92. Reprise; (cd) **WILD PLANET / B-52's** [ ] [ ]

Sep 95. Spectrum; (cd) **PLANET CLAIRE** [ ] [-]

FRED SCHNEIDER

solo, recorded 1984 and written with COTE.

Reprise Reprise

May 91. (cd)(c)(lp) **FRED SCHNEIDER** [ ] [ ]

– Monster / Out the concrete / Summer in Hell / Orbit / I'm gonna haunt you / It's time to kiss / This planet's a mess / Wave / Boonga (the New Jersey caveman).

Jun 91. (c-s)(cd-s) **MONSTER /** [-] [85]

Jello BIAFRA (see under ⇒ DEAD KENNEDYS)

BIG AUDIO DYNAMITE

Formed: London, England . . . 1984 by MICK JONES who still was under contract with 'CBS' records. Amongst others he recruits film-maker/friend and non-musician DON LETTS. Although their late 1985 debut 'THE BOTTOM LINE' soon became a favourite, it missed out on chart placing. However the follow-up 'E=Mc2', gave them near UK Top 10 hit in 1986, and resurrected sales of critically acclaimed but flop album. • **Style:** Punk/dub rock, mixed with samples and tapes. Because of Mick's unique punk vocals and his last band's break-up; circa 1985, their sound was not unlike a danceable CLASH. • **Songwriters:** Mainly JONES and LETTS, with other members contributing. Covers: DUELLING BANJOS (Arthur Smith's theme from 'Deliverance' Soundtrack) / BATTLE OF NEW ORLEANS (trad.). • **Trivia:** While recording 2nd album, JOE STRUMMER (Clash) came in to co-write and produce a couple of songs. For half a year in 1990, MICK was hospitalized while he recovered slowly from viral pneumonia and chicken pox. In 1991 he was credited guesting on AZTEC CAMERA top 20 UK hit 'GOOD MORNING BRITAIN'.

Recommended: THIS IS BIG AUDIO DYNAMITE (*8)

MICK JONES – vocals, guitar (ex-CLASH) / **DON LETTS** – effects, vocals / **DAN DONOVAN** – keyboards / **LEO WILLIAMS** – bass / **GREG ROBERTS** – drums.

C.B.S. Columbia

Sep 85. (7")(12")(ext-12") **THE BOTTOM LINE. / BAD** [ ] [ ]

Nov 85. (lp)(c) **THIS IS BIG AUDIO DYNAMITE** [ ] [ ]

– Medicine show / Sony / E=Mc2 / The bottom line / Sudden impact / Stone Thames / B.A.D. / A party. *(cd-iss.Jun86)*

Mar 86. (7")(12") **E=Mc2. / THIS IS BIG AUDIO DYNAMITE** [11] [ ]

May 86. (7") **MEDICINE SHOW. / A PARTY** [29] [ ]

(12") – ('A'extended). / ('B'dub)

(d12"+=) – E=Mc2 (remix) / Albert Einstein the human beatbox.

Oct 86. (7") **C'MON EVERY BEATBOX. / BADROCK CITY** [51] [ ]

(12"+=) – Beatbox's at dawn.

(12"++=) – The bottom line.

Oct 86. (lp)(c)(cd) **No.10 UPPING STREET** [11] [ ]

– C'mon every beatbox / Beyond the pale / Limbo the law / Sambadrome / V thirteen / Ticket / Hollywood boulevard / Dial a hitman / Sightsee M.C! (c+=)(cd+=) – Ice cool killer (dial a hitman-instrumental) / The big V (V thirteen – instrumental). *(re-iss.Oct89)*

Feb 87. (7") **V THIRTEEN. / HOLLYWOOD BOULEVARD** [49] [ ]

(12"+=) ('B'club)

Jul 87. (12"m) **SIGHTSEE MC! (radio cut) / ANOTHER ONE RIDES THE BUS / SIGHTSEE MC! / SIGHTSEE - WEST LONDON** [ ] [ ]

May 88. (7")(ext.12") **JUST PLAY MUSIC. / MUCH WORSE** [51] [ ]

Jun 88. (lp)(c)(cd) **TIGHTEN UP VOL.88** [33] [ ]

– Rock non stop (all night long) / Other 99 / Funny names / Applecart / Esquerita / Champagne / Mr.Walker said / The battle of All Saints Road, incorporating:- Battle of New Orleans – Duelling banjos / Hip neck and thigh / 2000 shoes / Tighten up vol.88 / Just play music. *(re-iss.cd+c Oct94 on 'Columbia')*

Jul 88. (7") **OTHER 99. / WHAT HAPPENED TO EDDIE?** [ ] [ ]

(12")(cd-s) – ('A'extended) / Just play music (club mix)

Sep 89. (lp)(c)(cd) **MEGATOP PHOENIX** [26] [85]

– Start / Rewind / All mink and no manners / Union, Jack / Contact / Dragon town / Baby don't apologise / Is yours working yet? / Around the girls in 80 ways / James Brown / Everybody needs a holiday / Mick's a hippie burning / House arrest / The green lady / London Bridge / Stalag 123 / End.

Oct 89. (7") **CONTACT. / IN FULL EFFECT** [ ] [ ]

(12"+=)(cd-s+=) – Who beats / If I were John Carpenter.

BIG AUDIO DYNAMITE II

was formed by **JONES** and **DONOVAN** (left mid'90) **NICK HAWKINS** – guitar / **GARY STONEDAGE** – bass / **CHRIS KAVANAGH** – drums (ex-SIGUE SIGUE SPUTNIK)all repl. others who formed SCREAMING TARGET in 1991. (album 'Hometown Hi-Fi')

Oct 90. (cd)(c)(lp) **KOOL-AID** [55] [ ]

– Change of atmosphere / Can't wait / Kickin' in / Innocent child / On one / Kool-aid / In my dreams / When the time comes.

Columbia Columbia

Jul 91. (cd)(c)(lp) **THE GLOBE** [63] [72]

– Rush / Can't wait (live) / I don't know / The globe / Innocent child / Green grass / Kool-aid / In my dreams / When the time comes / The tea party.

Jul 91. (7") **THE GLOBE (remix). / CITY LIGHTS** [ ] [76]

(12"+=)(cd-s+=) – ('A'dub).

Nov 91. (7")(c-s) **RUSH (New York mix). / (A3 version)** [ ] [32] Sep 91

(cd-s+=) – City lights (full version).

(12") – ('A'side) / ('A'-3 other mixes).

(above 'A'side was issued Feb91 on other side of CLASH single 'Should I Stay Or Should I Go')

BIG AUDIO

Nov 94. (c-s)(cd-s) **LOOKING FOR A SONG. / MODERN STONE AGE BLUES** [68] [ ]

(12"+=)(cd-s+=) – ('A'-Zonka remix) / ('A'-Shapps remix).

Nov 94. (cd)(c)(lp) **HIGHER POWER** [ ] [ ]

– Got to wake up / Harrow Road / Looking for a song / Some people / Slender Loris / Modern stoneage blues / Melancholy maybe / Over the rise / Why is it? / Moon / Lucan / Light up my life / Hope.

BIG AUDIO DYNAMITE

Radio-active M.C.A.

Jun 95. (c-s) **I TURNED OUT A PUNK / WHAT ABOUT LOVE**
(cd-s+=) – ('A'-Live fast, live fast mix).
(12") – ('A'side) / (A'-Live fast mix) / ('A'-Live fast instrumental) / ('A'-Feelin' lucky mix).

– compilations, others, etc. –

Nov 88. C.B.S.; (d-cd) **THIS IS BIG AUDIO DYNAMITE / No.10 UPPING STREET**
Sep 95. Columbia; (cd)(c) **PLANET B.A.D.**

BIG BLACK

Formed: Chicago, Illinois, USA . . . 1982 by STEVE ALBINI. Their first official release came late '82, when local independent label 'Ruthless' unleashed punk-inspired 'LUNGS' EP. Finally surfaced in the UK in 1986, when 'Homestead', issued the John Peel favourite 'ATOMIZER'. • **Style:** Abrasive but thought-provoking hardcore outfit. • **Songwriters:** ALBINI and group compositions except; HEARTBEAT (Wire) / HE'S A WHORE (Cheap Trick) / THE MODEL (Kraftwerk) / REMA REMA (Rema Rema). The controversial RAPEMAN covered JUST GOT PAID (ZZ Top). • **Trivia:** Their 'BULLDOZER' EP is now worth up to £300!

Recommended: ATOMIZER (*7) / SONGS ABOUT *!?KING (*8).

STEVE ALBINI – vocals, guitar

not issued Ruthless

1982. (c) **BIG BLACK LIVE (live)** [-]
– (UK-iss.Oct89 on 'Blast First')

— added **SANTIAGO DURANGO** – guitar (ex-NAKED RAYGUN, ex-SILVER ABUSE) / **JEFF PEZZATI** – bass (ex-NAKED RAYGUN) / **PAT BYRNE** – drums

Nov 82. (12"ep) **LUNGS** [-]
– Steelworker / Live in a hole / Dead Billy / I can be killed / Crack / R.I.P. *(re-iss.Nov92 on 'Touch & Go')*

Nov 83. (12"ep) **BULLDOZER** [-]
– Cables / Pigeon kill / I'm a mess / Texas / Seth / Jump the climb. *(re-iss.Nov92 on 'Touch & Go')*

Homestead Homestead

Apr 85. (m-lp) **RACER-X** 1984
– Racer-x / Shotgun / The ugly American / Deep six / Sleep! / Big payback. *(re-iss.Nov92 on 'Touch & Go')*

Sep 86. (7") **IL DUCE. / BIG MONEY** 1985
(re-iss.Nov92 on 'Touch & Go')

Sep 86. (lp) **ATOMIZER**
– Jordan, Minnesota / Passing complexion / Big money / Kerosene / Bad houses / Kerosene / Fists of love / Stinking drunk / Bazooka Joe / Strange things. *(re-iss.Nov86 on 'Blast First') (re-iss.+cd.Nov92 on 'Touch & Go')*

— **DAVE RILEY** – bass (ex-SAVAGE BELIEFS) repl. PEZZAM / drum machine replaced BYRNE.

Blast First Blast First

Jun 87. (12"ep)(c-ep) **HEADACHE**
– My disco / Grinder / Ready men / Pete, king of all detectives.
(free 7"w.a./tracks on c-ep) – HEARTBEAT. / THINGS TO DO TODAY / I CAN'T BELIEVE
(above 7" released on own 1986 on 'Touch & Go' US) *(UK re-iss.Nov92 on 'Touch & Go')*

Jul 87. (lp)(c)(cd) **SONGS ABOUT *!?KING**
– The power of independent trucking / The model / Bad penny / El doper / Precious thing / Columbian neck-tie / Kitty empire / Ergot / Kashmir S. Pulasiday / Fish fry / Pavement saw / Tiny, the king of the Jews / Bombastic intro. *(re-iss.+cd.Nov92 on 'Touch & Go', with 'He's A Whore')*

Blast First Touch & Go

Aug 87. (7") **HE'S A WHORE. / THE MODEL**

— Disbanded in 1988.

– compilations, etc. –

Mar 87. Homestead; (lp) **THE HAMMER PARTY** [-]
– (LUNGS + BULLDOZER) *(re-iss.+cd.Nov92 on 'Touch & Go' with 'RACER X')*

Jun 87. Not; (lp) **SOUND OF IMPACT (live bootleg)** [-]
(re-iss.1990)

1988. Blast First; (cd) **RICH MAN'S EIGHT TRACK TAPE** [-]
– (ATOMIZER + HEADACHE + HEARTBEAT) *(re-iss.+cd.Nov92 on 'Touch & Go')*

Oct 92. Touch & Go; (cd)(lp) **PIGPILE (live)**

RAPEMAN

were formed by **ALBINI** with **DAVID WM. SIMS** – bass / **REY WASHAM** – drums (both ex-SCRATCH ACID)

not issued Fierce

1988. (7") **HATED CHINEE. / MARMOSET** [-]

Blast First Blast First

Nov 88. (12"ep) **BUDD (live) / SUPERPUSSY (live). / LOG BASS (live) / DUTCH COURAGE**

Dec 88. (lp)(cd) **TWO NUNS AND BLACK MULE**
– Steak and black onions / Monobrow / Up beat / Cotition ignition mission / Kim Gordon's panties / Hated Chinee / Radar love wizard / Marmoset / Just got paid / Trouser minnow. *(cd+=)* Budd / Superpussy / Log brass / Dutch courage.

Sub Pop Sub Pop

Aug 89. (7")(7"clear) **INKI'S BUTT CRACK. / SONG NUMBER ONE**

— Had to split in Feb89, due to backlash against group name. SIMS returned to Austin, where he re-united with ex-SCRATCH ACID members to form JESUS LIZARD. They were produced by ALBINI who continued as a producer, noteably for others The PIXIES, The BREEDERS, NIRVANA, WEDDING PRESENT.

BIG BOPPER

Born: JAPE RICHARDSON, 29 Oct'32, Sabine Pass, Texas, USA. After sending demo to Pappy Dailey, he signed to 'Mercury' records 1956. Success came when he decided to name himself BIG BOPPER and release hit-to-be 'CHANTILLY LACE'. (see below for more details). • **Style:** Turned from hillbilly C&W to JERRY LEE LEWIS style rock'n'roll. • **Songwriters:** Writes own material. • **Trivia:** Early 1960, after his death, fellow Texan JOHNNY PRESTON hit top of US/UK charts with his 'RUNNING BEAR'.

Recommended: CHANTILLY LACE STARRING THE BIG BOPPER (*5)

JAPE RICHARDSON

(his real name) – vocals

Mercury Mercury

Nov 57. (7") **CRAZY BLUES. / BEGGAR TO A KING** [-]
May 58. (7") **THE MONKEY SONG. / TEENAGE MOON** [-]

The BIG BOPPER

Nov 58. (7")**CHANTILLY LACE. / THE PURPLE PEOPLE EATER MEETS THE WITCH DOCTOR** [12] [6] Jul 58
(re-iss.Mar83 on 'Swift', re-iss.Jan85 on 'Old Gold')

1958. (lp) **CHANTILLY LACE STARRING THE BIG BOPPER**
– Chantilly lace / Pink petticoats / The clock / Walking through my dreams / Someone watching over you / Old maid / Big Bopper's wedding / Little red riding hood / Preacher and the bear / It's the truth, Ruth / White lightning / Strange kisses. *(UK-iss.'59 on 'Contour', re-iss.'68 on 'Pickwick', US-re-iss.'81)*

Nov 58. (7") **LITTLE RED RIDING HOOD. / BIG BOPPER'S WEDDING** [38]
[72]

— On the 2nd Feb59, JAPE was killed in a plane crash, along with BUDDY HOLLY and RICHIE VALENS. Posthumous releases continue below

Feb 59. (7") **WALKING THROUGH MY DREAMS. / SOMEONE IS WATCHING OVER YOU** [-]
May 59. (7") **IT'S THE TRUTH RUTH. / THAT'S WHAT I'M TALKING ABOUT**
Aug 59. (7") **PINK PETTICOATS. / THE CLOCK** [-]

– compilations etc. –

1959. Mercury; (7"ep) **THE BIG BOPPER** [-]
– Chantilly lace / The purple people eater meets the witch doctor / Little Red Riding Hood / Big Bopper's wedding.

1959. Mercury; (7"ep) **PINK PETTICOATS** [-]
– Pink petticoats / Walking through my dreams / It's the truth Ruth / +1.

1977. Flyright; (lp) **LOUISIANA SWAMP POP (rare)** [-]
Mar 83. wift; (7"m) **CHANTILLY LACE. / MONKEY SONG / OLD MAID** [-]
Jan 85. Old Gold; (7") **CHANTILLY LACE. / ('B'by 'Freddy Bell')** [-]
1988. Rhino; (lp) **HELLOOO BABY: THE BEST OF THE BIG BOPPER** [-]

BIG BROTHER & THE HOLDING CO.

Formed: San Francisco, California, USA . . . 1966 by SAM ANDREW, etc. They recruited Texan JANIS JOPLIN who had just turned down opportunity to join 13th FLOOR ELEVATORS. They signed to 'Mainstream' records in Aug'66, and after excellent Monterey festival performance, released debut album. In 1968 when they signed to 'Columbia', where they had top selling US album 'CHEAP THRILLS', which hit No.1 for 7 weeks. When JANIS JOPLIN left with SAM ANDREW, this all but killed any further success for BIG BROTHER. • **Style:** Powerful bluesy rock, that gave light to tremendous vocal talent of JANIS JOPLIN. In the 70's, they mellowed with her absence. • **Songwriters:** Group compositions. • **Miscellaneous:** (see under; Janis JOPLIN).

Recommended: CHEAP THRILLS (*6)

SAM ANDREW (b.18 Dec'41, Taft, California) – guitar, vocals / **PETE ALBIN** (b. 6 Jun'44) – bass, vocals / **JAMES GURLEY** – guitar repl. DAVE ESKERSON (left Nov65) / **DAVID GETZ** – drums repl. CHUCK JONES (left Feb66) also on occasion / **ED BOGAS** – violin (left before Summer'66, to NEW RIDERS OF THE PURPLE SAGE)

— (Jun66) added **JANIS JOPLIN** (b.19 Jan'43, Port Arthur, Texas) – vocals

not issued Mainstream

Aug 67. (lp) **BIG BROTHER & THE HOLDING COMPANY** [-] [60] Aug 67
– Bye bye baby / Easy rider / Intruder / Light is faster than sound / Call on me / Coo

coo / Women is losers / Blind man / Down on me / Caterpillar / All is loneliness / The last time. *(UK-iss.'68 on 'Fontana') (re-iss.May71 on 'Columbia' 2 extra tracks 'Coo Coo' & 'The Last Mile' which were also 'A' & 'B' US single)(cd-iss.Apr93 as 'FIRST ALBUM' on 'Sony Europe')*

1967. (7") **BLIND MAN. / ALL IS LONELINESS** [-] [ ]

1967. (7") **DOWN ON ME. / CALL ME** [-] [ ]
(re-iss.Aug68 in US on 'Columbia' reached No.43) (UK-iss.'69)

Fontana / Mainstream

1967. (7") **BYE BYE BABY. / INTRUDER (US) / ALL IS LONELINESS (UK)** [ ] [ ]

1968. (7") **WOMEN IS LOSERS. / LIGHT IS FASTER THAN SOUND** [-] [ ]

C.B.S. / Columbia

Aug 68. (7") **PIECE OF MY HEART. / TURTLE BLUES** [ ] [12]

Sep 68. (lp) **CHEAP THRILLS** [ ] [1] Aug 68
– Combination of the two / I need a man to love / Summertime / Piece of my heart / Turtle blues / O sweet Mary / Ball and chain. *(re-iss.+c-Mar81) (cd-iss.Jan91 & Jun92)*

— Folded late 1968. JANIS JOPLIN went solo, taking SAM ANDREW. In Aug69 GETZ and ALBIN re-formed BIG BROTHER & THE HOLDING COMPANY with **NICK GRAVENITES** – vocals / **MIKE PRENDERGAST** – guitar / **TED ASHBURTON** – piano

— soon split again, GETZ was also in NU BUGALOO EXPRESS.

— **GETZ, GURLEY, ALBIN, SAM ANDREW** and **NICK GRAVENITES** – vocals re-grouped

— **BIG BROTHER & THE HOLDING COMPANY** with **KATHI McDONALD** – vocals and **MIKE FINNEGAN** – keyboards / **DAVID SCHALLOCK** – guitar (both ex-NU BUGALOO EXPRESS)

C.B.S. / Columbia

Jan 71. (lp)(c) **BE A BROTHER** [ ] [ ] Nov 70
– Keep on / Joseph's coat / Home on the strange / Someday / Heartache people / Sunshine baby / Mr.Natural / Funkie Jim / I'll change your flat tire Merle / Be a brother.

Sep 71. (lp)(c) **HOW HARD IT IS** [-] [ ] Aug 71
– How hard it is / You've been talkin' 'bout me, baby / House on fire / Black widow spider / Last band on side one / Nu Boogaloo jam / Maui / Shine on / Buried alive in the blues / Promise her anything but give her Arpeggio.

Sep 71. (7") **BLACK WIDOW SPIDER. / NU BOOGALOO JAM** [-] [ ]

— Split Feb72. ALBIN rejoined COUNTRY JOE (McDONALD) & THE FISH. He and GETZ were part of them in 1969. FINNEGAN played live with STEPHEN STILLS etc. GRAVENITES tried to revitalise ELECTRIC FLAG.

– compilations etc. –

Nov 68. Mainstream; (7") **COO COO. / ?** [-] [84]

Jun 83. Island; (12") **ADVENTURES IN SUCCESS (FIRST ADVENTURE). /** [ ] [ ]

1985. Edsel/ US= Making Waves; (lp) **CHEAPER THRILLS** (live 26th July '66) [-] [ ] Jan 84

Oct 84. Code; (7") **BIG BROTHER. / IF YOU TRY** [ ] [ ]

Apr 86. Edsel; (lp) **JOSEPH'S COAT** (best of 71's two albums) [ ] [-]

BIG COUNTRY

Formed: Dunfermline, Scotland ... Autumn 1981 by ADAMSON and WATSON. They recruited brothers PETER (keyboards) and ALAN WISHART (bass) plus CLIVE PARKER (drums, ex-SPIZZ ...). Early 1982 the latter three had been replaced by BRZEZICKI and BUTLER. After they turned down 'Ensign' contract, they signed to 'Mercury-Phonogram' Spring '82. They soon were based in London, England, and stormed the charts with 'FIELDS OF FIRE' & 'IN A BIG COUNTRY'. • **Style:** Anthemic heavy pop/rock, featuring live-like Scots 'bagpipe' sound from twin-guitars. • **Songwriters:** Mostly ADAMSON / WATSON, except TRACKS OF MY TEARS (Smokey Robinson & The Miracles) / HONKY TONK WOMAN (Rolling Stones) / AULD LANG SYNE (trad.) / ROCKIN' IN THE FREE WORLD (Neil Young) / FLY LIKE AN EAGLE (Steve Miller) / BLACK SKINNED BLUE EYED BOYS (Equals / Eddy Grant). OH WELL (Fleetwood Mac) / (DON'T FEAR) THE REAPER (Blue Oyster Cult) / WOODSTOCK (Joni Mitchell) / CRACKED ACTOR (David Bowie) / PARANOID (Black Sabbath). • **Trivia:** Their song 'ONE GREAT THING' was used on Tennent's lager advert. In August 1988, they tour major venues in Soviet Russia.

Recommended: THROUGH A BIG COUNTRY – GREATEST HITS (*8)

STUART ADAMSON (b.see SKIDS) – vocals, lead guitar, synthesizer (ex-SKIDS) / **BRUCE WATSON** (b.11 Mar'61, Ontario, Canada) – guitar (ex-DELINX) / **TONY BUTLER** (b. 3 Feb'59, London, England) – bass (ex-ON THE AIR) / **MARK BRZEZICKI** (b.21 Jun'57, Slough, England) – drums (ex-ON THE AIR)

Mercury / Mercury

Sep 82. (7") **HARVEST HOME. / BALCONY** [ ] [ ]
(12"+=)(12"clear+=) – Flag of nations (swimming).

Feb 83. (7") **FIELDS OF FIRE. / ANGLE PARK** [10] [52] Feb84
(7"sha-pic-d+=) – Harvest home.
(12"+=)(12"clear+=) – ('A'alternative mix).

May 83. (7") **IN A BIG COUNTRY. / ALL OF US.** [17] [17] Oct 83
(12"+=) ('A'pure mix)
(extra-12"++=) – Heart and soul.

Jun 83. (lp)(c) **THE CROSSING** [3] [18] Jul 83
– In a big country / Inwards / Chance / 1,000 stars / The storm / Harvest home / Lost patrol / Close action / Fields of fire / Porrohman. (c+=) 4 remixes. *(re-dist.+cd-Mar84) (re-cd.1986)*

Aug 83. (7") **CHANCE. / TRACKS OF MY TEARS (live)** [9] [ ]
(12")(12"pic-d) – ('A'extended) / The crossing.

Jan 84. (7") **WONDERLAND. / GIANT** [8] [86]
(12"+=)(12"clear+=) – ('A'extended).
(d7"+=) – Lost patrol (live – parts 1 & 2).

Apr 84 (m-lp) **WONDERLAND** [-] [65]
– Wonderland / Angle park / The crossing / All fall together.

Sep 84. (7") **EAST OF EDEN. / PRAIRIE ROSE.** [17] [ ]
(12"+=) – ('A'extended).

Oct 84. (lp)(c)(cd) **STEELTOWN** [1] [70]
– Flame of the west / East of Eden / Steeltown / Where the rose is sown / Come back to me / Tall ships go / Girl with grey eyes / Rain dance / The great divide / Just a shadow. *(re-cd.1986) (re-iss.cd+c.May93 on 'Spectrum')*

Nov 84. (7") **WHERE THE ROSE IS SOWN. / BELIEF IN THE SMALL MAN** [29] [ ]
(d7"+=) – Wonderland (live) / In a big country (live) / Auld Lang Syne (live).
(12"+=) – ('A'extended) / Bass dance.

Jan 85. (7") **JUST A SHADOW. / WINTER SKY.** [26] [ ]
(12"+=) – ('A'extended).

Apr 86. (7")(7"sha-pic-d) **LOOK AWAY. / RESTLESS NATIVES** [7] [ ]
(12") – ('A'-outlaw mix) / ('B'-soundtrack part 1).
(d7"+=) – Margo's theme / Highland scenery.

Jun 86. (7") **THE TEACHER. / HOME COME THE ANGELS** [28] [ ]
(12") – ('A'mystery mix) / Restless natives (part 2).

Jun 86. (lp)(c)(cd) **THE SEER** [2] [59]
– Look away / The seer / The teacher / I walk the hill / Eiledon / One great thing / Hold the heart / The seer / Remembrance day / The red fox / The sailor. *(re-iss.cd Aug94 on 'Vertigo')*

Sep 86. (7") **ONE GREAT THING. / SONG OF THE SOUTH** [19] [ ]
(12"+=) – ('A'mix).
(d7"+=) – Wonderland (live) / Chance (live).
(12"+=) – Look away (outlaw mix).
(c-s+=) – In a big country (pure mix) / Fields of fire (live).

Nov 86. (7")(12") **HOLD THE HEART. / HONKY TONK WOMAN (live)** [55] [ ]
(d12"+=) – (interview part 1 & 2).

added on tour **JOSS PHILIP-GORSE** – keyboards

Mercury / Reprise

Aug 88. (7") **KING OF EMOTION. / THE TRAVELLERS** [16] [ ]
(12"+=) – Starred & Crossed.
(c-s+=) – On the shore.
(cd-s++=) – Not waving but drowning.

Sep 88. (lp)(c)(cd) **PEACE IN OUR TIME** [9] [ ]
– King of emotion / Broken heart (thirteen valleys) / Thousand yard stare / From here to eternity / Everything I need / Peace in our time / Time for leaving / River of hope / In this place / I could be happy here. *(cd+=)* – The travellers.

Oct 88. (7") **KING OF EMOTION. / IN A BIG COUNTRY** [-] [ ]

Oct 88. (7") **BROKEN HEART (THIRTEEN VALLEYS). / SOAPY SOUTAR STRIKES BACK** [47] [ ]
(12"+=) – When a drum beats / On the shore.
(cd-s+=) – When a drum beats / Made in Heaven.
(cd-s+=) – Wonderland (12"mix).

Jan 89. (7") **PEACE IN OUR TIME. / PROMISED LAND** [39] [ ]
(12"+=) – The longest day / Over the border.
(extra-12"+=) – In a big country (live) / Chance (live).
(cd-s+=) – The longest day / Chance.

(Feb90) **PAT AHERN – drums** repl. BRZEZICKI who joined PRETENDERS

Apr 90. (7")(c-s) **SAVE ME. / PASS ME BY** [41] [ ]
(12"+=) Wonderland (live) / 1,000 yard stare (live) / Dead on arrival (live) *(not on cd)*
(cd-s++=) – World on fire.

May 90. (cd)(c)(lp) **THROUGH A BIG COUNTRY – GREATEST HITS** (compilation) [2] [ ]
– Save me / In a big country / Fields of fire / Chance / Wonderland / Where the rose is sown / Just a shadow / Look away / King of emotion / East of Eden / One great thing / The teacher / Broken heart (thirteen valleys) / Peace in our time. (c/cd+=) – Eiledon / The seer / Harvest home.

Jul 90. (7")(c-s) **HEART OF THE WORLD. / BLACK SKINNED BLUE EYED BOYS** [50] [ ]
(12"+=) – Broken heart (thirteen valleys) (acoustic) / Peace in our time (acoustic).
(cd-s+=) – Restless Natives.

Vertigo / Reprise

Aug 91. (7"ep) **REPUBLICAN PARTY REPTILE. / COMES A TIME / YOU, ME AND THE TRUTH** [37] [ ]
(7"ep)(12"ep)(10"ep) – Comes a time. *(re-iss.cd+c Feb93)*
(cd-ep+=) – ('A'side) / Freedom song / Kiss the girl goodbye / I'm only waiting.

Sep 91. (cd)(c)(lp) **NO PLACE LIKE HOME** [28] [ ]
– We're not in Kansas / Republican party reptile / Dynamic lady / Keep on dreaming / Beautiful people / The hostage speaks / Beat the Devil / Heap of faith / Ships / Into the fire. (cd+=) – You, me and the truth / Comes a time. *(re-iss.cd Aug94 on 'Vertigo')*

Oct 91. (7")(c-s) **BEAUTIFUL PEOPLE. / RETURN OF THE TWO HEADED KING** [72] [ ]
(cd-s+=) – Rockin' in the free world (live).
(12"pic-d+=) – Fly like an eagle.

— **ADAMSON, BUTLER + WATSON** were joined by session men **SIMON PHILLIPS** – drums / **COLIN BERWICK** – keyboards

Compulsion / Fox-RCA

Mar 93. (7")(c-s) **ALONE. / NEVER TAKE YOUR PLACE** [24] [ ]
(12"pic-d+=) – Winter sky / Look away.
(cd-s) – ('A'side) / Chance / Rockin' in the free world / Eastworld.

Mar 93. (cd)(c)(lp) **THE BUFFALO SKINNERS** [25] [ ]
– Alone / Seven waves / What are you working for / The one I love / Long way home / The selling of America / We're not in Kansas / Ships / All go together / Winding wind / Pink marshmallow moon / Chester's farm. *(re-iss.Sep94)*

Apr 93. (7")(c-s) **SHIPS (WHERE WERE YOU). / OH WELL** [29] [ ]
(12"+=)(cd-s+=) – (Don't fear) The reaper / Woodstock.
(cd-s+=) – The buffalo skinners / Cracked actor / Paranoid.

Jun 94. (cd)(c)(lp) **WITHOUT THE AID OF A SAFETY NET (live)** [35] [ ]

– Harvest home / Peace in our time / Just a shadow / Broken heart (thirteen valleys) / The storm / Chance / Look away / Steeltown / Ships / Wonderland / What are you working for / Long way home / In a big country / Lost patrol.

Transatla. not issued

May 95. (c-ep)(cd-ep) **I'M NOT ASHAMED / ONE IN A MILLION (1st visit) / MONDAY TUESDAY GIRL / ('A'edit)** [69] [-]
(cd-s) – ('A'side) / Crazytimes / In a big country / Blue on a green planet.

Jun 95. (cd)(c) **WHY THE LONG FACE?** [48] [ ]
– You dreamer / Message of love / I'm not ashamed / ail into nothing / Thunder & lightning / Send you / One in a million / God's great mistake / Wild land in my heart / Thank you to the Moon / Far from me to you / Charlotte / Post nuclear talking blues / Blue on a green planet.

Nov 95. (cd-ep) **NON!** [ ] [-]
– Post nuclear talking blues / Blue on a green planet / God's great mistake / All go together.

— above was an action awareness record for Greenpeace.

– compilations –

Aug 94. Nighttracks; (cd) **RADIO 1 SESSIONS** [ ] [-]
Aug 94. Legends In Music; (cd) **BIG COUNTRY** [ ] [-]
Aug 95. Spectrum; (cd) **IN A BIG COUNTRY** [ ] [-]
Oct 95. Windsong; (cd) **BBC LIVE IN CONCERT (live)** [ ] [-]

BIG STAR (see under ⇒ BOX TOPS)

BIOHAZARD

Formed: Brooklyn, New York, USA . . . 1988 by HAMBEL and SEINFELD. After 2 quickly dismissed albums in the early 90's, they finally cracked it with 'STATE OF THE WORLD ADDRESS' in '94 for major 'Warners'. • **Style:** A fusion of ONYX and CYPRESS HILL rap and New York hardcore metal. • **Songwriters:** Group compositions; except AFTER FOREVER (Black Sabbath). • **Trivia:** CYPRESS HILL's SEN DOG features on 'HOW IT IS'.

Recommended: STATE OF THE WORLD ADDRESS (*6)

BOBBY HAMBEL – vocals, guitar / **EVAN SEINFELD** – vocals, bass / **BILL GRAZIADEI** – guitar, keyboards / **DANNY SCHULER** – drums

Maze Maze

Dec 90. (cd)(lp) **BIOHAZARD** [ ] [ ]
– Retribution / Victory / Blue blood / Howard Beach / Wrong side of the tracks / Justified violence / Skinny song / Hold my own / ain / Panic attack / Survival of the fittest / There and back / Scarred for life.

Road-runner Maze

Oct 92. (cd)(c) **URBAN DISCIPLINE** [ ] [ ]
– Chamber spins three / Punishment / Shades of grey / Business / Black and white and red all over / Man with a promise / Disease / Urban discipline / Loss / Wrong side of the tracks / Mistaken identity / We're only gonna die (from our arrogance) / Tears of blood. (cd+=) Hold my own. (digi-cd+=) Shades of grey (live) / Punishment (live). *(re-iss.cd Oct94)*

Warners Warners

May 94. (cd)(c)(lp) **STATE OF THE WORLD ADDRESS** [ ] [48]
– State of the world address / Down for life / What makes us tick / Tales from the hard side / How it is / Remember / Five blocks to the subway / Each day / Failed territory / Lack there of / Pride / Human animal / Cornered / Love denied / Ink.

Jun 94. (7")(c-s) **TALES FROM THE HARD SIDE. / DOWN FOR LIFE** [47] [ ]
(10"+=)(cd-s+=) – State of the world address / ('A'video edit).

Jun 94. (7") **FEELING GOOD. / ?** [ ] [40]

— (above single on 'Mercury')

Aug 94. (10"colrd)(c-s) **HOW IT IS. / ('A'-Brooklyn bootleg 2 + 3)** [62] [ ]
(cd-s+=) – ('A'lethal MOD mix) / ('A'lethal instrumental mix).

BIRDLAND

Formed: near Coventry, Midlands, England . . . 1988 by VINCENT brothers, who earlier had been ZODIAC MOTEL. Late 1988, they signed to 'Lazy' once home of The PRIMITIVES, and scored with indie crossover 45 'SLEEP WITH ME'. In 1990, they were snapped up by MCA (US) and Toshiba (JAPAN), but this didn't prove fruitful. • **Style:** Bleached boys who 'Clash' through garage metal-punk. • **Songwriters:** All penned by the brothers, except ROCK'N'ROLL NIGGER (Patti Smith) / SEE NO EVIL (Television).

Recommended: BIRDLAND (*6)

ZODIAC MOTEL

(trio except ROGERS)

Swordfish not issued

Apr 87. (7") **SUNSHINE MINER. / CRESCENDO** [ ] [-]
(12"+=) – Inside my mind / Sugarblood.

— not known if VINCE brothers had departed, as RETRO / LIDD were main writers

Aug 87. (12"ep) **CRYSTAL INJECTION / (I CAN ONLY GIVE YOU) EVERYTHING. / DESTINY RANCH / STEPHANIE BLUE** [ ] [-]
1987. (lp) **THE STORY OF ROLAND FLAGG** [ ] [-]

BIRDLAND

ROBERT VINCE – vocals / **LEE VINCE** – guitar / **SID ROGERS** – bass / **GENE KALE** – drums

Lazy M.C.A.

Mar 89. (7") **HOLLOW HEART. / SUGAR BLOOD** [70] [-]
(7"ep+=)(12"ep+=) THE BIRDLAND EP – Crystal / Got to get away.

Jun 89. (7") **PARADISE. / WHITE** [70] [-]
(12"ep+=) EP 2 – Rage. (some mispressed – Stay)

Jan 90. (7"m) **SLEEP WITH ME / WANTED. / HOLLOW HEART (acoustic) / SLEEP WITH ME (acoustic)** [32] [-]

Sep 90. (7"m) **ROCK'N'ROLL NIGGER / FUN FUN FUN. / ROLLER COASTER / PROTECTION** [47] [-]

Jan 91. (7") **EVERYBODY NEEDS SOMEBODY. / DON'T HANG ON** [44] [ ]
(12"+=) – Shoot you down (acoustic) / Untitled *(12"only)*
(cd-s++=) – Twin sons.
(7"ep+=) – Twin sons / Exit (acoustic).

Feb 91. (cd)(c)(lp) **BIRDLAND** [44] [ ]
– Shoot you down / Sleep with me / Don't look back / Wake up dreaming / Letter you know / Rock'n'roll nigger / Everybody needs somebody / Beat me like a star / She belongs to me / Exit. (cd+=) – Hollow heart / Crystal / Got to get away.

— Disbanded soon after being dropped by record label.

BIRTHDAY PARTY

Formed: Caulfield, Melbourne, Australia . . . late 1977 as BOYS NEXT DOOR, by CAVE, HARVEY, PEW and CALVERT who knew each other since 1973. After over a year on 'Mushroom' records, they move to England as BIRTHDAY PARTY. They were soon snapped up mid 1980 by IVO on then new indie label '4ad'. In 1982, they achieved a Top 75 placing with lp 'JUNKYARD', but by the following year, all had splintered into other ventures. • **Style:** Avant-garde gothic/new wave, similar to PERE UBU or POP GROUP, but fronted by the near mental NICK CAVE. • **Songwriters:** Some CAVE / some HOWARD and others. BOYS NEXT DOOR cover; THESE BOOTS ARE MADE FOR WALKING (Nancy Sinatra). • **Trivia:** The band were miffed when 'Missing Link' released 'IT'S STILL LIVING' without their consent 1985. While PEW was in jail, others CAVE, HOWARD and HARVEY teamed up as TUFF MONKS with fellow Australians The GO-BETWEENS to issue one-off single 'AFTER THE FIREWORKS'.

Recommended: PRAYERS ON FIRE (*7) / HITS (*9)

BOYS NEXT DOOR

NICK CAVE – vocals / **MICK HARVEY** – guitar / **TRACY PEW** – bass / **PHIL CALVERT** – drums

Suicide not issued

May 78. (7") **THESE BOOTS ARE MADE FOR WALKING. / BOY HERO** [-] [-] Aussie

— (Dec78) added **ROWLAND S. HOWARD** – guitar (ex-YOUNG CHARLATANS)

Mushroom not issued

May 79. (7") **SHIVERS. / DIVE POSITION** [-] [-] Aussie
May 79. (lp) **DOOR DOOR** [-] [-] Aussie
– The nightwatchman / Brave exhibitions / Friends of my world / The voice / Roman Roman / Somebody's watching / After a fashion / Dive position / I mistake myself / Shivers. *(cd-iss.1987 Australia) (cd-iss.Mar93 on 'Grey Area-Mute')*

not issued Missing L.

Dec 79. (12"ep) **HEE-HAW** [-] [-] Aussie
– Catholic skin / The red clock / Faint heart / The hair shirt / Death by drowning. *(re-iss.Dec83 Australia; credited as BIRTHDAY PARTY)*

Feb 80. (7") **HAPPY BIRTHDAY. / THE RIDDLE HOUSE** [-] [-] Aussie

BIRTHDAY PARTY

(same line-up) (Australian record label in brackets)

Jul 80. (7") **MR.CLARINET. / HAPPY BIRTHDAY** (gig freebie) [-] [-]

4.a.d. not issued

Oct 80. Missing Link; (7"m) **THE FRIEND CATCHER. / WAVING MY ARMS / CATMAN** [-] [-] Aust.

Nov 80. Missing Link; (lp) **THE BIRTHDAY PARTY** [-] [-] Aust.
– (original copies by BOYS NEXT DOOR) – The friend catcher / Waving my arms / Catman / The red clock / Etc.+?

May 81. (lp) **PRAYERS ON FIRE** [ ] [-]
– Zoo music girl / Cry / Capers / Nick the stripper / Ho-ho / Figure of fun / King Ink / A dead song / Yard / Dull day / Just you and me.
(not iss.AUSTRALIA) *(cd-iss.Apr88)* (+=) – Blunder town / Kathy's kisses. *(also its first release in Australia on 'Virgin' red-lp + cd, also +=)*

Jun 81. Missing Link; (12"m) **NICK THE STRIPPER. / BLUNDER TOWN / KATHY'S KISSES** [-] [-] Aussie

Aug 81. (7") **RELEASE THE BATS. / BLAST OFF** [ ] [-]
(12"-issued Australia Apr83)

Oct 81. (7") **MR.CLARINET. / HAPPY BIRTHDAY** [ ] [-]

Feb 82. (m-lp) **DRUNK ON THE POPE'S BLOOD (live)** [ ] [-]
– Pleasure heads / king Ink / Zoo music girl / Loose.

(above other side by LYDIA LUNCH)

— (Dec81) while **TRACY PEW** was in jail for drunk driving he was replaced on tour only by either BARRY ADAMSON, CHRIS WALSH or **HARRY HOWARD**

May 82. (lp)(c) **JUNKYARD** [73] [-]
– She's hit / Dead Joe / Dim locator / Hamlet (pow-pow-pow) / Several sins / Big-Jesus-trash-can / Kiss me back / 6" gold blade / Kewpie doll / Junkyard. *(Australian release 1985, also iss.1991 on 'Virgin' pink-lp / +cd. +=) (cd-iss.Apr88)* (+=) – Release the bats / Blast off / Dead Joe (version).

1982. Missing LInk; (7") **NICK THE STRIPPER. / BLUNDERTOWN** [-] [-] Aust.

— Now quartet when **CALVERT** joined **PSYCHEDELIC FURS**. (HARVEY now drums)

Feb 83. (12"ep) **BAD SEED** [ ] [-]

– Sonny's burning / Wild world / Fears of gun / Deep in the woods.

— **JEFFREY WEGENER** – drums (ex-LAUGHING CLOWNS) repl. HARVEY Also **BLIXA BARGELD** – guitar (of EINSTURZENDE NEUBAUTEN) repl. absent HOWARD

Mute / not issued

Nov 83. (12"ep) **MUTINY** [ ] [-]
– Jennifer's evil / Mutiny in Heaven / Swampland / Says spell.

— Disbanded Autumn 1983. TRACY joined The SAINTS. (He was later to die late '86 of epileptic fit aged 28). ROWLAND HOWARD formed CRIME & THE CITY SOLUTION. NICK CAVE went solo, forming his BAD SEEDS taking with him MICK HARVEY.

– compilations, others, etc. – (all mostly UK)

Jun 83. 4 a.d.; (12"ep) **THE BIRTHDAY PARTY EP** [ ] [-]
– The friend catcher / Release the bats / Blast off / Mr.Clarinet / Happy birthday.
Aug 89. 4 a.d.; (cd) **HEE-HAW** [ ] [-]
(contains tracks from THE BIRTHDAY PARTY lp)
Aug 89. 4 a.d.; (cd) **MUTINY (ep) / THE BAD SEED (ep)** [ ] [-]
Oct 92. 4 a.d.; (cd)(c)(d-lp) **HITS** [ ] [-]
– The friend catcher / Happy birthday / Mr Clarinet / Nick the stripper / Zoo music girl / King Ink / Release the bats / Blast off / She's hit / 6" Gold blade / Hamlet (pow, pow, pow) / Dead Joe / Junkyard / Big-Jesus-Trash-Can / Wild world / Sonny's burning / Deep in the woods / Swampland / Jennifer's veil / Mutiny in Heaven.
Apr 85. MIssing Link; (d-lp) **IT'S STILL LIVING (live)** [-] [-] Aust.
(Australian re-iss.1991 on 'Virgin' green-lp +cd)
1985. Missing Link; (lp) **A COLLECTION – BEST AND RAREST** [-] [-] Aust.
(cd.iss.1991 Australia. w/diff 2nd side)
Feb 87. Strange Fruit; (12"ep) **THE PEEL SESSIONS** (21.4.81) [ ] [-]
– Release the bats / Rowland around in that stuff (sometimes) / Pleasure heads must burn / Loose. *(cd-s.iss.Aug88)*
Oct 88. (12"ep)(cd-ep) **THE PEEL SESSIONS** (2.12.81) [ ] [-]
– Big-Jesus-trash-can / She's hit / Bully bones / 6" gold blade.

ROWLAND S.HOWARD & LYDIA LUNCH

Sep 82. 4 a.d.; (12") **SOME VELVET MORNING. / I FELL IN LOVE WITH A GHOST** [ ] [-]

BJORK

Formed: 21 Oct'66, Reykjavik, Iceland. The SUGARCUBES were formed by BJORK and EINAR who had been part of KUKL. In 1987, they were signed by Derek Schulman (ex-Gentle Giant) to indie label 'One Little Indian'. Their classic debut 45 'BIRTHDAY', soon became a John Peel favourite, also making UK Top 75. • **Style:** SUGARCUBES; Underground avant-garde outfit featuring the tortured English speaking vocal talents of petite BJORK, intertwined with weird background squeaks of EINAR. Drew similarities to a futuristic SLITS minus the off-beat reggae. • **Songwriters:** All written by BJORK and EINAR, except TOP OF THE WORLD (Carpenters) / MOTOR-CYCLE MAMA (Sailcat). Solo BJORK with producer NELEE HOOPER also covered LIKE SOMEONE IN LOVE (J. Van Heusen & J. Burke) / IT'S OH SO QUIET (hit c.1948; Betty Hutton). • **Trivia:** BJORK issued her eponymous solo album in 1977 at the age of 10. She also made a number of homeland recordings with her group TAPPI TIKARRAS between 81-83. BJORK was married to THOR, but after they had child, he soon married new SUGARCUBE; MAGGA. SIGGI and BRAGI were former brother-in-laws who were married to twins. In 1989, they divorced and moved to Denmark to get married to each other!. The first openly gay marriage in rock/pop history.

Recommended: LIFE'S BEEN GOOD (SUGARCUBES; *9) / STICK AROUND FOR JOY (SUGARCUBES; *8) / HERE TODAY, TOMORROW, NEXT WEEK (SUGARCUBES; *8) / DEBUT (*10) / POST (*8)

KUKL

BJORK GUNDMUNDSDOTTIR – vocals, keyboards (ex-TAPPI TIKARRAS) / **EINAR ORN BENEDIKTSSON** – trumpet, vocals / **SIGTRYGGUR 'Siggi' BALDURESSON** – drums, percussion

Gramm / not issued

Sep 83. (7") **SONGULL / POKN FYRIR BYRJENDUR** [-] [-] ICELAND

Crass / not iss

Nov 84. (m-lp) **THE EYE** [ ] [-]
– Dismembered / Assassin / Anna. *(re-iss.Jun89)*
Mar 86. (m-lp) **HOLIDAYS IN EUROPE** [ ] [-]

SUGARCUBES

BJORK, EINAR + SIGGI recruited **THOR ELDON** – guitar / **BRAGI OLAFFSON** – bass / **EINAR MELLAX** – keyboards

O. L. Indian / Elektra

Sep 87. (7") **BIRTHDAY. / BIRTHDAY (Icelandic)** [65] [-]
(12"+=) – Cat.
Dec 87.(cd-s++=) – Motorcrash.
Feb 88. (7") **COLD SWEAT. / DRAGON (Icelandic)** [56] [-]
('A'remixed-12"+=) – Traitor (Icelandic) / Birthday (demo).
(cd-s+=) – Traitor (Icelandic) / Revolution.
Apr 88. (7") **DEUS. / LUFTGITAR** [51] [-]
(12"+=) – Steel of lift.
('A'remixed-10"+=) – Cowboy / Organic prankster.
(cd-s+=) – Organic prankster / Night of steel (Icelandic).
Apr 88. (lp)(c)(cd)(dat) **LIFE'S TOO GOOD** [14] [54] Jun 88
– Mama / Delicious demon / Birthday / Traitor / Blue eyed pop / Petrol / F***ing in rhythm and sorrow / Cold sweat / Deus / Sick for toys. (cd+=) – I want.
May 88. (12"ep)(cd-ep) **COLD SWEAT / COLD SWEAT (meat mix). / BIRTHDAY (Icelandic) / DELICIOUS DEMON / COLD SWEAT (instrumental)** [-] [ ]

— **MARGRET 'Magga' ORNOLFSDOTTIE** – keyboards repl. MELLAK

Sep 88. (7") **BIRTHDAY. / BIRTHDAY CHRISTMAS** [65] [-]
(12")(cd-s) – ('A'side) / Fucking in rhythm and sorrow (live) / Cowboy (live) / Cold sweat (live).
(12")(cd-s) **BIRTHDAY CHRISTMAS MIX**
– Christmas eve – Christmas day – Christmas present – Petrol (all live).
(US-green-ep title 'DELICIOUS DEMONS')

Above single was produced by The JESUS & MARY CHAIN brothers.

Dec 88. (c-s) **MOTORCRASH (live) / POLO** [-] [ ]
(12"+=)(3"cd-s+=) – Blue eyed pop.
Aug 89. (7") **REGINA. / REGINA (Icelandic)** [55] [ ]
(12")/ /(12"+=)(cd-s+=) – (2 different-12"mixes)./ / Hot meat.
Oct 89. (lp)(c)(cd)(silver-lp) **HERE TODAY, TOMORROW, NEXT WEEK** [15] [70]
– Tidal wave / Regina / Speed is the key / Dream T.V. / Nail / Pump / Eat the menu / Bee / Dear plastic / Shoot him / Water / Day called Zero / Planet. (cd+=) – Hey / Dark disco! / Hot meat.
Feb 90. (7") **PLANET. / PLANET (somersault version)** [ ] [ ]
(12"+=)(cd-s+=) – Planet (Icelandic) / Cindy.

Early 1991, BJORK contributed her vox to 2 songs on 808 STATE album EX-EL.

Dec 91. (7") **HIT. / HIT-INSTRUMENTAL** [17] [ ]
(12"+=) – Theft.
(cd-s++=) – Chihuahua – instrumental.
(7"ep++=) – Leash called love.
Feb 92. (cd)(c)(lp) **STICK AROUND FOR JOY** [16] [95]
– Gold / Hit / Leash called love / Lucky night / Happy nurse / I'm hungry / Walkabout / Hetero scum / Vitamin / Chihuahua.
Mar 92. (7") **WALKABOUT (remix). / STONEDRILL** [ ] [ ]
(12"++=)/ /(cd-s+=) – Top of the world./ / Bravo pop.
Aug 92. (12"ep)(cd-ep) **VITAMIN. / ('A'Babylon's Burning mix) / ('A'earth dub) / ('A'laser dub in Hell mix) / ('A'decline of Rome part 2 & 3) / ('A' meditation mix)** [ ] [ ]
(cd-ep+=) – ('A' E-mix).
Oct 92. (d-cd)(c)(lp) **IT'S IT** (remixes) [47] [ ]

— Officially disbanded late 1992.

– compilations, others, etc. –

Apr 90. One Little Indian; (ltd-7"box) **BOXED SET** [ ] [-]
Sep 92. One Little Indian; (12"ep)(c-ep) **BIRTHDAY REMIX EP** [64] [ ]
– ('A'-Robertson remix) / ('A'-Tommy D remix) / ('A'-Jesus & Mary Chain remix).
(cd-s+=) – ('A'other mix).
(cd-s+=) – Mama / Hit (remix).

BJORK

solo, with **MARIUS DE VRIES, PAUL WALLER, MARTIN VIRGO + GARRY HUGHES** – keyboards / **NELLEE HOOPER** (co-writer of some), **LUIS JARDIM** (also bass) + **BRUCE SMITH** – drums, percussion / **JON MALLISON** – guitar / **TALVIN SINGH** – tabla / **CORKI HALE** – harp / **JHELISA ANDERSON** – backing vocals / **OLIVER LAKE, GARY BARNACLE, MIKE MOWER** – brass.

O. L. Indian / Elektra

Jun 93. (c-s) **HUMAN BEHAVIOUR. / ATLANTIC** [36] [ ]
(12")(cd-s) – (3 or 4 'A'mixes)
Jul 93. (cd)(c)(lp) **DEBUT** [3] [61]
– Human behaviour / Crying / Venus as a boy / There's more to life than this recorded live at the Milk Bar toilets / Like someone in love / Big time sensuality / One day / Aeroplane / Come to me / Violently happy / The anchor song. – *(re-iss.cd+c Nov93+= Play dead).*
Aug 93. (7")(c-s) **VENUS AS A BOY. / ('A' dream mix)** [29] [ ]
(cd-s+=) – Violently happy / There's more to life than this (mix).
(cd-s) – ('A'side) / Stig du mig / Anchor song (black dog mix) / I remember you.
Oct 93. (7")(c-s) **PLAY DEAD. ("BJORK with DAVID ARNOLD") / ('A'mixes)** [12] [ ]
(12"+=)(cd-s+=) ('A' instrumental + film mixes).

— (above single on 'Island' and from film 'The Young Americans'. It featured JAH WOBBLE on bass & was remixed by TIM SIMENON (of BOMB THE BASS)

Nov 93. **BIG TIME SENSUALITY. / SiDASTA** [17] [88]
(cd-s+=) – Gloria / Come to me (black dog productions).
(12")(cd-s) – ('A'-Dave Morales def radio mix) / ('A'-Fluke mixes) / ('A'-Justin Robertson Lionrock wigout mix) / ('A'-Dom T. mix) / ('A'others).

— In Mar'94, BJORK was accused by SIMON FISHER (LOVEJOY) of not crediting him on 4 of her songs on her 'DEBUT' album.

Mar 94. (c-s) **VIOLENTLY HAPPY. / ('A'-Fluke mix)** [13] [ ]
(cd-s) – ('A'side) / Anchor song (acoustic) / Come to me (acoustic) / Human behavior (acoustic).
(d-cd-s) – ('B'side) / ('A'-5 other mixes).
Sep 94. (cd)(c)(lp) **BEST MIXES FROM THE ALBUM** [ ] [ ]
Apr 95. (c-s) **ARMY OF ME / ('A'-ABA All-Stars mix)** [10] [ ]
(cd-s) – ('A'side) / Cover me.
(cd-s+=) – You've been flirting again / Sweet intuition.
(cd-s+=) – ('A'-Massey mix) / ('A'-featuring SKUNK ANANSIE) / ('A'-ABA All-Stars instrumental).
(cd-s) – (all 4 mixes).
Jun 95. (cd)(c)(lp) **POST** [2] [32]
– Army of me / Hyper-ballad / The modern things / It's oh so quiet / Enjoy / You've been flirting again / Isobel / Possibly maybe / I miss you / Cover me / Headphones.
Aug 95. (c-s)(cd-s) **ISOBEL / CHARLENE (Black Dog mix) / I GO HUMBLE / VENUS AS A BOY (harpsicord version)** [23] [ ]
(cd-s) – ('A'side) / ('A'-Goldie mix) / ('A'-Eumir Deodato mix) / ('A'-Siggi mix).
Nov 95. (c-s) **IT'S OH SO QUIET / YOU'VE BEEN FLIRTING AGAIN (flat is a promise mix)** [4] [ ]

(cd-s+=) – Hyper-ballad (Over the edge mix) / Sweet sweet intuition.
(cd-s) – ('A'side) / Hyper-ballad (Girl's blouse mix) / Hyper-ballad (with The Brodsky Quartet) / My spine (featuring Evelyn Glennie).

BLACK

Formed: Liverpool, England . . . 1980 by mainstay COLIN VEARNCOMBE. They did debut gig as trio on New Years' Day 1981. Released 2 "indie" 45's before getting break 1983 for 'WEA' subsidiery 'Eternal', run by WAH! manager PETE FULWELL. Emerged again in 1986, when indie single 'WONDERFUL LIFE' broke into lower regions of UK chart. This prompted 'A&M' to give them major break, and they duly hit Top 3 the next year, with re-issue. • **Style:** Intelligent and moody romantic rock/pop not unlike early ASSOCIATES or The CHAMELEONS. • **Songwriters:** VEARNCOMBE with DICKIE on some, until latters departure. Covered SHADES (Iggy Pop / Bowie) / WHOLE WIDE WORLD (Wreckless Eric) / CONTROL (Janet Jackson) • **Trivia:** (45) SWEETEST SMILE was hit in Europe.

Recommended: WONDERFUL LIFE (*6)

COLIN VEARNCOMBE (b.26 May'61) – vocals, guitar, keyboards / **DAVE 'Dix' DICKIE** – keyboards, guitar (ex-LAST CHANT) plus 2 unknowns.

Rox | not issued

Jan 82. (7") **HUMAN FEATURES. / ELECTRIC CHURCH** [ ] [-]
(Jun82) trim to duo of **COLIN** and **DAVE**

W.W.O. | not issued

Oct 82. (7") **MORE THAN THE SUN. / JUMP** [ ] [-]

Eternal-WEA | not issued

Jan 84. (7") **HEY PRESTO. / STEPHEN.** [ ] [-]
(12"+=) – Liquid dream.

WEA | not issued

Jan 85. (7") **MORE THAN THE SUN (remix). / BUTTERFLY MAN** [ ] [-]
(12"+=) – I could kill you / Wide mouth / Stephen.

— **BLACK** are virtually **COLIN VEARNCOMBE,** with **DIX** now just engineer and on part-time keyboard sessions. Other contributions were from **ROY CORKHILL** – fretless bass / **MARTIN GREEN** – saxophone / **JIMMY HUGHES** – drums.

Uglyman | not issued

Aug 86. (7") **WONDERFUL LIFE. / BIRTHDAY NIGHT** [72] [-]
(d7"+=) – Sometimes for the asking / Everything's coming up roses.

A&M | A&M

Apr 87. (7")(7"white) **EVERYTHING'S COMING UP ROSES. / RAVEL IN THE RAIN** [ ] [ ]
(12"+=) – It's not like you Lady Jane.
Jun 87. (7") **SWEETEST SMILE. / SIXTEENS** [8] [ ]
(12"+=)(cd-s+=) – Leave yourself alone / Hardly star-crossed lovers.
Aug 87. (7")(c-s) **WONDERFUL LIFE. / LIFE CALLS** [8] [ ]
(12"+=)(cd-s+=) – Had enough / All we need is money.
Sep 87. (lp)(c)(cd) **WONDERFUL LIFE** [3] [ ]
– Wonderful life / Everything's coming up roses / Something for the asking / Finder / Paradise / I'm not afraid / I just grew tired / Blue / Just making memories / Sweetest smile. (c+=) – Sixteens.
(cd++=) – Hardly star-crossed lovers / Leave yourself alone / It's not like you Lady Jane / Ravel in the rain. *(cd.re-iss.Aug91)*
Oct 87. (7") **I'M NOT AFRAID. / HAVE IT YOUR OWN WAY** [ ] [ ]
(12"+=) – My love.
Dec 87. (7") **PARADISE. / DAGGER REELS** [38] [ ]
(12"+=)(cd-s+=) – Sometimes for the asking (new version).
Sep 88. (7") **THE BIG ONE. / YOU ARE THE ONE** [54] [ ]
(12"+=)(cd-s+=) – Scrapbook.
Oct 88. (lp)(c)(cd) **COMEDY** [32] [ ]
– The big one / I can laugh about it now / Whatever people say you are / You're a big girl now / Let me watch you make love / Hey, I was right, you were wrong / All we need is money / You don't always do what's best for you / Now you're gone / No one done nothing. (cd+=) – It's not over yet / Paradise lost.
Nov 88. (7") **YOU'RE A BIG GIRL NOW. / ENOUGH IS ENOUGH** [ ] [ ]
(12"+=) – Revroom.
Jan 89. (7") **NOW YOU'RE GONE. / ('A' Mardi gras version)** [66] [ ]
(12"+=)(cd-s+=) – Brother o' mine.

— **VEARNCOMBE** retained **GREEN** – (sax, guitar, clarinet) plus **ROY MARTIN** – drums / **BRAD LANG** – bass / **GORDON MORGAN** – guitar / **PETE DAVIS** – keys / **STEVE SIDWELL** – trumpet / **LUIS JARDIM** – perc. / **CAMILLA GRICHSEL-VEARNCOMBE** – b.vocals

Apr 91. (7"m) **FEEL LIKE CHANGE. / I NEVER WANTED TO WRITE THIS SONG / IT WON'T HELP WHAT'S GOING ON** [56] [ ]
(12"+=)(cd-s+=) – Wonderful life.
May 91. (cd)(c)(lp) **BLACK** [42] [ ]
– Too many times / Feels like change / Here it comes again / Learning how to hate / Fly up to the Moon / Let's talk about me / Sweet breath of your rapture / Listen / She's my best friend / This is life.
Jun 91. (7")(c-s) **HERE IT COMES AGAIN. / EVERY WAKING HOUR** [70] [ ]
(12"+=)(cd-s+=) – Shades / Wonderful life (88 Christmas recording).
Aug 91. (7")(c-s) **FLY UP TO THE MOON. / YOU LIFT ME UP / WHAT YOU ARE** [ ] [ ]
(cd-s+=) – Control.
(cd-s+=) – Whole wide world / Under wraps / What's right is right.

— (above featured **SAM BROWN** – vox

A&M – Polygram TV | not issued

Feb 94. (7")(c-s) **WONDERFUL LIFE. / SWEETEST SMILE** [42] [-]
(cd-s+=) – The big one / Feel the change.

Nero Schwarz | not issued

Mar 94. (cd-s) **(THAT'S) JUST LIKE LOVE / SURRENDER / PAPER CROWN** [ ] [-]
Apr 94. (cd)(c)(lp) **ARE WE HAVING FUN YET?** [ ] [-]
– Don't take the silence too hard / Swingtime / Wishing you were here / Leaving song / That's just like love / Ave Lolita / Wish the world awake / Paper crown / Change your mind / To take a piece.

– compilations, others, etc. –

Nov 87. W.E.A.; (m-lp)(c) **BLACK** (84-85 material) [ ] [ ]
Nov 92. A&M; (c-ep)(cd-ep) **WONDERFUL LIFE / NOW YOU'RE GONE / YOU'RE A BIG GIRL NOW** [ ] [-]

Frank BLACK (see under ⇒ PIXIES)

Pauline BLACK (see under ⇒ SELECTER)

BLACK CROWES

Formed: Atlanta, Georgia, USA ... 1988 originally as MR.CROWE'S GARDEN by ROBINSON brothers. Now as BLACK CROWES they signed worldwide to Rick Rubin's 'Def American' label May 1989. Their debut 1990 album 'SHAKE YOUR MONEY MAKER' eventually went platinum, climbing to US Top 5 a year later. • **Style:** Hard blues/glam rock band influenced by GUNS'N'ROSES, AEROSMITH or The FACES. • **Songwriters:** All written by ROBINSON brothers, except HARD TO HANDLE (Otis Redding) / RAINY DAY WOMAN NOS.12 & 35 (Bob Dylan) / TIME WILL TELL (Bob Marley) /DREAMS (Allman Brothers). • **Trivia:** Their father STAN ROBINSON had a minor US hit in '59 with 'BOOM-A-DIP-DIP'. Chuck Leavell (ex-ALLMANS) produced and guested on 1992 lp.

Recommended: SHAKE YOUR MONEY MAKER (*9) / THE SOUTHERN HARMONY AND MUSICAL COMPANION (*9) / AMORICA (*7)

CHRIS ROBINSON (b.20 Dec'66) – vocals 'Young' / **RICH ROBINSON** (b.RICHARD, 24 May'69) – guitar / **JEFF CEASE** (b.24 Jun'67, Nashville, USA) – guitar / **JOHNNY COLT** (b. 1 May'66, Cherry Point, NC.) – bass (repl. 2 earlier) / **STEVE GORMAN** (b.17 Aug'65, Hopkinsville, Kentucky) – drums (repl. 5 earlier)

Def Amer. | Def Amer.

May 90. (cd)(c)(lp) **SHAKE YOUR MONEY MAKER** [ ] [4] Oct 89
– Twice as hard / Jealous again / Sister luck / Could I've been so blind / Hard to handle / Seeing things / Thick'n'thin / She talks to angels / Struttin' blues / Stare it cold. *(finally hit UK No.36 Aug91) (re-dist.Sep92)*
Jun 90. (7") **JEALOUS AGAIN. / THICK'N'THIN** [ ] [75] May90
(12"+=)(cd-s+=)(12"pic-d+=) – Waitin' guilty.
Aug 90. (7")(c-s) **HARD TO HANDLE. / JEALOUS AGAIN (acoustic)** [45] [45] Jul 90
(12"+=)(12"sha-pic-d+=) – Twice as hard / Stare it cold (both live).
(cd-s+=) – Twice as hard (remix).
Jan 91. (7")(c-s) **TWICE AS HARD. / JEALOUS AGAIN (live)** [47] [ ]
(12"+=)(cd-s+=) – Jealous guy (live).
(12"pic-d+=) – Could have been so blind (live).
Mar 91. (c-s)(7") **SHE TALKS TO ANGELS. / ('A'live video version)** [-] [30]
Jun 91. (7") **JEALOUS AGAIN. / SHE TALKS TO ANGELS** [70] [ ]
(cd-s+=) – ('B'live) / Could I've been so blind.
(d12"+=) – ('A'&'B'acoustic) / Waitin' guilty / Struttin' blues.
Jun 91. (7") **HARD TO HANDLE. / WAITIN' GUILTY** [-] [26]
Aug 91. (7") **HARD TO HANDLE. / SISTER LUCK (live)** [39] [-]
(cd-s+=) – Sister Luck (live).
(12"+=) – Dreams.
(7"sha-pic-d) – ('A'side) / Stare it cold (live).
Oct 91. (7")(c-s) **SEEING THINGS. / COULD I'VE BEEN SO BLIND (live)** [72] [ ]
(12"+=) – She talks to angels (live) / Sister luck (live).
(cd-s) – ('A'side) / Hard to handle / Jealous again / Twice as hard.

— **MARK FORD** – guitar (ex-BURNING TREE) repl. CEASE added **EDDIE HAWRYSCH** – keyboards

Apr 92. (7")(c-s) **REMEDY. / DARLING OF THE UNDERGROUND PRESS** [24] [48]
(12"+=)(cd-s+=) – Time will tell.
May 92. (cd)(c)(lp) **THE SOUTHERN HARMONY AND MUSICAL COMPANION** [2] [1]
– Sting me / Remedy / Thorn in my pride / Bad luck blue eyes goodbye / Sometime salvation / Hotel illness / Black moon creeping / No speak, no slave / My morning song / Time will tell.
Sep 92. (c-s) **THORN IN MY PRIDE. / STING ME** [-] [80]
Sep 92. (7")(c-s) **STING ME. / RAINY DAY WOMEN NOS.12 & 35** [42] [-]
(live-cd-s) – ('A'side) / Jealous again / Seeing things / Boomer's story.
(live-ep-s) – ('A'side) / She talks to angels / Thorn in my pride / Darling of the underground press.
Nov 92. (7")(c-s) **HOTEL ILLNESS. / RAINY DAY WOMEN NOS.12 & 35** [47] [ ]
(12"clear+=) – Words you throw away.
(cd-s+=) – (interview 2 different with CHRIS or RICH).
Jun 93. (7")(c-s) **REMEDY / HARD TO HANDLE** [ ] [-]
(12"+=)(cd-s+=) – Hotel illness / Jealous again.
Nov 94. (cd)(c)(lp) **AMORICA** [8] [11]
– Gone / A conspiracy / High head blues / Cursed diamond / Non-fiction / She gave good sunflower / P.25 London / Ballad in urgency / Wiser time / Downtown money waster / Descending. *(cd+=)(c+=)* – Tied up and swallowed.
Jan 95. (7"blue) **HIGH HEAD BLUES. / A CONSPIRACY / REMEDY (live)** [25] [ ]
('A'extended/'B'live-12"+=) – Thick n' thin (live).
('B'live-cd-s+=) – P25 London (live).
(cd-s) – ('A'side) / A conspiracy / ('A'extended) / Thick n' thin (live).

Jul 95. (7") **WISER TIME. / CHEVROLET** 34
(cd-s+=) – ('A'-rock radio mix) / She talks to angels (acoustic).
(cd-s) – ('A'acoustic) / Jealous again (acoustic) / Non fiction (acoustic) / Thorn in my pride (acoustic).

BLACK FLAG

Formed: Los Angeles, California, USA . . . 1976 by GREG GINN and CHUCK DUKOWSKI. In 1977, their demo reached local indie 'Bomp', who decided after over 6 months, not to issue debut 45 'NERVOUS BREAKDOWN'. Instead GREG and CHUCK, with sound men MUGGER and SPOT, formed own label 'SST' (Solid State Tuners), and issued said 45 in 1978. By the time 1981's debut lp 'DAMAGED' had arrived, they had had severe label difficulties and numerous personnel changes. 'SST' had been offered distribution by 'Unicorn-MCA', but when they reneged, SST took them to court and won losing nearly $200,000!. HENRY ROLLINS from SOA, joined setup in the early 80's, and this was clearly their best period. • **Style:** Hardcore innovators of D.I.Y. punk rock & aggressive US idealogy. • **Songwriters:** GINN and DUKOWSKI, until latter's replacement by ROLLINS. Covered LOUIE LOUIE (Kingsmen). • **Trivia:** The 1984 lp FAMILY MAN was a spoken word / instrumental first.

Recommended: WASTED . . . AGAIN (*6)

KEITH MORRIS – vocals / **GREG GINN** – guitar / **CHUCK DUKOWSKI** – bass (ex-WURM) / **BRIAN MIGDOL** – drums

not issued S.S.T.

1978. (7"ep) **NERVOUS BREAKDOWN** -
– Nervous breakdown / Fix me / I've had it / Wasted. *(US 10"coloured+12"+cd-ep iss.1990)*

— **CHAVO PEDERAST** (aka RON REYES) – vocals (ex-RED KROSS) repl. KEITH who formed CIRCLE JERKS. **ROBO** – drums repl. MIGDOL

Mar 80. (12"ep) **JEALOUS AGAIN** -
– Jealous again / Revenge / White minority / No values / You bet we've got something personal against you. *(UK-iss.Mar83) (US 10"colrd-ep/12"ep/cd-ep iss.1990)*

— **DEZ CADENA** – vocals, guitar (ex-RED KROSS) repl. REYES

Jan 81. (7"ep) **SIX PACK** -
– Six pack / I've heard it before / American waste / etc. *(UK-iss.Dec81 on 'Alternative Tenticles') (US 10"colrd-ep/12"/ep/cd-ep iss.1990)*

— **HENRY ROLLINS** (b.13 Feb '61, Washington DC) – vocals (ex-SOA) repl. CHUCK who later formed SWA.

— Group now **ROLLINS, GINN, CADENA** (now rhythm guitar only) + **ROBO**

S.S.T. S.S.T.

Nov 81. (lp) **DAMAGED**
– Rise above / Spray paint / Six pack / What I see / TV party / Thirsty and miserable / Police story / Gimmie gimmie gimmie / Depression / Room 13 / Damaged II / No more / Padded cell / Life of pain / Damaged I.

In the US, 'Posh Boy' issued '79 recording 'LOUIE LOUIE'. / 'DAMAGED 1'. *(This was finally issued 10"coloured 1988 on 'SST' US) (re-iss.cd/c/lp Oct95)*

— **BILL STEVENSON** + guest **EMIL** – drums repl. ROBO

1982. (7"ep) **TV PARTY** -
– TV party / My rules / I've got to run. *(US 12"+cd-ep iss.1990)*

— guest on half **DALE NIXON** – bass repl. CADENA

Mar 84. (lp) **MY WAR**
– My war / Can't decide / Beat my head agaist the wall / I love you / The swinging man / Forever time / Nothing left inside / Three nights / Scream. *(cd-iss.1990) (re-iss.cd/c/lp Oct95)*

— added **KIRA ROESSLER** – bass

Sep 84. (lp) **FAMILY MAN**
– Family man / Salt on a slug / The pups are doggin' it / Let your fingers do the walking / Long lost dog of it / I won't stick any of you unless and until I can stick all of you / Hollywood diary / Armageddon man / Account for what? / Shred reading (rattus norvegicus) / No deposit, no return. *(cd-iss.1990) (re-iss.cd/c/lp Oct95)*

Oct 84. (12") **FAMILY MAN. / I WON'T STICK ANY OF YOU UNLESS AND UNTIL I CAN STICK ALL OF YOU**

Dec 84. (lp) **SLIP IT IN**
– Slip it in / Black coffee / Wound up / Rat's eyes / Obliteration / The bars / My ghetto / You're not evil. *(cd-iss.1990) (re-iss.cd/c/lp Oct95)*

Jan 85. (lp) **LIVE '84 (live)**
– The process of weeding out / My ghetto / Jealous again / I love you / Swinging man / Three nights / Nothing left inside / Black coffee. *(cd-iss.1990) (re-iss.cd/c/lp Oct95)*

Jun 85. (lp) **LOOSE NUT**
– Loose nut / Bastard in love / Annihilate this week / Best one yet / Modern man / This is good / I'm the one / Sinking / Now she's black. *(cd-iss.1990) (re-iss.cd/c/lp Oct95)*

— trimmed to of **GINN, KIRA + STEVENSON** when ROLLINS went solo

Sep 85. (m-lp) **THE PROCESS OF WEEDING OUT**
– Your last affront / Screw the law / The process of weeding out / Southern rise. *(US 10"colrd/m-cd iss.1990)*

Nov 85. (lp) **IN MY HEAD**
– Paralyzed / The crazy girl / Black love / Retired at 21 / Drinking and driving / White hot / In my head / Society's tease / It's all up to you / You let me down. *(cd-iss.1990) (re-iss.cd/c/lp Oct95)*
(cd+=) – Out of this world / I can see you.

May 86. (lp) **WHO'S GOT THE 10 1/2 (live in Portland 23/8/85)**
– I'm the one / Loose nut / Bastard in love / Slip it in / This is good / Gimmie gimmie gimmie / Drinking and driving / Modern man / My war. *(cd-iss.1990) (re-iss.cd/c/lp Oct95)* (cd+=) – Annihilate / Wasted / Sinking / Jam / Louie Louie / Best one yet.

— Had already, earlier in '86. KIRA continued with DOS, alongside MIKE WATT of The MINUTEMEN. GINN teamed up with DUKOWSKI again, and formed instrumental group GONE.

– compilations, others, etc. –

Mar 83. S.S.T.; (d-lp) **EVERYTHING WENT BLACK**(rare 78-81)
(re-iss.cd/c/lp Oct95)

1984. S.S.T.; (lp) **THE FIRST FOUR YEARS** -
(re-iss.cd/c/lp Oct95)

Dec 87. S.S.T.; (lp)(c)(cd) **WASTED . . . AGAIN**
– Wasted / TV party / Six pack / I don't care / I've had it / Jealous again / Slip it in / Annihilate this week / Loose nut / Gimme gimme / Louie Louie / Drinking and driving. *(re-iss.Oct95)*

GONE

— **GREG GINN, DUKOWSKI + band**

S.S.T. S.S.T.

Jul 86. (lp) **LET'S GET REAL, REAL GONE FOR A CHANGE**
– Insideous detraction / Get gone / Peter gone / Rosanne / Climbing Rat's wall / Watch the tractor / Last days of being stepped on / CH 69 / Lawndale Rock City / Hypercharge – the wait (the fifth force suite). *(re-iss.+cd+c 1993)*

Jan 87. (lp) **GONE II** – BUT NEVER TOO GONE!
– Jungle law / New vengeance / Unglued / Turned over stone / Drop the hat / Adams / Time of entry / Left holding the bag / GTV / Daisy strut / Cut off / Put it there / Utility hole / Yesterday is teacher / How soon they forget / Cobra XVIII.

Jan 94. (cd)(c)(lp) **THE CRIMINAL MIND**
– Poor losers / Punch drunk / Pull it out / Pump room / Snagglepuss / PS was wrong / Off the chains / Smoking gin in Wasco / Spankin' plank / Piled one higher / Row nine / Toggle / Big check / Ankle strap / Hand out / Freeny / Unknown calibar.

Apr 94. (12")(cd-s) **SMOKING GUN IN WASCO. / ?**

Aug 94. (cd)(c)(lp) **ALL THE DIRT THAT'S FIT TO PRINT**
–

GREG GINN

Cruz-S.S.T. Cruz-S.S.T.

Jun 93. (12") **PAYDAY. / ?**

Jun 93. (cd)(c)(lp) **GETTING EVEN**
– I've changed / Kill burn fluff / You drive me crazy / Pig MF / Hard thing / Payday / Nightmares / Torn / PF flyer / I can't wait / Short fuse / Not that simple / Yes officer / Crawling inside.

Sep 93. (cd)(c)(lp) **DICK**
– Never change baby / I want to believe / You wanted it / I won't give in / Creeps / Strong violent type / Don't tell me / You dirty rat / Disgusting reference / Walking away / Ignorant order / Slow fuse / You're gonna get it.

Mar 94. (12")(cd-s) **DON'T TELL ME. / ?**

Aug 94. (cd)(c)(lp) **LET IT BURN (BECAUSE I DON'T LIVE . . .)**

Sep 95. (12") **DAMAGE CONTROL. /**

BLACKFOOT

Formed: Jacksonville, Florida . . . 1968 by RICKY MEDLOCKE. Released two albums before getting more consistent contract with 'Atco'. Had to wait over 10 years for first taste of commercial success, when lp 'STRIKES' made US lists. • **Style:** Southern boogie blues band in the mould of LYNYRD SKYNYRD. • **Songwriters:** Group compositions, except I GOT A LINE ON YOU (Spirit) / THE STEALER (Free) / etc. BOBBY BARTH covered STOP IN THE NAME OF LOVE (Diana Ross & The Supremes) / TUPELO HONEY (Van Morrison) / THE ROAD'S MY MIDDLE NAME (Bonnie Raitt) / SITTIN' ON TOP OF THE WORLD (Howlin' Wolf). • **Trivia:** MEDLOCKE played drums on LYNYRD SKYNYRD album FIRST AND LAST. His grandfather SHORTY MEDLOCKE played banjo on early 80's albums. SIOGO stands for 'Suck It Or Get Out'. In 1984 BARTH is involved in crash which killed fellow AXE member MICHAEL OSBOURNE.

Recommended: HIGHWAY SONG – BLACKFOOT LIVE (*6).

RICKY MEDLOCKE – vocals, guitar / **CHARLIE HARGRETT** – guitar / **GREG T.WALKER** – bass / **JACKSON SPIRES** – drums, vocals

Island Epic

1976. (lp)(c) **FLYIN' HIGH** (UK-title 'NO RESERVATIONS')
– Feelin' good / Flyin' high / Try a little harder / Stranger on the road / Save your time / Dancin' man / Island of life / Junkie's dream / Madness / Mother.

M.C.A. M.C.A.

Jul 77. (7") **WHEN WILL I SEE YOU AGAIN. / LAY THE REAL THING ON ME** -

Atco Atco

Jul 79. (7") **HIGHWAY SONG. / TRAIN, TRAIN** -

Aug 79. (lp)(c) **STRIKES** 42 May 79
– Road fever / I got a line on you / Left turn on a red light / Pay my dues / Baby blue / Wishing well / Run and hide / Train, train / Highway song.

Sep 79. (7") **HIGHWAY SONG. / ROAD FEVER** - 26

Feb 80. (7") **TRAIN, TRAIN. / BABY BLUE** 38 Oct 79

May 80. (7") **STREET FIGHTER. / MY OWN LOVE** -

Jul 80. (lp)(c) **TOMCATTIN'** 50 Jun 80
– Warped / On the run / Dream on / Street fighter / Gimme, gimme, gimme / Every man should know (Queenie) / In the night / Reckless abandoner / Spendin' cabbage / Fox chase.

Jul 80. (7") **GIMME, GIMME, GIMME. / IN THE NIGHT**

Sep 80. (7") **ON THE RUN. / STREET FIGHTER** -

Nov 80. (7") **EVERY MAN SHOULD KNOW (QUEENIE). / HIGHWAY SONG** -

Jun 81. (7") **FLY AWAY. /** - 42

Jul 81. (lp)(c) **MARAUDER** [38] [48]
– Good morning / Payin' for it / Diary of a workingman / Too hard to handle / Fly away / Dry county / Fire of the dragon / Rattlesnake rock'n'roller / Searchin'.
Jul 81. (7") **GOOD MORNING. / PAYIN' FOR IT** [ ] [-]
Sep 81. (7") **SEARCHIN'. / PAYIN' FOR IT** [-] [ ]
Feb 82. (d7") **DRY COUNTY. / TOO HARD TO HANDLE / / ON THE RUN. / TRAIN, TRAIN** [43] [ ]
Aug 82. (lp)(c) **HIGHWAY SONG – BLACKFOOT LIVE (live)** [14] [ ]
– Gimme, gimme, gimme / Every man should know / Good morning / Dry county / Rollin' and tumblin' / Fly away / Road fever / Trouble in mind / Train, train / Highway song / Howay the lads.
Aug 82. (7"m) **HIGHWAY SONG (live). / ROLLIN' AND TUMBLIN' (live) / FLY AWAY (live)** [ ] [ ]

— added **KEN HENSLEY** – keyboards (ex-URIAH HEEP)

May 83. (lp)(c) **SIOGO** [28] [82]
– Send me an angel / Crossfire / Heart's grown cold / We're goin' down / Teenage idol / Goin' in circles / Run for cover / White man's land / Sail away / Drivin' fool.
May 83. (7")(12") **SEND ME AN ANGEL. / DRIVIN' FOOL** [66] [-]
Jun 83. (7")(12") **TEENAGE IDOL. / WE'RE GOIN' DOWN** [ ] [-]
Jun 83. (7") **TEENAGE IDOL. / RUN FOR COVER** [-] [ ]

— **BOBBY BARTH** – keyboards (ex-AXE) repl. HENSLEY

Sep 84. (lp)(c) **VERTICAL SMILES** [82] [ ]
– Morning dew / Living in the limelight / Ride with you / Get it on / Young girl / Summer days / A legend never dies / Heartbeat and heels / In for the kill.
Jan 85. (7")(12") **MORNING DEW. / LIVIN' IN THE LIMELIGHT** [ ] [ ]

— Disbanded Mar86, BARTH went solo and released Mar 87 album 'TWO HEARTS-ONE BEAT' for 'Atco'. In Aug'86 BLACKFOOT were again (with **MEDLOCKE, BARTH, WIZZARD** – bass (ex-MOTHER'S FINEST), **DOUG BARE, HAROLD SEAY** (ex-MOTHERS FINEST). **MEDLOCKE** reformed them again in 1989. Also in new line-up **NEAL CASAL** – guitar repl. DOUG BARE – keyboards (ex-MOTHER'S FIRST) / **RIKKI MEYER** – bass repl. MARK 'THE ANIMAL' MENDOZA (ex-TWISTED SISTER) / **GUNNER ROSS** – drums

M.F.N. | Loop

Nov 90. (cd)(c)(lp) **MEDICINE MAN** (US title 'CHILL TO THE BONE') [ ] [ ] Jun 89
– Doin' my job / The stealer / Sleazy world / Not gonna cry anymore / Runnin' runnin' / Chilled to d'bone / Guitar slingers song and dance.

— **RICK MEDLOCKE** – vocals, guitars, steel guitars, percussion / **MARK WOERPEL** – guitars, vocals / **TIM STUNSON** – bass / **BENNY RAPPA** – drums, percussion, vocals

M.F.N. | Bulletproof

Jul 94. (cd) **AFTER THE REIGN** [ ] [ ]
– Sittin' on top of the world / Rainbow / It's all over now / Tupelo honey / The road's my middle name / Hang time / Tonight / Nobody rides for free / Bandelero / After the reign.

BLACK GRAPE

Formed: Manchester, England . . .late 1994 by ex-HAPPY MONDAYS men SHAUN RYDER and BEZ. They were joined by KERMIT and JED from The RUTHLESS RAP ASSASSINS, plus a host of extras. SHAUN's brilliant return from oblivion was complete by summer 1995, when 'REVEREND BLACK GRAPE' returned him to Top 10 status. However the song and video were banned from TV, due to the Catholic church saying it condoned the Venezuelan terrorist Carlos The Jackal, which also angered the New York based ADL (Anti-Defamation League). Another Top 10 classic 'IN THE NAME OF THE FATHER' preceeded the No.1 album 'IT'S GREAT WHEN YOU'RE STRAIGHT'. During this time, they were one of the successes at Hamilton Park's 'T In The Park' 2-day festival (near Glasgow), even though KERMIT broke his leg and had to sit most of the time on a speaker! **•Style:** Groovy but controversial anthemic dance rap/rock featuring a new revamped, but not totally drug-free SHAUN RYDER. **•Songwriters:** SHAUN & KERMIT, although in October '95, INTASTELLA members MARTIN WRIGHT and MARTIN MITTLER served a writ, claiming they co-wrote with SHAUN on early demos before they departed.

Recommended: IT'S GREAT WHEN YOU'RE STRAIGHT . . . YEAH! (*9)

SHAUN RYDER – vocals (ex-HAPPY MONDAYS)/ **BEZ** – dancer (ex-HAPPY MONDAYS) / **KERMIT (PAUL LEVEREDGE)** – rapper (ex-RUTHLESS RAP ASSASINS)/ **JED BIRTWHISTLE** – (ex-RUTHLESS RAP ASSASSINS) / **WAGS** – guitar (ex-PARIS ANGELS) / **CRAIG GANNON** – guitar (ex-SMITHS) who replaced INTASTELLA guitarists **MARTIN WRIGHT + MARTIN MITTLER**

Radio-active | Radio-active

May 95. (c-s) **REVEREND BLACK GRAPE / STRAIGHT OUT OF TRUMPTON (BASEMENT TAPES)** [9] [ ]
(cd-s+=) – ('A'-dark side mix).
(12") – ('A'side) / ('A'-dub collar mix) / ('A'-dark side mix).
Jul 95. (7")(c-s) **IN THE NAME OF THE FATHER. / LAND OF A THOUSAND KAMA SUTRA BABIES** [8] [ ]
(cd-s+=) – ('A'-chopper's mix) / ('A'-chopper's instrumental).
(12") – ('A'side) / (above 2).
Aug 95. (cd)(c)(lp) **IT'S GREAT WHEN YOU'RE STRAIGHT . . .YEAH** [1] [ ]
– Reverend Black Grape / In the name of the father / Tramazi party / Kelly's heroes / Yeah yeah brother / Big day in the north / Shake well before opening / Shake your money / Little Bob.
Nov 95. (c-s) **KELLY'S HEROES / ('A'-The Milky Bar Kid mix)** [17] [ ]
(cd-s+=) – ('A'-The Archibald mix) / Little Bob (live).
(cd-s) – ('A'live) / In the name of the father (live) / Fat neck.

BLACKJACK (see under ⇒ BOLTON, Michael)

BLACKMORE's RAINBOW (see under ⇒ DEEP PURPLE)

BLACK OAK ARKANSAS

Formed: Black Oak, Arkansas, USA . . . mid 1971, by JIM DANDY. They had evolved from 60's band The KNOWBODY ELSE, but now had settled in Los Angeles. Signed to 'Atlantic-Atco' and gained reputation mainly in southern States. Early in 1974, they hit US Top 30 with eponymously titled 45 'JIM DANDY'. **• Style:** Long-haired bare-chested JIM DANDY, was main focal point of this heavy sounding swamp boogie. Unsuccessfully moved to a gospel-style rock'n'roll by the mid-70's. **• Songwriters:** All mostly by JIM DANDY, except GREAT BALLS OF FIRE (Jerry Lee Lewis) / SHAKIN' ALL OVER (Johnny Kidd) / RACE WITH THE DEVIL (Gun) / NOT FADE AWAY (Buddy Holly) / etc. **• Trivia:** MANGRUM (JIM DANDY) took his new name from 1950's song.

Recommended: HOT & NASTY (*6).

JIM DANDY (b.JAMES MANGRUM, 30 Mar'48, Black Oak, Arkansas, USA) – vocals / **HARVEY JETT** – guitar / **RICKIE REYNOLDS** (b.28 Oct'48, Manilla, Arkansas) – guitar, vocals / **STAN 'GOOBER' KNIGHT** (b.12 Feb'49, Little Rock, Arkansas) – guitar, vocals / **PAT DAUGHERTY** (b.11 Nov'47, Jonesboro, Arkansas) – bass, vocals / **WAYNE EVANS** – drums

not iss. | Enterprise

1970. (7") **KING'S ROW. / OLDER THAN GRANDPA** [-] [ ]

Atlantic | Atco

Sep 71. (lp) **BLACK OAK ARKANSAS** [-] [ ] Jul 71
– Uncle Lijiah / Memories at the window / The hills of Arkansas / I could love you / Hot and nasty / Singing the blues / Lord have mercy on my soul / When electricity came to Arkansas. *(UK-re-iss. around mid 70's) (re-iss.cd Jul92 on 'Repertoire')*
Sep 71. (7") **LORD HAVE MERCY ON MY SOUL. / UNCLE LIJAH** [-] [ ]
Nov 71. (7") **HOT AND NASTY. / SINGIN' THE BLUES** [-] [ ]
Mar 72. (lp) **KEEP THE FAITH** [-] [ ] Feb 72
– Keep the faith / Revolutionary all American boys / Feet on earth, head in sky / Fever in my mind / The big one's still coming / White-headed woman / We live on day to day / Short life line / Don't confuse what you don't know. *(cd-iss Jun95 on 'Repertoire' or 'Rhino-Sequel')*
1972. (7") **KEEP THE FAITH. / THE BIG ONE'S STILL COMING** [-] [ ]

— **TOMMY ALDRIDGE** (b.15 Aug'50, Nashville) – drums repl. WAYNE

Jul 72. (lp) **IF AN ANGEL CAME TO SEE YOU, WOULD YOU MAKE HER FEEL AT HOME?** [-] [93]
– Gravel roads / Fertile woman / Spring vacation / We help each other / Full Moon ride / Our minds eye / To make us what we are / Our eyes are on you / Mutants of the monster. *(cd-iss Jun95 on 'Rhino-Sequel')*
Aug 72. (7") **FULL BLOWN RIDE. / WE HELP EACH OTHER** [-] [ ]
Mar 73. (lp) **RAUNCH'N'ROLL – LIVE (live)** [ ] [90]
– Gettin' kinda cocky / When electricity came to Arkansas / Gigolo / Hot rod / Mutants of the monster / Hot and nasty / Up. *(cd-iss Aug93 on 'Rhino')*
Apr 73. (7") **HOT AND NASTY. / HOT ROD** [-] [ ]
Dec 73. (lp)(c) **HIGH ON THE HOG** [ ] [52] Nov 73
– Swimmin' in quicksand / Back to the land / Movin' / Happy hooker / Red hot lovin' / I'm Dandy / Moonshine sonata / Why shouldn't I smile / High'n'dry / Mad man. *(cd-iss Jun95 on 'Rhino-Sequel')*
Feb 74. (7") **JIM DANDY (TO THE RESCUE). / RED HOT LOVIN'** [ ] [25] Dec 73

— **RUBY STARR** – VOCALS repl. JETT.

Jul 74. (lp)(c) **STREET PARTY** [ ] [56]
– Dancing in the street / Sting me / Good good woman / Jail bait / Sure been workin' hard / Son of a gun / Brink of creation / I'm a man / Goin' home / Dixie / Everybody wants to see Heaven / Hey y'all. *(cd-iss Jun95 on 'Rhino-Sequel')*
Jul 74. (7") **DANCING IN THE STREET. / DIXIE** [ ] [ ]
Sep 74. (7") **HEY Y'ALL. / STING ME** [ ] [ ]
Dec 74. (7") **TAXMAN. / DIXIE** [-] [ ]

— **JIMMY HENDERSON** (b.20 May'54, Jackson, Missouri) – guitar repl. STARR.

Mar 75. (7") **TAXMAN. / JAILBAIT** [ ] [-]
May 75. (lp)(c) **AIN'T LIFE GRAND** [ ] [ ]
– Taxman / Fancy Nancy / Keep on / Good stuff / Rebel / Back door man / Love can be found / Diggin' for gold / Cryin' shame / Let life be good to you. *(cd-iss Jun95 on 'Rhino-Sequel')*
Apr 75. (7") **BACK DOOR MAN. / GOOD STUFF** [-] [ ]
Jun 75. (7") **FANCY NANCY. / KEEP ON** [ ] [ ]

— added 4 backing singers incl. **RUBY STARR** again.

M.C.A. | M.C.A.

Oct 75. (lp)(c) **X-RATED** [ ] [99]
– Bump'n'grind / Fightin' cock / Highway pirate / Strong enough to be gentle / Flesh needs flesh / Wild men from the mountains / High flyer / Ace in the hole / Too hot to stop.
Jan 76. (7") **STRONG ENOUGH TO BE GENTLE. / ACE IN THE HOLE** [-] [89]
May 76. (7") **GREAT BALLS OF FIRE. / HIGHWAY PIRATE** [ ] [ ]
Aug 76. (lp)(c) **BALLS OF FIRE** [ ] [ ] Jun 76
– Ramblin' gamblin' man / Fistful of love / Make that scene / Rock'n'roll / I can feel forever / Great balls of fire / Just to fall in love / Leather angel / Storm of passion / All my troubles. *(cd-iss Jun95 on 'Repertoire')*
Aug 76. (7") **FISTFUL OF LOVE. / STORM OF PASSION** [ ] [ ]
Sep 76. (7") **RAMBLIN' GAMBLIN' MAN. / STORM OF PASSION** [ ] [ ]

— **JIM DANDY & JIMMY HENDERSON** recruited new members **ANDY TANAS** – bass repl. PAT **JACK HOLDER** – guitar, etc. repl. STAN, RICKIE and RUBY. **JOEL WILLIAMS** – drums repl. TOMMY who joined PAT TRAVERS then OZZY OSBOURNE

Shaun Ryder BLACK GRAPE

Feb 77. (lp)(c) **10 YEARS OVERNIGHT SUCCESS**
– When the band was singin' "Shakin' all over" / Pretty, pretty / Can't blame it on me / Television indecision / Back it up / Bad boy's back in school / Love comes easy / You can't keep a good man down / Fireball.

Feb 77. (7") **WHEN THE BAND WAS SINGIN' "SHAKIN' ALL OVER". / BAD BOY'S BACK IN SCHOOL** -

BLACK OAK

GREG REDDING – guitar, keyboards repl. PAT.

Capricorn Capricorn

Dec 77. (lp)(c) **RACE WITH THE DEVIL**
– Race with the Devil / Freedom / One night stand / Daisy / Rainbow / Feels so good / Stand by your own kind / Not fade away.

1978. (7") **NOT FADE AWAY. / FEELS SO GOOD** -

1978. (lp) **I'D RATHER BE SAILING** -
– I'll take care of you / You keep me waiting / Ride with me / Made of stone / You can count on me / God bless the children / Innocent eyes / Daydreams / Wind in our sails.

1978. (7") **RIDE WITH ME. / WIND IN OUR SAILS** -

— Disbanded 1978.

JIM DANDY & BLACK OAK ARKANSAS

reformed 1984, with **DANDY** and **REYNOLDS** plus **STEVE NUNENMACHER** – guitar / **WILLIAM LEMUEL** – bass, vocals / **JON WELLS** – drums / **BILLY BATTLE** – keyboards

FM-Heavy Metal Hacienda

Nov 84. (lp) **READY AS HELL**
– Ready as Hell / Here comes the wind / The liberty rebellion / Don't tempt the Devil / Get ahead of your time / Black cat woman / Rude and crude / Space cadet / Fascination alley / Denouncement.

Aug 85. (7") **READY AS HELL. / BLACK CAT WOMAN**

1986. (lp)(c) **BLACK ATTACK IS BACK**
– Long distance runner / I'm on your side / The wanderer / I don't want much out of life / (I want a woman with) Big titties / etc.

– compilations, others, etc. –

not issued Stax

1975. (lp) **THE EARLY YEARS** (when as "KNOWBODY ELSE") -

Atlantic Atco

Oct 74. (lp)(c) **HOT & NASTY: THE BEST OF BLACK OAK ARKANSAS**
– Mean woman / Uncle Lijiah / Hot and nasty / Lord have mercy on my soul / When electricity came to Arkansas / Keep the faith / Fever in my mind / Hot rod / Gravel roads / Mutants of the monster / Jim Dandy / Happy hooker / Son of a gun / Dixie / Everybody wants to see heaven (nobody wants to die) / Diggin' for gold / Taxman / So you want to be a rock'n'roll star. *(re-iss.1977)*

Feb 76. (lp)(c) **LIVE! MUTHA (live 74-75)**
– Jim Dandy / Fancy Nancy / Lord have mercy on my soul / Cryin' shame / Fever in my mind / Hey y'all / Rebel / Taxman / Hot and nasty.

BLACK ROSE (see under ⇒ CHER)

BLACK SABBATH

Formed: Aston, Birmingham, England . . . early 1969 out of jazz fusion combo EARTH. (IOMMI had also filled in for 2 weeks as JETHRO TULL guitarist.) BLACK SABBATH name lifted from Dennis Wheatley novel. They signed to 'Fontana' late '69 and after flop single, they were shifted to progressive 'Vertigo' label 1970. Due to earlier constant gigging and press attention, their debut album immediately made inroads into UK Top 10. Their popularity grew even more, when they had classic UK Top 5 hit single PARANOID. Although they released more singles, they were mainly marketed as an album band, with most hitting Top 10. When OZZY finally departed in 1979, they seemed doomed, but with new wave of heavy-metal music taking off again, they/IOMMI managed to survive. • **Style:** Occult influenced heavy outfit, with IOMMI on doom-laden basic guitar riffs, fused with the banshee screech of OZZY. Lyrically morbid with futuristic / medieval outlook, part of their tongue-in-cheek protest against God. Not a band for the easily-led and weak-minded, as blame for suicide attempts were always laid at their door. Did have a softer track on each album (i.e. FLUFF / CHANGES / EMBRYO / DON'T START). • **Songwriters:** Mainly group compositions. Covered EVIL WOMAN (DON'T PLAY YOUR GAMES WITH ME) (Crow) / WARNING (Aynsley Dunbar). • **Trivia:** Group moved to Los Angeles in 1979 and recruited manager Don Arden who had replaced Patrick Meehan in 1974. The original SABBATH reunited on 13 Jul'85 for LIVE AID concert in Philadelphia. Now famous producer ROGER BAIN brought in RICK WAKEMAN to play keyboards on CHANGES from 'VOLUME 4'.

Recommended: WE SOLD OUR SOULS FOR ROCK'N'ROLL (*9) / BLACK SABBATH (*7) / PARANOID (*7) / MASTER OF REALITY (*8) / VOLUME 4 (*8) / SABBATH BLOODY SABBATH (*7) / SABOTAGE (*6).

OZZY OSBOURNE (b.JOHN, 3 Dec'48) – vocals / **TONY IOMMI** (b.19 Feb'48) – guitars / **TERRY 'GEEZER' BUTLER** (b.17 Jul'49) – bass / **BILL WARD** (b. 5 May'48) – drums

Fontana Warners

Jan 70. (7") **EVIL WOMAN (DON'T PLAY YOUR GAMES WITH ME). / WICKED WORLD**
(re-iss. Mar70 on 'Veritgo')

Vertigo Warners

Feb 70. (lp)(c) **BLACK SABBATH** 8 23 Jul 70
– Black Sabbath / The wizard / Behind the wall of sleep / N.I.B. / Evil woman (don't play your games with me) / Sleeping village / Warning. *(re-iss.Jun80 + Nov85 on 'NEMS', cd-iss.Dec86 += Wicked world)*

Aug 70. (7") **PARANOID. / THE WIZARD** 4 61

Sep 70. (lp)(c) **PARANOID** 1 12 Feb 71
– War pigs / Paranoid / Planet Caravan / Iron man / Electric funeral / Hand of doom / Rat salad / Fairies wear boots. *(re-iss.Jun80, hit 54/ + Nov85 + pic-d on 'NEMS') (cd-iss.Jun89 on 'Castle')* (cd+=) – Tomorrow's world (live).

Aug 71. (lp)(c) **MASTER OF REALITY** 5 8
– Sweet leaf / After forever / Embryo Children of the grave / Lord of this world / Solitude / Into the void / Orchid. *(re-iss.Jun80 + Nov85 on 'NEMS') (cd-iss.Jun89 on 'Castle')* (cd+=) – Killing yourself to live (live).

Jan 72. (7") **IRON MAN. / ELECTRIC FUNERAL** - 52
(re-iss. US 1974)

Sep 72. (7") **TOMORROW'S DREAM. / LAGUNA SUNRISE**

Sep 72. (lp)(c) **BLACK SABBATH VOL.4** 8 13 Oct 72
– Wheels of confusion / Tomorrow's dream / Changes / FX / Supernaut / Snowblind / Cornucopia / Laguna sunrise / St.Vitus' dance / Under the sun. *(re-iss.Jun80 on 'NEMS') (cd-iss.Jun89 on 'Castle')* (cd+=) – Children of the grave (live).

Oct 73. (7") **SABBATH BLOODY SABBATH. / CHANGES**

Nov 73. (lp)(c) **SABBATH BLOODY SABBATH** 4 11 Jan 74
– Sabbath bloody sabbath / A national acrobat / Fluff / Sabbra cadabra / Killing yourself to live / Who are you? / Looking for today / Spiral architect. *(re-iss.Jun80+Nov85 on 'NEMS') (cd-iss.Jun89 on 'Castle')* (cd+=) – Cornucopia (live).

(all lp's above moved to 'W.W.A.' Dec73)

N.E.M.S. Warners

Sep 75. (lp)(c) **SABOTAGE** 7 28
– Hole in the sky / Don't start (too late) / Symptom of the universe / Megalomania / Thrill of it all / Supertzar / Am I going insane (radio) / The writ. *(re-iss.Jan86) (cd-iss.Jun89 on 'Castle')* (cd+=) – Sweat leaf (live).

Feb 76. (7") **AM I GOING INSANE (RADIO). / HOLE IN THE SKY**

Oct 76. (lp)(c) **TECHNICAL ECSTACY** 13 51
– Back street kids / You won't change me / It's alright / Gypsy / All moving parts (stand still) / Rock'n'roll doctor / She's gone / Dirty women. *(re-iss.Aug83; cd-iss.Jun89)*

Nov 76. (7") **IT'S ALRIGHT. / ROCK'N'ROLL DOCTOR** -

— Late '77 OZZY leaves and is briefly repl. by **DAVE WALKER** (ex-SAVOY BROWN) Early 1978 **OZZY** returned.

May 78. (7") **NEVER SAY DIE. / SHE'S GONE** 21

Sep 78. (7")(7"purple) **HARD ROAD. / SYMPTOM OF THE UNIVERSE** 33

Oct 78. (lp)(c) **NEVER SAY DIE!** 12 69
– Never say die / Johnny Blade / Junior's eyes / Hard road / Shock wave / Air dance / Over to you / Breakout / Swinging the chain.. *(re-iss.May83)(re-iss.cd+c Sep93 on 'Spectrum')*

— **RONNIE JAMES DIO** (b.1949, New Hampshire, USA) – vocals (ex-(RITCHIE BLACKMORE'S) RAINBOW, ex-ELF etc.) repl.OZZY who went solo.

Apr 80. (lp)(c) **HEAVEN & HELL** 9 28 Jun 80
– Neon knights / Children of the sea / Lady evil / Heaven and Hell / Wishing well / Die young / Walk away / Lonely is the word. *(re-iss.May83, cd-iss.'87) (re-iss.cd+c May93 on 'Spectrum')*

Jun 80. (7") **NEON KNIGHTS. / CHILDREN OF THE SEA** 22

Nov 80. (7")(12") **DIE YOUNG. / HEAVEN AND HELL (live)** 41

— **VINNIE APPICE** – drums, percussion repl. WARD

Oct 81. (7")(12") **MOB RULES. / DIE YOUNG** 46

Nov 81. (lp)(c) **MOB RULES** 12 29
– Falling off the edge of the world / Voodoo / Mob rules / The sign of the southern cross / E 5150 / Slipping away / Turn up the night / Country girl / Over and over. *(re-iss.+cdJan85)*

Feb 82. (7")(12")(7"pic-d)(12"pic-d) **TURN UP THE NIGHT. / LONELY IS THE WORD** 37

Jan 83. (d-lp)(c) **LIVE EVIL (live)** 13 37
– E 5150 / Neon knights / N.I.B. / Children of the sea / Voodoo / Black Sabbath / War pigs / Iron man / Mob rules / Heaven and Hell / Sign of the southern cross / Paranoid / Children of the grave / Fluff. *(re-iss.Apr86)*

— **IAN GILLAN** – vocals (ex-DEEP PURPLE, ex-GILLAN) repl. RONNIE who formed DIO. **BILL WARD** – drums returned replacing VINNIE who also joined DIO. **BEV BEVAN** – drums (ex-ELECTRIC LIGHT ORCHESTRA) repl BILL, only originals in band were IOMMI and BUTLER

Sep 83. (lp)(c) **BORN AGAIN** 4 39
– Trashed / Stonehenge / Disturbing the priest / The dark / Zero the hero / Digital bitch / Born again / Hot line / Keep it warm.

Oct 83. (7") **STONEHENGE. / THRASHED** -

— **DAVE DONATO** – vocals repl. GILLAN who rejoined DEEP PURPLE

— **TONY IOMMI** recruited **GLENN HUGHES** – vocals (ex-DEEP PURPLE, etc.) repl. DONATO / **DAVE SPITZ** (b.New York) – bass repl. BUTLER / **ERIC SINGER** (b.Cleveland, Ohio) – drums repl. BEVAN / added **GEOFF NICHOLLS** (b.Birmingham) – keyboards (ex-QUARTZ) had toured '79.

Feb 86. (lp)(c)(cd) **SEVENTH STAR ("BLACK SABBATH with TONY IOMMI")** 78
– In for the kill / No stranger to love / Turn to stone / Sphinx (the guardian) / Seventh star / Danger zone / Heart like a wheel / Angry heart / In memory.
TONY IOMMI again added **BOB DAISLEY** – bass / **BEV BEVAN** – percussion / **TONY MARTIN** – vocals repl. HUGHES

Nov 87. (lp)(c)(cd) **THE ETERNAL IDOL** 66
– The shining / Ancient warrior / Hard life to love / Glory ride / Born to lose / Scarlet Pimpernel / Lost forever / The eternal idol.

— **IOMMI + MARTIN** recruited **COZY POWELL** – drums (ex-RAINBOW, ex-ELP) **LAURENCE COTTLE** – bass (on session)

I.R.S. I.R.S.

Apr 89. (7")(c-s) **HEADLESS CROSS. / CLOAK AND DAGGER** 62
(12"+=) – ('A'extended).

Apr 89. (lp)(c)(cd) **HEADLESS CROSS** 31

– The gates of Hell / Headless cross / Devil and daughter / When death calls / Kill in the spirit world / Call of the wild / Black moon / Nightwing. *(re-iss.cd Apr94)*

Jun 89. (7")(12")(7"pic-d) **DEVIL AND DAUGHTER. / (15 min.interview)** [ ] [ ]

— **NEIL MURRAY** – bass (ex-VOW WOW) joined mid'89 repl.COTTLE

Aug 90. (cd)(c)(lp) **TYR** [24] [ ]
– Anno Mundi / The lawmaker / Jerusalem / The sabbath stones / The battle of Tyr / Odin's court / Valhalla / Feels good to me / Heaven in black. *(re-iss.cd Apr94)*

Sep 90. (7") **FEELS GOOD TO ME. / PARANOID (live)** [ ] [ ]
(12"+=)(cd-s+=) – Heaven and Hell (live).

— The 1981-83 line-up reformed Oct91, **IOMMI, GEEZER, VINNIE** and **R.JAMES DIO.**

I.R.S. | Reprise

Jun 92. (cd)(c)(lp) **DEHUMANIZER** [28] [44]
– Computer god / After all (the dead) / TV crimes / Letters from Earth / Masters of insanity / Time machine / Sins of the father / Too late / I / Buried alive. *(re-iss.cd Apr94)*

Jun 92. (7") **TV CRIMES. / LETTERS FROM EARTH** [33] [ ]
(12"+=)(cd-s+=)(12"pic-d+=) – Paranoid (live).
(cd-s+=) – Mob rules (live).
(cd-s+=) Heaven and Hell (live).

— **TONY MARTIN** returned on vocals to repl.DIO

— **BOBBY RONDINELLI** – drums (ex-RAINBOW) repl.APPICE

Feb 94. (cd)(c)(lp) **CROSS PURPOSES** [41] [ ]
– I witness / Cross of thorns / Psychophobia / Virtual death / Immaculate deception / Dying for love / Back to Eden / The hand that rocks the cradle / Cardinal sin / Evil eye.

— The 1990 line-up was once again in force although COZY departed once again to be repl. by the returning RONDINELLI

Jun 95. (cd)(c)(lp) **FORBIDDEN** [71] [ ]
– The illusion of power / Get a grip / Can't get close enough / Shaking off the chains / I won't cry for you / Guilty as hell / Sick and tired / Rusty angels / Forbidden / Kiss of death.

- compilations etc. -

N.E.M.S. | Warners

Dec 75. N.E.M.S./ US= Warners; (d-lp)(c) **WE SOLD OUR SOULS FOR ROCK'N'ROLL** [35] [48] Feb 76
– Black sabbath / The wizard / Warning / Paranoid / Wicked world / Tomorrow's dream / Fairies wear boots / Changes / Sweet leaf / Children of the grave / Sabbath bloody sabbath / Am I going insane (radio) / Laguna sunrise / Snowblind / N.I.B. *(re-iss.Nov80) (re-iss.d-lp,c,cd.Apr86 on 'Raw Power')*

Dec 76. N.E.M.S.; (7") **PARANOID. / SABBATH BLOODY SABBATH** [ ] [ ]

Dec 77. N.E.M.S./ US= Warners; (lp)(c) **BLACK SABBATH'S GREATEST HITS** [ ] [ ]

Sep 78. N.E.M.S.; (7") **PARANOID. / SNOWBLIND** [14] [ ]
(re-iss.Jun80)

Jun 80. N.E.M.S./ US= Warners; (lp)(c) **LIVE AT LAST (live)** [5] [ ]
– Tomorrow's dream / Sweet leaf / Cornucopia / Wicked world / Killing yourself to live / Snowblind / Children of the grave / War pigs / Paranoid / Cornucopia.

Aug 82. N.E.M.S.; (7"pic-d) **PARANOID. / IRON MAN** [ ] [ ]
(12"+=) – Fairies wear boots / War pigs.

Dec 85. N.E.M.S.; (7xlp-box) **BOXED SET FIRST 6 LP'S + LIVE AT LAST)** [ ] [ ]

Aug 85. Castle; (d-lp)(cd) **THE COLLECTION** [ ] [ ]

Jun 86. Archive 4; (12"ep) **CLASSIC CUTS FROM THE VAULTS** [ ] [ ]
– Paranoid / War pigs / Iron man / Black sabbath.

Jun 88. Vertigo; (d-lp)(d-c)(d-cd) **SABBATH BLOODY SABBATH / BLACK SABBATH** [ ] [-]

Nov 89. Vertigo; (d-lp)(c)(cd) **BLACKEST SABBATH** [ ] [ ]

Jan 90. Masterpiece; (d-cd)(d-c)(d-lp) **BACKTRACKIN'** [ ] [-]

Mar 89. Old Gold; (cd-s) **PARANOID / ELECTRIC FUNERAL / SABBATH BLOODY SABBATH** [ ] [-]

Mar 90. Old Gold; (7") **PARANOID. / IRON MAN** [ ] [-]

May 91. Essential; (3xcd) **THE OZZY OSBOURNE YEARS** [ ] [-]
– (features first 6 albums)

Sep 94. Spectrum; (cd) **IRON MAN** [ ] [-]

Nov 95. EMI; (3xcd-box) **HEADLESS CROSS / TYR / DEHUMANISER** [ ] [-]

BLACK UHURU

Formed: Kingston, Jamaica . . . 1980 by MICHAEL ROSE and DUCKY SIMPSON. Later added American woman PUMA JONES. Big break came in the 80's, when Chris Blackwell of 'Island' records signed them. Had stemmed from earlier roots in UHURU who had releases on 'Third World'. In 1981, the 'RED' lp pushed its way into the UK charts, as they assumed the mantle of top reggae band. • **Style:** Harmony fuelled reggae, with militant Rastafarian roots. • **Songwriters:** Group compositions except HEY JOE (Jimi Hendrix) / NATURAL MYSTIC (Bob Marley). • **Trivia:** UHURU means 'Freedom'.

Recommended: RED (*5) / ANTHEM (*6)

MICHAEL ROSE – vocals / **DERRICK DUCKY SIMPSON.**

UHURU

not issued | Dynamic

1975. (7") **FOLK SONG. / ?** [-] [ ] JAMA

not issued | Third World

1977. (lp) **LOVE CRISIS** [-] [ ]

Jun 78. (lp) **WESTBOUND THING A SWING (as "BLACK U")** [-] [ ]

Mar 79. (12") **NATURAL MYSTIC. / SORRY FOR THAT MAN** [-] [ ]

BLACK UHURU

Greensleeves | not issued

1977. (lp) **BLACK SOUNDS OF FREEDOM** (UK Jul 81) [ ] [-]
– I love King Salassie / Satan / Army band / Time to unite / Eden and deh / Love crisis / African love / Hard ground / Will our tree / Sorry for that man. *(cd-iss.Feb87)*

— group now consisted of **MICHAEL ROSE, DUCKY SIMPSON** and **PUMA JONES** – vocals **RAD BRYAN** – guitar / **DOUGIE BRYAN** – guitar / **KEITH STERLING** – organ / **WINSTON WRIGHT** – organ / **ROBBIE SHAKESPEARE** – bass / **SLY DUNBAR** – drums

Butt | not issued

1980. (lp) **BLACK UHURU** [ ] [-]
– Shine eye girl / Leaving to Zion / General penitentiary / Guess who's coming to dinner / Abortion / Natural Reggae beat / Plastic smile. *(re-iss.Aug81 on 'Virgin', hit 81) (cd-iss.Jun89)*

— **ERROL RANCHEN McLEAN** – organ repl. WINSTON

Island | Island

Jul 80. (12") **SINSEMILLA. / GUESS WHO'S COMING TO DINNER** [ ] [-]

Feb 81. (lp)(c) **SINSEMILLA** [ ] [-]
– Happiness / World is Africa / Push push / There is a fire / No loafing / Sinsemilla / Endurance / Vampire. *(cd-iss.Mar89 + 1990)*

— added **BARRY REYNOLDS** – guitar / **MIKEY CHUNG** – guitar / **UZZIAH STICKY THIMPSON** – percussion / **ROBERT LYN** – percussion

Jun 81. (lp)(c) **RED** [28] [-]
– Youth of Eglington / Sponjii reggae / Sistren / Utternace / Journey / Puff she puff / Rockstone / Carbine. *(cd-iss.'88 & Jan91 on 'Mango')*

Jul 81. (12") **SPONJII REGGAE. / TRODDING** [ ] [-]

Feb 82. (lp)(c) **TEAR IT UP - LIVE** [ ] [-]
– Shine eye gal / Plastic smile / Abortion / General penitentiary / Guess who's coming to dinner / I love King Selassie / Sinsemilla / Leaving for Zion.

— **ANSEL COLLINS** – keyboards / **SKY JUICE** – percussion repl. STERLING

May 82. (7")(10") **DARKNESS. / YOUTH OF EGLINGTON** [ ] [-]

Jun 82. (lp)(c) **CHILL OUT** [38] [ ]
– Chill out / Darkness / Eye market / Right stuff / Mondays / Fleety foot / Wicked act / Moya (Queen of I jungle) / Emotional slaughter. *(cd-iss.Jul92)*

Jul 82. (7") **MONDAYS. / RIGHT STUFF** [ ] [-]
(10"+=) – Killer Tuesday.

— group were basically **MICHAEL ROSE, DUCKY SIMPSON, PUMA JONES** plus **SLY & ROBBIE** plus **DOUGIE & RAD BRYAN**

Aug 83. (7")(12") **PARTY NEXT DOOR. / PARTY IN SESSION** [ ] [-]

Dec 83. (lp)(c) **ANTHEM** [90] [-]
– What is life / Party next door / Try it / Black Uhuru anthem / Botanical roots / Somebody's watching you / Bull in the pen / Elements.

Aug 84. (7") **WHAT IS LIFE. / SOLIDARITY** [56] [-]
(12"+=)(12"pic-d+=) – Party next door.

— **JUNIO REID** – vocals repl. MICHAEL ROSE who went solo

Taxi | not issued

Jul 85. (12") **FIT U HAFFY FIT. / FITNESS** [ ] [-]

R.A.S. | not issued

Feb 86. (12") **CONVICTION OR FINE. / ?** [ ] [-]

Apr 86. (7")(12") **THE GREAT TRAIN ROBBERY. / ('A'dub version)** [62] [-]

May 86. (lp) **BRUTAL** [ ] [-]
– Let us pray / Dread in the mountain / Brutal / Great train robbery / City vibes / Uprown girl / Vision / Reggae with you / Conviction or fine / Fit you haffe fit. *(cd-iss.Feb87 & Jul95 +c)*

Nov 86. (lp)(c) **BRUTAL DUB** (dub versions of above) [ ] [-]

May 87. (12") **CONQUER THE TANKER. / REGGAE WITH YOU (vocal-dub - instrumental)** [ ] [-]

Oct 87. (lp)(c)(cd) **POSITIVE** [ ] [-]
– Positive / Dry weather house / I create / Concept / Cowboy town / Fire city / Space within my heart / Pain.

Oct 88. (lp)(c) **POSITIVE DUB** (dub versions of above) [ ] [-]

— SLY and ROBBIE continued their dual career.

Antler | Mesa

Jun 90. (12") **REGGAE ROCK. / HEY JOE** [ ] [-]

Jul 90. (cd)(c)(lp) **NOW** [ ] [ ] Mar 90
– Heathen / Peace and love / Army band / Take heed / Reggae rock / Thinking about you / Imposter / Freedom fighter / Word sound / Hey Joe.

East West | ???

Apr 93. (cd)(c) **MYSTICAL TRUTH** [ ] [ ]
– Questions / Baseline / Slippin' into darkness / Give my love / Don't you worry / Dreadlock pall bearers / One love (with LOUIE RANKIN) / Pay day / Ozone layer / Living in the city / Young school girl / Mercy Street / Tip of the iceberg (with ICE-T). *(re-iss.Apr94)*

- compilations, others etc. -

1979. D-Roy; (lp) **SHOWCASE** [-] [-] Jamaic

1979. D-Roy; (7") **SHINE EYE GAL. /** [-] [-] Jamaic

May 85. Island; (lp)(c) **REGGAE GREATS** [ ] [-]
(cd-iss.May88 & Jul89)

Dec 86. Sound; (lp)(c) **A DUB EXTRAVAGANZA (w/ JOHNNY ORBOURNE)** [ ] [-]
(cd-iss.Sep88)

Apr 88. Heartbeat; (lp)(c)(cd) **GUESS WHO'S COMING TO DINNER** [ ] [-]

Jun 88. J.R.; (12") **GET RICH AND SWITCH. / ('A'version)** [ ] [-]

Jun 88. Taxi-Island; (m-lp) **THE DUB FACTOR** [ ] [-]
(re-iss.cd/c.Sep91 & Jun92)

Jul 88. Rokit; (lp)(c)(cd) **LIVE IN NEW YORK (live)** [ ] [-]

Feb 94. Mango; (d-cd) **LIBERATION** – THE ISLAND ANTHOLOGY [ ] [-]

Apr 94. Mesa; (cd) **NOW DUB** - -
Apr 94. Mesa; (cd) **IRONSTORM** - -

BLACK WIDOW

Formed: England . . . 1969 by GANNON etc., out of PESKY GEE. Their debut lp 'SACRIFICE' for 'CBS', made it into UK Top 40, although their downfall was as quick as the climb. • **Style:** Heavy metal with occult overtones stamped with BLACK SABBATH imagary. • **Songwriters:** GANNON with others. • **Trivia:** Audiences were at times treated to a mock sacrifice at end of show.

Recommended: SACRIFICE (*6)

JIM GANNON – guitar / **ZOOT TAYLOR** – keyboards / **CLIVE JONES** – saxophone / **KIP TREVOR** – guitar, vocals / **BOB BOND** – bass, / **ROMEO CHALLENGER** – drums

C.B.S. Columbia

Mar 70. (lp)(c) **SACRIFICE** 32
– In ancient days / Way to power / Come to the sabbat / Conjuration / Seduction / Attack of the demon / Sacrifice. *(cd-iss.Jul93 on 'Repertoire')*
May 70. (7") **COME TO THE SABBAT. / WAY TO POWER**

— **FERNANDO SAUNDERS + FRANK LINX** – bass repl. NOSSOV

1971. (lp)(c) **BLACK WIDOW**
– Tears and wine / The gypsy / Bridge passage / When my mind was young / The journey / Poser / Mary Clark / Wait until tomorrow / An afterthought / Legend of creation.
Nov 71. (7") **WISH YOU WOULD. / ACCIDENT**

— **JOHN CULLEY** – guitar, vocals repl. GANNON

Jan 72. (lp)(c) **THREE**
– (a) The battle, (b) The onslaught, (c) If a man should die / Survival / Accident / Lonely man / The Sun / King of hearts / Old man.

— Disbanded 1972, ROMEO helped form SHOWADDYWADDY. (cd-iss.of all above were released 1991 or 1992)

BLANCMANGE

Formed: London, England . . . 1980 by NEIL ARTHUR and STEPHEN LUSCOMBE. Debut on own label as trio, until invitation to do 'SAD DAY' instrumental on 'Some Bizzare Album', which also featured DEPECHE MODE, SOFT CELL, THE THE, etc. This led to major contract with 'London' records early 1982, and a Top 10 third single 'LIVING ON THE CEILING'. Further success followed but all was forgotten by the mid-80's. • **Style:** Initially a synth-experimental outfit, progressing into Eastern influenced electro-pop disco. Many critics saw them as a cross between TALKING HEADS and SOFT CELL. • **Songwriters:** All by duo except, THE DAY BEFORE YOU CAME (Abba). • **Trivia:** Stage gimmick was to have usual background projection screen upfront.

Recommended: HAPPY FAMILIES (*7) / SECOND HELPINGS (*6)

NEIL ARTHUR (b.15 Jun'58, Darwen, Lancashire) – vocals / **STEPHEN LUSCOMBE** (b.29 Oct'54) – keyboards, synthesizers / **LAURENCE STEVENS** – drums

Blah Music not issued

1980. (7"ep) **IRENE & DAVIS** -
– Disco-a-bomb-bomb / Holiday camp / Overspreading / Art genius / Modichy in aneration / Concentration baby / Just another spectre.

— Trimmed to duo of **NEIL** and **STEPHEN** plus drum machine.

London Island

Mar 82. (7")(12") **GOD'S KITCHEN. / I'VE SEEN THE WORD** 65 -
Jul 82. (7")(12")(7"pic-d) **FEEL ME. / ('A'instrumental)** 46

— guests lp, **DAVID RHODES** – guitar / **MADELINE BELL + STEVE LANGE** – b.vox

Sep 82. (lp)(c)(pic-lp) **HAPPY FAMILIES** 30
– I can't explain / Feel me / I've seen the word / Wasted / Living on the ceiling / Waves / Kind / Feel me / Sad day / Cruel / God's kitchen.
Oct 82. (7")(12") **LIVING ON THE CEILING. / RUNNING THIN** 7
Feb 83. (7")(12") **WAVES. / GAMES ABOVE MY HEAD** 19
Apr 83. (7")(7"clear) **BLIND VISION. / HEAVEN KNOWS WHERE HEAVEN IS**
(12"+=) – ('A'version).
Nov 83. (7")(12")(7"pic-d) **THAT'S LOVE THAT IT IS. / VISHNU** 33
Apr 84. (7")(12")(7"pic-d) **DON'T TELL ME. / GET OUT OF THAT** 8

— 1983/84 added guests **PANDIT DINESH** – tablas / **DEEPAK KHAZANCHI** – sitar

May 84. (lp)(c)(cd)(pic-lp) **MANGE TOUT** 8
– Mange tout / Don't tell me / Games above my head / Blind vision / Time before the tide / That's love that it is / Murder / See the train / All things are nice / My baby / The day before you came.
Jul 84. (7")(7"pic-d) **THE DAY BEFORE YOU CAME. / ALL THINGS ARE NICE** 22
(12"+=)(12"pic-d+=) – Feel Me (live).
(d7"++=) – Feel me.

— added on session **DAVID RHOADS** – guitar

London Sire

Aug 85. (7") **WHAT'S YOUR PROBLEM?. / SIDE TWO ('A'instrumental)** 40
(12"+=) – Living on the ceiling.
Oct 85. (lp)(c)(cd) **BELIEVE YOU ME** 54
– Lose your love / What's your problem? / Paradise is / Why don't they leave things alone / 22339 / Don't you love it all / Believe / Lorraine's my nurse / Other animals / No wonder they never made it back / John.
Nov 85. (7")(12") **LOSE YOUR LOVE. / JOHN.**
(12"+=) – Mixing on the ceiling.
(d12"+=) – That's love that it is / Games above my head.
Apr 86. (7")(12") **I CAN SEE IT. / SCREAM DOWN THE HOUSE** 71

— They broke up 1986, **LUSCOMBE** wrote film scores with EAST INDIA COMPANY

– compilations, others, etc. –

1988. Old Gold; (12") **BLIND VISION. / LIVING ON THE CEILING** -
Oct 88. Old Gold; (7") **LIVING ON THE CEILING. / DON'T TELL ME** -
Dec 90. London; (cd)(c)(lp) **SECOND HELPINGS (THE BEST OF BLANCMANGE)** -
– God's kitchen / I've seen the word / Feel me / Living on the ceiling / Waves / Games above my head / Blind vision / That's love, that it is / Don't tell me / The day before you came / What's your problem. *(re-iss.Sep93)*
Dec 92. Elite; (cd)(c) **HEAVEN KNOWS – THE BLANCMANGE COLLECTION** -
(re-iss.May95)
Mar 94. Spectrum; (cd)(c) **THE THIRD COURSE** -
Jun 95. S.A.D.; (12") **SON OF CEILING. / ('A'mixes)** -

NEIL ARTHUR

went solo, augmented by CAROL KENYON

Chrysalis Chrysalis?

Sep 92. (7")(c-s) **ONE DAY, ONE TIME. / GOING ROUND IN TRIANGLES**
(12"+=) – (4 'A'mixes).
(cd-s+=) – ('A'mix) / Laughing in the rain.

NEIL also wrote several pieces for a Channel 4 documentary.

Jan 94. (c-s) **I LOVE, I HATE. / WENDY YOU'RE A BORE / LIVING ON THE CEILING (Blancmange)** 50
(cd-s) – (tracks 1 & 2) / Feel me (BLANCMANGE) / Oh no not yet.
(cd-s) – (tracks 1 & 3) / Festival.
(12") – ('A'side) / ('A'-Grid mixes).
Feb 94. (cd)(c)(lp) **SUITCASE**
– Breaking my heart / I love, I hate / Suitcase / Jumping like a kangaroo / I know these things about you / Heaven / That's love that it is / One day, one time / Jukebox theory / The beach.

BLIND FAITH

Formed: London, England . . . May69 . . . as supergroup of musicians. Played Hyde Park in June that year, supporting The ROLLING STONES. Their first and only album recorded virtually live in the studio, was massive seller on both sides of the Atlantic. Toured the States in the Autumn, but then aborted this project for pastures new. • **Style:** Roots blues, played with remarkable depth of feeling. • **Songwriters:** CLAPTON and WINWOOD, with cover WELL ALL RIGHT (Buddy Holly). • **Trivia:** GINGER BAKER's 11 year-old daughter was controversially used posing semi-naked on UK album sleeve. This was soon banned in USA.

Recommended: BLIND FAITH (*7)

STEVE WINWOOD – vocals, keyboards (ex-TRAFFIC, ex-SPENCER DAVIS GROUP) / **ERIC CLAPTON** – guitar, vocals (ex-CREAM, ex-JOHN MAYALL . . . , ex-YARDBIRDS, etc) / **RIC GRECH** – bass (ex-FAMILY) / **GINGER BAKER** – drums (ex-CREAM, ex-GRAHAM BOND ORGANISATION, ex-BLUES INC.)

Polydor Atlantic

Aug 69. (lp)(c) **BLIND FAITH** 1 1 Jul 69
– Had to cry today / Can't find my way home / Well all right / Presence of the Lord / Sea of joy / Do what you like. *(re-iss.Nov77 & Aug83 on 'RSO') (cd-iss.Apr86 & Sep95)* (cd+=) – Exchange and mart.

— Disbanded later 1969. GINGER BAKER formed AIRFORCE with STEVE WINWOOD. The latter returned to TRAFFIC before carving out a solo career. RIC GRECH went solo. As did ERIC CLAPTON who also formed DEREK & THE DOMINOES in 1970.

– compilations, others, etc. –

Obviously none were released but some BLIND FAITH tracks did surface on ERIC CLAPTON compilations CROSSROADS and THE HISTORY OF ERIC CLAPTON (see ⇒)

BLIND MELON

Formed: Newport Beach, Los Angeles, California, USA . . . 1989. Had to wait four years and a contract on 'Capitol', before breaking through, initially at home, where their eponymous debut album, made Top 3. Tipped for greater things in Britain 1994. • **Style:** Laid back 70's influenced jangly and at times funky hard rock outfit. • **Songwriters:** Group. • **Trivia:** Supported LENNY KRAVITZ on late '93 tour.

Recommended: BLIND MELON (*6).

SHANNON HOON – vocals / **ROGER STEVENS** – guitar / **CHRIS THORN** – guitar / **BRAD SMITH** – bass / **GLEN GRAHAM** – drums

Capitol Capitol

Jun 93. (12"pic-d-ep)(12"ep)(cd-ep) **TONES OF HOME / NO RAIN (live). / DRIVE (live) / SOAK THE SIN (live)** 62

Aug 93. (cd)(c) **BLIND MELON** 53 3
– Soak the sin / Tones of home / I wonder / Paper scratcher / Dear ol' dad / Change / No rain / Deserted / Sleepy house / Holyman / Seed to a tree / Drive / Time. *(re-iss.Jul94 free cd w /cd, hit UK 56)*

Dec 93. (7"yellow)(c-s) **NO RAIN. / NO BIDNESS (live)** 17 20 Aug 93
(cd-s)(12"pic-d) – ('A'live) / Soak the sin / Paper scratcher / Deserted.
(12"+=)(cd-s+=) – I wonder.

Jun 94. (7"green)(c-s) **CHANGE. / PAPER SCRATCHER (acoustic)** 35 □
(12"pic-d)(cd-s) – ('A'side) / No rain (live) / Candy says (live) / Time (live).

Jul 95. (cd-s) **GALAXIE / WILT / CAR SEAT (GOD'S PRESENT)** 37 □
(12"+=) – 2 x 4.
(cd-s) – (first 2 tracks) / Change.

Aug 95. (cd)(c) **SOUP** 48 28
– Galaxie / 2 x 4 / Vernie / Skinned / Toes across the floor / Walk / Dumptruck / Car seat (God's presents) / Wilt / The duke / St.Andrew's fall / New life / Mouthful of cavities / Lemonade.

— On October 21, frontman RICHARD SHANNON HOON died of drug overdose.

BLODWYN PIG

Formed: Luton, England . . . late 1968, by MICK ABRAHAMS, veteran of The HUSTLERS, SCREAMING LORD SUTCH, NEIL CHRISTIAN'S CRUSADERS and JETHRO TULL. Played bass on the latter for one album 'TIME WAS' before hre quickly decided where his roots lay. He remained on ex-band's label 'Island' for whom they had 2 surprise Top 10 album placings. • **Style:** Progressive roots blues, with touch of jazz experimentation, and similiar to JETHRO TULL and ROY HARPER. • **Songwriters:** ABRAHAMS except THE VICTIM (Dr.John-Doc Pomus). • **Trivia:** Albums now worth in excess of £30 each.

Recommended: AHEAD RINGS OUT (*7).

MICK ABRAHAMS – vocals, guitar (ex-JETHRO TULL, ex-McGREGOR'S ENGINE) / **JACK LANCASTER** – saxophone / **ANDY PYLE** – bass (ex-McGREGOR'S ENGINE) / **RON BERG** – drums

Island A&M

May 69. (7") **DEAR JILL. / SWEET CAROLINE** □ -
Aug 69. (lp) **AHEAD RINGS OUT** 9 □
– It's only love / Dear Jill / Walk on the water / The modern alchemist / See my way / Summer day / The change song / Backwash / Ain't ya coming home? *(re-iss.+cd.Mar89 on 'BGO') (cd re-iss.Oct94)*

Sep 69. (7") **SUMMER DAY. / WALK ON THE WATER** □ □

Chrysalis A&M

Jan 70. (7") **SAME OLD STORY. / SLOW DOWN** □ -
Apr 70. (lp)(c) **GETTING TO THIS** 8 96 Jun 70
– Drive me / Variations on Nainos / Meanie Morney / Long bomb blues / The squirreling must go on / San Francisco sketches:- (a) Beach scape, (b) Fisherman's wharf, (c) Telegraph hill, (d) Close the door I'm falling out of the room / Worry / Toys / Send your son to die. *(re-iss.Oct90 + cd on 'BGO'/ cd re-iss.Oct94)*

— (Sep70) **PETE BANKS** – guitar, vocals (ex-YES) repl. ABRAHAMS who went solo. Released two 'Chrysalis' lp's in 1971 and 1972 respectively; '(A MUSICAL EVENING WITH) THE MICK ABRAHAMS BAND' & 'AT LAST' (now both on cd). In 1974 he released another 'HAVE FUN LEARNING THE GUITAR WITH MICK ABRAHAMS'. In the 90's, he was back with 'ALL SAID AND DONE' for 'Elite'.

Meanwhile the remaining members changed group name to **LANCASTER'S BOMBER** (Dec70) **LARRY WALLIS** – guitar, vocals repl. BANKS who formed FLASH

— Disbanded again WALLIS joined UFO. ANDY PYLE joined SAVOY BROWN and then JUICY LUCY where he was reunited with RON BERG. They both rejoined SAVOY BROWN.

Early 1974 to mid '74, BLODWYN PIG reunited (LANCASTER, PYLE and ABRAHAMS) plus CLIVE BUNKER – drums (ex-JETHRO TULL). PYLE joined CHICKEN SHACK. They re-formed in Apr'89, with ABRAHAMS once again at the helm.

— Re-formed by **ABRAHAMS / MIKE SUMMERLAND** – bass (ex-GEORGIE FAME) / **GRAHAM WALKER** – drums (ex-GARY MOORE)

C.A.S. not issued

Jun 94. (cd) **LIES** □ -
– Lies / Tonight is gone / Recession blues / Latin girl / Gnatz / Funny money / Witness / Aby's lean / The victim (born in the country) / Won't let you down / Dead man's hill / Maggie Rose.

Indigo not issued

1995. (cd) **ALL TORE DOWN – LIVE (live)** □ -

BLONDIE

Formed: New York, U.S.A . . . August 1974, by former playboy bunny girl DEBBIE HARRY and boyfriend CHRIS STEIN. Other original members excluding female backing singers, were BILLY O'CONNOR – drums / FRED SMITH – bass (later to PATTI SMITH group) and IVAN KRAL – guitar (later TELEVISION). With a change of line-up they soon supported the likes of punk legend IGGY POP, issuing debut album on Richard Gottehrer's 'Private Stock' label early '77. 'Chrysalis' records reputidly bought the contract out for $500,000 in August that year. It payed off, when their first 45 for the label 'DENIS' rose to No.2 in UK. They surpassed this in early 1979, when 'HEART OF GLASS' went top. They had a further 4 No.1's in the next two years; ''SUNDAY GIRL', 'ATOMIC', 'CALL ME' & 'THE TIDE IS HIGH'. DEBORAH HARRY is still going strong as a solo artist, and is currently in 1993 hitting charts with 'I CAN SEE CLEARLY'. • **Style:** New wave pop, that later diversed into disco. Visual focus being the paroxide Marilyn Monroe of the seventies DEBBIE HARRY. • **Songwriters:** Most written by STEIN-HARRY except; DENIS (aka DENISE) (by Randy & The Rainbows) / HANGING ON THE TELEPHONE (Jack Lee; Nerves) / THE TIDE IS HIGH (Paragons; John Holt) / RING OF FIRE (Johnny Cash) / HEROES (David Bowie) / CALL ME (co-w / Giorgio Moroder) / her duet WELL, DID YOU EVAH (Cole Porter). Producers CHINN / CHAPMAN provided hit material 1978. • **Trivia:** DEBBIE HARRY filmography:- UNION CITY (1979) / ROADIE (1980) / VIDEODROME (1982) / HAIRSPRAY (1982) / Broadway play 'TEANECK TANZI: THE VENUS FLYTRAP' (1983), which bombed after one night. She also appeared on 'The Muppet Show' circa 1980. When she retired in 1983, it was to nurse STEIN through a long dehabilitating illness.

Recommended: THE COMPLETE PICTURE – THE VERY BEST OF DEBORAH HARRY & BLONDIE (*9) / PARALLEL LINES (*8).

DEBBIE HARRY (b.DEBORAH, 1 Jul'45, Miami, Florida) – vocals (ex-WIND IN THE WILLOWS) / **CHRIS STEIN** (b. 5 Jan'50, Brooklyn, New York) – guitar / **JIMMY DESTRI** (b.13 Apr'54) – keyboards (ex-KNICKERS) / **GARY VALENTINE** – bass / **CLEM BURKE** (b.CLEMENT, 24 Nov'55) – drums (ex-SWEET REVENGE)

Private Stock Private Stock

Dec 77. (7") **X-OFFENDER. / IN THE SUN** - □
Feb 77. (lp)(c) **IN THE FLESH. / MAN OVERBOARD** - □
Apr 77. (lp)(c) **BLONDIE** □ □ Feb 77
– X offender / Little girl lies / In the flesh / Look good in blue / In the sun / A shark in jet's clothing / Man overboard / Rip her to shreds / Rifle range / Kung Fu girls / The attack of the giant ants. *(re-iss.Sep77 on 'Chrysalis', re-iss.Mar79 hit UK 75) (re-iss.+c.Oct82 on 'Hallmark') (re-iss.+c.Apr85 on 'MfP')*

May 77. (7") **IN THE FLESH. / X OFFENDER** □ -

Chrysalis Chrysalis

Nov 77. (7")(12") **RIP HER TO SHREDS. / IN THE FLESH / X OFFENDER***(12"re-iss.Dec81)* □ □

— (Oct77) **FRANK INFANTE** – bass (ex-WORLD WAR III) repl. VALENTINE

Feb 78. (7")(12") **DENIS. / CONTACT IN RED SQUARE / KUNG FU GIRLS***(12"white; re-iss.Dec81)* 2 □
Apr 78. (lp)(c) **PLASTIC LETTERS** 10 72 Feb 78
– Fan mail / Denis / Bermuda Triangle blues (Flight 45) / Youth nabbed as sniper / Contact in Red Square / (I'm always touched by your) Presence dear / I'm on E / I didn't have the nerve to say no / Love at the pier / No imagination / Kidnapper / Detroit 442 / Cautious lip.

Apr 78. (7")(12") **(I'M ALWAYS TOUCHED BY YOUR) PRESENCE DEAR. / POET'S PROBLEM / DETROIT 442** 10 □
(12"re-iss.Dec81)

— (Nov77 on recording of 2nd lp) added **NIGEL HARRISON** – bass (b.England) now sextet with **INFANTE** – now on rhythm guitar

Aug 78. (7")(7"yellow) **PICTURE THIS. / FADE AWAY (AND RADIATE)** 12 □
Sep 78. (7") **I'M GONNA LOVE YOU TOO. / JUST GO AWAY** - □
Sep 78. (lp)(c)(white-lp) **PARALLEL LINES** 1 6
– Fade away (and radiate) / Hanging on the telephone / One way or another / Picture this / Pretty baby / I know but I don't know / 11:59 / Will anything happen / Sunday girl / Heart of glass / I'm gonna love you too / Just go away. *(re-iss.Jun88) (re-iss.+c+cd.Nov83 on 'Fame')*

Nov 78. (7") **HANGING ON THE TELEPHONE. / WILL ANYTHING HAPPEN** 5 -
Nov 78. (7") **HANGIN' ON THE TELEPHONE / FADE AWAY AND RADIATE** - □
Jan 79. (7") **HEART OF GLASS. / RIFLE RANGE** 1 - Feb 79
(12"+=) – ('A'instrumental). *(12"re-iss.Dec81)*
Mar 79. (7") **HEART OF GLASS. / 11:59** - 1
May 79. (7") **SUNDAY GIRL. / I KNOW BUT I DON'T KNOW** 1 □
(12"+=) – ('A' French version). *(12"clear;re-iss.Dec81)*
Jun 79. (7") **ONE WAY OR ANOTHER. / JUST GO AWAY** - 24
Sep 79. (7") **DREAMING. / SOUND ASLEEP** 2 27 Oct 79
Oct 79. (7") **DREAMIN'. / LIVING IN THE REAL WORLD** - □
Oct 79. (lp)(c) **EAT TO THE BEAT** 1 17
– Dreaming / The hardest part / Union city blue / Shayla / Eat to the beat / Accidents never happen / Die young stay pretty Slow motion / / Atomic / Sound-a-sleep / Victor / Living in the real world. *(re-iss.+cd.Jun87)*

Nov 79. (7") **UNION CITY BLUE. / LIVING IN THE REAL WORLD** 13 □
Dec 79. (7") **THE HARDEST PART. / SOUND-A-SLEEP** - 84
Feb 80. (7") **ATOMIC. / DIE YOUNG STAY PRETTY.** 1 39 May 80
(12"+=) – Heroes. *(12"re-iss.Dec81)*
Apr 80. (7")(12") **CALL ME. / ('A'instrumental)** 1 1 Feb 80
(12"+=) – ('A' Spanish).
Oct 80. (7") **THE TIDE IS HIGH. / SUZIE AND JEFFREY** 1 1 Nov 80
Nov 80. (lp)(c) **AUTOAMERICAN** 3 7
– Europa / Live it up / Here's looking at you / The tide is high / Angels on the balcony / Go through it / Do the dark / Rapture / Faces / Do the dark / T-Birds / Walk like me / Follow me.

Jan 81. (7") **RAPTURE. / WALK LIKE ME** 5 1
(12") – ('A'side) / Live it up.
Apr 82. (7")(12")(7"pic-d) **ISLAND OF LOST SOULS. / DRAGONFLY** 1 37 May 82
May 82. (lp)(c)(pic-lp) **THE HUNTER** 9 33
– Orchid club / Island of lost souls / Dragonfly / For your eyes only / The beast / War child / Little Caesar / Danceaway / (Can I) Find the right words (to say) / English boys / The hunter gets captured by the game.

Jul 82. (7")(12")(7"pic-d) **WAR CHILD. / LITTLE CAESAR** 39 □

— (Aug82) STEIN formed own 'Animal' label through 'Chrysalis'. CLEM BURKE joins EURYTHMICS and later RAMONES. He also teams up with HARRISON to form CHEQUERED PAST. A solo album HEART ON THE WALL was released by JIMMY DESTRI in 1982 and featured most of BLONDIE. DEBBIE (DEBORAH). HARRY continued solo career

– compilations, others, etc. –

Oct 81. Chrysalis; (lp)(c) **THE BEST OF BLONDIE** [4] [30]
(cd-iss.1983)
Dec 82. Chrysalis; (d-c) **EAT TO THE BEAT / AUTOAMERICAN** [ ] [-]
Nov 88. Chrysalis; (7") **DENIS (remix). / RAPTURE (remix)** [50] [ ]
(12"+=)(cd-s+=)(12"pic-d+=) – Heart of glass (remix) / Atomic (remix).
Dec 88. Chrysais; (lp)(c)(cd) **ONCE MORE INTO THE BLEACH (GREATEST HITS)** [50] [ ]
– Denis / Heart of glass / Call me / Rapture / Rapture (bonus beats) / The tide is high / The jam was moving (DEBBIE HARRY) / In love with love (DEBBIE HARRY) / Rush rush (DEBBIE HARRY) / French kissin' in the U.S.A. (DEBBIE HARRY) / Feel the spin (DEBBIE HARRY) / Backfired (DEBBIE HARRY) / Sunday girl (French version).

—— (above included DEBBIE HARRY solo material)

Feb 89. Chrysalis; (7") **CALL ME. / CALL ME (version)** [61] [ ]
(12"+=)(cd-s+=) – Backfired (DEBBIE HARRY).
Mar 91. Chrysalis; (cd)(c)(d-lp) **THE COMPLETE PICTURE – THE VERY BEST OF DEBORAH HARRY & BLONDIE** [3] [ ]
– Heart of glass / I want that man / Call me / Sunday girl / French kissin' in the USA / Denis / Rapture / Brite side / (I'm always touched by your) Presence dear / Well, did you evah! / The tide is high / In love with love / Hanging on the telephone / Island of lost souls / Picture this / Dreaming / Sweet and low / Union city blue / Atomic / Rip her to shreds.
Jan 94. Chrysalis; (cd)(c) **BLONDE AND BEYOND – RARITIES AND ODDITIES** [ ] [ ]
Aug 94. Chrysalis; (12")(c-s)(cd-s) **ATOMIC (remix). / ('A'mixes by Diddy & Alan Thompson)** [19] [ ]
(cd-s) – ('A'side) / Sunday girl / Union City blues.
Nov 94. Chrysalis; (d-cd) **THE PLATINUM COLLECTION** [ ] [ ]
Jun 95. Chrysalis; (12") **HEART OF GLASS. / CALL ME** [15] [ ]
(c-s) – ('A'side) / Rapture / Atomic.
(cd-s+=) – ('A'mixes).
Jul 95. Chrysalis; (cd)(c) **BEAUTIFUL – THE REMIX ALBUM** [25] [ ]
Oct 95. Chrysalis; (12"blue)(cd-s) **UNION CITY BLUE (remix) / I FEEL LOVE (live)** [31] [ ]
(cd-s) – (other mixes by Diddy / The Burger Queens / OPM / Vinny Vero & Jammin' Hot).
Re-issued /remastered all albums on cd (D.HARRY's) Sep94. PLASTIC LETTERS / AUTOAMERICAN / THE HUNTER + KOO KOO contained bonus tracks. PARALLEL LINES / EAT TO THE BEAT / DEBRAVATION + THE COMPLETE PICTURE were also on cassette, with the latter also released on vinyl & video.
Feb 87. Old Gold; (7") **DENIS. / PICTURE THIS** [ ] [-]
Feb 87. Old Gold; (7") **SUNDAY GIRL. / HANGING ON THE TELEPHONE** [ ] [-]
Feb 87. Old Gold; (7") **CALL ME. / UNION CITY BLUE** [ ] [-]
Feb 87. Old Gold; (7") **HEART OF GLASS. / THE TIDE IS HIGH** [ ] [-]
Feb 87. Old Gold; (7") **DREAMING. / ATOMIC** [ ] [-]
Mar 91. FM-Revolver; (lp) **BLONDIE HIT COLLECTION** [ ] [-]

DEBBIE HARRY

solo, with **NILE RODGERS** and **BERNARD EDWARDS** on production, etc.

Chrysalis Chrysalis

Jul 81. (7")(12") **BACKFIRED. / MILITARY RAP** [32] [43]
Aug 81. (lp)(c) **KOO KOO** [6] [23]
– Jump jump / The jam was moving / Chrome / Under arrest / Inner city spillover / Surrender / Backfired / Now I know you / Military rap / Oasis.
Sep 81. (7") **INNER CITY SPILLOVER. / THE JAM WAS MOVING** [ ] [ ]
(12"+=) – Chrome.

now worked with various session musicians.

Chrysalis Geffen

Jan 84. (7")(12") **RUSH RUSH. / RUSH RUSH (dub)** [ ] [ ]
(US b-side = DANCE, DANCE, DANCE)
Nov 86. (7")(12")(12"pic-d) **FRENCH KISSIN' IN THE U.S.A. / BUCKLE UP** [8] [ ]
Nov 86. (7") **FRENCH KISSIN' IN THE U.S.A. / ROCKBIRD** [-] [ ]
Nov 86. (lp)(c)(cd) **ROCKBIRD** [31] [ ]
– I want you / French kissin' in the U.S.A. / Buckle up / In love with love / You got me in trouble / Free to fall / Rockbird / Secret life / Beyond the limit.
Feb 87. (7")(12") **FREE TO FALL. / SECRET LIFE.** [46] [ ]
(12"+=) – Feel the spin.
Mar 87. (7") **IN LOVE WITH LOVE. / SECRET LIFE** [-] [ ]
Apr 87. (7")(12") **IN LOVE WITH LOVE. / FRENCH KISSIN' (in French)** [45] [ ]

not issued Reprise

1988. (7") **LIAR, LIAR. / QUEEN OF VOODOO (by "VOODOOIST CORPORATION"** [-] [ ]

DEBORAH HARRY

with **CHRIS STEIN** – guitar / **LEIGH FOXX** – bass / **TERRY BOZZIO** – drums / **TOMMY PRICE** – drums / **PHIL ASHLEY** – synthesizers / **STEVE GOLDSTEIN** – keyboards, etc.

Chrysalis Sire

Sep 89. (7") **I WANT THAT MAN. / BIKE BOY** [13] [ ]
(12")(12"pic-d) – ('A'side) / ('A'remix) / ('A'instrumental)
(cd-s+=) – (all 4 tracks above).
Oct 89. (lp)(c)(cd) **DEF, DUMB AND BLONDE** [12] [ ]
– I want that man / Lovelight / KIss it better / Bike boy * / Get your way / Maybe for sure / I'll never fall in love / Calmarie / Sweet and low / He is so / Bugeye / Comic books / Brite side / End of the run *. *(cd+=*)*
Nov 89. (7")(c-s) **BRITE SIDE. / BUGEYE** [59] [ ]
(12"+=) – In love with love.
(cd-s++=) – French kissin' in the U.S.A.

—— Her touring group at time included **STEIN** and **FOXX** plus **SUZY DAVIS** – keyboards / **CARLA OLLA** – rhythm guitar / **JIMMY CLARK** – drums

Mar 90. (7")(c-s) **SWEET AND LOW. / LOVELIGHT** [57] [ ]
(12")(cd-s) – ('A'side) / (2 other 'A'mixes).
May 90. (7")(c-s) **MAYBE FOR SURE. / GET YOUR WAY** [ ] [ ]
(12"+=)(cd-s+=) – ('A'extended).

one-off duet, which featured on Cole Porter tribute album 'Red Hot & Blue'.

Dec 90. (7")(12") **WELL, DID YOU EVAH (by "DEBORAH HARRY & IGGY POP"). /** ('B'by THOMPSON TWINS) [42] [ ]
(cd-s+=) – (track by 'Aztec Camera').

BLOOD, SWEAT & TEARS

Formed: New York, USA . . . Dec 1967 by KOOPER, KATZ, COLOMBY and FIELDER. Gained contract on 'Columbia' and soon were to become one of America's top ensembles. In 1969, they had 3 consecutive US No.2 hits with 'YOU'VE MADE ME SO VERY HAPPY', 'SPINNING WHEEL' & 'AND WHEN I DIE'. By 1973, they had failed to score with album 'NO SWEAT', and CLAYTON-THOMAS went solo. • **Style:** Brassy jazz-pop inspired rock with heavy soulful vox. • **Songwriters:** Most by KOOPER 'til CLAYTON-THOMAS took over. Covered AND WHEN I DIE (Laura Nyro) / YOU'VE MADE ME SO VERY HAPPY (Brenda Holloway) / MORNING GLORY (Tim Buckley) / HI-DE-HO (Goffin-King) / GOT TO GET YOU INTO MY LIFE (Beatles) / etc. • **Trivia:** JAMES WILLIAM GUERCIO was also their initial in-house producer.

Recommended: GREATEST HITS (*5)

AL KOOPER (b. 5 Feb'44, Brooklyn, New York) – vocals, keyboards (ex-BLUES PROJECT, ex-BOB DYLAN Band) / **STEVE KATZ** (b. 9 May'45, New York City) – vocals, guitar (ex-BLUES PROJECT) / **RANDY BRECKER** (b.27 Nov'44, Philadelphia) – trumpet, flugelhorn / **JERRY WEISS** (b. 1 May'46, New York City) – trumpet, flugelhorn / **FRED LIPSIUS** (b.19 Nov'43, New York City) – alto sax, piano / **DICK HALLIGAN** (b.29 Aug'43, Troy, New York) – trombone, flute, keyboards / **JIM FIELDER** (b. 4 Oct'47, Dallas, Texas) – bass (ex-BUFFALO SPRINGFIELD) / **BOBBY COLOMBY** (b.20 Dec'44, New York City) – drums

C.B.S. Columbia

Jun 68. (lp) **THE CHILD IS FATHER TO THE MAN** [40] [47] Apr 68
– Overture / I love you more than you'll ever know / Morning glory / My days are numbered / Without her / Just one smile / Meagan's gypsy eyes / House in the country / I can't quit her / Somethin' goin' on / The modern adventures of Plato, Diogenes and Freud / So much love / Underture. *(re-iss.Jul77 as 'FIRST ALBUM' on 'Embassy-CBS') (cd-iss.1988 & Nov95)*
Jun 68. (7") **I CAN'T QUIT HER. / HOUSE IN THE COUNTRY** [ ] [ ]

—— (Mar69) **DAVID CLAYTON-THOMAS** (b.DAVID THOMSETT, 13 Sep'41, Surrey, England, raised Canada) – vocals repl. KOOPER who went solo, etc.

—— **CHUCK WINFIELD** (b.5 Feb'43, Monessen, Pensylvania) – trumpet, flugelhorn repl. BRECKER who later formed BRECKER BROTHERS. **LEW SOLOFF** (b.20 Feb'44, Brooklyn, New York) – trumpet, flugelhorn and **JERRY HYMAN** (b.19 May'47, New York) – trombone repl. WEISS

Mar 69. (lp) **BLOOD, SWEAT & TEARS** [15] [1] Jan 69
– Variations on a theme by Eric Satie (1st & 2nd movements) / Smiling phases / Sometimes in winter / More and more / And when I die / God bless the child / Spinning wheel / You've made me so very happy / Blues (part 2) / Variations on a theme by Eric Satie (reprise). *(re-iss.+cd.Dec88 & Dec91 on 'B.G.O.')*
Apr 69. (7") **YOU'VE MADE ME SO VERY HAPPY. / THE BLUES (part 2)** [35] [2] Feb 69
Jun 69. (7") **SPINNING WHEEL. / MORE AND MORE** [ ] [2] May 69
Dec 69. (7") **AND WHEN I DIE. / SOMETIMES IN WINTER** [ ] [2] Oct 69
Jul 70. (lp)(c) **BLOOD, SWEAT & TEARS 3** [14] [1]
– Hi-de-ho / The battle / Lucretia Mac Evil / Lucretia's reprise / Fire and rain / Lonesome Suzie / Symphony for the Devil; Sympathy for the Devil – Emergence – Evil's game; (a) Labyrinth, (b) Satan's dance, (c) The demand – Submergence / Contemplation – Return / He's a miner / Somethin' comin' on / 40,000 headman. *(re-iss.May76)*
Jul 70. (7") **HI-DE-HO. / THE BATTLE** [ ] [14]
Oct 70. (7") **LUCRETIA MAC EVIL. / LUCRETIA'S REPRISE** [ ] [29]

—— **DAVID BARGERON** (b. 6 Sep'42, Massacusetts) – horns repl. HYMAN

Jul 71. (lp)(c) **B, S & T 4** [ ] [10]
– Go down gamblin' / Cowboys and Indians / John The Baptist (holy John) / Redemption / Lisa, listen to me / Look at my heart / High on a mountain / Valentine's day / Take me in your arms (rock me a little while) / For my lady / Mama gets high / Look to my heart.
Jul 71. (7") **GO DOWN GAMBLIN'. / VALENTINE'S DAY** [ ] [32]
Dec 71. (7") **LISA, LISTEN TO ME. / COWBOYS AND INDIANS** [ ] [73] Oct 71

—— **JERRY FISHER** (b. 1943, Texas) – vocals repl. **BOBBY DOYLE** who had repl. CLAYTON-THOMAS who went solo / **LOU MARINI Jr.** – saxophone repl. LIPSIUS / **LARRY WILLIS** – keyboards repl. HALLIGAN

Jul 72. (7") **SO LONG DIXIE. / KRAKBERGARNINGEN (CROWS FUNERAL)** [ ] [-]
Jul 72. (7") **SO LONG DIXIE. / ALONE** [-] [44]
Oct 72. (lp)(c) **NEW BLOOD** [ ] [32]
– Down in the flood / Touch me / Alone / Velvet / I can't move no mountains / Over the hill / So long Dixie / Snow queen / Maiden voyage.
Nov 72. (7") **TOUCH ME. / VELVET** [ ] [-]
Dec 72. (7") **I CAN'T MOVE NO MOUNTAINS. / VELVET** [-] [ ]
May 73. (7") **BACK UP AGAINST THE WALL. / OVER THE HILL** [ ] [-]
Aug 73. (7") **ROLLER COASTER. / INNER CRISIS** [-] [ ]
Aug 73. (lp)(c) **NO SWEAT** [ ] [72]
– Roller coaster / Save our ship / Django / Rosemary / Song for John / Almost sorry / Back up against the wall / Hip pickles / My old lady / Empty pages / Mary Miles / Inner crisis.
Oct 73. (7") **SAVE OUR SHIP. / SONG FOR JOHN** [-] [ ]
Nov 73. (7") **SAVE OUR SHIP. / INNER CRISIS** [ ] [-]

—— **DAVID CLAYTON-THOMAS** returned to repl. **JERRY LaCROIX** who had briefly replaced KATZ who was later to join AMERICAN FLYER / **TOM MALONE** – horns repl. WINFIELD

Jul 74. (7") **TELL ME THAT I'M WRONG. / ROCK REPRISE** [ ] [83] Jun 74

Sep 74. (lp)(c) **MIRROR IMAGE** [ ] [ ]
– Tell me that I'm wrong / Look up to the sky / Love looks good on you (you're candy sweet) / Hold on to me / Thinking of you / Are you satisfied / Rock reprise / She's coming home.

Oct 74. (7") **LOVE LOOKS GOOD ON YOU. / ARE YOU SATISFIED** [ ] [ ]

— **RON McCLURE** – bass repl. FIELDER / **BILL TILLMAN** – saxophone repl. SOLOFF

Jun 75. (lp)(c) **NEW CITY** [ ] [47] May 75
– Ride captain ride / Life / No show / I was a witness to a war / One room country shack / Applause / Yesterday's music / Naked man / Got to get you into my life / Takin' it home.

Jun 75. (7") **GOT TO GET YOU INTO MY LIFE. / NAKED MAN** [-] [62]

Sep 75. (7") **YESTERDAY'S MUSIC. / NO SHOW** [-] [ ]

— **CLAYTON-THOMAS, COLOMBY, BARGERON, WILLIS, TILLMAN & McCLURE** brought in guests **PATTI AUSTIN / CHAKA KHAN** – vocals plus newcomers **MIKE STERN** – guitar / **DON ALIAS** – perc. / **STEVE KHAN** – guitar / **F.BUCHTELL** – trumpet

Aug 76. (lp)(c) **MORE THAN EVER** [ ] [ ] Jul 766
– They / I love you more than ever / Kathy Bell / Sweet Sadie the savior / Hollywood / You're the one / Heavy blue / Saved by the grace of your love.

Jan 77. (7") **YOU'RE THE ONE. / HEAVY BLUE** [-] [ ]

— **DANNY TRIFAN** – bass repl. McCLURE / added **ROY McCURDY** – drums / **RANDY BERNSEN** – guitar repl. KHAN / **TONY KLATKA** – trumpet repl. ALIAS

A.B.C. A.B.C.

Nov 77. (lp)(c) **BRAND NEW DAY** [ ] [ ]
– Somebody I trusted / Dreaming as one / Same old blues / Lady put out the light / Womanizer / Blue street / Gimme that wine / Rock & roll queen / Don't explain.

Nov 77. (7") **BLUE STREET. / PUT ON THE LIGHT** [ ] [-]

Jan 78. (7") **BLUE STREET. / SOMEBODY I TRUSTED** [-] [ ]

— added **CHRIS ALBERT** – trumpet / **GREG HERBERT** – sax / **NEIL STUBENHAUS** – bass

— (1979) **CLAYTON-THOMAS** brought in new members **ROBERT PILTCH** – guitar / **RICHARD MARTINEZ** – keyboards / **BRUCE CASSIDY** – trumpet / **BOBBY ECONOMOU** – drums / **DAVID PILTCH** – bass / **EARL SEYMOUR** – sax, flute / **VERNON DORGE** – sax, flute

A.B.C. M.C.A.

Feb 80. (7") **NUCLEAR BLUES. / AGITATO** [-] [ ]

Feb 80. (7")(12") **NUCLEAR BLUES. / I'LL DROWN IN MY OWN TEARS** [ ] [-]

Mar 80. (lp)(c) **NUCLEAR BLUES** [ ] [ ]
– Agitato / Nuclear blues / Manic depression / I'll drown in my own tears / Fantasy stage / Spanish wine suite: La cantina – Spanish wine – Latin fire – The challenge – The duel – Amor – Spanish wine (reprise). *(re-iss.Sep89 on 'Big Time')*

— Break-up 1980, CLAYTON-THOMAS and COLOMBY did some reunion concerts, and even reformed varied line-up in 1988.

– compilations, others, etc. –

below on CBS-Columbia unless mentioned.

Jan 71. (lp) **THE OWL AND THE PUSSYCAT (Soundtrack)** [ ] [ ]

Mar 72. (lp)(c) **GREATEST HITS** [ ] [19]
(re-iss.Jul83, cd-iss. Nov 87) (quad-lp 1973)

Mar 73. (7") **SPINNING WHEEL. / AND WHEN I DIE** [ ] [ ]

1975. (7") **AND WHEN I DIE. / LUCRETIA MACEVIL** [ ] [ ]

Feb 78. (7") **YOU MADE ME SO VERY HAPPY. / SPINNING WHEEL** [ ] [ ]
(re-iss.Jul84)

May 80. (lp)(c) **CLASSIC BLOOD SWEAT & TEARS** [ ] [ ]

Jul 78. Pickwick; (lp) **BLOOD, SWEAT & TEARS** [ ] [-]

Nov 84. Astan; (lp)(c) **THE CHALLENGE** [ ] [-]

May 91. Elite; (cd)(c) **SMILING PHASES** [ ] [-]
(re-iss.cd Sep93)

Mike BLOOMFIELD (see under ⇒ELECTRIC FLAG)

BLOW MONKEYS

Formed: Based London, England. In 1981 Dr.ROBERT (HOWARD) employed cosmopolitan line-up, himself emigrating as a teenager to Australia. After an indie single and a year in the wilderness, they signed to 'RCA' late 1983. Broke through in 1986 when 'DIGGING YOUR SCENE' hit both UK & US Top 20's. • **Style:** Moved from brassy romantic type MARC BOLAN / ORANGE JUICE outfit in '84, to a disco-soul like ABC by 1986. • **Songwriters:** Mostly all by Dr.ROBERT, except IT'S NOT UNUSUAL (Tom Jones) / SUPERFLY (Curtis Mayfield) / FOLLOW THAT DREAM (Elvis Presley). • **Trivia:** They were banned from airwaves during election time 1987, when they released anti-Margaret Thatcher song '(CELEBRATE) THE DAY AFTER YOU'.

Recommended: CHOICES (*6).

Dr. ROBERT (b.BRUCE ROBERT HOWARD, 2 May'61, Scotland / raised Norfolk, England) – vocals, guitar, piano, computers / **NEVILLE HENRY** – saxophone / **MICK ANKER** (b. 2 Jul'57) – bass / **ANTHONY KILEY** (b.16 Feb'62) – drums, machines.

Parasol not issued

Jan 82. (7") **LIVE TODAY LOVE TOMORROW. / IN COLD BLOOD** [ ] [-]

R.C.A. R.C.A.

Mar 84. (7")(ext-12") **GO PUBLIC. / RUB A DUB SHANKA.** [ ] [-]

Jun 84. (7") **THE MAN FROM RUSSIA. / RESURRECTION LOVE.** [ ] [-]
(12"+=) – Slither.

Sep 84. (7") **ATOMIC LULLABY. / MY TWISTY JEWEL** [ ] [-]
('A'extended-12"+=) – Kill the pig.

Oct 84. (lp)(c) **LIMPING FOR A GENERATION** [ ] [ ]
– He's shedding skin / Wildflower / Atomic lullaby / Fat cat Belusha / Go public / Professor Supercool / Man from Russia / Waiting for Mr.Moonlight / Limping for a generation / Trashtown incident. *(re-iss.+cd.Oct87)*

Feb 85. (7") **WILDFLOWER. / WAITING FOR MR.MOONLIGHT (live)** [ ] [-]
(12"+=) – It's not unusual (live) / Trashtown incident (live).

Sep 85. (7") **FORBIDDEN FRUIT. / MY AMERICA.** [ ] [ ]
(12"+=) – The optimist.
(d12"+=) – Sweet murder (Eek-A-mix) / kill the pig (pig mix).

Feb 86. (7") **DIGGING YOUR SCENE. / I BACKED A WINNER (IN YOU)** [12] [14] May 86
(12"+=) – (2 'A'mixes).
(10"+=) – ('A'instrumental) / Man from Russia (remix).

Apr 86. (lp)(c)(cd) **ANIMAL MAGIC** [21] [35] Jun 86
– Digging your scene / Animal magic / Wicked ways / Sweet murder / Aeroplane city lovesong / I nearly died laughing / Don't be scared of me / Burn the rich / I backed a winner (in you) / Heaven is a place I'm moving to. (cd+=) – Walking the blue beat.

Apr 86. (7") **WICKED WAYS. / WALKING THE BLUE BEAT** [60] [ ]
(12"+=) – ('A'extended).
(d7"+=) – Digging your scene (scat mix) / Atomic lullaby.
(12") – ('A'side) / ('A'instrumental) / Wildflower.

Jul 86. (7") **DON'T BE SCARED OF ME. / SUPERFLY** [ ] [ ]
(12"+=) – ('A'extended).
(12"+=) – Wildflower / He's shedding skin.

Jan 87. (7") **IT DOESN'T HAVE TO BE THAT WAY. / ASK FOR MORE** [5] [ ]
(12"+=) – ('A'extended).

Mar 87. (7")(12") **OUT WITH HER. / THE GRANTHAM GRIZZLER** [30] [ ]
(d12"+=)(cd-s+=) – It doesn't have to be that way / Digging your scene.

Apr 87. (lp)(c)(cd) **SHE WAS ONLY A GROCER'S DAUGHTER** [20] [ ]
– It doesn't have to be that way / Some kind of wonderful / Out with her / How long can a bad thing last / Man at the end of his tether / Rise above / (Celebrate) The day after you / Checking out / Don't give it up / Cash / Beautiful child. (cd+=) – The Grantham grizzler (remix) / This is the way it has to be.

May 87. (7") **(CELEBRATE) THE DAY AFTER YOU. ("BLOW MONKEYS with CURTIS MAYFIELD") / BEAUTIFUL CHILD** [52] [ ]
(10"+=) – It's not unusual (live) / The smile on your face (sweet murder).
(12"+=) – ('A'extended).
(cd-s+=) – It's not unusual (live) / Don't give it up.

Jul 87. (7") **SOME KIND OF WONDERFUL. / SWEET OBSESSION** [67] [ ]
(12"+=) – Huckleberry.
(12") – ('A' side) / Worship you / It's got to be a hitch.

Aug 88. (7") **THIS IS YOUR LIFE. / THIS DAY TODAY** [70] [ ]
(cd-s+=) – ('A'extended).
(12"+=) – This is your house.
(12"+=) – Let the big bad dog.

Oct 88. (7") **IT PAYS TO BELONG. / THE LOVE OF WHICH I DARE NOT SPEAK** [ ] [ ]
(cd-s+=) – Digging your remix.
(12"++=)(cd-s++=) – It pays to be twelve / This is your house.

Dec 88. (7") **WAIT (edit)(as "ROBERT HOWARD & KIM MAZELLE"). / WAIT (bits and pieces)** [7] [ ]
(12"+=)(cd-s+=) – ('A'long version).

Feb 89. (7") **THIS IS YOUR LIFE. / ('A'accapella version)** [32] [ ]
(cd-s) – ('A'side) / Sweet talking rapist at home.
(12"+=)/ /(12"+=) – ('A'mix)/ / ('A'mix).

Feb 89. (lp)(c)(cd) **WHOOPS! THERE GOES THE NEIGHBOURHOOD** [46] [ ]
– This is your life / No woman is an island / It pays to belong / Mercy, pity, peace and love / Squaresville / Come on down / Sweet talking rapist at home / Bombed into the stoneage / Let's emigrate.

Jun 89. (7")(c-s) **CHOICE?. ("BLOW MONKEYS featuring SYLVIA TELLA") / OH YEAH** [22] [ ]
(12"+=)(cd-s+=) – (3 extra 'A'mixes only +'A').

Aug 89. (lp)(c)(cd) **CHOICES – THE SINGLES COLLECTION** [5] [ ]
(compilation)
– Wait / Choice? / Slaves no more / Celebrate (the day after you) / Wicked ways / Digging your scene / It doesn't have to be this way / Out with her / Don't be scared of me / This is your life / It pays to belong. *(cd+=)* – Wildflower / Forbidden fruit. *(re-iss.cd Apr93)*

Sep 89. (7")(c-s) **SLAVES NO MORE. / WHAT'S THAT?** [73] [ ]
(12"+=)(cd-s+=) – ('A'long version).

May 90. (7") **SPRINGTIME FOR THE WORLD. / LA PASSIONARA** [69] [ ]
(12"+=)(cd-s+=) – If you love somebody / The other side of you.

Jun 90. (cd)(c)(lp) **SPRINGTIME FOR THE WORLD** [ ] [ ]
– In too deep / Springtime for the world / Vibe alive! / Reflections '89 / Be not afraid / If you love somebody / La passionara / Let the people dance / Fruits of the Earth / As the dust settles. *(cd+=)* – Checking out / The other side of you.

Jul 90. (7") **LA PASSIONARA. ("BLOW MONKEYS featuring QUAN-T & BEZERK") / VIBE ALIVE!** [ ] [ ]
(12"+=)(cd-s+=) – ('A'-drums and rap mix) / ('A'-Tapas Rappers mix).

disbanded Sep'90.

– compilations, others, etc. –

Nov 92. Old Gold; (cd-ep) **DIGGING YOUR SCENE / IT DOESN'T HAVE TO BE THAT WAY / CHOICE?** [ ] [-]

Jun 93. Optima; (cd)(c) **THE BEST OF THE BLOW MONKEYS** [ ] [-]

Mar 94. R.C.A.; (cd)(c) **THE BEST OF THE BLOW MONKEYS** [ ] [ ]

DR. ROBERT

Re-gal Zono. / unissued?

Sep 91. (7")(c-s) **I'VE LEARNT TO LIVE WITH LOVE. / JUST US TONIGHT**
(12"+=)(cd-s+=) – ('A'dub version).

Apr 92. (7")(c-s) **A SIMPLER PLACE AND TIME. / ('A'instrumental)**
(12"+=)(cd-s+=) – ('A'original mix) / ('A'vocal mix) / (2 other 'A'mixes).

Apr 92. (cd)(c)(lp) **INTO THE REALMS OF GOLD** (withdrawn)

Heavenly / not issued

Nov 94. (7") **THE COMING OF GRACE. / LUCIFER'S FRIEND**

Nov 95. (7") **CIRCULAR QUAY. / GONE FISHING** [-]
(cd-s+=)(10"+=) – Bethesda (part 1) / Moments of madness (fearless version).

BLUE AEROPLANES

Formed: Bristol, England . . . 1983 out of ART OBJECTS and EXPLODING SEAGULLS by GERARD LANGLEY. After initial release on 'Abstract' they moved to another indie 'Fire' in 1985. By 1989, they had moved to major Irish label 'Ensign' and were on the verge of success, with next years' 'SWAGGER' album. • **Style:** A cross between FELT and The BYRDS, with early psychedelic and folk fused with poetry readings on stage. • **Songwriters:** GERARD LANGLEY and JACOBS with other members until latters' departure. Covered; UNSQUARE DANCE (Dave Brubeck) / BAD MOON RISING (Creedence Clearwater Revival) / BREAKING IN MY HEART (Tom Verlaine) / THE BOY IN THE BUBBLE (Paul Simon) / I WANNA BE YOUR LOVER (Bob Dylan) / TOP OF THE POPS (Smithereens). • **Trivia:** MICHAEL STIPE (R.E.M.) & BOO HEWERDINE (The Bible) guested on 1990 album.

Recommended: BEATSONGS (*8) / SWAGGER (*8).

ART OBJECTS

GERARD LANGLEY – vox / **JONATHAN KEY** – guitar, synth., vocals / **WILLIAM STAIR** – bass, guitar / **JOHN LANGLEY** – drums, vocals / **ROBIN KEY** – guitar, bass, keys / **WOJTEK** – dance, percussion.

Heartbeat / not issued

1980. (7") **SHOWING OFF TO IMPRESS THE GIRLS. / OUR SILVER SISTER (live)** [-]

1981. (lp) **BAGPIPE MUSIC** [-]
– Dumbness / Showing off to impress / Conversation / Who switches off the light / Landscape workers / Batpoem / Miraculous birth / 20th century composites / Magog / Passengers of fortune / What am I supposed to do? / Underground market / The paperweight flood.

Fried Egg / not issued

1981. (7") **HARD OBJECTS / BIBLIOTHEQUE / FIT OF PIQUE** [-]

BLUE AEROPLANES

GERARD LANGLEY – vocals / **NICK JACOBS** – rhythm guitar / **WOJTEK DMOCHOWSKI** – dancer / **with JOHN LANGLEY** – drums / **IAN KEARNEY** – bass (of OYSTER BAND), + guests **STAIR, J.KEY, R.KEY + MAXIMUM JOY members.**

Abstract / not issued

Apr 84. (lp) **BOP ART** [-]
– Control of embassies / Pinkies hit the union / Gunning the works / Owls / Outback jazz / Chelsea wallpaper / Bagpipe music / Built in a day. *(re-iss.Feb89 on 'Party')*

— added **ANGELO BRUSCHINI** – guitar, vocals (he was to leave and return soon) / **JOHN STAPLETON** – tapes / **RUTH COCHRANE** – bass, vocals / **DAVE CHAPMAN** – guitar, bass, vocals.

Fire / not issued

Mar 85. (12"ep) **ACTION PAINTING / LE PETIT CADEAU DE DON JUAN. / ASH TRAYS FROM MT. ETNA / POLICE (38 DIVINITY)** [-]

Mar 86. (12"ep) **LOVER AND CONFIDANTE PLUS OTHER STORIES** [-]
– Lover and confidante / Who built this station in the Midwest / Breaking in my heart / Weird heart.

Jun 86. (lp) **TOLERANCE** [-]
– Arriving / Journal of an airman / Rare flowers / Warhol's fifteen / 30 love / Lover and confidante / Tolerance / Ups / When the wave comes / Soul (seen and unseen). *(re-iss.+cd.Oct89 +cd.Sep91)*

Oct 86. (7") **TOLERANCE. / WHEN THE WAVE COMES** [-]
(12"+=) – Teaching English people through sex and death (remix) / And the couple in the next room / Complete blessing.

— added **CAROLINE HALCROW** guitar, a member in '87, became **CAROLINE TRETINE** but soon went solo.

Nov 87. (12"ep) **BURY YOUR LOVE LIKE TREASURE / KING OF THE SOAP BOX / VICE KING'S SON? CONTINUALLY TORN APART** [-]

Nov 87. (lp) **SPITTING OUT MIRACLES** [-]
– Goats / Cowardice and caprice / Julie / Spitting out miracles / Ceiling roses / In the mystery / Season ticket to a bad place / Bury your love like treasure / Days of 49 / Teaching English through sex and death / Winter Sun / What do you mean (what I said) / Do the dead know what time it is?. (free-7"flexi.w/a) COWARDICE AND CAPRICE Instrumental). / flexi *(re-iss.+cd.Oct89 + cd.Sep91)*

May 88. (12"ep) **VEILS OF COLOUR. / SPITTING OUT MIRACLES (remix) / ARRIVING / BUILT IN A DAY** [-]

— (mid'88) **RODNEY ALLEN** – vocals, rhythm guitar (ex-PRESS) repl. NICK. **ANDY McCREETH** – bass (ex-PRESS) repl. RUTH

— **GERARD, JOHN LANGLEY, RODNEY, ANDY, WOJTEK** and entourage, added **ALEX LEE** – guitar, keyboards, vocals (now 7-piece)

Ensign / Chrysalis

Jan 90. (7") **JACKET HANGS. / RAZOR WALK** [72]
(12"+=)(cd-s+=) – Different now / Big sky.

Feb 90. (cd)(c)(lp) **SWAGGER** [54]
– Jacket hangs / World view blues / Weightless / . . . and stones / Your ages / Love come around / The applicant / What it is / Anti-pretty / Careful boy / Picture framed / Cat-scan his'try.

May 90. (7")(c-s) **. . . AND STONES (remix). / ('A' lp version)** [63]
(12"+=)(cd-s+=) – ('A'vocal) / ('A'lovers mix).

Oct 90. (12"ep)(10"ep)(cd-ep) **LOVED**
– You (are loved) / You're going to need somebody / Sweet Jane / World view blue (acoustic).

— (Jan91) **PAUL MULREANY** – drums (ex-JAZZ BUTCHER CONSPIRACY) repl. JOHN **ANGELO BRUSCHINI** – guitar, accordion, vocals (returned from Saudi Arabia) guests on '91 album, **IAN KEARNEY** – multi / **ALEX ACUNA** – percussion / **DANNY TIMMS** – keyboards / **DAVID MANSFIELD** – violins, bouzouki / **J.J.KEY** – guitar / **JERRY MAROTTA** – drums / guest **JAZZ BUTCHER** – b.vocals / **ELAINE SUMMERS** – vocals.

Jul 91. (7")(c-s) **YR OWN WORLD. / PONY BOY**
(12"+=)(cd-s+=) – Mis-firing / Autumn journal XXII.

Aug 91. (cd)(c)(lp) **BEATSONGS** [33]
– Huh! / Yr own world / Angel words / Fun / cardboard box / My hurricane / Jack leaves & back spring / Aeroplane blues / Colour me / Streamers / The boy in the bubble / sixth continent.

Oct 91. (7") **THE BOY IN THE BUBBLE. / TALKIN' ON THE OTHER PHONE / DISNEY HEAD**
(12"+=) – Huh! (remix).
(cd-s++=) – Disneyhead.

— added on tour August '91 **HAZEL KEY** – guitar repl. injured ROBIN (JJ) and **MARCUS WILLIAMS** – bass (MIGHTY LEMON DROPS) repl. injured ANDY. / **SUSIE HUGG** – vocals (of KATYDIDS) repl. HAZEL Now a 5-piece in Sep92 after ANGELO left in Jul 92.

Beggar's B. / Beggar's B.

Jan 94. (12"ep)(cd-ep) **BROKEN AND MENDED / LOVE IS. / STAR CROSS'D / GET OUT!**

Mar 94. (cd)(c)(lp) **LIFE MODEL** [59]
– Broken & mended / (I'm a) Smart drug / Ghost-nets / Frightened at night / Daughter movie / Open / Honey I / Vade mecum gunslinger / Mercury (Hold / Protect / Love) / Fragile. *(re-iss.cd Sep95)*

Nov 94. (12"ep) **THE DETECTIVE SONG. / YOU'RE MINE AND ALWAYS WILL BE: JACK OF ALL HEARTS** – JEALOUS TOWN – IT'S ALRIGHT
(cd-ep+=) – A map below / Top of the pops.

Jan 95. (cd)(c)(lp) **ROUGH MUSIC**
– Detective song / Sugared almond / Scared / Worry beads / Contact high / A map below / James / Whatever hapened to our golden birds? / Wond'ring wild / Saint me and the Devil / Dark / Secret destination / Dear, though the night is gone. *(re-iss.cd Sep95)*

Mar 95. (cd-ep) **SUGARED ALMONDS EP**
– Sugared almonds (remix)/ Sacred (remix)/ Bad Moon rising/ Broken and mended (live).

– compilations, others, etc. –

Nov 88. Fire; (d-lp)(cd) **FRIENDLOVERPLANE** [-]
– Veils of colour / Complete blessing / Weird heart / Le petit cadeau de Don Juan / Severn beach / Police (36 divinity) / Action painting / Who built this station in the mid west / Old men sleeping on the bowery / 88 out / Ashtrays from Mt.Etna / Gunning the works / King of the soap box / Tolerance / Etiquette! / Continually torn apart / Days of 49 / I wanna be your lover / Warhol's fifteen / Shame / The couple in the next room / Stripped. (cd+=) 4 extra tracks.

Nov 92. Ensign; (cd)(c)(lp) **FRIENDLOVERPLANE 2 (UP IN A DOWNWORLD)** [-]
– You (are loved) / Pony boy / Different now / World view blue (acoustic version) / . . . .And stones (lovers all around mix) / Razor walk / Growing up, growing down / Autumn journal XV / Here it comes / For Tim Collins / Talkin' on the otherphone / You're going to need somebody / Missy Lane / Stranger / Trouble, tell me I'm alive / Big sky / Mis-firing / Disney head

Apr 88. Strange Fruit; (12"ep) **THE EVENING SHOW SESSIONS**
(15.2.87)
– Cowardice and Caprice / Coats / What do you mean / Shame.

GERARD LANGLEY & IAN KEARNEY

Fire / not issued

Feb 87. (m-lp) **SIAMESE BOYFRIENDS** [-]
– Nicknames / Snow-walking / Joe Taylor's / La marisque / Good weather / Dear through the night has gone / The famous aren't.

BLUE ANGEL (see under ⇒ LAUPER, Cyndi)

BLUE CHEER

Formed: San Francisco, California . . .early 1967 originally as a 6-piece; SAN FRANCISCO BLUES BAND. Trimmed to a trio (DICKIE PETERSON, LEIGH STEPHENS and PAUL WHALEY) soon after witnessing The JIMI HENDRIX EXPERIENCE at the Monterey Festival. Signed to 'Philips' that year and later moved to Boston. In 1968, they had resounding US Top 20 with version of 'SUMMERTIME BLUES'. Although its parent lp nearly made Top 10, they sadly never reinstated themselves as hit group. • **Style:** Claimed to be loudest band in the world, they had CREAM similarities that gained cult Hell's Angels following. • **Songwriters:** PETERSON and group, except SUMMERTIME BLUES (Eddie Cochran) / PARCHMENT FARM

(Mose Allison)/ (I CAN'T GET NO) SATISFACTION (Rolling Stones) / THE HUNTER (Booker T. & The MG's). • **Trivia:** Self-confessed drug takers who were managed by an ex-Hell Angel.

Recommended: THE BEST OF BLUE CHEER (*7)

DICKIE PETERSON (b.1946, Dakota) – vocals, bass (ex-GROUP 'B')/ **LEIGH STEPHENS** – guitar, vocals/ **PAUL WHALEY** – drums (ex-OXFORD CIRCLE)

Philips / Philips

Mar 68. (7") **SUMMERTIME BLUES. / OUT OF FOCUS** [ ] [14]
Jul 68. (lp) **VINCEBUS ERUPTUM** [ ] [11] Mar 68
– Summertime blues / Rock me baby / Doctor please / Out of focus / Parchment farm / Second time around. *(cd-iss.Aug92 on 'Line') (cd-iss.Nov94 on 'Repertoire')*
Jul 68. (7") **JUST A LITTLE BIT. / GYPSY BALL** [ ] [92]

— added on some **RALPH BURNS KELLOGG** – keyboards

Oct 68. (7") **FEATHERS FROM YOUR TREE. / SUN CYCLE** [ ] [ ]
Sep 68. (lp) **OUTSIDEINSIDE** [ ] [90]
– Feathers from your tree / Sun cycle / Just a little bit / Gypsy ball / Come and get it / (I can't get no) Satisfaction / The hunter / Magnolia caboose babyfinger / Babylon. *(cd-iss.Aug92 on 'Line') (cd-iss.Nov94 on 'Repertoire')*

— **RANDY HOLDEN** – guitar (ex-OTHER HALF, ex-SONS OF ADAM) repl. LEIGH due to his deafness. He later went solo before joining SILVER METRE and then PILOT (U.S.).

May 69. (7") **WHEN IT ALL GETS OLD. / WEST COAST CHILD OF SUNSHINE** [ ] [ ]
Jul 69. (lp) **NEW! IMPROVED! BLUE CHEER** [ ] [84] Apr 69
– When it all gets old / West Coast child of sunshine / I want my baby back / Aces'n eights / As long as I live / It takes a lot of love, it takes a train to cry / Peace of mind / Fruit & icebergs / Honey butter love. *(cd-iss.Nov94 on 'Repertoire')*

— **NORMAN MAYALL drums** repl. WHALEY

— **GARY YODER** – guitar, vocals (ex-OXFORD CIRCLE) repl. HOLDEN

Nov 69. (7") **ALL NIGHT LONG./ FORTUNES** [-] [ ]
Feb 70. (lp) **BLUE CHEER** [ ] [ ]
– Fool / You're gonna need someone / Hello L.A., bye bye, Birmingham / Saturday freedom / Ain't that the way (love's supposed to be) / Rock and roll queens / Better when we try / Natural man / Lovin' you's easy / The same old story.
Feb 70. (7") **NATURAL MAN. / HELLO L.A., BYE BYE, BIRMINGHAM** [-] [ ]
Jun 70. (7") **FOOL. / AIN'T THAT THE WAY (LOVE'S SUPPOSED TO BE)** [-] [ ]

— **BRUCE STEPHENS** – guitar + **RALPH** repl.YODER

Nov 70. (lp) **B.C. 5 THE ORIGINAL HUMAN BEINGS** [ ] [ ]
– Good times are hard to find / Love of a woman / Make me laugh / Pilot / Babaji (twilight raga) / Preacher / Black Sun / Tears by my bed / Man on the run / Sandwich / Rest at ease.
Apr 71. (7") **PILOT. / BABAJI (TWILIGHT RAGA)** [ ] [ ] Oct70
Nov 71. (lp) **OH! PLEASANT HOPE** [-] [ ]
– Highway man / Believer / Money troubles / Traveling man / Oh! pleasant hope / I'm the light / Ecological blues / Lester the arrester / Heart full of soul.

— Disbanded 1971, but briefly did reunions 1975 & 1979. In 1984 they return to studio. (WHALEY and PATERSON, + DUCK McDONALD)

not issued / Megaforce

1985. (lp) **THE BEAST IS BACK** [-] [ ]
– Nightmares / Summertime blues / Ride with me / Girl next door / Babylon / eart of the city / Out of focus / Parchment farm.

— Toured again in the late 80's/early 90's.

— now **PETERSON** plus **ANDREW DUCK McDONALD** – guitar / **DAVID SALCE** – drums

Thunderb.

Sep 90. (cd)(c)(lp) **BLITZKREIG ON NUREMBERG (live)** [ ] [-]
– Babylon – Girl next door / Ride with me / Just a little bit / Summertime blues / Out of focus / Doctor please / The hunter / Red house.

Nibelung / not issued

Nov 90. (cd)(c)(lp) **HIGHLIGHTS AND LOWLIVES** [-] [-] Germ'y
– (new recordings of old material?)
1991. (cd) **DINING WITH SHARKS** [-] [-] Germ'y
–

– compilations, others, etc. –

Oct 82. Philips; (lp)(c) **THE BEST OF BLUE CHEER** [-] [-] Europe
1986. Rhino; (lp) **LOUDER THAN GOD** [-] [-]

BLUE NILE

Formed: Glasgow, Scotland . . . 1981 by BUCHANAN, MOORE and BELL. After debut 45 on 'R.S.O.', they were offered unusual record contract by Scottish (East Lothian) label 'Linn', in which their sound/album was tested for hi-fi equipment. Later in 1984, with the album 'A WALK ACROSS THE ROOFTOPS' selling enough, due to rave reviews, 'Virgin' took over distribution. Although it took five years for the miraculous follow-up 'HATS', no momentum was lost and it was worth the wait. Currently in the studio again in 1993, so expect an album from them before the year 2000. • **Style:** Emotion riddled, atmospheric music that resurrects sophistication. Singer/crooner PAUL BUCHANAN has all the potential of being the next SINATRA. • **Songwriters:** All BUCHANAN penned with others contributing. • **Trivia:** As said before, basically a studio outfit, until they toured U.S.A. Spring 1990. The trio guested on ROBBIE ROBERTSON's 1991 solo album 'STORYVILLE'.

Recommended: A WALK ACROSS THE ROOFTOPS (*8) / HATS (1989 cd).

PAUL BUCHANAN – vocals, guitar, synthesizer / **PAUL JOSEPH MOORE** – keyboards, synthesizer, etc. / **ROBERT BELL** – bass, synthesizer, etc.

R.S.O. / not issued

Oct 81. (7") **I LOVE THIS LIFE. / SECOND ACT** [ ] [-]

— added guests **CALUM MALCOLM** – keyboards, vocals (ex-BADGER, ex-HEADBOYS) / **NIGEL THOMAS** – drums

Linn-Virgin / A&M

Apr 84. (7")(12") **STAY. / SADDLE THE HORSES** [ ] [ ] 1985
(re-iss.Jan89 also as (d7"+=) – Tinseltown in the rain / Heatwave.
Apr 84. (lp)(c) **A WALK ACROSS THE ROOFTOPS** [80] [ ] 1985
– A walk across the rooftops / Tinseltown in the rain / From rags to riches / Stay / Easter parade / Heatwave / Automobile noise. *(re-iss.+cdJan89)*
Jul 84. (7") **TINSELTOWN IN THE RAIN. / HEATWAVE (instrumental)** [ ] [-]
(12") – ('A'extended) / Regıet.

— Basic trio, plus session musicians.

Sep 89. (7") **THE DOWNTOWN LIGHTS. / THE WIRES ARE DOWN** [67] [ ]
(12"+=)(cd-s+=) – Halfway to Paradise (TV theme).
Oct 89. (lp)(c)(cd) **HATS** [12] [ ]
– Over the hillside / The downtown lights / Let's go out tonight / Headlights on the parade / From a late night train / Seven a.m. / Saturday night.
Sep 90. (7")(c-s) **HEADLIGHTS ON THE PARADE (Bob Clearmount mix). / ('A'-lp version)** [72] [ ]
(12"+=)(cd-s+=) – Easter parade (w / RICKIE LEE JONES)
Jan 91. (7")(c-s) **SATURDAY NIGHT. / ('A'version)** [50] [ ]
(12"+=)(cd-s+=) – Seven a.m. (live in the U.S.) / or / Our lives.

BLUE OYSTER CULT

Formed: Long Island, New York, USA . . . 1970 as SOFT WHITE UNDERBELLY by BUCK DHARMA, ALLEN LANIER and AL BOUCHARD. They became STALK-FORREST GROUP and signed to 'Elektra', where they had album rejected. Late 1971 they transformed to BLUE OYSTER CULT and gained contract to 'Columbia' through guru manager Sandy Pearlman. • **Style:** Heavy guitar-laden blues-influenced rock inspired by LED ZEPPELIN. By the mid 70's, on massive hit 'DON'T FEAR THE REAPER', they mellowed to a more mid-60's BYRDS feel. • **Songwriters:** Group compositions, except CAREER OF EVIL (written by LANIER's one-time girlfriend PATTI SMITH) / BLACK BLADE (co-written w / MICHAEL MOORCOCK – Hawkwind) / WE GOTTA GET OUT OF THIS PLACE (Animals) / BORN TO BE WILD (steppenwolf) / 2nd album contained lyrics by producer RICHARD MELTZER. • **Trivia:** AL BOUCHARD claimed on 1988 album 'IMAGINOS', he was inspiration.

Recommended: CAREER OF EVIL: THE METAL YEARS (*7).

ERIC BLOOM – vocals, "stun" guitar / **BUCK DHARMA** (b.DONALD ROSIER) – lead guitar, vocals / **ALLEN LANIER** – rhythm guitar, keyboards / **JOE BOUCHARD** – bass, vocals / **ALBERT BOUCHARD** – drums, vocals

C.B.S. / Columbia

1972. (7"ep) **LIVE BOOTLEG (live)** [-] [ ]
May 72. (lp)(c) **BLUE OYSTER CULT** [-] [ ]
– Transmaniacon / I'm on the lamb but I ain't no sheep / Then came the last days of May / Stairway to the stars / Before the kiss (a redcap) / Screams / She's as beautiful as a foot / Cities on flame with rock and roll / Workshop of the telescopes / Redeemed. *(re-iss.1981)*
Jun 72. (7") **CITIES ON FLAME WITH ROCK AND ROLL. / BEFORE THE KISS, A REDCAP** [-] [ ]
Mar 73. (7") **SCREAMING DIZ-BUSTERS. / HOT RAILS TO HELL** [-] [ ]
Mar 73. (lp)(c) **TYRANNY & MUTATION** [-] [ ]
– The red and the black / O.D.'d on life itself / Hot rails to Hell / 7 screaming diz-busters / Baby ice dog / Wings wetted down / Teen archer / Mistress of the Salman salt (quickline girl).
1974. (7") **CAREER OF EVIL. / DOMINANCE AND SUBMISSION** [-] [ ]
Sep 74. (lp)(c) **SECRET TREATIES** [ ] [53] Apr 74
– Career of evil / Subhuman / Dominance and submission / M.E. 262 / Cagey cretins / Harvester of eyes / Flaming telepaths / Astronomy. *(re-iss.Mar82)*
Nov 75. (d-lp) **ON YOUR FEET OR ON YOUR KNEES (live)** [ ] [22] Mar 75
– Subhuman / Harvester of eyes / Hot rails to Hell / The red and the black / 7 screaming diz-busters / Buck's boogie / Then came the last days of May / Cities on flame / M.E.262 / Before the kiss, a redcap / I ain't got you / Born to be wild. *(re-iss.Sep87)*
Nov 75. (7") **BORN TO BE WILD (live). / (part 2)** [-] [ ]
Jun 76. (lp)(c) **AGENTS OF FORTUNE** [26] [29]
– This ain't the summer of love / True confessions / (Don't fear) The reaper / E.T.I.(Extra Terrestrial Intelligence) / The revenge of Vera Gaming / Sinful love / Tattoo vampire / Morning final / Tenderloin / Debbie Denise. *(re-iss.1988) (cd-iss.Jun94 on 'Sony') (cd-iss.May95 on 'Columbia')*
Jul 76. (7") **(DON'T FEAR) THE REAPER. / TATTOO VAMPIRE** [ ] [12]
1976. (7") **DEBBIE DENISE. / THIS AIN'T THE SUMMER OF LOVE** [-] [ ]
Dec 77. (lp)(c) **SPECTRES** [60] [43] Nov 77
– Godzilla / Golden age of leather / Death valley nights / Searchin' for Celine / Fireworks / R U ready 2 rock? / Celestial the queen / Goin' through the motions / I love the night / Nosferatu. *(re-iss.Feb86)*
Dec 77. (7") **GOING THROUGH THE MOTIONS. / SEARCHIN' FOR CELINE** [ ] [ ]
May 78. (7")(12") **(DON'T FEAR) THE REAPER. / R U READY 2 ROCK** [16] [-]
Jun 78. (7") **GODZILLA. / GODZILLA (live)** [-] [ ]
Aug 78. (7") **I LOVE THE NIGHT. / NOSFERATU** [ ] [-]
Sep 78. (lp)(c) **SOME ENCHANTED EVENING (live)** [18] [44]
– R U ready 2 rock / E.T.I.(Extra Terrestrial Intelligence) / Astronomy (kick out the jams) / Godzilla / (Don't fear) The reaper / We gotta get out of this place.

Oct 78. (7") **WE GOTTA GET OUT OF THIS PLACE. / E. T. I. (EXTRA TERRESTRIAL INTELLIGENCE)** [-] [ ]
Nov 78. (7") **WE GOTTA GET OUT OF THIS PLACE (live). / STAIRWAY TO THE STARS** [ ] [-]
Aug 79. (lp)(c) **MIRRORS** [46] [44] Jul 79
– Dr.Music / The great Sun jester / In thee / Mirrors / Moon crazy / The vigil / I am the storm / You're not the one (I was looking for) / Lonely teardrops.
Aug 79. (7") **MIRRORS. / LONELY TEARDROPS** [ ] [ ]
Sep 79. (7") **IN THEE. / LONELY TEARDROPS** [-] [74]
Oct 79. (7") **IN THEE. / THE VIGIL** [ ] [-]
Feb 80. (7") **YOU'RE NOT THE ONE (I WAS LOOKING FOR). / MOON CRAZY** [-] [ ]
Jul 80. (lp)(c) **CULTOSAURUS ERECTUS** [12] [34]
– Black blade / Monsters / Divine wind / Deadlines / Here's Johnny (The Marshall plan) / Hungry boys / Fallen angel / Lips on the hills / Unknown tongue.
Jul 80. (7") **HERE'S JOHNNY (THE MARSHALL PLAN). / DIVINE WIND** [-] [ ]
Jul 80. (7") **FALLEN ANGEL. / LIPS IN THE HILLS** [ ] [ ]
Oct 80. (7") **DEADLINES. / MONSTERS** [ ] [ ]
Jul 81. (lp)(c) **FIRE OF UNKNOWN ORIGIN** [29] [24]
– Fire of unknown origin / Burnin' for you / Veteran of the psychic wars / Sole survivor / Heaven metal / The black and silver / Vengeance (the pact) / After dark / Joan Crawford / Don't turn your back.
Aug 81. (7") **BURNIN' FOR YOU. / VENGEANCE (THE PACT)** [-] [40]
Sep 81. (7") **BURNIN' FOR YOU. / THE BLACK AND SILVER** [ ] [-]
(12") – ('A'side) / Dr.Music / Flaming telepaths.
May 82. (d-lp)(d-c) **EXTRATERRESTRIAL LIVE (live)** [39] [29]
– Dominance and submission / Cities on flame / Dr.Music / The red and the black / Joan Crawford / Burnin' for you / Roadhouse blues / Black blade / Hot rails to Hell / Godzilla / Veteran of the psychic wars / E.T.I.(Extra Terrestrial Intelligence) / (Don't fear) the reaper.
Jun 82. (7") **BURNIN' FOR YOU (live). / (DON'T FEAR) THE REAPER (live)** [-] [ ]

— (late 1981) **RICK DOWNEY** – drums repl. ALBERT

Nov 83. (lp)(c) **THE REVOLUTION BY NIGHT** [95] [93]
– Take me away / Eyes on fire / Shooting shark / Veins / Shadows of California / Feel the thunder / Let go / Dragon lady / Light years of love.
Nov 83. (7") **TAKE ME AWAY. / FEEL THE THUNDER** [ ] [-]
(12"+=) – Burnin' for you / Dr.Music.
Feb 84. (7")(12") **SHOOTING SHARK. / DRAGON LADY** [ ] [83]
May 84. (7") **TAKE ME AWAY. / LET GO** [-] [ ]

— **TONY ZVONCHEK** – keyboards (ex-ALDO NOVA) repl. LANIER

— **TOMMY PRICE** – drums repl. DOWNEY.

Oct 85. (7") **DANCIN' IN THE RUINS. / SHADOW WARRIOR** [-] [ ]
Dec 85. (lp)(c)(cd) **CLUB NINJA** [ ] [63]
– White flags / Dancin' in the ruins / Rock not war / Perfect water / Spy in the house of the night / Beat 'em up / When the war comes / Shadow warrior / Madness to the method.
Dec 85. (7") **WHITE FLAGS. / ROCK NOT WAR** [ ] [ ]
(12"+=) – Shooting shark.
Feb 86. (7") **PERFECT WATER. / SPY IN THE HOUSE OF NIGHT** [-] [ ]

— added **ALBERT BOUCHARD** – guitar, percussion, vocals
ALLEN LANIER – keyboards returned to repl. TONY

Sep 88. (lp)(c)(cd) **IMAGINOS** [ ] [ ] Aug 88
– I am the one you warned me of / Les invisibles / In the presence of another world / Del Rio's song / Siege and investitune of Baron Von Frankenstein's castle / Astronomy (new version) / Magna of illusion.
Oct 88. (7") **ASTRONOMY. / MAGNA OF ILLUSION** [ ] [ ]
(12"+=) – ('A'wild mix).
(cd-s++=) – (Don't fear) The reaper.

— (early '89 tour) **JON ROGERS** – bass repl. JOE BOUCHARD / **RON RIDDLE** – drums repl. RICK DOWNEY

– compilations, others, etc. –

Below on 'CBS'/ 'Columbia' unless otherwise mentioned.
1984. (7") **(DON'T FEAR) THE REAPER. / I LOVE THE NIGHT** [ ] [ ]
Apr 90. (cd)(c)(lp) **CAREER OF EVIL: THE METAL YEARS** [ ] [ ]
– Cities on flame / The red and the black / Hot rails to Hell / Dominance and submission / Seven screaming Diz-busters / M.E. 262 / E.T.I. (Extra Terrestrial Intelligence) / Beat 'em up / Black blade / The harvester of eyes / Flaming telepaths / Godzilla / (Don't fear) The reaper.
Jun 84. Old Gold; (7") **(DON'T FEAR) THE REAPER. / R U READY TO ROCK** [ ] [-]
Jan 92. Castle; (cd) **LIVE 1976 (live)** [ ] [-]
Jun 94. Fragile; (cd)(c) **CULT CLASSICS** [ ] [-]
Jul 94. Fragile; (7")(c-s)(cd-s) **DON'T FEAR THE REAPER. / BURNIN' FOR YOU** [ ] [ ]

— Note: An recording EP was issued on 'Skydog' FRANCE, but very rare.

BLUESBREAKERS (see under ⇒ MAYALL, John)

BLUESOLOGY (see under ⇒ Elton John)

BLUES PROJECT

Formed: New York, USA ... mid-65 by STEVE KALB and ROY BLUMENFIELD. They made their live debut at CAFE AU GO GO, which was recorded for their first lp in 1966. Their second lp 'PROJECTIONS' gained entry into US Top 60, and was first to feature dual vocals of AL KOOPER and STEVE KATZ. Their appeal was short-lived and they disbanded in 1968. They re-unitd later and signed to 'Capitol', but KOOPER went off to pursue other activities. • **Style:** Country blues, using variations of folk and jazz fused with rock. • **Songwriters:** AL KOOPER or KATZ until former's departure. Cover VIOLETS OF DAWN (Eric Anderson) / CATCH THE WIND (Donovan) / I WANT TO BE YOUR DRIVER (Chuck Berry) / SPOONFUL (Willie Dixon) / TWO TRAINS RUNNING (Muddy Waters) / etc.

Recommended: THE BEST OF THE BLUES PROJECT (*6).

TOMMY FLANDERS – vocals / **STEVE KATZ** (b. 9 May'45) – guitar, vocals / **DANNY KALB** – guitar / **AL KOOPER** – organ, vocals / **ANDY KOLBERG** – bass, flute / **ROY BLUMENFELD** – drums

Verve Verve Folk
1965. (7") **BACK DOOR MAN. / VIOLETS OF DAWN** [-] [ ]
May 66. (lp) **LIVE AT THE CAFE AU GO GO (live)** [-] [77]
– Goin' down Louisiana / You go, and I'll go with you / Catch the wind / I want to be your driver / Alberta / The way my baby walks / Violets of dawn / Back door man / Jelly jelly blues / Spoonful / Who do you love.
1966. (7") **I WANT TO BE YOUR DRIVER. / CATCH THE WIND** [-] [ ]

— KATZ and KOOPER now share vocal duties, when FLANDERS leaves; later solo.

Oct 66. (lp) **PROJECTIONS** [ ] [52]
– I can't keep from crying / Steve's song / You can't catch me / Two trains running / Wake me, shake me / Cheryl's going home / Flute thing / Caress me baby / Fly away.
Nov 66. (7") **WHERE THERE'S SMOKE THERE'S FIRE. / GOIN' DOWN LOUISIANA** [-] [ ]
Jan 67. (7") **I CAN'T KEEP FROM CRYING. / THE WAY MY BABY WALKS** [ ] [ ]
Mar 67. (7") **NO TIME LIKE THE RIGHT TIME. / STEVE'S SONG** [-] [96]
Sep 67. (lp) **LIVE AT THE TOWN HALL** [-] [71]
– (introduction) / Electric flute thing / I can't keep from crying / Mean old Southern / No time like the right time / Love will endure / Where there's smoke, there's fire / Wake me, shake me.

— KOOPER went solo and then formed BLOOD, SWEAT AND TEARS. KATZ also leaves. The remaining members with KALB on a few tracks, brought in
JOHN GREGORY – guitar / RICHARD GREENE – violin

1968. (7") **GENTLE DREAMS. / LOST IN THE SHUFFLE** [-] [ ]
1968. (lp) **PLANNED OBSOLESCENCE** [-] [ ]
– If you gotta make a fool of somebody / Calypso / The endless sleep / Nairt aes hornpipe / Turtledove / Mojo Hanna / Frank and Curt incensed / She raised her hand / Dakota recollection.

— The rhythm section (KOLBERG & BLUMENFELD) became SEA TRAIN.

Aug 69. (lp)(c)(cd) **THE BEST OF THE BLUES PROJECT** (compilation) [-] [ ]
(re-iss.1989 on 'Rhino')

In 1971, BLUES PROJECT re-formed with BLUMENFELD and KALB. They recruit **DON KRETMAR – bass, saxophone**

Capitol Capitol
1971. (lp) **LAZARUS** [-] [ ]
– It's alright / Personal mercy / Black night / Visions of flowers / Yellow cab / Lazarus / Brown eyed handsome man / Reachings / Midnight rain / So far, so hear.

— added **DAVID COHEN** – piano / **TOMMY FLANDERS** – vox / **BILL LUSSENDEN** – guitar

1972. (lp) **THE BLUES PROJECT** [ ] [ ]
– Back door man / Danville dame / Railroad boy / Rainbow / Easy lady / Plain & fancy / Little rain / Crazy girl / I'm ready.
1972. (7") **CRAZY GIRL. / EASY LADY** [-] [ ]

— Disband again 1972, but originals minus FLANDERS re-unite mid'73.

M.C.A. M.C.A.
Jul 73. (d-lp) **REUNION IN CENTRAL PARK (live 24 Jun'73)** [ ] [ ]
– Louisiana blues / Steve's song / I can't keep from crying / You can't catch me / Fly away / Caress me baby / Catch the wind / Wake me, shake me / Two trains running / (closing audience).

— Same line-up re-kindle group for gig in New York 17 Mar'81. KATZ had joined AMERICAN FLYER earlier in the 70's.

Please note a 1964 album 'BLUES PROJECT' on 'Elektra' only featured KALB augmenting with DYLAN (aka BOB LANDY), JOHN SEBASTIAN, GEOFF MULDAUR, etc.

BLUES TRAVELER

Formed: New York, USA . . .mid 80's by JOHN POPPER. While at school in Connecticut, he became friends with BLUES BROTHERS keyboard player PAUL SHAFFER, who at the time was arranger for the DAVID LETTERMAN show. They soon appeared on his show (many times) as The BLUES BAND, but after moving from Princeton, New Jersey to New York, they opted for appropriate BLUES TRAVELER. By the late 80's, their distribution of demo tapes, helped BILL GRAHAM, set up fruitful support slots to SANTANA and The ALLMAN BROTHERS, which led to contract with 'A&M'. Further appearances on the LETTERMAN show, boosted sales of their 1990 debut. In the Autumn of '92, POPPER was seriously hurt in a motorcycle accident, but he returned just over half a year later, albeit on stage in a wheelchair!. Their biggest highlight came when celebrating the 25th year of WOODSTOCK Festival in August '94. The following year now signed to 'Polydor', saw them go Top 10 with album 'FOUR' and single 'RUN-AROUND'. •**Style:** Basic organic blues inspired by the film BLUES BROTHERS (especially late actor JOHN BELUSHI). •**Songwriters:** POPPER, some w/ SHEEHAN or others. •**Trivia:** GREGG ALLMAN (Allman Brothers) and close friend CHRIS BARRON (Spin Doctors) guested on their 2nd album.

Recommended: FOUR (*7)

JOHN POPPER (b.1967, Cleveland, Ohio) – vocals, harmonica, guitar / **CHAN KINCHLA** – guitar / **BOBBY SHEEHAN** – bass / **BRENDAN HILL** – drums, percussion

A&M A&M

Nov 90. (cd)(c)(lp) **BLUES TRAVELER** [ ] [ ]
– But anyway / Gina / Mulling it over / 100 years / Dropping some NYC / Slow change / Warmer days / Gotta get mean / Alone / Sweet talking hippie. (cd+=) – Crystal flame.

Sep 91. (cd)(c)(lp) **TRAVELERS & THIEVES** [ ] [ ]
– The tiding / Onslaught / Ivory tusk / What's for breakfast / I have my moments / Optimistic thoughts / The best part / Sweet pain / All in the groove / Support your local emperor / Bagheera / Mountain cry. *(w/ free cd)* ON TOUR FOREVER (live)

Apr 93. (cd)(c) **SAVE HIS SOUL** [ ] [72]
– Trina magna / Love and greed / Letter from a friend / Believe me / Go outside and drive / Defense and desire / Whoops / Manhattan Bridge / Love of my life / My prophesie / Save his soul / Bullshitter's lament / Conquer me / Fledgling.

Polydor Polydor

Mar 95. (c-s) **RUN-AROUND / SAVE HIS SOUL** [ ] [8]
(cd-s+=) – Escaping.

Apr 95. (cd)(c) **FOUR** [ ] [9] Sep94
– Run-around / Stand / Lok around / Fallible / The mountains win again / Freedom / Crash burn / Price to pay / Hook / The good the bad and the ugly / Just wait / Brother John.

Nov 95. (c-s)(cd-s) **HOOK /** [-] [41]

BLUETONES

Formed: Hounslow, London, England . . .1994 by brothers MARK and SCOTT MORRISS. Appeared on a 'Fierce Panda' compilation ep 'Return To Splendour', before being signed to A&M's 'Superior Quality' label early in 1995. •**Style:** Young Brit-pop pack influenced by STONE ROSES, CHARLATANS, The LA'S and even The SMITHS for songs. •**Songwriters:** Group.

Recommended: debut early '96 which will hit No.1 UK (*8)

MARK MORRISS – vocals / **ADAM DEVLIN** – guitar / **SCOTT MORRISS** – bass / **EDS CHESTERS** – drums

Superior not issued

Feb 95. (7"blue; mail order) **SLIGHT RETURN. / FOUNTAIN HEAD** [-] [-]

Jun 95. (7") **ARE YOU BLUE OR ARE YOU BLIND?. / STRING ALONG** [31] [ ]
(12"+=)(cd-s+=) – Driftwood.

Oct 95. (7")(c-s) **BLUETONIC. / GLAD TO SEE Y'BACK AGAIN?** [19] [ ]
(12"+=)(cd-s+=) – Colorado beetle.

BLUE VELVETS (see under ⇒ CREEDENCE CLEARWATER REVIVAL)

BLUR

Formed: Colchester, Essex, England. . . 1989. Initially were SEYMOUR then The GREAT WHITE HOPES, before succuming to name BLUR by 1990. They soon were on the books of David Balfe's Parlophone subsidiary label 'Food', where they secured first UK Top 10 hit 'THERE'S NO OTHER WAY'. They went from strength to strength with each release, peaking quite deservedly with 'PARKLIFE' from which their first UK Top 5 classic 'BOYS AND GIRLS' was lifted. The following year 1995, saw them win the battle to No.1 with 'COUNTRY HOUSE' over rivals OASIS, who were sharpening their tongues for an onslaught of media slagging. • **Style:** Groovy psychedelic pop influenced by rave and SYD BARRETT, which evolved into mod-ish pop/rock influenced by The SMALL FACES, The KINKS, due to DAMON's Cockney barra-boy delivery. • **Songwriters:** Group songs, ALBARN lyrics. Covered MAGGIE MAY (Rod Stewart) / LAZY SUNDAY (Small Faces). • **Trivia:** Producer – STEPHEN STREET. DAMON's father KEITH ALBARN used to be the manager of 60s rock outfit THE SOFT MACHINE.

Recommended: LEISURE (*7) / MODERN LIFE IS RUBBISH (*9) / PARKLIFE (*10) / THE GREAT ESCAPE (*8)

DAMON ALBARN (b.23 Mar'68, Whitechapel, London) – vocals / **GRAHAM COXON** (b.12 Mar'69, W.Germany) – guitars / **ALEX JAMES** (b.21 Nov'68, Dorset, England) – bass, vocals / **DAVE ROWNTREE** (b. 8 Apr'63) – drums

Food-EMI S.B.K.

Oct 90. (7")(c-s) **SHE'S SO HIGH. / I KNOW** [48] [-]
(12"+=) – ('A'definitive mix).
(cd-s+=) – Down.

Apr 91. (7")(c-s) **THERE'S NO OTHER WAY. / INERTIA** [8] [82] Dec 91
(12"+=) ('A'extended)
(12"+=)(cd-s+=) – Mr.Briggs / I'm all over.
(extra-12") – ('A'remix). / Day upon day (live).

Jul 91. (7")(c-s) **BANG. / LUMINOUS** [24] [ ]
(12"+=) – Explain / Uncle Love.
(cd-s++=) – Beserk.

Aug 91. (cd)(c)(lp) **LEISURE** [7] [ ]
– She's so high / Bang / Slow down / Repetition / Bad day / Sing / There's no other way / Fool / Come together / High cool / Birthday / Wear me down.

Mar 92. (7")(c-s) **POPSCENE. / MACE** [32] [ ]
(12"+=) – I'm fine / Garden central.
(cd-s++=) – Badgeman Brown.

Apr 93. (12")(c-s) **FOR TOMORROW. / INTO ANOTHER / HANGING OVER** [28] [ ]
(cd-s) – ('A'side) / Peach / Bone bag.
(cd-s) – ('A'side) / When the cows come home / Beachcoma / For tomorrow (acoustic).

May 93. (cd)(c)(lp) **MODERN LIFE IS RUBBISH** [15] [ ]
– For tomorrow / Advert / Colin Zeal / Pressure on Julian / Star shaped / Blue jeans / Chemical world / Sunday Sunday / Oily water / Miss America / Villa Rosie / Coping / Turn it up / Resigned.

Jun 93. (7"red)(c-s) **CHEMICAL WORLD. / MAGGIE MAY** [28] [ ]
(12")(cd-s) – ('A'mix) / Es schmecht / Young and lovely / My ark.
(cd-s) – ('A'side) / Never clever (live) / Pressure on Julian (live) / Come together (live).

Oct 93. (7") **SUNDAY SUNDAY. / TELL ME, TELL ME** [26] [ ]
(cd-s) – ('A'side) / Daisy bell / Let's all go to the Strand.
(cd-s) – ('A'side) / Dizzy / Fried / Shimmer.
(12") – ('A'side) / Long legged / Mixed up.

Mar 94. (7")(c-s) **GIRLS AND BOYS. / MAGPIE / PEOPLE IN EUROPE** [5] [59] Jun94
(cd-s) – (tracks 1 & 3) / Peter Panic.
(cd-s) – (tracks 1 & 2) / Anniversary waltz.

Apr 94. (cd)(c)(lp) **PARK LIFE** [1] [ ] Jun94
– Girls and boys / Tracy Jacks / End of a century / Park life / Bank holiday / Bad head / The debt collector / Far out / To the end / London loves / Trouble in the message centre / Clover over Dover / Magic America / Jubilee / This is a low / Lot 105.

May 94. (12")(c-s)(cd-s) **TO THE END. / GIRLS AND BOYS (Pet Shop Boys remix)** [16] [ ]
(cd-s) – ('A'side) / Threadneedle Street / Got yer!.

— Above 'A' featured LETITIA of STEREOLAB. Next 'A'; actor PHIL DANIELS.

Aug 94. (c-s)(cd-s) **PARKLIFE. / SUPA SHOPPA / THEME FROM AN IMAGINARY FILM** [10] [ ]
(12") – (1st 2 tracks) / To the end (French version).
(cd-s) – (1st track) / Beard / To the end (French version).

Nov 94. (7")(c-s) **END OF A CENTURY. / RED NECKS** [19] [ ]
(cd-s+=) – Alex's song.

Aug 95. (7")(c-s) **COUNTRY HOUSE. / ONE BORN EVERY MINUTE** [1] [ ]
(cd-s+=) – To the end (with FRANCOISE HARDY).
(live-cd-ep) ('A') / Girls and boys / Parklife / For tomorrow.

Sep 95. (cd)(c)(lp) **THE GREAT ESCAPE** [1] [ ]
– Stereotypes / Country house / Best days / Charmless man / Fade away / Top man / The universal / Mr. Robinson's quango / He thought of cars / It could be you / Ernold Same / Globe alone / Dan Abnormal / Entertain me / Yuko and Hiro.

Nov 95. (c-s) **THE UNIVERSAL / ENTERTAIN ME (the live it! remix)** [5] [ ]
(cd-s+=) – Ultranol / No monsters in me.
(cd-s) – ('A'side) / Mr.Robinson's quango (live) / It could be you (live) / Stereotypes (all live from the Beeb).

BMX BANDITS

Formed: Belshill, nr.Glasgow, Scotland . . .summer 1985 by DUGLAS T.STEWART with future SOUP DRAGONS; SEAN DICKSON and JIM McCULLOCH. In 1986, they released a couple of 45's for Stephen Pastel's '53rd & 3rd' label, noteably 'THE DAY BEFORE TOMORROW'. In 1986, DUGLAS was joined by FRANCIS McDONALD, but things slowed down, to let DUGLAS get out to gig solo, supporting The SHOP ASSISTANTS. (he was to mime Klaus Wunderlich on the organ, and later host a night-time pop-TV show). In 1989, their return was complete with debut lp 'C86'. Three years later, having signed to Tokyo-based 'Vinyl Japan', they issued follow-up 'STARWARS'. They've since been signed to 'Creation', where 'SERIOUS DRUGS' & 'KYLIE'S GOT A CRUSH ON US', have proved an indie treat. The latter having been used also by local friends TEENAGE FANCLUB. • **Style:** Soft jangly pop-rock. • **Songwriters:** DUGLAS, until 1990 when he co-wrote with NORMAN BLAKE. Covered DON'T FIGHT IT, FEEL IT (Primal Scream) / C'EST LA VENT BETTY (. . .Yared) / GREEN GROW (Rabbie Burns; trad) / YO YO SONG (trad) / THINKIN' 'BOUT YOU BABY (Beach Boys) / GIRL AT THE BUS STOP (Television Personalities) / COME AND GET IT (Badfinger) / KYLIE'S GOT A CRUSH ON US (Clydesmen) / LIKE A HURRICANE (Neil Young) / NAZI PUNKS FUCK OFF (Dead Kennedys) / CAST A SHADOW (Johnson-Lunsunda-Lewis) / I CAN'T STAY MAD AT YOU (Goffin-King) / THAT SUMMER FEELING (Jonathan Richman) / LITTLE RIVER OF SPRING (Okana-Takano). • **Trivia:** Took their name from children's bike film of the same name. 'KYLIE'S GOT A CRUSH ON US' was tongue-in-cheek humour about that lovely Australian singer!?

Recommended: LIFE GOES ON (*7)

DUGLAS STEWART – vocals / with **SEAN DICKSON** – bass / **JIM McCULLOCH** – guitar (both of SOUP DRAGONS) / **BILLY & WILLIE** (of SHOP ASSISTANTS?)

53rd & 3rd not issued

May 86. (7") **SAD?. / E102** [ ] [-]
(12"+=) – The cat from outer space (live) / Strawberry Sunday (live) / Groovy good luck friend (live).

— now w /out SEAN (B-side only for JIM)

Jan 87. (7") **WHAT A WONDERFUL WORLD. / THE DAY BEFORE TOMORROW** [ ] [-]
(12"+=) – Johnny Alucard / Sad? / Sandy's wallet.

— **DUGLAS** w / **FRANCIS McDONALD** – drums (ex-BOY HAIRDRESSERS, ex-PASTELS) / + **GORDON KEEN** – guitar / + **NORMAN BLAKE** – guitar, vocals (of TEENAGE FANCLUB)

Jan 88. (7") **FIGURE 4. / STARDATE 21.11.70.** [ ] [-]

Apr 88. (7") **IN HER HAIR. / BETTE BLUE** [ ] [-]
(12"ep'BMX BANDITS" +=) – Figure 4 / Stardate 21.11.70.

— now w / **NORMAN BLAKE + GERRY** (from TEENAGE FANCLUB)

Click — not issued

Mar 90. (lp) **C86** [ ] [-]
– Right across the street / Top Shop girl / Rimbaud and me / Yo yo song (1969) / Medley: Disco girl – Disco daze and disco knights / Your class / Disco girl II / Whirlpool / C86 / On somedays / But tonight / Let Mother Nature be your guide / Heaven's daughter. *(cd-iss.Nov92 as 'C86 PLUS' on 'Vinyl Japan')* (+=) – Stardate / Figure 4 / Strawberry sundae / C'est la vent Betty / Thinkin' 'bout you baby / Let Mother Nature be your guide (karaoke mix) / Your class.

Only — not issued

Dec 90. (lp) **TOTALLY GROOVY LIVE EXPERIENCE (live at Hattonrig Hotel)** [ ] [-]
– Whirlpool / Girl at the bus stop / Your class / In her hair / E102 / Bongo brains / Disco girl / The day before tomorrow / Like a hurricane / Nazi punks fuck off.

—— **DUGLAS** now w/**EUGENE KELLY** (ex-VASELINES, of CAPTAIN AMERICA + EUGENIUS) + **GORDON KEEN** / **JOE McLAUGHLIN** – guitar (of GROOVY LITTLE NUMBERS) / **F.McDONALD**

Vinyl Japan — not issued

Oct 91. (cd)(lp) **STARWARS** [ ] [-]
– Come clean / Think tank / Smile for me / Green grow / Retitled / Life goes on / The sailor's song (pt.1) / Disguise / Studcats of life / Extraordinary / Do you really love me? / The sailor's song / Stars Wars.

1992. (12"ep)(cd-ep) **COME CLEAN / LET MOTHER NATURE BE YOUR GUIDE. / RETITLED / ('A'-funky train mix)** [ ] [-]

Sunflower — not issued

Aug 92. (cd)(c)(m-lp) **GORDON KEEN AND HIS BMX BANDITS** [ ] [-]
– Kylie's got a crush on us / Come and get it / Girl at the bus stop / etc.

Creation — Creation

Nov 92. (12")(cd-s) **SERIOUS DRUGS / FUNNY FACE. / DON'T FIGHT IT FEEL IT (in concert) / SERIOUS DRUGS (demo)** [ ] [-]

Jul 93. (7")(c-s) **KYLIE'S GOT A CRUSH ON US. / HOLE IN MY HEART** [ ] [-]
(12"+=)(cd-s+=) – Thinkin' 'bout you baby / My generation.

Oct 93. (cd)(lp) **LIFE GOES ON** [ ] [ ]
– Little hands / Serious drugs / Space girl / Scar / I'll keep on joking / Hole in my heart / Cast a shadow / Cats and dogs / Your dreams / My friend / It hasn't ended / Intermission (bathing beauties) / Kylie's got a crush on us.

Nov 93. (12"ep)(cd-ep) **LITTLE HANDS / THE NEXT GIRL. / WITCHI TAI TO (home recording) / BUT TONIGHT (acoustic session)** [ ] [-]

Apr 94. (7"ep)(cd-ep) **SERIOUS DRUGS / LITTLE PONY. / I'LL KEEP ON JOKING / THE SAILOR'S SONG** [ ] [-]

Mar 95. (7") **GETTIN' DIRTY. / I CAN'T STAY MAD AT YOU** [ ] [ ]
(cd-s+=) – Tiny fingers, tiny toes / This guy's in love with you.

May 95. (cd)(lp) **GETTIN' DIRTY** [ ] [ ]
– Gettin' dirty / Hello again / Lost girl / Love come to me / No future / Konnichiva £2 / On the road to Heaven / Little river of spring.

Aug 95. (7") **LOVE COME TO ME. / THAT SUMMER FEELING** [ ] [ ]
(cd-s+=) – Come summer / Sunshine day.

BODY COUNT (see under ⇒ ICE-T)

Marc BOLAN

Born: MARK FELD, 30 Sep'47, London, England. After abandoning his performing name TOBY TYLER and career as a male model, he went solo 1965 signing to 'Decca'. In spring 1967 after 3 flop singles, he replaced GEOFF McLELLAND in JOHN'S CHILDREN. With him, they issued controversial DESDEMONA single on the 'Track' label. Early '68, he teamed up with STEVE PEREGRINE TOOK under TYRANNOSAURUS REX name. With airplay on John Peel's night-time show, they gained enough underground attention to hit pop charts. In 1970, with MICKEY FINN replacing TOOK, and under an abbreviated name T. REX, they had biggest hit 'RIDE A WHITE SWAN'. This was followed-up by 8 consecutive Top 3 hits, including 4 UK chart-toppers 'HOT LOVE', 'GET IT ON', TELEGRAM SAM' & 'METAL GURU'. • **Style:** Effeminate superstar, who glided through period of acoustic and electric psychedelia in the 60's, to blatant but excellent glam-rock pop in the 70's. • **Songwriters:** Most written by BOLAN, except SUMMERTIME BLUES (Eddie Cochran) / DO YOU WANNA DANCE (Bobby Freeman) / DOCK OF THE BAY (Otis Redding) / TO KNOW HIM IS TO LOVE HIM (Teddy Bears) / RIP IT UP (Little Richard) / ENDLESS SLEEP (Joey Reynolds) / A TEENAGER IN LOVE (Dion). • **Trivia:** At the end of 1973, he split with wife and assistant manager June Child, and soon became involved with coloured singer GLORIA JONES. She had been part of T. REX backing singers for some months. In '74 the pair virtually emigrated to Los Angeles and Monte Carlo as tax exiles. Moved back to London for comeback Granada TV show "MARC" in 1977. Gloria was seriously hurt when driving the car which hit a tree and killed MARC on 16 Sep'77. The tree which is said to be near Barnes Common, London has since become a shrine for fans. MARC BOLAN still has a fan club "MARC ON WAX" who are also responsible for numerous exploitation/high demand releases.

Recommended: THE ULTIMATE COLLECTION (*9) / MY PEOPLE WERE FAIR... (*6) / PROPHETS, SEERS... (*6) / UNICORN (*7) / A BEARD OF STARS (*6).

Marc BOLAN

solo, using session men

Decca — not issued

Nov 65. (7") **THE WIZARD. / BEYOND THE RISING SUN** [ ] [-]

Jun 66. (7") **THE THIRD DEGREE. / SAN FRANCISCO POET** [ ] [-]

Parlophone — not issued

Dec 66. (7") **HIPPY GUMBO. / MISFIT** [ ] [-]

—— BOLAN then joined JOHN'S CHILDREN before forming own band

TYRANNOSAURUS REX

MARC – vocals, guitars / **STEVE PEREGRINE TOOK** (b.28 Jul'49, London) – bongos, vocals

Regal Zono. — A&M

Apr 68. (7") **DEBORA. / CHILD STAR** [34] [ ]

Jun 68. (lp) **MY PEOPLE WERE FAIR AND HAD SKY IN THEIR HAIR . . . BUT NOW THEY'RE CONTENT TO WEAR STARS ON THEIR BROWS** [15] [ ]
– Red hot mama / Scenesof / Child star / Strange orchestras / Chateau in Virginia Waters / Dwarfish trumpet blues / Mustang Ford / Afghan woman / Knight / Graceful fat shake / Weilder of words / Frowning Atahuallpa. *(re-iss.May85+c. on 'Sierra')*

Regal Zono. — Blue Thumb

Aug 68. (7") **ONE INCH ROCK. / SALAMANDA PALAGANDA** [28] [ ]

Oct 68. (lp) **PROPHETS, SEERS AND SAGES, THE ANGELS OF THE AGES** [ ] [ ]
– Deboraarobed / Stacey grove / Wind quartets / Conesuala / Trelawny lawn / Aznagell the mage / The friends / Salamanda Palaganda / Our wonderful brownskin man / Oh Harley (the Saltimbanques) / Eastern spell / The travelling tragition / Juniper suction / Scenes of dynasty. *(re-iss.May85 on 'Sierra') (re-iss.cd Oct94 on 'Disky')*

Jan 69. (7") **PEWTER SUITOR. / WARLORD OF THE ROYAL CROCODILES** [ ] [ ]

May 69. (lp) **UNICORN** [12] [ ]
– Chariots of silk / 'Pon a hill / The seal of seasons / The throat of winter / Cat black (the wizard's hat) / Stones of Avalon / She was born to be my unicorn / Like a white star, tangled and far, Tulip that's what you are / Warlord of the royal crocodiles / Evenings of Damask / The sea beasts / Iscariot / Nijinsky hind / The pilgrim's tale / The misty coast of Albany / Romany soup. *(re-iss.May85+c. on 'Sierra')*

Jul 69. (7") **KING OF THE RUMBLING SPIRES. / DO YOU REMEMBER?** [44] [ ]

—— **MICKEY FINN** (b. 3 Jan'47) – bongos, vocals repl. TOOK who joined PINK FAIRIES (He died Nov80)

Jan 70. (7") **BY THE LIGHT OF THE MAGICAL MOON. / FIND A LITTLE WOOD** [ ] [ ]

Mar 70. lp,c) **A BEARD OF STARS** [21] [ ]
– Prelude / A day laye / The woodland bop / First heart mighty dawn dart / Pavillions of sun / Organ blues / By the light of the magical Moon / Wind cheetah / A beard of stars / Great horse / Dragon's ear / Lofty skies / Dove / Elemental child. *(US-import had free 7" BLUE THING)(UK re-iss.+c.May86 on 'Sierra')*

T.REX

Fly/E.M.I. — Reprise

Oct 70. (7"m) **RIDE A WHITE SWAN. / IS IT LOVE / SUMMERTIME BLUES** [2] [76] Jan 71

—— added **STEVE CURRY** (b.21 May'47, Grimsby, England) – bass / **BILL LEGEND** (b. 8 May'44, Essex, England) – drums

Dec 70. (lp)(c) **T.REX** [13] [ ]
– The children of Rarn / Jewel / The visit / Childe / The time of love is now / Diamond meadows / Root of star / Beltane walk / Is it love / One ich rock / Summer deep / Seagull woman / Sun eye / The wizard / The children of Rarn (reprise). *(re-iss.Mar78 + Oct81 on 'Cube', re-iss.May85 on 'Sierra') (cd-iss.May92 on 'Castle')*

Feb 71. (7"m) **HOT LOVE. / WOODLAND ROCK / KING OF THE MOUNTAIN COMETH** [1] [-]

Apr 71. (7") **HOT LOVE. / ONE INCH ROCK / SEAGULL WOMAN** [-] [72]

Jul 71. (7"m) **GET IT ON (BANG A GONG). / THERE WAS A TIME / RAW RAMP** [1] [10] Dec 71

Sep 71. (lp)(c) **ELECTRIC WARRIOR** [1] [32] Nov 71
– Mambo sun / Cosmic dancer / Jeepster / Monolith / Lean woman blues / Get it on (bang a gong) / Planet queen / Girl / The motivator / Life's a gas / Rip off. *(also iss.pic-lp) (re-iss.Mar78 + Oct81 on 'Cube',+cd.May85) (cd-iss.Apr90 on 'Castle') (cd+=)* – Hot love / Deborah.

Nov 71. (7") **JEEPSTER. / LIFE'S A GAS** [2] [-]

Nov 71. (7") **JEEPSTER. / RIP OFF** [-] [ ]

T.Rex-E.M.I. — Reprise

Jan 72. (7"m) **TELEGRAM SAM. / CADILLAC / BABY STRANGE** [1] [67] Apr 72
(re-iss.Mar82; hit 69)

E.M.I. — Reprise

May 72. (7"m) **METAL GURU. / LADY / THUNDERWING** [1] [ ]

Jul 72. (lp)(c) **THE SLIDER** [4] [17] Sep 72
– Metal guru / Mystic lady / Rock on / The slider / Baby boomerang / Spaceball ricochet / Buick MacKane / Telegram Sam / Rabbit fighter / Baby strange / Ballrooms of Mars / Chariot choogle / Main man. *(re-iss.Oct83 on 'Marc On Wax') (cd-iss.Nov89) (also on pic-lp) (re-iss.cd Jul94 on 'Demon')*

Jul 72. (7") **THE SLIDER. / ROCK ON** [-] [ ]

Sep 72. (7") **CHILDREN OF THE REVOLUTION. / JITTERBUG LOVE / SUNKEN RAGS** [2] [ ]

Dec 72. (7") **SOLID GOLD EASY ACTION. / BORN TO BOOGIE** [2] [ ]

Mar 73. (7") **20th CENTURY BOY. / FREE ANGEL** [3] [ ]

Mar 73. (lp)(c) **TANX** [4] [ ]
– Tenement lady / Rapids / Mister mister / Broken hearted blues / Shock rock / Country honey / Electric Slim and the factory man / Mad Donna / Born to boogie / Life is strange / The street and the babe shadow / Highway knees / Left hand Luke and the beggar boys. *(also iss.on pic-lp)(re-iss.Oct83, cd-iss.Nov89 on 'Marc On Wax') (re-iss.cd Jul94 on 'Demon')*

Jun 73. (7") **THE GROOVER. / MIDNIGHT** [4] [-]

Jun 73. (7") **THE GROOVER. / BORN TO BOOGIE** [-] [ ]

—— added **JACK GREEN** – guitar (plus 3 female b.singers inc.**GLORIA JONES)**

Nov 73. (7") **TRUCK ON (TYKE). / SITTING HERE** [12] [-]

with
my Les paul
I Know I'm SMALL
BUT I enjoy
living Anyway
Harry Horse

MARC BOLAN & T.REX

(T.REX = FINN, CURRIE, GREEN, JONES – keys, vocals) / **DAVY LUTTON** – drums (ex-HEAVY JELLY)repl. LEGEND (2 more female singers)

Feb 74. (7") **TEENAGE DREAM. / SATISFACTION PONY** [13] [ ]
Mar 74. (lp)(c) **ZINC ALLOY AND THE EASY RIDERS OF TOMORROW** [12] [ ]
– Venus loon / Sound pit / Explosive mouth / Galaxy / Orange / Nameless wildness / Teenage dream / Liquid gang / Carsmile Smith & the old one / You've got to jive to stay alive – Spanish midnight / Interstellar soul / Painless persuasion and the meathawk / Immaculate / The avengers (superbad) / The leopards (featuring Gardinia and The Mighty Slug). *(also iss.on pic-lp) (re-iss.Oct83, cd-iss.Nov89 on 'Marc On Wax') (re-iss.cd Jul94 on 'Demon')*

T.REX

(same line-up)

Jul 74. (7") **LIGHT OF LOVE. / EXPLOSIVE MOUTH** [22] [-]

—— added **DINO DINES** – keyboards

Nov 74. (7") **ZIP GUN BOOGIE. / SPACE BOSS** [41] [-]
Feb 75. (lp)(c) **BOLAN'S ZIP GUN** [ ] [-]
– Light of love / Solid baby / Precious star / Zip gun boogie / Token of my love / Think zine / 'Til dawn / Girl in the thunderbolt suit / I really love you baby / Golden belt. *(re-iss.Oct83, cd-iss. on 'Marc On Wax') (also iss.on pic-lp) (re-iss.cd Jul94 on 'Demon')*

—— members MICKEY FINN and JACK GREEN departed. The latter to PRETTY THINGS Now 5-piece band comprising **BOLAN, JONES, CURRIE, LUTTON** and **DINES.**

Jul 75. (7") **NEW YORK CITY. / CHROME SITAR** [15] [-]

—— next with **BILLY PRESTON** – keyboards

Oct 75. (7") **DREAMY LADY (as "T.REX DISCO PARTY"). / DO YOU WANNA DANCE / DOCK OF THE BAY** [30] [-]
Feb 76. (lp)(c) **FUTURISTIC DRAGON** [50] [ ]
– Futuristic dragon / Jupiter lion / All alone / Chrome sitar / New York City / My little baby / Calling all destroyers / Theme for a dragon / Sensation boulevard / Ride my wheels / Dreamy lady / Dawn storm / Casual agent. *(also on pic-lp) (re-iss.Oct83, cd-iss.Nov89 on 'Marc On Wax') (re-iss.cd Jul94 on 'Demon')*
Feb 76. (7") **LONDON BOYS. / SOLID BABY** [40] [-]
Jun 76. (7") **I LOVE TO BOOGIE. / BABY BOOMERANG** [13] [-]
Sep 76. (7") **LASER LOVER. / LIFE'S AN ELEVATOR** [41] [-]
Jan 77. (7") **TO KNOW YOU IS TO LOVE YOU (as "MARC BOLAN & GLORIA JONES"). / CITY PORT** [ ] [-]

—— now comprised BOLAN and DINES who brought in **MILLER ANDERSON** – guitar (ex-SAVOY BROWN) repl. GLORIA JONES who went solo / **HERBIE FLOWERS** – bass repl. CURRIE who went into sessions **TONY BRENNAN** – drums repl. LUTTON who joined WRECKLESS ERIC

Mar 77. (7") **THE SOUL OF MY SUIT. / ALL ALONE** [42] [-]
Mar 77. (lp)(c) **DANDY IN THE UNDERWORLD** [26] [ ]
– Dandy in the underworld / Crimson moon / Universe / I'm a fool for you / I love to boogie / Visions of Domino / Jason B. Sad / Groove a little / Hang-ups / The soul of my suit / Pain and love / Teen riot structure. *(also iss.pic-lp)(re-iss.Oct83, cd-iss.Nov89 on 'Marc On Wax') (pic-lp.Sep87) (re-iss.cd Jul94 on 'Demon')*
May 77. (7") **DANDY IN THE UNDERWORLD. / GROOVE A LITTLE** [ ] [-]
Aug 77. (7") **CELEBRATE SUMMER. / RIDE MY WHEELS** [ ] [-]

—— On 16 Sep77 MARC BOLAN died when his car driven by GLORIA hit a tree. ANDERSON joined SOUTHSIDE JOHNNY and FLOWERS formed SKY.

– compilations, others, etc. –

On 'Fly' UK / 'Reprise' US unless mentioned otherwise.

Jul 71. (lp)(c) **THE BEST OF T.REX** [21] [ ]
Mar 72. (d-lp) **PROPHETS, SEERS AND SAGES . . . / MY PEOPLE WERE FAIR . . .** (US-title 'TYRANNOSAURUS REX – A BEGINNING') [1] [ ]
Mar 72. (7"m) **DEBORA / ONE INCH ROCK. / WOODLAND BOP / SEAL OF SEASONS** [7] [ ]
May 72. (lp)(c) **BOLAN BOOGIE** [1] [ ]
– Get it on (bang a gong) / The king of the mountain cometh / She was born to be my unicorn / Dove / Woodland bop / Ride a white swan / Raw ramp / Jeepster / First heart mighty dawn dart / By the light of the magical Moon / Summertime blues / Hot love. *(re-iss.Mar78 on 'Cube-Pye', Oct81 on 'Cube-Dakota') (re-Feb85 on 'Sierra') (re-iss.+cd.Apr89 on 'Castle')*
1973. (7") **BANG A GONG. / TELEGRAM SAM** [-] [ ]
1973. (7") **METAL GURU. / JEEPSTER** [-] [ ]
1973. (7") **HOT LOVE. / RIP OFF** [-] [ ]
Apr 78. (7") **CRIMSON MOON. / JASON B. SAD** [ ] [ ]
Oct 72. M.F.P.; (lp)(c) **RIDE A WHITE SWAN** [ ] [-]
Nov 72. Cube; (d-lp) **A BEARD OF STARS / UNICORN** [44] [ ]
(re-iss.Mar78 + Oct81) (re-iss.d-lp,c,cd.Sep88 on 'That's Original') (re-iss.cd Oct94 on 'Disky')
Apr 76. Cube; (7") **HOT LOVE. / GET IT ON** [ ] [-]
Sep 77. Cube; (7"ep) **BOLAN'S BEST + 1** [ ] [-]
– Ride a white swan / Motivator / Jeepster / Demon queen.
Mar 78. Cube; (7"m) **HOT LOVE. / RAW RAMP / LEAN WOMAN BLUES** [ ] [-]
Apr 78. Cube; (d-lp)(c) **MARC, THE WORDS AND MUSIC OF MARC BOLAN** [ ] [-]
Jul 79. Cube; (12"ep) **LIFE'S A GAS / FIND A LITTLE WOOD. / BLESSED WILD APPLE GIRL / ONCE UPON THE SEAS OF ABYSSINIA** [ ] [-]
Aug 81. Cube; (7") **JEEPSTER. / GET IT ON** [ ] [-]
(re-iss.Aug82 on 'Old Gold')
Jun 84. Cube; (7") **RARE MAGIC: SAILOR OF THE HIGHWAY. / DO YOU REMEMBER** [ ] [-]
(12"+=) – Demon queen / Pewtor suitor / The wizard.
Sep 73. E.M.I.; (7") **BLACKJACK (as "BIG CARROT"). / SQUINT EYED MANGLE** [ ] [-]
Nov 73. E.M.I./ US= Reprise; (lp)(c) **GREAT HITS** [32] [ ]
Jun 79. E.M.I./ US= Reprise; (lp)(c) **SOLID GOLD T.REX** [51] [ ]
(re-iss.May82 on 'Fame')
Sep 80. E.M.I.; (lp)(c) **THE UNOBTAINABLE T.REX** [ ] [-]
Jul 82. E.M.I.; (7"ep) **CHILDREN OF THE REVOLUTION / I LOVE TO BOOGIE. / LONDON BOYS / SOLID GOLD EASY ACTION** [ ] [-]
Sep 82. E.M.I.; (7"ep) **TRUCK ON (TYKE) / ZIP GUN BOOGIE. / TEENAGE DREAM / LIGHT OF LOVE** [ ] [-]
Sep 82. E.M.I.; (7"ep) **TELEGRAM SAM / THE SOUL OF MY SUIT. / METAL GURU / LASER LOVE** [ ] [-]
Feb 74. Track; (lp)(c) **THE BEGINNING OF DOVES** [ ] [ ]
(re-iss.+cd.Sep89 on 'Media Motion') (re-iss.Oct91 on 'Receiver')
Jun 74. Track; (7"m) **JASPER C.DEBUSSY. / HIPPY GUMBO / THE PERFUMED GARDEN OF GULLIVER SMITH** [ ] [ ]
Nov 74. Sounds Superb; (lp) **GET IT ON** [ ] [-]
(re-iss.Jun86 on 'Fame')
Apr 78. Pickwick; (d-lp)(c) **THE T.REX COLLECTION / GREATEST HITS** [ ] [-]
Jun 78. Hallmark; (lp)(c) **GREATEST HITS VOL.1** [ ] [-]
(re-iss.Jan87 as 'THE VERY BEST OF VOLUME 1')
Oct 87. Hallmark; (lp)(c)(cd) **TEENAGE DREAM** [ ] [-]
Mar 81. Rarn; (7"ep)(12"ep)(12"clear-ep) **THE RETURN OF THE ELECTRIC WARRIOR** [50] [-]
– Sing me a song / Endless sleep / The lilac hand of Menthol Dan. *(re-iss.7"pic-d.Jul82)*
Jul 82. Rarn; (12")(12"blue) **DEEP SUMMER. / OH BABY / ONE INCH ROCK** [ ] [-]

below on 'Marc On Wax' until otherwise mentioned.

Aug 81. (lp)(c) **T.REX IN CONCERT (live)** [35] [-]
(re-iss.on pic-lp)
Jan 82. (7")(7"blue) **MELLOW LOVE. / FOXY BOX / LUNACY'S BACK** [ ] [-]
(12"+=) – Rock me.
Dec 82. (7"ep) **CHRISTMAS BOP. / SHY BOY / RIDE A WHITE SWAN** [ ] [-]
(12"ep)(12"pic-d-ep+=) – King of the rumbling spires / Savage Beethoven.
Jun 83. (7")(7"pic-d) **THINK ZINC. / MAGICAL MOON / TILL DAWN** [ ] [-]
(12") – ('A'side) – Rip it up / A teenager in love.
Sep 83. (lp)(c) **DANCE IN THE MOONLIGHT** [83] [-]
Oct 83. (lp)(c) **CHILDREN OF THE REVOLUTION** [ ] [-]
(free one-side 7".w/above) – MISTER MOTION
Aug 84. (red-lp)(c) **BILLY SUPER DUPER** [ ] [-]
(re-iss.lp Apr85)
Aug 84. (lp)(c) **T.REXTASY** [ ] [-]
(free 12"w/above) – JAM (live). / ELEMENTAL CHILD (live)
May 85. (7"ep) **MEGAREX 1 (MEDLEY). / CHARIOT CHOOGLE / LIFE'S AN ELEVATOR** [72] [-]
(12"+=) – Solid baby.
May 85. (12"ep) **MEGAREX 2 (MEDLEY). / TAME MY TIGER / CHROME SITAR / SOLID BABY** [ ] [-]

—— (MEGAREX 3: was a 7"sha-pic-d / + 12"pic-d)

Jul 85. (7"m) **SUNKEN RAGS. / JITTERBUG LOVE / DOWN HOME LADY** [ ] [-]
(12"+=) – Funky London / Childhood.
Nov 85. (lp)(c)(cd) **TILL DAWN** [ ] [-]
Feb 87. (7") **CHILDREN OF THE REVOLUTION (remix). / THE SLIDER(remix) / TEAR FOR THE HIGH STAR** (by 'Dave Ashby') [ ] [-]
(12"+=) – Free angel (TV remix).
May 87. (7") **GET IT ON. / JEEPSTER** [54] [-]
(12"+=)(c-s+=)(cd-s+=) – Cadillac.
Sep 87. (7") **I LOVE TO BOOGIE. / RIDE A WHITE SWAN / HOT LOVE** [ ] [-]
(12"+=)(cd-s+=) – Hot George.
Aug 89. (lp)(cd) **THE MARC SHOWS (Granada TV shows)** [ ] [-]
Aug 91. (7")(c-s) **20th CENTURY BOY. / MIDNIGHT / THE GROOVER** [13] [-]
(12"+=)(cd-s+=) – Telegram Sam.
Oct 91. (7")(c-s) **METAL GURU. / THUNDERWIND / BOLAN'S ZIP GUN** [ ] [-]
(12"+=)(cd-s+=) – Solid baby (remix).
Nov 91. (7") **SLEEPY MAURICE. / (1968 interview)** [ ] [-]
Dec 91. (cd)(c)(d-lp) **BORN TO BOOGIE (live & poetry)** [ ] [-]

– MARC BOLAN compilations, etc. –

Sep 81. Cherry Red; (7")(12")(7"pic-d) **YOU SCARE ME TO DEATH. / THE PERFUMED GARDEN OF GULLIVER SMITH** [51] [-]
Oct 81. Cherry Red; (lp) **YOU SCARE ME TO DEATH** [88] [-]
(re-iss.cd+c Nov94 on 'Emporio')
Oct 81. Cherry Red; (7") **CAT BLACK. / JASPER C.DEBUSSY** [ ] [-]
May 82. Cherry Red; (7"m) **THE WIZARD. / BEYOND THE RISING SUN / RINGS OF FORTUNE** [-] [ ]
Dec 91. Cherry Red; (cd) **LOVE AND DEATH** [ ] [-]
Dec 91. Essential; (3xcd) **ANTHOLOGY** [ ] [-]

– T.REX & MARC BOLAN compilations –

Nov 81. Dakota; (d-lp)(c) **THE PLATINUM COLLECTION OF T.REX** [ ] [-]
Jan 82. Dakota; (lp)(c)(pic-lp) **ACROSS THE AIRWAVES** [ ] [-]
Aug 82. Dakota; (7") **HOT LOVE. / JEEPSTER** [ ] [-]
Aug 82. Dakota; (7") **GET IT ON. / DEBORA** [ ] [-]
Aug 82. Dakota; (7") **RIDE A WHITE SWAN. / ONE INCH ROCK** [ ] [-]

below on 'Old Gold' until otherwise mentioned.

Aug 82. (7") **HOT LOVE. / RIDE A WHITE SWAN** [ ] [-]
Aug 82. (7") **DEBORA. / ONE INCH ROCK** [ ] [-]
(above was also iss.1,000 w/'B'side BELTANE WALK)
Jan 85. (7")(7"sha-pic-d) **METAL GURU. / CHILDREN OF THE REVOLUTION** [ ] [-]
Jan 85. (7") **TELEGRAM SAM. / I LOVE TO BOOGIE** [ ] [-]
Jan 85. (7") **SOLID GOLD EASY ACTION. / THE GROOVER** [ ] [-]
Feb 89. (7") **GET IT ON. / JEEPSTER** [ ] [-]
Mar 89. (cd-s) **TELEGRAM SAM / METAL GURU / CHILDREN OF THE REVOLUTION** [ ] [-]
May 89. (cd-s) **SOLID GOLD EASY ACTION / 20th CENTURY BOY / THE GROOVER** [ ] [-]
Oct 82. Countdown; (lp) **T.REX** [ ] [-]
Apr 84. Cambra; (d-lp)(d-c) **BEYOND THE RISING SUN** [ ] [-]
May 85. Cambra; (d-lp)(c) **THE MAIN MAN** [ ] [-]
(7"pic-d. w/above) – TEENAGE DREAM. / SOLID GOLD SEGUE
Nov 84. Sierra; (d-lp)(c) **OFF THE RECORD WITH T.REX** [ ] [-]
May 85. Sierra; (12"ep) **GET IT ON / THERE WAS A TIME. / RAW RAMP / ELECTRIC BOOGIE** *(re-iss.Apr86)* [ ] [-]
May 87. Sierra; (cd) **GREATEST HITS** [ ] [-]
Apr 85. K-Tel; (d-lp)(d-c) **THE BEST OF THE 20th CENTURY BOY** [5] [-]
Jul 85. Dojo; (lp) **A CROWN OF JEWELS** [ ] [-]
Dec 91. Dojo; (cd) **THE EARLY YEARS** [ ] [-]
(re-iss.+lp+c)
Jun 86. Archive 4; (12"ep) **CLASSIC CUTS** [ ] [-]
– Jeepster / Ride a white swan / Get it on / Hot love.
Mar 87. Castle; (d-lp)(d-c)(d-cd) **THE SINGLES COLLECTION** [ ] [-]
Aug 87. Strange Fruit; (12"ep) **THE PEEL SESSIONS (27.10.70)** [ ] [-]
– Jewel / Ride a white swan / Elemental child / Sun eye.
1987. Connoisseur; (lp)(c)(cd) **STAND BY ME** [ ] [-]
Jan 88. Special Edition; (3"cd-s) **HOT LOVE / GET IT ON / TELEGRAM SAM / METAL GURU** [ ] [-]
1988. Fun; (lp) **18 GREATEST HITS** [ ] [-]
Jul 88. Knight; (c) **NIGHTRIDING** [ ] [-]
1990. Rhino; (4xlp-box) **WHERE THERE'S CHAMPAGNE** [-] [ ]
Apr 91. S.P.S.; (lp)(cd) **RARITIES VOLUME ONE** [ ] [-]
Jun 91. Music Club; (cd) **THE VERY BEST OF MARC BOLAN & T.REX** [ ] [-]
Sep 91. Telstar; (cd)(c)(lp) **THE ULTIMATE COLLECTION** [4] [-]
– 20th century boy / Metal guru / I love to boogie / Deborah / New York City / Telegram Sam / Hot love / Dreamy lady / One inch rock / The soul of my suit / London boys / Ride a white swan / Get it on / Light of love / Children of the revolution / Jeepster / Laser love / Zip gun boogie / The groover / King of the rumbling spires / Plateau skull / Truck on (Tyke) / Solid gold easy action / Teenage dream. *(cd has 4 extra above)*
Apr 93. Windsong; (cd) **BBC RADIO 1 LIVE IN CONCERT (TYRANNOSAURUS REX live)** [ ] [-]
Apr 93. Deram; (cd-ep) **THE WIZARD / BEYOND THE RISIN' SUN / THE THIRD DEGREE / SAN FRANCISCO POET** [ ] [-]
Jun 93. Deram; (cd) **THE WIZARD** [ ] [-]
Jun 93. Zinc Alloy; (cd-ep) **BLOWIN' IN THE WIND / THE ROAD I'M ON (GLORIA) / BLOWIN' IN THE WIND (session version)** [ ] [-]
Apr 94. Remember; (cd) **20th CENTURY BOY** [ ] [-]
Jun 95. Edsel; (cd) **T.REX UNCHAINED: UNRELEASED RECORDINGS 1972 VOL.1** [ ] [-]
Jun 95. Edsel; (cd) **T.REX UNCHAINED: UNRELEASED RECORDINGS 1972 VOL.2** [ ] [-]
Aug 95. Old Gold; (cd-s) **TELEGRAM SAM / 20th CENTURY BOY** [ ] [-]
Sep 95. Polygram TV; (cd)(c) **THE ESSENTIAL COLLECTION** [24] [-]
Sep 95. Emporio; (cd)(c) **PREHISTORIC** [ ] [-]
Oct 95. Edsel; (cd) **T.REX UNCHAINED: VOLUME 3: 1973 PART 1** [ ] [-]
Oct 95. Edsel; (cd) **T.REX UNCHAINED: VOLUME 4: 1973 PART 2** [ ] [-]
Oct 95. Edsel; (cd) **CHANGE (THE ALTERNATIVE ZINC ALLOY)** [ ] [-]

Michael BOLTON

Born: MICHAEL BOLOTIN, 26 Feb'53, New Haven, Connecticut, USA. Signed to 'RCA' in the mid-70's, gaining reputation as powerful singer. However it took a slight change of name and a decade for his fortunes to change. After signing to 'Columbia', he released 'EVERYBODY'S CRAZY' in '85, and soon became singing star of the late 80's/early 90's. • **Style:** Adapted from many influences, from 'R&B' to AOR and most successfully, soul. His huge range of vocal depth, made him one of one largest sellers in the late 80's, which left behind wilderness years. • **Songwriters:** Writes own & some with MARK MANGOLD, except WHEN A MAN LOVES A WOMAN (Percy Sledge) / THE DOCK OF THE BAY (Otis Redding) / GEORGIA ON MY MIND (Hoagy Carmichael) / etc. TIMELESS (THE CLASSICS) album featured 10 cover versions:- SINCE I FELL FOR YOU (Lenny Welch) / TO LOVE SOMEBODY (Bee Gees) / REACH OUT I'LL BE THERE (Four Tops) / YOU SEND ME + BRING IT HOME TO ME (Sam Cooke) / YESTERDAY (Beatles) / HOLD ON, I'M COMING (Sam & Dave) / KNOCK ON WOOD (Eddie Floyd) / DRIFT AWAY (Dobie Gray) / WHITE CHRISTMAS (Irving Berlin) / BACK IN MY ARMS AGAIN (Holland-Dozier-Holland) / A LOVE SO BEAUTIFUL (Emerson-Lynne). • **Trivia:** His cousin CURTIS STIGERS is now in the 90's, carving out his own successful solo career.

Recommended: SOUL PROVIDER (*4).

Michael BOLOTIN

(solo) with **DAVID SANBORN** and **ANDY NEWMARK**

R.C.A. R.C.A.

1975. (lp)(c) **MICHAEL BOLOTIN** [-] [ ]
– Lost in the city / Everybody needs a reason / Your love it's just a feelin' / Dream while you can / Take me as I am / These eyes / You mean more to me / If I had your love / Give me a reason / Tell me how you feel / Time is on my side. *(cd-iss.Mar92 as 'THE EARLY YEARS')*
1976. (lp)(c) **EVERY DAY OF MY LIFE** [-] [ ]

BLACKJACK

were formed 1979 by **BOLOTIN** – vocals plus **BRUCE KULICK** – guitar / **JIMMY HASLIP** – bass / **SANDY GERMARRO** – drums

Polydor Polydor

Jul 79. (7") **LOVE ME TONIGHT. /** [-] [62]
Nov 79. (lp)(c) **BLACKJACK** [ ] [ ]
– Love me tonight / Heart of stone / The night has me calling for you / I'm aware of your love / Southern ballad / Fallin' / Without your love / Countin' on you / For you / Heart of mine.
1980. (7") **WITHOUT YOUR LOVE. / HEART OF MINE** [ ] [ ]
1980. (lp)(c) **WORLDS APART** [-] [ ]
– My world is empty without you / Love is hard to find / Stay / Airwaves / Maybe it's the power of love / Welcome to the world / Breakaway / Really wanna know / Sooner or later / She wants you back.

— Break-up 1981.

– compilation, others, etc. –

Nov 90. Polydor; (cd) **BLACKJACK / WORLDS APART** [ ] [ ]

MICHAEL BOLTON

went solo again, with band **BOB & BRUCE KULICK** – guitar / **CRAIG BROOKS** – guitar / **MARK MANGOLD** – keyboards (ex-TOUCH) / **MARK CLARKE** – bass (ex-MOUNTAIN, etc.) / **CHUCK BURGI** – drums (ex-BALANCE) / **ALDO NOVA + JAN MULLANEY** – keyboards

C.B.S. Columbia

Mar 83. (7") **FOOL'S GAME. / FIGHTING FOR MY LIFE** [-] [82]
Jul 83. (lp)(c) **MICHAEL BOLTON** [ ] [89] Mar 83
– Fool's game / She did the same thing / Home town hero / Can't hold on, can't let go / Fighting for my life / Paradise / Back in my arms again / Carrie / I almost believed you.
Sep 83. (7") **I ALMOST BELIEVED YOU. / SHE DID THE SAME THING** [-] [ ]

— now with **BRUCE + MARK,** plus newcomers **DENNIS FELDMAN** – bass / **MARK RIVERA** – saxophone / **LARRY FAST** – synthesizers / **PEPPY CASTRO** – guitar

Feb 85. (lp)(c) **EVERYBODY'S CRAZY** [ ] [ ] Jul 84
– Everybody's crazy / Save our love / Can't turn it off / Call my name / Start breaking my heart / Everytime / Desperate heart / You don't want me bad enough / Don't tell me it's over. *(re-iss.cd+c.May91)*
Nov 84. (7") **EVERYBODY'S CRAZY. / SHE DID THE SAME THING** [-] [ ]

— now with **JONATHAN CAIN / RANDY JACKSON / NEAL SCHON / MIKE BAIRD** and toured w / **ROSS VALORY** – bass / **DAN HILL** – saxophone / **STEF BURNHAM** – guitar / **MUGGS CAIN** – drums / **ROLF HARTLEY** – keyboards

Oct 87. (7") **THAT'S WHAT LOVE IS ALL ABOUT. / TAKE A LOOK AT MY FACE** [ ] [19] Aug 87
(12"+=)(cd-s+=) – Fool's game / Can't hold on, can't let go.
Oct 87. (lp)(c)(cd) **THE HUNGER** [ ] [46] Aug 87
– Hot love / Wait on love / (Sittin' on) The dock of the bay / Gina / That's what love is all about / The hunger / You're all I need / Take a look at my face / Walk away. *(UK re-iss.+cd.Aug90, reached No.44.)(re-iss.cd+c Sep93)*
Apr 88. (7") **(SITTIN' ON) THE DOCK OF THE BAY. / CALL MY NAME** [ ] [11] Jan 88
(12"+=)(cd-s+=) – ('A'acapella mix).
May 88. (7") **WAIT ON LOVE. / I ALMOST BELIEVED YOU** [-] [ ]
Aug 88. (7") **THE HUNGER. / WALK AWAY** [-] [ ]
Jul 89. (7") **SOUL PROVIDER. / THE HUNGER** [ ] [17] Jun 89
(12"+=)(cd-s+=) – ('A'version) / (Sitting on) The dock of the bay.
Aug 89. (lp)(c)(cd) **SOUL PROVIDER** [4] [3] Jul 89
– Soul provider / Georgia on my mind / It's only my heart / How am I supposed to live without you / How can we be lovers / You wouldn't know love / When I'm back on my feet again / From now on / Love cuts deep / Stand up for love.
Dec 89. (7")(c-s) **HOW AM I SUPPOSED TO LIVE WITHOUT YOU. / FOREVER EYES** [3] [1] Oct 89
(12"+=) – Soul provider.
(cd-s+=) – That's what love is all about / Can't hold on, can't let go.
Mar 90. (7")(c-s) **HOW CAN WE BE LOVERS. / THAT'S WHAT LOVE IS ALL ABOUT** [-] [3]
Apr 90. (7")(c-s) **HOW CAN WE BE LOVERS. / THE HUNGER** [10] [-] Mar 90
(12"+=)(cd-s+=) – Fool's game / Dock of the bay (live) / I almost believed you.
Aug 90. (7")(c-s) **WHEN I'M BACK ON MY FEET AGAIN. / I ALMOST BELIEVED YOU** [44] [7] May 90
(12"+=)(cd-s+=) – How am I supposed to live without you / Hometown hero / Walk away.
Sep 90. (7")(c-s) **GEORGIA ON MY MIND. / TAKE A LOOK AT MY FACE** [ ] [36] Aug 90
(12"+=)(cd-s+=) – That's what love is all about / (Sitting on) The dock of the bay.

Columbia Columbia

Apr 91. (7")(c-s) **LOVE IS A WONDERFUL THING. / SOUL PROVIDER** [23] [4]
(12"+=)(cd-s+=) – Georgia on my mind (ext.) / When I'm back on my feet again (remix).
Apr 91. (cd)(c)(lp) **TIME, LOVE & TENDERNESS** [2] [1]
– Love is a wonderful thing / Time, love & tenderness / Missing you now / Now that I found you / Forever isn't long enough / When a man loves a woman / We're

not makin' love anymore / New love / Save on / Steel bars.

Jun 91. (7") **TIME, LOVE AND TENDERNESS. / THAT'S WHAT LOVE IS ALL ABOUT** [-] [7]

Jul 91. (7")(c-s) **TIME, LOVE & TENDERNESS. / YOU WOULDN'T KNOW LOVE** [38] [ ]
(12"+=)(cd-s+=) – Love is a wonderful thing / The dock of the bay.

Oct 91. (7")(c-s) **WHEN A MAN LOVES A WOMAN. / SAVE ME** [8] [5]
(cd-s+=) – Love is such a wonderful thing (extended).
(cd-s) – ('A'side) / (Sitting on) The dock of the bay / Georgia on my mind.

Feb 92. (7")(c-s) **STEEL BARS. / HOW CAN WE BE LOVERS** [17] [ ]
(cd-s+=) – Take a look at my face / You wouldn't know love.

May 92. (7")(c-s) **MISSING YOU NOW. / IT'S ONLY MY HEART** [28] [12] Jan 92
(cd-s+=) – Love cuts deep / Walk away.

Oct 92. (cd)(c)(lp) **TIMELESS (THE CLASSICS)** [3] [5]
– Since I fell for you / To love somebody / Reach out I'll be there / You send me / Yesterday / Hold on, I'm coming / Bring it on home to me / Knock on wood / Drift away / White Christmas. *(re-iss.cd/c May95)*

Oct 92. (7")(c-s) **TO LOVE SOMEBODY. / NOW THAT I FOUND YOU** [16] [11]
(cd-s+=) – (Sitting on) The dock of the bay.
(cd-s) – ('A'side) / When a man loves a woman / Georgia on my mind.

Dec 92. (7")(c-s) **DRIFT AWAY. / WHITE CHRISTMAS** [18] [ ]
(cd-s+=) – Back in my arms again / Fool's case.

Mar 93. (7")(c-s) **REACH OUT I'LL BE THERE. / NEW LOVE** [37] [ ]
(cd-s+=) – Forever isn't long enough / Stand up for love.

Nov 93. (7")(c-s) **SAID I LOVED YOU ... BUT I LIED. / YOU SEND ME** [15] [6]
(cd-s+=)

Nov 93. (cd)(c)(lp) **THE ONE THING** [4] [3]
– Said I loved you...but I lied / I'm not made of steel / The one thing / Soul of my soul / Completely / Lean on me / Ain't got nothing if you ain't got love / A time for letting go / Never got enough of your love / In the arms of love. *(cd+c+=)* – The voice of my heart.

Feb 94. (7")(c-s) **SOUL OF MY SOUL. / THE VOICE OF MY HEART** [32] [ ]
(cd-s+=) – Steel bars (live).

Mar 94. (c-s)(cd-s) **COMPLETELY. / ?** [-] [32]

May 94. (7")(c-s) **LEAN ON ME. / TIME, LOVE AND TENDERNESS (live)** [14] [ ]
(cd-s+=) – To love somebody (live) / How can we be lovers (live).

Sep 95. (cd-s) **CAN I TOUCH YOU ...THERE? / THAT'S WHAT LOVE IS ALL ABOUT (live)** [6] [27] Aug95
(cd-s) – ('A'side) / (Sittin' on) The dock of the bay (live).

Sep 95. (cd)(c)(md) **GREATEST HITS 1985-1995** (compilation) [2] [5]
– Soul provider / (Sittin' on) The dock of the bay / How am I supposed to live without you / How can we be lovers / When I'm back on my feet again / Georgia on my mind / Time, love and tenderness / When a man loves a woman / Missing you now / Steel bars / Said I loved you . . . but I lied / Lean on me / Can I touch you . . .there / Promise you I found someone / A love so beautiful / This river.

Nov 95. (c-s) **A LOVE SO BEAUTIFUL / TO LOVE SOMEBODY** [27] [ ]
(cd-s+=) – Can I touch you there? (2 mixes).
(cd-s) – ('A'side) / Can I touch you there? (2 mixes).

– compilations, etc. –

1990. Columbia; (7") **GINA (remix) / WALK AWAY** [-] [ ]

Aug 93. Columbia; (3xcd-box) **MICHAEL BOLTON / EVERYBODY'S CRAZY / THE HUNGER** [ ] [ ]

Graham BOND

Born: 28 Oct'37, Romford, Essex, England. He was adopted from Dr.Bernardo's home. In 1962, he replaced CYRIL DAVIES in BLUES INCORPORATED (a group run by ALEXIS KORNER). BOND formed own outfit in 1964 and after one 45 on 'Decca', signed to 'Columbia', with help of new manager ROBERT STIGWOOD. His band went onto greater things after their departure. Had brief stay in the States in 1966, and broke through into UK charts in 1970 with lp 'SOLID BOND'. • **Style:** Switched from jazz, to being the Godfather of UK 'R&B'. In 1967, he brought in more Eastern mystical influences. This gave rise to his increasing obsession with the occult and Alistair Crowley, whom he believed he was the illegitimate son of. He married singer DIANE STEWART circa 1970-72. • **Songwriters:** Self/group penned, except GOT MY MOJO WORKING (Muddy Waters) / WHAT'D I SAY (Ray Charles) / etc. • **Trivia:** Appeared on 'B'side of original WHO single SUBSTITUTE under The WHO ORCHESTRA (Waltz For A Pig).

Recommended: THE SOUND OF '65 (*5)

GRAHAM BOND ORGANISATION

GRAHAM BOND – vocals, organ (ex-BLUES INCORPORATED, ex-DUFFY POWER) / **DICK HECKSTALL-SMITH** – saxophone repl. guitarist JOHN McLAUGHLIN / **JACK BRUCE** – bass, vocals / **PETER 'GINGER' BAKER** – drums

Decca / not issued

Jun 64. (7") **LONG TALL SHORTY. / LONG LEGGED BABY** [ ] [-]

Columbia / Columbia

Jan 65. (7") **WADE IN THE WATER. / TAMMY** [ ] [-]

Mar 65. (lp) **THE SOUND OF '65** [ ] [-]
– Hoochie coochie / Baby make love to me / Neighbour, neighbour / Early in the morning / Spanish blues / Oh baby / Little girl / I want you / Wade in the water / Got my mojo working / Train time / Baby, be good to me / Half a man / Tammy.

Mar 65. (7") **TELL ME. / LOVE COMES SHINING THROUGH** [ ] [-]

Jul 65. (7") **LEASE ON LOVE. / MY HEART'S IN LITTLE PIECES** [ ] [-]

Nov 65. (lp) **THERE'S A BOND BETWEEN US** [ ] [-]
– Who's afraid of Virgina Woolf / Hear me calling your name / The night time is the right time / Walkin' in the park / Last night / Baby it can't be true / What'd I say / Dick's instrumental / Don't let go / Keep-a-drivin' / Have you ever loved a woman / Camels and elephants.

— (Oct65) **NEIL HUBBARD** – guiter repl. BRUCE (to JOHN MAYALL and solo)

1966. (7") **ST. JAMES INFIRMARY. / SOUL TANGO** [ ] [-]

— BOND retained HECKSTALL-SMITH and HUBBARD plus **JOHN HISEMAH** – drums repl. BAKER who (with BRUCE) formed CREAM

Page One / not issued

Feb 67. (7") **YOU'VE GOT TO HAVE LOVE, BABY. / I LOVE YOU** [ ] [-]

— Split Sep67, HECKSTALL-SMITH and HISEMAN joined JOHN MAYALL then COLOSSEUM HUBBARD joined GREASE BAND then JUICY LUCY

GRAHAM BOND

moved to US & went solo, with **HARVEY MANDEL** – guitar / **HARVEY BROOKS** – bass / **EDDIE HOH** – drums

not issued / Pulsar

1968. (lp) **LOVE IS THE LAW** [-] [ ]
– Water, water / Oh shining on / Pictures in the fire / Baroque / Sisters and brothers / Stiffnecked chicken / Freaky beak / Walk onto me / Magic mojo / Brothers and sisters.

— (Dec69) returned to UK. He joined GINGER BAKER in AIRFORCE

— **GRAHAM BOND** also continues solo career with **BRUCE, BAKER, HECKSTALL-SMITH, HISEMAN** and **McLAUGHLIN**

Warners / Warners

Jan 70. (d-lp) **SOLID BOND** (compilation 63-66) [40] [ ]
– Green onions / Springtime in the city / Can't stand it / The grass is greener / Doxy / Only sixteen / Last night / Long legged baby / Walkin' in the park / It's not goodbye / Neighbour neighbour / Ho ho country kicking blues.

Feb 70. (7") **WALKING IN THE PARK. / SPRINGTIME IN THE CITY** [ ] [ ]

MAGICK

was formed by **GRAHAM BOND** plus **DIANNE STEWART** – vocals / **HENRY WILLIAMS** – guitar / **TERRY POOLE** – guitar / **STEVE GREGORY** – saxophone / **JOHN WEATHERS** – drums / **GASPER WILLIAMS** – percussion

Vertigo / Mercury

Feb 71. (lp) **HOLY MAGICK** [ ] [ ]
– Holy magick suite:- Meditation aumgn / The Qabalistic cross / The word of the Aeon / Invocation to the light / The pentagram ritual / The Qabablistic cross / Hymn of praise / Twelve gates to the city / The holy words Iao Saluco (these are the words) / Aquarius mantra (in Egyptian) / Enochian (Atlantean) call / Abrahadabra the word of the Aeon / Praise "city of light" / The Qabalistic cross aumgn / Return of Arthur / The magician / The judgement / An archangel Mikael. *(re-iss.Nov88 on 'B.G.O.')*

Apr 71. (7") **WATER WATER. / TWELVE GATES TO THE CITY** [ ] [-]

Dec 71. (lp) **WE PUT OUR MAGICK ON YOU** [ ] [-]
– Forbidden fruit (part 1) / Moving towards the light / Ajama / Druid / I put my magick on you / Time to die / Hail Ra Haraknite / Forbidden fruit (part 2). *(re-iss.'74 on 'Philips')*

GRAHAM BOND & PETE BROWN

Chapter One / not issued

Nov 72. (lp) **TWO HEADS ARE BETTER THAN ONE** [ ] [ ]
– Lost tribe / Ig the pig / Oobati / Amazing grass / Scunthorpe crabmeat train sideways boogie shuffle stomp / C.F.D.T. (Colonel Fright's dancing terrapins) / Mass debate / Looking for time.
(cd-iss.Dec92 with extra tracks on 'See For Miles') (also cd-iss.Dec92 including 'MALTAMOUR SOUNDTRACK' on 'Repertoire' +=)
– Milk is turning sour in my shoes / Macumbe / The beginning / Aeroplane drinking man / Italian song / Spend my nights in armour / Fury of war / Magpie man / Drum roll / Swing song / Sailor's song / The ending.

Greenwich-Decca / not issued

1972. (7") **LOST TRIBE / MILK IS TURNING SOUR IN MY SHOES / MACUMBA** [ ] [ ]

— They also both recorded for soundtrack 'MALTAMOUR'. In 1973 BOND forms MAGUS with folk singer CAROL ANNE PEGG. They split, and on 8th May74, after a bout of depression due to heroin addiction, he is found dead under a tube train in Finsbury. Mystery surrounds this as to whether it was suicide or a "cult" murder

– compilations etc. –

1964. Decca; (7"ep) **THE GRAHAM BOND ORGANISATION** [ ] [ ]
– Hoochie coochie man / High healed sneakers / Little girl / Long legged baby / Strut around.

1971. Mercury; (lp)(c) **BOND IN AMERICA** [ ] [ ]

1972. Philips; (lp)(c) **THIS IS GRAHAM BOND** [ ] [ ]

Jan 77. Charly; (lp) **THE BEGINNING OF JAZZ ROCK (Organisation live 1964)** [ ] [ ]

Oct 88. Charly; (lp)(c) **LIVE AT KLOOKS KLEEK (live)** [ ] [ ]

Mar 88. Edsel; (d-lp) **THE SOUND OF 65 / THERE'S A BOND BETWEEN US** [ ] [ ]

BON JOVI

Formed: Sayreville, New Jersey, USA . . . Spring '83, by JOHN and BRYAN. Signed worldwide by 'Phonogram' records who released RUNAWAY, a recent BONGIOVI solo effort which had been included on local radio station compilation lp. By 1986, they had become one of America's top selling rock bands, unleashing 'SLIPPERY WHEN WET' that year. • **Style:**

Hard hookline rock that slipped into mainstream metal, due to influence of BRUCE SPRINGSTEEN and 70's heavy rock. • **Songwriters:** All penned by BON JOVI, SAMBORA and some collaborations with DESMOND CHILDS. Covered: IT'S ONLY ROCK'N'ROLL (Rolling Stones) / WITH A LITTLE HELP FROM MY FRIENDS (Beatles) / I DON'T LIKE MONDAYS (Boomtown Rats). • **Miscellaneous:** April 1988 saw their manager DOC McGEE convicted for drug offences and sentenced to five years suspended, but doing community work. BONGIOVI married childhood sweetheart Dorothea Hurley on 29 April'89. He was given cameo role in film 'YOUNG GUNS II'.

Recommended: NEW JERSEY (*7) / SLIPPERY WHEN WET (*7) / CROSS-ROADS (*9)

JON BON JOVI (b.JOHN BONGIOVI, 2 Mar'62) – vocals, guitar / **RICHIE SAMBORA** (b.11 Jul'59) – lead guitar / **DAVID BRYAN** (b.DAVID RASHBAUM, 7 Feb'62) – keyboards / **ALEC JOHN SUCH** (b.14 Nov'56) – bass (ex-PHANTON'S OPERA) / **TICO 'Tar Monster' TORRES** (b. 7 Oct'53) – drums (ex-FRANKIE & THE KNOCKOUTS)

Vertigo Mercury

Apr 84. (lp)(c) **BON JOVI** [71] [43] Jan 84
– Runaway / Roulette / She don't know me / Shot through the heart / Love lies / Breakout / Burning for love / Come back / Get ready. *(cd-iss. 1986)*

May 84. (7")(12") **SHE DON'T KNOW ME. / BREAKOUT** [ ] [48]

Oct 84. (7")(12") **RUNAWAY. / BREAKOUT (live)** [ ] [39] Feb 84
(12"+=) – Runaway (live).

Apr 85 (7") **ONLY LONELY. /** [–] [54]

May 85. (lp)(c) **7800° FAHRENHEIT** [28] [37]
– In and out of love / The price of love / Only lonely / King of the mountain / Silent night / Tokyo road / The hardest part is the night / Always run to you / To the fire / Secret dreams. *(cd-iss. 1986)*

May 85. (7")(7"pic-d) **IN AND OUT OF LOVE. / ROULETTE (live)** [ ] [69]
(12"+=) – Shot through the heart (live).

Jul 85. (7") **THE HARDEST PART IS THE NIGHT. / ALWAYS RUN TO YOU** [68] [ ]
(12"+=) – Tokyo Road (live).
(d7"++=) – Shot through the heart (live).
(extra-12"red/clear) – ('A'side) / Tokyo Road (live) / In and out of love (live).

Aug 86. (7")(10"sha-pic-d) **YOU GIVE LOVE A BAD NAME. / LET IT ROCK** [14] [1] Sep 86
(12"+=) – Borderline.
(12"blue+=) – The hardest part is the night (live) / Burning for love (live).

Sep 86. (lp)(c)(cd) **SLIPPERY WHEN WET** [6] [1]
– Let it rock / You give love a bad name / Livin' on a prayer / Social disease / Wanted dead or alive / Raise your hands / Without love / I'd die for you / Never say goodbye / Wild in the streets. *(re-charted UK Dec90 hit 46, Jun91 No.42 , Sep92 re-issue) (re.pic-lp Aug88)*

Oct 86. (7")(7"pic-d) **LIVIN' ON A PRAYER. / WILD IN THE STREETS** [4] [1] Dec 86
(12"green+=) – Edge of a broken heart.
(d12"+=) – Only lonely (live) / Runaway (live).

Mar 87. (7") **WANTED DEAD OR ALIVE. / SHOT THROUGH THE HEART** [13] [7] Apr 87
(12"+=) – Social disease.
(12"silver++=) – Get ready (live).
(cd-s) – ('A'extended) / ('A'radio) / ('A'acoustic).

Aug 87. (7") **NEVER SAY GOODBYE. / RAISE YOUR HANDS** [21] [ ]
(12"+=)(c-s+=) – ('A'acoustic).
(12"yellow+=) – Wanted dead or alive (acoustic).

Sep 88. (7") **BAD MEDICINE. / 99 IN THE SHADE** [17] [1]
(12"+=)(cd-s+=) – Lay your hands on me.
(extra-12") – ('A'side) / You give love a bad name / Livin' on a prayer (live).

Sep 88. (lp)(c)(cd) **NEW JERSEY** [1] [1]
– Lay your hands on me / Bad medicine / Born to be my baby / Living in sin / Blood on blood / Stick to your guns / Homebound train / I'll be there for you / 99 in the shade / Love for sale / Wild is the wind / Ride cowboy ride. *(re-iss.cd+c Mar93)*

Nov 88. (7") **BORN TO MY BABY. / LOVE FOR SALE** [22] [3]
(12"+=)(12"pic-d+=) – Wanted dead or alive.
(cd-s++=) – Runaway / Livin' on a prayer.

Apr 89. (7") **I'LL BE THERE FOR YOU. / HOMEBOUND TRAIN** [18] [1] Mar 89
(12"+=) – Wild in the streets (live).
(cd-s+=) – Borderline / Edge of a broken heart.

Aug 89. (7")(c-s)(7"red/white/blue) **LAY YOUR HANDS ON ME. / BAD MEDICINE** [18] [7] May 89
(10"pic-d+=) – Blood on blood.
(12"+=)(cd-s++=) – Born to my baby (acoustic).

Nov 89. (7") **LIVING IN SIN. / LOVE IS WAR** [35] [9] Oct 89
(12"+=)(12"silver+=)(box-cd-s+=) – Ride cowboy ride / Stick to your guns.

JON BON JOVI

solo material inspired by the film 'Young Guns II'.

Aug 90. (7") **BLAZE OF GLORY. / YOU REALLY GOT ME NOW** [13] [1] Jul 90
(12"+=)(cd-s+=) – Blood money.

Aug 90. (cd)(c)(lp) **BLAZE OF GLORY** [2] [3]
– Billy get your guns / Miracle / Blaze of glory / Blood money / Santa Fe / Justice in the barrel / Never say die / You really got me now / Bang a drum / Dyin' ain't much of a livin' / Guano City. *(re-iss.cd/c Apr95)*

Nov 90. (7")(c-s) **MIRACLE. / BANG A DRUM** [29] [12] Oct 90
(12"+=)(cd-s+=) – Dyin' ain't much of a livin' / (interview).

RICHIE SAMBORA

(solo with **BRYAN** + **TORRES** + **TONY LEVIN** – bass)

Mercury Mercury

Aug 91. (7") **BALLAD OF YOUTH. / REST IN PEACE** [ ] [63]
(12"+=)(cd-s+=) – The wind cries Mary.

Sep 91. (cd)(c)(lp) **STRANGER IN THIS TOWN** [20] [36]
– Rest in peace / Church of desire / Stranger in this town / Ballad of youth / One light burning / Mr.Bluesman / Rosie / River of love / Father time / The answer. *(re-iss.cd/c Apr95)*

BON JOVI

were back for '92.

Mercury Jambco

Oct 92. (7")(c-s) **KEEP THE FAITH. / I WISH EVERYDAY COULD BE CHRISTMAS** [5] [29]
(cd-s+=) – Living in sin.
(cd-s+=) – Little bit of soul.

Nov 92. (cd)(c)(lp) **KEEP THE FAITH** [1] [5] Oct 92
– I believe / Keep the faith / I'll sleep when I'm dead / In these arms / Bed of roses / If I was your mother / Dry country / Woman in love / Fear / I want you / Blame it on the love of rock'n'roll / Little bit of soul.

Jan 93. (7")(c-s) **BED OF ROSES. / STARTING ALL OVER AGAIN** [13] [10]
(12"+=) – Lay your hands on me (live).
(cd-s) – Lay your hands on me (live) / I'll be there for you (live) / Tokyo road (live).

May 93. (7")(c-s) **IN THESE ARMS. / BED OF ROSES (acoustic)** [9] [27]
(cd-s) – ('A'side) / Keep the faith (live) / In these arms (live).
(c-s) – ('A'side) / Blaze of glory (acoustic).

Jul 93. (7")(c-s) **I'LL SLEEP WHEN I'M DEAD. / NEVER SAY GOODBYE (live acoustic)** [17] [97]
(cd-s) – ('A'side) / Blaze of glory / Wild in the streets (both live).
(cd-ep) 'HITS LIVE EP' ('A'side) / Blaze of glory / You give love a bad name / Bad medicine.

Sep 93. (7")(c-s) **I BELIEVE (Clearmountain mix). / ('A'live)** [11] [ ]
(cd-s) – ('A'side) / Runaway (live) / Livin' on the prayer (live) / Wanted dead or alive ('HITS LIVE PART 2 EP').
(cd-s) – ('A'side) / You give love a bad name (live) / Born to be my baby (live) / I'll sleep when I'm dead (live).

Mar 94. (7")(c-s) **DRY COUNTY. / STRANGER IN THIS TOWN (live)** [9] [ ]
(cd-s+=) – Blood money (live).
(cd-s) – ('A'side) / It's only rock'n'roll / Waltzing Matilda (all live).

Sep 94. (c-s) **ALWAYS. / THE BOYS ARE BACK IN TOWN** [2] [4]
(12"colrd) – ('A'side) / Prayer '94.
(cd-s) – ('A'side) / ('A'mix) / Edge of a broken heart.

Oct 94. (cd)(c)(lp) **CROSS ROAD – THE BEST OF BON JOVI** (compilation) [1] [8]
– Livin' on a prayer / Keep the faith / Someday I'll be Saturday night / Always / Wanted dead or alive / Lay your hands on me / You give love a bad name / Bed of roses / Blaze of glory / In these arms / Bad medicine / I'll be there for you / In and out of love / Runaway / Never say goodbye.

Dec 94. (7"pic-d)(c-s) **PLEASE COME HOME FOR CHRISTMAS / BACK DOOR SANTA** [7] [ ]
(cd-s+=) – I wish every day could be like Christmas.

Feb 95. (7"pic-d)(c-s) **SOMEDAY I'LL BE SATURDAY NIGHT. / GOOD GUYS DON'T ALWAYS WEAR WHITE (live)** [7] [ ]
(cd-s+=) – Always (live) / With a little help from my friends (live).
(cd-s+=) – ('A'mixes).

May 95. (c-s) **THIS AIN'T A LOVE SONG. / LONELY AT THE TOP** [6] [14]
(cd-s+=) – The end.
(cd-s) – ('A'side) / When she comes / Wedding day / Prostitute.

Jun 95. (cd)(c)(d-lp) **(THESE DAYS)** [1] [9]
– Hey God / Something for the pain / This ain't a love song / These days / Lie to me / Damned / My guitar lies bleeding in my arms / (It's hard) Letting you go / Hearts breaking even / Something to believe in / If that's what it takes / Diamond ring / All I want is everything / Bitter wine.

Sep 95. (c-s) **SOMETHING FOR THE PAIN / THIS AIN'T A LOVE SONG** [8] [76]
(cd-s+=) – I don't like Mondays.
(cd-s) – ('A'side) / Living on a prayer / You give love a bad name / Wild in the streets.

Nov 95. (c-s) **LIE TO ME / SOMETHING FOR THE PAIN (live)** [10] [ ]
(cd-s+=) – Always (live) / Keep the faith (live).
(cd-s) – ('A'side) / Something for the pain / Hey God (live) / I'll sleep when I'm dead (live).

BONZO DOG (DOO-DAH) BAND

Formed: London, England . . . 1965 by art students SLATER and SPEAR. After period on underground cabaret circuit, they signed to 'Parlophone' in 1966. By 1967 they released debut album GORILLA on 'Liberty' and performed on BEATLES' film 'MAGICAL MYSTERY TOUR'. Early 1968 they were seen every week on TV satire show 'Do Not Adjust Your Set'. By the end of the year, they were at No.5 with the surprise novelty hit 'I'M THE URBAN SPACEMAN'. • **Style:** Comic 1920's 'Dada' inspired outfit, with large extent of work filled with rib-tickling humour. • **Songwriters:** INNES and STANSHALL took most of credit to reproduce their blend of nostalgia. Covered ALLEY OOP (Hollywood Argyles) / Monster Mash (Bobby Pickett . . .) / etc. STANSHALL solo:- SUSPICION (Elvis Presley) / YOUNG ONES (Cliff Richard). • **Trivia:** PAUL McCARTNEY as APOLLO C.VERMOUTH produced hit 45.

Recommended: THE BEAST OF THE BONZO DOG BAND (*6) / SIR HENRY AT RAWLINSON'S END (*9)

VIVIAN STANSHALL (b.21 Mar'43, Shillingford, England) – vocals, trumpet / **NEIL INNES** (b. 9 Dec'44, Essex, England) – piano, vocals, guitar / **'LEGS' LARRY SMITH** (b.18 Jan'44, Oxford, England) – drums / **RODNEY SLATER** (b. 8 Nov'44, Lincolnshire, England) – horns / **ROGER RUSKIN SPEAR** (b.29 Jun'43, London) – tenor sax, kazoo, objects / **VERNON DUDLEY BOHAY-NOWELL** – bass, banjo, guitar / **SAM SPOONS** (b. MARTIN STAFFORD) – percussion

Stateside not issued

Apr 66. (7") **MY BROTHER MAKES THE NOISES FOR THE TALKIES. / I'M GONNA BRING A WATERMELON TO MY GAL TONIGHT** [ ] [–]

Sep 66. (7") **ALLEY OOP. / BUTTON UP YOUR RAINCOAT** [ ] [-]
Liberty Liberty
Oct 67. (lp) **GORILLA** [ ] [ ]
– Cool Britannia / Equestrian statue / Jollity farm / I left my heart in San Francisco / Look out, there's a monster coming / Jazz, delicious hot, disgusting cold / Death cab for Cutie / Narcissus / The intro and the outro / Mickey's son and daughter / Big shot / Music for head ballet / Piggy bank love / I'm bored / The sound of music. *(re-iss.Nov70 on 'Sunset') (re-iss.Aug80 on 'United Artists') (cd-iss.Jul95 on 'BGO')*
Nov 67. (7") **EQUESTRIAN STATUE. / THE INTRO AND THE OUTRO** [ ] [ ]

— **DENNIS COWAN** (b. 6 Mar'47, London) – bass repl. BOHAY-NOWELL Also SPOONS departed. For a short while BOB KERR "the nearly unknown" played sax.

Oct 68. (7") **I'M THE URBAN SPACEMAN. / THE CANYONS OF YOUR MIND** [5] [ ]

BONZO DOG BAND

Nov 68. (lp)**THE DOUGHNUT IN GRANNY'S GREENHOUSE** [40] [ ]
– We are normal / Postcard / Beautiful Zelda / Can blue men sing the whites / Hello Mabel / Kama Sutra / Humanoid boogie / The trouser press / My pink half of the drainpipe / Rockaliser baby / Rhinocratic oaths / Eleven mustachioed daughters. *(re-iss.Mar71 on 'Sunset') (re-iss.Mar87 on 'Edsel')*
Jul 69. (7") **MR. APOLLO. / READY MADES** [ ] [ ]
Aug 69. (lp) **TADPOLES** [36] [ ]
– Hunting tigers out in 'Indiah' / Shirt / Tubas in the moonlight / Dr. Jazz / Monster mash / I'm the urban spaceman / Ali Baba's camel / Laughing blues / By a waterfall / Mr.Apollo / Canyons of your mind. *(re-iss.Sep73 on 'Sunset', new title 'URBAN SPACEMAN')*
Nov 69. (7") **I WANT TO BE WITH YOU. / WE WERE WRONG** [ ] [ ]
Nov 69. (lp) **KEYNSHAM** [ ] [ ]
– You done my brain in / Keynsham / Quiet talks and summer walks / Tent / We were wrong / Joke shop man / The bride stripped bare by "The Bachelors" / Look at me, I'm wonderful / What do you do? / Mr. Slater's parrot / Sport (the odd boy) / I want to be with you / Noises for the leg / "Busted". *(re-iss.Nov75 on 'Sunset', re-iss.Dec80 on 'United Artists') (re-iss.Se87 on 'Edsel')*
Feb 70. (7") **YOU DONE MY BRAIN IN. / MR. SLATER'S PARROT** [ ] [ ]

— Split early 1970 with each member doing own disastrous projects. **STANSHALL, INNES, SMITH, RUSKIN-SPEAR and COWAN** re-formed late '71. Also using session people **HUGHIE FLINT** – drums / **BUBS WHITE** – guitar / **ANDY ROBERTS** – guitar / **DAVE RICHARDS** – bass / **DICK PARRY** – woodwind

United Art United Art
Mar 72. (lp)(c) **LET'S MAKE UP AND BE FRIENDLY** [ ] [ ]
– The strain / Turkeys / King of scurf / Waiting for the wardrobe / Straight from my heart / Rusty / Rawlinson End / Don't get me wrong / Fresh wound / Slush / Bad blood. *(re-iss.May78 on 'Sunsel') (re-iss.Jul86 & Apr87 on 'Awareness')*

– compilations, exploitation releases etc. –

Aug 70. Liberty; (lp) **THE BEAST OF THE BONZOS** [ ] [ ]
Oct 73. Liberty; (7") **THE INTRO AND THE OUTRO. / HELLO MABEL** [ ] [-]
Mar 74. Liberty; (7") **MR. SLATER'S PARROT. / NOISES FOR THE LEG** [ ] [ ]
Apr 74. Liberty; (d-lp)(c) **THE HISTORY OF THE BONZOS** [42] [ ]
May 78. Liberty; (7"m) **I'M THE URBAN SPACEMAN. / THE INTRO AND THE OUTRO / STRAIN** [ ] [ ]
Jul 84. E.M.I.; (7") **I'M THE URBAN SPACEMAN. / THE INTRO AND THE OUTRO** [ ] [-]
Apr 90. E.M.I.; (cd)(c) **THE BEASTIALITY OF THE BONZOS** [ ] [-]
– The intro and the outro / Canyons of your mind / Trouser press / Postcard / Mickey's son and daughter / Sport (the odd boy) / Tent / I'm the urban spaceman / Mr.Apollo / Shirt / Bad blood / Ready mades / Rhinocratic oaths / Can blue men sing the whites / Mr.Slater's parrot / The strain / We are normal / My pink half of the drainpipe / Jazz, delicious hot, disgusting cold / Big shot / Jollity farm / Humanoid boogie.
Aug 92. E.M.I.; (3xcd-box) **CORNOLOGY** [ ] [-]
Apr 92. China; (7") **NO MATTER WHO YOU VOTE FOR, THE GOVERNMENT ALWAYS GETS IN. / ?** [ ] [-]
Oct 84. M.F.P.; (lp)(c) **THE VERY BEST OF THE BONZO DOG DOO-DAH BAND** [ ] [-]
Jul 88. Strange Fruit; (12"ep) **THE PEEL SESSIONS (29.7.69)** [ ] [-]
– We're going to bring it on home / Sofa Head / Tent / Monster mash.
Jul 91. Rhino; (cd) **THE BEST OF THE BONZOS** [ ] [ ]
Jun 95. Strange Fruit; (cd) **UNPEELED** [ ] [-]

— NEIL INNES joined GRIMMS before going solo. He joined MONTY PYTHON team (part-time) before actually appearing in their films. He also created the Beatles spoof The RUTLES. He went on to host an under-5 children's TV show. LARRY SMITH went on tour with ELTON JOHN and ERIC CLAPTON. RUSKIN-SPEAR formed his KINETIC WARDROBE. SLATER had become a government officer. STANSHALL guest narrating on MIKE OLDFILED's "Tubular Bells" album,

VIVIAN STANSHALL

solo using session people

Liberty not issued
Feb 70 (7") **LABIO-DENTAL FRICATIVE. / PAPER ROUND (with SKIN HEAD SHOW BAND featuring ERIC CLAPTON)** [ ] [-]
Fly not issued
1970. (7"ep) **SUSPICION / BLIND DATE. / BIG GRUNT / GARGANTUAN CHUMS** [ ] [-]
Warners Warners
1974. (7") **LAKANGA. / BABA TUNDE** [ ] [ ]
1974. (lp) **MEN OPENING UMBRELLAS AHEAD** [ ] [ ]
– Afoju ti ole rirtan / Truck-track / Yelp, below, rasp et cetera / Prong / Redeye / How the zebra got his spots / Dwarf succulents / Bout of sobriety / Prong and Toots go steady / Strange tongues.

Harvest not issued
Nov 76. (7") **YOUNG ONES. / ARE YOU HAVIN' ANY FUN / QUESTION** [ ] [-]
Charisma Charisma
1978. (lp)(c) **SIR HENRY AT RAWLINSON END** [ ] [ ]
– Aunt Florrie's waltz / Interlewd / Wheelbarrow / Nice'n'tidy / Socks / The rub / Pigs 'ere purse / 6/8 hoodoo / Smeeton / Fool and bladder / Endroar / Jungle bunny / The beasht inshide / Rawlinsons & Maynards / Papadumb. *(cd-iss Jul91 & May95 on 'Virgin')*

(This comic concept was later made into feature film in which VIV appeared alongside TREVOR HOWARD as Sir Henry)

Jun 81. (lp)(c) **TEDDY BOYS DON'T KNIT** [ ] [ ]
– King Kripple / Slave Valse / Calypso to colapso / The tube / Biwilderbeeste / Ginger geezer / The cracks are showing / Flung a dummy / Possibly an armchair (and embodying) / Gums / Fresh faced boys / Terry keeps his clips on / Bass Macaw and broken bottles / Nose hymn / Everyday I have the blows / Smoke signals at night / Nouveau riffe. *(cd-iss.Jul91 on 'Virgin') (cd-iss.Mar94 on 'Virgin')*
Jun 81. (7") **TERRY KEEPS HIS CLIPS ON. / CALYPSO TO COLAPSO** [ ] [ ]

— next with **SEAN OLIVER** – bass / **BRUCE SMITH** – drums (both ex-POP GROUP, etc)

Demon not issued
Dec 84. (lp) **SIR HENRY AT NDIDI'S KRAAL** [ ] [ ]
– (further adventures of Sir Henry, this time in deepest Africa (in spoken word)) *(cd-iss.Jul92)*

— VIVIAN STANSHALL died in a fire in his London home mid 1995.

BOOKER T. & THE M.G.'S

Formed: Memphis, Tennessee, USA ... 1962 when 'Stax' in-house musicians recorded 2 tracks for label owner Jim Stewart. He released this on own label and after being flipped over, 'GREEN ONIONS' became Top 3 hit. All members were also part of MAR-KEYS backing band in the early 60's. They continued to sparkle for the rest of the 60's, with GREEN ONIONS becoming a mod classic. • **Style:** Instrumental bluesy dance combo, that helped give rise to 'Mod' phenomenon in the mid '60's. • **Songwriters:** BOOKER T, except GROOVIN' (Young Rascals) / McLENMORE AVENUE (Beatles: Abbey Road lp) / FOXY LADY (Jimi Hendrix) / THE HORSE (Jesse James) / LOVE CHILD (Richards-Sawyer-Taylor-Wilson) / SING A SIMPLE SONG (Pepper-Watt) / LADY MADONNA + MICHELLE (Beatles) / MRS.ROBINSON (Simon & Garfunkel) / THIS GUY'S IN LOVE WITH YOU (Bacharach-David) / LIGHT MY FIRE (Doors) / YOU'RE ALL I NEED TO GET BY (Ashford-Simpson) / IT'S YOUR THING (Isley Brothers) / and loads more. • **Trivia:** The MG's stood for MEMPHIS GROUP. Caribbean influenced SOUL LIMBO was/is used for theme tune to BBC TV's cricket coverage.

Recommended: GREATEST HITS (*7)

BOOKER T.JONES (b.12 Nov'44) – keyboards, multi (ex-MAR-KEYS) / **STEVE CROPPER** (b.21 Oct'41, Willow Springs, Missouri) – guitar (ex-MAR-KEYS) / **LEWIS STEINBERG** – bass / **AL JACKSON Jr.** (b.27 Nov'35) – drums (ex-ROY MILTON BAND)

not issued Volt
May 62. (7") **BEHAVE YOURSELF. / GREEN ONIONS** [-] [ ]
London Stax
Sep 62. (7") **GREEN ONIONS. / BEHAVE YOURSELF** [ ] [3] Jul62
(above 'A' side took 17 years and 'Atlantic' records to make hit UK Top 10)
Nov 62. (lp) **GREEN ONIONS** [ ] [33]
– Green onions / Rinky-dink / I got a woman / Mo' onions / Twist and shout / Behave yourself / Stranger on the shore / Lonely avenue / One who really loves you / You can't sit down / A woman, a lover, a friend / Comin' home baby. *(UK-re-iss Jul64 hit No.11. (UK re-iss.Feb80 on 'Atlantic')(cd-iss.Jul91 on 'Atco') (re-iss.cd Dec94) (re-iss.cd May93 on 'Atlantic') (re-iss.cd Sep95 on 'Warners')*
Feb 63. (7") **JELLY BREAD. / AW' MERCY** [ ] [82] Dec 62
May 63. (7") **HOME GROWN. / BIG TRAIN** [-] [ ]
Oct 63. (7") **CHINESE CHECKERS. / PLUM NELLIE** [ ] [78] Jul 63
Dec 63. (7") **MO' ONIONS. / TIC TAC TOE (or) FANNIE MAE** [-] [97]

— **DONALD 'DUCK' DUNN** (b.24 Nov'41) – bass (ex-MAR-KEYS) repl. LEWIS

Feb 64. (7") **SOUL DRESSING. / M.G. PARTY** [-] [95]
Mar 64. (lp)**SOUL DRESSING** [-] [ ]
– Soul dressing / Tic-tac-toe / Big train / Jelly bread / Aw' mercy / Outrage / Night owl walk / Chinese checkers / Home grown / Mercy, mercy / Plum Nellie / Can't be still. *(cd-iss.May93 on 'Atlantic') (cd-iss.Feb95 & Sep95 on 'Warners')*
Atlantic Stax
May 64. (7") **CAN'T BE STILL. / TERRIBLE THING** [-] [ ]
Jun 65. (7") **BOOT-LEG. / OUTRAGE** [ ] [58]
Jan 66. (7") **BE MY LADY. / RED BEANS & RICE** [-] [ ]
Jun 66. (lp) **AND NOW** [-] [ ]
– My sweet potato / Jericho / No matter what shape / One mint julep / In the midnight hour / Summertime / Working in the coal mine / Don't mess up a good thing / Think / Taboo / Soul jam / Sentimental journey. *(cd-iss.Jul92 and Aug 93 on 'Rhino')*
Oct 66. (7") **MY SWEET POTATO. / BOOKER LOO** [ ] [85] Aug 66
Dec 66. (7") **JINGLE BELLS. / WINTER WONDERLAND** [ ] [ ]
Dec 66. (lp) **IN THE CHRISTMAS SPIRIT** [ ] [ ]
– (festive recordings) *(cd-iss.Aug93 on 'Rhino') (re-iss.cd Dec95 on 'Warners')*
Apr 67. (7") **HIP HUG-HER. / SUMMERTIME** [ ] [37]
Jul 67. (lp) **HIP HUG-HER** [ ] [35] Jun 67
– Hip hug-her / Soul sanction / Get ready / More / Double or nothing / Carnaby St. / Slim Jenkins' joint / Pigmy / Groovin' / Booker's motive / Sunny. *(cd-iss.Aug93 on 'Rhino')*
Sep 67. (7") **GROOVIN'. / SLIM JENKINS' PLACE** [ ] [21] Aug 67
[70]
May 68. (lp) **DOIN' OUR THING** [-] [ ]
– I can dig it / Expressway (to your heart) / Doin' our thing / You don't love me / Never my love / The exodus song / The beat goes on / Ode to Billy Joe / Blue on

green / You keep me hanging on / Let's go get stoned. *(cd-iss.Aug93 on 'Rhino')*
Dec 67 (7") **SILVER BELLS. / WINTER SNOW** - -
Oct 68. (7") **SOUL-LIMBO. / HEADS OR TAILS** 30 17 Jul68
Oct 68. (lp) **SOUL-LIMBO**
– Be young, be foolish, be happy / La la means I love you / Hang 'em high / Willow weep for me / Over easy / Soul limbo / Eleanor Rigby / Heads or tails / (Sweet, sweet baby) Since you've been gone / Born under a bad sign / Foxy lady. *(re-iss.Feb88, cd-iss.1990)*
Nov 68. (7") **HANG 'EM HIGH. / OVER EASY** - 9
(re-iss. 1975 + Sep'87)
Mar 69. (7") **TIME IS TIGHT. / JOHNNY I LOVE YOU** - 6
Apr 69. (7") **TIME IS TIGHT. / HANG 'EM HIGH** 4 -
Apr 69. (lp) **UPTIGHT (Soundtrack)** 98 Feb 69
– Johnny, I love you / Cleveland now / Children, don't get weary / Tank's lament / Blues in the gutter / We've got Johnny Wells / Down at Ralph's joint / Deadwood Dick / Run tank run / Time is tight. *(re-iss.+cd.Jan90)*
Jul 69. (7") **MRS. ROBINSON. / SOUL CLAP '69** 35 37 Jun 69
Jul 69. (lp) **THE BOOKER T. SET** 53 Jun 69
– The horse / Love child / Sing a simple song / Lady Madonna / Mrs.Robinson / This guy's in love with you / Light my fire / Michelle / You're all I need to get by / I've never found a girl (to love me like you do) / It's your thing. *(re-iss.Dec86) (re-iss.+cd.May90) (US cd-iss.Dec86 on 'Stax-Fantasy')*
Sep 69. (7") **SLUM BABY. / MEDITATION** - 88
Nov 69. (7") **THE HORSE. / SLUM BABY**
May 70. (lp) **McLENMORE AVENUE** 70 Apr 70
– Golden slumbers – Carry that weight – The end – Here comes the Sun – Come together / Something / Because – You never give me your money / Sun king – Mean Mr. Mustard – Polythene Pam – She came in through the bathroom window – I want you – She's so heavy. *(re-iss.+cd.Dec88)*
Jul 70. (7") **SOMETHING. / SUNDAY SERMON** - 76
Sep 70. (7") **SOMETHING. / DOWN AT RALPH'S JOINT** -
Mar 71. (lp) **MELTING POT** 43 Feb 71
– Melting pot / Back home / Chicken pox / Fuquawi / Kinda easy like / Hi ride / L.A. jazz song / Sunny Monday.
– *(re-iss.Jun76) (cd-iss.Dec92 on 'Ace-Stax')*
Jun 71. (7") **MELTING POT. / KINDA EASY LIKE** 45 Mar 71
Sep 71. (7") **FUQUAWI. / JAMAICA THIS MORNING** -

—— May71, disbanded. JONES went solo and married singer PRISCILLA COOLIDGE (sister of RITA). He issued 3 albums with her **'BOOKER T. & PRISCILLA' / 'HOME GROWN' + 'CHRONICLES'** (for 'A&M'), plus **'EVERGREEN'** (for 'Epic' Feb75). CROPPER became workaholic session man and producer. **DUNN** and **JACKSON** continued as

The MG'S

with newcomers **BOBBY MANUEL** – guitar / **CARSON WHITSETT** – keyboards
Stax Stax
1972. (lp) **THE MG'S**

—— On the 1st October 1975, AL JACKSON was shot dead by a burglar.
1972. (7") **SUGARCANE. / BLACKRIDE** -
1973. (7") **BREEZY. / NECKBONE** -

BOOKER T. & THE MG'S

re-united (**BOOKER T., CROPPER and DUNN**) brought in **WILLIE HALL** – drums
Asylum Asylum
Mar 77. (lp)(c) **UNIVERSAL LANGUAGE**
– Sticky stuff / Grab bag / Space nuts / Love wheels / Motor cross / Last tango in Memphis / MG's salsa / Tie stick / Reincarnation.
Mar 77. (7") **STICKY STUFF. / TIE STICK** -
Jun 77. (7") **GRAB BAG. / REINCARNATION** -

—— Broke-up, again. CROPPER and DUNN were in backing band that featured in the film 'The BLUES BROTHERS' in 1980. They continued to work on session/production.
Columbia Columbia
Jun 94. (cd)(c) **THAT'S THE WAY IT SHOULD BE**
– Slip slidin' / Mo' greens / Gotta serve somebody / Let's wait awhile / That's the way it should be / Just my imagination (running away with me) / Camel ride / Have a heart / Cruisin' / I can't stand the rain / Sarasota sunset / I still haven't found what I'm looking for.

BOOKER T.

went solo, releasing 3 albums for 'A&M'; **TRY AND LOVE AGAIN**(Nov78),**THE BEST OF YOU** (Feb80), and **I WANT YOU** (1981). Also issued one single below.
Feb 79. (7") **LET'S GO DANCING. / KNOCKIN' ON HEAVEN'S DOOR**

– (band) compilations, others, etc. –

Aug 67. Stax; (lp) **BACK TO BACK (with MAR-KEYS)**
(re-iss.+cd.Jul91)
Nov 68. Stax; (lp) **THE BEST OF BOOKER T. & THE MG'S**
(re-iss.Jul84 on 'Atlantic') (cd-iss.Apr87 on 'London') (re-iss.+cd.May92 on 'Stax') (re-iss.cd May93 on 'Atlantic')
Nov 70. Stax; (lp)(c) **GREATEST HITS** *(re-iss.Aug74)*
1977 Stax; (7") **SHAFT. /?** -
Nov 74. Stax; (7") **TIME IS TIGHT. / SOUL LIMBO**
(re-iss.Nov77 & Mar82) (re-iss.Sep85 on 'Old Gold')
1974. Stax; (7"m) **TIME IS TIGHT. / BRING IT HOME TO ME / MY BABY SPECIALISES**
1975. Stax; (lp) **MEMPHIS SOUP**
Jul 75. Stax; (lp)(c) **BOOKER T. & THE MG'S**
(re-iss.May81)
Jan 76. Stax; (lp)(c) **UNION EXTENDED** (rare tracks)
Jul 76. Stax; (7") **SOUL LIMBO. / MRS. ROBINSON**
1977. Stax; (7") **SOUL LIMBO. / SOUL CLAP '69**
(re-iss.Aug82) (re-iss.Aug87 +7"pic-d)
May 80. Stax; (lp)(c) **TIME IS TIGHT**
Mar 67. Atlantic; (7") **GREEN ONIONS. / BOOTLEG** Jun 66
(re-iss.Jun72 + 74) (UK re-iss.Dec79-7" hit No.7, re-12"-Apr80)
Mar 80. Atlantic; (7") **HIP HUG HER. / SLIM JENKINS' PLACE**
Aug 87. Atlantic; (7")(12") **SOUL LIMBO. / HEADS OR TAILS**
1973. Warners; (d-lp) **STAR COLLECTION**
(re-iss.Jul78)
Jan 85. Old Gold; (7") **GREEN ONIONS. / CHINESE CHECKERS**
(re-iss.Jan86 on 'Atlantic')
Dec 77. Pye; (12"ep) **TIME IS TIGHT. / (3 other artists)** -

BOOMTOWN RATS

Formed: Don Laoghaire (near Dublin), Ireland . . . 1975 by ex-New Musical Express journalist BOB GELDOF and others (see below). Moved to England late 1976 and signed to newly formed 'Ensign' records. Numerous chart hits followed, with them peaking in 1979 with UK No.1 'I DON'T LIKE MONDAYS'. They had earlier been the first punks to hit No.1 with 'RAT TRAP'. • **Style:** Initially a new wave/punk outfit fused between EDDIE & THE HOT-RODS and The ROLLING STONES, due to GELDOF's energetic stage aura. They mellowed quickly into pop/rock field, hense their slow demise. • **Songwriters:** Most written by GELDOF except; BAREFOOTIN' (Robert Parker). GELDOF covered SUNNY AFTERNOON (Kinks). • **Trivia:** I DON'T LIKE MONDAYS was written about schoolgirl Brenda Spencer, who snipered/shot dead several of her school collegues. GELDOF starred in the feature films THE WALL (1982) & NUMBER ONE (1984). Late in 1984, BOB and MIDGE URE (of ULTRAVOX) masterminded BAND AID. They assembled together all the major stars of the time to sing DO THEY KNOW IT'S CHRISTMAS. It was top selling 45 making millions of pounds for famine relief in Ethiopia. Not content with this BOB and MIDGE assembled most of them again at Wembley Stadium for the LIVE AID concert on 13th July 85. This was simultaneously broadcast over the Atlantic at JFK Stadium, Philadephia. At the time it amassed well over £10m, and was spread around other needy charities as well as Ethiopia. The charity ended at the end of 1991 making over £100m. Already in June 1986, BOB was now Sir BOB GELDOF as he was knighted by the Queen. Two months later he married long-time fiancee PAULA YATES (a TV presenter and writer) who had had their child FIFI TRIXIBELLE and was soon in 1989 to give birth to another daughter PEACHES. They are now jointly responsible for 1992 Channel 4's 'Big Breakfast Show'. BOB had continued to work with BAND AID until the late '80s, while continuing less strenuous solo career.

Recommended: THE BOOMTOWN RATS (*6) / TONIC FOR THE TROOPS (*5) / LOUDMOUTH – THE BEST OF THE BOOMTOWN RATS AND BOB GELDOF (*8).

BOB GELDOF (b. 5 Oct'54, Dublin) – vocals / **JOHNNIE FINGERS** (b.JOHNNY MOYLETT) – keyboards, vocals / **GERRY COTT** – guitar / **PETE BRIQUETTE** (b.PATRICK CUSACK) – bass / **GERRY ROBERTS** – guitar, vocals / **SIMON CROWE** – drums, vocals
Ensign Mercury
Aug 77. (7"m)(12"m) **LOOKIN' AFTER No.1. / BORN TO BURN / BAREFOOTIN' (live)** 11 -
Sep 77. (lp)(c) **THE BOOMTOWN RATS** 18
– Lookin' after No.1 / Neon heart / Joey's on the street again / Never bite the hand that feeds / Mary of the 4th form / (She gonna) Do you in / Close as you'll ever be / I can make it if you can / Kicks. *(re-iss.Dec83 on 'Mercury')*
Nov 77. (7") **MARY OF THE 4th FORM. / DO THE RAT** 15 -
Ensign Columbia
Mar 78. (7") **SHE'S SO MODERN. / LYING AGAIN** 12
Jun 78. (7") **LIKE CLOCKWORK. / HOW DO YOU DO?** 6
Jul 78. (lp)(c) **A TONIC FOR THE TROOPS** 8
– Like clockwork / Blind date / (I never loved) Eva Braun / Living in an island / Don't believe what you read / She's so modern / Me and Howard Hughes / Can't stop * / (Watch out for) The normal people / Rat trap. *(US version repl.* w/ Joey) (UK re-iss.Dec83 on 'Mercury')*
Oct 78. (7") **RAT TRAP. / SO STRANGE** 1 -
(re-iss.Nov84 on 'Mercury')
Nov 78. (7") **RAT TRAP. / DO THE RAT** -
Jul 79. (7") **I DON'T LIKE MONDAYS. / IT'S ALL THE RAGE** 1 73 Jan 80
(re-iss.Nov84 on 'Mercury')
Oct 79. (lp)(c) **THE FINE ART OF SURFACING** 7
– Someone's looking at you / Diamond smiles / Wind chill factor (minus zero) / Having my picture taken / Sleep (Fingers' lullaby) / I don't like Mondays / Nothing happened today / Keep it up / Nice'n'neat / When the night comes. *(re-iss.Nov84 on 'Mercury')*
Nov 79. (7") **DIAMOND SMILES. / LATE LATE NIGHT** 13
Jan 80. (7")(12") **SOMEONE'S LOOKING AT YOU. / WHEN THE NIGHT COMES** 4
Feb 80. (7") **SOMEONE'S LOOKING AT YOU. / I DON'T LIKE MONDAYS (live)** -
Mercury Columbia
Nov 80. (7") **BANANA REPUBLIC. / MAN AT THE TOP** 3
Dec 80. (lp)(c) **MONDO BONGO** 6
– Please don't go / The elephant's graveyard (guilty) / Banana republic / Fall down / Hurt hurts / Whitehall 1212 * / Mood mambo / Straight up / This is my room / Another piece of red / Under their thumb . . .is under my thumb / Go man go. (US version repl.* w/ Don't talk to me)
Jan 81. (7") **THE ELEPHANT'S GRAVEYARD (GUILTY). / REAL DIFFERENT** 26

—— (Mar81) Trimmed to a quintet when GERRY COTT left to going solo.
Nov 81. (7") **UP ALL NIGHT. / ANOTHER PIECE OF RED** -
Nov 81. (7") **NEVER IN A MILLION YEARS. / DON'T TALK TO ME** 62

Mar 82. (7")(12") **HOUSE ON FIRE. / EUROPE LOOKED UGLY** 24
Mar 82. (lp)(c) **V DEEP** 64
– Never in a million years / The bitter end / Talking in code / He watches it all / A storm breaks / Charmed lives / House on fire / Up all night / Skin on skin / Little death.
Jun 82. (7") **CHARMED LIVES. / NO HIDING PLACE**
(d7"+=) – Nothing happened today (live) / A storm breaks (instrumental).
(12") – ('A'side) / A storm breaks.
Aug 82. (7") **CHARMED LIVES. / NEVER IN A MILLION YEARS** -
Jan 84. (7") **TONIGHT. / PRECIOUS TIME** 73
(12"+=) – Walking downtown.
May 84. (7") **DRAG ME DOWN. / AN ICICLE IN THE SUN** 50
(12"+=) – Rat trap / She's so modern.
Nov 84. (7")(7"pic-d) **DAVE. / HARD TIMES**
(d7"+=) – I don't like Mondays / It's all the rage.
(12"+=) – Banana republic (live) / Close as you'll ever be (live).
Dec 84. (lp)(c) **IN THE LONG GRASS**
– A hold of me / Drag me down / Dave / Over again / Another sad story / Tonight / Hard times / Lucky / Icicle in the Sun / Up or down.
Feb 85. (7") **A HOLD OF ME. / NEVER IN A MILLION YEARS**
(12"+=) – Say hi to Mick.
May 85. (7") **ICICLE IN THE SUN. / RAIN** -

— Had already split Nov'84. FINGERS and CROWE formed GUNG HO. BOB GELDOF, as I've said, pieced together BAND/LIVE AID before going solo. (see above/below)

– compilations, others, etc. –

Dec 83. Mercury; (7"box 6) **RAT PACK (6 best of singles pack)** -
Jan 88. Old Gold; (7") **I DON'T LIKE MONDAYS. / RAT TRAP** -

BOB GELDOF

solo, with guests **DAVE STEWART, ERIC CLAPTON**, etc.

Mercury Atlantic

Oct 86. (7")(12") **THIS IS THE WORLD CALLING. / TALK ME UP** 25 82
Nov 86. (lp)(c)(cd) **DEEP IN THE HEART OF NOWHERE** 79
– Love you like a rocket / In the pouring rain / This heartless night / Words from Heaven / Deep in the heart of nowhere / Night turns to day / I cry too / The beat of the night / When I was young / This is the world calling / August was a heavy month. (cd+=) – Pulled apart by horses / Good boys in the wrong / Truly true blue.
Jan 87. (7") **LOVE YOU LIKE A ROCKET. / THIS IS THE WORLD CALLING** 61
(12"+=) – ('A'extended).
(cd-s+=) – Pulled apart by horses / Truly true blue.
Mar 87. (7") **LOVE YOU LIKE A ROCKET. / PULLED APART BY HORSES** -
Jun 87. (7") **THE HEARTLESS NIGHT. / PULLED APART BY HORSES** -
Jun 87. (7") **I CRY TOO. / LET'S GO**
(12"+=) – Night turns to day / Deep in the heart of nowhere.

— He was now augmented by his **VEGETARIANS OF LOVE** backing band **GEOFF RICHARDSON** – viola, clarinet, etc. / **BOB LOVEDAY** – violin, bass, penny whistle / **PETE BRIQUETTE** – bass, keyboards / **PHIL PALMER** – guitars / **STEVE FLETCHER** – keyboard ALUN DUNN – accordion, organ / **RUPERT HINE** – keyboards, percussion, producer,

Jun 90. (7")(c-s) **THE GREAT SONG OF INDIFFERENCE. / HOTEL 75** 15
(12"+=)(cd-s+=) – In the pouring rain.
Jul 90. (cd)(c)(lp) **THE VEGETARIANS OF LOVE** 21
– A gospel song / Love or something / Thinking Voyager 2 type things / The great song of indifference / Crucified me / Big romance stuff / The chains of pain / A rose at night / Let it go / No small wonder / Walking back to happiness / The end of the world.
Aug 90. (7")(c-s) **LOVE OR SOMETHING. / OUT OF ORDER**
(12"+=) – The great song of indifference (mix) / Friends for life / One of these girls.
Nov 90. (7")(c-s) **A GOSPEL SONG. / VEGETARIANS OF LOVE**
(12"+=)(cd-s+=) – The warmest fire.

— now with The HAPPY CLUBSTERS (same as last)

Vertigo Mercury

Jun 92. (7")(c-s) **ROOM 19 (SHA LA LA LA LEE). / HUGE BIRDLESS SILENCE**
(cd-s+=) – The great song of indifference / Sweat for you (BRIQUETTE & SHARKEY CO.).
Sep 92. (7")(c-s) **MY HIPPY ANGEL. / MAYBE HEAVEN**
(cd-s+=) – Love or something / ('A'extended).
Oct 92. (cd)(c)(lp) **THE HAPPY CLUB**
– Room 19 (sha la la la lee) / Attitude chicken / The soft soil / A hole to fill / The song of the emergent nationalist / My hippy angel / The happy club / Like down on me / Too late God / Roads of Germany (after BD) / A sex thing / The house at the top of the world.
Apr 94. (7")(c-s) **CRAZY. / THE HAPPY CLUB** 65
(cd-s) – ('A'side) / Room 19 (sha la la la lee) (live) / The beat of the night (live) / Rat trap (live).
Note; below single by BOOMTOWN RATS (also compilation tracks *)
Jun 94. (7"colrd)(c-s) **I DON'T LIKE MONDAYS. / BORN TO BURN / DO THE RAT** 38
(cd-s) – ('A'side) / Looking after No.1 / Mary of the 4th form / She's so modern.
(cd-s) – ('A'side) / Rat trap / Someone's looking at you / Banana republic.
Jul 94. Vertigo; (cd)(c) **LOUDMOUTH – THE BEST OF THE BOOMTOWN RATS & BOB GELDOF** (compilation) 10
– I don't like Mondays * / This is the world calling / Rat trap * / The great song of indifference / Love or something / Banana republic * / Crazy / The elephant's graveyard (guilty) * / Someone's looking at you * / She's so modern * / House on fire * / The beat of the night / Diamond smiles * / Like clockwork * / Room 19 (sha la la la lee) / Mary of the 4th form * / Looking after No.1 *.

BOO RADLEYS

Formed: Liverpool, England . . . 1988, by SICE, etc (see below). Moved to 'Creation' late '91 and soon were favourites of the NME, etc, who praised the release of the masterful 'GIANT STEPS' album. • **Style:** Psychedelic and heavy BYRDS influenced outfit, full of flowing spicy jangly pop, fused with screeching guitars and brassic accompaniment. • **Songwriters:** CARR lyrics / group music, except TRUE FAITH (New Order) / ALONE AGAIN OR (Love) / ONE OF US MUST KNOW (Bob Dylan). • **Trivia:** MERIEL BARHAM of The PALE SAINTS provided vocals on 2 tracks for GIANT STEPS album.

Recommended: GIANT STEPS (*9) / EVERYTHING'S ALRIGHT FOREVER (*7) / WAKE UP! (*8)

SICE (b.18 Jun'69, Wallasey, Lancashire, England) – vocals, guitar / **MARTIN CARR** (b.29 Nov'68, Thurso, Highlands, Scotland) – guitar / **TIMOTHY BROWN** (b.26 Feb'69, Wallasey) – bass / **STEVE DREWITT** (b.Northwich, England) – drums

Action not issued

Jul 90. (lp) **ICHABOD AND I** -
– Eleanor everything / Bodenheim Jr. / Catweazle / Sweet salad birth / Hip clown rag / Walking 5th carnival / Kaleidoscope / Happens to us all.

— **ROBERT CIEKA** (b. 4 Aug'68, Birmingham, England) – drums repl. DREWITT to BREED

Rough Trade not issued

Oct 90. (12"ep)(cd-ep) **KALEIDOSCOPE** -
– Kaleidoscope / How I feel / Aldous / Swansong.
Apr 91. (12"ep)(cd-ep) **EVERY HEAVEN** -
– Finest kiss / Tortoise shell / Bluebird / Naomi.
Sep 91. (12"ep)(cd-ep) **BOO UP! (Peel sessions)**
– Sometime soon she said / Fosters van / Everybird / Song for up.

Creation Columbia

Feb 92. (12"ep)(cd-ep) **ADRENALIN**
– Lazy day / Vegas / Feels like tomorrow / Whiplashed.
Mar 92. (cd)(c)(lp) **EVERYTHING'S ALRIGHT FOREVER** 55
– Spaniard / Towards the light / Losing it (song for Abigail) / Memory babe / Skyscraper / I feel nothing / Room at the top / Does this hurt / Sparrow / Smile fades fast / Firesky / Song for the morning to sing / Lazy day / Paradise.
Jun 92. (7") **BOO! FOREVER / DOES THIS HURT** 67
(12"+=)(cd-s+=) – Buffalo Bill / Sunifly II: Walking with the kings.
Nov 92. (7") **LAZARUS. / LET ME BE YOUR FAITH**
(12"+=)(cd-s+=) – At the sound of speed / Petrolium.

— added **STEVE KITCHEN** – trumpet, flugel horn / **JACKIE ROY** – clarinet / **LINDSAY JOHNSTON** – cello

Jul 93. (7") **HANG SUSPENDED. / RODNEY KING (Saint Etienne mix)**
(12"+=)(cd-s+=) – As bound a stomorrow / I will always ask where you have been though I know the answer.
Jul 93. (cd)(c)(lp) **GIANT STEPS** 17
– Hang suspended / Upon 9th and Fairchild / Wish I was skinny / Leaves and sand / Butterfly McQueen / Rodney King (song for Lenny Bruce) / Thinking of ways / Barney (. . . and me) / Spun around / If you want it, take it / Best lose the fear / Take the time around / Lazarus / One is for / Run my way runway / I've lost the reason / The white noise revisited.
Oct 93. (7")(c-s) **WISH I WAS SKINNY / PEACH KEEN** 75
(12"+=)(cd-s+=) – Futhur / Crow eye
Feb 94. (7")(c-s) **BARNEY (. . .AND ME). / ZOOM** 48
(12"+=)(cd-s+=) – Tortoiseshell / Cracked lips, homesick.
May 94. (7")(c-s) **LAZARUS. / (I WANNA BE) TOUCHDOWN JESUS** 50
(cd-s+=) – ('A'acoustic) / ('A'-Saint Etienne mix) / ('A'-Secret Knowledge mix.
(12"+=) – ('A'-Ultramarine mix).
(cd-s) – ('A'-Secret Knowledge mix) / ('A'-Ultramarine mix) / ('A'-Augustus Pablo mix) / ('A'-12"mix).
Feb 95. (c-s) **WAKE UP BOO! / JANUS** 9
(cd-s+=) – Blues for George Michael / Friendship song.
(12") – Wake up Boo!: Music for astronauts / Janus / Blues for George Michael.
(cd-s) – Wake up Boo!: Music for astronauts / . . .And tomorrow the world / The history of Creation parts 17 & 36.
Mar 95. (cd)(c)(lp) **WAKE UP!** 1
– Wake up Boo! / Fairfax scene / It's Lulu / Joel / Find the answer within / Reaching out from here / Martin, Doom! it's 7 o'clock / Stuck on amber / Charles Bukowski is dead / 4am conversation / Twinside / Wilder.
May 95. (c-s) **FIND THE ANSWER WITHIN / DON'T TAKE YOUR GUN TO TOWN** 37
(cd-s+=) – Wallpaper.
(cd-s) – ('A'-High Llamas mix) / The only word I can find / Very together.
Jul 95. (c-s) **IT'S LULU / THIS IS NOT ABOUT ME** 25
(cd-s+=) – Reaching out from here (High Llamas mix / Martin, doom! it's seven o'clock (Stereolab mix).
(cd-s) – ('A'side) / Joel (Justin Warfield mix) / Tambo / Donkey.
Sep 95. (7")(c-s) **FROM THE BENCH AT BELVIDERE. / HI FALUTIN'** 24
(cd-s+=) – Crushed / Nearly almost time.

BOOTSY'S RUBBER BAND

Formed: USA . . .mid 70's by WILLIAM 'BOOTSY' COLLINS, former bassman for JAMES BROWN's The JB'S (1969-71), then GEORGE CLINTON's PARLIAMENT/ FUNKADELIC aggregation. Formed BOOTSY'S RUBBER BAND in the mid-70's and scored first of five hit albums early '76 with 'STRETCHIN' OUT IN . . .'. •**Style:** Funky bassman BOOTSY with brassy back-up from class line-up. •**Songwriters:** COLLINS.

Recommended: AHH . . .THE NAME IS BOOTSY, BABY! (*6) / BOOTSY? PLAY-

ER OF THE YEAR (*7) / THIS BOOT IS MADE FOR FONK-N (*5)

WILLIAM "BOOTSY" COLLINS (b.26 Oct'51, Cincinnati) – guitar, bass, vocals / **PHELPS "CATFISH" COLLINS** – bass, guitar / **GARY SHIDER + MIKE HAMPTON** – guitar / **GARY "MUD-BONE" COOPER + FRANKIE "KASH" WADDY + BOOGIE** – drums / **FRED WESLEY** – trombone / **MACEO PARKER + RANDY BRECKER** – sax / **MICHAEL BRECKER + RICK GARDNER** – trumpet / **CASPER** – bass, drums, guitar / **BERNIE WORRELL + FREDERICK ALLEN + SONNY TALBERT** – keyboards / **ROBERT "P-NUT" JOHNSON + LESLYN BAILEY** – vox

Warners Warners

Aug 76. (lp) **STRETCHIN' OUT IN BOOTSY'S RUBBER BAND** [ ] [59] Apr76
– Stretchin' out (in a rubber band) / Psychoticbumpschool / Another point of view / I'd rather be with you / Love vibes / Physical love / Vanish in our sleep.

—— **GLENN GOINS** – guitar / **JEROME BAILEY** – drums / **JOEL "RAZOR-SHARP" JOHNSON** – keyboards / **RICHARD GRIFFITH** – horns repl.BOOGIE, ALLEN, TARBERT + BAILEY

Jan 77. (lp) **AHH . . .THE NAME IS BOOTSY, BABY** [ ] [16]
– Ahh . . .the name is Bootsy, baby / The Pinocchio theory / Rubber duckie / Preview side too / What's a telephone bill? / Munchies for your love / Can't stay away / Reprise: We want Bootsy.

Jul 77. (7") **THE PINOCCHIO THEORY./ PSYCHOTICBUMPSCHOOL** [ ] [-]
(12"+=) – What's a telephone bill?.

—— now without HAMPTON, BAILEY, GOINS + BRECKER BROTHERS

Feb 78. (lp) **BOOTSY? PLAYER OF THE YEAR** [ ] [16]
– As in (I love you) / Bootsy (what's the name of this town?) / Bootzilla / Hollywood squares – Funk attack / May the force be with you / Roto-rooter / Very yes "Player of the year".

Jun 78. (7")(12") **BOOTZILLA./ HOLLYWOOD SQUARES** [43] [ ]

—— added **STARR-MON** – percussion, drums / **LARRY FRATANGELO** – percussion

Aug 79. (lp) **THIS BOOT IS MADE FOR FONK-N** [ ] [52] Jul79
– Under the influence of a groove / Bootsy get live / Oh boy gorl / Jam fan (hot) / Chug-a-lug (the bun patrol) / Shejam (almost Bootsy show).

BOOTSY

with **CATFISH/ RAZOR-SHARP/ MACEO/ FRED/ KUSH GRIFFIN + SHIDER + JOHNSON**

Dec 80. (lp) **ULTRA WAVE** [ ] [70]
– Mug push / F-Encounter / Is that my song? / It's a musical / Fat cat / Scared flower / Sound crack.

WILLIAM "BOOTSY" COLLINS

with usual array of friends incl. guest spot from GEORGE CLINTON

May 82. (lp) **THE ONE GIVETH, THE COUNT TAKETH AWAY** [ ] [ ]
– Shine-o-myte (rag popping) / Landshark (just when you thought it was safe) / Countracula (this one's for you) / £1 funkateer / Excon (of love) / So nice you name him twice / What's W-R-O-N-G radio / Music to smile by / Play on playboy / Take a lickin' and keep on kickin' / The funky funktioneer.

Bluebird ???

Aug 86. (12") **BODY SLAM. / ?** [ ] [ ]

C.B.S. Columbia

Sep 88. (7") **PARTY ON PLASTIC./ ?** [ ] [ ]
(12"+=) –

Nov 88. (lp)(c)(cd) **WHAT'S BOOTSY DOIN'?** [ ] [ ] Oct88
– Party on plastic (what's Bootsy doin'?) / Subliminal seduction (funk-me dirty) / Leakin' / Electro-cutie (shock-it-to-me) / 1st 1 2 the egg wins (the human race) / Love song / (I wannabee) Kissin' the "luv gun" / Yo-mama-loves ya / Save what's mine for me.

—— BOOTSY and his BOOTZILLA ORCHESTRA were credited on MALCOLM McLAREN's 1989 album 'Waltz Darling'. The RUBBER BAND were touring again in the early 90's and BOOTSY could be heard backing dance group DEEE-LITE.

BOOTSY COLLINS & BOOTSY'S NEW RUBBER BAND

featured BERNIE WORRELL

Rykodisc Rykodisc

Jan 95. (cd) **BLASTER OF THE UNIVERSE** [ ] [ ]
Aug 95. (cd) **KEEPIN' DAH FUNK ALIVE 4 1995** [ ] [ ]

BOSTON

Formed: 1975 by SCHOLZ who had set-up his own basement studio in Boston, Massachusetts, USA. He surrounded himself with local musicians and sent successful demo to 'Epic' in 1976. They released two massive selling albums, before going into hibernation for 8 years. They resurfaced on 'MCA', but only US public took notice, with album 'THIRD STAGE'. • **Style:** Mainstream hard rock, featuring twin lead guitars softened with light harmonies. • **Songwriters:** SCHOLZ wrote all. • **Trivia:** In their hiatus, SCHOLZ experimented on his 'Rockman', a device that amplified guitar sound at low volume for home recording.

Recommended: BOSTON (*6)

BRAD DELP (b.12 Jun'51) – vocals. guitar / **TOM SCHOLZ** (b.10 Mar'47, Toledo, Ohio) – guitar, keyboards, vocals / **BARRY GOUDREAU** (b.29 Nov'51) – guitar / **FRAN SHEENAN** (b.26 Mar'49) – bass / **SIB HASHIAN** (b.17 Aug'49) – drums repl. debut lp session drummer JIM MASDEA

Epic Epic

Dec 76. (7") **MORE THAN A FEELING. / SMOKIN'** [22] [5] Sep 76
Dec 76. (lp)(c) **BOSTON** [11] [3] Sep 76
– More than a feeling / Peace of mind / Foreplay / Long time / Rock and roll band / Smokin' / Hitch a ride / Something about you / Let me take you home tonight. *(re-iss.Apr81 hit UK 58) (cd-iss.Mar87)*

Feb 77. (7") **LONG TIME. / LET ME TAKE YOU HOME TONIGHT** [ ] [22] Jan 77
Jun 77. (7") **PEACE OF MIND. / FOREPLAY** [ ] [38] May 77
Aug 78. (7") **DON'T LOOK BACK. / THE JOURNEY** [43] [4]
Aug 78. (lp)(c)(US-pic-lp) **DON'T LOOK BACK** [9] [1]
– Don't look back / The journey / It's easy / A man I'll never be / Feelin' satisfied / Party / Used to bad news / Don't be afraid. *(re-iss.Jun81; cd-iss.Mar87)*

Dec 78. (7") **A MAN I'LL NEVER BE. / DON'T BE AFRAID** [ ] [31]
Mar 79. (7") **FEELIN' SATISFIED. / USED TO BAD NEWS** [ ] [46]

—— -(broke up for a while, after 3rd album was shelved / not completed) BARRY GOUDREAU made solo album late '80 before in '82 forming ORION THE HUNTER He was augmented by SCHOLZ and DELP. HASHIAN joined SAMMY HAGAR band.

BOSTON re-grouped around **SCHOLZ** and **DELP** plus **GARY PHIL** – guitar and the returning of **JIM MASDEA** – drums

M.C.A. M.C.A.

Oct 86. (7")(12") **AMANDA. / MY DESTINATION** [ ] [1] Sep 86
Oct 86. (lp)(c)(cd) **THIRD STAGE** [37] [1]
– Amanda / We're ready / The launch: Countdown – Ignition – Third stage separation / Cool the engines / My Destination / A new world / To be a man / I think I like it / Can'tcha say (you believe in me) / Still in love / Hollyann.

Jan 87. (7") **WE'RE READY. / ?** [-] [9]
Apr 87. (7") **CAN'TCHA SAY (YOU BELIEVE IN ME). / STILL IN LOVE** [ ] [20] Mar 87
(12"+=) – Cool the engines.
(cd-s+=) – The launch: Countdown – Ignition – Third stage separation.

—— Early in '90 SCHOLZ (aka BOSTON) won $million lawsuit against CBS.

RTZ

(RETURN TO ZERO)
were formed by **BRAD + BARRY** with **BRIAN MAES** – keyboards

Giant-Reprise Giant

Aug 91. (c-s)(cd-s) **FACE THE MUSIC /** [-] [49]
Apr 92. (cd)(c)(lp) **RETURN TO ZERO** [ ] [ ] Aug 91
– Face the music / Devil to pay / Hard time / Rain down on me / Livin' for the rock / Until your love comes around / This is my life / Return to zero.

Apr 92. (7")(c-s) **UNTIL YOUR LOVE COMES BACK AROUND. / EVERY DOOR IS OPEN** [ ] [26] Jan 92
(12"+=)(cd-s+=) – Return to zero / ('A'other mix).

Jun 92. (c-s)(cd-s) **ALL YOU'VE GOT / ?** [-] [ ]

BOSTON

—— Another comeback album.

M.C.A. M.C.A.

Jun 94. (cd)(c) **WALK ON** [56] [7]
– I need your love / Surrender to me / Livin' for you / Walkin' on the night / Walk on / Get organ-ized / Get re-organ-ized / Walk on (some more) / What's your name / Magdalene / We can make it.

Jul 94. (c-s) **I NEED YOUR LOVE / WE CAN MAKE IT** [ ] [51]
(cd-s+=) – The launch: The countdown – Ignition – Third stage separation.

– compilations etc. –

Sep 79. Epic; (7"m) **DON'T LOOK BACK. / MORE THAN A FEELING / SMOKIN'** [ ] [-]
Apr 83. Old Gold; (7") **MORE THAN A FEELING. / DON'T LOOK BACK** [ ] [-]
Aug 83. C.B.S.; (d-c) **BOSTON / DON'T LOOK BACK** [ ] [-]

David BOWIE

Born: DAVID ROBERT JONES, 8 Jan'47, Brixton, London. In 1964 he formed The KING BEES with schoolmate GEORGE UNDERWOOD. After one single they split after BOWIE joined The MANNISH BOYS. They too only lasted half a year and DAVID went solo with backing from The LOWER THIRD. Early 1966, he became DAVID BOWIE and signed to 'Pye', but still flopped. After three years trying he finally charted with 'SPACE ODDITY', a classic that introduced his character Major Tom. That year (1969) his father died, but he was compensated by his introduction to ANGIE, his future wife. Although he was regarded as one of top newcomers to rock/pop scene, it took him until 1972 to finally establish himself as *the* rock star. He formed his now famous backing band The SPIDERS and announced to the music press his bisexuality. The single 'STARMAN' and album 'ZIGGY STARDUST' (an archetype alter-ego) were to hit UK top 10. He was now on 'RCA' records, who re-issued past 3 albums, which broke into UK charts. His follow-up 'ALADDIN SANE' was his first of many albums to hit his No.1. • **Style:** Moved from 60's ANTHONY NEWLEY copyist, to innovator of risque glam-rock. He fashioned many styles including 'the feathercut' hairdo, make-up for men, and stage-mime (the latter being learnt from Lindsay Kemp). In 1975, his music dramatically diversed into Philadelphia soul/disco. This was thrown by the wayside for experimental/avant-garde type rock on (1977's) 'LOW', augmented by the obscure ENO. After HEROES album, same year, he returned to more conventional type rock, gaining another No.1 hit with his resurrection of Major Tom on 'ASHES TO ASHES'. After a virtual two and a half year hiatus he returned with CHIC producers for 'LET'S DANCE' album. It featured controversial video single 'CHINA GIRL' (once the co-

product of his great friend IGGY POP). In recent years the public have seen him slightly stumble from top 10 positions. When he introduced his TIN MACHINE project, it was regarded by many critics to be far from classic BOWIE. Unshifted by opinions, he carried on with this set-up in 1991, but could not substantiate any major hits. • **Songwriters:** He wrote all his own material even managing some for others (e.g. ALL THE YOUNG DUDES for (Mott The Hoople) / OH YOU PRETTY THINGS (Peter Noone) / THE MAN WHO SOLD THE WORLD / (Lulu) / PINK ROSE (Adrian Belew) / etc. He produced 'RCA' acts LOU REED (Transformer) / MICK RONSON (Slaughter on Tenth Avenue) / IGGY POP (The Idiot) / etc. BOWIE's cover album PIN-UPS featured SORROW (Merseys) / ROSALYN (Pretty Things) / HERE COMES THE NIGHT (Them) / SHAPES OF THINGS (Yardbirds) / FRIDAY ON MY MIND (Easybeats) / ANYWAY ANYHOW ANYWHERE + I CAN'T EXPLAIN (Who) / SEE EMILY PLAY (Pink Floyd) / WHERE HAVE ALL THE GOOD TIMES GONE (Kinks) / DON'T BRING ME DOWN + I WISH YOU WOULD (Pretty Things) / EVERYTHING'S ALRIGHT (Mojos) /. Other covers:- LET'S SPEND THE NIGHT TOGETHER (Rolling Stones) / KNOCK ON WOOD (Eddie Floyd) / ALABAMA SONG (Brecht-Weill) / DANCING IN THE STREET (Martha & The Vandellas). I FEEL FREE (Cream) / NITE FLIGHT (Scott Walker) / I KNOW IT'S GONNA HAPPEN SOMEDAY (Morrissey) / DON'T LET ME DOWN & DOWN (Tacha-Valmont) / THE SEEKER (Who). – TIN MACHINE :- He co-wrote with GABRELS except MAGGIE'S FARM (Bob Dylan) / WORKING CLASS HERO (John Lennon, who also co-wrote FAME for BOWIE in 1975) / IF THERE IS SOMETHING (Roxy Music). • **Trivia:** BOWIE'S acting career started in 1976 with the film 'THE MAN WHO FELL TO EARTH' and 'JUST A GIGOLO' (1978). After starring in stage production of ELEPHANT MAN in 1980, he returned to films THE HUNGER (1982) / MERRY XMAS MR. LAWRENCE (1983) / LABYRINTH (1986) / ABSOLUTE BEGINNERS (1986) / THE LAST TEMPTATION OF CHRIST (1989). In 1985, he was one of the major stars of LIVE AID concert, and co-sang on 'DANCIN' IN THE STREET' with MICK JAGGER.

Recommended: CHANGES ONE BOWIE (*10) / ZIGGY STARDUST *10) / ALADDIN SANE (*9) / THE MAN WHO SOLD THE WORLD (*9) / LOW (*10) / HUNKY DORY (*7) / HEROES (*9) / SPACE ODDITY (*6) / STATION TO STATION (*8) / SCARY MONSTERS (*7) / DIAMOND DOGS (*6) / PIN-UPS (*5) / YOUNG AMERICANS (*5) / LODGER (*4) / LET'S DANCE (*6) / TIN MACHINE (*4) / BLACK TIE, WHITE NOISE (*5).

DAVIE JONES with THE KING BEES

Vocalion | not issued

Jun 64. (7") **LIZA JANE. / LOUIE LOUIE GO HOME** [ ] [-]
(re-iss.Sep78 on 'Decca')

The MANNISH BOYS

Parlophone | not issued

Mar 65. (7") **I PITY THE FOOL. / TAKE MY TIP** [ ] [ ]

DAVIE JONES

with The LOWER THIRD

Aug 65. (7") **YOU'VE GOT A HABIT OF LEAVING. / BABY LOVES THAT WAY** [ ] [ ]
(above re-iss.Mar79 as 7"ep also cont. "MANNISH BOYS" 7" on 'EMI')

DAVID BOWIE with The LOWER THIRD

Pye | Warners

Jan 66. (7") **CAN'T HELP THINKING ABOUT ME. / AND I SAID TO MYSELF** [ ] [ ]

DAVID BOWIE

the name he was to keep forever

Pye | Warners

Apr 66. (7") **DO ANYTHING YOU SAY. / GOOD MORNING GIRL** [ ] [-]
Aug 66. (7") **I DIG EVERYTHING. / I'M NOT LOSING SLEEP** [ ] [-]

Deram | not issued

Dec 66. (7") **RUBBER BAND. / THE LONDON BOYS** [ ] [-]
Apr 67. (7") **THE LAUGHING GNOME. / THE GOSPEL ACCORDING TO TONY DAY** [ ] [-]
(above re-iss.Sep73 reaching No.6 in UK, re-iss.Jun82)
Jun 67. (lp) **LOVE YOU TILL TUESDAY** [ ] [-]
– Uncle Arthur / Sell me a coat / Rubber band / Love you till Tuesday There is a happy land / We are hungry men / When I live my dream / Little bombadier / Silly boy blue / Come and buy me toys / Join the gang / She's got medals / Maids of Bond Street / Please Mr. Gravedigger. *(cd-iss.Apr89)*
Jul 67. (7") **LOVE YOU TILL TUESDAY. / DID YOU EVER HAVE A DREAM** [ ] [-]

— (Jul68-Feb69) **BOWIE** formed FEATHERS with girlfriend **HERMOINE FARTHINGALE** and **JOHN HUTCHINSON** – bass. BOWIE went solo, recording solo album with session players **RICK WAKEMAN** – keyboards / etc.

Philips | Mercury

Jul 69. (7") **SPACE ODDITY. / THE WILD EYED BOY FROM FREECLOUD** [5] [-]
Nov 69. (lp) **DAVID BOWIE – MAN OF WORDS MAN OF MUSIC** [ ] [-]
– Space oddity / Unwashed and somewhat slightly dazed / Letter to Hermione / Cygnet committee / Janine / An occasional dream / The wild eyed boy from Freecloud / God knows I'm good / Memory of a free festival. *(re-iss.lp,c Nov72 on 'RCA' re-titled "SPACE ODDITY" reached No.17 UK, No.16 US, re-iss.+cd Apr90 hit 64 on 'EMI' += Conversation piece / Don't sit down)*

— **BOWIE** formed backing band **HYPE** with **TONY VISCONTI** – bass / **MICK RONSON** – guitar / **JOHN CAMBRIDGE** – drums

Mercury | Mercury

Mar 70. (7") **THE PRETTIEST STAR. / CONVERSATION PIECE** [ ] [-]

— **MICK 'Woody' WOODMANSEY** – drums repl. CAMBRIDGE

Jun 70. (7") **MEMORY OF A FREE FESTIVAL Pt.1. / Pt.2** [ ] [ ]
Jan 71. (lp) **THE MAN WHO SOLD THE WORLD** [ ] [ ]
– The width of a circle / All the madmen / Black country rock / After all / Running gun blues / Saviour machine / She took me cold / The man who sold the world / The supermen. *(re-iss.lp,c Nov72 on 'RCA' reached No.26 UK, re-iss.Apr83 on 'RCA' hit 64, cd-iss.Oct84, re-iss.+cd Apr90 hit 66 on 'EMI' +=)*– Lightning frightening / Moonage daydream / Holy holy / Hang on to yourself.
Jan 71. (7") **HOLY HOLY. / BLACK COUNTRY ROCK** [ ] [ ]

— Became **SPIDERS FROM MARS (BOWIE, RONSON, WOODMANSEY), TREVOR BOULDER** – bass repl. VISCONTI

R.C.A. | R.C.A.

Dec 71. (lp)(c) **HUNKY DORY** [ ] [93]
– Changes / Oh! you pretty things / Eight line poem / Life on Mars? / Kooks / Quicksand / Fill your heart – Andy Warhol / Song for Bob Dylan / Queen bitch / The Bewlay Brothers. *(re-dist.Sep72 reached No.3 UK)*,*(re-iss.Jan81 reached No.32 UK, cd-iss.Oct84, re-iss.+cd Apr90 on 'EMI' hit UK No.39 +=)*– Bombers / The supermen (alt.) / Quicksand (demo) / The Bewlay Brothers (alt.). *(pic-lp Mar84)*
Jan 72. (7") **CHANGES. / ANDY WARHOL** [ ] [66] Apr 72
(re-iss.Dec74 reached No.41 UK)
Apr 72. (7") **STARMAN. / SUFFRAGETTE CITY** [10] [65] Jun 72
Jun 72. (lp)(c) **THE RISE AND FALL OF ZIGGY STARDUST AND THE SPIDERS FROM MARS** [5] [75]
– Five years / Soul love / Moonage daydream / Starman / It ain't easy / Lady Stardust / Star / Hang on to yourself / Ziggy Stardust / Suffragette city / Rock'n'roll suicide. *(pic-lp Mar84) (re-iss.Jan81 reached No.33 UK, cd-iss.Oct84, re-iss.+cd Apr90 on 'EMI' hit No.25)*(cd+=) – John, I'm only dancing (demo) / Velvet goldmine / Sweet head / Ziggy Stardust (demo) / Lady Stardust (demo).
Sep 72. (7") **JOHN, I'M ONLY DANCING. / HANG ON TO YOURSELF** [12] [ ]
Nov 72. (7") **THE JEAN GENIE. / ZIGGY STARDUST** [2] [-]
Nov 72. (7") **THE JEAN GENIE. / HANG ON TO YOURSELF** [-] [71]
Apr 73. (7") **DRIVE-IN-SATURDAY. / ROUND AND ROUND** [3] [ ]

— with guests **MIKE GARSON** – piano / **KEN FORDHAM** and **BUX** – saxophone, flute

Apr 73. (lp)(c) **ALADDIN SANE** [1] [17] May 73
– Watch that man / Aladdin Sane (1913-1938-197?) / Drive-in Saturday / Panic in Detroit / Cracked actor / Time / The prettiest star / Let's spend the night together / The Jean genie / Lady grinning soul. *(re-iss.Feb82 reached No.49 UK, re-iss. pic.lp Jun84, cd-iss.Jun85)*(cd-iss.Jul90 hit 43 on 'EMI'+=) – other rare tracks
1973. (7") **TIME. / THE PRETTIEST STAR** [-] [ ]
1973. (7") **LET'S SPEND THE NIGHT TOGETHER. / LADY GRINNING SOUL** [-] [ ]
Jun 73. (7") **LIFE ON MARS. / THE MAN WHO SOLD THE WORLD** [3] [ ]

— **AYNSLEY DUNBAR** – drums repl. WOODY

Oct 73. (7") **SORROW. / AMSTERDAM** [3] [ ]
Oct 73. (lp)(c) **PIN-UPS** [1] [23]
– Rosalyn / Here comes the night / I wish you would / See Emily play / Everything's alright / I can't explain / Friday on my mind / Sorow / Don't bring me down / Shapes of things / Anyway anyhow anywhere / Where have all the good times gone!. *(re-iss.Sep81, re-iss.Apr83 hit UK 57, pic.lp-iss.Sep84, cd-iss.Jun85) (cd-iss.Jul90 hit 52 on 'EMI')*

— **DUNBAR** and **TONY NEWMAN** – drums / **HERBIE FLOWERS** – bass / **MIKE GARSON** – keys

Feb 74. (7") **REBEL REBEL. / QUEEN BITCH** [5] [64] May 74
May 74. (lp)(c) **DIAMOND DOGS (as "BOWIE")** [1] [ ]
– Future legend / Diamond dogs / Sweet thing / Candidate / Sweet thing (reprise) / Rebel rebel / Rock'n'roll with me / We are the dead / 1984 / Big brother (including 'Chant of the ever circling skeletal family'). *(re-iss.Feb81, re-iss.May83 hit 60, pic-lp+cd-iss.May84) (cd-iss.Jun90 hit 67 on 'EMI' +=) Dodo / Candidate.*
Jun 74. (7") **DIAMOND DOGS. / HOLY HOLY** [21] [ ]

— added **EARL SLICK** – guitar / **DAVID SANBORN** – saxophone

Sep 74. (7") **KNOCK ON WOOD (live). / PANIC IN DETROIT (live)** [10] [ ]
Nov 74. (d-lp)(c) **DAVID LIVE (live at the Tower theatre Philadelphia '74)** [2] [8]
– 1984 / Rebel rebel / Moonage daydream / Sweet thing / Changes / Suffragette city / Aladdin Sane (1913-1938-197?) / All the young dudes / Cracked actor / Rock'n'roll with me / Watch that man / Knock on wood / Diamond dogs/ Big brother / The width of a circle / The Jean genie / Rock'n'roll suicide. *(re-iss.May84) (cd-iss.Jun90 on 'EMI' +=)* – (band intro) / Here today, gone tomorrow / Time. *(re-iss.d-cd Jun95 on 'EMI')*

— **ANDY NEWMARK** – drums / **WILLIE WEEKS** – bass / **CARLOS ALOMAR** – guitar / **EARL SLICK** – guitar / guests **LUTHER VANDROSS and JOHN LENNON** – backing vocals

Feb 75. (7") **YOUNG AMERICANS. / SUFFRAGETTE CITY** [18] [28]
Mar 75. (lp)(c) **YOUNG AMERICANS** [2] [9]
– Young Americans / Win / Fascination / Right / Somebody up there like me / Across the universe / Can you hear me / Fame. *(re-iss.Sep81, re-iss.+cd Oct84) (c+cd.iss.Apr91 hit 54 on 'E.M.I.' +=) – Who can I be now? / John I'm only dancing again / It's gonna be me.*
Jul 75. (7") **FAME. / RIGHT** [17] [1] Jun 75

— retained **SLICK + ALOMAR**

— **GEORGE MURRAY** – bass + DENNIS DAVIS – drums repl. WEEKS + NEWMARK

Nov 75. (7") **GOLDEN YEARS. / CAN YOU HEAR ME** [8] [10]
Jan 76. (lp)(c) **STATION TO STATION** [5] [3]

– Station to station / Golden years / Word on a wing / TVC 15 / Stay / Wild is the wind. *(re-iss.Sep81, re-iss.+cd Nov84) (c+cd.iss.Apr91 hit 57 on 'E.M.I.'* – Word on the wing (live) / Stay (live).

May 76. (7") **TVC 15. / WE ARE THE DEAD** [33] [64]

Jul 76. (7") **SUFFRAGETTE CITY. / STAY** [ ] [ ]

— now collaborated with **BRIAN ENO** – synthesizers

— **RICKY GARDINER** – guitar repl. SLICK

Jan 77. (lp)(c) **LOW** [2] [11]

– Speed of life / Breaking glass / What in the world / Sound and vision / Always crashing in the same car / Be my wife / A new career in a new town / Warszawa / Art decade / Weeping wall / Subterraneans. *(re-iss.Jan81, re-iss.Jun83 hit 85, re-iss.+cd Nov84) (c+cd-iss.Aug91 hit 64 on 'E.M.I.')*

Feb 77. (7") **SOUND AND VISION. / A NEW CAREER IN A NEW TOWN** [3] [69]

Jun 77. (7") **BE MY WIFE. / SPEED OF LIFE** [ ] [ ]

— next guest **ROBERT FRIPP** – guitar who repl. RICKY GARDINER.

Oct 77. (7") **HEROES. / V2-SCHNEIDER** [24] [ ]

Oct 77. (lp)(c) **HEROES** [3] [35]

– Beauty and the beast / Joe the lion / Heroes / Sons of the silent age / Blackout / V-2 Schneider / Sense of doubt / Moss garden / Neukoln / Black out / The secret life of Arabia. *(re-iss.Jan81, re-iss.Jun83 hit 75, re-iss.+cd Nov84) (c+cd-iss.Apr91 on 'E.M.I.' +=)*– Joe the Lion (1991 remix) / Abolumajor.

— added **ADRIAN BELEW** – guitar / **SIMON HOUSE** – violin / **SEAN MAYES** – piano

Jan 78. (7") **THE BEAUTY AND THE BEAST. / SENSE OF DOUBT** [39] [ ]

Sep 78. (d-lp)(c) **STAGE (live)** [5] [44]

– Hang on to yourself / Ziggy Stardust / Five years / Soul love / Star / Station to station / Fame / TVC 15 / Warszawa / Speed of life / Art decade / Sense of doubt / Breaking glass / Heroes / What in the world / Blackout / Beauty and the beast. *(re-iss.+cd Jul84) (also on yellow vinyl) (cd-iss.Feb92 on 'EMI', w/ extra tracks)*

Oct 78. (7"ep) **BREAKING GLASS (live). / ZIGGY STARDUST (live) / ART DECADE (live)** [54] [ ]

Apr 79. (7") **BOYS KEEP SWINGING. / FANTASTIC VOYAGE** [7] [ ]

May 79. (lp)(c) **LODGER** [4] [20]

– Fantastic voyage / African night flight / Move on / Yassassin / Red sails / D.J. / Look back in anger / Boys keep swinging / Repitition / Red money. *(re-iss.Sep81, re-iss.+cd Oct84) (c+cd-iss.Aug91 on 'E.M.I.' – += 2 tracks)*

Jul 79. (7") **D.J. / REPITITION** [29] [ ]

Dec 79. (7")(12") **JOHN I'M ONLY DANCING (AGAIN). / JOHN I'M ONLY DANCING (1972)** [12] [ ]

Feb 80. (7") **ALABAMA SONG. / SPACE ODDITY** [23] [ ]

— guest **ROBERT FRIPP** – guitar repl. BRIAN ENO

Aug 80. (7") **ASHES TO ASHES. / MOVE ON** [1] [ ]

Sep 80. (lp)(c) **SCARY MONSTERS** [1] [12]

– It's no game (No.1) / Up the hill backwards / Scary monsters (and super creeps) / Ashes to ashes / Fashion / Teenage wildlife / Scream like a baby / Kingdom come / Because you're young / It's no game (No.2). *(re-iss.+cd Oct84) (re-iss.+cd.Jun92 on 'EMI', +=)*– Space oddity / Panic in Detroit / Crystal Japan / Alabama song.

Oct 80. (7")(12") **FASHION. / SCREAM LIKE A BABY** [5] [70]

Jan 81. (7")(c-s) **SCARY MONSTERS (AND SUPER CREEPS). / BECAUSE YOU'RE YOUNG** [20] [ ]

Mar 81. (7")(c-s) **UP THE HILL BACKWARDS. / CRYSTAL JAPAN** [32] [ ]

— (next single "UNDER PRESSURE" was a No.1 collaboration w/ "QUEEN".

Nov 81. (7")(12") **WILD IS THE WIND. / GOLDEN YEARS** [24] [ ]

Feb 82. (7"ep)**BAAL'S HYMN** [29] [ ]

– Baal's hymn / The drowned girl / Ballad of the adventurers / The dirty song / Remembering Marie.

Apr 82. (7")(12") **CAT PEOPLE (PUTTING OUT FIRE). / PAUL'S THEME** [26] [67]

— (above single taken from the feature film of the same name on 'MCA-UK' / 'Backstreet' US)

Nov 82. (7")(12") **LITTLE DRUMMER BOY ("DAVID BOWIE & BING CROSBY" rec. '77). / FANTASTIC BOY** [3] [ ]

— now with **NILE RODGERS + STEVIE RAY VAUGHAN** – guitar / **BERNARD EDWARDS + CARMINE ROJAS** – bass / **OMAR HAKIM + TONY THOMPSON** – drums / **SAMMY FIGUEROA** – perc.

EMI America — EMI America

Mar 83. (7")(12")(c-s) **LET'S DANCE. / CAT PEOPLE (PUTTING OUT FIRE)** [1] [1]

Apr 83. (lp)(pic-lp)(c) **LET'S DANCE** [1] [4]

– Modern love / China girl / Let's dance / China girl / Without you / Ricochet / Criminal world / Cat people (putting out fire) / Shake it. *(cd-iss.Jan84) (re-iss.cd Nov95 on 'Virgin')*

Jun 83. (7")(12")(7"pic-d) **CHINA GIRL. / SHAKE IT** [2] [10]

Sep 83. (7")(12") **MODERN LOVE. / MODERN LOVE (part 2)** [2] [14]

Feb 84. (7") **WITHOUT YOU. / CRIMINAL WORLD** [-] [73]

— retained **HAKIM, ROJAS, FIGUEROA** / brought back **ALOMAR** and recruited **DEREK BRAMBLE** – bass, snyths, etc.

Sep 84. (7")(12") **BLUE JEAN. / DANCING WITH THE BIG BOYS** [6] [8]

Sep 84. (lp)(c)(cd) **TONIGHT** [1] [11]

– Loving the alien / Don't look down / God only knows / Tonight / Neighbourhood threat / Blue Jean / Tumble and twirl / I keep forgetting / Dancing with the big boys. *(re-iss.cd Nov95 on 'Virgin')*

Nov 84. (7")(12") **TONIGHT. / TUMBLE AND TWIRL** [53] [53]

— next, from the film "Falcon And The Snowman")

Jan 85. (7")(12") **THIS IS NOT AMERICA ("DAVID BOWIE and The PAT METHANY GROUP"). / ('A'instrumental by The PAT METHANY GROUP)** [14] [32]

May 85. (7") **LOVING THE ALIEN. / DON'T LOOK DOWN** [19] [ ]

(12"+=)(12"sha-pic-d+=) – ('A' club mix).

Sep 85. (7") **DANCING IN THE STREET. ("DAVID BOWIE & MICK JAGGER") / ('A' instrumental)** [1] [7]

(12"+=) – ('A'dub) / ('A'extended).

(below single from film & album of the same name, cont. 3 BOWIE tracks, album reached No.19 UK) (the next, was from animated film of the same name)

Virgin — Virgin

Mar 86. (7")(12")(7"sha-pic-d) **ABSOLUTE BEGINNERS. / ('A'dub version)** [2] [53]

(cd-s+=) – ('A'versions).

Nov 86. (7")(12") **WHEN THE WIND BLOWS. / ('A'dub version)** [44] [ ]

— (below single from the feature film "Labyrinth" which cont. 5 BOWIE tracks, album reached No.38 UK)

— now with **ALOMAR, ROJAS + ERDAL KIZILCAY** – keyboards, etc. / **PHILIPPE SAISSE** – keyboards, etc. / **PETER FRAMPTON** – guitar

EMI America — EMI America

Jun 86. (7")(12")(7"sha-pic-d) **UNDERGROUND. / ('A'instrumental)** [21] [ ]

Mar 87. (7") **DAY-IN DAY-OUT. / JULIE** [17] [21]

(12"+=) – ('A'&'B'extended versions).

Apr 87. (lp)(c)(cd) **NEVER LET ME DOWN** [6] [34]

– Day-in day-out / Time will crawl / Beat of your drum / Never let me down / Zeroes / Glass spider / Shining star (makin' my love) / New York's in love / '87 and cry / Bang bang / Too dizzy. *(cd+=)* – Time will crawl (extended dance) / Never let me down (version) / Day-in day-out (Groucho mix).*(re-iss.cd Nov95 on 'Virgin')*

Jun 87. (7")(12") **TIME WILL CRAWL. / GIRLS** [33] [ ]

Aug 87. (7")(7"pic-d) **NEVER LET ME DOWN. / '87 AND CRY** [34] [27]

(12"+=) – Time will crawl (extended) / Day-in day-out (Groucho mix).

TIN MACHINE

was the name of **BOWIE's** next project/band. **DAVID BOWIE** – vocals, saxophone / **REEVES GABRELS** – lead guitar / **TONY SALES** – bass / **HUNT SALES** – drums (both ex-IGGY POP, ex-TODD RUNDGREN RUNT)plus p/t member **KEVIN ARMSTRONG** – guitar

EMI Manhattan — EMI Manhattan

May 89. (lp)(c)(cd) **TIN MACHINE** [3] [28]

– Heaven's in here / Tin machine / Prisoner of love / Crack city / I can't read / Under the god / Amazing / Working class hero / Bus stop / Pretty thing / Video crimes / Run * / Sacrifice yourself * / Baby can dance. *(cd+= *) (re-iss.cd Nov95 on 'Virgin')*

Jun 89. (7") **UNDER THE GOD. / SACRIFICE YOURSELF** [51] [ ]

(12"+=)(10"+=)(c-s+=)(cd-s+=) – (interview).

Aug 89. (7")(c-s)(7"pic-d)(7"sha-pic-d) **TIN MACHINE. / MAGGIE'S FARM (live)** [48] [ ]

(12"+=) – I can't read (live).

(cd-s++=) – Bus stop (live country version).

Oct 89. (7")(c-s)(7"pic-d)(7"sha-pic-d) **PRISONER OF LOVE. / BABY CAN DANCE (live)** [ ] [ ]

(12"+=)(cd-s+=) – Crack city (live)

London — Victory

Aug 91. (7")(12") **YOU BELONG IN ROCK'N'ROLL. / AMLAPURA** [33] [ ]

(pic-cd+=) – Stateside / Hammerhead.

Sep 91. (cd)(c)(lp) **TIN MACHINE II** [23] [ ]

– Baby universal / One shot / You belong in rock'n'roll / If there is something / Amlapura / Betty wrong / You can't talk / Stateside / Shopping for girls / Big hurt / I'm sorry / Goodbye Mr.Ed / Hammerhead.

Oct 91. (7")(c-s) **BABY UNIVERSAL. / YOU BELONG IN ROCK'N'ROLL** [48] [ ]

(12") – ('A'side) / A big hurt / ('A'new mix).

(cd-s) – ('A'side) / Stateside / Is there is something / Heaven's in here.

— In Feb'92, BOWIE's song 'SOUND AND VISION (remix)' was re-done with himself and 808 STATE on label 'Tommy Boy'.

Victory — Victory

Jul 92. (cd)(c)(lp) **OY VEY BABY (live)** [ ] [ ]

– If there is something / Amazing / I can't read / Stateside / Under the god / Goodbye Mr. Ed / Heaven's in here / You belong in rock'n'roll.

DAVID BOWIE

(solo again) and starred in the film 'THE LINGUINI INCIDENT'.

Warners — Warners

Jul 92. (7")(c-s) **REAL COOL WORLD. / ('A'instrumental)** [53] [ ]

(12") – ('A'club) / ('A'dub thing 1 & 2) / ('A'dub overture).

(cd-s+=) – (2 more 'A'mixes).

— with **NILE RODGERS** – guitar, co-producer / **DAVE RICHARDS + RICHARD HILTON + PHILIPPE SAISSE + RICHARD TEE** – keyboards / **BARRY CAMPBELL + JOHN REGAN** – bass / **PUGI BELL + STERLING CAMPBELL** – drums / **GERADO VELEZ** – percussion. Plus guests **MICK RONSON** – guitar / **LESTER BOWIE** – trumpet / **REEVES GABRELS** – guitar / **MIKE GARSON** – piano / **AL B.SURE!** – vocals / **WILD T.SPRINGER** – guitar

Savage-Arista — Savage-Arista

Mar 93. (7")(c-s) **JUMP THEY SAY. / PALLAS ATHENA (Don't Stop Praying Mix)** [9] [ ]

(cd-s) – ('A'side) / ('A'-Brothers In Rhythm mix) / ('A'-Brothers In Rhythm inst.) / ('A' Leftfield vocal).

(12") – ('A'side) / ('A'-Hard Hands mix) / ('A'-Leftfield vocal) / ('A'-dub oditty mix).

Apr 93. (cd)(c)(lp) **BLACK TIE, WHITE NOISE** [1] [39]

– The wedding / You've been around / I feel free / Black tie white noise / Jump they say / Nite flight / Pallas Athena / Miracle tonight / Don't let me down & down / Looking for Lester / I know it's gonna happen someday / The wedding song / Jump they say (alternate mix) / Lucy can't dance.

Jun 93. (7")(c-s) **BLACK TIE, WHITE NOISE. / YOU'VE BEEN AROUND (Meat Beat Manifesto mix)** [36] [ ]

(12"+=)(cd-s+=) – ('A'club mix with AL B.SURE!) / ('A'-John Waddell mix).

Oct 93. (7")(c-s) **MIRACLE TONIGHT. / LOKING FOR LESTER** [40] [ ]

(12")(cd-s) – ('A'mixes).

Nov 93. (7")(c-s) **BUDDHA OF SUBURBIA. / DEAD AGAINST IT** [35] [ ]

(cd-s+=) – South horizon / ('A'-Lenny Kravitz rock mix).

Nov 93. (cd)(c) **BUDDHA OF SUBURBIA (TV soundtrack)** [ ] [ ]

– Buddah of suburbia / Sex and the church / South horizon / The mysteries / Bleed like a craze, dad / Strangers when we meet / Read against it / Untitled No.1 / Ian Fish / UK heir / Buddah of suburbia (featuring LENNY KRAVITZ).

— now with **ENO** – synthesizers, co-writer (on most) / **REEVES GABRELS / ERDAL KIZILCAY / MIKE GARSON / STERLING CAMPBELL / CARLOS ALOMAR / JOEY BARON / YOSSI FINE**

R.C.A. — Arista

Sep 95. (c-s)(cd-s) **THE HEARTS FILTHY LESSON / I AM WITH NAME** [35] [92]
(cd-s+=) – ('A'-Bowie mix) / ('A'-Trent Reznor alt.remix) / ('A'-Tony Maserati remix).
(12"pic-d) – (5-'A'mixes; Bowie / alt. / Rubber / Simple text / Filthy).

Sep 95. (cd)(c)(d-lp) **OUTSIDE** [8] [21]
– THE NATHAN ADLER DIARIES: A Hyper Cycle:- Leon takes us outside / Outside / The hearts filthy lesson / A small plot of land / segue – Baby Grace (a horrid cassette) / Hello spaceboy / The motel / I have not been to Oxford Town / No control / segue Algeria touchshriek / The voyeur of utter destruction (as beauty) / segue – Ramona A. Stone – I am with name / Wishful beginnings / We prick you / segue – Nathan Adler / Strangers when we meet.

Nov 95. (7")(c-s) **STRANGERS WHEN WE MEET. / THE MAN WHO SOLD THE WORLD (live)** [39] [ ]
(cd-s+=) – ('A'side again) / Get real.
(12") – ('A'side) / The seeker / Hang ten high.

– compilations, exploitation, etc. –

Mar 70. Decca; (lp)(c) **THE WORLD OF DAVID BOWIE** [ ] [ ]
(re-iss.Feb73)
May 75. Decca; (d-lp)(c) **IMAGES 66-67** [ ] [ ]
May 75. Decca; (7") **LONDON BOYS. / LOVE YOU TILL TUESDAY** [ ] [ ]
Apr 81. Decca; (lp)(c) **ANOTHER FACE** [ ] [ ]
Oct 72. Pye; (7"ep) **DO ANYTHING YOU SAY / CAN'T HELP THINKING ABOUT ME. / I DIG EVERYTHING / I'M NOT LOSING SLEEP** [ ] [-]

Note; All below on 'RCA' unless otherwise mentioned.

Jan 73. (7") **SPACE ODDITY. / THE MAN WHO SOLD THE WORLD** [-] [15]
Apr 74. (7") **ROCK'N'ROLL SUICIDE. / QUICKSAND** [22] [ ]
Nov 75. (7"m) **SPACE ODDITY. / CHANGES / VELVET GOLDMINE** [1] [-]
Jun 76. (lp)(c) **CHANGESONEBOWIE** [2] [10]
Apr 81. (lp) **CHRISTIANE F. – WIR KINDER VOM BAHNHOF ZOO (soundtrack)** [-] [ ]
Nov 81. (lp)(c) **CHANGESTWOBOWIE** [24] [68]
(cd-iss.May84)
Dec 82. (10x7"pic-d) **FASHIONS** [ ] [ ]
– SPACE ODDITY / LIFE ON MARS / THE JEAN GENIE / REBEL REBEL / SOUND & VISION / DRIVE-IN SATURDAY / SORROW / GOLDEN YEARS / BOYS KEEP SWINGING / ASHES TO ASHES
Jan 83. (lp)(c) **RARE** [34] [ ]
Aug 83. (lp)(c) **GOLDEN YEARS (live recent)** [33] [99]
Oct 83. (d-lp)(d-c) **ZIGGY STARDUST – THE MOTION PICTURE (live '73 film)** [17] [89]
(re-iss./+cd.Sep92 on 'EMI')
Oct 83. (7") **WHITE LIGHT WHITE HEAT (live). / CRACKED ACTOR (live)** [46] [ ]
Jan 84. (7") **1984. / TVC 15** [-] [ ]
Apr 84. (lp)(c) **FAME AND FASHION (ALL TIME GREATEST HITS)** [40] [ ]
Dec 80. K-Tel; (lp)(c) **THE VERY BEST OF DAVID BOWIE** [3] [-]
Jun 81. P.R.T.; (10"mlp) **DON'T BE FOOLED BY THE NAME** [ ] [-]
Oct 87. P.R.T.; (m-lp)(c)(cd) **1966: DAVID BOWIE** [ ] [-]
(pic-lp Jun88) (re-iss.Dec89 on 'Castle')
1985. Castle; (d-lp)(c) **THE COLLECTION** [ ] [-]
(cd-iss.Aug92)
May 85. Krazy Kat; (12"ep) **HANG ON TO YOURSELF. / LOOKING FOR A FRIEND / MAN IN THE MIDDLE (by "ARNOLD CORNS & THE SPIDERS FROM MARS")** [ ] [-]
Apr 86. Krazy Kat; (lp)(c) **RARE TRACKS** [ ] [-]
Aug 86. Archive 4; (12"ep) **ARCHIVE 4** [ ] [-]
– London boys / Love you till Tuesday / Laughing gnome / Maid of Bond Street.
May 84. Deram; (lp)(c) **LOVE YOU TILL TUESDAY (soundtrack)** [53] [ ]
Jan 89. Deram; (cd) **CHAMELEON** [ ] [ ]
Sep 89. E.M.I./ US= Rykodisc; (cd) **SOUND + VISION** [ ] [97]
Mar 90. E.M.I./ US= Rykodisc; (7")(7"pic-d)(c-s) **FAME '90 (mix). / ('A'rap version)** [28] [ ]
(12"+=) – ('A'house mix) / ('A'hip hop mix).
(cd-s++=) – ('A'interminable variations/ mixes).
Apr 90. E.M.I./ US= Rykodisc; (cd)(c)(d-lp) **CHANGESBOWIE** [1] [39]
– Space oddity / John, I'm only dancing / Changes / Ziggy stardust / Suffragette city / The Jean genie / Diamond dogs / Rebel rebel / Young Americans / Fame ('90 remix) / Golden years / Heroes / Ashes to ashes / Fashion / Let's dance / China girl / Modern love / Blue Jean.
Nov 93. E.M.I./ US= Rykodisc; (cd)(c)(lp) **THE SINGLES COLLECTION** [9] [ ]
(re-iss.cd/c Nov95)
Apr 91. Rhino; (cd)(c) **EARLY ON (1964-66)** [-] [ ]
May 93. Spectrum; (cd)(c) **THE GOSPEL ACCORDING TO DAVID BOWIE** [ ] [-]
May 94. Trident; (cd)(c)(d-lp) **SANTA MONICA '72 (live)** [74] [-]
Jul 95. Trident; (cd) **RARESTONEBOWIE** [ ] [-]

BOW WOW WOW

Formed: London, England . . . late 1979 by extrovert entrepreneur manager MALCOLM McLAREN. He met 14 year-old ANNABELLA and took musicians from the split of ADAM & THE ANTS, and although he wasn't a member himself, he helped craft early sound, gaining experience for his own solo career later on. In 1980 the group signed to 'E.M.I.' and stir a little controversy with 'C'30, C'60, C'90, GO', a hit song about home-taping. This was followed by 'YOUR CASSETTE PET', a unique 20 min. EP tape, sleeved in cardboard pack. • **Style:** Like ADAM & THE ANTS, revivalists of 'Burundi' type drumming. This alongside ANNABELLA's adolescent sexual manner and artistic nude posing on the cover of SEE JUNGLE! SEE JUNGLE!, paved way for chart success. • **Songwriters:** Group compositions except; I WANT CANDY (Strangeloves) / FOOLS RUSH IN (Brook Benton) / FEVER (Peggy Lee). • **Trivia:** Late 1981, McLAREN nearly replaced ANNABELLA with BOY GEORGE. Her mother was furious at the unconsented(???) exploitation of her daughter, by McLAREN in his teen mag 'Chicken'.

Recommended: I WANT CANDY (*6)

ANNABELLA LWIN (b.MYANT MYANT AYE, 31 Oct'65, Rangoon, Burma) – vocals / **MATTHEW ASHMAN** – guitar / **LEROY GORMAN** – bass / **DAVE BARBEROSSA** – drums (all 3 men **ex-ADAM & THE ANTS**)

E.M.I. — not issued?

Jul 80. (c-s)(7") **C'30, C'60, C'90, GO. / SUN, SEA & PIRACY** [34] [-]
Nov 80. (c-ep) **YOUR CASSETTE PET** [58] [-]
– Louis Quatorze / Gold he said / Fools rush in / Giant sized baby thing / I want my baby on Mars / Uomo sex al Apache / Sexy Eiffel Towers / Radio G-string. *(cd-iss. Oct93)*
Mar 81. (7")(c-s) **W.O.R.K.(NE NO MY DADDY OH). / C'30, C'60, C'90, GO . . . ANDA!** [62] [-]

— added 2 female backing vocalists around 1981.

R.C.A. — R.C.A.

Jul 81. (7") **PRINCE OF DARKNESS. / ORANG UTANG** [58] [-]
(12") – ('A'side) / Sinner! sinner! sinner! (Prince of darkness).
Oct 81. (7")(12") **CHIHUAHUA. / GOLLY GOLLY GO BUDDY** [51] [-]
Oct 81. (lp)(c) **SEE JUNGLE! SEE JUNGLE! GO JOIN OUR CRAZY GANG YEAH CITY ALL OVER! GO APE CRAZY!** [26] [ ]
– Jungle boy / Chihuahua / Sinner! sinner! sinner! (Prince of darkness) / Mickey put it down / (I'm a) T.V. savage / Elimination dancing / Golly! golly! go buddy! / King Kong / Go wild in the country / I am not a know it all / Why are babies so wise? / Orang-utang / Hello, hello daddy (I'll sacrifice you). (c+=) – The joy of eating raw flesh. *(re-iss.+cd.Dec89 on 'Great Expectations')*
Jan 82. (7") **GO WILD IN THE COUNTRY. / EL BOSS DICKO** [7] [ ]
Apr 82. (7")(12") **SEE JUNGLE (JUNGLE BOY). / T.V. SAVAGE** [45] [ ]
May 82. (m-lp) **THE LAST OF THE MOHICANS** [-] [67]
– Cowboy / Louis Quatorze / I want candy / Mile High club.
May 82. (7") **I WANT CANDY. / (etched 1 side)** [9] [ ]
(7") – ('A'side) / King Kong.
Jul 82. (7") **LOUIS QUATORZE (remix). / MILE HIGH CLUB** [66] [ ]
Feb 83. (7")(7"pic-d) **DO YOU WANNA HOLD ME?. / WHAT'S THE TIME (HEY BUDDY)** [47] [ ]
Feb 83. (lp)(c) **WHEN THE GOING GETS TOUGH, THE TOUGH GET GOING** [ ] [ ]
– Aphrodisiac / Do you wanna hold me? / Roustabout / Lonesome tonight / Love me / What's the time (hey buddy) / Mario (your own way to Paradise) / Quiver (arrows in my) / Rikki Dee / Tommy Tucker / Love, peace and harmony.

— Disbanded mid '83. ASHMAN formed CHIEFS OF RELIEF with ex-SEX PISTOLS. Sadly he was to die on 21st Nov'95 of complications due to his diabetis.

– compilations, others, etc. –

Jul 82. E.M.I./ US= R.C.A.; (lp)(c) **I WANT CANDY** [ ] [ ] Sep 82
– I want Candy / Cowboy / Louis Quatorze / Mile high club / W.O.R.K. (ne no my daddy oh) / Fools rush in / I want my baby on Mars / Gold he said / Sexy Eiffel Towers / Radio G-string / C-30, C-60, C-90, go / Sun, sea & piracy / Uomo sex al apache / Giant sized baby thing / C-30, C-60, C-90, anda (Spanish version).
Sep 82. E.M.I.; (7") **FOOLS RUSH IN. / UOMO SEX AL APACHE** [ ] [-]
May 83. R.C.A.; (c-ep) **I WANT CANDY / SEE JUNGLE (JUNGLE BOY). / GO WILD IN THE COUNTRY / CHIHUAHUA** [ ] [-]
Nov 86. Old Gold; (7") **GO WILD IN THE COUNTRY. / I WANT CANDY** [ ] [-]
Aug 89. Receiver; (lp)(c)(cd) **THE BEST OF BOW WOW WOW** [ ] [-]

— There was also US-only release album **LAST OF THE MOHICANS** circa 1982.

Jun 94. R.C.A.; (cd) **THE BEST OF** [ ] [-]

ANNABELLA

R.C.A. — not issued

Oct 85. (7")(12") **DON'T DANCE WITH STRANGERS. / MAGDALENE** [ ] [-]
Apr 86. (7")(12") **WAR BOYS. / FEVER** [ ] [-]
May 86. (lp)(c) **FEVER** [ ] [-]
– Fever / School's out / Under the gun / Desire / Nightmare / War boys / High powered girl / Marry for love / Wild in me.

ANNABELLA retired from music scene. She's back in the studio '94 for forthcoming release.

Sony — Sony

Aug 94. (12")(c-s)(cd-s)(m-d) **CAR SEX. / ('A'remixes)** [ ] [ ]

— Above single had the acolade of being first ever mini-disc single release= m-d

Jan 95. (c-s)(cd-s) **DO WHAT YOU DO / L.O.V.E. / ('A'mix)** [68] [ ]
(cd-s+=)(12"+=) – Stone jumping / Hey you (don't bring me down).

BOX OF FROGS (see under ⇒ YARDBIRDS)

BOX TOPS

Formed: Memphis, Tennessee, USA . . . 1967 originally as DE VILLES. Signed to 'Bell' label offshoot 'Mala', and soon topped US chart with debut

45 'THE LETTER'. This was also to become well covered standard for many artists. Throughout the sixties, they had large number of hits, with CHILTON virtually taking over reigns in the 70's. • **Style:** Excellent white-soul orientated pop / rock, liked by past mods. • **Songwriters:** Producer DAN PENN and SPOONER OLDHAM wrote most, except THE LETTER and SOUL DEEP (penned by WAYNE THOMPSON). I SHALL BE RELEASED (Bob Dylan). BIG STAR saw CHILTON team up with songwriting partner CHRIS BELL. They now styled themselves with early BEATLES-type harmonies, that termed new description "Power-pop". • **Trivia:** TOMMY COGBILL produced later 60's & reunited 1974 work.

Recommended: THE BEST OF THE BOX TOPS (*5) / DOCUMENT (*5 ALEX CHILTON) / RECORD RADIO CITY (*7); BIG STAR

ALEX CHILTON (b.20 Dec'50) – vocals, guitar / **JOHN EVANS** – organ / **GARY TALLEY** (b.17 Aug'47) – guitar / **BILL CUNNINGHAM** (b.23 Jan'50) – bass, piano / **DANNY SMYTHE** – drums

Stateside / Mala

Sep 67. (7") **THE LETTER. / HAPPY TIMES** [5] [1] Jul 67
Nov 67. (7") **NEON RAINBOW. / SHE KNOWS HOW** [24]
Jan 68. (lp) **THE LETTER – NEON RAINBOW** [ ] [87] Nov 67
– The letter / She knows how / Trains & boats & planes / Break my mind / A whiter shade of pale / Everything I am / Neon rainbow / People make the world / I'm your puppet / Happy times / Gonna find somebody / I pray for rain.

Bell / Mala

Mar 68. (7") **CRY LIKE A BABY. / THE DOOR YOU CLOSED ON ME** [15] [2]
Apr 68. (lp) **CRY LIKE A BABY** [ ] [59]
– Cry like a baby / Deep in Kentucky / I'm the one for you / Weeping Analeah / Every time / Fields of clover / Trouble with Sam / Lost / Good morning dear / 727 / You keep me hanging on / The door you closed to me.
May 68. (7") **CHOO CHOO TRAIN. / FIELDS OF CLOVER** [ ] [26]

— **RICK ALLEN** – organ, drums repl. EVANS **TOM BOGGS** – drums repl. SMYTHE (both return to college)

Sep 68. (7") **I MET HER IN CHURCH. / PEOPLE GONNA TALK** [ ] [37]
Oct 68. (lp) **NON-STOP** [ ] [ ]
– Choo choo train / I'm movin' on / Sandman / She shot a hole in my soul / People gonna talk / I met her in church / Rock me baby / Rollin' in my sleep / I can dig it / Yesterday / Where's my mind / If I had let you in.
Dec 68. (lp) **THE BOX TOPS SUPER HITS** (compilation) [-] [45]
– The letter / Trains & boats & planes / Break my mind / A whiter shade of pale / She sot a hole in my soul / Neon rainbow / Cry like a baby / I'm your puppet / I met her in church / You keep me hanging on / Choo choo train.
Jan 69. (7") **SWEET CREAM LADIES, FORWARD MARCH. / SANDMAN** [ ] [28] Dec 68
Mar 69. (7") **I SHALL BE RELEASED. / I MUST BE THE DEVIL** [ ] [67]

— **JERRY RILEY** – guitar repl. TALLEY

Jul 69. (7") **SOUL DEEP. / HAPPY SONG** [22] [18]
Oct 69. (7") **TURN ON A DREAM. / TOGETHER** [ ] [58]
Oct 69. (lp) **DIMENSIONS** [ ] [77] Sep 69
– Soul deep / I shall be released / Midnight angel / Together / I'll hold out my hand / I must be the Devil / Sweet cream ladies, forward march / The happy song / Ain't no way / Rock me baby.
Feb 70. (7") **YOU KEEP TIGHTENING UP ON ME. / COME ON HONEY** [ ] [92]

— CHILTON (now the only original member), ALLEN, BOGGS and RILEY brought in **SWAIN SCHAEFER** – piano / **HAROLD CLOUD** – bass (both) repl. CUNNINGHAM

Sep 71. (lp) **BOX TOPS** [ ] [ ]
– The letter / Cry like a baby / Soul deep / I'm movin' on / Lost / A whiter shade of pale / Together / The happy song / Fields of clover / Weeping Analeah / I'll hold out my hand / I pray for rain.

– UK compilations etc. –

Jan 73. London; (7") **SUGAR CREEK WOMAN. / IT'S ALL OVER** [ ] [-]
Jun 74. M.F.P./ Sound Superb; (lp)(c) **THE BEST OF THE BOX TOPS** [ ] [-]
Mar 78. Stiff; (7") **CRY LIKE A BABY. / THE LETTER** [ ] [-]
(re-iss.Jul82 on 'Old Gold')
Jun 80. J.B.; (7") **THE LETTER. / CRY LIKE A BABY** [ ] [-]
Oct 80. Creole; (7") **THE LETTER. / (2 tracks by other artists)** [ ] [-]
(re-iss.Aug82)
Oct 80. Creole; (7") **CRY LIKE A BABY. / (2 tracks by other artists)** [ ] [-]
(re-iss.Aug82)
Nov 88. Decal; (lp)(c)(cd) **THE BEST OF THE BOX TOPS featuring ALEX CHILTON** [ ] [-]
– The letter / Neon rainbow / I pray for rain / The door you closed to me / Cry like a baby / Deep in Kentucky / Fields of clover / You keep me hangin' on / Choo choo train / I can dig it / Yesterday where's my mind / Soul deep / I shall be released / Together / I must be the Devil / Sweet cream ladies forward march / Happy song.
1988 Warners; (cd) **THE ULTIMATE BOX TOPS** [ ] [ ]
Jun 89. Arista; (cd-s) **THE LETTER. / HAPPY TIMES / CRY LIKE A BABY / THE DOOR YOU CLOSED ON ME** [ ] [-]

BIG STAR

was formed in 1972 by ALEX CHILTON plus **CHRIS BELL** (b.12 Jan'51) – guitar / **ANDY HUMMEL** (b.26 Jan'51) – bass / **JODY STEPHENS** – drums

Stax / Ardent

-Apr72. (lp) **£1 RECORD** [-] [ ]
– Feel / The ballad of El Goodo / In the street / Don't lie to me / Thirteen / The India song / When my baby's beside me / My life is right / Give me another chance / Try again / Watch the sunrise / St 100-6. *(re-iss.+c Nov86 on 'Big Beat')*
Apr 72. (7") **IN THE STREET. / WHEN MY BABY'S BESIDE ME** [-] [ ]
Jul 72. (7") **DON'T LIE TO ME. / WATCH THE SUNRISE** [-] [ ]

— now trio when BELL left to go solo, He's killed in car crash 27 Dec'78.

Feb 74. (lp) **RADIO CITY** [ ] [ ]
– O, my soul / Life is white / Way out west / What's going on / You got what you deserve / Mod Lang / Back of a car / Daisy glaze / She's a mover / September gurls / Morpha too – I'm in love with a girl. *(re-iss.Nov86 on 'Big Beat')*
Feb 74. (7") **O, MY SOUL. / MORPHATOO – I'M IN LOVE WITH A GIRL** [-] [ ]
May 74. (7") **SEPTEMBER GIRLS. / MOD LANG** [-] [ ]
(UK iss. Sep 78 on 'Stars')
1974. (7") **WILLOBEE AND DALE.(as "BOX TOPS") / I'M GONNA BE ALRIGHT** [-] [ ]

— ALEX CHILTON now sole BIG STAR with session people, incl. STEPHENS + STEVE CROPPER. In 1975, after recording below album, they disbanded. It was finally released.

Aura / P.V.C.

Jul 78. (lp) **BIG STAR'S THE THIRD ALBUM** [ ] [ ]
– Stroke it Noel / For you / Kizza me / You can't have me / Nightime / Blue moon / Take care / Jesus Christ / Femme fatale / O Dana / Big black car / Holocaust / Kangaroo / Thank you friends. *(cd-iss.Mar92 on 'Rykodisc')* (+=) – Nature boy / Till the end of the day / Dream lover / Downs / Whole lotta shakin' goin' on.
Jul 78. (7") **KIZZA ME. / DREAM LOVER** [ ] [ ]
Dec 78. (7") **JESUS CHRIST. / BIG BLACK CAR** [ ] [ ]

– (BIG STAR) compilations etc. –

Jul 78. Stax; (d-lp) **£1 RECORD / RADIO CITY** [ ] [ ]
(cd-iss.Jun87 omits 'In the street' + 'St 100-6')
Nov 87. Dojo/ US= P.V.C.; (lp)(c)(cd) **BIG STAR'S THIRD / SISTER LOVERS (rare)** [ ] [ ]

ALEX CHILTON

went solo in 1977, with **RICHARD ROSEBROUGH** – drums / etc.

not issued / Ork

1977. (lp) **ONE DAY IN NEW YORK** [-] [ ]

Aura / not issued

Feb 80. (lp) **LIKE FLIES ON SHERBET** [ ] [-]
– Boogie shoes / My rival / Hey little child / Hook or crook / I've had it / Rock hard / Girl after girl / Waltz across Texas / Alligator man / Like flies on sherbet. *(cd-iss.Sep92 on 'Great Expectations')* (+=) – No more the Moon shines on Lorena.
Jun 80. (7") **HEY LITTLE CHILD. / NO MORE THE MOON** [ ] [-]

— with **KNOX** – guitar / **MATTHEW SELIGMAN** – bass + **MORRIS WINDSOR** – drums

Dec 82. (lp) **LIVE IN LONDON (live)** [ ] [-]
– Bangkok / Tramp / In the street / Hey little child / Nightime / Rock hard / Alligator man / The letter / Train kept a rollin' / Kanga roo / My rival / Stranded on a dateless night / September gurls / No more the Moon shines on Lorena.

not issued / New Rose FRANCE

Jul 85. (lp) **FEUDALIST TARTS** [-] [-]
(cd-iss.1990 as 'STUFF' with 10 extra tracks)
May 86. (7") **NO SEX. / UNDERCRASS** [-] [-]
(12"+=) – Wild kingdom.
(d7"+=) – September gurls / I'm gonna make you mine (live Paris'85).
Nov 87. (7") **MAKE A LITTLE LOVE. / LONELY WEEKENDS** [-] [-]
Nov 87. (lp)(c) **HIGH PRIEST** [-] [-]
– Take it off / Let me get close to you / Dalai Lama * / Volare / Thing for you / Forbidden love / Make a little love / Trouble don't last / Don't be a drag / Nobody's fool / Come by here / Raunchy / Junkyard * / Lonely weekends / Margie * / Rubber room *. *(cd+= *)*
Feb 88. (d7"-ltd) **DALAI LAMA. / MARGIE / JUNKYARD. / RUBBER ROOM** [-] [-]
Feb 90. (cd)(m-lp) **BLACKLIST** [ ] [-]
– Little GTO / Guantanamerika / Jailbait / Baby baby baby / Nice and easy does it / I will turn your money green.

(above cont.some covers). In 1992 CHILTON resurrected BIG STAR (see below).

Feb 94. (cd) **CLICHES** [ ] [-]

– (ALEX CHILTON) compilations etc. –

Sep 85. Aura; (lp)(cd) **DOCUMENT** [ ] [ ]
– Kizza me / Downs / Holocaust / Big black car / Kangaroo / Dream lover / My rival / Hey little child / Hook or crook / Like flies on sherbet / Bangkok / September gurls / In the street.
Mar 86. Fan Club; (d-lp) **LOST DECADE (1969-77)** [-] [-] France
Feb 92. New Rose; (cd) **ALEX CHILTON** [-] [-]
Nov 87. Line; (cd) **BACH'S BOTTOM** (rec.1975) [-] [-] Germ'y
– Take me home / Make me like it / Everytime I close my eyes / All of the time / Oh baby I'm free / I'm so tired (parts 1 & 2) / Free again / Jesus Christ / The singer not the song / Summertime blues / Take me home again. *(originally rel. lp '81)*
May 91. Rhino; (cd) **19 YEARS (1969-87)** [ ] [ ]

BIG STAR

re-formation

Zoo / Zoo

Sep 93. (cd)(c) **LIVE AT MISSOURI UNIVERSITY (4.25.93) (live)** [ ] [ ]
– In the street / Don't lie to me / When my baby's beside me / I am the cosmos / The ballad of El Goodo / Back of a car / Way out west / Daisy glaze / Baby strange / For you / Fool / September gurls / Thank you friends / Slut / Jeepster.

BOY GEORGE

Born: GEORGE O'DOWD, 14 Jun'61, Eltham, Kent, England. In 1981 after a brief stage appearances with BOW WOW WOW, he formed IN PRAISE OF

LEMMINGS, which soon became CULTURE CLUB. After being previously turned down by EMI, they signed to 'Virgin' in 1982. After first two singles flopped, they had massive chart topper with 'DO YOU REALLY WANT TO HURT ME'. After many more hits, BOY GEORGE opted out for a lucrative solo career, which included another No.1 'EVERYTHING I OWN'. In the late 80's, he also sidelined with spiritual Hari Krishna outfit JESUS LOVES YOU. • **Style:** Mixed up a blend of white reggae and romantic teeny pop. Gender bender BOY GEORGE initially caused a stir in the media, when wearing dresses and make-up, which baffled most people originally to wonder what gender he was. He once stated he preferred having a cup of tea than having sex, and was the darling of the daily tabloids, until 1984 when they turned against his heroin addiction and extreme fashion. • **Songwriters:** All written by GEORGE and HAY. GEORGE solo covered EVERYTHING I OWN (Bread ; hit. Ken Boothe) / WHAT BECOMES OF THE BROKEN HEARTED (Jimmy Ruffin) / THE CRYING GAME (Dave Berry) / MY SWEET LORD (George Harrison) / FUNTIME (Iggy Pop) and co-wrote with DUST & THEWLIS. • **Trivia:** In 1988, BOY GEORGE protested about 'NO CLAUSE 28' law which the government used to ban homosexual literature. In 1989, he dueted with CONNIE FRANCIS on a version of Frank & Nancy Sinatra's 'Something Stupid'.

Recommended: THIS TIME: THE FIRST 4 YEARS (*6)

CULTURE CLUB

BOY GEORGE – vocals / **ROY HAY** (b.12 Aug'61) – guitar, keyboards (ex-RUSSIAN BOUQUET) repl. JOHN SUEDE / **MIKEY CRAIG** (b.15 Feb'60) – bass / **JON MOSS** (b.11 Sep'57) – drums, percussion (ex-EDGE, ex-DAMNED)

		Virgin	Epic
May 82.	(7")(12") **WHITE BOY. / LOVE TWIST**		
Jun 82.	(7")(12") **I'M AFRAID OF ME. / MURDER RAP TRAP**		
Sep 82.	(7") **DO YOU REALLY WANT TO HURT ME. / ('A' dub)**	1	-
	(12"+=) – Love is gold (You were never so good).		
Oct 82.	(lp)(c) **KISSING TO BE CLEVER**	5	14
	– White boy / You know I'm not crazy / I'll tumble 4 ya / Take control / Love twist / Boy boy (I'm the boy) / I'm afraid of me (remix) / White boys can't control it / Do you really want to hurt me. *(cd-iss.Jul87)*		
Nov 82.	(7")(7"pic-d) **TIME (CLOCK OF THE HEART). / WHITE BOYS CAN'T CONTROL IT**	3	2 Apr 83
	(12"+=) – Romance beyond the alphabet. (US 7" b-side)		
Dec 82.	(7") **DO YOU REALLY WANT TO HURT ME. / YOU KNOW I'M NOT CRAZY**	-	2
	(12") – ('A'side) / Love is cold (you were never no good)		
——	added guest vocalist **HELEN TERRY** in '83.		
Apr 83.	(7") **CHURCH OF THE POISON MIND. / MAN SHAKE**	2	10 Oct 83
	(12"+=) – Mystery boy. (US 7" b-side)		
Jun 83.	(7") **I'LL TUMBLE 4 YA. / MYSTERY BOY**	-	9
	(12"+=) – Man shake.		
Sep 83.	(7") **KARMA CHAMELEON. / THAT'S THE WAY**	1	1 Nov 83
	(12") – ('A'side) / I'll tumble 4 ya.		
Oct 83.	(lp)(c)(cd)(pic-lp) **COLOUR BY NUMBERS**	1	2
	– Karma chameleon / It's a miracle / Black money / Changing every day / That's the way (I'm only trying to help you) / Church of the poison mind / Miss me blind / Mister man / Stormkeeper * / Victims. *(c+= *)(cd+= *) (re-iss.+cd.1989)*		
Nov 83.	(7") **VICTIMS. / COLOUR BY NUMBERS**	3	
	(12"+=) – Romance revisited.		
Feb 84.	(7") **MISS ME BLIND. / COLOUR BY NUMBERS**	-	5
Mar 84.	(7")(7"pic-d) **IT'S A MIRACLE. / LOVE TWIST**	4	13 May 84
	(12"+=) – Miss me blind.		
Sep 84.	(7")(12") **WAR SONG. / LA CANCION DE GUERRA**	2	17
Oct 84.	(lp)(c)(cd)(pic-lp) **WAKING UP WITH THE HOUSE ON FIRE**	2	26
	– Dangerous man / War song / Unfortunate thing / Crime time / Mistake No.3 / The dive / The medal song / Don't talk about it / Mannequin / Hello goodbye. *(re-iss.1988)*		
Nov 84.	(7")(12") **THE MEDAL SONG. / DON'T GO DOWN THE STREET**	32	
Nov 84.	(7") **MISTAKE NO.3. / DON'T GO DOWN THAT STREET**	-	33
Mar 86.	(7")(5"pic-d) **MOVE AWAY. / SEXUALITY**	7	12
	(12"+=) – ('A'extended) / ('B'dub remix).		
Apr 86.	(lp)(c)(cd) **FROM LUXURY TO HEARTACHE**	10	32
	– Move away / I pray / Work on me baby / Gusto blusto / Heaven's children / Thank God you woman / Reasons / Too bad / Come clean / Sexuality. *(re-iss.1989)* (c+=) – Move away (remix) / Thank God you woman (remix). (cd++=) – Sexuality (remix).		
May 86.	(7")(12") **THANK GOD YOU WOMAN. / FROM LUXURY TO HEARTACHE**	31	

—— They split soon after autumn '86. MOSS formed HEARTBEAT UK. BOY GEORGE went solo.

– compilations etc. –

Apr 87.	Virgin/ US= Epic; (lp)(c)(cd) **THIS TIME: THE FIRST FOUR YEARS**	8	
	– Do you really want to hurt me / Move away / I'll tumble 4 ya / Love is love / Victims / Karma chameleon / Church of the poison mind / Miss me blind / Time (clock of the heart) / It's a miracle / Black money / War song. (cd+=) – I'll tumble 4 ya (US 12"remix) / Miss me blind (US 12"remix).		
Nov 88.	Virgin/ US= Epic; (7") **KARMA CHAMELEON. / IT'S A MIRACLE**		-
	(12"+=) – Miss me blind.		
1988.	Epic; (7") **CHURCH OF THE POISON MIND. / DO YOU REALLY WANT TO HURT ME**	-	
Sep 93.	Virgin/ US= Epic; (cd)(c) **AT WORST . . . THE BEST OF BOY GEORGE & CULTURE CLUB**	26	
	– (all hits from CULTURE CLUB 1982 – solo 1986 – JESUS LOVES YOU 1989, etc.)		
May 94.	Virgin; (cd)(c) **THE 12 INCH MIXES PLUS**		-
Sep 89.	V.I.P.; (lp)(c)(cd) **THE BEST OF CULTURE CLUB**		-
	(re-iss.cd/c Oct94)		
Nov 88.	Old Gold; (7") **DO YOU REALLY WANT TO HURT ME. / I'LL TUMBLE 4 YA**		-
	(12"+=) – Time (clock of the heart).		

BOY GEORGE

solo backed by WELL RED.

		Virgin	Virgin
Feb 87.	(7") **EVERYTHING I OWN. / USE ME**	1	
	(12"+=) – ('A'mix) / ('A'dub).		
May 87.	(7") **KEEP ME IN MIND. / STATE OF LOVE**	29	
	(12") – ('A'extended) / I pray.		
	(12"+=)(c-s+=)(12"pic-d+=) – Everything I own.		
Jun 87.	(lp)(c)(cd) **SOLD**	29	
	– Sold / I asked for love / Keep me in mind / Everything I own / Freedom / Just ain't enough / Where are you now? / Little ghost / Next time / We've got the right / To be reborn.		
Jul 87.	(7") **SOLD. / ARE YOU TOO AFRAID?**	24	
	(12"+=)(c-s+=) – Everything I own (go-go mix).		
Nov 87.	(7") **TO BE REBORN. / WHERE ARE YOU NOW**	13	
	(c-s+=)(cd-s+=) – ?		
Feb 88.	(7") **LIVE MY LIFE. / ('A'soul remix)**	62	40 Dec 87
	(12"+=) – ('A' club mix).		
Jun 88.	(7") **NO CLAUSE 28. / ('A'version)**	57	
	(12"+=) – ('A'version).		
Sep 88.	(7") **DON'T CRY. / LEAVE IN LOVE**		
	(12"+=) – ('A'&'B' versions).		
	(cd-s+=) – ('A'&'B' versions) / Boy called Alice.		
Oct 88.	(lp)(c)(cd) **TENSE NERVOUS HEADACHE**		
	– Don't cry / You are my heroin / I go where I go / Girl, with combination skin / Whisper / Something strange called love / I love you / Mama never knew / What becomes of the broken hearted?. (c+cd+=) – American boys / Happy family.		
Feb 89.	(7") **DON'T TAKE MY MIND ON A TRIP. / GIRLFRIEND**	68	
	(12"+=)(3"cd-s+=) – I go where I go.		

—— BOY GEORGE formed

JESUS LOVES YOU

		More Protein	More Protein
Nov 89.	(7") **AFTER THE LOVE. / ('A'version)**	68	
	(12"+=)(cd-s+=) – ('A'version).		
Jun 90.	(7")(c-s) **GENERATIONS OF LOVE. / ('A'dub version)**		
	(12"+=)(cd-s+=) – ('A' Sisters Of Mercy mix).		
Nov 90.	(7")(c-s) **ONE ON ONE. / ('A'Massive mix)**		
	(12"+=) – Generations of love (90's mix).		
	(cd-s++=) – After the love.		
Feb 91.	(7")(c-s) **BOW DOWN MISTER. / LOVE HURTS**	27	
	(12"+=) – ('A'mix).		
	(cd-s+=) – ('A'different mix).		
Apr 91.	(cd)(c)(lp) **THE MARTYR MANTRAS**	60	
	– Generations of love / One on one / Love's gonna let you down / After the love / I specialize in loneliness / No clause 28 / Love hurts / Siempre te amare / Too much love / Bow down mister. *(cd+=)* – Generations of love ('70 mix).		
May 91.	(7") **GENERATIONS OF LOVE. / ('A'mix)**	35	
	(12"+=) – ('A'love dub mix).		
	(cd-s++=) – ('A'different mixes).		
Sep 91.	(7") **AFTER THE LOVE '91. / ('A'version)**		
	(cd-s+=) – ('A'diff edit) / ('A' 10 glorious years mix).		
Nov 92.	(7")(c-s) **SWEET TOXIC THING. / AM I LOSING CONTROL**	65	
	(12"+=)(cd-s+=) – ('B'dizzy tequella mix) / Oh Lord.		

His label 'More Protein' was dropped by Virgin.

BOY GEORGE

(solo again)

		Spaghetti	S.B.K.
Sep 92.	(7")(c-s) **THE CRYING GAME. / I SPECIALIZE IN LONELINESS**	22	15 Feb 93
	(12"+=)(cd-s+=) – ('A'extended dance mix).		
		Virgin	Virgin
Mar 94.	(cd)(lp) **THE DEVIL IN SISTER GEORGE EP**	26	
	– Miss me blind / Generations of love / Am I losing control / Love hurts / Everything I own.		
——	GEORGE was credited on UK hit single 'More Than Likely' with PM DAWN.		
Mar 95.	(7")(c-s) **FUNTIME. / GENOCIDE PEROXIDE**	45	
	(12"+=)(cd-s+=) – ('A'mixes).		
May 95.	(cd)(c)(lp) **CHEAPNESS AND BEAUTY**	44	
	– Funtime / Satans butterfly ball / Sad / God don't hold a grudge / Genocide peroxide / If I could fly / Same thing in reverse / Cheapness and beauty / Evil is so civilised / Blind man / Your love is what I am / Unfinished business / Il adore.		
Jun 95.	(c-s) **IL ADORE / THESE BOOTS ARE MADE FOR WALKING**	50	
	(cd-s+=) – Sad / ('A'mixes).		
	(cd-s) – ('A'side) / Cheapness and beauty.		
——	In July '95, GEORGE was served a writ by one-time friend(?) KIRK BRANDON (Spear Of Destiny) for allegedly printing he was a closet homosexual in his book 'Take It Like A Man'.		
Sep 95.	(c-s) **SAME THING IN REVERSE / ('A'-Evolution radio screamer mix)**	56	
	(cd-s+=) – ('A'-Evolution brick in my hand mix) / ('A'-Clubzone).		
	(12") – (2 'A'-Clubzone mixes) / (2 'A'-Evolution mixes).		

BOY HAIRDRESSERS (see under ⇒ TEENAGE FAN CLUB)

BOYS NEXT DOOR (see under ⇒ BIRTHDAY PARTY)

Billy BRAGG

Born: STEVEN WILLIAM BRAGG, 20 Dec'57, Barking, Essex, England. In 1977, he formed PETERBOROUGH based R&B/punk band RIFF RAFF. When they split in 1981, he joined the army but bought himself out after 90 days. Complete with amplifier and guitar he busked around the cities, until he got studio time in 1983 by Charisma's indie subsidiary 'Utility'. LIFE'S A RIOT WITH SPY VS SPY was soon released and with help and distribution of new label 'Go! Discs' it finally hit UK top 30 early 1984. He continued with the label, issuing 45's for under a £1, due to initially not having to pay any band members. • **Style:** Socially aware rock that dubbed him 'the one-man Clash / Jam', mixing politics, love and basically songs about real people. • **Trivia:** He formed 'Red Wedge' in 1986 to help raise funds for the Labour Party through star gigs (i.e.STYLE COUNCIL, COMMUNARDS, himself, etc.). His stance with CND and anti-apartheid, anti-poll tax, etc, has often saw him on wrong side of the law. For the 90's it looks as though he will become a bit more cosmopolitan, but still ungagged. • **Songwriters:** Mostly all penned by himself except later collaborations with JOHNNY MARR, PETER BUCK and WIGGY. Covered; WALK AWAY RENEE (Four Tops) / SHE'S LEAVING HOME + REVOLUTION (Beatles) / JEANE (Smiths) / SEVEN AND SEVEN IS (Love) / THERE IS POWER IN A UNION (trad.new words) / THINK AGAIN (Dick Gaughan) / CHILE YOUR WATERS RUN RED THROUGH SOWETO (B.Johnson Reagan) / TRAIN TRAIN (Z.Delfeur) / DOLPHINS (Fred Neil) / EVERYWHERE (Sid Griffin-Greg Trooper) / JERUSALEM (William Blake) / WHEN WILL I SEE YOU AGAIN (Three Degrees).

Recommended: BACK TO BASICS (*9) / DON'T TRY THIS AT HOME (*8)

RIFF RAFF

(BILLY BRAGG – vocals, guitar) and other members

Chiswick | not issued

May 78. (7"ep) **I WANNA BE A COSMONAUT** [ ] [-]
– Cosmonaut / Romford girls / What's the latest? / Sweet as pie.

Geezer | not issued

Oct 80. (7") **EVERY GIRL AN ENGLISH ROSE. / U SHAPED HOUSE** [ ] [-]
Oct 80. (7") **KITTEN. / FANTOCIDE** [ ] [-]
Oct 80. (7") **LITTLE GIRLS KNOW. / SHE DON'T MATTER** [ ] [-]
Oct 80. (7") **NEW HOME TOWN. / RICHARD** [ ] [-]

BILLY BRAGG

went solo

Utility | not issued

Jun 83. (m-lp) **LIFE'S A RIOT WITH SPY VS.SPY** [30] [-]
– The milkman of human kindness / To have and have not / A new England / The man in the iron mask / The busy girl buys beauty / Lover's town revisited / Richard. *(re-iss.+c Jan84 on 'Go! Discs')*

— added for back-up **KENNY CRADDOCK** – organ / **DAVE WOODHEAD** – trumpet.

Go! Discs | Go! Discs

Oct 84. (lp)(c) **BREWING UP WITH BILLY BRAGG** [16] [-]
– It says here / Love gets dangerous / The myth of trust / From a Vauxhall Velox / The Saturday boy / Island of no return / St.Swithin's Day / Like soldiers do / This guitar says sorry / Strange things happen / A lover sings.
Feb 85. (7") **ST. SWITHIN'S DAY. / A NEW ENGLAND** [-] [ ] EURO
Mar 85. (7"ep) **BETWEEN THE WARS** [15] [-]
– Between the wars / Which side are you on? / World turned upside down / It says here.
Dec 85. (7"m) **DAYS LIKE THESE. / I DON'T NEED THIS PRESSURE RON / SCHOLARSHIP IS THE ENEMY OF ROMANCE** [43] [-]

— + guests **JOHNNY MARR** – guitar / **KIRSTY MacCOLL** – b.vocals / **KENNY JONES** – drums, co-producer / **JOHN PORTER** – bass, co-producer / **SIMON MORTEON** – perc. / **BOBBY VALENTINO** – violin.

Jun 86. (7"m) **LEVI STUBBS' TEARS. / THINK AGAIN / WALK AWAY RENEE** [29] [-]
(12"+=) – Between the wars (live).
Sep 86. (lp)(c) **TALKING WITH THE TAXMAN ABOUT POETRY** [8] [ ]
– Greetings to the new brunette / Train train / The marriage / Ideology / Levi Stubbs' tears / Honey, I'm a big boy now / There is power in a union / Help save the youth of America / Wishing the days away / The passion / The warmest room / The home front. *(cd-iss.May87)*
Nov 86. (7"m) **GREETINGS TO THE NEW BRUNETTE. / DEPORTEES / THE TATLER** [58] [-]
(12"+=) – Jeane / There is power in a union (instrumental).

Oct87 he is credited with OYSTER BAND backing **LEON ROSSELSON** on his single **BALLAD OF A SPYCATCHER** (Upside Down records)

— May88, he's credited with **CARA TIVEY** on 45 **SHE'S LEAVING HOME** the B-side of **WET WET WET** – With A little Help From My Friends. This UK No.1 single issued on 'Childline' gave all proceeds to children's charity, with backing including his usual friends.

May 88. (12"ep) **HELP SAVE THE YOUTH OF AMERICA (LIVE AND DUBIOUS)** [ ] [ ]
– Help save the youth of America / Think again / Chile your waters run red through Soweto / Days like these (DC mix) / To have and have not / There is power in a union (with The PATTERSONS).

Go! Discs | Elektra

Aug 88. (7"m) **WAITING FOR THE GREAT LEAP FORWARD. / WISHING THE DAYS AWAY / SIN CITY** [52] [ ]
Sep 88. (lp)(c)(cd) **WORKER'S PLAYTIME** [17] [ ]
– She's got a brand new spell / Must I paint you a picture / Tender comrade / The price I pay / Little timb-bomb / Rotting on demand / Valentine's day is over / Life with the lions / The only one / The short answer / Waiting for the great leap forward.
Nov 88. (7") **SHE'S GOT A BRAND NEW SPELL. / MUST I PAINT YOU A PICTURE** [ ] [-]
May 90. (cd)(c)(m-lp) **THE INTERNATIONALE** (on 'Utility' UK) [34] [ ]
– The internationale / I dreamed I saw Phil Ochs last night / The marching song of the convent battalions / Jerusalem / Nicaraguita / The red flag / My youngest son came home today.

— still holding on to **MARR, MacCOLL, TIVEY** (keyboards) and WOODHEAD. plus **WIGGY** – guitar, bass / **J.F.T.HOOD** – drums / **AMANDA VINCENT** – keyboards / etc.

Jun 91. (7") **SEXUALITY. / BAD PENNY** [27] [ ]
(12"+=)(cd-s+=) – (2 'A'mixes).
Aug 91. (7") **YOU WOKE UP MY NEIGHBOURHOOD. / ONTARIO, QUEBEC AND ME** [54] [ ]
(12"+=)(cd-s+=) – Bread and circuses / Heart like a wheel.

(above single 'A'featured **MICHAEL STIPE and PETER BUCK (R.E.M.)** with first 12"extra track with **NATALIE MERCHANT (10,000 MANIACS) – also b.vocals**

Sep 91. (cd)(c)(d-lp)(8x7"box) **DON'T TRY THIS AT HOME** [8] [ ]
– Accident waiting to happen / Moving the goalposts / Everywhere / Cindy of a thousand lives / You woke up my neighbourhood / Trust / God's footballer / The few / Sexuality / Mother of the bride / Tank park salute / Dolphins / North sea bubble / Rumours of war / Wish you were here / Body of water.
Feb 92. (7"ep) **ACCIDENT WAITING TO HAPPEN (Red Star version) / SULK. / THE WARMEST ROOM (live) / REVOLUTION** [33] [-]
(12"+=)(cd-s+=) – ('A'live version) / Levi Stubbs' tears / Valentine's day is over / North Sea bubble.

– compilations, others, etc. –

May 87. Strange Fruit; (12"ep) **THE PEEL SESSIONS** [ ] [-]
– A new England / Strange things happen / This guitar says sorry / Love gets dangerous / A13 trunk road to the sea / Fear . . .
Jun 87. Go! Discs; (d-lp)(d-c)(cd) **BACK TO BASICS** (best 83-85 material) [37] [-]
(re-iss.all albums Nov93 on 'Cooking Vinyl')
Feb 92. Strange Fruit; (cd)(lp) **THE PEEL SESSIONS ALBUM** [ ] [-]
Nov 93. Cooking Vinyl; (cd)(c)(d-lp) **VICTIM OF GEOGRAPHY** [ ] [-]

Delaney & Bonnie BRAMLETT (see under ⇒ DELANEY & BONNIE)

Kirk BRANDON'S 10:51 (see under ⇒ SPEAR OF DESTINY)

BREEDERS

Formed: Boston, USA . . . 1989 by TANYA DONNELLY (of THROWING MUSES) and KIM DEAL (of The PIXIES). Released an album 'Pod' in 1990, although TANYA was soon to leave for BELLY. In 1993, the BREEDERS were back with another gem album 'Last Splash' which sold massively in the States. • **Style:** Guitar-oriented but experimental indie rock act. • **Songwriters:** KIM DEAL wrote bulk from 1992 onwards. • **Covered:** HAPPINESS IS A WARM GUN (Beatles / George Harrison) / LORD OF THE THIGHS (Aerosmith). The AMPS covered JUST LIKE A BRIAR (Tasties).

Recommended: POD (*7) / LAST SPLASH (*9)

TANYA DONNELLY – rhythm guitar, vocals (of THROWING MUSES) with others **KIM DEAL** – guitar, vocals (of The PIXIES) / **JOSEPHINE WIGGS** – bass (of PERFECT DISASTER) repl. 2 from HUMAN SEXUAL RESPONSE. / **SHANNON DOUGHTY** – drums repl. NARCIZO.

4 a.d. | 4 a.d.

May 90. (cd)(c)(lp) **POD** [22] [ ]
– Glorious / Happiness is a warm gun / Oh! / Hellbound / When I was a painter / Fortunately gone / Iris / Opened / Only in 3's / Limehouse / Metal man.

— **DONNELLY, KIM DEAL, JO WIGGS + JON MATLOCK** (of SPIRITUALIZED)

Apr 92. (12"ep)(cd-ep) **SAFARI** [69] [ ]
– Safari / So sad about us / Do you love me now? / Don't call home.

— now **KIM** her sister **KELLEY DEAL** – guitar, vocals / **JO WIGGS** – bass, vox / **JIM MacPHERSON** – drums, vocals (living from 1989 Dayton, Ohio)

Aug 93. (12"ep)(cd-ep) **CANNONBALL. / CRO-ALOHA / LORD OF THE THIGHS / 900** [40] [44]
Sep 93. (cd)(c)(lp) **LAST SPLASH** [5] [33]
– New Year / Cannonball / Invisible man / No aloha / Roi / Do you love me now? / Flipside / I just wanna get along / Mad Lucas / Divine hammer / S.O.S./ Hag / Saints / Drivin' on 9 / Roi (reprise).
Oct 93. (7"clear)(c-s) **DIVINE HAMMER. / HOVERIN'** [59] [ ]
(10"ep+=)(cd-ep+=) – I can't help it (if I'm still in love with you) / Do you love me now Jr (J.Mascis remix).
Jul 94. (10"ep) **HEAD TO TOE. / SHOCKER IN GLOOMTOWN / FREED PIG** [68] [-]
(cd-ep+=) – Saints.

AMPS

KIM DEAL / JIM MacPHERSON / NATHAN FARLEY + LUIS LERMA

4 a.d. | 4 a.d.

Oct 95. (12"ep)(cd-ep) **TIPP CITY / JUST LIKE A BRIAR. / EMPTY GLASSES (Kim's basement 4 track version)** 61 |
Oct 95. (cd)(c)(lp) **PACER** 60 |
– Pacer / Tipp city / I am decided / Mom's drunk / Bragging party / Hoverin' / First revival / Full on idle / Breaking the split screen barrier / Empty glasses / She's a girl / Dedicated.

Edie BRICKELL & The NEW BOHEMIANS

Formed: Dallas, Texas, USA . . . 1985, when she drank enough to pluck up courage to venture onto stage next to band. Now a group, they signed to Geffen records, recording debut album with producer Pat Moran in Wales. This went platinum in the States, reaching Top 5, after release of 45 'WHAT I AM'. • **Style:** Soft-rock campus crooner with band leaning into muso/jazz, and her voice/range similar to RICKIE LEE JONES, JONI MITCHELL or MELANIE. • **Songwriters:** EDIE wrote most of material except some with WITHROW / and also BUSH. Covered; A HARD RAIN'S A-GONNA FALL (Bob Dylan) / WALK ON THE WILD SIDE (Lou Reed) / THE EARLY DAY (John Williams). • **Trivia:** In Dec'89, they collaborated on vinyl with SOUL II SOUL recording their own composition CIRCLE. EDIE married PAUL SIMON in Jun'92.

Recommended: SHOOTING RUBBERBANDS AT THE STARS (*6)

EDIE BRICKELL (b.'66) – vocals / with **KENNY WITHROW** – guitar / **BRAD HAUSER** – bass / **CHRIS WHITTON** – drums / **JOHN BUSH** – percussion / **WIX** – keyboards / (some keyboards by **BRENDAN ALY**)

Geffen | Geffen

Sep 88. (lp)(c)(cd) **SHOOTING RUBBERBANDS AT THE STARS** 25 | 4
– What I am? / Little Miss S. / Air of December / Love like we do / The wheel / Circle / Beat the time / She / Nothing / Now / Keep coming back. *(cd+=)* – I do. *(re-dist.Feb89) (re-iss.cd Mar95)*
Jan 89. (7") **WHAT I AM?. / I DO** 31 | 7 Nov 88
(12"+=)(cd-s+=) – Walk on the wild side.

—— **MARTIN** – keyboards repl. WIX

Apr 89. (7") **CIRCLE. / NOW (version)** 74 | 48
(12"+=)(cd-s+=) – Plain Jane.
Next 45, was from the film 'Born On The 4th Of July' on 'M.C.A.'
Mar 90. (7") **A HARD RAIN'S A-GONNA FALL. / THE EARLY DAY, MASSAPEQUA 1957** |
(12"+=)(cd-s+=) – ('A'version).
Nov 90. (cd)(c)(lp) **GHOST OF A DOG** 63 | 32
– Mama help me / Black and blue / Carmelito / He said / Times like this / Ghost of a dog / 10,000 angels / Strings of love / Woyaha / Oak cliff bra / Stwisted / This eye. *(re-iss.cd Mar95)*
Jan 91. (7")(c-s) **MAMA HELP ME. / OAK CLIFF BRA** |
(12"+=)(cd-s+=) – What I am / Beat the time (live).

EDIE BRICKELL

—— with **BILL DILLON, KENNY WITHROW, JOHN LEVENTHAL or BRIAN SOLTZ** – guitar / **TONY HALL, BAKIITHI KUMALO or BRAD HOUSER** – bass / **SHAWN PELTON or WILLIE GREEN** – drums / + guests hubby **PAUL SIMON + ART NEVILLE**

Geffen | Geffen

Aug 94. (cd)(c) **PICTURE PERFECT MORNING** 59 | 68
– Tomorrow comes / Green / When the lights go down / Good times / Another woman's dream / Stay awhile / Hard times / Olivia / In the bath / Picture perfect morning / Lost in the moment.
Sep 94. (c-s)(cd-s) **GOOD TIMES / PICTURE PERFECT MORNING / LOOK OUT FOR ME** 40 | 60

—— Above was a duet with BARRY WHITE!

BRIDGES (see under ⇒ A-HA)

BRINSLEY SCHWARZ

Formed: Turnbridge Wells, England . . . 1965 as KIPPINGTON LODGE by SCHWARZ and NICK LOWE. Released a number of singles in the 60's, before on Oct'69, took BRINSLEY SCHWARZ as group name. On 3rd Apr'70, their management team, with hype the theme, hired a plane to fly rock journalists to see them support VAN MORRISON in New York. This proved to be a six-figure sum disaster. 'United Art' released eponymous debut same time, but 'DESPITE IT ALL' (the name of that years' follow-up) they came to be regarded as large "pub-rock" attractions of the early 70's. This launched others into more lucrative pop careers (aka LOWE – solo / SCHWARZ and ANDREWS – The RUMOUR (see; GRAHAM PARKER). • **Style:** They fused heavy blues with CSN&Y harmonies, which grew into own basic R&B pub rock sound. • **Songwriters:** Until GOMM's arrival, LOWE had written near every song. They built up own dual writing team. Also covered (Beatles) I SHOULD HAVE KNOWN BETTER. / TELL ME WHY as 'The LIME-LIGHT' in '75. • **Trivia:** In 1974, they were featured as The ELECTRICIANS (with DAVE EDMUNDS; their sometimes producer) in the film 'Stardust'.

Recommended: SURRENDER TO THE RHYTHM (THE BEST OF . . .) (*6)

KIPPINGTON LODGE

BRINSLEY SCHWARZ – guitar, sax / **NICK LOWE** – vocals, bass / **BARRY LANDERMAN** – organ / **PETE WHALE** – drums

Parlophone | not iss.

Oct 67. (7") **SHY BOY. / LADY ON A BICYCLE** | -
Mar 68. (7") **RUMOURS. / AND SHE CRIED** | -
(above 4 tracks re-iss.Nov78.7"ep on 'EMI')

—— **BOB ANDREWS** (b.20 Jun'49) – organ, vox repl. BARRY to VANITY FARE

Aug 68. (7") **TELL ME A STORY. / UNDERSTAND A WOMAN** | -
Dec 68. (7") **TOMORROW TODAY. / TURN OUT THE LIGHT** | -
May 69. (7") **IN MY LIFE. / I CAN SEE HER FACE** | -

BRINSLEY SCHWARZ

(BRINSLEY, NICK and BOB) recruited **BILLY RANKIN** – drums to repl. PETE

United Art | Capitol

Apr 70. (lp) **BRINSLEY SCHWARZ** |
– Hymn to me / Shining brightly / Rock & roll women / Lady constant / What do you suggest / Mayfly / Ballad of a has-been beauty queen. *(cd-iss.Feb94 on 'Repertoire')*
1970. (7") **SHINING BRIGHTLY. / WHAT DO YOLU SUGGEST** | -

Liberty | not issued

1971 (7") **DESPITE IT ALL** | -
– Country girl / The slow one / Funk angel / Piece of home / Love song / Starship / Ebury down / Old Jarrow.
1970. (7") **COUNTRY GIRL. / FUNK ANGEL** | -

—— added **IAN GOMM** – guitar, vocals

United Art | United Art

Feb 72. (lp)(c) **SILVER PISTOL** |
– Dry land / Merry go round / One more day / Nightingale / Silver pistol / The last time I was fooled / Unknown number / Range war / Egypt / Niki Hoeke speedway / Ju ju man / Rockin' chair. *(re-iss.Apr86 on 'Edsel')*
Contributed 5 tracks to 'GREASY TRUCKERS' live lp, Apr72.
Sep 72. (lp)(c) **NERVOUS ON THE ROAD** |
– It's been so long / Happy doing what we're doing / Surrender to the rhythm / Don't lose your grip on love / Nervous on the road (but can't stay at home) / Feel a little funky / I like it like that / Brand new you, brand new me / Home in my hand / Why why why why why. *(re-iss.Dec80 on 'Liberty')*
May 73. (7") **THE HYPOCRITE. (as "The HITLERS") / ('A'version)** | -
Aug 73. (7") **SPEEDO. / I WORRY** | -
Oct 73. (lp)(c) **PLEASE DON'T EVER CHANGE** | -
– Hooked on love / Why do we hurt the one we love? / I worry ('bout you baby) / Don't ever change / Home in my hand / Play that fast thing (one more time) / I won't make it without you / Down in Mexico / Speedo / Hypocrite (the version). *(re-iss.Jan88 on 'Edsel')*
Mar 74. (7") **I'VE CRIED MY LAST TEAR. / (IT'S GONNA BE A) BRING DOWN** | -
May 74. (7") **(WHAT'S SO FUNNY 'BOUT) PEACE, LOVE AND UNDERSTANDING. / EVER SINCE YOU'RE GONE** | -
Jul 74. (lp)(c) **NEW FAVOURITES OF BRINSLEY SCHWARZ** | -
– Peace, love and understanding / Ever since you're gone / Ugly things / I got the real thing / Look what's in your eye tonight / Now's the time / Small town, big city / Trying to live my life without you / I like you I don't love you / Down in the dive. *(re-iss.Aug80 on 'Liberty')*
Jan 75. (7") **I LIKE YOU, I DON'T LOVE YOU. / EVERYBODY** | -
Jan 75. (7") **I SHOULD HAVE KNOWN BETTER. (as "The LIMELIGHT") / TELL ME WHY** | -

The BRINSLEYS

Mar 75. (7") **THERE'S A CLOUD IN MY HEART. / I GOT THE REAL THING** | -

—— Disbanded Mar75. SCHWARZ and RANKIN joined DUCKS DELUXE, The former later joining with ANDREWS in GRAHAM PARKER & THE RUMOUR. IAN GOMM later went solo, as did NICK LOWE (see ⇒)

– compilations, others, etc. –

Mar 74. United Artists; (lp)(c) **ORIGINAL GOLDEN GREATS** | -
Jun 76. United Artists; (7"m) **COUNTRY GIRL. / HOOKED ON LOVE / SURRENDER TO THE RHYTHM** | -
Jul 78. United Artists; (lp)(c) **FIFTEEN THOUGHTS OF BRINSLEY SCHWARZ** | -
Sep 78. United Artists; (7") **PEACE, LOVE AND UNDERSTANDING. / I'VE CRIED MY LAST TEAR** | -
May 88. Decal-Charly; (lp)(c)(cd) **IT'S ALL OVER NOW** | -
Jul 91. E.M.I.; (cd)(c)(lp) **SURRENDER TO THE RHYTHM (THE BEST OF BRINSLEY SCHWARZ)** | -
– Country girl / Surrender to the rhythm / Ugly things / Happy what we're doing / The look what's in your eyes / Last time I was fooled / Silver pistol / Nightingale / Hypocrite / Trying to live my life without you / I like it like that / Nervous on the road / Down in Mexico / I worry ('bout you baby) / Play that fast thing (one more time) / Don't lose your grip on love / Ju Ju man / Down in the dive / Home in my hand.
Jul 94. Beat Goes On; (cd) **BRINSLEY SCHWARZ / DESPITE IT ALL** | -
Dec 95. BGO; (cd) **NERVOUS ON THE ROAD / THE NEW FAVOURITES OF . . .** | -

BRITISH LIONS (see under ⇒ MOTT THE HOOPLE)

Dave BROCK (see under ⇒ HAWKWIND)

BRONSKI BEAT

Formed: Hackney, London, England . . . 1984 by STEVE, LARRY and JIMI. Form own 'Forbidden Fruit' label in conjunction with 'London' records and release debut hit single 'SMALLTOWN BOY', about a homosexual who has runaway to London. JIMI / others, were open gay activists who also supported 'Red Wedge' & Labour Party. • **Style:** Electro-pop/dance rock that first highlighted JIMI's falsetto vocal. • **Songwriters:** STEVE; music / JIMI; words (until his departure), except covers IT AIN'T NECESSARILY SO (Gershwin) / I FEEL LOVE – LOVE TO LOVE YOU BABY (Donna Summer / G. Moroder)/JOHNNY REMEMBER ME (Johnny Leyton) / I'M GONNA RUN AWAY FROM YOU (Tammi Lynn). • **Trivia:** Early '85, JIMI was fined £50 for gross indecency when he admited openly of being caught by police in a gay sexual act. The single 'HIT THAT PERFECT BEAT' was used on the film 'Letter To Brezhnev'.

Recommended: THE AGE OF CONSENT (*7).

JIMI SOMERVILLE (b.JIMMY, 22 May'61, Glasgow, Scotland) – vocals / **STEVE BRONSKI** (b.STEVE FORREST, 7 Feb'60, Glasgow) – synthesizer, piano / **LARRY STEINBACHEK** (b. 6 May'60, London) – synthesizer, keyboards

London | M.C.A.

May 84. (7")(7"sha-pic-d) **SMALLTOWN BOY. / MEMORIES** [3] [48] Dec 84
(12"+=) – Infatuation.

Sep 84. (7")(12") **WHY?. / CADILLAC CAR** [6] [ ]

Oct 84. (lp)(c)(cd) **THE AGE OF CONSENT** [4] [36] Jan 85
– Why? / It ain't necessarily so / Screaming / No more war / Love and money / Smalltown boy / Heatwave / Junk / Need a man blues / I feel love – Johnny remember me. (cd+=) – (12"mixes of first 2 singles).

Nov 84. (7") **IT AIN'T NECESSARILY SO. / CLOSE TO THE EDGE** [16] [ ]
(12"+=) – Red dance.

Apr 85. (7") **I FEEL LOVE (Medley) – I FEEL LOVE / LOVE TO LOVE YOU BABY / JOHNNY REMEMBER ME (as "BRONSKI BEAT & MARC ALMOND"). / PUIT D'AMOUR** [3] [ ]
(12+=)(10"+=) – ('A'instrumental).
(extra-12"+=) – The potato fields / Signs (and wonders).

— (May85) **JOHN JON FOSTER** (b.Newcastle, England) – vocals repl. JIMMY SOMERVILLE who formed COMMUNARDS, before going solo in 1989.

Sep 85 (m-lp)(c)(cd) **HUNDREDS AND THOUSANDS (re-mixes)** [24] [ ]
– Heatwave (remix) / Why (remix) / Run from love / Hard rain / Smalltown boy (remix) / Junk / Infatuation – Memories / Close to the edge / I feel love – Love to love you baby – Johnny remember me / Cadillac car. *(re-iss.cd+c May93 on 'Spectrum')*

Nov 85. (7")(12") **HIT THAT PERFECT BEAT. / I GAVE YOU EVERYTHING** [3] [ ]

Mar 86. (7") **C'MON, C'MON. / SOMETHING SPECIAL** [20] [ ]
(12"+=) – Drum majors.

May 86. (lp)(c)(cd) **TRUTHDARE DOUBLEDARE** [18] [ ]
– Hit that perfect beat / Truthdare doubledare / C'mon, c'mon / Punishment for love / We know how it feels / This heart / Do it / Dr.John / In my dreams. (cd+=) – What are you going to do about it? / I gave you everything. (c++=) – C'mon, c'mon (12"remix) / Hit that perfect beat (12"remix).

Aug 86. (7")(12") **THIS HEART. / WHAT ARE YOU GOING TO DO ABOUT IT?** [ ] [ ]

— (Oct88) **JONATHAN HELLYER** – vocals repl. JOHN who left late '86.

Arista | Arista

Jun 89. (7")(c-s) **CHA CHA HEELS (as "EARTHA KIT & BRONSKI BEAT"). / MY DISCARDED MEN** [ ] [ ]
(12"+=)(cd-s+=) – ('A'version).

Zed Beat | not issued

Nov 90. (7") **I'M GONNA RUN AWAY FROM YOU. / SWEET THING** [ ] [ ]
(12"+=)(cd-s+=) – ('A'extended).

Feb 91. (7")(c-s) **ONE MORE CHANCE. / BETTER TIMES** [ ] [ ]
(12"+=) – I'm gonna run away from you.
(cd-s++=) – ('A'version).

– compilations, others, etc. –

Jan 91. London (7")(12")(cd-s) **SMALLTOWN BOY.** [ ] [ ]
(other tracks by COMMUNARDS & JIMMY SOMERVILLE) BRONSKI BEAT tracks also on JIMMY SOMERVILLE compilation

Jan 91. (cd)(c)(lp) **THE SINGLES COLLECTION 1984-90**
(see under COMMUNARDS)

Gary BROOKER (see under ⇒ PROCOL HARUM)

Elkie BROOKS

Born: ELAINE BOOKBINDER, 25 Feb'45, Manchester, England. Her early years in the 60's consisted of several flop singles, but chose rock music when joining DADA in 1970. There she co-sang with future superstar ROBERT PALMER but they fragmented into VINEGAR JOE. After three albums for 'Island' in the early 70's, they disband. By 1975 she had landed contract with major 'A&M' label, and was soon on her way to the UK Top 10 with 'PEARL'S A SINGER'. She continued to sparkle for the next decade, and scored an even bigger hit in 1986 with 'NO MORE THE FOOL'. • **Style:** Her raunchy rock vocals, were compared to TINA TURNER or the late great JANIS JOPLIN. After initial success, she moved into more mellowed commercial MOR music. She was provided with • **Songwriters:** LEIBER & STOLLER (on TWO DAYS AWAY lp). Her many covers included:-SOMETHING'S GOT A HOLD ON ME (Etta James) / THE WAY YOU DO THE THINGS YOU DO / FOOL IF YOU THINK IT'S OVER (Chris Rea) / STAY WITH ME (Faces) / GASOLINE ALLEY (Rod Stewart) / ONLY LOVE CAN BREAK YOUR HEART (Neil Young) / NIGHTS IN WHITE SATIN (Moody Blues) / HE'S A REBEL (Crystals) / LOVE POTION No.9 (Clovers) / RESCUE ME (Fontella Bass) / SWEET NUTHIN'S (Brenda Lee) / The album SCREEN GEMS (was all film songs) / DANCE AWAY (Roxy Music) / STAIRWAY TO HEAVEN (Led Zeppelin) / PIECE OF MY HEART (Janis Joplin) / SAIL ON (Commodores) / WE'VE GOT TONIGHT (Bob Seger) / IF YOU LEAVE ME NOW (Chicago) / TOO BUSY THINKIN' 'BOUT MY BABY (Marvin Gaye) / etc. Her 1989 album was also totally covers, mainly Top 10. In 1986 she co-wrote with RUSS BALLARD and '88 with TREVER JORDAN. • **Trivia:** Late 1978, she married her sound engineer TREVOR JORDAN and later gave birth to baby JORDAN.

Recommended: PEARLS (*5)

ELKIE BROOKS

solo. – vocals, tambourine

Decca | Parrot

Jul 64. (7") **SOMETHING'S GOT A HOLD OF ME. / HELLO STRANGER** [ ] [-]

Sep 64. (7") **NOTHING LEFT TO DO BUT CRY. / STRANGE THO' IT SEEMS** [ ] [ ] Nov 64

Jan 65. (7") **THE WAY YOU DO THE THINGS YOU DO. / BLUE TONIGHT** [ ] [-]

H.M.V. | not issued

Jun 65. (7") **HE'S GOTTA LOVE ME. / WHEN YOU APPEAR** [ ] [-]

Oct 65. (7") **ALL OF MY LIFE. / CAN'T STOP THINKING OF YOU** [ ] [-]

1966. (7") **BABY LET ME LOVE YOU. / STOP THE MUSIC** [ ] [-]

— She spent the next 3 years, backing HUMPHREY LYTTLETON and ERIC DELANEY. She returned to record one more solo for

NEMS | not issued

Apr 69. (7") **COME SEPTEMBER. / IF YOU SHOULD GO** [ ] [-]

— In 1970, she joined

DADA

a jazz-fusion rock band based in London. also **PAUL KORDA** – vocals / **PETE GAGE** (b.31 Aug'47) – **guitar** (ex-G.WASHINGTON) / **STEVE LUKATHER** – guitar / **DON SHINN** – keyboards / **STEVE YORK** – bass / **MARTYN HARRYMAN** – drums / **MALCOLM CAPEWELL** – wind / **BARRY DUGGAN** – wind / **ERNIE LAUCHLAN** – horns

Atco | Atco

Jan 71. (lp) **DADA** [ ] [-]
– Big dipper / The last time / This is my song / Seed of peace / Organ interlude / Tonite is / She walks away / Aspen, Colorado / Eyes of the warren / Jasamin / Dada.

— **ROBERT PALMER** – vocals (ex-ALAN BOWN SET) repl. KORDA

VINEGAR JOE

late '71 **(BROOKS, PALMER, GAGE, YORK) were basic foursome, with sessioners.**

Island | Atco

Feb 72. (7") **NEVER MET A DOG. / SPEED QUEEN OF VENTURA** [ ] [-]

Apr 72. (lp)(c) **VINEGAR JOE** [ ] [-]
– Rusty red armour / Early Monday morning / Ride me easy rider / Circles / Leg up / See the world / Never met a dog / Avinu malkenu / Geetin' out / Live a little get somewhere.

1972. (7") **SEE THE WORLD. / CIRCLES** [-] [ ]

Nov 72. (7") **ROCK'N'ROLL GYPSIES. / SO LONG** [ ] [-]

Dec 72. (lp)(c) **ROCK'N'ROLL GYPSIES** [ ] [ ]
– So long / Charlie's horse / Rock'n'roll gypsies / Falling / It's getting to the point / Whole lotta shakin' goin' on / Buddy can you spare a line / Angel / No one ever does / Forgive us. *(cd-iss. Feb 90)*

Feb 73. (7") **ROCK'N'ROLL GYPSIES. / WHOLE LOTTA SHAKIN' GOIN' ON** [-] [ ]

Oct 73. (7") **BLACK SMOKE FROM THE CALUMET. / LONG WAY ROUND** [ ] [-]

Oct 73. (lp)(c) **SIX STAR GENERAL** [ ] [-]
– Proud to be / Food for thought / Dream of my own dreams / Lady of the rain / Stay true to yourself / Black smoke rising from the calumet / Giving yourself away / Talkin' 'bout my baby / Let me down easy / Fine thing.

— Disbanded early 1974, ROBERT PALMER goes solo (see ⇒)

ELKIE BROOKS

releases one-off for retainer

Island | not issued

Feb 74. (7") **RESCUE ME. / SWEET NUTHIN'S** [ ] [-]

— She moved to Macon, Georgia, USA for a year to back vox for WET WILLIE. Returned to England, to record for new label.

A&M | A&M

Oct 75. (7") **WHERE DO WE GO FROM HERE (RICH MAN'S WOMAN). / ?** [-] [ ]

Oct 75. (lp)(c) **RICH MAN'S WOMAN** [ ] [ ]
– Where do we go from here (rich man's woman) / Take cover / Jigsaw baby / Roll me over / He's a rebel / One step on the ladder / Rock'n'roll circus / Try a little love / Tomorrow. *(re-iss.May85 on 'Hallmark') (cd-iss.1989 on 'Pickwick')*

Jan 76. (7") **HE'S A REBEL. / TRY A LITTLE LOVE** [ ] [ ]

Mar 77. (7") **PEARL'S A SINGER. / YOU DID SOMETHING FOR ME** [8] [ ]

May 77. (lp)(c) **TWO DAYS AWAY** [16] [ ]
– Love potion No.9 / Spiritland / Honey, can I put on your clothes / Sunshine after the rain / Pearl's a singer / Mojo Hannah / Do right woman, do right man / You did something for me / Night bird / Saved. *(re-iss.1988)*
Jun 77. (7") **SAVED. / NIGHTBIRD** [ ] [-]
Aug 77. (7") **SUNSHINE AFTER THE RAIN. / SPIRIT LAND** [10] [-]
Aug 77. (7") **SUNSHINE AFTER THE RAIN. / YOU DID SOMETHING FOR ME** [-] [ ]
Oct 77. (7") **LOVE POTION NO. 9. / HONEY, CAN I PUT ON YOUR CLOTHES** [-] [ ]
Nov 77. (7") **DO RIGHT WOMAN, DO RIGHT MAN. / LOVE POTION No.9** [ ] [ ]
Feb 78. (7") **LILAC WINE. / LIVE, LAUGH & LOVE** [16] [ ]
Apr 78. (lp)(c) **SHOOTING STAR** [20] [ ]
– Only love can break your heart / Be positive / Since you went away / Putting my heart on the line / Stay with me / As / Learn to love / Too precious / Shooting star / Just an excuse.
Apr 78. (7") **ONLY LOVE CAN BREAK YOUR HEART. / JUST AN EXCUSE** [43] [ ]
Jul 78. (7") **SINCE YOU WENT AWAY. / TOO PRECIOUS** [ ] [ ]
Oct 78. (7") **DON'T CRY OUT LOUD. / GOT TO BE A WINNER** [12] [ ]
Apr 79. (7") **THE RUNAWAY. / ONE STEP OVER THE LADDER** [50] [ ]
Sep 79. (7") **HE COULD HAVE BEEN IN THE ARMY. / NOT ENOUGH LOVIN' LEFT** [ ] [-]
Sep 79. (lp)(c) **LIVE AND LEARN** [34] [ ]
– Viva la money / On the horizon / He could have been in the army / The rising cost of love / Dream dealer / Who's making love / If you can't beat me rockin' / The heartache is on / Not enough lovin' left / Falling star. *(re-iss.Mar82) (re-iss.May84 on 'Pickwick', cd-iss.1989)*
Nov 79. (7") **FALLING STAR. / DREAM DEALER** [ ] [-]
May 80. (7") **WHY DON'T YOU SAY IT. / WE ALL HAVE OUR DREAMS** [ ] [-]
Jul 80. (7") **PAINT YOUR PRETTY PICTURE. / PULL ON THE ROPE** [ ] [-]
Oct 80. (7") **DANCE AWAY. / PLAY THE WAY I FEEL** [ ] [-]
Oct 81. (7") **WARM AND TENDER LOVE. / THANK YOU FOR THE NIGHT** [ ] [-]
Nov 81. (lp)(c) **PEARLS** (part hits compilation) [2] [ ]
– Superstar / Fool if you think it's over / Givin' it up for love / Sunshine after the rain / Warm and tender love / Lilac wine / Pearl's a singer / Don't cry out loud / Too busy thinkin' 'bout my baby / If you leave me now / Paint your pretty picture / Dance away. *(cd-iss.Apr84)*
Dec 81. (7") **FOOL IF YOU THINK IT'S OVER. / GIVIN' IT UP FOR LOVE** [17] [ ]
Apr 82. (7") **OUR LOVE. / NOTHING IN THIS WORLD** [43] [ ]
Jul 82. (7") **NIGHTS IN WHITE SATIN. / LILAC WINE (live)** [33] [ ]
Oct 82. (lp)(c) **PEARLS II** [5] [ ]
– Goin' back / Our love / Gasoline alley / I just can't go on / Too much between us / Don't stop / Giving you hope / Money / Nights in white satin / Will you write me a song. *(cd-iss.Aug91) (re-iss.cd+c May93 on 'Spectrum')*
Nov 82. (7") **WILL YOU WRITE ME A SONG. / GIVING YOU HOPE** [ ] [-]
Dec 82. (7") **GASOLINE ALLEY. / LOVING ARMS** [52] [-]
Feb 83. (7") **I JUST CAN'T GO ON. / FORBIDDEN TERRITORY** [ ] [-]

— Her backing band now **DUNCAN MACKAY** – keyboards / **ZAL CLEMINSON** – guitar / **JOHN GIBLIN** – bass / **MATTHEW LATHLEY** – drums / **DUNCAN KINNELL** – percussion

Jun 84. (7") **MINUTES. / JUST ONE MORE DAY** [ ] [-]
Jun 84. (lp)(c) **MINUTES** [35] [-]
– Minutes / Driftin' / Night run / Take your freedom / Growing tired / Born lucky / I've been in love before / Too heavy too strong / Cross fire / Work pay.
Sep 84. (7") **DRIFTIN'. / ANY TIME** [ ] [-]

E.M.I. / Capitol

Oct 84. (7") **ONCE IN A WHILE. / WHAT'LL I DO** [ ] [-]
Nov 84. (lp)(c)(cd) **SCREEN GEMS** [35] [ ]
– Am I blue / Me and my shadow / Some of these days / You'll never know / My foolish heart / 3 o'clock in the morning / Once in a while / That old feeling / Blue Moon / Ain't misbehavin' / What'll I do / Love me or leave me.

Legend / not issued

Nov 86. (7") **NO MORE THE FOOL. / CITY LIGHTS** [5] [ ]
(12"+=) – Blue Jay.
Dec 86. (lp)(c)(cd) **NO MORE THE FOOL** [5] [ ]
– No more the fool / Only women bleed / No secrets (call of the wild) / break the chain / We've got tonight / All or nothing / Don't want to cry no more / Hiding inside yourself / Hold the dream.
Feb 87. (7") **BREAK THE CHAIN. / THE GROVE** [55] [-]
(12"+=) – ('A'extended) (7" w/free c-s. cont. diff. versions.
(cd-s++=) – No more the fool.
(d7"+=) – No more the fool / City lights.
Jun 87. (7") **WE'VE GOT TONIGHT. / HOLD THE DREAM (live)** [69] [ ]
(12"+=)(c-s+=) – ('A'live) / Piece of my heart.
Apr 88. (7") **SAIL ON. / THE DOOR** [ ] [-]
(12"+=)(cd-s+=) – ('A' extended).
Jun 88. (lp)(c)(cd) **BOOKBINDER'S KID** [57] [-]
– Sail on / Stairway to Heaven / You ain't leaving / Keep it a secret / When the hero walks alone / Only love will set you free * / What's the matter baby / Can't wait all night / Kiss me for the last time / Love is love / Foolish games / I can dream, can't I. (c+=*)(cd+=*)

Telstar / not issued

Sep 89. (7") **SHAME. / THE KI** [ ] [-]
(12"+=)(cd-s+=) – ('A'extended).
Oct 89. (lp)(c)(cd) **INSPIRATIONS** [58] [-]
– You're my inspiration / Shame / Broken wings / Hard habit to break / Every little bit hurts / Is this love / Maybe I'm amazed / In it for the same thing / Touch of Paradise / Black smoke / The ki / Tear it down / Three wishes. *(re-iss.cd+c Jul93 on 'Ronco')*
Feb 90. (7") **I'LL NEVER LOVE THIS WAY AGAIN. / DEDICATED TO YOU** [ ] [-]

Freestyle / not issued

Sep 91. (cd-s) **THE LAST TEARDROP / OFF THE BEATEN TRACK / FOR THE WORLD** [ ] [-]
Sep 91. (cd)(c)(lp) **PEARLS III – CLOSE TO THE EDGE** [ ] [-]

Castle / not issued

Mar 93. (cd)(c) **'ROUND MIDNIGHT** [27] [-]
– All night long / What kind of man are you / Since I fell for you / Cry me a river / Don't explain / Just for a thrill / 'Round midnight / Hard times / Black coffee / Travellin' light / Drinking again / Here's that rainy day / Save your love for me / Don't smoke in bed / Crazy he calls me / Spring can really hang you up the most.

— (all cover versions on above album, including WHAT KIND OF MAN ARE YOU (Ray Charles) + DON'T SMOKE IN BED (Smokey Robinson)

Castle / not issued

Apr 94. (cd)(c) **NOTHIN' BUT THE BLUES** (covers) [58] [-]
– I ain't got nothin' but the blues / Baby get lost / Blues for mama / Baby what you want me to do / Tell me more and then some / I'd rather go blind / I wonder who / Ain't no use / Nobody but you / I love your lovin' ways / Bad bad whiskey / Fine and mellow / Me and my gin / Mean and evil / Trouble in mind / Please send me someone to love.
Apr 95. (cd)(c) **CIRCLES** [ ] [ ]
– It all comes back on you / Live a little get somewhere / Circles / Mercedes Benz / Can't find my way home / Angel / Pearl's a singer / Live in peace / Butterfly bleu / You're gonna make me cry / Lilac wine.

– compilations, others, etc. –

Sep 85. Old Gold; (7") **PEARL'S A SINGER. / SUNSHINE AFTER THE RAIN** [ ] [-]
Oct 88. Old Gold; (7") **LILAC WINE. / DON'T CRY OUT LOUD** [ ] [-]
Feb 87. Telstar; (lp)(c)(cd) **THE VERY BEST OF ELKIE BROOKS** [10] [-]
1987. Castle; (d-lp)(cd) **THE COLLECTION** [ ] [-]
Nov 87. C5; (lp)(c) **THE EARLY YEARS 1964-66** [ ] [-]
Aug 88. A&M; (cd-ep) **COMPACT HITS** [ ] [-]
– Pearl's a singer / Sunshine after the rain / Only love can break your heart / Nights in white satin.
Oct 93. A&M; (cd) **PEARLS / TWO DAYS AWAY** [ ] [-]
Apr 93. Tring; (cd)(c) **PEARLS 3** [ ] [-]
Mar 93. Demon; (cd) **SIX STAR GYPSIES (VINEGAR JOE)** [ ] [-]
Aug 94. Pickwick; (cd)(c) **PRICELESS – HER VERY BEST** [ ] [-]
Jan 95. Spectrum; (cd) **WE'VE GOT TONIGHT** [ ] [-]
(re-iss.cd/c Jun95 on 'Truetrax')

Edgar BROUGHTON BAND

Formed: Warwick, England . . . 1968 by EDGAR and brother STEVE, although they moved to London in 1970. Already signed to 'Harvest', they began onsurge into British chart, with anthemic 'OUT DEMONS OUT'. Dogged by management problems and free festival inclinations, they soon dissolved. • **Style:** Hippie-metal, near to HAWKWIND, but with heavy occult overtones. • **Songwriters:** The BROUGHTONS, except OUT DEMONS OUT (Fugs). Their 'APACHE DROPOUT' was actually fused with The SHADOWS and CAPTAIN BEEFHEART songs. • **Trivia:** STEVE BROUGHTON drummed on MIKE OLDFIELD's 'Tubular Bells'.

Recommended: AS WAS (*6)

EDGAR BROUGHTON (b. ROBERT EDGAR BROUGHTON, 24 Oct'47) – vocals, guitar / **STEVE BROUGHTON** (b.20 May'50) – drums / **ARTHUR GRANT** (b.14 May'50) – bass, vocals / **VICTOR UNITT** (b. 5 Jul'46) – guitar

Harvest / Harvest

Jun 69. (7") **EVIL. / DEATH OF AN ELECTRIC CITIZEN** [ ] [ ]
Jul 69. (lp) **WASA WASA** [ ] [ ]
– Death of an electric citizen / American boy soldier / Why can't somebody love me / Neptune / Evil / Crying / Love in the rain / Dawn crept away. *(cd-iss.May92 on 'B.G.O.')*

— Became a trio early in 1970 when VICTOR joined The PRETTY THINGS

Mar 70. (7") **OUT DEMONS OUT. / MOMMA'S REWARD** [39] [ ]
May 70. (7") **UP YOURS. / OFFICER DAN** [ ] [ ]
Jun 70. (lp)(c) **SING BROTHER SING** [18] [ ]
– There's no vibrations but wait / The moth; (a) The moth, (b) People, (c) Peter / Momma's reward (keep them freaks a-rollin') / Refugee / Officer Dan / Old Gopher / Aphrodite / Granma / The psychopath; (a) The psychopath, (b) Is for butterflies / It's falling away. *(cd-iss.May92 on 'B.G.O.')*

— **VICTOR UNITT** – guitar, vocals returned.

Nov 70. (7") **APACHE DROPOUT. / FREEDOM** [33] [ ]
May 71. (lp)(c) **THE EDGAR BROUGHTON BAND** [28] [ ]
– Evening over rooftops / The birth / Piece of my own / Poppy / Don't even know which day it is / House of turnabout / Madhatter / Getting hard / What is a woman for / Thinking of you / For Dr.Spock (parts 1 & 2). *(cd-iss.Mar94 on 'Repertoire')*
Jun 71. (7") **HOTEL ROOM. / CALL ME A LIAR** [ ] [ ]
Mar 72. (7") **GONE BLUE / SOMEONE. / MR. CROSBY** [ ] [ ]
Jul 72. (lp)(c) **INSIDE OUT** [ ] [ ]
– Get out of bed / There's nobody there / Side by side / Sister Angela / I got mad / They took it away / Homes fit for heroes / Gone blue / Chilly morning momma / The rake / Totin' this guitar / Double agent / It's not you / Rock and roll. *(re-iss.Sep89 on 'B.G.O.') (cd-iss.Apr94 on 'Repertoire')*
May 73. (lp)(c) **OORA** [ ] [-]
– Hurricane man / Rock'n'roller / Roccococooler / Eviction / Oh you crazy noy! / Things on my mind / Exhibits from a new museum / Green lights / Face from a window / Pretty / Hijack boogie / Slow down / Capers. *(cd-iss.Sep91 & May92 on 'B.G.O.')*

— **JOHN THOMAS** – guitar repl. UNITT

NEMS / not issued

May 76. (lp)(c) **BANDAGES** [ ] [-]

– Get arise / Speak down the wires / John Wayne / The whale / Germany / Love gang / One to seven / Lady life / Signal injector / Fruehling flowers / I want to lie. *(cd-iss.May92 on 'Repertoire')*

— Disbanded Nov'76.

The BROUGHTONS

were formed by **EDGAR & STEVE** plus **ARTHUR GRANT** – bass / **RICHARD DeBASTION** – keyboards / **TOM NORDEN** – guitar / **PETE TOLSEN** – guitar

Harvest | Infinity

Oct 79. (lp)(c) **PARLEZ-VOUS ENGLISH?**
– Little one / Waiting for you / Drivin' to nowhere / Meglamaster / Didecoi / April in England / Revelations one / Anthem / Down in the jungle / Ventasong / Young boys / All I want to be.

Oct 79. (7") **LITTLE ONE. / DOWN IN THE JUNGLE** | | -

Jan 80. (7") **ALL I WANT TO BE. / MEGLAMASTER** | | -

— The BROUGHTONS were once again a trio, plus **NORDEN** + **DENNIS HAINES** – keyboards.

Sheet | not issued

Mar 82. (7") **ANCIENT HOMELANDS. / DO YOU WANNA BE IMMORTAL / LAST ELECTIONEER** | | -

Jun 82. (lp) **SUPERCHIP** | | -
– Metal Sunday / Superchip / Who only fade away / Curtain / Outrageous bahaviour / Not so funny farm / Nighthogs / Innocent bystanders / Pratfall / Overdose / Do you wanna / Immortal / Subway information / The last electioneer / Goodbye ancient homeland.

— EDGAR became a youth worker, until Spring '89 when he re-formed band with **STEVE** – drums / **ARTHUR GRANT** – guitar / **ANDREW BRISTOW** – bass

– compilations, others, etc. –

Apr 75. Harvest; (lp)(c) **A BUNCH OF 45's**

Apr 86. Harvest; (lp)(c) **OUT DEMONS OUT – THE BEST OF THE EDGAR BROUGHTON BAND** | | -

Sep 88. Harvest; (cd) **AS WAS – THE BEST OF . . .** | | -
– Out demons out / Love in the rain / Green lights / Sister Angela / I got mad / Hotel room / Thinking of you / For Dr.Spock (part 2) / American boy soldier / Call me a liar / Roccocockooler / Evening over rooftops / Momma's reward (keep them freaks a rollin') / Refugee / Evil / House of turnabout / Up yours / Apache drop out / Homes fit for heroes / Things on my mind.

1979. B.B.Records; (lp) **LIVE HITS HARDER (live)** | | -
(cd-iss.Dec95 on 'CTE')

Nov 92. Document; (cd) **PRESENTS . . . CLASSIC ALBUM & SINGLE TRACKS 1969-1973** | | -

Mar 93. Beat Goes On; (cd) **EDGAR BROUGHTON BAND / INSIDE OUT** | | -

Arthur BROWN

Born: 24 Jun'44, Whitby, Yorkshire, England. He formed The CRAZY WORLD OF ARTHUR BROWN in 1967, and after gigs at UFO Club in London, they signed to 'Track'. 2nd single 'FIRE' became No.1 in '68, but it was to be his only one, as outfit fell away into oblivion. • **Style:** Bizarre shock-rock, with ARTHUR's helmeted head theatrically ablaze for encore. His KINGDOM COME tried to recreate early antics but to no avail. • **Songwriters:** Member VINCENT CRANE wrote FIRE, etc., with ARTHUR the rest except covers: I PUT A SPELL ON YOU (Screamin' Jay Hawkins) / WE GOTTA GET OUT OF THIS PLACE (Animals: hit). • **Trivia:** ARTHUR portrayed the priest in the 1975 WHO film 'Tommy'.

Recommended: THE CRAZY WORLD OF ARTHUR BROWN (*5)

The CRAZY WORLD OF ARTHUR BROWN

ARTHUR BROWN – vocals with **VINCENT CRANE** – keyboards / **DRACHEN THEAKER** – drums (JON HISEMAN – on below 'A' side)

Track | Atlantic

Sep 67. (7") **DEVIL'S GRIP. / GIVE HIM A FLOWER**

— added **SEAN NICHOLAS** (aka NICK GREENWOOD) – bass (on tour)

Jun 68. (7") **FIRE. / REST CURE** | 1 | 2 Sep 68
(re-iss.'74, re-issJul84 on 'Old Gold')

Jun 68. (lp) **THE CRAZY WORLD OF ARTHUR BROWN** | 2 | 7 Sep 68
– Prelude – nightmare / Fanfare – fire poem / Fire / Come and buy / Time / I put a spell on you / Spontaneous / Apple creation / Rest cure / I've got money / Child of my kingdom. *(re-iss.Nov70 as "BACKTRACK") (cd-iss.Feb91 on 'Polydor')* (this album used session drummers AYNSLEY BUNBAR, JOHN MARSHALL or PAUL JONES)

— **JEFF CUTLER** – drums repl. THEAKER / **DICK HENNINGHAM** – organ repl. CRANE

— (Jul68) **BROWN and GREENWOOD** recruited **CARL PALMER** – drums repl. CUTLER

PETE SOLLEY – keyboards repl. HENNINGHAM

— (Oct68) **VINCENT CRANE** – organ returned to repl. SOLLEY

Nov 68. (7") **NIGHTMARE. / WHAT'S HAPPENING (or same track) MUSIC MAN**

— **JOHN MARSHALL** – drums repl. PALMER who formed ATOMIC ROOSTER: **McCULLOCH** – keyboards repl. CRANE who formed ATOMIC ROOSTER / **DENNIS TAYLOR** – bass repl. GREENWOOD / **ARTHUR BROWN** went solo for a while with GEORGE KHAN, BUTCH POTTER and JOHN MITCHELL in session. Recorded as "The PUDDLETOWN EXPRESS" and "RUSTIC HINGE" (see further on)

KINGDOM COME

ARTHUR BROWN – vocals / **ANDY DALBY** – guitar / **MICHAEL HARRIS** – keyboards / **PHIL SHUTT** – bass / **MARTIN STEER** – drums

Polydor | Polydor

Oct 71. (lp)(c) **GALACTIC ZOO DOSSIER**
– Internal messenger / Space plucks / Galactic zoo / Metal monster / Simple man / Night of the pigs / Sunrise / Trouble / Brains / Creep / Creation / Gypsy escape / No time. *(cd has extra tracks) (cd-iss.Apr93 on 'Voiceprint')*

1971. (7") **GENERAL MESSENGER. / I D SIDE TO BE B-SIDE THE C-SIDE**

Oct 72. (lp)(c) **ARTHUR BROWN'S KINGDOM COME**
– The teacher / A scientific experiment (featuring Lower colonic irrigation) / The whirlpool / The hymn / Water / City melody / Traffic light song / Love is (the spirit that will never die). *(cd-iss.Apr93 on 'Voiceprint')*

Jan 73. (7") **SPIRIT OF JOY. / COME ALIVE**

— **VICTOR PERAINO** – keyboards, synthesizer repl. HARRIS / **TONY UTER** – percussion repl. STEER

Polydor | Passport

Apr 73. (lp)(c) **JOURNEY**
– Time captives / Triangles / Gypsy / Superficial roadblocks (a)Lost time (b) Superficial roadblocks (c)Corpora supercelestia / Conception / Spirit of joy / Come alive. *(cd-iss.Apr93 on 'Voiceprint')*

ARTHUR BROWN

solo with loads of session people,incl. ANDY DALBY.

Gull | Gull

Sep 74. (7") **GYPSIES. / DANCE**

Sep 74. (lp) **DANCE**
– We gotta get out of this place / Helen with the sun / Take a chance / Crazy / Hearts and minds / Dance / Out of time / Quietly with tact / Soul garden / The Lord will find a way / Is there nothing beyond God. *(re-iss.May78)*

Mar 75. (7") **WE GOTTA GET OUT OF THIS PLACE. / HERE I AM**

— **VINCENT CRANE** rejoined

Feb 78. (lp) **CHISOLM IN MY BOSOM**
– Need to know / Monkey walk / I put a spell on you / She's on my mind / Let a little sunshine (into your life) / The lord is my saviour / Chisholm in my bosom.

— teamed up with KLAUS SCHULTZ on some recordings

WEA | not issued

1980. (lp) **FASTER THAN THE SPEED OF LIGHT ("ARTHUR BROWN & VINCENT CRANE")** | - | - Dutch
– Storm clouds / Nothing we can do / No / Bright gateway / Timeship / Come and join the fun / Stormwind / Storm / This is it / Tightrope / Balance / Faster than the speed of light.

— now with **SCOTT MORGAN** – synth / **STERLING SMITH** – mellotron / **D.ALDRIDGE** – percussion

Remote | not issued

1982. (lp) **REQUIEM (Dutch import)** | - | -
– Requiem / Mechanical masseur / Busha busha / 2024 / Chant-shades / Animal people / Spirits / Gabriel. *(cd-iss.Feb93 on 'Voiceprint')*

Voiceprint | not issued

Mar 94. (cd) **ORDER FROM CHAOS** – LIVE 1993 (live) | | -
– When you open the door (part 1 & 2) / King of England / Juices of love / Nightmare / Fire poem / Fire / Come and buy / Pick it up / Mandela / Time captains / I put a spell on you.

– compilations etc. –

Sep 77. Gull; (d-lp) **THE LOST EARS (by "ARTHUR BROWN'S KINGDOM COME")** | | -

May 88. Reckless; (lp)(c)(cd) **STRANGELANDS** | | -
(cd-iss.'89 incl. "RUSTIC HINGE" album)

Jul 88. Reckless; (lp) **RUSTIC HINGE** | | -

Feb 93. Voiceprint; (cd) **SPEAK NO TECH** | | -

Sep 95. See For Miles; (cd) **CHISHOLM IN MY BOSOM / DANCE** | | -

James BROWN

Born: 5 Mar'33, Augusta, Georgia, USA. At 15 he was sent to reform school for 4 years after breaking into cars. Interested in gospel music, he joined BOBBY BYRD in the GOSPEL STARLIGHTERS. In the mid 50's, he formed The FAMOUS FLAMES with BYRD, etc. They signed to Sid Nathan's 'King' records and released PLEASE PLEASE ME through (A&R man) Ralph Bass's insistence. His debut US chart entry came early in '59 with TRY ME, which began sparodic chart appearances throughout career. His output was phenomenal throughout the 50's and especially in 60's when he signed to 'King'. He even formed own label 'Smash' to release mostly instrumental 45's. • **Style:** Unique exhilarating live performer/dancer/singer dubbed 'The Godfather Of Soul'. His move through jazz-soul pop/gospel to R&B/funk rock in the late 60's marked him out as thee greatest black legends of all-time. He occasionally incorporated orchestra, fused with dynamic rhythm. His live backing team were excellent co-creaters of original funk and disco, that inspired many in the 70's. Lyrically he went through periods of emotional ballads, black power, dance routines and of course sex. He praised sound of ISAAC HAYES and CURTIS MAYFIELD in their soundtrack work, so he emulated this with BLACK CAESAR and SLAUGHTER . . . in 1973. His great comeback (LIVING IN AMERICA) in 1985 aged 52, saw him lose none of the stamina and stage presence of past era. (see further below for late 80's imprisonment). • **Songwriters:** Writes non-stop all material, collaborating with band of the time. He also covered

KANSAS CITY (Wilbert Harrison) / STAGGER LEE (Lloyd Price) / FEVER (Peggy Lee) / etc. • **Trivia:** After Martin Luther King was assassinated on 4th April 1968, he appealed to the people who were rioting in the streets to control energies and direct them positively elsewhere.

Recommended: THE BEST OF JAMES BROWN (THE GODFATHER OF SOUL) (*9) / LIVE AT THE APOLLO (*8)

JAMES BROWN & THE FAMOUS FLAMES

JAMES BROWN – vocals, multi / **BOBBY BYRD** – organ / **JOHNNY TERRY** – / **SYLVESTER KEELS** – / **NAFLOYD SCOTT** – guitar / **etc.**

not issued | Federal

Feb 56. (7") **PLEASE, PLEASE, PLEASE. / WHY DO YOU DO ME** | - |
1956. (7") **I DON'T KNOW. / I FEEL THAT OLD FEELING COMING ON** | - |
1956. (7") **NO, NO, NO, NO. / HOLD MY BABY'S HAND** | - |
1956. (7") **JUST WON'T DO ME RIGHT. / LET'S MAKE IT** | - |
1957. (7") **CHONNIE-ON-CHON. / I WON'T PLEAD NO MORE** | - |
1957. (lp) **PLEASE, PLEASE, PLEASE** | - |
– Please, please, please / Chonnie-On-chon / Hold my baby's hand / I feel that same old feeling coming on / Just won't do right / Baby cries over the ocean / I don't know / Tell me what I did wrong / Try me / That dood it / Begging, begging / I walked alone / No, no, no, no / That's when I lost my heart / Let's make it / Love or a game.
1957. (7") **CAN'T BE THE SAME. / GONNA TRY** | - |
1957. (7") **LOVE OR A GAME. / MESSING WITH THE BLUES** | - |
1957. (7") **YOU'RE MINE, YOU'RE MINE. / I WALKED ALONE** | - |
1958. (7") **THAT DOOD IT. / BABY CRIES OVER THE OCEAN** | - |
1958. (7") **BEGGING, BEGGING. / THAT'S WHEN I LOST MY HEART** | - |
Dec 58. (7") **TRY ME. / TELL ME WHAT I DID WRONG** | - | 48
1959. (7") **I WANT YOU SO BAD. / THERE MUST BE THE REASON** | - |
1959. (7") **I'VE GOT TO CHANGE. / IT HURTS TO TELL YOU** | - |
1959. (lp) **TRY ME** | - |
– Try me / There must be a reason / Strange things happen / Messing with the blues / Why do you do me / I've got to cry / Fine old foxy self / I want you so bad / It was you / I've got to change / Can't be the same / It hurts to tell you / I won't plead no more / You're mine, you're mine / Gonna try / Don't let it happen to me.
1959. (7") **GOOD GOOD LOVIN'. / DON'T LET IT HAPPEN TO ME** | - |
1959. (7") **IT WAS YOU. / GOT TO CRY** | - |

— Released MASHED POTATOES on 'Dade' label, as NAT KENDRICK & THE SWANS.

Feb 60. (7") **I'LL GO CRAZY. / I KNOW IT'S TRUE** | - |
1960. (lp) **THINK** | - |
– Think / Good good lovin' / Wonder when you're coming home / I'll go crazy / This old heart / I know it's true / Bewildered / I'll never never let you go / You've got the power / If you want me / Baby, you're right / So long.

Parlophone | Federal

Jun 60. (7") **THINK. / YOU'VE GOT THE POWER** | | 33 Apr60 / 86
Nov 60. (7") **THIS OLD HEART. / WONDER WHEN YOU'RE GOING HOME** | - | 79 Jul 60

Fontana | King

Nov60. (7") **THE BELLS. / AND I DO JUST WHAT I WANT** | | 68
(UK re-iss.Oct65 on 'Ember')
Jan 61. (7") **HOLD IT (instrumental). / THE SCRATCH (instrumental)** | - |
Feb 61. (7") **BEWILDERED. / IF YOU WANT ME** | - | 40
Apr 61. (7") **I DON'T MIND. / LOVE DON'T LOVE NOBODY** | - | 47
Jun 61. (7") **SUDS (instr.). / STICKY (instr.)** | - |
Aug 61. (7") **CROSS FIRING (instrumental). / NIGHT FLYING (instr.)** | - |
Sep 61. (7") **BABY YOU'RE RIGHT. / I'LL NEVER NEVER LET YOU GO** | - | 47
1961. (lp) **THE AMAZING JAMES BROWN** | - |
– I love you, yes I do / Lost someone / You don't have to go / Dancin' little thing / The bells / Tell me what you're gonna do / So long / Just you and me / And I do just what I want / Come over here / I don't mind / Love don't love nobody. *(cd-iss.Apr95 as 'TELL ME WHAT YOU'RE GONNA DO' on 'Charly')*
Nov 61. (7") **I LOVE YOU, YES I DO. / JUST YOU AND ME DARLING** | - |
Jan 62. (7") **LOST SOMEONE. / CROSS FIRING (instr.)** | - | 48

Parlophone | King

Jul 62. (7") **NIGHT TRAIN (instrumental). / WHY DOES EVERYTHING HAPPEN TO ME** | | 35 Apr 62
(re-iss.Dec64 on 'Sue')
Aug 62. (7") **SHOUT AND SHIMMY. / COME OVER HERE** | | 61
Sep 62. (7") **MASHED POTATOES U.S.A. / YOU DON'T HAVE TO GO** | - | 82
Dec 62. (7") **THREE HEARTS IN A TANGLE. / I'VE GOT MONEY** | - | 93

London | King

Dec 62. (lp) **LIVE AT THE APOLLO (live)** | | 2
– *(UK-iss.Sep64)* – I'll go crazy / Try me / Think / I don't mind / Lost someone (part 1 & 2) / Please, please, please / You've got the power / I found someone / Why do you do me like you do / I want you so bad / I love you yes I do / Why does everything happen to me / Bewildered / Please don't go / Night train. *(re-iss.Aug75 on 'Polydor') (cd-iss.Oct88) (cd-iss.Jan93)*
Jan 63. (7") **LIKE A BABY. / EVERY BEAT OF MY HEART (instrumental)** | - | 99
Apr 63. (7") **PRISONER OF LOVE. / CHOO CHOO (LOCOMOTION)** | | 18
Jun 63. (7") **THESE FOOLISH THINGS. / (CAN YOU) FEEL IT** | | 55

— (above 4 tracks were iss.on UK EP Jan84 'JAMES BROWN & THE FAMOUS FLAMES')

Oct 63. (7") **SIGNED, SEALED AND DELIVERED. / WAITING IN VAIN** | - | 77
Oct 63. (lp) **PRISONER OF LOVE** | - | 73 Sep 63
– Prisoner of love / Waiting in vain / Again / Lost someone / Bewildered / So long / Signed, sealed & delivered / Try me / (Can you) Feel it (pt.1) / How long darling / The thing in 'G'. *(re-iss.Nov83 on 'Polydor') (re-iss.Oct72 on 'Contour')*
Jan 64. (7") **I'VE GOT TO CHANGE. / THE BELLS** | - |
Feb 64. (7") **OH BABY DON'T YOU WEEP. / (pt.2)** | - | 23
Mar 64. (7") **PLEASE, PLEASE, PLEASE. / IN THE WEE WEE HOURS** | - | 95
Jul 64. (lp) **PURE DYNAMITE! LIVE AT THE ROYAL (live)** | | 10 Feb 64
– Shout and shimmy / These foolish things / Signed, sealed and delivered / Like a baby / I'll never let you go / Please, please, please / Oh, baby, don't you weep / Good, good lovin'.

— He signed to 'Smash' records in the US, and was also retained throughout on 'King'. In the UK, 'King' was licensed by 'London' until late '65 'Pye Int.'). The instrumental releases on 'Smash' were on 'Philips' UK, and marked *.

May 64. (7") * **CALEDONIA. / EVIL** | - | 95
Jun 64. (7") **AGAIN. / HOW LONG DARLING** | - |
Jul 64. (7") **SO LONG. / DANCIN' LITTLE THING** | - |
Aug 64. (7") * **THE THINGS I USED TO DO. / OUT OF THE BLUE** | - | 99
Sep 64. (7") **OUT OF SIGHT. / MAYBE THE LAST TIME** | | 24 Aug 64
Jun 64. (7") **TELL ME WHAT YOU'RE GONNA DO. / I DON'T CARE** | - |

— (above iss.UK-May65 on 'Ember', diff.'B'side – LOST SOMEONE)

Sep 64. (lp) * **SHOWTIME (live)** | | 61 May 64
Sep 64. (lp) **TELL ME WHAT YOU'RE GONNA DO** (on 'Ember') | | -
– Just you and me darling / I love, yes I do / I don't mind / Come over here / The bells / Love don't love nobody / Dancin' little thing / Lost someone / And I do just what I want / So long / You don't have to go / Tell me what you're gonna do.
Oct 64. (7") **THINK. / TRY ME** | - |
Oct 64. (7") **FINE OLD FOXY SELF. / MEDLEY** | - |
Dec 64. (7") **HAVE MERCY BABY. / JUST WON'T DO RIGHT** | - | 92
Mar 65. (7") * **DEVIL'S HIDEAWAY (instr.). / WHO'S AFRAID OF VIRGINIA WOOLF (instr.)** | - |
Apr 65. (lp) * **GRITS AND SOUL (instr.)** | |
– Grits / Tempted / There / After you're through / Devil's den / Who's afraid of Virginia Woolf / Infatuation / Wee wee / Mister hip / Headache.
Apr 65. (7") **THIS OLD HEART. / IT WAS YOU** | - |
Jul 65. (lp) **PLEASE, PLEASE, PLEASE** | |
– Try me / Please, please, please / I feel that old feeling coming on / That's when I lost my heart / Chonnie on chon / Hold my baby's hand / Tell me what I did wrong / Baby cries over the ocean / Begging, begging / No, no, no, no / That dood it / I don't know / I walked alone / Love or a game / Let's make it / Just won't do right. *(re-*

iss.Nov83)

— His UK touring band 1965 **BOBBY BYRD, BOBBY BENNETT, JAMES CRAWFORD and LLOYD STALLWORTH.**

Aug 65. (7") **PAPA'S GOT A BRAND NEW BAG. / (pt.2)** [25] [8] Jul 65
Sep 65. (lp) **PAPA'S GOT A BRAND NEW BAG** [ ] [26]
– Papa's got a brand new bag / Mashed potatoes U.S.A. / This old heart / Cross firing / Doin' the limbo / Baby, you're right / Love don't love nobody / Have mercy baby / And I do just what I want / I stay in the chapel every night / You don't have to go. *(UK-iss.Mar66, re-iss.May67) (re-iss.Nov83 on 'Polydor')*
Oct 65. (lp) **JAMES BROWN AND HIS FAMOUS FLAMES TOUR THE U.S.A. (live)** [-] [ ]
Dec 65. (7") * **TRY ME (instr.) / PAPA'S GOT A BRAND NEW BAG (instr.)** [ ] [63]
Dec 65. (lp) * **JAMES BROWN PLAYS JAMES BROWN TODAY AND YESTERDAY** [ ] [42] Nov 65
– Papa's got a brand new bag / Oh baby don't you weep / Every beat of my heart / Out of sight / Sidewinder / Maybe the last time / Hold it / Song for my father.
Nov 65. (7") **I GOT YOU (I FEEL GOOD). / I CAN'T HELP IT** [29] [3]
Jan 66. (lp) **I GOT YOU (I FEEL GOOD)** [ ] [36]
– I got you (I feel good) / Good good lovin' / Lost someone / I can't help it / You've got the power / Night train / I've got money / Dancin' little thing / Three hearts in a tangle / Suds / Love don't love nobody. *(UK-Apr66)*
Mar 66. (7") **LOST SOMEONE. / I'LL GO CRAZY** [-] [94] [73]
Apr 66. (7") **AIN'T THAT A GROOVE. / (pt.2)** [ ] [42]
Apr 66. (7") **PRISONER OF LOVE. / I'VE GOT TO CHANGE** [-] [ ]
May 66. (7") **COME OVER HERE. / TELL ME WHAT YOU'RE GONNA DO** [-] [ ]

— (above 4 songs were iss.as UK – EP Sep66 on 'Pye Int.')

Apr 66. (7") * **NEW BREED (instr.) / (pt.2)** [ ] [ ]
May 66. (lp) * **. . . PLAYS NEW BREED** [ ] [ ] Apr 66
– New breed / Slow walk / Fat bag / Vanshelia / Jabo / Lost in the mood of changes / All about my girl / Hooks / Something else.
Jun 66. (7") **IT'S A MAN'S, MAN'S, MAN'S WORLD. / IS IT YES OR IS IT NO?** [13] [8] Apr 66
Jun 66. (7") **JUST WON'T DO RIGHT. / I'VE GOT MONEY** [-] [ ]
Jun 66. (7") * **JAMES BROWN'S BOO-GA-LOO (instr.) / LOST IN A MOOD OF CHANGES** [-] [ ]
Jul 66. (lp) **IT'S A MAN'S, MAN'S, MAN'S WORLD** [ ] [90]
– It's a man's, man's, man's world / Is it yes or is it no? / Ain't that a groove (pt.1 & 2) / The scratch / Bewildered / The bells in the wee wee hours / Come over here / I don't mind / Just you and me / I love you, yes I do. *(re-iss.Nov83 on 'Polydor')*
Jul 66. (7") **IT WAS YOU. / I DON'T CARE** [-] [ ]
Aug 66. (7") **THIS OLD HEART. / HOW LONG DARLING** [-] [ ]
Sep 66. (7") **MONEY WON'T CHANGE YOU. / (pt.2)** [-] [53] Jul66
Nov 66. (7") **DON'T BE A DROP-OUT. / TELL ME THAT YOU LOVE ME** [-] [50]
Dec 66. (7") **THE CHRISTMAS SONG. / (pt.2)** [-] [ ]
Dec 66. (7") **SWEET LITTLE BABY BOY. / (pt.2)** [-] [ ]
Dec 66. (lp) **THE JAMES BROWN CHRISTMAS ALBUM** [-] [ ]
– (festive songs)
Dec 66. (7") **LET'S MAKE CHRISTMAS MEAN SOMETHING THIS YEAR. / (pt.2)** [-] [ ]
Feb 67. (7") **BRING IT UP. / NOBODY KNOWS** [ ] [29]
Feb 67. (lp) **MIGHTY INSTRUMENTALS** [ ] [ ]
– Papa's got a brand new bag (part 1) / Feel it / Hold it / Sticky / Scratch / James Brown's house party / Night train / Every beat of my heart / Cross firing / Suds / Doin' the limbo / Choo choo.
Mar 67. (7") * **LET'S GO GET STONED (instr.) / OUR DAY WILL COME (instr.)** [-] [ ]
Mar 67. (lp) * **HANDFUL OF SOUL** [ ] [ ] Nov 66
– Our day will come / Get loose / Oh Henry / Let's go get stoned / Hot mix / Hold on, I'm coming / King / When a man loves a woman / Message to Michael / 6345-789.
Apr 67. (7") **KANSAS CITY. / STONE FOX (instr.)** [ ] [55]
May 67. (lp) **RAW SOUL** [ ] [88] Apr 67
– Bring it up / Don't be a drop out / Till then / Tell me that you love me / Yours and mine / Money won't change you (part 1 & 2) / Only you / Let yourself go / The nearness of you / Nobody knows / Stone fox.
May 67. (7") **THINK (by 'JAMES BROWN & VICKI ANDERSON'). / ('B'side by VICKI ANDERSON)** [-] [100]
Nov 67. (lp) **LIVE AT THE GARDEN (live)** [ ] [41] Jun 67
Jul 67. (7") **LET YOURSELF GO. / GOOD ROCKIN' TONIGHT** [ ] [46]
Jul 67. (lp) **MR.EXCITEMENT** [ ] [ ]
– (recordings from 1962) *(re-iss.Nov83 on 'Polydor')*
Jul 67. (7") * **JIMMY MACK (instr.) / WHAT DO YOU LIKE (instr.)** [-] [ ]

— In mid'67, he released I LOVE YOU PORGY. / YOURS AND MINE on 'Bethlehem'.

— **ALFRED 'Pee-Wee' ELLIS** – repl. JONES new **JIMMY NOLEN** – guitar / **CLYDE STUBBLEFIELD** – drums / **MACEO PARKER** – tenor sax / **ST.CLAIR PINCKNEY** – tenor sax / **etc.**

Sep 67. (7") **COLD SWEAT. / (pt.2)** [ ] [7] Jul 67
Oct 67. (lp) **COLD SWEAT** [ ] [35] Sep 67
– Cold sweat (pt.1 & 2) / Nature boy / Come rain or come shine / I love you Porgy / Back stabbin' / Fever / Mona Lisa / I want to be around / Good rockin' tonight / Stagger Lee / Kansas City. *(re-iss.Nov83 on 'Polydor')*
Oct 67. (7") **IT WON'T BE ME. / MONA LISA** [-] [ ]
Nov 67. (lp) **THE JAMES BROWN SHOW (live)** [ ] [ ]
– I'll go crazy / Try me / Think / I don't mind / Lost someone / Please, please, please / You've got the power / I found someone / Why do you do me / I want you so bad / I love you yes I do / Why does everything happen to me / Bewildered / Please don't go / Night train.
Dec 67. (7") **GET IT TOGETHER. / (pt.2)** [ ] [40] Nov 67
Jan 68. (7") **FUNKY SOUL No.1 (instr.) / THE SOUL OF J.B.(instr.)** [-] [ ]

Polydor King

Dec 67. (7") **I CAN'T STAND MYSELF (WHEN YOU TOUCH ME). / THERE WAS A TIME** [ ] [28] [36]
Jan 68. (lp) **I CAN'T STAND MYSELF (WHEN YOU TOUCH ME)** [ ] [17]
– I can't stand myself (when you touch me) (part 1) / There was a time / Get it together (part 1) / Baby, baby, baby, baby / Time after time / The soul of J.B. (instrumental) / I can't stand myself (when you touch me) (part 2) / Get it together (part 2) / Why did you take your love away from me / Need your love so bad / You've got to change your mind / Fat Eddie (US) / Funky soul £1 (UK).

— Released 2 singles YOU'VE GOT TO CHANGE YOUR MIND and YOU'VE GOT THE POWER backing BOBBY BYRD and VICKI ANDERSON respectively on 'King' US.

May 68. (7") **I GOT THE FEELIN'. / IF I RULED THE WORLD** [ ] [6] Mar 68
Apr 68. (lp) **MR.DYNAMITE** [ ] [ ]
– Money won't change you (part 1 & 2) / I don't mind / Doin' the limbo / I stay in the chapel every night / Scratch / Night train / I can't help it / Is it yes or is it no / Come over here / In the wee wee hours / Choo choo.
Apr 68. (7") **MAYBE GOOD MAYBE BAD (instr.) / (pt.2)** [-] [ ]
May 68. (7") **SHHHHHHHH (FOR A LITTLE WHILE) (instr.) / HERE I GO (instr.)** [-] [ ]
Jun 68. (7") **LICKING STICK, LICKING STICK. / (pt.2)** [ ] [14] May 68
Jun 68. (lp) **I GOT THE FEELIN'** [-] [ ] May 68
– I got the feelin' / Maybe I'll understand – part 1 / You've got the power / Maybe good – Maybe bad – part 1 / Shhhhhhh (for a little while) / Just plain funk / If I ruled the world / Maybe I'll understand – part 2 / Stone fox / It won't be me / Maybe good – maybe bad – part 2 / Here I go.
Jun 68. (7") **AMERICA IS MY HOME. / (pt.2)** [-] [52]
Aug 68. (7") **I GUESS I'LL HAVE TO CRY CRY CRY. / JUST PLAIN FUNK (instr.)** [-] [55]

JAMES BROWN

solo, but still with The FAMOUS FLAMES

Sep 68. (7") **SAY IT LOUD – I'M BLACK AND I'M PROUD. / (pt.2)** [ ] [10]
Sep 68. (lp) **LIVE AT THE APOLLO VOL.2 (live)** [ ] [32]
– Introduction / Think / I want to be around / Thanks / That's life / Kansas City / Let yourself go / There was a time / I feel all right / Cold sweat / It may be the last time / I feel good / Prisoner of love / Out of sight / Try me / Bring it up / It's a man's man's world / Lost someone / Please, please, please. *(UK-iss.Jun69) (cd-iss.Dec88 on 'Polydor')(cd-iss. Jan 93)*
Nov 68. (7") **GOODBYE MY LOVE. / SHADES OF BROWN (instrumental)** [-] [31]
Nov 68. (7") **THAT'S LIFE. / PLEASE, PLEASE, PLEASE** [ ] [-]
Dec 68. (7") **SANTA CLAUS GOES STRAIGHT TO THE GHETTO. / YOU KNOW IT (instrumental)** [-] [ ]
Dec 68. (7") **TIT FOR TAT (AIN'T NO TAKING BACK). / BELIEVERS SHALL ENJOY** [-] [86]
Dec 68. (7") **LET'S UNITE THE WHOLE WORLD AT CHRISTMAS. / IN THE MIDDLE (pt.1)** [-] [ ]
Jan 69. (7") **GIVE IT UP OR TURN IT A LOOSE. / I'LL LOSE MY MIND** [-] [15]
Mar 69. (7") **ATTACK WITH THE NEWS. / SHADES OF BROWN (pt.2)** [-] [ ]

— Next 45, was a duet YOU'VE GOT TO HAVE A JOB with 'Marva Whitney'.

Mar 69. (7") **SOUL PRIDE. / (pt.2)** [-] [ ]
Apr 69. (7") **I DON'T WANT NOBODY TO GIVE ME NOTHIN' (OPEN UP THE DOOR, I'LL GET IT MYSELF). / (pt.2)** [ ] [20]
Apr 69. (lp) **SAY IT LOUD – I'M BLACK AND I'M PROUD** [ ] [53]
– Say it loud I'm black and proud (parts 1 & 2) / I guess I'll have to cry, cry, cry / Goodbye my love (parts 1 & 2) / Shades of brown / Licking stick / I love you / Then you can tell me goodbye / Let them talk / Maybe I'll understand / I'll lose my mind. *(UK-iss.Sep69)*
May 69. (7") **THE LITTLE GROOVE MAKER ME. / I'M SHOOK** [-] [ ]
Jun 69. (7") **THE POPCORN (instr.) / THE CHICKEN (instr.)** [-] [30]
Jul 69. (7") **MOTHER POPCORN (YOU GOT TO HAVE A MOTHER FOR ME). / (pt.2)** [ ] [11] Jun 69
Jul 69. (lp) **GETTIN' DOWN TO IT** [ ] [99] May 69
– Sunny / That's life / Strangers in the night / Willow weep for me / Cold sweat / There was a time / Chicago / For sentimental reasons / Time after time / All the way / It had to be you / Uncle. *(UK-iss.Jan70)*
Aug 69. (7") **LOWDOWN POPCORN (instr.) / TOP OF THE STACK (instr.)** [-] [41]
Aug 69. (lp) **JAMES BROWN PLAYS AND DIRECTS THE POPCORN** [-] [40]
– The popcorn / Why am I treated so bad / In the middle / Soul pride / A new shift / Sudsy / The chicken / The chase.
Sep 69. (7") **WORLD. / (pt.2)** [ ] [37]
Oct 69. (lp) **IT'S A MOTHER** [ ] [26] Sep 69
– Mother popcorn (you got to have a mother for me) (parts 1 & 2) / Mashed potato popcorn (parts 1 & 2) / I'm shook / Popcorn with a feeling / Little groove maker me (parts 1 & 2) / Any day now (my wild beautiful bird) / If I ruled the world / You're still out of sight / Top of the stack.
Oct 69. (7") **LET A MAN COME IN AND DO THE POPCORN (pt.1). / GETTIN' A LITTLE HIPPER (pt.1)** [-] [21] Sep 69
Dec 69. (7") **IT'S CHRISTMAS TIME. / (pt.2)** [-] [ ]
Jan 70. (7") **LET A MAN COME IN AND DO THE POPCORN (pt.2). / GETTIN' A LITTLE HIPPER (pt.2)** [ ] [40]
Jan 70. (7") **I CAN'T STAND MYSELF. / THERE WAS A TIME** [ ] [-]
Jan 70. (lp) **TURN IT LOOSE** [ ] [ ]
– Give it up, or turn it loose / I'll lose my mind / I don't want nobody to give me tonight (open up the door, I'll get it muself) (parts 1 & 2).
Mar 70. (lp) **THE POPCORN** [ ] [ ]
– Ain't it funky (parts 1 & 2) / Fat wood (parts 1 & 2) / Cold sweat / Give it up or turn it a loose / Nose job / Use your mother / After you done it.
Mar 70. (7") **AIN'T IT FUNKY NOW (instr.) / (pt.2)** [ ] [24] Nov 69
Mar 70. (lp) **AIN'T IT FUNKY** [ ] [43] Feb 70
– Ain't it funky (parts 1 & 2) / Fat wood (parts 1 & 2) / Cold sweat / Give it up or

turn it a loose / Nose job / Use your mother / After you done it. *(UK-iss.Aug70)*

Apr 70. (7") **FUNKY DRUMMER (instr.) / (pt.2)** [-] [51]

May 70. (7") **BROTHER RAPP (pt.1 & 2). / BEWILDERED** [-] [32]

Jul 70. (7") **IT'S A NEW DAY (pt.1 & 2). / GEORGIA ON MY MIND** [ ] [32] Feb 70

Jul 70. (lp) **IT'S A NEW DAY SO LET A MAN COME IN** [ ] [ ]
– It's a new day so let a man come in / Do the popcorn / World / Georgia on my mind / It's a man's man's world / Give it up or turn it a loose / If I ruled the world / The man in the glass / I'm not demanding.

(Also released lp SOUL ON TOP with The LOUIE BELLSON ORCHESTRA (Jul70)
Released another duet 7" with VICKI ANDERSON – Let It Be Me.

— He breaks up The FAMOUS FLAMES to introduce his new band The JB's. They included **BOOTSY COLLINS, FRED WESLEY, BOBBY BYRD, JIMMY PARKER**, etc.

Sep 70. (7") **GET UP I FEEL LIKE BEING A SEX MACHINE. / (pt.2)** [32] [15] Jul 70

— (released gospel 45, A MAN HAS TO GO BACK TO THE CROSSROADS on 'Bethlehem')

Nov 70. (7") **SUPERBAD. / (pt.2)** [ ] [13] Sep 70

Nov 70. (7") **HEY AMERICA (vocal). / (instr.)** [-] [ ]

Dec 70. (lp) **SEX MACHINE (live)** [ ] [29] Sep 70
– Get up I feel like being a sex machine / Brother Rapp (parts 1 & 2) / Bewildered / I got the feelin' / Give it up or turn it a loose / I don't want nobody / To give me nothing / Licking stick / Lowdown / Popcorn / Spinning wheel / If I ruled the world / There was a time / It's a man's man's world / Please, please, please / I can't stand myself / Mother popcorn.

Dec 70. (7") **SANTA CLAUS IS DEFINATELY HERE TO STAY. / (instr.)** [-] [ ]

Jan 71. (7") **GET UP, GET INTO IT, GET INVOLVED. / (pt.2)** [-] [34]

Feb 71. (7") **TALKING LOUD & SAYING NOTHING. / (pt.2)** [-] [ ]
(This was to hit US chart No.27 in Feb72 on 'Polydor')

Feb 71. (lp) **SUPERBAD** [ ] [61] Jan 71
– Superbad (parts 1 & 2) / Let it be me / Sometime a man has to go back to the crossroads / Giving out my juice / By the time I get to Phoenix. *(UK-iss.May71)*

Feb 71. (7") **SPINNING WHEEL (instr.) / (part 2)** [-] [90]

Mar 71. (7") **SOUL POWER. / (pt.2)** [ ] [29] Feb 71

May 71. (7") **I CRIED. / GET UP, GET INTO IT, GET INVOLVED** [ ] [50]

— Most of his band except WESLEY, joined PARLIAMENT/FUNKADELIC.

People Polydor

Jun 71. (7") **ESCAPE-ISM. / ?** [-] [35]

Jul 71. (7") **HOT PANTS (SHE GOT TO USE WHAT SHE GOT, TO GET WHAT SHE WANTS). / (pt.2)** [ ] [15]

Sep 71. (lp) **HOT PANTS** [ ] [22]
– Blues And Pants / Can't Stand It / Escape-Ism (Part 1) / Escape-Ism (Part 2) / Hot Pants (She Got To Use What She Got To Get What She Wants) / Escape-Ism

Polydor Polydor

Sep 71. (7") **MAKE IT FUNKY. / (pt.2)** [ ] [22]

Oct 71. (7") **MY PART: MAKE IT FUNKY PART 3. / (other version)** [-] [68]

Nov 71. (7") **I'M A GREEDY MAN. / (pt.2)** [ ] [35]

Feb 72. (d-lp) **REVOLUTION OF THE MIND – LIVE AT THE APOLLO, VOL.3 (live)** [ ] [39] Dec 71
– It's a new day so let a man come in and do the popcorn / Bewildered / Sex machine / Escape-ism / Make it funky / Try me / Fast medley: I can't stand myself – Mother popcorn – I got the feelin' / Give it up or turn it a loose / Call me Superbad / Get up, get into it, get involved (parts 1 & 2) / Soul power / Hot pants (she got to use what she got to get what she wants).

Feb 72. (7") **KING HEROIN. / THEME FROM KING HEROIN** [ ] [40]

Apr 72. (7") **THERE IT IS. / (pt.2)** [ ] [43]

Jun 72. (7") **HONKY TONK. / (pt.2)** [ ] [44]

Aug 72. (7") **GET ON THE GOOD FOOT. / (pt.2)** [ ] [18]

Nov 72. (lp)(c) **THERE IT IS** [ ] [ ] Jun 72
– There It Is (Parts 1 & 2) / King Heroin / I'm A Greedy Man (Parts 1 & 2) / Who Am I / Talkin' Loud And Sayin' Nothing / Public Enemy £1 (Part 1) / Public Enemy £1 (Part 2) / I Need Help (I Can't Do It Alone) / Never Can Say Goodbye

Nov 72. (7") **WHAT MY BABY NEEDS NOW IS A LITTLE MORE LOVIN'. / THIS GUY'S IN LOVE WITH YOU (by 'JAMES BROWN & LYN COLLINS')** [ ] [56]

Dec 72. (7") **I GOT A BAG OF MY OWN. / I KNOW IT'S TIME** [ ] [44]

Jan 73. (7") **I GOT ANTS IN MY PANTS (AND I WANT TO DANCE) (pt.1). / (pt.2)** [-] [27]

Jan 73. (d-lp) **GET ON THE GOOD FOOT** [ ] [68] Dec 72
– Get on the good foot (parts 1 & 2) / The whole world needs liberation / Your love was good for me / Cold sweat / Recitation by Hank Ballard / I got a bag of my own / Nothing beats a try but a fail / Lost someone / Funky side of town / Please, please, please / Ain't it a groove / My part – Make it funky (parts 3 & 4) / Dirty Harry / I know it's a true.

Mar 73. (7") **DOWN AND OUT IN NEW YORK CITY. / ?** [-] [50]

May 73. (lp)(c) **BLACK CAESAR (Soundtrack)** [ ] [31] Feb 73
– Down and out in New York city / Blind man can see it / Sportin' life / Dirty Harri / The boss / Make it good to yourself / Mama Feelgood / Mama's dead / White lightning (I mean moonshine) / Chase / Like it is, like it was.

Aug 73. (lp)(c) **SLAUGHTER'S BIG RIP-OFF OST** [ ] [92] Jul 73
– Slaughter Theme / Tryin' To Get Over / Transmografication / Happy For The Poor / Brother Rapp / Big Strong / Really, Really, Really / Sexy, Sexy, Sexy / To My Brother / How Long Can I Keep It Up / People Get Up And Drive Your Funky Soul / King Slaughter / Straight Ahea

Aug 73. (7") **SEXY SEXY SEXY. / (pt.2)** [-] [50]

Jan 74. (7") **STONED TO THE BONE. / SEXY SEXY SEXY** [-] [58]

Mar 74. (7") **THE PAYBACK. / (pt.2)** [-] [26]

Apr 74. (d-lp)(c) **THE PAYBACK MIX** [ ] [34] Jan 74
– The Payback Mix (Keep On Doing What You're Doing But MakeIt Funky) / Stone To The Bone (Part 1) / Give It Up Or Turnit A Loose (Remix) / Cold Sweat (Part 1)

Jun 74. (7") **MY THANG. / THE PAYBACK** [ ] [-]

Jul 74. (7") **MY THANG. / ?** [-] [31]

Sep 74. (7") **PAPA DON'T TAKE NO MESS. / (pt.2)** [-] [31]

Sep 74. (d-lp)(c) **(IT'S) HELL** [ ] [35] Jul 74
– Cold-blooded / Hell / My thang / Savin' it and doin' it / Please, please, please / When the saints go marching in / These foolish things / Storming Monday / A man has to go back to the cross road before he finds himself / Sometime / I can't stand it / Lost someone / Don't tell a lie about me and I won't tell the truth about you / Papa don't take no mess.
(re-iss.Jul88)

Jan 75. (7") **FUNKY PRESIDENT (PEOPLE IT'S BAD). / COLD BLOODED** [ ] [44] Nov 74

Feb 75. (7") **REALITY. / (pt.2)** [-] [80]

Mar 75. (lp)(c) **REALITY** [ ] [56] Jan 75
– Reality / Funky President (people it's bad) / Further on up the road / Check your body / Don't fence me in / All for one / I'm broken hearted / The twist / Who can I turn to.

Apr 75. (7") **SEX MACHINE (remix). / (pt.2)** [-] [ ]

May 75. (lp)(c) **SEX MACHINE TODAY** [ ] [ ]
– Sex machine (pt.1 & 2) / I feel good / Problems / Dood on it / Get up off of me / Dood on it.

Dec 75. (lp)(c) **EVERYBODY'S DOIN' THE HUSTLE AND DEAD ON THE DOUBLE BUMP** [ ] [ ] Oct 75
– Hustle (dead on it) / Papa's got a brand new bag / Your love / Turn on the heat and build some fire / Superbad, superslick / Calm & cool / Kansas City.

Jan 76. (7") **HOT. / SUPERBAD SUPERSLICK** [ ] [ ]

Mar 76. (lp)(c) **HOT** [ ] [ ]
– Hot / so long / For sentimental reasons / Try me / The future shock of the world / woman / Most of all / Goodnight my love / Please, please, please. *(re-iss.Jul88)*

Jul 76. (7") **GET UP OFFA THAT THING. / RELEASE THE PRESSURE** [22] [45]

Sep 76. (lp)(c) **GET UP OFFA THAT THING** [ ] [ ] Aug 76
– Get up offa that thing / Release the pressure / You took my heart / I refuse to lose / Can't take it with you / Home again / This feeling.

Jan 77. (7") **BODYHEAT. / (pt.2)** [36] [88]

Feb 77. (lp)(c) **BODYHEAT** [ ] [ ] Jan 77
– Bodyheat / Woman / Kiss in 77 / I'm satisfied / What the world needs now is love / Wake up and give yourself a chance / Don't feel it. *(re-iss.Jul88) (re-iss.Oct82 on 'Phoenix' diff.version?)*

Jul 77. (7") **HONKY TONK. / BROTHER RAPP** [ ] [ ]

Sep 77. (lp)(c) **MUTHA'S NATURE** [ ] [ ]
– Give me some skin / People who criticize / Have a happy day / Bessie / If you don't give a dogone about it / Summertime / People wake up and live / Take me higher and groove me.

— His backing group, left for a while, but soon returned. JIMMY NOLAN was to die of a heart attack 18 Dec'83.

May 78. (lp)(c) **JAM 1980's** [ ] [ ]
– Jam / The spank / Nature / Eyesight / I never never never will forget.

Jun 78. (7") **EYESIGHT. / NEVER, NEVER, NEVER WILL FORGET** [ ] [ ]

Oct 78. (7") **NATURE. / (pt.2)** [ ] [ ]

Jan 79. (7")(12") **FOR GOODNESS SAKES, LOOK AT THOSE CAKES. / GET UP I I FEEL LIKE BEING A SEX MACHINE** [ ] [ ]

Jan 79. (lp)(c) **TAKE A LOOK AT THOSE CAKES** [ ] [ ]
– For goodness sakes, take a look at those cakes / A man understands / As long as I love you / Someone to talk to / Spring.

Jul 79. (7")(12") **IT'S TOO FUNKY IN HERE. / ARE WE REALLY DANCING** [ ] [ ]

Aug 79. (lp)(c) **THE ORIGINAL DISCO MAN** [ ] [ ]
– It's too funky in here / Let the boogie do the rest / Still / The original disco man / Star generation / Women are something else.

Dec 79. (7")(12") **STAR GENERATION. / LET THE BOOGIE DO THE REST** [ ] [ ]

Feb 80. (7") **REGRETS. / STONE COLD DRAG** [ ] [ ]

Apr 80. (lp)(c) **PEOPLE** [ ] [ ]
– Regrets / Don't stop the funk / That's sweet music / Let the funk flow / Stone cold drag / Are we really dancing / Sometimes that's all there is. *(re-iss.Jul88)*

Oct 80. (d-lp)(c) **JAMES BROWN ... LIVE – HOT ON THE ONE (live)** [ ] [ ] Aug 80
– It's too funky for me in here / Gonna have a funky good time / Get up offa that thing / Body heat / I got the feelin' / Try me / Sex machine / It's a man's man's man's world / Get on the good foot / Papa's got a brand new bag / Please, please, please / Jam. *(cd-iss.Apr91)*

R.C.A. T.K.

Dec 80. (7")(12") **RAPP PAYBACK (WHERE IZ MOSES?). / (pt.2)** [39] [ ]

Dec 80. (lp)(c) **SOUL SYNDROME** [ ] [ ]
– Rapp payback / Mashed potatoes / Smokin' and drinkin' / Stay with me / Honky tonk. *(re-iss.Sep81)*

Feb 81. (7")(12") **STAY WITH ME. / SMOKIN' AND DRINKIN'** [ ] [ ]

Apr 81. (lp)(c) **THE THIRD COMING** [ ] [ ]
– Popcorn 80's / Give that bass player some / You're my only love / World cycle inc. / Superball / Superbad 80's / I go crazy.

May 81. (7") **FUNKY MAN. / (pt.2)** [ ] [ ]
(12"+=) – Mashed potatoes.

Jun 81. (7") **I GO CRAZY. / WORLD CYCLE INC.** [ ] [ ]

Sonet Augusta..

Jun 83. (7")(12") **BRING IT ON ... BRING IT ON. / NIGHT TIME IS THE RIGHT TIME** [45] [ ]

Sep 83. (lp)(c) **BRING IT ON** [ ] [ ]
– Bring it on ... bring it on / Today / You can't keep a good man down / Nighttime is the right time / Tennessee waltz / For your precious love.

— In Aug84, he teamed up with **AFRIKA BAMBAATAA** for one-off 7+12" **UNITY** (THE THIRD COMING) on 'Tommy Boy' (US No.49).

Scotti Bros Scotti Bros

Jan 86. (7")(12") **LIVING IN AMERICA. / FAREWELL (VINCE DI COLA)** [5] [4] Dec 85

— (above from the film 'Rocky IV', and written by DAN HARTMAN)

Oct 86. (7") **GRAVITY. / GRAVITY (dub)** [65] [93]
(12") – ('A'side) / The big G (dig this myth).

Oct 86. (lp)(c)(cd) **GRAVITY** [85] [ ]
– How do you stop / Turn me loose, I'm Dr.Feelgood / Living in America / Goliath / Repeat the beat (faith) / Return to me / Gravity.

Nov 86. (7") **HOW DO YOU STOP. / REPEAT THE BEAT (FAITH)** [ ] [ ]
(12"+=) – Living in America.

(12"+=) – ('A'house mix).
Nov 86. (7") **HOW DO YOU STOP. / HOUSE OF ROCK** -
1987. (7") **LET'S GET PERSONAL. / REPEAT THE BEAT** -
May 88. (7") **I'M REAL. / KEEP KEEPING** 31
(12"+=) – Tribute.
(cd-s++=) – ('A'hype mix).
May 88. (7") **I'M REAL. / TRIBUTE** -
Jun 88. (lp)(c)(cd) **I'M REAL** 27 96
– Tribute / I'm real / Static / Time to get busy / She looks types a good / Keep keeping / Can't git enuf / It's your money / Godfather runnin' the joint. *(cd-iss Jan93)*
Aug 88. (7") **STATIC. / GODFATHER RUNNIN' THE JOINT** -
Aug 88. (7") **STATIC. / I'M REAL (U.S.mix)**
(12"+=)(cd-s+=) – ('A'-Full Force mix).
1988. (7") **TIME TO GET BUSY. / BUSY JB** -
Feb 89. (7") **IT'S YOUR MONEY. / YOU AND ME** -
Jul 93. (cd)(c)(lp) **FUNKY PRESIDENT**
– Funky president (people it's bad) / Try me (I need you) / My thang / Body heat (Part 1) / Talkin' loud and sayin' nothing / There was a time / Doing it to death / The payback / Soul power (parts 1 & 2) / I got the feelin' / Honky tonk (part 1) / Get up, get into it and get involved / I got ants in my pants (part 1) / Funky drummer / It's a new day.

— He guested on ARETHA FRANKLIN single Nov88, 'GIMME YOUR LOVE'. In Apr-May'88, JAMES and his wife ADRIANNE were arrested for possession of substances and guns. She also filed for divorce and pleaded not guilty. Later that year, after resisting arrest in a car chase, etc., he was sentenced to 6 years. He was released on parole on 27th Feb'91, but had to return until late 1993 to serve full sentence. In 1992, he was awarded a special grammy award, for his contribution to music. He appeared there with his wife, to sing finale.

Polydor Polydor
Jul 91. (cd)(c)(lp) **LOVE OVERDUE**
– (So tired of standing still we got to) Move / Show me – dance, dance, dance / To the funk / Teardrops on your letter / Standing on higher ground / Later for dancing / You are my everything / It's time for love (put a little love).
Jul 91. (7") **(SO TIRED OF STANDING STILL WE GOT TO) MOVE ON / YOU ARE MY EVERYTHING**
(12"+=) – ('A' extended).
Mar 93. (cd)(c) **UNIVERSAL JAMES**
– Can't get any harder / Just do it / Mine all mine / Watch me / Georgia-Lina / Show me your friends / Everybody's got a thang / How long / Make it funky 2000 / Moments.
Apr 93. (7")(c-s) **CAN'T GET ANY HARDER (Radio Mix) / ('A' obc mix)** 59
(12"+=)(cd-s+=) – ?

– compilations, others, etc. –

Apr 65. London/ US= King; (lp) **16 UNBEATABLE HITS**
Oct 65. Ember; (7"ep) **I DO JUST WHAT I WANT** -
– I do just what I want / So long / Bells / I love you, yes I do.
May 66. Pye International; (7"ep) **I GOT YOU** -
– I got you / Good good loving / I can't help it.
Aug 66. Pye International; (7"ep) **I'LL GO CRAZY** -
– I'll go crazy / I've got money / Love don't love nobody / You've got the power.
Oct 66. Pye International; (7"ep) **HOW LONG DARLING** -
– How long darling / This old heart / Three hearts in a tangle / Lost someone.
May 67. Pye International; (7"ep) **BRING IT UP** -
– Bring it up / Tell me that you love me / Don't be a drop out / Nobody knows.
Apr 68. Polydor/ US= King; (lp) **JAMES BROWN'S GREATEST HITS**
Jan 69. Polydor/ US= King; (lp) **SOUL FIRE**
Mar 69. Polydor/ US= King; (lp) **KING OF SOUL**
Nov 69. Polydor/ US= King; (lp) **THE BEST OF JAMES BROWN**
(re-iss.Jul82)
Jan 70. Polydor; (7"ep) **GIVE IT UP OR TURN IT LOOSE** -
– Give it up or turn it loose / I'll lose my mind / I don't want nobody . . . / I'll get it myself.
May 71. Polydor/ US= King; (lp)(c) **SOUL BROTHER No.1**
(re-iss.+cd.May88 on 'Arcade')
Aug 72. Polydor; (lp)(c) **JAMES BROWN SOUL CLASSICS** 83
Feb 73. Polydor; (7"m) **PAPA'S GOT A BRAND NEW BAG. / OUT OF SIGHT / IT'S A MAN'S MAN'S MAN'S WORLD**
Mar 73. Polydor; (lp)(c) **SOUL CLASSICS VOL.2**
Apr 73. Polydor; (7") **THINK. / SOMETHING** 77
(re-iss.in US remixed Aug73, hit US No.80)
May 75. Polydor; (7") **SEX MACHINE (part 1). / (part 2)** - 61
May 75. Polydor; (lp)(c) **SOUL CLASSICS VOL.3**
May 77. Polydor; (lp)(c) **SOLID GOLD**
Oct 79. Polydor; (7") **PAPA'S GOT A BRAND NEW BAG. / OUT OF SIGHT**
Jun 82. Polydor; (lp)(c) **JAMES BROWN LIVE AND LOWDOWN AT THE APOLLO VOL.1**
(re-iss.Sep83)
Jul 82. Polydor; (lp)(c) **THE BEST OF JAMES BROWN**
Jul 82. Polydor; (12"ep) **PAPA'S GOT A BRAND NEW BAG / GET UP OFFA THAT THING / GET UP I FEEL LIKE BEING A SEX MACHINE / GET ON THE GOOD FOOT**
(re-iss.May87 on 'Perfect')
Nov 83. Polydor; (lp)(c) **PLEASE PLEASE PLEASE**
(re-iss.+cd. 1988 on 'Sing')
Jan 84. Polydor; (d-lp)(d-c) **ROOTS OF A REVOLUTION**
(d-cd.iss.Nov89)
Sep 85. Polydor; (cd) **THE COMPACT DISC OF JAMES BROWN**
Mar 86. Polydor; (lp)(c) **DEAD ON THE HEAVY FUNK 74-76**
May 86. Polydor; (lp)(c)(cd) **THE LP OF JB (SEX MACHINE & OTHER SOUL CLASSICS)**
Jan 88. Polydor; (lp)(c)(cd) **JAMES BROWN & FRIENDS (live)**
Jul 88. Polydor; (lp)(c) **NON STOP**
Feb 90. Polydor; (cd)(c)(lp) **DUETS**
(cd-iss. Jan93)
Jan 91. Polydor; (d-cd) **MESSIN' WITH THE BLUES** (rare R&B/ Blues)
May 91. Polydor; (4xcd)(4xc) **STARTIME**
Nov 91. Polydor; (cd)(c)(lp) **SEX MACHINE – THE VERY BEST OF JAMES BROWN** 19
(1991 Polydor) – (see K-Tel album except replacement of tracks marked * by:-) Night train / Out of sight / I'm a greedy man (pt.1) / Get up offa that thing / I'm real / It's too funky in here / Soul power (live).
Nov 91. Polydor; (7") **GET UP (I FEEL LIKE BEING A) SEX MACHINE (1991 EQ'd Version) / GET UP (I FEEL LIKE BEING A) SEX MACHINE**
(12"+=)(cd-s+=) – Think / I Got You (I Feel Good)
Feb 93. Polydor; (cd)(c) **MASTER SERIES** -
Apr 93. Polydor; (d-cd) **CHRONICLES – SOUL PRIDE**
Apr 85. Boiling Point/ US= Polydor; (7") **FROGGY MIX. / (pt.2)** 50
(12"+=) – (extra mixes).
Jun 85. Boiling Point; (7"ep) **GET UP, I FEEL LIKE BEING A SEX MACHINE (pt.2) / PAPA'S GOT A BRAND NEW BAG / GET UP OFFA THAT THING (RELEASE THE PRESSURE)** 47
(12"+=) – ('A'-pt.2) / Get on the good foot. *(re-iss.Feb86 hit UK-No.46)*
Apr 86. Boiling Point; (7") **SOUL POWER (pt.1). / IT'S A MAN'S, MAN'S, MAN'S WORLD**
(12"+=) – King Heroin / Don't tell it.
May 86. Urban-Polydor; (d-lp)(c) **IN THE JUNGLE GROOVE**
(UK-iss.May88 +cd)
Jan 88. Urban-Polydor; (7") **SHE'S THE ONE. / FUNKY PRESIDENT (PEOPLE IT'S BAD)** 45
(12"+=) – Funky drummer (edit) / Funky drummer (boms beat reprise).
Apr 88. Urban-Polydor; (7") **THE PAYBACK MIX (pt.1). / GIVE IT UP OR TURNIT A LOOSE**
(12") – ('A'side) / KEEP ON DOING WHAT YOU'RE DOING BUT KEEP IT FUNKY (+=) – Stoned to the bone / Cold sweat.
Feb 68. Philips/ US= Smash; (lp) **JAMES BROWN PLAYS THE REAL THING**
Nov 69. Philips; (lp)(c) **THIS IS JAMES BROWN** -
(re-iss.Feb72)
1969. Federal; (7") **SOUL PRESIDENT. / POPCORN WITH A FEELING** -
Dec 81. Audio Fidelity; (lp) **LIVE IN NEW YORK (live)** -
Oct 82. Phoenix; (lp) **MEAN ON THE STREETS** -
Jul 84. Old Gold; (7") **GET UP I FEEL LIKE BEING A SEX MACHINE. / GET UP OFFA THAT THING** -
(re-iss.Jul88)
Jan 90. Old Gold; (7") **IT'S A MAN'S, MAN'S, MAN'S WORLD. / PAPA'S GOT A BRAND NEW BAG** -
May 86. Konnexion; (12") **IT'S A MAN'S, MAN'S, MAN'S WORLD. / SEX MACHINE** -
Aug 86. People; (lp)(c) **JAMES BROWN'S FUNKY PEOPLE**
– (side 2 was by his JB's) *(re-iss.+cd.on 'Urban') (cd-iss Jan93)*

— **JAMES BROWN'S FUNKY PEOPLE 2** (cd-iss.Jan93)
Apr 87. Perfect; (lp) **COLD SWEAT (live)** -
Sep 87. K-Tel; (lp)(c)(cd) **THE BEST OF JAMES BROWN (THE GODFATHER OF SOUL)** 17 -
Living in America /* Body heat / Hey America / Please, please, please / Hot pants (pt.1) / Think / I got you (I feel good) / Say it loud, I'm black and proud (pt.1) / Get up (I feel like being a) sex machine / Make it funky (pt.1) / Papa's got a brand new bag (pt.1) / Get on the good foot / * Gonna have a funky good time / Cold sweat / * Honky tonk / It's a man's man's man's world / * Gravity.

— May88 'A&M' released I GOT YOU (I FEEL GOOD) hit UK 52, from the film 'Good Morning Vietnam', B-side by Martha Reeves & The Vandellas.
Aug 88. Charly; (lp)(c)(cd) **JAMES BROWN & THE SOUL G's – LIVE AT CHASTAIN PARK (live)** -
(cd-iss.Feb90 on 'Roots')
Oct 88. Lucky; (12") **LET'S GET SERIOUS. / ?** -
Feb 89. Mainline; (cd) **20 GREATEST HITS** -
Jul 84. Solid Smoke; (lp) **FEDERAL YEARS VOL.1** -
Jul 84. Solid Smoke; (lp) **FEDERAL YEARS VOL.2** -
Apr 90. Blue Moon; (cd)(lp) **SOUL JUBILEE**
Jul 91. Entelekeg; (cd)(c) **LIVE IN NEW YORK (live)** -
Sep 91. Rhino; (cd)(c)(lp) **SOUL SYNDROME**
Oct 92. F.B.I.; (7") **I GOT YOU (I FEEL GOOD) (remix). (as "JAMES BROWN V DAKEYNE") / PROCESSED B's** 72
(cd-s+=) – B-Funked.
Jul 93. Laserlight; (cd)(c) **LIVE (live)** -
Sep 93. Yesterday's Gold; (cd)(c) **GREATEST HITS** -
Nov 93. Fat Boy; (cd) **FATHER OF SOUL** -
Mar 94. Charly; (cd) **AT STUDIO 54** -
Jul 94. Charly; (cd) **LIVE AT CHASTAIN PARK** -
Jun 94. Javelin; (cd) **COLD SWEAT** -
Jul 94. Success; (cd)(c) **LIVE IN CONCERT (live)** -
Sep 94. Spectrum; (cd)(c) **THE GODFATHER RETURNS** -
Jan 95. Success; (cd) **SEX MACHINE – LIVE IN CONCERT** -
Feb 95. B.A.M.; (cd) **PEARLS OF THE PAST** -
Mar 95. Collection; (cd) **THE COLLECTION** -
Mar 95. Top Masters; (cd) **THE GODFATHER OF SOUL & FUNK** -
Apr 95. Wisepack; (d-cd) **THE ESSENTIAL COLLECTION** -
Sep 95. Summit; (cd) **LIVE** -
Nov 95. Polydor; (3xcd-box) **LIVE AT THE APOLLO 1 / & 2 / HOT ON THE ONE** -

Michael BROWN (see under ⇒ LEFT BANKE)

Pete BROWN

Born: 25 Dec'40, London, England. Poet and songwriter who was intergral part of CREAM as their lyricist. Went solo in 1969 after CREAM's demise, but never attained true potential, although working with the likes of GRAHAM BOND on dual lp 'TWO HEADS ARE BETTER THAN ONE' in 1972. • **Style:** Experimental rock, mixing many influences with blues being main inspiration. • **Songwriters:** BROWN with others from his groups contributing music. • **Trivia:** Still kept writing partnership with solo JACK BRUCE.

Recommended: BEFORE SINGING LESSONS – 1967-1977 (*5)

PETE BROWN & HIS BATTERED ORNAMENTS

PETE BROWN – vocals (ex-CREAM lyricist)with **CHRIS SPEDDING** – guitar, etc. / **CHARLIE HART** – organ / **PETE BAILEY** – percussion / **BUTCH POTTER** – bass / **GEORGE KHAN** – alto saxophone / **ROB TAIT** – drums.

Parlophone / not issued

Feb 69. (7") **THE WEEK LOOKED GOOD ON PAPER. / MORNING CALL** [ ] [-]

Harvest / not issued

Jul 69. (lp) **A MEAL YOU CAN SHAKE YOUR HANDS WITH IN THE DARK** [ ] [-]
– Dark lady / The old man / Station song / Politician / Morning call / Rainy taxi girl / Sandcastle / Travelling blues (or the new used Jew dues blues). *(cd-iss.Apr94 on 'Repertoire')*

PETE BROWN & PIBLOKTO

with **ROB,** and recruiting **JIM MULLEN** – guitar / **DAVE THOMPSON** – saxophone, keyboards / **ROGER BUNN** – bass

Oct 69. (7") **LIVING LIFE BACKWARDS. / HIGH FLYING ELECTRIC BIRD** [ ] [-]

Apr 70. (lp) **THINGS MAY COME AND THINGS MAY GO BUT THE ART SCHOOL DANCE GOES ON FOR EVER** [ ] [-]
– Things may come and things may go, but the artschool dance goes on forever / Someone like you / Country morning / High flying electric bird / Walk for charity, run for money / Then I must go and can I keep / My love's gone far away / Golden country kingdom / Firesong / Country morning. *(cd-iss.May94 on 'Repertoire')*

— **STEVE GLOVER** repl. BUNN

Jul 70. (7") **CAN'T GET OFF THIS PLANET. / BROKEN MAGIC** [ ] [-]

Nov 70. (lp) **THOUSANDS ON A RAFT** [ ] [-]
– Aeroplane head woman / Station song platform two / Highland song / If they could see me now (parts 1 & 2) / Got a letter from a computer / Thousands on a raft. *(cd-iss.May94 on 'Repertoire')*

— PETE retained GLOVER, added **BRIAN BREEZE** – lead guitar / **PHIL RYAN** – keyboards / **JOHN 'PUGWASH' WEATHERS** – drums (both ex-EYES OF BLUE)

Nov 70. (7") **FLYING HERO SANDWICH. / MY LAST BAND** [ ] [-]

— In 1972, Pete BROWN teamed up with GRAHAM BOND on lp 'TWO HEADS ARE BETTER THAN ONE' – single 'LOST TRIBE'.

— BROWN and BOND recorded for the film ''MALTAMOUR' but BOND died.

PETE BROWN & FRIENDS

with **ED SPEVOCK** – drums / **MAX MIDDLETON** – piano / **DEREK FOLEY** – guitar / **HENRY LOWTHER** – trumpet / **TAFF WILLIAMS** – guitar / **VIN STANSHALL** – tuba / **JEFF CLYNE** – bass / **etc.**

Deram / not issued

1973. (lp) **THE NOT FORGOTTEN ASSOCIATION (poems)** [ ] [-]

PETE BROWN & IAN LYNN

IAN – keyboards (ex-BACK TO FRONT)

Disc Int. / not issued

Aug 82. (lp) **PARTY IN THE RAIN** (recorded 1977) [ ] [-]
– Broken windscreen dance / White room / Big city cowboy / Walk into the Sun / Comeback / Still have the love / I read the funky times / Party in the rain. *(cd-iss.Jun91 on 'World Wide')*

– his compilations etc. –

Apr 77. Harvest; (lp)(c) **MY LAST BAND (with "PIBLOKTO")** [ ] [-]

Mar 87. Decal; (d-lp) **BEFORE SINGING LESSONS; 1967-1977** [ ] [-]
– The week looked good on paper / Station song / High flying electric bird / Things may come and things may go (but the art school dance goes on forever) / High sorrow / Raining pins and needles / Station song (platform 2) / Thousands on a raft / Broken magic / My last band / Aeroplane head woman / Lost tribe / Mass debate / Spend my nights in armour / Night at Joan and Rays / She used to come and see me when I slept on the floor / Late Fiona / Change of heart / The old rock singer / Barbed wire nightdress / Big city cowboy.

PETE BROWN & PHIL RYAN

Aura / not issued

Feb 91. (cd) **ARDOURS OF THE LOST RAKE** [ ] [-]

Voiceprint / not issued

Oct 93. (cd) **COALS TO JERUSALEM** [ ] [-]
– Ordinary man / Brain money / Armoured priest / Don't take your fish to the swimming pool / A hint of blonde / Pratinu rides again / Consuming passions / I begin with you / Holy smoke / Dark city / That's me, I'm a winner / International fear cocktail.

Jackson BROWNE

Born: 9 Oct'48, Heidelberg, W. Germany. His father was in US Army, but moved back to Orange County, California. In 1966 after brief stint with NITTY GRITTY DIRT BAND, Jackson went solo signing for 'Elektra', at first as house songwriter, then to David Geffen's new 'Asylum' label in 1971. Due to his songs being covered by many, 'DOCTOR MY EYES' (Jackson 5) / 'SHADOW DREAM SONG' (Tom Paxton), his eponymous debut album hit US Top 60. He continued to score with many more albums, and also several 45's. • **Style:** Singer-songwriter/balladeer with easy-listening but intelligent appeal. • **Songwriters:** Self penned, except STAY (Maurice Williams & the Zodiacs) / also co-wrote TAKE IT EASY with GLENN FREY (Eagles). • **Miscellaneous:** Disaster hit him when his wife PHYLLIS committed suicide on the 25th March 1976. He found new love in the 80's with actress girlfriend DARRYL HANNAH.

Recommended: THE PRETENDER (*6)

JACKSON BROWNE – vocals with **CRAIG DOERGE** – keyboards / **LELAND SKLAR** – bass / **RUSS KUNKEL** – drums / **CLARENCE WHITE** – guitar / **DAVID CROSBY** – b.vocals

Asylum / Asylum

Mar 72. (7") **DOCTOR MY EYES. / I'M LOOKING INTO YOU** [ ] [8]

Apr 72. (lp)(c) **JACKSON BROWNE** [ ] [53] Mar 72
– Jamaica say you will / A child in these hills / Song for Adam / Doctor my eyes / From Silver Lake / Something fine / Under the falling sky / Looking into you / Rock me on the water / My opening farewell. *(re-iss.Jun76) (cd-iss.Jan87)*

Aug 72. (7") **ROCK ME ON THE WATER. / SOMETHING FINE** [ ] [48]

— added **DAVID LINDLEY** – guitar, violin, etc. (ex-KALEIDOSCOPE)

Sep 73. (7") **REDNECK FRIEND. / THE TIMES YOU'VE COME** [-] [85]

Dec 73. (lp)(c) **FOR EVERYMAN** [ ] [43] Nov 73
– Take it easy / Our lady of the well / Colors of the sun / I thought I was a child / These days / Redneck friend / The times you've come / Ready or not / Sing my songs to me / For everyman. *(cd-iss.Jan87)*

Apr 74. (7") **TAKE IT EASY. / READY OR NOT** [ ] [ ]

— retained **LINDLEY** and brought in **JAI WINDING** – keyboards / **DOUG HAYWOOD** – bass, vocals / **LARRY ZACK** – drums

Nov 74. (7") **WALKING SLOW. / THE LATE SHOW** [ ] [-]

Oct 74. (7") **WALKING SLOW. / BEFORE THE DELUGE** [-] [ ]

Dec 74. (lp)(c) **LATE FOR THE SKY** [ ] [14] Oct 74
– Late for the sky / Fountain of sorrow / Farther on / The late show / The road and the sky / For a dancer / Walking slow / Before the deluge. *(quad-lp 1977) (cd-iss.Jan87)*

Mar 75. (7") **FOUNTAIN OF SORROW. / THE LATE SHOW** [ ] [ ]

— **KUNKEL, SKLAR, DOERGE and LINDLEY** plus **JEFF PORCARO** – drums / **JIM GORDON** – drums / **BOB GLAUB and CHUCK RAINEY** – bass / **ROY BITTAN and BILL PAYNE** – organ / **LUIS F.DAMIAN** – guitar / etc.

Nov 76. (lp)(c) **THE PRETENDER** [26] [5]
– The fuse / Your bright baby blues / Linda Paloma / Here come those tears again / Daddy's tune / The only child / Daddy's tune / Sleep's dark and silent gate / The pretender. *(cd-iss.Jan87)*

Feb 77. (7") **HERE COME THOSE TEARS AGAIN. / LINDA PALOMA** [ ] [23]

Jul 77. (7") **THE PRETENDER. / DADDY'S TUNE** [ ] [58] May 77

Jan 78 (7") **YOU LOVE THE THUNDER. / COCAINE** [ ] [ ]

Jan 78. (lp)(c) **RUNNING ON EMPTY** [28] [3]
– Running on empty / The road / Rosie / You love the thunder / Cocaine / Shaky town / Love needs a heart / Nothing but time / The load-out / Stay. *(cd-iss.Jan87)*

Mar 78. (7") **RUNNING ON EMPTY. / NOTHING BUT TIME** [ ] [11] Feb 78

Jun 78. (7") **STAY. / ROSIE** [12] [-]

Sep 78. (7") **STAY. / THE LOAD-OUT** [-] [20]

Nov 78. (7") **THE ROAD. / YOU LOVE THE THUNDER** [-] [ ]

Jul 80. (7") **BOULEVARD. / CALL IT A LOAN** [ ] [19]

Jul 80. (lp)(c) **HOLD OUT** [44] [1]
– Disco apocalypse / Hold out / That girl could sing / Boulevard / Of missing persons / Call it a loan / Hold on hold out. *(cd-iss.Jan87)*

Oct 80. (7") **DISCO APOCALYPSE. / BOULEVARD** [ ] [-]

Oct 80. (7") **THAT GIRL COULD SING. / OF MISSING PERSONS** [-] [22]

— next single was from "Fast Times at Ridgemont High" Soundtrack featuring **GRAHAM NASH + DAVID LINDLEY**

Aug 82. (7") **SOMEBODY'S BABY. / THE CROW ON THE CRADLE** [ ] [7] Jul 82

— **BROWNE** retained **KUNKEL, DOERGE, HAYWOOD, GLAUB RICK VITO** – guitar repl. LINDLEY

Jul 83. (7") **LAWYERS IN LOVE. / SAY IT ISN'T TRUE** [ ] [13]

Aug 83. (lp)(c)(cd) **LAWYERS IN LOVE** [37] [8]
– Lawyers in love / On the day / Cut it away / Downtown / Tender is the night / Knock on any door / For a rocker. *(cd-iss.Jul87)*

Oct 83. (7") **TENDER IS THE NIGHT. / ON THE DAY** [ ] [25] Sep 83

Jan 84. (7") **FOR A ROCKER. / DOWNTOWN** [-] [45]

— Early in '86, JACKSON was credited on US Top 20 single 'You're A Friend Of Mine', with CLARENCE CLEMONS (ex-BRUCE SPRINGSTEEN). His girlfriend DARRYL HANNAH guested, backing vocals.

Feb 86. (lp)(c)(cd) **LIVES IN THE BALANCE** [36] [23]
– For America / Soldier of plenty / In the shape of a heart / Candy / Lawless avenues / Lives in the balance / Till I go down / Black and white.

Feb 86. (7")(7"sha-pic-d) **FOR AMERICA. / TILL I GO DOWN** [ ] [30]

Elektra / Elektra

Oct 86. (7") **IN THE SHAPE OF A HEART. / VOICE OF AMERICA** [66] [70] Jun 86
(d7"+=) – Running on empty / The pretender.

Jan 87. (7")(12") **EGO MANIAC. / LOVE'S GONNA GET YOU** [ ] [ ]
(above single on 'Warners')

Jun 89. (lp)(c)(cd) **WORLD IN MOTION** [39] [45]
– World in motion / Enough of the night / Chasing you into the light / How long / Anything can happen / When the stone begins to turn / The word justice / My

personal revenge / I am a patriot / Lights and virtues. *(re-iss.cd Feb95)*
Jun 89. (7") **WORLD IN MOTION. / PERSONAL REVENGE** [-] [ ]
Oct 89. (7") **ANYTHING CAN HAPPEN. / LIGHTS AND VIRTUES** [-] [ ]
Jan 90. (7") **CHASING YOU INTO THE NIGHT. / HOW LONG** [-] [ ]

— with **DAVID LINDLEY, MARK GOLDENBERG, SCOTT THURSTON, MIKE CAMPBELL, WALLY WACHTEL** – guitars / **KEVIN McCORMICK** – bass / **BENMONT TENCH** – organ / **MAURICIO LEWAK** – drums / **LUIS CONTE + LENNY CASTRO** – percussion / plus guests **DAVID CROSBY / DON HENLEY / JENNIFER WARNES / SWEET PEA ATKINSON + SIR HARRY BOWENS**

Oct 93. (cd)(c) **I'M ALIVE** [35] [40]
– I'm alive / My problem is you / Everywhere I go / I'll do anything / Miles away / Too many angels / Take this rain / Two of me, two of you / Sky blue and black / All good things.
Nov 93. (7")(c-s) **I'M ALIVE / TOO MANY ANGELS** [ ] [ ]
(cd-s) – ('A' side) Late for the sky / Running on empty / The pretender.
Jun 94. (7")(c-s) **EVERYWHERE I GO. / I'M ALIVE (live)** [67] [ ]
(cd-s+=) – The pretender (live) / Running on empty (live).
(cd-s) – ('A'side) / Take it easy / Doctor my eyes / In the shape of a heart.
Nov 94. (c-s) **HAND IN HAND. / TENDER IS THE NIGHT** [ ] [ ]
(cd-s+=) – Everywhere I go.

– compilations etc. –

Sep 76. Asylum; (7") **DOCTOR MY EYES. / TAKE IT EASY** [ ] [ ]
Oct 82. Asylum; (d-c) **THE PRETENDER / LATE FOR THE SKY** [ ] [-]
Nov 83. Asylum; (d-c) **JACKSON BROWNE / RUNNING ON EMPTY** [ ] [-]

Jack BRUCE

Born: 14 May'43, Bishopbriggs, Lanarkshire, Scotland. At 17 he won scholarship to R.S.A. of music. He joined local band JIM McHARG'S SCOTSVILLE JAZZBAND, before moving to London to join BLUES INCORPORATED with ALEXIS KORNER. In 1963 he became member of GRAHAM BOND ORGANISATION. In Oct'65 he joined JOHN MAYALL'S BLUESBREAKERS, also releasing debut solo 45. Late 1965, MANFRED MANN recruited him for six months, until his greatest move co-forming CREAM. After their demise late 1968, he went solo with 'Polydor' retaining contract. His debut 'SONGS FOR A TAILOR' hit the UK Top 10, but thereafter this was his only commercial success. • **Style:** One of greatest bass players of all-time, his new blues, with jazzy improvisations alongside superior underated vocals, gave him unique appeal. • **Songwriters:** Wrote most work with PETE BROWN. • **Trivia:** During 1970, he was also part of US jazz-rock outfit TONY WILLIAMS' LIFETIME, releasing album of same name.

Recommended: GREATEST HITS (*6)

JACK BRUCE – vocals, bass (ex-BLUES INCORPORATED, ex-GRAHAM BOND ORGANISATION) with session people.

Polydor / not issued
Dec 65. (7") **I'M GETTIN' TIRED. / ROOTIN' AND TOOTIN'** [ ] [-]

— (see above for details between 1966 and 1968.) He brought in friends **JON HISEMAN** – drums / **DICK HECKSTALL-SMITH** – sax / **CHRIS SPEDDING** – guitar / etc.

Polydor / Atco
Sep 69. (lp)(c) **SONGS FOR A TAILOR** [6] [55]
– Never tell your mother she's out of tune / Theme of an imaginary western / Tickets to water falls / Weird of Hermiston / Rope ladder to the Moon / The ministry of bag / He the Richmond / Boston ball game, 1967 / To Isengard / The clearout. *(re-iss.May84) (cd-iss. May 88)*

— **JOHN McLAUGHLIN** – guitar (solo artist), repl. SPEDDING.

Apr 71. (lp)(c) **THINGS WE LIKE ("JACK BRUCE, JOHN McLAUGHLIN, DICK HECKSTALL-SMITH, JON HISEMAN")** [ ] [ ]
– Over the cliff / Statues / Sam enchanted Dick (medley:- Sam's back / Rill's thrills) / Born to be blue / Hchhh blues / Ballad of Arthur / Things we like. *(re-iss.1979)*

— retained some past musicians, bringing in **LARRY COYRELL** – guitar / **MIKE MANDEL** – keyboards / **MITCH MITCHELL** – drums

1971. (lp)(c) **HARMONY ROW** [ ] [ ]
– Can you follow? / Escape to the Royal wood (on ice) / You burned the tables on me / There's a forest / Morning story / Folk song / Smiles and grins / Post war / Letter of thanks / Victoria sage / The consul at sunset. *(cd-iss.1980's)*
1971. (7") **THE CONSUL AT SUNSET. / LETTER OF THANKS** [ ] [ ]

— In 1972/73, he became part of WEST, BRUCE & LAING (see; MOUNTAIN ⇒) He also collaborated on lp ESCALATOR OVER THE HILL with PAUL HAINES and CARLA.

— now with **MICK TAYLOR** – guitar / **CARLA BLEY** – piano / **RONNIE LEAHY** – keyboards / **BRUCE GARY** – drums

R.S.O. / R.S.O.
Oct 74. (7") **KEEP IT DOWN. / GOLDEN DAYS** [ ] [ ]
Nov 74. (lp)(c) **OUT OF THE STORM** [ ] [ ]
– Pieces of mind / Golden days / Running through our hands / Keep on wondering / Keep it down / Into the storm / One / Timeslip. *(cd-iss.!)*

— now with **SIMON PHILIPS** – drums / **HUGH BURNS** – guitar / **TONY HYMAS** – keyboards

Mar 77. (lp)(c) **HOW'S TRICKS ("JACK BRUCE BAND")** [ ] [ ]
– Without a word / Johnny B '77 / Times / Baby Jane / Lost inside a song / How's tricks / Madhouse / Waiting for the call / Outsiders / Something to live for.

— Friends: **DAVID SANCIOUS** – guitar, keyboards / **DAVE CLEMSON** – guitar / **BILLY COBHAM** – drums

Epic / Epic
Dec 80. (lp)(c) **I'VE ALWAYS WANTED TO DO THIS ("JACK BRUCE & FRIENDS").** [ ] [ ]
– Hit and run / Running back / Facelift 318 / In this way / Mickey the fiddler / Dancing on air / Livin' without ja / Wind and the sea / Out to lunch / Bird alone.

In 1981 he teamed up with BILL LORDAN and ROBIN TROWER to release lp 'B.L.T. Early the following year he and ROBIN TROWER (see ⇒ released TRUCE album).

— He returned to solo work after below 45 was featured on TV car advert.

Virgin / Virgin
Jun 86. (7")(12") **I FEEL FREE. / MAKE LOVE** [ ] [ ]

President / Intercord
Jan 87. (lp)(c) **AUTOMATIC** [ ] [ ]
– A boogie / Uptown breakdown / Travelling child / New world / Make love (part 2) / Green and blue / The swarm / Encore / Automatic pilot.

— next with **ANTON FIER** – drums (ex-PERE UBU) / **KENJI SUZUKI** – guitar

Epic / Epic
Jan 88. (lp)(c)(cd) **INAZUMA SUPER SESSION – ABSOLUTELY LIVE ("JACK BRUCE, ANTON FIER & KENJI SUZUKI" live)** [ ] [ ]
– Generation breakdown / White room / Out into the field / Working harder / Sittin' on top of the world / Sunshine of your love / Crossroads / Spoonful – Beat of rock.

— now with **VERNON REID, NICKY HOPKINS, ALLAN HOLDSWORTH, GINGER BAKER**

Jan 90. (cd)(c)(lp) **A QUESTION OF TIME** [ ] [ ]
– Life on Earth / Make love / No surrender! / Flying / Hey now princess / Blues you can't lose / Obsession / Kwela / Let me be / Only playing games / A question of time. *(re-iss.Feb91)*

— with **PETE BROWN** still lyricist / plus **ERIC CLAPTON** – lead guitar / **STUART ELLIOT** – drums / **PETER WIEHE** – rhythm guitar / **MAGGIE REILLY** – b.vocals / **CLEM CLEMPSON** – rhythm guitar, etc / **TRILOK GURTU** – percussion / and guests on 1 each **DICK HECKSTALL-SMITH + DAVID LIEBMAN** – saxophones

C.M.P. / C.M.P.
Mar 93. (cd)(c)(lp) **SOMETHIN ELS** [ ] [-]
– Waiting on a word / Willpower / Ships in the night / Peace of the East / Close enough for love / G.B. dawn blues / Criminality / Childsong / F.M.

— with **GARY MOORE** – guitar, vocals / **MAGGIE REILLY** – vocals / **GARY 'Mudbone' COOPER** – vocals, percussion / **GARY MOORE** – guitar, vocals / **CLEM CLEMPSON** – guitars / **DICK HECKSTALL-SMITH** – saxophone / **BERNIE WORRELL** – keyboards / **PETE BROWN** – vocals, percussion / **GINGER BAKER + SIMON PHILLIPS + GARY HUSBAND** – drums / **FRANCOIS GARNY** – bass / **MALCOLM BRUCE** – acoustic guitar, keyboards / **JONAS BRUCE** – keyboards / **ART THEMIN** – saxophone / **HENRY LOWTHER** – trumpet / **JOHN MUMFORD** – trombone / + **KIP HANRAHAN**

Mar 94. (d-cd)(d-c) **CITIES OF THE HEART (live)** [ ] [ ]
– Can you follow? / Running thro' our hands / Over the cliff / Statues / First time I met the blues / Smiles & grins / Bird alone / Neighbor, neighbor / Born under a bad sign // Ships in the night / Never tell your mother she's out of tune / Theme for an imaginary western / Golden days / Life on Earth / NSU / Sitting on top of the world / Politician / Spoonful / Sunshine of your love. *(re-iss.Aug94 + Nov94)*
Sep 95. (cd) **MONKJACK** [ ] [-]
– Third degree / The boy / Shouldn't we / David's harp / Know one blues / Time repairs / Laughing on music / Street / Folksong / Weird of Hermiston / Tightrope / The food / Immoral ninth.

BBM

(aka GINGER BAKER, JACK BRUCE & GARY MOORE) A near reformation of CREAM with MOORE taking the place of CLAPTON.

Virgin / Virgin
Jun 94. (cd)(c)(lp) **AROUND THE NEXT DREAM** [9] [ ]
– Waiting in the wings / City of God / Where in the world / Can't fool the blues / High cost of living / Glory days / Why does love (have to go wrong) / Naked flame / I wonder (why are you so mean to me?) / Wrong side of town.
Jul 94. (7")(c-s) **WHERE IN THE WORLD. / DANGER ZONE** [57] [ ]
(cd-s+=) – The world keeps on turnin'.
(cd-s) – ('A'side) / Sittin' on top of the world / I wonder (why are you so mean to me?).

– compilations, others, etc. –

1974. Polydor/ US= R.S.O.; (d-lp)(d-c) **AT HIS BEST** [ ] [ ]
Nov 80. Polydor; (lp) **GREATEST HITS** [ ] [ ]
Jul 89. Polydor; (d-lp)(c)(cd) **WILLPOWER** [ ] [ ]
(re-iss.cd Apr95)
May 92. Castle; (cd) **THE COLLECTION** [ ] [-]
May 94. Atonal; (cd) **THIS THAT ("HECKSTALL / BRUCE / STEVENS")** [ ] [-]
Sep 95. Windsong; (cd) **BBC LIVE IN CONCERT** [ ] [-]

B.T.O. (see under ⇒ BACHMAN-TURNER OVERDRIVE)

BUBONIQUE (see under ⇒ FATIMA MANSIONS)

Lindsey BUCKINGHAM / BUCKINGHAM-NICKS (see under ⇒ FLEETWOOD MAC)

Tim BUCKLEY

Born: 14 Feb'47, Washington DC, USA. In 1966 he signed to 'Elektra' after his California gigs were seen by Herb Cohen, manager of FRANK ZAPPA. With ZAPPA's musicians, he recorded eponymous debut, before moving to New York. Although he was regarded as great underground talent, his work never quite hit commercially. Tragically he died of an accidental drug overdose on 25 Jun'75. • **Style:** His spells took him through 60's folk-rock to free-form jazz and later funk-rock in the 70's. • **Songwriters:** Penned most himself, except SALLY GO ROUND THE ROSES (Jaynettes) / etc. • **Trivia:** His songs were later recorded by (This Mortal Coil) – SONG TO THE SIREN / (Blood, Sweat & Tears) – MORNING GLORY, etc..

Recommended: BEST OF TIM BUCKLEY (1983 US-import lp;*8)

TIM BUCKLEY – vocals, guitar with **LEE UNDERWOOD** – guitar, keyboards / **BILLY MUNDI** – drums / **JIM FIELDER** – bass / **VAN DYKE PARKS piano / JACK NITZSCHE** – string arrangements

Elektra Elektra

Nov 66. (7") **GRIEF IN MY SOUL. / WINGS** –

Dec 66. (lp) **TIM BUCKLEY** Oct 66
– I can't see you / Wings / Song of the magician / Strange street affair under blue / Valentine melody / Aren't you the girl / Song slowly sung / It happens every time / Song for Jainie / Grief in my soul / She is / Understand your man. *(re-iss.Jul71, re-iss.Mar75)*

Jan 67. (7") **AREN'T YOU THE GIRL. / STRANGE STREET AFFAIR UNDER BLUE**

— BUCKLEY retained only UNDERWOOD, recruiting **CARTER C. COLLINS** – congas

Sep 67. (7") **LADY GIVE ME YOUR HEART. / ONCE UPON A TIME** –

Nov 67. (7") **MORNING GLORY. / KNIGHT ERRANT**

Dec 67. (lp) **GOODBYE AND HELLO** Oct 67
– No man can find the war / Carnival song / Pleasant street / Hallucinations / I never asked to be your mountain / Once I was / Phantasmagoria in two / Knight-Errant / Goodbye and hello / Morning glory. *(re-iss.cd+c Mar93 on 'Pickwick') (re-iss.cd/c Sep95 on 'Warners')*

Jan 68. (7") **ONCE I WAS. / PHANTASMAGORIA IN TWO**

— added **JOHN MILLER** – acc. & elect.bass / **DAVID FREEDMAN** – vibes, percussion

Oct 68. (7") **PLEASANT STREET. / CARNIVAL STREET**

Jul 69. (lp) **HAPPY – SAD** 81
– Strange feeling / Buzzin' fly / Love from room 109 at the Islander (on Pacific Coast Highway) / Dream letter / Gypsy woman / Sing a song for you. *(re-iss.Jul71) (cd-iss.Feb93)*

— added **JIMMY MADISON** – drums

Straight Straight

Feb 70. (7") **HAPPY TIME. / SO LONELY**

Feb 70. (lp) **BLUE AFTERNOON**
– Happy time / Chase the blues away / I must have been blind / The river / So lonely / Cafe / Blue melody / Train.

— BUCKLEY retained only UNDERWOOD and COLLINS, recruiting **JOHN BLAKIN** – bass

Elektra Elektra

Oct 70. (lp) **LORCA**
– Lorca / Anonymous proposition / I had a talk with a woman / Driftin' / Nobody walkin'. *(re-iss.Jul71, re-iss.Mar75)*

— BUCKLEY retained only UNDERWOOD and BALKIN, recruiting co-write **LARRY BECKETT / MAURI BAKET** – timpani / **BUZZ GARDNER and BUNK GARDNER on wind and horns**

Straight Straight

Jan 71. (lp) **STARSAILOR**
– Come here woman / I woke up / Monterey / Moulin Rouge / Song to the siren / Jungle fire / Starsailor / The healing festival / Down by the borderline.

— from now on BUCKLEY used loads of session people plus past friends.

Warners Warners

Oct 72. (7") **MOVE WITH ME. / NIGHTHAWKIN'** –

Oct 72. (lp) **GREETINGS FROM L.A.**
– Move with me / Get on top / Sweet surrender / Nighthawkin' / Devil eyes / Hong Kong bar / Make it right.

Discreet Discreet

May 74. (lp) **SEFRONIA**
– Dolphins / Honey man / Because of you / Peanut man / Martha / Quicksand / I know I'd recognize your face / Stone in love / Sefron after Asklepiads, after Kafka / Sefronia – The King's chain / Sally go 'round the roses. *(re-iss.+cd. on 'Edsel')*

May 74. (7") **STONE IN LOVE. / QUICKSAND** –

Jul 74. (7") **HONEY MAN. / DOLPHINS** –

Nov 74. (lp) **LOOK AT THE FOOL**
– Bring it on up / Look at the fool / Ain't it peculiar / Freeway blues / Helpless / Tijuana Moon / Who could deny you / Mexicali voodoo / Wanda Lu / Down in the street. *(re-iss.+cd.Dec89 on 'Edsel')*

Nov 74. (7") **WANDA LU. / WHO COULD DENY YOU** –

— **TIM BUCKLEY** died 25 Jun '75 of accidental drug overdose. In 1994, his son JEFF BUCKLEY signed to 'Big Cat' and also appeared at Reading Festival in August. His debut album 'CLARE' cracked UK Top 50 around same time.

– compilations, etc. –

Mar 68. Elektra; (7") **WINGS. / I CAN'T SEE YOU**

Sep 76. Elektra; (7") **MORNING GLORY. / ONCE I WAS**

Jun 90. Demon; (cd)(d-lp) **DREAM LETTER**

Mar 94. Demon; (cd) **LIVE AT TROUBADOUR 1969 (live)** –

Aug 91. Strange Fruit; (12"ep)(cd-ep) **THE PEEL SESSIONS** –
– Morning glory / Coming home to you / Sing a song for you / Hallucinations / Troubadour / Once I was.

Aug 94. Band Of Joy; (cd) **MORNING GLORY** –

Harold BUDD, Elizabeth FRAZER, Robin GUTHRIE, Simon RAYMONDE (see under ⇒ COCTEAU TWINS)

BUDGIE

Formed: Cardiff, Wales . . . 1968 by SHELLEY. After local gigs, they signed to 'M.C.A.' where they finally gained recognition and a Top 30 album with 1974 'IN FOR THE KILL'. Fell away somewhat when they signed to 'A&M' in 1976, but always retained loyal following, which secured minor chart entries and on-the-road triumphs. • **Style:** Powerful but basic heavy-riffed rock, that laid down roots to many a new-wave metal band (e.g. METALLICA etc.). Bludgeoned guitar feasts were fused with SHELLEY's sharp high vox. • **Songwriters:** SHELLEY-BOURGE except:- BABY PLEASE DON'T GO (hit; Them). • **Trivia:** Never disbanded until 1987 when they had last gig. In the late 70's they moved to the States for 2 years, and this must have gained them recognition from new metal fans.

Recommended: THE BEST OF BUDGIE (*8)

BURKE SHELLEY – vocals, bass / **TONY BOURGE** – guitar, vocals / **RAY PHILLIPS** – drums

M.C.A. Kapp

1971. (7") **CRASH COURSE IN BRAIN SURGERY. / NUDE DISINTEGRATING PARACHUTIST WOMAN** –

1971. (lp) **BUDGIE** –
– Guts / Everything in my heart / The author / Nude disintegrating parachutist woman / Rape of the locks / All night petrol / You and I / Homicidal suicidal. *(re-iss.'74) (cd-iss.Jul93 on 'Repertoire')*

1972. (7") **WHISKEY RIVER. / GUTS**

1972. (lp) **SQUAWK**
– Whiskey river / Rockin' man / Rollin' home again / Make me happy / Hot as a docker's armpit / Drugstore woman / Bottled / Young is a world / Stranded. *(re-iss.'74, cd-iss.May90) (cd-iss.Jul93 on 'Repertoire')*

1972. (7") **WHISKEY RIVER. / STRANDED** –

M.C.A. M.C.A.

1973. (lp)(c) **NEVER TURN YOUR BACK ON A FRIEND**
– Breadfan / Baby please don't go / You know I'll always love you / You're the biggest thing since powdered milk / In the grips of a tyrefitter's hand / Riding my nightmare / Parents. *(re-iss.Jun87)(cd-iss.Jul93 on 'Repertoire')*

— **PETE BOOT** – drums repl. PHILLIPS (later to TREDEGAR)

May 74. (7") **ZOOM CLUB. / WONDERING WHAT EVERYONE KNOWS** –

Jun 74. (lp)(c) **IN FOR THE KILL** 29
– In for the kill / Crash course in brain surgery / Wondering what everyone knows / Zoom club / Hammer and tongs / Running from my soul / Living on your own.

— **STEVE WILLIAMS** – drums repl. BOOT

Feb 75. (7") **I AIN'T NO MOUNTAIN. / HONEY**

Sep 75. (lp)(c) **BANDOLIER** 36
– Breaking all the house rules / Slipaway / Who do want for love? / I can't see my feelings / Rock climbing / I ain't no mountain / Napoleon Bona-part one & two. *(cd-iss.Jul93 on 'Repertoire')*

A & M A & M

Apr 76. (lp)(c) **IF I WERE BRITANNIA I'D WAIVE THE RULES**
– Anne Neggan / If I were Brittannia I'd waive the rules / You're opening doors / Quacktors and bureaucrats / Sky high percentage / Heaven knows our name / Black velvet stallion. *(cd-iss.Jan94 on 'Repertoire')*

— added **MYF ISAACS** – 2nd guitar

Feb 78. (lp)(c) **IMPECKABLE**
– Melt the ice away / Love for you and me / All at sea / Dish it up / Pyramids / Smile boy smile / I'm a faker too / Don't go away / Don't dilute the water. *(cd-iss.Jan94 on 'Repertoire')*

Mar 78. (7") **SMILE BOY SMILE. / ALL AT SEA**

— **JOHN THOMAS** – guitar, slide, vocals (ex-GEORGE HATCHER BAND) repl. ROB KENDRICK (ex-TRAPEZE) who had repl. BOURGE. (He formed TREDEGAR). (ISAACS had also departed)

Active R.C.A.

Jul 80. (12"ep) **IF SWALLOWED DO NOT INDUCE VOMITING**
– Wild fire / High school kids.

Oct 80. (lp)(c) **POWER SUPPLY**
– Forearm smash / Hellbender / Heavy revolution / Gunslinger / Power supply / Secrets in my head / Time to remember / Crime against the world. *(cd-iss.Apr93 on 'Repertoire')*

Nov 80. (7") **CRIME AGAINST THE WORLD. / HELLBENDER**

R.C.A. R.C.A.

Sep 81. (7")(7"pic-d) **KEEPING A RENDEZVOUS. / APPARATUS** 71

Oct 81. (lp)(c) **NIGHT FLIGHT** 68
– I turned the stone / Keeping a rendezvous / Reaper of the glory / She used me up / Don't lay down and die / Apparatus / Superstar / Change your ways / Untitled lullaby. *(cd-iss.Feb93 on 'Repertoire')*

Nov 81. (7")(7"orange) **I TURNED TO STONE. / ('A'instrumental)**

— added **DUNCAN MACKAY** – keyboards (ex-COCKNEY REBEL, ex-10CC)

Sep 82. (7")(7"pic-d) **BORED WITH RUSSIA. / DON'T CRY**

Oct 82. (lp)(c) **DELIVER US FROM EVIL** 62
– Bored with Russia / Don't cry / Truth drug / Young girl / Flowers in the attic / N.O.R.A.D. (Doomsday city) / Give me the truth / Alison / Finger on the button / Hold on to love. *(cd-iss.Mar93 on 'Repertoire')*

— (disbanded late '82)

– compilations etc. –

Sep 76. M.C.A.; (lp)(c) **THE BEST OF BUDGIE**
– Whiskey river / Guts / Rolling home again / Homocidal suicide / Hot as a docker's armpit / Drugstore woman / Rocking man / You and I / Stranded / Breadfan / I ain't no mountain / I can't see my feelings / Baby please don't go / Zoom club / Breaking all the house rules / Parents / In for the kill / In the grip of a tyrefitter's hand. *(re-iss.Feb82) (cd-iss. Aug 89 with extra tracks)*

1981. Cube; (lp)(c) **THE BEST OF "BUDGIE" (early material)**

BUFFALO SPRINGFIELD

Formed: Los Angeles, California, USA . . . March 1966 by STEVE STILLS, NEIL YOUNG, RICHIE FUREY and BRUCE PALMER. They emigrated from various places and odd groups around North America (Canada) and soon signed to 'Atco' label releasing eponymous debut. Early in 1967, they scored a US Top 10 hit with classic 'FOR WHAT IT'S WORTH', but due to various changes in personnel, they didn't last long, and members went on to greater things (see below). • **Style:** Harmonious electric-rock that veered into protest and underground. • **Songwriters:** Mainly STILLS, YOUNG or FUREY. • **Trivia:** Took their name from type of steamroller.

Recommended: THE BEST OF . . . RETROSPECTIVE (*8)

STEPHEN STILLS (b. 3 Jan'45, Dallas, Texas) – lead guitar, vocals / **NEIL YOUNG** (b.12 Nov'45, Toronto, Canada) – lead guitar, vocals / **RICHIE FURAY** (b. 9 May'44, Dayton, Ohio) – vocals, guitar / **BRUCE PALMER** (b. 1944, Liverpool, Canada) – bass repl. KEN KOBLUN / **DEWEY MARTIN** (b.30 Sep'42, Chesterfield, Canada) – drums (ex-DILLARDS)

Atlantic Atco

1966. (7") **NOWADAYS CLANCY CAN'T EVEN SING. / GO AND SAY GOODBYE** [-] [ ]

Jan 67. (lp) **BUFFALO SPRINGFIELD** [ ] [80] Oct 66
– Don't scold me (*) / Go and say goodbye / Sit down I think I love you / Nowadays Clancy can't even sing / Everybody's wrong / Hot dusty roads / Flying on the ground / Burned / Do I have to come right out and say it? / Leave / Pay the price / Out of my mind. *(re-iss.'71 with below 'A' side repl. (*)) (cd-iss. Feb93)*

Jan 67. (7") **FOR WHAT IT'S WORTH. / DO I HAVE TO COME RIGHT OUT AND SAY IT?** [ ] [7]

— On stage **KEN KOBLUN** and **JIM FIELDER**, latter of The MOTHERS, repl. PALMER, although PALMER did return occasionally. / **DOUG HASTINGS** – guitar repl. YOUNG (also DAVID CROSBY guested at Monteray)

— **BOB WEST** – bass & CHARLIE CHIN – banjo deputise for above reshuffles

Jul 67. (7") **BLUEBIRD. / Mr.SOUL** [-] [58]

— **STILLS, FURAY, MARTIN** and the returning **YOUNG** recruit **JIM MESSINA** – bass repl. FIELDER who joined BLOOD SWEAT & TEARS

Oct 67. (7") **ROCK'N'ROLL WOMAN. / A CHILD'S CLAIM TO FAME** [ ] [44] Sep 67

Jan 68. (lp) **BUFFALO SPRINGFIELD AGAIN** [ ] [44] Nov 67
– Mr.Soul / A child's claim to fame / Everydays / Expecting to fly / Bluebird / Hung upside down / Sad memory / Good time boy / Rock'n'roll woman / Broken arrow. *(re-iss.'71)*

Feb 68. (7") **EXPECTING TO FLY. / EVERYDAYS** [ ] [98] Jan 68

Jun 68. (7") **UNO-MUNDO. / MERRY-GO-ROUND** [ ] [ ]

Aug 68. (7") **KIND WOMAN. / SPECIAL CARE** [-] [ ]

— with original line-up they recorded another album, but they had split May. MESSINA who had always been their sound recordist posthumously assembled

Sep 68. (lp) **LAST TIME AROUND** [ ] [42] Aug 68
– On the way home / It's so hard to wait / Pretty girl why / Four days gone / Carefree country day / Special care / The hour of not quite rain / Questions / I am a child / Merry-go-round / Uno mundo / Kind woman. *(re-iss.'71) (cd-iss.Mar94 on 'Atco')*

Oct 68. (7") **ON THE WAY HOME. / FOUR DAYS GONE** [-] [82]

— After their split, NEIL YOUNG went solo and joined STEPHEN STILLS in CROSBY, STILLS NASH & YOUNG. FURAY formed POCO adding later MESSINA. DEWEY MARTIN tried in vain to use BUFFALO SPRINGFIELD name.

– compilations etc. –

Mar 69. Atlantic/ US= Atco; (lp) **RETROSPECTIVE – THE BEST OF BUFFALO SPRINGFIELD** [ ] [42] Feb 69
– For what it's worth / Mr. Soul / Sit down I think I love you / Kind woman / Bluebird / On the way home / Nowadays Clancy can't even sing / Broken arrow / Rock and roll woman / I am a child / Go and say goodbye / Expecting to fly. *(cd-iss. Jul 88)*

Oct 69. Atlantic; (7"ep) **PRETTY GIRL WHY / QUESTIONS / BLUEBIRD / MR. SOUL / ROCK'N'ROLL WOMAN / EXPECTING TO FLY.** [ ] [-]

Oct 70. Atlantic; (lp) **EXPECTING TO FLY** [ ] [-]

Oct 72. Atlantic; (7"ep) **BLUEBIRD / MR.SOUL. / ROCK'N'ROLL WOMAN / EXPECTING TO FLY** [ ] [-]

Dec 73. Atlantic/ US= Atco; (d-lp)(d-c) **BUFFALO SPRINGFIELD** [ ] [ ]

— Some tracks appeared on NEIL YOUNG's comp.lp JOURNEY THROUGH THE PAST

BUFFALO TOM

Formed: Boston, Massachusetts, USA . . . 1986 by trio below. • **Style:** Like a grunge hybrid of HUSKER DU and VAN MORRISON. • **Songwriters:** Group except SHE BELONGS TO ME (Bob Dylan) / HEAVEN (Psychedelic Furs) / THE SPIDER AND THE FLY (Rolling Stones). • **Trivia:** Produced by J.MASCIS of DINOSAUR JR.

Recommended: (BIG RED LETTER DAY) (*7) / LET ME COME OVER (*8)

BILL JANOVITZ – vocals, guitar / **CHRIS COLBOURN** – bass / **TOM MAGINNIS** – drums

S.S.T. S.S.T.

Oct 89. (lp)(c)(cd) **BUFFALO TOM** [ ] [ ] Jul 89
– Sunflower suit / The plank / Impossible / 500,000 warnings / The bus / Racine / In the attic / Flushing stars / Walk away / Reason why. *(re-iss.Oct92 on 'Beggar's B.' with extra tracks) (+=) – Blue / Deep in the ground.*

Caff not issued

Feb 90. (7"ltd) **ENEMY. / DEEP IN THE GROUND** [ ] [-]

Megadisc ???

Jun 90. (12") **CRAWL. / ?** [ ] [-]

Situation 2 ???

Oct 90. (12"ep)(cd-ep) **BIRDBRAIN. / REASON WHY (live acoustic) / HEAVEN (live acoustic)** [ ] [ ]

Oct 90. (cd)(c)(lp) **BIRDBRAIN** [ ] [ ]
– Birdbrain / Skeleton key / Caress / Guy who is me / Enemy / Crawl / Fortune teller / Baby / Directive / Bleeding heart. *(cd+=)* Heaven / Reason why (acoustic). *(re-iss.cd Sep95)*

May 91. (12"ep)(cd-ep) **FORTUNE TELLER. / WAH WAH** [ ] [ ]

Feb 92. (12"ep)(cd-ep) **VELVET ROOF / SHE BELONGS TO ME. / CRUTCH / SALLY BROWN** [ ] [ ]

Mar 92. (cd)(c)(lp) **LET ME COME OVER** [49] [ ]
– Staples / Taillights fade / Mountains of your head / Mineral / Darry / Larry / Velvet roof / I'm not there / Stymied / Porch light / Frozen lake / Saving grace. (cd+=) – Crutch.

May 92. (10"ep)(12"ep)(cd-ep) **TAILLIGHTS FADE / BIRDBRAIN (live). / LARRY (live) / SKELETON KEY (live)** [ ] [ ]

Beggar's B Beggar's B

Oct 92. (7")(7"green) **MINERAL. / SUNFLOWER SUIT** [ ] [ ]
(cd-s+=) – Crawl / The bus.

Sep 93. (cd)(c)(lp) **(BIG RED LETTER DAY)** [17] [ ]
– Sodajerk / I'm Allowed / Tree House / Would Not Be Denied / Latest Monkey / My Responsibility / Dry Land / Torch Singer / Late At Night / Suppose / Anything That Way

Sep 93. (12"ep)(cd-ep) **SODA JERK / WOULD NOT BE DENIED. / WITCHES / THE WAY BACK** [ ] [ ]

Nov 93. (7") **TREEHOUSE. / ANYTHING THAT WAY (Acoustic)** [ ] [ ]
(12"+=)(cd-s+=) – Late At Night (Acoustic)

Apr 94. (12")(cd-s) **I'M ALLOWED. / FOR ALL TO SEE / BUTTERSCOTCH** [ ] [ ]

Jun 95. (10"ep)(cd-ep) **SUMMER. / CLOUDS / DOES THIS MEAN YOU'RE NOT MY FRIEND?** [ ] [ ]

Jul 95. (cd)(c)(lp) **SLEEPY EYED** [31] [ ]
– Tangerine / Summer / Kitchen door / Rules / It's you / When you discover / Sunday night / Your stripes / Sparklers / Clobbered / Sundress / Twenty-points (the ballad of sexual dependency) / Souvenir / Crueler.

Nov 95. (7") **TANGERINE. / BREATH** [ ] [ ]
(cd-s+=) – The spider and the fly.

The BUNCH (see under ⇒ FAIRPORT CONVENTION)

Eric BURDON (see under ⇒ ANIMALS)

Mark BURGESS (see under ⇒ CHAMELEONS)

J. J. BURNEL (see under ⇒ STRANGLERS)

JAKE BURNS & THE WHEEL (see under ⇒ STIFF LITTLE FINGERS)

BURRITO BROTHERS (see under ⇒ FLYING BURRITO BROTHERS)

BUSH

Formed: Kilburn, London, England . . .1994 although they soon re-located to the States, highlight being playing New York's CBGB's. Soon became million sellers there, when their 1995 album 'SIXTEEN STONE' hit the Top 20. •**Style:** Grunge rock; the English answer to NIRVANA or PEARL JAM. •**Songwriters:** Group except REVOLUTION BLUES (Neil Young).

Recommended: SIXTEEN STONE (*4)

GAVIN ROSSDALE – vocals, guitar / **NIGEL PULSFORD** – guitar / **DAVE PARSONS** – bass / **ROBIN GOODRIDGE** – drums

Atlantic Interscope

Apr 95. (c-s) **EVERYTHING ZEN. / BUD** [ ] [ ]
(12"+=)(cd-s+=) – Monkey.

May 95. (cd)(c) **SIXTEEN STONE** [ ] [17]
– Everything zen / Swim / Bomb / Little things / Comedown / Body / Machinehead / Testosterone / Monkey / Glycerine / Alien / X-girlfriend.

Jul 95. (5"ltd.)(c-s) **LITTLE THINGS / X-GIRLFRIEND** [ ] [ ]
(cd-s+=) – Swim.

Aug 95. (c-s) **COMEDOWN / REVOLUTION BLUES** [-] [30]
(cd-s+=) – Testosterone.

Kate BUSH

Born: CATHERINE BUSH, 30 Jul'58. Bexleyheath, Kent, England. In 1974, she formed own K.T.BUSH band with brother PADDY and future boyfriend DEL PALMER. By summer '76, with help from DAVE GILMOUR (Pink Floyd), she obtained contract with EMI. After a surprise No.1 hit early '78, she finally released 'THE KICK INSIDE', an album worked on for past 2+ years, which set her on the road to stardom. All her albums over the next decade or so made UK Top 10, and included nearly 20 Top 50 hits. • **Style:** A shy beauty, with dreamy childlike vocals to complement her innovative, experimental work. Her brilliant and extremely visual videos captured completely her imagination and choreography. • **Songwriters:** All or most written by KATE, except covers; ROCKET MAN + CANDLE IN THE WIND (Elton John) / I'M STILL WAITING (Diana Ross) / WHEN YOU WISH UPON A STAR (Walt Disney s/track). • **Trivia:** Her first major tour came in April'79, and although it was mildly successful, she only once appeared live again at 'The Secret Policeman's Third Ball' in 1987. She had always concentrated on studio work, but said she might tour soon. Actor Donald Sutherland appeared in her video for 'CLOUDBUSTING' 45.

Recommended: THE WHOLE STORY (*9) / THE SENSUAL WORLD (*7).

KATE BUSH – vocals, keyboards with **PADDY BUSH** – mandolin, etc. / **DEL PALMER** – bass / **IAN BAIRNSON** – guitar / **DUNCAN MACKAY** – keyboards / **ANDREW POWELL** – keyboards / **STUART ELLIOTT** – drums / **DAVID PATON** – bass / **MORRIS PERT** – percussion / **BRIAN BATH** – guitar / + others (her backing musicians changed from time to time, see 2nd edition)

E.M.I. | EMI America

Jan 78. (7") **WUTHERING HEIGHTS. / KITE** [1] [ ]
Feb 78. (lp)(c) **THE KICK INSIDE** [3] [ ]
– Moving / The saxophone song / Strange phenomena / Kite / The man with the child in his eyes / Wuthering heights / James and the cold gun / Feel it / Oh to be in love / L'amour looks something like you / Them heavy people / Room for the life / The kick inside. *(pic-lp iss.1979) (cd-iss.Jan84) (re-iss.Oct88 on 'Fame'+cd) (re-iss.cd+c Sep94)*
May 78. (7") **THE MAN WITH THE CHILD IN HIS EYES. / MOVING** [6] [85] Feb 79
Nov 78. (7") **HAMMER HORROR. / COFFEE HOMEGROUND** [44] [ ]
Nov 78. (lp)(c) **LIONHEART** [6] [ ]
– Symphony in blue / In search of Peter Pan (incl. When you wish upon a star) / Wow / Don't push your foot on the heartbrake / Oh England my lionheart / Fullhouse / In the warm room / Hammer horror / Kashka from Baghdad / Coffee homeground / Hammer horror. *(re-iss.Apr84 & Oct88 on 'Fame'+cd) (cd-iss.Jan85) (re-iss.cd+c Sep94)*
Mar 79. (7") **WOW. / FULLHOUSE** [14] [ ]
Sep 79. (d7"ep) **KATE BUSH ON STAGE (live)** [10] [ ]
– Them heavy people / Don't put you foot on the heartbrake / James and the cold gun / L'amour looks something like you.
Apr 80. (7") **DREAMING. / THE EMPTY BULLRING** [16] [ ]
Jun 80. (7") **BABOOSHKA. / RAN TAN WALTZ** [5] [ ]
Sep 80. (lp)(c) **NEVER FOR EVER** [1] [ ]
– Babooshka / Delius / Blow away / All we ever look for / Egypt / The wedding list / Violin / The infant kiss / Night scented stock / Army dreamers / Breathing. *(cd-iss.Mar87)*
Sep 80. (7"m) **ARMY DREAMERS. / DELIUS / PASSING THROUGH THE AIR** [16] [ ]
Nov 80. (7") **DECEMBER WILL BE MAGIC AGAIN. / WARM AND SOOTHING** [29] [ ]
Jul 81. (7") **SAT IN YOUR LAP. / LORD OF THE REEDY RIVER** [11] [ ]
Jul 82. (7") **THE DREAMING. / DREAMTIME (instrumental)** [48] [ ]
Sep 82. (lp)(c) **THE DREAMING** [3] [ ]
– Sat in your lap / There goes a tenner / Pull out the pin / Suspended in Gaffa / Leave it open / The dreaming / Night of the swallow Houdini / Get out of my house / All the love. *(cd-iss.Jan87) (re-iss.cd/c/lp.Mar91)*
Nov 82. (7") **THERE GOES A TENNER. / NE T'ENFUIS PAS** [ ] [ ]
Aug 85. (7") **RUNNING UP THAT HILL. / UNDER THE IVY** [3] [30]
(12"+=) – ('A'instrumental).
Sep 85. (lp)(c)(cd) **HOUNDS OF LOVE** [1] [30]
– Running up that hill / Hounds of love / The big sky / Mother stands for comfort / Cloudbusting / And dream of sheep / Under ice / Waking the witch / Watching you without me / Jig of life / Hello Earth / The morning fog. (cd+=) – Cloudbusting (extended).
Oct 85. (7") **CLOUDBUSTING. / BURNING BRIDGES** [20] [ ]
(12"+=) – My Lagan Love.
Feb 86. (7") **HOUNDS OF LOVE. / HANDSOME CABIN BOY** [18] [ ]
(12"+=) – ('A'instrumental) / Jig of life.
May 86. (7")(7"pic-d) **THE BIG SKY. / NOT THIS TIME** [37] [ ]
(12"+=) – The morning fog.
— In Oct 86, she did duet **DON'T GIVE UP** with **PETER GABRIEL** which hit for 'Geffen' UK No.9 / US No.72.
Nov 86. (7") **EXPERIMENT IV. / WUTHERING HEIGHTS (vocal)** [23] [ ]
(12"+=) – December will be magic again.
Nov 86. (lp)(c)(cd) **THE WHOLE STORY** [1] [ ]
– Wuthering heights / Cloudbusting / The man with the child in his eyes / Breathing / Wow / Hounds of love / Running up that hill / Army dreamers / Sat in your lap / Experiment IV / The dreaming / Babooshka.

E.M.I. | Columbia

Sep 89. (7")(c-s) **THE SENSUAL WORLD. / WALK STRAIGHT DOWN THE MIDDLE** [12] [ ]
(12")(cd-s) – ('A'extended)/ ('A'instrumental).
Oct 89. (lp)(c)(cd) **THE SENSUAL WORLD** [2] [43]
– The sensual world / Love and anger / The fog / Reaching out / Heads we're dancing / Deeper understanding / Between a man and a woman / Never be mine / Rocket's tail / This woman's work. (cd+=) – Walk straight down the middle.
Nov 89. (7")(7"pic-d) **THIS WOMAN'S WORK. / BE KIND TO MY MISTAKES** [25] [ ]
(12"+=)(cd-s+=) – ('A'version) / I'm still waiting.
Mar 90. (7")(c-s) **LOVE AND ANGER. / KEN** [38] [ ]
(12"+=) – The confrontation / Just one last look.
(cd-s++=) – One last look around the house before we go.
Apr 90. (7") **LOVE AND ANGER. / WALK STRAIGHT DOWN THE MIDDLE** [-] [ ]
Nov 91. (7")(c-s) **ROCKET MAN. / CANDLE IN THE WIND** [12] [ ]
(12"+=)(cd-s+=) – ('B'instrumental).
— (above single on 'Mercury')
— with **STUART ELLIOTT** – drums / **JOHN GIBLIN** – bass / **DANNY McINTOSH** – guitar / **GARY BROOKER** – hammond organ / **PADDY BUSH + COLIN LLOYD TUCKER** – vocals / **PAUL SPONG + STEVE SLOWER** – trumpet / **NEIL SIDWELL** – trombone / **NIGEL HITCHCOCK** – sax / **NIGEL KENNEDY** – violin / + guests **PRINCE + ERIC CLAPTON**
Sep 93. (7")(c-s) **RUBBERBAND GIRL. / BIG STRIPEY LIE** [12] [88]
(cd-s+=)(12"pic-d+=) – ('A'extended remix).
Nov 93. (cd)(c)(lp) **THE RED SHOES** [2] [28]
– Rubberband girl / And so is love / Eat the music / Moments of pleasure / The song of Solomon / Lily / The red shoes / Top of the city / Constellation of the heart / Big stripey lie / Why should I love you? / You're the one.
Nov 93. (7")(c-s) **MOMENTS OF PLEASURE. / SHOW A LITTLE DEVOTION** [26] [ ]
(12") – ('A'side) / ('A'instrumental) / Home for Christmas.
(cd-s) – ('A'side) / December will be magic again / Experiment IV.
Apr 94. (7")(c-s) **THE RED SHOES. / YOU WANT ALCHEMY** [21] [ ]
(cd-s+=) – Cloudbursting (video mix) / This woman's work.
(cd-s) – ('A'shoedance mix) / The big sky / Running up that hill.
— In Jul 94, KATE partnered LARRY ADLER on 'Mercury' single 'THE MAN I LOVE'. It hit UK No.27, and was from his tribute album 'The Glory Of Gershwin'.
Nov 94. (7"pic-d)(c-s) **AND SO IS LOVE. / RUBBERBAND GIRL (U.S.mix)** [26] [ ]
(cd-s+=) – Eat the music (U.S. mix).

– compilations, others, etc. –

Jun 83. EMI America; (m-lp) **KATE BUSH** [-] [ ]
Oct 83. Old Gold; (7") **WUTHERING HEIGHTS. / THE MAN WITH THE CHILD IN HIS EYES** [ ] [-]
Jan 84. E.M.I.; (7"x13) **THE SINGLES FILE** [ ] [-]
– (all previous singles +) NE T'ENFUIS PAS. / UN BAISER D'ENFANT
Oct 90. E.M.I.; (9xcd)(8xc)(8xlp)(box) **THIS WOMAN'S WORK – ANTHOLOGY 1978-1990** [ ] [ ]
Aug 94. E.M.I.; (cd)(cd-vid) **LIVE AT HAMMERSMITH ODEON (live)** [ ] [-]
— (a complete history of all her songs, re-issuing albums)
Oct 92. U.F.O.; (12"-box+cd) **NEVER FOREVER** [ ] [-]
(above issued w / free booklet & T-shirt)

Paul BUTTERFIELD BLUES BAND

Formed: Chicago, Illinois, USA . . . 1965 by PAUL. They signed to 'Elektra' that year, and released eponymous debut which reached minor US chart position. They contributed a number of tracks in 1966 to Elektra compilation 'What's Shakin''. Broke through at least critically, with the released in 1967 of lp 'EAST-WEST', which also reached US Top 75. • **Style:** Electric blues with second album leaning into Oriental experimental rock. • **Songwriters:** BUTTERFIELD and BISHOP except some covers. Time w / BETTER DAYS covered NEW WALKING BLUES (Robert Johnson) / TOO MANY DRIVERS (Big Bill Broonzy) / NOBODY'S FAULY BUT MINE (trad; Nina Simone) / BORN UNDER A BAD SIGN (Booker T.) / HIGHWAY 28 (Dan Hicks) / RULE THE ROAD (Von Schmidt) / BABY PLEASE DON'T GO (Big Joe Williams) / IF YOU LIVE (Mose Allison). • **Trivia:** In 1965 they did back-up on record for BOB DYLAN, on manager Albert Grossman's recommendation. Album ' . . . PIGBOY CRABSHAW' was actually ELVIN BISHOP's nick-name. BUZZ FIETON (a member in 1969) was later to resurface in US chart toppers Mr. Mister.

Recommended: GOLDEN BUTTER – THE BEST OF . . . (*5)

PAUL BUTTERFIELD (b.17 Dec'42) – vocals, harmonica (ex-MUDDY WATERS) / **MIKE BLOOMFIELD** (b.24 Jul'44) – slide guitar, lead guitar (ex-BOB DYLAN) / **ELVIN BISHOP** (b.21 Oct'42, Tulsa, Oklahoma) – guitar / **JEROME ARNOLD** – bass (ex-HOWLIN' WOLF) / **SAMMY LAY** – drums (ex-HOWLIN' WOLF)

Elektra | Elektra

May 66. (lp) **THE PAUL BUTTERFIELD BLUES BAND** [ ] [ ] Oct 65
– Born in Chicago / Shake your money-maker / Blues with a feeling / Thank you Mr. Poobah / I got my Mojo working / Mellow down easy / Screamin' / Our love is drifting / Mystery train / Last train / Look over yonders wall. *(re-iss.Mar85 on 'Edsel')(re-iss.cd+c Mar93 & Dec94 on 'Pickwick') (re-iss.Sep95 on 'Warners')*
1966. (7") **GOT MY MOJO WORKING. /** [-] [ ]
— added **BARTY GOLDBERG** – guitar and **AL KOOPER** (b.5 Feb'44, Brooklyn, New York) – keyboards (ex-BOB DYLAN)
— **MARK NAFTALIN** – organ (appears on debut 8-tracks) repl. GOLDBERG and KOOPER who went solo & etc.
Dec 66. (lp) **EAST-WEST** [ ] [65] Aug 66
– Walkin' blues / Get out of my life woman / I've got a mind to give up living / Work song / Never say no / Mary, Mary / Two trains running / All these blues / East west. *(re-iss.Feb71) (re-iss.Feb87 on 'Edsel') (cd-iss.+c Sep95 on 'Warners')*
Recorded EP with JOHN MAYALL BLUESBREAKERS see ⇒
1967. (7") **ALL THESE BLUES. / NEVER SAY NO** [ ] [ ]
1967.. (7") **COME ON IN. / I GOT A MIND TO GIVE UP LIVING** [-] [ ]
— **BILLY DAVENPORT** – drums repl. SAMMY LAY above now in 5-piece with **BUTTERFIELD, BISHOP, NAFTALIN** and **ARNOLD**
— then added brass section **GENE DINWIDDIE, DAVE SANBORN and KEITH JOHNSON / PHIL WILSON** – drums, vocals repl. DAVENPORT / **BUGSY MAUGH** – bass, vocals repl. ARNOLD
Nov 67. (7") **RUN OUT OF TIME. / ONE MORE HEARTACHE** [ ] [ ]
Feb 68. (lp) **THE RESURRECTION OF PIGBOY CRABSHAW** [ ] [52] Jan 68
– One more heartache / Driftin' and driftin' / Pity the fool / Born under a bad sign / Run out of time / Double trouble / Drivin' wheel / Droppin' out / Tollin' bells. *(re-iss.'71) (re-iss.Feb89 on 'Edsel')*
Apr 68. (7") **GET YOURSELF TOGETHER. / MINE TO LOVE** [ ] [ ]
— guest **AL KOOPER** – organ note; NAFTALIN aka NAFFY MARHAM
Sep 68. (lp) **IN MY OWN DREAMS** [ ] [79] Aug 68
– Last hope's gone / Mine to love / Get yourself together / Just be with you / Morning blues / Drunk again / In my own dreams. *(re-iss.'71)*
Nov 68. (7") **IN MY OWN DREAMS. /** [-] [ ]

— **BUZZ FEITON** – guitar, organ, French horn, vocals repl. BISHOP who went solo

Sep 69. (7") **WHERE DID MY BABY GO. / IN MY OWN DREAM**

Nov 69. (lp) **KEEP ON MOVING** Oct 69
– Love march / No amount of loving / Morning sunrise / Losing hand / Walking by myself / Except you / Love disease / Where did my baby go / All in a day / So far so good / Buddy's advice / Keep on moving *(re-iss.'71)*

Feb 70. (7") **LOVE MARCH. /** -

— **BUTTERFIELD** retained **HARRIS** and **DINWIDDIE** and brought in **RALPH WALSH** – guitar GEORGE DAVIDSON – drums TREVOR LAWRENCE – brass

Feb 71. (d-lp) **LIVE (live)** 72 Jan 71
– Everything going to be alright / Love disease / The boxer / No amount of loving / Driftin' and driftin' / Intro the musicians / Number nine / I want to be with you / Born under a bad sign / Get together again / So far, so good.

— **DENNIS WHITTED** – drums repl. DAVIDSON augmented by guests **BOBBY HALL** – congos BIG BLACK – bongos with **CLYDIE KING, MERRY CLAYTON, VENETTA FIELDS & ONA DRAKE** – vocal harmonies

Sep 71. (lp)(c) **SOMETIMES I JUST FEEL LIKE SMILING**
– Play on / 1000 ways / Pretty woman / Little piece of dying / Song for Lee / Trainman / Night child / Drowned in my own tears / Blind leading the blind.

— Disbanded late '71

– compilations etc –

Jun 72. Elektra; (d-lp)(d-c) **GOLDEN BUTTER – THE BEST OF THE PAUL BUTTERFIELD BLUES BAND** May 72
– Born in Chicago / Shake your moneymaker / Mellow down easy / Our love is drifting / Mystery train / Look over yonders wall / East West / Walkin' blues / Get out of my life / Woman / Mary, Mary / Spoonful / One more mile, one more heartache / Last hope's gone / In my own dreams / Love march / Driftin' and driftin' / Blind leading the blind.

1972. Red Lightnin; (lp) **AN OFFER YOU CAN'T REFUSE**
(recorded 1963)
(above 1/2 "PAUL BUTTERFIELD" – 1/2 "WALTER HORTON", re-iss.'82)

BETTER DAYS

were formed by **PAUL BUTTERFIELD** who recruited **GEOFF MULDAUR** – vocals, guitar, vibes (ex-JIM KWESKIN BAND) / **RONNIE BARRON** – keyboard, vocals, co-composer (ex-DR. JOHN) / **AMOS GARRETT** – guitar, bass (ex-JESSIE WINCHESTER BAND etc.) / **BILLY RICH** – bass / **CHRISTOPHER PARKER** – drums guests were **MARIA MULDAUR** – occ. violin & b.vocals / **DAVID SANDBORN** – horns / **BOBBY CHARLES** – b.vocals, co-composer, as was **DAVID WHITTED**

Bearsville Bearsville

Feb 73. (lp) **BETTER DAYS**
– New walkin' blues / Please send me home to love / Broke my baby's heart / Baby please don't go / Nobody's fault but mine / Done a lot of wrong things / Buried alive in the blues / Rule the road / Highway 28.

Nov 73. (lp) **IT ALL COMES BACK**
– It all comes back / Take your pleasure where you find it / Louisiana flood / Poor boy / If you live / It's getting harder to survive / Small town talk / Win or lose / Too many drivers. *(cd-iss.May93 on 'Rhino-Bearsville')*

— Split '74. GARRET joined MARIA MULDAUR and PARKER joined ARETHA FRANKLIN.

PAUL BUTTERFIELD

solo with sessioners

Bearsville Bearsville

Feb 76. (lp) **PUT IT IN YOUR EAR** 1975
– You can run but you can't hide / (If I never sing) My song / The animal / Breadline / Ain't that a lot of love? / I don't wanna go / Day to day / Here I go again / The flame / Watch 'em tell a lie.

— PAUL then toured with LEVON HELM's ALL-STARS, before teaming up with RICK DANKO. He realeased another solo effort (below) augmented by MICHAEL TOLES – multi

not issued Bearsville

1981. (lp) **NORTH SOUTH** -
– I get excited / Get some fun in your life / Footprints on the windshield / Upside down / Entch a train / Bread & Butterfield / Living in Memphis / Glow down / I let it go / Baby blue.

1981. (7") **LIVING IN MEMPHIS. / FOOTPRINTS ON THE WINDSHIELD** -

— went into session work in the 80's before making a come-back (below)

not issued Bearsville

1986. (lp) **THE LEGENDARY PAUL BUTTERFIELD RIDES AGAIN** -

— On 4 May87 PAUL BUTTERFIELD died of a long illness; peritonitis.

BUTTHOLE SURFERS

Formed: San Antonio, Texas, USA . . . 1980 originally as ASHTRAY BABY HEELS by ex-accountant GIBBY and PAUL who met at Trinity College, San Antonio. By 1983, they were signed to JELLO BIAFRA's (Dead Kennedys) label 'Alternative Tenticles'. Around the mid-80's, due to lack of US interest, they came to the UK, where with the help of airplay from John Peel, they made it into indie charts. • **Style:** Heavy psychedelia that mixes noise, confusion and futuristic punk with the manic GIBBY (complete with loudspeaker, etc). Always offensive and disturbing, their weird stage aura included nude dancer KATHLEEN who covered herself in green jello. • **Songwriters:** GIBBY and co., except AMERICAN WOMAN (Guess Who) / HURDY GURDY MAN (Donovan). • **Trivia:** PIOUHGD is Red Indian for 'pissed off'.

Recommended: LOCUST ABORTION TECHNICIAN (*8) / HAIRWAY TO STEVEN (*7)

GIBBY (b. GIBSON JEROME HAYNES) – vocals / **PAUL 'PABLO' LEARY WARTHALL** – guitar / **KING KOFFEE** – drums repl. ? / **ALAN ?** – bass

Alt. Tent. Alt. Tent.

Apr 84. (m-lp) **BUTTHOLE SURFERS (BROWN REASONS TO LIVE)** '83
– The Shah sleeps in Lee Harvey's grave / Hey / Something / Bar-b-que / Pope / Wichita cathedral / Suicide / The legend of Anus Presley. *(US title 'A BROWN REASON TO LIVE')(re-iss. Sep93)*

Jan 85. (12"ep) **LIVE PCPPEP (live 45rpm)**
– (contains most of last mlp)

— **TERENCE** – bass repl. ALAN (?)

not issued Touch & Go

Apr 85. (7") **LADY SNIFF. / ?** -

Fundament. Fundament.

Jul 85. (lp) **PSYCHIC . . . POWERLESS . . . ANOTHER MAN'S SAC** '84
– Concubine / Eye of the chicken / Dum dum / Woly boly / Negro observer / Butthole surfer / Lady sniff / Cherub / Mexican caravan / Cowboy Bob / Gary Floyd (cd-iss.Jan88.+=) – (includes below 12" CREAM CORN FROM THE SOCKET OF DAVIS)

— **MARK KRAMER** – bass (of SHOCKABILLY) repl. TREVOR who had repl. TERENCE

Oct 85. (12"ep) **CREAM CORN FROM THE SOCKET OF DAVIS**
– Moving to Florida / Comb – Lou Reed (two parter) / Tornadoes.

Red Rhino Touch & Go

Apr 86. (lp) **REMBRANDT PUSSYHORSE**
– Creep in the cellar / Sea ferring / American woman / Waiting for Jimmy to kick / Strangers die / Perry / Whirling hall of knives / Mark says alright / In the cellar.. *(cd-iss.May88)*

— **JEFF 'TOOTER' PINKUS** – bass repl. KRAMER who formed BONGWATER

Blast First Blast First

Mar 87. (lp)(cd) **LOCUST ABORTION TECHNICIAN**
– Sweet loaf / Graveyard 1 / Pittsburgh to Lebanon / Weber / Hay / Human cannonball / U.S.S.A. / Theoman / Kintz / Graveyard 2 / 22 going on 23 / The G-men.

— added **THERESA NAYLOR** – 2nd drummer / **KATHLEEN** – naked dancer(above with GIBBY, PAUL, COFFEY and PINKUS)

Apr 88. (lp)(c)(cd) **HAIRWAY TO STEVEN**
– Hairway Part 1 / Hairway Part 2 / Hairway Part 3 / Hairway Part 4 / Hairway Part 5 / Hairway Part 6 / Hairway Part 7 / Hairway Part 8 / Hairway Part 9
(9 tracks marked as rude symbols as titles)

Aug 89. (12"ep)(10"ep)(cd-ep) **WIDOWMAKER**
– Bong song / 1401 / Booze tobacco / Helicopter.

Rough Trade Capitol

Nov 90. (7") **THE HURDY GURDY MAN. / BARKING DOGS**
(12"+=)(cd-s+=) ('A'-Paul Leary remix)

Feb 91. (cd)(c)(lp) **PIOUHGD** 68
– Revolution pt.1 & 2 / Lonesome bulldog pt.1 & 2 / The hurdy gurdy man / Golden showers / Lonesome bulldog pt.3 / Blindman / No, I'm iron man / Something / P.S.Y. / Lonesome bulldog pt.IV. (cd+=) – Barking dogs. *(cd-iss.Dec 94 on 'Danceteria')*

In Apr'92, GIBBY guested for MINISTRY on single 'Jesus Built My Hotrod'.

Capitol Capitol

Mar 93. (cd)(c)(lp) **INDEPENDENT WORM SALOON** 73
– Who was in my room last night / The wooden song / Tongue / Chewin' George Lucas' chocolate / Goofy's concern / Alcohol / Dog inside your body / Strawberry / Some dispute over T-shirt sales / Dancing fool / You don't know me / The annoying song / Dust devil / Leave me alone / Edgar / The ballad of a naked man / Clean it up.

Nov 94. (7"pic-d) **GOOD KING WENCENSLAUS. / THE LORD IS A MONKEY**

– compilations, others, etc. –

Jun 89. Latino Bugger; (d-lp)(c)(cd) **DOUBLE LIVE (live ltd.)** -

Apr 95. Trance; (cd) **THE HOLE TRUTH & NOTHING BUTT**
(early demos)

JACK OFFICERS

off-shoot with **GIBBY, JEFF & KATHLEEN**

Naked Brain Shimmy DIsc

Dec 90. (cd)(c)(lp) **DIGITAL DUMP**
– Love-o-maniac / Time machine pt.1 & 2 / L.A.name peanut butter / Do it / Swingers club / Ventricular retribution / 6 / Don't touch that / An Hawaiian Christmas song / Flush.

PAUL LEARY

Rough Trade Capitol

Apr 91. (cd)(c)(lp) **THE HISTORY OF DOGS**
– The birds are dying / Apollo one / Dalhart down the road / How much longer / He's working overtime / Indians storm the government / Is it milky / Too many people / The city / Fine home.

DRAIN

aka KING COFFEY + DAVID McCREETH (ex-SQUID)

Synd. Trance Synd. Trance

Apr 91. (12")(cd-s) **A BLACK FIST**

BUZZCOCKS

Formed: Manchester, England . . . April 1976 by DEVOTO and SHELLEY who met at Bolton Institute Of Higher Education. First gig was on 20th

July'76 supporting SEX PISTOLS. Early '77, they released first ever non-Stiff punk "indie" 45 on 'New Hormones' in the form of SPIRAL SCRATCH EP. They suffered major bust up when DEVOTO departed, but carried on, signing to 'United Art' after featuring on the now famous 'LIVE AT THE ROXY' Various compilation ('Breakdown' + 'Love Battery'). Early 1978 they stormed the British charts with moping love gem 'WHAT DO I GET', which was followed by 3 bigger hits that year. More followed, but with the decline of new wave/pop, they disbanded in 1981. SHELLEY had mildly successful solo career, and BUZZCOCKS returned to good style but not the charts (yet!) early 1990. • **Style:** Punk rock/pop that had influences from STOOGES to RAMONES. Mellowed a little when SHELLEY took over with his romance'n'roll effeminate wordings. • **Songwriters:** DEVOTO wrote material until he left. SHELLEY took over with DIGGLE writing and vocalising on some. Covered HERE COMES THE NICE (Small Faces). • **Trivia:** In 1978, SHELLEY produced fun group ALBERTO Y LOST TRIOS PARANOIAS. His solo single 'HOMOSAPIAN' went No.1 in Australia.

Recommended: ANOTHER MUSIC IN A DIFFERENT KITCHEN (*9) / SINGLES – GOING STEADY (*9).

HOWARD DEVOTO (b.HOWARD TRAFFORD) – vocals / **PETE SHELLEY** (b.PETER McNEISH, 17 Apr'55) – guitar, vocals / **STEVE DIGGLE** – bass, vocals / **JOHN MAHER** – drums

New Hormones | not issued

Jan 77. (7"ep) **SPIRAL SCRATCH** [ ] [-]
– Breakdown / Times up / Boredom / Friends of mine. *(re-iss.Aug79 credited as "BUZZCOCKS with HOWARD DEVOTO" hit* No.31) *(re-iss.as 12"+cd-ep on 'Document')*

— (Mar77) **GARTH SMITH** – bass repl. DEVOTO who later formed MAGAZINE. **SHELLEY** now lead vocals, guitar / **DIGGLE** switched to guitar, vocals

United Art | not issued

Oct 77. (7") **ORGASM ADDICT. / WHATEVER HAPPENED TO . . . ?** [ ] [-]

— **STEVE GARVEY** – bass repl. GARTH (on tour at first)

Jan 78. (7") **WHAT DO I GET?. / OH SHIT** [37] [-]

United Art | I.R.S.

Mar 78. (lp)(c) **ANOTHER MUSIC IN A DIFFERENT KITCHEN** [15] [ ]
– Fast cars / No reply / You tear me up / Get on our own / Love battery / 16 / I don't mind / Fiction romance / Autonomy / I need / Moving away from the pulsebeat. *(re-iss.Aug85 on 'Liberty') (re-.blue-lp.Jun87 on 'Fan Club') (re-iss.lp/c/cd.May88 on 'Fame') (re-cd.Jul88 on 'E.M.I.')*

Apr 78. (7") **I DON'T MIND. / AUTONOMY** [55] [-]
Jul 78. (7") **LOVE YOU MORE. / NOISE ANNOYS** [34] [ ]
Sep 78. (7") **EVER FALLEN IN LOVE WITH SOMEONE YOU SHOULDN'T'VE. / JUST LUST** [12] [ ]
Sep 78. (lp)(c) **LOVE BITES** [13] [ ]
– Real world / Ever fallen in love with someone you shouldn't've / Operator's manuel / Nostalgia / Just lust / Sixteen again / Walking distance / Love is lies / Nothing left / E.S.P. / Late for the train. *(re-iss.Mar87 on 'Fame') (re-iss.blue-lp.Jun87 on 'Fan Club') (cd.iss.Jul88 on 'E.M.I.')*

Nov 78. (7") **PROMISES. / LIPSTICK** [20] [ ]
Mar 79. (7") **EVERYBODY'S HAPPY NOWADAYS. / WHY CAN'T I TOUCH IT?** [29] [ ]
Jul 79. (7") **HARMONY IN MY HEAD. / SOMETHING'S GONE WRONG AGAIN** [32] [-]
Sep 79. (7") **YOU SAY YOU DON'T LOVE ME. / RAISON D'ETRE** [ ] [-]
Sep 79. (lp)(c) **A DIFFERENT KIND OF TENSION** [26] [ ]
– Paradise / Sitting round at home / You say you don't love me / You know you can't help it / Mad mad Judy / Raison d'etre / I don't know what to do with my life / Money / Hollow inside / A different kind of tension / I believe / Radio Nine. *(re-iss.blue-lp.Jun87 on 'Fan Club') (cd-iss.Jul88 on 'E.M.I.')* (initial copies cont. previous 45)

Oct 79. (7") **I BELIEVE. / SOMETHING'S GONE WRONG AGAIN** [-] [ ]
Nov 79. (lp)(c) **GOING STEADY – THE SINGLES** (compilation) [-] [ ]
– Orgasm addict / What do I get / I don't mind / Love you more / Ever fallen in love with someone you shouldn't've / Promises / Everybody's happy nowadays / Harmony in my head / Whatever happened to . . . ? / Oh shit! / Autonomy / Noise annoys / Just luck / Lipstick / Why can't I touch it / Something's gone wrong again. *(UK-iss.Nov81 on 'Liberty', re-iss.Aug85) (cd-iss.Jun87 + Jun88 on 'E.M.I.')*

Liberty | I.R.S.

Aug 80. (7") **WHY SHE'S A GIRL FROM THE CHAINSTORE. / ARE EVERYTHING** [61] [ ]
Oct 80. (7") **STRANGE THING. / AIRWAVES DREAM** [ ] [ ]
Nov 80. (7") **RUNNING FREE. / WHAT DO YOU KNOW** [ ] [ ]

— (split Feb81) **DIGGLE** went solo and formed FLAG OF CONVENIENCE, with **MAHER**

PETE SHELLEY

solo, augmented by **STEVE GARVEY** – bass / **JIM RUSSELL** – drums.

Genetic-Island | Arista

Aug 81. (7")(12") **HOMOSAPIAN. / KEAT'S SONG** [ ] [ ]
Sep 81. (lp)(c) **HOMOSAPIAN** [ ] [ ] Jun 72
– Homosapian / Yesterday's here / I generate a feeling / Keat's song / Qu'est-ce que c'est que ca / I don't know what it is / Guess I must have been in love with myself / Pusher man / Just one of those affairs / It's hard enough knowing. *(re-iss.cd Sep94 on 'Grapevine')*

Nov 81. (d7")(12") **I DON'T KNOW WHAT IT IS. / WITNESS THE CHANGE/ / IN LOVE WITH SOMEBODY ELSE. / MAXINE** [ ] [ ]
Apr 82. (7")(12") **HOMOSAPIAN. / LOVE IN VAIN** [ ] [ ]

— **BARRY ADAMSON** – bass (ex-MAGAZINE, ex-BIRTHDAY PARTY) repl. GARVEY

added **MARTIN RUSHENT** – keyboards, producer

Island | Arista

Feb 83. (7")(12") **TELEPHONE OPERATOR. / MANY A TIME** [66] [ ]
Apr 83. (lp)(c) **XL-1** [42] [ ] Jul 83
– Telephone operator / If you ask me (I won't say no) / What was Heaven? / You better than I know / Twilight / (Millions of people) No one like you / Many a time / I just wanna touch / You and I / XL-1 *. (c+= dub tracks) (track* = only playable on ZX Spectrum computer) *(re-iss.cd Sep94 on 'Grapevine').*

Im-maculate | not issued

Nov 84. (7") **NEVER AGAIN. / ONE ONE ONE** [ ] [-]
(12"+=) Give it to me.

— **SHELLEY** brought in new **JOHN DOYLE** – drums / **MARK SANDERSON** – bass / **NORMAN FISCHER-JONES** – guitar / **GERARD COOKSON** – keyboards / **JIM GARDNER** – synth.

Mercury | Mercury?

Mar 86. (7")(12") **WAITING FOR LOVE. / DESIGNER LAMPS** [ ] [ ]
May 86. (7")(12") **ON YOUR OWN. / PLEASE FORGIVE ME . . . BUT I CANNOT ENDURE IT ANY LONGER** [ ] [ ]
Jun 86. (lp)(c)(cd) **HEAVEN AND THE SEA** [ ] [ ]
– Never again / My dreams / Blue eyes / You can't take that away / No Moon . . . / Waiting for love / On your own / They're coming for you / I surrender / Life without reason / Need a minit. *(re-iss.May88 on 'Line')*

Aug 86. (7")(12") **BLUE EYES. / NELSON'S RIDDLE** [ ] [ ]
Nov 86. (7")(12") **I SURRENDER. / I NEED A MINUTE** [ ] [ ]

— In 1988, **SHELLEY** formed **ZIP** with COOKSON and SANDERSON.

– his compilations, others, etc. –

Apr 80. Groovy; (12") **SKY YEN** (recorded 1974) [ ] [-]

Im-maculate | not issued

Apr 89. (7")(12") **HOMOSAPIAN. PETE SHELLEY VS. POWER, WONDER AND LOVE / ('A'mix)** [ ] [-]
(3"cd-s+=) – ('A'icon mix) / ('A'shower mix).

STEVE DIGGLE

Liberty | not issued

Feb 81. (7"m) **SHUT OUT THE LIGHTS. / 50 YEARS OF COMPARATIVE WEALTH / HERE COMES THE FIRE BRIGADE** [ ] [-]

FLAG OF CONVENIENCE

was formed by **DIGGLE, MAHER** and **DAVE FARROW** – bass / **D.P.** – keyboards

Sire | not issued

Sep 82. (7") **LIFE ON THE TELEPHONE. / OTHER MAN'S SIN** [ ] [-]

— **DIGGLE, MAHER** plus **GARY HAMER** – bass / **MARK** – keyboards.

Weird Systems | not issued

Dec 84. (7") **CHANGE. / LONGEST LIFE** [ ] [-]

— **JOHN CAINE** – drums repl. MAHER and MARK

M.C.M. | not issued

Apr 86. (7") **NEW HOUSE. / KEEP ON PUSHING** [ ] [-]

Flag of . . . | not issued

Apr 87. (12") **LAST TRAIN TO SAFETY. / ?** [ ] [-]

F.O.C.

M.C.M. | not issued

Oct 87. (12"ep) **SHOULD I EVER GO DEAF / PICTURES IN MY MIND. / THE GREATEST SIN / DROWNED IN YOUR HEARTACHES** [ ] [-]
Aug 88. (12"ep) **EXILES / I CAN'T STOP THE WORLD. / SHOT DOWN WITH YOUR GUN / TRAGEDY IN MARKET SQUARE** [ ] [-]

BUZZCOCKS F.O.C.

DIGGLE, HAMMER plus **ANDY COUZENS** – guitar / **CHRIS GOODWIN** – drums.

Thin Line | not issued

Jul 89. (12")(cd-s) **TOMORROW'S SUNSET. / LIFE WITH THE LIONS / ('A'version)** [ ] [-]

BUZZCOCKS

reformed in 1990 **SHELLEY, DIGGLE, GARVEY** and **MIKE JOYCE** – drums (ex-SMITHS) repl. ANDY and CHRIS who formed The HIGH.

Plan-et Pacific | not issued

Apr 91. (7"ep)(12"ep)(c-ep)(cd-ep) **ALIVE TONIGHT** [ ] [-]
– Alive tonight / Successful street / Serious crime / Last to know.

— **JOHN MAHER** – drums returned to repl. MIKE who joined PIL.

Essential | Rykodisc

Jun 93. (cd)(c)(lp) **TRADE TEST TRANSMISSION** [ ] [ ]
– Innocent / Smile / Palm of your hand / Last to know / Do it/ Who will help me to forget / Energy / Alive tonight / Inside / Isolation / Never gonna give it up / Crystal night / 369 / Chegga / It's unthinkable / Somewhere. (free 7"/12"/cd-s INNOCENT from Apr93)

Aug 93. (12")(cd-s) **DO IT. / TRASH AWAY / ALL OVER YOU** [ ] [ ]
Apr 94. (12")(cd-s) **LIBERTINE ANGEL. / ROLL IT OVER / EXCERPT FROM PRISON RIOT HOSTAGE** [ ] [-]

Dojo | not issued

Nov 95. (cd) **FRENCH (live in Paris 12th April 1995)** [ ] [-]

– I don't mind / Who'll help me to forget / Get on our own / Unthinkable / Strange thing / Energy / Breakdown / Innocent / Roll it over / Why she's a girl from the chainstore / Last to know? / Running free / Libertine angel / Why can't I touch it / Noise annoys / Isolation / Boredom / Do it / Harmony in my head / I believe.

– compilations, others, etc. –

Apr 87. Weird Systems; (lp)(c) **TOTAL POP** (c+=extra tracks) [ ] [-]
Jan 88. Strange Fruit; (12"ep) **THE PEEL SESSIONS** (7.9.77) [ ] [-]
– Fast cars / What do I get / Moving away from the pulsebeat.
Feb 90. Strange Fruit; (cd)(lp) **THE PEEL SESSIONS** [ ] [-]
Oct 88. R.O.I.R.; (c) **LEST WE FORGET (live)** [-] [ ]
(cd-iss.1990)
Sep 89. Absolutely Free; (lp)(cd) **LIVE AT THE ROXY CLUB, APRIL 1977 (live)** [ ] [-]
(cd= 1 extra track) *(re-iss.Jul90 on 'Receiver')*
Oct 89. E.M.I.; (7"ep) **THE FAB FOUR** [ ] [-]
– Ever fallen in love with someone you shouldn't've / Promises / Everybody's happy nowadays / Harmony in my head.
Nov 89. E.M.I.; (4xlp)(2xd-c)(2xd-cd) **PRODUCT** [ ] [-]
(above cont. first 3 albums + 1 live and rare) *(re-iss.May95)*
Sep 91. E.M.I.; (cd)(c)(d-lp) **OPERATOR'S MANUEL** [ ] [-]
May 92. E.M.I.; (cd) **ENTERTAINING FRIENDS** [ ] [-]
Oct 92. Old Gold; (cd-s) **EVER FALLEN IN LOVE WITH SOMEONE . . . / WHAT DO I GET / PROMISES** [ ] [-]
Feb 94. Anagram; (cd) **THE BEST OF . . . THE SECRET PUBLIC YEARS 1981-1989 ("STEVE DIGGLE & THE FLAG OF CONVENIENCE")** [ ] [-]
Apr 94. E.M.I.; (cd) **ANOTHER MUSIC IN A DIFFERENT KITCHEN / LOVE BITES** [ ] [-]
Jun 94. Strange Fruit; (cd) **THE PEEL SESSIONS ALBUM** [ ] [-]
Jul 95. Dojo; (cd) **TIME'S UP** [ ] [-]
Nov 95. Old Gold; (cd-s) **EVER FALLEN IN LOVE WITH SOMEONE YOU SHOULDN'T HAVE FALLEN IN LOVE WITH / PROMISES** [ ] [-]

STEVE DIGGLE

solo once more.

3:30 — not issued

Nov 93. (cd-ep) **HEATED AND RISING / OVER AND OUT / TERMINAL / WEDNESDAYS FLOWERS** [ ] [-]

Ax-s — not issued

Oct 95. (cd) **HERE'S ONE I MADE EARLIER** [ ] [-]

BYRDS

Formed: Los Angeles, California, USA . . . 1964 by McGUINN, CLARK and CROSBY. After one flop single on 'Elektra', they signed to 'CBS/Columbia' where they gained instant success with 'MR.TAMBOURINE MAN', which hit the top on both sides of the Atlantic. For the next 7 years, through many personnel changes, they became one of America's finest, hitting the charts many times. • **Style:** Initially influenced by The BEATLES and DYLAN, but by 1966 they had established own unique electric folk sound that many since have emulated. In 1968 they broke into country-rock territory, with help of new bluegrass method member GRAM PARSONS. • **Songwriters:** All had turns, mostly by 12-string Rickenbacker player McGUINN or CROSBY or HILLMAN. Covered:- MR.TAMBOURINE MAN + ALL I REALLY WANT TO DO + THE TIMES THEY ARE A-CHANGIN' + YOU AIN'T GOIN' NOWHERE + MY BACK PAGES + LAY LADY LAY + IT'S ALL OVER NOW, BABY BLUE + etc. (Bob Dylan) / TURN! TURN! TURN! + THE BELLS OF RHYMNEY (Pete Seeger) / WASN'T BORN TO FOLLOW + GOIN' BACK (Goffin-King a hit by Dusty Springfield) / COWGIRL IN THE SAND (Neil Young) / etc. • **Trivia:** McGUINN changed name to ROGER in 1967 due to his new-found Subud religion.

Recommended: THE BYRDS' GREATEST HITS (*9) / SWEETHEART OF THE RODEO (*8) / GREATEST HITS VOL.2 (*7)

BEEFEATERS

McGUINN, CLARK and CROSBY

Elektra — Elektra

Oct 64. (7") **PLEASE LET ME LOVE YOU. / DON'T BE LONG** [ ] [ ]

The BYRDS

GENE CLARK (b.HAROLD, 17 Nov'41, Missouri, USA) – vocals, tambourine / **JIM McGUINN** (b.13 Jul'42, Chicago, Illinois, USA) – guitar, vocals / **DAVID CROSBY** (b.14 Aug'41) – guitar, vocals / **CHRIS HILLMAN** (b. 4 Dec'42, L.A.) – bass, vocals (ex-HILLMEN) / **MICHAEL CLARKE** (b. 3 Jun'43, New York City) – drums

C.B.S. — Columbia

Jun 65. (7") **MR. TAMBOURINE MAN. / I KNEW I'D WANT TO** [1] [1] May 65
Aug 65. (7") **ALL I REALLY WANT TO DO. / I'LL FEEL A WHOLE LOT BETTER** [4] [40] Jul 75
Aug 65. (lp) **MR. TAMBOURINE MAN** [7] [6] Jun 65
– Mr.Tambourine man / I'll feel a whole lot better / Spanish Harlem incident / You won't have to cry / Here without you / The bells of Rhymney / All I really want to do / I knew I'd want you / It's no use / Don't doubt yourself, babe / Chimes of freedom / We'll meet again. *(re-iss.'74 on 'CBS Embassy', re-iss.Jul78)*
Oct 65. (7") **TURN! TURN! TURN!. / SHE DON'T CARE ABOUT TIME** [26] [1]
Feb66. (7") **SET YOU FREE THIS TIME. / IT WON'T BE WRONG** [ ] [79] / [63]
Mar 66. (lp) **TURN! TURN! TURN!** [11] [17] Dec 65
– Turn! Turn! Turn! / It won't be wrong / Set you free this time / Lay down your weary tune / He was a friend of mine / The world turns all around her / Satisfied mind / If you're gone / The times they are a-changin' / Wait and see / Oh! Susannah. *(re-iss.'76 on 'CBS Embassy', re-iss.Jul78)*

— trimmed to a quartet when GENE CLARK went solo

Apr 66. (7") **EIGHT MILES HIGH. / WHY?** [24] [14]
Jul 66. (7") **5D (FIFTH DIMENSION). / CAPTAIN SOUL** [ ] [44]
Sep 66. (lp) **FIFTH DIMENSION** [27] [24] Aug 66
– 5D (Fifth Dimension) / Wild mountain thyme / Mr. Spaceman / I see you / What's happening?!?! / I come and stand at every door / Eight miles high / Hey Joe / John Riley / Captain Soul / 2-4-2 Foxtrot (the Lear jet song). *(re-iss Jul83)*
Oct 66. (7") **MR. SPACEMAN. / WHAT'S HAPPENING?!?!** [ ] [36] Sep66
Feb 67. (7") **SO YOU WANT TO BE A ROCK'N'ROLL STAR. / EVERYBODY'S BEEN BURNED** [ ] [29] Jan 67
Apr 67. (lp) **YOUNGER THAN YESTERDAY** [37] [24] Mar 67
– So you want to be a rock'n'roll star / Have you seen her face / C.T.A. – 102 / Renaissance fair / Time between / Everybody's been burned / Thoughts and words / Mind gardens / My back pages / The girl with no name / Why. *(re-iss.+cd.Mar 87 on 'Edsel') (cd+c-iss.Oct 94 on 'Columbia')*
May 67. (7") **MY BACK PAGES. / RENAISSANCE MAN** [ ] [30] Mar 67
Jun 67. (7") **HAVE YOU SEEN HER FACE. / DON'T MAKE WAVES** [-] [74]
Sep 67. (7") **LADY FRIEND. / DON'T MAKE WAVES** [ ] [82]

— **GENE CLARK** – guitar, vocals returned to repl. DAVID who formed CROSBY, STILLS and NASH (JIM also changed name to ROGER McGUINN)

Dec 67. (7") **GOIN' BACK. / CHANGE IS NOW** [ ] [89] Nov 67
(re-iss Jun77)
Now a trio of **McGUINN, HILLMAN and CLARKE** (GENE continued solo career)
Apr 68. (lp) **THE NOTORIOUS BYRD BROTHERS** [12] [47] Jan 68
– Artificial energy / Goin' back / Natural harmony / Draft morning / Wasn't born to follow / Get to you / Change is now / Old John Robertson / Tribal gathering / Dolphin's smile / Space odyssey. *(re-iss.Aug88 on 'Edsel' +cd)*

— **KEVIN KELLEY** (b.1945, California) – drums (ex-RISING SONS) repl. MICHAEL who joined DILLARD & CLARK. Also added **GRAM PARSONS** – guitar, vocals, keyboards (ex-INTERNATIONAL SUBMARINE BAND) guests on album – **SNEAKY PETE** – pedal steel guitar / **DOUG DILLARD** – banjo

May 68. (7") **YOU AIN'T GOING NOWHERE. / ARTIFICIAL ENERGY** [45] [74]
Sep 68. (lp) **SWEETHEART OF THE RODEO** [ ] [77] Aug 68
– You ain't going nowhere / I am a pilgrim / The Christian life / You're still on my mind / Pretty Boy Floyd / You don't miss your water / Hickory wind / One hundred years from now / Blue Canadian Rockies / Life in prison / Nothing was delivered. *(re-iss.+cd Jun87 on 'Edsel')*
Oct 68. (7") **PRETTY BOY FLOYD. / I AM A PILGRIM** [ ] [ ]

— **CARLOS BERNAL** – guitar played on US tour replacing GRAM who joined FLYING BURRITO BROTHERS alongside HILLMAN and SNEAKY PETE. Soon McGUINN recruited entirely new members **CLARENCE WHITE** (b. 6 Jun'44, Lewiston, Maine, USA) – guitar, vocals (ex-NASHVILLE WEST) repl. BERNAL / **GENE PARSONS** (b.1944) – drums, vocals (ex-NASHVILLE WEST) repl. KELLEY / **JOHN YORK** – bass, vocals repl. HILLMAN

Mar 69. (7") **BAD NIGHT AT WHISKEY. / DRUG STORE TRUCK DRIVIN' MAN** [ ] [ ]
Apr 69. (lp) **DR. BYRDS AND MR. HYDE** [15] [ ] Mar 69
– This wheel's on fire / Old blue / Your gentle way of loving me / Child of the universe / Nashville West / Drug store truck drivin' man / King Apathy III / Candy / Bad night at the Whiskey / My back pages – B.J.blues – Baby what you want me to do.
Jun 69. (7") **LAY LADY LAY. / OLD BLUE** [ ] [ ]
Sep 69. (7") **WASN'T BORN TO FOLLOW. / CHILD OF THE UNIVERSE** [-] [ ]
Oct 69. (7") **THE BALLAD OF EASY RIDER. / WASN'T BORN TO FOLLOW** [-] [5]
Jan 70. (lp) **THE BALLAD OF EASY RIDER** [41] [36] Dec 69
– The ballad of Easy Rider / Fido / Oil in my lamp / Tulsa County / Jack Tarr the sailor / Jesus is just alright / It's all over now, baby blue / There must be someone / Gunga Din / Deportee (plane wreck at Los Gatos) / Armstrong, Aldrin and Collins.
Feb 70. (7") **JESUS IS JUST ALRIGHT. / IT'S ALL OVER NOW, BABY BLUE** [ ] [97]

— **SKIP BATTIN** (b. 2 Feb'34, Gallipolis, Ohio) – bass, repl. YORK

Nov 70. (d-lp) **UNTITLED (1/2 live)** [11] [40] Oct 70
– Lover of the bayou / Positively 4th Street / Nashville West / So you want to be a rock'n'roll star / Mr.Tambourine man / Mr.Spaceman / Eight miles high / Chestnut mare / Truck stop girl / All the things / Yesterday's train / Hungry planet / Just a season / Take a whiff (on me) / You all look alike / Well come back home.
Dec 70. (7") **CHESTNUT MARE. / JUST A SEASON** [19] [ ]
May 71. (7") **I TRUST (EVERYTHING'S GONNA WORK OUT FINE). / THIS IS MY DESTINY** [ ] [ ]
Aug 71. (lp) **BIRDMANIAX** [ ] [46] Jul 71
– Glory, glory / Pale blue / I trust / Tunnel of love / Citizen Kane / I wanna grow up to be a politician / Absolute happiness / Green apple quick step / My destiny / Kathleen's song / Jamaica say you will.
Oct 71. (7") **GLORY, GLORY. / CITIZEN KANE** [ ] [ ]
Jan 72. (lp) **FARTHER ALONG** [ ] [ ] Dec 71
– Tiffany queen / Get down your line / B.B. class road / Bugler / America's great national pastime / Antique Sandy / Precious Kate / So fine / Lazy waters / Bristol steam convention blues / Farther along.
Jan 72. (7") **AMERICA'S GREAT NATIONAL PASTIME. / FARTHER ALONG** [ ] [ ]

— They split mid '72, SKIP joined NEW RIDERS OF THE PURPLE SAGE. CLARENCE WHITE was killed in a road accident 14 Jul73. / **JOHN GUERRIN** – drums (session men) took over briefly when reforming

— **McGUINN** then re-formed the original **"BYRDS"** Himself, **CROSBY, CLARK,**

HILLMAN and **CLARKE**

Asylum Asylum

Apr 73. (lp)(c) **THE BYRDS** 31 20 Mar 73

– Full circle / Sweet Mary / Changing heart / For free / Born to rock'n'roll / Things will be better / Cowgirl in the sand / Long live the King / Borrowing time / Laughing / (See the sky) about to rain. *(re-iss.Feb93) (re-iss.May93 on 'Elektra')*

May 73. (7") **THINGS WILL BE BETTER. / FOR FREE** -

Jun 73. (7") **FULL CIRCLE. / LONG LIVE THE KING**

Jul 73. (7") **COWGIRL IN THE SAND. / LONG LIVE THE KING** -

—— McGUINN, HILLMAN and CLARK all went solo, later teaming up together on album. CROSBY re-formed CROSBY, STILL and NASH. Sadly, MICHAEL CLARKE was to die of liver failure 19th December '93.

– (BYRDS) compilations, etc. –

On 'CBS' / 'Columbia' unless mentioned otherwise.

Dec 65. (7"ep) **THE TIMES ARE A-CHANGING**

Oct 66. (7"ep) **EIGHT MILES HIGH**

Oct 67. (lp) **THE BYRDS' GREATEST HITS** 6 Aug 67

– Mr.Tambourine man / I'll feel a whole lot better / Bells of rhymney / Turn! turn! turn! / All I really want to do / Chimes of freedom / Eight miles high / Mr.Spaceman / 5D (Fifth Dimension) / So you want to be a rock'n'roll star / My back pages. *(re-iss.+c Jan84, re-iss.+cd Jun89) (REMASTERED cd.Feb91)*

Oct 71. (lp)(c) **THE BYRDS' GREATEST HITS VOL.2**

– The ballad of Easy rider / Jesus is just alright / Chestnut mare / You ain't goin' nowhere / I am a pilgrim / Goin' back / I trust / Lay lady lay / Wasn't born to follow / The times they are a-changin' / Drug store truck drivin' man / Get to you.

May 73. (d-lp)(c) **THE HISTORY OF THE BYRDS** 47 -

– Mr.Tambourine man / Turn! turn! turn! / She don't care about time / Wild mountain thyme / Eight miles high / Mr.Spaceman / 5D (Fifth Dimension) / So you want to be a rock'n'roll star / Time between / My back pages / Lady friend / Goin' back / Old John Robertson / Wasn't born to follow / You ain't goin' nowhere / Hickory wind / Nashville West / Drug store truck drivin' man / Gunga Din / Jesus is just alright / The ballad of Easy Rider / Chestnut mare / Yesterday's train / Just a season / Citizen Kane / Jamaica say you will / Tiffany queen / America's great national pastime. *(re-iss.Sep87)*

Jul 73. (7") **MR. TAMBOURINE MAN. / TURN! TURN! TURN!**

Feb 76. (7") **CHESTNUT MARE. / ALL I REALLY WANT TO DO**

Jul 76. (7") **TURN! TURN! TURN!. / YOU AIN'T GOIN' NOWHERE**

Jul 76. (d-lp)(c) **SWEETHEART OF THE RODEO / THE NOTORIOUS BYRD BROTHERS**

Feb 80. (lp)(c) **THE BYRDS PLAY DYLAN**

(cd+c-iss.Apr94 on 'Sony')

Aug 80. (lp)(c) **THE ORIGINAL SINGLES 1966-1967**

(re-iss.Nov81)

Feb 82. (lp)(c) **THE ORIGINAL SINGLES 1968-1969**

Jul 82. (7") **CHESTNUT MARE. / WASN'T BORN TO FOLLOW**

Jul 84. (7") **MR. TAMBOURINE MAN. / WASN'T BORN TO FOLLOW**

1989. (3"cd-ep) **MR. TAMBOURINE MAN / TURN! TURN! TURN!. / ALL I REALLY WANT TO DO / LAY LADY LAY**

Nov 90. Columbia; (4xcd-box) **THE BYRDS**

1990. Columbia; (7"ep) **FOUR DIMENSIONS**

– Eight miles high / Mr.Tambourine man / Turn! turn! turn! (to everything there is a season) / I feel a whole lot better

Oct 94. Columbia; (cd) **THE BEST**

Mar 93. Columbia; (cd)(c) **20 ESSENTIAL TRACKS**

Sep 73. Bumble/ US= Together; (lp) **PREFLYTE (demo recordings of '64)** Sep 69

Aug 75. Asylum; (7") **FULL CIRCLE. / THINGS WILL BE BETTER**

Sep 83. Scoop; (12"ep) **SIX TRACK HITS**

– Lay lady lay / Turn! turn! turn! / Goin' nowhere / So you want to be a rock'n'roll star / Chestnut mare / All I really want to do.

Sep 86. Castle; (d-lp)(c) **THE BYRDS COLLECTION** -

(cd-iss.1987, omits some tracks)

Jan 88. Old Gold; (7") **MR. TAMBOURINE MAN. / TURN! TURN! TURN!** -

May 88. Re-Flyte; (lp) **NEVER BEFORE (Import)** -

(cd-iss.Aug89 on 'Murray Hill')

Feb 91. Raven; (cd) **FULL FLYTE 1965-1970**

Dec 92. Edsel; (cd) **RETURN FLYTE (McGUINN, HILLMAN & CLARK)** -

Jul 93. Edsel; (cd) **RETURN 2 FLIGHT (McGUINN, HILLMAN & CLARK)** -

Oct 94. Edsel; (cd-ep) **TURN TURN TURN. / (other artists)**

(above from 'Epic' records soundtrack of 'Forrest Gump')

ROGER McGUINN

C.B.S. Columbia

Jun 73. (7") **DRAGGIN'. / TIME CUBE** -

Jun 73. (lp)(c) **ROGER McGUINN**

– I'm so restless / My new woman / Lost my drivin' wheel / Draggin' / Time cube / Bag full of money / Hanoi Hannah / Stone / Heave away / M'Linda / The water is wide. *(cd-iss.Feb91) (re-iss.Jul88 on 'Edsel')*

1974. (7") **SAME OLD SOUND. / GATE OF HORN** -

1974. (lp)(c) **PEACE ON YOU** 92

– Peace on you / Without you / Going to the country / One more time / Same old sound / Do what you want to / Together / Better change / Gate of horn / Lady.

Sep 74. (7") **PEACE ON YOU. / WITHOUT YOU**

1975. (lp)(c) **ROGER McGUINN AND BAND**

– Somebody loves you / Knockin' on Heaven's door / Bull Dog / Painted lady / Lover of the bayou / Lisa / Circle song/ So long / Easy does it / Born to rock and roll.

1975. (7") **SOMEBODY LOVES YOU / EASY DOES IT** -

1975. (7") **LOVER OF THE BAYOU. / EASY DOES IT** -

1976. (7") **TAKE ME AWAY. / FRIEND** -

Jun 76. (lp)(c) **CARDIFF ROSE**

– Jolly Roger / Take me away / Rock and roll time / Partners in crime / Friend / Up to me / Round table / Prettly Polly / Dream land.

1977. (lp)(c) **THUNDERBYRD**

– All night long / It's gone / Dixie highway / American girl / We can do it all over again / Why, baby why / I'm not lonely anymore / Golden loom / Russian Hill.

May 77. (7") **AMERICAN GIRL. / RUSSIAN HILL** -

May 77. (7") **AMERICAN GIRL. / I'M NOT LONELY ANYMORE** -

—— **McGUINN** used session people **STAN LYNCH** – drums / **GEORGE HAWKINS** – bass / **DAVID COLE** – acoustic guitar / **JOHN JORGENSEN** – guitar / **BELMONT TENCH** – keyboards / **MICHAEL THOMPSON** – acoustic guitar

Arista Arista

Feb 91. (cd)(c)(lp) **BACK FROM RIO** 44 Jan 91

– Someone to love / Car phone / You bowed down / Suddenly blue / The trees are all gone / king of the hill / Without your love / The time has come / Your love is a gold mine / If we never meet again.

Feb 91. (7") **KING OF THE HILL. / YOUR LOVE IS A GOLD MINE**

(cd-s+=) – The time has come.

Columbia Columbia

Mar 92. (cd)(c)(lp) **BORN TO ROCK AND ROLL** (his compilation)

GENE CLARK

(solo, after he left The BYRDS first time) with The **GODSIN BROTHERS (REX** and **VERN** – both guitars + vocals)

C.B.S. Columbia

Apr 67. (lp) **GENE CLARK & THE GODSIN BROTHERS**

– Echoes / Think I'm gonna feel better / Tried so hard / Is yours mine / Keep on pushing / I found you / So you say you lost your baby / Elevator operator * / The same one / Couldn't believe her / Needing someone. *(US remixed & re-iss.1972 as 'EARLY L.A. SESSIONS' extra track *) (re-iss.May88 on 'Edsel') (re-iss.1991 original) (CBS re-issued it as 'ECHOES' in 1991 w/ 6 extra BYRDS tracks)*

1967. (7") **ECHOES. / I FOUND OUT** - -

1967. (7") **SO YOU SAY YOU LOST YOUR BABY. / IS YOURS MINE** -

—— briefly in Oct67 he rejoined The BYRDS. In Aug68, GENE CLARK and occasional ex-BYRD; **DOUG DILLARD** – banjo formed

DILLARD & CLARK

MICHAEL CLARKE – drums (ed-BYRDS) / **DON BECK** – pedal steel / **BERNIE LEADON** – guitar, vocals / **DAVID JACKSON** – bass (both ex-HEARTS & FLOWERS)

A&M A&M

Oct 68. (lp) **THE FANTASTIC EXPEDITION OF DILLARD & CLARK**

– Out on the side / She darkened the sun / Don't come rollin' / Train leaves here this mornin' / With care from somewhere / The radio song / Git it on brother (git in line brother) / In the plan / Something's wrong / Why not your baby / Lyin' down the middle / Don't be cruel.

Nov 68. (7") **OUT ON THE SIDE. / TRAIN LEAVES HERE THIS MORNIN'** -

Feb 69. (7") **LYIN' DOWN THE MIDDLE. / DON'T BE CRUEL** -

May 69. (7") **WHY NOT YOUR BABY. / THE RADIO SONG** -

—— (Jan69) **JON CORNEAL** – drums (ex-FLYING BURRITO BROTHERS) repl. MICHAEL CLARKE who joined FLYING BURITTO BROTHERS / **DONNA WASHBURN** – guitar, vocals repl. BECK

—— (May69) **BYRON BERLINE** – fiddle repl. LEADON to FLYING BURRITO BROTHERS

Sep 69. (lp) **THROUGH THE MORNING, THROUGH THE NIGHT**

– No longer a sweetheart of mine / Through the morning, through the night / Rocky top / So sad / Corner street bar / I bowed my head and cried holy / Kansas city southern / Four walls / Polly / Roll in my sweet baby's arms / Don't let me down.

Nov 69. (7") **ROCKY TOP. / DON'T LET ME DOWN** -

—— DOUG DILLARD continued with other solo albums

GENE CLARK

after a rest period continued solo

A&M A&M

1971. (lp) **GENE CLARK (WHITE LIGHT)**

– The virgin / With tomorrow / White light / Because of you / One in a hundred / Spanish guitar / Where my love lies asleep / Tears of rage / 1975.

Ariola not issued

Dec 72. (lp) **ROADMASTER** - - Dutch

– She's the kind of girl / One in a hundred / Here tonight / Full circle song / In a misty morning / Rough and rocky / Roadmaster / I really don't want to know / I remember the railroad / She don't care about time / Shooting star. *(re-iss. 1988 on 'Edsel', cd-iss. Jun 90).*

Asylum Asylum

Oct 74. (lp) **NO OTHER**

– Life's greatest fool / Silver raven / No other / Strength of strings / From a silver phial / Some misunderstanding / The true one / Lady of the north. *(re-iss.1988 on 'Edsel')*

Jan 75. (7") **NO OTHER. / THE TRUE ONE**

Mar 75. (7") **LIFE'S GREATEST FOOL. / FROM A SILVER PHIAL**

Polydor R.S.O.

Mar 77. (lp) **TWO SIDES TO EVERY STORY**

– Home run King / Lonely Saturday / In the pines / Kansas city southern / Silent crusade / Give my love to Maria / Sister moon / Mary Lou / Hear the wind / Past address.

1977. (7") **HOME RUN KING. / LONELY SATURDAY** -

Spindrift Takoma

1984. (lp) **FIREBYRD**

– Mr. Tambourine man / Something about you / Rain song / Rodeo rider / Vanessa / If you could read my mind / Feel a whole lot better / Made for love / Blue raven. *(cd-iss.1995 as 'THIS BIRD HAS FLOWN' on 'Edsel'+=)* – C'est la Bonne Rue / Dixie flyer / All I want.

—— other solo (import) releases below **CARLA** – vocals of TEXTONES)

Demon Razor&Tie

Apr 87. (lp) **SO REBELLIOUS A LOVER (as "GENE CLARK & CARLA OLSON")**
– The drifter / Gypsy rider / Every angel in heaven / Del gato / Deportee / Fair and tender ladies / Almost Saturday night / I'm your toy / Are we still making love / Why did you leave me today / Don't it make you want to go home. *(cd+=)* – Lover's turnaround.

— GENE CLARK died of natural causes in Feb 1991.

1992. (cd) **SILHOUETTED IN LIGHT (live with CARLA OLSON)**
– Your fire burning / Number one is to survive / Love wins again / Fair and tender ladies / Photograph / Set you free this time / Last thing on my mind / Gypsy rider / Train leaves here this morning / Almost Saturday night / Delgato / Feel a whole lot better / She don't care about time / Speed of the sound of loneliness / Will the circle be unbroken.

CHRIS HILLMAN

Asylum Asylum

1977. (lp)(c) **SLIPPIN' AWAY**
– Step on out / Slippin' away / Falling again / Take it on the run / Blue morning / Witching hour / Down in the churchyard / Love is the sweetest amnesty / Midnight again / Lifeboat.

Jul 76. (7") **STEP ON OUT. / TAKE IT ON THE RUN**
May 77. (7") **SLIPPIN' AWAY. / YOUR LIFEBOAT**
1977. (lp)(c) **CLEAR SAILIN'**
– Nothing gets through / Fallen favourite / Quits / Hot dusty roads / Heartbreaker / Playin' the fool / Lucky in love / Rollin' and tumblin' / Ain't that peculiar / Clear sailin'.

McGUINN, CLARK & HILLMAN

(nearly a BYRDS reformation)

Capitol Capitol

1979. (7") **SURRENDER TO ME. / BYE BYE BABY** – –
Feb 79. (lp)(c) **McGUINN, CLARK & HILLMAN** 39
– Long long time / Little mama / Don't you write her off / Sad boy / Surrender to me / Backstage pass / Stopping traffic / Feeling higher / Release me girl / Bye bye baby.
Apr 79. (7") **DON'T YOU WRITE HER OFF. / SAD BOY** 33 Mar 79
(re-iss.Apr86)
Jun 79. (7") **SURRENDER TO ME. / LITTLE MAMA** –
Sep 79. (7") **BYE BYE BABY. / BACKSTAGE PASS** –
Jan 80. (lp)(c) **CITY ("CHRIS HILLMAN / ROGER McGUINN")**
– Who taught the night / One more chance / Won't let you down / Street talk / City / Skate date / Givin' herself away / Let me down easy / Deeper in / Painter fire.
Feb 80. (7") **STREET TALK. / ONE MORE CHANCE** –
Apr 80. (7") **CITY. / DEEPER** –
Mar 81. (lp)(c) **McGUINN / HILLMAN – MEAN STREETS (as "McGUINN & HILLMAN")**
– Mean streets / Entertainment / Soul shoes / Between you and me / Angel / Ain't no money / Love me tonight / King for a night / A secret side of you / Turn your radio on. *(cd-iss.Feb91)*
Mar 81. (7") **TURN YOUR RADIO ON. / MAKING MOVIES** –
May 81. (7") **LOVE ME TONIGHT. / KING FOR A NIGHT** –

McGUINN-HILLMAN

not issued Universal

1983. (7") **YOU AIN'T GOIN' NOWHERE. / DON'T YOU HEAR JERUSALEM MOAN** –

CHRIS HILLMAN

(solo again)

not issued Sugarhill

1982. (lp) **MORNING SKY** –
– Tomorrow is a long time / The taker / Here today and gone tomorrow / Morning sky / Ripple / Good time Charlie / Don't let your sweet love die / Mexico / It's happening to you / Hickory wind. *(UK-iss.Nov87 on 'Sundown', re-iss.Mar89)*

A&M Spindrift

Nov 84. (lp) **DESERT ROSE**
– Why you been gone so long / Somebody's back in town / Walk around your heart / Rough and rowdy ways / Desert rose / Running the roadblocks / I can't keep you in love with me / Treasure of love / Ashes of love / Turn your radio on. *(UK-iss.Nov87 on 'Sundown') (re-iss.Mar89)*

EVER READY CALL

CHRIS HILLMAN / BERNIE LEADON / AL PERKINS / DAVID MANSFIELD + JERRY SCHEFF

not issued A&M

1985. (lp) **EVER READY CALL** –
– River of Jordan / I'll be no stranger there / Don't let them take the bible out of our schoolroom / God loves his children / It's beginning to rain / Living in the name of love / Boat of love / Men are so busy / I'm using my bible for a roadmap / Panhandle rag.

DESERT ROSE BAND

HILLMAN with **HERB PEDERSON** – guitar, banjo, vocals (also on early-mid 80's lp's) / **J.D. MANESS** – pedal steel guitar (also on '84 lp) / **JOHN JORGENSON** – lead guitar, vocals / **BILL BRYSON** – bass / **STEVE DUNCAN** – drums

Curb-MCA Curb-MCA

Jan 87. (lp)(c)(US-cd) **DESERT ROSE BAND**
– One step forward / Love reunited / He's back and I'm blue / Leave this town / Time between / Ashes of love / One that got away / Once more / Glass hearts / Hard times.
Feb 87. (7") **ASHES OF LOVE. / LEAVE THIS TOWN** –
Jun 87. (7") **LOVE REUNITED. / HARD TIMES** –
Oct 87. (7") **ONE STEP FORWARD. / GLASS HEARTS** –
Feb 88. (7") **HE'S BACK AND I'M BLUE. / ONE THAT GOT AWAY** –

Jun 88. (lp)(c)(cd) **RUNNING**
– She don't love nobody / Running / Hello trouble / I still believe in you / Summer wind / For the rich man / Step on out / Homeless / Livin' in the house / Our songs.
Jul 88. (7") **SUMMER WIND. / OUR SONGS** –
Oct 88. (7") **I STILL BELIEVE IN YOU. / LIVIN' IN THE HOUSE** –
Mar 89. (7") **SHE DON'T LOVE NOBODY. / STEP ON OUT** –
May 89. (7") **HELLO TROUBLE. / HOMELESS** –
Oct 89. (7") **START ALL OVER AGAIN. / FOOLED AGAIN** –
Jan 90. (cd)(c) **PAGES OF LIFE**
– Story of love / Start all over again / Missing you / Just a memory / God's plane / Darkness in the playground / Our baby's gone / Time passes me by / Everybody's hero / In another lifetime / Desert rose.
Feb 90. (7") **IN ANOTHER LIFETIME. /** –
Jun 90. (7") **STORY OF LOVE. /** –
Jan 91. (7") **WILL THIS BE THE DAY. /** –
Mar 91. (cd)(c)(lp) **ONE DOZEN ROSES: GREATEST HITS** (compilation)
(re-iss.1994 as '16 ROSES' with extra tracks)

— also; **TOM BRUMLEY** – steel / **JEFF ROSS** – guitar / **TIM GROGAN** – drums repl.J.D., JORGENSON + DUNCAN

1992. (cd) **TRUE LOVE** –
– You can go home / It takes a believer / Twilight is gone / No-one else / A matter of time / Undying love (Alison Kravis duet) / Behind these walls / True love / Glory and power / Shades of blue.
1993. (cd) **LIFE GOES ON** –
– What about love / Night after night / Walk on by / Love refugees / Life goes on / That's not the way / Till it's over / Hold on / A little rain / Throw me a lifeline.

— Disbanded in 1993.

– other CHRIS HILLMAN recordings –

SCOTTSVILLE SQUIRREL BARKERS:- **HILLMAN / KENNY WERTZ / LARRY MURRAY**

1962. Crown; (lp) **BEST OF BLUEGRASS FAVOURITES (as "SCOTTSVILLE SQUIRREL BARKERS")** –
(re-iss.Dutch 1974 as 'THE KENTUCKY MOUNTAIN BOYS' on 'Ariola')

HILLMEN:- **HILLMAN / VERN + REX GROSDIN + DON PARSLEY**

1969. Together; (lp) **THE HILLMEN (as "The HILLMEN")** –
(re-iss.1988 on 'Sugarhill', cd-iss.Nov95)

David BYRNE (see under ⇒ TALKING HEADS)

David BYRON (see under ⇒ URIAH HEEP)

BYSTANDERS (see under ⇒ MAN)

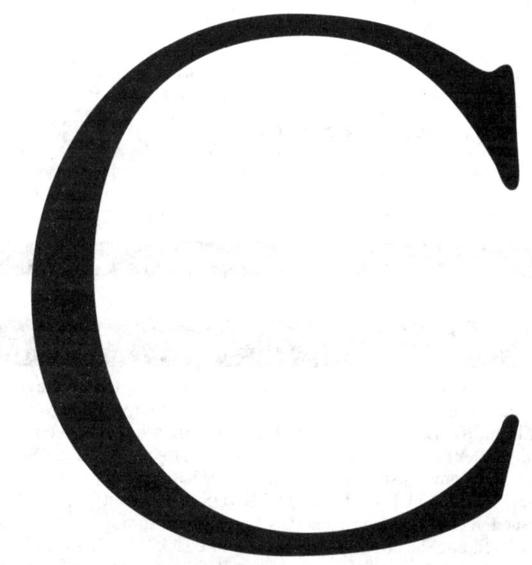

CABARET VOLTAIRE

Formed: Sheffield, England ... 1973 by MALLINDER, KIRK and WATSON. Named after experimental Parisian performances of the 20's. Contributed two songs to 'A FACTORY SAMPLER', then signed to Geoff Travis' new indie label 'Rough Trade' in 1978. Moved on in 1983 as a duo, to 'Some Bizzare'/'Virgin' label, and scored in UK charts with album 'THE CRACKDOWN'. • **Style:** Industrial avant-garde electronic outfit, who incorporated Eastern influences and hardcore dance. • **Songwriters:** All group compositions, except HERE SHE COMES NOW (Velvet Underground). • **Trivia:** Debut farcical gig was with taping of steamhammer and KIRK on clarinet. He had on a jacket covered by fairy lights and proceeded to be beaten up by audience.

Recommended: THE LIVING LEGENDS (*9) / THE CRACKDOWN (*8)

STEPHEN MALLINDER – vocals, bass, electronics, percussion, trumpet, piano / **RICHARD H.KIRK** – guitar, vocals, synthesizer, bongos, piano / **CHRISTOPHER R.WATSON** – electronics, tapes
(first issued cassette 25 copies LIMITED EDITION in 1976 on own label)

Rough Trade / not issued

Nov 78. (7"ep) **EXTENDED PLAY** [ ] [-]
– Talkover / Here she comes now / Do the Mussolini – headkick / The set up.

Jun 79. (7") **NAG NAG NAG. / IS THAT ME (FINDING SOMEONE AT THE DOOR)** [ ] [-]

Oct 79. (lp) **MIX-UP** [ ] [-]
– Kurlian photograph / No escape / 4th shot / Heaven and Hell / Eyeless sight (live) / Photophobia / On every other street / Expect nothing / Capsules. *(re-iss.+cd Jun90 on 'Mute')*

Dec 79. (7") **SILENT COMMAND. / EXCERPT FROM THE SOUNDTRACK CHANCE Vs CASUALITY** [ ] [-]

— added guest **MARK TATTERSALL** – drums

Jan 80. (lp) **LIVE AT THE Y.M.C.A. 27/10/79 (live)** [ ] [-]
– Untitled / On every other street / Nag nag nag / The set up / Havoc / Expect nothing / Here she comes now / No escape / Baader Meinhof. *(re-iss.+cd Jun90 on 'Mute')*

— now with guests **JOHN CLAYTON** – percussion / **JANE** – tapes

Mar 80. (m-lp) **THREE MANTRAS** [ ] [-]
– Eastern mantra / Western mantra. *(re-iss.+cd Jun90 on 'Mute')*

— with guest **HAYDN BOYES-WESTON** – drums (ex-2.3) (also on debut lp)

Jul 80. (lp) **THE VOICE OF AMERICA** [ ] [-]
– The voice of America / Damage is done / Partially submerged / Kneel to the boss / Premonition / This is entertainment / If the shadows could march? / Stay out of it / Obsession / News from nowhere / Messages received. *(re-iss.+cd Jun90 on 'Mute')*

Nov 80. (7") **SECONDS TOO LATE. / CONTROL ADDICT** [ ] [-]

— **NICK ALLDAY** – drums (ex-GRAPH) repl. HAYDN

Aug 81. (lp) **RED MECCA** [ ] [-]
– Touch of evil / Sly doubt / Landslide / A thousand ways / Red mask / Split second feling / Black mask / Spread the virus / A touch of evil (reprise). *(re-iss.+cd Jun90 on 'Mute')*

Sep 81. (c) **LIVE AT THE LYCEUM (live)** [ ] [-]
– Taxi music / Seconds too late / Your agent man / Split second feeling / Sluggin' for Jesus (part 1) / Kneel to the bass / Obsession / A thousand ways. *(re-iss.lp,cd Jun90 on 'Mute')*

Nov 81. (7") **JAZZ THE GLASS. / BURNT TO THE GROUND** [ ] [-]

Dec 81. (12") **EDDIE'S OUT. / WALLS OF JERICHO** [ ] [-]
(initial copies contained last 7" free)

— **ALAN FISH** – drums, percussion (of HULA) repl. **ALLDAY** / guest **ERIC RANDOM** – guitar (also a solo artist)

Jun 82. (2x12"lp) **2 x 45** [98] [-]
– Breathe deep / Yashar / Protection / War of nerves (T.E.S.) / Wait and shuffle / Get out of my face. *(re-iss.lp,cd Jun90 on 'Mute')*

Nov 82. (lp) **HAI! (live)** [-] [-] Germ'y
– Walls of Kyoto / 3 days monk / Yashar (version) / Over and over / Diskono / Taxi music (version). *(re-iss.+cd Jun90 on 'Mute')*

— trimmed to a duo (MALLINDER and **KIRK**) when WATSON departed. Retained **ALAN FISH** and brought in **DAVE BALL** – keyboards (of SOFT CELL)

Some Bizzare-Virgin / Virgin

Jul 83. (7") **JUST FASCINATION. / EMPTY WALLS** [ ] [-]
(12") – ('A'side) / Crackdown.

Aug 83. (lp)(c) **THE CRACKDOWN** [31] [ ]
– 24-24 / In the shadows / Talking time / Animation / Over and over / Just fascination / Why kill time (when you can kill yourself) / Haiti / Crackdown. *(re-iss.Apr86 +cd.with below tracks)*
(c.+=also 4 tracks below) (free 12"w/above) **MOSCOW / BADGE OF EVIL. / DISKONO / DOUBLE VISION**

Dec 83. (7")(12"ext.) **THE DREAM TICKET. / SAFETY ZONE** [ ] [ ]

Sep 84. (7")(12"ext'A') **SENSORIA. / CUT THE DAMN CAMERA** [ ] [ ]

Oct 84. (lp)(c)(cd) **MICROPHONIES** [69] [ ]
– Do right / The operative / Digital rasta / Spies in the wires / Theme from Earthshaker / James Brown / Slammer / Blue heat / Sensoria. (cd.+=) – Blue heat / Sensoria (12"mixes). *(re-iss.c+cd.Sep91 on 'Virgin')*

Jan 85. (7")(12") **JAMES BROWN. / BAD SELF (pt.1)** [ ] [ ]

Jun 85. (2x12"-lp) **DRINKING GASOLINE** [71] [ ]
– Kino / Sleepwalking / Big funk / Ghost talk. *(re-iss.c+cd.Sep91 on 'Virgin')*

Sep 85. (7")(12") **I WANT YOU. / DRINK YOUR POISON /** [ ] [ ]
(12"+=) C.O.M.A.

Oct 85. (lp)(c)(cd) **THE COVENANT, THE SWORD AND THE ARM OF THE LORD** [57] [ ]
– L21st / I want you / Hell's home / Kickback / The arm of the Lord / Warm / Golden halos / Motion rotation / Whip blow / The web. (cd.+=) – Sleepwalking / Big funk *(re-iss.c+cd.Sep91 on 'Virgin')*

— guest **DEE BOYLE** – drums (of CHAAK) repl. FISH

Doublevision / not issued

Jun 86. (12"ep) **THE DRAIN TRAIN** [ ] [-]
– Shakedown (the whole thing) / Menace / Electro-motive.
(12"w/above) **SHAKEDOWN (version). / SHAKEDOWN (dub)**

Parlophone / Capitol

Jul 87. (7") **DON'T ARGUE. / DON'T ARGUE (WHO'S ARGUING)** [69] [-]
(12"+=)(c-s+=) – ('A'extended / 'A'remix).
(12"+=) – ('A'dance) / ('A'dub).

Sep 87. (7") **HERE TO GO. / HERE TO GO (dub)** [ ] [ ]
(12"+=)(c-s+=) – ('A'extended).
(extra-12") – ('A'live drum remix) / ('A' 11-11 mix).

Oct 87. (lp)(c)(cd) **CODE** [ ] [ ]
– Don't argue / Sex, money, freaks / Thank you America / Here to go / TRouble (won't stop) / White car / No one here / Life slips by / Code. (cd+=) – Here to go (little dub) / Hey hey.

Oct 89. (7") **HYPNOTISED (Daniel Miller mix). / ('A'vocal mix)** [66] [ ]
(12"+=) – ('A'-Fon Force mix) / ('A'dub) / ('A'-Robert Gordon mix).
(cd-s) – ('A'-Fon Force mix) / ('A'-western works mix).
(extra-12") – (all above mixes except Daniel Miller mix).

Mar 90. (7") **KEEP ON (I GET THIS FEELING). / KEEP ON (Les dub)** [55] [ ]
(12") – ('A'-Sweet Exorcist mix) / ('A'-sleazy dog mix) / ('A'-mayday mix).
(cd-s) – ('A'-western works mix) / ('A'club mix).

Jun 90. (cd)(c)(lp) **GROOVY, LAIDBACK AND NASTY** [ ] [ ]
– Searchin' / Hypnotised / Minute by minute / Runaway / Keep on (I got this feeling) / Magic / Time beats / Easy life. (cd+=) – Rescue me (city lights). (free-12"ep.w/above) **(GROOVY, LAIDBACK AND NASTY)** (remixes) – Runaway / Magic / Searchin' / Rescue me (city lights) / Easy life.

Jul 90. (7") **EASY LIFE. / ('A'-Robert Gordon mix)** [61] [ ]
(12") – ('A'side) / Fluid / Positive I.D.
(cd-s) – ('A'side) / Fluid / ('A'-Jive Turkey mix).
(extra-12") – ('A'vocal) / ('A'strange mix) / ('A'very strange mix).

Crepescule / not issued

Feb 91. (12") **WHAT IS REAL. / ('A'virtual reality mix)** [ ] [ ]
(cd-s+=) – Legacy of a computer.

Mar 91. (cd)(c)(lp) **BODY AND SOUL** [ ] [-]
– No resistance / Shout / Happy / Decoy / Bad chemistry / Vibration / What is real / Western land. (cd.+=) – What is real (dreamtime mix).

Jul 91. (cd)(m-lp) **PERCUSSION FORCE** [ ] [-]
– Don't walk away / Keep on pushin' / Don't walk away (Robert Gordon mix) / Dynamic zone / Jazz the computer (part 1) / Keep on pushin' (version). (cd+=) – T.Phunk / Don't walk away (version) / Jazz the computer pt.2

Plastex / not issued

Oct 91. (cd)(c)(m-lp) **COLOURS** [ ] [-]

Oct 92. (cd)(c)(d-lp) **PLASTICITY** [ ] [-]

Jun 93. (cd) **INTERNATIONAL LANGUAGE** [ ] [-]
– Everything is true / Radical chic / Taxi mutant / Let it come down / Afterglow / The rest / Millenium / Belly of the beast (back in Babylon) / Other world.

Apollo-R&S / not issued

Jul 94. (d-cd)(q-lp) **THE CONVERSATION** [ ] [-]
– Exterminating angel / Brutal but clean / The message / Let's start / Night rider / Night rider / I think / The heat / Harmonic parallel / Project 80 (parts 1-4) / Exterminating angel (outro).

– compilations, others, etc. –

1980. Industrial; (c) **74-76** [ ] [-]
(cd-iss.Jun92 on 'Grey Area-Mute')

Jul 81. Crepescule Belguim; (12") **SLUGGIN' FOR JESUS (pt.1 & 2) / YOUR AGENT MAN** [ ] [-]

Feb 83. Crepescule Belguim; (12") **FOOL'S GAME (SLUGGIN' FOR JESUS pt.3). / GUT LEVEL** [ ] [-]

Feb 88. Crepescule Belgium; (lp)(cd) **8 CREPESCULE TRACKS** [ ] [-]

Jul 83. Factory Benelux; (12") **YASHAR (5.00). / YASHAR (7.20)** [ ] [-]

Nov 83. DoubleVision; (lp) **JOHNNY YES NO (Soundtrack)** [ ] [-]
– Taxi music / Hallucination sequence / DT's / Cold turkey / The quarry (in the

wilderness) / Title sequence / Taxi music dub. *(re-iss.+cd Jun90 on 'Mute')*

Nov 87. Rough Trade; (cd) **THE GOLDEN MOMENTS OF CABARET VOLTAIRE** [ ] [-]
– Do the Mussolini (Head Kick) / Nag nag nag / Photophobia / Expect nothing / Seconds Too late / This is entertainment / Obsession / Sluggin for Jesus / Landslide / Red mask / Get out of my face.

May 90. Mute; (cd-s) **NAG NAG NAG / YASHAR / YASHAR (John Robie remixes)** [ ] [-]

Jun 90. Mute; (cd)(c)(lp) **LISTEN UP WITH CABARET VOLTAIRE** (rare demos) [ ] [-]

Jun 90. Mute; (cd)(c)(lp) **THE LIVING LEGENDS . . . CABARET VOLTAIRE** (the 'Rough Trade' singles 'A'&'B') [ ] [ ]
– Do The Mussolini (Head Kick) / Talk Over / Here She Comes Now / The Set Up / Nag, Nag, Nag / Silent Command / Jazz The Glass / Walls Of Jericho / Seconds Too Late / Eddie's Out / Burnt To The Ground / Extract From : Chance Verses Causality / Control Addict / Is That Me (Finding Someone At The Door Again)

Jun 90. Mute; (c) **MIX-UP (lp) / LIVE AT THE Y.M.C.A. (lp)** [ ] [-]

Jun 90. Mute; (c) **2 x 45 (lp) / JOHNNY YES NO (soundtrack) (lp)** [ ] [-]

Jun 90. Mute; (c) **HAI! (lp) / RED MECCA (lp)** [ ] [-]

Jun 90. Mute; (c) **DRAINTRAIN (ep) / THREE MANTRAS (ep)** [ ] [-]

Jun 90. Mute; (c) **LIVE AT THE LYCEUM (lp) / THE VOICE OF AMERICA (lp)** [ ] [-]

Apr 92. Virgin; (12")(cd-s) **I WANT YOU. / KINO** [ ] [-]
– (Altern 8 remixes / Western re-works '92)

May 92. Virgin; (cd)(c)(lp) **TECHNOLOGY** (remixes late 70's & early 80's) [ ] [-]

Mar 82. Solidarity; (12"ep) **LIVE IN SHEFFIELD 19th JANUARY 1982 (live) (as "PRESSURE COMPANY")** [ ] [-]
– War of nerves / Wait & shuffle / Get out of my face / Vitrions China (paradox).

STEPHEN MALLINDER (solo)

Fetish / not issued

Nov 81. (12") **TEMPERATURE DROP. / COOL DOWN / LOVE STREET (with DAVE BALL & ROBERT GORDON)** [ ] [-]

1983. (m-lp) **POW WOW PLUS** [ ] [-]
– Temperature Drop / The Devil In Me / 0.58 / Pow Wow / Three Piece Swing / Cool Down / 1.37 / In Smoke / 1.59 / Length Of Time / Going Out / Del Sol *(re-iss. Oct85 as POW-WOW PLUS on 'Doublevision') (cd-iss.Jun92 on 'Grey Area-Mute')*

LOVE STREET

(aka **STEPHEN MALLINDER** solo)

Parlophone / not issued

Jun 88. (7")(12") **GALAXY. / COME ON DOWN TO LOVE STREET** [ ] [-]

RICHARD H.KIRK (solo)

Industrial / not issued

1981. (c) **DISPOSABLE HALF TRUTHS** [ ] [-]
– Synesthesia / Outburst / Information Therapy / Magic Words Command / Thermal Damage / Plate Glass Replicas / Insect Friends Of Allah / Scatalist / False Erotic Love / L.D. 50 / L.D. 60 / Amnesic Disassociation *(cd-iss.Jun92 on 'Grey Area-Mute')*

DoubleVision / not issued

Dec 83. (lp) **TIME HIGH FICTION** [ ] [-]

Rough Trade / not issued

Sep 86. (12") **HIPNOTIC. / MARTYRS OF PALESTINE** [ ] [-]

Sep 86. (lp) **BLACK JESUS VOICE** [ ] [-]
– Street gang / Hipnotic / Shala / Black Jesus voice / Martyrs of Palestine / This is the H-bomb sound / Short wave. *(cd-iss.Mar95 on 'Grey Area')*

Sep 86. (m-lp) **UGLY SPIRIT** [ ] [-]
– The emperor / Confession / Infantile / Frantic machine (part 1 & 2) / Hollywood Babylon / Thai voodoo. *(c-iss.Nov86 of all Sep86 releases) (cd-iss.Mar95 on 'Grey Area')*

PETER HOPE / RICHARD H.KIRK

(**HOPE**– of The **BOX**)

Doublevision / not issued

Oct 85. (12") **LEATHER HANDS (master mix). / ('A'radio) / ('A'crash)** [ ] [-]

Native / not issued

Nov 87. (lp,cd) **HOODOO TALK** [ ] [-]
– Intro / Numb skull / N.O. / Cop out / Surgeons / 50 tears / Leather hands / 50 tears (reprise).

Nov 88. (12") **SURGEONS / BEATS. / RESURGENCY / N.O.** [ ] [-]

SWEET EXORCIST

(aka **KIRK & DJ PARROTT**)

Warp / not issued

Feb 90. (12"m) **TEST ONE. / TEST TWO / TEST THREE** [ ] [-]
(extra-12"+=) – (remixes of above)

Jan 91. (cd)(lp) **CLONK' COMING** [ ] [-]

Plastex / not issued

1992. (12"ep) **POPCONE. /** [ ] [-]
– Mad Jack / Track Jack / Jack Jack / Trick Jack / Kick Jack / Psych Jack / Clonk' coming.

Touch / not issued

Aug 94. (cd) **SPIRIT GUIDE TO LOW TECH** [ ] [-]

XON

(aka **KIRK** with **ROBERT GORDON**)

Network / not issued

Jan 91. (7"ep) **THE MOOD SET** [ ] [-]

RICHARD H. KIRK

Warp / not issued

Jan 94. (cd)(c)(lp) **VIRTUAL STATE** [ ] [-]
– November x-ray Mexico / Frequency band / Come / Freezone / Clandestine transmission / The feeling (of warmth and beauty) / Velodrome / Soul catcher / World War Three / Lagoon west.

Jul 95. (cd)(c)(d-lp) **THE NUMBER OF MAGIC** [ ] [-]
– Lost souls on funk / Love is deep / So digital / Indole ring / East of Nina / Atomic / Poets saints revolutionaries / Monochrome dream / The number of magic.

Beyond / not issued

Sep 94. (d-cd)(q-lp-box) **ELECTRONIC EYE** [ ] [-]

CACTUS (see under ⇒ VANILLA FUDGE)

J.J. CALE

Born: JEAN-JACQUES CALE, 5 Dec'38, Oklahoma, USA). Having ventured to Nashville, then Los Angeles in the 60's while working with LEON RUSSELL and DELANEY & BONNIE, he returned home to record solo in own studio. After hearing demo LEON signed him to his new label 'Shelter' in 1969. Two years previously, also with LEON, he had been part of a psychedelic rock ensemble LEATHER COATED MINDS. His debut 'NATURALLY' finally issued in 1972, gave him near US Top 50 breakthrough. 20 years on and he was still treading the boards with superb comeback 'NUMBER 10'. • **Style:** Laid back and rhythmic, with his own brand of cajun / country. • **Songwriters:** All self penned except several covers. (ERIC CLAPTON charted with his 'AFTER MIDNIGHT' & 'COCAINE'). • **Trivia:** MARK KNOPFLER and RICHARD THOMPSON guested on his 8 album in 1983.

Recommended: SPECIAL EDITION (*8) / NUMBER 10 (*6).

J.J. CALE – vocals, guitar, piano with loads of session musicians, too numerous too mention, until next volume?

Liberty / Liberty

Jun 66. (7") **OUTSIDE LOOKING IN. / IN OUR TIME** [ ] [ ]

— In 1967 CALE and LEON RUSSELL formed LEATHER COATED MIND.

1968. (7") **AFTER MIDNIGHT. / SLOW MOTION** [-] [ ]

A & M / Shelter

Jan 72. (lp)(c) **NATURALLY** [ ] [51]
– Call me the breeze / Call the doctor / Don't go to strangers / Woman I love / Magnolia / Clyde / Crazy mama / Nowhere to run / After midnight / River runs deep / Bringing it back / Crying eyes. *(re-iss.Aug83 on 'Shelter') (cd-iss.on 'Mercury')*

Jan 72. (7") **CRAZY MAMA. / ?** [-] [22]

Aug 72. (7") **AFTER MIDNIGHT. / CRAZY MAMA** [ ] [42] May 72

Jan 73. (7") **LIES. / RIDING HOME** [ ] [42] Oct 72

Jan 73. (lp)(c) **REALLY** [ ] [92] Dec 72
– Lies / Everything will be alright / I'll kiss the world goodbye / Changes / Right down here / If you're ever in Oklahoma / Ridin' home / Going down / Soulin' / Playin' in the streets / Mo Jo / Louisiana women. *(re-iss.Apr76) (re-iss.Aug83 on 'Shelter') (cd-iss.on 'Mercury')*

Jun 74. (lp)(c) **OKIE** [ ] [ ]
– Crying / I'll be there (if you ever want me) / Everlovin' woman / Cajun moon / I'd like to love you baby / Starbound / Rock and roll records / The old man and me / Everlovin' woman / Cajun Moon / I'd like to love you baby / Anyway the wind blows / Precious memories / Okie / I got the same old blues. *(re-iss.Apr76) (re-iss.Aug83 on 'Shelter') (cd-iss.on 'Mercury')*

Jun 74. (7") **CAJUN MOON. / STARBOUND** [ ] [ ]

Sep 74. (7") **I'LL BE THERE (IF YOU EVER WANT ME). / PRECIOUS MEMORIES** [-] [ ]

Jan 75. (7") **I GOT THE SAME OLD BLUES. / ROCK AND ROLL RECORDS** [-] [ ]

Shelter-Island / Shelter

Sep 76. (lp)(c) **TROUBADOUR** [53] [84]
– Hey baby / Travelin' light / You got something / Ride me high / Hold on / Cocaine / I'm a gypsy man / The woman that got away / Super blue / Let me do it to you / Cherry / You got me on so bad. *(re-iss.Jan78 + Aug83) (cd-iss.! on 'Mercury')*

Oct 76. (7") **HEY BABY. / MAGNOLIA** [ ] [96]

Jan 77. (7") **TRAVELIN' LIGHT. / COCAINE** [ ] [ ]

Feb 78. (7") **I'M A GYPSY MAN. / CHERRY** [ ] [ ]

Jul 79. (lp)(c) **5** [40] [ ]
– Thirteen days / Boilin' point / I'll make love to you anytime / Don't cry sister / Too much for me / A sensitive kind / Friday / Lou-Easy-Ann / Let's go to Tahiti / Katy kool lady / Fate of a fool / Mona. *(re-iss.Oct83)*

Aug 79. (7") **KATY KOOL LADY. / JUAREZ BLUES** [ ] [ ]

Feb 81. (lp)(c) **SHADES** [44] [ ]
– Carry on / Deep dark dungeon / Wish I had not said that / Pack my jack / If you leave her / Mama don't / Runaround / What do you expect / Love has been gone / Cloudy day. *(re-iss. +cd May84 on 'Mercury')*

Feb 81. (7") **CARRY ON. / DEEP DARK DUNGEON** [-] [ ]

Mar 81. (7") **CARRY ON. / CLOUDY DAY** [ ] [ ]

May 81. (7") **MAMA DON'T. / WHAT DO YOU EXPECT** [ ] [ ]

Shelter-Island / Mercury

Jan 82. (7") **DEVIL IN DISGUISE. / DRIFTER'S WIFE** [-] [ ]

Mar 82. (lp)(c) **GRASSHOPPER** [36] [ ]
– City girls / Devil in disguise / One step ahead of the blues / You keep me hangin' on / Downtown L.A. / Can't live here / Grasshopper / Drifters wife / Don't wait / A thing going on / Nobody but you / Mississippi river / Does your mama like to reggae / Dr.Jive. *(re-iss.Nov84 on 'Ensign') (cd-iss. 1983)*

Mar 82. (7") **CITY GIRLS. / ONE STEP AHEAD OF THE BLUES** [ ] [ ]

Mercury / Mercury

Sep 83. (lp)(c) **£8** [47] [ ]
– Money talks / Losers / Hard times / Reality / Takin' care of business / People lie /

Unemployment / Trouble in the city / Teardrops in my tequila / Livin' here too. *(cd-iss. 1984)*

Sep 83. (7") **TEARDROPS IN MY TEQUILA. / AFTER MIDNIGHT**
(12"+=) – Cocaine.

Jun 84. (lp)(c) **LA FEMME DE MON POTE**
– Bringing it back / City girls / Mons (5) / Right down here / The woman that got away / Ride me high / Starbound (okie) / You keep me hangin' on / Super blue / Magnolia.

(above album was Soundtrack to French film MY BEST FRIEND'S GIRL)

— CALE retired from music business, writing only score for German film 50/50 around mid-1986. Below album took 5 years to record using backing band **TIM DRUMMOND + DOUG BELL** – bass / **JIM KARSTEIN** – drums, percussion / **JIM KELTNER** – drums, percussion, organ / **CHRISTINE LAKELAND** – guitar, organ, vocals / **SPOONER OLDHAM** – keyboards / **JAY MITTHAUER** – drums guests on * HOYT AXTON / **JAMES BURTON**

Silvertone Silvertone

Oct 89. (lp)(c)(cd) **TRAVEL-LOG** Mar90
– Shanghaid / Hold on baby / No time / Lady luck / Disadvantage / Lean on me / End of the line / New Orleans / Tijuana / That kind of thing / Who's talking / Change your mind / Humdinger / River boat song. *(re-iss.cd/c Apr95)*

Oct 89. (7") **SHANGHAID. / ARTIFICIAL PARADISE**
(cd-s+=) – Hang ups.

Mar 90. (7") **HOLD ON BABY. / ?**
(cd-s+=) – ?

Aug 92. (cd)(c)(lp) **NUMBER 10** 58
– Lonesome train / Digital blues / Feeling in love / Artificial paradise / Passion / Take out some insurance / Jailer / Low rider / Traces / She's in love / Shady grove / Roll on mama. *(re-iss.cd/c Apr95)*

Aug 92. (7") **LONESOME TRAIN. / LOW RIDER**
(cd-s+=) – Passion.

Virgin Virgin

Jun 94. (cd)(c) **CLOSER TO YOU**
– Long way home / Sho-biz blues / Slower baby / Devil's nurse / Like you used to / Borrowed time / Rose in the garden / Brown dirt / Hard love / Ain't love funny / Closer to you / Steve's song.

– compilations, others, etc. –

May 77. Shelter-Island; (7") **AFTER MIDNIGHT. / BRINGING IT BACK** -

Jun 84. Mercury; (lp)(c)(cd) **SPECIAL EDITION**
– Cocaine / Don't wait / Magnolia / Devil in disguise / A sensitive kind / Carry on / After midnight / Money talks / Call me the breeze / Lies / City girls / Cajun Moon / Don't cry sister / Crazy mama.

May 88. Mercury; (d-lp) **NATURALLY / OKIE** - -

Jul 88. Knight; (c)(cd) **NIGHTRIDING** -

John CALE

Born: 9 Mar'42, Garnant, Wales. Studied classical piano and later viola at London's Guildhall School Of Music. Aged only eight, he composed music for the BBC. In 1963, he moved to New York on a scholarship, and under JOHN CAGE and LaMONTE YOUNG's tuition, he experimented with avant-garde musak. In 1965, he met LOU REED, and they formed the legendary VELVET UNDERGROUND ⇒ . After recording their 2nd album, he was fired. In 1970, signed to 'Columbia', he released first of many solo albums, but lack of commercial success squeezed him into other directions. He sessioned for many, including ENO, and produced the STOOGES (IGGY POP), PATTI SMITH, MODERN LOVERS (JONATHAN RICHMAN), SQUEEZE, ++ • **Style:** Described initially as 'Baroque'n'roll', he drifted back into avant-garde. As an 'Island' artist, he shifted into more accessible rock forms, thus making him one of rock music's most gifted and influential artists. His vocal monotone not too dissimilar to stablemate NICK DRAKE or even KEVIN AYERS. • **Songwriters:** Writes mostly all work, but collaborated in 1971 with sax and keys man TERRY RILEY. In 1989 with DYLAN THOMAS text, scored Falkland theme and was accompanied by orchestra. 1990 saw him re-establish collaborations with past pals LOU REED then BRIAN ENO. CALE also covered HEARTBREAK HOTEL (Elvis Presley). • **Trivia:** A live performance in 1977, saw him decapitate a live chicken, which no doubt the 'Animal Liberation Front' must have missed.

Recommended: GUTS (*6) / PARIS (*7) / SLOW DAZZLE (*7)

JOHN CALE – vocals, viola, keyboards, bass, guitar with session people (not yet included)

C.B.S. Columbia

Nov 70. (7") **FAIRWEATHER FRIEND. / CLEO** -

Dec 70. (lp) **VINTAGE VIOLENCE**
– Hello there / Gideon's bible / Adelaide / Big white cloud / Cleo / Please / Charlemange / Bring it on up / Amsterdam / Ghost story / Fairweather friend. *(re-iss.+cd.May87 on 'Edsel') (cd-iss.Sep94 on 'Rewind')*

Jan 71. (7") **GIDEON'S BIBLE. / BIG WHITE CLOUD** -

Mar 71. (lp) **CHURCH OF ANTHRAX ("JOHN CALE & TERRY RILEY")**
– Church of anthrax / The hall of mirrors in the palace at Versailles / The soul of Patrick Lee / Ides of March / The protege. *(cd-iss.Oct93 on 'Sony Europe')*

Reprise Reprise

Apr 72. (lp)(c) **ACADEMY IN PERIL**
– The philosopher / Brahms / Legs Larry at Television Centre / Academy in peril / Intro: days of steam / 3 orchestral pieces: (a) Faust, (b) The balance, (c) Capt. Morgan's lament / King Harry / John Milton. *(re-iss.Apr86 on 'Edsel', cd-iss.Apr89) (cd-iss.Oct93 on 'Warners')*

May 72. (7") **DAYS OF STEAM. / LEGS LARRY AT TELEVISION CENTER** -

Mar 73. (lp)(c) **PARIS 1919**
– Child's Christmas in Wales / Hanky panky nohow / The endless plain of fortune / Andalucia / Macbeth / Paris 1919 / Graham Greene / Half past France / Antartica starts here. *(cd-iss.Oct93 on 'Warners')*

Around this time he contributed to album 'JUNE 1st, 1974' on 'Island' with others ENO, NICO, KEVIN AYERS.

— now with **ENO** – synth. / **PHIL MANZANERA** – guitar / **ARCHIE LEGGAT** – bass / **FRED SMITH** – drums guest on below 'A'side **JUDY NYLON** – vocals

Island A&M

Jul 74. (7") **THE MAN WHO COULDN'T AFFORD TO ORGY. / SYLVIA SAID** -

Sep 74. (lp)(c) **FEAR** -
– Fear is a man's best friend / Buffalo ballet / Barracuda / Emily / Ship of fools / Gun / The man who couldn't afford to orgy / You know more than I know / Momamma scuba. *(re-iss.cd+c.Aug91)*

— with **CHRIS SPEDDING + PHIL MANZANERA** – guitar / **PAT DONALDSON** – bass / **TIMI DONALD + GERRY CONWAY** – drums / **ENO** – synthesizer / **CHRIS THOMAS** – violin, electric piano

Apr 75. (lp)(c) **SLOW DAZZLE** -
– Mr.Wilson / Taking it all away / Dirty ass rock'n'roll / Darling I need you / Rollaroll / Heartbreak hotel / Ski patrol / I'm not the loving kind / Guts / The jeweller. *(cd-iss.1987) (cd-iss.Aug94)*

— **PHIL COLLINS** – drums repl. CONWAY, MANZANERA + THOMAS.

Nov 75. (lp)(c) **HELEN OF TROY** -
– My Maria / Helen of Troy / China sea / Engine / Save us / Cable Hogue / I keep a close watch / Pablo Picasso / Leaving it up to you / Baby what you want me to do? / Sudden death. *(cd-iss.Apr94)*

Feb 77. (lp)(c) **GUTS** (compilation) -
– Guts / Mary Lou / Helen of Troy / Pablo Picasso / Leaving it up to you / Fear is a man's best friend / Gun / Dirty ass rock 'n' roll / Heartbreak hotel. *(cd-iss.Aug94)*

— with **RITCHIE FLIEGLER** – lead guitar / **BRUCE BRODY** – mogg synthesizer / **JIMMY BAIN** – bass / **KEVIN CURRIE** – drums

Illegal not issued

Sep 77. (7"ep)(12"ep) **ANIMAL JUSTICE** -
– Chicken shit / Memphis / Hedda Gabbler.

— with **MARK AARON** – guitar / **JOE BIDWELL** – keyboards / **GEORGE SCOTT** – bass / **DOUG BROWN** – drums / **DEERFRANCE** – vocals

not issued Spy

Dec 79. (lp) **SABOTAGE (live)** -
– Mercenaries (ready for war) / Baby you know / Evidence / Dr.Mudd / Walkin' the dog / Captain Hook / Only time will tell / Sabotage / Chorale.

not issued I.R.S.

1980. (7") **MERCENARIES (READY FOR WAR). / ROSEGARDEN FUNERAL OF SORES** -

— with **STURGIS NIKIDES** – guitar, vocals / **JIM GOODWIN** – keyboards, synth. / **PETER MUNY** – bass / **ROBERT MEDECI** – drums

A&M A&M

Mar 81. (lp)(c) **HONI SOIT**
– Dead or alive / Strange times in Casablanca / Fighter pilot / Wilson Joliet / Streets of Laredo / Honi soit (la premiere Lecon de Francaise) / Riverbank / Russian roulette / Magic & lies. *(cd-iss.Jul94 on 'A&M')*

Apr 81. (7") **DEAD OR ALIVE. / HONI SOIT**

— now w / **ALAN LANIER** – keyboards / **D. J. YOUNG** – guitar / **DAVID LICHTENSTEIN** – drums / **JOHN WONDERLING** / **MIKE McCLINTOCK** / **ROBERT ELK**

Ze-Island Ze

Aug 82. (lp)(c) **MUSIC FOR A NEW SOCIETY**
– Taking your life in your hands / Thoughtless kind / Sanities / If you were still around / Close watch / Mama's song / Broken bird / Chinese envoy / Changes made / Damn life / Rise, Sam and Rimsky Korsakov. *(cd-iss.Mar94 on 'Yellow Moon')*

Apr 83. (7") **I KEEP A CLOSE WATCH. / CLOSE WATCH (instrumental)**

— **ANDY HEERMANS** – bass, vocals repl. LANIER

Jun 83. (lp)(c) **CARIBBEAN SUNSET**
– Hungry for love / Experiment number 1 / Model Beirut recital / Caribbean sunset / Praetorian underground / Magazines / Where there's a will / The hunt / Villa Albani.

Aug 84. (7") **OOH LA LA. / MAGAZINES**

Sep 84. (lp)(c) **JOHN CALE COMES ALIVE (live)**
– Ooh la la / Evidence / Dead or alive / Chinese envoy / Leaving it up to you / Dr.Mudd / Waiting for the man / Heartbreak hotel / Fear / Never give up on you.

— with **DAVID YOUNG** – guitar / **JAMES YOUNG** – keyboards / **GRAHAM DOWDALL** – percussion

Beggar's B. Warners

Jul 85. (7")(12") **DYING ON THE VINE. / EVERYTIME THE DOGS BARK** -

Nov 85. (lp)(c) **ARTIFICIAL INTELLIGENCE**
– Everytime the dogs bark / Dying on the vine / The sleeper / Vigilante lover / Chinese takeaway (Hong Kong 1997) (medley) / Song of the valley / Fade away tomorrow / Black rose / Satellite walk. *(re-iss.+cd.Jan89 on 'Lowdown-Beggar's Banquet')*

Nov 85. (12"m) **SATELLITE WALK. / DYING ON THE VINE / CRASH COURSE IN HARMONICS** -

— now w / **BRIAN ENO** – synth, keys / **NEIL CATCHPOLE** – viola, violin / **choir**

Oct 89. (lp)(c)(cd) **WORDS FOR THE DYING**
– The Falkland suite:- Introduction-There was a saviour – Interlude 1 / On a wedding anniversary – Interlude II – Lie still, sleep becalmed – Do not go gentle into that good night / Songs without words 1 & 2 / The soul of Carmen Miranda. *(re-iss.cd Oct95 on 'All Saints')*

Apr'90, CALE & Lou REED⇒, collaborated on Andy Warhol tribute album SONGS FOR DRELLA. On 'Sire' records, it was CALE's first excursion into the Top 30.

Oct'90, he teamed up with ENO ⇒ , on album WRONG WAY UP on 'Land' and a single 'ONE WORD'.

Delabel FRANCE not issued

Nov 91. (cd) **PARIS S'EVEILLE, SUIVI D'AUTRES COMPOSITIONS** -
– Paris S'eveille, suivi d'autres / Sanctus (four etudes for electronic orchestra) / Animals at night / The cowboy laughs at round-up / Primary motive 1) Factory

speech, 2) Strategy session, 3) Closing titles / Antartica starts here / Booker T. (by VELVET UNDERGROUND) *(UK-iss. Mar93 on 'Crepuscule') (re-iss.Nov95 on 'Yellow Moon')*

M.C.A. M.C.A.

May 94. (cd) **LAST DAY ON EARTH (Soundtrack) (JOHN CALE /BOB NEUWIRTH)**
– Overture- a) A tourist, b) A contract, c) A prisoner / Cafe Shabu / Pastoral angst / Who's in charge? / Short of time / Angel of death / Paradise Nevada / Old China / Ocean life / Instrumental / Modern world / Streets come alive / Secrets / Maps of the world / Broken hearts / The high and the mighty road.

– other compilations, etc. –

Jul 91. R.O.I.R.; (c) **EVEN COWBOYS GET THE BLUES (live 1978-79 at CBGB's)**
Oct 92. Hannibal; (cd) **FRAGMENTS OF A RAINY SEASON (live)** – –
Nov 93. Crepescule; (cd) **23 SOLO PIECES FOR LA NAISSANCE DE L'AMOUR** – –
(re-iss.Nov95 on 'Yellow Moon')
1994. Rhino; (d-cd) **SEDUCING THE DOOR** –

Randy CALIFORNIA (see under ⇒ SPIRIT)

Robert CALVERT (see under ⇒ HAWKWIND)

CAMEL

Formed: London, England . . . 1972 by R&B veteran PETE BARDENS. Their first recording 'GOD OF LIGHT REVISITED – PARTS ONE, TWO, THREE', featured on 1 side of a various d-lp 'Greasy Truckers – Live At Dingwalls'. Soon after in 1973, they issued eponymous debut on 'MCA', before they moved more successfully to 'Decca' and gave us interpretation of Paul Gallico's 'THE SNOW GOOSE'. Remained in the limelight before fading during the mid-80's. • **Style:** Concept and progressive rock group, whose instrumental work was similar to CARAVAN. • **Songwriters:** BARDENS, and group. • **Trivia:** Writer Gallico served writ on band for copyright infringement 1975. Their comeback album in '92 'DUST AND DREAMS', was inspired by John Steinbeck's book 'The Grapes Of Wrath'.

Recommended: THE SNOW GOOSE (*8) / THE COLLECTION (*7)

PETER BARDENS – keyboards, vocals (ex-THEM, ex-solo, ex-SHOTGUN EXPRESS) / **ANDY LATIMER** – vocals, guitar (ex-PHILIP GOODHAND-TAIT band) / **DOUG FERGUSON** – bass (ex-PHILIP GOODHAND-TAIT band) / **ANDY WARD** – drums, percussion (ex-PHILIP GOODHAND-TAIT band)

M.C.A. M.C.A.

1973. (7") **NEVER LET GO. / CURIOSITY**
Dec 73. (lp)(c) **CAMEL**
– Slow yourself down / Mystic queen / Six ate / Separation / Never let go / Curiosity / Arubaluba. *(re-iss.Aug81) (re-iss.Nov82 on 'Fame')(cd-iss.Jul93 on 'Camel')*

Deram Janus

1974. (lp)(c) **MIRAGE**
– Freefall / Supertwister / Nimrodel: – The procession – The white rider / Earthrise / Lady fantasy: – Encounter – Smiles for you – Lady fantasy. *(cd-iss.Jun89)*

Decca Janus

May 75. (lp)(c) **THE SNOW GOOSE** 22
– The great marsh – Rhayader – Rhayader goes to town – Sanctuary – Fritha – The snow goose – Friendship – Migration – Rhayader alone / Flight of the snow goose – Preparation – Dunkirk – Epitaph – Fritha alone – La princesse Perdue – The great marsh. *(re-iss.Nov76) (cd-iss.Jul '88)*
May 75. (7") **FLIGHT OF THE SNOW GOOSE. / RHAYADER**
Sep 75. (7") **THE SNOW GOOSE. / FREEFALL**
Apr 76. (lp)(c) **MOON MADNESS** 15
– Aristillus / Song within a song / Chord change / Spirit of the water / Another night / Air born / Lunar sea. *(cd-iss. 1983)*
Jun 76. (7") **ANOTHER NIGHT. / LUNAR SEA**

— **RICHARD SINCLAIR** – bass (ex-CARAVAN) repl. FERGUSON

Sep 77. (lp)(c) **RAIN DANCES** 20
– First light / Metrognome / Tell me / Highways of the sun / Unevensong / One of these days I'll get an early night / Elke / Skylines / Rain dances.
Sep 77. (7") **HIGHWAYS OF THE SUN. / TELL ME**

— added **MEL COLLINS** – saxophone (ex-KING CRIMSON etc.) / **DAVE SINCLAIR** – keyboards (ex-CARAVAN etc.)

Apr 78. (d-lp)(d-c) **A LIVE RECORD (live)**
– Never let go / Song within a song / Lunar sea / Skylines / Lady fantasy: Encounter – Smiles for you – Lady fantasy / The great marsh – Rhayader – Rhayader goes to town – Sanctuary – Fritha – The snow goose – Friendship – Migration – Rhayader alone / Flight of the snow goose: – Preparation – Dunkirk – Epitaph – Fritha alone – La princesse Perdue – The great marsh / Ligging at Louis'.*(re-iss.cd+c Jul93)*

Decca Arista

Sep 78. (lp)(c) **BREATHLESS** 26
– Breathless / Echoes / Wing and a prayer / Down on the farm / Starlight ride / Summer lightning / You make me smile / The sleeper / Rainbow's end.

— **COLIN BASS** – bass, vocals repl. RICHARD who later rejoined CARAVAN / **KIT WATKINS** – keyboards, flute repl. PETER who went solo then LATIMER, WARD

Sep 79. (lp)(c) **I CAN SEE YOUR HOUSE FROM HERE** 45
– Wait / Your love is no stronger than mine / Eye of the storm / Who are we / Survival / Hymn to her / Neon magic / Remote romance.
Oct 79. (7") **YOUR LOVE IS NO STRONGER THAN MINE. / NEON MAGIC**
Feb 80. (7") **REMOTE ROMANCE. / RAINBOW'S END / TELL ME**

— **DUNCAN MACKAY** – keyboards (ex-COCKNEY REBEL) repl. KIT

Jan 81. (lp)(c) **NUDE** 36
– City life / Nude / Drafted / Docks / Beached / Landscapes / Changing places / Pomp and circumstance / Please come home / Reflections / Captures / The homecoming / Lies / The last farewell / The birthday cake / Nude's return. *(cd-iss. 1987)*

— **JAN SCHELHAAS** – keyboards (ex-CARAVAN) repl. MACKAY who joined BUDGIE

Decca Passport

May 82. (lp)(c) **THE SINGLE FACTOR** 57
– No easy answer / You are the one / Heroes / Selva / Manic / Lullaby / Sasquatch / Camelogue / Today's goodbye / A heart's desire / End piece. *(cd-iss. 1983)*

— **PAUL BURGESS** – drums, percussion repl.WARD (joined MARILLION)

Mar 84. (lp)(c)(cd) **STATIONARY TRAVELLER** 57
– Pressure points / Refugee / Copos / Cloak and dagger man / Stationary traveller / West Berlin / Fingertips / Missing / Afterwords / Long goodbyes.
Mar 84. (7") **CLOAK AND DAGGER MAN. / PRESSURE POINTS**

— **LATIMER, BASS** and **BURGESS** with returning guests **MEL COLLINS & PETER BARDENS** brought in **TOM SCHERPENZEEL** – keyboards / **RICHIE CLOSE** – keys and **CHRIS RAINBOW** – vocals, keyboards

Nov 84. (lp)(c)(cd) **PRESSURE POINTS - CAMEL LIVE** (live 11 May84)
– West Berlin / Pressure points / Drafted / Captured / Lies / Rhayader goes to town / Sasquatch / Fingertips / Rhayader / Wait. *(cd-re-iss.'87 on 'London')*

— CAMEL disbanded in '84, but re-formed again in 1991.

Camel Prod. not issued

Sep 92. (cd)(c)(lp) **DUST AND DREAMS** –
– Dust bowl / Go west / Dusted out / Mother road / Needles / Rose of Sharon / End of the line / Storm clouds / Cotton camp / Broken ranks / Sheet rain / Whispers / Little rivers and little Rose / Hopeless anger / Whispers in the rain. *(cd-iss.Jul93)*

– compilations etc. –

Sep 81. Decca/ US= Arista; (lp)(c) **CHAMELEON**
Nov 85. Castle; (d-lp)(c)(cd) **THE COLLECTION** –
– Aristilus / Freefall / Supertwister / Spirit of the water / Lunar sea / The white rider / Earthrise / Song within a song / Rhayader – Rhayader goes to town – Migration – Rhayader alone – La princesse Perdue – The great marsh / Drafted / Captured / Sasquatch / Rain dances / Highways of the sun / First light.
May 91. Elite; (cd)(c) **LANDSCAPE** –
Jul 93. Camel; (cd) **CAMEL ON THE ROAD 1972 (live)** –

— In Jul 94, PETE BARDENS released cd 'BIG SKY' for 'H.T.D.'.

Patrick CAMPBELL-LYONS (see under ⇒ NIRVANA (Ire-UK))

CAMPER VAN BEETHOVEN

Formed: Redlands, Carifornia, USA . . . 1983 by DAVE LOWERY and DAVID McDANIELS, who had relocated to college in Santa Cruz. Signed to local indie label 'Pitch-A-Tent' label, where they issued eponymous lp in 1985. Arrived in Britain early 1987, after much airtime on John Peel Show for fave track 'TAKE THE SKINHEADS BOWLING'. Moved to 'Virgin' in 1988, although they never quite showed early appeal. • **Style:** Cow-punk outfit, influenced by BURRITO BROTHERS or JONATHAN RICHMAN, with witty and sarcastic avant-garde. • **Songwriters:** LOWERY except; I LOVE HER ALL THE TIME (Sonic Youth) / INTERSTELLAR OVERDRIVE (Pink Floyd) / PICTURES OF MATCHSTICK MEN (Status Quo). The MONKS OF DOOM covered; WHO ARE THE BRAIN POLICE? (Mothers Of Invention; Frank Zappa). • **Trivia:** Sessioned for EUGENE CHADBOURNE on his 1986 album.

Recommended: TELEPHONE FREE LANDSCAPE VICTORY (*6)

DAVE LOWERY – vocals, guitar, steel guitar / **JONATHAN SEGEL** – bass, guitar / **GREG LISHER** – guitar / **VICTOR KRUMMENBACKER** – bass / **CHRIS PEDERSON** – drums

Rough Trade Pitch A Tent

1985. (lp) **CAMPER VAN BEETHOVEN**
– Abundance / Cowboys from Hollywood / Sad lovers waltz / Turtlehead / I love her all the time / No flies on us / Down and out / No krugerrands for David / (Don't you go to) Goleta / 4 year plan / (We're a) Bad trip / Circles / Dustpan / Sometimes / Chain of circumstances / ZZ Top goes to Egypt.
Apr 86. (lp) **TELEPHONE FREE LANDSCAPE VICTORY**
– Cattle (reversed) / From another stone / No more bullshit / Take the skinheads bowling / Epigram No.2 / Cowboys from Hollywood / At Kuda? / Epigram No.1 / Colonel Enrique Adolfo Bermudas. *(above 2 lp's re-iss.1987 as d-lp)*
Aug 86. (7"ep)(12"ep) **TAKE THE SKINHEADS BOWLING. / ?**
(re-iss.Mar87)

— below featured **EUGENE CHADBOURNE** (of SHOCKABILLY)

Nov 86. (lp) **CAMPER VAN BEETHOVEN - THE 3RD LP** –
– Good guys, bad guys / Jo Stalin's Cadillac / Five sticks / Lulu land / Une fois / We saw Jerry's daughter / Surprise truck / Stairway to Heaven / The history of Utah / Still wishing to course / We love you / Hoe yourself down / Peace & love / Folly / Interstellar overdrive / Shut us down. *(cd-iss.Apr87)*
Oct 87. (12"ep) **GOOD GUYS, BAD GUYS. / ?**
Nov 87. (lp) **VAMPIRE CAN MATING OVEN** –
– Opi rides again / Club Med sucks / Oh no / Where the hell is Bill? / etc. *(on 'Pitch-A-Tent' US)*

— In Feb 88, they teamed up with EUGENE CHADBOURNE on lp 'CAMPER VAN CHADBOURNE' on 'Fundamental' records.

Virgin America Virgin

May 88. (lp)(c)(cd) **OUR BELOVED REVOLUTIONARY SWEET-HEART**

– Eye of Fatima (pt.1) / Turquoise jewelry / O death / She divines water / Devil song / One of these days / Waka / Change your mind / My path belated / Never go back / Eye of Fatima (pt.2) / Tania / Life is grand / The fool.

Sep 88. (7") **LIFE IS GRAND. / LOVE IS A WEED**
(12"+=)(cd-s+=) – Harmony in my head / Wade in the water.

—— **MORGAN FICHTER** – violin, vocals repl. SEGEL

Jan 90. (lp)(c)(cd) **KEY LIME PIE**
– Opening theme / Jack Ruby / Sweethearts / When I win the lottery / (I was born in a) Laundromat / Borderline / The light from a cake / June / All her favourite fruit / Interlude / Flowers / The humid press of days / Pictures of matchstick men / Come on darkness.

Jan 90. (7") **PICTURES OF MATCHSTICK MEN. / JACK RUBY**
(12"+=) – Closing theme / The humid press of days.

—— Disbanded after Spring 1990. LOWERY formed CRACKER, the others formed . . .

MONKS OF DOOM

SEGEL, PEDERSON, USHER + KRUMMENBACKER

C/Z C/Z

Aug 92. (cd)(m-lp) **THE INSECT GOD**

CAN

Formed: Cologne, Germany ... 1968 by CZUKAY, SCHMIDT and KAROLI. Signed to 'United Art' in 1970 and released debut lp 'MONSTER MOVIE', before unleashing the improvised beauty 'TAGO MAGO' (1971). Continued to be part of continental scene, and signed to Richard Branson's 'Virgin', where they had surprise UK Top 30 hit 45 with 'I WANT MORE' (1976). • **Style:** Avant-garde free-form experimental rock, that was influenced by JOHN CAGE, TERRY RILEY and The VELVET UNDERGROUND. The latter more so, in which hypnotic basic rhythms were interspersed with dour but effective vox. By 1977 they shifted into African /reggae style with introduction of ROSKO. • **Songwriters:** Group compositions, except I WANT MORE (David Gilmour) / CAN-CAN (Offenbach). • **Trivia:** The FALL payed homage to them by crediting a song as 'I AM DAMO SUZUKI'.

Recommended: CANNIBALISM (*8) / TAGO MAGO (*7)

IRMIN SCHMIDT – keyboards / **HOLGER CZUKAY** – bass, electronics / **DAVID JOHNSON** – flute / **MICHAEL KAROLI** (b.28 Apr'48) – guitar, violin / **JAKI LIEBZEIT** – drums / **MALCOLM MOONEY** – vocals

not issued Music Factory G'MANY

Nov 68. (7") **KAMA SUTRA. /**

—— Now a quintet when JOHNSON departed

Aug 69. (lp-500 copies) **DELAY 1968**
– Butterfly / Pnoom / 19th century man / Thief / Man named Joe / Uphill / Little star of Bethlehem. *(re-iss'81 on 'Spoon' GERMANY)(cd-iss.Jun89 on 'Spoon/Mute')*

United Art United Art G'MANY

May 70. (lp) **MONSTER MOVIE**
– Father cannot yell / Mary, Mary so contrary / You doo right / Outside my door. *(cd-iss.Jun89 on 'Mute')*

—— **KENJI 'DAMO' SUZUKI** – vocals repl.MOONEY who suffered nervous breakdown

not issued Liberty

Sep 70. (lp) **SOUNDTRACKS** Germ'y
– Deadlock / Tango whiskeyman / Don't turn the light off / Leave me alone / Soul desert / Mother sky / She brings the rain. *(UK-rel.Jun73 on 'United Artists') (cd-iss.Jun89 on 'Mute')*

1970. (7") **SOUL DESERT. / SHE BRINGS THE RAIN**

Feb 71. (d-lp) **TAGO MAGO** Feb 72
– Paperhouse / Mushroom / Oh yeah / Halleluwah / Aumgh / Peking O / Bring me coffee or tea. *(cd-iss.Jul89 on 'Mute')*

1971. (7") **TURTLES HAVE SHORT LEGS. / HALLELUWAH (edit)**

1971. (7") **SPOON. / SHIKAKO MARU TEN**
(from now just UK releases are mentioned to avoid confusion!?)

United Art United Art

Nov 72. (7") **SPOON. / I'M SO GREEN**

Nov 72. (lp) **EGE BAMYASI**
– Pinch / Sing swan song / One more night / Vitamin C / Soup / I'm so green / Spoon. *(cd-iss.Jun89 on 'Mute')*

Jun 73. (lp) **FUTURE DAYS**
– Future days / Spray / Moonshake / Bel Air. *(cd-iss.Jun89 on 'Mute')*

Oct 73. (7") **MOONSHAKE. / FUTURE DAYS (edit)**

—— Trimmed to a quartet when DAMO SUZUKI left to become Jehovah's witness. Now **SCHMIDT / KAROLI** (shared vocals) **CZUKAY** and **LIEBEZEIT**

Nov 74. (lp) **SOON OVER BABALUMA**
– Dizzy dizzy / Come sta la luna / Splash / Chain reaction / Quantum physics / Soon over Babaluma. *(cd-iss.Jun89 on 'Mute')*

Dec 74. (7") **DIZZY DIZZY (edit). / SPLASH (edit)**

Virgin Polydor

Sep 75. (lp) **LANDED**
– Full moon on the highway / Half past one / Hunters and collectors / Vernal equinox / Red hot Indians / Unfinished. *(cd-iss.Jun87)*

—— approx Mar76, tried two vocalists one a Malayan, the other **MICHAEL COUSINS** (English). added **DAVID GILMOUR** – guest/composer (3) b.vocals of PINK FLOYD

Jul 76. (7") **I WANT MORE. / ... AND MORE** 26
(re-iss.May81)

Oct 76. (lp) **FLOW MOTION**
– I want more / Cascade waltz / Laugh till you cry ... live till you die / ...And more / Babylonian pearl / Smoke (E.F.S. No.59) / Flow motion. *(cd-iss.Jun87)*

Nov 76. (7") **SILENT NIGHT. / CASCADE WALTZ**

—— added **ROSKO GEE** – bass (ex-TRAFFIC) (HOLGER now synths., samplers)

Mar 77. (lp) **SAW DELIGHT**
– Don't say no / Sunshine day and night / Call me / Animal waves / Fly by night. *(cd-iss.Jun87)*

Apr 77. (7") **DON'T SAY NO. / RETURN**

—— HOLGER went on a few holidays. The rest of the band below (**SCHMIDT, KAROLI, LIEBEZEIT & GEE**) recorded album. CZUKAY went solo

Lightning not issued

Jun 78. (7") **CAN-CAN. / CAN BE**

Jul 78. (lp) **OUT OF REACH**
– Serpentine / Pauper's daughter and I / November / Seven days awake / Give me no roses / Like Inobe God / One more day. *(re-iss.Jun86 on 'Thunderbolt')*

—— The split late '78. JAKI formed PHANTOM BAND and collaborated with HOLGER. IRMIN went solo and formed BRUNO SPOERRI. MICHAEL in '84 went solo. All their releases were mainly German only. **CAN** reformed 1969 line-up 20 years on.

Mercury not issued?

Oct 89. (lp)(c)(cd) **RITE TIME**
– On the beautiful side of a romance / The without law man / Below this level (patient's song) / Movin' right along / Like a new world / Hoolah hoolah / Give the drummer some. *(cd-iss.Oct94 on 'Spoon')*

White Label not issued

Sep 90. (cd)(c)(lp) **FISHERMAN'S FRIEND REMIXES**

– compilations etc. –

Aug 74. United Artists; (lp) **LIMITED EDITION** (ltd 15,000)

Oct 78. United Artists; (lp) **CANNIBALISM**
– Uphill / Pnoom / Connection / Mother Upduff / Little star / T.V. spot / Doko E. / Turtles have short legs / Shikaku maru ten / Gomorrha / Blue bag / Red hot Indians / Half past one / Flow motion / Smoke / I want more . . .and more / Laugh till you cry / Aspectacle animal waves / Sunshine day and night / E.P.S. No.7 / Melting away. *(cd-iss.Nov92 on Grey Area-Mute)*

May 76. Caroline; (d-lp) **UNLIMITED EDITION (early rare)**
(cd-iss.Nov91 on 'Spoon')

Nov 76. Sunset; (lp) **OPENER (71-74 material)**

Jul 79. Laser; (lp) **CAN**
(re-iss.Feb85 as 'INNER SPACE' on 'Thunderbolt', cd-iss.Jun87)

May 81. Virgin/ US= Polydor; (12") **I WANT MORE. / SILENT NIGHT / ... AND MORE**

Oct 81. Virgin/ US= Polydor; (lp) **INCANDESCENCE**

Mar 83. Cherry Red; (12"ep) **MOONSHAKE. / TURTLES HAVE SHORT LEGS / ONE MORE NIGHT**

Feb 95. Spoon; (cd) **CANNIBALISM III**

Sep 95. Strange Fruit; (cd) **LIVE AT THE BBC**

Oct 95. Strange Fruit; (cd) **THE PEEL SESSIONS**

HOLGER CZUKAY

Music Factory not issued

1968. (lp) **CANAXIS 5 ("HOLGER CZUKAY with ROLF DAMMERS")** Germ'y
– Boat woman song / Canaxis. *(cd-iss.Feb95 on 'Spoon')*

CZUKAY with other CAN members augenting

E.M.I. not issued

Nov 79. (7") **COOL IN THE POOL. / OH LORD GIVE US MORE MONEY** *(re-iss.Jul83)*

Jan 80. (lp)(c) **MOVIES**
– Cool in the pool / Oh Lord give us some money / Persian love / Hollywood symphony.

Feb 82. (lp)(c) **ON THE WAY TO THE PEAK OF NORMAL**
– Ode to perfume / On the way to the peak of normal / Witches multiplication table / Two bass shuffle / Hiss'n'listen.

Mar 82. (7") **ODE TO PERFUME. / PERSIAN LOVE**

—— next 2 as **HOLGER CZUKAY, JAKI LIEBEZEIT & JAH WOBBLE**

Virgin not issued

1982. (lp)(c) **FULL CIRCLE** Germ.

Island not issued

Jun 81. (12"ep) **HOW MUCH ARE THEY? / WHERE'S THE MONEY?. / TRENCH WARFARE / TWILIGHT WORLD**
(re-iss.1988 on 'Licensed')

Oct 82. (m-lp)(c) **SNAKE CHARMER (as "HOLGER CZUKAY, JAH WOBBLE & THE EDGE")**
– Snake charmer / Hold on to your dreams / It was a camel / Sleazy / Snake charmer (reprise).

Virgin not issued

May 84. (lp)(c) **DER OSTEN IST ROT**
– The photo song / Bankel rap '82 / Michy / Rhonrad / Collage / Esperanto socialiste / Der osten ist rot / Das massenmedium / Schave vertraucnsvdl in die zukunft / Traun mal wieder. *(re-iss.Apr86)*

May 84. (7") **THE PHOTO SONG. / DAS MASSENMEDIUM**
(12"+=) – Biomutanten.

Jan 87. (lp)(c)(cd) **ROME REMAINS ROME**
– Hey ba ba re bob / Blessed Easter / Sudentenland / Hit hit flop flop / Perfect world / Music in the air. (cd+=) – DER OSTEN IST ROT (lp)

collaborated next Mar88 on album PLIGHT AND PREMONITION with DAVID SYLVIAN (see: JAPAN ⇒).

—— Next with **SHELDON ANGEL** – vocals / **M.KAROLI** – guitar / **J.LIEBEZEIT** – drums

Jan 91. (cd)(c)(lp) **RADIO WAVE SURFER**
– Rhine, water / It ain't no crime / I got weird dreams / Saturday night movie / Dr.Oblivion / We can fight all night / Get it sweet / Ride a radio wave / Atmosphere tuning / Voice of Bulgaria / Late night radio / Through the freezing snow / Encore.

HOLGER CZUKAY also released in Germany 1980 with CONRAD PLANK & AXEL GROS, a 12"m LES VAMPYRETTES on 'Electrola' label.

JAKI LIEBEZEIT

with his group (who released on German labels)
PHANTOM BAND with others **DOMINIK VON SENGER** – guitar / **HELMUT ZERLETT** – keys / **ELEK GELBA** – percussion

Sky / not issued

1980. (lp) **PHANTOM BAND** [-] [-]
1981. (lp) **FREEDOM OF SPEECH** [-] [-]

Spoon / not issued

1984. (lp) **NOWHERE** [-] [-]

— In 1981 he and CZUKAY teamed up with PHEW on lp PHEW. ('Pass' label)

IRMIN SCHMIDT

(solo) on German labels

Spoon / not issued

1980. (lp) **FILM MUSIK** [-] [-]
1981. (lp) **TOY PLANET ("with BRUNO SPOERRI")** [-] [-]
1981. (lp) **FILM MUSIK VOL.2** [-] [-]
Jun 84. (d-lp) **FILM MUSIK VOLS. 3 & 4** [-] [-]

— In 1983 he issued other German album 'ROTE ERDE' on 'Teldec'.

W.E.A. / not issued

1987. (lp)(c) **MUSIC AT DUSK** [ ] [-]
– Left into silence / Love / Roll on, Euphrates / The great escape / Villa wunderbar / The child in history / Alcohol.

Venture / not issued

Apr 90 (cd)(c)(lp)**TOY PLANET** [ ] [-]
– The seven game / Toy Planet / Two dolphins go dancing / Yom tov / Spring lite rite / Rapido de noir / When the workers came to life.

Mute / not iss.

Nov 92. (cd) **IMPOSSIBLE HOLIDAYS** [ ] [ ]
– Dreamtime / Le weekend / Surprise / Shudder of love / Lullaby big / Time the dreamkiller / German ghast drift.

— Virgin issued 'FILM MUSIK VOL.5' in 1989.
MICHAEL KAROLI with **POLLY ESTES** also released DELUGE (lp) in 1984 on 'Spoon'
— **DAMO SUZUKI** with band DUNKEIZIFFER, released in 1984 (lp) **IN THE NIGHT**

CANADIAN SQUIRES (see under ⇒ BAND)

CANDLEBOX

Formed: Beverly Hills, California, USA . . . 1992 by (see below). Their eponymous debut album released on MADONNA's 'Maverick' label in mid-93, made a steady rise to the US Top 10 a year later. • **Style:** Grunge /hard rock. • **Songwriters:** MARTIN lyrics / group compositions except VOODOO CHILE (Jimi Hendrix). • **Trivia:** For Info write to; CANDLEBOX, 11012 Ventura Bl., Suite 299, Studio City, CA 91604.

Recommended: CANDLEBOX (*6)

KEVIN MARTIN – vocals / **PETER KLETT** – guitar / **BARDI MARTIN** – bass / **SCOTT MERCADO** – drums

Maverick-Sire / Maverick-Sire

Jul 93. (cd)(c) **CANDLEBOX** [ ] [7]
– Don't you / Change / You / No sense / Far behind / Blossom / Arrow / Rain / Mothers dream / Cover me / He calls home.
Mar 94. (c-s)(cd-s) **YOU. /** [-] [78]
Aug 94. (7")(c-s) **FAR BEHIND. / YOU (live)** [ ] [18]
(cd-s+=) – Live medley: Far behind – Voodoo chile (slight return).
Sep 95. (cd)(c) **LUCY** [ ] [11]
– Simple lessons / Drowned / Lucy / Best friend / Become (to tell) / Understanding / Crooked halo / Bothered / Butterfly / It's amazing / Vulgar before me / Butterfly (reprise).

CANNED HEAT

Formed: Los Angeles, USA . . . 1966 by HITE and WILSON. Appeared at 1967 Monterey Festival, which led them to sign for 'Liberty'. During the late 60's and early 70's, they clocked-up a few classic hit singles including 'ON THE ROAD AGAIN', 'GOING UP THE COUNTRY' and 'LET'S WORK TOGETHER'. • **Style:** Hard – rock boogie that evolved from jug-band music, and which featured HITE the very large bearded dual singer. His and WILSON's death put paid to any real kind of group reincarnation (see below). Inspired in almost every way by black bluesman JOHN LEE HOOKER. • **Songwriters:** HITE and WILSON, except LET'S WORK TOGETHER (Wilbert Harrison) / ROLLIN' AND TUMBLIN' (Muddy Waters) / WOOLY BULLY (Sam The Sham & The Pharoahs) / SUGAR BEE (Cleveland Crotchet) / BULLDOZE BLUES (Henry Thomas). • **Trivia:** 'Blind Owl' WILSON was so-called due to his bespectacled eyes.

Recommended: CANNED HEAT COOKBOOK (*9).

BOB 'THE BEAR' HITE (b.26 Feb'45, Torrance, California) – vocals, harmonica / **AL 'BLIND OWL' WILSON** (b. 4 Jul'43, Boston, Mass) – vocals, guitar, harmon.. / **HENRY VESTINE** (b.25 Dec'44, Washington DC) – guitar (ex-MOTHERS OF../**ZAPPA) / LARRY TAYLOR**(b.SAMUEL TAYLOR, 26 Jun'42, Brooklyn, New York) – bass repl. MARK ANDES who had repl. STUART BROTMAN (to KALEIDOSCOPE) / **FRANK COOK** – drums

Liberty / Liberty

Aug 67. (lp) **CANNED HEAT** [ ] [76]
– Rollin' and tumblin' / Bullfrog blues / Evil is going on / Goin' down slow / Catfish blues / Dust my broom / Help me / Big road blues / The story of my life / The road song / Rich woman. *(re-iss.Feb73 as 'ROLLIN' & TUMBLIN'' on 'Sunset') (re-iss.Jun89 on 'See for Miles' cd-iss.Aug90)*
1968. (7") **ROLLIN' AND TUMBLIN'. / BULLFROG BLUES** [ ] [ ]

— **FITO 'ADOLPHO' DE LA PARRA** (b. 3 Feb'46, Mexico) – drums (ex-BLUESBERRY JAM) repl. COOK

Mar 68. (7") **EVIL WOMAN. / THE WORLD IS A JUDGE** [-] [ ]
May 68. (7") **ON THE ROAD AGAIN. / BOOGIE MUSIC** [-] [16]
May 68. (7") **ON THE ROAD AGAIN. / THE WORLD IN A JUG** [8] [-]
(re-iss.Sep75 on 'United Art')
Jun 68. (lp) **BOOGIE WITH CANNED HEAT** [5] [16] Feb 68
– Evil woman / My crime / On the road again / World in a jug / Turpentine moan / Whiskey headed woman No.2 / Amphetamine Annie / An owl song / Marie Laveau / Fried hockey boogie. *(re-iss.Feb86 on 'See for Miles', cd-iss.Feb90)*
Dec 68. (7") **GOING UP THE COUNTRY. / ONE KIND FAVOUR** [19] [11]
Dec 68. (d-lp) **LIVING THE BLUES** [ ] [18]
– Pony blues / My mistake / Sandy's blues / Going up the country / Walking by myself / Boogie music / One kind favour / Parthenogenesis:- Nebulosity – Rollin' and tumblin' – Five owls – Bear wires – Snooky flowers – Sunflower power – Ragi Kafi – Icebag – Childhood's / Refried the boogie (part 1 – live) / Refried the boogie (part 2 – live). *(re-iss.Jul87 on 'See for Miles' cd-iss.Feb90)*
Apr 69. (7") **TIME WAS. / LOW DOWN** [ ] [67] Mar 69

— **HARVEY MANDEL** (b.1946, Detroit, Michegan) – guitar (+ solo artist) repl. VESTINE

Aug 69. (lp) **HALLELUJAH** [ ] [37]
– Same all over / Change my ways / Canned Heat / Sic 'em pigs / I'm her man / Time was / Do not enter / Big fat / Huautla / Get off my back / Down in the gutter, but free. *(re-iss.Feb89 on 'See for Miles', cd-iss.Aug90)*
Sep 69. (7") **POOR MAN. / SIC 'EM PIGS** [ ] [ ]
Dec 69. (7") **CHANGE MY WAYS. / GET OFF MY BACK** [-] [ ]
Jan 70. (lp) **CANNED HEAT COOKBOOK** (compilation) [8] [86]
– Bullfrog blues / Rollin' and tumblin' / Going up the country / Time was / Boogie music / On the road again / Same all over / Sic 'em pigs / Fried hockey boogie / I will wait for you. *(re-iss.Nov75 on 'Sunset')*
Jan 70. (7") **LET'S WORK TOGETHER. / I'M HER MAN** [2] [26] Oct 70
Jun 70. (7") **SUGAR BEE. / SHAKE IT AND BREAK IT** [49] [-]
Jun 70. (lp) **CANNED HEAT '70 CONCERT (live in Europe)** [15] [ ] Jul71
– That's all right mama / Bring it on home / Pulling hair blues / Back out on the road – On the road again / London blues / Let's work together / Goodbye for now. *(re-iss.1988)*

— **ANTONIO DE LA BARREDA** (aka TONY OLAV) – bass repl. LARRY TAYLOR

Sep 70. (7") **FUTURE BLUES. / SKAT** [ ] [-]
Sep 70. (lp)(c) **FUTURE BLUES** [27] [59]
– Sugar bee / Shake it and break it / That's all right mama / My time ain't long / Scat / Let's work together / London blues / So sad (the world's in a tangle) / Future blues. *(re-iss.+cd Jul89 on 'B.G.O.')*

— On 3rd Sep70, **AL WILSON** suffering depression died of drug o/d. He appeared on the releases below until stated.

Dec 70. (7") **CHRISTMAS BLUES. / DO NOT ENTER** [ ] [-]
Jan 71. (7") **WOOLY BULLY. / MY TIME AIN'T LONG** [ ] [ ]

— **HENRY VESTINE** – guitar returned to repl. MANDEL who returned to JOHN MAYALL.

Mar 71. (d-lp)(d-c) **HOOKER'N'HEAT ("CANNED HEAT / JOHN LEE HOOKER")** [ ] [73] Feb 71
– Messin' with the Hook / The feelin' is gone / Send me your pillow / Sittin' here thinkin' / Meet me in the bottom / Altmonia blues / Drifter / You talk too much / Burning Hell / Bottle up and go / The world today / I got my eyes on you / Whiskey and wimmen' / Just you and me / Let's make it / Peavine / Boogie chillen No.2. *(re-iss.Sep88 as lp 'THE BEST OF HOOKER'N'HEAT' on 'See for Miles') (also cd-iss.Aug89 as 'HOOKER'N'HEAT (THE BEST OF PLUS)')*

— **HOOKER** – blues guitarist

— **JOEL SCOTT HILL** – guitar, vocals finally repl. AL WILSON, now alongside **HITE, BARREDA, PARRA and VESTINE**

United Art / United Art

Mar 71. (7") **LET'S MAKE IT (w/JOHN LEE HOOKER). / WHISKEY AND WIMMEN** [-] [ ]
Sep 71. (7") **LONG WAY FROM L.A.. / HILL'S STOMP** [ ] [ ]

— **LITTLE RICHARD** – piano, vocals guested on next album

Mar 72. (lp)(c) **HISTORICAL FIGURES AND ANCIENT HEADS** [ ] [87]
– Sneakin' around / Hill's stomp / Rockin' with the king / I don't care what you tell me / Long way from L.A. / Cherokee dance / That's all right / Utah. *(re-iss.+cd.Aug90 on 'B.G.O.')*
Apr 72. (7") **ROCKIN' WITH THE KING. / I DON'T CARE WHAT YOU TELL ME** [ ] [88] Mar 72
Jul 72. (7") **CHEROKEE DANCE. / SNEAKIN' AROUND** [-] [ ]

— **RICHARD HITE** – bass (BOB's brother) (ex-POPPA HOP) repl. BARREDA. Added **JAMES SHANE** – guitar / **ED BEYER** – keyboards

Jun 73. (7") **KEEP IT CLEAN. / YOU CAN RUN, BUT YOU SURE CAN'T HIDE** [ ] [ ]
Sep 73. (lp)(c) **NEW AGE** [ ] [ ]
– Keep it clean / Harley Davidson blues / Don't deceive me / You can run, but you sure can't hide / Rock and roll music / Lookin' for my rainbow / Framed / Election blues / So long wrong *(cd-iss.May91 on 'B.G.O.')*
Sep 73. (7") **LOOKIN' FOR MY RAINBOW. / ROCK AND ROLL MUSIC** [-] [ ]
Nov 73. (7") **HARLEY DAVIDSON BLUES. /** [-] [ ]

Atlantic / Atlantic

Feb 74. (7") **ONE MORE RIVER TO CROSS. / HIGHWAY 401** [ ] [ ]
Mar 74. (lp) **ONE MORE RIVER TO CROSS** [ ] [ ]
– L.A. town / I need someone / Bagful of boogie / I'm a hog for you baby / You am what I am / Shake rattle & roll / Bright times are comin' / Highway 401 / We remember Fats.
1975. (7") **THE HARDER THEY COME. / ROCK 'N' ROLL SHOW** [-] [ ]

— **RICHARD HITE** and **FITO DE LA PARRA** took over control of band when BOB & HENRY got stoned. ED BAYER also departed. Recruited **CHRIS MORGAN** – guitar / **GENE TAYLOR** – keyboards (both ex-POPPA HOP)

Sonet Takoma

Dec 78. (lp) **THE HUMAN CONDITION**
– Strut my stuff / Hot money / House of blue lights / Just got to be there / You just got the rock / Human condition / She's lookin' good / Open up your backdoor / Wrapped up.

— (later in 70's) **BOB HITE** returned (he was to die of heart attack 4th Apr81)

— re-united + re-formed with **FITO, VESTINE,** and **TAYLOR** and others, **RAUL E. RODRIGUEZ + F.M. HALEY.**

not issued Destiny

1981. (lp) **KINGS OF THE BOOGIE** -
– Kings of the boogie / Stoned bad street fighting man / So fine / You just can't get close to me / Hell's just on down the road / I was wrong / Little crystal / Dog house blues / Sleepy hollow baby / Chicken shack.

not issued A.L.A.

1984. (12"ep) **THE HEAT BROS '84** -

— **JAMES THORNBERRY** – guitar repl. VESTINE.

Bedrock ?

Dec 87. (lp-blue) **THE BOOGIE ASSAULT (LIVE IN AUSTRALIA)**
– Kings of the boogie / Stoned bad street fighting man / So fine / You just can't get close to me / Hell's just on down the road / I was wrong / Little crystal / Dog house blues / Sleepy hollow baby / Chicken shack.

Topic Topic

Sep 93. (cd)(c) **BURNIN' (Recorded live in Australia 1990)**
– Let's work together / Gamblin' woman / Hucklebuck / Sunnyland / Rollin' and tumblin' / Nitwit / Gunstreet girl / One way out / J.J. jump / Mercury blues.

Aim Aim

Jul 95. (cd) **INTERNAL COMBUSTION**

– compilations etc. –

Aug 89. Liberty; (7") **LET'S WORK TOGETHER. / GOIN' UP THE COUNTRY**
(12"+=) – Rollin' and tumblin'.
(cd-s+=) – Amphetamine Annie.

Sep 89. Liberty; (lp)(c)(cd) **LET'S WORK TOGETHER (THE BEST OF CANNED HEAT)**
– On the road again / Bullfrog blues / Rollin' and tumblin' / Amphetamine / Annie / Fried hockey boogie / Sic 'em pigs / Poor Moon / Let's work together / Going up the country / Boogie music / Same all over / Time was / Sugar bee / Rockin' with the king / That's alright mama / My time ain't long.

Jan 70. Pye Int./ US= Janus; (lp) **VINTAGE HEAT**

Jun 70. Pye Int./ US= Janus; (7") **SPOONFUL. / BIG ROAD BLUES**

Jul 75. Barclay France; (lp) **MEMPHIS HEAT (with MEMPHIS SLIM)** - -

Nov 76. United Artists; (7"ep) **REMEMBER CANNED HEAT**
– On the road again / Let's work together / Going up the country.

Nov 76. D.J.M./ US= Scepter; (lp)(c) **LIVE AT TOPANGA CORRAL (live)**
(re-iss.'81 pic-lp as 'DOG HOUSE BLUES')

May 84. EMI-Golden; (7") **ON THE ROAD AGAIN. / LET'S WORK TOGETHER**

Nov 92. E.M.I.; (3xcd-box) **THE BIG HEAT**

1987. Rhino; (d-lp) **INFINITE BOOGIE** -

Feb 88. Rhino; (lp)(c)(cd) **HOOKER'N'HEAT VOL.2 (with JOHN LEE HOOKER)** -

Oct 88. Beat Goes On; (lp)(c) **70: LIVE IN EUROPE (live)**
(cd-iss.Sep89)

Feb 92. Thunderbolt; (cd) **STRAIGHT AHEAD** -

Apr 93. Pulsar; (cd) **BIG ROAD BLUES** -

Jul 94. Success; (cd)(c) **ROLLIN' AND TUMBLIN'** -

Aug 94. E.M.I.; (d-cd) **UNCANNED** -

Feb 95. B.A.M.; (cd) **PEARLS OF THE PAST** -

Jim CAPALDI (see under ⇒ TRAFFIC)

CAPTAIN AMERICA (see under ⇒ VASELINES)

CAPTAIN BEEFHEART & HIS MAGIC BAND

Formed: Los Angeles, California, USA . . . 1964 by VAN VLIET, former school mate of FRANK ZAPPA. Adopted his name from B-movie CAPTAIN BEEFHEART MEETS THE GRUNT PEOPLE. He and his band signed to 'A&M' in 1965 and recorded two singles before moving to 'Buddah' records to record seminal 'SAFE AS MILK' lp 1967. For the next 15 years, he and his band, became one of rock's most diverse acts. • **Style:** From early R&B roots, to weird and wonderful rock that held no barriers, supplanting new styles and imagery concocted by the grunting, HOWLIN' WOLF influenced BEEFHEART. The British public hailed 'TROUT MASK REPLICA' as one of all-time classics, although it verged between mad eccentricity or just alien being. • **Songwriters:** BEEFHEART with DRUMBO arranging/dictating instruments played. Covered: HARD WORKIN' MAN (Jack Nitzche). • **Trivia:** Championed by many bands as major influence (e.g. PERE UBU, STUMP, SHRUBS, MacKENZIES, etc., etc.).

Recommended: SAFE AS MILK (*9) / TROUT MASK REPLICA (*9) / MIRROR MAN (*8) / LICK MY DECALS OFF, BABY (*8) / THE SPOTLIGHT KID (*8) / CLEAR SPOT (*7).

CAPTAIN BEEFHEART (b.DON VAN VLIET, 15 Jan'41, Glendale, California, USA) – vocals, harmonica, occasional guitar, wind instruments / **ALEX ST.CLAIRE** – guitar / **DOUG MOON** – guitar / **JERRY HANDLEY** – bass / **PAUL BLAKELY** – drums

not issued A&M

1966. (7") **DIDDY WAH DIDDY. / WHO DO YOU THINK YOOU'RE FOOLING (*)** -

1966. (7") **MOONCHILD (*). / FRYING PAN** -
(these tracks became a UK 7"ep in '71. Also resurfacing as UK 12"ep Oct84 'THE LEGENDARY A&M SESSIONS' + 'Here I am, I always am' re-iss.Oct86 on 'Edsel', cd-iss.May92)*

— **The CAPTAIN** recruited an entire new band . . . **RY COODER** – slide guitar repl. MOON and ST.CLAIRE (they later joined DENNY KING) / **HERB BERMANN** – bass, co-composer repl. HANDLEY / **JOHN FRENCH** (DRUMBO) – drums repl. BLAKELY

Pye Int. Kama Sutra

Jan 68. (7") **YELLOW BRICK ROAD. / ABBA ZABA**

Feb 68. (lp) **SAFE AS MILK**
– Sure 'nuff 'n yes I do / Zig zag wanderer / Call on me / Dropout boogie / I'm glad / Electricity / Yellow brick road / Abba zaba / Plastic factory / Where there's woman / Plastic factory / Grown so ugly / Autumn's child. *(re-iss.'69, re-iss.Jan82 on 'PRT', re-iss.Jul85 on 'Buddah')*

— **JEFF COTTON** (ANTENNAE JIMMY SEMENS) **-guitar** repl. COODER who went solo

not issued Buddah

1968. (lp) **MIRROR MAN** (rec.1965) -
– Tarot plane / Kandy korn / 25th century Quaker / Mirror man. *(finally released UK May71, reached No.49)(re-iss.Aug74, re-iss.May82 on 'PRT', re-iss.Apr86 on 'Edsel')*

Liberty Blue Thumb

Dec 68. (lp) **STRICTLY PERSONAL**
– Ah feel like acid / Safe as milk / Trust us / Son of Mirror Man – Mere man / On tomorrow / Beatles bones 'n' smokin' stones / Gimme that harp boy / Kandy korn. *(cd-iss.Aug94 on 'EMI')*

— **The CAPTAIN** retained **DRUMBO** and **ANTANNAE** plus new members **ZOOT HORN ROLLO** (b.BILL HARKLEROAD) – brass, narrator, guitar, flute / **ROCKETTE NORTON** (b.MARK BOSTON) – bass, narrator repl. HERB / **THE MASCARA SNAKE** (b.VICTOR HAYDEN) – clarinet / guest **DOUG MOON** returned

Straight Straight

Nov 69. (d-lp) **TROUT MASK REPLICA** 21
– Frownland / The dust blows forward 'n dust blows back / Dachau blues / Ella guru / Hair pie: bake 1 / Moonlight on Vermont / Hair pie: bake 2 / Pena / Well / When big Joan sets up / Fallin' ditch / Sugar 'n spikes / Ant man bee / Pachuco cadaver / Bills corpse / Sweet sweet bulbs / Neon meate dream of an octafish / China pig / My human gets me blues / Dali's car / Orange claw hammer / Wild life / She's too much for my mirror / Hobo chang ba / The blimp (mousetrap replica) / Steal softly thru snow / Old fart at play / Veteran's day poppy. *(re-iss.May75 on 'Reprise') (re-iss.cd Sep94 on 'WEA')*

— **ED MARIMBA** (ART TRIPP) – marimba (ex-MOTHERS OF INVENTION) repl. THE MASCARA SNAKE

Jan 71. (lp) **LICK MY DECALS OFF BABY** 20
– Lick my decals off, baby / Doctor Dark / I love you, you big dummy / Peon / Bellerin' plain / Woe-is-uh-me-bop / Japan in a dishpan / I wanna find a woman that'll hold my big toe till I have a go / Petrified forest / One rose that I mean / The Buggy boogie woogie / The Smithsonian Institute blues (or the big dig) / Space-age couple / The clouds are full of wine (not whiskey or rye) / Flash Gordon's ape. *(re-iss.Jul73 on 'Reprise')*

— **THE WINGED EEL FINGERLING** (r.n. ELLIOT INGBER) – guitar, etc. (ex-MOTHERS etc.) repl. SEMENS who had already formed MU

Reprise Reprise

Jan 72. (7") **CLICK CLACK. / I'M GONNA BOOGLARIZE YOU BABY** -

Feb 72. (lp) **THE SPOTLIGHT KID ("CAPTAIN BEEFHEART")** 44
– I'm gonna booglarize you baby / White jam / Blabber 'n smoke / When it blows its stacks / Alice in Blunderland / The spotlight kid / Click clack / Grow fins / There ain't no Santa Claus on the evenin' stage / Glider.

— **ROY 'OREJON' ESTRADA** – bass (ex-LITTLE FEAT, ex-MOTHERS OF INVENTION) repl. INGBER. ROCKETTE moved to guitar, and augmented by backing vocals The **BLACKBERRIES / RUSS TITELMAN** – guitar (guested, as he did on "Safe as Milk")

Nov 72. (lp) **CLEAR SPOT**
– Low yo yo stuff / Nowadays a woman's gotta hit a man / Too much time / Circumstances / My head is my only house unless it rains / Sun zoom sparks / Clear spot / Crazy little thing / Long neck bottles / Her eyes are a blue million miles / Big eyed beans from Venus / Golden birdies. *(US re-iss.Jul87)*

Mar 73. (7") **TOO MUCH TIME. / MY HEAD IS MY ONLY HOUSE UNLESS IT RAINS**

— **ALEX ST.CLAIRE** – guitar returned to repl. ROY. Added **MARK MERCELLO** – keyboards

Virgin Mercury

Apr 74. (lp)(c) **UNCONDITIONALLY GUARENTEED**
– Upon the my-oh-my / Sugar bowl / New electric ride / Magic be / Happy love song / Full Moon, hot Sun / I got love on my mind / This is the day / Lazy music / Peaches. *(re-iss.Aug82+Aug85 on 'Fame') (cd-iss.Jun88)*

Apr 74. (7") **UPON THE MY-OH-MY. / MAGIC BE** -

Apr 74. (7") **UPON THE MY-OH-MY. / I GOT LOVE ON MY MIND** -

— **ELLIOT INGBER** – guitar returned to repl. ST.CLAIRE plus session men **MARK GIBBONS, MICHAEL SMOTHERMAN, JIMMY CARAVAN** – all keyboards repl. MARCELLO.

— **DEAN SMITH** – guitar / **BOB WEST** – bass / **GENE PELLO** – drums / **TV GRIMES** – percussion

Nov 74. (lp)(c) **BLUEJEANS AND MOONBEAMS**
– Party of special things do / Same old blues / Observatory crest / Pompadour swamp / Captain's holiday / Rock'n'roll's evil doll / Further than we've gone / Twist ah luck / Bluejeans and moonbeams. *(re-iss.Mar84) (cd-iss.Jun88)*

— Late '75 **BEEFHEART** collaborated with **FRANK ZAPPA** on **"BONGO FURY"** album. This was a near live album with 2 studio tracks.

— His new touring band featured past members **ELLIOT, INGBER** and **JOHN FRENCH** plus **DENNY WHALLEY** – slide guitar / **BRUCE FOWLER** – trombone (both on bongos)

— His '76 band were **DRUMBO, WHALLEY, JEFF MORRIS TEPPER** – guitar, and **JOHN THOMAS** – piano. They recorded first sessions for the next album

— **ERIC DREW FELDMAN** – keyboards, bass repl. THOMAS / **ROBERT WILLIAMS** – drums repl. DRUMBO / **RICHARD REDISS** – slide guitar repl. WHALLEY / **ART TRIPP** – marimba returned from MALLARD. **BRUCE FOWLER** also returned.

Virgin Warners

Feb 80. (lp)(c) **BAT CHAIN PULLER** (US-title 'SHINY BEAST')
– The floppy boot stomp / Tropical hot dog night / Ice rose / Harry Irene / You know you're a man / Bat chain puller / When I see mommy I feel like a mummy / Owed t'Alex / Candle mambo / Love lies / Suction prints / Apes-ma. *(re-iss.Aug85, re-iss+cd.Jun87)*

— **GARY LUCAS** – guitar repl. REDISS

Virgin Virgin

Aug 80. (lp)(c) **DOC AT RADAR STATION**
– Hot head / Ashtray heart / A carrot is as close as a rabbit gets to a diamond / Run paint run run / Sue Egypt / Brickbats / Dirty blue Gene / Best batch yet / Telephone / Flavour bud living / Sheriff of Hong Kong / Making love to a vampire with a monkey on my knee. *(re-iss.Aug85) (cd-iss.Jun88)*

— The CAPTAIN brought in **HATSIZE SNYDER, CLIFF MARTINEZ, WILLIAMS, LAMBOURNE FOWLER and DRUMBO**

Aug 82. (12") **LIGHT REFLECTED OFF THE OCEANS OF THE MOON. / ICE CREAM FOR CROW**

Virgin Epic

Sep 82. (lp)(c) **ICE CREAM FOR CROW** 90
– Ice cream for crow / The host, the ghost, the most holy-o / Semi-multi-(coloured) caucasian / Hey Garland, I dig your tweed coat / Evening bell / Cardboard cut-out sundown / The past is sure tense / Ink mathematics / The witch doctor life / "81" poop hatch / The thousand and tenth day of the human totem pole / Skeleton makes good. *(re-iss.Aug86) (cd-iss.Apr88)*

He retired from music business to concentrate on painting/sculpting in his recently bought Mojave desert home.

– compilations etc. –

Jul 70. Buddah; (lp) **DROPOUT BOOGIE**
(a re-iss. of "SAFE AS MILK" 2 tracks less)
1975. WRMB; (lp) **WHAT'S ALL THIS BOOGA-BOOGA MUSIC (live)** -
1978. Impossible; (d-lp) **EASY TEETH** -
Jan 78. Buddah; (7") **SURE 'NUFF 'N' YES I DO. / ELECTRICITY**
Aug 76. Reprise; (d-lp) **TWO ORIGINALS OF . . .**
(re-iss. of "DECALS" + "SPOTLIGHT KID")
Feb 91. Reprise; (d-cd) **THE SPOTLIGHT KID / CLEAR SPOT**
Nov 77. Pye; (d-lp) **THE CAPTAIN BEEFHEART FILE** (first 2-lp's) -

M.C.A. M.C.A.

May 78. M.C.A.; (7") **HARD WORKIN' MAN. / ('B'side by Jack Nitzche)**

— Above also features RY COODER – on guitar

1978. Virgin/ US= Warners; (7"pic-ep) **SIXPACK**
– Sugar bowl / Same old blues / Upon the My-Oh-My / Magic be / Rock'n'roll's evil doll / New electric ride.
Jul 83. P.R.T.; (10"lp) **MUSIC IN SEA MINOR** -
Jul 84. Breakaway; (lp)(pic-lp) **TOP SECRET** -
Jun 88. That's Original; (d-lp)(d-cd) **SAFE AS MILK / MIRROR MAN**
(re-iss.d-cd.May91 on 'Castle')
Jun 92. Sequel; (cd) **I MAY BE HUNGRY BUT I SURE AIN'T WEIRD – THE ALTERNATIVE CAPTAIN BEEFHEART** -
Jun 93. Flarenasch; (cd) **THE BEST BEEFHEART** -

CARAVAN

Formed: Canterbury, England . . . early 1968 by HASTINGS, COUGHLAN and the SINCLAIRS. They had stemmed from The WILDE FLOWERS which had included ROBERT WYATT and KEVIN AYRES (later of SOFT MACHINE). Signed to 'MGM' subsidiary 'Verve' releasing eponymous debut that year, before moving to 'Decca' 1970. Became durable outfit, although never attained much needed consistant chart status. • **Style:** At times whimsical eccentric outfit who bordered on underground and progressive rock. • **Songwriters:** All group compositions. • **Trivia:** Their 1973 album sleeve which depicted naked pregnant woman, was knocked back by record company for being too obscene.

Recommended: CANTERBURY TALES – THE BEST OF CARAVAN (*8) / IN THE LAND OF THE GREY AND PINK (*6).

RICHARD SINCLAIR – vocals, bass (ex-WILDE FLOWERS) / **PYE HASTINGS** – guitar, vocals (ex-WILDE FLOWERS) / **RICHARD COUGHLAN** – drums, precussion (ex-WILDE FLOWERS) / **DAVE SINCLAIR** – keyboard, vocals with guests **JIMMY HASTINGS** – flute, arrangements / **BRIAN HOPPER** – horns

Verve M.G.M.

Oct 68. (lp) **CARAVAN**
– Place of my own / Ride / Policeman / Love song with flute / Cecil runs / Magic man / Granma's lawn / Where but for Caravan would I be. *(re-iss.Jun72 on 'MGM') (re-iss.1979 on 'Polydor')*
1968. (7") **PLACE OF MY OWN. / RIDE**

Decca London

Sep 70. (7") **IF I COULD DO IT ALL OVER AGAIN, I'D DO IT ALL OVER YOU. / HELLO HELLO**
Oct 70. (lp)(c) **IF I COULD DO IT ALL OVER AGAIN, I'D DO IT ALL OVER YOU**
– If I could do it all over again, I'd do it all over you / And I wish I were stoned / Don't worry / As I feel I die / With an ear to the ground I can make it: Martinian – Only Cox – Reprise / Hello, hello / Asforteri / Can't be long now – Francoise – For Richard – Warlock / Limits. *(cd-iss.Jan 89) (re-iss.c Jul93)*
Feb 71. (7") **LOVE TO LOVE YOU (AND TONIGHT PIGS WILL FLY). / GOLF GIRL**

— with guests **JIMMY HASTINGS** – wind istr. / **DAVID GRINSTEAD** – persussion

Deram London

May 71. (lp)(c) **IN THE LAND OF GREY AND PINK**
– Golf girl / Winter wine / Love to love you (and tonight pigs will fly) / In the land of grey and pink / Nine feet underground: Nigel blows a tune – Love's a friend – Make it 76 – Dance of the seven paper hankies – Hold grandad by the nose – Honest I do – Disassociation – 100% proof. *(cd-iss.Apr89) (re-iss.c Jul93)*

— **STEVE MILLER** – keyboards (ex-'DYBLE, COXHILL & THE MILLER BROTHERS') repl. DAVE who joined ROBERT WYATT'S MATCHING MOLE / with guests **JIMMY HASTINGS, LOL COXHILL** – saxophone / **MIKE COTTON** – trumpet / **PHIL MILLER** – guitar

Apr 72. (lp)(c) **WATERLOO LILY**
– Waterloo Lily / Nothing at all – It's coming soon / Songs and signs / Aristocracy / The love in your eye / To catch me a brother / Subsultus – Debouchement – Tilbury kecks / The world is yours. *(re-iss.c Jul93)*

— **DEREK AUSTIN** – keyboards repl. STEVE MILLER who formed DELIVERY / **STUART EVANS** – bass repl. RICHARD SINCLAIR who joined HATFIELD & THE NORTH added **PETER GEOFFREY RICHARDSON** – electric viola to founders **HASTINGS & COUGHLAN. DAVE HASTINGS** returned to repl. AUSTIN / **JOHN G. PERRY** – bass, vocals (ex-SPREADEAGLE) repl. EVANS

Oct 73. (lp)(c) **FOR GIRLS WHO GROW PLUMP IN THE NIGHT**
– Memory Lain, Hugh / Headloss / Hoedown / Surprise, surprise / E'Thlu Thlu / The dog, the dog, he's at it again / Be all right / Chance of a lifetime / L'auberge du sanglier / A hunting we shall go / Pengola / Backwards / A hunting we shall go (reprise). *(cd-iss.Aug91) (re-iss.c Jul93)*

— **MARTYN FORD** – conducted orchestra, SIMON JEFFES – arrangements

Apr 74. (lp)(c) **CARAVAN AND THE NEW SYMPHONIA** (live at Drury Lane Oct73)
– (introduction) / Mirror of the day / The love in your eye / Virgin on the ridiculous / For Richard.

— **MIKE WEDGWOOD** – bass (ex-CURVED AIR) repl. PERRY (to QUANTUM JUMP)

Decca B.T.M.

Aug 75. (lp)(c) **CUNNING STUNTS** 50
– The show of your lives / Stuck in a hole / Lover / No back stage pass / Welcome the day / The Dabsong conshirtoe:- The mad Dabsong – Ben Karratt rides again – Pro's and con's / Wraiks and ladders – Sneakin' out the bare square – All sorts of unmentionable things / The fear and loathing in Tollington Park rag. *(cd-iss.Dec88 on 'BGO') (cd-iss.Sep94 on 'Repertoire')*
Sep 75. (7") **STUCK IN A HOLE. / LOVER**

— **JAN SCHELHAAS** – keyboards (ex-GARY MOORE) repl.DAVE SINCLAIR

B.T.M. Arista

Apr 76. (lp)(c) **BLIND DOG AT ST.DUNSTANS** 53
– Here I am / Chiefs and Indians / A very smelly, grubby little oik / Bobbing wide / Come on back / A very smelly, grubby little oik (reprise) / Jack and Jill / CAn you hear me / All the way (with John Wayne's single-handed liberation of Paris). *(cd-iss.Sep94 on 'Repertoire')*
Jul 76. (7") **ALL THE WAY (edit). / CHIEFS AND INDIANS**

— **DEK MESSECAR** – bass (ex-DARRYL WAY'S WOLF) repl. WEDGEWOOD who went solo (above now alongside **HASTINGS, COUGHLAN, RICHARDSON** and **SCHELHAAS**)

Arista Arista

May 77. (7") **BETTER BY FAR. / SILVER STRINGS**
Aug 77. (lp)(c) **BETTER BY FAR**
– Feelin' alright / Behind you / Better by far / Silver strings / The last unicorn / Give me more / Man in the car / Let it shine / Nightmare.

— **DAVE SINCLAIR** – keyboards returned from CAMEL (tour) to repl. DEK. Now a quartet when JAN joined CAMEL in '79

Kingdom not issued

Oct 80. (7") **HEARTBREAKER. / IT'S NEVER TOO LATE** -
Oct 80. (lp)(c) **THE ALBUM** -
– Heartbreaker / Corner of my eye / Watcha gonna tell me / Piano player / Make yourself at home / Golden mile / Bright shiny day / Piano player / Clera blue sky / Keepin' up de fences.

— **RICHARD SINCLAIR** – vocals, bass returned from CAMEL, joined all founders, repl. RICHARDSON who went into sessions etc.

also added **MEL COLLINS** – saxophone (ex-KING CRIMSON, etc., etc.,)

Jun 82. (lp) **BACK TO FRONT** -
– Back to Herne Bay front / Betcha wanna take it all / Hold on hold on / A.A. man / Videos of Hollywood / Sally don't change it / All aboard / Taken my breath away / Proper job / Back to front.

— Disband but reformed in 1990. In 1992, they became . . .

RICHARD SINCLAIR'S CARAVAN OF DREAMS

with also **DAVE SINCLAIR + JIMMY HASTINGS.** Plus **ANDY WARD** (ex-CAMEL)

H.T.D. not issued

Jul 92. (cd)(c) **CARAVAN OF DREAMS** -
– Going for a song / Cruising / Only the brave / Plan it Earth / Heather / Keep.
Jan 94. (d-cd) **AN EVENING OF MAGIC (live)** -

– In the land of grey and pink / Only the brave – Plan it Earth / Share it / Videos / Heather / Going for a song / O Caroline / Nine feet underground / Felafel shuffle / Keep on caring / Cruising / Emily / Halfway between Heaven and Earth / It didn't matter anyway / Golf girl.

RICHARD SINCLAIR

		Richard Sinclair Songs	not issued
Jul 94.	(cd) **R.S.V.P.**	[ ]	[-]

– compilations etc. –

Nov 76. Decca/ US= London; (d-lp)(c) **CANTERBURY TALES** [ ] [ ]
– If I could do it all over again I'd do it all over you / Aristocracy / Can't be long now – Francoise – For Richard – Warlock / Nine feet underground: Nigel blows a tune – Love's a friend – Make it 76 – Dance of the seven paper hankies – Hold grandad by the nose – Honest I do – Disassociation – 100 proof / Golf girl / Hoedown / The love in your eye / Subsultus – Debouchement – Tilbury kecks / Memory Laine, Hugh / Headloss / Virgin on the ridiculous / The dog, the dog, he's at it again.
Jul 81. Decca/ US= London; (lp)(c) **THE SHOW OF OUR LIVES** [ ] [ ]
Sep 84. Kingdom; (lp) **THE CANTERBURY COLLECTION** ('80-'82 material) [ ] [-]
(cd-iss. Jan 87)
Apr 85. See For Miles; (lp) **AND I WISH I WERE STONED, DON'T WORRY** [ ] [-]
Sep 87. C5; (c)(lp) **THE BEST OF CARAVAN** [ ] [-]
(cd-iss. 1990 + Apr93)
May 91. Elite; (cd)(c) **SONGS AND SIGNS** [ ] [-]
Oct 91. Windsong; (cd)(lp) **LIVE IN CONCERT (live)** [ ] [-]
Mar 93. Code 90; (cd) **LIVE 1990 (live)** [ ] [-]
CARAVAN re-formed with HASTINGS (not SINCLAIR)
Apr94. H.T.D.; (cd) **COOL WATER** [ ] [-]
– Cool water / Just the way you are / Tuesday is rock and roll nite / The crack of the willow / Ansaphone / Cold fright / Side by side / You woke me up in one of those / To the land of my fathers / Poor Molly / Send reinforcements.

Belinda CARLISLE (see under ⇒ GO-GO'S)

CARS

Formed: Boston, Massachusetts, USA . . . 1976 by ORR, HAWKES and EASTON who started out touring as CAP'N'SWING. Manager Fred Davis got demo of 'JUST WHAT I NEEDED' playlisted on US radio and they duly signed to 'Elektra' 1978. This was their first of many US Top 30 hits, and had best time in 1984 with 3 massive sellers 'YOU MIGHT THINK', 'MAGIC' & 'DRIVE'. • **Style:** Mainstream "new-wave" band, that drifted into fashionable pop/rock. • **Songwriters:** All written by OCASEK, ORR and EASTON, except THINK IT OVER and MAYBE BABY (Buddy Holly). • **Trivia:** The song 'DRIVE' was used for LIVE AID concert and re-released with proceeds to famine relief/BAND AID. Most members also produced bands noteably RIC OCASEK for SUICIDE ('81), BAD BRAINS ('83), etc.

Recommended: THE CARS' GREATEST HITS (*7)

RIC OCASEK (b.RICHARD OTCASEK, 23 Mar'49, Baltimore) – vocals, guitar / **BENJAMIN ORR** (b.ORZECHOWSKI, in Cleveland, Ohio) – vocals, bass / **ELLIOT EASTON** (b.ELLIOT SHAPIRO, 18 Dec'53, Brooklyn, New York) – guitar / **GREG HAWKES** – keyboards, saxophone (ex-MILKWOOD, with ORR and OCASEK) / **DAVID ROBINSON** – drums (ex-The POP, ex-DMZ, ex-MODERN LOVERS)

Elektra Elektra

Aug 78. (7") **JUST WHAT I NEEDED. / I'M IN TOUCH WITH YOUR WORLD** [-] [27]
Aug 78. (lp)(c) **THE CARS** [29] [18] Jun 78
– Good times roll / My best friend's girl / Just what I needed / I'm in touch with your world / Don't cha stop / You're all I've got tonight / Bye bye love / Moving in stereo / All mixed up. *(US-cd.-iss.Jan84)*
Oct 78. (7")(7"pic-d) **MY BEST FRIEND'S GIRL. / MOVING IN STEREO** [3] [-]
Oct 78. (7") **MY BEST FRIEND'S GIRL. / DON'T CHA STOP** [-] [35]
Jan 79. (7")(7"pic-d) **JUST WHAT I NEEDED. / I'M IN TOUCH WITH YOUR WORLD** [17] [-]
May 79. (7") **GOOD TIMES ROLL. / ALL MIXED UP** [ ] [41] Mar 79
Jun 79. (lp)(c) **CANDY-O** [30] [3]
– Let's go / Since I held you / It's all can do / Double life / Shoo be doo / Candy-O / Nightspots / You can't hold on too long / Lust for kicks / Got a lot on my head / Dangerous type. *(US-cd.iss.Jan84)*
Jul 79. (7")(7"pic-d) **LET'S GO. / THAT'S IT** [51] [14] Jun 79
Sep 79. (7")(7"pic-d) **DOUBLE LIFE. / COME AROUND** [ ] [-]
Oct 79. (7") **IT'S ALL I CAN DO. / GOT A LOT ON MY HEAD** [-] [41]
Jan 80. (7") **DOUBLE LIFE. / CANDY-O** [-] [ ]
Jan 80. (7") **IT'S ALL I CAN DO. / CANDY-O** [ ] [-]
Sep 80. (lp)(c) **PANORAMA** [ ] [5]
– Panorama / Touch and go / Gimme some slack / Don't tell me now / Getting through / Misfit kid / Down boys / You wear those eyes / Running to you / Up and down. *(re-iss.Nov81) (US-cd.iss.1987)*
Sep 80. (7") **TOUCH AND GO. / DOWN BOYS** [ ] [37]
Jan 81. (7") **DON'T TELL ME NO. / DON'T GO TO PIECES** [-] [ ]
Mar 81. (7") **GIMME SOME SLACK. / DON'T GO TO PIECES** [-] [ ]
Nov 81. (lp)(c) **SHAKE IT UP** [ ] [9]
– Since you're gone / Shake it up / I'm not the one / Victim of love / Cruiser / A dream away / This could be love / Think it over / Maybe baby. *(US-cd.iss.1986)*
Nov 81. (7")(7"grey/pink)(7"black/pink)(7"pic-d) **SHAKE IT UP. / CRUISER** [ ] [4]
Mar 82. (7") **SINCE YOU'RE GONE. / THINK IT OVER** [-] [41]
May 82. (7") **SINCE YOU'RE GONE. / MAYBE BABY** [37] [-]
Jun 82. (7") **THIS COULD BE LOVE. / VICTIM OF LOVE** [-] [ ]
Aug 82. (7") **THINK IT OVER. / I'M NOT THE ONE** [ ] [-]
Mar 84. (7") **YOU MIGHT THINK. / HEARTBEAT CITY** [-] [7]
Mar 84. (lp)(c) **HEARTBEAT CITY** [25] [3]
– Hello again / Magic / Stranger eyes / It's not the night / I refuse / Looking for love / Drive / You might think / Why can't I have you / Heartbeat city. *(US-cd.iss.Jul84)*
Apr 84. (7") **WHY CAN'T I HAVE YOU. / JACKIE** [ ] [-]
May 84. (7") **MAGIC. / I REFUSE** [-] [12]
Sep 84. (7") **DRIVE. / STRANGER EYES** [5] [3] Jul 84
(UK.re-iss.Jul85, hit No.4)
Oct 84. (7") **HELLO AGAIN. / ('A'-dub version)** [-] [20]
Nov 84. (7") **YOU MIGHT THINK. / I REFUSE** [ ] [-]
(12"+=) – Let's go.
Feb 85. (7") **WHY CAN'T I HAVE YOU. / HEARTBEAT CITY** [ ] [33] Jan 85
(12"+=) – Hello again (remix) / Moving in stereo.
Sep 85. (7") **HEARTBEAT CITY. / WHY CAN'T I HAVE YOU** [ ] [ ]
(12"+=) – Chemistry / Hello again.
Oct 85. (7") **TONIGHT SHE COMES. / JUST WHAT I NEEDED** [-] [7]
Nov 85. (7") **TONIGHT SHE COMES. / BREAKAWAY** [ ] [-]
(12"+=) – Just what I needed.
Nov 85. (lp)(c)(cd) **THE CARS' GREATEST HITS** (compilation) [27] [12]
– Just what I needed / Since you're gone / You might think / Good times roll / Touch and go / Drive / Tonight she comes / My best friend's girl / Heartbeat city / Let's go / Magic / Shake it up. (c+cd+=) – I'm not the one.
Jan 86. (7") **I'M NOT THE ONE. / HEARTBEAT CITY** [-] [32]
Mar 86. (7") **I'M NOT THE ONE (remix). / SINCE YOU'RE GONE** [ ] [-]
(12"+=) – Shake it up.
Aug 87. (lp)(c)(cd) **DOOR TO DOOR** [72] [26]
– Leave or stay / You are the girl / Double trouble / Fine line / Everything you say / Ta ta wayo wayo / Strap me in / Coming up you / Wound up on you / Go away / Door to door.
Sep 87. (7") **YOU ARE THE GIRL. / TA TA WAYO WAYO** [ ] [17] Aug 87
(12"+=) – Tonight she comes.
Nov 87. (7") **STRAP ME IN. / DOOR TO DOOR** [-] [ ]
Jan 88. (7") **COMING UP YOU. / DOUBLE TROUBLE** [-] [ ]
—— disbanded early 1988. OCASEK married Paulina Porizkova (23 Aug'89.)

RIC OCASEK

Geffen Geffen

Feb 83. (lp)(c) **BEATITUDE** [ ] [28]
– Jimmy Jimmy / Something to grab for / Prove / I can't wait / Connect up to me / A quick one / Out of control / Take a walk / Sneak attack / Time bomb. *(re-iss.Sep86)*
Mar 83. (7") **SOMETHING TO GRAB FOR. / CONNECT UP TO ME** [-] [47]
Jun 83. (7") **A QUICK ONE. / JIMMY JIMMY** [-] [ ]
Oct 86. (7") **EMOTION IN MOTION. / P.F.J.** [ ] [15]
(12"+=) – Step by step.
Nov 86. (lp)(c)(cd) **THIS SIDE OF PARADISE** [ ] [31]
– Keep on laughin' / True to you / Emotion in motion / Look in your eyes / Coming for you / Mystery / True love / P.F.J. / Hello darkness / This side of Paradise.
Jan 87. (7") **TRUE TO YOU. / HELLO DARKNESS** [-] [ ]

Sire Sire

Jul 91. (cd)(c)(lp) **FIREBALL ZONE** [ ] [ ]
– Rockaway / Touch down easy / Come back / The way you look tonight / All we need is love / Over and over / Flowers of evil / They tried / Keep that dream / Balance / Mister Meaner.

ELLIOT EASTON

Elektra Elektra

Apr 85. (lp)(c) **CHANGE NO CHANGE** [ ] [99]
– Tools of your labour / (Wearing down) Like a wheel / Shayla / Help me / (She made it) New for me / I want you / Change / The hard way / Fight my way to love / Wide awake.
Apr 85. (7") **THE HARD WAY. / (WEARING DOWN) LIKE A WHEEL** [-] [ ]
Jun 85. (7") **WEARING DOWN LIKE A WHEEL. / SHAYLA** [-] [ ]

BENJAMIN ORR

Elektra Elektra

Dec 86. (lp)(c) **THE LACE** [ ] [86]
– Too hot to stop / In circles / Stay the night / Skyline / When you're gone / Spinning / Hold on / The lace / That's the way / This time around.
Jan 87. (7")(12") **STAY THE NIGHT. / THAT'S THE WAY** [ ] [24]
Apr 87. (7") **THE LACE. / TOO HOT TO STOP** [-] [ ]

CARTER THE UNSTOPPABLE SEX MACHINE

Formed: Streatham, South London, England . . . 1988 by FRUITBAT and JIM BOB. They had been in early 80's outfit The BALLPOINTS, and after a lengthy period with real jobs, they formed the group JAMIE WEDNESDAY in 1984. They signed to 'Rough Trade' subsidiary label 'Pink', and released 2 singles before disbanding Feb87. The following year they became CARTER . . . and after more indie releases, they were contracted to 'Rough Trade' then 'Chrysalis' for whom they started to chart by 1991. • **Style:** D.I.Y. agit punk rock, with a little of the humour that HALF MAN HALF BISCUIT once had. • **Songwriters:** All penned by LES and JIM BOB, except RENT (Pet Shop Boys) / RANDY SCOUSE GIT (Monkees) / EVERYBODY'S HAP-

PY NOWADAYS (Buzzcocks) / BEDSITTER (Soft Cell) / THIS IS HOW IT FEELS (Inspiral Carpets) / PANIC (Smiths) / MANNEQUIN (Wire) / KING ROCKER (Generation X) / DOWN IN THE TUBE STATION AT MIDNIGHT (Jam) / ANOTHER BRICK IN THE WALL (Pink Floyd) / THE IMPOSSIBLE DREAM (Mitch Leigh/Joe Darion) / HIT (Sugarcubes) / SPEEED KING (These Animal Men) / SILVER DREAM MACHINE (David Essex). • **Trivia:** Surprizingly it was JONATHAN KING who gave them tabloid exposure in his 'Sun' column.

Recommended: 30 SOMETHING (*8) / 1992 THE LOVE ALBUM (*7) / POST-HISTORIC MONSTERS (*8) / 101 DAMNATIONS (*10).

JAMIE WEDNESDAY

JIM 'Jim Bob' MORRISON (b.22 Nov'60)– vocals, acoustic guitar / **LES 'Fruitbat' CARTER** (b.12 Feb'58)– bass / **LINDSEY HENRY** – trumpet / **SIMON LOWE** – brass / **DEAS LEGGETT** – drums

Pink / not issued

Nov 85. (12"ep) **VOTE FOR LOVE / THE WALL. / WHITE HORSES / BUTTONS AND BOWS** [ ] [-]

May 86. (12"ep) **WE THREE KINGS OF ORIENT AREN'T. / LAST NIGHT I HAD THE STRANGEST DREAM / I THINK I'LL THROW A PARTY FOR MYSELF** [ ] [-]

— disbanded Feb87.

CARTER THE UNSTOPPABLE SEX MACHINE

was duo formed by **JIM BOB & FRUITBAT** who now both played guitar with back-up of tape machines & **JIM BOB** – vocals

Big Cat / not issued

Aug 88. (12"m) **SHELTERED LIFE. / IS THIS THE ONLY WAY THROUGH TO YOU? / GRANNY FARMING IN THE U.K.** [ ] [-]
(re-iss. cd-ep Jul 94 on 'Southern')

Nov 89. (12"ep) **SHERIFF FATMAN / R.S.P.C.E. / TWIN-TUB WITH GUITAR / EVERYBODY'S HAPPY NOWADAYS** [ ] [-]

Jan 90. (lp)(c)(cd) **101 DAMNATIONS** [ ] [-]
– A perfect day to drop the bomb / Midnight on the murder mile / The road to Domestos / An all-American sport / 24 minutes to Tulsa Hill / Good grief / Charlie Brown / Everytime a churchbell rings / Good grief / Sheriff Fatman / G.I. blues. *(re-dist.Sep91, hit No.29)*

May 90. (12")(cd-s) **RUBBISH. / RENT / ALTERNATIVE ALF GARNET** [ ] [ ]

Rough Trade / not issued

Oct 90. (7") **ANYTIME, ANYPLACE, ANYWHERE. / RE-EDUCATING RITA** [ ] [-]
(12"+=)(cd-s+=) – Alternative title (randy sarf git).

Jan 91. (7")(c-s) **BLOODSPORTS FOR ALL. / 2001: A CLOCK-WORK ORANGE** [48] [-]
(12"+=)(cd-s+=) – Bedsitter.

Feb 91. (cd)(c)(lp) **30 SOMETHING** [8] [-]
– Surfin' USM / My second to last will and testament / Anytime anyplace anywhere / Prince in a pauper's grave / Shopper's paradise / Billy's smart circus / Bloodsport for all / Sealed with a Glasgow kiss / Say it with flowers / Falling on a bruise / The final comedown. *(US-iss.Aug91 on 'Chrysalis' / UK re-iss.Jan92 on 'Rough Trade', hit 21) (re-iss.cd/c Feb95)*

Chrysalis / Chrysalis

Jun 91. (7") **SHERIFF FATMAN. / R.S.P.C.E.** [23] [ ]
(12"+=)(c-s+=)(cd-s+=) – Twin-tub with guitar / Everybody's happy nowadays

Oct 91. (7")(c-s) **AFTER THE WATERSHED (EARLY LEARNING THE HARD WAY). / THE 90's REVIVAL / A NATION OF SHOPLIFTERS** [11] [ ]
(12"+=)(cd-s+=) – This is how it feels.

Dec 91. (7")(c-s) **RUBBISH. / ALTERNATIVE ALF GARNET** [14] [ ]
(12"+=)(cd-s+=) – Rent.

Apr 92. (7"ep)(12"ep)(c-ep)(cd-ep) **THE ONLY LIVING BOY IN NEW CROSS. / PANIC / WATCHING THE BIG APPLE TURN** [7] [ ]

May 92. (cd)(c)(lp) **1992 – THE LOVE ALBUM** [1] [ ]
– 1993 / Is wrestling fixed? / The only living boy in New Cross / Suppose you gave a funeral and nobody came / England / Do re mi, so far so good / Look mum, no hands / While you were out / Skywest and crooked / The impossible dream. *(re-iss.cd/c Mar94 & Feb95)*

Jun 92. (7"ep)(12"ep)(c-ep)(cd-ep) **DO RE MI, SO FAR SO GOOD / MANNEQUIN. / KING ROCKER / DOWN IN THE TUBE-STATION AT MIDNIGHT** [22] [ ]

Nov 92. (7"ep)(12"ep)(c-ep)(cd-ep) **THE IMPOSSIBLE DREAM / TURN ON, TUNE IN AND SWITCH OFF / WHEN THESAURUSES RULED THE WORLD / BRING ON THE GIRLS** [21] [ ]

Aug 93. (7")(c-s) **LEAN ON ME I WON'T FALL OVER. / HIT** [16] [ ]
(12"+=)(cd-s+=) – Always the bridesmaid never the bride.

Sep 93. (cd)(c)(lp) **POST HISTORIC MONSTERS** [5] [ ]
– 2 million years B.C. / The music that nobody likes / Mid day crisis / Cheer up, it might never happen / Stuff the jubilee! / A bachelor for Baden Powell / Spoilsports personality of the year / Suicide isn't painless / Being here / Evil / Sing fat lady sing / Travis / Lean on me I won't fall over / Lenny and Terence / Under the thumb and over the Moon. *(re-iss.Feb95)*

Feb 94. (7")(c-s) **GLAM ROCK COPS. / LEAN ON ME (I WON'T FALL OVER) (by The FAMILY CAT)** [24] [ ]
(12"+=)(cd-s+=) – ('A'-GRID mixes).
(cd-s) – ('A'side) / Bloodsports for all (by SULTANS OF PING F.C.) / Lenny and Terence (by BLADE) / Falling on a bruise (by PUBLIC WORKS).

Mar 94. (cd)(c)(lp) **STARRY EYED AND BOLLOCK NAKED (A COLLECTION OF B-SIDES)** (compilation) [22] [ ]
– Is this the only way to get through to you? / Granny farming in the UK / R.S.P.C.E. / Twin tub with guitar / Alternative Alf Garnett / Re educating Rita / 2001: A clock-work orange / The 90's revival / A nation of shoplifters / Watching the big apple turn over / Turn on, tune in and switch off / When Thesauruses ruled the Earth / Bring on the girls! / Always the bridesmaid never the bride / Her song / Commercial f**king suicide / Stuff the jubilee (1977) / Glam rock cops. *(re-iss.Feb95)*

— added **WEZ BOYNTON** – drums (ex-RESQUE)

Nov 94. (7")(c-s) **LET'S GET TATTOOS. / ESPECIALLY 4 U** [30] [ ]
(cd-s+=) – Speed king / Silver dream machine.
(cd-s) – ('A'side) / Turbulence / King for a day.

Jan 95. (7"colrd)(c-s) **THE YOUNG OFFENDER'S MUM. / TROUBLE** [34] [ ]
(cd-s+=) – This one's for me.
(cd-s) – ('A'side) / Rubbish (live) / Suicide isn't painless (live) / Falling on a bruise (live).

Feb 95. (d-cd)(c)(d-lp) **WORRY BOMB** [9] [ ]
– Cheap'n'cheesy / Airplane food – airplane fest food / The young offender's mum / Gas (man) / The life and soul of the party dies / My defeatest attitude / Worry bomb / Senile delinquent / Me and Mr.Jones / Let's get tattoos / Going straight / God, Saint Peter and the guardian angel / The only looney left in town / Ceasefire. **DOMA SPORTOVA . . . LIVE IN ZAGREB, 20/5/94** – Alternative Alf Garnett / Do re me so far so good / A bachelor pad for Baden Powell / Re-educating Rita / The only living boy in New Cross / Lean on me I won't fall over / Granny farming in the U.K. / Travis / Sing fat lady sing / Lenny and Terence / Commercial fucking suicide part 1.

Sep 95. (7"red)(c-s) **BORN ON THE 5th OF NOVEMBER. / D.I.V.O.R.C.E.F.G.** [35] [ ]
(cd-s) – ('A'side) / Tomorrow when you die / The aftertaste of Paradise / Air-plane food.

Oct 95. (cd)(c)(lp) **STRAW DONKEY . . .THE SINGLES** (compilation) [37] [ ]
– A sheltered life / Sheriff Fatman / Rubbish / Antime anyplace anywhere / Bloodsport for all / After the watershed (early learning the hard way) / The only living boy in New Cross / Do re mi, so far so good / The impossible dream / Lean on me (I won't fall over) / Lenny and Terence / Glam rock cops / Let's get tattoos / The young offender's mum / Born on the 5th of November.

– compilations, others, etc. –

Oct 90. Big Cat Export; (m-lp)(cd) **HANDBUILT FOR PERVERTS** [-] [ ]

Johnny CASH

Born: 26 Feb'32, Kingsland, Arkansas, USA. Raised on a Federal resettlement colony in Dyess, and after leaving school in 1950, he joined the US Air Force, who were based in Germany. After 3 years, he left Force and returned to America, becoming a door-to-door salesman in Memphis, Tennessee. In 1954, he joined The TENNESSEE THREE alongside MARSHALL GRANT – guitar & LUTHER PERKINS – guitar. On 7 Aug'54, he married Vivian Liberto, and she soon gave him on 24 May'55 a daughter ROSANNE. (She became from the late 70's, a star in her own right.) In 1955, having signed to Sam Phillips' 'Sun' records, he hit US country chart with debut single 'CRY CRY CRY'. After another country hit, he scored in the US Top 20 with 'I WALK THE LINE'. After 3 more Top 30 ventures, he signed to 'Columbia' in Autumn '58. Although his future successes were sporadic, he became top country artist until lean time in the 70's-80's. In 1967, he nearly died from drunkeness at the same time he divorced Vivian. In Mar'68, he married JUNE CARTER, after proposing to her on stage. **Style:** Country & western star, who near-narrated his way through many classic ballads, which annexed religion, country and rock-ing sound. **Songwriters:** CASH penned except; THE WAYS OF A WOMAN IN LOVE (Charlie Rich) / RING OF FIRE (Merle Haggard & June Carter) / IT AIN'T ME BABE + WANTED MAN (Bob Dylan) / A BOY NAMED SUE (Shel Silverstein) / IF I WERE A CARPENTER (Tim Hardin) / SUNDAY MORNING COMING DOWN (Kris Kristopherson) / JOHNNY 99 (Bruce Springsteen) / DADDY SANG BASS (Carl Perkins) / THE HIGHWAYMAN (Jimmy Webb) / BIRD ON A WIRE (Leonard Cohen) / THIRTEEN (Glenn Danzig) / THE BEAST IN ME (Nick Lowe) / THE MAN WHO COULDN'T CRY (Loudon Wainwright III). The 1964 album BITTER TEARS was written by PETER LA FARGE. **Trivia:** In 1969, he guested on BOB DYLAN's 'Nashville Skyline' lp track 'THE GIRL FROM NORTH COUNTRY'.

Recommended: THE MAN IN BLACK – THE DEFINITE . . . (*8) / AMERICAN RECORDINGS (*7)

JOHNNY CASH – vocals, guitar with **?**

London / Sun

Jun 55. (7") **CRY CRY CRY. / HEY PORTER** [-] [ ]
(UK-iss.Oct70 on 'Sun')

Jan 56. (7") **SO DOGGONE LONESOME. / FOLSOM PRISON BLUES** [-] [ ]

Jan 57. (7") **I WALK THE LINE. / GET RHYTHM** [ ] [17] May56

Jun 57. (7") **THERE YOU GO. / TRAIN OF LOVE** [ ] [ ] Nov56

Aug 57. (7") **NEXT IN LINE. / DON'T MAKE ME GO** [ ] [99] Jun 57

Oct 57. (lp) **JOHNNY CASH WITH HIS HOT & BLUE GUITAR** [-] [ ]
– The rock island line / I heard that lonesome whistle blow / Country boy / If the good Lord's willing and the creeks don't rise / Cry cry cry / Remember me / I'm so doggone lonesome / I was there when it happened / I walk the line / The wreck of the old 97 / Folsom Prison blues / Doin' my time. *(UK-iss.Feb81 on 'Charly')*

Dec 57. (7") **HOME OF THE BLUES. / GIVE MY LOVE TO ROSE** [ ] [88] Sep 57

Apr 58. (7") **BALLAD OF A TEENAGE QUEEN. / BIG RIVER** [ ] [14] Jan 58

May 58. (7") **COME IN STRANGER. / GUESS THINGS HAPEN THAT WAY** [-] [66]

Oct 58. (7") **THE WAYS OF A WOMAN IN LOVE. / YOU'RE THE NEAREST THING TO HEAVEN** [ ] [24] Aug 58

Philips Columbia

Nov 58. (7") **ALL OVER AGAIN. / WHAT DO I CARE** [ ] [38] [52]

Jan 59. (7") **DON'T TAKE YOUR GUNS TO TOWN. / I STILL MISS SOMEONE** [ ] [32]

Jan 59. (lp) **THE FABULOUS JOHNNY CASH** [ ] [19]
– Run softly, blue river / Frankie and Johnny / That's all over / The troubadour / One more ride/ That's enough / I still miss someone / Don't take your guns to town / I'd rather die young / Pickin' time / Shepherd of my heart / Suppertime. *(UK re-iss.Jun62 on 'CBS')*

May 59. (7") **FRANKIE'S MAN, JOHNNY. / YOU DREAMER YOU** [ ] [57] Apr59

Sep 59. (7") **I GOT STRIPES. / FIVE FEET HIGH AND RISING** [ ] [43]

—— recruited new drummer **W.S.HOLLAND** who stayed for next 30 years.

Nov 59. (7") **THE LITTLE DRUMMER BOY. / I'LL REMEMBER YOU** [ ] [63]

Jan 60. (lp) **SONGS OF OUR SOIL** [ ] [ ]
– Drink to me / Five feet high and rising / Man on the hill / Hank and Joe and me / Clementine / Don't step on mother's roses / Great speckled bird / I want to go home / Caretaker / Old Apache squaw / My grandfather's clock / It could happen to you.

Apr 60. (7") **SEASONS OF MY HEART. / SMILING BILL McCALL** [ ] [ ]

Jun 60. (lp) **HYMNS BY JOHNNY CASH** [ ] [ ]
– It was Jesus / I saw a man / Are all the children in / The old account / Lead me gently home / Swing low, sweet chariot / Snow in his hair / Lead me, father / I called him / These things shall pass / He'll be a friend / God will.

Jul 60. (7") **SECOND HONEYMOON. / HONKY TONK GIRL** [-] [ ]

Oct 60. (7") **GOING TO MEMPHIS. / LOADING COAL** [ ] [ ]

Oct 60. (lp) **NOW, THERE WAS A SONG** [ ] [ ]
– Seasons of my heart / I couldn't keep from crying / I feel better all over / My shoes keep walking back to you / Time changes everything / I'd just be a fool enough (to fall) / Why do you punish me / Transfusion blues / I will miss you when you go / I'm so lonesome, I could cry / Just one more / Honky tonk girl. *(re-iss.May62 on 'CBS') (cd-iss.Feb95)*

Dec 60. (lp) **RIDE THIS TRAIN** [ ] [ ]
– (as yet unknown)

May 61. (7") **THE REBEL THEME. / FORTY SHADES OF GREEN** [ ] [ ]

Nov 61. (7") **TENNESSEE FLAT-TOP BOX. / TALL MEN** [ ] [84]

Aug 62. (7") **BONANZA!. / PICK A BALL O' COTTON** [-] [94]

—— Since early 1961, JOHNNY lived on the road, after bouts of heavy drinking and pill poppin', which led to his estrangement from wife and 4 daughters.

C.B.S. Columbia

May 63. (lp) **BLOOD, SWEAT AND TEARS** [ ] [80] Apr 63
– The legend of John Henry's hammer / Tell him I'm gone / Another man done gone / Busted / Casey Jones / Nine pound hammer / Chain gang / Waiting for a train / Roughneck. *(cd-iss.Feb95)*

Jul 63. (7") **RING OF FIRE. / I'D STILL BE THERE** [ ] [17] Jun 63

Oct 63. (lp) **RING OF FIRE – THE BEST OF JOHNNY CASH – (compilation)** [ ] [26] Jul 63
– Ring of fire / I'd still be there / What do I care / I still miss someone / Forty shades of green / Were you there (when they crucified my Lord) / The rebel – Johnny Yuma / Bonanza / The big battle / Remember the Alamo / Tennessee top box / (There'll be) Peace in the valley (for me).

CASH now teamed up with JUNE CARTER for some gigs.

Nov 63. (7") **THE MATADOR. / STILL IN TOWN** [ ] [44] Oct63

Feb 64. (7") **UNDERSTAND YOUR MAN. / DARK AS A DUNGEON** [-] [35]

Sep 64. (lp) **I WALK THE LINE** [ ] [53]
– I walk the line / Bad news / Folsom Prison blues / Give my love to Rose / Hey Porter / I still miss someone / Understand your man / Wreck of old '97 / Still in town / Goodbye, little darlin' / Big river / Troublesome waters. (new versions of old recordings)

Nov 64. (lp) **THE CHRISTMAS SPIRIT – (festive songs)** [ ] [ ]

Jan 65. (lp) **BITTER TEARS (BALLADS OF THE AMERICAN INDIAN)** [ ] [47]
– As long as the grass shall grow / Apache tears / Custer / The talking leaves / The ballad of Ira Hayes / Drums / White girl / The vanishing race. *(cd-iss.Feb95)*

Mar 65. (7") **ORANGE BLOSSOM SPECIAL. / ALL GOD'S CHILDREN AIN'T FREE** [ ] [80] Feb 65

Apr 65. (lp) **ORANGE BLOSSOM SPECIAL** [ ] [49]
– Orange blossom special / The long black veil / It ain't me babe / The wall / Don't think twice, it's alright / You wild Colorado / Mama, you've been on my mind / When it's springtime in Alaska (it's forty below) / All of God's children ain't free / Danny boy / Wildwood flower / Amen.

May 65. (7") **IT AIN'T ME BABE. / TIME AND TIME AGAIN** [28] [58] Nov 64

Aug 65. (7") **RING OF FIRE. / STREETS OF LAREDO** [ ] [-]

Mar 66. (7") **THE ONE ON THE RIGHT IS ON THE LEFT. / COTTON PICKIN' HANDS** [ ] [46] Feb 66

Jul 66. (7") **EVERYBODY LOVES A NUT. / AUSTIN PRISON** [ ] [96]

Jul 66. (lp) **EVERYBODY LOVES A NUT** [28] [88]
– Everybody loves a nut / The one on the right is on the left / A cup of coffee / The bug that tried to crawl around the world / The singing star's queen / Austin Prison / Dirty old egg – Sucking dog / Take me home / Please don't play / Red river valley / Boa constrictor / Joe Bean.

Nov 66. (lp) **HAPPINESS IS YOU** [ ] [ ]
– Happiness is you / Guess things happen that way / Ancient history / You comb her hair / She came from the mountains / For lovin' me / No one will ever know / Is this my destiny / A wound time can't erase / Happy to be with you / Wabash cannonball.

Jan 67. (7") **YOU BEAT ALL I EVER SAW. / PUT THE SUGAR TO BED** [ ] [ ]

Mar 67. (lp) **FROM SEA TO SHINING SEA** (May68 hit-) [40] [ ]
– From sea to shining sea / Whirl anmd the suck / Call daddy from the mine / The frozen four-hundred-pound fair-to-middlin' cotton picker / The walls of a prison / The masterpiece / You and Tennessee / Another song to sing / The flint arrowhead / Cisco Clifton's fillin' station / Shrimpin' sailin' / From sea to shining sea (reprise).

Sep 67. (lp) **JOHNNY CASH'S GREATEST HITS, VOLUME 1 – (compilation)** [ ] [82] Jul 67
– Jackson (with JUNE CARTER) / I walk the line / Understand your man / Orange blossom special / The one on the right is on the left / Ring of fire / It ain't me babe / The balad of Ira Hayes / The rebel – Johnny Yuma / Five feet high and rising / Don't take your guns to town. *(cd+c.iss.Nov93 on 'Sony Europe')(UK hit No.23 Dec69)*

Nov 67. (lp) **CARRYIN' ON** [ ] [ ]
– Long-legged guitar pickin' man / Shantytown / It ain't me babe / Fast boat to Sydney / Pack up your sorrows / I got a woman / Jackson / Oh, what a good thing we had / You'll be all right / No, no, no / What'd I say.

Feb 68. (7") **ROSANNA'S GOING WILD. / LONG-LEGGED GUITAR-PICKIN' MAN** [ ] [91] Jan 68

Apr 68. (7") **A CERTAIN KIND OF HURTIN'. / ANOTHER SONG TO SING** [ ] [ ]

May 68. (lp)(c) **JOHNNY CASH AT FOLSOM PRISON (live prison gig)** [ ] [13]
– Folsom prison blues / Dark as a dungeon / I still miss someone / Cocaine blues / 25 minutes to go / Orange blossom special / The long black veil / Send a picture of mother / The wall / Dirty old egg sucking dog / Flushed from the bathroom of your heart / Jackson (with JUNE CARTER) / Give my love to Rose / I got stripes / Green green grass of home / Greystone chapel. *(cd/c-iss.Jan95 on 'Success')*

Jun 68. (7") **FOLSOM PRISON BLUES. / THE FOLK SINGER** [ ] [32]

Jan 69. (7") **DADDY SANG BASS. / HE TURNED THE WATER INTO WINE** [ ] [42]

May 69. (lp) **THE HOLY LAND** [ ] [54] Feb 69
– Prologue / Land of Israel / A mother's love / This is Nazareth / Nazareth town of Canaan / He turned the water into wine / My wife June at the sea of Galilee / Beautiful words / Our guide Jacob at Mount Tabor / The ten commandments / Daddy sang bass / At the wailing wall / Come to the wailing wall / In Bethlehem / In garden of Gethsemane / The fourth man / On the Via Dolorosa / Church of the holy / Sepulchre / At Calvary / God is not dead.

—— CASH guested on BOB DYLAN's country 1969 album 'Nashville Skyline'.

—— Jun69, he also began own self-titled TV show, with The CARTER FAMILY, CARL PERKINS, etc. **BOB WOTTON** – guitar repl. LUTHER who died in a house fire.

Aug 69. (lp)(c) **JOHNNY CASH AT SAN QUENTIN (live prison gig)** [2] [1] Jun 69
– Wanted man / Wreck of the old 97 / I walk the line / Darling companion / Starkville city jail / San Quentin / A boy named Sue / Peace in the valley / Folsom prison blues. *(cd-iss.Mar94 on 'Sony Collectors')*

Aug 69. (7") **A BOY NAMED SUE. / SAN QUENTIN** [4] [2] Jul69

Dec 69. (7") **BLISTERED. / SEE RUBY FALL** [ ] [50] [75] Nov 69

Feb 70. (7") **IF I WERE A CARPENTER. ("JOHNNY CASH & JUNE CARTER") / 'CAUSE I LOVE YOU** [ ] [36]

Feb 70. (lp)(c) **HELLO I'M JOHNNY CASH** [6] [6]
– Southwind / The Devil to pay / Cause I love you / See Ruby fall / If I were a carpenter / To beat the Devil / Blistered / Wrinkled, crinkled, wadded dollar bill / I've got a thing about trains / Jesus was a carpenter.

May 70. (7") **WHAT A TRUTH. / SING A TRAVELLING SONG** [21] [19] Apr 70

Aug 70. (d-lp) **THE WORLD OF JOHNNY CASH** [5] [ ]
– (as yet unknown)

Aug 70. (7") **SUNDAY MORNING COMING DOWN. / I'M GONNA TRY TO BE THAT WAY** [-] [46]

Oct 70. (7") **25 MINUTES TO GO. / I'M GONNA TRY TO BE THAT WAY** [ ] [ ]

Dec 70. (lp)(c) **THE JOHNNY CASH SHOW** [18] [ ]
– Sunday morning coming down / Come along and ride this train (medley): Six days on the road – There ain't no easy run – The sailor on a concrete sea / These hands / I'm gonna try to be that way / Come along and ride this train (medley): Mississippi Delta land – Detroit City – Uncloudy day – No setting sun – Mississippi Delta land / Here was a man (dialogue).

Jan 71. (7") **FLESH AND BLOOD. / THIS SIDE OF THE LAW** [ ] [54] Dec70

Mar 71. (lp) **LITTLE FAUSS AND BIG HALSEY (Soundtrack)** [ ] [ ]
– (as yet unknown)

Apr 71. (7") **MAN IN BLACK. / A LITTLE BIT OF YESTERDAY** [ ] [58] Mar71

Jun 71. (7"ep) **THE BALLAD OF LITTLE FAUSS & BIG HALSEY** [ ] [ ]
– (as yet unknown)

Sep 71. (7") **SINGING IN VIETNAM TALKING BLUES. / YOU'VE GOT A NEW LIGHT SHINING** [ ] [ ]

Sep 71. (lp) **THE MAN IN BLACK** [18] [56]
– The preacher said Jesus said / Orphan of the road / You've got a new light shining in your eyes / If not for love / The man in black / Singin' in Vietnam talkin' blues / Ned Kelly / Look for me / Dear Mrs. / I talk to Jesus every day. (included a duet with evangelist BILLY GRAHAM)

Oct 71. (lp)(c) **HIS GREATEST HITS, VOLUME II** (compilation) [43] [94]
(US title 'THE JOHNNY CASH COLLECTION'
(US title 'THE JOHNNY CASH COLLECTION (HIS GREATEST HITS, VOLUME II) [43] [ ]
– (compilation)

Early in 1972, he appeared in the film 'A Gunfight', and TV's 'Colombo'.

Mar 72. (7") **A THING CALLED LOVE. / DADDY** [4] [ ]

May 72. (lp)(c) **A THING CALLED LOVE** [8] [ ]
– Kate / Melva's wine / A thing called love / I promise you / Papa was a good man / Tear stained letter / Mississippi sand / Daddy / Arkansas lovin' man / The miracle man. *(re-iss.Dec85)*

Jun 72. (7") **KATE. / THE MIRACLE MAN** [ ] [75] May72

Nov 72. (lp)(c) **JOHNNY CASH: AMERICA (A 200-YEAR SALUTE IN STORY AND SONG)** [ ] [ ]
– (Opening dialogue) / Paul Revere / Begin West movement / The road to Kaintuck / To the shining mountains / The battle of New Orleans / Southwestward / Remember the Alamo / Opening the west / Lorena / The Gettysburg address / The west / Big foot / Like a young colt / Mister Garfield / A proud land / The big battle / On wheels and wings / Come take a trip in my airship / Reaching for the stars / These are my people.

Apr 73. (7") **ANY OLD WIND THAT BLOWS. / KENTUCKY STRAIGHT** [ ] [ ]

Apr 73. (lp)(c) **ANY OLD WIND THAT BLOWS** [ ] [ ]
– Any old wind that blows / Kentucky Straight / The loving gift / The good Earth / Best friend / Oney / The ballad of Annie Palmer / Too little, too late / If I had a hammer / Country trash / Welcome back Jesus.

Jun 73. (lp)(c) **THE GOSPEL ROAD** [ ] [ ]
– (double-lp of religious songs & narrations, etc.)

Sep 73. (7") **CHILDREN. / LAST SUPPER** [ ] [ ]

Oct 73. (lp)(c) **JOHNNY CASH AND HIS WOMAN** [ ] [ ]
– The color of love / Saturday night in Hickman County / Allegheny / Life has it's ups and downs / Matthew 24 (is knocking at the door) / The city of New Orleans /

Tony / The pine tree / We're for love / Godshine.

Nov 73. (7") **ALLEGHENY (w/JUNE CARTER CASH). / WE'RE FOR LOVE** [-] [ ]

Dec 73. (7") **JACKSON. / WE'RE FOR LOVE** [ ] [-]

Apr 74. (7") **RAGGED OLD FLAG. / DON'T GO NEAR THE WATER** [-] [ ]

May 74. (lp)(c) **RAGGED OLD FLAG** [ ] [ ]
– Ragged old flag / Don't go near the water / All I do is drive / Southern comfort / King of the hill / Pie in the sky / Lonesome to the bone / While I've got it on my mind / Good morning friend / I'm a worried man / Please don't let me out / What on Earth (will you do for Heaven's sake).

Jun 74. (7") **SOUTHERN COMFORT. / DON'T GO NEAR THE WATER** [ ] [ ]

Aug 74. (7") **CRYSTAL CHANDELIERS & BURGUNDY. / THE JUNKIE AND THE JUICEHEAD (MINUS ME)** [-] [ ]

Oct 74. (7") **FATHER AND DAUGHTER (w/ROSIE NIX). / DON'T TAKE YOUR GUNS TO TOWN** [-] [ ]

Oct 74. (lp)(c) **THE JUNKIE AND THE JUICEHEAD MINUS ME** [ ] [ ]
– The junkie and the juicehead (minus me) / Don't take your guns to town / Broken freedom song / I do believe / Ole slewfoot / Keep on the sunny side / Father and daughter (father and son) / Crystal chandeliers and burgundy / Friendly gates / Bily & Rex & Oral & Bob / Jesus / Lay back with my woman.

Jan 75. (7") **THE LADY CAME FROM BALTIMORE. / LONESOME TO THE BONE** [ ] [ ]

May 75. (lp)(c) **JOHN A. CASH** [ ] [ ]
– My old Kentucky home (turpentine and dandelion wine) / Hard times comin' / The lady came from Baltimore / Lonesome to the bone / The night they drove old Dixie down / Clean your own tables / Jesus was our saviour (cotton was our king) / Reason to believe / Cocaine Carolina / Smokey factory blues.

Aug 75. (7") **SMOKEY FACTORY BLUES. / CLEAN YOUR OWN TABLES** [ ] [-]

Nov 75. (lp)(c) **LOOK AT THEM BEANS** [ ] [ ]
– Texas-1947 / What have you got / Planned tonight, Diana / Look at them beans / No charge / I hardly ever sing / Beer drinking songs / Down the road I go / I never met a man like you before / All round cowboy / Gone / Down at Drippin' Springs.

Nov 75. (7") **LOOK AT THEM BEANS. / ALL AROUND COWBOY** [-] [ ]

Jan 76. (7") **TEXAS 1947. / I HARDLY EVER SING BEER DRINKING SONGS** [-] [ ]

Mar 76. (7") **STRAWBERRY CAKE. / I GOT STRIPES** [ ] [ ]

Mar 76. (lp)(c) **STRAWBERRY CAKE** [ ] [ ]
– (with dialogue) / Big river / Doin' my time / I still miss / Someone / I got stripes / Medley: Church in the wildwood – Lonesone valley / Strawberry cake / Rock Island Line / Navajo / Destination / Victoria Station / The fourth man.

May 76. (7") **ONE PIECE AT A TIME. / GO ON BLUES** [32] [29] Apr 76

— above + below credited to "JOHNNY CASH & THE TENNESSEE THREE"

Jun 76. (lp)(c) **ONE PIECE AT A TIME** [49] [ ]
– Let there be country / One piece at a time / In a young girl's mind / Mountain lady / Michegan city howdy do / Sold out of flagpoles / Committed to Parkview / Daughter of a railroad man / Love has lost again / Go on blues. *(re-iss.Mar81)*

Jul 76. (7") **MOUNTAIN LADY. / SOLD OUT OF FLAGPOLES** [-] [ ]

Sep 76. (7") **RIDIN' ON THE COTTON BELT. / IT'S ALL OVER** [-] [ ]

Nov 76. (7") **FAR SIDE BANKS OF JORDAN (w/JUNE CARTER CASH). / OLD TIME FEELING** [-] [ ]

Feb 77. (lp)(c) **THE LAST GUNFIGHTER BALLAD** [ ] [ ]
– I will dance with you / The last gunfighter ballad / Far side banks of Jordan (with JUNE CARTER CASH) / Ridin' on the cotton belt / Give it away / You're so close to me / City jail / Cindy / I love you / Ballad of Barbara / That silver haired daddy of mine.

Apr 77. (7") **THE LAST GUNFIGHTER BALLAD. / CITY JAIL** [ ] [ ]

Aug 77. (lp)(c) **THE RAMBLER** [ ] [ ]
– (with dialogue) / Hit the road and go / If it wasn't for the Wabash River / Lady / After the ball / No earthly good / A Wednesday car / My cowboy's last ride / Calilou.

Sep 77. (7") **LADY. / HIT THE ROAD AND GO** [ ] [ ]

Dec 77. (7") **CALILOU. / AFTER THE BALL** [-] [ ]

Apr 78. (7") **I WOULD LIKE TO SEE YOU AGAIN. / LATELY** [-] [ ]

Apr 78. (lp)(c) **I WOULD LIKE TO SEE YOU AGAIN** [ ] [ ]
– I would like to see you again / Lately / I wish I was crazy again / Who's Gene Autrey / Hurt so bad / I don't think I could take you back again / Abner Brown / After taxas / There ain't no good / Chain gang / That's the way it is / I'm alright now.

Jun 78. (7") **THERE AIN'T NO GOOD CHAIN GANG. ("JOHNNY CASH & WAYLON JENNINGS") / I WISH I WAS CRAZY AGAIN** [ ] [ ]

1979. (7") **GONE GIRL. / I'M ALRIGHT NOW** [-] [ ]

1979. (7") **IT'LL BE HER. / IT COMES AND GOES** [-] [ ]

Mar 79. (7") **I WILL ROCK AND ROLL WITH YOU. / A SONG FOR THE LIFE** [-] [ ]

Apr 79. (lp)(c) **GONE GIRL** [ ] [ ]
– Gone girl / I will rock and roll with you / Diplomat / No expectations / It comes and goes / It'll be her / Gambler / Cajun born / You and me / A song for the life.

Sep 79. (lp)(c) **SILVER** [ ] [ ]
– The L&N don't stop here anymore / Lonesome to the bone / Bull rider / I'll say it's true (with GEORGE JONES) / Ghost riders in the sky / Cocaine blues / Muddy waters / West Canterbury / Subdivision blues / Lately I been leanin' towards the blues / I'm gonna sit on the porch and pick on my old guitar.

Oct 79. (7") **GHOST RIDERS IN THE SKY. / I'M GONNA SIT ON THE PORCH** [ ] [ ]

Dec 79. (7") **I'LL SAY IT'S TRUE. / COCAINE BLUES** [-] [ ]

Mar 80. (7") **BULL RIDER. / LONESOME TO THE BONE.** [-] [ ]

Mar 80. (lp)(c) **A BELIEVER SINGS THE TRUTH** [ ] [ ]
– Wings in the morning / Gospel boogie (a wonderful time up there) / Over the next hill / He's alive / I've got Jesus in my soul / When he comes / I was there when it happened (so I guess I ought to know) / I'm a new born man / There are strange things happening every day / Children go where I send thee / I'm just an old chunk of coal (but I'll be a diamond someday) / Lay me down in Dixie / Don't take everybody for your friend / You'll get yours, I'll get mine / O come angel band / This train is bound for glory / I'm gonna try to be that way / What on Earth (will you do for Heaven's sake) / That's enough / The greatest cowboy of them all.

Dec 80. (lp)(c) **ROCKABILLY BLUES** [ ] [ ]
– Cold lonesome morning / Without love / W.O.M.A.N. / The cowboy who started the fight / The 20th century is almost over / Rockabilly blues (Texas 1955) / The last time / She's a go-er / It ain't nothin' new babe / One way rider.

Dec 80. (7") **COLD LONESOME MORNING. / THE COWBOY WHO STARTED TO FIGHT** [-] [ ]

Feb 81. (7") **THE LAST TIME. / ROCKABILLY BLUES (TEXAS 1965)** [-] [ ]

Apr 81. (7") **WITHOUT LOVE. / IT AIN'T NOTHIN' NEW BABE** [-] [ ]

Jun 81. (lp)(c) **THE BARON** [ ] [ ]
– The baron / Mobile boy / Magnolia blossoms / I learned the hard way / A ceiling, four walls and a floor / Hey hey train / The reverend Mr.Black / The blues keep gettin' bluer / Chattanooga city limit sign / Thanks to you / The greatest love affair.

Oct 81. (7") **THE BARON. / I WILL DANCE WITH YOU** [ ] [ ]

Jan 82. (7") **MOBILE BOY. / THE HARD WAY** [-] [ ]

Mar 82. (7") **THE REVEREND MR. BLACK. / CHATTANOOGA CITY LIMIT SIGN** [-] [ ]

May 82. (lp)(c) **THE SURVIVORS ("JOHNNY CASH, JERRY LEE LEWIS & CARL PERKINS")** [ ] [ ] Mar 82
– Get rhythm / I forgot to remember to forget / Goin' down the road feeling bad / That silver haired daddy of mine / Matchbox / I'll fly away / Whole lotta shakin' goin' on / Rockin' my life away / Blue suede shoes / There will be peace in the valley for me / Will the circle be unbroken / I saw the light. *(re-iss.Sep85 on 'Hallmark')*

Nov 82. (7") **I'VE BEEN TO GEORGIA ON A FAST TRAIN. / SING A SONG** [ ] [ ]

Nov 82. (lp)(c) **THE ADVENTURES OF JOHNNY CASH** [ ] [ ]
– I've been to Georgia on a fast train / John's fair weather friends / Paradise / we must believe in magic / Only love / Good old American guest / I'll cross over Jordan some day / Sing a song / Ain't gonna hobo no more.

Jan 83. (7") **AIN'T GONNA HOBO NO MORE. / FAIRWEATHER FRIENDS** [-] [ ]

Apr 83. (7") **I'LL CROSS OVER JORDAN SOME DAY. / WE MUST BELIEVE IN MAGIC** [-] [ ]

Oct 83. (7") **BRAND NEW DANCE (W/JUNE CARTER). / I'M RAGGED BUT RIGHT** [-] [ ]

Oct 83. (7") **JOHNNY 99. / BRAND NEW DANCE (w/ JUNE CARTER)** [ ] [-]

Nov 83. (lp)(c) **JOHNNY 99** [ ] [ ]
– Highway patrolman / That's the truth / God bless Robert E.Lee / New cut road / Johnny 99 / Ballad of the ark / Joshua gone to Barbados / Girl from the canyon / Brand new dance / I'm ragged but I'm right.

Jan 84. (7") **JOHNNY 99. / NEW CUT ROAD** [-] [ ]

Apr 84. (7") **THAT'S THE TRUTH. / JOSHUA GONE TO BARBADOS** [-] [ ]

Oct 84. (7") **CHICKEN IN BLACK. / BATTLE OF NASHVILLE** [ ] [ ]

The HIGHWAYMAN

were formed by country stars **JOHNNY CASH, WAYLON JENNINGS, WILLIE NELSON & KRIS KRISTOFFERSON** (same label)

Aug 85. (7") **THE HIGHWAYMAN. / THE HUMAN CONDITION** [ ] [ ]

Sep 85. (lp)(c) **THE HIGHWAYMAN** [ ] [ ]
– The highwayman / The last cowboy song / Jim, I wore a tie today / Big river / Committed to Parkview / Desperados waiting for the train / Deportees (plane wreck at Los Gatos) / Welfare line / Against the wind / The twentieth century is almost over. *(cd-iss.1987 & Apr90)*

They made a follow-up album for the same label in 1990.

Apr 90. (cd)(c)(lp) **THE HIGHWAYMAN 2** [ ] [ ]
– Silver stallion / Born and raised in black and white / Two stories wide / We're all in the corner / American remains / Anthem '84 / Angels love bad men / Songs that made a difference / Living legend / Texas. *(d-cd-iss.Oct93 on 'Sony Europe' incl. 1985 lp)*

Apr 90. (7") **SILVER STALLION. / AMERICAN DREAMS** [-] [ ]

Jun 90. (7") **BORN AND RAISED IN BLACK AND WHITE. / TEXAS** [-] [ ]

JOHNNY CASH

had continued with solo career.

Oct 85. (7") **DESPERADOES WAITING FOR A TRAIN. / THE TWENTIETH CENTURY IS ALMOST OVER** [-] [ ]

Dec 85. (7") **I'M LEAVING NOW. / EASY STREET** [-] [ ]

Dec 85. (lp)(c) **RAINBOW** [ ] [ ]
– I'm leaving now / Here comes that rainbow again / They're all the same to me / Easy street / Have you ever seen the rain / You beat all I ever saw / Unwed fathers / Love me like you used to / Casey's last ride / Borderline (a musical whodunit).

Jun 86. (lp)(c) **HEROES ("JOHNNY CASH & WAYLON JENNINGS")** [ ] [ ]
– Folks out on the road / I'm never gonna roam again / American by birth / Field of diamonds / Heroes / Even cowgirls get the blues / Love is the way / Ballad of forty dollars / I'll always love you in my own crazy way / One too many mornings.*(cd-iss.Nov93 on 'Sony Collectors')*

Jun 86. (7") **AMERICAN BY BIRTH. / EVEN COWGIRLS GET THE BLUES** [-] [ ]

(above and below singles also credited w/WAYLON JENNINGS)

Sep 86. (7") **THE BALLAD OF FORTY DOLLARS. / FIELD OF DIAMONDS** [-] [ ]

Mercury Mercury

May 87. (lp)(c)(cd) **JOHNNY CASH IS COMING TO TOWN** [ ] [ ]
– The big light / The ballad of Barbra / I'd rather have you / Let him roll / The night Hank Williams came to town / Sixteen tons / Letters from home / W.Lee O'Daniel and the light crust dough boys / Heavy metal (don't mean rock'n'roll to me) / My ship will sail.

Aug 87. (7") **THE NIGHT HANK WILLIAMS CAME TO TOWN (w/WAYLON JENNINGS). / I'D RATHER HAVE YOU** [ ] [ ]

Jan 88. (7") **THE BIG LIGHT. / SIXTEEN TONS** [ ] [-]

Jan 88. (7") **THE BALLAD OF BARBRA. / SIXTEEN TONS** [-] [ ]

— next feat. daughter and son **ROSANNE + JOHN** plus other guests **HANK WILLIAMS JR., PAUL McCARTNEY, EMMYLOU HARRIS, WAYLON JENNINGS and The**

EVERLYS

Oct 88. (lp)(c)(cd) **WATER FROM THE WELLS OF HOME** [ ] [ ]
– As long as I live / Ballad of a teenage queen / Last of the drifters / Where did we go right / Call me the breeze / That ole wheel / Sweeter than the flowers / Ballad of Robb MacDunn / New moon over Jamaica.

Nov 88. (7") **THAT OLE WHEEL. / THE LAST OF THE DRIFTERS** [ ] [ ] Jan 89

Feb 89. (7") **BALLAD OF A TEENAGE QUEEN. / GET RHYTHM** [ ] [ ] Oct 88

Feb 90. (cd)(c)(lp) **BOOM CHICKABOOM** [ ] [ ]
– A backstage pass / Farmer's almanac / Family bible / I love you, I love you / Monteagle mountain / Cat's in the cradle / Don't go near the water / Harley / Hidden shame / That's one you owe me.

Feb 90. (7") **CAT'S IN THE CRADLE. / I LOVE YOU, I LOVE YOU** [-] [ ]

Mar 91. (cd)(c)(lp) **THE MYSTERY OF LIFE** [ ] [ ]
– The greatest cowboy of them all / I'm an easy rider / The mystery of life / Hey porter / Beans for breakfast / Goin' by the book / Wanted man / I'll go somewhere and sing my songs again / The hobo song / The angel and the badman.

Apr 91. (7") **THE MYSTERY OF LIFE. / I'M AN EASY RIDER** [ ] [ ]
(cd-s+=) Veterans' day.

Spirit Of America | Spirit Of America

Oct 93. (cd)(c) **IT AIN'T ME BABE** [ ] [ ]

In 1993, JOHNNY guested on U2's 'Zooropa' album.

Def Amer. | Def Amer.

Oct 94. (cd)(c) **AMERICAN RECORDINGS** [ ] [ ] May94
Delia's gone / Let the train blow the whistle / The beast in me / Drive on / Why me / Thirteen / Oh bury me nought / Bird on a wire / Tennessee stud / Down there by the train / Like a soldier / The man who couldn't cry.

– other compilations, etc. –

Nov 58. London/ US= Sun; (7"ep) **JOHNNY CASH** [ ] [ ]

Jan 59. London/ US= Sun; (7") **IT'S JUST ABOUT TIME. / I JUST THOUGHT YOU'D LIKE TO KNOW** [ ] [47]
[85] Nov 58

Mar 59. London/ US= Sun; (7"ep) **JOHNNY CASH SINGS HANK WILLIAMS** [ ] [ ]

Apr 59. London/ US= Sun; (lp) **THE SONGS THAT MADE HIM FAMOUS** [ ] [ ]

May 59. London/ US= Sun; (7") **LUTHER PLAYED THE BOOGIE. / THANKS A LOT** [ ] [ ] Mar 59

Jun 59. London/ US= Sun; (7"ep) **COUNTRY BOY** [ ] [ ]

Jun 59. London/ US= Sun; (7"ep) **JOHNNY CASH No.2** [ ] [ ]

Jul 59. London/ US= Sun; (lp) **THE ROCK ISLAND LINE** [ ] [ ]

Aug 59. London/ US= Sun; (7") **KATY TOO. / I FORGOT TO REMEMBER TO FORGET** [ ] [66] Jul 59

Nov 59. London/ US= Sun; (7") **YOU TELL ME. / GOODBYE LITTLE DARLIN' GOODBYE** [ ] [ ] Sep 59

Mar 60. London/ US= Sun; (7") **STRAIGHT A'S IN LOVE. / I LOVE YOU BECAUSE** [ ] [84] Feb 60

Sep 60. London/ US= Sun; (7") **DOWN THE STREET TO 301. / THE STORY OF A BROKEN HEART** [ ] [85] Jun60

Mar 61. London/ US= Sun; (7") **OH LONESOME ME. / LIFE GOES ON** [ ] [93] Dec60

May 65. London/ US= Sun; (lp) **THE ORIGINAL SUN SOUND OF JOHNNY CASH** [ ] [ ]

Jan 66. London/ US= Sun; (lp) **LONESOME ME** [ ] [ ]

Nov 69. Sun; (7") **GET RHYTHM. / HEY PORTER** [-] [60]

Jan 70. Sun; (7") **ROCK ISLAND LINE. / NEXT IN LINE** [-] [93]

1970. Sun; (7") **BIG RIVER. / COME IN STRANGER** [-]

Dec 70. London/ US= Sun; (lp) **ORIGINAL GOLDEN HITS, VOL.1** [ ] [95] Sep 69

Dec 70. London/ US= Sun; (lp) **ORIGINAL GOLDEN HITS, VOL.2** [ ] [98] Sep 69

Mar 71. London/ US= Sun; (lp) **STORY SONGS OF THE TRAINS AND RIVERS** [ ] [ ]

Jul 71. London/ US= Sun; (lp) **SHOWTIME** [ ] [ ]

Jul 71. London/ US= Sun; (lp) **GET RHYTHM** [ ] [ ]
(cd-iss.Feb93 on 'Charity')

Sep 71. London/ US= Sun; (7"m) **I WALK THE LINE. / FOLSOM PRISON BLUES / WRECK OF THE OL' 97** [ ] [ ]

Oct 71. London/ US= Sun; (lp) **. . . SING HANK WILLIAMS (w / JERRY LEE LEWIS)** [ ] [ ]

Nov 71. London/ US= Sun; (d-lp) **THE MAN, HIS WORLD, HIS MUSIC** [ ] [ ]

Aug 72. London/ US= Sun; (lp) **ORIGINAL GOLDEN HITS, VOL.3** [ ] [ ]

Sep 72. London/ US= Sun; (7"m) **SUGARTIME / OH LONESOME ME. / HEY GOOD LOOKIN' / I FORGOT TO REMEMBER TO FORGET** [ ] [ ]

Nov 72. London/ US= Sun; (lp) **SUNDAY DOWN SOUTH (w / JERRY LEE LEWIS)** [ ] [ ]

Feb 74. London/ US= Sun; (d-lp) **THE GIANT OF COUNTRY AND WESTERN MUSIC** [ ] [ ]

Jun 60. Philips/ US= Columbia; (7"ep) **THE TROUBADOUR** [ ] [ ]

Nov 60. Philips/ US= Columbia; (7"ep) **SONGS OF OUR SOIL** [ ] [ ]

Dec 61. Philips/ US= Columbia; (7"ep) **STRICTLY CASH** [ ] [ ]

All C.B.S. releases below were issued for US counterpart 'Columbia'.

Apr 62. C.B.S.; (lp) **HYMNS FROM THE HEART** [ ] [ ]

Jul 62. C.B.S.; (lp) **THE SOUND OF JOHNNY CASH** [ ] [ ]

Sep 64. C.B.S.; (7"ep) **FORTY SHADES OF GREEN** [ ] [ ]

Sep 65. C.B.S.; (7"ep) **IT AIN'T ME BABE** [ ] [ ]

Nov 65. C.B.S.; (lp) **BALLADS OF THE TRUE WEST VOL.1** [ ] [ ]

Nov 65. C.B.S.; (lp) **BALLADS OF THE TRUE WEST VOL.2** [ ] [ ]

Jan 66. C.B.S.; (lp) **RIDE THIS TRAIN** [ ] [ ]

Jul 66. C.B.S.; (7"ep) **MEAN AS HELL** [ ] [ ]

Jan 69. C.B.S.; (lp) **JOHNNY CASH** [ ] [ ]

Dec 71. C.B.S.; (lp)(c) **A JOHNNY CASH PORTRAIT** [ ] [ ]

Sep 72. C.B.S.; (d-lp)(c) **STAR PORTRAIT** [16] [ ]

May 73. C.B.S.; (7") **A BOY NAMED SUE. / FOLSOM PRISON BLUES** [ ] [ ]

Aug 75. C.B.S.; (d-lp)(d-c) **RIDING THE RAILS** [ ] [ ]

Feb 76. C.B.S.; (7") **I WALK THE LINE. / RING OF FIRE** [ ] [ ]

Oct 76. C.B.S.; (lp)(c) **THE BEST OF JOHNNY CASH** [48] [ ]

Jun 78. C.B.S.; (lp)(c) **20 ITCHY FOOT TAPPING GREATS** [36] [ ]

1979. C.B.S.; (lp) **JOHNNY & JUNE (w / JUNE CARTER)** [ ] [-]
(re-iss.Sep84 on 'Bear Family')

Apr 82. C.B.S.; (7") **A BOY NAMED SUE. / FOLSOM PRISON BLUES** [ ] [ ]

Mar 83. C.B.S.; (lp)(c) **BIGGEST HITS** [ ] [ ]

Feb 85. C.B.S.; (lp)(c) **GREATEST HITS VOL.1** [ ] [ ]

Mar 86. C.B.S.; (lp)(c) **GREATEST HITS VOL.2** [ ] [ ]

Apr 87. C.B.S.; (lp)(c)(cd) **1958-1986 THE CBS YEARS** [ ] [ ]

Mar 89. C.B.S.; (lp)(c)(cd) **CLASSIC CASH** [ ] [ ] Dec 88

1965. Fontana; (c-ep) **JOHNNY CASH'S COUNTRY ROUND-UP** [ ] [-]

Jun 68. C.B.S./ US= Rollercoaster; (lp) **OLD GOLDEN THROAT** [37] [ ]
(re-iss.Sep82 on 'Bear Family')

Jul 69. C.B.S./ US= Rollercoaster; (lp) **MORE OF OLD GOLDEN THROAT** [ ] [ ]
(re-iss.Sep82 on 'Bear Family')

Dec 70. Hallmark; (lp)(c) **THE GREAT JOHNNY CASH** [ ] [-]

Mar 71. Hallmark; (lp)(c) **JOHNNY CASH** [ ] [-]

Mar 72. Hallmark; (lp)(c) **THE MAGNIFICENT JOHNNY CASH** [ ] [-]

Nov 72. Hallmark; (lp)(c) **THE MIGHTY JOHNNY CASH** [ ] [-]

Jun 74. Hallmark; (lp)(c) **FOLSOM PRISON BLUES** [ ] [-]

Jun 75. Hallmark; (lp)(c) **BALLAD OF A TEENAGE QUEEN** [ ] [-]

Nov 75. Hallmark; (lp)(c) **I FORGOT TO REMEMBER TO FORGET** [ ] [-]

Nov 76. Hallmark; (lp)(c) **THE STORY OF A BROKEN HEART** [ ] [-]

Apr 79. Hallmark; (lp)(c) **RING OF FIRE** [ ] [-]

Feb 80. Hallmark; (lp)(c) **I'M SO LONESOME I COULD CRY** [ ] [-]

Mar 76. Pickwick; (lp)(c) **THE JOHNNY CASH COLLECTION** [ ] [-]

Aug 78. Pickwick; (d-lp) **THE JOHNNY CASH COLLECTION VOL.2** [ ] [-]

Jul 79. Pickwick; (d-lp) **THE JOHNNY CASH COLLECTION VOL.3** [ ] [-]

Jul 80. Pickwick; (d-c) **THE JOHNNY CASH COLLECTION** [ ] [-]

Apr 86. Pickwick; (cd) **JOHNNY CASH – I LOVE COUNTRY** [ ] [-]
(re-iss.lp+c.Mar87 on'CBS')

Mar 74. Embassy-CBS; (lp)(c) **I WALK THE LINE** [ ] [ ]

Nov 74. Embassy-CBS; (lp)(c) **THE SOUND OF JOHNNY CASH** [ ] [ ]

Jul 77. Embassy-CBS; (lp)(c) **BALLADS OF THE TRUE WEST** [ ] [ ]

Jul 77. Embassy-CBS; (lp)(c) **JOHNNY CASH** [ ] [ ]

May 80. Embassy-CBS; (lp)(c) **A BOY NAMED SUE** [ ] [ ]

Mar 74. Contour; (lp) **THE ROUGH-CUT KING OF COUNTRY AND WESTERN** [ ] [-]

Oct 75. Charly; (lp) **OLD GOLDEN THROAT** [ ] [-]

Oct 76. Charly; (lp)(c) **THE ORIGINAL JOHNNY CASH** [ ] [-]

Dec 76. Charly; (7"ep) **BALLAD OF A TEENAGE QUEEN** [ ] [-]

Jul 77. Charly; (lp) **SUN SOUNDS SPECIAL** [ ] [-]

Jun 79. Charly; (7") **MEAN EYED CAT. / GET RHYTHM** [ ] [-]

Apr 84. Charly; (5xlp-box) **THE SUN YEARS** [ ] [-]

Apr 86. Charly; (cd) **COUNTRY BOY** [ ] [-]

Jul 79. Hammer; (lp) **JOHNNY CASH** [ ] [-]

Sep 79. Hammer; (7") **I WALK THE LINE. / ROCK ISLAND LINE** [ ] [-]

Mar 82. Ronco; (lp)(c) **COWBOYS (1-side w / MARTY ROBBINS)** [ ] [-]

Jul 82. Old Gold; (7") **A THING CALLED LOVE. / ONE PIECE AT A TIME** [ ] [-]

Jul 82. Old Gold; (7") **A BOY NAMED SUE. / SAN QUENTIN** [ ] [-]

Oct 82. Bear Family; (lp) **INSIDE A SWEDISH PRISON** [ ] [-]

Jul 84. Bear Family; (lp) **BITTER TEARS** [ ] [-]

Sep 84. Bear Family; (lp) **TALL MAN** [ ] [-]

Sep 84. Bear Family; (lp) **THE UNISSUED JOHNNY CASH** [ ] [-]

1985. Bear Family; (lp) **DESTINATION VICTORIA STATION** [ ] [-]

Nov 86. Bear FAmily; (cd) **UP THROUGH THE YEARS 1955-57** [ ] [-]

Aug 83. Peach River; (7") **LOVE ME TENDER. (with JULIE ANDREWS) / (other by her)** [ ] [-]

Oct 83. Scoop; (7"ep)(c-ep) **6 TRACK HITS** [ ] [-]
– A boy named Sue / I walk the line / Ring of fire / If I were a carpenter / Folsom Prison blues / What is truth?

Apr 84. Allegience; (lp)(c) **THE FIRST YEARS** [ ] [-]

Nov 84. Astan; (lp)(c) **GREAT SONGS OF JOHNNY CASH** [ ] [-]
(pic-lp Dec85)

Dec 84. Premier; (lp)(c) **18 LEGENDARY PERFORMANCES** [ ] [-]

Feb 87. Premier; (lp)(c) **LADY** [ ] [-]

Dec 85. Country STore; (lp)(c) **AT THE COUNTRY STORE** [ ] [-]

May 85. Wand; (lp)(c) **A DIAMOND IN THE ROUGH** [ ] [-]

May 85. Wand; (lp) **WELCOME FRIEND** [ ] [-]

Sep 86. Wand; (lp)(c) **BELIEVE IN HIM** [ ] [-]
(re-iss.Sep88 on 'MFP')

May 87. Topline; (cd) **HOME OF THE BLUES** [ ] [-]

May 88. Rhino; (cd-ep) **LIL BIT O' GOLD** [ ] [-]
– I walk the line / Folsom Prison blues / Guess things happen that way / Ballad of a teenage queen.

May 88. Big Country; (lp)(c)(cd) **THE ORIGINAL JOHNNY CASH** [ ] [-]

Jul 88. Connoisseur; (lp)(c) **COUNTRY BOOGIE** [ ] [-]
(cd-iss.Apr90)

Jul 88. Exel; (lp)(c) **BALLAD OF A TEENAGE QUEEN** [ ] [-]

1988. Starr; (cd) **20 GREATEST HITS** [ ] [-]

Nov 88. Sierra; (lp)(c) **REPLAY ON . . .** [ ] [-]

Jul 89. Instant; (lp)(c)(cd) **BORN TO LOSE** [ ] [-]
(re-iss.1992 on 'Charity')

Sep 92. Music Club; (cd)(c) **THE BEST OF THE SUN YEARS 1955-1961** [ ] [-]

Oct 93. Columbia; (7")(cd-s) **RING OF FIRE. / A THING CALLED LOVE** [ ] [-]

Oct 93. Sony Europe; (cd) **THE GOSPEL COLLECTION** [ ] [-]

Aug 94. Columbia; (cd)(c) **THE MAN IN BLACK – THE DEFINITIVE COLLECTION** [15] [ ]

– Ring of fire / I walk the line / Get rhythm (live) / It ain't me babe / I still miss someone / (Ghost) Riders in the sky / The baron / Sunday morning coming down / Daddy sang bass / Jackson (with JUNE CARTER) / One piece at a time / Orange blossom secial / Folsom prison blues (live) / San Quentin (live) / A boy named Sue (live) / A thing called love / Don't take your guns to town / Wanted man / Big river / Without love / No expectations / Highway patrolman / Singin' in Vietnam talkin' blues / Man in black.

Jan 94. Sony Europe; (cd) **20 FOOT-TAPPING GREATS** [ ] [ ]
Jan 94. Sony Europe; (cd) **JOHNNY 99** [ ] [ ]
Mar 94. Charly; (cd) **GUESS THINGS HAPPEN THAT WAY** [ ] [-]
Sep 94. Sixteen; (cd) **16 GREATEST HITS** [ ] [-]
Jan 95. Collection; (cd) **THE COLLECTION** [ ] [-]
Mar 95. Spectrum; (cd)(c) **RING OF FIRE** [ ] [-]
May 95. Columbia; (cd)(c) **ITCHY FEET – 20 FOOT TAPPIN' GREATS** [ ] [ ]
May 95. Pickwick; (cd)(c) **GET RHYTHM – THE BEST OF THE SUN YEARS** [ ] [-]
May 95. Marble Arch; (cd)(c) **THE BEST OF JOHNNY CASH** [ ] [-]
Jun 95. Truetrax; (cd)(c) **IN CONCERT** [ ] [-]
Jul 95. Charly; (cd) **RING OF FIRE – HIS GREATEST HITS LIVE** [ ] [-]
Jul 95. Summit; (cd) **LIVE IN THE RING OF FIRE** [ ] [-]
Jul 95. Charly; (cd) **FOLSOM PRISON BLUES** [ ] [-]
Sep 95. Hallmark; (cd)(c) **LIVE** [ ] [-]
Nov 95. Charly; (3xcd-box) **THE SUN YEARS** [ ] [-]
Nov 95. Columbia; (cd)(c) **PERSONAL CHRISTMAS COLLECTION** [ ] [-]
Nov 95. Bear Family; (6xcd-box) **THE MAN IN BLACK 1963-1969** [ ] [ ]

CAST

Formed: Liverpool, England . . .1994 by ex-LA'S guitarist JOHN POWER. Spent just under a year perfecting their rhythmic debut album 'ALL CHANGE', which was preceeded by two UK Top 20 hits 'FINETIME' & 'ALRIGHT'. • **Style:** Well-structured psychedelic rock likened to possibly OASIS. • **Songwriters:** JOHN POWER.

Recommended: ALL CHANGE (*7)

JOHN POWER – vocals, guitar (ex-LA'S) / **PETER WILKINSON** – bass / **KEITH O'NEILL** – drums / **LIAM 'SKIN' TYSON** – guitar

Polydor M.C.A.

Jul 95. (7"green)(c-s)(cd-s) **FINETIME. / BETTER MAN / SATELLITES** [17] [ ]
Sep 95. (7"blue)(c-s)(cd-s) **ALRIGHT. / FOLLOW ME DOWN / MEET ME** [13] [ ]
Oct 95. (cd)(c)(lp) **ALL CHANGE** [7] [ ]
– Alright / Promised land / Sandstorm / Mankind / Tell it like it is / Four walls / Finetime / Back of my mind / Walkaway / Reflections / History / Two of a kind.

CATCH (see under ⇒ EURYTHMICS)

CATHERINE WHEEL

Formed: Norwich & Great Yarmouth, England . . . Apr'90, by ROB DICKINSON and BRIAN FUTTER. They recorded demo on own 8-track in bedroom, which was sent to indie 'Wilde Club', who released debut EP 'SHE'S MY FRIEND'. Later in 1991, they went full-time and signed to 'Fontana', where they scored UK Top 40 album hit with Tim Friese-Greene (TALK TALK) produced 'FERMENT'. • **Style:** Guitar-based alternative shoe-gazing rock outfit, very reminiscent of TEARDROP EXPLODES. • **Songwriters:** Group penned except; DON'T WANT TO KNOW IF YOU ARE LONELY (Husker Du) / THAT'S WHEN I REACH FOR MY REVOLVER (Mission of Burma) / 30th CENTURY MAN (Scott Walker). • **Trivia:** ROB is the younger cousin of IRON MAIDEN singer BRUCE DICKINSON.

Recommended: FERMENT (*7).

ROB DICKINSON (b.23 Jul'65, Norwich) – vocals, guitar / **BRIAN FUTTER** (b. 7 Dec'65, London) – guitar, vocals / **DAVE HAWES** (b.10 Nov'65, Great Yarmouth) – bass / **NEIL SIMS** (b. 4 Oct'65, Norwich) – percussion, drums

Wilde Club not issued

Jan 91. (12"ep) **SHE'S MY FRIEND / UPSIDE DOWN. / WISH / SALT** [ ] [-]
May 91. (12"ep)(cd-ep) **PAINFUL THING / SHALLOW / SPIN / I WANT TO TOUCH YOU** [ ] [-]

Fontana Fontana

Nov 91. (7") **BLACK METALLIC. / LET ME DOWN AGAIN** [68] [-]
(12"+=)(cd-s+=) – Crawling over me / Saccharin.
Jan 92. (7") **BALLOON. / INTRAVENOUS** [59] [ ]
(12"+=)(cd-s+=) – Painful thing (live) / Let me down again (live).
Feb 92. (cd)(c)(lp) **FERMENT** [36] [ ]
– Texture / I want to touch you / Black metallic / Indigo is blue / She's my friend / Shallow / Ferment / Flower to hide / Tumbledown / Bill and Ben / Salt.
—— (incl.free 7"ep).
Apr 92. (d7")(12"ep)(cd-ep) **I WANT TO TOUCH YOU. / URSA MAJOR SPACE STATION/ / OUR FRIEND JOEY. / COLLIDEOSCOPE** [35] [ ]
(12") – (first 7") / Half life.
(cd-s) – (first 7") / Wish / Black metallic.
Nov 92. (12"ep)(cd-ep) **30th CENTURY MAN. / DON'T WANT TO KNOW IF YOU ARE LONELY / THAT'S WHEN I REACH FOR MY REVOLVER** [47] [ ]
Jul 93. (7")(c-s) **CRANK. / COME BACK AGAIN** [66] [ ]
(12") – ('A'side) / Black metallic / Painful ting.
(cd-s) – ('A'side) / La la la-la la / Something strange.
(cd-s) ('A' side) / Pleasure / Tongue twisted.
Sep 93. (7") **SHOW ME MARY. / FLOWER TO HIDE (live)** [62] [ ]
(cd-s+=) – Car / Girl stand still.
(cd-s) – ('A'side) / These four wheels / Smother.
(12") – ('A'side) / High heels / Mouth full of air.
Sep 93. (cd)(c)(lp) **CHROME** [58] [ ]
– Kill rhythm / I confess / Crank / Broken head / Pain / Strange fruit / Chrome / The nude / Ursa Major space station / Fripp / Half life / Show me Mary.
—— guests on album album:- TIM FRIESE-GREENE and AUDREY RILEY.
Jul 95. (10")(c-s) **WAYDOWN. / WISH YOU WERE HERE (XFM session)** [67] [ ]
(cd-s) – ('A'side) / Show me Mary (XFM sessions).
(pic-cd-s+=) – Kill rhythm.
(cd-s) – ('A'side) / Chrome / Broken head (XFM sessions).
Sep 95. (c-s)(cd-s) **JUDY STARING AT THE SUN / GOD INSIDE MY HEAD** [ ] [ ]
(cd-s+=) – Crank (live) / Waydown (live).
(cd-s+=) – Glitter / Capacity to change.
(cd-s+=) – Backwards guitar / Angelo Nero.
(above featured TANYA DONNELLY)
Nov 95. (cd)(c)(d-lp) **HAPPY DAYS** [ ] [ ]
– God inside my head / Waydown / Little muscle / Heal / Empty head / Receive / My exhibition / Eat my dust you insensitive fuck / Shocking / Love tips up / Judy staring at the sun / Hole / Fizzy love / Glitter / Kill my soul.

Felix CAVALIERE (see under ⇒ RASCALS)

Nick CAVE & The BAD SEEDS

Formed: Berlin, Germany . . . 1983 by Australian NICK CAVE, who at the time also lived in London. For a few gigs in '83, he was backed by The CAVEMEN until change of name. Around this time, CAVE had been credited on DIE HAUT album BURNIN' THE ICE, writing and singing 4 songs. CAVE was still contracted to the 'Mute' label from his BIRTHDAY PARTY days, so he stuck with them for release of UK Top 40 entry 'FROM HER TO ETERNITY'. • **Style:** Avant-garde alternative rock with CAVE'S weird but wonderful gruff vocals the forte. • **Songwriters:** All songs by CAVE, except IN THE GHETTO (Elvis Presley) / RUNNING SCARED (Roy Orbison) / BLACK BETTY (Ram Jam) / BY THE TIME I GET TO PHOENIX (Jim Webb) / MUDDY WATER (Johnny Rivers) / HEY JOE (Jimi Hendrix) / ALL TOMORROW'S PARTIES (Velvet Underground) / THE CARNIVAL IS OVER (Seekers) / SOMETHING'S GOTTEN HOLD OF MY HEART (Gene Pitney) / HELPLESS (Neil Young) / WHAT A WONDERFUL WORLD (Ray Charles) / etc. mainly from his covers album KICKING AGAINST THE PRICKS. • **Trivia:** He is the author of two books AND THE ASS SAW THE ANGEL and KING INK. By the late 80's, he had also starred in the film GHOSTS . . . OF THE CIVIL DEAD, also supplying soundtrack.

Recommended: THE FIRSTBORN IS DEAD (*7) / THE GOOD SUN (*8) / HENRY'S DREAM (*8) / LET LOVE IN (*8) / FROM HER TO ETERNITY (*6).

NICK CAVE – vocals (ex-BIRTHDAY PARTY, ex-BOYS NEXT DOOR)
MICK HARVEY – guitar, keyboards (ex-BIRTHDAY PARTY, ex-BOYS NEXT DOOR)
BLIXA BARGELD – guitar (of EINSTURZENDE NEUBAUTEN, ex-BIRTHDAY PARTY)
BARRY ADAMSON – bass, guitar (ex-MAGAZINE, ex-PETE SHELLEY)
HUGO RACE – drums

Mute Elektra

Jun 84. (7") **IN THE GHETTO. / THE MOON IS IN THE GUTTER** [ ] [ ]
—— added **ANITA LANE** – synthesizers (ex-solo artist)
Jun 84. (lp)(c) **FROM HER TO ETERNITY** [40] [ ]
– Avalanche / Cabin fever / Well of misery / From her to eternity / Wings of flies / Saint Huck / A box for black Paul. *(cd-1987 +=)* – In the ghetto / The Moon is in the gutter / From her to eternity (1987).
—— **THOMAS WYLDER** – drums (ex-DIE HAUT) repl. **HUGO and ANITA**
Jun 85. (lp)(c) **THE FIRSTBORN IS DEAD** [53] [ ]
– Tupelo / Say goodbye to the little girl tree / Train long suffering / Black crow king / Knockin' on Joe / Wanted man / Blind Lemon Jefferson. *(cd-iss.Apr88)*
Jul 85. (7") **TUPELO. / THE SIX STRINGS THAT DREW BLOOD** [ ] [-]
Jun 86. (7") **THE SINGER. / RUNNING SCARED.** [ ] [-]
(12"+=) – Black Betty.
Aug 86. (lp)(c)(cd) **KICKING AGAINST THE PRICKS** [89] [ ]
– Muddy water / I'm gonna kill that woman / Sleeping Annaleah / Long black veil / Hey Joe / The singer / Black Betty * / Running scared * / All tomorrow's parties / By the time I get to Phoenix / The hammer song / Something's gotten hold of my heart / Jesus met the woman at the well / The carnival is over. *(cd+= *)*
Nov 86. (lp)(c)(cd) **YOUR FUNERAL . . . MY TRIAL** [ ] [ ]
– Sad waters / The Carny / Your funeral . . . my trial / Stranger than kindness / Jack's shadow / Hard on for love / She fell away / Long time man. (cd+=) – Scum.
—— **CAVE** retained **HARVEY, BARGELD** and **WYDLER,** bringing in **ROLAND WOLF** – bass / **KID CONGO POWERS** – guitar (ex-CRAMPS, ex-GUN CLUB)
May 88. (7")(12") **THE MERCY SEAT. / NEW DAY** [ ] [-]
(12"+=) – ('A'video mix).
(cd-s+=) – From her to eternity (film version) / Tupelo (version).
Sep 88. (lp)(c)(cd) **TENDER PREY** [67] [ ]
– The mercy seat / Up jumped the Devil / Deanna / Watching Alice / Mercy / City of refuge / Slowly goes the night / Sunday's slave / Sugar, sugar, sugar / New morning. *(cd+=)* – The mercy seat (video mix). (free-12"ep.w/above) **AND THE ASS SAW THE ANGEL** (narration/book) – One Autumn / Animal static / Mah sanctum / Lamentation.

Sep 88. (12") **DEANNA. / THE GIRL AT THE BOTTOM OF MY GLASS** [ ] [-]
Mar 89. (lp)(c)(cd) **GHOSTS . . . OF THE CIVIL DEAD (Soundtrack w/ dialogue) ("NICK CAVE, MICK HARVEY, BLIXA BARGELD")** [ ] [-]
– The news / Introduction – A prison in the desert / David Hale – I've been a prison guard since I was 18 years old / Glover – I was 16 when they put me in prison / David Hale – you're danglin' us like a bunch of meat on a hook / Pop mix / Glover – we were united once / David Hale – the day of the murders / Lilly's theme ("A touch of warmth") / Maynard mix / David Hale – what I'm tellin' is the truth / Outro – The free world / Glover – one man released so they can imprison the rest of the world.

—— (now a 5-piece, without WOLF)
Mar 90. (7")(12")(cd-s) **THE SHIP SONG. / THE TRAIN SONG** [ ] [-]
Apr 90. (cd)(c)(lp) **THE GOOD SON** [47] [ ]
– Foi na cruz / The good son / Sorrow's child / The weeping song / The ship song / The hammer song / Lament / The witness song / Lucy.
(w/-7"/cd-s) **THE MERCY SEAT / CITY OF REFUGE / DEANNA (all acoustic)**
Sep 90. (7") **THE WEEPING SONG. / COCKS'N'ASSES** [ ] [-]
(12"+=)(cd-s+=) – Helpless.
Mar 92. (7") **STRAIGHT TO YOU. / JACK THE RIPPER (acoustic)** [68] [ ]
(12"+=)(cd-s+=) – Blue bird.
Apr 92. (cd)(c)(lp) **HENRY'S DREAM** [29] [ ]
– Papa won't leave you Henry / I had a dream, Joe / Straight to you / Brother, my cup is empty / Christina the astonishing / When I first came to town / John Finn's wife / Loom of the land / Jack the ripper.
Aug 92. (7") **I HAD A DREAM, JOE. / THE GOOD SON (live)** [ ] [ ]
(12"+=)(cd-s+=) – Henry's dream / The Carney (live) / The mercy seat (live) / The ship sons (live).
Nov 92. (7")(c-s) **WHAT A WONDERFUL WORLD. ("NICK CAVE & SHANE McGOWAN") / A RAINY NIGHT IN SOHO / LUCY 2** [72] [-]
Sep 93. (cd) **LIVE SEEDS (live)** [67] [ ]
– Mercy seat / Deanna / The ship song / Papa won't leave you Henry / Plain gold ring / John Finn's wife / Tupelo / Brother my cup is empty / The weeping song / Jack the ripper / The good son / From her to eternity.
Mar 94. (7")(12")(cd-s) **DO YOU LOVE ME? / CASSIEL'S SONG / SAIL AWAY** [68] [ ]
Apr 94. (cd)(c)(lp) **LET LOVE IN** [12] [ ]
– Do you love me? / Nobody's baby now / Loverman / Jangling Jack / Red right hand / I let love in / Thirsty dog / Ain't gonna rain anymore / Lay me low / Do you love me? (part 2).

—— **JAMES JOHNSON** – guitar (of GALLON DRUNK) repl. on tour only BLIXA
Jul 94. (7")(12")(cd-s) **LOVERMAN. / (I'LL LOVE YOU) TILL THE END OF THE WORLD** [ ] [ ]
Oct 94. (7"red) **RED RIGHT HAND. / THAT'S WHAT JAZZ IS TO ME** [ ] [ ]
(cd-s+=) – Where the action is.
Oct 95. (7")(c-s) **NICK CAVE AND THE BAD SEEDS + KYLIE MINOGUE:- WHERE THE WILD ROSES GROW. / BALLAD OF ROBERT MOORE & BETTY COLTRANE** [11] [ ]
(cd-s+=) – The willow garden.

C.C.S. (see under ⇒ KORNER, ALEXIS)

CHAMBERS BROTHERS

Formed: Lee County, Mississippi, USA . . . 1950's. The brothers moved to Los Angeles in 1961, and toured as black gospel singers. They signed to local 'Vault' records, but when they shifted to 'Columbia' in 1966, their • **Style:** dramatically changes with the times, into more soul-funk basic heavy blues. In 1968, they scored massive Stateside selling 'TIME HAS COME TODAY' 45 and lp. • **Songwriters:** The brothers, except SHOUT (Isley Brothers) / etc. • **Trivia:** LESTER had learned harmonica from the legendary SONNY TERRY.

Recommended: TIME HAS COME TODAY (*5)

LESTER CHAMBERS (b.13 Apr'40) – vocals, harmonica / **WILLIE CHAMBERS** (b. 2 Mar'38) – guitar, vocals / **JOE CHAMBERS** (b.22 Aug'52) – guitar, vocals / **GEORGE CHAMBERS** (b.26 Sep'31) – bass, vocals
Dec 64. (7") **CALL ME. / SEVENTEEN** [ ] [ ]
Mar 65. (7") **LOVE ME LIKE THE RAIN. / PRETTY GIRLS EVERYWHERE** [ ] [ ]
1965. (lp) **PEOPLE GET READY** [ ] [ ]
– Yes, yes, yes / Tore up over you / Reconsider baby / You've got me running / People get ready / Money / You can run / Hooka tooka / Call me / Summertime / Your old lady / It's all over now.
1967. (7") **SHOUT. / (part 2)** [-] [ ]
(re-iss.Dec68)

—— added **BRIAN KEENAN** (b.28 Jan'44) – drums (ex-MANFRED MANN)
1966. (lp) **THE CHAMBERS BROTHERS – NOW (live)** [ ] [ ]
– Introduction to / High heel sneakers / Baby, please don't go / What'd I say / Long tall Sally / Bony Moronie / It's groovin' time / You don't have to go / C.C.rider / So fine.

Direction-C.B.S. | Columbia

1966. (7") **TIME HAS COME TODAY. / DINAH** [-] [ ]
1967. (7") **PLEASE DON'T LEAVE ME. / I CAN'T STAND IT** [-] [ ]
1967. (7") **ALL STRUNG OUT OVER YOU. / FALLING IN LOVE** [ ] [ ]
Nov 67. (lp) **TIME HAS COME TODAY** (UK Nov 68) [ ] [4]
– All strung out over you / People get ready / I can't stand it / Romeo and Juliet / In the midnight hour / So tired / Uptown / Please don't leave me / What the world needs now is love / Time has come today.
Jan 68. (7") **UPTOWN. / LOVE ME LIKE THE RAIN** [ ] [ ]
Aug 68. (7") **THE TIME HAS COME TODAY. / PEOPLE GET READY** [ ] [11]
Nov 68. (7") **I CAN'T TURN YOU LOOSE. / DO YOUR THING** [ ] [37]
Nov 68. (lp) **A NEW TIME – A NEW DAY** [ ] [16]
– I can't turn you loose / Guess who / Do your thing / Where have all the flowers gone / Love is all I have / You got the power . . .to turn me on / I wish it would rain / Rock me mama / No, no, no, don't say goodbye / Satisfy you / A new time – a new day.
May 69. (7") **ARE YOU READY? / YOU GOT THE POWER TO TURN ME ON** [ ] [ ]
Jun 69. (7") **PEOPLE GET READY. / NO, NO, NO, DON'T SAY GOODBYE** [ ] [ ]
Aug 69. (7") **WAKE UP. / EVERYBODY NEEDS SOMEONE** [ ] [ ]

—— (above from the film 'The April Fools')
Dec 69. (d-lp) **LOVE, PEACE & HAPPINESS** [ ] [ ]
– Have a little faith / Let's do it / To love somebody / If you want me to / Wake up / Love, peace and happiness / Wade in the water / Everybody needs somebody / I can't turn you loose / People get ready / Bang bang / You're so fine / Medley: Undecided – Love love love. (1-lp= LIVE AT FILLMORE EAST, NEW YORK)
Oct 69. (7") **HAVE A LITTLE FAITH. / BABY TAKES CARE OF BUSINESS** [-] [ ]
Dec 69. (7") **MERRY CHRISTMAS, HAPPY NEW YEAR. / DID YOU STOP TO PRAY THIS MORNING** [-] [ ]
(re-iss. Dec 71)
Feb 70. (7") **LOVE, PEACE & HAPPINESS. / IF YOU WANT ME TO** [ ] [ ]
Jun 70. (7") **LET'S DO IT. / TO LOVE SOMEBODY** [ ] [ ]
Jan 71. (7") **FUNKY. / LOVE, PEACE & HAPPINESS** [ ] [ ]
Feb 71. (lp) **NEW GENERATION** [ ] [ ]
– Are you ready / Young girl / Funky / When the evening comes / Practice what you preach / Reflections / Pollution / New generation / Going to the mill.
Apr 71. (7") **NEW GENERATION. / WHEN THE EVENING COMES** [-] [ ]
Dec 71. (7") **(BY THE HAIR ON) MY CHINNY CHIN CHIN. / HEAVEN** [ ] [ ]
Mar 72. (lp) **OH MY GOD** [-] [ ]
– Mean old world / Which side / Heaven / Any old time / Man did it / Old doggone Devil / This little piece of land / Celebration of life / (By the hair on) My chinny chin chin.
1972. (7") **BOOGIE CHILDREN. / YOU MAKE THE MAGIC** [-] [ ]

—— Disbanded early 1972. KEENAN joined GENYA RAVAN's band. They reformed in 1973.

not issued | Aveo

1973. (lp) **UNBONDED** [-] [ ]
– Reflections / Let's go, let's go, let's go / The weight / 1-2-3 / If loving you is wrong I don't want to be right / Good vibrations / Gypsy woman / I (who have nothing) / Do you believe in magic / Looking back.
1973. (7") **LET'S GO, LET'S GO. / DO YOU BELIEVE IN MAGIC** [-] [ ]
1973. (7") **1-2-3. /** [-] [ ]

—— guest **JEROME BRAILEY** – drums repl. KEENAN
1974. (lp) **RIGHT MOVE** [-] [ ]
– Crazy 'bout the ladies / Pretty girls everywhere / Stop the train / Miss Lady Brown / Lotta fine mama / Smack dab in the middle / Stealin' watermelons (somethin' you got) / Who wants to listen / We'll sing together.
1974. (7") **MISS LADY BROWN. / STEALIN' WATERMELONS** [-] [ ]

—— Split again, but did some reunion gigs. **GREGG** – drums repl. BRAILEY

Roxbury | Chelsea

1977. (lp) **LIVE IN CONCERT ON MARS** [ ] [ ]
– Superstar / Me and your mother / Midnight blue (who are you) / Medley: Stealing watermelons (is something you got) – Mama your daughter (is not enough to burn water) – Bring it down front (pretty mama).

– compilations, others, etc. –

1968. Liberty/ US= Vault; (lp) **SHOUT** [ ] [ ]
1968. Vault; (7") **GIRLS WE LOVE YOU. / JUST A CLOSER WALK WITH THEE** [-] [ ]
1969. Vault; (7") **HOUSE OF THE RISING SUN. / BLUES GET OFF MY SHOULDER** [-] [ ]
1970. Liberty/ US= Vault; (lp) **FEELING THE BLUES** [ ] [ ]
Dec 70. Vault; (lp) **THE CHAMBERS BROTHERS' GREATEST HITS** [-] [ ]
Dec 71. C.B.S./ US= Columbia; (lp)(c) **GREATEST HITS** [ ] [ ]
– Funky / In the midnight hour / Time has come today / I can't turn you loose / People get ready / Let's do it / All strung out / Are you ready / Love, peace and happiness.
1975. C.B.S./ US= Columbia; (7") **THE TIME HAS COME TODAY. / I CAN'T TURN YOU LOOSE** [ ] [ ]

CHAMELEONS

Formed: Middleton, North Manchester, England . . . 1981 by BURGESS, FIELDING and SMITHIES. After brief disastrous spell with 'Epic' in 1982, they signed to 'Virgin' subsidiary 'Statik'. Their major break came late in 1985 when new manager and 5th member TONY FLETCHER encouraged David Geffen to sign them to his label. • **Style:** Filled the huge gap left by the demise of TEARDROP EXPLODES. Superb power-rock full of indie style mood/atmosphere. • **Songwriters:** All penned by band, except JOHN, I'M ONLY DANCING (Bowie) / TOMORROW NEVER KNOWS (Beatles) / SPLITTING IN TWO (Alternative TV) . REEGS covered; SEE MY FRIENDS (Kinks). MARK BURGESS covered YOU ONLY LIVE TWICE (John Barry) / FACADES (Philip Glass) / SOMETHING FOR THE GIRL WITH EVERYTHING + MOON OVER KENTUCKY (Sparks). • **Trivia:** Nothing whatsoever to do with LORI & THE CHAMELEONS. Below album 55 mins.

Recommended: THE SCRIPT OF THE BRIDGE (*9) / WHAT DOES ANYTHING MEAN? BASICALLY? (*8)

The YEARS

(**FIELDING /SMITHIES**) first band.

Tuff Gong not iss

1981. (7"m) **COME DANCING. / RED CHEVY / DON'T LEAVE** [ ] [-]

The CHAMELEONS

MARK 'Birdy' BURGESS – vocals, bass (ex-CLICHES) / **DAVE FIELDING** – guitar, strings (ex-YEARS) / **REG SMITHIES** – guitar (ex-YEARS) / **JOHN LEVER** – drums, percussion (ex-POLITICIANS) repl. BRIAN SCHOFIELD

Epic not issued

Mar 82. (7") **IN SHREDS. / LESS THAN HUMAN** [ ] [-]

— **JOHN LEVER** was replaced for a year by **MARTIN JACKSON** (ex-MAGAZINE)

Statik not issued

Feb 83. (7") **AS HIGH AS YOU CAN GO. / PLEASURE AND THE PAIN** [ ] [-]
(12"+=) – Paper tigers.

Jun 83. (7") **A PERSON ISN'T SAFE ANYWHERE THESE DAYS. / THURSDAY'S CHILD** [ ] [-]
(12"+=) – Prisoners of the Sun.

Aug 83. (lp)(c)(pic-lp) **THE SCRIPT OF THE BRIDGE** [ ] [-]
– Don't fall / Here today / Monkeyland / Second skin / Up the down escalator / Less than human / Pleasure and the pain / Thursday's child / As high as you can go / A person isn't safe anywhere these days / Paper tigers / View from a hill. *(cd+=)* – In shreds / Nostalgia. (re-iss.Oct85, cd-iss.Feb86 + Jun89) (re-iss.cd Jul95 on 'Dead Dead Good')

1983. (7") **UP THE DOWN ESCALATOR. / MONKEYLAND** [-] [-] Germ'y
(12"+=) – Prisoners of the sun.

Feb 85. (7") **IN SHREDS (live). / NOSTALGIA (live)** [ ] [-]
(12"+=) – Less than human (live).

— added on stage **ALISTAIR LEWTWAITE** – keyboards, but he was replaced by **ANDY CLEGG** – keyboards (ex-MUSIC FOR ABORIGINES)

May 85. (lp)(c) **WHAT DOES ANYTHING MEAN? BASICALLY?** [60] [-]
– Silence, sea and sky / Perfume garden / Intrigue in Tangiers / Return of the roughnecks / Singing rule Britannia (while the walls close in) / On the beach / Looking inwardly / One flesh / Home is where the heart is / P.S. goodbye. *(cd-iss.Feb86 + Jun89) (re-iss.cd Jul95 on 'Dead Dead Good')*

Aug 85. (7") **SINGING RULE BRITTANIA (WHILE THE WALLS CLOSE IN). / ('A'radio version)** [ ] [-]
(12"+=) – Pleasure and the pain (radio 1 version).

Geffen Geffen

Jun 86. (7") **TEARS. / PARADISO.** [ ] [ ]
(12"+=) – Inside out.
(d7"++=) – Swamp thing.

Sep 86. (lp)(c) **STRANGE TIMES** [44] [ ]
– Mad Jack / Caution / Tears / Soul in isolation / Swamp thing / Time – The end of time / Seriocity / In answer / Childhood / I'll remember. *(cd.iss.Mar87)* (+=) Tears (original version). (US-iss.was as lp w/free m-lp) – Tears (full arrangement)/ Paradiso/ Inside out/ Ever after/ John, I'm only dancing / Tomorrow never knows. *(re-iss.d-cd Jul93)*

Sep 86. (7") **SWAMP THING. / JOHN, I'M ONLY DANCING** [ ] [ ]
(12"+=) – Tears (original version).

— split after manager TONY FLETCHER died of a heart attack 1986. MARK and JOHN formed The SUN AND THE MOON with ANDY CLEGG and ANDY WHITAKER. In 1993, MARK BURGESS formed his SONS OF GOD. FIELDING and SMITHIES formed The REEGS in '88.

– compilations, others, etc. –

Mar 86. Hybrid; (ltd-lp) **THE FAN AND THE BELLOWS** (most rec. 1981) [ ] [-]
– The fan and the bellows / Nostalgia / Less than human / In shreds / Prisoners of the Sun / Nostalgia (7" version) / Turn to the vices / Love is / Everyday I'm crucified / Endlessly falling / Nathan's phase.

Oct 90. Glass Pyramid; (cd)(c)(lp) **TRIPPING DOGS** [ ] [-]
Dec 90. Strange Fruit; (cd)(c)(lp) **THE PEEL SESSIONS** [ ] [-]
Jun 92. Illusion; (cd)(c)(lp) **HERE TODAY . . . GONE TOMORROW** [ ] [-]
Jun 92. Illusion; (cd)(c)(lp) **LIVE IN TORONTO (live '87)** [ ] [-]
(above 2 re-iss.later in '92 as d-cd,d-lp)
Jan 93. Nighttracks; (cd) **RADIO 1 EVENING SHOW SESSIONS** [ ] [-]
Feb 93. Imaginary; (pic-cd) **FREE TRADE REHEARSAL (live)** [ ] [-]
May 93. Imaginary; (cd)(lp) **AUFFUHRUNG IN BERLIN (live)** [ ] [-]
May 93. Imaginary; (cd)(lp) **DALI'S PICTURE** [ ] [-]
May 93. Imaginary; (d-cd) **DALI'S PICTURE / LIVE IN BERLIN** [ ] [-]
1994. Glass Pyramid; (cd-ep) **TONY FLETCHER WALKED ON WATER . . . .LA LA LA LA LA – LA LA – LA-LA** [ ] [-]
– Is it any wonder / Free for all / The healer / Denims and curls.
(above was to have been issued as 7"ep Oct90)
Nov 94. Bone Idol; (cd) **NORTHERN SONGS** (w/ above EP) [ ] [-]

SUN AND THE MOON

MARK BURGESS + JOHN LEVER / + ANDY WHITAKER – keyboards (ex-MUSIC FOR ABORIGINES) / **ANDY CLEGG** – guitar (ex-MUSIC FOR ABORIGINES)

Geffen Geffen

May 88. (lp)(c)(cd) **THE SUN AND THE MOON** [ ] [ ]
– The speed of life / Death of imagination / Peace in our time / A matter of conscience / Dolphin / House on fire / The price of grain / Limbo-land / A picture of England / This passionate breed.

Jun 88. (7") **THE SPEED OF LIFE. / DEATH OF IMAGINATION** [ ] [ ]
(12"+=) – The boy who sees everything / I love you, you bastard.

Glass Pyr. not issued

Nov 88. (7"ep) **ALIVE; NOT DEAD. / ARABS AND AMERICANS / ELECTED** [ ] [-]
(re-iss.Feb89 as 12"ep/cd-ep on 'Midnight Music') (+=) – Adam's song.

— In 1991, LEVER, CLEGG + WHITAKER with ATKINSON formed WEAVEWORLD who released a 12" single for 'Sugarpussy'; DAVY JONES. / OUT AND DOWN / PATHETICAL TWAT

MARK BURGESS & THE SONS OF GOD

Imaginary not issued

Jul 93. (lp) **ZIMA JUNCTION** [ ] [-]
– World on fire / Waiting for a friend / Refugees / The great adventure / Beat the boat / When harmony comes / Our soul, dead soul, brother and fool / Happy new life / Up on the hill / Fascades / You only live twice.

Indigo not issued

Nov 94. (d-cd) **SPRING BLOOMS TRA-LA-LA** (solo) [ ] [-]
–

MARK BURGESS & YVES ALTANA

Dead Dead Good not issued

Aug 95. (7") **SIN. / HOLLIN HIGH** [ ] [-]
(cd-s+=) – Moon over Kentucky.

Sep 95. (7") **ALWAYS WANT. / STEPHANIE WEAVES** [ ] [-]
(cd-s+=) – Something for the girl with everything.

Oct 95. (cd)(c)(lp) **PARADYNING** [ ] [-]
– Sin / Always went / Adrian be / Silver / Money won't save our soul / You opened my mind (then the acid kicked in) / Inhaling / World without end / Hi Joe / Stop talking.

REEGS

FIELDING + SMITHIES

Imaginary not issued

Apr 89. (12"ep) **SEE MY FRIENDS / IS THERE. / A MOTHER-IN-LAW IN THE CLUB / THIS SAVAGE GARDEN** [ ] [-]

Oct 89. (12"ep) **CHORUS OF THE LOST. / POND LIFE / START TO SEE (instrumental)** [ ] [-]
(re-iss.Aug90)

— added drum machine + **GARY LAVERY** – vocals

Jul 91. (cd)(c)(lp) **RETURN OF THE SEA MONKEYS** [ ] [-]

— Split . . . FIELDING became producer noteably for The INSPIRAL CARPETS.

Harry CHAPIN

Born: 7 Dec'42, Greenwich Village, New York City, USA. Son of a big band drummer, he played in Brooklyn Heights Boys' Choir, before forming a trio with his brothers TOM and STEPHEN. Became a documentary film maker in the 60's and he directed in 1968 the Oscar-nominated 'Legendary Champions'. He formed own backing group and signed for 'Elektra' in 1971. Became multi-famous in the mid-70's for DJ song 'W-O-L-D', which went No.1 US in 1974. Another classic followed 'CAT'S IN THE CRADLE' (later a 90's hit for hard-rock act UGLY KID JOE), and he even wrote Broadway musical 'The Night That Made America Famous'. Sadly on the 16th July 1981, he was killed a automobile accident, while driving to a benefit concert. • **Style:** Narrative folk-rock balladeer with a message in every song. • **Songwriters:** Self-penned. • **Trivia:** His younger TOM CHAPIN released an album in 1988 for 'Flying Fish'; 'LET ME BACK INTO YOUR LIFE'.

Recommended: ANTHOLOGY (*7)

HARRY CHAPIN – vocals, guitar with **RON PALMER** – guitar / **TIM SCOTT** – cello / **JOHN WALLACE** – bass / **STEVE CHAPIN** – keyboards / **RUSS KUNKEL** – drums, percussion

Elektra Elektra

Feb 72. (7") **TAXI. / EMPTY** [-] [24]

Mar 72. (lp) **HEADS & TAILS** [ ] [60]
– Could you put your light on, please / Greyhound / Everybody's lonely / Sometime, somewhere wife / Empty / Taxi / Any old kind of day / Dogtown / Same sad singer.

Jul 72. (7") **COULD YOU PUT YOUR LIGHT ON, PLEASE. / ANY OLD KIND OF DAY** [ ] [ ]

Oct 72. (7") **SUNDAY MORNING SUNSHINE./ BURNING HERSELF** [-] [75]

Oct 72. (lp) **SNIPER AND OTHER LOVE SONGS** [ ] [ ]
– Sunday morning sunshine / Sniper / And the baby never cries / Burning herself / Barefoot boy / Better place to be (parts 1 & 2)/ Circle / Woman child / Winter song.

Jan 73. (7") **BETTER PLACE TO BE./ WINTER SONG** [-] [ ]

— **MICHAEL MASTERS** – cello / **PAUL LEKA** – keyboards / **JIM CHAPIN** – drums repl.SCOTT, brother STEVE CHAPIN + KUNKEL

Apr 74. (lp) **SHORT STORIES** [ ] [61] Dec73
– Short stories / W.O.L.D./ Song for myself / Song man / Changes / They call her easy / Mr.Tanner / Mail order Annie / There's a lot of lonely people tonight / Old College Avenue.

Apr 74. (7") **W.O.L.D. / SHORT STORIES** [34] [36] Dec 73

May 74. (7") **OLD COLLEGE AVENUE. / WHAT MADE AMERICA FAMOUS** [-] [ ]

— **STEVE CHAPIN** returned and added **ALLAN SCHWARTZBERG – drums**

Sep 74. (7") **CAT'S IN THE CRADLE. / VACANCY** [-] [1]

Sep 74. (lp) **VERITIES & BALDERDASH** [ ] [4]
– Cat's in the cradle / I wanna learn a love song / Shooting star / 30,000 pounds of bananas / She sings songs without words / What made America famous / Vacancy / Halfway to Heaven / Six-string orchestra.

Oct 74. (7") **CAT'S IN THE CRADLE. / SHOOTING STAR** [ ] [-]

Mar 75. (7") **I WANNA LEARN A LOVE SONG. / SHE SINGS SONGS WITHOUT WORDS** [ ] [44] Feb75

Jul 75. (7") **DREAMS GO BY. / SANDY** [ ] [ ]

Nov 75. (lp) **PORTRAIT GALLERY** [ ] [53] Sep75

– Dreams go by / Tangled up puppet / Star tripper / Babysitter / Someone keeps calling my name / The rock / Sandy / Dirt gets under the fingernails / Bummer / Stop singing those sad songs.

Jan 76. (7") **TANGLED UP PUPPET. / DIRT GETS UNDER THE FINGERNAILS** [ ] [ ]
Mar 76. (7") **THE ROCK. / STAR TRIPPER** [-] [ ]

HOWIE FIELDS – drums + **DOUG WALKER** – guitar were added

Apr 76. (d-lp) **GREATEST STORIES – LIVE (live)** [ ] [48]
– Dreams go by / W.O.L.D. / Saturday morning / I wanna learn a love song / Mr.Tanner / Better place to be / Let time go lightly / Cat's in the cradle / Taxi / Circle / 30,000 pounds of bananas / She is always seventeen / Love is just another word / The shortest story. *(cd-iss.1989)*
Jun 76. (7") **BETTER PLACE TO BE (live). / (part 2) (live)** [-] [86]
Aug 76. (7") **BETTER PLACE TO BE (live). / TAXI (live)** [ ] [-]

— now w/ **WALKER, WALLACE, FIELDS, S.CHAPIN + RON EVANUIK**

Oct 76. (lp)(c) **ON THE ROAD TO KINGDOM COME** [ ] [87]
– On the road to kingdom come / The parade's still passing by / The mayor of Candor lied / Laugh man / Corey's coming / If my Mary was here / Fall in love with him / Caroline / Roll down the river.
1977. (7") **IF MY MARY WAS HERE. / COREY'S COMING** [-] [ ]

— **KIM SCHOLES** – cello repl.EVANUIK

Sep 77. (7") **DANCE BAND ON THE TITANIC. / I WONDER WHAT HAPPENED TO HIM** [-] [ ]
Sep 77. (d-lp)(d-c) **DANCE BAND ON THE TITANIC** [ ] [58]
– Dance band on the Titanic / Why people should stay the same / My old lady / We grew up a little bit / Bluesman / Country dreams / I do it for you, Jane / I wonder what happened to him / Paint a picture of yourself (Michael) / Mismatch / Merceneries / Manhood / One light in a dark valley (an imitation spiritual) / There was only one choice.
Oct 77. (7") **DANCE BAND ON THE TITANIC. / (part 2)** [ ] [-]
May 78. (7") **MY OLD LADY. / I'D DO IT FOR YOU, JANE** [-] [ ]
Jun 78. (lp)(c):<lp> **LIVING ROOM SUITE** [ ] [ ]
– Dancin' boy / If you want to feel / Poor damned fool / I wonder what happened to this world / Jenny / It seems you only love me when it rains / Why do little girls / Flowers are red / Somebody said.
Aug 78. (7") **IF YOU WANT TO FEEL. / I WONDER WHAT WOULD HAPPEN TO THE WORLD** [ ] [ ]
May 79. (7") **FLOWERS ARE RED. / WHY DO LITTLE GIRLS** [ ] [-]

— w/ WALLACE, WALKER, FIELDS, S.CHAPIN + SCHOLES

Nov 79. (d-lp) **LEGENDS OF THE LOST AND FOUND – NEW GREATEST STORIES LIVE (live)** [ ] [ ] Oct79
– Stranger with the melodies / Copper / The day they closed the factory down / Pretzel man / Old folkie / Get on with it / We were three / Odd job man / Legends of the lost and found / You are the only song / Mail order Annie / Tangled up puppet / Poor damned fool / Corey's coming / If my Mary were here / Flowers are red.
Nov 79. (7") **FLOWERS ARE RED. / JENNY** [-] [ ]

— **YVONNE CABLE** – cello repl.SCHOLES

Boardwalk Boardwalk

Oct 80. (7") **SEQUEL. / I FINALLY FOUND IT SANDY** [ ] [23]

Above was the "sequel" to TAXI.

Epic Boardwalk

Apr 81. (7") **REMEMBER WHEN THE MUSIC. / NORTH WEST 222** [ ] [ ]
May 81. (lp) **SEQUEL** [ ] [58] Oct80
– Sequel / I miss America / Story of a life / Remember when the music / Up on the shelf / Salt and pepper / God babe, you've been good for me / Northwest 222 / I finally found it Sandy / Remember when the music (reprise).
Aug 81. (7") **STORY OF A LIFE. / SALT AND PEPPER** [-] [ ]

— HARRY was killed in a motor crash on 16 July 1981.

compilations, others

Jun 76. Elektra; (7") **W.O.L.D. / CAT'S IN THE CRADLE** [ ] [-]
Nov 85. Elektra; (lp)(c) **ANTHOLOGY** [ ] [-]
– W.O.L.D. / Any old kind of day / Cat's in the cradle / 30,000 pounds of bananas / Taxi / She is always seventeen / Sunday morning sunshine / I wanna learn a love song / Better place to be / Song man.
1989. Old Gold; (7") **CAT'S IN THE CRADLE. / W.O.L.D.** [ ] [-]
1989. Castle; (lp)(c)(cd) **THE LAST PROTEST SINGER** [ ] [-]
– Last of the protest singers / November rains / Basic protest song / Last stand / Sounds like America to me / Word wizard / Anthem / A quiet little love affair / I don't want to be president / Silly little girl / You only own the light.

Roger CHAPMAN (see under ⇒ FAMILY)

Tracy CHAPMAN

Born: 1964, Cleveland, Ohio, USA. After graduating from Medford University (Tufts), she signed to 'Elektra' records in 1986. She toured with stablemates 10,000 MANIACS, until her transatlantic US/UK No.1 eponymous debut album was released 1988. • **Style:** Folk balladeer who critics hailed as the new JOAN ARMATRADING. • **Songwriters:** All penned by TRACY, who started writing from age 8. She also interpreted traditional song HOUSE OF THE RISING SUN (Glenn Yarborough). • **Trivia:** She won 'Best New Artist, etc.' at the 1989 US grammy awards. She's also a supporter of human rights, and appeared at Nelson Mandela Concert on 11 June 1988.

Recommended: TRACY CHAPMAN (*7)

TRACY CHAPMAN – vocals, acoustic guitar / with **JACK HOLDER** – guitar, organ / **LARRY KLEIN** – bass / **DENNY FONGHEISER** – drums

Apr 88. (lp)(c)(cd) **TRACY CHAPMAN** [1] [1]
– Talkin' 'bout a revolution / Fast car / Across the lines / Behind the wall / Baby can I hold you / Mountains o' things / She's got her ticket / Why? / For my lover / If not now . . . / For you.
May 88. (7") **FAST CAR. / FOR YOU.** [5] [6]
(12"+=) – Behind the wall.
Aug 88. (7")(12") **TALKIN' 'BOUT A REVOLUTION. / IF NOT NOW . . .** [ ] [ ]
(cd-s+=) – She's got her ticket.
Nov 88. (7") **BABY CAN I HOLD YOU. / ACROOS THE LINES** [ ] [48]
(12"+=)(cd-s+=) – Mountain o' things.
Sep 89. (7") **CROSSROADS. / BORN TO FIGHT** [61] [ ]
(12"+=) – Fast car.
(cd-s+=) – Mountain o' things (live).
Oct 89. (lp)(c)(cd) **CROSSROADS** [1] [9]
– Crossroads / Bridges / Freedom now / Material world / Be careful of my heart / Subcity / Born to fight / A hundred years / This time / All that you have is your soul.
Feb 90. (7") **ALL THAT YOU HAVE IS YOUR SOUL. / SUBCITY** [ ] [-]
(12"+=) – Freedom now.
Feb 90. (7") **ALL THAT YOU HAVE IS YOUR SOUL. / MATERIAL WORLD** [-] [ ]
Apr 92. (7")(c-s) **BANG BANG BANG. / WOMAN'S WORK** [ ] [ ]
(12"+=)(cd-s+=) – House of the rising Sun.
May 92. (cd)(c)(lp) **MATTERS OF THE HEART** [19] [ ]
– Bang bang bang / So / I used to be a sailor / The love that you had / Woman's work / These are the things / Short supply / Dreaming on a world / Open arms / Matters of the heart. *(re-iss.cd+c Nov93)*
Jul 92. (7")(c-s) **DREAMING ON A WORLD. / WOMAN'S WORK** [ ] [ ]
(cd-s+=) – ('A'extended) / House of the rising Sun.
Nov 95. (cd)(c) **NEW BEGINNINGS** [ ] [58]
–

CHAPTERHOUSE

Formed: Reading, England . . . late '87 by ANDREW SHERRIFF, and others (see below). Soon moved to London, signing to newly formed label 'Dedicated' in 1990. Broke through in 1991 with hit album 'WHIRLPOOL'. • **Style:** Drew similarities between shoegazers MY BLOODY VALENTINE and RIDE, with psychedelic/noise pop feel. • **Songwriters:** All SHERRIFF or PATMAN or combined. Covered RAIN (Beatles) / LADY GODIVA'S OPERATION (Velvet Underground). • **Trivia:** First album below only 2 weeks in Top 50 chart.

Recommended: WHIRLPOOL (*6)

STEPHEN PATMAN (b. 8 Nov'68, Windsor, England) – vocals, guitar / **ANDREW SHERRIFF** (b. 5 May'69, Wokingham, England) – vocals, guitar / **SIMON ROWE** (b.23 Jun'69) – guitar / **ASHLEY BATES** (b. 2 Nov'71) – drums / **RUSSELL BARRETT** (b. 7 Nov'68, Vermont, USA) – bass repl. JON CURTIS

Dedicated not issued

Aug 90. (12"ep)(cd-ep) **FREEFALL** [ ] [-]
– Falling down / Need (somebody) / Inside of me / Sixteen years.
Nov 90. (12"ep)(cd-ep) **SUNBURST** (7" tracks*) [ ] [-]
– Something more* / Satin safe / Rain* / Feel the same.
Mar 91. (7") **PEARL. / COME HEAVEN** [67] [-]
(12"ep+=) – In my arms.
(cd-s++=) – Pearl (edit).
Apr 91. (cd)(c)(lp) **WHIRLPOOL** [23] [-]
– Brother / Pearl / Autosleeper / Treasure / Falling down / April / Guilt / If you want me / Something more. (free-ltd.12"w/lp)
– DIE DIE DIE. / (one sided)
Sep 91. (12"ep)(cd-ep) **MESMERISE. / PRECIOUS ONE / SUMMER CHILL / THEN WE'LL RISE** [60] [-]
Jul 93. (7"purple) **SHE'S A VISION. / DON'T LOOK NOW** [ ] [-]
(12"+=) – ('B' sitar trance mix) / For what it's worth (demo).
(12"+=) – ('B' sitar trance mix) / Deli (dark jester mix).
Aug 93. (7") **WE ARE THE BEAUTIFUL. / AGE** [ ] [ ]
(cd-s+=)(7"colrd+=) – Frost.
Sep 93. (cd)(c)(lp) **BLOOD MUSIC** [ ] [-]
– Don't look now / There's still life / we are the beautiful / Summer's gone / Everytime / Deli / On the way to fly / She's a vision / Greater power / Confusion trip / love forever.

CHARLATANS

Formed: Northwich, Cheshire, England . . . late 1989 as a quintet. Formed own 'Dead Good' records, which after their debut single, was taken over by 'Situation 2'. Following 2 major UK hits, they went in at No.1 with debut album 'SOME FRIENDLY' in 1990. • **Style:** Influenced by friends The STONE ROSES and also the 60's (i.e. PINK FLOYD). Organ-orientated Manchester inspired "rave" rock. • **Songwriters:** Group compositions except I FEEL MUCH BETTER ROLLING OVER (Small Faces). On their eponnymous 1995 album the track 'HERE COMES A SOUL SAVER' borrowed? a guitar riff from PINK FLOYD's 'Fearless'. • **Trivia:** Steve Harrison is the manager.

Recommended: SOME FRIENDLY (*8) / BETWEEN 10th & 11th (*6) / UP TO OUR HIPS (*7) / THE CHARLATANS (*8)

TIM BURGESS (b.30 May'68) – vocals (ex-ELECTRIC CRAYONS) repl. BAZ KETTLEY / **ROB COLLINS** (b.1967) – organ / **JON BAKER** (b.1969) – guitar / **JON-BOY BROOKS** (b.1969) – drums / **MARTIN BLUNT** (b.1965) – bass (ex-MAKIN' TIME, ex-TOO MUCH TEXAS w / TIM)

Dead Good not issued

Feb 90. (7") **INDIAN ROPE. / WHO WANTS TO KNOW** [89] [-]
(12"+=) – You can talk to me. *(re-iss.+cd-s.Jul 91, hit No. 57)*

Situation 2 Beggar's B

May 90. (7") **THE ONLY ONE I KNOW. / IMPERIAL 109** [9] [ ]
(12"+=) – Everything changed.
(cd-s+=) – You can talk to me (version).

Sep 90. (7") **THEN. / TAURUS MOANER** [12] [ ]
(12"+=)(cd-s+=) – ('A'alternative mix) / ('A'instrumental).

Oct 90. (cd)(c)(lp) **SOME FRIENDLY** [1] [73]
– You're not very well / White shirt / The only one I know * / Opportunity / Then / 109 pt.2 / Polar bear / Believe you me / Flower / Sonic / Sproston Green. *(cd+= *)*

Feb 91. (7"ep)(12"ep)(c-ep) **OVER RISING. / WAY UP THERE / HAPPEN TO DIE** [15] [ ]
(cd-s+=) – Opportunity Three (re-work).

— **MARK COLLINS** – guitar (ex-CANDLESTICK PARK) repl. BAKER

Oct 91. (7")(c-s) **ME IN TIME. / OCCUPATION H. MONSTER** [28] [ ]
(12"+=)(cd-s+=) – Subtitle.

Feb 92. (7")(c-s) **WEIRDO. / THEME FROM 'THE WISH'** [19] [ ]
(12"+=)(cd-s+=) – Sproston Green (remix) / ('A'remix).

Mar 92. (cd)(c)(lp) **BETWEEN 10th AND 11th** [21] [ ]
– I don't want to see the lights / Ignition / Page one / Tremelo song / The end of everything etc / Subtitle / Can't even be bothered / Weirdo / Chewing gum weekend / (No one) Not even the rain. *(re-iss.cd Sep95 on 'Beggar's Banquet')*

Jun 92. (7") **TREMELO SONG (alternative take). / HAPPEN TO DIE** [44] [ ]
(cd-s+=) – Normality swing (demo).
(cd-s+=) – Then (live) / Chewing gum weekend (live).
(12"+=) – (4 tracks, including 'A')

— ROB COLLINS was given a jail sentence in Sep'93 for his part in an armed robbery. He was released approximately 3-4 months later.

Beggar's B. Beggar's B.

Jan 94. (c-s) **CAN'T GET OUT OF BED. / WITHDRAWN** [24] [ ]
(7"+=)(12"+=)(cd-s+=) – Out.

Mar 94. (cd-ep) **I NEVER WANT AN EASY LIFE IF ME AND HE WERE EVER TO GET THERE. / ONLY A BOHO / SUBTERRAINIA / CAN'T GET OUT OF BED (demo)** [38] [ ]

Mar 94. (cd)(c)(lp) **UP TO OUR HIPS** [8] [ ]
– Come in number 21 / I never want an easy life / If me and he were ever to get there / Can't get out of bed / Feel flows / Autograph / Jesus hairdo / Up to our hips / Patrol / Another rider up in flames / Inside – looking out. *(re-iss.cd Sep95)*

Jun 94. (c-ep)(12"ep)(cd-ep) **JESUS HAIRDO / PATROL (Dust Brothers remix) / STIR IT UP – cd(or)12"- FEEL FLOWS (Van Basten remix)** [48] [ ]
(cd-s) – ('A'side) / I never want an easy life / Another rider up in flames / Up to our hips (BBC Radio 1 live sessions).

Dec 94. (7")(c-s) **CRASHIN' IN. / BACK ROOM WINDOW** [31] [ ]
(12"+=)(cd-s+=) Green flashing eyes.

May 95. (7")(c-s) **JUST LOOKIN'. / BULLET COMES** [32] [ ]
(cd-s+=) – Floor nine.

Aug 95. (c-s) **JUST WHEN YOU'RE THINKIN' THINGS OVER / FRINCK / YOUR SKIES ARE MINE** [12] [ ]
(cd-s+=) – Chemical risk (toothache remix).
(12") – (first 2 tracks) / Chemical risk dub / Nine acres (Dust Brothers mix).

Aug 95. (cd)(c)(d-lp) **THE CHARLATANS** [1] [ ]
– Nine acre court / Feeling holy / Just lookin' / Crashin' in / Bullet comes / Here comes a soul saver / Just when you're thinkin' things over / Tell everyone / Toothache / No fiction / See it through / Thank you. (d-lp+=) – Chemical risk (toothache remix).

Ray CHARLES

Born: RAY CHARLES ROBINSON, 23 Sep'30, Albany, Georgia, USA. Early on, after his family moved to Greenville, Florida, he was encouraged to play the piano, but aged 7 he suffered glaucoma (a blinding disease), due to witnessing the death of his brother. After leaving a school for the blind, where he had learnt classical piano, he moved to Jacksonville, Florida. In 1948, after both his parents had recently died, he started a new career as R.C.ROBINSON in Seattle with The McSON TRIO (the other 2 members being GOSSADY McGHEE – guitar / MILTON GARRAD – bass). In 1949, he signed to Jack Lauderdale's 'Downbeat' label, using only his two forenames RAY CHARLES, due to famous boxer at the time. He / they released 3 singles, until label was taken over by 'Swingtime'. After several more 78's, his contract was bought by 'Atlantic', where he built up wide R&B audiences. His first taste of success came when 'SWANEE RIVER ROCK', hit the US Top 40 late in 1957. After several follow-up's failed to be more than minor hits, he released what has become regarded as his classic song 'WHAT'D I SAY'. In the summer of 1959, it shot up into the Top 10, making him overnight star in the process. Throughout the 60's, with new contract for 'ABC Paramount', he had many fine moments including 3 US No.1's 'GEORGIA ON MY MIND', 'HIT THE ROAD JACK' & 'I CAN'T STOP LOVING YOU'. His albums also became million sellers, as a new generation of artists flocked to borrow his music. In 1964, he made debut acting appearance in the film 'Ballad In Blues', and went on to appear in many more. His use of heroin in the 60's, was curbed after his second court appearance in 1967, when a judge refrained from just sending him to prison. He was fined heavily, and put on 4 years probation. Around the mid-60's, he also formed own label 'Tangerine', which released several other artists' singles as well as his own. Having duetted with BETTY CARTER in the early 60's, the 70's & 80's saw him rely on collaborations with CLEO LAINE, CLINT EASTWOOD! (from the film 'Any Which Way You Can') / BILLY JOEL and a whole 1984 album's worth 'FRIENDSHIP' with major country stars HANK WILLIAMS JR., MICKEY GILLEY & a hit with WILLIE NELSON. In 1991, he won his 11th Grammy award, with 'I'LL BE GOOD TO YOU', which is credited as a duet with CHAKA KHAN and leader QUINCY JONES. • **Style:** Grew from a 50's NAT KING COLE impersonator, to creating a heavily mixed bag of R&B, soul, gospel or country. One of the few artists who could sell records with this extreme diversity. • **Songwriters:** RAY wrote most of material, although at times lending from others, i.e.- I'M MOVIN' ON (Hank Snow) / LET THE GOOD TIMES ROLL (Shirley & Lee) / GEORGIA ON MY MIND (Hoagy Carmichael) / HIT THE ROAD JACK (Percy Mayfield) / YOU ARE MY SUNSHINE (Jimmie Davis) / YOUR CHEATIN' HEART + TAKE THESE CHAINS FROM MY HEART (Hank Williams) / THAT LUCKY OLD SUN (?) / MAKIN' WHOOPEE (?) / CRY (Johnny Ray) / I'M A FOOL TO CARE (Joe Barry) / TOGETHER AGAIN (Buck Owens) / ELEANOR RIGBY + YESTERDAY (Beatles) / WHAT AM I LIVING FOR? (Chuck Willis) / LOOK WHAT THEY'VE DONE TO MY SONG, MA? (Melanie) / LIVING FOR THE CITY (Stevie Wonder) / PORGY & BESS album with CLEO LAINE (Gershwin) / etc. • **Miscellaneous:** Many didn't know at the time, but RAY was married to gospel singer DELLA REESE for 22 years, until they divorced late 1977. Also note that The Ray Charles Singers, who had US hits in the 60's, were in fact conducter Charles Ray Offenberg.

Recommended: THE COLLECTION (*6)

RAY CHARLES – vocals, piano / **GISADY McGHEE** – guitar / **MILTON GARRAD** – bass

not issued Downbeat

1949. (7") **CONFESSION BLUES. / I LOVE YOU, I LOVE YOU** [-] [ ]
1949. (7") **BLUES BEFORE SUNRISE. / HOW LONG BLUES** [-] [ ]
1949. (7") **A SENTIMENTAL BLUES. / YOU'LL ALWAYS MISS THE MATTER** [-] [ ]

not issued Swingtime

1949. (7") **ALONE IN THIS CITY. / CAN'T ANYONE ASK FOR MORE** [-] [ ]
1949. (7") **LET'S HAVE A BALL. / ROCKIN' CHAIR BLUES** [-] [ ]
(above 5 singles with The MAXIN TRIO)
1949. (7") **I'VE HAD MY FUN. / SITTIN' ON TOP OF THE WORLD** [-] [ ]
1949. (7") **AIN'T THAT FINE. / DON'T PUT YOUR DREAMS ALL IN ONE BASKET** [-] [ ]
1949. (7") **C.C. RIDER. / WHAT HAVE I DONE** [-] [ ]
1950. (7") **HONEY, HONEY. / SHE'S IN THE BALL** [-] [ ]
1950. (7") **LATE IN THE AFTERNOON BLUES. / THE EGO SONG** [-] [ ]
1950. (7") **I'LL DO ANYTHING BUT WORK. / SOMEDAY** [-] [ ]
1950. (7") **ALL TO MYSELF. / I WONDER WHO'S KISSING HER NOW** [-] [ ]
Jan 51. (7") **BABY LET ME HOLD YOUR HAND. / LONELY BOY** [-] [ ]
1951. (7") **KISS-A-ME BABY. / I'M GLAD FOR YOUR SAKE** [-] [ ]
1952. (7") **HEY NOW. / BABY WON'T YOU PLEASE COME HOME** [-] [ ]
1952. (7") **GUITAR BLUES. / BABY LET ME HEAR YOU CALL MY NAME** [-] [ ]
(re-iss.1952 on 'Sittin-In-With')

— **RAY** added sax / **+ 4 other horn players / + DAVID NEWMAN** – saxophone

not issued Atlantic

Jun 52. (7") **ROLL WITH MY BABY. / THE MIDNIGHT HOUR** [-] [ ]
1953. (7") **THE SUN'S GONNA SHINE AGAIN. / JUMPIN' IN THE MORNING** [-] [ ]
1953. (7") **MESS AROUND. / FUNNY BUT I STILL LOVE YOU** [-] [ ]
Jan 54. (7") **HEARTBREAKER. / FEELIN' SAD** [-] [ ]
Mar 54. (7") **IT SHOULD'VE BEEN ME. / SINNER'S PRAYER** [-] [ ]
1954. (7") **DON'T YOU KNOW (BABY). / LOSING HAND** [-] [ ]
1955. (7") **I'VE GOT A WOMAN. / COME BACK BABY** [-] [ ]
1955. (7") **THIS LITTLE GIRL OF MINE. / A FOOL FOR YOU** [-] [ ]
1955. (7") **BLACK JACK. / GREEN BACK** [-] [ ]
1956. (7") **DROWN IN MY OWN TEARS. / MARY ANN** [-] [ ]
1956. (7") **HALLELUJAH, I LOVE HER SO. / WHAT WOULD I DO WITHOUT YOU** [-] [ ]
1956. (lp) **HALLELUJAH, I LOVE HER SO** [-] [ ]
– Ain't that love / Drown in my own tears / Come back baby / Sinner's prayer / Funny / Losing hand / A fool for you / Hallelujah I love her so / Mess around / This little girl of mine / Mary Ann / Greenbacks / Don't you know / I got a woman. *(UK-iss.Mar67 on 'Atlantic')*
1956. (7") **LONELY AVENUE. / LEAVE MY WOMAN ALONE** [-] [ ]
1957. (7") **AIN'T THAT LOVE. / I WANT TO KNOW** [-] [ ]
1957. (7") **IT'S ALL RIGHT. / GET ON THE RIGHT TRACK BABY** [-] [ ]
Jul 57. (lp) **RAY CHARLES** [-] [ ]
– Honey honey / Ray Charles blues / You always miss the water when the well runs dry / She's on the ball / How long / Someday / Ain't that fine / Don't put all your dreams in one basket / Baby won't you please come home / Tell me baby. *(UK-iss.1965 on 'Society') (re-iss.1968 on 'Fidelity') (re-iss.1971 on 'Transatlantic') (re-iss.Sep80 on 'Pickwick') (re-iss.Oct84 on 'Audio Fidelity')*
Oct 57. (7") **SWANEE RIVER ROCK (TALKIN' 'BOUT THAT RIVER). / I WANT A LITTLE GIRL** [-] [34]
1958. (7") **TALKIN' 'BOUT YOU. / THAT'S ENOUGH** [-] [ ]
1958. (7") **YES INDEED. / I HAD A DREAM** [-] [ ]
1958. (lp) **YES INDEED** [-] [ ]
– What would I do without you / It's all right / I want to know / Yes indeed / Got on the right track baby / Talkin' 'bout you / Swanee River rock / Lonely Avenue / Blackjack / The sun's gonna shine again / I had a dream / I want a little girl / Heartbreaker / Leave my woman alone. *(UK-iss.Mar59 on 'London') (re-iss.1968 on 'Atlantic')*
1958. (7") **YOU BE MY BABY. / MY BONNIE** [-] [ ]

London Atlantic

Nov 58. (7") **ROCKHOUSE (Part 1). / (Part 2)** [ ] [79]
Nov 58. (lp) **RAY CHARLES AT NEWPORT (live)** [ ] [ ]
– The right time / In a little Spanish town / I got a woman / Blues waltz / Hot rod /

Talkin' 'bout you / Sherry / A fool for you. *(UK-iss.Mar59 on 'London-Jazz') (re-iss.Feb69 & Mar73 on 'Atlantic')*

Feb 59. (7") **(NIGHT TIME IS) THE RIGHT TIME. / TELL ALL THE WORLD ABOUT YOU** [-] [95]

(The following 2 albums were issued in UK 'London-Jazz')

Apr 59. (lp) **SOUL BROTHERS (w / "MILT JACKSON")** [ ] [ ] Feb 59
– How long blues / Cosmic Ray / The genius after hours / Charlesville / Bags of blues / 'Deed I do / Blue funk / Soul brothers / Bags' guitar blues / Soul meeting / Hallelujah I love her so / Blue genius / X-Ray blues / Love on my mind *(UK re-iss.as 'SOUL MEETING' Mar64 on 'London') (re-iss.1973 & Jul76 on 'Atlantic') (d-cd-iss.May93)*

May 59. (7") **THAT'S ENOUGH. / TELL ME HOW YOU FEEL** [-] [ ]

Jul 59. (7") **WHAT'D I SAY. / (Part 2)** [ ] [6]

Aug 59. (lp) **WHAT'D I SAY** [-] [ ]
– What'd I say (part 1&2) / Jumpin in the mornin' / You be my baby / Tell me how you feel / What kind of man are you / Rock house (part 1&2) / Roll with my baby / Tell all the world about you / My Bonnie / That's enough. *(UK-iss.Mar60 on 'London') (US re-iss.Aug61, hit No.20) (re-iss.Oct69)*

Dec 59. (7") **I'M MOVIN' ON. / I BELIEVE TO MY SOUL** [ ] [40] Nov 59

Feb 60. (7") **LET THE GOOD TIMES ROLL. / DON'T LET THE SUN CATCH YOU CRYIN'** [ ] [78]
[95] Jan 60

Feb 60. (lp) **THE GENIUS OF RAY CHARLES** [ ] [17]
– Let the good times roll / It had to be you / Alexander's ragtime band / Two years of torture / When your lover has gone / 'Deed I do / Just for a thrill / You won't let me go / Tell me you'll wait for me / Don't let the sun catch you crying / Am I blue? / Come rain or come shine *(cd-iss.Aug93)*

1960. (lp) **RAY CHARLES SEXTET** [-] [ ]

H.M.V. ABC Para..

1960. (7") **WHO YOU GONNA LOVE. / MY BABY** [-] [ ]

Aug 60. (7") **STICKS AND STONES. / WORRIED LIFE BLUES** [ ] [40] Jul 60

Oct 60. (lp) **THE GENIUS HITS THE ROAD** [ ] [9] Sep 60
– Alabama bound / Georgia on my mind / Basin Street blues / Mississippi mud / Moonlight in Vermont / New York's my home / California, here I come / Moon over Miami / Deep in the heart of Texas / Carry me back to Old Virginny / Blue Hawaii / Chattanooga choo choo.

Nov 60. (7") **GEORGIA ON MY MIND. / CARRY ME BACK TO OLD VIRGINITY** [24] [1] Sep 60

Feb 61. (7") **RUBY. / HARD-HEARTED HANNAH** [ ] [28]
[55] Dec60

May 61. (7") **THEM THAT GOT. / I WONDER** [ ] [58] Oct 60

Jun 61. (7") **I'VE GOT NEWS FOR YOU. / I'M GONNA MOVE TO THE OUTSKIRTS OF TOWN** [-] [66]
[84]

Jul 61. (7") **ONE MINT JULEP (inst.). / LET'S GO** [ ] [8] Apr 61
(Above 2 singles were actually released in US 'ABC-Impulse')

Sep 61. (lp) **DEDICATED TO YOU** [ ] [11] Mar 61
– Hard hearted Hannah / Nancy / Margie / Ruby / Rosetta / Stella by starlight / Cherry / Josephine / Candy / Marie / Diane / Sweet Georgia Brown.

Sep 61. (7") **HIT THE ROAD JACK. / THE DANGER ZONE** [6] [1]

Nov 61. (lp) **GENUIS + SOUL = JAZZ** [ ] [4] Mar 61
– From the heart / I've got news for you / Moanin' / Let's go / One mint julep / I'm gonna move to the outskirts of town / Stompi' room only / Mister C / Strike up the band / Birth of the blues. *(re-iss.+c+cd.Sep89 on 'Essential') (re-iss.cd Jul95 on 'Actual Jazz')*

Jan 62. (7") **UNCHAIN MY HEART. / BUT ON THE OTHER HAND BABY** [ ] [9]
[72] Dec 61

(The following 2 releases were by "RAY CHARLES & BETTY CARTER")

Feb 62. (7") **BABY IT'S COLD OUTSIDE. / WE'LL BE TOGETHER AGAIN** [-] [91]
(an EP of the same name was issued UK Jun63)

Mar 62. (lp) **RAY CHARLES AND BETTY CARTER** [ ] [52] Sep 61
– Everytime we say goodbye / You and I / Intro; Goodbye / We'll be together again / People will say we're in love / Cocktails for two / Side by side / Baby it's cold outside / Together / For all we know / It takes twoo to tango / Alone together. *(re-iss.c+cd.Nov89 on 'Essential')*

Apr 62. (7") **HIDE NOR HAIR. / AT THE CLUB** [ ] [20]
[44]

May 62. (lp) **MODERN SOUNDS IN COUNTRY AND WESTERN MUSIC** [6] [1] Apr 62
– Bye bye love / You don't know me / Half as much / I love you so much it hurts / Just a little lovin' / Born to lose / Worried mind / It makes no difference now / You win again / Careless love / I can't stop loving you / Hey, good lookin'.

May 62. (7") **I CAN'T STOP LOVING YOU. / BORN TO LOSE** [1] [1]
[41]

Sep 62. (7") **YOU DON'T KNOW ME. / CARELESS LOVE** [9] [2]
[60] Jul 62

Nov 62. (7") **YOUR CHEATIN' HEART. / YOU ARE MY SUNSHINE** [13] [29]
[7]

Feb 63. (lp) **MODERN SOUNDS IN COUNTRY AND WESTERN MUSIC VOL.2** [15] [2] Nov 62
– You are my sunshine / No letter today / Someday (you'll want me to want you)/ Don't tell me your troubles / Midnight / Oh, lonesome me / Take these chains from my heart / Your cheating heart / I'll never stand in your way / Making believe / Teardrops in my heart / Hang your head in shame.

Mar 63. (7") **DON'T SET ME FREE. / THE BRIGHTEST SMILE IN TOWN** [37] [20]
[92] Feb 63

May 63. (7") **TAKE THESE CHAINS FROM MY HEART. / NO LETTER TODAY** [5] [8] Apr 63

Jul 63. (7") **NO ONE. / WITHOUT LOVE (THERE IS NOTHING)** [35] [21]
[29]

Oct 63. (7") **BUSTED. / MAKE BELIEVE** [21] [4] Sep 63

Oct 63. (lp) **INGREDIENTS IN A RECIPE FOR SOUL** [ ] [9] Sep 63
– Busted / Where can I go / Born to the blue / That lucky old sun / Ol' man river / In the evening / A stranger in town / Ol' man time / Over the rainbow / You'll never walk alone. *(cd-iss.Jun95 on 'Personality') (re-iss.cd Jul95 on 'Actual Jazz')*

Jan 64. (7") **THAT LUCKY OLD SUN. / OL' MAN TIME** [ ] [20]

Mar 64. (7") **BABY, DON'T YOU CRY. / MY HEART CRIES FOR YOU** [ ] [39]
[38]

May 64. (lp) **SWEET AND SOUR TEARS** [ ] [9] Mar 64
– Cry / Guess I'll hang my tears out to dry / A tear fell / No one to cry to / You've got me crying again / After my laughter came tears / Teardrops from my eyes / Don't cry baby / Cry me a river / Baby, don't you cry / Willow weep for me / I cried for you.

Jun 64. (7") **MY BABY DON'T DIG ME. / SOMETHING'S WRONG** [ ] [51] May 64

Sep 64. (7") **NO ONE TO CRY TO. / A TEAR FELL** [38] [50]
[55] Jul 64

Nov 64. (lp) **HAVE A SMILE WITH ME** [ ] [36] Sep 64
– Smack dab in the middle / Feudin' and fightin' / Two ton Tessie / I never see Maggie alone / Move it on over / Ma (she's making eyes at me) / The thing / The man with the weird beard / The naughty lady of Shady Lane / Who cares (for me).

Dec 64. (7") **SMACK DAB IN THE MIDDLE. / I WAKE UP CRYING** [ ] [52] Sep 64

Dec 64. (7") **MAKIN' WHOOPEE. / ('A'instrumental)** [-] [46]

Jan 65. (7") **MAKIN' WHOOPEE. / MOVE IT ON OVER** [42] [-]

Mar 65. (7") **CRY. / TEARDROPS FROM MY EYES** [ ] [58]

Apr 65. (7") **LIGHT OUT OF DARKNESS. / PLEASE FORGIVE & FORGET** [ ] [-]

Apr 65. (lp) **RAY CHARLES LIVE IN CONCERT (live)** [ ] [80] Mar 65
– Opening (introduction) / Swing a little taste / I gotta woman / Margie / You don't know me / Hide nor hair / Baby, don't you cry / Makin' whoopee / Hallelujah I love her so / Don't set me free / What'd I say / Finale. *(cd-iss.Aug93)*

Apr 65. (7") **I GOTTA WOMAN (live). / (Part 2)** [-] [79]

May 65. (7") **WITHOUT A SONG. / (Part 2)** [-] [ ]

Jul 65. (7") **I GOTTA WOMAN (live). / WITHOUT A SONG** [ ] [-]

Aug 65. (7") **LOVE'S GONNA LIVE HERE. / I'M A FOOL TO CARE** [ ] [84] B-side

Oct 65. (7") **THE CINCINNATI KID. / THAT'S ALL I AM TO YOU** [ ] [ ]

Nov 65. (lp) **TOGETHER AGAIN – COUNTRY AND WESTERN MEETS RHYTHM & BLUES** [ ] [ ] Aug 65
– Together again / I like to hear it sometime / I've got a tiger by the tail / Please forgive and forget / I don't care / Next door to the blues / Blue Moon of Kentucky / Light out of darkness / Maybe it's nothing at all / All night long / Don't let her know / Watch it baby.

Dec 65. (7") **CRYING TIME. / WHEN MY DREAM BOAT COMES HOME** [ ] [6]

Apr 66. (7") **TOGETHER AGAIN. / YOU'RE JUST ABOUT TO LOSE YOUR CLOWN** [48] [19]
[91]

May 66. (lp) **CRYING TIME** [ ] [15] Mar 66
– Crying time / No use crying / Let's go get stoned / Going down slow / Peace of mind / Tears / Drifting blues / We don't see eye to eye / You're in for a big surprise / You're just about to lose your crown / Don't you think I ought to know / You've got a problem.

Jun 66. (7") **LET'S GO GET STONED. / THE TRAIN** [ ] [31]

Sep 66. (7") **I CHOOSE TO SING THE BLUES. / HOPELESSLY** [ ] [32]

Nov 66. (lp) **RAY'S MOODS** [ ] [52] Sep 66
– What-cha doing in there (I wanna know) / Please say you're fooling / By the light of the silvery Moon / You don't understand / Maybe it's because of love / Chitlins with candied yams / Granny wasn't grinning that day / She's lonesome again / Sentimental journey / A born loser / It's a man's world / A girl I used to know.

Nov 66. (7") **PLEASE SAY YOU'RE FOOLING. / I DON'T NEED NO DOCTOR** [ ] [64]
[72]

Feb 67. (7") **I WANT TO TALK ABOUT YOU. / PLEASE SAY YOU'RE FOOLING** [ ] [98]

Apr 67. (7") **YOU WIN AGAIN. / BYE BYE BYE** [ ] [-]

H.M.V. ABC-Tangerine

Jun 67. (7") **HERE WE GO AGAIN. / SOMEBODY OUGHT TO WRITE A BOOK ABOUT IT** [38] [15]

Sep 67. (lp) **RAY CHARLES INVITES YOU TO LISTEN** [ ] [76] Jul 67
– She's funny that way (I got a woman crazy for me) / How deep is the ocean (how high is the sky) / You made me love you (I didn't wanna do it) / Yesterday / I'll be seeing you / Here we go again / All for you / Love walked in / Gee, baby ain't I good to you / People.

Sep 67. (7") **IN THE HEAT OF THE NIGHT. / SOMETHING'S GOT TO CHANGE** [ ] [33] Aug 67

Stateside ABC-Tangerine

Dec 67. (7") **YESTERDAY. / NEVER HAD ENOUGH OF NOTHING YET** [44] [25] Nov 67

Mar 68. (7") **THAT'S A LIE. / GO ON HOME** [ ] [64] Feb 68

Jul 68. (7") **ELEANOR RIGBY. / UNDERSTANDING** [36] [35]
[46]

Nov 68. (7") **SWEET YOUNG THING LIKE YOU. / LISTEN, THEY'RE PLAYING OUR SONG** [ ] [83]
[92] Aug 68

Jan 69. (7") **IF IT WASN'T FOR BAD LUCK. (w / JIMMY LEWIS) / WHEN I STOP DREAMING** [-] [77]

Feb 69. (lp) **A PORTRAIT OF RAY** [ ] [51] Apr 68
– Eleanor Rigby / Am I blue / Never say naw / Sun died / Yesterday / When I stop dreaming / I won't leave / Sweet young thing like you / Bright lights and you girl / Understanding.

Mar 69. (7") **I'LL BE YOUR SERVANT. / I DIDN'T KNOW WHAT TIME IT WAS** [-] [ ]

May 69. (7") **LET ME LOVE YOU. / I'M SATISFIED** [-] [94]

Jul 69. (lp) **I'M ALL YOURS – BABY!** [ ] [ ] Mar 69
– Yours / I didn't know what the time was / Love is here to stay / Memories of you / Till the end of time / I had the craziest dream / Someday / Indian love call / I dream of you (more than you dream I do) / Gloomy Sunday

Sep 69. (7") **WE CAN MAKE IT. / BABY I CAN'T STOP LOVING YOU** [ ] [ ]

Nov 69. (7") **CLAUDIE MAE. / SOMEONE TO WATCH OVER ME** [-] [ ]

Feb 70. (lp) **DOING HIS THING** [ ] [ ] Jul 69

– The same thing that can make you laugh (can make you cry) / Finders keepers, losers weepers / You ought to change your ways / Baby please / Come and get it / We can make it / I'm ready / That thing called love / If it wasn't for bad luck / I told you so.

Feb 70. (7") **LAUGHIN' AND CLOWNIN'. / THAT THING CALLED LOVE** - 98

Apr 71. (7") **IF YOU WERE MINE. / TILL I CAN'T TAKE IT ANYMORE** -

Tangerine Tangerine

Jul 70. (lp) **MY KIND OF JAZZ (instrumental)**
– Golden boy / Booty butt / This here / I remember Clifford / Sidewinder / Bluesette / Pas-se-o-ne blues / Zig zag / Senior blues. *(UK-iss. 1971)*

Probe ABC-Tang

Oct 70. (7") **TILL I CAN'T TAKE IT ANYMORE. / IF YOU WERE MINE** 41

Nov 70. (lp) **LOVE COUNTRY STYLE** Aug 70
– f you were mine / Ring of fire / Your love is so doggone good / Don't change on me / Till I can't take it anymore / You've still got a place in my heart / I keep it hid / Sweet memories / Good morning dear / Show me the sunshine.

Mar 71. (7") **DON'T CHANGE ON ME. / SWEET MEMORIES** - 36

May 71. (7") **BOOTY BUTT (instrumental). / ZIG ZAG (instrumental)** 36

— (Above single by "RAY CHARLES ORCHESTRA" was issued 1972 on 'Tangerine')

Jul 71. (lp)(c) **VOLCANIC ACTION OF MY SOUL** 52 May 71
– See you then / What am I living for / Feel so bad / The long and winding road / The three bells / All I ever need is you / Wichita lineman / Something / I may be wrong (but I think you're wonderful) / Down in the valley.

Oct 71. (7") **FEEL SO BAD. / YOUR LOVE IS SO DOGGONE GOOD** - 68 Aug71

Dec 71. (7") **WHAT AM I LIVING FOR?. / TIRED OF MY TEARS** - 54

May 72. (lp)(c) **A MESSAGE FOR THE PEOPLE** 52 Apr 72
– Lift every voice and sing / Seems like I gotta do wrong / Heaven help us all / There'll be no peace without all men as one / Hey mister / What have they done to my song, ma / Abraham, Martin and John / Take me home, country road / Every Saturday night / America the beautiful.

Jun 72. (7") **LOOK WHAT THEY'VE DONE TO MY SONG, MA. / AMERICA THE BEAUTIFUL** - 65

1972. (7") **HEY MISTER. / THERE'LL BE NO PEACE WITHOUT ALL MEN AS ONE** -

1972. (7") **EVERY SATURDAY NIGHT. / TAKE ME HOME COUNTRY ROADS** -

Feb 73. (lp)(c) **THROUGH THE EYES OF LOVE** Nov 72
– My first night alone without you / I can make it thru the days (but oh those lonely nights) / Someone to watch over me / A perfect love / If you wouldn't be help us my lady / You leave me breathless / Never ending song of love / Rainy night in Georgia.

Jun 73. (7") **I CAN MAKE IT THROUGH THE DAYS (BUT OH THOSE LONELY NIGHTS). / RING OF FIRE** - 81

London Crossover

Sep 73. (7") **COME LIVE WITH ME. / EVERYBODY SING** 82

1974. (lp)(c) **COME LIVE WITH ME**
– Till there was you / If you go away / It takes so little time / Somebody / Come live with me / Problems, problems / Louise / Where was he / Everybody sing.

1974. (7") **LOUISE. / SOMEBODY** -

Aug 75. (lp)(c) **RENAISSANCE** Jun 75
– Living for the city / Then I'll be home / My God and I / We're gonna make it / For mama / Sunshine / Bein' green / Sail away.

Aug 75. (7") **LIVING FOR THE CITY. / THEN I'LL BE HOME** - 91

Sep 75. (7") **LIVING FOR THE CITY. / FOR MAMA** -

1976. (7") **AMERICA THE BEAUTIFUL. / SUNSHINE** -

— (All 'RCA' by "RAY CHARLES & CLEO LAINE")

London R.C.A.

Oct 76. (7") **OH LAWD, I'M ON MY WAY. / OH BESS, WHERE'S MY BESS**

Dec 76. (d-lp)(c) **PORGY AND BESS ("RAY CHARLES & CLEO LAINE")**
– Summertime (instrumental) / Summertime / My man's gone now / A woman is a sometimes thing / They pass by singing / What you want wild Bess / I got plenty o' nothin' (instrumental) / I got plenty o' nothing / Buzzard song / Bess, you is a woman / Oh doctor Jesus / Crab man's call / Here come de honey man / Strawberry woman's call / It ain't necessarily so (instrumental) / It ain't necessarily so / There's a boat dat's leaving for New York (instrumental) / There's a boat dat's leaving for New York / Oh Bess, oh where's my Bess / Oh lawd I'm on my way.

London Atlantic

Nov 77. (7") **I CAN SEE CLEARLY NOW. / ANONYMOUS LOVE**

Jan 78. (lp)(c) **TRUE TO LIFE** 78 Nov 77
– I can see clearly now / The jealous kind / Oh what a beautiful morning / How long has this been goin' on / Be my love / Anonymous love / Heavenly music / Game number nine / Let it be.

1978. (7") **ENJOY A PEACE THAT WE NEVER COULD. / GAME NUMBER 9** -

1979. (7") **YOU FORGET YOUR MEMORIES. / RIDING THUMB** -

Sep 79. (lp)(c) **AIN'T IT SO**
– Some enchanted evening / Blues in the night / Just because / What'll I do / One of these days / Love me or set me free / Drift away / Love me tonight.

1980. (7") **SOME ENCHANTED EVENING. / 20TH CENTURY FOX** -

1980. (7") **LOVE ME OR SET ME FREE. / JUST BECAUSE** -

Oct 80. (7") **BEERS TO YOU (w/CLINT EASTWOOD). / COTTON-EYED CLINT (by the TEXAS OPERA COMPANY)** -

— (above from the Clint Eastwood movie 'Any Which Way You Can')

Dec 80. (7") **COMPARED TO WHAT. / NOW THAT WE FOUND EACH OTHER**

— (Oct80, issued SHAKE YOUR TALL FEATHER. / MINNIE THE MOOCHER with "CAB CALLOWAY")

C.B.S. Columbia

Mar 83. (7") **STRING BEAN. / BORN TO LOVE ME** -

Mar 83. (lp)(c) **WISH YOU WERE HERE TONIGHT?**
– 3-4 times / Ain't your memory got no pride at all / I don't want no stranger sleepin' in my bed / Born to love me / Let your love flow / Shakin' your head / String bean / I Wish you were here tonight? / You've got the longest leaving act / You feel good all over. *(cd-iss.Apr90 on 'Pickwick')*

1983. (7") **YOU FEEL GOOD ALL OVER. / 3-4 TIMES** -

1983. (7") **AIN'T YOUR MEMORY GOT NO PRIDE AT ALL. / I DON'T WANT NO STRANGERS SLEEPIN' IN MY BED** -

1983. (7") **I WISH YOU WERE HERE TONIGHT (w/GEORGE JONES & CHET ATKINS). / WE DIDN'T SEE A THING** -

1984. (7") **DO I EVER CROSS YOUR MIND. / THEY CALL IT LOVE** -

Jul 84. (lp)(c) **DO I EVER CROSS YOUR MIND**
– I had it all / Do I ever cross your mind / Woman sensuous woman / Then I'll be over you / Lay around and love on you / Love of my life / They call it love / If I were you / Workin' man's woman / I was on Georgia time.

1984. (7") **WOMAN SENSUOUS WOMAN. / I WAS ON GEORGIA TIME** -

Oct 84. (lp)(c) **FRIENDSHIP** 75
– Two old cats like us / This old heart / We didn't see a thing / Who cares / Rock and roll shoes / Friendship / It ain't gonna worry my mind / Little hotel room / Crazy old soldier / Seven Spanish angels.

1984. (7") **ROCK AND ROLL SHOES (w/B. J. THOMAS). / THEN I'LL BE OVER YOU** -

(Above featured duets w / country acts, incl. WILLIE NELSON for below 45)

Mar 85. (7") **SEVEN SPANISH ANGELS. / WHO CARES (w/JANE FRICKIE)**

1985. (7") **IT AIN'T GONNA WORRY MY MIND (w/MICKEY GILLEY). / CRAZY OLD SOLDIER (w/JOHNNY CASH)** -

1985. (7") **TWO OLD CATS LIKE US (w/HANK WILLIAMS). / LITTLE HOTEL ROOM (w/MERLE HAGGARD)** -

Dec 85. (lp)(c) **THE SPIRIT OF CHRISTMAS**
– What child is this / Little drummer boy / Santa Claus is coming to town / This time of the year / Rudolph the red-nosed reindeer / That spirit of Christmas / All I want for Christmas / Christmas in my heart / Winter wonderland / Christmas time.

Aug 86. (7") **FROM THE PAGES OF MY MIND. / SLIP AWAY** -

Aug 86. (lp)(c) **FROM THE PAGES OF MY MIND**
– From the pages of my mind / Slip away / Anybody wit the blues / Class reunion / Caught a touch of your love / A little bit of Heaven / Dixie Moon / Over and over (again) / Beaucoup love / Love is worth the pain.

Nov 86. (7") **DIXIE MOON. / A LITTLE BIT OF HEAVEN** -

— He's credited on BILLY JOEL's 'Baby Grand' 45 (Apr87). Semi-retired from music biz, but continued acting mainly on 'Moonlighting' and 'St.Elsewhere'.

Sep 88. (lp)(c)(cd) **JUST BETWEEN US**
– Nothing like a hundred miles/ / I wish I'd never loved you at all / Too hard to love you / Now I don't believe that anymore / Let's call the whole thing off / Stranger in my own hometown / Over the top / I'd walk a little more for you / If that's what cha want / Save the bones for Henry Jones.

In the early 90s he featured on QUINCY JONES + CHAKA KHAN hit 'I'll Be Good To You'.

Warners Warners

Mar 93. (cd)(c) **MY WORLD**
– My world / A song for you / None of us are free / So help me God / Let me take over / One drop of love / If I could / Love has a mind of its own / I'll be there / Still crazy after all these years.

— All written for him, and covered **A SONG FOR YOU** (Leon Russell) / **STILL CRAZY AFTER ALL THESE YEARS** (Paul Simon). BILLY PRESTON appeared on keyboards.

In Nov93, RAY teamed up with INXS on their hit 'Please (You Got That . . .)'.

– compilations, others, etc. –

1953. Swingtime; (7") **MISERY IN MY HEART. / THE SNOW IS FALLING** -

1952. Sittin-In-With; (7") **I CAN'T DO MORE. / ROLY POLY** -

1952. Rockin'; (7") **WALKIN' AND TALKIN' WITH MYSELF. / I'M WONDERIN' AND WONDERIN'** -

1950s Rockin'; (7") **HARD TIMES. / (part 2)** -

1950s Rockin'; (7") **DOODLIN. / (part 2)** -

Mar 59. London-Jazz; (lp) **THE GREAT RAY CHARLES** -
(cd-iss.Aug93)

Note; All 'London' UK releases were issued in US on 'Atlantic'.

1960. London; (7") **JUST FOR A THRILL. / HEARTBREAKER** -

Jul 60. London; (lp) **RAY CHARLES IN PERSON (live)** 13
(re-iss.Apr69 on 'Atlantic')

Sep 60. London; (7") **TELL THE TRUTH. / SWEET 16 BARS**

Dec 60. London; (7") **COME RAIN OR COME SHINE. / TELL ME YOU'LL WAIT FOR ME** 98
(re-iss.Jan68)

Jun 61. London; (7") **EARLY IN THE MORNING. / A BIT OF SOUL**

1961. London; (7") **AM I BLUE?. / IT SHOULD'VE BEEN ME** -

Oct 61. London; (7") **HARD TIMES. / I WONDER WHO** -

Oct 61. London; (7"ep) **WHAT'D I SAY** -

Nov 61. London; (7"ep) **RAY CHARLES AT NEWPORT** -

Jan 62. London; (lp) **DO THE TWIST** (early work) 11

1962. London; (7") **CARRYING THAT LOAD. / FEELIN' SAD** -

Mar 62. London-Jazz; (lp) **THE GENIUS SINGS THE BLUES** 73 Nov 61

Nov 62. London; (7"ep) **THE ORIGINAL** -

Jan 63. London; (lp) **THE RAY CHARLES STORY** 11 Sep 62

Jan 63. London; (7") **THE RAY CHARLES STORY VOL.2** -

Mar 63. London; (lp) **THE GENIUS AFTER HOURS** 49 Aug 61

Nov 63. London; (7"ep) **THE ORIGINAL VOL.1** -

Nov 63. London; (7"ep) **THE ORIGINAL VOL.2** -

Nov 63. London; (7"ep) **THE ORIGINAL VOL.3** -

1964. London; (7") **TALKIN' 'BOUT YOU. / IN A LITTLE SPANISH TOWN** -

Sep 75. London; (lp) **FOCUS ON RAY CHARLES** -

Jun 77. London; (lp) **WHAT HAVE I DONE TO THEIR SONGS** [ ] [-]
1978. London; (lp)(c) **LOVE AND PEACE** [ ] [-]
Aug 80. London; (lp)(c) **HEART TO HEART – 20 RAY CHARLES' HOTTEST HITS** [29] [-]
Dec 80. London; (lp) **BROTHER RAY** [ ] [ ]
1960. Time; (7") **I FOUND MY BABY. / GUITAR BLUES** [-] [ ]
1962. Time; (7") **BACK HOME. / WHY DID YOU GO** [-] [ ]
1965. Concert Hall; (lp) **THE AUTHENTIC RAY CHARLES** [ ] [-]
1965. Summit; (lp) **THE INCOMPARABLE RAY CHARLES** [ ] [-]
1963. Baronet; (7") **C.C.RIDER. / I USED TO BE SO HAPPY** [-] [ ]
Apr 63. H.M.V./ US= Atlantic; (lp) **RAY CHARLES' GREATEST HITS** [16] [5] Sep62
Note; All 'H.M.V.' records below were issued in US on 'ABC Paramount'
Feb 62. H.M.V.; (7"ep) **HIT THE ROAD JACK** [ ] [-]
Dec 62. H.M.V.; (7"ep) **I CAN'T STOP LOVING YOU** [ ] [-]
Feb 63. H.M.V.; (7"ep) **BALLAD STYLE OF RAY CHARLES** [ ] [-]
May 63. H.M.V.; (7"ep) **THE SWINGING STYLE OF RAY CHARLES** [ ] [-]
Sep 63. H.M.V.; (7"ep) **TAKE THESE CHAINS** [ ] [-]
Feb 64. H.M.V.; (7"ep) **BUSTED** [ ] [-]
Jun 64. H.M.V.; (7"ep) **RAY CHARLES SINGS** [ ] [-]
Feb 66. H.M.V.; (7"ep) **LIVE IN CONCERT (live)** [ ] [-]
Jul 66. H.M.V.; (7"ep) **RAY CHARLES SINGS SONGS OF BUCK OWENS** [ ] [-]
Mar 67. H.M.V.; (d-lp) **A MAN AND HIS SOUL** [ ] [77]
1964. Realm; (7"ep) **THE YOUNG RAY CHARLES** [ ] [-]
1965. Arc/ Summit; (7"ep) **RAY CHARLES** [ ] [-]
Sep 68. Stateside/ US= Atlantic; (lp) **GREATEST HITS VOL.2** [24] [ ]
Dec 71. Atlantic/ US= A.B.C.; (d-lp)(c) **A 25th ANNIVERSARY IN SHOW BUSINESS SALUTE TO RAY CHARLES** [ ] [ ]
Nov 72. Atlantic/ US= A.B.C.; (7"ep) **WHAT'D I SAY / YES INDEED. / I GOT A WOMAN / DON'T LET THE SUN CATCH YOU CRYING** [ ] [-]
Jun 73. Atlantic/ US= A.B.C.; (d-lp)(c) **RAY CHARLES LIVE (Newport & Herndon)** [ ] [ ]
Jul 87. Atlantic; (lp)(c)(cd) **THE RIGHT TIME** [ ] [ ]
May 93. Atlantic; (cd) **THE BEST OF RAY CHARLES** [ ] [ ]
Jun 72. Probe/ US= A.B.C.; (7") **HIT THE ROAD JACK. / GEORGIA ON MY MIND** [ ] [-]
Jun 72. Probe/ US= A.B.C.; (7") **WHAT HAVE THEY DONE TO MY SONG, MA. / AMERICA** [ ] [-]
Apr 73. Probe/ US= A.B.C.; (lp)(c) **ALL-TIME GREAT C&W HITS** [ ] [-]
1972. Boulevard; (lp) **THE ORIGINAL RAY CHARLES** [ ] [-]
Aug 74. Decca; (lp)(c) **THE WORLD OF RAY CHARLES** [ ] [-]
May 75. Decca; (lp)(c) **THE WORLD OF RAY CHARLES VOL.2** [ ] [-]
1978. Ember; (lp) **RAY CHARLES' BLUES** [ ] [-]
Apr 81. Joker; (lp) **RAY CHARLES VOL.2** [ ] [ ]
1988. Joker; (lp) **RAY CHARLES** [ ] [ ]
1988. Joker; (lp) **ROCKIN' WITH RAY** [ ] [ ]
Apr 79. Flyover/ US= A&M; (lp) **SUPER DISC OF RAY CHARLES** [ ] [ ]
Sep 79. Ampro; (c) **KING OF THE BLUES** [ ] [-]
Sep 79. Bulldog; (lp) **20 GOLDEN PIECES OF RAY CHARLES** [ ] [ ]
(re-iss.Jul82)
Sep 80. Pickwick; (lp)(c) **I CAN'T STOP LOVING YOU** [ ] [-]
Sep 93. Pickwick; (cd)(c) **GEORGIA TIME** [ ] [-]
May 80. Manhattan; (lp) **SIMPLY RAY** [ ] [-]
Aug 80. Manhattan; (lp) **A RAY OF HOPE** [ ] [-]
Sep 80. Manhattan; (lp) **EVERYTHING** [ ] [-]
Sep 81. Ampro; (c) **KING OF THE BLUES** [ ] [-]
Oct 82. Phoenix; (lp) **GREAT HITS** [ ] [-]
Jun 84. Meteor; (lp) **GOING DOWN SLOW** [ ] [-]
Nov 84. Astan; (lp) **JAMMIN' THE BLUES** [ ] [-]
Jun 85. Premier; (lp)(c) **C.C. RIDER** [ ] [-]
Mar 84. Charly; (lp)(c) **TELL THE TRUTH** [ ] [-]
Feb 87. Charly; (7")(12") **I WONDER WHO'S KISSING HER NOW. / SHE'S ON THE BALL / BABY WON'T YOU PLEASE COME HOME** [ ] [-]
May 94. Musidisc; (cd) **TWO ON ONE** (w / NAT KING COLE) [ ] [-]
Mar 85. Charly; (d-lp) **THE FANTASTIC RAY CHARLES** [ ] [-]
Aug 85. Deja Vu; (lp)(c) **COLLECTION (20 GOLDEN GREATS)** [ ] [-]
(cd-iss.Sep87)
Jun 88. Deja Vu; (lp)(c)(cd) **COLLECTION: RAY CHARLES (THE LOVE SONGS)** [ ] [-]
Apr 93. Deja Vu; (cd)(c) **THE GOLD COLLECTION** [ ] [-]
(re-iss.Jun95)
Apr 86. Starjazz; (lp)(c) **THE COLLECTION** [ ] [-]
Apr 86. Arcade; (lp)(c) **THE COUNTRY SIDE OF RAY CHARLES** [ ] [-]
May 88. Arcade; (cd) **THE LEGEND LIVES** [ ] [-]
Mar 90. Arcade; (cd)(c)(lp) **THE COLLECTION** [36] [-]
– Your cheatin' heart / Hit the road Jack / Georgia on my mind / Unchain my heart / One mint julep / Take these chains from my heart / I can't stop loving you / Busted / You are my sunshine / Making whoopee / Let's go get stoned / My heart cries for you / Feel so bad / The lucky old Sun / Smack dab in the middle / Crying time / If it wasn't for bad luck / In the heat of the night / Eleanor Rigby / Born to lose / No one / Hard hearted / Hannah / Yesterday.
Mar 93. Arcade; (d-cd)(d-c) **THE LIVING LEGEND** [48] [-]
Apr 87. Topline; (lp)(c)(cd) **THIS LOVE OF MINE** [ ] [-]
Sep 87. Timeless; (c) **16 ORIGINAL HITS** [ ] [-]
Mar 88. Exel; (lp)(c)(cd) **THE GENIUS** [ ] [-]
Mar 88. King; (lp) **14 ORIGINAL GREATEST HITS** [-] [-]
May 88. Commander; (lp)(c)(cd) **HITS OF A GENIUS** [ ] [-]
Jun 88. Spectrum; (cd) **CLASSIC DUO ("& PERRY COMO")** [ ] [-]
1988. Zeta; (lp) **THE EARLY YEARS** [ ] [-]
May 89. Object; (lp) **BLUES IS MY MIDDLE NAME** [ ] [-]
Jan 90. Mainline; (cd)(c) **16 GREATEST HITS** [ ] [-]
Feb 90. Sequel; (cd) **GREATEST COUNTRY & WESTERN HITS** [ ] [-]
(re-iss.Jun95 on 'Personality')
1990. Castle; (cd)(c)(d-lp) **RAY CHARLES: THE COLLECTION** [ ] [-]
Jul 92. Castle; (cd)(c) **THE RAY CHARLES COLLECTION VOLUME 2** [ ] [-]
Jun 91. Essential; (3xcd-set) **THE CLASSIC YEARS** [ ] [-]
Mar 94. Traditional LIne; (cd) **INGREDIENTS IN A RECIPE FOR SOUL** [ ] [-]
Mar 94. Rhino; (d-cd) **THE BLUES & JAZZ ANTHOLOGY** [ ] [-]
Jul 94. Rhino; (cd) **THE BEST OF RAY CHARLES: THE ATLANTIC YEARS** [ ] [-]
Apr 94. Jazz Door; (cd) **LIVE '93 (live)** [ ] [-]
Apr 94. Castle; (cd) **RAY CHARLES & BETTY CARTER** [ ] [-]
Jul 94. Prestige; (cd)(c) **THE CLASSIC YEARS** [ ] [-]
Aug 94. Dynamite; (cd) **RAY CHARLES** [ ] [-]
Apr 95. Wisepack; (d-cd) **THE ESSENTIAL COLLECTION** [ ] [-]

CHEAP AND NASTY (see under ⇒ HANOI ROCKS)

CHEAP TRICK

Formed: Rockford, Illinois, USA . . . 1973 after periods as FUSE / NAZZ and The SICK MAN OF EUROPE. In 1976, they finally recorded eponymous debut album on 'Epic'. In 1979, they scored first major US hit with 'I WANT YOU TO LOVE ME'. A year earlier they had taken Japan by storm, after concerts at Budokan. Became international sensations during the rest of the 70's & most of 80's. • **Style:** Rock band with a hint of CARS-like new wave, which drifted into light metal pop. • **Songwriters:** RICK NEILSEN was main pen-smith. They covered AIN'T THAT A SHAME (Fats Domino) / DON'T BE CRUEL (Elvis Presley) / DANCING THE NIGHT AWAY (Motors) / SPEAK NOW (Terry Reid) / MONEY (Barrett Strong) / MAGICAL MYSTERY TOUR (Beatles) / etc? • **Trivia:** TODD RUNDGREN produced their 1983 album 'NEXT POSITION PLEASE'.

Recommended: THE GREATEST HITS (*5)

GRIM REAPERS

RICK NEILSEN (b.22 Dec'46, Rockford)– guitar / **JOE SUNDBERG** – vocals / **CRAIG MYERS** – guitar / **TOM PETERSSON** (b.1950)– bass / **CHIP GREENMAN** – drums

not issued — Smack
1968. (7") **HOUND DOG. / CRUISIN' FOR BURGERS** [-] [ ]
(re-rel.'68 by "FUSE" in US on 'CBS', same line-up)

not issued — Epic
Dec 68. (lp) **FUSE (as "FUSE") (w/ drawn)** [-] [ ]

— split soon after above **NEILSEN** and **PETERSSON** teamed up invariably as NAZZ and FUSE with ex-NAZZ members **ROBERT 'STEWKEY' ANTONI** – vocals / **THOM MOONEY** – drums In '72 they became **"SICK MAN OF EUROPE"** and moved to Philadelphia **BUN E.CARLOS** (b.BRAD CARLSON, 12 Jun'53) – drums (ex-PAGANS) repl. MOONEY / **XENO** (r.n. RANDY HOGAN) – vocals repl. STEWKEY / **RICK SZELUGA** – bass repl. PETERSSON for a short while, until they became in '73 . . .

CHEAP TRICK

in '73. (NEILSEN, PETERSSON, CARLOS and **XENO**)

— Oct74 **ROBERT ZANDER** (b.23 Jan'53) – vocals, guitar (ex-TOONS) repl. XENO who joined STRAIGHT UP.

Epic — Epic
Mar 77. (7") **OH CANDY. / DADDY SHOULD HAVE STAYED IN HIGH SCHOOL** [-] [ ]
Mar 77. (lp) **CHEAP TRICK** [ ] [ ] Jan 77
– Hot love / Speak now (or forever hold your peace) / He's a whore / Mandocello / The ballad of TV violence / Elo kiddies / Daddy should have stayed in high school / Taxman, Mr Thief / Cry cry / Oh, Candy. *(re-iss.Nov81)(cd-iss.Jun88 on 'Collector's Choice')*
Nov 77. (7") **I WANT YOU TO WANT ME. / OH BOY (instrumental)** [ ] [ ]
Nov 77. (lp)(c) **IN COLOR** [ ] [73] Aug 77
– Hello there / Big eyes / Downed / I want you to want me / You're all talk / Oh Caroline / Clock strikes ten / Southern girls / Come on, come on / So glad to see you. *(cd-iss.Jun88 on 'Collector's Choice') (cd-iss.Oct93 on 'Sony Europe')*
Nov 77. (7") **SOUTHERN GIRLS. / YOU'RE ALL TALK** [-] [ ]
Mar 78. (7") **SO GOOD TO SEE YOU. / YOU'RE ALL TALK** [ ] [ ]
May 78. (7") **SURRENDER. / AUF WIEDERSEHEN** [ ] [62]
May 78. (lp)(c) **HEAVEN TONIGHT** [ ] [48]
– Surrender / On top of the world / California man / High roller / Auf wiedersehen / Takin' me back / On the radio / Heaven tonight / Stiff competition / How are you. *(cd-iss.Sep93 on 'Sony Europe')*
Jul 78. (7") **CALIFORNIA MAN. / STIFF COMPETITION** [ ] [-]
Aug 78. (7") **CALIFORNIA MAN. / I WANT YOU TO WANT ME** [-] [ ]
Feb 79. (lp)(c)(yellow-lp) **AT BUDOKAN (live)** [29] [4]
– Hello there / Come on, come on / Look out / Big eyes / Need your love / Ain't that a shame / I want you to want me / Surrender / Goodnight now / Clock strikes ten. *(re-iss.as d-lp.Nov81) (cd-iss.Feb86) (cd-re-iss.Jul91 on 'Castle')*
Feb 79. (7") **VOICES (live). / SURRENDER (live)** (withdrawn UK after 1 week) [ ] [32] Dec 78
Mar 79. (7")(7"orange) **I WANT YOU TO WANT ME (live). / CLOCK STRIKES TEN (live)** [29] [7]
Jul 79. (7") **SURRENDER (live). / AUF WIEDERSEHEN (live)** [ ] [ ]
Sep 79. (7") **AIN'T THAT A SHAME (live). / ELO KIDDIES** [ ] [35] Jul 79
Sep 79. (lp)(c) **DREAM POLICE** [41] [6]
– Dream police / Way out of the world / House is rockin' / Gonna raise Hell / I'll be with you tonight / Writing on the wall / I know what I want / Need your love. *(also on pic-lp)*

Oct 79. (7") **DREAM POLICE. / HEAVEN TONIGHT** [ ] [26] Sep 79
Jan 80. (7") **WAY OF THE WORLD. / OH CANDY** [73] [-]
Mar 80. (7"ep) **I'LL BE WITH YOU TONIGHT. / HE'S A WHORE / SO GOOD TO SEE YOU** [ ] [-]
Apr 80. (7") **EVERYTHING WORKS IF YOU LET IT. / WAY OF THE WORLD** [-] [44]
Jul 80. (7") **EVERYTHING WORKS IF YOU LET IT. / HEAVEN TONIGHT** [ ] [-]
Oct 80. (7") **STOP THIS GAME. / WHO D'KING** [ ] [48]
Oct 80. (lp)(c) **ALL SHOOK UP** [ ] [24]
– Stop this games / Just got back / Baby loves to rock / Can't stop it but I'm gonna try / World's greatest lover / High Priest of rhythmic noise / Love comes a-tumblin' down / I love you honey but I hate your friends / Go for the throat (use your own imagination) / Who d'king. *(cd-iss.Jun88 on 'Collector's Choice')*
Jan 81. (7") **WORLD'S GREATEST LOVER. / HIGH PRIEST OF RHYTHMIC NOISE** [ ] [ ]

— **PETE COMITA** – bass repl. PETERSSON who formed own group with wife

Aug 81. (7") **REACH OUT. / I MUST BE DREAMING** [-] [ ]

— (above single from the film 'Heavy Metal'. issued on 'Full Moon-Asylum') now alongside **NEILSEN** (some bass),**ZANDER** and **CARLOS**

(late '81) JOHN BRANT – bass (on three songs) repl. COMITA

May 82. (7") **IF YOU WANT MY LOVE. / FOUR LETTER WORD** [57] [45]
May 82. (lp)(c) **ONE ON ONE** [95] [39]
– I want you / One on one / If you want my love / Oo la la la / Lookin' out for number one / She's tight / Time is runnin' / Saturday at midnight / Love's gotta hold on me / I want be man / Four letter word. *(also on re-lp & pic-lp) (re-iss.Jun85)*
Sep 82. (7") **SHE'S TIGHT. / ALL I REALLY WANT TO DO** [-] [65]
Aug 83. (7") **DANCING THE NIGHT AWAY. / DON'T MAKE OUR LOVE A CRIME** [-] [ ]
Sep 83. (lp)(c) **NEXT POSITION PLEASE** [ ] [61]
– I can't take it / Borderline / I don't love her anymore / Next position please / Younger girls / Dancing the night away / 3-D / You say jump / Y.O.Y.O.Y. / Won't take no for an answer / Heaven's falling / Invaders of the heart. *(US-c+=/cd+=)* – You take too much / Don't make our love a crime.
Sep 83. (12"ep) **DANCING THE NIGHT AWAY. / AIN'T THAT A SHAME / I WANT YOU TO WANT ME / SURRENDER** [ ] [-]
Nov 83. (7") **I CAN'T TAKE IT. / YOU TALK TOO MUCH** [-] [ ]
Feb 84. (7") **SPRING BREAK. / GET READY** [-] [ ]
(above from the film 'Spring Break'. issued on 'Warner Bros.')
Sep 85. (7") **TONIGHT IT'S YOU. / WILD WILD WOMEN** [ ] [44] Jul 85
(12"+=) – I want you to want me / If you want my love.
Oct 85. (lp)(c) **STANDING ON THE EDGE** [ ] [35] Aug 85
– Little sister / Tonight it's you / She's got motion / Love comes / How about you / Standing on the edge / This time around / Rock all night / Cover girl / Wild wild women.
Jun 86. (7") **MIGHTY WINGS. / (other artist)** [-] [ ]
Nov 86. (lp)(c) **THE DOCTOR** [ ] [ ] Oct 86
– It's up to you / Rearview mirror romance / The doctor / Are you lonely tonight / Name of the game / Kiss me red / Take me to the top / Good girls go to heaven (bad girls go everywhere) / Man-u-lip-u-later / It's only love.
Nov 86. (7") **IT'S ONLY LOVE. / NAME OF THE GAME** [-] [ ]

— **TOM PETERSSON** – bass, vocals returned to repl. BRANT

May 88. (7")(7"sha-pic-d) **THE FLAME. / THROUGH THE NIGHT** [ ] [1] Apr 88
(12"+=)(cd-s+=) – I want you to want me / If you want my love. *(re-iss.Dec88)*
May 88. (lp)(c)(cd) **LAP OF LUXURY** [ ] [18]
– Let go / No mercy/ The flame / Space / Never had a lot to lose / Don't be cruel / Wrong side of love / All we need is a dream / Ghost town / All wound up. *(cd-iss.Oct93 on 'Sony Europe')*
Aug 88. (7")(7"sha-pic-d)(US c-s) **DON'T BE CRUEL. / I KNOW WHAT I WANT** [ ] [4] Jul 88
(12"+=)(cd-s+=) – California man / Ain't that a shame.
(3"cd-s+=) – Dream police / Way of the world.
Oct 88. (7")(c-s) **GHOST TOWN. / WRONG SIDE OF LOVE** [-] [33]
Jan 89. (7")(c-s) **NEVER HAD A LOT TO LOSE. / ALL WE NEED IS A DREAM** [-] [75]

— In Feb89, ZANDER dueted with Heart's ANN WILSON on US Top 10 single 'SURRENDER TO ME'.

Aug 90. (7")(c-s) **CAN'T STOP FALLING INTO LOVE. / YOU DRIVE, I'LL STEER** [ ] [12] Jul 90
(12"+=)(cd-s+=) – The flame.
Sep 90. (cd)(c)(lp) **BUSTED** [ ] [48] Jul 90
– Back'n'blue / I can't understand it / Wherever would I be / If you need me / Can't stop falling into love / Busted / Walk away / You drive, I'll steer / When you need someone / Had to make you mine / Rock'n'roll tonight.
Oct 90. (7")(c-s) **WHEREVER WOULD I BE. / BUSTED** [ ] [50]
Apr 91. (7")(c-s) **IF YOU NEED ME. / BIG BANG (withdrawn)** [-] [ ]

Warners Warners

Mar 94. (cd)(c) **WOKE UP WITH A MONSTER** [ ] [ ]
– My gang / Woke up with a monster / You're all I wanna do / Never run out of love / Didn't know I had it / Ride the pony / Girlfriends / Let her go / Tell me everything / Cry baby / Love me for a minute.

– compilations etc. –

Apr 80. Epic; (10"ep) **FOUND ALL THE PARTS (rare '76-'79)** [-] [39]
– Day tripper (live) / Can't hold on / Such a good girl /
Oct 91. Epic; (cd)(c)(lp) **THE GREATEST HITS** [ ] [ ]
– Magical mystery tour / Dream police / Don't be cruel / Tonight it's you / She's tight / I want you to want me (Live) / If you want my love / Ain't that a shame / Surrender / The flame / I can't take it / Can't stop fallin' into love / Voices *(re-iss.May94)*
Feb 92. Castle; (cd)(c)(lp) **THE COLLECTION** [ ] [-]

CHEMICAL BROTHERS

Formed: North London, England . . .1992 by resident DJ's ED SIMONS and TOM ROWLANDS. Both had been students at Manchester University, where they worked under the borrowed name of The DUST BROTHERS (US rap producers) to work on versions of 'Song to The Siren' and 'Chemical Beats'. Due to an objection by said rap artists, they became The CHEMICAL BROTHERS and appeared on numerous production work for the likes of CHARLATANS, PRIMAL SCREAM and The MANICS. They finally unleashed their debut album 'EXIT PLANET DUST', which made UK Top 10 lists. • **Style:** Young techno wizards of distorted hip-hop and a wide variety of sounds. • **Songwriters:** ROWLANDS-SIMONS except samples of Blake Baxters 'Brothers Gonna Work It Out' on 'LEAVE HOME'/ Borrowed Swallow's; 'Peekaboo' & 'Follow Me Down'.

Recommended: EXIT PLANET DUST (*8)

TOM ROWLANDS + ED SIMONS with voices by **TIM BURGESS** (CHARLATANS) + **BETH ORTON** (PORTISHEAD)

Junior Boy's Own Virgin

Jun 95. (d12")(cd-s) **LEAVE HOME (Sabres Of Paradise mix). / LEAVE HOME (Underworld mix) / LET ME IN MATE** [17] [ ]
Jun 95. (cd)(c)(d-lp) **EXIT PLANET DUST** [9] [ ]
– Leave home / In dust we trust / Song to he siren / Three little birdies down beats / Fuck up beats / Chemical beats / Chico's groove / One too many mornings / Life is sweet / Playground for a wedgeless firm / Alive alone.
Aug 95. (12")(cd-s) **LIFE IS SWEET. / ('A'-daft punk remix) / ('A'remix 1) / (A'remix 2)** [25] [ ]
(cd-s) – (A-remix 1, repl.by) Leave home (terror burns).
(cd-s) – ('A'remix 1) / If you kling to me I'll klong to you / Chico's groove (mix 2).

CHER

Born: CHERILYN SARKASIAN LA PIER, 20 May'46, El Centro, California, USA. In 1963 she moved to LA to attend acting classes and met SONNY BONO. Through him she did backing vocals for Phil Spector group The RONETTES. The following year she married SONNY, and released number of duet 45's as CAESAR & CLEO. These were JUST YOU and BABY DON'T GO. Later at the height of their success late'65, more early recordings were given light of day on 'Reprise'. In 1964, Phil Spector issued her BEATLES tribute 45 RINGO I LOVE YOU on his own 'Annette' records. Her debut solo single as CHERILYN bombed, but by mid'65, now as CHER, she was in Top 20 with ALL I REALLY WANT TO. Signed to 'Atco', SONNY & CHER also had many hits, starting with I GOT YOU BABE which hit No.1 on both sides of the Atlantic. She would continue her solo and duo work simultaneously having large but sporadic hits mostly in the States. • **Style:** She moved through folk influenced pop in the 60's. She split from SONNY in Mar '74, and soon married GREGG ALLMAN, but this too did not last. In 1979, she became involved with GENE SIMMONS (Kiss), and he introduced her to hard rock music while signing for 'Casablanca'. Her fashion too, throughout each year was to say the least outrageous. By the late 80's her controversial scantilly dressed videos were competing with arch rival MADONNA. The music too had become more raunchier, using heavies such as RICHIE SAMBORA (Bon Jovi), etc. • **Songwriters:** Wrote several herself, but mostly collaborated with others. Covered ALL I REALLY WANT TO DO + BLOWIN' IN THE WIND + LIKE A ROLLING STONE (Bob Dylan) / ALFIE (hit: Cilla Black) / SONNY (Bobby Hebb) / DARK LADY (Johnny Durill) / GYPSIES, TRAMPS AND THIEVES (Robert Stone) / HALF BREED (Mary Dean & Al Capps) / NEEDLES AND PINS (Searchers) / IT'S NOT UNUSUAL (Tom Jones) / TWELTH OF NEVER (Johnny Mathis) / ELUSIVE BUTTERFLY (Bob Lind) / UNTIL IT'S TIME FOR YOU TO GO (Elvis Presley) / CATCH THE WIND (Donovan) / PIED PIPER (Crispan St.Peters) / YOU DON'T HAVE TO SAY YO LOVE ME (Dusty Springfield) / GIRL FROM IPANEMA (Stan Getz) / OUR DAY WILL COME (Ruby & The Romantics) / OLD MAN RIVER (Paul Robeson) / I WALK ON GILDED SPLINTERS (Dr.John) / FOR WHAT IT'S IT'S WORTH (Buffalo Springfield) / BABY I LOVE YOU (Ronettes) / LOVE HURTS (Everly Brothers) / I FOUND SOMEONE (Michael Bolton-Mark Mangold) / WE ALL SLEEP ALONE (Bon Jovi-Child) / OH NO NOT MY BABY (Goffin-King) / THE SHOOP SHOOP SONG (IT'S IN HIS KISS) (Rudy Clark) / Around this time in the 90's, DESMOND CHILD & DIANE WARREN wrote her material. HEART OF STONE (was originally written for BUCKS FIZZ! by Pete Sinfield & Andy Hill). • **Trivia:** In 1981, she dueted with MEAT LOAF on his DEAD RINGER FOR LOVE (45). She appeared with SONNY on many TV specials in the 60's/70's. She appeared in 60's films GOOD TIMES and CHASTITY, but was given starring parts in the 80's. **Filmography:-** COME BACK TO THE FIVE & DIME, JIMMY DEAN, JIMMY DEAN (1982) / SILKWOOD (1983) / MASK (1985) / WITCHES OF EASTWICK (1987) / MOONSTRUCK (1987) / SUSPECT (1987) / MERMAIDS (1991).

Recommended: GREATEST HITS 1965-1992 (*6)

CHER – vocals with session people (no band at this time)

Liberty Imperial

Mar 65. (7") **DREAM BABY. / STAN QUETZAL** [-] [ ]
Jun 65. (7") **ALL I REALLY WANT TO DO. / I'M GONNA LOVE YOU** [9] [15]

Sep 65. (lp) **ALL I REALLY WANT TO DO** 7 16
– All I really want to do / I go to sleep / Needles and pins / Don't think twice / She thinks I still care / Dream baby / The bells of Rhymney / Girl don't come / See see rider / Come and stay with me / Cry myself to sleep / Blowin' in the wind.
Oct 65. (7") **WHERE DO YOU GO. / SEE SEE RIDER** 25
Mar 66. (7") **BANG BANG (MY BABY SHOT ME DOWN). / OUR DAY WILL COME** 3 2
May 66. (lp) **THE SONNY SIDE OF CHER** 11 26 Apr 66
– Bang bang (my baby shot me down) / Elusive butterfly / Where do you go / Our day will come / The girl from Ipanema / It's not unusual / Like a rolling stone / Time / Come to your window / Old man river / Milord / A young girl (une enfante).
Jul 66. (7") **ALFIE. / SHE'S NOT BETTER THAN ME** - 32
Aug 66. (7") **I FEEL SOMETHING IN THE AIR. / COME TO YOUR WINDOW** 43
—— (above US-title MAGIC IN THE AIR)
Sep 66. (7") **SUNNY. / SHE'S NO BETTER THAN ME** 32 -
Oct 66. (lp) **CHER** 59 Sep 66
– Sunny / Twelth of never / You don't have to say you love me / I feel something in the air (magic in the air) / Will you love me tomorrow/Until it's time for you to go / Cruel war / Catch the wind / Pied piper / Homeward bound / I want you before.
Nov 66. (7") **MAMA (WHEN MY DOLLIES HAVE BABIES). / BEHIND THE DOOR** 97 B-side
Sep 67. (7") **HEY JOE. / OUR DAY WILL COME** - 94
Dec 67. (lp) **WITH LOVE – CHER** 47 Nov 67
– You better sit down, kids / But I can't love you more / Hey Joe / Mama (when my dollies have babies) / Behind the door / Sing for your supper / Look at me / There but for fortune / I will wait for you / The times they are a-changin'.
Feb 68. (7") **YOU BETTER SIT DOWN KIDS. / ELUSIVE BUTTERFLY** 9 Oct 67
1968. (lp) **BACKSTAGE (live)**
– Go now / Carnival (manha de carnaval) (cancion de orfeo) / It all adds up now / Reason to believe / Masters of war / Do you believe in magic / I wasn't ready / A house is not a home / Take me for a little while / The impossible dream (the quest) / The click song / Song called children.

Atlantic Atco

Feb 69. (7") **YOURS UNTIL TOMORROW. / VERY THOUGHT OF YOU** -
Apr 69 (7") **CHASTITY'S SONG. / I WALK ON GILDED SPLINTERS** -
Jun 69. (7") **I WALK ON GILDED SPLINTERS. / TONIGHT I'LL BE STAYING HERE WITH YOU** -
Jul 69. (lp) **3614 JACKSON HIGHWAY**
– For what it's worth / (Just enough to keep me) Hangin' on / (Sittin' on) The dock of the bay / Tonight I'll be staying here with you / I threw it all away / I walk on guilded splinters / Lay baby lay / Please don't tell me / Cry like a baby / Do right woman, do right man / Save the children.
Sep 69. (7") **FOR WHAT IT'S WORTH. / (JUST ENOUGH TO KEEP ME) HANGIN' ON**
Nov 69. (7") **YOU MADE ME SO VERY HAPPY. / FIRST TIME** -
1970. (7") **SUPERSTAR. / FIRST TIME** -
1971. (7") **LAY LADY LAY. / (JUST ENOUGH TO KEEP ME) HANGIN' ON** -

M.C.A. Kapp

May 71. (7") **DON'T PUT IT ON ME. / CLASSIFIED A1**
Sep 71. (7") **GYPSYS, TRAMPS AND THIEVES. / HE'LL NEVER KNOW** 4 1
Nov 71. (lp)(c) **CHER (US title 'GYPSYS, TRAMPS & THIEVES')** 16
– The way of love / Gypsies, tramps and thieves / He'll never know / Fire and rain / When you find out where you're goin' let me know / He ain't heavy, he's my brother / I hate to sleep alone / I'm in the middle / Touch and go / One honest man *(re-iss.Aug81 on 'MFP')*
Jan 72. (7") **THE WAY OF LOVE. / DON'T PUT IT ON ME** - 7
Feb 72. (7") **THE WAY OF LOVE. / FIRE AND RAIN** -
Jun 72. (7") **LIVING IN A HOUSE DIVIDED. / ONE HONEST MAN** 22 May 72
Aug 72. (lp)(c) **FOXY LADY** 43 Jul 72
– Living in a house divided / It might as well stay Monday (from now on) / Song for you / Down, down, down / Don't try to close a rose / The first time / Let me down easy / If I knew then / Don't hide your love / Never been to Spain

M.C.A. M.C.A.

Nov 72. (7") **DON'T HIDE YOUR LOVE. / THE FIRST TIME** 46 Sep 72
May 73. (lp)(c) **BITTERSWEET WHITE LIGHT** Apr 73
– By myself / I got it bad and that ain't good / Am I blue / How long has this been going on / The man I love / Jolson medley: Sonny boy – My mammy – Rock-a-bye your baby with a Dixie melody / More than you know / Why was I born / The man that got away.
Jun 73. (7") **AM I BLUE. / HOW LONG WAS THIS BEEN GOING ON**
Oct 73. (7") **HALF BREED. / MELODY** 1 Aug 73
Oct 73. (lp)(c) **HALF BREED** 28 Sep 73
– My love / Two people clinging to a thread / Half breed / The greatest song I ever heard / How can you mend a broken heart / Carousel man / David's song / Melody / The long and winding road / This God-forsaken day / Ruby Jean & Billie Lee.
Jan 74. (7") **DARK LADY. / TWO PEOPLE CLINGING TO A THREAD** 36 1
May 74. (7") **TRAIN OF THOUGHT. / DIXIE GIRL** 27
Jun 74. (lp)(c) **DARK LADY** 69 May 74
– Train of thought / I saw a man and he danced with his wife / Make the man love me / Just what I've been lookin' for / Dark lady / Miss Subway of 1952 / Dixie girl / Rescue me / What'll I do (from The Great Gatsby) / Apples don't fall from the tree.
Aug 74. (7") **I SAW A MAN WHO DANCED WITH HIS WIFE. / I HATE TO SLEEP ALONE** 42

Warners Warners

Jul 75. (7") **A LOVE LIKE YOURS (DON'T COME KNOCKING EVERY DAY). / (JUST ENOUGH TO KEEP ME) HANGIN' ON** Apr 75
(above credited with **HARRY NILSSON**)
May 75. (lp)(c) **STARS**
– Love enough / Bell bottom blues / These days / Mr.Soul / Just this one time / Geronimo's Cadillac / The bigger they come the harder they fall / Love hurts / Rock and roll doctor / Stars.
1975. (7") **GERONIMO'S CADILLAC. / THESE DAYS** -
Mar 76. (7") **A WOMAN'S STORY. / BABY I LOVE YOU** Feb 76
Oct 76. (7") **LONG DISTANCE LOVE AFFAIR. / BORROWED TIME** -
Oct 76. (lp)(c) **I'D RATHER BELIEVE IN YOU**
– Long distance love affair / I'd rather believe in you / I know (you don't love me) / Silver wings and golden rings / Flashback / It's a cryin' shame / Early morning strangers / Knock on wood / Spring / Borrowed time.
Jan 77. (7") **PIRATE. / SEND THE MAN OVER** - 93
Apr 77. (lp)(c) **CHERISHED**
– Pirate / He was beautiful / War paint and soft feathers / Love the devil out of ya / She loves to hear the music / L.A. plane / Again / Dixie / Send the man over / Thunderstorm.
1977. (7") **WAR PAINT AND SOFT FEATHERS. / SEND THE MAN OVER** -
She collaborated with husband GREGG ALLMAN late '77 on lp TWO THE HARD WAY.

Casablanca Casablanca

Mar 79. (7") **TAKE ME HOME. / MY SONG (GONE TOO FAR)** 8 Feb 79
Apr 79. (lp)(c) **TAKE ME HOME** 25 Feb 79
– Take me home / Wasn't it good / Say the word / Happy was the day we met / Git down (guitar groupie) / Pain in my heart / Let this be a lesson to you / It's too late to love me now / My song (too far gone). *(also on pic-lp)*
Jul 79. (7") **WASN'T IT GOOD. / IT'S TOO LATE TO LOVE ME NOW** 49 May 79
(12") – ('A'side) / Take me home.
Oct 79. (7")(12") **HELL ON WHEELS. / GIT DOWN (GUITAR GROUPIE)** 59 Sep 79
Mar 80. (lp)(c) **PRISONER** Oct 79
– Prisoner / Holdin' out for love / Shoppin' / Boys and girls / Mirror image / Hell on wheels / Holy smoke / Outrageous.
Mar 80. (7") **IT'S TOO LATE TO LEAVE ME NOW. / SHOPPIN'** -
Mar 80. (7") **HOLDING OUT FOR LOVE. / BOYS AND GIRLS** -
Mar 80. (7") **HOLDIN' OUT FOR LOVE. / OUTRAGEOUS**

BLACK ROSE

CHER vocalist, with boyfriend **LES DUDEK** – guitar (ex-STEVE MILLER BAND) / **MIKE FINNEGAN** – keyboards, vocals / **GARY FURGASON** – drums / **TREY THOMPSON** – bass / **RON RITCHOTTE** – guitar

Casablanca Casablanca

Nov 80. (lp)(c) **BLACK ROSE**
– Never should've started / Julie / Take it from the boys / We all fly home / 88 degrees / You know it / Young and pretty / Fast company.
Nov 80. (7") **YOUNG AND PRETTY. / TAKE IT FROM THE BOYS** -
Feb 81. (7") **NEVER SHOULD'VE STARTED. / YOUNG AND PRETTY** -
—— split almost immediately.

CHER

went solo again

C.B.S. Columbia

Mar 82. (7") **RUDY. / DO I EVER CROSS YOUR MIND**
Aug 82. (7") **I PARALYZE. / WALK WITH ME**
Nov 82. (lp)(c) **I PARALYZE**
– Rudy / Games / I paralyze / When the love is gone / Say what's on your mind / Back on the street again / Walks with me / The book of love / Do I ever cross your mind.
She turned to acting, and appeared in many films (see above Filmography)

Geffen Geffen

Oct 87. (7") **I FOUND SOMEONE. / DANGEROUS TIMES** 5 10
(12"+=) – ('A'version).
Oct 87. (lp)(c)(cd) **CHER** 26 32
– I found someone / We all sleep alone / Bang bang (my baby shot me down) / Main man / Give our love a fightin' chance / Perfection / Dangerous times / Skin deep / Working girl / Hard enough getting over you. *(re-iss.Jan91) (re-iss.Mar93)*
Apr 88. (7") **WE ALL SLEEP ALONE. / WORKING GIRL** 47 14
(12"+=)(cd-s+=) – I found someone.
Sep 88. (7")(12") **SKIN DEEP. / PERFECTION** 79 Jul 88
(ext-12"+=)(ext.-cd-s+=) – ('A'dub version).
May 89. (7")(c-s) **AFTER ALL. ("CHER & PETER CETERA") / DANGEROUS TIMES** 6 Mar 89
(12"+=)(cd-s+=) – I found someone / Main man.
Jul 89. (lp)(c)(cd) **HEART OF STONE** 7 10
– If I could turn back time / Just like Jesse James / You wouldn't know love / Heart of stone / Still in love with you / Love on a rooftop / Emotional fire / All because of you / Does anybody really fall in love anymore? / Starting over / Kiss to kiss / After all. *(re-iss.Jan91, charts again UK.49, May92-No.43)*
Jul 89. (7")(c-s)(7"pic-d) **IF I COULD TURN BACK TIME. / SOME GUYS** 6 3
(12"+=) – Kiss to kiss.
(cd-s+=) – ('A'remix) / ('A'rock guitar mix) / I found someone.
Jan 90. (7")(c-s) **JUST LIKE JESSE JAMES. / STARTING OVER** 11 8 Oct 89
(12"+=)(cd-s+=) – I found someone.
Mar 90. (7")(c-s) **HEART OF STONE. / ALL BECAUSE OF YOU** 43 20 Feb 90
(12"+=)(cd-s+=) – Working girl.
Jul 90. (7")(c-s) **YOU WOULDN'T KNOW LOVE. / KISS TO KISS** 55
(12"+=) – Bang bang / Heart of stone.
(7"ep)(cd-ep) – ('A'side) /If I could turn back time / I found someone / We all sleep alone (remix).
Oct 90. (7")(c-s) **BABY I'M YOURS. / (IT'S BEEN) HARD ENOUGH GETTING OVER YOU**
(12"+=)(cd-s+=) – Just like Jesse James.
Apr 91. (7")(c-s) **THE SHOOP SHOOP SONG (IT'S IN HIS KISS). / BABY I'M YOURS** 1 33 Nov 90
(12"+=)(cd-s+=) – We all sleep alone.
(above single was from the film 'Mermaids' and released on 'Epic'.)
Jun 91. (cd)(c)(lp) **LOVE HURTS** 1 48

– Save up all your tears / Love hurts / Love and understanding / Fires of Eden / I'll never stop loving you / The shoop shoop song (it's in his kiss) / One small step / A world without heroes / Could've been you / When love calls your name / When lovers become strangers / Who you gonna believe. *(re-iss.cd Mar 95)*

Jul 91. (7")(c-s) **LOVE AND UNDERSTANDING. / TRAIL OF BROKEN HEARTS** 10 17 Jun 91

(12"+=)(cd-s+=) – If I could turn back time.

Sep 91. (7")(c-s) **SAVE UP ALL YOUR TEARS. / A WORLD WITHOUT HEROES** 37 37

(12"+=)(cd-s+=) – Love and understanding.

Nov 91. (7")(c-s) **LOVE HURTS. / ONE SMALL STEP** 43

(12"+=)(cd-s+=) – Just like Jesse James.

Mar 92. (7"+c-s+7"pic-d) **COULD'VE BEEN YOU. / LOVE AND UNDERSTANDING** 31

(12"sha-pic-d+=)(cd-s+=) – Save up all your tears.

Nov 92. (cd)(c)(d-lp) **GREATEST HITS 1965-92** (compilation) 1

– Oh no not my baby / Whenever you're near / Many rivers to cross (live) / Love and understanding / Save up all your tears / The shoop shoop song (it's in his kiss) / If I could turn back time / Just like Jesse James / Heart of stone / I found someone / We all sleep alone / Bang bang (my baby shot me down) (with SONNY) / Dead ringer for love (with MEAT LOAF) / Dark lady / Gypsys, tramps and thieves / I got you babe (with SONNY).

Nov 92. (7")(c-s) **OH NO NOT MY BABY. / LOVE HURTS** 33

(cd-s+=) – Love on a rooftop / Main man.

Jan 93. (7")(c-s) **MANY RIVERS TO CROSS. / WHO YOU GONNA BELIEVE** 37

(cd-s+=) – ?

Feb 93. (7")(c-s) **WHENEVER YOU'RE NEAR. / COULD'VE BEEN YOU** 72

(12"pic-d+=)(cd-s+=) – You wouldn't know love / I'll never stop loving you.

Jan 94. (c-s)(cd-s) **I GOT YOU BABE. ("CHER with BEAVIS & BUTT-HEAD") / I GOT YOU BABE ("SONNY & CHER")** 35

— BEAVIS & BUTT-HEAD are cult TV cartoon characters, who have already carved up a lot of parental hysteria, by their use of foul language and violence. In Mar'95 alongside CHRISSIE HYNDE, NENEH CHERRY and ERIC CLAPTON, she hit UK No.1 with charity Comic Relief song 'LOVE CAN BUILD A BRIDGE'.

Oct 95. (c-s) **WALKING IN MEMPHIS / ANGELS RUNNING** 11

(cd-s+=) – The fall.
(cd-s+=) – ('A'-Shut up and dance instrumental).
(cd-s) – ('A'-4 mixes).

Nov 95. (cd)(c) **IT'S A MAN'S WORLD** 28

– Walking in Memphis / Not enough love in the world / One by one / I wouldn't treat a dog (the way you treated me) / Angels running / Paradise is here / I'm blowin' away / Don't come around tonite / What about the moonlight / The same mistake / The gunman / The sun ain't gonna shine anymore / Shape of things to come / It's a man's, man's, man's world.

– other compilations, etc. –

Nov 68. Sunset/ US= Imperial; (lp) **CHER'S GREATEST HITS**
(re-iss.Mar75 + May82 on 'M.C.A.')

Jan 72. Imperial; (d-lp) **CHER SUPERPAK** -

Nov 75. Sunset; (lp)(c) **GOLDEN HITS** -

1970's. Imperial; (lp)(c) **THIS IS CHER** -

Jan 72. United Artists; (d-lp) **CHER SUPERPAK** - 92

Oct 72. United Artists; (d-lp) **CHER SUPERPAK, VOL.II** - 95

1972. United Artists; (lp)(c) **HITS OF CHER** -

1970's. Springboard; (lp) **SINGS THE HITS** -

Apr 75. M.C.A.; (7") **RESCUE ME. / DIXIE GIRL**

Jul 80. M.C.A.; (7") **GYPSIES, TRAMPS & THIEVES. / DARK LADY**

Oct 85. M.C.A.; (lp)(c) **GOLDEN GREATS**

Jul 93. M.C.A.; (cd)(c) **CHER / FOXY LADY**

Jul 93. M.C.A.; (cd)(c) **HALF BREED / DARK LADY**

Jul 82. Old Gold; (7") **GYPSIES, TRAMPS & THIEVES. / HALF BREED** -
(re-iss.!) (as cd-ep+=) – All I really want to do.

Jul 84. EMI Gold; (7") **BANG BANG (MY BABY SHOT ME DOWN). / ALL I REALLY WANT TO DO** -

Mar 91. Liberty; (cd)(c)(lp) **BANG BANG (MY BABY SHOT ME DOWN) – THE BEST OF CHER**

1966. Liberty; (7"ep) **THE HITS OF CHER** -

Sep 85. Liberty; (lp)(c) **THE BEST OF CHER** -

Apr 93. Pulsar; (cd) **HOLDIN' OUT FOR LOVE** -

May 93. Spectrum; (cd)(c) **TAKE ME HOME / PRISONER** -

Apr 93. Movieplay Gold; (cd) **GYPSIES, TRAMPS & THIEVES** -

Nov 95. EMI; (3xcd-box) **ALL I REALLY WANT TO DO / SONNY SIDE / CHER** -

SONNY & CHER

(first 2 singles originally credited to CAESAR & CLEO)

Reprise Reprise

Oct 64. (7") **JUST YOU. / SING C'EST LA VIE** -
(re-iss.US Aug65 credited as "SONNY & CHER", hit No.20)

Feb 65. (7") **BABY DON'T GO. / WALKING THE QUETZEL**
(re-iss.US Aug65 credited as "SONNY & CHER", hit No.8) (UK-ep, above four hit No.11) (SONNY AND CHER AND CAESAR AND CLEO)

Atlantic Atco

Jul 65. (7") **I GOT YOU BABE. / IT'S GONNA RAIN** 1 1

— In Sep65, she contributed vox to BONNIE + THE TREASURES 7" Home Of The Brave

Oct 65. (7") **BUT YOU'RE MINE. / HELLO** 17 15

Oct 65. (lp) **LOOK AT US** 7 2 Aug 65

– I got you babe / Unchained melody / Then he kissed me / Sing c'est la vie / It's gonna rain / 500 miles / Just you / The letter / Let it be me / You don't love me / You've really got a hold on me / Why don't they let us fall in love.

Feb 66. (7") **WHAT NOW MY LOVE. / I LOOK FOR YOU** 13 16 Jan 66

Jun 66. (7") **HAVE I STAYED TOO LONG. / LEAVE ME BE** 42 49

May 66. (lp) **THE WONDEROUS WORLD OF SONNY & CHER** 15 34 Apr 66

– Summertime / Tell him / I'm leaving it all up to you / But you're mine / ring it on home to me / Set me free / What now my love / Leave me be / I look for you / Laugh at me / Turn around / So fine.

Sep 66. (7") **LITTLE MAN. / MONDAY** 4 21

Nov 66. (7") **LIVING FOR YOU. / TURN AROUND** 44 -

Nov 66. (7") **LIVING FOR YOU. / LOVE DON'T COME** - 87

Jan 67. (7") **THE BEAT GOES ON. / LOVE DON'T COME** 29 6

Apr 67. (lp) **IN CASE YOU'RE IN LOVE** 45 Mar 66

– The beat goes on / Groovy kind of love / You baby / Monday / Love don't come / Podunk / Little man / We'll sing in the sunshine / Misty roses / Stand by me / Living for you / Cheryl's goin' home.

May 67. (7") **A BEAUTIFUL STORY. / PODUNK** 53 Apr 67

May 67. (lp) **GOOD TIMES** - 73

Aug 67. (7") **PLASTIC MAN. / IT'S THE LITTLE THINGS** 74 Jun 67

Sep 67. (7") **IT'S THE LITTLE THINGS. / DON'T TALK TO STRANGERS** - 50

Dec 67. (7") **GOOD COMBINATIONS. / YOU AND ME** 56

— (above 'B'side by 'SONNY')

Feb 68. (7") **CIRCUS. / I WOULD MARRY YOU TODAY**

Sep 68. (7") **YOU GOTTA HAVE A THING OF YOUR OWN. / I GOT YOU BABE**

1969. (7") **YOU'RE A FRIEND OF MINE. / I WOULD MARRY YOU TODAY** -

Jul 70. (7") **GET IT TOGETHER. / HOLD YOU TIGHTER**

M.C.A. Kapp

Jun 71. (7") **REAL PEOPLE. / SOMEBODY**

Oct 71. (lp)(c) **SONNY AND CHER LIVE (live)** 35

– What now my love / The beat goes on / Once in a lifetime / More today than yesterday / Gotta get you into my life / Someday (you'll want me to want you) / Danny boy / Laugh at me / Something / Hey Jude / I got you babe.

Nov 71. (7") **ALL I EVER NEED IS YOU. / I GOT YOU BABE** 8 7 Oct 71

Jun 72. (lp)(c) **ALL I EVER NEED IS YOU** 14 Feb 72

– All I ever need is you / Here comes that rainy day feeling / More today than yesterday / Crystal clear waters / United we stand / A cowboy's work is never done / I love what you did with the love I gave you / You better sit down kids / We'll watch the Sun coming up / Somebody. *(re-iss.May74)*

Apr 72. (7") **A COWBOY'S WORK IS NEVER DONE. / SOMEBODY** 8 Feb 72

Aug 72. (7") **WHEN YOU SAY LOVE. / CRYSTAL CLEAR – MUDDY WATERS** 32 Jul 92

M.C.A. M.C.A.

Feb 73. (lp)(c) **MAMA WAS A ROCK AND ROLL SINGER** Jun 73

– It never rains in Southern California / I believe in you / I can see clearly now / Rhythm of your heartbeat / Mama was a rock and roll singer, papa used to write all her songs (parts 1 & 2) / By love I mean / Brother Love's travelling salvation show / You know darn well / The greatest show on Earth / Listen to the music.

Apr 73. (7") **MAMA WAS A ROCK AND ROLL SINGER, PAPA USED TO WRITE ALL HER SONGS. / (part 2)** 77 Mar 73

Jul 73. (7") **GREATEST SHOW ON EARTH. / YOU KNOW DARN WELL I DO**

May 74. (d-lp)(c) **LIVE IN LAS VEGAS VOL.2 (live)** Dec 73

– All I ever need is you / I can see clearly now / You've got a friend / Where you lead / You'd better sit down kids / A cowboy's work is never done / I got you babe / Gypsies, tramps and thieves / Brother Love's travelling salvation show / You and I / Superstar / Bang bang (my baby shot me down).

They release 2 more US singles on 'Warner Bros.' but they decide to end partnership as they seperated and divorced 26th June 74. (see biography above) Professionally they did re-unite in 1976-77 on US TV 'SONNY & CHER SHOW' again.

– their compilations, others, etc. –

Oct 65. Reprise; (lp) **BABY DON'T GO (+other artists)** - 69

All below on UK 'Atlantic' released in US on 'Atco'.

Mar 67. Atlantic; (7") **I GOT YOU BABE. / BUT YOU'RE MINE**

Oct 67. Atlantic; (lp) **THE BEST OF SONNY & CHER** 23 Aug 67
(re-iss.lp/c.Aug72)

Sep 72. Atlantic; (d-lp) **THE TWO OF US (LOOK AT US + IN CASE YOU'RE IN LOVE)** -

Jan 74. Atlantic; (7"m) **I GOT YOU BABE. / THE BEAT GOES ON / LITTLE MAN** -

Jun 72. Atlantic; (7") **I GOT YOU BABE. / THE BEAT GOES ON**
(re-iss.Jul81)

1975. Atlantic; (lp)(c) **THE BEAT GOES ON – THE BEST OF . . .** -
(cd-iss.Jun93 on 'Atco')

Jan 75. M.C.A.; (lp)(c) **GREATEST HITS** Sep 74

Jun 81. Hallmark; (lp)(c) **THE VERY BEST OF SONNY & CHER** -

Sep 85. Old Gold; (7") **I GOT YOU BABE. / WHAT NOW MY LOVE** -

Dec 90. W.E.A.; (cd)(c)(lp) **THE SONNY & CHER COLLECTION**

May 93. Epic; (7")(c-s) **I GOT YOU BABE. / ?**
(cd-s+=) – ?

— (SONNY had solo releases, noteably Top 10 UK/US hit LAUGH AT ME)

Neneh CHERRY

Born: 10 Aug'64, Stockholm, Sweden. Mother Swedish / father African, she was raised and educated by her mother and stepfather DON CHERRY (famous jazz trumpeter) in Manhattan New York. In 1981 she moved to London, augmented The SLITS, before joining RIP, RIG & PANIC. They made 3 albums; GOD (1981), I AM COLD (1982) and ATTITUDE (1983), before she left to form FLOAT UP CP. • **Songwriters:** In 1986, she met and later married (1990), CAMERON McVEY (aka BOOGA BEAR). They started writing partnership and launched her solo career in 1988, with McVEY as producer /

musician. In 1990, she covered I'VE GOT YOU UNDER MY SKIN (Cole Porter). Sampled BORN TO BE WILD (Steppenwolf) / FOR THE LOVE OF MONEY (O'Jays) / SUGAR FREE (Juicy). • **Trivia:** She guested duet on THE THE – Slow Train To Dawn, on his/their 1986 Infected album. She gave birth to her second child in Mar'89. • **Style:** Vocalist/rapper with off-beat avant-garde rock background that laid foundations to her modern soul/pop.

Recommended: RAW LIKE SUSHI (*6)

NENEH – vocals / **CAMERON** – keyboards

Circa / Virgin

Nov 88. (7") **BUFFALO STANCE. / ('A'-electro ski mix)** 3 | 3 Mar 89
(12"+=) – ('A'extended).
(3"cd-s++=) – ('A'scratchappela mix).
May 89. (7")(c-s) **MANCHILD. / ('A'version)** 5
(12"+=)(3"cd-s+=) – Buffalo stance.
(12"+=) – ('A'versions).
Jun 89. (lp)(c)(cd) **RAW LIKE SUSHI** 2 | 40
– Buffalo stance * / Manchild * / Kisses on the wind / Inna city mama / The next generation / Love ghetto / Heart * / Phoney ladies / Outre risque locomotive / So here I come. *(cd+=)* – My bitch / (tracks marked * = extra remixes).
Aug 89. (7")(c-s) **KISSES ON THE WIND. / BUFFALO BLUES** 20 | 8
(12"+=)(3"cd-s+=) – ('A'extended).
Dec 89. (7")(c-s) **INNA CITY MAMA. / THE NEXT GENERATION** 34 | -
(12"+=) – Kisses on the wind.
(cd-s++=) – So here I come.
Dec 89. (c-s) **HEART. / ?** -
Sep 90. (7") **I'VE GOT YOU UNDER MY SKIN. / ('A'version)** 25
(12"+=)/ /(12"+=) – ('A'long version)/ / ('A'different mix).
Sep 92. (7")(c-s) **MONEY LOVE. / TWISTED** 23
(ext-12"+=)(cd-s+=) – ('A'-Paul Oakenfield) / ('A'perfecto mix).
Below album featured guests GURU from GANGSTARR / J$ / MICHAEL STIPE / etc.
Oct 92. (cd)(c)(lp) **HOMEBREW** 27
– Sassy / Money love / Move with me / I ain't gone under yet / Twisted / Buddy X / Somedays / Trout / Peace in mind / Red paint. *(re-iss.Jul93)*
Jun 93. (7")(c-s) **BUDDY X (What's Up Mix) / BUDDY X (Falcon & Fabian Remix)** 35 | 43 Apr 93
(12"+=)(cd-s+=) – (4 other 'A' mixes)

— In May 94, she was credited on UK Top 3 single '7 SECONDS' with YOUSSOU N'DOUR. In Mar95, alongside CHER, CHRISSIE HYNDE and ERIC CLAPTON, she hit No.1 UK with Comic Relief charity song 'LOVE CAN BUILD A BRIDGE'.

CHERRY BOMBZ (see under ⇒ HANOI ROCKS)

CHIC

Formed: New York, USA . . . 1972 as The BIG APPLE BAND by NILE, BERNARD & TONY. They worked together sessioning for disco acts (i.e. NEW YORK CITY hit 'I'm Doin' Fine' and CAROL DOUGLAS), before forming CHIC in 1976. They added singer NORMA JEAN WRIGHT, who had recently made a 'Bearsville' album with CHIC at the controls. They were finally signed by 'Atlantic', after company president listened to their demo. Late 1977, 'DANCE DANCE DANCE (YOWSAH YOWSAH YOWSAH)' hit the charts, eventually to peak at No.6 on both sides of the Atlantic. With change of vocalists the following year, they issued 'LE FREAK', which gave them their first US No.1. In 1979, RODGERS and EDWARDS produced other disco act SISTER SLEDGE on their hits 'He's The Greatest Dancer' & 'We Are Family'. Later in the year, they had their second No.1 with 'GOOD TIMES'. Meanwhile, offers poured in for production work from the likes of DIANA ROSS (Diana) / DEBBIE HARRY (Koo Koo) / DAVID BOWIE (Let's Dance). They split CHIC in 1982, to concentrate on other projects, etc. (see further below) • **Style:** Introduced recognizable rhythmical bass-line beat to the disco scene, which in the 80's set new trend for their contemporaries. • **Songwriters:** RODGERS-EDWARDS wrote all material. • **Trivia:** In 1980, The SUGARHILL GANG's 'Rapper's Delight', was found guilty of plagiarising CHIC's 'Good Times', and were ordered to pay writers royalties.

Recommended: GREATEST HITS (*7).

NILE RODGERS (b.19 Sep'52, New York, USA) – guitar / **BERNARD EDWARDS** (b.31 Oct'52, Greenville, New Connecticut, USA) – bass / **TONY THOMPSON** – drums / **NORMA JEAN WRIGHT** – vocals

Atlantic / Atlantic

Nov 77. (7") **DANCE DANCE DANCE (YOWSAH YOWSAH YOWSAH). / SAO PAULO** 6 | 6 Oct 77
Feb 78. (lp)(c) **CHIC** | 27 Dec 77
– Dance dance dance (yowsah yowsah yowsah) / Sao paulo / You can get by / Everybody dance / Est ce que c'est Chic / Falling in love with you / Strike up the band. *(cd-iss.Nov93)*
Mar 78. (7") **EVERYBODY DANCE. / YOU CAN GET BY** 9 | 38

— **ALFA ANDERSON + LUCI MARTIN** – vocals repl. NORMA JEAN WRIGHT

Nov 78. (7") **LE FREAK. / SAVIOR FAIRE** 7 | 1 Oct 78
(12"+=) – Chic (everybody say).
Dec 78. (lp)(c) **C'EST CHIC** 2 | 4 Nov 78
– Chic cheer / Le freak / I want your love / Happy man / Dance dance dance / Savoir faire / At last I am free / Sometimes you win / Funny bone / Everybody dance. *(cd-iss.Nov93)*
Feb 79. (7") **I WANT YOUR LOVE. / FUNNY BONE** 4 | 7
(12") – ('A'side) / – Chic cheer / Le freak.
Jun 79. (7")(12") **GOOD TIMES. / A WARM SUMMER NIGHT** 5 | 1
Aug 79. (lp)(c) **RISQUE** 29 | 5
– Good times / A warm summer night / My feet keep dancing / My forbidden lover / Can't stand to love you / Will you cry when you hear this song / What about me. *(cd-iss.Nov93)*
Sep 79. (7") **MY FORBIDDEN LOVER. / WHAT ABOUT ME** 15 | 43
Nov 79. (7") **MY FEET KEEP DANCING. / WILL YOU CRY WHEN YOU HEAR THIS SONG** 21
Dec 79. (lp)(c) **LES PLUS GRANDS SUCCES DE CHIC – GREATEST HITS** (compilation) 30 | 88
Jul 80. (7")(12") **REBELS ARE WE. / OPEN UP** | 61
Jul 80. (lp)(c) **REAL PEOPLE** | 30
– Real people / Rebels are we / You can't do it alone / Chip off the old block / I got protection / Open up / 26.
Sep 80. (7")(12") **26. / CHIP OFF THE OLD BLOCK**
Nov 80. (7") **REAL PEOPLE. / CHIP OFF THE OLD BLOCK** | 79
Nov 81. (lp)(c) **TAKE IT OFF**
– Flashback / Take it off / Just out of reach / Telling lies / Stage fright / So fine / Baby doll / Your love is cancelled / Burn hard / Would you be my baby.
Jun 82. (7") **STAGE FRIGHT. / SO FINE** - | 80

— (above from the film 'Soup For One' for which NILE & RODGERS wrote s-track on 'Mirage')

Nov 82. (lp)(c) **TONGUE IN CHIC**
– Hangin' / I feel your love comin' on / When you love someone / Chic (everybody say) / Hey fool / Sharing love / City lights.
Jan 83. (7")(12") **HANGIN'. / CITY LIGHTS** 64 | -
Jan 83. (7") **HANGIN'. / CHIC (EVERYBODY SAY)** -
Dec 83. (lp)(c) **BELIEVER**
– Believer / You are beautiful / Take a closer look / Give me the lovin' / Show me your light / You got some love for me / In love with music / Party everybody.
Dec 83. (7") **YOU GOT SOME LOVE FOR ME. / GIVE ME THE LOVIN'** -

— Early in 1983, they had already split. EDWARDS and THOMPSON later joined The POWER STATION with ROBERT PALMER and members of DURAN DURAN ⇒ .

NILE RODGERS

went solo, also augmented by EDWARDS and THOMPSON

Mirage-WEA / Mirage-WEA

Feb 83. (lp)(c) **ADVENTURES IN THE LAND OF THE GOOD GROOVE**
– The land of the good groove / Yum yum / Beat / Get her crazy / It's all in your hands / Rock bottom / My love song for you / Most down.
Mar 83. (7")(12") **THE LAND OF GOOD GROOVE. / MY LOVE SONG FOR YOU**
May 83. (7")(12") **YUM YUM. / GET HER CRAZY**

— After spell with The HONEYDRIPPERS (see LED ZEPPELIN), he continued solo.

Warners / Warners

Jun 85. (lp)(c) **B-MOVIE MATINEE**
– Groove master / Let's go out tonight / Same wavelength / Plan number 9 / State your mind / Face in the window / Doll squad.
Jun 85. (7")(12") **LET'S GO OUT TONIGHT. / DOLL SQUAD**
Jan 86. (7") **STATE OF MIND. / STAY OUT OF THE LIGHT**

— In 1987, RODGERS formed The OUTLOUD with PHILLIPE SAISSE + FELICIA COLLINS.

CHIC

reformed 1991 and signed to . . .

W.E.A. / W.E.A.

Jan 92. (7")(c-s) **CHIC MYSTIQUE. / ('A'lovely without rap mix)** 48
(12"+=) – ('A'-4 a.m. mix) / ('A'lovely mix).
(cd-s++=) – ('A'extended) / ('A'accapella mix).
Mar 92. (cd)(c)(lp) **CHIC-ISM**
– Chic mystique / Your love / Jusagroove / Something you can feel / One and only one / Doin' that thing to me / Chicism / In it to win it / My love's for real / Take my love / High / M.M.F.T.C.F. *(re-iss.cd Feb95)*
May 92. (7") **YOUR LOVE. / ('A'mix)**
(12"+=)(cd-s+=) – ('A'extended).

– other compilations, others, etc. –

Nov 84. Atlantic; (7") **CHIC CHEERS. / SAVOIR FAIRE**
(12"+=) – Dance, dance, dance (yowsah, yowsah, yowsah).
Aug 86. Atlantic; (12"ep) **LE FREAK. / SAVOIR FAIRE / CHIC (EVERYBODY SAY)**
Sep 87. Atlantic; (7")(12") **JACK LE FREAK. / SAVOIR FAIRE** 19 | -
Jul 90. Atlantic; (7")(c-s) **MEGACHIC (Chic Medley). / LE FREAK** 58 | -
(12"+=)(cd-s+=) – ('A'edit).
Nov 87. Telstar; (lp)(c)(cd) **FREAK OUT** (half album with SISTER SLEDGE) 72 | -
Jun 93. Atlantic; (cd) **THE BEST OF CHIC – VOLUME 2**
Jul 91. Dino; (cd)(c)(d-lp) **GREATEST HITS – SIDE BY SIDE** | -

— (half album by ROSE ROYCE) *(re-iss.cd+c.Apr93)*

CHICAGO

Formed: Chicago, Illinois, USA . . . 1966 as CHICAGO TRANSIT AUTHORITY on the idea of friend/manager/producer James William Guercio. The band (KATH and PARAZAIDER, etc.) moved to Los Angeles and recorded hit debut eponymous album for 'CBS/Columbia' 1969. That year, due to legal threats, they shortened name to CHICAGO. They became one of America's top bands of the 70's & 80's, and scored 2 US No.1's with 'IF

YOU LEAVE ME NOW' (1976) & 'HARD TO SAY I'M SORRY' (1982). • **Style:** Brass-laden jazz-pop rock in the 60's, moving into soft-AOR in the mid 70's. Due to this new guaranteed formula for hits, they stayed with this style throughout the 80's. • **Songwriters:** LAMM wrote lyrics, KATH and group the music. Covered I'M A MAN (Spencer Davis Group). • **Trivia:** 80's newcomer JASON SCHEFF was son of Elvis Presley's bassman JERRY.

Recommended: CHICAGO IX GREATEST HITS (*6).

ROBERT LAMM (b.13 Oct'44, Brooklyn, New York) – vocals, keyboards / **TERRY KATH** (b.31 Jan'46) – vocals, guitar / **PETER CETERA** (b.13 Sep'44) – vocals, bass / **DAN SERAPHINE** (b.28 Aug'48) – drums / **LEE LOUGHNANE** (b.21 Oct'46) – trumpet, vocals / **JAMES PANKOW** (b.20 Aug'47) – trombone / **WALTER PARAZAIDER** (b.14 Mar'48) – reeds

C.B.S. Columbia

Sep 69. (d-lp) **CHICAGO TRANSIT AUTHORITY** (as "CHICAGO TRANSIT AUTHORITY") [9] [17] May69
– (introduction) / Does anybody really know what time it is? / Beginnings / Questions 67 and 68 / Listen / Poem 58 / Free form guitar / South California purples / I'm a man / (prologue, August 29, 1968) / Someday / Liberation. *(re-iss.+c+cd.Sep87) (cd-iss.Oct93 on 'Sony Europe') (re-iss.cd+c Jun94 on 'Columbia')*

Jul 69. (7") **QUESTIONS 67 AND 68. / LISTEN** [ ] [71]

Dec 69. (7") **I'M A MAN. / DOES ANYBODY REALLY KNOW WHAT THE TIME IS?** [8] [ ]

Mar 70. (d-lp) **CHICAGO II** [6] [4] Feb 70
– Movin' in / The road / Poem for the people / In the country / Wake up sunshine (ballet for a girl in Buchannon) / Make me smile / So much to say, so much to give / Anxiety's moment / West Virginia fantasies / Colour my world / To be free / Now more than ever / Fancy colours / 25 or 6 to 4 / (prelude) / A.M. mourning / P.M. mourning / Memories of love / It better end soon (movements 1-5) / Where do we go from here. *(cd-iss.Oct93 on 'Sony Europe')*

Apr 70. (7") **MAKE ME SMILE. / COLOUR MY WORLD** [ ] [9]

Jul 70. (7") **25 OR 6 TO 4. / WHERE DO WE GO FROM HERE** [7] [4]

Nov 70. (7") **DOES ANYBODY REALLY KNOW WHAT THE TIME IS?. / LISTEN** [-] [7]

Feb 71. (7") **FREE. / FREE COUNTRY** [ ] [20]

Mar 71. (d-lp) **CHICAGO III** [31] [2] Jan 71
– Sing a mean tune kid / Loneliness is just a word / What else can I say / I don't want your money / Flight 602 / Motorboat to Mars / Free / Free country / At the sunrise / Happy 'cause I'm going home / Mother / Lowdown / A hard risin' morning without breakfast / Off to work / Fallin' out / Morning blues again / When all the laughter dies in sorrow / Canon / Once upon a time / Progress? / The approaching storm / Man vs. man / The end. *(cd-iss.Oct93 on 'Sony Europe')*

May 71. (7") **LOWDOWN. / LONELINESS IS JUST A WORD** [ ] [35]

Jul 71. (7") **BEGINNINGS. / COLOUR MY WORLD** [ ] [7] Jun 71

Nov 71. (q-lp) **LIVE AT CARNEGIE HALL (live)** [ ] [3]
– In the country / Fancy colours / Does anybody really know what time it is? / Free form guitar / South California purples / Questions 67 and 68 / Sing a mean tune kid / Beginnings / It better end soon (5 movements) / (introduction) / Mother / Lowdown / Flight 602 / Motorboat to Mars / Where do we go from here / I don't want your money / Happy 'cause I'm going home / Wake up sunshine (ballet for a girl in Buchannon) / Make me smile / So much to say, so much to give / Anxiety's moment / West Virginia fantasies / Colour my world / To be free / Free / Now more than ever / A song for Richard and his friends / 25 or 6 to 4 / I'm a man. *(cd-iss.Apr89)*

Jan 72. (7") **QUESTIONS 67 AND 68 (live). / I'M A MAN (live)** [-] [ ]

Aug 72. (7") **SATURDAY IN THE PARK. / ALMA MATER** [ ] [3]

Sep 72. (lp)(c) **CHICAGO V** [24] [1] Jul 72
– Saturday in the park / A hit by Varese / All is well / Now that you've gone / Dialogue (part 1 & 2) / While the city sleeps / State of the union / Alma mater / Goodbye. *(re-iss.Apr84 on 'Hallmark') (cd-iss.1988) cd-iss.Nov93 on 'Sony Collectors')*

Nov 72. (7") **DIALOGUE (pt.1 & 2). / NOW THAT YOU'VE GONE** [ ] [24] Oct 72

Aug 73. (7") **FEELIN' STRONGER EVERY DAY. / JENNY** [ ] [10] Jun 73

Aug 73. (lp)(c) **CHICAGO VI** [ ] [1] Jul 73
– Critic's choice / Just you 'n' me / Darlin' dear / Jenny / What's this world comin' to / Something in this city changes people / Hollywood / Jenny / In terms of two / Rediscovery / Feelin' stronger every day.

Sep 73. (7") **JUST YOU 'N' ME. / CRITIC'S CHOICE** [-] [4]

Oct 73. (7") **JUST YOU 'N' ME. / FEELIN' STRONGER EVERY DAY** [ ] [-]

Apr 74. (7") **(I'VE BEEN) SEARCHIN' SO LONG. / BYBLOS** [ ] [9] Mar 74

May 74. (lp)(c) **CHICAGO VII** [ ] [1] Mar 74
– (prelude to Aire) / Aire / Devil's sweet / Halian from New York / Hanky panky / Life saver / Happy man / (I've been) Searchin' so long / Mongonucleosis / Song of the evergreens / Byblos / Wishing you were here / Call on me / Woman don't want to love me / Skinny boy. *(cd-iss.May88)*

Oct 74. (7") **CALL ON ME. / AIRE** [ ] [6] Jun74

Oct 74. (7") **WISHING YOU WERE HERE. / LIFE SAVER** [-] [11]

Nov 74. (7") **WISHING YOU WERE HERE. / SONG OF THE EVERGREENS** [ ] [-]

Mar 75. (7") **HARRY TRUMAN. / TILL WE MEET AGAIN** [ ] [13] Feb 75

Apr 75. (lp)(c) **CHICAGO VIII** [ ] [1]
– Anyway you want / Brand new love affair (pt.I & II) / Never been in love before / Hideaway / Till we meet again / Harry Truman / Oh, thank you great spirit / Long time no see / Ain't it blue / Old days.

Jun 75. (7") **OLD DAYS. / HIDEAWAY** [ ] [5] Apr 75

Aug 75. (7") **NEVER BEEN IN LOVE BEFORE. / (part 2)** [ ] [ ]

Oct 75. (7") **BRAND NEW LOVE AFFAIR. / HIDEAWAY** [ ] [61]

Oct 75. (lp)(c) **CHICAGO IX GREATEST HITS** (compilation) [ ] [1]
– 25 or 6 to 4 / Does anybody really know what time it is? / Colour my world / Just you 'n' me / Saturday in the park / Feelin' stronger every day / Make me smile / Wishing you were here / Call on me / (I've been) Searchin' so long / Beginnings. *(re-iss.Nov84) (cd-iss.Jul87)*

Jul 76. (7") **ANOTHER RAINY DAY IN NEW YORK. / HOPE FOR LOVE** [ ] [32] Jun 76

Jul 76. (lp)(c) **CHICAGO X** [21] [3]
– Once or twice / You are on my mind / Skin tight / If you leave me now / Together again / Another rainy day in New York City / Mama mama / Scrapbook / Gently I'll wake you / You get it up / Hope for love. *(cd-iss.1988)*

Sep 76. (7") **IF YOU LEAVE ME NOW. / TOGETHER AGAIN** [1] [1]

Feb 77. (7") **YOU ARE ON MY MIND. / GENTLY I'LL WAKE YOU** [-] [49]

Sep 77. (lp)(c) **CHICAGO XI** [ ] [6]
– Mississippi Delta queen blues / Baby, what a big surprise / Policeman / Till the end of time / Take me back to Chicago / Vote for me / Takin' it on uptown / This time / The inner struggles of a man / (prelude) / Little one. *(cd-iss.1988)*

Sep 77. (7") **BABY, WHAT A BIG SURPRISE. / TAKIN' IT ON UPTOWN** [41] [4]

Jan 78. (7") **TAKE ME BACK TO CHICAGO. / POLICEMAN** [ ] [63] May 78

Mar 78. (7") **LITTLE ONE. / TILL THE END OF TIME** [ ] [44] Feb 78

—— On the 23rd Jan'78, TERRY KATH died, accidentally shooting himself in the head. Later in year, he was repl. by **DONNIE DACUS** – guitar (ex-STEPHEN STILLS)

Sep 78. (lp)(c) **HOT STREETS** [ ] [12]
– Alive again / The greatest love on Earth / Little Miss Lovin' / Hot streets / Take a chance / Gone long gone / Ain't it time / Love was new / No tell lover / Show me the way. *(re-iss.cd+c May93 on 'Sony Collectors')*

Oct 78. (7") **ALIVE AGAIN. / LOVE WAS NEW** [ ] [14]

Mar 79. (7") **NO TELL LOVER. / TAKE A CHANCE** [ ] [14] Dec 78

Apr 79. (7") **GONE LONG GONE. / THE GREATEST LOVE ON EARTH** [-] [73]

Aug 79. (7") **MUST HAVE BEEN CRAZY. / CLOSER TO YOU** [ ] [83]

Sep 79. (lp)(c) **CHICAGO 13 – STREET PLAYER** [ ] [21] Aug 79
– Street player / Mama take / Must have been crazy / Window dreamin' / Paradise alley / Aloha mama / Reruns / Loser with a broken heart / Life is what it is / Run away.

Oct 79. (7") **MAMA TAKE. / WINDOW DREAMIN'** [ ] [-]

Apr 80. (7") **STREET PLAYER. / WINDOW DREAMIN'** [ ] [ ]

—— **CHRIS PINNICK** – guitar repl. DACUS

Jun 80. (7") **THUNDER AND LIGHTNING. / I'D RATHER BE RICH** [-] [56] Aug 80

Aug 80. (7") **SONG FOR YOU. / I'D RATHER BE RICH** [-] [ ]

Sep 80. (7") **THE AMERICAN DREAM / SONG FOR YOU** [ ] [-]

Sep 80. (lp)(c) **CHICAGO XIV** [ ] [71] Aug 80
– Manipulation / Upon arrival / Song for you / Where did the lovin' go / Birthday boy / Hold on / Overnight cafe / Thunder and lightning / I'd rather be rich / The American dream.

Dec 81. (lp)(c) **CHICAGO – GREATEST HITS, VOLUME II** (compilation) [ ] [ ]
– Baby, what a big surprise / Dialogue (part 1 & 2) / No tell lover / Alive again / Old days / If you leave me now / Questions 67 and 68 / Happy man / Gone long gone / Take me back to Chicago.

—— added **BILL CHAMPLIN** – vocals, bass, guitar (ex-SONS OF CHAMPLIN)

Full Moon Full Moon

Jun 82. (lp)(c) **CHICAGO 16** [44] [9]
– What you're missing / Waiting for you to decide / Bad advice / Chains / Hard to say I'm sorry / Get away / Follow me / Sonny think twice / Rescue you / What can I say / Love me tomorrow. *(cd-iss.1983)*

Aug 82. (7") **HARD TO SAY I'M SORRY. / SONNY THINK TWICE** [4] [1] Jun 82

Nov 82. (7") **LOVE ME TOMORROW. / BAD ADVICE** [ ] [22] Sep 82

Jan 83. (7") **WHAT YOU'RE MISSING. / RESCUE YOU** [-] [81]

Jun 84. (7") **STAY THE NIGHT. / ONLY YOU** [ ] [16] Apr84

Jul 84. (lp)(c)(cd) **CHICAGO 17** [24] [4] May 84
– Stay the night / We can stop the hurtin' / Hard habit to break / Only you / Remember the feeling / Along comes a woman / You're the inspiration / Please hold on / Prima Donna / Once in a lifetime.

Oct 84. (7") **HARD HABIT TO BREAK. / REMEMBER THE FEELING** [8] [3] Aug 84

Jan 85. (7") **YOU'RE THE INSPIRATION. / LOVE ME TOMORROW** [14] [3] Nov 84
(12"+=) – Once in a lifetime. (US B-side)

Mar 85. (7")(12") **ALONG COMES A WOMAN. / WE CAN STOP THE HURTIN'** [ ] [14] Feb 85

—— **JERRY SCHEFF** – bass repl. CETERA who goes solo.

Oct 86. (7") **25 OR 6 TO 4 (remix). / ONE MORE DAY** [ ] [48] Sep 86
(12"+=) – Hard habit to break.

Oct 86. (lp)(c)(cd) **CHICAGO 18** [ ] [35]
– Niagara Falls / Forever / If she would have been faithfull / 25 or 6 to 4 / Will you still love me? / Over and over / It's alright / Nothin's gonna stop us now / I believe / One more day. *(re-iss.cd Feb93)*

Nov 86. (7") **WILL YOU STILL LOVE ME? / 25 OR 6 TO 4** [-] [3]

Feb 87. (7") **WILL YOU STILL LOVE ME? / FOREVER** [ ] [-]
(12"+=) – Hard habit to break.

Jul 87. (7") **NIAGARA FALLS. /** [-] [91]

Oct 87. (7") **IF SHE WOULD HAVE BEEN FAITHFUL. / FOREVER** [ ] [17] Mar 87
(12"+=) – 25 or 6 to 4.

Warners Reprise

Jun 88. (lp)(c)(cd) **CHICAGO 19** [ ] [43]
– Heart in pieces / I don't want to live without your love / I stand up / We can last forever / Come in from the night / Look away / What kind of man would I be? / Runaround / You're not alone / Victorious.

Aug 88. (7")(c-s) **I DON'T WANNA LIVE WITHOUT YOUR LOVE. / I STAND UP** [ ] [3] Jun 88
(12"+=) – 25 or 6 to 4.
(cd-s+=) – Will you still love me?.

Sep 88. (7")(c-s) **LOOK AWAY. / COME IN FROM THE NIGHT** [ ] [1]
(12"+=)(cd-s+=) – 25 or 6 to 4.

Jan 89. (7")(c-s) **YOU'RE NOT ALONE. / IT'S ALRIGHT** [-] [10]

May 89. (7")(c-s) **WE CAN'T LAST FOREVER. / ONE MORE DAY** [-] [55]

Jan 90. (cd)(c)(lp) **GREATEST HITS 1982-1989** (compilation) [ ] [37] Dec 89

Feb 90. (7") **WHAT KIND OF MAN WOULD I BE? / 25 OR 6 TO 4** [ ] [5] Dec 89
(12"+=)(cd-s+=) – You're the inspiration / Hard to say I'm sorry.

Jul 90. (7") **HEART'S IN TROUBLE. / ('B'side by 'Hans Zimmer')** [ ] [75]
(12"+=)(cd-s+=) – (track by other artist) *(above on 'D.G.C.' US)*

—— Trimmed when SERAPHINE departed Aug90.

Jan 91. (c-s) **CHASIN' THE WIND. / ONLY TIME CAN HEAL THE WOUNDED** [-] [39]

May 91. (cd)(c)(lp) **TWENTY 1** [ ] [66] Feb 91
– Explain to my heart / If it were you / You come to my senses / Somebody somewhere / What does it take / One from the heart / Chasin' the wind / God save the Queen / Man to woman / Only time can heal the wounded / Who do you love / Holdin' on.

		not issued	Giant
Jun 95.	(cd)(c) **NIGHT AND DAY**	-	90

– other compilations, etc. –

(all 'C.B.S.' releases were on 'Columbia' counterpart in US)

Apr 73.	C.B.S.; (7") **25 OR 6 TO 4. / MAKE ME SMILE** *(re-iss.Mar75 & 76)*		
1975.	C.B.S.; (7") **BEGINNINGS. / QUESTIONS 67 AND 68**		
1975.	C.B.S.; (7") **COLOUR MY WORLD. / I'M A MAN**		
1975.	C.B.S.; (7") **DOES ANYBODY REALLY KNOW WHAT THE TIME IS? / FREE**		
1975.	C.B.S.; (7") **SATURDAY IN THE PARK. / DIALOGUE**		
Aug 75.	C.B.S.; (7") **WISHING YOU WERE HERE. / LIFESAVER**		
Jan 77.	C.B.S.; (7") **WISHING YOU WERE HERE. / GENTLY I'LL WAKE YOU**		
Mar 79.	C.B.S.; (7") **I'M A MAN. / 25 OR 6 TO 4**		
Nov 82.	C.B.S.; (7") **IF YOU LEAVE ME NOW. / 25 OR 6 TO 4**		
Nov 82.	C.B.S.; (lp)(c) **IF YOU LEAVE ME NOW** *(re-iss.Apr86, cd-iss.Dec92)*		
Jan 83.	C.B.S.; (c-ep) **GREATEST ORIGINAL HITS**		-

– If you leave me now / 25 or 6 to 4 / Baby, what a big surprise / Wishing you were here.

Aug 88.	C.B.S.; (3"cd-s) **25 OR 6 To 4. / MAKE ME SMILE**	-	
Nov 82.	Virgin TV; (lp)(c) **LOVE SONGS**	42	-
Dec 83.	Meteor; (lp) **BEGINNINGS** *(re-iss.Jan85 on 'Topline') (cd-iss.Feb93 on 'Charly')*		-
Jul 84.	Design; (pic-lp) **TORONTO ROCK'N'ROLL REVIVAL (live)** *(cd-iss.Jul91 on 'Thunderbolt')*		-
Apr 86.	Showcase; (lp)(c) **CHICAGO LIVE (live)** *(cd-iss.Dec88 on 'Spectrum')*		-
Feb 89.	Crusader; (lp) **THE BEST OF CHICAGO**		-
May 89.	That's Original; (d-lp(c)(cd) **THE COLLECTION** – (CHIGAGO XIII / STREET PLAYER)		-
Nov 89.	Warners; (lp)(c)(cd) **THE HEART OF CHICAGO** – (c/cd+=3 extra) *(re-iss.cd+c Feb94, re-hit UK No.6)*	9	
Apr 93.	Pulsar; (cd) **I'M A MAN & OTHER GREAT HITS LIVE (live)**		-
May 94.	Columbia-Legacy; (4xcd-box)(4xc-box) **GROUP PORTRAIT**		
Aug 94.	Legends In Music; (cd) **CHICAGO**		-
Sep 94.	Prestige; (cd) **25 OR 6 TO 4**		-

ROBERT LAMM

		C.B.S.	Columbia
1974.	(lp)(c) **SKINNY BOY**		

– Temporary Jones / Love song / Crazy ways to spend a year / Until the times run out / Skinny boy / One step forward, two steps back / Fireplace and Ivy / Someday I'm gonna go / A lifetime we / City living / Crazy brother John.

CHICKEN SHACK

Formed: Birmingham, England ... 1965 as The SOUNDS OF BLUE. Changed to CHICKEN SHACK in 1967 and signed to 'Blue Horizon'. Their debut album in 1968, nearly hit the UK Top 10, setting them up for next years' classic re-indition of 'I'D RATHER GO BLIND'. Success eluded them after the departure in 1971 of CHRISTINE PERFECT to FLEETWOOD MAC. • **Style:** Blues great, led by STAN WEBB. By the mid-70's they had drifted into pub-rock mould. • **Songwriters:** WEBB penned. Covered I'D RATHER GO BLIND (Etta James) / HOLD ON (Jennings-Sample) / I'M TORN DOWN (...Thompson) / EVIL (Willie Dixon) / EVERY DAY I HAVE THE BLUES (...Chapman) / etc. • **Trivia:** CHRISTINE was voted Best Female singer in NME for 1969 material.

Recommended: THE COLLECTION (*8) / 40 BLUE FINGERS...(*7) / O.K. KEN (*7).

STAN WEBB – vocals, guitar / **CHRISTINE PERFECT** – vocals, keyboards / **ANDY SILVESTER** – bass / **DAVE BIDWELL** – drums repl. AL SYKES

		Blue Horizon	Epic
Dec 67.	(7") **IT'S O.K. WITH ME BABY. / WHEN MY LEFT EYE JUMPS**		-
Jun 68.	(lp) **40 BLUE FINGERS FRESHLY PACKED AND READY TO SERVE**	12	

– The letter / Lonesone whistle blues / When the train comes back / San-ho-say / King of the world / See see baby / First time I met the blues / Webbed feet / You ain't no good / What you did last night. *(cd-iss.Oct93 on 'B.G.O.') (cd-iss.Sep94 on 'Rewind')*

Sep 68.	(7") **WORRIED ABOUT MY WOMAN. / SIX NIGHTS IN SEVEN**		
Dec 68.	(7") **WHEN THE TRAIN COMES BACK. / HEY BABY**		-
Feb 69.	(lp) **O.K. KEN**	9	

– Baby's got me crying / The right way is my way / Get like you used to be / Pony and trap / Tell me / I wanna see my baby / Remington ride / Fishing in your river / Mean old world / Sweet sixteen. *(cd-iss.Jul93 on 'B.G.O.')*

Apr 69.	(7") **I'D RATHER GO BLIND. / NIGHT LIFE**	14	

—— **PAUL RAYMOND** – keyboards repl. CHRISTINE who later joined FLEETWOOD MAC

Aug 69.	(7") **TEARS IN THE WIND. / THE TEARS YOU PUT ME THROUGH**	29	
Nov 69.	(lp) **100 TON CHICKEN**		

– The road of love / Look ma, I'm crying / Evelyn / Reconsider baby / Weekend love / Midnight hour / Tears in the wind / Horse & cart / The way it is / Stiil worried about my woman / Anji. *(cd-iss.Jun94 on 'Sony Europe')*

Jan 70.	(7") **MAUDIE. / ANDALUCIAN BLUES**		-
Jul 70.	(lp) **ACCEPT**		

– Diary of your life / Pocket / Never ever / Sad clown / Maudie / Telling your fortune / Tired eyes / Some other time / Going round / Andalucian blues / You knew you did / She didn't use her loaf / Apple tart.

Jul 70.	(7") **SAD CLOWN. / TIRED EYES**		-

—— **JOHN GLASCOCK** – bass (ex-GODS) repl. SILVESTER and RAYMOND
PAUL HANCOX – drums repl. BIDWELL who joined SAVOY BROWN with above 2

		Deram	London
Apr 72.	(lp)(c) **IMAGINATION LADY**		

– Crying won't help you now / Going down / The loser / Telling your fortune / Daughter of the hillside / Poor boy / If I were a carpenter. *(cd-iss.Dec94 on 'Deram')*

—— **BOB DAISLEY** – bass repl. GLASCOCK who joined JETHRO TULL

Mar 73.	(7") **AS TIME GOES PASSING BY. / POOR BOY**		-
May 73.	(lp)(c) **UNLUCKY BOY**		

– You know you could be right / Revelation / Prudence's party / Too late to cry / Stan the man / Unlucky boy / As time goes passing by / Jammin' with the ash / He knows the rules. *(cd-iss.Dec94 on 'Deram')*

Jul 73.	(7") **YOU KNOW YOU COULD BE RIGHT. / THE LOSER**		

—— original **STAN WEBB** recruited new members **DAVE WILKINSON** – keyboards / **BOB HULL** – bass repl. DAISLEY who joined RAINBOW / **ALAN POWELL** – drums repl. HANCOX

Feb 74.	(lp)(c) **GOODBYE CHICKEN SHACK (live)**		

– Every day I have the blues / The thrill is gone / Going down / You take me down / Webb's boogie / You're mean / Poor boy / Webb's guitar shuffle / Tutti frutti. *(cd-iss.Dec94 on 'Deram')*

—— Disbanded late 1973 when STAN WEBB joined SAVOY BROWN. ALAN POWELL joined HAWKWIND. BOB HULL joined MUNGO JERRY. DAVE WILKINSON to STRETCH. 1977.

—— **STAN** re-formed with **ROBBIE BLUNT** – guitar, vocals (ex-SILVERHEAD) / **PAUL MARTINEZ** – bass / **DAVE WINTHROP** – saxophone (ex-SUPERTRAMP) / **ED SPEVOCK** – drums

		WEA	not issued
Aug 78.	(lp) **THE CREEPER**		-

– The creeper / Delilah / Riding with the Devil / Think / Stop knocking my door / Blue vein / It's easy if you're lonely / The guitar playing derelict / Dr.Brown / Red haired lady.

—— **STEVE YORK** – bass repl. PAUL MARTINEZ

		Shark	not issued
Jul 79.	(lp) **THAT'S THE WAY WE ARE**		-

– The end (prisoner) / High cost of love / Doesn't matter about your size / It wasn't me / You'll be mine / Sillyness / Little bird / Rich man's blues / Emily / Let me love / Shake your money maker.

CHICKEN SHACK featuring STAN WEBB

with **PAUL BUTLER** – guitar, vocals / **ALAN SCOTT** – bass / **RIC LEE** – drums / **TONY ASHTON** – keyboards.

		R.C.A.	not issued
Apr 81.	(lp)(c) **ROADIE'S CONCERTO (live)**		-

– Tell me / Why I sing the blues / Back door man / Black night / So far back / The end (prisoner) / Poor boy / Shake your money maker / Hideaway.

—— STAN broke up CHICKEN SHACK until mid-80s.

—— **STAN** now with **DAVID WILKEY** – keyboards, percussion / **JAN CAMPBELL** – bass / **DAVID WINTHROP** – saxophone / **JOHN GUNZELL** – drums

		Bellaphon G'MANY	not issued
1986.	(lp) **39 BARS**	-	-

– Runnin' and hidin' / I'd rather go blind / Who cares / Ev'ry little bit of my heart / Hold on / A blues song / Tore down / Every day I have the blues / The millionairess.

		S.P.V.	not issued
Jan 90.	(cd)(lp) **SIMPLY LIVE (live)**		-

		In-Akustik	not issued
Dec 93.	(cd) **PLUCKING GOOD**		-
Sep 95.	(cd) **CHANGES**		-

STAN WEBB'S CHICKEN SHACK

		Indigo	not issued
Dec 94.	(cd) **WEBB'S BLUES**		-

– I'm torn down / A blues song / Every little bit of my heart / Sweet nothin's / Crying again / Who cares / Hold on / Webb's blues instrumental / Homework / Evil / Set me free / Every day I have the blues.

Dec 95.	(cd) **STAN THE MAN LIVE (live)**		-

– compilations, others, etc. –

Aug 74.	C.B.S.; (7") **I'D RATHER GO BLIND. / SAD CLOWN**		-
Nov 77.	C.B.S.; (lp)(c) **GOLDEN ERA OF POP MUSIC**		-
May 80.	C.B.S.; (lp)(c) **IN THE CAN**		-
Jul 82.	Old Gold; (7") **I'D RATHER GO BLIND. / TEARS IN THE WIND**		-
Jun 88.	Castle; (d-lp)(c) **THE COLLECTION**		-

– The letter / When the train comes back / Lonesome whistle blues / You ain't no good / Baby's got me crying / The right way is my way / Get like you used to be / A woman is blues / Remington ride / Mean old world / San-ho-zay / The way it is / Tears in the wind / Maudie / Some other time / Andalucian blues / Crazy 'bout you baby / Close to me / I'd rather go blind.

Dec 91.	Band Of Joy; (cd)(lp) **ON AIR (live)**		-
Jun 95.	Deram; (cd) **GO LIVE**		-

CHIEFTAINS

Formed: Dublin, Ireland . . .1963; all ex-CEOLTEOIRI CHAULANN (SEAN O'RAIDA's folk orchestra). First album was recorded in 1964, which although only released low-key in Ireland, gained attention in mainland Britain. The became full-time in the mid-70's, due to Chris Blackwell's 'Island' signing them. 'CHIEFTAINS 5' led to MOLONEY composing for Stanley Kubrick's 1975 film 'Barry Lyndon'. They also guested on MIKE OLDFIELD's 'Ommadawn' album. Enjoyed growing reputations on both sides of the Atlantic, culminating in 1995 with trans-atlantic Top 30 collaboration album 'THE LONG BLACK VEIL', which featured among others The ROLLING STONES (great fans!), SINEAD O'CONNOR, STING, VAN MORRISON and MARIANNE FAITHFUL. • **Style:** Multi-talented traditional Celtic-folk band. • **Songwriters:** As said with arrangements & songs from others.

Recommended: CHIEFTAINS 5 (*6) / BOIL THE BREAKFAST EARLY (*6) / LONG BLACK VEIL (*7)

PADDY MOLONEY (b.1938, Donnycarney, Dublin) – Uilleann pipes, tin whistle / **SEAN POTTS** (b.1930) – tin whistle / **MARTIN FAY** (b.1936) – fiddle, bones / **MICK TUBRIDY** (b.1935) – flute, concertina / plus **DAVID FALLON** – bodhran

Claddagh not issued

Feb65. (lp) **THE CHIEFTAINS** – – Ire
– Se fath mo bhuartha / The lark on the Strand / An fhallaingin mhuimhneach / Trim the velvet / An comhra donn, Murphy's hornpipe / Cailin na gruaige doinne / Comb your hair and curl it, the boys of Ballisadare / The musical priest, the Queen of May / The walls of Liscarroll jig / A dhruim donn dilis / The Connemara stocking / The limestone rock, Dan Breen's / Casadh an tSugain / The boy in the gap / Saint Mary's, Church Street / Garrett Barry, the battering ram, Kitty goes a-milking, Rakish Paddy. *(re-iss.lp/c Jan79) (UK-iss.Jan74 on 'Island') (cd-iss.1994)*

1966. (7") **COTTON EYED JOE./ THE GOLD RING** –

— **SEAN KEANE** (b.1947) **-fiddle + PAEDAR MERCIER** (b.1914) **-bodhran, bones** repl.FALLON

1969. (lp) **THE CHIEFTAINS 2** – – Ire
– Banish misfortune / Gillian's apples / Planxty George Brabazon / Bean an fhir rua / Pis fhliuch / An paistin fionn / Mrs.Crotty's reel / Fox hunt / The mountain top / An Mhaigdean Mhara / Tie the bonnet / O'Rourke's reel / Byrnes hornpipes / Pigtown / Tie the ribbons / The bag of potatoes / The humours of whiskey / Hardiman the fiddler / Donal Og / Brian Boru's march / Polkas: Sweeney's- Murphy's- The Scarborough polka. *(re-iss.lp/c Jan79) (UK-iss.Jan74 on 'Island')*

1971. (lp) **THE CHIEFTAINS 3** – – Ire
– Strike the gay harp / Lord Mayo / The lady on the island / Sailor on the rock / Sonny's muzurka / Tommy Hunt's jig / Eibhi gheai chiuin no chearbhaill / Delahunty's hornpipe / Hunter's purse / March of the King Of Laois / Caro Lan's concerto / Tom Billy's reel / Road to Lisdoonvarna / Merry sisters / An ghaoth aneas / Lord Inchquin / Trip to Sligo / An raibh tu ag an Gcarraig / John Kelly's slide / Merrily kiss the quaker. *(UK-iss.Jan74 on 'Island') (re-iss.Aug78 on 'CBS') (cd-iss.Oct88 on 'Shanachie')*

— added **DEREK BELL** (b.1935, Belfast, N.Ireland) **-harps**

1973. (lp) **THE CHIEFTAINS 4** – – Ire
– Drowsey Maggie / Morgan Magan / Tip of the whistle / The bucks of Oranmore / The battle of Aughrim / Morning dew / Carrick Fergus / Hewlett / Cherish the ladies / Lord Mayo / Mha nah Eireann / O'Keefe's slide / An Suisan ban / Star above the garter / Weavers. *(UK-iss.Jan74 on 'Island') (re-iss.Aug78 on 'CBS') (cd-iss.Oct88)*

— added **RONNIE McSHANE – percussion**

— British releases from now on . . .

Island Island

Nov 75. (lp):<lp> **THE CHIEFTAINS 5** Feb76
– The Timpan reel / Tabhair dom do lamh / Three Kerry polkas / Ceol bhriotanach / The Chieftains knock on the door / The robbers glen / An gheagus gra geal / The humours of Carolan / Samhradh, Samhradh. *(re-iss.Aug88 on 'CBS') (cd-iss.Oct88 on 'Claddagh')*

Nov 75. (7") **THE TIMPAN REEL. / SAMHRADH, SAMHRADH** –

Jan 76. (7") **WOMEN OF IRELAND. / MORNING DEW** –

Jan 76. (lp) **WOMEN OF IRELAND** –
–

— **KEVIN CONNEFF – bodhran + DOLORES KEANE – vocals** repl.MERCIER

1976. (lp) **BONAPARTE'S RETREAT**
– The chattering Magpie / An chead Mhairt den Fhomhar (the first Tuesday of Autumn) / Green grow the rushes o / Bonaparte's retreat / Away with ye / Caledonia / Inion Nic Diarmada (Miss MacDermott) / Or the Princess Royal / Maire dhall (Blind Mary) / John Drury / The rights of man / Round the house and mind the dresser. *(re-iss.lp/c Aug78 on 'CBS') (cd-iss.1994)*

— now without RONNIE McSHANE + DOLORES KEANE

1977. (lp) **THE CHIEFTAINS LIVE (live)**
– Morning dew / George Brabazon / Kerry slides / Carolan's concerto / Carrick Fergus / The Fox hunt / Round the house and mind the dresser / Solos: (a) Caitlin trail, (b) For the sake of old decency, (c) Carolan''s farewell to music, (d) Banish misfortune, (e) The tarboltan- The pinch of snuff, (f) The star of Munster / The flogging reel / Limerick's lamentation / O'Neill's march / Ril mhor. *(re-iss.lp/c Aug78 on 'CBS') (cd-iss.1989 on 'Claddagh')*

C.B.S. C.B.S.

Dec 77. (lp) **THE CHIEFTAINS 7** –
– Away we go again / Dochas / Hedigan's fancy / John O'Connor and the ode to whiskey / Friel's kitchen / No.6 the coombe / O'Sullivan's march / The ace and deuce of pipering / The fairies lamentation & dance / O, the breeches full of stitches.

Dec 78. (lp) **THE CHIEFTAINS 8** –
– The session / Doctor John Hart / Sean sa cheo / An tsean bhean bhocht / The fairies hornpipe / Sea image / If I had Maggie in the wood / An speic seoigheach / The dogs among the bushes / Miss Hamilton / The job of journeywork / The wind that shakes the barley / The reel with the Beryle.

— **MATT MOLLOY** (b.Ballaghaderreen, Roscommon, Ireland) **-flute (ex-PLANXTY, ex-BOTHY BAND)** repl.TUBRIDY

Feb 80. (lp)(c) **BOIL THE BREAKFAST EARLY**
– Mrs.Judge / March from Oscar and Malvina / When a man's in love / Bealach an doirin / Ag taisteal na blarnan / Up against the buachalawns / Boil the breakfast early / Gol na mhan san ar / Carloan's welcome / Chase around the windmill / Toss the feathers / Ballinasloe fair / Cailleach an airgid / Pretty girl / Cuil aodha slide. *(cd-iss.1988 & May95 on 'Columbia')*

1981. (lp)(c) **THE CHIEFTAINS 10**
– The Christmas reel / Salut a la compagnie / My love is in America / Manx music / Master Crowley's reels / The pride of Pimlico / An faire / An durzhune / Sir Arthur Shaen and Madam Cole / Garech's wedding / Cotton-eyed Joe. *(re-iss.lp/c/cd Aug88) (cd-iss.1994)*

Shanachie not issued

Jun 85. (lp) **BALLAD OF THE IRISH HORSE (soundtrack)**
– (re-iss.lp/c 1987 on 'Claddagh')

Claddagh not issued

Aug 85. (lp)(c)(cd) **LIVE IN CHINA (live)**
–

R.C.A. R.C.A.

Mar 87. (lp)(c) **JAMES GALWAY & THE CHIEFTAINS IN IRELAND**
– Roche's favourite / Down by the Sally Gardens / She moved through the fair / O'Carolan's concerto / Danny boy / Crowley's reel / Avondale / Up and about / Humours of Kilfenora / Carrickfergus.

Aug 87. (lp)(c) **CELTIC WEDDING**
– Dans mod koh a vaod / A breton carol / Dans-tro fisel / Marches / Dans bro-leon / Heuliadenn toniou breizh-izel / Ev chistr ta lauo! / Jabadaw / Celtic wedding. *(cd-iss.Aug89)*

— In Jul'88, they teamed up with VAN MORRISON for album 'IRISH HEARTBEAT'.

Aug 88. (lp)(c) **THE YEAR OF THE FRENCH (soundtrack)**
–

Apr 89. (lp)(c)(cd) **A CHIEFTAINS CELEBRATION**
– O'Mahoney's frolics / Galicia / Coolin medley / Here's a health to the company / Planxty Brown / The William Davis's / Lady Wrixon / Boffyflow and Spike / The strayaway child / Iron man / The Wexford carol / Gaftai baile bui / Millenium Celtic suite.

Jun 90. (cd)(c)(lp) **THE CELTIC CONNECTION ("JAMES GALWAY & THE CHIEFTAINS")**
– Carolan's quarrel with the landlord / Three hornpipes / Eugene Stratton / The banks / Arthur seat / Over the sea to Skye / A slip and a double jig / Cath cheim an thia / The Rowan tree / Bonnie Prince Charlie / Lilibulero / The dark island / Skibbereen / A fanfare / The last rose of summer / Dance in the morning early / The three sea captains / Full of joy (Chinese folk tune) / Solo salutes (finale).

— now with JACKSON BROWNE, ELVIS COSTELLO, MARIANNE FAITHFUL, NANCI GRIFFITH, RICKIE LEE JONES, KATE & ANNA McGARRIGLE + BURGESS MEREDITH

Dec 91. (cd)(c) **THE BELLS OF DUBLIN** (festive)
– The bells of Dublin / Christmas eve / Past three o'clock / St.Stephe's Day murders / Il est ne – Ca berger / Don oiche ud I mBeithil / I saw three ships a sailing / A Berton carol / Carols medley: O the holly she bears a berry – God rest ye merry gentlemen – The boar's head / The Wexford carol / The rebel Jesus / Skyline jig / O holy night / Medley "The wren! the wren!" – The arrival of the Wren boys / The dingle set – dance – The wren in the furze / A dance duet – reels – Brafferton village- Walsh's hornpipe / The farewell: The piper through the meadow strayed – This is the season to be merry / Once in Royal David's City / Ding dong merrily on high / O come all ye faithful.

— now with vocals by ROGER DALTREY or NANCI GRIFFITH

Mar 92. (cd)(c) **AN IRISH EVENING – LIVE AT THE GRAND OPERA HOUSE (live)**

— below with CHET ATKINS / EMMYLOU HARRIS / COLIN JAMES / WILLIE NELSON / NITTY GRITTY DIRT BAND / RICKY SCAGGS / DON WILLIAMS

1992. (cd)(c)(lp) **ANOTHER COUNTRY**
– Happy to meet / I can't stop loving you / Wabash cannonball / Heartbreak hotel / Goodnight Irene / Cunla / Nobody's darlin' but mine / Cotton-eyed Joe / Tahitian skies / Killybegs / Paddy's green shamrock shore / Finale.

1993. (cd)(c)(lp) **THE CELTIC HARP (with The BELFAST HARP ORCHESTRA)**
–

Jan 95. (cd)(c) **THE LONG BLACK VEIL** 17 22
– Mo ghile mear – "Our hero" (with STING) / The long black veil (with MICK JAGGER) / The foggy dew (with SINEAD O'CONNOR) / Have I told you lately that I love you? (with VAN MORRISON) / Changing your demeanour / The lily of the west (with MARK KNOPFLER) / Coast of Malabar (with RY COODER) / Dunmore lassies (instrumental) (with RY COODER) / Love is teasin' (with MARIANNE FAITHFULL) / He moved through the fair (with SINEAD O'CONNOR) / Ferny Hill (instrumental) / Tennessee waltz – Tennessee Mazurka (with TOM JONES) / The rocky road to Dublin (with The ROLLING STONES).

Mar 95. (c-s)(cd-s) **HAVE I TOLD YOU LATELY THAT I LOVE YOU? (with Van Morrison) / LOVE IS TEASIN' (with Marianne Faithfull) / FERNY HILL (instrumental)** 71

compilations, others

1989. Castle; (lp)(c)(cd) **THE COLLECTION** –

Jul 91. Claddagh; (cd)(c)(lp) **REEL MUSIC: THE FILMSCORES**

1992. Legacy-Sony; (cd)(c) **THE BEST OF THE CHIEFTAINS**
– Up against the Buachalawas / Boil the breakfast early / Friel's kitchen / No.6 the coombe / O'Sullivan's march / Sea image / An speic seoigheach / The dogs among the bushes / The job of journeywork / Oh! the breeches full of stitches / Medley: Chase around the windmill- Toss the feathers- Ballinasloe fair- Cailleach an airgid- Cuil aodha slide- The pretty girl / Medley: The wind that shakes the barley- The reel with the beryle.

DEREK BELL

Claddagh not issued

Mar 77. (lp)(c) **CAROLAN'S RECEIPT** –
(re-iss.Oct88 on 'Shanachie')

Aug 88. (lp)(c) **CAROLAN'S FAVOURITE** –
(also iss.UK Oct88 on 'Shanachie')

Aug 88. (lp)(c) **DEREK BELL'S MUSICAL IRELAND** [ ] [-]

SEAN KEANE

Claddagh / not issued

Aug 88. (lp)(c) **GUSTY'S FROLICS** [ ] [-] Ire

Also released in 1988 '(FIDDLE & VIOLA)' on 'Ogham'.

Jul 90. (cd)(c) **JIG IT IN STYLE** [ ] [-]

Mar 93. (cd)(c) **THE FIRE AFLAME** [ ] [ ]

– The wheels of the world – The pinch of snuff – Micho Russell's reel; reels / The Belharbour hornpipe – The old ruined cottage in the glen; hornpipe and reel / The geese in the bog – The little fair Cannavans – Whelan's old sow; jigs / The maid of Ballingarry – The stack of barley; air and hornpipe / The J.B. reel – The lads of Laois – The rambling Thatcher; reels / The drunken sailor; hornpipe / Night fishing 30th January 1972 the rights of man; hornpipe / Johnny 'Watt' Henry's reel – Jerry McMahons reel; reels / Pat Ward's jig – The dusty miller – Ask my father – The Connaught heifer; jigs and reel / Casadh na nGeanna (the turning of the geese); air / The ace and the deuce of pipering; set dance / Eire; air / Sean Ryan's reel – The Grand Spey; reels.

(above by SEAN KEANE, MATT MOLLOY & LIAM O'FLYNN)

Cross Border

Nov 93. (cd)(c) **ALL HEART NO ROSES** [ ] [-]

Westmoor

Sep 94. (cd)(c) **21 IRISH ACCORDION FAVOURITES** [ ] [-]

SEAN POTTS

Claddagh

Oct 88. (lp)(c) **BAKERSWELL** [ ] [-] Ire

MATT MOLLOY also released a few solo albums; 'MATT MOLLOY' Sep79 Ireland (Mulligan)/ 'CONTENTMENT IS WEALTH' w/ SEAN KEANE – Mar87 US lp/c (Green Linnet)/ 'STONY STEPS' Jul87 Ireland lp/c/cd (Claddagh)/ 'HEATHERY BREEZE' Oct89 (Shanachie). Also recorded an album with PAUL BRADY & TOMMY PEOPLES for 'Mulligan'.

Alex CHILTON (see under ⇒ BOX TOPS)

CHINA CRISIS

Formed: Kirkby, Merseyside, England . . . late 1979 by DALY and LUNDON. After one 45 on local indie label, they signed to 'Virgin' Spring '82. Charted soon with re-issue of 'AFRICAN AND WHITE', which was pursued by higher hits and a number of fine top selling albums. • **Style:** Inoffensive romantic pop/rock influenced by STEELY DAN, (Walter Becker produced 3rd album). • **Songwriters:** All written by DALY / LUNDON, until 1985 with JOHNSON. Covered 98.6 (Keith). • **Trivia:** In Jan'85 they were lucky to escape serious injury when their car overturned on icy road. Became first major band to play in Gibraltar early '86.

Recommended: THE CHINA CRISIS COLLECTION (*8) / DIFFICULT SHAPES (*7) / WORKING WITH FIRE AND STEEL (*8) / FLAUNT THE IMPERFECTION (*6).

GARRY DALY (b. 5 May'62) – vocals, keyboards / **EDDIE LUNDON** (b. 9 Jun'62) – guitar, vocals

Inevitable / unissued

Feb 82. (7") **AFRICAN AND WHITE. / RED SAILS** [ ] [-]

— added **GAZZA JOHNSON** – bass / **ROBERT LYTHGOE** – keys / **GARY O'TOOLE** – drums

Virgin / Warners

May 82. (7")(12") **SCREAM DOWN AT ME. / CUCUMBER GARDEN** [ ] [-]

Jul 82. (7") **AFRICAN AND WHITE. / DE SUSPICOIUS** [45] [-]

Oct 82. (7") **NO MORE BLUE HORIZONS. / NO ORDINARY LOVER** [ ] [-]

(12"+=) – Watching our burning fields.

Nov 82. (lp)(c) **DIFFICULT SHAPES & PASSIVE RHYTHMS: SOME PEOPLE THINK IT'S FUN TO ENTERTAIN** [21] [ ]

– Seven sports for all / No more blue horizons / Feel to be driven away / Some people I know to lead fantastic lives / Christian / African and white / Are we a worker / Red sails / You never see it / Temptations big blue eyes / Jean walks in fresh fields. *(cd-iss.Jul87) (re-iss.cd Mar94)*

Jan 83. (7") **CHRISTIAN. / GOLDEN HANDSHAKE** [12] [ ]

(12")(12"pic-d) – ('A'side) / Green acre bay / Performing seals.

— **KEVIN WILKINSON** – drums (ex-HOLLY & THE ITALIANS) repl. O'TOOLE added guest **BRYAN McNEILL** – keyboards repl. LYTHGOE

May 83. (7")(12") **TRAGEDY AND MYSTERY. / GOLDEN SHAKEDOWN** [46] [ ]

Oct 83. (7") **WORKING WITH FIRE AND STEEL. / DOCKLAND** [48] [ ]

(12"+=) – Forever and I.

Oct 83. (lp)(c) **WORKING WITH FIRE AND STEEL** [20] [ ]

– Working with fire and steel / When the piper calls / Hanna Hanna / Animals in jungles / Here comes a raincloud / Wishful thinking / Tragedy and mystery / Papua / The gates of door to door / The soul awakening. *(cd-iss.Sep84)*

Dec 83. (7")(7"red) **WISHFUL THINKING. / THIS OCCUPATION** [9] [ ]

(12"+=) – Some people I know to lead fantastic lives.

Feb 84. (7") **HANNA HANNA. / AFRICAN AND WHITE (live)** [44] [ ]

(12"+=) – Here comes a raincloud.

— 4-piece added guests **WALTER BECKER** – synthesizer, percussion / **NICK MAGNUS** – piano, synth., keys / **TIM RENWICK** – guitars / **STEVE GREGORY** – sax.

Mar 85. (7")(12")(7"sha-pic-d) **BLACK MAN RAY. / ANIMALISTICS (A DAY AT THE ZOO)** [14] [ ]

May 85. (lp)(c) **FLAUNT THE IMPERFECTION** [9] [ ]

– The highest high / Strength of character / You did cut me / Black man Ray / Wall of God / Gift of freedom / King in a Catholic style / Bigger the punch I'm feeling / The world spins, I'm part of it / Blue sea. *(cd-'87) (re-iss.1989)*

May 85. (7") **KING IN A CATHOLIC STYLE (WAKE UP). / BLUE SEA** [19] [ ]

(12"+=) – ('A'extended).

Aug 85. (7")(7"pic-d) **YOU DID CUT ME. / ('A'version)** [54] [ ]

(12"+=) – Christian.

(d7"++=) – Seven sports for all (live).

Nov 85. (7") **THE HIGHEST HIGH. / 96.8** [ ] [ ]

(12"+=) – Orange mutt mutt dance.

Virgin / A&M

Oct 86. (7") **ARIZONA SKY. / TRADING IN GOLD** [47] [ ]

(12"+=) – ('A'extended).

Nov 86. (lp)(c)(cd) **WHAT PRICE PARADISE** [63] [ ]

– It's everything / Arizona sky / Safe as houses / Worlds apart / Hampton beach / The understudy / Best kept secret / We do the same / June bride / A day's work for a dayo's done. *(cd.+=)* – Trading in gold.

Jan 87. (7") **BEST KEPT SECRET. / THE INSTIGATOR** [36] [ ]

(12"+=) – Little Italy.

(cd-s+=) – Black man Ray / You did cut me / Arizona sky.

Mar 89. (7") **ST. SAVIOR'S SQUARE. / BACK HOME** [ ] [ ]

(12"+=)(3"cd-s+=) – ('A'version).

May 89. (lp)(c)(cd) **DIARY OF A HOLLOW HORSE** [58] [ ]

– St. Savior's Square / Stranger by nature / Sweet charity in adoration / Day after day / Diary of a hollow horse / Red letter day / In northern skies / Singing the praises of finer things / All my prayers / Age old need.

May 89. (7") **RED LETTER DAY. / DIARY OF A HOLLOW HORSE** [ ] [ ]

(12"+=)(3"cd-s+=) – Strength of character.

— Split from Virgin in 1990.

— Reformed in 1994.

Stardumb / not issued

Aug 94. (c-s)(12")(cd-s) **EVERY DAY THE SAME. / TELL ME WHAT IT IS** [ ] [-]

Telegraph / not issued

Sep 95. (cd)(c) **ACOUSTICALLY YOURS** [ ] [-]

– African and white / No more blue horizons / Wishful thinking / Everyday the same / It's everything / Christian / Good again / Hands on the wheel / Black man Ray / King in a Catholic style / Thank you / Singing the praise of finer things / Working with fire and steel / Diary of a hollow horse.

– compilations, others, etc. –

Nov 88. Old Gold; (7")(12") **CHRISTIAN. / WISHFUL THINKING** [ ] [-]

Nov 88. Old Gold; (7") **BLACK MAN RAY. / KING IN A CATHOLIC STYLE (WAKE UP)** [ ] [-]

Jun 88. Virgin; (3"cd-ep) **BLACK MAN RAY / ANIMALISTIC (A DAY AT THE ZOO) / HAMPTON BEACH** [ ] [ ]

Aug 90. Virgin; (d-cd)(c)(lp) **THE CHINA CRISIS COLLECTION** [32] [ ]

– African and white / No more blue horizons / Christian / Tragedy and mystery / Working with fire and steel / Wishful thinking / Hanna Hanna / Black man Ray / King in a Catholic style / You did cut me / Arizona sky / Best kept secret / It's everything / St.Saviour Square. *(cd+=)* Scream down at me / Cucumber garden / A golden handshake for every daughter / Some people I know to lead fantastic lives / The instigator (Italian fuzzbox version) / Little Italy / Greenacre Bay / No ordinary lover / Dockland / Forever and I / Performing seals / This occupation / Watching our burning fields.

CHRISTIANS

Formed: Liverpool, England . . . 1984 by the brothers with caucasian mate PRIESTMAN. In 1974 the brothers as NATURAL HIGH, appeared on TV show 'Opportunity Knocks'. 12 years later, they got a deal with 'Island' records. From the outset though, the brothers always argued, and ROGER soon left because of focal limelight going to shaven-headed cool looking GARRY. 'FORGOTTEN TOWN' was the first of many UK hits, which was lifted from eponymous parent No.1 album. • **Style:** Harmonising, near accapella outfit, mixing social lyrics with soul-rock. • **Songwriters:** GARRY, RUSSELL or HENRY penned after the departure of ROGER. Covered HARVEST FOR THE WORLD (Isley Brothers) / PEOPLE GET READY + SMALL AXE (Bob Marley) / WORDS (trad.) / THE BOTTLE (Gil Scott-Heron) / WHAT ABOUT US (Leiber-Stoller). • **Trivia:** The HARVEST FOR THE WORLD single proceeds were given to Famine Relief. In May 1989, the group featured on the No.1 – FERRY ACROSS THE MERSEY single, for Hillsborough football disaster.

Recommended: THE CHRISTIANS (*6)

GARRY CHRISTIAN (b.1955) – vocals / **ROGER CHRISTIAN** (b.1950) – vocals / **RUSSELL CHRISTIAN** (b. 8 Jul'56) – vocals, saxophone / **HENRY PRIESTMAN** (b.21 Jun'55) – keyboards, vocals, guitar (ex-IT'S IMMATERIAL, ex-WAH!, ex-YACHTS, etc.)

Island / Island

Jan 87. (7") **FORGOTTEN TOWN. / WHY WALTZ** [22] [ ]

(12"+=) – Heading for a hard time.

(cd-s+=) – One in a million / Man oh man / Look around.

— Became a trio when GARRY left to pursue solo career.

May 87. (7") **HOOVERVILLE (THEY PROMISED US THE WORLD). / NO REASON** [21] [ ]

(12"+=) – The losing game.

(c-s+=) – Born again / Drip drop.

Sep 87. (7")(12") **WHEN THE FINGERS POINT. / REBECCA** [34] [ ]

(cd-s+=) – Every town waltz / Throw a farewell kiss.

Oct 87. (lp)(c)(cd) **THE CHRISTIANS** [1] [ ]

– Forgotten town / When the fingers point / Born again / Ideal world / Save a soul in every town / . . .And that's why / Hooverville (they promised us the world) / One in a million / Sad songs. *(cd+=)* – Why waltz / Forgotten town (12"version) / When the fingers point (12"version). *(re-iss.cd Mar93)*

Nov 87. (7") **IDEAL WORLD. / ROCKIN' CHANT BLUES** [14] [ ]
(10"+=)(12"+=)(cd-s+=) – ('A'mix) / Say it isn't so (part 1).

Apr 88. (7") **BORN AGAIN. / FORGOTTEN TOWN (U.S.mix)** [25] [ ]
(12"+=)(pic-cd-s+=) – A lover's question.

Oct 88. (7") **HARVEST FOR THE WORLD. / ('A'version)** [8] [ ]
(12"+=) – Small axe / People get ready.

Dec 89. (7")(c-s) **WORDS. / LONG GONE** [18] [ ]
(12"+=)(3"cd-s+=) – Funny money.
(d7"+=) – ?

Jan 90. (cd)(c)(lp) **COLOUR** [1] [ ]
– Man don't cry / I found out / Greenback Drive / All talk / Words / Community of spirit / There you go again / One more baby in black / In my hour of need. *(re-iss.cd+c Apr94)*

Mar 90. (7")(c-s) **I FOUND OUT. / SAVE US FROM OUR FRIENDS** [56] [ ]
(10"+=)(12"+=)(cd-s+=) – Sent here to shine.

Aug 90. (7") **GREENBACK DRIVE. / FROM THE WATER'S EDGE** [63] [ ]
(12"+=)(cd-s+=) – ('A'dance version).

Sep 92. (7")(c-s) **WHAT'S IN A WORD. / HAPPY IN HELL** [33] [ ]
('A'extended-12"+=) – You never know.
(cd-s++=) – ('A'version).

Oct 92. (cd)(c)(lp) **HAPPY IN HELL** [18] [ ]
– What's in a word / Uninvited guest / Garden of love / Say it isn't so (pt.2) / Father / The bottle / Storms / Slip away / Learn to love / Still small voice / Happy in Hell (acappella). *(re-iss.cd+c Apr94)*

Nov 92. (7")(c-s) **FATHER. / WORLD** [55] [ ]
(cd-s+=) – Forgotten town / Ideal world.
(cd-s) – ('A'side) / Harvest for the world / Hooverville (they promised us the world) / What about us.

Feb 93. (7")(c-s) **THE BOTTLE. / TRUE TO YOURSELF** [39] [ ]
(12"+=)(cd-s+=) – ('A'mixes).

Nov 93. (cd)(c) **THE BEST OF THE CHRISTIANS** (compilation) [22] [ ]
– Forgotten town / Harvest for the world / The perfect moment / What's in a word / Born again / Words / Ideal world / The bottle / When the fingers point / Father / Greenbank Drive (remix) / Hooverville (and they promised us the world) / Small axe.

Nov 93. (7")(c-s) **THE PERFECT MOMENT. / VILLAGE GHETTOLAND** [ ] [ ]
(12"+=)(cd-s+=) – A farewell kiss.

CHUMBAWAMBA

Formed: Burnley /Barnsley, Yorkshire, England ... 1980 by sextet who shacked up in Leeds commune (see below). In 1982, they appeared as SKIN DISEASE on a single 'BACK ON THE STREETS'. CHUMBAWAMBA toured a year later with CRASS, while releasing 3 cassettes independently. In 1985 /86, they caused controversy by issuing records arguing the merits of the BAND /LIVE AID charity causes. Needless to say, these were banned from radio airplay. More publicity surrounded them around this time, when they poured red paint over The CLASH, when they arrived in Leeds for their 'Busking Britain Tour'. The early 90's saw them finally appreciated by the new hippy crustie scene, culminating in their 1994 album 'ANARCHY' cracking the Top 30. • **Style:** Vegan / non-smoking politicised and animal-rights outfit, like MADDY PRIOR (Steeleye Span) fusing with CRASS. • **Songwriters:** Group, except some traditional Hungarian folk tunes. Also sampled JOHN LENNON (Imagine), ELVIS, ALTERNATIVE TV, GANG OF FOUR, CRASS, FALL, X-RAY SPEX, STIFF LITTLE FINGERS, DAGMAR KRAUSE and GERSHWIN!. The lp 'ENGLISH REBEL SONGS' were all traditional. Covered on 'JESUS H CHRIST'; ALRIGHT NOW (Free) / MONEY, MONEY, MONEY (Abba) / SOLID GOLD EASY ACTION (T.Rex) / HEY YOU GET OFF MY CLOUD (Rolling Stones) / STAIRWAY TO HEAVEN (Led Zeppelin) / BIGMOUTH STRIKES AGAIN (Smiths) / I SHOULD BE SO LUCKY (Kylie Minogue)/ MANNEQUIN (Wire) / HUNCHBACK OF NOTRE DAME (Frantic Elevators; Mick Hucknall). • **Trivia:** In 1982, track 'THREE YEARS LATER' appeared on 'Crass' label album 'BULLSHIT DETECTOR 2'. ALICE NUTTER was named after a 17th century witch. DANBERT NOBACON released a single before he joined them, which featured a picture of his utensil on the cover!. 'NEVER SAY DI' single (proceeds to charity) was surprisingly in support of Princess Diana, as they were anti-royalists. 'BEHAVE!' was a tribute ha!, about 'The Hit Man And Her' (aka PETE WATERMAN & MICHAELA).

Recommended: PICTURES OF STARVING CHILDREN SELL RECORDS (*7) / SHHH (*8) / ANARCHY (*9)

ALICE NUTTER – vocals / **ALAN WHALLEY** – guitar, vocals / **(FRANK) BOFF** – guitar, vocals / **LOUISE MARY WATTS** – keyboards, vocals / **MAVIS DILLON** – brass / **BILLY McCOID** – drums

— (released 3 cassettes before the mid-80's)

Agit Prop / not issued

Sep 85. (7"ep) **REVOLUTION** [ ] [-]
–

Apr 86. (7") **WE ARE THE WORLD. / A STATE OF MIND** [ ] [-]

In 1986, they issued DESTROY FASCISM as The ANTIDOTE; alongside The EX.

Oct 86. (lp) **PICTURES OF STARVING CHILDREN SELL RECORDS** [ ] [-]
– How to get your band on television / British colonialism and the BBC – flicking pictures hypnotise / Commercial break / Unilever / More whitwashing / . . .An interlude: Beginning to take it back / Dutiful servants and political masters / Cocoa colanisation / . . .And in a nutshell 'food aid is our most powerful weapon' / Invasion.

Jul 87. (lp) **NEVER MIND THE BALLOTS: HERE'S THE REST OF YOUR LIFE** [ ] [-]
– Always tell the voter what he voter wants to hear / Come on baby (let's do the revolution) / The wasteland / Today's sermon / Ah-men / Mr. Heseltine meets his public / The candidates find common ground / Here's the rest of your life.

— Under the name SCAB AID, they issued 'Let It Be' on the 'Scum' label.

Jul 88. (7") **FIGHT THE ALTON BILL. / SMASH CLAUSE 28** [ ] [-]

Oct 88. (10"lp) **ENGLISH REBEL SONGS 1381-1914** [ ] [-]
– The Cutty wren / The diggers song / Colliers march / The triumph of General Ludd / Chartist anthem / Song of the times / Smashing of the van / World turned upside down / Poverty knock / Idris strike song / Hanging on the old barbed wire / The Cutty wren (reprise). *(re-iss.lp Nov89) (re-iss.+cd Feb93 & Feb95 on 'One Little Indian')*

— In Dec89; they appeared on 'Agit Prop' Various Artists (SPORTCHESTRA) lp '101 SONGS ABOUT SPORT'. Another Various 'THIS SPORTING LIFE' was iss.Aug90.

Jul 90. (cd)(lp) **SLAP!** [ ] [-]
– Ulrike / Tiananmen Square / Car trouble / Chase PC's flee attack by own dog / Rubens has been shot! / I never gave up (Rappoport's testament) / Gave up / Slap! / That's how grateful we are / Meinhof. *(re-iss.+c Feb95 on 'One Little Indian')*

— In Mar91, CHUMBAWAMBA AND OTHER SUBVERSIVES released 7"; GREATEST HITS for 'Peasant Revolt'. At the same time ALICE and LOUISE (I think?) as The PASSION KILLERS released mail-order EP 'FOUR WAR IS SHIT SONGS' featuring tracks 'Shipbuilding', 'Reuters' + 2 for 'Rugger Bugger' records.

— now a 8-piece group **ALICE, LOUISE, BOFF** (NIGEL HUTTER), **ALAN** (DANBERT BACON) plus **DUNSTON BRUCE** – vocals, percussion / **HARRY** (DARREN HAMMER) – drums, percussion / **MAVE** (MAVIS DILLON) – keyboards / **PAUL GRECO** – bass w / **MATTY** (MC FUSION) – vocals (of CREDIT TO THE NATION) / **COMMON KNOWLEDGE** – keyboards, accordion, vocals / **NEIL FERGUSON** – guitar, keys

Jan 92. (7") **I NEVER GAVE UP (RAPPAPORT'S TESTAMENT). / LAUGHING** [ ] [ ]
(12") – ('A'-Rondo mix) / ('A'cass mix).
(cd-s) – (all 4 tracks). *(re-iss Jul94 on 'Southern')*

Jun 92. (cd)(c)(lp) **SHHH** [ ] [-]
– Shhh / Big mouth strikes again / Nothing that's new / Behave! / Snip snip snip / Look! no strings! / Happiness is just a chant away / Pop star kidnap / Sometimes plunder / You can't trust anyone nowadays / Stitch that. *(re-iss.Nov94 on 'Southern')*

Jul 92. (7") **NEVER SAY DI. / FOR THE LOVE OF A PRINCESS** [ ] [-]

Nov 92. (12")(cd-s) **SOMEONE'S ALWAYS TELLING YOU HOW TO BEHAVE!. / (2-'A'mixes by PAPA BRITTLE)** [ ] [-]

Dec 92. (cd)(c)(lp) **JESUS H CHRIST** [ ] [ ]
– Alright now / Money, money, money / Solid gold easy action / Silly love songs / Hey you get off my cloud / Stairway to Heaven / Bigmouth strikes again / I should be so lucky.

O. L. Indian / Elektra?

Sep 93. (12"ep)(c-ep)(cd-ep) **ENOUGH IS ENOUGH. / HEAR NO BULLSHIT (on fire mix) / THE DAY THE NAZI DIED (1993 mix)** [56] [ ]

— (above was with CREDIT TO THE NATION)

Nov 93. (12"ep)(c-ep)(cd-ep) **TIMEBOMB. / TECHNO THE BOMB / THE WORLD TURNED UPSIDE DOWN** [59] [ ]

Dec 93. (12"ep)(c-ep)(cd-ep) **LOVE IS ON THE WAY. / ?** [59] [ ]

May 94. (cd)(c)(lp) **ANARCHY** [29] [ ]
– Give the anarchist a cigarette / Timebomb / Homophobia / On being pushed / Heaven – Hell / Love me / Georgina / Doh! / Blackpool rock / This year's thing / Mouthful of shit / Never do what you are told / Bad dog / Enough is enough / Rage.

— Next credited with The SISTERS OF PERPETUAL INDULGENCE

May 94. (12"ep)(c-ep)(cd-ep) **HOMOPHOBIA (with The SISTERS OF PERPETUAL INDULGENCE). / MORALITY PLAY IN THREE ACTS / ('A'acappella mix) / SONG FOR DEREK JARMEN** [ ] [ ]
(cd-s) – ('A'side) / Enough is enough (w / CREDIT TO THE NATION) / The day the Nazi died (w / CREDIT TO THE NATION) / Morality play in three acts.

Mar 95. (cd)(c)(lp) **SHOWBUSINESS! CHUMBAWAMBA LIVE (live)** [ ] [-]
– Never do what you are told / I never gave up / Give the anarchist a cigarette / Heaven-Hell / That's how grateful we are / Homophobia / Morality play in three acts / Bad dog / Stitch that / Mouthful of shit / The day the Nazi died / Time bomb (Jimmy Echo vocal) / Slag aid.

Oct 95. (7")(c-s) **UGH! YOUR UGLY HOUSES!. / THIS GIRL** [ ] [-]
(cd-s+=) – Mannequin / Hunchback of Notre Dame.

Oct 95. (d-cd)(c)(d-lp) **SWINGIN' WITH RAYMOND** [70] [ ]
– This girl / Never let go / Just look at me now / Not the girl I used to be / The morning after (the night before) / Love can knock you over / All mixed up / This dress kills / Salome (let's twist again) / Oxymoron / Waiting, shouting / Hey you! outside now! / Ugh! your ugly houses.

– compilations, others, etc. –

Feb 92. Agit Prop; (cd)(lp) **FIRST 2** [ ] [-]
– (as said 1st 2 albums, originally Aug89 as '100 SONGS ABOUT SPORT') (re-iss.d-cd/d-c Feb95 on 'One Little Indian')

CHURCH

Formed: Canberra, Australia ... 1980 by STEVE KILBEY. Popular in homeland, they signed to 'Capitol' in US, ('Carrere' for UK-releases). It took them seven years to finally get recognition with a US Top 30 single 'UNDER THE MILKY WAY'. • **Style:** Cult psychedelic/new wave outfit, with grey melancholy side that reflected both BOWIE and The PSYCHEDELIC FURS. • **Songwriters:** KILBEY wrote nearly all songs until '86 when others contributed too. • **Trivia:** L.A. producer WOODY WATCHEL worked on their 1988 and 1990 albums, and led to breakthrough.

Recommended: CONCEPTION (*7)

STEVE KILBEY – vocals, bass, occasional keyboards / **PETER KOPPES** – guitar / **MARTY WILLSON-PIPER** (b. Sweden) – guitar / **NICK WARD** – drums, percussion

—— first releases on Australian 'Parlophone' label.

1981. (7") **SHE NEVER SAID. / IN A HEARTBEAT** [-] [-]

1981. (lp) **OF SKINS AND HEART** [-] [-]
– For a moment we're strangers / Chrome injury / The unguarded moment / Memories in future tense / Bel-Air / Is this where you live / She never said / Fighter pilot * / Korean war * / Don't open the door to strangers. *(UK-iss.Sep87 on 'Arista' += *+)* / Too fast for you / Tear it all away / Sisters.

1981. (d7") **TWO FAST FOR YOU. / SISTERS/ / TEAR IT ALL AWAY. / YOU'VE GOT TO GO / FRAULEIN** [-] [-]

Carrere Capitol

Mar 82. (7") **UNGUARDED MOMENT. / BUSDRIVER** [ ] [ ]

Mar 82. (lp)(c) **THE CHURCH** [ ] [ ]
-(same as 'OF SKINS AND HEART' except **Tear it all away** repl. *) *(re-iss.Apr85) (cd-iss.May88)*

Sep 82. (7") **ALMOST WITH YOU. / LIFE SPEEDS UP** [ ] [ ]

—— **RICHARD PLOOG** – drums(on most tracks) repl. WARD

Oct 82. (lp)(c) **THE BLURRED CRUSADE** [ ] [-]
– Almost with you / When you were mine / Field of Mars / An interlude / Secret corners / Just for you / A fire burns / To be in your eyes / You Took / Don't look back. *(re-iss.Mar85) (cd-iss.Aug88)*

Nov 82. (7"m) **UNGUARDED MOMENT. / INTERLUDE / GOLDEN DAWN** [ ] [ ]
(10"ep+=) – Sisters.

Mar 83. (7") **A DIFFERENT MAN. / I AM A ROCK** [ ] [-]
(12"ep) **SING SONGS** (on 'Capitol'UK) (+=) – Ancient history / Night is very soft / In this room.

May 84. (lp)(c) **SEANCE** [ ] [ ]
– Fly / One day / Electric / It's no reason / Travel by thought / Disappear? / Electric lash / Now I wonder why / Dropping names / It doesn't change. *(re-iss.May85)*

Jun 84. (7") **IT'S NO REASON. / SOMEONE SPECIAL** [ ] [ ]
(12"+=) – Autumn soon.

Feb 85. (lp)(c) **REMOTE LUXURY** [ ] [ ]
– Constant in opal / Violet town / No explanation / 10,000 miles / Maybe these boys / Into my hands / A month of Sundays / Volumes / Shadow cabinet / Remote luxury. *(re-iss.+cd.Jun89 on 'Arista')*

—— note: they were still signed to 'Parlophone' Australia.

E.M.I. Warners

Feb 86. (7") **COLUMBUS. / AS YOU WILL** [-] [ ]

May 86. (7") **TANTALIZED. / THE VIEW.** [ ] [ ]
(12"+=) – As you will.

Jun 86. (lp)(c)(cd) **HEYDAY** [ ] [ ]
– Myrrh / Tristesse / Already yesterday / Columbus / Happy hunting ground / Tantalized / Disenchanted / Night of light / Youth worshipper / Roman. (c-s+=)(cd-s+=) – As you will / The view.

Sep 86. (7") **DISENCHANTED. / TRANCE ENDING** [ ] [ ]
(12"+=) – You've got to go.

Arista Arista

Feb 88. (7") **UNDER THE MILKY WAY. / MUSK** [ ] [24]
(12"+=)(cd-s+=) – Warm spell.

Mar 88. (lp)(c)(cd) **STARFISH** [ ] [41]
– Destination / Under the Milky Way / Blood money / Lost / North, south, east and west / Spark / Antenna / Reptile / A new season / Hotel womb. (free 12"w/ lp) **ANNA MIRANDA / MUSK. / PERFECT CHILD / FROZEN AND DISTANT / TEXAS MOON**

Mar 90. (cd)(c)(lp) **GOLD AFTERNOON FIX** [ ] [66]
– Pharoah / Metropolis / Terra Nova Cain / City / Russian Autumn heart / Essence / You're still beautiful / Disappointment / Transient / Fading away / Grind. (cd+=) – Monday morning / Laughing.

Apr 90. (7")(c-s) **METROPOLIS. / MONDAY MORNING** [ ] [ ]
(12"+=)(cd-s+=) – Much too much.

Jun 90. (cd-ep) **RUSSIAN AUTUMN HEART / HUNTER / FEAST / DESERT / RIDE INTO THE SUNSET** [-] [ ]

—— **JAY DEE DAUGHERTY** – drums (ex-PATTI SMITH GROUP) repl. PLOOG / **WILLSON-PIPER** joined ALL ABOUT EVE in 1990.

Mar 92. (cd)(c)(lp) **PRIEST = AURA** [ ] [ ]
– Aura / Ripple / Paradox / Lustre / Swan lake / Feel Mistress / Kings / Dome / Witch hunt / The disillusionist / Old flame / Chaos / Film.

—— now a basic duo of **KILBEY + WILLSON-PIPER** plus **TIM POWELL** – drums / **LINDA NEIL** – violin / **SANDY CHICK** – female voice / **CAROL BROCA-WANDER** – French female voice / **BORIS GOUDENOV** – drumloops / **DARREN RYAN** – loops, + drums on 1

May 94. (d-cd)(c)(lp) **SOMETIME ANYWHERE** [ ] [ ]
– Days of the dead / Lost my touch / Loveblind / My little problem / The maven / Angelica / Lullaby / Eastern / Two places at once / Business woman / Authority / Fly home / The dead man's dream. (d-cd+=) Drought / The time being / Leave your clothes on / Cut in two / The myths you made / Freeze to burn / Macabre tavern.

– compilations, others, etc. –

Apr 88. Carrere; (lp)(c)(cd) **CONCEPTION** [ ] [-]
– When you were mine / Chrome injury / A different man / To be in your eyes / Is this where you live / Unguarded moment / Just for you / Memories and future tense / Almost with you / You took.

May 88. Carrere; (7") **UNGUARDED MOMENT. / BEL-AIR** [ ] [-]
(12") – ('A'side) / Temperature drop / Downtown / Winterland.

Jan 95. Raven; (cd) **ALMOST YESTERDAY 1981-1990** [ ] [-]

HEX

KILBEY + DONETTE THAYER (of GAME THEORY)

Demon Rykodisc

Mar 90. (cd)(c)(lp) **HEX** [ ] [ ]
– Diviner / Hermaphrodite / Ethereal message / Mercury towers / Out of the pink / Fire island / In the net / Silvermine / Elizabeth Green / An arrangement.

Feb 91. (cd)(c)(lp) **VAST HALOS** [ ] [ ]
– Monarch / Shelter / March / Centaur / Antelope / Hollywood in winter / Orpheus circuit / Aquamarine / Hell / Vast halos.

JACK FROST

formed by **STEVE KILBEY & GRANT McLENNAN** (ex-GO-BETWEENS)

Arista Arista

Mar 91. (cd)(c)(lp) **JACK FROST** [ ] [ ]
– Every hour God sends / Birdowner (as seen on TV) / Civil war lament / Geneva 4 a.m. / Trapeze boy / Providence / Thought I was over you / Threshold / Number eleven / Didn't know where I was / Rauble / Everything takes forever.

STEVE KILBEY

solo, with brother **RUSSELL** and fiancee **KARIN JANSSON**

—— In Australia, he was signed to 'Red Eye', except for debut on 'E.M.I.'

1986. (7"m) **ASPHALT EDEN. / NEVER COME BACK / SHELL** [-] [-]

Enigma Rykodisc

Aug 87. (lp)(cd) **UNEARTHED** [ ] [ ]
– Out of this world / Guilty / Pretty ugly, pretty sad / Swampdrome / Judgement day / Rising son / Tyrant / Transference / My birthday the moon festival / Design error / Nothing inside / Other time / Heliopolis / Famine.

Nov87. (lp) **EARTHED** (instrumental) [-] [ ]
– The dawn poems / Dreambeings / Memory / The white plague / A love letter from Sydney / City of women / Carthage / Hotel / The empire mourns her sun without tears / Cornucopia / Aphrodite / Sad little piano piece / The reality generators malfunctioned / Napoleon's army, Christmas eve, outside Moscow / Atlantis / Pan / The woman who was married to love / Agog / Earthed. *(cd-iss.Mar94 on 'Rykodisc')*

1988. (7") **FIREMAN. / FORGETFULNESS / NONAPOLOGY** [-] [-]

1989. (12"ep) **TRANSACTIONS** [-] [-]

1990. (d-lp) **REMINDLESSNESS** [-] [-]

Tomata-Du not issued

1989. (lp)(cd) **THE SLOW CRACK** [ ] [-]

Red Eye Sony

1991. (cd-ep) **NARCOSIS** [ ] [ ]

PETER KOPPES

solo, featuring his wife **MELODY, KILBEY** and **PLOOG.**

1984. EMI; (7") **LOVE CAN'T IMAGINE. / SHOW ME THAT** [-] [-] Aussie

1987. Session; (12") **WHEN REASON FORBIDS. /** [-] [-] Aussie

May 88. Session; (lp) **MANCHILD & MYTH** [ ] [-]
– Take a vow / These three things / The wise and the wicked / What's the matter? / Quest / Comes as no surprise / Opus / Sahara / The Colosseum / A drink from the cup / Into the bright light / Let you walk away / Our love. *(cd-iss.Mar94 on 'Rykodisc')*

1989. T.N.T.; (lp) **FROM THE WELL** [-] [-] Aussie

MARTY WILLSON-PIPER

1987. Chase (lp) **IN REFLECTION** [-] [-] Aussie

1988. Survival (7") **SHE'S KING. / FRIGHTENED JUST BECAUSE OF YOU** [-] [-] Aussie

1988. Survival; (lp) **ART ATTACK** [-] [-] Aussie
(cd-iss.Mar94 on 'Rykodisc')

1989. Borderline; (lp) **RHYME** [-] [-] Aussie
(cd-iss.Mar94 on 'Rykodisc')

CICCONE YOUTH (see under ⇒ SONIC YOUTH)

CINDERELLA

Formed: Philadelphia, Pennsylvania, USA ... 1983 by KEIFER, LaBAR and BRITTINGHAM. Through help of BON JOVI seeing a gig, they signed worldwide to 'Phonogram' records in 1985 and soon added COURY. Their 1986 debut album 'NIGHT SONGS', broke them big in the States, and climbed to No.3. • **Style:** Bluesy heavy-metal influenced by AC/DC and AEROSMITH, but sounding like NAZARETH and LED ZEPPELIN. • **Songwriters:** All KIEFER compositions, except MOVE OVER (Janis Joplin). • **Trivia:** Andy Johns produced 2nd lp.

Recommended: NIGHT SONGS (*5)

TOM KEIFER – vocals, guitar, piano / **JEFF LaBAR** – guitar / **ERIC BRITTINGHAM** (b. 8 May'60) – bass / **FRED COURY** (b.20 Oct'65) – drums repl. KELLY SMITH who joined BRITNY FOX

Vertigo Mercury

Aug 86. (lp)(c) **NIGHT SONGS** [ ] [3] Jul 86
– Night songs / Shake me / Nobody's fool / Nothin' for nothin' / Once around the ride / Hell on wheels / Somebody save me / In from the outside / Push, push / Back home again. *(cd-iss.Jan87)*

Feb 87. (7") **SHAKE ME. / NIGHT SONGS** [ ] [ ]
(12"+=) – Hell on wheels.

Apr 87. (7") **SOMEBODY SAVE ME. /** [-] [66]

May 87. (7") **NOBODY'S FOOL. / SHAKE ME (live)** [ ] [13] Nov 86
(12"+=) – The galaxy blues.

Jun 88. (lp)(c)(cd) **LONG COLD WINTER** [30] [10]
– Bad seamstress blues – Falling apart at the seams / Gypsy road / Don't know what you've got (till it's gone) / The last mile / Second wind / Long cold winter / If you don't like it / Coming home / Fire and ice / Take me back.

Jul 88. (7") **GYPSY ROAD. / SECOND WIND** [54] [51] Aug 89
(12"+=)(12"white+=) – Somebody save me.
(cd-s+=) – Nobody's fool / Shake me.

Jan 89. (7") **THE LAST MILE. / ?** [-] [36]

Feb 89. (7") **DON'T KNOW WHAT YOU GOT (TILL IT'S GONE). / FIRE AND ICE** [54] [12] Sep 88

(12"+=) – Push, push (live) / Once around the ride.
(cd-s+=) – Push, push (live) / Long cold winter.
Apr 89. (7") **COMING HOME. / ?** [-] [20]
Nov 90. (7")(c-s) **SHELTER ME. / LOVE GONE BAD** [55] [36]
(12"+=)(cd-s+=) – Electric love.
(12"colrd+=) – Rock me baby / Bring it on love / Second wind (live).
Nov 90. (cd)(c)(lp) **HEARTBREAK STATION** [36] [19]
– The more things change / Love's got me doin' time / Shelter me / Sick for the cure / Heartbreak station / One for rock and roll / Dead man's road / Make your own way / Electric love / Love gone bad / Winds of change.
Apr 91. (7")(7"sha-pic-d) **HEARTBREAK STATION. / SICK FOR THE CURE** [63] [44] Mar 91
(12"+=) – Falling apart at the seams.
(10"sha-pic-d+=) – Move over.
(pic-cd-s+=) – Gypsy road / Shake me / Somebody save me.

— **KEVIN VALENTINE** – drums (ex-SHADOW KING) repl. COURY
Nov 94. (cd)(c) **STILL CLIMBING** [ ] [ ]
– Bad attitude shuffle / All comes down / Talk is cheap / Hard to find the words / Blood from a stone / Still climbing / Freewheelin' / Through the rain / Easy come easy go / The road's still long / Hot and bothered.

CITY (see under ⇒ KING, Carole)

CLANNAD

Formed: Dublin, Ireland . . . 1976, the offspring of Irish bandleader LEE O.BRAONAIN. CLANNAD means "Family" in Gaelic. After noteable Irish album releases in the 70's and early 80's, they signed worldwide to 'RCA', where they hit the charts with TV 'Theme from HARRY'S GAME'. It received an Ivor Novello award in 1983, with 1984's ROBIN OF SHERWOOD also gaining British Academy Award. BONO of U2, a great fan, provided dual vocals on their 1986/89 Top 20 hit IN A LIFETIME. • **Style:** Traditional folk group, that moved into well crafted mystical folk rock for the 80's. • **Songwriters:** POL and CIARAN penned most except covers I SEE RED (Jim Rafferty) / and lots of traditional Irish tunes. • **Trivia:** In 1987, American producers RUSS KUNKEL and GREG LADANYI were used on SIRIUS album, which also featured guests J.D. SOUTHER, BRUCE HORNSBY and STEVE PERRY.

Recommended: PASTPRESENT (*8)

MAIRE NI BHRAONAIN – vocals, harp / **POL O. BRAONAIN** – guitar, keyboards, vocals / **CIARAN O. BRAONAIN** – bass, synthesizer, vocals / **NOEL O. DUGAIN** – guitar, vocals / **PANDRAIG O. DUGAIN** – mandolin, guitar, vocals(twin uncles)

Phillips IRELAND / not issued

1973. (lp) **CLANNAD** [-] [-]
– Nil se ina la / Thois chois na tra domh / Brian Boru's march / Siobhan ni dhuibhir / An mhaighdean mhara / Liza / An toilean ur / Mrs.McDermott / The pretty maid / An phairc / Harvest home / Morning dew.. *(re-iss. 1982 as 'THE PRETTY MAID').*
1974. (lp) **CLANNAD II** [-] [ ]
– An gabhar ban / Eleanor Plunkett / Coinleach ghlas an fhomain / Rince philib a' cheoil / By chance it was / Rince briotanach / Dheanainn sugradh / Gaoth barra na dtonn / Teidhir abhaile riu / Fairly shot of her / Chuargh me ha. *(re-iss.May79, UK re-iss.+cd Jan89 on 'Shanachie')*

Gael-Linn IRELAND

1976. (lp) **DULAMAN** [-] [-]
– Dulaman / Cumha coghain vi Neill / Two sisters / Eirirgh suas a stoirin / The Galtee hunt / Eirigh ic cui ort do chuid eadaigh soiriu / Siuil a run / Mo Mhaire / Dtig eas a damhsa / Cucanandy – The Jug of brown ale.*(re-iss.May79, UK re-iss.+cd.Jan89 on 'Shanachie')*

Ogham / not issued

Sep 79. (lp) **CLANNAD IN CONCERT (live)** [-] [-]
– Bhean a ti / Fairies hornpipe off to California / Neansai mhile gra / Mhaire Bruineall / Planxty Burke / An giobog / Down by the Sally gardens / Nil se'n la. *(re-iss.'82 on 'Tara', UK-iss.+cd.1987+Jan89 on 'Shanachie')*

Tara IRELAND / not issued

1980. (lp) **CRANN ULL** [-] [-]
– Ar A Ghabhail 'n A 'chuain Damh / The Last Rose Of Summer / Cruscin LÆn / Bacach Shile Andai / La Coimhtioch Fan Dtuath / Crann Ull / Gathering Mushrooms / Bunan Bui / Planxty Browne. *(re-iss.'80 on 'Tara', UK re-iss.Nov82 on 'Phillips')*

— added **ENYA NI BHRAONAIN** – vocals, keyboards
1982. (lp) **FUAIM** [-] [-]
– Na buachailli alainh / Mheall si lena ghoithai me / Bruach na carraige baine / La brea fan btuath / An tull / Strayed away / Ni la na gaoithe la na scoilb? / Lish young buy-a-broom / Mhroag's na horo gheallaidh / The green fields of Gaothdobhair / Buai reamh phosta. *(re-iss.cd/c/lp Apr90 on 'Cooking Vinyl')*

— reverted to original quintet when ENYA went solo

R.C.A. / Atlantic

Oct 82. (7") **THEME FROM HARRY'S GAME. / STRAYED AWAY** [5] [ ]
Feb 83. (lp)(c) **MAGICAL RING** [26] [ ]
– Theme from 'Harry's Game' / Tower hill / Seachran charn siall / Passing time / Coinleach glasan fhomhair / I see red / Ta me no shui / Newgrange / The fairy queen / Thios fa'n chosta. *(re-iss.May84, hit 91) (re-iss.+cd Oct87)*
Mar 83. (7") **I SEE RED. / TA ME NO SHUI** [ ] [ ]
May 83. (7") **NEWGRANGE. / SEARCHRAN AND TISAIL** [65] [ ]
Apr 84. (7") **ROBIN (THE HOODED MAN). / LADY MARIAN** [42] [ ]
May 84. (lp)(c) **LEGEND (MUSIC FROM ROBIN OF SHERWOOD)** [15] [ ]
– Robin (the hooded man) / Now is here / Herne / Together we / Dark mere / Strange land / Scarlet inside / Lady Marian / Battles / Ancient forest. *(cd-iss.'87)*

Jun 84. (7") **NOW IS HERE. / TOGETHER WE** [ ] [ ]
Mar 85. (7") **SCARLET INSIDE. / ROBIN (THE HOODED MAN)** [ ] [ ]
(12"+=) – Theme from Harry's Game.

R.C.A. / R.C.A.

Sep 85. (7") **CLOSER TO YOUR HEART. / BUACHAILL AN EIREN** [ ] [ ]
(12"+=) – Theme from Harry's Game / Robin (The hooded man). *(re-iss.Feb86)*
Oct 85. (lp)(c) **MACALLA** (means 'Echo') [33] [ ]
– Caislean oir / The wild cry / Closer to your heart / In a lifetime / Almost seems (too late to turn) / Indoor / Buachaill on Eirne / Blackstairs / Journey's end / Northern skyline. *(cd-iss.'87) (re-iss.cd Sep93)*
Nov 85. (7") **ALMOST SEEMS (TOO LATE TO TURN). / JOURNEY'S END** [ ] [ ]
(12"+=) – Theme from Harry's Game / Robin (The hooded man).
Jan 86. (7") **IN A LIFETIME ("CLANNAD featuring BONO"). / INDOOR** [20] [ ]
(12"+=) – Northern skyline / Newgrange.
Sep 87. (7") **SOMETHING TO BELIVE IN. / SECOND NATURE** [ ] [ ]
(12"+=) – In a lifetime.
Oct 87. (lp)(c)(cd) **SIRIUS** [34] [ ]
– White fool / Something to believe in / Live and learn / Many roads / Sirius / In search of a heart / Second nature / Turning tide / Skelig / Stepping stone.
Jan 88. (7") **WHITE FOOL. / MANY ROADS** [ ] [ ]
(12"+=) – Closer to your heart.
Jan 89. (lp)(c)(cd) **ATLANTIC REALM (BBC soundtrack)** [41] [ ]
– Atlantic realm / Predator / Moving thru / The Berbers / Signs of life / In flight / Ocean of light / Drifting / Under Neptune's cape / Voyager / Primeval sun / Child of the sea / The kirk pride. *(issued on 'BBC' records)*
Feb 89. (7") **THE HUNTER. / ATLANTIC REALM** [ ] [ ]
(12"+=) – Skelig / Turning tide.
Apr 89. (lp)(c)(cd) **PAST PRESENT** (compilation) [5] [ ]
– Theme from Harry's Game / Closer to your heart / Almost seems (too late to turn) / The hunter / Lady Marian / Sirius / Coinleach glas an fhomair / World of difference / In a lifetime / Robin (the hooded man) / Something to believe in / Newgrange / Buachaille an Eirne / White fool.
(cd/c+=) – Second stone / Stepping stone. *(re-iss.cd Oct95)*
May 89. (7")(c-s) **IN A LIFETIME. ("CLANNAD featuring BONO") / SOMETHING TO BELIEVE IN** [17] [ ]
(12"+=) – Caislean Oir / The wild cry.
(cd-s++=) – Atlantic realm.
Jul 89. (7")(c-s)**HOURGLASS. / THEME FROM HARRY'S GAME** [ ] [ ]
(12"+=) – World of difference.
(cd-s++=) – Journey's end.
Nov 89. (7")(c-s)(cd-s) **A DREAM IN THE NIGHT. / THE PIRATES AND THE SOLDIER BOY** [ ] [ ]
Dec 89. (lp)(c)(cd) **THE ANGEL AND THE SOLDIER BOY (narrator; Tom Conti)** [ ] [ ]
– A dream in the night / The pirates / The soldier boy / The angel / The flies / The spider / The cat / The Jolly Rodger / Into the picture / Pirates merrymaking / Finding the key / Pirates on the island / Sea and storm / The love theme / The chase / The toys / The rescue / Back to the door / A dream in the night (instrumental). *(re-iss.cd Apr95)*

— now quartet, when POL left
Oct 90. (cd)(c)(lp) **ANAM** [14] [ ]
– Mi na cruinne / Anam / In fortune's hand / The poison glen / Wilderness / Why worry? / Uirchill an chreagain / Love and affection / You're the one / Dobhar. *(re-iss.US Apr93 hit No.46)*
Nov 90. (7") **IN FORTUNE'S HAND. / DOBHAR** [ ] [ ]
(12"+=)(cd-s+=) – An mhaighdean mhara.

— In mid-'91 teamed up with PAUL YOUNG on 'MCA' single 'BOTH SIDES NOW' which hit UK No.74.

— usual quartet plus guests **ANTO DRENNAN** – guitar / **JOHN DONNELLY** – drums / **MEL COLLINS** – sax, flute / **IAN PARKER** – keyboards / **FRANKIE KENNEDY** – flute, whistle / **BRIDIN BRENNAN** – vocals / **DENIS WOODS** – keyboards, synth prog.
May 93. (cd)(c)(lp) **BANBA** [5] [ ]
– Na laethe bhi / Banba oir / There for you / Mystery game / Struggle / I will find you / Soul searcher / Ca de sin do'n te sin / The other side / Sunset dreams / A gentle place.

– compilations etc. –

May 86. R.C.A.; (7"ep) **ROBIN OF SHERWOOD. / CAISLEAN OIR / NOW IS HERE / HERNE** [ ] [ ]
Sep 92. R.C.A.; (7") **THEME FROM HARRY'S GAME. / ROBIN (THE HOODED MAN)** [ ] [ ]
Jul 86. Starblend; (lp)(c)(cd) **ROBIN OF SHERWOOD** [ ] [-]
Dec 88. K-Tel Ireland; (lp)(c)(cd) **THE COLLECTION** [ ] [-]

Eric CLAPTON

Born: ERIC CLAPP, 30 Mar'45, Ripley, Surrey, England. Raised by grandparents, due to parents' separation. He became a busker until he joined The ROOSTERS in 1963, but he left after six months, joining CASEY JONES & THE ENGINEERS. In October that year, he replaced ANTHONY TOPHAM in The YARDBIRDS. Their manager Giorgio Gomelsky nicknamed him "Slowhand", due to relaxed guitar style. With his roots still in blues, he joined JOHN MAYALL'S BLUESBREAKERS in Mar65, but finally departed Jun'66 to form CREAM with JACK BRUCE and GINGER BAKER. After their demise late '68, ERIC soon formed another supergroup BLIND FAITH. They were around for a year, making Transatlantic No.1 album. After a brief spell with DELANEY & BONNIE, mainly on tour, he went solo in 1970. Later in the year he formed DEREK & THE DOMINOES. In his time with the said groups, he also sessioned for GEORGE HARRISON, playing lead on WHILE MY GUITAR GENTLY WEEPS. He had previously guested on his

WONDERWALL album. In 1971 he retired from the music scene as his drug addiction took over. He marked his return 13 Jan'73 at The Rainbow, London by releasing hit album that year. In 1974, he signed to Robert Stigwood's label 'RSO', and soon released 461 OCEAN BOULEVARD, his first in the studio for 4 years. He had already beaten his drug addiction by electro-acupuncture. In the mid-70's, he married PATTI ex-wife of Beatle GEORGE HARRISON, who he had been going out with for some time. They divorced in the late 80's, and tragically his 4 year old son CONOR fell to his death, from the open window of a 53rd storey building. • **Style:** Greatest living guitarist, who is described by fans as GOD. His heavy blues style in the 60's, was nearly abandoned, with his laid back mainstream rock in the mid 70's. His live shows though, were always filled with all his old work, as well as new. • **Songwriters:** CLAPTON wrote most (even attributing LAYLA and WONDERFUL TONIGHT to his wife Patti). Covered AFTER MIDNIGHT + COCAINE + I'LL MAKE LOVE TO YOU ANYTIME (J.J. Cale) / I SHOT THE SHERIFF (Bob Marley) / MAY YOU NEVER (John Martyn) / KNOCKIN' ON HEAVEN'S DOOR (Bob Dylan) / SWING LOW SWEET CHARIOT (spiritual/gospel trad.) / FURTHER ON UP THE ROAD (?) / WILLIE AND THE HAND JIVE + CRAZY COUNTRY HOP (Johnny Otis) / HAVE YOU EVER LOVED A WOMAN (Billy Myles) / NOBODY KNOWS YOU WHEN YOU'RE DOWN AND OUT (Jimmy Cox) / KEY TO THE HIGHWAY (Sager/Broonzy) / KNOCK ON WOOD (Eddie Floyd) BEHIND THE MASK (Yellow Magic Orchestra) / WATCH YOURSELF (Buddy Guy) / WORRIED LIFE BLUES (Mecio Merryweather) / HOODOO MAN (Sonny Boy Williamson) / HOUND DOG (hit; Elvis Presley) / DOUBLE TROUBLE (Otis Rush) / SIGN LANGUAGE (Bob Dylan) / FLOATING BRIDGE and EVERYBODY OUGHTA (Sleepy John Estes) / LEAD ME ON (Womack/Womack) / BEFORE YOU ACCUSE ME (Bo Diddley) / RUNNING ON FAITH + PRETENDING (Williams) / RUN SO FAR (Wilbert Harrison) / DON'T KNOW WHICH WAY TO GO (Willie Dixon) / etc. • **Trivia:** In 1966, with JACK BRUCE, PAUL JONES, STEVE WINWOOD and PETE YORK, he briefly formed The POWERHOUSE which recorded 3 songs for 'Elektra' compilation WHAT'S SHAKIN'. This biography is in no way an attempt to wholly register every detail, but is a summary of his notable work. This job must be left to another biographer, who would do justice to this legend.

Recommended: BACKTRACKIN' (*9)

ERIC CLAPTON (solo) – vocals, guitar (ex-DELANEY & BONNIE, ex-BLIND FAITH ex-CREAM, ex-JOHN MAYALL'S BLUESBREAKERS, ex-YARDBIRDS, etc) featured his **DOMINOES** musicians plus **STEPHEN STILLS** – guitar.

Polydor / Atco

Aug 70. (lp)(c) **ERIC CLAPTON** — 17 / 13 Jul 70
– Slunky / Bad boy / Lonesome and a long way from home / After midnight / Easy now / Blues power / Bottle of red wine / Lovin' you lovin' me / I've told you for the last time / I don't know why / Let it rain. *(re-iss.Nov82 & Feb83)*

— In Oct 70, CLAPTON guested on KING CURTIS single 'TEASIN'. / **SOULIN'**

Nov 70. (7") **AFTER MIDNIGHT. / EASY NOW** — [ ] / 18 Oct 70

DEREK AND THE DOMINOES

ERIC CLAPTON – vox, guitar with **BOBBY WHITLOCK** – keyboards, vocals / **CARL RADLE** – bass / **JIM GORDON** – drums / **and guest DUANE ALLMAN** – guitar

Sep 70. (7") **TELL THE TRUTH. / ROLL IT OVER** — [ ] / [ ]
Dec 70. (7") **LAYLA. / BELL BOTTOM BLUES** — [ ] / 51 Mar 71
Dec 70. (d-lp)(c) **LAYLA & OTHER ASSORTED LOVE SONGS** — [ ] / 16 Nov 70
– I looked away / Bell bottom blues / Keep on growing / Nobody knows you when you're down and out / I am yours / Anyday / Key to the highway / Tell the truth / Why does love got to be so sad? / Have you ever loved a woman / Little wing / It's too late / Layla / Thorn tree in the garden. *(re-iss.Aug74 + Feb77) (re-iss.Jan84) (cd-iss.Mar91)*
Feb 71. (7") **BELL BOTTOM BLUES. / KEEP ON GROWING** — - / 91
Jul 72. (7") **LAYLA. / I AM YOURS** — 7 / 10 Apr72

— They split Spring '71 but left behind posthumous album below, etc

R.S.O. / R.S.O.

Sep 72. (7") **LET IT RAIN. / EASY NOW** — - / 48
Mar 73. (d-lp)(d-c) **DEREK AND THE DOMINOES - IN CONCERT (live)** — 36 / 20 Jan 73
– Why does love got to be so sad? / Got to get better in a little while / Let it rain / Presence of the Lord / Tell the truth / Bottle of red wine / Roll it over / Blues power / Have you ever loved a woman.
Apr 73. (7") **WHY DOES LOVE GOT TO BE SO SAD? (live). / PRESENCE OF THE LORD (live)** — [ ] / [ ]
Jun 73. (7") **BELL BOTTOM BLUES. / LITTLE WING** — [ ] / 78 Feb 73

— In '71 ERIC had virtually retired into session work. He appeared in GEORGE HARRISON's Bangla Desh concert, 1 Aug71.

ERIC CLAPTON

returned for a one-off concert at the Rainbow, 13Jan73 with **PETE TOWNSHEND** – guitar / **RON WOOD** – guitar / **STEVE WINWOOD** – keyboards / **JIMMY KARSTEIN & JIM CAPALDI** – drums / **REE BOP** – percussion / **RIC GRECH** – bass

Polydor / R.S.O.

Sep 73. (lp)(c) **THE RAINBOW CONCERT** — 19 / 18
– Badge / Roll it over / Presence of the Lord / Pearly queen / After midnight / Little wing. *(re-iss.Aug83) (cd-iss.1988 & May95)*

ERIC CLAPTON went solo again with **GEORGE TERRY** – guitar (ex-sessions) / **CARL RADDLE** – bass (ex-DEREK AND THE DOMINOES, ex-DELANEY & BONNIE) / **DICK SIMS** – keyboards (ex-BOB SEGER) / **JAMIE OLDAKER** – drums (ex-BOB SEGER) / **MARCY LEVY** – b.vocals (ex-BOB SEGER) / **YVONNE ELLIMAN**

R.S.O. / R.S.O.

Jul 74. (7") **I SHOT THE SHERRIF. / GIVE ME STRENGTH** — 9 / 1
Aug 74. (lp)(c) **461 OCEAN BOULEVARD** — 3 / 1 Jul 74
– Motherless children / Give me strength / Willie and the hand jive / Get ready / I shot the sheriff / I can't hold out / Please be with me / Steady rollin' man / Mainline Florida. *(re-iss.Aug83) (cd-iss.Nov89)*
Oct 74. (7") **WILLIE AND THE HAND JIVE. / MAINLINE FLORIDA** — [ ] / 26

— added **MARCY LEVY** – vocals, tambourine

Apr 75. (7") **SWING LOW SWEET CHARIOT. / PRETTY BLUE EYES** — 19 / [ ]
Apr 75. (lp)(c) **THERE'S ONE IN EVERY CROWD** — 15 / 21
– We've been told (Jesus' coming soon) / Swing low sweet chariot / Little Rachel / Don't blame me / The sky is crying / Singing the blues / Better make it through today / Pretty blue eyes / High / Opposites. *(re-iss.Mar85) (cd-iss.Nov86)*
Aug 75. (7") **KNOCKIN' ON HEAVEN'S DOOR. / SOMEONE LIKE YOU** — 38 / [ ]
Sep 75. (lp)(c) **E.C. WAS HERE (live)** — 14 / 20
– Have you ever loved a woman / Presence of the Lord / Drifting blues / Can't find my way home / Ramblin' on my mind / Farther on up the road. *(re-iss.Aug83)*

— added **SERGIO PASTORA** – percussion (ex-BOB SEGER)

Aug 76. (lp)(c) **NO REASON TO CRY** — 8 / 15 Sep 76
– Beautiful thing / Carnival / Sign language / County jail blues / All our past times / Hello old friend / Double trouble / Innocent times / Hungry / Black summer rain. *(re-iss.Aug83) (cd-iss.Dec86)*
Oct 76. (7") **HELLO OLD FRIEND. / ALL OUT PAST TIMES** — [ ] / 24
Feb 77. (7") **CARNIVAL. / HUNGRY** — [ ] / [ ]

— Augmented by five piece when ELLIMAN then PASTORA both went solo.

Nov 77. (7") **LAY DOWN SALLY. / COCAINE** — 39 / 3
Nov 77. (lp)(c) **SLOWHAND** — 23 / 2
– Cocaine / Wonderful tonight / Lay down Sally / Next time you see her / We're all the way / The core / May you never / Mean old Frisco / Peaches and diesel. *(re-iss.+cd Aug83)*
Mar 78. (7") **WONDERFUL TONIGHT. / PEACHES AND DIESEL** — [ ] / 16 May 78

— **ERIC CLAPTON & HIS BAND**

ERIC now backed up only by **SIMS, OLDAKER** and **RADLE** when MARCY LEVY went solo and GEORGE TERRY went into sessions.

Sep 78. (7") **PROMISES. / WATCH OUT FOR LUCY** — 37 / 9, 40
Nov 78. (lp)(c) **BACKLESS** — 18 / 8
– Walk out in the rain / Watch out for Lucy / I'll make love to you anytime / Roll it / Tell me that you love me / If I don't be there by morning / Early in the morning / Promises / Golden ring / Tulsa time. *(re-iss.Aug83) (cd-iss.Jan89)*
Mar 79. (7") **IF I DON'T GET THERE BY MORNING. / TULSA TIME** — [ ] / [ ]

— added **ALBERT LEE** – guitar (ex-solo artist, etc.) to complete new band, **DAVE MARKEE** – bass repl.CARL / **HENRY SPINETTI drums** repl.JAMIE

May 80. (d-lp)(d-c) **JUST ONE NIGHT (live at Budokhan)** — 3 / 2
– Tulsa time / Early in the morning / Lay down Sally / Wonderful tonight / If I don't be there by morning / Worried life blues / All our past times / After midnight / Double trouble / Setting me up / Blues power / Ramblin' on my mind / Cocaine / Farther on up the road. *(cd-iss.Nov88)*
Jul 80. (7") **TULSA TIME (live). / COCAINE (live)** — [ ] / 30 Jun 80
Oct 80. (7") **BLUES POWER (live). / EARLY IN THE MORNING (live)** — - / 76

— **GARY BROOKER & CHRIS STAINTON** – keyboards repl. DICK

Feb 81. (7") **I CAN'T STAND IT. / BLACK ROSE** — [ ] / 10
Feb 81. (lp)(c) **ANOTHER TICKET** — 18 / 7 Mar 81
– Something special / Black rose / Blow wind blow / Another ticket / I can't stand it / Hold me Lord / Floating bridge / Catch me if you can / Rita Mae. *(re-iss.Apr84) (cd-iss.Feb87)*
Apr 81. (7") **ANOTHER TICKET. / RITA MAE** — [ ] / 78

— **ERIC CLAPTON** retained **LEE** and recruited **RY COODER, ROGER HAWKINS, DONALD 'DUCK' DUNN** plus backing vocalists **JOHN SAMBATAO** and **CHUCK KIRKPATRICK**

Duck-Warners / Duck

Feb 83. (7") **I'VE GOT A ROCK'N'ROLL HEART. / MAN OVERBOARD** — [ ] / 18 Jan 83
(12"+=) – Everybody oughta make a change.
Feb 83. (lp)(c) **MONEY AND CIGARETTES** — 13 / 16
– Everybody outta make a change / The shape you're in / Ain't going down / I've got a rock'n'roll heart / Man overboard / Pretty girl / Man in love / Crosscut saw / Slow down Linda / Crazy country hop. *(cd-iss. 1984 & Feb95)*
Apr 83. (7")(7"pic-d) **THE SHAPE YOU'RE IN. / CROSSCUT SAW** — 75 / [ ]
(12"+=) – Pretty girl.
May 83. (7") **SLOW DOWN LINDA. / CRAZY COUNTRY HOP** — [ ] / [ ]
(12"+=) – The shape you're in.

— **CLAPTON** put together a new band. **TIM RENWICK** – guitar (ex-SUTHERLAND BROTHERS & QUIVER) / **CHRIS STAINTON** – keyboards (ex-solo, ex-JOE COCKER) / **DONALD 'DUCK' DUNN** – bass (ex-BOOKER T. AND THE M.G.'s) / **JAMIE OLDAKER** – drums (returned) **MARCY LEVY** (returned) **& SHAUN MURPHY** – backing vocals

Mar 85. (7") **FOREVER MAN. / TOO BAD** — 51 / 26
(12"+=) – Something's happening.
(12"+=) – Heaven is one step away.
Mar 85. (lp)(c)(cd) **BEHIND THE SUN** — 8 / 34
– She's waiting / See what love can do / Same old blues / Knock on wood / Something's happening / Forever man / It all depends / Tangled in love / Never make you cry / Just like a prisoner / Behind the sun. *(re-iss.cd Feb95)*
May 85. (7") **SEE WHAT LOVE CAN DO. / SHE'S WAITING** — - / 89
Jul 85. (7") **SHE'S WAITING. / JAILBAIT** — [ ] / -
Dec 85. (7") **EDGE OF DARKNESS (by "ERIC CLAPTON & MICHAEL KAMEN"). / SHOOT OUT** — 65 / -
(12"+=) – ('A'side) / Escape from North Moor.
(c-s+=) – (all 3 tracks). *(re-iss.cd-s.Feb89)*
(above from 'BBC' TV Edge Of Darkness on 'BBC' records.

Nov 86. (lp)(c)(cd) **AUGUST** 3 37 Dec 86
– It's in the way that you use it / Run / Tearing us apart / Bad influence / Hung up on your love / Take a chance / Hold on / Miss you / Holy mother / Behind the mask. (cd+=) – Grand illusion. *(re-iss.cd Feb95)*
Jan 87. (7") **BEHIND THE MASK. / GRAND ILLUSION** 15
(12"+=) – Wanna make love to you.
(d7"+=) – White room (live) / Crossroads (live).
Mar 87. (7") **IT'S IN THE WAY THAT YOU USE IT. / BAD INFLUENCE**
(d7+=)(12"+=) – Old ways / Pretty girl.

— **GREG PHILLINGANES** also joined
Jun 87. (7") **TEARING US APART. (by "ERIC CLAPTON & TINA TURNER") / HOLD ON** 56
(12"+=) – Run.
Nov 87. (7") **HOLY MOTHER. / TANGLED IN LOVE**
(12"+=) – Behind the mask / Forever man.

— now backed in concert by BUCKWHEAT ZYDECO
Feb 89. (lp)(c)(cd) **HOMEBOY (Soundtrack w/ others on 'Virgin' records UK)**
– Travelling east / Johnny / Call me if you need me (MAGIC SAM) / Bridge / Pretty baby (J.B. HUTTO & THE NEW HAWKS) / Dixie / Ruby's loft / I want to love you baby (PEGGY SCOTT / JO JO BENSON) / Bike ride / Ruby / Living in the real world (The BRAKES) / Final flight / Dixie / Homeboy. (cd+=) – Country bikin' / Party / Training / Chase.

— now with **ALAN CLARKE, ROBERT CRAY, GEORGE HARRISON, PHIL COLLINS,** etc
Nov 89. (lp)(c)(cd) **JOURNEYMAN** 3 16
– Pretending / Anything for your love / Bad love / Running on faith / Hard times / Hound dog / No alibis / Run so far / Old love / Breaking point / Lead me on / Before you accuse me.
Jan 90. (7") **BAD LOVE. / BEFORE YOU ACCUSE ME** 88 Mar 90
(12")(cd-s)(c-s) – ('A'side) / Badge / Let it rain (both live).
Mar 90. (7")(c-s) **NO ALIBIS. / RUNNING ON FAITH** 53
(12"+=) – Behind the mask (live) / Cocaine (live).
(cd-s+=) – No alibis / Cocaine (live).
Jun 90. (7") **PRETENDING. / HARD TIMES** 55 Nov 89
(12"+=) – Knock on wood.
(cd-s++=) – Behind the Sun.

— with **ALAN CLARKE** – keyboards / **NATHAN EAST** – bass / **STEVE FERRONE** – drums / **PHIL PALMER** – guitar / **RAY COOPER** – guitar / **RICHARD TEE** – piano / **CRAIG PHILLINGAMES** – keyboards, synths. and The NATIONAL PHILHARMONIC ORCHESTRA.
Oct 91. (cd)(c)(lp) **24 NIGHTS (live)** 17 38
– Badge / Running on faith / White room / Sunshine of your love / Watch yourself / Have you ever loved a woman / Worried life blues / Hoodoo man / Pretending / Bad love / Old love / Wonderful tonight / Bell bottom blues / Hard times / Edge of darkness.
Nov 91. (7") **WONDERFUL TONIGHT (live). / EDGE OF DARKNESS (live)** 30
(12")(cd-s)(c-s) – ('A' side) / Layla (band version) / Cocaine.
Jan 92. (cd)(c) **RUSH (Soundtrack)** 24
– Tears in Heaven / Will Gaines / Tracks and lines / Realization / New recruit / Preludia fugue / Kristen and Jim / Help me up / Cold turkey / Don't know which way to go. *(re-iss.cd Feb95)*

— **CHUCK LEAVELL** – keyboards (ex-ALLMANS) repl. CRAIG and RICHARD / **ANDY FAIRWEATHER-LOW** – guitar (ex-AMEN CORNER, ex-solo) repl. PHIL backing singers **KATIE KISSOON + TESSA MILES**
Jan 92. (7")(c-s) **TEARS IN HEAVEN. / WHITE ROOM (live)** 5 2
(12"+=)(cd-s+=) – Tracks & lines / Bad love (live).
In Jul92, ERIC teamed up with ELTON JOHN on single 'RUNAWAY TRAIN'. A month later, STING was his co-collaborator on another hit 'IT'S PROBABLY ME'.
Sep 92. (7")(c-s) **LAYLA (acoustic). / TEARS IN HEAVEN (acoustic)** 45 12
(cd-s+=) – (MTV unplugged interview).
Sep 92. (cd)(c)(lp) **UNPLUGGED (acoustic)** 2 1
– Signe / Before you accuse me / Hey hey / Tears in Heaven / Lonely stranger / Nobody knows when you're down & out / Layla / Running on faith / Walkin' blues / Alberta / San Francisco Bay blues / Malted milk / Old love / Rollin' & tumblin'.
Sep 94. (cd)(c)(lp) **FROM THE CRADLE** 1 1
– Third degree / Hoochie coochie man / Standin' round cryin' / Groanin' the blues / Blues before sunrise / Reconsider baby / Five long years / I'm tore down / How long blues / Goin' away baby / Blues leave me alone / Sinner's prayer / Motherless child / It hurts me too / Someday after a while.
Oct 94. (c-s) **MOTHERLESS CHILD. / DRIFTIN'** 63
(12"+=)(cd-s+=) – County jail blues / 32-20 blues.

— In Mar'95, alongside CHER, CHRISSIE HYNDE and NENEH CHERRY, he hit UK No.1 with charity Comic Relief single 'LOVE CAN BUILD A BRIDGE'.

– more compilations, etc –

Note that 'Polydor' releases were issued on 'Atco' US.
Aug 72. Polydor; (lp)(c) **THE HISTORY OF ERIC CLAPTON** 20 6 Apr 72
Feb 73. Polydor; (lp)(c) **CLAPTON** - 67
Apr 73. Polydor; (lp)(c) **AT HIS BEST** 87 Oct 72
1970. Polydor; (7") **TEASIN'.(by "ERIC CLAPTON & KING CURTIS") / SOULIN'** -
Jan 82. R.S.O.; (7")(12") **LAYLA 'Derek and the Dominoes'. / WONDERFUL TONIGHT** 4
Mar 82. R.S.O.; (7") **I SHOT THE SHERIFF. / COCAINE** 64
(12"+=) – Knockin' on Heaven's door (live).
Apr 82. R.S.O.; (d-lp)(d-c) **TIME PIECES – THE BEST OF ERIC CLAPTON** 20
(cd-iss.1983, re-iss.Dec92 & Apr95)
Aug 82. R.S.O.; (d-c) **SLOWHAND / BACKLESS**
Nov 82. R.S.O.; (t-lp-set) **461 OCEAN BOULEVARD / BACKLESS / SLOWHAND**
May 83. R.S.O.; (lp)(c) **TIME PIECES VOL.II – 'LIVE' IN THE SEVENTIES**
(cd-iss.1985)
Jun 83. R.S.O.; (d-c) **461 OCEAN BOULEVARD / ANOTHER TICKET**

Polydor R.S.O.

Apr 84. Polydor/ US= R.S.O.; (7") **WONDERFUL TONIGHT. / COCAINE**
(re-iss.Aug87)
Aug 87. Polydor; (7") **WONDERFUL TONIGHT. / I SHOT THE SHERIFF**
(12"+=) – Layla (full version).
(cd-s++=) – Swing low sweet chariot.
Sep 87. Polydor; (d-lp)(c)(cd) **THE CREAM OF ERIC CLAPTON** 9
(re-charted Sep92, hit UK No.49) (re-iss.cd/c Mar94, US re-iss.Mar95 hit No.80)
Apr 88. (6xlp)(4xc)(4xcd) **CROSSROADS** 34

— (above features all his work of past 25 years) (YARDBIRDS to solo)
Jul 88. Polydor; (7") **AFTER MIDNIGHT. / I CAN'T STAND IOT**
(12"+=) – What you doing today.
(cd-s++=) – Sunshine of your love (by "CREAM").
Nov 90. Polydor; (cd)(c) **THE LAYLA SESSIONS (Derek & The Dominoes)**
Jul 91. Polydor; (7") **LAYLA. (Edit) / BELL BOTTOM BLUES**
Nov 91. Polydor; (cd)(c)(d-lp) **THE BEST OF ERIC CLAPTON (w /CREAM)**
(re-iss.cd/cJul93)
Mar 94. Polydor; (d-cd)(d-c) **LIVE AT FILLMORE (DEREK & THE DOMINOES)**
May 84. Starblend; (d-lp)(d-c) **BACK TRACKIN'** 29
– I shot the sheriff / Knockin' on Heaven's door / Lay down Sally / Promises / Swing low sweet chariot / Wonderful tonight / Sunshine of your love (CREAM) / Tales of brave Ulysses (CREAM) / Badge (CREAM) / Little wing (DEREK & THE DOMINOES) / Layla (DEREK & THE DOMINOES) / Cocaine / Strange brew (CREAM) / Spoonful (CREAM) / Let it rain / Have you ever loved a woman? (DEREK & THE DOMINOES) / Presence of the Lord (BLIND FAITH) / Crossroads (CREAM) / Roll it over (DEREK & THE DOMINOES live) / Can't find my way home (live) / Blues power (live) / Further on up the road (live).
(re-iss.+d-cd Feb85 on 'Polydor') (re-iss.all formats. Feb91)
Nov 84. Astan; (lp)(c) **TOO MUCH MONKEY BUSINESS**
Mar 86. Thunderbolt; (lp)(c) **SURVIVOR**
(re-iss.Mar88)
Jul 84 Old Gold; (7") **LAYLA (Derek & the Dominoes) / ONLY YOU KNOW AND I KNOW**
Mar 86. Old Gold; (7") **I SHOT THE SHERIFF. / KNOCKIN' ON HEAVEN'S DOOR** -
Apr 86. Arcade; (lp)(c) **GREATEST HITS** -
1987. Castle; (d-lp)(c)(cd) **THE CLAPTON COLLECTION** -
(cd re-iss.Jun92)
1992. Castle; (cd)(c)(lp) **THE EARLY COLLECTION** -
May 88. Big Time; (lp)(c) **FIVE LONG YEARS** -
Jun 81. Decca; (lp)(c) **STEPPIN' OUT (live)** -
Feb 89. Venus; (lp)(c) **THE MAGIC OF ERIC CLAPTON** -
(re-iss.cd+c.Jun93 on 'Royal Collection')
Apr 93. Pulsar; (cd) **MISTER SLOWHAND** -
Dec 93. Immediate; (cd) **THE EARLY YEARS** -
Aug 94. Charly; (cd) **BEGINNINGS** -
Sep 95. Polydor; (d-cd) **LIVE AT THE FILLMORE (DEREK & THE DOMINOES)**
Nov 95. Polydor; (3xcd-box) **SLOWHAND / 461 OCEAN BOULEVARD / THERE'S ONE IN EVERY CROWD**
(also see under CREAM)

Gary CLARK (see under ⇒ DANNY WILSON)

Gene CLARK (see under ⇒ BYRDS)

Allan CLARKE (see under ⇒ HOLLIES)

John Cooper CLARKE

Born: 25 Jan'49, Salford, Manchester, England. In 1977 he embarked on a solo career, signing one-off indie deal with local 'Rabid' label. The following year he gained contract with 'Epic'. He toured with reggae poet LINTON KWESI JOHNSON and appeared 1980 in The Poetry Olympics at Westminster Abbey. • **Style:** A quick-fire humourous punk poet/ranter with BOB DYLAN looks. His venture into singing, was not wholly appreciated by music critics, who saw him as an alternative answer to stand-up comedy. • **Songwriters:** All penned by himself. • **Trivia:** In 1982, his docu-film TEN YEARS IN AN OPEN NECKED SHIRT was seen on UK-TV Channel 4. It was based on his book of the same name.

Recommended: ME AND MY BIG MOUTH (*7)

JOHN COOPER CLARKE & The INVISIBLE GIRLS

with **MARTIN HANNETT** – bass, producer / **PAUL BURGESS** – drums / **JOHN SCOTT** – guitar / some with **LYN OAKLEY** – guitar, etc. / guest **PETE SHELLEY** – bass

Rabid not issued

Oct 77. (7"ep) **INNOCENTS** -
– Psycle sluts (part 1 & 2) / Innocents / Suspended sentence. *(re-Sep82)*

JOHN COOPER CLARKE

solo with backing musicians, (INVISIBLE GIRLS)

Epic / not issued

Aug 78. (7") **POST-WAR GLAMOUR GIRLS. / KUNG FU INTERNATIONAL (live)** [ ] [-]

Oct 78. (lp)(c) **DISGUISE IN LOVE** [ ] [-]
– I don't want to be nice / Psycle sluts 1 & 2 / (I've got a brand new) Tracksuit / Teenage werewolf / Readers wives / Post war glamour girl / (I married a) Monster from Outer Space / Salome Maloney / Health fanatic / Strange bed fellows / Valley of the lost women. *(cd-iss.Jun95 on 'Columbia')*

Feb 79. (7")(7"sha-orange) **GIMMIX! (PLAY LOUD). / I MARRIED A MONSTER FROM OUTER SPACE (version)** [39] [-]

Jun 79. (10"lp) **WALKING BACK TO HAPPINESS** [ ] [-]
– Gaberdine Angus / Majorca / Bronze adonis / Twat / The pest / Who stole the marble index / Gimmix! (play loud) / Nothing / Split beans.

1979. (7"clear) **WALKING BACK TO HAPPINESS (live). /** [ ] [-]

Oct 79. (7") **SPLAT. / TWAT. / SLEEPWALK** [ ] [-]
(above 'A'side was double grooved to play 2 tracks)

Apr 80. (lp)(c) **SNAP, CRACKLE & BOP** [26] [-]
– Evidently Chickentown / Conditional discharge / Sleepwalk / 23rd / Beasley Street / 36 hours / Belladonna / The it man / Limbo / A distant relation. *(cd-iss.Sep94 on 'Rewind')*

May 80. (7") **THE IT MAN. / 36 HOURS** [ ] [-]

Apr 82. (7") **THE DAY MY PAD WENT MAD. / A DISTANT RELATION** [ ] [-]

May 82. (lp)(c) **ZIP STYLE METHOD** [97] [-]
– Midnight shift / The new assassin / Face behind the scream / I travel in biscuits / The day the world stood still / A heart disease called love / The ghost of Al Capone / Ninety degrees in the shade / The day my pad went mad / I wanna be yours / Drive she said / Night people.

Jun 82. (7") **NIGHT PEOPLE. / FACE BEHIND THE SCREAM** [ ] [-]

– compilations, others, etc –

Jul 80. Rabid; (lp) **OU EST LA MAISON DE FROMAGE** [ ] [-]
(re-iss.Mar89 on 'Receiver')

May 81. Epic; (lp) **ME AND MY BIG MOUTH** [ ] [-]
– I married a monster from Outer Space / I don't want to be nice / Valley of the lost women / 36 hours / The it man / Kung Fu international / Twat / Majorca / Bronze Adonis / Gimmix! (play loud) / Beasley Street.

—— He retired from recording, but still recited occasionally. He lived with American girlfriend/singer NICO until her death on 18th July 1988. He went into TV-advertisements for Sugar Puffs, etc.

Stanley CLARKE

Born: 30 Jun'51, Philadelphia, USA. Classically trained at 13, he left local Musical Academy in 1970 moving to New York, where he joined HORACE SILVER and then JOE HENDERSON BAND. He soon met CHICK COREA, and after guesting on his CHILDREN OF FOREVER album in 1972, they decided to form RETURN TO FOREVER. With LENNY WHITE and AL DiMEOLO also in ranks, they signed to 'Polydor' and made 4 instrumental albums (LIGHT AS A FEATHER – 1972 / HYMN OF THE SEVENTH GALAXY – 1973 / WHERE HAVE I KNOWN YOU BEFORE – 1974, hit US No.32 / NO MYSTERY – 1975, hit US No.39). In 1976, they shifted to 'CBS' where they issued more of the same kind of albums (ROMANTIC WARRIOR – 1976, hit US No.35 / MUSIC MAGIC – 1977, hit No.38 / RETURN TO FOREVER LIVE – 1978). Late 1974 he also went solo releasing many albums for 'Epic'. • **Style:** Jazz-rock bass virtuoso, who inspired many a young thumb-slapper including MARK KING (Level 42). His inventive techniques, gave the bass new forefront in the world of rock & jazz. • **Songwriters:** Himself, and early in 1981 with GEORGE DUKE. Covered LOUIE LOUIE (Kingsmen) / HEROES (David Bowie) / OVERJOYED (Stevie Wonder) / BORN IN THE USA (Bruce Springsteen) / • **Trivia:** In the early 80's, he also was part of The NEW BARBARIANS, a host of star musicians (i.e.KEITH RICHARDS, RON WOOD, BOBBY KEYS) who played live.

Recommended: THE COLLECTION (*6)

STANLEY CLARKE with many guest musicians, mostly from 2nd **JEFF BECK** – guitar / **GEORGE DUKE** – keyboards (ex-FRANK ZAPPA) / **STEVE GADD** – drums / plus many others

Epic / Nemperor

Nov 74. (lp)(c) **STANLEY CLARKE** [ ] [59]
– Vulcan princess / Yesterday princess / Lopsy Lu / Power / Spanish phases for strings and bass / Life suite (pt.I, II, III, IV). *(re-iss.Nov81 on 'Nemperor')*

Jan 75. (7") **VULCAN PRINCESS. / LOPSY LU** [-] [ ]

Oct 75. (lp)(c) **JOURNEY TO LOVE** [ ] [34]
– Silly putty / Journey to love / Hello Jeff / Song to John / Concerto for jazz – Rock orchestra. *(re-iss.Nov81 on 'Nemperor')*

Jan 76. (7") **SILLY PUTTY. / HELLO JEFF** [ ] [ ]

Aug 76. (lp)(c) **SCHOOL DAYS** [ ] [34]
– School days / Quiet afternoon / The dancer / Desert song / Hot fun / Life is just a game. *(re-iss.Mar82 on 'Nemperor') (cd-iss. Mar 87)*

Feb 77. (7") **HOT FUN. / LIFE IS JUST A GAME** [ ] [ ]

May 78. (lp)(c) **MODERN MAN** [ ] [57] Apr 78
– (opening statement) / He lives on (story about the last journey of a warrior) / More hot fun / Slow dance / (interlude) / A serious occasion / Got to find my own place / Dayride / (interlude) / It's what she didn't say / Modern man / A relaxed occasion / Rock'n'roll jelly / (closing statement). *(re-iss.Feb84 on 'CBS') (cd-iss. Mar 87)*

May 78. (7") **MORE HOT FUN. / SLOW DANCE** [ ] [ ]

May 78. (7") **ROCK'N'ROLL JELLY. / SLOW DANCE** [-] [ ]

Jul 79. (7") **JAMAICAN BOY (live). / ROCK'N'ROLL JELLY (live)** [-] [ ]

Aug 79. (d-lp)(c) **I WANNA PLAY FOR YOU (live)** [ ] [62] Jul 79
– Rock'n'roll jelly / All about / Jamaican boy / Christopher Ivanhoe / My greatest hits / Strange weather / I wanna play for you / Just a feeling / The streets of Philadelphia / School days / Quiet afternoon / Together again / Blues for Mingus / Off the planet / Hot fun / (closing). *(cd-iss.Dec94)*

Aug 79. (7") **JUST A FEELING (live). / THE STREETS OF PHILADELPHIA (live)** [-] [ ]

Oct 79. (7") **TOGETHER AGAIN. / (part 2)** [-] [ ]

Oct 79. (7") **TOGETHER AGAIN (live). / ROCK'N'ROLL JELLY (live)** [ ] [ ]

Epic / Epic

Jun 80. (lp)(c) **ROCKS, PEBBLES & SAND** [42] [95]
– Danger street / All hell broke loose / Rocks, pebbles & sand / Underestimation / You/me together / We supply / The story of a man and a woman: She thought I was Stanley Clarke – A fool again – I nearly went crazy (until I realised what had occured). *(re-iss.Mar83)*

Jul 80. (7") **WE SUPPLY. / TOGETHER AGAIN** [ ] [-]

Jul 80. (7") **WE SUPPLY. / UNDERESTIMATION** [-] [ ]

Sep 80. (7") **YOU/ME TOGETHER. / ROCKS, PEBBLES & SAND** [ ] [ ]

—— In 1980, he and a host of jazz superstars (ERIC GALE, GEORGE BENSON, WYNTON MARSALIS, MARCUS MILLER, TOM BROWNE, NDUGU CHANCLER, STANLEY TURRENTINE, DAVE VALENTINE & RONNIE FOSTER) were part of FUSE ONE, who released one lp for 'CTI' called 'SILK'; Feb81.

STANLEY CLARKE & GEORGE DUKE

with **JOHN ROBINSON** – drums / etc.

Epic / Epic

Apr 81. (lp)(c) **THE CLARKE / DUKE PROJECT** [ ] [33]
– Wild dog / Louie Louie / Sweet baby / I just want to love you / Winners / Touch and go / Never judge a cover by it's book / Let's get started / Finding my way.

Apr 81. (7") **SWEET BABY. / NEVER JUDGE A COVER BY IT'S BOOK** [ ] [19]

Jun 81. (7") **I JUST WANT TO LOVE YOU. / NEVER JUDGE A COVER BY IT'S BOOK** [ ] [-]

Oct 81. (7") **I JUST WANT TO LOVE YOU. / FINDING MY WAY** [-] [ ]

Dec 81. (7") **TOUCH AND GO. / WILD DOG** [-] [ ]

Nov 83. (lp)(c) **THE CLARKE / DUKE PROJECT II** [ ] [ ]
– Put it on the line / Heroes / Try me baby / Every reason to smile / Great Danes / The good times / You're gonna love it / Trip you in love / Atlanta.

Nov 83. (7")(12") **HEROES. / ATLANTA** [ ] [ ]

Apr 84. (7") **THE GOOD TIMES. / GREAT DANES** [-] [ ]

STANLEY CLARKE

Epic / Epic

Aug 82. (lp)(c) **LET ME KNOW YOU** [ ] [ ]
– Straight to the top / Let me know you / You are the one for me / I just want to be your brother / The force of love / Play the bass / Secret to my heart / New York City.

Aug 82. (7") **STRAIGHT TO THE TOP. / THE FORCE OF LOVE** [ ] [ ]

Nov 82. (7") **YOU ARE THE ONE FOR ME. / PLAY THE BASS** [-] [ ]

May 84. (lp)(c) **TIME EXPOSURE** [ ] [ ] Apr 84
– Play the bass / Are you ready (for the future) / Speedball / Heaven sent you / Time exposure / Future shock / Future / Spacerunner / I know just how you feel.

May 84. (7") **SPEEDBALL. / ARE YOU READY (FOR THE FUTURE)** [-] [ ]

Jun 84. (7") **HEAVEN SENT YOU. / SPEEDBALL** [-] [ ]

Nov 84. (7") **FUTURE. / SPACERUNNER** [-] [ ]

Jun 85. (7") **BORN IN THE U.S.A. / CAMPO AMERICANO** [ ] [ ]

Jul 85. (lp)(c)(cd) **FIND OUT** [ ] [ ]
– Find out / What if I should fall in love / Born in the U.S.A. / The sky's the limit / Don't turn the lights out / Campo Americano / Stereotypics / Psychedelic / My life.

Jul 85. (7") **WHAT IF I SHOULD FALL IN LOVE. / STEREOTYPICS** [-] [ ]

Oct 86. (7") **I'M HERE TO STAY. / BOYS OF JOHNSON STREET** [-] [ ]

Nov 86. (lp)(c)(cd) **HIDEAWAY** [ ] [ ]
– Hideaway / Overjoyed / My love, her inspiration / Where do we go / Boys of Johnston Street / Old friends / When it's cold outside / Listen to the beat of your heart / Basketball / I'm here to stay.

Jan 87. (7") **LISTEN TO THE BEAT OF YOUR HEART. / WHERE DO WE ALL GO** [-] [ ]

Aug 88. (lp)(c)(cd) **IF THIS BASS COULD ONLY TALK** [ ] [ ]
– If this bass could only talk / Goodbye pork pie hat / I wanna play for ya / Stories to tell / Funny how time flies (when you're having fun) / Workin' man / Tradition / Come take my hand / Bassically taps.

ANIMAL LOGIC

STANLEY CLARKE – bass, with **STEWART COPELAND** – drums (ex-POLICE) / **DEBORAH HOLLAND** – vocals

Virgin / Virgin

May 89. (7") **THERE'S A SPY (IN THE HOUSE). / SOMEONE TO COME HOME TO** [ ] [ ]
(12"+=) – Night owls.

Jun 89. (lp)(c)(cd) **ANIMAL LOGIC** [ ] [ ]
– There's a spy (in the house) / Someday we'll understand / Winds of Santa Ana / I'm through with love / As soon as the Sun goes down / I still feel for you / Elijah / Firing up the sunset gun / Someone to come home to / I'm sorry baby (I want you in my life).

Aug 89. (7") **SOMEDAY WE'LL UNDERSTAND. / LOPSY LU (live)** [ ] [ ]
(12"+=)(cd-s+=) – Chasing the guard.

STANLEY CLARKE / GEORGE DUKE

Epic / Epic

1990. (7") **DUKE LADY. / FINDOUT WHO YOU ARE** [-] [ ]

1990. (cd)(c)(lp) **THE CLARKE DUKE PROJECT III** [ ] [ ]

1990. (c-s)(12") **MOTHERSHIP CONNECTION. / ('A' instrumental)** [-] [ ]

Stanley CLARKE

Epic Epic

Aug 93. (cd)(c) **EAST RIVER DRIVE** [ ] [ ]
– Justice's groove (from Poetic Justice) / Fantasy love / Zabadoobeede (yabadoobeeda) / East River Drive / I'm home Africa / Funk is it's own reward (theme from Boyz In The Hood) / Christmas in Rio / What if I forget the champagne / Never lose your heart / There lies the passion / Illegal / Lords of the low frequencies.

Nov 94. (cd) **LIVE AT THE GREEK (live)** [ ] [ ]
– Minute by minute / Stratus / Buenos Aires / All blues / Goodbye pork pie hat / Her favourite song / School days.

– compilations, others, etc. –

1987. Nemperor; (7") **ROCK 'N' ROLL JELLY. / JAMAICAN BOY** [-] [ ]
Oct 87. Optimistic; (lp)(cd) **SHIELDSTONE (w / BILL SHIELDS)** [-] [ ]
1990. Castle; (cd)(c)(d-lp) **THE COLLECTION** [ ] [-]
– Vulcan princess / Journey to love / Silly putty / Stories to tell / School days / Quiet afternoon / The dancer / Rock'n'roll jelly / Jamaican boy / I wanna play for you / Off the planet / Time exposure / Hideaway / Goodbye pork pie hat.

Feb 94. Jazz Door; (cd) **LIVE IN MONTREAUX (live by The STANLEY CLARKE / GEORGE DUKE BAND)** [ ] [-]

Vince CLARKE & PAUL QUINN (see under ⇒ YAZOO)

Dave CLARK FIVE

Formed: London, England . . . 1958 by drummer DAVE CLARK and original bass player CHRIS WALSH. After loads of personnel changes, DAVE finally settled for complete new line-up in 1961 (see below). After a few instrumental singles for 'Piccadilly' in 1962, they signed to 'Columbia' early '63. By the following year, they were at No.1 with 'GLAD ALL OVER'. This also broke them into the US chart, where they provided ammunition for the British Invasion (i.e. BEATLES / ANIMALS / HERMAN'S HERMITS). • **Style:** Beat-pop combo who stomped their way to stardom in the 60's. • **Songwriters:** CLARK and vocalist MIKE SMITH. Covered (singles only); THE MULBURY BUSH (nursery rhyme) / DO YOU LOVE ME (Contours) / I LIKE IT LIKE THAT (Chris Kenner) / OVER AND OVER (Bobby Day) / YOU GOT WHAT IT TAKES (Marv Johnson) / YOU MUST HAVE BEEN A BEAUTIFUL BABY (Bobby Darin) / EVERYBODY KNOWS (Les Reed & Barry Mason) / RED BALLOON (Raymond Froggatt) / PUT A LITTLE LOVE IN YOUR HEART (Jackie DeShannon) / BRING IT ON HOME TO ME (Sam Cooke) / PARADISE (Amen Corner) / GOOD OLD ROCK'N'ROLL (Cat Mother & The All-Night Newsboys) / EVERYBODY GET TOGETHER (Youngbloods) / DRAGGIN' THE LINE (Tommy James) / SWEET CITY WOMAN (Stampeders) / SOUTHERN MAN (Neil Young) / etc. • **Trivia:** Featured in a few films in the 60's 'Get Yourself A College Girl' & 'Catch Us If You Can' (US-title 'Having A Wild Weekend').

Recommended: 25 THUMPING HITS (*7)

DAVE CLARK (b.15 Dec'42, Tottenham, London, England) – drums, vocals / **MIKE SMITH** (b.12 Dec'43, Edmunton, London) – vocals, keyboards / **LENNY DAVIDSON** (b.30 May'44, Enfield, London) – guitar, vocals / **RICK HUXLEY** (b. 5 Aug'42, Dartford, Kent, England) – bass, vocals / **DENNY PAYTON** (b. 8 Aug'43, Walthamstow, London) – saxophone, etc.

Piccadilly Congress

Jun 62. (7") **I KNEW IT ALL THE TIME. / THAT'S WHAT I SAID** [ ] [-]
(US re-iss.May64, hit No.53)

(Aug62) 'Ember' records, who had rights to early recordings, released 7" **CHAQUITA. / IN YOUR HEART** (it virtually went unoticed, but it was issued US May64 on 'Jubilee')

Piccadilly Laurie

Dec 62. (7") **FIRST LOVE. / I WALK THE LINE** [ ] [-] Jul 63
(US re-iss.& flipped over, Mar64 on 'Rust')

Columbia Epic

Mar 63. (7") **THE MULBERRY BUSH. / CHAQUITA** [ ] [-]
Sep 63. (7") **DO YOU LOVE ME. / DOO-DAH** [30] [-]
Nov 63. (7") **GLAD ALL OVER. / I KNOW YOU** [1] [6] Feb 64
Feb 64. (7") **BITS AND PIECES. / ALL OF THE TIME** [2] [4] Mar 64
Apr 64. (7") **DO YOU LOVE ME. / CHAQUITA** [-] [11]
Apr 64. (lp) **A SESSION WITH THE DAVE CLARK FIVE** [3] [5] Jun 64
– Can't you see that she's mine / I need you, I love you / I love you no more / Rumble / Funny / On Broadway / Zip-a-dee-doo-dah / Can I trust you / Forever and a day / Theme without a name / She's all mine / Time (track not on US version titled THE DAVE CLARK FIVE RETURN!). *(re-iss.'68 on 'MFP')*

Apr 64. (lp) **GLAD ALL OVER (as above)** [-] [3]
May 64. (7") **CAN'T YOU SEE THAT SHE'S MINE. / BECAUSE** [10] [-]
Jun 64. (7") **CAN'T YOU SEE THAT SHE'S MINE. / NO TIME TO LOSE** [-] [4]
Jul 64. (7") **BECAUSE. / THEME WITHOUT A NAME** [-] [3]
Aug 64. (7") **THINKING OF YOU BABY. / WHENEVER YOU'RE AROUND** [26] [-]
Aug 64. (lp) **AMERICAN TOUR (live)** [-] [11]
– Because / Who does he thinks he is / Move on / Whenever you're around / I want you still / Long ago / Come on over / Blue Monday / Sometimes / Any time you want love / I cried over you / Ol' soul.

Oct 64. (7") **ANYWAY YOU WANT IT. / CRYING OVER YOU** [25] [14] Nov 64
Oct 64. (7") **EVERYBODY KNOWS. / OL' SOL** [-] [15]
Jan 65. (7") **EVERYBODY KNOWS. / SAY YOU WANT ME** [37] [-]
Jan 65. (7") **COME HOME. / YOUR TURN TO CRY** [-] [14]
Jan 65. (lp) **COAST TO COAST** [-] [6]
– Any way you want it / Give me love / I can't stand it / I'm left without you / Say you want me / Everybody knows / I still love you / Crying over you / Say you want me / When / Don't you know me / It's not true.

Mar 65. (7") **REELIN' AND ROCKIN'. / LITTLE BITTY PRETTY ONE** [24] [23] Apr 65
May 65. (7") **COME HOME. / MIGHTY GOOD LOVING** [16] [-]
Apr 65. (lp) **WEEKEND IN LONDON** [-] [24]
– Come home / We'll be running / Blue suede shoes / Hurting inside / I'll never know / 'Til the right one comes along / I'm thinking / Your turn to cry / Little bitty pretty one / Remember, it's me / Mighty good loving.

Jun 65. (7") **I LIKE IT LIKE THAT. / HURTING INSIDE** [-] [7]
Jul 65. (7") **CATCH US IF YOU CAN. / ON THE MOVE** [5] [4] Aug 65
Aug 65. (lp) **CATCH US IF YOU CAN (Soundtrack)** [8] [15]
– Catch us if you can / On the move / If you come back / Long ago / Any time you want love / I can't stand it / Your turn to cry / Hurtin' inside / Don't be taken in / Don't you realize / I cried over you / Sweet memories. *(US-title 'HAVING A WILD WEEKEND')*

Nov 65. (7") **OVER AND OVER. / I'LL BE YOURS** [45] [1]
Nov 65. (lp) **I LIKE IT LIKE THAT** [-] [32]
– I like it like that / Pumping / I need love / Maybe it's you / That's how long our love will last / A little bit of love / I'll be yours my love / Please love me / Goodbye my friends / I am on my own / She's loving girl / You know you're lying.

Feb 66. (7") **AT THE SCENE. / I MISS YOU** [-] [18]
Mar 66. (7") **TRY TOO HARD. / ALL NIGHT LONG** [ ] [12]
May 66. (7") **LOOK BEFORE YOU LEAP. / PLEASE TELL ME WHY** [50] [28] Jun 66
(US-'A')

Jun 66. (lp) **TRY TOO HARD** [-] [77]
– Try too hard / Today / I never will / Looking in / Ever since you've been away / Somebody find a new love / I really love you / It don't feel good / Scared of falling in love / I know.

Aug 66. (7") **SATISFIED WITH YOU. / DON'T LET ME DOWN** [-] [50]
Sep 66. (lp) **SATISFIED WITH YOU** [-] [ ]
– Satisfied with you / Go on / Do you still love me / I meant you / Look before you leap / Please tell me why / You never listen / I still need you / It'll only hurt for a little while / Good lovin'.

Oct 66. (7") **NINETEEN DAYS. / I NEED LOVE** [ ] [-]
Oct 66. (7") **NINETEEN DAYS. / SITTING HERE BABY** [-] [48]
Jan 67. (7") **I'VE GOT TO HAVE A REASON. / GOOD TIME WOMAN** [-] [44]
Mar 67. (7") **YOU GOT WHAT IT TAKES. / SITTING HERE BABY** [28] [-]
Mar 67. (7") **YOU GOT WHAT IT TAKES. / DOCTOR RHYTHM** [-] [7]
Apr 67. (lp) **5 BY 5 = GO!** [-] [ ]
– Just a little bit now / Maze of love / Return my love / Best day's work / Who do you think you're talking to / Got love if you want it / Red ballooon / Please stay / Devoted to me / 3406 / Away from the noises / When I am alone / I still need you / No one can break a heart like you.

May 67. (7") **TABATHA TWITCHIT. / MAN IN A PIN-STRIPED SUIT** [ ] [-]
Jun 67. (7") **YOU MUST HAVE BEEN A BEAUTIFUL BABY. / THE MAN IN THE PIN-STRIPE SUIT** [-] [35]
Jun 67. (7") **A LITTLE BIT NOW. / YOU DON'T PLAY ME AROUND** [-] [67]
Aug 67. (lp) **YOU GOT WHAT IT TAKES** [-] [ ]
– You've got what it takes / I've got to have a reason / You won't play me around / Thinkin' of you baby / Lovin' so good / Doctor Rhythm / Play with me / Let me be / Blueberry Hill / Tabatha twitchit.

Oct 67. (7") **RED AND BLUE. / CONCENTRATION BABY** [-] [89]
Nov 67. (7") **EVERYBODY KNOWS. / CONCENTRATION BABY** [2] [-]
Dec 67. (7") **EVERYBODY KNOWS. / INSIDE AND OUT** [-] [43]
Feb 68. (lp) **EVERYBODY KNOWS** [-] [ ]
– Everybody knows / Little bit now / At the place / Inside and out / Red and blue / You must have been a beautiful baby / Good love is hard to find / Lost in his dreams / Hold on tight / I'll do the best I can / Concentration baby.

Feb 68. (7") **NO ONE CAN BREAK A HEART LIKE YOU. / YOU DON'T WANT MY LOVIN'** [28] [ ]
May 68. (7") **PLEASE STAY. / FORGET** [-] [ ]
Sep 68. (7") **THE RED BALLOON. / MAZE OF LOVE** [7] [ ]
Nov 68. (7") **LIVE IN THE SKY. / CHILDREN** [38] [ ]
Feb 69. (7") **THE MULBERRY TREE. / SMALL TALK** [ ] [ ]
Mar 69. (lp) **14 TITLES BY DAVE CLARK FIVE (5 BY 5 1964-1969)**(compilation) [ ] [-]
May 69. (7") **(IF) PARADISE (WAS HALF AS NICE). / 34-06** [-] [ ]
Jul 69. (7") **IF SOMEBODY LOVES YOU. / BEST DAY'S WORK** [-] [ ]
Oct 69. (7") **PUT A LITTLE LOVE IN YOUR HEART. / 34-06** [31] [ ]
Dec 69. (7") **BRING IT ON HOME TO ME. / DARLING I LOVE YOU** [-] [ ]
Dec 69. (7") **GOOD OLD ROCK'N'ROLL / SWEET LITTLE SIXTEEN / LONG TALL SALLY / WHOLE LOTTA SHAKIN' GOIN' ON / BLUE SUEDE SHOES / LUCILLE / REELIN' AND ROCKIN' / MEMPHIS TENNESSEE (medley)** [7] [ ]
Feb 70. (7") **EVERYBODY GET TOGETHER / DARLING I LOVE YOU** [8] [ ]
Apr 70. (7") **JULIA. / FIVE BY FIVE** [ ] [-]
Jun 70. (7") **HERE COMES SUMMER. / BREAK DOWN AND CRY** [44] [ ] Sep 70
(re-iss.Jun75 on 'EMI')

Oct 70. (7") **MORE GOOD OLD ROCK'N'ROLL (medley):-Rock and roll music / Blueberry hill / Good golly Miss Molly / My blue Heaven / Keep a knockin' / Loving you / One night / Lawdy Miss Clawdy** [34] [ ]
Dec 70. (7") **SOUTHERN MAN. / IF YOU WANNA SEE ME CRY** [ ] [ ]
Dec 70. (lp) **IF SOMEBODY LOVES YOU** [ ] [-]
If somebody loves you / It ain't what you do / Live in the sky / 5 by 5 / Here comes summer / How do you get to Heaven / Everybody get together / July / Break down and cry / I'm on my own / Red and blue / If you wanna see me cry / Worried time / Darling I love you.

Jun 71. (7") **WON'T YOU BE MY LADY. / INTO YOUR LIFE** [ ] [ ]

— They had already officially disbanded.

DAVE CLARK & FRIENDS

Columbia Epic

Oct 71. (7") **DRAGGIN' THE LINE. / ONE EYED, BLUES SUITED, GUN TOTIN' MAN** [ ] [-]
Feb 72. (7") **THINK OF ME. / RIGHT OR WRONG** [ ] [-]

Jun 72. (7") **RUB IT IN. / I'M SORRY BABY** [ ] [ ]
(re-iss.Aug74)
Sep 72. (lp)(c) **DAVE CLARK & FRIENDS** [ ] [-]
– Southern man / Bring it on home to me / Signs / Won't you be my lady / The time has come / If you've got a little love to give / Officer McKirk / Paradise (is half as nice) / Draggin' the line / Think of me / One-eyed, blue-suited, gun-totin' man / Right or wrong / I don't know / Put a little love in your heart.

E.M.I. — not issued

Mar 73. (7") **SWEET CITY WOMAN. / LOVE COMES BUT ONCE** [ ] [-]
Oct 73. (7") **SHA-NA-NA-NA. / I DON'T KNOW** [ ] [-]

—— CLARK ended musical career, and concentrated on his business. In 1986 he co-wrote musical TIME, which featured many superstars including CLIFF RICHARD, FREDDIE MERCURY, DIONNE WARWICK, LEO SAYER, STEVIE WONDER, etc. DAVID CASSIDY replaced CLIFF in the lead role.

May 86. (d-lp)(d-c) **DAVE CLARK'S TIME – THE ALBUM** [21] [-]
– (various artists album)

Mooncrest — not issued

Nov 90. (cd)(c)(lp) **IT'S ONLY ROCK'N'ROLL ("DAVE CLARK")** [ ] [ ]

– compilations, others, etc. –

Note; All 'Columbia' releases were issued on 'Epic' US.

Jan 64. Columbia; (7"ep) **THE DAVE CLARK FIVE** [28] [-]
– I know you / Poison Ivy / Twist and shout / No time to lose.
Apr 64. Congress; (7") **I KNEW IT ALL THE TIME. / THAT'S WHAT I SAID** [-] [53]
Mar 65. Columbia; (7"ep) **THE HITS OF THE DAVE CLARK FIVE** [ ] [-]
Sep 65. Columbia; (7"ep) **WILD WEEKEND** [ ] [-]
Mar 66. Columbia; (lp) **DAVE CLARK FIVE'S GREATEST HITS** [-] [9]
Dec 66. Columbia; (lp) **DAVE CLARK FIVE'S: MORE GREATEST HITS** [-] [ ]
Mar 67. Columbia; (lp) **GREATEST HITS** [ ] [-]
Mar 71. Columbia; (d-lp) **THE DAVE CLARK FIVE** [-] [ ]
Dec 72. Columbia; (7") **ALL TIME GREATS MEDLEY. / WILD WEEKEND** [ ] [-]
Mar 75. Columbia; (d-lp) **GLAD ALL OVER AGAIN: THE DAVE CLARK FIVE'S GREATEST HITS** [-] [ ]
1964. Ember; (lp) **THE DAVE CLARK FIVE AND THE WASHINGTON DC's** [ ] [-]
1975. Epic; (7") **BECAUSE. / DO YOU LOVE ME** [ ] [-]
1975. Epic; (7") **CATCH US IF YOU CAN. / OVER AND OVER** [ ] [-]
1975. Epic; (7") **GLAD ALL OVER. / BITS AND PIECES** [ ] [-]
1975. Epic; (7") **YOU GOT WHAT IT TAKES. / COME HOME** [ ] [-]
1970. Regal Starline; (lp)(c) **THE BEST OF THE DAVE CLARK FIVE** [ ] [-]
Oct 75. M.F.P.; (lp)(c) **PLAYS GOOD OLD ROCK'N'ROLL** [ ] [-]
Feb 77. Polydor; (d-lp)(c) **25 THUMPING GREAT HITS** [7] [-]
– Glad all over / Do you love me? / Bits and pieces / Can't you see / Catch us if you can / Because / Over and over / Reelin' and rockin' / You got what it takes / Everybody knows / Good old rock'n'roll / Sweet little sixteen / Long tall Sally / Chantilly lace / Whole lotta shakin' goin' on / Blue suede shoes / Wild weekend / Here comes summer / Live in the sky / Red balloon / Come home / Sweet city woman / Sha-na-na / Put a little love in your heart / Everybody get together.
Nov 77. Polydor; (7") **EVERYBODY KNOWS. / ALWAYS ME** [ ] [-]
Apr 93. E.M.I./ US= Hollywood; (cd)(c)(d-lp) **GLAD ALL OVER AGAIN** [28] [ ]
(US title 'THE HISTORY OF')
Apr 93. E.M.I./ US= HOllywood; (12"ep)(c-ep)(cd-ep) **GLAD ALL OVER EP** [37] [ ]

Gary CLARK (see under ⇒ DANNY WILSON)

CLASH

Formed: London, England . . . mid'76, by JONES, SIMONEN, STRUMMER and CHIMES. KEITH LEVENE future PIL member also had a brief spell with them in '76. Manager BERNIE RHODES attained deal with 'C.B.S.' early '77, and soon hit charts with 2 minute classic 'WHITE RIOT'. • **Style:** Punk rock, raw with energy, fuelled by politics and mixed with sporadic dub reggae. After two attempts (1978/1979 lp's) to go near commercial and "sell-out" punk roots, they returned with budget triple album SANDINISTA!, that experimented with all musical styles. In 1982 they achieved major success in America, but when most of band dispersed into new ventures in 83/84, their long-awaited return CUT THE CRAP virtually didn't. • **Songwriters:** Either STRUMMER / – JONES until 1980 group penned, except POLICE AND THIEVES (Junior Murvin / LEE PERRY) / PRESSURE DROP (Maytals) / I FOUGHT THE LAW (Sonny Curtis) / POLICE ON MY BACK (Equals) / ARMAGIDEON TIME (Willie Williams) / JUNCO PARTNER + ENGLISH CIVIL WAR (unknown trad) / EVERY LITTLE BIT HURTS (Ed Cobb) / BRAND NEW CADILLAC (Vince Taylor). • **Trivia:** Early 1980, the band featured live in the docu-film 'Rude Boy' about a fictionalized CLASH roadie. JOE STRUMMER went into acting 1986 (Straight To Hell) / 1989 (Lost In Space). A surprise return to the charts in 1991, with re-issue SHOULD I STAY OR SHOULD I GO was due to a TV-ad for Levi jeans.

Recommended: THE CLASH (*10) / THE STORY OF THE CLASH (*9) / GIVE 'EM ENOUGH ROPE (*7) / LONDON CALLING (*8) / SANDINISTA! (*7) / COMBAT ROCK (*6)

JOE STRUMMER (b.JOHN MELLORS, 21 Aug'52, Ankara, Turkey./ raised London) – vocals, guitar (ex-101'ers) / **PAUL SIMONEN** (b.15 Dec'55, Brixton, England) – bass, vocals / **MICK JONES** (b.MICHAEL JONES, 26 Jun'55, Brixton) – guitar, vocals / **TORY CRIMES** (b.TERRY CHIMES, 25 Jan'55) – drums

C.B.S. — not issued

Mar 77. (7") **WHITE RIOT. / 1977** [38] [-]
Apr 77. (lp)(c) **THE CLASH** [12] [-]
– Janie Jones / Remote control / I'm so bored with the U.S.A. / White riot / Hate and war / What's my name / Deny / London's burning / Career oportunities / Cheat / Protex blue / Police and thieves / 48 hours / Garage land. *(re-iss.Nov82)(cd-iss.May89 + Jun91)(US-release Jul79 on 'Epic' tracks differed, cont free 7"* **GROOVY TIMES. / GATES OF THE WEST.** *This lp version iss.UK – Jan91 on cd)*

—— (Jan77) (NICKY) **TOPPER HEADON** (b.30 May'57, Bromley, Kent, England) – drums repl. CHIMES who later joined COWBOYS INTERNATIONAL and GENERATION X.

May'77. (7") **REMOTE CONTROL. / LONDON'S BURNING (live)** [ ] [-]
Sep 77. (7") **COMPLETE CONTROL. / THE CITY OF THE DEAD** [28] [-]
Feb 78. (7") **CLASH CITY ROCKERS. / JAIL GUITAR DOORS** [35] [-]
Jun 78. (7") **WHITE MAN IN HAMMERSMITH PALAIS. / THE PRISONER** [32] [-]

C.B.S. — Epic

Nov 78. (lp)(c) **GIVE 'EM ENOUGH ROPE** [2] [ ] Mar 79
– Safe European home / English civil war / Tommy gun / Julie's been working for the drug squad / Guns on the roof / Drug-stabbing time / Stay free / Cheapstakes / All the young punks (new boots and contracts). *(re-iss.1984) (cd-iss.May89 + Jan91)*
Nov 78. (7") **TOMMY GUN. / 1-2, CRUSH ON YOU** [19] [ ]
Feb 79. (7") **ENGLISH CIVIL WAR. / PRESSURE DROP** [25] [ ]
May 79. (7"ep) **THE COST OF LIVING** [22] [ ]
– I fought the law / Groovy times / Gates of the west / Capital radio.
Jul79. (7") **I FOUGHT THE LAW. / WHITE MAN IN HAMMERSMITH PALAIS** [-] [ ]

—— added on tour 5th member **MICKEY GALLAGHER** – keyboards (ex-IAN DURY)

Dec 79. (7") **LONDON CALLING. / ARMAGIDEON TIME** [11] [ ]
(12"+=) – Justice tonight ('B'version) / Kick it over ('B'version).
Dec 79. (d-lp)(c) **LONDON CALLING** [9] [27] Jan 80
– London calling / Brand new Cadillac / Jimmy Jazz / Hateful / Rudie can't fail / Wrong 'em Boyd / Death or glory / Koka Kola / The card cheat / Spanish bombs / The right profile / Lost in the supermarket / The guns of Brixton / Lover's rock / Four horsemen / I'm not down / Revolution rock / Train in vain. *(cd-May88)*
Feb 80. (7") **TRAIN IN VAIN (STAND BY ME). / LONDON CALLING** [-] [27]
Aug 80. (7") **BANKROBBER. / ROCKERS GALORE . . . UK TOUR** [12] [ ]
Nov 80. (7") **THE CALL-UP. / STOP THE WORLD** [40] [-]
Dec 80. (t-lp,d-c) **SANDINISTA!** [19] [24]
– The magnificent seven / Hitsville UK / Junco partner / Ivan meets G.I. Joe / The leader / Something about England / Rebel waltz / Look here / The crooked beat / Somebody got murdered / One more time / One more dub / Lightning strikes (not once but twice) / Up in Heaven (not only here) / Corner soul / Let's go crazy / If music could talk / The sound of the sinners / Police on my back / Midnight log / The equaliser / The call up / Washington bullets / Broadway / Lose this skin / Charlie don't surf / Mensforth Hill / Junkie slip / Kingston advice / The street parade / Version city / Living in fame / Silicone on sapphire / Version pardner / Career opportunites (version) / Shepherds delight. *(iss.as lp in US)(d-cd.iss.1989)*
Jan 81. (7") **HITSVILLE UK. / RADIO ONE** [56] [-]
Feb 81. (7") **HITSVILLE UK. / POLICE ON MY BACK** [-] [ ]
Mar 81. (7") **THE CALL-UP. / THE MAGNIFICENT SEVEN** [-] [ ]
(12"+=) – The magnificent dance / The cool-out.
Apr 81. (7") **THE MAGNIFICENT SEVEN. / THE MAGNIFICENT DANCE** [34] [-]
(12"+=) – (2-'A'extra mixes).
Nov 81. (7") **THIS IS RADIO CLASH. / RADIO CLASH** [47] [ ]
(12"+=) – Outside broadcast / Radio 5.

—— **TERRY CHIMES** returned to replace HEADON who later went solo.

Apr 82. (7") **KNOW YOUR RIGHTS. / FIRST NIGHT BACK IN LONDON** [43] [ ]
May 82. (lp)(c) **COMBAT ROCK** [2] [7]
– Know your rights / Car jamming / Should I stay or should I go / Rock the Casbah / Red angel dragnet / Straight to Hell / Overpowered by funk / Atom tan / Sean Flynn / Ghetto defendant / Inoculated city / Death is a star. *(re-iss.Nov86) (cd-iss.Sep88 + Jan91)*
Jun 82. (7") **ROCK THE CASBAH. / INOCULATED CITY** [-] [8]
Jun 82. (7") **ROCK THE CASBAH. / LONG TIME JERK** [30] [ ]
(12") – ('A'side) / Mustapha dance.
Jul 82. (7") **SHOULD I STAY OR SHOULD I GO. / COOL CONFUSION (or) FIRST NIGHT BACK IN LONDON** [-] [45]
Sep 82. (7")(12")(7"pic-d) **SHOULD I STAY OR SHOULD I GO. / STRAIGHT TO HELL** [17] [-]

—— (Feb83-Jan84) **STRUMMER & SIMONEN** brought in new musicians **PETE HOWARD** – drums (ex-COLD FISH),repl. CHIMES who later joined HANOI ROCKS. / **NICK SHEPHERD** – guitar (ex-CORTINAS) + **VINCE WHITE** – guitar repl. JONES who formed BIG AUDIO DYNAMITE

Sep 85. (7") **THIS IS ENGLAND. / DO IT NOW** [24] [ ]
(12"+=) – Sex mad roar.
Nov 85. (lp)(c) **CUT THE CRAP** [16] [88]
– Dictator / Dirty punk / We are The Clash / Are you red..Y / Cool under heat / Movers and shakers / This is England / Three card trick / Play to win / Fingerpoppin' / North and south / Life is wild. *(cd-iss.Dec92 on 'Columbia')*

—— disbanded Dec'85. STRUMMER went solo (see below). SHEPHERD formed HEAD. In the 90's, SIMONEN formed HAVANA 3 a.m.

– compilations, others, etc. –

Oct 80. Epic; (10"m-lp) **BLACK MARKET CLASH** [-] [74]
– Time is tight / Capital radio / Bank robber / Presure drop / The prisoner / City of the dead / Justice tonight – kick it over (version). *(UK-iss.c+cd.Sep91+Nov93 on 'Columbia')*
Nov 82. C.B.S.; (7"ep) **COMPLETE CONTROL / LONDON CALLING. / BANKROBBER / CLASH CITY ROCKERS** [ ] [-]
Sep 86. C.B.S.; (c-ep) **THE 12" TAPE** [ ] [-]
– London calling / The magnificent dance / This is Radio Clash / Rock the Casbah /

This is England / Last dance.
Mar 88. C.B.S./ US= Epic; (7") **I FOUGHT THE LAW. / THE CITY OF THE DEAD / 1977** [29] [ ]
(12"+=)(cd-s+=) – Police on my back / 48 hours.
Mar 88. (d-lp)(c)(cd) **THE STORY OF THE CLASH** [7] [ ]
– The magnificent seven / Rock the Casbah / This is Radio Clash / Should I stay or should I go / Straight to Hell / Armagideon time / Clampdown / Train in vain / Guns of Brixton / I fought the law / Somebody got murdered / Lost in the supermarket / Bank robber / White man in Hammersmith Palais / London's burning / Janie Jones / Tommy gun / Complete control / Capital radio / White riot / Career opportunities / Clash city rockers / Safe European home / Stay free / London calling / Spanish bombs / English civil war / Police and thieves. *(re-iss.cd/c/lp.Mar91 as THE STORY OF THE CLASH VOL.1, on 'Columbia', UK charted 13.)*
Apr 88. C.B.S.; (7") **LONDON CALLING. / BRAND NEW CADILLAC** [46] [ ]
(12"+=) – Rudie can't fail.
(cd-s+=) – The street parade.
Jul 90. C.B.S.; (7")(c-s) **RETURN TO BRIXTON (remix). / ('A'-SW2 mix)** [57] [ ]
(12"+=)(cd-s+=) – The guns of Brixton.
Feb 91. Columbia; (7")(c-s) **SHOULD I STAY OR SHOULD I GO. / Rush (by "BAD II")** [1] [ ]
(12"+=)(cd-s+=) – ('B'dance mix) / Protex blue.
(cd-s) – ('A'side) / London calling / Train in vain / I fought the law.
Apr 91. Columbia; (7")(c-s) **ROCK THE CASBAH. / MUSTAPHA DANCE** [15] [ ]
(12"+=)(cd-s+=) – The magnificent dance / This is Radio Clash.
(cd-s) – ('A'side) / Tommy gun / White man in Hammersmith Palais / Straight to Hell.
Jun 91. Columbia; (7") **LONDON CALLING. / BRAND NEW CADILLAC** [64] [ ]
(12"+=) – Return to Brixton (remix).
(cd-s++=) – The call-up.
Oct 91. Columbia; (7")(c-s) **TRAIN IN VAIN (STAND BY ME). / THE RIGHT PROFILE** [ ] [ ]
(cd-s+=) – Groovy times / Gates to the west.
(pic-cd-s+=) – ('A'remix) / Death or glory.
Nov 91. Columbia; (cd)(c)(lp) **THE SINGLES COLLECTION** [68] [ ]
May 94. Columbia; (3xcd)(3xc) **ON BROADWAY** [ ] [ ]
The CLASH also appeared under different guises for singles below
May 83. Celluloid; (12") **ESCAPADES OF FUTURA 2000 ("FUTURA 2000 featuring The CLASH")** [ ] [-]
Dec 83. Big Beat; (7") **HOUSE OF THE JU-JU QUEEN. / SEX MACHINE ("JANIE JONES & THE LASH")** [ ] [-]
— They can also be heard backing **TYMON DOGG** on 45; Lose This Skin (May80)

JOE STRUMMER

C.B.S. Epic
Oct 86. (7")(12") **LOVE KILLS. / DUM DUM CLUB** [69] [ ]
Virgin Virgin
Feb 88. (lp)(c)(cd) **WALKER (Soundtrack)** [ ] [ ]
– Filibustero / Omotepe / Sandstorm / Machete / Viperland / Nica libre / Latin romance / The brooding side of madness / Tennessee rain / Smash everything / Tropic of no return / The unknown immortal / Musket waltz.
Epic Epic
Jun 88. (7") **TRASH CITY. / THEME FROM A PERMANENT RECORD** [ ] [ ]
(12"+=)(pic-cd-s+=) – Norfitili rock.
— He's augmented by new band **JACK IRONS** – drums (of RED HOT CHILI PEPPERS) **ZANDON SCHLOSS** – guitar (ex-CIRCLE JERKS) / **RONNIE MARSHALL** – bass (of TONE LOC)
Aug 89. (7")(c-s) **GANGSTERVILLE. / JEWELLERS AND BUMS** [ ] [ ]
(7"ep+=) – Passport to Detroit / Punk rock blues.
(12"+=)(cd-s+=) – Don't tango with my django.
Sep 89. (lp)(c)(cd) **EARTHQUAKE WEATHER** [58] [ ]
– Gangsterville / King of the bayou / Island hopping / Slant six / Dizzy's goatee / Shouting street / Boogie with your children / Leopardskin limousines / Sikorsky parts / Jewellers and bums / Highway on zero street / Ride your donkey / Passport to Detroit / Sleepwalk.
Oct 89. (7") **ISLAND HOPPING. / CHOLO VEST** [ ] [ ]
(12"+=)(cd-s+=) – Mango street / Baby o' boogie.
STRUMMER joined The POGUES on tour, deputising when SHANE McGOWAN was under the bottle. At the start of 1992, he had begun writing with them, so who knows? At least it will quell the dogged persistent rumours of a CLASH reformation.

Jimmy CLIFF

Born: JAMES CHAMBERS, 1948, St.Catherine, Jamaica. Moved to Kingston in 1962, where he made a few 45's for a label run by Leslie Kong. One of them 'HURRICANE HATTY' hit No.1 there that year. In 1965, Chris Blackwell (boss of 'Island' records) took him to England, where he became a backing singer as well as solo star for 'Fontana'. His records finally got issued on 'Island', where he signed a longer contract in '67. After a few hits late in the 60's, he starred in the semi-autobiographical film 'The Harder They Come', released 1972. Always around in the music biz, during the next 2 decades. • **Style:** Moved from ska and R&B to be popular reggae star between 1968 to the 80's. • **Songwriters:** Penned most himself, except covers WILD WORLD (Cat Stevens) / etc. • **Trivia:** In the early 70's, JIMMY wrote DESMOND DEKKER's hit 'YOU CAN GET IT IF YOU REALLY WANT' & The PIONEERS' 'LET YOUR YEAH BE YEAH'. In 1985, he wrote 'TRAPPED' for BRUCE SPRINGSTEEN, who sang it on charity album 'USA FOR AFRICA'.

Recommended: THE BEST OF JIMMY CLIFF (*6) / THE HARDER THEY COME (*6)

Island JAMAICA
1962. (7") **HURRICAN HATTY. / DEAREST BEVERLEY** [-] [-]
1962. (7") **MISS JAMAICA. / GOLD DIGGER** [ ] [-]
1962. (7") **SINCE LATELY. / I'M FREE** [ ] [-]
1963. (7") **MY LUCKY DAY. / ONE EYED JACKS** [ ] [-]
1963. (7") **KING OF KINGS. / ('B'by SIR PERCY)** [ ] [-]
1963. (7") **MISS UNIVERSE. / THE PRODIGAL** [ ] [-]
Stateside not issued
Sep 64. (7") **ONE EYED JACKS. / KING OF KINGS** [ ] [-]
Fontana not issued
Jan 66. (7") **CALL ON ME. / PRIDE AND PASSION** [ ] [-]
Black Swan not issued
1963. (7") **THE MAN. / YOU ARE NEVER TOO OLD** [ ] [-]
Blue Beat not issued
1966. (7") **I'M SORRY. / ('B'by RED PRICE & THE BLUE BEATS)** [ ] [-]
Island not issued
Feb 67. (7") **AIM AND AMBITION. / GIVE AND TAKE** [ ] [-]
1967. (lp) **HARD ROAD TO TRAVEL** [ ] [-]
– Reward / Let's dance / Can't get enough of it / I've got a feeling / All I know about you / Give and take / Pride and passion / Searchin' for my baby / Hard road to travel / White shade of pale / Call on me / Aim and ambition.
1967. (7") **I GOT A FEELING. / HARD ROAD TO TRAVEL** [ ] [-]
1967. (7") **THAT'S THE WAY LIFE GOES. / THANK YOU** [ ] [-]
Jul 68. (7") **WATERFALL. / REWARD** [ ] [-]
Jun 68. (7") **SET ME FREE. ("JACKIE EDWARDS & JIMMY CLIFF") / HERE I COME** [ ] [-]
Trojan A & M
Oct 69. (7") **WONDERFUL WORLD, BEAUTIFUL PEOPLE. / HARD ROAD TO TRAVEL** [6] [-]
Nov 69. (7") **WONDERFUL WORLD, BEAUTIFUL PEOPLE. / WATERFALL** [-] [25]
Dec 69. (lp) **JIMMY CLIFF** [ ] [ ]
– Many rivers to cross / Vietnam / My ancestors / Hard road to travel / Hello sunshine / Wonderful world, beautiful people / Sufferin' in the land / Use what I got / That's the way it goes / Come into my life. *(re-iss.Mar77 on 'Island') (re-iss.1983, cd-iss.1988) (cd-iss.Mar94 on 'Trojan')*
Feb 70. (7") **VIETNAM. / SHE DOES IT RIGHT** [46] [ ]
Mar 70. (7") **COME INTO MY LIFE. / VIETNAM** [ ] [89]
May 70. (7") **YOU CAN GET IT IF YOU REALLY WANT. / BE AWARE** [-] [ ]
Island A & M
Jul 70. (7") **WILD WORLD. / BE AWARE** [8] [-]
Feb 71. (7") **GOODBYE YESTERDAY./ BREAKDOWN** [ ] [-]
1971. (7") **SITTING IN LIMBO. / THE BIGGER THEY COME** [ ] [ ]
1971. (lp)(c) **ANOTHER CYCLE** [ ] [ ]
– Take a look at yourself / Please tell me why / Rap / Opportunity only knocks once / My friend's wife / Another cycle / Sitting in limbo / Oh, how I miss you / Inside out, upside down / One thing is over.
1971. (7") **TRAPPED. / STRUGGLIN' MAN** [ ] [-]
— In 1972, he appears and contributes some tracks to 'THE HARDER THEY COME' film soundtrack on 'Island'. In US, released early 1975. (cd-iss.Sep86) (cd-re-iss.Oct90 on 'Mango')
1972. (7") **THE HARDER THEY COME. / MANY RIVERS TO CROSS** [ ] [ ]
E.M.I. Reprise
1973. (7") **BORN TO WIN. / BLACK QUEEN** [-] [ ]
Jul 73. (7") **OH MY LOVE. / OH JAMAICA** [ ] [ ]
1973. (lp)(c) **UNLIMITED** [ ] [ ]
– Under the Sun, Moon and stars / Fundamental reggay / World of peace / Black queen / Be true / Oh Jamaica / Commercialization / The price of peace / On my life / I see the light / Rip off / Poor slave / Born to win. *(re-iss.+cd Oct90)*
Oct 73. (7") **FUNDAMENTAL REGGAY. / THE MONEY VERSION** [ ] [-]
May 74. (7") **LOOK WHAT YOU DONE TO MY LIFE. / I'VE BEEN DEAD 400 YEARS** [ ] [ ]
1974. (lp)(c) **STRUGGLING MAN** [ ] [ ]
– Struggling man / When you're young / Better days are coming / Sooner or later / Those good old days / Can't stop worrying, can't stop loving you / Let's seize the time / I can't live without you / Going back west / Come on people.
Jul 74. (7") **MONEY WON'T SAVE YOU. / YOU CAN'T BE WRONG AND GET IT RIGHT** [ ] [-]
Nov 74. (7") **DON'T LET IT DIE. / ACTIONS SPEAK LOUDER THAN WORDS** [ ] [ ]
1974. (lp)(c) **HOUSE OF EXILE** [ ] [ ]
– Brother / I want to know / House of exile / Foolish pride / No.1 rip-off man / Long time no see / Music maker / My love is solid as a rock / You can't be wrong and get it right / Look what you do to my life, devil woman / Money won't save you / I've been dead 400 years. (US-title:- MUSIC MAKER) *(cd-iss.Dec95 on 'EMI Europe')*
1974. (7") **MUSIC MAKER. / YOU CAN'T BE WRONG AND GET RIGHT** [-] [ ]
1975. (lp)(c) **BRAVE WARRIOR** [ ] [-]
– My people / Bandwagon / Every tub / Don't let it die / Actions speak louder than words / A million teardrops / Brave warrior / Save a little loving / My people (reprise).
Sep 75. (7") **OH JAMAICA. / MILLION TEARDROPS** [ ] [-]
Reprise Reprise
Nov 75. (lp)(c) **FOLLOW MY MIND** [ ] [ ]
– Look at the mountains / The news / I'm gonna live, I'm gonna love / Going mad / Dear mother / Who feels it, knows it / Remake the world / No woman no cry / Wahjahka man / Hypocrite / If I follow my mind / You're the only one.
Apr 76. (7") **LOOK AT MY MOUNTAINS. / NO WOMAN NO CRY** [ ] [ ]
1976. (lp)(c) **LIVE IN CONCERT (live)** [ ] [ ]
– You can get it if you really want / Vietnam / Fountain of life / Many rivers to cross /

Wonderful world, beautiful people / Under the Sun, Moon and stars / Wild world / Sitting in limbo / Struggling man / The harder they come.

1976. (7") **HARDER THEY COME (live). / VIETNAM (live)** [-] [ ]

Warners Warners

1978. (lp)(c) **GIVE THANKX** [ ] [ ]
– Bongo man / Stand up and fight back / She is a woman / You left me standing by the door / Footprints / Medley in Afrika / Wanted man / Lonely street / Love I need / Universal love (beyond the boundaries).

Jan 79. (7") **STAND UP AND FIGHT BACK. / FOOTPRINTS** [ ] [ ]

Jun 80. (7") **ALL THE STRENGTH WE GOT. / LOVE AGAIN** [ ] [ ]

Jul 80. (lp)(c) **I AM THE LIVING** [ ] [ ]
– I am the living / Another summer / All the strength we got / It's the beginning of the end / Gone clear / Love again / Morning train / Satan's kingdom.

Oct 80. (7") **ANOTHER SUMMER. / SATAN'S KINGDOM** [ ] [ ]

Jan 81. (7") **ANOTHER SUMMER. / IT'S THE BEGINNING OF THE END** [-] [ ]

Sep 81. (lp)(c) **GIVE THE PEOPLE WHAT THEY WANT** [ ] [ ]
– Son of man / Give the people what they want / Experience / Shelter of your love / Majority rule / Let's turn the tables / Material world / World in trap / What are you doing with your life / My philosophy.

Sep (7") **MY PHILOSOPHY. / SHELTER OF YOUR LOVE** [-] [ ]

—— 1982 with backing group **ONENESS**

C.B.S. Columbia

Feb 82. (7")(12") **ROOTS RADICAL. / RUB-A-DUB PARTNER** [ ] [ ]

Jun 82. (7")(12") **PEACE OFFICER. / SPECIAL** [-] [ ]

Jul 82. (lp)(c) **SPECIAL** [ ] [ ]
– Special / Love is all / Peace officer / Treat the youths right / Keep on dancing / Rub-a-dub partner / Roots radical / Love heights / Originator / Rock children / Where there is love.

Jul 82. (7")(12") **MIDNIGHT ROCKERS. / TRUE LOVERS** [ ] [-]

Sep 82. (7") **SPECIAL. / KEEP ON DANCING (dub)** [ ] [-]

Jan 83. (7") **LOVE IS ALL. / ORIGINATOR / ROOTS RADICAL** [ ] [-]

Oct 83. (7") **REGGAE NIGHTS. / LOVE HEIGHTS** [ ] [-]
(12"+=) – ('A' instrumental)

Oct 83. (lp)(c) **THE POWER AND THE GLORY** [ ]
– We all are one / Sunshine in the music / Reggae nights / Piece of the pie / American dream / Roots woman / Love solution / The power and the glory / Journey. *(cd-iss.1988)*

Jan 84. (7") **WE ALL ARE ONE. / ROOTS WOMAN** [-] [ ]

Jan 84. (7") **WE ARE ALL ONE. / NO APOLOGY** [ ] [-]
(12"+=) – Piece of the pie.

Aug 84. (7") **REGGAE MOVEMENT. / TREAT THE YOUTHS RIGHT** [ ] [-]
(12"+=) – ('A'dub movement).

Jul 85. (7") **HOTSHOT. / MODERN WORLD** [ ] [-]
(12"+=) – Reggae night / ('A'instrumental).

Aug 85. (lp)(c)(cd) **CLIFF HANGER** [ ] [ ]
– Hitting with music / American sweet / Arrival / Brown eyes / Reggae street / Hot shot / Sunrise / Dead and awake / Now and forever / Nuclear war.

Aug 85. (7") **AMERICAN SWEET. / REGGAE MOVEMENT** [-] [ ]

1986. (7") **7-DAY WEEKEND (w/ ELVIS COSTELLO & THE ATTRACTIONS). / BRIGHTEST STAR** [-] [ ]

1986. (7") **CLUB PARADISE. / THIRD WORLD PEOPLE** [-] [ ]

In 1986, JIMMY starred in the film 'Club Paradise', and cont. on soundtrack.

Mar 88. (lp)(c)(cd) **HANGING FIRE** [ ] [ ]
– Love me love me / Hanging fire / Girls and cars / She was so right for me / It's time / Reggae down Babylon / Hold tight (eye for an eye) / Soar like an angel.

Mar 88. (7") **LOVE ME LOVE ME. / SUNSHINE IN THE MUSIC** [-] [ ]

Cliff not issued

Oct 89. (lp)(c)(cd) **IMAGES** [ ] [ ]

—— Below from the film 'Cool Runnings', featuring recently deceased John Candy. It was a UK No.5 hit in 1972 for JOHNNY NASH.

Columbia Chaos

Mar 94. (7")(c-s) **I CAN SEE CLEARLY NOW. / ('A'mix)** [23] [18] Oct93
(cd-s+=) – ('A'mix).

– compilations, others, etc. –

Note; All 'Island' releases below were issued on 'A&M' US.

1973. Island; (7") **MANY RIVERS TO CROSS. / WONDERFUL WORLD, BEAUTIFUL PEOPLE** [-] [ ]

Mar 76. Island; (lp)(c) **THE BEST OF JIMMY CLIFF** [ ] [ ]
– Hard road to travel / Sooner or later / Sufferin' in the land / Keep your eye on the sparrow / Struggling man / Wild world / Vietnam / Another cycle / Wonderful world, beautiful people / The harder they come / Let your yeah be yeah / Synthetic world / I'm no immigrant / Give and take / Many rivers to cross / Going back west / Sitting in limbo / Come into my life / You can get it if you really want / Goodbye yesterday. *(cd-iss.1988 on 'Mango')*

1976. Island; (7") **THE HARDER THEY COME. / LET YOUR YEAH BE YEAH** [ ] [-]

May 77. Island; (7") **YOU CAN GET IT IF YOU REALLY WANT. / MANY RIVERS TO CROSS** [ ] [-]

Jul 81. Island; (7") **WILD WORLD. / BE AWARE** [ ] [ ]

1985. Island; (lp)(c) **REGGAE GREATS** [ ] [-]
(cd-issJan91 on 'Mango')

May 88. Mango; (7") **WILD WORLD. / HARD ROAD TO TRAVEL** [ ] [-]

Apr 83. Old Gold; (7") **WONDERFUL WORLD, BEAUTIFUL PEOPLE. / ('Suzanne Beware Of The Devil' by Dandy Livingstone)** [ ] [-]

1983. Trojan; (12") **MANY RIVERS TO CROSS. / ?** [ ] [-]
(cd-issJun94 on 'Trojan')

Feb 87. See For Miles; (lp) **FUNDAMENTAL REGGAY** [ ] [-]
(re-iss.+cdJan91, extra tracks)

Feb 89. Greensleeves; (12") **PRESSURE (version). / ('B'by JOSEY WALES)** [ ] [-]

1971. Chrysalis; (7") **GOODBYE YESTERDAY. / BREAKDOWN** [ ] [-]

1971. Chrysalis; (7") **SYNTHETIC WORLD. / I GO TO PIECES** [ ] [-]

Jan 93. Ammi-JMS; (cd) **BREAKOUT** [ ] [-]

Feb 93. EMI; (cd)(c) **BORN TO WIN** [ ] [-]

Aug 94. Rhino; (cd) **LIVE (live)** [ ] [ ]

Feb 95. More Music; (cd) **THE COOL RUNNER LIVE IN LONDON** [ ] [-]

Aug 95. Sony Europe; (cd) **GOLD COLLECTION** [ ] [-]

CLIMAX BLUES BAND

Formed: Stafford, England . . . 1968 as sextet (see below). Signed to 'EMI' subsidiaries 'Parlophone' & 'Harvest' in 1969/70, but big break came in the mid 70's when the laid back COULDN'T GET IT RIGHT hit UK/US Top 10. Peaked at this time, but couldn't, at least in the UK, emulate success. • **Style:** As early group name suggests, they relied heavily on blues, but fused this with COOPER'S gruff, bassy type vocals and interspersed with HOLT's falsettos. Became very Americanised in the mid 70's and were most suitable for FM radio stations. • **Songwriters:** HAYCOCK, and group. Don't know of any covers. • **Trivia:** When JONES departed in 1969, he attained degree at Cambridge, also in theatre.

Recommended: COULDN'T GET IT RIGHT (*6)

PETER HAYCOCK (b. 4 Apr'52) – vocals, guitar / **RICHARD JONES** – bass / **ARTHUR WOODS** – keyboards / **COLIN COOPER** (b. 7 Oct'39) – vocals, saxophone / **DEREK HOLT** (b.26 Jan'49) – vocals / **GEORGE NEWSOME** (b.14 Aug'47) – drums

CLIMAX CHICAGO BLUES BAND

Parlophone Sire

Feb 69. (lp) **THE CLIMAX CHICAGO BLUES BAND** [ ] [ ]
– Mean old world / Insurance / Going down this road / You've been drinking / Don't start me takin' / Wee baby blues / Twenty past one / A stranger in your town / How many more years / Looking for my baby / And lonely / The entertainer. *(re-iss.+cdJun90)*

Aug 69. (7") **LIKE UNCLE CHARLIE. / LOVING MACHINE** [ ] [ ]

Jan 70. (lp)**PLAYS ON** [ ] [ ]
– Flight / Hey baby everything's gonna be alright yeah yeah yeah / Cubano chant / Little girl / Mum's the word / Twenty past two / Temptation rag / So many roads / City ways / Crazy 'bout my baby. *(re-iss.+cdJun90 on 'C5')*

—— **PETER FILLEUL** – keyboards repl. JONES (**HOLT** now on bass)

Harvest Sire

Nov 70. (7") **REAP WHAT I'VE SOWED. / SPOONFUL** [ ] [ ]

Dec 70. (lp) **A LOT OF BOTTLE** [ ] [ ]
– Country hat / Reap what I've sowed / Brief case / Alright blues? / Seventh son / Please don't help me / Morning, noon and night / Long lovin' man / Louisiana blues / Cut you loose. *(re-iss.+cdJun90+Apr93 on 'C5')*

CLIMAX CHICAGO

now without FILLEUL.

Aug 71. (7") **TOWARDS THE SUN. / EVERYDAY** [ ] [-]

Oct 71. (lp)(c) **TIGHTLY KNIT** [ ] [ ]
– Hey mama / Shoot her if she runs / Towards the Sun / Come on in my kitchen / Who killed McSwiggen / Little link / St.Michael's blues / Bide my time / That's all. *(re-iss.+cdJun90 on 'C5')*

Nov 71. (7") **HEY MAMA. / THAT'S ALL** [-] [ ]

—— **JOHN CUFFLEY** – drums repl. NEWSOME + WOOD.

Nov 72. (7") **MOLE ON THE DOLE. / LIKE UNCLE CHARLIE** [ ] [-]

Dec 72. (lp) **RICH MAN** [ ] [ ]
– Rich man / Mole on the dole / You make me sick / Standing by a river / Shake your love / All the time in the world / If you wanna know / Don't you mind people grinning in your face. *(re-iss.+cdJun90 on 'C5')*

Apr 73. (7") **SHAKE YOUR LOVE. / YOU MAKE ME SICK** [ ] [-]

May 73. (7") **SHAKE YOUR LOVE. / MOLE ON THE DOLE** [-] [ ]

CLIMAX BLUES BAND

Polydor Sire

Nov 73. (lp)(c) **FM LIVE (live)** [ ] [ ]
– All the time in the world / Flight / The seventh son / So many roads / So many trains / You make me sick / Shake your love / Goin' to New York. *(re-iss.+cd.Sep89 on 'See For Miles'+=) I am constant / Mesopopmania / Country hat / Let's work together.*

Jan 74. (7") **GOIN' TO NEW YORK. / I AM CONSTANT** [-] [ ]

Sep 74. (7") **SENSE OF DIRECTION. / BIRD TO WHISTLE** [ ] [-]

Sep 74. (7") **SENSE OF DIRECTION. / LOSIN' THE HUMBLES** [-] [ ]

Sep 74. (lp)(c) **SENSE OF DIRECTION** [ ] [37] Jun 74
– Amerita / Sense of direction / Losin' the humbles / Shopping bag people / Noagales / Reaching out / Right now / Before you reach the grave / Milwaukee truckin' blues.

Nov 74. (7") **REACHING OUT. / MILWAUKEE TRUCKIN' BLUES** [-] [ ]

—— **RICHARD JONES** – keyboards, guitar, vocals, returned.

B.T.M. Sire

Sep 75. (7") **USING THE POWER. / RUNNING OUT OF TIME** [-] [ ]

Sep 75. (lp)(c) **STAMP ALBUM** [ ] [69]
– Using the power / Mr.Goodtime / I am constant / Running out of time / Sky high / Rusty nail / The Devil knows / Loosen up / Spirit returning / Cobra.

Sep 76. (7") **COULDN'T GET IT RIGHT. / FAT MAYBELLENE** [10] [-]

Sep 76. (lp)(c) **GOLD-PLATED** [56] [27]
– Together and free / Mighty fire / Chasing change / Berlin blues / Couldn't get it right / Rollin' home / Sav'ry gravy / Extra.

Feb 77. (7") **SENSE OF DIRECTION. / LOSIN' THE HUMBLES** [-] [3]

Apr 77. (7") **GOIN' TO NEW YORK. / I AM CONSTANT** [-] [ ]

—— added the returning FILLEUL.

Warners Sire

Mar 78. (7") **WHEN TALKING IS TOO MUCH TROUBLE. / TAKE A HAND** [ ] [ ]

May 78. (lp)(c) **SHINE ON** | | 71 Apr 78
– Makin' love / Mistress moonshine / When talking is too much / The gospel singer / Watche feel / Teardrops / Like a movie / Champagne & rock and roll.
Jul 78. (7") **MAKIN' LOVE. / GOSPEL SINGER** | - | 91
Sep 78. (7") **MISTRESS MOONSHINE. / TEARDROPS** | - |

— Trimmed again (HAYCOCK, COOPER, HOLT, FILLEUL & CUFFLEY),when JONES left.

Apr 79. (7") **LONG DISTANCE LOVE. / CHILDREN OF THE NIGHTTIME** | - |
Jun 79. (lp)(c) **REAL TO REAL** | |
– Summer rain / Money in your pocket / Children of the nightime / Long distance love / Lovin' wheel / Fallen in love (for the very last time) / Fat city / Crazy world.
Jun 79. (7") **SUMMER RAIN. / MONEY IN YOUR POCKET** | - |

— FILLEUL now left again.

Warners | Warners

Nov 80. (7") **GOTTA HAVE MORE LOVE. / ONE FOR ME AND YOU** | |
Feb 81. (lp)(c) **FLYING THE FLAG** | | 75
– Gotta have more love / So good after midnight / Horizontalized / I love you / Hold on to your heart / Dance the night away / Money talking / Black Jack and me / Nothing but starlight / One for me and you.
Feb 81. (7") **DANCE THE NIGHT AWAY. / BLACKJACK AND ME** | |
Jun 81. (7") **I LOVE YOU. / HORIZONTALIZED** | | 12 Feb 81
Oct 81. (lp)(c) **LUCKY FOR SOME** | |
– Victim / Cutting up rough / Shake it lucky / Oceans apart / Breakdown / Darlin' / This time you're the singer / Last chance saloon / They'd never believe us.
Nov 81. (7") **DARLIN'. / THIS TIME YOU'RE THE SINGER** | - |
Feb 82. (7") **BREAKDOWN. / SHAKE IT LUCY** | - |

— **COOPER, HAYCOCK** were joined by **GEORGE GLOVER** – keyboards / **HENRY SPINETTI** – drums / **DAVE MARKEE** – bass. HOLT teamed up with STEWART COPELAND (The POLICE).

Virgin | Virgin

Feb 83. (7") **LISTEN TO THE NIGHT. / CHURCH** | |
Mar 83. (lp)(c) **SAMPLE AND HOLD** | |
– Friends in high places / Sign of the times / Walking on sunset / Shine / Movie queen / Heaven and Hell / Listen to the night / Doin' alright / I'm ready / The end of the seven seas.

PETER HAYCOCK'S CLIMAX

w/**GEOFF CASTLE** – keyboards / **LIVINGSTONE BROWNE** – bass / **PETE THOMPSON** – drums.

Nu Disk | not issued

Jun 85. (7") **SUNBIRD. / IRRESISTABLE FORCES** | | -
Jun 85. (lp)(c) **TOTAL CLIMAX** | | -
Oct 85. (7") **YOUNG EXECUTIVE. / MEAN STREAK** | | -
1986 (lp)(cd) **THE SOFT SPOT** | | -
– The soft spot / Voodoo lady / Big fish / (Give me back my) honey / Tell me that you want me / Love's just (a part of the blues) / A matter of timing / The hurt stays home / Communication.

PETER HAYCOCK

I.R.S. | I.R.S.

Feb 88. (lp)(c)(cd) **GUITAR AND SON** | |
– Liberty / Lucienne / Spikes / Terry Anne / Dr. Brown I pressume / Down to Bay six / The claymore / Rebecca / The New York stakes / Follow that fog.
May 88. (7") **LUCIENNE. / THE CLAYMORE** | | -

— In Apr'89, HAYCOCK appeared on Various Artists live d-lp,c,cd,video 'NIGHT OF THE GUITAR', which incl. 'LUCIENNE' & 'DR.BROWN I PRESSUME', etc.

CLIMAX BLUES BAND

together in the studio again, after still constantly touring. Their new guitarist is **LES HUNT**

Clay | not issued

Aug 88. (7") **COULDN'T GET IT RIGHT ('88 mix). / THE DECEIVER** | | -
Dec 88. (lp)(c)(cd) **DRASTIC STEPS** | | -
– California sunshine / Lonely avenue / The deceiver / Ordinary people / The winner / Couldn't get it right / Fool for the bright times / Good times / Trouble / American dream. (cd+=) *(red-lp iss.Jul89 on 'Sonic') (cd-iss.Dec92 on 'C5' w/extra tracks) – Couldn't get it right (88 mix).*
May 89. (7") **THE WINNER. / ?** | | -

— Disbanded again, after above. HAYCOCK joined ELO II in the early 90's

PETE HAYCOCK BAND

New Note | New Note

Nov 92. (cd) **LIVIN' IT** | |
– Come on in my kitchen – Country hatslide solo (medley) / Liberty / So many roads / Communication / The thrill is gone / Lucienne / Dr.Brown, I pressume / Blackjack and me.

– compilations, others, etc. –

1975. Harvest; (lp)(c) **THE HARVEST YEARS 1969-1972** | | -
(cd-iss.Jul91 w.extra tracks)
1983. R.C.A.; (lp) **THE BEST OF . . .(TAKE OFF)** | | -
Mar 84. See For Miles; (lp)(c) **LOOSEN UP 1974-1976** | | -
Nov 86. Old Gold; (7") **COULDN'T GET IT RIGHT. / (B side by 'Al Stewart')** | | -
Nov 87. C5; (lp)(c)(cd) **COULDN'T GET IT RIGHT** | | -
– Couldn't get it right / Berlin blues / Chasing change / Losin' the humbles / Shopping bag people / Sense of direction / Before you reach the grave / Sky high / Loosen up / Running out of time / Mr.Goodtime / I am constant / Mighty fire. (cd+=) – Reaching out / Right now / Cobra / Rollin' home / Sav'ry gravy.
Jun 93. Optima; (cd)(c) **LIVE AND DANGEROUS (live)** | | -
Jan 94. H.T.D.; (cd)(c) **BLUES FROM THE ATTIC** | |
Nov 94. Repertoire; (cd) **25 YEARS** | | -

George CLINTON

Born:22 Jul'40, Kannapolis, N.Carolina, USA, but raised in Newark, New Jersey. Released a couple of singles in the 1955 with doo-wop PARLIAMENTS before moving to Detroit and recording for 'Gordy (Tamla Motown)' in 1962. Unsuccessful to land deal, they issued one-off 45 'THAT WAS MY GIRL' for 'Golden World' in 1965. CLINTON also continued to write material for Motown, until 1967, when he added new image and musicians to line-up. Signed to 'Revilot' in the States, they then hit Top20 with single '(I WANNA) TESTIFY'. After a series of flops, he was stopped temporarily by Motown writers HOLLAND-DOZIER-HOLLAND from using PARLIAMENT'S name. By the late 60's, the group had evolved into FUNKADELIC. They signed to 'Westbound' and after a few minor hits, CLINTON also re-actified PARLIAMENT set-up, with nearly the same musicians. In 1971, they signed to 'Invictus' label, and simultaneously issued own releases under that name. Over the next several years The 'Parliafunkadelicament Thang', grew into large musical corporation that featured over 35 members. In the mid-late 70's, PARLIAMENT (now on 'Casablanca' records), scored with 5 US Top30 albums, initiated by their 1976 single 'TEAR THE ROOF OFF THE SUCKER'. Meanwhile in '78, FUNKADELIC (now on 'Warners') scored with hit album title track 'ONE NATION UNDER A GROOVE'. Throughout the 80's, they/CLINTON were synonymous with giving new attitude to funk and rock. • **Style:** As said, but with also extravagant stage shows, featuring sci-fi technical effects combining with cartoon-strip like characters/musicians. • **Songwriters:** CLINTON was main inspiration, producer, arranger, etc. CLINTON also wrote/co-wrote most of material. He covered SUNSHINE OF YOUR LOVE (Cream). • **Trivia:** In 1985, he collaborated with THOMAS DOLBY on 'DOLBY'S CUBE' single 'May The Cube Be With You'. Breakaway splinter groups were another part of saga: In the 70's, FRED WESLEY had been part of The JB'S (ex-JAMES BROWN musicians). FUNKADELIC bassist BOOTSY COLLINS, formed BOOTSY'S RUBBER BAND in 1976, and they released several albums before disarming. Note: – An entirley different George Clinton surprised us with 'ABC' release 'Please Don't Run From Me'.

Recommended: PARLIAMENT LIVE – P FUNK EARTH TOUR (*7) / FUNKADELIC (*7) /

The PARLIAMENTS

GEORGE CLINTON – vox / **CHARLES BUTCH DAVIS** – vocals / **CALVIN SIMON** – vocals repl. GENE BOYKIN / **ROBERT LAMBERT** – vocals repl. HERBIE JENKINS / **GRADY THOMAS** – vocals repl. DANNY MITCHELL

not iss. | Hull-/Apt

May 59. (7") **POOR WILLIE. / PARTY BOYS** | - |

— **JOHNNY MURRAY** repl. LAMBERT

not issued | Flipp

1959. (7") **LONELY ISLAND. / (YOU MAKE ME WANNA) CRY** | - |

not issued | Symbol

1961. (7") **I'LL GET YOU YET. / YOU'RE CUTE** | - |

not issued | U.S.A.

1961. (7") **MY ONLY LOVE. / TO BE ALONE** | - |

— Spent 4 years writing for Motown . . . then sign to (see below)

— **CLARENCE 'Fuzzy' HASKINS** – vocals repl. JOHNNY MURRAY + CALVIN SIMON **RAYMOND DAVIS** – vocals repl. BUTCH DAVIS

not issued | Golden World

1966. (7") **HEART TROUBLE. / THAT WAS MY GIRL** | - |

— added **EDDIE HAZEL** – lead guitar / **TAWL ROSS** – rhythm guitar / **BILLY NELSON** – bass / **MICKEY ATKINS** – organ (on some) / **TIKI FULWOOD** – drums

not issued | Revilot

Jun 67. (7") **(I WANNA) TESTIFY. / I CAN FEEL THE ICE MELTING** | - | 20
Sep 67. (7") **ALL YOUR GOODIES ARE GONE (THE LOSER'S SEAT). / DON'T BE SORE AT ME** | - | 80
Nov 67. (7") **THE GOOSE (THAT LAID THE GOLDEN EGG). / LITTLE MAN** | - |
Jan 68. (7") **LOOK AT WHAT I ALMOST MISSED. / WHAT YOU BEEN GROWING** | - |
Nov 68. (7") **A NEW DAY BEGINS. / I'LL WAIT** | - |
(re-iss.Jan69 on 'Atco', hit US No.44)

ROSE WILLIAMS

with GEORGE CLINTON & FUNKEDELICS.
12 years later, this song was to give CLINTON rights to group name.

not issued | Funkedelic

1969. (7") **WHATEVER MAKES MY BABY FEEL GOOD. / ('A'instrumental)** | - |

FUNKADELIC

BERNIE WORRELL – keyboards repl. ATKINS

Pye Int. | Westbound

1969. (7") **MUSIC FOR MY MOTHER. / ('A'instrumental)** | - |

Sep 69. (7") **I'LL BET YOU. / QUALIFY AND SATISFY** - 63

Apr 70. (7") **I GOT A THING, YOU GOT A THING, EVERYBODY'S GOT A THING. / FISH, CHIPS & SWEAT** 80 Feb 70

Sep 70. (lp) **FUNKADELIC** Mar 70
– Mommy, what's a Funkadelic? / I'll bet you / What is soul? / Music for my mother / I got a thing, you got a thing, everybody's got a thing / Good old music / Quality and satisfaction / What is soul?. *(re-iss.+c+cd.Aug89 on 'Westbound')*

Dec 70. (7") **I WANNA KNOW IF IT'S GOOD TO YOU. / ('A'instrumental)** - 81

1971. (lp) **FREE YOUR MIND ... AND YOUR ASS WILL FOLLOW** 92 Oct 70
– Free your mind and your ass will follow / Friday night, August 14th / Funky dollar bill / I wanna know if it's good to you / Some more / Eulogy and light. *(re-iss.+cd+c.Feb90 on 'Westbound')*

Apr 71. (7") **YOU AND YOUR FOLKS, ME AND MINE. / FUNKY DOLLAR BILL** 91 Feb 71

PARLIAMENT

(i.e. **CLINTON & FUNKADELIC** musicians) + **R.DAVIS / G.THOMAS / F.HASKINS / C.SIMON**

Invictus Invictus

1971. (7") **I CALL MY BABY PUSSYCAT. / LITTLE OLE COUNTRY BOY** -
(UK-iss.Dec84 on 'H.D.H.')

Apr 71. (lp) **OSMIUM** Dec 70
– The breakdown / Call my baby Pussycat / Little ole country boy / Moonshine Heather / Oh Lord – why Lord – prayer / Red hot mama / My automobile / Nothing before me but thang / Funky woman / Come on in out of the rain / The silent boatman. *(re-iss.+cd.Feb90 as 'RHENIUM' on 'H.D.H.' label with extra tracks)(cd-iss.Jul93).*

May 71. (7") **LIVIN' THE LIFE. / THE SILENT BOATMAN** Dec 70

Jul 71. (7") **THE BREAKDOWN. / LITTLE OLE COUNTRY BOY** -

Sep 71. (7") **COME IN OUT OF THE RAIN. / LITTLE OLE COUNTRY BOY**

FUNKADELIC

Now without NELSON + ROSS. Replaced by **GARY SHIDER** – guitar

Westbound Westbound

Sep 71. (7") **CAN YOU GET TO THAT. / BACK IN OUR MINDS** - 93

Sep 71. (lp) **MAGGOT BRAIN** Aug 71
– Maggot brain / Can you get to that / Hit it and quit it / You and your folks, me and mine / Super stupid / Back in our minds / Wars of armageddon. *(re-iss.+c+cd.Aug89)*

— added **WILLIAM BOOTSY COLLINS** – bass / **CATFISH COLLINS** – guitar / **FRANKIE 'Kash' WADDY** – drums (all of The J.B.'s, ex-JAMES BROWN)

Jul 72. (d-lp) **AMERICA EATS IT'S YOUNG** -
– You hit the nail on the head / If you don't like the effects / Don't produce the cause / Everybody is going to make it this time / A joyful process / We hurt too / Loose booty / Philmore / I call my baby Pussycat / America eats its young / Biological speculation / That was my girl / Balance / Miss Lucifer's love / Wake up. *(cd-iss.Jul90 on 'Westbound-Ace')*

1972. (7") **I MISS MY BABY. / BABY I OWE YOU SOMETHING GOOD** -

1972. (7") **HIT AND QUIT IT. / A WHOLE LOT OF BS** -

1973. (7") **LOOSE BOOTY. / A JOYFUL PROCESS** -

Jul 73. (lp) **COSMIC SLOP** -
– Happy dug out / You can't miss what you can't measure / March to the witches castle / Let's make it last / Cosmic slop / No compute (alias spit don't make no babies) / Broken heart / Trash a go-go / Can't stand the strain. *(re-iss.+cd+c.Feb91)*

1973. (7") **COSMIC SLOP. / YOU DON'T LIKE THE EFFECTS, DON'T PRODUCE THE CAUSE** -

— added **FRED WESLEY & MACEO PARKER** – horns (both of J.B.'s)

Nov 74. (lp) **STANDING ON THE VERGE OF GETTING IT ON** - Sep 74
– Red hot mama / Alice in my fantasies / I'll stay / Sexy ways / Standing on the verge of getting it on / Jimmy's got a little bit of bitch in him / Good thoughts, bad thoughts. *(re-iss.+cd+c.Aug91)*

Nov 74. (7") **(STANDING) ON THE VERGE OF GETTING IT ON. / JIMMY'S GOT A LITTLE BIT OF BITCH IN HIM** -

1975. (7") **RED HOT MAMA. / VITAL JUICES** -

1975. (lp) **FUNKADELIC'S GREATEST HITS** (compilation) - Jul 74

20th Cent Westbound

Jun 75. (lp) **LET'S TAKE IT TO THE STAGE**
– Good to your earhole / Better by the pound / Be my beach / No head no backstage pass / Let's take it to the stage / Get off your ass and jam / Baby I owe you something good / Stuffs & things / The song is familiar / Atmosphere. *(cd-iss.Mar92 on 'Westbound-Ace')*

Oct 75. (7") **BETTER BY THE POUND. / STUFFS AND THINGS** - 99

Jan 76. (7") **LET'S TAKE IT TO THE STAGE. / BIOLOGICAL SPECULATION** -

— **MIKE HAMPTON** – guitar repl. EDDIE HAZEL who went solo

1976. (lp) **TALES OF KIDD FUNKADELIC** -
– Butt to butt resuscitation / Let's take it to the people / Undisco kid / Take your dead ass home / I'm never gonna tell it / Takes of Kidd Funkadelic / How do yeaw view you. *(cd-iss.Mar93)*

1976. (7") **UNDISCO KIDD. / HOW DO YEAW VIEW YOU** -

— After one more compilation 'THE BEST OF FUNKADELIC EARLY YEARS, VOL.1' in 1977, COLLINS continued with BOOTSY'S RUBBER BAND. Also leaving were HASKINS, SIMON and DAVIS who were to form own FUNKADELIC in the early 80's. They and 'Lax' label issued album CONNECTIONS AND DISCONNECTIONS (without CLINTON).

— Meanwhile in the mid-70's,

PARLIAMENT

(**CLINTON, etc.**) were signed to . . .

Casablanca Casablanca

Dec 74. (7") **THE GOOSE (pt.1). / (pt.2)** -

Dec 74. (lp)(c) **UP FOR THE DOWN STROKE** Aug 74
– Up for the down stroke / (I wanna) Testify / The goose / I can move you (if you let me) / I just got back / All your goodies are gone / Whatever makes baby feel good / Presence of a brain. *(re-iss.May77 & Nov78)*

Feb 75. (7") **UP FOR THE DOWN STROKE. / PRESENCE OF A BRAIN** 63 Aug 74

1975. (7") **TESTIFY. / I CAN MOVE YOU (IF YOU LET ME)** -

May 75. (7") **CHOCOLATE CITY. / ('A'long version)** - 94

Jun 75. (lp)(c) **CHOCOLATE CITY** 91 Apr 75
– Chocolate city / Ride on / Together / Side effects / What comes funky / Let me be / If it don't fit (don't force it) / Misjudged you / Big footin'. *(re-iss.May77)*

1975. (7") **RIDE ON. / BIG FOOTIN'** -

Jun 76. (7") **P.FUNK (WANTS TO GET FUNKED UP). / NIGHT OF THE THUMPASORUS PEOPLES** -

Jun 76. (lp)(c) **MOTHERSHIP CONNECTION** 13 Feb 76
– P.Funk (wants to get funked up) / Mothership connection (star child) / Unfunky UFO / Supergroovalisticprosifunkstication (the thumps bump) / Handcuffs / Tear the roof off the sucker (give up the funk) / Night of the thumpasorus people. *(re-iss.May77 & Aug87)*

Jun 76. (7") **TEAR THE ROOF OFF THE SUCKER (GIVE UP THE FUNK). / P.FUNK (WANTS TO GET FUNKED UP)** 15 May 76

1976. (7") **STAR CHILD. / SUPERGROOVALISTICPROSIFUNKSTACATION (THE THUMPS BUMB)** -

Oct 76. (7")(12") **DO THAT STUFF. / HANDCUFFS** -

May 77. (lp)(c) **THE CLONES OF DR.FUNKENSTEIN** 20 Oct 76
– Prelude / Gamin' on ya / Dr.Funkenstein / Children of productions / Gettin' to know you / Do that stuff / Everything is on the one / I've been watching you (move your sexy body) / Funkin' for fun. *(re-iss.+cd.Feb91)*

Jan 77. (7") **DR.FUNKENSTEIN. / CHILDREN OF PRODUCTION** -

May 77. (7"m) **TEAR THE ROOF OFF THE SUCKER (GIVE UP THE FUNK). / DR.FUNKENSTEIN / P.FUNK (WANTS TO GET FUNKED UP)** -

Jun 77. (d-lp)(d-c) **PARLIAMENT LIVE - P.FUNK EARTH TOUR (live)** 29 May 77
– P.Funk (wants to get funked up) / Dr.Funkenstein's supergroovalisticprosifunkstication / Medley (a) Let's take it to the stage (b) Take your dead ass home (c) Say som'n nasty / Do that stuff / The landing (of the holy mothership) / The undisco Kidd (the girl is bad) / Children of production / Mothership connection (star child) / Swing down, sweet chariot / This is the way we funk with you (featuring Mike Hampton; lead snare) / Dr.Funkenstein / Gamin' on you / Tear the roof off the sucker medley:- (a) Give up the funk (tear the roof off the sucker) (b) Get off your ass and jam / Night of the thumpasorus people / Fantasy is reality.

1977. (7") **FANTASY IS REALITY. / THE LANDING (OF THE HOLY MOTHERSHIP)** -

Dec 77. (lp)(c) **FUNKENTELECHY VS. THE PLACEBO SYNDROME** 13
– Bop gun (endangered species) / Sir Nose D'voidoffunk / Pay attention B-3M / Wizard of finance / Funkentelechy / Placebo syndrome / Flash light.

Jan 78. (7") **BOP GUN (ENDANGERED SPECIES). / I'VE BEEN WATCHING YOU (MOVE YOUR SEXY BODY)** Nov 77
(12"+=) – Do that stuff. *(US 12" has 2 'A'mixes)*

Apr 78. (7") **FLASH LIGHT. / SWING DOWN SWEET CHARIOT (live)** - 16 Feb 78
(US-12") – (2 'A'mixes).

1978. (7") **FUNKENTELECHY (part 1). / (part 2)** -

— Early '78, other PARLIAMENT / FUNKADELIC off-shoots "PARLET" (vocalists MALLIA FRANKLIN, JEANETTE WASHINGTON and SHIRLEY HAYDEN) released album 'THE PLEASURE PRINCIPLE'. Another album 'INVASIONS OF THE BODY SNATCHERS' was further issued Jul 79. "The BRIDES OF FUNKENSTEIN" (vocalists LYNN MABRY and DAWN SILVA) released album 'FUNK OR WALK' on 'Atlantic' late 1978.

FUNKADELIC

meanwhile had reappeared signing to . . .

Warners Warners

1977. (7") **COMIN' ROUND THE MOUNTAIN. / IF YOU GOT FUNK, YOU GOT STYLE** -

Feb 78. (lp)(c) **HARDCORE JOLLIES** 96 Nov 77
– Osmosis phase one / Comin' round the mountain / Smokey / If you got funk, you got style / Hardcore jollies / Terribitus phase two / Sould mate / Cosmic slop / You scared the lovin' outta me / Adolescent funk. *(re-iss.+cd.Jul93 on 'Charly')*

Feb 78. (7") **SMOKEY. / SOUL MATE** -

— add **JEROME BRAILEY** – drums (who had joined PARLIAMENT mid '76) / **WALTER 'JUNIE' MORRISON** – keyboards (ex-OHIO PLAYERS)

Nov 78. (7") **ONE NATION UNDER A GROOVE (part 1). / (part 2)** 9 28 Oct 78

Dec 78. (lp)(c) **ONE NATION UNDER A GROOVE** 56 16 Sep 78
– One nation under a groove / Groovallegience / Who says a funk band can't play rock / Promentalashitbackwashipsychosisenema squad / Into you / Cholly (funk getting ready to roll) / Lunchmeat and phobia / P.E.squad / Doodoo chasers / Maggot brain. *(re-iss.+cd.Jul93 on 'Charly')*

Apr 79. (7") **CHOLLY (GETTING READY TO ROLL). / INTO YOU**
(US-12") – (2 'A'mixes).

— drummer BRAILEY left to form own group MUTINY.

Oct 79. (lp)(c) **UNCLE JAM WANTS YOU** 18
– Freak of the week / (Not just) Knee deep / Uncle Jam / Field manoeuvres / Cholly wants to go to California / Foot soldiers.

Jan 80. (7") **(NOT JUST) KNEE DEEP. / (part 2)** 77 Oct 79

1980. (7") **UNCLE JAM. / (part 2)** -

Aug 81. (12") **THE ELECTRIC SPANKING OF WAR BABIES. / THE ELECTRIC SPANKING (instrumental)**

Apr 81. (lp)(c) **THE ELECTRIC SPANKING OF WAR BABIES**

– The electric spanking of war babies / Electrocuties / Funk gets stronger / Brettino's bounce / She loves you / Shockwaves / Oh, I / Laka-prick.

1981. (7") **SHOCKWAVES. / BRETTINO'S BOUNCE** [-] [ ]

— (above featured CLINTON's long-time friend SLY STONE)

— The FUNKADELIC project had now been abandoned, due to splinter band.

PARLIAMENT

were still around simultaneously with FUNKADELIC and continued throughout the 80's.

Casablanca Casablanca

Dec 78. (7") **AQUA BOOGIE (A PSYCHOALPHADISCOBETABIOQUADOLOOP). / (YOU'RE A FISH AND I'M A) WATER SIGN** [ ] [89]

Dec 78. (lp)(c)(pic-lp) **MOTOR-BOOTY AFFAIR** [ ] [23]
– Mr.Wiggles / Rumpopsteelskin / (You're a fish and I'm a) Water sign / Aqua boogie (a psychoalphadiscobetabioquadoloop) / One of those funky things / Liquid sunshine / Motor-booty affair / Deep. *(re-iss.+cd.Feb91)*

1979. (7") **RUMPOPSTEELSKIN. / LIQUID SUNSHINE** [-] [ ]

Jul 79. (7")(12") **DEEP. / FLASH LIGHT** [ ] [-]

Dec 79. (lp)(c) **GLORYHALLASTOOPID – OR PIN THE TALE ON THE FUNKY** [-] [44]
– Party people / Big bang theory / Freeze (sizzaleenmean) / Colour me funky / Theme from the black hole / May we bang you / Gloryhallastoopid (or pin the tale on the funky).

Jan 80. (12") **THEME FROM THE BLACK HOLE. / THE BIG BANG THEORY** [ ] [-]

Apr 80. (7") **PARTY PEOPLE. / ('A'reprise)** [ ] [ ] 1979
(12") – ('A'side) / Tear the roof off the sucker (give up the funk) / Flash light.

Apr 81. (7")(12") **AGONY OF DE FEET. / THE FREEZE (SIZZALEENMEAN)** [ ] [ ]

Apr 81. (lp)(c) **TROMBIPULATION** [-] [61] Jan 81
– Trombipulation / crush it / Long way round / Agony of de feet / Now doo review / Let's play house / Body language / Peck-a-groove. *(re-iss.+cd.Feb91)*

— PARLIAMENT were also defunkt, leaving behind a few exploitation releases

1981. (12") **CRUSH IT. / BODY LANGUAGE** [-] [ ]

GEORGE CLINTON

(solo) with numerous session people and **BOOTSY COLLINS / FRED WESLEY**

A.B.C. not iss?

Apr 75. (7") **PLEASE DON'T RUN FROM ME. / LIFE AND BREATH** [ ] [ ]

Capitol Capitol

Nov 82. (lp)(c) **COMPUTER GAMES** [ ] [40]
– Get dressed / Man's best friend / Loopzilla / Pot sharing tots / Computer games / Atomic dog / Free alterations / One fun at a time.

Nov 82. (7") **LOOPZILLA. / POT SHARING TOTS** [57] [ ]
(12"+=) – ('A'broadcast version). (US-12") – (2 'A'version)

Feb 83. (7") **ATOMIC DOG. / MAN'S BEST FRIEND** [ ] [ ]
(12"+=) – ('A'instrumental). (US B-side ='A'instrumental). *(US re-iss.1984)*

1983. (7") **GET DRESSED. / FREE ALTERATIONS** [-] [ ]

Dec 83. (7")(12") **NIBIAN NUT. / FREE ALTERATIONS** [ ] [ ]

Jan 84. (lp)(c) **YOU SHOULDN'T NUF BIT FISH** [ ] [ ] Dec83
– Nubian nut / Quickie / Last dance / Silly millameter / Stingy / You shouldn't – Nuf bit fish. *(cd-iss.Sep91 on 'E.M.I.')*

1984. (7")(12") **QUICKIE. / LAST DANCE** [-] [ ]

1984. (7")('A'extended-12") **LAST DANCE. / LAST DANCE (version)** [-] [ ]

Jul 85. (7") **DOUBLE OH-OH. / BANGLADESH** [ ] [ ]
(12"+=) – ('A'version).

Sep 85. (lp)(c) **SOME OF MY JOKES ARE FRIENDS** [ ] [ ] Aug 85
– Some of my best jokes are friends / Double oh-oh / Bulletproof / Pleasures of exhaustion (do it till I drop) / Bodyguard / Bangladesh / Thrashin' / Some of my best jokes are friends – reprise.

Dec 85. (7")(12") **BULLETPROOF. / SILLY MILLAMETER** [-] [ ]

Apr 86. (7") **DO FRIES GO WITH THAT SHAKE. / PLEASURES OF EXHAUSTION (DO IT TILL I DROP)** [57] [ ]
(UK-12"+=) – Scratch medley. (US-12") – (2 'A'versions).

Did he release IRON EAGLE (Soundtrack) album around this time?

May 86. (7")('A'ext.-12") **HEY GOOD LOOKIN'. / ('A'mix)** [-] [ ]

May 86. (lp)(c) **R&B SKELETONS (IN THE CLOSET)** [-] [ ]
– Hey good looking / Do fries go with that shake / Mix master suite – Startin' from scratch – Counter irritant – Nothing left to burn – Electric Pygmies – Intense – Cool Joe – R&B Skeleton (in the closet). *(cd-iss.Sep91 on 'E.M.I.')*

1986. (7") **R&B SKELETONS IN THE CLOSET. / NUBIAN NUT** [-] [-]

1987. (lp)(c) **THE BEST OF GEORGE CLINTON & THE MOTHERSHIP CONNECTION LIVE FROM HOUSTON (live)** [-] [ ]
– Atomic dog / R&B Skeleton (in the closet) / Quickie / Do fries go with that shake / Hey good lookin' / Double oh-oh / Nubian nut / Last dance.

Paisley P. Paisley P.

Jul 89. (7")(12") **WHY SHOULD I DOG U OUT (part 1). / (part 2)** [ ] [ ]

Aug 89. (lp)(c)(cd) **THE CINDERELLA THEORY** [ ] [ ]
– Airbound / Tweakin' / The Cinderella theory / Why should I dog you out? / Serious slammin' / There I go again / (She's got it) Goin' on / The banana boat song / French kiss / Rita bewitched / Kredit-Kard / Airbound (reprise).

1989. (7") **TWEAKIN'. / FRENCH KISS** [-] [ ]
(12") – ('A'side) / Hysterical / ('A'remix).

Oct 93. (cd)(c) **HEY MAN, SMELL MY FINGER** [ ] [ ]
– Martial law / Paint the White House black / Way up / Dis beat disrupts / Get satisfied / Hollywood / Rhythm and rhyme / The big pump / If true love / High in my hello / Maximumisness / Kickback / The flag was still there / Martial law (hey man . . . smell my finger) (single version). *(re-iss.Mar95 on 'NPG')*

— CLINTON guested for PRIMAL SCREAM on their early 1994 album 'GIVE OUT BUT DON'T GIVE UP'. To start the second half of '94, he featured on ICE CUBE single 'BOP GUN (ONE NATION) ', a re-indition of his old FUNKADELIC number.

Essential Rykodisc

Feb 95. (cd) **FIFTH OF FUNK** [ ] [ ]

PARLIAMENT, FUNKADELIC & THE P-FUNK ALL STARS

Hot Hands Hot Hands

Apr 95. (12")(c-s)(cd-s) **FOLLOW THE LEADER. / ('A'-D&S radio mix) / ('A'-Kool az phuk mix)** [ ] [ ]

May 95. (cd)(c) **DOPE DOGS** [ ] [ ]

– (GEORGE CLINTON compilations) –

Aug 92. Castle; (cd)(c)(lp) **FAMILY SERIES – VOL.1** [ ] [-]

Jun 93. Essential; (cd)(c)(lp) **FAMILY SERIES PART 3 – P IS THE FUNK** [ ] [ ]
– (his productions, etc.)

Feb 93. M.O.L.; (cd)(lp) **SAMPLE A BIT OF DISC AND A BIT OF DAT** [ ] [ ]

Oct 93. M.O.L.; (cd)(lp) **SAMPLE SOME OF DISC II** [ ] [ ]

– (PARLIAMENT) compilations –

Sep 86. Club; (lp)(c) **UNCUT FUNK – THE BOMB (THE BEST OF PARLIAMENT)** [ ] [-]

May 93. Mercury; (d-cd) **TEAR THE ROOF OFF: 1974-80** [ ] [ ]
(re-iss.Sep95)

Oct 94. Goldmine; (cd) **I WANNA TESTIFY** [ ] [ ]

Apr 95. Hot Hands; (cd)(c)(d-lp) **HOT HANDS** (PARLIAMENT / FUNKADELIC / P FUNK ALL STARS) [ ] [-]

Jun 95. Westbound; (cd)(lp) **HYDRAULIC FUNK** [ ] [-]

Sep 95. Mercury; (cd) **GIVE UP THE FUNK** [ ] [-]

FUNKADELIC

not issued M.C.A.

1989. (12") **BY THE WAY OF THE DRUM. / ('A'edit) / ('A'instrumental)** [-] [ ]

– (FUNKADELIC) compilations –

Mar 94. Westbound; (4xpic-cd-box) **PICTURE DISC BOXED SET VOLUME 2** [ ] [ ]

Mar 94. Charly; (cd)(c) **THE BEST OF FUNKADELIC 1976-1981** [ ] [-]

Nov 94. Charly; (cd) **HARDCORE FUNK JAM** [ ] [-]

Oct 94. Sequel; (4xcd-box) **PARLIAMENT /FUNKADELIC LIVE (live)** [ ] [-]

COAL PORTERS (see under ⇒ LONG RYDERS)

Billy COBHAM

Born: 16 May'44, Panama. Raised in New York City, where in 1967 he gigged with BILLY TAYLOR and The NEW YORK JAZZ SEXTET. He soon joined MILES DAVIS group, and played on 3 lp's, before joining DREAMS. This outfit who included MICHAEL & RANDY BRECKER, EDWARD VERNON and BARRY ROGERS, released 2 albums for 'Columbia'; DREAMS (1970) + IMAGINE MY SURPRISE (1971). He also sessioned for many artists and fitted time in for a spell with JOHN McLAUGHLIN's MAHAVISHNU ORCHESTRA. COBHAM's first solo outing in 1973 'SPECTRUM', gave him first of several US hit albums. • **Style:** Jazz-rock power drummer percussionist, with identifiable sound, which has been employed by many. • **Songwriters:** Own compositions. • **Trivia:** In the 70s, he produced AIRTO (Virgin Land) + DAVID SANCIOUS (Forest of Feelings).

Recommended: THE BEST OF BILLY COBHAM (*6).

BILLY COBHAM – percussion, drums (ex-MAHAVISHNU ORCHESTRA, ex-LARRY CORYELL) with **TOMMY BOLIN** – guitar / **JOHN TROPEA** – guitar / **JAN HAMMER** – keyboards / **RON CARTER** – bass / **JOE FARRELL** – wind / **RAY BARRETTO** – congas

Atlantic Atlantic

Jan 74. (lp)(c) **SPECTRUM** [ ] [26] Nov 73
– Quadrant 4 / Searching for the right door / Spectrum – Anxiety / Taurian matador / Stratus / To the women in my life – Le lis – Snoopy's search / Red baron. *(re-iss.1988) (cd-iss.Feb93)*

Feb 74. (7") **STRATUS (pt.1). / STRATUS (pt.2)** [ ] [ ]

— now with **JOHN ABERCROMBIE** – guitar / **MILCHO LEVIEV** – keyboards / **ALEX BLAKE** – bass / **RANDY + MICHAEL BRECKER** – horns / **GLEN FERRIS** – trombone

May 74. (lp)(c) **CROSSWINDS** [ ] [23] Apr 74
– Spanish moss: (A sound portrait – Savannah the serene – Storm – Flash flood / The pleasant pheasant / Heather / Crosswinds. *(re-iss.1988)*

Jul 74. (7") **CROSSWINDS. / LE LIS** [-] [ ]

Nov 74. (lp)(c) **TOTAL ECLIPSE** [ ] [36]
– Solarization:- Solarization – Second phase – Crescent Sun – Voyage – Solarization recapitulation / Lunarputations / Total eclipse / Bandits / Moon germs / The Moon ain't made of green cheese / Sea of tranquility / Last frontier.

Jan 75. (7") **BANDIT. / MOON GERMS** [-] [ ]

May 75. (lp)(c) **SHABAZZ (live in Europe)** [ ] [74]
– Shabazz / Taurian matador / Red baron / Tenth pinn.

— **JOHN SCOFIELD** – guitar repl. ABERCROMBIE

Oct 75. (lp)(c) **A FUNKY THIDE OF SINGS** [ ] [79]
– Panhandler / Sorcery / A funky thide of sings / Thinking of you / Some skunk funk / Light at the end of the tunnel / A funky kind of thing / Moody modes.

— with **SCOFIELD / PHIL BODNER** – flute / **DAWILLI GONGA** – keyboards / **ALLAN**

ZAVOD – organ / **RICHARD DAVIS + DOUG RAUCH** – bass / **+ string trio**

Mar 76. (lp)(c) **LIFE AND TIMES**
– Life & times / 29 / Siesta – Wake up!!!!!! that's what you said / East bay / Earthlings / Song for a friend (pt.1) / On a natural high / Song for a friend (pt.2).

—— Next credited with The **GEORGE DUKE BAND**

Dec 76. (lp)(c) **LIVE ON TOUR IN EUROPE (live)** 99
– Hip pockets / Ivory tattoo / Space lady / Almustafa the beloved / Do what cha wanna / Frankenstein goes to the disco / Sweet wine / Juicy.

Dec 76. (7") **DO WHAT CHA WANTA. / HIP POCKETS** -

C.B.S. Columbia

Dec 77. (lp)(c) **MAGIC**
– On a magic carpet ride / AC-DC / Leeward winds / Puff'n'stuff / "Anteres" the star / Magic / Reflections in the clouds / Magic recapitulation.

Oct 78. (lp)(c) **SIMPLICITY OF EXPRESSION – DEPTH OF THOUGHT**
– Bolinas / La Guernica / Pocket change / Indigo / Opelousas / Early libra.

1978. (7") **BOLINAS. / INDIGO** -

1978. (lp)(c) **A LIVE MUTHA FOR YA (live)**
– Anteres the star / Bahama mama / Shadows / Some punk funk / Spindrift / On a magic carpet ride.

1979. (7") **DANA. / WHAT IS YOUR FANTASY** -

Oct 79. (lp)(c) **B.C.**
– Mendocino / Dana / What is your fantasy / Little travellin' music / Lonely bull / I don't want to be without you / Bring up the house lights / Vlaster on encounter.

1979. (7") **WHAT IS YOUR FANTASY. / BRIGHT UP THE HOUSE LIGHTS** -

Jun 80. (lp)(c) **THE BEST OF BILLY COBHAM** (compilation)
– On a magic carpet ride / Bolinas / Pocket change / Puff'n'stuff / What is your fantasy / Anteres the star / Indigo / Mendocino.

—— with **BARRY FINERTY** – guitar / **DON GROLNICK** – keyboards / **TIM LANDERS** – bass

??? Sandim

Jun 80. (lp)(c) **FLIGHT TIME (live 1980)** -
– Flight time / Anterries / 6 Persimmins / Days grace / The whisper / Princess / Jackhammer. *(US cd-iss.1988 on 'Inak')*

—— **MIKE STERN** – guitar + MICHAEL URBANIAK – elec. violin repl. BARRY + DON

Mar 81. (lp) **STRATUS**
– Drum solo intro / Stratus / AC-DC / Kasia / All hallows eve / Wrapped in a cloud / Drum solo / Total eclipse / Brooze. *(US cd-iss.1988 on 'Inak')*

BILLY COBHAM'S GLASS MANAGERIE

with **DEAN BROWN** – guitar / **GIL GOLDSTEIN** – keyboards / **TIM LANDER** – bass

Elektra Musician Elektra Musician

Jun 82. (lp)(c) **OBSERVATIONS & REFLECTIONS**
– Jailbait / M.S.R. / Arroyo / Chiquita Linda / Take it to the sky / Observations & reflections.

Jun 83. (lp)(c) **SMOKIN'**
– Some other kind / Chiquita Linda / Looks bad, feel good / Red baron / Situation comedy.

BILLY COBHAM

with **DEAN BROWN / GERRY ETKINS** – keyboards / **BARON BROWNE** – bass / **SA DAVIS** – percussion

G.N.P. G.N.P.

Sep 85. (lp)(cd) **WARNING**
– Moziak / Red and yellow cabriolet / Slow body poppin' / Unknown Jeromes / The dancer / Stratus / Come join me / Go for it.

—— added **ONAJE ALLAN GUMBS** – keyboards

Jun 86. (lp)(c)(cd) **POWER PLAY**
– Times of my life / Zanzibar breeze / Radioactive / A light shines in your eyes / Summit Afrique / The foundation – Isisekulozulu / Dance of the blue men / The nomads / The debate (indabe) / The little one (omncane) / Dessicated coconuts / Tinseltown.

—— with **ETKINS / DAVIS / RANDY BRECKER** – flugelhorn / **GROVER WASHINGTON** – sax / **MICHAEL ABENE** – piano / **TOM SCOTT** – lyricon / **RON CARTER** – bass / **VICTOR BAILEY + ABRAHAM LABORIEL** – bass

Sep 87. (lp)(c)(cd) **PICTURE THIS**
– Two for Juan / Same ole love / Taurian matador / You within me within you / This one's for Armando / Sign of the times / The juggler / Dance for Noh masque.

Oct 87. (7") **SAME OLE LOVE. / THE JUGGLER**
(12"+=) – Mozaik.

—— now with **LARRY CORYELL + DEAN BROWN** – guitar / **ERNIE WATTS** – wind / **BRIAN BROMBERG** – bass / **SHEILA ESCOVEDO** – piano

New Note New Note

Dec 92. (cd) **BY DESIGN**
– Kinky Dee / Slidin' by / Panema / Do you mean to imply / Mirror image / Serengetti Plains / Layed back lifestyle / Permanent jet-lag / Mirror image (reprise) / Dream / Street urchin / Rendez-vous at studio gimmick / Dream (reprise).

F.N.A.C. F.N.A.C.

May 94. (cd) **THE TRAVELER**
– Alfa waves / All that your soul provides / Balancing act / What if / Dipping the biscuits in the soup / Fragolino / Just one step away / Mushu Creole blues / On the inside track / Soul provider.

– other compilations, etc. –

May 78. Atlantic; (lp) **CONFLICTS** -
– Arroyo / El Barrio / Inner conflicts / Muffin talks back / Nickels and dimes.

1988. Atlantic Jazz; (lp)(c)(cd) **THE BEST OF BILLY COBHAM**
– Quadrant 4 / Snoopy's search / Red baron / Spanish moss – A sound portrait / Moon germs / Stratus / The pleasant pheasant / Solo panhandler / Do what cha wanna. *(cd-iss.May93)*

Oct 88. G.N.P.; (lp)(c)(cd) **BILLY'S BEST HITS**
(cd+=) – (3 extra tracks).

Eddie COCHRAN

Born: EDWARD RAY COCHRANE, 3 Oct'38, Oklahoma City, Oklahoma. He was raised in Albert Lea, Minnesota, but moved with Irish parents in 1951 to Bell Gardens, Los Angeles. Four years later, he formed The COCHRANS with friend HANK COCHRAN and they soon issued records for 'Ekko'. Songwriter JERRY CAPEHEART joined the duo early in '56 on a single 'WALKIN' STICK BOOGIE'. Several months after its recording, HANK split with EDDIE, when the former moved to Nashville. CAPEHEART became solo EDDIE's new writing partner, but their first collaboration 'SKINNY JIM' flopped. Later in the year, EDDIE was asked to sing 'TWENTY FLIGHT ROCK', in the up and coming Jayne Mansfield film 'The Girl Can't Help It'. In Apr'57, he had first Top 20 hit with 'SITTIN' IN THE BALCONY'. After a couple of flops and minor hits during the next year, he finally advanced again when 'SUMMERTIME BLUES' gave him another Top20 hit. He followed this gem with 'C'MON EVERYBODY', which got him higher acolade in the UK. Around this time (Jan-Feb'59), he took part in the Alan Freed/Hal Roach film 'Go, Johnny Go!', but had to withdraw from a winter tour alongside good friend BUDDY HOLLY. He went into prolonged shock, after hearing of his death in the plane crash which also killed other stars RICHIE VALENS and BIG BOPPER. Returning to the studio in Mar'59, he brought in Irish group The KELLY FOUR to also augment him on stage. After 'TEENAGE HEAVEN' (from his current film) flops, he released what was to be his 3rd greatest hit 'SOMETHIN' ELSE'. Although this only managed to scrape into the US 60, it hit UK No.22. Early in 1960, he made his final recordings 'THREE STEPS TO HEAVEN' & 'HALLELUJAH I LOVE HER SO', with the latter being lifted for a UK Top 30 hit. On the strength of his UK success, he toured around the country with co-bill topper GENE VINCENT for 10 weeks. He accepted an extension to stay for further shows, and invited girlfriend SHARON SHEELEY to come over for her birthday. On the 17th April, they and GENE were involved in a car crash, when a London cab they were travelling in, skidded off the road. SHARON and GENE suffered broken bones, but EDDIE died after he had been propelled through the windscreen. Two months later, the appropriately titled 'THREE STEPS TO HEAVEN' hit UK No.1. More records were posthumously issued, most selling well enough to again hit the UK charts. • **Style:** Rebellious rocker, whose leather-clad appearance, conjured up image of being a rock'n'roll James Dean. His poetical sometimes poignant lyrics, reflected on the youth of the 50's. • **Songwriters:** As said above plus covers: SITTIN' IN THE BALCONY (Johnny Dee) / SOMETHIN' ELSE + LONELY (c.Sharon Sheeley) / HALLELUJAH I LOVE HER SO (Ray Charles) / MY WAY (Paul Anka) / WEEKEND (Post-Post) / CUT ACROSS SHORTY (Wilkin-Walker) / NERVOUS BREAKDOWN (. . . Roccuzzo) / etc. • **Trivia:** Made his UK TV debut in Jan'60 on the Jack Good show 'Boy Meets Girl'.

Recommended: THE VERY BEST OF EDDIE COCHRAN (30th ANNIVERSARY ALBUM) (*9)

COCHRAN BROTHERS

EDDIE – guitar, vocals / **HANK COCHRAN** (no relation) – vocals, guitar / with **CONNIE 'GUMBO' SMITH** – bass / **HAROLD HENSLEY** – fiddle

not issued Ekko

Jul 55. (7") **MR.FIDDLE. / TWO BLUE SINGIN' STARS** -

Nov 55. (7") **GUILTY CONSCIENCE. / YOUR TOMORROW MAY NEVER COME** -

—— (Next 7", Feb56 **WALKIN' STICK BOOGIE. / ROLLIN'** was credited to **JERRY CAPEHEART with The COCHRAN BROTHERS** on 'Cash' records.

Jun 56. (7") **TIRED AND SLEEPY. / FOOL'S PARADISE** -

EDDIE COCHRAN

not issued Crest

Oct 56. (7") **SKINNY JIM. / HALF LOVED** -

London Liberty

Apr 57. (7") **TWENTY FLIGHT ROCK. / DARK LONELY HEART** -

Jul 57. (7") **SITTIN' IN THE BALCONY. / DARK LONELY HEART** 18 Mar 57

Jun 57. (7") **MEAN WHILE I'M MAD. / ONE KISS** -

Aug 57. (7") **DRIVE IN-SHOW. / AM I BLUE** - 82

Nov 57. (7") **TWENTY FLIGHT ROCK. / CRADLE BABY** -

Jan 58. (7") **JEANIE, JEANIE, JEANIE. / POCKET FULL OF HEARTACHES** - 94

Apr 58. (7") **PRETTY GIRL. / THERESA** -

Aug 58. (lp) **SINGING TO MY BABY** 1957
– Sittin' in the balcony / Completely sweet / Undying love / I'm alone because I love you / Lovin' time / Proud of you / Am I blue / Twenty flight rock / Drive-in show / Mean when I'm mad / Stockin's 'n' shoes / Tell me why / Have I told you lately that I love you / Cradle baby / One kiss. *(UK re-iss.Jul60 hit No.19. (re-iss.Sep63 on 'Liberty' hit No.20 re-iss.Nov68)*

Sep 58. (7") **SUMMERTIME BLUES. / LOVE AGAIN** 18 8 Aug 58

Jan 59. (7") **C'MON EVERYBODY. / DON'T EVER LET ME GO** 6 35 Dec 58
(re-iss.Jul79 on 'United Art')

—— Augmented by **The KELLY FOUR: JIM STIVERS** – piano / **MIKE HENDERSON** – sax / **DAVE SCHRIEBER** – bass / **GENE RIDGIO** – drums

Jun 59. (7") **TEENAGE HEAVEN. / I REMEMBER** 99 Jan 59

Sep 59. (7") **SOMETHIN' ELSE. / BOLL WEEVIL SONG** 22 58 Aug59
(re-iss.Sep79 on 'United Artists')

Jan 60. (7") **HALLELUJAH I LOVE HER SO. / LITTLE ANGEL** 22 Dec 59

Tragedy struck, 17th April, 1960 . . . when in a London cab with GENE VINCENT and girlfriend SHARON SHEELEY, he was killed after a 70 m.p.h. crash. Below release was

already recorded and due out.
May 60. (7") **THREE STEPS TO HEAVEN. / CUT ACROSS SHORTY** [1] [ ]

– others, plus compilations, exploitation, etc. –

Note below releases on 'London' were issued US 'Liberty'.
May 59. London; (7"ep) **C'MON EVERYBODY** [ ] [-]
– (re-iss.Sep63)
Feb 60. London; (7"ep) **SOMETHIN' ELSE** [ ] [-]
– (re-iss.Nov63 on 'Liberty')
Sep 60. London; (lp) **THE EDDIE COCHRAN MEMORIAL ALBUM** [9] [ ]
– (re-iss.Apr63 on 'Liberty', hit No.11. re-Aug87)
Sep 60. London; (7") **SWEETIE PIE. / LONELY** [38] [ ]
(above was flipped over after 3 weeks and hit UK No.41)
Nov 60. London; (7"ep) **EDDIE'S HITS** [ ] [-]
– (re-iss.Nov63 on 'Liberty')
Dec 60. Liberty; (7") **WEEKEND. / LONELY** [-] [ ]
Jun 61. London; (7") **WEEKEND. / CHERISHED MEMORIES** [15] [-]
Nov 61. London; (7") **PRETTY GIRL. / TERESA** [ ] [ ]
Nov 61. London; (7") **JEANNIE, JEANNIE, JEANNIE. / POCKETFUL OF HEARTS** [31] [ ]
Nov 61. London; (7"ep) **CHERISHED MEMORIES OF EDDIE COCHRAN** [ ] [-]
– (re-iss.Nov63 on 'Liberty')
Dec 61. London; (7") **STOCKINGS AND SHOES. / UNDYING LOVE** [ ] [ ]
Nov 62. Liberty; (7") **THINK OF ME. / NEVER** [ ] [ ]
Nov 62. Liberty; (7"ep) **NEVER TO BE FORGOTTEN** [ ] [-]
Dec 62. Liberty; (lp) **CHERISHED MEMORIES** [15] [ ]
– Cherished memories / I've waited so long / Never / Skinny Jim / Half loved / Weekend / Nervous breakdown / Let's go together / Rock and roll blues / Dark lonely street / Pink pegged slacks / That's my desire / Sweetie pie / Think of me. *(re-iss.Nov67 & Sep83) (re-iss.Feb72 on 'Sunset')*
Dec 62. Liberty; (7"ep) **CHERISHED MEMORIES VOL.1** [ ] [-]
Apr 63. Liberty; (7") **MY WAY. / ROCK AND ROLL BLUES** [23] [ ]
Sep 63. Liberty; (7") **DRIVE-IN SHOW. / I ALMOST LOST MY MIND** [ ] [-]
Jul 64. Liberty; (7") **SKINNY JIM. / NERVOUS BREAKDOWN** [ ] [ ]
Sep 64. Liberty; (lp) **MY WAY** [ ] [ ]
(re-iss.Apr68)
Nov 64. Liberty; (7"ep) **STOCKINGS AND SHOES** [ ] [-]
Jun 65. Liberty; (7"ep) **C'MON AGAIN** [ ] [-]
Apr 66. Liberty; (7") **C'MON EVERYBODY. / SUMMERTIME BLUES** [ ] [ ]
Sep 66. Liberty; (7") **THREE STARS. / SOMETHIN' ELSE** [ ] [ ]
Feb 67. Liberty; (7") **EDDIE'S BLUES. / THREE STEPS TO HEAVEN** [ ] [ ]
Apr 68. Liberty; (7") **SUMMERTIME BLUES. / LET'S GET TOGETHER** [34] [ ]
Aug 68. Liberty; (7") **MILK COW BLUES. / SOMETHIN' ELSE** [ ] [ ]
Apr 70. Liberty; (d-lp)(d-c) **THE VERY BEST OF EDDIE COCHRAN (10th ANNIVERSARY ALBUM)** [34] [ ]
– Summertime blues / Teresa / Weekend / Teenage cutie / Never / Completely sweet / Sittin' in the balcony / Think of me / Hallelujah I love her so / Am I blue / My love to remember / Three steps to Heaven / Eddie's blues / Little Lou / Cut across Shorty / Long tall Sally / C'mon everybody / Mean while I'm mad / Pretty girl / Rock and roll blues / Milk cow blues / Boll weevil song / Somethin' else / Teenage Heaven / Twenty flight rock / Love again / Jeannie, Jeannie / Cherished memories / Little angel / Sweetie pie / My way / I remember.
(re-iss.Apr75 '15th . . . ' re-iss.Apr80 '20th . . . ') (re-iss.May82 on 'Fame, cd – May90) (re-Apr85 as '25th . . . ') (re-iss.Apr90 as '30th . . . '
Aug 70. Liberty; (7") **C'MON EVERYBODY. / MEAN WHEN I'M MAD** [ ] [ ]
Oct 85. Liberty; (lp)(c) **THE BEST OF EDDIE COCHRAN** [ ] [ ]
(cd-iss.1987 on 'EMI America')
Jan 88. Liberty; (7") **C'MON EVERYBODY. / DON'T EVER LET ME GO** [14] [ ]
(12"+=)(cd-s+=) – Skinny Jim / Jeannie, Jeannie, Jeannie.
Oct 88. Liberty; (d-lp)(d-c)(d-cd) **EDDIE COCHRAN BOX SET** [ ] [-]
Nov 70. Sunset; (lp) **C'MON EVERYBODY** [ ] [-]
1971. Union Pacific; (lp) **A LEGEND IN OUR TIME** [ ] [-]
Note; Below releases on 'United Artists' were on US 'Liberty'.
Jun 71. U.A.; (lp)(c) **THE LEGENDARY EDDIE COCHRAN** [ ] [ ]
Apr 72. U.A.; (lp)(c) **LEGENDARY MASTERS** [ ] [ ]
Jul 72. U.A.; (7") **SUMMERTIME BLUES. / COTTON PICKER** [ ] [ ]
Sep 72. U.A.; (lp)(c) **ON THE AIR** [ ] [ ]
Jun 76. U.A.; (7") **C'MON EVERYBODY. / MILK COW BLUES** [ ] [ ]
Aug 79. U.A.; (lp)(c) **THE EDDIE COCHRAN SINGLES ALBUM** [39] [ ]
Mar 80. U.A.; (7") **TWENTY FLIGHT ROCK. / TEENAGE CUTIE** [ ] [ ]
May 79. Rockstar; (lp)(c) **THE MANY SIDES OF EDDIE COCHRAN** [ ] [-]
(re-iss.Dec85 on 'Conifer')
Sep 79. Rockstar; (7") **WHAT'D I SAY. / MILK COW BLUES** [ ] [-]
1979. Rockstar; (7"ep) **LET'S COAST AWHILE (w/BO DAVIS)** [ ] [-]
1979. Rockstar; (7"ep) **WALKIN' STICK BOOGIE** [ ] [-]
1979. Rockstar; (7"ep) **TIRED AND SLEEPY** [ ] [-]
1979. Rockstar; (7"ep) **COUNTRY STYLE** [ ] [-]
Apr 80. Rockstar; (7"ep) **20th ANNIVERSARY SPECIAL** [ ] [-]
Jan 82. Rockstar; (lp)(c) **ROCK'N'ROLL HEROES** [ ] [-]
Sep 82. Rockstar; (lp)(c) **THE YOUNG EDDIE COCHRAN** [ ] [-]
May 84. Rockstar; (lp)(c) **COUNTRY STYLE** [ ] [-]
1984. Rockstar; (7"ep) **PINK PEGGED SLACKS** [ ] [-]
Mar 85. Rockstar; (lp)(c) **WORDS AND MUSIC** [ ] [-]
Apr 85. Rockstar; (lp)(c) **PORTRAIT OF A LEGEND** [ ] [-]
1985. Rockstar; (7"ep) **MORE SIDES OF EDDIE COCHRAN** [ ] [-]
1985. Rockstar; (7") **I WANT ELVIS FOR CHRISTMAS. / ?** [ ] [-]
— (above by 'The HOLLY TWINS')
Dec 85. Rockstar; (lp)(c) **THE HOLLYWOOD SESSIONS** [ ] [-]
Apr 87. Rockstar; (cd) **ROCK'N'ROLL LEGEND** [ ] [-]
May 88. Rockstar; (lp)(c) **LET'S COAST AWHILE** [ ] [-]
May 88. Rockstar; (7"ep) **RARE ITEMS** [ ] [-]
May 88. Rockstar; (lp)(c) **WALKIN'** [ ] [-]
Sep 89. Rockstar; (lp)(c) **THRU' ABOUT YOU** [ ] [-]
May 84. EMI Gold; (7") **SUMMERTIME BLUES. / TWENTY FLIGHT ROCK** [ ] [-]
Apr 86. M.F.P.; (lp)(c) **EDDIE COCHRAN** [ ] [-]
Jul 87. Capeheart; (lp) **SOMETHIN' ELSE** [ ] [-]
Jan 88. Ace; (lp)(c)(cd) **THE EARLY YEARS** (c/cd+=4) [ ] [-]
Apr 88. Sunjay; (lp) **HOLLYWOOD ROCKER** [ ] [-]
Jun 86. Card; (cd) **A LEGEND LIVES ON** [ ] [-]
Apr 88. Liberty; (cd)(c)(lp) **C'MON EVERYBODY** [53] [ ]
May 88. Rhino; (cd-ep) **LIL' BIT OF GOLD** [ ] [ ]
– Summertime blues / Somethin' else / C'mon everybody / Nervous breakdown.
Jul 88. Hydra; (lp) **RECORD DATE** [ ] [-]
Sep 89. See For MIles; (lp)(c) **THE EP COLLECTION** [ ] [-]
(cd-iss.Mar91)
May 92. Sunjay; (cd) **GUITAR PICKIN' RARITIES ("EDDIE COCHRAN & GARY LAMBERT")** [ ] [ ]
Sep 92. Old Gold; (cd-s) **THREE STEPS TO HEAVEN / SUMMERTIME BLUES / HALLELUJAH I LOVE HER SO** [ ] [-]
Oct 92. Old Gold; (cd-s) **C'MON EVERYBODY / SOMETHIN' ELSE / WEEKEND** [ ] [-]
Apr 93. Remember; (cd)(c) **SUMMERTIME BLUES** [ ] [-]
May 95. Rockstar; (cd) **MIGHTY MEAN** [ ] [-]
— Also see under: Gene VINCENT ⇒ for joint release Nov81)

Joe COCKER

Born: JOHN ROBERT COCKER, 20 May'44, Sheffield, England. In 1964, he issued one flop single 'I'LL CRY INSTEAD', before forming his GREASE BAND with CHRIS STAINTON, etc. In 1968, he returned to the studio for solo career with band, and had classic UK No.1 'WITH A LITTLE HELP FROM MY FRIENDS'. (see discography.) Continued to be a major star for the next 2 decades. • **Style:** Often compared to RAY CHARLES, he used powerful vox chords to supplant himself as great white blues singer. In the mid-70's, like so many of his contemporaries he shifted music and body to the West Coast. • **Songwriters:** Pens some with band (GREASE BAND) member CHRIS STAINTON. Covers:- I'LL CRY INSTEAD + WITH A LITTLE HELP FROM MY FRIENDS + SHE CAME IN THROUGH THE BATHROOM WINDOW + YOU'VE GOT TO HIDE YOUR LOVE AWAY (Beatles) / DELTA LADY (Leon Russell) / THE LETTER (Box Tops) / YOU ARE SO BEAUTIFUL (Billy Preston-Jim Price) / JUST LIKE A WOMAN + I SHALL BE RELEASED + WATCHING THE RIVER FLOW (Bob Dylan) / DON'T LET ME BE MISUNDERSTOOD (Nina Simone) / DARLING BE HOME SOON (Lovin' Spoonful) / BIRD ON THE WIRE + I'M YOUR MAN (Leonard Cohen) / HONKY TONK WOMEN (Rolling Stones) / I'VE BEEN LOVING YOU TOO LONG (Otis Redding) / GIVE PEACE A CHANCE (John Lennon) / ST.JAMES INFIRMARY (Graham Bond) / LAWDY MISS CLAWDY (Little Richard) / A WHITER SHADE OF PALE (Procol Harum) / MANY RIVERS TO CROSS (Jimmy Cliff) / I HEARD IT THROUGH THE GRAPEVINE (Barrett Strong) / TALKING BACK TO THE NIGHT (Steve Winwood) / INNER CITY BLUES (Marvin Gaye) / UNCHAIN MY HEART (Ray Charles) / UP WHERE WE BELONG (Buffy Sainte Marie-Will Jennings-Jack Nitzchse) / DON'T LET THE SUN GO DOWN ON ME (Elton John) / CAN'T FIND MY WAY HOME (Blind Faith) / THE MOON IS A HARSH MISTRESS (Jimmy Webb) / FIVE WOMEN (Prince)/TWO WRONGS DON'T MAKE A RIGHT (Bendith-Schwartz) / TEMPTED (Squeeze) / I STILL CAN'T BELIEVE IT'S TRUE (. . . Cadd) / LET THE HEALING BEGIN (Tony Joe White) / HAVE A LITTLE FAITH IN ME (John Hiatt) / THE SIMPLE THINGS (Shanks-Neigher-Roy) / SUMMER IN THE CITY (Lovin' Spoonful) / THE GREAT DIVIDE (J.D. Souther) / HIGHWAY HIGHWAY (Steven Allen Davis) / TOO COOL (G.Sutton-K.Fleming) / SOUL TIME (Will Jennings-Frankie Miller) / OUT OF THE BLUE (Robbie Robertson) / HELL AND HIGHWATER (John Miles) / STANDING KNEE DEEP IN A RIVER (Bob McDill-Dickey Lee-Bucky Jones) / TAKE ME HOME (Kipner-Capek-Jordan) / and many more. • **Trivia:** 'UP WHERE WE BELONG' won a Grammy for best song in 1983.

Recommended: THE LEGEND: THE ESSENTIAL COLLECTION (*7)

"JOE COCKER" – vocals, (touring band JOE COCKER'S BIG BLUES) with **DAVE HOPPER** – guitar / **VERNON NASH** – piano / **DAVE GREEN** – bass / **DAVE MEMMOT** – drums Record company used session men instead incl. **BIG JIM SULLIVAN** – guitar

Decca / not issued
Oct 64. (7") **I'LL CRY INSTEAD. / PRECIOUS WORDS** [ ] [-]
— He formed **The GREASE BAND** in '67 retaining **NASH** and **MEMMOTT** and recruited **CHRIS STAINTON** – bass, and **FRANK MYLES** – guitar. But once again opted for session musicians incl. **CLEM CATTINI** – drums / **J. PAGE & A. LEE** – guitar. Although STAINTON did appear. (JIMMY PAGE also appeared on next 45)

Regal Zono. / A & M
Sep 68. (7") **MARJORINE. / THE NEW AGE OF LILY** [48] [ ]
— **JOE COCKER & THE GREASE BAND** with **STAINTON** brought in new guys **TOMMY EYRE** – keyboards / **MICKEY GEE** – guitar / **TOMMY REILLY** – drums
Sep 68. (7") **WITH A LITTLE HELP FROM MY FRIENDS. / SOMETHING'S COMING ON** [1] [68]
— **MENRY McCULLOCH** – guitar repl. MICKEY GEE (he later joined SHAKIN' STEVENS) **KENNY SLADE** – drums repl. REILLY Plus of course a huge selection

of session people

May 69. (lp) **WITH A LITTLE HELP FROM MY FRIENDS** [ ] [35]
– Feeling alright / Bye bye blackbird / Change in Louise / Marjorine / Just like a woman / Do I still figure in your life / Sandpaper Cadillac / Don't let me be misunderstood / With a little help from my friends / I shall be released. *(re-iss.Oct81, cd-iss.1988 on 'Cube') (re-iss.Feb90 on 'Castle')*

Jun 69. (7") **FEELING ALRIGHT. / SANDPAPER CADILLAC** [-] [69]
(re-iss.Dec71 on 'A&M')

— **JOE'S GREASE BAND** retained **STAINTON** – now keyboards and **McCULLOCH ALAN SPENNER** – bass repl. TOMMY EYRE who joines AYNSLEY DUNBAR, etc.

BRUCE ROWLANDS – drums repl. KENNY SLADE who went into sessions

Sep 69. (7") **DELTA LADY. / SHE'S GOOD TO ME** [10] [69]

Nov 69. (lp)(c) **JOE COCKER!** [ ] [11]
– Dear landlord / Bird on the wire / Lawdy Miss Clawdy / She came in through the bathroom window / Hitchcock railway / That's your business now / Something / Delta lady / Hello little friend / Darling be home soon. *(cd-iss.May91 on 'Castle')*

Dec 69. (7") **SHE CAME IN THROUGH THE BATHROOM WINDOW. / CHANGE IN LOUISE** [-] [ ]

Jun 70. (7") **THE LETTER. / SPACE CAPTAIN** [39] [7] Apr 70

— Early '70 he retained **STAINTON** and assembled his **MAD DOGS AND ENGLISHMEN** entourage which included **LEON RUSSELL & THE SHELTER PEOPLE** – guitar, piano / **DON PRESTON** – guitar CARL RADLE – bass / **BOBBY KEYS** – sax / **JIM PRICE** – trumpet / **JIM KELTNER** – drums plus even more session people, over 10, which was documented on film in '71.

A&M A&M

Sep 70. (d-lp)(c) **MAD DOGS & ENGLISHMEN (live)** [16] [2]
– (introduction) / Honky tonk women / Sticks and stones / Cry me a river / Bird on the wire / Feeling alright / Superstar / Let's go get stoned / Blue medley: I'll drown in my own tears – When something is wrong with my baby – I've been loving too long / Girl from North Country / Give peace a chance / She came in through the bathroom window / Space captain / The letter / Delta lady. *(re-iss.1983, cd-iss.1988)*

Fly A&M

Oct 70. (7") **CRY ME A RIVER (live). / GIVE PEACE A CHANCE (live)** [ ] [11]

— JOE retained **STAINTON** and some of his past session men

May 71. (7") **HIGH TIME WE WENT. / BLACK EYED BLUES** [ ] [22]

— now with the CHRIS STAINTON BAND" (a 12-piece) retaining **KEYS, PRICE** and **KELTNER.** (also had loads of session men)

Cube A&M

Aug 72. (7") **MIDNIGHT RIDER. / WOMAN TO WOMAN** [ ] [27] [56]

Dec 72. (lp)(c) **SOMETHING TO SAY** [ ] [30]
– Pardon me sir / High time we went / She don't mind / Black eyed blues / Something to say / Midnight rider / Do right woman / Woman to woman / St.James infirmary. *(US title 'JOE COCKER') (UK re-iss.May85 on 'Sierra') (UK re-iss.+cd.Dec90 on 'Castle')*

Feb 73. (7") **PARDON ME SIR. / SHE DON'T MIND** [ ] [-]

Feb 73. (7") **PARDON ME SIR. / ST. JAMES INFIRMARY** [-] [51]

— now (complete new line-up) **STAINTON** joined TUNDRA / **HENRY McCULLOCH** – guitar / **MICK WEAVER** (aka WYNDER K. FROG) – keyboards / **BUFFALO GELBER** – bass / **JIMMY KARSTEIN** – drums

Jun 74. (7") **PUT OUT THE LIGHT. / IF I LOVE YOU** [ ] [46]

Aug 74. (lp)(c) **I CAN STAND A LITTLE RAIN** [ ] [11]
– Put out the light / I can stand a little rain / I get mad / Sing me a song / The moon is a harsh mistress / Don't forget me / You are so beautiful / It's a sin when you love somebody / Performance / Guilty. *(re-iss.Oct81) (re-iss.+cd.Apr89 on 'Castle')*

Dec 74. (7") **YOU ARE SO BEAUTIFUL. / I GET MAD** [ ] [-]

Jan 75. (7") **YOU ARE SO BEAUTIFUL. / IT'S A SIN WHEN YOU LOVE SOMEBODY** [-] [5]

— He then formed **JOE COCKER & The COCK'N'BULL BAND** with **WEAVER** plus **ALBERT LEE** – guitar / **PETER GAVIN** – drums / **ANDY DENNO** – bass

JOE COCKER retained **LEE, GAVIN** plus touring band **RICHARD TEE** – keyboards / **GORDON EDWARDS** – bass / **CORNELL DUPREE** – guitar / **KENNY SLADE** – percussion and three girl backing singers

Jul 75. (7") **I THINK IT'S GONNA RAIN TODAY. / OH MAMA** [-] [ ]

Aug 75. (lp)(c) **JAMAICA SAY YOU WILL** [ ] [42]
– (That's what I like) In my woman / Where am I now / I think it's going to rain today / Forgive me now / Oh mama / Lucinda / If I love you / Jamaica say you will / It's all over but the shoutin' / Jack-a-diamonds.

Oct 75. (7") **IT'S ALL OVER BUT THE SHOUTIN'. / SANDPAPER CADILLAC** [ ] [ ]

Oct 75. (7") **JAMAICA SAY YOU WILL. / IT'S ALL OVER BUT THE SHOUTIN'** [-] [ ]

— **JOE COCKER & STUFF** retained **TEE, EDWARDS** and **DUPREE** added **ERIC GALE** – guitar repl. LEE who went solo **STEVE GADD drums** repl. GAVIN

A&M A&M

Apr 76. (7") **THE MAN IN ME. / (part 2)** [-] [ ]

Apr 76. (lp)(c) **STINGRAY** [ ] [70]
– The jealous kind / I broke down / You came along / Catfish / Moon dew / The man in me / She is my lady / Worrier / Born thru indifference with you / A song for you.

Jul 76. (7") **THE JEALOUS KIND. / YOU CAME ALONG** [ ] [ ]

Sep 76. (7") **I BROKE DOWN. / YOU CAME ALONG** [ ] [ ]

— JOE then joined **KOKOMO** for a month late '76 (no recordings). Took a long time off from studio & stage. Returned with a host of session people

Asylum Asylum

Sep 78. (7") **FUN TIME. / WATCHING THE RIVER FLOW** [-] [ ]

Sep 78. (lp)(c)(pic-lp) **LUXURY YOU CAN AFFORD** [ ] [76]
– Fun time / Watching the river flow / Boogie baby / A white shade of pale / I can't say no / Southern lady / I know (you don't want me no more) / What you did to me last night / Lady put the light out / Wasted years / I heard it through the grapevine.

Sep 78. (7") **FUN TIME. / I CAN'T SAY NO** [ ] [-]

Jan 79. (7") **A WHITER SHADE OF PALE. / WATCHING THE RIVER FLOW** [ ] [ ]

— In Sep81 JOE was credited on a single 'I'm So Glad I'm Standing Here Today' and guested on 'Standing Still' by the CRUSADERS.

JOE COCKER returned to solo work '82, (first w/SLY DUNBAR + ROBBIE SHAKESPEARE)

Island Island

Jun 82. (7")(12") **SWEET LITTLE WOMAN. / LOOK WHAT YOU'VE DONE** [ ] [ ]

Jul 82. (lp)(c) **SHEFFIELD STEEL** [ ] [ ]
– Look what you've done / Shocked / Sweet little woman / Seven days / Marie / Ruby Lee / Many rivers to cross / So good so right / Talking back to the night / Just like always.

Aug 82. (7") **MANY RIVERS TO CROSS. / TALKING BACK TO THE NIGHT** [ ] [ ]

below from the film 'An Officer and a Gentleman'

Jan 83. (7") **UP WHERE WE BELONG.(by "JOE COCKER & JENNIFER WARNES") / SWEET LITTLE WOMAN** [7] [1] Aug 82

Jun 83. (7") **THREW IT AWAY. / EASY RIDER** [ ] [ ]

Capitol Capitol

Jun 84. (7") **CIVILIZED MAN. / A GIRL LIKE YOU** [ ] [ ]

Jun 84. (lp)(c)(cd) **CIVILIZED MAN** [100] [ ] May 84
– Civilized / There goes my baby / Come on in / Tempted / Long drag off a cigarette / I love the night / Crazy in love / A girl like you / Hold on (I feel our love is changing) / Even a fool would let go. *(re-iss.Jul88)*

Nov 84. (7") **EDGE OF A DREAM (from film 'Teachers'). / TEMPTED** [ ] [69] Oct 84

Jan 85. (7") **CRAZY IN LOVE. / COME ON IN** [-] [ ]

Feb 86. (7") **SHELTER ME. / TELL ME THERE'S A WAY** [-] [91]

Mar 86. (7") **SHELTER ME. / ONE MORE TIME** [ ] [-]
(12"+=) – If you have love, give me some.

Apr 86. (lp)(c)(cd) **COCKER** [ ] [50]
– Shelter / A to Z / Don't you love me anymore / Living without your love / Don't drink the water / You can leave your hat on / Heart of the matter / Inner city blues / Love is on a fade / Heaven. *(re-iss.Oct89 on 'Fame') (re-iss.cd+c Jul94)*

Apr 86. (7")(12") **YOU DON'T LOVE ME ANYMORE. / TELL ME THERE'S A WAY** [ ] [-]
(re-iss.May88) (12"+=) – All our tomorrows.
(cd-s++=) – With a little help from my friends.

May 86. (7") **DON'T YOU LOVE ME ANYMORE. / DON'T DRINK THE WATER** [-] [ ]

Jun 86. (7")(12") **YOU CAN LEAVE YOUR HAT ON. / LONG DRAG OFF THE CIGARETTE** [ ] [ ]

1987. (7") **LOVE LIVES ON. / ON MY WAY TO YOU** [-] [ ]
(above on 'MCA')

Oct 87. (7")(12") **UNCHAIN MY HEART. / YOU CAN LEAVE YOUR HAT ON** [46] [-]
(12") – ('A'side) / ('A'rock mix) / The one.
(cd-s+=) – ('A'dance mix). *(re-iss.Jun92, hit UK No.17)*

Oct 87. (7") **UNCHAIN MY HEART. / SATISFIED** [-] [ ]

Oct 87. (lp)(c)(cd) **UNCHAIN MY HEART** [ ] [89]
– Unchain my heart / Two wrongs (don't make a right) / I stand in wonder / The river's rising / Isolation / All our tomorrows / A woman loves a man / Trust in me / The one / Satisfied. *(re-iss.Jun89)*

Dec 87. (7")(12") **LOVE LIVE ON. / MY WAY TO YOU** [ ] [-]

Dec 87. (7") **TWO WRONGS (DON'T MAKE A RIGHT). / ISOLATION** [-] [ ]

— (above from 'Bigfoot & The Hendersons' US title 'Harry & The Hendersons', on 'M.C.A.')

Jul 89. (lp)(c)(cd) **ONE NIGHT OF SIN** [ ] [52]
– When the night comes / I will live for you / I've got to use my imagination / Letting go / Just to keep from drowning / The unforgiven * / Another mind gone / Fever / You know it's gonna hurt / Bad bad sign / I'm your man / One night of sin. *(cd+= *) (re-iss.cd+c Mar94)*

Oct 89. (c-s) **WHEN THE NIGHT COMES. / ONENIGHT OF SIN** [-] [11]

Nov 89. (7") **WHEN THE NIGHT COMES. / RUBY LEE** [65] [-]
(12"+=)(cd-s+=) – ('A'extended).

— **JOE COCKER BAND** is **DERIC DYER** – sax, keys, perc. / **STEVE HOLLEY** – drums / **PHIL GRANDE** – lead guitar / **JEFF LEVINE** – keys / **KEITH MACK** – rhythm guitar / **CHRIS STAINTON** – keys / **T.M. STEVENS** – bass, vocals / **DOREEN CHANTER** – vocals / **MAXINE GREEN** – vocals / **CRYSTAL TALIEFERO** – vocals, perc. / **The MEMPHIS HORNS:- WAYNE JACKSON, ANDREW LOVE, GARY GAZAWAY**

Jun 90. (cd)(c)(d-lp) **JOE COCKER LIVE (live)** [ ] [95]
– Feeling alright? / Shelter me / Hitchcock railway / Up where we belong / You can leave your hat on / Guilty / When the night comes / Unchain my heart / With a little help from my friends / You are so beautiful / The letter / She came in through the bathroom window / High time we went / What are you doing with a fool like me (studio) / Living in the promise land (studio).

May 90. (c-s) **WHAT ARE YOU DOING WITH A FOOL LIKE ME? / ANOTHER MIND GONE** [-] [96]

(studio:- **KENNY RICHARDS** – drums / **EARL SLICK** – guitar / **BASHARI JOHNSON** – perc. / backing vocals – **TAWATHA AGEE, VANEESE THOMAS & FONZI THORNTON.**)

Oct 91. (cd)(c)(lp) **NIGHT CALLS** [ ] [ ]
– Love is alive / Little bit of love / Please no more / There's a storm coming / You've got to hide your love away / I can hear the river / Don't let the Sun go down on me / Night calls / Five women / Can't find my way home / Not too young to die of a broken heart / Out of the rain. *(re-iss.Apr92, hit UK No.25)*

Oct 91. (7")(c-s) **NIGHT CALLS. / OUT OF THE RAIN** [ ] [ ]
(12"+=)(cd-s+=) – Not too young to die of a broken heart.

Mar 92. (7")(c-s) **(ALL I KNOW) FEELS LIKE FOREVER. / WHEN THE NIGHT COMES** [25] [ ]
(cd-s+=) – Up where we belong / With a little help from my friends.

May 92. (7")(c-s) **NOW THAT THE MAGIC HAS GONE. / FIVE WOMEN** [28] [ ]
(12"+=)(cd-s+=) – Two wrongs don't make a right / The letter.

Nov 92. (7")(c-s) **WHEN THE NIGHT COMES. / YOU'VE GOT TO HIDE YOUR LOVE AWAY** [61] [ ]
(cd-s+=) – Tempted / I still can't believe it's true.
(cd-s) – ('A'side) / The Moon is a harsh mistress / I'm your man / She came in

through the bathroom window.

— now w / **JACK BRUNO** – drums / **BOB FEIT + TONY JOE WHITE + TIM PIERCE** – guitar / **CHRIS STAINTON** – keyboards / **LENNY CASTRO** – percussion / **C.J. VANSTON** – organ

Aug 94. (c-s) **THE SIMPLE THINGS. / SUMMER IN THE CITY** 17 □
(cd-s+=) – With a little help from my friends (live).
(cd-s) – ('A'side) / Angeline / My strongest weakness.

Sep 94. (cd)(c)(lp) **HAVE A LITTLE FAITH** 9 □
– Let the healing begin / Have a little faith in me / The simple things / Summer in the city / The great divide / Highway highway / Too cool / Soul time / Out of the blue / Angeline / Hell and highwater / Standing knee deep in a river / Take me home.

Oct 94. (7")(c-s)(cd-s) **TAKE ME HOME. (featuring BEKKA BRAMBLETT) / TEMPTED / UNCHAIN MY HEART (90's version)** 41 □
(cd-s) – ('A'side) / Up where we belong / You can leave your hat on.

Dec 94. (7")(c-s)(cd-s) **LET THE HEALING BEGIN. / SUMMER IN THE CITY (2-mixes)** 32 □
(cd-s) – ('A'side) / You are so beautiful (live) / The letter (live).

Jun 95. (c-s) **HAVE A LITTLE FAITH IN ME / THE SIMPLE THINGS (live) / LET THE HEALING BEGIN (live)** □ □
(cd-s) – ('A'side) / Summer in the city (live) / Angeline (live).
(re-iss.Sep95, hit No.67 UK)

– compilations etc. –

Apr 71. Flyover/ US= A&M; (lp)(c) **COCKER HAPPY** □ □
(re-iss.May85 on 'Sierra') (cd-iss.Oct94 on 'Disky')

Note; All releases on 'Cube' were issued on 'A&M' US.

Apr 72. Cube; (d-lp) **WITH A LITTLE HELP FROM MY FRIENDS / JOE COCKER!** 29 □

Dec 76. Cube; (lp)(c) **LIVE IN L.A. (live)** □ □
(re-iss.May86 on 'Sierra')

1977. Cube; (7") **CRY ME A RIVER. / FEELING ALRIGHT** - □

Oct 81. Cube; (d-lp)(d-c) **THE JOE COCKER PLATINUM COLLECTION** □ □

Dec 81. Cube; (7") **LET IT BE. / MARJORINE** □ □

Apr 82. Cube; (lp)(c) **SPACE CAPTAIN (live)** □ □

Oct 82. Cube; (lp)(c) **COUNTDOWN JOE COCKER** □ □

May 83. Cube; (7") **YOU ARE SO BEAUTIFUL. / MARJORINE** □ □

May 78. Hallmark; (lp)(c) **GREATEST HITS VOL.I** □ □ Nov 77

Jul 82. Old Gold; (7") **WITH A LITTLE HELP FROM MY FRIENDS. / DELTA LADY** □ -

Nov 84. Sierra; (d-lp)(c) **OFF THE RECORD** □ □

May 86. Sierra; (lp)(c) **REPLAY ON . . .** □ □

Apr 86. Castle; (d-lp)(d-c)(cd) **THE COLLECTION** □ □

May 86. Telstar; (lp)(c)(cd) **THE VERY BEST OF JOE COCKER** □ □

Sep 86. Archive 4; (12"ep) **WITH A LITTLE HELP FROM MY FRIENDS / MARJORINE / THE LETTER / DELTA LADY (live).**
(3"cd-iss.'88)

Mar 88. That's Original; (d-lp)(c) **JAMAICA SAY YOU WILL / COCKER HAPPY** □ □
(d-cd.iss-Sep91)

1988. Knight; (cd) **THE BEST OF JOE COCKER** □ □

Jul 88. Knight; (c) **NIGHTRIDING** □ □

1988. Fun; (lp) **16 GREATEST HITS** □ -

Jan 92. Raven-Topic; (cd) **CONNOISSEUR'S COCKER** □ -

Jun 92. Polygram TV; (cd)(c)(d-lp) **THE LEGEND** 4 -
– Up where we belong (with JENNIFER WARNES) / With a little help from my friends / Delta lady / The letter / She came in through the bathroom window / A whiter shade of pale / Love the one you're with (live) / You are so beautiful / Let it be / Just like a woman / Many rivers to cross / Talking back to the night / Fun time / I heard it through the grapevine / Please give peace a chance (live) / Don't let me be misunderstood / Honky tonk woman (live) / Cry me a river (live).

Oct 93. Spectrum; (cd)(c) **THE FIRST TIME** □ -

Jul 94. BR Music; (cd)(c) **THE VERY BEST OF JOE COCKER** □ -

Oct 94. BR Music; (cd) **FAVOURITE RARITIES** □ -

Aug 94. E.M.I.; (cd)(cd-vid) **THE BEST OF JOE COCKER – LIVE (live)** □ -

Oct 94. Woodford; (cd) **MIDNIGHT RIDER** □ -

Oct 94. Woodford; (cd) **SIMPLY THE BEST** □ -

Sep 95. Spectrum; (cd)(c) **THE ESSENTIAL JOE COCKER** □ -

Dec 95. A&M; (4xcd-box) **THE LONG VOYAGE HOME** □ -

COCKNEY REBEL

Formed: London, England . . . early 1973 by ex-journalist STEVE HARLEY. After initially flopping commercially that year, they broke through in '74, when 'JUDY TEEN' hit UK Top 5. This was followed by a hit second album 'THE PSYCHOMODO' and another Top 10 single 'MR.SOFT', before HARLEY and group fell-out and split. Early the next year, STEVE HARLEY & COCKNEY REBEL were at the top of the charts with 'MAKE ME SMILE (COME UP AND SEE ME)'. • **Style:** Clever pop-rock combo influenced initially by ROXY MUSIC and DAVID BOWIE. The first split was mainly caused by HARLEY's self-indulgent occupation with niggling the UK music press. • **Songwriters:** HARLEY written material, except HERE COMES THE SUN (Beatles; George Harrison). • **Miscellaneous:** Early in 1986, HARLEY dueted with SARAH BRIGHTMAN on Top 10 single from 'Phantom Of The Opera', but was surprised when MICHAEL CRAWFORD was chosen for the lead role in the musical version. An ex-original member JEFFREYS died in the Lockerbie plane crash 21 Dec'88.

Recommended: MAKE ME SMILE – BEST OF STEVE HARLEY &.. (*6)

STEVE HARLEY (b. STEVEN NICE, 27 Feb'51, London, England) – vocals, guitar / **MILTON REAME-JAMES** – keyboards / **JEAN-PAUL** (b. JOHN) **CROCKER** – violin / **PAUL AVRON JEFFERIES** – bass / **STUART ELLIOT** – drums

E.M.I. E.M.I.

Aug 73. (7") **SEBASTIAN. / ROCK AND ROLL PARADE** □ □

Nov 73. (lp)(c) **THE HUMAN MENAGERIE** □ □
– Hideaway / What Ruthy said / Loretta's tale / Crazy raver / Sebastian / Mirror freak / My only vice / Muriel the actor / Chameleon / Death trip. *(cd-iss.Jul90 w/• tracks)*

Mar 74. (7") **JUDY TEEN. / SPACED OUT** 5 □

Jun 74. (lp)(c) **THE PSYCHOMODO** 8 □
– Sweet dreams / Psychomodo / Mr. Soft / Singular band / Ritz / Cavaliers / Bed in the corner / Sling it / Tumbling down. *(cd-iss.Jul90 w/ tracks)* – Big big deal / Such a dream.

Jul 74. (7") **MR. SOFT. / SUCH A DREAM** 8 □

Nov 74. (7") **BIG BIG DEAL.(by "STEVE HARLEY") / BED IN THE CORNER** □ -

Nov 74. (7") **SINGULAR BAND. / TUMBLING DOWN** - □

STEVE HARLEY & COCKNEY REBEL

retained only **ELLIOT** with **JIM CREGAN** – guitar (ex-FAMILY)repl. CROCKER / **DUNCAN MACKAY** – keyboards repl. REAME-JAMES / **GEORGE FORD** – bass repl. JEFFERIES (he died early '89 in the Lockerbie disaster).

Feb 75. (7") **MAKE ME SMILE (COME UP AND SEE ME). / ANOTHER JOURNEY** 1 96 Feb 76

Mar 75. (lp)(c) **THE BEST YEARS OF OUR LIVES** 4 □
– (introducing the best years) / Mad mad moonlight / Mr. Raffles (man it was mean) / It wasn't me / Panorama / Make me smile (come up and see me) / Back to the farm / 49th parallel / The best years of our lives. *(re-iss.+cd.Mar91)*

May 75. (7") **MR. RAFFLES (MAN IT WAS MEAN). / SEBASTIAN (live)** 13 □

— now a quartet when JIM CREGAN left to join ROD STEWART's band

Nov 75. (7") **BLACK OR WHITE. / MAD MAD MOONLIGHT (live)** □ □

Feb 76. (7") **WHITE, WHITE DOVE. / THROW YOUR SOUL DOWN HERE** □ □

Feb 76. (lp)(c) **TIMELESS FLIGHT** 18 □
– Red is a mean, mean colour / White, white dove / Understand / All men are hungry / Black or white / Everything changes / Nothing is sacred / Don't go, don't cry. *(re-iss.+cd.Mar91)*

STEVE HARLEY

E.M.I. Capitol

Jul 76. (7") **HERE COMES THE SUN. / LAY ME DOWN** 10 -

Aug 76. (7") **HERE COMES THE SUN. / ALL MEN ARE HUNGRY** - □

Oct 76. (7") **LOVE'S A PRIMA DONNA. / SIDETRACK ONE** 41 □

Oct 76. (lp)(c) **LOVE'S A PRIMA DONNA** 28 □
– Seeking a love / G.I. valentine / Finally a card game / Too much tenderness / Love compared with you / (I believe) Love's a prima donna / Seeking a love (pt.2) / (If this is love) Give me more / Carry me again / Here comes the Sun / Innocence and guilt / Is it true what they say.

Nov 76. (7") **LOVE COMPARED WITH YOU. / G.I. VALENTINE** □ -

Dec 76. (7") **LOVE COMPARED WITH YOU. / TOO MUCH TENDERNESS** - □

Jun 77. (lp)(c) **FACE TO FACE – A LIVE RECORDING (live)** 40 □
– Here comes the sun / (I believe) Love's a prima donna / Mad, mad moonlight / Red is a mean, mean colour / The best years of our lives / Love compared with you / Mr.Soft / Sebastian.

Aug 77. (7")(12") **THE BEST YEARS OF OUR LIVES (live). / TUMBLING DOWN (live)** □ □

Jul 78. (7") **ROLL THE DICE. / WAITING** □ □

Jul 78. (lp)(c) **HOBO WITH A GRIN** □ □
– Roll the dice / America the brave / Living in a rhapsody / I wish it would rain / Riding the waves (with Virginia Woolf) / Someone's coming / Hot youth / (I don't believe) God is an anarchist / Faith, hope and charity.

Sep 79. (7") **FREEDOM'S PRISONER. / ONE MORE TIME** 58 □

Sep 79. (lp)(c) **THE CANDIDATE** □ □
– Audience with the man / Woodchopper / Freedom's prisoner / Love on the rocks / Who's afraid / One more time / How good it feels / From here to eternity / Young hearts (the candidate).

— In Mar'81, HARLEY did duet 45 'I Can't Even Touch You' w / MIDGE URE.

Stiletto-RCA not issued

Jul 83. (7") **BALLERINA (PRIMA DONNA). / FACE TO FACE** 51 □
(12"+=) – ('A'extended) / Sebastian (new version).

Polydor not issued

Dec 85. (7")(12") **PHANTOM OF THE OPERA. ("SARAH BRIGHTMAN & STEVE HARLEY") / OVERTURE (From the Musical)** 7 □

— now solo with a backing band.

R.A.K. not issued

Jan 86. (7") **IRRESISTABLE. / SUCH IS LIFE** □ -
(12") – ('A'extended) / Sebastian (by COCKNEY REBEL).

Apr 86. (7")(12") **HEARTBEAT LIKE THUNDER. / WARM MY COLD HEART** □ -

Jun 86. (7")(12") **IRRESISTABLE. / LUCKY MAN** □ -

ANDERSON, HARLEY & BATT

(**JON ANDERSON** of YES / **MIKE BATT** – solo artist)

Epic not issued

Nov 88. (7") **WHATEVER YOU BELIEVE. / ('A' live version)** □ □
(12"+=) – Morning has broken (instrumental by RAF BAND).

STEVE HARLEY

solo again

Vital Vinyl | not issued

Jun 89. (7") **WHEN I'M WITH YOU. / THEME FROM BABBACOMBE LEE** [ ] [ ]

— In Apr'90, STEVE HARLEY and several ex-COCKNEY REBEL members re-formed as RAFFLES UNITED, and played 4 consecutive Sunday nights live in a Sudbury pub.

Realisation | not issued

Nov 93. (cd)(c) **LIVE IN THE UK (live)** [ ] [-]

CTE | not issued

Dec 95. (cd) **YES YOU CAN** [ ] [-]

– others, compilations, etc. –

Note; All releases on 'EMI' were issued on 'Capitol' US.

Apr 76. Capitol; (lp)(c) **A CLOSER LOOK** [-] [ ]

Sep 80. E.M.I.; (lp)(c) **THE BEST OF STEVE HARLEY AND COCKNEY REBEL** [ ] [ ]
(re-iss.May82 on 'Fame')

Oct 80. E.M.I.; (7") **MAKE ME SMILE (COME UP AND SEE ME). / SEBASTIAN** [ ] [ ]

Sep 83. E.M.I.; (d-lp) **THE HUMAN MENAGERIE / THE PSYCHOMODO** [ ] [ ]

Feb 88. E.M.I.; (7") **MR. SOFT. / MAD MAD MOONLIGHT** [ ] [ ]

May 88. E.M.I.; (lp)(c)(cd) **GREATEST HITS: STEVE HARLEY AND COCKNEY REBEL** [ ] [ ]

Apr 92. E.M.I.; (7")(c-s) **MAKE ME SMILE (COME UP AND SEE ME). / MR.SOFT** [46] [-]
(cd-s+=) – Spaced out / (Love) Compared with you.

May 92. E.M.I.; (cd) **MAKE ME SMILE – THE BEST OF STEVE HARLEY & COCKNEY REBEL** [ ] [-]
– Mr.Soft / Riding the waves (for Virginia Woolf) / Irresistable (remix) / Mr. Raffles / Freedoms prisoner / Hideaway / Judy Teen / Best years of our lives (live) / Make me smile (come up and see me) / If this is love (give me more) (live) / Here comes the Sun / Sebastian / Roll the dice / Understand / I believe (love's a prima donna) / Tumbling down.

Oct 83. Old Gold; (7") **MAKE ME SMILE (COME UP AND SEE ME). / JUDY TEEN •** [ ] [ ]

1988. Connoisseur; (lp)(c) **MR. SOFT** [ ] [-]

1988. Castle; (lp)(c) **THE COLLECTION** [ ] [-]

May 94. Magnum; (cd) **MAKE ME SMILE** [ ] [-]

Jul 95. Windsong; (cd) **LIVE AT THE BBC (live)** [ ] [-]

Nov 95. Old Gold; (cd-s) **MAKE ME SMILE (COME UP AND SEE ME) / JUDY TEEN** [ ] [-]

Dec 95. Premier; (7")(c-s) **MAKE ME SMILE (COME UP AND SEE ME). / JUDY TEEN** [33] [-]
(cd-s+=) – Another journey / (I believe) Love's a prima donna.

COCTEAU TWINS

Formed: Grangemouth, Scotland . . . late 1981 when the then trio visited London to give DJ John Peel a demo tape. He booked them for sessions on his Radio 1 night time show, and they signed to IVO's indie label '4 a.d.'. Throughout the 80's, they refused many "big deal" offers and issued albums at their own unrushed pace. • **Style:** Pastel and picturesque beauty, fused with LIZ's intentionally incoherent but heart-felt vox. • **Songwriters:** All by COCTEAU TWINS. • **Trivia:** In 1983, LIZ and ROBIN guested for THIS MORTAL COIL (Ivo/4.a.d. assembly of musicians) on SONG TO THE SIREN (45). ROBIN has since produced many '4.a.d.' outfits, and also The GUN CLUB in 1987. An item for some time, LIZ and ROBIN became parents in 1989. Early in 1991, LIZ was surprisingly but not undeservedly nominated for Best Female Vocalist at the 'Brit' awards.

Recommended: TREASURE (*9) / VICTORIALAND (*8) / GARLANDS (*7) / HEAD OVER HEELS (*8) / BLUE BELL KNOLL (*7) / HEAVEN OR LAS VEGAS (*7) / THE PINK OPAQUE (*8).

ELIZABETH FRASER – vocals / **ROBIN GUTHRIE** – guitar, drum programming, keyboards / **WILL HEGGIE** – bass

4 a.d. | not issued

Jul 82. (lp) **GARLANDS** [ ] [-]
– Blood bitch / Wax and wane / But I'm not / Blind dumb deaf / Grail overfloweth / Shallow than halo / The hollow men / Garlands. *(c-iss.Apr84 +=)* – Dear heart / Blind dumb deaf / Hearsay please / Hazel. *(cd-iss.1986 ++=)* – Speak no evil / Perhaps some other acon.

Sep 82. (12"ep) **LULLABIES** [ ] [-]
– It's all but an ark lark / Alas dies laughing / Feathers-Oar-Blades.

Mar 83. (7")**PEPPERMINT PIG. / HAZEL** [ ] [-]
(12"+=) – Laugh lines.

— Trimmed to a duo, when HEGGIE left to form LOWLIFE.

Oct 83. (lp) **HEAD OVER HEELS** [51] [-]
– When mama was moth / Sugar hiccup / In our anglehood / Glass candle grenades / Multifoiled / In the gold dust rush / The tinderbox (of a heart) / My love paramour / Musette and drums / Five ten fiftyfold. *(c-iss.Apr84, cd-iss.1986)* (c/cd+=) – Sunburst And Snowblind EP

Oct 83. (12"ep) **SUNBURST AND SNOWBLIND** [ ] [-]
– Sugar hiccup / From the flagstones / Because of whirl-Jack / Hitherto.

— added **SIMON RAYMONDE** – bass, keyboards, guitar (ex-DROWNING CRAZE)

Apr 84. (7") **PEARLY DEWDROPS DROP. / PEPPER-TREE** [29] [-]
(12"+=) – The spangle maker.

4 a.d. | Relativity

Nov 84. (lp)(c) **TREASURE** [29] [-]
– Ivo / Lorelei / Beatrix / Persephone / Pandora – for Cindy / Amelia / Aloysius / Cicely / Otterley / Donimo. *(cd-iss.1986)*

Mar 85. (7") **AIKEA-GUINEA. / KOOKABURRA** [41] [-]
(12"+=) – Rococo / Quiquose.

Nov 85. (12"ep) **TINY DYNAMITE** [52] [-]
– Pink orange red / Ribbed and veined / Sultitan Itan / Plain tiger.

Nov 85. (12"ep) **ECHOES IN A SHALLOW BAY** [65] [-]
– Great spangled fritillary / Melonella / Pale clouded white / Eggs and their shells *(cd.iss.Oct86 contains TINY DYNAMITE ep)*

— **RICHARD THOMAS** – saxophone, bass (of DIF JUZ) repl. SIMON who fell ill.

Apr 86. (lp)(c)(cd) **VICTORIALAND** [10] [ ]
– Lazy calm / Fluffy tufts / Throughout the dark months of April and May / Whales tales / Oomingmak / Little Spacey / Feet-like fins / How to bring a blush to the snow / The thinner the air.

— **SIMON RAYMONDE** returned replacing temp. RICHARD (back to DIF JUZ)

Oct 86. (7") **LOVE'S EASY TEARS. / THOSE EYES, THAT MOUTH** [53] [-]
(12"+=) – Sigh's smell of farewell.

— next a COCTEAU TWINS one-off collaboration with '4.a.d' new signing **HAROLD BUDD** – piano

Nov 86. (lp)(c)(cd) **THE MOON AND THE MELODIES (as HAROLD BUDD, ELIZABETH FRASER, ROBIN GUTHRIE, SIMON RAYMONDE)** [46] [-]
– Sea, swallow me / Memory gongs / Why do you love me? / Eyes are mosaics / She will destroy you / The ghost has no home / Bloody and blunt / Ooze out and away, one how.

4 a.d. | Capitol

Sep 88. (lp)(c)(cd) **BLUE BELL KNOLL** [15] [ ]
– Blue bell knoll / Athol-brose / Carolyn's fingers / For Phoebe still a baby / The itchy glowbo blow / Cico buff / Suckling the mender / Spooning good singing gum / A kissed out red floatboat / Ella megablast burls forever.

Oct 88. (7") **CAROLYN'S FINGERS. / BLUE BELL KNOLL** [-] [ ]

— In Apr 90, **LIZ** was heard on IAN McCulloch's (ex-ECHO & THE BUNNYMEN) 'Candleland' single.

Aug 90. (7")(c-s) **ICEBLINK LUCK. / MIZAKE THE MIZAN** [38] [ ]
(12"+=)(cd-s+=) – Watchiar.

Sep 90. (cd)(c)(lp) **HEAVEN OR LAS VEGAS** [7] [99]
– Cherry coloured funk / Pitch the baby / Iceblink luck / Fifty-fifty clown / Heaven or Las Vegas / I wear your ring / Fotzepolitic / Wolf in the breast / Road, river and rail / Frou-frou foxes in midsummer fires.

— on U.S. tour, augmented by **MITSUO TATE & BEN BLAKEMAN** – guitars

Fontana | Capitol

Sep 93. (7")(c-s) **EVANGELINE. / MUD AND LARK** [34] [ ]
(12"pic-d+=)(cd-s+=) – Summer-blink.

Oct 93. (cd)(c)(lp) **FOUR CALENDAR CAFE** [13] [78]
– Know who you are ate every age / Evangeline / Blue beard / Theft and wandering around lost / Oil of angels / Squeeze-wax / My truth / Essence / Summerhead / Pur.

Dec 93. (cd-s) **WINTER WONDERLAND. / FROSTY THE SNOWMAN** [58] [ ]

— (above festive tracks, were thankfully deleted after 1 week in UK Top60)

Feb 94. (7")(c-s) **BLUEBEARD. / THREE SWEPT** [33] [ ]
(12"+=) – Ice-pulse.
(cd-s++=) – ('A'acoustic).

Sep 95. (d7"ep)(cd-ep) **TWINLIGHTS** [59] [ ]
– Rilkean heart / Golden-vein / Pink orange red / Half-gifts.

Oct 95. (cd-ep) **OTHERNESS** (An Ambient EP) [59] [ ]
– Feet like fins / Seekers who are lovers / Violaine / Cherry coloured funk.

– compilations, others, etc. –

1985. 4 a.d./ US= Relativity; (cd) **THE PINK OPAQUE** [ ] [ ] Sep85
– The spangle maker / Millimillenary / Wax and wane / Hitherto / Pearly-dewdrops' drops (12" Version) / From the flagstones / Aikea-Guinea / Lorelei / Pepper-tree / Musette and drums.

Nov 91. Capitol; (cd-s-box-10) **THE SINGLES COLLECTION** [ ] [-]

— (above featured previous 9 singles + new 1) (all sold separately Mar92)

Leonard COHEN

Born: 21 Sep'34, Montreal, Canada. In the 50's and early 60's he wrote poetry which was later to become lyrics for his songs. In 1963 COHEN published first novel THE FAVOURITE GAME, before attending Columbia Uni. In 1966 he signed to 'Columbia', after songs (most notably SUZANNE for JUDY COLLINS) had been covered. Around the same period, his second novel BEAUTIFUL LOSERS was published, and a film documentary 'LADIES & GENTLEMEN . . . ' was issued. In 1968, his debut album 'THE SONGS OF LEONARD COHEN' gained lots of interest, mostly in the UK where it hit Top 20. Relying on mostly album sales, his work though never massive, made him most respected and enduring artists of all-time. He was back in 1992, when 'THE FUTURE' gave him another album success. • **Style:** Droning narrative-like vocals, not unlike LOU REED in tone, made him loved by college beatnik circuit, although parodied and panned by music press critics. However, in recent years he has become more appreciated. I'M YOUR FAN Various Artists tribute album released late 1991. • **Songwriters:** He penned all material. Also covered; ALWAYS (Irving Berlin) / THE PARTISAN (A.Marly & H.Zaret-Bernard) / BE FOR REAL (Frederick Knight). • **Trivia:** His long-time dual backing singer and solo artist JENNIFER WARNES released album 'FAMOUS BLUE RAINCOAT' which contained all songs written by COHEN.

Recommended: GREATEST HITS (*9)

LEONARD COHEN – vocals, guitar(with various session people)

C.B.S. Columbia

Feb 68. (lp) **THE SONGS OF LEONARD COHEN** 13 83
– Suzanne / Master song / Winter lady / The stranger song / Sisters of mercy / So long, Marianne / Hey, that's no way to say goodbye / Stories of the street / Teachers / One of us cannot be wrong. *(re-iss.+cd.Nov91)*

May 68. (7") **SUZANNE. / SO LONG, MARIANNE**

Apr 69. (lp)(c) **SONGS FROM A ROOM** 2 63
– Bird on the wire / Story of Isaac / Bunch of lonesome heroes / The partisan / Seems so long ago, Nancy / Old revolution / The butcher / You know who I am / Lady midnight / Tonight will be fine. *(re-iss.Nov81) (cd-iss.Feb88)*

May 69. (7") **BIRD ON THE WIRE. / SEEMS SO LONG AGO, NANCY**

Mar 71. (lp)(c) **SONGS OF LOVE AND HATE** 4
– Avalanche / Last year's man / Dress rehearsal rag / Diamonds in the mine / Love call you by your first name / Famous blue raincoat / Sing another song / Boys / Joan of Arc. *(re-iss.Sep82) (re-iss.cd+c Jun94 on 'Columbia')*

Jul 71. (7") **JOAN OF ARC. / DIAMONDS IN THE MINE**

Jul 72. (7"ep) **McCABE & MRS. MILLER**
– Sisters of mercy / Winter lady / The stranger song.

— w / **RON CORNELIUS** – guitar / **BOB JOHNSTON** – organ, guitar, harmonica / **CHARLIE DANIELS** – bass, fiddle / **ELKIN FOWLER** – banjo, guitar / **JENNIFER WARNES** – vocals / **PETER MARSHALL** – bass / **DAVID O'CONNOR** – guitar

Apr 73. (lp)(c) **LEONARD COHEN: LIVE SONGS (live)**
– (minute prologue) / Passing through / You know who I am / Bird on the wire / Nancy / Improvisation / Story of Isaac / Please don't pass me by (a disgrace) / Tonight will be fine / Queen Victoria. *(re-iss.Mar84, cd-iss. May88)*

Apr 73. (7") **NANCY (live). / PASSING THROUGH (live)** -

Jul 74. (7") **BIRD ON THE WIRE (live). / TONIGHT WILL BE FINE (live)**

— now w/ loads of sessioners

Aug 74. (lp)(c) **NEW SKIN FOR THE OLD CEREMONY** 24
– Is this what you wanted / Chelsea hotel No.2 / Lover lover lover / Field Commander Cohen / Why don't you try / There is a war / A singer must die / I tried to leave you / Who by fire / Take this longing / Leaving Green sleeves. *(cd-iss.Feb88)*

Nov 74. (7") **LOVER LOVER LOVER. / WHO BY FIRE**

Nov 75. (lp)(c) **GREATEST HITS**
– Suzanne / Sisters of mercy / So long, Marianne / Bird on the wire / Lady Midnight / The partisan / Hey, that's no way to say goodbye / Famous blue raincoat / Last year's man / Chelsea hotel No.2 / Who by fire / Take this longing. *(re-iss.+cd.Apr85) (re-iss.Jul88, hit UK 99)*

Nov 77. (lp)(c) **DEATH OF A LADIES MAN** 35
– True love leaves no traces / Iodine / Paper thin hotel / Memories / I left a woman waiting / Don't go home with your hard-on / Fingerprints / Death of a ladies man. *(cd-iss.Feb88 & May95 +c)*

Dec 77. (7") **MEMORIES. / DON'T GO HOME WITH YOUR HARD-ON**

Oct 78. (7") **TRUE LOVE LEAVES NO TRACES. / I LEFT A WOMAN WAITING**

Sep 79. (lp)(c) **RECENT SONGS**
– The guests / Humbled in love / The window / Came so far for beauty / The lost Canadian (un Canadien errant) / The traitor / Our lady of solitude / The gypsy's wife / The smokey life / The ballad of absent mare. *(cd-iss.May88) (re-iss.cd.Dec93 on 'Sony Europe') (re-iss.cd+c May94 on 'Columbia')*

C.B.S. Passport

Feb 85. (lp)(c) **VARIOUS POSITIONS** 52
– Dance me to the end of love / Come back to you / The law / Night comes on / Hallelujah / The captain / Hunter's lullaby / Heart with no companion / If it be your will. *(cd-iss.Feb88)*

Feb 85. (7") **DANCE ME TO THE END OF LOVE. / THE LAW**

Jan 88. (7") **FIRST WE TAKE MANHATTAN. / SISTERS OF MERCY**
(12"+=)(cd-s+=) – Bird on the wire / Suzanne.

Feb 88. (lp)(c)(cd) **I'M YOUR MAN** 48
– First we take Manhattan / Ain't no cure for love / Everybody knows / I'm your man / Take this waltz / Jazz police / I can't forget / Tower of song. *(re-iss.cd Dec95)*

May 88. (7") **AIN'T NO CURE FOR LOVE. / JAZZ POLICE**
(12"+=)(cd-s+=) – Hey that's no way to say goodbye / So long, Marianne.

Columbia Columbia

Nov 92. (cd)(c)(lp) **THE FUTURE** 36
– The future / Waiting for the miracle / Be for real / Closing time / Anthem / Democracy / Light as the breeze / Always / Tacoma trailer.

Dec 92. (cd-ep) **THE FUTURE EP**

May 93. (cd-ep) **CLOSING TIME / FIRST WE TAKE MANHATTAN / FAMOUS BLUE RAINCOAT / WINTER LADY** -

– compilations etc. –

Note; on 'CBS/ Columbia' until otherwise stated.

Mar 73. (7") **SUZANNE. / BIRD ON THE WIRE**

May 76. (7") **SUZANNE. / TAKE THIS LONGING**

May 88. (cd) **THE BEST OF LEONARD COHEN** (UK-iss.Oct94)

Aug 83. Pickwick; (7"ep)(c-ep) **SCOOP 33** -
– Suzanne / Hey, that's no way to say goodbye / Joan of Arc / Bird on the wire / Paper thin hotel / Lady midnight.

Sep 92. Sony-Columbia; (d-cd) **NEW SKIN FOR THE OLD CEREMONY / SONGS FROM A ROOM**

Oct 93. Sony-Columbia; (3xcd-box) **SONGS OF LEONARD COHEN / SONGS OF LOVE & HATE / LIVE**

Nov 93. Sony Collectors; (cd)(c) **SO LONG, MARIANNE** -
(re-iss.Dec95 on 'Columbia')

Feb 95. Columbia; (d-cd) **SONGS FROM A ROOM / SONGS OF LOVE & HATE** -

Marc COHN

Born: Cleveland, Ohio, USA. Discovered by CARLY SIMON, and founded The SUPREME COURT; a 14-piece band from New York. • **Style:** Bearded balladeer in mould of CHRISTOPHER CROSS or an FM made JOE COCKER. • **Songwriters:** All penned by himself, a few with LEVENTHAL. • **Trivia:** Harmony was provided by guests CROSBY & NASH on his 1993 album.

Recommended: MARC COHN (*5).

MARC COHN – vocals, piano with **JOHN LEVENTHAL** – organ, keyboards, guitar / **JIM KELTNER** – drums / with session people

Atlantic Atlantic

May 91. (7")(c-s) **WALKING IN MEMPHIS. / DIG DOWN DEEP** 66 13 Mar 91
(cd-s+=) – Saving the best for last (live) / 29 ways (inc.)

Jun 91. (cd)(c)(lp) **MARC COHN** 27 38 Apr 91
– Walking in Memphis / Ghost train / Silver Thunderbird / Dig down deep / Walk on water / Miles away / Saving the best for last / Strangers in a car / 29 ways / Perfect love / True companion.

Jul 91. (7")(c-s) **SILVER THUNDERBIRD. / ANGEL SONG** 54
(cd-s+=) – Walking in Memphis (live).

Sep 91. (7")(c-s) **WALKING IN MEMPHIS. / SILVER THUNDER-BIRD / 29 WAYS (live)** 22 -
(cd-s) – (1st 2 tracks) / Ghost train (live).

Dec 91. (7" c-s) **TRUE COMPANION. / MILES AWAY** -
(cd-s+=) – ('A' live) / Silver Thunderbird.
(cd-s+=) – Strangers in a car / Walking in Memphis (live)

Feb 92. (7") **STRANGERS IN A CAR. / WALKING IN MEMPHIS**
(c-s+=)(cd-s+=) – True companion (live) / Silver Thunderbird.

— still with **LEVANTHAL + KELTNER** plus **JAMES HUTCHINSON** – bass / **BELMONT TENCH** – piano, keyboards / **RICK DEPOFI** – tenor sax / **ADAM KOLKER** – baritone sax

May 93. (7")(c-s) **WALK THROUGH THE WORLD. / FROM THE STATION** 37
(cd-s+=) – One thing of beauty / Walking in Memphis (live).
(cd-s) – ('A'side) / The calling / Old soldier / Nowhere fast.

Jun 93. (cd)(c)(lp) **THE RAINY SEASON** 24 63
– Walk through the world / Rest for the weary / The rainy season / Mama's in the Moon / Don't talk to her at night / Paper walls / From the station / Medicine man / Baby king / She's becoming gold / The things we've handed down. *(re-is.cd Feb95)*

Lloyd COLE

Formed: Glasgow, Scotland . . . Summer '83, COLE and BLAIR COWAN formed LLOYD COLE & THE COMMOTIONS. They recruited CLARK, ex-jailbird DONEGAN and Scots lightweight boxing champ IRVINE. They almost immediately signed with 'Polydor', becoming college circuit darlings by the mid 80's. They/he had enduring string of albums accompanied by several hit singles, starting with 'PERFECT SKIN'. • **Style:** Intelligent laid-back rock with looks/image courtesy of COLE. • **Songwriters:** COLE penned, except GLORY (Television) / MYSTERY TRAIN (Elvis Presley) / I DON'T BELIEVE YOU (Bob Dylan) / CHILDREN OF THE REVOLUTION (T.Rex). • **Trivia:** 60's chanteuse/singer SANDIE SHAW had minor UK chart hit in 1986 with their 'Rattlesnakes' lp track, 'ARE YOU READY TO BE HEART-BROKEN?'. By 1990, COLE had flitted to New York, also beginning a brief modelling career.

Recommended: 1984-1989 (*8)

LLOYD COLE & THE COMMOTIONS

LLOYD COLE (b.31 Jan'61, Derbyshire, England) – vocals, guitar / **NEIL CLARK** (b. 3 Jul'55) – guitar / **BLAIR COWAN** – keyboards, vocals / **LAWRENCE DONEGAN** (b.13 Jul'61) – bass (ex-BLUEBELLS) / **STEPHEN IRVINE** (b.16 Dec'59) – drums

Polydor Geffen

Apr 84. (7") **PERFECT SKIN. / THE SEA AND THE SAND** 26
(12"+=) – You will never be so good.

Aug 84. (7") **FOREST FIRE. / ANDY'S BABIES** 41
(12"+=) – Glory

Oct 84. (lp)(c)(cd) **RATTLESNAKES** 13
– Perfect skin / Speedboat / Rattlesnakes / Down on Mission Street / Forest fire / Charlotte Street / 2CV / Four flights up / Patience / Are you ready to be heartbroken?. (cd.+=) – The sea and the sand / You will never be no good / Sweetness / Andy's babies. *(re-iss.c+cd. 1991)*

Oct 84. (7") **RATTLESNAKES. / SWEETNESS** 65
(12"+=) – Four flights up

Aug 85. (7") **BRAND NEW FRIEND. / HER LAST FLING** 19
(12"+=) – Speedboat (live) / 2CV (live).

Oct 85. (7")(10") **LOST WEEKEND. / BIG WORLD** 17
(12"+=) – Never ends.

Nov 85. (lp)(c)(cd) **EASY PIECES** 5
– Rich / Why I love country music / Pretty gone / Grace / Cut me down / Brand new friend / Lost weekend / James / Minor characters / Perfect blue. *(c+=)* – Her last fling / Big world. *(cd++=)* – Never ends. *(re-iss.c+cd.1991) (re-iss.cd+c May93 on 'Spectrum')*

Jan 86. (7") **CUT ME DOWN (remix). / ARE YOU READY TO BE HEARTBROKEN? (live)** 38
(12"+=) – Forest fire (live).
(d7"++=) – Perfect blue (instrumental).

— Trimmed to studio quartet, when COWAN became only part-time (gigs only)

Polydor Capitol

Sep 87. (7") **MY BAG. / JESUS SAID** 46
(12"+=)(cd-s+=) – Perfect skin.

Oct 87. (lp)(c)(cd) **MAINSTREAM** 9
– My bag / From the hip / 29 / Mainstream / Jennifer she said / Mister malcontent / Sean Penn blues / Big snake / Hey Rusty / These days.

Oct 87. (7") **MY BAG. / LOVE YOUR WIFE** -

Jan 88. (7") **JENNIFER SHE SAID. / PERFECT BLUE** 31

(12"+=) – Mystery train (live) / I don't believe you (live).
(cd-s+=) – My bag (mix).

Apr 88. (7"ep)(12"ep)(cd-ep) **FROM THE HIP** [59] [ ]
– From the hip / Please / Lonely mile / Love you wife.

Mar 89. (lp)(c)(cd) **1984-1989** (compilation) [14] [ ]
– Perfect skin / Are you ready to be heartbroken? / Forest fire / You will never be so good / Rattlesnakes / Perfect blue / Brand new friend / Cut me down / Lost weekend / Her last fling / Mr.Malcontent / My bag / Jennifer she said / From the hip.

Apr 89. (7") **FOREST FIRE ('89 remix). / PERFECT BLUE** [ ] [ ]
(12"+=)(cd-s+=) – ('A'&'B'extended).

— DONEGAN decided to leave, and the group folded Apr'89.

LLOYD COLE

went solo with **BLAIR COWAN** – keyboards / **DARYLL SWEET** – bass / **ROBEDRT QUINE** – guitar / **FRED MAHER** – drums, etc / **NICKY HOLLAND and PARKER DU LANY backing vocals.** / (on tour; DAN McCARROLL repl. MAHER / **DAVID BALL repl. SWEET)**

Jan 90. (7")(c-s) **NO BLUE SKIES. / SHELLY I DO** [42] [ ]
(10"+=)(12"+=)(cd-s+=) – Wild orphan.

Feb 90. (cd)(c)(lp) **LLOYD COLE** [11] [ ]
– Don't look back / What do you know about love? / Loveless / No blue skies / Sweetheart / To the church / Downtown / A long way down / Ice cream girl / I hate to see you baby doing that shift / Undressed / Waterline / Mercy killing. *(re-iss.cd Apr95)*

Mar 90. (7")(c-s) **DON'T LOOK BACK. / BLAME MARY JANE** [59] [ ]
(10"+=)(12"+=)(cd-s+=) – Witching hour.

Oct 90. (7")(c-s) **DOWNTOWN. / A LONG WAY DOWN (live)** [ ] [ ]
(12"+=)(cd-s+=) – Sweetheart (live).

— **COLE** now with **COWAN & CLARK**

Aug 91. (7") **SHE'S A GIRL AND I'M A MAN. / WEIRD ON ME** [55] [ ]
(12"+=)(cd-s+=) – Children of the revolution.

Sep 91. (cd)(c)(lp) **DON'T GET WEIRD ON ME BABE** [21] [ ]
– Butterfly / Theme for her / Margo's waltz / Half of everything / Man enough / What he doesn't know / Tell your sister / Weeping wine / To the lions / Pay for it / The one you never had / She's a girl and I'm a man.

Oct 91. (7") **WEEPING WINE. / TELL YOUR SISTER** [ ] [ ]
(12"+=)(cd-s+=) – Somewhere out in the east.

Mar 92. (7")(c-s) **BUTTERFLY. / JENNIFER SHE SAID** [ ] [ ]
(12"+=)(cd-s+=) – ('A'the Planet Anne Charlotte mix).

Fontana Fontana

Sep 93. (7")(c-s) **SO YOU'D LIKE TO SAVE THE WORLD. / VICIOUS** [72] [ ]
(cd-s+=) – Mystic lady.
(cd-s) – ('A'side) / For your pleasure for your company / 4 M.B.

Oct 93. (cd)(c)(lp) **BAD VIBES** [38] [ ]
– Morning is broken / So you'd like to save the world / Holier than thou / Love you so what / Wild mushrooms / My way to you / Too much of a good thing / Fall together / Mister Wrong / Seen the future / Can't get arrested.

— above w/ **ADAM PETERS, ANN CHARLOTTE VENGSGAARD, JOHN MICCO, JOHN CARRUTHERS, NEIL CLARK, MATTHEW SWEET, DAN McCARROLL, ANTON FIER, CURTIS WATTS, FRED MAHER, DANA VLCEK, Lightning BOB HOFFNAR + PETER MARK**

Nov 93. (7")(c-s) **MORNING IS BROKEN. / RADIO CITY MUSIC HALL** [ ] [ ]
(cd-s+=) – Radio City music hall / Eat your greens.
(cd-s+=) – The slider / Mannish girl.

Mercury Mercury

Sep 95. (c-s) **LIKE LOVERS DO / I WILL NOT LEAVE YOU ALONE** [24] [ ]
(cd-s+=) – Rattlesnakes.
(cd-s) – ('A'side) / Brand new baby blues (demo) / Perfect skin.
(cd-s) – ('A'side) / Traffic / Forest fire.
(cd-s) – ('A'side) / Forest fire / Rattlesnakes / Perfect skin.

Sep 95. (cd)(c) **LOVE STORY** [27] [ ]
– Trigger happy / Sentimental fool / I didn't know that you cared / Love ruins everything / Baby / Be there / The June bride / Like lovers do / Happy for you / Traffic / Let's get lost / For crying out loud.

Nov 95. (c-s) **SENTIMENTAL FOOL / BRAND NEW FRIEND** [73] [ ]
(cd-s+=) – Lost weekend / Cut me down.
(cd-s) – ('A'side) / Most of the time / Millionaire / Sold.

COLLECTIVE SOUL

Formed: Stockbridge, Georgia, USA . . .late 80's by ED ROLAND, who had studied at Boston's Berklee School Of Music. After numerous rejections from major record companies, he split band in 1992. He continued to try his hand at writing songs for other artists and made songwriting demo for some radio stations. Interest in the song 'SHINE' let 'Atlantic' take note and they duly signed him/them in 1993. He brought in musicians, including his brother DEAN and original drummer SHANE EVANS. SHINE became a near Top 10 hit in the States, as did debut album 'HINTS . . .', helped by playing the Woodstock 25th Anniversary Festival '94. • **Style:** Catchy hard and sometimes alternative rock act. • **Songwriters:** ED ROLAND.

Recommended: HINTS, ALLEGATIONS AND THINGS LEFT UNSAID (*6)

ED ROLAND – vocals, guitar / **ROSS CHILDRESS** – lead guitar / **DEAN ROLAND** – guitar / **WILL TURPIN** – bass / **SHANE EVANS** – drums

Atlantic Atlantic

May 94. (c-s) **SHINE / LOVE LIFTED ME / BURNING BRIDGES** [ ] [11]
(12"+=)(cd-s+=) – ('A'version).

Sep 94. (cd)(c) **HINTS, ALLEGATIONS AND THINGS LEFT UNSAID** [ ] [18] May 94
– Shine / Goodnight, good guy / Wasting time / Sister don't cry / Love lifted me / In a moment / Heaven's already here / Pretty Donna / Reach / Breathe / Scream / Burning bridges / All.

Oct 94. (c-s)(cd-s) **BREATHE /** [-] [ ]

May 95. (c-s)(cd-s) **GEL /** [-] [ ]

— (above was featured in the comedy film 'The Jerky Boys')

May 95. (cd)(c) **COLLECTIVE SOUL** [ ] [23] Mar95

May 95. (c-s)(cd-s) **DECEMBER /** [-] [20]

Dec 95. (cd-s) **THE WORLD I KNOW /** [-] [40]

Albert COLLINS

Born: 1 Oct'32, Leona, Texas, USA. After his sharecropping family moved to the ghettos of Houston, he was taught guitar by his cousin LIGHTNIN' HOPKINS (who was already a blues recording artist). ALBERT then went on the road with CLARENCE 'Gatemouth' BROWN and by the age of 17 had formed own group The RHYTHM ROCKERS. In the 50's he became a session player and had the (future!) acolade of replacing a young JIMI HENDRIX in LITTLE RICHARD's band. His debut solo outing was in 1958 when 'Kangaroo' records issued instrumental 'FREEZE'. Sparodical instrumentals followed in the 60's, due to Texans being overshadowed at the time by the Chicago blues scene. However his first real break came about when CANNED HEAT's BOB HITE recommended him to his label 'Imperial', who duly signed him and issued debut lp 'LOVE CAN BE FOUND ANYWHERE EVEN IN A GUITAR'. Another two Nashville-based albums saw light and he even moved to Chicago to join the short-lived 'Tumbleweed' stable run by BILL SZYMCZYK. In the mid-70's he toured constantly and finally found a home at BRUCE IGLAUER'S 'Alligator' records in 1978, where he has stayed ever since. He was nominated for Grammy awards during the 80's, and is now well known for influencing a young ROBERT CRAY, with whom he shared an album /and JOHNNY COPELAND in 1985. With a couple of early 90's revival albums for 'Virgin' behind him, he tragically died of lung cancer on 1st December 1993. • **Style:** Powerful but cool blues master of the Telecaster guitar, who is well regarded by his contemporaries and peers. • **Songwriters:** Self-penned except several covers. • **Trivia:** Played alongside GEORGE THOROGOOD at 1985's LIVE AID show.

Recommended: DON'T LOSE YOUR COOL (*7) / ICE PICKIN' (*8)

ALBERT COLLINS – guitar with various personnel

not issued Kangaroo

1958. (7"w / HIS RHYTHM ROCKERS) **FREEZE. / COLLINS SHUFFLE** [-] [ ]

not issued Great Scot

1962. (7") **ALBERT'S ALLEY. / DEFROST** [-] [ ]
(re-iss.on 'Hall-Way' 1963 + 'Smash')

not issued Hall-Way

1962. (7") **HOMESICK. / SIPPIN' SODA** [-] [ ]

1962. (7") **FROSTY. / TREMBLE** [-] [ ]

1962. (7") **THAWOUT. / BACKSTROKE** [-] [ ]

not issued 20th Cent Fox

1963. (7") **SNO-CONE (part 1). / SNO-CONE (part 2)** [-] [ ]

1963. (7") **DYIN' FLU. / HOT'N'COLD** [-] [ ]

1963. (7") **FROST BITE. / DON'T LOSE YOUR COOL** [-] [ ]

1968. (7") **TAKING MY TIME. / COOKIN' CATFISH** [-] [ ]

not issued Tracie

1968. (7") **(WHAT'D I SAY) I DON'T KNOW. / SOULROAD** [-] [ ]

— **COLLINS** now vocals, guitar with Nashville musicians

Liberty Imperial

1968. (lp) **LOVE CAN BE FOUND ANYWHERE EVEN IN A GUITAR** [ ] [ ]
– Got a good thing goin' / Ain't got time / Do the sissy / Turnin' on / Collins mix / Let's get it together / Left overs / Doin' my thing / Whatcha say (I don't know) / Pushin' / Stom poker.

1968. (7") **GOT A GOOD THING GOIN'. / AIN'T GOT TIME** [-] [ ]

1968. (7") **TURNIN' ON. / DO THE SISSY** [-] [ ]

1969. (lp) **TRASH TALKIN'** [-] [ ]
– Harris County line / Conversation with Collins / Jawing / Grapeland gossip / Chatterbox / Trash talkin' / Baby what you want me to do / Rock me baby / Lip service / Talking Slim blues / Back-yard back-talk / Tongue lashing / And then it started raining.

1970. (lp) **THE COMPLEAT** [-] [ ]
– Do what you want to do / Cool'n collards / Soul food / Jam it up / Black bottom bayou / Junkey monkey / 69 Underpass roadside / I need you so / Blend down and jam / Sweet'n sour / Bitsey / Swamp sauce.

1970. (7") **COOL 'N COLLARDS. / DO WHAT YOU WANT TO DO** [-] [ ]

Tumble-weed Tumble-weed

Jan 72. (lp) **THERE'S GOTTA BE A CHANGE** [ ] [ ]
– There's gotta be a change / In love wit'cha / Stickin' / Today ain't like yesterday / Somethin' on my mind / Frog jumpin' / I got a mind to travel / Get your business straight / Fade away.

— his live band were around 1980; **A.C. REED** – tenor sax / **ALLAN BATTS** – keyboards / **MARVIN JACKSON** – guitar / **JOHNNY B. GAYDEN** – bass / **CASEY JONES** – drums

Sonet Alligator

Jan 79. (lp) **ICE PICKIN'** [ ] [ ]
– Honey hush / When the welfare turns it's back on you / Ice pick / Cold, cold feeling / Too tired / Master charge / Conversation with Collins / Avalanche. *(cd-iss.Oct86 + Jul88) (re-iss.cd+c May93 on 'Alligator')*

Jun 80. (lp) **FROSTBITE** [ ] [ ]
– If you love me like you say / Blue Monday hangover / I got a problem / The highway is like a woman / Brick / Don't go reaching across my plate / Give me the

blues / Snowed in. *(cd-iss.Aug90) (re-iss.cd+c May93 on 'Alligator')*

Nov 81. (lp) **FROZEN ALIVE (live)**
– Frosty / Angel of mercy / I got that feeling / Caldonia / Things I used to do / Got a mind to travel / Cold cuts. *(cd-iss.Aug90) (re-iss.cd+c May93 on 'Alligator')*

— **LARRY BURTON** – guitar repl. MARVIN / guest **CHRIS FOREMAN** – keyboards repl. BATTS / added **ABE LOCKE + DINO SPELLS** – saxes

Jul 83. (lp) **DON'T LOSE YOUR COOL**
– Get to gettin' / My mind is trying to leave me / Broke / Don't lose your cool / When a guitar plays the blues / . . .But I was cool / Melt down / Ego trip / Quicksand. *(cd-iss.Aug90) (re-iss.cd+c May93 on 'Alligator')*

Mar 85. (lp) **LIVE IN JAPAN (live)**
– Listen here / Tired man / If trouble was money / Jealous man / Stormy Monday / Skatin' / All about my girl. *(cd-iss.Aug90) (re-iss.cd+c May93 on 'Alligator')*

— next with also **ALLEN BATTS** – organ / **JOHNNY B. GAYDEN** – bass / **CASEY JONES** – drums

Nov 85. (lp) **SHOWDOWN! (with JOHNNY COPELAND & ROBERT CRAY)**
– T-Bone shuufle / The Moon is full / Lion's den / The dream / She's into something / Bring your fine self home / Black cat bone / Albert's alley / Blackjack. *(cd-iss.Oct87) (re-iss.cd+c May93 on 'Alligator')*

Jan 87. (lp) **COLD SNAP**
– Cash talkin' / Bending like a willow tree / A good fool is hard to find / Lights are on but nobody's home / I ain't drunk / Hooked on you / Too many dirty dishes / Snatchin' it back / Fake I.D. *(re-iss.cd+c Aug90) (re-iss.cd+c May93 on 'Alligator')*

Feb 88. (7") **BABYSITTIN' BLUES. / ?**
(above from the film he appeared in 'Adventures In Babysitting')

Virgin Virgin

Feb 91. (cd)(c)(lp) **ICEMAN**
– Mr.Collins, Mr.Collins / Iceman / Don't mistake kindness for weakness / Travelin' south / Put the shoe on the other foot / I'm beginning to wonder / Head rag / Hawk / Blues for Gabe / Mr.Collins, Mr.Collins (reprise).

Nov 93. (cd)(c) **COLLINS MIX**
– There's gotta be a change / Honey hush / Mastercharge / If trouble was money / Don't lose your cool / If you love me like you say / Frosty / Tired man / The Moon is full / Collins mix / Same old thing.

— ALBERT died of lung cancer on the 1st Dec'93 aged 61.

Pointblack Pointblank

Sep 95. (cd) **LIVE '92-'93 (live)**
–

– compilations, etc –

Sep 82. Red Lightnin'; (lp) **ALIVE & COOL (live)** -
1992. Red Lightnin'; (cd) **MOLTEN ICE** -
Jun 85. Crossgates; (lp) **THE COOL SOUND OF ALBERT COLLINS** -
1986. Charly; (lp)(c) **ICE COLD BLUES** -
Oct 91. Imperial; (cd) **THE COMPLETE IMPERIAL RECORDINGS** -
Nov 95. Charly; (cd) **LIVE** -

Allen COLLINS BAND (see under ⇒ LYNYRD SKYNYRD)

Edwyn COLLINS

Born: 23 Aug'59, Edinburgh, Scotland. Formed ORANGE JUICE in Glasgow, Scotland . . . 1977 initially as the NU-SONICS. In 1979, ORANGE JUICE signed to local indie label 'Postcard'. After 4 well-received 45's, they transferred to 'Polydor', helped by manager Ian Crann. After 2 minor hits, they progressed early 1982 with debut Top 30 album 'YOU CAN'T HIDE YOUR LOVE FOREVER'. They split in 1984 and after a few singles in the mid 80's, EDWYN finally issued his debut album in 1989 'HOPE AND DESPAIR'. However, it took just over half a decade for him to climb back into the charts with his gorgeous hit single 'A GIRL LIKE YOU'. • **Style:** Jangly alternative pop outfit, fronted by throaty deep vox of COLLINS. He and Nigerian newcomer ZEKE MANYIKA moved into a more funkier territory in 1982. • **Songwriters:** Most written by COLLINS, some with MANYIKA. Note that KIRK was the writer of FELICITY, and Ross provided PUNCH DRUNK. Covered L.O.V.E. (Al Green). COLLINS solo covered MY GIRL HAS GONE (Smokey Robinson) + TIME OF THE PREACHER (Willie Nelson). • **Trivia:** COLLINS was raised in Dundee while of school age, until he moved to Bearsden, near Glasgow.

Recommended: THE ESTEEMED ORANGE JUICE (THE VERY BEST OF ORANGE JUICE) (*9) / GORGEOUS GEORGE (*8)

EDWYN COLLINS – vox, guitar, occ.violin / **JAMES KIRK** – guitar, vocals / **DAVID McCLYMONT** – bass, synths repl. ALAN DUNCAN/ **STEPHEN DALY** – drums

Postcard not issued

Feb 80. (7") **FALLING AND LAUGHING. / MOSCOW** -
(free 7"flexi) – FELICITY (live).
Aug 80. (7") **BLUE BOY. / LOVE SICK** -
Dec 80. (7") **SIMPLY THRILLED HONEY. / BREAKFAST TIME** -
Mar 81. (7") **POOR OLD SOUL. / (part 2)** -

Polydor Polydor

Oct 81. (7") **L.O.V.E . . . LOVE. / INTUITION TOLD ME** 65 -
(12"+=) – Moscow.
Jan 82. (7") **FELICITY. / IN A NUTSHELL** 63 -
(12"+=) – You old eccentric.
Feb 82. (lp)(c) **YOUR LOVE CAN'T LAST FOREVER** 21
– Tender object / L.O.V.E . . . love / Falling and laughing / Wan light / Untitled melody / Dying day / Upwards and onwards / Felicity / Three cheers for our side / Intuition told me / Satellite city / In a nutshell / Consolation prize.

— **MALCOLM ROSS** – guitar (ex-JOSEF K) repl. KIRK who formed MEMPHIS / **ZEKE MANYIKA** (b. Nigeria) – percussion, vocals, synths repl. DALY to above

Jul 82. (7")(10") **TWO HEARTS TOGETHER. / HOKOYO** 60 -
Oct 82. (7") **I CAN'T HELP MYSELF. / TONGUES BEGIN TO WAG** 42
(12"+=) – Barbeque.
Nov 82. (lp)(c) **RIP IT UP** 39
– Rip it up / Turn away / I can't help myself / Breakfast time / Tender hook / A million pleading places / Flesh of my flesh / Mud in your eye / Louise Louise. *(re-iss.Jul89)*
Feb 83. (7") **RIP IT UP (remix). / SNAKE CHARMER** 8
(12") – ('A'extended) / A sad lament.
(d7"++=) – (all tracks).
May 83. (7")(7"pic-d) **FLESH OF MY FLESH. / LORD JOHN WHITE AND THE BOTTLENECK TRAIN** 41

— basically now a duo of **COLLINS + MANYIKA** with session people replacing ROSS (who joined AZTEC CAMERA) and McCLYMONT (to The MOODISTS)

Feb 84. (7") **BRIDGE. / OUT FOR THE COUNT** 67
(12"+=) – ('A' Summer '83 mix).
(free 7"flexi w/7") – Poor old soul (live).
Feb 84. (m-lp)(c) **TEXAS FEVER** 34
– A sad lament / Craziest feeling / A place in my heart / The day I went down to Texas / Punch drunk / Bridge.
Apr 84. (7") **WHAT PRESENCE?!. / A PLACE IN MY HEART** 47
(12"+=) – ('A'extended).
(free c-s w/7") – In a nutshell (live) / Simply thrilled honey (live) / Dying day (live).
Oct 84. (7") **LEAN PERIOD. / BURY MY HEAD IN MY HANDS** 74
(12"+=) – ('A'extended).
(free 7"flexi w/7") – Rip it up / What presence?!.
Nov 84. (lp)(c) **THE ORANGE JUICE – THE THIRD ALBUM**
– Get while the goings good / Salmon fishing in New York / I guess I'm just a little sensitive / Burning desire / The artisan / Lean period / What presence?! / Out for the count / All that mattered / Searchager. (c+=) – (extra versions)

— Disbanded after above album. MANYIKA went solo, as did EDWYN COLLINS. He had already in Aug84 hit UK 72 with PAUL QUINN on 7"/12" 'PALE BLUES EYES' (a Velvet Underground cover) released on 'Swamplands'.

– compilations, others, etc. –

Jul 85. Polydor; (lp)(c) **IN A NUTSHELL** -
(w/free 7"flexi) – FELICITY.
Jan 91. Polydor; (cd)(c) **THE ORANGE JUICE / YOU CAN'T HIDE YOUR LOVE FOREVER** -
Jul 92. Polydor; (cd)(c)(lp) **THE VERY BEST OF ORANGE JUICE (THE ESTEEMED ORANGE JUICE)** -
– Falling and laughing / Consolation prize (live) / Old encentric / L.O.V.E. love / Felicity / In a nutshell / Rip it up / I can't help myself / Flesh of my flesh / Tenterhook / Bridge / The day I went down to Texas / Punch drunk / A place in my heart / A sad lament / Lean period / I guess I'm just a little too sensitive / The artisans / Salmon fishing in New York / What presence?! / Out for the count. *(re-iss.cd Sep95)*
Jul 92. Postcard; (cd)(c)(lp) **OSTRICH CHURCHYARD (live in Glasgow)** -
(re-iss.cd Oct95)
May 93. Postcard; (7") **BLUEBOY. / LOVESICK** -
(cd-s+=) – Poor old soul (French version) / Poor old soul (instrumental).
Jul 93. Postcard; (cd)(lp) **THE HEATHER'S ON FIRE** -
– Falling and laughing / Moscow / Moscow Olympics / Blue boy / Love sick / Simply thrilled honey / Breakfast time / Poor old soul / Poor old soul pt.2 / Felicity / Upwards and onwards / Dying day / Holiday hymn. *(re-iss.cd Oct95)*

EDWYN COLLINS

solo, with **DENNIS BOVELL, MALCOLM ROSS, ALEX GRAY + CHRIS TAYLOR**

Creation Elevation

May 87. (7") **DON'T SHILLY SHALLY. / IF EVER YOU'RE READY** -
(12"+=) – Queer fish.

Elevation not issued

Nov 87. (7")(12") **MY BELOVED GIRL. / CLOUDS (FOGGING UP MY MIND)** -

— now with **BERNARD CLARKE** – keys / **DENNIS BOVELL** – bass / **DAVE RUFFY** – drums

Demon not issued

Jun 89. (lp)(c)(cd) **HOPE AND DESPAIR** -
– Coffee table song / 50 shades of blue / You're better than you know / Pushing it to the back of my mind / The wheels of love / Darling, they want it all / The beginning of the end / The measure of the man / Testing time / Let me put my arms around you / The wide eyed child in me / Ghost of a chance. *(re-iss.cd Sep95)*
Jul 89. (7") **THE COFFEE TABLE SONG. / JUDAS IN BLUE JEANS** -
(12"+=) – Out there.
Oct 89. (7") **50 SHADES OF BLUE (new mix). / IF EVER YOU'RE READY** -
(12"+=) – Kindred spirit / Just call her name / Ain't that always the way.

— (on cd-s last track repl. by) – Judas in blue jeans.

Oct 90. (cd)(c)(lp) **HELLBENT ON COMPROMISE** -
– Means to an end / You poor deluded fool / It might as well be you / Take care of yourself / Graciously / Someone else besides / My girl has gone / Everything and more / What's the big idea? / Hellbent medley:- Time of the preacher – Long time gone. *(re-iss.cd Oct95)*

EDWYN COLLINS

w / **STEVEN SKINNER** – guitar / **PHIL THORNALLEY** – bass / **PAUL COOK** – drums

Setanta not issued

Aug 94. (cd)(c)(lp) **GEORGEOUS GEORGE** -
– The campaign for real rock / A girl like you / Low expectations / Out of this world / If you could love me / North of Heaven / Georgeous George / It's right in front of you / Make me feel again / You got it all / Subsidence / Occupy your mind. *(re-*

iss.Jul95, hit UK No.8)

Nov 94. (12"ep)(c-ep)(cd-ep) **EXPRESSLY** [42] [ ]
– A girl like you / Out of this world / Don't shilly shally (spotter's '86 demo). (cd-ep) – A girl like you / A girl like you (Macrame remix by Youth) / Out of this world (I hear a new world) remixed by St.Etienne / Occupy your mind.

Mar 95. (12"ep) **IF YOU COULD LOVE ME (radio edit). / IN A BROKEN DREAM / INSIDER DEALING / ('A'-MC Esher mix)** [ ] [ ]
(cd-s) – (first 3 tracks) / Hope and despair.
(cd-s) – ('A'side) / If ever you're ready / Come to your senses / A girl like you (mix).

Jun 95. (7") **A GIRL LIKE YOU. / YOU'RE ON YOUR OWN** [4] [32]
(c-s+=) – If you could love me (acoustic version).
(cd-s++=) – Don't shilly shally (Spotter's 86 demo version).

Judy COLLINS

Born: 1 May'39, Denver, Colorado, USA . . . daughter of a blind radio celebrity and musician Chuck Collins. In her teenage years, she studied classical piano but left college in Jacksonville, to get married in Denver 1957. Two years later, she began singing professionally also reciting poetry on the New York folk scene. In 1961, she was noticed by Jac Holzman, who signed her to his new 'Elektra' label. She made many critically acclaimed albums before breaking through in the mid-60's. In 1968, she had first Top 10 US hit 'BOTH SIDES NOW'. In 1971, she seemed like a resident in the UK Top 50, with classic acappella 45 'AMAZING GRACE'. The 1975 hit 'SEND IN THE CLOWNS' gave her more success, but this was to prove to be her last UK single. • **Style:** Folk-rock/pop singer, who like DYLAN and BAEZ, also used politics and protest themes. She was active in the movement to give black people the right to vote in US elections. In the 70's, her beautiful vox mainly covered contemporary ballads. • **Songwriters:** Wrote songs/lyrics herself and many covers by BOB DYLAN, LEONARD COHEN, JONI MITCHELL, The BYRDS, etc. Others included; WHO KNOWS WHERE THE TIME GOES (Sandy Denny) / IN MY LIFE (Beatles) / CATS IN THE CRADLE (Harry Chapin) / FROM A DISTANCE (Julie Gold) / WIND BENEATH MY WINGS (Henley/Silbar) / I PITY THE POOR IMMIGRANT (Bob Dylan) / THE AIR THAT I BREATHE (Hollies). • **Trivia:** Her 1969 boyfriend STEPHEN STILLS, wrote a song inspired by her 'SUITE: JUDY BLUE EYES'. ROGER McGUINN played on her third album.

Recommended: SO EARLY IN THE SPRING (*5)

JUDY COLLINS – vocals, guitar(with session people)

not issued / Elektra

Oct 61. (lp) **A MAID OF CONSTANT SORROW** [-] [ ]
– Maid of constant sorrow / The prickle bush / Wild mountain thyme / Tim Evans / Sailor's life / Bold Fenian men / Wars of Germany / O daddy be gay / I know where I'm going / John Riley / Pretty Savo / The rising of the moon. *(UK-iss.1975 on 'Elektra')*

Jul 62. (lp) **GOLDEN APPLES OF THE SUN** [-] [ ]
– Golden apples of the Sun / Bonnie ship the Diamond / Little brown dog / Twelve gates to the city / Christ child lullaby / Great Selchie of Shule Skerry / Tell me who I'll marry / Fannerio / Crow on the cradle / Lark in the mornign / Sing hallelujah / Shule Aaron. *(UK-iss.1975 on 'Elektra')*

Mar 64. (lp) **£3** [-] [ ]
– Anathea / Bullgine run / Farewell / Hey, Nelly, Nelly / Ten o'clock all is well / The dove / Masters of war / In the hills of Shiloh / The bells of Rhymney / Deportee / Come away Melinda / Turn turn turn.

1964. (7") **TURN TURN TURN. / FAREWELL** [-] [ ]

Oct 64. (lp) **IN CONCERT – TOWN HALL (live)** [-] [ ]
– Winter sky / That was the last thing on my mind / Tear down the walls / Bonnie boy is young / Me & my uncle / Wild ripping water / The lonesome death of Hattie Carroll / My ramblin' boy / Redwinged blackbird / Coal tattoo / Cruel mother / Bottle of wine / Medgar Evers lullaby / Hey, Nelly, Nelly.

London / Elektra

Oct 65. (lp) **FIFTH ALBUM** [ ] [69] Sep 65
– Pack up your sorrows / The coming of the roads / So early, early in the Spring / Tomorrow is a long time / Daddy you've been on my mind / Thirsty boots / Mr.Tambourine man / Lord Gregory / In the heat of the summer / Early morning rain / Carry it on / It isn't nice. *(US re-iss.Apr76)*

Mar 66. (7") **I'LL KEEP IT WITH MINE. / THIRSTY BOOTS** [ ] [ ]

Dec 66. (lp) **IN MY LIFE** [ ] [46]
– Tom Thumb's blues / Hard lovin' loser / Pirate Jenny / Suzanne / La Colombe / Marat / Sade / I think it's going to rain today / Sunny Goodge Street / Liverpool lullaby / Dress rehearsal rag / In my life.

Dec 66. (7") **HARD LOVIN' LOSER. / IN MY LIFE** [ ] [-]

Dec 66. (7") **HARD LOVIN' LOSER. / I THINK IT'S GOING TO RAIN TODAY** [-] [ ]

Elektra / Elektra

Jan 68. (lp) **WILDFLOWERS** [ ] [5]
– Both sides now / Michael from the mountains / Since you asked / Sisters of mercy / A ballata of Francesco Landini / Lasso di Donna / La chanson des vieux amants (the song of old lovers) / Sky fell / Albatross / Hey that's no way to say goodbye. *(re-iss.May87 +cd US)*

Nov 68. (7") **BOTH SIDES NOW. / WHO KNOWS WHERE THE TIME GOES** [ ] [8]

Dec 68. (lp) **WHO KNOWS WHERE THE TIMES GOES** [ ] [29]
– Hello, hurray / Story of Isaac / My father / Someday soon / Who knows where the time goes / I pity the poor immigrant / The first boy I loved / Bird on the wire / Pretty Polly. *(cd-iss.Feb93 & Mar95)*

Feb 69. (7") **SOMEDAY SOON. / MY FATHER** [ ] [55]

Oct 69. (7") **CHELSEA MORNING. / PRETTY POLLY** [ ] [78] Jul 69

Nov 69. (7") **TURN! TURN! TURN! – THE EVERYTHING THERE IS A SEASON. / MR.TAMBOURINE MAN** [-] [69]

Jan 70. (7") **PACK UP YOUR SORROWS. / TURN, TURN, TURN** [ ] [-]

Nov 70. (7") **AMAZING GRACE. / I PITY THE POOR IMMIGRANT** [5] [15]
(Scraped back into UK Top 40 Sep71, In Apr72 dented UK Top 20, re-iss.Nov76)

Jan 71. (lp)(c) **WHALES AND NIGHTINGALES** [37] [17] Nov 70
– Farewell to Tarwathie / Song for David / Sons of / The patriot game / Oh had I a golden thread / Prothalmum / Gene's song / Time passes slowly / Maricke / Nightingale I / Nightingale II / Simple gifts / Amazing Grace.

Nov 71. (7") **OPEN THE DOOR (SONG FOR JUDITH). / INNISFREE** [ ] [90]

Jan 72. (lp)(c) **LIVING** [ ] [64] Nov 71
– Joan of Arc / Four strong winds / Vietnam love song / Innisfree / Song for Judith (open the door) / All things are quite silent / Easy times / Chelsea morning / Famous blue raincoat / Just like Tom Thumb's blues.

Feb 73. (7") **COOK WITH HONEY. / SO BEGINS THE TASK** [ ] [32]

Mar 73. (lp)(c) **TRUE STORIES & OTHER DREAMS** [ ] [27] Feb 72
– Che / Song for Martin / Cook with honey / So begins the task / Fisherman song / Dealer (done and losin') / The secret gardens / Holly Ann / The hostage song.

1973. (7") **THE SECRET GARDENS. / THE HOSTAGE** [-] [ ]

May 75. (7") **SEND IN THE CLOWNS. / HOUSES** [6] [36]
(re-iss.1976, US re-iss.Sep77 hit No.19)

May 75. (lp)(c) **JUDITH** [7] [17] Apr 75
– Born to the breed / Send in the clowns / The Moon is a harsh mistress / Angel spread your wings / Houses / The loving of the game / Song for Duke / Salt of the Earth / Brother can you spare a dime / City of New Orleans / I'll be seeing you / Pirate ships. *(re-iss.Nov76 quad)*

Jul 75. (7") **I'LL BE SEEING YOU. / BORN TO THE BREED** [ ] [-]

Sep 75. (7") **SALT OF THE EARTH. / SONG FOR DUKE** [ ] [-]

Sep 76. (lp)(c) **BREAD AND ROSES** [ ] [25]
– Bread and roses / Everything must change / Special delivery / Out of control / Plegaria del labrador / Come down in time / Spanish is the loving tongue / I didn't know about you / Take this longing / Love hurts / Marjorie / King David.

Oct 76. (7") **BREAD AND ROSES. / OUT OF CONTROL** [-] [ ]

Nov 76. (7") **BREAD AND ROSES. / KING DAVID** [ ] [-]

Feb 77. (7") **SPECIAL DELIVERY. / EVERYTHING MUST CHANGE** [-] [ ]

May 77. (7") **BORN TO THE BREED. / SPECIAL DELIVERY** [-] [ ]

Mar 79. (7") **DOROTHY. / WHERE OR WHEN** [-] [ ]

Mar 79. (lp)(c) **HARD TIMES FOR LOVERS** [ ] [54]
– Hard times for lovers / Marie / Happy ending / Desperado / I remember sky / Theme from 'The Promise' (I'll never say goodbye) / Starmaker / Dorothy / Theme from 'The Ice Castle' (Through the eyes of love) / Where or when. *(cd-iss.Dec94) (re-iss.Sep95 on 'Warners')*

Mar 79. (7") **HARD TIMES FOR LOVERS. / HAPPY ENDING** [ ] [66]

May 80. (lp)(c) **RUNNING FOR MY LIFE** [ ] [ ]
– Running for my life / Bright morning star / Green Finch & Linnet bird / Marieke / Pretty woman / Almost free / I could really show you around / I've done enough dying for today / Anyone would love you / Rainbow connection / This is the day.

May 80. (7") **BRIGHT MORNING STAR. / ALMOST FREE** [-] [ ]

Jul 80. (7") **THE RAINBOW CONNECTION. / RUNNING FOR MY LIFE** [-] [ ]

Jan 82. (7") **MEMORY. / THE LIFE YOU DREAM** [-] [ ]

Mar 82. (lp)(c) **THE TIME OF OUR LIVES** [ ] [ ]
– Great expectations / The rest of your life / Grandaddy / It's gonna be one of those nights / Memory / Sun son / Mama mama / Drink a round to Ireland / Don't say goodbye love.

May 82. (7") **GREAT EXPECTATIONS. / MEMORY** [ ] [-]

1982. (7") **MAMA MAMA. / IT'S GONNA BE ONE OF THOSE NIGHTS** [-] [ ]

Nov 84. (7") **HOME AGAIN (w/ T.G. SHEPHERD). / DREAM ON** [-] [ ]

Jan 85. (lp)(c) **HOME AGAIN** [ ] [ ] Nov 84
– Only you / Sweetheart on parade / Everybody works in China / Yellow kimono (Tokyo time) / From where I stand / Home again / Shoot first / Don't say love / Dream on / The best is yet to come.

Feb 85. (7") **ONLY YOU. / ?** [-] [ ]

Goldcastle / Goldcastle

Nov 88. (lp)(c) **TRUST YOUR HEART** [ ] [ ] Nov 87
– Amazing Grace / Trust your heart / Jerusalem / Day by day / The life you dream / The rose / Moonfall / Morning has broken / When a child is born / When you wish upon a star. *(re-iss.c+cd.Aug91)*

Jun 89. (lp)(c)(cd) **SANITY AND GRACE (live)** [ ] [ ]
– History / Wind beneath my wings / Lovin' and leavin' / From a distance / Sanity and grace / daughters of time / Cats in the cradle / Pretty Polly / Born to the breed. *(re-iss.c+cd.Aug91)*

Columbia / Columbia

Feb 91. (cd)(c)(lp) **FIRES OF EDEN** [ ] [ ]
– The blizzard / Fortune of soldiers / Test of time / Fires of Eden / Home before dark / The air that I breathe / City of cities / Dreaming / Queen of the night / From a distance / The blizzard – reprise.

– compilations, others, etc. –

Nov 69. Elektra; (lp)(c) **RECOLLECTIONS (THE BEST OF . . .)** [ ] [29] Sep 69

Jan 70. Elektra; (7") **BOTH SIDES NOW. / HEY THAT'S NO WAY TO SAY GOODBYE** [14] [ ]
(re-iss.Oct 73 + Sep 76)

1972. Elektra; (7") **SUZANNE. / SOMEDAY SOON** [-] [ ]

1972. Elektra; (7") **IN MY LIFE. / SUNNY GOODGE STREET** [-] [ ]

Jul 72. Elektra; (lp)(c) **COLORS OF THE DAY – THE BEST OF JUDY COLLINS** [ ] [37] May 72
– Somebody soon / Since you've asked / Both sides now / Sons of Susan / Farewell / Tarwathie / Who knows where the time goes / Sunny Goodge Street / My father always promised / Albatross / In my life. (US title:- AMAZING GRACE – THE BEST OF JUDY COLLINS) *(re-iss.Nov76 quad) (cd-iss.1989)*

Aug 77. Elektra; (lp)(c) **SO EARLY IN THE SPRING: THE FIRST 15 YEARS** [ ] [42]
– Pretty Polly / So early, early in the Spring / Pretty Saro / Golden apples of the Sun / Bonnie ship the diamond / Farewell to Tarwathie / The hostage / La Colombe / Coal tattoo / Carry it on / Bread and roses / The Marat-Sade / Special delivery / The lovin' of the game / Both sides now / Marieke / Send in the clowns / Bird on the wire / Since you've asked / Born to the breed / My father / Holly Ann / Houses / Secret gardens.

1977. Elektra; (lp)(c) **MOST BEAUTIFUL SONGS OF . . .** [ ] [ ]

Nov 77. Elektra; (7"ep) **AMAZING GRACE / SEND IN THE CLOWNS. / HOSTAGE / BOTH SIDES NOW**

Jul 81. Elektra; (7") **AMAZING GRACE. / BOTH SIDES NOW** [ ] [ ]
Oct 82. Hallmark; (lp)(c) **BOTH SIDES NOW** [ ] [-]
Sep 85. Old Gold; (7") **AMAZING GRACE. / SEND IN THE CLOWNS** [ ] [-]
(cd-iss. Jul 87)
Dec 85. Telstar; (lp)(c) **AMAZING GRACE** [34] [-]
(re-iss.cd/c Mar93 on 'Pickwick')
Sep 95. Warners; (cd)(c) **AMAZING GRACE** [ ] [-]
Oct 95. Vanguard; (cd) **LIVE AT NEWPORT 1959-1966 (live)** [ ] [ ]

— next album covers by BOB DYLAN.

Mar 94. Geffen; (cd) **JUDY SINGS DYLAN . . JUST LIKE A WOMAN** [ ] [ ]
– Like a rolling stone / It's all over now, baby blue / Simple twist of fate / Sweetheart like you / Gotta serve somebody / Dark eyes / Love minus zero – No limit / Just like a woman / I believe in you / With God on our side / Bob Dylan's dream.

Phil COLLINS (see under ⇒ GENESIS)

William "Bootsy" COLLINS (see under ⇒ BOOTSY'S RUBBER BAND)

COLOSSEUM

Formed: London, England . . . Sep'68 by HISEMAN, etc. Gained contract on 'Philips' subsidiary labels, on which they had 2 Top 20 albums. They soon had split, but re-united again in the mid-70's as COLOSSEUM II, which featured GARY MOORE. • **Style:** Pioneers of the UK jazz-rock fusion scene. All accomplished musicians, who later moved into heavier rock field with TEMPEST. • **Songwriters:** Each contributed music with HISEMAN lyrics. Initial lyrics were by poet PETE BROWN, who also went solo. They covered WALKING IN THE PARK (Graham Bond). TEMPEST covered PAPERBACK WRITER (Beatles). • **Trivia:** In 1969, COLOSSEUM appeared in the rock film 'Supersession'.

Recommended: EPITAPH (*6)

JON HISEMAN (b.21 Jun'44) – drums (ex-GRAHAM BOND, ex-JOHN MAYALL) / **DAVE GREENSLADE** – keyboards (ex-CHRIS FARLOWE's THUNDERBIRDS) / **TONY REEVES** – bass (ex-JOHN MAYALL'S BLUESBREAKERS) / **DICK HECKSTALL-SMITH** (b.26 Sep'34, Ludlow) – sax (ex-G.BOND, ex-J.MAYALL) / **JAMES LITHERLAND** – guitar, vocals repl. JIM ROCHE

Fontana Dunhill

Mar 69. (lp) **THOSE WHO ARE ABOUT TO DIE WE SALUTE YOU** [15] [-]
– Walking in the park / Plenty hard luck / Mandarin / Debut / Beware the Ides of March / The road she walked before / Backwater blues / Those who are about to die.
May 69. (7") **WALKING IN THE PARK. / THOSE WHO ARE ABOUT TO DIE** [ ] [-]

Vertigo Dunhill

Nov 69. (lp) **VALENTYNE SUITE** [15] [-]
– The kettle / Elegy / Butty's blues / The machine demands a sacrifice / The Valentyne suite: a) January's search, b) February's Valentyne, c) The grass is always greener. *(re-iss.Oct77 on 'Bronze')*
Nov 69. (7") **THE KETTLE. / PLENTY HARD LUCK** [-] [ ]
Jan 70. (lp) **THE GRASS IS GREENER** [-] [ ]
– Jumping off the sun / Lost Angeles / Elegy / Butty's blues / Rope ladder to the Moon / Bolero / The machine demands a sacrifice / The grass is greener.

— **DAVE CLEMPSON** (b. 5 Sep'49) (had played on US version of 2nd lp) **-guitar, vocals** (ex-BAKERLOO) repl. LITHERLAND who joined MOGUL THRASH

In 1970, DICK + GEN were credited on lp 'THINGS WE LIKE' with JACK BRUCE + JOHN McLAUGHLIN.

— (Sep70) **MARK CLARKE** – bass, vocals repl. REEVES (later to GREENSLADE) / added **CHRIS FARLOWE** (b.JOHN DEIGHTON) – vocals (ex-Solo artist)

Nov 70. (lp)(c) **DAUGHTER OF TIME** [23] [ ]
– Three score and ten, amen / Time lament / Take me back to Doomsday / The daughter of time / Theme for an imaginary western / Bring out your dead / Downhill and the shadows / The time machine. *(re-iss.cd+c Jul94 on 'Success')*

Bronze Warners

Jun 71. (d-lp) **COLOSSEUM LIVE (live)** [17] [ ]
– Rope ladder to the Moon / Walking in the park / Skellington / Tanglewood 63 / Encore / Stormy Monday blues / Lost Angeles. *(re-iss.Oct77) (re-iss.Mar87 on 'Castle') (cd-iss.Jun92 on 'Sequel')*
Nov 71. (lp)(c) **COLLECTOR'S COLOSSEUM** (compilation) [ ] [-]
– Jumping off the Sun / Those about to die / I can't live without you / Beware the Ides Of March / Walking in the park / Bolero / Rope ladder to the Moon / The grass is greener. *(re-iss.Oct77 on 'Bronze')*

— Disbanded Oct'71. DAVE formed GREENSLADE. CLEMPSON joined HUMBLE PIE and FARLOWE joined ATOMIC ROOSTER. CLARKE joined URIAH HEEP until mid 1972.

other compilations, etc.

Apr 86. Raw Power; (lp)(c)(cd) **EPITAPH** [ ] [-]
– Walking in the park / Bring out your dead / Those about to die / Beware the ides of March / Daughter of time / Valentine suite.
Jun 90. Knight; (cd) **THE GOLDEN DECADE OF COLOSSEUM** [ ] [-]
Jan 91. Sequel; (cd) **THOSE WHO ARE ABOUT TO DIE . . . / VALENTYNE SUITE** [ ] [-]
May 91. Castle; (cd)(d-lp) **THE COLLECTION** [ ] [-]
May 95. Spectrum; (cd) **THE IDES OF MARCH** [ ] [-]

TEMPEST

were formed by **HISEMAN & CLARKE** plus **PAUL WILLIAMS** – vocals (ex-JUICY LUCY, ex-ZOOT MONEY, ex-JOHN MAYALL) / **ALLAN HOLDSWORTH** – guitar

Island not issued

Jan 73. (lp)(c) **JON HISEMAN'S TEMPEST** [ ] [-]
– Gorgon / Foyers of fun / Dark house / Brothers / Up and on / Grey and black / Strange her / Upon tomorrow.

— **OLLIE HALSALL** – guitar repl. WILLIAMS (HOLDSWORTH joined SOFT MACHINE)

Mar 74. (lp)(c) **LIVING IN FEAR** [ ] [-]
– Funeral empire / Paperback writer / Stargazer / Dance to my tune / Living in fear / Yeah, yeah, yeah / Waiting for a miracle / Turn around.
(both above on cd Feb91 on 'Sequel')

COLOSSEUM II

was formed by **HISEMAN** in May75. **MIKE STARR** – vocals / **DON AIREY** – keyboards / **NEIL MURRAY** – bass / **GARY MOORE** – guitar, vocals (ex-THIN LIZZY, ex-SKID ROW)

Island Warners

Apr 76. (lp)(c) **STRANGE NEW FLESH** [ ] [-]
– Dark side of the moog / Down to you / Gemini and Leo / Secret places / On second thoughts / Winds. *(re-iss.+cd.Apr86 on 'Castle Comm.')*

— with MOORE now on some lead vocals, **NEIL MOLE** – bass repl. STARR who joined LUCIFER'S FRIEND. Also NEIL MURRAY left (later to WHITESNAKE)

M.C.A. M.C.A.

Jan 77. (lp)(c) **ELECTRIC SAVAGE** [ ] [ ]
– Am I / Intergallactic strut / Put it this way / All skin and bone / Rivers / The scorch / Lament / Desperado. *(re-iss Jul82)*
Aug 77. (7") **LAMENT. / THE SCORCH** [ ] [-]
Oct 77. (lp)(c) **WAR DANCE** [ ] [ ]
– War dance / Put it that way / Major key / Castles / Fighting talk / Quaser / Inquisition / Star maidens / Mysteriouso / Last exit. *(re-iss.Aug81)*

— **KEITH AIREY** – guitar repl. GARY MOORE who joined THIN LIZZY. But they soon split late 1978. DON AIREY joined RAINBOW. HISEMAN joined his wife BARBARA THOMPSON in the band PARAPHERNALIA.

JON HISEMAN

Kuckluck

1981. (lp) **NIGHT IN THE SUN** [-] [-] Germ.
– Tropeiro / The hearts of carnival / Sun roof / A night in the sun / Eunice / Makenna Beach / Walking on air.

Temple not issued

Sep 86. (lp,cd) **ABOUT TIME TOO!** [ ] [-]
– Solo Berlin: Ganz schon heiss, man / Solo Hanover: Ganz schon heiss, man

COLOSSEUM

— **FARLOWE / HECKSTALL-SMITH + CLARKE** re-formed in 1994

Intuition not issued

May 95. (cd) **THE REUNION CONCERTS 1994 (live)** [ ] [-]
– January's search – February's valentyne – The grass is always greener (the valentyne suite) / Those about to die we salute you / Elegy / Theme for an imaginary western / The machine demands another sacrifice / Solo Colonia / Lost Angeles / Stormy Monday blues.

COLOUR FIELD (see under ⇒ HALL, Terry)

COMMUNARDS

Formed: London, England . . . 1985, briefly as 'The COMMITEE' (until another band objected) by JIMMY SOMERVILLE and friend RICHARD COLES who was an ex-student of Royal School of Church Music and occasional stage member of BRONSKI BEAT. Their eponymous hit debut album on 'London' (SOMERVILLE's Bronski Beat label) was produced by STEPHEN HAGUE (New Order fame). • **Style:** Pro-gay dance-synth orientated pop, fused with the soulful voice of SOMERVILLE. • **Songwriters:** All written by COLES / SOMERVILLE, except covers NEVER CAN SAY GOODBYE (Gloria Gaynor) / DON'T LEAVE ME THIS WAY (Harold Melvin & The Blue Notes) / ZING WENT THE STRINGS OF MY HEART (Trammps) / YOU MAKE ME FEEL (Sylvester) / ADIEU (Francois Hardy). SOMERVILLE writes with guitarist GARY BUTCHER except; TO LOVE SOMEBODY (Bee Gees) / FROM THIS MOMENT ON (Cole Porter) / HURTS SO GOOD (hit; Susan Cadogan) / SOMEDAY WE'LL BE TOGETHER (Johnny Bristol). • **Trivia:** The 45 'FOR A FRIEND' was dedicated to friend MARK ASHTON who died of AIDS. They also gave support to the Labour Party 'Red Wedge' tour, instigated by BILLY BRAGG.

Recommended: THE SINGLES COLLECTION 1984-1990 (*7)

JIMMY SOMERVILLE (b.22 Jun'61, Glasgow, Scotland) – vocals (ex-BRONSKI BEAT) / **RICHARD COLES** (b.23 Jun'62, Northampton, England) – keyboards, programming

London M.C.A.

Sep 85. (7") **YOU ARE MY WORLD. / BREADLINE BRITAIN** [30] [ ]
(10"+=)(12"+=) – Sentimental journey.
(d7"++=) – Heaven's above.

— augmented by **SARAH JANE MORRIS** – b.vocals / **DAVID RENWICK** – bass / **AUDREY RILEY** – cello / **JO PRETZEL** – keys / **ANNE STEPHENSON** – violin / **JOCELYN POOK** – viola/

May 86. (7") **DISENCHANTED. / JOHNNY VERSO** [29] [ ]

(12"+=) – ('A'dance mix).
(12"+=)(12"pic-d+=) – Annie.

Jul 86. (lp)(c)(cd) **THE COMMUNARDS** 7 90 Sep 86
– Don't leave me this way / La Dolarosa / Disenchanted / Reprise / So cold the night / You are my world / Lover man / Don't slip away / Heaven's above / Forbidden love. *(cd+=)* – Breadline Britain.

Aug 86. (7")(7"pic-d)(7"sha-pic-d) **DON'T LEAVE ME THIS WAY. (as "COMMUNARDS featuring SARAH JANE MORRIS") / SANCTIFIED** 1 40
(12"+=) – ('A'versions).

Nov 86. (7") **SO COLD THE NIGHT. / WHEN THE WALLS COME TUMBLING DOWN** 8
(12"+=) – Never no more.
(12"+=) – Sanctified.
(d7"+=)(c-s+=) – Don't leave me this way / Sanctified.

Feb 87. (7") **YOU ARE MY WORLD ('87). / JUDGEMENT DAY** 21
(12"+=) – ('A'version).
(12"+=) – Czardas (live).
(12"+=) – The message.
(c-s+=) – Czardas (live) / Reprise / When the walls come tumbling down.

— **JUNE MILES-KINGSTON** – b.vocals (ex-MO-DETTES) repl. SARAH who went solo

Aug 87. (7")(7"red)(10") **TOMORROW. / I JUST WANT TO LET YOU KNOW** 23
(12"+=) – Romance for violin, piano and hedgehog / Seat.

Oct 87. (lp)(c)(cd) **RED** 4
– Tomorrow / T.M.T. .T.B.M.G. / Matter of opinion / Victims / For a friend / Never can say goodbye / Lovers and friends / Hold on tight / If I could tell you / C minor.

Oct 87. (7") **NEVER CAN SAY GOODBYE. / '77 THE GREAT ESCAPE** 4 51
(12"+=) – Piece of saxophone.
(cd-s+=) – I do it all for you.

Feb 88. (7")(12") **FOR A FRIEND. / VICTIMS (live)** 28
(cd-s+=) – Don't leave me this way (live) / Heaven's above.

May 88. (7") **THERE'S MORE TO LOVE. / ZING WENT THE STRINGS OF MY HEART** 20
(12"+=)(cd-s+=) – Spanish rap (el amar no es solo un hombre y una mayor / When the boy in your heart is the boy in your arms.
(extra-12"+=) – ('A'version).

JIMMY SOMERVILLE

(after partnership broke up in '88)
went solo, with **JUNE MILES-KINGSTON** – b.vocals / etc.

Oct 89. (7") **(COMMENT TE DIRE) ADIEU!. / TELL THE WORLD** 14
(7"+=)(12"+=)(c-s+=)(cd-s+=) – Smalltown boy / Don't leave me this way / You are my world.

Dec 89. (lp)(c)(cd) **READ MY LIPS** 29
– (Comment te dire) Adieu! / You make me feel (mighty real) / Heaven here (on Earth) with your love / Don't know what to do (without you) / My heart is in your hands / Control / And you never thought this could happen to you / Rain / Read my lips (enough is enough) *(re-iss.cd+c May93 on 'Spectrum')*.

Jan 90. (7")(c-s) **YOU MAKE ME FEEL (MIGHTY REAL). / NOT SO GOD ALMIGHTY** 5
(12"+=)(cd-s+=) – Stranger.

Mar 90. (7")(c-s) **READ MY LIPS (ENOUGH IS ENOUGH). / AND YOU NEVER THOUGHT THIS COULD HAPPEN TO YOU** 26
(12")(cd-s) – ('A'side) / Stranger.

Oct 90. (7")(c-s) **TO LOVE SOMEBODY. / RAIN** 8
(12"+=)(cd-s+=) – Why?

Aug 91. (7")(c-s) **RUN FROM LOVE. / DESIRE**
(12"+=)(cd-s+=) – To love somebody.

Jan 95. (12")(cd-s) **HEARTBEAT (club mixes by E-Smoove / Armand Van Helden / Media Records)** 24

May 95. (c-s)(cd-s) **HURT SO GOOD / ('A'-Beatmasters mix)** 15
(cd-s+=) – Love you forever / Been so long.
(cd-s+=) – ('A'-Stevie & Clevie dub) / ('A'-2 Sly & Robbie mixes).

Jun 95. (cd)(c)(lp) **DARE TO LOVE** 38
– Heartbeat / Hurts so good / Cry / Lovething / By your side / Dare to love / Someday we'll be together / Alright / Too much of a good thing / A dream gone wrong / Come lately / Safe in these arms / Because of him.

Oct 95. (c-s) **BY YOUR SIDE / NOTHING SAID, NOTHING DONE** 41
(12") – ('A'-The shining mix) / ('A'-Miss you like crazy mix).
(cd-s) – (all 4 tracks above).

– JIMMY SOMMERVILLE compilations, others, etc. –

Nov 90. London/ US= M.C.A.; (cd)(c)(lp) **THE SINGLES COLLECTION 1984-1990** 4
– Smalltown boy (BRONSKI BEAT) / Don't leave me this way / Ain't necessarily so (BRONSKI BEAT) / (Comment te dire) Adieu! / Never can say goodbye / Why? (BRONSKI BEAT) / You are my world / For a friend / I feel love (BRONSKI BEAT & MARC ALMOND) / So cold the night / Mighty real / To love somebody / Run from love (remix)/ There's more to love. *(cd+=)* Tomorrow / Disenchanted.

— (above features BRONSKI BEAT 84-85, COMMUNARDS 85-88, JIMMY SOMERVILLE 89)

Jan 91. London; (7")(c-s) **SMALLTOWN BOY ("JIMMY SOMMERVILLE with BRONSKI BEAT"). / THERE'S MORE TO LOVE** 32
(12"+=)(cd-s+=) – To love somebody ('B'side "COMMUNARDS")

Oct 93. Spectrum; (cd)(c) **HEAVEN** -

COMSAT ANGELS

Formed: Sheffield, England . . . 1978 initially as "RADIO EARTH" but due to contractual problems never recorded until change to COMSAT ANGELS. After one indie single they signed to 'Polydor' late 1979, but deserved more success than a near UK Top 50 album 'SLEEP NO MORE'. • **Style:** Anti-war new wave rock/pop that lay somewhere between COSTELLO, PETTY or counterparts The SOUND. • **Songwriters:** All group compositions. • **Trivia:** They were named the CS ANGELS in the States, after communications conglomorate COMSAT threatened to take legal action. ROBERT PALMER produced and guested on 1987 album 'CHASING SHADOWS'.

Recommended: WAITING FOR A MIRACLE (*8)

STEVEN FELLOWS – vocals, guitar / **ANDY PEAKE** – keyboards, synthesizers / **KEVIN BACON** – bass / **MIC GLAISHER** – drums

Junta not issued

Mar 79. (red-7"m) **RED PLANET. / I GET EXCITED / SPECIMEN No.2** -

Polydor M.C.A.

May 80. (7") **TOTAL WAR. / WAITING FOR A MIRACLE**
(12"+=) – Home on the range.

Jul 80. (7") **INDEPENDENCE DAY. / WE WERE**

Sep 80. (lp)(c) **WAITING FOR A MIRACLE**
– Missing in action / Baby / Independence day / Waiting for a miracle / Total war / On the beach / Monkey pilot / Real story / Map of the world / Postcard.

Mar 81. (7") **EYE OF THE LENS. / AT SEA**
(d12"+=) – Another world / Gone.

Aug 81. (lp)(c) **SLEEP NO MORE** 51
– Eye dance / Slep no more / Be brave / Gone / Dark parade / Diagram / Restless / Goat of the west / Light years / Our secret.

Oct 81. (d7") **DO THE EMPTY HOUSE. / NOW I KNOW // RED PLANET REVISITED**

May 82. (7") **IT'S HISTORY. / ZINGER**

Aug 82. (lp)(c) **FICTION** 94
– After the rain / Zinger / Now I know / Not a word / Ju ju money / More / Pictures / Birdman / Don' t look now / What else.

Oct 82. (7") **AFTER THE RAIN. / PRIVATE PARTY**

Jive-CBS Jive-CBS

Jul 83. (7") **WILL YOU STAY TONIGHT. / SHINING HOUR**
(12"+=) – A world away.

Sep 83. (lp)(c)(pic-lp) **LAND** 91
– Will you stay tonight / Alicia (can you hear me) / A world away / Independence day / Nature trails / Mister memory / Island heart / I know that feeling / As above so below.

Oct 83. (7")(12") **ISLAND HEART. / SCISSORS AND STONES**

Jan 84. (7") **INDEPENDENCE DAY. / MISTER MEMORY** 71
(12"+=) – Intelligence.
(d7"+=)(d12"+=) – Total war / After the rain.

Apr 84. (lp) **ENZ** (Dutch compilation) - -

May 84. (7") **YOU MOVE ME. / ESCAPE FROM WILLESDEN**
(12") – ('A'side) / Land / Eye of the lens (live)

Sep 84. (7") **DAY ONE. / WILL YOU STAY TONIGHT**
(12"+=) – Independence day.

— added guest **PAUL ROBERTSON** – keyboards

Aug 85. (7") **I'M FALLING. / NEW HEART AND MIND**
(12"blue+=) – ('A'extended).

Sep 85. (lp)(c) **7 DAY WEEKEND**
– Day one / You're the heroine / High tide / New heart and hand / Still it's not enough / Believe it / Forever young / You move me / I'm falling / Close your eyes.

Oct 85. (7") **FOREVER YOUNG. / STILL IT'S NOT ENOUGH**
(12"+=) – Sign.

— reverted to original quartet, when ROBERTSON departed.

Island Island

Jan 87. (lp)(c)(cd) **CHASING SHADOWS**
– The thought that counts / The cutting edge / Under the influence / Carried away / You'll never know / Lost continent / Flying dreams / Pray for rain.

Feb 87. (7") **THE CUTTING EDGE. / SOMETHING'S GOT TO GIVE**
(12"+=) – Our secret.
(12"+=) – Flying dreams.

— Broke-up 1987, although the original line-up re-formed in 1992. They signed to 'Crisis' (Benelux) & 'Normal' (Germany). FELLOWS had recently written several songs for the HARBOUR KINGS. They had emerged in 1990 as The HEADHUNTERS, until this fell through.

Thunderbird not issued

Jun 92. (7") **DRIVING. / ?** -
(12"+=)(cd-s+=) There is no enemy / My mind's eye / Driving (mix).

Sep 92. (cd)(lp) **MY MIND'S EYE** -
– Driving / Beautiful monster / Shiva descending / My mind's eye / I came from the sun / Field of tall flowers / Always hear / Route 666 / Mystery plane / And all the stars.

Jul 93. (7") **FIELD OF TALL FLOWERS (remix). / ?** -
(cd-s+=) – Too much time / Storm of change / ('A'acoustic).

1993. (cd-ep) **SHIVA DESCENDING / MAFONIA / JU-JU MONEY / GOAT OF THE WEST** - - Germ'y

— now without BACON repl.by **SIMON ANDERSON** – guitar/ **SIMON TERRY** – bass

Crisis not issued

1994. (cd) **UNRAVELLED** -
– After the rain / Beautiful monster / The cuting edge / Field of all flowers / SS 100X / Our secret / Always near / Eye of the lens / Storm of change / Audrey in denim / Citadel.

Jun 95. (cd) **THE GLAMOUR** -
– Psychedelic dungeon / The glamour / Audrey in denim / Oblivion / Web of sound / Breaker / SS100X / Sailor / Demon lover / Pacific ocean blues / Anjelica / Valley of the Nile / Spaced.

– more compilations, etc. –

Nov 92. R.P.M.; (cd) **TIME CONSIDERED (BBC sessions 1979-1984)** [ ] [-]
Jul 94. R.P.M.; (cd) **UNRAVELLED – THE DUTCH RADIO SESSIONS** [ ] [-]

CONTRABAND (see under ⇒ SCHENKER, Michael)

Ry COODER

Born: RYLAND COODER, 15 Mar'47, Los Angeles, California, USA. He sessioned for likes of JACKIE DE SHANNON and TAJ MAHAL, before moving on to CAPTAIN BEEFHEART in '67. He nearly replaced BRIAN JONES in The ROLLING STONES, but chose to only guest on their LET IT BLEED album, before going solo. He signed to 'Reprise' in 1970, and was used on debut album by LITTLE FEAT and STONES' 'Sticky Fingers'. • **Style:** His repertoire shifted through folk / blues, Tex-Mex, and jazz with his bottleneck style a feature. • **Songwriters:** All by COODER except; VIGILANTE MAN (Woody Guthrie) / GET RHYTHM (Johnny Cash) / HE'LL HAVE TO GO (hit; Jim Reeves) / LITTLE SISTER (Pomus-Shuman) / 13 QUESTION METHOD (Chuck Berry) / MONEY HONEY (hit; Drifters) / STAND BY ME (Ben E.King) / IT'S ALL OVER NOW (Bobby Womack) / GOODNIGHT IRENE (Leadbelly) / NEED A WOMAN (Bob Dylan) / BLUE SUEDE SHOES (Carl Perkins) / ALL SHOOK UP (Elvis Presley) / and loads more. The JAZZ album had early 1940's covers, etc. • **Trivia:** He also wrote score for 1980 film SOUTHERN COMFORT which sadly was not issued on soundtrack.

Recommended: WHY DON'T YOU TRY ME TONIGHT (*7)

RY COODER – vocals, guitar (ex-CAPTAIN BEEFHEART & HIS MAGIC BAND) plus session people too numerous to mention

Reprise Reprise

Oct 70. (7") **GOIN' TO BROWNSVILLE. / AVAILABLE SPACE** [-] [ ]
Dec 70. (7") **ALIMONY. / PIGMEAT** [-] [ ]
Jan 71. (lp)(c) **RY COODER** [ ] [ ] Dec70
– Alimony / France dance / One meat ball / Do re mi / Old Kentucky home / How can a poor man stand such times and live? / Available space / Pig meat / Police dog blues / Goin' to Brownsville / Dark is the night. *(cd-iss.May95 on 'Warners')*
May 71. (7") **HOW CAN A POOR MAN STAND SUCH TIMES AND LIVE. / GOIN' TO BROWNSVILLE** [ ] [ ]
Feb 72. (7") **ON A MONDAY. / DARK IS THE NIGHT** [-] [ ]
Feb 72. (lp)(c) **INTO THE PURPLE VALLEY** [ ] [ ]
– How can you keep on moving / Billy the kid / Money honey / F.D.R. in Trinidad / Teardrops will fall / Denomination blues / On a Monday / Hey porter / Great dreams from heaven / Taxes on the farmer feeds us all / Vigilante man.
Feb 72. (7") **MONEY HONEY. / ON A MONDAY** [-] [ ]
Apr 72. (7") **MONEY MONEY. / BILLY THE KID** [-] [ ]
Oct 72. (7") **BOOMER'S STORY. / BILLY THE KID** [-] [ ]
Nov 72. (lp)(c) **BOOMER'S STORY** [ ] [ ]
– Boomer's story / Cherry ball blues / Crow black children / Axe sweet mama / Maria Elena / Dark end of the street / Rally 'round the flag / Comin' in on a wing and a prayer / President Kennedy / Good morning Mr. Railroad man.
May 74. (lp)(c) **PARADISE AND LUNCH** [ ] [ ]
– Tamp 'em up solid / Tattler / Married man's a fool / Jesus on the mainline / It's all over now / Fool about a cigarette – Feelin' good / If walls could talk / Mexican divorce / Ditty wa ditty.

— next with **FLACO JIMINEZ** – accordion / **GABBY PAHINHI** – steel guitar / **BOBBY KING** – gospel vocals

Oct 76. (lp)(c) **CHICKEN SKIN MUSIC** [ ] [ ]
– The bourgeois blues / I got mine / Always lift him up / He'll have to go / Smack dab in the middle / Stand by me / Yellow roses / Chloe / Goodnight Irene.
Mar 77. (7") **HE'LL HAVE TO GO. / THE BOURGEOIS BLUES** [ ] [ ]

Warners Warners

Aug 77. (lp)(c) **SHOW TIME (live)** [ ] [ ]
– School is out / Alimony / Jesus on the mainline / ark end of the street / Viva sequin – Do re mi / Volver, volver / How can a poor man stand such times and live? / Smack dab in the middle. *(cd-iss.Nov93)*
Aug 77. (7") **SCHOOL IS OUT (live). / JESUS ON THE MAINLINE (live)** [-] [ ]
Jun 78. (lp)(c) **JAZZ** [ ] [ ]
– Face to face I shall meet him / Davenport blues / In a mist / Big bad Bill is sweet William now / Happy meeting in glory / We shall be happy / Nobody / Shine / Flashes / Dream / Pearls / Tia Juana.
Jun 79. (7") **LITTLE SISTER. / DOWN IN HOLLYWOOD** [ ] [ ]
Aug 79. (lp)(c) **BOP TILL YOU DROP** [36] [62]
– Little sister / Go home girl / The very thing that makes you rich (makes me poor) / I think it's gonna work out fine / Down in Hollywood / Look at granny run run / Trouble, you can't fool me / Don't mess up a good thing / I can't win.
Aug 79. (7") **LITTLE SISTER. / GO HOME GIRL** [ ] [ ]
Oct 79. (7") **THE VERY THING THAT MAKES YOU RICH (MAKES ME POOR). / LITTLE SISTER** [-] [ ]
Jun 80. (lp) **THE LONG RIDERS (Soundtrack)** [ ] [ ]
– (main title) The long riders / I'm a good old rebel / Seneca square dance / Archie's funeral (hold to God's unchanging hand) / I always knew that you were the one / Rally 'round the flag / Wildwood boys / Better things to talkabout / My grandfather / Cole Younger polka / Escape from Northfield / Leaving Missouri / Jesse James.
Oct 80. (lp)(c) **BORDERLINE** [35] [43] Jan81
– 634-5789 / Speedo / Why don't you try me / Down in the Boondocks / Johnny Porter / The way we make a broken heart / Crazy 'bout an automobile (every woman I know) / The girls from Texas / Borderline / Never make a move too soon.
Oct 80. (7") **BORDERLINE. / THE GIRLS FROM TEXAS** [-] [ ]
Oct 80. (7") **634-5789. / THE GIRLS FROM TEXAS** [-] [-]
Dec 80. (7") **CRAZY 'BOUT AN AUTOMOBILE. / BORDERLINE** [-] [ ]
Aug 81. (7") **CRAZY 'BOUT AN AUTOMOBILE (EVERY WOMAN I KNOW). / THE VERY THING THAT MAKES YOU RICH (MAKES ME POOR)** [ ] [ ]
(12"+=) – If wall could talk / Look at granny run run.
Mar 82. (lp) **THE BORDER (Soundtrack)**(on 'Backstreet-MCA') [ ] [ ]
– Earthquake / Across the borderline / Maria / Building fires / Texas bop / Highway 23 / Palomita / Rio Grande / Too late / No quiro / Skin game / El Scorcho / Nino.
Apr 82. (lp)(c) **THE SLIDE AREA** [18] [ ]
– UFO has landed in the ghetto / I need a woman / Gypsy woman / Blue suede shoes / Mama, don't treat your daughter mean / I'm drinking again / Which came first / That's the way love turned out for me.
May 82. (d7") **GYSPY WOMAN. / ALIMONY / TEARDROPS WILL FALL / IT'S ALL OVER NOW** [ ] [ ]
Feb 85. (lp)(c) **PARIS, TEXAS (Soundtrack)** [ ] [ ]
– Paris, Texas / Brothers / Nothing out there / Cancion Mixteca / No safety zone / Houston in two seconds / She's leaving the bank / On the couch / I knew these people / Dark was the night.

London Slash

Aug 85. (lp) **MUSIC FROM ALAMO BAY (Soundtrack)** [ ] [ ]
– Theme from Alamo Bay / Gooks on main street / Klan meeting / Too close / Sailfish evening / The last stand / Glory / Search and destroy / Quatro vicios.

Warners Warners

Mar 86. (lp)(c)(cd) **WHY DON'T YOU TRY ME TONIGHT (THE BEST OF RY COODER)** (compilation) [ ] [ ]
– How can a poor man stand such times and live? / Available space / Money honey / Tattler / He'll have to go / Smack dab in the middle / Dark end of the street / Down in Hollywood / Little sister / I think it's gonna work out fine / Crazy 'bout an automobile (every woman I know) / 634-5789 / Why don't you try me tonight.
Jul 86. (lp)(c) **BLUE CITY (Soundtrack)** [ ] [ ]
– Blue city down / Elevation 13 foot / True believers – Marianne / Nice bike / Greenhouse / Billy and Annie / Pops and 'timer – Tell me something slick / Blue city / Don't take your guns to town / A leader of men / Not even Key West.
Jul 86. (7") **BILLY AND ANNIE. / TELL ME SOMETHING SLICK** [-] [ ]
Jul 86. (7") **CROSSROADS. / FEEL IT (BAD BLUES)** [-] [ ]
Jul 86. (lp)(c) **CROSSROADS** [ ] [85] May 86
– Crossroads / Down in Mississippi / Cotton needs pickin' / Viola Lee blues / See you in Hell, blind boy / Walkin' away blues / Nitty gritty Mississippi / He made a woman out of me / Feelin' bad blues / Somebody's callin' my name / Willie Brown blues.
Dec 87. (lp)(c) **GET RHYTHM** [75] [ ] Nov 87
– Get rhythm / Low-commotion / Going back to Okinawa / 13 question method / Women will rule the world / All shook up / I can tell by the way you smell / Across the borderline / Let's have a ball.
Jan 88. (7") **GET RHYTHM. / GOING BACK TO OKINAWA** [-] [ ]
Apr 88. (7") **ALL SHOOK UP. / GET YOUR LIES STRAIGHT** [-] [ ]
Apr 88. (7")(10") **GET RHYTHM. / GET YOUR LIES STRAIGHT** [ ] [ ]
(3"cd-s+=)(12"+=) – Down in Hollywood.
Oct 89. (lp)(c)(cd) **JOHNNY HANDSOME (Soundtrack)** [ ] [ ]
– Main theme / I can't walk this time – The prestige / Angola / Clip joint rhumba / Sad story / Fountain walk / Cajun metal / First week at work / Greasy oysters / Smells like money / Sunny's tune / I like your eyes / Adios Donna / Cruising wife Rafe / How's my face / End theme. *(re-iss.cd Feb95)*

— In 1991 he recorded Soundtrack for Robin Williams film PECOS BILL. He also teamed up with NICK LOWE, JOHN HIATT and JIM KELTNER in band LITTLE VILLAGE.

Sire Sire

Jan 93. (cd) **TRESPASS** (soundtrack w/ other artists) [ ] [82]
– Video drive-by / Trespass / East St.Louis toodle-oo / Orgil Bros. / Goose and lucky / You think it's on now / Solid gold / Heroin / Totally boxed in / Give 'm cops / Lucy in the trunk / We're rich / King of the street / Party lights. *(re-iss.Feb95)*

RY COODER & V.M. BHATT

RY – bottle neck guitar with **VISHWA MOHAN BHATT** – mohan vina / **JOACHIM COODER**(14 year old son) / **SUKHVINDER** – tabla

Water lily Water Lily

Dec 93. (cd) **A MEETING BY THE RIVER** [ ] [ ]
– A meeting by the river / Longing / Ganges Delta blues / Isa Lei.

ALI FARKA TOURE / RY COODER

World Circuit World Circuit

Mar 94. (cd)(c) **TALKING TIMBUKTU** [44] [ ]
– Blonde / Soukora / Gomni / Sega / Amandrai / Lasidan / Keito / Banga / Ai du / Diaraby.

– (RY COODER) compilations, etc. –

May 93. Columbia; (cd) **THE RISING SONS ("The RISING SONS featuring RY COODER & TAJ MAHAL")** [ ] [ ]

Sam COOKE

Born: SAMUEL COOK, 22 Jan'31, Chicago, Illinois, USA. He had religious upbringing as son of a reverend who had seven other children. He progressed through gospel choir groups, to become lead tenor in 1951 with The SOUL STIRRERS. They signed to 'Speciality' records, but by 1956, SAM as DALE COOK, got out his solo debut 'LOVEABLE'. In 1957, he relinquished said contract and any royalties to sign for 'Keen' records. His first hit 'YOU SEND ME' (written by his brother Charles), was released late '57, and after guesting on the 'Ed Sullivan Show', peaked at No.1. He became overnight star/idol, and continued having several more US Top 30 hits for 'Keen'. In 1960, he moved stables to 'R.C.A.', and nearly hit No.1 again with his classic 'CHAIN GANG'. Early the next year, he co-launched record label 'S.A.R.', who signed

The SIMMS TWINS and The VALENTINOS. Tragedy happened to him in Jul'63, when his son Vincent, drowned in their swimming pool. A year and a half later, with his career still on a high, SAM was shot dead by motel owner Bertha Franklin. She claimed that he had attempted to rape his escort and assaulted her in the process. The coroner returned a verdict of justifiable homocide, but his funeral was still attended by a reported 200,000 fans, most of them women. • **Style:** Gospel-tinged soul legend, who mixed soft ballads with up-tempo classics. • **Songwriters:** COOKE wrote mostly all material, except SEND ME SOME LOVIN' (Little Richard) / LIITLE RED ROOSTER (Willie Dixon) / FRANKIE AND JOHNNY (Brook Benton) / and a few other lp tracks. ONLY SIXTEEN was written by Barbara Campbell, which was actually a pseudonym for the collective pens of SAM, LOU ADLER and HERB ALPERT. His songs have been covered by numerous doyens of the rock-pop world. • **Trivia:** CASSIUS CLAY (aka. MOHAMMED ALI) once descibed him as the "The world's greatest rock'n'roll singer . . . ".

Recommended: THE MAGIC OF SAM COOKE (*6)

SAM COOKE – vocals, with session people

		not issued	Speciality
1956.	(7") **LOVEABLE. (as "DALE COOK") / FOREVER**	-	
1956.	(7") **I'LL COME RUNNING BACK TO YOU. / FOREVER**	-	
	(hit US chart Dec57 at No.18 + 60)		
1957.	(7") **THAT'S ALL I NEED TO KNOW. / I DON'T WANT TO CRY**	-	
	(above and below finally released in UK on 'London' circa 1958)		
1957.	(7") **I NEED YOU NOW. / HAPPY IN LOVE**	-	
1957.	(lp) **TWO SIDES OF SAM COOKE**	-	
	– The last mile of the way / Touch the hem of his garment / Jesus gave me water / Were you there / Pilgrim of sorrow / He's my guide / I'll come running back to you / I don't want to cry / Loveable / That's all I need to know / Forever / Happy in love. *(re-iss.!)*		
		London	Keen
Dec 57.	(7") **YOU SEND ME. / SUMMERTIME**	29	1
			81 Oct 57
Dec 57.	(7") **(I LOVE YOU FOR) SENTIMENTAL REASONS. / DESIRE ME**		17
		H.M.V.	Keen
Feb 58.	(lp) **SAM COOKE**		
	– You send me / The lonesome road / Tammy / Ol' man river / Moonlight in Vermont / Canadian sunset / Summertime / Around the world / Ain't misbehavin' / The bells of St.Mary's / So long / Danny boy / That lucky old Sun. *(re-iss.+c.1982 on 'Dakota') (re-iss.Jan87 on 'Deja Vu') (cd-iss.Dec93 on 'Entertainers')*		
Mar 58.	(7") **LONELY ISLAND. / YOU WERE MADE FOR ME**		26
			39
——	(above 2 singles, could have been released just before YOU SEND ME in '57)		
1958.	(7") **ALL OF MY LIFE. / STEALING KISSES**		
Aug 58.	(7") **WIN YOUR LOVE FOR ME. / LOVE SONG**	-	22
Nov 58.	(7") **LOVE YOU MOST OF ALL. / WIN YOUR LOVE FOR ME**		-
Nov 58.	(lp) **ENCORE**		
	– When I fall in love / I cover the waterfront / My foolish heart / Today I sing the blues / The gypsy / It's the talk of the town / Oh look at me now / Someday (You'll want me to want you) / Along the Navajo Trail / Running wild / Ac-cent-tchu-aet the positive / Mary, Mary Lou.		
Dec 58.	(7") **LOVE YOU MOST OF ALL. / BLUE MOON**	-	26
Mar 59.	(7") **EVERYBODY LIKES TO CHA CHA. / THE LITTLE THINGS YOU DO**		31
Jun 59.	(7") **ONLY SIXTEEN. / LET'S GO STEADY AGAIN**	23	28
1959.	(7") **SUMMERTIME. / (pt.2)**	-	
Oct 59.	(7") **THERE, I'VE SAID IT AGAIN. / ONE HOUR AHEAD OF THE POSSE**		81
Dec 59.	(7") **NO ONE. / 'T AIN'T NOBODY'S BIZNESS**		
——	(below 4 singles were belatedly released on 'Keen' US)		
Jun 60.	(7") **WONDERFUL WORLD. / ALONG THE NAVAJO TRAIL**	27	12 May 60
1960.	(lp) **WONDERFUL WORLD OF SAM COOKE**		
	– (cd-iss.Apr87 on 'Card')		
1960.	(7") **WITH YOU. / I THANK GOD**	-	
1960.	(7") **STEAL AWAY. / SO GLAMOUROUS**	-	
1960.	(7") **MARY, MARY LOU. / EE-YI-EE-YI-OH**	-	
——	Orchestration by his new producers **HUGO & LUIGI**		
		R.C.A.	R.C.A.
Mar 60.	(7") **TEENAGE SONATA. / IF YOU WERE THE ONLY GIRL**		50
May 60.	(7") **YOU UNDERSTAND ME. / I BELONG TO YOUR HEART**		
1960.	(lp) **COOKES TOUR (live)**	-	
	– Faraway places / Under Paris skies / South of the border / Bali Ha'l / The coffeee song / Arrivederci Roma / London by night / Jamaica farewell / Galway bay / Sweet Leilani / The Japenese farewell song / The house I live in.		
Sep 60.	(7") **CHAIN GANG. / I FALL IN LOVE EVERY DAY**	9	2 Aug 60
1960.	(lp) **THE ONE & ONLY**	-	
Dec 60.	(7") **SAD MOOD. / LOVE ME**		29
Mar 61.	(7") **THAT'S IT - I QUIT - I'M MOVIN' ON. / WHAT DO YOU SAY**		31
1961.	(lp) **HITS OF THE 50's**	-	
	– Hey there / Mona Lisa / Too young / The great pretender / You, you, you / Unchained melody / The wayward wind / Secret love / The song from Moulin Rouge / I'm walking behind you / Cry / Venus.		
Jul 61.	(7") **CUPID. / FAREWELL MY DARLING**	7	17 Jun61
Sep 61.	(7") **FEEL IT. / IT'S ALL RIGHT**		56
			93
Feb 62.	(lp) **MY KIND OF BLUES**	-	
	– Don't get around much anymore / Little girl blue / Nobody knows you when you're down and out / Out in the cold again / But not for me / Exactly like you / I'm just a lucky so and so / Since I met you baby / Baby, won't you please come home / Trouble in mind / You're always on my mind / The song is ended.		
Feb 62.	(7") **TWISTIN' THE NIGHT AWAY. / ONE MORE TIME**	6	9
May 62.	(lp) **TWISTIN' THE NIGHT AWAY**		72
	– Twistin' the night away / Sugar dumpling / Twistin' in the kitchen with Dinah / Somebody's gonna miss me / A whole lotta woman / The twist / Twistin' in the old town tonight / Movin' and a-groovin' / Camptown twist / Somebody have mercy / Soothe me / That's it – I quit – I'm movin' on. *(re-iss.Jul76 on 'Starcall') (re-iss.1984 on 'Premier')*		
Jun 62.	(7") **HAVING A PARTY. / BRING IT ON HOME TO ME**		17
			13
Oct 62.	(7") **NOTHING CAN CHANGE THIS LOVE. / SOMEBODY HAVE MERCY**		12
			70
Nov 62.	(lp) **THE BEST OF SAM COOKE** (compilation)		22
Jan 63.	(7") **SEND ME SOME LOVIN'. / BABY, BABY, BABY**		13
			60
Mar 63.	(lp) **MR.SOUL**		94
	– I wish you love / Willow weep for me / Chains of love / Smoke rings / All the way / Send me some lovin' / Cry me a river / Driftin' blues / (I love you for) Sentimental reasons / Nothing can change this love / Little girl / These foolish things. *(re-iss.1980)*		
Apr 63.	(7") **ANOTHER SATURDAY NIGHT. / LOVE WILL FIND A WAY**	23	10
Aug 63.	(7") **FRANKIE AND JOHNNY. / COOL TRAIN**	30	11
Sep 63.	(lp) **NIGHT BEAT**	-	62
	– Nobody knows the trouble I've seen / Lost and lookin' / Mean old world / Please don't drive me away / I lost everything / Get yourself another fool / Little red rooster / Laughin' and clownin' / Trouble blues / You gotta move / Fool's Paradise / Shake, rattle and roll.		
Oct 63.	(7") **LITTLE RED ROOSTER. / YOU'VE GOTTA MOVE**	-	11
Nov 63.	(7") **LITTLE RED ROOSTER. / SHAKE RATTLE AND ROLL**		-
Feb 64.	(7") **(AIN'T THAT) GOOD NEWS. / BASIN STREET BLUES**		11
May 64.	(lp) **AIN'T THAT GOOD NEWS**		34 Mar 64
	– Ain't that good news / Meet me at Mary's place / Good times / Rome wasn't built in a day / Another Saturday night / Tennessee waltz / change is gonna come / Falling in love / Home / Sittin' in the Sun / No second time / The riddle song.		
Jun 64.	(7") **GOOD TIMES. / TENNESSEE WALTZ**		11
			35
Oct 64.	(7") **COUSIN OF MINE. / THAT'S WHERE IT'S AT**		31
			93
Jan 65.	(lp) **AT THE COPA (LIVE)**		29 Oct 64
	– (Opening introduction) / The best things in life are free / Bill Bailey / Nobody knows you when you're down and out / Frankie and Johnny / Medley: Try a little tenderness – (I love you) For sentimental reasons – You send me / If I had a hammer / When I fall in love / This little light of mine / Blowin' in the wind / Tennessee waltz.		

On 11th Dec'64, COOKE was shot dead by motel manager Bertha Franklin. She claimed he had attempted to rape his female guest, and then turned on her. A coroner's verdict of 'Justifiable Homocide', was declared before burial on the 18th.

– posthumous, compilations, etc. –

——	Released 2 EP's in the 60's:- HEART AND SOUL / SWING SWEETLY		
Jan 65.	R.C.A.; (7") **SHAKE. / A CHANGE IS GONNA COME**		7
			31
Feb 65.	R.C.A.; (lp) **SHAKE!**		44
	– Shake / Yeah man / Win your love for me / Love you most of all / Meet me at Mary's place / I've got the whole world shakin' / A change is gonna come / I'm in the mood for love / I'm just a country boy / You're nobody 'til somebody loves you / Comes love / Ease my troublin' mind.		
Mar 65.	R.C.A.; (7") **IT'S GOT THE WHOLE WORLD SHAKIN'. / EASE MY TROUBLED MIND**		41
May 65.	R.C.A.; (7") **WHEN A BOY FALLS IN LOVE. / THE PIPER**		52
Jun 65.	R.C.A.; (lp) **THE BEST OF SAM COOKE VOL.2**		
Sep 65.	R.C.A.; (7") **SUGAR DUMPLING. / BRIDGE OF TEARS**		32 Aug 65
Oct 65.	R.C.A.; (lp) **TRY A LITTLE LOVE**		
	– Try a little love / Don't cry on my shoulder / Bridge of tears / I fall in love every day / You're always on my mind / Almost in your arms / When a boy falls in love / To each his own / Tammy / The gypsy / The little things you do / You send me.		
Jan 66.	R.C.A.; (7") **FEEL IT. / THAT'S ALL**		95
Mar 66.	R.C.A.; (7") **LET'S GO STEADY AGAIN. / TROUBLE BLUES**		97
1967.	R.C.A.; (7") **MEET ME AT MARY'S PLACE. / IF I HAD A HAMMER**		
Mar 76.	R.C.A.; (lp)(c) **INTERPRATES BILLIE HOLIDAY**		
Oct 76.	R.C.A.; (lp)(c) **THE GOLDEN AGE OF SAM COOKE**		
Jun 80.	R.C.A.; (7"ep) **ANOTHER SATURDAY NIGHT. / SOOTHE ME / +2**		-
Feb 86.	R.C.A.; (7") **WONDERFUL WORLD. / CHAIN GANG**	2	
	(12"+=) – Cupid / A change is gonna come.		
Apr 86.	R.C.A.; (d-lp)(d-c)(d-cd) **A MAN AND HIS MUSIC**	8	
Apr 86.	R.C.A.; (7") **ANOTHER SATURDAY NIGHT. / LITTLE RED ROOSTER**	75	
	(12"+=) – Frankie & Johnny.		

1971. Cherie; (7") **DARLING I NEED YOU NOW. / WIN YOUR LOVE FOR ME** | - | |
1971. Speciality; (7") **CHRIST IS ALL. / JUST ANOTHER DAY** | - | - |
Aug 79. EMI-Nut; (lp)(c) **WHEN I FALL IN LOVE** | | - |
(re-iss.Feb87 on 'Arena')
Feb 85. Golden Grooves; (7") **YOU SEND ME. / ONLY SIXTEEN** | | - |
1985. Cambra; (lp)(c) **THE FABULOUS SAM COOKE** | | - |
1985. Cambra; (lp)(c) **SOLITUDE** | | - |
1986. Perfect; (12") **YOU SEND ME. / +?** | | - |
1986. Topline; (lp)(c)(cd) **YOU SEND ME** | | - |
(re-iss.cd+cJul93 on 'Charity')
Apr 87. Topline; (lp)(c) **SWING OUT BROTHER** | | - |
Sep 87. Conifer; (cd) **20 GREATEST HITS** | | - |
Nov 89. Instant; (c)(cd) **THE WORLD OF SAM COOKE** | | - |

— (next credited with The SOUL STIRRERS)

Jul 88. C5; (lp)(cd) **HEAVEN IS MY HOME** | | - |
Dec 89. Ace; (lp)(cd) **IN THE BEGINNING** | | - |

— (above & below with The SOUL STIRRERS)

1991. Ace; (cd) **SAM COOKE WITH THE SOUL STIRRERS** | | - |
Jun 91. Music Club; (cd) **THE MAGIC OF SAM COOKE** | | - |
– You send me / Only sixteen / Stealing kisses / Talk of the town / I love you most of all / Comes love / Lover come back to me / Everybody loves to cha cha cha (cha-cha) / The little things you do / Good morning heartache / Win your love for me / Moonlight in Vermont / There I've said it again / Stealaway / All of my life / That lucky old Sun / God bless the child / When I fall in love.
May 94. Charly; (cd) **TWO ON ONE** (w/ JACKIE WILSON) | | - |
Jan 95. Ariola Express; (cd)(c) **SAM COOKE** | | - |
Jun 95. RCA; (cd) **HITS OF THE 50's** | | - |
Sep 95. London; (cd) **SAM COOKE'S NIGHT BEAT** | | - |

COOLIO

Born: Compton, California, USA. Hip hop rapper with distinctive spiky braided hair, he started out early 80's with DR DRE in the WORLD CLASS WRECKIN' CREW. Signed briefly to 'Ruthless' records, but this too was unproductive in the recording studios. His debut 'WHATCHA GONNA DO' was one of first rap records out of L.A., but for the next several years he struggled in and out of rehab centres, due to his cocaine addiction. After obtaining a job as a fire-fighter, he drifted back into music through working with WC & THE MADD CIRCLE then 40 THIEVZ. In 1993, he teamed up with fellow writer WINO and finally debutted (album-wise) with 'HOME ALONE'. In 1995, all his hard work paid off, when he hit No.1 on both sides of the Atlantic with classic rap single 'GANGSTA'S PARADISE' taken from the film 'Dangerous Minds' starring Michelle Pfiefer. • Miscellaneous: Not sure of real name (surname could be IVEY).

Recommended: IT TAKES A THIEF (*7) / GANGSTA'S PARADISE (*7)

COOLIO – vocals (with WINO, etc) (from 1994 only)

Tommy Boy | M.C.A.

1994. (c-s)(cd-s) **COUNTY LINE /** | - | |
1994. (cd)(c)(lp) **HOME ALONE** | - | |
Jul 94. (c-s) **FANTASTIC VOYAGE / ('A'-timer radio mix)** | 41 | 3 |
(12"+=)(cd-s+=) – ('A'-Dave Bellochio street mix) / ('A'-QD III remix) / ('A'-QD III bonus beats) / ('A'-Funk master flex).
Oct 94. (c-s) **I REMEMBER / ('A'mix)** | 73 | |
(cd-s+=) – (3 other mixes).
Oct 94. (cd)(c)(lp) **IT TAKES A THIEF** | 67 | 8 | Aug94
– Fantastic voyage / County line / Mama I'm in love with a gangsta / Hand on my nutsac / Ghetto cartoon / Smokin' stix / Can o'corn / U know hoo / It takes a thief / Bring back somethin' fo da hood / N da closet / On my way to Harlem / Sticky fingers / Thought you knew / Ugly women / I remember.
Oct 95. (7")(c-s) **GANGSTA'S PARADISE ('COOLIO featuring L.V."). / FANTASTIC VOYAGE** | 1 | 1 | Aug95
(cd-s+=) – Mama I'm in love with a gangsta (clean radio mix) / ('A'instrumental).
(cd-s) – ('A'side) / The worry come up (final mix) / Gangsta's paradise (Barr 9 version) / ('A'instrumental).
Nov 95. (cd)(c)(lp) **GANGSTA'S PARADISE** | 18 | 11 |
– That's how it is / Geto highlites / Gangsta's paradise / Too hot / Cruisin' / Exercise yo' game / Sumpin' new / Smilin' / Fucc Coolio / Kinda high, kinda drunk / For my sistas / Is this me? / A thing goin' on / Bright as the sun / Recoup this / The revolution / Get up, get down.
Nov 95. (c-s)(cd-s) **TOO HOT /** | - | 37 |

Alice COOPER

Formed: Phoenix, Arizona ... 1965 as The EARWIGS, by VINCENT FURNIER son of a preacher. The following year, they became The SPIDERS, and gained good airplay for 45 'DON'T BLOW YOUR MIND', released on local record label 'Santa Cruz'. In '68 they briefly took NAZZ for a name, but dropped it for ALICE COOPER when they signed to FRANK ZAPPA's 'Straight' records. In the 70's, VINCENT adopted group name, when he virtually went solo. By 1971, they sealed a deal with 'Warners', and soon appeared on Top of the Pops, with teen anthem 'SCHOOL'S OUT'. Hits continued throughout the 70's, with ALICE taking time off to recuperate in a mental home. By the late 80's, ALICE was back in the Top 20 with new heavy-metal assault. • **Style:** From 60's garage rock, to gory/glam shocking stage shows in the 70's (his use of pet snake, simulated hangings & guillotine, bloody toy babies, was well documented at the time). In the late 70's, due to alcohol addiction, he mellowed into soft AOR, leaving true fans and burgeoning punks stunned. By the 80's he had backtracked into past themes, culminating in hard-rock image in 1989. • **Songwriters:** ALICE wrote / co-wrote with band most of material, also using producer BOB EZRIN. DICK WAGNER to BERNIE TAUPIN also contributed in the 70's. On 'CONSTRICTOR' album, ALICE co-wrote with ROBERTS, some with KELLY and WEGENER. Collaborated with DESMOND CHILD in '89 and JACK PONTI, VIC PEPE, BOB PFEIFER in 1991. Covered:- SUN ARISE (trad. Rolf Harris) / SEVEN AND SEVEN IS (Love) / FIRE (Jimi Hendrix). **Trivia** Film cameo appearances have been DIARY OF A HOUSEWIFE (1970) / SGT.PEPPER'S LONELY HEARTS CLUB BAND (1978) / ROADIE (1980) / PRINCE OF DARKNESS (1987) / FREDDIE'S DEAD: THE FINAL NIGHTMARE (1991 also acted). In 1975 he sang 'I'M FLASH' on Various Artists concept album 'FLASH FEARLESS VS.THE ZORG WOMEN Pts.5 & 6'. VINCENT PRICE guest narrated on concept 1975 album 'WELCOME TO MY NIGHTMARE'. On 7 Apr'88 during a stage rehearsal he nearly hung himself with noose/prop.

Recommended: BEAST OF ALICE COOPER (*8) / WELCOME TO MY NIGHTMARE (*8) / KILLER (*8) / LOVE IT TO DEATH (*8) / BILLION DOLLAR BABIES (*7).

The SPIDERS

ALICE COOPER (b.VINCENT DAMON FURNIER, 4 Feb'48, Detroit) – vocals / **GLEN BUXTON** (b.17 Jun'47, Washington DC) – lead guitar / **MICHAEL BRUCE** (b.21 Nov'48, California) – rhythm guitar, keyboards / **DENNIS DUNAWAY** (b.15 Mar'46, California) – bass / **NEAL SMITH** (b.10 Jan'48, Washington DC) – drums

not issued | Santa Cruz

1967. (7") **DON'T BLOW YOUR MIND. / NO PRICE TAG** | - | |

not issued | Very

1967. (7") **WONDER WHO'S LOVING HER NOW. / LAY DOWN AND DIE, GOODBYE** | - | |

ALICE COOPER

Straight | Straight

Dec 69. (lp) **PRETTIES FOR YOU** | | | Jul 69
– Titanic overture / 10 minutes before the worm / Sing low sweet cheerio / Today Mueller / Living / Fields of regret / No longer umpire / Levity ball / B.B. on Mars / Reflected / Apple bush / Earwigs to eternity / Changing, arranging.
Jan 70. (7") **LIVING. / REFLECTED** | - | |
Jun 70. (lp) **EASY ACTION** | | |
– Mr. and Misdemeaner / Shoe salesman / Still no air / Below your means / Return of the spiders / Still no air / Laughing at me / Refridgerator Heaven / Beautiful flyaway / Lay down and die, goodbye.
Jun 70. (7") **CAUGHT IN A DREAM. / EIGHTEEN** | - | |
Nov 70. (7") **RETURN OF THE SPIDERS. / SHOE SALESMAN** | - | |

Straight | Warners

Mar 71. (7") **EIGHTEEN. / IS IT MY BODY** | | 21 | Feb 71
Jun 71. (lp)(c) **LOVE IT TO DEATH** | | 35 | Mar 71
– Caught in a dream / Eighteen / Long way to go / Black Juju / Is it my body / Hallowed be thy name / Second coming / Ballad of Dwight Fry / Sun arise. *(UK re-iss.Dec71 on 'Warner Bros.', Sep72 hit 28.*

Warners | Warners

Jun 71. (7") **CAUGHT IN A DREAM. / HALLOWED BE THY NAME** | - | 94 |
Dec 71. (7") **UNDER MY WHEELS. / DESPERADO** | | 59 |
(re-iss.Aug74)
Dec 71. (lp)(c) **KILLER** | 27 | 21 | Nov 71
– Under my wheels / Be my lover / Halo of flies / Desperado / You drive me nervous / Yeah yeah yeah / Dead babies / Killer. *(cd-iss.Sep89 on 'WEA')*
Feb 72. (7") **BE MY LOVER. / YOU DRIVE ME NERVOUS** | | 49 |
Jul 72. (7") **SCHOOL'S OUT. / GUTTER CAT** | 1 | 7 | Jun 72
Jul 72. (lp)(c) **SCHOOL'S OUT** | 4 | 2 |
– School's out / Luney tune / Gutter cat vs. the jets / Street fight / Blue Turk / My stars / Public animal No.9 / Alma mater / Grande finale. *(re-iss.+cd.Sep89 on 'WEA')*
Oct 72. (7") **ELECTED. / LUNEY TUNE** | 4 | 26 |
Feb 73. (7") **HELLO HURRAY. / GENERATION LANDSLIDE** | 6 | 35 |
Mar 73. (lp)(c) **BILLION DOLLAR BABIES** | 1 | 1 |
– Hello hurray / Raped and freezin' / Elected / Billion dollar babies / Unfinished sweet / No more Mr. Nice guy / Generation landslide / Sick things / Mary Ann / I love the dead.
Apr 73. (7") **NO MORE MR. NICE GUY. / RAPED AND FREEZIN'** | 10 | 25 |
Jul 73. (7") **BILLION DOLLAR BABIES. / MARY ANN** | - | 57 |
Jan 74. (lp)(c) **MUSCLE OF LOVE** | 34 | 10 | Dec 73
– Muscle of love / Woman machine / Hard hearted Alice / Man with the golden gun / Big apple dreamin' (hippo) / Never been sold before / Working up a sweat / Crazy little child / Teenage lament '74.
Jan 74. (7") **TEENAGE LAMENT '74. / HARD HEARTED ALICE** | 12 | 48 | Dec 73
Mar 74. (7") **MUSCLE OF LOVE. / CRAZY LITTLE CHILD** | - | |
Jun 74. (7") **MUSCLE OF LOVE. / EIGHTEEN** | - | |

— **ALICE** sacked rest of band, who became BILLION DOLLAR BABIES. He brought in **DICK WAGNER** – guitar, vocals / **STEVE** (DEACON) **HUNTER** – guitars / **PRAKASH JOHN** – bass / **PENTII 'Whitey' GLAN** – drums / **JOSEF CHIROWSKI** – drums. (all ex-LOU REED band)

Anchor | Atlantic

Feb 75. (7") **DEPARTMENT OF YOUTH. / COLD ETHYL** | | 67 | Aug 75
Mar 75. (lp)(c) **WELCOME TO MY NIGHTMARE** | 19 | 5 |
– Welcome to my nightmare / Devil's food / The black widow / Some folks / Only women bleed / Department of youth / Cold Ethyl / Years ago / Steven / The awakening / Escape. *(re-iss.+cd.Sep87 on 'Atlantic')*
Apr 75. (7") **ONLY WOMEN BLEED. / COLD ETHYL** | - | 12 |
Jun 75. (7") **ONLY WOMEN BLEED. / DEVIL'S FOOD** | | - |
Aug 75. (7") **DEPARTMENT OF YOUTH. / SOME FOLKS** | | - |
Oct 75. (7") **WELCOME TO MY NIGHTMARE. / COLD ETHYL** | - | 45 |
Nov 75. (7") **WELCOME TO MY NIGHTMARE. / BLACK WIDOW** | | - |

Warners Warners

Jun 76. (lp)(c) **ALICE COOPER GOES TO HELL** [23] [27]
– Go to Hell / You gotta dance / I'm the coolest / Didn't we meet / I never cry / Give the kid a break / Guilty / Wake me gently / Wish you were here / I'm always chasing rainbows / Going home.
Jul 76. (7") **I NEVER CRY. / GO TO HELL** [ ] [12]
Apr 77. (7") **YOU AND ME. / IT'S HOT TONIGHT** [-] [9]
May 77. (7") **(NO MORE) LOVE AT YOUR CONVENIENCE. / IT'S HOT TONIGHT** [44] [ ]
May 77. (lp)(c) **LACE AND WHISKEY** [33] [42]
– It's hot tonight / Lace and whiskey / Road rats / Damned if I do / You and me / King of the silver screen / Ubangi stomp / (No more) Love at your convenience / I never wrote those songs / My God.
Jul 77. (7") **YOU AND ME. / MY GOD** [ ] [-]

— **FRED MANDEL** – keyboards repl. JOSEF

Dec 77. (lp)(c) **THE ALICE COOPER SHOW (live)** [ ] [ ]
– Under my wheels / Eighteen / Only women bleed / Sick things / Is it my body / I never cry / Billion dollar babies / Devil's food – The black widow / You and me / I love the dead / Go to Hell / Wish you were here / School's out.

— **Alice COOPER** now basically a solo artist with session people, which retaining **MANDEL, DAVEY JOHNSTONE** – guitar (ex-ELTON JOHN) / **MARK VOLMAN + HOWARD KAYLAN** – backing vocals (ex-TURTLES)

Dec 78. (7") **HOW YOU GONNA SEE ME NOW. / NO TRICKS** [61] [12] Oct 78
Dec 78. (lp)(c) **FROM THE INSIDE** [68] [60]
– How you gonna see me now / Wish I were born in Beverley Hills / The quiet room / Nurse Rozetta / Millie and Billie / Serious / How you gonna see me now / For Veronica's sake / Jacknife Johnny / Inmates (we're all crazy).
Jan 79. (7") **FROM THE INSIDE. / NURSE ROZETTA** [-] [ ]

— above w / **JOHN LO PRESTI** – bass / **DENNIS CONWAY** – drums

May 80. (lp)(c) **FLUSH THE FASHION** [56] [44]
– Talk talk / Clones (we're all) / Pain / Leather boots / Aspirin damage / Grim facts / Nuclear infected / Model citizen / Dance yourself to death / Headlines.
Jun 80. (7") **CLONES (WE'RE ALL). / MODEL CITIZEN** [ ] [40] May 80
Sep 80. (7") **DANCE YOURSELF TO DEATH. / TALK TALK** [-] [ ]

— now w / **MIKE PINERA + DAVEY JOHNSTONE** – guitar / **DUANE HITCHINGS** – keyboards / **ERIC SCOTT** – bass / **CRAIG KRAMPF** – drums

Sep 81. (7") **WHO DO YOU THINK WE ARE. / YOU WANT IT, YOU GOT IT** [-] [ ]
Sep 81. (lp)(c) **SPECIAL FORCES** [96] [ ]
– Who do you think we are / Seven and seven is / Skeletons in the closet / You're a movie / You want it, you got it / Vicious rumours / Perfect cop on the block / Generation landslide '81 / You look good in rags / Don't talk old to me.
Feb 82. (7") **SEVEN AND SEVEN IS (live). / GENERATION LANDSLIDE '81 (live)** [62] [ ]
May 82. (7")(7"pic-d) **FOR BRITAIN ONLY. / UNDER MY WHEELS (live)** [66] [ ]
(12"+=) – Who do you think we are (live) / Model citizen (live).

— now w / **MIKE PINERA + DAVEY JOHNSTONE** – guitar / **DUANE HITCHINGS** – keyboards / **ERIC SCOTT** – bass / **CRAIG KRAMPF** – drums

Oct 82. (7") **I LIKE GIRLS. / ZORRO'S ASCENT** [-] [ ]
Oct 82. (lp)(c) **ZIPPER CATCHES SKIN** [ ] [ ]
– Zorro's ascent / Make that money / I am the future / No baloney homosapiens / Adaptable (anything for you) / I like girls / Remarkably insincere / Tag, you're it / I better be good / I'm alive (that was the day my dead pet returned to save my life).

— **COOPER + WAGNER** re-united w / **EZRIN + PRAKASH** and recruited **GRAHAN SHAW** – synth / **JOHN ANDERSON + RICHARD KOLINGA** – drums

Mar 83. (7") **I AM THE FUTURE (remix). / ZORRO'S ASCENT** [ ] [ ]
Mar 83. (7") **I AM THE FUTURE. / TAG, YOU'RE IT** [-] [ ]
Nov 83. (lp)(c) **DADA** [93] [ ]
– Dada / Enough's enough / Former Lee Warner / No man's land / Dyslexia / Scarlet and Sheba / I love America / Fresh blood / Pass the gun around.
Nov 83. (12"m) **I LOVE AMERICA. / FRESH BLOOD / PASS THE GUN AROUND** [ ] [ ]

— Band now consisted of **KANE ROBERTS** (b.16 Jan'59) – guitar, vocals / **DAVID ROSENBERG** – drums / **PAUL DELPH** – keyboards, vocals / **DONNIE KISSELBACK** – bass, vocals, **+ KIP WINGER.**

M.C.A. M.C.A.

Oct 86. (7") **HE'S BACK (THE MAN BEHIND THE MASK). / BILLION DOLLAR BABIES** [61] [ ]
(12"+=) – I'm eighteen.
Oct 86. (lp)(c) **CONSTRICTOR** [41] [59]
– Teenage Frankenstein / Give it up / Thrill my gorilla / Life and death of the party / Simple disobedience / The world needs guts / Trick bag / Crawlin' / The great American success story / He's back (the man behind the mask).
Apr 87. (7") **TEENAGE FRANKENSTEIN. / SCHOOL'S OUT (live)** [ ] [ ]
(12"+=) – Only women bleed.

— **KEN K. MARY** – drums repl.ROSENBERG / **PAUL HOROWITZ** – keyboards, repl. DELPH + KISSELBACH.

Oct 87. (lp)(c) **RAISE YOUR FIST AND YELL** [48] [73]
– Freedom / Lock me up / Step on you / Give the radio back / Step on you / Not that kind of love / Prince of darkness / Time to kill / Chop, chop, chop / Gail / Roses on white lace. *(cd-iss.+pic-lp.May88)*
Mar 88. (7") **FREEDOM. / TIME TO KILL** [50] [ ]
(12"+=) – School's out (live).

— retained **KIP WINGER** bringing in guests **JON BON JOVI, RICHIE SAMBORA** plus **JOE PERRY, TOM HAMILTON, JOEY KRAMER** etc.

— **COOPER + WAGNER** re-united w / **EZRIN + PRAKASH** and recruited **GRAHAN SHAW** – synth / **JOHN ANDERSON + RICHARD KOLINGA** – drums

Epic Epic

1988. (7") **I GOT A LINE ON YOU. / LIVIN' ON THE EDGE** [-] [ ]
Jul 89. (7") **POISON. / TRASH** [2] [7]
(12"+=) – The ballad of Dwight Fry / Cold Ethyl (live) =(12"only)
(cd-s+=) – I got a line on you (live).
Aug 89. (lp)(c)(cd) **TRASH** [2] [20]
– Poison / Spark in the dark / House of fire / Why trust you / Only my heart talkin' / Bed of nails / This maniac's in love with you / Trash / Hell is living without you / I'm your gun. *(re-iss.cd+c Sep93)*
Sep 89. (7")(c-s)(7"green)(7"red)(7"blue) **BED OF NAILS. / I'M YOUR GUN** [38] [ ]
(12"+=)(12"pic-d+=) – Go to Hell (live).
(cd-s++=) – Only women bleed (live).
Dec 89. (7")(c-s) **HOUSE OF FIRE. / POISON (live)** [65] [56]
(7"red)(7"yellow)(7"sha-pic-d) – ('A'side) / This maniac's in love with you.
(12"+=)(cd-s+=) – Billion dollar babies (live) / Under my wheels (live).
(12"+=) – Spark in the dark (live) / Under my wheels (live).
(12"pic-d+=) – Poison (live).
Apr 90. (c-s)(cd-s) **ONLY MY HEART TALKIN'. / UNDER MY WHEELS** [-] [89]

— (Mar90) touring band **PETE FRIEZZEN** – guitar / **AL PITRELLI** – guitar / **TOMMY CARADONNA** – bass / **DEREK SHERINIAN** – keyboards / **JONATHAN MOVER** – drums

— (1991 sessions) **STEVE VAI, JOE SATRIANI, STEF BURNS** (on tour), **VINNIE MOORE, MICK MARS, SLASH** – guitars / **HUGH McDONALD, NIKKI SIXX** – bass / **MICKEY CURRY** – drums / **ROBERT SALLEY, JOHN WEBSTER** – keyboards / **STEVE CROES** – synclaiver

Jun 91. (7") **HEY STOOPID. / IT RAINED ALL NIGHT** [-] [78]
Jun 91. (7") **HEY STOOPID. / WIND-UP TOYS** [21] [-]
(12"+=)(cd-s+=)(12"pic-d+=) – It rained all night.
Jun 91. (cd)(c)(lp) **HEY STOOPID** [4] [47]
– Hey stoopid / Love's a loaded gun / Snakebite / Burning our bed / Dangerous tonight / Might as well be on Mars / Feed me Frankenstein / Hurricane years / Die for you / Little by little / Dirty dreams / Wind-up toys.
Sep 91. (7")(c-s)(7"pic-d) **LOVE'S A LOADED GUN. / FIRE** [38] [ ]
(12"+=)(12"pic-d+=) – Eighteen (live '91).
(cd-s+=) – Love gun.
Jun 92. (7") **FEED ME FRANKENSTEIN. / BURNING OUR BED** [27] [ ]
(cd-s+=)(12"pic-d+=) – Poison / Only my heart talkin'.
(cd-s+=) – Hey stoopid / Bed of nails.

— w / **STEF BURNS** – guitar, vocals / **GREG SMITH** – bass, vocals / **DEREK SHERINIAN** – keyboards, vocals / **DAVID VOSIKKINEN** – drums

May 94. (c-s) **LOST IN AMERICA. / HEY STOOPID (live)** [22] [ ]
(12"pic-d+=)(pic-cd-s+=) – Billion dollar babies / No more Mr.Nice Guy (both live).
Jun 94. (cd)(c)(lp) **THE LAST TEMPTATION** (w /free comic) [6] [68]
– Sideshow / Nothing free / Lost in America / Bad place alone / You're my temptation / Stolen prayer / Unholy war / Lullaby / It's me / Cleansed by fire.
Jul 94. (c-s) **IT'S ME. / BAD PLACE ALONE** [34] [ ]
(12"pic-d+=)(pic-cd-s+=) – Poison / Sick things.
Oct 95. (cd)(c) **CLASSICKS** (compilation) [ ] [ ]
– Poison / Hey stoopid / Feed my Frankenstein / Love's a loaded gun / Stolen prayer / House of fire / Lost in America / It's me / Under my wheels (live) / Billion dollar babies (live) / I'm eighteen (live) / No more Mr. Nice guy (live) / Only women bleed (live) / School's out (live) / Fire.

– compilations, others, etc. –

Jun 73. Warners; (d-lp)(d-c) **SCHOOLDAYS** (1st-2 lp's) [ ] [ ]
Mar 73. Warners; (7") **BE MY LOVER. / UNDER MY WHEELS** [-] [ ]
Sep 74. Warners; (lp)(c) **ALICE COOPER'S GREATEST HITS** [ ] [8] Aug 74
(cd-iss.Jun89)
Feb 75. Warners; (7"ep) **SCHOOL'S OUT / NO MORE MR.NICE GUY. / BILLION DOLLAR BABIES / ELECTED** [ ] [ ]
Feb 76. Warners; (7") **SCHOOL'S OUT. / ELECTED** [ ] [ ]
(re-iss.Dec80) (re-iss.Sep85 on 'Old Gold')
1978. Warners; (7") **I'M EIGHTEEN. / SCHOOL'S OUT** [-] [ ]
Dec 77. Anchor; (12"ep) **DEPARTMENT OF YOUTH** [ ] [-]
– Department of youth / Welcome to my nightmare / Black widow / Only women bleed.
Apr 84. Design; (pic-lp) **ROCK'N'ROLL REVIVAL: TORONTO LIVE '69 (live)** [ ] [ ]
(above re-iss.Apr86 as **FREAKOUT SONG** on 'Showcase')
Apr 87. Thunderbolt; (m-lp)(c) **LADIES MAN (live'69)** [ ] [ ]
(cd-iss.Aug88) (re-cd.Jun91)
Dec 89. W.E.A.; (lp)(c)(cd) **THE BEAST OF ALICE COOPER** [ ] [ ]
– School's out / Under my wheels / Billion dollar babies / Be my lover / Desperado / Is it my body? / Only women bleed / Elected / I'm eighteen / Hello hurray / No more Mr.Nice guy / Teenage lament '74 / Muscle of love / Department of youth.
May 92. Edsel; (cd) **LIVE AT THE WHISKEY, 1969 (live)** [ ] [ ]
Apr 93. Pulsar; (cd) **NOBODY LIKES ME** [ ] [-]

Julian COPE

Born: 21 Oct'57, Bargeld, Wales, raised Liverpool, England. In the Autumn of 1978 TEARDROP EXPLODES formed, originally as A SHALLOW MADNESS by ex-CRUCIAL THREE member COPE, FINKLER and SIMPSON. Late '78, they attained deal with local indie label 'Zoo', and became TEARDROP EXPLODES. After three critically acclaimed singles, they transferred to major label 'Mercury' in July 1980. They captured first hit with 'WHEN I DREAM', which was cut from classic album 'KILIMANJARO'. He ventured solo in 1983 sticking with 'Mercury' records, for whom he released 2 albums in 1984. He signed for 'Island' in 1985 leaving behind unissued (until 1990) SKELLINGTON lp. Around the same time he suffered marriage break-up and drug problems, but soon recovered when he re-married in 1986. • **Style:** Keyboard-biased (TEARDROP EXPLODES) and mostly influenced by 60's pop psychedelia, and sounds like a modern post new wave SCOTT WALKER. Public stage antics cutting (IGGY POP-like) his stomach in 1984, and singing perched on high pole in 1986, saw rise to new but weird character. Although it was sometimes his alter-ego (SQWUBBSY a seven foot giant) at work. • **Songwriters:** COPE penned except; READ IT IN BOOKS (co-with; Ian McCulloch, ex-CRUCIAL THREE). He wrote all material, except NON-ALIGNMENT PACT (Pere Ubu) / BOOKS (Teardrop Explodes) / RAVE ON (Buddy Holly). • **Trivia:** The album DROOLIAN, was released for campaign to free from jail ROKY ERICKSON (ex-13th FLOOR ELEVATORS). In '90, COPE marched on Anti-Poll tax march from Brixton to Trafalgar Square.

Recommended: PEGGY SUICIDE (*8) / SAINT JULIAN (*7) / FLOORED GENIUS...(*9) / WORLD SHUT YOUR MOUTH (*7) / FRIED (*7) / MY NATION UNDERGROUND (*6) / JEHOVAHKILL (*7) / TEARDROP EXPLODES:- KILIMANJARO (*9) / WILDER (*7).

TEARDROP EXPLODES

JULIAN COPE (b.21 Oct'57, Bargoed, Wales) – vocals, bass / **PAUL SIMPSON** – keyboards / **MICK FINKLER** – guitar / **GARY DWYER** – drums

Zoo / not issued

Feb 79. (7"m) **SLEEPING GAS. / CAMERA CAMERA / KIRBY WORKERS' DREAM FADES** [ ] [-]

— **GERARD QUINN** – keyboards repl. SIMPSON who formed The WILD SWANS

May 79. (7") **BOUNCING BABIES. / ALL I AM IS LOVING YOU** [ ] [-]

— **DAVID BALFE** – keyboards (ex-LORI & THE CHAMELEONS, ex-BIG IN JAPAN, ex-THOSE NAUGHTY LUMPS) repl. QUINN who also joined The WILD SWANS

Mar 80. (7") **TREASON (IT'S JUST A STORY). / READ IT IN BOOKS** [ ] [-]

— **ALAN GILL** – guitar (ex-DALEK I) repl. FINKLER now (COPE, DWYER, BALFE + GILL)

Mercury / Mercury

Sep 80. (7") **WHEN I DREAM. / KILIMANJARO** [47] [ ]

Oct 80. (lp)(c) **KILIMANJARO** [24] [ ]
– Ha, ha, I'm drowning / Sleeping gas / Treason (it's just a story) / Second head / Poppies in the field / Went crazy / Brave boys keep their promises / Bouncing babies / Books / Thief of Baghdad / When I dream. *(re-iss.Mar81+=)* – Reward. *(re-iss.Jul84, re-iss.+cd.May89)*

(below trumpet by – **RAY MARTINEZ**)

Jan 81. (7") **REWARD. / STRANGE HOUSE IN THE SNOW** [6] [ ]

Apr 81. (7") **TREASON (IT'S JUST A STORY). / USE ME** [18] [ ]
(12"+=) – Traison (French remix).

Jun 81. (7") **POPPIES IN THE FIELD. / HA HA I'M DROWNING** [ ] [ ]
(d7"+=) – Bouncing babies / Read it in books.

— **TROY TATE** – guitar, vocals (ex-INDEX, ex-SHAKE) repl. GILL

Sep 81. (7") **PASSIONATE FRIEND. / CHRIST VS. WARHOL** [25] [ ]

— on session/**gigs ALFIE ALGIUS** (b.Malta) – bass / **JEFF HAMMER** – keyboards

Nov 81. (lp)(c) **WILDER** [29] [ ]
– Bent out of shape / Tiny children / The culture bunker / Falling down around me / Passionate friend / Colours fly away / Pure joy / Seven views of Jerusalem / The great dominions / Like Leila Khaled said / . . .And the fighting takes over. *(re-iss.Jun87, cd-iss.1989)*

Nov 81. (7") **COLOURS FLY AWAY. / WINDOW SHOPPING FOR A NEW CROWN OF THORNS** [54] [ ]

— **DAVID BALFE** returned. **RON FRANCOIS** – bass (ex-SINCEROS) repl. guests

Jun 82. (7") **TINY CHILDREN. / RACHEL BUILT A STEAMBOAT** [44] [ ]
(12"+=) – Sleeping gas.

— now a trio of **COPE, DWYER + BALFE** plus sessionman **FRANCOIS.** TROY TATE went solo and joined FASHION.

Mar 83. (7") **YOU DISAPPEAR FROM VIEW. / SUFFOCATE** [41] [ ]
(12"+=)(d7"+=) – Soft enough for you / Ouch monkeys / The in-psychlopedia.

— Disbanded early '83. BALFE went into producing films. JULIAN COPE went solo augmented by DWYER.

– compilations, others, etc. –

Jun 85. Mercury; (7") **REWARD (remix). / TREASON (IT'S JUST A STORY)** [ ] [-]
(12"+=) – Strange house in the snow / Use me.

Jan 90. Fontana; (7") **SERIOUS DANGER. / SLEEPING GAS** [ ] [-]
(12"+=)(cd-s+=) – Seven views of Jerusalem.

Mar 90. Fontana; (cd)(c)(lp) **EVERYBODY WANTS TO SHAG THE TEARDROP EXPLODES** – (Their long lost 3rd album) [72] [-]
– Ouch monkeys / Serious danger / Metranil Vavin / Count to ten and run forever / In-psychiopaedia / Soft enough for you / You disappear from view / The challenger / Not only my friend / Sex / Terrorist / Strange house in the snow.

Apr 90. Fontana; (7") **COUNT TO TEN AND RUN FOR COVER. / REWARD** [ ] [-]
(12"+=)(cd-s+=) – Poppies / Khaled said.

Jan 91. Document; (cd)(lp) **PIANO** [ ] [-]
– (early 'Zoo' material)

Dec 93. Windsong; (cd)(lp) **BBC RADIO 1 LIVE IN CONCERT (live)** [ ] [-]

JULIAN COPE

JULIAN COPE – vocals, bass, rhythm guitar, organ (ex-TEARDROP EXPLODES) with **GARY DWYER** (ex-TEARDROP EXPLODES), **STEVE CREASE + ANDREW EDGE** – drums / **STEPHEN LOWELL** – lead guitar / **RON FRANCOIS** – bass / **KATE ST.JOHN** – oboe.

Mercury / Mercury

Nov 83. (7") **SUNSHINE PLAYROOM. / HEY HIGH CLASS BUTCHER** [64] [ ]
(12"+=) – Wreck my car / Eat the poor.

Feb 84. (lp)(c) **WORLD SHUT YOUR MOUTH** [40] [ ]
– Bandy's first jump / Metranil Vavin / Strasbourg / An elegant chaos / Quizmaster / Kolly Kibber's birthday / Sunshine playroom / Head hang low / Pussy face / The greatness and perfection of love / Lunatic and fire pistol. *(cd-iss. 1986)*

Mar 84. (7") **THE GREATNESS AND PERFECTION OF LOVE. / 24a VELOCITY CRESCENT** [52] [ ]
(12"+=) – Pussy face.

Nov 84. (lp)(c) **FRIED** [87] [ ]
– Reynard the fox / Bill Drummond said / Laughing boy / Me singing / Sunspots / Me singing / Bloody Assizes / Search party / O king of chaos / Holy love / Torpedo. *(cd-iss. 1986)*

Feb 85. (7") **SUNSPOTS. / I WENT ON A CHOURNEY** [ ] [ ]
(d7"+=) – Mick mack mock / Land of fear.

— **COPE** recruited Americans **DONALD ROSS SKINNER** – guitar / **JAMES ELLER** – bass / **DOUBLE DE HARRISON** – keyboards / **CHRIS WHITTEN** – drums

Island / Island

Sep 86. (7") **WORLD SHUT YOUR MOUTH. / UPTEENTH UNNATURAL BLUES** [19] [84] Feb 87
(d7"+=) – Non-alignment pact / Transportation.
(c-s+=) – I've got levitation.
(12"++=) – (all extra 3 above).
(12"+=) ('A'version).

Jan 87. (7") **TRAMPOLENE. / DISASTER** [ ] [ ]
(7"ep+=)(12"ep+=) – Mock Turtle / Warwick the kingmaker.
(12"+=) – ('A' version).

Feb 87. (m-lp) **JULIAN COPE** [-] [ ]
– World shut your mouth / Transportation / Umpteenth unnatural blues / Non-argument pact / I've got levitation.

Mar 87. (lp)(c)(cd) **SAINT JULIAN** [11] [ ]
– Trampolene / Shot down / Eve's volcano (covered in sin) / Spacehopper / Planet ride / Trampolene / World shut your mouth / Saint Julian / Pulsar NX / Space hopper / Screaming secrets / A crack in the clouds. *(re-iss.c+cd.Aug91)*

Apr 87. (7") **EVE'S VOLCANO (COVERED IN SIN). / ALMOST BEAUTIFUL CHILD** [ ] [ ]
(12"+=) – Pulsar NX (live) / Shot down (live).
(12"+=) – Spacehopper-annexe.
(cd-s++=) – (all 3 extra above).

— **DAVE PALMER** – drums (studio) / **MIKE JOYCE** – drums (tour) repl. WHITTEN / added **RON FAIR** – keyboards / **ROOSTER COSBY** – percussion, some drums

Sep 88. (7") **CHARLOTTE ANNE. / CHRISTMAS MOURNING** [35] [ ]
(12"+=) – Question of temperatures / Books.

Oct 88. (lp)(c)(cd) **MY NATION UNDERGROUND** [42] [ ]
– 5 o'clock world / Vegetation / Charlotte Anne / My nation underground / China doll / Someone like me / Easter everywhere / I'm not losing sleep / The great white hoax. *(re-iss.c+cd.Aug91)*

Nov 88. (7") **5 O'CLOCK WORLD. / S.P.Q.R.** [42] [ ]
(12"+=)(cd-s+=) – Reynard in Tokyo (live 12 minute version).

Jun 89. (7") **CHINA DOLL. / CRAZY FARM ANIMAL** [53] [ ]
(cd-s+=) – Desi.
(10"+=)(12"+=) – Rave on.

— **COPE** retained **SKINNER & COSBY** plus **J.D.HASSINGER** – drums / **TIM** – keyboards / **BRAN** – bass (both of Guernsey)

Jan 91. (7")(c-s) **BEAUTIFUL LOVE. / PORT OF SAINTS** [32] [ ]
(12"+=)(cd-s+=) – Love (L.U.V.) / Unisex cathedral.

Mar 91. (cd)(c)(d-lp) **PEGGY SUICIDE** [23] [ ]
– Pristeen / Double vegetation / East easy rider / Promised land / Hanging out & hung up on the line / Safesurfer / If you loved me at all / Drive, she said / Soldier blue / You . . . / Not raving but drowning / Head / Leperskin / Beautiful love / Uptight / Western Front 1992 CE / Hung up & hanging out to dry / The American Lite / Las Vegas basement. *(re-iss.cd Aug94)*

Apr 91. (7")(c-s) **EAST EASY RIDER. / BUTTERFLY E** [51] [ ]
(12"+=)(cd-s+=) – Almost live / Little donkey.
(12"pic-d+=) – Easty Risin' / Ravebury stones.

Jul 91. (7") **HEAD. / BAGGED - OUT KEN** [57] [ ]
(12"+=)(cd-s+=) – Straw dogs / Animals at all.

Oct 92. (7")(c-s) **FEAR LOVES THE SPACE. / SIZEWELL B** [42] [ ]
(12"pic-d+=) – I have always been here before / Gogmagog.

Oct 92. (cd)(c)(d-lp) **JEHOVAHKILL** [20] [ ]
– Soul desert / No harder shoulder to cry on / Akhenaten / The mystery trend / Upwards at 45° / Cut my friends down / Necropolis / Slow rider / Gimme back my flag / Poet is priest / Julian H Cope / The subtle energies commission / Fa-fa-fa-fine / Fear loves this place / Peggy Suicide is missing. *(re-iss.cd Aug94)*

— Next was last in the 90's album trilogy about pollution. Its theme this time was the car, (coincidentally he had just passed his driving test). It featured usual musicians.

Echo / Def Amer.

Jul 94. (cd)(c)(lp) **AUTOGEDDON** [16] [ ]
– Autogeddon blues / Don't call me Mark Chapman / Madmax / I gotta walk / Ain't no gettin' round gettin' round / Paranormal in the West Country / Paranormal / Archdrude's roadtrip / Kar-ma-kanik / Ain't but the one way / Starcar.

Aug 95. (7"ep)(c-ep)(cd-ep) **TRY TRY TRY / WESSEXY. / BABY, LET'S PLAY VET / DON'T JUMP ME, MOTHER** [24] [ ]

Aug 95. (cd)(c)(d-lp) **20 MOTHERS** [20] [ ]
– Wheelbarrow man / I wandered lonely as a child / Try try try / Stone circles 'n' you / Queen – Mother / I'm your daddy / Highway to the sun / 1995 / By the light of he Silbury moon / Adam and Eve hit the road / Just like Pooh Bear / Girl-call / Greedhead detector / Don't take roots / Senile get / The lonely guy / Cryingbabiessleeplessnights / Leli B. / Road of dreams / When I walk through the land of fear.

– compilations, others, etc. –

May 90. Capeco-Zippo; (cd)(lp) **SKELLINGTON** (1985 lost lp) [ ] [-]
– Doomed / Beaver / Me & Jimmy Jones / Robert Mitchum / Out of my mind on dope and speed / Don't crash here / Everything playing at once / Little donkey / Great white wonder / Incredibly ugly girl / No how, no why, no way, no where, no when / Comin' soon.

Jul 90. Mofoco-Zippo; (lp) **DROOLIAN** [ ] [-]

Feb 85. Bam Caruso; (7") **COMPETITION (as "RABBI JOSEPH GORDON"). / BELIEF IN HIM** [ ] [-]

Jul 92. Island; (7")(c-s) **WORLD SHUT YOUR MOUTH (remix). / DOOMED** [44] [ ]

(12"+=)(cd-s+=) – Reynard the fox / The elevators / Levitation.
Aug 92. (cd)(c)(d-lp) **FLOORED GENIUS – THE BEST OF JULIAN COPE AND THE TEARDROP EXPLODES 1981-1991** 22
– Reward / Treason / Sleeping gas / Bouncing babies / Passionate friend / The great dominions (all TEARDROP EXPLODES) / The greatness & perfection of love / An elegant chaos / Sunspots / Reynard the fox / World shut your mouth / Trampolene / Spacehopper / Charlotte Anne / China doll / Out of my mind on dope & speed / Jellypop perky Jean / Beautiful love / East easy rider / Safesurfer.
Nov 92. (d-cd) **SAINT JULIAN / MY NATION UNDERGROUND**

Stewart COPELAND (see under ⇒ POLICE)

Chick COREA

Born: ANTHONY ARMANDO COREA, 12 Jun'41, Chelsea, Massachusetts, USA. Cut jazz teeth with STAN GETZ, HERBIE MANN and MONGO SANTAMARIA. In 1967, he released his debut solo lp 'TONES FOR JOAN'S BONES' prior to joining MILES DAVIS on his jazz-rock spell lp's 'In A Silent Way', 'Bitches Brew' and 'Live At The Fillmore'. He then formed free-improvising group of musicians CIRCLE, before settling for tighter outfit RETURN TO FOREVER, which was the title of 1972 album. It featured STANLEY CLARKE on bass and also FLORA PLURIM. After their demise, many solo works followed and COREA moonlighted with HERBIE HANCOCK on many sessions. • Style: Jazz-rock pianist whose instrumental albums of the 70's (either solo or with his RETURN TO FOREVER), embraced romance with Latin-rock. • Songwriters: Composed himself.

Recommended: RETURN TO FOREVER (*8) / WHERE HAVE I KNOWN YOU BEFORE (*7) / NO MYSTERY (*6) / ROMANTIC WARRIOR (*6) / MUSICMAGIC (*6) / THE LEPRECHAUN (*7) / THE MAD HATTER (*6)

CHICK COREA – piano / **STEVE SWALLOW** – bass / **JOE CHAMBERS** – drums / **JOE FARRELL** – tenor sax, flute / **WOODY SHAW** – trumpet

not issued Vortex
1967. (lp) **TONES FOR JOAN'S BONES** -
– Litha / This is new / Tones for Joan's bones / Straight up and down. *(UK-iss.Mar77 on 'Atlantic')*

now with **MIROSLAV VITUOUS** – bass / **ROY HAYNES** – drums

not issued Solid State
1968. (lp) **NOW HE SINGS, NOW HE SOBS** -
– Steps – What was / Matrix / Now he sings – Now he sobs / Now he beats the drums – Now he stops / The law of falling and catching up. *(re-iss.1988 lp/cd on 'Blue Note') (US cd-iss.1989 on 'Blue Note')*

— with **WOODY SHAW** – trumpet / **DAVE HOLLAND** – bass / **HORACE ARNOLD + JACK DeJOHNETTE** – drums / **HUBERT LAWS** – flute

1969. <lp> **"IS"** -
– Is / Jamala / This / It.

— with **CIRCLE:- DAVE HOLLAND** – bass / **BARRY ALTSCHUL** – drums

Blue Note Blue Note
1971. (lp) **THE SONG OF SINGING**
– Toy room / Ballad 1 / Rhymes / Flesh / Ballad 3 / Nerfertitti. *(US re-iss.1978) (UK-iss.lp/cd Apr85)*

E.C.M. E.C.M.
Feb 71. (lp) **A.R.C.**
– Nerfetitti / Ballad for Tillie / A.R.C. / Vedana / Thanatos / Games. *(re-iss.Jul87) (cd-iss.Mar88)*
May 71. (lp) **PIANO IMPROVISATIONS**
– Noon song / Song for Sally / Ballad for Anna / Song of the wind / Sometime ago / Where are you now- A suite of eight pictures. *<US cd-iss.1988)*

— added **ANTHONY BRAXTON** – reeds, percussion

1972. (d-lp) **CIRCLE – PARIS CONCERT (live as "COREA & BRAXTON & HOLLAND")**
– Nerfertitti / Song for the newborn / Duet / Lookout farm / 73 Kalvin (variation 3) / Toy room- Q & A / No greater love.
1972. (lp) **PIANO IMPROVISATIONS VOL.2**
– Afternoon song / Song for Lee Lee / Song for Thad / Trinkle tinkle / Masquellero / Preparation 1 & 2 / Departure from Planet Earth / A new place / Arrival / Scenery / Imps walk / Rest. *(cd-iss.1988)*

— now w/ **STANLEY CLARKE** – bass / FLORA PURIM – vocals, percussion / JOE FARRELL – flute, soprano sax / **AIRTO MOREIRA** – drums, percussion

1972. (lp) **RETURN TO FOREVER**
– Return to forever / Crystal silence / What game shall we play today / Sometime ago – La fiesta. *(cd-iss.Mar88)*

RETURN TO FOREVER

CHICK COREA – keyboards / **FLORA PURIM** – vocals, percussion / **JOE FARRELL** – wind / **STANLEY CLARKE** – bass

Polydor Polydor
Oct 72. (lp) **LIGHT AS A FEATHER**
– You're everything / Light as a feather / Captain Marvel / 500 miles high / Children's song / Spain. *(re-iss.Jun81) (cd-iss.1988 on 'ECM')*
1972. (7") **CAPTAIN MARVEL. / SPAIN** -

— **CHICK COREA** – piano, organ, percussion / **STANLEY CLARKE** – bass (ex-MILES DAVIS) / **LENNY WHITE** – drums, percussions (ex-MILES DAVIS, ex-SANTANA) / **BILL CONNORS** – guitar

Feb 74. (lp) **HYMN OF THE SEVENTH GALAXY** Dec73
– Hymn of the seventh galaxy / After the cosmic rain / Captain Senor Mouse / Theme to the mothership / Space circus (parts I & II) / The game maker.

— **AL DiMEOLA** (b.22 Jul'54, Jersey City, New Jersey, USA) – guitar (ex-LENNY COYRELL) repl.BILL

Nov 74. (lp) **WHERE HAVE I KNOWN YOU BEFORE** 32 Sep74
– Beyond the seventh galaxy / Earth juice / The shadow of Lo / Song to the Pharoah kings / Vulcan worlds / Where have I dreamed with you before / Where have I known you before / Where have I loved you before. *(re-iss.Jun81) (cd-iss.Mar88)*
Jan 75. (7") **EARTH JUICE. / BEYOND THE SEVENTH GALAXY**
Mar 75. (lp) **NO MYSTERY** 39
– Dayride / Jungle waterfall / Flight of the newborn / Sofistifunk / Excerpt from the first movement of heavy metal / No mystery / Interplay / Celebration suite (part 1 & 2). *(cd-iss.Mar88; 827 149-2)*
Apr75. (7") **JUNGLE WATERFALL. / EXCERPT FROM THE FIRST MOVEMENT OF HEAVY METAL** -

C.B.S. Columbia
May 76. (lp) **ROMANTIC WARRIOR** 35 Mar76
– Medieval overture / Sorceress / Romantic warrior / Majestic dance / The magician / Duel of the jester and the tyrant (part I & II).

— **COREA + CLARKE** now with **GAYLE MORAN** – keyboards, synths / **JOE FARRELL** – saxes, flute / **GERRY BROWN** – drums / **JOHN THOMAS** – trumpet, flugelhorn / **JAMES TINSLEY** – trumpet / **JIM PUGH** – trombone / **HAROLD GARRETT** – trombone, horns

Apr 77. (lp) **MUSICMAGIC** 38 Mar77
– The musician / Hello again / Musicmagic / So long Mickey Mouse / Do you ever / The endless night.
Feb 79. (lp) **RETURN TO FOREVER LIVE (live)**
– So long Mickey Mouse / The musician / Chick's piano solo / Music magic / The Moorish warrior and Spanish princess / Come rain or come shine / The endless night (part 1 & 2).

CHICK COREA

with RETURN TO FOREVER; **STANLEY CLARKE, JOE FARRELL, ANTHONY BRAXTON, DAVE HOLLAND, AIRTO MOREIRA, BARRY ALTSCHUL**

not issued Oxford
1975. (lp) **LIVE IN NEW YORK (live)** -
– Some time ago / Nerfertitti.

— with **ROY HAYNES + MIROSLAV VITUOUS**

not issued Blue Note
1976. (d-lp) **CIRCLING IN** -
– Bossa / Gemini / My one and only love / Fragments / Windows / Samba Yanta / I don't know / Pannonica / Blues connotation / Duet for bass and piano / Starp / 73 degree – A Kelvin / Ballad / Danse for clarinet and piano.

— with **GAYLE MORAN** – vocals / **EDDIE GOMEZ + ANTHONY JACKSON** – bass / **JOHN GATCHELL + BOB MILIKAN + DANNY KAHN** – trumpet / **WAYNE ANDRE + BILL WATRONS** – trombone

Polydor Polydor
Apr 76. (lp) **THE LEPRECHAUN** 42 Feb76
– Imp's welcome / Lenore / Reverie / Looking at the world / Nite sprite / Soft and gentle / Pixieland rag / The leprechaun's dream.

— with **JEAN LUC PONTY** – violin / **NARADA MICHAEL WALDEN** – drums / **STANLEY CLARKE** – bass / **GAYLE** / **DON ALIAS** – percussion / **JOHN THOMAS – trumpet**

Feb 77. (d-lp) **MY SPANISH HEART** 55 Jan77
– Love castle / The gardens / Day danse / My Spanish heart / Night streets / The hilltop / The sky medley / Wind danse / Armando's rhumba / La Bozo (parts I-III) / Spanish fantasy (parts I-IV). *(cd-iss.Mar88)*

— **STEVE GADD** – drums + **EDDIE GOMEZ** – bass repl.WALDEN + CLARKE

Apr 78. (lp) **THE MAD HATTER** 61 Mar78
– The woods / Tweedle dee / The trial / Humpty Dumpty / Falling Alice / Tweedle dum / Dear Alice / The mad hatter / Rhapsody.
Aug 78. (lp) **FRIENDS** -
-
Jan 79. (lp) **SECRET AGENT**
– The golden dawn / Slinky / Mirage / Drifting / Glebe St. blues / Fickle funk / Bagatelle / Hot news blues / Central Park.
Jan 79. (7") **CENTRAL PARK. / BAGATELLE No.4** -

In Mar79, COREA was credited with HERBIE HANCOCK on live d-lp 'AN EVENING WITH HERBIE HANCOCK & CHICK COREA'; Columbia.

Aug 79. (lp) **DELPHI 1** -
– Delphi 1-8 / Children's song £20 / Stride time 1-7.
Nov 79. (d-lp) **AN EVENING WITH CHICK COREA & HERBIE HANCOCK (live with HERBIE HANCOCK)**
– Homecoming / Ostinato / The hook / Bouquet / Maiden voyage / La fiesta.

Warners Warners
Jun 80. (lp) **TAP STEP** May 80
– Samba L.A. / The embrace / Tap step / Magic carpet / The slide / Grandpa blues / Flamenco.

— with **MICHAEL BRECKER** – sax / **EDDIE GOMEZ** – bass / **STEVE GADD** – drums

Jul 81. (lp) **THE THREE QUARTETS**
– Quartet No.1-3; No.2 in 2 parts (dedicated to Duke Ellington) – (dedicated to John Coltrane).

— w/ **PACO DE LUCIA + AL DiMEOLA** – guitar / **CARLOS BENAVENT + STANLEY CLARKE** – bass / **DON ALIAS + ALEX ACUNA** – percussion / **LENNY WHITE** – drums / **GAYLE MORAN** – vocals

1982. (lp) **TOUCHSTONE** -
– Touchstone: a) Procession, b) Ceremony, c) Departure / The yellow nimbus / Duende / Compadres / Estancia / Dance of chance.

— with **GARY BURTON** – vibraphone

E.C.M. E.C.M.
Oct 81. (d-lp) **IN CONCERT, ZURICH OCT.28, 1980 (live)**
– Senor Mouse / Bud Powell / Crystal silence / Tweak / I'm your pal / Hullo Bolinas / Love castle / Falling Grace / Mirror mirror / Song to Gayle / Endless trouble, endless pleasure. *(cd-iss.1984)*

— with **MIROSLAV + ROY**

Oct 82. (d-lp) **TRIO MUSIC** (Thelonius Monk tribute)
– Trio improvisation 1-3 / Duet improvisation 1 & 2 / Trio improvisation 4 / Slippery when wet / Rhythm-a-ning / 'Round midnight / Eronel / Think of one / Little rootie tootie / Reflections / Hackenshack. *(d-cd iss.May87)*

IMS Polydor / not issued

Oct 82. (lp) **FIESTA** [-] [-] Germ'y
– Sea journey / Moments notice / Come rain or shine / Fiesta piano solo / I ain't mad at you.

— with **CARLOS + DON + TOM BRECHTLEIN** – drums / **STEVE KUJALA** – flute, saxes

Elektra / Elektra

Feb 83. (lp) **AGAIN AND AGAIN** (The Jo'Burg sessions)
– Quintet 3 / Waltze / Again and again / 1-2-1234 / Diddle diddle / Twang. *(cd-iss.Jun84)*

— with sextet; **GARY BURTON** – vibes / **FRED SHERRY** – cello / **KAREN DREYFUSS** – viola / **CAROL SHIVE + IKWHAN BAE** – violin

E.C.M. / E.C.M.

Oct 83. (lp) **LYRIC SUITE FOR SEXTET**
– Lyric suite for sextet: Overture – Waltz – Sketch – Rollercoaster – Brasilia – Dream – Finale.

Apr 84. (lp)(cd) **CHILDREN'S SONGS**
– Children's songs Nos.1-11 / Nos.12-20.

— with **STEVE KUJALA** – flute

Mar 85. (lp)(cd) **VOYAGE**
– Mallorca / Diversions / Star island / Free fall / Hong Kong.

Dec 85. (lp)(cd) **SEPTET**
– 1st- 2nd- 3rd- 4th- 5th movement / The temple of Ishafan.

— with **MIROSLAV VITUOUS** – bass / **ROY HAYNES** – drums

Dec 86. (lp)(cd) **TRIO MUSIC, LIVE IN EUROPE (live in '84)**
– The loop / I hear a rhapsody / Summer night / Night and day / Prelude No.2 / Mock up / Transformation / Hittin' it / Mirovisions.

The CHICK COREA ELEKTRIC BAND

w/ **JOHN PATITUCCI** – bass / **DAVE WECKL** – drums, percussion / **CARLOS RIOS** – guitar

G.R.P. / G.R.P.

Apr 86. (lp)(c) **THE CHICK COREA ELEKTRIC BAND**
– Rumble / Side walk / Cool weasel boogie / Got a match / Elektic city / No zone / King Cockroach / India song. *(cd-iss.Apr88)* (cd+=) – City gate / All love / Silver temple.

— **ERIC MARIENTHAL** – sax / **FRANK GAMBORE** – guitar repl.RIOS

May 87. (lp)(c)(cd) **LIGHT YEARS**
– Light years / Second sight / Flamingo / Prism / Time track / Starlight / Your eyes / The dragon / View from the outside / Smokescreen / Hymn of the heart / Kaleidoscope. *(dat-iss.Jul88; GRT 9546)*

Jul 88. (lp)(c)(cd) **EYE OF THE BEHOLDER**
– Home universe / Eternal child / Forgotten past / Passage / Beauty / Cascade (1 & 2) / Trance dance / Eye of the beholder / Ezinda / Amnesia.

Feb 89. (lp)(c)(lp) **THE AKOUSTIC BAND**
– Autumn leaves / So in love / Morning sprite / Circles / Spain.

Feb 90. (cd)(c)(lp) **INSIDE OUT**
– Inside out / Make a wish (part 1 & 2) / Stretch it (part 1 & 2) / Kicker / Child's play / Tale of daring (chapters 1, 2, 3 & 4).

Aug 91. (cd)(c)(lp) **BENEATH THE MASK**
– Beneath the mask / Little things that count / One of us is over 40 / A wave goodbye / Lifescape / Jammin' E. Cricket / Charged particles / Free step / 99 flavors / Illusions.

Stretch / Stretch

Aug 95. (cd) **TIME WARP**

compilations, others

with on below **DAVE HOLLAND** – bass / **JACK DeJOHNETTE + HORACE ARNOLD** – drums / **WOODY SHAW** – trumpet / **HUBERT LAWS** – flute

People / Groove Merchant

1974. (lp) **SUNDANCE**
– The brain / Song of wind / Converge / Sundance.

Sep 74. Atlantic; (lp) **INNER SPACE** (1966-68)

1974. Epic; (lp) **ROUND TRIP (w/ S.WATANABE)** [-]

1975. Verve; (lp) **CAPTAIN MARVEL (w/ STAN GETZ)** [-]

Jun 77. Muse; (lp) **WITH UNDERSTANDING** (w/ RON DAVIS) [-]

1977. CBS; (q-lp) **LIVE – THE COMPLETE CONCERT (live)** [-]

1978. Muse; (lp) **BLISS!**

Oct 79. ECM; (lp) **CRYSTAL SILENCE** [-]

May 81. MPS Jazz; (lp) **MIRROR MIRROR (w/ JOE HENDERSON)** [-]

Jan 82. Gateway; (lp)(c) **CHICK & LIONEL LIVE AT MIDEM, 1978** (with LIONEL HAMPTON) [-]
– Sea breeze / Moments notice / Come rain or shine / Fiesta piano solo / I ain't mad at you.

1984. Philips; (lp) **THE MEETING** (w/ FRIEDRICH GULDA)
– Someday my prince will come / Put your little foot out / Poem No.3 / Wiegenlied.

Nov 83. ECM; (c) **WORKS** (1971-1984)
(lp/cd-iss.Jun89)

Apr 89. Denon; (cd)(c) **EARLY DAYS**

Jun 86. Polydor; (c)(cd) **CHICK COREA** [-]

Hugh CORNWALL (see under ⇒ STRANGLERS)

Elvis COSTELLO

Born: DECLAN McMANUS, 25 Aug'55, Paddington, London, England. Grew up in Liverpool the son of bandleader ROSS McMANUS. He took his mother's maiden name and in the 70's played live as D.P. McMANUS. In Dec'76, he signed to Jake Riviera's new indie label 'Stiff', recording debut album under the wing of stablemate producer NICK LOWE. His success from then on was similar to DYLAN, in the way he had mostly UK-Top 10 albums, and at times sporadic UK-Top30 45's. By the late 70's, RIVIERA had taken him to new labels 'Radar' then 'F-Beat'. He continued to impress the buying public during the 80's and early 90's. • **Style:** On the crest of the "new-wave", but branched out into country-rock, melodic pop and even melancholy soul. His musical directions have held no limitations or barriers to most styles of rock music. • **Songwriters:** All penned by COSTELLO, bar NEAT NEAT NEAT (Damned) / I CAN'T STAND UP FOR FALLING DOWN (Sam & Dave) / SWEET DREAMS (Patsy Cline) / A GOOD YEAR FOR THE ROSES (Jerry Chestnut) / DON'T LET ME BE MISUNDERSTOOD (Nina Simone) / I WANNA BE LOVED (Farnell Jenkins) / THE UGLY THINGS (Nick Lowe) / YOU'RE NO GOOD (Swinging Blue Jeans) / FULL FORCE GALE (Van Morrison) / YOU'VE GOT TO HIDE YOUR LOVE AWAY (Beatles) / STEP INSIDE LOVE (Cilla Black) / STICKS & STONES (Ray Charles) / FROM HEAD TO TOE (Smokey Robinson) / CONGRATULATIONS (Paul Simon) / STRANGE (Screaming Jay Hawkins) / HIDDEN CHARMS (Willie Dixon) / REMOVE THIS DOUBT (Supremes) / I THREW IT ALL AWAY (Bob Dylan) / LEAVE MY KITTEN ALONE (Little Willie John) / EVERY-BODY'S CRYIN' MERCY (Mose Allison) / I'VE BEEN WRONG BEFORE (Randy Newman) / BAMA LAMA BAMA LOO (Little Richard) / MUST YOU THROW DIRT IN MY FACE (Louvin Bros.) / POURING WATER ON A DROWNING MAN (James Carr) / THE VERY THOUGHT OF YOU (Ray Noble) / PAYDAY (Jesse Winchester) / PLEASE STAY (Bacharach-David) / RUNNING OUT OF FOOLS (Jerry Ragavoy) / DAYS (Kinks) / etc. • **Trivia:** He has also produced The SPECIALS (1979) / SQUEEZE (1981) / POGUES (1985) retaining a latter acquaintance in CAIT O'RIORDON, whom he married on 16 May'86. He acted (played bit-parts) in most of playwright / friend Alan Bleasdale's work including SCULLY (1985 TV series), NO SUR-RENDER (1988 film). He provided score for the film 'The Courier' in 1987 alongside HOTHOUSE FLOWERS. Around the same time he collaborated with PAUL McCARTNEY writing BACK ON MY FEET for McCartney, and VERONICA for himself in 1989. Costello was produced by T-BONE BURNETT on his 'KING OF AMERICA' + 'SPIKE' albums.

Recommended: THE BEST OF ELVIS COSTELLO THE MAN (*8) / THIS YEAR'S MODEL (*9) / MY AIM IS TRUE (*8) / ARMED FORCES (*7) / GOT HAPPY! (*6) / TRUST (*6) / ALMOST BLUE (*5) / IMPERIAL BEDROOM (*6) / PUNCH THE CLOCK (*8) / GOODBYE CRUEL WORLD (*6) / KING OF AMERICA (*7) / SPIKE (*6) / BLOOD AND CHOCOLATE (*7) / MIGHTY LIKE A ROSE (*5).

"ELVIS COSTELLO" (solo) – vocals, guitar with backing band The **SHAMROCKS,** (alias CLOVER) / **JOHN McFEE** – guitar / **ALEX CALL** – guitar, vocals / **SEAN HOPPER** – keyboards / **JOHN CIAMBOTTI** – bass / **MICHAEL SHINE** – drums

Stiff / Columbia

Mar 77. (7") **LESS THAN ZERO. / RADIO SWEETHEART** [-]

May 77. (7") **ALISON. / WELCOME TO THE WORKING WEEK**
(US 'B'side of above= **MIRACLE MAN**)

Jul 77. (7") **(THE ANGELS WANNA WEAR MY) RED SHOES. / MYSTERY DANCE** [-]

Jul 77. (lp)(c) **MY AIM IS TRUE** [14] [32] Nov 77
– Welcome to the working week / Miracle man / No dancing / Blame it on Cain / Alison / Sneaky feelings / (The angels wanna wear my) Red shoes / Less than zero / Mystery dance / Pay it back / I'm not angry / Waiting for the end of the world. (US version included **Watching the detectives.**) *(UK re-iss.+cd.Jul86 on 'Demon') (re-iss.cd Mar93 w/extra tracks)*

ELVIS COSTELLO & THE ATTRACTIONS

STEVE NIEVE (b.NASON)– keys repl. HOPPER to HUEY LEWIS & THE NEWS
BRUCE THOMAS – bass, vocals (ex-QUIVER)repl. CIAMBOTTI, CALL and McFEE
PETE THOMAS (b.9 Aug'54, Sheffield, England)– drums (ex-CILLI WILLI, ex-WILKO JOHNSON)repl. SHINE

Oct 77. (7"m) **WATCHING THE DETECTIVES. / BLAME IT ON CAIN (live) / MYSTERY DANCE (live)** [15]

Radar / Columbia

Mar 78. (7") **(I DON'T WANT TO GO TO) CHELSEA. / YOU BELONG TO ME** [16]

Mar 78. (lp)(c) **THIS YEAR'S MODEL** [4] [30]
– No action / This year's girl / The beat / Pump it up / Little Triggers / You belong to me / Hand in hand / (I don't want to go to) Chelsea / Lip service / Living in Paradise / Lipstick vogue / Night rally. *(re-iss.1984/ cd-iss.1986/ Mar93/ Feb95 on 'Demon' w/extra tracks)* (free-7"w/above) **STRANGER IN THE HOUSE. / NEAT NEAT NEAT**

May 78. (7") **PUMP IT UP. / BIG TEARS** [24]

Oct 78. (7") **RADIO RADIO. / TINY STEPS** [29]

Jan 79. (lp)(c) **ARMED FORCES** [2] [10]
– Senior service / Oliver's army / Big boys / Green shirt / Party girl / Goon squad / Busy bodies / Sunday's best / Moods for moderns / Chemistry class / Two little Hitlers / Accidents will happen. (free 7"w/ above) WATCHING THE DE-TECTIVES. / ALISON / ACCIDENTS WILL HAPPEN *(re-iss.1984/ cd-iss.Jan86/ Mar93/ Feb95 on 'Demon' w/extra tracks)*

Feb 79. (7") **OLIVER'S ARMY. / MY FUNNY VALENTINE** [2]

May 79. (7"m) **ACCIDENTS WILL HAPPEN. / TALKING IN THE DARK / WEDNESDAY WEEK** [28]

ELVIS COSTELLO

solo, but still used ATTRACTIONS

F-Beat / Columbia

Feb 80. (7") **I CAN'T STAND UP FOR FALLING DOWN. / GIRLS TALK** [4]

Feb 80. (lp)(c) **GET HAPPY!** [2] [11]
– Love for tender / Opportunity / The imposter / Secondary modern / King Horse / Possession / Man called Uncle / Clowntime is over / New Amsterdam / High fidelity / I can't stand up for falling down / Black and white world / Five years in reverse / B

movie / Motel matches / Human touch / Beaten to the punch / Temptation / I stand accused / Riot act. *(re-iss.1984,cd-iss.Jan86, re-iss.cd Mar93 on 'Demon') (re-iss.cd May94 on 'Demon' w/extra tracks)*

Apr 80. (7") **HIGH FIDELITY. / GETTING MIGHTY CROWDED** 30 –
(12"+=) – Clowntime is over.

Jun 80. (7")(7"pic-d) **NEW AMSTERDAM. / DR.LUTHER'S ASSISTANT** 36 –
(7"pic-d-ep+=) – Ghost train / Just a memory.

ELVIS COSTELLO & THE ATTRACTIONS

(same line-up)

Dec 80. (7"m) **CLUBLAND. / CLEAN MONEY / HOOVER FACTORY** 60 –

Jan 81. (lp)(c) **TRUST** 9 28
– Clubland / Lovers walk / You'll never be a man / Pretty words / Strict time / Luxembourg / Watch your step / New lace sleeves / From a whisper to a scream / Different finger / White knuckles / Shot with his own gun / Fish'n'chip paper / Big sister's clothes. *(re-iss.1984,cd-iss.Jan86,re-iss.cd Mar93 on 'Demon') (re-iss.cd May94 on 'Demon' w/extra tracks)*

Feb 81. (7") **FROM A WHISPER TO A SCREAM. / LUXEMBOURG** – –

Sep 81. (7") **GOOD YEAR FOR THE ROSES. / YOUR ANGEL STEPS OUT OF HEAVEN** 6 –

Oct 81. (lp)(c) **ALMOST BLUE** 7 50
– Why don't you love me (like you used to do) / Sweet dreams / Success / I'm your toy / Tonight the bottle let me down / Brown to blue / Good year for the roses / Sittin' and thinkin' / Colour of the blues / Too far gone / Honey hush / How much I lied. *(re-iss.1984, cd-iss.Jan86, re-iss.cd Mar93 on 'Demon' w/extra tracks)*

Dec 81. (7") **SWEET DREAMS. / PSYCHO** 42 –

Apr 82. (7"m) **I'M YOUR TOY (live). / CRY CRY CRY / WONDERING** 51 –
(12") – ('A'side) / My shoes keep walkin' back to you / Blues keep calling / Honky tonk girl. (with The ROYAL PHILHARMONIC ORCHESTRA)

Jun 82. (7"m) **YOU LITTLE FOOL. / BIG SISTER / THE STAMPING GROUND** (3rd track credited to **The EMOTIONAL TOOTHPASTE**) 52 –

Jul 82. (lp)(c) **IMPERIAL BEDROOM** 6 30
– Beyond belief / Tears before bedtime / Shabby doll / The long honeymoon / Man out of time / Almost blue / . . . And in every home / The loved ones / Human hands / Kid about it / Little savage / Boy with a problem / Pidgin English / You little fool / Town cryer. *(re-iss.1984, cd-iss.Jan86, re-iss.cd Mar93 on 'Demon' w/extra tracks)*

Jul 82. (7") **MAN OUT OF TIME. / TOWN CRYER** 58 –
(12"+=) – Imperial bedroom.

Sep 82. (7") **FROM HEAD TO TOE. / THE WORLD OF BROKEN HEARTS** 43 –

—— (below from the film 'Party Party')

A & M / A & M

Nov 82. (7") **PARTY PARTY. / IMPERIAL BEDROOM** 48 –

Imp-Demon / Columbia

May 83. (7") **PILLS AND SOAP.(as "The IMPOSTER") / ('A'extended version)** 16 –

F-Beat / Columbia

Jul 83. (7") **EVERYDAY I WRITE THE BOOK. / HEATHEN TOWN** 28 36
(12"+=) – Night time.

Jul 83. (lp)(c) **PUNCH THE CLOCK** 3 24
– Let them all talk / Everyday I write the book / The greatest thing / The element within her / Love went mad / Shipbuilding / T.K.O. (boxing day) / Charm school / The invisible man / Mouth almighty / King of thieves / Pills and soap / The world and his wife. *(re-iss.+cd.Sep84/ Jan88 on 'Demon') (cd-iss. Mar93/ Feb95 on 'Demon' w/extra tracks)*

Sep 83. (7")(12") **LET THEM ALL TALK. / KEEP IT CONFIDENTIAL** 59 –

Apr 84. (7") **PEACE IN OUR TIME.(as "The IMPOSTER") / WITHERED AND DEAD** 48 –

Jun 84. (7") **I WANNA BE LOVED. / TURNING THE TOWN RED** 25 –
(12"+=) – ('A'extended).

Jun 84. (lp)(c) **GOODBYE CRUEL WORLD** 10 35
– The only flame in town / Room with no number / Inch by inch / Worthless thing / Love field / I wanna be loved / The comedians / Joe Porterhouse / Sour milk cow blues / The great unknown / The deportees club / Peace in our time. *(re-iss.Jan87,cd-iss.Mar86 + Oct87, re-iss.cd Mar93 & Mar95 on 'Demon' w/extra tracks)*

Aug 84. (7") **THE ONLY FLAME IN TOWN. / THE COMEDIANS** 71 56 Jul 84
(12"+=) – Pump it up (dance mix).

Imp-Demon / Columbia

Jul 85. (7") **THE PEOPLE'S LIMOUSINE.(as "The COWARD BROTHERS" feat. T-BONE BURNETT) / THEY'LL NEVER TAKE THEIR LOVE FROM ME** – –

The COSTELLO SHOW

featuring The ATTRACTIONS and The CONFEDERATES
added **JAMES BURTON** – guitar / **MITCHELL FROOM** – keyboards / **JERRY SCHEFF** – bass / **JIM KELTNER** – drums / **RON TUTT** – drums (i.e.The CONFEDERATES)

F-Beat / Columbia

Jan 86. (7") **DON'T LET ME BE MISUNDERSTOOD. / BABY'S GOT A BRAND NEW HAIRDO** 33 –
(12"+=) – Get yourself another girl.

Demon-Imp / Columbia

Feb 86. (lp)(c)(cd) **KING OF AMERICA** 11 39
– Brilliant mistake / Loveable / Our little angel / Don't let me be misunderstood / Glitter gulch / Indoor fireworks / Little palaces / I'll wear it proudly / American without tears / Eisenhower blues / Poisoned rose / The big light / Jack of all parades / Suit of lights / Sleep of the just. *(re-iss.Jan87) (cd-iss.Mar93/ Feb95 w/extra tracks)*

ELVIS COSTELLO & THE ATTRACTIONS

(ELVIS, BRUCE, STEVE & PETE) plus guest **NICK LOWE** – guitar

Imp Demon / Columbia

Aug 86. (7") **TOKYO STORM WARNING. / (part 2)** 73 –
(12"+=) – Black sails in the sunset.

Sep 86. (lp)(c)(cd) **BLOOD AND CHOCOLATE** 16 84
– Uncomplicated / I hope you're happy now / Tokyo storm warning / Home is anywhere you hang your head / I want you / Honey are you straight or are you blind? / Blue chair / Battered old bird / Crimes of Paris / Poor Napoleon / Next time around. *(re-iss.cd Mar93/ Feb95 w/extra tracks)*

Nov 86. (7") **I WANT YOU. / I HOPE YOU'RE HAPPY NOW (acoustic)** – –
(12"+=) – I want you (part 2).

Jan 87. (7") **BLUE CHAIR. / AMERICA WITHOUT TEARS No.2** – –
(10"+=) – I want you.
(12"+=) – Shoes without heels.

May 87. (7")(12") **A TOWN CALLED BIG NOTHING.(as "McMANUS GANG" featuring SY RICHARDSON) / RETURN TO BIG NOTHING** – –

ELVIS COSTELLO

solo, with mostly **FROOM, KELTNER, PETE THOMAS** (2), **MICHAEL BLAIR** – percussion / **MARC RIBOT** – guitar / **JERRY MAROTTA** – drums / **PAUL McCARTNEY, ROGER McGUINN, CAIT O'RIORDAN, T-BONE BURNETT, CHRISSIE HYNDE** on 1 or 2, plus **The**

DIRTY DOZEN BRASS BAND (GREGORY DAVIS, EFREM TOWNS, ROGER LEWIS, KEVIN HARRIS, KIRK JOSEPH, C.JOSEPH plus loads more).

Warners Warners

Feb 89. (lp)(c)(cd) **SPIKE** 5 32
– . . . This town . . . / Let him dangle / Deep dark truthful mirror / Veronica / God's comic / Chewing gum / Tramp the dirt town / Stalin Malone / Satellite / Pads, paws and claws / Baby plays around / Miss Macbeth / Any king's shilling / Coal train robbers * / Last boat leaving. *(cd.+= *) (re-iss.cd Nov93 w/extra tracks)*
Feb 89. (7") **VERONICA. / YOU'RE NO GOOD** 31 19
(12"+=)(cd-s+=) – The room nobody lives in / Coal train robbers.
May 89. (7")(c-s) **BABY PLAYS AROUND. / POISONED ROSE** 65
(7"ep+=)(10"+=)(cd-s+=) – Almost blue / My funny valentine.
(12")(cd-s) – ('A'side) / (++=) – Point of no return.
Apr 91. (7")(c-s) **THE OTHER SIDE OF SUMMER. / COULDN'T CALL IT UNEXPECTED No.4** 43
(12"+=)(cd-s+=) – The ugly things.
May 91. (cd)(c)(lp) **MIGHTY LIKE A ROSE** 5 55
– The other side of summer / How to be dumb / All grown up / Invasion hit parade / Harpers bizarre / Hurry down doomsday (the bugs are taking over) / After the fall / Georgie and her rival / So like Candy / Interlude: couldn't call it unexpected No.2 / Playboy to a man / Sweet pear / Broken / Couldn't call it unexpected No.4. *(re-iss.cd Feb95)*
Oct 91. (7")(c-s) **SO LIKE CANDY. / VERONICA (demo)**
(12"+=)(cd-s+=) – Couldn't call it unexpected (live) / Hurry down doomsday (the blues are taking over).
In 1992, he wrote material for WENDY JAMES (Transvision Vamp)

ELVIS COSTELLO / THE BRODSKY QUARTET

with **MICHAEL THOMAS + IAN BELTON** – violins / **PAUL CASSIDY** – viola / **JACQUELINE THOMAS** – violincello (all co-wrote music with him)
Jan 93. (cd)(c) **THE JULIET LETTERS** 18
– Deliver us / For other eyes / Swine / Expert rites / Dead letter / I almost had a weakness / Why? / Who do you think you are? / Taking my life in your hands / This offer is unrepeatable / Dear sweet filthy world / The letter home / Jacksons, Monk and Rowe / This sad burlesque / Romeo's seance / I thought I'd write to Juliet / Last post / The first to leave / Damnation's cellar / The birds will still be singing.
Feb 93. (c-ep)(cd-ep) **JACKSON MONK AND ROE / THIS SAD BURLESQUE / (interview excerpts)**

Elvis COSTELLO

Mar 94. (7")(c-s) **SULKY GIRL. / A DRUNKEN MAN'S PRAISE OF SOBRIETY** 22
(cd-s+=) – Idiophone (with the ATTRACTIONS).
Mar 94. (cd)(c) **BRUTAL YOUTH** 2 34
– Pony St. / Kinder murder / 13 steps lead down / This is Hell / Clown strike / You tripped at every step / Still too soon to know / 20% amnesia / Sulky girl / London's brilliant parade / My science fiction twin / Rocking horse road / Just about glad / All the rage / Favourite hour.
Apr 94. (7")(c-s) **13 STEPS LEAD DOWN. / DO YOU KNOW WHAT I'M SAYING?** 59
(cd-s) – ('A'side) / Puppet girl / Basement kiss / We despise you.
Jul 94. (7")(c-s) **YOU TRIPPED AT EVERY STEP. / YOU'VE GOT TO HIDE YOUR LOVE AWAY**
(cd-s+=) – Step inside love / Sticks & stones.
Nov 94. (c-s) **LONDON'S BRILLIANT PARADE. / NEW AMSTERDAM** 48
(cd-ep+=) – Beyond belief / Shipbuilding.
(cd-ep+=) – From head to toe / The loved ones.
(12") – ('A'side) / My resistance is low / Congratulations.
May 95. (cd)(c) **KOJAK VARIETY** 21
– Strange / Hidden charms / Remove this doubt / I threw it all way / Leave my kitten alone / Everybody's cryin' mercy / I've been wrong before / Bama lama bama loo / Must you throw dirt in my face / Pouring water on a drowning man / The very thought of you / Payday / Please stay / Running out of fools / Days.

– compilations, others, etc. –

Mar 82. Old Gold; (7") **OLIVER'S ARMY. / GOOD YEAR FOR THE ROSES** -
Apr 85. Telstar; (lp)(c)(cd) **THE BEST OF ELVIS COSTELLO – THE MAN** 8 -
– Watching the detectives / Oliver's army / Alison / Accidents will happen / Pump it up / High fidelity / Pills and soap (THE IMPOSTER) / (I don't want to go to) Chelsea / New lace sleeves / A good year for the roses / I can't stand up for falling down / Clubland / Beyond belief / New Amsterdam / Green shirt / Everyday I write the book / I wanna be loved / Shipbuilding (THE IMPOSTER). *(re-iss.Jan87, re-iss.cd Mar93 on 'Demon')*
Nov 80. Columbia; (lp)(c) **TAKING LIBERTIES** - 28
Apr 85. F-Beat; (7")(7"green) **GREEN SHIRT. / BEYOND BELIEF** 68 -
(12"+=)(12"green+=) – ('A'extended).
Nov 85. Stiff; (12"ep) **WATCHING THE DETECTIVES / RADIO SWEETHEART. / LESS THAN ZERO / ALISON** -
Mar 80. Imp-Demon; (lp)(c) **TEN BLOODY MARY'S & TEN HOW'S YOUR FATHERS** -
(re-iss.1984, cd-iss.1986) (re-iss.cd Mar93)
Oct 87. Imp-Demon; (lp)(c) **OUT OF OUR IDIOT**
— (above credited to "VARIOUS ARTISTS" but all by his pseudonyms) *(re-iss.cd Mar93)*
Oct 89. Imp-Demon; (lp)(c)(cd)(dat) **GIRLS GIRLS GIRLS** 67 -
Jul 91. Imp-Demon; (cd)(c)(lp) **GBH SOUNDTRACK** -
— (above was credited to "ELVIS COSTELLO & RICHARD HARVEY")
Nov 94. Imp-Demon; (cd)(c) **THE VERY BEST OF ELVIS COSTELLO** 57 -
Nov 95. Demon; (4xcd-box) **2 1/2 YEARS**
The first 4 singles were also re-issued together around 1980 and could be found on 'Stiff' 10-pack Nos.11-20).

The ATTRACTIONS released two singles and an album (Aug80) **MAD ABOUT THE WRONG BOY** on 'F-Beat'.

ELVIS COSTELLO & BILL FRISELL

Nonesuch Nonesuch

Aug 95. (cd) **DEEP DEAD BLUE**
– Weird nightmare / Love field / Shamed into love / Gigi / Poor Napoleon / Baby plays around / Deep dead blue.

John COUGAR

(see under ⇒ MELLENCAMP, John Cougar)

COUNT FIVE

Formed: San Jose, California, USA . . .1965 by (see below). Signed to L.A. label 'Double Shot' and released their debut single 'PSYCHOTIC REACTION', which soon hit US Top 5 late 1966. Were reputed to have given up $1,000,000 worth of bookings, so that they could return to school!. In 1967, after their same titled album failed to hit Top 100, they remained as one hit wonders. • **Style:** YARDBIRDS inspired and psychedelic/garage outfit, who initially attired themselves in Dracula capes. • **Songwriters:** Group. • **Trivia:** In the early 80's, The CRAMPS revived 'PSYCHOTIC REACTION'.

Recommended: PSYCHOTIC REACTION (*7)

KEN ELLNER (b.1948, Brooklyn, New York, USA) – vocals, harmonica / **SEAN BYRNE** (b.1947, Dublin, Ireland) – guitar, vocals / **JOHN MICHALSKI** (b.1949, Cleveland, Ohio, USA) – lead guitar / **ROY CHANEY** (b.1948, Indianapolis, USA) – bass / **CRAIG ATKINSON** (b.1947, Springfield, Missouri, USA) – drums

Pye Inter. Double Shot

Oct 66. (7") **PSYCHOTIC REACTION. / THEY'RE GONNA GET YOU** 5 Sep66
Nov 66. (lp) **PSYCHOTIC REACTION** -
– Double-decker bus / Pretty big mouth / The world / My generation / She's fine / Psychotic reaction / Peace of mind / They're gonna get you / The morning after / Can't get your lovin' / Out in the street.
Jan 67. (7") **PEACE OF MIND. / THE MORNING AFTER** -
1967. (7") **YOU MUST BELIEVE ME. / TEENY BOPPER, TEENY BOPPER** -
1967. (7") **MERRY-GO-ROUND. / CONTRAST** -
1968. (7") **DECLARATION OF INDEPENDENCE. / RELELATION IN SLOW MOTION** -
1968. (7") **MAILMAN. / PRETTY BIG MOUTH** -
— Disbanded in 1968. BYRNE returned to Ireland and joined PUBLIC FOOT THE ROMAN for one album in 1973. Five years later his group LEGOVER issued album 'WAIT TILL NIGHTIME'.

compilations, others

Oct 87. dsel (lp) **PSYCHOTIC REACTION** -
– PSYCHOTIC REACTION lp tracks + / You must believe me / Teeny bopper, teeny bopper / Merry-go-round / Contrast / Revelation in slow motion / Declaration of independence. *(cd-iss.Mar91) (re-iss.cd May92 on 'Repertoire')*

COUNTING CROWS

Formed: Bay Area, San Francisco, USA . . . 1992 out of early 90's outfit SORDID HUMOR. This band cut an album 'LIGHT MUSIC FOR DYING PEOPLE' for 'Capricorn', which remained unreleased until after COUNTING CROWS became massive in 1994. A year earlier the much-lauded album 'AUGUST AND EVERYTHING AFTER' had breeched the US charts. • **Style:** Melodic rock similar to JAYHAWKS. • **Songwriters:** DURITZ; some w /BRYSON, except THE GHOST IN YOU (Psychedelic Furs). • **Trivia:** Debut was produced by T-BONE BURNETT, and featured MARIA McKEE on backing vocals.

Recommended: AUGUST AND EVERYTHING AFTER (*8)

ADAM DURITZ – vocals, piano, harmonica (ex-SORDID HUMOR) / **DAVID BRYSON** – guitar, vocals (ex-SORDID HUMOR) / **MATT MALLEY** – bass, guitar, vocals / **CHARLIE GILLINGHAM** – piano, organ, accordion, chamberlain, vocals / **STEVE BOWMAN** – drums, vocals

Geffen Geffen

Oct 93. (cd)(c)(lp) **AUGUST AND EVERYTHING AFTER** 16 4
– Round here / Omaha / Mr.Jones / Perfect blue buildings / Anna begins / Time and time again / Rain king / Sullivan Street / Ghost train / Raining in Baltimore / A murder of one.
— added **DAN VICKREY** – guitar
Apr 94. (7")(c-s) **MR.JONES. / RAINING IN BALTIMORE** 28
(cd-s+=) – Rain king / ('A'acoustic).
Jun 94. (7")(c-s) **ROUND HERE. / GHOST TRAIN** 70
(cd-s+=) – The ghost in you (live).
Oct 94. (c-s) **RAIN KING. / ?** 49
(cd-s+=) –

COUNTRY JOE AND THE FISH

(see under ⇒ McDONALD, Country Joe)

Dave COUSINS (see under ⇒ STRAWBS)

COVERDALE PAGE (see under ⇒ WHITESNAKE)

COWBOY JUNKIES

Formed: Toronto, Canada . . . 1985 by MICHAEL TIMMINS, with young brother PETER and sister MARGO. In the late 70's and early 80's, MICHAEL had been in groups HUNGER PROJECT and GERMINAL, before moving to New York and London in the process. In the mid 80's, The COWBOY JUNKIES recorded debut lp WHITES OFF EARTH NOW! in garage releasing it on their own Canadian indie label 'Latent'. By 1988 they were on the roster of 'R.C.A.', with 'Cooking V.' licensing them in UK. In 1990, they achieved major international success with album 'THE CAUTION HORSES'. • **Style:** Minimalist country/blues rock, influenced by SPRINGSTEEN, described as EMMYLOU HARRIS meeting The VELVET UNDERGROUND. • **Songwriters:** MICHAEL wrote & produced songs, except SHINING MOON (Lightning Hopkins) / STATE TROOPER (Bruce Springsteen) / ME AND THE DEVIL + CROSSROADS (Robert Johnson) / DECORATION DAY + I'LL NEVER GET OUT OF THESE BLUES ALIVE + FORGIVE ME (John Lee Hooker) / BABY PLEASE DON'T GO (Bukka White) / POWDERFINGER (Neil Young) / SWEET JANE (Velvet Underground) / COWBOY JUNKIES LAMENT + TO LIVE IS TO FLY (Townes Van Zandt) / IF YOU'VE GOTTA GO, GO NOW (Bob Dylan) / LOST MY DRIVING WHEEL (Wiffen). • **Trivia:** Their second lp 'THE TRINITY SESSION' was recorded one day in a church, and eventually sold over a million worldwide. They used many session people for the 90's albums.

Recommended: THE TRINITY SESSION (*6)

MICHAEL TIMMINS (b.21 Apr'59, Montreal, Canada) – guitar / **MARGO TIMMINS** (b.27 Jun'61, Montreal) – vocals / **PETER TIMMINS** (b.29 Oct'65, Montreal) – drums / **ALAN ANTON** (b.ALAN ALIZOJVODIC, 22 Jun'59, Montreal) – bass

not issued / Latent

1986. (lp) **WHITES OFF EARTH NOW!** [-] [ ] CAN
– Shining Moon / State trooper / Me and the Devil / Decoration day / Baby please don't go / I'll never get out of these blues alive / Take me / Forgive me / Crossroads. *(UK-iss.cd,c,lp.Feb91 on 'RCA')*

Jan 88. (lp) **THE TRINITY SESSIONS** [-] [ ]
– Mining for gold / Misguided angel / Blue moon revisited (song for Elvis) * / I don't get in / I'm so lonesome I could cry / To love is to bury / 200 more miles / Dreaming my dreams with you / Working on a building * / Sweet Jane / Postcard blues / Walking after midnight. *(UK-iss.lp/c/cd.Mar89 on 'Cooking Vinyl') (re-iss.cd Feb94) (US iss. Jan89 on 'RCA', hit No.26)*

Cooking V. / R.C.A.

Mar 89. (7") **SWEET JANE. / 200 MORE MILES** [ ] [ ] Nov 88
(12"+=) – Postcard blues.

May 89. (7") **MISGUIDED ANGEL. / POSTCARD BLUES** [-] [ ]

Jul 89. (7") **BLUE MOON REVISITED (SONG FOR ELVIS). / TO LOVE IS TO BURY** [ ] [ ]
(12"+=)(cd-s+=) – ('A'live version).
(10"+=) – You won't be loved again / Shining moon / Waking after midnight.

R.C.A. / R.C.A.

Feb 90. (7") **SUN COMES UP, IT'S TUESDAY MORNING. / WITCHES** [ ] [ ]
(12"+=) – Powderfinger.
(c-s+=) – Dead ponies.
(cd-s+=) – Misguided angel.

Mar 90. (cd)(c)(lp) **THE CAUTION HORSES** [33] [47]
– Sun comes up, it's Tuesday morning / 'Cause cheap is how I feel / Thirty summers / Mariner's song / Powderfinger / Where are you tonight / Witches / Rock and bird / Escape is so easy / You will be loved again. *(re-iss.cd Feb94)*

Jun 90. (7") **'CAUSE CHEAP IS HOW I FEEL. / THIRTY SUMMERS** [ ] [ ]
(12"+=)(cd-s+=) – Declaration day / State trooper / Take me.

Sep 90. (c-s) **ROCK AND BIRD. / ?** [-] [ ]

Jan 92. (cd-ep) **SOUTHERN RAIN / MURDER, TONIGHT, IN THE TRAILER PARK / LOST MY DRIVING WHEEL / IF YOU'VE GOTTA GO, GO NOW** [ ] [ ]

Feb 92. (cd)(c)(lp) **BLACK EYED MAN** [21] [76]
– Southern rain / Oregon hill / This street, that man, this life / A horse in the country / If you were the woman and I was the man / Murder, tonight, in the trailer park / Black eyed man / Winter's song / The last spike / Cowboy Junkies lament / Townes' blues / To live is to fly. (w/ free cd-cp) DEAD FLOWERS / CAPTAIN KIDD / TAKE ME / 'CAUSE CHEAP IS HOW I FEEL.

Mar 92. (7") **A HORSE IN THE COUNTRY. / OREGON HILL** [ ] [ ]
(cd-s+=) – Five room love story.

Nov 93. (cd)(c) **PALE SUN, CRESCENT MOON** [ ] [ ]
– Crescent Moon / First recollection / Ring of the sill / Anniversary song / White sail / Seven years / Pale Sun / The past / Cold tea blues / Hard to explain / Hunted / Floorboard blues.

Kevin COYNE

Born: 27 Jan'44, Derby, England. At 19, he went to work at a mental hospital in Preston and in 1969, he moved to London and joined SIREN. They gained contract on 'Dandelion' label owned by DJ John Peel. In 1972 COYNE left said band, and his job as a Camden social worker to go solo full-time. In 1973 he shifted to Richard Branson's new 'Virgin' label, where he released several fine albums. • **Style:** Mannered throaty vocals in the mould of ROGER CHAPMAN (Family) or JOE COCKER, with approach very anti-commercial. • **Songwriters:** COYNE wrote all, except some with CLAGUE. In 1980 he wrote with WICKENS. Covered KNOCKIN' ON HEAVEN'S DOOR (Bob Dylan) / OL' MAN RIVER (Paul Robeson) / ONE FINE DAY (Chiffons). • **Trivia:** He married in 1965, and has 2 now grown-up children.

Recommended: THE DANDELION YEARS (*8) / SIGN OF THE TIMES (*7).

COYNE-CLAGUE

Dandelion / not issued

1970. (7") **BOTTLE UP AND GO. / MANDY LEE** [ ] [-]

1970. (7") **THE STRIDE. / I WONDER WHERE** [ ] [-]

SIREN

KEVIN COYNE – vocals, guitar / **DAVID CLAGUE** – bass, guitar, producer / **NICK CUDWORTH** – guitar, piano / **JOHN CHICHESTER** – lead guitar / **TAT MEAGER** – drums / with guests **COLIN WOOD** – keyboards, flute / **DAVID GIBBONS / ALISTAIR CAMPBELL**

Dandelion / Elektra

1970. (7") **ZE-ZE-ZE-ZE. / AND I WONDER** [-] [ ]

1970. (lp) **SIREN** [ ] [ ]
– Ze-ze-ze-ze / Get right church / Rock me baby / Wake up my children / Wasting my time / Sixteen women / First time I saw your face / Gardener man / And I wonder / The war is over / Asylum / Bertha Lee / I wonder where.

— **MICK GRATTON** – guitar, repl. CHICHESTER.

1971. (lp) **STRANGE LOCOMOTION** [ ] [ ]
– Relaxing with Bonnie Lou / Some dark day / Hot potato / Soon / Gigolo / I'm all aching / Strange locomotion / Shake my hand / Lonesome ride / Fetch me my woman / Fat moaning Minnie / Squeeze me.

1971. (7") **STRANGE LOCOMOTION. / I'M ALL ACHING** [ ] [-]

KEVIN COYNE

went solo, retaining **CLAGUE**, with session people

1972. (lp) **CASE HISTORY** [ ] [-]
– God bless the bride / White horse / Uggy's song / Need somebody / Evil Island home / Araby / Mad boy / My message to the people / Sand all yellow. *(cd-iss.Sep94 as ' . . .PLUS' on 'See For Miles')*

Polydor / not issued

1972. (7") **CHEAT ME. / FLOWERING CHERRY** [ ] [-]

Virgin / Virgin

1973. (d-lp) **MARJORY RAZORBLADE** [ ] [ ]
– Marjory Razorblade / Marlene / Talking to no one / Eastbourne ladies / Old soldiers / I want my crown / Nasty, lonesome valley / House on the hill / Cheat me / Jackie and Edna / Everybody says / Mummy / Heaven in my view / Karate king / Dog Latin / This is Spain / Chairman's ball / Good boy / Chicken wing. *(cd-iss.Apr91)* (cd+=) – Lovesick fool / Sea of love. *(US-iss.single lp)*

Aug 73. (7") **MARLENE. / EVERYBODY SAYS** [ ] [ ]

Nov 73. (7") **LOVESICK FOOL. / SEA OF LOVE** [ ] [ ]

1974. (lp)(c) **BLAME IT ON THE NIGHT** [ ] [ ]
– River of sin / Sign of the times / I believe in love / Don't delude me / Wanting you is not easy / Take a train / Blame it on the night / Poor swine / Light up you little light / Choose / Witch / Right on her side. *(cd-iss.Apr91)*

1974. (7") **I BELIEVE IN LOVE. / QUEENIE QUEENIE CAROLINE** [ ] [-]

— His band were **GORDON SMITH** – slide guitar / **ANDY SUMMERS** – guitar / **TIM PENN** – keyboards / **PETER WOOLF** – drums / **ARCHIE LEGGAT** – bass

Apr 75. (lp)(c) **MATCHING HEAD AND FEET** [ ] [-]
– Saviour / Lucy / Lonely lover / Sunday morning sunrise / Rock'n'roll hymn / Mrs.Hooley go home / It's not me / Turpentine / Tulip / One fine day. *(cd-iss.Apr91)*

Apr 75. (7") **ROCK'N'ROLL HYMN. / IT'S NOT ME** [ ] [-]

— **STEVE THOMPSON** – bass repl. LEGGAT who went solo. **ZOOT MONEY** – keyboards, vocals (ex-ERIC BURDON) repl. PENN and SMITH

Nov 75. (7") **LORNA. / SHANGRI-LA** [ ] [-]

Feb 76. (7") **DON'T MAKE WAVES. / MONA WHERE'S MY TROUSERS** [ ] [-]

Feb 76. (lp)(c) **HEARTBURN** [ ] [-]
– Strange locomotion / Don't make waves / Happy band / I love my mother / Shangri-la / America / Big white bird / Games games games / My mother's eyes / Daddy. *(cd-iss.Apr91)*

May 76. (7") **WALK ON BY. / SHANGRI-LA** [ ] [-]

— ZOOT & ANDY joined KEVIN AYERS. The latter formed The POLICE.

Oct 76. (7") **FEVER. / DADDY** [ ] [-]

Jan 77. (d-lp) **IN LIVING BLACK AND WHITE (live)** [ ] [-]
– Case history No.2 / Fat girl / Talking to no-one / My mother's eyes / Ol' man river / Eastbourne ladies / Sunday morning sunrise / One fine day / Marjory Razorblade / Coconut Island / Turpentine / House on the hill / Knockin' on Heaven's door / Saviour / Mummy / Big white bird / America. *(cd-iss.Apr91)*

Apr 77. (7") **MARLENE. / ENGLAND IS DYING** [ ] [-]

Jan 78. (7") **AMSTERDAM. / I REALLY LOVE YOU** [ ] [-]

Feb 78. (lp)(c) **DYNAMITE DAZE** [ ] [-]
– Dynamite daze / Brothers of mine / Lunatic / Are we dreaming / (Take me back to) Dear old Blighty / I really live round here (fake friends) / I am / Amsterdam / I only want to see you smile / Juliet and Mark / Woman, woman, woman / Cry / Dance of the bourgeoisie. *(cd-iss.Apr91),(cd-iss.Mar94)*

1978. (lp)(c) **MILLIONAIRES AND TEDDYBEARS** [ ] [-]
– People / Having a party / I'll go too / I'm just a man / Pretty park / Let me be with you / Marigold / Don't blame Mandy / Little Miss Portobello / Wendy's dream / The world is full of fools. *(cd-iss.Ap91)*

Mar 79. (7") **I'LL GO TOO. / HAVING A PARTY** [ ] [-]

Aug 79. (lp)(c) **BABBLE ("KEVIN COYNE & DAGMAR KRAUSE")** [ ] [-]
– Are you deceiving me? / Come down here / Dead, dying, gone / Stand up / Lonely man / I really love you / Sun shines down on me / I confess / Sweetheart / Shaking hands with the Sun / My mind's joined forces / It's my mind / Love together / Happy homes / It really doesn't matter / We know who we are. *(cd-iss.Mar91)*

Feb 80. (lp)(c) **BURSTING BUBBLES** [ ] [-]
– The only one / Children's crusade / No melody / Learn to swim – learn to drown /

Mad boy No.2 / Dark dance hall / Don't know what to do / A little piece of Heaven / Day to day / Golden days / The old fashioned love song. *(cd-iss.Mar91)*

— next release had backing by punk group The **RUTS.**

1980. (lp)(c) **SANITY STOMP** [ ] [-]
– Fat man / The monkey man / How strange / When (see you again) / Taking on the world / No romance / Too dark (one for the hero) / Admit you're wrong / Formula eyes / New motorway / A lovin' hand / Fear of breathing / In silence / Take on the Bowers / Wonderful wilderness / My wife says / The world speaks / You can't kill us. *(cd-iss.Apr91)* (cd+=) – Somewhere in my mind.

— with **BRIAN GODDING** – guitar / **STEVE BULL** – synthesizers / **STEVE LAMB** – bass / **DAVE SHEEN** – drums, vocals

Cherry Red / not issued

Oct 81. (lp) **POINTING THE FINGER** [ ] [-]
– There she goes / As I recall / Children of the deaf / One little moment / Let love reside / Sleeping – Waking / Pointing the finger / You can't do that / Song of the womb / Old lady.

— **PETER KIRTLEY** – guitar + **JIM WOODLAND** – vocals repl.GODDING / LAMB + SHEEN although the latter 2 returned in 1983

1982. (lp) **POLITICZ** [ ] [-]
– Your holiness / Liberation / Fun flesh / Flashing back / Tell the truth / Banzai / Poisoning you / Magnolia street / I've got the photographs.

Nov 82. (7") **SO STRANGE. / FATHER DEAR FATHER** [ ] [-]

Jan 83. (lp) **BEAUTIFUL EXTREMES ET CETERA** [ ] [-]
– Something gone wrong / Looking for the river / Roses in your room / Face in the mirror / All the battered babies / Right in hand / Love in your heart / Hello friends, hello everyone / Mona, where's my trousers / So strange / Rainbow curve / Fool fool fool.

Collapse / not issued

Feb 84. (lp) **LEGLESS IN MANILA** [ ] [-]
– Big money man / Gina's song / Money machine / Raindrop on the river / Nigel in Napoli / Zoo wars / Black clouds / Legless in Manila / Don't raise an argument / Cycling. *(cd-iss.Nov94 on 'Golden Hind')*

On GER-Imp. / not issued

1985. (lp) **ROUGH – LIVE (live)** [-] [-]
– The house on the hill / Singing the blues / Gina's song / Lucille / Pretty park / Dark dance hall / A loving hand / The monkey man / The old fashioned love song / I wander (poem).

KEVIN COYNE BAND

— with **HANS PUKKE** – guitar / **ROBERT STEINHART** – bass / **FALK STEFFEN** – drums

Line / not issued

1987. (lp)(cd) **STUMBLING ON TO PARADISE** [-] [-] Germ'y
– I'm still here / Pack of lies / How is your luck / Sunshine home / Tear me up / No revolution / Victoria smiles / Charming / Winter into summer / Love for five minutes / Back home boogie. *(re-iss.cd Nov 94 on 'Golden Hind')*

KEVIN COYNE & THE PARADISE BAND

Ind.M.S. / not issued

1989. (lp)(cd) **EVERYBODY'S NAKED** [ ] [-]
– The millionaires song / I couldn't love you / Not the way / We don't talk too much / Here comes the morning / City crazy / Take me back in your arms / Last time blues / The slave / Old hippie / Radio / Everybody's naked. *(re-iss.cd Dec 94 on 'Zabo')*

Golden Hind / not issued

Jun 94. (cd) **TOUGH AND SWEET** [ ] [-]
– Little Miss Dynamite / Precious love / Burning head II / Really in love / Pony tail song / Elvis is dead / Totally naked II / Walls have ears / Baby blue / Talking money / Slow burner / All the loving / No lullabies / It's amazing II / Tell me Tony / Now's the time / Getting old / Some day / Love and money / Let's get romantic / Creeper.

Nov 94. (cd) **WILD TIGER LOVE** [ ] [-]
– The bungalow / Sensual / Cafe crazy / Looking in your eyes / Open up the gates / Go Sally go / American girls / Fish brain / Fooled again / Don't you look (that way) / Raindrops on the window / Passion's pleasure.

Dec 94. (cd) **ROMANCE** – ROMANCE [ ] [-]
– Ready for love / Happy, happy / Chances / It's all over / The 17th floor / Theresa / No kindness, no pity / The Heaven song / Lovers and friends / Wild eyes / Best friend / Impossible child / Neighbourhood girl.

Oct 95. (cd) **THE ADVENTURES OF CRAZY FRANK** [ ] [-]
–

– compilations, others, etc. –

Feb 81. Butt; (3xlp-box) **THE DANDELION YEARS** [ ] [-]
– (SIREN / STRANGE LOCOMOTION / CASE HISTORY lp's)

Feb 91. Virgin; (d-cd) **MARJORY RAZORBLADE / MILLIONAIRE AND TEDDY BEARS** [ ] [-]

Mar 91. Strange Fruit; (cd)(lp) **THE PEEL SESSIONS (73-79)** [ ] [-]
– Marlene / Cheat me / By up me duck / The miner's song / Evil island home / Araby / Dance of the bourgenoise / Do not shout at me father / Need somebody / Poor swine / Rivers of blood / Lunatic / I only want to see you smile / That's rock'n'roll / A leopard never changes its spots / I couldn't love you.

Mar 94. Virgin; (cd) **SIGN OF THE TIMES** [ ] [ ]
– Marjory razor blade / Marlene / Eastbourne ladies / House on the hill / Dog Latin / Good boy / Karateking / Fat girl / Saviour / Brothers of mine / Dynamite daze / Having a party / I'm just a man / The only one / Children's crusade / Mona, where's my trousers / Sign of the times / Witch / Blame it on the night.

Oct 94. Voiceprint; (cd) **RABBITS (w / SIREN)** [ ] [-]

Dec 94. See For Miles; (cd) **STRANGE LOCOMOTION / SIREN** [ ] [-]

Mar 95. Golden Hind; (cd) **ELVIRA: SONGS FROM THE ARCHIVES 1979-83** [ ] [-]

CRACKER

Formed: North Carolina, California, USA . . . 1990 by LOWERY and LOVERING (former members of top cult US acts). While LOVERING had been sidekick of FRANK BLACK in The PIXIES, LOWERY had been in CAMPER VAN BEETHOVEN, who were famous for 5 albums for 'Rough Trade' in the 80's and the classic track 'TAKE THE SKINHEADS BOWLING'. • **Style:** Acoustic laid-back hard rockin' grunge cowpunks, fusing TOM PETTY or IAN HUNTER like songs with twanging country rock. • **Songwriters:** LOWERY or LOWERY-HICKMAN-FARAGHER on second album. Covered LOSER (Grateful Dead). • **Trivia:** Produced by DON SMITH.

Recommended: KEROSENE HAT (*7)

DAVID LOWERY – vocals, guitars (ex-CAMPER VAN BEETHOVEN) / **JOHNNY HICKMAN** – guitar, vocals / **BOB RUPE** – bass (ex-SILOS)/ **DAVE LOVERING** – drums (ex-PIXIES)

Virgin America / Virgin

Mar 92. (7") **TEEN ANGST (WHAT THE WORLD NEEDS NOW). / CAN I TAKE MY GUN TO HEAVEN** [ ] [ ]
(12"+=) – China.
(cd-s++=) – ('A'version).

Apr 92. (cd)(c)(lp) **CRACKER** [ ] [ ]
– Teen angst (what the world needs now) / Happy birthday to me / This is Cracker soul / I see the light / St.Cajetan / Mr.Wrong / Someday / Can I take my gun to Heaven / Satify you / Another song about the rain / Don't f*** me up (with peace and love) / Dr.Bernice.

— **DAVEY FARAGHER** – bass, vocals repl. RUPE

— **MICHAEL URBANO** – drums repl. LOVERING

May 94. (7")(c-s) **LOW. / TEEN ANGST (WHAT THE WORLD NEEDS NOW)** [43] [64]
(cd-s) – ('A'side) / I ride my bike / Sunday train / Whole lotta trouble.
(10") – ('A'side) / River Euphrates / Euro-trash girl / Bad vibes everybody.
(all above single re-iss.Nov94, hit 54 UK)

Jun 94. (cd)(c)(lp) **KEROSENE HAT** [44] [59] Sep93
– Low / Movie star / Get off this / Kerosene hat / Take me down to the infirmary / Nostalgia / Sweet potato / Sick of goodbyes / I want everything / Lonesome Johnny blues / Let's go for a ride / Loser.
(cd+=) – No songs: Eurotrash girl + I ride my bike / Hi-desert biker meth lab. (c+=) – No songs; Euro-trash girl + I ride my bike / Kerosene hat (acoustic).

Jul 94. (c-s)(cd-s) **GET OFF THIS / HAPPY BIRTHDAY TO ME / CHINA / DR.BERNICE** [41] [ ]
(cd-s) – ('A'side) / Fucking up (live) / Blue Danube / Don't fuck me up (with peace and love).
(10") – ('A'side) / Steve's hornpipe / Mr.Wrong / I want everything (acoustic).

CRAMPS

Formed: Ohio, U.S.A . . . 1975 by LUX INTERIOR and POISON IVY. After two singles on US indie label, they signed to Miles Copeland's 'Illegal' label 1979. Legal wrangles dogged them throughout the 80's, and output was never massive. Their early 1986 lp 'A DATE WITH ELVIS', gave them deserved UK chart entry, hitting Top 40. • **Style:** Bass-less "psychobilly" punk rock'n'roll, fusing 50's rockabilly and 60's garage punk. Frontman LUX and his female sidekicks seemed to wear less and less with each passing phase. • **Songwriters:** Most written by LUX and IVY except SURFIN' BIRD (Trashmen) / FEVER (Little Willie John) / THE WAY I WALK (Robert Gordon) / GREEN DOOR (Jim Lowe) / JAILHOUSE ROCK (Elvis Presley) / MULESKINNER BLUES (Fendermen) / PSYCHOTIC REACTION (Count Five) / LONESOME TOWN (Ricky Nelson) / HARD WORKIN' MAN (Jack Nitzche) / HITSVILLE 29 B.C. (Turnbow) / WHEN I GET THE BLUES (Larry Mize) / HOW COME YOU DO ME? (. . .Joiner) / STRANGE LOVE (. . .West) / BLUES BLUES BLUES (. . .Thompson) / TRAPPED LOVE (Kohler-Fana) / SINNERS (. . .Aldrich) / ROUTE 66 (. . .Troup) / etc. • **Trivia:** Produced by former BOX TOPS singer ALEX CHILTON in 1979/1980. Their fan club surprisingly was based in Grangemouth, Scotland.

Recommended: OFF THE BONE (*9) / A DATE WITH ELVIS (*7) / SMELL OF FEMALE (*6)

LUX INTERIOR (b.ERICK LEE PURKHISER) – vocals / **POISON IVY RORSCHACH** (b.KIRSTY MALANA WALLACE) – guitar / **BRIAN GREGORY** – guitar / **NICK KNOX** (b.NICK STEPHANOFF) – drums repl. MIRIAM LINNA who had repl. PAM BALAM GREGORY

not issued / Vengeance

Apr 78. (7") **THE WAY I WALK. / SURFIN' BIRD** [-] [ ]

Nov 78. (7") **HUMAN FLY. / DOMINO** [-] [ ]

Illegal / I.R.S.

Jul 79. (12"ep) **GRAVEST HITS** [ ] [-]
– Human fly / The way I walk / Domino / Surfin' bird / Lonesome town. *(re-iss.Sep82- 7"blue-ep) (re-iss.Mar83- 7"red-ep)*

Mar 80. (7") **GARBAGEMAN. / FEVER** [ ] [-]

Mar 80. (lp)(c) **SONGS THE LORD TAUGHT US** [ ] [ ]
– TV set / Rock on the Moon / Garbageman / I was a teenage werewolf / Sunglasses after dark / The mad daddy / Mystery plane / Zombie dance / What's behind the mask / Strychnine / I'm cramped / Tear it up / Fever. *(re-iss.+cd.Feb90)*

Jul 80. (7"m) **DRUG TRAIN. / LOVE ME / I CAN HARDLY STAND IT** [ ] [-]

Jul 80. (7") **DRUG TRAIN. / GARAGEMAN** [-] [ ]

— **KID CONGO POWERS** (b.BRIAN TRISTAN) – guitar repl. JULIEN BOND who had repl. GREGORY for two months mid 1980.

I.R.S. I.R.S.

May 81. (7")(7"yellow) **GOO GOO MUCK. / SHE SAID**

May 81. (lp)(c) **PSYCHEDELIC JUNGLE**
– Green fuzz / Goo goo muck / Rockin' bones / Voodoo idol / Primitive / Caveman / The crusher / Don't eat stuff off the sidewalk / Can't find my mind / Jungle hop / The natives are restless / Under the wires / Beautiful gardens / Green door.

Sep 81. (7") **THE CRUSHER. / SAVE IT** [ ] [-]
(12+=) – New kind of kick.

— (LUX, IVY & NICK were joined by . . .) **IKE KNOX** (Nick's cousin) – guitar repl. KID CONGO who returned to GUN CLUB (appeared on live tracks 83-84)

New Rose New Rose

Mar 83. (7")(7"brown)(7"clear)(7"green)(7"orange) **I AIN'T NUTHIN' BUT A GOREHOUND. / WEEKEND ON MARS** [ ] [-] France

Big Beat New Rose

Nov 83. (m-lp)(red-lp)(pic-lp) **SMELL OF FEMALE (live)** [74] [ ] France
– Faster pussycat / I ain't nuthin' but a gorehound / Psychotic reaction / The most exhalted potentate of love / You got good taste / Call of the wig hat. *(cd-iss.May87) (re-iss.lp,c,cd.Feb90)* (cd+=) – Beautiful gardens / She said / Surfin' dead.

— **CANDY FUR** (DEL-MAR) – guitar repl. IKE

Nov 85. (7")(7"orange) **CAN YOUR PUSSY DO THE DOG?. / BLUE MOON BABY** [68] [ ]
(10")(12")(10"red)(10"blue) Georgia Lee Brown.

Feb 86. (lp)(c)(cd) **A DATE WITH ELVIS** [34] [ ]
– How far can too far go / The hot pearl snatch / People ain't too good / What's inside a girl? / Can your pussy do the dog? / Kizmiaz / Cornfed dames / Chicken / (Hot pool of) Woman need / Aloha from Hell / It's just that song.

May 86. (7") **WHAT'S INSIDE A GIRL?. / GET OFF THE ROAD**
(12"+=) – Give me a woman.
(cd-s++=) – Scene / Heart of darkness.

Enigma Enigma

Jan 90. (7")(c-s)(7"sha-pic-d) **BIKINI GIRLS WITH MACHINE GUNS. / JACKYARD BACKOFF** [35] [ ]
(12"+=)(cd-s+=) – Her love rubbed off.

Feb 90. (cd)(c)(lp) **STAY SICK** [62] [ ]
– Bop pills / Goddam rock'n'roll / Bikini girls with machine guns / All woman are bad / Creature from the black leather lagoon / Shortenini' bread / Daisy's up your butterfly / Everything goes / Journey to the centre of a girl / Mama oo pow pow / Saddle up a buzz buzz / Muleskinner blues (cd.+=) – Her love rubbed off. *(re-iss.cd Feb94)*

Apr 90. (7")(c-s) **ALL WOMAN ARE BAD. / TEENAGE RAGE (live)**
(12"+=)(cd-s+=)(12"pic-d+=) – King of the drapes (live) / High school hell-cats (live).

Aug 90. (7") **CREATURES FROM THE BLACK LEATHER LAGOON. / JAILHOUSE ROCK**
(12"+=)(cd-s+=) – Beat out my love.

— **LUX & IVY** are joined by **SLIM CHANCE** – guitar (ex-PANTHER BURNS) / **JIM SCLAVUNOS** – drums

Big Beat Enigma

Sep 91. (7") **EYEBALL IN MY MARTINI. / WILDER WILDER FASTER FASTER**
(12"+=)(cd-s+=) – Wilder wilder faster faster.

Sep 91. (cd)(c)(lp)(pic-lp)(cd) **LOOK MOM, NO HEAD!**
– Dames, booze, chains and boots / Two headed sex change / Blow up your mind / Hard workin' man / Miniskirt blues / Alligator stomp / I wanna get in your pants Bend over, I'll drive / Don't get funny with me / Eyeball in my Martini / Hipsville 29 B.C. / When I get the blues (the strangeness in me).

— **NICKY ALEXANDER** – drums (ex-WEIRDOS) repl. JIM

— **HARRY DRUMDINI** – drums repl. NICKY

Creation

Oct 94. (7") **ULTRA TWIST!. / CONFESSIONS OF A PSYCHO CAT**
(12"+=)(cd-s+=) – No club love wolf.

Oct 94. (cd)(c)(lp) **FLAME JOB**
– Mean machine / Ultra twist / Let's get f*cked up / Nest of the cuckoo bird / I'm customized / Sado country auto show / Naked girl falling down the stairs / How come you do me? / Inside out and upside down (with you) / Trapped love / Swing the big eyed rabbit / Strange love / Blues blues blues / Sinners / Route 66 (get your kicks on).

Feb 95. (7") **NAKED GIRL FALLING DOWN THE STAIRS. / LET'S GET F*CKED UP**
(cd-s+=) – Surfin' bird.

– compilations, others, etc. –

Illegal I.R.S.

May 83. I.R.S.; (lp)(c)(pic-lp) **OFF THE BONE** [44] [ ]
– Human fly / The way I walk / Domino / Surfin' bird / Lonesome town / Garbageman / Fever / Drug train / Love me / I can't hardly stand it / Goo goo muck / She said / The crusher / Save it / New kind of kick.
(US-title-BAD MUSIC FOR BAD PEOPLE) *(UK cd-iss.Jan87) (re-iss. cd 1992 on 'Castle' +=) – Uranium Rock / Good taste (live)*

Feb 84. New Rose France; (7")(7"pic-d) **FASTER PUSSYCAT. / YOU GOT GOOD TASTE** [-] [-]

1984. New Rose; (4x7") **I AIN'T NUTHIN' BUT A GOREHOUND. / WEEKEND ON MARS / FASTER PUSSYCAT. / YOU GOT GOOD TASTE / CALL OF THE WIGHAT. / THE MOST EXHALTED POTENTATE OF LOVE / PSYCHOTIC REACTION. /** (one sided) (all 4 either blue/white/black/green) [-] [-]

May 86. New Rose France; (7") **KIZMIAZ. / GET OFF THE ROAD** [-] [-]
(12"+=) – Give me a woman.

Nov 87. Vengeance; (lp) **ROCKIN' AND REELIN' IN AUCKLAND, NEW ZEALAND (live)** [-] [ ]
(cd-iss.Sep94 on 'Ace')

1989. Big Beat; (4x7"diff.colours) (singles from Mar83/ Feb84/ Nov85/ May86) [ ] [-]

CRANBERRIES

Formed: Limerick, Ireland . . . 1990, initially as covers band The CRANBERRY SAW US, until the inclusion of DOLORES. An independent single 'UNCERTAIN' on 'Xeric' appeared late 1991. They went into the studio late in 1991, and soon re-surfaced on 'Island' in 1992 /3 with 'DREAMS', 'LINGER' and 'PUT ME DOWN'. These were tracks featured on 1993's debut album 'EVERYBODY ELSE IS DOING IT . . .', which went on to sell a million in the US initially, and a year later in the slow-warming UK. • **Style:** An indie style major outfit, initially described as The Irish SUNDAYS, although DOLORES maintains her Heavenly deep-rooted Irish accent in song. • **Songwriters:** DOLORES / N.HOGAN, except (THEY LONG TO BE) CLOSE TO YOU (Carpenters). • **Trivia:** Supported MOOSE in the summer of '91. DOLORES guested on MOOSE's 1992 album 'XYZ'. In the summer of '95, 'ZOMBIE' was discofied into the UK Top 20 by pop/rave artist AMY . . .'nough said.

Recommended: EVERYBODY ELSE IS DOING IT . . . (*8) / NO TIME TO ARGUE (*6).

DOLORES O'RIORDAN (b.1971) – vocals, acoustic guitar / **NOEL HOGAN** – guitar / **MIKE HOGAN** – bass / **FERGAL LAWLER** – drums

Xeric not issued

Oct 91. (12"ep)(cd-ep) **UNCERTAIN / NOTHING LEFT AT ALL. / PATHETIC SENSES / THEM** [ ] [-]

Island Island

Sep 92. (7") **DREAMS. / WHAT YOU WERE**
(12"+=)(cd-s+=) – Liar.

Feb 93. (7")(c-s) **LINGER. / REASON** [74] [8]
(12"+=)(cd-s+=) – How (radical mix).

Mar 93. (cd)(c)(lp) **EVERYBODY ELSE IS DOING IT, SO WHY CAN'T WE?** [64] [18]
– I still do / Dreams / Sunday / Pretty / Waltzing black / Not sorry / Linger / Wanted / Still can't . . . / I will always / How / Put me down. *(re-iss.Nov93) (re-iss.Mar94, hit UK No.1)*

Jan 94. (7")(c-s) **LINGER. / PRETTY (live)** [14] [-]
(cd-s+=)(10"+=) – Waltzing black (live) / I still do (live).

Apr 94. (7")(c-s) **DREAMS. / WHAT YOU WERE** [27] [42]
(cd-s+=) – Liar.
(cd-s) – ('A'live) / Liar (live) / Not sorry (live) / Wanted (live).

— Jun 94; DOLORES featured on JAH WOBBLE's Top 50 hit 'The Sun Does Rise'.

Sep 94. (7")(c-s) **ZOMBIE. / AWAY** [14] [ ]
(cd-s+=) – I don't need.
(cd-s) – ('A'side) / Waltzing black (live) / Linger (live).

Oct 94. (cd)(c)(lp) **NO NEED TO ARGUE** [2] [6]
– Ode to my family / I can't be with you / 21 / Zombie / Empty / Everything I said / The icicle melts / Disappointment / Ridiculous thoughts / Dreaming my dreams / Yeat's grave / Daffodil lament / No need to argue.

Nov 94. (7")(c-s) **ODE TO MY FAMILY. / SO COLD IN IRELAND** [29] [ ]
(cd-s+=) – No need to argue / Dreaming my dreams.
(cd-s) – ('A'side) / Dreams (live) / Ridiculous thoughts (live) / Zombie (live).

Feb 95. (7")(c-s) **I CAN'T BE WITH YOU. / (THEY LONG TO BE) CLOSE TO YOU** [23] [ ]
(cd-s+=) – Empty.
(cd-s) – ('A'side) / Zombie (acoustic) / Daffodil lament (live).

Jul 95. (7")(c-s) **RIDICULOUS THOUGHTS. / LINGER** [20] [ ]
(cd-s+=) – Twenty one (live) / Ridiculous thoughts (live).

compilations, etc

Nov 95. (d-cd) **EVERYBODY ELSE IS DOING IT . . . / NO NEED TO ARGUE** [ ] [ ]

CRANES

Formed: Portsmouth, England . . .1986 by sister and brother ALISON and JIM SHAW. In 1987, they sold privately a cassette 'FUSE', and after issuing 1989 debut on own label, they moved up to 'Dedicated' for the 90's, and broke through in 1993 after supporting The CURE. • **Style:** A new breed of gothic minimalists featuring ALISON's vox fusion of LYDIA LUNCH and CLARE GROGAN, backed with COCTEAU TWINS-like energy. • **Songwriters:** ALISON lyrics / plus JIM on songs. • **Trivia:** Another group to be helped by airplay from DJ JOHN PEEL.

Recommended: WINGS OF JOY (*7) / FOREVER (*8).

ALISON SHAW – vocals / **MARK FRANCOME** – guitar / **MATT COPE** – guitar / **JIM SHAW** – drums

Bite Back not issued

May 89. (m-lp) **SELF NON SELF** [ ] [-]
– One from the slum / Beach mover / Joy lies within / Focus breathe / Heaven or bliss / Fuse / Reach / Nothing in the middle nothing at the end. *(cd-iss.Nov92 on 'Dedicated' w /2 extra)*

Dedicated B.M.G.

Aug 90. (12"ep) **INESCAPABLE EP** [ ] [-]
– Inescapable / Give / Dada 331 / Inescapable II.

Nov 90. (12"ep)(cd-ep) **ESPERO EP** [ ] [-]
– I hope / EG shining / Cha cha esqueta.

May 91. (12")(cd-s) **BRIGHTER. / ADORATION** [ ] [-]

Sep 91. (12"ep)(cd-ep) **TOMORROW'S TEARS / CASA BLANCA. / SIXTH OF MAY / DREAMLESS** [ ] [-]

Sep 91. (cd)(c)(lp) **WINGS OF JOY** [52] [ ]
– Watersong / Thursday / Living and breathing / Leaves of summer / Starblood / Wish / Tomorrow's tears / Beautiful sadness / Hopes are high / Adoration. (cd+=) –

Sixth of May. *(re-iss.Nov92, w /free 5" cd-s)*
Mar 93. (12"ep)(cd-ep) **ADRIFT. / EVERYWHERE / UNDERWATER**
May 93. (cd)(c)(lp) **FOREVER** 40
– Everywhere / Cloudless / Jewel / Far away / Adrift / Clear / Sun and sky / And ever / Golden / Rainbows.
Sep 93. (7") **JEWEL (remix). / CLEAR (scalpicin mix)** 29
(7") – ('A'side) / Cloudless (Thai mix).
(7") – ('A'side) / Love her to Heaven (II).
(cd-ep) – (all 4 tracks).
Aug 94. (7"m) **SHINING ROAD. / LILLIES / SEPTEMBER** 57
(cd-s+=) – Green song 7.
(7"m) – ('A'braver mix) / Lillies (Flood mix) / Don't close our eyes.
Sep 94. (cd)(c)(lp) **LOVED**
– Shining road / Pale blue sky / Reverie / Lillies / Are you gone? / Loved / Beautiful friend / Bewildered / Gone this far / Paris and Rome.

CRASH TEST DUMMIES

Formed: Winnepeg, Canada . . . early 90's by ROBERTS and brother DAN. Released initially in Canada-only the eventually platinum selling 'THE GHOST THAT HAUNT ME', which hosted US Hot 100 breakthrough single 'SUPERMAN'S SONG'. They finally released the acclaimed return in 1994, with the deliciously titled 'MMM MMM MMM MMM', which went world-wide Top 3. • **Style:** Angst lyrically, although BRAD's deep vox fuses in well with semi-acoustic backing. • **Songwriters:** BRAD ROBERTS except ALL YOU PRETTY GIRLS (Xtc). • **Trivia:** Co-produced w/ JERRY HARRISON (ex-TALKING HEADS).

Recommended: GOD SHUFFLED HIS FEET (*6)

BRAD ROBERTS – vocals, guitars / **ELLEN REID** – keyboards, accordion / **BENJAMIN DARVILL** – mandolin, harmonicas / **DAN ROBERTS** – bass / **MITCH DORGE** – drums, percussion

Arista Arista
Sep 91. (c-s)(cd-s) **SUPERMAN'S SONG. / THE VOYAGE** 56
Nov 91. (cd)(c) **THE GHOSTS THAT HAUNT ME**
– Winter song / Comin' back soon (the bereft man's song) / Superman's song / The country life / Here on Earth (I'll have my cake) / The ghosts that haunt me / Thick-necked man / Androgynous / The voyage / At my funeral. *(re-iss.cd Oct95)*

R.C.A. Arista
Apr 94. (7")(c-s) **MMM MMM MMM MMM. / HERE I STAND BEFORE ME (live)** 2 4 Jan94
(cd-s+=) – Superman's song (live).
May 94. (cd)(c)(lp) **GOD SHUFFLED HIS FEET** 2 9 Feb94
– God shuffled his feet / Afternoons & coffee spoons / Mmm mmm mmm mmm / In the days of the caveman / Swimming in your ocean / Here I stand before me / I think I'll disappear now / How does a duck know? / When I go out with artists / The psychic / Two knights and maidens / Untitled.
Jun 94. (7")(c-s) **AFTERNOONS & COFFEE SPOONS. / IN THE DAYS OF THE CAVEMAN (live)** 23 66
(cd-s+=) – The ghosts that haunt me / Androgynous (live).
(cd-s) – ('A'side) / Mmm mmm mmm mmm (live) / God shuffled his feet (live).
Oct 94. (7")(c-s)(cd-s) **GOD SHUFFLED HIS FEET. / AFTERNOONS & COFFEE SPOONS (live)**
(12"+=)(cd-s+=) – Winter song / Mmm mmm mmm mmm.
Below feat. vocals by ELLEN REID
Apr 95. (c-s) **THE BALLAD OF PETER PUMPKINHEAD. / GOD SHUFFLED HIS FEET** 30
(cd-s+=) – Afternoons and coffeespoons (live) / Swimming in your ocean.
(cd-s) – ('A'side) / Afternoons and coffeespoons (live) / When I go out with artists (live) / Swimming in your ocean (live).

CRASS

Formed: North Weald, Essex, England . . . 1978 by communal dwellers PENNY, JOY, etc. After debut 45 on indie 'Small Wonder', they formed own named label 1979. Fluctuated line-up to whoever was living with them at the time. Surprised many when their 1982 budget priced double lp 'YES SIR, I WILL', hit UK Top 30. • **Style:** Punk rock hippies, who protested in song against the establishment (i.e. the bomb, police, media, government, etc.). • **Songwriters:** Group compositions. 'BIG A LITTLE A' (was adapted from a children's learning book). • **Trivia:** During the Falklands conflict, they had tapes confiscated by the Thatcher government, and were charged under The Obscene Publications Act. Not surprisingly, no records were ever given a release outside the U.K.

Recommended: THE FEEDING OF THE FIVE THOUSAND (*8) / BEST BEFORE 1984 (*7)

EVE LIBERTINE – vocals / **JOY DE VIVRE** – vocals / **STEVE IGNORANT** – vocals / **PHIL FREE** – lead guitar / **N.A. PALMER** – guitar, vocals / **PENNY RIMBAUD** – drums / **PETE WRIGHT** – bass / **MICK G.** (DUFFIELD) – flute, film-maker /

Small Wonder not issued
Dec 78. (m-lp) **THE FEEDING OF THE FIVE THOUSAND** -
– Asylum / Do they owe us a living? / End result / They've got a bomb / Punk is dead / Reject of society / General Bacardi / Banned from The Roxy's / G's song / Fight war, not wars / Women / Securicor / Sucks / You pay / Angels / What a shame / So what / Well? . . .do they. *(re-iss.Nov80 as 'FEEDING OF THE 5,000 EP (2nd SITTING)', re-iss Oct81 + Dec87 on 'Crass') (cd-iss.Oct90.+=)*

Crass not issued
May 79. (7")(c-s) **REALITY ASYLUM. / SHAVED WOMAN** -
(7"-re-iss.Dec80)
Sep 79. (d-lp) **STATIONS OF THE CRASS** -
– Mother Earth / White punks on hope / You've got big hands / Darling / System / Big man, big M.A.N. / Hurry up Garry / Fun going on / Crutch of society / Heard too much about / Chairman of the bored / Tired / Walls / Uptight citizen / Time out / The gasman cometh / Democrats / Contaminational power / I ain't thick it's just a trick. // live:- System / Big man, big M.A.N. / Banned from the Roxy / Hurry up Garry / Time out / They've got a bomb / Fight war, not wars / Women / Shaved women / You pay / Heard too much about / Angels / What a shame / So what / G's song / Do they owe us a living? / Punk is dead. *(re-iss.Oct81 + Dec87, cd-iss.Oct90)*
May 80. (7") **BLOODY REVOLUTIONS. / ('B'side by the "Poison Girls")** -
(re-iss.Dec80 + May81 as above on 'Crass/Xntrix' joint label outing)
Feb 81. (7") **NAGASAKI NIGHTMARE. / BIG A LITTLE A** -
(re-iss.Oct81)
Oct 81. (lp) **PENIS ENVY** -
– Bat a motel / Systematic death / Poison in a pretty pill / What the fuck / Where next Columbus / Berkertex bribe / Smother love / Health surface / Dry weather. *(re-iss.+c.Dec87, cd-iss.Oct90)*
Dec 81. (7") **MERRY CRASSMAS. / MERRY CRASSMAS – HAVE FUN** -
Aug 82. (d-lp) **CHRIST THE ALBUM (some live)** 26 -
– Have a nice day / Mother love / Nineteen eighty bore / I know there is love / Beg your pardon / Birth control 'n' rock'n'roll / Reality white-wash / It's the greatest working class rip-off / Deadhead / You can be who / Buy no pay as you go / Rival tribal revel rebel part 2 / Bumhooler / Sentiment / Major General despair / Banned from the Roxy / The sound of one hand / Punk is dead / Nagasaki nightmare / Bat a motel blues / Berkertex bribe / Fold it in half / Big hands / Heart-throb of the mortuary / Bumhooler / Big A little A / First woman / Arlington 73 / Bomb plus bomb tape / Contaminational power / I ain't thick / G's song / Securicor / I can't stand it / Shaved women / A part of life / Do they owe us a living? / So what / Salt'n'pepper. *(cd-iss.Oct90)*
Oct 82. (7") **HOW DOES IT FEEL (TO BE THE MOTHER OF A THOUSAND DEAD) . / THE IMMORTAL DEATH / DON'T TELL ME YOU CARE** -
May 83. (lp) **YES SIR, I WILL** -
– Yes sir, I will / The pig's head controversy – the aesthetics of anarchy.
May 83. (7") **SHEEP FARMING IN THE FALKLANDS. / GOTCHA! (live)** -
(free-7"brown.w/above) **WHO DUNNIT? / WHO DUNNIT (part 2)**
Jan 84. (7") **YOU'RE ALREADY DEAD. / DON'T GET CAUGHT / NAGASAKI IS YESTERDAY'S DOG END** -

—— broke up 1984. STEVE joined CONFLICT.

– compilations, others, etc. –

Jul 86. Crass; (d-lp) **BEST BEFORE 1984** -
– Intro / Do they owe us a living? / Major general despair / Angela Rippon / Reality asylum / Shaved women / Bloody revolutions / Nagasaki nightmare / Big a little a / Rival tribal rebel revel – Sheep farming in the Falklands (Flexidisc version) / How does it feel / The immortal death / Don't tell me that you care / Sheep farming in the Falklands / Gotcha / Nagasaki is yesterdays dogend / Don't get caught / Smash the mac / Do they owe us a living? (live) *(re-iss.Dec87)*
Nov 86. Crass; (12") **TEN NOTES ON A SUMMER'S DAY. / (instrumental mix)**
Dec 93. omona-Crass; (cd) **YOU'LL RUIN IT FOR EVERYONE (live '81)** -

JOY DE VIVRE

Crass not issued
May 81. (7"white) **OUR WEDDING. / (one-sided)** -

PENNY RIMBAUD & EVE LIBERTINE

Crass not issued
Jun 85. (lp) **ACT OF LOVE** -
– (short poems written by Joy's deceased friend WALLY HOPE between 68-73)

PENNY RIMBAUD

Crass not issued
Jul 92. (cd)(c)(lp) **CHRIST'S REALITY ASYLUM** -
– (spoken word)

Robert CRAY

Born: 1 Aug'53, Columbus, Georgia, USA. He later moved to Tacoma, Washington and toured West Coast 1973, alongside high school idol ALBERT COLLINS. This led to CRAY forming own band in 1975. They cut album in 1978, but WHO'S BEEN TALKIN' finally saw light 1980 on 'Tomato' records. After another long wait, the 'Hightone' label, licensed to 'Demon' for UK, and released follow-up BAD INFLUENCE. From then on, he won many awards, including Best Blues Guitarist / Album for 1984 and '86 respectively, leading to contract with 'Mercury'. His 1986 album 'STRONG PERSUADER' was first to give UK chart status, which continued into the 90's. • **Style:** Black blues guitarist, influenced by Texas style, and heroes ELMORE JAMES, B.B.KING, STEVE CROPPER and ALBERT COLLINS. • **Songwriters:** Mostly CRAY compositions with group collaborations. 1992 producer DENNIS WALKER wrote most with CRAY or PUGH. The same album saw CRAY co-write with BOZ SCAGGS and STEVE CROPPER on 'A PICTURE OF A BROKEN HEART' & 'ON THE ROAD DOWN' respectively. Covered; GOT TO MAKE A COMEBACK (Eddie Floyd) / DON'T TOUCH ME (Johnny 'Guitar' Watson) / TOO MANY COOKS (Willie

Dixon) / YOU'RE GONNA NEED ME (Albert King) etc. • **Trivia:** In 1980 he and band appeared in the film 'Animal House' as OTIS DAY's house group.

Recommended: DON'T BE AFRAID OF THE DARK (*7) / MIDNIGHT STROLL (*7) / BAD INFLUENCE (*6) / FALSE ACCUSATIONS (*6) / STRONG PERSUADER (*6)

ROBERT CRAY – vocals, guitar / **RICHARD COUSINS** – bass / **DAVE OLSON** – drums / also **MIKE VANNICE** – sax, keyboards / **WARREN RAND** – sax / **CURTIS SALADO** – guest harmonica

ROBERT CRAY BAND

Tomato / not issued

1980. (lp) **WHO'S BEEN TALKIN'** [-] [ ]
– Too many cooks / The score / The welfare (turns its back on you) / That's what I'll do / I'd rather be a wino / Who's been talkin' / Sleeping in the ground / I'm gonna forget about you / Nice as a fool can be / If you're thinkin' what I'm thinkin'. *(UK-iss.+c.Oct86 on 'Charly') (US-re-iss.lp,c,cd.May88) (re-iss.cd/c 1992 as 'THE SCORE' on 'Charly')*

Demon / Hightone

Mar 84. (lp) **BAD INFLUENCE** [ ] [ ] 1983
– Phone booth / The grinder / Got to make a comeback / So many women, so little time / Where do I go from here / Waiting for a train / March on / Don't touch me / No big deal. *(US-re-lp,c,cd.Mar87.) (UK-re-lp/cd.Jul87)* (cd+=) – I got loaded / Share what you've got, Keep what you need.

— **PETER BOE** – keyboards, vocals repl. SALADO, VANNICE and RAND.

Oct 85. (lp)(c) **FALSE ACCUSATIONS** [68] [ ]
– Porch light / Change of heart, change of mind (S.O.F.T.) / She's gone / Playin' in the dirt / I've slipped her mind / False accusations / The last time (I get burned like this) / Payin' for it now / Sonny. *(cd-iss.1986)*

Nov 85. (12"ep) **CHANGE OF HEART, CHANGE OF MIND (soft) / I GOT LOADED. / PHONE BOOTH / BAD INFLUENCE** [ ] [ ]

Mercury / Mercury

Oct 86. (7") **I GUESS I SHOWED HER. / DIVIDED HEART** [ ] [ ]
(12"+=) – Got to be a comeback / Share what you've got, keep what you need.

Nov 86. (lp)(c)(cd) **STRONG PERSUADER** [34] [13]
– Smoking gun / I guess I showed her / Right next door (because of me) / Still around / More than I can stand / Foul play / I wonder / Fantasized / New blood.

Feb 87. (7") **SMOKING GUN. / FANTASIZED** [ ] [22]
(12"+=) – Divided heart.

May 87. (7") **RIGHT NEXT DOOR (BECAUSE OF ME). / NEW BLOOD** [50] [80]
(12"+=) – Share what you've got, keep what you need.
(10"+=) – I wonder / Smoking gun.

Aug 87. (7") **NOTHIN' BUT A WOMAN. / I WONDER** [ ] [ ]
(12"+=) – Still around / New blood.
(10"+=) – Right next door (because of me).

Aug 88. (7") **DON'T BE AFRAID OF THE DARK. / AT LAST** [ ] [74]
(12"+=) – Without a trace.

Aug 88. (lp)(c)(cd) **DON'T BE AFRAID OF THE DARK** [13] [32]
– Don't be afraid of the dark / Don't you even care? / Your secret's safe with me / I can't go home / Night patrol / Acting this way / Gotta change the rules / Across the line / At last / Laugh out loud.

Oct 88. (7") **NIGHT PATROL. / MORE THAN I CAN STAND** [ ] [ ]
(12"+=) – Divided heart.
(cd-s+=) – I wonder.

Jan 89. (7")(12") **ACTING THIS WAY. / LAUGH OUT LOUD** [ ] [ ]
(cd-s+=) – ('A'guitar version) / Smoking gun.

ROBERT CRAY

solo, retained only **COUSINS** plus **JIMMY PUGH** – keyboards / **KEVIN HAYES** – drums, percussion / **TIM KAIHATSU** – guitar / **& MEMPHIS HORNS: WAYNE JACKSON** – trumpet, trombone / **ANDREW LOVE** – tenor saxophone credited later as **ROBERT CRAY BAND with The MEMPHIS HORNS**

Aug 90. (12"ep)(cd-ep) **THE FORECAST (CALLS FOR PAIN) / HOLDIN' COURT. / LABOUR OF LOVE / MIDNIGHT STROLL** [ ] [ ]

Sep 90. (cd)(c)(lp) **MIDNIGHT STROLL** [19] [51]
– The forecast (calls for pain) / These things / My problem / Labour of love / Bouncin' back / Consequences / The things you do to me / Wall around time / Move a mountain / Midnight stroll. (cd.+=) – Holdin' court. *(re-iss.cd/c Mar93)*

Jan 91. (7") **CONSEQUENCES. / SMOKING GUN** [ ] [ ]
(12"+=)(cd-s+=) – Right next door (because of me).

— **KARL SEVAREID** – bass repl. COUSINS

Aug 92. (cd)(c)(lp) **I WAS WARNED** [29] [ ]
– Just a loser / I'm a good man / I was warned / The price I pay / Won the battle / On the road down / A whole lotta pride / A picture of a broken heart / He don't live here anymore / Our last time. *(re-iss.cd Apr95)*

— **EDWARD MANION** – saxophone / **MARK PENDER** – trumpet repl. horn section

Oct 93. (cd)(c) **SHAME + A SIN** [48] [ ]
– 1040 blues / Some pain, some shame / I shiver / You're gonna need me / Don't break this ring / Stay go / Leave well enough alone / Passing by / I'm just lucky that way / Well I lied / Up and down.

Nov 93. (7")(c-s) **I HATE TAXES. / SMOKING GUN** [ ] [ ]
(cd-s+=) – 1040 blues / Right next door.

— with **PUGH / SEVAREID / HAYES**

May 95. (cd)(c) **SOME RAINY MORNING** [63] [ ]
– Moan / I'll go on / Steppin' out / Never mattered much / Tell the landlord / Little boy big / Enough for me / Jealous love / Will you think of me / Holdin' on / Love well spent.

– compilations, others, etc. –

Nov 85. Sonet/ US= Alligator; (lp) **SHOWDOWN!** [ ] [ ]

— above by **"ROBERT CRAY, ALBERT COLLINS & JOHNNY COPELAND"**

Jan 92. Tomato-Rhino; (cd)(lp) **TOO MANY COOKS** (1978 session) [ ] [ ]
(cd re-iss.Jun93)

CRAZY HORSE

Formed: California, USA ... 1962 as DANNY & THE MEMORIES by WHITTEN, TALBOT and MOLINA. Recorded one 45 for 'Valiant' before finally settling for name The ROCKETS in 1967. Released one album early in 1968 which led to them joining forces with NEIL YOUNG. They were credited on 2 of his albums EVERYBODY KNOWS THIS IS NOWHERE (1969) and AFTER THE GOLDRUSH (1970). They then recorded debut solo album CRAZY HORSE, which received rave reviews but only just broke them into US Top 100. After 2 more group albums, they recorded TONIGHT'S THE NIGHT and ZUMA with Neil Young for release in 1975. In between this, DANNY WHITTEN had died on 18 Nov'72 of a self-enduced drug overdose. • **Style:** Country-flavoured rock which lent heavily on influence of NEIL YOUNG. • **Songwriters:** WHITTEN with others. • **Miscellaneous:** ROD STEWART hit No.1 with WHITTEN's 'I Don't Want To Talk About It'. Their roadie and friend BRUCE BERRY also overdosed in 1973.

Recommended: CRAZY HORSE (*6)

The ROCKETS

DANNY WHITTEN – vocals, guitar / **BILLY TALBOT** – bass / **RALPH MOLINA** – drums / with **LEON WHITSELL** – guitar, vocals / **GEORGE WHITSELL** – guitar, vocals / **BOBBY NOTKOFF** – violin.

not issued / White Whale

Mar 68. (lp) **THE ROCKETS** [-] [ ]

CRAZY HORSE

(**WHITTEN, TALBOT & MOLINA**) plus **JACK NITZSCHE** – keyboards, with **NILS LOFGREN** – guitar / **RY COODER** – steel guitar / **BOB GUILBEAU** – fiddle

Reprise / Reprise

Feb 71. (7") **DOWNTOWN. / CROW JANE LADY** [-] [ ]

Apr 71. (lp)(c) **CRAZY HORSE** [ ] [84] Feb71
– Gone dead train / Dance, dance, dance / Look at all the things / Beggars day / I don't want to talk about it / Downtown / Carolay / Dirty, dirty / Nobody / I'll get by / Crow Jane lady. *(re-iss.Mar86 on 'Edsel') (cd-iss.Apr94)*

Apr 71. (7") **DANCE, DANCE, DANCE. / LOOK AT ALL THE THINGS** [ ] [-]

1971. (7") **DANCE, DANCE, DANCE. / CAROLAY** [-] [ ]

1971. (7") **BEGGAR'S DAY. / DIRTY DIRTY** [-] [ ]

— **GREG LEROY** – guitar, vocals repl. WHITTEN (He later died, see above) **JOHN BLANTON** – keyboards / **GEORGE WHITSELL** – guitar repl. NITZSCHE (producer)

Apr 72. (lp)(c) **LOOSE** [ ] [ ] Jan 72
– Hit and run / Try / One thing I love / Move / All alone now / All the little things / Fair weather friend / You won't miss me / Going home / I don't believe it / Kind of woman / One sided love / And she won't even blow smoke in my direction.

Apr 72. (7") **ALL ALONE NOW. / ONE THING I LOVE** [ ] [ ]

— **RICK CURTIS** – guitar, vocals repl. WHITSELL. **MICHAEL CURTIS** – keyboards, guitar repl. BLANTON

Epic / Epic

Jan 73. (lp)(c) **AT CROOKED CREEK** [ ] [ ]
– Rock and roll band / Love is gone / We ride / Outside lookin' in / Don't keep me burning / Vehicle / Your song / Lady soul / Don't look back / 85 El Paso's.

Feb 73. (7") **ROCK AND ROLL BAND. / OUTSIDE LOOKIN' IN** [-] [ ]

Jun 73. (7") **WE RIDE. / OUTSIDE LOOKING IN** [ ] [-]

— Now concentrated on working for NEIL YOUNG.

— **FRANK SAMPEDRO** – guitar, vox had now been recruited by TALBOT and MOLINA. CRAZY HORSE re-united for one more studio album.

R.C.A. / R.C.A.

Apr 79. (lp)(c) **CRAZY MOON** [ ] [ ] Nov 78
– She's hot / Going down again / Lost and lonely / Dancin' lady / End of the line / New Orleans / That day.

— As a trio, they continued to augment NEIL YOUNG well into the 90's.

CRAZY WORLD OF ARTHUR BROWN (see under ⇒ BROWN, Arthur)

CREAM

Formed: London, England ... mid'66 as earliest ever supergroup by ERIC CLAPTON, GINGER BAKER and JACK BRUCE. All had initial experience with top early 60's bands (see below). This stature, made Robert Stigwood of new 'Reaction' records ('Atco' US), give them contract after seeing them debut at The National Jazz & Blues Festival on 3rd Jul'66. Their initial single 'WRAPPING PAPER', gave them first of many Top 40 hits on both sides of the Atlantic. They played their farewell tour in Nov'68, ending at a sell-out Royal Albert Hall. All members went on to more success from 1969 onwards. • **Style:** Improvised ,blues-rock mixed at times with superb and subtle heavy pop. One of the first bands to introduce long solo pieces, featuring GINGER's superb drumming and of course ERIC's legendary axe-playing, best seen live. • **Songwriters:** Bulk of material written by JACK BRUCE with lyrics by poet/non-member PETE BROWN. They also covered; ROLLIN' AND TUMBLIN' (Muddy Waters) / I'M SO GLAD (Skip James) / FROM FOUR TILL LATE + CROSSROADS (Robert Johnson) / BORN UNDER A BAD SIGN (Booker T. Jones ?)/ made famous by Albert King) / SPOONFUL (Howlin' Wolf) / etc. GEORGE HARRISON co-wrote 'BADGE' with ERIC CLAPTON. • **Trivia:** Producer FELIX PAPPALARDI became unofficial 4th member in 1968.

Recommended: DISRAELI GEARS (*8) / STRANGE BREW – THE VERY BEST OF CREAM (*9) / WHEELS OF FIRE (*7) / (also CREAM tracks on CLAPTON comps.)

ERIC CLAPTON (b.ERIC PATRICK CLAPP, 30 May'45, Ripley, Surrey, England) – guitar, vocals (ex-YARDBIRDS, ex-JOHN MAYALL'S BLUESBREAKERS); **JACK BRUCE** (b.JOHN BRUCE, 14 May'43, Glasgow, Scotland) – vocals, bass (ex-GRAHAM BOND, ex-JOHN MAYALL'S BLUESBREAKERS, ex-MANFRED MANN) / **GINGER BAKER** (b.PETER BAKER, 19 Aug'39, Lewisham, London, England) – drums (ex-GRAHAM BOND ORGANISATION, ex-ALEXIS KORNER'S BLUES INCORPORATED)

		Reaction	Atco
Oct 66.	(7") **WRAPPING PAPER. / CAT'S SQUIRREL**	34	
Dec 66.	(lp) **FRESH CREAM**	6	39

– N.S.U. / Sleepy time time / Dreaming / Sweet wine / Spoonful / Cat's squirrel / Four until late / Rollin' and tumblin' / I'm so glad / Toad. *(re-iss.Jan69, reached No.7 UK, re-iss Oct70 as 'FULL CREAM' & Mar75 as 'CREAM'+ 2 tracks on 'Polydor') (cd-iss.Jan84)* (+=) – Wrapping paper / The coffee song.

Dec 66.	(7") **I FEEL FREE. / N.S.U.**	11	
Jun 67.	(7") **STRANGE BREW. / TALES OF BRAVE ULYSSES** *(re-iss.Jul84 on 'Old Gold')*	17	
Nov 67.	(7") **SPOONFUL. / (part 2)**	-	
Nov 67.	(lp) **DISRAELI GEARS**	5	4

– Strange brew / Sunshine of your love / World of pain / Dance the night away / Blue condition / Tales of brave Ulysses / S.W.L.A.B.R. / We're going wrong / Outside woman blues / Take it back / Mother's lament. *(re-iss.Nov77 on 'RSO', cd-iss.Jan 84 on 'Track')*

Jan 68.	(7") **SUNSHINE OF YOUR LOVE. / SWLABR** *(UK-iss.Sep68 hit No.25.)*	-	5
		Polydor	Atco
May 68.	(7") **ANYONE FOR TENNIS. / PRESSED RAT AND WARTHOG**	40	64

— **FELIX PAPPALARDI** – producer, instr. guested as 4th p/t member

Aug 68.	(d-lp) **WHEELS OF FIRE**	3	1 Jul 68

(re-iss.'72)(re-iss.Jan84 on 'RSO')(above lp was released as d-lp & 2 lp's) (cd-iss.Jan84 & Feb89)

Aug 68.	(lp) **WHEELS OF FIRE – IN THE STUDIO**	7	

– White room / Sitting on top of the world / Passing the time / As you said / Pressed rat and warthog / Politician / Those were the days / Born under a bad sign / Deserted cities of the heart. *(re-iss.Nov77 on 'R.S.O.')*

Aug 68.	(lp) **WHEELS OF FIRE – LIVE AT THE FILLMORE (live)**		

– Crossroads / Spoonful / Traintime / Toad. *(re-iss.Nov77 on 'R.S.O.')*

Jan 69.	(7") **WHITE ROOM. / THOSE WERE THE DAYS**	28	6 Oct 68

— They split around mid-'68. The rest of their releases were posthumous and CLAPTON went solo after forming BLIND FAITH with BAKER. He also went solo. JACK BRUCE went solo, etc.

– compilations, others, etc. –

Note; Below 'Polydor' releases issued on 'Atco' in the US.

Jan 69.	Atco; (7") **CROSSROADS. / PASSING THE TIME**	-	28
Mar 69.	Polydor; (lp)(c) **GOODBYE**	1	2

– I'm so glad * / Politician * / Sitting on top of the world * / Badge / Doing that scrapyard thing / What a bringdown. *(* – live, re-iss.Nov77 & Aug84 on 'RSO') (cd-iss.Jan84. +=) – Anyone for tennis)*

Apr 69.	Polydor; (7") **BADGE. / WHAT A BRINGDOWN** *(re-iss.Oct72)*	18	60
Nov 69.	Polydor; (lp)(c) **BEST OF CREAM** *(re-iss.Nov77 on 'RSO') (re-iss.Apr86 on 'Arcade')*	6	3 Jul 69
Jun 70.	Polydor; (lp)(c) **LIVE CREAM (live)**	4	15 Apr 70

– N.S.U. / Sleepy time time / Lawdy mama / Sweet wine / Rollin' and tumblin'. *(re-iss.Nov77 & Mar85 on 'RSO') (cd-iss.May88)*

Jul 70.	Polydor; (7") **LAWDY MAMA (live). / SWEET WINE (live)**	-	
Jul 71.	Polydor; (7") **I FEEL FREE. / WRAPPING PAPER** *(re-iss. Jul84 on 'Old Gold')*		
Jun 72.	Polydor; (lp)(c) **LIVE CREAM VOL.2**	15	27 Mar 72

– Deserted cities of the heart / White room / Politician / Tales of brave Ulysses / Sunshine of your love. *(re-iss.Nov77 on 'RSO')(cd-iss.May88)*

Apr 73.	Polydor; (d-lp)(c) **HEAVY CREAM**		Oct 72
Oct 80.	Polydor; (lp-box) **CREAM BOX SET**		
Oct 83.	Polydor; (lp)(c) **THE STORY OF CREAM VOL.1**		
Oct 83.	Polydor; (lp)(c) **THE STORY OF CREAM VOL.2**		-
Apr 78.	R.S.O.; (lp)(c) **CREAM VOLUME TWO**		
Feb 83.	R.S.O.; (lp)(c) **STRANGE BREW – THE VERY BEST OF CREAM**		

– Badge / Sunshine of your love / Crossroads / White room / Born under a bad sign / Swlabr / Strange brew / Anyone for tennis / I feel free / Tales of brave Ulysses / Politician / Spoonful. *(cd-iss.Nov87 on 'Polydor')*

Aug 82.	R.S.O.; (7") **BADGE. / TALES OF BRAVE ULYSSES** (12"+=) – White room.		
Jul 86.	R.S.O.; (7") **I FEEL FREE. / BADGE**		
Jul 84.	Old Gold; (7") **WHITE ROOM. / BADGE**		-
Jul 84.	Old Gold; (7") **SUNSHINE OF YOUR LOVE. / ANYONE FOR TENNIS**		-
Feb 89.	Koine; (cd) **LIVE 1968 (live)**		-
Dec 91.	U.F.O.; (cd) **IN GEAR (w/ booklet)**		-
Nov 92.	I.T.M.; (cd) **THE ALTERNATIVE ALBUM**		-
Dec 92.	Pickwick; (cd)(lp) **DESERTED CITIES: THE CREAM COLLECTION**		-
Feb 95.	Polydor; (cd)(c) **THE VERY BEST OF CREAM**		

CREATION

Formed: Hertfordshire, England ... 1961 as 5-piece! MARK FOUR by KENNY PICKETT, JACK JONES and EDDIE PHILLIPS. Under the guidance of manager ROBERT STIGWOOD, they released a couple of flop singles for 'Mercury'. After two more for others, they changed their line-up in mid-66 and became The CREATION. They also employed new manager TONY STRATTON-SMITH, who found American producer SHEL TALMY and a new label 'Planet'. They unleashed 2 superb 45's in 1966 'MAKING TIME' and 'PAINTER MAN', which both hit UK Top 50, helped by alleged chart hyping from TONY. The latter also gave them a bit pocket money by hitting No.1 in Germany. However, when they moved to 'Polydor' in 1967 they ran out of steam and split the year after. Unfortunately their only lp release had been in Germany, where they had found some other success. • **Style:** Pop-art loud + heavy mods similar to The WHO or The KINKS. PHILLIPS was the first person to play guitar with a violin bow, a feat later achieved by JIMMY PAGE of LED ZEPPELIN. • **Songwriters:** PICKETT or PHILLIPS plus covers:- ROCK AROUND THE CLOCK (Bill Haley) / TRY IT BABY (Marvin Gaye) / LIKE A ROLLING STONE (Bob Dylan) / BONY MORONIE (Larry Williams). • **Trivia:** In 1970, PICKETT co-wrote UK No.1 hit 'Grandad' for CLIVE DUNN (Dad's Army) with HERBIE FLOWERS. PICKETT was later to write 'TEACHER TEACHER' for DAVE EDMUNDS, before he co-wrote some more songs with BILLY BREMNER. **Legacy:** PAINTER MAN was a 1979 UK Top 10 hit for BONEY M, while much later The GODFATHERS (in 1990) and RIDE (in 1994) covered HOW DOES IT FEEL TO FEEL. Many have been inspired by them including TELEVISION PERSONALITIES / TIMES / BIFF BANG POW and the label 'Creation'.

Recommended: HOW DOES IT FEEL TO FEEL (*8)

MARK FOUR

KENNY PICKETT (b. 3 Sep'47, Ware, England) – vocals / **EDDIE PHILLIPS** (b.EDWIN, 15 Aug'45, Leytonstone, England) – lead guitar / **MICK THOMPSON** – rhythm guitar / **JOHN DALTON** – bass / **JACK JONES** (b. 8 Nov'44, Northampton, England) – drums

		Mercury	not issued
May 64.	(7") **ROCK AROUND THE CLOCK. / SLOW DOWN**		-
Aug 64.	(7") **TRY IT BABY. / CRAZY COUNTRY HOP**		-
		Decca	not issued
Aug 65.	(7") **HURT ME IF YOU WILL. / I'M LEAVING**		-
		Fontana	not issued
Feb 66.	(7") **WORK ALL DAY (SLEEP ALL NIGHT). / GOING DOWN FAST**		-

— Split after final gig on 6th June 1966. DALTON joined The KINKS.

CREATION

BOB GARNER – bass (ex-TONY SHERIDAN BAND) repl. THOMPSON

		Planet	Planet
Jun 66.	(7") **MAKING TIME. / TRY AND STOP ME**	49	-
Oct 66.	(7") **PAINTER MAN. / BIFF BANG POW**	36	-

KIM GARDNER – bass (ex-BIRDS) repl. GARNER

		Polydor	not issued
Jun 67.	(7") **IF I STAY TOO LONG. / NIGHTMARES**		-
Oct 67.	(7") **LIFE IS JUST BEGINNING. / THROUGH MY EYES**		-
Feb 68.	(7") **HOW DOES IT FEEL TO FEEL. / TOM TOM**		-

RON WOOD – guitar (ex-BIRDS) repl. DIGGER who had briefly repl. PICKETT

— **PICKETT** returned to repl. PHILLIPS + GARDNER

May 68.	(7") **MIDWAY DOWN. / THE GIRLS ARE NAKED**		-

— Disbanded soon after above. PICKETT continued to write for SHEL TALMY and he also became road manager for LED ZEPPELIN in America. RON WOOD joined The FACES and later became a member of The ROLLING STONES. GARDNER co-formed ASHTON, GARDNER & DYKE who had a 1970 Top 3 hit with 'RESURRECTION SHUFFLE'. He later formed BADGER. JACK JONES drifted into cabaret session work.

— CREATION re-formed in the mid-80's with **PHILLIPS, PICKETT, NOBBY DALTON** – bass (ex-KINKS) + **MICK AVORY** – drums (ex-KINKS).

		Jet	not issued
Apr 87.	(12"ep) **A SPIRIT CALLED LOVE. / MAKING TIME / MUMBO JUMBO**		-

— **PHILLIPS**, etc, without PICKETT formed pub band CUCKOOS NEST. In 1994, The CREATION re-formed with **PICKETT, JONES + PHILLIPS.**

		Creation	not issued
Jul 94.	(7"+cd-s) **CREATION. / SHOCK HORROR / POWER SURGE**		-

– compilations, etc. –

Sep 73.	Charisma; (lp) **CREATION '66-67**		-
Oct 73.	Charisma; (7") **MAKING TIME. / PAINTER MAN** *(re-iss.Nov77 on 'Raw')*		-
Sep 82.	Edsel; (lp) **HOW DOES IT FEEL TO FEEL**		-

– How does it feel to feel / Life is just beginning / Through my eyes / Ostrich man / I am the walker / Tom Tom / The girls are naked / Painter man / Try and stop me / Biff bang pow / Making time / Cool jerk / For all that I am / Nightmares / Midway down / Can I join your band?. *(cd-iss.Aug90)*

May 84.	Edsel; (7") **MAKING TIME. / UNCLE BERT**		-
Feb 84.	Line; (lp) **WE ARE PAINTERMEN**	-	- GERM

— (bove originally released in Germany 1967)
Feb 84. Line; (lp) **RECREATION** [-] [-]
1985. Bam Caruso; (7"ep) **LIVE AT THE BEAT SCENE CLUB** [ ] [-]

CREATURES (see under ⇒ SIOUXSIE & THE BANSHEES)

CREDIT TO THE NATION

Formed: Bristol, England ... by 17 year-old MC FUSION (MATTHEW HANSON). Deposited a minor hit in 1993, when 'CALL IT WHAT YOU WANT' was also NME's single of the week. • **Style:** Described as the black rapping Dennis The Menace. • **Songwriters:** HANSON w / MARTIN & COULTER, except sampled riffs from SMELLS LIKE TEEN SPIRIT (Nirvana) on 'CALL IT WHAT YOU WANT'.

Recommended: TAKE DIS (*7)

MC FUSION – vocals (also of CHUMBAWAMBA) / **MARTIN / COULTER**

Agit Prop / not issued

Jan 92. (12") **PAY THE PRICE. / STOP FOOLING AROUND / MAKE IT A BETTER DAY** [ ] [-]
(re-iss.May93)

One Little Indian / Elektra?

May 93. (7")(c-s) **CALL IT WHAT YOU WANT. / THE LADY NEEDS RESPECT** [57] [ ]
(12"+=)(cd-s+=) – ('A'mix).
Aug 93. (12")(c-s)(cd-s) **HEAR NO BULLSHIT SEE NO BULLSHIT SAY NO BULLSHIT. / OLD HIM SELECTOR / TIME TO GET HYPE (remix)** [ ] [ ]
— (In Sep 93 were credited on 'ENOUGH IS ENOUGH' with CHUMBAWAMBA; hit UK 56)
Feb 94. (12"ep)(c-ep)(cd-ep) **TEENAGE SENSATION / PUMP YOUR FIST. / CALL IT WHAT YOU WANT (live) / ENOUGH IS ENOUGH** [24] [ ]
Mar 94. (cd)(c)(lp) **TAKE DIS** [20] [ ]
– Pressure / Hear no bullshit, see no bullshit, say no bullshit / The lady needs respect / Raggamonarchy / Man made / Honey / Teenage sensation / Teen groove / Sowing the seeds of hatred / Filth / Rising tide / Old him selector / Money talks / Call it what you want / Puppet.
May 94. (7"red)(c-s)(12")(cd-s) **SOWING THE SEEDS OF HATRED. / MR.EGO TRIP** [72] [ ]
— Early in 1995, MATTY suffered two nervous breakdowns and sectioned under the mental health act. COMMON KNOWLEDGE (SIMON LANZON) was sacked mid-95 and duly took legal action.
Jul 95. (c-s) **LIAR LIAR / Y'AIN'T GOTTA CLUE** [60] [ ]
(12"+=)(cd-s+=) – Liar liar inda jungle / Liar liar (12"remix).
Sep 95. (c-s) **MAD DOG / MAD DOG (original)** [ ] [ ]
(12"+=)(cd-s+=) – Free ya mind / Mad dog – pedigree chum mix.

CREEDENCE CLEARWATER REVIVAL

Formed: California, USA . . . late 1959 as schoolgroup The BLUE VELVETS by JOHN FOGERTY, STU COOK and DOUG CLIFFORD. JOHN soon invited other multi-instrumentalist and brother TOM. After one 45 on a local label, they became The GOLLIWOGS in 1964. They signed to 'Fantasy' records by boss Hy Weiss. Around mid-1967, they became CREEDENCE CLEARWATER REVIVAL after JOHN and DOUG were earlier drafted. Late in 1968, their first single 'SUSIE Q', helped by live stature, broke them into the US Top 20. The following 2 years, saw them hit No.1 in the US with single 'BAD MOON RISING', and peak on both sides of the Atlantic with album chart topper 'COSMO'S FACTORY' in 1970. • **Style:** Fused swamp rock with traditional country blues and basic rock'n'roll. The GOLLIWOGS had been influenced by British beat combos of '63-64. • **Songwriters:** JOHN wrote most of material. Also covered; SUSIE Q (Dale Hawkins) / I PUT A SPELL ON YOU (Screamin' Jay Hawkins) / I HEARD IT THROUGH THE GRAPEVINE (hit; Marvin Gaye) / OOBY DOOBY (Roy Orbison) / HELLO MARY LOU (Ricky Nelson) / etc. • **Miscellaneous:** TOM FOGERTY was to die of tuberculosis on 6 Sep'90.

Recommended: CREEDENCE GOLD (*8)

The BLUE VELVETS

JOHN FOGERTY (b.28 May'45, Berkeley, California)– vocals, guitar / **TOM FOGERTY** (b. 9 Nov'41, Berkeley)– rhythm guitar, piano / **STU COOK** (b.25 Apr'45, Portland, California)– bass / **DOUG 'COSMO' CLIFFORD** (b.24 Apr'45, Palo Alto, California)- **drums**

not issued / Orkhestra

1962. (7") **HAVE YOU EVER BEEN LONELY. / BONITA** [-] [ ]

The GOLLIWOGS

same line-up (TOM sang lead on first)

not issued / Fantasy

Nov 64. (7") **DON'T TELL ME NO LIES. / LITTLE GIRL** [-] [ ]
1965. (7") **YOU CAME WALKING. / WHERE YOU BEEN** [-] [ ]
1965. (7") **YOU CAN'T BE TRUE. / YOU GOT NOTHIN' ON ME** [-] [ ]

Vocalion / Scorpio

Jan 66. (7") **BROWN-EYED GIRL. / YOU BETTER BE CAREFUL** [ ] [ ]
Mar 66. (7") **FRAGILE CHILD. / FIGHT FIRE** [ ] [ ]
Dec 66. (7") **WALKING ON THE WATER. / YOU BETTER GET IT** [-] [ ]
Nov 67. (7") **PORTERVILLE. / CALL IT PRETENDING** [ ] [ ]
(above single was soon later credited to below group name)*(also a compilation album of some singles above was released in '74 on 'Fantasy')*

CREDENCE CLEARWATER REVIVAL

same line-up

Liberty / Fantasy

Sep 68. (7") **SUZIE Q (Pt.1). / SUZIE Q (Pt.2)** [-] [11]
Nov 68. (7") **I PUT A SPELL ON YOU. / WALK ON THE WATER** [-] [ ]
Apr 69. (lp) **CREEDENCE CLEARWATER REVIVAL** [ ] [52] Jul 68
– I put a spell on you / Suzie Q / The working man / Ninety-nine and a half (won't do) / Get down woman / Porterville / Gloomy / Walk on the water. *(re-iss.Mar73 & Jul84 & Aug87 +cd.on 'Fantasy')*
May 69. (7") **PROUD MARY. / BORN ON THE BAYOU** [8] [2] Jan 69
Jun 69. (lp) **BAYOU COUNTRY** [ ] [7] Feb 69
– Born on the bayou / Bootleg / Graveyard train / Good golly Miss Molly / Penthouse pauper / Keep on chooglin' / Proud Mary. *(hit UK 62 May70) (re-iss.Mar73 & Aug87 on 'Fantasy' +cd)*
Aug 69. (7") **BAD MOON RISING. / LODI** [1] [2] / [52] May 69
Nov 69. (7") **GREEN RIVER. / COMMOTION** [19] [2] Jul 69 / [30]
Dec 69. (lp)(c) **GREEN RIVER** [20] [1] Sep 69
– Green river / Commotion / Tombstone shadow / Wrote a song for everyone / Bad moon rising / Lodi / Cross-tie walker / Sinister purpose / Lodi / Wrote a song for everyone / Night time is the right time. *(re-iss.Mar73, Jul84, & cd Aug87 on 'Fantasy')*
Feb 70. (7") **DOWN ON THE CORNER. / FORTUNATE SON** [31] [3] Oct 69 / [14]
Mar 70. (lp)(c) **WILLY AND THE POOR BOYS** [10] [3] Dec 69
– Down on the corner / It came out of the sky / Cotton fields / Poor boy shuffle / Feelin' blue / Fortunate son / Don't look now (it ain't you or me) / The midnight special / Side of the road / Effigy. *(re-iss.Mar73 & Jul84 & Aug87 +cd on 'Fantasy')*
Mar 70. (7") **TRAVELLIN' MAN. / WHO'LL STOP THE RAIN** [8] [2] Jan 70
Jun 70. (7") **UP AROUND THE BEND. / RUN THROUGH THE JUNGLE** [3] [4] Apr 70
Aug 70. (7") **LONG AS I CAN SEE THE LIGHT. / LOOKIN' OUT MY BACK DOOR** [20] [2] B-side
Sep 70. (lp)(c) **COSMO'S FACTORY** [1] [1] Jul 70
– Ramble tamble / Before you accuse me / Travelin' band / Ooby dooby / Lookin' out my back door / Run through the jungle / Up around the bend / My baby left me / Who'll stop the rain / I heard it through the grapevine / Long as I can see the light. *(re-iss.Mar73, Jul84, & cd.Aug87 on 'Fantasy')*
Jan 71. (lp)(c) **PENDULUM** [23] [5] Dec 70
– Pagan baby / Sailor's lament / Chameleon / Have you ever seen the rain / (Wish I could) Hideaway / Born to move / Hey tonight / It's just a thought / Molina / Rude awakening No.2. *(re-iss.Mar73 & Nov89 +cd. on 'Fantasy')*
Mar 71. (7") **HAVE YOU EVER SEEN THE RAIN / HEY TONIGHT** [36] [8] Jan 71
— now a trio when TOM FOGERTY departed to go solo (Feb 71).

United Art / Fantasy

Jul 71. (7") **SWEET HITCH-HIKER. / DOOR TO DOOR** [36] [6]
Jul 71. (lp)(c) **MARDI GRAS** [ ] [12] Apr 71
– Lookin' for a reason / Take it like a friend / Need someone to hold / Tearin' up the country / Hello Mary Lou / Someday never comes / What are you gonna do / Hello Mary Lou / Door to door / Sweet hitch-hiker. *(re-iss.Mar73) (re-iss.Jul84 & cd-iss.Nov89 on 'Fantasy')*
Apr 72. (7") **SOMEDAY NEVER COMES. / TEARIN' UP THE COUNTRY** [-] [25]
— Split Oct72.

– compilations etc. –

Mar 72. Fantasy; (d-lp)(d-c) **COSMO'S FACTORY / WILLY AND THE POOR BOYS** [ ] [ ]
Dec 72. Fantasy; (7") **BORN ON THE BAYOU. / I PUT A SPELL ON YOU** [ ] [ ]
Jan 73. Fantasy; (lp)(c) **CREEDENCE GOLD** [ ] [15] Nov 72
(cd-iss.Sep91)
– Proud Mary / Down on the corner / Bad Moon rising / I heard it through the grapevine / Midnight special / Have you ever seen the rain / Born on the bayou / Suzie Q.
Mar 73. Fantasy; (7") **IT CAME OUT OF THE SKY. / SIDE O' THE ROAD** [ ] [ ]
Sep 73. Fantasy; (lp)(c) **MORE CREEDENCE GOLD** [ ] [61] Jul 73
(cd-iss.Sep91)
– Hey tonight / Run through the jungle / Fortunate son / Bootleg / Lookin' out my back door / Molina / Who'll stop the rain / Sweet hitch-hiker / Good golly Miss Molly / I put a spell on you / Don't look now / Lodi / Porterville / Up around the bend.
May 74. Fantasy; (lp)(c) **LIVE IN EUROPE (live)** [ ] [ ] Nov 73
– Born on the bayou / Green river / It came out of the sky / Door to door / Travellin' band / Fortunate son / Porterville / Up around the bend / Suzie Q / Commotion / Lodi. *(re-iss.+cd.Feb90)*
Mar 76. Fantasy; (d-lp)(c) **CREEDENCE CHRONICLE** [ ] [ ]
– Suzie Q / I put a spell on you / Proud Mary / Bad Moon rising / Lodi / Green river / Commotion / Down on the corner / Fortunate son / Travellin' band / Who'll stop the rain / Up around the bend / Run through the jungle / Lookin' out my back door / Long as I can see the light / Have you ever seen the rain? / Hey tonight / Sweet hitch-hiker / Someday never comes.
(cd-iss.Jun87 on 'Big Beat' += I heard it through the grapevine)
Mar 76. Fantasy; (7") **I HEARD IT THROUGH THE GRAPEVINE. / GOOD GOLLY MISS MOLLY** [ ] [43] Dec 75

Jul 77. Fantasy; (7") **BAD MOON RISING. / PROUD MARY / GREEN RIVER** [ ] [ ]
Nov 78. Fantasy; (7") **WHO'LL STOP THE RAIN. / PROUD MARY / HEY TONIGHT** [ ] [ ]
Jun 79. Fantasy; (lp)(c) **GREATEST HITS (20 GOLDEN)** [35] [ ]
Jul 79. Fantasy; (7") **I HEARD IT THROUGH THE GRAPEVINE. / (ROCKIN' ALL OVER THE WORLD ("JOHN FOGERTY")** [ ] [43]
(12") ('A'side) / Keep on chooglin' (extended).
Feb 81. M.F.P./ US= Fantasy; (lp)(c) **LIVE AT THE ROYAL ALBERT HALL (live)** [ ] [62] Dec 80
(re-iss.+cd.Aug89 as 'THE CONCERT')
Feb 82. M.F.P./ US= Fantasy; (lp)(c) **THE HITS ALBUM** [ ] [ ]
Aug 81. Golden Grooves; (7") **PROUD MARY. / UP AROUND THE BEND** [ ] [ ]
Oct 81. Golden Grooves; (7") **BAD MOON RISING. / GOOD GOLLY MISS MOLLY** [ ] [ ]
Sep 85. Old Gold; (7") **BAD MOON RISING. / GOOD GOLLY MISS MOLLY** [ ] [-]
Sep 85. Old Gold; (7") **PROUD MARY. / TRAVELLIN' BAND** [ ] [-]
Oct 85. Impression; (d-lp)(c) **THE CREEDENCE COLLECTION** [68] [ ]
Jun 88. Ace-Fantasy; (7") **BAD MOON RISING. / HAVE YOU EVER SEEN THE RAIN?** [ ] [ ]
(12"+=) – Keep on chooglin'.
Jun 88. Ace-Fantasy; (lp)(c) **THE BEST OF – VOLUME 1** [ ] [ ]
1988. Ace-Fantasy; (cd) **CHOOGLIN'** [-] [ ]
(re-iss.Nov92)
Aug 88. Ace-Fantasy; (lp)(c) **THE BEST OF – VOLUME 2** [ ] [ ]
Dec 92. Ace-Fantasy; (cd) **CREEDENCE COUNTRY** [ ] [ ]
May 88. Arcade; (cd) **THE COMPLETE HITS ALBUM VOL.1** [ ] [-]
May 88. Arcade; (cd) **THE COMPLETE HITS ALBUM Vol.2** [ ] [-]
Apr 92. Epic; (7") **BAD MOON RISING. / AS LONG AS I CAN SEE THE LIGHT** [71] [ ]
(cd-s+=) –
Aug 95. Old Gold; (cd-s) **TRAVELIN' BAND. / WHO'LL STOP THE RAIN** [ ] [-]
Sep 95. Old Gold; (cd-s) **UP AROUND THE BEND / RUN THROUGH THE JUNGLE** [ ] [-]

BLUE RIDGE RANGERS

was JOHN FOGERTY's first total solo venture

Fantasy / Fantasy

Dec 72. (7") **JAMBALAYA (ON THE BAYOU). / WORKING ON A BUILDING** [ ] [16]
Apr 73. (lp)(c) **BLUE RIDGE RANGERS** [ ] [47]
– Blue ridge mountain blues / Somewhere listening (for my name) / You're the reason / Jambalaya (on the bayou) / She thinks I still care / California blues (blue yodel #4) / Workin' on a building / Please help me I'm falling / Have thine own way, Lord / I ain't never / Hearts of stone / Today I started loving you. *(re-iss.Sep87, + cd-iss. 1991)*
May 73. (7") **HEARTS OF STONE. / SOMEWHERE LISTENING (FOR MY NAME)** [ ] [37] Mar 73
Oct 73. (7") **YOU DON'T OWE ME. / BACK IN THE HILLS** [-] [ ]

JOHN FOGERTY

solo, plays, sings everything

not issued / Fantasy

Mar 74. (7") **COMING DOWN THE ROAD. / RICOCHET** [-] [ ]

Asylum / Asylum

Sep 75. (7") **ROCKIN' ALL OVER THE WORLD. / THE WALL** [ ] [27]
Oct 75. (lp)(c) **JOHN FOGERTY** [ ] [78]
– Rockin' all over the world / You rascal you / The wall / Travelin' high / Lonely teardrops / Almost Saturday night / Where the river flows / Sea cruise / Dream – Song / Flyin' away. *(re-iss.+cd.Sep87 on 'Ace-Fantasy')*
Dec 75. (7") **ALMOST SATURDAY NIGHT. / SEA CRUISE** [-] [78]
May 76. (7") **YOU GOT THE MAGIC. / EVIL THING** [ ] [87]

JOHN FOGERTY

returned after 9 years complete with new session people.

Warners / Warners

Jan 85. (7") **THE OLD MAN DOWN THE ROAD. / BIG TRAIN (TO MEMPHIS)** [ ] [10] Dec 84
Feb 85. (lp)(c) **CENTERFIELD** [48] [1] Jan 85
– The old man down the road / Rock and roll girls / Big train (from Memphis) / I saw it on T.V. / Mr. Greed / Searchlight / Centerfield / I can't help myself / Zant Kant danz. *(cd-iss.Nov93)*
Jun 85. (7") **ROCK AND ROLL GIRLS. / CENTERFIELD** [ ] [20/44] Mar 85

—— now with **JOHN ROBINSON** – drums, percussion / **NEIL STUBENHAUS** – bass

Aug 86. (7") **CHANGE IN THE WEATHER. / MY TOOT TOOT** [-] [ ]
Oct 86. (lp)(c)(cd) **EYE OF THE ZOMBIE** [44] [26]
– Goin' back home / Eye of the zombie / Headlines / Knockin' on your door / Change in the weather / Violence is golden / Wasn't that a woman / Soda pop / Sail away.
Oct 86. (7") **EYE OF THE ZOMBIE. / CONFESS** [ ] [81]
(12"+=) – I can't help myself.

CRICKETS

Formed: Lubbock, Texas, USA . . . Feb'57 as back-up musicians to augment rising star BUDDY HOLLY. They consisted of NIKI SULLIVAN, JOE MAUDLIN and JERRY ALLISON, with the latter having been part of HOLLY's band since 1955. As a marketing ploy, BUDDY sang solo, and with group crediting latter as "CRICKETS". Their first record (a re-recording of a past HOLLY solo cut) 'THAT'LL BE THE DAY', hit US + UK No.1 in the Autumn of '57, and bolted HOLLY to overnight stardom. The CRICKETS' next song 'OH BOY!', hit both Top 10's once again. In Oct'58, after 2 more Top 30 triumphs 'MAYBE, BABY' & 'THINK IT OVER', BUDDY decided to set up base in New York, leaving them CRICKETS group name. Chaos in the ranks ensued, as members came and went as easy as they arrived (see further below). The tragedy of HOLLY's death on 2nd Feb'59, didn't help much too, as they were about to re-unite for live work in the UK. In Apr'59, they had first hit 'LOVE'S MADE A FOOL OF YOU' without HOLLY. Their appeal lay mainly in the UK at this time, where they were still enjoying minor hits. In 1962, they recorded covers album with BOBBY VEE, and this partnership led to the lp making No.2 in the UK. Prior to this, they had achieved a return to UK Top 5, with 'DON'T EVER CHANGE'. After a few more successes and with the advent of The BEATLES, they decided to disband in Mar'65. JERRY ALLISON reformed them many times, but with no great deal of fortune. • **Style:** Rock'n'roll was put aside in the 60's for pop, and then 70's country. • **Songwriters:** From 1959 onwards, ALLISON and CURTIS were main contributors. Selective covers were:- DON'T EVER CHANGE (Goffin-King) / A FOOL NEVER LEARNS (hit.Andy Williams) / RIGHT OR WRONG (Sharon Sheeley-Jackie DeShannon) / LONELY AVENUE (Ray Charles) / LOVESICK BLUES (Hank Williams) / I WANT TO HOLD YOUR HAND (Beatles) / etc. • **Trivia:** SONNY & JERRY played on 60's session with EVERLY BROTHERS and EDDIE COCHRAN. Their sessions also included ERIC CLAPTON, LEON RUSSELL, BILLY PRESTON, etc.

Recommended: ROCK'N'ROLL MASTERS – THE BEST OF . . . (*6)

"The CRICKETS". BUDDY HOLLY – vocals, guitar / **NIKI SULLIVAN** – rhythm guitar / **JOE B. MAUDLIN** – bass / **JERRY J.I. ALLISON** (b.31 Aug'39, Hillsboro) – drums (also of BUDDY HOLLY's solo back-up)

Vogue Coral / Brunswick

Sep 57. (7") **THAT'LL BE THE DAY. / I'M LOOKING FOR SOMEONE TO LOVE** [1] [1] May 57
(re-iss.Jul82 on 'Old Gold')

Coral / Brunswick

Dec 57. (7") **OH BOY!. / NOT FADE AWAY** [3] [10] Oct 57
(re-iss.Jul82 on 'Old Gold')
Feb 58. (lp) **THE CHIRPING CRICKETS** [ ] [ ] Nov 57
– Oh boy! / Not fade away / You've got to love / Maybe baby / It's too late / Tell me how / That'll be the day / I'm looking for someone to love / An empty cup (and a broken date) / Send me some lovin' / Last night / Rock me baby. *(US re-iss.Feb62 as 'BUDDY HOLLY & THE CRICKETS' on 'Coral') (UK re-iss.Dec69, Feb74 + Jul75 on 'Coral') (re-iss.Mar83 + Nov86 on 'M.C.A.') (cd-iss.Oct92 on 'Sequel')*
Feb 58. (7") **MAYBE BABY. / TELL ME HOW** [4] [17]
(re-iss.Jul82 on 'Old Gold')
Jul 58. (7") **THINK IT OVER. / FOOL'S PARADISE** [11] [27/58] May 58
Sep 58. (7") **REAL WILD CHILD. /** [-] [68]
Oct 58. (7") **IT'S SO EASY. / LONESOME TEARS** [ ] [ ] Sep58

—— Split Oct58, when SULLIVAN then HOLLY departed. BUDDY HOLLY continued his solo career, until his untimely death 2 Feb'59.

—— JERRY & JOE re-formed The CRICKETS in '59 with new recruits **EARL SINKS** – vocals / **SONNY CURTIS** – guitar, vocals (same label)

Apr 59. (7") **LOVE'S MADE A FOOL OF YOU. / SOMEONE, SOMEONE** [26] [ ]

—— briefly **TOMMY ALLSUP** – guitar (on tour only) repl. CURTIS, who returned

Dec 59. (7") **WHEN YOU ASK ABOUT LOVE. / DEBORAH** [27] [ ]

—— SONNY CURTIS took over vocals when EARL SINKS split.

Apr 60. (7") **MORE THAN I CAN SAY. / BABY MY HEART** [42] [ ]

—— **DAVID BOX** – vocals repl. CURTIS who was drafted into the US army added **ERNIE HALL** – drums (on 'B' side) (ALLISON now on guitar)

1960. (7") **PEGGY SUE GOT MARRIED. / DON'TCHA KNOW** [ ] [ ]

—— trimmed to just ALLISON and MAUDLIN, (BOX went solo before dying in a plane crash)

1960. (7") **I FOUGHT THE LAW. / A SWEET LOVE** [ ] [ ]
Mar 61. (lp) **IN STYLE WITH THE CRICKETS** [13] [ ] '60
– More than I can say / Rockin' pneumonia and the boogie woogie flu / Great balls of fire / Ting-a-ling / Just this once / Deborah / Baby my heart / When you ask about love / Time will tell / A sweet love / I fought the law / Love's made a fool of you / Someone, someone / Doncha know / Why did you leave? / Smooth guy / So you're in love / Peggy Sue got married *(re-iss.Sep75 on 'M.C.A.') (re-iss.cd+c May94 on 'MCA')*

—— JERRY ALLISON now alone because MAUDLIN quit, recruited sessioners **EARL PALMER** – drums / **ERNIE FREEMAN** – piano / **RED CALLENDER** – guitar / **TOMMY ALLSUP** – guitar returned (ALLISON – vocals backed by BOBBY VEE)

London / Liberty

1961. (7") **HE'S OLD ENOUGH TO KNOW BETTER. / I'M FEEELING BETTER** [ ] [ ]

—— (solo artist **BOBBY VEE** – vocals) **VEE, ALLISON,** the house sessioners plus **JERRY NAYLOR and JOE B. MAUDLIN**

Liberty / Liberty

Oct 61. (lp) **BOBBY VEE MEETS THE CRICKETS (as "BOBBY VEE & THE CRICKETS")** [2] [ ] Jul 61
– Peggy Sue / Bo Diddley / Someday (When i'm gone from you) / Well . . . all right / I gotta know / Lookin' for love / Sweet little sixteen / When you're in love / Lucille / Girl of my best friend / Little Queenie / The girl can't help it / Lonely weekends (version 1) / It's too late (version 1) / Come on baby / Mountain of love / No one knows / Shanghaied / Keep a knockin' / Lonely weekends (version 2) / It's too late (version 2) / Buddy Holly medley / What to do / Crying, waiting, hoping / Learning the game *(hit UK chart Oct62) (re-iss.1977 on 'Sunset')*

— **ALLISON + NAYLOR** brought in guest **GLEN CAMPBELL** – guitar, vocals

Liberty Liberty

Jun 62. (7") **DON'T EVER CHANGE. / I'M NOT A BAD GUY** [5] [ ]

— **NAYLOR** (now lead vocals) was joined by **SONNY CURTIS** – vocals, guitar (from EVERLY BROTHERS) / **GLEN D.HARDIN** – piano, piano bass added on tour **DON GROOM** – drums (of MIKE BERRY'S – OUTLAWS)

Nov 62. (7") **LITTLE HOLLYWOOD GIRL. / PARISIAN GIRL** [ ] [ ]

Nov 62. (lp) **SOMETHING OLD, SOMETHING NEW, SOMETHING BLUE, SOMETHING ELSE!** [ ] [ ]
– What'd I say / Searchin' / Willie and the hand jive / Love is strange / Don't ever change / Little Hollywood girl / He's old enough to know better / Parisian girl / Pretty blue eyes / Blue, blue day / Summertime blues / Blue Monday.

Jan 63. (7") **MY LITTLE GIRL. / TEARDROPS FALL LIKE RAIN** [17] [ ]

Mar 63. (7") **DON'T SAY YOU LOVE ME. / APRIL AVENUE** [-] [ ]

May 63. (7") **DON'T TRY TO CHANGE ME. / LOST AND ALONE** [37] [-]

1963. (7") **RIGHT OR WRONG. / YOU CAN'T BE INBETWEEN** [ ] [-]

— augmented by **JAMES BURTON** – guitar / **LEON RUSSELL** – piano

1964. (7") **LONELY AVENUE. / YOU CAN'T BE IN-BETWEEN** [-] [ ]

1964. (7") **LONELY AVENUE. / PLAYBOY** [ ] [-]

— **JERRY ALLISON** – vocals, guitar returned to repl. NAYLOR (heart attack) added **BUZZ CASON** – multi (drums, guitar)

Jun 64. (7") **(THEY CALL HER) LA BAMBA. / ALL OVER YOU** [21] [ ]

— Disbanded when CURTIS re-joined EVERLY BROTHERS. HARDIN and BURTON formed The SHINDIGS. Others now

JERRY ALLISON & THE CRICKETS

with **CASON** and the fully recovered **NAYLOR**. (same label)

1964. (7") **I THINK I'VE CAUGHT THE BLUES. / WE GOTTA GET TOGETHER** [ ] [ ]

Feb 65. (7") **NOW HEAR THIS. / EVERYBODY'S GOT A LITTLE PROBLEM** [ ] [ ]

The CRICKETS

re-formed with **JERRY ALLISON / LARRY TRIDER** – vocals / **LARRY WELBORN** – guitar / Note: next 45 rec.'63 with **SONNY CURTIS** – vocals

Apr 66. (7") **APRIL AVENUE. / DON'T SAY YOU LOVE ME** [ ] [-]

— In 1968 they were now **ALLISON, CURTIS + HARDIN**

not issued Music Fac.

1968. (7") **MILLION DOLLAR MOVIE. / A MILLION MILES APART** [-] [ ]
(UK-iss.Mar84 on 'Rollercoaster')

— now with guest **BONNIE BRAMLETT**

C.B.S. Barnaby

1971. (lp) **ROCKIN' 50's, ROCK'N'ROLL** (new recordings) [ ] [ ]

— added **RICK GRECH** – bass (ex-FAMILY, ex-BLIND FAITH, ex-TRAFFIC)

Philips Philips

1972. (7") **LOVESICK BLUES. / MY ROCKIN' DAYS** [ ] [ ]

Feb 73. (lp)(c) **BUBBLEGUM, POP, BALLADS & BOOGIES** [ ] [ ]
– I can make you feel it / Hayride / Wasn't it nice in New York City / Rockin' pneumonia and boogie woogie flu / Lovesick blues / My rockin' days / I've got a thing about you baby / On the outside looking in / Keep a knockin' / Day gig / Destiny's child.

1973. (7") **WASN'T IT NICE IN NEW YORK CITY. / HAYRIDE** [ ] [ ]

— now quintet when added **ALBERT LEE** – guitar (ex-HEADS, HANDS & FEET) soon guest **STEVE KRIKORIAN** – vocals repl. HARDIN (re-to ELVIS PRESLEY)

Mercury Vertigo

1974. (7") **OOH LAS VEGAS. / RHYME AND TIME** [ ] [ ]

1974. (lp) **REMNANTS** [ ] [ ]
– Find out what's happening / Lay lady lay down / Rock and roll man / I'm gonna ruin your health / Rhyme and time / Decoy baker / Losin' streak / Atmore / The truth is still the same / Hitchhike out to Venus / Ooh Las Vegas / Draggin' chains.

1974. (lp) **A LONG WAY BACK FROM LUBBOCK** [ ] [-]
– Ain't protestin' / An American love affair / Bony Moronie / Decoy Baker / Find out what's happening / He's got a way with women / I got a thing about you baby / I like your music / Lay lady lay down / Now and then it's gonna rain / Ooh Las Vegas / Rhyme and time / You make it way too hard

— (late '74) LEE joined JOE COCKER Band and GRECH joined JOHNNY RIVERS tour. The other trio carried on until 1976 when bass player JOE OSBOURNE repl. STEVE. In 1977, still touring; **ALLISON** and **CURTIS** were joined by **JOE B.MAUDLIN.**

Roller-coaster Roller-coaster

Jul 79. (7") **CRUISIN' IT. / ROCK AROUND WITH OLLIE VEE** [ ] [ ]

— Between 1978 + 1983, The CRICKETS backed WAYLON JENNINGS.

— (1985-88+) **GORDON PAYNE** – vocals, guitar (ex-W.JENNINGS) repl. CURTIS who went solo.

C.B.S. Columbia

Sep 88. (7") **T-SHIRT. / HOLLY WOULD** [ ] [ ]
(12"+=)(cd-s+=) – Forever in mind.

Oct 88. (lp)(c)(cd) **T-SHIRT** [ ] [ ]
– Your m-m-memory is t-t-torturing me / Rockin' socks / The weekend / Holly would / T-shirt / Forever in mind / Cruisin' it / True piece / Don't tell me that you can't come out tonight / That's all she wrote.

– compilations, others, etc. –

Jan 58. Brunswick; (7"ep) **THE CHIRPING CRICKETS** [-] [ ]
– That'll be the day / Oh! boy / Looking for someone to love / Not fade away.

Sep 58. Brunswick; (7"ep) **THE SOUND OF THE CRICKETS** [-] [ ]
– Maybe baby / Rock me baby / Send me some lovin' / Tell me how.

Sep 58. Coral; (7"ep) **THE SOUNDS OF THE CRICKETS** [ ] [-]
– Oh! boy / Not fade away / Maybe baby / Tell me how.

Jan 59. Coral; (7"ep) **IT'S SO EASY** [ ] [-]
– It's so easy / Lonesome tears / Think it over / Fool's Paradise.

May 60. Coral; (7"ep) **FOUR MORE BY THE CRICKETS** [ ] [-]
– Last night / Send me some lovin' / You've got love / Rock me my baby.

Nov 60. Coral; (7"ep) **THAT'LL BE THE DAY** [ ] [-]
– That'll be the day / Looking for someone to love / It's too late / An empty cup.

Jun 62. Coral; (7"ep) **THE CRICKETS DON'T EVER CHANGE** [ ] [ ]

1963. Liberty; (7"ep) **JUST FOR FUN** [ ] [-]

1963. Liberty; (7"ep) **STRAIGHT FOR STRINGS** [ ] [-]

1963. Liberty; (7"ep) **BOBBY VEE MEETS THE CRICKETS** [ ] [-]

1963. Liberty; (7"ep) **BOBBY VEE MEETS THE CRICKETS VOL.2** [ ] [-]

1964. Liberty; (7"ep) **COME ON** [ ] [-]

May 65. Liberty; (lp) **THE CRICKETS – A COLLECTION** [ ] [ ]

1968. Liberty; (7") **MY LITTLE GIRL. / LONELY AVENUE** [ ] [-]

— (below one as "BUDDY HOLLY & THE CRICKETS")

May 68. M.C.A.; (7") **OH! BOY. / THAT'LL BE THE DAY** [ ] [-]

Sep 84. M.C.A.; (7") **THINK IT OVER. / IT'S SO EASY** [ ] [-]

1971. Sunset; (lp) **ROCK REFLECTIONS** [ ] [-]

1972. United Artists; (7") **DON'T EVER CHANGE. / PLAYBOY** [ ] [-]

Nov 77. Rollercoaster; (7"ep) **MILLION DOLLAR MOVIE** (rec.'68) [ ] [ ]
– Million dollar movie / A million miles apart / Rock and roll.

Mar 88. Rollercoaster; (lp)(c) **THREE PIECE** [ ] [ ]

May 90. Rollercoaster; (7"ep) **BACK HOME IN TENNESSEE** [ ] [ ]
– Blackmail / I can't hold it / We helped each other out / Back home in . . .

Dec 93. Rollercoaster; (cd) **DOUBLE EXPOSURE** [ ] [ ]

Feb 84. Charly; (lp) **THE COMPLETE CRICKETS** [ ] [-]

Feb 87. See For Miles; (lp) **THE CRICKETS FILE 1961-1965** [ ] [-]
(cd-iss.Feb90)

Aug 89. E.M.I.; (lp)(c)(cd) **ROCK'N'ROLL MASTERS – THE BEST OF THE CRICKETS** [ ] [ ]
– My little girl / Teardrops fall like rain / Lost and alone / Little Hollywood girl / What'd I say / Right or wrong / Blue Monday / La bamba / Lonely avenue / Don't ever change / Willie and the hand jive / I think I've caught the blues / Summertime blues / Love is strange / I'm not a bad guy / Now hear this. (cd+=) – Thoughtless / Slippin' and slidin' / Someday / I believe in you.

Apr 91. E.M.I.; (cd) **THE LIBERTY YEARS** [ ] [ ]

— (see also under ⇒ Buddy HOLLY, for other releases under his name)

May 92. Rockstar; (cd) **RAVIN' ON – FROM CALIFORNIA TO CLOVIS** [ ] [ ]

Jun 92. Bear Family; (cd) **STILL IN STYLE** [ ] [-]

Jun 94. Pickwick; (cd)(c) **THE SINGLES COLLECTION 1957-1960** [ ] [-]

Apr 95. BGO; (cd) **A COLLECTION / CALIFORNIA SUN / SHE LOVES YOU** [ ] [-]

Peter CRISS (see under ⇒ KISS)

Jim CROCE

Born: 10 Jan'43, Philadelphia, Pennsylvania, USA, although he moved to New York in 1967 with wife INGRID. In the early 60's, he had already started to play guitar, developing skills, while working on loads of jobs, including broadcasting a university campus radio show in 1963. In 1970, he returned to Pennsylvania to write more songs for a new demo. In 1972 'ABC' records gave him contract and by end of year, he was surprisingly top of the US album charts. He had many Top 10 hits, including No.1 'BAD, BAD LEROY BROWN', before sadly, he and 4 others were killed in a chartered plane crash on 20 Sep'73. • **Style:** Ever-lasting singer-songwriter similar to JAMES TAYLOR, and who was more appreciated after his death, outside the USA. • **Songwriters:** CROCE except, SALON SALOON (Maury Meuhleisen) / THURSDAY (S.Joseph) / I GOT A NAME (Fox-Gimbel) / CHAIN GANG (Sam Cooke) / HE DON'T LOVE YOU (Impressions) / SEARCHIN' (Coasters) / OLD MAN RIVER (Kern-Hammerstein) / etc. • **Miscellaneous:** In 1974, FRANK SINATRA paid tribute, by recording BAD BAD LEROY BROWN, which also hit the US Hot 100. All albums were produced by TOMMY WEST and TERRY CASHMAN, and also featured his long-time friend MAURY, who was also killed in same plane crash.

Recommended: THE JIM CROCE COLLECTION (*6).

INGRID & JIM CROCE

(Husband & wife, INGRID (b.27 Apr'47)

not issued Capitol

1968. (lp) **APPROACHING DAY** [-] [ ]
– Age / Spin spin spin / I am who I am / What do people do / Another day, another town / Vespers / Big wheel / Just another day / The next man that I marry / What the hell / The man that is me. *(UK-iss.as 'ANOTHER DAY' 1977 on 'Pickwick')*

In 1970, JIM guested on MAURY MUEHLIESEN's debut album 'Gingerbread'.

JIM CROCE

went solo.

Vertigo A.B.C.

Apr 72. (lp)(c) **YOU DON'T MESS AROUND WITH JIM** [ ] [1]
– You don't mess around with Jim / Tomorrow's gonna be a brighter day / New York's not my home / Hard time losin' man / A long time ago / Walkin' back to Georgia / Operator (that's not the way it feels) / Time in a bottle / Rapid Roy (the stock car boy) / Box 10 / Photographs and memories / Hey tomorrow.

Jul 72. (7") **YOU DON'T MESS AROUND WITH JIM. / PHOTOGRAPHS AND MEMORIES** [ ] [8]

Oct 72. (7") **OPERATOR (THAT'S NOT THE WAY IT FEELS). / RAPID BOY** [ ] [17]

Jan 73. (7") **ONE LESS SET OF FOOTSTEPS. / IT DOESN'T HAVE TO BE THAT WAY** [-] [37]
Apr 73. (7") **BAD BAD LEROY BROWN. / A GOOD TIME MAN LIKE ME AIN'T GO NO BUSINESS (SINGIN' THE BLUES)** [-] [1]
Jul 73. (lp)(c) **LIFE AND TIMES** [ ] [7] Feb 73
– One less set of footsteps / Roller derby queen / Dreamin' again / Careful man / Alabama rain / A good time man like me ain't got no business (singin' the blues) / Next time, this time / Bad, bad Leroy Brown / These dreams / Speedball Tucker / It doesn't have to be that way. *(re-iss.Nov76)*
May 73. (7") **BAD, BAD LEROY BROWN. / ROLLER DERBY QUEEN** [ ] [1] Apr 73
Nov 73. (7") **I GOT A NAME. / ALABAMA RAIN** [ ] [10] Sep73

— JIM was killed 20 Sep'73, when his chartered plane crashed on take-off. His guitarist MAURY MUEHLEISEN was also to die with another 3 in fatality.

– compilations, exploitation, etc. –

Nov 73. A.B.C.; (7") **TIME IN A BOTTLE. / HARD TIME LOSIN' MAN** [-] [1]
Dec 73. A.B.C.; (7") **IT DOESN'T HAVE TO BE THAT WAY. /** [-] [64]
Feb 74. Vertigo; (7") **TIME IN A BOTTLE. / HEY TOMORROW** [ ] [-]
Feb 74. A.B.C.; (7") **ROLLER DERBY QUEEN. / IT DOESN'T HAVE TO BE THAT WAY** [-] [ ]
Apr 74. Vertigo/ US= A.B.C.; (lp)(c) **I GOT A NAME** [ ] [2] Nov 73
– I got a name / Lover's cross / Five short minutes / Ages / Workin' at the carwash blues / I'll have to say I love you in a song / Salon & saloon / Thursday / Top hat bar and grill / Recently / The hard way / Every time.
Mar 74. A.B.C.; (7") **I'LL HAVE TO SAY I LOVE YOU IN A SONG. / SALON & SALOON** [-] [9]
Mar 74. Lifesong; (7") **I'LL HAVE TO SAY I LOVE YOU IN A SONG. / PHOTOGRAPHS AND MEMORIES** [ ] [-]
(re-iss.Jan77 on 'Lifesong-GTO')
Sep 74. Lifesong/ US= A.B.C.; (lp)(c) **PHOTOGRAPHS AND MEMORIES – HIS GREATEST HITS** [ ] [2]
(re-iss.+cd.Jun88 on 'Castle Comm.')
Jun 74. A.B.C.; (7") **WORKIN' AT THE CAR WASH BLUES. / THURSDAY** [-] [32]
Jul 75. Lifesong/ US= A.B.C.; (d-lp)(c) **THE FACES I'VE BEEN** [ ] [87]
Sep 75. Lifesong/ US= A.B.C.; (7") **LOVER'S CROSS. / SPEEDBALL TUCKER** [ ] [ ]
Dec 75. Lifesong; (7") **CHAIN GANG MEDLEY: CHAIN GANG – HE DON'T LOVE YOU – SEARCHIN'. /** [-] [63]
Jul 77. Lifesong; (lp)(c) **TIME IN A BOTTLE: JIM CROCE'S GREATEST LOVE SONGS** [ ] [ ] Feb 77
(re-iss.+cd.1986 on 'Castle')
1978. Lifesong; (lp)(c) **BAD, BAD LEROY BROWN: JIM CROCE'S GREATEST CHARACTER SONGS** [ ] [ ]
Mar 80. K-Tel; (lp)(c) **HIS GREATEST HITS** [ ] [-]
(cd-iss.Sep87 on 'Commander')
Sep 86. Castle; (lp)(c)(cd) **DOWN THE HIGHWAY** [ ] [-]
Dec 86. (d-lp)(c)(cd) **THE JIM CROCE COLLECTION** [ ] [-]
– Time in a bottle / Operator (that's not the way it feels) / Salon saloon / Alabama rain / Dreamin' again / It doesn't have to be that way / I'll have to say I love you in a song / Lover's cross / Thursday / These dreams / A long time ago / Photographs and memories / I got a name / Mississippi lady / New York's not my home / Chain gang medley:- Chain gang – He don't love you – Searchin' / You don't mess around with Jim / Old man river / Which way are you goin' / Bad, bad Leroy Brown / Walkin' back to Georgia / Box 10 / Speedball Tucker / Rapid boy (the stock car boy).
May 88. Commander; (d-lp)(d-c) **SONGBOOK** [ ] [-]
May 88. Commander; (lp)(c)(cd) **GREATEST HITS** [ ] [-]
1988. Roadrunner; (cd) **THE LEGEND OF JIM CROCE** [ ] [-]
Feb 90. Essential; (cd)(c)(lp) **THE FINAL TOUR (live)** [ ] [-]
Nov 92. Essential; (d-cd-box) **50th ANNIVERSARY COLLECTION** [ ] [-]
May 94. Castle; (cd) **LIVE** – THE FINAL TOUR (live) [ ] [-]
Oct 94. Woodford; (cd) **SIMPLY THE BEST** [ ] [-]

CROSBY, STILLS, NASH (& YOUNG)

Formed: Los Angeles, California, USA ... Summer 1968 as a superband trio (DAVID) CROSBY, (STEPHEN) STILLS and (GRAHAM) NASH. Their eponymous first offering, came out in Summer '69 and soon broke into US Top 10. After lifting 2 US Top 30 hits, later in the year, they were joined by another semi-star at the time, NEIL YOUNG, who had already played an electric set on their mid-69 gigs. The 4 supported The ROLLING STONES on their ill-fated Altamont concert (when a fan was murdered) on 6 Dec'69. In 1970, after lifting the coveted Best Newcomers award at the Grammys, they released their magnum-opus 'DEJA VU', which hit US No.1 and UK Top 5. Internal disruption and friction between the 4, led to them parting for solo ventures late 1970 (see below discography for all details). • **Style:** Critically acclaimed supergroup, experimental in both vocal harmony, and laid back folk and country rock. A band that inspired many others, including POCO, EAGLES, etc, etc. • **Songwriters:** All 4 took a hand individually and later together in all songs. Also covered; WOODSTOCK (Joni Mitchell) / DEAR MR.FANTASY (Traffic) / and a few more. • **Miscellaneous:** CROSBY's late 60's drug problem was to rear its ugly head again in 1982, when he was arrested twice for possessing cocaine and a gun. The following year, he was convicted and sentenced to 5 years, but after an appeal was sent to a drug rehabilitation center to recover. In Mar'85, he reneged on agreement and was sent to jail. He was released a couple of years later and soon married long-time girlfriend Jan Dance. Early in 1989, he was back again with a solo album 'OH YES WE CAN', which followed a re-union CROSBY, STILLS, NASH & YOUNG comeback album 'AMERICAN DREAM'.

Recommended: DEJA VU (*8) / THE BEST OF CROSBY & STILLS, (*5) / STILL STILLS – THE BEST OF STEPHEN STILLS (*6) / (best solo:-) GRAHAM NASH – SONGS FOR BEGINNERS (*7)
For NEIL YOUNG, albums and reviews, see own discography ⇒.

CROSBY, STILLS & NASH

DAVID CROSBY (b.DAVID VAN CORTLAND, 14 Aug'41, Los Angeles, California) – vocals, guitar (ex-BYRDS) / **STEPHEN STILLS** (b. 3 Jan'45, Dallas, Texas)– vocals, guitar, bass, keyboards (ex-BUFFALO SPRINGFIELD) / **GRAHAM NASH** (b. 2 Feb'42, Blackpool, England)– vocals, guitar (ex-HOLLIES)
with **DALLAS TAYLOR** – drums

Atlantic Atlantic

Jun 69. (lp) **CROSBY, STILLS & NASH** [25] [6]
– Suite: Judy blue eyes / Marrakesh express / Guinnevere / You don't have to cry / Pre-road downs / Wooden ships / Lady of the island / Helplessly hoping / Long time gone / 49 bye-byes. *(re-iss.'72) (re-iss.+cd.Jul87)*
Jul 69. (7") **MARRAKESH EXPRESS. / HELPLESSLY HOPING** [17] [28]
Oct 69. (7") **SUITE: JUDY BLUE EYES. / LONG TIME GONE** [ ] [21]

CROSBY, STILLS, NASH & YOUNG

— added **NEIL YOUNG** – guitar, vocals (ex-solo, ex-BUFFALO SPRINGFIELD) also **GREG REEVES** – bass

Mar 70. (lp)(c) **DEJA VU** [5] [1]
– Carry on / Teach your children / Almost cut my hair / Helpless / Woodstock / Deja vu / Our house / 4 + 20 / Country girl: Whiskey boot hill – Down, down, down – Country girl / Everybody I love you. *(re-iss.'72) (re-iss.+cd.May87)*
Apr 70. (7") **TEACH YOUR CHILDREN. / COUNTRY GIRL** [ ] [16] Jun 70
May 70. (7") **WOODSTOCK. / HELPLESS** [ ] [11] Mar 70
Jun 70. (7") **TEACH YOUR CHILDREN. / CARRY ON** [-] [ ]
Aug 70. (7") **OHIO. / FIND THE COST OF FREEDOM** [ ] [14]
Nov 70. (7") **OUR HOUSE. / DEJA VU** [ ] [30] Sep 70

— (May70) **CALVIN 'FUZZY' SAMUELS** – bass repl. REEVES **JOHN BARBATA** – drums (ex-TURTLES) repl. TAYLOR

— (Aug70) split before release of posthumous album below with last line-up

Apr 71. (d-lp)(d-c) **FOUR-WAY STREET (live)** [5] [1]
– On the way home / Teach your children / Triad / The Lee shore / Chicago / Right between the eyes / Cowgirl in the sand / Don't let it bring you down / 49 bye-byes / Love the one you're with / Pre-road downs / Long time gone / Southern man / Ohio / Carry on / Find the cost of freedom. *(re-iss.'72) (re-iss.+cd.Jul87) (d-cd-iss.Aug92)*

— Their solo recordings, excluding NEIL YOUNG's, are below

STEPHEN STILLS

– solo, – vocals, guitar with **STEPHEN FROMHOLTZ** – guitar / **PAUL HARRIS** – keyboards / **DALLAS TAYLOR** – drums / **CALVIN SAMUELS** – bass / **plus Memphis Horns**

Atlantic Atlantic

Nov 70. (lp)(c) **STEPHEN STILLS** [30] [3]
– Love the one you're with / Do for the others / Church (part of someone) / Old times, good times / Go back home / Sit yourself down / To a flame / Black queen / Cheroke / We are not helpless. *(re-iss.'73) (cd-iss.Oct95)*
Dec 70. (7") **LOVE THE ONE YOU'RE WITH. / TO A FLAME** [37] [14]
May 71. (7") **SIT YOURSELF DOWN. / WE ARE NOT HELPLESS** [ ] [37] Mar 71
Jul 71. (lp)(c) **STEPHEN STILLS II** [22] [8]
– Change partners / Nothin' to do but today / Fishes and scorpions / Sugar babe / Know you got to run / Open secret / Relaxing town / Singin' call / Ecology song / Word game / Marianne / Bluebird revisited. *(re-iss.'78)*
Jul 71. (7") **CHANGE PARTNERS. / RELAXING TOWN** [ ] [43] Jun 71
Sep 71. (7") **MARIANNE. / NOTHIN' TO DO BUT TODAY** [ ] [42] Aug 71

STEPHEN STILLS & MANASSAS

STILLS retained **SAMUELS, HARRIS** and **TAYLOR,** brought in **CHRIS HILLMAN** – guitar, vocals / **AL PERKINS** – steel guitar, guitar / **JOE LALA** – percussion / **KENNY PASSARELLI** – bass (ex-JOE WALSH)repl. SAMUELS.

Atlantic Atlantic

May 72. (d-lp)(d-c) **MANASSAS** [30] [4] Apr 72
– Fallen eagle / Jesus gave love away for free / Colorado / So begins the task / Hide to the deep / Don't look at my shadow / It doesn't matter / Johnny's garden / Bound to fall / How far / Move around / The love gangster / Song of love / Rock'n'roll crazies – Cuban bluegrass / Jet set (sigh) / Anyway / Both of us (bound to lose) / What to do / Right now / The treasure (take one) / Blues man. *(cd-iss.Feb93 & Oct95)*
May 72. (7") **IT DOESN'T MATTER. / ROCK'N'ROLL CRAZIES – CUBAN BLUEGRASS** [-] [61]
Aug 72. (7") **IT DOESN'T MATTER. / FALLEN ANGEL** [ ] [ ]
Nov 72. (7") **ROCK'N'ROLL CRAZIES. / COLORADO** [-] [92]
May 73. (lp)(c) **DOWN THE ROAD** [33] [26]
– Isn't it about time / Lies / Pensamiento / So many times / Business on the street / Do you remember the Americans / Down the road / City junkies / Guaguanco de Vero / Rollin' my stone. *(cd-iss.Nov93)*
May 73. (7") **ISN'T IT ABOUT TIME. / SO MANY TIMES** [ ] [56] Apr 73
Jul 73. (7") **GUAGUANCO DE VERO. / DOWN THE ROAD** [ ] [ ]

— (Sep73) **HARRIS, PERKINS and HILLMAN joined SOUTHERN HILLMAN FURAY BAND. STEPHEN STILLS** formed his own band, retaining **PASSARELLI** and **LALA** plus **DONNIE DACUS** – guitar / **JERRY AIELLO** – keyboards / **HUSS KUNKEL** – drums

CROSBY, STILLS NASH & YOUNG

(May74) re-formed, mainly for concerts. Augmented by **TIM DRUMMOND** – bass / **RUSS**

KUNKEL – drums / **JOE LALA percussion**

STEPHEN STILLS

went solo again (Feb75) with new band **LALA, DACUS, AIELLO** plus **GEORGE PERRY** – bass / **RONNIE ZIEGLER** – drums

C.B.S. Columbia

Jun 75. (lp)(c) **STILLS** 31 19
– Turn back the pages / My favorite changes / My angel / In the way / Love story / To mama Christopher and the old man / First things first / New mama / As I come of age / Shuffle just as bad / Cold cold world / Myth of Sisyphus.

Jul 75. (7") **TURN BACK THE PAGES. / SHUFFLE JUST AS BAD** 84

— added **RICK ROBERTS** – guitar, vocals (of FIREFALL)

Apr 76. (7") **BUYIN' TIME. / SOLDIER** -

May 76. (lp)(c) **ILLEGAL STILLS** 54 30
– Buyin' time / Midnight in Paris / Different tongues / Closer to you / Soldier / The loner / Stateline blues / No me nieges / Ring of love / Circlin'.

Jul 76. (7") **THE LONER. / STATELINE BLUES**

STILLS-YOUNG BAND

STEPHEN STILLS – vocals, guitar / **NEIL YOUNG** – vocals, guitar with **AIELLO, PERRY, VITALE** and **LALA.**

Reprise Reprise

Sep 76. (7") **LONG MAY YOU RUN. / 12:8 BLUES**

Oct 76. (lp)(c) **LONG MAY YOU RUN** 12 26
– Long may you run / Make love to you / Midnight on the bay / Black coral / Ocean girl / Let it shine / 12/8 blues (all the same) / Fontainebleau / Guardian angel. *(cd-iss.Jul93)*

Dec 76. (7") **MIDNIGHT ON THE BAY. / BLACK CORAL** -

— CROSBY, STILLS & NASH re-formed in '77 (see further on for more solo STILLS)

DAVID CROSBY

with loads of session people, too numerous to mention.

Atlantic Atlantic

Feb 71. (lp)(c) **IF I COULD ONLY REMEMBER MY NAME** 12 12
– Music is love / Cowboy movie / Tamalpais High (at about 3) / Laughing / What are their names / Traction in the rain / Song with no name (tree with no leaves) / Orleans / I'd swear there was somebody here. *(cd-iss.Nov93)*

Apr 71. (7") **MUSIC IS LOVE. / LAUGHING** - 95

Jul 71. (7") **ORLEANS. / TRACTION IN THE RAIN** -

CROSBY & NASH

duo (DAVID & GRAHAM with more sessioners and left over GRATEFUL DEAD members which were included on DAVID's debut solo album.

May 72. (lp)(c) **GRAHAM NASH & DAVID CROSBY** 13 4 Apr 72
– Southbound train / Whole cloth / Black notes / Strangers room / Where will I be / Page 43 / Frozen smiles / Games / Girl to be on my mind / The wall song / Immigration man.

May 72. (7") **IMMIGRATION MAN. / WHOLE CLOTH** - 36

Jul 72. (7") **SOUTHBOUND TRAIN. / WHOLE CLOTH**

Jul 72. (7") **SOUTHBOUND TRAIN. / THE WALL SONG** - 99

— after CROSBY, STILLS, NASH & YOUNG reunion May74-Feb75

— resurrected partnership, with steady band members **CRAIG DOERGE** – keyboards / **LEE SKLAR & TIM DRUMMOND** – bass / **DANNY KOOTCH & RUSS KUNKEL** – drums / **DAVID LINDLEY** – guitar, violin.

Polydor A.B.C.

Jan 76. (lp)(c) **WIND ON THE WATER** 6 Oct 75
– Carry me / Mama lion / Bittersweet / Take the money and run / Naked in the rain / Love work out / Low down payment / Cowboy of dreams / Homeward through the haze / Fieldworker / To the last whale. *(cd-iss.Nov91 on 'Thunderbolt')*

Nov 75. (7") **CARRY ME. / MAMA LION** 52

Mar 76. (7") **TAKE THE MONEY AND RUN. / BITTERSWEET** -

May 76. (7") **LOVE WORK OUT. / BITTERSWEET** -

Jul 76. (lp)(c) **WHISTLING DOWN THE WIRE** 26
– Spotlight / Broken bird / Time after time / Dancer / Mutiny / J.B.'s blues / Marguerita / Taken at all / Foolish man / Out of the darkness.

Aug 76. (7") **OUT OF THE DARKNESS. / LOVE WORK OUT** -

Aug 76. (7") **OUT OF THE DARKNESS. / BROKEN BIRD** - 89

Oct 76. (7") **SPOTLIGHT. / FOOLISH MAN** -

— CROSBY STILLS & NASH reformed '77 (see further on)

GRAHAM NASH

solo using C,S & N past members plus GRATEFUL DEAD main men

Atlantic Atlantic

Jun 71. (lp)(c) **SONGS FOR BEGINNERS** 13 15
– Military madness / Better days / Wounded bird / I used to be a king / Be yourself / Simple man / Man in the mirror / There's only one / Sleep song / Chicago / We can change the world. *(cd-iss.Feb93)*

Jun 71. (7") **CHICAGO. / SIMPLE MAN** 35 May 71

Sep 71. (7") **MILITARY MADNESS. / I USED TO BE A KING** -

Sep 71. (7") **MILITARY MADNESS. / SLEEP SONG** - 73

Nov 71. (7") **I USED TO BE A KING. / WOUNDED BIRD** -

Nov 73. (7") **PRISON SONG. / HEY YOU (LOOKING AT HTE MOON)** -

Mar 74. (lp)(c) **WILD TALES** 34 Dec 73
– Wild tales / Hey you (looking at the Moon) / Prison song / You'll never be the same / And so it goes / Oh! Camil (the winter soldier) / I miss you / On the line / Another sleep song.

Mar 74. (7") **ON THE LINE. / I MISS YOU**

Aug 74. (7") **GRAVE CONCERN. / ANOTHER SLEEP SONG**

— GRAHAM rejoined below and had more solo releases later.

CROSBY, STILLS & NASH

reformed in '77, with various session men.

Atlantic Atlantic

Jun 77. (lp)(c) **CSN** 23 2
– Shadow captain / See the changes / Carried away / Fair game / Anything at all / Cathedral / Dark star / Just a song before I go / Cold rain / In my dreams / I give you give blind. *(cd-iss.Oct94)*

Jun 77. (7") **JUST A SONG BEFORE I GO. / DARK STAR** 7 May 77

Oct 77. (7") **FAIR GAME. / ANYTHING AT ALL** 43 Sep 77

Dec 77. (7") **CARRIED AWAY. / I GIVE YOU GIVE BLIND** -

STEPHEN STILLS

more solo releses with session people & his tour band **DALLAS TAYLOR** – drums / **GEORGE PERRY** – bass / **MIKE FINNEGAN** – keyboards / **JERRY TOLMAN & BONNIE BRAMLETT** – b.vocals

C.B.S. Columbia

Sep 78. (7") **CAN'T GET NO BOOTY. / LOWDOWN**

Oct 78. (lp)(c) **THOROUGHFARE GAP** 83
– You can't dance alone / Thoroughfare gap / We will go / Beaucoup yumbo / What's the game / Midnight rider / Woman Lleva / Lowdown / Not fade away / Can't get no booty.

Nov 78. (7") **THOROUGHFARE GAP. / LOWDOWN** -

GRAHAM NASH

solo, with usual and past session people + CROSBY, STILLS & YOUNG

Capitol Capitol

Jan 80. (7") **IN THE 80'S. / T.V. GUIDE** -

Mar 80. (7") **OUT ON THE ISLAND. / HELICOPTER SONG** -

Mar 80. (lp)(c) **EARTH & SKY**
– Earth & sky / Love has come / Out on the island / Skychild / Helicopter song / Barrel of pain / T.V. guide / It's alright / Magical child / In the 80's.

May 80. (7") **EARTH & SKY. / MAGICAL CHILD** -

CROSBY, STILLS & NASH

reformed mid '82, with session men.

Atlantic Atlantic

Jun 82. (7") **WASTED ON THE WAY. / DELTA** 9

Jul 82. (lp)(c) **DAYLIGHT AGAIN** 8
– Turn your back on love / Wasted on the way / Southern cross / Into the darkness / Delta / Since I met you / Too much love to hide / Song for Susan / You are alive / Might as well have a good time / Daylight again. *(cd-iss.Oct94)*

Nov 82. (7") **SOUTHERN CROSS. / INTO THE DARKNESS** 18 Sep 82

Jan 83. (7") **TOO MUCH LOVE TO HIDE. / SONG FOR SUSAN** - 69

Jun 83. (lp)(c) **ALLIES (live)** 43
– War games / Raise a voice / Turn your back on love / Barrel of pain / Shadow captain / Dark star / Blackbird / He played real good for free / Wasted on my way / For what it's worth. *(cd-iss.1984)*

Jul 83. (7") **WAR GAMES (live). / SHADOW CAPTAIN (live)** 45 Jun 83
(12") – ('A'side) / Dark Star (live) / Keep your . . .

Sep 83. (7") **RAISE A VOICE (live). / FOR WHAT IT'S WORTH (live)** -

— Split Aug82, when CROSBY is sentenced to 5 years for drugs. He gets leniency when he agrees to rehabilitate himself in drug hospital Dec84.

STEPHEN STILLS

solo again (2nd single featured WALTER FINNEGAN)

W.E.A. Atlantic

Sep 84. (lp)(c) **RIGHT BY YOU** 75
– 50/50 / Stranger / Flaming heart / Love again / No problem / Can't let go / Grey to green / Only love can break your heart / No hiding place / Right by you. *(cd-iss.Nov93)*

Aug 84. (7") **STRANGER. / NO HIDING PLACE** - 61

Oct 84. (7") **CAN'T LET GO. / GREY TO GREEN** - 67

(above as STEPHEN STILLS featuring MICHAEL FINNIGAN)

Dec 84. (7") **ONLY LOVE CAN BREAK YOUR HEART. / LOVE AGAIN** -

not issued Goldhill

1990. (cd) **STILLS ALONE** -
– Isn't it so / Everybody's talkin' / Just isn't like you / In my life / Ballad of Hollis Brown / Singin call / The right girl / Blind fiddler medley / Amazonia / Treetop flyer.

GRAHAM NASH

solo, he had rejoined The HOLLIES between Sep81-Apr83.

Atlantic Atlantic

Apr 86. (7") **INNOCENT EYES. / I GOT A ROCK** 84

Apr 86. (lp)(c) **INNOCENT EYES**
– See you in Prague / Keep away from me / Innocent eyes / Chippin' away / Over the wall / Don't listen to the rumours / Sad eyes / Newday / Glass and steel / I got a rock.

Jul 86. (7") **SAY EYES. / NEWDAY** -

Oct 86. (7") **CHIPPIN' AWAY. / NEWDAY** -

CROSBY, STILLS, NASH & YOUNG

reformed yet again

Atlantic Atlantic

Nov 88. (7") **GOT IT MADE. / THIS OLD HOUSE** - 69

Nov 88. (lp)(c)(cd) **AMERICAN DREAM** 16
– American dream / Got it made / Name of love / Don't say goodbye / This old house / Nighttime for the generals / Shadowland / Drivin' thunder / Clear blue skies / That

girl / Compass / Soldiers of peace / Feel your love / Night song.
Jan 89. (7") **AMERICAN DREAM. / COMPASS** [55] [ ]
(12"+=) – Soldiers of peace.

DAVID CROSBY

solo again

A & M A & M

Feb 89. (lp)(c)(cd) **OH YES I CAN** [ ] [ ]
– Drive my car / Melody / Monkey and the underdog / In the wide ruin / Tracks in the dust / Drop down mama / Lady of the harbour / Distances / Flying man / Oh yes I can / My country 'tis of thee.
Feb 89. (7") **DRIVE MY CAR. / TRACKS IN THE DUST** [ ] [ ]
(12"+=) – Flying men.
Apr 89. (7")(12") **LADY OF THE HARBOR. / DROP DOWN MAMA** [ ] [ ]

— with band **LELAND SKLAR** – bass / **RUSSELL KUNKEL + JEFF PORCARO** – drums / **CRAIG DOERGE** – keyboards / **ANDY FAIRWEATHER-LOWE** – guitar / **DEAN PARKS** – guitar, flute / **BERNIE LEADON** – acoustic guitar / **C.J. VANSTON** – keyboards / with many guests **JACKSON BROWNE + DON WAS** plus outside writers + on session **PHIL COLLINS, JONI MITCHELL, MARC COHN, JIMMY WEBB, PAUL BRADY, STEPHEN BISHOP, JOHN HIATT, BONNIE HAYES + NOEL BRAZIL.**

Atlantic Atlantic

May 93. (7")(c-s) **HERO. ("DAVID CROSBY featuring PHIL COLLINS") / COVERAGE** [ ] [44]
(cd-s+=) – Fare thee well.
Jun 93. (cd)(c) **THOUSAND ROADS** [ ] [ ]
– Hero / Too young to die / Old soldier / Through your hands / Yvette in English / Thousand roads / Columbus / Helpless heart / Coverage / Natalie.
Mar 95. (cd)(c) **IT'S ALL COMING BACK TO ME NOW (live '93)** [ ] [ ]
– In my dreams / Rusty and blue / Hero / Till it shines on you / 1000 roads / Cowboy movie / Almosy cut my hair / Deja vu / Long time gone / Wooden ships.

CROSBY, STILLS & NASH

with **JOE VITALE** – drums, organ, synth bass / **LELAND SKLAR** – bass / **CRAIG DOERGE** – keyboards / **MIKE LANDAU** – guitar / **MIKE FISHER** – percussion.

East West Atlantic

Jun 90. (cd)(c)(lp) **LIVE IT UP** [ ] [57]
– Live it up / If anybody had a heart / Tomboy / Haven't we lost enough / Yours and mine / (Got to keep) Open / Straight line / House of broken dreams / Arrows / After the dolphin.
Aug 94. (cd)(c) **AFTER THE STORM** [ ] [98]
– Only waiting for you / Find a dream / Camera / Unequal love / Till it shines / It won't go away / These empty days / In my life / Street to lean on / Bad boyz / After the storm / Panama.

– their compilations etc. –

Aug 74. Atlantic; (d-lp)(c) **SO FAR – THE BEST OF . . .** [25] [1]
– Woodstock / Marrakesh express / You don't have to cry / Teach your children / Love the one you're with / Almost cut my hair / Wooden ships / Dark star / Helpless / Chicago – We can change the world / Cathedral / 4 + 20 / Our house / Change partners / Just a song before I go / Ohio / Wasted on the way / Southern cross / Suite: Judy blue eyes / Carry on – Questions / Horses through a rainstorm / Johnny's garden / Guinnevere / Helplessly hoping / The Lee Shore / Taken it all / Shadow captain / As I come of age / Drive my car / Dear Mr.Fantasy / In my dreams / Yours and mine / Haven't we lost enough? / After the dolphin / Find the cost of freedom. *(cd-iss.Oct94)*
(re-iss.+cdJan87)
Nov 80. Atlantic; (lp)(c) **REPLAY** [ ] [ ]
(cd-iss.Oct94)
Dec 91. East West; (4xcd)(4xc) **CROSBY, STILLS & NASH** [ ] [ ]
Feb 92. East West; (7")(c-s) **OUR HOUSE. / MARRAKESH EXPRESS** [ ] [ ]
(12"+=)(cd-s+=) – Carry on / Dear Mr.Fantasy (STEPHEN STILLS / GRAHAM NASH
(above was re-actified on a famous building society TV ad).
Feb 92. East West; (d-cd)(d-c) **THE BEST OF CROSBY, STILLS & NASH** [ ] [-]
Oct 75. Atlantic; (d-lp) **TWO ORIGINALS OF STEPHEN STILLS (1st 2 lp's)** [ ] [ ]
Dec 75. Atlantic; (lp)(c) **STEPHEN STILLS – LIVE (live)** [ ] [ ]
Jan 77. Atlantic; (lp)(c) **STEPHEN STILLS – THE BEST OF STEPHEN STILLS** [ ] [ ]
– Love the one you're with / It doesn't matter / We are not helpless / Marianne / Bound to fall / Isn't it about time / Change partners / Go back home / Johnny's garden / Rock and roll crazies – Cuban bluegrass / Sit yourself down.
STEPHEN STILLS was credited on Aug68 lp 'SUPER SESSION' alongside AL KOOPER & MIKE BLOOMFIELD.
Nov 77. Polydor/ US= A.B.C.; (lp)(c) **LIVE (live)) ("CROSBY & NASH")** [ ] [52]
Jan 79. Polydor/ US= A.B.C.; (lp)(c) **THE BEST OF CROSBY & NASH** [ ] [ ] Oct 78
(re-iss.Nov80)

CROSS (see under ⇒ QUEEN)

Christopher CROSS

Born: CHRISTOPHER GEPPART, 3 May'51, San Antonio, Texas, USA. In 1971, he was part of heavy rock group FLASH, who never quite made it onto record although were support band for LED ZEPPELIN and DEEP PURPLE. He quit them in '73, but continued writing songs. He toured with new band (see below) in 1976, and finally got recording contract with 'Warners' in 1978, at the same time of moving to Los Angeles. His eponymous debut album, produced by MICHAEL OMARTIAN (also retained for later work), stayed in the U.S.chart for over two years, but waited until early 1981 to hit UK Top 20. This was due to resurgence of the single SAILING. Declined steadily during the 80's, and faded into run-of-the-mill act. • **Style:** Mainstream AOR, but with a touch of sophistication. Virtually unknown facially, due to his beard /plumpness and naive label fear of failure. • **Songwriters:** Wrote own material, collaborated mainly with OMARTIAN, and others. ARTHUR'S THEME (co-written with BURT BACHARACH, CAROLE BAYER SAGER and PETER ALLEN). • **Trivia:** In the Grammys US 1981, he cleaned up top awards. Heavies SAXON later covered his 'RIDE LIKE THE WIND'.

Recommended: CHRISTOPHER CROSS (*5)

CHRISTOPHER CROSS – vocals, guitar / **ROB MEURER** – keyboards / **ANDY SALMON** – bass / **TOMMY TAYLOR** – drums

Warners Warners

Feb 80. (lp)(c) **CHRISTOPHER CROSS** [ ] [6]
– Say you'll be mine / I really don't know anymore / Spinning / Never be the same / Poor Shirley / Ride like the wind / The light is on / Sailing / Minstrel gigolo. *(UK-re-dist.Feb81 No.14) (cd-iss. 1984)*
Feb 80. (7") **RIDE LIKE THE WIND. / MINSTREL GIGOLO** [69] [2]
Jun 80. (7") **SAILING. / POOR SHIRLEY** [-] [1]
Aug 80. (7") **SAILING. / THE LIGHT IS ON** [ ] [-]
(UK-iss.Feb81 hit 48)
Oct 80. (7") **NEVER BE THE SAME. / THE LIGHT IS ON** [ ] [15]
(UK-re-iss.Mar82)
Mar 81. (7") **SAY YOU'LL BE MINE. / SPINNING** [-] [20]
Apr 81. (7") **SAY YOU'LL BE MINE. / POOR SHIRLEY** [ ] [-]
Oct 81. (7") **ARTHUR'S THEME (BEST THAT I CAN DO). / MINSTREL GIGOLO** [56] [1] Aug 81
(UK-re-issJan82 hit No.7)

— basic 4-piece added **STEVE LUKATHER** – guitar / **MICHAEL CHARMAN** – keyboards / **STEVE GADD, JEFF PORCARO** – drums / **ABRAHAM LABORIEL, MIKE PORCARO** – bass / **MICAEL OMARTIAN, PAULINHO DA COSTA, LENNY CASTRO** – percussion.

Jan 83. (7") **ALL RIGHT. / LONG WORLD** [51] [12]
(12"+=) – Arthur's theme.
Feb 83. (lp)(c) **ANOTHER PAGE** [4] [11]
– No time for talk / Baby says no / What am I supposed to believe / Deal 'em again / Think of Laura / All right / Talking in my sleep / Nature of the game / Long world / Words of wisdom. *(cd-iss. 1984)*
Apr 83. (7")(12") **NO TIME FOR TALK. / WORDS OF WISDOM** [ ] [33]
Jun 83. (7")(12") **DEAL 'EM AGAIN. / BABY SAYS NO** [ ] [ ]
Sep 83. (7") **ALL RIGHT. / RIDE LIKE THE WIND** [ ] [ ]
Mar 84. (7") **THINK OF LAURA. / WORDS OF WISDOM** [ ] [9] Dec 83
Jun 84. (7") **A CHANCE FOR HEAVEN. / TALKING IN MY SLEEP** [ ] [76]
(above rel. on 'Columbia' from Los Angeles Olympic Games)

— CROSS completely changed line-up, except from OMARTIAN. He brought in **JOE CHERNAY** – bass / **JOHN ROBINSON** – drums / **GARY HERBIG, HUTCHROFT** – saxophone / **JERRY HEY, CHUCK FINDLEY, GARY GRANT** – trumpet.

Oct 85. (7") **CHARM THE SNAKE. / OPEN YOUR HEART** [ ] [68]
Oct 85. (lp)(c)(cd) **EVERY TURN OF THE WORLD** [ ] [ ]
– Every turn of the world / Charm the snake / I hear you call / Don't say goodbye / It's you that really matters / Love is love (in any language) / Swing street / Love found a home / That girl / Open your heart.
Dec 85. (7") **EVERY TURN OF THE WORLD. / OPEN YOUR HEART** [-] [ ]
Feb 86. (7") **FOUND LOVE A HOME. / LOVE IS LOVE (IN ANY LANGUAGE)** [-] [ ]
Feb 86. (7") **THAT GIRL. / OPEN YOUR HEART** [ ] [ ]
(12"+=) – I really don't know anymore.

Reprise Reprise

Aug 88. (lp)(c)(cd) **BACK OF MY MIND** [ ] [ ]
– Someday / Never stop believing / Swept away / Any old time / I will (take you forever) / She told me so / Back of my mind / I'll be alright / Just one look.
Aug 88. (7") **I WILL (TAKE YOU FOREVER). ("CHRISTOPHER CROSS with FRANCIS RUFFELLE") / JUST ONE LOOK** [ ] [ ]
(12"+=) – Ride like the wind.
Oct 88. (7") **SWEPT AWAY. / ?** [-] [ ]

Ariola Ariola

Sep 92. (7")(cd-s) **IN THE BLINK OF AN EYE. / RENDEZVOUS** [ ] [ ]

Sheryl CROW

Born: Feb'62, Kennett, Missouri, USA. She left university where she studied classical music and moved to St.Louis. In the mid-80's, she set off to L.A and finally cut her teeth as SHIRLEY CROW on MICHAEL JACKSON's 1988 'Bad' tour. She then earned her crust singing back-up for ROD STEWART, DON HENLEY and JOE COCKER. Always wanting to be a solo singer, she handed a demo to producer HUGH PADGHAM, who with a recommendation from STING, got her signed to 'A&M' in '91. An album of unproductive songs was shelved, but with the help of a second producer BILL BOTTRILL, they emerged late in 1993 with debut 'TUESDAY NIGHT MUSIC CLUB'. Although it didn't sparkle immediately, it became a deserved smash a year later after a support slot to the re-formed EAGLES and a well-received appearance at WOODSTOCK II. Suddenly her album turned gold and a single 'ALL I WANNA DO' was nearly hitting peak spot. • **Style:** Storyteller songstress like EDIE BRICKELL or ROSIE VELA. • **Songwriters:** Writes lyrics mainly / songs by BILL BOTTRELL or BAERWALD-GILBERT-McLEOD, etc. except I'M GONNA BE A WHEEL SOMEDAY (Fats Domino) / D'YER

MAKER (Led Zeppelin). • **Trivia:** The track 'HUNDREDS OF TEARS' featured on 'Pointbreak' soundtrack. Another 2 'STRONG ENOUGH' and 'NO ONE SAID IT WOULD BE EASY' appeared in the 1994 film 'Kalifornia'.

Recommended: TUESDAY NIGHT MUSIC CLUB (*6)

SHERYL CROW – vocals + sessioners incl. **BILL BOTTRILL**

A & M A & M

Sep 93. (7")(c-s) **RUN BABY RUN. / ALL BY MYSELF** [ ] [ ]
(cd-s+=) – The na-na song / Reach around jerk.

Oct 93. (cd)(c) **TUESDAY NIGHT MUSIC CLUB** [68] [3]
– Run baby run / Leaving Las Vegas / Strong enough / Can't cry anymore / Solidify / The na-na song / No one said it would be easy / What I can do for you / All I wanna do / We do what we can / I shall believe. *(re-dist.US Feb94) (re-dist.Sep94 hit UK No.22 & 8 early '95) (re-iss.cd May95 w/ free cd '6 TRACK LIVE MINI-ALBUM')*

Feb 94. (7")(c-s) **WHAT I CAN DO FOR YOU. / VOLVO COWGIRL 99** [ ] [ ]
(cd-s+=) – ('A'version) / I shall believe.

Apr 94. (7")(c-s) **RUN BABY RUN. / LEAVING LAS VEGAS (acoustic)** [ ] [ ]
(cd-s+=) – All by myself / Reach around jerk.

Jun 94. (7")(c-s) **LEAVING LAS VEGAS. / ('A'live)** [66] [60] Apr94
(cd-s) – ('A'side) / I shall believe (live) / What I can do for you.
(cd-s) – ('A'side) / No one said it would be easy (live) / The na-na song (live).

Oct 94. (7")(c-s) **ALL I WANNA DO. / SOLIDIFY** [5] [2]
(cd-s+=) – I'm gonna be a wheel someday.
(cd-s) – ('A'side) / Run baby run / Leaving Las Vegas.

Jan 95. (7")(c-s) **STRONG ENOUGH. / NO ONE SAID IT WOULD BE EASY** [33] [5]
(cd-s+=) – All I wanna do.
(cd-s) – ('A'side) / ('A'mix) / All by myself / Reach around jerk.

May 95. (c-ep)(cd-ep) **CAN'T CRY ANYMORE / ALL I WANNA DO / STRONG NOUGH (U.S.version) / WE DO WHAT WE CAN** [33] [36]
(cd-ep) – ('A'side) / What I can do for you (live) / No one said it would be easy (live) / I shall believe (live).

Jul 95. (c-s) **RUN, BABY, RUN / LEAVING LAS VEGAS** [24] [ ]
(cd-s) – ('A'side) / Can't cry anymore / Reach around jerk / I shall believe (the live Nashville sessions).
(cd-s) – ('A'side) / Strong enough / No one said it would be easy / The na na song (the live Nashville sessions).

Oct 95. (c-s) **WHAT I CAN DO FOR YOU / LEAVING LAS VEGAS (live)** [43] [ ]
(cd-s) – ('A'side) / D'yer maker / I'm gonna be a wheel someday / No one said it would be easy.
(cd-s) – ('A'live) / All I wanna do (live) / Strong enough (live) / Can't cry anymore (live).

CROWDED HOUSE

Formed: virtually as SPLIT ENDS in Oct'72 by TIM FINN and PHIL JUDD. Soon slightly altered their name to SPLIT ENZ, stylising their own brand of humour pop fused somewhere between SPARKS and ROXY MUSIC. In fact PHIL MANZANERA of ROXY produced and remixed their 'SECOND THOUGHTS' album in 1976. They were soon joined by brother NEIL FINN, which became nucleus of CROWDED HOUSE, although TIM didn't join until later. CROWDED HOUSE were based in Melbourne, Australia . . . 1985 (NEIL FINN, PAUL HESTER and NICK SEYMOUR). They moved to Los Angeles, California 1986 and signed to 'Capitol', working with MITCHELL FROOM for eponymous US hit debut the following year. • **Style:** From once zany men from SPLIT ENZ, to mainstream romantic pop / rock. In 1991 CROSBY, STILLS & NASH were cited as influence. • **Songwriters:** NEIL FINN penned except MR. TAMBOURINE MAN (Bob Dylan) + EIGHT MILES HIGH + SO YOU WANT TO BE A ROCK'N'ROLL STAR (Byrds). SPLIT ENZ; either NEIL or TIM. • **Trivia:** SIX MONTHS IN A LEAKY BOAT was banned by the BBC in 1982, due to the Argentian / Falklands conflict. Big brother TIM married actress GRETA SCAACHI in 1985. The FINN brothers were awarded OBE's for their services to New Zealand's music industry. NICK is brother of MARK SEYMOUR, vox of other Aussie band HUNTERS + COLLECTORS.

Recommended: WOODFACE (*9) / TOGETHER ALONE (*8) / HISTORY NEVER REPEATS (*7)

SPLIT ENZ

TIM FINN – vocals, piano / **PHIL JUDD** – vocals, guitar / **JON CHUNN** – bass / **MILES GOLDING** – violin / **MICHAEL HOWARD** – drums

Vertigo not issued

Apr 73. (7") **FOR YOU. / ?** [ ] [-]

SPLIT ENZ

EDDIE RAYNOR – keyboards repl. MILES / **WALLY WILKINSON** – guitar + **NOEL CROMBIE** – percussion repl. **HOWARD**

Mushroom AUSTRALIA not issued

Jun 75. (lp) **MENTAL NOTES** [-] [-]
– Late last night / Walking down a road / Titus / Lovey dovey / Sweet dreams / Stranger than fiction / Time for a change / Matinee idyll / The woman who loves you / Mental notes. *(UK-iss.Aug76 on 'Chrysalis')*

Jun 75. (7") **TITUS. / ?** [-] [-]

Sep 75. (7") **LOVEY DOVEY. / ?** [-] [-]

May 76. (lp) **SECOND THOUGHTS** (re-mixes of debut lp) [-] [-]
– (In 1977, UK 'Chrysalis' issued it)

— **NEIL FINN** – vocals, guitar repl. JUDD. WALLY, JON and drummer PAUL CROWTHER were repl. by Englishmen **NIGEL GRIGGS** – bass / **MALCOLM GREEN** – drums

(next iss. Australia; May77 on 'Mushroom')

Chrysalis Mush-room AUST

1977. (7") **LATE LAST NIGHT. / WALKING DOWN THE ROAD** [ ] [ ] 1976

1977. (7") **ANOTHER GREAT DIVIDE. / STRANGER THAN FICTION** [ ] [-]

Oct 77. (lp) **DIZRHYTHMIA** [ ] [ ]
– Bold as brass / My mistake / Parrot fashion love / Sugar and spice / Without a doubt / Crosswords / Charley / Nice to know / Jambouree. *(re-iss.1983)*

Oct 77. (7") **MY MISTAKE. / CROSSWORDS** [ ] [ ]
(12"+=) – The woman who loves you.

— JUDD re-joined but quit again

Mushroom AUSTRALIA not issued

1978. (lp) **FRENZY** [-] [ ]

1978. (7") **I SEE RED. / ?** [-] [ ]

Illegal not issued

Nov 79. (7"m) **I SEE RED. / GIVE IT A WHIRL / HERMIT McDERMOTT** [ ] [-]

— Initial A&M material iss.Australia 1979 'Mushroom'.

A & M A & M

Aug 80. (lp)(c) **TRUE COLOURS** [42] [40]
– Shark attack / I got you / What's the matter with you / I hope I never / Nobody takes me seriously / Missing persons / Poor boy / How can I resist her / The choral sea. *(re-iss.Nov85, cd-iss.1988)*

Aug 80. (7") **I GOT YOU. / DOUBLE HAPPY** [12] [53]

Nov 80. (7") **NOBODY TAKES ME SERIOUSLY. / THE CHORAL SEA** [ ] [-]

Jan 81. (7") **POOR BOY. / MISSING PERSON** [-] [ ]

Jan 81. (7") **I HOPE I NEVER. / THE CHORAL SEA** [-] [ ]

Mar 81. (7") **NOBODY TAKES ME SERIOUSLY. / WHAT'S THE MATTER WITH YOU** [-] [ ]

Mar 81. (lp)(c) **WAIATA** [ ] [45] May 81
– Hard act to follow / One step ahead / I don't wanna dance / Iris / Whale / Clumsby / History never repeats / Walking through the ruins / Ships / Ghost girl / Albert of India.

Apr 81. (7"m) **HISTORY NEVER REPEATS. / SHARK ATTACK / WHAT'S THE MATTER WITH YOU** [63] [ ]

Jun 81. (7") **ONE STEP AHEAD. / IN THE WARS** [ ] [ ]

— MALCOLM GREEN left and NOEL now on drums.

Apr 82. (7") **SIX MONTHS IN A LEAKY BOAT. / MAKE SOME SENSE OF IT** [ ] [ ]

Apr 82. (lp)(c) **TIME AND TIDE** [71] [58]
– Dirty creature / Giant heartbeat / Hello Sandy Allen / Never ceases to amaze me / Lost for words / Small world / Take a walk / Pioneer / Six months in a leaky boat / Haul away / Log cabin fever / Make some sense of it.

Aug 84. (7") **MESSAGE TO THE GIRL. / BON VOYAGE (KIAKATIA)** [ ] [ ]

Aug 84. (lp)(c) **CONFLICTING EMOTIONS** [ ] [ ] Jul 84
– Strait old line / Bullett brain and cactus head / Message to my girl / Working up an appetite / Our day / No mischief / The devil you know / I wake up every night / Conflicting emotions / Bon voyage. *(cd-iss.1988)*

— Now a quartet (**EDDIE RAYNOR, NEIL FINN, NIGEL GRIGGS + NOEL CROMBIE**) when TIM FINN married actress Greta Saatchi and went solo.

1985. (m-lp) **SEE YOU ROUND** (live) [ ] [ ]

— Disbanded 1985, NEIL formed CROWDED HOUSE, which later included TIM.

– compilations, others, etc. –

Dec 80. Chrysalis; (lp)(c) **BEGINNING OF THE ENZ** [ ] [-]

1992. Chrysalis; (cd) **HISTORY NEVER REPEATS (THE BEST OF SPLIT ENZ)** [ ] [ ]
– I got you / Hard act to follow / Six months in a leaky boat / What's the matter with you / One step ahead / I see red / Message to my girl / History never repeats / I hope I never / Dirty creature / Poor boy.

Sep 87. Concept; (d-lp) **COLLECTION: 1973-1984 . . . THE BEST OF SPLIT ENZ** [ ] [-]

— (above issued in Australia with diff.track listing)

Feb 94. Chrysalis; (cd)(c) **THE BEST OF SPLIT ENZ** [ ] [ ]

CROWDED HOUSE

NEIL FINN (b.27 May'58, Te Awamutu, New Zealand) – vocals, guitar, piano (ex-SPLIT ENZ) / **NICHOLAS SEYMOUR** – bass / **PAUL HESTER** – drums, vocals with many guests **TIM PIERCE** – guitar / **MITCHELL FROOM** – keyboards, producer / **JOE SATRIANI** – b.vox / **JORGE BERMUDEZ** – percussion etc.

Capitol Capitol

Aug 86. (7") **WORLD WHERE YOU LIVE. / THAT'S WHAT I CALL LOVE** [ ] [ ]
('A'ext.12"+=) – Can't carry on.
('A'ext.c-s+=)(cd-s+=) – Something so strong / Don't dream it's over.

Mar 87. (7") **DON'T DREAM IT'S OVER. / THAT'S WHAT I CALL LOVE** [27] [2] Jan 87
(12"+=)(c-s+=) – ('A'extended).

Mar 87. (7") **LOVE YOU 'TIL I DIE. / MEAN TO ME** [-] [ ]

Mar 87. (lp)(c)(cd) **CROWDED HOUSE** [ ] [12] Aug 86
– World where you live / Now we're getting somewhere / Don't dream it's over / Mean to me / Love you 'til the day I die / Something so strong / Hole in the river / I walk away / Tombstone / That's what I call love. (cd+=) – Can't carry on. *(re-iss.cd+c Mar94)*

Jun 87. (7") **SOMETHING SO STRONG. / I WALK AWAY** [ ] [7] Apr 87
(12"+=) – Don't dream it's over (live).

Aug 87. (7") **WORLD WHERE YOU LIVE. / HOLE IN THE RIVER** - 65
Nov 87. (7") **NOW WE'RE GETTING SOMEWHERE. / TOMBSTONE** -
Jun 88. (7") **BETTER BE HOME SOON. / KILL EYE** 42
(12"+=)(cd-s+=) – Don't dream it's over (live).
Jul 88. (lp)(c)(cd) **TEMPLE OF LOW MEN** 40
– I feel possessed / Kill eye / Into temptation / Mansion in the slums / When you come / Never be the same / Love this life / Sister madly / In the lowlands / Better be home soon.
Aug 88. (7") **INTO TEMPTATION. / BETTER BE HOME SOON** -
Aug 88. (7")(c-s) **SISTER MADLY. / MANSION IN THE SLUMS**
(12"+=)(cd-s+=) – Something so strong (live).
Nov 88. (7") **I FEEL POSSESSED. /** -

— added **TIM FINN** (b.25 Jun'52, New Z.) – vocals, piano (ex-SPLIT ENZ)

Jun 91. (cd)(c)(lp) **WOODFACE** 34 83
– Chocolate cake / It's only natural / Fall at your feet / Tall trees / Four seasons in one day / Weather with you / Whispers and moans / There goes God / Fame is / All I ask / As sure as I am / Italian plastic / She goes on / How will you go. *(above album hit UK No.6 after Feb92 single)*
Jun 91. (7")(c-s) **CHOCOLATE CAKE. / AS SURE AS I AM** 69
(12"+=)(cd-s+=) – Anyone can tell.
Oct 91. (7")(c-s) **FALL AT YOUR FEET. / DON'T DREAM IT'S OVER** 17 75
(cd-s) – ('A'side) / Six months in a leaky boat (live) / Now we're getting somewhere (live) / Something so strong (lp version). (extra cd-s+=) – Sister madly / Better be home soon.

— reverted to a trio again, when TIM departed Autumn '91. He was replaced on tour by US session man **MARK HART**

Feb 92. (7")(c-s) **WEATHER WITH YOU. / INTO TEMPTATION** 7
(cd-s) – ('A'side) / Mr.Tambourine man / Eight miles high / So you want to be a rock'n'roll star (all live).
(cd-s) – ('A'side) / Fall at your feet / When you come / Walking on the spot (all live).
Jun 92. (7")(c-s) **FOUR SEASONS IN ONE DAY. / THERE GOES GOD** 26
(cd-s) ('A'side) / Dr.Livingstone / Recurring dream / Anyone can tell (all live).
(cd-s) – ('A'side) / Weather with you / Italian plastic / Message to my girl (all live).
Sep 92. (7")(c-s) **IT'S ONLY NATURAL. / CHOCOLATE CAKE** 24
(cd-s+=) (7 minute songs medley) It's only natural – Six months in a leaky boat – Hole in the river / The burglar's song.
Sep 93. (7")(c-s) **DISTANT SUN. / WALKING ON THE SPOT** 19
(cd-s+=) – Throw your arms around me (live) / One step ahead (live).
(cd-s) – ('A'side) / This is massive (live) / When you come (live).
Oct 93. (cd)(c)(lp) **TOGETHER ALONE** 4 73
– Kare Kare / In my command / Nails in my feet / Black & white boy / Fingers of love / Pineapple head / Locked out / Private universe / Walking on the spot / Distant Sun / Catherine wheels / Skin feeling / Together alone.
Nov 93. (7")(c-s) **NAILS IN MY FEET. / ZEN ROXY** 22
(cd-s+=) – Don't dream it's over (live).
Feb 94. (c-s) **LOCKED OUT. / DISTANT SUN (live)** 12
(cd-s+=) – Hole in the river (live) / Sister Madly (live).
(10"+=) – Private universe (live) / Fall at your feet (live).
(cd-s) – ('A'side) / (above 2-10" tracks) / Better be home soon (live).
Jun 94. (c-s) **FINGERS OF LOVE (live). / NAILS IN MY FEET (live)** 25
(cd-s) – ('A'side) / Skin feeling / Kare Kare (live) / In my command (live).
(10") – ('A'side) / Love u till the day I die (live) / Whispers and moans (live) / It's only natural (live).
(cd-s) – ('A'side) / Catherine wheels / Pineapple head (live) / Something so strong (live).
Sep 94. (c-s) **PINEAPPLE HEAD (live). / WEATHER WITH YOU** 27
(10"+=)(cd-s+=) – Don't dream it's over / Together alone.

— NEIL and TIM were awarded O.B.E.'s in Queen's birthday honours.

compilations, etc

Nov 95. EMI; (3xcd-box) **CROWDED HOUSE / TEMPLE OF LOW MEN / WOODFACE**

TIM FINN

(solo with SPLIT ENZ members)

Epic A&M

Nov 83. (7") **GRAND ADVENTURE. / THROUGH THE YEARS** -
Nov 83. (7") **FRACTION TOO MUCH FRICTION. / BELOW THE PAST** Apr 84
Jan 84. (7") **MADE MY DAY. / GRAND ADVENTURE** -
Jun 84. (lp)(c) **ESCAPADE** Sep 83
– Fraction too much friction / Staring at the embers / Through the years / Not for nothing / In a minor key / Made my day / Wait and see / Below the belt / I only want to know / Growing pains. *(re-iss.cd Oct93 on 'Sony Europe') (re-iss.cd+c Jun94 on 'Epic')*

Virgin Virgin

Mar 86. (7") **NO THUNDER NO FIRE NO CAR. / SEARCHING FOR THE STREETS**
Apr 86. (lp)(c) **BIG CANOE**
– Are we one or are we two? / Searching the streets / Hole in my heart / Spiritual hung / Don't bury my heart / Timmy / So into wine / Hyacinth / Big canoe. *(re-iss.cd Mar94 on 'Virgin')*
Jun 86. (7")(12") **CARVE YOU IN MARBLE. / HOLE IN MY HEART**

Capitol Capitol

Apr 89. (lp)(c)(cd) **TIM FINN**
– Young mountain / Not even close / How'm I gonna sleep / Parihaka / Tears inside / Birds swim fish fly / Suicide on Downing Street / Show a little mercy / Crescendo / Been there, done that. *(re-iss.Oct92)*
Jul 89. (7") **HOW'M I GONNA SLEEP. / CRUEL BLACK CROW**
(12"+=)(cd-s+=) – Six months in a leaky boat.

— with **RICHARD THOMPSON / ANDY WHITE / LIAM O'MAONLAI**

Jun 93. (c-s) **PERSUASION. / STRANGENESS AND CHARM (version)** 43
(cd-s) – ('A'side) / Parihaka / Secret heart / ('A'acoustic).
(cd-s) – ('A'side) / Six months in a leaky boat (live) / Not even close (live) / Protected (live).
Jun 93. (cd)(c) **BEFORE AND AFTER** 29
– Hit the ground running / Protected / In love with it all / Persuasion / Many's the time (in Dublin) / Funny way / Can't do both / In your sway / Strangeness in charm / Always never now / Walk you home / I found it *(re-iss.Sep94)*
Sep 93. (7")(c-s) **HIT THE GROUND RUNNING. / NO MORE TEARS** 50
(cd-s+=) – Not made of stone / You've changed.
(cd-s) – ('A'side) / Walk you home (live) / Charlie (live w / PHIL MANZANERA) / ('A'live).

ALT

— **TIM FINN** / + **ANDY WHITE** – vocals, guitar (former solo artist) / **LIAM O'MAONLAI** – vocals, guitar (ex-HOTHOUSE FLOWERS). ALT (ANDY, LIAM & TIM) recorded in Australia, although initiated in Dublin.

Parlophone Capitol

Jun 95. (cd)(c) **ALTITUDE** 67
– We're all men / Penelope tree / When the winter comes / Favourite girl / Swim / The refugee tree / What you've done / Second swim / Girlfriend guru / Mandala / I decided to fly / The day you were born / Halfway round the world.

FINN

TIM + NEIL duo

Parlophone Capitol

Oct 95. (c-s) **SUFFER NEVER / WEATHER WITH YOU (demo)** 29
(cd-s+=) – Prodigal son (demo) / Catherine wheel (demo).
(cd-s) – ('A'side) / Strangeness and charm (demo) / In love with it all (demo) / Four seasons in one day.
Oct 95. (cd)(c) **FINN** 15
– Only talking sense / Eyes of the world / Mood swinging man / Last day of June / Suffer never / Angels heap / Niwhai / Where is my soul / Bullets in my hairdo / Paradise ((wherever you are) / Kiss the road of Rarotonga.
Nov 95. (c-s)(cd-s) **ANGELS HEAP / IT'S ONLY NATURAL (demo) / CHOCOLATE CAKE (demo)** 41
(cd-s) – ('A'side) / There goes God (demo) / How will you go (demo).

CRUNT (see under ⇒ BABES IN TOYLAND)

CRUSADERS

Formed: Houston, Texas, USA . . . 1960. Originally called The MODERN JAZZ SEXTET in the mid 1950's, before becoming The NIGHT HAWKS in 1958 and moving to L.A. In 1961, the 4 (FELDER, SAMPLE, HOOPER & HENDERSON) transformed into The JAZZ CRUSADERS and signed to 'Pacific J.'. They recorded over a dozen albums in the 60's, and enjoyed loads of session work. In 1971, they altered group name to The CRUSADERS, also signing new deal with 'Blue Thumb'. By late 1974, their fortunes changed when album 'SOUTHERN COMFORT' reached the US Top 40. This led to an invitation to open for The ROLLING STONES on their UK tour. In 1979, they moved to 'M.C.A.' and had first major cross-over hit 'STREET LIFE'. It also helped guest lead vocalist RANDY CRAWFORD, to get initial recognition. Unfortunately, this period saw them peak commercially, but critics still regarded them with high esteem throughout the 80's. All 4 members were always in work, either with group, solo projects or numerous session albums. • **Style:** Exponents of wide range of jazz elements, including free-form and jazz-funk. Instrumental at first, but after success with RANDY CRAWFORD, produced more material with guest singers (i.e. BILL WITHERS, JOE COCKER, etc). • **Songwriters:** SAMPLE and group compositions, covered many songs (selective):- UPTIGHT (Stevie Wonder) / ELEANOR RIGBY + HEY JUDE + GET BACK (Beatles) / etc. • **Trivia:** Without a bassist, they were augmented in the mid 70's by POPS POWELL and white guitarist LARRY CARLTON who was virtually a member.

Recommended: THE BEST OF CRUSADERS (*6)

JAZZ CRUSADERS

WILTON FELDER (b.31 Aug'40) – tenor sax / **JOE SAMPLE** (b. 1 Feb'39) – keyboards / **NESBERT 'Stix' HOOPER** (b.15 Aug'58) – percussion / **WAYNE HENDERSON** (b.24 Sep'39) – trombone **ROY GAINES** – guitar / **JIMMIE BOND** – bass

Fontana Pacific J.

1961. (lp) **FREEDOM SOUND** -
– The geek / M.J.S. funk / Coon / Freedom sound / Theme from Exodus / That's it. *(cd-iss.!91 or 92 has extra takes of tracks 2 & 3)*
1962. (7") **THE GEEK** -
1962. (lp) **LOOKING AHEAD**
– Song of India / Big hunk of funk / Tonight / 507 Neyland / Till all ends / Tortoise and the hare / In a dream / Sinnin' Sam / The young rabbits.
1962. (7") **SINNIN' SAM. / TONIGHT** -
1962. (7") **THE YOUNG RABBITS. / SONG OF INDIA** -

— **VICTOR GASKIN** – bass repl. BOND

1963. (lp) **AT THE LIGHTHOUSE (live)** -
– Congolese sermon / Cathy's dilemma / Blues for Ramona / Weather beat / Scandalizing / Appointment in Ghana.
1963. (7") **CONGOLESE SERMON. / WEATHER BEAT** -

— **BOBBY HAYNES** – bass repl. GAINES + GASKIN

1964. (lp) **TOUGH TALK** [-] [ ]
– Deacon Brown / Turkish black / Brahms lullaby / Boopie / Tough talk / No name samba / Lazy canary / Lonely horn / Brother Bernard.
1964. (7") **NO NAME SAMBA. / TOUGH TALK** [-] [ ]
—— Note: the label 'Pacific J.' changed to 'World Pacific' in 1964.
1965. (7") **BOOPIE. / TURKISH BLACK** [-] [ ]
1965. (lp) **HEAT WAVE** [-] [ ]
– On Broadway / Green back dollar / Close shave / Free sample / Mr.Sandman / Heat wave / Sassy / Theme from The L-Shaped Room / Some samba / Stix march / Purple onion
1965. (7") **HEATWAVE. / ON BROADWAY** [-] [ ]
—— added **MONK MONTGOMERY** – bass / **JOE PASS** – guitar
1965. (lp) **STRETCHIN' OUT** [-] [ ]
– Long John / Robbin's nest / You are only sometimes rain / Out back / Bacha fillen / I'll remember tomorrow / Polka dots and moonbeams / Sweetwater.
1965. (7") **LONG JOHN. / I'LL REMEMBER TOMORROW** [-] [ ]
—— now a sextet again, after PASS departed
1965. (lp) **THE THING** [ ] [ ]
– The thing / Sunset in mountains / White cobra / New time shuffle / While the city sleeps / Para mi espoza / Soul kosher.
1965. (7") **THE THING. / TOUGH TALK** [-] [ ]
—— **AL McKIBBON** – bass / **CLARE FISHER** – organ / **HUNGARIA GARCIA** – percussion / **HUBERT LAWS** – flute / **CARLOS VIDAL** – congas repl. MONK + VICTOR
1966. (lp) **CHILI CON SOUL** [-] [ ]
– Aqua dulce / Soul bourgeoisie / Ontem a note / Tough talk / Tacos / Latin bit / The breeze and I / Dulzura.
1966. (7") **AQUA DULCE. / SOUL BOURGEOISE** [-] [ ]
Mar 66. (7") **UPTIGHT (EVERYTHING'S ALRIGHT). / ?** [-] [95]
—— **LEROY VINNEGAR** – bass repl. last newcomer
Jun 66. (lp) **LIVE AT THE LIGHTHOUSE '66 (live)** [-] [ ]
– Aleluia / Blues up tight / You don't know what love is / Miss it / Scratch / Doin' that thing / Milestones.
Dec 66. (lp) **TALK THAT TALK** [-] [ ]
– Walkin' my cat named Dog / Studewood I can't believe you love me / There is a time / Hey girl / Uptight / Arrastao / Mohair Sam / Walk on by / 1, 2, 3 / The shadow do / Turkish black.
—— **HERBIE LEWIS + JIMMIE BOND** – bass repl. LEROY
1967. (lp) **LIVE AT NEWPORT – LIVE AT PACIFIC JAZZ FESTIVAL (live)** [-] [ ]
– Young rabbits / Freedom sound / Trance dance / A summer madness.
1968. (lp) **UH HUH** [-] [ ]
– Airwaves / Blue Monday / Uh huh / Watts happening / Ice water / Night theme.
—— **CHARLES BUSTER WILLIAMS** – bass repl. LEWIS + BOND
1968. (lp) **LIGHTHOUSE '68 (live)** [-] [ ]
– Ooga-boo-ga-loo / Eleanor Rigby / Native had it so good / The emperor impressions.
1968. (7") **ELEANOR RIGBY. / OOGA BOOGALOO** [-] [ ]
1968. (7") **HEY JUDE. / LOVE AND PEACE** [-] [ ]
Dec 68.. (lp) **POWERHOUSE** [-] [ ]
– Promises, promises / Love and peace / Hey Jude / Sting Ray / Fancy dance / Love is blue (l'amour est bleu) / Cookie / Upstairs / Fire water. *(cd-iss.Sep91)*
1969. (lp) **LIGHTHOUSE '69 (live)** [-] [ ]
– Inside the outside / Ruby P'Gonia / It's your thing / Reflections / Willie and Laura Mae Jones / It's gotta be real / Get back / Svenska Flicka.
1969. (7") **GET BACK. / WILLIE AND LAURA MAE JONES** [-] [ ]
1970. (lp) **THE BEST OF THE JAZZ CRUSADERS** [-] [ ]
– (compilation)
—— **ARTHUR ADAMS + FREDDIE ROBINSON** – guitar repl. WILLIAMS

Rare Earth | Chisa

Oct 70. (lp) **OLD SOCKS, NEW SHOES . . . NEW SOCKS, OLD SHOES** [ ] [90]
– Thank you / Funny shuffle / Why do you laugh at me / Jackson / Rainy night in Georgia / Golden slumbers / Jazz / Time has no ending / Hard times / Way back home. *(cd-iss.Dec94 on 'Mo Jazz')*
Nov 71. (7") **WAY BACK HOME. / JACKSON** [ ] [90]

The CRUSADERS

Rare Earth | Chisa

Jun 71. (lp) **PASS THE PLATE** [-] [ ]
(cd-iss.Dec94 on 'Mo Jazz')(cd-iss.Dec94 on 'Mo Jazz')(cd-iss.Dec94 on 'Mo Jazz')(cd-iss.Dec94 on 'Mo Jazz')
SAMPLE, HOOPER, FELDER, HENDERSON + ADAMS recruited **LARRY CARLTON + DAVID T.WALKER** – guitar / **CHUCK RAINEY** – bass guest

Island | Blue Thumb

Mar 72. (d-lp)(c) **CRUSADERS 1** [ ] [96]
– That's how I feel / So far away / Put it where you want it / Mystique blues / Full Moon / Sweet revival / Mud hole / It's just gotta be that way / Georgia cottonfield / A shade of blues / Three children / Mosadi (woman).
(re-iss.Jul76 on 'A.B.C.')
Jul 72. (7") **PUT IT WHERE YOU WANT IT. / MOSADI WOMAN** [ ] [52]

A.B.C. | Blue Thumb

Mar 73. (d-lp)(c) **THE 2ND CRUSADE** [ ] [45]
– Don't let it get you down / Take it or leave it / Gotta get it on / Where there's a will there's a way / Look beyond the hill / Journey from within / Ain't gonna change a thing / A message from the inner city / A search of soul / No place to hide / Tomorrow where are you / Tough talk / Do you remember when. *(re-iss.Jul76 on 'A.B.C.')*
Apr 73. (7") **DON'T LET IT GET YOU DOWN. / JOURNEY FROM WITHIN** [-] [86]
—— **MAX BENNETT** – bass repl. WALKER
Dec 73. (lp)(c) **UNSUNG HEROES** [ ] [ ]
– Unsung heroes / Lay it on the line / Crossfire / Hard times / Let's boogie / Freedom sound / In the middle of the river / Heavy up / Night time / How I lay me down to sleep. *(re-iss.Jul76 on 'A.B.C.')*
—— now without ADAMS + BENNETT
Apr 74. (lp)(c) **SCRATCH** (live) [ ] [73]
– Scratch / Eleanor Rigby / Hard times / So far away / Way back home. *(re-iss.Sep82 on 'M.C.A.')*
Apr 74. (7") **SCRATCH (live). / WAY BACK HOME (live)** [ ] [81]
Nov 74. (d-lp)(c) **SOUTHERN COMFORT** [ ] [31] Oct 74
– Stomp and buck dance / Greasy spoon / Get on the soul ship / Super stuff / Double bubble / The well's gone dry / Southern comfort / Time bomb / When there's love around / Lillies of the Nile / Whispering pines / A ballad for Joe.

Anchor | Blue Thumb

Apr 75. (7") **STOMP & BUCK DANCE. / BALLAD FOR JOE (LOUIS)** [ ] [ ]
Aug 75. (lp)(c) **CHAIN REACTION** [ ] [26]
– Creole / Chain reaction / I felt the love / Mellow out / Rainbow visions / Hallucinate / Give it up / Hot's it / Sugar cane / Soul caravan / Spiral / Keep that same old feeling / My Mama told me so / 'Til the sun shines / And then there was the blues / Serenity / Feeling funky *(re-iss.Mar77 on 'A.B.C.') (re-iss.Jun79 on 'Flyover' / Mobile')*
Nov 75. (7") **CREOLE. / I FELT THE LOVE** [ ] [ ]
—— the quintet added **ROBERT POPWELL** – bass / **ARTHUR ADAMS** – guitar
May 76. (lp)(c) **THOSE SOUTHERN NIGHTS** [ ] [38]
– Spiral / Keep that same old feeling / My mama told me so / Till the Sun shines / And then there was the blues / Serenity / Feeling funky. *(re-iss.Feb82 on 'M.C.A.')*
Jun 76. (7") **KEEP THAT SAME OLD FEELING. / TILL THE SUN SHINES** [ ] [ ]
Sep 76. (7") **PUT IT WHERE YOU WANT IT. / DON'T LET IT GET YOU DOWN** [ ] [ ]
Dec 76. (d-lp)(c) **THE BEST OF THE CRUSADERS**(compilation) [ ] [ ]
– Put it where you want it / Stomp and buck dance / Greasy spoon / Scratch / So fare away / Hard times / So far away (live) / Don't let it get you down / Keep that same old feeling / That's how I feel / Soul caravan / Chain reaction / Ballad for Joe (Louis) / Do you remember when / Way back home.*(re-iss.Oct81 on 'M.C.A.') (re-iss.cd+c Dec94 on 'Pickwick')*
—— WAYNE HENDERSON had already vacated (late '75) to venture solo. They proceeded to employ session musicians and singers to cover his absence.
—— next was first of many to feature **ROLAND BAUTISTA + DEAN PARKS** – guitar / **PAULINHO DA COSTA** – percussion
Jul 77. (lp)(c) **FREE AS THE WIND** [ ] [41] Jun 77
– Free as the wind / I felt the love / The way we was / Nite crawler / Feel it / Sweet'n'sour / River rat / It happens every day. *(re-iss.1983 on 'M.C.A.')*
Jul 77. (7") **FEEL IT. / THE WAY WE WAS** [ ] [ ]
—— **BILLY ROGERS** – guitar repl. ADAMS
Jul 78. (lp)(c) **IMAGES** [ ] [34]
– Fair tales / Marcella's dream / Bayou bottoms / Merry go round / Cosmic reign / Covert action / Snow flake. *(re-iss.Aug81 on 'M.C.A.')*
Jul 78. (7") **BAYOU BOTTOMS. / COVERT ACTION** [ ] [ ]

M.C.A. | M.C.A.

Jun 79. (lp)(c) **STREET LIFE** [10] [18]
– Street life / My lady / Rodeo drive / Carnival of the night / The hustler / Night faces. *(re-iss.+cd.Sep86)*
Aug 79. (7") **STREET LIFE. / THE HUSTLER** [5] [36]
—— (above featured **RANDY CRAWFORD** – vocals (see also ⇒) (re-iss.12"-Jul82)
—— now basic trio (**SAMPLE, HOOPER + FELDER**) plus 1977 accompaniment
Jul 80. (lp)(c) **RHAPSODY AND BLUES** [40] [29]
– Soul shadows / Honky tonk strutting / Elegant evening / Rhapsody in blues / Last call / Sweet gentle love. *(re-iss.1983)*
Jul 80. (7")(12") **SOUL SHADOWS. / PUT IT WHERE YOU WANT IT** [ ] [-]
Jul 80. (7") **SOUL SHADOWS. / SWEET GENTLE LOVE** [-] [ ]
—— (above featured **BILL WITHERS** – vocals (solo artist)
Jan 81. (7")(12") **LAST CALL. / HONKY TONK STRUTTING** [ ] [ ]
Aug 81. (7") **I'M SO GLAD I'M STANDING HERE TODAY. / STANDING TALL (w/ JOE COCKER)** [61] [97]
(re-iss.Apr83)
Sep 81. (lp)(c) **STANDING TALL** [47] [59]
– Standing tall / I'm so glad I'm standing here today / Sunshine in your eyes / This old world's too funky for me / Luckenbach Texas / Longest night / I'm so glad I'm standing here today (reprise). (album featured and credited **JOE COCKER – vocals**)
Nov 81. (7")(12") **THIS OLD WORLD'S TOO FUNKY FOR ME. / I'M SO GLAD I'M STANDING HERE TODAY (w/JOE COCKER)** [ ] [ ]
Apr 82. (lp) **ONGAKU DA – LIVE IN JAPAN (live)** [ ] [ ]
– (introduction) / Rainbow seeker / The hustler / Sweet gentle love / (drum introduction) / Spiral / In all my wildest dreams / Carmel / Put it where you want it. *(cd-iss.Nov93 on 'GRP')*
Jun 82 (7") **(w/ B.B. KING) STREETLIFE. / OVERTURE** [-] [ ]
Jun 82. (d-lp)(d-c) **ROYAL JAM (live at Royal Festival Hall with B.B. King & Orchestra)** [ ] [ ]
– Overture: I'm so glad I'm standing here today / One day I'll fly away / Fly with wings of love / Burnin' up the carnival / Last call / The thrill is gone / Better not look down / Hold on / Street life / I just can't leave your love alone / Never make a move too soon. *(cd-iss.Jul87)*
Jul 82. (7")(12") **SCRATCH (live). / ?** [ ] [-]
—— (1983) **LEON 'Ndugu' CHANCLER** – drums repl. HOOPER
Mar 84. (7")(12") **NIGHT LADIES. / MEGASTREET (Megamix)** [55] [ ]
Apr 84. (7") **NEW MOVES. / MR. COOL** [-] [ ]
Mar 84. (lp)(c) **GHETTO BLASTER** [46] [79]
– Dead end / Gotta lotta shakalada / New moves / Zalal'e mini (take it easy) / Night ladies / Mr. Cool / Dream start.
Jun 84. (7") **DEAD END. / DREAM STREET** [-] [ ]
Jul 84. (7") **NEW MOVES. / DEAD END** [ ] [-]
(12"+=) – 1984 Street Life.

Nov 84. (7") **GOTTA LOTTA SHAKALADA. / ZALAL'E MINI (TAKE IT EASY)** [-] [ ]
Nov 86. (lp)(c)(cd) **THE GOOD AND BAD TIMES** [ ] [ ]
– Good times / The way it goes / Sweet dreams / Michievous ways / Sometimes you can take it or leave it / Three wishes.
(above featured **LARRY CARLTON & NANCY WILSON**)
Jan 87. (7") **THE WAY IT GOES. / GOOD TIMES** [-] [ ]

— **SAMPLE + FELDER** added **MICHAEL LANDAU** – guitar / **NATHAN EAST** – bass / **JOHN ROBINSON** – drums / + sessioners

Jun 88. (lp)(c)(cd) **LIFE IN THE MODERN WORLD** [ ] [ ]
– Passion fruit / Let me prove myself / A.C. "Alternative Currents" / Destiny / Life in the modern world / Coulda, woulda, shoulda / Samplin' / Some people just never learn / Mulholland nights.

G.R.P. G.R.P.

May 91. (cd)(c)(lp) **HEALING THE WOUNDS** [ ] [ ]
– Pessimisticism / Mercy, mercy, mercy / Little things can mean a lot / Cause we've ended as lovers / Shake dance / Maputo / Running man / Healing the wounds.
Oct 92. (cd)(c) **IMAGES** [ ] [ ]
– Fairy tales / Marcella's dream / Bayou bottoms / Merry-go-round / Cosmic reign / Covert action / Snowflake.

– more compilations, etc. –

1973. Mowest; (lp) **HOLLYWOOD** [-] [ ]
(cd-iss.Dec94 on 'MoJazz')
1970'S. Mowest; (lp) **AT THEIR BEST** (compilation) [-] [ ]
Aug 83. M.C.A.; (lp)(c) **THE VOCAL ALBUM / TAPE** (The 12"mixes) [ ] [ ]
Sep 84. M.C.A.; (d-c) **RHAPSODY AND BLUES / STREET LIFE** [ ] [ ]
Oct 87. M.C.A.; (cd) **RHAPSODY AND BLUES / STANDING TALL** [ ] [ ]
1989. M.C.A.; (cd) **CHAIN REACTION / THOSE SOUTHERN NIGHTS** [-] [ ]
Apr 87. Old Gold; (7") **STREET LIFE. / INHERIT THE WIND (by 'WILTON FELDER')** [ ] [-]
(re-iss.12"-May88)
Jan 89. Connoisseur; (cd)(cd)(d-lp) **SAMPLE A DECADE** [ ] [-]
– So far away / Chain reaction / Bayou bottoms / Streetlife / Don't let it get you down / Hold on (w / R.P.O. & B.B.KING) / My mama told me so / Snow flake / (I'm so glad) I'm standing here today / Rhapsody and blues / Sweet'n'sour / Nite crawler / Night ladies / Rodeo drive (high steppin') / Honky tonk struttin'. (d-lp/c+=) – And then there was the blues / Soul shadows / Soul caravan / Fairy tales / Free as the wind.
Sep 92. G.R.P.; (3xcd) **THE GOLDEN YEARS** [ ] [ ]
Jul 94. Music Club; (cd)(c) **AND BEYOND ...** [ ] [-]
Feb 95. Calibre; (d-cd)(d-c) **THE GREATEST CRUSADE** [ ] [-]
Mar 95. Connoisseur; (cd) **SOUL SHADOWS** [ ] [-]
Mar 95. Nectar; (cd)(c) **THE ULTIMATE COLLECTION** [ ] [-]
Apr 95. Castle; (cd) **THE COLLECTION** [ ] [-]
Aug 95. Sin-Drome/ Via; (cd) **HAPPY AGAIN (JAZZ CRUSADERS)** [ ] [-]

JOE SAMPLE

A.B.C. A.B.C.

Feb 78. (lp)(c) **RAINBOW SEEKER** [ ] [62]
– Rainbow seeker / In all my wildest dreams / There are many stops along the way / Melodies of love / Fly with wings of love / As long as it lasts / Islands in the rain / Together we'll find a way. *(re-iss.Aug81 on 'M.C.A.', cd-iss.Jul87)*
Feb 79. (lp)(c) **CARMEL** [ ] [56]
– Carmel / Painting / Cannery Row / A rainy day in Monterey / Sunrise / Midnight and mist / More beautiful each day. *(re-iss.May82 on 'M.C.A.')*

M.C.A. M.C.A.

Sep 79. (7") **CARMEL. / RAINY DAY IN MONTEREY** [ ] [ ]
Feb 81. (lp)(c) **VOICES IN THE RAIN** [ ] [65] Jan 81
– Voices in the rain / Burnin' up the carnival / Greener grasses / Eye of the hurricane / Dream of dreams / Shadows / Sonata in solitude. *(re-iss.1983)*
Feb 81. (7")(12") **BURNIN' UP THE CARNIVAL. / DREAM OF DREAMS** [ ] [ ]
Apr 82. (lp)(c) **SWING STREET CAFE ("JOE SAMPLE & DAVIS T. WALKER")** [ ] [ ]
– Hallelujah I lover her so / Rock house / Honest I do / Next time u see me / Woke up this morning / C.C.rider / Honky tonk / After hours. *(re-iss.Aug86, cd-iss.Jul87)*
Mar 83. (lp)(c) **THE HUNTER** [ ] [ ]
– The hunter / Blue ballet / Beauty and the beast / Wings of fire / Just a little higher / Night flight. *(cd-iss.Jun88)*
Oct 85. (lp)(c)(cd) **OASIS** [ ] [ ]
– Oasis / New places, new faces / Teardrops / Asian eyes / The survivor / Love's paradise / Wonderful / Mirage. *(cd-iss.Oct87)*
Oct 85. (7")(12") **THE SURVIVOR. / WONDERLAND** [ ] [ ]
Jun 87. (lp)(c)(cd) **ROLES** [ ] [ ]
– Woman, you're driving me mad / The gifted / Friends and lovers / Ego maniac mambo / Fortune hunter / Ship of fools.

W.E.A. Warners

Jan 89. (lp)(c)(cd) **SPELLBOUND** [ ] [ ]
– Seven years of good luck / Spellbound / Somehow our love survives / All God's children / Leading me back to you / U-turn / Bones jive / Luna in New York / Serialized / Looking glass.
Feb 89. (7") **U-TURN. / SERIALIZED** [-] [ ]
Apr 89. (7")(c-s) **SPELLBOUND. / LEADING ME BACK TO YOU** [-] [ ]

Warners Warners

Sep 94. (cd) **DID YOU FEEL THAT? (w / The SOUL COMMITTEE)** [ ] [ ]

– his compilations, others, etc. –

Jan 79. Sonet; (lp) **FANCY DANCE** [ ] [-]
– Children's song / Fancy dance / All the lonely years / Another blues / Svenska flicka / Old town. *(cd-iss.Oct86)*
Oct 83. M.C.A.; (d-c) **CARMEL / RAINBOW SEEKER** [ ] [ ]
(cd-iss.Apr87)

WILTON FELDER

solo.

A.B.C. A.B.C.

Nov 78. (lp)(c) **WE ALL HAVE A STAR** [ ] [ ]
– We all have a star / I know who I am / Why believe / The cycles of time / Let's dance together / My name is love / You and me and ecstasy. *(re-iss.Feb82 on 'M.C.A.')*
Jan 79. (7") **LET'S DANCE TOGETHER. / RIDE ON** [ ] [ ]

— (below lp + '45 feat. **BOBBY WOMACK** – vocals)

M.C.A. M.C.A.

Oct 80. (7") **INHERIT THE WIND. / UNTIL THE MORNING COMES** [39] [ ]
Nov 80. (lp)(c) **INHERIT THE WIND** [ ] [ ]
– Inherit the wind / Someday we'll all be free / Until the morning comes / Insight / L.A.light / I've got a secret I'm gonna tell.
Jan 81. (7")(12") **INSIGHT. / I KNOW WHO I AM** [ ] [-]
Jan 81. (7") **INSIGHT. / L. A. LIGHT** [-] [ ]
1982. (7") **INHERIT THE WIND (w/ BOBBY WOMACK). / SOMEDAY WE'LL ALL BE FREE** [-] [ ]
Apr 83. (lp)(c) **GENTLE FIRE** [ ] [ ]
– Gentle fire / Driftin' on a dream / Only for those who care / I got to feel like you do / Summer nights in Rio / Somewhere in my past.
1983. (7") **GENTLE FIRE (w/ TASTE OF HONEY). / (part 2)** [-] [ ]
Jan 85. (7")(12") **(NO MATTER HOW HIGH I GET) I'LL STILL BE LOOKIN' UP TO YOU. / LA LUZ** [63] [ ]

— (above 45 + below lp once again featured **BOBBY WOMACK** – vocals)

Feb 85. (lp)(c) **SECRETS** [77] [81]
– Secrets / (No matter how high I get) I'll still be lookin' up to you / La Luz / The truth song / I found you.
Feb 85. (7") **SECRETS. / SOMEDAY WE'LL ALL BE FREE** [-] [ ]

STIX HOOPER

M.C.A. M.C.A.

Oct 79. (7") **RUM OR TEQUILA. / BRAZOS RIVER BREAKDOWN** [-] [ ]
Nov 79. (7") **CORDON BLEU. / BRAZOS RIVER BREAKDOWN** [ ] [-]
Nov 79. (lp)(c) **THE WORLD WITHIN** [ ] [ ]
– Brazos river breakdown / African spirit / Rum or tequila / Passion / Cordon bleu / Jasmine breeze / Little drummer boy. *(re-iss.Nov83)*
Jan 80. (7") **CORDON BLEU. / PASSION** [-] [ ]

After he departed from band, he issued album TOUCH THE FEELING in Nov 82 + singles 'GIMME SOME SPACE' / 'I TOUCHED A DREAM' / 'LET'S TALK IT OVER' / 'ESPECIALLY FOR YOU' (w/Jerry Butler).

CRYSTALS

Formed: Brooklyn, New York, USA ... 1961 when they met songwriter LEROY BATES, whose daughter CRYSTAL gave the group its name. They almost immediately signed to producer PHIL SPECTOR's new label 'Philles', gaining first US Top 20 hit with 'B'side THERE'S NO OTHER (LIKE MY BABY). Controversially, SPECTOR decided to use other singers mainly DARLENE LOVE on lead, when their fourth 45, HE'S A REBEL hits US top slot late in '62. The following year, with originals bar MARY back at the helm, they had another two Top 10 transatlantic hits; DA DOO RON RON and THEN HE KISSED ME. But for another US Top 40 hit in 1964, they virtually disappeared into semi-retirement and golden oldies circuit. • **Style:** SPECTOR created his "wall of sound" around them and The RONETTES, using their voices rather than them as artists. It worked for a while until the "beat" groups took over in 1964. • **Songwriters:** UPTOWN (Mann/Weill) / HE'S A REBEL (Gene Pitney) / etc. • **Miscellaneous:** They appeared on PHIL SPECTOR's seasonal Christmas 1963 lp 'A CHRISTMAS GIFT FOR YOU', contributing 'Santa Claus Is Coming To Town' & 'Rudolph The Red Nosed Reindeer'.

Recommended: THE BEST OF THE CRYSTALS (*6)

BARBARA ALSTON – vocals / **MARY THOMAS** – vocals / **DEE DEE KENNIBREW** – vocals / **LALA BROOKS** – vocals / **PAT WRIGHT** – vocals

Parlophone Philles

Feb 62. (7") **THERE'S NO OTHER (LIKE MY BABY). / OH YEAH, MAYBE BABY** [ ] [20] Oct 61
(above was originally released in US Jul61, flipped over)
Feb 62. (7") **UPTOWN. / WHAT A NICE WAY TO TURN SEVENTEEN** [-] [13]
May 62. (lp) **TWIST UPTOWN** [-] [ ]
– Uptown / Another country, another world / Frankenstein twist / Oh yeah, maybe baby / Please hurt me / There's no other (like my baby) / On Broadway / What a nice way to turn seventeen / No one ever tells you / Gee whiz, look at my eyes / I love you Eddie.
Jun 62. (7") **HE HIT ME (AND IT FELT LIKE A KISS). / NO ONE EVER TELLS YOU** [-] [ ]

— (Oct62)Now a quartet, when MARY left to get married. The next two 45's saw SPECTOR using bogus CRYSTALS (**DARLENE LOVE** – lead vocals & **FANITA JAMES and GRACIA NITZSCHE** – b.vocals ex-BLOSSOMS)

London Philles

Oct 62. (7") **HE'S A REBEL. / I LOVE YOU EDDIE** [19] [1] Aug 62
(re-iss.Jun75 on 'Phil Spector Int.')
Jan 63. (7") **HE'S SURE THE BOY I LOVE. / WALKIN' ALONG** [ ] [11] Dec 62
Feb 63. (lp) **HE'S A REBEL** [ ] [ ]
– He's a rebel / Uptown / Another country, another world / Frankenstein twist / Oh yeah, maybe baby! / He's sure the boy I love / There's no other like my baby / On Broadway / What a nice way to turn seventeen / No one ever tells you / He hit me / I love you Eddie.

— **LALA** now on lead vocals, with other 3 originals.

May 63. (7") **DA DOO RON RON. / GIT IT** [5] [3] Apr 63
Sep 63. (7") **THEN HE KISSED ME. / BROTHER JULIUS** [2] [6] Aug 63

— **FRANCES COLLINS** – vocals repl. PAT who also gets married.

Jan 64. (7") **LITTLE BOY. / HARRY (FROM W.V.) AND MILT** [-] [92]
Feb 64. (7") **I WONDER. / LITTLE BOY** [36] [-]
Jul 64. (7") **ALL GROWN UP. / IRVING (JAGGERED SIXTEENTHS)** [ ] [98]

United Art United Art

Oct 65. (7") **MY PLACE. / YOU CAN'T TIE A GIRL DOWN** [ ] [ ]
Feb 66. (7") **ARE YOU TRYING TO GET RID OF ME, BABY?. / I GOT A MAN** [-] [ ]

— In 1966, they were discarded by record company, and retired to domesticity. After a few out of retirement gigs, they appeared mid '71, at New York's 'Rock'n 'roll revival show'. Depleted somewhat in line-up, they continued throughout the 70's & 80's on the 'Golden Oldies' circuit.

- compilations, others, etc. -

1963. London; (7"ep) **THE CRYSTALS** [ ] [-]
1963. Philles; (lp) **THE CRYSTALS SING THE GREATEST HITS VOLUME 1** [-] [ ]
(UK-iss.Oct75 as '. . . SING THEIR GREATEST HITS' on 'Phil Spector Int.')
Jan 69. London; (7") **DA DOO RON RON. / HE'S A REBEL** [ ] [-]
Oct 74. Phil Spector; (7"blue) **DA DOO RON RON. / THEN HE KISSED ME** [15] [ ]
(re-iss.7" Jan76 & Aug77)
Dec 74. London/ US= Philles; (7") **SANTA CLAUS IS COMING TO TOWN. / RUDOLPH THE RED NOSED REINDEER** [ ] [ ]

— (below was boxed-set)

Oct 75. Phil Spector; (lp)(c) **PHIL SPECTOR WALL OF SOUND VOL.3** [ ] [ ]
Apr 77. Phil Spector; (7") **ALL GROWN UP. / THE TWIST** [ ] [-]
Oct 80. Creole; (7"m) **DA DOO RON RON. / AND THEN HE KISSED ME / HE'S A REBEL** [ ] [-]
(re-iss.Aug82)
Aug 87. Raise The Roof; (7") **DA DOO RON RON. / THEN HE KISSED ME** [ ] [-]
(12"+=) – He's a rebel.
Nov 92. E.M.I.; (cd)(c)(lp) **THE BEST OF THE CRYSTALS** [ ] [ ]
– There's no other (like my baby) / Oh yeah, maybe baby / Uptown / What a nice way to turn 17 / He hit me (and it felt like a kiss) / No one ever tells you / He's a rebel / I love you Eddie / Another country, another world / Please hurt me / He's sure the boy I love / Look in my eyes / Da doo ron ron / Heartbreaker / Then he kissed me / I wonder / Little boy / Girls can tell / All grown up.
Apr 93. Sixteen; (cd) **16 GREATEST HITS** [ ] [-]

CUD

Formed: Leeds, England . . . 1987 by CARL PUTTNAM and STEVE 'CUD' GOODWYN. After a long period on indie labels, they were found by 'A&M' in the early 90's, and hit charts with 'OH NO, WON'T DO' single. • **Style:** Described themselves as a cross between LED ZEPPELIN and INXS, a combination of funk and alternative fun new wave. • **Songwriters:** Group compositions, except YOU SEXY THING (Hot Chocolate) / LIVING IN THE PAST (Jethro Tull) / PRICE OF LOVE (Everly Brothers) / DOWN DOWN (Status Quo). • **Trivia:** Initiated after finding discarded drum-kit in a skip!

Recommended: LEGGY MAMBO (*7) / ASQUARIUS (*6)

CARL PUTTNAM (b.1967, Ilford, Essex) – vocals / **MIKE DUNPHY** (b.1967, Northumberland, England) – guitar, keyboards / **WILLIAM POTTER** (b.1968, Derby, England) – bass / **STEVE GOODWIN** (b.1967, Croydon, Surrey, England) – drums

Reception not issued

Oct 87. (12"ep) **YOU'RE THE BOSS / MIND THE GAP. / VAN VAN VAN / YOU'RE THE BOSS (Out To Lunch mix)** [ ] [-]

Ediesta not issued

Apr 88. (12"ep) **UNDER MY HAT. / PUNISHMENT-REWARD RELATIONSHIP / ART!** [ ] [-]

Dug-Nightime not issued

Sep 88. (12"ep) **SLACK TIME. / I'VE HAD IT WITH BLONDES / MAKE NO BONES** [ ] [-]

Imaginary not issued

Apr 89. (7") **LOLA. / THE DAY CRIME PAID** [ ] [-]
Jun 89. (lp)(cd) **WHEN IN ROME, KILL ME** [ ] [-]
– When in Rome, kill me: (i) When in Rome, kill me (ii) Only a prawn in Whitby (iii) Bibi couldn't see (iv) Strange kind of love (v) Push and shove / (vi) The day crime paid (vii) When in Rome, kill me again / I've had it with blondes / Van van van / Vocally speaking / Wobbly jelly / Alison springs / Epicurean's answer.
Sep 89. (12"ep) **ONLY A PRAWN IN WHITBY / (other version) / LIVING IN THE PAST / EVERYBODY WORKS SO HARD** [ ] [-]
May 90. (7"one-sided-ltd.) **HEYWIRE.** [ ] [-]
(12"+=)(cd-s+=) Purple love baloon. / Possession.
Sep 90. (7") **ROBINSON CRUSOE. / PLANTATION ISLAND** [86] [-]
(cd-s+=) – L.O.P.H.E. / ('A'-Friday mix).
Oct 90. (cd)(c)(lp) **LEGGY MAMBO** [ ] [-]
– Now / Heart / Hey, boots / Love in a hollow tree / Love mandarin / Not exactly D L E R C / Robinson Crusoe / Eau water / Carl's 115th coach trip nightmare / Magic / Syrup and sour grapes / Brain on a slow train.
Mar 91. (7") **MAGIC (Farsley mix). / MAGIC (Stockport mix)** [80] [-]
(12"+=)(cd-s+=) – Marjorie. / Beyond hair.

A&M A&M

Oct 91. (7") **OH NO WON'T DO. / ARIEL** [49] [ ]
(12"+=)(cd-s+=) – Procession / Price of love.
Mar 92. (7") **THROUGH THE ROOF. / UNDOUBTABLY THOMAS** [44] [ ]
(12"+=)(cd-s+=) – Prime cut.
May 92. (7")(7"pic-d) **RICH AND STRANGE. / LOVE MANDARIN (acoustic)** [24] [ ]
(12")(cd-s) – ('A'side) / Do it again / A song called that.
Jun 92. (cd)(c)(lp) **ASQUARIUS** [30] [ ]
– Rich and strange / Easy / Sometimes rightly sometimes wrongly / Spanish love story / Magic Alex / Beyond hair / Pink flamingo / Possession / Through the roof / Soul food / Once again / No smoking. *(re-iss.cd May95)*
Jul 92. (7")(c-s)(7"pic-d) **PURPLE LOVE BALLOON. / SPANISH LOVE SONG (acoustic)** [27] [ ]
(12")(cd-s)(12"pic-d) – ('A'side) / ('A'killer rabbit mix-omatosis) / ('A'-US mix) / Remember what it is that your love.
Oct 92. (7")(c-s) **ONCE AGAIN. / DAY BY DAY** [45] [ ]
(12"+=)(cd-s+=) – Eau water (acoustic) / Soul food (acoustic).
Jan 94. (7") **NEUROTICA. / MIDNIGHT RIDE** [37] [ ]
(c-s)(cd-s) – ('A'side) / Brand name skin / Juicy eureka / 1 W.G.S.
(12"++=) – Neurotica (remix).
Mar 94. (7") **STICKS AND STONES. / SKI BUM** [68] [ ]
(cd-s+=) – My need to hurry.
(cd-s) – ('A'side) / Down the plug / My keyhole don't keep secrets anymore.
Apr 94. (cd)(c)(lp) **SHOWBIZ** [46] [ ]
– Somebody snatched my action / E.S.P. / Waving and drowning / Sticks and stones / Mystery deepens / Slip away / One giant love / I reek of chic / Not necessarily evil / You lead me / Tourniquet / Neurotica. *(re-is.cd May95)*
Aug 94. (c-s)(cd-s) **ONE GIANT LOVE / LOOK ON UP AT THE BOTTOM / FIND IT** [52] [ ]
(12") – ('A'side) / Robinson Crusoe (live) / Strange kind of love (live) / Purple love balloon (live).
(cd-s) – ('A'live) / Slip away (live) / Magic (live) / Neurotica (live).

- compilations, others, etc. -

Jan 88. Strange Fruit; (12"ep) **THE PEEL SESSIONS (16.6.87)** [ ] [-]
– Mind the gap / You're the boss / Don't bank on it / You sexy thing.
Jul 90. Imaginary; (cd)(c)(lp) **ELVIS BELT** (1989-1991 label product) [ ] [-]

CULT

Formed: Bradford, England . . . 1982 as SOUTHERN DEATH CULT by IAN ASTBURY who was then called IAN LINDSAY. He and his family had once stayed in Scotland before emigrating to Canada. By Spring '83, they had become DEATH CULT, leaving only a single FAT MAN, and demo album behind them. They stuck with 'Beggar's B.' subsidiary label 'Situation 2' for a couple more singles, and moved to Manchester. Early in 1984, they shortened name again to become The CULT, also relocating to London, with 'Beggar's B.' now taking full reins. Soon became one of Britain's biggest crowd-pullers worldwide, setting up home in Los Angeles 1988. • **Style:** Initially "gothic"-punks, which shifted into LED ZEPPELIN-ish heavy-metal by '85. ASTBURY always focal point as Red Indian influenced warrior of rock. • **Songwriters:** From '83 onwards, all by ASTBURY / DUFFY. Covered WILD THING (Troggs) / LOUIE LOUIE (Kingsmen) / CONQUISTADOR ? / FAITH HEALER (Alex Harvey). • **Trivia:** RICK RUBIN (Def Jam boss) produced ELECTRIC lp.

Recommended: LOVE (*8) / DREAMTIME (*6) / SOUTHERN DEATH CULT (*6) / ELECTRIC (*6) / PURE CULT (*7)

The SOUTHERN DEATH CULT

IAN LINDSAY (b.ASTBURY, 14 May'62, Heswell, Cheshire, England)– vocals / **BUZZ BURROWS** – guitar / **BARRY JEPSON** – bass / **AKY (NAWAZ QUERESHI)** – drums

Situation 2 not issued

Dec 82. (7") **FATMAN. / MOYA** [ ] [-]
(12"+=) – The girl.

Beggar's B. not issued

Jun 83. (lp)(c) **SOUTHERN DEATH CULT** [43] [-]
– All glory / Fatman / Today / False faces / The crypt / Crow / Faith / Vivisection / Apache / Moya.

— (Apr'83) (as BUZZ, AKY and BARRY formed GETTING THE FEAR)

DEATH CULT

with now **IAN ASTBURY** recruited new people– BILLY DUFFY (b.12 May'61)– lead guitar (ex-THEATRE OF HATE, ex-NOSEBLEEDS) / **JAMIE STUART** – bass (ex-RITUAL, ex-CRISIS) / **RAY MONDO** (r.n.SMITH)– drums (ex-RITUAL)

Situation 2 not issued

Jul 83. (12"ep) **BROTHERS GRIMM / HORSE NATION. / GHOST DANCE / CHRISTIANS** [ ] [-]

— **NIGEL PRESTON** – drums (ex-SEX GANG CHILDREN) repl. MONDO

Nov 83. (7")(12") **GOD'S ZOO. / GOD'S ZOO (THESE TIMES)** [ ] [ ]
(re-iss.Nov88)

The CULT

(same line-up)

Situation 2 not issued

May 84. (7") **SPIRITWALKER. / FLOWER IN THE DESERT** [ ] [-]
(12"+=) – Bone bag.

Beggar's B. Sire

Aug 84. (lp)(c)(pic-lp) **DREAMTIME** [21] [ ]
– Horse nation / Spiritwalker / 83rd dream / Butterflies / Go west (crazy spinning

circles) / Flower in the desert / Dreamtime / Rider in the snow / Bad medicine waltz. *(re-iss.Oct88.+cd+=) – Bone bag / Sea and sky / Resurrection Joe. (free live-lp.w/above, also cont. on c)* **DREAMTIME AT THE LYCEUM** – 83rd dream / God's zoo / Bad medicine / Dreamtime / Horse nation / Bone bag / Brother Grimm / Moya.

Sep 84. (7") **GO WEST (CRAZY SPINNING CIRCLES). / SEA AND SKY** [ ] [-]
(12"+=) – Brothers Grimm (live).

Dec 84. (7")(12") **RESURRECTION JOE. / ('A' hep cat mix)** [74] [-]

May 85. (7") **SHE SELLS SANCTUARY. / NUMBER 13** [15] [ ]
(12"+=) – The snake.
(c-s+=) – Assault sanctuary.

— **MARK BRZEZICKI** – drums (of BIG COUNTRY) deputised repl. PRESTON

Sep 85. (7") **RAIN. / LITTLE FACE** [17] [ ]
(12"+=) – Here comes the rain.

Oct 85. (lp)(c)(cd) **LOVE** [4] [87]
– Nirvana / Big neon gliter / Love / Brother Wolf, Sister Moon / Rain / The phoenix / The hollow man / Revolution / She sells sanctuary / Black angel. (cd+=) – Judith / Little face.

— **LES WARNER** (b.13 Feb'61) – drums (ex-JOHNNY THUNDERS, etc) repl. MARK

Nov 85. (7") **REVOLUTION. / ALL SOULS AVENUE** [30] [ ]
(d7"+=)(12"+=) – Judith / Sunrise.

Feb 87. (7") **LOVE REMOVAL MACHINE. / WOLF CHILD'S BLUES** [18] [ ]
(c-s+=) – ('A'extended).
(d7"+=)(12"+=) – Conquistador / Groove Co.

Apr 87. (lp)(c)(cd) **ELECTRIC** [4] [38]
– Wild flower / Peace dog / Lil' devil / Aphrodisiac jacket / Electric ocean / Bad fun / King contrary man / Love removal machine / Born to be wild / Outlaw / Memphis hipshake. *(also on gold-lp)*

Apr 87. (7") **LIL' DEVIL. / ZAP CITY** [11] [ ]
(12"+=) – Bonebag (live) / She sells sanctuary (live).
(d12"+=)(c-s+=) – Wild thing (live) / Louie Louie (live) / The phoenix (live) / She sells sanctuary (live). (cd-s+=) – Love removal machine (live) / The phoenix (live) / She sells sanctuary (live).

Aug 87. (7")(7"pic-d) **WILDFLOWER. / LOVE TROOPER** [24] [ ]
(12"+=) – ('A'dub version).
(d7"+=)(cd-s+=) – Horse nation (live) / She sells sanctuary (live) / Outlaw (live).

— **MICKEY CURRY** – (on session) drums repl. WARNER and KID CHAOS

Mar 89. (7") **FIRE WOMAN. / AUTOMATIC WOMAN** [15] [46]
(12"+=)(cd-s+=) – Messin' up the blues.

Apr 89. (lp)(c)(cd) **SONIC TEMPLE** [3] [10]
– Sun king / Fire woman / American horse / Edie (ciao baby) / Sweet soul sister / Soul asylum / New York City / Automatic blues / Soldier blue / Wake up time for freedom. *(cd+=)* – Medicine train.

— **ASTBURY, DUFFY and STUART** were joined by **MATT SORUM** – drums / **MARK TAYLOR** – keyboards (on tour)

Jun 89. (7")(c-s) **EDIE (CIAO BABY). / BLEEDING HEART GRAFFITI** [32] [93]
(12"+=) – Medicine train / Love removal machine (live).
(c-s+=)(cd-s+=) – Revolution (live) / Love removal machine (live).
(pic-cd+=) – Lil' devil (live).

Nov 89. (7") **SUN KING. / EDIE (CIAO BABY)** [39] [ ]
(12"+=) – She sells sanctuary.
(cd-s++=) – ('A'version).

Feb 90. (7")(c-s) **SWEET SOUL SISTER. / THE RIVER** [42] [ ]
(12"+=)(cd-s+=)(12"pic-d+=) American horse (live) / Soul asylum (live).

— (Apr-Oct90) **MARK MORRIS** – bass (ex-BALAAM AND THE ANGEL) repl. STUART

— (1991) **ASTBURY and DUFFY** brought in **CHARLIE DRAYTON** – bass / **MICKEY CURRY** – drums / **RICHIE ZITO** – keyboards, producer / **BELMONT TENCH** – piano, mellotron / **TOMMY FUNDERBUCK** – backing vocals

Sep 91. (7") **WILD HEARTED SON. / INDIAN** [40] [ ]
(12"+=) – Red Jesus.
(cd-s++=) – ('A'extended version).

Sep 91. (cd)(c)(lp) **CEREMONY** [9] [25]
– Ceremony / Wild hearted son / Earth mofo / White / If / Full tilt / Heart of soul / Bangkok rain / Indian / Sweet salvation / Wonderland.

Feb 92. (12"ep)(cd-ep) **HEART OF SOUL / HEART OF SOUL (acoustic) / EARTH MOFO (radio mix) / EDIE (CIAO BABY) (radio mix)** [51] [ ]

Jan 93. (cd-ep) **SHE SELLS SANCTUARY (DOG STAR RADIO) / ('A'live) / ('A'slutnostic mix) / ('A'sundance mix)** [15] [ ]
(12") – ('A'side) / ('A'original mix).
(cd-s+=) – ('A'-Phlegmatic mix) / ('A'-Flustersquish mix).

Feb 93. (d-cd)(c)(d-lp)(4x12") **PURE CULT** compilation) [1] [ ]
– She sells sanctuary / Fire woman / Lil' devil / Spiritwalker / The witch / Revolution / Wild hearted Sun / Love removal machine / Rain / Edie (ciao baby) / Heart of soul / Love / Wildflower / Go west / Ressurection Joe / Sun king / Sweet soul ister / Earth mofo. *(d-lp w/other d-lp)* LIVE AT THE MARQUEE '91

Sep 94. (c-s) **COMING DOWN. / ('A'remix)** [50] [ ]
(12"+=)(cd-s+=) – Gone.

Oct 94. (cd)(c)(lp) **THE CULT** [21] [69]
– Gone / Coming down / Real girl / Black Sun / Naturally high / Joy / Star / Sacred life / Be free / Universal you / Emperor's new horse / Saints are down.

Dec 94. (c-s) **STAR. / BREATHING OUT** [65] [ ]
(12"+=)(cd-s+=) – The witch (extended).

— In Apr'95, they cancelled tour, due to new guitarist JAMES STEVENSON returning to the re-formed GENE LOVES JEZEBEL.

– compilations, others, etc. –

Dec 88. Beggar's Banquet; (cd) **THE MANOR SESSIONS** [ ] [-]

Dec 89. Beggar's Banquet; (pic-cd-ep) **THE LOVE MIXES** [ ] [-]

Dec 89. Beggar's Banquet; (pic-cd-ep) **THE ELECTRIC MIXES** [ ] [-]

Aug 91. Beggar's Banquet; (10xcd-ep) **1984-1990** [ ] [-]

— (above 10 ep's later sold seperately)

Jun 92. Beggar's Banquet; (video w/free cd-ep) **FAITH HEALER / FULL TILT (live) / LOVE REMOVAL MACHINE (live)** [ ] [ ]

CULTURE CLUB (see under ⇒ BOY GEORGE)

Burton CUMMINGS (see under ⇒ GUESS WHO)

CUPOL (see under ⇒ WIRE)

CURE

Formed: Crawley, Sussex, England . . . 1976 initially as The EASY CURE until 1977 (see below line-ups). In 1978, after a brief liason with the 'Hansa' label the previous year, they recorded one-off 45 'KILLING AN ARAB' for 'Small Wonder'. Around the same time (Jul78), they signed to Chris Parry's new 'Fiction' label who re-released debut early '79. They soon broke into the UK 50 with first album 'THREE IMAGINARY BOYS'. Six years later on 'Elektra', they began inroads into burgeoning US market, culminating in a near chart topper in 1989 with 'LOVESONG'. • **Style:** Moved quickly from punky new wave to experimental pop-rock, which combined elements of danceable sensual alternative music. • **Songwriters:** Group compositions, except cover of FOXY LADY (Jimi Hendrix), HELLO I LOVE YOU (Doors). • **Trivia:** SMITH married childhood sweetheart Mary Poole on 13 Aug'88.

Recommended: STANDING ON THE BEACH / STARING AT THE SEA (*9) / THREE IMAGINARY BOYS (*8) / THE TOP (*7) / DISINTIGRATION (*8) / THE HEAD ON THE DOOR (*6) / PORNOGRAPHY (*6) / WISH (*6) / KISS ME, KISS ME, KISS ME (*7) / SEVENTEEN SECONDS (*5) / FAITH (*5).

ROBERT SMITH (b.21 Apr'59) – vocals, lead guitar / **LAWRENCE TOLHURST** – drums, keyboards / **MICHAEL DEMPSEY** – bass

Small Wonder / not issued

Aug 78. (7") **KILLING AN ARAB. / 10.15 SATURDAY NIGHT** [ ] [-]

Fiction-Polydor / not issued

Jan 79. (7") **KILLING AN ARAB. / 10.15 SATURDAY NIGHT** [ ] [-]

May 79. (lp)(c) **THREE IMAGINARY BOYS** [44] [-]
– 10.15 Saturday night / Accuracy / Grinding halt / Another day / Object / Subway song / Foxy lady / Meat hook / So what / Fire in Cairo / It's not you / Three imaginary boys. *(cd-iss.Apr90)*

May 79. (7") **BOYS DON'T CRY. / PLASTIC PASSION** [ ] [-]

— **SIMON GALLUP** – bass, keyboards repl. DEMPSEY who joined The ASSOCIATES

Oct 79. (7") **JUMPING SOMEONE ELSE'S TRAIN. / I'M COLD** [ ] [-]

— added **MATHIEU HARTLEY** – keyboards, synthesizers

Nov 79. (7") **I'M A CULT HERO (as "CULT HEROES"). / I DIG YOU** [ ] [-]

Mar 80. (7")(12") **A FOREST. / ANOTHER JOURNEY BY TRAIN** [31] [-]

Apr 80. (lp)(c) **SEVENTEEN SECONDS** [20] [-]
– The final sound / A forest / M / At night / Seventeen seconds / A reflection / Play for today / Secrets / In your house / Three . . . *(cd-iss.Jan86)*

— reverted back to trio of **SMITH, TOLHURST & GALLUP** when HARTLEY left forming CRY.

Mar 81. (7")(12") **PRIMARY. / DESCENT** [43] [-]

Fiction-Polydor / P.V.C.

Apr 81. (lp)(c) **FAITH** [14] [ ]
– The holy hour / Primary / Other voices / All cats are grey / The funeral party / Doubt / The drowning man / Doubt / Faith. *(cd-iss.Jan86)* (c+=) – ('CARNAGE VISORS' film soundtrack)

Oct 81. (7") **CHARLOTTE SOMETIMES. / SPLINTERED IN HER HEAD** [44] [ ]
(12"+=) – Faith (live).

Fiction-Polydor / Sire

Apr 82. (lp)(c) **PORNOGRAPHY** [8] [ ]
– One hundred years / A short term effect / The hanging garden / Siamese twins / The figurehead / A srange day / Cold / Pornography. *(cd-iss.Jan86)*

Jul 82. (7") **THE HANGING GARDEN. / KILLING AN ARAB (live)** [34] [ ]
(d7"+=)(12"+=) – One hundred years (live) / A forest (live).

— **STEVE GOULDING** – bass repl. GALLUP who also joined CRY. (LOL now keyboards)

Nov 82. (7")(12") **LET'S GO TO BED. / JUST ONE KISS** [44] [ ]

— Trimmed to duo of **SMITH & TOLHURST**

Jul 83. (7")(7"pic-d) **THE WALK. / THE DREAM** [12] [ ]
(12"+=) – Lament.
(free 12"w/12") – Let's go to bed / Just one kiss.

— added **PHIL THORNALLEY** – bass / **ANDY ANDERSON-drums** (ex-BRILLIANT)

Oct 83. (7")(7"pic-d) **THE LOVECATS. / SPEAK MY LANGUAGE** [7] [ ]
(12"+=) – Mr. Pink eyes.

Dec 83. (m-lp)(c) **JAPANESE WHISPERS** [26] [ ]
– Let's go to bed / The walk / The lovecats / The dream / Just one kiss / The upstair's room / Lament / Speak my language.

Mar 84. (7")(7"pic-d) **THE CATERPILLAR. / HAPPY THE MAN** [14] [ ]
(12"+=) – Throw your foot.

Apr 84. (lp)(c)(cd) **THE TOP** [10] [ ]
– The caterpillar / Piggy in the mirror / The empty world / Bananafishbones / The top / Shake dog shake / Birdman girl / Wailing wall / Give me it / Dressing up.

— added **PORL THOMSON** – guitar, saxophone, keyboards (a member in '77)

Oct 84. (lp) **CONCERT-THE CURE LIVE (live)** [26] [ ]
(d-c) **CONCERT AND CURIOSITY-CURE ANOMALIES 1977-1984**
– Shake dog shake / Primary / Charlotte sometimes / The hanging garden / Give me it / The walk / One hundred years / A forest / 10.15 Saturday night / Killing an Arab. CURE ANOMILIES – Heroin face / Boys don't cry / Subway song / At night / In your house / The drowning man / Other voices / The funeral party / All mine / Forever.

— **SIMON GALLUP** returned to repl. PORL. **BORIS WILLIAMS** – drums (ex-THOMPSON TWINS) repl. ANDERSON who joined JEFFREY LEE PIERCE (of The GUN CLUB)

Fiction-Polydor | Elektra

Jul 85. (7") **IN BETWEEN DAYS. / EXPLODING BODY** [15] [-]
(12"+=) – A few hours after this.

Aug 85. (lp)(c)(cd) **THE HEAD ON THE DOOR** [7] [59]
– In between days / Kyoto song / The blood / Six different ways / Push / The baby screams / Close to me / A night like this / Screw / Sinking.

Sep 85. (7") **CLOSE TO ME. / A MAN INSIDE MY MOUTH** [24] [-]
(10"+=)(12"+=) – Stop dead / New day.

Jan 86. (7") **IN BETWEEN DAYS. / STOP DEAD** [-] [99]

Mar 86. (7") **CLOSE TO ME. / SINKING** [-] [ ]

Apr 87. (7")(12") **WHY CAN'T I BE YOU. / A JAPANESE DREAM** [21] [54]
(d7"+=) – Six different ways (live) / Push (live).

May 87. (d-lp)(c)(cd) **KISS ME, KISS ME, KISS ME** [6] [35]
– The kiss / Catch / Torture / If only tonight we could sleep / Why can't I be you / How beautiful you are / Snakepit / Hey you / Just like heaven / Hot hot hot!!! / All I want / One more time / Like cockatoos / Icing sugar The perfect girl / A thousand hours / Shiver and shake / Fight. *(pic-lp iss.Dec87)* (free-ltd.12"orange / or green,w/cd) – A Japanese dream / Breathe / Chain of flowers / Sugar girl / Snow in summer / Icing sugar (remix).

— added **ROBERT O'CONNELL** – keyboards (ex-PSYCHEDELIC FURS (on tour).

Jul 87. (7")(7"clear) **CATCH. / BREATHE** [27] [ ]
(12"+=) – Chain of flowers.
(7"+=)(12"ep+=) – Night like this (live) / Kyoto song (live).

Oct 87. (7")(7"white)(7"pic-d) **JUST LIKE HEAVEN. / SNOW IN SUMMER** [29] [-]
(12"+=) – Sugar girls.

Oct 87. (7") **JUST LIKE HEAVEN. / BREATHE** [-] [40]

Feb 88. (7") **HOT HOT HOT!!!. / HEY YOU** [45] [65]
(12"+=)(cd-s+=) – ('A'remix).

Apr 89. (7")(7"clear) **LULLABY (remix). / BABBLE** [5] [-]
(12"+=)(12"pink+=)(3"cd-s+=) – Out of mind / ('A'extended).

Apr 89. (c-s) **LULLABY (remix). / HOMESICK** [-] [74]

May 89. (lp)(c)(cd) **DISINTIGRATION** [3] [12]
– Plainsong / Pictures of you / Closedown / Lovesong / Lullaby / Fascination street / Prayers for rain / The same deep water as you /Disintigration / Untitled. (cd+=) – Last dance / Homesick. *(pic-lp Apr90)*

May 89. (7") **FASCINATION STREET. / BABBLE** [-] [46]

Aug 89. (7") **LOVESONG. / 2 LATE** [18] [2]
(12"+=)(c-s+=) – Fear of ghosts.
(cd-s+=) – ('A'-12"mix).

— (Mar89) reverted to a quintet when TOLHURST left **SMITH, GALLUP, THOMPSON, WILLIAMS and PERRY BAMONTE** – keyboards

Mar 90. (7")(c-s)(7"green)(7"purple) **PICTURES OF YOU (remix). / PRAYERS FOR RAIN (live)** [24] [71]
(some 'B'sides repl. above with – LAST DANCE (live)
(12"+=)(12"green+=)(12"purple+=) – Disintigration (live).
(cd-s+=) – Fascination street (live). (W.H. Smith's released ENTREAT (May90) a live EP, which featured the 5 tracks +=) – Closedown / Homesick / Untitled.

Sep 90. (7")(12") **NEVER ENOUGH. / HAROLD AND JOE** [13] [ ]
(12"+=)(cd-s+=)(12"pic-d+=) – Let's go to bed (milk mix).

Oct 90. (7") **CLOSE TO ME (closet remix). / JUST LIKE HEAVEN** [13] [97] Jan 91
(12"+=)(cd-s+=) – ('A'dizzy mix) / Primary (red mix).
(cd-s+=) – Why can't I be you (extended).

Nov 90. (cd)(c)(d-lp) **MIXED UP (remix album)** [8] [14]
– Lullaby (extended mix) / Close to me (closer mix) / Fascination Street (extended mix) / The walk (everything mix) / Lovesong (extended mix) / A forest (tree mix) / Pictures of you (extended dub mix) / Hot hot hot!!! (extended mix) / The caterpillar (flicker mix) / Inbetween days (shiver mix) / Never enough (big mix).

Apr 91. (cd)(c)(lp) **ENTREAT (live)** (see above) [10] [ ]
– (finally nationally released)

Mar 92. (7")(c-s) **HIGH. / THIS TWILIGHT GARDEN** [8] [42]
(12"+=) – Play.
(cd-s+=) – High (higher mix).

Apr 92. (12"clear) **HIGH (trip mix). / OPEN (fix mix)** [44] [43]

Apr 92. (cd)(c)(d-lp) **WISH** [1] [2]
– Open / High / Apart / From the edge of the deep green sea / Wendy time / Doing the unstuck / Friday I'm in love / Trust / A letter to Elise / Cut / To wish impossible things / End.

May 92. (7")(c-s) **FRIDAY I'M IN LOVE. / HALO** [6] [18]
(12"+=)(cd-s+=) – Scared as you.
(cd-s++=) – ('A'-Strangelove mix).

Oct 92. (7")(c-s) **A LETTER TO ELISE. / THE BIG HAND** [28] [ ]
(12"+=) – A foolish arrangement.
(cd-s++=) – ('A'version).

Sep 93. (d-cd)(d-c)(d-lp) **SHOW (live)** [29] [42]
– Tape / Open / High / Pictures of you / Lullaby / Just like Heaven / Fascination Street / A night like this / Trust / Doing the unstuck / The walk / Let's go to bed / Friday I'm in love / In between days / From the edge of the deep green sea / Never enough / Cut / End.

— PORL departed after the above.

Oct 93. (cd)(c)(d-lp) **PARIS (live Oct'93)** [56] [ ]
– The figurehead / One hundred years / At night / Play for today / Apart / In your house / Lovesong / Catch / A letter to Elise / Dressing up / Charlotte sometimes / Close to me.

— about to return in '96.

– compilations, etc. –

Aug 80. Fiction/ US= P.V.C.; (c) **BOYS DON'T CRY** [ ] [ ]
(lp – re-iss.Aug83 hit 71) (cd-iss. early 1986)

Apr 86. Fiction; (7") **BOYS DON'T CRY. / PILLBOX BLUES** [22] [-]
(12"+=) – Do the Hansa.

May 86. P.V.C.; (7") **BOYS DON'T CRY. / LET'S GO TO BED** [-] [ ]

May 86. Fiction/ US= Elektra; (lp)(cd)(d-c) **STANDING ON THE BEACH** ('A'45's) / **STARING AT THE SEA** ('B'45's) [4] [48]
– Killing an Arab / Boys don't cry / Jumping someone else's train / A forest / Primary / Charlotte sometimes / The hanging garden / Let's go to bed / The walk / The lovecats / The caterpillar / In between days / Close to me. (cd+=) – 10.15 Saturday night / Play for today / Other voices / A night like this. *(re-iss.Feb91)*

Oct 88. Fiction; (vid-cd) **WHY CAN'T I BE YOU (video) / JAPANESE DREAM / HEY YOU / WHY CAN'T I BE YOU** [ ] [-]

Oct 88. Fiction; (vid-cd) **IN BETWEEN DAYS (video) / SIX DIFFERENT WAYS (live) / PUSH (live)** [ ] [-]

Oct 88. Fiction; (vid-cd) **CATCH (video) / CATCH / BREATHE / A CHAIN OF FLOWERS / ICING SUGAR (new mix)** [ ] [-]

May 88. Strange Fruit; (12"ep) **THE PEEL SESSIONS** [ ] [-]
– Killing an Arab / Boys don't cry / 10:15 Saturday night / Fire in Cairo.

CURVE

Formed: London, England . . . 1991 by TONI HALLIDAY and her partner DEAN GARCIA. They had previously been in STATE OF PLAY, before TONI went solo. As CURVE, they broke through commercially, after signing to DAVE STEWART's 'Anxious' label. GARCIA was a friend of DAVE's since playing on EURYTHMICS' albums 'Touch' & 'Be Yourself Tonight'. • **Style:** Gothic alternative rock act, gathering together the sultry dark looks and distinctive vox of TONI, with the dreamy guitar-playing of DEAN. • **Songwriters:** HALLIDAY-GARCIA except cover; I FEEL LOVE (Donna Summer). • **Trivia:** TONI sang backing vox on ROBERT PLANT'S 'Shaken Not Stirred' & RECOIL's 'Bloodline' albums.

Recommended: DOPPELGANGER (*6).

STATE OF PLAY

TONI HALLIDAY (b.1965, Sunderland, England) – vocals (ex-UNCLES) / **DEAN GARCIA** (half Hawaiian, lives Kentish Town) – bass / **ROMO / BAVIN**

Virgin | not issued

Apr 86. (7") **NATURAL COLOURS. / LOST SOULS** [ ] [-]
(12"+=) – ('A'extended).

Jun 86. (7") **ROCKABYE BABY. / METROPOLIS** [ ] [-]
(12"+=) – ('A'extended).

Jul 86. (lp)(c)(cd) **BALANCING THE SCALES** [ ] [-]
– Naked as the day you were born / Natural colour (remix) / Rockabye baby / Workman / Human kind / Winds of change / we go under / Take me to the king / Lost souls. (c+=) – The trout / Strange air. (cd++=) – Rescue.

TONI HALLIDAY (solo)

Anxious | not iss.

Apr 88. (7") **WEEKDAY. / TOP OF THE TREE** [ ] [-]
(12"+=) – ('A'extended).
(cd-s++=) – Get out of the rain.

Jul 88. (7") **LOVE ATTRACTION. / CHILD** [ ] [-]
(12"+=) – ('A'sub culture mix).
(cd-s++=) – ('A'instrumental).

Mar 89. (7") **TIME TURNS AROUND. / DULL MAN** [ ] [-]
(12"+=)(cd-s+=) – ('A'mix).

Jul 89. (lp)(c)(cd) **HEARTS AND HANDSHAKES** [ ] [-]
– Time turns around / Cut up / Love attraction / Make a wish / Welcome to Heaven / Ode to Anna / Woman in mind / Weekday / I want more / Tales of tomorrow / The price you have to pay / Hearts and handshakes. (cd+=) – Dull man / Child.

Jul 89. (7") **WOMAN IN MIND. / CHEMICAL COMEDOWN** [ ] [ ]
(12")(cd-s) – ('A'&'B'-thicker version) / ('A'live version).

CURVE

(HALLIDAY & GARCIA) with **CHRIS SHEEHAN** – guitar / **MONTI** – drums

Anxious | Virgin

Mar 91. (7"ep)(12"ep)(cd-ep) **THE BLINDFOLD EP** [68] [-]
– Ten little girls / I speak your every word / Blindfold / No escape from Heaven.

May 91. (7")(c-s) **THE COAST IS CLEAR. / FROZEN** [34] [-]
(12")(cd-s) – THE FROZEN EP (+=) – The colour hurs / Zoo.

Oct 91. (7")(c-s) **CLIPPED. / DIE LIKE A DOG** [36] [-]
(12"+=)(cd-s+=) – THE CHERRY EP – Galaxy / Cherry.

Feb 92. (7")(c-s) **FAIT ACCOMPLI. / ARMS OUT** [22] [ ]
(12"+=)(cd-s+=) – Sigh.
(12") – ('A'extended) / Coast is clear (live) / Die like a dog (live).

Mar 92. (cd)(c)(lp) **DOPPELGANGER** [11] [ ]
– Already yours / Horror head / Wish you dead / Doppelganger / Lillies dying / Ice that melts the tips / Split into fractions / Think & act / Fait accompli / Sandpit.

— **DEBBIE SMITH + ALEX** – guitar repl. CHRIS

Jul 92. (7")(c-s) **HORROR HEAD (remix). / MISSION FROM GOD** [31] [ ]
(12"+=)(cd-s+=) – Today is not the day / Falling free.

Jun 93. (cd)(c)(lp) **RADIO SESSIONS** [72] [ ]
– Ten little girls / No escape from Heaven / The colour hurts / The coast is clear / Die like a dog / Horror head / Arms out / Split into fractions.

— with **MONTI** – ever faithful drummer / and guest **SALLY HERBERT** – violin

Aug 93. (12"ep)(c-ep)(cd-ep) **BLACKERTHREETRACKER EP** [39] [ ]
– Missing link / On the wheel / Triumph.
(cd-s) – Missing link (screaming bird mix) / Rising (mix) / Half the time (mix).

Sep 93. (cd)(c)(lp) **CUCKOO** [29] [ ]
– Missing Link / Crystal / Men Are From Mars Woman From Venus / All Of One / Unreadable Communication / Turkey Crossing / Super Blaster / Left Of Mother / Sweetest Pie / Cuckoo

— Split in Jul 94.

CURVED AIR

Formed: London, England . . . early 1970 by Royal College of Music violinist DARRYL WAY and FRANCIS MONKMAN (ex-SISYPHUS). When asked to perform the musical 'Who The Murderer Was', the band found ex-British 'Hair' musical singer SONJA KRISTINA (who had also recently spent time playing solo folk festivals). Took the name CURVED AIR from a Terry Riley album, and after another tour signed to 'Warners'. Late 1970 they issued debut album 'AIR CONDITIONING' (the first ever rock picture disc lp), and this, due to new marketing ploy, crashed into the Top 10. Their 1971 US tour, was followed quickly by their first UK single success 'BACK STREET LUV'. After a third album, the public abandoned them for flash-rock and glam. • **Style:** At first regarded as a gimmick band. Live their quasi-classical sound featured DARRYL WAY's electric perspex violin and of course the beautiful SONJA. Later with the addition of 17 year-old EDDIE JOBSON, they branched out into eclectic synth sound tinged with a little jazz. • **Songwriters:** Group compositions. VIVALDI was a fusion of classical & rock inspired by the composer's 'Four Seasons'. • **Trivia:** SONJA later married 1975 newcomer and POLICE drummer STUART COPELAND.

Recommended: THE BEST OF CURVED AIR (*5)

SONJA KRISTINA – vocals / **DARRYL WAY** – violin, vocals / **FRANCIS MONKMAN** – keyboards (ex-SISYPHUS) / **ROBERT MARTIN** – bass / **FLORIAN PILKINTON-MISKA** – drums (both ex-SISYPHUS)

Warners Warners

Nov 70. (lp)(c)(pic-lp) **AIR CONDITIONING** 8
– It happened today / Stretch / Screw / Blind man / Vivaldi / Hide and seek / Propositions / Rob one / Situations / Vivaldi with cannons.

Jan 71. (7"m) **IT HAPPENED TODAY. / VIVALDI / WHAT HAPPENS WHEN YOU BLOW YOURSELF UP?**

— **IAN EYRE** – bass repl. ROBERT

Jul 71. (7") **BACK STREET LUV. / EVERDANCE** 4

Sep 71. (lp)(c) **SECOND ALBUM** 11
– Young mother / Back street luv / Jumbo / You know / Puppets / Everdance / Bright summer's day '68 / Piece of mind.

— **MIKE WEDGWOOD** – bass repl. IAN

Mar 72. (7") **SARAH'S CONCERN. / PHANTASMAGORIA**

Apr 72. (lp)(c) **PHANTASMAGORIA** 20
– Marie Antoinette / Melinda (more or less) / Not quite the same / Cheetah / Ultra-Vivaldi / Phantasmagoria / Whose shoulder are you looking over anyway / Over and above / One a ghost, always a ghost.

— **SONJA & MIKE** brought in new members **EDDIE JOBSON** – violin, synthesizers repl. DARRYL who formed hi WOLF

— **KIRBY GREGORY – guitar** repl. FRANCIS who went into sessions

— **JIM RUSSEL – drums** repl. FLORIAN who joined KIKI DEE

Apr 73. (lp)(c) **AIR CUT**
– The purple speed queen / Elfin boy / Metamorphosis / World / Armin / U.H.F. / Two-three-two / Easy.

— Split mid-'73. Re-formed Autumn '74. SONJA the sole survivor recruited past members **DARRYL WAY** – violin returned to repl. JOBSON who joined ROXY MUSIC in '73. **FRANCIS MONKMAN** – keyboards repl. GREGORY / **FLORIAN PILKINTON-MISK** – drums repl. RUSSEL and **PHIL KOHN** – bass repl. WEDGWOOD who joined CARAVAN.

Deram London

Feb 75. (lp)(c) **CURVED AIR LIVE (live)**
– It happened today / Marie Antoinette / Back street luv / Propositions / Young mother / Vivaldi / Everdance. *(cd-iss.Jul88) (cd-iss.Jan95 on 'Repertoire')*

Mar 75. (7") **BACK STREET LUV (live). / IT HAPPENED TODAY (live)**

— **MICK JAQUES** – guitar repl. FRANCIS MONKMAN who joined 801, then SKY **STEWART COPELAND** – drums repl. FLORIAN. **JOHN PERRY** – bass (ex-CARAVAN) repl. PHIL / also guest **PETE WOODS** – keyboards.

B.T.M. R.C.A.

Sep 75. (lp)(c) **MIDNIGHT WIRE**
– Woman on a one night stand / Day breaks my heart / The fool / Pipe of dreams / Orange Street blues / Dance of love / Midnight wire. *(cd-iss.Jan95 on 'Repertoire')*

— **TONY REEVES** – bass (ex-GREENSLADE) repl. PERRY who joined QUANTUM JUMP (above now with **SONJA, DARRYL, STEWART and MICK**)

B.T.M. B.T.M.

Jun 76. (lp)(c) **AIRBORNE**
– Desiree / Kids to blame / Broken lady / Juno / Touch of tequila / Moonshine / Heaven (never seemed so far away) / Hot and bothered / Dazed. *(cd-iss.Sep94 on 'Repertoire')*

Aug 76. (7") **DESIREE. / KIDS TO BLAME**

Oct 76. (7") **BABY PLEASE DON'T GO. / BROKEN LADY**

— **ALEX RICHMAN** – keyboards (ex-BUTTS BAND) repl. DARRYL WAY who went solo They split early '77. STEWART COPELAND formed The POLICE, TONY REEVES re-formed GREENSLADE, SONJA KRISTINA went solo forming group ESCAPE. In the 80's she toured Scotland with heavy band TUNIS who were based in High Wycombe.

SONJA KRISTINA

(solo with said band?) and featuring DARRYL WAY, etc,etc.

Chopper not issued

Apr 80. (7") **ST.TROPEZ. / MR.SKIN** -

Aug 80. (lp) **SONJA KRISTINA** -
– Street run / Man the colour / Colder than a rose in the snow / Breaking out in smiles / Mr.Skin / Roller coaster / Full time woman / The comforter / St.Tropez / Fade away.

— In '84 **SONJA** and **DARRYL** re-formed

CURVED AIR

Pearl Key not issued

Jul 84. (7") **RENEGADE. / WE'RE ONLY HUMAN**

— They again re-formed for some gigs in 1988 & Summer 1990.

Essential not issued

Aug 90. (cd)(c)(lp) **LOVECHILD** -
– Exsultate jubilate / Lovechild / Seasons / The flasher / Joan / The dancer / The widow / Paris by night. *(re-iss.cd May94 on 'Castle')*

– compilations, etc. –

Apr 76. Warners; (lp)(c) **THE BEST OF CURVED AIR**
– It happened today / Vivaldi / You know / Back street luv / Melinda (more or less) / Cheetah / Metamorphosis / The purple speed queen.

Mar 82. Decca; (7") **BACK STREET LUV. / IT HAPPENED TODAY**
(re-iss.Oct81)

Dec 95. Band Of Joy; (cd) **LIVE AT THE BBC** -

As "SONJA KRISTINA with TY-LOR & FRIENDS", she issued May91 cd album 'SONGS FROM THE ACID FOLK' on label 'Fruithouse'. In May95, another 'CLOUD 10 – HARMONICA OF LOVE' for 'HTD' records.

CYPRESS HILL

Formed: Los Angeles, California, USA . . . 1991 by MUGGS, B.REAL and SEN DOG. In the early 90's, after signing to US 'Ruffhouse' label, they cracked the Top 40 their with eponymous debut. After many tours alongside other rappers HOUSE OF PAIN, they smashed straight into US top slot, with 2nd album 'BLACK SUNDAY'. • **Style:** Hardcore rapping Latinos, who were renowned for liking a joint. • **Songwriters:** Group penned. • **Trivia:** MUGGS also produced HOUSE OF PAIN, BEASTIE BOYS and ICE CUBE.

Recommended: BLACK SUNDAY (*8) / CYPRESS HILL (*7).

B-REAL (b.LOUIS FREESE, 1970) – MC, lead rapper / **SEN DOG** (b.SENEN REYES, 1965) – MC / **DJ MUGGS** (b.LARRY MUGGERUD, 1969) – DJ, producer

Columbia Ruffhouse

Dec 91. (c-s) **HAND ON THE PUMP. / REAL ESTATE** -
(12"+=) – ('A'instrumental).

Jan 92. (cd)(c)(lp) **CYPRESS HILL** 31 Nov 91
– Pigs / How I could just kill a man / Hand on the pump / Hole in the head / Ultraviolet dreams / Light another / The phuncky feel one / Break it up / Real estate / Stoned is the way of the walk / Psycobetabuckdown / Something for the blunted / Latin lingo / The funky Cypress Hill shit / Tres equis / Born to get busy. *(re-iss.May94)*

Feb 92. (7") **HOW I COULD JUST KILL A MAN. / THE PHUNKY FEEL ONE** - 77

1992. (12"ep)(cd-ep) **HAND ON THE PUMP (Mugg's extended mix) / ('A' instrumental) / HAND ON THE GLOCK** -

1992. (12"ep)(cd-ep) **LATIN LINGO (Prince Paul mix) / STONED IS THE WAY OF THE WALK (reprise) / HAND ON THE GLOCK** -

Jul 93. (12")(cd-s) **INSANE IN THE BRAIN (Radio version). / WHEN THE SHIP GOES DOWN (Radio version)** 32 19

Jul 93. (cd)(c)(lp) **BLACK SUNDAY** 13 1
– I wanna get high / I ain't goin' out like that / Insane in the brain / When the shit goes down / Lick a shot / Cock the hammer / Interlude / Lil' putos / Legalize it / Hits from the bong / What go around come around, kid / A to the K / Hand on the glock / Break 'em off some.

Sep 93. (12")(cd-s) **WHEN THE SHIT GOES DOWN** (extended). / **('A'-instrumental) / The Phuncky feel one (extended) / How could I just kill a man (the Killer mix)** 19

Dec 93. (12"ep)(c-ep)(cd-ep) **I AIN'T GOIN' OUT LIKE THAT. / HITS FROM THE BONG / WHEN THE S**T GOES DOWN (Diamond D mix)** 15 65

Feb 94. (c-s) **INSANE IN THE BRAIN. / STONED IS THE WAY OF THE WALK** 21
(12"+=) – Latin lingo (Prince Paul mix).
(cd-s) – ('A'side) / Something for the blunted.

Apr 94. (c-s) **LICK A SHOT (Baka Boys remix). / I WANNA GET HIGH** 20
(12"+=)(cd-s+=) – Scooby Doo.

Sep 95. (c-s) **THROW YOUR SET IN THE AIR / KILLA HILL NIGGAS** 15 45
(12"+=)(cd-s+=) – ('A'-Slow roll remix) / ('B'instrumental).

Oct 95. (cd)(c)(d-lp) **III (TEMPLES OF BOOM)** 11 3
– Spark another owl / Throw your set in the air / Stoned raiders / Illusions / Killa hill niggas / Boom biddy bye bye / No rest for the wicked / Make a move / Killafornia / Funk freakers / Locotes / Red light visions / Strictly hip hop / Let it rain / Everybody must get stoned. (w/ free cd or lp) DJ MUGGS BUDDHA MIX:- Hole in the head – How could I just kill a man – Insane in the brain – Stoned is the way of the walk – Hits from the bong – Hand on the pump – Real estate – I wanna get high.

Holger CZUKAY (see under ⇒ CAN)

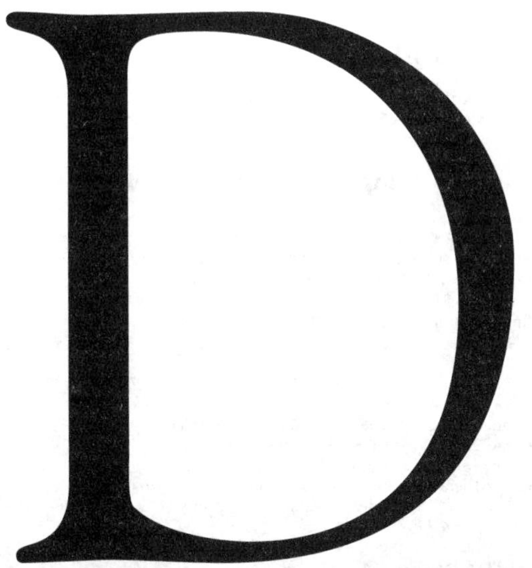

DADA (see under ⇒ BROOKS, Elkie)

D.A.F.

Formed: Dusseldorf, Germany . . . 1979 by DELGADO and GORL. Took name DEUTSCHE AMERIKANISCHE FREUNDSCHAFT from local posters depicting German-US friendship. After debut German lp, they signed to Daniel Miller's UK indie 'Mute' label, but soon moved onto 'Virgin'. With diverse airplay from John Peel and underground discos, they supplied label with excellent 'ALLES IST GUT' lp. • **Style:** Macho experimentation with electro-disco, filled with sexual harsh angst warbled in German, that drew similarities between SUICIDE and KRAFTWERK. • **Songwriters:** DELGADO and GORL. • **Trivia:** In 1981, they guested on EURYTHMICS debut album 'In The Garden'. ANNIE LENNOX returned compliment by contributing backing vox to GORL's 'DARLING DON'T LEAVE ME' single.

Recommended: D.A.F. (*7)

DEUTSCHE AMERIKANISCHE FREUNDSCHAFT

GABI DELGADO-(LOPEZ) – vocals (ex-MITTAGSPAUSE) / **MICHAEL KEHMER** – bass / **ROBERT GORL** – synthesizers, drums / **CHRISLO HAAS** – synthesizers
(HAAS left 1980, later to CRIME AND THE CITY SOLUTION)

Warning / not issued

1979. (lp) **PRODUKT** - -

Mute / not issued.

Mar 80. (7") **KEBAB TRAUME. / GEWALT (VIOLENCE)** -
Aug 80. (lp) **DIE KLEINEN UND DIE BOSEN** (means 'THE SMALL AND THE EVIL') -
– Osten wahrt am langsten / Essen dann schlafen / Co co Pino / Kinderfunk / Nachtarbeit / Ich gebe dir ein Stuck von mir / Die Panne / Gewalt / Gib's mir / Auf wiedersehen / Das ist Liebe / Was ist eine Weele / Anzufassen und anzufassen / Volkstanz / Die lustigen Stiefel / Die kleinen und die Bosen / Ich bin die fesche Lola / El Basilon / Y la gracia. *(cd-iss.Nov92)*
Oct 80. (7")(12") **DER RAUBER UND DER PRINZ. / TANZ MIT MUR** -

— trimmed to duo (DELGANO and **GORL)** when MICHAEL departed.

Virgin / not issued.

Mar 81. (lp)(c) **ALLES IST GUT** -
– Ich und die Wirklichkeit (Me and reality) / Als wars das letzte mal (As if it were the last time) / Verlier nicht den Kopf (Don't loose your head) / Alle gegen all (Everybody fights everybody) / Alles ist gut (Everything is good) / Sato-sato / Der Mussolini (The Mussolini) / Rote Lippen (Red lips) / Mein Herz macht bum (My heart goes boom) / Der rauber und der Prinz (The robber and the Prince). *(re-iss.Mar84)(cd-iss.1987)*
May 81. (12") **DER MUSSOLINI. / DER RAUBER UND DER PRINZ** -
Nov 81. (7")(12") **GOLDENES SPIELZEUG. / EL QUE** -
Nov 81. (lp)(c) **GOLD UND LIEBE** -
– Ich will / Muskel / Absolute Korperkontrolle / Verschwende deine Jugend / Greif nach den Sternen / Liebe auf den ersten Blick / El Que / Sex unter wasser / Was ziehst du an heute nacht / Ich will / Sex unter wasser / Goldenes Spielzeug. *(re-iss.Aug88) (cd-iss.Apr88 w/extra B-sides)*
Feb 82. (7") **SEX UNTER WASSER. / KNOCHEN AUF KNOCHEN** -
Sep 82. (12") **VERLIEB DICH IN MICH. / EIN BISSCHEN KRIEG** -
Oct 82. (lp)(c) **FUR IMMER** -
– Kebab traume / Prinzessin / Die Lippe / Verehrt euren Haaarschnitt / Wer schon sein will muss leiden / Im Dschungel der Liebe / Ein bisschen Krieg / Die Gotter sind weiss / Verlieb dich in mich / Geheimnis. *(re-iss.Aug88, cd-iss.Apr88)*

— split late '82

GABI DELGADO

went solo with **RAOUL WALTON, STEPHAN WITTNER & EDWARD LOPEZ.**

Mar 83. (7")(12") **HISTORY OF A KISS. / SEX GODDESS** -
Mar 83. (lp)(c) **MISTRESS** -
– Sex goddess / History of a kiss / Amor / Young lions / Victims / Mistress.. *(re-iss.1988)*
Jul 83. (12") **AMOR. / SEX AND SOUL** -

ROBERT GORL

also went solo.

Mute / Elektra

Mar 83. (7") **MIT DIR (WITH YOU). / BERUHRT VERFUHT** -
Feb 84. (7")(12") **DARLING DON'T LEAVE ME. / IST WEIDER DA**
Mar 84. (lp)(c) **NIGHT FULL OF TENSION**
– Playtime / I love me / Charlie Cat / Gewinnen wir die beste der Frauen / Queen King / Love in mind / Darling don't leave me / Wind in hair. *(cd+=)* Mit dir (extended) / Beruhrt verfuhrt (remix) / Darling don't leave me (extended) / Ist wieder da / Eckhardt's party.

— **DELGADO** and **GORL** reformed

D.A.F.

the abbreviation people always used.

Il-luminated / not issued

Aug 85. (12") **ABSOLUTE BODY CONTROL. / 1st TRIP TO HEAVEN** -
Nov 85. (7")(12") **BROTHERS (Robert's mix). / BROTHERS (Gabi's mix)** -

Ariola / not issued

Jan 86. (lp)(c)(cd) **1st STEP TO HEAVEN** - - Germ'y
– Voulez vous coucher avec moi (part 1) / Pure joy / Blond hair, dark brown hair / Sex up / Absolute body control / Voulez vous coucher avec moi (part 2) / Crazy crazy / Brothers (opium mix) / 1st step to Heaven (mix).

— (split again)

– compilations etc. –

May 84. Music For Midgets; (c) **LIVE IN LONDON 1980 (live)** -
Jun 88. Virgin; (lp)(c)(cd) **D.A.F.** -
– Verschwende deine Jugend / Der Mussolini (remix) / Mein Herz macht bum / El que / Ich und die Wirklichkeit / Die gotter sind weiss / Der Rauber und der Prinz / Liebe auf der ersten Blick (remix) / Im Dschungel der Liebe / Prinzessin / Greif nach den Sternen / Kebab traume / Die Lippe / Als wars das letzte mal.

ROBERT GORL

Disko B / not issued

May 93. (12") **PSYCHO SAFE. / ?** -
Aug 94. (cd)(lp) **THERAPIE** -
Mar 95. (12") **HAPPY GATHERING./** -

DAINTEES (see under ⇒ STEPHENSON, Martin)

DALI'S CAR (see under ⇒ BAUHAUS)

Roger DALTREY (see under ⇒ The WHO)

DAMNED

Formed: London, England . . . May 1976 by BRIAN JAMES and RAT SCABIES who soon found The CAPTAIN and former undertaker VANIAN. They were signed to new UK indie label 'Stiff' by JAKE RIVERA, and released classic song NEW ROSE produced by stablemate NICK LOWE. Became first "New Wave punks" to release and chart with an album (Mar'77). A number of bust-ups dogged their career until 1985 when major label 'M.C.A.' gave them new pop sensibility. • **Style:** Punk pioneers with extrovert members giving live appeal. Like the STRANGLERS they moved into slight experimental 80's new wave, before drifting into pop-rock and final obscurity. • **Songwriters:** Most written by JAMES, until he left, when group took over. Covered:- HELP! (Beatles) / I FEEL ALRIGHT (Stooges / Iggy Pop) / JET BOY JET GIRL (New York Dolls) / CITADEL (Rolling Stones) / ELOISE (Paul & Barry Ryan) / WHITE RABBIT (Jefferson Airplane) / ALONE AGAIN OR (Love) / WILD THING (Troggs) / LET THERE BE RATS (aka DRUMS) (Sandy Nelson). • **Trivia:** NICK MASON (Pink Floyd drummer) produced disappointing 2nd album MUSIC FOR PLEASURE. CAPTAIN SENSIBLE had UK-No.1 in 1982 with (Rogers-Hammerstein's) HAPPY TALK, and although briefly, became a top disco/pop act abroad.

Recommended: DAMNED DAMNED DAMNED (*8) / BEST OF THE DAMNED (*8)

DAVE VANIAN (b.DAVE LETTS) – vocals / **BRIAN JAMES** (b.BRIAN ROBERTSON) – guitar (ex-LONDON S.S.) / **CAPTAIN SENSIBLE** (b.RAY BURNS, 23 Apr'55) – bass, vocals / **RAT SCABIES** (b.CHRIS MILLER, 30 Jul'57) – drums (ex-LONDON S.S.)

Stiff / not issued

Nov 76. (7") **NEW ROSE. / HELP!** -
Feb 77. (7") **NEAT NEAT NEAT. / STAB YOR BACK. / SINGALONGASCABIES** -
Feb 77. (lp)(c) **DAMNED DAMNED DAMNED** 36 -
– Neat neat neat / Fan club / I fall / Born to kill / Stab yor back / Feel the pain / New

rose / Fish / See her tonite / 1 of the 2 / So messed up / I feel alright. *(re-iss.+cd.Apr87 on 'Demon',+pic-lp 1988 + 1991)*

— added (ROBERT) **LU EDMUNDS** – guitar

Sep 77. (7") **PROBLEM CHILD. / YOU TAKE MY MONEY** [ ] [-]
Nov 77. (lp)(c) **MUSIC FOR PLEASURE** [ ] [-]
– Problem child / Don't cry wolf / One way love / Politics / Stretcher case / Idiot box / You take my money / Alone / Your eyes / Creep (you can't fool me) / You know. *(re-iss.coloured lp +cd.Apr88. on 'Demon')*
Dec 77. (7")(7"pink) **DON'T CRY WOLF. / ONE WAY LOVE** [ ] [-]

— **DAVE BERK** – drums (ex-JOHNNY MOPED) repl. SCABIES who formed various bands.

— **JOHN MOSS** – drums replaced BERK. They split Feb 78. VANIAN joined DOCTORS OF MADNESS. SENSIBLE formed SOFTIES then KING. EDMUNDS & MOSS formed THE EDGE. MOSS later joined ADAM & THE ANTS then CULTURE CLUB. EDMUNDS later joined ATHLETICO SPIZZ 80, The MEKONS, SHRIEKBACK, PIL. etc. BRIAN JAMES formed TANZ DER YOUTH, then The HELLIONS. Later he formed LORDS OF THE NEW CHURCH. Reformed Autumn '78 as The **DOOMED** with LEMMY of MOTORHEAD on bass. (1 gig) **HENRY BADOWSKI** – bass (ex-CHELSEA) replaced LEMMY.

— Group reverted to name The **DAMNED** with originals VANIAN, SENSIBLE (now guitar, keyboards) **& SCABIES. ALGY WARD** – bass (ex-SAINTS) replaced BADOWSKI who went solo.

Chiswick not isssued.

Apr 79. (7")(7"red) **LOVE SONG. / NOISE NOISE NOISE / SUICIDE** [20] [-]
(re-iss.7"blue Feb82 on 'Big Beat')
Oct 79. (7") **SMASH IT UP. / BURGLAR** [35] [-]
(re-iss.7"red Mar82 on 'Big Beat')
Nov 79. (lp)(c) **MACHINE GUN ETIQUETTE** [31] [-]
– Love song / Machine gun etiquette / I just can't be happy today / Melody Lee / Anti-Pope / These hands / Plan 9 channel 7 / Noise noise noise / Looking at you / Smash it up (parts 1 & 2). *(re-iss.Jun85 on 'Big Beat', 1986 cd)* (cd+=) – Ballroom blitz / Suicide / Rabid (over you) / White rabbit.
Nov 79. (7") **I JUST CAN'T BE HAPPY TODAY. / BALLROOM BLITZ / TURKEY SONG** [46] [-]

— **PAUL GRAY** – bass, vocals (ex-EDDIE AND THE HOT RODS) repl. WARD who formed TANK.

Jun 80. (7") **WHITE RABBIT. / RABID OVER YOU** [ ] [-]
(12"+=) – Seagulls / Curtain Call (version).
Sep 80. (7")(12") **THE HISTORY OF THE WORLD (part 1). / I BELIEVE THE IMPOSSIBLE / SUGAR AND SPITE** [ ] [-]
Nov 80. (d-lp)(c) **UNTITLED (THE BLACK ALBUM)** [29] [-]
– Wait for the blackout / Lively arts / Silly kids games / Drinking about my baby / Hit and miss / Doctor Jekyll and Mr. Hyde / 13th floor vendetta / Twisted nerve / Sick of this and that / History of the world (part 1) / Therapy // Curtain call / live side:- Love song / Second time around / Smash it up (parts 1 & 2) / New rose / I just can't be happy today / Plan 9 Channel 7. (1/2 studio, 1/4 live, 1/4 concept) *(re-Aug82 on'Big Beat' as lp) (c-iss.Jun85, cd-iss.Mar90 omits live tracks)*
Nov 80. (7") **THERE AINT NO SANITY CLAUS. / LOOKING AT YOU** [ ] [-]
(12"+=) – Anti-Pope.

N.E.M.S. not issued.

Nov 81. (d7"ep) **FRIDAY THE 13th** [50] [-]
– Disco man / The limit club / Citadel / Billy bad breaks.

Bronze not issued.

Jul 82. (7") **LOVELY MONEY. / I THINK I'M WONDERFUL** [42] [-]
Sep 82. (7") **DOZEN GIRLS. / TAKE THAT** [ ] [-]
Oct 82. (lp)(c) **STRAWBERRIES** [15] [-]
– Ignite / Generals / Stranger on the town / Dozen girls / The dog / Gun fury / Pleasure and the pain / Life goes on / Bad time for Bonzo / Under the floor again / Don't bother me. *(re-iss.Mar86 in red vinyl +c. on 'Legacy') (re-iss.+cd.Dec86 on 'Dojo') (cd-iss.Apr94 on 'Cleopatra')*
Nov 82. (7") **GENERALS. / DISGUISE / CITADEL ZOMBIES** [ ] [-]

Damned not issued.

Nov 83. (lp)(pic-lp) **LIVE IN NEWCASTLE (live) – ltd 5000** [ ] [-]
(cd-iss.Jan94 on 'Receiver')
May 84. (7")(7"pic-d)(7"red)(7"blue)(7"white)(12")(12"marble) (12"multi-colrd)(12"sha-pic-d) **THANKS FOR THE NIGHT. / NASTY** [ ] [-]
(re-iss.12"-ltd.1985 +=) – Do the blitz)

— **VANIAN** and **SCABIES** recruited new guys **ROMAN JUGG** – guitar, keyboards / who replaced the CAPTAIN who carried on with solo career. **BRYN GUNN** – bass repl. GRAY

M.C.A. M.C.A.

Mar 85. (7")(7"pic-d) **GRIMLY FIENDISH. / EDWARD THE BEAR** [21] [ ]
(12"+=) – ('A'version).
Jun 85. (7")(10") **SHADOW OF LOVE. / NIGHTSHIFT** [25] [ ]
(12"+=) – Would you.
(d7"+=) – Let there be Rats / Wiped out.
Jul 85. (lp)(c)(pic-lp)(colrd-lp) **PHANTASMAGORIA** [11] [ ]
– Street of dreams / Shadow of love / There'll come a day / Sanctum sanctorium / Is it a dream / Grimly fiendish / Edward the bear / The eighth day / Trojans. *(free 7" w.a.-)* I JUST CAN'T BE HAPPY TODAY *(re-iss.'86 cont.free 12"blue ELOISE)*
Sep 85. (7") **IS IT A DREAM?. / STREET OF DREAMS(live)/** [34] [ ]
(12"+=) – Wild thing (live).
Jan 86. (7")(12") **ELOISE. / TEMPTATION /** [3] [ ]
(12"+=) – Beat girl.
Nov 86. (7") **ANYTHING. / THE YEAR OF THE JACKAL** [32] [ ]
(12"+=)(10"+=) – Thanks for the night.
Nov 86. (lp)(c)(cd) **ANYTHING** [40] [ ]
– Anything / Alone again or / The portrait / Restless / In dulce decorum / Gigolo / The girl goes down / Tightrope walk / Psychomania.
Feb 87. (7"clear)(12"clear) **GIGOLO. / PORTRAIT** [29] [-]
Apr 87. (7") **ALONE AGAIN OR. / IN DULCE DECORUM** [27] [-]
(12"+=) – Psychomania.
(d7"++=) – Eloise.
Nov 87. (7") **IN DULCE DECORUM. / PSYCHOMANIA** [72] [-]
(12"+=) – ('A' dub version.)

— Disbanded in the late 80's, although re-union gigs were forthcoming.

Essential not issued

Aug 89. (lp)(c) **FINAL DAMNATION** (live '88 reunion) [ ] [-]
– See her tonite / Neat neat neat / Born to kill / I fall / Fan club / Fish / Help / New rose / I feel alright / I just can't be happy today / Wait for the blackout / Melody Lee / Noise noise noise / Love song / Smash it up (parts 1 & 2) / Looking at you / The last time. *(cd-iss.Apr94 on 'Castle')*

– compilations, others, etc. –

Nov 85. Stiff; (12"ep) **NEW ROSE / NEAT NEAT NEAT. / STRETCHER CASE / SICK OF BEING SICK** [ ] [-]
Jul 86. Stiff; (blue-lp) **NOT THE CAPTAIN'S BIRTHDAY PARTY – LIVE AT THE ROUNDHOUSE** [ ] [-]
(re-iss.Nov91 on 'Demon')
Jun 86. Strange Fruit; (12"ep) **THE PEEL SESSIONS (10.5.77)** [ ] [-]
– Sick of being sick / Stretcher case / Feel the pain / Fan club. *(c-ep.iss.1987, cd-ep.iss.May88)*
Jul 87. Strange Fruit; (12"ep) **THE PEEL SESSIONS (30.11.76)** [ ] [-]
– Stab yor back / Neat neat neat / New rose / So messed up / I fall.
Nov 93. Strange Fruit; (cd) **SESSIONS OF THE DAMNED** [ ] [-]
Nov 81. Chiswick; (lp)(c) **THE BEST OF THE DAMNED** [43] [-]
– New rose / Neat neat neat / I just can't be happy today / Jet boy jet girl / Hit or miss / There ain't no sanity claus / Smash it up (parts 1 & 2) / Plan 9 channel 7 / Rabid (over you) / Wait for the blackout / History of the world (part 1). *(cd-iss.Oct87 on 'Big Beat')*
May 82. Big Beat; (7")(7"pic-d) **WAIT FOR THE BLACKOUT. / JET BOY JET GIRL** [ ] [-]
Nov 82. Big Beat; (lp) **LIVE AT SHEPPERTON 1980 (live)** [ ] [-]
– Love song / Second time around / I just can't be happy today / Melody Lee / Help / Neat neat neat / Looking at you / Smash it up (parts 1 & 2) / New rose / Plan 9 channel 7. *(c-iss.Jun85) (cd-iss.Jun88)*
Jun 88. Big Beat; (lp)(c)(cd) **THE LONG LOST WEEKEND: BEST OF VOL.1/2** [ ] [-]
Oct 87. I.D.; (lp)(cd) **MINDLESS, DIRECTIONLESS, ENEMY (live)** [ ] [-]
Oct 82. Nems import; (7")(10")(7"green) **LIVELY ARTS. / TEENAGE DREAM** [ ] [-]
Jan 86. Dojo; (lp)(c)(cd) **DAMNED BUT NOT FORGOTTEN** [ ] [-]
Dec 91. Dojo; (cd) **TOTALLY DAMNED (live + rare)** [ ] [-]
Dec 87. M.C.A.; (d-lp)(c)(cd) **THE LIGHT AT THE END OF THE TUNNEL** [87] [-]
Dec 90. Castle; (d-lp)(c)(cd) **THE COLLECTION** [ ] [-]
Jan 91. Deltic; (7") **FUN FACTORY ('82). / A RIOT ON EASTBOURNE PIER** [ ] [-]
May 93. Receiver; (cd) **SCHOOL BULLIES** [ ] [-]
Jun 94. M.C.I.; (cd)(c) **ETERNALLY DAMNED – THE VERY BEST OF . . .** [ ] [-]
Jul 94. Success; (cd)(c) **LIVE (live)** [ ] [-]
Dec 94. Cleopatra; (cd) **TALES FROM THE DAMNED** [ ] [-]
May 95. Spectrum; (cd) **FROM THE BEGINNING** [ ] [-]
Sep 95. Emporio; (cd)(c) **NOISE – THE BEST OF: LIVE** [ ] [-]

DAVE VANIAN & THE PHANTOM CHORDS

Big Beat not issued

Mar 95. (cd) **BIG BEAT PRESENTS . . .** [ ] [-]
– Voodoo doll / Screamin' kid / Big town / This house is haunted / You and I / Whiskey and me / Fever in my blood / Frenzy / Shooting Jones / Jezebel / Tonight we ride / Johnny Guitar / Chase the wild wind / Swamp thing.

DAMN YANKEES (see under ⇒ NUGENT, Ted)

DAMON & NAOMI (see under ⇒ GALAXIE 500)

Charlie DANIELS

Born: 28 Oct'36, Wilmington, North Carolina, USA. Turned semi-professional in the late 50's, and moved to Nashville in the mid-60's to session for BOB DYLAN, LEONARD COHEN, RINGO STARR, etc. In 1970, he signed to 'Kama Sutra' records and released 2 solo albums, before forming band in 1973, with his past session players. That year, they hit the US Top 10 with 'UNEASY RIDER' (a post-script anti-redneck pun of film EASY RIDER). Went from strength to strength, especially after signing to 'Epic' late 1975. However in the 80's, all was lost to a new breed of country stars. • **Style:** Southern rock-boogie with usual twin-guitar & drum musicians. The bearded big man never lost his country roots which were exemplified on Country Grammy winner 'THE DEVIL WENT DOWN TO GEORGIA'. • **Songwriters:** DANIELS wrote most material. • **Trivia:** Played at President Carter's inaugural ball in 1975.

Recommended: A DECADE OF HITS (*5)

CHARLIE DANIELS – vocals, lead guitar, fiddle with **JOEL DiGREGORIO** – keyboards / **EARL GRIGSBY** – bass / **JEFF MYER** – drums

Kama Sutra Kama Sutra

1970. (lp) **TE JOHN GREASE & WOLFMAN** [ ] [ ]
– Great big bunches of love / I'll trug again tomorrow / Parchman farm / Tomorrow's gonna be another day / Black Autumn / In the city / New York City / King size Rosewood bed / Evil / Billy Joe Young / Drinking wine spo-dee-o-dee. *(re-iss.1978 on 'Epic')*
1971. (7") **GREAT BIG BUNCHES OF LOVE. / ?** [-] [ ]

— **FRED EDWARDS** – drums repl. MYER

Jul 73. (lp) **HONEY IN THE ROCK** [-] [ ]
– Funky junky / Big man / Why can't people / Revelations / Uneasy rider / Midnight lady / Somebody loves you / No place to go.

— now as CHARLIE DANIELS BAND

Jul 73. (7") **UNEASY RIDER. / FUNKY JUNKY** [-] [9]
(UK-iss.Apr80 on 'Epic')

— **CHARLIE** retained **JOEL** and **FRED.** Added **BARRY BARNES** – lead guitar / **MARK FITZGERALD** – bass / **GARY ALLEN** – 2nd drummer

1974. (7") **WHISKEY. /** [-] [ ]
1974. (lp)(c) **WAY DOWN YONDER** [-] [ ]
– I've been down / Give this fool another try / Lay down lady / Land of opportunity / Way down yonder / Whiskey / I'll always remember that song / Looking for Mary Jane.
1974. (7") **WAY DOWN YONDER. / I'VE BEEN DOWN** [-] [ ]
1974. (7") **LAND OF OPPORTUNITY. / ?** [-] [ ]
Feb 75. (7") **THE SOUTH'S GONNA DO IT. / NEW YORK CITY, KING SIZE ROSEWOOD BED** [ ] [29]
Feb 75. (lp)(c) **FIRE ON THE MOUNTAIN** [ ] [38] Dec 74
– Cabello diablo / Long haired country boy / Trudy / Georgia / Feeling free / The South's gonna do it / New York City, kingsize rosewood bed / No place to go / Orange blossom special. *(re-iss.Jun80 on 'C.B.S./Embassy')*
May 75. (7") **LONG HAIRED COUNTRY BOY. / I'VE BEEN DOWN** [-] [56]

— **TOM CRAIN** – guitar, vocals repl. BARNES / **DON MURRAY** – drums repl. ALLEN

Nov 75. (7") **TOMORROW'S GONNA BE ANOTHER DAY. / EVIL** [ ] [-]
Nov 75. (7") **DAMN GOOD COWBOY. / BIRMINGHAM BLUES** [-] [ ]
Nov 75. (lp)(c) **NIGHTRIDER** [ ] [57] Sep 74
– Texas / Willie Jones / Franklin limestone / Evil / Everything is kinda' alright / Funky junky / Birmingham blues / Damn good cowboy / Tomorrow's gonna be another day. *(re-iss.1979 on 'Epic')*
Feb 76. (7") **TEXAS. / EVERYTHING IS KINDA' ALRIGHT** [-] [91]

— (DANIELS, DiGREGORIO, EDWARDS, CRAIN & MURRAY) brought in **CHARLES HAYWARD** – bass repl. FITZGERALD

Capricorn Capricorn

1976. (d-lp) **VOLUNTEER JAM** (live with extra musicians) [ ] [ ]
– Whiskey / Birmingham blues / The south's gonna do it / The thrill is gone / Sweet mama / Mountain dew.

Epic Epic

Aug 76. (lp)(c) **SADDLE TRAMP** [ ] [35] May 76
– Dixie on my mind / Saddle tramp / Sweet Louisiana / Wichita jail / Cumberland mountain number nine / It's my life / Sweetwater Texas.
Sep 76. (7") **WICHITA JAIL. / IT'S MY LIFE** [-] [ ]
Feb 77. (lp)(c) **HIGH LONESOME** [ ] [83] Nov 76
– Billy the kid / Carolina / High lonesome / Running with the crowd / Right now Tennessee blues / Roll Mississippi / Slow song / Tennessee / Turned my head around.
Mar 77. (7") **BILLY THE KID. / SLOW SONG** [-] [ ]
Dec 77. (lp)(c) **MIDNIGHT WIND** [ ] [ ] Nov 77
– Midnight wind / Sugar Hill Saturday night / Heaven can be anywhere (Twin Pines theme) / Maria Teresa / Indian man / Grapes of wrath / Redneck fiddlin' man / Ode to sweet Smoky / Good ole boy / Black bayou.
Dec 77. (7") **GOOD OLE BOY. / HEAVEN CAN BE ANYWHERE (TWIN PINES THEME)** [-] [ ]
1978. (7") **SUGAR HILL SATURDAY NIGHT. / MARIA TERESA** [-] [ ]
1978. (7") **SWEET LOUISIANA. / TRUDY** [-] [ ]
1979. (d-lp) **VOLUNTEER JAM III & IV (live with others)** [ ] [ ]
– (other artists= GRINDERSWITCH / JOHNNY & EDGAR WINTER / WET WILLIE / SEA LEVEL / PAPA JOHN CREACH / MARSHALL TUCKER BAND)

— **JAMES MARSHALL** – drums repl. MURRAY

Sep 79. (7") **THE DEVIL WENT DOWN TO GEORGIA. / RAINBOW RIDE** [14] [3] Jun 79
Oct 79. (lp)(c) **MILLION MILE REFLECTIONS** [74] [ ] May 79
– Passing lane / Blue star / Jitterbug / Behind your eyes / Reflections / The Devil went down to Georgia / Mississippi / Blind man / Rainbow ride. *(re-iss.cd+c Apr94 on 'Sony')*
Nov 79. (7") **JITTERBUG. / BLUE STAR** [ ] [ ]
Jan 80. (7") **MISSISSIPPI. / PASSING LANE** [-] [ ]
Apr 80. (7") **UNEASY RIDER. / MIDNIGHT LADY** [ ] [-]
Apr 80. (7") **BLUE STAR. / BEHIND YOUR EYES** [-] [ ]
Jun 80. (7") **IN AMERICA. / BLUE STAR** [ ] [11] May 80
Sep 80. (d-lp) **VOLUNTEER JAM V & VI (live)** [ ] [ ]
– Rich kids / New Orleans lady / The night they drove old Dixie down / Same old story (same old song) / Funky junky / Amazing Grace / Will the circle be unbroken / Keep on smilin' / So long / Down home blues / Carol / Do the funky chicken / Lady luck.
Sep 80. (7") **THE LEGEND OF WOOLEY SWAMP. / MONEY** [ ] [31] Aug 80
Oct 80. (lp)(c) **FULL MOON** [ ] [ ] Aug 80
– The legend of Wooley Swamp / Carolina (I remember you) / Lonesome boy from Dixie / No potion for the pain / El Toreador / South sea song / Dance gypsy dance / Money / In America.
Nov 80. (7") **CAROLINA (I REMEMBER YOU). / SOUTH SEA SONG** [-] [ ]
Jan 81. (7") **THE LEGEND OF WOOLY SWAMP. / IN AMERICA** [-] [ ]
Apr 81. (7") **SWEET HOME ALABAMA. / FALLING IN LOVE FOR THE NIGHT** [-] [ ]
Apr 81. (lp) **VOLUNTEER JAM VII (live)** [ ] [ ]
– Sweet home Alabama / Standing on shakey ground / Falling in love for the night / Marie Laveau / (Your love has lifted me) Higher and higher / Mississippi queen / Around and around / A change is gonna come / Can't you see.
Apr 82. (7") **STILL IN SAIGON. / BLOWING ALONG THE WIND** [ ] [22] Mar 82
Apr 82. (lp)(c) **WINDOWS** [ ] [ ] Mar 82
– Still in Saigon / Ain't no ramblers anymore / The lady in red / We had it all one time / Partyin' gal / Ragin' cajun / Makes you want to go home / Blowing along with the wind / Nashville Moon / The universal hand.
1982. (7") **RAGIN' CAJUN. / UNIVERSAL MIND** [-] [ ]
1982. (7") **WE HAD IT ALL ONE TIME. / MAKES YOU WANT TO COME HOME** [-] [ ]
Aug 83. (lp)(c) **A DECADE OF HITS** [ ] [84] Jul 83
– The Devil went down to Georgia / The South's gonna do it again / Stroker's theme / Uneasy rider / Let it roll / In America / Still in Saigon / Long haired country boy / The legend of Wooley Swamp / Everytime I see him.

— now without MARSHALL

Nov 85. (7") **STILL HURTIN' ME. / BLOWIN' ALONG WITH THE KIDS** [ ] [-]
Nov 85. (7") **STILL HURTIN' ME. / AMERICAN ROCK AND ROLL** [-] [ ]
Jan 86. (lp)(c) **ME AND THE BOYS** [ ] [ ]
– Me and the boys / Still hurtin' me / Talking to the Moon / Class of '63 / American farmer / M.I.A. / American rock and roll / Ever changing lady / Louisiana fai dodo / Drinkin' my baby goodbye.
1986. (7") **DRINKIN' MY BABY GOODBYE. / EVER CHANGING LADY** [-] [ ]
Jun 87. (7") **BOGGED DOWN IN LOVE WITH YOU. / TRAPPED IN THE CITY** [-] [ ]
Sep 87. (lp)(c) **POWDER KEG** [ ] [ ]
– Bogged down in love with you / Bottom line / Love pouring out of me / Saturday night U.S.A. / Dance with me / Powder keg / What she do to me / Trapped in the city / Stay with me / Juanita.
Sep 87. (7") **POWDER KEG. / BOTTOM LINE** [-] [ ]
Nov 88. (7") **UNEASY RIDER '88. / BOOGIE WOOGIE FIDDLE COUNTRY BLUES** [-] [ ]
Nov 88. (lp)(c)(cd) **HOMESICK HEROES** [-] [ ]
– Alligator / Big bad John / Uneasy rider '88 / You can't pick cotton / Midnight train / Ill wind / Get me back to Dixie / Cowboy hat in Dallas / Boogie woogie fiddle country blues / Boogie woogie man / Honky tonk avenue.
Jan 89. (7") **COWBOY HAT IN DALLAS / EASY RIDER** [-] [ ]
May 89. (7") **MIDNIGHT TRAIN. / GET ME BACK TO DIXIE** [-] [ ]
Mar 90. (cd)(c)(lp) **SIMPLE MAN** [ ] [82] Nov 89
– (What this world needs is) A few more rednecks / Was it 26 / Oh Atlanta / Midnight wind / Saturday night down south / Play me some fiddle / Simple man / Old rock'n'roller / Mister DJ / It's my life.
Mar 90. (7") **SIMPLE MAN. / ILL WIND** [-] [ ]
May 90. (7") **MISTER D. J. / IT'S MY LIFE** [-] [ ]
Jul 90. (7") **(WHAT THE WORLD NEEDS IS) A FEW MORE REDNECKS. / IT'S MY LIFE** [-] [ ]
Oct 90. (7") **OH ATLANTA. / WHAT IS 26** [-] [ ]
May 91. (7") **WILLIE JONES. / HONKY TONK LIFE** [-] [ ]
May 91. (cd)(c) **RENEGADE** [-] [ ]
– Willie Jones / Fathers and sons / Honky tonk life / What my baby sees in me / Renegade / Little folks / Let freedom ring / Layla.
Jul 91. (7") **THIS TWANG FACTOR. / OLD ROCK 'N' ROLL** [-] [ ]
1991. (7") **LET FREEDOM RING. / LITTLE FOLKS** [-] [ ]

CHARLIE DANIELS

Liberty Liberty

May 93. (cd) **AMERICA, I BELIEVE IN YOU** [ ] [ ]
– All night long / troubles of my own / Tennessee two step / The girl next door / America, I believe in you / Oh Juanita / Sweet little country girl / Alley cat / What you gonna do about me / San Miguel.

– compilations, others, etc. –

1976. Kama Sutra; (lp) **THE ESSENTIAL CHARLIE DANIELS** [-] [ ]
1980. Epic; (7") **SWEET LOUISIANA. / LONG HAIRED COUNTRY BOY** [-] [ ]
Jan 88. Old Gold; (7") **THE DEVIL WENT DOWN TO GEORGIA. / JITTERBUGGIN'** [ ] [-]
Oct 93. Sony Europe; (cd) **ALL-TIME GREATEST HITS** [ ] [-]

DANNY & DUSTY (see under ⇒ GREEN ON RED)

DANNY WILSON

Formed: Dundee, Scotland . . . 1986 by brothers GARY and KIT plus friend GED. After originally calling themselves SPENCER TRACY, they took their name from a Frank Sinatra film. They signed to 'Virgin' and soon became hits on both sides of the Atlantic. • **Style:** Intelligent pop/rock influenced by STEELY DAN or a softer ASSOCIATES. • **Songwriters:** GARY CLARK was main composer, except cover KNOWING ME KNOWING YOU (Abba). GARY CLARK covered SARA SMILE (Hall&Oates) / MY LOVE IS LIKE A RED RED ROSE (trad.). • **Trivia:** On their debut album they introduced LESTER BOWLES BRASS FANTASY with DAVID PALMER, RODDY LORIMER, GEOFF DUGMORE, etc.

Recommended: SWEET DANNY WILSON (*8)

GARY CLARK – vocals, guitar / **KIT CLARK** – keyboards, perc. / **GED GRIMES** – bass.

Virgin Virgin

Feb 87. (7") **MARY'S PRAYER. / ('A' instrumental)** [ ] [-]
(12"+=) – ('A' version.)
Apr 87. (lp)(c)(cd) **MEET DANNY WILSON** [65] [79]
– Davy / Aberdeen / Mary's prayer / Lorraine parade / Nothing ever goes to plan / Broken china / Steam trains to the milky way / You remain an angel / Ruby's golden wedding / A girl I used to know / Five friendly aliens / I wont be here when you get home. *(Apr88 hit No.65.)*
May 87. (7") **DAVY. / I WON'T FORGET** [ ] [ ]
(12"+=) – Pleasure to pleasure.
Aug 87. (7") **MARY'S PRAYER. / MONKEY'S SKINNY DAY** [42] [23] May 87

(12"+=) – ('A' version) *(re-iss.Mar88 hit UK No.3)*
(cd-s+=)(7"box+=) – Kooks / Mary's prairie.
(10"+=) – Broken china / Steam trains to the milky way.

Oct 87. (7") **A GIRL I USED TO KNOW. / I WONT FORGET** | |
(12"+=) – Pleasure to pleasure.
(cd-s++=) – Mary's prayer.

Jun 88. (7") **DAVY. / LIVING TO LEARN** | |
(12"+=) – Aberdeen (The way it should have been) / Kathleen.

Jun 89. (7") **THE SECOND SUMMER OF LOVE. / I'LL BE WAITING** | 23 |
(12"+=) – Growing emotional.

Jul 89. (lp)(c)(cd) **BEBOP MOPTOP** | 24 |
– Imaginary girl / The second summer of love / I can't wait / Desert hearts / If you really love me (let me go) / If everything you said was true / Loneliness / I was wrong / Charlie boy / Never gonna be the same / N.Y.C. shanty / Goodbye shanty town / The ballad of me and Shirley MacLaine.

Aug 89. (7") **NEVER GONNA BE THE SAME. / NOTHING EVER GOES TO PLAN** | 69 |
(12"+=)(cd-s+=)(10"+=) – The lonesome road / Get happy.

Nov 89. (7") **I CAN'T WAIT. / STEAMTRAINS TO THE MILKY WAY (live)** | |
(12"+=)(cd-s+=) – Knowing me knowing you.

— Disbanded Feb90.

– compilations, others, etc. –

Aug 88. Virgin; (cd-ep) **A GIRL I USED TO KNOW / DAVY / MARY'S PRAYER** | | - |

Jul 91. Virgin; (7") **IF YOU REALLY LOVE ME (LET ME GO) (New York mix). / THE SECOND SUMMER OF LOVE** | | - |
(12"+=)(cd-s+=) – I can't wait (live) / Mary's prayer (live).

Aug 91. Virgin; (cd)(c)(lp) **SWEET DANNY WILSON** | 54 |
– Never gonna be the same / The ballad of me and Shirley MacLaine / If you really love me (let me go) (New York mix) / Mary's prayer / A girl I used to know / Pleasure to pleasure / Davy / Ruby's golden wedding / I can't wait / I won't be here when you get home / Second summer of love / From a boy to a man / Get happy / Kathleen (house mix) / Growing emotional / I'll be waiting / Living to learn / I won't forget / Kooks / Broken China (live) / Aberdeen (live) / Steamtrains (to the Milky Way) (live) / Knowing me knowing you (live) / Don't know who I am (live) / I was wrong (live) / Loneliness (live).

Dec 95. VIP Virgin; (cd) **THE BEST OF DANNY WILSON** | | - |

ELEVEN

was formed by **GARY CLARK** and an ex-member of PREFAB SPROUT.

Seven | not issued

Nov 91. (12") **YOU CAN'T TURN AROUND TO ME. / A PLACE TO STAY** | | - |

GARY CLARK

with **GARY THOMPSON** – horns / **KARLOS EDWARDS** – percussion

Circa | Virgin

Jan 93. (7")(c-s) **WE SAIL ON STORMY WATERS. / THE LETTER** | 34 |
(cd-s+=) – Sara Smile. / We can love again
(cd-s)('A'side) My love is like a red red rose / You can't turn around to me / Now do you stop!

Mar 93. (7")(c-s) **FREEFLOATING. / A RED RICKENBACKER GUITAR** | 50 |
(cd-s+=) – Where will I live (demo).
(cd-s+=) – ???

Apr 93. (cd)(c)(lp) **TEN SHORT SONGS ABOUT LOVE** | 25 |
– This is why J. / We sail on stormy waters / St.Jude / A short song about love / Make a family / Freefloating / Baby blue No.2 / Nancy any Sunday morning / Making people cry / Sail on! / A Jackson in your kitchen.

Jun 93. (7")(c-s) **MAKE A FAMILY. / THE SECOND SUMMER OF LOVE (live)** | 70 |
(cd-s+=) – Learning to do without me (live) / Saturday night (live).
(cd-s) – ('A'side) / We sail on stormy waters (live) / Baby blue No.2 (live) / Mary's prayer (live).

KING L

GARY CLARK / NEIL MacCOLL / ERIC PRESSLEY / MATT LANG

Circa | Virgin

Aug 95. (cd-ep) **TRAGEDY GIRL / TON DRIVER / BACK TO LOVING ARMS / TWO CARS COLLIDE** | | - |

Sep 95. (cd)(c) **GREAT DAY FOR GRAVITY** | | |
– Tragedy girl / Dumbest story / Ton driver / Greedy / All hail the alien queen / Back to loving arms / Life after you / That's how it works / Hoping they'll be open / First man on the sun / Two cars collide / Don't believe in Hollywood / Lost and found and lost again / My last cigarette.

Oct 95. (c-ep)(cd-ep) **LIFE AFTER YOU / BREAKDOWN / GREEDY** | | - |

DANZIG

Formed: New York, USA … 1987 by ex-MISFITS frontman GLENN DANZIG. Signed by Rick Rubin in 1988 to boost his new more heavier orientated label 'Def American', where they unleashed eponymous album. • **Style:** Satanic heavy rock outfit, fronted by howling muscleman GLENN DANZIG. Influenced by METALLICA, The CULT and 50's rock'n'roll. • **Songwriters:** All by GLENN, who also produced them. Covered TROUBLE (Elvis Presley).

Recommended: DANZIG III – HOW THE GODS KILL (*6)

MISFITS

— **GLENN DANZIG** – vocals / **JOEY IMAGE** (DOYLE) – guitar / **JERRY ONLY** – bass / **ARTHUR GOOGY** (MR.JIM) – drums

Cherry Red | Planet 9

Jul 81. (12"ep) **BEWARE EP** | | |

Ruby-WEA

1982. (lp) **WALK AMONG US** | | |
– 20 eyes / I turned into a Martian / All Hell breaks loose / Vampira / Nike a go-go / Hate breeders / Mommy, can I go out & kill tonight / Night of the living dead / Skulls / Violent world / Devils whorehouse / Astro zombies / Brain eaters. *(re-iss.+cd Sep88 on 'Ruby-WEA')*

Agressive Rock

1983. (lp) **EVIL – LIVE (live)** | - | |
– 20 eyes / Night of the living dead / Astro zombies / Horror business / London dungeon / All Hell breaks loose / We are 138. *(re-iss.Sep87 on 'Caroline')*

— **ROBO** (BOBBY STEELE) – drums repl. ARTHUR

Feb 84. (lp) **WOLF'S BLOOD** | - | |
– Earth a.d. / Queen wasp / Devilrock / Death comes ripping / Green Hell / Wolf's blood / Demonomania / Bloodfeast / Hellhound / Die die my darling / We bite.

UK-Revolver | Plan 9

1986. (lp,cd) **LEGACY OF BRUTALITY** | - | |
– Angelfuck / Who killed Marilyn / Where eagles dare / She / Halloween / American nightmare / Static age / T.V. casualty / Hybrid moments / Spinal remains / Come back / Some kinda hate / Theme for a jackal.

Jul 86. (lp) **BEST OF . . .** | | - |

Nov 87. (12") **DIE DIE MY DARLING. / ?** | - | |

Oct 95. Plan 9; (cd)(c)(lp) **COLLECTION VOLUME 2** (compilation) | | |

DANZIG

GLENN DANZIG – vocals (ex-MISFITS) / **JOHN CHRIST** – guitar / **EERIE VON** – bass / **CHUCK BISCUITS** – drums (ex-BLACK FLAG)

Def Amer. | Def Amer.

Sep 88. (lp)(c)(cd) **DANZIG** | | |
– Twist of Cain / Not of this world / She rides / Soul on fire / Am I demon / Mother / Possession / End of time / The hunter / Evil thing.

Jun 90. (cd)(c)(lp) **DANZIG II – LUCIFUGE** | | 74 |
– Long way back from Hell / Snakes of Christ / Killer wolf / Tired of being alive / I'm the one / Her black wings / Devil's plaything / 777 / Blood and tears / Girl / Pain in the world.

Sep 90. (c-s) **HER BLACK WINGS. /** | - | |

May 92. (7") **DIRTY BLACK SUMMER. / WHEN DEATH HAD NO NAME** | | |
(12"+=)(cd-s+=) – Bodies.

Jul 92. (cd)(c)(lp) **DANZIG III – HOW THE GODS KILL** | | 24 | Jun92
– Godless / Anything / Bodies / How the gods kill / Dirty black summer / Left hand black / Heart of the Devil / Sistines / Do you wear the mark / When the dying calls.

May 93. (cd)(c)(lp) **THRALL-DEMONSWEATLIVE (live)** | | 54 |
– It's coming soon / The violent fire / Trouble / Snakes of Christ / Am I demon / Sistines / Mother.

May 94. (10"sha-pic-d) **MOTHER. / MOTHER (live)** | 62 | 43 | Jan94
(12"+=) – When death had no name.
(cd-s++=) – How the gods kill.

Oct 94. (cd)(c)(lp) **DANZIG IV** | | 29 |
– Brand new god / Little whip / Cantspeak / Going down to die / Until you call on the dark / Dominion / Bringer of death / Sadistikal / Son of the morning star / I don't mind the pain / Stalker song / Let it be captured.

Terence Trent D'ARBY

Born: 15 Mar'62, Manhattan, New York, USA. Moved to East Orange, Chicago with preacher father. Enlisted in the army in 1980, and was based in Germany, where in 1982 joined funk band TOUCH. After some recordings he left for London in 1984, where after two years making demos, etc., he signed to CBS helped by manager Klaus Pieter 'KP' Schleinitz. With promotional help on UK TV Channel 4's 'The Tube', he hit charts immediately with 'IF YOU LET ME STAY', followed soon by acclaimed debut album. However, after terrible album reviews in 1989 for his second, his commercial success plummeted. • **Style:** Funk/soul romantic who fashioned himself between PRINCE, STEVIE WONDER and SMOKEY ROBINSON. A self-obsessed/opinionated outlook didn't help surprise downfall in the late 80's. • **Songwriters:** Writes own material, except:- HEARTBREAK HOTEL (Elvis Presley) / UNDER MY THUMB and JUMPIN' JACK FLASH (Rolling Stones) / WONDERFUL WORLD (Sam Cooke). • **Trivia:** His debut album was produced by MARTYN WARE (Heaven 17).

Recommended: INTRODUCING THE HARDLINE ACCORDING TO . . . (*7)

C.B.S. | Columbia

Feb 87. (7") **IF YOU LET ME STAY. / LOVING YOU IS ANOTHER WORD FOR LONELY.** | 7 | 68 | Oct 87
(12"+=) – ('A' extra mixes).

Jun 87. (7") **WISHING WELL. / ELEVATORS AND HEARTS** | 4 | 1 | Jan 88
(12"+=) – ('A' mix).
(12"+=) – Wonderful world.

Jul 87. (lp)(c)(cd) **INTRODUCING THE HARDLINE ACCORDING TO TERENCE TRENT D'ARBY** | 1 | 4 | Oct 87
– If you all get to Heaven / If you let me stay / Wishing well / I'll never turn my back on you / Dance little sister / Seven more days / Let's go forward / Rain / Sign your name / As yet untitled / Who's loving you?. *(pic-lp/cd.Dec87) (re-iss.cd/c May95)*

Sep 87. (7") **DANCE LITTLE SISTER. / (part 2)** | 20 | 30 | Aug 88

(12"+=) – Sunday jam (one woman man).
(c-s+=) – Heartbreak hotel.

Dec 87. (7") **SIGN YOUR NAME. / GREASY CHICKEN (live)** 2 | 4 May 88
(12"+=)(12"pic-d+=) – Under my thumb (live) / Jumpin' Jack Flash (live).
(10"+=) – Rain (remix)/If you all get to heaven (remix).
(cd-s-pic+=) – Dance little sister.

Oct 89. (lp)(c)(cd) **NEITHER FLESH NOR FISH** 12 | 61 Nov 89
– Declaration / Neither flesh nor fish / I have faith in these desolate times / It feels so good to love someone like you / I'll be alright / Billy don't fall / This side of love / You will pay tomorrow / Roly Poly / I don't want to bring your gods down / And I need to be with someone tonight.

Nov 89. (7")(c-s) **THIS SIDE OF LOVE. / SAD SONG FOR SISTER SARAH**
(12"+=) – Sign your name (live).
(cd-s+=) – Seven more days.

Jan 90. (7")(7"pic-d) **TO KNOW SOMEONE DEEPLY IS TO LOVE SOMEONE SOFTLY. / LOOSE VARIATIONS ON A DEAD MAN'S VIBE IN CM** 55
(12"+=)(cd-s+=) – ('A'mix) / Rain (live).

—— now with **TIM PIERCE** – guitar / **NEIL STUBENHAUSEN or KEVIN WYATT** – bass plus various guests.

Columbia | Columbia

Apr 93. (c-s) **DO YOU LOVE ME LIKE YOU SAY?. / READ MY LIPS (I DIG YOUR SCENE) / PERFUMED PAVILLION (THE MOTION OF MY MEMORIES)** 14
(cd-s+=) – ('A'original).
(cd-s) – ('A'side) / Wishing well / If you let me stay / To know someone is to love someone.
(12")(cd-s) – (3 'A'mixes) / Read my lips (I dig your scene).

May 93. (cd)(c)(lp) **SYMPHONY OR DAMN** 4
– PART I _ CONFRONTATION; Welcome to my monastery / She kissed me / Do you love me like you say? / Baby let me share my love / Delicate / Neon messiah / Penelope please / Wet your lips / Turn the page
– PART II – RECONCILIATION; Castilian blue / "T.I.T.S." – "F & J" / Are you happy? / Succumb to me / I still love you / Seasons / Let her down easy.

Jun 93. (7")(c-s) **DELICATE. / SHE'S MY BABY** 14 | 74
(cd-s+=) – Dance little sister (extended) / Survivor.

Sep 93. (7")(c-s) **SHE KISSED ME. / DO YOU LOVE ME LIKE YOU SAY? (Masters At Work 12" Mix)** 16
(12"+=)(cd-s+=) – (2-'B' mixes)

Nov 93. (7")(12")(c-s) **LET HER DOWN EASY. / DO YOU LOVE ME LIKE YOU SAY** 18
(cd-s) – ('A'side) / Turn the page / Sign your name / Delicate.

—— with **LOUIS METOYER** – guitar / **KEVIN WYATT** – bass / **EPHEN THEARD (STEVO)** – drums / etc.

Mar 95. (c-s) **HOLDING ON TO YOU / ANGELS FLY BECAUSE** 20
(cd-s+=) – Your love is indecipherable / Epilog.
(cd-s) – ('A'side) / Sign your name / Delicate (feat. DES'REE) / To know someone deeply is to know someone softly.

Apr 95. (cd)(c) **TTD'S VIBRATOR** 11
– Vibrator / Supermodel sandwich / Holding on to you / Read my lips (I dig your scene) / Undeniably / We don't have that much time together / C.Y.F.M.L.A.Y.? / If you go before me / Surrender / TTD's recuring dream / Supermodel sandwich w/cheese / Resurrection / It's been said.

Aug 95. (c-s) **VIBRATOR / SURRENDER (Brooklyn mix)** 57
(cd-s+=) – Surrender (MK mix) / I realy want you.
(cd-s) – ('A'side) / Do you love me like you say? / She kissed me / Attracted to you.

– others, etc. –

THE INCREDIBLE E.G. O'REILLY

Sep 89. Polydor; (7") **THE BIRTH OF MAUDIE. / AN CHUILEANN** | -

TOUCH

(featuring **TERENCE TRENT D'ARBY** – vocals) **MIKE WILLIAMS, MARK BURTON** – guitar / **FRANK 'Babyface' ITT** – bass / **STEFAN LUPP** – keyboards / **DETLEF VOGEL** – guitar / **BENNY BRACIN** – drums

Aug 89. Polydor; (lp)(c) **TOUCH** (early works rec.'83).
– I want to know (international lady) / Eggs and coffee / Don't call me up / Long way / Weekends / Passion / Immaterial / Somebody else / Get up and run / Cross my heart.

DARLING BUDS

Formed: Cardiff, Wales ... 1986 by ANDREA and HARLEY, who were soon based in Gwent, Wales. After debut release on own label, they signed to Doncaster based indie 'Native' run by Kevin Donaghue. Played nightly on JOHN PEEL's Radio 1 show, they were soon snatched up by major 'Epic' summer 1988. • **Style:** Punk pop fronted by blonde bombshell ANDREA, with sound similar to BLONDIE, RAMONES or The PRIMITIVES. • **Songwriters:** ANDREA lyrics / HARLEY music. • **Trivia:** In Sep'92, their album 'EROTICA', competed forlornly with MADONNA's same titled cd

Recommended: POP SAID (*6)

ANDREA LEWIS (b.25 Mar'67) – vocals / **HARLEY FARR** (b. 4 Jul'64, Singapore) – guitar / **CHRIS McDONOGH** (b. 6 Mar'62, Newport, Wales) – bass / **BLOSS** – drums

Darling Buds | not issued.

Feb 87. (7") **IF I SAID. / JUST TO BE SEEN** | -

Native | not issued.

Mar 88. (7") **SHAME ON YOU. / VALENTINE** | -
(12"+=) – That's the reason.
(7"ltd.+=) – Spin.

Epic | Epic

Sep 88. (7") **BURST. / BIG HEAD** 50
(12"+=)(cd-s+=) – Shame on you (psychedelic version)

Dec 88. (7") **HIT THE GROUND. / PRETTY GIRL** 27
(12"+=)(cd-s+=) – ('A' version) / If I said.

Jan 89. (lp)(c)(cd) **POP SAID** 23
– Hit the ground / Burst / Uptight / The other night / Big head / Let's go round there / She's not crying / Shame on you / You've got to choose / Spin / When it feels good / The things we do for love.

Mar 89. (7")(7"yellow) **LET'S GO ROUND THERE. / TURN YOU ON** 49
(12"+=)(cd-s+=) – Different daze.
(7"ep++=) – It's all up to you.

Jun 89. (7")(c-s) **YOU'V GOT TO CHOOSE. / MARY'S GO TO GO** 45
(12"+=)(cd-s+=) – I'll never stop.

—— **JIMMY HUGHES** – drums (ex-BLACK) repl. BLOSS

May 90. (7")(c-s) **TINY MACHINE. / ME? SATISFIED?** 60 | -
(12"+=)(cd-s+=) – ('A'mix).

Aug 90. (7") **CRYSTAL CLEAR. / TINY MACHINE** | -
(12"+=) – ('A'version).
(cd-s+=) – Tripped up.

Sep 90. (c-s) **CRYSTAL CLEAR. / YOU WON'T MAKE ME DIE** - |

Sep 90. (cd)(c)(lp) **CRAWDADDY** | -
– It makes no difference / Tiny machine / Crystal clear / Do you have to break my heart / You won't make me die / A little bit of Heaven / Fall / Honey suckle / So close / The end of the beginning.

Feb 91. (7")(c-s) **IT MAKES NO DIFFERENCE. / OFF MY MIND** | -
(12"+=) – Love and death / If.

Aug 92. (7")(c-s) **SURE THING. / BABYHEAD** 71
(12"+=)(cd-s+=) – Suffer / What goes around (or 'PLease Yourself' on US-cd).

Sep 92. (cd)(c)(lp) **EROTICA**
– One thing leads to another / Sure thing / Off my mind / Gently fall / Please yourself / Angels fallen / Isolation / Long day in the universe / Wave / If.

Dave DAVIES (see under ⇒ KINKS)

Martha DAVIS (see under ⇒ MOTELS)

Miles DAVIS

Born: 25 May 1926, Alton, Illinois, USA, but raised in East St.Louis. In 1944, after a period with bandleader BILLY ECKSTINE, he moved to New York and Harlem with new wife, where he joined singer RUBBERLEGS WILLIAMS. Around this time, he also recorded and played with saxophonist CHARLIE PARKER. In 1948, DAVIS assembled his own 9-piece band dubbed The TUBA BAND, which included saxophonists GERRY MULLIGAN and LEE KONITZ. They issued a number of radical 78's (singles), which were later (1957) coupled together on 'THE BIRTH OF THE COOL' lp. Through the early to mid-50's, with various personnel, DAVIS worked on some fine albums, gaining recognition from every jazz critic. By 1955, after a bout of illness due to drug addiction, he formed his now famous MILES DAVIS QUINTET which included JOHN COLTRANE, RED GARLAND, PAUL CHAMBERS and PHILLY JOE JONES. This period, saw them highly regarded by polls and jazz critics alike. In 1963, after earlier moving to 'Columbia-CBS', he formed a new combo of young musicians HERBIE HANCOCK, RON CARTER, TONY WILLIAMS and WAYNE SHORTER. This line-up, produced enough brilliance to enthuse a new buying public, to give them US chart albums. In 1968 they shocked the jazz and rock market, when MILES IN THE SKY introduced electric instrumentation. Other new talent also came through from this fusion, like JOHN McLAUGHLIN, JOE ZAWINUL, CHICK COREA to name but a few. Their next 2 albums 'IN A SILENT WAY' & 'BITCHES' BREW', saw them universally peaking, both critically and commercially (the latter hitting the US Top40, his only effort ever to do so). After a heavy car crash in 1972, MILES worked reclusively, away from mainstream music business. In the 80's, his return was heralded, although only by music journalists and past jazz fanatics. Broke a 27-year partnership with 'Columbia' when he moved to 'Warners' in 1986. MILES died on the 27th Dec'91, after contracting AIDS some years earlier. • **Style:** After being initially influenced by bop/jazz pioneers DIZZY GILLESPIE and CHARLIE PARKER, this innovative jazz/rock trumpeter, struck onto new stylistic type of jazz, that revolutionised jazz music in its day. His classic musicians, moved through a period of self-indulgent, but creative jazz/bop, to a more picturesque embryonic rock-jazz fusion by the late 1960's. Gave the unfashionable trumpet, a new character for the non-chart loving beatnik fraternity. • **Songwriters:** DAVIS wrote most of the material, except PORGY & BESS (Gershwin) / TIME AFTER TIME (Cyndi Lauper) / PERFECT WAY (Scritti Politti) / etc? • **Trivia:** He married actress CICELY TYSON in 1982. MILES also featured on many recordings by CHARLIE PARKER.

Recommended: IN A SILENT WAY (*7) / BITCHES' BREW (*8) / BIRTH OF THE COOL (*9) / WORKIN' / STEAMIN' / COOKIN' / RELAXIN' (all 6) / SKETCHES OF SPAIN (*7) / KIND OF BLUE (*10) / MILES SMILES (*9) / MILESTONES (*8) / SOMEDAY MY PRINCE WILL COME (*7) / E.S.P. (*7) / TUTU (*7) / JACK JOHNSON (*8)

(1948) **MILES DAVIS** – trumpet / **GIL EVANS, GERRY MULLIGAN, LEE KONITZ, JOHN LEWIS, JOHNNY CARISI, GUNTHER SCHULLER, SANDY SIEGELSTEIN** – saxophones /

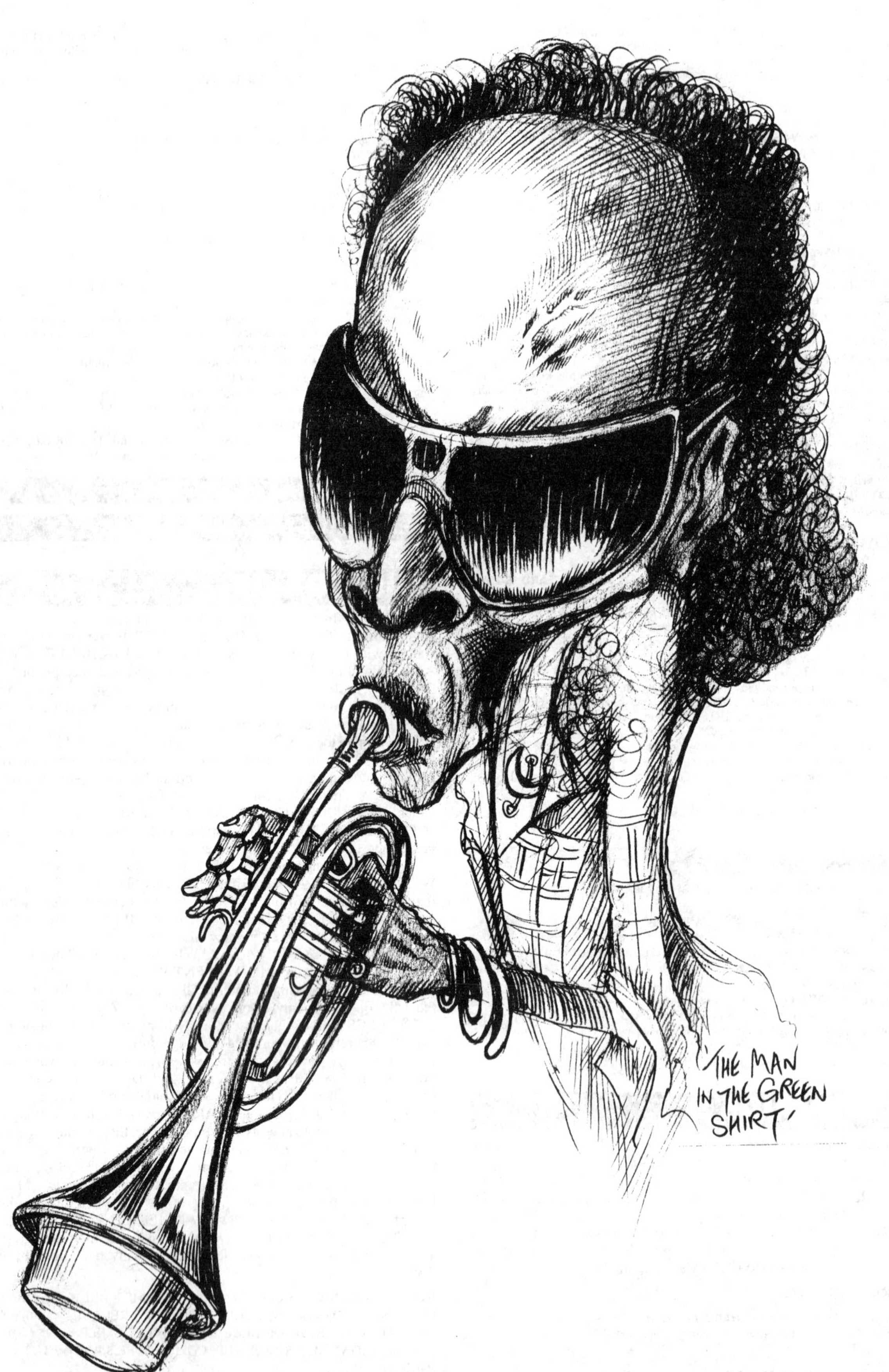
'THE MAN
IN THE GREEN
SHIRT'

JAY JAY JOHNSON – trombone / **JOHN 'Bill' BARBER** – tuba / **MAX ROACH** (or) **KENNY CLARKE** – drums / with on some **JUNIOR COLLINS** – French horn / **MIKE ZWERIN.**

not issued Capitol

1950. (lp) **BIRTH OF THE COOL**
– Move / Jeru / Moon dreams / Venus De Milo / Budo / Deception / Godchild / Boplicity / Rocker / Israel / Rouge.

— (May52 with) **JOHNSON + CLARKE** plus **JACKIE McLEAN** – alto sax / **GIL COGGINS** – piano / **OSCAR PETTIFORD** – bass

not issued Blue Note

Oct 51. (lp) **DIG**
– Dig / It's only a paper moon / Dental / Bluing / Out of the blue. *(UK-iss.1958 on 'Esquire')*

May 52. (lp) **MILES DAVIS VOL.1**
– How deep is the ocean / Dear old Stockholm / Chance it / Yesterdays / Donna / Woody 'n you.

— (Apr53) **PERCY HEATH** – bass repl. PETTIFORD / **ART BLAKEY** – drums repl. CLARKE / **JIMMY HEATH** – tenor sax repl. McLEAN

Tracks recorded: – Tempes fugit / Kelo / Enigma / Ray's idea / C.T.A. / I waited for you.

Sep 53. (lp) **AT LAST! MILES DAVIS AND THE LIGHTHOUSE ALL STARS**

— (Mar54) **HORACE SILVER** – piano repl. JIMMY, JAY JAY + GIL

Mar 54. (lp) **MILES DAVIS VOL. 2**

Tracks recorded: – Take-off / Weirdo / Well you needn't / The leap / Lazy Susan / It never entered my mind.

They also recorded tracks: – Four / Old Devil Moon / Blue haze.

— He formed The MILES DAVIS QUARTET earlier (May53) with **PERCY HEATH** – bass **JOHN LEWIS** – piano / **MAX ROACH** – drums with guest **CHARLIE MINGUS** – piano (1)

Albums issued at this time:- BAGS GROOVE / . . . & HORNS / MILES DAVIS Tracks recorded: – When lights are low / Tune up / Miles ahead / Smooch.

— The first incarnation of **MILES DAVIS QUINTET** appeared with **MILES, HORACE, PERCY, KENNY CLARKE** plus **DAVEY SCHILDKRAUT** – alto sax

MILES DAVIS ALL-STARS

were **CLARKE, JOHNSON, SILVER, PERCY HEATH & LUCKY THOMPSON**

not issued Prestige

Apr 54. (lp) **WALKIN'**
– Walkin' / Blues'n'boogie / Solar / You don't know what love is / Love me or leave me. *(cd-iss.Aug93 + Nov93 on 'Jazz Hour')*

— (Jun55) **MILES** – trumpet + **RED GARLAND** – piano / **PHILLY JOE JONES** – drums / **OSCAR PETTIFORD** – bass

1955. (lp) **THE MUSING OF MILES**
– I didn't / Will you still be mine? / Green haze / I see your face before me / A night in Tunisia / A gal in Calico. *(re-iss.Jun84)*

— (Nov55) **JOHN COLTRANE** – tenor sax + **PAUL CHAMBERS** – bass repl. OSCAR

MILES DAVIS QUINTET

Nov 55. (lp) **MILES**
– Just squeeze me / There is no greater love / How am I to know? / S'posin' / The theme / Stablemates. *(Above 2 albums issued as 'MILES' in 1958)*

Oct 56. (lp) **WORKIN'**
– It never entered my mind / Four / In your own sweet way / The theme (take 1 + 2) / Treme's blues / Ahmad's blues / Half Nelson.

Oct 56. (lp) **STEAMIN'**
– Surrey with the fringe on top / Salt peanuts / Something I dreamed last night / Diane / Well you needn't / When I fall in love.

Oct 56. (lp) **COOKIN' (live)**
– If I were a bell / Stella by starlight / Walkin' / Miles.

Oct 58. (lp) **RELAXIN'**
– You're my everything / I could write a book / Cleo / It could happen to you / Woodyn' you.

Others albums:- ODYSSEY / MODERN JAZZ GIANTS / CONCEPTION / CLEO / etc?

— **BILL EVANS** – piano + **JIMMY COBB** – drums repl. GARLAND + JONES / added **CANNONBALL ADDERLEY** – alto sax

C.B.S. Columbia

May 57. (lp) **MILES AHEAD**
– Springsville / Maids of Cadiz / Duke / My ship / Miles ahead / Blues for Pablo / New rhumba / Meaning of the blues / Lament / I don't wanna be kissed. *(UK-iss. 1966)*

Apr 58. (lp) **MILESTONES**
– Doctor Jekyll / Sid's ahead / Two bass hits / Miles / Billy Boy / Straight no chaser. *-(cd-iss. 1992)*

— added on below lp **JOHN COLTRANE** – tenor sax

May 59. (lp) **KIND OF BLUE**
– So what / Freddie Freeloader / Blue in green / All blues / Flamenco sketches. *(cd-iss.Sep93)*

(released 5 unknown singles-US in 1959)

Nov 59. (lp) **PORGY AND BESS**
– The buzzard song / Bess, you is my woman / Gone, gone, gone, gone / Summertime / Bess, oh where's my Bess / Prayer / Objector Jesus / Fisherman / Strawberry and Devil crab / My man's gone now / It ain't necessarily so / Here comes de honey man / I love you Porgy / There's a boat that's leaving soon for New York. *(re-iss.Sep82) (re-iss.+cd.Feb88)*

Jan 60. (7") **IT AIN'T NECESSARILY SO. / I LOVE YOU PORGY**

(above + below lp's credited arranger GIL EVANS ORCHESTRA)

Apr 60. (lp) **SKETCHES OF SPAIN**
– Concerto de Aranjuez / Will o' the wisp / The pan piper / Saeta / Solea. *(re-iss.Mar81 + Apr88, cd-iss.Dec85 + Apr92)*

— In Autumn 1960, **SONNY STITT** – saxophone repl. COLTRANE in Sweden. Later in the year **SAM RIVERS** then **WAYNE SHORTER** repl. SONNY

Sep 61. (d-lp) **IN PERSON (AT THE BLACKHAWK)** – 68
– Fran-dance / So what / Cleo / If I were a bell / Neo / Round midnight. *cd-iss.Jun 93 on 'Giants of Jazz')*

— **HANK MOBLEY** – saxophone repl. CONTRANE

Mar 62. (lp) **SOMEDAY MY PRINCE WILL COME**
– Someday my prince will come / Old folks / Pfrancing / Drad-dog / Teo / I thought about you.*(re-iss.Jul75 on 'Code-CBS') (cd-iss.Jan86 + Apr92)*

1963. (7") **NEW RHUMBA. / SLOW SAMBA**

Sep 62. (lp) **MILES DAVIS AT CARNEGIE HALL 1961 (live)** – 59
– So what / Spring is here / No blues / Cleo / Someday my prince will come / The meaning of the blues / Lament / New rhumba. *(cd-iss. Apr93 on 'Sony Europe')*

Dec 62. (lp) **ROUND ABOUT MIDNIGHT**
– Round about midnight / Ah leucha / All of you / Bye bye blackbird / Tadd's delight / Dear old Stockholm.

(above recorded 1956). *(cd-iss.Apr92)*

1963. (7") **BUDD. / TADD'S DELIGHT**

— Above issued on 'Philips'? at this time.

— now with **HERBIE HANCOCK** – piano / **TONY WILLIAMS** – drums / **RON CARTER** – bass / **GEORGE COLEMAN** – tenor sax

Sep 63. (lp) **SEVEN STEPS TO HEAVEN** 62
– Basin street blues / Seven steps to Heaven / I fall in love too easily / So near so far / Baby won't you please come home / Joshun. *(re-iss.Jul75 on 'Code-CBS')*

1963. (7") **SEVEN STEPS TO HEAVEN. / THE DEVIL MAY CARE**

Apr 64. (lp) **QUIET NIGHTS** – 93
– Once upon a summertime / Aos pes da cruz / Song No.1 / Wait till you see her / Corrovado / Summer night.
– *(re-iss.Jul75 on 'Code-CBS') (cd-iss. Jul 89)*

1964. (lp) **MILES AND MONK AT NEWPORT ("MILES DAVIS & THEOLONIUS MONK")**
– Ah-leu-cha / Straight, no chaser / Fran-dance / Two bass hit / Nutty / Blue Monk. *(re-iss.Jul75 on 'Code-CBS')*

Sep 64. (lp) **MILES DAVIS IN EUROPE (live)**
– Untitled medley:- Agitation / Footprints / Round midnight / No blues / Masqualero / All of you. *(re-iss.Jul75 on 'Code-CBS')*

Line-up now **DAVIS, WILLIAMS, HANCOCK, CARTER + SHORTER**

Jan 65. (lp) **E.S.P.**
– E.S.P. / Eighty one / Little one / R.J. / Agitation / Iris / Mood. *(re-iss.Jul75 on 'Code-CBS') (cd-iss.Apr92)*

Apr 65. (lp) **MY FUNNY VALENTINE: MILES DAVIS LIVE IN CONCERT (live)**
– My funny valentine / All of you / Stella by starlight / All blues / I thought about you. *(re-iss.Jul75 on 'Code-CBS') (cd-iss.May87 on 'CBS')*

— credited his QUINTET, (**SHORTER** repl. COLEMAN)

1966. (lp) **MILES SMILES**
– Orbits / Circle / Footprints / Dolores / Freedom jazz dance / Ginger bread boy. *(re-iss.Aug75 on 'Code-CBS')*

1967. (lp) **THE SORCERER**
– Prince of darkness / Vonetta / Limbo / Masquealero / Pee wee / The sorcerer. *(re-iss.Aug76) (re-iss.Jul87)(re-iss.cd Sep93)*

1967. (lp) **NEFERTITI**
– Nefertiti / Fall / Hand jive / Madness / Riot / Pinocchio. *(re-iss.Aug76) (cd-iss.Apr92)*

1968. (lp) **FILLES DE KILIMANJARO**
– Frelon burn (Brown hornet) / Tout de suite / Petits machins (little stuff) / Filles de Kilimanjaro (girls of . . .) / Mademoiselle Mabry. *(cd-iss.Apr92)*

Nov 68. (lp) **MILES IN THE SKY**
– Stuff / Paraphernalia / Black comedy / Country son. *(re-iss.Aug75 on 'Code-CBS')*

MILES DAVIS

with past members **HERBIE HANCOCK** – electric piano / **WAYNE SHORTER** – soprano sax / **TONY WILLIAMS** – drums. New:- **DAVE HOLLAND** – bass repl. CARTER / **CHICK COREA** – electric piano / **JOSEF ZAWINUL** – electric piano & organ / **JOHN McLAUGHLIN** – guitar

Aug 69. (lp) **IN A SILENT WAY**
– Ssh-Peaceful / In a silent way / It's about that time.

1970. (7") **GREAT EXPECTATIONS. / LITTLE BLUE FROG**

— **LARRY YOUNG** – electric piano repl. HANCOCK who cont. solo work / **JACK DeJOHNETTE + LENNY WHITE** – drums repl. WILLIAMS who formed his LIFETIME / added **JIM RILEY** – perc. / **HARVEY BROOKS** – Fender bass / **BENNIE MAUPIN** – clarinet

Jun 70. (d-lp) **BITCHES BREW** 71 35 May 70
– Pharoah's dance / Bitches brew / Spanish key / John McLaughlin / Miles runs the voodoo down / Sanctuary. *(re-iss.Sep87, d-cd-iss.Apr92)*

Jul 70. (7") **MILES RUNS THE VOODOO DOWN (edit). / SPANISH KEY**

Jan 71. (d-lp) **MILES DAVIS AT FILLMORE (live)** Dec 70
– Wednesday Miles / Thursday Miles / Friday Miles / Saturday Miles. *(re-iss.Jul75 on 'Code-CBS')*

Feb 71. (7") **SATURDAY MILES. / FRIDAY MILES**

— Other members at this time **BILLY COBHAM** – percusion / **KEITH JARRETT** – keyboards

May 71. (lp) **A TRIBUTE TO JACK JOHNSON (Soundtrack)** Apr 71
– Right off / Yesternow. *(re-imported Jan76)(cd-iss.Sep93)*

May 71. (7") **RIGHT OFF. / (part 2)**

Dec 71. (d-lp) **LIVE-EVIL**
– Sivod / Little church / Medley: Gemini-Double image / What I say / Nem um talvez / Selim / Funky tonk / Inamorata.

Sep 72. (7") **MOLESTER. /**

Nov 72. (7") **VOTE FOR MILES. / (part 2)**

Nov 72. (lp) **ON THE CORNER**
– On the corner / New York girl / Thinkin' one thing and doin' another / Vote for Miles / Black satin / One and one / Helen Butte / Mr.Freedom

X. *(re-iss.Jan87) (re-iss.Dec88 on 'B.G.O.', cd-iss.Apr92) (re-iss.cd Feb94 on 'Sony')*

Apr 73. (d-lp) **IN CONCERT (live)**

Jun 74. (lp)(c) **BIG FUN**
– Go ahead, John / Lonely fire / Great expectations / Mulher Laranja / Ife.

Jun 74. (7") **BIG FUN. / HOLLYWOOD** -

Oct 74. (7") **GREAT EXPECTATIONS. / GO AHEAD JOHN** -

Oct 74. (lp)(c) **BLACK BEAUTY**

Jan 75. (lp)(c) **GET UP WITH IT**
– He loved him madly / Maiysha / Honky tonk / Rated X / Calypso frelimo / Red China blues / Mtume / Billy Preston.

Jan 75. (7") **CHINA BLUES. / MAIYSHA** -

Nov 75. (d-lp)(c) **AGHARTA (live)**
– Prelude (pt.1 & 2) / Maiysha / Interlude / Theme from Jack Johnson. *(re-iss.Jan87)(re-iss.d-cd Sep93)*

1976. (d-lp)(c) **PANGAEA** (live) -
– Zimbabwe (parts 1-3). *(d-cd-iss. Sep93 on 'Warners')*

In the mid-70's, he suffered from injuries sustained in a car crash. He recuperated, with record co. issuing some recordings/out-takes.

Jan 77. (lp)(c) **WATER BABIES**
– Water babies / Capricorn / Sweet pea / Two-faced / Dual Mr.Tillman Anthony. *(re-iss.Jul86)*

Nov 77. (lp)(c) **PARIS FESTIVAL INTERNATIONAL (live)**
– Rifftide / Good bait / Don't blame me / Lady bird / Wah'hoo / Allen's alley / Embraceable you / Ornithology / All the things you are.

Jan 80. (d-lp)(c) **CIRCLE IN THE ROUND (rec 55-70)**
– Two bars hit / Love for sale / Blues No.2 / Circle in the round / Ted's bag / Side car 1 + 2 / Splash / Sanctuary / Guinnevere. *(re-iss.May82)(re-iss.cd Sep93)*

— DAVIS returned tour/studio with **MARCUS MILLER** – bass / **MIKE STERN** – guitar / **BILL EVANS** – soprano + tenor sax / **AL FOSTER** – drums / **MINO CINELU** – percussion

Jul 81. (7") **FAT TIME. / SHORT** -

Jul 81. (lp)(c) **THE MAN WITH THE HORN** 53
– Fat time / Back seat Betty / Short / Aida / The man with the horn / Urasula. *(cd-iss.1983)(re-iss.cd Sep93)*

Jun 82. (d-lp)(d-c) **WE WANT MILES (live Boston/Tokyo)** May 82
– Jean Pierre / Back seat Betty / Fast track / My man's gone now / Kix. *(re-iss.cd Sep93)*

— added **JOHN SCOFIELD** – electric guitar / **TOM BARNEY** – electric bass

May 83. (7") **STAR ON CICELY. / IT GETS BETTER** -

May 83. (lp)(c) **STAR PEOPLE**
– Come get it / It gets better / Speak / Star people / U'il / Star on Cicely. *(cd-iss.May87)(re-iss.cd Sep93)*

— **DARYLL 'The Munch' JONES** – electric bass repl. MILLER to SCRITTI POLITTI / **ROBERT IRVING III** – synthesizers, co-composer repl. MIKE STERN + TOM BARNEY / **BRANFORD MARSALIS** shared sax duties with **EVANS**

Jun 84. (7") **DECOY. / CODE M. D.** -

Jun 84. (lp)(c)(cd) **DECOY**
– Decoy / Robot 415 / Code M.D. / Freaky Deaky / What it is / That's right / That's what happened. *(re-iss.cd Sep93)*

— **VINCE WILBURN JR.** – drums + **STEVE THORNTON** – percussion repl. CINELU / **BOB BERG** – soprano sax repl. MARSALIS + EVANS / guest on 2 tracks **JOHN McLAUGHLIN** – guitar

May 85. (7")(12") **TIME AFTER TIME. / KATIA**

Jun 85. (lp)(c)(cd) **YOU'RE UNDER ARREST** 88 May 85
– One phone call – Street scenes / Human nature / Intro: MD1 – Something's on your mind- MD2 / Ms. Morrisine / Katia prelude / Katia / Time after time / You're under arrest medley: Jean Pierre – You're under arrest – Then there were none. *(re-iss.cd Sep93)*

— **MILES DAVIS** now with basic line-up of **MILLER, GEORGE DUKE** – multi / **PAULINHO DA COSTA** – synthesizers / plus **JASON MILES** – synth.prog. / **ADAM HOLZMAN** – synth.prog. / **STEVE REID** – percusson / **OMAR HAKIM** – drums, perc / etc.

Warners Warners

Oct 86. (lp)(c)(cd) **TUTU** 74
– Tutu / Tomaas / Portia / Splatch / Backyard ritual / Perfect way / Don't lose your mind / Full Nelson.

Oct 86. (7") **TUTU. / PORTIA** -

Feb 87. (7") **TOMAAS. / FULL NELSON** -

May 87. (7") **BACKYARD RITUAL. / TOMAAS** -

Feb 88. (lp)(c)(cd) **SIESTA (Soundtrack)**
– Lost in Madrid (pt.1): Siesta – Kitt's kiss / Lost in Madrid (part 2): / Theme for Augustine – Wind – Seduction – Kiss / Submission / Lost in Madrid (pt.3): Conchita – Lament / Lost in Madrid (pt.4): Rat dance – The call / Claire – Lost in Madrid (pt.5): Afterglow / Los Feliz.

In 1988, he appeared on albums by JONI MITCHELL and SCRITTI POLITTI.

— Next included loads of musicians, including **MILLER, DUKE, CINELU, MILES, FOSTER, DA COSTA, HAKIM, KENNY GARRETT** – soprano sax / **DON ALIAS** – percussion /

May 89. (lp)(c)(cd) **AMANDLA** 49
– Catembe / Cobra / Big time / Hannibal / Jo Jo / Amandla / Jilli / Mr.Pastorius.

MILES, due to heroin addiction, lost his battle against AIDS on 28 Sep'91.

Nov 91. (cd)(c)(lp) **DINGO (Music From The Motion Picture)**
– Kimberley trumpet / The arrival / Concert on the runway / The departure / Dingo howl / Letter as hero / Trumpet cleaning / The dream / Paris walking I & II / Knight trumpet in Paris / The music room / Club entrance / The jam session / Going home / Surprise. (album w / MICHAEL LEGRAND).

Next had been a collaboration with **EAZY MO BEE** – rapper, writer, etc.

May 92. (cd)(c)(lp) **DOO-BOP**
– Mystery / The doo-bop song / Chocolate chip / High speed chase / Blow / Sonya / Fantasy / Duke Booty / Mystery (reprise).

– (some) compilations, others, etc. –

1957. Capitol; (lp) **BIRTH OF THE COOL** -
– Move / Jeru / Moon dreams / Venus De Milo / Budo / Decepetion / Godchild / Boplivity / Rocker / Israel / Rouge. *(UK-iss.Jul78 on 'Capitol') (cd-iss.Apr90)* (+=) – Darn that dream. *(cd-iss.Mar95 on 'Blue Note')*

1966. Xtra; (lp) **EZZ THETIC (w / LEE KONITZ)** -
(US re-iss. Feb86 on 'Fantasy')

1966. Transatlantic; (d-lp) **COLLECTORS ITEMS**
(re-iss.1973 on 'Prestige')

All CBS releases below were issued 'Columbia' in the US.

1973. C.B.S.; (lp) **THE ESSENTIAL MILES DAVIS** -

Aug 74. C.B.S.; (lp) **JAZZ AT THE PLAZA (live)** -

1976. C.B.S.; (d-lp) **LIVE AT THE PLUGGED NICKEL**
(re-iss.Dec82)

May 76. C.B.S.; (d-lp)(c) **CLASSICS**

1976. C.B.S.; (7") **ROUND MIDNIGHT. / SOLEA**

1979. C.B.S.; (lp) **MILES DAVIS WITH JOHN COLTRANE QUINTET (live)**

Mar 81. C.B.S.; (d-lp)(c) **DIRECTIONS** -

Feb 83. C.B.S.; (d-c) **SKETCHES OF SPAIN / IN A SILENT WAY** -

May 83. C.B.S.; (lp)(c) **BLUES AT CHRISTMAS** -

Jan 84. C.B.S.; (d-lp)(d-c) **HEARD 'ROUND THE WORLD** -

Feb 88. C.B.S.; (lp)(c) **A PORTRAIT OF MILES DAVIS** -

1988. C.B.S.; (lp) **FOUR & MORE**
(cd-iss. Apr93 on 'Sony Europe')

Apr 89. Columbia; (lp)(c)(cd) **BALLADS** -

Oct 89. C.B.S.; (d-lp)(c)(cd) **AURA**

Apr 92. Columbia; (cd) **MELLOW MILES** -

May 93. Columbia; (d-cd) **COMPLETE CONCERT '64 (live)**

Nov 94. Columbia; (d-cd) **AT THE FILLMORE**

Nov 94. Columbia; (d-cd) **IN CONCERT**

Jun 76. Beppo; (lp) **MILES DAVIS' ALL-STARS & GIL EVANS**

Jun 76. Beppo; (lp) **AT THE BIRDLAND '51 (live)**

Nov 76. Vogue; (d-lp) **DAVIS, PARKER & GILLESPIE**

1973. Prestige; (d-lp) **TALLEST TREES** -

May 74. Prestige; (d-lp) **WORKIN' AND STEAMIN'** -
(re-iss.Oct93, 4xcd)

Nov 76. Prestige; (d-lp) **GREEN HAZE**
– (lp's:- THE MUSING OF MILES + MILES)

May 79. Prestige; (d-lp) **TUNE UP**

Dec 80. Prestige; (12xlp-box) **CHRONICLE – THE COMPLETE PRESTIGE RECORDINGS 1951-1956**
(re-issJun92 as 8xcd-box)

Aug 84. Prestige; (lp) **BLUE HAZE**
(cd-iss.Apr93)

Jul 75. D.J.M.; (lp) **EARLY MILES** -

Nov 76. D.J.M.; (lp) **BIRD AND MILES (with CHARLIE PARKER)** -

Jan 91. D.J.M.; (cd) **COOKIN' AND RELAXIN'** -

May 79. Blue Note; (lp) **SOMETHING ELSE WITH CANNONBALL ADDERLEY**

Jul 82. Blue Note; (lp) **VOLUME 1**

Jul 82. Blue Note; (lp) **VOLUME 2**

Jun 80. Manhattan; (lp) **MILES OF FUN**

Jul 80. Manhattan; (lp) **WORLD OF JAZZ**

1979. Joker; (lp) **MILES DAVIS IN L.A. 1946 (live)** -

Apr 81. Joker; (lp) **A NIGHT IN TUNISIA (live)** -

Apr 81. V.G.M.; (lp) **MILES AT ST.LOUIS (live with QUINTET 1963)** -

Apr 81. Jazz Horizons; (lp) **PRE-BIRTH OF THE COOL** (with HIS TUBA BAND 1948) -

Apr 81. Unique Jazz; (lp) **LIVE (with "JOHN COLTRANE")** -

Aug 81. Kingdom Of Jazz; (lp) **MILES DAVIS & STAN GETZ** -

Jul 82. Kingdom Of Jazz; (lp) **AT HIS RARE OF ALL RAREST PERFORMANCES VOL.1** -

Aug 85. Deja Vu; (lp) **THE MILES DAVIS COLLECTION** -
(cd-iss.Sep87)

Apr 93. Deja Vu; (d-cd)(d-c) **THE GOLD COLLECTION** -
(re-iss.Jun95)

May 87. J.V.C.; (cd) **ARTISTRY IN JAZZ (GREATEST HITS)**

Jan 89. J.V.C.; (cd) **MILES DAVIS & THE MODERN JAZZ GIANTS** -
(re-iss. Oct93 on 'Fantasy')

Sep 87. Giants Of Jazz; (lp) **1954 – THE MASTERPIECES** -

1988. Giants Of Jazz; (cd) **EVOLUTION OF A GENUIS 1945-1954** -

Jun 88. Black Lion; (lp)(cd) **BOPPIN' THE BLUES** (rec.Oct'46) -

Jun 90. Castle; (cd)(c)(d-lp) **THE COLLECTION** -

Dec 90. Flyright; (cd)(lp) **LIVE IN 1958 (live)** -

Dec 90. Regal Jazz; (cd) **LIVE-NONET 1948 / JAM 1949 (live)** -

Aug 91. Magnetic; (cd)(c)(lp) **FREE TRADE HALL 1960, VOL.1 & 2** -

Feb 93. O.M.D.; (cd) **LIVE IN EUROPE 1988** -

Mar 93. Original Jazz; (cd) **CONCEPTION** -

Nov 93. Original Jazz; (cd) **BLUE MOODS** -

May 93. Royal Collection; (cd)(c) **SUPER HORNS ("& FREDDIE HUBBARD")** -

Sep 93. Natasha; (cd) **WHY DO I LOVE YOU? – RARE BROAD-CASTS 1947-48** -

Nov 93. Jazz Door; (cd) **MILES IN MONTREUX** -

Dec 93. Sony Europe; (cd) **ESSENTIAL JEAN-PIERRE**

— See also QUINCY JONES for release in Aug'93 'LIVE AT MONTREUX'.

Mar 94. Le Jazz; (cd) **THE BIRDLAND SESSIONS** -

May 94. J.M.Y.; (cd) **WHAT I SAY? VOLUME 1** -

May 94. J.M.Y.; (cd) **WHAT I SAY? VOLUME 2**

Aug 94. Jazz Roots; (cd) **MILESTONES 1945-1954** -

Nov 94. Jazz Roots; (cd) **CONCIERTO DE ARANJUEZ (live)** -

Aug 94. Jazz Portrait; (cd) **1954-1955** [ ] [-]
Aug 94. Jazz Portrait; (cd) **1956-1958** [ ] [-]
Aug 94. Jazz Portrait; (cd) **1958-1960** [ ] [-]
Oct 94. Jazz Door; (cd) **LIVE IN NEW YORK (1957-59 w /JOHN COLTRANE)** [ ] [ ]
Mar 95. RTE; (cd) **IN CONCERT (1960)** [ ] [-]
Jun 95. Collection; (cd) **THE COLLECTION** [ ] [-]
Jul 95. Le Jazz; (cd) **AT THE ROYAL ROOST 1948, AT BIRDLAND 1950/1, 1953** [ ] [-]
Jul 95. Sony Jazz; (8xcd-box) **LIVE AT PLUGGED NICKEL 1965** [ ] [-]
Oct 95. Sony Jazz; (cd) **HIGHLIGHTS FROM THE PLUGGED NICKEL** [ ] [-]
Oct 95. Sony Jazz; (5xcd-box) **THE COMPLETE COLUMBIA STUDIO SESSIONS (with GIL EVANS)** [ ] [ ]
Oct 95. Sony Jazz; (d-cd) **HIGHLIGHTS FROM THE COMPLETE COLUMBIA STUDIO SESSIONS (with GIL EVANS)** [ ] [-]
Nov 95. Blue Note; (3xcd-box) **BIRTH OF THE COOL / VOLUME 1 / VOLUME 3** [ ] [-]
Dec 95. Music De-Luxe; (cd) **COOL** [ ] [-]

Spencer DAVIS GROUP

Formed: Birmingham, England . . . August 1963, when DAVIS met YORK and the WINWOOD brothers at local jazz clubs. After a year on the circuit they signed to 'Fontana' records, helped by owner of 'Island' label CHRIS BLACKWELL who had recommended act. They soon became one of the top hitmakers of 1966, although the following year the young WINWOOD joined TRAFFIC. SPENCER DAVIS soldiered on but original momentum was lost. • **Style:** Basic 'R&B' outfit, with STEVE's vox heavily influenced by 'Motown' sound. After his departure, they unsuccessfully turned to psychedelia 1967. • **Songwriters:** Most surprisingly written by 16-17 year old STEVE. They also covered DIMPLES (John Lee Hooker) / EVERY LITTLE BIT HURTS (Brenda Holloway) / KEEP ON RUNNING (Jackie Edwards) / etc. • **Trivia:** Late 1967, they made small cameo appearance as the group in the film 'HERE WE GO ROUND THE MULBURRY BUSH'.

Recommended: THE BEST OF THE SPENCER DAVIS GROUP (*7)

SPENCER DAVIS (b.17 Jul'42, Swansea, Wales) – guitar (ex-SAINTS) / **STEVE WINWOOD** (b.12 May'48, Birmingham) – vocals, keyboards, guitar / **MUFF WINWOOD** (b.Mervyn, 14 Jun'43, Birmingham) – bass, vocals / **PETER YORK** (b.15 Aug'42, Redcar, Cleveland, England) – drums

Fontana Fontana

Aug 64. (7") **DIMPLES. / SITTIN' AND THINKIN'** [ ] [-]
Oct 64. (7") **I CAN'T STAND IT. / MIDNIGHT TRAIN** [47] [ ] Mar 65
Jan 65. (7") **EVERY LITTLE BIT HURTS. / IT HURTS ME SO** [41] [-]
May 65. (7") **STRONG LOVE. / THIS HAMMER** [44] [-]
Jul 65. (lp) **FIRST ALBUM** (hit-Jan66) [6] [-]
– My babe / Dimples / Searchin' / Every little bit hurts / I'm blue (gong gong song) / Sittin' and thinkin' / I can't stand it / Here right now / Jump back / It's gonna work out fine / Midnight train / It hurts me so. *(re-iss.1980's on 'Wing')*

Fontana United A..

Nov 65. (7") **KEEP ON RUNNING. / HIGH TIME BABY** [1] [76]
Jan 66. (lp) **SECOND ALBUM** [2] [-]
– Look away / Keep on running / This hammer / Georgia on my mind / Please do something / Let me down easy / Strong love / I washed my hands in muddy water / Since I met you baby / You must believe me / Hey darling / Watch your step.
Mar 66. (7") **SOMEBODY HELP ME. / STEVIE'S BLUES** [1] [47] Jun 67
Aug 66. (7") **WHEN I GET HOME. / TRAMPOLINE** [12] [ ]
Sep 66. (lp) **AUTUMN '66** [4] [-]
– Together till the end of time / Take this hurt off me / Nobody knows you when you're down and out / Midnight special / When a man loves a woman / When I come home / Mean woman blues / Dust my blues / On the green light / Neighbour, neighbour / High time baby / Somebody help me.
Oct 66. (7") **GIMME SOME LOVIN'. / BLUES IN F** [2] [7] Jan 67
— (above 'A'side was different remix in the States)
Jan 67. (7") **I'M A MAN. / CAN'T GET ENOUGH OF IT** [9] [10] Mar 67
Mar 67. (lp) **GIMME SOME LOVIN'** [-] [54]
– Keep on running / When a man loves a woman / Take this hurt off me / Georgia on my mind / You must believe me / Here right now / When I get home / I'm a man. *(UK-iss 1988 on 'Capitol')*

— **EDDIE HARDIN** (b.EDWARD HARDING, 19 Feb'49) – organ, vocals replaced STEVE who joined TRAFFIC and later BLIND FAITH then solo. / **PHIL SAWYER** (b.8 Mar'47) – lead guitar replaced MUFF who became A&R man, / also **CHARLIE McCRACKEN** – bass (guest).

Jul 67. (lp) **I'M A MAN** [-] [83]
– Dimples / Every little bit hurts / Stevie's blues / On the green light / Searchin' / Midnight train / My babe / Georgia on my mind / I can't get enough of it / I'm a man / I can't stand it / Look away.
Jul 67. (7") **TIME SELLER. / DON'T WANT YOU NO MORE** [30] [100]

United Art United Art

Dec 67. (7") **MR. SECOND CLASS. / SANITY INSPECTOR** [35] [ ]
Mar 68. (7") **AFTER TEA. / MOONSHINE** [ ] [ ]
1968. (lp) **WITH THEIR NEW FACE ON** [-] [ ]
– With his new face on / Mr.Second class / Alec in transitland / Sanity inspector / Feel your way / Morning sun / Moonshine / Don't want you no more / Time seller / Stop me, I'm fallin'.
1968. (7") **SHORT CHANGE. / PICTURE OF HEAVEN** [-] [ ]

— (Nov68) **DEE MURRAY** – bass / **NIGEL OLSSON** – drums repl. HARDIN & YORK who formed self named duo.

1969. (lp) **HEAVIES** [-] [ ]
– Please do something / Waltz for lum umba / I'm blue (gong gong song) / Hey darling / Mean woman blues / Watch your step / Drown in my own tears / Together til' the end of time / Take this hurt off me / Back into my life again.

— Split mid '69. MURRAY and OLSSON joined ELTON JOHN's Band.

SPENCER DAVIS & PETER JAMESON

United Art United Art

1970. (lp) **IT'S BEEN SO LONG** [ ] [ ]
– It's been so long / Crystal river / One hundred years ago / Balkan blues / Brother can you make up your mind / Mountain lick / Jav's tune / King of her / It's too late now.

SPENCER DAVIS

1972. (lp) **MOUSETRAP** [ ] [ ]
– Rainy season / Listen to the rhythm / What can I be / Tried / Easy rider / Tumbledown tenement row / Sunday walk in the rain / I washed my hands in muddy water / Sailor's lament / Hollywood Joe / In the hills of Tennessee / Ella speed.
1972. (7") **LISTEN TO THE RHYTHM. / SUNDAY WALK IN THE RAIN** [-] [ ]
1972. (7") **RAINY SEASON. / TUMBLEDOWN TENEMENT ROW** [-] [ ]

— now re-united w / **HARDIN, YORK, FENWICK + CHARLIE McCRACKEN** – bass

Vertigo Mercury

1972. (7") **CATCH YOU ON THE REBOB. / THE EDGE** [ ] [ ]
1973. (lp) **GLUGGO** [ ] [ ]
– Catch you on the Moon / Don't it let it bring you down / Alone / Today Gluggo, tomorrow the world / Feeling rude / Legal eagle shuffle / Trouble in mind / Mr.Operator / Tumbledown tenement row.
1973. (7") **MR OPERATOR / TOUCHING CLOTH** [ ] [ ]
Oct 73. (7") **LIVING IN A BACKSTREET. / SURE NEED A HELPING HAND** [ ] [ ]
1974. (lp) **LIVING IN A BACKSTREET** [ ] [ ]
– Living in a backstreet / One night / Hanging around / No reason / Fasted thing / On four wheels / Backstreet boys / Another day / Sure need a helping hand / We can give it a try / Let's have a party.

— SPENCER retired from solo work until 1983.

Allegience not issued

May 84. (7") **PRIVATE NUMBER. (by "SPENCER DAVIS & DUSTY SPRINGFIELD") / DON'T WANT YOU NO MORE** [ ] [-]
Apr 84. (lp)(c) **CROSSFIRE** [ ] [-]
– Blood runs hot / Don't want you no more / Love is on a roll / Crossfire / Private number / Just a gigolo / Careless love / A pretty girl is like a melody / When the day is done / Hush-a-bye.

SPENCER became an executive at Island records in the mid 70's. In 1990 **SPENCER DAVIS GROUP** reformed with others **DON KIRKPATRICK, EDDIE TREE** – guitars / **RICK SERATTE** – keys / **CHARLIE HARRISON** – bass / **BRYAN HITT** – drums (ex-WANG CHUNG).

– compilations, others, etc. –

1964. Fontana; (7"ep) **YOU PUT THE HURT ON ME** [ ] [-]
1965. Fontana; (7"ep) **EVERY LITTLE BIT HURTS** [ ] [-]
1966. Fontana; (7"ep) **SITTIN' AND THINKIN'** [ ] [-]
Mar 68. United Artists; (lp) **SPENCER DAVIS' GREATEST HITS** [-] [-]
1969. Philips; (c-ep) **THE HITS OF THE SPENCER DAVIS GROUP** [ ] [-]
1972. Island; (lp)(c) **THE BEST OF THE SPENCER DAVIS GROUP** [ ] [-] *(re-iss.Oct 86)*
Aug 76. Island; (7") **GIMME SOME LOVIN'. / WHEN I GET HOME** [ ] [-]
May 78. Island; (7"ep) **KEEP ON RUNNING** [ ] [-]
– Gimme some lovin' / Somebody help me / Every little bit hurts / I'm a man.
May 91. Island; (7")(c-s) **KEEP ON RUNNING. / HIGH TIME BABY** [ ] [ ]
(12"+=)(cd-s+=) – Somebody help me / This hammer.
1984. Inak; (cd) **LIVE TOGETHER** [ ] [-]
1985. Inak; (cd) **24 HOURS – LIVE IN GERMANY** [ ] [-]
May 93. Royal Collection; (cd)(c) **KEEP ON RUNNING** [ ] [-]
Jun 94. R.P.M.; (cd) **TAKING OUT TIME 1967-69** [ ] [-]
Oct 94. Charly; (cd) **KEEP ON RUNNING** [ ] [-]
Jun 95. RPM; (cd) **CATCH YOU ON THE REBOP – LIVE IN EUROPE 1973** [ ] [-]

Brian DEACON (see under ⇒ QUEEN)

DEACON BLUE

Formed: Glasgow, Scotland . . . 1985, by former remedial teacher RICKY ROSS who finds four other guys, who soon took name from a STEELY DAN song. By sheer accident/inspiration ROSS invited girlfriend LORRAINE to sing/accompany his vocals, and she soon became sixth member. By this time they had already been signed to 'CBS' by their manager MUFF WINWOOD (ex-SPENCER DAVIS GROUP). Their first division breakthrough came in 1989, when that year's album hit No.1. • **Style:** Classy rock-pop, slightly similar to early PREFAB SPROUT. • **Songwriters:** All written by ROSS, except covers ANGELIOU (Van Morrison) / TRAMPOLENE (Julian Cope) / I'M DOWN (Beatles) / I'LL NEVER FALL IN LOVE AGAIN and the 3 others on 1990 EP (Bacharach & David). • **Trivia:** Their re-issue of WHEN WILL YOU (MAKE MY TELEPHONE RING) featured future LONDON BEAT group.

Recommended: OUR TOWN (*9)

RICKY ROSS (b.22 Dec'57, Dundee) – vocals / **JAMES PRIME** (b. 3 Nov'60, Kilmarnock) – keyboards (ex-ALTERED IMAGES) / **GRAEME KELLING** (b. 4 Apr'57, Paisley) – guitar / **EWAN VERNAL** (b.27 Feb'64, Glasgow) – bass, keyboard bass / **DOUGLAS VIPOND** (b.15

Oct'66, Johnstone) – drums, percussion / **LORRAINE McINTOSH** (b.13 May'64, Glasgow) – vocals

C.B.S. Columbia

Mar 87. (7") **DIGNITY. / RICHES**
(12"+=) – Ribbons and bow.
(c-s+=) – (edit, excerpts 'RAINTOWN' lp)

Jun 87. (7")(c-s) **LOADED. / LONG DISTANCE FROM ACROSS THE ROAD**
(12"+=) – Which side of the world are you on / Kings of the western world.

Aug 87. (7") **WHEN WILL YOU (MAKE MY TELEPHONE RING). / CHURCH**
(12") – ('A'side) / A town to be blamed (live) (US B-side) / Angeliou (live).

Jan 88. (7") **DIGNITY. / SUFFERING** [31]
(10"+=) – Shifting sands.
(cd-s++=) – Just like boys.
(7"ep+=) – Ronnie Spector / Raintown (piano).
(12"+=) – Ronnie Spector / Just like boys.

Feb 88. (lp)(c)(cd) **RAINTOWN** [14]
– Born in a storm / Raintown / Ragman / He looks like Spencer Tracy now / Loaded / When will you (make my telephone ring) / Chocolate girl / Dignity / The very thing / Love's great fears / Town to be blamed. *(re-packaged Aug88 free with above lp+c)* RICHES – Which side are you on / King of the western world * / Riches * / Angeliou / Just like boys / Raintown / Church / Suffering / Shifting sand / Ribbons and bows / Dignity. *(cd+= *)*

Mar 88. (7") **WHEN WILL YOU (MAKE MY TELEPHONE RING). / THAT BRILLIANT FEELING** [34]
(12"+=)(cd-s+=)(pic-cd-s+=) – Punch and Judy man / Disneyworld.

Jul 88. (7") **CHOCOLATE GIRL. / S.H.A.R.O.N.** [43]
(7"ep+=)(cd-ep+=) – The very thing / Love's great fears.
(12"+=) – Loves great fears (live) / Dignity (live).

Oct 88. (7") **REAL GONE KID. / LITTLE LINCOLN** [8]
(7"ep+=)(cd-ep+=) – Born again / It's not funny.
(12"+=) – ('A'extended).

Feb 89. (7") **WAGES DAY. / TAKE ME TO THE PLACE** [18]
(7"ep+=)(cd-ep+=) – Take the saints away / Trampolene.
(12"+=) – ('A'extended).

Apr 89. (lp)(c)(cd) **WHEN THE WORLD KNOWS YOUR NAME** [1]
– Queen of the New Year / Wages day / Real gone kid / Love and regret / Circus lights / This changing light / Fergus sings the blues / Sad loved girl / The world is hit by lightning / Silhouette / One hundred things / Your constant heart / Orphans.

May 89. (7") **FERGUS SINGS THE BLUES. / LONG WINDOW TO LOVE** [14]
(12"+=) – ('A'extended).
(7"ep+=)(c-ep+=) – London A-Z.
(10"++=)(cd-ep++=) – Back here in Beano land.

Sep 89. (7")(c-s) **LOVE AND REGRET. / DOWN IN THE FLOOD** [28]
(12"+=) – Undeveloped heart.
(10")(cd-s) – ('A'side) / Spanish moon – Down in the flood (live) / Dark end of the street (live) / When will you make my telephone ring (live).

Dec 89. (7") **QUEEN OF THE NEW YEAR. / MY AMERICA** [21]
(12"+=) – Circus light (acoustic).
(7"ep+=)(c-ep+=)(cd-ep+=) – Sad loved girl (extended) / Las Vegas.
(7"ltd.) – ('A'side) / Chocolate girl.
(12")(c-s) – (above 2) / Undeveloped heart / A town to be blamed.

Aug 90. (7"ep)(12"ep)(cd-ep) **FOUR BACHARACH AND DAVID SONGS** [2]
– I'll never fall in love again / The look of love / Message to Michael / Are you there (with another girl).

Columbia Columbia

Sep 90. (d-cd)(c)(d-lp) **OOH LAS VEGAS** ('B'sides, sessions) [3]
– Disneyworld / Ronnie Spector / My America / S.H.A.R.O.N. / Undeveloped heart / Souvenirs / Born again / Down in the flood / Back here in Beanoland / Love you say / Let your hearts be troubled/ / Gentle teardrops / Little Lincoln / That country / Is it cold beneath the hill? / Circus lights / Trampolene / Las Vegas / Killing the blues / Long window to love / Christine / Take me to the place / Don't let the teardrops start.

May 91. (7")(c-s) **YOUR SWAYING ARMS. / FOURTEEN YEARS** [23]
(cd-s+=) – Faifley.
(12"++=) – ('A'extended).
(10") – ('A'-12"alternative mix) / ('A'-Drumapella mix) / ('A'-7"mix) / ('A'-dub mix).

May 91. (cd)(c)(lp) **FELLOW HOODLUMS** [2]
– James Joyce soles / Fellow hoodlums / Your swaying arms / Cover from the sky / The day that Jackie jumped the jail / The wildness / A brighter star than you will shine / Twist and shout / Closing time / Goodnight Jamsie / I will see you tomorrow / One day I'll go walking.

Jul 91. (7")(c-s) **TWIST & SHOUT. / GOOD** [10]
(12"+=) – ('A'extended) / I'm down.
(cd-s+=) – Golden bells.

Sep 91. (7")(c-s) **CLOSING TIME. / I WAS LIKE THAT** [42]
(cd-s+=) – Into the good night.
(12"++=) – Friends of Billy the bear.

Dec 91. (7")(c-s) **COVER FROM THE SKY. / WHAT DO YOU WANT THE GIRL TO DO / CHRISTMAS (BABY PLEASE COME HOME)** [31]
(12"+=) – Real gone kid / Loaded / One hundred things.
(cd-s+=) – Wild mountain thyme / Silhouette / I'll never fall in love again.

Sony-Columbia Sony-Columbia

Nov 92. (7")(c-s) **YOUR TOWN. / ALMOST BEAUTIFUL** [14]
(cd-s+=) – I've been making such a fool.
(12") – ('A'perfecto mix) / ('A'extended)

Feb 93. (7")(c-s) **WILL WE BE LOVERS. / SLEEPER** [31]
(cd-s+=) – Paint it red.
(12") – ('A'side) / (4 other 'A' mixes)

Mar 93. (cd)(c)(lp) **WHATEVER YOU SAY, SAY NOTHING** [4]
– Your town / Only tender love / Peace and jobs and freedom / Hang your head / Bethlehem's gate / Last night I Dreamed of Henry Thomas / Will we be lovers / Fall so freely down / Cut lip / All over the world.

Apr 93. (7")(c-s) **ONLY TENDER LOVE. / RICHES** [22]
(cd-s+=) – Which side are you on? / Shifting sand.
(12") – ('A'side) / Pimp talking / Cracks you up.
(cd-s) – (above 3) / Your town (perfecto mix).

Jul 93. (c-ep)(cd-ep) **HANG YOUR HEAD EP** [21]
– Hang your head – freedom train (live) / Here on the wind / Indigo sky.
(cd-ep) – (1st track) / Ribbons & bows / Just like boys / Church.

Mar 94. (7")(c-s) **I WAS RIGHT AND YOU WERE WRONG. / MEXICAN RAIN** [32]
(cd-s+=) – Goin' back / Wages day.
(cd-s) – ('A'extended) / Kings of the western world / Suffering / Raintown (piano version).

Apr 94. (cd)(c)(d-lp) **OUR TOWN – THE GREATEST HITS** (compilation) [1]
– Dignity / Wages day / Real gone kid / Your swaying arms / Fergus sings the blues / I was right and you were wrong / Chocolate girl / I'll never fall in love again / When will you (make my telephone ring) / Twist and shout / Your town / Queen of the New Year / Only tender love / Cover from the sky / Love and regrets / Will we be lovers / Loaded / Bound to love / Still in the mood. (d-lp+=) – Beautiful stranger.

May 94. (7")(c-s) **DIGNITY. / BEAUTIFUL STRANGER** [20]
(cd-s+=) – Waves of sorrow / Bethlehem's gate.
(cd-s) – ('A'side) / Fergus sings the blues (live) / Loaded (live) / Chocolate girl (live).

— Disbanded after above release, as it looks certain ROSS will go solo. VIPOND has already secured a spot on a Scottish TV news programme.

DEAD KENNEDYS

Formed: San Francisco, California, USA . . . 1978 by BIAFRA. Formed own label 'Alternative Tenticles', which was initially licensed to 'Fast' then 'Cherry Red' in the UK 1979-81. • **Trivia:** Always the height of controversy, their FRANCHENCHRIST album with free "penis landscape" poster by Swiss artist HR Giger, led to BIAFRA being tried in court for distributing harmful material to minors. The case was dropped, and since then BIAFRA has protested on spoken word albums against his treatment. He was later to stand for mayor of San Francisco, coming 4th!. • **Style:** Raw hard-core politically aware punks, who scathed their attack on US imperialism and power hunger. They were pro-animal rights campaigners, and also anti-nuclear, anti-abortion, etc. • **Songwriters:** All/most written by BIAFRA, except RAWHIDE (Link Wray – hit) / TAKE THIS JOB AND SHOVE IT (Coe) / CESSPOOLS IN EDEN (?). **More trivia:** A 'DEAD KENNEDYS' tribute album by Various Artists was released May'92 on their own label.

Recommended: GIVE ME CONVENIENCE OR GIVE ME DEATH (*7)

JELLO BIAFRA (b.ERIC BOUCHER, Bolder, Colorado) – vocals / **EAST BAY RAY** (VALIUM) – guitar, (synthesisers-later 80's) / **KLAUS FLUORIDE** – bass, vocals / **TED** – drums

Fast Alt.Tent.

Oct 79. (7") **CALIFORNIA UBER ALLES. / MAN WITH THE DOGS**

Cherry Red Alt.Tent.

Jun 80. (7")(12") **HOLIDAY IN CAMBODIA. / POLICE TRUCK**
(also on I.R.S. in US) *(re-iss.Sep81) (re-iss.7"/cd-s Jun88 & Mar95)*

Sep 80. (lp)(c) **FRESH FRUIT FOR ROTTING VEGETABLES** [33]
– Kill the poor / Forward to death / When ya get drafted / Let's lynch the landlord / Drug me / Your emotions / Chemical warfare / Calilfornia uber alles / I kill children / Stealing people's mail / Funland at the beach / Ill in my head / Holiday in Cambodia / Viva Las Vegas. *(re-iss.'82) (cd-iss.Mar95)*

Oct 80. (7")(12") **KILL THE POOR. / IN SIGHT** [49]
(re-iss.7"/cd-s Mar95)

May 81. (7")(12") **TOO DRUNK TO F***. / THE PREY** [36]
(re-iss.7"/cd-s.May88 & Mar95)

— **BRUCE SLEZINGER** – drums repl. TED

Alt.Tent. Alt.Tent.

Dec 81. (10"ep) **IN GOD WE TRUST INC.**
– Religious vomit / Moral majority / Kepone factory / Dog bite / Nazi punks f*** off / We've got a bigger problem now / Rawhide.

1981. (7") **NAZI PUNKS F*** OFF. / MORAL MAJORITY**

— **J.H. PELIGRO** – drums, vocals repl. BRUCE

Jul 82. (7")(12") **BLEED FOR ME. / LIFE SENTENCE**

Nov 82. (lp)(c) **PLASTIC SURGERY DISASTERS**
– Government flu / Terminal preppie / Trust your mechanic / Well paid scientist / Buzzbomb / Forest fire / Halloween / Winnebago warrior / Riot / Bleed for me / I am the owl / Dead end / Moon over Marin. *(re-iss.Oct85 on 'Static')* (cd-iss.Nov86 +=) – IN GOD WE TRUST (ep)

Nov 82. (7")(12") **HALLOWEEN. / SATURDAY NIGHT HOLOCAUST**

— meanwhile other projects included

KLAUS FLUORIDE

May 82. (12") **SHORTNING BREAD. / DROWNING COWBOY**

Aug 84. (12"ep) **CHA CHA CHA WITH MR. FLUORIDE**
– Ghost riders / etc.

EAST BAY RAY

Jun 84. (7") **TROUBLE IN TOWN. / POISON HEART**

DEAD KENNEDYS

(regrouped, see last line-up)

Dec 85. (lp)(cd) **FRANKENCHRIST**
– Soup is good food / Hellnation / This could be anywhere (this could be everywhere) / A growing boy needs his lunch / Chicken farm / Macho-rama (invasion of the beef-patrol) / Goons of Hazzard / At my job / M.T.V. – Get off the air / Stars

and stripes of corruption.

Dec 86. (lp)(c) **BEDTIME FOR DEMOCRACY**
– Take this job and shove it / Hop with the jet set / Dear Abby / Rambozo the clown / Fleshdunce / The great wall / Shrink / Triumph of the swill / I spy / Macho insecurity / Cesspools in Eden / One-way ticket to Pluto / Do the slag / Gone with the wind / A commercial / Anarchy for sale / Chickenshit conformist / Where do ya draw the line / Potshot heard round the world / D.M.S.O. / Lie detector.

Split Dec86 when RAY departed. KLAUS FLUORIDE went solo (lp) BECAUSE I SAY SO.

– compilations, etc. –

Jun 87. Alternative Tentacles; (lp)(cd) **GIVE ME CONVENIENCE OR GIVE ME DEATH** [84]
– Police truck / Too drunk to f*** / California uber alles / Man with the dogs / In sight / Life sentence / A child and his lawnmower / Holiday in Cambodia / Night of the living rednecks / I fought the law / Saturday night holocaust / Pull my strings / Short songs / Straight A's / Kinky sex makes the world go round / The prey / Buzzbomb from Pasadena (free flexi with above)

Feb 92. Alternative Tentacles; (cd-ep's re-iss) **IN GOD WE TRUST / HALLOWEEN / BLEED FOR ME**

Jun 92. Alternative Tentacles; (cd) **PLASTIC SURGERY DISASTERS / IN GOD WE TRUST** [-]

Jun 93. Subterranean; (7"ep) **NAZI PUNKS **** OFF / ARYANISMS. / ('A'live) / CONTEMPTUOUS** [-]

JELLO BIAFRA

(solo)(first 2 albums were spoken word)

Alt.Tent. Alt.Tent.

Nov 87. (d-lp) **NO MORE COCOONS**
(re-iss.cd Mar93)

1988. (lp) **HIGH PRIEST OF HARMFUL MATTER (TALES OF THE TRIALS, LIVE)** *(re-iss.cd Mar93)*

LARD

BIAFRA, AL JOURGENSEN + PAUL BARKER (Ministry) / **JEFF WARD** – drums

Alt.Tent. Alt.Tent.

1989. (12"ep)(c-ep)(cd-ep) **THE POWER OF LARD / HELL FUDGE. / TIME TO MELT (31 mins.)**

Jul 90. (cd)(lp) **THE LAST TEMPTATION OF LARD** [69]
– Forkboy / Pineapple face / Hate, spawn and dic / Drug raid at 4a.m. / Can God fill teeth? / Bozo skeleton / Sylvestre Matuschka / They're coming to take me away / I am your clock.

JELLO BIAFRA & D.O.A.

— w/ **JOE KEITHLEY + CHRIS PROHOM** – guitar, vocals / **BRIAN GORLE** – bass, vocals / **JON CARD** – drums

Alt.Tent. Alt.Tent.

May 90. (cd)(lp) **THE LAST SCREAM OF THE MISSING NEIGHBOURS**
– That's progress / Attack of the peacekeepers / Wish I was in El Salvador / Power is boring / We gotta get out of this place / Full metal jackoff.

JELLO BIAFRA & NO MEANS NO

with **TIPPER GORE BOB WRIGHT** – guitar / **JOHN WRIGHT** – drums / **JON CARD** – percussion

Alt.Tent. Alt.Tent.

Mar 91. (cd)(c)(lp) **THE SKY IS FALLING AND I WANT MY MOMMY**
– The sky is falling and I want my mommy (falling space junk) / Jesus was a terrorist / Bruce's diary / Sad / Ride the flume / Chew / Sparks in the Gene pool / The myth is real – let's eat.

JELLO BIAFRA

Alt.Tent. Alt.Tent.

Jun 91. (cd)(c)(d-lp) **BLOW MINDS FOR A LIVING**
– Pledge of allegience / Talk on censorship – let us prey / Die for oil, sucker – higher octane version / I was a teenage pacifist / If voting changed anything . . . / Running for mayor / Grow more pot / Lost orgasm / Talk on censorship-Better living through new world orders + Fear of a free planet.

TUMOR CIRCUS

— **DARREN MOR-X / DALE FLAT-UM + MIKE MDRASKOID** (of STEEL POLE BATH TUB) / **KING GRONG CHARLIE (TOLNAY)** (of LUBRICATED GOAT) + **J.BIAFRA**

Alt.Tent. Alt.Tent.

Nov 91. (cd)(c)(lp) **TUMOR CIRCUS – HIGH VOLTAGE CONSPIRACY FOR RADICAL FREEDOM**
– Hazing for success / Human cyst / The man with the corkscrew eyes / Fireball / Calcutta a-go-go / Turn off the respirator. (cd+=) Swine flu / Take me back or I'll drown our dog / Meathook up my rectum.

Feb 92. (7") **MEATHOOK UP MY RECTUM. / (etched side)**
(12"+=)(cd-s+=) – Take me back or I'll drown the dog / Swine flu / Fireball.

JELLO BIAFRA & MOJO NIXON

Alt.Tent. Alt.Tent.

Nov 93. (7") **WILL THE FETUS BE ABORTED?. / THE LOST WORLD**
(cd-s+=) – Drinkin' with Jesus / Achey raky heart.

Feb 94. (cd)(lp) **PRAIRIE HOME INVASION**
– Buy my snake oil / Where are we gonna work (when the trees are gone) / Convoy in the sky / Atomic power / Are you drinkin' with me Jesus / Love me, I'm a liberal / Burgers of wrath / Nostalgia for an angel that never existed / Hammer chicken plant disaster / Mascot mania / Let's go burn de Nashville down / Will the fetus be aborted / Plastic Jesus.

DEAD OR ALIVE

Formed: Liverpool, England . . . May 1980 by PETE BURNS after a year as NIGHTMARES IN WAX. He had been a member of trio The MYSTERY GIRLS that once included PETE WYLIE and JULIAN COPE. After releases on local and own indie labels, they finally got worldwide contract with 'Epic' early in 1983. • **Style:** Their fusion of dance-orientated white glam-funk, and PETE's over-the-top gender-bender image, made them in the mid 80's, one of top disco-rock pop acts. BURNS & CO. at this period were produced by STOCK-AITKEN-WATERMAN famous for KYLIE and JASON, etc. They were also large hits in Japan, where they toured constantly, retaining cult following in homeland London. • **Songwriters:** BURNS compositions, except THAT'S THE WAY I LIKE IT (K.C. & the Sunshine Band). • **Trivia:** PETE BURNS' parents were German.

Recommended: SOPHISTICATED BOOM BOOM (*6)

NIGHTMARES IN WAX

PETE BURNS (b. 5 Aug'59) – vocals (ex-MYSTERY GIRLS) / **MARTIN HEALY** – keyboards / **MICK REID** – guitar / **PHIL HURST** – drums / **PETE** – bass repl. AMBROSE (ex-BIG IN JAPAN) who repl. WALTER OGDEN

Inevitable not issued

Feb 80. (7") **BLACK LEATHER. / GIRL SONG**
(re-iss.Jan84 & Jun85)

— In May80, **PETE BURNS, HEALY+REID** formed

DEAD OR ALIVE

with **SUE JAMES** – bass / **JOE MUSKER** – drums

Inevitable not issued

May 80. (7") **I'M FALLING. / FLOWERS** [-]

Feb 81. (7") **NUMBER ELEVEN. / NAME GAME (live)** [-]

— **WAYNE HUSSEY** – guitar (ex-HAMBI AND THE DANCE, etc) repl. MICK / **MIKE PERCY** (b.11 Mar'61) – bass repl. SUE

Black Eyes not issued

Feb 82. (12"ep) **IT'S BEEN HOURS NOW. / WHIRLPOOL / NOWHERE TO NOWHERE / IT'S BEEN HOURS NOW (version)** [-]

Jul 82. (7")(12") **THE STRANGER. / SOME OF THAT** [-]

Epic Epic

May 83. (7")(7"pic-d) **MISTY CIRCLES. / ('A'instrumental)** [-]
(12") – ('A'dance) ('A'dub) / Selfish side.

Aug 83. (7")(12") **WHAT I WANT. / THE STRANGER**
(re-iss.& remixed. Jun84 different cat.no.)

— now a 4-piece **BURNS, HEALY, PERCY** and **MUSKER.** WAYNE HUSSEY left to join SISTERS OF MERCY and later The MISSION. (He appeared on lp below).

Jan 84. (7") **I'D DO ANYTHING. / ANYTHING (dub)**
(10"+=) – Give it to me.
(12"+=) – What I want / Misty circles.

— **TIM LEVER** – keyboards, saxophone (ex-MODERN EON) repl. HEALY / **STEVE COY** (b.15 Mar'62) – drums, repl. MUSKER

Mar 84. (7")(12")(7"pic-d) **THAT'S THE WAY (I LIKE IT). / KEEP THE BODY STRONG (THAT'S THE WAY)** [22]

Apr 84. (lp)(c) **SOPHISTICATED BOOM BOOM** [29]
– I'd do anything / That's the way (I like it) / Absolutely nothing / What I want / Far too hard / You make me wanna / Sit on it / Wish you were here / Misty circles / Do it. (c.+=) – Anything (dub) / Keep that body strong (that's the way) / Misty circles (instrumental). *(re-iss.Nov86)*

Oct 84. (7") **YOU SPIN ME ROUND (LIKE A RECORD). / MISTY CIRCLES** [1] [11] May 85
(12") – ('A'murder mix) / ('B'extended)
(d7"+=) – ('A' mighty mix part 1) / (part one continued).
(d12"+=) – Misty Circles (dance mix) / The stranger.
(extra 12") – ('A'performance mix) / Wish you were here / What I want / Do it / Misty circles (mighty mix part two).

Apr 85. (7")(12")(7"sha-pic-d) **LOVER COME BACK TO ME. / FAR TOO HARD** [11] [75] Sep 85
(12"+=) ('A'extra mix).

May 85. (lp)(c) **YOUTHQUAKE** [19] [31]
– You spin me round (like a record) / I wanna be a toy / D.J. hit that button / In too deep / Big daddy of the rhythm / Cake and eat it / Lover come back to me / My heart goes bang / It's been a long time. (c+=)(cd+=) – You spin (performance mix) / Lover (extended). *(re-iss.cd Oct94 on 'Rewind')*

Jun 85. (7") **IN TOO DEEP. / I'D DO ANYTHING** [14]
(12") – ('A'-off yer mong mix) / ('B'side) / ('A'instrumental).
(12") – ('A'-off yer mong mix) / ('B'side) / You make me wanna.

Sep 85. (7") **MY HEART GOES BANG (GET ME TO THE DOCTORS). / BIG DADDY OF THE RHYTHM (live)** [23]
(d7"+=) – Cake and eat it (live) / In too deep (live).
(12"+=) – ('A' extended).
(12") – ('A'-American mix) / ('B'side) / ('A'instrumental).

— now a trio of **BURNS, PERCY** and **COY** plus live band. **CHRIS PAYNE** – keyboards, / **RUSSELL BELL** – guitar, (both ex-GARY NUMAN)

Sep 86. (7")(7"pic-d) **BRAND NEW LOVER. / IN TOO DEEP (live)** [31] [15] Nov 86
(12") – ('A'club mix) / ('B'side) / – ('A'instrumental).
(12") – ('A'mix) / ('B'side) / – Cake and eat it (live).

Dec 86. (7") **SOMETHING IN MY HOUSE. / DJ HIT THAT BUTTON** 12 85 Apr 87
(d7"+=) – In too deep (live) / Brand new lover.
(12"+=) – ('A' Flamenco version).
(12") – ('A'-U.S.mix pt.2) / ('B'side) / ('A'house mix).
Feb 87. (lp)(c)(cd) **MAD BAD AND DANGEROUSE TO KNOW** 27 52
– Brand new lover / I'll save you all my kisses / Son of a gun / Then there was you / Come inside / Something in my house / Hooked on love / I want you / Special star. *(re-iss.Nov89)*
Mar 87. (7") **HOOKED ON LOVE. / YOU SPIN ME ROUND (LIKE A RECORD) (live)** 69
(d7"+=) – Something in my house / D.J. hit that button.
(12"+=) – Something in my house (US mix pt.2).
Sep 87. (7") **I'LL SAVE YOU ALL MY KISSES. / LOVER COME BACK TO ME**
(12") – ('A'mix) / ('B'side) / I wanna be a toy.
(12") – ('A'long wet slippy mix) / ('B'side) / Whirlpool / Nowhere to nowhere.
Jul 88. (cd)(c)(lp) **RIP IT UP** (remixes) -
Aug 88. (7") **TURN AROUND AND COUNT 2 TEN. / SOMETHING IN MY HOUSE (instrumental)** 70
(cd-s+=) – ('A' Pearl & Dean mix) / ('B'instrumental).
(12") – (above 2 tracks only, nothing else).
(12"+=) – Then there was you / Come inside.
Jul 89. (7") **COME HOME WITH ME BABY. / I'LL SAVE YOU ALL MY KISSES** 62 69
(12"+=) – I want you (mix).
(12")(cd-s) – ('A'side) / ('A' dub) / ('A'other version).
Aug 89. (lp)(c)(cd) **NUDE**
– Turn around and count 2 ten / Give it back that love is mine / Baby don't say goodbye / Stop kicking my heart around / Come home with me baby / I don't wanna be your boyfriend / Get out of my house / I cannot carry on / My forbidden lover.

not issued Epic-Japan

Sep 89. (12") **BABY DON'T SAY GOODBYE (power mix). / ('A'club mix)** -
(3"cd-s+=) – ('A'-lp version).
(3"cd-s) – ('A'extended) / ('A'house mix).
Dec 90. (3"cd-ep) **YOUR SWEETNESS IS YOUR WEAKNESS / BLUE CHRISTMAS / YOUR SWEETNESS IS YOUR WEAKNESS (instrumental)** -
Dec 90. (cd) **FAN THE FLAME (PART 1)** - -
– (as yet unknown and not released in any other country than Japan)
Apr 91. (3"cd-ep) **GONE 2 LONG / TURN AROUND AND COUNT 2 TEN (live) / BLUE CHRISTMAS (live) / YOUR SWEETNESS IS YOUR WEAKNESS (live) / BEATS 2 LONG** -
Aug 91. (3"cd-ep) **UNHAPPY BIRTHDAY (edit) / TOTAL STRANGER (remix) / UNHAPPY BIRTHDAY (Ninja mix)** -

DEATH CULT (see under ⇒ CULT)

Chris DeBURGH

Born: CHRISTOPHER JOHN DAVIDSON, 15 Oct'50, Argentina. Son of British parents (father in diplomatic corps), who lived in most parts of the globe, and finally settled in Dublin, Ireland. In 1973-74, in between support slots to HORSLIPS and SUPERTRAMP, he signed to A&M. His first hit was a No.1 in Brazil with double A-side FLYING / TURNING AROUND. Had to wait 'til the 80's for minor UK/US success, culminating in 1986 when THE LADY IN RED gave him first but only No.1 in Britain. • **Style:** Easy listening soft romantic pop-rock. • **Songwriters:** All self penned. • **Trivia:** THE GETAWAY album was produced by RUPERT HINE.

Recommended: FROM A SPARK TO A FLAME – THE VERY BEST OF . . . (*5).

CHRIS DE BURGH – vocals, piano (with various session people)

A & M A & M

Jan 75. (lp)(c) **FAR BEYOND THESE CASTLE WALLS** •
– Hold on / The key / Windy night / Sin city / Turning around / New moon / Watching the world / Sat on green shutters / Lonesome cowboy / Goodnight. *(re-iss.Mar82, cd-iss.1988) (re-iss.'84 'Pickwick')*
Feb 75. (7") **HOLD ON. / SIN CITY**
Jul 75. (7") **FLYING. / WATCHING THE WORLD**
Nov 75. (lp)(c) **SPANISH TRAIN & OTHER STORIES**
– Spanish train / Lonely sky / This song for you / The painter / Patricia the stripper / A spaceman came travelling / I'm going home / Old friend / The tower / Just another poor boy. *(re-iss.Aug85, hit UK 78) (cd-iss.Feb89)*
Jan 76. (7") **LONELY SKY. / THIS SONG FOR YOU**
Apr 76. (7") **PATRICIA THE STRIPPER. / OLD FRIEND** -
Nov 76. (7") **A SPACEMAN CAME TRAVELLING. / JUST A POOR BOY** Nov 77
Aug 77. (7") **SUMMER RAIN. / RAINY NIGHTS IN PARIS**
Aug 77. (lp)(c) **AT THE END OF A PERFECT DAY**
– Broken wings / Round and around / I will / Summer rain / Discovery / Brazil / In a country churchyard / Rainy nights in Paris / If you love her, let her go . Perfect day. *(cd-iss.1988)*
Oct 77. (7") **BROKEN WINGS. / I WILL**
Jan 78. (7") **DISCOVERY. / ROUND AND AROUND**
Mar 78. (7") **PERFECT DAY. / SPANISH TRAIN**
Jan 79. (lp)(c) **CRUSADER**
– Carry on / I had the love in my eyes / Something else again / The girl with April in her eyes / Just in time / The Devils eyes / It's such a long way home / Old fashioned people / Quiet moments / Crusader: a) The fall of Jerusalem, b) In the court of Saladin, c) The battlefield, d) Finale / You and me. *(re-iss.Sep86, hit 72) (cd-iss.1988)*
Feb 79. (7") **CARRY ON. / THE GIRL WITH APRIL IN HER EYES** -
Feb 79. (7") **I HAD THE LOVE IN MY EYES. / JUST IN TIME**
Apr 79. (7") **THE DEVILS EYES. / IT'S SUCH A LONG WAY HOME**
Jul 80. (7") **SHADOWS AND LIGHTS. / WALLS OF SILENCE**
Jul 80. (lp)(c) **EASTERN WIND**
– The traveller / The record company bash / Tonight / Wall of silence / Flying home / Shadows and lights / Sailor / Some things never change / Tourist attraction / Eastern wind. *(cd-iss.1988)*
Oct 80. (7") **THE TRAVELLER. / EASTERN WIND** -
Nov 80. (7") **THE TRAVELLER. / WALL OF SILENCE** -
Aug 81. (7") **WAITING FOR THE HURRICANE. / BROKEN WINGS (live)**
Sep 82. (7") **DON'T PAY THE FERRYMAN. / ALL THE LOVE I HAVE INSIDE** 48 34 Apr 83
Oct 82. (lp)(c) **THE GETAWAY** 30 43 Apr 83
– Don't pay the ferryman / Living on the island / Crying and laughing / I'm counting on you / The getaway / Ship to shore / All the love I have inside / Borderline / Where peaceful waters flow / The revolution / Light a fire / Liberty. *(cd-iss.Apr84 & May95 +c)*
Nov 82. (7") **THE GETAWAY. / LIVING ON THE ISLAND** -
Feb 83. (7") **SHIP TO SHORE. / CRYING AND LAUGHING** -
Aug 83. (7") **SHIP TO SHORE. / THE GETAWAY** - 71
Apr 84. (7") **HIGH ON EMOTION. / MUCH MORE THAN THIS** 44 44 Jun 84
May 84. (lp)(c)(cd) **MAN ON THE LINE** 11 69
– The ecstasy of flight (I love the night) / Sight and touch / Taking it to the top / The head and the heart / The sound of a gun / High on emotion / Much more than this / Man on the line / Moonlight and vodka / Transmission ends.*(re-iss.cd+c Mar93)*
Jul 84. (7") **THE ECSTASY OF FLIGHT (I LOVE THE NIGHT). / MOONLIGHT AND VODKA** -
(12"+=) – Don't pay the ferryman / A spaceman came travelling.
Feb 85. (7") **SIGHT AND TOUCH / TAKING IT TO THE TOP** -
Mar 86. (7") **FIRE ON THE WATER. / THE VISION**
(12"+=) – The leader / What about me.
May 86. (lp)(c)(cd) **INTO THE LIGHT** 1 25 Sep 86
– Last night / Fire on the water / The ballroom of romance / The lady in red / Say goodbye to it all / The sirit of man / Fatal hesitation / One word (straight to the heart) / For Rosanna / The leader / The vision / What about me. *(re-iss.cd/c May95)*
Jun 86. (7") **THE LADY IN RED. / SAY GOODBYE TO IT ALL** 1 3 Feb 87.
(12"+=) – Don't pay the ferryman.
Sep 86. (7")(12") **FATAL HESITATION. / ECSTACY OF FLIGHT (I LOVE THE NIGHT)** 44 -
Nov 86. (7") **FATAL HESITATION. / THE BALLROOM ROMANCE** -
Dec 87. (7") **THE SIMPLE TRUTH (A CHILD IS BORN). / LOVE IS MY DECISION** -
Dec 87. (7") **THE SIMPLE TRUTH (A CHILD IS BORN). / THE SPIRIT OF MAN** 55 -
(12"+=) – Head and the heart (live).
Oct 88. (7")(12") **MISSING YOU. / THE RISEN LORD** 3
(cd-s+=) – The last time I cried. (US b-side)
Nov 88. (lp)(c)(cd) **FLYING COLOURS** 1
– Sailing away / Carry me (like a fire in your heart) / Tender hands / A night on the river / Leather on my shoes / Suddenly love / Missing you / I'm not scared anymore / Don't look back / Just a word away / The risen lord / The last time I cried. (cd+=) – The simple truth (A child is born). *(re-iss.cd/c May95)*
Dec 88. (7") **TENDER HANDS. / A NIGHT ON THE RIVER** 43
(12"+=)(cd-s+=) – The simple truth (a child is born).
Feb 89. (7") **SAILING AWAY. / THE HEAD AND THE HEART**
(12"+=)(cd-s+=) – ('A'extended).
Sep 89. (7") **THIS WAITING HEART. / CARRY ME (LIKE A FIRE IN YOUR HEART)** 59
(12"+=)(cd-s+=) – The spirit of man.
Oct 89. (lp)(c)(cd) **FROM A SPARK TO A FLAME – THE VERY BEST OF CHRIS DE BURGH** (compilation) 4
– This waiting heart / Don't pay the ferryman / Much more than this / Sailing away / The lady in red / Borderline / Say goodbye to it all / One word (straight to the heart) / A spaceman came travelling / Ship to shore / Missing you / Diamond in the dark / Tender hands / The getaway / Where peaceful waters flow / High on emotion. *(cd+=)* – Spanish train / Fatal hesitation. *(re-entered UK chart Apr92, peaked 43)*
Nov 89. (7") **DIAMOND IN THE DARK. / LAST NIGHT**
(12"+=)(cd-s+=) – Transmission ends.
Sep 90. (cd)(c)(d-lp) **HIGH ON EMOTION – LIVE FROM DUBLIN (live)** 15
– Last night / Sailing away / The revolution / I'm not scared anymore / Spanish train / Borderline / The risen Lord / The last time I cried / The lady in red / Lonely sky / A spaceman came travelling / Patricia the stripper / The ballroom of romance / Say goodbye to it all / Don't pay the ferryman / High on emotion. *(re-iss.cd/c May95)*
Apr 92. (7")(c-s) **SEPARATE TABLES. / MAKING THE PERFECT MAN (extended)** 30
(cd-s+=) – The Connemara coast (instrumental).
May 92. (cd)(c)(lp) **POWER OF TEN** 3
– Where we will be good / By my side / Heart of darkness / In your eyes / Separate tables / Talk to me / Brother John / The Connemara coast / Shine on / A celebration / She means everything to me / Making the perfect man. *(re-iss.cd/c May95)*
Jul 92. (7")(c-s)(cd-s) **MAKING THE PERFECT MAN. / SAY GOODBYE TO IT ALL (live) / BORDERLINE (live)**
Sep 92. (7")(c-s) **SHINE ON. / HEART OF DARKNESS**
(12"+=)(cd-s+=) – I'm not scared anymore (live).

—— now w / **VIC MARTIN** – keyboards / **NEIL TAYLOR** – guitar / **PHIL SPALDING** – bass, rhythm guitar, vocals / **JIMMY COPLEY** – drums

May 94. (7")(c-s) **BLONDE HAIR, BLUE JEANS. / YOU ARE THE REASON** 51
(cd-s+=) – Strangers on a train.
May 94. (cd)(c) **THIS WAY UP** 5
– This silent world / This is love / This weight on me / Here is your Paradise / Oh my brave hearts / Blonde hair, blue jeans / The son and the father / The snows of New York / Love's got a hold on me / You are the reason / Up here in Heaven.
Jul 94. (7")(c-s) **THIS SILENT WORLD. / ON MY BRAVE HEARTS**
(cd-s+=) – When I see you tonight.

Oct 94. (7")(c-s) **HERE IS YOUR PARADISE. / THE SNOWS OF NEW YORK** [ ] [ ]
(cd-s+=) – Shine on.

Nov 95. (cd)(c) **BEAUTIFUL DREAMS** [33] [ ]
– Missing you / Carry me / Discovery / The snows of New York / In love forever / Shine on / Lady in red / In dreams / I'm not crying over you / Always on my mind / Say goodbye to it all / One more mile to go.

Dec 95. (c-s)(cd-s) **THE SNOWS OF NEW YORK / GIRL / MISSING YOU** [60] [-]

– compilations, others, etc –

Aug 81. A&M; (lp)(c) **BEST MOVES** [65] [ ]
(cd-iss.1988 & May95)

Nov 81. A&M; (7") **A SPACEMAN CAME TRAVELLING. / PATRICIA THE STRIPPER** [ ] [ ]

Dec 84. A&M; (7") **A SPACEMAN CAME TRAVELLING. / BORDERLINE** [ ] [ ]

Nov 86. A&M; (7") **A SPACEMAN CAME TRAVELLING. / BALLROOM OF ROMANCE** [40] [ ]
(12"+=) – Getaway.
(d7"++=) – Borderline.

Aug 88. A&M; (cd-ep) **COMPACT HITS** [ ] [ ]
– The ecstacy of flight (I love the night) / The lady in red / Don't pay the ferryman / High on emotion.

May 90. A&M; (d-lp) **INTO THE LIGHT / FLYING COLOURS** [ ] [-]

May 91. A&M; (7")(c-s) **THE SIMPLE TRUTH. / THE SPIRIT OF MAN** [36] [ ]
(12"+=)(cd-s+=) – The head and the heart (live).

Oct 93. A&M; (cd) **FLYING COLOURS / INTO THE LIGHT** [ ] [-]

Dec 84. Telstar; (lp)(c)(cd) **THE VERY BEST OF CHRIS DE BURGH** [6] [ ]

DEEP FOREST

Formed: France by keyboard kings MOUQUET and SANCHEZ, who moved to USA in 1993. Were a hit in Australia, before single 'SWEET LULLABY' took Europe by storm early '94. • **Style:** Ambient club sound, using haunting voices of the Central African Pygmies, plus Baka chants of Cameroun, Borundi and Senegal. A little similar in conceptual idea to ENIGMA with INCANTATION panpipes. • **Songwriters:** MOUQUET / SANCHEZ. • **Trivia:** They also do their bit to save the Rain Forests of the Pygmies.

Recommended: DEEP FOREST (*8)

ERIC MOUQUET – keyboards, claviers, programming / **MICHEL SANCHEZ** – keyboards, claviers, programming; additional vocals **MICHEL VILLAIN**

Columbia Epic

Dec 92. (7")(c-s) **SWEET LULLABY. / ('A'mix)** [ ] [ ] Jun93
(12"+=) – (2 more remixes).
(cd-s++=) – (2 more remixes; now 6 in total). *(re-iss.Jan94, hit UK No.10 & US No.78)*

Feb 94. (cd)(c)(lp) **DEEP FOREST** [15] [59] Aug93
– Deep forest / Sweet lullaby / Hunting / Night bird / The first twilight / Savana dance / Desert walk / White whisper / The second twilight / Sweet lullaby (ambient mix) / Forest hymn.

May 94. (c-s) **DEEP FOREST. / ('A'mix)** [20] [ ]
(12"+=)(cd-s+=) – (4 more remixes).

Jul 94. (c-s) **SAVANNA DANCE. / ('A'mix)** [28] [ ]
(cd-s+=) – (4 more remixes).

May 95. (cd)(c)(lp) **BOHEME** [12] [76]
– Anathasia / Bohemian ballet / Marta's song / Gathering / Lament / Bulgarian melody / Deep folk song / Freedom cry / Twosome / Cafe Europa / Katharina / Boheme.

Jun 95. (c-s) **MARTA'S SONG / SWEET LULLABY** [26] [ ]
(cd-s+=) – ('A'-Into the deep mix) / ('A'-Arnand's Muslim mix).
(12") – (6 'A'mixes).

DEEP PURPLE

Formed: London, England ... 1968 intially as ROUNDABOUT, by then member CHRIS CURTIS. He recruited JON LORD and RITCHIE BLACKMORE, who was living in Germany at the time. By Spring '68, they had become DEEP PURPLE, soon signing to 'Parlophone UK', and 'Tetragrammation' (US label run by comedian Bill Cosby). HUSH gave them near immediate chart success in the States, but had to wait until summer 1970 with BLACK NIGHT for a home Top-3 hit. From then on, but for a few other hits, albums became their tour de force. • **Style:** DEEP PURPLE Mk.I were initially influenced by VANILLA FUDGE, but by the late 60's and Mk.II moved into a more powerful riff heavy rock. Mk.III saw their sound mellow into bluesy funk rock due to new vox of DAVID COVERDALE. Easily the best line-up (Mk.II) reformed in 1984 but they did nothing to resurrect past glories, although albums did net some cash. • **Songwriters:** Mk.I:-Mostly BLACKMORE / EVANS / LORD. Mk.II:- Group. Mk.III:- BLACKMORE / COVERDALE, adding at times LORD and PAICE. Mk.IV:- Permutation 2 of COVERDALE, BOLIN or HUGHES. Covered HUSH (Joe South) / WE CAN WORK IT OUT + HELP (Beatles) / KENTUCKY WOMAN (Neil Diamond) / RIVER DEEP MOUNTAIN HIGH (Ike & Tina Turner) / HEY JOE (Jimi Hendrix) / I'M SO GLAD (Cream). GILLAN covered; LUCILLE (Little Richard) / LIVING FOR THE CITY (Stevie Wonder) / SOUTH AFRICA (Bernie Marsden). RAINBOW; STILL I'M SAD (Yardbirds). • **Trivia:** In the Guinness Book of Records, according to decibel reading meter, they were recorded as "The Loudest Rock Group In the World". To obtain charity monies for the Armenian earthquake disaster late 1989, BLACKMORE, GILLAN and others (i.e. BRUCE DICKINSON, ROBERT PLANT, BRIAN MAY etc.) contributed to Top 40 new version of SMOKE ON THE WATER.

Recommended: MACHINE HEAD (*7) / MADE IN JAPAN (*8) / DEEPEST PURPLE (*9) / COME HELL OR HIGH WATER (*7). RAINBOW:- THE BEST OF RAINBOW (*6) GILLAN:- THE VERY BEST OF GILLAN (*6)

RITCHIE BLACKMORE (b.14 Apr'45, Weston-Super-Mare, Avon, England) – guitar (ex-MANDRAKE ROOT, ex-OUTLAWS, ex-SCREAMING LORD SUTCH, etc.) / **JON LORD** (b.9 Jun'41, Leicester, England) – keyboards (ex-FLOWERPOT MEN) / **NICK SIMPER** (b. 1946, Southall, London) – bass (ex-JOHNNY KIDD & PIRATES) / **ROD EVANS** (b. 1945, Edinburgh, Scotland) – vocals (ex-MAZE, ex-MI5) / **IAN PAICE** (b.29 Jun'48, Nottingham, England) – drums (ex-MAZE, ex-MI5)

Parlophone Tetragramme

Jun 68. (7") **HUSH. / ONE MORE RAINY DAY** [ ] [4]

Sep 68. (lp) **SHADES OF DEEP PURPLE** [ ] [24]
– And the address / Hush / One more rainy day / (prelude) Happiness – I'm so glad / Mandrake root / Help / Love help me / Hey Joe. *(re-iss.Feb77 on 'EMI Harvest') (cd-iss.Mar89) (cd-iss.Feb95 on 'Fame')*

Nov 68. (7") **KENTUCKY WOMAN. / WRING THAT NECK** [ ] [38]

Jan 69. (7") **RIVER DEEP – MOUNTAIN HIGH. /** [-] [53]

Feb 69. (7") **EMMARETTA. / WRING THAT NECK** [ ] [ ]

Harvest Tetragramme

Jun 69. (lp) **BOOK OF TALIESYN** [ ] [54]
– Listen, learn, read on / Wring that neck / Kentucky woman / Shield / Anthem / Exposition / We can work it out / River deep – mountain high. *(re-iss.Jun85 on 'EMI') (re-iss.+cd Aug89)*

Nov 69. (lp)(c) **DEEP PURPLE** [ ] [ ]
– Chasing shadows / Blind / Lalena: (a) Faultline, (b) The painter / Why didn't Rosemary? / The bird has flown / April. *(re-iss.Jun85 on 'EMI') (re-iss.lp/c/cd.Mar89) (re-iss.cd May95 on 'Fame')*

(In Jun69 below two were used on session for 'HALLELUJAH'. They became regular members after the recording of 'DEEP PURPLE' album.) / **IAN GILLAN** (b.19 Aug'45, Hounslow, London) – vocals (ex-EPISODE SIX) replaced EVANS who joined CAPTAIN BEYOND. / **ROGER GLOVER** (b.30 Nov'45, Brecon, Wales) – bass (ex-EPISODE SIX) replaced SIMPER who later formed WARHORSE.

Harvest Warners

Jul 69. (7") **HALLELUJAH (I AM THE PREACHER). / APRIL (part 1)** [ ] [ ]

Jan 70. (lp) **CONCERTO FOR GROUP AND ORCHESTRA WITH THE ROYAL PHILHARMONIC ORCHESTRA (live)** [26] [ ]
– First Movement: Moderato – Allegro / Second Movement: Andante (part 1) – Andante conclusion / Third Movement: Vivace – Presto. *(cd-iss.Aug 90 +=)* – Wring that neck / Child in time.

Jun 70. (7") **BLACK NIGHT. / SPEED KING** [2] [-]

Jun 70. (lp)(c) **IN ROCK** [4] [ ]
– Speed king / Blood sucker / Child in time / Flight of the rat / Into the fire / Speed king / Living wreck / Hard lovin' man. *(re-iss.May82 on 'Fame', cd-iss.Apr88) (pic-lp Jun85) (re-iss.cd Jun95)*

Jul 70. (7") **BLACK NIGHT. / INTO THE FIRE** [-] [66]

Feb 71. (7") **STRANGE KIND OF WOMAN. / I'M ALONE** [6] [ ]

Sep 71. (lp)(c) **FIREBALL** [1] [32]
– Fireball / No no no / Demon's eye / Anyone's daughter / The mule / Fools / No one came. *(re-iss.Mar84 on 'Fame') (re-iss.+cd Jan88 on 'EMI') (pic-lp Jun85 on 'EMI')*

Oct 71. (7") **FIREBALL. / DEMON'S EYE** [15] [-]

Nov 71. (7") **FIREBALL. / I'M ALONE** [-] [ ]

Purple Warners

Mar 72. (7") **NEVER BEFORE. / WHEN A BLIND MAN CRIES** [35] [ ]

Apr 72. (lp)(c) **MACHINE HEAD** [1] [7]
– Highway star / Maybe I'm a Leo / Pictures of home / Never before / Smoke on the water / Lazy / Space truckin'. *(re-iss.Jun85 on 'EMI') (re-iss.Oct86, cd-iss Mar89 on 'Fame', cd-iss.Mar87 on 'EMI')*

Jun 72. (7") **LAZY. / WHEN A BLIND MAN CRIES** [-] [ ]

Oct 72. (7") **HIGHWAY STAR. / (part 2)** [-] [ ]

Dec 72. (d-lp)(d-c) **MADE IN JAPAN (live)** [16] [6] May 73
– Highway star / Child in time / Smoke on the water / The mule / Strange kind of woman / Lazy / Space truckin'. *(cd-iss.Sep88 on 'EMI')*

Feb 73. (lp)(c) **WHO DO YOU THINK WE ARE!** [4] [15]
– Woman from Tokyo / Mary Long / Super trouper / Smooth dancer / Rat bat blue / Place in line / Our lady. *(re-iss.Jun85, cd-iss.Oct87 on 'EMI')*

Apr 73. (7") **WOMAN FROM TOKYO. / SUPER TROUPER** [-] [60]
(re-iss.Sep73)

May 73. (7") **SMOKE ON THE WATER. / (part 2)** [-] [4]

— **BLACKMORE, LORD** and **PAICE** brought in new members / **DAVID COVERDALE** (b.22 Sep'49, Saltburn-by-the-sea, Cleveland, England) – vocals replaced GILLAN who later formed own band. / **GLENN HUGHES** (b.Penkridge, England) – bass (ex-TRAPEZE) repl. GLOVER who became top producer.

Feb 74. (lp)(c) **BURN** [3] [9]
– Burn / Might just take your life / Lay down stay down / Sail away / You fool no one / What's goin' on here / Mistreated / "A" 200. *(re-iss.Jun85) (cd-Jul89)*

Mar 74. (7") **MIGHT JUST TAKE YOUR LIFE. / CORONARIAS REDIG** [ ] [91]

May 74. (7") **BURN. / CORONARIAS REDIG** [-] [ ]

Nov 74. (lp)(c) **STORMBRINGER** [6] [20]
– Stormbringer / Love don't mean a thing / Holy man / Hold on / Lady double dealer / You can't do it right / High ball shooter / The gypsy / Soldier of fortune. *(re-iss.Jun85) (re-iss.+cd.Oct88 on 'EMI')*

Nov 74. (7") **HIGH BALL SHOOTER. / YOU CAN'T DO IT RIGHT** [-] [ ]

Jan 75. (7") **STORMBRINGER. / LOVE DON'T MEAN A THING** [-] [ ]

— **TOMMY BOLIN** (b.1951, Sioux City, Iowa, USA) – guitar (ex-JAMES GANG, ex-ZEPHYR) repl. BLACKMORE who formed RAINBOW. (see further below)

Oct 75. (lp)(c) **COME TASTE THE BAND** [19] [43]
– Coming home / Lady luck / Gettin' together / The dealer / I need love / Drifter /

Love child / This time around – Owed to the 'G' / You keep on moving. *(re-iss.Jun85 on 'EMI') (cd-iss.Jul95 on 'Fame')*

Mar 76. (7") **YOU KEEP ON MOVING. / LOVE CHILD** [ ] [-]
Mar 76. (7") **GETTIN' TIGHTER. / LOVE CHILD** [-] [ ]
Nov 76. (lp)(c) **MADE IN EUROPE (live)** [12] [ ]
– Burn / Mistreated (interpolating 'Rock me baby') / Lady double dealer / You fool no one / Stormbringer / Mistreated. (US album title DEEP PURPLE LIVE)

— They split Spring 76. TOMMY BOLIN went solo. He died (of an overdose) 4 Dec 76. HUGHES reformed TRAPEZE. COVERDALE formed WHITESNAKE, he was later joined by LORD and PAICE, after they had been in PAICE, ASHTON and LORD. Remarkably **DEEP PURPLE** reformed 8 years later with early 70's line-up. **GILLAN, BLACKMORE, LORD, PAICE** and **GLOVER.**

Polydor Mercury

Nov 84. (lp)(c)(cd)(pic-lp) **PERFECT STRANGERS** [5] [17]
– Knocking at your back door / Under the gun / Nobody's home / Mean streak / Perfect strangers / A gypsy's kiss / Wasted sunsets / Hungry days. *(cd+=)* – Not responsible.
Jan 85. (7")(7"pic-d) **PERFECT STRANGERS (edit). / A GYPSY'S KISS** [48] [ ] Mar 85
(12"+=) – Wasted sunsets / Hungry daze.
Jun 85. (7")(12") **KNOCKING AT YOUR BACK DOOR. / PERFECT STRANGERS** [68] [61] Jan 85
Jan 87. (lp)(c)(cd) **THE HOUSE OF BLUE LIGHT** [10] [34]
– Bad attitude / The unwritten law / Call of the wild / Mad dog / Black and white / Hard lovin' woman / The Spanish archer / Strangeways / Mitzi Dupree / Dead or alive.
Jan 87. (7")(12") **CALL OF THE WILD. / STRANGEWAYS** [ ] [ ]
(12")(12"pic-d) – ('A'side) / ('B' long version).
Jun 88. (7") **HUSH (live). / DEAD OR ALIVE** [62] [ ]
(12"+=)(cd-s+=) – Bad attitude.
Jun 88. (d-lp)(c)(cd) **NOBODY'S PERFECT (live)** [38] [ ]
– Highway star / Strange kind of woman / Perfect strangers / Hard lovin' woman / Bad attitude / Knocking on your back door / Child in time / Lazy / Space truckin' / Black night / Woman from Tokyo / Smoke on the water / Hush. *(re-iss.Mar91 all formats on 'EMI')*

— **JOE LYNN TURNER** – vocals (ex-RAINBOW, ex-YNGWIE J.MALMSTEEN'S RISING FORCE) repl. GILLAN who continued solo.

R.C.A. Giant-Reprise

Oct 90. (7") **KING OF DREAMS. / FIRE IN THE BASEMENT** [70] [ ]
(12"+=)(cd-s+=) – ('A'version).
Nov 90. (cd)(c)(lp) **SLAVES AND MASTERS** [45] [87]
– King of dreams / The cut runs deep / Fire in the basement / Truth hurts / Breakfast in bed / Love conquers all / Fortune teller / Too much is not enough / Wicked ways. *(re-iss.cd Apr94)*
Feb 91. (7")(c-s) **LOVE CONQUERS ALL. / TRUTH HURTS** [57] [ ]
(12"+=)(cd-s+=) – Slow down sister.

— early 70s line-up again after TURNER was sacked.

Jul 93. (cd)(c)(lp) **THE BATTLE RAGES ON** [21] [ ]
– The battle rages on / Lick it up / Anya / Talk about love / Time to kill / Ramshackle man / A twist in the tale / Nasty piece of work / Solitaire / One man's meat. *(re-iss.cd Oct95)*
Nov 94. (cd)(c)(d-lp) **COME HELL OR HIGH WATER (live mid-93)** [ ] [ ]
– Highway star / Black night / Twist in the tail / Perfect strangers / Anyone's daughter / Child in time / Anya / Speed king / Smoke on the water.

— **STEVE MORSE** – guitar (ex-DIXIE DREGGS) repl. JOE SATRIANI who repl. BLACKMORE on European tour late '93-mid '94

– compilations, exploitation releases, etc. –

Note; All releases on 'Purple' issued on 'Warners' US.

Sep 72. Warners; (lp) **PURPLE PASSAGES** [-] [57]
Oct 72. Warners; (7") **HUSH. / KENTUCKY WOMAN** [-] [ ]
Jun 75. Purple; (lp)(c) **24 CARAT PURPLE (1970-73)** [14] [ ]
– Woman from Tokyo / Fireball / Strange kind of woman / Never before / Black night / Speed king / Smoke on the water / Child in time. *(re-iss.Sep85, cd-iss.Oct87 on 'Fame')*
Mar 77. Purple; (7"m) **SMOKE ON THE WATER. / CHILD IN TIME / WOMAN FROM TOKYO** [21] [ ]
Sep 77. Purple; (7"ep) **NEW LIVE & RARE** [31] [ ]
– Black night (live) / Painted horse / When a blind man cries.
Jan 78. Purple; (lp)(c) **POWERHOUSE** (early 70's line-up) [ ] [ ]
(re-iss.Jun85)
Sep 78. Purple; (7"ep) **NEW LIVE & RARE VOL.2** [45] [ ]
– Burn (edit) / Coronarias redig / Mistreated (live).
Apr 79. Purple; (lp)(c) **THE MARK II PURPLE SINGLES** [24] [ ]
(singles 'A' & 'B's – 1970-1973)
(re-iss.+cd.Nov88 on 'Fame')
Jan 93. Harvest; (cd) **SINGLES A'S AND B'S** [ ] [-]

Note; All releases on 'Harvest' issued on 'Warners' in US.

Apr 79. Harvest; (7")(12") **BLACK NIGHT. / STRANGE KIND OF WOMAN** [ ] [ ]
Jul 80. Harvest; (lp)(c) **DEEPEST PURPLE** [1] [ ]
– Black night / Speed king / Fireball / Strange kind of woman / Child in time / Woman from Tokyo / Highway star / Space truckin' / Burn / Demon's eye / Stormbringer / Smoke on the water.
(cd-iss.Aug84, re-iss.all formats 1989 on 'EMI')
Jul 80. Harvest; (7") **BLACK NIGHT. / SPEED KING (live)** [43] [ ]
Oct 80. Harvest; (7"ep) **NEW LIVE & RARE VOL.3** [48] [ ]
– Smoke on the water (live) / The bird has flown / Grabsplatter.
Dec 80. Harvest; (lp)(c) **IN CONCERT 1970-1972 (live)** [30] [ ]
– Speed king / Child in time / Wring that neck / Mandrake root / Highway star / Strange kind of woman / Maybe I'm a Leo / Never before / Lazy / Space truckin' / Smoke on the water / Lucille.
Aug 82. Harvest; (lp)(c) **DEEP PURPLE LIVE IN LONDON (live '74)** [23] [ ]
– Burn / Might just take your life / Lay down, stay down / Mistreated / Smoke on the water / You fool no one / The mule.
Jun 85. Harvest; (d-lp)(d-c) **THE ANTHOLOGY** [50] [ ]
(cd-iss.1990+=) – *(3 extra tracks).*
May 92. Harvest; (d-cd) **IN CONCERT 1970-72 (live)** [ ] [-]
Nov 87. Telstar; (lp)(c)(cd) **THE BEST OF DEEP PURPLE** [ ] [-]
(cd+=) – (1 extra track).
1989. Connoisseur; (d-lp)(c)(d-cd) **SCANDINAVIAN NIGHTS (live)** [ ] [-]
Aug 91. Connoisseur; (d-cd)(d-c)(d-lp) **KNEBWORTH '85 (live)** [ ] [-]
Jul 93. Connoisseur; (cd) **THE DEEP PURPLE FAMILY ALBUM** [ ] [-]
(associated releases)
Mar 91. E.M.I.; (d-cd)(d-c)(t-lp) **ANTHOLOGY** [ ] [-]
Sep 91. E.M.I.; (cd)(c)(lp) **PURPLE RAINBOWS** [ ] [-]
– (all work including RAINBOW, GILLAN, WHITESNAKE, etc.)
Nov 93. E.M.I.; (3xcd-box) **LIVE IN JAPAN (live)** [ ] [-]
Apr 92. Polygram; (cd) **KNOCKING AT YOUR BACK DOOR** [ ] [-]
May 93. Spectrum; (cd)(c) **PROGRESSION** [ ] [-]
Jun 95. EMI; (12")(cd-s) **BLACK NIGHT (remix). / SPEED KING (remix)** [66] [-]
Sep 95. Spectrum; (cd) **CHILD IN TIME** [ ] [-]
Nov 95. EMI; (3xcd-box) **BOOK OF TALIESYN / SHADES OF DEEP URPLE / DEEP PURPLE IN CONCERT** [ ] [-]

JON LORD

solo (first 3 albums while still a **DEEP PURPLE** member) with the **LONDON SYMPHONY ORCHESTRA** and guests.

Purple Warners

Apr 72. (lp)(c) **GEMINI SUITE** [ ] [ ]
– Guitar / Piano / Drums / Vocals / Bass guitar / Organ. *(re-iss.Nov84 on 'Safari')*

— now with the MUNICH CHAMBER OPERA ORCHESTRA and guests.

Apr 74. (lp)(c) **WINDOWS** [ ] [ ]
– Continuo on B.A.C.H. / Windows: Renga – Gemini – Alla Marcia – Allegro.

TONY ASHTON & JON LORD

ASHTON – keyboards,vocals (ex-ASHTON GARDNER and DYKE, ex-FAMILY, ex-REMO FOUR, ex-CHRIS FARLOWE)

Apr 74. (lp)(c) **FIRST OF THE BIG BANDS** [ ] [ ]
– We're gonna make it / I've been lonely / Silly boy / The jam / Downside upside down / Shut up / Ballad of Mr.Giver / Celebration / The resurrection shuffle. *(cd-iss.Jun93 on Windsong)*
1974. (7") **WE'RE GONNA MAKE IT. / BAND OF THE SALVATION ARMY BAND** [ ] [-]

JON LORD

solo again, plus guests.

Sep 76. (7") **BOUREE. / ARIA** [ ] [ ]
Nov 76. (lp)(c) **SARABANDE (live)** [ ] [ ]
– Fantasia / Sarabande / Aria / Gigue / Bouree / Pavane / Caprice / Finale. *(cd-iss.1989 on 'Line')*

PAICE, ASHTON and LORD

formed Aug76 and recruited **BERNIE MARSDEN** – guitar (ex-BABE RUTH) / **PAUL MARTINEZ** – bass (ex-STRETCH)

Oyster Oyster

Feb 77. (lp)(c) **MALICE IN WONDERLAND** [ ] [ ]
– Ghost story / Remember the good times / Arabella / Silas and Jerome / Dance with me baby / On the road again / Sneaky rivate Lee / I'm gonna stop drinking / Malice in Wonderland. *(cd-iss.Jul95 on 'Repertoire')*

— When this bunch split up MARTINEZ joined JOHN OTWAY and more sessions. ASHTON became noted producer. MARSDEN was followed by LORD and then PAICE into WHITESNAKE.

JON LORD

and more solo work. (with **MARSDEN, PAICE, NEIL MUNRO, COZY POWELL** and **BAD COMPANY** most of group.

Harvest Harvest

May 82. (7") **BACH INTO THIS. / GOING HOME** [ ] [ ]
Jul 82. (lp) **BEFORE I FORGET** [ ] [ ]
– Chance on a feeling / Tender babes / Hollywood rock and roll / Bach onto this / Before I forget / Say it's alright / Burntwood / Where are you. *(cd-iss.Mar93 on 'R.P.M.')*

Safari not issued

Mar 84. (lp)(c) **COUNTRY DIARY OF AN EDWARDIAN LADY** [ ] [-]
Mar 84. (7") **COUNTRY DIARY OF AN EDWARDIAN LADY. / ?** [ ] [-]

RITCHIE BLACKMORE'S RAINBOW

RITCHIE BLACKMORE – guitar with (ex-ELF) men **RONNIE JAMES DIO** – vocals / **MICKEY LEE SOULE** – keyboards / **CRAIG GRUBER** – bass / **GARY DRISCOLL** – drums

Oyster Oyster

Aug 75. (lp)(c) **RITCHIE BLACKMORE'S RAINBOW** [11] [30]
– Man on the silver mountain / Self portrait / Black sheep of the family / Catch the rainbow / Snake charmer / The temple of the king / If you don't like rock'n'roll / Sixteenth century Greensleeves / Still I'm sad. *(re-iss.Feb78, Aug81 – hit UK 91- & Aug83 on 'Polydor') (cd-iss.1988 on 'Polydor')*
Oct 75. (7") **MAN ON THE SILVER MOUNTAIN. / SNAKE CHARMER** [ ] [ ]

— RITCHIE only retained **DIO**, recruiting new members **TONY CARBY** – keyboards / **JIMMY BAIN** – bass / **COZY POWELL** – drums.

Polydor Oyster

May 76. (lp)(c) **RAINBOW RISING (as "BLACKMORE'S RAIN-BOW")** [11] [48]

– Tarot woman / Run with the wolf / Starstruck / Do you close your eyes / Stargazer / A light in the black. *(re-iss.Aug83) (cd-iss.Nov86)*

RAINBOW

Jul 77. (d-lp)(c) **RAINBOW ON STAGE** (live) [7] [65]
– Kill the king: (a) Man on a silver mountain, (b) Blues, (c) Starstruck / Catch the rainbow / Mistreated / Sixteenth century Greensleeves / Still I'm sad. *(re-iss Jan84) (cd-iss.Nov86)*

Aug 77. (7") **KILL THE KING: MAN ON THE SILVER MOUNTAIN. / MISTREATED** [44] [ ]
(re-iss Jul81. reached 41)

—— **MARK CLARKE** – bass (ex-COLOSSEUM, ex-URIAH HEEP) repl. BAIN who joined WILD HORSES / **BOB DAISLEY** – bass (ex-WIDOWMAKER, ex-CHICKEN SHACK) repl. CLARKE / **DAVID STONE** – keyboards (ex-SYMPHONIC SLAM) repl. CAREY

Polydor Polydor

Mar 78. (7") **LONG LIVE ROCK'N'ROLL. / SENSITIVE TO LIGHT** [33] [ ]
(re-iss Jul81)

Apr 78. (lp)(c) **LONG LIVE ROCK'N'ROLL** [7] [89]
– Long live rock'n'roll / Lady of the lake / L.A. connection / Gates of Babylon / Kill the king / The shed / Sensitive to light / Rainbow eyes. *(re-iss.Aug83)*

Sep 78. (7"red) **L.A. CONNECTION. / LADY OF THE LAKE** [40] [ ]
(re-iss.7"black Jul81)

—— **BLACKMORE** retained only **COZY POWELL / GRAHAM BONNET** – vocals (ex-Solo artist, ex-MARBLES) repl. DIO who went solo / **ROGER GLOVER** – bass, vocals (ex-DEEP PURPLE) repl. DAISLEY / **DON AIREY** – keyboards repl. STONE

Aug 79. (lp)(c)(clear-lp) **DOWN TO EARTH** [6] [66]
– All night long / Eyes of the world / No time to lose / Makin' love / Since you've been gone / Love's no friend / Danger zone / Lost in Hollywood. *(re-iss.Apr84) (cd-iss.Dec86)*

Aug 79. (7") **SINCE YOU'VE BEEN GONE. / BAD GIRLS** [6] [57]
(re-iss Jul81)

Feb 80. (7") **ALL NIGHT LONG. / WEISS HEIM** [5] [ ]
(re-iss Jul81)

—— **JOE LYNN TURNER** – vocals, repl. BONNET who continued solo career. / **BOBBY RONDINELLI** – drums repl. POWELL who later joined E.L.P.

Jan 81. (7") **I SURRENDER. / MAYBE NEXT TIME** [3] [50]
(re-iss Jul81)

Feb 81. (lp)(c) **DIFFICULT TO CURE** [3] [50]
– I surrender / Spotlight kid / No release / Vielleicht das nachster zeit (Maybe next time) / Can't happen here / Freedom fighter / Midtown tunnel vision / Difficult to cure. *(re-iss.+cd.Aug84)*

Jun 81. (7") **CAN'T HAPPEN HERE. / JEALOUS LOVER** [20] [ ]

Nov 81. (m-lp) **JEALOUS LOVER** [-] [ ]
– Jealous lover / Can't happen here / I surrender / Weiss Helm.

—— **DAVE ROSENTHAL** – keyboards repl. AIREY who joined OZZY OSBOURNE.

Polydor Mercury

Mar 82. (7"blue)(12"blue) **STONE COLD. / ROCK FEVER** [34] [40]

Apr 82. (lp)(c) **STRAIGHT BETWEEN THE EYES** [5] [30]
– Death alley driver / Stone cold / Bring on the night / Tite squeeze / Tearin' out my heart / Power / Miss Mistreated / Rock fever / Eyes of fire. *(cd-iss.1983) (cd-iss.Apr94)*

—— **BLACKMORE** still had in his ranks **GLOVER, TURNER, ROSENTHAL, /** and **CHUCK BURGI** – drums (ex-BRAND X) repl. RONDINELLI

Aug 83. (7")(7"pic-d) **STREET OF DREAMS. / ANYBODY THERE** [52] [60]
(12"+=) – Power (live)

Sep 83. (lp)(c)(cd) **BENT OUT OF SHAPE** [11] [34]
– Stranded / Can't let you go / Fool for the night / Fire dance / Anybody there / Desperate heart / Street of dreams / Drinking with the devil / Snowman / Make your move.

Oct 83. (7")(7"sha-pic-d) **CAN'T LET YOU GO. / ALL NIGHT LONG** [43] [ ]
(12"+=) – Stranded (live).

—— Split late '83 . . .BLACKMORE and GLOVER as said reformed DEEP PURPLE

RITCHIE BLACKMORE'S RAINBOW

—— re-formed for comeback concerts & an album. His new band:- **DOOGIE WHITE** – vocals / **PAUL MORRIS** – keyboards / **GREG SMITH** – bass / **JOHN O'REILLY** – drums

Arista Arista

Sep 95. (cd)(c) **STRANGER IN ALL OF US** [ ] [ ]
– Wolf to the Moon / Cold hearted woman / Hunting humans (insatiable) / Stand and fight / Ariel / Too late for tears / Black masquerade / Silence / Hall of the mountain king / Still I'm sad.

RAINBOW – compilations etc. –

Sep 78. Polydor; (d-lp) **RITCHIE BLACKMORE'S RAINBOW. / RAINBOW RISING** [ ] [ ]

Nov 81. Polydor; (d-lp)(d-c) **THE BEST OF RAINBOW** [14] [ ]
– All night long / Man on the silver mountain / Can't happen here / Lost in Hollywood / Since you've been gone / Stargazer / Catch the rainbow / Kill the king / 16th century Greensleeves / I surrender / Long live rock'n'roll / Eyes of the world / Starstruck / A light in the black / Mistreated. *(cd-iss.1983)*

Feb 85. Polydor; (d-c) **DOWN TO EARTH / DIFFICULT TO CURE** [ ] [ ]

Feb 86. Polydor; (d-lp)(d-c)(d-cd) **FINYL VINYL (live 80's material)** [ ] [87]

Feb 88. Old Gold; (7") **SINCE YOU'VE BEEN GONE. / ALL NIGHT LONG** [ ] [-]

Jun 93. Old Gold; (cd-s) **I SURRENDER / SINCE YOU'VE BEEN GONE / ALL NIGHT LONG** [ ] [-]

1989. Connoisseur; (d-lp)(c)(cd) **ROCK PROFILE VOL.1** [ ] [-]
(above credited to RITCHIE BLACKMORE contains early sessions and PURPLE work) (cd.omits interview tracks + 1 song)

Dec 90. Connoisseur; (d-cd)(c)(d-lp) **LIVE IN GERMANY 1976 (live)** [ ] [-]

Jul 91. Connoisseur; (cd)(d-lp) **ROCK PROFILE VOLUME 2** [ ] [-]
(above also credited to RITCHIE BLACKMORE contains RAINBOW material, etc.)

Jan 94. R.P.M.; (cd) **SESSION MAN** [ ] [-]

Jun 94. R.P.M.; (cd) **TAKE IT!** – SESSIONS 63-68 [ ] [-]

IAN GILLAN BAND

GILLAN – vocals / **RAY FENWICK** – guitar (ex-SPENCER DAVIS GROUP, ex-AFTER TEA) **MIKE MORAN** – keyboards / **JOHN GUSTAFSON** – bass (ex-BIG THREE, ex-EPISODE SIX, ex-QUATERMASS) / **MARK NAUSEEF** – drums (ex-ELF)

Oyster-Polydor Oyster

Jul 76. (lp)(c) **CHILD IN TIME** [55] [ ]
– Lay me down / You make me feel so good / Shame / My baby loves me / Down the road / Child in time / Let it slide. *(cd-iss.Apr90 on 'Virgin') (cd-iss.Mar94)*

—— **COLIN TOWNS** – keyboards repl. MICKEY LEE SOULE who had briefly repl. MIKE TOWNS also contributed some songs.

Island Antilles

Apr 77. (lp)(c) **CLEAN AIR TURBULANCE** [ ] [ ]
– Clean air turbulance / Five moons / Money lender / Over the hill / Goodhand Liza / Angel Manchenio. *(re-iss Jun82, Aug88 on 'Virgin', cd-iss.Apr90)*

Oct 77. (lp)(c) **SCARABUS** [ ] [ ]
– Scarabus / Twin exhausted / Poor boy hero / Mercury high / Pre release / Slags to bitches / Apathy / Mad Elaine / Country lights / Fool's mate. *(re-iss Jun82, Aug88 on 'Virgin', cd-iss.Apr90 +=)* – My baby loves me.

Feb 78. (7") **MAD ELAINE. / MERCURY HIGH** [ ] [ ]
This band also recorded LIVE AT BUDOKAN VOL 1 & 2, only released in Japan.– Clear air turbulence / My baby loves me / Scarabus / Money lender / Twin exhausted / Over the hill / Child in time / Smoke on the water / Mercury high / Woman from Tokyo. *(UK-issue 1987 on 'Virgin. cd-iss.Nov89) (re-iss.cd Sep93 as 'GILLAN – THE JAPANESE ALBUM' on 'R.P.M.')*

GILLAN

he only retained TOWNS and brought in **STEVE BYRD** – guitar / **JOHN McCOY** – bass / **PETE BARNACLE** – drums. An album GILLAN was released in Japan (only May78).

—— (May79) **BERNIE TORME** – guitar (ex-solo artist) repl. BYRD / **MICK UNDERWOOD** – drums (ex-EPISODE SIX, ex-QUATERMASS, ex-STRAPPS, etc.) repl. BARNACLE

Acrobat Arista

Sep 79. (lp)(c) **MR. UNIVERSE** [11] [ ]
– Second sight / Secret of the dance / She tears me down / Roller / Mr Universe / Vengence / Puget sound / Dead of the night / Message in a bottle / Fighting man. *(re-iss Jan83 on Fame)*

Oct 79. (7") **VENGENCE. / SMOKE ON THE WATER** [ ] [ ]

Virgin Virgin/RSO

Jun 80. (7") **SLEEPIN' ON THE JOB. / HIGHER AND HIGHER** [55] [ ]

Jul 80. (7"m) **NO EASY WAY. / HANDLES ON HER HIPS / I MIGHT AS WELL GO HOME** [ ] [ ]

Aug 80. (lp)(c) **GLORY ROAD** [3] [ ]
– Unchain your brain / Are you sure? / Time and again / No easy way / Sleepin' on the job / On the rocks / If you believe me / Running, white face, city boy / Nervous / Your mother was right. *(re-iss.Mar84)* (free lp w.a.) **FOR GILLAN FANS ONLY** (limited 15000) *(cd-iss.Nov89) (containing free album)* – Redwatch / Abbey of Thelema / Trying to get to you / Come tomorrow / Dragon's tongue / ost fade brain damage / Egg timr / Harry Lime theme.

Sep 80. (7") **TROUBLE. / YOUR SISTER'S ON MY LIST** [14] [ ]
(free live-7"w.a.) **MR.UNIVERSE. / VENGEANCE / SMOKE ON THE WATER**

Feb 81. (7") **MUTUALLY ASSURED DESTRUCTION. / THE MAELSTROM** [32] [ ]

Mar 81. (7") **NEW ORLEANS. / TAKE A HOLD OF YOURSELF** [2] [ ]

Apr 81. (lp)(c) **FUTURE SHOCK** [2] [ ]
– Future shock / Night ride out of Phoenix / The ballad of Lucitania express / No laughing in Heaven / Sacre bleu / New Orleans / Bite the bullet / If I sing softly / Don't want the truth / For your dreams. *(re-iss.Aug88) (re-iss.cd/c May95 on 'Virgin-VIP')*

Jun 81. (7"ep) **NO LAUGHING IN HEAVEN / ONE FOR THE ROAD. / LUCILLE / BAD NEWS** [31] [ ]

—— **JANICK GERS** – guitar (ex-WHITE SPIRIT) repl. TORME (later to DESPERADO)

Oct 81. (7") **NIGHTMARE. / BITE THE BULLET (live)** [36] [ ]

Nov 81. (d-lp)(d-c) **DOUBLE TROUBLE (live)** [12] [ ]
– I'll rip your spine out / Restless / Men of war / Sunbeam / Nightmare / Hadely bop bop / Life goes on / Born to kill / No laughing in Heaven / No easy way / Trouble / Mutally assured destruction / If you believe me / New Orleans. *(cd-iss.Nov89)*

Jan 82. (7")(7"pic-d) **RESTLESS. / ON THE ROCKS (live)** [25] [ ]

Aug 82. (7") **LIVING FOR THE CITY. / BREAKING CHAINS** [50] [ ]
(7"pic-d) – ('A'side). / PURPLE SKY

Sep 82. (lp)(c)(pic-lp) **MAGIC** [17] [ ]
– What's the matter / Bluesy blue sea / Caught in a trap / Long gone / Driving me wild / Demon driver / Living a lie / You're so right / Living for the city / Demon driver (reprise). *(re-iss.Aug88 +cd.Aug89) (cd-iss.Mar94)*

Oct 82. (7") **LONG GONE. / FIJI** [ ] [ ]

—— **IAN GILLAN** then joined BLACK SABBATH, before the reformation of DEEP PURPLE in Nov84. GILLAN left PURPLE again to go solo

Jun 88. (7") **SOUTH AFRICA. / JOHN** [ ] [ ]
(12"+=) – ('A'extended).

After GILLAN's departure from DEEP PURPLE in late 80's, he made 2 other albums (Jul 90) NAKED THUNDER for 'East West' records, and a year later 'TOOLBOX'. He re-joined DEEP PURPLE late '92

– GILLAN compilations etc. –

Aug 84. Thunderbolt; (lp) **ROCKS ON! (by GILLAN / DEAN)** [ ] [ ]

Jun 86. 10-Virgin; (d-lp)(c)(cd) **WHAT I DID ON MY VACATION** [ ] [ ]

– On the rocks / Scarabus / Puget sound / No easy way / If I sing softly / I'll rip your spine out / New Orleans / Mutally assured destruction / You're so right / Long gone / If you believe in me / Bluesy blue sea / Lucille. (d-lp+=) – Mad Elaine / Time and again / Vengeance / Unchain your brain / No laughing in Heaven.

Dec 90. Raw Fruit; (cd)(c)(lp) **LIVE AT READING ROCK FESTIVAL 1980 (live)** -

May 91. V.I.P.; (cd)(c) **TROUBLE – (THE BEST OF GILLAN)** -
– Trouble / New Orleans / Fighting man / Living for the city / Helter skelter / Mr.Universe / Telephone box / Dislocated (GILLAN-GLOVER) / Sleeping on the job / MAD (Mutally Assured Destruction) / No laughing in Heaven / Nightmare / Restless / Purple sky / Born to kill (live) / Smoke on the water (live). *(re-iss.cd+c Dec93 on 'Virgin-VIP')*

Sep 91. Music Club; (cd)(c) **THE VERY BEST OF GILLAN** -

1992 R.P.M.; (cd) **CHERKAZOO AND OTHER STORIES** -

Jul 95. Connoisseur; (cd) **ROCK PROFILE** -

ROGER GLOVER

(solo)

Purple UK

Dec 74. (lp)(c) **BUTTERFLY BALL (Soundtrack)** Jan 76
– Dawn / Get ready / Saffron doormouse and Lizzy bee / Harlequin hare / Old blind mole / Magician moth / No solution / Behind the smile / Fly away / Arena / Sitting in a dream / Waiting / Sir Maximus mouse / Dreams of Sir Bedivere / Together again / Watch out for the bat / Little chalk blue / The feast / Love is all / Homeward. *(re-iss.Nov84 on 'Safari') (cd-iss.1989 on 'Line') (re-iss.cd Jul95 on 'Repertoire')*

Aug 76. (7") **LOVE IS ALL. / OLD BLIND MOLE**

Polydor Polydor?

Apr 78. (lp)(c) **ELEMENTS**
– The first ring made of clay / The next a ring of fire / The third ring's water flow / The fourth ring's with the wind / Finale.

May 84. (lp)(c) **MASK**
– Divided world / Getting stranger / The mask / Fake it / Dancin' again / (You're so) Remote / Hip level / Don't look down. *(cd-iss.Apr93 w/ ELEMENTS on 'Connoisseur')*

Polydor 21 records

Jun 84. (7") **THE MASK. / (YOU'RE SO) REMOTE**

— **GLOVER** also rejoined DEEP PURPLE (late '84)

GILLAN / GLOVER

10-Virgin Virgin?

Jul 87. (7") **DISLOCATED. / CHET**
(12"+=) – Purple people eater.

Jan 88. (7")(12") **SHE TOOK MY BREATH AWAY. / CAYMAN ISLAND**

Feb 88. (lp)(c)(cd) **ACCIDENTALLY ON PURPOSE**
– Cloud and rain / She took my breath away / Can't believe you wanna leave / Dislocated / Viva! Miami / I can't dance to that / Lonely avenue / Telephone box / I thought no. (cd+=) – Cayman Island / Purple people eater / Chet.

DEEP WOUND (see under ⇒ DINOSAUR JR.)

DEFINITION OF SOUND

Formed: Home Counties, England ... late 80's by former graffiti artist KEV WEEKES and DON CLARK, out of TOP BILLIN! • **Style:** Modern daisy age rap duo, with added superior guitar style by BROUGH. • **Songwriters:** CLARK and WEEKES words adding BROUGH for music sample DONOVAN + The HOMBRES. • **Trivia:** KEV guested on KRUSH'S 1987 hit 'House Arrest'.

Recommended: LOVE AND LIFE (*7).

TOP BILLIN!

DON CLARK – vocals / **TAYLOR** – vocals / **KEV WON WEEKES** – vocals

Danceyard not iss.

Sep 88. (7")(12") **NATURALLY. / NEVER** -

Jan 89. (7")(12") **STARLIGHT FROM MY SOUL** -

May 89. (7") **MY THING. / SURPRISE** (w/ P.P.Arnold) -
(12"+=) ('A'-sunrise mix)

DEFINITION OF SOUND

— **REX BROUGH** (The Roo King) – guitar (repl. TAYLOR) plus **COXON.** Also most dual vocals by **ELAINE VASSELL and ASHANTI.**

Circa Cardiac

Nov 90. (7")(c-s) **NOW IS TOMORROW. / MOIRA JANE'S CAFE**
(12"+=)(cd-s+=) – ('A' experiments in funk pt.1).

Feb 91. (7") **WEAR YOUR LOVE LIKE HEAVEN. / ('A'live)** 17
(12") – ('A'side) / ('A'uptown mix).
(cd-s) – ('A'extended) / ('A'kingdom mix) / I don't know 'bout daisies.

May 91. (7") **NOW IS TOMORROW. / MOIRA JANE'S CAFE** 46
(12"+=) – ('A' Mr.Mojo rising mix).
(12"+=) – ('A'mix) / Won your lovin'.
(12")(cd-s) – (3 different 'A'mixes)

Jun 91. (cd)(c)(lp) **LOVE AND LIFE** 38
– Now is tomorrow / Passion and pain / Wear your love like Heaven / Reality / Rise like the Sun / Dream girl / Change / The blues / Moira Jane's cafe / City lights / Time is running out.

Aug 91. (7")(c-s) **DREAM GIRL. / THE GOD IN ME**
(12"+=) – The Don Mon mix.
(12") – ('A'side) – (4 'A' mixes).
(12") – ('A'brighter mix / 'A'ubiquity mix).

Jan 92. (7")(c-s) **MOIRA JANE'S CAFE. / ('A'live)** 34
(12"+=)(cd-s+=) – (5 other radical remixes).

Aug 92. (7")(c-s) **WHAT ARE YOU UNDER?. / AIN'T SAYING NOTHING** 68
(12"+=)(cd-s+=) – (3 other mixes).

Sep 92. (cd)(c)(lp) **THE LICK**
– Looking good / Can I get over / What are you under / Together / Move your body / She hangs out / Sunshine and rain / Too young to know / Travellin' man / Cry.

Nov 92. (7")(c-s)(12"pic-d) **CAN I GET OVER. / REVERSE THE HEARSE** 61
(12"+=)(12"pic-d+=) – ('B'instrumental) / ('A'acappella).
(cd-s+=) – In deep / Rise like the Sun.

Apr 95. (c-s) **BOOM BOOM / DEIRDRE** 59
(cd-s) – (3 'A'mixes).

Nov 95. (c-s) **PASS THE VIBES / ('A'-C Swing mix)** 23
(cd-s+=) – Set up.
(12") – (5-'A'mixes).

DEF LEPPARD

Formed: Sheffield, England ... 1977 by youngsters initially as ATOMIC MASS (see below). In 1978, ELLIOT's dad loaned them money to issue debut EP on own indie label 'Bludgeon Riffola'. The following year, after tours supporting AC/DC, etc., they were signed to 'Vertigo' by Roger Bain. This also prompted a move to London, and in 1980, their debut album 'ON THROUGH THE NIGHT', broke the UK 20, and also nearly hit the US 50, where they soon became massive attraction. • **Style:** Heavy metal, that through the years has mellowed into glam-metal pop. The most easy listening metal band of the time, hated by critics, but loved by their loyal ever growing legion of teen-age fans. • **Songwriters:** Group compositions, except ONLY AFTER DARK (Mick Ronson) / ACTION (Sweet) / YOU CAN'T ALWAYS GET WHAT YOU WANT (Rolling Stones) / LITTLE WING (Jimi Hendrix) / ELECTED (Alice Cooper). Roadie STUMPUS MAXIMUS sung; PLEASE RELEASE ME (Engelbert Humperdink). • **Miscellaneous:** The group has been dogged by accidents and deaths (see discography for correct details).

Recommended: VAULT 1980-1995 – DEF LEPPARD'S GREATEST HITS (*8).

JOE ELLIOT (b. 1 Aug'59) – vocals / **PETE WILLIS** – lead guitar / **STEVE CLARK** (b.23 Apr'60) – guitar / **RICK SAVAGE** (b. 2 Dec'60) – bass / **FRANK NOON** – drums.

Bludgeon not issued

Jan 79. (7"m) **OVERTURE. / RIDE INTO THE SUN / GETCHA ROCKS OFF** -

— **RICK ALLEN** (b. 1 Nov'63) – drums, repl. FRANK who later joined LIONHEART, then WAYSTED.

Vertigo Mercury

Feb 79. (7"ep) **OVERTURE. / GETCHA ROCKS OFF / RIDE INTO THE SUN**

Nov 79. (7") **WASTED. / HELLO AMERICA** 61

Feb 80. (7") **HELLO AMERICA. / GOOD MORNING FREEDOM** 45

Mar 80. (lp)(c) **ON THROUGH THE NIGHT** 15 51
– Rock brigade / Hello America / Sorrow is a woman / It could be you / Answer to the master / When the walls came tumbling down / Wasted / Rocks off / It don't matter / Satellite / Overture. *(re-iss.+cd Jan89)*

1980. (7") **ROCK BRIGADE. / WHEN THE WALLS COME TUMBLING DOWN** -

Jul 81. (lp)(c) **HIGH'N'DRY** 26 38
– High 'n' dry (Saturday night) / You got me runnin' / Let it go / Another hit and run / Lady Strange / Mirror, mirror (look into my eyes) / No no no / Bringin' on the heartbreak / Switch 625. *(US re-iss.May84 +=)*– Bringin' on the heartbreak (remix) / Me and my wine. *(re-iss.+cd Jan89)* (cd+=) – You got me runnin' (remix) / Me and my wine.

Aug 81. (7") **LET IT GO. / SWITCH 625**

Jan 82. (7") **BRINGIN' ON THE HEARTACHE (remix). / ME AND MY WINE**
(12"+=) – You got me runnin'.

Jan 83. (7") **PHOTOGRAPH. / BRINGIN' ON THE HEARTBREAK** 66 12 Mar 83
(12"+=) – Mirror, Mirror (look into my eyes).

— **PHIL COLLEN** (b. 8 Dec'57) – lead guitar (ex-GIRL) repl. PETE

Mar 83. (lp)(c)(cd) **PYROMANIA** 18 2
– Rock! rock! (till you drop) / Photograph / Stagefright / Too late for love / Die hard the hunter / Foolin' / Rock of ages / Comin' under fire / Action! not words / Billy's got a gun.

Aug 83. (7")(12")(7"pic-d)(7"sha-pic-d) **ROCK OF AGES. / ACTION! NOT WORDS** 41 16 Jun 83

Nov 83. (7") **FOOLIN'. / TOO LATE FOR LOVE** 28 Aug 83
(12"+=) – High'n'dry.

Jun 84. (7") **BRINGIN' ON THE HEARTBREAK (remix). / ?** - 61

Aug 85. (7") **PHOTOGRAPH. / BRINGIN' ON THE HEARTBREAK** -
(12"+=) – Mirror, mirror.

— Remained a 5-piece although **RICK ALLEN** lost an arm in a car crash (31 Dec84). He now used specially adapted programmable drum pads and foot pedals.

Jul 87. (7") **ANIMAL. / TEAR IT DOWN** 6 19 Oct 87
(12"+=)(12"red+=) – ('A'extended).
(cd-s++=) – Women.

Aug 87. (lp)(c)(cd)(pic-lp) **HYSTERIA** 2 1
– Women / Rocket / Animal / Love bites / Pour some sugar on me / Armageddon it / Gods of war / Don't shoot shotgun / Run riot / Hysteria / Excitable / Love and affection. *(cd+=)* – I can't let you be a memory.

Aug 87. (7") **WOMEN. / ?** - 80

Sep 87. (7")(c-s)(7"sha-pic-d) **POUR SOME SUGAR ON ME. / I WANNA BE YOUR HERO** 18 2 Apr 88

(12"+=)(12"pic-d+=) – ('A'extended mix).

Nov 87. (7")(c-s) **HYSTERIA. / RIDE INTO THE SUN ('87 version)** 26 10 Jan 88
(12"+=) – Love and affection (live).
(cd-s++=) – I wanna be your hero.

Apr 88. (7") **ARMAGEDDON IT!. / RING OF FIRE** 20 3 Nov 88
(12"+=) – ('A'atomic mix).
(pic-cd-s++=) – Animal / Pour some sugar on me.

Jul 88. (7") **LOVE BITES. / BILLY'S GOT A GUN (live)** 11 1
(12"+=)(cd-s+=) – Excitable (orgasmic mix).

Jan 89. (7") **ROCKET. / RELEASE ME** 15 12
(12"+=)(cd-s+=)(12"pic-d+=) – ('A'rock mix) / Rock of ages (live).

— **STEVE CLARK** was found dead 8 Jan'91 after drinking/drugs session. Replaced by **VIV CAMPBELL** – guitar (ex-DIO, ex-WHITESNAKE, ex-SHADOWKING)

Mar 92. (7")(c-s) **LET'S GET ROCKED. / ONLY AFTER DARK** 2 15
(12"pic-d+=) – Too late for love (live).
(pic-cd-s+=) – Women (live).

Apr 92. (cd)(c)(lp) **ADRENALIZE** 1 1
– Let's get rocked / Heaven is / Make love like a man / Tonight / White lightning / Stand up (kick love into motion) / Personal property / Have you ever needed someone so bad / I wanna touch u / Tear it down. *(pic-lp iss.Dec92, w / 2 extra tracks)*

Jun 92. (7")(c-s) **MAKE LOVE LIKE A MAN. / MISS YOU IN A HEARTBEAT** 12 36
(12"+=) – Two steps behind (acoustic).
(cd-s++=) – Action.

Sep 92. (7")(c-s) **HAVE YOU EVER NEEDED SOMEONE SO BAD. / FROM THE INSIDE** 16 12 Aug 92
(cd-s+=) – You can't always get what you want / Little wing.

Dec 92. (c-s) **STAND UP (KICK LOVE INTO MOTION). / ?** - 34

Jan 93. (7"etched)(c-s) **HEAVEN IS. / SHE'S TOO TOUGH** 13
(pic-cd-s+=) – Let's get rocked (live) / Elected (live).
(12"pic-d) – ('A'side) / Let's get rocked (live) / Tokyo road (live).

Apr 93. (7")(c-s) **TONIGHT. / NOW I'M HERE (live)** 34 62
(cd-s+=) – ('A'demo).
(cd-s+=) – Photograph (live).

Sep 93. (c-s)(cd-s) **TWO STEPS BEHIND. / TONIGHT (demo)** 32 12 Aug 93
(12"+=)(cd-s+=) – S.M.C.

(above single from the film 'Last Action Hero' on 'Columbia')

Oct 93. (cd)(c)(lp) **RETRO ACTIVE** 6 9
– Desert song / Fractured love / Two steps behind (acoustic) / Only after dark / Action / She's too tough / Miss you in a heartbeat (acoustic) / Only after dark (acoustic) / Ride into the Sun / From the inside / Ring of fire / I wanna be your hero / Miss you in a heartbeat / Two steps behind.

Jan 94. (7")(c-s) **ACTION. / MISS YOU IN A HEARTBEAT** 14
(cd-s+=) – She's too tough.

Oct 95. (c-s) **WHEN LOVE & HATE COLLIDE / POUR SOME SUGAR ON ME (remix)** 2 59
(cd-s+=) – Armageddon it (remix).
(cd-s++=) – ('A'demo).
(cd-s) – ('A'side) / Rocket (remix) / Excitable (remix).
(cd-s) – ('A'side) / Excitable (remix) / ('A'demo).

Oct 95. (cd)(c)(lp) **VAULT 1980-1995 DEF LEPPARD GREATEST HITS** (compilation) 3 15
– Pour some sugar on me / Photograph / Love bites / Let's get rocked / Two steps behind / Animal / Heaven is / Rocket / When love & hate collide / Action / Make love like a man / Armageddon it / Have you ever needed someone / So bad / Rock of ages / Hysteria / Bringin' on the heartbreak. (cd w/free cd) **LIVE AT DON VALLEY, SHEFFIELD (live)**

DEL AMITRI

Formed: Glasgow, Scotland . . . 1983 by JUSTIN CURRIE, etc. (see below). Made one single on indie label 'No Strings' before signing to major 'Chrysalis' records in 1984. Finally broke through early in the 90's on 'A&M', with hit 45 'NOTHING EVER HAPPENS'which was lifted from the Top 10 album 'THE WAKING HOUR'. • **Style:** Intelligent acoustic outfit, led by CURRIE, drawing on similarities to Scottish 'Postcard' era. • **Songwriters:** CURRIE-HARVIE composed except covers; DON'T CRY NO TEARS (Neil Young) / BYE BYE PRIDE (Go-Betweens) / CINDY INCIDENTLY (Faces). • **Trivia:** Means 'from the womb' in Greek.

Recommended: THE WAKING HOUR (*8) / CHANGE EVERYTHING (*6)

JUSTIN CURRIE (b.11 Dec'64) – vocals, bass, acoustic guitar / **IAIN HARVIE** (b.19 May'62) – guitar / **BRYAN TOLLAND** – guitar / **PAUL TYAGIS** – drums, percussion

No Strings not issued

Aug 83. (7") **SENSE SICKNESS. / THE DIFFERENCE IS** -

Chrysalis not issued

May 85. (lp)(c) **DEL AMITRI**
– Heard through a wall / Hammering heart / Former owner / Sticks and stones girl / Deceive yourself (in ignorant Heaven) / I was here / Crows in a wheatfield / Keepers / Ceasefire / Breaking bread. *(re-iss.cd+c Mar93)*

Jul 85. (7") **STICKS AND STONES GIRL. / THE KING IS POOR** -
(12"+=) – The difference is.

Oct 85. (7")(12") **HAMMERING HEART. / LINES RUNNING NORTH** -

— **MICK SLAVEN** – guitar (ex-BOURGIE BOURGIE) repl. TOLLAND / sessions from **ANDY ALSTON** – keyboards / **ROBERT CAIRNS** – violin / **BLAIR COWAN** – accordion / **STEPHEN IRVINE** – drums / **JULIAN DAWSON** – harmonica / **JAMES O'MALLEY** – bass / **CAROLINE LEVELLE** – cello / **WILL MOWAT** – seq, keyboards

A & M A & M

Jul 89. (7") **KISS THIS THING GOODBYE. / NO HOLDING ON** 59
(12"+=)(cd-s+=) – Slowly / It's coming back.

Jul 89. (lp)(c)(cd) **THE WAKING HOUR** 6 95 Mar 90
– Kiss this thing goodbye / Opposite view / Move away Jimmy Blue / Stone cold sober / You're gone / When I want you / This side of the morning / Empty / Hatful of rain / Nothing ever happens. *(re-iss.cd/c Mar95)*

Oct 89. (7") **STONE COLD SOBER. / THE RETURN OF MAGGIE BROWN**
(12"+=)(cd-s+=) – Talk it to death.

Jan 90. (7")(c-s) **NOTHING EVER HAPPENS. / SO MANY SOULS TO CHANGE** 11
(12"+=)(cd-s+=) – Don't I look like the kind of guy you used to hate? / Evidence.

Mar 90. (7")(c-s) **KISS THIS THING GOODBYE. / NO HOLD-ING ON** 43 35 Mar 90
(12"+=)(cd-s+=) – *(all a straight re-issue of Jul89 diff.cat.no.)*

Jun 90. (7")(c-s) **MOVE AWAY JIMMY BLUE. / ANOTHER LETTER HOME** 36
(12"+=) – April the first / This side of the morning.
(12"+=)(cd-s+=) – April the first / More than you'd ever know.

Oct 90. (7")(c-s) **SPIT IN THE RAIN. / SCARED TO LIVE** 21
(10"+=)(12"+=)(cd-s+=) – The return of Maggie Brown / Talk it to death.

— **DAVID CUMMINGS** – guitar repl. SLAVEN / **BRIAN McDERMOTT** – drums (who guested on last) repl. TYGANI

Apr 92. (7")(c-s) **ALWAYS THE LAST TO KNOW. / LEARN TO CRY** 13 30 Jul 92
(12"+=)(cd-s+=) – Angel on the roof / The whole world is quiet.

Jun 92. (cd)(c)(lp) **CHANGE EVERYTHING** 2
– Be my downfall / Just like a man / When you were young / Surface of the Moon / I won't take the blame / The first rule of love / The ones that you love lead you nowhere / Always the last to know / To last a lifetime / As soon as the tide comes in / Behind the fool / Sometimes I just have to say your name. *(re-iss.cd/c Mar95)*

Jun 92. (7")(c-s) **BE MY DOWNFALL. / WHISKEY REMORSE** 30
(10"+=)(cd-s+=) – Lighten up the load / The heart is a bad design.

Aug 92. (7")(c-s) **JUST LIKE A MAN. / SPIT IN THE RAIN (remix)** 25
(cd-s) – ('A'side) / Don't cry no tears / Bye bye pride / Cindy incidentally.
(cd-s) – ('A'side) / Carry on Colombus / I want to take the blame (acoustic) / Scared to live.

Jan 93. (7")(c-s) **WHEN YOU WERE YOUNG. / THE ONES THAT YOU LOVE LEAD YOU NOWHERE** 20
(cd-s+=) – Kiss this thing goodbye (live) / Hatful of rain (live).
(cd-s) – ('A'side) / Long journey home / The verb to do / Kestral road.

Feb 95. (c-s) **HERE AND NOW / SOMEONE ELSE WILL** 21
(cd-s)(10") – ('A'side) / Long way down / Queen of false alarms / Crashing down.
(cd-s) – ('A'side) / Always the last to know (live) / When I want you / Stone cold sober (live).

Feb 95. (cd)(c) **TWISTED** 3
– Food for songs / Start with me / Here and now / One thing left to do / Tell her this / Being somebody else / Roll to me / Crashing down / It might as well be you / Never enough / It's never too late to be alone / Driving with the brakes on. *(re-iss.d-cd Aug95)*

Apr 95. (7")(c-s) **DRIVING WITH THE BRAKES ON. / LIFE BY MISTAKE** 18
(cd-s+=) – A little luck / In the meantime.
(cd-s) – ('A'side) / Nothing ever happens / Kiss this thing goodbye / Always the last to know.

Jun 95. (c-s) **ROLL TO ME / IN THE FRAME** 22 10
(cd-s+=) – Food for songs (acoustic) / One thing left to do (acoustic).
(cd-s) – ('A'side) / Spit in the rain / Stone cold sober / Move away Jimmy Blue.

Oct 95. (c-s) **TELL HER THIS / A BETTER MAN** 32
(cd-s+=) – The last love song / When you were young (alt.version).
(cd-s) – ('A'side) / Whiskey remorse / Fred Partington's daughter / Learn to cry.

DELANEY & BONNIE

Formed: Los Angeles, California, USA . . . 1967 by recently married (after a week courting) DELANEY BRAMLETT and BONNIE LYNN. DELANEY had released solo singles as well as being part of The SHINDIGS, while BONNIE was formerly with IKE & TINA TURNER's backing singers The IKETTES. In mid-'69, after a stint with 'Stax' (the first white act to do so), they signed to 'Elektra', where they issued 'ACCEPT NO SUBSTITUTE' album. By the end of the year, both were touring with JOHN LENNON & THE PLASTIC ONO BAND and started up friendship with ERIC CLAPTON, who even joined aggregation of friends early 1970. After a successful single 'COMIN' HOME', 2nd album plus tour, ERIC left to go solo, but duo continued fortunes during the early 70's, until their divorce in 1972. • **Style:** A blend of gospel & soul mixed with country rock, which featured them alongside many friends/stars incl. DUANE ALLMAN, LEON RUSSELL, GEORGE HARRISON, all DEREK & THE DOMINOES, RITA COOLIDGE. • **Songwriters:** Both penned material. Leon Russell wrote GROUPIE (SUPERSTAR), which later became a hit for The CARPENTERS. • **Trivia:** Their Top 20 US hit 'NEVER ENDING SONG OF LOVE' became a UK Top 3 hit for NEW SEEKERS. In 1979, BONNIE argued then punched ELVIS COSTELLO, allegedly about racial remarks.

Recommended: THE BEST OF DELANEY & BONNIE (*5)

DELANEY BRAMLETT

Vocallion Vocallion

Apr 65. (7") **LIVERPOOL LOU. / YOU HAVE NO CHOICE**

Nov 65. (7") **YOU NEVER LOOKED SWEETER. / HEARTBREAK HOTEL**

DELANEY & BONNIE

duo **DELANEY BRAMLETT** (b. 1 Jul'39, Pontotoc Co., Missouri, USA) – vocals / **BONNIE BRAMLETT** (b.BONNIE LYNN, 8 Nov'44, Acton, Illinois, USA) – vocals with back-up from BOOKER T. & THE MG'S. **BOBBY WHITLOCK** – keyboards

Stax Stax

1967. (7") **IT'S BEEN A LONG TIME COMING. /** [-] [ ]

1968. (lp) **HOME** [-] [ ]
– It's been a long time coming / A right now love / We can love / My baby specializes / Everybody loves a winner / Things get better / Just plain beautiful / Hard to say goodbye / Pour your love on me / Piece of my heart. *(not-iss. until 1974) (cd-iss.May90 on 'Stax-Ace')*

1968. (7") **JUST PLAIN BEAUTIFUL. / HARD TO SAY GOODBYE** [ ] [ ]
(UK-iss.1970)

not issued Independence

1968. (lp) **DELANEY & BONNIE** [-] [ ]
– What the world needs now is love / You've lost that loving feeling / Heartbreak Hotel / Tomorrow never comes / I can't take it much longer / I got a woman / Lonely me / Without your love / Better than me / Liverpool Lou / You never looked sweeter / You have no choice.*(re-iss.1971 as 'GENESIS' on 'London' UK + 'Crescendo' US)*

— back-up from future DEREK & THE DOMINOES (see; Eric CLAPTON). Also incl. **WHITLOCK, JERRY McGEE** – guitar / **DAVE MASON, DUANE ALLMAN**, etc.

Apple Elektra

Jul 69. (lp) **ACCEPT NO SUBSTITUTE – THE ORIGINAL DELANEY & BONNIE** [ ] [ ]
– Get yourselves together / Someday / The ghetto / When the battle is over / Dirty old man / Love me a little bit longer / I can't take it much longer / Do right woman – do right man / Soldiers of the cross / The gift of love. *(re-iss.1971 on 'Elektra') (re-iss.+cd.Feb88 on 'Thunderbolt')*

Elektra Elektra

Oct 69. (7") **GET YOURSELVES TOGETHER. / SOLDIERS OF THE CROSS (withdrawn)** [-] [ ]

Feb 70. (7") **SOMEDAY. / DIRTY OLD MAN** [ ] [ ]

DELANEY & BONNIE & FRIENDS

with **DEREK & THE DOMINOES**, plus **GEORGE HARRISON** guest

Atlantic Atco

Dec 69. (7") **COMIN' HOME. (as "DELANEY & BONNIE & FRIENDS FEATURING ERIC CLAPTON") / GROUPIE (SUPERSTAR)** [16] [84]

May 70. (lp)(c) **DELANEY & BONNIE & FRIENDS ON TOUR WITH ERIC CLAPTON** [39] [29] Apr 70
– Things get better / Poor Elijah – Tribute to Johnson (medley) / Only you know and I know / I don't want to discuss it / That's what my man is for / Where there's a will, there's a way / Coming home / Little Richard medley: Tutti Frutti – The girl can't help it – Long tall Sally – Jenny Jenny. *(re-iss.Jul87, cd-iss.Feb93) (re-iss.cd Jun93 on 'Atco')*

— Broke from DEREK & THE DOMINOES & CLAPTON when they teamed up again The BRAMLETT's brought numerous session people.

Jun 70. (7") **FREE THE PEOPLE. / SOUL SHAKE** [ ] [75]
[43]

Oct 70. (lp)(c) **TO BONNIE FROM DELANEY** [ ] [58]
– Hard luck and troubles / God knows I love you / Lay down my burden / Medley: Come on in my kitchen – Mama, he treats your daughter mean – Going down the road feeling bad / The love of my man / They call it rock and roll music / Soul shake / Miss Ann / Alone together / Living on the open road / Let me be your man / Free the people.

— In 1970 they with ERIC CLAPTON featured on KING CURTIS style 'TEASIN' / SOULIN'

Nov 70. (7") **MISS ANN. / THEY CALL IT ROCK AND ROLL MUSIC** [-] [ ]

Mar 71. (7") **MISS ANN. / LET ME BE YOUR MAN** [ ] [-]

Apr 71. (lp)(c) **MOTEL SHOT** [ ] [65]
– Where the soul never dies / Will the circle be unbroken / Rock of ages / Long road ahead / Faded love / Talkin' about Jesus / Come on in my kitchen / Don't deceive me (please don't go) / Never ending song of love / Sing my way home / Going down the road feeling bad / Lonesome and a long way from home.

Jun 71. (7") **NEVER ENDING SONG OF LOVE. / DON'T DECEIVE ME** [ ] [13] May 71

DELANEY & BONNIE

with sessioners.

Oct 71. (7") **ONLY YOU KNOW AND I KNOW. / GOD KNOWS I LOVE YOU** [ ] [20] Sep 71

Nov 71. (lp)(c) **COUNTRY LIFE** [ ] [ ]
– Only you know and I know / Sound of the city / I'm on fire / Superstargroupie song / Well well / I know something good about you / Coming home / Country life / Big change comin' / Wade in the River Jordan / Your kind of kindness / Try a little harder.

Jan 72. (7") **MOVE 'EM OUT. / SING MY WAY HOME** [-] [59]

Mar 72. (7") **WHERE THERE'S A WILL THERE'S A WAY. / LONESOME AND A LONG WAY FROM HOME** [-] [99]

C.B.S. Columbia

Apr 72. (lp)(c) **D & B TOGETHER** [ ] [ ]
– Only you know and I know / Wade in the river Jordan / Sound of the city / Well, well / I know how it feels to be lonely / Comin' home / Move 'em out / Big chance comin' / A good thing (I'm on fire) / Groupie (superstar) / I know something good about you / Country life.

— Divorced and dissolved partnership after above.

– compilations, others, etc. –

Atlantic Atco

Jun 72. (7"m) **THEY CALL IT ROCK & ROLL. / SOUL SHAKE / WHERE THERE'S A WILL THERE'S A WILL** [ ] [ ]

1973. (lp)(c) **THE BEST OF DELANEY & BONNIE** [ ] [ ]
– When the battle is over / Dirty old man / Only you know and I know / We've got to get ourselves together / Where there's a will, there's a way / Never ending song of love / Coming home / The love of my man / Soul shake / Come on in my kitchen / Mama, he treats your daughter mean / Goin' down the road feeling bad / Free the people. *(re-iss.1987)*

1973. (7") **WILL THE CIRCLE BE UNBROKEN. / SING MY WAY HOME** [-] [ ]

DELANEY BRAMLETT

went solo.

C.B.S. Columbia

1972. (lp)(c) **SOMETHING'S COMING** [ ] [ ]
– Over and over / Thank God / Please accept my love / Keep it going / Something's coming (heartbeat) / Down by the riverside / Sit right down / I'm not your lover, I'm your lovee / Try a little harder.

1972. (7") **OVER AND OVER. / I'M NOT YOUR LOVER, I'M YOUR LOVEE** [-] [ ]

1972. (7") **THANK GOD. / WE CAN'T BE SEEN TOGETHER** [-] [ ]

1973. (lp)(c) **MOEBIUS STRIP** [ ] [ ]
– Are you a Beatle or a Rolling Stone / What am I doin' (in a place like this) / A young girl / Big ol' piece of blues / Circles / When a man is in need of a woman / I'm a M-A-N / B.B.'s blues / A little bit of you in me / California rain.

Nov 73. (7") **THAT'S WHAT GOD SAID. / I FOUND JESUS** [ ] [-]

1974. (7") **ARE YOU A BEATLE OR A ROLLING STONE. / CALIFORNIA RAIN** [-] [ ]

not issued M.G.M.

1975. (lp)(c) **GIVING BIRTH TO A SONG** [-] [ ]
– Giving birth to a song / I get high / So much in love / My lover's prayer / I wanna stay home with you / The plug / Nothing without you / Never no more blues / Lonesome long gone, and so long / Over you / I get away.

DELANEY AND FRIENDS

(ERIC CLAPTON, LEON RUSSELL, RINGO STARR, BILLY PRESTON, GEORGE HARRISON, etc.

Prodigal Prodigal

1977. (lp)(c) **CLASS REUNION** [ ] [ ]
– Looked up in Alabama / Every day's a holiday / I wish it would rain / It's a touchy situation / You can't measure my love / I think I got it / Invitation to a heartbreak / For old times sake / Who you gonna blame it on / You were the light.

— DELANEY retired from music scene, around same time.

BONNIE BRAMLETT

solo.

C.B.S. Columbia

1973. (lp)(c) **SWEET BONNIE BRAMLETT** [ ] [ ]
– Able, qualified and ready / Singer man / Crazy 'bout my baby / Got to get down / Good vibrations / Rollin' / Celebrate life / The sorrow of love / (You don't know) How glad I am / Don't wanna go down there.

1973. (7") **GOOD VIBRATIONS. / HOW GLAD I AM** [-] [ ]

Capricorn Capricorn

Feb 75. (lp)(c) **IT'S TIME** [ ] [ ]
– Your kind of kindness / Atlanta, Georgia / It's time / Cover me / Higher and higher / Where you come from / Cowboys and Indians / (Your love has brought me from a) Mighty long way / Since I met you baby / Oncoming traffic.

1975. (7") **IT'S TIME. / HIGHER AND HIGHER** [-] [ ]

1976. (lp)(c) **LADY'S CHOICE** [ ] [ ]
– Think / Hold on I'm coming / You send me / Never gonna give you up / Let's go get stoned / Two steps from the blues / If I were your woman / Ain't that lovin' you baby / You really got a hold on me / Let's go, let's go, let's go / Forever young.

Nov 76. (7") **HOLD ON I'M COMING. / IT'S TIME** [ ] [ ]

Jan 77. (7") **NEVER GONNA GIVE YOU UP. ("BONNIE BRAMLETT & DOBIE GRAY") / YOU SEND ME** [ ] [ ]

Mar 77. (7") **NEVER GONNA GIVE YOU UP ("BONNIE BRAMLETT & DOBIE GRAY. / LET'S GO, LET'S GO, LET'S GO** [-] [ ]

Apr 77. (7") **LET'S GO, LET'S GO, LET'S GO. / THINK** [ ] [-]

1978. (lp)(c) **MEMORIES** [ ] [ ]
– Holdin' on to you / Writing on the wall / Except for real / Lies / I've just seen a face / Can't find my way home / The flame blurts the moth / Can't stay / Memories.

1978. (7") **I'VE JUST SEEN A FACE. / EXCEPT FOR REAL** [-] [ ]

— BONNIE became back-up session singer for many including STEPHEN STILLS.

DE LA SOUL

Formed: Amityville, nr.New York, USA . . . 1987 by JOLICEUR, MERCER & MASON. After two disastrous singles for 'Tommy Boy', they moved to 'Big Life' late '88, where they produced the critically acclaimed cross-Atlantic debut album '3 FEET HIGH AND RISING'. Their well-anticipated but disappointing follow-up in 1991, already predicted their fate 'DE LA SOUL IS DEAD'. • **Style:** Hip-hop rappers & samplers influenced a little by The JUNGLE BROTHERS. Dressed in sportswear, they deposited a near flower-power attitude to lyrics, termed as 'daisy-age'. Sample everything from JAMES BROWN (again!) to STEELY DAN, the latter on debut hit 'ME MYSELF AND I'. • **Trivia:** Produced by PRINCE PAUL.

Recommended: 3 FEET HIGH AND RISING (*9)

TRUGOY THE DOVE (b.DAVID JOLICEUR, 21 Sep'58) – vocals / **POSDNUOS** (b.KELVIN MERCER, 17 Aug'69) – vocals / **PACEMASTER MASE** (b.VINCENT MASON, 24 Mar'70) – discjockey

Tommy Boy Tommy Boy

1988. (7") **PLUG TUNIN'. / FREEDOM OF SPEAK** [-] [ ]

Oct 88. (7") **JENIFA (TAUGHT ME). / ?** [-] [ ]

Big Life Tommy Boy

Mar 89. (7") **ME MYSELF AND I. / BRAIN WASHED FOLLOWER** [22] [34]

(12"+=) – Ain't hip to be labelled a hippie / What's more.
(cd-s+=) – Ain't hip to be labeled a hippie / ('A'version).

Mar 89. (lp)(c)(cd) **3 FEET HIGH AND RISING** [26] [24]
– Intro / The magic number / Change in speak / Cool breeze on the rocks / Can you kep a secret / Jenifa (taught me) / Ghetto thang / Transmitting live from Mars / Eye know / Take it off / A little bit of soap / Tread water / Say no go / Do as De La does / Plug tunin' / De La orgee / Buddy / Description / Me myself and I / This is a recording for living in a fulltime era I can do anything / D.A.I.S.Y. age / Potholes in my lawn.

Jun 89. (7") **SAY NO GO. / THEY DON'T KNOW THAT THE SOUL DON'T GO FOR THAT** [18] [ ]
(12"+=)(cd-s+=) – ('A'versions).

Sep 89. (7")(c-s)(7"pic-d) **EYE KNOW. / THE MACK DADDY ON THE LEFT** [14] [ ]
(12"+=)(cd-s+=) – ('A'versions).

Nov 89. (7")(c-s) **THE MAGIC NUMBER. / BUDDY** [7] [ ]
(12"+=)(cd-s+=) – Ghetto thang.

In Mar'90, DE LA SOUL guested & were credited on QUEEN LATIFAH's Top 20 single 'MAMA GAVE BIRTH TO THE SOUL CHILDREN'.

Apr 91. (7")(c-s) **RING RING RING (HA HA HEY). / PILES AND PILES OF DEMO TAPES BI DA MILES** [10] [ ]
(12") – ('A'extended) / Afro connection of a mis / ('A'sax version).
(cd-s+=) – ('A'party mix).

May 91. (cd)(c)(d-lp) **DE LA SOUL IS DEAD** [7] [26]
– Intro / Oodles of O's / Talking 'bout hey love / Pease porraige / Skit 1 / Johnny's dead aka Vincent Mason (live from the BK lounge) / A roller skating jam named 'Saturday's' (disco fever edit) / WRMS' dedication to the bitty / Bitties in the BK lounge / Skit 2 / Let, let me in / Rap de rap show / Millie pulled a pistol on Santa / Skit 3 / Pass the plugs / Ring ring ring (ha ha hey) / WRMS: Cats in control / Skit 4 / Scwingalokate / Fanatic of the B word / Keepin' the faith / Skit 5.

Jul 91. (7")(c-s) **A ROLLER SKATING JAM CALLED 'SATURDAY'S'. / WHAT YOUR LIFE CAN TRULY BE** [22] [ ]
(12"+=)(cd-s+=) – ('A'disco version) / Who's skatin'.

Nov 91. (7")(c-s) **KEEPIN' THE FAITH (remix). / ('A'instrumental)** [50] [ ]
(12"+=) – Roller skating jam called 'Saturday's' / Ring ring ring (ha ha hey).
(cd-s) – (2 'A'versions) / ('A'instrumental) / ('A' funky mix).

Sep 93. (7")(c-s) **BREAKADAWN. / EN FOCUS (vocal version)** [39] [76]
(12"+=)(cd-s+=) – (2 other 'A' mixes)

Sep 93. (cd)(c)(lp) **BUHLOONE MIND STATE** [37] [40]
– Intro / Eye patch / En focus / Patti Dooke / I be blowin' / Long Island wildin' / Ego trippin' / Paul Revere / Three days later / Area / I am I be / In the woods / Breakadawn / Dave has a problem . . . seriously / Stone age / Lonely days.

— In Mar'94. they teamed up with TEENAGE FANCLUB on the single 'FALLIN''. Taken from the rap-rock album 'Judgement Night' on 'Epic'.

Gabi DELGADO (see under ⇒ D.A.F.)

Sandy DENNY

Born: ALEXANDRA (ELENE MacLEAN) DENNY, 6 Jan'41, London, England. After leaving Kensington Art College, she became folk singer, joining The STRAWBS in 1967 for one co-credited lp. In Summer '68, she moved to FAIRPORT CONVENTION and soon secured herself as one of top female singers of that era. At the end of the 60's, she left FAIRPORT to form own outfit FOTHERINGAY with future husband TREVOR LUCAS. Following their split early in 1971, she went solo, releasing her debut 'THE NORTH STAR GRASSMAN . . . ' to critical acclaim. After a few more solo albums, she returned to FAIRPORT, and was re-actifying a new solo career, when she tragicaly died of a brain haemorrhage on 21 Apr'78. • **Style:** Crystal clear vocalist, who shifted between folk roots and classicly rich melancholy ballads. • **Songwriters:** She penned own material, except covers TOMORROW IS A LONG TIME (Bob Dylan) / LET'S JUMP THE BROOMSTICK (Brenda Lee) / SILVER THREADS AND GOLDEN NEEDLES (Springfields) / CANDLE IN THE WIND (Elton John) and some traditional tunes. FOTHERINGAY covered; TOO MUCH OF NOTHING (Bob Dylan). • **Trivia:** JUDY COLLINS covered her song 'WHO KNOWS WHERE THE TIME GOES' as title track to her 1969 lp.

Recommended: THE BEST OF SANDY DENNY (*7)

SANDY DENNY solo – vocals (with below artists **JOHNNY SILVO & A. CAMPBELL**)

Saga | not issued

1970. (lp) **SANDY DENNY** [ ] [ ]
(recorded '67. (comp. ALEX CAMPBELL & FRIENDS and SANDY & JOHNNY albums '67) *(re-iss.'78 as 'THE ORIGINAL SANDY DENNY' on 'Mooncrest')*

FOTHERINGAY

SANDY DENNY – vocals (ex-FAIRPORT CONVENTION, ex-STRAWBS) plus **JERRY DONAHUE** – guitar, vocals / **TREVOR LUCAS** – guitar, vocals (ex-ECLECTION) / **GERRY CONWAY** – drums (ex-ECLECTION) / **PAT DONALDSON** – bass

Island | A&M

Jun 70. (lp)(c) **FOTHERINGAY** [18] [ ]
– Nothing more / The sea / The ballad of Ned Kelly / Peace in the end / Winter winds / The way I feel / The pond down the stream / Too much of nothing / Banks of the Nile. *(re-iss.+cd.Sep89 on 'Hannibal')*

1970. (7") **PEACE IN THE END. / WINTER WINDS** [ ] [ ]

1970. (7") **THE BALLAD OF NED KELLY. / THE SEA** [-] [ ]

Split early '71. CONWAY, DONALDSON and DONAHUE then backed MICK GREENWOOD with the latter joining LUCAS (now a producer) to FAIRPORTS.

SANDY DENNY

went solo.

Island | A&M

Sep 71. (lp)(c) **THE NORTH STAR GRASSMAN AND THE RAVENS** [31] [ ]
– Late november / Black waterside / The sea captain / Down in the flood / John the gun / Next time around / The optimist / Let's jump the broomstick / Wretched Wilbur / The north star grassman and the ravens / Crazy lady blues. *(re-iss.Nov86) (re-iss.c+cd.Aug91)*

Feb 72. (7") **CRAZY LADY BLUES. / LET'S JUMP THE BROOMSTICK** [-] [ ]

Sep 72. (7"ep) **PASS OF ARMS** [ ] [ ]
– Man of iron / Here in silence. (also includes poem not by her)

Sep 72. (lp)(c) **SANDY** [ ] [ ]
– It'll take a long time / Sweet Rosemary / For nobody to hear / Tomorrow is a long time / Quiet joys of brotherhood / Bushes and friars / The lady / Listen listen / It sets me wild / The music weaver. *(re-iss.c+cd.Aug91)*

Sep 72. (7") **LISTEN LISTEN. / TOMORROW IS A LONG TIME** [ ] [ ]

Nov 73. (7") **WHISPERING GRASS. / FRIENDS** [ ] [ ]

Jun 74. (lp) **LIKE AN OLD FASHIONED WALTZ** [ ] [ ]
– Solo / Whispering grass / Like an old fashioned waltz / Friends / Carnival / Dark of the night / At the end of the day / Until the real thing comes along / No end. *(re-iss.May88 on 'Carthage')*

She had returned to FAIRPORT CONVENTION between Mar74-Jan76. After a years rest she returned in '77. (note in '72 she was also in The BUNCH.)

May 77. (lp)(c) **RENDEZVOUS** [ ] [ ]
– I wish I was a fool for you / Gold dust / Candle in the wind / Take me away / One way donkey ride / I'm a dreamer / All our days / Silver threads and golden needles / No more sad refrains. *(re-iss.Jan87 on 'Hannibal')*

— **SANDY** tragically died on 21 Apr78 of a brain haemorrhage after a fall.

– compilations, others, etc –

1973. Hallmark; (lp) **ALL OUR OWN WORK (by SANDY DENNY & THE STRAWBS)** [ ] [ ]
(re-iss.lp,c,cd.Jul91 on 'Hannibal')

Jan 86. Hannibal; (4xlp-box) **WHO KNOWS WHERE THE TIME GOES?** [ ] [ ]
– (best material from 1967-1977, including live, out-takes, demos, and group work with STRAWBS, FAIRPORT CONVENTION, FOTHERINGAY, & The BUNCH) *(re-iss.May89)*

Aug 87. Island/ US= A&M; (lp)(cd) **THE BEST OF SANDY DENNY** [ ] [ ]
– Listen, listen / One way donkey ride / It'll take a long time / Farewell, farewell / Tam Lin / The pond and the stream / Late November / The sea / Banks of the Nile / Next time around / For shame of doing wrong / Stranger to himself / I'm a dreamer / Who knows where the time goes? *(re-iss.+cd.Sep89 on 'Hannibal')*

Feb 91. Mooncrest; (cd)(c)(lp) **THE ORIGINAL SANDY DENNY** [ ] [-]

Jul 95. Special Delivery; (cd) **THE ATTIC TRACKS 1972-1984 (with TREVOR LUCAS & FRIENDS)** [ ] [-]

DEPECHE MODE

Formed: Basildon, Essex, England . . . 1980 by CLARKE, GORE and FLETCHER. First appeared on Various Artists lp 'Some Bizzare Album' early '81, having already been signed to Daniel Miller's 'Mute' label. Their second single 'NEW LIFE', nearly reached the UK Top 10, and was the first of 24 consecutive Top 30 hits. Became worldwide Euro + US stars from the mid-80's onwards. • **Style:** Socially aware electronic rock-pop outfit, initially influenced by KRAFTWERK. • **Songwriters:** MARTIN GORE wrote music after the departure of YAZOO then ERASURE bound VINCE CLARKE. Covered: ROUTE 66 (hit; Nat King Cole) • **Trivia:** MARTIN GORE's solo album contained 6 cover versions incl. NEVER TURN YOUR BACK ON MOTHER EARTH (Sparks). He later re-done Leonard Cohen's COMING BACK TO YOU.

Recommended: THE SINGLES 1981-1985 (*9) / VIOLATOR (*8) / CONSTRUCTION TIME AGAIN (*7) / BLACK CELEBRATION (*8) / SOME GREAT REWARD (*7) / MUSIC FOR THE MASSES (*7) / SPEAK AND SPELL (*6) / A BROKEN FRAME (*7).

VINCE CLARKE (b. 3 Jul'60) – keyboards, synthesiser / **DAVID GAHAN** (b. 9 May'62) – vocals / **MARTIN GORE** (b.23 Jul'61) – keyboards, synthesiser, vocals / **ANDY FLETCHER** (b. 8 Jul'61) – guitar, synthesiser, drum machine

Mute | Sire

Mar 81. (7") **DREAMING OF ME. / ICE MACHINE** [57] [ ]

Jun 81. (7") **NEW LIFE. / SHOUT** [11] [ ]
(12"+=) – (extended versions).

Sep 81. (7") **JUST CAN'T GET ENOUGH. / ANY SECOND NOW** [8] [-]
(12"+=) – (extended versions).

Oct 81. (lp)(c) **SPEAK & SPELL** [10] [ ]
– New life / Just can't get enough / I sometimes I wish I was dead / Puppets / Boys say go / No disco / What's your name / Photographic / Tora! Tora! Tora! / Big Muff / Any second now. *(re-iss.+cd.Apr88)* (cd+=) – Dreaming of me / New life (extended) / Shout (Rio mix) / Any second now (altered mix).

Nov 81. (7") **JUST CAN'T GET ENOUGH. / TORA! TORA! TORA!** [-] [ ]

— **ALAN WILDER** (b. 1 Jun'59) – electronics (ex-HITMEN) repl. VINCE who formed YAZOO.

Jan 82. (7") **SEE YOU. / NOW, THIS IS FUN** [6] [ ] Aug 82
(12"+=) – (extended versions).

Apr 82. (7") **THE MEANING OF LOVE. / OBERKORN** [12] [ ]
(12"+=) – (extended versions).

Aug 82. (7") **LEAVE IN SILENCE. / EXCERPT FROM MY SECRET GARDEN** [18] [ ]
(12"+=) – ('A' version).

Sep 82. (lp)(c) **A BROKEN FRAME** [8] [ ]

– Leave in silence / My secret garden / Monument / Nothing to fear / See you / Satellite / The meaning of love / A photograph of you / Shouldn't have done that / The sun and the rainfall. *(re-iss.+cd.Jul88)*

Feb 83. (7") **GET THE BALANCE RIGHT. / THE GREAT OUTDOORS** [13] [ ]
(12"+=) – Tora! Tora! Tora! (live).
(12") – ('A'side) (live +=) – My secret garden / See you / Satellite / Tora! Tora! Tora!.

Jul 83. (7") **EVERYTHING COUNTS. / WORK HARD** [6] [ ]
(12"+=) – (extended versions).
(12") – ('A'side) / Boys say go (live) / New life (live) / Nothing to fear (live) / The meaning of love (live).

Aug 83. (lp)(c) **CONSTRUCTION TIME AGAIN** [6] [ ]
– Love in itself / More than a party / Pipeline / Everything counts / Two minute warning / Shame / The landscape is changing / Told you so / And then . . . *(re-iss.+cd.Jul88)*

Sep 83. (7") **LOVE IN ITSELF 2. / FOOLS** [21] [ ]
(12"+=) – (extended versions).
(12") – ('A'side) (live+=) – Just can't get enough / Photograph / A photograph of you / Shout.

Mar 84. (7") **PEOPLE ARE PEOPLE. / IN YOUR MEMORY** [4] [13] May 85
(12"+=) – ('A' On-U-Sound remix).

Jul 84. (lp)(c) **PEOPLE ARE PEOPLE** [-] [71]
– People are people / Everything counts / Get the balance right / Love in itself / Now this is fun / Leave in silence / Told you so / Work hard.

Aug 84. (7") **MASTER AND SERVANT. / SET ME FREE (RENOVATE ME)** [9] [ ] Sep 85
(12"+=) – (extended versions).
(12") – ('A' On-U-Sound mix) – Are people people.

Sep 84. (lp)(c) **SOME GREAT REWARD** [5] [51] Jul 85
– Something to do / Lie to me / People are people / It doesn't matter / Stories of old / Somebody / Master and servant / If you want to / Blasphemous rumours. *(re-iss.+cd.Sep87)*

Nov 84. (7") **BLASPHEMOUS RUMOURS. / SOMEBODY** [16] [ ]
(d7"+=) – Told you so (live) / Everything counts (live).
(12"+=) – Ice machine / Two minute warning.

May 85. (7") **SHAKE THE DISEASE. / FLEXIBLE** [18] [ ]
(12"+=) – (extended versions).
(12"+=) – Master and servant (live) / Something to do (metal mix).

Sep 85. (7") **IT'S CALLED A HEART. / FLY ON THE WINDSCREEN** [18] [ ]
(12"+=) – (extended versions).
(extra-d12"+=) – (versions).

Oct 85. (lp)(c) **THE SINGLES 1981-1985** (compilation) [6] [ ]
– People are people / Master and servant / It's called a heart / Just can't get enough / See you / Shake the disease / Everything counts / New life / Blasphemous rumours / Leave in silence / Get the balance right / Love in itself / Dreaming of me. *(cd-iss.Sep87 with 2 extra tracks, as cass.)* (above US-title 'CATCHING UP WITH DEPECHE MODE')

Feb 86. (7") **STRIPPED. / BUT NOT TONIGHT** [15] [ ]
(12"+=) – Breathing in fumes / Fly on the windscreen / Black day.

Mar 86. (lp)(c)(cd) **BLACK CELEBRATION** [4] [90]
– Black celebration / Fly on the windscreen – final / A question of tlust / Sometimes / It doesn't matter two / A question of time / Stripped / Here is the house / World full of nothing / Dressed in black / New dress. (cd+=) – But not tonight / Breathing in fumes / Black day.

Apr 86. (7") **A QUESTION OF LUST. / CHRISTMAS ISLAND** [28] [ ]
(12"+=) – (versions) / It doesn't matter / People are people (live).
(free c-s. w/7") – ('A' Flood mix) / If you want (live) / Shame (live) / Blasphemous rumours (live).

Aug 86. (7") **A QUESTION OF TIME. / BLACK CELEBRATION** [17] [ ]
(12") – ('A'+'B'diff.mixes) – More than a party (live).
(12"+=) – Stripped (live) / Something to do (live).

Apr 87. (7") **STRANGELOVE. / PIMPF** [16] [76]
(12"+=) – ('A'mix).
(12"++=)(cd-s++=) – Agent orange.

Aug 87. (7") **NEVER LET ME DOWN AGAIN. / TREASURE LITTLE PLEASURE** [22] [63]
(c-s+=) – ('A' aggro mix).
(12"+=)(cd-s+=) – ('A'+'B'mixes) / To have and to hold (Spanish taster).

Sep 87. (lp)(d-c)(cd)(clear-lp) **MUSIC FOR THE MASSES** [10] [35]
– Never let me down again / The things you said / Strangelove / Sacred / Little 15 / Behind the wheel / I want you now / To have to hold / Nothing / Pimpf. *(cd+=)* – Agent orange / Never let me down again (aggro mix) / To have and to hold (Spanish) / Pleasure the treasure (glitter mix). *(d-c+=)* – BLACK CELEBRATION (album)

Dec 87. (7") **BEHIND THE WHEEL. / ROUTE 66** [21] [61]
(12") – ('A'+'B' versions).
(cd-s++=) – ('A'-lp version).

Jan 88. (7") **BEHIND THE WHEEL. / (part 2)** [-] [ ]
Mar 88. (7") **STRANGELOVE. / NOTHING** [-] [ ]
May 88. (7"import) **LITTLE 15. / ?** [60] [ ]
Feb 89. (7") **EVERYTHING COUNTS (live). / NOTHING (live)** [22] [ ]
(12"+=) – Sacred (live) / A question of lust (live).
(10") – ('A' absolute mix) / ('B' US mix)/ ('A'-1983 mix)
(12")(cd-s) – ('A'+'B' diff.mixes) – Strangelove (remix).

Mar 89. (d-lp)(d-c)(d-cd) **101 (live)** [5] [45]
– Pimpf / Behind the wheel / Strangelove / Sacred * / Something to do / Blasphemous rumours / Stripped / Somebody / Things you said / Black generation / Shake the disease / Nothing * / Pleasure little treasure / People are people / A question of time / Never let me down again / A question of lust * / Master and servant / Just can't get enough / Everything counts *. *(c+=*)(cd+=*)*

Aug 89. (7")(US-c-s) **PERSONAL JESUS. / DANGEROUS** [13] [28] Dec 89
(12"+=)(c-s+=)(3"cd-s+=) – ('A'acoustic mix).

Feb 90. (7") **NOTHING. / ('A' instrumental)** [-] [ ]
Feb 90. (7")(c-s) **ENJOY THE SILENCE. / MEMPHISTO** [6] [8] Apr 90
(12"+=)(cd-s+=) – ('A'bassline) ('A'harmonium) ('A'Rikki Tavi) mixes.

Mar 90. (cd)(c)(lp) **VIOLATOR** [2] [7]
– World in my eyes / Sweetest perfection / Personal Jesus / Halo / Waiting for the night / Enjoy the silence / Policy of truth / Blue dress / Clean.

May 90. (7")(c-s) **POLICY OF TRUTH. / KALEID (remix)** [16] [15] Aug 90
(12"+=)(cd-s+=) – ('A'-Pavlov's dub mix).

Sep 90. (7")(12")(cd-s) **WORLD IN MY EYES. / HAPPIEST GIRL / SEA OF SIN** [17] [52] Nov 90
(12") – (first 2 tracks) / ('A'remix).
(c-s+=)(cd-s+=) – Meaning of love / Somebody.

— In Nov 91.(re-iss.all singles on cd-s.3 ltd.box sets of 6)

Feb 93. (7")(c-s) **I FEEL YOU. / ONE CARESS** [8] [37]
(12"+=)(cd-s+=) – ('A'throb mix) / ('A'Babylon mix).
(12")(cd-s) – ('A'side) / ('A'swamp mix) / ('A'-Renegade Soundwave mix) / ('A'-Helmut mix).

Mar 93. (cd)(c)(lp) **SONGS OF FAITH AND DEVOTION** [1] [1]
– I feel you / Walking in my shoes / Condemnation / Mercy in you / Judas / In your room / Get right with me / Rush / One caress / Higher love.

May 93. (c-s)(cd-s) **WALKING IN MY SHOES. / MY JOY** [14] [69]
Sep 93. (c-ep)(12"ep) **CONDEMNATION. / PERSONAL JESUS (live) / ENJOY THE SILENCE (live) / HALO (live)** [9] [ ]
(cd-s) – ('A'Paris mix) / Death's door (jazz mix) / Rush (spiritual mix) / Rush (amylnitrate mix).
(12") – ('A'side) / Rush.

Dec 93. (cd)(c)(lp) **SONGS OF FAITH AND DEVOTION LIVE . . . (live)** [ ] [ ]
– (see last album)

Jan 94. (c-s)(cd-s) **IN YOUR ROOM / ('A'mixes) / HIGHER LOVE (adrenaline mix)** [8] [ ]
(cd-s)(12") – ('A'side) / ('A'mixes) / Never let me down again / Death's door.
(cd-s)(12") – ('A'side) / Policy of truth / World in my eyes / Fly on the windscreen.

— ANDREW FLETCHER departed to take over groups' business affairs.

— On the 17th August '95, GAHAN was thought by the music press, to have attempted suicide by cutting at his wrists after his wife left him. His record company however said this had been an accident and was over-hyped by the media.

MARTIN L. GORE

Mute Sire

Jun 89. (m-lp)(c)(cd) **COUNTERFEIT** [51] [ ]
– Smile in the crowd / Never turn your back on Mother Earth / Gone / Motherless child / Compulsion / In a manner of speaking.

DEREK & THE DOMINOES (see under ⇒ CLAPTON, Eric)

Rick DERRINGER

Born: RICHARD ZEHRINGER, 5 Aug'47, Colina, Ohio, USA. With brother RANDY, he formed Indiana based teenage band The McCOYS in 1962. After many gigs, supporting the likes of The FOUR SEASONS, The BEACH BOYS and CHUCK BERRY, they were spotted by Bert Berns, who wrote their chart-topper 'HANG ON SLOPPY' in 1965. After more mid-60's success, and an early 70's back-up career with JOHNNY & EDGAR WINTER, he went solo as RICK DERRINGER. His initial releases in '74 hit the charts, but soon he faded into obscurity, only re-appearing commercially as live guitarist with CYNDI LAUPER!. • **Style:** The McCOYS shifted from bubblegum pop to flower-power pop-rock in 1968. In the 70's, his music and his lead guitar progressed with the advent of new heavy metal sound. • **Songwriters:** Writes own material except when with The McCOYS who covered loads incl. RUNAWAY (Del Shannon) / FEVER (Little Willie John) / COME ON LET'S GO (Richie Valens) / STUBBORN KIND OF FELLOW (Marvin Gaye) / ALL I REALLY WANT TO DO (Bob Dylan) / HIGH HEEL SNEAKERS (Tommy Tucker) / PAPA'S GOT A BRAND NEW BAG (James Brown). DERRINGER solo:- MY MY HEY HEY . . . (Neil Young) / etc. • **Trivia:** He also produced many albums, including EDGAR WINTER's chart topping album 'They Only Come Out At Night'.

Recommended: LIVE (*5)

RICK Z COMBO

RICK ZEHRINGER (aka DERRINGER) – vocals, lead guitar / **RANDY ZEHRINGER** – drums / **RONNIE BRANDON** – keyboards / **DENNIS KELLY** – bass

not issued not known

1965. (7") **YOU KNOW THAT I LOVE YOU. / ?** [-] [ ]

McCOYS

BOBBY PETERSON – organ repl. BRANDON / **RANDY JO HOBBS** – bass repl. KELLY

Immediate Bang

Aug 65. (7") **HANG ON SLOOPY. / I CAN'T EXPLAIN IT** [5] [1]
Nov 65. (7") **FEVER. / SORROW** [44] [7]
Dec 65. (lp) **HANG ON SLOOPY** [ ] [44] Nov 65
– Hang on Sloopy / Fever / If you tell a lie / I don't mind / Stubborn kind of fellow / I can't help fallin' in love / All I really want to do / Papa's got a brand new bag / I can't explain it / High heel sneakers / Stormy Monday blues. *(re-iss.Mar89 ' . . . PLUS' cd extra tracks on 'See For Miles')*

Mar 66. (7") **UP AND DOWN. / IF YOU TELL A LIE** [ ] [46]
May 66. (7") **COME ON LET'S GO. / LITTLE PEOPLE** [-] [22]
Jun 66. (7") **COME ON LET'S GO. / RUNAWAY** [ ] [-]
Aug 66. (7") **(YOU MAKE ME FEEL) SO GOOD. / RUNAWAY** [-] [53]
Aug 66. (7") **(YOU MAKE ME FEEL) SO GOOD. / EVERYDAY I HAVE TO CRY** [ ] [-]
Aug 66. (lp) **(YOU MAKE ME FEEL) SO GOOD** [-] [ ]
– Say those magic words / Everyday I have to cry / (You make me feel) So good / The dynamite / Drive my car / Mr.Summer / Stagger Lee / Sweets for my sweet /

Smokey Joe's cafe / Little people / Runaway / C'mon let's go.

Oct 66. (7") **DON'T WORRY MOTHER, YOUR SON'S HEART IS PURE. / KO-KO** [ ] [67]

Dec 66. (7") **I GOT TO GO BACK (AND WATCH THAT LITTLE GIRL DANCE). / DYNAMITE** [ ] [69]

Apr 67. (7") **BEAT THE CLOCK. / JUST LIKE YOU DO TO ME** [-] [92]

London Bang

Sep 67. (7") **SAY THOSE MAGIC WORDS. / I WONDER IF SHE REMEMBERS ME** [ ] [ ]

—— **RANDY BRECKER** – trumpet / **JERRY WEISS** – trumpet / **FRED LIPSIUS** – saxophone / **DICK HALLIGAN** – trombone repl. PETERSON

Mercury Mercury

1968. (lp) **HUMAN BALL** [ ] [ ]
– Human ball blues / Only human / Epilogue / All over you / Daybreak / It really doesn't matter / Love don't stop / Clergy lies / Stormy Monday blues.

Oct 68. (7") **JESSE BRADY. / RESURRECTION** [ ] [98]

Oct 68. (lp) **INFINITE McCOYS** [ ] [ ]
– Faces / Jesse Brady / Resurrection / Rosa Rodriguez / Hell / Genesis through a window / Song for Janie / He likes it / Open your eyes / Eldorado / Melodrama / Union City waltz.

—— ZEHRINGER becomes DERRINGER and with others join JOHHNY WINTER group. DERRINGER also became producer for said artist and his brother EDGAR. His session work included STEELY DAN, TODD RUNDGREN and RICHIE HAVENS.

– compilations, others, etc. –

Immediate not issued

1966. (7"ep) **McCOYS** [ ] [-]

1966. (7"ep) **McCOYS 2** [ ] [-]

Immediate not issued

Feb 69. (7") **HANG ON SLOOPY. / THIS IS WHERE I CAME IN** [ ] [-]

London Mercury

1974. (d-lp) **OUTSIDE STUFF** [-] [-]

Feb 75. (7") **HANG ON SLOOPY. / FEVER** [ ] [-]
(re-iss. Oct 76 on 'Bang') (re-iss.Sep85 on 'Old Gold')

RICK DERRINGER

(solo) with **BOBBY CALDWELL** – drums / **EDGAR WINTER** – keys / **KENNY PASSARELLI** – bass / plus other guests.

Epic Blue Sky

Feb 74. (lp)(c) **ALL AMERICAN BOY** [ ] [25] Nov 73
– Rock and roll hoochie koo / Joy ride / Teenage queen / Cheap tequila / Hold / Uncomplicated / The airport giveth (the airport taketh away) / Teenage love affair / It's raining / Slide on over Slinky / Time warp / Jump, jump, jump.

Feb 74. (7") **TEENAGE LOVE AFFAIR. / JOY RIDE** [ ] [-]

Apr 74. (7") **ROCK AND ROLL HOOCHIE KOO. / TIME WARP** [ ] [23] Jan 74

Apr 74. (7") **TEENAGE LOVE AFFAIR. / SLIDE ON OVER SLINKY** [-] [80]

Jul 74. (7") **CHEAP TEQUILA. / IT'S RAINING** [-] [ ]

—— **JOHNNY SIEGLER** – bass repl. KENNY

Blue Sky Blue Sky

Apr 75. (7") **HANG ON SLOOPY. / SKYSCRAPER BLUES** [ ] [94]

Apr 75. (lp)(c) **SPRING FEVER** [ ] [ ]
– Gimme more / Tomorrow / Don't ever say goodbye / Still alive and well / Rock / Hang on Sloopy / Roll with me / Walkin' the dog / He needs some answers / Skyscraper blues.

Aug 75. (7") **DON'T EVER SAY GOODBYE. / GIMME MORE** [ ] [ ]

—— Dec'75 he is credited on lp **THE EDGAR WINTER GROUP WITH RICK DERRINGER**

DERRINGER

formed by **RICK** plus **DANNY JOHNSON** – guitar / **KENNY AARONSON** – bass / **VINNIE APPICE** – drums

Aug 76. (lp)(c) **DERRINGER** [ ] [ ] Jul 76
– Let me in / You can have it / Loosen up your grip / Envy / Comes a woman / Sailor / Beyond the universe / Goodbye again *(cd-iss.Jul93 on 'Sony Europe')*

Oct 76. (7") **LET ME IN. / YOU CAN HAVE ME** [ ] [86] Aug 76

Mar 77. (lp)(c) **SWEET EVIL** [ ] [ ] Feb 77
– Don't stop loving me / Sittin' by the pool / Keep on makin' love / One-eyed Jack / Let's make it / Sweet evil / Drivin' sideways / I didn't ask to be born.

Mar 77. (7") **DON'T STOP LOVING ME. / LET'S MAKE IT** [-] [ ]

Aug 77. (lp)(c) **DERRINGER LIVE (live)** [ ] [ ] Jul 77
– Let me in / Teenage love affair / Sailor / Beyond the universe / Sittin' by the fool / Uncomplicated / Still alive and well / Rock and roll hoochie koo.

RICK DERRINGER

(solo) retained AARONSON and brought in newcomers / **MARK CUNNINGHAM** – guitar to repl. JOHNSON who later formed AXIS / **MYRON GROOMBACHER** – drums repl. APPICE who also formed AXIS. (with KENNY also)

Sep 78. (7") **LAWYERS, GUNS AND MONEY. / SLEEPLESS** [-] [ ]

Sep 78. (lp)(c) **IF I WEREN'T SO ROMANTIC, I'D SHOOT YOU** [ ] [ ]
– It ain't funny / Midnight road / If I weren't so romantic, I'd shoot you / EZ action / Lawyers, Guns and money / Power of love / Sleepless / Tonight / Rocka rolla / Attitude / Monomania.

Nov 78. (7") **MIDNIGHT ROAD. / ROCKA ROLLA** [-] [ ]

—— session players from **TODD RUNDGREN / UTOPIA** repl. CUNNINGHAM

Oct 79. (lp)(c) **GUITARS & WOMEN** [ ] [ ]
– Something warm / Guitars & women / Everything / Man in the middle / It must be love / Desires of the heart / Timeless / Hopeless romantic / Need a little girl (just like you) / Don't ever say goodbye.

Oct 79. (7") **SOMETHING WARM. / NEED A LITTLE GIRL (JUST LIKE YOU)** [-] [ ]

Apr 80. (7") **TIMELESS. / DON'T EVER SAY GOODBYE** [ ] [ ]

—— **RICK** with **BENJY KING** – keys / **DON KISSELBACH** – bass / **JIMMY WILCOX** – drums

Dec 80. (lp)(c) **FACE TO FACE** [ ] [ ]
– Runaway / You'll get yours / Big city loneliness / Burn the midnight oil / Let the music play / Jump jump / I want a lover / My my, hey hey (out of the blue)

Dec 80. (7") **RUNAWAY. / TEENAGE LOVE AFFAIR** [-] [ ]

Feb 81. (7") **LET THE MUSIC PLAY. / YOU'LL GET YOURS** [-] [ ]

—— RICK returned to production work in the early 80's.

Polydor Passport

1983. (lp) **GOOD DIRTY FUN** [ ] [ ]
– Shake me / Party at the hotel / White heat / Just wanna dance / Doo wah diddy / When love attacks / I play guitar / Take it like a man / Numb / Hardball. *(cd-iss.1988)*

DNA

were formed by **RICK DERRINGER & CARMINE APPICE** – drums (ex-VANILLA FUDGE, ex-CACTUS, etc) **DUANE HITCHINGS** – keyboards / **JIMMY JOHNSON** – bass

Polydor Passport

Dec 83. (lp)(c) **PARTY TESTED** [ ] [ ]
– Doctors of the universe / Intellectual freedom for the masses / Rock'n'roll (part 2) / The song that wrote itself / Party tested / The recipe for life / What about.

Jan 84. (7") **DOCTORS OF THE UNIVERSE. / RECIPE OF LIFE** [ ] [ ]
(12"+=) – Intellectual freedom for the masses.

—— RICK became producer for WEIRD AL JANKOVIC (Eat It) and BONNIE TYLER. He also became live guitarist for CYNDI LAUPER in 1986.

Rick DERRINGER

Road-runner Road-runner

Aug 93. (cd)(c) **BACK TO THE BLUES** [ ] [ ]
– Trouble in Paradise / Blue suede shoes / Blues all night long / Meantown blues / Sorry for your heartache / Sink or swim / Diamond / Crybaby / Unsolved mystery / Blue velvet / Time to go.

Road-runner Road-runner

Oct 94. (cd) **ELECTRA BLUES** [ ] [ ]

DESERT ROSE BAND (see under ⇒ BYRDS)

DETROIT (see under ⇒ RYDER, Mitch)

Marcella DETROIT (see under ⇒ SHAKESPEAR'S SISTER)

dEUS

Formed: Antwerp, Belguim ... early 1994 by (see below). Signed to 'Island' that year and quickly found an audience with British public after an appearance at Glastonbury Festival 24 June. • **Style:** Heavy art-rock, fusing BEEFHEART or WAITS with early BIG BLACK, BLACK FLAG or even the lighter VIOLENT FEMMES. • **Songwriters:** Group (CARLENS + BARMAN with SERGEY) or (TROUVE + JANZOONS with VERMEERSCH + VERVLOESEM) except a sample of FRANK ZAPPA on their 1994 album.

Recommended: WORST CASE SCENARIO (*8)

TOM BARMAN – vocals / **KLAUS JANZOONS** – / **RUDY TROUVE** – / **JULLE DE BORGHER** – / **STEF CARLENS** –

Island Island

Jul 94. (7") **SUDS AND SODA. / SECRET HELL** [ ] [ ]
(12"+=)(cd-s+=) – Texan coffee / It. furniture in the Far East.

Sep 94. (7") **VIA. / VIOLINS / HAPPY ENDINGS** [ ] [ ]
(12"+=)(cd-s+=) – Great American nude (strip mix) / Niche.

Oct 94. (cd)(c)(lp) **WORST CASE SCENARIO** [ ] [ ]
– Intro / Suds and soda / W.C.S. / Jigsaw you / Morticiahair / Via / Right as rain / Mute / Let's get lost / Hotel lounge (be the death of me) / Shake you up / Great American nude / Secret hell / Dive bomb djingle.

Jan 95. (7")(c-s) **HOTELLOUNGE (BE THE DEATH OF ME). / JIGAW YOU (live)** [55] [ ]
(cd-s+=) – Whose Vegas (is it anyway).

DEUTSCHE AMERIKANISCHE FREUNDSCHAFT (see under ⇒ D.A.F.)

DEVIANTS (see under ⇒ PINK FAIRIES)

Willy DeVILLE (see under ⇒ MINK DeVILLE)

DEVO

Formed: Akron, Ohio, USA ... Sep'76 by 2 sets of brothers MOTHERSBAUGH and CASALE. From the early 70''s, they had been known as The DE-EVOLUTION BAND. Released 2 singles on own indie label 'Booji Boy', which became licensed to 'Stiff' UK in 1977. The following year, they signed to 'Warners'US & 'Virgin'UK, where they had Top 20 debut album inspiringly titled 'Q: ARE WE NOT MEN? A: WE ARE DEVO!'. Broke the US pop charts in 1980, when 'WHIP IT' made No.14. • **Style:** Comic strip, quirky new wave futurists, who experimented with electronic melody and intelligent pop-rock. Extreme dress sense brought a little light humour back into late 70's pop, and contrasted with the more serious German outfit KRAFTWERK. • **Songwriters:** JERRY & MARK wrote most of material, except the second best ever version of SATISFACTION (Rolling Stones) / ARE U EXPERIENCED (Jimi Hendrix) / WORKING IN A COALMINE (Lee Dorsey). • **Trivia:** In 1982, DEVO had contributed services to choreographer TONI BASIL on her debut solo album 'WORD OF MOUTH'. In the late 70's, MARK had appeared on HUGH CORNWALL (of The STRANGLERS) and ROBERT WILLIAMS collaboration 'Nosferatu'.

Recommended: HOT POTATOES: THE BEST OF DEVO (*8)

BOB MOTHERSBAUGH – vocals, guitar / **MARK MOTHERSBAUGH** – keyboards, synthesisers / **BOB CASALE** – guitar / **JERRY CASALE** – bass, vocals / **ALAN MYERS** – drums repl. JIM MOTHERSBAUGH

Stiff / Booji Boy

Feb 78. (7") **MONGOLOID. / JOCKO HOMO** [62] [ ] Dec 76
Apr 78. (7")(12") **(I CAN'T GET ME NO) SATISFACTION. / SLOPPY (I SAW MY BABY GETTING)** [41] [ ] Jul 77

Stiff / not issued

Jul 78. (7"clear)(7"lemon) **BE STIFF. / SOCIAL FOOLS** [71] [ ]

Virgin / Warners

Aug 78. (7")(12")(7"grey) **COME BACK JONEE. / SOCIAL FOOLS** [60] [-]
Sep 78. (lp)(c) **Q: ARE WE NOT MEN? A: WE ARE DEVO!** [12] [78]
– Uncontrollable urge / (I can't get no) Satisfaction / Praying hands / Space junk / Mongoloid / Jocko homo / Too much paranoias / Gut feeling – (slap your mammy) / Come back Jonee / Sloppy (I saw my baby getting) / Shrivel-up. *(re-iss.Mar84) (also on pic-lp, w/free flexi-7")*
Sep 78. (7") **(I CAN'T GET NO) SATISFACTION. / UNCONTROLLABLE URGE** [-] [ ]
Nov 78. (7") **COME BACK JONEE. / PRAYING HANDS** [-] [ ]
Jun 79. (7") **THE DAY ME BABY GAVE ME A SURPRIZE. / PENETRATION IN THE CENTREFOLD** [ ] [ ]
Jun 79. (lp)(c) **DUTY NOW FOR THE FUTURE** [49] [73]
– Devo corporate anthem / Clockout / Timing X / Wiggly world / Blockhead / Strange pursuit / S.I.B. (Swelling Itching Brain) / Triumph of the will / The day my baby gave me a surprize / Pink pussycat / Secret agent man / Smart patrol – Mr. DNA / Red eye. *(re-iss.Mar84)*
Jul 79. (7") **SECRET AGENT MAN. / RED EYE** [-] [ ]
Aug 79. (7") **SECRET AGENT MAN. / 500 BAWLS** [ ] [-]
May 80. (7") **GIRL U WANT. / MR. B'S BALLROOM** [-] [ ]
May 80. (7") **GIRL U WANT. / TURN AROUND** [ ] [-]
May 80. (lp)(c) **FREEDOM OF CHOICE** [47] [22]
– Girl u want / It's not right / Whip it / Snowball / Ton o' luv / Freedom of choice / Gates of steel / Cold war / Don't you know / That's Pep! / Mr.B's ballroom / Planet Earth. *(re-iss.Mar84)*
Nov 80. (7") **WHIP IT. / TURN AROUND** [51] [14]
Feb 81. (7") **FREEDOM OF CHOICE. / SNOWBALL** [-] [ ]
May 81. (7") **GATES OF STEEL. / BE STIFF (live)** [-] [ ]
May 81. (m-lp)(c) **DEVO LIVE (live)** [ ] [49] Apr 81
– Freedom of choice (theme song) / Whip it / Girl u want / Gates of steel / Be stiff / Planet Earth.
Aug 81. (7") **THROUGH BEING COOL. / GOING UNDER** [-] [ ]
Aug 81. (7") **THROUGH BEING COOL. / RACE OF DOOM** [ ] [-]
Aug 81. (lp)(c) **NEW TRADITIONALISTS** [50] [24]
– Through being cool / Jerkin' back 'n' forth / Pity you / Soft things / Going under / Race of doom / Love without anger / The super thing / Beautiful world / Enough said. *(re-iss.Aug88)*
Oct 81. (7") **WORKING IN A COALMINE. / PLANET EARTH** [-] [ ]
Oct 81. (7") **WORKING IN A COALMINE. / ENOUGH SAID** [ ] [-]
(above iss. US on 'Asylum')
Nov 81. (7") **BEAUTIFUL WORLD. / ENOUGH SAID** [-] [ ]
Jan 82. (7") **BEAUTIFUL WORLD. / THE SUPER THING** [ ] [-]
Mar 82. (7") **JERKIN' BACK 'N' FORTH. / MECHA MANIA BOY** [-] [ ]
Oct 82. (7")(US-12") **PEEK-A-BOO. / FIND OUT** [ ] [ ]
Oct 82. (lp)(c) **OH NO! IT'S DEVO!** [ ] [47]
– Time out for fun / Peek-a-boo / Out of synch / Explosions / That's good / Patterns / Big mess / Speed racer / What I must do / I desire / Deep sleep. *(re-iss.Aug88)*
Jan 83. (7") **THAT'S GOOD. / WHAT MUST I DO** [-] [ ]

M.C.A. / Warners

Jun 83. (7")(12") **THEME FROM 'DOCTOR DETROIT'. / KING OF SOUL** [ ] [59]

Warners / Warners

Oct 84. (7") **ARE YOU EXPERIENCED?. / GROWING PAINS** [-] [ ]
Oct 84. (lp)(c) **SHOUT!** [ ] [83]
– Shout / The satisfied mind / Don't rescue me / The 4th dimension / C'mon / Here to go / Jurisdiction of love / Puppet boy / Please please / Are you experienced?.
Mar 85. (7") **SHOUT. / C'MON** [ ] [ ]
(d7"+=) – Mongloid / Jocko homo.

— **DAVID KENDRICK** – drums, repl. MYERS.

Enigma / Enigma

Jul 88. (lp)(c)(cd) **TOTAL DEVO** [ ] [ ] Jun 88
– Baby doll / Disco dancer / Some things never change / Plain truth / Happy guy / Don't be cruel / I'd cry if you died / Agitated / Man turned inside out / Blow up. *(re-iss.cd Mar95 on 'Restless')*
Oct 90. (7") **POST-POST MODERN MAN. / WHIP IT (live)** [ ] [ ]
(12"+=) – ('A'-ultra post mix).
(cd-s++=) – Baby doll (mix).
Oct 90. (cd)(c)(lp) **SMOOTH NOODLE MAPS** [ ] [ ]
– Stuck in a loop / Post-post modern man / When we do it / Spin the wheel / Morning dew / A chance is gonna cum / The big picture / Pink jazz trancers / Devo has feelings too / Jimmy / Danghaus. *(re-iss.cd Mar95 on 'Restless')*

– compilations etc. –

Jan 79. Stiff; (m-lp) **BE STIFF** (1st 3 singles 'A'&'B') [ ] [-]
May 83. Virgin; (12"ep) **COME BACK JONEE. / WHIP IT / + 2** [ ] [-]
Aug 87. Warners; (cd) **E-Z LISTENING DISC** [-] [ ]
Jul 89. Virgin; (d-lp)(cd) **NOW IT CAN BE TOLD** [ ] [-]
(re-iss.cd Mar95 on 'Restless')
Jun 93. Virgin; (cd) **Q: ARE WE NOT MEN? A: WE ARE DEVO / DEVO LIVE** [ ] [ ]
Jun 93. Virgin; (cd) **DUTY NOW FOR THE FUTURE / NEW TRADITIONALISTS** [ ] [ ]
Jun 93. Virgin; (cd) **OH NO! IT'S DEVO / FREEDOM OF CHOICE** [ ] [ ]
Sep 93. Virgin; (cd)(c) **HOT POTATOES: THE BEST OF DEVO** [ ] [ ]
– Jocko homo / Mongoloid / Satisfaction (I can't get me no) / Whip it / Girl u want / Freedom of choice / Peek-a-boo / Thru being cool / That's good / Working in a coalmine / Devo corporate anthem / Be stiff / Gates of steel / Come back Jonee / Secret agent man / The day my baby gave me a surprise / Beautiful world / Big mess / Whip it (HMS & M remix).
Oct 90. Fan Club /US= Rykodisc; (cd)(lp) **HARD CORE DEVO** [ ] [-]
(demos 74-77)
(re-iss.c Mar94 on 'Rykodisc')
Dec 91. Rykodisc; (cd) **HARDCORE DEVO VOLUME 2: 1974-1977**
(re-iss.c Mar94 on 'Rykodisc')
Sep 92. Rykodisc; (cd) **LIVE: THE MONGOLOID YEARS (live)** [ ] [ ]
Oct 94. Virgin; (3xcd-box) **THE COMPACT COLLECTION** [ ] [ ]

Howard DEVOTO (see under ⇒ MAGAZINE)

DEXY'S MIDNIGHT RUNNERS

Formed: Birmingham, England ... Jul'78 by ex-KILLJOYS members KEVIN ROWLAND and AL ARCHER. Named themselves after a frequently used pep-pill Dexerine. In 1979, new (ex-CLASH) manager Bernie Rhodes, obtained deal with 'Parlophone' records, and they scraped into the Top 40 with 'DANCE STANCE'. The following year, they became the darlings of the music press, after 'GENO' hit top spot. • **Style:** Initial image inspired from 'Mean Streets' film (i.e. New York dockers). Influenced by mid-60's brassy soul scene & GENO WASHINGTON whom they attributed on said No.1. In 1982, they took diverse new direction in acquiring scruffy dungareed attire,to accompany gypsy-folk pop music. • **Songwriters:** All penned by ROWLAND, except BURNING DOWN THE WALLS OF HEARTACHE (Johnny Johnson & The Bandwagon) / ONE WAY LOVE (Russell-Meade) / SOUL FINGER (?) / JACKIE WILSON SAID (Van Morrison). • **Trivia:** In 1986, 'BECAUSE OF YOU', was used on TV sit-com 'Brush Strokes'.

Recommended: THE VERY BEST OF DEXY'S MIDNIGHT RUNNERS (*8)

KEVIN ROWLAND – vocals, guitar (b.17 Aug'53, Wolverhampton, England) (ex-KILLJOYS, as **KEVIN ROLAND) / AL ARCHER** – guitar, vocals (ex-KILLJOYS) / **PETE SAUNDERS** – keyboards / **PETE WILLIAMS** – bass, vocals / **JIMMY PATTERSON** – trombone / **J.B. BLYTE** – tenor, saxophone / **STEVE 'BABYFACE' SPOONER** – alto sax / **ANDY 'STOKER' GROWCOTT** – drums repl. BOBBY JUNIOR

Parlophone / not issued

Nov 79. (7") **DANCE STANCE. / I'M JUST LOOKING** [40] [-]

— **MICK TALBOT** – keyboards (ex-MERTON PARKAS) repl. SAUNDERS.

Mar 80. (7") **GENO. / BREAKING DOWN THE WALLS OF HEARTACHE** [1] [-]
Jun 80. (7") **THERE THERE MY DEAR. / THE HORSE** [7] [-]
Jul 80. (lp)(c) **SEARCHING FOR THE YOUNG SOUL REBELS** [6] [-]
– Burn it down / Tell me when my light turns green / The teams that meet in caffs / I'm just looking / Geno / Seven days too long / I couldn't help it if I tried / Thankfully not living in Yorkshire, it doesn't apply / Keep it / Love (pt.1) / There, there my dear. *(re-iss.1982 on 'Fame')*
Nov 80. (7") **KEEP IT. / ONE WAY LOVE** [ ] [-]
Mar 81. (7") **PLAN B. / SOUL FINGER** [58] [-]

— **ROWLAND and PATTERSON** recruited new guys **BILLY ADAMS** – guitar / **MICKEY BILLINGHAM** – keyboards / **PAUL SPEARE** – tenor sax / **BRIAN MAURICE** – alto sax / **SEB SHELTON** – drums (ex-SECRET AFFAIR) / **STEVE WYNNE** – bass (replaced ARCHER, GROWCOTT and TALBOT who formed BUREAU)

Mercury / Mercury

Jun 81. (7") **SHOW ME. / SOON** [16] [ ]
Nov 81. (7") **LIARS A TO E. / . . . AND YES, WE MUST REMAIN THE WILDHEARTED OUTSIDERS** [ ] [ ]

— Kept **ADAMS, SHELTON, PATTERSON** and **GIORGIO KILKENNY** – bass repl. WYNNE.

DEXY'S MIDNIGHT RUNNERS & EMERALD EXPRESS

added **HELEN O'HARA** – violin, vocals repl. BILLINGHAM / **STEVE BRENNAN** – violin / **ROGER MacDUFF** – violin

Mar 82. (7") **THE CELTIC SOUL BROTHERS. / LOVE (part.2)** [45] [ ]
Jun 82. (7") **COME ON EILEEN. / DUBIOUS** [1] [1] Jan 83
(12"+=) – Liars A to E (remix).
Jul 82. (lp)(c) **TOO-RYE-AY** [2] [14] Feb 83
– The Celtic soul brothers / Let's make this precious / All in all / Jackie Wilson said (I'm in Heaven when you smile) / Old / Plan B – I'll show you / Liars A to E / Until I believe in my soul / Come on Eileen. *(cd-iss.Jan83)*

KEVIN ROWLAND & DEXY'S MIDNIGHT RUNNERS

PATTERSON left Jun82, MAURICE & SPEARE left Jul82.

Sep 82. (7") **JACKIE WILSON SAID. / LET'S MAKE THIS PRECIOUS** [5] [ ]
(12"+=) – TSOP.
Nov 82. (7") **LET'S GET THIS STRAIGHT FROM THE START. / OLD (live)** [17] [ ]

(12"+=) – Respect (live).
Mar 83. (7") **THE CELTIC SOUL BROTHERS. / REMINISCE (pt.1)** [20] [86]
(12"+=) – Show me.

DEXY'S MIDNIGHT RUNNERS

again. Line-up **ROWLAND, O'HARA & ADAMS / JIMMY PATTERSON** – trombone (returned) + new part-time sessioners / **NICKY GATFIELD** – saxophone / **JULIAN LITTMAN** – mandolin / **JOHN EDWARDS** – bass / **TOMMY EVANS** – steel guitar / **TIM DANCY** – drums / **ROBERT NOBLE** – keyboards, synthe / and special guest star **VINCENT CRANE** – piano (ex-ATOMIC ROOSTER)

Sep 85. (lp)(c)(cd) **DON'T STAND ME DOWN** [22] [ ]
– The occasional flicker / This is what she's like / Knowledge of beauty / One of those things / Reminisce (pt.2) / Listen to this / The waltz. *(cd+=)* – This is what's she's like (instrumental).
Nov 85. (7") **THIS IS WHAT SHE'S LIKE. / ('A'instrumental)** [ ] [ ]
(12"+=) – Reminisce (part 1).
(10") – ('A'side) / Marguerita time.
(d12"+=) – ('A'+'B' versions).
Oct 86. (7") **BECAUSE OF YOU. / KATHLEEN MAVOUREEN** [13] [ ]
(12"+=) – Sometimes theme.

– compilations, others, etc. –

Feb 83. E.M.I.; (7") **DANCE STANCE. / THERE THERE MY DEAR** [ ] [ ]
Mar 83. E.M.I.; (lp)(c) **GENO** [79] [ ]
(re-iss.Oct87, cd-iss.Jun88 on 'Fame')
Mar 90. Old Gold; (7") **COME ON EILEEN. / JACKIE WILSON SAID** [ ] [-]
Sep 92. Old Gold; (cd-s) **GENO / THERE THERE MY DEAR / DANCE STANCE** [ ] [-]
Jun 91. Mercury; (cd)(c)(lp) **THE VERY BEST OF DEXY'S MIDNIGHT RUNNERS** [12] [ ]
– Come on Eileen / Jackie Wilson said (i'm in heaven when you smile) / Let's get this straight (from the start) / Because of you / Show me / The celtic soul brothers (more, please, thank you) / Liars a to e / One way love / Old / Geno / There there my dear / Breakin' down the walls of heartache / Dance stance / Plan b / Keep it / I'm just looking / Soon / This is what she's like / Soul finger. (cd+=) – (5 extra tracks) *(re-iss.Jul92)*
Jun 91. Mercury; (7") **COME ON EILEEN. / BECAUSE OF YOU** [ ] [-]
(12"+=)(cd-s+=) – Let's get this straight (from the start).
May 93. Spectrum; (cd)(c) **BECAUSE OF YOU** [ ] [-]
Nov 93. Windsong; (cd) **BBC RADIO 1 LIVE IN CONCERT – NEWCASTLE (live)** [ ] [-]
ul 95. Nighttracks; (cd) **1980-1982 – THE RADIO SESSIONS** [ ] [-]

KEVIN ROWLAND

Mercury / Mercury

Apr 88. (7") **WALK AWAY. / EVEN WHEN I HOLD YOU** [ ] [ ]
(12"+=) – ('A' version) / The way you look tonight.
(cd-s+=) – The way you look tonight / Because of you.
Jun 88. (lp)(c)(cd) **THE WANDERER** [ ] [ ]
– Young man / Walk away / You'll be the one for me / Heartaches by the number / I am a wanderer / Tonight / When you walk alone / Age can't wither you / I want / Remember me.
Jul 88. (7") **TONIGHT. / KEVIN ROWLAND'S BAND** [ ] [ ]
(12"+=) – Come on Eileen.
Oct 88. (7") **YOUNG MAN. / ONE WAY TICKET TO PALOOKAHVILLE** [ ] [ ]
(12"+=) – Jackie Wilson said (I'm in Heaven when you smile).
(cd-s+=) – Show me.

Dennis DeYOUNG (see under ⇒ STYX)

Neil DIAMOND

Born: NOAH KAMINSKY, 24 Jan'41, Brooklyn, New York, USA. After a couple of years in the early 60's, as part of duo NEIL & JACK (with Jack Parker), he signed for 'Columbia' records. Hired mainly as an apprentice songwriter, he didn't really go solo until 1966, after his songs were being covered by stars like CLIFF RICHARD, JAY & THE AMERICANS, etc. That year he signed contract for Bert Berns' 'Bang' label, retaining heads of publishing company Jeff Barry and Ellie Greenwich as producers. His first success came when 'CHERRY CHERRY' made the US Top 10, and was followed by a string of hits during the 60's, culminating in a Top 5 smash 'SWEET CAROLINE'. In between this, his songs written for The MONKEES; 'I'M A BELIEVER' & 'A LITTLE BIT ME, A LITTLE BIT YOU', had raced to the top of the charts. LULU had also hit the UK Top 10 with his 'THE BOAT THAT I ROW'. In the 70's, his acolade as a superstar was unquestionable, as he piled on hit after hit. In 1979, he starred in the film re-make of 'THE JAZZ SINGER' alongside Laurence Olivier. Although this was a great success mainly due to his hit-riddled soundtrack, NEIL would not return to the silver screen. • **Style:** Powerful vocalist, who mixed beautiful love ballads and uptempo melodic rock-pop tunes with live visual aura. At times in the early 70's, he was unfairly condemned by critics for mingling with experimental pop. • **Songwriters:** Wrote 99% of material for himself and for loads of others. He also squeezed in a few covers himself:- NEW ORLEANS (Gary U.S.Bonds) / UNTIL IT'S TIME FOR YOU TO GO (Buffy Sainte-Marie) / HE AIN'T HEAVY, HE'S MY BROTHER (Hollies) / HEARTLIGHT + FRONT PAGE STORY (Bacharach/Bayer-Sager) / I'M ALIVE (co-with David Foster) / MORNING HAS BROKEN (Cat Stevens) / etc. • **Trivia:** ROBBIE ROBERTSON (of The BAND) produced his 1976 album 'BEAUTIFUL NOISE'. In the 60's, he also wrote 'RED RED WINE', later a No.1 smash for UB40.

Recommended: THE GREATEST HITS 1966-1992 (*7) / JONATHAN LIVINGSTON SEAGULL (*6) / BEAUTIFUL NOISE (*6) / TAP ROOT MANUSCRIPT (*6).

NEIL & JACK

not issued / Duel

1960. (7") **WHAT WILL I DO. / YOU ARE MY LOVE AT LAST** [-] [ ]
1961. (7") **I'M AFRAID. / TILL YOU'VE TRIED LOVE** [-] [ ]

NEIL DIAMOND

not issued / Columbia

1963. (7") **CLOWN TOWN. / AT NIGHT** [-] [ ]

— He then began writing for JAY & THE AMERICANS, CLIFF RICHARD and later The MONKEES. Returned to the studio early 1966.

London / Bang

May 66. (7") **SOLITARY MAN. / DO IT** [ ] [55]
Sep 66. (7") **CHERRY CHERRY. / I'LL COME RUNNING** [ ] [6] Aug 66
Oct 66. (lp) **THE FEEL OF NEIL DIAMOND** [-] [ ]
– Solitary man / Red rubber ball / La bamba / Do it / Hanky panky / Monday Monday / New Orleans / Someday baby / I got the feelin' / I'll come running / Love to love / Cherry, Cherry.
Nov 66. (7") **I GOT THE FEELIN' (OH NO NO). / THE BOAT THAT I ROW** [ ] [16]
Feb 66. (7") **YOU GOT TO ME. / SOMEDAY BABY** [ ] [18] Jan67
Apr 66. (7") **GIRL, YOU'LL BE A WOMAN SOON. / YOU'LL FORGET** [ ] [10]
Jul 67. (7") **I THANK THE LORD FOR THE NIGHT. / LONG WAY HOME** [ ] [13]
Sep 67. (lp) **JUST FOR YOU** [-] [80]
– Girl, you'll be a woman soon / The long way home / Red red wine / You'll forget / The boat that I row / Cherry, Cherry / I'm a believer / Shilo / You got to me / Solitary man / Thank the Lord for the night time.
Nov 67. (7") **KENTUCKY WOMAN. / THE TIME IS NOW** [ ] [22] Oct 67
Jan 68. (7") **NEW ORLEANS. / HANKY PANKY** [ ] [51] Dec 67
Apr 68. (7") **RED RED WINE. / RED RUBBER BALL** [ ] [62]

Uni / Uni

May 68. (7") **BROOKLYN ROADS. / HOLIDAY INN BLUES** [ ] [58]

M.C.A. / Uni

Jun 68. (lp) **VELVET GLOVES AND SPIT** [ ] [ ]
– Two bit manchild / A modern day version of love / Honey dripping times / The pot smoker's song / Brooklyn roads / Shilo / Sunday sun / Holiday inn blues / Practically newborn / Knackerffeng / Merry-go-round. *(re-iss.1974 & Feb82)*
Jul 68. (7") **TWO-BIT MANCHILD. / BROAD OLD WOMAN (9 a.m. INSANITY)** [ ] [66]
Sep 68. (7") **SUNDAY SUN. / HONEY DRIPPING TIMES** [-] [68]
Apr 69. (7") **BROTHER LOVE'S TRAVELLING SALVATION SHOW. / MODERN DAY VERSION OF LOVE** [ ] [22] Mar 69
Apr 69. (lp) **BROTHER LOVE'S TRAVELLING SALVATION SHOW** [ ] [82] Mar 69
– Brother Love's travelling salvation show / Dig in / River runs, newgrown plums / Juliet / Long gone / And the grass won't pay you no mind / Memphis street / Glory road / Deep in the morning / If I ever knew your name / You're so sweet horseflies keep hanging round your face / Hurtin' / You don't come easy. *(re-iss.+c.1970 on 'Uni')* (+=) – Sweet Caroline. *(re-iss.1974)*
Jul 69. (7") **SWEET CAROLINE (GOOD TIMES NEVER SEEMED SO GOOD). / DIG IN** [ ] [4]

Uni / Uni

Nov 69. (7") **HOLLY HOLY. / HURTIN' YOU DON'T COME EASY** [ ] [6] Oct 69
Jan 70. (lp)(c) **TOUCHING YOU, TOUCHING ME** [ ] [30] Dec69
– Sweet Caroline (good times never seemed so good) / Until it's time for you to go / Everybody's talkin' / Mr.Bojangles / Smokey lady / Holly holy / Both sides now / And the singer sings his song / Ain't no way / New York boy. *(re-iss.74)*
Feb 70. (7") **UNTIL IT'S TIME FOR YOU TO GO. / AND THE SINGER SINGS HIS SONG** [-] [53]
May 70. (7") **SOOLAIMON (AFRICAN TRILOGY II). / AND THE GRASS WON'T PAY YOU NO MIND** [ ] [30]
Aug 70. (7") **CRACKLIN' ROSIE. / LORDY** [3] [1]
(re-iss.1974)
Sep 70. (lp)(c) **GOLD (live at Troubador)** [23] [10]
– Lordy / Both sides now / Solitary man / Holly holy / Cherry, cherry / Kentucky woman / Sweet Caroline / Thank the Lord for the night time / And the singer sings his songs / Brother Love's travelling salvation show. *(re-iss.1974 on 'MCA') (re-iss.Oct87 on 'MFP')*
Nov 70. (7") **HE AIN'T HEAVY HE'S MY BROTHER. / FREE LIFE** [-] [20]
Mar 71. (lp)(c) **TAPROOT MANUSCRIPT** [19] [13] Nov 70
– Cracklin' Rosie / Free life / Coldwater morning / Done too soon / He ain't heavy he's my brother / The African trilogy (a folk ballet: I am the lion / Madrigal / Soolamain / Missa / African smile / Childsong (reprise). *(re-iss.1974 on 'MCA', cd-iss.1987)*
Apr 71. (7") **I AM . . . I SAID. / DONE TOO SOON** [4] [4]
[65] Mar 71
Nov 71. (7") **STONES. / CRUNCHY GRANOLA SUITE** [ ] [14]
Nov 71. (lp)(c) **STONES** [18] [11]
– I am . . . I said / The last thing on my mind / Husbands and wives / Chelsea morning / Crunchy granola suite / Stones / If you go away / Suzanne / I think it's going to rain today / I am . . . I said (reprise). *(re-iss.1974 on 'M.C.A.')*
Apr 72. (7") **SONG SUNG BLUE. / GITCHY GOOMY** [14] [1]
Jul 72. (lp)(c) **MOODS** [7] [5]
– Walk on water / Song sung blue / Porcupine pie / High rolling man / Canta libre / Captain Sunshine / Play me / Gitchy goomy / Theme / Prelude in E major / Morning side. *(cd-iss.1987 on 'M.C.A.')*
Aug 72. (7") **PLAY ME. / PORCUPINE PIE** [ ] [11]
Nov 72. (7") **WALK ON WATER. / HIGH ROLLING MAN** [ ] [17]

Uni M.C.A.

Apr 73. (7") **CHERRY CHERRY (live). / MORNINGSIDE (live)** [ ] [31]

Dec 73. (d-lp)(d-c) **HOT AUGUST NIGHTS (live)** [32] [5] Dec 72
– Prologue / Crunchy granola suite / Done too soon / Dialogue / Solitary man / Cherry cherry / Sweet Caroline / Porcupine pie / You're so sweet / Red red wine / Soggy pretzels / And the grass won't pay you no mind / Shilo / Girl you'll be a woman soon / Play me / Canta libre / Morningside / Song sung blue / Cracklin' Rosie / Holly holy / I am . . . I said / Soolamain / Brother Love's travelling salvation show / Encore. *(re-iss.1975 on 'MCA')*

C.B.S. Columbia

Nov 73. (7") **BE. / FLIGHT OF THE GULL** [ ] [ ]

Jan 74. (lp)(c) **JONATHAN LIVINGSTON SEAGULL (Film Soundtrack)** [35] [2] Nov 73
– Prologue / Be / Flight of the gull / Dear father / Skybird / Lonely looking sky / The odyssey: Be – Lonely looking sky – Dear father / Anthem / Be / Skybird / Dear father / Be. *(cd-iss.1986)*

Apr 74. (7") **SKYBIRD. / LONELY LOOKING SKY** [ ] [75] Feb74

Oct 74. (lp)(c) **SERENADE** [11] [3]
– I've been this way before / Rosemary's wine / Lady Magdalene / The last Picasso / Longfellow serenade / Yes I will / Reggae strut / The gift of song. *(re-iss.Jun81) (cd-iss.May87) (re-iss.+cd.1989 on 'Pickwick')(re-iss.cd+c Sep93 on 'Sony Collectors')*

Nov 74. (7") **LONGFELLOW SERENADE. / ROSEMARY'S WINE** [ ] [5]

Feb 75. (7") **I'VE BEEN THIS WAY BEFORE. / REGGAE STRUT** [ ] [34]

Jun 75. (7") **THE LAST PICASSO. / THE GIFT OF SONG** [ ] [ ]

Jun 76. (7") **IF YOU KNOW WHAT I MEAN. / STREET LIFE** [35] [11]

Jul 76. (lp)(c) **BEAUTIFUL NOISE** [10] [4]
– Beautiful noise / Stargazer / Lady oh / Don't think . . . Feel / Surviving the life / If you know what I mean / Street life / Home is a wounded heart / Jungletime / Signs / Dry your eyes. *(re-iss.+cd.Apr87 & Mar91)*

Sep 76. (7") **DON'T THINK . . . FEEL. / HOME IS A WOUNDED HEART** [-] [43]

Sep 76. (7") **BEAUTIFUL NOISE. / HOME IS A WOUNDED HEART** [13] [-]

Feb 77. (d-lp)(d-c) **LOVE AT THE GREEK (live)** [3] [8]
– Street life / Kentucky woman / Sweet Caroline (good times never seem so good) / The last Picasso / Longfellow serenade / Beautiful noise / Lady-oh / Stargazer / If you know what I mean / Surviving the life / Glory road / Song sung blue / Holly holy / Brother Love's travelling salvation show / Jonathan Livingstone Seagull / Be / Dear father / Lonely looking sky / Sanctus / Skybird / Be (encore) / I've been this way before. *(cd-iss.May87)(re-iss.cd+c Apr93 on 'Columbia')*

Mar 77. (7") **STARGAZER (live). / JUNGLE LIFE (live)** [ ] [-]

Jun 77. (7") **I'VE BEEN THIS WAY BEFORE (live). / SURVIVING THE LIFE (live)** [ ] [-]

Jul 77. (7") **DON'T THINK . . . FEEL. / SIGNS** [ ] [-]

Dec 77. (7") **DESIREE. / ONCE IN A WHILE** [39] [16]

Dec 77. (lp)(c) **I'M GLAD YOU'RE HERE WITH ME TONIGHT** [16] [6]
– God only knows / Let me take you in my arms / Once in a while / Let the little boy sing / I'm glad you're here with me tonight / Lament in D minor / Dance of the sabres / Desiree / As if / Free man in Paris. *(cd-iss.May87)(re-iss.cd+c Oct93 on 'Sony Collectors')(re-iss.Nov93)*

Feb 78. (7") **GOD ONLY KNOWS. / ONCE IN A WHILE** [ ] [-]

Mar 78. (7") **I'M GLAD YOU'RE HERE WITH ME TONIGHT. / DANCE OF SABRES** [-] [ ]

Apr 78. (7") **I'M GLAD YOU'RE HERE WITH ME TONIGHT. / AS IF** [ ] [-]

Sep 78. (7") **LET ME TAKE YOU IN MY ARMS. / AS IF** [ ] [-]

Nov 78. (7") **YOU DON'T BRING ME FLOWERS. (w / "BARBRA STREISAND") / (instrumental)** [5] [1]
(re-iss.Apr82)

Dec 78. (lp)(c) **YOU DON'T BRING ME FLOWERS** [15] [4]
– The American popular song / Forever in blue jeans / Remember me / You've got your troubles / You don't bring me flowers / The dancing bumble-bee-bumble boogie / Mothers and daughters, fathers and sons / Memphis flyer / Say maybe / Diamond girls. *(cd-iss.May87) (re-iss.c+cd.Aug91 on 'Columbia')*

Feb 79. (7") **FOREVER IN BLUE JEANS. / REMEMBER ME** [16] [20]

May 79. (7") **SAY MAYBE. / DIAMOND GIRLS** [-] [55]

May 79. (7") **THE AMERICAN POPULAR SONG. / DIAMOND GIRLS** [ ] [-]

Jan 80. (7") **SEPTEMBER MORN. / I'M A BELIEVER** [ ] [17]

Jan 80. (lp)(c) **SEPTEMBER MORN** [14] [10] Dec 79
– September morn / Mama don't know / That kind / Jazz time / The good Lord loves you / Dancing in the street / The shelter of your arms / I'm a believer / The Sun ain't gonna shine anymore / Stagger Lee. *(cd-iss.May87)*

Mar 80. (7") **THE GOOD LORD LOVES YOU. / JAZZ TIME** [-] [67]

Mar 80. (7") **DANCING IN THE STREET. / JAZZ TIME** [ ] [-]

Capitol Capitol

Oct 80. (7") **LOVE ON THE ROCKS. / ACAPULCO** [17] [2]

Nov 80. (lp)(c) **THE JAZZ SINGER (Soundtrack)** [14] [3]
– America / Adon o lume / You baby / Love on the rocks / Amazed and confused / The Robert E.Lee / Summer love / Hello again / Acapulco / Hey Louise / Songs of life / Jerusalem / Kol ridre / My name is Yussef (theme) / America (reprise). *(cd-iss.Jul84)*

Jan 81. (7") **HELLO AGAIN. / AMAZED AND CONFUSED** [51] [6]

Apr 81. (7") **AMERICA. / SONGS OF LIFE** [ ] [8]

C.B.S. Columbia

Oct 81. (lp)(c) **ON THE WAY TO THE SKY** [39] [17]
– Yesterday's songs / On the way to the sky / Right by you / Only you / Save me / Be mine / The drifter / Fear of the market place / Rainy day song / Guitar Heaven / Love burns. *(cd-iss.Jul87)*

Nov 81. (7") **YESTERDAY'S SONGS. / GUITAR HEAVEN** [ ] [11]

Jan 81. (7") **RAINY DAY SONGS. / BE MINE TONIGHT** [ ] [-]

Feb 82. (7") **ON THE WAY TO THE SKY. / SAVE ME** [-] [27]

Jun 82. (7") **BE MINE TONIGHT. / RIGHT BY YOU** [ ] [35]

Sep 82. (7") **HEARTLIGHT. / YOU DON'T KNOW ME** [47] [5]

Oct 82. (lp)(c) **HEARTLIGHT** [43] [9]
– Heartlight / I'm alive / I'm guilty / Hurricane / Lost amongst the stars / A fool for you / In enserada / Star flight / Front page story / Comin' home / First you have to say you love me. *(cd-iss.May87) (re-iss.cd Mar94 on 'Sony Collectors')*

Jan 83. (7") **FRONT PAGE STORY. / LOVE AMONG THE STARS** [ ] [-]

Feb 83. (7") **I'M ALIVE. / LOST AMONGST THE STARS** [-] [35]

Apr 83. (7") **FRONT PAGE STORY. / I'M GUILTY** [-] [65]

Jul 84. (7") **TURN AROUND. / BROOKLYN ON A SATURDAY NIGHT** [ ] [62]

Aug 84. (lp)(c) **PRIMITIVE** [7] [35]
– Turn around / Primitive / Fire on the tracks / Brooklyn on a Saturday night / Sleep with me tonight / Crazy / My time with you / Love's own song / It's a trip (go for the Moon) / You make it feel like Christmas / One by one. *(cd-iss.May87)*

Sep 84. (7") **PRIMITIVE. / IT'S A TRIP** [ ] [-]

Sep 84. (7") **SLEEP WITH ME TONIGHT. / ONE BY ONE** [-] [ ]

Nov 84. (7") **YOU MAKE IT FEEL LIKE CHRISTMAS. / CRAZY** [-] [ ]

Nov 84. (7") **YOU MAKE IT FEEL LIKE CHRISTMAS. / ONE BY ONE** [ ] [-]

May 86. (7") **HEADED FOR THE FUTURE. / ANGEL** [-] [53]

May 86. (lp)(c)(cd) **HEADED FOR THE FUTURE** [36] [20]
– Headed for the future / The man you need / I'll see you in the radio (Laura / Stand up for love / It should have been me / Lost in Hollywood / The story of my life / Angel / Me beside you / Love doesn't live here anymore.

Jul 86. (7")(12") **STAND UP FOR LOVE. / THE STORY OF MY LIFE** [ ] [-]

Jul 86. (7") **THE STORY OF MY LIFE. / LOVE DOESN'T LIVE HERE ANYMORE** [-] [ ]

Nov 87. (7")(cd-s) **I DREAMED A DREAM. / SWEET CAROLINE** [ ] [ ]

Dec 87. (d-lp)(c)(cd) **HOT AUGUST NIGHT II (live)** [74] [59] Nov 87
– Song of the whales (fanfare) / Headed for the future / September morn / Thank the Lord for the night time / Cherry cherry / Sweet Caroline / Hello again / Love on the rocks / America / Forever in blue jeans / You don't bring me flowers / I dreamed a dream / Back in L.A. / Song sung blue / Crackling Rosie / I am . . . I said / Holly holy / Soolamain / Brother Love's travelling salvation show / Heartlight. *(re-iss.cd+c Sep93 on 'Columbia')*

Jan 88. (7") **CHERRY CHERRY (live). / AMERICA (live)** [-] [ ]

Feb 89. (lp)(c)(cd) **THE BEST YEARS OF OUR LIVES** [42] [46] Jan 89
– The best years of our lives / Hard times for young lovers / This time / Everything's gonna be fine / Hooked on a memory of you / Take care of me / Baby can I hold you / Carmelita's eyes / Courtin' disaster / If I couldn't see you again / Long hard climb.

1989. (7") **THIS TIME. / IF I COULDN'T SEE YOU AGAIN** [-] [ ]

Jun 89. (7")(c-s) **THIS TIME. / BABY CAN I HOLD YOU** [ ] [-]
(12"+=) – Hooked on the morning of you.
(cd-s+=) – Beautiful noise / If you know what I mean.

1989. (7") **THE BEST YEARS OF OUR LIVES. / CARMELITA'S EYES** [-] [ ]

Columbia Columbia

Oct 91. (cd)(c)(lp) **LOVESCAPE** [36] [44] Sep 91
– If there were no dreams / Mountains of love / Don't turn around / Someone who believes in you / When you miss your love / Fortune of the night / One hand, one heart / Hooked on the memory of you / Wish everything was alright / The way / Sweet L.A. days / All I really need is you / Lonely lady 17 / I feel you / Common ground.

Nov 92. (7")(c-s) **MORNING HAS BROKEN. / SANTA CLAUS IS COMING TO TOWN** [36] [ ]
(cd-s) – ('A'side) / Happy xmas (war is over) / Silver bells / Love on the rocks.

Nov 92. (cd)(c)(lp) **THE CHRISTMAS ALBUM** [50] [8]
(festive songs & recent single)

Sep 93. (cd)(c)(lp) **ON THE ROOF – SONGS OF THE BRILL BUILDING** [28] [28]
– You've lost that lovin' feelin' (duet with DOLLY PARTON) / Up on the roof / Love potion number nine / Will you love me tomorrow/ Don't be cruel / Do wah diddy diddy (with MARY'S DANISH) / I (who have nothing) / Do you know the way to San Jose? / Don't make me over / River deep mountain high / A groovy kind of love / Spanish Harlem / Sweets for my sweet / Happy birthday sweet sixteen / Ten lonely guys / Save the last dance for me

Aug 94. (d-cd)(d-c) **LIVE IN AMERICA (live)** [ ] [93]
– America / Hello again / Kentucky woman / You got to me / Cherry cherry / I'm a believer / Sweet Caroline / Love on the rocks / Hooked on the memory of you (with LINDA PRESS) / Lady oh / Beautiful noise / Play me / Up on the roof / You've lost that lovin' feelin' (with RAVEN KANE) / River deep, mountain high / I (who have nothing) / Missa / Soolaimon / Holly holy / And the grass won't pay you no mind / You don't bring me flowers (with RAVEN KANE) / September morn / Havah nagilah / Solitary man / Red red wine / Song sung blue / Forever in blue jeans / Heartlight / Cracklin' Rose / I am . . .I said / Crunchy Granola suite / Brother Love's traveling salvation show.

– compilations, others, etc. –

1968. Bang; (7") **SHILO. / LA BAMBA** [-] [ ]
(re-iss.Mar70 hit US No.24)

Jul 68. Bang; (lp) **GREATEST HITS** [-] [ ]

Sep 70. Bang; (lp)(c) **SHILO** [-] [52]

Aug 70. Bang; (7") **SOLITARY MAN. / THE TIME IS NOW** [-] [21]

Dec 70. Bang; (7") **DO IT!. / HANKY PANKY** [-] [36]

Feb 71. Bang; (lp)(c) **DO IT!** [-] [100]

1971. President; (7") **SOLITARY MAN. / HANKY PANKY** [ ] [-]

1971. President; (7"m) **KENTUCKY WOMAN. / CHERRY CHERRY / I THANK THE LORD FOR THE NIGHT** [ ] [-]

Jun 71. President/ US= Bang; (7") **I'M A BELIEVER. / CROOKED STREET** [ ] [51]

Feb 71. Uni; (7") **SWEET CAROLINE. / BROTHER LOVE'S TRAVELLING SALVATION SHOW** [8] [-]
(re-iss.Aug74 on 'MCA')

1971. Joy; (lp)(c) **GREATEST HITS** [ ] [-]

1971. Joy; (lp)(c) **I'M A BELIEVER** [ ] [-]

Feb73. Bang; (d-lp) **DOUBLE GOLD** [-] [36]

Aug 73. London/ US= Bang; (7") **THE LONG WAY HOME. / MONDAY MONDAY** [ ] [91]

1973. London; (lp)(c) **GOLD DIAMOND** [ ] [-]

Sep 74. London; (lp)(c) **GOLD DIAMOND VOL.2** [ ] [-]

Sep 75. London; (d-lp) **FOCUS ON NEIL DIAMOND** [ ] [-]

Aug 73. M.C.A.; (7") **THE LAST THING ON MY MIND. / CANTA LIBRE** [-] [56]

Feb 74. M.C.A.; (lp)(c) **RAINBOW** [39] [35] Dec 73
May 74. M.C.A.; (7") **SHILO. / BROOKLYN ROADS** [ ] [-]
Jun 74. M.C.A.; (lp)(c) **HIS 12 GREATEST HITS** [13] [29]
(cd-iss.May87)
Aug 74. M.C.A.; (7") **HOLLY HOLY. / SOOLAIMON (AFRICAN TRILOGY II)** [ ] [-]
Oct 75. M.C.A.; (d-lp)(c) **DIAMONDS** [ ] [ ]
(re-iss.Oct81 & Oct87)
Nov 76. M.C.A.; (lp)(c) **AND THE SINGER SINGS HIS SONG** [ ] [ ]
(re-iss.Aug81)
Jun 77. M.C.A.; (7"ep) **LIVE DIAMONDS EP (live)** [ ] [-]
– Shilo / Brother Love's travelling salvation show / Cherry Cherry.
Nov 77. M.C.A.; (7") **AND THE GRASS WON'T PAY YOU NO MIND. / MERRY-GO-ROUND** [ ] [-]
Nov 78. M.C.A.; (lp)(c) **20 GOLDEN GREATS** [2] [-]
(cd-iss.Feb91) (re-iss.Jul92, hit UK No.48)
Jan 81. M.C.A.; (lp)(c) **LOVE SONGS** [43] [ ]
Apr 82. M.C.A.; (lp)(c) **LIVE DIAMONDS (live)** [ ] [-]
Jan 83. M.C.A.; (c-ep) **CASSETTE EP** [ ] [-]
– You don't bring me flowers / If you know what I mean / September morn / Beautiful noise.
Sep 84. M.C.A.; (d-c) **LOVE SONGS / GOLD** [ ] [-]
Apr 82. M.C.A.; (d-c) **TOUCHING ME TOUCHING YOU / MOODS** [ ] [-]
Note; All CBS releases were issued in US on 'Columbia'.
Mar 76. C.B.S.; (7") **BE. / LONGFELLOW SERENADE** [ ] [-]
Jan 82. C.B.S.; (lp)(c) **12 GREATEST HITS VOLUME 2** [32] [48]
(cd-iss.May87)
Jan 83. C.B.S.; (lp)(c) **CLASSICS – THE EARLY YEARS** [ ] [ ]
(cd-iss.May87 & Apr89)
Jun 92. Columbia; (cd)(c)(d-lp) **THE GREATEST HITS 1966-1992** [1] [90]
– Solitary man / Cherry, Cherry / I get the feelin' (oh no, no) / Thank you Lord for the night time / Girl, you'll be a woman soon / Kentucky woman / Shilo / You got to me / Brooklyn roads / Red, red wine / I'm a believer / Sweet Caroline / Soolaimon / Cracklin' Rose / Song sung blue / lay me / Holly holy / Morningside / Crunchy granola suite/ / Brother Love's travelling salvation show / I am . . . I said / Be / Longfellow serenade / Beautiful noise / If you know what I mean / Desiree / September morn / You don't bring me flowers (w / BARBRA STREISAND) / Forever in blue jeans / Hello America / Love on the rocks / Yesterday's songs / Heartlight / Headed for the future / Heartbreak Hotel (w / KIM CARNES) / All I really need is you.
Aug 93. Columbia; (3xcd-box) **I'M GLAD YOU'RE HERE WITH ME TONIGHT / BEAUTIFUL NOISE / YOU DON'T SEND ME FLOWERS** [ ] [ ]
Sep 79. M.F.P.; (lp)(c) **NEIL DIAMOND** [ ] [-]
Sep 81. Hallmark; (lp)(c) **SOLITARY MAN** [ ] [-]
Sep 86. Hallmark; (lp)(c) **THE BEST OF NEIL DIAMOND** [ ] [-]
Feb 88. Hallmark; (lp)(c) **RED RED WINE** [ ] [-]
Dec 81. W.R.C.; (4xlp-box) **THE BEST OF NEIL DIAMOND** [ ] [-]
Jul 82. Old Gold; (7") **SONG SUNG BLUE. / I AM . . . I SAID** [ ] [-]
Apr 83. Old Gold; (7") **CRACKIN' ROSIE. / SWEET CAROLINE** [ ] [-]
1989. Old Gold; (cd-ep) **CRACKIN' ROSIE / I AM . . . I SAID / SONG SONG BLUE** [ ] [-]
Dec 83. K-Tel; (lp)(c) **THE VERY BEST OF NEIL DIAMOND** [33] [-]
Jan 89. Pickwick; (cd) **THE BEST OF NEIL DIAMOND** [ ] [-]
(re-iss.c May95)
May 95. Pickwick; (cd) **THE VERY BEST OF NEIL DIAMOND** [ ] [-]
May 95. Pickwick; (cd) **RED RED WINE** [ ] [-]

DIAMOND HEAD

Formed: Stourbridge, Midlands, England . . . 1976 by HARRIS and TATLER. After a number of singles in the early 80's, and an obscure German album on 'Woolfe', they signed to 'MCA'. Their debut album 'BORROWED TIME', gave them a UK top 30 placing, but by 1985 the dream was over, after a disastrous 'Monsters Of Rock' concert. • **Style:** One of the pioneers of the 'New Wave of British Heavy Metal'. They were acclaimed by 'Sounds' journalists as the new LED ZEPPELIN, and were later cited as the main influence of METALLICA. • **Songwriters:** HARRIS-TALER compositions. • **Trivia:** Their 1991 'WILD ON THE STREETS' track, was actually written in 1978.

Recommended: CANTERBURY (*6) / BORROWED TIME (*7)

SEAN HARRIS – vocals, guitar / **BRIAN TATLER** – guitar / **COLIN KIMBERLEY** – bass / **DUNCAN SCOTT** – drums

Happy Face — not issued
Mar 80. (7") **SHOOT OUT THE LIGHTS. / HELPLESS** [ ] [-]
1980. (lp) **LIGHTNING TO THE NATIONS** (sold at gigs) [ ] [-]
– Lightning to the nations / The prince / Sucking my love / Am I evil / Sweet and innocent / It's electric / Helpless.
Media — not issued
Aug 80. (7") **SWEET AND INNOCENT. / STREETS OF GOLD** [ ] [-]
Windsong — not issued
Mar 81. (7") **PLAY IT LOUD. / WAITED TOO LONG** [ ] [-]
Aug 81. (12"ep) **DIAMOND LIGHTS / WE WON'T BE BACK. / I DON'T GOT / IT'S ELECTRIC** [ ] [-]
M.C.A. — M.C.A.
Apr 82. (7"ep)(12"ep) **FOUR CUTS** [ ] [-]
– Dead reckoning / +3.
Sep 82. (7")('A'extended-12") **IN THE HEAT OF THE NIGHT. / PLAY IT LOUD (live)** [67] [-]
(d7"+=) – Sweet and innocent (live) / (interview with Tommy Vance).
Oct 82. (lp)(c) **BORROWED TIME** [24] [-]
– In the heat of the night / To Heaven from Hell / Call me / Lightning to the nations / Borrowed time / Don't you ever leave me / Am I evil. *(re-iss.Feb84)*
Nov 82. (7")(12") **CALL ME. / TRICK OR TREAT** [ ] [-]
Aug 83. (7")(12") **MAKIN' MUSIC. / (Andy Peebles interview)** [ ] [-]
Sep 83. (lp)(c) **CANTERBURY** [32] [-]
– Makin' music / Out of phase / The king maker / One more night / To the Devil his due / Knight of the swords / Ishmael / I need your love / Canterbury.
Oct 83. (7")(7"pic-d) **OUT OF PHASE. / THE KING MAKER** [ ] [-]
(12"+=) – Sucking my love.

—— (Dec83) **DAVID WILLIAMSON** – bass repl. MERVYN GOLDSWORTHY who had repl. KIMBERLEY. / **ROBBIE FRANCE** – drums repl. SCOTT

FM-Revolver — not issued
May 87. (lp)(c)(cd) **AM I EVIL?** (compilation) [ ] [-]
– Am I evil? / Heat of the night / Don't you ever leave me / Borrowed time / To Heaven from Hell / Dead reckoning / Lightning to the nations / Sucking my love. *(pic-lp. May88) (re-iss.cd,c,lp Oct94 on 'Heavy Metal')*

—— Later 1987, HARRIS formed new band NOTORIOUS with guitarist ROBIN GEORGE. They released quickly deleted eponynous album that year on 'Geffen'. Meanwhile TATLER worked with RADIO MOSCOW who issued 1 lp WORLD SERVICE.

Transmogrified mid'91, when **TATLER** and **HARRIS** changed from new adopted group name MAGNETIC AKA to **DIAMOND HEAD.** brought in newcomers **EDDIE CHAOS** – bass / **CARL WILCOX** – drums

Bronze — not iss?
Nov 91. (7")(1-sided 12") **WILD ON THE STREETS. / ?** [ ] [ ]
Jan 92. (m-lp) **RISING UP** [ ] [-]
– Feels good / Can't help myself / Rising up / Kiss of fire / Calling your name / Wild on the streets.
Esssential — not issued
Jun 93. (cd)(c)(lp) **DEATH & PROGRESS** [ ] [ ]
– Star crossed (lovers of the night) / Truckin' / Calling your name / I can't help myself / Paradise (featuring BILLY & SARAH GAINES) / Dust / Run / Wild on the streets / Damnation Street / Home.

– compilations, others, etc. –

Apr 86. Metal Masters; (lp) **BEHOLD THE BEGINNING** [ ] [-]
(re-iss.+cd.May91) (re-iss.cd,c,lp Oct94 on 'Heavy Metal')
1988. Metal Masters; (cd) **SWEET AND INNOCENT** [ ] [-]
Feb 91. FM-Revolver; (cd)(c)(lp) **IN THE BEGINNING** [ ] [-]
Feb 92. Raw Fruit; (cd) **FRIDAY ROCK SHOW SESSIONS (live '86)** [ ] [-]

Bruce DICKINSON

Born: 7 Aug'58, Sheffield, England. Vocalist BRUCE BRUCE had cut his teeth in heavyweights SAMSON between 1978-1981. They released 2 albums 'HEAD ON' (1980) and 'SHOCK TACTICS', before he opted to join IRON MAIDEN. Now using his real surname, he became Britain's top heavy voxman, which helped boost all albums over the next 11 years to UK Top 3. Early in 1990 while still an IRON MAIDEN member, he unleashed his debut solo outing 'TATTOOED MILLIONAIRE'. While a little lighter and more commercial, it still gathered enough hard-rock support, even when rehashing classic MOTT THE HOOPLE number 'ALL THE YOUNG DUDES'. Surprisingly he opted to leave IRON MAIDEN in 1993 and released second hit album the following year.

Recommended: BALLS TO PICASSO (*5)

solo, with **JANICK GERS** – guitar, co-composer / **FABIO DEL RIO** – drums (ex-JAGGED EDGE)

E.M.I. — Columbia
Apr 90. (7")(c-s)(7"sha-pic-d) **TATTOOED MILLIONAIRE. / BALLAD OF MUTT** [18] [ ]
(12"+=)(cd-s+=) – Winds of change.
May 90. (cd)(c)(lp) **TATTOOED MILLIONAIRE** [14] [100]
– Son of a gun / Tattooed millionaire / Born in '58 / Hell on wheels / Gypsy road / Dive! dive! dive! / All the young dudes / Lickin' the gun / Zulu Lulu / No lies.
Jun 90. (7")(c-s)(7"sha-pic-d) **ALL THE YOUNG DUDES. / DARKNESS BE MY FRIEND** [23] [ ]
(12"+=)(cd-s+=) – Sin city.
Aug 90. (7")(c-s) **DIVE! DIVE! DIVE!. / RIDING WITH THE ANGELS (live)** [45] [ ]
(12"+=)(cd-s+=)(12"pic-d+=) – Sin city / Black night.
Mar 91. (7")(c-s) **BORN IN '58. / TATTOOED MILLIONAIRE (live)** [ ] [ ]
(12"+=)(cd-s+=) – Son of a gun (live).

—— feature backing from gangstas TRIBE OF GYPSIES.

May 94. (7"clear) **TEARS OF THE DRAGON. / FIRE CHILD** [28] [ ]
(7"pic-d) – ('A'side) / Elvis has left the building.
(cd-s+=) – Breeding house / No way out . . .to be continued.
(cd-s+=) – Winds of change / Spirit of joy.
Jun 94. (cd)(c)(lp) **BALLS TO PICASSO** [21] [ ]
– Cyclops / Hell no / Gods of war / 1000 points of light / Laughing in the hiding bush / Change of heart / Shoot all the clowns / Fire / Sacred cowboy / Tears of the dragon.
Sep 94. (7") **SHOOT ALL THE CLOWNS. / OVER AND OUT** [37] [ ]
(cd-s) – ('A'side) / Tibet / Tears of the dragon: The first bit . . .
(cd-s) – ('A'side) / Cadillac gas mask / No way out – continued.
(12") – ('A'side) / Laughing in the hiding bush (live) / The post alternative Seattle fallout (live).
Castle — Rykodisc
Mar 95. (cd)(c) **ALIVE IN STUDIO A (live)** [ ] [ ]
– Surrender to the city / She's the one that I adore / Wasted / D F dogs / The shipyard song / The past is another country.

DICTATORS

Formed: New York, USA . . . mid 70's by MANITOBA and ROSS THE BOSS. After a mildly received debut for 'Epic', they nearly broke through in 1977 with 'Asylum' lp 'MANIFEST DESTINY', which contained UK Top 50 breaker 'SEARCH & DESTROY'. • **Style:** Fast hard rock in the mould of MOTORHEAD, but influenced by late 60's garage punk (i.e.STOOGES, etc.). • **Songwriters:** Group penned except covers SEARCH AND DESTROY (Iggy Pop / Stooges) / I GOT YOU BABE (Sonny & Cher). • **Trivia:** In UK, were one initial punk bands to realise the potential hype of the 12" single.

Recommended: MANIFEST DESTINY (*5)

'HANDSOME' DICK MANITOBA (b.RICHARD BLUM, 29 Jan'54) – vocals / **ROSS THE BOSS** (b.FUNICELLO) – guitar, vocals / **ANTHONY SHERNOFF** – keyboards, bass, vocals / **MARK 'THE ANIMAL' MENDOZA** – bass / **STU BOY KING** – drums

Epic | Epic

Dec 75. (lp)(c) **GO GIRL CRAZY** [ ] [ ]
– The next big thing / Back to Africa / California Sun / I got you babe / Teengenerate / Weekend (I live for) / Cars and girls / Master race / Two tag man. *(re-iss.Dec77) (cd-iss.Jul93 on 'Sony Europe')*

— **RITCHIE TEETER** – drums repl. STU

Asylum | Asylum

Jun 77. (7") **DISEASE. / HEY BOYS** [-] [ ]
Jun 77. (lp)(c) **MANIFEST DESTINY** [ ] [ ]
– Exposed / Heartache / Sleepin' with the T.V. on / Disease / Hey boys / Steppin' out / Science gone too far / Young, fast, scientific / Search and destroy.
Aug 77. (7") **SLEEPIN' WITH THE T.V. ON. / SCIENCE GONE TOO FAR** [-] [ ]
Sep 77. (7")(12") **SEARCH AND DESTROY. / SLEEPIN' WITH THE T.V. ON** [49] [ ]
Aug 78. (lp)(c) **BLOOD BROTHERS** [ ] [ ]
– Faster and louder / Baby let's twist / No tomorrow / The Minnesota strip / Stay / I stand tall / Borneo Jimmy / What is it / Slow death.
Aug 78. (7") **I STAND TALL. / TOO MUCH FUN** [-] [ ]

not issued | Pro Tempore

1980. (lp) **DICTATORS** [-] [ ]
– Next big thing / Disease / Hey boys / Two tub man / The Moon upstairs / Weekend / New York, New York / I stand tall / Slow death.

— Disbanded 1980. ROSS formed SHAKIN' STREET and later MANOWAR. MARK later joined TWISTED SISTER. DICK later formed MANITOBA'S WILD KINGDOM.

– compilations, others, etc. –

1981. R.O.I.R.; (c) **FUCK 'EM IF THEY CAN'T TAKE A JOKE** [-] [ ]
(re-iss.lp Mar91) (cd-iss.Feb 95)

Bo DIDDLEY

Born: ELLIS BATES, 30 Dec 1928, McComb, Missouri, USA. As a toddler, he was re-surnamed McDANIEL, when he was adopted by mother's Chicago cousin. In the early 50's, he gave up boxing (where he acquired new professional name), moving from street busking to sign for 'Checker' records in 1955. His debut recording 'BO DIDDLEY', sold well enough in the R&B circuit to give him break later in the year on the 'Ed Sullivan Show'. By the late 50's, he was having well deserved success with US Top 20 hit 'SAY MAN'. Late in 1963, after a tour of Britain, his re-issued albums 'BO DIDDLEY', 'GUNSLINGER' & 'RIDES AGAIN' hit the UK Top 20. He continued to have varied degrees of fortune throughout the rest of the 60's, reviving rock'n'roll in the 70's. • **Style:** His Chicago-influenced R&B "jungle" rock, was heavily indebted to CHUCK BERRY or the older LOUIS JORDAN. DIDDLEY virtually created the beat boom of the 60's, when groups The WHO, YARDBIRDS, MANFRED MANN and especially The ROLLING STONES borrowed his material. • **Songwriters:** All DIDDLEY penned, except some covers. • **Trivia:** He also played on a number of songs with friend/stablemate CHUCK BERRY.

Recommended: CHESS MASTERS (*6)

BO DIDDLEY – vocals, guitar.

London | Checker

Jun 55. (7") **BO DIDDLEY. / I'M A MAN** [-] [ ]
(re-iss. 1962)

— **BILLY BOY ARNOLD** – harmonica / **JEROME GREEN** – bass, maracas, etc. / **FRANK KIRKLAND** – drums / guest **OTIS SPANN** – piano

Jun 56. (7") **DIDDLEY DADDY. / SHE'S FINE, SHE'S MINE** [-] [ ]
Jun 56. (7"ep) **RHYTHM & BLUES WITH BO DIDDLEY** [ ] [-]
– (above 4 tracks)
Sep 56. (7") **BRING IT TO JEROME. / PRETTY THING** [-] [ ]
Dec 56. (7") **DIDDY WAH DIDDY. / I'M LOOKING FOR A WOMAN** [-] [ ]
1957. (7") **WHO DO YOU LOVE. / IN BAD** [-] [ ]
1957. (7") **COPS AND ROBBERS. / DOWN HOME SPECIAL** [-] [ ]
1957. (7") **HEY! BO DIDDLEY. / MONA** [-] [ ]
1958. (7") **SAY! (BOSS MAN). / BEFORE YOU ACCUSE ME** [-] [ ]
1958. (7") **HUSH YOUR MOUTH. / DEAREST DARLING** [-] [ ]
Aug 58. (7") **WILLIE AND LILLIE. / LET'S MEET THE MONSTER** [-] [ ]
Oct 58. (lp) **GO BO DIDDLEY** [ ] [ ]
– Crackin' up / I'm sorry / Bo's guitar / Willie and Lillie / You don't love me (you don't care) / Say man / The great grandfather / Oh, yea! / Don't let it go / Little girl / Dearest darling / The clock struck twelve.
1959. (7") **I'M SORRY. / OH YEA!** [-] [ ]

— Recorded and released other 45's between 57-58, all in the US.

Sep 59. (7") **CRACKIN' UP. / THE GREAT GRANDFATHER** [ ] [62] Jul 59
Oct 59. (7") **SAY MAN. / THE CLOCK STRIKES TWELVE** [ ] [20]
Jan 60. (7") **SAY MAN, BACK AGAIN. / SHE'S ALRIGHT** [ ] [ ]
Apr 60. (7") **ROADRUNNER. / MY STORY** [ ] [75]
1960. (7") **CRAWDADDY. / WALKIN' AND TACKIN'** [-] [ ]
1960. (7") **GUNSLINGER. / SIGNIFYING BLUES** [-] [ ]
1961. (7") **NOT GUILTY. / AZTEC** [-] [ ]
1961. (7") **CALL ME. / PILLS** [-] [ ]

— added half-sister **THE DUCHESS** – guitar

Pye Jazz | not issued

Sep 61. (lp) **BO DIDDLEY IS A GUNSLINGER** [ ] [ ]
– Gunslinger / Ride on Josephine / Doing the craw-daddy / Cadillac / Somewhere / Whoa mule / Sixteen tons / Cheyenne / No more lovin' / Diddling. *(UK re-dist.Nov63, hit No.20)*

Pye Int. | Checker

Oct 62. (7") **YOU CAN'T JUDGE A BOOK BY THE COVER. / I CAN TELL** [ ] [48] Jul 62
(UK re-iss.Sep63)
Nov 62. (lp) **BO DIDDLEY** (hit in Nov63=) [11] [ ]
– You can't judge a book by the cover / Mama don't allow no twistin' / Mr. Khruschev / Sad sack / You all green / Diddling / Who may your lover be / Babes in the wood / Bo's bounce / Bo's twist / I can tell / Give me a break. *(re-iss.Apr87) (cd-iss.Dec86)*
May 63. (lp) **HEY! BO DIDDLEY** [ ] [ ]
– Mess around / Somebody's crying / Hong Kong / Can I go home with you / I'm going home / Rhyme song / Cracklin' / Rockin' on. *(cd-iss.May94 on 'Charly')*
Jun 63. (7") **WHO DO YOU LOVE?. / BO DIDDLEY IS A TWISTER** [ ] [-]
Jul 63. (7") **BO DIDDLEY. / DETOUR** [ ] [-]
Sep 63. (7") **PRETTY THING. / ROADRUNNER** [34] [-]
Oct 63. (7") **GREATEST LOVER IN THE WORLD. / SURFER'S LOVE CALL** [-] [ ]
Nov 63. (lp) **BO DIDDLEY RIDES AGAIN** [19] [ ]
– Bring it to Jerome / Cops and robbers / Mumblin' guitar / Oh, yea! / You don't love me / Down home special / Bo Diddley is loose / Help out / Call me (Bo's blues) / Don't let it go / Nursery rhyme / Dearest darling.
(cd-iss.Feb94 on 'See For Miles')
Nov 63. (7") **BO DIDDLEY IS A LOVER. / DOIN' THE JAGUAR** [ ] [-]
Jan 64. (lp) **BO DIDDLEY'S BEACH PARTY** [13] [ ]
– Memphis / Gunslinger / Hey Bo Diddley / Old Smokey / Bo Diddley's dog / I'm all right / Mr.Custer / Bo's waltz / What's buggin' you / Roadrunner. *(re-iss.1989)*
Feb 64. (7") **MEMPHIS. / MONKEY DIDDLEY** [ ] [ ]
May 64. (7") **MONA. / GIMME GIMME** [ ] [ ]
Jun 64. (lp) **IN THE SPOTLIGHT** [ ] [ ]
– Gimme, gimme / Not guilty / Scuttle bug / Say, man / Let me in / Hong Kong / Mississippi / Craw-dad / Bo's a lumber Jack / Walkin' and talkin' / I need you, baby / You're looking good / She's alright.
Aug 64. (7") **MAMA KEEP YOUR BIG MOUTH SHUT. / JO-ANN** [ ] [ ]
1964. (lp) **ROADRUNNER** [-] [ ]
– Bo Diddley / I'm a man / Pretty thing / Who do you love / Mona (I need you baby) / Say man / Hush your mouth / Road runner / You can't judge a book by looking at the cover / Cops and robbers / Hey Bo Diddley / Crackin' up / Diddley daddy / Bring it to Jerome. *(UK-iss.Jul84 on 'Black Lion') (cd-iss.Nov89 on 'Instant-Charly')*

Chess | Chess

Mar 65. (7") **HEY GOOD LOOKIN'. / YOU AIN'T AS BAD AS YOU CLAIM TO BE** [39] [ ]
Mar 65. (lp) **HEY GOOD LOOKIN'** [ ] [ ]
– Mess around / Somebody's crying / King Kong / Can I go home with you / I'm going home / Rhyme song / Crackin' / Rockin' on. *(re-iss.Aug86 on 'Magnum F.') (re-iss.+cd.May88 on 'Jazz Life')*
May 65. (7") **SOMEBODY BEAT ME. / MUSH MOUTH MILLIE** [ ] [ ]
Sep 65. (7") **LET THE KIDS DANCE. / LET ME PASS** [ ] [-]
Sep 65. (lp) **LET ME PASS (. . .PLUS)** [ ] [ ]
– Let me pass / Stop my monkey / Greasy spoon / Tonight is ours / Root hoot / Stinkey / Hey red riding hood / Let the kids dance / He's so mad / Soul food / Corn bread / Somebody beat me / 500% more man / Mama, keep your big mouth shut / We're gonna get married / Easy *(cd-iss.Feb94 on 'See For Miles')*
Nov 65. (7") **500% MORE MAN. / LET THE KIDS DANCE** [-] [ ]
Dec 65. (7") **500% MORE MAN. / SOMEBODY BEAT ME** [ ] [-]
1966. (lp) **500% MORE MAN** [-] [ ]
– 500% more man / Let me pass / Stop my monkey / Greasy spoon / Tonight is ours / Root hoot / Hey Red Riding Hood / Let the kids dance / He's so mad / Soul food / Corn bread / Somebody beat me.

— JEROME and The DUCHESS left his band.

Apr 66. (7") **WE'RE GONNA GET MARRIED. / DO THE FROG** [-] [ ]
Jun 66. (7") **WE'RE GONNA GET MARRIED. / EASY** [ ] [-]
Jan 67. (lp) **THE ORIGINATOR** [ ] [ ]
– Pills / Jo Ann / Two flies / Yakky doodle / What do you know about love / Lazy woman / You ain't bad / Love you baby / Limbo / Background to a music / Puttentang / Africa speaks.
May 67. (7") **OOH BABY. / BACK TO SCHOOL** [ ] [88] Jan 67
Feb 68. (7") **WRECKING MY LOVE LIFE. / BOO-GA-LOO BEFORE YOU GO** [ ] [ ]
Jun 68. (7") **ANOTHER SUGAR DADDY. / I'M HIGH AGAIN** [ ] [ ]
Mar 69. (lp) **SUPERBLUES** [ ] [ ]
– (above w / MUDDY WATERS and LITTLE WALTER)
Apr 69. (7") **BO DIDDLEY '69. / SOUL TRAIN** [ ] [ ]
1970. (7") **THE SHAPE I'M IN. / POLLUTION** [-] [ ]

— BO virtually retired from business, but released comebacks below. He surfaced periodically on live work.

Chess | Chess

Oct 71. (lp) **ANOTHER DIMENSION** [-] [ ]
– The shape I'm in / I love you more than you'll ever know / Pollution / Bad Moon rising / Down on the corner / Said shut up woman / Bad side of the Moon / Lodi / Go for broke.

1972. (7") **I SAID SHUT UP WOMAN. / I LOVE YOU MORE THAN YOU'LL EVER KNOW**
1972 (7") **BO DIDDLEY-ITIS. / INFATUATION** [-]
1972. (7") **HUSBAND-IN-LAW. / BO-JAM** [-]
1973. (7") **DON'T WANT NO LYIN' WOMAN. / MAKE A HIT RECORD** [-]
1972. (d-lp) **GOT ANOTHER BAG OF TRICKS** (compilation)

R.C.A. R.C.A.

1970s (7") **DRAG ON. / NOT FADE AWAY** [-]

Magnum F. not issued

Apr 86. (lp)(c) **HEY . . BO DIDDLEY IN CONCERT** [-]
– Intro/Bo Diddley Vamp / Doctor Jeckyll / Everleen / I Don't Know Where I've Been / You Can't Judge A Book By The Cover / Road Runner / I'm A Man / Bubble Bo Diddley
– (with band MAINSQUEEZE)

New Rose not issued

Jun 84. (7") **AIN'T IT GOOD TO BE FREE. / BO DIDDLEY PUT THE ROCK IN ROCK'N'ROLL** [-] France
Jun 84. (lp) **AIN'T IT GOOD TO BE FREE** [-]
– Bo Diddley / Bo Diddley put the rock in rock'n'roll / Gotta be a change / I don't want your welfare / Mona, where's your sister / Stabilize yourself / I don't know where I've been / I ain't gonna force it on you / Evil woman / Let the fox talk. *(re-iss.+cd.Feb88)*
Sep 89. (lp,cd) **LIVING LEGEND** [-]
– Turbo Diddley 2000 / R.U.Serious? / Jeanette Jeanette / I Broke The Chain / Bo-Pop Quake / The Best / I'll Lick Yo' Face / U Killed It / Going Home To McComb

– compilations, others, etc. –

Sep 63. Pye; (7"ep) **CHUCK BERRY AND BO DIDDLEY VOLUME 1** [-]
Nov 63. Pye; (7"ep) **CHUCK BERRY AND BO DIDDLEY VOLUME 2** [-]
Feb 64. Pye; (7"ep) **CHUCK BERRY AND BO DIDDLEY VOLUME 3** [-]
Nov 64. Pye; (7") **CHUCK'S BEAT. (w/CHUCK BERRY) / BO'S BEAT** [-]
Nov 64. Pye/ US= Chess; (lp) **TWO GREAT GUITARS**

— (above comp. credited w / **CHUCK BERRY**)

Nov 63. Pye; (7"ep) **HEY BO DIDDLEY** [-]
Apr 64. Pye; (7"ep) **THE BO DIDDLEY STORY** [-]
Oct 64. Pye; (7"ep) **BO DIDDLEY IS A LUMBERJACK** [-]
Nov 64. Pye; (7"ep) **DIDDLING** [-]
Dec 64. Pye/ US= Chess; (lp) **16 ALL TIME HITS** [-]
Nov 65. Chess; (7"ep) **I'M A MAN** [-]
Jul 66. Chess; (7"ep) **ROOSTER STEW** [-]
May 82. Chess; (lp)(c) **CHESS MASTERS VOLUME 1** [-]
(re-iss.+cd.Mar88 on 'Stylus')
May 83. Chess; (lp)(c) **CHESS MASTERS VOLUME 2** [-]
Jul 85. Chess; (7"ep) **BO DIDDLEY / PRETTY THING. / ROAD RUNNER / SAY MAN** [-]
Aug 88. Chess; (cd) **DIDDLEY DADDY** [-]
Jul 73. London; (lp) **THE LONDON BO DIDDLEY SESSIONS** [-]
(cd-iss.Jun90)
Nov 89. Charly; (3xlp)(2xc)(2xcd-box) **BO DIDDLEY BOX SET** [-]
Feb 89. Charly; (cd-ep) **BO DIDDLEY / ROAD RUNNER / YOU CAN'T JUDGE A BOOK BY THE COVER / MONA (I NEED YOU BABY)** [-]
Feb 93. Charly; (cd) **I'M A MAN** [-]
Jul 93. Charly; (cd)(c) **SIGNIFYING BLUES** [-]
Nov 93. Charly; (12xcd-box) **THE CHESS YEARS** [-]
Aug 65. Marble Arch; (lp) **SURFIN' WITH BO DIDDLEY** [-]
(above issued in the US earlier on 'Checker')
Jun 85. Red Lightnin'; (12"ep) **IT'S GREAT TO BE RICH** [-]

— (above credited w / **BILLY BOY ARNOLD**)

Aug 91. Provogue; (cd) **ROADRUNNER VOL.2** [-]
Jun 91. See For Miles; (cd)(c)(lp) **THE EP COLLECTION** [-]
1991. Edsel/ US= R.C.A.; (cd)(lp) **THE 20th ANNIVERSARY OF ROCK'N'ROLL** 1976
Sep 93. Ace; (cd) **BO'S BLUES** [-]
Jul 95. BGO; (cd) **HEY! BO DIDDLEY / BO DIDDLEY** [-]
Aug 95. Triple X; (cd) **THIS SHOULD NOT BE** [-]
Aug 95. Triple X; (cd) **LIVE** [-]
Aug 95. Triple X; (cd) **PROMISES** [-]
Aug 95. Triple X; (cd) **THE MIGHTY BO DIDDLEY** [-]

DIFFORD & TILBROOK (see under ⇒ SQUEEZE)

DIGA RHYTHM BAND (see under ⇒ GRATEFUL DEAD)

Steve DIGGLE (see under ⇒ BUZZCOCKS)

DILLARD & CLARK (see under ⇒ BYRDS)

DIM STARS (see under ⇒ HELL, Richard)

Dion DiMUCCI (see under ⇒ DION)

DINOSAUR JR.

Formed: Amherst, Massachusetts, USA . . . 1983 by J.MASCIS. After brief spell recording for US indie labels, they finally made it big in the 90s, landing contract for 'WEA' subsidiaries; Blanco Y Negro (UK) / Sire (US). • **Style:** Punk / hard-core rock, with flowing melodic psychedelia, not unlike HUSKER DU or MEAT PUPPETS, with MASCIS definitely influenced by NEIL YOUNG. • **Songwriters:** MASCIS wrote all, except JUST LIKE HEAVEN (Cure) / LOTTA LOVE (Neil Young) / QUICKSAND (David Bowie) / I FEEL A WHOLE LOT BETTER (Byrds) / GOIN' BLIND (Kiss) / HOT BURRITO 2 (Gram Parsons). • **Trivia:** In Jun'91, MASCIS as drummer, splintered with Boston satanic hard-core group UPSIDE DOWN CROSS, who made one self-titled album Autumn '91 on 'Taang!'. He also wrote songs and made a cameo appearance in the 1992 film 'Gas, Food, Lodging'.

Recommended: BUG (*7) / YOU'RE LIVING ALL OVER ME (*6) / GREEN MIND (*7) / WHERE YOU BEEN? (*7).

LOU BARLOW – guitar / **J.MASCIS** – drums / **CHARLIE NAKAJIMA** – vox / **SCOTT HELLAND** – bass

DEEP WOUND

not issued Radiobeat

Dec 83. (7"ep) **I SAW IT** [-]
– I saw it / Sisters / In my room / Don't need / Lou's anxiety song / Video prick / Sick of fun / Deep wound / Dead babies.

— **J.MASCIS** – vocals, guitar, percussion / **LOU BARLOW** – bass, ukelele, vocals

DINOSAUR

added **MURPH** (b.PATRICK MURPHY) – drums (ex-ALL WHITE JURY)

not issued Homestead

Jun 85. (lp) **DINOSAUR** [-]
– Forget the swan / Cats in a bowl / The leper / Does it float / Pointless / Repulsion / Gargoyle / Several lips / Mountain man / Quest / Bulbs of passion.
Mar 86. (7") **REPULSION. / BULBS OF PASSION** [-]

DINOSAUR JR.

S.S.T. S.S.T.

Mar 87. (12"ep) **DINOSAUR JR.** [-]
– Little fury things / In a jar / Show me the way. *(cd-ep iss.Dec88)*
Jul 87. (m-lp)(c) **YOU'RE LIVING ALL OVER ME**
– Little fury things / Kracked / Sludgefeast / The lung / Raisans / Tarpit / In a jar / Lose / Poledo / Show me the way. *(cd-iss.Oct95)*

Blast First Blast First

Sep 88. (7") **FREAK SCENE. / KEEP THE GLOVE**
(US-iss.7"/7"green)
Oct 88. (lp)(c)(cd) **BUG**
– Freak scene / No bones / They always come / Yeah we know / Let it ride / Pond song / Budge / The post / Don't.

— **DONNA BIDDELL** – bass (ex-SCREAMING TREES) repl. BARLOW

Apr 89. (7")(12"one-sided)(cd-s) **JUST LIKE HEAVEN / THROW DOWN / CHUNKS** 78 Feb 90
(US version 7"+=/7"green+=/12"ep+=/cd-ep+= Freak scene / Keep the glove)

— BARLOW was sacked Jun'89, at the same time DONNA left. They were repl. by **DON FLEMING** – guitar + **JAY SPIEGEL** – drums (both B.A.L.L.)

not issued Sub Pop

Jun 90. (7")(7"purple) **THE WAGON. / BETTER THAN GONE** [-]

— In Oct 90, J.MASCIS and other ex-DINOSAUR JR member FLEMING + SPIEGEL, made an album 'RAKE' as VELVET MONKEYS (aka B.A.L.L. + friends).

Blanco Y Negro Sire

Jan 91. (7")(c-s) **THE WAGON. / THE LITTLE BABY** 49
(12"+=)(cd-s+=) – Pebbles and weeds / Quicksand.
Feb 91. (cd)(c)(lp) **GREEN MIND** 36
– The wagon / Puke and cry / Blowing it – I live for that look / Flying cloud / How'd you pin that one on me / Water / Muck / Thumb / Green mind.
Aug 91. (7")(c-s) **WHATEVER'S COOL WITH ME. / SIDEWAYS**
(12"+=)(cd-s+=) – Thumb (live) / Keep the glove (live).

— **MASCIS + MURPH** introduced new member **MIKE JOHNSON** – bass

Nov 92. (7") **GET ME. / HOT BURRITO 2** 44
(12"+=)(c-s+=)(cd-s+=) – Qwest (live).
Jan 93. (7") **START CHOPPIN'. / TURNIP FARM** 20
(12"+=)(cd-s+=)(10"pic-d+=) – Forget it.
Feb 93. (cd)(c)(lp) **WHERE YOU BEEN?** 10 50
– Out there / Start choppin' / What else is new? / On the way / Not the same / Get me / Drawerings / Hide / Goin' home / I ain't sayin'.
Jun 93. (7")(12")(c-s) **OUT THERE. / KEEBLIN' (live) / KRACKED (live)** 44
(10"+=) – Post.
(cd-s++=) – Quest (live).
(cd-s) – ('A'side) / Get me / Severed lips / Thumb (radio sessions).
Aug 94. (7")(c-s)(10"etched)(cd-ep) **FEEL THE PAIN / GET OUT OF THIS / REPULSION (acoustic)** 25
Sep 94. (cd)(c)(lp) **WITHOUT A SOUND** 24 44
– Feel the pain / I don't think so / Yeah right / Outta hand / Grab it / Even you / Mind glow / Get out of this / On the brink / Seemed like the thing to do / Over your shoulder.
Feb 95. (7"green)(c-s) **I DON'T THINK SO. / GET ME (live)** 67
(cd-s+=) – What else is new? / Sludge.

DIO

Formed: By American RONNIE JAMES DIO, Oct'82 after basing himself in London, England. He recruited Irishman VIVIAN CAMPBELL and 2

Englishmen JIMMY BAIN and VINNY APPICE (brother of CARMINE). DIO's previous expreience, stretched back to the 1962, when he ran his own school group RONNIE & THE PROPHETS, who managed to issue a number of singles starting with 'LOVE PAINS. / OOH POO PAH DOO for 'Atlantic US'. In 1967, RONNIE and his cousin DAVID FEINSTEIN formed The ELECTRIC ELVES, who in the early 70's, became ELF. In 1972, they signed to 'Purple' records, and soon supported label boss's DEEP PURPLE. They made a couple of well-received albums, before he and most of others, took off in April 1975, to join RITCHIE BLACKMORE'S RAINBOW. In May'79, RONNIE took the place of OZZY OSBOURNE in BLACK SABBATH, and stayed with them until he formed own DIO group. Became successful albums orientated band throughout the 80's and early 90's. • **Style:** With dynamic vocal range, he obviously carried on where RAINBOW left off, portraying his anthemic tunes, to mystical themes backed with tight heavy metal backing. • **Songwriters:** DIO compositions, although he wrote material in ELF with MICKEY SOULE. • **Trivia:** RONNIE was also a fair player of the piano and bass in his early years.

Recommended: DIAMONDS – THE BEST OF DIO (*5)

RONNIE JAMES DIO (b.RONALD PADAVONA, 10 Jul'47, Portsmouth, New Hampshire, USA, raised Portland, NY) – vocals (ex-ELF, ex-RAINBOW, ex-BLACK SABBATH) / **VIVIAN CAMPBELL** – guitar (ex-SWEET SAVAGE) / **JIMMY BAIN** – bass (ex-RAINBOW, ex-WILD HORSES) / **VINNIE APPICE** – drums (ex-BLACK SABBATH) / **CLAUDE SCHNELL** – keyboards

Vertigo | Warners

Jun 83. (lp)(c) **HOLY DIVER** 13 | 56
– Stand up and shout / Holy diver / Gypsy / Caught in the middle / Don't talk to strangers / Straight through the heart / Invisible / Rainbow in the dark / Shame on the night. *(re-iss.Mar88)*

Aug 83. (7") **HOLY DIVER. / EVIL EYES** 72 | □
(12"+=) – Don't talk to strangers.

Oct 83. (7") **RAINBOW IN THE DARK. / STAND UP AND SHOUT (live)** 46 | □
(12"+=) – Straight through the heart.

Oct 83. (7") **RAINBOW IN THE DARK. / GYPSY** - | □

Jul 84. (7") **MYSTERY. / I SPEED AT NIGHT** - | □

Jul 84. (lp)(c) **THE LAST IN LINE** 4 | 23
– We rock / The last in line / Breathless / I speed at night / One night in the city / Evil eyes / Mystery / Eat your heart out / Egypt (the chains are on). *(cd-iss. 1985)(re-iss.cd Mar93 on 'Polygram')*

Jul 84. (7") **WE ROCK. / HOLY DIVER (live)** 42 | □
(12"+=) – Shame on the night / Rainbow in the dark.

Sep 84. (7")(7"pic-d) **MYSTERY. / EAT YOUR HEART OUT** 34 | □
(12"+=) – Don't talk to strangers.

Aug 85. (7") **ROCK'N'ROLL CHILDREN. / SACRED HEART** □ | □
(12"+=) – Last in line (live) / We rock (live).

Aug 85. (lp)(c)(cd) **SACRED HEART** 4 | 29
– King of rock'n'roll / Sacred heart / Another lie / Hungry for heaven / Rock'n 'roll children / Like the beat of a heart / Just another day / Fallen angels / Shoot shoot. *(re-iss.cd Mar93 on 'Polygram')*

Oct 85. (7")(7"sha-pic-d) **HUNGRY FOR HEAVEN. / KING OF ROCK'N'ROLL** 72 | □
(12"+=) – ?

May 86. (7")(7"pic-d) **HIDING (FROM) THE RAINBOW. / HUNGRY FOR HEAVEN** 56 | □
(d7"+=)(12"+=)(12"pic-d+=) – Shame on the night / Egypt (the chains are on).

— **CRAIG GOLDIE** – guitar (in the studio) repl. CAMPBELL

Jun 86. (m-lp)(c) **INTERMISSION (live except *)** 22 | 70
– King of rock'n'roll / Rainbow in the dark / Sacred heart / Time to burn* / Rock'n'roll children / We rock. *(re-iss.cd Mar93 on 'Polygram')*

Jul 87. (7") **I COULD HAVE BEEN A DREAMER. / NIGHT PEOPLE** 69 | □
(12"+=) – Sunset superman.

Aug 87. (lp)(c)(cd) **DREAM EVIL** 8 | 43
– Night people / Dream evil / Sunset superman / All the fools sailed away / Naked in the rain / Over love / I could have been a dreamer / Faces in the window / When a woman cries.

Aug 87. (7") **I COULD HAVE BEEN A DREAMER. / OVER LOVE** - | □

— **DIO** recruited entire new line-up; **ROWAN ROBERTSON** (b.1971, Cambridge, England) – guitar repl. GOLDIE / **JENS JOHANSSON** (b.Sweden) – keyboards repl. SCHNELL / **TEDDY COOK** (b.New York, USA) – bass repl. BAIN / **SIMON WRIGHT** (b.19 Jun'63, England) – drums (ex-AC/DC) repl. APPICE

May 90. (cd)(c)(lp) **LOCK UP THE WOLVES** 28 | 61
– Wild one / Born on the sun / Hey angel / Between two heats / Night music / Lock up the wolves / Evil on Queen street / Walk on water / Twisted / My eyes. *(cd+=)* – Why are they watching me.

Jun 90. (7") **HEY ANGEL. / WALK ON WATER** □ | □
(12"+=) – Rock'n'roll children / Mystery.
(cd-s++=) – We rock.
(12"+=) – We rock / Why are they watching me.

Mar 92. (cd)(c)(lp) **DIAMONDS – THE BEST OF DIO** (compilation) □ | □
– Holy Diver / Rainbow In The Dark / Don't Talk To Strangers / We Rock / The Last In Line / Rock 'n' Roll Children / Sacred Heart / Hungry For Heaven / Hide In The Rainbow / Dream Evil / Wild One / Lock Up The Wolves

Oct 93. (cd)(c)(lp) **STRANGE HIGHWAYS** □ | □
– Jesus, Mary & the holy ghost / Fire head / Strange highways / Hollywood black / Evilution / Pain / One foot in the grave / Give her the gun / Blood from a stone / Here's to you / Bring down the rain. *(re-iss.cd Apr95)*

– early material below –

ELECTRIC ELVES

RONNIE JAMES DIO – vocals, bass / **DAVE FEINSTEIN** – guitar / **DOUG THALER** – keyboards / **GARY DRISCOLL** – drums / **NICK PANTAS** – guitar

M.G.M. | M.G.M.

Dec 67. (7") **HEY LOOK ME OVER. / IT PAYS TO ADVERTISE** □ | □

The ELVES

Decca | ?

Sep 69. (7") **IN DIFFERENT CIRCLES. / SHE'S NOT THE SAME** □ | □

M.C.A. | ?

Feb 70. (7") **AMBER VELVET. / WEST VIRGINIA** □ | □

— Mid'70, all were involved in a car crash, PANTAS was killed and THALER hospitalised for a year.

ELF

were formed mid'71, by DIO, THALER (now guitar), **FEINSTEIN, DRISCOLL** and **MICKEY LEE SOULE** – keyboards, guitar

Epic | Epic

Aug 72. (lp)(c) **ELF** □ | □
– Hoochie coochie lady / First avenue never more / I'm coming back for you / Sit down honey / Dixie Lee junction / Love me like a woman / Gambler gambler. *(re-iss.Sep86 on 'CBS')In Jul93, 'ELF' was issued on cd, by 'Sony Europe'.*

Sep 72. (7") **HOOCHIE KOOCHIE LADY. / FIRST AVENUE** □ | □

— Early'73, moved to England. Added **CRAIG GRUBER** – bass STEVE EDWARDS – guitar replaced FEINSTEIN

Purple | M.G.M.

Mar 74. (lp)(c) **CAROLINA COUNTRY BALL (US-title; L.A.59)** □ | □
– Carolina country ball / L.A.59 / Ain't it all amusing / Happy / Anmorte New Orleans / Rockin' chair rock'n'roll blues / Rainbow / Do the same thing / Blanche. *(re-iss.Aug84 on 'Safari')*

Apr 74. (7") **LA. 59. / AIN'T IT ALL AMUSING** □ | □

1975. (7") **SITTING IN A DREAM** ("RONNIE DIO & GUESTS") / ('B' by JOHN LAWTON) □ | -

— Added **MARK NAUSEEF** – percussion (ex-VELVET UNDERGROUND)

M.G.M. | M.G.M.

Jun 75. (lp)(c) **TRYING TO BURN THE SUN** □ | □
– Black swan water / Prentice wood / When she smiles / Good time music / Liberty road / Shotgun boogie / Wonderworld / Streetwalker. *(re-iss.Aug84 on 'Safari')*

— Apr'75. NAUSEEF joined GILLAN then THIN LIZZY. The rest with DIO joined (RITCHIE BLACKMORE'S) RAINBOW. DIO joined BLACK SABBATH in 1979.

– compilations, others, etc. –

May 87. Safari; (cd) **THE GARGANTIAN ELF ALBUM** □ | □
– (1974 + 1975 albums, minus a few tracks)

DION

Born: DION DiMUCCI, 18 Jul'39, The Bronx, New York, USA. In 1957, he formed DION & THE TIMBERLAINES, who after one flop single, became DION & THE BELMONTS in 1958. That year, they had their first US hit, when 'I WONDER WHY' hit the 30. After a couple of more successes, their greatest 2+ minutes, 'A TEENAGER IN LOVE', gave them first UK hit, and a new line in designer college sweat shirts. Late in 1960, advice from his manager, encouraged DION to embark on solo career. The following year, his best work 'RUNAROUND SUE' & 'THE WANDERER', became US million-sellers, and also big hits in the UK. Throughout the early 60's, with a new contract on 'Columbia', he continued to have fruitful US chart run. His career took a dive in 1964 with the onslaught of the British invasion (i.e. BEATLES, etc). After a flop reformation of him and the BELMONTS, his career took off again in diverse directions, when signing to 'Warners' in 1968. He also kicked his drug habit in the same year. • **Style:** Moved from teenybop rock'n'roll to mid-60's roots blues. By the late 60's, his sound had found folk-rock. His many comebacks, were helped by PHIL SPECTOR in 1975 and Christianity in the early 80's. In 1989, he returned to harder-edged rock'n'roll, which led back into minor chart placings. • **Songwriters:** Penned some of own material, except several by ERNIE MARESCA. The group worked in the late 1950's with writers DOC POMUS and MORT SHUMAN. Covered; WHERE OR WHEN (Rodgers & Hart) / WHEN YOU WISH UPON A STAR (?) / IN THE STILL OF THE NIGHT (Cole Porter). DION solo covered RUBY BABY + DRIP DROP (Lieber-Stoller) / COME GO WITH ME (Del Vikings) / I'M YOUR HOOCHIE COOCHIE MAN (Muddy Waters) / JOHNNY B.GOODE (Chuck Berry) / SPOONFUL (Willie Dixon) / ABRAHAM, MARTIN & JOHN (Dick Holler) / PURPLE HAZE (Jimi Hendrix) / BOTH SIDES NOW (Joni Mitchell) / AND THE NIGHT STOOD STILL (Diane Warren) / SAN DIEGO SERENADE (Tom Waits) / etc. In 1989, he co-wrote with TUCHY, and covered; SERENADE (Tom Waits). • **Trivia:** DION is featured on the sleeve of the BEATLES' 'Sgt.Pepper' album in 1967.

Recommended: THE FABULOUS DION & THE BELMONTS (*5) / THE FABULOUS DION (*5).

DION & THE TIMBERLANES

DION DIMUCCI – lead vocals / **CARLO MASTRANGELO** (b. 5 Oct'39) – vocals / **FRED MILANO** (b.26 Aug'40) – vocals / **ANGELO D'ALEO** (b. 3 Feb'41) – vocals not issued Mohawk

1957. (7") **THE CHOSEN FEW. / OUT IN COLORADO** [-] [ ]
(re-iss. later on 'Jubilee')

BELMONTS

1957. (7") **TEEN-AGE CLEMENTINE. / SANTA MARGUERITA** [-] [ ]

DION & THE BELMONTS

(same line-up)

1958. (7") **WE WENT AWAY. / TAG ALONG** [-] [ ]

London Laurie

Jul 58. (7") **I WONDER WHY. / TEEN ANGEL** [ ] [22] May 58
Oct 58. (7") **NO ONE KNOWS. / I CAN'T GO ON (ROSALIE)** [ ] [19] Aug 58
Feb 59. (7") **DON'T PITY ME. / JUST YOU** [ ] [40] Dec 58
Jun 59. (7") **A TEENAGER IN LOVE. / I'VE CRIED BEFORE** [28] [5] Apr 59
1959. (lp) **PRESENTING DION & THE BELMONTS** [-] [ ]
– I wonder why / Teen angel / Where or when / You better not do that / Just you / I got the blues / Don't pity me / A teenager in love / Wonderful girl / Funny feeling / I've cried before / That's my desire / No one knows / I can't go on (Rosalie). *(UK-iss.1984 on 'Ace', cd-iss.1989)*

— Now a trio when D'ALEO was conscripted to US navy.

Nov 59. (7") **EVERY LITTLE THING I DO. / A LOVER'S PRAYER** [ ] [48] [73] Sep 59

(above single on 'Pye Int.' UK)

Jan 60. (7") **WHERE OR WHEN. / THAT'S MY DESIRE** [ ] [3] Dec 59

Top Rank Laurie

Apr 60. (7") **WHEN YOU WISH UPON A STAR. / WONDERFUL GIRL** [-] [30]
May 60. (7") **WHEN YOU WISH UPON A STAR. / MY PRIVATE JOY** [ ] [-]
Jul 60. (7") **IN THE STILL OF THE NIGHT. / A FUNNY FEELING** [-] [38]
Sep 60. (7") **IN THE STILL OF THE NIGHT. / SWINGING ON A STAR** [ ] [-]
1964. (lp) **TOGETHER WITH THE BELMONTS** [-] [ ]
– We belong together / Every little thing I do / Meant to be / Come take a walk with me / Tag along / Teen angel / Such a long way / We went away / I can't go on / That's how I need you / Will you love me still / Faith.

DION

went solo. The BELMONTS signed to 'Sabina' and issued own 45's.

Top Rank Laurie

Nov 60. (7") **LONELY TEENAGER. / LITTLE MISS BLUE** [47] [12] [96]
Feb 61. (7") **HAVIN' FUN. / NORTH-EAST END OF THE CORNER** [ ] [42]
Apr 61. (7") **KISSIN' GAME. / HEAVEN HELP ME** [-] [82]
Jul 61. (7") **SOMEBODY NOBODY WANTS. / COULD SOMEBODY TAKE MY PLACE TONIGHT** [-] [ ]
Oct 61. (7") **RUNAROUND SUE. / RUNAWAY GIRL** [11] [1] Sep 61
(re-iss.Aug76 on 'Philips') (re-iss.Aug82 on 'EMI Gold')
Dec 61. (lp) **RUNAROUND SUE** [-] [11] Nov 61
– Runaround Sue / Somebody wants me / Dream lover / Life is but a dream / The wanderer / Runaway girl / I'm gonna make it somehow / The majestic / Could somebody take my place tonight / Little star / Lonely world / In the still of the night / Kansas City / Take good care of my baby. *(re-iss.1985 on 'Ace', cd-iss.1989)*

H.M.V. Laurie

Feb 62. (7") **THE WANDERER. / THE MAJESTIC** [10] [2] Dec 61 [36]
May 62. (7") **LOVERS WHO WANDER. / (I WAS) BORN TO CRY** [ ] [3] Apr 62 [42]

Stateside Laurie

Aug 62. (7") **LITTLE DIANE. / LOST FOR SURE** [ ] [8] Jul 62
Aug 62. (lp) **LOVERS WHO WANDER** [-] [8] Jul 62
– Lovers who wander / Come go with me / King without a queen / So long friend / Twist / Little Diane / Mi muchacha / Stagger Lee / Shout / Tonight, tonight / Born to cry / Queen of the hop / Candy man / Sandy / Lost for sure / Love came to me. *(UK-iss.Jan86 on 'Ace')*
Nov 62. (7") **LOVE CAME TO ME. / LITTLE GIRL** [ ] [10]

C.B.S. Columbia

Jan 63. (7") **RUBY BABY. / HE'LL ONLY HURT YOU** [ ] [2]
Mar 63. (lp) **RUBY BABY** [ ] [20]
– Ruby baby / The end of the world / Go away little girl / Gonna make it alone / Fever / My mammy / Will love ever come my way / The loneliest man in the world / You made me love you (I didn't want to do it) / He'll only hurt you / You're nobody 'til somebody loves you / Unloved, unwanted me.
May 63. (7") **THIS LITTLE GIRL. / THE LONELIEST MAN IN THE WORLD** [ ] [21] Apr 63
Jul 63. (7") **BE CAREFUL OF STONES THAT YOU THROW. / I CAN'T BELIEVE (THAT YOU DON'T LOVE ME ANYMORE)** [ ] [31]

DION DIMUCCI

Sep 63. (7") **DONNA THE PRIMA DONNA. / YOU'RE MINE** [ ] [6]
Sep 63. (lp) **DONNA THE PRIMA DONNA** [-] [ ]
– Donna the prima donna / Can't we be sweethearts / Sweet, sweet baby / This little girl of mine / Flim flam / Troubled man / This little girl / Oh happy days / You're mine / Donna / I can't believe (that you don't love me anymore) / Be careful of stones that you throw.
Nov 63. (7") **DRIP DROP. / NO ONE'S WAITING FOR ME** [ ] [6]
Mar 64. (7") **I'M YOUR HOOCHIE COOCHIE MAN. / THE ROAD I'M ON (GLORIA)** [ ] [ ]
Oct 64. (7") **JOHHNY B.GOODE. / CHICAGO BLUES** [ ] [71]
Mar 65. (7") **SWEET SWEET BABY. / UNLOVED, UNWANTED ME** [ ] [ ]
1965. (lp) **WONDER WHERE I'M BOUND** [-] [ ]
– I can't help but wonder where I'm bound / It's all over now, baby blue / A Sunday kind of love / Knowing I won't go back there / 900 miles / Now / Southern train / The seventh son / Farewell / Wake up baby / Baby, please don't go.
Jun 65. (7") **SPOONFUL ("DION"). / KICKIN' CHILD** [ ] [ ]

— In 1966, he formed folk-pop outfit

DION & THE WANDERERS

not issued Columbia

1966. (7") **YOU MOVE ME BABE. / TOMORROW WON'T BRING THE RAIN** [-] [ ]
1966. (7") **TIME IN MY HEART FOR YOU. / WAKE UP BABY** [-] [ ]
1966. (7") **SO MUCH YOUNGER. / TWO TON FEATHER** [-] [ ]

DION & THE BELMONTS

(see past line-up)

H.M.V. ABC Para

Nov 66. (7") **BERIMBAU (MY GIRL). / THE MONTH OF MAY** [ ] [ ]
Mar 67. (7") **MOVIN' MAN. / FOR BOBBIE** [ ] [ ]
May 67. (lp) **TOGETHER AGAIN** [ ] [ ]
– Movin' man / Berimbau / Come to my side / All I wanna do / But not for me / New York town / Loserville / For Bobbie / Jump back baby / Baby you've been on my mind / My girl / The month of May

DION

(solo)

London Laurie

Nov 68. (7") **ABRAHAM, MARTIN AND JOHN. / DADDY ROLLIN'** [ ] [4] Oct 68
(re-iss.Mar75 on 'UK Decca')
Dec 68. (lp) **DION** [ ] [ ]
– Abraham, Martin and John / Purple haze / Tomorrow is a long time / Everybody's talkin' / Sonny boy / The dolphins / He looks a lot like me / Sun fun song / From both sides now / Sisters of mercy / Loving you is sweeter than ever. *(re-iss.Feb87 as 'ABRAHAM, MARTIN & JOHN' on 'Ace')*
Feb 69. (7") **PURPLE HAZE. / THE DOLPHINS** [-] [63]
Apr 69. (7") **FROM BOTH SIDES NOW. / SUN FUN SONG** [-] [91]

Warners. Warners

Jun 69. (7") **LOVING YOU IS SWEETER THAN EVER. / HE LOOKS A LOT LIKE ME** [-] [ ]
Jun 69. (7") **BOTH SIDES NOW. / SONNY BOY** [ ] [-]
Jan 70. (7") **IF WE ONLY HAVE LOVE. / NATURAL MAN** [ ] [ ]
1970. (lp) **SIT DOWN OLD FRIEND** [ ] [ ]
– Natural man / I don't believe my race is run / Jammed up blues / Little pink pony / You can't judge a book by the cover / If we only have love / Sweet pea / Just a little girl / Let go, let God / King con man / Sit down old friend.
Aug 70. (7") **YOUR OWN BACK YARD. / SIT DOWN OLD FRIEND** [ ] [75]
Apr 71. (7") **CLOSE TO IT ALL. / LET IT BE** [ ] [ ]
1971. (lp) **YOU'RE NOT ALONE** [ ] [ ]
– Close to it all / Sunniland / Windows / The visitor / Peaceful place / Let it be / The stuff I got / Blackbird / Josie / Attraction works better than promotion.
Jun 71. (7") **JOSIE. / SUNNILAND** [-] [ ]
Jul 71. (7") **SUNNILAND. / PEACEFUL PLACE** [ ] [ ]
Dec 71. (lp) **SANCTUARY (some live)** [ ] [ ]
– Sunshine lady / Sanctuary / Willigo / Harmony sound / Gotta get up / Please be my friend / Take a little time / The wanderer / Abraham, Martin and John / Almond joy / Ruby baby / Brand new morning.
May 72. (7") **SANCTUARY. / BRAND NEW MORNING** [ ] [ ]
Nov 72. (lp) **SUITE FOR LATE SUMMER** [ ] [ ]
– Seagull / Wedding song / Jennifer knew / It all fits together / To dream tomorrow / Didn't you change / Tennessee Madonna / Traveler in the rain / Running close behind you.
Nov 72. (7") **RUNNING CLOSE BEHIND YOU. / SEAGULL** [-] [ ]

On the 2nd Jun'72, he re-united with The BELMONTS for live one-off.

Feb 73. (lp)(c) **REUNION (live at Madison Square Garden)** [ ] [ ]
– The wanderer / No one knows / I wonder why / Teenager in love / Ruby baby / That's my desire / Drip drop / Where or when / Runaround Sue / Little Diane.
1973. (7") **DOCTOR ROCK AND ROLL. / SUNSHINE LADY** [-] [ ]
1973. (7") **NEW YORK CITY SONG. / RICHER THAN A RICH MAN** [-] [ ]
1974. (7") **HEY MY LOVE. / LOVER BOY SUPREME** [-] [ ]
1974. (7") **LOVER BOY SUPREME. / THE WAY YOU DO THE THINGS YOU DO** [-] [ ]
1974. (7") **QUEEN OF '59. / OH THE NIGHT** [-] [ ]
1975. (7") **YOUNG VIRGIN EYES (I'M ALL WRAPPED UP). / OH THE NIGHT** [-] [ ]

Phil Spector Int. Phil Spector Int.

1975. (7") **BORN TO BE WITH YOU. / RUNNING CLOSE BEHIND YOU** [-] [ ]
Jun 75. (7") **MAKE THE WOMAN LOVE ME. / RUNNING CLOSE BEHIND YOU** [ ] [ ]
Oct 75. (lp)(c) **BORN TO BE WITH YOU** [ ] [ ]
– Born to be with you / ake the woman love me / Your own backyard / He's got the whole world in his hands / Only you know / New York City song / In and out of showers / Good vin' man.
Feb 76. (7") **BORN TO BE WITH YOU. / GOOD LOVIN' MAN** [ ] [-]
Aug 76. (7") **BABY LET'S STICK TOGETHER. / NEW YORK CITY SONG** [ ] [ ]

Warners. Warners

Aug 76. (lp)(c) **STREETHEART**
– Runaway man / Streetheart / Hey my love / On the night / Lover boy supreme / Queen of '59 / You showed me what love is / More to you / If I can just get through the night.
Aug 76. (7") **YOU SHOWED ME WHAT LOVE IS. / LOVER BOY SUPREME** [ ] [ ]

Lifesong Lifesong

1978. (lp) **RETURN OF THE WANDERER** [ ] [ ]
– Lookin' for the heart of Saturday night / Midtown American main street gang / You've awakened something in me / Guitar queen / The pattern of my lifeline / (I used to be a) Brooklyn Dodger / Streetheart theme / The power of love within / Spanish Harlem incident / Do you believe in magic. *(cd-iss.Jun90 on 'Ace')*

1978. (7") **LOOKING FOR THE HEART OF SATURDAY NIGHT. / YOU'VE AWAKENED SOMETHING IN ME** [-] [ ]

1978. (7") **GUITAR QUEEN. / MIDTOWN AMERICAN MAIN STREET GANG** [-] [ ]

1978. (7") **(I USED TO BE A) BROOKLYN DODGER. / STREETHEART THEME** [-] [ ]

not issued Dayspring

1982. (lp) **INSIDE JOB** [-] [ ]
– I believe / He's the one / Centre of my life / Truth will set you free / Gonna be ready / Old souvenirs / New Jersey wife / Man in the glass / Sweet Surrender.

Aura Dayspring

Oct 83. (7") **WE DON'T TALK ANYMORE. / MIDNIGHT LOVER** [ ] [-]

Aug 84. (7") **THE WAY YOU DO THE THINGS YOU DO. / HEY MY LOVE** [ ] [ ]

1984. (lp) **I PUT AWAY MY IDOLS** [-] [ ]
– Here is my servant / Trust in my Lord / Day of the Lord / I put away my idols / Daddy / Very soon / He won't tell you / Healing / Give up and surrender / My prayer for you.

1985. (lp) **KINGDOM IN THE STREETS** [-] [ ]

DION DiMUCCI

with **DAVE EDMUNDS** – guitar, bass / **JIM HORN** – sax / **PHIL CHEN** – bass / **CHUCK LEAVELL** – keyboards / **DAVE CHARLES** – percussion

Arista Arista

Jun 89. (7") **AND THE NIGHT STOOD STILL. / TOWER OF LOVE** [ ] [75]
(12"+=)(cd-s+=) – The wanderer.

Jun 89. (lp)(c)(cd) **YO FRANKIE** [ ] [ ]
– King of the New York streets / And the night stood still / Yo Frankie (she's all right with me) / I've got to get to you / Medley:- Written on the subway wall – Little star / Drive all night / Always in the rain / Loving you is killing me / Tower of love / Serenade.

Jul 89. (7") **KING OF THE NEW YORK STREETS. / THE WANDERER** [74] [ ]
(12"+=)(cd-s+=) – ???

Feb 90. (7"ep)(cd-ep) **WRITTEN ON THE SUBWAY WALL – LITTLE STAR (medley) / KING OF THE NEW YORK STREETS. / AND THE NIGHT STOOD STILL / TOWER OF LOVE** [ ] [ ]

– compilations, others, etc. (* w/BELMONTS) –

Note; All 'Stateside' releases were issued on 'Laurie' US.

Dec 62. Laurie; (lp) **DION SINGS HIS GREATEST HITS *** [-] [29]
Mar 63. Stateside; (7") **SANDY. / FAITH** [ ] [21]
Jun 63. Laurie; (lp) **DION SINGS TO SANDY (AND ALL HIS OTHER GIRLS)** [-] [ ]
Jul 63. Stateside; (7") **COME GO WITH ME. / KING WITHOUT A QUEEN** [ ] [48]
1964. Laurie; (7") **LONELY WORLD. / TAG ALONG** [-] [ ]
1965. Laurie; (7") **THEN I'LL BE TIRED OF YOU. / AFTER THE DANCE** [-] [ ]
1965. Laurie; (7") **SHOUT. / LITTLE GIRL** [-] [ ]
1966. Laurie; (7") **(I WAS) BORN TO CRY. / I GOT THE BLUES** [-] [ ]
Mar 73. Columbia; (lp) **DION'S GREATEST HITS** [-] [ ]
(re-iss.Apr74 & Dec81 on 'R.C.A.'-UK / 'Laurie'-US)
Apr 76. Philips; (7") **THE WANDERER. / LITTLE DIANE** [16] [ ]
Oct 76. Philips; (7") **A TEENAGER IN LOVE.* / I CAN'T GO ON (ROSALIE)*** [ ] [ ]
Oct 80. Philips; (7"m) **THE WANDERER. / RUNAROUND SUE / I WONDER WHY *** [ ] [ ]
Jul 76. Sonic; (lp) **PICK HITS OF THE RADIO GOOD GUYS VOL.1** [ ] [-]
Jul 76. Sonic; (lp) **PICK HITS OF THE RADIO GOOD GUYS VOL.2** [ ] [-]
Jul 76. Sonic; (lp) **PICK HITS OF THE RADIO GOOD GUYS VOL.3** [ ] [-]
May 79. Ensign; (lp)(c) **DION & THE BELMONTS *** [ ] [-]
Mar 80. K-Tel; (lp)(c) **DION AND THE BELMONTS' 20 GOLDEN GREATS** [31] [-]
Aug 81. RCA-Gold; (7") **A TEENAGER IN LOVE.* / I WONDER WHY *** [ ] [-]
Aug 81. RCA-Gold; (7") **THE WANDERER. / LOVE COME BACK TO ME** [ ] [-]
Jun 84. Old Gold; (7") **THE WANDERER. / LOVERS WHO WANDER** [ ] [-]
Jun 84. Old Gold; (7") **RUNAROUND SUE. / LONELY TEENAGER** [ ] [-]
Jun 84. Old Gold; (7") **A TEENAGER IN LOVE.* / WHERE OR WHEN *** [ ] [-]
Feb 89. Old Gold; (cd-ep) **THE WANDERER / RUNAROUND SUE / A TEENAGER IN LOVE *** [ ] [-]
1985. Ace; (lp) **WISH UPON A STAR** [ ] [-]
1985. Ace; (lp) **ALONE WITH DION** [ ] [-]
Nov 85. Ace; (lp) **SO WHY DIDN'T YOU DO THAT THE FIRST TIME** [ ] [-]
Aug 86. Ace; (lp) **HITS** [ ] [-]
Sep 90. Ace; (cd) **WISH UPON A STAR / ALONE WITH DION** [ ] [-]
Feb 91. Ace; (cd) **LOVERS WHO WANDER / SO WHY DIDN'T YOU DO THAT THE FIRST TIME** [ ] [-]
Mar 91. Ace; (cd) **PRESENTING DION & THE BELMONTS * / RUNAROUND SUE** [ ] [-]
Sep 91. Ace; (cd) **THE FABULOUS DION & THE BELMONTS *** [ ] [-]
– Where or when / A teenager in love / I wonder why / No one knows / Don't pity me / Every little thing I do / A lover's prayer / When you wish upon a star / In the still of the night / I can't go on (Rosalie) / That's my desire / Wonderful girl.
Sep 91. Ace; (cd) **THE FABULOUS DION** [ ] [-]
– Runaround Sue / The wanderer / Lovers who wander / Little Diane / Love came to me / Lonely teenager / Little Miss Blue / The majestic / (I was) Born to cry / Sandy / Come go with me / Havin' fun.
Apr 92. Legacy; (cd) **BRONX BLUES (THE COLUMBIA RECORDINGS 1962-1965)** [ ] [-]

DIRE STRAITS

Formed: Deptford, London, England . . . mid-77 by ex-teacher and journalist MARK KNOPFLER, brother DAVID and JOHN ILLSLEY. In Oct'77, Radio 1 DJ Charlie Gillett gave their demo an airing, and soon A&R man John Stainze found and signed them to 'Vertigo' records. In May78, their debut single 'SULTANS OF SWING' missed chart, but eponymous album made the UK 40, after great live reviews and a major signing to 'Warners' in the States. After a sell-out US tour the single re-gained momentum again early the following year, re-peaking at US No.4 & UK 8. This enormously re-actified debut album sales, which shot it up to cross-Atlantic million selling Top 5 placings. BOB DYLAN invited MARK KNOPFLER to augment him on his 'Slow Train Coming' album of 1979. Meanwhile DIRE STRAITS were becoming worldwide rock stars, and by 1985 had one of the biggest selling albums of all-time, 'BROTHERS IN ARMS'. • **Style:** MARK was certainly influenced by laid back rock legends such as BOB DYLAN or JJ CALE. But DIRE STRAITS and virtuso guitarist MARK KNOPFLER were certainly treading most of their own ground all through the 80's. • **Songwriters:** KNOPFLER compositions, except when he formed a sort of TRAVELING WILBURYS style band The NOTTING

HILLBILLIES, who based music on country folk-roots and covered FEEL LIKE GOING HOME (Charlie Rich). • **Trivia:** MARK penned 'PRIVATE DANCER' for TINA TURNER in 1983, and also produced to name but a few; 'Infidels' for BOB DYLAN and 'Knife' for AZTEC CAMERA.

Recommended: MONEY FOR NOTHING (*8).

MARK KNOPFLER (b.12 Aug'49, Glasgow, Scotland) – vocals, lead guitar / **DAVID KNOPFLER** (b.1951) – guitar / **JOHN ILLSLEY** (b.24 Jun'49, Leicester, England) – bass / **PICK WITHERS** – drums

Vertigo Warners

May 78. (7") **SULTANS OF SWING. / EASTBOUND TRAIN** [ ] [ ]
(re-iss.Jan79, hit UK No.8 + US No.4) (re-iss. 12" – Jan 83)

Jun 78. (lp)(c) **DIRE STRAITS** [5] [2] Oct 78
– Down to the waterline / Water of love / Setting me up / Six blade knife / Southbound train / Sultans of swing / Wild West End / Lions / In the gallery. *(cd-iss.1987)(re-iss.cd+c May93)*

Jul 79. (7") **LADY WRITER. / WHERE DO YOU THINK YOU'RE GOING?** [ ] [45]

Aug 79. (lp)(c) **COMMUNIQUE** [5] [11] Jun 79
– Once upon a time in the west / News / Where do you think you're going? / Communique / Lady writer / Angel of mercy / Portobello belle / Single-handed sailor / Follow me home. *(cd-iss.1987)(re-iss.cd+c May93)*

Oct 79. (7") **ONCE UPON A TIME IN THE WEST. / NEWS** [-] [ ]

—— **HAL LINDES** (b.30 Jun'53, Monterey, California, USA) – guitar repl. DAVID who later went solo, also added **ROY BITTAN** – keyboards / (ex-E-STREET BAND BRUCE SPRINGSTEEN).

Oct 80. (lp)(c) **MAKING MOVIES** [4] [19]
– Tunnel of love / Romeo and Juliet / Skateaway / Expresso love / Hand in hand / Solid rock / Les boys. *(master deition Apr82) (cd-iss.1987)(re-iss.cd+c May93)*

Nov 80. (7") **ROMEO AND JULIET / SOLID ROCK** [8] [ ]

Dec 80. (7") **SKATEAWAY. / SOLID ROCK** [-] [58]

Mar 81. (7") **SKATEAWAY. / EXPRESSO LOVE** [37] [-]

Sep 81. (7") **TUNNEL OF LOVE. / TUNNEL OF LOVE (part 2)** [54] [ ]

—— **ALAN CLARK** (b. 5 Mar'52, Durham, England) – keyboards repl ROY.

Aug 82. (7")(10") **PRIVATE INVESTIGATIONS. / BADGES, POSTERS, STICKERS, T-SHIRTS** [2] [ ]

Sep 82. (lp)(c)(cd) **LOVE OVER GOLD** [1] [19]
– Telegraph road / Private investigations / Industrial disease / Love over gold / It never rains / If I had you / Twisting by the pool / Two young lovers / Badges, posters, stickers, T-shirts. *(re-iss.cd+c May93)*

Nov 82. (7") **INDUSTRIAL DISEASE. / BADGES, POSTERS, STICKERS, T-SHIRT** [-] [75]

Jan 83. (7"m)(12"m) **TWISTING BY THE POOL. / TWO YOUNG LOVERS / IF I HAD YOU** [14] [53]
(above iss.US Mar83 as m-lp, += Badges, Posters, Stickers, T-shirts)

—— **IOMAR HAKIM** – drums, percussion repl. PICK / above was replaced by **TERRY WILLIAMS** – drums ex-MAN, ex-MOTORS, ex-ROCKPILE. / (both played on album below alongside **MARK, JOHN, HAL** and **ALAN).**

Feb 84. (10")(12") **LOVE OVER GOLD (live). / SOLID GOLD (live)** [50] [ ]

Mar 84. (d-lp)(c)(cd) **ALCHEMY – LIVE** [3] [46]
– Once upon a time in the west / Romeo and Juliet / Expresso love / Private investigations / Sultans of swing / Two young lovers / Tunnel of love / Telegraph road / Solid rock / Going home (theme from "Local Hero"). *(c+=)(cd+=)* – Love over gold (live). *(re-iss.cd.1988)*

—— added **GUY FLETCHER** – keyboards / also **JACK SONNI** – guitar (on tour)

Apr 85. (7")(10")(12") **SO FAR AWAY. / WALK OF LIFE** [20] [-]

May 85. (lp)(c)(cd) **BROTHERS IN ARMS** [1] [1]
– So far away / Money for nothing / Walk of life / Your latest trick / Why worry? / Ride across the river / The man's too strong / One world / Money for nothing / Brothers in arms. *(c+=)(cd+=)* – So far away / Money for nothing / Your latest trick / Why worry? (extended versions). *(also available oblong pic-d)*

Jun 85. (7")(10")(12")(7"pic-d) **MONEY FOR NOTHING. / LOVE OVER GOLD (live)** [4] [1]

Oct 85. (7") **WALK OF LIFE. / ONE WORLD** [-] [7]

Oct 85. (7")(10") **BROTHERS IN ARMS. / GOING HOME (live)** [16] [ ]
(12"+=) – Why worry.
(d7"++=)(ltd-cd-s+++=) – ('A'version).

Jan 86. (7") **WALK OF LIFE. / TWO YOUNG LOVERS (live)** [2] [-]
(12"+=) – Sultans of swing.
(d7"++=) – Eastbound train (live).

Feb 86. (7") **SO FAR AWAY. / IF I HAD YOU** [-] [19]

Apr 86. (7") **YOUR LATEST TRICK. / IRISH BOY** [26] [ ]
(12"+=) – The long road.

Oct 88. (lp)(c)(cd) **MONEY FOR NOTHING** (compilation) [1] [62]
– Sultans of swing / Down to the waterline / Portobello belle (live) / Twisting by the pool / Tunnel of love / Romeo and Juliet / Where do you think you're going? / Walk of life / Private investigations / Telegraph Road (live) / Money for nothing / Brothers in arms.

Nov 88. (7") **SULTANS OF SWING (re-issue). / PORTOBELLO BELLE** [62] [ ]
(12"+=)(cd-s+=) – Romeo and Juliet / Money for nothing.

Aug 91. (7")(c-s) **CALLING ELVIS. / IRON HAND** [21] [ ]
(12"+=)(cd-s+=) – Millionaire blues.

Sep 91. (cd)(c)(lp) **ON EVERY STREET** [1] [12]
– Calling Elvis / On every street / When it comes to you / Fade to black / The bug / You and your friend / Heavy fuel / Iron hand / Ticket to Heaven / My parties / Planet of New Orleans / How long.

Oct 91. (7") **HEAVY FUEL. / PLANET OF NEW ORLEANS** [55] [ ]
(12"+=)(cd-s+=) – Kingdom come.

Feb 92. (7")(c-s) **ON EVERY STREET. / ROMEO AND JULIET** [42] [ ]
(cd-s+=) – Private investigations / Sultans of swing.

Jun 92. (7")(c-s) **THE BUG. / TWISTING BY THE POOL** [67] [ ]
(cd-s+=) – ('A'version) ???

—— added touring band 91-93 **DANNY CUMMINGS** – percussion / **PHIL PALMER** – guitar / **PAUL FRANKLIN** – pedal steel / **CHRIS WHITE** – sax, flute / **CHRIS WHITTEN** – drums

May 93. (cd)(c)(lp) **ON THE NIGHT (live)** [4] [ ]
– Calling Elvis / Walk of life / Heavy fuel / Romeo & Juliet / Your latest trick / Private investigations / On every street / You and your friend / Money for nothing / Brothers in arms.

May 93. (12"ep)(c-ep)(cd-ep) **ENCORES LIVE EP (live)** [31] [ ]
– Your latest trick / The bug / Solid rock / Local hero (wild theme).

Oct93; MARK was credited on HANK MARVIN's single 'Wonderful Land'.

compilations, etc.

Jul 95. Windsong; (cd)(c)(lp) **LIVE AT THE BBC (live)** [71] [-]

MARK KNOPFLER

(first with **CLARK, LINDES** plus **MIKE BRECKER** – sax)

Vertigo Warners

Feb 83. (7")(12") **GOING HOME. / SMOOCHING** [56] [ ]

Apr 83. (lp)(c) **MUSIC FROM THE FILM SOUNDTRACK 'LOCAL HERO'** [14] [ ]
– The rocks and the water / Wild theme / Freeway flyer / Boomtown / The way it always starts / The rocks and the thunder / The ceilidh and the northern lights / The mist covered mountains / The ceilidh: Louis' favourite Billy's tune / Whistle theme / Smooching / The rocks and the thunder / Going home (theme from "Local Hero"). *(cd-iss.Jun89)*

Jul 84. (12") **COMFORT (THEME FROM COMFORT AND JOY. / FISTFUL OF ICE-CREAM** [ ] [ ]

Sep 84. (7")(12") **LONG ROAD. / IRISH BOY** [ ] [ ]

Oct 84. (lp)(c)(cd) **CAL (MUSIC FROM THE FILM)** [65] [ ]
– Irish boy / The road / Waiting for her / Irish love / A secret place / Where will you go? / Father and son / Meeting under the trees / Potato picking / in a secret place / Fear and hatred / Love and guilt / The long road.

Oct 86. (7")(12") **GOING HOME. / WILD THEME** [ ] [ ]
(cd-s+=) – Comfort (theme from Comfort And Joy).
(re-iss.7"/c-s Oct 93)

Nov 87. (lp)(c)(cd) **MUSIC FROM THE FILM SOUNDTRACK 'THE PRINCESS BRIDE'** [ ] [ ]
– Once upon a time . . . storybook love / I will never love again / Florin dance / Morning ride / The friends' song / The cliffs of insanity / The sword fight / Guide my sword / The fireswamp and the rodents of unusual size / Revenge / A happy ending / Storybook love.

Mar 88. (7") **STORYBOOK LOVE. / THE FRIENDS SONG** [ ] [ ]
(c-s+=)(cd-s+=) – ('A'version) / Once upon a time.

Nov 89. (lp)(c)(cd) **LAST EXIT TO BROOKLYN (Soundtrack)** [ ] [ ]
– Last exit to Brooklyn / Victims / Think fast / A love idea / Tralala / Riot / The reckoning / As low as it gets / Last exit to Brooklyn – finale

NOTTING HILLBILLIES

MARK KNOPFLER – guitar, vocals, producer / **GUY FLETCHER** – guitar, vocals, producer / **BRENDAN CROKER** – guitar, vocals / **STEVE PHILLIPS** – guitar, vocals / with **PAUL FRANKLIN** – pedal steel guitar

Vertigo Warners

Feb 90. (7")(c-s) **YOUR OWN SWEET WAY. / BEWILDERED** [ ] [ ]
(12"+=)(cd-s+=) – That's where I belong.

Mar 90. (cd)(c)(lp) **MISSING . . . PRESUMED HAVING A GOOD TIME** [2] [52]
– Railroad worksong / Bewildered / Your own sweet way / Run me down / One way gal / Blues stay away from me / Will you miss me / Please baby / Weapon of prayer / That's where I belong / Feel like going home.

Apr 90. (7")(c-s) **FEEL LIKE GOING HOME. / LONESOME WIND BLUES** [ ] [ ]
(12"+=)(cd-s+=) – One way gal.

Jun 90. (7")(c-s) **WILL YOU MISS ME. / THAT'S WHERE I BELONG** [ ] [ ]
(12"+=)(cd-s+=) – Lonesome wind blues.

CHET ATKINS & MARK KNOPFLER

C.B.S. Columbia

Oct 90. (7") **POOR BOY BLUES. / ?** [ ] [ ]

Nov 90. (cd)(c)(lp) **NECK AND NECK** [41] [ ]
– Poor boy blues / Sweet dreams / There'll be some changes made / Just one time / So soft / Your goodbye / Yakety axe / Tahitian skies / Tears / I'll see you in my dreams / The next time I'm in town. *(re-iss.cd/c May93)*

JOHN ILLSLEY

Vertigo Warners

Jun 84. (7")(12") **NEVER TOLD A SOUL. / HYPNOTISED** [ ] [ ]

Jun 84. (lp)(c)(cd) **NEVER TOLD A SOUL**
– Boy with Chinese eyes / The night cafe / Never told a soul / Jimmy on the central line / Northern land / Another alibi / Let the river flow.

May 88. (7") **I WANT TO SEE THE MOON. / WORDS** [ ] [ ]
(12"+=)(cd-s+=) – The world is made of glass.

May 88. (lp)(c)(cd) **GLASS** [ ] [ ]
– High stakes / I want to see the Moon / Papermen / All I want is you / The world is full of glass / Red turns to blue / Let's dance / She wants everything / Star for now.

DISCHARGE

Formed: Stoke-On-Trent, England . . . 1980 by CAL, BONES and RAINY. That year, they founded own indie label 'Clay', to discharge EPs during the early 80's. In 1982, their debut album 'HEAR NOTHING, . . . ' sold well enough to stay in the Top 50 for 5 weeks. • **Style:** Hard-core 'oi' protest punk outfit, who were innovators of incomprehensible vocals, which inspired many mid-80's groups such as NAPALM DEATH and EXTREME NOISE TERROR. By this time DISCHARGE had shifted into more heavier pursuits. • **Songwriters:** Group compositions. • **Trivia:** 3 members were fined by the DHSS for earning while on tour.

Recommended: DISCHARGE 1980-1986 (*6)

CAL (b.KELVIN MORRIS) – vocals / **BONES** (b. A.ROBERTS) – guitar (gutarist changed often) / **RAINY WAINWRIGHT** – bass / **GARRY MALONEY** – drums
(others at various times **NICK BUSHELL – guitar / STEPHEN BROOKS – ?** (last 2 were to later join DEMON)

Clay / not issued

Apr 80. (7"ep) **REALITIES OF WAR / THEY DECLARE IT / BUT AFTER THE GIG / SOCIETY'S VICTIM.** [ ] [-]
(re-iss.Feb87)

Jul 80. (7"ep) **FIGHT BACK / WAR'S NO FAIRY TALES / ALWAYS RESTRICTIONS / YOU TAKE PART IN CREATING THIS SYSTEM / RELIGIOUS INSTIGATES** [ ] [-]

Dec 80. (7"ep) **DECONTROL / IT'S NO TV SKETCH / TOMORROW BELONGS TO US** [ ] [-]

May 81. (12"ep) **WHY** [ ] [-]
– Visions of war / Does the system work / A look at tomorrow / Why / Maimed and slaughtered / Mania for conquest / Ain't no feeble bastard / Is this to be / Massacre of innocents (air attack). *(re-iss.+cd.Jan90)* (cd+=) – State violence – state control / Doomsday.

Oct 81. (7") **NEVER AGAIN. / DEATH DEALERS / TWO MONSTROUS NUCLEAR STOCK-PILES** [64] [-]

May 82. (lp) **HEAR NOTHING, SEE NOTHING, SAY NOTHING** [40] [-]
– Hear nothing, see nothing, say nothing / The nightmare continues / The final blood bath / Protest and survive / I won't subscribe / Drunk with power / Meanwhile / A hell on earth / Cries of help / The possibility of life's destruction / Q – and children?, A – and children / The blood runs red / Free speech for the dumb / The end. *(re-iss.+cd.Jan90)*

Oct 82. (7") **STATE VIOLENCE – STATE CONTROL. / DOOMSDAY** [ ] [-]

— (Nov82) **POOCH PURTILL** – guitar repl. BONES who formed BROKEN BONES

Feb 83. (lp) **NEVER AGAIN (1/2 live)** [ ] [-]
– Warning / Never again / Hear nothing, see nothing, say nothing / The nightmare continues / The final bloodbath / Drunk with power / Where there's a will / Anger burning / Two monstrous nuclear stockpiles / The price of silence / Protest and survive / Born to die in the gutter / Doomsday / The more I see / State violence – state control / Decontrol / In defence of our future. *(re-iss.Jun84) (re-iss.+cd.Jan90)*

Mar 83. (7") **PRIDE OF SILENCE. / BORN TO DIE IN THE GUTTER** [ ] [-]

Sep 83. (12"ep) **WARNING – H.M. GOVERNMENT: WARNING / WHERE THERE'S A WILL / IN DEFENCE OF OUR FUTURE / ANGER BURNING.** [ ] [-]

May 84. (7") **THE MORE I SEE. / PROTEST AND SURVIVE** [ ] [-]
(12"+=) – ('A' extended).

May 85. (7") **IGNORANCE. / NO COMPROMISE** [ ] [-]
(12"+=) – ('A' extended).

Jul 86. (lp) **GRAVE NEW WORLD** [ ] [-]
– Grave new world / In love believe / DTY/AYF / Time is kind / We dare speak (a moment only) / Sleep in hope / The downward spiral

— (Feb87) **ROCKY SHADES** (b.ROB BERKELEY) – guitar (ex-WRATHCHILD) repl. CAL

— (note:- DAVE ELLESMERE an early member later joined FLUX and DR.& CRIPPENS)

— **DISCHARGE** reformed 1991, with **CAL** and long-standing **ANDY GREEN** – guitar. Newcomers were **ANTHONY MORGAN** – bass / **GERRY MALONEY** – drums.

Nov 91. (cd)(lp) **MASSACRE DIVINE** [ ] [-]
– City of fear / F.E.D. / Lost tribe rising / Challenge the terrior / White knuckle ride / New age / Terror police / Kiss tomorrow goodbye / Sexplosion / Dying time / E£ 2.30 / F.E.D. (F2 mix) / Terror police (F2 mix).

Oct 93. (cd) **SHOOTIN' UP THE WORLD** [ ] [-]
– Manson's Child / Lost In You / Shootin' Up The World / Psycho Active / Leaders Deceivers / Fantasy Overload / Down And Dirty / Never Came To Care / Real Life Snuff / Exiled In Hell / Manson's Child (Reprise)

Nu-clear Blast / not issued

Jan 94. (cd)(c)(lp) **SEEING, FEELING, BLEEDING** [ ] [-]
–

– compilations etc. –

Jul 87. Clay; (lp) **DISCHARGE THE SINGLES COLLECTION 1980-1986** [ ] [-]
(cd-iss.Aug95)

Feb 90. Clay; (cd)(lp) **LIVE AT CITY GARDEN (live)** [ ] [-]

H3DISCO 2000 (see under ⇒ KLF)

DISPOSABLE HEROES OF HIPHOPRISY

Formed: Bay Area, San Francisco, USA . . . 1987 as The BEATNIGS, by MICHAEL FRANTI, a 6'6" ethnic rapper (who was adopted by a middle class family), and Oriental RONO TSE. The BEATNIGS with 3 others, had a few releases in the late 80's for JELLO BIAFRA's 'Alternative Tentacles', including 'TELEVISION'. This in 1992, became a Top 50 hit, when issued by their new project DISPOSABLE HEROES OF HIPHOPRISY. • **Style:** Rapping meta political trio, with punk / industrial credentials. • **Songwriters:** FRANTI penned except; CALIFORNIA UBER ALLES (Dead Kennedys). • **Trivia:** Befriended BILLY BRAGG after supporting him on US tour.

Recommended: HIPHOPRISY THE GREATEST LUXURY (*8).

BEATNIGS

MICHAEL FRANTI – vocals / **RONO TSE** – percussion, metal-bashing / **HENRY / KEVIN / ANDRE**

Alt.Tent. / Alt.Tent.

Oct 88. (12"ep) **TELEVISION** (extended). / **('A' dub) / 'A' radio) / JAZZY BEATS** [ ] [ ]
(re-iss.May92)

— Above remixed by ADRIAN SHERWOOD & TACKHEAD.

1989. (lp)(c)(cd) **BEATNIGS** [ ] [ ]
– (Welcome) Television / C.I.A. / (Instructions) When you wake up in the morning / (The experience of us all) Street fulla nigs / (Re-classification) Control / Malcolm X / Nature / Burritos / Rooticus sporaticus / Who is doin' this to all my people / Rules / Jazzy beats / Pre-war America. *(cd-iss.1992 +=)* Television (radio edit) / Television (remix). *(re-iss.cd Sep95)*

DISPOSABLE HEROES OF HIPHOPRISY

FRANTI + TSE + CHARLIE HUNTER – jazz guitar, bass, piano, organ

Worker's P. / Alter.Tent

Oct 90. (12"ep) **(WHAT WILL WE DO TO BECOME) FAMOUS AND DANDY JUSTKE AMOS AND ANDY** (as 'HIPHOPRISY') [ ] [ ]
– Famous and dandy (extended) / Satanic reverses / Financial leprosy / Famous and dandy (steal our heat mix) / Financial reverses (steal our heat mix)
(cd-s+=) – (2 extended title tracks) *(re-iss.Jun92)*

4th & Bro. / 4th & Bro.

Mar 92. (7")(c-s) **TELEVISION; THE DRUG OF THE NATION. / WINTER OF THE LONG HOT SUMMER** [57] [ ]
(cd-s+=) – Financial leper (live) / California uber alles (live) / It's a crime to be broke in England / America (live).
(12"+=) – Langling. *(re-iss.Dec92, hit UK No.44)*

May 92. (cd)(c)(d-lp) **HIPOCRISY THE GREATEST LUXURY** [40] [ ]
– Satanic reverses / Famous and dandy (like Amos'n'Andy) / Television, the drug of the nation / Language of violence / The winter of the long hot summer / Hypocrisy is the greatest luxury / Everyday life has become a health risk / Ins greencard A-19 191 500 / Socio-genetic experiment / Music and politics / Financial leprosy / California uber ales / Water pistol man.

May 92. (7")(c-s) **LANGUAGE OF VIOLENCE. / FAMOUS AND DANDY (LIKE AMOS AND ANDY)** [68] [ ]
(cd-s+=) – ('A'instrumental) / Waterpistol man (live).

Sep 92. (7")(c-s) **FAMOUS AND DANDY (LIKE AMOS AND ANDY). / POSITIVE** [ ] [ ]
(12"+=)(cd-s+=) – Language of violence (jazz version).

SPEARHEAD

MICHAEL FRANTI / + MARY HUNTER – vocals / **KRAVITZ / STORCH** (RONO was to form BLACK CHINA)

Capitol / Capitol

Oct 94. (cd)(c)(d-lp) **HOME** [ ] [ ]
– People in the middle / Love is da shit / Piece o' peace / Positive / Of course you can / Hole in my bucket / Home / Dream team / Runfayalife / Crime to be broke in America / 100,000 miles / Red beans and rice / Caught without an umbrella.

Dec 94. (c-s) **OF COURSE YOU CAN. / POSITIVE / WATER PISTOL MAN (acoustic)** [74] [ ]
(cd-s+=) – Booty and the beats.

Apr 95. (12"ep)(c-ep) **HOLE IN THE BUCKET / RUNFAYLIFE (Franti mix) / ('A'-Sensimi Street mix) / ('A'-Adrian Sherwood mix)** [55] [ ]
(cd-ep) – ('A'-Slave ship mix) – (repl.) ('A'-Adrian Sherwood mix).

Jun 95. (12")(cd-s) **PEOPLE IN THA MIDDLE / ('A'-Mello madness mix) / ('A'-Angel remix) / ('A'-album mix) / ('A'-Adrian Sherwood remix)** [49] [ ]
(cd-s) – ('A'side) / Hole in the bucket / 100,000 miles (live) / Positive (live).

Willie DIXON

Born: 1 July 1915, Vicksburg, Missouri. As a young teenager, he moved to Chicago, where he learned bass. In 1936, he won the Golden Gloves Amateur Heavyweight Boxing title. The next year, under the guidance of LEONARD CASTON (aka blues singer BABY DOO), he was taught bass and guitar. He soon turned pro, and worked with CASTON in The FIVE BREEZES, then The BIG THREE TRIO in the mid-40's. In the early 50's to mid-50's, he house sessioned and composed for the 'Chess' label. He contributed on many recordings by the future greats BO DIDDLEY, HOWLIN' WOLF, MUDDY WATERS, OTIS RUSH, etc, and even became local talent scout. He became right-hand man of LEONARD CHESS, and soon was churning out his own much appraised material, although his solo outings were too few and far between. He departed from CHESS at the end of '56, due to 2 families he had to support (he was earlier divorced). At this, he joined 'Cobra' label, run by ELI TOSCANO, but this lasted for only 3 years, and he reluctantly returned to 'Chess', when the label folded. That same year, TOSCANO was to drown under suspicious circumstances, as it was thought he was murdered by creditors. DIXON was to have an even greater effect in the 60's. In the 70's, he featured on films 'Chicago Blues' & 'Out Of The Blacks And Into

The Blues'. After a slight return in the late 80's he fell ill and died of heart failure 29 Jan'92. • **Blues style:** Bassist, singer & guitarist, who learned style from BABY DOO. • **Songwriters:** Self-penned gems. • **Legacy:** Wrote for other blues artists MUDDY WATERS (I'm Ready / I Just Want To Make Love To You / Walking Blues / I'm Your Hoochie Coochie Man / Don't Go No Further / I Love The Life I Live, I Live The Life I Love / Close To You / My Captain / Same Thing / When The Eagle Flies); HOWLIN' WOLF (Spoonful / Wang Dang Doodle / Little Baby / The Red Rooster / Shake For Me / Built For Comfort / Do The Do / I Ain't Superstitious / Evil); LITTLE WALTER (My Babe); OTIS RUSH (I Can't Quit You Baby); LITTLE MILTON (I Can't Quit You Baby / Country Style / Too Late); BO DIDDLEY (You Can't Judge A Book By The Cover); KOKO TAYLOR (I Got What It Takes / Don't Mess With The Messer / Whatever I Am, You Made Me / Blue Heaven / (I Got) All You Need / Wang Dang Doodle / What Came First: The Egg Or The Hen? / Fire / Insane Asylum / I Don't Know Who Cares / Separate Or Integrate / Yes, It's Good For You); BUDDY GUY (co:-I Dig Your Wig / Crazy Love (Crazy Music) / Too Many Ways / Goin' Home / I Cry And Sing The Blues / Every Girl I See (DIXON-MURPHY); ETTA JAMES (Fire); EDDIE BOYD (Third Degree); JIMMY WITHERSPOON (Everything But You / Crazy Mixed Up World); ALBERT KING (Howlin' For My Darling / Down In The Bottom); SONNY BOY WILLIAMSON (co:- BUDDY GUY- I Dig Your Wig);

Recommended: THE CHESS BOX (*9)

WILLIE DIXON – vocals, bass / **LAFAYETTE LEAKE** – piano / **FRED BELOW** – drums / **HAROLD ASHBY** – tenor sax

		not issued	Checker
Aug 55.	(7" – . . .& THE ALL-STARS-) **WALKING THE BLUES. / IF YOU'RE MINE**	-	
Jan 56.	(7") **CRAZY FOR MY BABY. / I AM THE LOVER MAN**	-	
Aug 57.	(7" – . . .& THE ALL-STARS-) **TWENTY NINE WAYS. / THE PAIN IN MY HEART**	-	

WILLIE DIXON – vocals, bass / **MEMPHIS SLIM** – piano / **WALLY RICHARDSON** – guitar / **HAROLD ASHBY** – tenor sax / **GUS JOHNSON** – drums

		Prestige	Bluesville
Feb 60.	(7") **NERVOUS. / SITTIN' AND CRYIN' THE BLUES**	-	
1960.	(lp) **WILLIE'S BLUES ("WILLIE DIXON & MEMPHIS SLIM")**		

– Nervous / Good understanding / That's my baby / Slim's thing / That's all I want baby / Don't you tell nobody / Youth to you / Sittin' and cryin' the blues / Built for comfort / I got a razor / Go easy / Move me. *(re-iss.Feb84 on 'O.B.C.', cd-iss.Jun92)*

— now with – LUCKY THREE TRIO – (DIXON / **LEAKE + CLIFTON JAMES** – drums)

		not issued	Tuba
1962.	(7") **BACK HOME IN INDIANA. / WRINKLES**	-	

WILLIE with drummer – **PHILIPPE COMBELLE**

		Polydor	not issued
1963.	(lp) **WILLIE DIXON & PHILIPPE COMBELLE**		-

– African hunch with a boogie beat / Baby, baby, baby / Cold blooded / Do de do / Just you and I / New way to love / Shame, pretty girls / The way she loves a man.

		Pye Int.	not issued
Oct 64.	(7") **WALKING THE BLUES. / CRAZY FOR MY BABY**		-

now with The CHICAGO ALL-STARS: **WALTER HORTON** (aka SHAKY JAKE) – harmonica / **SUNNYLAND SLIM** – piano / **JOHNNY SHINES** – guitar / **CLIFTON JAMES** – drums

		not issued	Columbia
1969.	(lp) **I AM THE BLUES**	-	

– Back door man / I can't quit you, baby / The seventh son / Spoonful / I ain't superstitious / You shook me / I'm your hoochie coochie man / The little red rooster / The same thing. *(cd-iss.1986 on 'Mobile Fidelity')*

— now with **BUSTER BENTON + DENNIS MILLER** – guitar / **LAFAYETTE LEAKE** – piano / **FREDDIE DIXON** – bass / **CLIFTON JAMES** – drums / **CARRIE BELL HARRINGTON** – harmonica

		Ovation	not issued
1976.	(lp) **CATALYST**		-
1978.	(lp) **WHAT HAPPENED TO MY BLUES**	-	

– Moon cat / What happened to my blues / Pretty baby / Got to love you baby / Shakin' the shack / Hold me baby / It's so easy to love you / Oh Hugh baby / Put it all in there / Hey hey pretty mama.

		not issued	Spivey
1970's.	(lp) **WILLIE DIXON AND THE CHICAGO BLUES BAND**	-	
		not issued	**Pausa**
1980's.	(lp) **MIGHTY EARTHQUAKE AND HURRICANE**	-	
1980's.	(lp) **BACKSTAGE ACCESS (live)**	-	
		Colosseum	**Colosseum**
Oct 89.	(lp)(c)(cd) **GINGER ALE AFTERNOON**		
		Silvertone	**Silvertone**
Apr 91.	(cd)(c)(lp) **HIDDEN CHARMS** (rec.1988)		

– Blues you can't lose / I don't trust myself / Jungle swing / Don't mess with the messer / Study war no more / I love the life I live / I cry for you / Good advice / I do the job. *(re-iss.cd/c Mar94 & Apr95)*

— On 29 Jan'92, WILLIE died of heart failure at St.Thomas' Hospital, California.

– compilations, etc –

Jan 87.	Deja Vu; (lp)(c) **WILLIE DIXON: 20 BLUES GREATS**		-

– Little red rooster / Built for comfort / Wang dang doodle / Ain't superstitious / Evil / Walking the blues / Fiery love / Alone / Mannish boy / All aboard / Rock me / I love the life I live / Sugar sweet / Thunderbird / One more / Teenage beat / Snake dancer / Temperature / Rock bottom / Black angel blues.

1988.	M.C.A.; (d-cd)(d-c)(t-lp) **THE CHESS BOX** *(contains other artists' versions) (re-iss.Sep90)*		
Oct 90.	Columbia; (cd)(c) **THE BIG THREE TRIO**		
Nov 92.	Chess; (cd) **TRIBUTE TO WILLIE DIXON**		
Mar 93.	Blues Encore; (cd) **I AM THE BLUES**		-

Note; Below releases on 'Roots' were his songs by various artists

Jun 93.	Roots; (cd)(c) **THE BLUES DIXONARY VOL.1**		
Jun 93.	Roots; (cd)(c) **THE BLUES DIXONARY VOL.2**		
Jun 93.	Roots; (cd)(c) **THE BLUES DIXONARY VOL.3**		
Jun 93.	Roots; (cd)(c) **THE BLUES DIXONARY VOL.4**		
Jun 93.	Roots; (cd)(c) **THE BLUES DIXONARY VOL.5**		

DNA (see under ⇒ DERRINGER, Rick)

DODGY

Formed: Hounslow, London, England . . .early 1990 as a trio. With DJ CHRIS SLADE, they set up The Dodgy Club in the summer, where they gained local support. Did first national tour in September '91 termed the 'Word Of Mouth' tour, as they didn't know where they were playing until their fans phoned up prospective promoters and venues. A year later, they were snapped up by 'A&M', who released 2 quickfire singles in Spring '93. • **Style:** Pop-rock; The BEATLES and SQUEEZE rolled into one. • **Songwriters:** Basic trio, except I CAN'T MAKE IT (Small Faces). • **Trivia:** Guests on second album were ROB LORD – keyboards / CAROLINE LAVELLE + SONIA SLANY – strings. It was produced by HUGH JONES.

Recommended: THE DODGY ALBUM (*7) / HOMEGROWN (*6)

NIGEL CLARK – vocals, bass / **ANDY MILLER** – lead guitar, vocals / **MATHEW PRIEST** – drums, vocals, percussion

		Bostin'	not issued
Sep 91.	(12") **SUMMER FAYRE. / ST.LUCIA**		-
Nov 91.	(7") **EAST WAY. / SEEMS LIKE A BAD DAY** (cd-s+=) – Groove song (St.Lucia demo) / Smeasy way.		-
Apr 92.	(7"white)(7")(12")(12"white) **THE BLACK AND WHITE SINGLE-black side: JUNGLE DARK DANCE BATH / ELEVATORS GOIN' UP (WORTH THE BLOOD). / white side: 4am NOCTURNAL / WATCH THE SUN GO DOWN (THE ELEPHANT)** (cd-s+=) – D-Club (versions).		-

— added 4th member **CHRIS SLADE** – DJ, keyboards

		A & M	A & M
Mar 93.	(7")(c-s) **WATER UNDER THE BRIDGE. / IT'S BEEN SO LONG** (12"+=)(cd-s+=) – She wants my loving / Valuable fool.		
Apr 93.	(7")(c-s) **LOVEBIRDS. / BIG BROWN MOON** (12"+=)(cd-s+=) – Sylvia's bedroom / Smashed up in a flat.	65	
Jun 93.	(cd)(c)(lp) **THE DODGY ALBUM**	75	

– Water under the bridge / I need another / Lovebirds / Satisfied / Grand old English oak tree / Stand by yourself / As my time goes by / Never again / Cold tea / We're not going to take this anymore.

Jun 93.	(7"mustard-ep)(c-ep) **I NEED ANOTHER. / IF I FALL / HENDRE DHU** (12"ep+=)(cd-ep+=) – Never again (campfire version).	67	
Oct 93.	(12"ep)(cd-ep) **HOMEGROWN E.P.**		

– Don't go back (to the beaten track) / Home grown / Let's wait till we get there.

— now without CHRIS and back to trio

Jul 94.	(7"ep)(c-ep) **THE MELOD-E.P.: MELODIES HAUNT YOU. / THE SNAKE** (10"+=) – Don't go back (to the beaten track). (cd-s++=) – Summer fayre.	53	
Sep 94.	(7"blue)(c-s) **STAYING OUT FOR THE SUMMER. / LOVEBIRDS (original)** (cd-s+=) As time goes by (demo) / Back to life. (cd-s) ('A'side) / A summer's day in mid-January / Don't you think / Colour me with paints.	38	
Oct 94.	(cd)(c)(lp) **HOMEGROWN**	43	

– Staying out for the summer / Melodies haunt you / So let me go far / Crossroads / One day / We are together / Whole lot easier / Making the most of / Waiting for the day / What have I done wrong? / Grassman. *(re-iss.Jun95, hit No.28)*

Dec 94.	(c-s) **SO LET ME GO FAR. / DON'T GET LOW, DON'T GET LOW (U.K.R.I.P.)** (12"+=)(cd-s+=) – The elephant / So let me wobble jah. (cd-s) – ('A'side) / I need another (live) / Satisfied (live) / Melodies haunt you (live).	30	

— below featured The KICK HORNS

Feb 95.	(7"pic-d)(c-s) **MAKING THE MOST OF. / FAISONS AU MIEUX (YES, IT'S IN FRENCH)** (cd-s+=) – The Ludlow sessions part 1: Spent all my time running / All the time in the world. (cd-s) – ('A'extended) / The Ludlow sessions part 2: Watch out watcha doin' / This is ours / (Get off your) High horse.	22	
May 95.	(c-s) **STAYING OUT FOR THE SUMMER (mixed up in 95) / SATISFIED (live)** (cd-s) – ('A'side) / (Your love keeps lifting me) Higher and higher / Crossroads (live) / Melodies haunt you (live). (cd-s) – ('A'side) / Waiting for the day (live) / One day (live) / (Get off your) High horse (live).	19	

John DOE (see under ⇒ X)

DOGS D'AMOUR

Formed: Birmingham, England . . . early 1983 by TYLA. In 1984, they recorded lp for Finnish label 'Kumibeat', before they were briefly contracted to

Japanese label 'Watanabe'. Early in 1988, they gained deal with semi-major label 'China', for whom they achieve UK Top 30 status a year later, helped by the production of Mark Dearnley. • **Style:** Heavy glam-metal outfit, influenced by HANOI ROCKS, MOTT THE HOOPLE and The FACES. • **Songwriters:** All lyrics and even the comic sleeve designs by TYLA, with music by group. • **Trivia:** STEVE JAMES married Kathryn Shaw 16 Jun'90.

Recommended: DOG HITS AND BOOTLEG ALBUM (*6)

TYLA – vocals, guitar / **CARL** – bass / **DAVE KUSWORTH** – guitar repl. NICK HALLS & NED CHRISTIE – vocals (Sep83) / **PAUL HORNBY** – drums repl. BAM-BAM.

Kumibeat FINLAND — not issued

Apr 84. (7") **HOW DO YOU FALL IN LOVE. / THE STATE I'M IN** [-] [-]
Sep 84. (lp) **THE STATE WE'RE IN** [-] [-]

— **BAM-BAM** – drums returned to repl. HORNBY **JO-DOG** – guitar repl. DAVE KUSWORTH who with NIKKI SUDDEN became JACOBITES. (above later went solo in 1987, at this time TYLA, while having no contract, also joined JACOBITES)

— (Aug85) **MARK DRAX** – bass repl. MARK DUNCAN (ex-DOLL BY DOLL) who repl. CARL

— (Jan87) **STEVE JAMES** – bass repl. DRAX in new line-up – **STEVE, TYLA, BAM-BAM & JO DOG.**

China — China

Feb 88. (7")(12") **HOW COME IT NEVER RAINS. / SOMETIMES / LAST BANDIT** [ ] [ ]
(originally issued Dec 87 on 'Supertrade')
May 88. (7") **THE KID FROM KENSINGTON. / EVERYTHING I WANT** [ ] [ ]
(12"+=)(12"yellow+=) – The state I'm in.
Jul 88. (lp)(c) **THE (UN)AUTHORISED BOOTLEG** (ltd.3,000) [ ] [ ]
– Firework girl / Chains / Gold / Pourin' out my heart / Wait until I'm dead / How do you fall in love again? / Kiss this joint / Heroine / Tales of destruction / Dynamite jet saloon / Swingin' the bottle.
Sep 88. (7") **I DON'T WANT YOU TO GO. / HEROINE** [ ] [ ]
(12"+=)(12"pink+=) – Ugly.
Sep 88. (lp)(c)(cd) **IN THE DYNAMITE JET SALOON** [97] [ ]
– Debauchery / I don't want you to go / How come it never rains / Last bandit / Medicine man / Gonna get it right / Everything I want / Heatbreak / Billy Two rivers / Wait until I'm dead. (cd+=) – The kid from Kensington / Sometimes / The state I'm in.
Jan 89. (7") **HOW COME IT NEVER RAINS (remix). / BABY GLASS (live)** [44] [ ]
(12"+=)(12"pic-d+=) – Kirsten Jet (live).
(cd-s++=) – ('A'extended).
Mar 89. (10"m-lp)(lp)(c)(cd) **A GRAVEYARD OF EMPTY BOTTLES** [16] [ ]
– I think it's (love again) / So once I was / Comfort of the Devil / Saviour / Errol Flynn / The bullet proof poet / When the dream has come / Angel.
Jun 89. (7")(7"pic-d) **SATELLITE KID. / SHE THINKS TOO MUCH OF ME / DRUNK LIKE ME** [26] [ ]
(12"+=)(12"pic-d+=) – Things he'd do.
(cd-s+=) – As I see the poppies fall.
Sep 89. (lp)(c)(cd) **ERROL FLYNN** (US-title "KING OF THIEVES") [22] [ ]
– Drunk like me / Goddess from the gutter / Hurricane / Satellite kid / Errol Flynn / Planetary Pied Piper / Princess Valium / Dogs hair / Trail of tears / Ballad of Jack / The prettiest girl in the world / Girl behind the glass. (cd+=) – Things seem to go wrong / Baby glass.
Oct 89. (7")(c-s) **TRAIL OF TEARS. / POURIN' OUT MY HEART** [24] [ ]
(cd-s+=) – In the dynamite set saloon / Swingin' the bottle.
(12"+=)(12"pic-d+=) – As I see the poppies fall.
Jun 90. (7")(c-s) **VICTIMS OF SUCCESS. / BILLY TWO RIVERS** [36] [ ]
(12")(cd-s) – ('A'extended) / Ballad of Jack (live).
Sep 90. (7")(c-s) **EMPTY WORLD. / LADY NICOTINE** [61] [ ]
(12"+=)(cd-s+=) – Chiva / Heading for the target of insanity.
Sep 90. (cd)(c)(lp) **STRAIGHT** [32] [ ]
– Cardboard town / Kiss my heart goodbye / Lie in this land / You can't beat the Devil / Gypsy blood / Empty world / Back on the juice / Evil / Flyin' solo / Victims of success / Heroine. *(cd+=)(c+=)* – Chiva / Lady Nicotine.
Nov 90. (7")(c-s) **BACK ON THE JUICE. / VICTIMS OF SUCCESS (live)** [ ] [ ]
(12"+=) – Bullet proof poet (live).
(cd-s+=) – Lie in this land.
Aug 91. (cd)(c)(d-lp) **DOGS HITS AND BOOTLEG ALBUM** (compilation) [58] [ ]
– How come it never rains / The kid from Kensington / I don't want you to go (extended) / Satellite kid / Trail of tears / Victims of success / Empty world / Back on the juice / I think it's (love again)/ (BOOTLEG ALBUM tracks).

— Disbanded Jul'91 after TYLA had slashed himself on stage with a broken bottle. He received over 30 stitches to an open chest wound. BAM BAM joined The WILD HEARTS and STEVE JAMES forms The LAST BANDITS. Re-formed again late 1992.

Mar 93. (12"ep)(c-ep)(cd-ep) **ALL OR NOTHING EP** [53] [ ]
– All or nothing / When nobody loves you / What's happening here (acoustic) / Hard to leave this world. *(re-iss.+remixed.Jun93)*
May 93. (cd)(c)(lp) **THE MORE UNCHARTED HEIGHTS OF DISGRACE** [30] [ ]
– What's happening here? / What you do / Pretty, pretty once / World's different now (an ode to Drug Hill) / Mr.Addiction / Johnny Silvers / Cach / More uncharted heights of disgrace / Scared of dying / Mr.Barfly / Put it in her arm.
Aug 93. (7"m) **PRETTY PRETTY ONCE. / EVERYTHING I WANT (live) / HEARTBREAK (live)** [illegible] [ ]
(7"m) – ('A'side) / Trail of tears (live) / Medicine man (live).
(7"m) – ('A'side) / Drunk like me (live) / I don't want to go (live).
(cd-s) – ('A'side) / Mr.Addiction (live) / Last bandit (live) / How come it never rains (live).

– compilations, etc. –

Jun 93. China; (5xcd-box) **DOGS BOLLOX** (all albums) [ ] [-]

DOKKEN

Formed: Los Angeles, California, USA . . . 1981 by DON DOKKEN. Alongside future members of self-named band, he had refused solo lp 'BACK IN THE STREETS' around early 80's. After he contributed backing vox for The SCORPIONS on their 'BLACKOUT' album, he signed to French based label 'Carrere' in 1982. Broke through in the mid-80's with giant American album 'UNDER LOCK AND KEY'. • **Style:** Hard rock metal outfit. • **Songwriters:** DAN DOKKEN. • **Trivia:** Produced by MICHAEL WAGENER and ROY THOMAS-BAKER at various times.

Recommended: BEAST FROM THE EAST (*5)

DON DOKKEN (b.29 Jun'53) – vocals, guitar / **GEORGE LYNCH** (b.28 Sep'54) – guitar / **JUAN CROUCIER** – bass / **MICK BROWN** – drums

Carrere — Elektra

Apr 82. (7") **WE'RE ILLEGAL. / PARIS** [ ] [ ]
May 82. (lp)(c) **BREAKIN' THE CHAINS** [ ] [ ] 1981
– Breakin' the chains / Seven thunders / I can see you / We're illegal / In the middle / Paris / Stick to your guns / Young girl / Felony / Night rider.
1983. (7") **BREAKIN' IN THE CHAINS. / FELONY** [-] [ ]

— **JEFF PILSON** – bass repl. JUAN CROUCIER who later formed RATT.

Elektra — Elektra

Oct 84. (7") **BULLETS TO SPARE. / INTO THE FIRE** [-] [ ]
Oct 84. (lp)(c) **TOOTH AND NAIL** [ ] [49]
– Without warning / Tooth and nail / Just got lucky / Don't close your eyes / Heartless heart / When Heaven comes down / Into the fire / Bullets to spare / Alone again / Turn on the action.
Jan 85. (7") **JUST FOR LUCKY. / DON'T CLOSE YOUR EYES** [-] [ ]
Apr 85. (7") **ALONE AGAIN. / TOOTH AND NAIL** [-] [ ]
Mar 86. (7") **IN MY DREAMS. / TELL THE LIVING END** [ ] [77] Feb 86
(12"+=) – Alone again.
Mar 86. (lp)(c)(cd) **UNDER LOCK AND KEY** [ ] [32] Dec 85
– Unchain the night / The hunter / In my dreams / Lightning strikes again / Slippin' away / It's not love / Jaded heart / Don't lie to me / Will the Sun rise? / 'Til the livin' end.
Jun 86. (7") **LIGHTNING STRIKES AGAIN. / IT'S NOT LOVE** [-] [ ]
May 87. (7") **BACK FOR THE ATTACK. / DREAM WARRIORS** [-] [ ]
Nov 87. (lp)(c)(cd) **BACK FOR THE ATTACK** [96] [13]
– Kiss of death / The prisoner / Night by night / Standing in the shadows / Heaven sent / Mr. Scary / So many tears / Lost behind the wall / Burning like a flame / Stop fighting love / Cry of the gypsy / Sleepless nights / Dream warriors.
Feb 88. (7") **BURNING LIKE A FLAME. / LOST BEHIND THE WALL** [ ] [72] Dec 87
(12"+=)(12"pic-d+=) – Back for the attack.
Apr 88. (7") **HEAVEN SENT. / MR. SCARY** [-] [ ]
Jun 88. (7") **SO MANY TEARS. / MR. SCARY** [-] [ ]
Dec 88. (d-lp)(c)(cd) **BEAST FROM THE EAST (live)** [ ] [33] Nov 88
– Unchain the night / Kiss of death / Tooth and nail / When heaven comes down / Into the fire / Mr. Scary / Heaven sent / Dream warriors / It's not love / Alone again / Breaking the chains / Just got lucky / In my dreams / Walk away. (d-lp+c+=) – Standing in the shadows / Sleepless nights / Turn on the action.
Dec 88. (7") **ALONE AGAIN (live). / IT'S NOT LOVE (live)** [-] [ ]
Feb 89. (7") **WALK AWAY (live). / UNCHAIN THE NIGHT (live)** [-] [ ]

— (DOKKEN had split earlier in the year) **LYNCH** and **BROWN** formed **LYNCH MOB.**

DON DOKKEN

went solo, augmented by **JOHN NORTON** – guitar (ex-EUROPE) / **BILLY WHITE** – guitar (ex-WATCHTOWER) / **PETER BALTES** – bass (of ACCEPT) / **MIKKEY DEE** – drums (ex-KING DIAMOND)

Geffen — Geffen

Sep 90. (cd)(c)(lp) **UP FROM THE ASHES** [ ] [50]
– Crash'n'burn / 1,000 miles away / Whern some nights / Forever / Living a lie / When love finds a fool / Give it up / Mirror mirror / Stay / Down in the flames / The hunger. *(re-dist.Aug91)*

DOKKEN

re-formed (on same label)
May 95. (cd)(c) **DYSFUNCTIONAL** [-] [47]

– compilations, etc. –

Jul 93. Repertoire; (cd) **BACK IN THE STREETS** (rec.1979) [ ] [-]
– Back in the streets / Felony / Day after day / We're going wrong / Liar / Prisoner.

Thomas DOLBY

Born: THOMAS ROBERTSON, 14 Oct'58, Cairo, Egypt. Became regular session man in the early 80's for FOREIGNER, DEF LEPPARD, LENE LOVICH, etc., while also issuing one-off 45 for indie 'Armageddon'. Previous to this, he had made his name working as a live sound mixer and part-time member of BRUCE WOOLLEY & THE CAMERA CLUB plus The FALL-OUT CLUB. In mid-81, he signed major solo deal to 'Parlophone', which soon incorporated his own independent label 'Venus In Peril'. He broke the UK 50 that year with 'EUROPA AND THE PIRATE TWINS'. In 1983, after a mildly successful UK debut album 'THE GOLDEN AGE OF WIRELESS', he smashed the US Top 5 with single 'SHE BLINDED ME WITH SCIENCE'. • **Style:** Eccentric electronic wizard, experimenting with all aspects of popular music (i.e. ballad, funk, film, etc.). • **Songwriters:** Dolby penned, except I SCARE MYSELF (Dan Hicks & The Charlatans; US) / HOT SAUCE (George Clinton). • **Trivia:** In 1987, THOMAS moved to Los Angeles, California, and soon married 'Dynasty' soap star Kathleen Beller. DOLBY was also producer for PREFAB SPROUT.

Recommended: THE BEST OF THOMAS DOLBY – RETROSPECTIVE (*6)

THOMAS DOLBY – vocals, keyboards, synthesizers (ex-BRUCE WOOLLEY & THE CAMERA CLUB, ex-SW9, ex-LENE LOVICH, ex-FALLOUT CLUB) used various friends as backing.

Armageddon | not issued

Feb 81. (7") **URGES. / LEIPZEIG** | | -

Parlophone | Capitol

Aug 81. (7") **EUROPA AND THE PIRATE TWINS. / THERAPY** | 48 | 67 Jun 83
(12"+=) – Growth / Leipzig.

Venus In Peril | Capitol

Jan 82. (7")(12") **AIRWAVES. / THE WRECK OF THE FAIRCHILD**
Apr 82. (7")(12") **RADIO SILENCE. / ('A' version)**
May 82. (lp)(c) **THE GOLDEN AGE OF WIRELESS** | 65 | 13 Mar 83
– The wreck of the Fairchild / Airwaves / Radio silence / Cloudburst at Shingle Street / Flying north / Commercial break-up / Weightless / Europa and the pirate twins / Windpower. *(re-iss.Aug83, includes – She blinded me with science / One of our submarines is missing.* replacing – The wreck of the Fairchild. *US-iss.Jan83 titled* **'SHE BLINDED ME WITH SCIENCE'** *reached No.20) (cd-iss.May95 on 'Fame')*
Jul 82. (7")(12") **WINDPOWER. / FLYING NORTH** | 31 |
Oct 82. (7")(12") **SHE BLINDED ME WITH SCIENCE. / JUNGLE LINE** | 49 |
Jun 83. (7")(12") **SHE BLINDED ME WITH SCIENCE. / ON OF OUR SUBMARINES IS MISSING** | 56 | 5

Parlophone | Capitol

Oct 83. (7")(12") **GET OUT OF MY MIX. (as "DOLBY'S CUBE") / GET ON OUT OF MY MIX**
Jan 84. (7") **HYPERACTIVE. / WHITE CITY** | 17 | 62
(12"+=) – ('A' mix)
Feb 84. (lp)(c)(cd) **THE FLAT EARTH** | 14 | 35
– Dissidents / The flat earth / Screen kiss / White city / Mulu the rain forest / I scare myself / Hyperactive. *(re-iss.+cd.Jun87)*
Mar 84. (7") **I SCARE MYSELF. / CLOUDBURST AT SHINGLE STREET** | 46 | -
(12"+=) – Puppet theatre.
Apr 84. (7") **I SCARE MYSELF. / DISSIDENTS** | - |
Jun 84. (7") **DISSIDENTS (Pt.1). / THE SEARCH FOR TRUTH – DISSIDENTS (Pt.2)**
(12"+=) – Urges / One of our submarines is missing.
Jul 85. (7") **MAY THE CUBE BE WITH YOU. (as "DOLBY'S CUBE") / GOO GOO PLEXUS**
(12"+=) – ('A' 3D mix) / Cube Creature Cavier.

— In Feb86, teamed up with RYUICHI SAKAMOTO on 7" FIELD WORK.

M.C.A. | M.C.A.

Nov 86. (7")(12") **HOWARD THE DUCK (film soundtrack). / DON'T TURN AWAY**

Virgin | Virgin

Feb 87. (lp)(c)(cd) **GOTHIC (original soundtrack)**
– Fantasmagoria / Byronic love / Shelleymania / Mary's theme / Party games / Gipsy girl / Crucifix / The fundamental source / Sin and buggery / Impaleuent / Leech juice / Restless sleep / 1,2 & 3 / It's his / Coitus per stigmata / Once we vowed eternal love / Riddled with guilt / The final seance / Funeral by the lake / No ghosts in daylight / To the grave / The Devil is an Englishman featuring Screaming Lord Byron / Skull pulse / A trickle of blood.
Feb 87. (7")(12") **THE DEVIL IS AND ENGLISHMAN. / FANTASMAGORIA**

— with **The LOST TOY PEOPLE: LARRY TREADWELL** – guitar / **DAVID OWENS** – drums / **TERRY JACKSON** – bass / **MIKE KAPITAN** – synthesizer / **LAURA CREAMER** – vocals, percussion

Manhattan-EMI | Manhattan

Mar 88. (7") **AIRHEAD. / BUDAPEST BY BLIMP** | 53 |
(12"+=) – Hyperactive.
(cd-s+=) – Airhead (extended).
Apr 88. (lp)(c)(cd) **ALIENS ATE MY BUICK** | 30 | 70
– The key to the Ferrari / Airhead / Hot sauce / Pulp culture / My brain is like a sieve / The ability to swing / Budapest by blimp. (cd+=) – May the cube be with you.
Dec 88. (7") **HOT SAUCE. / SALSA PICANTE**
(12"+=) – (2 'A' mixes).
(cd-s+=) – Get out of my mix.
Feb 89. (7") **MY BRAIN IS LIKE A SIEVE. / ('A'instrumental)**
(12"+=)(cd-s+=) – ('A'extended) / Ravivor foire.

Virgin | Giant

May 92. (7")(c-s) **CLOSE, BUT NO CIGAR. / NEON SISTERS** | 22 |
(cd-s+=) – ('A'side) / Hyperactive / She blinded me with science / I scare myself.
(cd-s+=) – Beauty of a dream / ('A'version).
Jul 92. (cd)(c)(lp) **ASTRONAUTS AND HERETICS** | 35 |
– I love you goodbye / Cruel / Silk pyjamas / I live in a suitcase / Eastern Bloc / Close but no cigar / That's why people fall in love / Neon sisters / Beauty of a dream.
Jul 92. (7")(c-s) **I LOVE YOU GOODBYE. / EASTERN BLOC (SEQUEL TO 'EUROPA AND THE PIRATE TWINS')** | 36 |
(cd-s+=) – ('A'version) / Eastern Bloc (version).
(cd-s) – ('A'side) / Windpower / Europa and the pirate twins.
Sep 92. (7")(c-s) **SILK PYJAMAS. / FIELDWORK (w / RYUICHI SAKAMOTO)** | 62 |
(cd-s) – ('A'side) / Airhead / Urges / Leipzig.
(cd-s+=) – Puppet theatre / Get out of my mix.

E.M.I. | Capitol

Jan 94. (c-s) **HYPERACTIVE (heavy brother subversion). / SHE BLINDED ME WITH SCIENCE (U.S.mix)** | 23 |
(12"+=) – Windpower.
(cd-s+=) – One of our submarines is missing / Dissidents (the search for the truth part 2).
(cd-s) – ('A'side) / Windpower / Dissidents / Puppet theatre.
Feb 94. (cd)(c) **THE BEST OF THOMAS DOLBY – RETROSPECTABLE** (compilation)
– Europa and the pirate twins / Urges / Leipzig / Windpower / Airwaves / She blinded me with science / One of our submarines is missing / Screen kiss / Hyperactive / I scare myself / The flat earth / Pulp culture / Budapest by blimp / Cruel / Close but no cigar / I love you goodbye.

Mickey DOLENZ (see under ⇒ MONKEES)

DOLPHIN BROTHERS (see under ⇒ JAPAN)

DOME (see under ⇒ WIRE)

Fats DOMINO

Born: ANTOINE DOMINO, 26 Feb 1928, New Orleans, Louisiana, USA. In 1948, after working in honky tonk clubs, he signed to 'Imperial'. Around the same time, he was nicknamed 'Fats' by his bassist Billy Diamond, because of his 16 stone stature. His first record 'THE FAT MAN', hit the R&B chart only, but by 1953 was a million seller. He toured throughout the early 50's, and was rewarded in 1955, when 'AIN'T THAT A SHAME' hit the US Top 10. By late 1956, he had appeared in 2 films 'Shake, Rattle & Roll' & 'The Girl Can't Help It', which enabled worldwide access to more late 50's/early 60's hits including 'I'M IN LOVE AGAIN', 'BLUEBERRY HILL', 'BLUE MONDAY', 'I'M WALKIN'', 'WHOLE LOTTA LOVIN'', 'BE MY GUEST' & 'WALKIN TO NEW ORLEANS'. • **Style:** R&B pianist, whose simplistic boogie rock'n'roll spawned from New Orleans' cosmopolitan roots. In the early 60's, he pioneered form of reggae/ska with the song 'IT KEEPS RAININ''. • **Songwriters:** Wrote with bandleader DAVE BARTHOLOMEW until circa 1956. He penned own material, at times collaborating with others. WHEN THE SAINTS GO MARCHING IN (trad.) / JAMBALAYA + YOU WIN AGAIN (Hank Williams) / I HEAR YOU KNOCKIN' (Smiley Lewis) / DID YOU EVER SEE A DREAM WALKIN' (Eddy Duchin) / RED SAILS IN THE SUNSET (Platters) / I CAN'T STOP LOVING YOU (Ray Charles) / I LEFT MY HEART IN SAN FRANCISCO (Tony Bennett) / LADY MADONNA + LOVELY RITA + EVERYBODY'S GOT SOMETHING TO HIDE EXCEPT ME AND THE MONKEY (Beatles) / etc. • **Trivia:** He married childhood sweetheart Rosemary in the late 40's, bringing up 8 children in homeland New Orleans.

Recommended: MY BLUE HEAVEN: THE BEST OF FATS DOMINO (*6)

FATS DOMINO – vocals, piano with **DAVE BARTHOLOMEW** – trumpet / **RED TYLER** – bass / **EARL PALMER** – drums

not issued | Imperial

Apr 50. (7") **THE FAT MAN. / DETROIT CITY BLUES** | - |
1950. (7") **BOOGIE WOOGIE BABY. / LITTLE BEE** | - |
1950. (7") **SHE'S MY BABY. / HIDE AWAY BLUES** | - |
1950. (7") **HEY LA BAS BOOGIE. / BRAND NEW BABY** | - |

— (above 3 singles were on 78 rpm. only) (In the 50's, all 45 & 78 rpm)

Nov 50. (7") **KOREA BLUES. / EVERY NIGHT ABOUT THIS TIME** | - |

— FATS now finds own musicians.

1951. (7") **TIRED OF CRYING. / WHAT'S THE MATTER BABY** | - |
1951. (7") **DON'T LIE TO ME BABY. / SOMETIMES I WONDER** | - |
1951. (7") **NO NO BABY. / RIGHT FROM WRONG** | - |
Nov 51. (7") **ROCKIN' CHAIR. / CARELESS LOVE** | - |
Jan 52. (7") **YOU KNOW I MISS YOU. / I'LL BE GONE** | - |
Mar 52. (7") **GOIN' HOME. / REELIN' AND ROCKIN'** | - |
1952. (7") **POOR POOR ME. / TRUST IN ME** | - |
1952. (7")(7"red) **HOW LONG. / DREAMING** | - |
1953. (7")(7"red) **NOBODY LOVES ME. / CHEATIN'** | - |
May 53. (7")(7"red) **GOING TO THE RIVER. / MARDI GRAS IN NEW ORLEANS** | - |
Jul 53. (7") **PLEASE DON'T LEAVE ME. / THE GIRL I LOVE** | - |

— added **LEE ALLEN** – saxophone

London | Imperial

Feb 54. (7") **ROSEMARY. / YOU SAID YOU LOVED ME** | | Oct 53
Jul 54. (7") **YOU DONE ME WRONG. / (HEY) LITTLE SCHOOL GIRL** | | Feb 54
Nov 54. (7") **DON'T LEAVE ME THIS WAY. / SOMETHING'S WRONG** | | Dec 53
1954. (7") **BABY PLEASE. / WHERE DID YOU STAY** | - |
1954. (7") **YOU CAN PACK YOUR SUITCASE. / I LIVED MY LIFE** | - |
Feb 55. (7") **LOVE ME. / DON'T YOU HEAR ME CALLIN' YOU** | | 1954
Apr 55. (7") **I KNOW. / THINKIN' OF YOU** | | Jan 55
1955. (7") **DON'T YOU KNOW. / HELPING HAND** | - |

— now with **WALTER NELSON** – guitar / **CORNELIUS COLEMAN** – drums.

Sep 55. (7") **AIN'T THAT A SHAME. / LA-LA-LA** | | 10 Jun 55
(above single hit UK chart No.23 in Jan57)
1955. (lp) **CARRY ON ROCKIN'**
– The fat man / Tired of crying / Goin' home / You said you love me / Going to the river / Please don't leave me / Rose Mary / All by myself / Ain't that a shame / Poor

me / Bo Weevil / Don't blame it on me.

Sep 55. (7") **ALL BY MYSELF. / TROUBLES OF MY OWN** -

Nov 55. (7") **POOR ME. / I CAN'T GO ON (ROSALIE)** -

Mar 56. (7") **BO WEEVIL. / DON'T BLAME IT ON ME** 35

May 56. (7") **I'M IN LOVE AGAIN. / MY BLUE HEAVEN** 12 3 / 21

Aug 56. (lp) **FATS DOMINO – ROCK & ROLLIN'** 18

– The fat man / Tired of crying / Goin' home / You said you love me / Going to the river / Please don't leave me / Rose Mary / All by myself / Ain't that a shame / Poor me / Bo Weevil / Don't blame it on me.

Aug 56. (7") **WHEN MY DREAMBOAT COMES HOME. / SO LONG** 14 Jul 56

Sep 56. (7") **BLUEBERRY HILL. / HONEY CHILE** - 5

Oct 56. (7") **BLUEBERRY HILL. / I CAN'T GO ON (ROSALIE)** 6 -

Jan 57. (7") **HONEY CHILE. / DON'T YOU KNOW** 29 -

Feb 57. (lp) **THIS IS FATS DOMINO!** 19

– Blueberry hill / Honey chile / What's the reason I'm not pleasing you / Blue Monday / So long / La la / Troubles of my own / You done me wrong / Reeling and rocking / The fat man's hop / Poor poor me / Trust in me.

Mar 57. (7") **BLUE MONDAY. / WHAT'S THE REASON (I'M NOT PLEASING YOU)** 23 5 Dec 56

Apr 57. (7") **I'M WALKIN'. / I'M IN THE MOOD FOR LOVE** 19 4 Feb 57

Jun 57. (7") **VALLEY OF TEARS. / IT'S YOU I LOVE** 25 6 / 22 May 58

1957. (lp) **HERE STANDS FATS DOMINO**

– Detroit City blues / Hide away blues / She's my baby / New baby / Little bee / Every night about this time / I'm walkin' / I'm in the mood for love / Cheatin' / You can pack your suitcase / Hey fat man / I'll be gone.

Aug 57. (7") **WHEN I SEE YOU. / WHAT WILL I TELL MY HEART** 29 / 64

Nov 57. (7") **WAIT AND SEE. / I STILL LOVE YOU** 23 / 79 Oct 57

—— sessions incl. **ALLEN TOUSSAINT** – piano

Mar 58. (7") **THE BIG BEAT. / I WANT YOU TO KNOW** 20 26 / 48 Dec 57

Feb 58. (7") **YES MY DARLING. / DON'T YOU KNOW I LOVE YOU** - 55

1958. (lp) **THIS IS FATS**

– The rooster song / My happiness / As time goes by / Hey la bas / ove me / Don't you hear me calling you / It's you I love / Valley of tears / Where did you stay / Baby please / Thinking of you / You know I miss you. *(re-iss.Apr79 on 'Flyover') (re-iss.US Jan83)*

Jun 58. (7") **SICK AND TIRED. / NO, NO** 26 22 / 55 Apr 58

Jul 58. (7") **LITTLE MARY. / PRISONER'S SONG** 48 Jun 58

Oct 58. (7") **YOUNG SCHOOL GIRL. / IT MUST BE LOVE** 92 Aug 58

Nov 58. (7") **WHOLE LOTTA LOVING. / COQUETTE** 6 / 92

1958. (lp) **THE FABULOUS MR.D**

– The big beat / I'll be glad when you're dead you rascal you / What will I tell my heart / Barrelhouse / Little Mary / Sick and tired / I want you to know / "44" / Mardi Gras in New Orleans / I can't go on / Long lonesome journey / Young school girl *(re-iss.US Jan83)*

Mar 59. (7") **WHEN THE SAINTS GO MARCHING IN. / TELLING LIES** 50

May 59. (7") **I'M READY. / MARGIE** (UK-'A') 18 16 / 51

(re-iss.Jul76 on 'United Art')

1959. (lp) **FATS DOMINO SWINGS** -

– The fat man / Blue Monday / Blueberry Hill / I'm in love again / Going to the river / My blue Heaven / Bo Weevil / Goin' home / Please don't leave me / Ain';t that a shame / I'm walkin' / Whole lotta lovin'.

Sep 59. (7") **I WANT TO WALK YOU HOME. / I'M GONNA BE A WHEEL SOMEDAY** 14 8 / 17 Jul 59

Dec 59. (7") **BE MY GUEST. / I'VE BEEN AROUND** 11 8 Oct 59 / 33

1959. (lp) **LET'S PLAY FATS DOMINO**

– You left me / Ain't it good / Howdy podner / Stack & Billy / Would you / Margie / Hands across the table / When the saints go marching in / Ida Jane / Lil' Liza Jane / I'm gonna be a wheel some day / I want to walk you home.

Mar 60. (7") **COUNTRY BOY. / IF YOU NEED ME** 19 25 / 98 Jan 60

Jun 60. (7") **TELL ME THAT YOU LOVE ME. / BEFORE I GROW TOO OLD** 51 / 84 Apr 60

1960. (lp) **FATS DOMINO SINGS MILLION RECORD HITS** -

– You said you love me / I still love you / Be my guest / Country boy / If you need me / I want to walk you home / It's you I love / I've been around / I'm gonna be a wheel some day / I'm ready / Margie / I want you to know.

Jul 60. (7") **WALKING TO NEW ORLEANS. / DON'T COME KNOCKIN'** 19 6 / 21 Jun 60

Oct 60. (7") **THREE NIGHTS A WEEK. / PUT YOUR ARMS AROUND ME HONEY** 45 15 / 58 Aug 60

1960. (lp) **A LOT OF DOMINO'S**

– Put your arms around me honey / Three nights a week / Shurah / Rising Sun / My girl Josephine / The sheik of Araby / Walking to New Orleans / Don't come knockin' / Magic isles / You always hurt the one you love / It's the talk of the town / Natural born lover.

Dec 60. (7") **MY GIRL JOSEPHINE. / NATURAL BORN LOVER** 32 14 / 38 Oct 60

Mar 61. (7") **WHAT A PRICE. / AIN'T THAT JUST LIKE A WOMAN** 22 / 33 Jan 61

Apr 61. (7") **SHU-RAH. / FELL IN LOVE ON MONDAY** 32

1961. (lp) **I MISS YOU SO**

– I miss you so / It keeps rainin' / Ain't that just like a woman / Once in a while / I hear you knockin' / Isle of Capri / What a price / When I was young / Fell in love on Monday / My bleeding heart / Easter parade / I'll always be in love with you.

Jun 61. (7") **IT KEEPS RAININ'. / I JUST CRY** 49 23

Sep 61. (7") **LET THE FOUR WINDS BLOW. / GOOD HEARTED MAN** 15 Jul 61

1961. (lp) **LET THE FOUR WINDS BLOW**

– Along the Navajo trail / You win again / One night / I'm alone because I love you / Won't you come on back / Trouble blues / I can't give you anything but love / Good hearted man / Your cheating heart / Let the four winds blow / In a shanty in Old Shanty Town / Am I blue.

Nov 61. (7") **WHAT A PARTY. / ROCKIN' BICYCLE** 22 / 83 Oct 61

Nov 61. (lp) **WHAT A PARTY**

– Did you ever see a dream / Walking rockin' bicycle / Before I grow too old ain't gonna do it / Bad luck and trouble / Hold hands / Trouble in mind / Coquette / What a party / I just cry / I've been calling / Tell me that you love me.

Dec 61. (7") **JAMBALAYA (ON THE BAYOU). / I HEAR YOU KNOCKIN'** - 30 / 67

Mar 62. (7") **JAMBALAYA. / YOU WIN AGAIN** 41 -

Mar 62. (7") **YOU WIN AGAIN. / IDA JANE** - 22 / 90

1962. (lp) **TWISTIN' THE STOMP**

– Twistin' the spots / The twist set me free / I know / Every night / Town talk / Wait and see / Twistin' the stomp / Don't deceive me / A long way from home / The girl I love / Do you know what it means to miss New Orleans / South of the border.

Jun 62. (7") **MY REAL NAME. / MY HEART IS BLEEDING** 59 May 62

Aug 62. (7") **DANCE WITH MR.DOMINO. / NOTHING NEW (SAME OLD THING)** 98 77 Jul 62

Oct 62. (7") **STOP THE CLOCK. / DID YOU EVER SEE A DREAM WALKING** Sep 62

Dec 62. (7") **WON'T YOU COME ON BACK. / HANDS ACROSS THE TABLE** -

1963. (7") **THOSE EYES. / HUM-DIDDY-DOO** -

H.M.V. ABC Para

May 63. (7") **THERE GOES (MY HEART AGAIN). / CAN'T GO ON WITHOUT YOU** 59

Jul 63. (7") **WHEN I'M WALKING (LET ME WALK). / I'VE GOT A RIGHT TO CRY**

Sep 63. (7") **RED SAILS IN THE SUNSET. / SONG FOR ROSEMARY** 34 35

Sep 63. (lp) **HERE COMES FATS DOMINO**

– When I'm walking / I got a right to cry / There goes my heart again / Just a lonely man / Red sails in the sunset / Bye baby, bye, bye / Forever, forever / I'm livin' right / Can't go on without you / Land of 1000 dances / Song for Rosemary / Tell me the truth, baby. *(cd-iss.Sep92 + Jul93 on 'Repertoire')*

Jan 64. (7") **WHO CARES. / JUST A LONELY MAN** 63 Dec 63

Mar 64. (7") **LAZY LADY. / DON'T WANT TO SET THE WORLD ON FIRE** 86 Feb 64

1964. (lp) **FATS ON FIRE**

– I don't want to set the world on fire / You know I miss you / Fats on fire / Land of make believe / Old man trouble / Love me / Mary, oh Mary / Gotta get a job / The fat man / Valley of tears / Fats shuffle / I'm a fool to care.

May 64. (7") **SOMETHING YOU GOT BABY. / IF YOU DON'T KNOW WHAT LOVE IS**

Jul 64. (7") **MARY OH MARY. / PACKIN' UP**

Sep 64. (7") **SALLY WAS A GOOD OLD GIRL. / FOR YOU** 99

1964. (lp) **FANTASTIC FATS**

Nov 64. (7") **HEARTBREAK HILL. / KANSAS CITY** 99

Apr 65. (7") **WHY DON'T YOU DO RIGHT. / WIGS**

Jun 65. (lp) **GETAWAY WITH FATS DOMINO**

– When the dreamboat comes home / Wigs / Trouble in mind / Man that's all / Kansas City / Reelin' and rockin' / On a slow boat to China / Monkey business / Heartbreak hill / Girl I'm gonna marry you / Why don't you do right / Ballin' the jack. *(re-iss.Dec83 on 'Ace')*

1965. (7") **LET ME CALL YOU SWEETHEART. / GOODNIGHT SWEETHEART** -

1965. (7") **I DON'T WANT TO SET THE WORLD ON FIRE. / I'M LIVIN' RIGHT** -

Mercury Mercury

Sep 65. (7") **I LEFT MY HEART IN SAN FRANCISCO. / I DONE GOT FOR YOU**

Nov 65. (7") **WHAT'S THAT YOU GOT. / IT'S NEVER TOO LATE**

Dec 65. (lp) **'65 (live)**

– (Introduction) / Blueberry hill / Please don't leave me / Domino twist / Let the four winds blow / I'm gonna be a wheel someday / I'm in the mood for love / Jambalaya (on the bayou) / Oh, what a price / Ain't that a shame / So long.

not issued Broadmoor

Dec 67. (7") **THE LADY IN BLACK. / WORK MY WAY UP STEADY** -

1968. (7") **BIG MOUTH. / WAIT TILL IT HAPPENS TO YOU** -

Valient Reprise

1968. (7") **ONE FOR THE HIGHWAY. / HONEST PAPAS LOVE THEIR MAMAS BETTER** -

Aug 68. (7") **LADY MADONNA. / ONE FOR THE HIGHWAY** 100

Sep 68. (lp) **FATS IS BACK**

– My old friends / I'm ready / So swell when you're well / Wait till it happens to you / I know / Lady Madonna / Honest papas love their mamas better / Make me belong to you / One for the highway / Lovely Rita / One more song for you.

1968. (7") **LOVEY RITA. / WAIT TILL IT HAPPENS TO YOU** -

1969. (7") **EVERYBODY'S GOT SOMETHING TO HIDE EXCEPT ME AND THE DONKEY. / SO SWELL WHEN YOU'RE WELL** -

1970. (7") **MAKE ME BELONG TO YOU. / HAVE YOU SEEN MY BABY** -

1970. (lp) **FATS** -

– I'm going to cross that river / Big mouth / It's a sin to tell a lie / Wait till it happens to you / I'm going to help a friend / The lady in black / Another mule / When you're smiling (the whole world smiles with you) / These old shoes / Lawdy Miss Clawdy /

Work my way up steady.

1970. (7") **NEW ORLEANS AIN'T THE SAME. / SWEET PATOOTIE** [-] [ ]

Atlantic / Atlantic

Jun 74. (lp) **LIVE AT MONTREAUX – HELLO JOSEPHINE (live '73)** [ ] [ ]
– Hello Josephine / I'm in love again / Blueberry hill / Jambalaya / Walking to New Orleans / I'm gonna be a wheel someday / Blue Monday / Mardi Gras in New Orleans / Stagger Lee / I want to walk you home / Let the four winds blow / I'm walking / When the saints go marching in / Sentimental journey.

Sonet / Polydor

May 79. (lp) **SLEEPING ON THE JOB** [ ] [ ]
– Sleeping on the job / After hours / When I lost my baby / Something about you baby / Move with the groove / Any old time / Shame on you / I just can't get the girl I love / Love me.

Nov 78. (7") **SLEEPING ON THE JOB. / AFTER HOURS** [ ] [-]

not issued / Warners

Jan 81. (7") **WHISKEY HEAVEN. / BEERS TO YOU (by the Texas Opera Company)** [-] [ ]

— Retired from music, to spend time with family, although he made comeback album in 1985.

not issued / Toot Toot

1985. (7") **MY TOOT TOOT-ONE (w/Doug Kershaw). / MY TOOT TOOT-THREE** [-] [ ]

— He was backed by many session men.

not issued / M.C.A.

1986. (lp)(c) **HIS GREATEST HITS (live)** [-] [ ]
– My girl Josephine / The fat man / I'm gonna be a wheel someday / Blue Monday / Jambalaya (on the bayou) / Blueberry Hill / Going to the river / I'm ready / I want to walk you home / Whole lotta loving / Poor me / Ain't that a shame / I almost lost my mind / I'm in love again / I'm walkin' / Walking to New Orleans / Let the four winds blow / Shake, rattle and roll / My toot toot / I can't go on.

– compilations, others, etc. –

Note; Some below releases on 'London' were issued on 'Imperial' US.

Jul 62. London; (lp) **MILLION SELLERS BY FATS** [ ] [ ]
Jun 63. London; (7") **YOU ALWAYS HURT THE ONE YOU LOVE. / TROUBLE BLUES** [ ] [ ]
1963. London; (lp) **WALKIN' TO NEW ORLEANS** [ ] [ ]
1963. Imperial; (7") **ISLE OF CAPRI. / TRUE CONFESSION** [-] [ ]
1963. Imperial; (7") **ONE NIGHT. / I CAN'T GO ON THIS WAY** [-] [ ]
1964. Imperial; (lp) **LET'S DANCE** [-] [ ]
1964. Imperial; (7") **I CAN'T GIVE YOU ANYTHING BUT LOVE. / GOIN' HOME** [-] [ ]
1964. Imperial; (7") **YOUR CHEATIN' HEART. / WHEN I WAS YOUNG** [-] [ ]
1964. Imperial; (lp) **HERE HE COMES AGAIN** [-] [ ]
Apr 65. Liberty; (lp) **MILLION SELLERS BY FATS VOL.2** [ ] [ ]
1968. Liberty; (7") **WALKING TO NEW ORLEANS. / BLUEBERRY HILL** [ ] [ ]
Jul 74. Liberty; (6xlp-box) **THE FATS DOMINO STORY** [ ] [ ]
Oct 85. Liberty; (lp)(c) **THE BEST OF FATS DOMINO** [ ] [ ]
(cd-iss. Jul 88 on 'E.M.I.')
Nov 90. Liberty; (7") **MY BLUE HEAVEN. / BLUEBERRY HILL** [ ] [ ]
(12"+=) – Walking to New Orleans.
(cd-s++=) – The fat man.
1967. ABC-Paramount; (7") **I DON'T WANT TO SET THE WORLD ON FIRE. / I'M LIVING RIGHT** [-] [ ]
1969. Mercury; (7") **JAMBALAYA. / WHAT'S THAT YOU GOT** [ ] [-]
Apr 70. U.A.; (lp)(c) **THE VERY BEST OF FATS DOMINO: PLAY IT AGAIN FATS** [56] [ ]
Jun 71. U.A.; (7") **BLUE MONDAY. / DON'T YOU KNOW I LOVE YOU** [ ] [ ]
1971. U.A.; (lp)(c) **RARE DOMINOES VOL.2** [ ] [ ]
1972. U.A.; (lp)(c) **LEGENDARY MASTERS** [ ] [ ]
Feb 75. U.A.; (7") **BLUEBERRY HILL. / WALKIN' TO NEW ORLEANS** [ ] [ ]
Feb 76. U.A.; (7") **BLUEBERRY HILL. / IT KEEPS RAININ'** [41] [-]
Mar 77. U.A.; (lp)(c) **20 GREATEST HITS** [ ] [-]
May 77. U.A.; (d-lp) **THE FATS DOMINO STORY VOLS.1 & 2** [ ] [-]
Jul 77. U.A.; (d-lp) **THE FATS DOMINO STORY VOLS.3 & 4** [ ] [-]
Oct 77. U.A.; (d-lp) **THE FATS DOMINO STORY VOLS.5 & 6** [ ] [-]
Mar 78. U.A.; (lp)(c) **LIVE IN EUROPE (live)** [ ] [-]
May 79. U.A.; (7") **WALKIN' TO NEW ORLEANS. / THE FAT MAN** [ ] [-]
May 84. E.M.I.; (7") **AIN'T THAT A SHAME. / THE FAT MAN** [ ] [-]
Feb 91. E.M.I.; (cd) **MY BLUE HEAVEN: THE BEST OF FATS DOMINO** [ ] [-]
– My blue Heaven / The fat man / Please don't leave me / Ain't that a shame / I'm in love again / When my dreamboat comes home / Blueberry hill / Blue Monday / I'm walkin' / Valley of tears / Big beat / Yes my darling / Whole lotta loving / I'm ready / I'm gonna be a wheel someday / I want to walk you home / Be my guest / Walking to New Orleans (undubbed) / Let the four winds blow / What a party.
Nov 91. E.M.I.; (4xcd-box) **THEY CALL ME THE FAT MAN** [ ] [-]
Jun 84. S.M.P.; (7"ep) **BLUEBERRY HILL / AIN'T THAT A SHAME. / I WANT TO WALK YOU HOME / THE FAT MAN** [ ] [-]
1985. Magnum Force; (7") **MY TOOT TOOT ("FATS DOMINO & DOUG KERSHAW"). / DIGGY IGGY TO** [ ] [-]
Sep 91. Charly; (cd) **BE MY GUEST – LIVE (live)** [ ] [-]
Feb 93. Charly; (cd) **ROCKIN' WITH FATS** [ ] [-]
Jul 93. Repertoire; (cd) **KINGS OF BEAT** [ ] [-]
Aug 93. Tomato; (cd) **ANTOINE FATS DOMINO** [ ] [-]
Nov 93. Fat Boy; (cd) **HIS GREATEST HITS** [ ] [-]
Nov 93. Bear Family; (cd) **OUT OF NEW ORLEANS** [ ] [-]
Mar 94. Spectrum; (cd) **JAMBALAYA** [ ] [-]
May 94. Laserlight; (cd)(c) **WHEN I'M WALKING** [ ] [-]
Jul 94. Success; (cd)(c) **GREATEST HITS LIVE (live)** [ ] [-]
Aug 94. Dynamite; (cd) **FATS DOMINO** [ ] [-]
Oct 94. Kenwest; (cd) **BLUEBERRY HILL** [ ] [ ]
Dec 94. See For Miles; (cd) **THE E.P. COLLECTION** [ ] [-]
Feb 95. Marble Arch; (cd)(c) **THE BEST OF FATS DOMINO** [ ] [-]
Apr 95. Muskateer; (cd)(c) **HIS GREATEST HITS** [ ] [-]

— Also released number of UK-EP's on 'London'. **BLUES FOR LOVE / BLUES FOR LOVE** (VOL.2) / **FATS / HERE COMES FATS / HERE COMES FATS** (VOL.2) / **CARRY ON ROCKIN' / CARRY ON ROCKIN'** (VOL.2) / **BLUES FOR LOVE** (VOL.3) / **BLUES FOR LOVE** (VOL.4) / **HERE COMES FATS** (VOL.3) / **THE ROCKIN' MR.D / THE ROCKIN' MR.D** (VOL.2) / **BE MY GUEST / THE ROCKIN' MR.D** (VOL.3) / **WHAT A PARTY. / RED SAILS IN THE SUNSET** (on 'H.M.V.)

Lonnie DONEGAN

Born: ANTHONY JAMES DONEGAN, 29 Apr'31, Glasgow, Scotland. Moved to East London in 1952 after a period in the army. He joined KEN COLYER'S JAZZMEN as a guitar/banjo player and re-united with army pal CHRIS BARBER. He took the name LONNIE, after a compere wrongly mixed his name with the top of the bill blues guitarist LONNIE JOHNSON. Early in 1954, BARBER left COLYER, to form own band which featured DONEGAN. The following year, CHRIS BARBER'S JAZZ BAND as The LONNIE DONEGAN SKIFFLE GROUP, released a 10"lp 'NEW ORLEANS JOY' on 'Decca' records. Early 1956, a track, the US trad.song 'ROCK ISLAND LINE', was re-recorded from the lp, which surprisingly climbed into the UK + US Top10. With fame on the ascendency, he signed to 'Pye-Nixa', and his official follow-up 'LOST JOHN' / 'STEWBALL', hit UK No.2. The following year, after a few more hits, LONNIE was at No.1 with 'CUMBERLAND GAP'. He continued to have string of hits, until the arrival of The BEATLES. • **Style:** His early jazz and folk roots evolved into 'skiffle' (a hybrid of US folk/blues, mixed with D.I.Y. instrumentation and comic attitude). Virtually overnight, he started new 'skiffle' craze, with mothers having to buy a separate washboard just for their offspring. • **Trivia:** His comic novelty song 'MY OLD MAN'S A DUSTMAN', was the first ever record to go straight to No.1 in Britain. On reflection though, this change in direction, led to his steady downfall. • **Songwriters:** DONEGAN mainly adapted old negro songs, and traditional folk songs including that of WOODY GUTHRIE (GAMBLIN' MAN / GRAND COOLIE DAM). He also covered TOM DOOLEY (Kingston Trio) / DOES YOUR CHEWING GUM . . . (c.Breur-Rose-Bloom) / BATTLE OF NEW ORLEANS (Johnny Horton) / YANKEE DOODLE DONEGAN EP (Lieber & Stoller) / I WANNA GO HOME (c.Sandburg-Hayes; was 'Wreck Of The John B.', later a hit for BEACH BOYS as 'Sloop John B.') / HAVE A DRINK ON ME + BRING A LITTLE WATER, SYLVIE (Huddie Ledbetter- . . . Campbell) / MICHAEL ROW THE BOAT (Highwaymen).

Recommended: THE HIT SINGLES COLLECTION (1987 compilation cd)

LONNIE DONEGAN – vocals, guitar, banjo with his Skiffle Group: **DENNY WRIGHT** – lead guitar / **MICKY ASHMAN** – upright bass / **NICK NICHOLS** – drums

Decca / London

1955. (10"lp) **NEW ORLEANS JOY** [ ] [-]
(above by "The LONNIE DONEGAN SKIFFLE GROUP")
Dec 55. (7") **ROCK ISLAND LINE. / JOHN HENRY** [8] [8]
Feb 56. (7") **DIGGIN' MY POTATOES. / BURY MY BODY** [ ] [ ]

Pye-Nixa / London

Apr 56. (7") **LOST JOHN. / STEWBALL** [2] [58]
Jun 56. (7"ep) **SKIFFLE SESSION** [20] [ ]
– Railroad Bill / Stockalee / Ballad of Jessie James / Ol' Riley.
Aug 56. (7") **BRING A LITTLE WATER, SYLVIE. / DEAD OR ALIVE** [7] [ ]

— (below lp actually hit singles chart, due to non-existence of UK lp chart)

Dec 56. (10"lp) **LONNIE DONEGAN SHOWCASE** [26] [ ]
– Wabash cannonball / How long how long blues / Nobody's child / I shall not be moved / I'm Alabammy bound / I'm a rambling man / Wreck of the old '97 / Frankie and Johnny. *(re-iss.1968 on 'Marble A.')*
Jan 57. (7") **DON'T YOU ROCK ME, DADDY-O. / I'M ALABAMMY BOUND** [4] [ ]
Mar 57. (7") **CUMBERLAND GAP. / LOVE IS STRANGE** [1] [ ]
May 57. (7") **PUTTING ON THE STYLE (live). / GAMBLIN' MAN** [1] [ ]
Sep 57. (7") **MY DIXIE DARLING. / I'M JUST A ROLLING STONE** [10] [ ]
1957. (lp) **LONNIE** [ ] [ ]
– Lonesome traveller / The sunshine of his love / Ain't no more cane on the Brazos / Ain't you glad you've got religion / Times are getting hard, boys / Lazy John / Light from the lighthouse / I've got my rocks in my bed / Long summer day.
Dec 57. (7") **JACK O'DIAMONDS. / HAM'N'EGGS** [14] [ ]
Apr 58. (7") **THE GRAND COOLEE DAM. / NOBODY LOVES LIKE AN IRISHMAN** [6] [ ]
1958. (lp) **TOPS WITH LONNIE** [ ] [ ]
– Don't you rock me, daddy-o / Puttin' on the style / Gamblin' man / My Dixie darling / Bring a little water, Sylvie / Cumberland gap / Grand Coulee Dam / Saly, don't you grieve / Nobody loves likes an Irishman / Lost John / Does your chewing gum lose it's flavour / Tom Dooley.
Jun 58. (7") **SALLY, DON'T YOU GRIEVE. / BETTY BETTY BETTY** [11] [ ]
Sep 58. (7") **LONESOME TRAVELLER. / THINGS ARE GETTING HARD BOYS** [28] [ ]
Nov 58. (7") **LONNIE'S SKIFFLE PARTY (Medley Pt.1: LITTLE LIZA JANE-PUTTING ON THE STYLE-CAMPTOWN RACES-KNEES UP MOTHER BROWN. / (Medley Pt.2: SO LONG-ON TOP OF OLD SMOKEY-DOWN IN THE VALLEY-SO LONG** [23] [ ]
Nov 58. (7") **TOM DOOLEY. / ROCK O' MY SOUL** [3] [ ]

Pye-Nixa / Dot

Jan 59. (7") **DOES YOUR CHEWING GUM LOSE IT'S FLAVOUR (ON THE BEDPOST OVERNIGHT). / AUNT RILEY** [3] [5] Jul 61
Apr 59. (7") **FORT WORTH JAIL. / WHOA BUCK** [14] [ ]

Pye London

Jun 59. (7") **BATTLE OF NEW ORLEANS. / DARLING COREY** 2
Aug 59. (7") **MY LAGAN LOVE. / KEVIN BARRY**
Sep 59. (7") **SAL'S GOT A SUGAR LIP. / CHESAPEAKE BAY** 13
Nov 59. (7") **SAN MIGUEL. / TALKING GUITAR BLUES** 19
1959. (lp) **LONNIE RIDES AGAIN**
– Fancy talking tinker / Miss Otis regrets / Jimmie Brown the newsboy / Mr.Froggy / Take this hammer / The gold rush is over / You pass me by / Talking guitar blues / John Hardy / House of the rising Sun / San Miguel. *(re-iss.1969 on 'Marble Arch')*
Mar 60. (7") **MY OLD MAN'S A DUSTMAN. / THE GOLDEN VANITY** 1
May 60. (7") **I WANNA GO HOME. / JIMMIE BROWN THE NEWSBOY** 5
Aug 60. (7") **LORELEI. / IN ALL MY WILDEST DREAMS** 10
1960. (lp) **MORE TOPS WITH LONNIE**
– Battle of New Orleans / Lorelei / Lively! / Sal's got a sugar lip / I wanna go home / Leave my woman alone / My old man's a dustman / Fort Worth jail / Have a drink on me / (Bury me) Beneath the willow / Little Liza Jane / Puttin' on the style / Camptown races / Knees up, Mother Brown / On top of Old Smokey / Down in the valley / So long.
Nov 60. (7") **LIVELY. / BLACK CAT (CROSS MY PATH TODAY)** 13
Dec 60. (7") **VIRGIN MARY. / BEYOND THE SUNSET** 27
Jan 61. (7") **(BURY ME) BENEATH THE WILLOW. / LEAVE MY WOMAN ALONE**
May 61. (7") **HAVE A DRINK ON ME. / SEVEN DAFFODILS** 8
Aug 61. (7") **MICHAEL ROW THE BOAT. / LUMBERED** 6
Jan 62. (7") **THE COMMANCHEROS. / RAMBLIN' ROUND** 14
Mar 62. (7") **THE PARTY'S OVER. / OVER THE RAINBOW** 9
Jun 62. (7") **I'LL NEVER FALL IN LOVE AGAIN. / KEEP ON THE SUNNYSIDE**
Aug 62. (7") **PICK A BALE OF COTTON. / STEAL AWAY** 11
Oct 62. (7") **THE MARKET SONG. / TITBITS (live)** -

Pye A.B.C.

1962. (lp) **SING HALLELUJAH**
– Sing hallelujah / We shall walk through the valley / No hiding place / Good news, Chariot's a-comin' / Noah found grace in the eyes of the Lord / Joshua fit the battle of Jericho / His eye is on the sparrow / Born in Bethlehem / This train / New burying ground / Steal away / Nobody knows the trouble I've seen.
Dec 62. (7") **LOSING MY HAIR. / TRUMPET SOUNDS** -
1963. (7") **IT WAS A VERY GOOD YEAR. / RISE UP** -
1963. (7") **LEMON TREE. / I'VE GOTTA GIRL SO FINE** -
1963. (7") **500 MILES AWAY FROM HOME. / THIS TRAIN** -
1964. (7") **BEANS IN MY EARS. / IT'S A LONG ROAD TO TRAVEL** -
1964. (7") **FISHERMAN'S LUCK. / THERE'S A BIG WHEEL** -
1965. (7") **GET OUT OF MY LIFE. / WON'T YOU TELL ME** -
1965. (7") **LOUISIANA MAN. / BOUND FOR ZION** -
1965. (lp) **THE FOLK ALBUM** -
– I'm gonna be a bachelor / Interstate forty / After taxes / Where in the world are we going / Diamonds of dew / Bound for Zioln / She was T-bone talking woman / Wedding bells / Reverend Mr.Black / The doctor's daughter / Blistered / Farewell.
Jan 66. (7") **WORLD CUP WILLIE. / WHERE IN THIS WORLD ARE WE GOING** -
Nov 66. (7") **AUNTIE MAGGIE'S REMEDY. / MY SWEET MARIE** -
Nov 69. (7") **MY LOVELY JUANITA. / WHO KNOWS WHERE THE TIME GOES** -
1970. (lp) **LONNIEPOPS** -
– Little green apples / Hey! hey! / First of May / Both sides now / If you go away / Love song to a princess / Who knows where the times goes / What the world needs now is love / My lovely Juanita / Windmills of your mind / Long haired lover from Liverpool / And you need me.

Black Lion not issued

Jul 76. (7") **LOST JOHN. / JENNY'S BALL** -

Decca not issued

Aug 76. (7") **I'VE LOST MY LITTLE WILLIE. / CENSORED** -

— next releases included such stars as **RINGO STARR, ELTON JOHN, BRIAN MAY,** and most 'Chrysalis' artists.

Chrysalis United Art

Feb 78. (lp)(c) **PUTTING ON THE STYLE** 51
– Rock Island line / Have a drink on me / Ham'n'eggs / I wanna go home / Diggin' my potatoes / Nobody's child / Puttin' on the style / Frankie and Johnny / Drop down baby / Lost John.
1978. (7") **ROCK ISLAND LINE. / HAM'N'EGGS**
1978. (7") **PUTTIN' ON THE STYLE. / DROP DOWN BABY**
May 79. (lp)(c) **SUNDOWN**
– I'm all out and down / Home / Streamline train / Sundown / Mama's got the know how / Morning light / Louisiana Sun / The battle of New Orleans / Cajun / Dreaming my dreams with you.

In 1981, he teamed up with Scots group SHAKIN' PYRAMIDS on a single. In the 80's he suffered from heart attacks, but recovers enough in 1986 to put together resurrection outfit

DONEGAN'S DANCING SUNSHINE BAND

Rosie not issued

Jul 87. (7") **DONEGAN'S DANCING SUNSHINE BAND. / LEAVING BLUES** -

— In 1987 he became actor, noteably in 'Rockcliffe's Babies'. He had emigrated to California in 1976, returning frequently for small gigs, appearances, etc.

– compilations, others, etc. –

1955. Polygon; (7"ep) **BACKSTAIRS SESSION** -
– Midnight special / When the Sun goes down / New burying ground / Worried man blues. *(re-iss.1956 on 'Pye-Nixa')*
1957. Columbia; (7") **ON A CHRISTMAS DAY. / TAKE MY HAND PRECIOUS LORD** -
1968. Columbia; (7") **TOYS. / RELAX YOUR MIND** -
1957. Pye-Jazz; (7") **MIDNIGHT SPECIAL. / WHEN THE SUN GOES DOWN**
Aug 62. Golden Guinea; (lp) **THE GOLDEN AGE OF DONEGAN** 3 -
(re-iss.1965 on 'Marble Arch')
Jan 63. Golden Guinea; (lp) **THE GOLDEN AGE OF DONEGAN VOL.2** 15 -
(re-iss.1967 on 'Marble Arch')
Apr 66. Pye; (7") **I WANNA GO HOME. / BLACK CAT (CROSS MY PATH TODAY)** -
1970. Pye; (7") **SPEAK TO THE SKY. / GET OUT OF LIFE** -
1971. Pye; (lp) **GOLDEN HOUR OF LONNIE DONEGAN** -
1973. Pye; (lp) **GOLDEN HOUR VOL.2** -
Nov 77. Pye; (lp)(c) **THE LONNIE DONEGAN FILE** -
1977. Pye; (12"ep) **DOES YOUR CHEWING GUM LOSE IT'S FLAVOUR (ON THE BEDPOST OVERNIGHT) / MY OLD MAN'S A DUSTMAN. / THE BATTLE OF NEW ORLEANS / TOM DOOLEY** -
Jul 78. Pye; (7") **MY OLD MAN'S A DUSTMAN. / I WANNA GO HOME** -
Jul 78. Pye; (7") **TOM DOOLEY. / THE BATTLE OF NEW ORLEANS** -
May 79. Flashback; (7") **MY OLD MAN'S A DUSTMAN. / DOES YOUR CHEWING GUM LOSE IT'S FLAVOUR (ON THE BEDPOST OVERNIGHT)** -
Oct 85. Flashback; (lp)(c) **ROCK ISLAND LINE** -
1957. Pye-Nixa; (7"ep) **HIT PARADE** -
– Lost John / Stewball / Bring a little water / Dead or alive.
1957. Pye-Nixa; (7"ep) **HIT PARADE VOL.2** -
– Cumberland gap / Love is strange / Don't you rock me, daddy-o / I'm Alabammy bound.
1958. Pye-Nixa; (7"ep) **HIT PARADE VOL.3** -
– Putting on the style / My Dixie darling / Gamblin' man / I'm just a rolling stone.
1958. Pye-Nixa; (7"ep) **DONEGAN ON STAGE (live)** -
– Mule skinner blues / Old Hannah / On a Monday / Glory.
1958. Pye-Nixa; (7"ep) **HIT PARAE VOL.4** -
– Grand Coolee Dam / Ham'n'eggs / Nobody loves like an Irishman / Jack O'Diamonds.
1959. Pye-Nixa; (7"ep) **HIT PARADE VOL.5** -
– Tom Dooley / Rock o' my soul / Sally don't you grieve / Betty Betty Betty.
1959. Pye-Nixa; (7"ep) **RELAX WITH LONNIE** -
– Bewildered / Kevin Barry / It's no secret / My lagan love.
1959. Pye-Nixa; (7"ep) **HIT PARADE VOL.6** -
– The battle of New Orleans / Fort Worth jail / Does your chewing gum lose the flavour (on the bedpost overnight) / Darling Corey.
1960. Pye-Nixa; (7"ep) **YANKEE DOODLE DONEGAN** -
– Corrine Corrina / Junko partner / Nobody understands me / Sorry but I'm gonna have to pass.
1961. Pye-Nixa; (7"ep) **HIT PARADE VOL.7** -
– My old man's a dustman / The golden vanity / Sal's got a sugar lip / Talking guitar blues.
1961. Pye-Nixa; (7"ep) **HIT PARADE VOL.8** -
– Michael row the boat / I wanna go home / Lumbered / Have a drink on me.
1970. Pye; (7") **BURNING BRIDGES. / TILL I CAN'T TAKE ANYMORE** -
Jan 76. Pye; (7") **THE BATTLE OF NEW ORLEANS. / PUTTIN' ON THE STYLE** -
1971. Hallmark; (lp)(c) **MY OLD MAN'S A DUSTMAN** -
1970's. Hallmark; (lp) **LONNIE DONEGAN** -
1978. M.F.P.; (lp)(c) **HITS OF LONNIE DONEGAN** -
Feb 80. Ronco; (c) **GREATEST HITS** -
Nov 81. Dakota; (lp) **JUBILEE CONCERT (live)** -
Jul 82. Old Gold; (7") **GAMBLIN' MAN. / PUTTIN' ON THE STYLE** -
1989. Old Gold; (7") **ROCK ISLAND LINE. / LAST TRAIN TO SAN FERNANDO** -
Jun 85. Bear Family; (lp) **RARE AND UNISSUED GEMS** -
Oct 93. Bear Family; (cd) **MORE THAN PIE IN THE SKY** -
Sep 87. P.R.T.; (d-lp)(c)(cd) **THE HIT SINGLES COLLECTION** -
– Rock island line / Stewball / Lost John / Railroad Bill / Old Riley / Bring a little water, Sylvie / Dead or alive / Don't you rock me, daddy-o / Cumberland gap / Gamblin' man / Putting on the style / My Dixie darling / Jack o'diamonds / Grand Coolee dam / Sally don't you grieve / Betty, Betty, Betty / Lonesome traveller / Tom Dooley / Does your chewing gum lose its flavour on the bed-post overnight / Fort Worth jail / The battle of New Orleans / Sal's got a sugar lip / San Miguel / My old man's a dustman / I wanna go home / Lorelei / Lively / Virgin Mary / Have a drink on me / Michael row the boat / umbered / The Comancheros / The party's over / Pick a bale of cotton / Lonnie's skiffle party (parts 1 & 2).
Jan 89. Pickwick; (cd) **THE BEST OF LONNIE DONEGAN** -
Sep 89. Castle; (lp)(c)(cd) **LONNIE DONEGAN: THE COLLECTION** -
Apr 92. See For Miles; (cd) **THE ORIGINALS** -
Aug 92. See For Miles; (cd) **THE EP COLLECTION** -
Oct 93. See For Miles; (cd) **THE EP COLLECTION VOLUME 2** -
Dec 92. Sequel; (3xcd-box) **PUTTIN' ON THE STYLES** -
Mar 95. Spectrum; (cd)(c) **FAVOURITE FLAVOURS** -
Nov 95. Old Gold; (cd-s) **DOES YOUR CHEWING GUM LOSE IT'S FLAVOUR ON THE BEDPOST OVERNIGHT / CUMBERLAND GAP** -

DONOVAN

Born: DONOVAN PHILIP LEITCH, 10 May'46, Maryhill, Glasgow, Scotland. At age 10, his family had moved to Hatfield, England. In 1964, while playing small gigs in Southend, he was noticed by Geoff Stephens and Peter Eden, who became his managers. Late 1964, while playing 3 consecutive weeks on 'Ready Steady Go!' pop show, he signed to 'Pye'. His debut single 'CATCH THE WIND', released the same time as DYLAN's 'The Times They

Are A-Changin'', broke him into the UK Top 5, and later reached No.23 in the US, where he also had burgeoning career. • **Style:** Initially Britain's answer to BOB DYLAN, who retained folk/pop roots which progressed into flower-power in 1966. Dressed himself in denim cap and jeans which led to beatnik/hippie tag. A peace loving anti-war activist, guided in the studio by enigmatic producer MICKIE MOST. In 1968, he was yet another star (i.e.The BEATLES), to seek the inspiration and transcendental meditation of the Maharishi Mahesi Yogi. In 1971, he recorded a double album of children's songs 'H.M.S. DONOVAN', which led to a critical backlash from the music press. After a 3-year exile in Ireland due to tax purposes, he set up home in California 1974, with wife Linda Lawrence and daughters Astrella and Oriole. He has 2 other children to American ENID; DONOVAN LEITHCH JNR. (star of film 'Gas, Food, Lodging') and IONE SKYE, although the latter is said nt to bother too much about her famous father. • **Songwriters:** Self-penned except, UNIVERSAL SOLDIER (Buffy Sainte-Marie) / LONDON TOWN (Tim Harding) / REMEMBER THE ALAMO (Jane Bowes) / CAR CAR (Woody Guthrie) / GOLDWATCH BLUES (Mick Softley) / DONNA DONNA (Kevess-Secunda-Secanta-Schwartz-Zeitlin) / OH DEED I DO+ DO YOU HEAR ME NOW (Bert Jansch) / CIRCUS OF SOUR (Paul Bernath) / LITTLE TIN SOLDIER (Shawn Phillips / LORD OF THE DANCE (Sydney Carter) / ROCK'N'ROLL WITH ME (David Bowie-Warren Peace) / MY SONG IS TRUE (Darell Adams) / NO MAN'S LAND (Eric Bogle) / WIND IN THE WILLOWS (Eddie Hardin) / NEWEST BATH GUIDE + MOIRA McCAVENDISH (John Betjeman) / THE SENSITIVE KIND (J. J. Cale) / traditional:- KEEP ON TRUCKIN' + YOU'RE GONNA NEED SOMEBODY + CANDY MAN + THE STAR + COULTER'S CANDY + HENRY MARTIN + THE HEIGHTS OF ALMA + YOUNG BUT GROWING + STEALIN'. He also put music to words/poetry by; William Shakespeare (UNDER THE GREENWOOD TREE) / Gypsy Dave (A SUNNY DAY) / Lewis Carroll (WALRUS AND THE CARPENTER + JABBERWOCKY) / Thora Stowell (THE SELLER OF STARS + THE LITTLE WHITE ROAD) / Fifida Wolfe (LOST TIME) / Lucy Diamond (THE ROAD) / Agnes Herbertson (THINGS TO WEAR) / Edward Lear (THE OWL AND THE PUSSYCAT) / Eugene Field (WYNKEN, BLYNKEN AND NOD) / W. B. Yeats (THE SONG OF WANDERING AENGUS) / Natalie Joan (A FUNNY MAN) / Thomas Hood (QUEEN MAB) / Astella Leitch (MEE MEE I LOVE YOU) / Warwick Embury (ONE NIGHT IN TIME) / Note; HURLEY GURLEY MAN originally had a verse by GEORGE HARRISON but this was not recorded and he only added this for live appearences. • **Trivia:** Sang co-lead on title track from ALICE COOPER's 1973 lp 'Billion Dollar Babies'.

Recommended: GREATEST HITS AND MORE (*8)

DONOVAN – vocals, acoustic guitar, harmonica with **BRIAN LOCKING** – bass / **SKIP ALLEN** – drums / **GYPSY DAVE** (b. DAVID MILLS) – kazoo, etc.

P.Y.E. Hickory

Mar 65. (7") **CATCH THE WIND. / WHY DO YOU TREAT ME LIKE YOU DO** 4 23 Apr 65

May 65. (7") **COLOURS. / TO SING FOR YOU** 4 61 Jun 65

May 65. (lp) **WHAT'S BIN DID AND WHAT'S BIN HID** 3 30

– Josie / Catch the wind / Remember the Alamo / Cuttin' out / Car car * (riding in my car) / Keep on truckin' / Goldwatch blues / To sing for you / You're gonna need somebody on your bond / Tangerine puppet / Donna Donna * / Ramblin' boy *(re-iss.Jul68 on 'Marble Arch' omiting *)*

Sep 65. (7") **UNIVERSAL SOLDIER. / DO YOU HEAR ME** - 53

Sep 65. (7"ep) **THE UNIVERSAL SOLDIER EP** 13 -

– Universal soldier* / The ballad of a crystal man / Do you hear me now* / The war drags on.

Oct 65. (lp) **FAIRY TALE** 20 85 Dec 65

– Colours * / I'll try for the Sun / Sunny Goodge street / Oh deed I do / Circus of sour / The summer day reflection song / Candy man / Jersey Thursday / Belated forgiveness plea / Ballad of a crystal man / Little tin soldier * / Ballad of Geraldine. *(re-iss.Mar69 on 'Marble Arch' omitting *) (re-iss.cd+c.Feb91 on 'Castle')*

Nov 65. (7") **TURQUOISE. / HEY GYP (DIG THE SLOWNESS)** 30 -

Nov 65. (7") **YOU'RE GONNA NEED SOMEBODY ON YOUR BOND. / THE LITTLE TIN SOLDIER**

Jan 66. (7") **I'LL TRY FOR THE SUN. / TURQUOISE** -

Feb 66. (7") **JOSIE. / LITTLE TIN SOLDIER** -

Apr 66. (7") **REMEMBER THE ALAMO. / THE BALLAD OF A CRYSTAL MAN** -

— **DONOVAN** plus **JOHN CAMERON** – piano, harpsicord / **HAROLD McNAIR** – flute

P.Y.E. Epic

Jul 66. (7") **SUNSHINE SUPERMAN. / THE TRIP** 2 1 Jun 66

Sep 66. (lp) **SUNSHINE SUPERMAN** - 11

– Sunshine Superman / Legend of a girl child Linda / The observation / Guinevere / Celeste / Writer in the Sun / Season of the witch / Hampstead incident / Sand and foam / Young girl blues / Three kingfishers / Bert's blues. *(UK-iss.Feb91 on 'BGO')(re-iss.cd+c Sep93 on 'Remember')*

Nov 66. (7") **MELLOW YELLOW. / SUNNY SOUTH KENSINGTON** - 2

Jan 67. (7") **EPISTLE TO DIPPY. / PREACHIN' LOVE** - 19

Feb 67. (7") **MELLOW YELLOW. / PREACHIN' LOVE** 8 -

Feb 67. (lp) **MELLOW YELLOW** - 14

– Mellow yellow / Writer in the Sun / Sand and foam / The observation / Bleak city woman / House of Jansch / Young girl blues / Museum / Hampstead incident / Sunny South Kensington. *(cd-iss.Oct93 on 'Sony Europe')*

Jun 67. (lp) **SUNSHINE SUPERMAN** 25 -

– (compilation of last 2 US albums)

Oct 67. (7") **THERE IS A MOUNTAIN. / SAND AND FOAM** 8 11 Sep 67

— **DONOVAN** retained **HAROLD** and in came **TONY CARR** – percussion / **CANDY JOHN CARR** – bongos **CLIFF BARTON** – bass / **KEITH WEBB** – drums / **MIKE O' NEIL** – keyboards / **MIKE CARR** – vibraphone / **ERIC LEESE** – electric guitar

Dec 67. (7") **WEAR YOUR LOVE LIKE HEAVEN. / OH GOSH** - 23

Dec 67. (lp) **WEAR YOUR LOVE LIKE HEAVEN** - 60

– Wear your love like Heaven / Mad John's escape / Skip-a-long Sam / Sun / There was a time / Oh gosh / Little boy in corduroy / Under the greenwood tree / The land of doesn't have to be / Someone's singing / Song of the naturalist's wife / The enchanted gypsy.

— **KEN BALDOCK** – bass repl. BARTON, LEESE, WEBB, O'NEIL + MIKE CARR.

Dec 67. (lp) **FOR LITTLE ONES** -

– Voyage into the golden screen / Isle of Islay / The mandolin man and his secret / Lay of the last tinker / The tinker and the crab / Widow with shawl (a portrait) / The lullaby of spring / The magpie / Starfish-on-the-toast / Epistle to Derroll.

Feb 68. (7") **JENNIFER JUNIPER. / POOR COW** 5 26

Apr 68. (d-lp-box) **A GIFT FROM A FLOWER TO A GARDEN** 13 19

(contains 2 US Dec67 albums boxed) *(cd-iss.Jul 93 on 'B.G.O.')*

May 68. (7") **HURDY GURDY MAN. / TEEN ANGEL** 4 5

Sep 68. (lp) **DONOVAN IN CONCERT (live)** 18 Jul68

– Isle of Islay / Young girl blues / There is a mountain / Poor cow / Celeste / The fat angel / Guinevere / Widow with shawl (a portrait) / Preachin' love / The lullaby of Spring / Writer in the Sun / Rules and regulations / Pebble and the man / Mellow yellow. *(re-iss.+c+cd.May91 on 'BGO') (cd-iss.Nov94 on 'Start')*

Oct 68. (7") **LALENA. / AYE, MY LOVE** - 33

Oct 68. (lp) **HURDY GURDY MAN** - 20

– Jennifer Juniper / Hurdy gurdy man / Hi, it's been a long time / Peregrine / The entertaining of a shy girl / Tangier / As I recall it / Get thy bearings / West Indian lady / Teas / The river song / The Sun is a very magic fellow / A sunny day.

Nov 68. (7") **ATLANTIS. / I LOVE MY SHIRT** 23 -

Feb 69. (7") **ATLANTIS. / TO SUSAN ON THE WEST COAST WAITING** - 7

35

DONOVAN with The JEFF BECK GROUP

[illegible]

Jun 69. (7") **GOO GOO BARABAJAGAL (LOVE IS HOT). / BED WITH ME** 12 -

Sep 69. (7") **GOO GOO BARABAJAGAL (LOVE IS HOT). / TRUDI** - 36

Sep 69. (lp) **BARABAJAGAL** -

– Barabajagal / Superlungs my supergirl / I love my shirt / The love song / To Susan on the West Coast waiting / Atlantis / Trudi / Pamela Jo / Happiness runs. *(cd-iss.Oct93 on 'Sony Europe')*

DONOVAN AND THE OPEN ROAD

with **JOHN CARR** – drums, vocals / **MIKE THOMPSON** – bass, vocals / **MIKE O'NEILL** – piano

Dawn Epic

Sep 70. (lp) **OPEN ROAD** 30 16 Jul 70

– Changes / Song for John / Curry land / Joe Bean's theme / People used to / Celtic rock / Riki tiki tavi / Clara clairvoyant / Roots of oak / Season of farewell / Poke at the Pope / New Year's resovolution.

Sep 70. (7") **RIKI TIKI TAVI. / ROOTS OF OAK** 55

DONOVAN WITH DANNY THOMPSON

(DANNY – double bass)

Dec 70. (7") **CELIA OF THE SEALS. / MR.WIND** -

DONOVAN

was now solo again.

Feb 71. (7") **CELIA OF THE SEAS. / THE SONG OF THE WANDERING AENGUS** - 84

Jul 71. (d-lp) **H.M.S. DONOVAN**

– The walrus and the carpenter / Jabberwocky / The seller of the stars / Lost time / The little white road / The star / Coulter's candy / The road / Things to wear / The owl and the pussycat / Homesickness / Fishes in love / Mr.Wind / Wynken, Bylnken and Nod / Celia of the seas / The pee song / The voyage to the Moon / The unicorn / Lord of dance / Little Ben / Can ye dance / In an old fashioned picture book / The song of the wandering Aengus / A funny man / Lord of the reedy river / Henry Martin / Queen Mab / La moor.

— with guests **CHRIS SPEDDING** – guitar / **JOHN 'RABBIT' BUNDRICK** – keyboards / **JIM HORN** – bass / **COZY POWELL** – drums

Epic Epic

Mar 73. (lp)(c) **COSMIC WHEELS** 15

– Cosmic wheels / Earth sign man / Sleep / / Maria Magenta / Wild witch lady / Sleep / The music makers / The intergallactic laxative / I like you / Only the blues / Appearances. *(cd-iss.Sep94 on 'Rewind')*

Apr 73. (7") **I LIKE YOU. / EARTH SIGN MAN** 66

Jun 73. (7") **MARIA MAGENTA. / THE INTERGALLACTIC LAXATIVE**

— now with **STEVE MARRIOT, PETER FRAMPTON** and **NICKY HOPKINS**

Nov 73. (7") **SAILING HOMEWARD. / LAZY DAZE** -

Dec 73. (lp)(c) **ESSENCE TO ESSENCE**

– Operating manual for spaceship Earth / Lazy daze / Life goes on / There is an ocean / Dignity of man / Yellow star / Divine daze of deathless delight / Boy for every girl / Saint Valentine's angel / Life is a merry-go-round / Sailing homeward.

Jan 74. (7") **SAILING HOMEWARD. / YELLOW STAR** -

— Mainly used session musicians from now on.

Sep 74. (7") **ROCK'N'ROLL WITH ME. / THE DIVINE DAZE OF DEATHLESS DELIGHT** Nov 74

Nov 74. (lp)(c) **7-TEASE**

– Rock and roll souljer / Your broken heart / Salvation stomp / The ordinary family / Ride-a-mile / Sadness / Moon rok / Love of my life / The voice of protest / How silly / The great song of the sky / The quest.

Jan 75. (7") **ROCK AND ROLL SOULJER. / HOW SILLY** -

Feb 75. (7") **ROCK AND ROLL SOULJER. / LOVE OF MY LIFE** -

Jun 76. (lp)(c) **SLOW DOWN WORLD**

– Dark-eyed blue jean angel / Cryin' shame / The mountain / Children of the world / My love is true (love song) / A well known has-been / Black widow / Slow down world / Liberation rag.

Jun 76. (7") **A WELL-KNOWN HAS-BEEN. / DARK EYED BLUE JEAN ANGEL** [-] [ ]

Rak Arista

Aug 77. (7") **DARE TO BE DIFFERENT. / THE INTERNATIONAL MAN** [-] [ ]
Oct 77. (lp)(c) **DONOVAN** [ ] [ ]
– Brave new world / Local boy chops wood / Kalifornia kids / International man / Lady of the stars / Dare to be different / Mijah's dance / The light / Astral angel.
Nov 77. (7") **THE LIGHT. / THE INTERNATIONAL MAN** [ ] [-]
Feb 78. (7") **DARE TO BE DIFFERENT. / SING MY SONG** [ ] [-]

— (note:- on above US singles [Jan 73, Jan 75, Jun 76, Aug 77] the 'B' side was mono version on 'A').

not issued R.A.

Aug 80. (lp) **NEUTRONICA** [-] [-] Germ.
– Shipwreck / Only to be expected / Comin' to you / No hunger / Neutron / Mee Mee I love you / The heights of Alma / No man's land / We are one / Madrigalinda / Harmony.

— with **DANNY THOMPSON** – double bass / **JOHN STEPHENS** – drums / **TONY ROBERTS** – multi-wind instruments / and his 9 year-old daughter **ASTELLA** – dual vocals

Luggage-RCA not issued

Oct 81. (lp)(c) **LOVE IS ONLY FEELING** [ ] [-]
– Lady of the flowers / Lover o lover / The actor / Half Moon bay / The hills of Tuscany / Lay down Lassie / She / Johnny Tuff / Love is only feeling / Marjorie Margerine.
Oct 81. (7") **LAY DOWN LASSIE. / LOVE IS ONLY FEELING** [ ] [-]

R.C.A. Allegiance

Jan 84. (lp)(c) **LADY OF THE STARS** [ ] [ ]
– Lady of the stars / I love you baby / Seasons of the witch / Bye bye girl / Every reason / Boy for every girl / Local boy chops wood / Sunshine superman / Til I see you again / Living for the lovelight.

After nearly 7 years in the wilderness, he returned on new label

Permanent Permanent

Nov 90. (cd)(c)(lp) **DONOVAN RISING** [ ] [ ]
– Jennifer Juniper / Catch the wind / The hurdy gurdy man / Sunshine superman / Sadness / Universal soldier / Cosmic wheels / Atlantis / Wear your love like heaven / Colours / To Susan on the west coast waiting / Young girl blues / Young but growing / Stealing / Sailing homeward / Love will find a way / Lalena.

— He had also credited on The SINGING CORNER's (Nov90) single version of his JENNIFER JUNIPER.

Silhouette not issued

Apr 92. (7"m) **NEW BATH GUIDE / MOIRA McCAVENDISH / BROTHER SUN, SISTER MOON** [ ] [-]

– compilations, others, etc. –

Dec 65. Pye; (7"ep) **COLOURS** [ ] [-]
– Catch the wind / Why do you treat me like you do / Colours / To sing for you.
Mar 66. Pye; (7"ep) **DONOVAN VOL.1** [ ] [-]
– Sunny Goodge Street / Oh deed I do / Jersey Thursday / Hey Gyp (dig the slowness).
Jul 66. Hickory; (7") **HEY GYP (DIG THE SLOWNESS). / THE WAR DRAGS ON** [-] [ ]
Oct 66. Hickory; (7") **SUNNY GOODGE STREET. / SUMMER DAY REFLECTION SONG** [-] [ ]
Sep 66. Hickory; (lp) **THE REAL DONOVAN** [-] [96]
Feb 68. Pye; (7"ep) **CATCH THE WIND** [ ] [-]
– Catch the wind / Remember the Alamo / Josie / Rambling Rose.
Apr 68. Hickory; (lp) **LIKE IT IS, WAS AND EVERMORE SHALL BE** [-] [ ]
1968. Hickory; (7") **DO YOU HEAR ME NOW. / WHY DO YOU TREAT ME LIKE YOU DO** [-] [ ]
Aug 68. Pye; (7"ep) **HURDY GURDY DONOVAN** [ ] [-]
– Jennifer juniper / Hurdy gurdy man / Mellow yellow / There is a mountain. *(re-iss.Nov71)*
Jan 69. Hickory; (7") **CATCH THE WIND. / UNIVERSAL SOLDIER** [-] [ ]
Mar 69. Pye/ US= Epic; (lp) **DONOVAN'S GREATEST HITS** [ ] [4]
(re-iss.1973) (re-iss.Sep79 on 'CBS-Embassy') (cd-iss.Aug90 on 'Epic')
1973. Pye/ US= Epic; (4xlp-set) **FOUR SHADES OF DONOVAN / OPEN ROAD / DONOVAN'S GREATEST HITS/ / H.M.S. DONOVAN** [ ] [ ]
Nov 77. Pye; (d-lp) **THE DONOVAN FILE** [ ] [-]
1978. Epic; (7") **SUNSHINE SUPERMAN. / MELLOW YELLOW** [-] [ ]
Jul 78. Epic; (7") **COLOURS. / UNIVERSAL SOLDIER** [-] [ ]
Oct 67. Marble Arch; (lp) **UNIVERSAL SOLDIER** [5] [-]
(re-iss.Feb83 on 'Spot')
1969. Marble Arch; (lp)(c) **THE WORLD OF DONOVAN** [ ] [-]
Mar 69. United Artists; (lp) **IF IT'S TUESDAY IT MUST BE BELGUIM (Soundtrack)** [ ] [ ]
Oct 70. Janus; (7") **COLOURS. / JOSIE** [-] [ ]
Oct 70. Janus; (7") **CATCH THE WIND. / WHY DO YOU TREAT ME LIKE YOU DO** [-] [ ]
Oct 70. Janus; (7") **CANDY MAN. / HEY GYP (DIG THE SLOWNESS)** [-] [ ]
Nov 70. Janus; (d-lp) **DONOVAN P.LEITCH** (early work) [-] [ ]
1971. Golden Hour; (lp)(c) **THE GOLDEN HOUR OF DONOVAN** [ ] [-]
Nov 69. Hickory; (lp) **THE BEST OF DONOVAN** [-] [ ]
1971. Hallmark; (lp)(c) **CATCH THE WIND** [ ] [-]
(re-iss.Apr86 on 'Castle')
1972. Hallmark; (lp) **COLOURS** [ ] [-]
(re-iss.+cd.Oct87 on 'P.R.T.')
1972. Memory Lane; (7") **SUNSHINE SUPERMAN. / MELLOW YELLOW** [-] [ ]
1972. Memory Lane; (7") **JENNIFER JUNIPER. / HURDY GURDY MAN** [-] [ ]
Jul 80. Flashback; (7"ep) **EP** [ ] [-]
– Catch the wind / Turquoise / Colours / Universal soldier.
Oct 81. P.R.T.; (lp)(c) **SPOTLIGHT ON DONOVAN** [ ] [-]
Jul 83. P.R.T.; (10"lp) **MINSTREL BOY** [ ] [-]
Jul 82. Old Gold; (7") **CATCH THE WIND. / COLOURS** [ ] [-]
Feb 85. E.M.I.; (7") **MELLOW YELLOW. / SUNSHINE SUPERMAN** [ ] [-]
Aug 89. E.M.I.; (7") **SUNSHINE SUPERMAN. / JENNIFER JUNIPER** [ ] [-]
('A'extended-12"+=) – Wear your love like Heaven.
(cd-s++=) – Mellow yellow.
Sep 89. E.M.I.; (lp)(c)(cd) **GREATEST HITS AND MORE** [ ] [-]
– Sunshine Superman / Wear your love like Heaven / Jennifer Juniper / Barabajagal (love is hot) / Hurdy gurdy man / Epistle to Dippy / To Susan on the West Coast waiting / Catch the wind / Mellow yellow / There is a mountain / Happiness runs / Season of the witch / Colours / Superlungs-My Supergirl / Lalena / Atlantis.
(cd+=) – Preachin' love / Poor cow / Teen angel / Aye my love.
Feb 91. E.M.I.; (d-cd)(d-c)(d-lp) **THE TRIP** (1964-1968 material) [ ] [ ]
Nov 94. E.M.I.; (4xcd-box) **ORIGINALS** [ ] [ ]
Oct 90. See For Miles; (lp)(c)(cd) **THE EP COLLECTION** [ ] [-]
Mar 91. Gulf Peace Team; (7") **UNIVERSAL SOLDIER. / CATCH THE WIND** [ ] [ ]
(12"+=) I'll try for the sun.
Jun 91. Mammoth; (cd)(c) **THE HITS** [ ] [-]
Dec 93. Disky; (cd) **GOLD: GREATEST HITS** [ ] [-]
May 94. Magnum; (cd) **COLOURS** [ ] [-]
Jul 94. Success; (cd)(c) **JOSIE** [ ] [-]
Jul 94. Success; (cd)(c) **TILL I SEE YOU AGAIN** [ ] [-]
Jan 95. Spectrum; (cd) **UNIVERSAL SOLDIER** [ ] [-]
Dec 95. Javelin; (cd) **SUNSHINE SUPERMAN** [ ] [-]

DOOBIE BROTHERS

Formed: San Jose, California, USA . . . 1970 as PUD, by JOHN HARTMAN, TOM JOHNSTON and DAVE SHOGREN. In 1971, they signed to 'Warner Bros.' and released unsuccessful eponymous Ted Templeton produced album. Their second album 'TOULOUSE STREET', gave them their first gold disc, with cut from it 'LISTEN TO THE MUSIC', nearly hitting US Top 10 in 1972. • **Style:** Typical West Coast soft-rock outfit with boogie feel, described as an easy-listening ALLMANS. They blended together a fine harmonious (near gospel) backing, with funky soulful rock. In 1978, their sound had encompassed aspects of dance beat AOR. • **Songwriters:** JOHNSTON or SIMMONS penned until MICHAEL McDONALD contributed on his 1975 arrival. JESUS IS JUST ALRIGHT (Byrds) / TAKE ME IN YOUR ARMS (Holland-Dozier-Holland) / LITTLE DARLIN' (I NEED YOU) (Marvin Gaye) / etc. WHAT A FOOL BELIEVES was co-written by McDONALD and KENNY LOGGINS. • **Trivia:** They took the name 'DOOBIE' from the slang for a joint.

Recommended: LISTEN TO THE MUSIC – THE VERY BEST OF THE DOOBIES (*7) / THE BEST OF THE DOOBIES, VOL.II (1981 compilation lp)

TOM JOHNSTON (b. Visalia, California, USA) – vocals, guitar / **PAT SIMMONS** (b.23 Jan'50, Aberdeen, Washington, USA) – guitar, vocals / **DAVE SHOGREN** (b. San Francisco, California, USA) – bass / **JOHN HARTMAN** (b.13 Mar'50, Falls Church, Virginia, USA) – drums

Warners Warners

Apr 71. (lp)(c) **THE DOOBIE BROTHERS** [ ] [ ]
– Nobody / Slippery St. Paul / Greenwood creek / It won't be right / Travellin' man / Feelin' down farther / The master / rowin' a litle each day / Beehive state / Closer every day / Chicago. *(re-iss.Jul87) (cd-iss.May95)*
Apr 71. (7") **NOBODY. / SLIPPERY ST. PAUL** [-] [ ]
Jul 71. (7") **TRAVELIN' MAN. / FEELIN' DOWN FARTHER** [-] [ ]
Sep 71. (7") **BEEHIVE STATE. / CLOSER EVERY DAY** [-] [ ]

— **TIRAN PORTER** (b. Los Angeles) – bass, vocals repl. SHOGREN.
added 2nd drummer **MICHAEL HOSSACK** (b.18 Sep'50, Paterson, New York, USA)

Jul 72. (lp)(c) **TOULOUSE STREET** [ ] [21]
– Listen to the music / Don't start me talkin' / Mamaloi / Toulouse Street / Rockin' down the highway / Jesus is just alright / White sun / Cotton mouth / Disciple / Snake man. *(quad-lp 1976) (cd-iss.Jul88)(cd-iss.May93)*
Aug 72. (7") **LISTEN TO THE MUSIC. / TOULOUSE STREET** [29] [11]
Dec 72. (7") **JESUS IS JUST ALRIGHT. / ROCKIN' DOWN THE HIGHWAY** [ ] [35]
Mar 73. (lp)(c) **THE CAPTAIN AND ME** [ ] [7]
– Natural thing / Long time runnin' / China Grove / Dark-eyed Cajun woman / Clear as the driven snow / Without you / South city midnight lady / Evil woman / Busted down around O'Connelly corners / Ukiah / The captain and me. *(cd-iss.Oct87 & Feb95)*
Apr 73. (7") **LONG TRAIN RUNNIN'. / WITHOUT YOU** [ ] [8]
Aug 73. (7") **CHINA GROVE. / EVIL WOMAN** [ ] [15]

— **KEITH KNUDSON** (b.18 Oct'52, Ames, Iowa) – drums (ex-MANDELBAUM) repl. HOSSACK / added **BILL PAYNE** – keyboards (ex-LITTLE FEAT)

Feb 74. (lp)(c) **WHAT WERE ONCE VICES ARE NOW HABITS** [19] [4]
– Song to see you through / Spirit / Pursuit on 53rd street / Black water / Eyes of silver / Road angel / You just can't stop it / Tell me what you want / Down in the track / Another park, another Sunday / Flying cloud. *(quad-lp US 1976) (cd-iss.Jul88)(cd-iss.May93)*
Apr 74. (7") **ANOTHER PARK, ANOTHER SUNDAY. / BLACK WATER** [ ] [32]
Jul 74. (7") **EYES OF SILVER. / YOU JUST CAN'T STOP IT** [ ] [52]
Oct 74. (7") **FLYING CLOUD. / NOBODY** [ ] [58] B-side
Dec 74. (7") **BLACK WATER. / SONG TO SEE YOU THROUGH** [ ] [1]

— **JEFF BAXTER** (b.13 Dec'48, Washington DC) – guitar (ex-STEELY DAN) repl. PAYNE who rejoined LITTLE FEAT.

Apr 75. (lp)(c) **STAMPEDE** 14 4
– Sweet Maxine / Neal's fandango / Texas lullaby / Music man / Slat key sequel rag / Take me in your arms / I cheat the hangman / Precis / Rainy day crossroad blues / I've been workin' on you / Double dealin' four flusher. *(cd-iss.Jun89)(cd-iss.May93)*
Apr 75. (7") **TAKE ME IN YOUR ARMS. / SLAT KEY SEQUEL RAG** 29
Jul 75. (7") **SWEET MAXINE. / DOUBLE DEALIN' FOUR FLUSHER** 40
Nov 75. (7") **I CHEAT THE HANGMAN. / MUSIC MAN** 60

— **MICHAEL McDONALD** (b.1952, St.Louis, Missouri) – keyboards, vocals (ex-STEELY DAN) repl. JOHNSTON who fell ill.

Mar 76. (lp)(c) **TAKIN' IT TO THE STREETS** 42 8
– Wheels of fortune / Takin' it to the streets / 8th Avenue shuffle / Losin' end / Rio / For someone special / It keeps you runnin' / Turn it loose / Carry me away. *(cd-iss.Jun89)*
Mar 76. (7") **TAKIN' IT TO THE STREETS. / FOR SOMEONE SPECIAL** 13
Aug 76. (7") **WHEELS OF FORTUNE. / SLAT KEY SEQUEL RAG** 87
Nov 76. (7") **IT KEEPS YOU RUNNIN'. / TURN IT LOOSE** 37

— **TOM JOHNSTON** returned but left again early '77 to go solo.

Jul 77. (7") **LITTLE DARLING (I NEED YOU). / LOSING END** 48
Aug 77. (lp)(c) **LIVIN' ON THE FAULT LINE** 25 10
– You're made that way / Echoes of love / Little darling (I need you) / You belong to me / Livin' on the fault line / Nothin' but a heartache / Chinatown / There's a light / Need a lady / Larry the logger two-step. *(cd-iss.Jun89)*
Sep 77. (7") **ECHOES OF LOVE. / THERE'S A LIGHT** 66
Mar 78. (7") **LIVIN' ON THE FAULT LINE. / NOTHIN' BUT A HEARTACHE** -
Dec 78. (lp)(c) **MINUTE BY MINUTE** 1
– Sweet feelin' / Open your eyes / Dependin' on you / Here to love you / Minute by minute / You never change / What a fool believes / Steamer lane breakdown / How do the fools survive? / Don't stop to watch the wheels. *(cd-iss. 1988 & Feb95)*
Jan 79. (7"+12") **WHAT A FOOL BELIEVES. / DON'T STOP TO WATCH THE WHEELS** 31 1
Apr 79. (7") **MINUTE BY MINUTE. / SWEET FEELIN'** - 14
Apr 79. (7") **MINUTE BY MINUTE. / HOW DO THE FOOLS SURVIVE?** -
Jul 79. (7") **DEPENDIN' ON YOU. / HOW DO THE FOOLS SURVIVE?** 25
Aug 79. (7") **OPEN YOUR EYES. / STEAMER LANE BREAKDOWN**

— **JOHN McFEE** (b.18 Nov'53, Santa Cruz, California) – guitar, vocals repl. BAXTER / **CHET McCRACKEN** (b.17 Jul'52, Seattle, Washington) – drums, vibes (ex-session man) repl. HARTMAN / added **CORNELIUS BUMPUS** (b.13 Jan'52) – keys, sax (ex-MOBY GRAPE) / (now septet alongside **SIMMONS, McDONALD, PORTER and KNUDSEN**).

Aug 80. (7") **REAL LOVE. / THANK YOU LOVE** 5
Oct 80. (lp)(c) **ONE STEP CLOSER** 53 3
– Dedicate this heart / Real love / No stoppin' us now / Thank you love / One step closer / Keep this train a-rollin' / Just in time / South bay strut / One by one.
Nov 80. (7") **ONE STEP CLOSER. / SOUTH BAY STRUT** 24
Dec 80. (7") **WYNKEN, BLYNKEN AND NOD. / IN HARMONY** 76

— (above credited w/ KATE + SIMON TAYLOR)

Jan 81. (7") **KEEP THIS TRAIN A-ROLLIN'. / JUST IN TIME** 62

— **WILLIE WEEKS** – bass repl. PORTER.

They split Mar82, recorded final concert album Sep82.

Jun 83. (d-lp)(d-c) **THE DOOBIE BROTHERS FAREWELL TOUR (live)** 79
– Slippery St. Paul / Takin it to the streets / Jesus is just alright / Minute by minute / Can't let it get away / Listen to the music / Echoes of love / What a fool believes / Black water / You belong to me / Slat key sequel rag / Streamer lane breakdown / South city / Midnight lady / Olana / Don't start me to talking / Long train runnin' / China grove. *(re-iss.Aug84)*
Jul 83. (7") **YOU BELONG TO ME. / SOUTH CITY MIDNIGHT LADY** 79

— By this time MICHAEL McDONALD had gone solo, as did PATRICK SIMMONS. **DOOBIE BROTHERS** reformed mid'88. (JOHNSTON, HARTMAN, SIMMONS, PORTER) plus **MICHAEL HOSSACKS** – drums / **BOBBY LAKIND** – percussion

Capitol Capitol

Jul 89. (lp)(c)(cd) **CYCLES** 17 Jun 89
– The doctor / One chain (don't make no prison) / Take me to the highway / South of the border / Time is here and gone / Need a little taste of love / I can read your mind / Wrong number / Tonight I'm coming through (the border) / Too high a price.
Jul 89. (7") **THE DOCTOR. / TOO HIGH A PRICE** 73 9 May 89
(12"+=)(cd-s+=) – Anything for love.
Sep 89. (7") **NEED A LITTLE TASTE OF LOVE. / I CAN READ YOUR MIND** 45 Aug 89
(12"+=)(cd-s+=) – The doctor.
Apr 91. (cd)(c)(lp) **BROTHERHOOD** 82
– Something you said / Is love enough / Dangerous / Our love / Divided highway / Under the spell / Excited / This train I'm on / Showdown / Rollin' on.

– compilations etc. –

Nov 76. Warners; (lp)(c) **THE BEST OF THE DOOBIES** 5
– China Grove / Long train runnin' / Takin' it to the streets / Listen to the music / Black water / Rockin' down the highway / Jesus is just alright / It keeps you runnin' / South city midnight lady / Take me in your arms (rock me a little while) / Without you. *(cd-iss.1988)*
Nov 81. Warners; (lp)(c) **THE BEST OF THE DOOBIES VOL.2** 39
– Little darlin' / Echoes of love / You belong to me / One step closer / What a fool believes / Dependin' on you / Here to love you / One by one / Real love / Minute by minute.
Jan 82. Warners; (7") **HERE TO LOVE YOU. / WYNKEN, BLYNKEN AND NOD** 65
1984. Warners; (d-c) **TAKIN' IT TO THE STREETS. / LIVIN' ON THE FAULT LINE**
Jan 87. Warners; (7") **WHAT A FOOL BELIEVES. / MINUTE BY MINUTE** 57
(12"+=) – Real love.
May 93. Warners; (cd)(c) **LISTEN TO THE MUSIC – THE VERY BEST OF THE DOOBIE BROTHERS**
(re-iss. May 94)
Nov 93. Warners; (7")(c-s) **LONG TRAIN RUNNIN'. / ('A'mix)** 7
(12"+=)(cd-s+=) – ('A' mix).
Apr 94. Warners; (7")(c-s) **LISTEN TO THE MUSIC ('94 remix). / ('A'mix)** 37
(12"+=)(cd-s+=) – ('A'remixes by MOTIV8 / RAMP . . . / DEVELOPMENT CORPORATION)
Mar 86. Old Gold; (7") **LISTEN TO THE MUSIC. / WHAT A FOOL BELIEVES** -
May 93. F.N.A.C.; (cd) **INTRODUCING . . .** -

— JOHN HARTMAN who was a reserve fireman /policeman, was refused promotion by his home state court, due to his alleged drug-taking past.

PATRICK SIMMONS

Elektra Elektra

Mar 83. (7") **SO WRONG. / IF YOU WANT A LITTLE LOVE** 30
Apr 83. (lp)(c) **ARCADE** 52
– Out on the streets / So wrong / Don't make me do it / Why you givin' up / Too long / Knocking at your door / If you want a little love / Have you seen her / Sue sad / Dream about me.
Jun 83. (7") **DON'T MAKE ME DO IT. / SUE SAD** - 75

DOOR AND THE WINDOW (see under ⇒ ALTERNATIVE TV)

DOORS

Formed: Los Angeles, California, USA . . . July 1965 by RAY MANZAREK and JIM MORRISON. In 1966 after some personnel changes, they soon settled with JOHN DENSMORE and ROBBIE KREIGER, to become The DOORS. They were released from a 'Columbia' recording contract, when ARTHUR LEE (of LOVE), recommended them to his 'Elektra' label boss Jac Holzman. Early in 1967, their eponymous debut lp was issued, and soon climbed to US No.2, after an edited version of 'LIGHT MY FIRE' hit No.1 in Jul'67. This classic lp contained an extremely disturbing 11 minute gem 'THE END' (which was later used on the 1979 Francis Ford Coppola film 'Apocalypse Now'). After another US Top 3 album at the end of '67, things looked bleak as MORRISON's drink and drugs antics were increasing. He was arrested many times on stage and off, mostly for lewd simulation of sexual acts and indecent exposure. In the late summer of '68, they were top of the US charts again with 45 'HELLO I LOVE YOU' and lp 'WAITING FOR THE SUN'. More controversy was aroused when in Nov'69, MORRISON was accused of interfering with a stewardess while a flight was in progress. He was later acquitted, but the following year, he was given 8 months hard labour, etc., after being found guilty of indecent exposure and profanity. He was freed on appeal, but moved to Paris in March '71, where he was to be found dead in his bathtub on the 3rd July 1971. Speculation was rife at the time, but it seemed he died from a drugs/drink induced heart attack. He was also buried in Paris, his grave becoming a shrine to all but his parents, who disowned him in '67. Two months prior to his death, The DOORS had issued their 6th studio US Top 10 album 'L.A.WOMAN'. It was a remarkable return to form, and featured a superb title track and 2 classic US Top 20 hits, 'LOVE HER MADLY' & 'RIDERS ON THE STORM'. The others continued as a trio for the next 2 years, but sadly the public refused to acknowledge them as the real DOORS. • **Style:** Theatrical rock and blues, which diversified dramatically from organ orientated rock'n'roll to experimental but classic pop. MORRISON's stage energy and sexual aura although controversial, was group's forte. Many groups have copied, but few have sustained any lasting god-like credibility. • **Songwriters:** MORRISON – words/poetry (under the influence of explorative narcotics), Group/MANZAREK compositions. Covered; ALABAMA SONG (Brecht-Weill) / BACK DOOR MAN (Howlin' Wolf) / WHO DO YOU LOVE (Bo Diddley) / CRAWLING KING SNAKE (John Lee Hooker) / LITTLE RED ROOSTER (Willie Dixon). • **Trivia:** In 1968, they featured on a UK TV documentary 'The Doors Are Open', which was later issued on video. In 1991, Oliver Stone released a feature film 'THE DOORS', with Val Kilmer playing the role of MORRISON.

Recommended: THE DOORS (*10) / STRANGE DAYS (*8) / ABSOLUTELY LIVE (*7) / L.A. WOMAN (*9) / WEIRD SCENES INSIDE THE GOLDMINE (*8).

JIM MORRISON (b. 8 Dec'43, Melbourne, Florida, USA) – vocals / **RAY MANZAREK** (b.12 Feb'35, Chicago, Illinois, USA) – keyboards, bass pedal / **ROBBIE KRIEGER** (b. 8 Jan'46, Los Angeles, California, USA) – guitar / **JOHN DENSMORE** (b. 1 Dec'45, Los Angeles, California, USA) – drums / also guest **DOUG LABAHN** – bass (of CLEAR LIGHT)

Elektra Elektra

Feb 67. (7") **BREAK ON THROUGH (TO THE OTHER SIDE). / END OF THE NIGHT** Jan 67
Mar 67. (lp) **THE DOORS** 1 Mar 67
– Break on through (to the other side) / Soul kitchen / The crystal ship / Twentieth century fox / Alabama song (whiskey song) / Light my fire / Back door man / I looked at you / End of the night / Take it as it comes / The end. *(re-iss.+c.Nov71) (cd-iss.Jan84 & Feb89) (re-iss.Apr91 hit UK No.43)*
May 67. (7") **ALABAMA SONG (WHISKEY BAR). / TAKE IT AS IT COMES**

Lizard King

Jul 67. (7") **LIGHT MY FIRE (edit). / THE CRYSTAL SHIP** 49 1 Jun 67
(re-iss.Jul71)

Sep 67. (7") **PEOPLE ARE STRANGE. / UNHAPPY GIRL** 12

Dec 67. (lp) **STRANGE DAYS** 3 Nov 67
– Strange days / You're lost little girl / Love me two times / Unhappy girl / Horse latitudes / Moonlight drive / People are strange / My eyes have seen you / I can't see your face in my mind / When the music's over. *(re-iss.+c.Nov71) (cd-iss.Jan86 & Feb89)*

Dec 67. (7") **LOVE ME TWO TIMES. / MOONLIGHT DRIVE** 25

Apr 68. (7") **THE UNKNOWN SOLDIER. / WE COULD BE SO GOOD TOGETHER** 39 Mar 68

Aug 68. (7") **HELLO I LOVE YOU. / LOVE STREET** 15 1 Jul 68

—— **LEROY VINEGAR** – acoustic bass repl. LABAHN

Sep 68. (lp) **WAITING FOR THE SUN** 16 1 Aug 68
– Hello I love you / Love street / Not to touch the Earth / Summer's almost gone / Wintertime love / The unknown soldier / Spanish caravan / My wild love / We could be so good together / Yes, the river flows / Five to one. *(re-iss.+c.Nov71) (cd-iss.Jan86 & Feb89)*

Dec 68. (7") **TOUCH ME. / WILD CHILD** 3

May 69. (7") **WISHFUL SINFUL. / WHO SCARED YOU** 44 Mar 69

Aug 69. (7") **TELL ALL THE PEOPLE. / EASY RIDE** 57 Jun 69

Sep 69. (lp) **THE SOFT PARADE** 6 Aug 69
– Tell all the people / Touch me / Shaman's blues / Do it / Easy ride / Wild child / Runnin' blue / Wishful sinful / The soft parade. *(re-iss.+c.Nov71) (cd-iss.Feb89)*

Sep 69. (7") **RUNNIN' BLUE. / DO IT** - 64

—— guest **LONNIE MACK** – bass repl. LABAHN

Apr 70. (7") **YOU MAKE ME REAL. / ROADHOUSE BLUES** - 50

Apr 70. (7") **YOU MAKE ME REAL. / THE SPY** -

Apr 70. (lp)(c) **MORRISON HOTEL / HARD ROCK CAFE** 12 4 Mar 70
– Land ho! / The spy / Queen of the highway / Indian summer / Maggie McGill / Roadhouse blues / Waiting for the sun / You make me real / Peace frog / Blue Sunday / Ship of fools. *(re-iss.+c.Nov71) (cd-iss.Apr86 & Feb89)*

Jul 70. (7") **ROADHOUSE BLUES. / BLUE SUNDAY** -

Sep 70. (d-lp)(c) **ABSOLUTELY LIVE (live)** 69 8 Aug 70
– Who do you love medley: Alabama song – Back door man – Love hides – Five to one / Build me a woman / When the music's over / Close to you / Universal mind / Break on through (to the other side) / The celebration of the lizard / Soul kitchen. *(re-iss.Nov71) (d-cd-iss.Mar87)*

Oct 70. (7") **UNIVERSAL MIND. / THE ICEWAGON FLEW** -

—— guest **JERRY SCHEFF** – bass repl. MACK

May 71. (7") **LOVE HER MADLY. / (YOU NEED MEAT) DON'T GO NO FURTHER** 11 Apr 71

Jun 71. (lp)(c) **L.A. WOMAN** 26 9 May 71
– The changeling / Love her madly / Been down so long / Cars hiss by my window / L.A. woman / L'America / Hyacinth house / Crawling KIng Snake / The wasp (Texas radio and the big beat) / Riders on the storm. *(re-iss.+cd.1984) (cd-iss.Feb89) (re-iss.Apr91)*

Jul 71. (7") **RIDERS ON THE STORM (edit). / THE CHANGELING** 22 14

—— **RAY** – vocals, ROBBIE and JOHN carried on when JIM MORRISON died 3rd Jul'71 of a mysterious heart attack. The trio continued (MANZAREK now on vox). Used guest session bassmen **WILLIE RUFF, WOLFGANG MERTZ** and **JACK CONRAD**

Nov 71. (7") **TIGHTROPE RIDE. / VARIETY IS THE SPICE OF LIFE** 71

Dec 71. (lp)(c) **OTHER VOICES** 31 Nov 71
– In the eye of the sun / Variety is the spice of life / Ships w.sails / Tightrope ride / Down on the farm / I'm horny, I'm stoned / Wandering musician / Hang on to your life

May 72. (7") **SHIP W. SAILS. / IN THE EYE OF THE SUN**

—— bass sessions **J. CONRAD, CHARLES LARKEY, LEE SKLAR and CHRIS ETHRIDGE.**

Aug 72. (7") **GET UP AND DANCE. / TREE TRUNKS**

Sep 72. (lp)(c) **FULL CIRCLE** 68
– Get up and dance / Four billion souls / Verdilac / Hardwod floor / Good rockin' / The mosquito / The piano bird / It slipped my mind / The Peking King and the New York Queen.

Sep 72. (7") **THE MOSQUITO. / IT SLIPPED MY MIND** - 85

Dec 72. (7") **THE PIANO BIRD. / GOOD ROCKIN'** -

—— They finally split 1973. MANZAREK went solo and KRUGER & DENSMORE formed The BUTTS BAND. With JESS RODEN as lead singer / **PHILIP CHEN** – bass / **ROY DAVIS** – keyboards, they made 2 albums for ~'Blue Thumb' records; 'THE BUTTS BAND' (1974) / **'HEAR AND NOW'** (1975).

– compilations, etc. –

Note; All on 'Elektra' until mentioned.

Mar 71. (lp)(c) **13** 25 Dec 70

Mar 72. (d-lp)(c) **WEIRD SCENES INSIDE THE GOLDMINE** 50 55
– Break on through (to the other side) / Strange days / Shaman's blues / Love street / Peace frog / Blue Sunday / The wasp (Texas radio and the big beat) / End of the night / Love her madly / Ship of fools / The spy / The end / Take it as it comes / Running blue / L.A. woman / Five to one / Who scared you? / Don't go no further / Riders on the storm / Maggie McGill / Horse latitudes / When the music's over.

Oct 74. (lp)(c) **THE BEST OF THE DOORS**

Feb 76. (7") **RIDERS ON THE STORM. / L.A. WOMAN** 33

Sep 76. (7") **LIGHT MY FIRE. / THE UNKNOWN SOLDIER**

Sep 76. (7") **LOVE HER MADLY. / TOUCH ME**

Jan 79. (d7") **LOVE ME TWO TIMES. / HELLO I LOVE YOU / GHOST SONG / ROADHOUSE BLUES**

Jan 79. (7") **ROADHOUSE BLUES. / AN AMERICAN PRAYER** -

Jan 80. (12") **THE END. / (b-side 'Delta' not by The DOORS.)**

Oct 80. (lp)(c) **GREATEST HITS** 17
(cd-iss.Oct95)

Oct 80. (7") **PEOPLE ARE STRANGE. / NOT TO TOUCH THE EARTH** -

Aug 82. (d-c) **THE SOFT PARADE / AN AMERICAN PRAYER**

Oct 83. (12") **GLORIA (live). / LOVE ME TWO TIMES (live)** 71

Oct 83. (lp)(c) **ALIVE SHE CRIED (live)** 36 23
– Gloria / Light my fire / You make me real / The wasp (Texas radio and the big beat) / Love me two times / Little red rooster / Moonlight drive. *(cd-iss.Jul84)*

Oct 83. (7") **GLORIA (live). / MOONLIGHT DRIVE (live)** -

Jun 85. (lp)(c) **CLASSICS**

Nov 85. (d-lp)(c)(cd) **BEST OF THE DOORS** (diff.to '74 version)
– Break on through (to the other side) / Light my fire / The crystal ship / People are strange / Strange days / Love me two times / Five to one / Waiting for the Sun / Spanish caravan / When the music's over / Hello, I love you / Roadhouse blues / L.A. woman / Riders on the storm / Touch me / Love her madly / The unknown soldier / The end. (cd+=) – Alabama song (whiskey bar). *(re-iss.Apr91 hit UK No.17 & US No.32)*

Jun 87. (m-lp)(c)(cd) **LIVE AT THE HOLLYWOOD BOWL (live)**
– Wake up / Light my fire / The unknown soldier / A little game / The hill dwellers / Spanish caravan.

Mar 91. (cd)(c)(lp) **THE DOORS: A FILM BY OLIVER STONE – MUSIC FROM THE ORIGINAL SOUNDTRACK** 11 8

Apr 91. (7")(c-s) **BREAK ON THROUGH. / LOVE STREET** 64
(12"+=)(cd-s+=) – Hello I love you / Touch me.

May 91. (7") **LIGHT MY FIRE (edit). / PEOPLE ARE STRANGE** 7
(12"+=)(cd-s+=) – Soul kitchen.

May 91. (d-cd)(d-c)(t-lp) **THE DOORS: IN CONCERT (live)** 24 50

Jul 91. (7")(c-s) **RIDERS ON THE STORM. / LOVE ME TWO TIMES (live)** 68
(12"+=)(cd-s+=) – Roadhouse blues (live).

Sep 85. Old Gold; (7") **RIDERS ON THE STORM. / LIGHT MY FIRE** -

Jun 95. Elektra; (c-s) **THE GHOST SONG. ("JIM MORRISON & THE DOORS") / (interview)**
(cd-s+=) – Love me two times / Roadhouse blues (live).

JIM MORRISON

poetry with sparse musical accompaniment-

Elektra Elektra

Nov 78. (lp) **AN AMERICAN PRAYER** (recorded 8 Nov '70) 54
– Awake / Ghost song / Dawn's highway / Newborn awakening / To come of age / Black polished chrome / Latino chrome / Angels and sailors / Stoned immaculate / The poet's dreams / The movie / Curses invocations / World on fire / American night / Roadhouse blues / Lament / The hitchhiker / An American prayer. *(re-iss.cd/c/lp May95)*

DOROTHY (see under ⇒ RAINCOATS)

Ray DORSET (see under ⇒ MUNGO JERRY)

DRAIN (see under ⇒ BUTTHOLE SURFERS)

NICK DRAKE

Born: 19 Jun'48, Burma. By mid'50's, his family moved to Tamworth-in-Ardon then Stratford, England. Discovered by ASHLEY HUTCHINGS (Fairport Convention) who after seeing him gig in Cambridge, where he was at college, got him signed to 'Island'. From then on his work was heralded by critics, but commercial success never came, setting NICK off into a depression which led to his untimely death in '74. He did however leave behind at least one great classic album in 1970, 'BRYTER LAYTER'. • **Style:** Broody melancholic melodies, that were at first compared with ASTRAL WEEKS (Van Morrison), but later with more jazz feel. He quit gigging around the early 70's, and the 6'3" genius opted out from the music world. **Songwriters:** All work penned by himself. • **Trivia:** His sister Gabrielle was semi-successful TV actress in the 70's/80's, noteably on 'Crossroads' soap.

Recommended: BRYTER LAYTER (*9) / FIVE LEAVES LEFT (*7) / PINK MOON (*5)

NICK DRAKE – vocals, guitar, piano with **RICHARD THOMPSON** – guitar / **DANNY THOMPSON** – double bass / **PAUL HARRIS** – keyboards / **CLAIRE LOWTHER** and **ROCKY DZIDZORNU,** plus 15-piece orchestra.

Island Antilles

Sep 69. (lp) **FIVE LEAVES LEFT** - 1976
– Time has told me / River man / Three hours / Day is done / Way to blue / Cello song / The thoughts of Mary Jane / Man in a shed / Fruit tree / Saturday sun. *(c-iss.1974) (re-iss.+cd.Feb87) (re-cd.May89)*

—— retained **RICHARD** bringing in other (FAIRPORT CONVENTION members: **DAVE PEGG** – / **DAVE MATTACKS** – . Also sessioned **PAUL HARRIS, RAY WARLEIGH, CHRIS McGREGOR.**

Nov 70. (lp) **BRYTER LAYTER** - 1977
– Introduction / Hazey Jane II / At the chime of a city clock / One of these things first / Hazey Jane I / Bryter layter / Fly / Poor boy / Northern sky / Sunday. *(c-iss.1974) (re-iss.+cd.May87 + Oct89)*

—— **NICK DRAKE** – vocals, guitar (totally solo)

Feb 72. (lp) **PINK MOON** -
– Pink moon / Place to be / Road / Which will / Horn / Things behind the sun / Know / Parasite / Ride / Harvest breed / From the morning / Voice from the mountain / Rider on the wheel / Black eyed dog / Hanging on a star. *(c-iss.1974) (cd-iss.Apr90)*

He had put down some tracks for new album, when in 25 Nov'74 he overdosed on medication/drugs. Questionable coroner's verdict was 'Death by suicide'.

– compilations, others, etc. –

1972. Antilees; (lp) **NICK DRAKE** (69-70 material) -

Apr 79. Island; (3xlp-box) **FRUIT TREE – THE COMPLETE RECORDED WORKS**

(contains all 3 albums)
May 85. Island; (lp)(c) **HEAVEN IN A WILD FLOWER** *(cd-iss.Apr90)*
Aug 86. Hannibal/ US= Rykodisc; (4xlp-box)(US-4xcd-box) **FRUIT TREE**
(all 3 lp's, plus TIME OF NO REPLY rec.1973) *(cd-iss.Dec91)* (all.+=) – Fruit tree / Fly / Man in a shed / Thoughts of Mary Jane.
Jan 87. Hannibal/ US= Rykodisc; (lp) **TIME OF NO REPLY** *(c+cd-iss.May89)*
Jun 94. Island; (cd)(c) **WAY TO BLUE – AN INTRODUCTION TO NICK DRAKE**

DR. DRE (see under ⇒ N.W.A.)

DREADZONE

Formed: London, England . . .1992 by GREG ROBERTS and TIM BRAN. Were a surprise signing to major indie 'Creation', where they released debut '360°'. After appearing on the bill at many rave concerts, they signed to 'Virgin' and album chart debutted with 'SECOND LIGHT'. From it came the catchy Top 20 hit 'LITTLE BRITAIN', now used on TV sports features. • **Style:** Thumping bassy trance-dub. Described unfairly in the NME as sea shanty techno. Use samples from B-movies / cult film. • **Songwriters:** Group or ROBERTS. • **Trivia:** Appeared in the dance tent at 1995's 'T In The Park' in Hamilton, Scotland.

Recommended: 360° (*5) / SECOND LIGHT (*6)

GREG ROBERTS – drums (ex-SCREAMING TARGET, ex-BIG AUDIO DYNAMITE) / **TIM BRAN** – samples, keyboards, etc

Creation / not issued

May 93. (12"ep)(cd-ep) **THE WARNING / AFRICA. / NO JUSTICE NO PEACE (the Warning remix) / HEART OF DARKNESS (Africa remix)** — [ ] [-]
Jul 93. (12")(cd-s) **THE GOOD, THE BAD AND THE DREAD** — [ ] [-]
– mixes; (part one, the good) / (part two, the bad) / (part three, the dread) / (a fistful of dub).
Oct 93. (cd)(c)(lp) **360°** — [ ] [-]
– House of Dread / L.O.V.E. / Chinese ghost story / The good, the bad and the Dread / The warning / Dream on / Far encounter / Skeleton at the feast / Rastafarout.

— added **LEO WILLIAMS** – bass (ex-BIG AUDIO DYNAMITE)

Totem / not issued

Oct 94. (m-cd)(m-lp) **PERFORMANCE, DREADZONE** — [ ] [-]
– Africa / House of Dread / Far encounter / Dream on / The warning.
Oct 94. (12"ep)(cd-ep) **FIGHT THE POWER. / (Drum club mix) / (DJ Evolution) / (Dread Zone dub)** — [ ] [-]
In 1994, they mixed TRANS-GLOBAL UNDERGROUND for 'Lookee Here' EP.

Virgin / Virgin

Apr 95. (c-ep)(12"ep)(cd-ep) **ZION YOUTH. / ('A'-Underworld mix) / ('A'-Dan Donovan mix) / ('A'-Digidub mix)** — [49] [ ]
Jun 95. (cd)(c)(d-lp) **SECOND LIGHT** — [37] [ ]
– Life, love & unity / Litle Britain / A Canterbury tale / Captain Dread / Cave of angels / Zion youth / One way / Shining path / Out of Heaven.
Jul 95. (c-s) **CAPTAIN DREAD / ('A'-Zexos free troupe mix)** — [49] [ ]
(12"+=)(cd-s+=) – ('A'-Walk the plank mix) / ('A'-X-Press 2 mix).
(cd-s++=) – ('A'-Zexos citizen mix) / Epilogue.
Sep 95. (12"ep)(cd-ep) **MAXIMUM EP** — [56] [ ]
– Fight the power / One way / Maximum.
Dec 95. (c-s) **LITTLE BRITAIN / ('A'vocal mix)** — [31] [ ]
(12"+=)(cd-s+=) – ('A'-Eon mix) / ('A'-Black Star Liner mix) / ('A'-More Rockers mix).

DREAM (see under ⇒ EXTREME)

DREAM SYNDICATE

Formed: California, USA ... 1981 by STEVE WYNN and KARL PREGODA. After an untitled mini-lp on US label, they caught interest of UK indie 'Rough Trade' in 1983, who released debut 'DAYS OF WINE AND ROSES'. Although moving onto bigger labels by the mid 80's, they never quite let go underground status. • **Style:** New wave / country-rock outfit, influenced by NEIL YOUNG and VELVET UNDERGROUND. They broke new ground alongside contemporaries GREEN ON RED. • **Songwriters:** Most written by WYNN, except CINNAMON GIRL (Neil Young) / MR.SOUL (Buffalo Springfield). • **Trivia:** STEVE WYNN was also in DANNY & DUSTY duo Feb 85 album see GREEN ON RED.

Recommended: DAYS OF WINE AND ROSES (*7).

STEVE 'DUSTY' WYNN – vocals / **KARL PREGODA** – guitar / **TOM ZVONCHECK** – keyboards / **MARK WALTON** – bass, vocals / **KENDRA SMITH** – drums

not issued / Down There

1982. (m-lp) **UNTITLED** — [-] [ ]
– Sure thing / Some kinda itch / That's what you always say / When you smile. *(UK-iss.Jun85 as 'DREAM SYNDICATE' on 'Demon', cd-iss.Aug92)*

Rough Trade / Slash

Nov 83. (lp) **DAYS OF WINE AND ROSES** — [ ] [ ]
– Tell me when it's over / Definitely clean / That's what you always say / Then she remembers / Halloween / When you smile / Until lately / Too little, too late / Days of wine and roses. *(re-iss.Jan87 on 'Slash') (cd-iss.Jan95 on 'Normal')*
Dec 83. (12"ep) **TELL ME WHEN IT'S OVER. / SOME KINDA ITCH (live) / MR. SOUL (live) / SURE THING (live)** — [ ] [ ]

— **DENNIS DUCK** – drums repl. KENDRA who joined RAINY DAY then OPAL (recorded live album early '84) / **DAVE PROVOST** – bass repl. TOM and MARK.

A&M / A&M

Jun 84. (lp)(c) **MEDICINE SHOW** — [ ] [ ]
– Still holding on to you / Daddy's girl / Burn / Armed with an empty gun / Bullet with my name on it / The medicine show / John Coltrane stereo blues / Merrittville.

— added **PAUL B. CUTLER** – lead guitar

Chrysalis / Chrysalis

Jun 86. (lp)(c) **OUT OF THE GREY** — [ ] [ ]
– Out of the grey / Forest for the trees / 50 in a 25 zone / Boston / Slide away / Dying embers / Now I ride alone / Dancing blind / You can't forget. *(re-iss.+cd.Oct87 on 'Big Time')*
Sep 87. (12"ep) **50 IN A 25 ZONE. / DRINKING PROBLEM / BLOOD MONEY / THE LONELY BULL** — [ ] [ ]

— trimmed to a quartet (WYNN, CUTLER, PROVOST and DUCK) when PREGODA left

Enigma / Enigma

Sep 88. (lp)(c)(cd) **GHOST STORIES** — [ ] [ ]
– The side I'll never show / My old haunts / Loving the sinner, hating the sin / Whatever you please / Weathered and torn / See that my grave is kept clean / I have faith / Some place better than this / Black / When the curtain calls. *(re-iss.cd Sep95 on 'Restless')*
Nov 88. (7") **I HAVE FAITH. / NOW I RIDE ALONE** — [ ] [ ]
(12"+=) – I ain't living like this.

— split 1988

– compilations etc. –

Feb 85. A&M; (lp) **IT'S NOT THE NEW DREAM SYNDICATE ALBUM (live rec.'84)** — [ ] [ ]
– Tell me when it's over / Bullet with my name on it / Armed with an empty gun / The medicine show / John Coltrane stereo blues.
Jun 89. Enigma; (lp) **LIVE AT RAJA'S (live at Hollywood Jan85)** — [ ] [ ]
– Still holding on to you / Forest for the trees / Until lately / That's what you always say / Burn / Merritville / The days of wine and roses / The medicine show / Halloween / Boston / John Coltrane stereo blues.
Jun 90. Enigma; (cd)(d-lp) **LIVE AT RAJAS / GHOST STORIES** — [ ] [ ]
Sep 89. Another Cowboy; (lp) **IT'S TOO LATE TO STOP NOW** — [ ] [ ]

STEVE WYNN

World Service / Rhino

May 90. (cd)(lp) **KEROSENE MAN** — [ ] [ ]
– Tears won't help / Carolyn / The blue drifter / Younger / Under the weather / Here on Earth as well / Something to remember me by / Killing time / Conspiracy of the heart / Kerosene man / Anthem. *(re-iss.cd. May93 on 'Rhino')*
May 93. (cd) **DAZZLING DISPLAY** — [ ] [ ]

Return To Sender / Return To Sender

Nov 94. (cd) **TAKE YOUR FLUNKY AND DANGLE** — [ ] [ ]

KENDRA SMITH

4 a.d. / 4 a.d.

May 95. (cd)(lp) **FIVE WAYS OF DISAPPEARING** — [ ] [ ]
– Aurelia / Bohemian Zebulon / Temporarily Lucy / In your head / Space: Unadorned / Maggots / Drunken boat / Interlude: Dirigible / Valley of the morning sun / Judge not / Get there / Interlude: Saturn / Bold marauder.

DR.FEELGOOD

Formed: Canvey Island, Essex, England . . . mid-71 by BRILLEAUX and JOHNSON, taking their name from a 50's bluesman. In 1974, they signed to 'United Art', and had hit with Top 20 second album 'MALPRACTICE'. Their loyal support had all but abandoned them in the 80's, after a riotous late 70's chart period. • **Style:** Progressed from pub rock R&B revivalists influenced by The PIRATES, to becoming classy raw edged rockers, loved by even new wave punks. BRILLEAUX's image was complete with crushed suit, which combined neatly with his gruff vox. • **Songwriters:** BRILLEAUX and JOHNSON, and later MAYO. Covered:- BONY MORONIE (Larry Williams) / TEQUILLA (Champs) / ROUTE 66 (Nelson Riddle) / DUST MY BROOM (Elmore James) / MAD MAN BLUES + DIMPLES (John Lee Hooker) / ROCK ME BABY (B.B. King) / MY BABY (Willie Dixon) / SOMETHING YOU GET (Kenner) / CAN'T FIND THE LADY (Larry Wallis) / GOING DOWN (Don Nix) / NO TIME (JJ Cale) / STANDING AT THE CROSSROADS AGAIN (Mickey Jupp) / BEEN DOWN SO LONG (Doors) / DON'T WORRY BABY (Ritchie Valens) / YOU'VE GOT MY NUMBER (Undertones) / GET RHYTHM (Johnny Cash) / I'M A REAL MAN (John Hiatt) / AS LONG AS THE PRICE IS RIGHT (Larry Wallis) / GREAT BALLS OF FIRE (Jerry Lee Lewis) / etc. • **Trivia:** In 1977, NICK LOWE produced and co-wrote some material.

Recommended: STUPIDITY (*6) / SINGLES (*7)

LEE BRILLEAUX (b.1948, London, England) – vocals, harmonica / **WILKO JOHNSON** (b.JOHN WILKINSON, 1947) – guitar (ex-ROAMERS) / **JOHN B.SPARKS** – bass / **THE BIG FIGURE** (aka.JOHN MARTIN, 1947) – drums (ex-ROAMERS)

United Art / Columbia

Nov 74. (7") **ROXETTE. / ROUTE 66** — [ ] [-]

Dec 74. (lp)(c) **DOWN BY THE JETTY** [ ] [-]
– She does it right / Boom boom / The more I give / Roxette / One weekend / That ain't the way to behave / I don't mind / Twenty yards behind / Keep it out of sight / All through the city / Cheque book / Oyeh / Bonie Moronie / Tequila. *(re-iss.Dec78) (re-iss.May82 on 'Fame') (re-iss.Oct85 on 'Edsel')*
Mar 75. (7") **SHE DOES IT RIGHT. / I DON'T MIND** [ ] [-]
Oct 75. (lp)(c) **MALPRACTICE** [17] [ ]
– I can tell / Going back home / Back in the night / Another man / Rolling and tumbling / Don't let your daddy know / Watch your step / Don't you just know it / Riot in cell block No.9 / Becaue you're mine / You shouldn't call the doctor (if you can't afford the bill). *(re-iss.cd. 1991)*
Nov 75. (7") **BACK IN THE NIGHT. / I'M A MAN** [ ] [ ]
Sep 76. (lp)(c) **STUPIDITY (live)** [1] [ ]
– I'm talking about you / Twenty yards behind / Stupidity / All through the city / I'm a man / Walking the dog / She does it right / Going back home / I don't mind / Back in the night / I'm a hog for you baby / Checkin' up on my baby / Roxanne. (free 7"-w.a.) **ENCORE (live)** – Riot in cell block No.9 / Johnny B.Goode *(re-iss.Apr91 as d-lp,c,cd. 'STUPIDITY +' +=) (2 tracks above)*
Sep 76. (7") **ROXETTE (live). / KEEP IT OUT OF SIGHT (live)** [ ] [ ]
May 77. (7") **SNEAKIN' SUSPICION. / LIGHTS OUT** [47] [ ]
May 77. (lp)(c) **SNEAKIN' SUSPICION** [10] [ ]
– Sneakin' suspicion / Paradise / Nothin' shakin' (but the leaves and trees) / Walking on the edge / Lights out / Lucky 7 / All my love / You'll be mine / Time and the Devil / Hey mama / Keep your big mouth shut. *(re-iss.May87 on 'Fame') (cd-iss.Jan92 on 'Grand')*

—— (Mar77) **JOHN 'GYPIE' MAYO** (b.JOHN CAWTHRA) – guitar replaced HENRY McCULLOCH who had for 2 months repl. WILKO JOHNSON who went solo.

Sep 77. (7"m)(12"m) **SHE'S A WIND-UP. / HI-RISE / HOMEWORK** [34] [ ]
Sep 77. (lp)(c) **BE SEEING YOU** [55] [ ]
– Ninety-nine ana a half (won't do) / She's a wind-up / I thought I had it made / I don't wanna know / That's it, I quit / As long as the price is right / Hi-rise / My buddy buddy friends / Baby Jane / The blues had a baby, and they named it rock'n'roll / Looking back / 60 minutes of our love. *(re-iss.Oct87 on 'Edsel') (cd-iss.Jan92 on 'Grand')*
Nov 77. (7") **BABY JANE. / LOOKING BACK** [ ] [ ]
(12"+=) – You upset me baby.
Sep 78. (7") **DOWN AT THE DOCTORS. / TAKE A TIP** [48] [ ]
Oct 78. (lp)(c) **PRIVATE PRACTICE** [41] [ ]
– Down at the doctors / Every kind of vice / Things get better / Milk and alcohol / Night time / Let's have a party / Take a tip / It wasn't me / Greaseball / Sugar shaker. *(re-iss.+cd.Oct88 on 'Grand')*
Jan 79. (7")(7"milky)(7"beer-coloured) **MILK AND ALCOHOL. / EVERY KIND OF VICE** [9] [ ]
Apr 79. (7")(7"blue)(7"brown)(7"purple) **AS LONG AS THE PRICE IS RIGHT (live). / DOWN AT THE DOCTORS (live)** [40] [-]
May 79. (lp)(c) **AS IT HAPPENS (live)** [42] [-]
– Take a tip / Every kind of vice / Down at the doctors / Baby Jane / Sugar shaker / Things get better / She's a wind-up / Ninety-nine and a half (won't do) / My buddy buddy friends / Milk and alcohol / Matchbox / As long as the price is right / Night time. (free 7"ep) – Riot In Cell Block No.9 / Blues Had A Baby And They Named It Rock'n' Roll / Lights Out / Great Balls Of Fire. *(cd-iss.Dec92 on 'Grand' with free EP tracks)*
Aug 79. (7") **PUT HIM OUT OF YOUR MIND. / BEND YOUR EAR** [73] [-]
Sep 79. (lp)(c) **LET IT ROLL** [ ] [-]
– Java blue / Feels good / Put him out of your mind / Bend your ear / Hong Kong money / Keeka smeeka / Shotgun blues / Pretty face / Riding on the L & N / Drop everything and run.
Jan 80. (7") **HONG KONG MONEY. / KEEKA SMEEKA** [ ] [-]
Aug 80. (7") **NO HO DOYA KAMO. / BEST IN THE WORLD** [ ] [-]
Sep 80. (lp)(c) **A CASE OF THE SHAKES** [ ] [-]
– Jumping from love to love / Going some place else / Best in the world / Punch drunk / King for a day / Violent love / No mo do Yakamo / Love hound / Coming to you / Who's winning / Drives me wild / A case of the shakes. *(re-iss.Aug86 on 'Edsel')*
Nov 80. (7") **JUMPING FROM LOVE TO LOVE. / LOVE HOUND** [ ] [-]
Jan 81. (7") **VIOLENT LOVE. / A CASE OF THE SHAKES** [ ] [-]

Liberty / not issued

Aug 81. (lp)(c) **ON THE JOB (live)** [ ] [-]
– Drives me wild / Java blue / Jumping from love to love / Pretty face / No mo do Yakomo / Love hound / Shotgun blues / Best in the world / Who's winning / Riding on the L'&'N / Shotgun blues / Goodnight Vienna. *(cd-iss.Dec92 on 'Grand')*

—— (early'81) **JOHNNY GUITAR** – guitar (ex-COUNT BISHOPS) repl. MAYO

Oct 81. (7") **WAITING FOR SATURDAY NIGHT. / EILEEN** [ ] [-]

—— **LEE & JOHNNY** recruited **PAT McMULLEN** – bass (ex-COUNT BISHOPS) repl. SPARKS / **BUZZ BARWELL** – drums (ex-LEW LEWIS BAND) repl. THE BIG FIGURE

Chiswick / not issued

Sep 82. (7") **TRYING TO LIVE MY LIFE WITHOUT YOU. / MURDER IN THE FIRST DEGREE** [ ] [-]
Oct 82. (lp)(c) **FAST WOMEN AND SLOW HORSES** [ ] [-]
– She's the one / Monkey / Sweet sweet lovin' (gone sour on me) / Trying to live my life without you / Rat race / Baby Jump / Crazy about girls / Sugar bowl / Educated fool / Bum's rush / Baby why do you treat me this way / Beautiful Delilah. *(re-iss.+cd.May88 on 'Grand')*
Mar 83. (7") **CRAZY ABOUT GIRLS. / SOMETHING OUT OF NOTHING** [ ] [-]

—— (1983) **GORDON RUSSELL** – guitar repl. JOHNNY GUITAR/ **PHIL MITCHELL** – bass repl. McMULLEN (1984) / **KEVIN MORRIS** – drums repl. BUZZ

Demon / not issued

Sep 84. (7") **DANGEROUS. / CAN'T FIND THE LADY** [ ] [-]
Oct 84. (lp) **DOCTOR'S ORDERS** [ ] [-]
– Close but no cigar / So long / You don't give me / My way / Neighbour, neighbour / Talk of the Devil / Hit git and split / I can't be satisfied / Saturday night fish fry / Drivin' wheel / It ain't right / I don't worry about a thing / She's in the middle / Dangerous. *(re-iss.1986) (re-iss.+cd.Jan90 on 'Grand')*
Dec 84. (7") **MY WAY. / SHE'S IN THE MIDDLE** [ ] [-]

I.D. / not issued

Oct 85. (lp) **MAD MAN BLUES** [ ] [-]
– Dust my broom / Something you got / Dimples / Living on the highway / Tore down / Mad man blues / I've got news for you / My babe / Can't find the lady / Rock me baby. *(re-iss.Oct88 on 'Grand')*

Stiff / not issued

Aug 86. (7")(12") **DON'T WAIT UP. / SOMETHING GOOD** [ ] [-]
(d7"+=) – Back in the night / Milk & alcohol.
Nov 86. (7")(12") **SEE YOU LATER ALLIGATOR. / I LOVE YOU SO YOU'RE MINE** [ ] [-]
Jun 87. (7")(12") **HUNTING SHOOTING FISHING. / BIG ENOUGH** [ ] [-]
Sep 87. (lp)(c)(cd) **CLASSIC** [ ] [-]
– Hunting shooting fishing / Break these chains / Heartbeat / (I wanna) Make love to you / Hurricane / See you later alligator / Quit while you're behind / Nothing like it / Spy vs. spy / Highway 61 / Crack me up.
Apr 89. (7") **MILK AND ALCOHOL (new recipe). / SHE'S GOT HER EYES ON YOU** [ ] [ ]
(12"+=) – Mad man blues.

Grand / not issued

May 89. (lp)(c)(cd) **BRILLEAUX** [ ] [-]
– I love you, so you're mine / You've got my number / Big enough / Don't wait up / Get rhythm / Here is the next one? / Play dirty / Grow too old / Rough ride / I'm a real man / Come over here / Take what you can get.

—— **BRILLEAUX + MITCHELL + MORRIS** recruited **STEVE WALWYN** – guitar (ex-STEVE MARRIOTT group)

May 90. (cd)(c)(lp) **LIVE IN LONDON (live)** [ ] [-]
– King for a day / You upset me baby / As long as the price is right / Mad man blues / She does it right / Baby Jane / Quit while you're behind / Back in the night / Milk and alcohol / See you later alligator / Down at the doctors / Route 66 / Going back home / Bony Moronie / Tequila.
Jun 91. (cd)(c)(lp) **PRIMO** [ ] [ ]
– Heart of the city / My sugar turns to alcohol / Going down / No time / World in a jug / If my baby quit me / Primo blues / Standing at the crossroads again / Been down so long / Don't worry baby / Down by the jetty blues / Two times nine.
Jul 93. (cd)(c)(lp) **THE FEELGOOD FACTOR** [ ] [-]
– The feelgood factor / Tranqueray / Tell me no lies / Styrofoam / I'm in the mood for you / Double crossed / Lying about the blues / She moves me / Wolfman calling / One step forward / One to ten / Fool for you.

—— In Apr 94; LEE BRILLEAUX died of throat cancer.

– compilations, others, etc. –

Nov 81. United Artists; (lp)(c) **CASEBOOK** [ ] [-]
Apr 87. Emus; (cd) **CASE HISTORY – THE BEST OF DR.FEELGOOD** [ ] [-]
May 89. Liberty; (d-lp)(c)(cd) **SINGLES (THE U.A. YEARS)** [ ] [-]
– Roxette / She does it right / Back in the night / Going back home / Riot in cell block 9 / Sneakin' suspicion / She's a wind-up / Baby Jane / Down at the doctors / Milk and alcohol / As long as the price is right / Put him out of your mind / Hong Kong money / No modo Yakama / Jumping from love to love / Violent love / Waiting for Saturday night / Monkey / Trying to live my life without you / Crazy about girls / My way / Mad man blues / See you later alligator / Hunting shooting fishing.(d-lp+c+=) – Don't wait up / Milk and alcohol (new recipe).
Sep 91. Grand; (cd)(d-lp) **SNEAKIN' SUSPICION / BE SEEING YOU** [ ] [-]
Nov 91. Grand; (d-lp) **SNEAKIN' SUSPICION / LIGHTS OUT** [ ] [-]
May 94. Grand; (cd)(c)(lp) **DOWN AT THE DOCTORS** [ ] [-]
Oct 95. EMI; (5xcd-box) **LOOKING BACK** [ ] [-]

DRIFTERS

Formed: New York, USA ... May'53, by CLYDE McPHATTER who had just been fired from The DOMINOES. He signed to 'Atlantic' records and finally found friends from The THRASHER WONDERS to augment him in The DRIFTERS. With help from producers / writers Jerry Wexler and 'Atlantic' boss Ahmet Ertegun, their first song 'MONEY HONEY' became a million seller & R&B No.1, but didn't crossover into US pop charts!. Their initial batch of singles during this time, followed on same path. In 1954, CLYDE was drafted into the army, and was replaced by DAVID BAUGHAN and then JOHNNY MOORE in 1955. On his return in Apr'56, he did not re-join them, but went solo, having the first of 8 US Top40 hits with 'TREASURE OF LOVE'. Although the group had minor hits during this time, their varied line-up of lead vocalists, gave them no identity. In June 1958, their manager (since mid-54), GEORGE TREADWELL who owned group name, fired them all and brought in new line-up featuring BEN E.KING. His arrival gave them a new lease of life which sparked off a number of hits starting with 'THERE GOES MY BABY'. They had a US No.1 in Oct'1960 with 'SAVE THE LAST DANCE FOR ME', but after a complaint about wages to manager TREADWELL, he too was ousted. They found RUDY LEWIS in 1961, and continued successfully, until his surprise fatal heart attack in Jun'64. JOHNNY MOORE returned to the fold, but after several more hits, group's commercial appeal lagged. In 1971, GEORGE TREADWELL died, leaving his wife FAYE to take over management. After a re-issue hits the UK Top 3, she initiated them a deal with 'Bell' records. They churned out some fine pop tunes, which became hits only in Britain. From 1977 onwards, they continued with many different line-up variations, mostly on the cabaret circuit. • **Style:** They moved from R&B and doo-wop PLATTERS influence, to a more pre-Motown black pop formula during the 60's. • **Songwriters:** MONEY HONEY (Jesse Stone) / Lieber & Stoller wrote RUBY BABY and other material until Pomus-Shuman added their repertoire in the early 60's. Gerry Goffin & Carole King became their writing hitmakers from 1961. Lieber & Stoller opted out in Sep'63, when they formed own record co. There were other sources at this time, too numerous to mention. Their 70's revival included songs by Cook-Greenaway and Tony MacAuley, to name but a few. • **Trivia:** In the late 50's, they were augmented by a female backing group which included DIONNE WARWICK, CISSY HOUSTON and DORIS TROY.

Recommended: THE VERY BEST OF THE DRIFTERS (*5)

CLYDE McPHATTER & THE DRIFTERS

CLYDE McPHATTER (b.13 Nov'33, Durham, North Carolina, USA) – lead vocals / **GERHART THRASHER** – tenor vocals / **ANDREW THRASHER** – baritone vocals / **BILL PINCKNEY** – bass vocals repl. WILLIE FERBEE

Date	Release	not issued	Atlantic
Sep 53.	(7") **MONEY HONEY. / WHY I FEEL**	-	
Mar 54.	(7") **LUCILLE. / SUCH A NIGHT**	-	
Sep 54.	(7") **HONEY LOVE. / WARM YOUR HEART**	-	
Nov 54.	(7") **BIP BAM. / SOMEDAY YOU'LL WANT ME TO WANT YOU**	-	
Dec 54.	(7") **WHITE CHRISTMAS. / BELLS OF ST.MARY'S** *(US re-iss.Dec55 hit No.80/ hit No.88 Dec62) (UK-iss.Dec74)*	-	
May 55.	(7") **WHATCHA GONNA DO. / GONE**	-	
1955.	(lp) **CLYDE McPHATTER & THE DRIFTERS** – Without love / I make believe / Thirty days / Treasure of love / Someday you'll want me to want you / Seven days / I'm not worthy of you / Bells of St.Mary's / White Christmas / Warm your heart / Money honey / What'cha gonna do / Such a night / Honey love.	-	
1955.	(7") **EVERYONE'S LAUGHING. / HOT ZIGGETY**	-	
1955.	(7") **ADORABLE. / STEAMBOAT**	-	

— **DAVID BAUGHAN** – lead vocals repl. McPHATTER who had been drafted. /(Aug55) **JOHHNY MOORE** – lead vocals repl. BAUGHAN / **CHARLIE HUGHES** – baritone vocals repl. ANDREW

DRIFTERS

Date	Release	not issued	Atlantic
Jan 56.	(7") **RUBY BABY. / YOUR PROMISE TO BE MINE**	-	

— In Apr'56, McPHATTER was discharged from the army, but went solo instead.

Date	Release	not issued	Atlantic
Nov 56.	(7") **SOLDIER OF FORTUNE. / I GOTTA GET MYSELF TOGETHER**	-	
Jan 57.	(7") **FOOLS FALL IN LOVE. / IT WAS A TEAR**	-	69
May 57.	(7") **HYPNOTIZED. / DRIFTING AWAY FROM YOU**	-	79
Jul 57.	(7") **I KNOW. / YODEE YANKEE**	-	

— **BOBBY HENDRICKS** – tenor vocals (of The FLYERS) repl. MOORE (drafted). The following couple of years saw various members come and go.

— Group now **HENDRICKS, GERHART THRASHER, JIMMY MILLENDER & TOMMY EVANS**

Date	Release	not issued	Atlantic
Jun 58.	(7") **MOONLIGHT BAY. / DRIP DROP**	-	72 / 58
1958.	(lp) **ROCKIN' AND DRIFTIN'** – Moonlight bay / Ruby baby / Drip drop / I gotta get myself a woman / Fools fall in love / Hypnotized / Yodee yakee / I know / Soldier of fortune / Drifting away from you / Your promise to be mine / It was a tear / Adorable / Steamboat.	-	

— Manager GEORGE TREADWELL fired all the group, He replaced them with The CROWNS who featured **BEN E.KING** – lead vocal / **CHARLIE THOMAS / DOC GREEN** and **ELSBEARY HOBBS.**

Date	Release	London	Atlantic
Jun 59.	(7") **THERE GOES MY BABY. / OH MY LOVE**		2
Oct 59.	(7") **DANCE WITH ME. / (IF YOU CRY) TRUE LOVE, TRUE LOVE**	17	15 / 33

— (above 'B'side featured JOHNNY LEE WILLIAMS – lead vocals)

Date	Release	London	Atlantic
Mar 60.	(7") **THIS MAGIC MOMENT. / BALTIMORE**		16
May 60.	(7") **LONELY WINDS. / HEY SENORITA**		54
Oct 60.	(7") **SAVE THE LAST DANCE FOR ME. / NOBODY BUT ME**	2	1 Sep 60
Feb 61.	(7") **I COUNT THE TEARS. / SADIE MY LADY**	28	17 Dec 60
1961.	(lp) **SAVE THE LAST DANCE FOR ME** – Saturday night at the movies / Come on over to my place / Save the last dance for me / At the club / I count the tears / When my little girl is smiling / Up on the roof / Dance with me / Under the boardwalk / I've got sand in my shoes / There goes my baby / On Broadway / I'll take you home / This magic moment / Some kind of wonderful / I'll take you where the music's playing. *(re-iss.compilation +cd.extra tracks; May87)*	-	

— **RUDY LEWIS** – lead vocals (ex-CLARA WARD . . .) repl. BEN E. who went solo

Date	Release	London	Atlantic
Mar 61.	(7") **SOME KIND OF WONDERFUL. / HONEY BEE**		32
Jun 61.	(7") **PLEASE STAY. / NO SWEET LOVIN'**		14
Sep 61.	(7") **SWEETS FOR MY SWEET. / LONELINESS OR HAPPINESS**		16
Feb 62.	(7") **ROOM FULL OF TEARS. / SOMEDAY NEW DANCIN' WITH ME**		72 Nov 61
Mar 62.	(7") **WHEN MY LITTLE IS SMILING. / MEXICAN DIVORCE**	31	28
May 62.	(7") **STRANGER ON THE SHORE. / WHAT TO DO**		73
Jul 62.	(7") **SOMETIMES I WONDER. / JACKPOT**	-	
Nov 62.	(7") **UP ON THE ROOF. / ANOTHER NIGHT WITH THE BOYS**		5
Mar 63.	(7") **ON BROADWAY. / LET MUSIC PLAY**		5
May 63.	(lp) **UP ON THE ROOF** (comp.recent 45's) – Up on the roof / There goes my baby / Sweets for my sweet / This magic moment / Mexican divorce / Stranger on the shore / What to do / Save the last dance for me / Loneliness or happiness / Another night with the boys / (If you cry) True love, true love / When my little girl is smiling / Room full of tears / Ruby baby.		
Jul 63.	(7") **RAT RACE. / IF YOU DON'T COME BACK**		71 May 63
Sep 63.	(7") **I'LL TAKE YOU HOME. / I FEEL GOOD ALL OVER**	37	25
Jan 64.	(7") **VAYA CON DIOS. / IN THE LAND OF MAKE BELIEVE**		43
Apr 64.	(7") **ONE WAY LOVE. / DIDN'T I**		56

— **JOHNNY MOORE** returned to replace LEWIS who died June 1964.

Date	Release	Atlantic	Atlantic
Jun 64.	(7") **UNDER THE BOARDWALK. / I DON'T WANT TO GO ON WITHOUT YOU**	45	4
Sep 64.	(7") **(I'VE GOT) SAND IN MY SHOES. / HE'S JUST A PLAYBOY**		33
Oct 64.	(lp) **UNDER THE BOARDWALK** (comp.recent 45's)		40 Aug 64
Nov 64.	(7") **SATURDAY NIGHT AT THE MOVIES. / SPANISH LACE**		18
Dec 64.	(7") **CHRISTMAS SONG. / I REMEMBER CHRISTMAS**	-	
Feb 65.	(7") **AT THE CLUB. / ANSWER THE PHONE**	35	43
Apr 65.	(7") **COME ON OVER TO MY PLACE. / CHAINS OF LOVE**	40	60 / 90
Jun 65.	(lp) **THE GOOD LIFE WITH THE DRIFTERS** – Quando quando quando / On the street where you live / I wish you love / Tonight / More / What kind of fool am I / The good life / As long as she needs me / Desafinado / Who can I turn to / Saturday night at the movies / Temptation.		Feb 65
Jul 65.	(7") **FOLLOW ME. / THE OUTSIDE WORLD**		91 Jun65
Aug 65.	(7") **I'LL TAKE YOU WHERE THE MUSIC'S PLAYING. / FAR FROM THE MADDING CROWD**		51
Oct 65.	(lp) **I'LL TAKE YOU WHERE THE MUSIC'S PLAYING** – I'll take you where the music's playing / I've got sand in my shoes / At the club / I don't want to go on without you / Answer the phone / He's just a playboy / Follow me / Spanish lace / Chains of love / Far from the maddening crowd / The outside world / Come on over to my place		
Jan 66.	(7") **WE GOTTA SING. / NYLON STOCKINGS**		
Mar 66.	(7") **MEMORIES ARE MADE OF THIS. / MY ISLANDS IN THE SUN**		48
Jul 66.	(7") **UP IN THE STREETS OF HARLEM. / YOU CAN'T LOVE 'EM ALL**		
Dec 66.	(7") **BABY WHAT I MEAN. / ARETHA** *(re-iss.1972)*	49	62
1967.	(7") **AIN'T IT THE TRUTH. / UP JUMPED THE DEVIL**	-	
Jun 68.	(7") **STILL BURNING IN MY HEART. / I NEED YOU NOW**	-	
1969.	(7") **YOUR BEST FRIEND. / STEAL AWAY**	-	
Jun 68.	(7") **YOU GOT TO PAY YOUR DUES. / BLACK SILK**	-	
Mar 71.	(7") **ROSE BY ANY OTHER NAME. / BE MY LADY**		

— In 1971, GEORGE TREADWELL died. His wife FAYE now took control of group. Past member CYLDE McPHATTER also died (heart failure, due to drugs) 13 Jun'72.

– 'Atlantic' compilations, others, etc.- (up to 1972)

Date	Release	UK	US
1960.	(lp) **DRIFTERS' GREATEST HITS**	-	
Jan 65.	(lp) **OUR BIGGEST HITS**		
Feb 68.	(lp) **GOLDEN HITS** *(re-iss.+c.May72, hit UK No.26) (re-iss.1974, cd-iss.1987)(re-iss.cd Feb93)*	27	
Feb 68.	(7") **I'LL TAKE YOU WHERE THE MUSIC'S PLAYING. / ON BROADWAY** *(re-iss.1972)*		
Feb 69.	(7") **SATURDAY NIGHT AT THE MOVIES. / UNDER THE BOARDWALK**		
Jul 71.	(7") **WHEN MY LITTLE GIRL IS SMILING. / SWEETS FOR MY SWEET**		
Mar 72.	(7"m) **AT THE CLUB. / MEMORIES ARE MADE OF THIS / SATURDAY NIGHT AT THE MOVIES**	3	
Jul 72.	(7"m) **COME ON OVER TO MY PLACE. / UP ON THE ROOF / I DON'T WANT TO GO ON WITHOUT YOU** *(re-iss.Oct80 & Sep86)*		
Sep 72.	(7"m) **I'LL TAKE YOU HOME. / (I'VE GOT) SAND IN MY SHOES / HE'S JUST A PLAYBOY**		

— **JOHNNY MOORE** – still on **lead vocals.**

Date	Release	Bell	Bell
Nov 72.	(7") **EVERY NIGHT. / SOMETHING TELLS ME**		
Feb 73.	(7") **YOU'VE GOT YOUR TROUBLES. / I'M FEELING SAD**	-	
Jul 73.	(7") **LIKE SISTER AND BROTHER. / THE SONGS WE USED TO SING**	7	
1973.	(lp)(c) **THE DRIFTERS NOW** – You've got your troubles / Four and twenty hours (seven days of every week I love you) / Sweet Caroline (good times never seemed so good) / Love me more the life I lead / Save the last dance for me / Always something there to remind me / Every night / Something tells me (something's gonna happen tonight) / Deep down inside (beats a heart of gold) / I'm feeling sad (and oh so lonely) / Say goodbye to Angelina / The songs we used to sing.		
Jan 74.	(7") **I'M FREE. / SAY GOODBYE TO ANGELINA**		
Jun 74.	(7") **KISSIN' IN THE BACK ROW OF THE MOVIES. / I'M FEELING SAD**	2	
Oct 74.	(7") **DOWN ON THE BEACH TONIGHT. / SAY GOODBYE TO ANGELINA**	7	
Dec 74.	(7") **LOVE GAMES. / THE CUT IS DEEP**	33	
Mar 75.	(lp)(c) **LOVE GAMES** – Love games / Like sister and brother / I'm ready (to make a fool of myself again) / If you're gonna love me / The cut is deep / I can't get away from you / Kissin' in the back row of the movies / I'm free for the rest of your life / I can't live without you / If it feels good, do it / A blessing in disguise / Down on the beach tonight.		
Aug 75.	(7") **THERE GOES MY FIRST LOVE. / DON'T CRY ON THE WEEKEND**	3	
Nov 75.	(7") **CAN I TAKE YOU HOME LITTLE GIRL. / ?**	10	
Dec 75.	(lp)(c) **THERE GOES MY FIRST LOVE** – Hello happiness / Harlem child / The juggler / Lovin' you is easy / And with no regrets / If only I could start again / I've got you on my mind / You chose a fine time / Don't cry on the weekend / Please help me down / Can I take you home little girl / There goes my first love. *(re-iss.Nov77 on 'M.F.P.')*		
Mar 76.	(7") **HELLO HAPPINESS. / I CAN'T GET AWAY FROM YOU**	12	
Aug 76.	(7") **EVERY NITE'S A SATURDAY NIGHT WITH YOU. / I'LL GET TO KNOW YOUR NAME ALONG THE WAY**	29	

		Arista	Arista
Nov 76.	(lp)(c) **EVERY NITE'S A SATURDAY NIGHT**		

– Every nite's a Saturday night with you / I'll get to know your name along the way / Do you have to go now / Like a movie I've seen before / Twice a week / Another kind of sorrow / Sweet little rock'n'roller / Midnight cowboy / Another lonely weekend / I know when true love really passes by / Summer in the city.

Nov 76.	(7") **YOU'RE MORE THAN A NUMBER IN MY LITTLE RED BOOK. / DO YOU HAVE TO GO NOW**	5	
Mar 77.	(7") **I KNOW WHEN TRUE LOVE PASSES BY. / A GOOD SONG NEVER DIES**		
Jul 77.	(7") **IT LOOKS LIKE I'M THE CLOWN AGAIN. / I CAN'T BELIEVE IT'S OVER**		
Mar 78.	(7") **HONEY YOU'RE HEAVEN TO ME. / WHEN YA COMIN' HOME**		
Jul 78.	(7") **CLOSE GUARDED SECRET. / I CAN'T BELIEVE IT'S OVER**		
		Epic	Epic
Aug 79.	(7") **POUR YOUR LITTLE HEART OUT. / (version)**		
Apr 80.	(7") **I'M NOT THAT KIND OF GUY. / WHAT AM I DOING FALLING IN LOVE**		

— In the mid 80's, BEN E.KING returned as sidekick of JOHNNIE MOORE who had briefly departed. Others were mostly past members who permutated as DRIFTERS on their mainly cabaret tours.

– more compilations, others, etc. –

Note; Below all on 'Atlantic' until stated.

Aug 74.	(7") **SATURDAY NIGHT AT THE MOVIES. / TAKE ME WHERE THE MUSIC'S PLAYING**		
Nov 74.	(lp)(c) **THE DRIFTERS' STORY**		
Aug 75.	(7") **BABY WHAT I MEAN. / ANOTHER NIGHT WITH THE BOYS**		
Nov 75.	(7") **UNDER THE BOARDWALK. / ON BROADWAY**		
Nov 75.	(d-lp)(c) **24 ORIGINAL HITS**	2	
Jan 76.	(7") **YOU GOTTA PAY YOUR DUES. / BLACK SILK**		
Apr 80.	(12") **UNDER THE BOARDWALK. / AT THE CLUB**		
Aug 82.	(7") **YOU BETTER MOVE ON. / SAVE THE LAST DANCE FOR ME**		
Jul 87.	(lp)(c)(cd) **SAVE THE LAST DANCE FOR ME – THE DEFINITIVE COLLECTION**		
Aug 93.	(d-cd) **BOOGIE WOOGIE ROLL – GREATEST HITS 1953-58**		
Aug 93.	(d-cd) **GREATEST HITS & MORE 1959-1965**		
Sep 75.	Sounds Superb; (lp) **SAVE THE LAST DANCE FOR ME**		-
Apr 79.	Lightning; (7") **SAVE THE LAST DANCE FOR ME. / WHEN MY LITTLE GIRL IS SMILING**	69	-
Jul 79.	Old Gold; (7") **SAVE THE LAST DANCE FOR ME. / WHEN MY LITTLE GIRL IS SMILING**		-
Jul 82.	Old Gold; (7") **LIKE SISTER AND BROTHER. / THERE GOES MY FIRST LOVE**		-
Jul 84.	Old Gold; (7") **KISSING IN THE BACK ROW. / YOU'RE MORE THAN A NUMBER..**		-
May 82.	Audio Fidelity; (lp) **JUKE BOX GIANTS**		-
Aug 82.	Creole; (7") **SATURDAY NIGHT AT THE MOVIES. / UNDER THE BOARDWALK**		-

(12"+=) – Up on the roof / Save the last dance for me.

Apr 80.	Pickwick; (lp)(c) **SATURDAY NIGHT AT THE CLUB**		-
Sep 83.	Scoop; (7"ep)(c-ep) **6 TRACK HITS**		-

– Can I take you home little girl / Something tells me / Love games / Down on the beach tonight / Say goodbye to Angelina / Like sister and brother.

1984.	Astan; (lp) **THIS MAGIC MOMENT**		-
Nov 84.	Astan; (lp) **GREATEST HITS LIVE (live)**		-
Oct 85.	M.F.P.; (lp)(c) **GREATEST**		-
Apr 86	Showcase; (lp)(c) **LIVE AT HARVARD UNIVERSITY (live December 1972)** *(cd-iss.Nov92 on 'Fan Club')*		-
Jul 86.	Timeless; (c) **THEIR TOP HITS**		-
Oct 86.	Telstar; (lp)(c)(cd) **THE VERY BEST OF THE DRIFTERS**	24	-

– Saturday night at the movies / You're more than a number in my little red book / At the club / Can I take you home little girl / When my little girl is smiling / Like sister and brother / Down on the beach tonight / Love games / Hello happiness / Save the last dance for me / Come on over to my place / Kissin' in the back row of the movies / Spanish Harlem / Up on the roof / There goes my first love / Dance with me / Every night a Saturday night with you / Sweet Caroline / On Broadway / Under the boardwalk. *(re-iss.cd Jul93 on 'Rhino')*

Oct 90.	Telstar; (cd)(c)(lp) **THE BEST OF BEN E.KING & THE DRIFTERS**	15	-
Apr 87.	Magnum Force; (lp) **SOME KIND OF WONDERFUL**		-
Apr 87.	Object; (cd) **THE DRIFTERS**		-
1988.	Gusto; (cd) **18 GREATEST HITS**	-	-
Apr 88.	Diamond-CBS; (cd) **THE DRIFTERS**		-
Jun 88.	Spectrum; (cd) **ON BROADWAY**		-
Nov 88.	Castle; (d-lp)(c)(cd) **THE COLLECTION**		-
Mar 89.	Crusader; (lp) **SOME KIND OF WONDERFUL**		-
Mar 93.	Crusader; (cd)(c) **KISSIN' IN THE BACK ROW: THE 70'S CLASSICS**		-
Jul 94.	Success; (cd)(c) **GREATEST HITS**		-
Aug 94.	Dynamite; (cd) **DRIFTERS**		-
Dec 94.	Warners; (cd)(c) **UP ON THE ROOF, ON BROADWAY & UNDER THE BOARDWALK** *(re-iss.Sep95)*		
Feb 95.	B.A.M.; (cd) **PEARLS OF THE PAST**		-
Apr 95.	Prestige; (cd)(c) **GREATEST HITS**		-
Apr 95.	Wisepack; (d-cd) **THE ESSENTIAL COLLECTION**		-
May 95.	Rhino; (d-cd) **BOOGIE WOOGIE ROLL – GREATEST HITS 1953-1958**		
Jun 95.	Collection; (cd) **THE COLLECTION**		-
Jul 95.	Charly; (cd) **GREATEST HITS LIVE**		-
Jul 95.	Pickwick; (cd)(c) **KISSING IN THE BACK ROW**		-

DR. JOHN

Born: MALCOLM REBENNACK, 21 Nov'40, New Orleans, USA. He became noted session man in 1957, and soon branched out on his own that year. In 1960, he wrote a US Top 20 hit for LLOYD PRICE (Lady Luck). He became known as DR.JOHN but his session work was now on piano after one of his fingers was shot off in a bar room brawl. In 1967, he signed to 'Atco' and bemused the critics with superb experimental album 'GRIS GRIS'. In 1973, he tasted first fruits of success, when the Allen Toussaint produced album 'IN THE RIGHT PLACE' hit US Top 30. He was still out and about in the 90's with own typical album. • **Style:** R&B experimentation that returned always faithfully into Bayou type jazz piano music. • **Songwriters:** REBENNACK compositions except; IKO IKO (Dixie Cups) / THE WAY YOU DO THE THINGS YOU DO (Smokey Robinson) / YESTERDAY (Beatles) / IT'S ALL RIGHT WITH ME (Cole Porter) / BLUE SKIES (Irving Berlin) / etc. • **Trivia:** His organ playing featured heavily on ARETHA FRANKLIN's 1971 single 'Spanish Harlem'.

Recommended: GRIS GRIS (*6) / IN THE NIGHT (*5)

MAC REBENNACK

		not issued	Rex
Nov 57.	(7") **STORM WARNING. / FOOLISH LITTLE GIRL**	-	
1958.	(lp) **DR.JOHN AND HIS NEW ORLEANS CONG..**	-	
		not iss.	A.F.O.
1960.	(7") **THE POINT. / ONE NAUGHTY FLAT**	-	

He becomes session man in the early 60's. He also forms numerous bands, including ZU ZU. Around 1963 he adopts name of DR.JOHN THE NIGHT TRIPPER.

		not issued	A & M
1965.	(lp) **ZU ZU MAN** (demos ?)	-	

– Cat and mouse game / She's just a square / Bald headed / In the night / Helpin' hand / Zu zu man / Mean cheatin' woman / Woman's the root of all evil / Trader John / Shoo-ra / Tipatina / One night late. *(cd-iss.Apr87 on 'Topline')(re-iss.May89 on 'Thunderbolt')(re-iss.cd+c. Jul93 on 'Charly')*

DR.JOHN THE NIGHT TRIPPER

– vocals, piano with various sessioners

		Atlantic	Atco
1968	(7") **I WALK ON GUILDED SPLINTERS (part 2)**	-	
1968.	(lp) **GRIS GRIS**		

– Gris gris gumbo ya ya / Danse kalinda ba boom / Mama roux / Danse fambeaux / Croker court bullion / Jump steady / I walk on gilded splinters. *(re-iss.Aug87 on 'Sonet') (cd-iss.Nov93)*

Feb 69.	(7") **MAMA ROUX. / JUMP STEADY**	-	
Apr 69.	(7") **PATRIOTIC FLAG WAVER. / ('A'-long version)**	-	
Apr 69.	(lp) **BABYLON**		

– Babylon / Glowin' / Black Widow spider / Barefoot lady / Twilight zone / The patriotic flag-waver / The lonesome guitar strangler. *(cd-iss.Nov93)*

May 70.	(7") **WASH MAMA WASH. / LORD GAROO**		-
Jun 70.	(7") **WASH MAMA WASH. / MAMA ROUX**		-
Aug 70.	(lp) **REMEDIES**		

– Loop garoo / What goes around comes around / Wash, mama, wash / Chippy, chippy / Mardi Gras day / Angola anthem. *(cd-iss.Nov93)*

DR. JOHN

Nov 71.	(lp) **SUN, MOON AND HERBS**		Oct 71

– Black John the conqueror / Where ya at mule / Cranet crow / Familiar reality (opening) / Pots on fiyo / Zu Zu mama / Familiar reality (reprise). *(cd-iss.Nov93)*

Apr 72.	(7") **IKO IKO. / HUEY SMITH MEDLEY**		71
Jul 72.	(lp) **DR.JOHN'S GUMBO**		May 71

– Iko Iko / Blow wind blow / Big chief / The lock / Mess around / Let the good times roll / Junko partner / Stack-a-lee / Tipitina / Those lonely lonely nights / Huey Smith medley / High blood pressure / Don't you just know it / Well I'll be John Brown / Little Liza Jane. *(re-iss.Nov87 on 'Alligator')*

Jul 72.	(7") **WANG DANG DOODLE. / BIG CHIEF**		-
1972.	(7") **LET THE GOOD TIMES ROLL. / STACK-A-LEE**	-	
Mar 73.	(7") **RIGHT PLACE, WRONG TIME. / I BEEN HOODOOED**		9
Mar 73.	(lp)(c) **IN THE RIGHT PLACE**		24

– Right place, wrong time / Same old same old / Just the same / Qualified / Travelling mood / Peace brother peace / Life / Such a nite / Shoo fly marches on / I been hoodooed / Cold cold cold. *(cd-iss.Jun93)*

Jun 73.	(7") **SUCH A NITE. / LIFE**		-
Jun 73.	(7") **SUCH A NITE. / COLD COLD COLD**	-	42

— In Aug'73 he was credited on album TRIUMVIRATE with JOHN HAMMOND and MIKE BLOOMFIELD.

Mar 74.	(lp)(c) **DESITIVELY BONNAROO**		

– Quitters never win / Stealin' / What comes around / Me-You-Loneliness / Mosscocious / Rite away / Let's make a better world / Ru four real / Sing along song / Can't git enuff / Go tell the people / Desitively Bonnaroo. *(cd-iss.Nov93)*

Apr 74.	(7") **(EVERYBODY WANNA GET RICH) RITE AWAY. / MOS'SCOCIOUS**		92
Aug 74.	(7") **LET'S MAKE A BETTER WORLD. / ME, YOU =LONELINESS**		
		D.J.M.	Spring-board
Sep 75.	(lp)(c) **CUT ME WHILE I'M HOT (ANYTIME ANYPLACE)**		

– Woman is the root of all evil / Shoo ra / Tipatina / One night late / Cat and mouse game / She's just a square / Bald headed / In the night / Helpin' hand / Mean cheatin' woman. *(cd-iss.Feb95 on 'Thunderbolt')*

United Art United Art

Dec 76. (lp)(c) **HOLLYWOOD BE THY NAME**
– New island soiree / Reggae doctor / The way you do the things you do / Swanee river boogie / Yesterday / Babylon / Back by the river / Medley: It's all right with me – Blue skies – Will the circle be unbroken / Hollywood be thy name / I wanna rock. *(cd-iss.Oct89 on 'B.G.O.')*

In 1977, he joined The R.C.O. ALL STARS with LEVON HELM and others.

— now with **STEVE GADD** – drums / **WILL LEE** – bass / **RICHARD TEE** – keyboards / **JOHN TROPEA** – guitar / **HUGH McCRACKEN** – guitar / **ARTHUR JENKINS** – percussion

Horizon A & M

Oct 78. (lp)(c) **CITY LIGHTS**
– Dance the night away with you / Street side / Wild honey / Rain II snake eyes / Fire of love / Senata – he's a hero / City lights.

1979. (lp) **TANGO PALACE** -
– Keep the music simple / Discotherapy / Renegade / Fonky side / Bon steps rouler / Something you got / I thought I heard New Orleans say / Tango palace / Louisiana lullabye.

— Early in 1981, DR. JOHN w/ LUBBY TITUS & AL JARREAU released 'Warner Bros' single, SAILOR AND THE MERMAID. / ONE GOOD TURN.

Demon Clean Cuts

Sep 82. (7") **THE NEARNESS OF YOU. / MAC'S BOOGIE**

Oct 82. (lp) **DR.JOHN PLAYS MAC REBENNACK**
– Dorothy / Mac's boogie / Memories of Professor Longhair / The nearness of you / Delicado / Honeydripper / Big Mac / New island midnight / Saints / Pinetop. *(cd-iss. 1992+=)* Silent night / Dance a la Negras / Wade in the water.

Nov 83. (lp) **THE BRIGHTEST SMILE IN TOWN**
– Saddled the cow / Boxcar boogie / The brightest smile in town / Waiting for a train / Monkey puzzle / Average kind of guy / Pretty Libby / Marie Le Veau / Come rain or shine / Suite home New Orleans. *(cd-iss. 1992+=)* Didn't he ramble / Touro infirmary / Closer walk with thee.

Beggar's B. Streetwise

Mar 84. (7")(12") **JET SET. / ('A'dub version)**

Spindrift ?

Jun 84. (lp)(c) **SUCH A NIGHT – LIVE IN LONDON (live)**

Topline not issued

Jan 85. (lp)(c) **IN THE NIGHT** -
– Bald head / Bring your love / Did she mention my name / Go ahead / Grass is greener / I pulled the cover off you two lovers / In the night / Just like America / Tipitina / Zuzu man / Mean cheatin' woman / New Orleans / Shoo-ra / The time has come / Noe night late / The ear is on strike. *(re-iss.+cd.May89 on 'Thunderb.')*

Warners. Warners

Apr 89. (lp)(c)(cd) **IN A SENTIMENTAL MOOD**
– Makin' whoopee / Candy / Ac-cent-tchu-ste the positive / My buddy / In a sentimental mood / Black night / Don't let the Sun catch you cryin' / Love for sale / More than you know.

Jun 89. (7") **MAKIN' WHOOPEE. / MORE THAN YOU KNOW**
(12"+=) – In a sentimental mood.

(above 'A'side feature RICKIE LEE JONES)

Jul 92. (cd)(c)(d-lp) **GOIN' BACK TO NEW ORLEANS**
– Litanie des saints / Careless love / My red Indian / Milneburg joys / I thought I heard Buddy Bolden say / Basin Street blues / Didn't he ramble / Do you call that a buddy? / How come my dog don't bark (when you come around) / Good night, Irene / Fess up / Since I fell for you / I'll be glad when you're dead, you rascal you / Cabbage head / Goin' home tomorrow / Blue Monday / Scald dog medley – I can't go on – Goin' back to New Orleans.

— next with **HUGH McCRACKEN** – guitar, harmonica / **GEORG WADENIUS** – guitar / **DAVID BARARD** – bass / **FREDDIE STAHLE** – drums

GRP-MCA GRP-MCA

Apr 94. (cd)(c) **TELEVISION**
– Television / Lissen / Limbo / Witchy red / Only the shadow knows / Shut d. fonk up / Thank you / Spaceship relationship / Hold it / Money / U lie too much / Same day service.

Jul 95. (cd)(c) **AFTERGLOW**
– I know what I've got / Gee baby, ain't I good to you / I'm just a lucky so and so / Blue skies / So long / New York City blues / Tell me you'll wait for me / There must be a better world somewhere / I still think about you / I'm confessin' (that I love you).

– compilations, others, etc. –

1975. Rare Earth; (lp) **NIGHT TRIPPER AT HIS BEST** -
(UK-iss.Jul88 on 'Bellaphon')

Jan 77. Atlantic; (7") **RIGHT PLACE, WRONG TIME. / SUCH A NIGHT** -

1970's. Trip; (lp) **16 GREATEST HITS** -

1970's. Trip; (lp) **DR.JOHN SUPERPAH** -

1982 Fontana; (lp) **LOSER FOR YOU BABY (1960's material)**
– The time had come / Loser for you baby / The ear is on strike / A little closer to my home / I pulled a cover off you two lovers / New Orleans / Go ahead on / Just like a mirror / Bring your love / Bald head. *(re-iss.+cd.Nov88 on 'Thunderbolt', w/2 extra tracks)*

Feb 83. Black LIon; (d-lp) **TAKE ME BACK TO NEW ORLEANS (w / "CHRIS BARBER")**

May 89. Timeless/ US= Great Southern; (lp)(c)(cd) **MARDI GRAS AT THE MARQUEE (live) (w / "CHRIS BARBER")** Jan 91
(US-title 'ON A MARDI GRAS DAY')

Jul 84. Edsel/ US= Atco; (lp) **I BEEN HOODOOED** ('73+'74)

Feb 86. Demon; (d-c) **MAC REBENNACK / BRIGHTEST SMILE IN TOWN** -

Feb 86. Milestone; (lp) **ROADHOUSE SYMPHONY (w / "HANK CRAWFORD")**
– Roadhouse symphony / Track magick / Jubilee / Say it isn't so / Time is our side / Precious Lord / Sugar ditch.

Jun 88. Warners; (cd) **THE ULTIMATE DR.JOHN**

Feb 94. Rhino; (d-cd) **MOS'SCOCIOUS – THE DR.JOHN ANTHOLOGY**
– Bad neighborhood (RONNIE & DELINQUENTS) / Morgus The Magnificent (MORGUS & THE 3 GHOULS) / Storm warning (MAC REBENNACK) / Sahara (MAC REBENNACK & HIS ORCHESTRA) / Down the road (ROLAND STONE) / Gris-gris gumbo ya ya / Mama Roux / Jump sturdy / I walk on guilded splinters / Black widow spider / Loop garoo / Wash, mama, wash / Mardi Gras day / Familiar reality – opening / Zu zu mamou / Mess around / Somebody changed the lock / / Iko iko / Junko partner / Tipitina / Huey Smith medley; a) High blood pressure, b) Don't you just know it, c) Well I'll be John Brown / Right place wrong time / Traveling mood / Life / Such a night / I been hoodood / Cold cold cold / Quitters never win / What comes around (goes around) / Mos'scocious / Let's make a better world / Back by the river / I wanna rock / Memories of Prof. Longhair / Honey dripper / Pretty Libby / Makin' whoopee! / Accentuate the positive / More than you know.

May 95. Rhino; (cd) **THE VERY BEST OF DR.JOHN**

DR. ROBERT (see under ⇒ BLOW MONKEYS)

DRUGSTORE

Formed: London-based, England ...1992 by Brazilian born ISOBEL MONTEIRO and L.A. born MIKE CHYLINSKI. They were joined a year later by DARREN ROBINSON. Two singles on 'Honey' 1 for 'Rough Trade', were followed by a signing for 'Go! Discs' in 1994. Eponymous debut in Spring of '95, just missed out on a UK Top 30 placing. • **Style:** Smokey-voxed female fronted alternative rock outfit. MAZZY STAR like. • **Songwriters:** MONTEIRO main writer/ some with group except SHE DON'T USE JELLY (Flaming Lips) / TEENAGE KICKS (Undertones).

Recommended: DRUGSTORE (*6)

ISOBEL MONTEIRO – vocals, bass/ **DARON ROBINSON** – guitar / **MIKE CHYLINSKI** – drums

Honey not issued

1994. (7") **ALIVE. /** -

Honey – Go! Discs Go! Discs

Sep 94. (7") **STARCROSSED. / ACCELERATE** -
(10"+=)(cd-s+=) – Fader.

Dec 94. (7") **NECTARINE. / ANAESTHASIA** -
(10"+=)(cd-s+=) – She don't use jelly.

Mar 95. (7") **SOLITARY PARTY GROOVER. / ELECTRIC LIGHT / STARCROSSED (demo)**
(12")(cd-s) – (first 2 tracks) / Get inside my head / Spacegirl.

Apr 95. (cd)(c)(lp) **DRUGSTORE** 31
– Speaker 12 / Favourite sinner / Alive / Solitary party groover / If / Devil / Saturday sunset / Fader / Super glider / Baby astrolab / Gravity / Nectarine / Accelerate. (lp w/free 7")(cd w/free cd-s) SOLITARY PARTY GROOVER (acoustic). / BABY ASTROLAB (acoustic)

May 95. (7") **FADER. / REBOUND / UNDER THE MOON** 72
(12")(cd-s) – ('A'side) / French devil / Slide / Sugar sugar.

Oct 95. (7"ep)(cd-ep) **INJECTION / HEART OF HONEY. / SHE DON'T USE JELLY (electric version) / GRAVITY (Terry Edwards mix)**

Bill DRUMMOND (see under ⇒ KLF)

DUBSTAR

Formed: Sheffield, England ...1994 by ex-JOANS members; WILKIE and HILLIER, who soon met with SARAH BLACKWOOD. With help from manager Graham Robinson, they secured a deal with Parlophone outlet 'Food' (home to BLUR). In June 1995, they had debut chart appearance with 'STARS' and grew to be an alternative pop favourite of '95. • Style: Dreamy experimental Euro-pop lying somewhere between SAINT ETIENNE and The PET SHOP BOYS. • Songwriters: Group. • Trivia: Produced by STEPHEN HAGUE.

Recommended: DISGRACEFUL (*7)

SARAH BLACKWOOD – vocals / **CHRIS WILKIE** – guitar / **STEVE HILLIER** – programmer

Food ???

Jun 95. (c-s) **STARS / ('A'mixes)** 40

Sep 95. (c-s)(cd-s)(12") **ANYWHERE / DON'T BLAME ME** 37

Oct 95. (cd)(c)(lp) **DISGRACEFUL** 33
– Stars / Anywhere / Just a girl she said / Elevator song / The day I see you again / Week in week out / Not so manic now / opdorian / Not once not ever / St. Swithin's Day / Disgraceful.

Dec 95. (c-s) **NOT SO MANIC NOW / IF IT ISN'T YOU** 18
(cd-s+=) – Song No.9 / Certain sadness.

Anne DUDLEY & Jaz COLEMAN (see under ⇒ ART OF NOISE)

DUET EMMO (see under ⇒ WIRE)

DUKES OF STRATOSPHEAR (see under ⇒ XTC)

SLY DUNBAR (see under ⇒ SLY & ROBBIE)

Francis DUNNERY (see under ⇒ IT BITES)

DURAN DURAN

Formed: Birmingham, England ... 1978 by NICK RHODES, JOHN TAYLOR, STEPHEN DUFFY and clarinetist SIMON COLLEY. They took group name from a character in the 60's sci-fi/fantasy film 'Barbarella'. In 1979, ANDY WICKETT and ROGER TAYLOR replaced DUFFY and COLLEY respectively (the former going on to have successful pop solo career). Soon a new guitarist was added to take the place of brief newcomer JOHN CURTIS. In April 1980, they recruited new vocalist SIMON LE BON to complete the line-up, after WICKETT had left late 1979. Their first UK tour supporting HAZEL O'CONNOR, was rewarded late 1980 when 'E.M.I.' signed them up. Their debut 45 in 1981, broke them into the UK Top 20, where they became resident throughout the 80's and 90's. • **Style:** Latched onto the 'new romantic' boom period in the early 80's. Their electronic dance sound and photogenic looks helped sell to a new video age audience. Progressed to a more adult rock based synth sound with each new album release. • **Songwriters:** LE BON – lyrics / RHODES – music. Covered; MAKE ME SMILE (Steve Harley & Cockney Rebel) / WHITE LINES (Grandmaster Flash) / I WANNA TAKE YOU HIGHER (Sly & The Family Stone) / PERFECT DAY (Lou Reed) / WATCHING THE DETECTIVES (Elvis Costello) / LAY LADY LAY (Bob Dylan) / 911 IS A JOKE (Public Enemy) / SUCCESS (Iggy Pop) / CRYSTAL SHIP (Doors) / BALL OF CONFUSION (Temptations) / THANK YOU (Led Zeppelin). POWER STATION covered GET IT ON (T.Rex). • **Trivia:** SIMON LE BON married top-model Yasmin Parvanah on 27 Dec'85. In mid-84, other two ROGER and NICK had also married cosmopolitan models.

Recommended: DECADE (*8).

(1980) **SIMON LE BON** (b.27 Oct'58, Bushley, Hertfordshire, England) – vocals / **ANDY TAYLOR** (b.16 Feb'61, Newcastle, England) – guitar / **NICK RHODES** (b. NICHOLAS BATES, 8 Jun'62) – keyboards / **JOHN TAYLOR** (b.20 Jul'60, Solihull, England) – bass / **ROGER TAYLOR** (b.26 Apr'60) – drums.

E.M.I. / Harvest

Jan 81. (7") **PLANET EARTH. / LATE BAR** [12] [ ]
(12"+=) – Planet earth (night version). *(re-iss.Aug83 7+12")*

Apr 81. (7")(12") **CARELESS MEMORIES. / KHANDA** [37] [ ]
(re-iss.Aug83 7"/12" (+=) – Fame.

Jun 81. (lp)(c) **DURAN DURAN** [3] [10] Feb 83
– Girls on film / Planet Earth / Anyone out there / To the shore / Careless memories / (Waiting for the) Night boat / Sound of thunder / Friends of mine / Tel Aviv. *(re-iss.Aug83) (cd-iss.Oct84) (re-iss.Sep87 on 'Fame') (re-iss.d-cd Jan94)*

Jul 81. (7") **GIRLS ON FILM. / FASTER THAN LIGHT** [5] [ ]
(12"+=) – ('A' instrumental). *(re-iss.Aug83, 7"/12")*

Nov 81. (7") **MY OWN WAY. / LIKE AN ANGEL** [14] [ ]
(12"+=) – ('A'night version) *(re-iss.Aug83, 7"/12")*

May 82. (7")(12") **HUNGRY LIKE THE WOLF. / CARELESS MEMORIES (live)** [5] [3] Jan 83
(re-iss.Aug83, 7"/12")

E.M.I. / Capitol

May 82. (lp)(c) **RIO** [2] [6] Jan 83
– Rio / My own way / Lonely in your nightmare / Hungry like the wolf / Hold back the rain / New religion / Last chance on the stairway / Save a prayer / The chauffeur. *(re-iss.Aug83) (cd-iss.Jan84) (re-iss.+cd.Mar90)(re-iss.cd+c Sep93 on 'Parlophone')*

Aug 82. (7")(12") **SAVE A PRAYER. / HOLD BACK THE RAIN (remix)** [2] [16] Feb 85
(re-iss.Aug83, 7+12")

Sep 82. (m-lp; on 'Harvest-US) **CARNIVAL** [-] [98]
– My own way / Hold back the rain / Girls on film / Hungry like the wolf.

Nov 82. (7") **RIO. / THE CHAUFFEUR (BLUE SILVER)** [9] [14] Mar 83
(12") – ('A'side) / Rio / (pt.2) / My own way. *(re-iss.Aug83 7+12")*

Mar 83. (7")(12") **IS THERE SOMETHING I SHOULD KNOW. / FAITH IN THIS COLOUR** [1] [4] May 83
(re-iss.Aug83 7"/12")

Oct 83. (7") **UNION OF THE SNAKE. / SECRET OKTOBER** [3] [3]
(12"+=) – ('A' monkey remix).

Nov 83. (lp)(c) **SEVEN AND THE RAGGED TIGER** [1] [8]
– The reflex / New Moon on Monday / (I'm looking for) Cracks in the pavement / I take the dice / Of crime and passion / Union of the snake / Shadows on your side / Tiger tiger / The seventh stranger. *(cd-iss.Mar84) (re-iss.+cd.Aug88 on 'Fame') (re-iss.cd+c Sep93)*

Jan 84. (7")(12") **NEW MOON ON MONDAY. / TIGER TIGER** [9] [10]

Apr 84. (7")(12")(12"pic-d) **THE REFLEX. / MAKE ME SMILE (COME UP AND SEE ME) (live)** [1] [1]

Parlophone / Capitol

Oct 84. (7")(12") **THE WILD BOYS. / (I'M LOOKING FOR) CRACKS IN THE PAVEMENT** [2] [2]

Nov 84. (lp)(c)(cd) **ARENA (live)** [6] [4]
– Is there something I should know / Hungry like the wolf / New religion / Save a prayer / The wild boys / The seventh stranger / The chauffeur / Union of the snake / Planet Earth / Careless memories. *(re-iss.+cd.Oct89 on 'Fame')*

May 85. (7")(12")(7"white) **A VIEW TO A KILL. / ('A' instrumental)** [2] [1]

— After taking time off for own solo projects (see below) only 3 returned. **SIMON, NICK** and **JOHN.** (ANDY went solo). (ROGER quits music)

E.M.I. / Capitol

Oct 86. (7")(12") **NOTORIOUS. / WINTER MARCHES ON** [7] [2]
(c-s+=) – ('A' extra mix).

Nov 86. (lp)(c)(cd) **NOTORIOUS** [16] [12]
– Notorious / American science / Skin trade / A matter of feeling / Hold me / Vertigo (do the demolition) / So misled / Meet el Presidente / Winter marches on / Proposition.

Feb 87. (7")(12")(c-s) **SKIN TRADE. / WE NEED YOU** [22] [39]

Apr 87. (7")(12") **MEET EL PRESIDENTE. / VERTIGO (DO THE DEMOLITION)** [24] [70]
(cd-s+=) – Meet el Beat.

— added **WARREN CUCCURULLO** – guitar (ex-FRANK ZAPPA, ex-MISSING PERSONS) / **STEVE FERRONE** – drums (ex-BRIAN AUGER, ex-AVERAGE WHITE BAND) (both on last lp

Sep 88. (7") **I DON'T WANT YOUR LOVE. / ('A' instrumental)** [14] [4]
(12"+=)(cd-s+=) – ('A'version).

Oct 88. (lp)(c)(cd) **BIG THING** [15] [24]
– Big thing / I don't want your love / All she wants is / Too late Marlene / Drug (it's just a state of mind) / Do you believe in shame? / Palomino / Interlude one / Land / Flute interlude / The edge of America / Lake shore driving. *(re-iss.+cd.Mar90)(re-iss.cd+c Sep93 on 'Parlophone')*

Dec 88. (7") **ALL SHE WANTS IS. / I BELIEVE** [ ] [22]
(12"+=) – ('A'-US mix) / All you need to know.
(cd-s+=) – Skin trade.

Apr 89. (7")(7"pic-d) **DO YOU BELIEVE IN SHAME?. / KRUSH BROTHERS (l.s.d. mix)** [30] [72]
(12"+=) – Palomino (edit) / Drugs (it's just a state of mind).
(10"+=) – Notorious (live).
(3"cd-s+=) – God.

Nov 89. (lp)(c)(cd) **DECADE** [5] [67]
– Planet Earth / Girls on film / Hungry like the wolf / Rio / Save a prayer / Is there something I should know / Union of the snake / The reflex / Wild boys / A view to a kill / Notorious / Skin trade / I don't want your love / All she wants is.

Dec 89. (7") **BURNING THE GROUND. / DECADENCE** [31] [ ]
(12"+=)(cd-s+=) – ('B' extended).

— **STERLING CAMPBELL** – drums repl. FERRONE

Parlophone / Capitol

Jul 90. (7") **VIOLENCE OF SUMMER (LOVE' TAKING OVER). / ('A'mix)** [20] [64]
(12"+=) – ('A'extended).
(cd-s+=) – Throb.

Aug 90. (cd)(c)(lp) **LIBERTY** [8] [46]
– Violence of summer (love's taking over) / Liberty / Hothead / Serious / All along the water / My Antartica / Read my lips / First impression / Can you deal with it / Venice drowning / Downtown. *(re-iss.cd+cSep93)*

Nov 90. (7")(c-s) **SERIOUS. / YOU BAD AZIZI** [48] [ ]
(12"+=)(cd-s+=) – Water babies.

Jan 93. (7")(c-s)(7"pic-d) **ORDINARY WORLD. / MY ANTARTICA** [6] [3]
(cd-s+=) – Save a prayer / Skin trade.
(cd-s) – ('A'side) / The reflex / Hungry like the wolf / Girls on film.

Feb 93. (cd)(c)(lp) **DURAN DURAN** [4] [7]
– Too much / Information / Ordinary world / Love voodoo / Drowning man / Shotgun / Come undone / Breath after breath / UMF / Home of the above / Femme fatale / Shelter / To whom it may concern.

Mar 93. (7")(c-s) **COME UNDONE. / ORDINARY WORLD (acoustic)** [13] [7]
(cd-s+=) – ('A'mixes).
(cd-s) – ('A'side) / ('A'version) / Rio / Is there something I should know / A view to a kill.

Aug 93. (c-s)(12") **TOO MUCH INFORMATION. / COME UNDONE (live)** [35] [45]
(12"+=) – Come undone (12"mix Coming together) / Notorious (live).
(cd-s) – ('A'side) / Drowning man.

Mar 95. (7")(c-s) **PERFECT DAY. / FEMME FATALE (alt.mix)** [28] [ ]
(cd-s+=) – Make me smile (come up and see me) / Perfect day (acoustic).
(cd-s) – ('A'side) / Love voodoo / Needle and the damage done / 911 is a joke (alternative mix).

Mar 95. (cd)(c) **THANK YOU** [12] [19]
– White lines / I wanna take you higher / Perfect day / Watching the detectives / Lay lady lay / 911 is a joke / Success / Crystal ship / Ball of confusion / Thank you / Drive by / I wanna take you higher again.

below actually featured GRANDMASTER FLASH

Jun 95. (c-s) **WHITE LINES (DON'T DO IT) / SAVE A PRAYER / NONE OF THE ABOVE (Drizabone mix)** [17] [ ]
(cd-s+=) – Ordinary world (acoustic).
(12") – ('A'side) / ('A'-Junior Vasquez mix) / ('A'-Oakland fonk mix) / ('A'-70's club mix).

The POWER STATION

(ANDY and JOHN TAYLOR) / **ROBERT PALMER** – vocals (solo artist see under own listing) **/ TONY THOMPSON** – drums (ex-CHIC)

E.M.I. / Capitol

Mar 85. (7")(7"pic-d) **SOME LIKE IT HOT. / THE HEAT IS ON** [14] [6]
(12"+=)(12"pic-d+=) – ('A'extended).

Apr 85. (lp)(c) **THE POWER STATION** [12] [6]
– Some like it hot / Murderess / Lonely tonight / Communication / Get it on (bang a gong) / Go to zero / Harvest for the world / Still in your heart. *(re-iss.cd+c Aug93 on 'Parlophone')*

May 85. (7")(12") **GET IT ON. / GO TO ZERO** [22] [9]

Nov 85. (7")(12") **COMMUNICATION. / MURDERESS** [75] [34]

— **MICHAEL DES BARNES** – vocals repl.PALMER on tour.

JOHN TAYLOR

Mar 86. (7")(12") **I DO WHAT I DO (theme from 9 1/2 weeks). / JAZZ** [42] [23]

ARCADIA

(**SIMON LE BON** – vocals / **NICK RHODES** – keyboards / **ROGER TAYLOR** – drums) with session people

Oct 85. (7") **ELECTION DAY. / SHE'S MOODY AND SHE'S MEAN AND SHE'S RESTLESS** [7] [6]
(12"+=) – (2 – 'A' mixes).

Dec 85. (lp)(c)(cd) **SO RED THE ROSE** [30] [23]
– Election day / Keep me in the dark / Goodbye is forever / The flame / Missing / Rose Arcana / The promise / El Diablo / Lady Ice. *(re-iss.cd+c Aug93 on 'Parlophone')*

Dec 85. (7") **GOODBYE IS FOREVER. / MISSING** - 33
Feb 86. (7") **THE PROMISE. / ROSE ARCANE** 37
(12"+=) – ('A' extended).
Jul 86. (7") **THE FLAME. / FLAME AGAIN** 58
(12"+=) – Election day.

DURUTTI COLUMN

Formed: Manchester, England . . . early 1978 by VINI REILLY, CHRIS JOYCE and DAVE ROWBOTHAM. That year they signed to Tony Wilson's indie label 'Factory', but split mid-79 leaving VINI REILLY to pick up pieces. They/he released many fine lp's throughout the 80's, starting with Martin Hannett produced debut 'THE RETURN OF . . . '. • **Style:** Picturesque and dreamy jazzy guitar-based outfit, led by skinny VINI, accompanied by now stalwart percussion man BRUCE MITCHELL. • **Songwriters:** All composed by REILLY, except cover; I GET ALONG WITHOUT YOU VERY WELL (Hoagy Carmichael). • **Trivia:** The name stemmed from a political cartoon strip, once used in the 60's by the SI in Strasbourg. • **Miscellaneous:** On 8 Nov'91, original member DAVE ROWBOTHAM was axed to death by an as yet undiscovered murderer.

Recommended: THE RETURN OF (*9) / VALUABLE PASSAGES (*8) / L.C. (*7) / DOMO ARIGATO (*7) / SEX AND DEATH (*7).

VINI REILLY (b. Aug'53) – guitar (ex-NOSEBLEEDS, ex-V2) / **DAVE ROWBOTHAM** – guitar / **CHRIS JOYCE** – drums / **BRUCE MITCHELL** – percussion / also **TONY BOWERS** – bass / **PHIL RAINFORD** – vocals (left Jul78)
recorded for Various Artists EP – A FACTORY SAMPLER. Split mid'79, DAVE, CHRIS and TONY joined The MOTHMEN. **VINI REILLY** now brought in **MARTIN HANNETT** – switches, producer (ex-INVISIBLE GIRLS (JOHN COOPER CLARKE) with **PETER CROOKS** – bass / **TOBY** (b.PHILIP TOMANOV) – drums / **GAMMER** – melody

Factory / not issued

Feb 80. (lp) **THE RETURN OF THE DURUTTI COLUMN** -
– Sketch for Summer / Requiem for a father / Katherine / Conduct / Beginning / Jazz / Sketch for winter / Collette / In "D". *(c-iss.Nov84)(re-iss.Jul80 with free testcard flexi by MARTIN HANNETT.*
FIRST ASPECT OF THE SAME THING. / SECOND ASPECT OF THE SAME THING

— **VINI** on his own, featured **PHIL RAYNHAM** – vocals

Factory Ben. / not issued

Nov 80. (12") **LIPS THAT WOULD KISS (FORM PRAYERS TO BROKEN STONE). / MADELEINE** -
(cd-s.iss.Mar91)
Next single on Italian label 'Sordid Sentimental')
Mar 81. (7") **ENIGMA. / DANNY** - -

— now just a duo when **VINI** – guitars, now on extra vocals & keyboards / added **BRUCE MITCHELL** – percussion (ex-ALBERTOS Y LOST TRIOS PARANOIAS)

Factory / not issued

Sep 81. (lp) **LC** -
– Sketch for dawn 1 / ~Portrait for Frazier / Jacqueline / Messidor / Sketch for dawn 2 / Never known / The act committed / Detail for Paul / The missing boy / The sweet cheat gone. *(c-iss.Nov84)*

— VINI completely solo.

Factory Ben. / not issued

1982. (7") **FOR PATTI. / WEARINESS AND FEVER** -
Mar 82. (12"ep) **DEUX TRIANGLES**
– Favourite painting / Zinni / Piece for out of tune grand piano. *(re-iss.Aug87 on 'Crepescule')*

— added guests **LINDSAY WILSON** – vocals / **MAUNAGH FLEMING** – cor anglais

Factory / not issued

Aug 82. (7") **I GET ALONG WITHOUT YOU VERY WELL. / PRAYER**

— **VINI** now augmented by **MERVYN FLETCHER** – saxophone / **TONY BOWERS** – bass / **CHRIS JOYCE** – drums / **TIM KELLETT** – trumpet (all ex-MOTHMEN)

Aug 83. (lp)(c) **ANOTHER SETTING** -
– Prayer / Bordeaux / The beggar / The response / For a western / Francesca / Smile in the crowd / Dream of a child / Spent time / You've heard it before / Second family.

— **VINI** retained **MERVYN** and **TIM.**(TONY & CHRIS later joined SIMPLY RED with TIM). **BRUCE MITCHELL** rejoined (he had always been part of live set-up) / **MAUNAGH FLEMING** rejoined with new guests **CAROLINE LAVELLE** – cello / **RICHARD HENRY** – trombone / **BLAINE REININGER** – viola/violin (of TUXEDO MOON)

Dec 84. (lp)(c) **WITHOUT MERCY** -
– Face 1 / Face 2. *(re-iss.Nov86)*

— Now just basically **VINI** with **BRUCE** with old friends augmenting

Mar 85. (12"ep) **SAY WHAT YOU MEAN, MEAN WHAT YOU SAY**
– Goodbye / The room / E.E. / A little mercy / Silence / Hello.

Factory Ben. / not issued

Mar 86. (7") **TOMORROW. / TOMORROW (live)**
(12"+=) – All that love and maths can do.
Mar 86. (lp)(c)(cd) **CIRCUSES AND BREAD**
– Pauline / Tomorrow / Dance 2 / For Hilary / Street fight / Royal infirmary / Black horses / Dance 1 / Blind elevator girl – Osaka. *(cd+=) – (last 45). (cd-iss.Nov93 on 'Crepescule')*

— **VINI** with **MITCHELL, KELLETT, JOHN METCALFE**

Factory / not issued

Jul 86. (vid-cd) **DOMO ARIGATO (live Japan)**
– Sketch for Summer / Mercy theme / Sketch for dawn / E.E. / Little mercy / Jacqueline / Dream of a child / Mercy dance / The room / Blind elevator girl / Tomorrow / Belgian friends / Missing boy / Self-portrait / (audience noise).

(next single on Italian label 'Materoli Sonori')
Oct 86. (12") **GREETINGS THREE** - -
– Florence sunset / All that love and maths can do / San Giovanni dawn / For friends in Italy.

— now credited with **DEBI DIAMOND** – vocals

Factory / not issued

Aug 87. (12"ep) **THE CITY OF OUR LADY**
– Our lady of the angels / White rabbit* / Coctos con guantes. *(re-cd-ep Dec87.* When the world repl. *)

— **VINI** and **BRUCE** were joined by guests **TIM KELLETT** (of SIMPLY RED) (1 track.) / **STANTON MIRANDA** – vocals (solo artist – 2 tracks.) **POL** – vocals (3 tracks.) / **STEPHEN STREET** – bass (1 track.) **JOHN METCALFE** – viola (1 track.) / **ROB GREY** – mouth organ

Nov 87. (lp)(c)(cd)(dat) **THE GUITAR AND OTHER MACHINES**
– When the world / Arpeggiator / What is it to me (woman) / U.S.P. / Red shoes / Jongleur grey / Bordeaux sequence / Miss Haynes / Don't think you're funny / English tradition landscape / Pol in 'B'.
Dec 87. (7"flexi) **THE GUITAR AND OTHER MARKETING DEVICES** -
– Jangular grey / Bordeaux sequence / English tradition landscape / U.S.P.

— added **ROBERT NEWTON** plus **DV8 PHYSICAL THEATRE**

Factory / Factory

Apr 88. (vid-s) **WHEN THE WORLD (soundtrack) / WHEN THE WORLD (lp) / FINAL CUT / WHEN THE WORLD (video)**
Dec 88. (3"cd-ep) **WOMAD LIVE (live)** -
– Otis / English landscape tradition / Finding the sea / Bordeaux.
(VINI joined MORRISSEY for a period in 1988)
Mar 89. (lp)(c)(cd)(dat) **VINI REILLY**
– Homage to Catalonea / Opera II / People's pleasure park / Pol in G / Love no more / Opera I / Finding the sea / Otis / They work every day / Requiem again / My country.
Included sampled voices of OTIS REDDING, ANNIE LENNOX and TRACY CHAPMAN. **VINI** added **PAUL MILLER**
Dec 90. (cd)(c)(lp) **OBEY THE TIME**
– Vino della easa Bianco / Fridays / Home / Art and freight / Spanish reggae / Neon / The warmest rain / Contra-indictions / Vino della casa rossa.
Feb 91. (12"ep)(cd-ep) **THE TOGETHER MIX. / CONTRA DICTIONS (version) / FRIDAYS (up-person mix)** -

Materiali Sonori / not issued

Jun 91. (cd)(lp) **DRY** - Italy

— **VINI, BRUCE** w / guests **PETER HOOK** – bass + **MARTIN JACKSON** – keyboards

Factory too / not issued

Nov 94. (cd) **SEX AND DEATH**
– Anthony / The rest of my life / For Colette / The next time / Beautiful lies / My irasable friend / Believe in me / Fermina / Where I should be / Fado / Madre mio / Blue period.

– compilations, imports, etc. –

1983. V.U.; (lp) **LIVE AT THE VENUE (live VINI & BRUCE)**
– Sketch for summer / Conduct / Never known / Jacqueline / Party / etc.
Dec 85. Fundacao Atlantica Portugal; (lp) **AMIGOS EM PORTUGAL / DEDICATIONS FOR JACQUELINE** - -
– Friends in Portugal / Small girl by a pool / Crumpled dress / Sara and Tristana / Nighttime Estoril / Lisbon / To end with / Wheels turning / Favourite descending intervals / Saudade / Games of rhythm / Lies of mercy.
Dec 86. Factory; (lp)(cd)(d-c) **VALUABLE PASSAGES**
– Sketch for summer / Conduct / Sketch for winter / Lips that would kiss / Belgian friends / Danny / Piece for out-of-tune piano / Never know / Jacqueline / Missing boy / Prayer / Spent time / Without mercy stanzas 2-8 & 12-15 / Room / Blind elevator girl / Tomorrow / LFO MOD.
Mar 88. Factory; (4xcd-box) **THE DURUTTI COLUMN – THE FIRST FOUR ALBUMS** -
Jan 87. Materali Senori Italy; (12") **GREETINGS THREE** - -
(re-iss. of "Deux Triangles")
Nov 87. R.O.I.R.; (c) **LIVE AT THE BOTTOM LINE (live)**
(re-iss.cd/c.May93 & Feb95)
Dec 89. Spora; (cd) **THE SPRADIC RECORDINGS (ltd.)** -

Ian DURY

Born: 12 May'42, Upminster, Essex, England. At age 7 he became partially crippled from contracting polio. In 1970, he was employed as a teacher / lecturer at Canterbury College. The following year, he formed KILBURN & THE HIGH ROADS, who embarked on pub/college circuit in London. After 1 album in the mid-70's and many line-up changes, they disbanded, leaving DURY and manager DAVE ROBINSON to create solo deal for DURY. Signing to Jake Riviera's new indie label 'Stiff', he soon raced up album charts in 1977 with the new wave favourite 'NEW BOOTS AND PANTIES!'. • **Style:** DURY's articulate patter and intelligent lyrics, fused well with funky/jerky group backing, that diversed between rock'n'roll and disco. He also developed many areas of Cockney rhyme-slang into rude but clever lyrics. • **Songwriters:** DURY – words / JANKEL – music, until his departure from The BLOCKHEADS. • **Trivia:** After he semi-retired in the mid-80's, he started acting career in films:- NUMBER ONE (1985) / PIRATES (1986) / HEARTS OF FIRE (1987), and TV plays:- KING OF THE GHETTOS (1986) / TALK OF THE DEVIL (1986) / NIGHT MOVES (1987). His other work on TV was mainly on commercials, etc.

Recommended: NEW BOOTS AND PANTIES (*8) / SEX AND DRUGS AND ROCK AND ROLL (*7).

KILBURN & THE HIGH ROADS

IAN DURY – vocals / **KEITH LUCAS** – guitar / **DAVEY PAYNE** – sax / **CHARLIE SINCLAIR** – bass repl. HUMPHREY OCEAN who had repl. CHARLIE HART / **LOUIS LAROSE** then **GEORGE BUTLER** – drums

Early 1974, recorded lp for 'Raft', which was shelved after 'Warners' took over label. It was later issued by them in Oct'78 as 'WOTABUNCH', after DURY was top of the charts.

— (mid-74) **DAVID ROHOMAN** – drums repl. BUTLER / **ROD MELVIN** – piano repl. HARDY

Dawn-Pye not issued

Nov 74. (7") **ROUGH KIDS. / BILLY BENTLEY** -

Feb 75. (7") **CRIPPLED WITH NERVES. / HUFFETY PUFF** -

Jun 75. (lp) **HANDSOME** -
– The roadette song / Pam's mood / Crippled with nerves / Broken skin / Upminster kid / Patience / Father / Thank you mum / Rough kids / The badger and the rabbit / The mumble rumble and the cocktail rock / The call up. *(re-iss.+c.Nov85 on 'Flashback')*

— Disbanded mid-75, although IAN gigged at times with a new line-up as IAN DURY & THE KILBURNS. KEITH LUCAS was later to become NICK CASH and form 999.

There were also other KILBURN material re-released after DURY's success.

IAN DURY

– vocals solo with **CHAZ JANKEL** – guitar, keys (ex-BYZANTIUM) plus session men that became The BLOCKHEADS (see below)

Stiff Stiff

Aug 77. (7")(7"orange) **SEX AND DRUGS AND ROCK AND ROLL. / RAZZLE IN MY POCKET** -

Sep 77. (lp)(c)(gold-lp) **NEW BOOTS AND PANTIES** 5 Apr 78
– Sweet Gene Vincent / ake up and make love with me / I'm partial to your abracadabra / My old man / Billericay Dickie / Clevor Trever / If I was with a woman / Plainstow Patricia / Blockheads / Blackmail man. *(re-iss.+cd.Sep86 on 'Demon')* (cd+=) – (interview). *(re-iss.cd May95 on 'Disky')*

Nov 77. (7") **SWEET GENE VINCENT. / YOU'RE MORE THAN FAIR** -

IAN DURY AND THE BLOCKHEADS

with **JANKEL** plus **NORMAN WATT-ROY** – bass (ex-LOVING AWARENESS, ex-GLENCOE) / **CHARLEY CHARLES** – drums (ex-LOVING AWARENESS, ex-GLENCOE) / **MICKEY GALLAGHER** – keyboards (ex-LOVING AWARENESS, ex-FRAMPTON'S CAMEL) / **JOHN TURNBULL** – guitar (ex-LOVING AWARENESS) / **DAVEY PAYNE** – saxophone (ex-WRECKLESS ERIC)

Apr 78. (7")(12") **WHAT A WASTE. / WAKE UP AND MAKE LOVE WITH ME** 11
(re-iss. 1981)

Nov 78. (7") **HIT ME WITH YOUR RHYTHM STICK. (as "Ian & THE BLOCKHEADS" one-off) / THERE AIN'T HALF BEEN SOME CLEVER BASTARDS** 1

May 79. (lp)(c) **DO IT YOURSELF** 2 Jul 79
– Inbetweenies / Quiet / Don't ask me / Sink my boats / Waiting for your taxi / This is what we find / Uneasy sunny hotsy totsy / Mischief / Dance of the screamers / Lullaby for Francies. *(re-iss.+cd.Feb90 on 'Demon') (re-iss.cd May95 on 'Disky')*

Jul 79. (7")(12") **REASONS TO CHEERFUL (pt.3). / COMMON AS MUCK** 3

Aug 80. (7")(12") **I WANT TO BE STRAIGHT. / THAT'S NOT ALL HE WANTS** 22

— **WILKO JOHNSON** – guitar (ex-DR. FEELGOOD, solo artist) repl. JANKEL who went solo

Oct 80. (7") **SUPERMAN'S BIG SISTER. / FUNKY ADA** 51
(12"+=) – You'll see glimpses.

Nov 80. (lp)(c) **LAUGHTER** 48 Jan 81
– Sueperman's big sister / Pardon / Delusions of grandeur / Yes and no (Paula) / Dance of the crackpots / Over the points / (Take your elbow out of the soup you're sitting on the chicken) / Uncoolohol / Hey, hey, take me away / Manic depression / Oh, Mr. Peanut / Fucking Ada. *(cd-iss.May95 on 'Disky')*

— IAN DURY now brought in the services of rhythm boys **SLY & ROBBIE** plus **JANKEL + TYRONE DOWNIE** – keyboards.

Polydor Polydor

Aug 81. (7")(12") **SPASTICUS AUSTICIOUS. / ('A'instrumental)**

Sep 81. (lp)(c) **LORD UPMINSTER** 53
– Funky disco pops / Red letter / Girls watching / Wait for me / The body song / Lonely town / Trust is a must / Spasticus austicious. *(re-iss.+cd.Dec89 on 'Great Expectations')*

IAN DURY & THE MUSIC STUDENTS

with many musicians incl. **JANKEL, PAYNE + RAY COOPER**

Polydor Polydor

Nov 83. (7")(12") **REALLY GLAD YOU CAME. / INSPIRATION**

Jan 84. (lp)(c) **4,000 WEEKS HOLIDAY** 54
– (You're my) Inspiration / Friends / Tell your daddy / Peter the painter / Ban the bomb / Percy the poet / Very personal / Take me to the cleaners / The man with no face / Really glad you came. *(re-iss.+cd.Dec89 on 'Great Expectations')*

Feb 84. (7") **VERY PERSONAL. / BAN THE BOMB**
(12"+=) – The sky's the limit.

IAN DURY

solo, with **PAYNE, GALLAGHER, COOPER** plus **STEVE WHITE** – drums / **MICHAEL McEVOY** – bass, synth / **MERLIN RHYS-JONES** – guitar / **FRANCES RUFELLE** – vocals / etc.

E.M.I. not issued

Oct 89. (7")(7"pic-d) **PROFOUNDLY IN LOVE WITH PANDORA (theme from 'ADRIAN MOLE' TV series). / EUGENIUS (YOU'RE A GENIUS)** 45 -

WEA WEA

Oct 89. (7") **APPLES. / BYLINE BROWN**

Oct 89. (lp)(c)(cd) **APPLES**
– Apples / Love is all / Byline Browne / Bit of kit / Game on / Looking for Harry / England's glory / Bus driver's prayer / P.C.Honey / The right people / All those who say okay / Riding the outskirts of fantasy.

In Sep90 he reforms IAN DURY & THE BLOCKHEADS for two reunion gigs. Credited to

IAN DURY

Demon not issued

Oct 92. (cd)(c) **THE BUS DRIVERS PRAYER & OTHER STORIES** -
– That's enough of that / Bill Haley's last words / Poor Joey / Quick quick slow / Fly in the ointment / O'Donegal / Poo-poo in the prawn / Ave a word / London talking / D'orine the cow / Your horoscope / No such thing as love / Two old dogs without a name / Bus driver's prayer.

– compilations etc. –

Nov 81. Stiff; (lp)(c) **JUKE BOX DURIES**
(re-iss.Sep82 as 'GREATEST HITS' on 'Fame') (cd-iss.May95 on 'Disky')

May 85. Stiff; (7") **HIT ME WITH YOUR RHYTHM STICK (Paul Hardcastle mix). / SEX AND DRUGS AND ROCK AND ROLL** 55
(12"+=) – Reasons to be cheerful / Wake up and make love to me (Paul Hardcastle mix).

Apr 87. Demon; (lp)(c)(cd) **SEX AND DRUGS AND ROCK AND ROLL**
– Hit me with your rhythm stick / I want to be straight / There ain't half been some clever bastards / What a waste! / Common as muck / Reasons to be cheerful part 3 / Sex and drugs and rock and roll / Superman's big sister / Razzle in my pocket / You're more than fair / Inbetweenies / You'll see glimpses.

Apr 91. Demon; (cd)(c)(lp) **WARTS'N'AUDIENCE (live)**

Aug 91. Demon; (cd)(c)(lp) **IAN DURY & THE BLOCKHEADS** -

1991. Demon; (cd-set) **NEW BOOTS AND PANTIES / DO IT YOURSELF / SEX AND DRUGS AND ROCK AND ROLL** -

Jul 91. Flying; (7")(c-s) **HIT ME WITH YOUR RHYTHM STICK '91 (The Flying Remix Version) / HIT ME WITH YOUR RHYTHM STICK** 73 -
(12"+=)(cd-s+=)

Nov 94. Repertoire; (cd) **THE BEST OF IAN DURY** -

— The BLOCKHEADS also released their own singles and lp early 80's.

Bob DYLAN

Born: ROBERT ALLAN ZIMMERMAN, 24 May'41, Duluth, Minnesota, USA. In 1960, he left his local university and changed name to BOB DYLAN. He also began trek to New York, where he played first gig supporting JOHN LEE HOOKER on 11 Apr'61 at Gerde's Folk City. Soon after this, he enjoyed harmonica session work for folk songstress Caroline Hester. Her employers 'Columbia' records, through John Hammond Snr., signed him Oct'61. His eponymous debut album in 1962, gained sparse attention, although his live work created critical appraisal. In 1963 he unleashed 'THE FREEWHEELIN' BOB DYLAN', and after PETER, PAUL & MARY lifted a million seller from it 'BLOWIN' IN THE WIND', it gained enough respect to give him US Top 30 album. In 1965, at the peak of his career, the album was to make the top spot in the UK. Many up and coming and already established artists were successfully covering his material (see below). • **Style:** Idolized folk legend WOODY GUTHRIE who was to die 3 Sep'67 of a paralyzing hereditary disease. In 1966, DYLAN stunned folk purists, by employing an electric band The HAWKS (later The BAND) to augment his live and studio work. (A year earlier, he had introduced electric sound with band on half of No.1 album 'BRINGING IT ALL BACK HOME'.) After a motorcycle accident later in '66, he sustained severe neck injuries and retired for 2 years. This was of course after laying down tracks for legendary double lp 'BLONDE ON BLONDE'. He returned with slight change of vocal chords to release more country-rock orientated music. In the mid-70's, he returned with two harder edged rock classics 'BLOOD ON THE TRACKS' & 'DESIRE', which gave him needed regained credibility from critics and buying public alike. From 1979 and throughout the 80's, his work mellowed into more spiritual themes, due to his new-found Christianity. • **Songwriters:** 99% DYLAN compositions except, HOUSE OF THE RISING SUN + IN MY TIME OF DYIN' (trad.) / TAKE A MESSAGE TO MARY (Everly Brothers) / THE BOXER (Simon & Garfunkel) / EARLY MORNIN' RAIN (Gordon Lightfoot) / A FOOL SUCH AS I + CAN'T HELP FALLING IN LOVE (hits; Elvis Presley) / BIG YELLOW TAXI (Joni Mitchell) / MR.BOJANGLES (Jerry Jeff Walker) / LET'S STICK TOGETHER (Wilbert Harrison) / SPANISH IS THE LOVING TONGUE + SHENANDOAH (trad.) / ANGELS FLYING TOO CLOSE TO THE GROUND (Willie Nelson) / etc. **Writing credits/hits:** BLOWIN' IN THE WIND + DON'T THINK TWICE, IT'S ALRIGHT (Peter, Paul & Mary; 1963) / ALL I REALLY WANT TO DO (Cher; 1965) / IT AIN'T ME BABE (Turtles; 1965) / MR.TAMBOURINE MAN + ALL I REALLY WANT TO DO + MY BACK PAGES (Byrds; 1965-1967) / IT'S ALL OVER NOW, BABY BLUE + FAREWELL ANGELINA (Joan Baez; 1965) / IF YOU GOTTA GO, GO NOW + JUST LIKE A WOMAN + MIGHTY QUINN (Manfred Mann; 1965/66/68) / TOO MUCH OF NOTHING (Peter, Paul & Mary; 1967) / THIS WHEEL'S ON FIRE (Julie Driscoll, Brian Auger & The Trinity; 1968) / ALL ALONG THE WATCHTOWER (Jimi Hendrix; 1968) / IF NOT FOR

YOU (Olivia Newton-John; 1971) / A HARD RAIN'S A-GONNA FALL (Bryan Ferry; 1973) / KNOCKIN' ON HEAVEN'S DOOR (Eric Clapton; 1975 / Guns'n'Roses; 1992) / I'LL BE YOUR BABY TONIGHT (UB40 & Robert Palmer; 1990) / & some minor hits. **Filmography:** DON'T LOOK BACK (1965 documentary) / EAT THE DOCUMENTARY (1971 docu-film) / PAT GARRETT & BILLY THE KID (1973) / RENALDO AND CLARA (1978) / HEARTS OF FIRE (1987). • **Trivia:** On the 22 Nov'65, BOB married Sara Lowndes, but she divorced him in 1977. (Band members in discography are selectful.)

Recommended: DESIRE (*10) / BLOOD ON THE TRACKS (*9) / BLONDE ON BLONDE (*10) / THE FREEWHEELIN' BOB DYLAN (*9) / BRINGING IT ALL BACK HOME (*9) / ANOTHER SIDE OF BOB DYLAN (*7) / THE TIMES THEY ARE A-CHANGIN' (*7) / HIGHWAY 61 REVISITED (*10) / MORE BOB DYLAN'S GREATEST HITS (*7) / BOB DYLAN (*5) / GREATEST HITS (*10) / JOHN WESLEY HARDING (*5) / NASHVILLE SKYLINE (*5) / SELF PORTRAIT (*4) / NEW MORNING (*3) . PAT GARRETT AND BILLY THE KID (*3) / PLANET WAVES (*6) / DYLAN (*3) / BEFORE THE FLOOD (*7) / THE BASEMENT TAPES (*7) / HARD RAIN (*6) / STREET LEGAL onwards *5s and under.

BOB DYLAN – vocals, guitar, harmonica

C.B.S. Columbia

Mar 62. (7") **MIXED UP CONFUSION. / CORRINA CORRINA** [-] [ ]

Jun 62. (lp) **BOB DYLAN** [ ] [ ] Mar 62
– She's no good / Talkin' New York / In my time of dyin' / Man of constant sorrow / Fixin' to die blues / Pretty Peggy-o / Highway 51 blues / Gospel plow / Baby, let me follow you down / House of the risin' sun / Freight train blues / Song to Woody / See that grave is kept clean. *(re-dist.May65, hit No.13) (re-iss.+c.Mar81) (cd-iss.Nov89)*

— added musicians **HOWARD COLLINS** – guitar / **GEORGE BARNES** – bass / **HERB LOVELL** – drums / **LEONARD GASKIN** – bass / etc.

Nov 63. (lp) **THE FREEWHEELIN' BOB DYLAN** [16] [22] May 63
– Blowin' in the wind / Girl from the North Country / Masters of war / Down the highway / Bob Dylan's blues / A hard rains a-gonna fall / Don't think twice, it's all right / Bob Dylan's dream / Oxford Town / / Talking World War III blues / Corrina, Corina / Honey, just allow me one more chance / I shall be free. *(re-dist.Apr65, hitNo.1) (re-iss.+c.Mar81) (cd-iss.Nov89)*

Jun 64. (lp) **THE TIMES THEY ARE A-CHANGING** [20] [20] Mar 64
– The times they are a-changin' / Ballad of Hollis Brown / With God on our side / One too many mornings / North country blues / Only a pawn in their game / Boots of Spanish leather / When the ship comes in / The lonesome death of Hattie Carroll / Restless farewell. *(re-dist.Apr65, hit No.4) (re-iss.+c.Mar81) (cd-iss.Nov89)*

Nov 64. (lp) **ANOTHER SIDE OF BOB DYLAN** [8] [43] Sep 64
– All I really want to do / Black crow blues / Spanish Harlem incident / Chimes of freedom / I shall be free No.10 / To Ramona / Motorpsycho nitemare / I don't believe you / To Ramona / Ballad in plain D / It ain't me babe. *(re-iss.+c.Mar81) (cd-iss.Nov89)*

Mar 65. (7") **THE TIMES THEY ARE A-CHANGING. / HONEY, JUST ALLOW ME ONE MORE CHANCE** [9] [ ]

— with **BOBBY GREGG** – drums / **JOHN SEBASTIAN** – bass / **BRUCE LANGHORNE** – guitar

Apr 65. (7") **SUBTERRANEAN HOMESICK BLUES. / SHE BELONGS TO ME** [9] [ ]

May 65. (lp) **BRINGING IT ALL BACK HOME** [1] [6] Mar 65
– Subterranean homesick blues / She belongs to me / Maggie's farm / Love minus zero – No limit / Outlaw blues / On the road again / Bob Dylan's 115th dream / Mr. Tambourine man / Gates of Eden / It's alright, ma (I'm only bleeding) / It's all over now, baby blue. *(re-iss.+c.Jul83) (cd-iss.Jul89 as 'SUBTERRANEAN HOMESICK BLUES')*

Jun 65. (7") **MAGGIE'S FARM. / ON THE ROAD AGAIN** [22] [-]

— now with **AL KOOPER** – organ / **PAUL BUTTERFIELD** – guitar / **PAUL GRIFFIN** – keys / **CHARLIE McCOY** – guitar / **RUSS SAVAKUS** – bass /

Aug 65. (7") **LIKE A ROLLING STONE. / GATES OF EDEN** [4] [2] Jul 65

Sep 65. (lp) **HIGHWAY 61 REVISITED** [4] [3] Aug 65
– Like a rolling stone / Tombstone blues / It takes a lot to laugh, it takes a train to cry / From a Buick 6 / Ballad of a thin man / Queen Jane approximately / Highway 61 revisited / Just like Tom Thumb's blues / Desolation row. *(re-iss.+c.Dec85) (cd-iss.Nov89)*

Oct 65. (7") **POSITIVELY 4TH STREET. / FROM A BUICK 6** [8] [7] Sep 65

Jan 66. (7") **CAN YOU PLEASE CRAWL OUT YOUR WINDOW. / HIGHWAY 61 REVISITED** [17] [58] Nov 65

Apr 66. (7") **ONE OF US MUST KNOW (SOONER OR LATER). / QUEEN JANE APPROXIMATELY** [33] [ ] Feb 66

— Now augmented by members of The **BAND:- ROBBIE ROBERTSON** – guitar / **RICHARD MANUEL** – keyboards / **LEVON HELM** – drums / **RICK DANKO** – bass / **GARTH HUDSON** – keyboards plus also **KENNY BUTTREY** – drums

May 66. (7") **RAINY DAY WOMEN NOS.12 & 35. / PLEDGING MY TIME** [7] [2] Apr 66

Jul 66. (7") **I WANT YOU. / JUST LIKE TOM THUMB'S BLUES (live)** [16] [20] Jun 66

Aug 66. (d-lp) **BLONDE ON BLONDE** [3] [9] May 66
– Rainy day women # 12 & 35 / Pledging my love / Visions of Johanna / One of us must know (sooner or later) / Most likely you go your way (and I'll go mine) / Temporary like Achilles / Absolutely sweet Marie / 4th time around / Obviously 5 believers / I want you / Stuck inside of Mobile with the Memphis blues again / Leopard-skin pill-box hat / Just like a woman / Sad eyed lady of the lowlands. *(re-iss.+d-c.May82) (cd-iss.Jul87 + Jun89 + Feb95)*

Sep 66. (7") **JUST LIKE A WOMAN. / OBVIOUSLY 5 BELIEVERS** [-] [33]

Jan 67. (lp) **GREATEST HITS** (US diff.tracks) [6] [10] Dec 66
– Blowin' in the wind / It ain't me babe / The times they are a-changin' / Mr.Tambourine man / She belongs to me / It's all over now, baby blue / Subterranean homesick blues / One of us must know (sooner or later) / Like a rolling stone / Just like a woman / Rainy day women Nos. 12 & 35. *(re-iss.Mar88, hit UK 99) (cd-iss.Nov89) (cd+c-iss.Feb91 on 'Columbia') (re-iss.cd Oct94 as 'BEST OF . . .')*

May 67. (7") **LEOPARD SKIN PILL-BOX HAT. / MOST LIKELY YOU GO YOUR WAY (AND I'LL GO MINE)** [ ] [81] Mar 67

— now with **BUTTREY, McCOY** and **PETE DRAKE** – sitar, guitar

Feb 68. (lp) **JOHN WESLEY HARDING** [1] [2]
– John Wesley Harding / As I went out one morning / I dreamed I saw St. Augustine / All along the watchtower / The ballad of Frankie Lee and Judas Priest / Drifter's escape / Dear landlord / I am a lonesome hobo / I pity the poor immigrant / The wicked messenger / Down along the cove / I'll be your baby tonight. *(c-iss.1969) (cd-iss.Nov89)*

— next featured **CHARLIE DANIELS** – bass, guitar / **etc.**

May 69. (7") **I THREW IT ALL AWAY. / DRIFTER'S ESCAPE** [30] [85]

May 69. (lp)(c) **NASHVILLE SKYLINE** [1] [3]
– Girl from the North country (with JOHNNY CASH) / Nashville skyline rag / To be alone with you / I threw it all away / Pegy Day / Lady lady lay / One more night / Tell me that it isn't true / Country pie / Tonight I'll be staying here with you. *(re-iss.May87) (cd-iss.Jan86) (quad-lp 1970's)*

Sep 69. (7") **LAY LADY LAY. / PEGGY DAY** [5] [7] Jul 69

Dec 69. (7") **TONIGHT I'LL BE STAYING HERE WITH YOU. / COUNTRY PIE** [ ] [50] Oct 69

Jul 70. (dlp,d-c) **SELF PORTRAIT** [1] [4]
– All the tired horses / Alberta #1 / I forgot more than you'll ever know / Days of 49 / Early mornin' rain / In search of little Sadie / Let it be me / Little Sadie / Woogie boogie / Belle isle / Living the blues / Like a rolling stone (version) / Copper kettle (the pale moonlight) / Gotta travel on / Blue Moon / The boxer / The mighty Quinn (Quinn, the eskimo) / Take me as I am / Take a message to Mary / It hurts me too / Minstrel boy / She belongs to me / Wigwam / Alberta #2. *(re-iss.Sep87) (cd+c-iss.Feb91 on 'Columbia')*

Jul 70. (7") **WIGWAM. / COPPER KETTLE (THE PALE MOONLIGHT)** [ ] [41]

Nov 70. (lp)(c) **NEW MORNING** [1] [7]
– If not for you / Day of the locusts / Time passes slowly / Went to see the gypsy / Winterlude / If dogs ran free / New morning / Sign on the window / One more weekend / The man in me / Three angels / Father of the night. *(re-iss.Sep83) (cd+c-iss.Feb91 on 'Columbia') (re-iss.cd+c Feb94 on 'Columbia')*

Mar 71. (7") **IF NOT FOR YOU. / NEW MORNING** [ ] [ ]

Jun 71. (7") **WATCHING THE RIVER FLOW. / SPANISH IS THE LOVING TONGUE** [24] [41]

Dec 71. (7") **GEORGE JACKSON (Acoustic). / GEORGE JACKSON (big band version)** [ ] [33]

Dec 71. (d-lp)(d-c) **MORE BOB DYLAN GREATEST HITS** [12] [14]
– Watching the river flow / Don't think twice, it's alright / Lay lady lay / Stuck inside Mobile with the Memphis blues again / I'll be your baby tonight / All I really want to do / My back pages / Maggie's farm / Tonight I'll be staying here with you / Positively 4th Street / All along the watchtower / The mighty Quinn (Quinn, the eskimo) / Just like Tom Thumb's blues / A hard rain's a-gonna fall / If not for you / New morning / Tomorrow is a long time / When I paint my masterpiece / I shall be released / You ain't goin' nowhere / Down in the flood.
(US-title BOB DYLAN'S GREATEST HITS, VOL.II) *(cd-iss.Oct87) (cd-re-iss.Aug92 on 'Columbia')(re-iss.cd+cMar93 on 'Columbia')*

Sep 73. (lp)(c) **PAT GARRETT AND BILLY THE KID (Soundtrack)** [29] [16]
– Mmain title theme / Cantina theme (working for the law) / Billy 1 / Bunkhouse theme / River theme / Turkey chase / Knockin' on Heaven's door / Final theme / Billy 4 / Billy 7. *(re-iss.Mar82) (cd+c-iss.Feb91 on 'Columbia')*

Sep 73. (7") **KNOCKIN' ON HEAVEN'S DOOR. / TURKEY CHASE** [14] [12]

Nov 73. (lp)(c) **DYLAN** (recorded 1970) [ ] [17]
– Lily of the west / Can't help falling in love / Sarah Jane / The ballad of Ira Hayes / Mr. Bojangles / Mary Ann / Big yellow taxi / A fool such as I / Spanish is the loving tongue. *(re-iss.Mar83) (cd+c-iss.Feb91 on 'Columbia')*

Jan 74. (7") **A FOOL SUCH AS I. / LILY OF THE WEST** [ ] [55]

Island Asylum

Feb 74. (lp)(c) **PLANET WAVES** [7] [1]
– On a night like this / Going going gone / Tough mama / Hazel / Something there is about you / Forever young / Dirge / You angel you / Never say goodbye / Wedding song. *(re-iss.Sep82) (cd-iss.Nov89 on 'CBS' + Jun88 on 'Collector's Choice')(quad-lp US 1970's)*

Feb 74. (7") **ON A NIGHT LIKE THIS. / YOU ANGEL YOU** [ ] [-]

Feb 74. (7") **ON A NIGHT LIKE THIS. / FOREVER YOUNG** [ ] [-]

Apr 74. (7") **SOMETHING THERE IS ABOUT YOU. / GOING GOING GONE** [-] [ ]

Asylum Asylum

Jul 74. (d-lp)(d-c) **BEFORE THE FLOOD (live) ("BOB DYLAN / The BAND")** [8] [3]
– Most likely you go your way (and I'll go mine) / Lay lady lay / Rainy day women #12 & 35 / Knockin' on Heaven's door / It ain't me babe / The ballad of a thin man / Up on Cripple Creek * / I shall be released / Endless highway * / The night they drove old Dixie down * / Stage fright * / Don't think twice, it's all right / Just like a woman / It's alright ma (I'm only bleeding) / The shape I'm in * / When you awake * / The weight * / All along the watchtower / Highway 61 revisited / Like a rolling stone / Blowin' in the wind. (* tracks by The BAND) *(re-iss.Sep82) (cd-iss.Jul87 + Nov89)*
The BAND had been his backing group from the mid '60's.

Aug 74. (7") **MOST LIKELY YOU GO YOUR WAY (AND I'LL GO MINE) (live). / SATGE FRIGHT (The BAND live)** [-] [66]

Nov 74. (7") **ALL ALONG THE WATCHTOWER (live). / IT AIN'T ME BABE (live)** [-] [ ]

C.B.S. Columbia

Feb 75. (lp)(c) **BLOOD ON THE TRACKS** [4] [1]
– Tangled up in blue / Simple twist of fate / You're a big girl now / Idiot wind / You're gonna make me lonesome when you go / Meet me in the morning / Lily, Rosemary and the Jack of Hearts / If you see her, say hello / Shelter from the storm / Buckets of rain. *(re-iss.May82) (cd-iss.Dec85)(re-iss.cd+cSep93 on 'Columbia')*

Mar 75. (7") **TANGLED UP IN BLUE. / IF YOU SEE HER, SAY HELLO** [-] [31]

Jul 75. (d-lp)(d-c) **THE BASEMENT TAPES** (recorded 1967) [8] [7]
– Odds and ends / Orange juice blues (blues for breakfast) / Million dollar bash / Yazoo street scandal / Goin' to Acapulco / Katie's been gone / Lo and behold / Bessie Smith / Clothes line saga / Apple suckling tree / Please Mrs.Henry / Tears of rage / Too much of nothing / Yea! heavy and a bottle of wine / Ain't no more Cane / Crash on the levee (down in the flood) / Ruben Remus / Tiny Montgomery / You ain't goin' nowhere / Don't ya tell Henry / Nothing was delivered / Open the

doors, Homer / Long distance operator. *(cd-iss.Nov89)*
Oct 75. (7") **MILLION DOLLAR BASH. / TEARS OF RAGE** [ ] [ ]

—— next featured **EMMYLOU HARRIS** – vocals / **SCARLET RIVIERA** – violin / **RONNE BLAKELY** – vocals / **HOWIE WYTHE** – drums / **ROB STONER** – bass / **STEVEN SOLES** – guitar

Jan 76. (7") **HURRICANE (part 1). / HURRICANE (full version)** [43] [33] Dec 75
Jan 76. (lp)(c) **DESIRE** [3] [1]
– Hurricane / Isis / Mozambique / One more cup of coffee / Oh, sister / Joey / Romance in Durango / Black diamond bay / Sara. *(re-iss.Apr85) (cd-iss.Jul87 + Jun89) (quad-lp rel.1976)*
Apr 76. (7") **MOZAMBIQUE. / OH, SISTER** [ ] [54]

—— His HARD RAIN tour added **MICK RONSON** – guitar / **DAVID MANSFIELD** – keys

Sep 76. (lp)(c) **HARD RAIN (live)** [3] [17]
– Maggie's farm / One too many mornings / Stuck inside of Mobile with the Memphis blues again / Lay lady lay / Shelter from the storm / You're a big girl now / I threw it all away / Idiot wind. *(re-iss.Apr83) (cd-iss.Nov89)*
Feb 77. (7") **RITA MAY. / STUCK INSIDE OF MOBILE WITH THE MEMPHIS BLUES AGAIN (live)** [ ] [ ]
May 78. (7")(12") **BABY STOP CRYING. / NEW PONY** [13] [ ]
Jun 78. (lp)(c) **STREET-LEGAL** [2] [11]
– Changing of the guards / New pony / No time to think / Baby stop crying / Is your love in vain / Senor (tales of Yankee power) / True love tends to forget / We better talk this over / Where are you tonight (journey through dark heat). *(cd-iss.Mar86 & May95 +c)*
Oct 78. (7")(12") **IS YOUR LOVE IN VAIN. / WE BETTER TALK THIS OVER** [56] [ ]
Dec 78. (7") **CHANGING OF THE GUARDS. / SENOR (TALES OF YANKEE POWER)** [ ] [ ]
1978. (7"ep) **4 SONGS FROM "RENALDO AND CLARA"** [-] [ ]
– People get ready / Never let me go / Isis / It ain't me babe.
May 79. (d-lp)(d-c) **BOB DYLAN AT BUDOKAN (live)** [4] [13]
– Mr.Tambourine man / Shelter from the storm / Love minus zero – No limit / Ballad of a thin man / Don't think twice, it's all right / Maggie's farm / One more cup of coffee / Like a rolling stone / I shall be released / Oh sister / Is your love in vain? / Going going gone / Blowin' in the wind / Just like a woman / Simple twist of fate / All along the watchtower / I want you / All I really want to do / Knockin' on Heaven's door / It's alright ma (I'm only bleeding) / Forever young / The times they are a-changin'. *(cd-iss.Jul87)(re-iss.d-cd+d-c Apr93 on 'Columbia')*
Jun 79. (7") **FOREVER YOUNG (live). / ALL ALONG THE WATCHTOWER (live)** [ ] [-]
Aug 79. (7") **PRECIOUS ANGEL. / TROUBLE IN MIND** [ ] [-]
Aug 79. (lp)(c) **SLOW TRAIN COMING** [2] [3]
– Gotta serve somebody / Precious angel / I believe in you / Slow train / Gonna change my way of thinking / Do right to me baby (do unto others) / When you gonna wake up / Man gave names to all the animals / When he returns. *(re-iss.Nov85, cd-Mar86 +Apr89)*
Sep 79. (7") **GOTTA SERVE SOMEBODY. / TROUBLE IN MIND** [-] [24]
Oct 79. (7") **MAN GAVE NAMES TO ALL THE ANIMALS. / WHEN HE RETURNS** [ ] [-]
Jan 80. (7") **MAN GAVE NAMES TO THE ANIMALS. / WHEN YOU GONNA WAKE UP** [-] [ ]
Jan 80. (7") **GOTTA SERVE SOMEBODY. / GONNA CHANGE MY WAY OF THINKING** [ ] [-]
Mar 80. (7") **SLOW TRAIN. / DO RIGHT TO ME BABY (DO UNTO OTHERS)** [-] [ ]
May 80. (7") **SOLID ROCK. / COVENANT WOMAN** [-] [ ]
Jun 80. (lp)(c) **SAVED** [3] [24]
– A satisfied mind / Saved / Covenant woman / What can I do for you? / Solid rock / Pressing on / In the garden / Saving Grace / Are you ready. *(cd+c-iss.Feb91 on 'Columbia')(re-iss.cd+c Mar93 on 'Columbia')*
Jun 80. (7") **SAVED. / ARE YOU READY** [ ] [ ]
Jun 81. (7") **HEART OF MINE. / THE GROOM'S STILL WAITING AT THE ALTAR** [-] [ ]
Jul 81. (7") **HEART OF MINE. / LET IT BE ME** [ ] [-]
Aug 81. (lp)(c) **SHOT OF LOVE** [6] [33]
– Shot of love / Heart of mine / Property of Jesus / Lenny Bruce / Watered down love / Dead man, dead man / In the summertime / Trouble / Every grain of sand. *(cd+c-iss.Feb91 on 'Columbia' +=)– The groom's still waiting at the altar. (re-iss.cd Jun94 on 'Sony Europe')*
Sep 81. (7") **LENNY BRUCE. / DEAD MAN, DEAD MAN** [ ] [ ]
Oct 83. (7") **UNION SUNDOWN. / I AND I** [ ] [ ]
Nov 83. (lp)(c) **INFIDELS** [9] [20]
– Jokerman / Sweetheart like you / Neighbourhood bully / License to kill / Man of peace / Union sundown / I and I / Don't fall apart on me tonight. *(cd-iss.Jul87) (re-iss.+cd.Dec89)*
Dec 83. (7") **SWEETHEART LIKE YOU. / UNION SUNDOWN** [-] [55]
May 84. (7") **JOKERMAN. / ISIS** [-] [ ]
Jun 84. (7") **JOKERMAN. / LICENSE TO KILL** [ ] [-]
Dec 84. (lp)(c)(cd) **REAL LIVE (live)** [54] [ ]
– Highway 61 revisited / Maggie's farm / I and I / License to kill / It ain't me babe / Tangled up in blue / Masters of war / Ballad of a thin man / Girl from the North country / Tombstone blues. *(cd+c-iss.Feb91 on 'Columbia')*
Jan 85. (7") **HIGHWAY 61 REVISITED (live). / IT AIN'T ME BABE (live)** [ ] [ ]
Jun 85. (7") **TIGHT CONNECTION TO MY HEART. / WE'D BETTER TALK THIS OVER** [ ] [ ]
Jun 85. (lp)(c)(cd) **EMPIRE BURLESQUE** [11] [33]
– Tight connection to my heart (has anybody seen my love) / Seeing the real you at last / I'll remember you / Clean cut kid / Never gonna be the same again / Trust yourself / Emotionally yours / When the night comes falling from the sky / Something's burning, baby / Dark eyes. *(re-cd.1988) (cd+c-iss.Feb91 on 'Columbia')*
Aug 85. (7")(12") **WHEN THE NIGHT COMES FALLING FROM THE SKY. / DARK EYES** [ ] [-]

—— Apr86, was credited next on TOM PETTY ⇒ single BAND OF THE HAND.

Oct 85. (7") **WHEN THE NIGHT COMES FALLING FROM THE SKY. / EMOTIONALLY YOURS** [-] [ ]
Jul 86. (lp)(c)(cd) **KNOCKED OUT LOADED** [35] [53]
– You wanna ramble / They killed him / Driftin' too far from shore / Precious memories / Maybe someday / Brownsville girl / Got my mind made up / Under your spell. *(cd+c-iss.Feb91 on 'Columbia')(re-iss.cd+c Mar93 on 'Columbia')*
Oct 86. (7") **THE USUAL. / GOT MY MIND MADE UP** [ ] [ ]
(12"+=) – They killed him.
Jun 88. (lp)(c)(cd) **DOWN IN THE GROOVE** [32] [61]
– Let's stick together / When did you leave Heaven? / Sally Sue Brown / Death is not the end / Had a dream about you, baby / Ugliest girl in the world / Silvio / Ninety miles an hour (down a dead end street) / Shenandoah / Rank strangers to me.
Jul 88. (7") **SILVIO. / WHEN DID YOU LEAVE HEAVEN?** [ ] [ ]
(12"+=) – Driftin' too far from shore. (US; b-side)

Later in 1988 onwards he was also part of supergroup TRAVELLING WILBURYS

Feb 89. (lp)(c)(cd) **DYLAN & THE DEAD (live) ("BOB DYLAN & GRATEFUL DEAD")** rec. Summer '87 [38] [37]
– Slow train / I want you / Gotta serve somebody / Queen Jane approximately / Joey / All along the watchtower / Knockin' on Heaven's door. *(re-iss.cd+c May94 on 'Columbia')*
Sep 89. (lp)(c)(cd) **OH MERCY** [6] [30]
– Political world / Where teardrops fall / Everything is broken / Ring them bells / Man in the long black coat / Most of the time / What good am I? / Disease of conceit / What was it you wanted / Shooting star.
Oct 89. (7") **EVERYTHING IS BROKEN. / DEAD MAN, DEAD MAN** [-] [ ]
Oct 89. (7") **EVERYTHING IS BROKEN. / DEATH IS NOT THE END** [ ] [-]
(12") – ('A'side) / Dead man, dead man / I want you (live)
(cd-s) – ('A'side) / Where the teardrops fall / Dead man, dead man / Ugliest girl in the world.
Feb 90. (7") **POLITICAL WORLD. / RING THEM BELLS** [ ] [ ]
(12"+=)(cd-s+=) – Silvio / All along the watchtower (live).
(cd-s) – ('A'side) /Caribbean wind / You're a big girl now / It's all over now, baby blue.
Sep 90. (cd)(c)(lp) **UNDER THE RED SKY** [13] [38]
– Wiggle wiggle / Under the red sky / Unbelievable / Born in time / TV talkin' time / 10,000 men / 2x2 / God knows / Handy Dandy / Cat's in the well.
Sep 90. (7") **UNBELIEVABLE. / 10,000 MEN** [ ] [ ]
(cd-s+=) – In the summertime / Jokerman.
Feb 91. (7")(c-s) **SERIES OF DREAMS. / SEVEN CURSES** [ ] [ ]
(cd-s+=) – Tangled up in blue / Like a rolling stone.

—— totally solo DYLAN

Columbia Columbia
Nov 92. (cd)(c)(lp) **GOOD AS I BEEN TO YOU** [18] [51]
– Frankie & Albert / Jim Jones / Blackjack Davey / Canadee-i-o / Sittin' on top of the world / Little Maggie / Hard times / Step it up and go / Tomorrow night / Arthur McBride / You're gonna quit me / Diamond Joe / Froggie went a courtin'.

In Aug93, a host of artists released a live tribute d-cd,d-c 'ANNIVERSARY CONCERT', which hit US No.30. Below all traditional tunes.

Nov 93. (cd)(c) **WORLD GONE WRONG** [35] [70]
– World gone wrong / Ragged and dirty / Love Henry / Blood in my eyes / Delia / Broke down engine / Two soldiers / Stack A Lee / Jack A Roe / Love pilgrim.

—— with **TONY GARNIER** – bass / **JOHN JACKSON** – guitar / **BUCKY BAXTER** – pedal steel, dobro / **WINSTON WATSON** – drums / **BRENDAN O'BRIEN** – hammond organ

Apr 95. (cd)(c)(lp) **MTV UNPLUGGED** [10] [23]
– Tombstone blues / Shooting star / All along the watchtower / The times they are a-changin' / John Brown / Desolation row / Rainy day women £ 12 & 35 / Love minus zero – No limit / Dignity / Knockin' on Heaven's door / Like a rolling stone / With God on our side.
May 95. (c-s) **DIGNITY / JOHN BROWN** [33] [ ]
(cd-s+=) – It ain't me babe (live).
(cd-s) – ('A'side) / A hard rain's a-gonna fall.

– compilations, others, etc. –

Apr 66. C.B.S.; (7"ep) **ONE TOO MANY MORNINGS** [ ] [-]
– One too many mornings / Spanish Harlem incident / Oxford town / She belongs to me.
Jun 66. C.B.S.; (7"ep) **DON'T THINK TWICE IT'S ALRIGHT** [ ] [-]
– Don't think twice it's alright / Blowin' in the wind / Corrina, Corrina / When the ship comes.
Oct 66. C.B.S.; (7"ep) **MR.TAMBOURINE MAN** [ ] [-]
– Mr.Tambourine man / Subterranean homesick blues / It's all over now, baby blue.
Mar 73. C.B.S.; (7") **JUST LIKE A WOMAN. / I WANT YOU** [ ] [ ]
Feb 76. C.B.S.; (7") **LAY LADY LAY. / I THREW IT ALL AWAY** [ ] [ ]
(re-iss.Feb79)
Nov 85. C.B.S./ US= Columbia; (5xlp-box)(3xc-box)(3xcd-box) **BIOGRAPH** [ ] [33]

—— (above contains 16 unreleased tracks)

1988. C.B.S.; (d-c) **DESIRE / BLOOD ON THE TRACKS** [ ] [-]
Apr 91. Columbia; (3xcd)(3xc)(6xlp) **THE BOOTLEG SERIES VOLUMES 1-3 (RARE & UNRELEASED) 1961-1991** [32] [49]
Aug 92. Columbia; (d-cd) **HIGHWAY 61 REVISITED / JOHN WESLEY HARDING** [ ] [ ]
Oct 93. Columbia; (3xcd-box) **BLONDE ON BLONDE / JOHN WESLEY HARDING / SELF PORTRAIT** [ ] [ ]
Oct 83. Go Int.; (lp)(c) **HISTORICAL ARCHIVES VOL.1** [ ] [ ]
Oct 83. Go Int.; (lp)(c) **HISTORICAL ARCHIVES VOL.2** [ ] [ ]
Sep 87. Compact Collection; (cd) **THE GASLIGHT TAPES** [ ] [ ]
1988. Joker; (lp) **THE BEST OF BOB DYLAN** [ ] [-]
May 88. Big Time; (lp)(c) **BLOWIN' IN THE WIND** [ ] [-]
May 88. Big Time; (lp)(c) **DON'T THINK TWICE, IT'S ALRIGHT** [ ] [-]
Nov 94. Columbia; (cd)(c)(d-lp) **GREATEST HITS VOLUME III** [ ] [ ]
– Tangled up in blue / Changing the guards / The groom's still waiting at the altar / Hurricane / Forever young / Jokerman / Dignity / Silvio / Ring them bells / Gotta serve somebody / Series of dream / Brownsville girl / Under the red sky / Knockin' on Heaven's door.

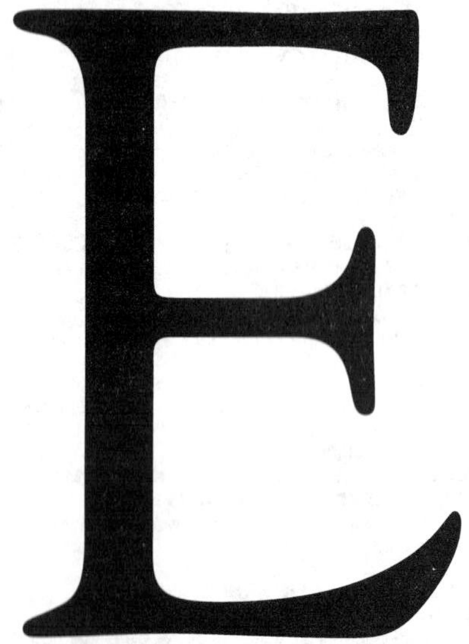

EAGLES

Formed: Los Angeles, California, USA . . . 1972, by FREY and HENLEY. Signed to 'Asylum' records that year, and soon issued eponymous debut album which hit US Top 30. By 1975, they had become America's top rock-pop band when album and single ONE OF THESE NIGHTS shot to top slot. The following year (1976) saw them release their classic all-time great HOTEL CALIFORNIA. For another 4 years, they enjoyed an unrivalled reign as easy-listening FM rock stars, until they split. All continued solo, with most success stemming from HENLEY and FREY. HENLEY's career was set back somewhat in Nov'80, when a 16 year-old female was found naked and drugged in his Californian home. He was fined and ordered to attend a drug counselling scheme. The next year, he recorded debut album with DANNY KORTCHMAR and GREG LADANYI, but this lay dormant until late 1982. In the meantime, he was credited on US Top 10 single by STEVIE NICKS 'Leather And Lace'. His debut album titled 'I CAN'T STAND STILL', hit US Top 30, helped by an appropriately titled Top 3 single 'DIRTY LAUNDRY'. In '84, he moved to 'Geffen' label, and secured cross-Atlantic Top 20 single 'THE BOYS OF SUMMER' & album 'BUILDING THE PERFECT BEAST'. FREY first dueted on STEVIE NICKS (Fleetwood Mac) early '82 hit single 'Leather And Lace'. That same year, still contracted to 'Asylum' records, he issued US Top 40 album 'NO FUN ALOUD'. In 1984, his next Top 40 album 'THE ALLNIGHTER', which prompted NBC TV to feature 'SMUGGLER'S BLUES' and FREY, on their 'Miami Vice' cop series. This gave him a cross-Atlantic Top 30 hit in 1985, and was proceeded by another hit song from the series 'YOU BELONG TO THE CITY'. After a quiet 2 years, FREY returned to business, with 1988's 'SOUL SEARCHIN' album. • **Style:** West-coast country AOR rock, that hardened up somewhat with the entry of JOE WALSH in '76. • **Songwriters:** All took turns writing. Covered; OL'55 (Tom Waits) / TAKE IT EASY (co-written by FREY and Jackson Browne) / PLEASE COME HOME FOR CHRISTMAS (Charles Brown). HENLEY covered EVERYBODY KNOWS (Leonard Cohen). • **Trivia:** HOTEL CALIFORNIA track won a Grammy award in 1977. A few years later, FREY, HENLEY and WALSH appeared on RANDY NEWMAN's 'Little Criminals'. In 1990, FREY was honoured by the Rock'n'charity foundation for his work to prevent against AIDS and cancer.

Recommended: THEIR GREATEST HITS 1971-1975 (*9) / ONE OF THESE NIGHTS (*8) / HOTEL CALIFORNIA (*8).

GLEN FREY (b. 6 Nov'48, Detroit, Michigan, USA) – guitar, vocals (ex-LINDA RONSTADT Band, ex-LONGBRANCH PENWHISTLE) / **BERNIE LEADON** (b.19 Jul'47, Minneapolis, Minnesota, USA) – guitar, vocals (ex-LINDA RONSTADT Band, ex-FLYING BURRITO BROTHERS) / **RANDY MEISNER** (b. 8 Mar'47, Scottsbluff, Nebraska, USA) – bass, vocals (ex-LINDA RONSTADT Band, ex-POCO, ex-RICK NELSON) / **DON HENLEY** (b.22 Jul'47, Gilmer, Texas, USA) – drums, vocals (ex-LINDA RONSTADT Band, ex-SHILOH)

		Asylum	Asylum
Jun 72.	(7") **TAKE IT EASY. / GET YOU IN THE MOOD**		12 May 72
Sep 72.	(7") **WITCHY WOMAN. / EARLY BIRD**		9
Oct 72.	(lp)(c) **EAGLES** – Take it easy / Witchy woman / Chug all night / Most of us are sad / Nightingale / Train leaves here this morning / Take the Devil / Early bird / Peaceful easy feeling / Tryin'. *(re-iss.Jun76) (cd-iss.Feb87 + 1989)*		22 Jun 72
Dec 72.	(7") **PEACEFUL EASY FEELING. / TRYIN'**	-	22
Feb 73.	(7") **TRYIN'. / CHUG ALL NIGHT**		
Apr 73.	(lp)(c) **DESPERADO** – Doolin-Dalton / Twenty-one / Out of control / Tequila sunrise / Desperado / Certain kind of fool / Outlaw man / Saturday night / Bitter creek. *(re-iss.Aug75, hit UK No.39) (re-iss.Jun76) (cd-iss.1989)*		41
Jul 73.	(7") **TEQUILA SUNRISE. / TWENTY-ONE**		64 Jun 73
Oct 73.	(7") **OUTLAW MAN. / CERTAIN KIND OF FOOL**		59 Sep 73

— added **DON FELDER** (b.21 Sep'47, Topanga, California, USA) – guitar, vocals (ex-FLOW)

Apr 74.	(lp)(c) **ON THE BORDER** – Already gone / You never cry like a lover / Midnight flyer / My man / On the border / James Dean / Ol' 55 / Is it true / Good day in Hell / Best of my love. *(re-iss.Jun76) (quad-lp 1977) (cd-iss.1989)*	28	17
Apr 74.	(7") **ALREADY GONE. / IS IT TRUE**	-	32
May 74.	(7") **JAMES DEAN. / IS IT TRUE**		77
Jul 74.	(7") **ALREADY GONE. / OL' 55**		-
Sep 74.	(7") **JAMES DEAN. / GOOD DAY IN HELL**	-	
Nov 74.	(7") **BEST OF MY LOVE. / OL' 55**	-	1
Dec 74.	(7") **BEST OF MY LOVE. / MIDNIGHT FLYER**		-
May 75.	(7"m) **MY MAN. / TAKE IT EASY / TEQUILA SUNRISE**		-
Jun 75.	(lp)(c) **ONE OF THESE NIGHTS** – One of these nights / Too many hands / Hollywood waltz / Journey of the sorceror / Lyin' eyes / Take it to the limit / Visions / After the thrill is gone / I wish you peace. *(re-iss.Jun76) (quad-lp 1977) (cd-iss.1989)*	8	1
Jun 75.	(7") **ONE OF THESE NIGHTS. / VISIONS**	23	1 May 75
Sep 75.	(7") **LYIN' EYES. / TOO MANY HANDS**	-	2
Oct 75.	(7") **LYIN' EYES. / JAMES DEAN**	23	-
Dec 75.	(7") **TAKE IT TO THE LIMIT. / AFTER THE THRILL IS GONE**	-	4
Feb 76.	(7") **TAKE IT TO THE LIMIT. / TOO MANY HANDS**	12	-
Feb 76.	(lp)(c) **THEIR GREATEST HITS 1971-1975 (compilation)** – Take it easy / Witchy woman / Lyin' eyes / Already gone / Desperado / One of these nights / Tequila sunrise / Take it to the limit / Peaceful easy feeling / Best of my love. *(cd-iss.May87)*	2	1

— **JOE WALSH** (b.20 Nov'47, Wichita, Kansas, USA) – guitar, vocals (ex-Solo artist, ex-JAMES GANG),repl. LEADON who formed own duo band

Dec 76.	(lp)(c) **HOTEL CALIFORNIA** – Hotel California / New kid in town / Life in the fast lane / Wasted time / Wasted time (reprise) / Victim of love / Pretty maids all in a row / Try and love again / The last resort. *(cd-iss.May87) (re-iss.Jun91)*	2	1
Jan 77.	(7") **NEW KID IN TOWN. / VICTIM OF LOVE**	20	1 Dec 76
Apr 77.	(7") **HOTEL CALIFORNIA. / PRETTY MAIDS ALL IN A ROW**	8	1 Feb 77
Jun 77.	(7") **LIFE IN THE FAST LANE. / THE LAST RESORT**		11 May 77

— **TIMOTHY B. SCHMIT** (b.30 Oct'47, Sacramento, California, USA) – bass, vocals (ex-POCO) repl. MEISNER who went solo.

(SCHMIT now alongside FREY, HENLEY, WALSH and FELDER)

Dec 78.	(7") **PLEASE COME HOME FOR CHRISTMAS. / FUNKY NEW YEAR**	30	18

— added p/t **JOE VITALE** – keyboards

Sep 79.	(7") **HEARTACHE TONIGHT. / TEENAGE JAIL**	40	1
Sep 79.	(lp)(c) **THE LONG RUN** – The long run / I can't tell you why / In the city / The disco strangler / King of Hollywood / Heartache tonight / Those shoes / Teenage jail / The Greeks don't want no freaks / The sad cafe. *(cd-iss.1986)*	4	1
Nov 79.	(7") **THE LONG RUN. / THE DISCO STRANGLER**	66	8
Jan 80.	(7") **I CAN'T TELL YOU WHY. / THE GREEKS DON'T WANT NO FREAKS**		8
May 80.	(7") **THE SAD CAFE. / THOSE SHOES**		
Nov 80.	(d-lp)(d-c) **THE EAGLES LIVE (live)** – Hotel California / Heartache tonight / I can't tell you why / The long run / New kid in town / Life's been good / Seven bridges road / Wasted time / Take it to the limit / Doolin-Dalton / Desperado / Saturday night / All night long / Life in the fast lane / Take it easy. *(d-cd-iss.Feb93)*	24	6
Dec 80.	(7") **SEVEN BRIDGES ROAD (live). / THE LONG RUN (live)**	-	21
Jan 81.	(7") **TAKE IT TO THE LIMIT (live). / SEVEN BRIDGES ROAD (live) / TAKE IT EASY (live)**		
		not issued	Full Moon
Mar 81.	(7") **I CAN'T TELL YOU WHY. / AMBROSIA OUTSIDE**	-	

— By this time they had all mutually agreed to disband. All five went on to individual solo careers.

– more compilations etc. –

Note; All releases on 'Asylum' until mentioned.

Sep 76.	(7") **TAKE IT EASY. / WITCHY WOMAN**		
Sep 76.	(7") **PEACEFUL EASY FEELING. / OL'55**		
Sep 76.	(7") **TEQUILA SUNRISE. / ON THE BORDER**		
Oct 82.	(lp)(c) **EAGLES GREATEST HITS – VOL.2** – Hotel California / Heartache tonight / Life in the fast lane / Seven bridges road / The sad cafe / I can't tell you why / New kid in town / The long run / Victim of love / After the thrill is gone.		52
Oct 83.	(d-c) **DESPERADO / ONE OF THESE NIGHTS**		
Nov 83.	(d-c) **HOTEL CALIFORNIA / THE LONG RUN**		
May 85.	(lp)(c)(cd) **THE BEST OF THE EAGLES** – Tequila sunrise / Lyin' eyes / Take it to the limit / Hotel California / Life in the fast lane / Heartache tonight / The long run / Take it easy / Peaceful easy feeling / Desperado / Best of my love / One of these nights / New kid in town. *(re-iss.Aug88 hit UK No.8)*	10	
Jun 88.	(7") **HOTEL CALIFORNIA. / PRETTY MAIDS ALL IN A ROW** (12"+=) – The sad cafe. (cd-s++=) – Hotel California (live).		
Jun 89.	(cd-ep) **TAKE IT EASY / ONE OF THESE NIGHTS / DESPERADO / LYIN' EYES**		
Jan 91.	(cd)(c)(lp) **BEST OF EAGLES**		
Jul 94.	(cd)(c) **THE VERY BEST OF EAGLES**	5	
Sep 85.	Old Gold; (7") **TAKE IT TO THE LIMIT. / BEST OF MY LOVE**		-
Sep 85.	Old Gold; (7") **HOTEL CALIFORNIA. / DESPERADO**		-
Oct 85.	Old Gold; (7") **LYIN' EYES. / ONE OF THESE NIGHTS**		-

Don HENLEY

Asylum Asylum

Aug 82. (lp)(c) **I CAN'T STAND STILL** [ ] [24]
– I can't stand still / You better hang up / Long way home / Nobody's business / Talking to the Moon / Dirty laundry / Johnny can't read / Them and us / La Eile / Lilah / The uncloudy day. *(cd-iss.1988)*

Sep 82. (7") **JOHNNY CAN'T READ. / LONG WAY HOME** [ ] [42] Aug 82
Dec 82. (7") **DIRTY LAUNDRY. / LILAH** [59] [3] Oct 82
(12"+=) – Them and us. *(re-iss.Jun85)*
Jan 83. (7") **I CAN'T STAND STILL. / THEM AND US** [-] [48]
May 83. (7") **THE UNCLOUDED DAY. / LONG WAY HOME** [ ] [ ]
(12"+=) – I can't stand still.
Jul 83 (7") **NOBODY'S BUSINESS. / LONG WAY HOME** [-] [ ]

Geffen Geffen

Dec 84. (7") **THE BOYS OF SUMMER. / A MONTH OF SUNDAYS** [12] [5] Nov 84
Feb 85. (lp)(c) **BUILDING THE PERFECT BEAST** [14] [13] Dec 84
– The boys of summer / You can't make love / Man with a mission / You're not drinking enough / Not enough love in the world / Building the perfect beast / All she wants to do is dance / Sunset grill / Drivin' with your eyes closed / Land of the living. *(cd+=)* – A month of Sundays. *(re-iss.Sep86) (cd-iss.Feb87 & 1988) (re-iss.+cd.Jan91 & Mar95)*

Apr 85. (7") **SUNSET GRILL. / BUILDING THE PERFECT BEAST** [ ] [-]
Jun 85. (7") **ALL SHE WANTS TO DO IS DANCE. / BUILDING THE PERFECT BEAST** [ ] [9] Feb 85
Jul 85. (7") **NOT ENOUGH LOVE IN THE WORLD. / MAN WITH A MISSION** [ ] [34] May 85
Aug 85. (7") **SUNSET GRILL. / MAN WITH A MISSION** [-] [22]

— His basic back-up consisted of **DANNY KORTCHMAR** – guitar, keyboards / **STAN LYNCH** – drums / **PINO PALLADINO** – bass / **JAI WINDING** – keyboards / **MIKE CAMPBELL** –

Jun 89. (lp)(c)(cd) **THE END OF THE INNOCENCE** [17] [8]
– The end of the innocence / How bad do you want it? / I will not go quietly / The last worthless evening / New York minute / Shangri-la / Little tin god / Gimme what you got / If dirt were dollars / The heart of the matter. *(re-iss.+cd.Jan91 & Oct95)*

Jul 89. (7") **THE END OF THE INNOCENCE. / IF DIRT WERE DOLLARS** [48] [8] Jun 89
(12"+=)(cd-s+=) – The boys of summer.
Oct 89. (7")(c-s) **NEW YORK MINUTE. / GIMME WHAT YOU GOT** [ ] [48] Nov 90
(10"+=)(12"+=)(cd-s+=) – Sunset grill (live).
Oct 89. (7") **THE LAST WORTHLESS EVENING. / GIMME WHAT YOU GOT** [-] [21]
Feb 90. (7")(c-s) **THE LAST WORTHLESS EVENING. / ALL SHE WANTS TO DO IS DANCE** [ ] [-]
(12"+=) – You can't make love.
(cd-s++=) – ('A'version).
Feb 90. (c-s) **THE HEART OF THE MATTER. / LITTLE TIN GOD** [-] [21]
Jul 90. (c-s) **HOW BAD DO YOU WANT IT?. / ?** [-] [48]

— In Sep 92, HENLEY charted US No.2 / UK No.22 with SOMETIMES LOVE JUST AIN'T ENOUGH.

— In Mar'93, DON featured on TRISH YEARWOOD's single 'Walkaway Joe'.

Nov 95. (cd)(c) **ACTUAL MILES: HENLEY'S GREATEST HITS** (compilation + 2 new *) [ ] [48]
– Dirty laundry / The boys of summer / All she wants to do is dance / Not enough love in the world / Sunset grill / The end of the innocence / The last worthless evening / New York minute / The heart of the matter / The garden of Allah * / You don't know me at all *. *(cd+=)*– I get the message.

Glenn FREY

Asylum Asylum

Jun 82. (lp)(c) **NO FUN ALOUD** [ ] [32]
– I found somebody / The one you love / Party town / I volunteer / I've been born again / Sea cruise / That girl / All those lies / She can't let go / Don't give up.

Jul 82. (7") **I FOUND SOMEONE. / SHE CAN'T LET GO** [ ] [31] Jun 82
Oct 82. (7") **THE ONE YOU LOVE. / ALL THOSE LIES** [-] [15]
Jan 83. (7") **ALL THOSE LIES. / THAT GIRL** [-] [41]

M.C.A. M.C.A.

Jul 84. (lp)(c) **THE ALLNIGHTER** [ ] [37]
– The allnighter / Sexy girl / I got love / Somebody else / Lover's moon / Smuggler's blues / Let's go home / Better in the U.S.A. / The heat is on / New love. *(re-act.Jun85 reached UK No.31) (cd-iss.Aug89)*

Aug 84. (7") **SEXY GIRL. / BETTER IN THE U.S.A.** [ ] [20]
Oct 84. (7") **THE ALLNIGHTER. / SMUGGLER'S BLUES** [-] [54]
Nov 84. (7") **SMUGGLER'S BLUES. / NEW LOVE** [ ] [12] Apr 85
Jan 85. (7")(12") **THE HEAT IS ON. / ('B'side by Harold Faltermeyer)** [12] [2] Dec 84

— Above was used for the film 'Beverly Hills Cop', starring Eddie Murphy.

— Below was issued on 'BBC' records in Britain only.

Jun 85. (7") **SMUGGLER'S BLUES. / NEW LOVE** [22] [-]
(12"+=) – Living in darkness.
Jul 85. (7") **SEXY GIRL. / BETTER IN THE U.S.A.** [ ] [-]
(12"+=) – The heat is on (dub) / New love.
Sep 85. (7") **YOU BELONG TO THE CITY. / SMUGGLER'S BLUES** [-] [2]
Oct 85. (7") **YOU BELONG TO THE CITY. / I GOT LOVE** [ ] [2] Sep 85
(12"+=) – ('A' version).
Sep 88. (7") **TRUE LOVE. / WORKING MAN** [ ] [13] Aug 88
(12"+=)(cd-s+=) – The heat is on.
Oct 88. (lp)(c)(cd) **SOUL SEARCHING** [ ] [36] Aug 88
– Soul searchin' / Livin' right / True love / I did it for your love / Working man / Two hearts / Some kind of blue / Can't put out this fire / Let's pretend we're still in love / It's your life.

Jan 89. (7") **SOUL SEARCHIN'. / IT'S COLD DOWN HERE** [ ] [ ]
(12"+=)(cd-s+=) – True love.
Mar 89. (7") **LIVIN' RIGHT. / SOUL SEARCHIN'** [-] [90]
May 89. (7") **TWO HEARTS. / SOME KIND OF BLUE** [-] [ ]

— Now writes with keyboard player **JAY OLIVER** or **JACK TEMPCHIN**

Apr 91. (c-s) **PART OF ME, PART OF YOU. /** [-] [55]

— (above taken from the film 'Thelma And Louise')

Jul 92. (7")(c-s) **I'VE GOT MINE. / PART OF ME, PART OF YOU** [ ] [91]
(cd-s+=) – A walk in the dark. (US; b-side)
Aug 92. (cd)(c)(lp) **STRANGE WEATHER** [ ] [ ]
– Silent spring / Long hot summer / Strange weather / Agua tranquillo / Love in the 21st century / He took advantage / River of dreams / Before the ship goes down / I've got mine / Rising sun / Brave new world / Delicious / A walk in the dark / Big life / Part of me, part of you.

Sep 92. (7") **RIVER OF DREAMS. / HE TOOK ADVANTAGE** [-] [ ]
May 93. (cd)(c) **LIVE (live)** [ ] [ ]
– Peaceful easy feeling / New kid in town / The one you love / Wild mountain thyme / Strange weather / I've got mine / Lyin' eyes – Take it easy (medley) / River of dreams / True love / Love in the 21st century / Smuggler's blues / The heat is on / Heartache tonight / Desperado.

Apr 95. (cd) **SOLO CONNECTION** [ ] [ ]
–

EAGLES

re-formed **HENLEY/ FREY/ WALSH/ FELDER + SCHMIDT**

Geffen Geffen

Nov 94. (cd)(c) **HELL FREEZES OVER** [28] [1]
– Get over it / Love will keep us alive / The girl from yesterday / Learn to be still / Tequila sunrise / Hotel California / Wasted time / Pretty maids all in a row / I can't tell you why / New York minute / The last resort / Take it easy / In the city / Life in the fast lane / Desperado.

Nov 94. (c-s)(cd-s) **GET OVER IT. / ?** [-] [31]

Steve EARLE

Born: 17 Jan'55, Fort Monroe, Virginia, USA but moved to Schertz, Texas, then Nashville. In 1981 he went solo and after one-off single on US indie, signed to 'Epic'. Gained hard reputation and with his DUKES signed worldwide to 'M.C.A.' in 1986. • **Style:** Country rock'n'roll with a social conscience that was influenced by SPRINGSTEEN or MELLENCAMP. • **Songwriters:** Himself except covers THE DEVIL'S RIGHT HAND MAN (Waylon Jennings) / DEAD FLOWERS (Rolling Stones) / TECUNSEH VALLEY (Steve Van Zandt) / RIVERS OF BABYLON (trad.) / etc. MARIA McKEE (ex-LONE JUSTICE) co-wrote 2 songs on his 1990 album. • **Trivia:** Late 1987 EARLE was attacked by policeman LONNIE ALLEN, but was sentenced to probation himself.

Recommended: COPPERHEAD ROAD (*6)

STEVE EARLE – vocals, guitar + sessions

not issued L.S.I.

1982. (7"ep) **PINK AND BLACK** [-] [ ]

not issued Epic

Aug 83. (7") **NOTHING BUT YOU. / CONTINENTAL TRAILWAY BLUES** [-] [ ]
Feb 84. (7") **SQUEEZE ME IN. / THE DEVIL'S RIGHT HAND** [-] [ ]
Jun 84. (7") **WHAT'LL YOU DO ABOUT ME. / CRY MYSELF TO SLEEP** [-] [ ]
Oct 84. (7") **A LITTLE BIT IN LOVE. / THE CRUSH** [-] [ ]

— (a couple more 45's were released Stateside, not known yet) **STEVE EARLE** – vocals, guitar (with The **DUKES**) **BUCKY BAXTER** – steel guitar, vocals / **RICHARD BENNETT** – guitars / **KEN MOORE** – organ, synthesizers, vocals / **HARRY STINSON** – drums, vocals / **EMORY GORDY JR.** – bass, mand plus **JOHN JARVIS** – piano / **STEVE NATHAN** – synth. / **PAUL FRANKLIN** – pedal steel

M.C.A. M.C.A.

Aug 86. (7") **SOMEDAY. / GUITAR TOWN** [ ] [ ]
Aug 86. (lp)(c) **GUITAR TOWN** [ ] [89]
– Guitar town / Goodbye's all we've got left / Hillbilly highway / Good ol' boy (gettin' tough) / My old friend the blues / Someday / Think it over / Fearless heart / Little rock'n'roller / Down the road. *(cd-iss.Apr87 / Jan90 +=) – Good ol' boy (gettin' tough) (live).*

Feb 87. (7") **SOMEDAY. / GUITAR TOWN** [ ] [ ]
(12"+=) – Good ol' boy (gettin' tough).
(cd-s++=) – Goodbye's all we've got.

— credited on sleeve to "STEVE EARLE & THE DUKES" (EARLE, BAXTER, MOORE, STINSON plus **RENO KING** – bass / **MIKE McADAM** – guitars. Others included **BENNETT, GORDY JR. / JARVIS** and **K-MEAUX BOUDIN** – accordion

Apr 87. (7") **FEARLESS HEART. / LITTLE ROCK'N'ROLLER** [ ] [ ]
(12"+=) – ('A'long version).
Apr 87. (lp)(c)(cd) **EXIT 'O'** [77] [90]
– Nowhere road / Sweel little '66' / No.29 / Angry young man / San Antonio girl / The rain came down / I ain't ever satisfied / The week of living dangerously / I love you too much / It's all up to you.

May 87. (7")(12") **I AIN'T EVER SATISFIED. / NOWHERE ROAD** [ ] [ ]
Nov 87. (d7") **THE RAIN CAME DOWN. / GUITAR TOWN (live)/ / I LOVE YOU TOO MUCH (live). / No.29 (live)** [ ] [ ]
Jun 88. (7") **I AIN'T EVER SATISFIED. / MY OLD FRIEND THE BLUES** [ ] [ ]
(12"+=) – I love you too much.

M.C.A. Uni

Sep 88. (7") **COPPERHEAD ROAD. / LITTLE SISTER** [45] [ ]
(12"+=) – No.29.
(cd-s+=) – San Antonio girl / I ain't ever satisfied.
Oct 88. (lp)(c)(cd) **COPPERHEAD ROAD** [44] [56]
– Copperhead road / Snake oil / Back to the wall / You belong to me / Devil's right hand / Johnny come lately / Even when I'm blue / Waiting on you / Once you love /

Nothing but a child. *(re-iss.cd+cAug93)*
Dec 88. (7") **JOHNNY COME LATELY. / NOTHING BUT A CHILD** 75
(12"+=) – Nebraska (live).
(cd-s++=) – Copperhead Road (live).
Feb 89. (7") **BACK TO THE WALL (edit). / SNAKE OIL**
(12"+=)(cd-s+=) – State trooper.

STEVE EARLE AND THE DUKES

He retained **BAXTER, MOORE** and p/t **JARVIS.** Newcomers = **ZIP GIBSON** – guitar, vocals / **KELLY LEONEY** – bass, vocals / **CRAIG WRIGHT** – drums. plus **PATRICK EARLE** – percussion and other guests
May 90. (7") **THE OTHER KIND. / WEST NASHVILLE BOOGIE**
(12"+=)(cd-s+=) – Guitar town (live) / Dead flowers (live).
Jun 90. (cd)(c)(lp) **THE HARD WAY** 22 100
– The other kind / Promise you anything / Hopeless romantics / Esmeralda's Hollywood / This highway's mine (roadmaster) / Billy Austin / Justice in Ontario / Have mercy / Country girl / When the people find out / Regular guy / Close your eyes / West Nashville boogie.
Sep 90. (7")(c-s) **JUSTICE IN ONTARIO. / THIS HIGHWAY'S MINE (ROADMASTER)**
(12"+=)(cd-s+=) – Copperhead road (live) / I ain't ever satisfied (live).
— **STACEY EARLE-MIMS** – b.vocals, acoustic percussion repl. JARVIS
Sep 91. (cd)(c)(d-lp) **SHUT UP AND DIE LIKE AN AVIATOR (live)** 62
– Good ol' boy (gettin' tough) / Devil's right hand / I ain't ever satisfied / Someday / West Nashville boogie / Snake oil / Blue yodel #9 / The other kind / Billy Austin / Copperhead road / Fearless heart / Guitar town / I love you too much / The rain came down / She's about a mover / Dead flowers.
— EARLE was dropped by record label, after being busted for heroin possession. He was sentenced to a year in prison and to attend a rehab centre. He was released in 1994 and was straight back to recording.
— with PETER ROWAN / NORMAN BLAKE / ROY HUSKEY + EMMYLOU HARRIS

Tranatlantic Winter Har
Jul 95. (cd)(c) **TRAIN a COMIN'**
– Mystery train part II / Hometown blues / Sometimes she forgets / Mercenary song / Goodbye / Tom Ames' prayer / Nothin' without you / Angel is the Devil / I'm looking through you / Northern winds / Ben McCulloch / Rivers of Babylon / Tecumseh Valley.

– compilations etc. –

Jul 87. Epic; (lp)(c) **EARLY TRACKS** Oct 86
– Nothin' but you / If you need a fool / Continental trailway blues / Open up your door / Breakdown lane / Squeeze me in / Annie, is tonight the night / My baby worships me / Cadillac / Devil's right hand. *(cd-iss.Jul91 on 'Pickwick') (was to have been released '83 as 'CADILLAC')*
Oct 93. Pickwick; (cd)(c) **THIS HIGHWAY'S MINE**

Elliott EASTON (see under ⇒ CARS)

EARTH, WIND & FIRE

Formed: Chicago, Illinois, USA . . . 1969 as The SALTY PEPPERS by ex-session man MAURICE WHITE. In 1970, they became EARTH, WIND & FIRE and signed to 'Warners'. They released 2 albums before WHITE sacked most of group to employ others, and signed to 'Columbia' in 1972. By the mid 70's, after a US No.1 'SHINING STAR', they had risen to be one of America's top pop soul attractions. Continued to maintain chart status, with PHILIP BAILEY even managing some mid-80's solo hits, one a No.1 with PHIL COLLINS 'EASY LOVER'. • **Style:** Progressive black rock band that shifted into funk and disco pop by mid 70's. • **Songwriters:** WHITE penned with others, except covers MAKE IT WITH YOU (Bread) / WHERE HAVE ALL THE FLOWERS GONE (Pete Seeger) / GOT TO GET YOU INTO MY LIFE (Beatles) / AFTER THE LOVE HAS GONE (c.David Foster, Bill Champlin + Jay Graydon) / etc. • **Trivia:** Backing female group The EMOTIONS, also scored a few hits, hitting big in 1977 with US No.1 'BEST OF MY LOVE'.

Recommended: THE BEST OF EARTH, WIND & FIRE VOL.1 (*6)

MAURICE WHITE (b.19 Dec'41, Memphis, USA) – vocals, drums, percussion, etc (ex-RAMSEY LEWIS TRIO, also sessioned for IMPRESSIONS / JACKIE WILSON / etc.) /**VERDINE WHITE** (b.25 Jul'51) – bass / **WADE FLEMONS** – keyboards, vocals / **DON WHITEHEAD** – piano, vocals / **MICHAEL BEAL** – guitar, etc. / **SHERRY SCOTT** – vocals / **YACKOV BEN ISRAEL** – congas, etc. / **CHET WASHINGTON** – t.sax / **ALEX THOMAS** – trombone

SALTY PEPPERS

not issued Capitol
1969. (7") **LA LA TIME. / (part II)** -
1969. (7") **YOUR LOVE IS LIFE. / UH HUH YEAH** -

EARTH, WIND & FIRE

Warners Warners
Jan 71. (7") **THIS WORLD TODAY. / FAN THE FIRE** -
Mar 71. (7") **LOVE IS LIFE. / THIS WORLD TODAY** - 93
Mar 71. (lp) **EARTH, WIND AND FIRE** -
– Help somebody / Moment of truth / Love is life / Fan the fire / C'mon children / The world today / Bad tune. *(re-iss.Sep80 on 'Pickwick')*
May 71. (7") **LOVE IS LIFE. / HELP SOMEBODY** 93
Nov 71. (7") **C'MON CHILDREN. / I THINK ABOUT LOVIN' YOU** -
Jan 72. (lp)(c) **THE NEED OF LOVE** - 89
– Energy / Beauty / I can feel it in my bones / I think about lovin' you / Everything is everything.
— **WHITE** retains only brother **VERDINE,** and recruited/**employed new line-up PHILIP BAILEY** (b.8 May'51, Denver, Colorado, USA) – vocals, percussion / **LARRY DUNN** (b.19 Jun'53, Colorado) – keyboards, clavinet /**RALPH JOHNSON** (b. 4 Jul'51, California) – drums, percussion / **ROLAND BAUTISTA** – guitar / **RONALD LAWS** – saxophone, flute / **JESSICA CLEAVES** – vocals

C.B.S. Columbia
Oct 72. (lp)(c) **LAST DAYS AND TIME** 87
– Time is on your side / They don't see / Make it with you / Power / Remember the children / Where have all the flowers gone / I'd rather have you / Mom. *(re-iss.Oct79)*
— **AL McKAY** (b. 2 Feb'48, Louisiana, USA) – guitar repl. BAUTISTA / **ANDREW WOODFOLK** (b.11 Oct'50, Texas) – horns repl. LAWS who went solo / added **JOHNNY GRAHAM** (b. 3 Aug'51, Kentucky, USA)
May 73. (lp)(c) **HEAD TO THE SKY** 27
– Evil / Keep your head to the sky / Build your nest / The world's masquerade / Clover / Zanzibar. *(re-iss.1975 & Mar81)(re-iss.cd+cSep93 on 'Sony Collectors')*
Oct 73. (7") **EVIL. / CLOVER** 50 Jul 73
Feb 74. (7") **KEEP YOUR HEAD TO THE SKY. / BUILD YOUR NEST** 53 Nov 73
— now w/out JESSICA
May 74. (7") **MIGHTY MIGHTY. / DRUM SONG** 29 Mar 74
Jun 74. (lp)(c) **OPEN OUR EYES** 15 Mar 74
– Mighty mighty / Devotion / Fair but so uncool / Feelin' blue / Kalimba story / Drum song / The nine chee bit / Spasmodic mood / Caribou / Open our eyes. *(re-iss.Mar81)*
Sep 74. (7") **DEVOTION. / ?** - 33
Nov 74. (7") **KALIMBA STORY. / THE NINE CHEE BIT** 55 Jul 74
— added other brother **FRED WHITE** (b.13 Jan'55, Chicago) – drums
Early 1975, E, W & F were credited on 2 singles by RAMSEY LEWIS – 'Hot Dawgit' No.50 / 'Sun Goddess' No.44 (both US).
Apr 75. (lp)(c) **THAT'S THE WAY OF THE WORLD** 1 Mar75
– Shining star / That's the way of the world / Happy feelin' / All about love / Yearnin' learnin' / Reasons / Africano / See the light. *(re-iss.Nov81) (cd-iss. 1988?)*
Apr 75. (7") **SHINING STAR. / YEARNIN' LEARNIN'** 1 Feb 75
Jul 75. (7") **THAT'S THE WAY OF THE WORLD. / AFRICANO** 12
Nov 75. (7") **SHININ' STAR (live). / HAPPY FEELIN'** -
Dec 75. (d-lp)(c) **GRATITUDE (most live)** 1 Nov 75
– (introduction) / Sing a song / Gratitude / Celebrate / Can't hide love / Sunshine / Shining star / Sun Goddess / reasons / Sing a message to you / Devotion / Medley: Africano – Power / Yearnin' learnin'. *(re-iss.May82) (cd-iss. 1987)*
Apr 76. (7") **SING A SONG (live). / ('A' instrumental)** 5 Nov 75
Mar 76. (7") **CAN'T HIDE LOVE. / GRATITUDE** - 39
May 76. (7") **REASONS (live). / GRATITUDE** -
Aug 76. (7") **GETAWAY. / ('A' instrumental)** 12 Jul 76
Nov 76. (lp)(c) **SPIRIT** 2 Sep 76
– Getaway / On your face / Imagination / Spirit / Saturday nite / Earth, wind and fire / Departure / Biyo / Burnin' bush. *(re-iss.Apr84 on 'Pickwick')*
Jan 77. (7") **SATURDAY NITE. / DEPARTURE** 17 21 Nov 76
Apr 77. (7") **BIYO. / ON YOUR FACE** -
Jun 77. (7") **ON YOUR FACE. / DEPARTURE** -
Dec 77. (7") **SERPENTINE FIRE. / ('A' instrumental)** 13 Oct 77
Jan 78. (lp)(c) **ALL'N'ALL** 13 3 Nov 77
– Serpentine fire / Fantasy / In the market place / Jupiter / Love's holiday / Brazillian rhyme / I'll write a song for you / Master mind / Runnin' / Be ever wonderful. *(re-iss.Mar83) (cd-iss.1987)*
Jan 78. (7") **FANTASY. / RUNNIN'** - 32
Feb 78. (7") **FANTASY. / BOOGIE WONDERLAND** 14 32
Apr 78. (7") **JUPITER. / RUNNIN'** 41
Jul 78. (7") **MAGIC MIND. / LOVE'S HOLIDAY** 54 -
Sep 78. (7") **GOT TO GET YOU INTO MY LIFE. / I'LL WRITE A SONG FOR YOU** 33 9 Jul 78
Oct 78. (7") **SEPTEMBER. / LOVE'S HOLIDAY** - 8
Nov 78. (7") **SEPTEMBER. / CAN'T HAVE LOVE** 3 8
Dec 78. (lp)(c) **THE BEST OF EARTH, WIND & FIRE, VOL.1** 6 6 Nov 78
(compilation)
– Got to get you into my life / Fantasy / Can't hide love / Saturday night / Love music / Getaway / That's the way of the world / September / Shining star / Reasons / Singasong. *(re-iss.Nov84) (cd-iss.1987)*
May 79. (7")(12") **BOOGIE WONDERLAND. ("EARTH, WIND & FIRE with The EMOTIONS") / ('A'instrumental)** 4 6
Jun 79. (lp)(c) **I AM** 5 3
– In the stone / Can't let go / After the love has gone / Let your feelings show / Boogie wonderland / Star / Wait / Rock that / You and I. *(re-iss.Jun85) (cd-iss.1987)*
Jul 79. (7") **AFTER THE LOVE HAS GONE. / ROCK THAT** 4 2
Sep 79. (7") **STAR. / YOU AND I** 16 64 Dec 79
Oct 79. (7") **IN THE STONE. / YOU AND I** - 58
Dec 79. (7") **CAN'T LET GO. / LOVE MUSIC** 46 -
Feb 80. (7") **IN THE STONE. / AFRICAN BIYO** 53 -
Sep 80. (7") **LET ME TALK. / ('A'instrumental)** 29 44
Oct 80. (d-lp)(c) **FACES** 10 10
– Let me talk / Turn it into something good / Pride / You / Sparkle / Back on the road / Song in my heart / You went away / And love goes on / Sail away / Take it to the sky / Win or lose / Share your love / In time / Faces. *(re-iss.cdOct93 on 'Sony Europe')*
Nov 80. (7") **YOU. / SHARE YOUR LOVE** -
Dec 80. (7")(12") **BACK ON THE ROAD. / TAKE IT TO THE SKY** 63
Jan 80. (7") **AND LOVE GOES ON. / WIN OR LOSE** - 59
Feb 81. (7")(12") **AND LOVE GOES ON. / FACES** -
May 81. (7") **YOU. / PRIDE** -
— **ROLAND BAUTISTA** – guitar rejoined repl. McKAY who went into production.
Oct 81. (7")(12") **LET'S GROOVE. / ('A'instrumental)** 3 3
Nov 81. (lp)(c) **RAISE** 14 5
– Let's groove / Lady Sun / My love / Evolution orange / Kalimba tree / You are a winner / I've had enough / Wanna be with you / The changing times. *(re-*

iss.+cd.Aug86)

Jan 82. (7")(12") **I'VE HAD ENOUGH. / KALIMBA TREE** 29 -
Jan 82. (7") **WANNA BE WITH YOU. / KALIMBA TREE** - 51
Mar 82. (7") **WANNA BE WITH YOU. / MY LOVE** -
Jan 83. (7")(12") **FALL IN LOVE WITH ME. / LADY SUN** 47 17
Feb 83. (lp)(c) **POWERLIGHT** 22 12
– Fall in love with me / Spread your love / Side by side / Straight from the heart / The speed of love / Freedom of choice / Something special / Heart to heart / Miracles. *(cd-iss.1988)(re-iss.cd Oct93 on 'Sony Europe')*
Mar 83. (7") **SPREAD YOUR LOVE. / HEART TO HEART** -
May 83. (7") **SIDE BY SIDE. / SOMETHING SPECIAL** - 76
Jul 83. (7")(12") **SPREAD YOUR LOVE. / FREEDOM OF CHOICE** -

— Still a member, PHIL BAILEY also takes on solo career.

Nov 83. (7")(12") **MAGNETIC. / SPEED OF LOVE** 57
Dec 83. (lp)(c) **ELECTRIC UNIVERSE** 40
– Magnetic / Touch / Moonwalk / Could it be right / Spirit of a new world / Sweet sassy lady / We're living in our own time / Electic nation. *(cd-iss.1988)*
Feb 84. (7") **TOUCH. / SEPTEMBER** -
Feb 84. (7") **TOUCH. / SWEET SASSY LADY** -
May 84. (7") **MOONWALK. / WE'RE LIVING IN OUR OWN TIME** -
(12"+=) – After the love has gone / Boogie wonderland.

— Disbanded Mar'84,

MAURICE WHITE

solo.

C.B.S. Columbia

Sep 85. (7")(12") **STAND BY ME. / CAN'T STOP LOVE** 50
Dec 85. (lp)(c) **MAURICE WHITE** 61
– Switched on your radio / Jamboree / Stand by me / Sea of glass / I need you / Believe in magic / Lady is love / Invitation / Sleeping flame / Alpha dance / Children of Afrika.
Jan 86. (7") **BELIEVE IN MAGIC. / I NEED YOU** - 95 B-side
Mar 86. (7") **INVITATION. / LADY IS LOVE** -

EARTH, WIND & FIRE

re-formed (**MAURICE WHITE, VERDINE WHITE, PHILIP BAILEY, ANDREW WOODFOLK**)plus new man **SHELDON REYNOLDS** – guitar + loads of session people.

Oct 87. (7") **SYSTEM OF SURVIVAL. / WRITING ON THE WALL** 54 60
(12"+=) – ('A'accapella) / ('A'dub).
(12"+=)(cd-s+=) – ('A'-12"version).
Nov 87. (lp)(c)(cd) **TOUCH THE WORLD** 33
– System of survival / Evil boy / Thinking of you / You and I / Musical interlude new horizons / Mon ey tight / Every now and then / Touch the world / Here today and gone tomorrow / Victim of the modern heart.
Dec 87. (7") **MUSICAL INTERLUDE: NEW HORIZONS. / YOU AND I** -
Feb 88. (7") **THINKING OF YOU. / MONEY TIGHT** 67
(12"+=) – ('A'version).
(cd-s+=) – ('A'house mix).
Feb 88 (7") **EVIL BOY. / (part 2)** -
1989. (7") **TURN ON (THE BEAT BOX). / (part 2)** -

— added **RALPH JOHNSON** – percussion / **SONNY EMORY** – drums / **+ session people**

Feb 90. (7")(c-s) **HERITAGE. / GOTTA FIND OUT**
(12"+=) – ('A'acapella) / Let's groove (extended).
(cd-s+=) – Fantasy / September / ('A'extended).
(cd-s+=) – Brazillian rhyme (interlude) / Got to get you into my life / I've had enough.
Mar 90. (cd)(c)(lp) **HERITAGE** Feb 90
– Soweto / Takin' chances / Heritage / Good time / Body wrap / Anything you want / Bird / Wanna be the man / Close to home / Daydreamin' / King of the groove / I'm in love / For the love of you / Gotta find out / Motor / Faith / Welcome / Soweto (reprise).
Apr 90. (7") **FOR THE LOVE OF YOU. / MOTOR** -
Sep 90. (7")(c-s) **WANNA BE THE MAN. / WELCOME** -
('A'extended-12"+=)(cd-s+=) – ('A'dub version).

Columbia Columbia

May 91. (cd)(c) **THE BEST OF EARTH, WIND & FIRE, VOL.2**
– (compilation)

Reprise Reprise

Sep 93. (cd)(c) **MILLENIUM, YESTERDAY, TODAY** 39
– Even if you wonder / Sunday morning / Blood brothers / Kalimba interlude / Spend the night / Divine / Two hearts / Honor the magic / Love is the greatest story / The L word / Just another lonely night / Super hero / Wouldn't change a thing about you / Love across the wire / Chicago (Chitown) blues / Kalimba blues.
Oct 93. (7")(c-s) **SUNDAY MORNING. / THE L WORD** 53 Aug 93
(cd-s+=) – Just another lonely heart.

Avex Avex

Nov 95. (cd)(c) **LIVE AND UNPLUGED (live)**
–

– other compilations, others, etc. –

Sep 74. Warners; (d-lp) **ANOTHER TIME** (first 2 lp's)
Note; All 'CBS' releases on US counterpart 'Columbia'.
1975. CBS; (7") **KEEP YOUR HEAD TO THE SKY. / EVIL** -
Apr 77. CBS; (7") **SING A SONG. / BIYO** -
Oct 79. CBS; (t-lp-box) **EARTH, WIND & FIRE** -
– (3 early albums)
1980. CBS; (7") **FANTASY. / BOOGIE WONDERLAND** -
Aug 80. CBS; (7") **AFTER THE LOVE HAS GONE. / THAT'S THE WAY OF THE WORLD** -
Apr 82. CBS; (7") **SEPTEMBER. / AFTER THE LOVE HAS GONE** -
1982. CBS; (c-ep) **SING A SONG / BIYO / SHINING STAR / THAT'S THE END OF THE WORLD** -
Jun 86. CBS; (7")(12") **BOOGIE WONDERLAND. / LET'S GROOVE** -
Jul 89. CBS; (cd) **GREATEST HITS** -
Dec 90. CBS; (3xcd-box) **I AM / ALL'N'ALL / RAISE** -
Sep 85. Old Gold; (7") **FANTASY. / SEPTEMBER** -
Sep 85. Old Gold; (7") **BOOGIE WONDERLAND. / LET'S GROOVE** -
Feb 86. Old Gold; (12"ep) **STAR / SATURDAY NITE. / AFTER THE LOVE HAS GONE / I'VE HAD ENOUGH** -
May 86. K-Tel; (lp)(c)(cd) **THE COLLECTION** -
May 88. Arcade; (cd) **THE VERY BEST OF . . . VOL.1** -
May 88. Arcade; (cd) **THE VERY BEST OF . . . VOL.2** -
Oct 94. Columbia; (cd) **THE BEST**
Dec 95. Columbia; (cd)(c) **THE LOVE SONGS**

PHILIP BAILEY

C.B.S. Columbia

Aug 83. (7")(12") **I KNOW. / THE GOOD GUYS ARE SUPPOSED TO GET THE GIRLS**
Sep 83. (lp)(c) **CONTINUATION** 71
– I know / It's our time / Desire / I'm waiting for your love / Vaya (go with love) / The good guys supposed to get the girls / Your boyfriend's back. *(re-iss.Feb86)*
Oct 83. (7")(12") **WAITING FOR YOUR LOVE. / VAYA (GO WITH LOVE)**
Nov 83. (7") **VAYA (GO WITH LOVE). / TRAPPED** -
Oct 84. (7")(12") **CHILDREN OF THE GHETTO. / SHOW YOU THE WAY TO LOVE**
Oct 84. (lp)(c) **CHINESE WALL** 29 22
– Photogenic memory / I go crazy / Walking on the Chinese wall / For every heart that's been broken / Go / Easy lover / Show you the way to love / Time is a woman / Woman / Children of the ghetto. *(re-iss.+cd.Nov86) (cd-iss.Nov93 on 'Sony Collectors') (cd-iss.May95 on 'Columbia')*
Jan 85. (7") **WALKING ON THE CHINESE WALL. / WOMAN**
(12"+=) – I know.
Mar 85. (7")(12") **EASY LOVER. ("PHILIP BAILEY & PHIL COLLINS") / WOMAN** 2 1 Dec 84
(12"+=) – ('A'extended).
Jun 85. (7") **WALKING ON THE CHINESE WALL. / CHILDREN OF THE GHETTO** - 46
May 85. (7") **WALKING ON THE CHINESE WALL. / TRAPPED** 34 -
Jul 85. (7")(12") **CHILDREN OF THE GHETTO. / SHOW YOU THE WAY TO LOVE**
May 86. (7")(12") **STATE OF THE HEART. / TAKE THIS WITH YOU**
May 86. (lp)(c)(cd) **INSIDE OUT** 84
– Welcome to the club / State of the heart / Long distance love / Echo my heart / Don't leave me baby / Special effect / Because of you / Back it up / Take this with you / The day will come.
Jun 86. (7") **ECHO MY HEART. / SPECIAL EFFECT** -
Jul 86. (7") **ECHO MY HEART. / TAKE THIS WITH YOU** -
(12"+=) – Walking on the Chinese wall / Children of the ghetto.
In Mar89, he teamed up with LITTLE RICHARD on film single 'TWINS'.

– others by BAILEY on religious label 'Myrrh' –

Feb 85. (lp)(c) **WONDERS OF HIS LOVE** Nov 84
(cd-iss.Jul88)
Nov 86. (lp)(c)(cd) **TRIUMPH**
Feb 90. (cd)(c)(lp) **FAMILY AFFAIR**

EASYBEATS

Formed: Sydney, Australia ... 1963 by 3 ex-UK compatriots WRIGHT, YOUNG and FLEET, plus Dutch immigrants VANDA and DIAMONDE, who all met in a migrant youth hostel. Took group name from a Brian Matthews titled radio show, and were soon signed by Ted Albert of 'Parlophone' Australia. Their second 45 'SHE'S SO FINE' hit No.1 down under, and was followed by a string of Australian chartbusters. In mid-66, they signed worldwide deal with 'United Art', and were soon Top 20 UK/US with 'FRIDAY ON MY MIND'. They found it hard to emulate this classic pop song, and by the late 60's, had parted company (see below). • **Style:** Ranged from being easy-listening pop to dippy psychedelic rock-pop. • **Songwriters:** WRIGHT-YOUNG or VANDA-YOUNG, except HIT THE ROAD JACK (Ray Charles) / CAN'T TAKE MY EYES OFF YOU (Frankie Valli; hit) / etc. • **Trivia:** After moving back to Australia, GEORGE YOUNG produced JOHN PAUL YOUNG, who had UK + US Top 10 hit with 'Love Is In The Air'. GEORGE had previously, instigated two of his other brothers ANGUS & MALCOLM to form own heavy-metal outfit AC/DC.

Recommended: THE COLLECTION (*5)

LITTLE STEVIE WRIGHT (b.20 Dec'48, Leeds, England) – vocals / **HARRY VANDA** (b.HARRY VANDAN, 22 Mar'47, Holland) – guitar (ex-STARFIGHTERS) / **GEORGE YOUNG** (b. 6 Nov'47, Glasgow, Scotland) – guitar / **DICK DIAMONDE** (b.28 Dec'47, Holland) – bass / **GORDON 'SNOWY' FLEET** (b.16 Aug'45, Liverpool, England) – drums (ex-MOJOS)

Parlophone AUSTRALIA not issued

Mar 65. (7") **FOR MY WOMAN. / SAY THAT YOU'RE MINE** - -
May 65. (7") **SHE'S SO FINE. / THE OLD OAK TREE** - -
Jun 65. (lp) **EASY** - -
– It's so easy / I'm a madman / I wonder / She said alright / I'm gonna tell everybody / Hey girl / She's so fine / You got it off me / Cry, cry, cry / A letter / Easy beat / You'll come back again / Girl on my mind / Ya can't do that.
Jul 65. (7") **WEDDING RING. / ME OR YOU** - -

Sep 65. (7") **EASY AS CAN BE. / SAD & LONELY & BLUE** - -
Jan 66. (7") **WOMEN. / IN MY BOOK** - -
Jan 66. (lp) **IT'S 2 EASY** - -
– Let me be / You are the light / Women (make you feel alright) / Come and see her / I'll find somebody to take your place / Someway, somewhere / Easy as can be / I can see / Sad and lonely blue eyes / Somethin' wrong / In my book / What about our love / Then I'll tell you goodbye / Wedding ring. *cd-iss.Mar93 on 'Repertoire')*
Jun 66. (lp) **VOLUME 3** - -
– Sorry / Funny feeling / Say you want me / You said that / Goin' out of my mind / Not in love with you / Promised things / The last day of Mary / Today / My my my / Dance of the lovers / What do you want babe / Can you leave her?. *(cd-iss.Mar93 on 'Repertoire')*
Aug 66. (7") **SORRY. / FUNNY FEELING** - -

— Group had earlier moved to London, England. Still signed to 'Parlophone' Australia.

United Art United Art

Jun 66. (7") **COME AND SEE HER. / WOMEN** -
Oct 66. (7") **FRIDAY ON MY MIND. / MADE MY BED, GONNA LIE ON IT** 6 16 Mar 67
Mar 67. (7") **WHO'LL BE THE ONE?. / SATURDAY NIGHT**

— (In Australia, above 'B'side was DO YOU HAVE A SOUL)

Apr 67. (lp) **GOOD FRIDAY**
– Saturday night / Happy is the man / Do you have a soul / River deep mountain high / Hound dog / Pretty girl / Friday on my mind / Who'll be the one / Made my bed gonna lie in it / Remember Sam. *(US-title* **'FRIDAY ON MY MIND', Seeline woman** repl.) *(US version re-iss+cd.Nov85 on 'Fan Club', re-cd-iss.Feb92 on 'Repertoire' US title)*

— (Mar67) **FREDDIE SMITH** – drums repl. FLEET who returned to Australia. Later **TONY CAHILL** repl. SMITH more permanently after recording of below lp.

Jun 67. (7") **HEAVEN AND HELL. / PRETTY GIRL**
Nov 67. (7") **FALLING OFF THE EDGE OF THE WORLD. / REMEMBER SAM** - -
Jan 68. (7") **MUSIC GOES ROUND MY HEAD. / COME IN YOU'LL GET PNEUMONIA** - -
Mar 68. (7") **HELLO, HOW ARE YOU? / FALLING OFF THE EDGE OF THE WORLD** 20 -
Mar 68. (7") **HELLO, HOW ARE YOU? / COME IN YOU'LL GET PNEUMONIA** -
May 68. (lp) **VIGIL**
– Good times / What in the world / Falling off the edge of the world / Music goes round my head / Can't take my eyes off you / Sha la la / Come on in you'll get pneumonia / See saw / Land of make believe / Fancy seeing you here / Hello how are you / Hit the road Jack / We all live happily together / I can't stand it. *(cd-iss.Feb92 on 'Repertoire')(US-title 'FALLING OFF THE EDGE OF THE WORLD')*
Jun 68. (7") **THE LAND OF MAKE BELIEVE. / WE ALL LIVE HAPPILY TOGETHER** -
Sep 68. (7") **GOOD TIMES. / LAY ME DOWN AND DIE**

— (Aussie 'B'side, THE LAND OF MAKE BELIEVE)

Dec 68. (7") **LAY ME DOWN AND DIE. / SEE LINE WOMAN** - -

Polydor Rare Earth

Oct 69. (7") **ST.LOUIS. / CAN'T FIND LOVE** 100
Nov 69. (lp) **FRIENDS**
– St.Louis / Who are my friends / Watching the world go by / Can't find love / Holding on / I love Marie / Rock and roll boogie / Tell your mother / Train song / What becomes of you my love / Woman you're on my mind. *(cd-iss.Nov92 on 'Repertoire')*
Jan 70. (7") **I LOVE MARIE. / GONNA MAKE IT** -

— (above credited to "HARRY VANDA" in the UK)

Apr 70. (7") **FRIENDS. / ROCK'N'ROLL BOOGIE** -

— Disbanded early 1970. CAHILL joined PYTHON LEE JACKSON then RAY CHARLES.

- compilations, others, etc. -

on 'Parlophone' Australia until mentioned.

1965. (7"ep) **SHE'S SO FINE** - -
1965. (7"ep) **EASY AS CAN BE** - -
1965. (7"ep) **EASY FEVER** - -
1966. (7"ep) **FRIDAY ON MY MIND** - -
1966. (lp) **THE BEST OF THE EASYBEATS, PLUS PRETTY GIRL** - -
1967. (7"ep) **HEAVEN AND HELL** - -
1967. (7"ep) **EASY FEVER VOLUME 2** - -
1970. (7") **PECULIAR HOLE IN THE SKY. / ?** - -
1970s. Raven Australia; (7"ep) **MEAN OLD LOVIN'** - -
1970s. Raven Australia; (7"ep) **SON OF EASY FEVER** - -
1978. Albert Australia; (lp) **THE SHAME JUST DRAINED** - -
– (cd-iss.Mar93 on 'Repertoire')
1980. Albert Australia; (d-lp) **ABSOLUTE ANTHOLOGY** - -
1985. New Rose; (7") **FRIDAY ON MY MIND. / HELLO, HOW ARE YOU** -
Jan 87. Fan Club; (lp) **EASY AS CAN BE – THE BEST OF THE EASYBEATS VOLUME 2** -
Jan 86. Rhino; (lp) **THE BEST OF THE EASYBEATS** -
(cd-iss.May95 on 'Repertoire')
Feb 85. EMI Gold; (7") **FRIDAY ON MY MIND. / HELLO, HOW ARE YOU** -
(re-iss.Jun88 on 'Old Gold')
(above 'A'side also on flip of ZOMBIES 45)
Dec 89. Impact; (cd) **THE COLLECTION** -

PAINTBOX

are formed by **GEORGE and HARRY.**

Youngblood Youngblood

Oct 71. (7") **GET READY FOR LOVE. / CAN I GET TO KNOW YOU** -

— They then become TRAMP then WHATWHAT.

HAFFY'S WHISKY SOUR

Deram not issued

Nov 71. (7") **SHOT IN THE HEAD. / BYE BYE BLUEBIRD** -

— Yet again they change name to

MARCUS HOOK ROLL BAND

after brief spell as GRAPEFRUIT with GEORGE ALEXANDER.

Regal Zono. Capitol

Aug 72. (7") **NATURAL MAN. / BOOGALOOING IS FOR WRONG**
Mar 73. (7") **LOUISIANA LADY. / HOOCHIE COOCHIE HAR KAU**
1973. (lp) **FEATURING VANDA & YOUNG** -
– Can't stand the heat / Goodbye Jane / Quick reaction / Silver shoes / Watch her do it now / People and the power / Red revolution / Shot in the head / Ape man / Louisiana lady.

E.M.I. not issued

Mar 74. (7") **CAN'T STAND THE HEAT. / MOONSHINE BLUES** -

— VANDA and YOUNG returned to Australia, where YOUNG also became producer for little brothers band AC/DC. He also sessioned for them in 1974.

FLASH AND THE PAN

were formed by GEORGE and HARRY.

Ensign Epic

Apr 77. (7") **HEY ST.PETER. / WALKING IN THE RAIN** -
(re-iss.Aug79, hit US No.76)
Jul 78. (7") **AND THE BAND PLAYED ON (DOWN AMONG THE DEAD MEN). / MAN WHO KNEW THE ANSWER** 54
Mar 79. (7") **CALIFORNIA. / HOLE IN THE MIDDLE**
Jun 79. (7") **AFRICAN SHUFFLE. / FIRST AND LAST**
Jul 79. (lp)(c) **FLASH AND THE PAN** 80
– African shuffle / And the band played on (down among the dead men) / California / First and last / Hey, St.Peter / Hole in the middle / Lady killer / Man in the middle / Man who knew the answer / Walking in the rain.

— added **LEE KARSKI** – bass / **RAY ARNOTT** – drums / **WARREN MORGAN** – piano.

Jun 80. (7") **MEDIA MAN. / MAKE YOUR OWN CROSS**
Aug 80. (lp)(c) **LIGHTS IN THE NIGHT**
– Media man / Headhunter / Restless / Welcome to the universe / Make your own cross / Lights in the night / Captain beware / Atlantis calling.

— **LYNDSAY HAMMOND** – vocals / **RALPH WHITE** – horns repl. KARSKI + MORGAN

1982. (lp)(c) **HEADLINES**
– Jetsetter's ball / Don't vote / Waiting for a train / War games / Where were you? / Love is a gun / Up against the wall / Psychos in the street / Hey Jimmy / Phil the creole.
1982. (7") **HEY JIMMY. / WHERE WERE YOU** -

Easy Beat Epic

Apr 83. (7") **WAITING FOR A TRAIN. / ('A" instrumental)** 7
Jul 83. (lp)(c) **PAN-ORAMA** 69
– (cd-iss.1988 on 'De-Lite')

Epic Epic

Nov 84. (7")(12") **MIDNIGHT MAN. / FAT NIGHT**

— now duo of **VANDA + YOUNG** again

Feb 85. (lp)(c) **EARLY MORNING WAKE UP CALL**
– Early morning wake up call / Communication breakdown / Barking at the Moon / Downtown too long / Opera singers / Midnight man / On the road / Look at that woman go / Fat night / Believe in yourself.
May 88. (lp)(c)(cd) **NIGHTS IN FRANCE**
– Money don't lie / Nights in France / Ayla / Yesterday's gone / Drawn by the light / Hard livin' / Savior man / Bones.
Jul 88. (7") **AYLA. / YOUR LOVE IS STRANGE**
(12"+=) – ('A'disco).
(cd-s++=) – ('A'original out of town mix).

- compilations, others, etc. -

1983. Easybeat; (7") **AND THE BAND PLAYED ON (DOWN AMONG THE DEAD MEN). / MAN IN THE MIDDLE** -
1989. Cha Cha; (7")(12")(cd-s) **WAITING FOR A TRAIN. / ('A'-'89 version)** -
Jun 91. Old Gold; (12") **WAITING FOR A TRAIN. / DOWN AMONG THE DEAD MEN** -

EAT STATIC (see under ⇒ OZRIC TENTACLES)

EAZY-E (see under ⇒ N.W.A.)

ECHO AND THE BUNNYMEN

Formed: Liverpool, England . . . Autumn 1978 by McCULLOCH, SERGEANT and PATTINSON. McCULLOCH had once been in The CRUCIAL THREE alongside JULIAN COPE and PETE WYLIE. McCULLOCH and COPE formed A SHALLOW MADNESS, and together they co-wrote 'READ IT IN BOOKS' (the b-side of debut single 'PICTURES ON MY WALL'). The BUNNYMEN, complete with drum machine ECHO, released this one-off for local 'Zoo' label, before signing to 'W.E.A.' subsidiary 'Korova' late in '79. By the following year, they'd had a Top 10 album and were soon breaking

into singles chart. • **Style:** Very much DOORS influenced, but with fresher up-tempo appeal, that was very much part of a new Merseyside-based sound of the early 80's. • **Songwriters:** Mainly group compositions except PEOPLE ARE STRANGE (Doors) / PAINT IT BLACK (Rolling Stones) / ALL YOU NEED IS LOVE (Beatles) / FRICTION (Television) / RUN RUN RUN (Velvet Underground) / SHIP OF FOOLS (John Cale). McCULLOCH covered: SEPTEMBER SONG (Kurt Weill) / RETURN TO SENDER (Elvis Presley) / LOVER, LOVER, LOVER (Leonard Cohen). • **Trivia:** DAVE BALFE (of DALEK I LOVE YOU) played keyboards on their first JOHN PEEL session in August 1979.

Recommended: CROCODILES (*9) / HEAVEN UP HERE (*9) / SONGS TO LEARN AND SING (*9) / PORCUPINE (*7) / OCEAN RAIN (*7) / ECHO & THE BUNNYMEN (*5) / CANDLELAND (Ian McCulloch) (*6).

IAN McCULLOCH (b. 5 May'59) – vocals, guitar (ex-CRUCIAL THREE) **WILL SERGEANT** (b.12 Apr'58) – lead guitar / **LES PATTINSON** (b.18 Apr'58) – bass (& 'ECHO' a drum machine)

Zoo | not issued

Mar 79. (7") **PICTURES ON MY WALL. / READ IT IN BOOKS** | | -
(re-iss.Mar91 on 'Document')

— **PETE DE FREITAS** (b. 2 Aug'61, Port Of Spain, Trinidad) – drums repl. 'ECHO'

Korova | Sire

Apr 80. (7") **RESCUE. / SIMPLE STUFF** | 62 | -
(12"+=) – Pride.

Jul 80. (lp)(c) **CROCODILES** | 17 |
– Going up / Stars are stars / Pride / Monkeys / Crocodiles / Rescue / Villier's terrace / Pictures on my wall / All that jazz / Happy death men. *(re-iss.Dec80 + below) (re-iss.+cd.1989 on 'WEA')* (free-7" w/a) – **DO IT CLEAN. / READ IT IN BOOKS**

Sep 80. (7") **THE PUPPET. / DO IT CLEAN**

Apr 81. (12"ep) **SHINE SO HARD (live)** | 37 |
– Crocodiles / All that jazz / Over the wall / Zimbo (All my colours).

May 81. (lp)(c) **HEAVEN UP HERE** | 10 |
– Show of strength / With a hip / Over the wall / It was a pleasure / A promise / Heaven up here / The disease / All my colours / No dark things / Turquoise days / All I want. *(cd-iss.Jul88 on 'WEA')*

Jul 81. (7")(12") **A PROMISE. / BROKE MY NECK** | 49 |

May 82. (7") **THE BACK OF LOVE. / THE SUBJECT** | 19 |
(12"+=) – Fuel.

Jan 83. (7") **THE CUTTER. / WAY OUT** | 8 | 8
(12"+=) – Zimbo.
(c-s) – ('A'side) / Villier's terrace / Ashes to ashes / Monkeys / Read it in books.

Jan 83. (lp)(c) **PORCUPINE** | 2 |
– The cutter / The back of love / My white devil / Clay / Porcupine / Heads will roll / Ripeness / Higher hell / Gods will be gods / In bluer skies. (free ltd.c-s w/a) – 'JOHN PEEL SESSIONS' (see below Nov88 version) *(re-iss.+cd.Jul88 on 'WEA')*

Feb 83. (7") **THE CUTTER. / GODS WILL BE GODS** | - |

Jul 83. (7") **NEVER STOP. / HEADS WILL ROLL** | 15 |
('A'disco 12"+=) – The original cutter (A drop in the ocean).

Jan 84. (7") **THE KILLING MOON. / DO IT CLEAN** | 9 |
(12"+=) – ('A'extended).

Jan 84. (m-lp) **ECHO AND THE BUNNYMEN** | - |
– Back of love / Never stop / Rescue / The cutter / Do it clean.

Apr 84. (lp)(c)(cd) **OCEAN RAIN** | 4 | 87 Jun 84
– Silver / Nocturnal me / Crystal days / The yo yo man / Thorn of crowns / The killing moon / Seven seas / My kingdom / Ocean rain.

Apr 84. (7") **SILVER. / ANGELS AND DEVILS** | 3 |
(12"+=) – Silver (Tidal wave).

Jun 84. (7") **SEVEN SEAS. / ALL YOU NEED IS LOVE** | 16 |
(12"+=)(d7"+=) – Killing Moon / Starts and stars (acoustic) / Villier's terrace (acoustic).

Oct 85. (7")(7"pic-d) **BRING ON THE DANCING HORSES. / OVER MY SHOULDER** | 21 |
(extended 12"+=) – Beds, bugs and ballyhoo.
(d7"+=) – Villier's terrace / Monkeys.

Nov 85. (lp)(c)(cd) **SONGS TO LEARN AND SING** (compilation) | 6 |
– Rescue / The puppet / Do it clean / The promise / The back of love / The cutter / Never stop / The killing moon / Silver / Seven seas / Bring on the dancing horses. (c/cd+=) – Pride / Simple stuff / Read it in books / Angels and devils. (free ltd.c-s w/ same extra tracks)

— (Feb86) temp. **MARK FOX** – drums (ex-HAIRCUT 100) repl. DE FREITAS until return Sep'86.

WEA | Sire

Jun 87. (7") **THE GAME. / SHIP OF FOOLS** | 28 |
(12"+=) – Lost And Found.

Jul 87. (lp)(c)(cd) **ECHO AND THE BUNNYMEN** | 4 | 51
– The game / Over you / Bedbugs and ballyhoo / All in your mind / Bombers bay / Lips like sugar / Lost and found / New direction / Blue blue ocean / Satellite / All my life. *(re-iss.cd Nov94)*

Jul 87. (7") **LIPS LIKE SUGAR. / ROLLERCOASTER** | 36 |
(12"+=) – People are strange.

Feb 88. (7")(c-s) **PEOPLE ARE STRANGE. / RUN RUN RUN** | 29 |
(12"+=) – Paint it black / Friction. *(re-iss.Feb91 on 'East-West' hit No.34)*

— They split some unofficial time in '88. Re-formed after McCULLOCH went solo. PETE DE FREITAS joined SEX GODS. He died in motorcycle accident 14 Jun '89.

— **SERGEANT** and **PATTINSON** reformed group early 1990, with newcomers **NOEL BURKE** – vocals / **JACK BROCKMAN** – keyboards / **DAMON REECE** – drums

Korova | not issued

Oct 90. (7")(c-s) **ENLIGHTEN ME. / LADY, DON'T FALL BACKWARDS**
(12"+=)(cd-s+=) – ('A'extended).

Nov 90. (cd)(c)(lp) **REVERBERATION**
– Freaks dwell / Cut and dried / Revilment / Flaming red / Salvatore / Fine thing / Gone, gone, gone / Enlighten me / King of your castle / Senseless / Thick skinned world. (cd+=) – False goodbyes.

Euphoric / not issued

Oct 91. (12"ep)(cd-ep) **PROVE ME WRONG. / FINE THING / REVERBERATION** [ ] [-]

Mar 92. (12")(cd-s) **INSIDE ME, INSIDE YOU. / WIGGED OUT WORLD** [ ] [-]

— The BUNNYMEN disbanded soon after the above and LES joined TERRY HALL'S backing group.

- compilations etc. -

Strange Fruit / not issued

Nov 88. Strange Fruit; (12"ep)(c-ep)(cd-ep) **THE PEEL SESSIONS (15.8.79)** [ ] [-]
– Read it in books / Stars are stars / I bagsy yours / Villier's terrace. *(re-iss.cd-ep Dec94)*

Jul 90. Old Gold; (7") **THE CUTTER. / THE BACK OF LOVE** [ ] [-]

Jul 90. Old Gold; (7") **THE KILLING MOON. / SEVEN SEAS** [ ] [-]

Nov 91. Windsong; (cd) **BBC RADIO 1 LIVE IN CONCERT (live)** [ ] [-]

Mar 93. Pickwick; (cd)(c) **THE CUTTER** [ ] [-]
(re-iss.Sep95 on 'Warners')

Ian McCULLOCH

IAN McCULLOCH – vocals while still a member of The BUNNYMEN

Korova / not issued

Nov 84. (7")(10") **SEPTEMBER SONG. / COCKLES AND MUSCLES** [51] [-]
(12"+=) – ('A'extended).

— Now solo his back-up came from **RAY SHULMAN** – keyboards, programmer, bass, producer / plus guests **MICHAEL JOBSON** – bass / **BORIS WILLIAMS** – drums / **OLLE REMO** – drum programmer / **LIZ FRASER** – vox (of COCTEAU TWINS)

W.E.A. / Sire

Aug 89. (7")(c-s) **PROUD TO FALL. / POTS OF GOLD** [51] [ ]
(12") – ('A' side) / ('A'extended) / The dead end (long version).
(cd-s++=) – ('A'version).
(12") ('A' side / Everything is real / The circle game.

Sep 89. (lp)(c)(cd) **CANDLELAND** [18] [ ]
– The flickering wall / The white hotel / Proud to fall / The cape / Candleland / Horse's head / Faith and healing / I know you well / In bloom / Start again.

Nov 89. (7")(c-s) **FAITH AND HEALING (remix). / TOAD** [ ] [ ]
(12"+=) – Fear of the known.
(cd-s++=) Rocket ship.
(12") – ('A' side) / Fear of the known / Rocket ship.

Apr 90. (7")(c-s) **CANDLELAND (THE SECOND COMING). / THE WORLD IS FLAT** [75] [ ]
(12"+=)(cd-s+=) – Big days / Wassailing in the night.

His backing band from late '89, were The PRODIGAL SONS (**MIKE MOONEY** – guitar / **JOHN McEVOY** – r.guitar, keys / **EDGAR SUMMERTIME** – bass / **STEVE HUMPHRIES** – drums)

East West / East West

Feb 92. (7")(c-s) **LOVER, LOVER, LOVER. / WHITE HOTEL (acoustic) / THE GROUND BELOW** [47] [ ]
(12"+=) – ('A'-Indian dawn mix).
(cd-s++=) – Vibor blue (acoustic).

Apr 92. (cd)(c)(lp) **MYSTERIOSO** [46] [ ]
– Mayreal world / Close your eyes / Dug for love / Honeydrip / Damnation / Lover, lover, lover / Webbed / Pomegranate / Vibor blue / Heaven's gate / In my head.

Apr 92. (7")(c-s) **DUG FOR LOVE. / DAMNATION (live)** [ ] [ ]
(12"+=)(cd-s+=) – Do it clean / Pomegranate / In my head (all live).

WILL SERGEANT

Jul 82. Korova; (7") **FAVOURITE BRANCHES. / (b-side by RAVI SHANKER & BILL LOVELADY)** [ ] [-]

Mar 82. 92 Happy Customers; (lp) **THEMES FOR GRIND** [ ] [ ]

ELECTRAFIXION

— **IAN McCULLOCH** – vocals, guitar / **WILL SERGEANT** – guitar / **LEON DE SYLVA** – bass / **TONY McGUIGAN** – drums

W.E.A. / Warners

Nov 94. (12"ep)(c-ep)(cd-ep) **THE ZEPHYR EP** [47] [ ]
– Zephyr / Burned / Mirrorball / Rain on me.

Sep 95. (7"red-ep)(c-ep)(12"ep)(cd-ep) **LOWDOWN / HOLY GRAIL. / LAND OF THE DYING SUN / RAZORS EDGE** [54] [ ]

Sep 95. (cd)(c) **BURNED** [38] [ ]
– Feel my pulse / Sister pain / Lowdown / Timebomb / Zephyr / Never / Too far gone / Mirrorball / Who's been sleeping in my head? / Hit by something / Bed of nails.

Oct 95. (c-s) **NEVER / NOT OF THIS WORLD** [58] [ ]
(cd-s+=) – Subway train / Lowdown (rest of the trash mix).
(cd-s) – ('A'side) / Lowdown / Work it on out / Never (Utah Saints blizzard on mix) / Sister pain.

ECHOBELLY

Formed: London, England by Anglo-Asian SONYA aged 27. In 1994, toured in the States with fan MORRISSEY; the injured GLENN was replaced by Curve's DEBBIE SMITH. • **Style:** Like BLONDIE vox on a SMITHS-type backing. • **Songwriters:** MADDEN / JOHANSSON.

Recommended: EVERYONE'S GOT ONE (*5)

SONYA AURORA MADAN – vocals / **GLENN JOHANSSON** – guitar / **ALEX KEYSER** – bass, piano / **ANDY HENDERSON** – drums

Pande-monium / not issued

Nov 93. (12"ep)(cd-ep) **BELLYACHE** [ ] [-]
– Give her a gun / Call me names / England swings.

Jan 94. (12"ep)(cd-ep) **BELLYACHE / SLEEPING HITLER. / GIVE HER A GUN / I DON'T BELONG HERE** [ ] [ ]
(re-iss.May94)

Fauve-Rhythm King / not issued

Mar 94. (7")(c-s) **INSOMNIAC. / TALENT** [47] [ ]
(12"+=) – ('A'mix).
(cd-s+=) – Centipede.

— added **DEBBIE SMITH** – guitar noise

Jun 94. (7")(c-s) **I CAN'T IMAGINE THE WORLD WITHOUT ME. / VENUS WHEEL** [39] [ ]
(12"+=)(cd-s+=) – Sober.

Aug 94. (cd)(c)(lp) **EVERYONE'S GOT ONE** [8] [ ]
– Today tomorrow sometime never / Father, ruler, king, computer / Give her a gun / I can't imagine the world without me / Bellyache / Taste of you / Insomniac / Call me names / Close . . .but / Cold feet warm heart / Scream.

Oct 94. (7")(12")(c-s) **CLOSE . . .BUT. / SO LA DI DA** [59] [ ]
(cd-s+=) – I can't image the world without me (live) / Cold feet warm heart (live).

Aug 95. (7")(c-s) **GREAT THINGS. / HERE COMES THE SCENE** [13] [ ]
(cd-s+=) – God's guest list / On turn off.
(cd-s) – ('A'side) / On turn on / Bunty / One after 5 a.m.

Sep 95. (cd)(c)(lp) **ON** [4] [ ]
– Oar fiction / King of the kerb / Great things / Natural animal / Go away / Pantyhose and roses / Something hot in a cold country / Four letter word / Nobody like you / In the year / Dark therapy / Worms an angels.

Oct 95. (c-s) **KING OF THE KERB / CAR FICTION (French)** [25] [ ]
(cd-s+=) – On turn on (acoustic) / Natural animal (acoustic).
(cd-s) – ('A'live) / I can't imagine the world without me (live) / Insomniac (live) / Great things (live).

EDDIE & THE HOT RODS

Formed: Canvey Island & Southend, Essex, England . . . 1975 by former amateur boxer BARRIE MASTERS. Manager / producer / lyricist ED HOLLIS found them contract with 'Island' label, as they set about on London pub circuit. Throughout the "punk" years they had success in UK, but this had fizzled out by the late 70's. • **Style:** R&B punks, whose energy was reminiscent of DR. FEELGOOD or The WHO. • **Songwriters:** Group with HOLLIS lyrics, except covers of 96 TEARS (? & The Mysterians) / GET OUT OF DENVER (Bob Seger) / THE KIDS ARE ALRIGHT (Who) / YOU BETTER RUN (Rascals) / WOOLY BULLY (Sam The Sham & The Pharoahs) / GLORIA (Them) / SATISFACTION (Rolling Stones) / etc. • **Miscellaneous:** One-time member LEW LEWIS was jailed for 7 years in 1987, due to his part in a P.O. robbery.

Recommended: TEENAGE DEPRESSION (*5) / LIFE ON THE LINE (*5)

BARRIE MASTERS – vocals / **DAVE HIGGS** – guitar / **PAUL GRAY** – bass / **STEVE NICOL** – drums / plus **LEW LEWIS** – mouth harp

Island / not issued

Jan 76. (7") **WRITING ON THE WALL. / CRUISIN'** [ ] [-]

Jun 76. (7") **WOOLY BULLY. / HORSEPLAY** [ ] [-]

Aug 76. (7"ep) **LIVE AT THE MARQUEE (live)** [43] [-]
– 96 tears / Get out of Denver / Medley: Gloria- Satisfaction.

Oct 76. (7") **TEENAGE DEPRESSION. / SHAKE** [35] [-]

Dec 76. (lp)(c) **TEENAGE DEPRESSION** [43] [-]
– Teenage depression / The kids are alright / Why can't it be / Horseplay (wearier of the Schmatlz) / On the run / Show me / Been so long / Shake / All I need is money / Double checkin' woman.

— **GRAEME DOUGLAS** – guitar (ex-KURSAAL FLYERS) repl. LEW who went solo

Apr 77. (7") **I MIGHT BE LYING. / IGNORE THEM** [44] [-]

Jun 77. (7"ep) **LIVE AT THE SPEED OF SOUND (live)** [ ] [-]
– Hard driving man / etc.

Aug 77. (7") **DO ANYTHING YOU WANNA DO. (as "The RODS") / SCHOOLGIRL LOVE** [9] [-]

Nov 77. (lp)(c) **LIFE ON THE LINE** [27] [-]
– Do anything you wanna do / Beginning of the end / Quit this town / (I don't know) what's really going on / We sing the cross / Life on the line / Telephone girl / Ignore them (still life) / (And) don't believe your eyes.

Jan 78. (7") **QUIT THIS TOWN. / DISTORTION MAY BE EXPECTED** [36] [-]

Mar 78. (7") **LIFE ON THE LINE. / DO ANYTHING YOU WANNA DO** [ ] [-]
(12"+=) – What's going on / Why can't it be.

Oct 78. (7") **MEDIA MESSIAHS. / HORROR THROUGH THE STRAIGHTNESS** [ ] [-]

Mar 79. (7") **POWER AND THE GLORY. / HIGHLANDS ONE, HOPEFULS TWO** [ ] [-]

Mar 79. (lp)(c) **THRILLER** [50] [-]
– Power and the glory / Media Messiahs / Circles / Take it or leave it / Echoes / Out to lunch / Strangled on the payphone / Breathless / He does it with mirrors / Living dangerously.

E.M.I. / not issued

Mar 80. (7") **AT NIGHT. / YOU BETTER RUN / LOOKING AROUND** [ ] [ ]

— now a quartet of **MASTERS, HIGGS, DOUGLAS** and **T.C.** – bass, (GRAY joined DAMNED)

Nov 80. (7") **WIDE EYED KIDS. / LEAVE US ALONE** [ ] [ ]

— guests **RUFUS JENKINS** – accordion AL KOOPER – keyboards, guitar, vocals

Apr 81. (7") **FARTHER ON DOWN THE ROAD. / FISH'N'CHIPS** [ ] [ ]

Apr 81. (lp)(c) **FISH AND CHIPS** [ ] [ ]

– Fish'n'chips (pt.1 & 2) / This is today / Time wont let me / Farther on down the road (you will accompany me) / Wide eyed kids / You better run / Another party / Unfinished business / Call it quits / We want more.

— split '81 **BARRIE MASTERS** joined The INMATES, until he reformed **EDDIE & THE HOTRODS** '84 with **TEX AXILE** – drums

Waterfront / not issued

Feb 85. (7") **FOUGHT FOR YOU. / HEY TONIGHT** [ ] [-]
Sep 85. (m-lp) **ONE STORY TOWN (live)** [ ] [-]

— Split finally '85. AXILE later joined TRANSVISION VAMP

– compilations, others, etc. –

— next as "ROB TYNER & THE HOT RODS" (TYNER – vocals, harmonica (ex-MC5)

Dec 77. Island; (7") **'TIL THE NIGHT IS GONE. / FLIPSIDE ROCK** [ ] [-]
Dec 92. Link; (cd) **CURSE OF THE HOT RODS** [ ] [-]
Sep 93. Receiver; (cd) **LIVE AND RARE (live)** [ ] [-]
Mar 94. Dojo; (cd) **TIES THAT BIND** [ ] [-]
Jul 94. Windsong; (cd) **BBC RADIO 1 LIVE IN CONCERT (live)** [ ] [-]
Aug 94. Island; (cd) **THE END OF THE BEGINNING – THE BEST OF . . .** [ ] [-]

Duane EDDY

Born: 26 Apr'38, Corning, New York, USA. His family moved to Arizona, where he took up guitar after leaving Coolidge High School. In 1958, he formed his REBELS, and with help from DJ's Lee Hazlewood & Lester Still, they signed to 'Jamie' records. After an initial minor hit, they credited DUANE to front them on next smash hit 'REBEL ROUSER'. This began a string of major hits during the late 50's & early 60's, the best of which being; 'PETER GUNN THEME', 'FORTY MILES OF BAD ROAD' & 'BECAUSE THEY'RE YOUNG'. • **Style:** Catchy instrumental tunes, based around guitar & saxophone. His hits from 'DANCE WITH THE GUITAR MAN' onwards, featured vocal accompaniment from The REBELETTES. • **Songwriters:** DUANE and echo-chamber producer LEE HAZLEWOOD penned most of the songs until early 1961. He re-united with HAZLEWOOD late 1962. Other writers were:- Henry Mancini (PETER GUNN) / Trad 'My Bonnie Lies Over The Ocean' (BONNIE COME BACK) / (Al Casey (CARAVAN) / trad. (DEEP IN THE HEART OF TEXAS) / etc. • **Trivia:** His handsome features, gained him acting experience in the 1960 film 'Because They're Young' (also the title of song). A few years later he appeared in the films 'The Savage Seven' & 'Kona'. In 1973, he produced PHIL EVERLY's solo album 'Star Spangled Springer'. In 1986, he re-appeared on 'Top Of The Pops', when ART OF NOISE were re-working a hit version of 'PETER GUNN'.

Recommended: MOVIN' 'N' GROOVIN' (*6)

The REBELS

featuring **DUANE EDDY** – guitar / **AL CASEY** – guitar, piano / **BUDDY WHEELER** – bass / **DONNIE OWENS** – guitar / **CORKY CASEY** – guitar / **MIKE BERMANI** – drums / **PIAS JOHNSON** – saxophone

not issued / Ford

Jan 58. (7") **RAMROD. / CARAVAN** [-] [ ]

DUANE EDDY & THE REBELS

London / Jamie

Apr 58. (7") **MOVIN'N'GROOVIN'. / UP AND DOWN** [-] [72]
Aug 58. (7") **REBEL-ROUSER. / STALKIN'** [19] [6] Jun 58
Oct 58. (7") **RAMROD. / WALKER** [ ] [27] Aug 58
Dec 58. (7") **CANNONBALL. / MASON-DIXON LINE** [22] [15] Nov 58
Mar 59. (7") **THE LONELY ONE. / DETOUR** [ ] [23] Jan 59
Apr 59. (7") **YEP!. / THREE-30 BLUES** [-] [30]
Jun 59. (lp) **HAVE TWANGY GUITAR WILL TRAVEL** [6] [5] Jan59

– Lonesome road / I almost lost my mind / Rebel-rouser / Three-30-blues / Cannon-ball / The lonely one / Detour / Stalkin' / Ramrod / Anytime / Movin' and Groovin' / Loving you.

Jun 59. (7") **PETER GUNN THEME. / YEP!** [6] [ ] Jun 59 [17]
Aug 59. (7") **FORTY MILES OF BAD ROAD. / THE QUIET THREE** [11] [9] [46] Jun 59
Oct 59. (lp) **ESPECIALLY FOR YOU** [6] [24] Aug 59

– Peter Gunn / Only child / Lover / Fuzz / Yep! / Along the Navajo trail / Just because / Quiniela / TRouble in mind / Tuxedo Junction / Hard times / Along came Linda.

Dec 59. (7") **SOME KIND-A EARTHQUAKE. / FIRST LOVE, FIRST TEARS** [12] [37] [59] Oct 59
Dec 59. (7") **BONNIE CAME BACK. / LOST ISLAND** [-] [26]
Feb 60. (7") **BONNIE CAME BACK. / MOVIN' & GROOVIN'** [12] [-]
Apr 60. (lp) **THE "TWANG'S" THE THANG** [2] [18] Jan 60

– My blue Heaven / Tiger love and turnip greens / The last minute of innocence / Route No.1 / You are my sunshine / St.Louis blues / Night train to Memphis / The battle / Trombone / Blueberry hill / Rebel walk / Easy.

— His touring REBELS were now **AL CASEY** – bass / **JIM HORN** – sax / **LARRY KNECHTEL** – piano / **JIMMY TROXEL** – drums

Apr 60. (7") **SHAZAM!. / SECRET SEVEN** [4] [45] Mar 60
Jul 60. (7") **BECAUSE THEY'RE YOUNG. / REBEL WALK** [2] [4] May 60
Sep 60. (7") **(WHY MUST I DIE) THE GIRL ON DEATH ROW. / WORDS MEAN NOTHING** [-] [ ]
Oct 60. (7") **KOMMOTION. / THEME FOR MOON CHILDREN** [13] [78] Aug 60
Oct 60. (7") **PETER GUNN. / ALONG THE NAVAJO TRAIL** [-] [27]
Dec 60. (lp) **SONGS OF OUR HERITAGE** [13] [ ]

– Cripple Creek / Riddle song / John Henry / Streets of Laredo / Prisoner's song / In the pines / Ole Joe Clark / Wayfarin' stranger / Top of Old Smokey / Mule train / Scarlet ribbons.

Jan 61. (7") **PEPE. / LOST FRIEND** [2] [18] Dec 60
Apr 61. (7") **THEME FROM DIXIE. / BATTLE** [7] [ ]
Mar 61. (7") **THEME FROM DIXIE. / GIDGET GOES HAWAIIAN** [-] [39]
May 61. (7") **RING OF FIRE. / BOBBY** [-] [84]
Jun 61. (7") **RING OF FIRE. / GIDGET GOES HAWAIIAN** [17] [ ] May 61
Aug 61. (7") **DRIVIN' HOME. / TAMMY** [-] [87]
Aug 61. (7") **DRIVIN' HOME. / MY BLUE HEAVEN** [30] [-]
Aug 61. (lp) **GIRLS GIRLS GIRLS** [ ] [93] Jul 61

– Brenda: I want to be wanted that's all you gotta do / I'm sorry / Sioux City Sue / Tommy / Big 'liza / Mary Ann / Annette / Tuesday / Sweet Cindy / Patricia / Mona Lisa / Connie / Carol.

Sep 61. (7") **CARAVAN. / (part 2)** [42] [ ]
(above iss. on 'Parlophone' UK / 'Gregmark' US)

Oct 61 (7") **MY BLUE HEAVEN. / ALONG CAME LINDA** [-] [50] Aug 61

London / Jamie

Jan 62 (7") **THE AVENGER. / LONDONDERRY AIR** [ ] [ ]
Feb 62 (7") **THE BATTLE. / TROMBONE** [-] [ ]
Apr 62 (7") **RUNAWAY PONY. / JUST BECAUSE** [-] [ ]

DUANE EDDY

(solo)

R.C.A. / R.C.A.

May 62. (7") **DEEP IN THE HEART OF TEXAS. / SAINTS AND SINNERS** [19] [78] Apr 62
Aug 62. (lp) **TWISTIN' N' TWANGIN'** [8] [82] May 62

– The peppermint twist / Twistin' 'n' twangin' / Let's twist again / Miss Twist / Sugartime twist / Exactly like you / Walkin' 'n' twistin' (I'm walkin') / Dear lady twist / Moanin' 'n' twistin' / Country twist / The twist / Twisting off a cliff.

Aug 62. (7") **THE BALLAD OF PALADIN. / THE WILD WESTERNER** [10] [33] Jul 62

DUANE EDDY & THE REBELETTES

(REBELETTES were female singers)

Oct 62. (7") **(DANCE WITH THE) GUITAR MAN. / STRETCHIN' OUT** [4] [12]
Nov 62. (lp) **TWANGY GUITAR – SILKY STRINGS** [13] [72] Oct 62

– High noon / Born to be with you / Secret love / Unchained melody / When I fall in love / Mirriam / Moon river / Bali Ha'I / Hi-lili, hi-lo / Angel on my shoulder / Memories of Madrid / Love me tender.

Jan 63. (lp) **DANCE WITH THE GUITAR MAN** [ ] [47]

– Dance with the guitar man / Limbo rock / Wild Watusi / The scrape / New Hully Gully / Popeye (the hitchhiker) / Spanish twist / The climb / Loco-locomotion / Nashville stomp / Creamy mashed potatoes / Waltz of the wind. *(cd-iss.Apr93)*

Feb 63. (7") **BOSS GUITAR. / THE DESERT RAT** [27] [28]

DUANE EDDY

(solo)

May 63. (7") **LONELY BOY, LONELY GUITAR. / JOSHIN'** [35] [82]
Aug 63. (7") **YOUR BABY'S GONE SURFIN'. / SHUCKIN'** [49] [93]
Aug 63. (lp) **TWANG A COUNTRY SONG** [ ] [ ]

– Sugar foot rag / Weary blues / Fireball mail / Please help me I'm falling / Wildwood flower / Precious memories / Crazy arms / Have you ever been lonely / The window up above / A satisfied mind / Making believe / Peace in the valley.

Oct 63. (7") **MY BABY PLAYS THE SAME OLD SONG ON HIS GUITAR ALL NIGHT. / GUITAR'D AND FEATHERED** [ ] [ ]
Oct 63. (lp) **TWANGIN' UP A STORM** [ ] [93]

– Guitar child / All you gave to me / Giddy goose / Walk right in / He's so fine / Beach bound / Mr.Guitar man / Blowin' up a storm / My baby plays the same old song on his guitar all night long / Guitar'd and feathered / Soldier boy / Soul twist.

Nov 63. (7") **THE SON OF REBEL ROUSER. / THE STORY OF THREE LOVERS** [ ] [97]
Dec 63 (7") **GUITAR CHILD. / JERKY JALOPY** [-] [ ]
Apr 64. (lp) **LONELY GUITAR**

– I'm so lonesome I could cry / Long lonely days of winter / Along came Linda / Someday the rainbow / Gunsmoke / A home in the meadow / Danny boy / Shenandoah / Summer kiss / My destiny / Cryin' happy tears / Annie Laurie.

Jan 64 (7") **THEME FROM A SUMMER PLACE. / WATER SKIING** [-] [ ]
Jul 64. (lp) **WATER SKIING**

– Water skiing / Slalom rooster tail / The backward swan / Whip off / Jitterboard / Deep-water start / The wake ballet / Toe-hold side slide / Banana peels / In gear / Jumping the wake.

Oct 64. (7") **GUITAR STAR. / THE IGUANA** [ ] [ ]
Jan 65 (7") **MOONSHOT. / ROUGHNECK** [-] [ ]

Colpix / Colpix

Aug 65. (7") **TRASH. / SOUTH PHOENIX** [ ] [ ]
Oct 65. (lp) **DUANE A-GO-GO-GO!** [ ] [ ]

– Trash / Puddin' / Movin'n'groovin' / Choo choo a go go – toot toot! / Just to satisfy you / Around the block in 80 days (march in 'A') / Cottonmouth / If you've seen one, you've seen them all! / South Phoenix / Dream lover / Busted / I'm blue.

Dec 65. (7") **THE HOUSE OF THE RISING SUN. / DON'T THINK TWICE IT'S ALRIGHT** [ ] [ ]
Mar 66. (lp) **DUANE GOES BOB DYLAN** [ ] [ ]

– Don't think twice / House of the rising sun / It ain't me babe / Not the loving kind / She belongs to me / All I really want to do / Houston / Love minus zero – no limit / Mr.Tambourine man / Blowin' in the wind / Swing low sweet chariot / Eve of destruction.

1966 (7") **EL RANCHO GRANDE. / POPPA'S MOVIN' ON (I'M MOVIN' ON)** [-] [ ]
1966 (7") **GUITAR ON MY MIND. / WICKED WOMAN FROM WICKENBURG** [-] [ ]

		Valient	Reprise
1966.	(7") **DAYDREAM. / THIS GUITAR WAS MADE FOR TWANGIN'**		
1966.	(7") **MONSOON. / ROARIN'**		
1966.	(7") **GUITAR ON MY MIND. / WICKED WOMAN FROM WICKENBURG**	-	
1966.	(lp) **THE BIGGEST TWANG OF THEM ALL**		

– This guitar was / Made for twangin' / Batman / Monday Monday / Strangers in the night / Night train / Ballad of the green berets / Daydream / What now my love / Younger girl / Where were you when I needed you / A groovy kind of love / Mame.

1967.	(7") **NIKI HOEKY. / VELVET NIGHTS**		
1967.	(lp) **THE ROARING TWANGIES**		

– Bye bye blues / Roarin' / A happy girl / Goofus / American patrol / Out on the town / Undecided / Born free / St.Louis blues march / Hello, Dolly / A string of pearls / Wicked woman from Wickenburg.

1967	(7") **THIS TOWN. / THERE IS A MOUNTAIN**	-	
		C.B.S.	Columbia
1969.	(7") **BREAK MY MIND. / ?**	-	
		not iss.	Congress
1970	(7") **PUT ALITTLE LOVE IN YOUR HEART. / FREIGHT TRAIN**	-	
		not iss.	Uni
1970	(7") **THE FIVE-SEVENTEEN. / SOMETHING**		
		not iss.	Big Tree
1970	(7") **RENEGADE. / NIGHTLY NEWS**		

DUANE EDDY & THE REBELETTES

		G.T.O.	G.T.O.
Feb 75.	(7") **PLAY ME LIKE YOU PLAY YOUR GUITAR. / BLUE MONTANA SKY**	9	
Apr 75.	(lp)(c) **GUITAR MAN**		

– Rock'n'roll guitar man / Night prowler / Son of a guitar man / Love theme from Romeo & Juliet / Play me like you play your guitar / Mark of Zorro / The man with the gold guitar / (Last night) I didn't get to sleep at all / Cannon ball rag / Blue Montana sky / Dance with the guitar man. *(re-iss.Apr78 on 'Hallmark')*

Jun 75.	(7") **THE MAN WITH THE GOLDEN GUITAR. / MARK OF ZORRO**		
			Target
Oct 75.	(7") **LOVE CONFUSION. / LOVE IS A WARM EMOTION**		
		Elektra	Elektra
1978.	(7") **YOU ARE MY SUNSHINE. / 7 TO 8**	-	

—— Made live comeback in 1983. In May'86 he featured on ART OF NOISE single version of PETER GUNN. This hit UK No.8 / US No.50, enabling him to return to solo work.

		Capitol	Capitol
Sep 87.	(7") **ROCKESTRA THEME. / BLUE CITY** (12"+=) – ('A'&'B'version).		
Sep 87.	(lp)(c)(cd) **DUANE EDDY**		
Nov 78	(7") **SPIES. / ROCKABILLY HOLIDAY**	-	

– Kickin' asphalt / Rockestra theme / Theme for something reading important / Spies / Blue city / The trembler / Los campaneros / Lost innocence / Rockabilly holiday / Last look back.

– compilations, others, etc. –

All releases on 'London' below, were on US 'Jamie'.

1958.	London; (7"ep) **REBEL ROUSER**		-	
1959.	London; (7"ep) **THE LONELY ONE**		-	
1959.	London; (7"ep) **YEP!**		-	
1960.	London; (7"ep) **BECAUSE THEY'RE YOUNG**		-	
1960.	London; (7"ep) **TWANGY**		-	
Feb 61.	London; (lp) **A MILLION DOLLAR'S WORTH OF TWANG**	5	11	Dec 60
1961.	London; (7"ep) **PEPE**		-	
1961.	London; (7"ep) **DUANE EDDY PLAYS MOVIE THEMES**		-	
1962.	London; (7"ep) **TWANGY No.2**		-	
Jun 62.	London; (lp) **A MILLION DOLLAR'S WORTH OF TWANG VOL.2**	18		
May 68.	London; (7") **PETER GUNN. / REBEL ROUSER**			
May 70.	London; (lp) **MOVIN' N' GROOVIN'**			

– Peter Gunn / Rebel rouser / Thirty three blues / Movin 'n groovin' / Forty miles of bad road / Shazam! / Some kinda earthquake / Only child / Blueberry hill / Hard times / The avenger / Because they're young.

1963.	R.C.A.; (7"ep) **A COUNTRY TWANG**		-
1963.	R.C.A.; (7"ep) **MR.TWANG**		-
1963.	R.C.A.; (7"ep) **TWANGIN' UP A STORM**		-
1965.	R.C.A.; (lp) **TWANGIN' THE GOLDEN HITS**		
Nov 65.	R.C.A.; (lp) **TWANGSVILLE**		
Jan 79.	R.C.A.; (lp) **DUANE EDDY**		
Nov 80.	R.C.A.; (lp)(c) **20 TERRIFIC TWANGIES**		
Jul 86.	R.C.A.; (d-lp)(d-c) **FOREVER**		
1970.	Camden; (lp) **TWANGY GUITAR**		-
May 75.	Deram; (d-lp) **LEGEND OF ROCK**		-
1965.	Colpix; (7"ep) **COTTONMOUTH**		-
Aug 78.	Pickwick; (d-lp) **THE COLLECTION**		-
Oct 80.	Creole; (7") **REBEL ROUSER. / ?**		-
Oct 80.	Creole; (7") **FORTY MILES OF BAD ROAD. / ?**		-
May 83.	Cambra; (lp)(c) **THE FABULOUS DUANE EDDY**		-
Sep 84.	Nouveaux; (lp)(c)(cd) **THE BEST OF DUANE EDDY**		-
Nov 84.	Magnum Force; (lp) **REBEL ROUSIN'**		-
Sep 86.	M.F.P.; (lp)(c) **GUITAR MAN**		-
Feb 87.	Arena; (lp)(c) **DANCE WITH THE GUITAR MAN**		-
Feb 88.	Motown; (cd) **COMPACT COMMAND PERFORMANCES**		-
Apr 88.	Diamond; (cd) **DUANE EDDY**		-
May 89.	Performance; (cd) **THE GUITAR MAN (20 CLASSIC TRACKS)**		-
Jun 91.	R.C.A.; (cd)(c)(lp) **TWANGY PEAKS**		-

– (DUANE A GO-GO / DYLAN GOES BOB DYLAN)

May 94.	Bear Family; (cd) **THAT CLASSIC TWANG**		
May 94.	Bear Family; (cd) **ESPECIALLY FOR YOU / GIRLS GIRLS GIRLS**		
May 94.	Bear Family; (cd) **THE TWANG'S THE THANG / SONGS OF OUR HERITAGE**		-
Dec 94.	Bear Family; (7xcd-box) **TWANGIN' FROM PHOENIX TO L.A.**		
May 94.	B.R.Music; (cd)(c) **BECAUSE THEY'RE YOUNG**		-
Jun 94.	Ronco; (cd)(c) **20 TWANGY HITS**		-
Dec 94.	See For MIles; (cd) **HIS TWANGY GUITAR AND THE REBELS**		-

The EDGE (see under ⇒ U2)

Graeme EDGE (see under ⇒ MOODY BLUES)

Dave EDMUNDS

Born: 15 Apr '44, Cardiff, Wales. After being in two local bands: The 99'ers & The RAIDERS in the mid-60's, he joined The IMAGE in 1966. He and their drummer broke away the following year, to form The HUMAN BEANS. In 1968, they evolved into LOVE SCULPTURE, smashing the UK Top 5 with 'SABRE DANCE'. Exactly 2 years later and now solo, EDMUNDS topped the UK charts with 'I HEAR YOU KNOCKIN' ', which also broke the US Top 10. Became a well-respected singles artist for the next decade, with late 70's-early 80's jaunts into the UK Top 40 album lists. In 1974, he featured in the film 'STARDUST', alongside DAVID ESSEX and KEITH MOON. • **Style:** Rock'n'roll revivalist, re-creating production techniques, reminiscent of Phil Spector's 'wall of sound'. • **Songwriters:** EDMUNDS penned material. In ROCKPILE he co-wrote songs with NICK LOWE. The HUMAN BEANS covered MORNING DEW (Tim Rose). LOVE SCULPTURE covered WANG DANG DOODLE (Willie Dixon) / SABRE DANCE (Khachaturian) / ON THE ROAD AGAIN (Wilbert Harrison) / SUMMERTIME (Gershwin). EDMUNDS solo; I HEAR YOU KNOCKIN' (Smiley Lewis) / BLUE MONDAY (Fats Domino) / BABY I LOVE YOU (Ronettes) / BORN TO BE WITH YOU (Chordettes) / GET OUT OF DENVER (Bob Seger) / HEY GOOD LOOKIN' (Hank Williams) / GIRLS TALK (Elvis Costello) / CRAWLING FROM THE WRECKAGE (Graham Parker) / SINGING THE BLUES (Guy Mitchell) / WRONG WAY (Difford-Tilbrook of Squeeze) / ALMOST SATURDAY NIGHT (John Fogerty) / FROM SMALL THINGS BIG THINGS COME (Bruce Springsteen) / OUTLAW BLUES (Bob Dylan) / etc. • **Trivia:** EDMUNDS produced many artists, including SHAKIN' STEVENS & THE SUNSETS in 1970, BRINSLEY SCHWARZ (1974) / FLAMIN' GROOVIES (1976) / FABULOUS THUNDERBIRDS (1980-81) / EVERLY BROTHERS (1983-86) / k.d.LANG (1988) / NICK LOWE (1989) / DION (1989) / STRAY CATS (1980 + 1989).

Recommended: THE BEST OF DAVE EDMUNDS (*6)

HUMAN BEANS

DAVE EDMUNDS – vocals, guitar / **TOMMY RILEY** – drums / **JOHN WILLIAMS** – bass

		Columbia	not issued
Jul 67.	(7") **MORNING DEW. / IT'S A WONDER**		

LOVE SCULPTURE

(same line-up)

		Parlophone	Rare
Feb 68.	(7") **RIVER TO ANOTHER DAY. / BRAND NEW WOMAN**		-

—— **BOB 'CONGO' JONES** – drums repl. RILEY

Sep 68.	(7") **WANG DANG DOODLE. / THE STUMBLE**		
Nov 68.	(7") **SABRE DANCE. / THINK OF LOVE**	5	
Dec 68.	(lp) **BLUES HELPING**		

– The stumble / 3 o'clock blues / I believe to my soul / Blues helping / Summertime (from Porgy and Bess) / Don't answer the door / So unkind / On the road again / Wang dang doodle / Come back baby / Shake your hips.

Feb 69.	(7") **FARENDOLE. / SEAGULL**		
		Parlophone	Parrot
Jan 70.	(lp) **FORMS AND FEELINGS**		

– In the land of the few / Seagull / Nobody's talking / People people / Why (how now) / Sabre dance (from 'Gayaneh-Ballet') / You can't catch me / Farandole.

Feb 70.	(7") **IN THE LAND OF THE FEW. / PEOPLE PEOPLE**		

—— **TERRY WILLIAMS** – drums (ex-DREAM) repl. JONES who joined SASSAFRASS / added **MICKEY GEE** – guitar (ex-JOE COCKER'S GREASE BAND ex-TOM JONES)

—— split soon after, GEE and WILLIAMS later joined MAN.

DAVE EDMUNDS' ROCKPILE

EDMUNDS – multi-instr. retained **JOHN WILLIAMS**

		M.A.M.	M.A.M.
Nov 70	(7") **I HEAR YOU KNOCKING. / BLACK BILL**	1	4

ROCKPILE

		Regal Zono.	M.A.M.

Mar 71. (7") **I'M COMING HOME. / COUNTRY ROLL** [ ] [75]
Jul 71. (7") **BLUE MONDAY. / I'LL GET ALONG** [ ] [ ]

—— guests included **TERRY WILLIAMS** – drums / **B.J. COLE** – pedal steel guitar / **ANDY FAIRWEATHER-LOW** – guitar (ex-AMEN CORNER)

Jun 72. (lp)(c) **ROCKPILE** [ ] [ ]
– Down down down / It ain't easy / I hear you knockin' / Hell of a pain / You can't catch me / Dance dance dance / Outlaw blues / Egg or the hen.
Jul 72. (7") **DOWN DOWN DOWN. / IT AIN'T EASY** [ ] [ ]

DAVE EDMUNDS

went solo playing nearly every instrument himself

Rockfield R.C.A.

Dec 72. (7") **BABY I LOVE YOU. / MAYBE** [8] [ ]
May 73. (7") **BORN TO BE WITH YOU. / PICK AXE BLUES** [5] [ ]
Sep 74. (7") **NEED A SHOT OF RHYTHM AND BLUES. / LET IT BE ME** [ ] [ ]
Feb 75. (7") **I AIN'T NEVER. / SOME OTHER GUY** [ ] [ ]

—— **EDMUNDS** added guests **BRINSLEY SCHWARTZ** – guitar and some of his band **NICK LOWE** – bass / **BOB ANDREWS** – keyboards / **IAN GOMM** – guitar / **PICK WITHERS, TERRY WILLIAMS and BILLY RANKIN** – drums

Apr 75. (lp)(c) **SUBTLE AS A FLYING MALLET** [ ] [ ]
– Baby I love you / Leave my woman alone / Maybe / Let it rock / Let it be me / Da doo ron ron / No money down / I ain't never / Billy the kid / Shot of rhythm and blues / She's my baby / Born to be with you. *(re-iss.1978+Oct81 on 'R.C.A.')*

Swan Song Swan Song

Aug 76. (7") **HERE COMES THE WEEKEND. / AS LOVERS DO** [ ] [ ]
Oct 76. (7") **WHERE OR WHEN. / NEW YORK'S A LONELY TOWN** [ ] [ ]

—— Now DAVE's band was **LOWE, T. WILLIAMS** and **BILLY BREMNER** – guitar plus session people as guests

Apr 77. (lp)(c) **GET IT** [ ] [ ]
– Get out of Denver / Back to schooldays / Hey good lookin' / I knew the bride (when she used to rock'n'roll) / get it / Here comes the weekend / Worn out suits and brand new pockets. / Where or when / Ju-ju man / Let's talk about us / What did I do last night? / My baby left me / Little darlin'.
Apr 77. (7") **JU-JU MAN. / WHAT DID I DO LAST NIGHT?** [ ] [ ]
Jun 77. (7") **I KNEW THE BRIDE. / BACK TO SCHOOLDAYS** [26] [ ]
Aug 78. (7") **DEBORAH. / WHAT LOOKS BEST ON YOU** [ ] [ ]
Sep 78. (lp)(c) **TRACKS ON WAX** [ ] [ ]
– Trouble boys / Never been in love / Not a woman, not a child / Television / What looks best on you / Readers wives / Deborah / Thread your needle / A.1 on the jukebox / It's my own business / Heart of the city.
Oct 78. (7") **TELEVISION. / NEVER BEEN IN LOVE** [ ] [ ]
Feb 79. (7") **A-1 ON THE JUKEBOX. / IT'S MY OWN BUSINESS** [ ] [ ]
Jun 79. (7")(7"clear) **GIRLS TALK. / BAD IS BAD** [4] [65]
Jun 79. (lp)(c) **REPEAT WHEN NECESSARY** [39] [54]
– Girls talk / Crawling from the wreckage / Sweet little Lisa / The creature from the black lagoon / Home in my hand / Take me for a little while / Queen of hearts / We were both wrong / Bad is bad / Dynamite / Goodbye Mr Good Guy.
Sep 79. (7") **QUEEN OF HEARTS. / CREATURE FROM THE BLACK LAGOON** [11] [ ]
Nov 79. (7") **CRAWLING FROM THE WRECKAGE. / AS LOVERS DO** [59] [ ]
Jan 80. (7") **SINGIN' THE BLUES. / BOYS TALK** [28] [ ]

CARLENE CARTER / DAVE EDMUNDS

one-off 'A'side, CARLENE on 'B'side

F-Beat Columbia

Aug 80. (7") **BABY RIDE EASY. / TOO BAD ABOUT SANDY** [ ] [ ]

ROCKPILE

(EDMUNDS, LOWE, BREMNER and T. WILLIAMS)

F-Beat Columbia

Sep 80. (7")(7"yellow) **WRONG WAY. / NOW AND ALWAYS** [ ] [ ]
Oct 80. (lp)(c) **SECONDS OF PLEASURE** [34] [27]
– Teacher teacher / If sugar was as sweet as you / Wrong way / Now and always / Knife and fork / When I write the book / Pet you and hold you / Oh what a thrill / Play that fast thing (one more time) / For too long / Heart / (You ain't nothing but) Fine fine fine. *(re-iss.Jun84 on 'Demon')* (free 7"ep w/above **NICK LOWE & DAVE EDMUNDS SING THE EVERLY BROTHERS**
Nov 80. (7") **TEACHER TEACHER. / FOOL TOO LONG** [ ] [51]
Mar 81. (7") **TAKE A MESSAGE TO MARY. / ROCKPILE HEART** [-] [ ]

DAVE EDMUNDS

solo again. NICK LOWE continued his solo career also WILLIAMS later joined DIRE STRAITS. BREMNER joined ? **DAVE** now used session people including past friends

Swan Song Swan Song

Mar 81. (7") **ALMOST SATURDAY NIGHT. / YOU'LL NEVER GET ME UP** [58] [54]
Apr 81. (lp)(c) **TWANGIN'** [37] [48]
– (I'm gonna start) Living again if it kills me / The race is on / Almost Saturday night / Singin' the blues / Something happens / It's been so long / Cheap talk, patter and jive / You'll never get me up / I'm only human / Baby let's play house.
Jun 81. (7") **THE RACE IS ON. ("DAVE EDMUNDS & The STRAY CATS") / (I'M GONNA START) LIVING AGAIN IF IT KILLS ME** [34] [ ]

—— His touring band consisted of **MICKEY GEE** – guitar / **JOHN DAVID** – bass and **DAVID CHARLES** – drums. (They appear on album alongside sessioners)

Arista Columbia

Feb 82. (7") **WARMED OVER KISSES (LEFT OVER LOVE). / LOUISIANA MAN** [ ] [ ]
Mar 82. (lp)(c) **DE 7th** [60] [46]
– From small things big things come / Dear dad / Me and the boys / Bail you out / Generation number / Other guy's girls / Warmed over kisses (left over love) / Paula meet Jeanne / One more night / Deep in the heart of Texas / Louisiana man. (free 7"ep w/a) – LIVE AT THE VENUE (live) *(re-iss.Mar84 on 'Fame')*
Apr 82. (7") **ME AND THE BOYS. / QUEEN OF HEARTS (live)** [ ] [ ]
Jul 82. (7") **FROM SMALL THINGS BIG THINGS COME. / YOUR TRUE LOVE (live)** [ ] [-]
Jul 82. (7") **FROM SMALL THINGS BIG THINGS COME. / WARMED OVER KISSES (LEFT OVER LOVE)** [-] [ ]

—— plus **JEFF LENNY** – bass, synthesizers and production

Mar 83. (7")(12") **SLIPPING AWAY. / DON'T CALL ME TONIGHT** [60] [39]
Apr 83. (lp)(c) **INFORMATION** [92] [51]
– Slipping away / Don't you double / I want you bad / Wait / The watch on my wrist / The shape I'm in / Feels so right / What have I got to do to win / Have a heart / Information / Don't call me tonight.
May 83. (7")(12") **INFORMATION. / WHAT HAVE I GOT TO DO TO WIN** [ ] [ ]

—— **DAVE EDMUNDS** retained **JOHN DAVID /RICHARD TANDY** – keyboards (ex-ELECTRIC LIGHT ORCHESTRA) repl. GEE **TERRY WILLIAMS** – drums returned to repl. DAVID CHARLES

Jul 84. (7") **SOMETHING ABOUT YOU. / CAN'T GET ENOUUGH** [ ] [ ]
(12"+=) – Slipping away / Warmed over kisses (left over love) / From small things big things come.
Sep 84. (7") **BREAKING OUT. / HOW COULD I BE SO WRONG** [-] [ ]
Sep 84. (lp)(c) **RIFF RAFF** [ ] [ ]
– Something about you / Breaking out / Busted loose / S.O.S. / Far away / Rules of the game / Steel claw / Can't get enough / How could I be so wrong / Hang on.
Sep 84. (7") **STEEL CLAW. / HOW COULD I BE SO WRONG** [ ] [ ]
Jul 85. (7") **HIGH SCHOOL NIGHTS. / PORKY'S REVENGE** [ ] [91] Apr 85

—— (above from film 'Porky's Revenge', lp featured 3 more EDMUNDS tracks) 'RUN RUDOLPH RUN' appeared on 2 various comps. 'CHRISTMAS AT THE PATTI (live) and 'PARTY PARTY' soundtrack. They also appeared on 'STARDUST' soundtrack on 'CBS'/'Columbia'.

Aug 85. (7") **DO YOU WANT TO DANCE. / DON'T CALL ME TONIGHT** [-] [ ]
Jan 87. (lp)(c)(cd) **I HEAR YOU ROCKIN' – LIVE: DAVE EDMUNDS BAND (live)** [ ] [ ]
– I hear you knocking / Down down down / Hell of a pain / I'll get along / It ain't easy / Country roll / Blue Monday / The promised land / Dance, dance, dance / Lover not a fighter / Egg or the hen / Sweet little rock and roller / Black bill / Outlaw blues / Sabre dance.
Jan 87. (7") **HERE COMES THE WEEKEND. / PARALYZED** [-] [ ]
Apr 87. (7") **THE WANDERER (live). / INFORMATION (live)** [-] [ ]

—— next featured **LEE ROCKER / BRIAN SETZER** (Stray Cats)

Capitol Capitol

Mar 90. (7") **KING OF LOVE. / STAY WITH ME TONIGHT** [68] [ ]
(10"+=)(12"+=)(cd-s+=) – Everytime I see her.
Apr 90. (cd)(c)(lp) **CLOSER TO THE FLAME** [ ] [ ]
– King of love / Don't talk to me / Everytime I see her / Test of love / Closer to the flame / Stockholm / Fallin' through a hole / Never take the place of you / I got your number / Sincerely. *(re-iss.Mar91)*

Columbia Columbia

Aug 94. (cd)(c)(lp) **PLUGGED IN** [ ] [ ]
– Chutes and ladders / New step back / I love music / Halfway down / Beach Boy blood (in my veins) / The claw / I got the will / Better word for love / Standing at the crossroads / It doesn't really matter / Sabre dance.

– compilations etc. –

—— (*DAVE EDMUNDS, **ROCKPILE, ***LOVE SCULPTURE, ****HUMAN BEANS)

May 80. R.C.A.; (7"ep) **BABY I LOVE YOU** (*) [ ] [ ]
Aug 80. Harvest; (lp)(c) **THE SINGLES A's & B's** (**) + (****) [ ] [ ]
Aug 87. Harvest; (lp)(c) **THE ORIGINAL ROCKPILE VOL.II** (**) [ ] [ ]
Nov 81. Swan Song; (lp)(c) **THE BEST OF DAVE EDMUNDS** (*) + (**) + (***) [ ] [ ]
– Deborah / Girls talk / I knew the bride / A1 on the jukebox / The race is on / I hear you knockin' / Almost Saturday night / Sabre dance / Queen of hearts / Crawling from the wreckage / Here comes the weekend / Trouble boys / Ju ju man / Singing the blues / Born to be with you.
May 82. RCA Gold; (7") **BABY I LOVE YOU. / BORN TO BE WITH YOU** (*) [ ] [ ]
Oct 83. Old Gold; (7") **SABRE DANCE** (***) **/ My white Bicycle (by 'Tomorrow')** [ ] [ ]
Aug 87. Old Gold; (7") **I HEAR YOU KNOCKIN'. / SHE'S ABOUT A MOVER / SABRE DANCE** [ ] [ ]
Jul 91. E.M.I.; (d-cd)(d-c) **THE EARLY YEARS** [ ] [ ]
Dec 94. Connoisseur; (cd) **CHRONICLES** [ ] [-]

8 EYED SPY (see under ⇒ LUNCH, Lydia)

808 STATE

Formed: Manchester, England ... 1987 by PRICE and MASSEY. All met while working next to, and frequenting MARTIN PRICE's 'Eastern Bloc' record shop. After 2 albums on indie label 'Creed', they signed to 'Island' offshoot 'ZTT' in 1989. Their first single PACIFIC STATE (co-written with A GUY CALLED GERALD) breeched UK Top 10, and began onslaught into Europe. • **Style:** Techno-dance rave-rock using sampling, sparse anthemic vocals, once described as TANGERINE DREAM on speed. • **Songwriters:** Group compositions, except ONE IN TEN (UB40). • **Trivia:** Composed theme tune in 1990 for TV pop/chat programme 'The Word'. Remixed many, including

QUINCY JONES!?! (mid 91).

Recommended: EX:EL (*7).

GRAHAM MASSEY (b. 4 Aug'60) – prog., saxophone, engineer (ex-BITING TONGUES) / **MARTIN PRICE** (b.26 Mar'55) – programming, keyboards

Creed / not issued

Sep 88. (lp) **NEWBUILD** [ ] [-]

Nov 88. (12") **LET YOURSELF GO (303 mix). / LET YOURSELF GO (D50 mix) / DEEPVILLE** [ ] [-]

— **ANDREW BARKER** – DJ, drum prog., keys + **DARREN PARTINGTON** – DJ, drum prog., replaced GERALD SIMPSON who formed solo project A GUY CALLED GERALD.

Jul 89. (m-lp) **QUADRASTATE** [ ] [-]
– Pacific state / 106 / State ritual / Disco state / Fire cracker / State to state.

Z.T.T. / Tommy Boy

Oct 89. (7")(c-s) **PACIFIC STATE. / ('A' version)** [10] [ ]
(12"+=) – Pacific 707 / Pacific 202.

Dec 89. (12"+=)(cd-s+=) **PACIFIC STATE (9 minute version). / COBRA BORA (6 minutes)**

Dec 89. (lp)(c)(cd) **90** [57] [ ]
– Magical dream / Ancodia / Cobra bora / Pacific 202 / Donkey doctor / Sunrise / 808080808 / The fat shadow (pointy head mix). (US-title 'UTD.STATE '90').

Mar 90. (12"ep)(cd-ep) **THE EXTENDED PLEASURE OF DANCE** [56] [ ]
– Cobra bora (call the cops mix) / Cubik / Ancodia (deep nittater funky beat mix)

Oct 90. (7")(c-s) **CUBIK. / OLYMPIC (mix)** [10] [ ]
(12"+=)(cd-s+=) – ('A' Pan-Am mix) / ('B' Eir bass mix).

Feb 91. (7")(c-s) **IN YER FACE. / LEO LEO** [9] [ ]
(12"+=)(cd-s+=) – ('A'version) / ('B'mixes).

— next featured **BJORK** (Sugarcubes) – vocals (*)

Mar 91. (cd)(c)(lp)(2xlp-on 45 r.p.m.) **EX: EL** [4] [ ]
– San Francisco / Spanish heart / Leo Leo / Qwart * / Nephatiti / Lift / Ooops * / Empire / In yer face / Cubik / Lambrusco cowboy / Techno ball. (cd+=) – Olympic.

Apr 91. (7")(c-s) **OOOPS. / THE SKI FAMILY** [42] [ ]
(12"+=)(cd-s+=) – 808091 (live).
(12") – (2 'A'mixes).

Aug 91. (7")(c-s) **LIFT. / OPEN YOUR MIND** [38] [ ]
(12"+=)(cd-s+=) – ('A'open version) / ('B'sound galore mixes).

— MARTIN PRICE departed Oct'91.

In Feb'92, they collaborated with DAVID BOWIE on a version of 'SOUND AND VISION'. Below single as "808 STATE featuring BJORK".

Aug 92. (7")(c-s) **TIME BOMB. / NIMBUS** [ ] [ ]
('A'-Fon mix) (12"+=)(cd-s+=) – Reaper repo (short mix) / Reaper repo.

Nov 92. (7")(c-s) **ONE IN TEN 808. / ('A'vocal)** [17] [ ]
(12"+=) – ('A'-fast Fon mix) / ('A'-forceable lobotomy mix).
(cd-s++=) – ('A'instrumental).

Jan 93. (7")(c-s) **PLAN 9. / OLYMPIC '93 (The word mix)** [50] [ ]
('A'choki galaxy mix-12"+=) – ('A'guitars on fire mix).
(cd-s++=) – Bbambi (the April showers mix).

Feb 93. (cd)(c)(lp) **GORGEOUS** [17] [ ]
– Plan 9 / Moses / Contrique / 10 X 10 / Timebomb / One in ten / Europa / Orbit / Black morpheus / Southern cross / Nimbus / Colony.

Jun 93. (c-s) **10 X 10 (radio mix). / LA LUZ (chunky funky mix)** [67] [ ]
(12"+=) – ('A'black eye mix) / ('A'trace mix).
('A'hit man's club-10"+=) – ('A'instrumental).
(cd-s) – (3 'A'mixes above) / ('A'rockathon mix) / ('A'vox mix) / ('A'beats mix) / ('A'hit man's acapella mix).

Aug 94. (12")(c-s)(cd-s) **BOMBADIN. / MARATHON** [67] [ ]

MC TUNES Versus 808 STATE

(MC =NICHOLAS LOCKETT – English rapper)

May 90. (7")(c-s) **THE ONLY RHYME THAT BITES. / ('A'version)** [10] [ ]
(12"+=)(cd-s+=) – (other versions).

Sep 90. (7")(c-s) **TUNES THAT SPLIT THE ATOM. / DANCE YOURSELF TO DEATH** [18] [ ]
(12"+=) – (other versions)
(cd-s++=) – (1 extra version).

Oct 90. (cd)(c)(lp) **NORTH AT IT'S HEIGHT** [26] [ ]
– The only rhyme that bites / This ain't no fantasy / Dance yourself to death / Own worst enemy / The north at it's heights / Tunes splits the atom / Mancunian blues / The sequel / Primary rhyming / Dub at it's heights.

MC TUNES also released own single Nov90.- PRIMARY RISING

Mark EITZEL (see under ⇒ AMERICAN MUSIC CLUB)

ELASTICA

Formed: London, England . . . Oct'92 by JUSTINE, who had been an embryonic member of SUEDE with then boyfriend BRETT ANDERSON. Signed for new 'Deceptive' label in 1993 and collected critical acclaim from music press for their debut 45 'STUTTER'. Their follow-up 'LINE UP' early '94 stretched them into the UK Top 20 and made US labels take note. The 'Geffen' label soon took up the option for worldwide sales as all awaited 1995's tip for the top and their first album. • **Style:** New wave of the new wave featuring fuzzgun WIRE-like guitars. However this blatant plagiarism didn't go without notice, when they had to settle out of court with WIRE, for the use of 'Three Girl Rhumba' riff on 'CONNECTION' hit. Soon after this The STRANGLERS were paid out for 'No More Heroes' backing on another hit 'WAKING UP'. However bassist JEAN-JAQUES BURNEL is said to be a great fan. • **Songwriters:** FRISCHMANN lyrics / group compositions. • **Trivia:** In 1993-96, JUSTINE was the girlfriend of DAMON ALBARN (Blur). As DAN ABNORMAL (anagram) he played keyboards on their debut album and with them on Top Of The Pops.

Recommended: ELASTICA (*9)

JUSTINE FRISCHMANN (b.1968, Twickenham) – vocals, rhythm guitar (ex-SUEDE) / **DONNA MATTHEWS** (b. Newport, Wales) – vocals, guitar / **ANNIE HOLLAND** (b.Brighton, England) – bass / **JUSTIN WELCH** (b. Nuneaton, England) – drums (ex-SUEDE)

Deceptive / Sub Pop

Oct 93. (7") **STUTTER. / PUSSYCAT** [ ] [ ] Aug94

Jan 94. (7") **LINE UP. / VASELINE** [20] [ ]
(12"+=)(cd-s+=) – Rockunroll / Annie (John Peel sessions).

Deceptive / Geffen

Oct 94. (7")(c-s) **CONNECTION. / SEE THAT ANIMAL** [17] [53] Feb95
(12"+=)(cd-s+=) – Blue (demo) / Spastica.

Feb 95. (7")(c-s) **WAKING UP. / GLORIA** [13] [ ]
(12"+=)(cd-s+=) – Car wash / Brighton rock.

Mar 95. (cd)(c)(lp) **ELASTICA** [1] [66] Apr95
– Line up / Annie / Connection / Car song / Smile / Hold me now / S.O.F.T. / Indian song / Blue / All-nighter / Waking up / 2:1 / Vaseline / Never here / Stutter.

— In Jul'95, they guested on 'Sub Pop' 4x7"box-set 'HELTER SHELTER'.

Jun 95. (10"gold-ep) **STUTTER / ROCKUNROLL. / 2:1 (1 F.M. evening session) / ANNIE (John Peel session)** [-] [67]

— ANNIE departed in August.

ELECTRAFIXION (see under ⇒ ECHO & THE BUNNYMEN)

ELECTRIC FLAG

Formed: Chicago, USA . . . Apr'67 by MIKE BLOOMFIELD (see below), an ex-session man of BOB DYLAN, OTIS REDDING and WILSON PICKETT. They made their debut at the famous Monterey Festival in 1967, and soon signed to 'Columbia'. After a well-received album in 1968, MIKE left to set up partnerships with AL KOOPER and STEVE STILLS, then the latter, on 2 US Top 20 albums. The ELECTRIC FLAG continued, but not for long as they disbanded in '69. BLOOMFIELD continued on the solo front until his untimely death on 15 Feb'81 of a drug overdose. • **Style:** Brassy blues ensemble whom exploded too soon. • **Songwriters:** Group compositions? except some covers KILLING FLOOR (Howlin' Wolf) / YOU THREW YOUR LOVE ON ME TOO STRONG (Albert King) / IT TAKES A LOT TO LAUGH, IT TAKES A LOT TO CRY (Bob Dylan) / etc. KGB covered I'VE GOT A FEELING (Beatles). • **Trivia:** THE TRIP was written and directed by Jack Nicholson and starred PETER FONDA.

Recommended: MICHAEL BLOOMFIELD – A RETROSPECTIVE (*6) / A LONG TIME COMIN' (*6)

MICHAEL BLOOMFIELD (b.28 Jul'44, Chicago, USA) – guitar, percussion (ex-PAUL BUTTERFIELD BLUES BAND) / **NICK GRAVENITES** – vocals, guitar / **BARRY GOLDBERG** – keyboards / **BUDDY MILES** – drums, percussion / **HARVEY BROOKS** – bass, guitar / **MARCUS DOUBLEDAY** – trumpet, percussion / plus **PETER STRAZZA** – tenor sax / **HERBIE RICH** – guitar, saxophone

not issued / Sidewalk

Jun 67. (lp) **THE TRIP (by "The ELECTRIC FLAG, AN AMERICAN MUSIC BAND")** [-] [ ]
– Peter's trip / Joint passing / Psyche soap / M-23 / Synethesia / A little head / Hobbit / Inner pocket / Fewghh / Green and gold / The other Ed Norton / Flash, bam pow / Home room / Peter gets off / Practice music / Fine jung thing / Senior citizen / Gettin' hard. *(UK-iss.Mar87 on 'Edsel')*

C.B.S. / Columbia

Jul 68. (lp) **A LONG TIME COMIN'** [ ] [31] Mar 68
– Killing floor / Groovin' is easy / Over-lovin' you / She should have just / Wine / Texas / Sittin' in circles / You don't realise / Another country / Easy rider. *(re-iss.Aug74 on 'Embassy-CBS')*

Jul 68. (7") **GROOVIN' IS EASY. / OVER-LOVIN' YOU** [ ] [ ]

— BLOOMFIELD left to to go solo & collaborate with AL KOOPER, etc.

Jan 69. (lp) **ELECTRIC FLAG** [ ] [76]
– Soul searchin' / Sunny / With time there is change / Nothing to do / See to your neighbor / Qualified / Hey, little girl / Mystery / My woman that hangs around the house.

Mar 69. (7") **SUNNY. / SOUL SEARCHIN'** [ ] [ ]

— Disband '69, GOLDBERG went solo and BROOKS joined FABULOUS RHINESTONES. BUDDY MILES formed his own EXPRESS and joined JIMI HENDRIX's BAND OF GYPSIES.

MIKE BLOOMFIELD, AL KOOPER & STEVE STILLS

(AL KOOPER ex-BLUES PROJECT) / (STEVE STILLS of-CROSBY, STILLS & NASH)

C.B.S. / Columbia

Sep 68. (lp) **SUPER SESSION** [ ] [12] Aug 68
– Albert's shuffle / Stop / Man's temptation / His holy modal majesty / Really / It takes a lot to laugh, it takes a train to cry / Seasons of the witch / You don't love me / Harvey's tune. *(re-iss.1973 on 'Embassy-CBS') (cd-iss.Aug91 on Essential) (cd issued 1992 on 'Castle')*

MIKE BLOOMFIELD & AL KOOPER

also feat. **ELVIN BISHOP + CARLOS SANTANA**

C.B.S. / Columbia

Feb 69. (d-lp) **THE LIVE ADVENTURES OF MIKE BLOOMFIELD & AL KOOPER (live)** [ ] [18]

– The 59th Street Bridge song / I wonder who / Her holy modal highness / The weight – Mary Ann / Together 'til the end of time / That's all right – Green onions / Sonny Boy Williamson / No more lonely night / Dear Mr.Fantasy / You threw your love on me so strong / Finale – Refugee. *(re-iss.May88 on 'Edsel') (re-iss.d-cd Jun94 on 'Sony Europe')*

Mar 69. (7") **THE WEIGHT. / THE 59th STREET BRIDGE SONG**

— BLOOMFIELD then (Apr69) on MUDDY WATERS live album 'Fathers And Sons'.

MIKE BLOOMFIELD

solo **NICK GRAVENITES** – vocals / **JOHN KAHN** – bass / **MARK NAFTKAN** – keyboards / **IRA KAMIN** – keyboards / **BOB JONES** – drums

C.B.S. Columbia

Nov 69. (lp) **IT'S NOT KILLING ME** — Oct 69
– If you see my baby / For anyone you meet / Good old guy / Far too many nights / It's not killing me / Next time you see me / Michael's lament / Why must my baby / The ones I loved are gone / Don't think about it, baby / Goofers.

1970. (lp) **LIVE AT BILL GRAHAM'S FILLMORE EAST (live)**
– It takes time / Oh mama / Love got me / Blues on a westside / One more mile to go / It's about time / Carmelita skiffle.

— MIKE back into session work, until helping out NICK GRAVENITES on his soundtrack album 'Steelyard Blues' 1973. The same year he collaborates below

BLOOMFIELD / HAMMOND / DR.JOHN

(**HAMMOND** – vocals / **DR.JOHN** – piano, vocals)

C.B.S. Columbia

Aug 73. (lp)(c) **TRIUMVIRATE** — Jun 73
– Cha-dooky-doo / Last night / I yi yi / Just to be with you / Baby let me kiss you / Sho bout to drive me wild / It hurts me too / Rock me baby / Ground hog blues / Pretty thing. *(re-iss.May87 on 'Edsel') (re-iss.cd Jun94 on 'Sony Europe')*

ELECTRIC FLAG

BLOOMFIELD with **GRAVENITES, GOLDBERG + MILES,** plus new man **ROGER TROY** – bass

Atlantic Atlantic

Nov 74. (lp)(c) **THE BAND KEPT PLAYING**
– Sweet soul music / Every now and then / Sudden change / Earthquake country / Doctor oh doctor / Lonely song / Make your love / Inside information / Talkin' won't get it / The band kept playing.

1974. (7") **SWEET SOUL MUSIC. / EVERY NOW AND THEN** -

1975. (7") **THE BAND KEPT PLAYING. / DOCTOR OH DOCTOR** -

— Break-up again finally 1975.

– compilations, others, etc. –

C.B.S. Columbia

1971. (lp)(c) **THE BEST OF THE ELECTRIC FLAG**

Thunderb. not issued

Nov 83. (lp) **GROOVIN' IS EASY (live)** -
(cd-iss.Nov88)

KGB

BLOOMFIELD + GOLDBERG with **RAY KENNEDY** – vocals / **RICK GRECH** – bass / **CARMINE APPICE** – drums

M.C.A. M.C.A.

Jun 76. (lp)(c) **KGB** — Mar 76
– Let me love you / Midnight traveler / I've got a feeling / High roller / Sail on sailor / Workin' for the children / You got the notion / Baby should I stay or go / It's gonna be a hard night / Magic in your touch.

— **GREG SUTTON** – bass repl. GRECH **BEN SCHULTZ** – guitar repl. BLOOMFIELD who went solo again (see further below)

1976. (lp)(c) **MOTION**
– Woman, stop watcha doin' / I only need a next time / My serene Coleene / Lookin' for a better way / Lay it all down / Treading water / Goin' through the motions / Je t'aime / Determination.

MICHAEL BLOOMFIELD

with **NICK GRAVENITES** – guitar, vocals / **ROGER TROY + DOUG KILMER** – bass / **IRA KAMIN** – keyboards / **TOM DONLINGER + DAVE NEDITCH** – drums / **ERIC KRISS** – piano

Sonet Guitar P..

Aug 77. (lp) **IF YOU LOVE THESE BLUES, PLAY 'EM AS YOU PLEASE**
– If you love these blues / Hey foreman / India / Death cell rounder blues / City girl / Kansas City / Mama lion / Thrift shop rag / Death in the family / East Colorado blues / Blue ghost blues / The train is gone / The alter song.

— now w / **GRAVENITES / TROY + BOB JONES** – drums / **MARCIA ANN TAYLOR + ANNA RIZZO** – vocals

Sonet Takoma

Dec 77. (lp) **ANALINE**
– Peepin' an a moanin' / Mr.Johnson & Mr.Dunn / Frankie and Johnny / At the cross / Big 'C' blues / Hilo waltz / Effionna rag / Mood indingo / Analine.

T.K. Clouds

1978. (lp) **COUNT TALENT AND THE ORIGINALS**
– Love walk / You was wrong / Peach tree man / Sammy knows how to party / When I need you / I need your loving / Bad man / Saturday night / You're changin' / Let the people dance.

— **DAVID SHOREY** – bass, vocals repl. TROY

Sonet Takoma

1978. (lp) **MICHAEL BLOOMFIELD** -
– Guitar king / Knockin' myself out / My children, my children / Women loving each other / Sloppy drunk / You took my money / See that my grave is kept clean / The gospel truth.

— **ROGER TROY** – bass returned to replace SHOREY

1979. (lp) **BETWEEN THE HARD PLACE AND THE GROUND** -
– Lights out / Between the hard place and the ground / Big chief from New Orleans / Kid man blues / Orphans blues / Juke joint / Your friends.

— now w / **HENRY ODEN** – bass / **TOM RIZZO** – drums / **JONATHAN CRAMER** – keyboards / **HART McNEE** – baritone sax / **KING PERKOFF + DERRICK WALKER** – tenor sax

1981. (lp) **CRUISIN' FOR A BRUISIN'**
– Cruisin' for a bruisin' / Linda Lu / Papa mama rompah stompah / Jurker's blues / Midnight / It'll be me / Motorized blues / Mathilda / Winter bird / Snowblind.

— He brought back a near 1977 line-up.

not issued Waterhouse

Apr 82. (lp) **LIVING IN THE FAST LANE** -
– Maudie / Shine on love / Roots / Let them talk / Watkin's rag / Andy's bad / When I get home / Used to it / Big "C" blues / The dizz rag.

Above was his last album, recorded just before his death of a drug overdose 15 Feb'81.

– (MIKE BLOOMFIELD) compilations –

Apr 80. Sonet/ US= Kicking Mule; (lp) **BLOOMFIELD & HARRIS ("w / WOODY HARRIS")**

1981. Sonet/ US= KIcking Mule; (d-lp) **INITIAL SHOCK (live)**
– Eyesight to the blind / Woman lovin' each other / Linda Lu / Kansas City / Blues in B-flat / Medley: Darktown strutters ball – Mop top – Call me a dog / I'm glad I'm Jewish / Great gifts from Heaven / Lo, though I am thee / Jockey blues / Between the hard place and the ground / Don't lie to me / Cherry red / Uncle Bob's barrelhouse blues / Wee wee hours / Vamp in C / One of these days.

Jan 84. CBS/ US= Columbia; (d-lp)(d-c) **BLOOMFIELD – (A RETROSPECTIVE)**
– I've got my mojo working / Born in Chicago / Texas / Groovin' is easy / Killing floor / You don't realise / Wine / Albert's shuffle / Stop / I wonder who / You're killing my love / Goofers / It hurts me too / Relaxin' blues / Blues for Jimmy Yancey / Sunnyland Slim and Otis Spann / Woodyard street / Midnight on my radio / Why Lord, oh why? / Easy rider.

Apr 84. Thunderbolt; (lp) **AMERICAN HERO** -
(cd-iss.Mar88)

Jun 87. Demon; (lp) **I'M WITH YOU ALWAYS** (rare) -
(cd-iss. 1992)

Mar 94. Shanachie; (cd)(c) **BLUES, GOSPEL AND RAGTIME GUITAR INSTRUMENTALS** -

Jun 94. Columbia; (cd)(c) **ESSENTIAL BLUES 1964-69**

ELECTRIC LIGHT ORCHESTRA

Formed: Birmingham, England . . . 1968 by ROY WOOD, as alternative/idea to his other group The MOVE, who were drifting into slight cabaret circuit band. In 1969, he offered close friend JEFF LYNNE a place in The MOVE, but he declined, waiting until ROY came up with E.L.O. in 1971. The two outfits co-existed at this time, and the ELO debut finally hit the shops later that year. Highly regarded by the critics, it didn't hit No.32 until single '10538 OVERTURE', made the Top 10 in August 1972. WOOD soon departed ELO and The MOVE to form glam/flash rockers WIZZARD, which left JEFF LYNNE as the main man. The new line-up rejuvenated a past Chuck Berry classic 'ROLL OVER BEETHOVEN' to the heights of the Top 10. By the mid-70's, they had signed a new deal with 'Jet', where they took off to become massive international band. In the early 90's, an ELO PART II should have never been, as JEFF LYNNE had by now gone solo releasing hit album 'ARMCHAIR THEATER'. • **Style:** Creative BEATLES influenced rock-pop outfit, who relied heavily on string-laden themes, and a romanticised lyrical future. • **Songwriters:** JEFF LYNNE compositions (bar debut). Covered DO YA (Move). In the 90's, TROYER, HAYCOCK, BEVAN, etc, co-wrote songs after the departure of JEFF LYNNE. • **Trivia:** JEFF LYNNE also produced DAVE EDMUNDS (1981-84) / BRIAN WILSON (1988) / TOM PETTY (1989) / etc.

Recommended: OUT OF THE BLUE (*7) / THE GREATEST HITS (*8) / FACE THE MUSIC (*6) / A NEW WORLD RECORD (*6)

ROY WOOD (b. 8 Nov'46) – cello, vocals, multi (ex-The MOVE) / **JEFF LYNNE** (b.30 Dec'47) – vocals guitar (ex-The MOVE, ex-IDLE RACE) / **BEV BEVAN** (b. BEVERLEY, 24 Nov'46) – **drums, vocals**(ex-The MOVE) / **RICHARD TANDY** – bass, keyboards, vocals(ex-BALLS, ex-UGLYS) / **BILL HUNT** – keyboards, French horn / **WILF GIBSON** – violin / **HUGH McDOWELL** – cello / **ANDY CRAIG** – cello

Harvest United Art

Dec 71. (lp)(c) **THE ELECTRIC LIGHT ORCHESTRA** 32
– 10538 overture / Look at me now / Nellie takes her bow / The battle of Marston Moor (July 2nd, 1644) / First movement (jumpin' biz) / Mr.Radio / Manhattan rumble (49th Street massacre) / Queen of the hours / Whisper in the night. *(re-iss.Nov83 on 'Fame') (quad-lp 1972)*

Jul 72. (7") **10538 OVERTURE. / FIRST MOVEMENT (JUMPIN' BIZ)** 9 -

Sep 72. (7") **10538 OVERTURE. / THE BATTLE OF MARSTON MOOR (JULY 2ND, 1644)** -

— **MIKE EDWARDS** – cello repl. ROY WOOD who formed WIZZARD (Also went solo) / **MICHAEL DE ALBUQUERQUE** – bass repl. HUNT and McDOWELL who joined WIZZARD / **COLIN WALKER** – cello repl. ANDY CRAIG

Jan 73. (7") **ROLL OVER BEETHOVEN. / QUEEN OF THE HOURS** 6 42 Apr 73

Feb 73. (lp)(c) **E.L.O. 2** 35 62
– In old England town (boogie £2) / Momma / Roll over Beethoven / From the sun to the world (boogie £1) / Kuiama. *(re-iss.May82 on 'Fame')*

Sep 73. (7") **SHOWDOWN. / IN OLD ENGLAND TOWN (BOOGIE £2)** [12] [53] Nov 73
(US re-iss.Jul76)

— **MIK KAMINSKI** – violin repl. GIBSON / **HUGH McDOWELL** – cello returned to repl. WALKER (Above 2 in septet with **LYNNE, BEVAN, TANDY, WALKER ALBUQUERQUE** and **EDWARDS.**

Warners United Art

Dec 73. (lp)(c) **ON THE THIRD DAY** [ ] [52]
– Ocean breakup – King of the universe / Daybreaker / Bluebird is dead / Oh no, not Susan / New world rising / Ocean breakup (reprise) / Showdown / Daybreaker / Ma-Ma-Ma belle / Dreaming of 4000 / In the hall of the Mountain King. *(re-iss.1976 on 'Jet') (clear-lp iss.1978) (re-iss.'76 on 'Jet' & '78 clear vinyl)*

Mar 74. (7") **MA-MA-MA BELLE. / CAN'T FIND THE TITLE** [22] [-]

Mar 74. (lp) **THE NIGHT THE LIGHT WENT OUT IN LONG BEACH (live)** [-] [ ]
– Daybreaker / Showdown / Daytripper / 10538 overture / Mik's solo / Orange blossom special / Medley: In the hall of the mountain king – Great balls of fire / Roll over Beethoven. *(UK-iss.Nov85)*

Apr 74. (7") **DAYBREAKER (live). / MA-MA-MA BELLE (live)** [-] [87]

Jun 74. (7") **CAN'T GET IT OUT OF MY HEAD. / ILLUSIONS IN G MAJOR** [ ] [9] Dec 74

Oct 74. (lp)(c) **ELDORADO – A SYMPHONY BY THE ELECTRIC LIGHT ORCHESTRA** [ ] [16]
– Eldorado – overture / Can't get it out of my head / Boy blue / Larendo tornado / Poor boy (the greenwood) / Mister Kingdom / Nobody's child / Illusions in G major / Eldorado – finale. *(re-iss.'76 on 'Jet' & '78 yellow vinyl)*

Nov 74. (7") **ELDORADO. / BOY BLUE** [-] [ ]

— **KELLY GROUCUTT** – bass, vocals repl. ALBUQUERQUE / **MELVYN GALE** – cello repl. EDWARDS

Jet United Art

Oct 75. (lp)(c) **FACE THE MUSIC** [ ] [8]
– Fire on high / Waterfall / Evil woman / Night rider / Poker / Strange magic / Down home town / One summer dream. *(re-iss.'78 green vinyl) (re-iss.Jun85 on 'Epic') (re-iss.cd Mar94 on 'Sony Collectors') (re-iss.cd on 'Columbia')*

Dec 75. (7") **EVIL WOMAN. / 10538 OVERTURE (live)** [10] [10] Nov 75

Mar 76. (7") **NIGHT RIDER. / DAYBREAKER** [ ] [-]

Mar 76. (7") **STRANGE MAGIC. / NEW WORLD RECORD** [-] [14]

Jun 76. (7") **STRANGE MAGIC. / SHOWDOWN (live)** [38] [-]

Jul 76. (7") **SHOWDOWN (live). / DAYBREAKER (live)** [-] [59]

Oct 76. (7")(7"blue)(12"blue) **LIVIN' THING. / FIRE ON HIGH** [4] [-]

Oct 76. (7") **LIVIN' THING. / MA-MA-MA BELLE** [-] [13]

Nov 76. (lp)(c) **A NEW WORLD RECORD** [6] [5] Oct 76
– Tightrope / Telephone line / Rockaria! / Mission (a new world record) / So fine / Livin' thing / Above the clouds / Do ya / Shangri-la. *(re-iss.1978 on red-vinyl) (re-iss.Nov84 on 'Epic', cd-ss.Mar87) (re-iss.Aug88 on 'Jet', cd-iss.Apr89) (re-iss.+cd.Sep89 on 'Pickwick')*

Jan 77. (7") **DO YA. / NIGHTRIDER** [-] [24]

Feb 77. (7") **ROCKARIA!. / POKER** [9] [ ]
(re-iss.May78)

May 77. (7") **TELEPHONE LINE. / CALL BOY** [8] [-]
(re-iss.May78)

Jun 77. (7") **TELEPHONE LINE. / POOR BOY (THE GREENWOOD)** [-] [7]

Oct 77. (7") **TURN TO STONE. / MISTER KINGDOM** [18] [13] Nov 77
(re-iss.May78)

Nov 77. (d-lp)(d-c) **OUT OF THE BLUE** [4] [4]
– Turn to stone / It's over / Sweet talkin' woman / Across the border / Night in the city / Starlight / Jungle / Believe me now / Steppin' out / Standing in the rain / Summer and lightning / Mr. Blue Sky / Sweet is the night / The whale / Wild west hero / Birmingham Blues. *(re-iss.blue-lp 1978) (re-iss.+cd.May87 & Jun91 on 'Epic')*

Jan 78. (7")(7"blue) **MR. BLUE SKY. / ONE SUMMER DREAM** [6] [35] Jun 78
(re-iss.May78)

Feb 78. (7") **SWEET TALKIN' WOMAN. / FIRE ON HIGH** [-] [17]

Jun 78. (7")(12"yellow) **WILD WEST HERO. / ELDORADO** [6] [ ]

Oct 78. (7") **IT'S OVER. / THE WHALE** [-] [75]

Sep 78. (7")(7"mauve)(12"mauve) **SWEET TALKING WOMAN. / BLUEBIRD IS DEAD** [6] [17] Feb 78

May 79. (7")(12"white) **SHINE A LITTLE LOVE. / JUNGLE** [6] [8]

Jun 79. (lp)(c) **DISCOVERY** [1] [5]
– Shine a little love / Confusion / Need her love / The diary of Horace Wimp / Last train to London / Midnight blue / On the run / Wishing / Don't bring me down. *(re-iss.+cd.Nov86 & Jun91 on 'Epic')*

Jul 79. (7") **THE DIARY OF HORACE WIMP. / DOWN HOME TOWN** [6] [ ]

Aug 79. (7")(12") **DON'T BRING ME DOWN. / DREAMING OF 4000** [3] [4]

Oct 79. (7") **CONFUSION. / POKER** [-] [37]

Nov 79. (7") **CONFUSION. / LAST TRAIN TO LONDON** [8] [-]

Jan 80. (7") **LAST TRAIN TO LONDON. / DOWN HOME TOWN** [-] [39]

— Now trimmed basic quartet of **LYNNE, BEVAN, TANDY** and **GROUCUTT** (KAMINSKI formed VIOLINSKI) (McDOWELL and GALE also departed). For below album / singles they shared billing with OLIVIA NEWTON JOHN (ONJ) (E.L.O. tracks (***) / ELO and ONJ tracks (**) / ONJ tracks (*).

May 80. (7") **I'M ALIVE (***). / DRUM DREAMS (***)** [2] [16]

Jun 80. (7")(10"pink) **XANADU (**). / FOOL COUNTRY (*)** [1] [ ]

Jun 80. (7") **XANADU (*). / (other track by GENE KELLY & OLIVIA NEWTON JOHN)** [-] [8]

Jul 80. (lp)(c) **XANADU (film Soundtrack)** [2] [4]
– Xanadu ** / I'm alive (***) / All over the world (***) / etc

Jul 80. (7")(10"blue) **ALL OVER THE WORLD(***). / MIDNIGHT BLUE (***)** [11] [ ]

Jul 80. (7") **ALL OVER THE WORLD (***). / DRUM DREAMS (***)** [-] [ ]

Nov 80. (7") **DON'T WALK AWAY (***). / ACROSS THE BORDER (***)** [21] [-]

E.L.O

Jul 81. (7") **HOLD ON TIGHT. / WHEN TIME STOOD STILL** [4] [10]

Aug 81. (lp)(c) **TIME** [1] [16]
– Prologue / Twilight / Yours truly, 2095 / Ticket to the Moon / The way life's meant to be / Another heart breaks / Rain is falling / From the end of the world / The lights go down / Here is the news / 21st century man / Hold on tight / Epilogue. *(re-iss.+cd.Feb88) (c+cd.re-iss.Jun91)*

Oct 81. (7") **TWILIGHT. / JULIE DON'T LIVE HERE** [30] [33]

Dec 81. (7")(12"pic-d) **TICKET TO THE MOON. / HERE IS THE NEWS** [24] [-]

Jan 82. (7") **RAIN IS FALLING. / ANOTHER HEART BREAKS** [-] [ ]

Mar 82. (7") **THE WAY LIFE'S MEANT TO BE . / WISHING** [ ] [ ]

Jun 83. (7")(12") **ROCK'N'ROLL IS KING. / AFTER ALL** [13] [19]

Jun 83. (lp)(c)(cd) **SECRET MESSAGES** [4] [36]
– Secret messages / Loser gone wild / Bluebird / Take me on and on / Four little diamonds / Stranger / Danger ahead / Letter from Spain / Train of gold / Rock'n'roll is king. *(cd-iss.May87)* (cd+=) – Time after time. *(c/cd.re-iss.Jun91, re-iss.cd+c.Mar93)*

Aug 83. (7")(7"pic-d) **SECRET MESSAGES. / BUILDINGS HAVE EYES** [48] [36]

Oct 83. (7")(12") **FOUR LITTLE DIAMONDS. / LETTER FROM SPAIN** [ ] [86] Sep 83

Jan 84. (7") **STRANGER. / TRAIN OF GOLD** [-] [ ]

ELECTRIC LIGHT ORCHESTRA

After a brief spell in BLACK SABBATH, **BEVAN** rejoined ELO with others **JEFF LYNNE** and the returning **MICK KAMINSKI**

Epic C.B.S.

Feb 86. (7")(12") **CALLING AMERICA. / CAUGHT IN A TRAP** [28] [18] Jan 86

Mar 86. (lp)(c) **BALANCE OF POWER** [9] [49] Feb 86
– Heaven only knows / So serious / Getting to the point / Secret lives / Is it alright? / Sorrow about to fall / Without someone / Calling America / Endless lies / Send it. *(cd-iss.May87) (c+cd.re-iss.Jun91)(re-iss.cd/c.Mar93)*

Apr 86. (7") **SO SERIOUS. / A MATTER OF FACT** [ ] [-]
(12"+=) – ('A' alternative mix).

May 86. (7") **SO SERIOUS. / ENDLESS LIES** [-] [ ]

Jul 86. (7")(12") **GETTING TO THE POINT. / SECRET LIVES** [ ] [ ]

— continued without LYNNE! who went solo and joined TRAVELING WILBURYS

ELECTRIC LIGHT ORCHESTRA PART II

now with **BEVAN, KAMINSKI, McDOWELL, GROUCUTT, LOUIS CLARK, PETE HAYCOCK** – vocals (ex-CLIMAX BLUES BAND) / session **NEIL LOCKWOOD, ERIC TROYER.**

Telstar not issued

Apr 91. (7")(c-s) **HONEST MAN. / LOVE FOR SALE** [60] [ ]
(12"+=)(cd-s+=) – ('A'extended).

May 91. (cd)(c)(lp) **PART II** [34] [ ]
– Hello / Honest man / Every night / Once upon a time / Heartbreaker / Thousand eyes / For the love of a woman / Kiss me red / Heart of hearts / Easy street.

— **ERIC TROYER + PHIL BATES** – guitar, vocals repl. HAYCOCK (now solo again)

Ultrapop Ultrapop

Aug 94. (c-s)(cd-s) **POWER OF A MILLION LIGHTS. / ?** [ ] [-]

Oct 94. (cd)(c) **MOMENT OF TRUTH** [ ] [ ]
– Moment of truth (overture) / Breakin' down the walls / Power of a million lights / Interlude / One more tomorrow / Don't wanna / Voices / Interlude 2 / Vixen / The fox / Love or money / Blue violin / Whiskey girls / Interlude / Twist of the knife / So glad you said goodbye / Underture / The leaving.

Oct 94. (c-s)(cd-s) **BREAKIN' DOWN THE WALLS. / ?** [ ] [-]

– compilations etc. –

Note; All 'Harvest' releases were issued on 'United Artists' US.

Oct 74. Harvest; (lp)(c) **SHOWDOWN** [ ] [ ]

Apr 77. Harvest; (lp)(c) **THE LIGHT SHINES ON** [ ] [ ]

Mar 79. Harvest; (lp)(c) **THE LIGHT SHINES ON (VOL.2)** [ ] [ ]

Apr 86. Harvest; (lp)(c)(cd) **FIRST MOVEMENT** [ ] [ ]

Note; All 'Jet' releases were issued on 'United Artists' US.

Jun 76. Jet; (lp)(c) **OLE ELO** [ ] [32]

Dec 78. Jet; (7"ep) **E.L.O. EP** [34] [ ]
– Can't get it out of my head / Strange magic / Evil woman / Ma-ma-ma-belle.

Dec 78. Jet; (3xlp-box) **THREE LIGHT YEARS** [38] [ ]
(first 3 albums boxed)

Nov 79. Jet; (lp)(c) **ELO'S GREATEST HITS** [7] [30]
(re-iss.Jan87 on 'Epic', cd-iss. 1986)

1980. Jet; (4xlp-box) **FOUR LIGHT YEARS** [ ] [ ]
(first 4 albums boxed)

1988. Jet; (cd) **A PERFECT WORLD OF MUSIC** [ ] [-]

Dec 92. Epic; (3xcd-box) **ELDORADO / A NEW WORLD RECORD / OUT OF THE BLUE** [ ] [-]
(re-iss.cd+c Jun94)

May 84. Old Gold; (7") **ROLL OVER BEETHOVEN. / 10538 OVERTURE** [ ] [-]

May 88. Arcade; (cd) **ALL OVER THE WORLD** [ ] [-]

Dec 89. Telstar; (lp)(c)(cd) **THE GREATEST HITS** [13] [-]
– Evil woman / Livin' thing / Can't get it out of my head / Showdown / Turn to stone / Rockaria! / Sweet talkin' woman / Telephone line / Ma ma ma belle / Strange magic / Mr blue sky *(re-iss.Oct90 as 'THE VERY BEST OF THE ELECTRIC LIGHT ORCHESTRA', hit 28)*

Aug 91. E.M.I.; (cd)(c)(d-lp) **EARLY ELO** [ ] [ ]
– (first 2 albums, plus bonus tracks)

Jun 93. Sony Europe; (cd) **THE DEFINITIVE COLLECTION** [ ] [-]

Jun 94. Dino; (cd)(c) **THE VERY BEST OF THE ELECTRIC LIGHT ORCHESTRA** [4] [-]

Jul 94. Legacy; (3xcd-box) **AFTERGLOW** [ ] [-]

Oct 94. Epic; (cd) **THE BEST VOLUME 1** [ ] [ ]

Oct 94. Epic; (cd) **THE BEST VOLUME 2**
Oct 94. Epic; (3xcd-box) **TIME / SECRET MESSAGES / DISCOVERY**

JEFF LYNNE

(solo, while a ELO member)

Jet Jet

Jul 77. (7")(12") **DOIN' THAT CRAZY THING. / GOIN' DOWN TO RIO**

not issued Epic

Aug 84. (7") **VIDEO. / SOONER OR LATER** [-]
(above from the film 'Electric Dreams')

BEV BEVAN

Jet not issued

May 76. (7") **LET THERE BE DRUMS. / HEAVY HEAD** [-]

ELECTRIC PRUNES

Formed: Seattle, Washington, USA . . . 1965 by (see below). That year they also moved to Los Angeles, where they signed to 'Reprise'. After an initial flop, they soon broke into the charts late 1966 with 'I HAD TOO MUCH TO DREAM LAST NIGHT'. Another Annette Tucker & Nancie Mantz written song 'GET ME TO THE WORLD ON TIME', also charted on both sides of the Atlantic in Spring 1967. When their albums failed to show any commercial promise, their new 1968 member DAVID AXELROD took over, but with no originals left, they soon folded. • **Style:** Cult psychedelic rock outfit, who briefly surfaced from the underground. • **Songwriters:** LOWE-TULIN, except as mentioned and AXELROD in '68. • **Trivia:** Their 1968 album 'MASS IN F MINOR', was a concept piece of music based on Catholic transposition and sung in Latin.

Recommended: LONG DAY'S FLIGHT (*6).

JIM LOWE (b. San Luis Obispo, California) – vocals / **KEN WILLIAMS** (b. Long Beach, California) – lead guitar / **WEASEL SPANGOLA** (b. Cleveland, Ohio) – rhythm guitar / **MARK TULIN** (b. Philadelphia, Pennsylvania) – bass / **PRESTON RITTER** (b. Stockton, California) – drums

Reprise Reprise

May 66. (7") **AIN'T IT HARD. / LITTLE OLIVE** [-]
Nov 66. (7") **I HAD TOO MUCH TO DREAM (LAST NIGHT). / LUVIN'** [49] [11]
(re-iss.Mar79 UK on 'Radar')
Apr 67. (7") **GET ME TO THE WORLD ON TIME. / ARE YOU LOVIN' ME MORE (BUT ENJOYING IT LESS)** [42] [27] Mar 67
Apr 67. (lp) **I HAD TOO MUCH TO DREAM LAST NIGHT**
– I had too much to dream last night / Bangles / Onie / Are you lovin' me more / Train for tomorrow / Sold to the highest bidder / Get me to the world on time / About a quarter to nine / The king is in the counting house / Luvin' / Try me on for size / The Toonerville trolley.

— **QUINT** – drums repl. RITTER

1967. (7") **DR. DOGOOD. / HIDEAWAY** [-]
Jul 67. (7") **THE GREAT BANANA HOAX. / WIND-UP TOYS** [-]
Aug 67. (lp) **UNDERGROUND** [-]
– The great banana hoax / Children of rain / Wind-up toys / Antique doll / It's not fair / I happen to love you / Dr.Dogood / I / Hideaway / Big city / Capt.Glory / Long day's flight.
Dec 67. (7") **LONG DAY'S FLIGHT. / THE KING IN HIS COUNTING HOUSE** [-]
1968. (7") **EVERYBODY KNOWS YOU'RE IN LOVE. / YOU NEVER HAD IT BETTER** [-]

— added **DAVID AXELROD** – conductor / **RON MORGAN** – guitar repl. SPANGOLA / **BRETT WADE** (b. Vancouver, Canada) – bass, vocals repl. / **MARK TULIN and RICHARD WHETSTONE** (b. Hutchison, Kansas) – drums (on session until '69) repl. QUINT

— **MARK KINCAID** (b. Topeka, Kansas) – vocals, guitar repl. JIM LOWE / also **JIM HERREN** (b. Elk City, Oklahoma) – keyboards repl. WILLIAMS (above 2 amalgamating with **MORGAN, WADE** and **WHETSTONE)** There were now no original members left, even AXELROD went solo

Mar 68. (lp) **MASS IN F MINOR** Jan 68
– Kyrie Eleison / Gloria / Credo / Sanctus / Benedictus / Agnus Dei.
Nov 68. (lp) **RELEASE OF AN OATH**
– Kol Nidre / Holy are you / General confession / Individual confessional / Our father, our king / Adoration / Closing hymn.
Jun 69. (7") **HEY MR. PRESIDENT. / FLOWING SMOOTHLY** [-]
Jun 69. (lp) **JUST GOOD OLD ROCK'N'ROLL** [-]
– Tracks / 14 year old funk / Sell / Sing to me / Silver passion mine / Love grows / So many people to tell / Finders keepers, losers weepers / Giant sunhouse / Violent rose / Thorjan.

– compilations etc. –

May 86. Edsel; (lp) **LONG DAY'S FLIGHT** (66-67) [-]
– Ain't it hard / Little Olive / I had too much to dream last night / Luvin' / Get me to the world on time / Are you lovin' me more (but enjoying it less) / Bangles / Train for tomorrow / Sold to the highest bidder / Try me on for size / Doctor Do-good / Hideaway / The great banana hoax / Children of rain / Antique doll / I happen to love you / Long days flight / You never had it better.

ELECTRONIC (see under ⇒ NEW ORDER)

ELEVEN (see under ⇒ DANNY WILSON)

ELF / (ELECTRIC) ELVES) (see under ⇒ DIO)

Cass ELLIOT (see under ⇒ MAMAS & THE PAPAS)

E.L.O. (see under ⇒ ELECTRIC LIGHT ORCHESTRA)

Joe ELY

Born: 9 Feb'47, Amarillo, Texas, USA, although his family later moved to Lubbock, Texas. Went solo in 1976, after being one-time member of The FLATLANDERS from 1972. He signed to 'M.C.A.' and released well-received albums that even attracted interest from The CLASH, who invited him on support tour late 70's. • **Style:** Bar-room "honky-tonk" blues that brought together blends of "Tex-Mex" and basic country rock. Briefly, on HI-RES lp 1984, he changed style bringing in 'electro-pop'. • **Songwriters:** Writes own material except some covers. • **Trivia:** Appeared on CLASH album COMBAT ROCK '82.

Recommended: LETTER TO LAREDO (*6)

JOE ELY – vocals, guitar (ex-FLATLANDERS) with backing band **JESSE TAYLOR** – guitar / **GREGG WRIGHT** – bass / **PONTI BONE** – keyboards / **STEVE KEETON** – drums / **LLOYD MAINES** – steel guitar / **JOHN KEISTER** – keyboards

M.C.A. M.C.A.

Jul 77. (7") **MARDI GRAS WALTZ. / ALL MY LOVE** [-]
Sep 77. (lp)(c) **JOE ELY**
– I had my hopes up high / Mardi Gras waltz / She never spoke Spanish to me / Gambler's pride / Suckin' a big bottle of gin / Tennessee's not got the state I'm in / If you were a bluebird / Treat me like a Saturday night / All my love / Johnny blues. *(re-iss.Aug81)*
Sep 77. (7") **GAMBLER'S PRIDE. / TENNESSEE'S NOT THE STATE I'M IN**
Mar 78. (7") **FINGERNAILS. / BECAUSE OF THE WIND**
Mar 78. (lp)(c) **HONKY TONK MASQUERADE**
– Cornbread moon / Because of the wind / Box cars / Tonight I think I'm gonna go downtown / Honky tonk masquerade / Honky tonkin' / Jerico (your walls must come tumblin' down) / I'll be your fool / Fingernails / West Texas waltz.
May 78. (7") **BOXCARS. / HONKY TONK MASQUERADE**
Apr 79. (7") **DOWN ON THE DRAG. / IN ANOTHER WORLD**
May 79. (lp)(c) **DOWN ON THE DRAG**
– Fools fall in love / B.B.Q. and foam / Standin' at the big hotel / Crazy lemon / Crawdad train / In another world / She leaves you where you are / Down on the drag / Time for travellin' Maria.
Mar 80. (7"ep) **FINGERNAILS. / SUCKIN' A BIG BOTTLE OF GIN / STANDIN' AT THE BIG HOTEL**
May 80. (lp)(c) **LIVE SHOTS (live)**
– Fingernails / Midnight shift / Honky tonk masquerade / Honky tonkin' / Long snake Moon / I had my hopes up high / She never spoke Spanish to me / Johnny's blues / Fools fall in love / Boxcars.

— **ELY** retained **TAYLOR, BONE** and **MAINES.**(STEVE KEETON mysteriously died 1981). Recruited **ROBERT MARQUAM** – drums / **MICHAEL ROBERTSON** – bass / **REESE WYNANS** – keyboards / **SMOKEY JOE MILLER** – saxophone / **JAMES FENNER** – percussion. note:- 13 year-old **CHARLIE SEXTON** played guitar on some live gigs.

Mar 81. (7") **MUSTA NOTTA GOTTA LOTTA. / WISHIN' FOR YOU**
May 81. (lp)(c) **MUSTA NOTTA GOTTA LOTTA**
– Musta notta gotta lotta / Dallas / Wishin' for you / Old on / Rock me my baby / I keep gettin' paid the same / Road hawg / Good rockin' tonight / Hard livin' / Damn of my heart / Bet.
Jun 81. (7") **DALLAS. / HARD LIVIN'**

— **ELY** now with **BONE, MILLER** plus **ROSCOE BECK** – bass / **STEVE MEADOR** – drums / **MITCH WATKINS** – guitar, synth. / **BILL GINN** – synth. / **MICHAEL RAMOS** – synth. / **etc.**

Apr 84. (lp)(c) **HI-RES**
– What's shakin' tonight / Cod rockin' Loretta / Madam Wo / Dream camera / Letter to Laredo / She gotta get the gettin' / Lipstick in the night / Imagine Houston / Dame tu mano / Locked in a boxcar with the queen of Spain.

— now w/**BOBBY KEYES** – saxophone / **DAVID GRISSOM** – guitar / **DAVE McCLARY** – drums

Demon Hightone

Sep 87. (lp)(c)(cd) **LORD OF THE HIGHWAY**
– Lord of the highway / (Don't put a) lock on my heart / Are you listening Lucky / Me and Billy the kid / Letter to L.A. / No rope, Daisy-o / Thinks he's French / Row of dominoes / Everybody got hammered / Silver city.
Oct 88. (lp)(cd) **DIG ALL NIGHT**
– Settle for love / For your love / My eyes got lucky / Maybe she'll find me / Drivin' me / Dig all night / Grandfather blues / Jazz street / Rich man, poor boy / Behind the bamboo shade.

Sunstorm Sunstorm

Nov 88. (m-lp) **MILKSHAKES AND MALTS (live)**
– She never spoke Spanish to me / Boxcars / West Texas waltz / Down in the drag.
Sep 89. (lp)(cd) **WHATEVER HAPPENED TO MARIA**

M.C.A. M.C.A.

Nov 90. (7")(12") **ROW OF DOMINOES. / ME AND BILLY THE KID**
(cd-s+=) – Are you listening Lucky.
Dec 90. (cd)(c)(lp) **LIVE AT LIBERTY LUNCH (live)**
– Me and Billy the kid / Are you listening Lucky / Grandfather blues / B.B.Q. and foam / Row of dominoes / Dallas / Where is my love? / She gotta get the gettin' / Drivin' to the powerhouse in a limousine / Cool rockin' Loretta / Musta notta gotta

lotta / Letter to L.A. / If you were a bluebird.

—— He and his band toured in Oct'92.

Demon Rykodisc?

Apr 95. (cd) **NO BAD TALK OR LOUD TALK** (compilation?) ☐ ☐
– Honky tonk masquerade / If you were a bluebird / Dallas / Fingernails / Boxcars / Tonight I think I'm gonna go downtown / I had my hopes up high / Fools fall in love / Treat me like a Saturday night / Maria / Down on the drag / Hard livin' / Musta notta gotta lotta / Suckin' a big bottle of gin / Johnny's blues / She never spoke Spanish to me / Because of the wind / West Texas waltz.

compilations, etc. –

Nov 95. Transatlantic; (cd) **LETTER TO LAREDO** ☐ -
– All just to get to you / Gallo del cielo / Run preciosa / Saint Valentine / Ranches and rivers / Letter to Laredo / I saw it in you / She finally spoke Spanish to me / I ain't been here long / hat ain't enough / I'm a thousand miles from home.

– compilations, etc. – (FLATLANDERS)

—— **JOE ELY** – guitar, vocals / **BUTCH HANCOCK** – vocals / **TOMMY HANCOCK** – fiddle / **JIMMY DALE GILMORE** – guitar / **SYLVESTER RICE** – bass / **STEVE WESSON** – drums

Charly Rounder

1980. (lp) **ONE MORE ROAD** (rec.1972) ☐ ☐ 1989
US title: MORE A LEGEND THAN A BAND.

EMERSON LAKE & PALMER

Formed: London, England . . . mid-1970. Soon signed to 'Island' records, after featuring on the Isle Of Wight festival 29 Aug'70. Their eponymous debut later in the year, made the UK/US Top 20, with 1971 follow-up hitting Top spot in UK. Early singles were issued at this time, but only in America where they were signed to 'Atlantic' subsidiary 'Cotillion'. In 1977, an edited version of FANFARE FOR THE COMMON MAN nearly gave them a surprise UK No.1. This however was to mark the end of ELP, at least commercially. They re-formed in '86, with the P of the band taken up by new veteran drummer COZY POWELL. The original group re-formed again in 1991, but were found floundering on past glories with 'BLACK MOON' album in '92. • **Style:** Techno-rock supergroup with considerable musical ability appreciated in most polls, although they were accused of flashy over-indulgence. Their concept pieces, although slightly mechanical, revived their classical inhibitions in the progressive rock world. • **Songwriters:** GREG LAKE compositions / PETE SINFIELD words. Covered complete PICTURES AT AN EXHIBITION (Mussorgsky) / NUT ROCKER (Tchaikovsky) / JERUSALEM (trad.hymn) / FANFARE FOR THE COMMON MAN (Aaron Copeland / PETER GUNN (Henry Mancini). KEITH EMERSON solo:- HONKY TONK TRAIN BLUES (Meade Lux Lewis). • **Trivia:** 'Manticore' their label formed in 1973, also signed PETE SINFIELD, P.F.M. and LITTLE RICHARD!

Recommended: TRILOGY (*8) / BRAIN SALAD SURGERY (*8)

KEITH EMERSON (b. 2 Nov'44) – keyboards (ex-NICE, ex-GARY FARR & THE T-BONES / **GREG LAKE** (b.10 Nov'48) – vocals, guitar, bass (ex-KING CRIMSON) / **CARL PALMER** (b.20 Mar'47) – drums, percussion (ex-ATOMIC ROOSTER, ex-CRAZY WORLD OF ARTHUR BROWN)

Island Cotillion

Nov 70. (lp)(c) **EMERSON LAKE & PALMER** 4 18
– The barbarian / Take a pebble / Knife edge / The three fates:- Clotho – Lachesis – Acropus / Tank / Lucky man. *(re-iss.'74 on 'Manticore') (cd-iss.1988 on 'WEA')(re-iss.cd Dec93 on 'Victory')*

Mar 71. (7") **LUCKY MAN. / KNIFE EDGE** - 48
(US re-iss.Jan73 hit No.51)

Jun 71. (lp)(c) **TARKUS** 1 9
– Tarkus:- Eruption – Stones of years – Iconoclaust – The mass – Manticore – Battlefield – Aquatarkus – (conclusion) / Jeremy Bender / Bitches crystal / The only way / Infinite space / A time and a place / Are you ready Eddy?. *(re-iss.'74 on 'Manticore') (cd-iss.Sep89 on 'WEA') (re-iss.cd Dec93 on 'Victory')*

Sep 71. (7") **STONES OF YEARS. / A TIME AND A PLACE** - ☐

Nov 71. (lp)(c) **PICTURES AT AN EXHIBITION** 2 10
– Promenade: The gnome – Promenade – The sage – The old castle – Blues variation – Promenade / The hut of Baba Yaga – The curse of Baba Yaga – The hut of Baba Yaga – The great gates of Kiev – Nutrocker. *(re-iss '74 on 'Manticore') (cd-iss.1988 on 'Cotillion' & Sep89 on 'WEA')(re-iss. Dec93 on 'Victory')*

Mar 72. (7") **NUTROCKER. / THE GREAT GATES OF KIEV** - 70

Jul 72. (lp)(c) **TRILOGY** 2 5
– The endless enigma (part 1) – Fugue – The endless enigma (part 2) / From the beginning / The sheriff / Hoedown / Trilogy / Living sin / Abaddon's bolero. *(re-iss.'74 on 'Manticore') (cd-iss.Jun89 on 'Atlantic')(re-iss.cd Dec93 on 'Victory')*

Aug 72. (7") **FROM THE BEGINNING. / LIVING SIN** - 39

Manticore Manticore

Dec 73. (lp)(c) **BRAIN SALAD SURGERY** 2 11
– Jerusalem / Toccata / Still . . .you turn me on / Benny the bouncer / Karn evil 9. 1st impression – part 1 & 2 – 2nd impression – 3rd impression. *(cd-iss.Jun89 on 'WEA') (re-iss.cd Dec93 on 'Victory')*

Dec 73. (7") **JERUSALEM. / WHEN THE APPLE BLOSSOM BLOOMS IN THE WINDMILLS OF YOUR MIND, I'LL BE YOUR VALENTINE** ☐ ☐

Aug 74. (t-lp)(d-c) **WELCOME BACK MY FRIENDS TO THE SHOW THAT NEVER ENDS – LADIES AND GENTLEMEN . . . EMERSON, LAKE & PALMER (live)** 5 4
– Howdown / Jerusalem / Toccata / Tarkus:- Eruption – Stones of years – Iconoclaust – The mass – Manticore – Battlefield – Epitaph – Aquatarkus – (conclusion) / Take a pebble – Piano improvisations – Take a pebble (conclusion) / Jeremy Bender / The sheriff / Karn evil 9. 1st impression – 2nd impression – 3rd impression. *(re-iss.cd Dec93 on 'Victory')*

– solo projects –

GREG LAKE

Nov 75. (7") **I BELIEVE IN FATHER CHRISTMAS. / HUMBUG** 2 ☐
(re-iss.Nov82 hit 72 & Dec83 hit 65)

KEITH EMERSON

with **KENDALL STUBBS** – bass / **FRANK SCULLY** – drums

Apr 76. (7") **HONKY TONK TRAIN BLUES. / BARREL HOUSE SHAKE DOWN** 21 ☐

EMERSON, LAKE & PALMER

Atlantic Atlantic

Mar 77. (d-lp)(d-c) **WORKS 1** 9 12
– Piano concerto No.1 – 1st movement: Allegro giojoso / 2nd movement: Andante molto cantabile / 3rd movement: Toccata con fuoco / Lend your love to me tonight / C'est la vie / Hallowed by thy name / Nobody loves you like I do / Closer to believing / The enemy God dances with the black spirits / L.A. nights / New Orleans / Bach: Two part invention in D minor / Food for your soul / Tank / Fanfare for the common man / Pirates. *(cd-iss.Jun89)(re-iss.d-cd Dec93 on 'Victory')*

Jun 77. (7")(12") **FANFARE FOR THE COMMON MAN (edit). / BRAIN SALAD SURGERY** 2 ☐

Aug 77. (7") **C'EST LA VIE (as "GREG LAKE" solo). / JEREMY BENDER** ☐ ☐

Nov 77. (lp)(c) **WORKS 2** (compilation of rare and demo work) 20 37
– Tiger in a spotlight / When the apple blossoms bloom in the windmills of your mind I'll be your valentine / Bullfrog / Brain salad surgery / Barrelhouse shakedown / Watching over you / So far to fall / Maple leaf rag / I believe in Father Christmas / Close but not touching / Honky tonk train blues / Show me the way to go home. *(cd-iss.Jun89) (re-iss.cd Dec93 on 'Victory')*

Jan 78. (7") **WATCHING OVER YOU ("GREG LAKE" solo). / HALLOWED BE THY NAME** ☐ ☐

Nov 78. (lp)(c) **LOVE BEACH** 48 55
– All I want is you / Love beach / Taste of my love / The gambler / For you / Canario / Memoirs of an officer and a gentleman – Prologue – The education of a gentleman / Love at first sight / Letters from the front / Honourable company. *(cd-iss.Jun89) (re-iss.cd Dec93 on 'Victory')*

Nov 78. (7") **ALL I WANT IS YOU. / TIGER IN A SPOTLIGHT** ☐ ☐

—— (disbanded Dec78)

KEITH EMERSON

(solo)

Atlantic Atlantic

Sep 80. (7") **TAXI RIDE. / MATER TENEBARUM** ☐ ☐

Atlantic Cinevox

Dec 80. (lp) **INFERNO (Soundtrack)** ☐ ☐
– Inferno / Rose's descent into a cellar / The taxi ride / The library / Sarah in the library vaults / Bookbinder's delight / Rose leaves the apartment / Rose gets it / Elisa's story / A cat attic attack / Kazanian's tarantella / Mark's discovery / Matter tenebarum / Inferno (finals) / Ices, cigarettes, etc. *(re-iss.Mar90 on 'Silva Screen')*

—— added **NEIL SYMONETTE** – drums / **TRISTAN FRY** – percussion / **GREG BOWEN** – trumpet / **JEROME RICHARDSON** – sax / **PAULETTE McWILLIAMS** – vocals

M.C.A. Backstreet

Apr 81. (7") **I'M A MAN. / NIGHTHAWKS** ☐ ☐

Apr 81. (lp) **NIGHTHAWKS (Soundtrack)** ☐ ☐
– Nighthawks – main title theme / Mean stalkin' / The bust / Nighthawking / The chase / I'm a man / The chopper / tramway / I'm comin' in / Face to face / The flight of the hawk.

Red Bus not issued

Dec 83. (7") **UP THE ELEPHANT AND ROUND THE CASTLE. / ('A'version)** ☐ -

Chord not issued

Mar 85. (lp) **ARMAGEDDON** ☐ -
– Theme from Floi / Joe and Micheko / Children of the light / Funny's skate state / Zamedy stomp / Challenge of the psonic fighters. *(re-iss.Feb87)*

—— **MOTT** – guitar / **DICK MORRISSEY + ANDREW BRENNAN + PETE KING** – saxophone

Apr 85. (cd) **HONKY** ☐ -
– Hello sailor / Bach before the mast / Salt cay / Green ice / Intro-juicing / Big horn breakdown / Yancey special / Rum-a-thing / Jesus loves me.
(lp-iss.Mar86)

—— Some with **DOREEN CHANTER** – vocals / **MIKE SEBBAGE** – vocals / **TOM NICOL + DEREK WILSON** – drums / **MICHAEL SHEPPARD** – bass, guitar, co-producer

May 86. (lp)(cd) **MURDEROCK** ☐ -
– Murderock / Tonight is your night / Streets to blame / Not so innocent / Prelude to Candice / Don't go in the shower / Coffee time / Candice / New York dash / Tonight is not your night / The spill one.

—— next with The National Philharmonic Orchestra, plus **BRAD DELP, L.HELM.**

Oct 86. (lp)(cd) **BEST REVENGE (Film Soundtrack) (by "KEITH EMERSON & JOHN COLEMAN")** ☐ ☐
– Dream runner / The runner / Wha 'dya mean / Straight between the eyes / Orchestral suite to "Best Revenge" / Playing for keeps (main title theme).

Priority not issued

Nov 88. (lp)(c)(cd) **EMERSON – THE CHRISTMAS ALBUM** ☐ ☐
(cd-iss.Jun93 on 'A.M.P.') (re-iss.cd Dec95 on 'Amp')

Emerson not issued

Dec 88. (7") **WE THREE KINGS OF ORIENT ARE. / CAPTAIN STARSHIP HOPKINS** ☐ -

– (KEITH EMERSON) compilations etc. –

Feb 87. Chord; (d-lp) **ARMAGEDDON. / CHINA FREE FALL (with "DEREK AUSTIN")** [ ] [ ]
Oct 88. Chord; (lp)(cd) **THE KEITH EMERSON COLLECTION** [ ] [ ]
Dec 95. Amp; (cd-s) **TROIKA (THE CHRISTMAS SINGLE). /** [ ] [-]

GREG LAKE BAND

GREG LAKE – vocals, guitar, bass with **TOMMY EYRE** – keyboards / **GARY MOORE** – guitar (ex-solo artist ex-THIN LIZZY ex-COLOSSEUM) / **TRISTRAM MARGETTS** – bass / **TED McKENNA** – drums (ex-SENSATIONAL ALEX HARVEY BAND)

Chrysalis Chrysalis

Sep 81. (7") **LOVE YOU TOO MUCH. / SOMEONE** [ ] [ ]
Oct 81. (lp)(c) **GREG LAKE** [62] [62]
– Nuclear attack / Love you too much / It hurts / One before you go / Loving goodbye / Retribution drive / Black and blue / Let me love you once / The lies / For those who dare.
Dec 81. (7") **LET ME LOVE YOU ONCE. /** [-] [48]
Feb 82. (7") **IT HURTS. / RETRIBUTION DRIVE** [ ] [ ]

E.M.I. not issued

Jul 83. (lp)(c) **MANOEUVRES** [ ] [ ]
– Manoeuvres / Too young to love / Paralysed / A woman like you / I don't want to lose your love tonight / It's you, you've got to believe / Famous last words / Slave to love / Haunted / I don't know why I still love you.

— LAKE joined ASIA with PALMER

P.M.

CARL PALMER with **TODD COCHRAN** – keyboards / **BARRY FINNERTY** – guitar, vocals / **JOHN NITZINGER** – guitar, vocals / **ERIK SCOTT** – bass, vocals

Ariol Ariola

May 80. (lp)(c) **1 P.M.** [ ] [ ]
– Dynamite / You've got me rockin' / Green velvet splendour / Dreamers / Go on carry on / D'ya go all the way / Go for it / Madeleine / You're too much / Children of the air age.
Apr 80. (7") **YOU GOT ME ROCKIN'. / GO FOR IT** [ ] [ ]
Jul 80. (7") **DYNAMITE. / D'YA GO ALL THE WAY** [ ] [ ]

— (Jan81) PALMER joined ASIA.

EMERSON, LAKE & POWELL

are the new set up **COZY POWELL** – drums, (ex-solo artist, ex-RAINBOW, etc.)

Polydor Polydor

Jul 86. (lp)(c)(cd) **EMERSON, LAKE & POWELL** [35] [23] Jun 86
– Mars to the bringer of war / Score / Learning to fly / Touch and go / Miracle / Love blind / Step aside / Lay down your guns.
Jul 86. (7") **TOUCH AND GO. / LEARNING TO FLY** [ ] [60] Jun 86
(12"+=) – The locomotion.
1986. (7") **LAY DOWN YOUR GUNS. / ?** [-] [ ]

— (1987 originals reformed but disbanded Oct87)

3

was unit formed by **EMERSON, PALMER** and American **ROBERT BERRY** – vocals (ex-HUSH)

Geffen Geffen

Feb 88. (lp)(c)(cd) **TO THE POWER OF THREE** [ ] [ ]
– Talkin' about / Lover to lover / Chains / Desde la vida / Eight miles high / Runaway / You do or you don't / On my way home.
Feb 88. (7") **TALKIN' ABOUT. / LA VISTA** [-] [ ]

EMERSON, LAKE & PALMER

re-formed 1992.

Victory Victory

Apr 92. (cd)(c)(lp) **BLACK MOON** [ ] [78]
– Black Moon / Paper blood / Affairs of the heart / Romeo and Juliet / Farewell to arms / Changing states / Burning bridges / Close to home / Better days / Footprints in the snow.
May 92. (7") **BLACK HOLE. / MILES IZ DEAD** [ ] [ ]
(12")(cd-s) – ('A'side) / ('A'version) / A blade of grass.

London London

Nov 92. (7")(c-s) **AFFAIRS OF THE HEART. / BETTER DAYS** [ ] [ ]
(cd-s+=) – A blade of grass / Black moon.
Feb 93. (cd)(c) **LIVE AT THE ROYAL ALBERT HALL (live)** [ ] [ ]
– 1st impression part 2 / Tarkus: Eruption – Stones of years – Iconoclast / Knife edge / Paper blood / Romeo & Juliet / Creole dance / Still . . . you turn me on / Lucky man / Black moon / The pirates / Finale / Fanfare for the common man / America / Blue rondo A la Turk
Sep 94. (cd)(c) **IN THE HOT SEAT** [ ] [ ]
– Hand of truth / Daddy / One by one / Heart on ice / Thin line / Man in the long black coat / Change / Give me a reason to stay / Gone too soon / Street war. *(cd+=)* – Pictures at an exhibition: a) Promenade- b) The gnome- c) Promenaded) The sage- e) The hut of Baba Yaga- f) The great gates of Kiev.

– compilations, others, etc. –

Oct 79. Atlantic; (lp)(c) **EMERSON, LAKE & PALMER IN CONCERT (live 1978)** [ ] [73]
– (introductory fanfare) / Peter Gunn / Tiger in a spotlight / C'est la vie / The enemy god dances with the black spirits / Knife edge / Piano concerto No.1 / Pictures at an exhibition.
Dec 79. Atlantic; (7") **PETER GUNN (live). / KNIFE EDGE (live)** [ ] [ ]
Nov 80. Atlantic; (lp)(c) **THE BEST OF EMERSON, LAKE & PALMER** [ ] [ ]
– Hoedown / Lucky man / Karn evil 9 / Trilogy / Fanfare for the common man / Still . . .you turn me on / Tiger in a spotlight / Jerusalem / Peter Gunn. *(cd-iss.1983)*
Jul 92. Atlantic; (cd)(c)(lp) **THE ATLANTIC YEARS** [ ] [ ]
Dec 93. Victory; (4xcd-box) **THE RETURN OF THE MANTICORE** [ ] [ ]
Dec 93. Victory; (d-cd) **WORKS LIVE (live)** [ ] [ ]

EMF

Formed: Forest of Dean, Gloucestershire, England . . . early 1990 by the older Oxford graduate IAN DENCH (23) and 4 other teenagers (19). After 4th gig, they were found by ABBO (ex-UK DECAY) and his girlfriend LINDA who got them signed to 'E.M.I.' sub. 'Parlophone' Mar90. Debut single, UNBELIEVABLE broke into UK Top 3, and in '91 they set about taking both sides of the Atlantic by storm. • **Style:** Similar to JESUS JONES or a high speed DEPECHE MODE. • **Songwriters:** Group compositions except LOW SPARK OF THE HIGH HEELED BOYS (Traffic) / SHADDAP YOU, FACE (Joe Dolce) / I'M A BELIEVER (Monkees). • **Trivia:** EMF stands for ECSTASY MOTHER FUCKERS.

Recommended: SCHUBERT DIP (*5) / STIGMA (*7)

JAMES ATKIN – vocals / **IAN DENCH** – guitar, keyboards (ex-APPLE MOSAIC) / **DERRY BROWNSON** – samples, percussion (ex-LAC's) / **ZAC FOLEY** – bass (ex-IUC's) / **MARK DE CLOEDT** – drums (ex-ZU) / plus **MILF** – DJ scratcher

Parlophone E.M.I.

Oct 90. (7")(c-s) **UNBELIEVABLE. / EMF (live)** [3] [1] Feb91
(12"+=)(cd-s+=) – ('A' Sin City sex mix).
Jan 91. (7")(c-s) **I BELIEVE. / WHEN YOU'RE MINE** [6] [ ]
(12"+=)(cd-s+=) Unbelievable (funk mix).
Apr 91. (7")(c-s) **CHILDREN. / STRANGE BREW (live remix)** [19] [ ]
(12"+=) – Children (mix).
(cd-s++=) – Children – Battle for the minds of North Amerika.
(7"ep+=) – (live versions)
May 91. (cd)(c)(lp) **SCHUBERT DIP** [3] [12]
– Children / Long summer days / When you're mine / Travelling not running / I believe / Unbelievable / Girl of an age / Admit it / Lies / Long time. *(re-iss.cd+c Mar94)*
Aug 91. (7")(c-s) **LIES. / HEAD THE BALL** [28] [21]
(12"+=)(cd-s+=) – ('A'mix).
Apr 92. (7"ep) **UNEXPLAINED** [18] [ ]
– Getting through / Far from me / The same.
(12"ep+=)(cd-ep+=) – Search and destroy.
Sep 92. (7")(c-s) **THEY'RE HERE. / PHANTASMAGORIC** [29] [ ]
(12"+=) – ('A'remix).
(cd-s+=) – Low spark of the high heeled boys.
Sep 92. (cd)(c)(lp) **STIGMA** [19] [ ]
– They're here / Arizona / It's you that leaves me dry / Never know / Blue highs / Inside / Getting through / She bleeds / Dog / The light that burns twice as bright . . .
Nov 92. (cd-ep) **IT'S YOU (3 Butch Vig mixes) / DOF (Foetus mix)** [23] [ ]
(cd-ep) – It's you (Orbital mix) / The light that burns twice as bright . . . (mix) / They're here (mix).
Feb 95. (c-s) **PERFECT DAY / ANGEL** [27] [ ]
(cd-s+=) – I won't give into you / Kill for you (lo-fi mix).
(12"+=) – ('A'-Temple of boom remix) / ('A'-Chris & James epic).
(cd-s) – ('A'side) / ('A'-Chris & James mix) / ('A'-Black One mix) / ('A'-Toytown mix).
Mar 95. (cd)(c) **CHA CHA CHA** [30] [ ]
– Perfect day / La plage / The day I was born / Secrets / Shining / Bring me down / Skin / Slouch / Bleeding you dry / Patterns / When will you come / West of the Cox / Ballad o' the bishop / Glass smash Jack.
Apr 95. (c-s) **BLEEDING YOU DRY / TOO MUCH / EASY / PERFECT DAY (acoustic)** [ ] [ ]
(cd-s) – (first 3 tracks) / Shining (acoustic).
(cd-s) – ('A'side) / I pushed the boat out so far it sank / Patterns (acoustic).
Jun 95. (7")(c-s) **I'M A BELIEVER. ("EMF with REEVES & MORTIMER") / AT LEAST WE'VE GOT OUR GUITARS** [3] [-]
(cd-s) – ('A'side) / At this stage I couldn't say / ('A'-Unbelievable mix) / La plage (mix).
Oct 95. (c-s) **AFRO KING / UNBELIEVABLE** [51] [ ]
(cd-s+=) – Children / I believe.
(cd-s) – ('A'side) / Too much / Easy / Bring me down.

ENIGMA

Formed: German-based duo of MICHAEL CRETU and wife SANDRA, who quickly found themselves with unusual worldwide hit SADENESS' early 1991. • **Style:** Gregorian chant musak, sampled from Munich's Kapelle Antiqua Choir,-over a hip-hop dance beat. • **Songwriters:** MICHAEL CRETU, who also produces-album. Sampled: SONGS FROM THE VICTORIOUS CITY (Anne Dudley & Jaz Coleman) + THE CALLING (Mind Over Rhythm).

Recommended: MCMXC a.D. (*6) / THE CROSS OF CHANGES (*5).

CURLY M.C. (b.MICHAEL CRETU, 18 May'57, Bucharest, Romania) – electronics / **F.GREGORIAN** (SANDRA, b.France) – vocals / **DAVID-FAIRSTEIN** – etc.

Virgin Int Charisma

Nov 90. (7")(c-s) **SADENESS (part 1). / ('A'-Mediterranean mix)** [1] [5]
(12"+=)(cd-s+=) – ('A'extended) / ('A'violent US mix).
Dec 90. (cd)(c)(lp) **MCMXC a.D.** [1] [6]
– The voice of Enigma / Principles of lust (a) Sadeness (b) Find love (c) Sadeness-(reprise) / Callas went away / Mea culpa / The voice & the snake / Knocking on-forbidden doors / Back to the rivers of belief (a) Way to eternity (b) Hallelujah-(c) The rivers of belief. *(re-iss.Nov91)*

Mar 91. (7")(c-s) **MEA CULPA (part II). / ('A'-Catholic mix)** [55] [ ]
(12"+=)(cd-s+=) – ('A' fading shades mix).
Sep 91. (7")(c-s) **PRINCIPLES OF LUST. / SADENESS (pt.2 radio mix)** [59] [ ]
(12"+=) – ('A'extended) / ('A'-Owen mix).
(cd-s+=) – ('A'jazz mix) / ('A'-Owen mix).
Jan 92. (7")(c-s) **THE RIVERS OF BELIEF. / KNOCKING ON FORBIDDEN-DOORS** [68] [ ]
(12"cd-s) – ('A'-mixes).
Jan 94. (7")(c-s) **RETURN TO INNOCENCE. / ('A'mix)** [3] [4]
(12"+=) – ('A'extended mix).
(cd-s++=) – ('A'mix).
Feb 94. (cd)(c)(lp) **THE CROSS OF CHANGES** [1] [9]
– Second chapter / The eyes of truth / Return to innocence / Love you . . .I'll kill you / Silent warrior / The dream of the dolphin / Age of loneliness (Carly's song) / Out from the deep / The cross of changes. *(gold-cd-iss.Nov94)*
May 94. (7")(c-s) **THE EYES OF TRUTH. / ('A'mix)** [21] [ ]
(cd-s+=) – (2 other 'A'mixes).
(cd-s) – ('A'side) / Sadeness (part I) / Mea culpa (part II) / Principles of lust.
Aug 94. (12") **AGE OF LONELINESS. / ('A'-Jam & Spoon mix)** [21] [ ]
(cd-s+=) – Return to innocence (mix) / Sadeness part 1 (mix) / Principles of lust (everlasting lust).

Brian ENO

Born: BRIAN PETER GEORGE ST.JOHN LE BAPTISTE DE LA SALLE ENO, 15 May'48, Suffolk, England. After leaving art school, where he fronted heavy group MAXWELL DEMON, he joined ROXY MUSIC in 1971. After contributing greatly to their image and sound on albums 'ROXY MUSIC' & 'FOR YOUR PLEASURE', he left them, due to dispute over new pop-rock direction. His first post-ROXY venture was '(NO PUSSYFOOTING)' in 1973 with ROBERT FRIPP (of KING CRIMSON). This was nothing more than extreme experimentation of synth-electronics and treated guitar. However it did provide art lovers, with a photo-shot of ENO & FRIPP in a multi-mirrored room. His first solo work in early 1974 'HERE COME THE WARM JETS', disappointed the critics, who gave it the thumbs down, bar one gem 'BABY'S ON FIRE'. He released 2 more greatly improved efforts for 'Island', before he formed own label in '75 appropriately titled 'Obscure'. Preceeding this in a fit of depression, he joined The WINKIES for a short tour Feb-Mar74, but departed after being diagnosed with a collapsed lung. Recovered to find himself, on an 'Island records' concert bill on '1st JUNE, 1974', alongside stablemates KEVIN AYERS, NICO and JOHN CALE. The following year, he was hit by a car, which caused slight, but not lasting brain damage. In the late 70's & 80's, he concentrated more on specialist albums, collaborations, soundtracks and production work (see below). • **Style:** The balding genius once described himself as a non-musician, who just turned dials and switches. Technically brilliant ambient experimentalist, whose new obscure musak is possibly a direct link to what listeners will appreciate in the 21st century. (Martin the prophet!? – ed). • **Songwriters:** All composed by ENO. • **Trivia:** His 1977 song 'KING'S LEAD HAT' was in fact an anagram of TALKING HEADS. In the mid-80's, his work was featured on an BBC2 'Arena Special', and included paintings by RUSSELL MILLS, and 'ANOTHER GREEN WORLD' title track, which had become the programme's theme tune. ENO has also done session and production work for JOHN CALE (1974-75), ROBERT WYATT (1975), ROBERT CALVERT (1975), DAVID BOWIE (1977) / DEVO (1978) / TALKING HEADS (1978-80) / U2 (1985-91 with Daniel Lanois) / etc.

Recommended: DESERT ISLAND SELECTION (*7) / HERE COME THE WARM JETS (*6) / ANOTHER GREEN WORLD (*9) / TAKING TIGER MOUNTAIN BY STRATEGY (*7) / NERVE NET (*6) / MY LIFE IN THE BUSH OF GHOSTS (*8) with DAVID BYRNE / APOLLO (*8) / WRONG WAY UP (*7) with JOHN CALE.

FRIPP & ENO

ROBERT FRIPP – guitar of KING CRIMSON / **BRIAN ENO** – synthesizers, instruments

Island-Help / Antilles

Nov 73. (lp) **(NO PUSSYFOOTING)** [ ] [ ]
– The heavenly music corporation / Swastika girls. *(re-iss.Oct77 on 'Polydor', re-issJan87 on 'EG')*

ENO

now solo with guest session people, including ROXY MUSIC musicians and ROBERT FRIPP, CHRIS SPEDDING, PAUL RUDOLPH and others.

Island / Island

Jan 74. (lp)(c) **HERE COME THE WARM JETS** [26] [ ]
– Needles in the camel's eye / The paw paw Negro blowtorch / Baby's on fire / Cindy tells me / Driving me backwards / On some faraway beach / Black rank / Dead finks don't talk / Some of them are old / Here come the warm jets. *(re-iss.Mar77 on 'Polydor', re-iss.'87 on 'EG')*
Mar 74. (7")**SEVEN DEADLY FINNS. / LATER ON** [ ] [ ]
—— guests incl. PORTSMOUTH SINFONIA ORCHESTRA, PHIL COLLINS – drums / etc.
Nov 74. (lp)(c) **TAKING TIGER MOUNTAIN (BY STRATEGY)** [ ] [ ]
– Burning airlines give you so much more / Back in Judy's jungle / The fat lady of Limbourg / Mother whale eyeless / The great pretender / Third uncle / Put a straw under baby / The truth wheel / China my China / Taking tiger mountain. *(re-iss.Mar77 on 'Polydor') (re-issJan87 on 'EG')*
Aug 75. (7") **THE LION SLEEPS TONIGHT. /** [-] [ ]
—— now with **FRIPP** (3) / **COLLINS** (3) / **JOHN CALE** – viola (2) / **PAUL RUDOPLH** (3) / **PERCY JONES** – bass (3) / **ROD MELVIN** – piano (3) / **BRIAN TURRINGTON** – bass, piano (1)
Sep 75. (lp)(c) **ANOTHER GREEN WORLD** [ ] [ ]
– Sky saw / Over Fire Island / St. Elmo's fire / In dark trees / The big ship / I'll come running / Another green world / Sombre reptiles / Little fishes / Golden hours / Becalmed / Zawinul – Lava / Everything merges with the night. *(re-iss.Mar77 on 'Polydor', re-iss.+cd Jan87 on 'EG')*

Obscure / Antilles

Nov 75. (lp)(c) **DISCREET MUSIC** [ ] [ ]
– Discreet music 1 & 2 / Three Variations on canon in D major; a) Fullness of wind – b) French catalogues – c) Brutal ardour.

FRIPP & ENO

collaborate again.

Help-Island / not issued

Dec 75. (lp)(c) **EVENING STAR** [ ] [-]
– Wind on water / Evening star / Evensong / Wind on wind / An index of metals. *(re-iss.Oct77 on 'Polydor') (re-iss.+cd.Jan87 on 'EG')*
—— For the next couple of years he worked with 801 (PHIL MANZANERA's band). He also produced his own 'Obscure' label, discovering people including PENGUIN CAFE ORCHESTRA, MICHAEL NYMAN, MAX EASTLEY & DAVID TOOP, HAROLD BUDD plus JAN STEELE / JOHN CAGE. More commercially he also played on and produced 1977 albums by DAVID BOWIE, TALKING HEADS, ULTRAVOX.

BRIAN ENO

solo once more

Polydor / Island

Dec 77. (lp)(c) **BEFORE AND AFTER SCIENCE** [ ] [ ]
– No one receiving / Backwater / Kurt's rejoiner / Energy fools the magician / King's lead hat / Here he comes / Julie with . . . / By this river / Through hollow lands / Spider and I.
Jan 78. (7") **KING'S LEAD HAT. / R.A.F. ('B'side credited to "ENO & SNATCH")** [ ] [ ]
Sep 78. (lp)(c) **MUSIC FOR FILMS** [55] [ ]
– M386 / Aragon / From the same hill / Inland sea / Two rapid formations / Slow water / Sparrowfall 1 / Sparrowfall 2 / Sparrowfall 3 / Quartz / Events in dense fog / There is nobody / A measured room / Patrolling wire borders / Task force / Alternative 3 / Strange light / Final sunset. *(re-iss.+cd Jan87 on 'EG')*

Ambient-EG / P.V.C.

Mar 79. (lp)(c) **AMBIENT 1: MUSIC FOR AIRPORTS** [ ] [ ]
– Side 1 / Side 2. *(re-iss.+cd Jan87 on 'EG')*

HAROLD BUDD & BRIAN ENO

(BUDD – piano)

Ambient / E.G.

Apr 80. (lp)(c) **AMBIENT 2: THE PLATEAUX OF MIRROR** [ ] [ ]
– First light / Steal away / The plateau of mirror / Above Chiangmai / An arc of doves / Not yet remembered / The chill air / Among fields of crystal / Wind in lonely fences / Failing light. *(re-issJan87 on 'EG')*

JON HASSELL & BRIAN ENO

(HASSELL – trumpet)

Editions / E.G.

Apr 80. (lp) **FOURTH WORLD VOL.1: POSSIBLE MUSICS** [ ] [ ]
– Chemistry / Delta rain dream / Griot (over contageous magic) / Ba-Benzele / Rising thermal 14 degrees 16n, 32 degrees 28e / Charm (over Borundi cloud). *(re-issJan87 on 'EG')*

BRIAN ENO & DAVID BYRNE

BYRNE of TALKING HEADS

EG / Sire

Feb 81. (lp)(c) **MY LIFE IN THE BUSH OF GHOSTS** [29] [44]
– America is waiting / Mea culpa / Regiment / Help me somebody / The Jezebel spirit / Qu'ran / Moonlight in glory / The carrier / A secret life / Come with us / Mountain of needles. *(re-issJan87 on 'EG')*
May 81. (7") **THE JEZEBEL SPIRIT. / REGIMENT** [ ] [ ]
(12"+=) – Very very hungry (Qu'ran).

BRIAN ENO

Editions-EG / Sire

Mar 82. (lp)(c) **AMBIENT (4): ON LAND** [93] [ ]
– Lizard point / The lost day / Tal coat / Shadow / Lantern marsh / Unfamiliar wind / A clearing / Dunwich Beach, Autumn 1960. *(re-issJan87 on 'EG')*

BRIAN ENO with DANIEL LANOIS & ROGER ENO

E.G. / Sire

Jul 83. (lp)(c) **APOLLO: ATMOSPHERES & SOUNDTRACKS** [ ] [ ]
– Under stars / The secret place / Matta / Signals / An ending (ascent) / Under stars II / Drift / Silver morning / Deep blue day / Weightless / Always returning / Stars. *(re-iss.+cd Jan87 on 'EG')*

HAROLD BUDD & BRIAN ENO with DANIEL LANOIS

Editions-EG / Sire

Aug 84. (lp)(c) **THE PEARL**
– Late October / A stream with bright fish / The silver ball / Against the sky / Lost in the humming air / Dark-eyed sister / Their memories / The pearl / Foreshadowed / An echo of night / Still return. *(re-iss.+cdJan87)*

ENO

E.G. Sire

Oct 85. (cd) **THURSDAY AFTERNOON**
– Thursday afternoon. *(1 track only)*

MICHAEL BROOK with BRIAN ENO & DANIELS LANOIS

Editions-EG Sire

Aug 85. (lp)(c) **HYBRID**
– Hybrid / Distant village / Mimosa / Pond life / Ocean motion / Midday / Earth floor / Vacant.

ROGER ENO with BRIAN ENO

did guest appearance

Editions-EG Sire

Aug 85. (lp)(c) **VOICES**
– A place in the wilderness / The day after / At the water's edge / Grey promenade / A paler sky / Through the blue / Evening tango / Recalling winter / Voices / The old dance / Reflections on I.K.B. *(re-issJan87)*

ENO / CALE

(collaboration **JOHN CALE** – vocals, multi-)with **ROBERT AHWAI** – rhythm guitar / **DARYL JOHNSON** – bass / **NEIL CATCHPOLE** – violin / **RONALD JONES** – drums, tabla / **DAVE YOUNG** – guitars, bass

Land Sire

Oct 90. (cd)(c)(lp) **WRONG WAY UP**
– Lay my love / One word / In the backroom / Empty frame / Cordoba / Spinning away / Footsteps / Been there done that / Crime in the desert / The river.

Nov 90. (12"ep)(cd-ep) **ONE WORLD. / GRANDFATHER'S HOUSE / PALAQUIN** | -

BRIAN ENO

Opal-WEA Opal-WEA

Jul 92. (7") **FRACTIAL ZOOM. / ('A'-Moby mix)**
(12"+=) – (4 mixes).
(cd-s++=) – (another mix) / The roil, the choke.

Sep 92. (cd)(c)(lp) **NERVE NET** 70
– Fractial zoom / Wire shock / What actually happened? / Pierre in mist / My squelchy life / Decentre / Juju space jazz / The roil, the choke / Ali click / Distributing being / Web.

Oct 92. (7") **ALI CLICK (Beirut mix). / ('A'rural mix)**
(12"+=) – ('A'-Markus Draws + Grid mix).
(cd-s) – ('A'side) / (++=) – ('A'trance long darkly mad mix) / ('A'trance instrumental).

Nov 92. (cd)(c) **THE SHUTOV ASSEMBLY**
– (music inspired by Moscow painter Sergei Shutov)

Around the same time as above, he lectured at Sadler's Wells, and is the brunt of NME jokes as Professor Eno.

All Saints not iss?

Jun 93. (cd) **:NEROLI:** | -
– :Neroli:.

— Above long piece of music, was used in hospitals for childbirth!

— Sep 94; he was credited on JAMES' ltd.album 'WAH WAH'.

BRIAN ENO / JAH WOBBLE

All Saints not issued

Oct 95. (cd)(c)(lp) **SPINNER** 71 | -
– Where we lived / Like organza / Steam / Garden recalled / Marine radio / Unusual balance / Space diary 1 / Spinner / Transmitter and trumpet / Left where it fell.

– (ENO) compilations, others, etc. –

1982. E.G.; (d-c) **NO PUSSYFOOTIN' + EVENING STAR ("FRIPP & ENO")** | -

Nov 83. E.G.; (10xlp-box) **WORKING BACKWARDS 1983-1973**
– (first 9 lp's, plus MUSIC FOR FILMS VOL.2 / + RARITIES m-lp:- Seven deadly finns / The lion sleeps tonight / Strong flashes of light / More volts / Mist rhythm)

Mar 86. E.G.; (lp)(c) **MORE BLANK THAN FRANK**

Jan 87. E.G.; (cd) **DESERT ISLAND SELECTION**
– Here he comes / Everything merges with the night / I'll come running (edit) / On some faraway beach (edit) / Spirits drifting / Back in Judy's jungle / St Elmo's fire / No one receiving / Julie with . . . / Taking tiger mountain (edit).

Jan 87. E.G.; (lp)(c) **MUSIC FOR FILMS 2**
– The dove / Roman twilight / Matta / Dawn, marshland / Climate study / The secret place / An ending (ascent) / Always returning 1 / Signals / Under stars / Drift / Study / Approaching Taidu / Always returning 2.

Mar 89. E.G.; (cd-s) **ANOTHER GREEN WORLD / DOVER BEACH / DEEP BLUE DAY / 2-1** | -

Dec 89. E.G.; (t-lp)(t-c)(t-cd) **ISLAND VARIOUS ARTISTS** | -
– (with other artists / ANOTHER GREEN WORLD / BEFORE AND AFTER SCIENCE / APOLLO)

Nov 93. Virgin; (3xcd-box) **BRIAN ENO (collaborations)**

Nov 93. Virgin; (3xcd-box) **BRIAN ENO 2 (collaborations)**

Feb 94. Venture; (cd)(c) **THE ESSENTIAL FRIPP AND ENO**

Oct 94. Virgin; (3xcd-box) **THE COMPACT COLLECTION**

ENO contributed 2 tracks on live lp 'JUNE 1st, 1974' with KEVIN AYERS, NICO and JOHN CALE. He also with brother ROGER and DANIEL LANOIS provided one track to DUNE film (1984).

CLUSTER & ENO

CLUSTER (see below members), had released several German albums in 70's on 'Sky'.

May 78. (lp) **CLUSTER AND ENO** | -

Mar 79. (lp) **AFTER THE HEAT** (ENO, MOEBIUS & ROEDELIUS) | -

Apr 84. (lp)(cd) **BEGEGNUNGEN** (ENO, MOEBIUS, ROEDILIUS & PLANK) | -

1985. (lp)(cd) **BEGEGNUNGEN II** (ENO, MOEBIUS, ROEDILIUS & PLANK) | -

Jan 86. (lp) **OLD LAND** (CLUSTER AND ENO) | -

JOHN ENTWISTLE (see under ⇒ WHO)

ENYA

Born: EITHNE NI BHRAONAIN, 17 May '61, Gweadore, County Donegal, Ireland. Classically a trained pianist, she went solo, after 2 appearances in the early 80's on her family's (CLANNAD) album 'FUAIM'. Her first solo project in 1985, was an 'Island' records film soundtrack 'THE FROG PRINCE'. The following year, she was commissioned by the BBC, to write the TV score to documentary 'THE CELTS'. It's minor success, and the rise of CLANNAD, enabled 'WEA' records in 1988 to give her record deal. Her first single for the label 'ORINOCO FLOW', became surprise UK No.1 later in October. • **Style:** Beautiful vocalist with atmospheric and dreamy landscapes that cannot be pigeonholed into pop or rock. • **Songwriters:** ENYA pens songs and collaborates with her backing musicians ROMA and NICKY RYAN (her producer from 1988). • **Trivia:** Her father LED BRENNAN was a member of showband SLIEVE FOY BAND.

Recommended: WATERMARK (*7) / SHEPHERD MOONS (*6).

ENYA – vocals, keyboards, percussion (ex-CLANNAD)

Island not issued

Oct 85. (lp)(c) **THE FROG PRINCE** | -

B.B.C. not issued

Feb 87. (lp)(c) **THE CELTS** (recorded 1980) 69 | -
– The Celts / Aldebaran / I want tomorrow / March of the Celts / Deireadh on tuath / The Sun in the stream / To go beyond (1) / Epona / Fairytale / Epona Triad: St. Patrick Cu Chulainn-oisin / Boadicea / Bard dance / Dan y dur / To go beyond (II). *(re-iss.Dec88 as 'ENYA') ('THE CELTS' re-iss.+cd.Nov92 on 'WEA', hit UK No.10, extra track 'Portrait (out of the blue)').*

Feb 87. (7") **I WANT TOMORROW. / THE CELTS THEME**
(12"+=)(cd-s+=) – To Go Beyond I + II. *(re-issNov88)*

W.E.A. Geffen

Sep 88. (lp)(c)(cd) **WATERMARK** 5 | 25 Mar 89
– Watermark / Cursum perficio / On your shore / Storms in Africa / Exile / Miss Clare remembers / Orinoco flow / Evening falls / River / The longships / Na laetha geal m'oige / Storms in Africa (part II). *(re-iss.Oct91 hit No.44, Jul92-No.43)*

Oct 88. (7") **ORINOCO FLOW. / OUT OF THE BLUE** 1 | 24 Feb 89
(12"+=) – Smaotin.

Dec 88. (7") **EVENING FALLS. / OICHE CHIUN (SILENT NIGHT)** 20
(12"+=)(cd-s+=) – Morning glory.

Feb 89. (7") **STORMS IN AFRICA (pt.II)./STORMS IN AFRICA** 41
(12"+=)(3"cd-s+=) – The Celts / Aldebaran. *(re-dist.May89)*

May 91. (7")(c-s) **EXILE. / ON YOUR SHORE**
(12"+=)(cd-s+=) – Watermark / River.

W.E.A. Reprise

Oct 91. (7") **CARIBBEAN BLUE. / ORINOCO FLOW** 13 | 79 Feb92
(cd-s+=) – Angels.
(cd-s++=) – As baile / Oriel window.

— album guests **ROMA RYAN** – percussion / **STEVE SIDWELL** – cornet / **NICKY RYAN** and **ANDY DUNCAN** – perc. / **LIAM O'FLIONN** – vulcan pipes / **ROY JEWITT** – clarinet

Nov 91. (cd)(c)(lp) **SHEPHERD MOONS** 1 | 17
– Shepherd moons / Caribbean blue / How can I keep from singing? / Ebudae / Angeles / No holly for Miss Quinn / Book of days / Evacuee / Lothlorien / Marble halls / Afer Ventus / Smaonte . . .

Dec 91. (7") **HOW CAN I KEEP FROM SINGING?. / ORCHE CHIUN (SILENT NIGHT)** 13
(12"+=)(cd-s+=) – 'S Fagain mo baile.

Jul 92. (7") **BOOK OF DAYS. / AS BAILE** 10
(cd-s) – ('A'side) / Watermark / On your shoe / Exile.

Nov 92. (7")(c-s) **THE CELTS. / OFCHE CHIUN** 29
(cd-s+=) – S'fagain mobhaile.

Nov 95. (7")(c-s)(cd-s) **ANYWHERE IS. / BOADICEA** 7
(cd-s+=) – Oriel window.
(cd-s) – ('A'side) / Book of days / Caribbean blue / Orinoco flow.

Nov 95. (cd)(c) **THE MEMORY OF TREES** 5 | 21
– The memory of trees / Anywhere is / Pax deorum / Athair ar neamh / From where I am / China roses / Hope has a place / Tea-house moon / Once you had gold / La sonadora / On my way home.

EQUALS (see under ⇒ GRANT, Eddy)

ERASURE

Formed: London, England . . . 1985 by VINCE CLARKE and one-time choirboy ANDY BELL, who answered a Melody Maker "vocalist wanted" ad.

CLARKE's lucrative past had included spearheading other outfits; DEPECHE MODE ('81), YAZOO (82-83) and the one-off ASSEMBLY ('84) with FEARGAL SHARKEY and E.C.RADCLIFFE. In June 1985, he teamed up with PAUL QUINN (ex-Bourgie Bourgie) on another one-off 'ONE DAY'. All were released on Daniel Miler's indie label 'Mute', as were his new outfit. ERASURE's debut single in Sep85 'WHO NEEDS LOVE LIKE THAT', only finds a No.55 placing, and things looked bleak, when their 2 follow-ups only managed to scrape into the Top 100. One of them 'OH L'AMOUR', later became a Top 10 hit in late '87 for pop duo DOLLAR. ERASURE finally broke through from the indie scene in Oct86, when 'SOMETIMES' made UK No.2. From then on they were a safe bet to reach the UK Top 20 (a further consecutive 18 in fact), with each album from 'THE INNOCENTS' onwards peaking at No.1. • **Style:** Electronic pop-rock, with extrovert showman BELL, sounding not too disimiliar to VINCE's ex-YAZOO partner ALISON MOYET. • **Songwriters:** CLARKE writes all material except; RIVER DEEP MOUNTAIN HIGH (Phil Spector) / GIMME GIMME GIMME + ABBA-ESQUE EP (Abba) / TOO DARN HOT (Cole Porter). • **Trivia:** In 1991, BLUE SAVANNAH is named as Most Performed Song at the Ivor Novello awards.

Recommended: POP! THE FIRST 20 HITS (*9)

VINCE CLARKE (b. 3 Jul'60, Basildon, Essex) – keyboards / **ANDY BELL** (b.25 Apr'64, Peterborough) – vocals (ex-The VOID)

		Mute	Sire
Sep 85.	(7") **WHO NEEDS LOVE LIKE THAT. / PUSH ME SHOVE ME** (12") – ('A'&'B' mixes) ('A'instrumental) *(re-iss.cd-s Sep93).*	55	
Nov 85.	(7") **HEAVENLY ACTION. / DON'T SAY NO** (12"+=) – ('A'&'B' mixes) / My heart . . . so blue. (d12"+=) – Who needs love like that (Mex. mix) / Push me shove me. *(re-iss.cd-s Sep93)*		
Apr 86.	(7") **OH L'AMOUR. / MARCH ON DOWN THE LINE** (12"+=) – Gimme gimme gimme (a man after midnight). *(re-iss.cd-s Sep93)*		
Jun 86.	(lp)(c)(cd) **WONDERLAND** – Who needs love like that / Reunion / Cry so easy / Push me shove me / Heavenly action / Say what / Love is a loser / My heart . . . so blue / Oh l'amour / Pistol. (ltd-12"-w/lp) – OH L'AMOUR / MARCH ON DOWN THE LINE / GIMME GIMME GIMME. (cd+=) – (remixes); Say what / Senseless / March on down the line.	71	
Oct 86.	(7") **SOMETIMES. / SEXUALITY** (12"+=) – ('A'&'B' mixes) / Say what. (d7"+=) – Oh l'amour / March on down the line. (c-s+=) – Oh l'amour / Who needs love like that / Heavenly action. *(re-iss.cd-s Sep93)*	2	
Feb 87.	(7") **IT DOESN'T HAVE TO BE. / IN THE HALL OF THE MOUNTAIN KING** (12"+=//+12"+=) – Who needs love like that// / Heavenly action. (d7"+=) – Sometimes / Sexuality. (cd-s++=) – Oh l'amour / Gimme gimme gimme. *(re-iss.cd-s Sep93)*	12	
Apr 87.	(lp)(c)(cd) **THE CIRCUS** – It doesn't have to be / Hideaway / Don't dance / If I could / Saxuality / Victim of love / Leave me to bleed / Sometimes / The circus / Spiralling. (ltd-d-c) – Includes 'WONDERLAND'. (cd+=) – Sometimes (remix) / It doesn't (mix) / In the hall of the mounain king.	6	
May 87.	(7")(7"pic-d) **VICTIM OF LOVE (remix). / THE SOLDIER'S RETURN** (12"+=)(12"pic-d+=) – ('A' dub). (12"+=) – If I could help (Jap.mix). (cd-s+=) – ('A' dub) / Safety in numbers (live) / Don't dance (live) / Leave me to bleed (live).	7	
Sep 87.	(7") **THE CIRCUS (remix). / THE CIRCUS (version)** (live-12"+=) – Victim of love / If I could / Spiralling. (live-12"+=) – It doesn't have to be / Who needs love like that / Gimme gimme gimme. (live-12"+=) – Sometimes / Say what / Oh l'amour. *(re-iss.cd-s Sep93)*	6	
Dec 87.	(2x12"lp)(c)(cd) **THE TWO RING CIRCUS** *(re-iss. last lp)* (cd+=) – Victim of love / The Circus / Spiralling / Sometimes / Gimme gimme gimme / Oh l'amour / Who needs love like that.		
Feb 88.	(7") **SHIP OF FOOLS. / WHEN I NEEDED YOU** (12"+=)(3"cd-s+=) – River deep mountain high (mix).	6	
Apr 88.	(lp)(c)(cd) **THE INNOCENTS** – A little respect / Ship of fools / Phantom bride / Chains of love / Sixty-five thousand / Heart of stone / Yahoo! / Imagination / Witch in the ditch / Weight of the world. (cd+=) – River deep mountain high (mix) / When I needed you (mix).	1	49
May 88.	(7") **CHAINS OF LOVE. / I DON'T SUPPOSE** (12"+=)(cd-s+=) – The good the bad and the ugly (mix).	11	12 Jul 88
Sep 88.	(7") **A LITTLE RESPECT. / LIKE ZSA ZSA GABOR** (12"+=)(cd-s+=) – Love is cooler than death.	4	14 Dec 88
Dec 88.	(7"ep)(12"ep)(cd-ep) **CRACKERS INTERNATIONAL: EP** – Stop / Knocking on your door / She won't be home / The hardest part. (d3"cd-ep+=)(pic-cd-ep+=)(12"+=) – Stop / Knocking on your door / God rest ye merry gentlemen. (US= 12"m-lp +cd Jul89, hit No.97)	3	73
Sep 89.	(7")(c-s) **DRAMA. / SWEET SWEET BABY** (12"+=)(cd-s+=) – ('A'&'B'mixes) / Paradise (mix).	4	
Oct 89.	(lp)(c)(cd) **WILD!** – You surround me / Drama! / How many times? / Crown of thorns / Piano song (instrumental) / Blue savannah / Star / La Gloria / Brother and sister / 2,000 miles / Piano song.	1	57
Nov 89.	(7")(c-s) **YOU SURROUND ME. / 91 STEPS** (12"+=)(cd-s+=) – ('A' mix) / Supernature. (12"+=)(cd-s+=) – (different mixes of above 3)	15	
Feb 90.	(7")(c-s) **BLUE SAVANNAH. / NO G.D.M. (unfinished mix)** (12"+=)(cd-s+=) – Runaround on the underground. (extra 12") – ('A' der Deutche mix 1 & 2).	3	
Jun 90.	(7")(c-s) **STAR. / ('A'soul mix)** (12"+=)(cd-s+=) – ('A'dreamlike state 24 hour technicolour mix).	11	
Jun 91.	(7") **CHORUS. / ('A'mix)** (12"+=) – (2 'A'mixes) / Snappy. (cd-s+=) – Over the rainbow.	3	83
Sep 91.	(7")(c-s) **LOVE TO HATE YOU. / VITAMIN C** (12"+=) – La la la. (cd-s++=) – ('A'version).	4	
Oct 91.	(cd)(c)(lp) **CHORUS** – Chorus / Waiting for the day / Joan / Breath of life / Am I right? / Love to hate you / Turns the love to anger / Siren song / Perfect stranger / Home.	1	29
Nov 91.	(7")(12")(cd-ep) **AM I RIGHT?** – Am I right? / Carry on clangers / Let it flow / Waiting for sex.	15	
Jan 92.	(7"ep-ltd.15,000) **REMIX EP** – Am I right? (The Grid remix) / Love to hate you (Mark Saunders remix) / Chorus (Moby remix). (12"+=//+cd-s+=) – B3./ / Perfect stranger.	22	
Mar 92.	(7")(c-s) **BREATH OF LIFE. / ('A'version)** (12"+=)(cd-s+=) – (3 other 'A'versions).	8	
Jun 92.	(7"ep)(12"ep)(c-ep)(cd-ep) **ABBA-ESQUE** – Lay your love on me / S.O.S. / Take a chance on me / Voulez vous. (US-m-lp +cd on 'Mute')	1	85
Oct 92.	(12")(c-s)(cd-s) **WHO NEEDS LOVE LIKE THAT (Hanbury mix). / SHIP OF FOLLS (Orb mix) / SOMETIMES (remix)** (cd-s)('A' side) Don't say no / Soldier's return / The circus (remix).	10	
Nov 92.	(cd)(c)(d-lp) **POP! THE FIRST 20 HITS** (compilation) – Who needs love like that / Heavenly action / Oh l'amour / Sometimes / It dooesn't have to be like that / Victim of love / The circus / Ship of fools / Chains of love / A little respect / Stop! / Drama! / You surround me / Blue Savannah / Star / Chorus / Love to hate you / Am I right? / Breathe of life / Take a chance on me. (c+=) – Who needs love like that (Hamburg mix).	1	
Apr 94.	(7")(c-s)(cd-s) **ALWAYS. / ('A'mix)** (12"+=)(cd-s+=) – 2 more 'A'mixes.	4	20
May 94.	(cd)(c)(lp) **I SAY I SAY I SAY** – Take me back / I love Saturday / Man in the Moon / So the story goes / Run to the Sun / Always / All through the years / Blues away / Miracle / Because you're so sweet.	1	18
Jul 94.	(7"yellow)(c-s) **RUN TO THE SUN. / TENDEREST MOMENT** (cd-s+=) – ('A'-Beatmasters mix). (cd-s++=) – ('A'-Andy Bell remix).	6	
Nov 94.	(c-s) **I LOVE SATURDAY / DODO / BECAUSE YOU'RE SO SWEET** (cd-s) – ('A'side) / Ghost / Truly, madly, deeply / Tragic (vocal version). (cd-s) – ('A'side) / ('A'radio mix) / ('A'-JX mix) / ('A'-Beatmasters dub mix) / Dodo. (cd-s) – ('A'-Beatmasters club mix) / ('A'-Andy Bell mixes) / Always (x cut dub).	21	
Sep 95.	(7")(c-s) **STAY WITH ME. / TRUE LOVE WARS** (cd-s+=) – ('A'-Flow mix) / ('A'guitar mix) / ('A'-Castaway mix).	15	
Oct 95.	(cd)(c)(d-lp)(m-d) **ERASURE** – Guess I'm into feeling / Rescue me / Sono luminous / Fingers & thumbs (cold summer's day) / Rock me gently / Grace / Stay with me / Love the way you do so / Angel / I love you / A long goodbye.	14	82
Nov 95.	(c-s)(cd-s) **FINGERS & THUMBS (COLD SUMMER'S DAY) / HI NRG** (cd-s+=) – ('A'-Tin Tin Out mix) / ('A'-Francois Kevorkian mix) / ('A'-Wire mix).	20	

Roky ERICKSON (see under ⇒ 13th FLOOR ELEVATORS)

Melissa ETHERIDGE

Born: 1961, Leavenworth, Kansas, USA. Studied guitar at Boston's Berklee College Of Music, before being found playing live at Long Beach, California (where she now lives) by CHRIS BLACKWELL of 'Island' records. Her eponymous debut album released in 1988, made headway with growing audience. It finally hit US Top 30 a year later and was nominated for a Grammy. • **Style:** Soft-rock blonde with vox similiar to BONNIE TYLER, although looking a touch LITA FORD of late. • **Songwriters:** Self penned except a few each album with co-producer and bass player KEVIN McCORMICK. • **Trivia:** After writing for 'Weeds' film in 1988, she provided backing vox for DON HENLEY's 'New York Minute'. BONO of U2 guested on her second album 'BRAVE AND CRAZY'.

Recommended: NEVER ENOUGH (*6)

MELISSA ETHERIDGE – vocals, guitar, piano / **KEVIN McCORMICK** – bass / **CRAIG KRAMPF** – drums, percussion / **WADDY WACHTEL + JOHNNY LEE SCHELL** – guitars / **SCOTT THURSTON + WALLY BADAROU** – keyboards

		Island	Island
Apr 88.	(7") **SIMILIAR FEATURES. / I WANT YOU** (12"+=)(cd-s+=) – Don't you need.		
May 88.	(lp)(c)(cd) **MELISSA ETHERIDGE** – Similiar features / Chrome plated heart / Like the way I do / Precious pain / Don't you need / The late September dogs / Occasionally / Watching you / Bring me some water / I want you.		22
Jun 88.	(7") **DON'T YOU NEED. / PRECIOUS PAIN** (12"+=) – ('A'live). (cd-s++=) – Similiar features.		
Feb 89.	(7") **BRING ME SOME WATER. / OCCASIONALLY** (12"+=)(cd-s+=) – I want you.		
Mar 89.	(7") **SIMILAR FEATURES. / BRING ME SOME WATER**	-	94

— **MAURICIO FRITZ LEWAK** – drums + **BERNIE LARSEN** – guitar repl. SCHELL + BADAROU

Jul 89.	(7") **NO SOUVENIRS. / ('A'live)** (12"+=)(cd-s+=) – Brave and crazy (live).		95
Sep 89.	(lp)(c)(cd) **BRAVE AND CRAZY** – No souvenirs / Brave and crazy / You used to love to dance / The angels / You can sleep while I drive / Testify / Let me go / My back door / Skin deep / Royal	63	22 Aug89

Station 4-16.
Nov 89. (7") **THE ANGELS. / ('A'live)** [ ] [ ]
(12"+=)(cd-s+=) – Chrome plated heart. *(re-iss.May90)*
1990. (7") **YOU CAN SLEEP WHILE I DRIVE. / THE LATE SEPTEMBER DOGS (live)** [ ] [ ]
(12"+=) – ('A'live).

—— **STEUART SMITH + MARK GOLDENBERG** – guitars repl. LARSEN + WACHTEL

1992. (7")(c-s) **DANCE WITHOUT SLEEPING. / AIN'T IT HEAVY** [ ] [ ]
(12"+=)(cd-s+=) – Similiar features.
Apr 92. (cd)(c)(lp) **NEVER ENOUGH** [56] [21]
– Ain't it heavy / 2001 / Dance without sleeping / Place your hand / Must be crazy for me / Meet me in the back / The boy feels strange / Keep it precious / The letting go / It's for you.
Apr 92. (7") **AIN'T IT HEAVY. / THE BOYS FEEL STRANGE** [ ] [ ]
(12"+=)(cd-s+=) – Royal Station 4-16 (live).
Jul 92. (7")(c-s) **2001. / ('A'remix)** [ ] [ ]
(12"+=) – Meet me in the back / Testify.
(cd-s+=) – Meet me in the back / ('A'-12"remix).
Oct 93. (cd)(c)(lp) **YES I AM** [ ] [15]
– I'm the only one / If I wanted to / Come to my window / Silent legacy / I will never be the same / All American girl / Yes I am / Resist / Ruins / Talking to my angel. *(re-iss.Apr94)*
Nov 93. (c-s) **I'M THE ONLY ONE. / ('A'version)** [ ] [8]
(12"+=)(cd-s+=) – Yes I am.
Apr 94. (c-ep)(cd-ep) **COME TO MY WINDOW / AIN'T IT HEAVY / THE LETTING GO / I'M THE ONLY ONE** [ ] [22]
Feb 95. (c-s)(cd-s) **IF I WANTED TO / LIKE HIS . . .** [-] [16]
Oct 95. (c-s) **YOUR LITTLE SECRET / ALL AMERICAN GIRL** [ ] [ ]
(cd-s+=) – Bring me some water / Skin deep.
Nov 95. (cd)(c) **YOUR LITTLE SECRET** [ ] [6]
– Your little secret / I really like you / Nowhere to go / An unusual kiss / I want to come over / All the way to Heaven / I could have been you / Shriner's Park / Change / This war is over.

EUGENIUS (see under ⇒ VASELINES)

EUROPE

Formed: Upplands-Vasby, Stockholm, Sweden . . . 1980 by TEMPEST, NORUM and LEVEN as FORCE. In 1982, they appropriately changed name to EUROPE, and after a number of homeand triumphs on 'Hot', they signed to 'Epic' in 1986. Their first 45 'THE FINAL COUNTDOWN', gave them breakthrough internationally, peaking at No.1 in the UK. • **Style:** Heavy metal rock, likened to TOTO, RUSH or RAINBOW. • **Songwriters:** TEMPEST wrote English lyrics. • **Trivia:** Producers were KEVIN ELSON (1st album) / RON NEVISON (2nd) / BEAU HILL (3rd).

Recommended: 1982-92 (*5)

JOEY TEMPEST (b. JOAKIM LARSSON, 19 Aug'63) – vocals / **JOHN NORUM** – guitar / **JOHN LEVEN** – bass / **JOHN RENO** – drums

not issued Hot

Mar 83. (lp) **EUROPE** [-] [8] Sweden
– In the future to come / Female / Seven doors hotel / The king will return / Boyazant / Children of the time / Memories / Words of wisdom / Paradise beach. *(UK-iss.+c.Jan87 on 'Chord')*
Apr 84. (lp)(c) **WINGS OF TOMORROW** [-] [-] Sweden
– Stormwind / Scream of anger / Open your heart / Treated bad again / Aphasia / Wings of tomorrow / Wasted time / Dreamer / Lyin' eyes / Dance the night away. *(UK-iss.Mar88 on 'Epic')*

—— **IAN HAUGHLAND** – drums, vocals repl. RENO / **KEE MARCELLO** – guitar (ex-EASY ACTION) repl. NORUM / added **MIC MICHAELI** – keyboards

Epic Epic

Oct 86. (7")(12") **THE FINAL COUNTDOWN. / ON BROKEN WINGS** [1] [8] Jan 87
(3"cd-s+=) – Heart of stone.
Nov 86. (lp)(c)(cd) **THE FINAL COUNTDOWN** [9] [8]
– The final countdown / Rock the night / Carrie / Danger on the track / Ninja / Cherokee / Time has come / Heart of stone / On the loose / Love chaser. *(re-iss.+cd.Mar90)*
Jan 87. (7")(7"colrd) **ROCK THE NIGHT. / SEVEN DOORS HOTEL** [12] [30] May 87
(12"+=) – Storm wind / Wings of tomorrow.
Apr 87. (7")(7"colrd) **CARRIE. / LOVE CHASER** [22] [3] Jul 87
(12"+=) – Danger on the track.
(d7"+=) – Open your heart / Dance the night away.
Jan 88. (7") **CHEROKEE. / HEART OF STONE** [ ] [72] Nov 87
(12"+=)(cd-s+=) – ?
Aug 88. (7") **SUPERSTITIOUS. / LIGHTS AND SHADOWS** [34] [31]
(12"+=)(cd-s+=) – Towers calling / The final countdown.
Aug 88. (lp)(c)(cd) **OUT OF THIS WORLD** [12] [19]
– Superstitious / Let the good times rock / Open your heart / More than meets the eye / Coast to coast / Ready or not / Sign of the times / Just the beginning / Never say die / Lights and shadows / Towers callin' / Tomorrow.
Oct 88. (7") **OPEN UP YOUR HEART. / TOWER'S CALLING** [-] [ ]
Oct 88. (7") **OPEN YOUR HEART. / JUST THE BEGINNING** [ ] [-]
(12"+=)(cd-s+=) – Rock the night / Lyin' eyes.
Mar 89. (7") **LET THE GOOD TIMES ROCK. / NEVER SAY DIE** [ ] [ ]
(12"+=)(cd-s+=) – Carrie / Seven doors hotel.
Oct 91. (cd)(c)(lp) **PRISONERS IN PARADISE** [61] [ ]
– All or nothing / Halfway to Heaven / I'll cry for you / A little bit of lovin' / Talk to me / Seventh sign / Prisoners in Paradise / Bad blood / Homeland / Get your mind in the gutter / 'Til my heart beats down your door / Girl from Lebanon. *(pic-lp Feb92)*
Jan 92. (7")(c-s) **I'LL CRY FOR YOU. / BREAK FREE** [28] [ ]
(12"+=//+cd-s++=) – ('A'acoustic)./ / Prisoners in Paradise.
Mar 92. (7") **HALFWAY TO HEAVEN. / YESTERDAY'S NEWS** [42] [ ]
(12"+=) – Superstitious / Got your mind in the gutter.
(cd-s+=) – The final countdown / Open your heart (acoustic mix).

– compilations, others, etc. –

Sep 90. Old Gold; (7") **THE FINAL COUNTDOWN. / CARRIE** [ ] [-]
Apr 93. Epic; (cd)(c)(lp) **1982-1992** [ ] [ ]
– In the future to come / Seven doors hotel / Stormwind / Open your heart / Scream of anger / Dreamer / The final countdown / On broken wings / Rock the night / Carrie / Cherokee / Superstitious / Ready or not / Prisoners in Paradise / I'l cry for you / Sweet love child / Yesterday's news.

EURYTHMICS

Formed: By LENNOX and STEWART in London, England . . . where they met in 1976. They formed The CATCH in 1977 with PETE COOMBES, but by 1979 they had evolved into The TOURISTS. They signed to 'Logo' records, and scored Top 10 hits with some fine pop singles (i.e.'I ONLY WANT TO BE WITH YOU' & 'SO GOOD TO BE BACK HOME'), before breaking with COOMBES late in 1980. The duo, now The EURYTHMICS became live-in lovers, and after a flop Conny Plank produced debut album 'IN THE GARDEN', they registered in the 1983 charts with No.2 single 'SWEET DREAMS'. They went on to hit No.1 in the States, and secured a regular place in both charts throughout the 80's until they split in 1990. In 1992 ANNIE LENNOX went solo, and disappointed no-one with her appropriately titled album 'ANNIE LENNOX – DIVA', which later received Best Album award. • **Style:** Innovative pop-rock, that shifted between electronic dance-rock and melancholy romantic pop. ANNIE became the queen chameleon of video, changing visually with each new acting out portrayal. In 1985, she acted (approx. 10 lines) alongside Al Pacino and Donald Sutherland in the flop film 'Revolution'. • **Songwriters:** COOMBES penned songs in The TOURISTS, except I ONLY WANT TO BE WITH YOU (Dusty Springfield). DAVE and ANNIE wrote together in The EURYTHMICS. Now a solo writer, ANNIE LENNOX covered KEEP YOUNG AND BEAUTIFUL (Al Dubin-Harry Warren) / FEEL THE NEED (Detroit Emeralds) / RIVER DEEP MOUNTAIN HIGH (Phil Spector) / DON'T LET ME DOWN (Beatles) / NO MORE "I LOVE YOU'S" (The Lover Speaks) / TAKE ME TO THE RIVER (Al Green) / A WHITER SHADE OF PALE (Procol Harum) / DON'T LET IT BRING YOU DOWN (Neil Young) / TRAIN IN VAIN (Clash) / I CAN'T GET NEXT TO YOU (Strong-Whitfield) / DOWNTOWN LIGHTS (Blue Nile) / THE THIN BLUE LINE BETWEEN LOVE AND HATE (Pretenders; hit) / WAITING IN VAIN (Bob Marley) / SOMETHING SO RIGHT (Paul Simon) / LADIES OF THE CANYON (Joni Mitchell) / I'M ALWAYS TOUCHED BY YOUR PRESENCE DEAR (Blondie). DAVE STEWART's VEGAS covered SHE (Charles Aznavour). • **Trivia:** In Mar'84 ANNIE, now not involved intimately with DAVE, married German Hare Krishna RADHA RAMAR, but this only lasted 6 months. She married again in the late 80's?, and gave birth to first child in Spring 1993. On 1st of August, DAVE married SHAKESPEAR'S SISTER & ex-BANANARAMA singer SIOBHAN FAHEY. He has also produced many artists including FEARGAL SHARKEY, MARIA McKEE, DARYL HALL, BOB GELDOF, BOB DYLAN. TOM PETTY, MICK JAGGER, BORIS GREBENSHIKOV (Russian rocker) and LONDONBEAT.

Recommended: EURYTHMICS GREATEST HITS (*8). ANNIE LENNOX solo:- ANNIE LENNOX – DIVA (*7).

The CATCH

ANNIE LENNOX (b. 25 Dec'54, Aberdeen, Scotland) – vocals, keyboards, flute / **DAVE STEWART** (b. 9 Sep'52, Sunderland, England) – guitar, keyboards, etc. (ex-LONGDANCER) / **PETE COOMBES** – guitar, vocals

Logo not issued

Nov 77. (7") **BORDERLINE. / BLACK BLOOD** [ ] [-]

TOURISTS

adding **EDDY CHIN** – bass / **JIM TOOMEY** – drums

Logo R.C.A.

May 79. (7") **BLIND AMONG THE FLOWERS. / HE WHO LAUGHS LAST LAUGHS LONGEST** [52] [ ]
(d7"+=) – The golden lamp / Wrecked
Jun 79. (lp)(c) **THE TOURISTS** [72] [ ]
– Blind among the flowers / Save me / Fool's paradise / Can't stop laughing / Don't get left behind / Another English day / Deadly kiss / Ain't no room / The loneliest man in the world / Useless duration of time / He who laughs last laughs longest / Just like you. *(re-iss.Jun81 on 'R.C.A.')*
Aug 79. (7")(7"pic-d) **THE LONELIEST MAN IN THE WORLD. / DON'T GET LEFT BEHIND** [32] [ ]
Oct 79. (lp)(c) **REALITY EFFECT** [23] [ ]
– It doesn't have to be this way / I only want to be with you / In the morning / All life's tragedies / Everywhere you look / So good to be back home / Nothing to do / Circular fever / In my mind / Something in the air tonight / Summers night.
Oct 79. (7") **I ONLY WANT TO BE WITH YOU. / SUMMER NIGHT** [4] [83] Apr 80
Jan 80. (7") **SO GOOD TO BE BACK HOME. / CIRCULAR SAW** [6] [ ]

R.C.A. R.C.A.

Sep 80. (7") **DON'T SAY I TOLD YOU SO. / STRANGE SKY** [40] [ ]
Oct 80. (lp)(c) **LUMINOUS BASEMENT** [75] [ ]
– Walls and foundations / Don't say I told you so / Week days / So you want to go away now / One step nearer the edge / Angels and demons / Talk to me / Round

round blues / Let's take a walk / Time drags so slow / I'm going to change my mind. *(free-7"yellow-w/a)* **FROM THE MIDDLE ROOM. / INTO THE FUTURE**

— After The TOURISTS split late '80.

EURYTHMICS

were formed by **ANNIE LENNOX** and **DAVE STEWART** with guests **ROBERT GORL** and **GABI DELGADO** of D.A.F. / **JAKI LIEBEZEIT** – percussion and **HOLGER CZUKAY** – bass (both ex-CAN)

R.C.A. R.C.A.

Jun 81. (7")(12") **NEVER GONNA CRY AGAIN. / LE SINISTRE** [63] [ ]
Aug 81. (7") **BELINDA. / HEARTBEAT, HEARTBEAT** [ ] [ ]
Oct 81. (lp)(c) **IN THE GARDEN** [ ] [ ]
– English summer / Belinda / Take me to your heart / She's invisible now / Your time will come / Caveman head / Never gonna cry again / All the young (people of today) / Sing sing / Revenge. *(re-iss.Mar84) (cd-iss.Jan87 & Sep91)*

— **ANNIE** and **DAVE** now augmented with synthesisers, also guests **CLEM BURKE** – drums (ex-BLONDIE, who later joined RAMONES in '87)

Mar 82. (7") **THIS IS THE HOUSE. / HOME IS WHERE THE HEART IS** [ ] [ ]
(12") – ('A'side) / Take me to your heart (live) / 4-4 In leather (live) / Never gonna cry again (live) / Your time will come (live).
Jun 82. (7") **THE WALK. / STEP ON THE BEAST / THE WALK (pt.2)** [ ] [ ]
(12") – The walk (pt.1 & 2) / – Invisible hands / Dr.Trash.
Sep 82. (7")(7"pic-d) **LOVE IS A STRANGER. / MONKEY MONKEY** [54] [ ]
(12"+=) – Let's just close our eyes. *(re-iss.Apr83 reached no.6, US re-iss.Sep83 reached 23)*
Jan 83. (7")(7"pic-d) **SWEET DREAMS (ARE MADE OF THIS). / I COULD GIVE YOU (A MIRROR)** [2] [1] May 83
(12"+=) – Baby's gone blue.
Feb 83. (lp)(c)(pic-lp) **SWEET DREAMS (ARE MADE OF THIS)** [3] [15] May 83
– Sweet dreams (are made of this) / Jennifer / This city never sleeps / This is the house / Somebody told me / The walk / I've got an angel / Love is a stranger / Wrap it up / I could give you (a mirror). *(re-iss.Aug84) (cd-iss.Jan84 & re-iss.Oct87)*
Jul 83. (7")(7"pic-d) **WHO'S THAT GIRL. / YOU TAKE SOME LENTILS . . . AND YOU TAKE SOME RICE** [3] [-]
(12"+=) – A.B.C. (freeform).
Oct 83. (7")(7"pic-d) **RIGHT BY YOUR SIDE. / ('A'party mix)** [10] [29] Jul 84
(12"+=) – ('A'&'B' special mix) / Plus something else.
(free-c-s.with 7") – Intro speech / Step on the beast / Invisible hands / Angel (dub) / Satellite of love.

— **ANNIE** and **DAVE** were augmented on album by **CLEM** – drums plus **DICK CUTHELL** – brass MARTIN DOBSON – horns / **DEAN GARCIA** – bass(above 3 also went on tour adding) **VIC MARTIN** – synthesizers / **PETE PHIPPS** – drums / and backing singers **GILL O'DONOVAN, SUZIE O'LISZT and MAGGIE RYDER**

Nov 83. (lp)(c) **TOUCH** [1] [7] Jan 84
– Here comes the rain again / Regrets / Right by your side / Cool blue / Who's that girl? / The first cut / Aqua / No fear, no hurt, no pain (no broken hearts) / Paint a rumour. *(cd-iss.Sep84) (re-iss.+cd.Sep89) (also iss.pic-lp)*
Jan 84. (7")(7"pic-d) **HERE COMES THE RAIN AGAIN. / PAINT A RUMOUR** [8] [4]
(12"+=) – This city never sleeps (live).
Apr 84. (7") **WHO'S THAT GIRL?. / AQUA** [-] [21]
Jun 84. (m-lp)(c)(cd) **TOUCH DANCE** (remixes) [31] [ ]
– The first cut (instrumental) / Cool blue (instrumental) / Paint a rumour (instrumental) / The first cut / Cool blue / Paint a rumour / Regrets. *(cd-iss.Dec91)*

Virgin R.C.A.

Oct 84. (7") **SEXCRIME (NINETEEN EIGHTY-FOUR). / I DID IT JUST THE SAME** [4] [81]
(12")(12"pic-d) – ('A'extended).
Nov 84. (lp)(c)(cd) **1984 – FOR THE LOVE OF BIG BROTHER (soundtrack)** [23] [93]
– I did it just the same / Julia / Sexcrime (nineteen eighty-four) / Doubleplusgood / For the love of big brother / Ministry of love / Winston's diary / Room 101 / Greetings from a dead man. *(re-iss.Jan88) (cd-iss.Apr89 & Dec95)*
Jan 85. (7")(7"pic-d) **JULIA. / MINISTRY OF LOVE** [44] [ ]
(12"+=) – ('A'extended).

R.C.A. R.C.A.

Apr 85. (7")(12")(12"red)(12"yellow)(12"blue) **WOULD I LIE TO YOU? / HERE COMES THAT SINKING FEELING** [11] [5]
(also available on d7"red / blue / or yellow)
May 85. (lp)(c)(cd) **BE YOURSELF TONIGHT** [3] [9]
– It's alright (baby's coming back) / Would I lie to you / There must be an angel (playing with my heart) / I love you like a ball and chain / Sisters are doin' it for themselves / Conditioned soul / Adrian / Here comes that sinking feeling / Better to have lost in love (than never to have loved at all). *(re-iss.+cd.May90)*
Jun 85. (7") **THERE MUST BE AN ANGEL (PLAYING WITH MY HEART). / GROWN UP GIRLS** [1] [22]
(12"+=) – ('A'dance mix).
Oct 85. (7")(12") **SISTERS ARE DOIN' IT FOR THEMSELVES. ("EURYTHMICS & ARETHA FRANKLIN") / I LOVE YOU LIKE A BALL AND CHAIN** [9] [18]
Jan 86. (7") **IT'S ALRIGHT (BABY'S COMING BACK). / CONDITIONED SOUL** [12] [78]
(12"+=) – Tous les garcons et les filles.
Jun 86. (7") **WHEN TOMORROW COMES. / TAKE YOUR PAIN AWAY** [30] [ ]
(12"+=) – ('A'orchestral).
Jul 86. (lp)(c)(cd) **REVENGE** [3] [12]
– Let's go / Take your pain away / A little of you / Thorn in my side / In this town / I remember you / Missionary man / The last time / When tomorrow comes / The miracle of love.
Aug 86. (7") **THORN IN MY SIDE. / IN THIS TOWN** [5] [68] Oct 86
(12"+=) – ('A'extended).
Aug 86. (7")(12") **MISSIONARY MAN. / TAKE YOUR PAIN AWAY** [-] [14]
Nov 86. (7")(7"pic-d) **THE MIRACLE OF LOVE. / WHEN TOMORROW COMES (live)** [23] [ ]
(12"+=) – Who's that girl (live).
(12"pic-d+=) – Don't ask me why.
Feb 87. (7") **MISSIONARY MAN. / THE LAST TIME (live)** [31] [-]
(12"+=) – ('A'extended).
Oct 87. (7") **BEETHOVEN (I LOVE TO LISTEN TO). / HEAVEN** [25] [ ]
(10"+=)(12"+=)(cd-s+=) – ('A'dance mix).
Nov 87. (lp)(c)(cd) **SAVAGE** [7] [41]
– Beethoven (I love to listen to) / I've got a lover (back in Japan) / Do you want to break up? / You have placed a chill in my heart / Shame / Savage / I need a man / Put the blame on me / Heaven / Wide eyed girl / I need you / Brand new day. *(re-iss.cd May93)*
Dec 87. (7") **SHAME. / I'VE GOT A LOVER (BACK IN JAPAN)** [41] [ ]
(12"+=) – ('A'dance mix).
(cd-s+=) – There must be an angel (playing with my heart).
Dec 87. (7") **I NEED A MAN. / HEAVEN** [-] [46]
Mar 88. (7") **I NEED A MAN. / I NEED YOU** [26] [-]
(12"+=) – ('A'macho mix).
(cd-s++=) – Missionary man (live).
(10"+=) – There must be an angel (playing with my heart).
(7"m+=) – I need a man (live).
May 88. (7") **YOU HAVE PLACED A CHILL IN MY HEART. / ('A'acoustic mix)** [16] [64]
(12"+=) – ('A'dance).
(cd-s++=) – Do you want to break up / Here comes the rain again (live).

In Oct'88, ANNIE was credited on AL GREEN ⇒ single PUT A LITTLE LOVE IN YOUR HEART

R.C.A. Arista

Aug 89. (7")(c-s) **REVIVAL. / PRECIOUS** [26] [ ]
(12"+=)(cd-s+=) – ('A'extended-ET dance mix).
Sep 89. (lp)(c)(cd) **WE TOO ARE ONE** [1] [34]
– We two are one / The King and Queen of America / (My my) Baby's gonna cry / Don't ask me why / Angel / Revival / You hurt me (and I hate you) / Sylvia / How long? / When the day goes down. *(re-iss.cd Jun94)*
Oct 89. (7")(c-s) **DON'T ASK ME WHY. / RICH GIRL** [25] [40] Sep 89
(12"+=)(cd-s+=)(12"pic-d+=) – Sylvia.
(12"+=)(cd-s+=) – ('A'version) / When the day goes down.
Jan 90. (7")(c-s) **KING AND QUEEN OF AMERICA (remix). / SEE NO EVIL** [29] [ ]
(12") – ('A'dance mix) / ('B'side) / ('A'dub mix).
(12"+=)(cd-s+=) – There must be an angel (playin' with my heart) (live) / I love you like a ball and chain (live).
(12"++=)(cd-s++=) – ('A'dub mix).
Apr 90. (7")(c-s) **ANGEL. / ANGEL (choir version)** [23] [-]
(12"+=)(cd-s+=) – Missionary man (acoustic).
(12") – ('A'remix) / Sweet dreams (are made of this) mix
Apr 90. (c-s) **ANGEL / PRECIOUS** [-] [ ]
Jun 90. (c-s) **(MY MY) BABY'S GONNA CRY / ('A'acoustic)** [-] [ ]

— Disbanded after last album.

– compilations, others, etc. –

Nov 88. Virgin; (3"cd-ep)(5"cd-ep) **SEXCRIME (1984 extended mix) / JULIA (extended) / I DID IT JUST THE SAME** [ ] [ ]
Mar 89. R.C.A.; (3"cd-ep) **SWEET DREAMS (ARE MADE OF THIS) / I COULD GIVE YOU (A MIRROR) / HERE COMES THE RAIN AGAIN / PAINT A RUMOUR** [ ] [ ]
Mar 91. R.C.A.; (cd)(c)(lp) **EURYTHMICS' GREATEST HITS** [1] [72]
– Love is a stranger / Sweet dreams (are made of this) / Who's that girl? / Right by your side / Here comes the rain again / There must be an angel (playing with my heart) / Sisters are doin' it for themselves / It's alright (baby's coming back) / When tomorrow comes / You have placed a chill in my heart / Sexcrime (nineteen eighty-four) / Thorn in my side Don't ask me why. *(cd/c+=)* – Miracle of love / Angel / Would I lie to you? / Missionary man / I need a man.
Mar 91. R.C.A.; (7")(c-s) **LOVE IS A STRANGER. / JULIA** [46] [ ]
(12"+=)(cd-s+=) – ('A'obsession mix) / There must be an angel (playin' with my heart).
(12") – ('A'diff.mix) / ('A'instrumental) / ('A'-Coldcut mix).
Nov 91. R.C.A.; (7")(c-s) **SWEET DREAMS (ARE MADE OF THIS) '91. / KING AND QUEEN OF AMERICA** [48] [ ]
(12") – ('A'side) / ('A'house mix) / ('A'nightmare mix) / ('A'hot remix).
(cd-s) – ('A'side) / Beethoven (I love to listen to) / Shame / This city never sleeps.
Nov 93. R.C.A.; (d-cd)(d-c) **EURYTHMICS LIVE 1983-1989 (live)** [22] [ ]
– Never gonna cry again / Love is a stranger / Sweet dreams (are made of this) / This city never sleeps / Somebody told me / Who's that girl? / Right by your side / Here comes the rain again / Sex crime / I love you like a ball and chain / There must be an angel (playing with my heart) / Thorn in my side / Let's go / Missionary man / The last time / Miracle of love / I need a man / We two are one / (My my) Baby's gonna cry / Don't ask me why / Angel. *(cd includes free 7 track EP) (re-iss.Oct95)*
Apr 95. R.C.A.; (cd) **BE YOURSELF TONIGHT / REVENGE** [ ] [-]

ANNIE LENNOX

in 1992 with **STEPHEN LIPSON** – guitars, prog., keyboards / **PETER-JOHN VITTESE** – keyboards, prog., recorder / **MARIUS DE VRIES** – prog., keys/ also **LOUIS JARDIM** – percussion / **ED SHEARMUR** – piano / **KEITH LeBLANC** – drums / **DOUG WIMBUSH** – bass / **KENJI JAMMER** – guitar / **STEVE JANSON** – drum pro / **DAVE DeFRIES** – trumpet / **GAVON WRIGHT** – violin / **PAUL MOORE** – keyboards (co-writer on 1)

R.C.A. Arista

Mar 92. (7")(c-s) **WHY. / PRIMITIVE** [5] [34]
(12"+=//+cd-s+=) – Keep young and beautiful./ / ('A'instrumental).
Apr 92. (cd)(c)(lp) **ANNIE LENNOX – DIVA** [1] [27]
– Why / Walking on broken glass / Precious / Legend in my living room / Cold / Money can't buy it / Little bird / Primitive / Stay by me / The gift.
May 92. (7")(c-s) **PRECIOUS. / ('A'version)** [23] [ ]
(cd-s+=) – Step by step / Why.
Aug 92. (7")(c-s)(cd-s) **WALKING ON BROKEN GLASS. / LEGEND IN MY LIVING ROOM** [8] [14]

(12"+=)(cd-s+=) – Don't let me down.

Oct 92. (7")(c-s) **COLD. / ('A'live)** [26] [ ]
(c-s+=) – River deep mouintain high / You have placed a chill in my heart.
(cd-s) – ('A'side) / Why / The gift / Walking on broken glass.
(cd-s) – ('A'side) / It's alright / Here comes the rain again / You have placed a chill in my heart.

Feb 93. (7")(c-s)(12")(cd-s) **LITTLE BIRD. / LOVE SONG FOR A VAMPIRE** [3] [49]
(cd-s+=)/ /(cd-s+=)/ /(cd-s+=) – Feel the need (live). / / River deep mountain high (live). / / Don't let me down (live).

— with **STEPHEN LIPSON** – programmer, guitar, keyboards, bass

Feb 95. (7")(c-s) **NO MORE I LOVE YOU'S. / LADIES OF THE CANYON** [2] [23]
(cd-s+=) – Love song for a vampire.
(cd-s) – ('A'side) / Why (acoustic) / Cold (acoustic) / Walking on broken glass (acoustic).

Mar 95. (cd)(c)(lp) **MEDUSA** [1] [11]
– No more "I love you's" / Take me to the river / A whiter shade of pale / Don't let it bring you down / Train in vain / I can't get next to you / Downtown lights / The thin line between love and hate / Waiting in vain / Something so right. *(re-iss.d-cd Dec95 w/ free 'LIVE IN CENTRAL PARK')*

May 95. (c-s) **A WHITER SHADE OF PALE / HEAVEN** [16] [ ]
(cd-s+=) – I'm always touched by your presence dear / Love song for a vampire.
(cd-s) – ('A'side) / Don't let it bring you down / You have placed a chill in my heart / Here comes the rain again.

Sep 95. (12")(c-s)(cd-s) **WAITING IN VAIN. / NO MORE "I LOVE YOU'S"** [31] [ ]
(cd-s+=) – Train in vain.
(cd-s+=) – (interview) / ('A'-Strong body mix).
(cd-s) – ('A'side) / ('A'-Strong body mix) / ('A'-Howie B mix).
(cd-s) – ('A'side) / Train in vain (3 mixes).

(below feat.PAUL SIMON)

Nov 95. (c-s)(cd-s) **SOMETHING SO RIGHT / SWEET DREAMS (ARE MADE OF THIS)** [44] [ ]
(cd-s+=) – Who's that girl / I love you like a ball and chain.
(cd-s) – ('A'side) / Waiting in vain live) / Something so right (live) / Money can't buy it.

— as DAVID A. STEWART he recorded single 'AVENUE D' with ETTA JAMES (May89)

DAVID A. STEWART & CANDY DULFER

(CANDY solo artist and ex-PRINCE)

Anxious-RCA | R.C.A.

Feb 90. (7")(c-s) **LILY WAS HERE. / LILY ROBS THE BANK** [7] [11] Apr 91
(12"+=)(cd-s+=) – ('A'space centre medical unit mix).

Apr 90. (cd)(c)(lp) **LILY WAS HERE (Soundtrack)** [35] [ ]
– Lily was here / The pink building / Lily robs the bank / Toyshop robbery / Toys on the sidewalk / The good hotel / Second chance / Here comes the rain again / Alone in the city / Toyshop (part one) / The coffin / Teletype / Inside the pink building / Percussion jam / Peaches / Lily was here (reprise).

DAVID A. STEWART

R.C.A. | R.C.A.

Oct 91. (cd)(c)(lp) **JUTE CITY** (BBC Soundtrack) [ ] [ ]
– Jute City / Dead planets / Last love / In Duncan's arms / Black wedding / Jute City revisited / Contaminated / See no evil / Jigula / The lords theme / Hats off to Hector / Deep waters / Dark wells.

Oct 91. (7")(c-s) **JUTE CITY. / JUTE CITY (Caroline's mix)** [ ] [ ]
(cd-s+=) – Dead planet / Black wedding.
(12") – ('A'remix) / (above extra 2).

DAVE STEWART AND THE SPIRITUAL COWBOYS

with **IZZY MAE DOORITE** – guitar, vocals / **WILD MONDO** – keyboards, vocals / **CHRISTOPHER D.JAMES** – bass, vocals / **MARTIN O'DALE** – drumwarp, vocals / **ZAC BARTEL** – drum prog. / **JOHN TEXAS TURNBULL** – electric bow semi-acoustic

R.C.A. | R.C.A.

Aug 90. (7")(c-s) **JACK TALKING. / SUICIDE SID** [69] [ ]
(12"+=)(cd-s+=) – Love calculator.

Sep 90. (cd)(c)(lp) **DAVE STEWART AND THE SPIRITUAL COWBOYS** [38] [ ]
– Soul years / King of the hypocrites / Diamond avenue / This little town / On fire / Heaven and Earth / Love shines / Party town / Mr.Reed / Fashion bomb / Jack talking / Hey Johnny / The Devil's just been using you / Spiritual love.

Oct 90. (7")(12")(c-s) **LOVE SHINES. / MARIANNE** [ ] [-]
(10"+=)/ /(cd-s+=) – Instant karma (live). / / Victim of fate.

Feb 91. (c-s) **PARTY TOWN (party on down mix). / PARTY TOWN (politico mix)** [-] [ ]
(cd-s+=) Love calculator. / Suicidal Sid

May 91. (c-s) **LOVE SHINES. / INSTANT KARMA** [-] [ ]

Sep 91. (7")(c-s) **CROWN OF MADNESS. / FRUSTRATION** [ ] [ ]
(12"+=)(cd-s+=) – If that's love.
(cd-s) – ('A'side) / Honest (live) / On fire (live) / Motorcycle mystics (live).

Oct 91. (cd)(c)(lp) **HONEST** [ ] [ ]
– Honest / Whole wide world / Count of madness / Out of reach / You've lost / Fool's parradise / Motorcycle mystery / Impossible / Here we go again / Here she comes / Fade away / Cat with a tale / R U satisfied

Nov 91. (7")(c-s) **OUT OF REACH. / DAY OF THE DEAD** [ ] [ ]
(12"+=)(cd-s+=) – The ballad of Michael Pain.

— DAVE STEWART teamed up with TERRY HALL to form VEGAS.

DAVE STEWART

with **BOOTSY COLLINS** – bass, space bass / **BERNIE WORRELL** – keyboards / **JEROME 'BIG FOOT' BRAILEY** – drums + guests **LAURIE ANDERSON** (electric violin, vox on 'Kinky Sweetheart') / **LOU REED** (guitar solo on 'You Talk a lot' w /saxophone **DAVE SANBORN**) / **CARLY SIMON** (argumented w/**SANBORN;** last track) / **TERRY DISLEY** – keyboards

East West | Warners

Aug 94. (c-s)(cd-s) **HEART OF STONE / PEACE IN WARTIME / COAL NIGHTS** [36] [ ]
(12"+=)(cd-s+=) – Sure is Pure (remixes).

Sep 94. (cd)(c) **GREETINGS FROM THE GUTTER** [ ] [ ]
– Heart of stone / Greetings from the gutter / Jealousy / St.Valentine's day / Kinky sweetheart / Damien save me / Crazy sister / You talk a lot / Tragedy Street / Chelsea lovers / Oh no, not you again.

Apr 95. (c-s) **JEALOUSY / BLIND LEADING THE BLIND** [ ] [ ]
(cd-s+=) – Tragedy Street.

Oct 95. (c-s) **SECRET / ('A'-SPS vocal mix)** [ ] [ ]
(cd-s+=) – Kinky sweetheart.
(12"+=) – ('A'-Posterity mix) / ('A'-SPS mad club mix).

EVERLAST (see under ⇒ HOUSE OF PAIN)

EVERLY BROTHERS

Formed: Kentucky, USA . . . 1955 by brothers DON and PHIL. That year they went to Nashville, hoping that country artists would buy their songs. In 1956, they gained deal with 'Columbia' records, who released one single before opting out. After a short struggle trying to find another label, their father IKE contacted old friend CHET ATKINS, who got them signed as songwriters for Roy Acuff and Wesley Rose. The latter became their manager and persuaded Archie Bleyer of 'Cadence' records, to sign them in 1957. Their first song 'BYE BYE LOVE', became a million seller, peaking at US No.2 in Jul'57. They appeaed on many TV shows (ie. 'Ed Sullivan'& 'Perry Como', etc.). During the next year, 3 of their 4 singles, hit the US peak spot. In 1960, they signed to 'Warners', scored with debut 'CATHY'S CLOWN', which had to fight off own 'Cadence' label singles in competition. More hits followed until onslaught of 1963-64 British Invasion. In 1965, the UK public were their greatest asset, as their classic 'THE PRICE OF LOVE' hit No.2, after floundering in the States. But for a few 70's & 80's reunions, their work in the future, was mainly as solo artists. • **Style:** Harmonising vocal duo, who took country-hillbilly roots, and blended it into their blend of popular melodious rock'n'roll. • **Songwriters:** B.& F. BRYANT wrote most of their work until 1959. DON and PHIL began writing sperately on most others from then on. Also covered:- CLAUDETTE (Roy Orbison) / LET IT BE ME (Gilbert Becaud) / BE-BOP-A-LULA (Gene Vincent) / LUCILLE (Little Richard) / WALK RIGHT BACK (Sonny Curtis; of Crickets) / EBONY EYES + IT'S MY TIME (John D. Loudermilk) / TEMPTATION (Bing Crosby) / CRYING IN THE RAIN (Carole King & Howard Greenfield) / BOWLING GREEN (Terry Slater) / ABANDONED LOVE (Bob Dylan) / THE GIRL SANG THE BLUES + LOVE HER (Mann-Weill) / YVES (Scott McKenzie). After an inter-label rift between Wesley Rose was rectified, The BRYANTS returned on late 1964's 'GONE GONE GONE'. The album 'ROCK'N'SOUL' featured many classic rock'n'roll oldies. • **Trivia:** Many famous musicians have passed through their ranks, including FLOYD CHANCE – bass (1957) / JOEY PAGE – guitar (1962) / JIM GORDON and BILLY PRESTON. Other 60's sessioners stemmed from The BYRDS, The HOLLIES and LED ZEPPELIN!.

Recommended: THE VERY BEST OF THE EVERLYS (*7)

DON EVERLY (b.ISAAC DONALD EVERLY, 1 Feb'37, Brownie, Kentucky, USA) – vocals, guitar / **PHIL EVERLY** (b.19 Jan'39, Chicago, Illinois, USA) – vocals, guitar

not issued | Columbia

Feb 56. (7") **KEEP A LOVIN' ME. / THE SUN KEEPS SHINING** [-] [ ]

London | Cadence

Jun 57. (7") **BYE BYE LOVE. / I WONDER IF I CARE AS MUCH** [6] [2] May 57
(re-iss.Jul82 on 'Old Gold')

Oct 57. (7") **WAKE UP LITTLE SUSIE. / MAYBE TOMORROW** [2] [1] Sep 57
(re-iss.Oct80 on 'Old Gold')

Feb 58. (7") **THIS LITTLE GIRL OF MINE. / SHOULD WE TELL HIM** [ ] [26]

Mar 58. (lp) **THE EVERLY BROTHERS – THEY'RE OFF AND RUNNING!** [ ] [16] Jan 58
– This little girl of mine / Maybe tomorrow / Bye bye love / Brand new Heartache / Keep a knockin' / Be-bop-a-lula / Rip it up / I wonder if I care as much / Wake up little Susie / Leave my woman alone / Should we tell him / Hey doll baby.

May 58. (7") **ALL I HAVE TO DO IS DREAM. / CLAUDETTE** [1] [1] / [30] Apr 58
(US re-iss.Jul61, A-side hit No.96) (re-iss.Oct80, Jul82, Jun88 on 'Old Gold')

Sep 58. (7") **BIRD DOG. / DEVOTED TO YOU** [2] [1] / [10] Jul58
(re-iss.Jul82 on 'Old Gold')

Nov 58. (lp) **SONGS OUR DADDY TAUGHT US** [ ] [ ] Sep 58
– Roving gambler / Down in the willow garden / Longtime gone / Lightning express / That silver haired daddy of mine / Who's gonna shoe your pretty little feet / Barbara Allen / Oh so many years / I'm here to get my baby out of jail / Rockin' alone (in an old rocking chair) / Kentucky / Put my little shoes away. *(re-iss.Aug83 on 'Ace' UK / 'Barclay' US)*

Jan 59. (7") **PROBLEMS. / LOVE OF MY LIFE** [6] [2] / [40] Nov 58
(re-iss.Oct80 on 'Old Gold')

May 59. (7") **POOR JENNY. / TAKE A MESSAGE TO MARY** [14] [22] / **20** [16] Apr 59
(re-iss.Oct80 on 'Old Gold')

Sep 59. (7") **TILL I KISSED YOU. / OH WHAT A FEELING** [2] [4] Aug 59

(re-iss.Oct80 on 'Old Gold')
Feb 60. (7") **LET IT BE ME. / SINCE YOU BROKE MY HEART** 13 7 Jan 60
(re-iss.Jul82 on 'Old Gold')

Warners Warners

Apr 60. (7") **CATHY'S CLOWN. / ALWAYS IT'S YOU** 1 1
56
Jun 60. (lp) **IT'S EVERLY TIME!** 2 9 May 60
– So sad / Just in case / Memories are made of this / That's what you do to me / Sleepless nights / What kind of girl are you / Oh true love / Carol Jane / Some sweet day / Nashville blues / You thrill me / I want you to know. *(re-iss.May85 on 'Rollercoaster')*
Sep 60. (7") **LUCILLE. / SO SAD (TO WATCH GOOD LOVE GO BAD)** 4 21
7 Aug 60
Jan 61. (7") **WALK RIGHT BACK. / EBONY EYES** 1 7
8
Feb 61. (lp) **A DATE WITH THE EVERLY BROTHERS** 3 9 Nov 60
– Made to love / That's just too much / Stick with me baby / Baby what you want me to do / Sigh cry almost die / Always it's you / Love hurts / Lucille / So how come / Donna Donna / A change of heart / Cathy's clown. *(re-iss.May85 on 'Rollercoaster')*
Jun 61. (7") **TEMPTATION. / STICK WITH ME BABY** 1 27
41
Sep 61. (7") **DON'T BLAME ME. / MUSKRAT** 20 20
82
1961. (lp) **BOTH SIDES OF AN EVENING**
– My mamma / Muskrat / My gal Sal / My grandfather's clock / Bully of the town / Chloe / Mention my name in Sheboygan / Hi Lili hi lo / Wayward wind / Don't blame me / Now is the hour / Little old lady / When I grow too old to dream / Love is where you find it.
Jan 62. (7") **CRYIN' IN THE RAIN. / I'M NOT ANGRY** 6 6
May 62. (7") **HOW CAN I MEET HER. / THAT'S OLD FASHIONED (THAT'S THE WAY LOVE SHOULD BE)** 12 75
9
Jul 62. (lp) **INSTANT PARTY** 20
– Jezebel / Oh my papa / Step it up and go / True love / Bye bye blackbird / Trouble in mind / Love makes the world go round / Long lost John / Autumn leaves / Party's over / Ground hawg / When it's night time in Italy. *(re-iss.+cd.Oct86)*
Sep 62. (lp) **THE GOLDEN HITS OF THE EVERLY BROTHERS** 35
– (compilation of hits since April'60)
– That's Old Fashioned (That's The Way Love Should Be) / How Can I Meet Her? / Crying In The Rain / I'm Not Angry / Don't Blame Me / Ebony Eyes / Cathy's Clown / Walk Right Back / Lucille / So Sad (To Watch Good Love Go Bad)/ Muskrat / Temptation. *(re-iss.Dec65) (cd+c-iss 1991 on 'WEA')*
Oct 62. (7") **NO ONE CAN MAKE MY SUNSHINE SMILE. / DON'T ASK ME TO BE FRIENDS** 11 48 B-side
Dec 62. (lp) **CHRISTMAS WITH THE EVERLY BROTHERS AND THE BOYS TOWN CHOIR**
– (traditional Xmas songs)
Mar 63. (7") **SO IT WILL ALWAYS BE. / NANCY'S MINUET** 23
1963. (lp) **THE EVERLY BROTHERS SING GREAT COUNTRY HITS**
– Oh lonesome me / Born to lose / Just one time / Send me the pillow you dream on / Release me / Please help me I'm falling / I walk the line / Lonely street / Silver threads and golden needles / I'm so lonesome I could cry / Sweet dreams / This is the last song I'm ever going to sing. *(re-iss.Jul67 + Dec85)*
Jun 63. (7") **IT'S BEEN NICE. / I'M AFRAID** 26
Oct 63. (7") **THE GIRL SANG THE BLUES. / LOVE HER** 25
Apr 64. (7") **AIN'T THAT LOVIN' YOU BABY. / HELLO AMY**
Jun 64. (7") **THE FERRIS WHEEL. / DON'T FORGET TO CRY** 22 72
Jan 65. (lp) **THE VERY BEST OF THE EVERLY BROTHERS** Jul 64
– (re-recorded hits) Bye bye love / (Til) I kissed you / Wake up little Susie / Crying in the rain / Walk right back / Cathy's clown / Bird dog / All I have to do is dream / Devoted to you / Lucille / So sad (to watch good love go bad) / Ebony eyes. *(re-iss.+c.May74, hit No.43)*
1964. (7") **RING AROUND MY ROSIE. / YOU'RE THE ONE I LOVE** -
Nov 64. (7") **GONE GONE GONE. / TORTURE** 36 31
Dec 64. (lp) **GONE GONE GONE**
– Donna Donna / The lovely island / Facts of life / Ain't that lovin' you baby / Love is all I need / Torture / The drop out / Radio and TV / Honolulu / It's been a long dry spell / The ferris wheel / Gone gone gone. *(re-iss.1970 on 'Valient')*
Feb 65. (7") **YOU'RE MY GIRL. / DON'T LET THE WHOLE WORLD KNOW**
Apr 65. (7") **THAT'LL BE THE DAY. / GIVE ME A SWEETHEART** 30
May 65. (lp) **ROCK'N'SOUL**
– That'll be the day / So fine / Maybelline / Dancing in the street / Kansas City / I got a woman / Love hurts / Slippin' and slidin' / Susie Q / Hound dog / I'm gonna move to the out-skirtsd of town / Lonely weekends. *(re-iss.May85 on 'Rollercoaster')*
May 65. (7") **THE PRICE OF LOVE. / IT ONLY COSTS A DIME** 2
Aug 65. (7") **I'LL NEVER GET OVER YOU. / FOLLOW ME** 35
Sep 65. (lp) **BEAT AND SOUL**
– Love is strange / Money / What am I living for / High heel sneakers / C.C. rider / Lonely avenue / Man with money / People get ready / My babe / Walking the dog / I almost lost my mind / The girl can't help it. *(re-iss.Dec85)*
Oct 65. (7") **LOVE IS STRANGE. / MAN WITH MONEY** 11
Mar 66. (7") **THE POWER OF LOVE. / LEAVE MY GIRL ALONE**
Mar 66. (lp) **IN OUR IMAGE**
– Leave my girl alone / Chained to a memory / I'll never get over you / The doll house is empty / Glitter and gold / The power of love / The price of love / It's all over / I used to love you / Lonely Kravezit / June is as cold as December / It only cost a dime. *(re-iss.May85 on 'Rollercoaster')*
Mar 66. (7") **I USED TO LOVE YOU. / IT'S ALL OVER** -
1966. (7") **THE DOLL HOUSE IS EMPTY. / LONELY KRAVEZIT** -
Jul 66. (lp) **TWO YANKS IN ENGLAND**
– Somebody help me / So lonely / Kiss your man goodbye / Signs that will never change / Like everytime before / Pretty flamingo / I've been wrong before / Have you ever loved somebody / The collector / Don't run and hide / Fifi the flea / Hard, hard year. *(re-iss.Feb89 on 'Edsel')*
Aug 66. (7") **SOMEBODY HELP ME. / HARD, HARD YEAR** -
Aug 66. (7") **I'VE BEEN WRONG BEFORE. / HARD, HARD YEAR** -
1966. (7") **FIFI THE FLEA (by "DON"). / LIKE EVERYTIME BEFORE (by "PHIL")** -
1967. (7") **OH BOY. / GOOD GOLLY MISS MOLLY**
Feb 67. (lp) **THE HIT SOUND OF THE EVERLY BROTHERS**
– Blueberry Hill / Movin' on / Devil's child / Trains and boats and planes / Sea of heartbreak / Oh boy / (I'd be a) Legend in my time / Let's go get stoned / Sticks and stones / The house of the rising Sun / She never smiles anymore / Good golly Miss Molly.
1967. (7") **THE DEVIL'S CHILD. / SHE NEVER SMILES ANYMORE** -
Jun 67. (7") **BOWLING GREEN. / I DON'T WANT TO LOVE YOU** 40
Sep 67. (7") **MARY JANE. / TALKING TO THE FLOWERS**
Nov 67. (7") **LOVE OF THE COMMON PEOPLE. / A VOICE WITHIN**
Apr 68. (7") **IT'S MY TIME. / EMPTY BOXES** 39
Aug 68. (7") **MILK TRAIN. / LORD OF THE MANOR**
Nov 68. (lp) **ROOTS** (new & re-old material)
– Introduction: The Everly family / Mama tried / Less of me / T for Texas / I wonder if I care as much / Ventura boulevard / Shady grove / Illinois / Living too close to the ground / You done me wrong / Turn around / Sing me back home / Montage : The Everly family-Shady grove-Kentucky. *(re-iss.Sep86) (cd-iss.May95 on 'Warners')*
Apr 69. (7") **I'M ON MY WAY HOME AGAIN. / THE CUCKOO BIRD** -
1969. (7") **T – FOR TEARS. / I WONDER IF I CARE AS MUCH** -
1969. (7") **CAROLINA ON MY MIND. / MY LITTLE YELLOW BIRD** -
Feb 70. (d-lp) **THE EVERLY BROTHERS SHOW (live at The Grand Hotel)**
– Mama tried / Kentucky / Bowling green / Till I kissed you / Wake up little Susie / Cathy's clown / Bird dog / Maybelline / Lord of the manor / I wonder if I care as much / Love is strange / Let it be me / Give peace a chance / Rock and roll music / The end / Aquarius / If I were a carpenter / The price of love / The thrill is gone / Games people play / Baby what you want me to do / All I have to do is dream / Walk right back / Susie Q / Hey Jude.
Oct 70. (7") **YVES. / HUMAN RACE** Feb 70

RCA Victor RCA Victor

1972. (7") **RIDIN' HIGH. / STORIES WE COULD TELL**
Jun 72. (lp)(c) **STORIES WE COULD TELL**
– All we really want to do / Breakdown / Green river / Mandolin wind / Up in Mabel's room / Del Rio Dan / Ridin' high / Brand new Tennessee waltz / Stories we can tell / Christmas eve can kill you / I'm tired of singing my songs in Las Vegas.
1972. (7") **PARADISE. / LAY IT DOWN** -
1973. (7") **NOT FADE AWAY. / LADIES LOVE OUTLAWS** -
1973. (7") **NOT FADE AWAY. / LAY IT DOWN** -
Feb 73. (lp)(c) **PASS THE CHICKEN AND LISTEN**
– Lay it down / Husbands and wives / Woman don't you try to tie me down / Sweet memories / Ladies love outlaws / Not fade away / Watchin' it go / Paradise / Somebody nobody knows / Good-hearted woman / A nickel for the fiddler / Rocky top. *(re-iss.+cdJul91 on 'Edsel')*

— Announced their break-up at a 14 Jul'73 concert. PHIL went solo later.

DON EVERLY

with one lp under his belt, also continued with solo career.

A & M Ode

1971. (7") **TUMBLIN' TUMBLEWEEDS. / ONLY ME** -
1971. (lp)(c) **DON EVERLY**
– Don't drink the water / Eyes of Asia / February 15th / My baby / My friend / Omaha / Safari / Sweet dreams of you / Tumbling tumbleweed / Thinking it over / When I stop dreaming.

— His next album featured group HEADS, HANDS & FEET
Aug 74. (7") **WARMIN' UP THE BAND. / EVELYN SWING**
Oct 74. (lp)(c) **SUNSET TOWERS**
– Melody train / Jack Daniels Old No.7 / Warmin' up the band / Helpless when you're gone / Did it rain / Brand new rock and roll band / Takin' shots / The way you remain / Evelyn swing / Southern California.

D.J.M. Hickory

Jul 76. (7") **YESTERDAY JUST PASSED MY WAY AGAIN. / NEVER LIKE THIS**
Mar 77. (7") **SO SAD TO WATCH GOOD LOVE GO BAD. / LOVE AT LAST SIGHT** -
1976. (7") **OH, I'D LIKE TO GO AWAY. / LOVE AT LAST SIGHT** -
1976. (7") **DEEP WATER. / SINCE YOU BROKE MY HEART** -
Mar 77. (lp)(c) **BROTHER JUKE BOX**
– Brother juke box / Love at last sight / So sad to watch good love go bad / Lettin' go / Since you broke my heart / Never like this / Deep water / Yesterday just passed my way again / Oh I'd like to go away / Oh what a feeling / Turn the memories back again. *(re-iss.1983 + May88 on 'Sundown') (cd-iss.Aug94 on 'Sundown')*
Mar 78. (7") **BROTHER JUKE BOX. / OH, WHAT A FEELING**

Polydor Polydor

Aug 81. (7") **LET'S PUT OUR HEARTS TOGETHER. / SO SAD TO WATCH GOOD LOVE GO BAD**

Sundown Sundown

Nov 85. (7") **BROTHER JUKE BOX. / NEVER LIKE THIS**

PHIL EVERLY

solo with **JAMES BURTON / WARREN ZEVON, JIM HORN and EARL PALMER**

R.C.A. R.C.A.

Sep 73. (7") **THE AIR THAT I BREATHE. / GOD BLESS OLD LADIES**
Sep 73. (lp)(c) **STAR SPANGLED SPRINGER**
– The air that I breathe / Sweet grass country / God bless older ladies (for they made

rock and roll) / It pleases me to please you / Lady Anne / Red, white and blue / Our song / Poisonberry pie / La divorce / Snowflake bombadier.

Pye Pye

1974. (7") **OLD KENTUCKY RIVER. / SUMMERSHINE** [-] [ ]
1974. (7") **NEW OLD SONG. / BETTER THAN NOW** [-] [ ]
Aug 74. (7") **INVISIBLE MAN. / IT'S TRUE** [ ] [-]
Nov 74. (7") **SWEET MUSIC. / GOODBYE LINE** [ ] [-]
Jan 75. (lp)(c) **THERE'S NOTHING TOO GOOD FOR MY BABY** [ ] [ ]

– Sweet music / Goodbye line / Feather bed / Summershine / Too blue / There's nothing too good for my baby / Invisible man / Caroline / We're running out / It's true / New old song. *(US title – 'PHIL'S DINER')*

Oct 75. (7") **BETTER THAN NOW. / YOU AND I ARE A SONG** [ ] [ ]
Nov 75. (lp)(c) **MYSTIC LINE** [ ] [ ]

– Patiently / Lion and the lamb / Mystic line / Jammy butterfly / You and I are a song / Worlds in your eyes / Better than now / When will I be loved / Back when the bands played in ragtime / Friends.

1976. (7") **WORLDS IN YOUR EYES. / BACK WHEN THE BAND PLAYED IN RAGTIME** [-] [ ]
1976 (7") **GOD BLESS OLDER LADIES. / SWEET GRASS COUNTRY** [-] [ ]

not issued Elektra

1979. (lp)(c) **LIVING ALONE** [-] [ ]

– It was too late for the party / Ich bin dein (I am yours) / You broke it / Living alone / Buy me a beer / California gold / Love will pull us through / I just don't feel like dancing / Charleston guitar / The fall of '59.

—— guested on SANDRA LOCKE single 'Don't Say You Don't Love Me No More'

1979 (7") **LIVING ALONE. / I JUST DON'T FEEL LIKE DANCING** [-] [ ]
1979. (7") **YOU BROKE IT. / BUT ME A BEER** [-] [ ]

Epic Curb

Mar 81. (7") **DARE TO DREAM AGAIN. / LONELY DAYS LONELY NIGHTS** [ ] [ ]
1981. (7") **SWEET SOUTHERN LOVE. / IN YOUR EYES** [-] [ ]

Capitol Capitol

Oct 82. (7") **LOUISE. / SWEET SUZANNE** [47] [ ]
Jan 83. (7") **SHE MEANS NOTHING TO ME. ("PHIL EVERLY and CLIFF RICHARD") / A WOMAN AND A MAN** [9] [-]
1983. (7") **WHO'S GONNA KEEP ME WARM. / ONE WAY LOVE ON A TWO WAY STREET)** [-] [ ]
Apr 83. (lp)(c) **PHIL EVERLY** [61] [ ]

– She means nothing to me / I'll mend your broken heart / God bless older ladies / Sweet pretender / Never gonna dream again / Better than now / A woman and a man / Louise / When I'm dead and gone / Sweet Suzanne / Oh baby oh (you're the star). *(re-iss.Aug87 as 'LOUISE', + cd-iss.Jan88 on 'Magnum Force')(cd-iss.Oct93 & Feb95 on 'B.G.O.')*

Apr 83. (7") **SWEET PRETENDER. / BETTER THAN NOW** [ ] [ ]
Jun 83. (7") **OH BABY OH (YOU'RE THE STAR). / GOD BLESS OLDER LADIES** [ ] [-]

EVERLY BROTHERS

re-united.

Impression Passport

Nov 83. (7"ep)(12"ep) **DEVOTED TO YOU / EBONY EYES. / LOVE HURTS / THE PRICE OF LOVE (all live)** [ ] [ ]
Dec 83. (lp)(c) **EVERLY BROTHERS' REUNION CONCERT** (Royal Albert Hall – Sep'83) [47] [ ]

– The price of love / Walk right back / Claudette / Crying in the rain / Love is strange / Live medley / Take a message to mary / Maybe tomorrow / I wonder if I care as much / When will I be loved / Bird dog / Live medley; Devoted to you – Ebony eyes – Love hurts / Barbara Allen / Lightning Express / Put my little shoes away / Long time gone / Down in the willow garden / Step it up and go / Cathy's clown / Gone, gone, gone / You send me / So sad (to watch good love go bad) / Blues (stay away from me) / Bye bye love / All I have to do is dream / Wake up little Susie / ('Til) I kissed you / Temptation / Be-bop-a-lula / Lucille / Let it be me / Good golly Miss Molly. *(cd-iss.May86 on 'Mercury') (re-iss.cd in 2 parts Jul95 on 'Charly') (re-iss.cd/c Sep95 on 'Emporio')*

Mercury Mercury

Aug 84. (7") **ON THE WINGS OF A NIGHTINGALE. / ASLEEP** [41] [50]
Oct 84. (lp)(c)(cd) **THE EVERLY BROTHERS** [36] [38]

– Danger, danger / The first in line / On the wings of a nightingale / The story of me / I'm taking my time / Lay lady lay / Following the Sun / You make it seem so easy / More than I can handle / Asleep. *(US title 'EB 84')(UK re-iss.Jun87)*

Nov 84. (7") **THE STORY OF ME. / FOLLOWING THE SUN** [ ] [ ]
Nov 84. (7") **THE STORY OF ME. / THE FIRST IN LINE** [-] [ ]
Oct 85. (7") **AMANDA RUTH. / BORN YESTERDAY** [ ] [ ]
Oct 85. (7") **BORN YESTERDAY. / DON'T SAY GOODNIGHT** [-] [ ]
Nov 85. (lp)(c)(cd) **BORN YESTERDAY** [ ] [ ]

– Amanda Ruth / I know love / Born yesterday / These shoes / Arms of Mary / That uncertain feeling / Thinkin' about you / Why worry / Abandoned love / Don't say goodnight / Always drive a Cadillac. (c-cd+=) – You send me.

Feb 86. (7') **I KNOW LOVE. / THESE SHOES** [-] [ ]
(Below 'A'side featured The BEACH BOYS).
Nov 88. (7") **DON'T WORRY BABY. / BORN YESTERDAY** [ ] [-]
(cd-s+=) – On the wings of a nightingale.
Apr 89. (lp)(c)(cd) **SOME HEARTS** [ ] [ ] Nov 88
Apr 89. (7") **DON'T WORRY BABY. / RIDE THE WIND** [-] [ ]

– Some hearts / Ride the wind / Can't get it over / Brown eyes / Julianne / Don't worry baby / Be my love again / Angel of the darkness / Three bands of steel / Any single – solitary heart.

– compilations, others, etc. –

Note; All below 'London' were released on US 'Cadence'.

1958. London; (7"ep) **THE EVERLY BROTHERS** [ ] [ ]
1958. London; (7"ep) **THE EVERLY BROTHERS No.2** [ ] [ ]
1958. London; (7"ep) **THE EVERLY BROTHERS No.3** [ ] [ ]
Jan 59. London; (7"ep) **SONGS OUR DADDY TAUGHT US (Part 1)** [ ] [ ]
Feb 59. London; (7"ep) **SONGS OUR DADDY TAUGHT US (Part 2)** [ ] [ ]
Mar 59. London; (7"ep) **SONGS OUR DADDY TAUGHT US (Part 3)** [ ] [ ]
1959. London; (7"ep) **THE EVERLY BROTHERS No.4** [ ] [ ]
1960. London; (7"ep) **THE EVERLY BROTHERS No.5** [ ] [ ]
Jul 60. London; (7") **WHEN WILL I BE LOVED. / BE-BOP-A-LULA** [4] [8] / [74] Jun 60
(re-iss.Oct80 on 'Old Gold')
1960. London; (m-lp) **ROCKIN' WITH THE EVERLY BROTHERS** [-] [ ]
Oct 60. London; (lp) **THE FABULOUS STYLE OF THE EVERLY BROTHERS** [4] [23] Aug 60
(re-iss.Jan86 on 'Rhino') (cd-iss.Dec91 on 'Ace')
Nov 60. Cadence; (7") **LIKE STRANGERS. / BRAND NEW HEARTACHE** [-] [22]
Dec 60. London; (7") **LIKE STRANGERS. / LEAVE MY WOMAN ALONE** [11] [-]
1961. London; (7"ep) **THE EVERLY BROTHERS No.6** [ ] [ ]
Oct 62. Cadence; (7") **I'M HERE TO GET MY BABY OUT OF JAIL. / LIGHTNING EXPRESS** [-] [76]
1961. Warners; (7"ep) **ESPECIALLY FOR YOU** [ ] [ ]
1961. Warners; (7"ep) **FOR EVERLY YOURS** [ ] [-]
1962. Warners; (7"ep) **IT'S EVERLY TIME!** [ ] [-]
1962. Warners; (7"ep) **A DATE WITH THE EVERLY BROTHERS Vol.1** [ ] [-]
1962. Warners; (7"ep) **A DATE WITH THE EVERLY BROTHERS Vol.2** [ ] [-]
1962. Warners; (7"ep) **INSTANT PARTY (Vol.1)** [ ] [-]
1962. Warners; (7"ep) **INSTANT PARTY (Vol.2)** [ ] [-]
1963. Warners; (7"ep) **BOTH SIDES OF AN EVENING – FOR DANCING** [ ] [ ]
1963. Warners; (7"ep) **BOTH SIDES OF AN EVENING – FOR DREAMING** [ ] [-]
1964. Warners; (7"ep) **... SING GREAT COUNTRY HITS Vol.1** [ ] [-]
1964. Warners; (7"ep) **... SING GREAT COUNTRY HITS Vol.2** [ ] [-]
1964. Warners; (7"ep) **... SING GREAT COUNTRY HITS Vol.4** [ ] [-]
1964. Warners; (7"ep) **BOTH SIDES OF AN EVENING – FOR FUN** [ ] [-]
1965. Warners; (7"ep) **THE PRICE OF LOVE** [ ] [-]
1965. Warners; (7"ep) **ROCK'N'SOUL Vol.1** [ ] [-]
1965. Warners; (7"ep) **ROCK'N'SOUL Vol.2** [ ] [-]
1966. Warners; (7"ep) **LOVE IS STRANGE** [ ] [-]
1966. Warners; (7"ep) **PEOPLE GET READY** [ ] [-]
1966. Warners; (7"ep) **WHAT AM I LIVING FOR** [ ] [-]
1967. Warners; (7"ep) **LEAVE MY GIRL ALONE** [ ] [-]
1967. Warners; (7"ep) **SOMEBODY HELP ME** [ ] [-]
1967. Warners; (7") **CATHY'S CLOWN. / WALK RIGHT BACK** [ ] [ ]
(re-iss.Jul81)
1974. Warners; (7") **CATHY'S CLOWN. / CRYIN' IN THE RAIN** [ ] [ ]
1974. Warners; (7") **WAKE UP LITTLE SUSIE. / BYE BYE LOVE** [ ] [ ]
1975. Warners; (7") **CATHY'S CLOWN. / ALL I HAVE TO IS DREAM** [ ] [ ]
Oct 75. Warners; (lp)(c) **WALK RIGHT BACK WITH THE EVERLYS** [10] [ ]
1976. Warners; (7") **WALK RIGHT BACK. / FERRIS WHEEL** [ ] [ ]
Mar 76. Warners; (7") **EBONY EYES. / WAKE UP LITTLE SUSIE** [ ] [ ]
Mar 77. Warners; (lp)(c) **LIVING LEGENDS** ('Cadence' hits) [12] [ ]
Sep 77. Warners; (lp)(c) **THE NEW ALBUM** (from vaults) [ ] [ ]
Sep 77. Warners; (7") **SILENT TREATMENT. / DANCING ON MY FEET** [ ] [ ]
Nov 83. Warners; (lp)(c) **THE BEST OF THE EVERLY BROTHERS** [ ] [ ]
May 93. Warners; (cd)(c) **THE GOLDEN YEARS OF THE EVERLY BROTHERS – THEIR 24 GREATEST HITS** [26] [ ]
Sep 70. C.B.S./ US= Barnaby; (d-lp) **THE EVERLY BROTHERS ORIGINAL GREATEST HITS** [7] [ ]
Dec 70. C.B.S./ US= Barnaby; (lp) **END OF AN ERA** [ ] [ ]
Jun 75. Janus; (7") **ALL I HAVE TO DO IS DREAM. / WAKE UP LITTLE SUSIE** [-] [ ]
Dec 82. K-Tel; (lp)(c) **LOVE HURTS** [31] [-]
(re-iss.Sep84)
Jul 82. Revival; (7") **YOU'RE JUST WHAT I WAS LOOKING FOR. / WHATEVER HAPPENED TO JUDY** [ ] [-]
Jul 80. Old Gold; (14x7"box) **(14 singles boxed)** [ ] [-]
Jul 82. Old Gold; (7") **LIKE STRANGERS. / SHOULD WE TELL HIM** [ ] [-]
Jul 82. Old Gold; (7") **CATHY'S CLOWN. / TEMPTATION** [ ] [-]
Jul 82. Old Gold; (7") **THE PRICE OF LOVE. / CRYING IN THE RAIN** [ ] [-]
Nov 87. Old Gold; (7") **TILL I KISSED YOU. / BIRD DOG** [ ] [-]
Feb 89. Old Gold; (cd-ep) **ALL I HAVE TO DO IS DREAM / BYE BYE LOVE / WAKE UP LITTLE SUSIE** [ ] [-]
Mar 90. Old Gold; (7") **WALK RIGHT BACK. / EBONY EYES** [ ] [-]
Sep 83. Scoop; (7"ep)(c-ep) **6 TRACK HITS** [ ] [-]

– All I have to do is dream / Wake up little Susie / Bye bye love / Bird dog / Problems / Till I kissed you.

Sep 84. Magnum Force; (lp) **NICE GUYS** [ ] [-]
Jul 87. Magnum Force; (lp)(c) **SUSIE Q** [ ] [-]
(cd-iss.Jun88)
Feb 85. Hallmark; (lp)(c) **GREATEST HITS Vol.1** [ ] [-]
May 85. Hallmark; (lp)(c) **GREATEST HITS Vol.2** [ ] [-]
Oct 88. Hallmark; (lp)(c)(cd) **THE VERY BEST OF THE EVERLY BROTHERS** [ ] [-]

– Bye bye love / This little girl of mine / Should we tell him / Claudette / Devoted to you / Problems / Love of my life / Poor Jenny / Since you broke my heart / Let it be me / Wake up little Susie / I wonder if I care as much / Maybe tomorrow / All I have to do is dream / Bird dog / Brand new heartache / Take a message to Mary / ('Til) I kissed you / When will I be loved / Like strangers.

(cd-iss. 'Pickwick')

1988. Neon; (cd) **GREATEST HITS** -
Feb 83. Ace-Charly; (lp) **RIP IT UP** -
Oct 84. Ace-Charly; (lp) **PURE HARMONY** -
Nov 85. Ace-Charly; (lp) **IN THE STUDIO** -
Feb 86. Ace-Charly; (lp)(c) **ROCKIN' IN HARMONY** -
May 86. Ace-Charly; (lp)(c)(cd) **GREAT RECORDINGS** -
1989. Ace-Charly; (d-c) **RIP IT UP / PURE HARMONY** -
Sep 89. Ace-Charly; (lp) **HIDDEN GEMS** -
May 89. Ace-Charly; (lp) **THE WARNER BROTHERS YEARS Vol.1** -
Oct 89. Ace; (lp) **THE WARNER BROTHERS YEARS Vol.2** -
Apr 90. Ace; (cd) **THE EVERLY BROTHERS (debut) / THE FABULOUS STYLE OF ...** -
Jan 85. V.F.M.; (c) **BYE BYE LOVE** -
(re-iss.+cd.Sep87 on 'Entertainers')
Dec 85. Astan; (pic-lp) **GREATEST HITS** -
Jan 86. Rhino; (lp) **ALL THEY HAVE TO DO IS DREAM** -
Jan 87. Muskateer; (lp) **IN GERMANY & ITALY (live)** -
May 86. Castle; (lp)(c) **THE COLLECTION** -
(cd-iss.1988)
1986. Creole; (cd) **CADENCE CLASSICS – 20 GREATEST HITS** -
May 88. (cd-ep) **LIL' BIT OF GOLD** -
– Wake up little Susie / Bird dog / Let it be me / All I have to do is dream.
Jul 86. Spectrum; (cd) **20 GREATEST HITS** -
Jul 86. Spectrum; (cd) **20 GOLDEN LOVE SONGS** -
May 93. Spectrum; (cd)(c) **DREAMING** -
May 88. Mercury; (d-lp) **EB 84 / BORN YESTERDAY** -
Feb 90. Mainline; (cd)(c)(lp) **SO MANY YEARS** -
Jun 91. Sequel; (cd) **THE LONDON SESSIONS (PHIL EVERLY)** -
Apr 92. Bear Family; (3xcd-box) **CLASSIC EVERLY BROTHERS** -
Apr 93. Sony Europe; (cd)(c) **THE RARE SOLO CLASSICS** -
Jun 93. Sequel; (3xcd) **THE PERFECT HARMONY** -
Dec 93. Disky; (cd) **GOLD: GREATEST HITS** -
Jan 94. Disky; (cd) **THE BEST OF THE EVERLY BROTHERS** -
Oct 94. Woodford; (cd) **SIMPLY THE BEST** -
Dec 94. Ace; (cd) **THE ORIGINAL BRITISH HIT SINGLES** -
Feb 95. More Music; (cd)(c) **RE-UNION AT THE ROYAL ALBERT HALL (live)** -
Apr 95. Mercury; (cd) **GREATEST HITS** -
May 95. Spectrum; (cd)(c) **WILL I BE LOVED? (PHIL EVERLY)** -
May 95. Pickwick; (cd)(c) **THE BEST OF THE EVERLY BROTHERS – RARE SOLO CLASSICS** -
Jul 95. Music Club; (cd) **THE BEST OF THE EVERLY BROTHERS** -

EVER READY CALL (see under ⇒ BYRDS)

EVERYTHING BUT THE GIRL

Formed: Hull, England ... mid 1982 by ex-Hull university graduates TRACEY THORN and BEN WATT. They had both recorded solo for indie label 'Cherry Red', before venturing in 1983 onto 'WEA' subsidiary 'Blanco Y Negro' run by Geoff Travis & Mike Alway. They immediately struck gold, with 'EACH AND EVERY ONE', making the UK Top 30. It's parent album 'EDEN', was their first of 5 to hit or nearly hit, the UK Top 20. These were obviously helped to do so, by the large experienced ensemble of musicians the duo employed. • **Style:** Publicly shy melancholy duo, who blended together light jazz, folk and agitpop. Their influences ranged from COLE PORTER to the modern day JOHN MARTYN. • **Songwriters:** Most written by duo or individually, except the covers; NIGHT AND DAY (Cole Porter) / I DON'T WANT TO TALK ABOUT IT (c.Danny Whitten, of Crazy Horse; Rod Stewart hit) / KID (Pretenders) / ALFIE (hit; Cilla Black) / DOWNTOWN TRAIN (Tom Waits) / I FALL TO PIECES (Patsy Cline) / TAKE ME (Womack And Womack) / ON MY MIND (?) / NO PLACE LIKE HOME (from 'Wizard Of Oz') / LOVE IS STRANGE (Everly Brothers) / TOUGHER THAN THE REST (Bruce Springsteen) / TIME AFTER TIME (Cyndi Lauper) / ALISON (Elvis Costello) / MY HEAD IS MY ONLY HOUSE UNLESS IT RAINS (Captain Beefheart) / THESE DAYS (Jackson Browne). TRACEY THORN solo:- FEMME FATALE (Velvet Underground). • **Trivia:** EVERYTHING BUT THE GIRL was the name of a local second hand store in Hull.

Recommended: HOME MOVIES (*7)

BEN WATT

solo releases

Cherry Red / not issued

Jun 81. (7") **CAN'T. / AUBADE / TOWER OF SILENCE** -
Apr 82. (12"ep) **SUMMER INTO WINTER (by "BEN WATT & ROBERT WYATT")** -
– Walter and John / Aquamarine / Slipping slowly / Another conversation with myself / A girl in winter.
Feb 83. (7") **SOME THINGS DON'T MATTER. / ON BOX HILL** -
Feb 83. (lp)(c) **NORTH MARINE DRIVE** -
– On Boxhill / Some things don't matter / Lucky one / Empty bottles / North marine drive / Waiting like mad / Thirst for knowledge / Long time no sea / You're gonna make me lonesome when you go. *(cd-iss.Jul93)*

TRACEY THORN

solo releases

Cherry Red / not issued

Aug 82. (m-lp) **A DISTANT SHORE** -
– Smalltown girl / Simply couldn't care / Seascape / Femme fatale / Dreamy / Plain sailing / New opened eyes / Too happy. *(re-iss.+cd+c.Aug93)*
Dec 82. (7") **PLAIN SAILING. / GOODBYE JOE** -

EVERYTHING BUT THE GIRL

TRACEY THORN (b.26 Sep'62) – vocals, guitar (ex-MARINE GIRLS, ex-solo) / **BEN WATT** (b. 6 Dec'62) – vocals, guitar, piano (ex-solo artist)

Jun 82. (7"m)(12"m) **NIGHT AND DAY. / FEELING DIZZY / ON MY MIND** -
(re-iss.12"/cd-s/7"-Jul93)

— with **SIMON BOOTH** – guitar (of WORKING WEEK, ex-WEEKEND) / **CHUCHO MERCHAN** – double bass / **CHARLES HAYWARD** – drums / **BOSCO DE OLIVEIRA** – percuss / **PETER KING** – alto saxophone / **NIGEL NASH** – tenor saxophone / **DICK PEARCE** – flugel trumpet

Blanco Y Negro / Sire

Apr 84. (7") **EACH AND EVERY ONE. / LAUGH YOU OUT THE HOUSE** 28
(12"+=) – Never have been worse.
Jun 84. (lp)(c) **EDEN** 14
– Each and every one / Bittersweet / Tender blue / Another bridge / The spice of life / The dustbowl / Crabwalk / Even so / Frost and fire / Fascination / I must confess / Soft touch. *(US-title EVERYTHING BUT THE GIRL)*
Jul 84. (7") **MINE. / EASY AS SIN** 58
(12"+=) – Gun coloured love.
Sep 84. (7") **NATIVE LAND. / RIVER BED DRY** 73
(12"+=) – Don't you go.

— now with **NEIL SCOTT** – guitars / **PHIL MOXHAM** – bass (ex-The GIST ex-YOUNG MARBLE GIANTS) / **JUNE MILES KINGSTON** – drums, vocals (ex-MODETTES, ex-FUN BOY THREE) and the wind section above

Mar 85. (7") **WHEN ALL'S WELL. / HEAVEN HELP ME**
(12"+=) – Kid.
Apr 85. (lp)(c)(cd) **LOVE NOT MONEY** 10
– When all's well / Uglt little dreams / Shoot me down / Are you trying to be funny / Sean / Ballad of the times / Anytown / This love (not for sale) / Trouble and strife / Angel. *(c+=)* – Heaven help me / Kid.
May 85. (7") **ANGEL. / PIGEONS IN THE ATTIC ROOM / CHARMLESS CALLOW WAYS**
(12"+=) – Easy as sin.

— now **BEN** and **TRACEY** used new session people below plus an orchestra **CARA TIVEY** – keyboards / **MICKEY HARRIS** – bass / **PETER KING** – alto sax / **ROBERT PETERS** – drums (ex-DANGEROUS GIRLS)

Jul 86 (7") **COME ON HOME. / DRAINING THE BAR** 44
(12"+=) – I fall to pieces / ('A' version).
Aug 86. (lp)(c)(cd) **BABY THE STARS SHINE BRIGHT** 22
– Come on home / Don't leave me behind / A country mile / Cross my heart / Don't let the teardrops rust your shining heart / Careless / Sugar Finney / Come hell or high water / Fighting talk / Little Hitler.
Sep 86. (7") **DON'T LEAVE ME BEHIND. / ALFIE** 72 -
(12"+=) – Where's the playground Suzie.
Feb 87. (7") **DON'T LEAVE ME BEHIND. / DRAINING THE BAR** -

— **BEN and TRACEY** now with **PETER KING / IAN FRASER** – tenor saxophone / **STEVE PEARCE** – bass / **JAMES McMILLAN** – trumpet / **DAMON BUTCHER** – piano, synth.

Feb 88. (7") **THESE EARLY DAYS. / DYED IN THE GRAIN** 75
(12"+=) – No place like home.
(12"+=) – ('A' demo) / Another day another dollar.
Mar 88. (lp)(c)(cd) **IDLEWILD** 13
– Love is here where I live / These early days / I always was your girl / Oxford Street / The night I heard Caruso sing / Goodbye Sunday / Shadow on a harvest moon / Blue moon rose / Tears all over town / Lonesome for a place I know / Apron strings. *(re-issJul88 +=)* – I don't wanna talk about it. *(re-iss.cd Nov94)*
Mar 88. (7") **I ALWAYS WAS YOUR GIRL. / HANG OUT THE FLAGS**
(12"+=) – Home from home.
(cd-s++=) – Almost blue.
Jun 88. (7") **I DON'T WANNA TALK ABOUT IT. / OXFORD STREET** 3
(12"+=) – ('A' instrumental) / Shadow on a harvest moon.
(cd-s+=) – Come on home.
Sep 88. (7") **LOVE IS WHERE I LIVE. / LIVING ON A HONEYCOMB**
(12"+=) – Each and every one / How about me.
Dec 88. (7")(12") **THESE EARLY DAYS (remix). / DYED IN THE GRAIN**
(cd-s+=) – No place like home / Another day another dollar.

— duo now with **OMAR HAKIM** – drums / **JOHN PATITUCCI** – bass / **LARRY WILLIAMS** – synth.prog., piano / **LENNY CASTRO** – percussion / **MICHAEL LANDAU** – guitar / etc.

Jan 90. (7")(c-s) **DRIVING. / ME AND BOBBY D** 54
(12"+=) – Easy as sin / I don't want to talk about it.
(cd-s+=) – ('A'version) / Downtown train.
Feb 90. (cd)(c)(lp) **THE LANGUAGE OF LIFE** 10 77
– Driving / Get back together / Meet me in the morning / Take me / Me and Bobby D / The language of life / Imagining America / My baby don't love me / Letting love go / The road. *(re-iss.cd Feb95)*
Mar 90. (7")(c-s) **TAKE ME. / DRIVING (acoustic)**
(12"+=)(cd-s+=) – ('A'remix).

— now with **GEOFF GISCOYNE and STEVE PEARCE** – bass / **DICK OATTS** – saxophone / **RALPH SALMINS** – drums, percussion

Aug 91. (7") **OLD FRIENDS. / APRON STRINGS (live)**
(cd-s+=) – Politics aside (instrumental) / Back to the old house (live).
Sep 91. (cd)(c)(lp) **WORLDWIDE** 29
– Old friends / Understanding / You lift me up / Talk to me like the sea / British

summertime / Twin cities / Frozen river / One place / Politics aside / Boxing and pop music / Feel alright. *(re-iss.cd Feb95)*

Nov 91. (7") **TWIN CITIES. / MEET ME IN THE MORNING (live)** [ ] [ ]
(12"+=)(cd-s+=) – ('A'acapella) / Mine.

Feb 92. (7"ep)(12"ep)(c-ep)(cd-ep) **THE COVERS EP** [13] [ ]
– Love is strange / Tougher than the rest / Time after time / Alison.

Apr 93. (7")(c-s) **THE ONLY LIVING BOY IN NEW YORK. / BIRDS / HORSES IN THE ROOM** [42] [ ]
(12"+=)(cd-s+=) – Gabriel / Horses in the room.

May 93. (cd)(c)(lp) **HOME MOVIES – THE BEST OF EVERYTHING BUT THE GIRL** (compilation) [5] [ ]
– Each and every one / Another bridge / Fascination / Native land / Come on home / Cross my heart / Apron strings / I don't want to talk about it / The night I heard Caruso sing / Driving / Imagining America / Understanding / Twin cities / Love is strange / I didn't know I was looking for love / The only living boy in New York.

Jun 93. (7"ep)(c-ep)(cd-ep) **I DIDN'T KNOW I WAS LOOKING FOR LOVE. / MY HEAD IS MY ONLY HOUSE UNLESS IT RAINS / POLITICAL SCIENCE / A PIECE OF MY MIND** [72] [ ]

— with **DAVE MATTACKS** – drums / **DANNY THOMPSON** – double bass (both ex-FAIRPORT CONVENTION) / **MARTIN DITCHAM** – percussion / (guests) **RICHARD THOMPSON** – guitar / **PETER KING** – alto sax / **KATE ST.JOHN** – cor anglais

May 94. (7"ep)(c-ep)(cd-ep) **THE ROLLERCOASTER EP** [65] [ ]
– Rollercoaster / Straight back to you / Lights of Te Touan / I didn't know I was looking for love (demo).

Jun 94. (cd)(c)(lp) **AMPLIFIED HEART** [20] [ ]
– Rollercoaster / Troubled mind / I don't understand anything / Walking to you / Get me / Missing / Two star / We walk the same line / 25th December / Disenchanted. *(re-iss.cd/c Nov95)*

Aug 94. (c-ep)(cd-ep) **MISSING / EACH & EVERY ONE (live) / I DON'T WANT TO TALK ABOUT IT (live) / THESE DAYS (live)** [69] [ ]
(12"ep)(cd-ep) – ('A'side) / ('A'-Chris & James remix) / ('A'-Little Joey remix) / ('A'-Ultramarine remix).

Aug 95. (c-ep)(cd-ep) **MISSING – THE LIVE EP (live)** [69] [ ]
– Missing / Each and every one (live) / I don't want to talk about it (live) / These days (live).
(12")(cd-s) THE REMIX EP – ('A'-Chris & James full on club mix) / ('A'-Little Joey remix) / ('A'-Ultramarine mix.

Oct 95. (c-s) **MISSING (Todd Terry club mix) / ('A'-Amplified Heart album mix)** [3] [14]
(cd-s+=) – ('A'-radio edit) / ('A'-Rockin' blue mix) / ('A'-Chris & James full on club mix) / ('A'-Todd Terry's piece).
(12") – (all above except 'B'side).

– compilations, etc. –

1991. W.E.A.; (cd) **ACOUSTIC** [-] [ ]

EXPLOITED

Formed: East Kilbride & Edinburgh, Scotland ... 1979 by BIG JOHN, WATTIE, GARY and DRU. Later moved to Edinburgh after issuing a number of 45's on own label, they moved to another indie 'Secret', where they surprisingly scored with 2 Top 20 albums between 81 + 82. • **Style:** Anti-establishment punk revivalists, whose 100 mph oi anthems and mohawk hair-dos, even made it onto Top Of The Pops. • **Songwriters:** Group compositions except; GOD SAVE THE QUEEN (Sex Pistols). • **Trivia:** . In 1992/93, BIG JOHN was the tour replacement for KURT COBAIN (Nirvana) when he went missing.

Recommended: TOTALLY EXPLOITED (*5).

WATTIE BUCHAN – vocals / **'BIG' JOHN DUNCAN** – guitar, vocals / **GARY McCORMICK** – bass, vocals (ex-JOSEF K) / **DRU STIX (GLEN CAMPBELL)** – drums, vocals

Exploited / not issued

Aug 80. (7") **ARMY LIFE. / FUCK THE MODS / CRASHED OUT** [ ] [-]
(re-iss.Apr81 on 'Secret')

Nov 80. (7") **EXPLOITED BARMY ARMY. / I BELIEVE IN ANARCHY / WHAT YOU WANNA DO** [ ] [-]
(re-iss.Apr81 on 'Secret')

1981. (7"ep) **EXTRACTS FROM EDINBURGH NIGHT CLUB (live)** [ ] [-]

Secret / not issued

Apr 81. (7") **DOGS OF WAR. / BLOWN TO BITS (live)** [63] [-]

May 81. (lp)(c) **PUNK'S NOT DEAD** [20] [-]
– Punk's not dead / Mucky pup / Exploited barmy army / S.P.G. / Cop cars / Free flight / Army life (Pt.2) / Dole q / Out of control / Ripper / Blown to bits / Son of a copper / Sex and violence / Royalty / I believe in anarchy. *(re-iss.Jun82) (re-iss.Feb89 on 'Link')*

Oct 81. (7") **DEAD CITIES. / HITLER'S IN THE CHARTS AGAIN / CLASS WAR** [31] [-]

Superville / not issued

Nov 81. (lp) **EXPLOITED LIVE-ON STAGE (live)** [52] [-]
– Cop cars / Crashed out / Dole Q / Dogs of war / Army life / Out of control / Ripper / F*** the mods / Exploited barmy army / Royalty / Sex & violence / Punks not dead / I believe in anarchy. *(cd-iss.Oct92 on Continium (re-iss.1987 on 'Dojo')*

Nov 81. (12"ep) **DON'T LET 'EM GRIND YOU DOWN** [70] [-]
(other side 2 songs by ANTI-PASTI)

Secret / not issued

Apr 82. (7") **ATTACK. / ALTERNATIVES** [50] [-]

Jun 82. (lp)(c) **TROOPS OF TOMORROW** [17] [-]
– Jimmy Boyle / Daily news / Disorder / Alternatives (remix) / Germs / Rapist / UK'82 / War / Troops of tomorrow / Sid Vicious was innocent / They won't stop / So tragic. *(re-iss.Feb89 on 'Link')*

Oct 82. (7") **COMPUTERS DON'T BLUNDER. / ADDICTION** [ ] [-]

— **BILLY DUNN**– guitar (ex-SKROTEEZ) repl. BIG JOHN who formed BLOOD UNCLES before joining GOODBYE MR MCKENZIE.

Blurg-Pax / not issued

Oct 83. (7") **RIVAL LEADERS. / ARMY STYLE / SINGALONGABUSHELL** [ ] [-]

Pax / Combat

Dec 83. (lp) **LET'S START A WAR (SAID MAGGIE ONE DAY)** [ ] [ ]
– Let's start a war / Insanity / Safe below / Eyes of the vulture / Should we can't we / Rival leaders (remix) / God saved the Queen / Psycho / Kidology / False hopes / Another day to go nowhere / Wankers. *(cd-iss.Mar94 on 'Dojo')*

— **DEPTFORD JOHN** repl. WAYNE / **MAD MICK** repl. EGGHEAD / **also with WATTIE, KARL, WILLIE BUCHAN** – drums / **CAPTAIN SCARLETT** – guitar
McCORMICK formed ZULU SYNDICATE, while STIX struggled with a drug addiction and then was sentenced to seven years for armed robbery.

Konnexion / not issued

Mar 85. (lp)(c) **HORROR EPICS** [ ] [-]
– Horror epics / Don't forget the chaos / Law and order / I hate you / No more idols / Maggie / Dangerous vision / Down below / Treat you like shit / Forty odd years ago / My life. *(cd-iss.Mar94 on 'Dojo')*

Rough Justice / not issued

Apr 86. (12"ep) **JESUS IS DEAD. / POLITICIANS / DRUG SQUAD / PRIVACY INVASION** [ ] [-]

Skunx / not issued

Jul 88. (12"ep) **PUNK'S ALIVE** [ ] [-]
– Alternative / Let's start a war / Horror epics / Troops of tomorrow / Dogs of war.

Rough Justice / not issued

Nov 88. (12") **WAR NOW. / UNITED CHAOS AND ANARCHY / SEXUAL FAVOURS** [ ] [-]

Aug 89. (lp)(c)(cd) **DEATH BEFORE DISHONOUR** [ ] [ ]
– Anti UK / Power struggle / Scaling the Derry wall / Barry Prossitt / Don't really care / No forgiveness / Death before dishonour / Adding to their fears / Police informer / Drive me insane / Pulling us down / Sexual favours. *(cd+=)* Drug squad man / Privacy invasion / Jesus is dead / Politicians / War now / United chaos and anarchy / Sexual favours (dub version).

— **WATTIE** – vocals / **SMEGS** – bass, vocals / **GOGS** – guitar / **TONY** – drums

Jan 91. (lp)(c) **THE MASSCRE** [ ] [-]
– The massacre / Sick bastard / Porno slut / Now I'm dead / Boys in blue / Dog soldier / Don't pay the poll tax / F . . . religion / About to die / Blown out of the city / Police shit / Stop the slaughter.

— new line-up mid-90's; **WATTIE** – vocals / **ARTHUR** – guitar / **BILLY** – bass / **WULLIE** – drums

Dec 95. (cd)(c)(lp) **BEAT THE BASTARDS** [ ] [-]
– (could have put back 'til Mar96)

– compilations etc. –

Dec 84. Dojo; (lp) **TOTALLY EXPLOITED** [ ] [-]
– Punk's not dead / Army life / F**k a mod / Barmy army / Dogs of war / Dead cities / Sex and violence / Yops / Daily news / Dole Q / Believe in anarchy / God save the Queen / Psycho / Blown to bits / Insanity / S.P.G. / Jimmy Boyle / U.S.A. / Attack / Rival leaders. *(re-iss.+cd.Apr86)*

Mar 94. Dojo; (cd) **LIVE IN JAPAN** [ ] [-]

Aug 91. Dojo; (cd) **LIVE ON STAGE 1981 / LIVE AT THE WHITEHOUSE 1985** [ ] [-]

Jan 85. Chaos; (c) **LIVE ON THE APOCALYPSE TOUR '81 (live)** [ ] [-]
(lp-iss.Feb87)

Feb 86. Suck; (lp) **LIVE AT THE WHITHOUSE (live)** [ ] [-]

Aug 86. Archive 4; (12"ep) **DEAD CITIES. / PUNK'S NOT DEAD / ARMY LIFE / EXPLOITED BARMY LIFE** [ ] [-]

Mar 87. Snow; (lp) **INNER CITY DECAY** [ ] [-]

Dec 87. Link; (lp) **LIVE AND LOUD (live)** [ ] [-]
(cd-iss.Oct93 on 'Anagram')

1989. Roadrunner; (d-c) **PUNK'S NOT DEAD / TROOPS OF TOMORROW** [ ] [-]

1989. Grand Slam; (lp) **LIVE, LEWD, LUST (live)** [-] [ ]

Dec 91. Streetlink; (cd) **THE SINGLES COLLECTION** [ ] [-]

Apr 94. Cleopatra; (cd) **THE SINGLES COLLECTION** [ ] [-]

EXPLORERS (see under ⇒ ROXY MUSIC)

EXTREME

Formed: Boston, Massachusetts, USA ... 1988 initially as The DREAM. Soon became EXTREME signing to A&M in 1987 through A&R man Bryan Huttenhower. Cracked charts early in '91, when single MORE THAN WORDS hit US No.1. In 1992, they paid tribute to recently deceased by playing QUEEN numbers at his benefit concert. • **Style:** Heavy ballad rock similiar to CHEAP TRICK with danceable appeal and image. Initially influenced by QUEEN and KISS. • **Songwriters:** BETTENCOURT (also producer) and CHERONE. Cover on record LOVE OF MY LIFE (Queen), STRUTTER (Kiss). • **Trivia:** Unlike others of their genre, they were pro-Christian.

Recommended: PORNOGRAFFITTI (*5) / III SIDES TO EVERY STORY (*6)

THE DREAM

GARY CHERONE (b.26 Jul'61, Malden, Massachusetts) – vocals / **NUNO BETTENCOURT** (b.20 Sep'66, Azores, Portugal) – guitar, keyboards, vocals / **PAT BADGER** (b.22 Jul'67, Boston) – bass, vocals / **PAUL GEARY** (b.24 Jul'61, Medford, Massachusetts) – drums, percussion

not issued / Toppe

1985. (lp) **THE DREAM** [-] [ ]

– Take your time / The tender touch / Makes no sense / All over again / Tipsy on the brink of love / You / Here is the love / Desires / Suzanne / Wonderful world / Last Monday.

EXTREME

		A&M	A&M	
Mar 89.	(lp)(c)(cd) **EXTREME**		80	
	– Little girls / Wind me up / Kid ego / Watching, waiting / Mutha (don't wanna go to school today) / Teachers pet / Big boys don't cry / Smoke signals / Flesh'n'blood / Rock a bye bye. *(cd+=)* – (1 track).			
Apr 89.	(7") **KID EGO. / FLESH'N'BLOOD**			
	(12"+=) – Smoke signals. *(US; b-side)*			
May 91.	(7")(c-s) **GET THE FUNK OUT. / LIL' JACK HORNY**	19		
	(12"+=) – Little girls (edit).			
	(12"pic-d+=) – Nice place to visit.			
	(cd-s+=) – Mutha (don't wanna go to school today).			
Jun 89.	(7") **TEACHER'S PET. / MUTHA (DON'T WANNA GO TO SCHOOL TODAY)**	-		
Feb 91.	(7") **MORE THAN WORDS. / GET THE FUNK OUT**	-	1	
May 91.	(cd)(c)(lp) **PORNOGRAFFITTI**	12	10	Aug 90
	– Decadence dance / Li'l Jack Horny / When I'm president / Get the funk out / More than words / Money (in God we trust) / It ('s a monster) / Pornograffitti / When I first missed you / Suzi (wants her all day what?) / He-man woman hater / Song for love. *(originally released UK Sep90)*			
Jul 91.	(7")(c-s) **MORE THAN WORDS. / NICE PLACE TO VISIT**	2	-	
	(cd-s+=) – Little girls.			
	(12"++=) – Mutha (don't wanna go to school today).			
Aug 91.	(7")(c-s) **HOLE HEARTED. / SUZI (WANTS HER ALL DAY WHAT?)**	-	4	
Sep 91.	(7") **DECADENCE DANCE. / MONEY (IN GOD WE TRUST)**	36		Mar 91
	(12"+=)(cd-s+=) – ('A'version) / More than words (acapella with congas).			
Nov 91.	(7")(c-s) **HOLE HEARTED. / GET THE FUNK OUT (remix)**	12	-	
	(12"box+=)(cd-s+=) – Suzi (wants her all day what?) / Sex'n'love.			
Apr 92.	(7")(12")(c-s)(cd-s) **SONG FOR LOVE. / LOVE OF MY LIFE (feat. BRIAN MAY)**	12		
Aug 92.	(7")(c-s) **REST IN PEACE. / PEACEMAKER DIE**	13	96	
	(etched-12"+=) – ('A'album version).			
	(cd-s++=) – Monica.			
Sep 92.	(cd)(c)(d-lp) **III SIDES TO EVERY STORY**	2	10	
	– Warheads / Rest in peace / Politicalamity / Color me blind / Cupid's dead / Peacemaker die/ / Seven Sundays / Tragic comic / Our father / Stop the world / God isn't dead/ / Everything under the Sun (I) Rise'n shine / (II) Am I ever gonna change / (III) Who cares?			
Nov 92.	(7")(c-s) **STOP THE WORLD. / CHRISTMAS TIME AGAIN**	22	95	
	(12"+=) – Warheads.			
	(cd-s++=) – Don't leave me alone.			
Jan 93.	(7"etched) **TRAGIC COMIC. / HOLEHEARTED (horn mix)**	15		
	(12"pic-d+=)(cd-s+=) – ('A'version) / Rise'n'shine (acoustic).			
	(cd-s) – ('A'side) / Help! / When I'm president (live).			
Feb 95.	(cd)(c) **WAITING FOR THE PUNCHLINE**	10	40	
	– There is no God / Cynical / Tell me something I don't know / Hip today / Naked / Midnight express / Leave me alone / No respect / Evilangelist / Shadow boxing / Unconditionally / Fair-weather friend.			
Mar 95.	(7"sha-pic-d) **HIP TODAY. / THERE IS NO GOD**	44		
	(cd-s+=) – Better off dead / Kid ego (live).			
	(cd-s+=) – Never been funked / When I'm president (live) / Strutter.			
	(12") – ('A'side) / Wind me up (1987 demo).			
Jul 95.	(c-s) **UNCONDITIONALLY /**			
	(cd-s) –			

– compilations, etc. –

Oct 93.	A&M; (cd) **EXTREME / PORNOGRAFFITTI**			

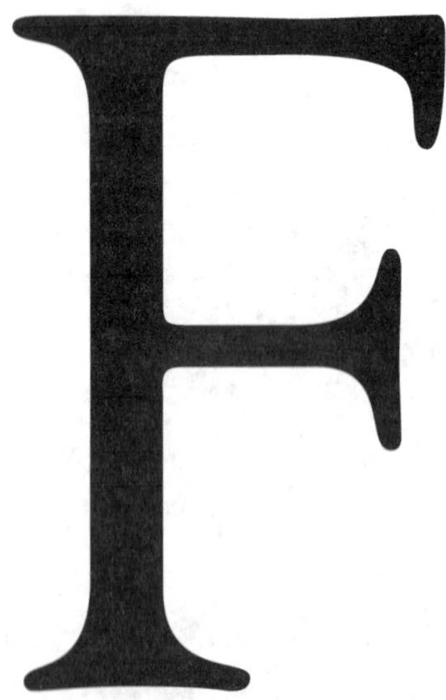

FABULOUS THUNDERBIRDS

Formed: Austin, Texas ... 1975 by JIMMIE VAUGHAN (brother of STEVIE RAY VAUGHAN), WILSON, FERGUSON and BUCK. In 1979, they signed to 'Chrysalis', and released eponymous debut. In 1986, the T-BIRDS as they are sometimes known, had Top 10 hit in the US with 'TUFF ENUFF'. • **Style:** Straight and basic R&B rock' n'roll outfit, who had excellent live reputation. • **Songwriters:** All written by WILSON or WILSON-FERGUSON-VAUGHAN, except THE CRAWL (Shuler-Victorica) / DIDDY WAH DIDDY (Bo Diddley) / SHE'S TUFF (... McCain) / YOU AIN'T NOTHIN' BUT FINE (Simien-Soileau) / MARKED DECK (... Wright) / MATHILDA (Knowry-Thiery) / FULL-TIME LOVER (Jones-Scott) / HOW DO YOU SPELL LOVE (Strickland-Patterson-Boxley) / SUGAR COATED LOVE (Rice Miller) / TIP ON IN (Moore-Holmes) / THE MONKEY (BB King) / MY BABE (Dixon-McDaniel) / ROLL, ROLL, ROLL (Shuler-Baker) / SCRATCH MY BACK (Slim Harpo) / CHERRY PINK & APPLE BLOSSOM WHITE (US+UK No.1 for; Perez Prado) / WRAP IT UP (Isaac Hayes) / HERE COMES THE NIGHT (Them; hit) / etc. • **Trivia:** NICK LOWE produced their 1982 album, before DAVE EDMUNDS took over.

Recommended: PORTFOLIO (*6).

KIM WILSON (b. 6 Jan'51) – vocals, harmonica / **JIMMIE VAUGHAN** (b.20 May'51, Dallas, Texas, USA) – guitar / **KEITH FERGUSON** (b.23 Jul'46, Houston, Texas) – bass / **MIKE BUCK** (b.17 Jun'52) – drums

Chrysalis Takoma

Oct 79. (lp) **THE FABULOUS THUNDERBIRDS** [ ] [ ]
– Wait on time / Scratch my back / Rich woman / Full time lover / Rocket rocket / She's tuff / Marked deck / Wakin' to my baby / Rock with me / C-boy's blues / Let me in. *(US title 'GIRLS GO WILD', re-iss.Jul89 on 'Epic')*

1980. (7"m) **YOU AIN'T NOTHING BUT JIVE. / SHE'S TUFF / SCRATCH MY BACK** [ ] [ ]

— **FRAN CHRISTINA** (b. 1 Feb'51, Westerley) – drums (ex-ROOMFUL OF BLUES, ex-ASLEEP AT THE WHEEL) repl. BUCK who joined FOUR BIG GUITARS FROM TEXAS (both drummers shared duties on below album)

Chrysalis Chrysalis

Apr 80. (7") **THE CRAWL. / LAST CALL FOR ALCOHOL** [ ] [ ]

May 80. (lp)(c) **WHAT'S THE WORD** [ ] [ ]
– Running shoes / You ain't seen nothin' but fine / The crawl / Low down woman / Extra jimmies / Sugar coated love / Jumping bad / Last call for alcohol / I'm a good man it / You learn to treat me right / Dirty work / That's enough of that stuff / Los Fabulous Thunderbirds.

Jun 80. (7") **SUGAR COATED LOVE. / LOS FABULOUS THUNDERBIRDS** [ ] [ ]

Mar 81. (lp)(c) **BUTT ROCKIN'** [ ] [ ]
– I believe I'm in love / One's too many / Me all your lovin / Roll roll roll / Cherry pink and apple blossom white / I'm sorry / I hear you knockin' / Tipon it / Mathilda / Tell me why / On orbit.

Apr 81. (7") **CHERRY PINK & APPLE BLOSSOM WHITE. / I BELIEVE I'M IN LOVE** [ ] [ ]

Oct 82. (lp)(c) **T-BIRD RHYTHM** [ ] [ ]
– Can't tear it up enuff / How do you spell love / Neighbour tend to your business / You're humbuggin' me / The monkey / My babe / Diddy wah diddy / Lover's crime / Poor boy / Gotta have some – just got some / Tell me (pretty baby).

— (dropped by 'Chrysalis' records, gigged constant for 3 years) **PRESTON HUBBARD** – bass (ex-ROOMFUL OF BLUES) repl. FERGUSON who joined FOUR BIG GUITARS FROM TEXAS / added **JUNIOR BRANTLEY** – keyboards later left '86 to join ROOMFUL OF BLUES (above 2 now joining **WILSON, VAUGHAN and CHRISTINA)**

Epic CBS Assoc.

Jun 86. (lp)(c) **TUFF ENUFF** (recorded '85) [ ] [13] Mar 86
– Tuff enuff / Tell me / Look at that, look at that / Two time for lovin' / Amnesia / Wrap it up / True love / Why get up / I don't care / Down at Antones.

Aug 86. (7") **WRAP IT UP. / TRUE LOVE** [-] [50]

Oct 86. (7")(12") **TUFF ENUFF. / LOOK AT THAT, LOOK AT THAT** [ ] [10] Apr 86

Nov 86. (7") **I DON'T CARE. / WHY GOT UP** [-] [ ]

Jul 87. (7") **STAND BACK. / IT TAKES A BIG MAN TO CRY** [ ] [76]

Aug 87. (lp)(c) **HOT NUMBER** [ ] [49] Jul 86
– Stand back / Hot number / Wasted tears / Love in common / How do you spell love / It comes to me naturally / Sofa circuit / Streets of gold / Don't bother tryin' to steal her love / It takes a big man to cry.

Nov 87. (7") **HOW DO YOU SPELL LOVE. / LOVE IN COMMON** [-] [ ]

Feb 88. (7") **WASTED TEARS. / IT COMES TO ME NATURALLY** [-] [ ]

Aug 88 (7") **POWERFUL STUFF** (b-side LITTLE RICHARD – 'Tutti Frutti') [-] [65]

— (above single from 'Cocktail' soundtrack on 'Elektra')

Apr 89. (7") **KNOCK YOURSLEF OUT. / EMERGENCY** [-] [ ]

Apr 89. (lp)(c)(cd) **POWERFUL STUFF** [ ] [ ]
– Rock this place / Knock yourself out / Mistake number 1 / One night stand / Emergency / Powerful stuff / Close together / Now loosen up baby / She's hot / Rainin' in my heart.

In 1990, JIMMIE joined brother STEVIE RAY as The VAUGHANS, and just previously featured in film 'Great Balls of Fire'.

— next featured new guitarists **DUKE ROBILARD & KID BANGAM** who repl. JIMMIE

Dec 91. (cd)(c)(lp) **WALK THAT WALK, TALK THAT TALK (live)** [ ] [ ]
– Twist of the knife / Ain't that a lot of love / Work together / Born to love you / Need somebody to love / Feelin' good / Sweet thang / Can't stop rockin' / When I get home / Paralyzed.

— line-up **KIM WILSON / FRAN CHRISTINA / GENE TAYLOR** – keyboards / **HARVEY BROOKS** – bass / **DANNY KORTCHMAR** – rhythm guitar / **DAVID GRISSOM + KID RAMOS** – guitar

Private Private

Sep 95. (cd) **ROLL OF THE DICE** [ ] [ ]
– Roll of the dice / Too many irons in the fire / How do I get you back? / Here comes the night / Takin' it too easy / I don't wanna be the one / Mean love / I can't win / Memory from Hell / Lookin' forward to lookin' back / Do as I say / Zip a dee do dah.

– compilations etc. –

Jul 87. Chrysalis; (d-lp)(c)(cd) **PORTFOLIO (1972-1982)** [ ] [ ]
– The crawl / She's tuff / Scratch my back / Tip on in / That's enough of that stuff / Full time lover / Sugar-coated love / Wait on time / Los Fabulosos Thunderbirds / I'm a good man if you treat me right / You ain't nothin' but fine / Walkin' to my baby / Marked deck / Learn to treat me right / I believe I'm in love / How do you spell love / Mathilda / One's too many / Dirty work / Can't tear it up enuff / Cherry pink and apple blossom white / The monkey / Give me all your lovin' / Diddy wah diddy / My babe / Roll roll roll.

Jul 93. B.G.O.; (cd) **THE FABULOUS THUNDERBIRDS / WHAT'S THE WORD** [ ] [-]

Aug 93. B.G.O.; (cd) **BUTT ROCKIN' / T-BIRD RHYTHM** [ ] [-]

Dec 93. Sony Europe; (cd) **HOT STUFF – GREATEST HITS** [ ] [-]

JIMMIE VAUGHAN

Epic Epic

May 94. (cd)(c) **STRANGE PLEASURE** [ ] [ ]

FACES (see under ⇒ SMALL FACES)

Donald FAGEN (see under ⇒ STEELY DAN)

FAIRFIELD PARLOUR (see under ⇒ KALEIDOSCOPE (UK)

FAIRGROUND ATTRACTION (see under ⇒ READER, Eddi)

FAIRPORT CONVENTION

Formed: Muswell Hill, London, England ... mid-1967 by THOMPSON, NICOL, HUTCHINGS, DYBLE and original drummer SHAUN FRATER. By the end of the year, FRATER was ousted by LAMBLE, and after a debut 45 for 'Polydor', they added IAN MATTHEWS. This new sextet with Joe Boyd on production, made 1968 eponymous debut lp, but after its release, JUDY left and was replaced by SANDY DENNY. They signed to 'Island' at the same time, and issued 2nd lp 'WHAT WE DID ON OUR HOLIDAYS', which was the last to feature MATTHEWS. He was soon at UK No.1 in 1970, with his SOUTHERN COMFORT version of 'Woodstock'. After the completion of their 3rd lp 'UNHALFBRICKING' and while on tour, tragedy struck on 14 May'69, when MARTIN LAMBLE was killed when their tour van crashed. With the help of their Top 30 French version 'SI TU DOIS PARTIR' of a Dylan song, their 3rd lp was the first of 4 consecutive UK Top 20 sellers. They continued with various personnel during the next 2 decades. • **Style:** Initially Britain's answer to US West Coast folk-rock, they moved into more traditional folk sounds in the 70's, which influenced many others to follow suit. • **Songwriters:** Mainly group compositions, with numerous renditions of traditional English folk tunes. Other writers:- IF I HAD A RIBBON BOW (Maxine Sullivan) / NOTTAMUN

TOWN + SHE MOVED THROUGH THE FAIR + loads more (trad.) / MILLION DOLLAR BASH + SI TU DOIS PARTIR (IF YOU GOTTA GO, GO NOW – Bob Dylan) / etc. The 1972 lp as The BUNCH, was full of covers. • **Trivia:** In 1970, their 'B'side 'SIR B.McKENZIE's DAUGHTER, etc . . . ' got into The Guinness Book Of Records, for having longest song title ever.

Recommended: THE HISTORY OF FAIRPORT CONVENTION (*8).

RICHARD THOMPSON (b. 3 Apr'49, London, England) – guitar, vocals / **SIMON NICOL** (b.13 Oct'50) – guitar, vocals / **JUDY DYBLE** (b. 1948) **vocals, autoharp / ASHLEY HUTCHINGS** (b.Jan'45) – bass / **MARTIN LAMBLE** (b.Aug'49) – drums repl. SHAUN FRATER

Polydor Cotillion

Nov 67. (7") **IF I HAD A RIBBON BOW. / IF (STOMP)**

— added **IAN MATTHEWS** (b.IAN McDONALD, 16 Jun'46, Scunthorpe, England) – vocals (ex-PYRAMIDS)

Jun 68. (lp) **FAIRPORT CONVENTION**
– Time will show the wiser / I don't know where I stand / If (stomp) / Decameron / Jack O'Diamonds / Portfolio / Chelsea morning / Sun shade / The lobster / It's alright ma, it's only witchcraft / One sure thing / M1 breakdown. *(re-iss.Jul75)*

— **SANDY DENNY** (b. 6 Jan'41) – vocals (ex-STRAWBS, etc) repl. JUDY who joined GILES, GILES and FRIPP

Island A&M

Nov 68. (7) **MEET ON THE LEDGE. / THROWAWAY STREET PUZZLE** [-]

Jan 69. (lp) **WHAT WE DID ON OUR HOLIDAYS** [-]
– Fotheringay / Mr. Lacey / Book song / The Lord is in his place / No man's land / I'll keep it with mine / Eastern rain / Mr. Lacey / Nottamun town / Tale in hard time / She moves through the fair / Meet on the ledge / End of a holiday. *(re-iss.May89 on 'Carthage') (cd-iss.Feb90)*

1969. (7") **FOTHERINGAY. / I'LL KEEP IT WITH MINE** [-]

— Trimmed to a quintet when IAN formed MATTHEW'S SOUTHERN COMFORT

Jul 69. (7") **SI TU DOIS PARTIR. / GENESIS HALL** [21]

Jul 69. (lp)(c) **UNHALFBRICKING** [12]
– Genesis Hall / Si tu dois partir / Autopsy / A sailor's life / Cajun woman / Who knows where the time goes / Percy's song / Million dollar bash. *(re-iss.May89 on 'Carthage') (cd-iss.Nov89)*

— **DAVE MATTACKS** (b.Mar'48, London) – drums repl. MARTIN LAMBLE who died 14 May'69 in tour bus crash / also added **DAVE SWARBRICK** (b. 5 Apr'41, London) – fiddle, vocals

Dec 69. (lp)(c) **LIEGE & LIEF** [17]
– Come all ye / Reynardine / Matty Groves / Farewell farewell / The deserter / The lark in the morning / Tamlin / Crazy man Michael / Rakish Paddy / Foxhunters jigs / Toss the feathers. *(re-iss.+cd.Sep86)*

— **DAVE PEGG** (b. 2 Nov'47, Birmingham, England) – bass, vocals (ex-UGLYS) repl HUTCHINGS who joined STEELEYE SPAN (**PEGG** now in quintet with **THOMPSON, NICOL, MATTACKS** and **SWARBRICK** because SANDY DENNY also departed to form FOTHERINGAY)

Jul 70. (lp)(c) **FULL HOUSE** [13]
– Walk awhile / Dirty linen / Sloth / Sir Patrick Spens / Flatback caper / Doctor of physick / Flowers of the forest. *(re-iss.Jul87 on 'Hannibal', + cd-iss.Jan92)*

Oct 70. (7") **NOW BE THANKFUL. / SIR B. McKENZIE'S DAUGHTER'S LAMENT FOR THE 77th MOUNTED LANCERS' RETREAT FROM THE STRAITS OF LOCH KOMBE IN THE YEAR OF OUR LORD 1727, ON THE LAIRD OF KINLEAKIE**

— Now a quartet when RICHARD THOMPSON left to go solo

Jun 71. (7") **THE JOURNEYMAN'S GRACE. / THE WORLD HAS SURELY LOST IT'S HEAD** [-]

Jun 71. (lp)(c) **ANGEL DELIGHT** [8]
– Lord Marlborough / Sir William Gower / Bridge over the River Ash / Wizard of the worldly game / The journeyman's grace / Angel delight / Banks of the sweet primroses / Instrumental medley:- Cuckoo's nest – Hardiman the fiddler – Papa stoor / The bonny black hare / Sickness and diseases. *(cd-iss.Mar93)*

Sep 71. (7") **JOHN LEE. / THE TIME IS NEAR**

Nov 71. (lp)(c) **BABBACOMBE LEE**
– John Babbacombe Lee: (John's reflection of his boyhood / His struggle with his family / Then the happiest period of his life, the Navy / Returning reluctantly to his job after being invalided out of the service / And the senseless murder of his mistress and the three attempts to hang him – Hanging song).

— **ROGER HILL** – guitar, vocals repl. NICOL who joined ALBION COUNTRY BAND / **TOM FARNAL** – drums repl. MATTACKS who joined ALBION COUNTRY BAND

— In Jun72, **DAVID REA** – guitar repl. ROGER HILL until Aug72 when **MATTACKS** returned to repl. FARNALL / **TREVOR LUCAS** (b.Dec'43, Melbourne, Australia) – guitar, vocals (ex-FOTHERINGAY) repl. REA / **adding JERRY DONAHUE** (b.24 Sep'46, New York City, USA) – guitar, vocals (ex-FOTHERINGAY)

Mar 73. (7") **ROSIE. / KNIGHTS OF THE ROAD**

Mar 73. (lp)(c) **ROSIE**
– Rosie / Matthew, Mark, Luke and John / Knights of the road / Peggy's pub / The plainsman / Hungarian rhapsodie / My girl / Me with you / The hen's march through the midden & the four-poster bed / Furs and feathers.

Oct 73. (lp)(c) **NINE**
– The Hexamshire lass / Polly on the shore / The brilliancy medley and Cherokee shuffle / To Althea from prison / Tokyo / Bring 'em down / Big William / Pleasure and pain / Possibly Parsons Green.

— added the returning **SANDY DENNY** – vocals (who had had solo career)

Oct 74. (lp)(c) **LIVE CONVENTION (live)** [-]
– Matty Groves / Rosie / Fiddlestix / John the gun / Something you got / Sloth / Dirty linen / Down in the flood / Sir B. MacKenzie . . .

— **PAUL WARREN** – drums repl. MATTACKS who rejoined ALBION DANCE BAND

— **BRUCE ROWLANDS** – drums (ex-RONNIE LANE, ex-JOE COCKER) repl. WARREN

Island Island

Jul 75. (7") **WHITE DRESS. / TEARS** [-]

Jul 75. (lp)(c) **RISING FOR THE MOON** [52]
– Rising for the Moon / Restless / White dress / Let it go / Stranger to himself / What is true? / Iron lion / Dawn / After halloween / Night-time girl / One more chance.

— FAIRPORT Basic trio **SWARBRICK, PEGG** and **ROWLANDS** recruited new folks **DAN AR BRAS** – guitar repl. SANDY DENNY who went solo again. (She later died of a brain haemorrage on 21 Apr78 after falling down her stairs) **BOB BRADY** – piano (ex-WIZZARD) repl. LUCAS who became producer. **ROGER BURRIDGE** – mandolin, fiddle repl. DONAHUE who became session man

Island Antilles

May 76. (lp)(c) **GOTTLE O'GEER (as "FAIRPORT")**
– When first into this country / Our band / Lay me down easy / Cropedy capers / The frog up the pump / Don't be late / Sandy's song / Come and get it / Limey's lament.

— **FAIRPORT CONVENTION** again because founder member **SIMON NICOL** – guitar returned to repl. BRADY, BRAS and BURRIDGE

Vertigo not issued

Feb 77. (lp)(c) **THE BONNY BUNCH OF ROSES** [-]
– James O'Donnell's jig / The Eynsham poacher / Adieu adieu / The bonny bunch of roses / The poor ditching boy / General Taylor / Run Johnny run / The last waltz / Royal Selection No.13. *(re-iss.+cd.Oct88 on 'Woodworm')*

May 78. (lp)(c) **TIPPLERS TALES** [-]
– Ye mariner's all / Three drunken maidens / Jack O'rion / Reynard the fox / Lady of pleasure / Bankruptured / The widow of Westmorland / The hair of the dogma / As bitme / John Barleycorn. *(re-iss.+cd.1989 on 'B.G.O.')*

Simon's not issued

Oct 79. (7") **RUBBER BAND. / BONNY BLACK HARE** [-]

Nov 79. (lp) **FAREWELL FAREWELL (live)** [-]
– Matty Groves / Orange blossom special / John Lee / Bridge over the River Ash / Sir Patrick Spens / Mr.Lacey / Walk awhile / Bonny black hare / Journeyman's grace / Meet on the ledge. *(re-iss.cd+c Jun94 on 'Terrapin Truckin')*

Woodworm Varrick

1982. (lp) **MOAT ON THE LEDGE – LIVE AT BROUGHTON CASTLE 1981 (live)** [-]
– Walk awhile / Country pie / Rosie / Matty Groves / Both sides now / Poor Will and the hangman / The brilliancy medley – Cherokee shuffle / Woman or man / High school confidential.

— **DAVE MATTACKS and DAVE PEGG** returned to repl. SWARBRICK and ROWLAND **NICOL** also recruited sessioners **MARTIN ALLCOCK** (b. 5 Jan'57, Manchester, England) – strings / **RIC SAUNDERS** – violin (ex-SOFT MACHINE)

Woodworm Rounder

Aug 85. (lp)(c)(cd) **GLADYS LEAP** 1988
– How many times / Bird from the mountain / Honour and praise / The hiring fair / Instrumental medley '85: The riverhead – Glady's leap – The wise maid / My feet are set for dancing / Wat Tyler / Head in a sack. *(cd-iss.Mar93)*

1986. (lp)(c) **EXPLETIVE DELIGHTED** [-]
– Medley; The Rutland reel – Sack the juggler / Medley; The cat on the mixer – Three left feet / Bankruptured / Portmeirion / James O'Donnell's jig / Expletive delighted / Sigh beg sigh mor / Innstuck / The gas almost works / Hanks for the memory; Shazam – Pipeline – Apache – Peter Gunn. *(cd-iss.Mar93)*

— now 7-piece of **ALLCOCK, SAUNDERS, PEGG, MATTACKS, NICOL, DONAHUE** and **RICHARD THOMPSON**

New Routes not issued

Jan 89. (lp)(c)(cd) **RED AND GOLD** [74] [-]
– Set me up / The noise club / Red and gold / The beggars song / The battle / Dark eyed Molly / The rose hip / Summer before the war / Open the door Richard. *(re-iss.cd Dec95 on 'HTD')*

Dec 90. (cd)(c)(lp) **THE FIVE SEASONS** [-]
– Cloudy beats: medley – Cup of tea! – A loaf of bread – Miss Monahan's / All your beauty / Sock in it / Gold / Ginnie / Mock Morris '90:- The green man – The cropedy badger – Molly on the jetty / Medley:- The card song – Shuffle the pack – The wounded whale.

— **NICOL, ALLCOCK, PEGG, MATTACKS + SAUNDERS**

Woodworm not issued

Jan 95. (cd)(c) **JEWEL IN THE CROWN**
– Jewel in the crown / Slip jigs and reels / A surfeit of lampreys / Kind of fortune / Diamonds and gold / The naked highwayman / The islands / The youngest daughter / London Danny / Summer in December / Travelling by steam / (Travel by steam) / She's like the swallow / Red tide / Home is where the heart is / Closing time.

– compilations etc. –

Nov 72. Island/ US= A&M; (d-lp)(c) **THE HISTORY OF FAIRPORT CONVENTION**
– Meet on the ledge / Fotheringay / Mr.Lacey / Book song / Sailor's life / Si tu dois partir / Who knows where the time goes / Matty Groves / Crazy man Michael / Now be thankful (medley) / Walk awhile / Sloth / The bonny black hare / Angel delight / Bridge over the river Ash / John Lee / Breakfast in Mayfair / Hanging song / The hen's march through the midden / The four-poster bed. *(re-iss.+cd Jul91. omits 2 tracks)*

1976. A&M; (lp) **FAIRPORT CHRONICLES** [-]

May 87. Island; (7") **MEET ON THE LEDGE. / SIGH BEG SIGH MORE**
(12"+=) – John Barleycorn.

Nov 87. Island; (lp)(c)(cd) **IN REAL TIME**

Apr 88. Island; (cd) **THE BEST OF FAIRPORT CONVENTION**

Jul 70. Polydor; (7") **IF (STOMP). / CHELSEA MORNING**

Dec 76. Help-Island/ US= Antilees; (lp) **LIVE AT THE L.A. TROUBADOUR 1970 (live)**
(re-iss.Jan87 as HOUSE FULL on 'Hannibal', + cd-iss.Jan92)

Sep 84. Woodworm; (c) **THE AIRING CUPBOARD TAPES** [-]

1992. Woodworm; (cd) **THE WOODWORM YEARS** [-]

Sep 87. Hannibal; (lp)(c) **HEYDAY (BBC sessions '68-'69)** [-]

The BUNCH

TREVOR LUCAS (his idea), **SANDY DENNY, RICHARD THOMPSON, ASHLEY HUTCHINGS, DAVE MATTACKS** and session people

Island | A&M

Apr 72. (lp) **ROCK ON** [ ] [ ]
– That'll be the day / Love's made a fool of you / When will I be loved / Willie and the hand jive / Learning the game / My girl in the month of May / Don't be cruel / The locomotion / Jambalaya (on the bayou) / Sweet little rock'n'roller / Nadine / Crazy arms. *(7"flexi w/a)* **-LET THERE BE DRUMS (1 sided)** *(re-iss.+c May88 on 'Carthage')*

Apr 72. (7") **WHEN WILL I BE LOVED. / WILLIE AND THE HAND JIVE** [ ] [ ]

Marianne FAITHFULL

Born: 29 Dec'46, Hampstead, London, England. Daughter of a university lecturer and an Austrian baroness, who had sent her to St.Joseph's convent school in Reading, Berkshire. While attending a London party with artist boyfriend John Dunbar in 1964, she was snapped up by (ROLLING STONES manager) ANDREW LOOG OLDHAM, who signed her to 'Decca' records. Her debut 45 'AS TEARS GO BY', soon made the UK Top 10 and US Top 30. She flopped with follow-up, but had another Top 10 hit early in '65 with 'COME AND STAY WITH ME'. This was followed by 2 simultaneously issued lp's 'COME MY WAY' & 'MARIANNE FAITHFULL', which both hit UK Top 20. In Nov'65, she gave birth to son Nicholas, but separated from Dunbar. Later that year, she began much-publicised affair with MICK JAGGER, after allegedly bedding the other 3! (except WATTS). She was busted for drugs with JAGGER and The STONES on many occasions, with the couple visiting Maharishi Yogi in '68. At this time, she also began acting; 'The Three Sisters' (Chekhov play) & on film 'Girl On A Motorcycle' with Alain Delon. In late 1968, she miscarried with JAGGER's baby, and 6 months later, both were arrested in their London home for possession of marijuana. In mid-69, while on the set of film 'Ned Kelly' alongside JAGGER, she was found in a coma, after an overdose of barbituates (100+ Tuinal). She was dropped from the film and went into hospital for heroin addiction and depression. In 1970, after a season playing Ophelia in 'Hamlet' alongside Nicol Williamson, her suspected suicide bids were reported by press, as was her divorce from Dunbar and split with JAGGER. After 5 years, in the wilderness, she returned on 'Nems' in 1975 with single 'DREAMING MY DREAMS'. After 2 albums for label, she signed to 'Island' in 1979 and had returned to Top 50 with 'THE BALLAD OF LUCY JORDAN'. On 23 Nov'79, she married BEN BRIERLY of punk rock band The VIBRATORS, but her future was always marred by drug intake. In 1987 still surprisingly contracted to 'Island' and now living in Cambridge, Massachusetts, USA with new husband writer Girgio Della, she issued album 'STRANGE WEATHER'. The next year, she was deported from the States, but settled in Ireland. • **Style:** Light-folk singer, whose pop stardom, might have been bigger, but for her drug addiction. In 1978, she moved into C&W, with little acclaim. A year later though she was the leather-clad punk mistress diva when she sang the explicit 'WHY DYA DO IT' from classy 'BROKEN ENGLISH' album. • **Songwriters:** Penned some herself with MARK but she mostly covered others; AS TEARS GO BY + SISTER MORPHINE (music; M.Jagger) / BLOWIN' IN THE WIND + I'LL BE YOUR BABY TONIGHT (Bob Dylan) / GREENSLEEVES + HOUSE OF THE RISING SUN + SCARBOROUGH FAIR (trad.) / COME AND STAY WITH ME (Jackie DeShannon) / GREEN ARE YOUR EYES (Bert Jansch) / THE LAST THING ON MY MIND (Tom Paxton) / THE FIRST TIME EVER I SAW YOUR FACE (Ewan MacColl) / SALLY FREE AND EASY (. . . Tannery) / COCKLESHELLS (. . . Taylor) / THIS LITTLE BIRD (John D.Loudermilk) / SUNNY GOODGE STREET + THE MOST OF WHAT IS LEAST (Donovan) / YESTERDAY (Beatles) / SOMETHING BETTER (Goffin-King) / IS THIS WHAT I GET FOR LOVING YOU (Ronettes) / THE BALLAD OF LUCY JORDAN (Stel Silverstein) / DREAMING MY DREAMS (Waylon Jennings) / WORKING CLASS HERO (John Lennon) / STRANGE WEATHER (Tom Waits) / MADAME GEORGE (Van Morrison) / GHOST DANCE (Patti Smith), etc. In 1979, she began writing partnership with guitarist BARRY REYNOLDS. • **Trivia:** In 1967, she provides guest appearance & backing vocals for The BEATLES on their 'All You Need Is Love' 45 & TV video.

Recommended: THE VERY BEST OF MARIANNE FAITHFULL (*7) / BROKEN ENGLISH (*7).

MARIANNE FAITHFULL – vocals (with session people)

Decca | London

Jul 64. (7") **AS TEARS GO BY. / GREENSLEEVES** [9] [22] Sep 64

Oct 64. (7") **BLOWING IN THE WIND. / THE HOUSE OF THE RISING SUN** [ ] [ ]

Feb 65. (7") **COME AND STAY WITH ME. / WHAT HAVE I DONE WRONG** [4] [26] Jan 65

Apr 65. (7") **THIS LITTLE BIRD. / MORNING SUN** [6] [32] Jun 65

May 65. (lp) **COME MY WAY** [12] [-]
– Come my way / Jabberwock / Portland town / House of the rising sun / Spanish is a loving tongue / Fare thee well / Lonesome traveller / Down in the Salley garden / Mary Ann / Full fathom five / Four strong winds / Black girl / Once I had a sweetheart / Bells of freedom. *(re-iss.+cd.Sep91 on 'Deram' +=)* – Blowin' in the wind / Et maintenant (what now my love) / That's right baby / Sister Morphine.

May 65. (lp) **MARIANNE FAITHFULL** [15] [12]
– Come and stay with me / They will never leave you *(UK-only)* / / What have they done to the rain / In my time of sorrow / What have I done wrong / I'm a loser / As tears go by / If I never get to love you / Time takes time / He'll come back to me / Paris bells / Plasir d'amour. *(re-iss.Aug84) (re-iss.1988 on 'Castle' cd-iss.Jun89 w / extra +=)* – Can't you hear my heartbeat? / Downtown.

Jul 65. (7") **SUMMER NIGHTS. / THE SHA LA LA SONG** [10] [24] Aug 65

Oct 65. (7") **YESTERDAY. / OH LOOK AROUND YOU** [36] [ ]

Nov 66. (7") **GO AWAY FROM MY WORLD. / ?** [-] [89]

Dec 65. (lp) **GO AWAY FROM MY WORLD** [-] [81]
– Go away from my world / Yesterday / Come my way / Last thing on my mind / How should true love / Wild mountain time / Summer nights / Mary Ann / Scarborough Fair / Lullabye / North country maid / Sally free and easy.

Apr 66. (lp) **NORTH COUNTRY MAID** [ ] [-]
– Green are your eyes / Scarborough fair / Cockleshells / The last thing on my mind / The first time ever I saw your face / Sally free and easy / Sunny Goodge Street / How should your true love know / She moved through the fair / North country maid / Lullaby / Wild mountain thyme. *(cd-iss.1992, with +=)* – The most of what is least / Come my way / Mary Ann.

May 66. (7") **TOMORROW'S CALLING. / THAT'S RIGHT BABY** [ ] [ ]

Jul 66. (7") **COUNTING. / I'D LIKE TO DIAL YOUR NUMBER** [ ] [ ]

Nov 66. (lp) **FAITHFULL FOREVER** [-] [ ]
– Counting / Tomorrow's calling / The first time / With you in mind / In the night time / Ne me quitte pas (love theme from Umbrellas of Cherbourg) / Monday Monday / Some other Spring / That's right baby / Lucky girl / I'm the sky / I have a love.

Feb 67. (7") **IS THIS WHAT I GET FOR LOVING YOU. / TOMORROW'S CALLING** [43] [ ]

Feb 67. (lp) **LOVE IN A MIST** [ ] [-]
– Yesterday / You can't go where the roses go / Our love has gone / Don't make promises / In the night time / This little bird / Ne me quite pas / Counting / Reason to believe / Conquillage / With you in mind / Young girl blues / Good guy / I love a love. *(cd-iss.Oct88 +=)* – Rosie, Rosie.

Feb 69. (7") **SOMETHING BETTER. / SISTER MORPHINE** [ ] [ ]

—— She retired from music business, and when she and MICK JAGGER broke up, attempted to commit suicide many times. She had period of hospitalisation, due to increasing heroin addiction early in the 70's. By Autumn 1975, she had recovered and was back in the studio.

NEMS | not issued

Nov 75. (7") **DREAMIN' MY DREAMS. / LADY MADELAINE** [ ] [-]

Sep 76. (7") **ALL I WANNA DO IN MY LIFE. / WRONG ROAD AGAIN** [ ] [-]

Jan 77. (lp)(c) **DREAMIN' MY DREAMS** [ ] [-]
– Fairy tale hero / This time / I'm not Lisa / he way you want me to be / Wrong road again / All I wanna do in life / I'm looking for blue eyes / Somebody loves you / Vanilla O'lay / Dreamin' my dreams / Lady Madelaine / Sweet little sixteen.

—— She was now backed by **The GREASE BAND**

Mar 78. (lp)(c) **FAITHLESS** [ ] [-]
– Dreamin' my dreams / Vanilla O'Lay / Wait for me down by the river / I'll be your baby tonight / Lady Madelaine / All I wanna do in life / The way you want me to be / Wrong road again / This was the day (Nashville) / This time / I'm not Lisa / Honky tonk angels. *(re-iss.+cd.Apr89)*

—— now with **BARRY REYNOLDS** – guitar, co-producer / **STEVE YORK** – bass / **TERRY STANNARD** – drums / **JOE HAVETY** – keys / etc.

Island | Island

Oct 79. (7") **THE BALLAD OF LUCY JORDAN. / BRAIN DRAIN** [48] [ ]

Oct 79. (lp)(c) **BROKEN ENGLISH** [57] [82]
– Broken English / Witches song / Brain drain / Guilt / The ballad of Lucy Jordan / What's the hurry / Working class hero / Why d'ya do it?. *(re-iss.Sep86) (re-iss.lp Jan94 + May94)*

Jan 80. (7") **BROKEN ENGLISH. / BRAIN DRAIN** [ ] [ ]

Jan 80. (7") **BROKEN ENGLISH. / WHAT'S THE HURRY** [ ] [-]

Oct 81. (7") **INTRIGUE. / FOR BEAUTY'S SAKE** [ ] [ ]

Oct 81. (lp)(c) **DANGEROUS ACQUAINTANCES** [45] [ ]
– Sweetheart / Intrigue / Easy in the city / Strange one / Tenderness / For beautie's sake / So sad / Eye communication / Truth bitter truth. *(cd-iss.May95)*

Nov 81. (7") **SWEETHEART. / OVER HERE** [ ] [-]

Jan 82. (7") **SWEETHEART. / FOR BEAUTIE'S SAKE** [-] [ ]

May 82. (7")(12") **BROKEN ENGLISH. / SISTER MORPHINE** [ ] [ ]

—— **BEN BRIERLEY + MIKEY CHUNG** – guitar repl. MAVETY **FERNANDO SAUNDERS** – bass + **WALLY BADAROU** – keyboards repl. YORK

Feb 83. (lp)(c) **A CHILD'S ADVENTURE** [99] [ ]
– Times Square / The blue millionaire / Falling from grace / Morning come / Ashes in my hand / Running for our lives / Ireland / She's got a problem. *(re-iss.Apr87) (cd-iss.May95)*

Mar 83. (7") **RUINING OF OUR LIVES. / SHE'S GOT A PROBLEM** [ ] [ ]

—— now w/ **many on session, incl. SAUNDERS.**

Jun 87. (7") **AS TEARS GO BY. / TROUBLE IN MIND (THE RETURN)** [ ] [ ]
(12"+=) – This hawk el Gavian.

Jul 87. (lp)(c)(cd) **STRANGE WEATHER** [78] [ ]
– Stranger intro / Boulevard of broken dreams / I ain't goin' down to the well no more / Yesterdays / Sign of judgement / Strange weather / Love, life and money / I'll keep it with mine / Hello stranger / Penthouse serenade / As tears go by / A stranger on Earth.

—— now with **BARRY REYNOLDS** – guitar / **MARC RIBOT / LEW SOLOFF / GARTH HUDSON**

May 90. (cd)(c)(lp) **BLAZING AWAY (live + 1 studio)** [ ] [ ]
– Les prisons du roi / Guilt / Sister morphine / Why d'ya do it? / The ballad of Lucy Jordan / Blazing away / Broken English / Strange weather / Working class hero / As tears go by / When I find my life / Times Square / She moved through the fair. *(re-iss.cd May95)*

Sep 94. (cd)(c) **FAITHFULL – A COLLECTION OF HER BEST RECORDINGS (compilation)** [ ] [ ]
– Broken English / The ballad of Lucy Jordan / Working class hero / Guilt / Why d'ya do it? / Ghost dance / Trouble in mind (the return) / Times Square (live) / Strange weather / She / As tears go by.

—— below from a VAN MORRISON tribute album on 'Exile-Polydor' / 'M.C.A.'

Sep 94. (c-s) **MADAME GEORGE. / ('b'side by Brian Kennedy)**
(cd-s+=) – (other by Brian Kennedy + Shana Morrison).

—— below with composer ANGELO BADALEMENTI

Apr 95. (cd)(c) **A SECRET LIFE**
– Prologue / Sleep / Love in the afternoon / Flaming September / She / Bored by dreams / Losing / The wedding / The stars line up / Epilogue.

– compilations, others, etc. –

May 65. Decca; (7"ep) **MARIANNE FAITHFULL** | -
– Go away from my world / The most of what is least / El main tenant (what now my love) / The sha la la song.

Feb 69. Decca; (lp) **THE WORLD OF MARIANNE FAITHFULL** | -

Apr 69. London; (lp) **MARIANNE FAITHFULL'S GREATEST HITS** - |
(same tracks as above)

Jul 80. Decca; (7") **AS TEARS GO BY. / COME AND STAY WITH ME** | -
(re-iss.Oct83 on 'Old Gold')

Feb 81. Decca; (lp)(c) **AS TEARS GO BY** | -

Mar 84. Decca; (lp)(c) **SUMMER NIGHTS** | -

Nov 85. Castle; (d-lp)(c)(cd) **RICH KID BLUES** | -

Mar 87. London; (cd) **THE VERY BEST OF MARIANNE FAITHFULL** | -
– As tears go by / Come and stay with me / Scarborough Fair / Monday, Monday / Yesterday / The last thing on my mind / What have they done to the rain / This little bird / Something better / In my time of sorrow / Is this what I get for loving you? / Tomorrow's calling / Reason to believe / Sister Morphine / Go away from my world / Summer nights *(lp/c.iss.Jun87 + Sep87)*

Oct 87. Hannibal; (lp) **HEYDAY** (BBC sessions 1968-69) | -

Oct 93. Spectrum; (cd)(c) **THIS LITTLE BIRD** | -

FAITH NO MORE

Formed: Los Angeles & San Francisco, California, USA ... 1980 by MOSELEY and GOULD, although they only started gigging 1982. In 1985, they issued eponymous debut lp on local indie 'Mordam' label. Early in 1987, they moved on to 'Slash' records, who unleashed 'INTRODUCE YOURSELF'. In 1988, due to musical differences and off-beat stage humour, MOSELEY was discharged from band. By the end of the year, he was succeeded by 20 year-old MIKE PATTON. Their 1989 album 'THE REAL THING', went cross-Atlantic Top 30, and hosted a string of hits, the best and biggest being 'EPIC'. • **Style:** Funk-metal rap with diverse heavy image similar in vein to RED HOT CHILI PEPPERS or DAN REED NETWORK. • **Songwriters:** Group compositions (PATTON took over lyric duties from MOSELEY in 1989). Covered WAR PIGS (Black Sabbath) / THE RIGHT STUFF (Edwin Starr) / MIDNIGHT COWBOY (John Barry) / MALPRACTICE (sampled: Kronos Quartet No.8) / LET'S LYNCH THE LANDLORD (Dead Kennedys) / I'M EASY (Commodores) / I STARTED A JOKE (Bee Gees) / GREENFIELDS (Gilykson-Dehr-Miller). • **Trivia:** Their 1987 album was produced by MATT WALLACE and STEVE BERLIN (of LOS LOBOS).

Recommended: ANGEL DUST (*9) / THE REAL THING (*8) / INTRODUCE YOURSELF (*7).

CHUCK MOSELEY – vocals / **BILLY GOULD** (b.24 Apr'63) – bass / **RODDY BOTTUM** (b. 1 Jul'63) – keyboards / **JIM MARTIN** (b.21 Jul'61) – guitar / **MIKE BORDIN** (b.27 Nov'62) – drums

not issued | Mordam

1985. (lp) **FAITH NO MORE** - |
– We care a lot / The jungle / Mark Bowen / Jim / Why do you bother / Greed / Pills for breakfast / As the worm turns / Arabian disco / New beginnings. *(iss.UK Feb88 as 'WE CARE A LOT')*

Slash-London | Slash

Oct 87. (lp)(c)(cd) **INTRODUCE YOURSELF**
– Faster disco / Anne's song / Introduce yourself / Chinese arithmetic / Death march / We care a lot / R'n'r / Crab song / Blood / Spirit.

Jan 88. (7") **WE CARE A LOT. / SPIRIT** 53 |
(12"+=) – Chinese Arithmetic (radio mix).

Apr 88. (7")(12")(7"pic-d) **ANNE'S SONG (remix). / GREED**

—— **MIKE PATTON** (b.27 Jan'68) – vocals (ex-MR. BUNGLE) repl. CHUCK who later (1991) joined BAD BRAINS

Jul 89. (lp)(c) **THE REAL THING** 30 | 11
– From out of nowhere / Epic / Falling to pieces / Surprise, you're dead / Zombie eaters / The real thing / Underwater love / The morning after / Woodpecker from Mars. (cd+=) – Edge of the world / War pigs. *(re-iss.Sep92)*

Oct 89. (7") **FROM OUT OF NOWHERE. / COWBOY SONG**
(12"+=) – The grave.

Jan 90. (7")(7"sha-pic-d) **EPIC. / WAR PIGS (live)** 37 |
(12"+=)(cd-s+=) – Chinese arithmetic.
(7"m+=) – Surprise you're dead (live).

Apr 90. (c-s) **FROM OUT OF NOWHERE. / WOODPECKER FROM MARS (live)** 23 |
(7"m+=) – Epic (live).
(12"+=)(cd-s+=)(12"pic-d+=) – The real thing (Live).

Jul 90. (7") **FALLING TO PIECES. / WE CARE A LOT (live)** 41 | 92 Nov 90
(7"m+=)(c-s+=) – Underwater love (live).
(12"+=)(cd-s+=) – From out of nowhere.

Sep 90. (7"sha-pic-d) **EPIC. / FALLING TO PIECES (live)** 25 | 9 Jun 90
(7"m+=)(c-s+=) – Epic (live).
(12"++=)(cd-s++=) – As the worm turns.

Feb 91. (cd)(c)(m-lp) **LIVE AT BRIXTON ACADEMY (live)** 20 | -
– Falling to pieces / The real thing / Pump up the jam / Epic / War pigs / From out of nowhere / We care a lot / The right stuff / Zombie eaters / Edge of the world. (cd/c+=) – The grade / The cowboy song.

Slash-London | Slash-Reprise

May 92. (7")(c-s)(7"colrd) **MIDLIFE CRISIS. / JIZZLOBER / CRACK HITLER** 10 |
(12"pic-d+=)(pic-cd-s+=) – Midnight cowboy.

Jun 92. (cd)(c)(lp) **ANGEL DUST** 2 | 10
– Land of sunshine / Caffeine / Midlife crisis / RV / Smaller and smaller / Everything's ruined / Malpractice / Kindergarten / Be aggressive / A small victory / Crack Hitler / Jizzlober / Midnight cowboy. (lp +free-12"ep 'MIDLIFE CRISIS (remix)' / (2). *(re-iss.Feb93)* (+=) I'm easy.

Jul 92. (7") **A SMALL VICTORY. / LET'S LYNCH THE LANDLORD** 29 |
(12"+=)(12"pic-d+=) – Malpractise.
(cd-s++=) – ('A'full version).

Sep 92. (12"ep)(cd-ep) **A SMALL VICTORY (Youth remix) / R-EVOLUTION 23 (full Moon mix) / SUNDOWN (mix) / SUNDOWN (instrumental).** | -

Nov 92. (7")(c-s) **EVERYTHING'S RUINED. / MIDLIFE CRISIS (live)** 28 |
(cd-s+=) – Land of sunshine (live).
(cd-s) – ('A'side) / Edge of the world (live) / RV (live).

Jan 93. (7")(12")(cd-s) **I'M EASY. / BE AGGRESSIVE** 3 | 58

Oct 93. (12"ep)(cd-ep) **ANOTHER BODY MURDERED. ("FAITH NO MORE / BOO-YA TRIBE") / Just Another Victim (by "HELMET / HOUSE OF PAIN")** 26 |

—— (above from the film 'Judgement Day')

Mar 95. (7")(c-s) **DIGGING THE GRAVE. / UGLY IN THE MORNING** 16 |
(12"blue+=) – Absolute zero / Get out.
(cd-s+=) – Absolute zero / Cuckoo for Caca.
(cd-s) – ('A'side) / I started a joke / Greenfields.

Mar 95. (cd)(c)(lp)(5x7"box) **KING FOR A DAY – FOOL FOR A LIFETIME** 5 | 31
– Get out / Ricochet / Evidence / The great art of making enemies / Star A.D. / Cuckoo for Caca / Caralho Voador / Ugly in the morning / Digging the grave / Take this bottle / King for a day / What a day / The last to know / Just a man. (7"box-set feat. interviews).

May 95. (c-s) **RICOCHET / SPANISH EYES** 27 |
(cd-s+=) – I wanna f**k myself.
(cd-s) – ('A'side) / Midlife crisis (live) / Epic (live) / We care a lot (live).

Jul 95. (c-s) **EVIDENCE / EASY (live)** 32 |
(cd-s+=) – Digging the grave (live) / From out of nowhere (live).
(cd-s) – ('A'side) / Das schutzenfest / (interview).

MR.BUNGLE

PATTON also still a member of

Slash | Slash

Sep 91. (cd)(c)(lp) **MR.BUNGLE** 57 |
– Quote unquote / Slowly growing deaf / Squeeze me macaroni / Carousel / Egg / Stubb (a dub) / The girls of porn / Love is a fist / Dead goon.

FALL

Formed: Salford, Manchester, England ... Dec'76 by MARK E.SMITH, MARTIN BRAMAH and TONY FRIEL. After 1977 session on The John Peel Radio 1 show, they were signed to indie label 'Step Forward'. Their debut release 'BINGO-MASTERS BREAK-OUT! EP', was issued in Jun78, and was soon followed by Bob Sargeant produced first studio lp 'LIVE AT THE WITCH TRIALS'. Advanced steadily throughout the next decade, and had first taste of commercial success, when album 'BEND SINISTER' hit UK Top 40. • **Style:** Repetitive and uncompromising punk rock, that progressed experimentally incorporating rockabilly, alternative rock and poetic punk. MARK E.SMITH became unlikely cult figure in the 80's, fusing his sharp acid-tongue screach with CAN-like backing from ever-changing group personnel. • **Songwriters:** All lyrics by MARK E. and music by MARK E. & various group members, especially SCANLON or wife of 5 years BRIX E. Started doing covers from 1986:- ROLLIN' DANY (Gene Vincent) / THERE'S A GHOST IN MY HOUSE (R.Dean Taylor) / VICTORIA (Kinks) / MR. PHARMACIST (Other Half) / JERUSALEM (William Blake) / POPCORN DOUBLE FEATURE (Searchers) / WHITE LIGHTNING (Big Bopper) / A DAY IN THE LIFE (Beatles) / LEGEND OF XANADU (Dave Dee, Beaky, Mick and Tich) / TELEPHONE THING (Cold Cut) / BLACK MONK THEME (Monks) / JUST WAITING (Hank Williams) / LOST IN MUSIC (Sister Sledge) / I'M GOING TO SPAIN (S. Bent) / WHY ARE PEOPLE GRUDGEFUL? (Lee Perry – unknown) / SHUT UP! (Monks) / JUNK MAN (McFree) / WAR (Blegvad-Moore) / I'M NOT SATISFIED (Frank Zappa) / ROADHOUSE (John Barry). • **Trivia:** MARK's ex-wife BRIX appeared on new boyfriend NIGEL KENNEDY's 1991 'This Is Your Life'. His classical violin virtuoso, had featured on album 'BEND SINISTER'?. MARK E. featured on TACKHEAD b-side of 'Dangerous Sex' in mid 1990, alongside ADRIAN SHERWOOD and GARY CLAIL. Just previous to this, he had a solo track 'ERROR-ORROR I' for Various Artists compilation 'HOME'.

Recommended: THIS NATION'S SAVING GRACE (*9) / BEND SINISTER (*8) / LIVE AT THE WITCH TRIALS (*9) / EXTRICATE (*8) / SHIFT-WORK (*8) / THE WONDERFUL AND FRIGHTENING WORLD OF ... (*8) / DRAGNET (*8) / PERVERTED BY LANGUAGE (*8) / I AM KURIOUS ORANJ (*8) / THE FRENZ EXPERIMENT (*7) / HEX ENDUCTION HOUR (*7) / THE FALL LIVE (*7) / GROTESQUE (*7) / SLATES (*6) / ROOM TO LIVE (*6) / MIDDLE CLASS REVOLT (*6) / CODE : SELFISH (*5) / SEMINAL LIVE (*4) / CELEBRAL CAUS-

TIC (*6)

MARK E. SMITH (b. Mar'57) – vocals / **TONY FRIEL** – bass / **MARTIN BRAMAH** – guitar / **UNA BAINES** – electric piano / **KARL BURNS** – drums

Step Forward | I.R.S.

Jun 78. (7"ep) **BINGO-MASTERS BREAK-OUT!** –
– Psycho Mafia / Bingo-Master / Repitition.

— **MARC RILEY** – bass repl. (ERIC and JOHNNIE BROWN) who had repl. FRIEL (He formed The PASSAGE) / **YVONNE PAWLETT** – keyboards repl. BAINES who formed BLUE ORCHIDS

Nov 78. (7") **IT'S THE NEW THING. / VARIOUS TIMES** –

Jan 79. (lp) **LIVE AT THE WITCH TRIALS**
– Frightened / Crap rap 2 – Like to blow / Rebellious jukebox / No Xmas for John Quays / Mother-sister! / Industrial estate / Underground medecin / Two steps back / Live at the Witch Trials / Futures and pasts / Music scene.

— **MARK E.** (now sole founder), **RILEY** (now guitar) and **PAWLETT** recruited **STEVE HANLEY** (b. 1959, Dublin, Ireland) – bass repl. BRAMAH who also joined BLUE ORCHIDS / **MIKE LEIGH** – drums repl. BURNS who also joine The PASSAGE and P.I.L.

Jul 79. (7") **ROWCHE RUMBLE. / IN MY AREA** –

— **CRAIG SCANLON** – guitar (RILEY now guitar, keyboards) repl. PAWLETT

Oct 79. (lp) **DRAGNET**
– Psykick dancehall / A figure walks / Printhead / Dice man / Before the Moon falls / Your heart out / Muzorewi's daughter / Flat of angles / Choc-stock / Spectre vs. rector / Put away. *(re-iss.+cd.Dec90 on 'I.R.S.')*

Jan 80. (7") **FIERY JACK. / SECOND DARK AGE / PSYKICK DANCEHALL II** –

Rough Trade | not issued

May 80. (lp) **THE FALL LIVE – TOTALE'S TURNS (IT'S NOW OR NEVER) (live)** –
– (intro) – Fiery Jack / Rowche rumble / Muzorewi's daughter / In my area / Choc-stock / Spectre vs. rector 2 / Cary Grant's wedding / That man / New puritan / No Xmas for John Quays. *(cd-iss.Nov92 on 'Dojo')*

— **PAUL HANLEY** – drums repl. LEIGH

Jun 80. (7") **HOW I WROTE ELASTIC MAN. / CITY HOBGOBLINS** –

Sep 80. (7") **TOTALLY WIRED. / PUTTA BLOCK** –

— **KAY CARROLL** their manager augmented p/t on backing vocals, kazoo

Nov 80. (lp) **GROTESQUE (AFTER THE GRAMME)**
– Pay your rates / English scheme / New face in Hell / C'n'c Smithering / The container drivers / Impression of J. Temperance / In the park / W.M.C. – Blob 59 / Gramme Friday / The N.W.R.A. *(re-iss.cd Sep93 on 'Castle')*

Apr 81. (10"m-lp) **SLATES** –
– Middle mass / An older lover etc. / Prole art threat / Fit and working again / Slates, slags, etc. / Leave the capitol.

— **KARL BURNS** – drums returned now alongside **SMITH, RILEY, SCANLON, S & P HANLEY**

Kamera | not issued

Nov 81. (7") **LIE DREAM OF A CASINO SOUL. / FANTASTIC LIFE**

Mar 82. (lp) **HEX ENDUCTION HOUR** 71 –
– The classical / Jaw-bone and the air-rifle / Hip priest / Fortress – Deer park / Mere psued mag. ed / Winter / Winter 2 / Just step s'ways / Who makes the Nazis? / Iceland / And this day. *(re-iss.1987 on 'Line', cd-iss.Sep89)*

Apr 82. (7") **LOOK KNOW. / I'M INTO C.B.** –

Nov 82. (lp) **ROOM TO LIVE** –
– Joker hysterical face / Marquee cha-cha / Hard life in the country / Room to live / Detective instinct / Solicitor in studio / Papal visit. *(re-iss.Oct87 on 'Line')*

— Reverted to quintet when RILEY left to form MARC RILEY & THE CREEPERS (note that their manager and p/t member KAY CARROLL also departed)

Rough Trade | not issued

Jun 83. (7") **THE MAN WHOSE HEAD EXPANDED. / LUDD GANG** –

Oct 83. (d7") **KICKER CONSPIRACY. // WINGS / CONTAINER DRIVERS (live) / NEW PURITANS (live)** –

— added **LAURA-ELISE** (now BRIX E. SMITH) (b.USA) – guitar, vocals (ex-BANDA DRATSING) P. HANLEY added keyboards and BURNS added lead bass to their repertoire

Dec 83. (lp)(c) **PERVERTED BY LANGUAGE** –
– Eat y'self fitter / Neighbourhood of infinity / Garden / Hotel Bloedel / I feel voxish / Tempo house / Hexen definitive / strife knot. *(re-iss.Oct87 on 'Line', cd-iss.Sep89)* (cd+=) – Oh! brother / God-box / C.R.E.E.P. / Pat-trip dispenser. *(re-iss.cd.Sep93 on 'Castle')*

Begger's Banquet | P.V.C.

Jun 84. (7") **OH BROTHER. / GOD-BOX** –
(12"+=) – ('A' instrumental).

Aug 84. (7")(7"pic-d) **C.R.E.E.P. / PAT-TRIP DISPENSER** –
(12"+=)(12"green+=) – ('A'extended).

— added **GAVIN FRIDAY** – some vocals (of VIRGIN PRUNES) (on next 2 releases)

Sep 84. (lp)(c) **THE WONDERFUL AND FRIGHTENING WORLD OF . . .** 62
– Lay of the land / 2 x 4 / Copped it / Elves / Slang king / Bug day / Stephen song / Craigness / Disney's dream debased. *(re-iss.+cd.Jul88)* (cd+=) – Oh! brother / Draygo's guilt / God-box / Clear off! / C.R.E.E.P. / Pat-trip dispenser / No bulbs.

Oct 84. (12"ep) **CALL FOR ESCAPE ROUTE** –
– Draygo's Guilt / No bulbs / Clear Off!. (with free-7") **NO BULBS 3. / SLANG KING**

— **SIMON ROGERS** – bass, keyboards repl. P. HANLEY (he cont. with KISS THE BLADE) (GAVIN returned to VIRGIN PRUNES and S. HANLEY took a holiday)

Jul 85. (7") **COULDN'T GET AHEAD. / ROLLIN' DANY**
(12"+=) – Petty (thief) lout.

— **STEVE HANLEY** returned to join **MARK E., BRIX, CRAIG, KARL and SIMON**

Sep 85. (lp)(c) **THIS NATION'S SAVING GRACE** 54
– Mansion / Bombast / Barmy / What you need / Spoilt Victorian child / L.A. / Out of the quantifier / My new house / Paintwork / I am Damo Suzuki / To nkroachment: yarbles. *(re-iss.+cd.Feb90 +=)* – Vixen / Couldn't get ahead / Pretty (thief) lout / Rollin' Dany / Cruiser's creek.

Oct 85. (7") **CRUISER'S CREEK. / L.A.**
(12"+=) – Vixen.

Jul 86. (7") **LIVING TOO LATE. / HOT AFTER-SHAVE BOP**
(12"+=) – Living too long.

— **JOHN S. WOOLSTENCROFT** – drums (ex-WEEDS) repl. BURNS who formed THIRST

Sep 86. (7") **MR. PHARMICIST. / LUCIFER OVER LANCASHIRE** 75
(12"+=) – Auto-tech pilot.

Oct 86. (lp)(c)(cd) **BEND SINISTER** 36
– R.O.D. / Dktr. Faustus / Shoulder pads £1 / Mr. Pharmicist / Gross chapel – British grenadiers / U.S. 80's-90's / Terry Waite sez / Bournemouth runner / Riddler / Shoulder pads £2. *(cd-iss.Jan88 +=)* – Living too late / Auto-tech pilot.

Nov 86. (7") **HEY! LUCIANI. / ENTITLED** 59
(12"+=) – Shoulder pads.

Apr 87. (7") **THERE'S A GHOST IN MY HOUSE. / HAF FOUND, BORMAN** 30
(12"+=)(c-s+=) – Sleepdebt / Snatches / Mark'll sink us.

— added **MARSHA SCHOFIELD** – keyboards, vocals of ADULT NET, (ex BANDA DRATSING)

Oct 87. (7")(7"pic-d) **HIT THE NORTH. / Pt.2** 57
(12"+=) – Australians in Europe.
(cd-s+=) – Northerns in Europe / (Hit the north versions).

— reverted back to sextet of **MARK E., BRIX, CRAIG, JOHN S., STEVE** and **MARSHA** when **SIMON** became their producer & studio guitarist only

Jan 88. (7") **VICTORIA. / TUFF LIFE BOOGIE** 35

(12"+=) – Guest informant / Twister.

Mar 88. (lp)(c)(cd) **THE FRENZ EXPERIMENT** [19] [ ]
– Frenz / Carry bag man / Get a hotel / Victoria / Athlete cured / In these times / The steak place / Bremen nacht / Guest informant (excerpt) / Oswald defence lawyer. *(c/cd+=)* – Tuff life boogie / Guest informant / Twister / There's a ghost in my house / Hit the north (part 1).

Below album was a MICHAEL CLARK and company ballet, first premiered in Amsterdam 11 Jun'88. Dancer MICHAEL had been a long-time fan and friend.

Oct 88. (lp)(c)(cd) **I AM KURIOUS, ORANJ** [54] [ ]
– New big prinz / Overture from 'I Am Curious, Orange' / Dog is life – Jerusalem / Wrong place, right time / Guide me soft * / C.D. win fall 2088 ad / Yes, o yes / Van plague? / Bad news girl / Cab it up! / Last nacht * / Big new priest *. *(c/cd+= *)*

Nov 88. (d7"ep)(d3"cd-ep) **JERUSALEM / ACID PRIEST 2088. / BIG NEW PRINZ / WRONG PLACE, RIGHT TIME** [59] [ ]

Jun 89. (7") **CAB IT UP. / DEAD BEAT DESCENDENT (out take from ballet** [ ] [ ]
(12"+=) – Kurious oranj (live) / Hit the north (live).

Jun 89. (lp)(c)(cd) **SEMINAL LIVE (some studio)** [40] [ ]
– Dead beat descendant / Pinball machine / H.O.W. / Squid law / Mollusc in Tyrol / 2 x 4 / Elf prefix – L.A. / Victoria / Pay your rates / Cruiser's creek. *(c/cd+=)* – Kurious oranj / Hit the north / In these times / Frenz.

— **MARTIN BRAMAH** – guitar returned to repl. BRIX E. who continued with ADULT NET.

Cog Sinister-Fontana | Fontana

Jan 90. (7")(c-s) **TELEPHONE THING. / BRITISH PEOPLE IN HOT WEATHER** [58] [ ]
(12"+=)(cd-s+=) – Telephone (dub).

Feb 90. (cd)(c)(lp) **EXTRICATE** [31] [ ]
– Sing! Harpy / I'm Frank / Bill is dead / Black monk theme part 1 / Popcorn double feature / Telephone thing / Hilary / Chicago, now! / The littlest rebel / British people in hot weather / And therein. (c+cd+=) – Arms control poseur / Black monk theme part II / Extricate.

Mar 90. (7") **POPCORN DOUBLE FEATURE. / BUTTERFLIES 4 BRAINS** [ ] [ ]
(12"+=) – Arms control poseur.
(12"+=)(cd-s+=) – Zandra / Black monk theme part II.

— trimmed to basic quartet of **MARK E, CRAIG, STEVE and JOHN.**

Aug 90. (7") **WHITE LIGHTNING. / BLOOD OUTTA STONE** [56] [ ]
(12"+=) – Zagreb.
(12"ep)(cd-ep) – THE DREDGER EP (++=) – Life just bounces.

Dec 90. (7") **HIGH TENSION LINE. / XMAS WITH SIMON** [ ] [ ]
(12"+=)(cd-s+=) – Don't take the pizza.

— added guest **KENNY BRADY** – violin

Apr 91. (cd)(c)(lp) **SHIFT-WORK** [17] [ ]
– EARTH'S IMPOSSIBLE DAY :-So what about it? / Idiot joy showland / Edinburgh man / Pittsville direkt / The book of lies / High tension line / The war against intelligence/ / NOTEBOOKS OUT PLAGLARISTS :-Shift-work / You haven't found it yet / The mixer / White lightning / A lot of wind / Rose / Sinister waltz.

— **DAVID BUSH** – keyboards, machines repl. BRADY

Mar 92. (7") **FREE RANGE. / EVERYTHING HURTZ** [40] [ ]
(12"+=)(pic-cd-s+=) – Dangerous / Return.

Mar 92. (cd)(c)(lp) **CODE: SELFISH** [21] [ ]
– The Birmingham school of business school / Free range / Return / Time enough at last / Everything hurtz / Immorality / Two-face! / Jusy waiting / So-called dangerous / Gentlemen's agreement / Married, 2 kids / Crew filth. *(re-iss.cd Aug93)*

Jun 92. (12"ep)(cd-ep) **ED'S BABE / PUMPKIN HEAD XSCAPES / THE KNIGHT, THE DEVIL AND DEATH / ARID'S AL'S DREAM / FREE RANGER** [ ] [ ]

Permanent-Permanent | Cog Sinister

Apr 93. (7") **WHY ARE PEOPLE GRUDGEFUL?. / GLAM-RACKET** [43] [ ]
(12"+=)(cd-s+=) – The Re-Mixer / Lost In Music

Apr 93. (cd)(c)(lp) **THE INFOTAINMENT SCAN** [9] [ ]
– Ladybird (green grass) / Lost in music / Glam-racket / I'm going to Spain / It's a curse / Paranoia man in cheap sh*t room / Service / The league of bald-headed men / A past gone mad / Light fireworks / League Moon monkey mix. (cd+=) – Why are people grudgeful?.

— added the returning **KARL BURNS** – percussion(now 6-piece yet again)

Dec 93. (d-cd-ep)(d12"ep) **BEHIND THE COUNTER EP** [75] [ ]
– Behind the counter / War / M5 / Happy holiday / Cab driver / (1).

— Feb 94; MARK guested for INSPIRAL CARPETS on their single 'I Want You'.

Apr 94. (10"clear-ep)(12"ep)(cd-ep) **15 WAYS. / HEY! STUDENT / THE $500 BOTTLE OF WINE** [65] [ ]

May 94. (cd)(c)(lp) **MIDDLE CLASS REVOLT (aka THE VAPOURISATION OF REALITY** [48] [ ]
– 15 ways / The reckoning / Behind the counter / M5£1 / Surmount all obstacles / Middle class revolt! / You're not up to much / Symbol of Mordgan / Hey! student / Junk man / The $500 bottle of wine / City dweller / War / Shut up!.

— added on tour the returning **BRIX SMITH**

Feb 95. (cd)(c)(lp) **CEREBRAL CAUSTIC** [67] [-]
– The joke / Don't call me darling / Rainmaster / Feeling numb / Pearl city / Life just bounces / I'm not satisfied / The aphid / Bonkers in Phoenix / One day / North west fashion show / Pine leaves.

Aug 95. (d-cd)(d-c)(d-lp) **THE TWENTY-SEVEN POINTS (live)** [ ] [-]
– Mollusc in Tyrol / Return / Lady bird (green grass) / Idiot – Walk-out / Ten points / Idiot – Walk-out / Big new prinz / Intro: Roadhouse / The joke / ME's jokes – The British people in hot weather / Free range / Hi-tension line / The league of the bald headed men / Glam racket: Star / Lost in music / Mr. Pharmacist / Cloud of black / Paranoia man in cheap shit room / Bounces / Outro / Passable / Glasgow advice / Middle class revolt: Simon, Dave and John / Bill is dead / Strychnine / War! / Noel's chemical effluence / Three points – Up too much.

– compilations, etc. –

Sep 81. Step Forward; (lp) **77-EARLY YEARS-79** [ ] [-]

Mar 82. Chaos; (c) **LIVE AT ACKLAM HALL, LONDON 1980** [ ] [-]

Nov 82. Cottage; (lp) **A PART OF AMERICA THEREIN** [-] [-]

Nov 83. Kamera; (7") **MARQUEE CHA-CHA. / ROOM TO LIVE/ / (PAPAL VISIT orig. 'B')** [ ] [-]

Mar 85. Situation 2; (lp)(c) **HIP PRIESTS AND KAMERADS** (81-82 material) [ ] [-]
(c+=) – (has 4 extra tracks) *(cd-iss.Mar88 += same 4) (re-iss.cd Sep95 on 'Beggar's Banquet')*

May 87. Strange Fruit; (12"ep) **THE PEEL SESSIONS** (28.11.78) [ ] [-]
– Put away / No Xmas for John Quay / Like to blow / Mess of my.

Mar 93. Strange Fruit; (12"ep) **KIMBLE** [ ] [-]
– Kimble / C'n'c hassle schmuk / Spoilt Victorian child / Words of expectation.

Nov 87. Cog Sinister; (lp)(c)(cd) **IN PALACE OF SWORDS REVERSED (80-83)** [ ] [-]

Sep 90. Cog Sinister; (cd)(c)(lp) **458489** ('A'sides; 1984-89) [47] [ ]
– Oh! brother / C.R.E.E.P. / No bulbs 3 / Rollin' Dany / Couldn't get ahead / Cruiser's creek / L.A. / Living too late / Hit the north (part 1) / Mr.Pharmacist / Hey! Luciani / There's a ghost in my house / Victoria / Big new prinz / Wrong place, right time No.2 / Jerusalem / Dead beat descendant. // God-box / Pat-trip dispenser / Slang king 2 / Draygo's guilt / Clear off! / No bulbs / Petty thief lout / Vixen / Hot aftershave bop / Living too long / Lucifer over Lancashire / Auto tech pilot / Entitled / Shoulder pads £1 / Sleep debt snatches / Mark'll sink us / Haf found Bormann / Australians in Europe / Northerns in Europe / Hit the north (part 2) / Guest informant / Tuff life boogie / Twister / Acid priest 2088 / Cab it up.

Dec 90. Cog Sinister; (cd)(c)(d-lp) **458489** (B'sides; 1984-89) [ ] [ ]
– God-box / Pat-trip dispenser / Slang king 2 / Draygo's guilt / Clear off! / No bulbs / Petty thief lout / Vixen / Hot aftershave bop / Living too long / Lucifer over Lancashire / Auto tech pilot / Entitled / Shoulder pads £1 / Sleep debt snatches / Mark'll sink us / Haf found Bormann / Australians in Europe / Northerns in Europe / Hit the north (part 2) / Guest informant / Tuff life boogie / Twister / Acid priest 2088 / Cab it up. *(cd+=)* Bremen nache run out / Mark'll sink us (live) / Kurious oranj.

Apr 93. Castle; (cd)(c) **THE COLLECTION** [ ] [-]

Aug 93. Windsong; (cd) **BBC RADIO 1 LIVE IN CONCERT** [ ] [-]

Agnetha FALTSKOG (see under ⇒ ABBA)

FAMILY

Formed: Leicester, England . . . 1967 by WHITNEY, CHAPMAN, KING and GRECH. The 4 originally stemmed from The FARINAS, who were on the go for 5 years, and who issued 'Fontana' 45 in Aug'64; 'YOU'D BETTER STOP. / I LIKE IT LIKE THAT'. As FAMILY, they moved to London, and made their debut at The Royal Albert Hall in Jul'67 supporting TIM HARDIN. After a one-off 7" vinyl debut for 'Liberty', they signed to 'Reprise' in 1968. Their DAVE MASON & JIMMY MILLER produced first lp 'MUSIC FROM A DOLL'S HOUSE', made the UK Top 40. Their next 5 lp's, all hit Top 20, and they also ventured into singles chart with classics 'NO MULE'S FOOL', 'STRANGE BAND', 'IN MY OWN TIME' & 'BURLESQUE'. • **Style:** Excellent progressive power-rock outfit, fronted by the manic 'frog-in-throat', but prolific voxist ROGER CHAPMAN. Their last album 'IT'S ONLY A MOVIE' (1973), saw a divertion to more commercial good-time rock, although it suffered undeserved critical panning. • **Songwriters:** CHAPMAN-WHITNEY penned most of material, except ROGER CHAPMAN solo covers LET'S SPEND THE NIGHT TOGETHER (Rolling Stones) / I'M YOUR HOOCHIE COOCHIE MAN + THAT SAME THING (Willie Dixon) / KEEP A KNOCKIN' (Little Richard) / I'M A KING BEE (Sam Moore) / STONE FREE (Jimi Hendrix) / LOVE LETTERS IN THE SAND (Pat Boone?) / SLOW DOWN (Hank Williams) / BUSTED LOOSE (Paul Brady) / KEEP FORGETTING (Leiber-Stoller) / TALKING ABOUT YOU (Chuck Berry). • **Trivia:** In 1968, their exploits on tour, were given light in Jenny Fabian's obscure novel 'Groupie'.

Recommended: THE BEST OF FAMILY (*9) / MUSIC IN A DOLL'S HOUSE (*7) / ENTERTAINMENT (*6) / A SONG FOR ME (*6) / FEARLESS (*6) / BAND-STAND (5) / THE BEST OF STREETWALKERS (*5) / KICK IT BACK (*4) (ROGER CHAPMAN).

ROGER CHAPMAN (b. 8 Apr'44, Leicester, England) – vocals / **CHARLIE WHITNEY** (b. 4 Jun'44, Leicester) – guitar, vocals / **JIM KING** – saxophone, flute / **RIC GRECH** (b. 1 Nov'46, Bordeaux, France) – bass / **HARRY OVENALL** – drums

Liberty | not issued

Sep 67. (7") **SCENE THROUGH THE EYE OF A LENS. / GYPSY WOMAN** [ ] [-]

— **ROB TOWNSEND** (b. 7 Jul'47) – drums repl. HARRY

Reprise | Reprise

Jun 68. (7") **ME AND MY FRIEND. / HEY MR. POLICEMAN** [ ] [ ]

Jul 68. (7") **OLD SONGS NEW SONGS. / HEY MR. POLICEMAN** [-] [ ]

Jul 68. (lp) **MUSIC IN A DOLL'S HOUSE** [35] [ ]
– The chase / Mellowing grey / Never like this / Me and my friend / Variation on a theme of Hey Mr. Policeman / Winter / Old songs new songs / Variation on a theme of the breeze / Hey Mr. Policeman / See through windows / Variation on a theme of me and my friend / Peace of mind / Voyage / The breeze / 3 x time. *(re-iss.+cd.Sep87 on 'See For Miles')*

Nov 68. (7") **SECOND GENERATION WOMAN. / HOME TOWN** [ ] [ ]

Mar 69. (lp) **ENTERTAINMENT** [6] [ ]
– The weaver's answer / Observations from a hill / Hung up down / Summer '67 / How-hi-the-li / Second generation woman / From past archives / Dim / Processions / Face in the crowd / Emotions. *(re-iss.+cd.Sep87 on 'See For Miles')*

— **JOHN WEIDER** (b.21 Apr'47) – bass, violin (ex-ERIC BURDON & ANIMALS)

repl. GRECH who joined BLIND FAITH

Oct 69. (7") **NO MULE'S FOOL. / GOOD FRIEND OF MINE** 29

— **POLI PALMER** (b. JOHN, 25 May'43) – keyboards, vibes (ex-ECLECTION) repl. KING who joined RING OF TRUTH

Jan 70. (lp)(c) **A SONG FOR ME** 4
– Drowned in wine / Some poor soul / Love is a sleeper / Stop for the traffic (through the heart of me) / Wheels / Song for sinking lovers / Hey let it rock / The cat and the rat / 93's ok J. / A song for me. *(re-iss.+cd.Nov88 on 'See For Miles')*

Apr 70. (7") **TODAY. / SONG FOR SINKING LOVERS**

Aug 70. (7"m) **STRANGE BAND. / THE WEAVER'S ANSWER / HUNG UP DOWN** 11

Reprise United A..

Nov 70. (lp)(c) **ANYWAY . . .** (half live) 7
– Good news bad news / Holding the compass / Strange band / Willow tree / Part of the load / Anyway / Normans / Lives and Ladies. *(re-iss.+cd.Nov88 on 'See For Miles') (re-iss.cd May94 on 'Castle')*

Mar 71. (lp)(c) **OLD SONGS NEW SONGS** (compilation remixed)
– Hung up down / Today / Observations from a hill / Good friend of mine / Drowned in wine / Peace of mind / Home town / The cat and the rat / No mule's fool / See through windows / The weaver's answer.

Jun 71. (7") **IN MY OWN TIME. / SEASONS** 4

— **JOHN WETTON** (b.12 Jul'49, Derby, England) – bass, vocals (ex-MOGUL THRASH) repl. WEIDER who joined STUD

Oct 71. (lp)(c) **FEARLESS** 14
– Between blue and me / Sat'd'y barfly / Larf and sing / Spanish tide / Save some for thee / Take your partners / Children / Crinkly grin / Blind / Burning bridges. *(re-iss.+cd Nov88 on 'See For Miles') (re-iss.cd May94 on 'Castle')*

Sep 72. (7") **BURLESQUE. / THE ROCKIN' R'S** 13

Sep 72. (lp)(c) **BANDSTAND** 15
– Burlesque / Bolero babe / Coronation / Dark eyes / Broken nose / My friend the sun / Glove / Ready to go / Top of the hill. *(re-iss.+cd.Nov88 on 'See For Miles') (cd-iss.Mar94 on 'Castle')*

Jan 73. (7") **MY FRIEND THE SUN. / GLOVE**

— CHAPMAN, WHITNEY and TOWNSEND were joined by **JIM CREGAN** – bass, guitar (ex-STUD) repl. WETTON who joined KING CRIMSON / **TONY ASHTON** (b. 1 Mar'46, Blackburn, England) – keyboards (ex-ASHTON, GARDNER and DYKE) repl. PALMER

Raft United Art

Apr 73. (7") **BOOM BOOM. / STOP THIS CAR**

Sep 73. (7") **SWEET DESIREE. / DRINK TO YOU**

Sep 73. (lp)(c) **IT'S ONLY A MOVIE** 30
– It's only a movie / Leroy / Buffet tea for two / Boom bang / Boots 'n' roots / Banger / Sweet Desiree / Suspicion / Check out.

— They split late '73 with TOWNSEND joining MEDICINE HEAD and CREGAN went to COCKNEY REBEL, ASHTON went into production. ROGER and CHARLIE formed CHAPMAN / WHITNEY STREETWALKERS

– compilations, others, etc. –

Note; All below releases on 'Reprise' issued in US 'United Artists'

Sep 74. Reprise; (lp)(c) **THE BEST OF FAMILY**
– Burlesque / My friend the Sun / The chase / Old songs, new songs / Part of the load / In my own time / It's only a movie / Sweet desiree / Sat'd'y barfly / Children / No mule's fool / The weaver's answer. *(re-iss.+cd.Nov91 on 'See For Miles', with extra tracks)(re-iss.cd+cApr93 on 'Castle')*

Nov 74. Reprise; (7") **MY FRIEND THE SUN. / BURLESQUE**

May 78. Reprise; (7"ep) **BURLESQUE. / IN MY OWN TIME / THE WEAVER'S ANSWER**

Oct 81. Rebecca; (lp) **RISE** -

Jan 82. Rebecca; (7") **BURLESQUE. / MY FRIEND THE SUN** -

Nov 88. Strange Fruit; (12"ep)(cd-ep) **THE PEEL SESSIONS (8.5.73)** -

Aug 89. That's Original; (d-lp)(c)(cd) **IT'S ONLY A MOVIE / FEARLESS** -

Nov 92. Castle; (cd) **A's & B's** -

Mar 93. Dutch East India; (cd) **THE PEEL SESSIONS** -

STREETWALKERS

ROGER CHAPMAN – vocals / **CHARLIE WHITNEY** – guitar / **BOBBY TENCH** – guitar, vocals (ex-JEFF BECK) / **PHILIP CHEN** – bass / **TIM HINKLEY** – keyboards / **MEL COLLINS** – saxophone, flute / **IAN WALLACE** – drums (both ex-KING CRIMSON)

Reprise Mercury

May 74. (lp)(c) **STREETWALKERS**
– Parisienne high heels / Roxianna / Systematic stealth / Call ya / Creature feature / Sue and Betty Jean / Showbiz Joe / Just four men / Tokyo rose / Hangman.

Jun 74. (7") **ROXIANNA. / CRACK**

— **JON PLOTEL** – bass (ex-CASABLANCA) repl. CHEN & HINKLEY (to sessions) / **NICKO McBAIN** – drums repl. WALLACE & COLLINS (to ALVIN LEE ⇒ TEN YEARS AFTER)

Vertigo Mercury

Oct 75. (lp)(c) **DOWNTOWN FLYERS**
– Downtown flyers / Toenail draggin' / Raingame / Miller / Crawfish / Walking on waters / Gypsy moon / Burn it down / Ace o'spades.

Oct 75. (7") **RAINGAME. / MILLER**

May 76. (red-lp)(c) **RED CARD** 16
– Run for cover / Me an' me horse an' me rum / Crazy charade / Daddy rolling stone / Roll up, roll up / Between us / Shotgun messiah / Decadence code.

Jun 76. (7") **DADDY ROLLING STONE. / HOLE IN YOUR POCKET**

— **CHAPMAN, WHITNEY + TENCH** were joined by **MICKY FEAT** – bass / **DAVID DOWLE** – drums / **BRIAN JOHNSON** – keyboards (**McBAIN** joined **PAT TRAVERS** and later **IRON MAIDEN**)

Jan 77. (lp)(c) **VICIOUS BUT FAIR**
– Mama was mad / Chili con carne / Dice man / But you're beautiful / Can't come in / Belle star / Sam (maybe he can come to some arrangement) / Cross time woman. *(cd-iss.Aug92 on 'See For Miles' ' . . . PLUS' +=)*– Downtown flyers / Gypsy Moon / Crawfish / Raingame / Crazy charade / Shotgun Messiah / Decadence code / Daddy rolling stone.

Dec 77. (lp)(c) **LIVE (live)**
– Chilli con carne / Crazy charade / Walking on waters / Dice man / My friend the Sun / Toenail draggin' / Mama was mad / Me an' me horse an' me rum / Run for cover / Burlesque / Can't come in.

— Had already split, TENCH and FEAT joined VAN MORRISON. JOHNSON and DOWLE joined DAVID COVERDALE'S WHITESNAKE.

– (STREETWALKERS) compilations, etc. –

Dec 90. Phonogram; (cd) **THE BEST OF STREETWALKERS** -

Jun 94. Windsong; (cd) **BBC RADIO 1 LIVE IN CONCERT** -

ROGER CHAPMAN

went solo, augmented by MICKEY JUPP

Arista Arista

Mar 79. (lp)(c) **CHAPPO**
– Midnite child / Moth to a flame / Keep forgettin' / Shape of things / Face of stone / Who pulled the nite down / Always gotta pay in the end / Hang on to a dream / Pills / Don't give up. *(re-iss.+cd.1988 on 'Maze') (cd-iss.Jul92 on 'Castle')*

Acrobat not issued

Mar 79. (7") **MIDNITE CHILD. / MOTH TO A FLAME** -

May 79. (7") **WHO PULLED THE NIGHT DOWN. / SHORTLIST** -

Jul 79. (7") **LET'S SPEND THE NIGHT TOGETHER. / SHAPE OF THINGS** -

Dec 79. (lp)(c) **LIVE IN HAMBURG (live w/ The SHORTLIST)** -
– Moth to a flame / Keep forgettin' / Midnite child / Who pulled the nite down / Talking about you / Shortlist / Can't get in / Keep a knockin' / I'm your hoochie coochie man / Let's spend the night together. *(re-iss.+cd.1988 on 'Maze') (cd-iss.Dec92 on 'Castle')*

B.B.C. not issued

Oct 80. (7") **SPEAK FOR YOURSELF. / SWEET VANILLA** -

— with **PALMER / HINKLEY / WHITEHORN**

Kamera not issued

Sep 80. (lp)(c) **MAIL ORDER MAGIC** -
– Unknown soldier (can't get to Heaven) / He was, she was / Barman / Right to go / Duelling man / Making the same mistake / Another little hurt / Mail order magic / Higher ground / Ground floor. *(re-iss.+cd.1988 on 'Maze') (cd-iss.Dec92 on 'Castle')*

Polydor not issued

Dec 81. (lp)(c) **HYENAS ONLY LAUGH FOR FUN** -
– Prisoner / Hyenas only laugh for fun / Killing time / Want's nothing chained / The long goodbye / Blood and sand / Common touch / Goodbye (reprise) / Hearts on the floor / Step up – Take a bow / Jukebox mama.

Oct 82. (d-lp)(c) **HE WAS SHE WAS YOU WAS WE WAS (live)** -
– Higher ground / Ducking down / Making the same mistake / Blood and sand / Medley:- I'm a king bee – That same thing – Face of stone / Hyeanas only laugh for fun / Prisoner / Medley:- Slow down – Common touch / Jukebox mama No.3 / He was, she was / Stone free / Bitches brew / Unknown soldier. *(re-iss.+cd.1988 on 'Maze') (re-iss.cd Apr94 on 'Castle')*

Mar 83. (lp)(c) **MANGO CRAZY** -
– Mango crazy / Toys: Do you? / I read your file / Los dos Bailadores / Blues breaker / Turn it up loud / Let me down / Hunt the man / Rivers run dry / I really can't go straight / Room service / Hegoshegoyougoamigo. *(re-iss.+cd.1988 on 'Maze') (cd-iss.Dec92 on 'Castle')*

(CHAPMAN provided vocals for MIKE OLDFIELD on single 'Shadow On The Wall')

Apr 84. (7") **HOW HOW HOW. / HOLD THAT TIDE BACK** -

R.C.A. not issued

May 85. (lp)(c)(cd) **THE SHADOW KNOWS** -
– Busted loose / Leader of men / Ready to roll / I think of you now / The shadow knows / How how how / Only love is in the red / Sweet vanilla / I'm a good boy now. *(re-iss.cd Mar94 on 'Castle')*

1986. (lp)(c)(cd) **ZIPPER** -
– Zipper / Running with the flame / On do die day / Never love a rolling stone / Let the beat get heavy / It's never too late to do-ron-ron / Woman of destiny / Hoodoo me up.

1987. (lp)(c) **TECHNO-PRISONERS** -
– The drum / Wild again / Techno-prisoner / Black forest / We will touch again / Run for your love / Slap bang in the middle / Who's been sleeping in my bed / Ball of confusion. *(re-iss.cd Mar94 on 'Castle')*

1989. (lp)(c)(cd) **WALKING THE CAT** -
– Kick it back / Son of Red Moon / Stranger than strange / Just a step away (let's go) / The fool / Walking the cat / J & D / Come the dark night / Hands off / Jivin' / Saturday night kick back.

Maze not issued

Nov 89. (m-lp) **LIVE IN BERLIN (live)** -
– Shadow on the wall / Let me down / How how how / Mango crazy. *(cd-iss.Dec92 on 'Castle')*

Castle not issued

1992. (cd) **KICK IT BACK** -
– Walking the cat / Cops in shades / House behind the Sun / Chicken fingers / Kick it back / Son of red Moon / Someone else's clothes / Hideaway / Toys: Do you? / Hot night to rhumba / Stranger than strange / Just a step away (let's go) / Jesus and the Devil.

FAMILY CAT

Formed: Yeovil, Somerset, England . . . 1988 by FRED, JELB, TIM, JOHN and KEV, who soon moved to South London. They released surprise indie success 'TOM VERLAINE', just prior to late 1989 lp 'TELL 'EM WE'RE SURFIN''. • **Style:** Indie hippies of twang, fronted by the TEARDROP EXPLODES influenced but introverted FRED. • **Songwriters:** Group except; BUS STOP (Hollies) / I MUST HAVE BEEN BLIND (Tim Buckley) / LEAN

ON ME (I WON'T FALL OVER) (Carter The Unstoppable Sex Machine). • **Trivia:** 'COLOUR ME GREY' featured POLLY HARVEY on backing vocals. Renowned to be SONIC YOUTH's fave UK band.

Recommended: FURTHEST FROM THE SUN (*7) / MAGIC HAPPENS (*8)

PAUL FREDERICK – vocals, guitar / **STEPHEN JELBERT** – guitar / **TIM McVAY** – guitar / **JOHN GRAVES** – bass / **KEVIN DOWNING** – drums

Bad Girl · not issued

Jul 89. (7"flexi) **TOM VERLAINE (demo).** — -
(12"ep+=) – Gabriel's weakness / Octopus Jr.

Sep 89. (m-lp) **TELL 'EM WE'RE SURFIN'** — -
– Albert Hoffman's bike / Final mistake / Sandbag your heart / Slept in clothes / From the city to the sea / Taken by surprise / Endless cigarette / Gabriel's wings. *(cd-iss.Mar90)*

May 90. (7")(12")(cd-s) **REMEMBER WHAT IT IS THAT YOU LOVE. / PUSH COMES TO SHOVE** — -

Aug 90. (12"ep)(cd-ep) **A PLACE WITH NO NAME. / CONCRETE / PASSAWAY / THEME FROM THE FAMILY CAT** — -

Sep 91. (12"ep)(cd-ep) **COLOUR ME GREY. / I MUST HAVE BEEN BLIND / GREAT UGLY FACES** — -

—— (below deleted in one day and issued on 'Clawfist')

Dec 91. (7")(12")(cd-ep) **JESUS CHRIST. / CHILL OUT YE MERRY GENTLEMEN / CHRIST JESUS / JESUS KARAOKE CHRIST (instrumental)** — -

Dedicated · Big Cat

May 92. (7") **STREAMROLLER (pt.1). / STEAMROLLER (pt.2) / WHAT WE TALK ABOUT WHEN WE TALK ABOUT LOVE**
(12"+=)(cd-s+=) – What we talk about when we talk about love / Across the universe.

Jun 92. (cd)(c)(lp) **FURTHEST FROM THE SUN** 55
– Too many late nights / Colour me grey / Prog one / Furthest from the Sun / Steamroller / Keep it to yourself / With a war / River of diamonds / Gameshow / Fire music.
(free-7"w /a + cd+) – Kolombus / Montague Terrace (in blue).

Sep 92. (12"ep)(cd-ep) **RIVER OF DIAMONDS (re-navigated). / SANDBAG YOUR HEART (re-bagged) / TOM VERLAINE (re-bereted)**
– (free7"w.a) – Tom Verlaine.

Aug 93. (7"purple)(c-s) **AIRPLANE GARDENS. / ATMOSPHERIC ROAD** 69
(12"+=)(cd-s+=) – Amazing hangover.

Oct 93. (7") **SPRINGING THE ATOM. / PROG 4**
(12"+=)(cd-s+=) – Happy to be here.

May 94. (7"clear)(c-s) **WONDERFUL EXCUSE. / UNWIELDY WORLD** 48
(cd-s+=) – Sign of the bloodcell / Propeller blades.
(12") – ('A'side) / Counting crosses (acoustic) / Gameshow (acoustic) / ('A'acoustic).

May 94. (cd)(c)(lp) **MAGIC HAPPENS**
– Wonderful excuse / Amazing hangover / Move over I'll drive / Your secrets will stay mine / Airplane gardens / Gone, so long / Hamlet for now / Goldenbook / Rockbreaking / Springing the atom / Blood orange / Nowhere to go but down.

Jul 94. (7"green-ep)(c-ep) **GOLDEN BOOK EP** 42
– Bring me the head of Michael Portillo / Springing the atom (acoustic) / River of diamonds (acoustic).
(7"gold-ep) – (1st track) / Goldenboot / Old faithful.
(cd-s) – (1st track) / Blood orange (acoustic) / Gone to Heaven.

Chris FARLOWE

Born: JOHN HENRY DEIGHTON, 13 Oct'40, London, England. In 1957, he and his teenage band The JOHN HENRY SKIFFLE GROUP won a skiffle competition. In the late 50's, he formed The THUNDERBIRDS and after a one-off 45 for 'Decca', they signed to 'Columbia' in 1963. Contracted to Andrew Loog Oldman's 'Immediate' in 1965, they had a flop 45, before transferring to solo ventures. Early in 1966, he had first UK Top 40 hit with 'THINK', which was soon followed by a No.1 JAGGER-RICHARD re-indition of 'OUT OF TIME'. He had 4 more UK hits during the next 18 months, but he decided in the early 70's to join jazz-rock outfit COLOSSEUM and then heavies ATOMIC ROOSTER. In 1975, his 'OUT OF TIME' 45, returned him to the charts, although his future was left to be a guest vocalist and make further comebacks. • **Style:** Powerful blues R&B singer, whom many thought in the 60's, sounded black. • **Songwriters:** Wrote some himself, but mainly borrowed from others; HOUND DOG (Leiber-Stoller) / THINK + OUT OF TIME + PAINT IT BLACK (Rolling Stones) / MY WAY OF GIVING (Small Faces) / WE CAN WORK IT OUT (Beatles) / ONLY WOMEN BLEED (Alice Cooper) / AFTER MIDNIGHT (JJ Cale) / LET THE HEARTACHES BEGIN (Long John Baldry) / MOANING (Timous-Hendrix) / etc. • **Trivia:** Used to collect Nazi memorabilia to sell in his London shop.

Recommended: GREATEST HITS (*5).

CHRIS FARLOWE – (solo) vocals, guitar with sessioners

Decca · not issued

Nov 62. (7") **AIR TRAVEL. / WHY DID YOU BREAK MY HEART** — -

CHRIS FARLOWE & THE THUNDERBIRDS

with **RICKY CHARMAN** – bass / **JOHNNY WISE** – drums / **DAVE GREENSLADE** – organ

Columbia · Columbia

Sep 63. (7") **I REMEMBER. / PUSH PUSH** — -

Feb 64. (7") **GIRL TROUBLE. / ITTY BITTY PIECES** — -

—— (May64) added **ALBERT LEE** (b.21 Dec'43) – guitar (ex-MIKE HIRST)

Jul 64. (7") **JUST A DREAM. / WHAT YOU GONNA DO** — -

Oct 64. (7") **HEY, HEY, HEY, HEY. / HOUND DOG** — -

1965. (lp) **CHRIS FARLOWE & THE THUNDERBIRDS** (comp.)
– Stormy Monday blues (part 1&2) / Reelin' and rockin' / Just a dream / Hey hey hey hey / Hound dog / What you gonna do / I remeber / Itty bitty pieces / Girl trouble / Push push / Voodoo. *(re-iss. 1967 as 'STORMY MONDAY' on 'M.F.P.')*

—— **BUGS WADDELL** – bass repl. CHARMAN / **IAN HAGUE** – drums repl. WISE

The BEAZERS

(reggae style)

Decca · not issued

1964. (7") **THE BLUE BEAT. / I WANNA SHOUT** — -

LITTLE JOE COOK

under pseudonym

Sue · not issued

Aug 65. (7") **STORMY MONDAY BLUES. / (part 2)** — -

CHRIS FARLOWE

(solo again & see last line-up of THUNDERBIRDS)

Immediate · Immediate

Oct 65. (7") **THE FOOL. / TREAT HER GOOD** — -

Jan 66. (7") **THINK. / DON'T JUST LOOK AT ME** 37

Mar 66. (lp) **14 THINGS TO THINK ABOUT** 19
– Think / My colouring book / Lipstick traces / Summertime / That's no big thing / Don't play that song / Looking for you / It's all over now, baby blue / I just don't know what to do with myself / Rockin' pneumonia / Why don't you change your ways / My girl Josephine / Yesterday / Don't just look at me. *(cd-iss.Apr93 on 'Repertoire')*

Jun 66. (7") **OUT OF TIME. / BABY MAKE IT SOON** 1

Oct 66. (7") **RIDE ON BABY. / HEADLINES** 31

Dec 66. (lp) **THE ART OF CHRIS FARLOWE** 37
– What becomes of the broken hearted / We're doing fine / Paint it black / Cuttin' in / Open the door to your heart / North south east west / You're so good for me / Out of time / I'm free / I've been loving you too long / Life is but nothing / It was easier to hurt her / Reach out I'll be there / Ride on baby.

Jan 67. (7") **MY WAY OF GIVING. / YOU'RE SO GOOD TO ME** 48

Apr 67. (7") **YESTERDAY'S PAPERS. / LIFE IS BUT NOTHING**

Jun 67. (7") **MOANIN'. / WHAT HAVE I BEEN DOIN'** 46

Jul 67. (7") **PAINT IT BLACK. / YOU'RE SO GOOD TO ME** -

Dec 67. (7") **HANDBAGS AND GLADRAGS. / EVERYONE MAKES A MISTAKE** 33

Dec 67. (lp) **THE BEST OF CHRIS FARLOWE, VOLUME 1** (compilation)
– Satisfaction / The last goodbye / Mr.Pitiful / Life is but nothing / What have I been doing / I'm free / In the midnight hour / Everyone makes a mistake / You're so good for me / Who can I turn to / What becomes of the broken hearted / Ride on baby.

—— **CARL PALMER** – drums repl. HAGUE & WADDELL / **PETE SOLLEY** – keyboards repl. DAVE GREENSLADE who later formed COLOSSEUM

Apr 68. (7") **THE LAST GOODBYE. / PAPERMAN FLY IN THE SKY ('B'side by "CHRIS FARLOWE & THE THUNDERBIRDS")**

—— ALBERT LEE now departed to form COUNTRY FEVER. In 1969, he formed POET & THE ONE-MAN BAND who became HEADS, HANDS & FEET. He later joined The CRICKETS / JOE COCKER / his own band with CHAS & DAVE / ERIC CLAPTON and many sessions.

Jun 68. (7") **PAINT IT BLACK. / WHAT HAVE I BEEN DOING** -

Jul 68. (7") **PAINT IT BLACK. / I JUST NEED YOUR LOVIN'**

1968. (7") **DAWN. / APRIL WAS THE MONTH**

1969. (lp) **THE LAST GOODBYE** — -
– The last goodbye / Think / In the midnight hour / Mr.Pitiful / (I can't get no) Satisfaction / Who can I turn to / You're so good for me / Dawn / Looking for you / It was easier to hurt her / Don't just look at me / April was the month / Handbags and gladrags / Life is but nothing.

1969. (7") **OUT OF TIME. / RIDE ON BABY**

—— He had already disbanded The THUNDERBIRDS. CARL PALMER had already joined The CRAZY WORLD OF ARTHUR BROWN, then ATOMIC ROOSTER, before co-forming EMERSON, LAKE & PALMER.

CHRIS FARLOWE & THE HILL

with **BRUCE WADDELL** – bass / **COLIN DAVY** – drums / **STEVE HAMMOND** – guitar / **PETER ROBINSON** – keyboards / **PAUL BUCKMASTER** – cello

Polydor · Polydor

1970. (7") **BLACK SHEEP. (solo) / FIFTY YEARS** — -

Sep 70. (lp) **FROM HERE TO MAMA ROSA** — -
– Travelling into make believe / Fifty years / Where do we go from here / Questions / Head in the clouds / Are you sleeping / Black sheep / Winter of my life / Mama Rosa.

1970. (7") **PUT THE LIGHT OUT. / QUESTIONS** — -

—— In late 1970, he joined COLOSSEUM and made 1 album 'DAUGHTER OF TIME'. He left them in Oct'71 and joined ATOMIC ROOSTER. They made 2 albums together 'MADE IN ENGLAND' (1972) & 'NICE 'N' GREASY' (1973), before he left. He and their leader VINCENT CRANE also issued dual 45 'CAN'T FIND A REASON'.

CHRIS FARLOWE

went solo again in 1975, after OUT OF TIME re-hit.

Polydor · M.C.A.

Oct 75. (7") **WE CAN WORK IT OUT. / ONLY WOMEN BLEED** — -

Nov 75. (lp)(c) **CHRIS FARLOWE & HIS BAND – LIVE (live)** — -
– We're gonna make it / Rhyme and time / Peace of mind / After midnight / Only women bleed / Mandy / Hot property / Handbags and gladrags / You haven't done nothin' / It ain't no use.

—— Early in 1978, he sings on 'GANGSTERS' TV theme serial alongside DAVE

GREENSLADE, who wrote the incidental track for the BBC.
In 1982, FARLOWE guested on JIMMY PAGE's (ex-LED ZEPPELIN) film soundtrack album 'Death Wish II'. He also went solo again

C.B.S. | not issued

Oct 82. (7") **LET THE HEARTACHES BEGIN. / BARRYMORE** | | -

— In late 1983, he went to jail for 30 days for not paying his shop rates.

CHRIS FARLOWE & THE THUNDERBIRDS

re-formed w / **TIM HINKLEY** – keyboards / **MO WITHAM** – guitar / **BIG GEORGE WEBLEY** – bass / **JOHN 'THE BIG FIGURE' MARTIN** – drums / **STEVE GREGORY** – sax, flute

Thunderb. | not issued

Jan 86. (lp) **OUT OF THE BLUE** | | - | 1984
I ain't superstitious / Gambler's blues / Them that's got (I ain't got nothin' yet) / Ain't no love in the heart of the city / It's all wrong / Key to my kingdom / The thrill is gone / Watch your step / All the way lover / (Standing on) Shakey ground.

— **TEX COMER** – bass / **MARTYN C.WINNING** – tenor sax repl. WEBLEY + GREGORY

1986. (lp)(cd) **LIVE IN HAMBURG (live)** | | -
– Satisgy Susie / Going back to Luisiana / Under suspicion / (I've been) Born again.

Oct 86. (lp)(c) **BORN AGAIN** | | -
– Into the night / Starting all over again / Lonely eyes / One night stand / Ain't got no money / I'm yours / I've been born again / Living ain't easy without you / Never too old / End of the line / I stayed away too long. *(re-iss.Nov88 on 'Unicorn')*

— In 1988, he again featured on a JIMMY PAGE album 'Outrider'.

– compilations, others, etc. –

1963. Decca; (7"ep) **CHRIS FARLOWE (AIR TRAVEL)** | | -
1966. Columbia; (7") **JUST A DREAM. / HEY, HEY, HEY, HEY** | | -
1966. Island; (7"ep) **STORMY MONDAY** | | -
1967. Immediate; (7"ep) **FARLOWE IN THE MIDNIGHT HOUR** | | -
1967. Immediate; (7"ep) **CHRIS FARLOWE HITS** | | -
Sep 75. Immediate; (7") **OUT OF TIME. / MY WAY OF GIVING** | 44 | -
(re-iss.Oct82)
Dec 75. Immediate; (lp)(c) **OUT OF TIME** | | -
Jan 78. Immediate; (lp)(c) **GREATEST HITS** | | -
– Satisfaction / Ride on baby / What becomes of the broken hearted / The fool / Think / Handbags and gladrags / Paint it black / Yesterday's papers / In the midnight hour / Reach out I'll be there / Moaning / Out of time.
Dec 93. Immediate; (cd) **THE BEST OF CHRIS FARLOWE - OUT OF TIME** | |
Nov 77. Charly; (7") **ONLY WOMEN BLEED. / AFTER MIDNIGHT** | | -
Nov 77. Charly; (lp) **CHRIS FARLOWE & THE THUNDERBIRDS (feat. ALBERT LEE)** | | -
Aug 78. Charly; (lp) **OUT OF TIME - PAINT IT BLACK** | | -
Jul 80. Virgin; (d7") **OUT OF TIME. / HANDBAGS AND GLADRAGS/ / YESTERDAY'S PAPERS. / RIDE ON BABY** | | -
Oct 83. Taurus; (7") **LIVING AIN'T EASY WITHOUT YOU. / DON'T TALK TO ME** | | -
Jan 85. Old Gold; (7") **OUT OF TIME. / THINK** | | -
Sep 86. Showcase; (lp)(c) **MR.SOULFUL** | | -
(cd-iss.Dec87)
Aug 87. Decal; (lp) **BUZZ WITH FUZZ** | | -
Mar 94. See For Miles; (cd) **I'M THE GREATEST** | | -

FARM

Formed: Liverpool, England . . . early '83 by PETE HOOTEN and STEVE GRIMES. Appeared on BBC2 TV's 'Oxford Road Show', and met MADNESS man SUGGS McPHERSON, who produced their 1984 debut 45 'HEARTS AND MINDS'. Struggled early on and suffered tragedy when drummer ANDY McVANN died in a car crash late '86. Things got decidedly better, when they started own label 'Produce' in 1990. Their first single that year 'STEPPING STONE', hit No.56, and was followed by 2 classy UK Top 10 hits 'GROOVY TRAIN' & 'ALL TOGETHER NOW'. • **Style:** At first influenced by brassy DEXY's or REDSKINS sound, but opted in the late 80's for new rave/dance scene. • **Songwriters:** All written by HOOTEN-GRIMES, except covers of STEPPING STONE (hit; Monkees) / DON'T YOU WANT ME (Human League) / SHAKE SOME ACTION (Flamin' Groovies). • **Miscellaneous:** In 1990, their live technician RAY TOOMEY, was jailed for 30 months for his part in the Risley remand centre rooftop protest.

Recommended: SPARTACUS (*7).

PETE HOOTEN (b.28 Sep'62) – vocals / **STEVE GRIMES** (b. 4 Jun'62) – guitar / **JOHN MELVIN** – guitar / **PHILIP STRONGMAN** – bass / **ANDY McVANN** – drums / plus **TONY EVANS** – trombone / **GEORGE MAHER** – trumpet / **STEVE 'SNOWY' LEVY** – saxophone / **and occasional live JOE MUSKER** – percussion

Skysaw | not issued

Nov 84. (12"ep) **HEARTS AND MINDS. / ('A'dub version) / INFORMATION MAN / SAME OLD STORY** | | -

Admirality | not issued

Nov 85. (7") **STEPS OF EMOTION. / MEMORIES** | | -
(12") – ('A'side) / Power over me / No man's land / Better / Living for tomorrow.

Fire | not issued

Sep 86. (7") **SOME PEOPLE. / STANDING TOGETHER** | | -
(12"+=) – Sign of the times / The Moroccan.
Oct 86. (lp) **PASTURES OLD AND NEW** | | -
– Hearts and minds / Information man / Same old story / Hearts and minds (dub) / Steps of emotion / Power over me / No man's land / Better / Worn out sayings / Some people / Little old wine drinker me. *(comp. of Radio 1 sessions) (re-iss.Aug89)*

— (early '87) **MICK HANRATTY** – drums (on tour) repl. ANDY McVANN who died in a crash Dec86. Late 1987; **ROY BOULTER** (b. 2 Jul'64) – drums repl. HANRATTY and the horn section /**KEITH MULLEN** (DR. KEITH LOVE) (b.Bootle) – guitar repl. MELVIN / **CARL HUNTER** (b.14 Apr'65, Bootle, England) – bass repl. PHILLIP

— (early '89) **HOOTEN, GRIMES, HUNTER, MULLEN, and BOULTER** added **BEN LEACH** (b. 2 May'69) – keyboards

Foresight | not issued

Jul 89. (7") **BODY AND SOUL. / COLONELS AND HEROES** | | -
(12"+=) – Stuck on you.

Produce | Sire

Apr 90. (12")(7") **STEPPING STONE. / FAMILY OF MAN** | 58 | -
Sep 90. (7") **GROOVY TRAIN. / ('A' 3:30 a.m. mix)** | 6 | 41 | Aug 91
(12"+=)(cd-s+=) – ('A'bottle mix).
Nov 90. (7")(c-s) **ALL TOGETHER NOW. (featuring PETE WYLIE) / ('A' Terry Farley mix)** | 4 |
(12"+=)(cd-s+=) – ('A'Rocky & Diesel mix).

— added guest backing vocalist **PAULA DAVID**

Mar 91. (cd)(c)(lp) **SPARTACUS** | 1 |
– Hearts and minds / How long / Sweet inspiration / Groovy train / Higher and higher / Don't let me down / Family of man / Tell the story / Very emotional / All together now. *(initial copies, incl.free remix lp)*
Apr 91. (7")(c-s) **DON'T LET ME DOWN. / ('A' Terry Farley mix)** | 36 |
(12"+=)(cd-s+=) – ('A'-Rocky & Diesel mix).
Aug 91. (7")(c-s) **MIND. / STEPPING STONE** | 31 |
(12"+=)(cd-s+=) – ('A'new mix).
Dec 91. (7") **LOVE SEE NO COLOUR (Suggs mix). / ('A' Noel Watson mix)** | 58 |
(d12"+=)(cd-s+=) – (6 other remixes).

— In October 1991, KEITH MULLEN was attacked and stabbed needing over 80 stitches. 'ALL TOGETHER NOW' is used by The Labour Party in their General election campaign.

End Product-Sony | Sony

Jun 92. (7")(c-s) **RISING SUN. / CREEPERS** | 48 |
(12"+=)(cd-s+=) – ('A'-Mark Saunders mix) / ('A'-Steve Spiro mix).
Oct 92. (7")(c-s) **DON'T YOU WANT ME. / OBVIOUSLY** | 18 |
(cd-s+=) – Groovy train (US mix).
Dec 92. (7")(c-s) **LOVE SEE NO COLOUR. / ALL TOGETHER NOW** | 35 |
(12"+=) – Anytown / (other 'A'side).
(cd-s) – ('A'side) / ('A'original) / Rain / Don't you want me (mixes).

Produce | not issued

Feb 93. (5x12"box)(cd-box-ep) **STEPPING STONE. / ALL TOGETHER NOW (mix)/ / GROOVY TRAIN. / (mix)/ / ALL TOGETHER NOW. / (mix)/ / MIND. / (mix)/ / DON'T LET ME DOWN. / (mix)/ /** | | -

Sire-Reprise | Sire-Reprise

Jul 94. (7")(c-s) **MESSIAH. / ONE MORE FOOL** | |
(cd-s+=) – Somewhere (acoustic) / Love made up my mind.
Aug 94. (cd)(c) **HULLABALOO** | |
– Messiah / Shake some action / Comfort / The man who cried / Hateful / Golden vision / To the ages / All American world / Distant voices / Echoes.

Mark FARNER (see under ⇒ GRAND FUNK RAILROAD)

Mick FARREN (see under ⇒ PINK FAIRIES)

FATIMA MANSIONS

Formed: London, England; based 1989 Irish born (ex-MOCRODISNEY frontman) CATHAL COUGHLAN. Were well-received by music press & indie minded public alike after the release of debut album 'AGAINST NATURE'. • **Style:** Creative indie/alternative outfit, energised by the genius of CATHAL COUGHLAN. • **Songwriters:** Most by CATHAL, except NITE FLIGHTS (Scott Walker) / SHINY HAPPY PEOPLE (R.E.M.) / EVERYTHING I DO (Bryan Adams).

Recommended: BERTIE'S BROCHURE (*8) / VALHALLA AVENUE (*8)

CATHAL COUGHLAN – vocals, keyboards, composer with **ANDREAS 'GRIMMO' O'GRUNIA** – guitar / **ZAK** – keyboards / **HUGH BUNKER** – bass / **NICHOLAS TIOMPAN ALLUM** – drums, wind

Kitchen-ware | not issued

Nov 89. (lp)(c)(cd) **AGAINST NATURE** | | -
– Only losers take the bus / The day I lost everything / Wilderness on time / You won't get me here / 13th century boy / Bishop of Babel / Valley of the dead ass / Big madness – Monday club Carol.
Feb 90. (12"m) **ONLY LOSERS TAKE THE BUS. / ('A'version) / WHAT?** | | -
Jun 90. (7") **BLUES FOR CEAUSESCU. / 13th CENTURY BOY** | | -
(12"+=)(cd-s+=) – Suicide bridge.
Sep 90. (cd)(c)(lp) **VIVA DEAD PONIES** | | -
– Angel's delight / Concrete block / Mr.Bailey / The door-to-door inspector / Start the week / You're a rose / Legoland 3 / Thursday / Ceausescu flashback / Broken radio No.1 / Look what I stole for us darling / Farewell Ontario / The white knuckle express / Chemical cosh / Tima Mansio speaks / A pack of lies / Viva dead ponies / More smack vicar. *(re-iss.Mar91) (re-iss.cd+c Sep94)*
Feb 91. (12"ep) **HIVE / STIGMATA. / CHEMICAL COSH / THE HOLY MUGGER** | | -
Apr 91. (7")(c-s) **YOU'RE A ROSE. / BLUES FOR CEAUSESCU** | | -
(cd-s+=) – Against nature.
(12"+=) – Only losers take the bus.

Sep 91. (cd)(m-lp) **BERTIE'S BROCHURES** (acoustic) [ ] [-]
– Behind the man / Bertie's brochures / Long about now / The great Valerio / Shiny happy people / VN (apology) / Mario Vargas Yoni / Smiling. *(re-iss.cd/c Sep94)*

— **DUKE O MALAITHE** – keyboards repl. ZAK.

Kitchen-ware | Radio-active

Apr 92. (12"m) **EVIL MAN. / THE SCARECROW / EVIL MAN II** [59] [ ]
(12"m) – EVIL MAN I & II / Blues for Ceausescu (mix) / Chemical cosh.
(d-cd-s) – EVIL MAN I & II / Only losers take the bus (dump the dead) / Hive.

May 92. (cd)(c)(lp) **VALHALLA AVENUE** [52] [ ]
– Evil man / Something bad / Valhalla avenue / 1000% / North Atlantic wind / Purple window / Go home bible Mike / Perfumes of Paradise / Greyhair / C7 – breakfast with Bandog / Ray of hope, hope of rape / Be dead. *(re-iss.cd+c Sep94)*

Jul 92. (12"m) **1,000 %. / HIVE (live) / 1,000,000 %** [61] [ ]
(cd-s) – Paper thin hotel (repl. 'Hive').
(cd-s) – Angel's delight (repl. '1,000,000').
(cd-s) – ('A'side) / Behind the Moon (live) / Evil man (live) / White knuckles express (live).

Sep'92, covered a version of Bryan Adams' 'EVERYTHING I DO' on B-side of MANIC STREET PREACHERS UK Top10 hit version of 'Suicide Is Painless'.

Feb 93. (cd)(c)(lp) **COME BACK MY CHILDREN** (compilation) [ ] [-]
– Only losers take the bus / The day I lost everything / Wilderness on time / You won't get me home / 13th century you / Bishop of Babel / Valley of the dead cars / Big madness / What? / Blues for Ceausescu / On Suicide Bridge / Hive / The holy mugger / Stigmata / Lady Godiva's operation.

Jul 94. (7")(c-s) **THE LOYALISER. / GARY NUMAN'S PORSCHE** [58] [ ]
(12"+=)(cd-s+=) – Arnie's love / Into thinner air with the loyaliser.

Sep 94. (cd)(c)(colrd-lp) **LOST IN THE FORMER WEST** [ ] [ ]
– Belong nowhere / The loyaliser / Popemobile to Paraguay / Walk yr. way / Bruncelings's song / Lost in the former west / Nite flights / Your world customer / Sunken cities / Brain blister / A walk in the woods / Humiliate me.

Oct 94. (c-s) **NITE FLIGHTS. / IGNORANCE IS PISS** [ ] [ ]
(10")(cd-s) – ('A'side) / As I washed the blood off / Diamonds, fur coat, champagne / It's so cold . . . I think.

BUBONIQUE

CATHAL's alter-ego featuring Irish comedian **SEAN HUGHES**

Kitchen-ware | not issued

Mar 92. (7") **SCREW. / MONOGAMY I'M GOING TO KICK YOUR HEAD IN** [ ] [-]

Nov 92. (7")(cd-s) **SUMMER THE FIRST TIME. / FREE CHARLES MANSON** [ ] [-]

Apr 93. (cd)(c) **20 GOLDEN SHOWERS** [ ] [-]
– Summer the first time / Think you're cool / Play that funky music / Cop lover / Cod-sucker blues / My baby gave me rabiers / Release the bats / Elvis '93 / Chicken arse (theme) / Iron child / Yoda lady / Anytime anyplace it's ok / 2 J.G. / Stock Hausen and Waterman / East sheep station / Love me deadly kiss me Headley / DLT 666 no idea / The bubonique America Top 10 / Frank is Frank / Jellypop porky Jean / Dildo neighbour / Love camp 7 / Nation of Bubonique / Closedown.

Sep 95. (cd) **TRANCE ARSE VOLUME 3** [ ] [-]
– You can't fool the dead / Cod is love / The pianna / Truck Turner / The sermon / Freestyle masterclass 1; Sawing / Talkin' about talkin' about / Freebird / I've always liked hunting / Oi copper / Return of the nice age / What's e saying / Hey, handsome / Industrial woman / Rainbow buffalo cornwoman / Freestyle masterclass; Drilling / Q magazine / Kind of pue / 'George' aid suite / Abbabortion / Swan of Newcastle.

FAT LADY SINGS

Formed: Dublin, Ireland . . . mid 80's by NICK KELLY, etc (see below). For 4 years they plodded on for indie labels, until 'East West' came along early in 1990. Much loved by music press, especially after 1991 debut album 'TWIST'. • **Style:** Similiar sound to The BLUE NILE, The BIBLE or even a mellower U2. • **Songwriters:** KELLY, except ME AND JULIO DOWN BY THE SCHOOLYARD (Paul Simon) / IT'S A HARD LIFE WHEREVER YOU GO (Nanci Griffith).

Recommended: TWIST (*7) / JOHN SON (*6)

NICK KELLY – vocals, guitars, keyboards / **TIM BRADSHAW** – guitar, keyboards, violin, harmonica, vocals / **DERMOT LYNCH** – bass, keyboards, vocals / **ROBERT HAMILTON** – drums

Good Vibrations | not issued

Dec 86. (7") **FEAR AND FAVOUR. / WISHING WELL** [ ] [-]

Har-bour Base | not issued

Mar 88. (7") **BE STILL. / KING OF FREEDOM** [ ] [-]

Fourth Base | not issued

Sep 89. (7") **ARCLIGHT. / BEHIND YOUR BACK** [ ] [-]
(12"+=) – Fear and favour.

Jan 90. (7") **DRONNING MAUD LAND. / A MESSAGE (live)** [ ] [-]
(12"+=) – Heavy duty.

East West | East West

Oct 90. (7"+c-ep) **MAN SCARED. / BE STILL / BROKEN INTO** [ ] [ ]
(12"ep+=) – Not to touch.
(cd-ep) – (first 2 tracks) / Not to touch / Grand country wedding.

Mar 91. (7")(c-s) **ARCLIGHT. / BEHIND YOUR BACK** [ ] [ ]
(10"+=)(12"+=)(cd-s+=) – Fear and flavour.

May 91. (7")(c-s) **TWIST. / HEAVY DUTY** [ ] [ ]
(12"+=)(cd-s+=) – Is this all there is?
('A'acoustic-10"+=) – Call me dirt / Toytown.

May 91. (cd)(c)(lp) **TWIST** [50] [ ]
– Broken into / Arclight / Who wants you? / Twist / Love turned upside down / Deborah / Man scared / Be still / Gravy train / Contact / Dronning Maud land.

Aug 91. (7"ep)(c-ep)(10"ep)(12"ep)(cd-ep) **DEBORAH (alternative version) / GRAND COUNTRY WEDDING (acoustic tuba-laden version). / ME AND JULIO DOWN BY THE SCHOOLYARD (cajunified whistleicious) / GRAVY TRAIN (alternative rap intro mix)** [ ] [ ]

— HAMILTON replaced by additional members **NIC FRANCE** – drums, percussion / **STEVE OSBOURNE** – keyboards, percussion, vocals

May 93. (7")(c-s) **SHOW OF MYSELF. / EVERYWOMAN** [ ] [ ]
(cd-s+=) – Border keep.
(cd-s) – ('A'mix) / Broken promised land / Creepy baby.

Jul 93. (7")(c-s) **DRUNKARD LOGIC. / WHAT ARE YOU LIKE?** [56] [ ]
(cd-s+=) – Twist (live).
(cd-s) – ('A'side) / Contact (live) / Arclight (live).

Jul 93. (cd)(c)(lp) **JOHN SON** [ ] [ ]
– Boil / Show of myself / Alien / Drunkard logic / World exploding touch / Horse water wind / This guitar / Johnny Sunrise / Stealing a plane / Colourblind / But / Providence.

Oct 93. (7")(c-s)(cd-s) **WORLD EXPLODING TOUCH. / JOHN SON** [ ] [ ]
(cd-s+=) – Boil.
(cd-s) – ('A'side) / Alien (live) / Be still (live).

FAUST

Formed: Hamburg, Germany ... Spring 1971 by producer UWE NETTELBECK, who brought in musicians to his Wumme studios (see below). Became part of the burgeoning 'krautrock' underground scene alongside compatriots CAN, KRAFTWERK and TANGERINE DREAM. Unfortunately they were the ones left behind by public, although 'THE FAUST TAPES' ('Virgin' sampler of unreleased tunes) sold well enough, but was barred from the charts due to its 49 pence pricetag!. They had already unleashed 2 early 70's lp's for 'Polydor' and in 1973 they toured Europe after Richard Branson's 'Virgin' issued 'FAUST IV'. In 1974, they made an album with TONY CONRAD, who had earlier been a member of JOHN CALE's pre-VELVET days outfit The DREAM SYNDICATE (not the 80's US group). Eventually FAUST faded away into obscurity, but were re-called for one-off gig at London's Marquee 25th Oct'92. • **Style:** Avant-garde STOCKHAUSEN / VELVETS inspired outfit, who left conventional songs at the starting gate and opted for new usually untitled concept pieces /sides of interactive play. • **Songwriters:** Group & producer penned. • **Trivia:** UWE also produced for SLAPP HAPPY. Were and still are one of JULIAN COPE's (ex-TEARDROP EXPLODES) fave bands.

Recommended: SO FAR (*8) / THE FAUST TAPES (*5 at the time / *8 now!)

RUDOLF SOSNA – guitar/ **HANS JOACHIM IRMLER** – guitar/ **WERNER DIERMAIER** – drums/ **JEAN HERVE PERON** – bass/ **GUNTHER WUSTHOFF** – saxophone/ **A. MEIFERT** – other instruments

Polydor | not issued

1972. (lp) **FAUST** [ ] [-]
– Why don't you eat carrots / Meadow meal / Miss Fortune. *(re-iss.Oct79 on 'Recommended')*

— MEIFERT departed around same time, but still contributed later

1972. (lp) **SO FAR** [ ] [-]
– It's a rainy day, sunshine girl / On the way to Abamae / No harm / So far / Mamie is blue / I've got my car and my T.V. / Picnic on a frozen river / Me back space . . . /. . . In the spirit. *(re-iss.Oct79 on 'Recommended')*

Caroline | not issued

1973. (lp) **OUTSIDE DREAM SYNDICATE** ("FAUST & TONY CONRAD") [ ] [-]
(cd-iss.Feb94 on 'Lithium')

— added **PETER BLEGVAD** – guitar, clarinet, vocals

Virgin | Virgin

1973. (lp) **FAUST IV** [ ] [-]
– Krautrock / The sad skinhead / Jennifer / Just a second / Picnic on a picnic river / Deuxieme tableux / Giggy smile / Laeuft . . . heisst dass es laeuft oder es kommt bald . . . laeuft / It's a bit of a pain. *(cd-iss.Oct92)*

1973. (lp) **THE FAUST TAPES** (rec.1971-73) [ ] [-]
– (no song titles) *(cd-iss.Apr91 + Feb94 on 'R.E.R.')*

— Disbanded in 1973. PETER BLEGVAD went solo. However, they did re-form for London Marquee gig on 25 Oct'92.

– compilations, etc –

Mar 80. Recommended; (7") **EXTRACTS FROM FAUST PARTY 3** [ ] [-]
1980. Recommended; (lp) **CASABLANCA MOON** [ ] [-]
Apr 91. R.E.R.; (lp) **THE LAST LP** [ ] [-]
Nov 92. R.E.R.; (cd) **THE FAUST TAPES / 71 MINUTES OF FAUST** [ ] [-]
Feb 94. R.E.R.; (cd) **71 MINUTES OF FAUST** [ ] [-]

FEAR FACTORY

Formed: Los Angeles, USA . . .1991 by (see below). Completed two BILL GOULD (Faith No More) tracks for compilation album 'L.A. Death Metal' before being snapped up by 'Roadrunner'. Their debut album 'SOUL OF A NEW MACHINE' was produced by COLIN RICHARDSON and they ended 1992 on a tour supporting BIOHAZARD. They then teamed up with Canadian industrialists FRONT LINE ASSEMBLY who remixed their debut as 'FEAR IS THE MINDKILLER'. 1995 saw them grow into frontrunners of new electronic industrial death-metal brigade. • **Style:** As said. • **Songwriters:** BELL /

CAZARES / HERRERA, except DOG DAY SUMMR (Head Of David).

Recommended: DEMANUFACTURE (*6)

BURTON C. BELL – vocals / **DINO CAZARES** – guitar (of BRUJERIA) / **ANDREW SHIVES** – bass / **RAYMOND HERRERA** – drums

Road-runner Road-runner

Sep 92. (cd) **SOUL OF A NEW MACHINE**
– Martyr / Leechmaster / Scapegoat / Crisis / Crash test / Flesh hold / Lifeblind / Scumgrief / Natividad / Big god – Raped souls / Arise above oppression / Self immolation / Suffer age / W.O.E. / Desecrate / Escape confusion / Manipulation.

Apr 93. (m-cd) **FEAR IS THE MINDKILLER** -
– Martyr (suffer bastard mix) / Self immolation (vein tap mix) / Scapegoat (pigf*** mix) / Scumgrief (deep dub trauma mix) / Self immolation (liquid sky mix) / Self immolation (album version).

— **WELBERS** – bass repl.SHIVES

Jun 95. (cd)(c)(lp) **DEMANUFACTURE** 27
– Demanufacture / Self bias register / Zero signal / Replica / New breed / Dog day sunrise / Body hammer / Flashoint / H-K (Hunter-Killer) / Pisschrist / A therapy for pain / Your mistake / Resistancial! / New breed (revolutionary designed mix).

Nov 95. (12"ep)(cd-ep) **DOG DAY SUNRISE / ('A'version) / CONCRETO / REPLICA (electric sheep mix)**

Wilton FELDER (see under ⇒ CRUSADERS)

FELT

Formed: Birmingham, England . . . 1979 by LAWRENCE HAYWARD, who after debut 45 'INDEX', brought in NICK GILBERT. NICK issued his own 45 'NEWTRITION' / 'BLIMP' as The VERSATILE NEWTS for 'Shanghai' label in 1980. The same year, FELT brought in 2 new guys MAURICE DEEBANK and GARY AINGE, and signed to indie label 'Cherry Red'. Their next single 'SOMETHING SENDS ME TO SLEEP' appeared in 1981, and was soon followed by debut mini-lp 'CRUMBLING THE ANTISEPTIC BEAUTY'. FELT continued to be integral part of the 80's, although mainly only appealing to underground following. With LAWRENCE's new 1992 glam-rock project DENIM, maybe this will change. • **Style:** Guitar-picking pieces of romantic delight, played by TOM VERLAINE influenced LAWRENCE, augmented equally greatly by MAURICE until 1984. • **Songwriters:** LAWRENCE or MAURICE or together. • **Trivia:** ROBIN GUTHRIE produced them in 1985.

Recommended: ABSOLUTE CLASSIC MASTERPIECES (*8) / BUBBLEGUM PERFUME (*6) / BACK IN DENIM (*8; DENIM).

LAWRENCE HAYWARD – guitar, vocals

Shanghai not issued

Sep 79. (7") **INDEX. / BREAK IT** -

— added **MAURICE DEEBANK** – guitar / **GARY AINGE** – drums / **NICK GILBERT** – bass

Cherry Red not issued

Jul 81. (7") **SOMETHING SENDS ME TO SLEEP. / RED INDIANS** -

Feb 82. (m-lp) **CRUMBLING THE ANTISEPTIC BEAUTY** -
– Birdmen / Cathedral / I worship the sun / Templeroy / Fortune / Evergreen dazed.

— NICK GILBERT decided to leave. Also DEEBANK left for a short while

Sep 82. (7") **MY FACE IS ON FIRE. / TRAILS OF COLOUR DISSOLVE** -

— added **MICK LLOYD** – bass and the returning **DEEBANK**

Jun 83. (7") **PENELOPE TREE. / A PREACHER IN NEW ENGLAND** -
(12"+=) – Now Summer's spread its wings again.

Feb 84. (m-lp,c) **THE SPLENDOUR OF FEAR** -
– The stagnant pool / Red Indians / The world is as soft as lace / Mexican bandits / The optimist and the poet / Preacher in New England. *(re-iss.+1st m-lp as cd+c Sep86)(re-iss.cd Feb93)*

Mar 84. (7") **MEXICAN BANDITS. / THE WORLD IS AS SOFT AS LACE** -

Jul 84. (7") **SUNLIGHT BATHED THE GOLDEN GLOW. / FORTUNE** -
(12"+=) – Sunlight strings.

Oct 84. (lp) **THE STRANGE IDOLS PATTERN AND OTHER SHORT STORIES** -
– Roman litter / Sempiternal darkness / Spanish Louise / Vasco da Gama / Sunlight bathed the golden glow / Crucifix heaven / Whirlpool vision of shame / Dismantled King is off the throne / Imprint / Crystal ball.

— **MARTIN DUFFY** – organ repl. LLOYD (below b-side was above line-up) / **MARCO THOMAS** – bass guested with **ELIZABETH FRAZER** – vocals (COCTEAU TWINS) ROBIN GUTHRIE of The COCTEAUS produced 1985 material.

Aug 85. (12") **PRIMITIVE PAINTERS. / CATHEDRAL (rec.'84)** -
(pic-cd-s iss.Aug88)

— Band consisted of interchanging lead guitarists LAWRENCE and MAURICE, MARTIN and LIZ on some vocals, MARCO on nearly all bass, plus GARY – drums

Sep 85. (lp) **IGNITE THE SEVEN CANNONS** -
– My darkest light will shine / The day the rain came down / Scarlet servants / I don't know which way to turn / Serpent shade / Primitive painters / Elegance of an only dream / Black ship in the harbour / Textile ranch / Caspian see / Southern state tapestry. (c+=) – (incl.previous lp). *(cd-iss.Jul89 +1992, with last album)*

— guest **TONY WILLE** – guitar repl. MAURICE DEEBANK (MARCO now full member)

Creation not issued

May 86. (7") **BALLAD OF THE BAND. / I DIDN'T MEAN TO HURT YOU** -
(12"+=) – Candles in a church / Ferdinand Magellan.

Jun 86. (lp) **LET THE SNAKES CRINKLE THEIR HEADS TO DEATH** -
– Song for William S. Harvey / Ancient city where I lived / The seventeenth century / The palace / Indian scriptures / The Nazca plain / Voyage to illumination / Jewel sky / Viking dress / Sapphire mansions. *(cd-iss.Mar91)*

— **TONY WILLE** – guitars guested again

Sep 86. (lp)(c) **FOREVER BREATHES THE LONELY WORD** -
– Down but not yet out / Hours of darkness have changed my mind / All the people I like are those that are dead / Grey streets / Gather up your wings and fly / Rain of crystal spires / A wave crashed on rocks / September lady. (c+=) – (includes previous lp). *(cd-iss.Oct90)*

Sep 86. (7") **RAIN OF CRYSTAL SPIRES. / I WILL DIE WITH MY HEAD IN FLAMES** -
(12"+=) – Gather up your wings and fly / Sandman's on the rise again.

— added 6th guest member **NEIL SCOTT** – Fender jazzmaster retained guest **TONY WILLE** to augment **LAWRENCE, GARY, MARTIN** and **MARCO**

Jun 87. (m-lp) **POEM OF THE RIVER** -
– Declaration / She lives by the castle / Riding on the equator / Stained glass windows in the sky / Dark red birds / Silver plane. *(cd-iss.Mar91)*

— **FELT** are **LAWRENCE, MARTIN DUFFY, MARCO THOMAS, GARY AINGE** but album features 1. LAWRENCE with guest **RICHARD THOMAS** – soprano saxophone (of DIF JUZ) 2. DUFFY – solo / 3. LAWRENCE – solo guitar / 4. LAWRENCE with **MICK TRAVIS** – bass 5. LAWRENCE, DUFFY and TRAVIS – instrumental

Jul 87. (12"ep) **1.-THE FINAL RESTING PLACE OF THE ARK / 2.-Autumn / 3.-Fire circle / 4.-There's no such thing as victory / 5.-Buried wild blind.** -

— added **MICK BUND** – bass (MARCO now lead guitar & LAWRENCE added organ)

May 88. (lp) **THE PICTORIAL JACKSON REVIEW** -
– Apple boutique / Ivory past / Christopher St. / Bitter end / Until the fools get wise / How spook got her man / Don't die on my doorstep / Under a pale light / Sending lady Lord / The darkest ending.

— Next album was down to just DUFFY and AINGE. Others were rested

Aug 88. (lp) **TRAIN ABOVE THE CITY** -
– On Weegee's sidewalk / Train above the city / Run Chico run / Press sofltly on the brakes Holly / Seahorses on Broadway / Spectral morning / Book of swords / Teargardens. *(cd-iss.Oct88, with last album)*

— Full group again, + **ROSE McDOWELL** – vocals (ex-STRAWBERRY SWITCHBLADE)

Oct 88. (7") **SPACE BLUES. / Tuesdays secret** -
(12"+=) – Be still / Female star.

— **JOHN MOHAN** – guitar (ex-SERVANTS) repl. ROSE who was only guest.

El not issued

Oct 89. (7"free-flexi) **GET OUT OF MY MIRROR. /** -

Nov 89. (lp)(cd) **ME AND A MONKEY ON THE MOON** -
– I can't make love to you anymore / Mobile shack / Free / Budgie jacket / Carton sky / New day dawning / Down an August path / Never let you go / She deals in crosses / Get out of my mirror.

— They split late 1989, having been together for 10 years. LAWRENCE moved to New York, having flitted to Brighton a year earlier. DUFFY joined PRIMAL SCREAM.

– compilations, etc. –

Sep 87. Cherry Red; (lp)(c)(cd) **GOLD MINE THRASH** -
(c+=) – (includes 7 extra tracks).

May 88. Cherry Red; (cd) **POEM OF THE RIVER / FOREVER BREATHES THE LONELY WORD** -

Mar 92. Cherry Red; (12"ep)(cd-ep) **PRIMITIVE PAINTERS / DISMANTLED KING IS OFF THE THRONE. / SUNLIGHT BATHED THE GOLDEN GLOW** -

Apr 92. Cherry Red; (cd) **ABSOLUTE CLASSIC MASTERPIECES** -
– Primitive painters / The day the rain came down / My darkest light will shine / Textile ranch / Sunlight bathed the golden glow / Crystal ball / Dismantled king is off the throne / Fortune / Dance of deliverance / The stagnant pool / Red Indians / The world is as soft as lace / Penelope Tree / Trails of colour dissolve / Evergreen dazed / Templeroy / Something sends me to sleep / Index *(re-iss.cd/d-cd. Sep93)*

Jun 90. Creation; (cd)(c)(lp) **BUBBLEGUM PERFUME** -
– I will die with my head in flames / Stained glass windows in the sky / I Didn't mean to hurt you / Space blues / Autumn / Be still / There's no such thing as victory / Magellan / The final resting of the ark / Sandman's on the rise again / Don't die on my doorstep / A wave crashed on rocks / Book of swords / Declaration / Gather up your wings and fly / The darkest ending / Bitter end / Rain of crystal spires / Voyage of illumination / Ballad of the band

DENIM

were formed by **LAWRENCE** – vocals, guitar, keyboards with **SIOBHAN** – bass / **GERRY SHEPHERD** – drums (ex-GLITTER BAND)

Boy's Own not issued

Nov 92. (cd)(c)(lp) **BACK IN DENIM** -
– Back in denim / Fish and chips / Bubble head / Middle of the road / The Osmonds / I saw the glitter on your face / American rock / Livin' on the streets / Here is my song for Europe / I'm against the eighties.

Jan 93. (7")(c-s) **MIDDLE OF THE ROAD. / APE HANGERS** -
(12"+=)(cd-s+=) – Robin's nest / The great grape ape hangers.

MAURICE DEEBANK

also released a solo album while a FELT member. Augmented by **JOHN A. RIVERS** – producer, keyboards, percussion / **DA'AVE ELSON** – bass

Cherry Red not issued

Aug 84. (m-lp) **INNER THOUGHT ZONE** -
– The watery song / Four corners of the Earth / Study No.1 / Golden hills / Silver mountain of Paradise Square / So serene. *(cd-iss.Nov92 +=)* Dance of deliverance /

Pavanne / A tale from Seriabins lonely trail / Meastoso con anima *(cd-iss.1992, with extra tracks)*

Jay FERGUSON (see under ⇒ JO JO GUNNE)

Bryan FERRY (see under ⇒ ROXY MUSIC)

FFWD (see under ⇒ ORB)

FIELDS OF THE NEPHILIM

Formed: Stevenage, Hertfordshire, England . . . 1983 by CARL McCOY, etc (see below). After a debut 45 on 'Tower' in 1985, they signed to Beggar's B. off-shoot 'Situation 2'. A hit in the indie charts for a couple of years, they finally broke into big-time, when 'MOONCHILD' single hit UK Top 30 in 1988. It was quickly pursued a few months later, when second album 'THE NEPHILIM' made Top 20. • **Style:** Post-punk raiders of the apocalypse, fronted by gravel-voxed goth McCOY, whose image wasn't that far removed from SISTERS OF MERCY. • **Songwriters:** Group compositions except; IN EVERY DREAM HOME A HEARTACHE (Roxy Music). • **Trivia:** Their 1990 lp was produced by Andy Jackson.

Recommended: DAWNRAZOR (*6) / THE NEPHILIM (*6).

CARL McCOY – vocals / **PAUL WRIGHT** – guitar / **PETER YATES** – guitar / **TONY PETTIT** – bass / **NOD WRIGHT** – drums

Tower / not issued

Aug 85. (12"ep) **BURNING THE FIELDS** [ ] [-]
– Back in the Gehenna / Trees come down / Dark cell / Laura. *(re-iss.Jul87 on 'Situation 2')*

Situation 2 / not issued

Aug 86. (12"m) **POWER. / SECRETS / THE TOWER** [ ] [ ]
(above 2 re-iss. cd Dec 91 as 'LAURA' on 'Contempo')

Mar 87. (7") **PREACHER MAN. / LAURA II** [ ] [ ]
(12"+=) – ('A' contaminated).

May 87. (lp)(c) **DAWNRAZOR** [62] [ ]
– Intro (The harmonica man) / Slow kill / Volcane (Mr. Jealousy has returned) / Vet for the insane / Dust / Reanimator / Dawnrazor / The sequel. *(c+=)* – Preacher man / Power. *(cd++=)* – Laura II / Secrets / The Tower. *(cd-iss.Sep95 on 'Beggar's Banquet')*

Oct 87. (7") **BLUE WATER. / IN EVERY DREAM HOME A HEARTACHE** [75] [ ]
(12") – ('A'electrostatic mix) / ('A' hot wire version).

May 88. (7") **MOONCHILD (first seal). / SHIVA** [28] [ ]
(12"+=) – ('A'-Longevity).
(12"+=) – Power (live) / Vet for the insane (live).

Sep 88. (lp)(c)(cd) **THE NEPHILIM** [14] [ ]
– Endemoniada / The watchman / Phobia / Moonchild / Chord of souls / Shiva / Celebrate / Love under will / Last exit for the lost. *(re-iss.Jun89 as 2x12") (re-iss.Sep95 on 'Beggar's Banquet')*

May 89. (7")(12") **PSYCHONAUT (Lib.II). / CELEBRATE (second seal)** [35] [ ]
(cd-s+=) – Psychonaut (Lib.IV).
(12") – Psychonaut (Lib.III) / Psychonaut (Lib.I) / Psychonaut (Lib.IV).

Beggar's B. / Beggar's B

Jul 90. (7") **FOR HER LIGHT. / SUBMISSION** [54] [ ]
(12"+=)(cd-s+=) – ('A'&'B'extended).

Sep 90. (cd)(c)(lp) **ELIZIUM** [22] [ ]
– (Dead but dreaming) For her light (At the gates of silent memory) Paradise regained / Submission / Sumerland (what dreams may come) / Wail of summer / And there will your heart be also. *(re-iss.cd Sep95)*

Nov 90. (7") **SUMERLAND (DREAMED). / THE WATCHMAN (live)** [37] [ ]
(12"+=)(cd-s+=) – Blue water (live) / Phobia (live).

— In 1990, for live work they added **PAUL CHOWSER** – keyboards

Mar 91. (cd)(c)(d-lp) **EARTH INFERNO** (live Aug-Nov'90) [39] [ ]
– Intro (Dead but dreaming) For her light (at the gates of silent memory) Paradise regained / Moonchild / Submission / Preacher man / Love under will / Sumerland / Last exit for the lost / Psychonaut / Dawnrazor. *(re-iss.cd Sep95)*

— CARL McCOY departed Oct'91.

– compilations, etc. –

Jul 93. Beggar's Banquet; (d-cd)(c)(d-lp) **REVELATIONS** [ ] [ ]
– Moonchild / Chord of souls / Last exit for the lost / Preacher man / Love under will / Power / Psychonaut lib III / For her light / Blue water / Vet for the insane / The watchman / Dawnrazor. *(re-iss.cd Sep95)*

Nov 93. Supporti; (cd-ep) **RETURN TO GEHENNA** [ ] [-]
– Power (new version) / Laura (new version) / Secrets / The tower / Returning to Gehenna new version).

RUBICON

(aka FIELDS OF THE NEPHILIM)
with new vocalist **ANDY DELANEY** replacing McCOY

Beggar's B. / Beggar's B.

Aug 92. (12"ep)(cd-ep) **WATCH WITHOUT PAIN. / WATCH WITHOUT PAIN (full version) / KILLING TIME (demo version)** [ ] [-]

Oct 92. (12"ep)(cd-ep) **CRAZED. / CHAINS ARE GONE / BRAVE HEARTS (CELLAR TAPE)** [ ] [-]

Oct 92. (cd)(c)(lp) **WHAT STARTS, ENDS** [ ] [ ]
– Before my eyes / Crazed / Watch without pain / Brave hearts / Killing time / Inside your head / Unspoken / Hand for you / Rivers / What starts, ends. *(re-iss.cd+cApr93)*

Mar 93. (12"ep)(cd-ep) **BEFORE MY EYES / STANDING ALONE. / ON YOUR SIDE / HARD FOR YOU** [ ] [ ]

Apr 95. (cd-ep) **INSATIABLE / BURY MY GOLD / PRIME** [ ] [ ]

Apr 95. (cd)(c) **ROOM 101** [ ] [ ]
– Ageless / Rest a while / Doubt all / Insatiable / Cut down / On your side / This drenching night / Bury my gold / Empty hands / Eat with me.

FINE YOUNG CANNIBALS

Formed: Midlands, England . . . late '84 by COX and STEELE, who found vocalist ROLAND GIFT playing in a blues group in London. The trio took their name from a 1960 movie title, and signed to 'London' early 1985. Their debut 45 'JOHNNY COME HOME', with heavy promotion on Channel 4's 'The Tube', hit UK Top 10. After another Top 50 hit 'BLUE', they scored at UK No.11 with self-titled debut album late '85. In 1987, they contributed songs to 'Something Wild' film, and from it, had another Top 10 hit 'EVER FALLEN IN LOVE'. For the next 2 years, ROLAND starred in feature films 'Sammy And Rosie Get Laid' (1987) & 'Scandal' (1989). The group returned with a bang early in 1989, when album 'THE RAW AND THE COOKED', hit top spot in both UK & US. • **Style:** Intelligent pop-soul outfit, mixed with disco-rock beat, fronted by emotional AL JOLSON sounding ROLAND GIFT. • **Songwriters:** All written by COX-STEELE, except; SUSPICIOUS MINDS (hit; Elvis Presley) / EVER FALLEN IN LOVE (Buzzcocks). • **Trivia:** Singer JIMMY SOMERVILLE guested on their 'SUSPICIOUS MINDS' single.

Recommended: FINE YOUNG CANNIBALS (*6) / RAW AND THE COOKED (*6)

ROLAND GIFT (b.Birmingham, England) – vocals (ex-AKRYLYKX) / **ANDY COX** (b.25 Jan'60, Birmingham) – rhythm guitar (ex-BEAT) / **DAVID STEELE** (b. 8 Sep'60, Birmingham) – bass, keyboards (ex-BEAT) / with **MARTIN PARRY** – percussion / **GRAEME HAMILTON** – trumpet

London / I.R.S.

May 85. (7")(12")(7"pic-d) **JOHNNY COME HOME. / GOOD TIMES AND BAD** [8] [76] Mar 86

Oct 85. (7") **BLUE. / WADE IN THE WATER** [41] [ ]
(12"+=) – ('A'remix).
(d7"+=) – ('A'version) / Love for sale. (US; b-side)

Dec 85. (lp)(c)(cd) **FINE YOUNG CANNIBALS** [11] [49]
– Johnny come home / Couldn't care more / Don't ask me to choose / Funny how love is / Suspicious minds / Blue / Move to work / On a promise / Time isn't kind / Like a stranger.

Dec 85. (7")(7"pic-d) **SUSPICIOUS MINDS. / PRICK UP YOUR EARS** [8] [ ]
(12"+=) – ('A'live) / Time isn't kind.
(12") – ('A'live) / (US & remix-versions).

Mar 86. (7")(7"pic-d) **FUNNY HOW LOVE IS. / MOTHERLESS CHILD** [58] [ ]
(12"+=) – Johnny come home (live).

Apr 87. (7") **EVER FALLEN IN LOVE. / COULDN'T CARE MORE** [9] [-]
(12"+=) – ('A'dub).
(12") – ('A'club mix) / ('A'rare mix).
(c-s)(cd-s) – ('A'club mix) / Blue (live).

May 87. (7") **EVER FALLEN IN LOVE. / MOVE TO WORK** [-] [ ]

Jan 89. (7") **SHE DRIVES ME CRAZY. / PULL THE SUCKER OFF** [5] [1]
(12"+=)(cd-s+=) – ('A'remix).

Feb 89. (lp)(c)(cd) **THE RAW AND THE COOKED** [1] [1]
– She drives me crazy / Good thing / I'm not the man I used to be / I'm not satisfied / Tell me what / Don't look back / It's OK (it's alright) / Don't let it get you down / As hard as it is / Ever fallen in love.

Apr 89. (7")(10") **GOOD THING. / SOCIAL SECURITY** [7] [1]
(12"+=) – ('A'instrumental).
(cd-s+=) – ('A'remix) / She drives me crazy (remix).

Aug 89. (7")(c-s) **DON'T LOOK BACK. / YOU NEVER KNOW** [34] [11]
(12"+=)(cd-s+=) – ('A'remix).

Nov 89. (7")(c-s) **I'M NOT THE MAN I USED TO BE. / MOTHERLESS CHILD** [20] [ ]
(12")(cd-s) – ('A'side) / She drives me crazy / Good thing / Don't look back.
(extra-12"+=) – ('A' 3 versions) / ('A'instrumental). /

Feb 90. (7")(c-s) **I'M NOT SATISFIED. / ('A' Nicci mix)** [46] [ ]
(12"+=)(cd-s+=) – ('A'versions).

Dec 90. (cd)(c)(lp) **THE RAW & THE REMIX** ('89 lp remixed) [61] [ ]

TWO MEN, A DRUM MACHINE & A TRUMPET

(**COX** and **STEEL** one-off)

London / I.R.S.

Jan 88. (12") **I'M TIRED OF GETTING PUSHED AROUND. / MAKE IT FUNNY** [18] [ ]

FINI TRIBE

Formed: Edinburgh, Scotland . . . 1984 by CHRIS CONNELLY and JOHN VICKI and 4 others. In 1986 with 2 singles under their belt, they virtually threw away all conventional instruments and bought a sampler, thus opting out of live gigs. Signed to Chicago label 'Wax Trax' in '87, where they issued 2 better selling singles 'I WANT MORE' & 'MAKE IT INTERNAL'. Returned to some live work in '87 and resurrected label 'Finiflex', although 3 members were soon to leave. Finally released debut lp 'NOISE, LUST AND FUN' late '88, which featured ANNIE ANXIETY BANDEZ, plus ROSAGHN (Bop'sh'bam), WILF PLUM (Dog Faced Hermans) and JESS HOPKINS (World Reknowned

Fame). Ran into threatened court action in September '91, when ELECTRIBE 101 objected to them using FINITRIBE 101 on a single. • **Style:** Electro art terrorists mixing baleric classical and soundtrack-like technology with scientist dance-rock appeal. Were one of main pioneers of the acid-house and balearic beat scene in 1986. • **Songwriters:** Group penned. Sampled nursery rhyme 'OLD McDONALD' on 'ANIMAL FARM'! • **Trivia:** Their group name derives from 'finny Tribe'; fish in Rosicruscians, Ireland. In the first half of 1989, The FINIS can be heard on TOTAL and ABSTRACT recordings.

Recommended: NOISE, LUST AND FUN (*7) / AN UNEXPECTED GOOVY TREAT (*8)

CHRIS CONNELLY / JOHN VICKI (b. 6 Nov '65) / **DAVID MILLAR** (b. 20 Jul '62, Moffat, Scotland) / + 3 others.

Finiflex — not issued

Jun 84. (12") **CURLING & STRETCHING EP** — -
(re-iss.1988)

Cathexis — not issued

Oct 86. (12"ep) **LET THE TRIBE GROW** — -
– De testimony (collapsing edit) / Throttle hearts (rising mix) / Adults absolved / Monimail. *(re-iss. Oct 88 on 'Finiflex')*

1980's? (lp) **YOU BET WE'VE GOT** (compilation) — -

Wax Trax — Wax Trax

Oct 87. (12") **I WANT MORE / IDIOT STRENGTH. / I WANT MORE (row, row, row the mix)**

—— 5-piece **CHRIS CONNELLY / JOHN VICKI / PHILIP PINSKY / SIMON McGOWAN / DAVID MILLAR**

Feb 88. (12") **MAKE IT INTERNAL (integrity mix) / LITTLE VISITORS. / MAKE IT INTERNAL (here we go round the mulberry mix)**

—— CONNELLY joined The REVOLTING COCKS in 1988 before embarking on solo career.

Finiflex — not issued

Nov 88. (lp) **NOISE, LUST & FUN**
– Electrolux / Disturb / Swans / Finis / Throttlehearts / Zulus / Fluke / Electrolux / Swans / Disturb / Ultra. *(cd-iss.Oct89 on 'O. L. Indian')*

Nov 88. (12"ep) **ZULUS EP**
– The crunchy mix / The rhythmix / Noise (pick'n'mix).

Oct 88. (12"ep) **DE TESTIMONY EP** — -
– The batter mix / Micromix / Pick'n'mix.

Dec 88. (12"ep) **ELECT-ROLUX EP** — -
– Electrolux (pick'n'mix) / Electrolux (minimix) / Disturb (cement mix).

One Little Indian — Rough Trade

Nov 89. (12"ep)(cd-ep) **ANIMAL FARM EP**
Chicken mix / Ouch ya go (ouchtakes) / Monkey mix / Animal farm (meatymix).

Dec 89. (lp)(c)(cd) **GROSSING 10K**
– Eyeball / Instant access / An Earth creature / Whale of a tail / Ask a silly question / Monster in the house / Asstrax / 3 AAA's / Put your trunk in it / Built in monster / Animal farm / Ouch ya go.

Mar 90. (12"ep) **MONSTER IN THE HOUSE EP**
– Monster club / Monster in the wireless / Eyeball / Built in monsters

—— Trimmed to a trio of **VICKI, PINSKY + MILLAR**

Jul 91. (7")(12")(cd-s) **101. (by "FINITRIBE 101") / SONIC SHUFFLE (mixed by Andy Weatherall)**
(12") – 101 (mixed by Graham Massey of 808 State).

Nov 91. (12"ep)(cd-ep) **ACE* LOVE* DEUCE (Steve Osbourne mix). / ('A'-Justin Robertson mix)** — -

Jun 92. (3x12"ep)(c-ep)(cd-ep) **FOREVERGREEN (2 Justin Robertson mixes) / ('A'-Youth mixes) / ('A'-Andy Weatherall mix)** — 51

Sep 92. (cd)(c)(lp) **AN UNEXPECTED GROOVY TREAT**
– Forevergreen / 101 (sonic shuffle edit) / Come and get it / Mellowman / Yer crazy / Bagomatix II (there can only be one) / Ace* love* deuce* / Hypnopaedia / Glisten / An unexpected groovy treat / Forevergreen (forevermost excellent) / Ace love deuce / Forevergreen (foreverdreaming).

Ffrr-London — London

Nov 94. (12"ep)(cd-ep) **BRAND NEW EP** — 69
– Tip top tune / Tip top.

Mar 95. (c-s) **LOVE ABOVE / ('A'-Sheigra 5 mix)**
(12"+=) – ('A'-Cheeky Vee half mix) / ('A'-Analogue mix).
(cd-s++=) ('A'-original mix).

Apr 95. (d-cd)(c)(d-lp) **SHEIGRA**
– Dark / Sunshine / Brand new (tip-top tune) / Mushroom shaped / Sheigra 5 / Truth / Catch the whistle / We have come / Mesmerise / Off on a slow one / Love above (Analogue mix).

Tim FINN / FINN (see under ⇒ CROWDED HOUSE)

FIRE ENGINES

Formed: Edinburgh, Scotland . . . 1979 by DAVEY HENDERSON, etc (see below). After a single and album on own indie labels, they signed to Bob Last's 'Pop Aural' label in 1981. Their next 2 gems 'CANDY SKIN' & 'BIG GOLD DREAM', became music press favourites, although their demise was imminent. In 1984, HENDERSON and BURN were back with more commercially fruitful WIN. They soon signed to Alan Horne's 'Swamplands' label, and when this was taken over by 'London' in 1986, they had near UK Top 50 hit album 'UH! TEARS BABY (A TRASH ICON)'. • **Style:** Funk-punk outfit, similar to The POP GROUP and A CERTAIN RATIO. WIN were a more intellectual soul-pop based outfit, with slices of funk. • **Songwriters:** All written by HENDERSON, except FASCIST GROOVE (Heaven 17). NECTARINE No.9 covered INSIDE OF YOUR HEART (Velvet Underground) / FROWNLAND (Captain Beefheart) / PULL MY DAISY (Ginsberg-Kerouac). • **Trivia:** WIN's 'YOU'VE GOT THE POWER' was featured on a McEwan's lager TV ad.

Recommended: FOND (*9) / UH! TEARS BABY WIN (WIN *7).

DAVEY HENDERSON – vocals, guitar (ex-DIRTY REDS) / **MURRAY SLADE** – guitar / **GRAHAM MAIN** – bass / **RUSSELL BURN** – drums

Codex — not issued

Dec 80. (7") **GET UP AND USE ME. / EVERYTHING'S ROSES** — -

Accessory — Fast

Jan 81. (m-lp) **LUBRICATE YOUR LIVING ROOM** — - 1982
– Plastic gift / Get up and use me / Hungry beat / Lubricate your living room pt.1 & 2 / New thing in the cartons / Sympathetic anaesthetic / Discord. *(US title 'AUFGELADEN UND BEREIT FUR ACTION UNDER SPASS')*

Pop Aural — not issued

May 81. (7") **CANDY SKIN. / MEAT WHIPLASH** — -

—— added guests **SIMON BEST** – keyboards / **HI-RAY** (b. HILARY MORRISON) – vocals (of FLOWERS) / **KAREN BROWN** – b. vocals

Nov 81. (7") **BIG GOLD DREAM. / SYMPATHETIC ANAESTHETIC** — -
(12"+=) – New thing in cartons.

Band folded 31 Dec'81. DAVEY and HILARY formed HEARTBEAT. (1 track on NME-c)

– compilations, etc. –

Aug 92. Revola-Creation; (cd) **FOND** (all work, etc) — -

EVEREST THE HARD WAY

were formed by **RUSSELL** with others **IAN STODDART** – bass / **STEPHEN LIRONI** – guitar, keyboards (later ALTERED IMAGES)

Do-It — not issued

Apr 82. (7")(12") **TIGHTROPE. / WHEN YOU'RE YOUNG** — -

—— They split later that year. RUSSELL joined DIRTY REDS before forming below.

WIN

DAVEY HENDERSON – vocals, guitar / **RUSSELL BURN** – drums / **IAN STODDART** – bass

Swamplands — not issued

Mar 85. (7")(12") **UNAMERICAN BROADCASTING pt.1. / UNAMERICAN BROADCASTING pt.2** — -

Jun 85. (7") **YOU'VE GOT THE POWER. / IN HEAVEN (LADY IN THE RADIATOR SONG)** — -
(12") – ('A'side) / Unamerican broadcasting pt.1 & 2.
(d7") – (all 4 tracks).

London — London

Mar 86. (7") **SHAMPOO TEARS. / EMPTY HOLSTERS** — -
(12"+=) – The slider / ('A'dub version).

Mar 87. (7") **SUPER POPOID GROVE. / BABY CUTTING** — 63 -
(12"+=) – You've got the power.
(d7"++=) – In Heaven (the lady in the radiator song).

Apr 87. (lp)(c)(cd) **UH! TEARS BABY (A TRASH ICON)** — 51
– Super popoid groove / Shampoo tears / Binding love spell / Unamerican broadcasting / Hollywood Baby too / Empty holsters / You've got the power / Charms of powerful trouble / It may be a beautiful sky tonight but it's only a shelter for a world at risk / Charms (reprise) / Baby cutting. *(c+cd+=)* – Shampoo tears (extended) / You've got the power (extended).

—— added **MANNY SCHONIVVA** – guitar / **WILLIE PERRY** – keyboards / **SIMON SMEETON** – guitar(appeared on last album alongside EMANUEL SHONIWA.)

Virgin — Virgin

Nov 88. (7")(12") **WHAT'LL YOU DO TILL SUNDAY, BABY. / TRIGGER HAPPY** — -

Jan 89. (7") **LOVE UNITS. / SCARY SCARY**
(12"+=) – ('A'version).
(cd-s++=) – Pull my daisy.

Mar 89. (lp)(c)(cd) **FREAKY TRIGGER**
– What'll you do til' Sunday baby / Taboo / Love units / Rainbow / Truckee river / How do you do / What's love if you can kill for chocolate / Mind the gravy / Dusty heartfelt / We can cover up the "C". *(c++)(cd+=)* – Love units (12"mix) / What's love if you can kill for chocolate (12"mix).

May 89. (7") **DUSTY HEARTFELT. / PEACE ON EGG**
(12"+=)(3"cd-s+=) – ('A'version).

—— Disbanded late 1989, and HENDERSON went onto form . . .

NECTARINE No.9

DAVEY HENDERSON +

Postcard — not issued

Feb 93. (cd)(lp) **A SEA WITH THREE STARS** — -
– Pop's love thing / She's a nicer word to sing / The holes of Corpus Christi / Beautiful car / 22 blue / Peanut brain / Smiths new automatic / A sea with three stars / The No. you mean / Don't worry babe, you're not the only one awake / Trace nine / Chocolate swastika.

Oct 93. (cd-ep) **UNLOADED FOR YOU** — -
– Pop's new thing / Chocolate swastika / Going off someone / Don't worry babe you're not the only one awake.

Apr 94. (cd-ep) **GUITAR THIEVES** (on 'Nightracks') — -
– Frownland / Pull my daisy / Inside of your heart / +.

Jun 95. (cd-ep) **PREGNANT WITH POSSIBILITIES ("PAUL QUINN / NECTARINE No.9 / JOCK SCOTT")** — -
– Tiger tiger / Will I ever be inside of you / Just another f***ed-up little druggy on the scene / Grunge girl groan.

Jul 95. (cd) **SAINT JACK** — -

– Saint Jack / Curdled fragments / Fading memory babe / Can't scratch out / This arsehole's been burned too many times before / It's not my baby putting me down / My trapped lightning / Just another f***ed-up little druggy on the scene / Couldn't phone potatoes / Dead horse a rum / Firecrackers / Unloaded for you / Clipped wings and power stings / Tape your head on.

FIREHOSE (see under ⇒ MINUTEMEN)

FIRM (see under ⇒ LED ZEPPELIN)

FISH

Born: DEREK WILLIAM DICK, 25 Apr'58, Dalkeith, Lothian, Scotland. After leaving MARILLION in Sep'88, he released debut single 'STATE OF MIND', a year later. This hit UK Top 40, as did his early 1990 follow-up 'BIG WEDGE'. A Top 5 album 'VIGIL IN A WILDERNESS OF MIRRORS' was soon in chart, and he continued further fruitful activities on 'Polydor'. He had now moved back to Scotland, after living in London. • **Style:** FISH sported a more commercial guitar-based sound, although his vox always was indebted to PETER GABRIEL. • **Songwriters:** He co-wrote most of material with MICKEY SIMMONDS. He covered; THE FAITH HEALER (Sensational Alex Harvey Band). In early 1993, he released full covers album with tracks: QUESTION (Moody Blues) / BOSTON TEA PARTY (Sensational Alex Harvey Band) / FEARLESS (Pink Floyd) / APEMAN (Kinks) / HOLD YOUR HEAD UP (Argent) / SOLD (Sandy Denny) / I KNOW WHAT I LIKE (Genesis) / JEEPSTER (T.Rex) / FIVE YEARS (David Bowie) / ROADHOUSE BLUES (Doors). • **Trivia:** October '86, FISH was credited on TONY BANKS (Genesis) single 'Short Cut To Nowhere'.

Recommended: VIGIL IN A WILDERNESS OF MIRRORS (*6).

FISH – vocals (ex-MARILLION) with guest musicians on debut album **FRANK USHER** – guitar / **HAL LINDES** – guitar / **MICKEY SIMMONDS** – keyboards / **JOHN GIBLIN** – bass / **MARK BRZEZICKI** – drums / **CAROL KENYON** – backing vocals / plus **LUIS JARDIM** – percussion / **JANICK GERS** – guitar

E.M.I. E.M.I.

Oct 89. (7")(c-s) **STATE OF MIND. / THE VOYEUR (I LIKE TO WATCH)** 32
(12"+=)(cd-s+=) – ('A'version).
Dec 89. (7")(c-s) **BIG WEDGE. / JACK AND JILL** 25
(12"+=)(cd-s+=)(12"pic-d+=) – Faith healer (live).
Feb 90. (cd)(c)(lp)(pic-lp) **VIGIL IN A WILDERNESS OF MIRRORS** 5
– Vigil / Big wedge / State of mind / The company / A gentleman's excuse me / The voyeur (I like to watch) / Family business / View from the hill / Cliche.
Mar 90. (7")(c-s)(7"sha-pic-d)(7"red) **A GENTLEMAN'S EXCUSE ME. / WHIPLASH** 30
(12"+=)(cd-s+=)(12"pic-d+=) – ('A'demo version).

— retained SIMMONDS and USHER, and brought in **ROBIN BOULT** – lead guitar, vocals / **DAVID PATON** – bass / **ETHAN JOHNS** – drums, perc. / guest drummer **TED McKENNA**

Polydor Polydor

Sep 91. (7") **INTERNAL EXILE. / CARNIVAL MAN** 37
(12"+=)(12"pic-d+=) – ('A' karaoke mix).
(cd-s++=) – ('A'other mix).
Oct 91. (cd)(c)(lp) **INTERNAL EXILE** 21
– Shadowplay / Credo / Just good friends (close) / Favourite stranger / Lucky / Dear friend / Tongues / Internal exile. *(re-iss.cd Apr95)*
Dec 91. (7")(c-s) **CREDO. / POET'S MOON** 38
(12"+=)(cd-s+=) – ('A'mix).
(12"+=) – (2 'A'versions) / Tongues (demo).
Jun 92. (7")(c-s) **SOMETHING IN THE AIR. / DEAR FRIEND** 51
(12"+=) – ('A'-Teddy bear mix).
(cd-s++=) – ('A'radio mix).
(cd-s) – ('A'&'B'diff.mixes) / Credo / Shadowplay.

— **FOSTER PATTERSON** – keyboards, vocals repl. SIMMONS / **KEVIN WILKINSON** – drums, percussion repl. JOHNS.

Jan 93. (cd)(c)(lp) **SONGS FROM THE MIRROR** (covers) 46
– Question / Boston tea party / Fearless / Apeman / Hold your head up / Solo / I know what I like / Jeepster / Five years. *(re-iss.cd Apr95)*

Dick Bros not issued

Mar 94. (d-cd) **SUSHI (live)** -
– Fearless / Big wedge / Boston tea party / Credo / Family business / View from a hill / He knows you know / She chameleon / Kayleigh / White Russian / The company / / Just good friends / Jeepster / Hold your head up / Lucky / Internal exile / Cliche / Last straw / Poets Moon / 5 years.
Apr 94. (c-s)('A'ext-12"pic-d) **LADY LET IT LIE / OUT OF MY LIFE. / BLACK CANAL** 46
(cd-s) – ('A'extended) / ('B'live) / Emperors song (live) / Just good friends.
May 94. (cd)(c)(pic-lp)(d-lp) **SUITS** 18
– 1470 / Lady let it lie / Emperor's song / Fortunes of war / Somebody special / No dummy / Pipeline / Jumpsuit city / Bandwagon / Raw meat.
Sep 94. (cd-ep) **FORTUNES OF WAR (edit) / SOMEBODY SPECIAL (live) / STATE OF MIND (live) / LUCKY (Live)** 67
(cd-ep) – ('A'live) / Warm wet circles / Jumpsuit city / The company (all live).
(cd-ep) – ('A'acoustic) / Kayleigh (live) / Internal exile (live) / Just good friends (acoustic).
(cd-ep) – ('A'acoustic) / Sugar mice (live) / Dear friend (live) / Lady let it lie (acoustic).

— Above 4-cd single (nearly 90 mins.) (can be fitted in together as 1 package.

Aug 95. (c-s) **JUST GOOD FRIENDS. ("FISH featuring SAM BROWN") / SOMEBODY SPECIAL** 63
(cd-s+=) – State of mind.
(cd-s) – ('A'side) / Raw meat (live) / Roadhouse blues (live).
Sep 95. (cd)(c) **YIN** (THE BEST OF FISH & '95 remixes) 58 -
– Incommunicado / Family business / Just good friends / Pipeline / Institution waltz / Tongues / Favourite stranger / Boston tea party / Raw meat / Time & a word / Company / Incubus / Solo.
Sep 95. (cd)(c) **YANG** (THE BEST OF FISH & '95 remixes) 52 -
– Lucky / Big wedge / Lady let it lie / Lavender / Credo / A gentleman's excuse me / Kayleigh / State of mind / Somebody special / Sugar mice / Punch & Judy / Internal exile / Fortunes of war.

FIXX

Formed: London, England . . . late 1979 as The PORTRAITS by CURNIN, GREENHALL and WOODS. After 1 single 'HAZARD IN THE HOME' for 'Ariola', they became The FIX, a year later. Another 45 followed, and after its flop, they decided to add an X to group name. They set up own label late 1981, which was endorsed by major 'MCA'. Their first entry to UK chart, came in Spring '82, when 'STAND OR FALL', breached in Top 60. After a minor hit album 'SHUTTERED ROOM', they cracked US market in 1983, when 45 'SAVED BY ZERO' hit Top 20. • **Style:** Relaxing sophisticated rock-pop, that suited American AOR audiences. • **Songwriters:** All written by CURNIN & WEST-ORAM. • **Trivia:** The pair penned hit single 'BETTER BE GOOD TO ME' for TINA TURNER in 1984.

Recommended: REACT (*5)

The PORTRAITS

CY CURNIN (b.12 Dec'57) – vocals, piano / **RUPERT GREENHALL** – keyboards / **ADAM WOODS** – drums, percussion

Ariola not issued

Feb 80. (7") **HAZARD IN THE HOME. / NEVER LET GO** -

The FIX

added **JAMES WEST-ORAM** – guitars (ex-The DOLL, ex-PHIL RAMBOW BAND) / **CHARLES BARRETT** – bass

101-Polydor not issued

Apr 81. (7") **LOST PLANES. / I'VE BEEN HERE BEFORE** -

The FIXX

Fixx-M.C.A. M.C.A.

Jan 82. (7") **SOME PEOPLE. / I FOUND YOU**
Mar 82. (7")(12") **STAND OR FALL. / THE STRAIN** 54 -
Apr 82. (lp)(c) **SHUTTERED ROOM** 54 Sep 82
– Stand or fall / Red skies / Some people / The fool / Cameras in Paris / Shuttered room / Lost planes / I live / Time in a glass / Sinking island. *(US cd-iss.Jun88)*
Jun 82. (7")(7"pic-d) **RED SKIES. / IT IS BY INSTINCT** 57
(12") – ('A'side) / – Sinking island.
Oct 82. (7") **STAND OR FALL. / SINKING ISLAND** - 76

— **ALFIE AGIES** – bass (ex-TEARDROP EXPLODES) repl. BARRETT

Apr 83. (7") **SAVED BY ZERO. / GOING OVERBOARD** 20
(12"+=) – The fool.
May 83. (lp)(c) **REACH THE BEACH** 91 8
– Reach the beach / Saved by zero / Outside / The sign of fire / Running / Opinions / Changing / One thing leads to another / Liner / Privilege. *(cd-iss.1986, US cd-iss.Jun88)*
Aug 83. (7") **ONE THING LEADS TO ANOTHER. / OPINIONS** - 4
Aug 83. (7")(12") **ONE THING LEADS TO ANOTHER. / REACH THE BEACH** -
(d7") – ('A'side) / – Red skies / Stand or fall / Opinions
Nov 83. (7") **THE SIGN OF FIRE. / SAVED BY ZERO (live)** - 32

— **DAN K. BROWN** – bass repl. ALGIES

Jul 84. (7") **ARE WE OURSELVES? / DEEPER AND DEEPER** - 15
Aug 84. (7")(12") **LESS CITIES MORE MOVING PEOPLE. / DEEPER AND DEEPER** -
Sep 84. (lp)(c)(cd) **PHANTOMS** 19
– Less cities more moving people / Lose face / Sunshine in the shade / Woman on a train / Wish / In suspense / Lost in the battle / Facing the wind / Are we ourselves? / Questions / Lost in the battle overseas / I will / Phantom living. *(cd-iss.Jan85) (US cd-iss.Jun88)*
Sep 84. (7") **LESS CITIES, MORE MOVING PEOPLE. / WOMAN ON A TRAIN** -
Oct 84. (7")(12") **ARE WE OURSELVES. / QUESTIONS** -
Nov 84. (7") **SUNSHINE IN THE SHADE. /** - 69
Mar 85. (7")(12") **I WILL. / QUESTIONS**
Jun 86. (7") **SECRET SEPARATION. / SENSE OF ADVENTURE** 19 May 86
(12"+=) – Rediscover.
Sep 86. (lp)(c)(cd) **WALKABOUT** 30 Jun 86
– Secret separation / Built for the future / Treasure it / One look up / Chase the fire / Can't finish / Walkabout / Campher / Read between the lines / Sense of adventure.
Oct 86. (7") **BUILT FOR THE FUTURE. / CAMPHER** -
1987. (7") **RED SKIES (live). / BUILT FOR THE FUTURE (live)** -
Jun 87. (lp)(c)(cd) **REACT** (live) -
– Red Skies / Big wall / Don't be afraid / Rules and schemes / Deeper and deeper / Stand or fall / Built for the future / Saved by zero / Are we ourselves / One thing leads to another.

— Split for a while. WEST-ORAM had joined TINA TURNER '85. Re-formed 1988

R.C.A. R.C.A.

Feb 89. (lp)(c)(cd) **CALM ANIMALS** 72

– I'm life / Driven out / Subterranean / Precious stone / Gypsy fat / Calm animals / Shred of evidence / The flow / World weary / Cause to be alarmed.

Mar 89. (7") **DRIVEN OUT. / SHRED OF EVIDENCE** [ ] [55] Feb 89
(12"+=)(cd-s+=) – The flow.

E.M.I. / Impact-MCA

Mar 91. (cd)(c)(lp) **INK** [ ] [ ]
– All is fair / How much is enough / No one has to cry / Crucified / Shut it out / Still around / All the best things / Yesterday, today / One jungle / Climb the hill. (cd+=) – Make no plans. (c++=) – Falling in love.

Apr 91. (7"ep)(c-ep) **HOW MUCH IS ENOUGH / ALL IS FAIR. / CRUCIFIED / STILL AROUND** [ ] [35] Mar 91
(12"ep+=)(cd-ep+=) – ('A'dance mix).

FLAG OF CONVENIENCE / F. O. C. (see under ⇒ BUZZCOCKS)

FLAMIN' GROOVIES

Formed: Bay Area, San Francisco, California, USA ... 1966 originally as The CHOSEN FEW and then The LOST AND FOUND, by CYRIL JORDAN, ROY LONEY, GEORGE ALEXANDER and TIM LYNCH. In 1967, they issued self-financed debut lp, the 10" 'SNEAKERS', which resulted in a deal with 'Epic'. After one poorly promoted lp 'SUPERSNAZZ', they left to join ranks of 'Kama Sutra', helped by producer Richard Robinson in 1970. They issued 2 well-received lps 'FLAMINGO' & 'TEENAGE HEAD', before again moving stables to 'United Art' in '72. The following years were spent changing personnel, touring Europe, and finally getting released another DAVE EDMUNDS produced 'Sire' comeback 'SHAKE SOME ACTION'. He had worked on their previous lp 'SLOW DEATH' in 1972. • **Style:** High energy rock'n'roll, which updated 50's material into late 60's style garage punk rock. Were at home in new wave scene at its 1976 initiation period. • **Songwriters:** JORDAN-LONEY, until latters' departure in '71. Recorded many covers including; SOMETHIN' ELSE (Eddie Cochran) / PISTOL PACKIN' MAMA (Gene Vincent) / SHAKIN' ALL OVER (Johnny Kidd) / THAT'LL BE THE DAY (Buddy Holly) / KEEP A KNOCKIN' (Little Richard) / MOVE IT (Cliff Richard) / FEEL A WHOLE LOT BETTER (Byrds) / PAINT IT BLACK + JUMPIN' JACK FLASH + 19th NERVOUS BREAKDOWN (Rolling Stones) / MARRIED WOMAN (Frankie Lee Sims) / TEENAGE CONFIDENTIAL (Jerry Lee Lewis) / WEREWOLVES OF LONDON (Warren Zevon) / ABSOLUTELY SWEET MARIE (Bob Dylan) / TALLAHASSEE LASSIE (Freddy Cannon) / KICKS (Mann-Weill) / CALL ME LIGHTNING (Who) / MONEY (Barrett Strong) / PLEASE PLEASE ME + MISERY + THERE'S A PLACE (Beatles) / etc. • **Trivia:** Long-time fan GREG SHAW, issued 1975 single 'YOU TORE ME DOWN', for his own 'Bomp' magazine label.

Recommended: GROOVIES GREATEST GROOVES (*6)

ROB LONEY (b.13 Apr'46) – vocals / **CYRIL JORDAN** (b. 1948) – lead guitar / **TIM LYNCH** (b.18 Jul'46) – rhythm guitar / **GEORGE ALEXANDER** (b.18 May'46, San Mateo, Calif.) – bass / **DANNY MIHM** – drums (ex-WHISTLING SHRIMP) repl. RON GRECO

not issued / Snazz

1967. (10"mlp) **SNEAKERS** [-] [ ]
– The slide / I'm drowning / Babes in the sky / Love time / My yada / Golden clouds / Prelude in A flat to afternoon of a plad.

not issued / Epic

1968. (7") **ROCKIN' PNEUMONIA AND THE BOOGIE WOOGIE FLU. / THE FIRST ONE'S FREE** [-] [ ]

1968. (7") **SOMETHIN' ELSE. / LAURIE DID IT** [-] [ ]

1969. (lp) **SUPERSNAZZ** [-] [ ]
– Love have mercy / The girl can't help it / Laurie did it / Apart from that / Rockin' pneumonia and the boogie woogie flu / The first one's free / Pagan Rachel / a) Somethin' else, b) Pistol packin' mama / Brushfire / Bam balam / Around the corner. *(UK-rel.Feb86 on 'Edsel')*

Kama Sutra / Kama Sutra

1970. (lp) **FLAMINGO** [-] [ ]
– Roadhouse / Headin' for the Texas border / Gonna rock tonite / Comin' after you / Sweet roll me on down / Keep a knockin' / Second cousin / Childhood's end / Jailbait / She's falling apart / Walking the dog / Somethin' else / My girl Josephine / Louie Louie / Rockin' pnumonia and the boogie woogie flu / Going out there (version).

1971. (7") **TEENAGE HEAD. / EVIL HEARTED ADA** [ ] [ ]

1971. (d-lp) **TEENAGE HEAD** [-] [ ]
– Teenage head / Whiskey women / Yesterday's numbers 32:20 / High flyin' baby / City lights / Have you seen my baby / Evil hearted Ada / Doctor Boogie / Rumble / Shakin' all over / That'll be the day / Round and round / Going out theme. *('FLAMINGO' + 'TEENAGE HEAD' iss.UK as 'FLAMIN' GROOVIES' on 'Kama Sutra')*

1972. (7") **GONNA ROCK TONITE. / KEEP ON ROCKIN' (by 'Sha Na Na')** [ ] [ ]

— **CHRIS WILSON** (b.10 Sep'52, Waltham, Massacusetts, USA) – vocals (ex-LOOSE GRAVEL) repl. LONEY / **JAMES FARRELL** – guitar (ex-LOOSE GRAVEL) repl. LYNCH who formed HOT KNIVES. — Reverted to same group name after changing to The DOGS for a short while.

United Art / United Art

1972. (7") **SLOW DEATH. / TALAHASSIE LASSIE** [ ] [ ]

Jun 72. (lp) **SLOW DEATH** [ ] [ ]
– Sweet little rock'n'roller / Doctor Boogie / Walking the dog / Roadhouse / Teenage head / Slow death / Shakin' all over / Louie Louie / Have you seen my baby / Can't explain.

Jan 73. (7") **MARRIED WOMAN. / A SHOT OF RHYTHM & BLUES** [ ] [ ]

— **JORDAN, WILSON, FARRELL and ALEXANDER** recruited new member **DAVID WRIGHT** – drums repl. TERRY RAE who had repl. MIHM (to HOT KNIVES)

Skydog / not issued

1974. (7") **JUMPIN' JACK FLASH. / BLUES FROM PHILLYS** [ ] [-] France
(re-iss.'77 on 12")

1974. (7"ep) **GREASE** [ ] [-]
– Let me rock / Dog meat / Sweet little rock'n'roller.

Philips / not issued

1975. (7") **LET THE BOY ROCK'N'ROLL. / YES IT'S TRUE** [ ] [-] France

not issued / Bomp

1975. (7") **YOU TORE ME DOWN. / HIM OR ME** [-] [ ]

Sire / Sire

Jun 76. (lp)(c) **SHAKE SOME ACTION** [ ] [ ]
– Shake some action / Sometimes / Yes it's true / St. Louis blues / You tore me down / Please please girl / Let the boy rock'n'roll / Don't you lie to me / She said yeah / I'll cry alone / Misery / I saw her / Teenage confidential / I can't hide. *(re-iss.Sep78)*

Jul 76. (7") **DON'T YOU LIE TO ME. / SHE SAID YEAH / SHAKE SOME ACTION** [ ] [ ]

Nov 76. (7") **SHAKE SOME ACTION. / TEENAGE CONFIDENTIAL** [ ] [ ]

Nov 76. (7") **TEENAGE CONFIDENTIAL. / I CAN'T HIDE** [-] [ ]

— **MIKE WILHELM** – guitar repl. FARRELL who joined PHANTOM MOVERS

Apr 78. (lp) **THE FLAMIN' GROOVIES NOW** [ ] [ ]
– Feel a whole lot better / Bewteen the lines / Ups and downs / There's a place / Take me back / Reminiscing / Good laugh man / Yeah my baby / House of blue lights / All I wanted / Blue turns to grey / When I heard your name / Move it / Don't put me on. *(re-iss.Sep78)*

Apr 78. (7") **FEEL A WHOLE LOT BETTER. / PAINT IT BLACK / SHAKE SOME ACTION** [ ] [ ]
(12"+=) – Blue turns to grey / When I heard your name.

Aug 78. (7") **MOVE IT. / WHEN I HEARD YOUR NAME** [ ] [ ]

Jun 79. (lp)(c) **JUMPING IN THE NIGHT** [ ] [ ]
– Please please girl / Next one crying / Down down down / Tell me again / Absolutely sweet Marie / (You're my) Wonderful one / Jumpin' in the night / 19th nervous breakdown / Boys / 5D / First plane home / Lady friend / In the U.S.A. *(US-different tracks)*

1979. (7") **ABSOLUTELY SWEET MARIE. / WEREWOLVES OF LONDON / NEXT ONE CRYING** [ ] [ ]

— **DANNY MIHM** – drums (ex-PHANTOM MOVERS) re-repl. WRIGHT before split CHRIS WILSON joined BARRACUDAS in '82, **CYRIL JORDAN** re-formed **FLAMIN' GROOVIES** in May87

A.B.C. / A.B.C.

Jul 87. (7") **SHAKE SOME ACTION (live). / ?** [ ] [ ]

Jul 87. (lp) **ONE NIGHT STAND (live)** [ ] [ ]
– Kicks / Bittersweet / I can't hide / Money / Call me Lightning / Shake some action / Slow death / Teenage head / Slow down / Tallahassee lassie.

– compilations etc. –

May 84. Skydog France; (lp) **SUPERGREASE** [-] [-]

1980's. Skydog (7") **I CAN'T EXPLAIN. / LITTLE QUEENIE** [-] [-]

Nov 84. Eva; (lp) **'68 (live)** [ ] [ ]

Nov 84. Eva; (lp) **'70 (live)** [ ] [ ]

Jul 85. Buddah; (lp)(c) **STILL SHAKIN'** [-] [ ]

Jun 77. Kama Sutra; (7") **TEENAGE HEAD. / HEADIN' FOR TEXAS BORDER** [ ] [ ]

Nov 76. United Artists; (7"ep) **SLOW DEATH. / TALAHASSIE LASSIE / MARRIED WOMAN. / A SHOT OF RHYTHM & BLUES** [ ] [ ]

May 86. Edsel; (lp) **ROADHOUSE** [ ] [-]
(comp of 'FLAMINGO' + 'TEENAGE HEAD')

Aug 89. Sire; (c)(cd) **GROOVIES GREATEST GROOVES** [ ] [ ]
– Shake some action / Teenage head / Slow death / Tallahassie lassie / Yeah my baby / Yes it's true / First plane home / In the U.S.A. / Between the lines / Don't you lie to me / Down down down / I'll cry alone / You tore me down / Please please girl / Yes I am / Teenage confidential / I can't hide / Absolutely sweet Marie / Don't put me on / I saw her / All I wanted / Jumpin' in the night / There's a place / River deep, mountain high

Apr 93. Marilyn; (cd)(lp) **RARE DEMOS & LIVE RECORDINGS** [ ] [-]

Nov 93. Mystery; (cd) **ROCKIN' AT THE ROUNDHOUSE – LIVE IN LONDON 1976/78 (live)** [ ] [-]

Nov 94. Bomp; (10"lp) **EP** [ ] [ ]

Apr 95. Aim; (cd) **LIVE AT THE FESTIVAL OF THE SUN** [ ] [-]

Apr 95. EMI; (cd) **A BUCKET OF BRAINS** [ ] [-]

ROY LONEY

solo with all original FLAMIN' GROOVIES

not issued / Sol-id Smoke

1978. (7"ep) **ARTISTIC AS HELL** [ ] [ ]

— **ROY** formed **PHANTOM MOVERS** with **DANNY, MIHM** and **JAMES FARRELL + LARRY LEA** – guitar, vocals / **MAURICE TANI** – bass / **NICK BUCK** – keyboards.

Sep 79. (lp) **OUT AFTER DARK** [-] [ ]
– Born to be your fool / Used hoodoo / Phantom mover / Neat petite / Return to sender / People people / Rockin' in the graveyard / I love it / Scum city / Trophy / She run away / San Francisco girls.

1980. (lp) **PHANTOM TRACKS** [-] [ ]
– Emmy Emmy / Down the road apiece / Act of love / You ain't gettin' out / Hundred miles an hour / I must behave / Don't believe those lies / Poor tuxedo.

— **JOHN KALDOR** – guitar / **JOHNNY SURRELL** – drums repl. FERRELL + MIHM

not issued / War Bride

1981. (lp) **CONTENTS UNDER PRESSURE** [-] [ ]
– Sorry / We're all heroes / Dead ringer / Different kind / Swinging single / Too funky to live / She's no lady / Heart full of soul / Cinema girls / Last time I'll cry / Intrigue indeed / Contents under pressure.

not issued Rockhouse

Nov 82. (lp) **ROCK & ROLL DANCE PARTY** [-] [ ]
– Ain't got a thing / My baby comes to me / Gonna rock tonite / Magdalena / Slip, slide and stomp / Doctor Boogie / Panic to a manic degree / Oh pretty woman / Double dare / Lovin' machine / Lana Lee / Don't start cryin' now / Goodnight Alcatraz.

Marilyn Marilyn

Sep 93. (cd)(c) **ACTION SHORTS** [ ] [ ]

FLAMING LIPS

Formed: Oklahoma City, USA . . . early 80's by COYNE brothers WAYNE and MARK, who reputedly stole instruments from church hall. Received their break in 1985, when 'Enigma' took them onto books. Signed to 'Warners' in 1992, and the following 2 years appeared at the Reading Festivals. • **Style:** Avant-garde psychedelic BARRETT /FLOYD inspired, whose barrage of sound was described as JAMC meeting BLACK FLAG or DEAD KENNEDYS. • **Songwriters:** Coyne-English-Ivins except; SUMMERTIME BLUES (Eddie Cochran) / WHAT'S SO FUNNY 'BOUT PEACE, LOVE & UNDERSTANDING (Brinsley Schwarz) / STRYCHNINE (Sonics).

Recommended: TELEPATHIC SURGERY (*6)

MARK COYNE – vocals / **WAYNE COYNE** – guitar / **MICHAEL IVINS** – bass / **RICHARD ENGLISH** – drums

not issued L.S.D.

1985. (7"green-ep) **THE FLAMING LIPS E.P.** [ ] [ ]
– Bag full of thoughts / Out for a walk / Garden of eyes – Forever is a long time / Scratching the door / My own planet. *(re-iss.1986 red-ep) (re-iss.1987 +c-ep on 'Pink Dust')*

— **WAYNE** now on vox, when MARK departed

Nov 86. (lp)(cd) **HEAR IT IS** [ ] [ ]
– With you / Unplugged / Trains, brains and rain / Jesus shootin' heroin / Just like before / She is death / Charles Manson blues / Man from Pakistan / Godzilla flick / Staring at sound – With you.
(cd+=) – Summertime blues / FLAMING LIPS E.P.

Nov 87. (lp)(cd)(clear-lp) **OH MY GAWD!!!** [-] [ ]

Feb 89. (lp)(c)(cd) **TELEPATHIC SURGERY** [ ] [ ]
– Drug machine / Michael time to wake up / Miracle on 42nd Street / UFO story / Shaved gorilla / Begs and achin' / Right now / Hare Krishna stomp wagon / Chrome plated suicide / Redneck school of technology / Spontaneous combustion of John / The last drop of morning dew.

— **JONATHAN PONEMANN** – guitar + **JOHN DONAHUE** – guitar

Glitterhouse Sub Pop

Jun 89. (7"m) **STRYCHNINE / DRUG MACHINE. / (WHAT'S SO FUNNY ABOUT) PEACE, LOVE AND UNDERSTANDING** [ ] [ ] Jan89

— **NATHAN ROBERTS** – drums repl. ENGLISH

City Slang Sub Pop

Jan 91. (12"ep) **UNCONSCIOUSLY SCREAMING E.P.** [ ] [ ]
–

Feb 91. (cd)(c)(lp)(pink-lp) **IN A PRIEST DRIVEN AMBULANCE** [ ] [ ]
– Shine on sweet Jesus – Jesus song No.5 / Unconsciously screaming / Rainin' babies / Take Meta Mars / Five stop Mother Superior rain / Stand in line / God walks among us now / Jesus song No.6 / There you are / Jesus song No.7 / Mountain song / Wonderful world.

Warners Warners

Aug 92. (cd)(c)(lp) **HIT TO DEATH IN THE MAJOR HEAD** [ ] [ ]
– Talkin' about the deathporn immorality (everyone wants to live forever) / Hit me like you did the first time / The Sun / Felt good to burn / Gingerale afternoon (the astrology of a Saturday) / Halloween on the Barbary Coast / The magician vs. the headache / You have to be joking (autopsy of the Devil's brain) / Frogs / Hold your head. *(re-iss.Apr95)*

— **RONALD JONES** – guitar repl. JOHN who joined MERCURY REV

— **STEVEN DROZD** – drums repl. NATHAN

Jun 93. (cd)(c)(lp) **TRANSMISSIONS FROM THE SATELLITE HEART** [ ] [ ]
– Turn it on / Pilot can at the queer of God / Oh my pregnant head (labia in the sunlight) / She don't use jelly / Chewin' the apple of your eye / Superhumans / Be my head / Moth in the incubator / Plastic Jesus / When yer twenty-two / Slow nerve action.

Aug 94. (7")(c-s) **SHE DON'T USE JELLY. / TURN IT ON (bluegrass version)** [ ] [55]
(cd-s+=) – Translucent egg.
(cd-s) – ('A'side) / The process / Moth in the incubator.

Sep 95. (cd)(c)(lp) **CLOUDS TASTE METALLIC** [ ] [ ]
– The abandoned hospital ship / Psychiatric explorations of the fetus with needles / Placebo headwood / This here giraffe / Brainville / Guy who lost a headache and accidentally saves the world / When you smile / Kim's watermelon gun / They punctured my yolk / Lightning strikes the postman / Christmas at the zoo / Evil will prevail / Bad days (aurally excited version).

Dec 95. (c-s) **BAD DAYS / GIRL WITH HAIR LIKE AN EXPLOSION** [ ] [ ]
(cd-s+=) – She don't use jelly / Giraffe (demo).
(cd-s) – ('A'side) / Ice drummer / When you smiled I lost my only idea / Put the water bug in the policeman's ear.

FLASH AND THE PAN (see under ⇒ EASYBEATS)

FLEETWOOD MAC

Formed: London, England . . . July 1967, by MICK FLEETWOOD, PETER GREEN and BOB BRUNNING. They quickly inducted JEREMY SPENCER and made live debut at prestigeous Windsor Jazz & Blues Festival on 12 Aug'67. They replaced BRUNNING with another ex-BLUESBREAKERS member JOHN McVIE, and signed to 'Blue Horizon'. Billed at first as PETER GREEN'S FLEETWOOD MAC, they flopped late '67 with first 45 'I BELIEVE MY TIME AIN'T LONG'. Around the same time, they became in-house band for blues artists like OTIS SPANN and DUSTER BENNETT. Early in '68, their debut lp 'PETER GREEN'S FLEETWOOD MAC', hit the Top 5, and was soon pursued by Top 40 singles 'BLACK MAGIC WOMAN' & 'NEED YOUR LOVE SO BAD'. Their 2nd lp 'MR. WONDERFUL', also cracked the UK Top 10, and was followed by million-selling UK No.1 instrumental 'ALBATROSS'. Out of contract, they signed one-off deal with 'Immediate', who issued another Top 3 gem 'MAN OF THE WORLD' early '69. In the Autumn, yet another classic 'OH WELL' (in 2 parts), hit No.2 for new label 'Reprise', and at the same time lp 'THEN PLAY ON' made UK Top 10. On Apr'70, GREEN departed group, due to increasing state of mental health. He left behind another haunting Top 10 single 'THE GREEN MANALISHI', which showed his deep lyrical attitude at the time. Without him, the group failed to emulate earlier success, and had rough period until the mid-70's. Newcomers LINDSEY BUCKINGHAM and STEVIE NICKS, came into the fold alongside CHRISTINE McVIE (member and wife of JOHN McVIE since Aug'70) and MICK FLEETWOOD. Early in 1976 now residents of California, USA, they had 3 US Top 20 hits, and a self-titled album, that eventually rose to the top that year. Their much anticipated 1977 follow-up 'RUMOURS' surpassed its predecessor, topping both US & UK charts, before going on to sell over 15 million copies. Although the McVIE's separation quickly followed, the break-up of BUCKINGHAM and NICKS sealed the band's fate. The group, however, continued to be massive attraction for the rest of the 70's & 80's. All had own solo sideline, with the beautiful STEVIE being the most prolific in the 80's until her departure. • **Style:** Pioneers of the white blues boom of the late 60's, they progressed into sophisticated husband-wife AOR team, ready-made for FM radio. • **Songwriters:** GREEN compositions, except early covers; NEED YOUR LOVE SO BAD (Little Willie John) / NO PLACE TO GO (Howlin' Wolf) / DUST MY BROOM (Robert Johnson) / etc. • **Trivia:** Late 1973, their manager Clifford Davis, put together a bogus FLEETWOOD MAC, which resulted in a legal court battle, in which they won. The bogus group became STRETCH, and had a late '75 UK Top 20 hit with 'Why Did You Do It'.

Recommended: GREATEST HITS (*9 1971) / RUMOURS (*8) / FLEETWOOD MAC'S GREATEST HITS (*9 1988).

JEREMY SPENCER (b. 4 Jul'48, Hartlepool, England) – guitar, vocals / **PETER GREEN** (b. PETER GREENBAUM, 29 Oct'49) – guitar, vocals (ex-JOHN MAYALL'S BLUESBREAKERS, ex-SHOTGUN EXPRESS) / **MICK FLEETWOOD** (b.24 Jun'42) – drums (ex-JOHN MAYALL'S BLUESBREAKERS) / **JOHN McVIE** (b.26 Nov'45) – bass (ex-JOHN MAYALL'S BLUESBREAKERS) repl. BOB BRUNNING who formed SUNFLOWER BLUES BAND after recording B-side)

Blue Horizon Epic

Nov 67. (7") **I BELIEVE MY TIME AIN'T LONG. / RAMBLING PONY** [ ] [-]

Feb 68. (lp) **(PETER GREEN'S) FLEETWOOD MAC** [4] [ ]
– My heart beat like a hammer / Merry go round / Long grey mare / Shake your moneymaker / Looking for somebody / No place to go / My baby's good to me / I love another woman / Cold black night / The world keep on turning / Got to move. *(re-iss.Oct73 on 'CBS/Embasssy' & Jul77 on 'CBS') (cd-iss.May88 on 'Line')(cd-iss.Nov93 on 'B.G.O.')*

Mar 68. (7") **BLACK MAGIC WOMAN. / THE SUN IS SHINING** [37] [-]

Apr 68. (7") **BLACK MAGIC WOMAN. / LONE GREY MARE** [-] [ ]

Jul 68. (7") **NEED YOUR LOVE SO BAD. / STOP MESSIN' ROUND** [31] [-]

Aug 68. (lp) **MR. WONDERFUL** [10] [-]
– Stop messin' round / Coming home / Rollin' man / Dust my broom / Love that burns / Doctor Brown / Need your love tonight / If you be my baby / Evenin' boogie / Lazy poker blues / I've lost my baby / Trying so hard to forget. *(re-iss.+c,cd.Nov89 on 'Essential')*

— added **DANNY KIRWAN** (b.13 Mar'50) – guitar, vocals (ex-BOILERHOUSE)

Nov 68. (7") **ALBATROSS. / JIGSAW PUZZLE BLUES** [1] [-]

Feb 69. (lp) **ENGLISH ROSE** [-] [ ]
– Stop messin' round / Jigsaw puzzle blues / Doctor Brown / Something inside of me / Evenin' boogie / Love that burns / Black magic woman / I've lost my baby / One sunny day / Without you / Coming home / Albatross.

Immediate not issued

Apr 69. (7") **MAN OF THE WORLD. / SOMEBODY'S GONNA GET THEIR HEAD KICKED IN TONIGHT (B-side by "EARL VINCE & THE VINCENTS")** [2] [-]

Reprise Reprise

Sep 69. (7") **OH WELL (Pt.1). / OH WELL (Pt.2)** [2] [55] Jan 70

— (note that SPENCER, for some reason did not play on the below album)

Sep 69. (lp) **THEN PLAY ON** [6] [ ]
– Coming your way / Closing my eyes / Showbiz blues / Underway / Oh well / Although the sun is shining / Rattlesnake shake / Searching for Madge / Fighting for Madge / Closing my eyes / When you say / One sunny day / Although the sun is shining / Like crying / Before the beginning. *(re-iss.Apr77)*

Oct 69. (7") **COMING YOUR WAY. / RATTLESNAKE SHAKE** [-] [ ]

May 70. (7") **THE GREEN MANALISHI (WITH THE TWO PRONGED CROWN). / WORLD IN HARMONY** [10] [ ]

— Now a quartet of **FLEETWOOD, McVIE, SPENCER and KIRWAN** when GREEN went solo

Sep 70. (lp)(c) **KILN HOUSE** [39] [69]
– This is the rock / Station man / Blood on the floor / Hi ho silver / Jewel eyed Judy / Buddy's song / Earl Grey / One together / Tell me all the things you do / Mission

bell. *(re-iss.cd.Feb93 on 'Warners')*

Jan 71. (7") **JEWEL EYED LADY. / STATION MAN** [-] [ ]

— added **CHRISTINE** (PERFECT) **McVIE** – keyboards, vocals (ex-CHICKEN SHACK) (she had already guested on 'MR. WONDERFUL' album)

Mar 71. (7") **DRAGONFLY. / PURPLE DANCER** [ ] [ ]

— **BOB WELCH** (b.31 Jul'46, California, USA) – guitar, vocals (ex-HEAD WEST) repl. SPENCER who formed CHILDREN OF GOD

Sep 71. (lp)(c) **FUTURE GAMES** [ ] [91]
– Women of 1000 years / Morning rain / What a shame / Future games / Sands of time / Sometimes / Lay it all down / Show me a smile. *(re-iss.Apr77)*

Sep 71. (7") **SANDS OF TIME. / LAY IT ALL DOWN** [-] [ ]

Apr 72. (lp)(c) **BARE TREES** [ ] [70]
– Child of mine / The ghost / Homeward bound / Sunny side of Heaven / Bare trees / Sentimental lady / Danny's chant / Spare me a little of your love / Dust / Thoughts on a grey day. *(re-iss.Apr77)*

Aug 72. (7") **SENTIMENTAL LADY. / SUNNY SIDE OF HEAVEN** [-] [ ]

— **DAVE WALKER** – vocals (ex-SAVOY BROWN) repl. KIRWAN who went solo / added **BOB WESTON** – guitar, vocals (ex-LONG JOHN BALDRY) (above two now with FLEETWOOD, J. McVIE, C. McVIE and WELCH)

May 73. (7") **REMEMBER ME. / DISSATISFIED** [-] [ ]

May 73. (lp) **PENGUIN** [ ] [49] Apr 73
– Remember me / Bright fire / Dissatisfied / (I'm a) Road runner / The derelict / Revelation / Did you ever love me / Night watch / Caught in the rain. *(re-iss.Apr77)*

Jun 73. (7") **DID YOU EVER LOVE ME. / THE DERELICT** [ ] [-]

Jun 73. (7") **DID YOU EVER LOVE ME. / REVELATION** [-] [ ]

— Reverted to a quintet when WALKER departed forming HUNGRY FIGHTER

Jan 74. (lp)(c) **MYSTERY TO ME** [ ] [67] Nov 73
– Emerald eyes / Believe me / Just crazy love / Hypnotised / Forever / Keep on going / The city / Miles away / Somebody / The way I feel / Good things come to those who wait / Why. *(re-iss.Apr77) (re-iss.cd.Feb93 on 'Warners')*

— Trimmed to quartet when WESTON also left

Mar 74. (7") **FOR YOUR LOVE. / HYPNOTISED** [ ] [ ]

Sep 74. (lp)(c) **HEROES ARE HARD TO FIND** [ ] [34]
– Heroes are hard to find / Coming home / Angel / The Bermuda Triangle / Come a little bit closer / She's changing me / Bad loser / Silver heels / Prove your love / Born enchanter / Safe harbour. *(re-iss.cd.Feb93 on 'Warners')*

Feb 75. (7") **HEROES ARE HARD TO FIND. / BORN ENCHANTER** [ ] [ ]

— **LINDSEY BUCKINGHAM** (b. 3 Oct'47. Palo Alto, USA) – guitar, vocals (as below; ex-BUCKINGHAM-NICKS) repl. WELCH / added **STEVIE NICKS** (b.26 May'48, Phoenix, Arizona, USA) – vocals

Aug 75. (lp)(c)(white-lp) **FLEETWOOD MAC** [ ] [1]
– Monday morning / Warm ways / Blue letter / Rhiannon / Over my head / Crystal / Say you love me / Landslide / World turning / Sugar daddy / I'm so afraid. *(reached UK No.23 Nov76) (cd-iss.Dec85) (re-iss.cd Sep94 on 'Rewind')*

Oct 75. (7") **WARM WAYS. / BLUE LETTER** [ ] [ ]

Feb 76. (7") **OVER MY HEAD. / I'M SO AFRAID** [ ] [20] Nov 75

Apr 76. (7"m) **RHIANNON. / WILL YOU EVER WIN / SUGAR DADDY** [ ] [11] Mar 76
(re-iss.Feb78 reached UK-No.46)

Sep 76. (7") **SAY YOU LOVE ME. / MONDAY MORNING** [40] [11] Jul 76

Warners Warners

Jan 77. (7") **GO YOUR OWN WAY. / SILVER SPRINGS** [38] [10]

Feb 77. (lp)(c) **RUMOURS** [1] [1]
– Second hand news / Dreams / Never going back again / Don't stop / Go your own way / Songbird / The chain / You make loving fun / I don't want to know / Oh daddy / Gold dust woman. *(re-iss.Jun88) (cd-iss.Dec83)*

Apr 77. (7") **DON'T STOP. / GOLD DUST WOMAN** [32] [3] Jul77

Jun 77. (7") **DREAMS. / SONGBIRD** [24] [1] Apr 77

Sep 77. (7") **YOU MAKE LOVING FUN. / NEVER GOING BACK AGAIN** [45] [-]

Oct 77. (7") **YOU MAKE LOVING FUN. / GOLD DUST WOMAN** [-] [9]

Mar 79. (7") **THINK ABOUT ME. / SAVE ME A PLACE** [-] [20]

Sep 79. (7") **TUSK. / NEVER MAKE ME CRY** [6] [8]

Oct 79. (d-lp)(c) **TUSK** [1] [4]
– Over & over / The ledge / Think about me / Save me a place / Sara / What makes you think you're the one / That's all for everyone / Not that funny / Sisters of the Moon / Angel / That's enough for me / Brown eyes / Never make me cry / I know I'm not wrong / Honey hi / Beautiful child / Walk a thin line / Tusk / Never forget. *(cd-iss.Mar87)*

Dec 79. (7") **SARA. / THAT'S ENOUGH FOR ME** [37] [7]

Feb 80. (7") **NOT THAT FUNNY. / SAVE ME A PLACE** [ ] [ ]

Mar 80. (7") **THINK ABOUT ME. / HONEY HI** [ ] [-]

Mar 80. (7") **THINK ABOUT ME. / SAVE ME A PLACE** [-] [20]

Jun 80. (7") **SISTERS OF THE MOON. / WALK A THIN LINE** [-] [86]

Nov 80. (d-lp)(c) **FLEETWOOD MAC LIVE (live)** [31] [14]
– Monday morning / Say you love me / Dreams / Oh well / Over & over / Sara / Not that funny / Never going back again / Landslide / Fireflies / Over my head / Rhiannon / Don't let me down again / One more night / Go your own way / Don't stop / I'm so afraid / The farmer's daughter. *(cd-iss.May88 on 'Commander')*

Jan 81. (7") **FIREFLIES. / OVER MY HEAD** [-] [60]

Feb 81. (7") **THE FARMER'S DAUGHTER (live). / DREAMS (live)** [ ] [-]

Mar 81. (7") **THE FARMER'S DAUGHTER (live). / MONDAY MORNING (live)** [-] [ ]

Jul 82. (7") **HOLD ME. / EYES OF THE WORLD** [ ] [4] Jun 82

Jul 82. (lp)(c) **MIRAGE** [5] [1]
– Love in store / Can't go back / That's alright / Book of love / Gypsy / Only over you / Empire state / Straight back / Hold me / Oh Diane / Eyes of the world / Wish you were here. *(cd-iss.Dec83 + 1989)*

Sep 82. (7") **GYPSY. / COOL CLEAN WATER** [46] [12]

Nov 82. (7") **LOVE IN STORE. / CAN'T GO BACK** [-] [22]

Dec 82. (7")(7"pic-d) **OH DIANE. / ONLY OVER YOU** [9] [-]
(12"+=) – The chain.

Feb 83. (7") **OH DIANE. / THAT'S ALRIGHT** [-] [ ]

Apr 83. (7") **CAN'T GO BACK. / THAT'S ALRIGHT** [ ] [ ]
(12"+=) – Rhiannon / Tusk.

Mar 87. (7") **BIG LOVE. / YOU AND I (Pt.1)** [9] [5]
(12"+=)(12"pic-d) – ('A'extended).
(d7"+=) – The chain / Go your own way.

Apr 87. (lp)(c)(cd) **TANGO IN THE NIGHT** [1] [7]
– Big love / Seven wonders / Everywhere / Caroline / Tango in the night / Mystified / Little lies / Family man / Welcome to the room . . . Sara / Isn't it midnight / When I see you again / You and I, part II.

Jun 87. (7") **SEVEN WONDERS. / BOOK OF MIRACLES** [56] [19]
(12"+=)(12"pic-d+=) – ('A'dub).

Aug 87. (7") **LITTLE LIES. / RICKY** [5] [4]
(12"+=)(c-s+=)(12"pic-d+=) – ('A'dub).

Nov 87. (7") **FAMILY MAN. / DOWN ENDLESS STREET** [54] [90] Mar 88
(12") – ('A'side) / You and I (Pt.2) / Family party.

Feb 88. (7") **EVERYWHERE. / WHEN I SEE YOU AGAIN** [4] [14] Nov 87
(12"+=) – ('A'version) / ('A'dub).

Jun 88. (7")(12") **ISN'T IT MIDNIGHT. / MYSTIFIED** [60] [ ]
(3"cd-s+=) – Say you love me / Gypsy.

Nov 88. (7")(12") **AS LONG AS YOU FOLLOW. / OH WELL (live)** [66] [43]
(cd-s+=) – Gold dust woman.

Nov 88. (lp)(c)(cd) **FLEETWOOD MAC'S GREATEST HITS** (compilation) [3] [14]
– As long as you follow / No questions asked / Rhiannon / Don't stop / Go your own way / Hold me / Everywhere / Gypsy / Say you love me / Dreams / Little lies / Sara / Tusk. *(cd+c+=)* – Oh Diane / Big love / You making loving fun / Seven wonders.

Feb 89. (7") **HOLD ME. / NO QUESTIONS ASKED** [ ] [ ]
(12"+=)(cd-s+=) – I loved another woman (live).

— (Jul88) When BUCKINGHAM departed, he was repl. by **RICK VITO** – guitar / **BILLY BURNETT** – guitar

Feb 90. (7") **THE SKIES THE LIMIT. / THE SECOND TIME** [-] [ ]

Apr 90. (7") **SAVE ME. / I LOVED ANOTHER WOMAN (live)** [53] [33]
(12"+=)(cd-s+=) – Everywhere (live).

Apr 90. (cd)(c)(lp) **BEHIND THE MASK** [1] [18]
– The skies the limit / In the back of my mind / Do you know / Save me / Affairs of the heart / When the Sun goes down / Behind the mask / Stand on the rock / Hard feelings / Freedom / When it comes to love / The second time. *(re-iss.cd Feb95)*

Aug 90. (7")(c-s) **IN THE BACK OF MY MIND. / LIZARD PEOPLE** [58] [ ]
(12") – ('A'side) / Little lies (live) / The chain (live).
(cd-s) (all 4 tracks).

Nov 90. (7")(c-s) **SKIES THE LIMIT. / LIZARD PEOPLE** [ ] [ ]
(12")(cd-s) – ('A'side) / Little lies (live) / The chain (live).

— STEVIE NICKS left to go solo, and CHRISTINE departed due to MICK's new book allegations.

— **MICK FLEETWOOD, JOHN McVIE, CHRISTINE McVIE + BILLY BURNETTE** added **DAVE MASON** – vocals, guitars (ex-TRAFFIC, ex-solo artist)/ **BEKKA BRAMLETT** – vocals (daughter of DELANEY & BONNIE)

Oct 95. (cd)(c) **TIME** [47] [ ]
– Talkin' to my heart / Hollywood (some other kind of town) / Blow by blow / Winds of change / I do / Nothing without you / Dreamin' the dream / Sooner or later / I wonder why / Nights in Estoril / I got it in for you / All over again / These strange times.

– compilations etc. –

Note all 'Blue Horizon' releases were on 'Epic' US.

Jul 69. Blue Horizon; (7") **NEED YOUR LOVE SO BAD. / NO PLACE TO GO** [32] [ ]

Aug 69. Blue Horizon; (lp)(c) **PIOUS BIRD OF GOOD OMEN** [18] [ ]
– Need your love so bad / Coming home / Rambling pony / The big boat / I believe my time ain't long / The sun is shing / Albatross / Black magic woman / Just the blues / Jigsaw puzzle blues / Looking for somebody / Stop messin' around. *(re-iss.Jun81 on 'CBS') (cd-iss.Jun95 on 'Rewind')*

Dec 69. Blue Horizon; (d-lp) **BLUES JAM AT CHESS (-with other artists)** [ ] [ ]
– *(re-iss.d-cd.Oct93 on 'Sony Europe')*

Oct 71. Epic; (d-lp) **BLACK MAGIC WOMAN** [-] [ ]
(UK-iss.Feb80 on 'C.B.S.')

Note all CBS releases were on 'Epic' US.

May 71. C.B.S.; (lp) **THE ORIGINAL FLEETWOOD MAC BEFORE THE SPLIT** [ ] [ ]
(re-iss.+c/cd.Jun90 on 'Castle')

Nov 71. C.B.S.; (lp)(c) **GREATEST HITS** [36] [ ]
– The green Manalishi (with the two-pronged crown) / Oh well (part 1 & 2) / Shake your moneymaker / Need your love so bad / Rattlesnake shake / Dragonfly / Black magic woman / Albatross / Man of the world / Stop messin' around / Love that burns. *(re-iss.cd Dec94 on 'Columbia')*

Mar 72. C.B.S.; (7") **ALBATROSS. / I NEED YOUR LOVE SO BAD** [2] [ ]
(re-iss.Feb78)

Aug 73. C.B.S.; (7") **BLACK MAGIC WOMAN. / STOP MESSIN' ROUND** [ ] [ ]

1974. Epic; (d-lp) **ENGLISH ROSE** (incl.extra rare tracks) [-] [ ]

Jun 75. C.B.S.; (d-lp)(d-c) **THE ORIGINAL FLEETWOOD MAC / ENGLISH ROSE** [ ] [ ]
(re-iss.Jun76) (re-iss.cd May94 on 'Castle')

Mar 77. C.B.S.; (lp)(c) **VINTAGE YEARS** [ ] [ ]
(re-iss.May82 as THE HISTORY OF FLEETWOOD MAC)

Aug 77. C.B.S.; (lp)(c) **ALBATROSS (1 side by 'CHRISTINE PERFECT')** [ ] [ ]
(re-iss.+cd.Feb91 on 'Columbia')

Sep 78. C.B.S.; (lp)(c) **MAN OF THE WORLD** [ ] [ ]

Feb 89. C.B.S.; (7") **ALBATROSS. / MAN OF THE WORLD** [ ] [-]
(12"+=)(cd-s+=) – Black magic woman / Love that burns.

Jul 71. Blue Horizon; (d-lp) **FLEETWOOD MAC IN CHICAGO (rec. Jan69) (live)** [ ] [ ]

Mar 73. Reprise; (7") **THE GREEN MANALISHI. / OH WELL (Pt.1)** [ ] [ ]

1978. Reprise; (lp)(c) **THE BEST OF FLEETWOOD MAC** [ ] [ ]

Oct 75. D.J.M.; (7") **MAN OF THE WORLD. / SECOND CHAPTER ('B' side 'DANNY KIRWAN')** [ ] [ ]

(re-iss.Feb76 on 'Epic')
Jun 79. Flyover; (lp)(c) **FLEETWOOD MAC**
Nov 86. Thunderbolt; (lp)(c)(cd) **LONDON LIVE '68 (live)**
Jul 87. Castle; (d-lp)(c)(cd) **THE COLLECTION** — -
Apr 89. Castle; (lp)(c)(cd) **THE BLUES COLLECTION** — -
1988. Varrick; (lp)(c) **JUMPING AT SHADOWS** - -
May 88. Mainline; (lp)(c)(cd) **GREATEST HITS LIVE (live)**
(re-iss.Dec89 on 'Commander')
Dec 89. Mainline; (lp)(c)(cd) **OH WELL** — -
Oct 82. Warners; (d-c) **RUMOURS / FLEETWOOD MAC**
Nov 92. Warners; (4xcd)(4xc) **25 YEARS – THE CHAIN**
Jan 93. Warners; (7"ep)(c-ep)(cd-ep) **LOVE SHINES. / THE CHAIN (alternate mix) / ISN'T IT MIDNIGHT (alternate mix)**
Jan 85. Shanghai; (lp)(c) **LIVE IN BOSTON (live)** — -
(re-iss.May88 on 'Line', cd-iss.Oct89 on 'Castle')
Aug 85. Shanghai; (d-lp)(c) **CERULEAN** — -
Oct 85. Shanghai; (cd) **RATTLESNAKE SHAKE** — -
Sep 85. Old Gold; (7") **MAN OF THE WORLD. / ('B'side by Humble Pie)** — -
Nov 89. Pickwick; (lp)(c)(cd) **LOOKING BACK AT FLEETWOOD MAC** — -
Feb 91. Essential; (3xcd)(5xlp) **THE ORIGINAL FLEETWOOD MAC: THE BLUES YEARS**
(re-iss.May93 on 'Castle')
Jun 91. Elite; (cd)(c) **LIKE IT THIS WAY** — -
(re-iss.Sep93)
Jun 92. Sunflower; (cd) **LIVE AT THE MARQUEE (live by "PETER GREEN'S FLEETWOOD MAC")** — -
Sep 92. Dojo; (cd) **THE EARLY YEARS ("PETER GREEN'S FLEETWOOD MAC")** — -
Jul 94. Success; (cd)(c) **LIVE (live)** — -
Jun 95. Savanna; (cd)(c) **LIVE** — -
Sep 95. Essential; (d-cd)(d-c) **LIVE AT THE BBC** 48 -

MICK FLEETWOOD

R.C.A. R.C.A.
Jun 81. (lp)(c) **THE VISITOR** — 43
– Rattlesnake shake / You weren't in love / O'Niamali / Super brains / Don't be sorry (just be happy) / Walk a thin line / Not fade away / Cassiopeia surrender / The visitor / Amelle (come on show me your heart).
Aug 81. (7") **YOU WEREN'T IN LOVE. / AMELLE (COME ON SHOW ME YOUR HEART)**

ZOO

MICK FLEETWOOD with BILLY BURNETTE – guitar, vocals / **STEVE ROSS** – guitar, vocals / **GEORGE HAWKINS** – bass, keyboards, vocals + **CHRISTINE + LINDSEY + TODD SHARP** (main writer in '92)
Nov 83. (lp)(c) **I'M NOT ME**
– Angel come home / You might need somebody / I want you back / Tonight / I'm not me / State of the art / I give / This love / Put me right / Just because / Tear it up.
Oct 83. (7") **I WANT YOU BACK. / PUT ME RIGHT**
Feb 84. (7") **ANGEL COME HOME. / I GIVE** -
Capricorn Capricorn
Jun 92. (cd)(c) **SHAKIN' THE CAGE**
– Reach out / God created woman / Night life / Shakin' the cage / Voodoo / How does it feel / The night and you / Takin' it out to the people / Breakin' up / In your hands.

CHRISTINE PERFECT

solo with **DANNY KIRWAN** and **JOHN McVIE** plus **CHRIS HARDING** – drums / **TONY TOPHAM** – guitar / **MARTIN DUNSFORD** – guitar and RICK HAYWARD – guitar
Blue Horizon Sire
Oct 69. (7") **WHEN YOU SAY. / NO ROAD IS THE RIGHT ROAD**
Mar 70. (7") **I'D RATHER GO BLIND. / CLOSE TO ME** -
Apr 70. (7") **I'M TOO FAR GONE. / CLOSE TO ME** — -
Jun 70. (lp) **CHRISTINE PERFECT**
– Crazy 'bout you / I'm on my way / Let me go (leave me alone) / Wait and see / Close to me / I'd rather go blind / I want you / When you say / And that's saying a lot / No road is the right road / For you / I'm too far gone (to turn around) / I want you. *(re-iss.'82 on 'CBS') (re-iss.Oct93 on 'B.G.O.') (re-iss.Aug76 as 'THE LEGENDARY CHRISTINE PERFECT ALBUM' on 'Sire' US)*
C.B.S. C.B.S.
1974. (7") **I'D RATHER GO BLIND. / SAD CLOWN**

CHRISTINE McVIE

with **TODD SHARP** – guitar / **GEORGE HAWKINS** – bass, vocals / **STEVE FERRONE** – drums, percussion / + guests **LINDSEY, MICK + STEVE WINWOOD, ERIC CLAPTON, EDDY QUINTELA + RAY COOPER**
Warners Warners
Jan 84. (7"pic-d)(12"pic-d) **GOT A HOLD ON ME. / WHO'S DREAMING THIS DREAM** — 10
Feb 84. (lp)(c)(cd) **CHRISTINE McVIE** 58 26
– Love will show us how / The challenge / One in a million / So excited / Ask anybody / Got a hold on me / Who's dreaming this dream / I'm the one / Keeping secrets / The smile I live for.
May 84. (7") **LOVE WILL SHOW US HOW. / THE CHALLENGE** — 30
Jul 84. (7") **I'M THE ONE. / THE CHALLENGE** -

BUCKINGHAM-NICKS

duo (recorded before MAC members) **with TOM MONCREIFF** – bass / **GARY HODGES and BOB GEARY** – drums

Polydor Polydor
Apr 74. (7") **DON'T LET ME DOWN AGAIN. / RACES ARE RUN**
Jun 76. (7") **DON'T LET ME DOWN AGAIN. / CRYSTAL**
Feb 77. (lp) **BUCKINGHAM NICKS** 1973
– Crying in the night / Stephanie / Without a leg to stand on / Crystal / Long distance winner / Don't let me down again / Django / Races are run / Lola / Frozen love.
Mar 77 (7") **CRYING IN THE NIGHT. / STEPHANIE** -

LINDSEY BUCKINGHAM

solo with MICK FLEETWOOD and CHRISTINE McVIE as guests
Mercury Asylum
Nov 81. (lp)(c) **LAW AND ORDER** — 32
– Bwana / Trouble / Mary Lee Jones / I'll tell you now / It was I / September song / Shadow of the west / That's how we do it in L.A. / Johnny Stew / Love from here, love from there / A satisfied mind. *(cd-iss. 1984)*
Dec 81. (7") **TROUBLE. / THAT'S HOW WE DO IT IN L.A.** 31 -
Dec 81. (7") **TROUBLE. / MARY LEE JONES** - 9
Feb 82. (7") **IT WAS I. / LOVE FROM HERE, LOVE FROM THERE** -
Mar 82. (7") **THE VISITOR. / A SATISFIED MIND** — -
May 82. (7") **MARY LEE JONES. / SEPTEMBER SONG** — 43
Jul 83. (7") **HOLIDAY ROAD. / MARY LEE JONES**
—— (above from film 'Vacation')
Mercury Elektra
Aug 84. (lp)(c)(cd) **GO INSANE** — 45
– I want you / Go insane / Slow dancing / I must go / Play in the rain (part 1 & 2) / Loving cup / Bang the drum / D.W. suite.
Sep 84. (7")(12") **GO INSANE. / PLAY IN THE RAIN** — 23
Dec 84. (7") **SLOW DANCING. / D.W. SUITE**
—— Left FLEETWOOD MAC in '87 + released 1992 album 'OUT OF THE CRADLE'.

FLO & EDDIE (see under ⇒ TURTLES)

FLOWERED UP

Formed: London, England . . . mid-89 by LIAM MAHER, who brought in young brother JOE + other 3. Made their breakthrough in the early 90's, after signing to 'Heavenly Records'. • **Style:** Happy Mondays cockney clones with excellent alternative pop appeal. • **Songwriters:** Group. • **Trivia:** TAKE IT was co-written with JOE STRUMMER. Their flowery dancer BARRY MOONCULT covered WILD THING (Troggs).

Recommended: A LIFE WITH BRIAN (*6)

LIAM MAHER – vocals / **TIM DORNEY** – keyboards (repl. SIMON, who formed SLY & LOVECHILD) / **JOE MAHER** – guitar / **JOHN TUVEY** – drums (repl. other JOHN) / **ANDY JACKSON** – bass
Heavenly not issued
Jul 90. (7")(12") **IT'S ON. / IT'S ON – SONIA** 54 -
(12") – ('A'side) / It's bloody on (it's on mix) / It's still on (dub).
(10"one-sided) – IT'S ON – FEEL PAIN
(cd-s) – ('A'side) / It's on and on (not much like the Happy Mondays mix) / It's on John.
Nov 90. (12")(cd-s) **PHOBIA (extended). / FLAPPING / PHOBIA (paranoid mix)** 75 -
(7"iss.May91; 1st two tracks)
Heavenly-London London
Apr 91. (7")(c-s) **TAKE IT. / I'LL BE YOUR DOG** 34
(12"+=//+12"+=) – Phobia (live).// ('A'mixes).
May 91. (cd)(c)(lp) **A LIFE WITH BRIAN** 23
– Sunshine / Take it / Mr.Happy reveller / Hysterically blue / It's on / Silver plan / Phobia / Egg rush / Doris . . . is a little bit partial / Crackerjack.
Aug 91. (7")(c-s) **IT'S ON (re-recorded). / EGG RUSH (vox ANNA HAIGH)** 38
(12"+=)(cd-s+=) – Take it (live).
—— **MICKEY LEADER** – bass repl. ANDY
Heavenly-Columbia Columbia
Apr 92. (c-s)(cd-s) **WEEKENDER. (one 12min.track only)** 20
(12"+=) – ('A'-Andy Weatherall mix).
In Oct'92, they did a version of RIGHT SAID FRED's 'DON'T TALK JUST KISS' on an 'Heavenly' artists EP. Proceeds were given to the Terence Higgins trust. Other tracks 'DEEPLY DIPPY' (Rockingbirds) + 'I'M TOO SEXY' (St.Etienne). Disbanded sometime in 1993, MAHER went back to work as a cassette seller in Camden market.
Jul 94. (7") **BETTER LIFE. / ('A'mix)** — -

FLUKE

Formed: Beaconsfield, Buckinghamshire, England . . .mid 1989 by trio of MIKE BRYANT, MICHAEL TOURNIER and JONATHAN FUGLER. They emerged with white label 12" 'THUMPER!', before creating a stir with dancehall favourite 'JONI', which sampled her 'BIG YELLOW TAXI' single. In 1990, after a debut gig at a 'Boy's Own' label rave, they signed to major indie 'Creation'. Early the following year saw the release of their first album 'THE TECHNO ROSE OF BLIGHTY', which paved the way for a major signing to Virgin subsidiary 'Circa'. In 1993, their 3rd album nearly made UK Top 40 lists. • **Style:** Electronic dance pop/rock similiar to the CABS or YELLO. • **Songwriters:** Group – sampled many including TALK TALK's 'Life's What You Make It'/ STEVE HILLAGE's 'Hello Dawn'/ BILL NELSON's 'When

Your Dream Of Perfect Beauty Comes True'/ etc. • **Trivia:** Have been house remixers for TEARS FOR FEARS, TALK TALK, WORLD OF TWIST, etc.

Recommended: SIX WHEELS ON MY WAGON (*7) / OTO (*6)

MIKE BRYANT (b. 1 May'60, High Wycombe) – synthesizer/ **MICHAEL TOURNIER** (b.24 May'63, High Wycombe) – synthesizer/ **JONATHAN FUGLER** (b.13 Oct'2, St.Austell, Cornwall, England) – synthesizer

white label / not issued

Sep 89. (12") **THUMPER! (mixes)** [-] [-]

Taxi / not issued

May 90. (12") **JONI (mixes)** [ ] [-]

Creation / not issued

Oct 90. (7") **PHILLY. / TAXI** [ ] [-]
(12")(cd-s) – ('A'side) / ('A'-amorphous mix) / ('A'-Jamoeba mix) / ('A'-Jameteur mix).

Feb 91. (cd(c)(lp) **THE TECHNO ROSE OF BLIGHTY** [ ] [-]
– Philly / Glorious / Cool hand Fluke / Joni / Easy peasy / Phin / Jig / Taxi / Coolest.

Circa / Circa

Nov 91. (12"ep)(cd-ep) **THE BELLS. / (other mixes)** [ ] [-]

Nov 91. (12"ep)(cd-ep)(c-ep) **OUT (IN ESSENCE)** [ ] [ ]
– Pan Am into Philly / Pearls of wisdom / The bells:- Heresy – Garden of Blighty.

—— added **JULIAN NUGENT** – synthesizer

Mar 93. (12"ep)(cd-ep) **SLID (glid). / (4 other mixes; No guitars / Glidub / PDFMIX / Scat and sax frenzy mix)** [59] [ ]

Jun 93. (12"ep)(c-ep) **ELECTRIC GUITAR (vibrochamp). / ('A'-superhound mix) / ('A'-headstock mix)** [58] [ ]
(cd-ep+=) – ('A'-sunburst mix) / ('A'-hot tube mix).

Sep 93. (7"ep)(c-ep) **GROOVY FEELING (Toni Bell's single scoop) / ('A'-Make mine a 99 mix) / ('A'-Nutty chip cornet mix)** [45] [ ]
(12"ep+=)(cd-ep+=) – ('A'-Lolly gobble choc bomb) / ('A'-screwball mix).

Oct 93. (cd)(c)(lp) **SIX WHEELS ON MY WAGON** [41] [ ]
– Groovy feeling – Make mine a 99 / Letters / Glidub / Electric guitar – Humbucker / Top of the world / Slid – PDFMONE / Slow motion / Spacey (Catch 22 dub) / Astrosapiens / Oh yeah / Eko / Life support. (cd w/free cd) THE TECHNO ROSE OF BLIGHTY

Apr 94. (c-ep)(cd-ep) **BUBBLE (speakbubble). / ('A'-stuntbubble mix) / ('A'-burstbubble mix)** [37] [ ]
(12"+=) – ('A'-Braillbubble mix).

Jul 95. (12"ep)(cd-ep) **BULLET / ('A'-Dust Brothers (US) mix) / ('A-Empirion mix) / ('A'-Atlas space odyssey mix)** [23] [ ]
(cd-ep+=) – ('A'-Bullion mix) / ('A'-percussion cap mix) / ('A'-cannonball mix) / ('A'-bitter mix).

Aug 95. (cd)(c)(lp) **OTO** [44] [ ]
– Bullet / Tosh / Cut / Freak / Wobbler / Squirt / O.K. / Setback.

Nov 95. (12"ep) **TOSH / (mixes; gosh / mosh / cosh / posh)** [32] [ ]
(cd-s) – ('A'mixes; Nosh / Dosh / Josh / Shriekbackwash).
(12") – ('A'mixes; Mosh / Gosh / Nosh / Dosh).

compilations, etc –

Dec 95. Strange Fruit; (cd-ep) **THE PEEL SESSIONS** [ ] [-]
– Thumper / Taxi / Jig / Our definition of jazz / The bells / The allotment of Blighty / Time keeper.

FLYING BURRITO BROTHERS

Formed: Los Angeles, California, USA . . . late 1968 by ex-BYRDS members GRAM PARSONS, CHRIS HILLMAN, SNEAKY PETE KLEINOW and CHRIS ETHRIDGE. This line-up made one 'A&M' lp 'THE GILDED PALACE OF SIN', which made US Top 200. They recorded another lp 'BURRITO DELUXE' in 1970, before PARSONS departed due to physical drug abuse. He was to go on to solo career, but died a mysterious death on 19 Sep'73. The group continued, but only to be further dismissed by public. • **Style:** Harmonious sounding country-rock outfit, taking off where The BYRDS' classic 'Sweetheart Of The Rodeo' left-off. • **Songwriters:** PARSONS wrote most, until his premature departure after 2nd lp. Group took over writing credits, from then on. Covered; DO RIGHT WOMAN (Aretha Franklin) / WILD HORSES (Rolling Stones) / IF YOU GOTTA GO, GO NOW (Bob Dylan) / etc. • **Trivia:** DAVID CROSBY guested harmonies on their 1969 track 'DO RIGHT WOMAN'.

Recommended: DIM LIGHTS, THICK SMOKE AND LOUD MUSIC (*6)

GRAM PARSONS (b.CECIL CONNOR, 5 Nov'46, Florida) – vocals, guitar (ex-BYRDS) / **CHRIS HILLMAN** (b. 4 Dec'42) – guitar, vocals (ex-BYRDS) / **SNEAKY PETE KLEINOW** (b.1935) – pedal steel guitar (ex-BYRDS part-time) / **CHRIS ETHERIDGE** – bass / **JON CORNEAL** – drums (half) / other guest drummers **POPEYE PHILLIPS / EDDIE HOH + SAM GOLDSTEIN**

A & M / A & M

Apr 69. (lp) **THE GILDED PALACE OF SIN** [ ] [ ] Mar 69
– Christine's tune / Sin city / Do right woman / Dark end of the street / My uncle / Wheels / Juanita / Hot burrito £1 / Hot burrito £2 / Do you know how it feels / Hippie boy. *(re-iss.1975) (re-iss.+c.Jul86 on 'Edsel', cd-iss.1988)*

Jun 69. (7") **THE TRAIN SONG. / HOT BURRITO £1** [ ] [ ]

—— **BERNIE LEADON** – guitar, vocals (ex-DILLARD & CLARK) repl. ETHERIDGE / **MICHAEL CLARKE** – drums (ex-DILLARD & CLARK) repl. CORNEAL (ex-changed to D&C) (HILLMAN now switched to bass, vocals)

Apr 70. (7") **IF YOU GOTTA GO, GO NOW. / CODY, CODY** [-] [ ]

May 70. (lp) **BURRITO DELUXE** [ ] [ ]
– Lazy day / Image of me / High fashion queen / If you gotta go, go now / Man in the fog / Further along / Older guys / Cody, Cody / God's own singer / Down in the churchyard / Wild horses. *(re-iss.Jul86 on 'Edsel', cd-iss.Jun90)*

Jul 70. (7") **OLDER GUYS. / DOWN IN THE CHURCHYARD** [ ] [ ]

—— **RICK ROBERTS** – guitar, vocals repl. PARSONS (went solo, died 19 Sep'73)

Dec 70. (7") **TRIED SO HARD. / LAZY DAY** [ ] [ ]

Jun 71. (lp)(c) **THE FLYING BURRITO BROTHERS** [ ] [ ]
– White line fever / Colorado / Hand to mouth / Tried so hard / Just can't be / To Romana / Four days of rain / Can't you hear me calling / All alone / Why are you crying.

Jul 71. (7") **COLORADO. / WHITE LINE FEVER** [-] [ ]

—— **HILLMAN, ROBERTS, CLARKE** bring in new members **AL PERKINS** – pedal steel (ex-SHILOH) repl. SNEAKY PETE who went into sessions / **KENNY WERTZ** – guitar, vocals (ex-DILLARD & CLARK) repl. LEADON (later EAGLES) / added **ROGER BUSH** – bass / **BYRON BERLINE** – drums (both ex-COUNTRY GAZETTE)

Feb 72. (lp)(c) **LAST OF THE RED HOT BURRITOS (live)** [ ] [ ]
– Devil in disguise / Six days on the road / My uncle / Dixie breakdown / Don't let your deal go down / Orange blossom special / Ain't that a lot of love / High fashion queen / Don't fight it / Hot burrito £2 / Losing game. *(cd-iss.Apr89)*

—— Had already split late '71. HILLMAN and PERKINS joined STEPHEN STILLS band. **ROBERTS** Enlisted **BUSH, BERLINE, WERTZ, DON BECK, ALAN MUNDE + ERIC DALTON.** They tour Europe and the Netherlands release 2 live albums for 'Ariola'; 'LIVE IN AMSTERDAM' (d-lp; Feb73) & 'BLUEGRASS SPECIAL' (1974). **KLEINOW** returned but they made no recordings.

—— **SNEAKY PETE + ETHERIDGE** re-formed band with **FLOYD 'GIB' GUILBEAU** – fiddle / **GENE PARSONS** – drums (ex-BYRDS) / **JOEL SCOTT HILL** – bass (ex-CANNED HEAT) ROBERTS & CLARKE later formed FIREFALL.

C.B.S. / Columbia

Nov 75. (7") **BUILDING FIRES. / HOT BURRITO £3** [ ] [ ]

Dec 75. (lp)(c) **FLYING AGAIN** [ ] [ ] Oct 75
– Easy to get on / Wind and rain / Why baby why / Dim lights, thick smoke (and loud, loud music) / You left the water running / Building fires / Desert childhood / Bon soir blues / River road / Hot burrito £3.

1976. (7") **BON SOIR BLUES. / HOT BURRITO £3** [-] [ ]

—— **SKIP BATTIN** – bass (ex-BYRDS, ex-NEW RIDERS OF THE . . .) repl. ETHERIDGE

Jul 76. (lp)(c) **AIRBORNE** [ ] [ ] Jun 76
– Waitin' for love to begin / Out of control / Big bayou / Toe tappin' music / Linda Lu / Walk on the water / Northbound bus / Jesus broke the wild horse / She's a sailor / Quiet man / Border town.

1976. (7") **BIG BAYOU. / WAITIN' FOR LOVE TO BEGIN** [-] [ ]

—— disbanded when BATTIN re-joined NEW RIDERS . . . / His replacement ED PONDERS also departed as did PARSONS.

SIERRA

were formed by **GUILBEAU, KLEINOW & HILL** plus **THAD MAXWELL** – bass / **MICKEY McGEE** – drums / **BOBBY COCHRAN**

not issued / Mercury

1977. (lp) **SIERRA** [-] [ ]
– Gina / Farmer's daughter / Honey dew / I found love / Strange here in the night / I'd rather be with you / If I could only get to you / She's the tall one / Don't plant roses / You give me lovin' / Let me live.

1977. (7") **GINA. / STRANGE HERE IN THE NIGHT** [-] [ ]

FLYING BURRITO BROTHERS

were once again with **GUILBEAU, KLEINOW + GREG HARRIS** – guitar / **ED PONDER + SKIP BATTIN**

Sundown / Regency

Jun 79. (lp) **LIVE IN TOKYO (live)** [-] [ ]
– Big bayou / White line fever / Dim lights, thick smoke / There'll be no teardrops tonight / Roll in my sweet baby's arms / Hot burrito £2 / Colorado / Rocky top / Six days on the road / Truck drivin' man. *(re-iss.+cd.Jan86 on 'Sundown')*

Dec 79. (7") **WHITE LINE FEVER (live). / BIG BAYOU (live)** [-] [ ]

The BURRITO BROTHERS

JOHN BELAND – vocals, guitar (ex-SWAMPWATER) repl. HARRIS and PONDER

not issued / Curb

Dec 80. (7") **SHE'S A FRIEND OF A FRIEND. / ?** [-] [ ]

Jan 81. (lp) **HEARTS ON THE LINE** [-] [ ]
– That's the way you know it's over / She's a friend of a friend / Isn't that just like love / She belongs to everyone but me / Why must the ending be so sad / Family tree / Damned if I'll be lonely tonight / Does she wish she was single again / Too much honky tonkin' / Oh lonesome me.

Apr 81. (7") **DOES SHE WISH SHE WAS SINGLE AGAIN. / OH LONESOME ME** [-] [ ]

Jul 81. (7") **SHE BELONGS TO EVERYONE BUT ME. / WHY MUST THE ENDING ALWAYS BE SO SAD** [-] [ ]

—— Trimmed to a duo of **BELAND + GUILBEAU**

Dec 81. (7") **IF SOMETHING SHOULD COME BETWEEN US (LET IT BE LOVE). / DAMNED IF I'LL BE LONELY TONIGHT** [-] [ ]

Jan 82. (lp) **SUNSET SUNDOWN** [-] [ ]
– If something should come between us / Louisiana / I'm drinkin' Canada dry / When you're giving yourself to a stranger / What's one more time / Run to the night / How'd we ever get this way / Coast to coast / Closer to you / Save the wild life.

Apr 82. (7") **CLOSER TO YOU. / COAST TO COAST** [-] [ ]

Jul 82. (7") **I'M DRINKIN' CANADA DRY. / HOW'D WE EVER GET THAT WAY** [-] [ ]

Nov 82. (7") **BLUE AND BROKEN HEARTED ME. / OUR ROOTS ARE COUNTRY MUSIC** [-] [ ]

M.C.A. / Curb

1983. (7" w/ EARL SCRUGGS) **COULD YOU LOVE ME ONE MORE TIME. / ROLLER COASTER** [-] [ ]

—— The duo cut another lp for 'Curb', but this was shelved.

Jan 84. (7") **ALMOST SATURDAY NIGHT. / JUKEBOX KIND OF NIGHT** [-] [ ]

May 84. (7") **MY KIND OF LADY. / DREAM CHASER** [-] [ ]

— Signed to LEON RUSSELL's 'Paradise', but album was shelved until '95.

The FLYING BROTHERS

with **SNEAKY PETE, SKIP BATTIN, GREG HARRIS + JIM GOODALL**

not issued | Relix

Oct 85. (lp) **CABIN FEVER (live)** [-] [ ]
– Wheels / Hot burrito £2 / Hickory wind / Do right woman / Uncle Penn / Louisiana man / She belongs to me / Six days on the road / Mr. Spaceman / Bugles.

1986. (lp) **LIVE FROM EUROPE (live)** [-] [ ]
– Streets of Baltimore / Cash on the barrelhead / Help is on it's way / Roll on brother / Come a little closer / Star of the show / Spitting image / Sin city / Christin's tune / Foggy mountain breakdown / Steam-powered airplane / Mystery train.

The FLYING BURRITO BROTHERS

reformed by **GUILBEAU + BELAND**

Disky | Disky

Dec 87. (d-lp)(c)(cd) **BACK TO THE SWEETHEARTS OF THE RODEO** [ ] [ ]
– Back to the sweethearts of the rodeo / Burning embers / Red shoes / Shoot for the Moon / Moonlight raider / Gold guitar / True true love / I'm impressed / Let's do something crazy / Like a shadow / I don't believe you met my baby / My heart stops a beat / Take a message to Mary / Last call / You're running wild / This could be the night / My shoes keep walking back to you / You should know my name by now / I've got a new heartache / Roadmaster. *(cd/c-iss.Mar88 on 'Magnum') (re-iss.d-cd Jul95 on 'Appalosa' +=)* – Carry me / Baby won't you let me be the one / You're a fool to love / Mean streets / Burn the midnight oil / Should we tell him / One man woman / Do you know Mary Lou.

— **KLEINOW, GUILBEAU & BELAND** added **GEORGE GRANTHAM** – bass (ex-POCO)

Voodoo | not issued

1990. (cd) **SOUTHERN TRACKS** [-] [-] France
– Crazy horses / Born for honky tonkin' / Armed and dangerous / Shelly's little girl / Thunder road / Matchbox / She's your lover now / Love minus zero / They want to hang a bad boy / My believing heart / Christine's tune (live) / My bucket's got a hole in it (live). *(UK-iss.Oct93)*

— **LARRY PATTON + RICK LANOW** – bass + drums repl.GRANTHAM

Sundown | not issued

May 91. (cd) **ENCORE – LIVE IN EUROPE (live)** [ ] [-]
– Dim lights, thick smoke / You ain't goin' nowhere / Hickory wind / White line fever / Sweet little Colette / Big bayou / Sweet Suzanna / Wild horses / Silverwings / Help wanted / Cannonball rag / When it all comes down to love / Wheels.

— **CHRIS ETHERIDGE / BRIAN CADD** (b.Australia) – keyboards / **RONNIE TUTT** – drums repl.PATTON + LANOW

Oct 93. (cd) **EYE OF THE HURRICANE** [ ] [-]
– Wheel of love / Like a thief in the night / Bayou blues / Angry words / Rosetta knows / Heart highway / I sent your saddle home / Jukebox Saturday night / Arizona moon / Wild wild west / Eye of a hurricane / Sunset boulevard / Smile.

– compilations, etc. –

1971. A&M; (cd) **GRASS ROOTS** (half by DILLARD & CLARK) [-] [ ]

1973. Pye/ US= Bumble; (lp) **SIX DAYS ON THE ROAD – LIVE IN AMSTERDAM** [ ] [ ]

Jul 74. (d-lp)(c) **CLOSE UP THE HONKY TONKS** [ ] [ ]
– (out-takes from past albums)

Mar 87. Edsel/ US= A&M; (lp)(cd) **DIM LIGHTS, THICK SMOKE AND LOUD, LOUD MUSIC** [ ] [ ]
– Train song / Close up the honky tonks / Sing me back home / Tonight the bottle let me down / Your angel steps out of Heaven / Crazy arms / Together again / Honky tonk women / Green, green grass of home / Dim lights / Bony Moronie / To love somebody / Break my mind / Dim lights, thick smoke and loud music. *(re-iss.Jul93)*

1989. A&M; (cd) **FARTHER ALONG** [-] [-]

May 90. Sundown; (cd)(lp) **HOLLYWOOD NIGHTS** (demos 1979-81) [ ] [-]

May 91. Sundown; (cd)(c)(lp) **FROM ANOTHER TIME** (live 1975) [ ] [-]

1992. Relix; (cd) **SIN CITY (live 1976)** [-] [ ]

Nov 94. Start; (cd) **IN CONCERT** [ ] [-]

Dec 95. Sundown; (cd) **DOUBLE BARREL** (rec.1984) [ ] [ ]
– She's single again / New shade of blue / Price of love / Ain't love just like the rain / One more time / Sailor / No easy way out / Tonight / Hearts in my eyes / Ain't worth the powder / Late in the night / I'm confessing / Let your heart do the talking.

FOCUS

Formed: Amsterdam, Holland . . . late 1969 by THIJS VAN LEER, HANS CLEUVER and MARTIN DRESDEN, who became backing band for Dutch version of 'Hair' musical, after they recruited JAN AKKERMAN in 1970. They signed to 'Bovema' label in Holland and issued debut lp 'IN AND OUT OF FOCUS'. From it, their European hit 'HOUSE OF THE KING', made label 'Blue Horizon' release it in UK. Their 2nd album 'MOVING WAVES', was released late 1971, and contained long version of 'HOCUS POCUS', which gave them a UK Top 20 hit for new label 'Polydor' late '72. With its success, the lp shot up to No.2, and promted a quick 45 follow-up 'SYLVIA', which hit UK Top 5. The next year, their 3rd album (a double), made UK Top 10, and issued on 'Sire' in the US, hit Top40, due mainly to 'HOCUS POCUS' making Top 10 there. After a live album, and disappointing 'HAMBURGER CONCERTO' (1974) album, which both made UK top 30 lists, the band went into sharp commercial decline. • **Style:** Improvised neo-classical rock outfit, that gathered together virtuoso guitarist AKKERMAN and talented flautist/organist VAN LEER. The latter took the group into more jazz-rock field, which was disliked by the 1976 departing AKKERMAN. • **Songwriters:** AKKERMAN & VAN LEER, except TOMMY (Tom Barlage). • **Trivia:** On Apr'90, FOCUS of late'72 re-formed for Dutch TV special.

Recommended: MOVING WAVES (*7) / FOCUS III (*6)

THIJS VAN LEER (b.31 Mar'48) – organ, flute, some vocals / **JAN AKKERMAN** (b.24 Dec'46) – lead guitar, lute (ex-BRAINBOX, ex-HUNTERS) / **MARTIN DRESDEN** – guitar / **HANS CLEUVER** – drums

Polydor | Sire

Jan 71. (lp)(c) **IN AND OUT OF FOCUS** [ ] [ ]
– Focus (instrumental) / Why dream / Happy nightmare (mescaline) / Anonymous / Black beauty / Sugar Island / House of the king / Focus (vocal). *(re-iss.Dec73 + Jun73 US)*

Jan 71. (7") **HOUSE OF THE KING. / BLACK BEAUTY** [ ] [ ]

— **PIERRE VAN DER LINDEN** (b.19 Feb'46) – drums (ex-BRAINBOX, ex-HUNTERS) repl. CLEUVER / **CYRIL HAVERMANS** – bass, vocals repl. DRESDEN

Blue Horizon | Sire

Oct 71. (lp)(c) **MOVING WAVES** [ ] [8] Jan 73
– Hocus pocus / Le clochard ("bread") / Janus / Moving waves / Focus II / Eruption: Orpheus – Pupilla – Tommy – Pupilla – Answer – The bridge – Euridice – Dayglow – Endless road – Answer – Orfeus – Euridice. *(re-iss.Nov72 on 'Polydor' hit UK No.2.)*

Oct 71. (7") **HOCUS POCUS. / JANIS** [ ] [-]
(re-iss.Oct72 on 'Polydor', hit No.20 UK.)

1972. (7") **TOMMY. / FOCUS II** [ ] [-]

— **BERT RUITER** (b.26 Nov'46) – bass, vocals repl. CYRIL who went solo

Polydor | Sire

Nov 72. (d-lp)(c) **FOCUS III** [6] [35] Apr 73
– Round goes the gossip / Love remembered / Sylvia / Carnival fugue / Focus III / Answers? questions! questions? answers! / Anonymous II (part 1) / Elspeth of Nottingham / House of the king.

Dec 72. (7") **SYLVIA. / HOUSE OF THE KING** [4] [89] Jul 73

Feb 73. (7") **HOCUS POCUS (pt.1). / HOCUS POCUS (pt.2)** [-] [9]

Oct 73. (lp)(c) **FOCUS AT THE RAINBOW (live)** [23] [ ]
– Focus III / Answers? questions! questions? answers! / Focus II / Eruption: Orfeus – Answer – Pupilla – Tommy – Pupilla / Hocus pocus / Sylvia / Hocus pocus (reprise).

— (Oct73) **COLIN ALLEN** – drums (ex-STONE THE CROWS, ex-JOHN MAYALL) repl. LINDEN (He later briefly returned)

Polydor | Atco

Apr 74. (7") **HAREM SCAREM. / EARLY BIRTH** [ ] [ ]

May 74. (lp)(c) **HAMBURGER CONCERTO** [20] [66]
– Delitiae musicae / Harem scarem / La cathedrale de Strasbourg / Birth / Hamburger concerto:- Starter – Rare – Medium I – Medium II – Well done – One for the road.

— (mid'75) **DAVID KEMPER** (b.USA) – drums repl. ALLEN

Oct 75. (lp)(c) **MOTHER FOCUS** [ ] [ ]
– Mother Focus / I need a bathroom / Bennie Helder / Soft vanilla / Hard vanilla / Tropic bird / Focus IV – Someone's crying . . .what! / All together . . .oh that! / No hang ups / My sweetheart / Father Bach.

Mar 76. (7") **HOUSE OF THE KING (new). / O AVENDROOD** [ ] [-]

— (Mar76) **PHILIP CATHERINE** (b.27 Oct'42, London) – guitar (ex-JEAN LUC PONTY, ex-JOHN McLAUGHLIN) repl. JAN AKKERMAN who went solo. / **STEVE SMITH** – drums (ex-JEAN LUC PONTY) repl. VAN DER LINDEN / added **EEF ALBERS** – guitar They split around the same time but managed to leave a collaboration with 60's pop star **P.J.PROBY.**

Harvest | not issued

Jan 78. (lp)(c) **FOCUS CON PROBY** [ ] [-]
– Wingless / Orion / Night flight / Eddy / Sneezing bull / Brother / Tokyo Rose / Maximum / How long.

— **RICHARD JAMES** – drums repl. SMITH who joined JOURNEY. THIJS VAN LEER continued his solo career, further below.

– compilations, others, etc. –

Feb 75. Sire; (lp)(c) **DUTCH MASTERS – A SELECTION . . .** [-] [ ]

Jul 75. Polydor; (lp)(c) **FOCUS** [23] [-]
(cd-iss.Aug85 on 'Mercury')

Sep 77. Harvest/ US= Sire; (lp)(c) **SHIP OF MEMORIES (rare 1973)** [ ] [ ]
– P's march / Can't believe my eyes / Focus V / Out of Vesuvius / Glider / Red sky at night / Spoke the Lord Creator / Crackers / Ship of memories.

Sep 84. Fame; (lp)(c) **GREATEST HITS OF FOCUS** [ ] [-]

1986. E.M.I.; (cd) **THE BEST OF FOCUS** [ ] [-]

Feb 85. EMI-Gold; (7") **SYLVIA. / HOUSE OF THE KING** [ ] [-]

Mar 87. Old Gold; (7") **SYLVIA. / HOCUS POCUS** [ ] [-]

May 94. E.M.I.; (cd) **HOCUS POCUS – THE BEST OF FOCUS** [ ] [-]

THIJS VAN LEER

C.B.S. | Columbia

Nov 72. (lp)(c) **INTROSPECTION** [ ] [ ]
– Pavane / Rondo / Agnus dei / Focus 1 / Erbarme dich / Focus 2 / Introspection.

— next arranged by **ROGER VAN OTTERLOO** / voice by **LETTY DE JONG**

Dec 75. (lp)(c) **INTROSPECTION 2** [ ] [-]
– Goyeseas No.IV / Rondo II / Introduction / Siciliano / Focus III / Larghetto & Allegro / Introspection II / Sheep may safely graze / Mild wild Rose / Bist du bei hair / Carmes elysium.

Dec 75. (7") **RONDO. / SICILIANO** [ ] [-]

— In Apr76, he also issued 'O MY LOVER' album on 'Philips'.

Dec 76. (lp) **MUSICA PER LA NOTTE DI NATALE** [ ] [-]
– O Jesulein suess / Coventry carol / Hark, the herald angels sing / Es ist ein Ros' entsprungen / Mafia die zoude naaar Bethlehem gaan / Vom Himmel hoch, da komm ich her / Er is een Kindeke Geboren Op Aard / Away in a manger / Ich steh' an deiner Krippe hier / Hoe leit dit kindeke / God rest ye merry gentleman.

Nov 77. (7") **PAVANE. / COVERNTY CAROL** [ ] [-]

Feb 79. (lp)(c) **INTROSPECTION 3** [ ] [ ]

– Reigen se liger / Rondeau / Adagio / Elazotta / Brother / Siciliano / Rondo III / He shall feed his flock / Focus V.

Aug 79. (lp)(c) **NICE TO HAVE MET YOU** [ ] [-]
– My sweetheart / Nice to have met you (concrete) / Pastorale / Bahama mama / Hocus pocus / Tonight beneath the sky / Rosebud / Super frishell.

1979. (7") **BAHAMA MAMA. / ?** [ ] [-]

PEDAL POINT

was formed by **THIJS VAN LEER / TATO GOMEZ** – vocals, bass, percussion / **PAUL SHICIHARA** – guitar / **MARIO AREANDONAG** – drums, percussion, vocals.

C.B.S.Euro not issued

1981. (lp) **DONA NOBIS PACEM** [-] [-]
– Kyrie, kyrie Eleison 1 – Christe Eleison – Kyrie Eleison 2 / Credo: introduction Credo 1 & 2 – Et in umum – Et incarnatus est – Crucifixus / Credo (continued): Et resuurexit – Et resurrexit 2 – Et in spiritum sanctum: Sanctus – Osanna / Agnus dei / Pater noster.

VAN LEER BAND

Co-produced by PHIL WARD-LARGE, who now works for BBC on Johnnie Walker show.

Ariola not issued

1987. (lp)(c) **I HATE MYSELF** [ ] [-]

JAN AKKERMAN

In 1972 'EMI' re-iss.1969 Dutch lp, 'TALENT FOR SALE' as 'GUITAR FOR SALE'.

Harvest Sire

Apr 73. (7") **BLUE BOY. / MINSTREL-FARMERS DANCE** [ ] [ ]

May 73. (lp)(c) **PROFILE** [ ] [ ]
– Fresh air / Must be my land / Wrestling to get out / Back again / The fight / Fresh air – blue notes for listening / Water and skies are telling me / Happy Gabriel / Andante sostenute / Maybe just a dream / Elude / Kemps jig / Blue boy / Minstrel-farmers dance / Stick. *(rel.Holland 1972)*

Atlantic Atco

Jan 74. (lp)(c) **TABERNAKEL** [ ] [ ]
– Brittania / Coranto for Mrs.Muircroft / The Earl of Derby / Hid galliard / House of the king / A galliard / A pavan / Javeh / A fantasy / Lammy / I am asleep, half asleep / Awak – she is Lammy / We are / The last will and testament / Amen.

Jan 74. (7") **HOUSE OF THE KING. / JAVEH** [ ] [ ]

Feb 77. (lp)(c) **ELI ("JAN AKKERMAN with KAZ LUX")** [ ] [ ]
– Eli / Guardian angel / Tranquilizer / Can't fake a good time / There he still goes / Striadberg / Wings of strings / Naked actress / Fairytale.

Feb 78. (7") **CRACKERS. / WINGS OF STRINGS** [ ] [-]

Feb 78. (lp)(c) **JAN AKKERMAN** [ ] [ ]
– Crackers / Angel watch / Pavane / Street walker / Skydancer / Floatin' / Gate to Europe.

May 78. (7") **CRACKERS. / ANGELS WATCH** [ ] [-]

Aug 78. (lp) **ARANJUEZ ("JAN AKKERMAN & CLAUS OGERMANN"** [ ] [-]
– Adagio from 'Concerto de Aranjuez' / Nightwings / Madinha / Espandeta / Pavane pour une infante defunte / Love remembered / The seed of God / Bachranas Brasileiras No.5.

Mar 79. (lp) **LIVE (live)** [ ] [-]
– Transitory / Skydancer / Pavane / Crackers / Tommy / Azimuth.

Dec 79. (lp) **3** [ ] [-]
– Stingray / Wait and see / She's so divine / Funk me / This is the one / Night prayer / Time out of mind.

Jan 80. (7") **SHE'S SO DEVINE. / SKYDANCER** [ ] [-]

Polydor not issued

1980. (lp) **TRANSPARENTAL (w / KAZ LUX)** [ ] [-]
– Inspiration / Apocalypso / Concentrate don't hesitate / Transparental / I don't make it much longer / Marsha / You're not the type / The party is over.

C.N.R. G'MANY not issued

1981. (lp) **OIL IN THE FAMILY** [-] [-]
– Oil in the family / Formula none / Discoasis / No doubt about it / Family – reprise / Blue in the shadow.

W.E.A. W.E.A.

1982. (lp) **PLEASURE POINT** [ ] [ ]
– Valdez / Heavy pleasure / Cool in the shadow / Visions of blue / C.S. / Bird island. *(UK-iss.+c+cd Jul87 on 'Decal') (re-iss.cd Nov91 on 'Charly')*

Polydor not issued

1982. (lp) **IT COULD HAPPEN TO YOU** [-] [-]
– Old tennis shoe / Come closer / Funkology: (a) Baby start (b) One way (c) Free / It could happen to you. *(UK-iss.Dec85 on 'Charly')*

Metrognome G'MANY not issued

1983. (lp) **CAN'T STAND NOISE** [-] [-]
– Pietons / Everything must change / Back to the factory / Journey (a real elegant gipsy) / Heavy treasure / Just because / Who knows. *(UK-iss.May86 on 'Charly') (above 2 lp's issued on cd Jun86 as THE COMPLETE GUITARIST) (cd-iss.1992)*

1984. (lp) **FOCUS (w / THIJS VAN LEER)** [-] [-]
– Russian roulette / King Kong / Le tango / Indian summer / Beethoven's revenge / Ole Judy / Who's calling.

C.B.S. Columbia

1985. (lp) **FROM THE BASEMENT** [ ] [ ]
– Headbanger / All along the watchtower / Dark rose / Wallenberg / From the basement / P.C.B. chicken / Status quo.

Sound Pro. not issued

1987. (lp,cd) **HEARTWARE** [-] [-]
– My pleasure / Just because, so / Lost & found / Heartware / Winter born / Lyric / Lonely street of dreams / Firenze.

Inak not issued

1988. (cd) **LIVE! (live "JAN AKKERMAN & JOACHIM KUEHN")** [ ] [-]
– (part 1 in Kiel / part 2 in Stutgart)

FORCEFIELD II

AKKERMAN with **RAY FENWICK & COZY POWELL + MO FOSTER** – bass / **PETE PRESENT** – vocals..

— Covered TIRED OF WAITING . . . (Kinks) + many others.

President not issued

Aug 88. (lp)(cd) **THE TALISMAN** [ ] [-]
– The talisman / Year of the dragon / Tired of waiting for you / Heartache / Good is good / Carrie / Without your love / I lose again / The mercenary. (cd+=extra instrumental tracks).

Sep 88. (7") **HEARTACHE. / I LOSE AGAIN (instrumental)** [ ] [-]

Sep 89. (lp)(cd) **TO OZ AND BACK** [ ] [-]
– Hit and run / Always / Stay away / Desire / Tokyo / Who'll be next in line / Wings on my feet / Fire power / hold on / Rendezvous.

JAN AKKERMAN

(solo)

I.R.S. E.M.I.

Jun 90. (cd)(c)(lp) **THE NOISE OF ART** [ ] [ ]
– Trojan horse / You can't keep a bad man up / Bonnaville / Shame on you / Prelude: friends always / Prima Donna / Having fun / Akkerman's sombrero / My pleasure / Quiet storm.

Inak Inak

Dec 94. (cd) **PUCCINI'S CAFE** [ ] [ ]

– (JAN AKKERMAN) compilations –

1979. Bovena Negrum Holland; (lp) **A PHENOMENON** [-] [-]

John FOGERTY (see under ⇒ CREEDENCE CLEARWATER REVIVAL)

FOGHAT

Formed: England . . . late 1970 by former SAVOY BROWN members PEVERETT, STEVENS and EARL, who brought in ROD PRICE. In 1972, they issued eponymous debut lp for 'Bearsville', which included Top 100 single 'I JUST WANT TO MAKE LOVE TO YOU'. Their 3rd album 'ENERGIZED' in 1974, became first of 7 albums to hit US Top 40. Due to their popularity there, they emigrated to New York around the mid-70's. • **Style:** Hard & bluesy boogie rock outfit, not far removed from sound of previous band SAVOY BROWN. • **Songwriters:** Group penned, except; I JUST WANT TO MAKE LOVE TO YOU (Willie Dixon) / MAYBELLENE (Chuck Berry) / THAT'LL BE THE DAY (Buddy Holly) / etc. • **Trivia:** They first worked together as WARREN PHILLIPS & THE ROCKETS, who issued US only lp 'FOCKED OUT' on 'Parrot' records.

Recommended: THE BEST OF FOGHAT (*6)

'LONESOME' DAVE PEVERETT – vocals, guitar (ex-SAVOY BROWN) / **ROD PRICE** – guitar, vocals / **TONE STEVENS** – bass (ex-SAVOY BROWN) / **ROGER EARL** – drums (ex-SAVOY BROWN)

Bearsville Bearsville

Jun 72. (7") **WHAT A SHAME. / HOLE TO HIDE IN** [ ] [-]

Jul 72. (lp) **FOGHAT** [ ] [ ]
– I just want to make love to you / Trouble, trouble / Leavin' again (again!) / Fools hall of fame / Sarah Lee / Highway (killing me) / Maybellene / Hole to hide in / Gotta get to know you. *(re-iss.Jun74) (cd-iss.May93 on 'Rhino-Bearsville')*

Oct 72. (7") **I JUST WANT TO MAKE LOVE TO YOU. / HOLE TO HIDE IN** [-] [83]

Mar 73. (lp) **FOGHAT (- ROCK'N'ROLL)** [ ] [67]
– Ride, ride, ride / Feel so bad / Long way to go / It's too late / What a shame / Helping hand / Road fever / She's gone / Couldn't make her stay. *(cd-iss.May93 on 'Rhino-Bearsville')*

Apr 73. (7") **WHAT A SHAME. / HELPING HAND** [-] [82]

Feb 74. (7") **LONG WAY TO GO. / RIDE, RIDE, RIDE** [-] [ ]

May 74. (7") **THAT'LL BE THE DAY. / WILD CHERRY** [-] [ ]

Jul 74. (lp)(c) **ENERGIZED** [ ] [34] Jan 74
– Wild cherry / Step outside / Home in my hand / Nothin' I won't do / That'll be the day / Golden arrow / Fly by night / Honey hush. *(cd-iss.May93 on 'Rhino-Bearsville')*

Jul 74. (7") **STEP OUTSIDE. / MAYBELLENE** [ ] [ ]

Oct 74. (lp)(c) **ROCK AND ROLL OUTLAWS** [ ] [40]
– Eight days on the road / Hate to see you go / Dreamer / Trouble in my way / Rock and roll outlaw / Shirley Jean / Blue spruce woman / Chateau lafitte '59 boogie.

— **NICK JAMESON** (b. Missouri, USA) – bass, keyboards repl. STEVENS (later to MIDNIGHT FLYER)

Dec 75. (7") **SLOW RIDE. / SAVE YOUR LOVIN' FOR ME** [ ] [20]

Feb 76. (lp)(c) **FOOL FOR THE CITY** [ ] [23] Oct 75
– Fool for the city / Save your loving (for me) / Drive me home / Take it or leave it / Terraplane blues / My babe / Slow ride. *(cd-iss.Jun93 on 'Rhino-Bearsville')*

Jun 76. (7") **FOOL FOR THE CITY. / TAKE IT OR LEAVE IT** [-] [45]

— **CRAIG MacGREGOR** – bass repl. NICK

Nov 76. (7") **DRIVIN' WHEEL. / NIGHT SHIFT** [ ] [34]

Dec 76. (lp)(c) **NIGHT SHIFT** [ ] [36] Nov 76
– Night shift / Drivin' wheel / I'll be standing by / Burning the midnight oil / Take me to the river / Hot shot love / New place to call home / Don't run me down.

Mar 77. (7") **I'LL BE STANDING BY. / TAKE ME TO THE RIVER** [-] [67]

Sep 77. (lp)(c) **FOGHAT LIVE (live)** [ ] [11]
– Fool for the city / Home in my hand / I just want to make love to you / Road fever / Honey hush / Slow ride. *(cd-iss.May93 on 'Rhino-Bearsville')*

Jan 78. (7") **I JUST WANT TO MAKE LOVE TO YOU (live). / FOOL FOR THE CITY (live)** [ ] [33] Sep 77

May 78. (7") **STONE BLUE. / CHEVROLET** [ ] [36]
Jun 78. (lp)(c) **STONE BLUE** [ ] [25] May 78
– Stone blue / Sweet home Chicago / Easy money / Midnight madness / It hurts me too / High on love / Chevrolet / Stay with me. *(cd-iss.May93 on 'Rhino-Bearsville')*
Sep 78. (7") **SWEET HOME CHICAGO. / HIGH ON LOVE** [-] [ ]
Oct 79. (lp)(c) **BOOGIE MOTEL** [ ] [35]
– Somebody's been sleepin' in my bed / Third time lucky (first time I was a fool) / Comin' down with love / Paradise alley / Boogie Motel / Love in motion / Nervous release.
Nov 79. (7") **THIRD TIME LUCKY (FIRST TIME I WAS A FOOL). / LOVE IN MOTION** [-] [23]
Mar 80. (7") **THIRD TIME LUCK (FIRST TIME I WAS A FOOL). / SOMEBODY'S BEEN SLEEPIN' IN MY BED** [ ] [-]

— added guests **COLIN EARL** – keyboards / **JIMMY AMBROSIA** – keyboards (PRICE departed after following album)

Island Bearsville
Jul 80. (7") **STRANGER IN MY HOME TOWN. / BE MY WOMAN** [-] [81]
Aug 80. (lp)(c) **TIGHT SHOES** [ ] [ ] Jun 80
– Stranger in my home town / Loose ends / Full time lover / Baby can I change your mind / Too late the hero / Dead end street / Be my woman / No hard feelings.

— **ERIK CARTWRIGHT** – bass repl. CRAIG

Avatar Bearsville
Jul 81. (7") **LOVE ZONE. / WIDE BOY** [-] [ ]
Jan 82. (lp)(c) **GIRLS TO CHAT, AND BOYS TO BOUNCE** [ ] [92] Jul 81
– Second childhood / Wide boy / Let me get close to you / Weehand driver / Live now – pay later / Delayed reaction / Sing about love / Love zone.

— added **ELI JENKINS** – keyboards, bass

— (to DAVE, ROGER and ERIK)

Oct 82. (7") **SLIPPED, TRIPPED, FELL IN LOVE. / AND I DO JUST WHAT I WANT** [-] [ ]
Nov 82. (lp) **IN THE MOOD FOR SOMETHING RUDE** [-] [ ]
– Love rustler / Rustin' up or bustin' out / Slipped, tripped, fell in love / Ain't livin' long like this / There ain't no man that can't be caught / Take this heart of mine / Back for a taste of your love / And I do just what I want.
Jul 83. (lp) **ZIG-ZAG WALK** [-] [ ]
– Zig-zag walk / Choo choo ch'boogie / Down the road apiece / It'll be late / Linda Lou / Three wheel Cadillac / Silent treatment / Seven day weekend / Jenny don't mind.
Jul 83. (7") **SEVEN DAY WEEKEND. / THAT'S WHAT LOVE CAN DO** [-] [ ]

— Disbanded around 1984.

– compilations, others, etc. –

Mar 91. Sequel; (cd) **THE BEST OF FOGHAT** [ ] [-] Jun 89
– I just want to make love to you / Night shift / Ride ride ride / Take it or leave it / Home in my hand / Drivin' wheel / Fool for the city / Eight days on the road / Stone blue / Honey hush / Maybelline / Wild cherry / Third time lucky (first time I was a fool) / Easy money / Chateau Latiffe '59 boogie / Slow ride. *(cd-iss.Aug93 on 'Rhino-Bearsville')*
May 92. Sequel; (cd) **THE BEST OF FOGHAT VOL.2** [ ] [-]
(cd-iss.Aug93 on 'Rhino-Bearsville')

FOLK IMPLOSION (see under ⇒ SEBADOH)

FOO FIGHTERS (see under ⇒ NIRVANA)

FORCEFIELD II (see under ⇒ FOCUS)

Lita FORD

Born: 23 Sep'59, London, England. After leaving California band The RUNAWAYS in 1979, she went solo signing to 'Mercury' in 1982. The following year, she and her band issued debut album 'OUT FOR BLOOD'. She broke through in 1988, when single 'KISS ME DEADLY' hit US Top 20. • **Style:** Rated the best female guitarist in the world, she mixed heavy rock and her sex appeal, although her music generally slid into typical American AOR. • **Songwriters:** All composed by LITA, with many collaborations (mid-80's with LEIB and LACHOON, 1988 with MIKE CHAPMAN & HOLLY KNIGHT, and late with GROMBACHER and KISSELBACH, plus DAVID EZRIN) except covers; ONLY WOMEN BLEED (Alice Cooper). FALLING IN AND OUT OF LOVE was co-written with NIKKI SIX of POISON. • **Trivia:** On Jun'89, she married WASP guitarist CHRIS HOLMES.

Recommended: THE BEST OF LITA FORD (*5)

LITA FORD BAND

LITA – vocals, lead guitar (ex-RUNAWAYS)with **BRIAN MERRYWEATHER** – bass, vocals, producer / **DUSTY WATSON** – drums, vocals

Mercury not issued
Jul 83. (lp)(c) **OUT FOR BLOOD** [ ] [-]
– Out for blood / Stay with me baby / Just a feeling / Die for me only / Ready willing and able / Rock'n'roll made me what I am today / If you can't live it / On the run / Any way that you want me / I can't stand it.

LITA FORD

solo with **HUGH McDONALD** – bass / **RANDY CASTILLO** – drums

Vertigo Mercury
Apr 84. (7") **GOTTA LET GO. / RUN WITH THE MONEY** [ ] [-]
(12"+=) – Lady killer.
May 84. (lp)(c) **DANCIN' ON THE EDGE** [96] [66]
– Gotta let go / Dancing on the edge / Dressed to kill / Hit'n'run / Lady killer / Still waitin' / Five in my heart / Don't let me down tonight / Run with the $.

— **ERIC SINGER** – drums repl. CASTILLO who joined OZZY OSBOURNE / **TOMMY CALABONNA** – bass repl. McDONALD

R.C.A. R.C.A.
Apr 88. (lp)(c)(cd) **LITA** [ ] [29] Feb 88
– Fatal passion / Under the gun / Broken dreams / Close my eyes forever / Can't catch me / Blueberry / Kiss me deadly / Falling in and out of love. *(re-iss.cd Mar94)*
May 88. (7")(7"pic-d) **KISS ME DEADLY. / BROKEN DREAMS** [ ] [12] Apr 88
(12"+=) – ('A'instrumental). *(re-iss.Nov88, reached No.75-UK)*
Nov 88. (7") **BACK TO THE CAVE (remix). / UNDER THE GUN** [-] [ ]
May 89. (7")(7"pic-d) **CLOSE MY EYES FOREVER. ("LITA FORD with OZZY OSBOURNE") / UNDER THE GUN** [47] [8] Feb 89
(12"+=)(cd-s+=) – Blueberry.
Jul 90. (7") **HUNGRY. / BIG GUN** [ ] [98]
(12"+=)(cd-s+=) – Aces and eights.
Jul 90. (cd)(c)(lp) **STILETTO** [66] [52] Jun 90
– Your wake up call / Hungry / Dedication / Stiletto / Lisa / The ripper / Big gun / Only women bleed / Bad boy / Aces and eights / Cherry red / Outro.
Dec 91. (7") **SHOT OF POISON. / LARGER THAN LIFE** [63] [ ] Oct91
(12"+=)(12"pic-d+=)(cd-s+=) – ('A'remixed).

B.M.G.-RCA B.M.G.-RCA
Jan 92. (cd)(c)(lp) **DANGEROUS CURVES** [51] [ ] Nov 91
– Larger than life / What do you know about love / Shot of poison / Bad love / Playin' with fire / Hellbound train / Black widow / Little too early / Holy man / Tambourine dream / Little black spider. *(re-iss.cd Mar94)*
Aug 92. (cd)(c)(lp) **THE BEST OF LITA FORD** – (compilation) [ ] [ ]
– What do you know about love / Kiss me deadly / Shot of poison / Hungry / Gotta let go / Close my eyes forever / Larger than life / Only women bleed / Playin' with fire / Back to the cave / Lisa.

ZYX Pyramid
Jan 95. (cd)(c) **BLACK** [ ] [ ]
–
Apr 95. (c-s)(cd-s) **A FUTURE TO HIS LIFE. ("JOE WALSH & LITA FORD") /** [-] [ ]

FOREIGNER

Formed: New York, USA . . . early 1976 by English expatriots JONES, McDONALD and ELLIOTT, who linked up with New Yorkans GRAMM, GREENWOOD and GAGLIARI. After a year in the studio, they unleashed eponymous debut lp for 'Atlantic'. Although it did not chart in the UK, it hit Top 5 in the States. This was boosted by 2 hit cuts from it, 'FEELS LIKE THE FIRST TIME' & 'COLD AS ICE'. They remained constant hitmakers during the next several years, peaking early in 1985 with cross-Atlantic No.1 single 'I WANT TO KNOW WHAT LOVE IS'. • **Style:** Radio FM aimed AOR band, with leanings to hard-rock empire. • **Songwriters:** JONES penned some with GRAMM, until his 1987 departure. • **Trivia:** Saxist JUNIOR WALKER guested on their 1981 single 'URGENT', which with its parent album '4', was produced by THOMAS DOLBY & ROBERT 'MUTT' LANGE.

Recommended: GREATEST HITS (*6).

LOU GRAMM (b. 2 May'50, Rochester, New York) – vocals (ex-BLACK SHEEP) / **MICK JONES** (b.27 Dec'47, London, England) – guitar (ex-SPOOKY TOOTH) / **IAN McDONALD** (b.25 Jun'46, London) – guitar, keyboards (ex-KING CRIMSON) / **AL GREENWOOD** (b. New York) – keyboards / **ED GAGLIARI** (b.13 Feb'52, New York) – bass (ex-STORM) / **DENNIS ELLIOTT** (b.18 Aug'50, London) – drums (ex-IAN HUNTER BAND)

Atlantic Atlantic
Apr 77. (7") **FEELS LIKE THE FIRST TIME. / WOMAN OH WOMAN** [39] [4] Mar 77
Apr 77. (lp)(c) **FOREIGNER** [ ] [4] Mar 77
– Feels like the first time / Cold as ice / Starrider / Headknocker / The damage is done / Long, long way from home / Woman oh woman / At war with the world / Fool for the anyway / I need you. *(cd-iss.1988 & Oct95)*
Jul 77. (7")(7"clear) **COLD AS ICE. / I NEED YOU** [24] [6]
Dec 77. (7") **LONG, LONG WAY FROM HOME. / THE DAMAGE IS DONE** [-] [20]
Apr 78. (7"m) **LONG, LONG WAY FROM HOME. / FEELS LIKE THE FIRST TIME / COLD AS ICE** [ ] [-]
Aug 78. (lp)(c) **DOUBLE VISION** [32] [3] Jul 78
– Back where you belong / Blue morning, blue day / Double vision / Hot blooded / I have waited so long / Lonely children / Spellbinder / Tramontane / You're all I am. *(cd-iss.1988 & Oct95)*
Oct 78. (7")(7"red) **HOT BLOODED. / TRAMONTANE** [42] [3] Jun 78
Jan 79. (7")(7"pic-d) **BLUE MORNING, BLUE DAY. / I HAVE WAITED SO LONG** [45] [15]
Jul 79. (7") **DOUBLE VISION. / LONELY CHILDREN** [ ] [2] Sep 78

— **RICK WILLS** – bass (ex-ROXY MUSIC, ex-SMALL FACES) repl. AL (joined SPYS)

Sep 79. (7") **DIRTY WHITE BOY. / REV ON THE RED LINE** [ ] [12]
Sep 79. (lp)(c) **HEAD GAMES** [ ] [5]
– Dirty white boy / Love on the telephone / Women / I'll get even with you / Seventeen / Head games / The modern day / Blinded by science / Do what you like / Rev on the red line. *(cd-iss.Nov85) (re-iss.cd Feb93 on 'Atco') (re-iss.cd Oct95)*
Feb 80. (7") **HEAD GAMES. / DO WHAT YOU LIKE** [ ] [14] Nov79
Apr 80. (7") **WOMEN. / THE MODERN DAY** [ ] [41] Feb 80
Sep 80. (7") **I'LL GET EVEN WITH YOU. / BLINDED BY SCIENCE** [ ] [ ]

— Trimmed to quartet, when GAGLIARI and McDONALD leave.

Jul 81. (7") **URGENT. / GIRL ON THE MOON** [54] [4] Jun 81
Jul 81. (lp)(c) **4** [5] [1]

– Night life / Juke box hero / Break it up / Waiting for a girl like you / Luanne / Urgent / I'm gonna win / Woman in black / Urgent / Girl on the Moon / Don't let go. *(cd-iss.1988 & Oct95)*

Sep 81. (7") **JUKE BOX HERO. / I'M GONNA WIN** [48] [26] Feb 82
Oct 81. (7") **WAITING FOR A GIRL LIKE YOU. / I'M GONNA WIN** [-] [2]
Nov 81. (7"m) **WAITING FOR A GIRL LIKE YOU. / FEELS LIKE THE FIRST TIME / COLD AS ICE** [8] [-]
Mar 82. (7") **DON'T LET GO. / FOOL FOR YOU ANYWAY** [ ] [ ]
Apr 82. (7") **BREAK IT UP. / LUANNE** [-] [26]
Apr 82. (7") **URGENT. / HEAD GAMES (live)** [45] [-]
(12") – ('A'side) / Hot Blooded (live).
Jul 82. (7") **LUANNE. / FOOL FOR YOU ANYWAY** [-] [75]
Dec 82. (lp)(c)(cd) **RECORDS (THE BEST OF . . .)** (compilation) [58] [10]
– Cold as ice / Double vision / Head games / Waiting for a girl like you / Feels like the first time / Urgent / Dirty white boy / Jukebox hero / Long, long way from home / Hot blooded. *(re-iss.cd Oct95)*
Nov 84. (7")(7"sha-pic-d) **I WANT TO KNOW WHAT LOVE IS. / STREET THUNDER** [1] [1]
(12"+=) – Urgent.
Dec 84. (lp)(c)(cd) **AGENT PROVOCATEUR** [1] [4] Nov 84
– Tooth and nail / That was yesterday / I want to know what love is / Growing up the hard way / Reaction to action / Stranger in my own house / A love in vain / Down on love / Two different worlds / She's too tough. *(re-iss.cd Oct95)*
Mar 85. (7") **THAT WAS YESTERDAY (remix). / TWO DIFFERENT WORLDS** [28] [12]
(12"+=) – ('A'orchestral version).
May 85. (7") **REACTION TO ACTION. / SHE'S TOO TOUGH** [-] [54]
Aug 85. (7") **DOWN ON LOVE. / GROWING UP THE HARD WAY** [-] [54]

—— LOU GRAMM left to go solo.

Jul 87. (7") **SAY YOU WILL. / A NIGHT TO REMEMBER** [71] [6] Nov 87
(12"+=)(cd-s+=) – Hot blooded (live).
Dec 87. (lp)(c)(cd) **INSIDE INFORMATION** [64] [15]
– Heart turns to stone / Can't wait / Say you will / I don't want to live without you / Counting every minute / Inside information / The beat of my heart / Face to face / Out of the blue / A night to remember.
May 88. (7") **I DON'T WANT TO LIVE WITHOUT YOU. / FACE TO FACE** [ ] [5] Mar 88
(12"+=) – ('A'extended).
(cd-s++=) – Urgent.
Jul 88. (7") **HEART TURNS TO STONE. / COUNTING EVERY MINUTE** [-] [56]

—— (1990) added **JOHNNY EDWARDS** – vocals to join **JONES + THOMAS**

Jun 91. (7")(c-s) **LOWDOWN AND DIRTY. / FLESH WOUND** [ ] [ ]
(12"+=)(cd-s+=) – No hiding place.
Jul 91. (cd)(c)(lp) **UNUSUAL HEAT** [56] [ ]
– Only Heaven knows / Lowdown and dirty / I'll fight for you / Moment of truth / Mountain of love / Ready for the rain / When the night comes down / Safe in my heart / No hiding place / Flesh wound / Unusual heat. *(cd-iss.Nov93)*
Aug 91. (7")(c-s) **I'LL FIGHT FOR YOU / MOMENT OF TRUTH** [ ] [ ]
(12"+=)(cd-s+=) – Dirty white boy (live).

Arista Arista

Oct 94. (7")(c-s) **WHITE LIE. / UNDER THE GUN** [58] [ ]
(cd-s+=) – ('A'mixes).
Nov 94. (cd)(c) **MR. MOONLIGHT** [59] [ ]
–
Mar 95. (c-s) **UNTIL THE END OF TIME / HAND ON MY HEART** [ ] [42]
(cd-s+=) – ('A'mix).

– compilations, others, etc. –

Nov 88. Atlantic; (7") **JUST WANNA HOLD. / YOU ARE MY FRIEND** [-] [ ]
Jun 85. Atlantic; (7") **COLD AS ICE (remix). / REACTION TO ACTION** [64] [ ]
(12"+=) – Head games (live).
(d7"++=) – Hot blooded (live).
Apr 92. Atlantic; (cd)(c)(lp) **GREATEST HITS** [19] [ ]
– Feels like the first time / Cold as ice / Starrider / Hot blooded / Blue morning, blue day / Double vision / Dirty white boy / Women / Head games / Juke Box hero / Waiting for a girl like you / Urgent / That was yesterday / I want to know what love is / Say you will / I don't want to live without you. *(re-iss Dec 92 as 'THE VERY BEST AND BEYOND')*
Apr 92. Atlantic; (7")(c-s) **WAITING FOR A GIRL LIKE YOU. / COLD AS ICE** [ ] [ ]
(12"+=)(cd-s+=) – That was yesterday / Feels like the first time.
Dec 93. Atlantic; (cd)(c) **CLASSIC HITS LIVE (live)** [ ] [ ]

MICK JONES

Atlantic Atlantic

Nov 88. (7") **JUST WANNA HOLD. / YOU ARE MY FRIEND** [-] [ ]
Jan 89. (7") **EVERYTHING THAT COMES AROUND. / THE WRONG SIDE OF THE LAW** [ ] [ ]
(12"+=) – ('A'extended).
Aug 89. (lp)(c)(cd) **MICK JONES** [ ] [ ]
– Just wanna hold / Save me tonight / That's the way my love is / The wrong side of the law / 4 wheels turnin' / Everything that comes around / You are my friend / Danielle / Write tonight / Johnny (part 1).

Robert FORSTER (see under ⇒ GO-BETWEENS)

FOTHERINGAY (see under ⇒ FAIRPORT CONVENTION)

4 NON BLONDES

Formed: San Francisco, California, USA . . . 1990 by LINDA PERRY, etc. After signing to 'Atlantic' off-shoot label 'Intercord', they smashed the US Top 20 with classic 'WHAT'S UP' single, which also broke them into Top 3 in Britain. • **Style:** Loud and eccentric looking 3 girl / 1 guy hard-edged rock outfit, with sense of political lyrical awareness. PERRY's paint-stripping vox was described as the female equivalent of AXL ROSE. • **Songwriters:** PERRY or group penned.

Recommended: BIGGER, BETTER, FASTER, MORE! (*5).

LINDA PERRY – vocals / **ROGER ROCHA** – guitar repl. LOUIS METOYER after 1st lp / **CHRISTA HILLHOUSE** – bass, vocals / **DAWN RICHARDSON** – drums / and 1 track guests

Interscope Interscope

Jun 93. (7")(c-s) **WHAT'S UP. / THE TRAIN** [2] [14] Apr 93
(cd-s+=) – ('A'mixes).
Jun 93. (cd)(c) **BIGGER, BETTER, FASTER, MORE!** [4] [14] May 93
– Train / Superfly / What's up / Pleasantly blue / Morphine & chocolate / Spaceman / Old Mr. Heffer / Calling all the people / Dear Mr. President / Drifting / No place like home.
Oct 93. (7")(c-s) **SPACEMAN. / STRANGE** [53] [ ]
(12"+=)(cd-s+=) – What's up (remix or piano version).
Dec 93. (7")(c-s) **DEAR MR.PRESIDENT. / SUPERFLY** [ ] [ ]
(cd-s+=) – Drifting.

—— In Aug 94, 'WHAT'S UP' was ripped off by charting dance / pop terrorist DJ MIKO.

FOUR TOPS

Formed: Detroit, Michegan, USA . . . 1953 initially as The FOUR AIMS. In 1956 they changed name to FOUR TOPS and released one-off single for 'Chess'. More flop 45's followed, but fortune smiled in Mar'63, when the growing 'Tamla Motown' took them on board. Their first recordings that year could have been on new 'Tamla' specialist jazz label 'Workshop', but they spent it as back-up to label acts like The SUPREMES. In 1964, producers HOLLAND-DOZIER-HOLLAND decided to give them some songs to record, and by the end of the year 'BABY I NEED YOUR LOVING' is No.11 in US charts. After a couple of more hits, they hit big time in 1965 with US No.1 'I CAN'T HELP MYSELF'. They soon became household names on both sides of the Atlantic, with the Motown industry churning out hit after hit in the 60's and early 70's. In 1981 on their new label 'Casablanca', they found renewed success, with hit singles 'WHEN SHE WAS MY GIRL' & 'DON'T WALK AWAY'. To end the 80's, they were enjoying another comeback for 'Arista', when 'LOVE IN ACAPULCO' hit the UK Top10. • **Style:** Classy Motown soul outfit, who fused storming vocals with great lyrical content. They moved into disco land in the 80's. • **Songwriters:** From 1964 to 1967, most of their songs were from HOLLAND-DOZIER-HOLLAND. In 1972, 'Dunhill' records furnished them with 2 other writers DENNIS LAMBERT and BRIAN POTTER. The FOUR TOPS also covered:- WALK AWAY RENNE (Left Banke) / IF I WERE A CARPENTER (Tim Hardin) / DO WHAT YOU GOTTA DO + MacARTHUR PARK (Jim Webb) / IT'S ALL IN THE GAME (Tommy Edwards) / A SIMPLE GAME + SO DEEP WITHIN YOU (Moody Blues) / WONDERFUL BABY (Smokey Robinson) / LAST TRAIN TO CLARKSVILLE (Boyce-Hart) / I'M A BELIEVER (Neil Diamond) / etc. • **Trivia:** BILLY BRAGG made one Four Top famous again, after singing about LEVI STUBBS' TEARS on a 1986 single. That year LEVI also provided the voice for the man-eating plant in the film musical 'Little Shop Of Horrors'.

Recommended: THE SINGLES COLLECTION (*6)

LEVI STUBBS (b.STUBBLES) – lead vocals (ex-ROYALS) / **RENALDO 'OBIE' BENSON** – vocals / **LAWRENCE PAYTON** – vocals / **ABDUL 'DUKE' FAKIR** – vocals

not issued Chess

Jul 56. (7") **KISS ME BABY. / COULD IT BE YOU** [-] [ ]

—— (In 1958. released another unknown 45 on 'Red Top')

not issued Columbia

Oct 60. (7") **AIN'T THAT LOVE. / LONELY SUMMER** [-] [ ]
(re-iss.Jul65, hit No.93)

not issued Riverside

1962. (7") **WHERE ARE YOU?. / PENNIES FROM HEAVEN** [-] [ ]
(US re-iss.Jul65 on 'Columbia')

Stateside Motown

Sep 64. (7") **BABY I NEED YOUR LOVING. / CALL ON ME** [ ] [11] Aug 64
Jan 65. (7") **WITHOUT THE ONE YOU LOVE. / LOVE HAS GONE** [ ] [43] Nov 64

Tamla Motown Motown

Mar 65. (7") **ASK THE LONELY. / WHERE DID YOU GO?** [ ] [24] Feb 65
Jun 65. (7") **I CAN'T HELP MYSELF (SUGAR PIE, HONEY BUNCH). / SAD SOUVENIRS** [23] [1] May 65
Jun 65. (lp) **THE FOUR TOPS** [ ] [63] Feb 65
– Baby I need your loving / Without the one you love / Where did you go / Ask the lonely / Your love is amazing / Sad souvenirs / Don't turn away / Tea house in Chinatown / Left with a broken heart / Love has gone / Call on me. *(re-iss.Mar77 + Feb82)*
Aug 65. (7") **IT'S THE SAME OLD SONG. / YOUR LOVE IS AMAZING** [34] [5] Jul 65
Nov 65. (7") **SOMETHING ABOUT YOU. / DARLING I HUM OUR SONG** [ ] [19]
Mar 66. (lp) **THE FOUR TOPS' SECOND ALBUM** [ ] [20] Nov 65

– Baby I need your loving / Without the one you love / Where did you go / Ask the lonely / Your love is amazing / Sad souvenirs / Tea house in China / Left with a broken heart / Love has gone / Call on me / I can't help myself / Love feels like fire / Is there anything that I can do / Something about you / It's the same old song. *(re-iss.Jan80 + Oct82)*

Mar 66. (7") **SHAKE ME, WAKE ME (WHEN IT'S OVER). / JUST AS LONG AS YOU NEED ME** [ ] [18]

Jul 66. (7") **LOVING YOU IS SWEETER THAN EVER. / I LIKE EVERYTHING ABOUT YOU** [21] [45] May 66

Oct 66. (7") **REACH OUT I'LL BE THERE. / UNTIL YOU LOVE SOMEONE** [1] [1] Sep 66

Nov 66. (lp) **ON TOP** [9] [32] Aug 66
– I got a feeling / Brenda / Loving you is sweeter tha ever / Shake me, wake me (when it's over) / Until you love someone / There's no one left / Matchmaker / Michelle / In the still of the night / Bluesette / Quiet nights of quiet stars / Then.

Jan 67. (7") **STANDING IN THE SHADOWS OF LOVE. / SINCE YOU'VE BEEN GONE** [6] [6] Dec 66

Feb 67. (lp) **FOUR TOPS LIVE! (live)** [4] [17] Dec 66
– (Introduction) / It's the same old song / It's not unusual / Baby I need your loving / Reach out I'll be there / I'll turn to stone / I left my heart in San Francisco / You can't hurry love / Ask the lonely / Climb ev'ry mountain / The girl from Ipanema / If I had a hammer / I can't help myself / I like everything about you. *(re-iss.Apr85)*

Mar 67. (7") **BERNADETTE. / I GOT A FEELING** [8] [4]

Apr 67. (lp) **FOUR TOPS ON BROADWAY** [-] [79]
–

Jun 67. (7") **7 ROOMS OF GLOOM. / I'LL TURN TO STONE** [12] [14] [76] May 66

Oct 67. (lp) **FOUR TOPS REACH OUT** [4] [11] Aug 67
– What else is there to do (but think about you?) / If I were a carpenter / Reach out, I'll be there / Walk away Renee / 7 nights of gloom / Last train to Clarksville / I'll turn to stone / I'm a believer / Standing in the shadows of love / Bernadette / Cherish / Wonderful baby. *(cd-iss.Sep95)*

Oct 67. (7") **YOU KEEP RUNNING AWAY. / IF YOU DON'T WANT MY LOVE** [26] [19] Sep 67

Nov 67. (7") **WALK AWAY RENEE. / YOUR LOVE IS WONDERFUL** [-] [14]

Dec 67. (7") **WALK AWAY RENEE. / MAME** [3] [14]

Jan 68. (lp) **THE FOUR TOPS GREATEST HITS** (compilation) [1] [4] Sep67
– Baby i need your loving / It's the same old song / Reach out i'll be there / Ask the lonely / Standing in the shadows of love / Loving you is sweeter than ever / I can't help myself / Without the one you love (life's not worthwhile) / 7 rooms of gloom / Something about you / Bernadette / Shake me, wake me (when it's over)

Feb 68. (7") **IF I WERE A CARPENTER. / WONDERFUL BABY** [-] [20]

Mar 68. (7") **IF I WERE A CARPENTER. / YOUR LOVE IS WONDERFUL** [7] [-]

Aug 68. (7") **YESTERDAY'S DREAMS. / FOR ONCE IN MY LIFE** [23] [49]

Nov 68. (7") **I'M IN A DIFFERENT WORLD. / REMEMBER WHEN** [27] [51] Oct 68

Jan 69. (lp) **YESTERDAY'S DREAM** [37] [91] Sep 68
– Yesterday's dream / Can't seem to get you out of my mind / I'm in a different world / We've got a strong love (on our side) / By the time I get to Phoenix / Remember when / Sunny / Never my love / Daydream believer / Once upon a time / The sweetheart tree / A place in the Sun.

May 69. (7") **WHAT IS A MAN?. / DON'T BRING BACK MEMORIES** [16] [53]

Sep 69. (lp) **FOUR TOPS NOW!** [ ] [74] Jul 69
– The key / What is a man / My past just crossed my future / Don't let him take your love from me / Eleanor Rigby / Little green apples / Do what you gotta do / MacArthur Park / Don't bring back memories / Wish I don't love you so / Opportunity knock (for me) / The fool on the hill.

Sep 69. (7") **DO WHAT YOU GOTTA DO. / CAN'T SEEM TO GET YOU OUT OF MY MIND** [11] [ ]

Sep 69. (7") **DON'T LET HIM TAKE YOUR LOVE FROM ME. / THE KEY** [-] [ ]

Feb 70. (lp) **SOUL SPIN** [ ] [ ] Dec 69
– Look out your window / Barbara's boy / Lost in a pool of red / Got to get you into my life / Stop the world / Nothing / This guy's in love with you / Light my fire / Honey / The look of love / California dreamin'.

Mar 70. (7") **I CAN'T HELP MYSELF. / BABY I NEED YOUR LOVING** [10] [-]

May 70. (7") **IT'S ALL IN THE GAME. / LOVE IS THE ANSWER** [5] [24]

Jun 70. (lp)(c) **STILL WATERS RUN DEEP** [29] [21] Apr 70
– Still water (love and peace) / Reflections / It's all in the game / Everybody's talkin' / Love is the answer / I wish I were your mirror / Elusive butterfly / Ring me together / L.A. (my town) / I'm a believer / Standing in the shadows of love / Cherish / Bernadette / Wonderful baby. *(re-iss.Jun82)(re-iss.+cd.Mar91)*

Sep 70. (7") **STILL WATER (LOVE). / STILL WATER (PEACE)** [10] [11]

—— (With The SUPREMES ⇒ , they release (Nov70) album THE MAGNIFICENT 7, this was issued UK May71 hit No.6. At same time 7" – RIVER DEEP MOUNTAIN HIGH hit US No.14, and UK No.11 in Jun71.

Jan 71. (lp)(c) **CHANGING TIMES** [ ] [ ] Oct 70
– In these changing times / Just seven numbers / Raindrops keep fallin' on my head / Right before my eyes / I almost had her / Try to remember / Something's tearing at the edges of time / Sing a song of yesterday / The long and winding road.

May 71. (7") **JUST SEVEN NUMBERS (CAN STRAIGHTEN OUT OF LIFE). / I WISH I WERE YOUR MIRROR** [36] [40] Feb 71

Jun 71. (7") **IN THESE CHANGING TIMES. / RIGHT BEFORE MY EYES** [-] [70]

—— Again with The SUPREMES, issued (Jun71) album RETURN OF THE MAGNIFICENT 7 and single YOU GOTTA HAVE LOVE IN YOUR HEART. UK releases both Nov 71.

Aug 71. (7") **MACARTHUR PARK (part II). / (part 1)** [-] [38]

Sep 71. (7") **A SIMPLE GAME. / YOU STOLE MY LOVE** [3] [-]

Oct 71. (7") **A SIMPLE GAME. / L. A. (MY TOWN)** [-] [90]

Nov 71. (lp)(c) **FOUR TOPS' GREATEST HITS VOLUME 2** (compilation) [25] [ ] Sep 71
– In these changing times / Still water (love) / Still water (peace) / Don't let him take your love from me / It's all in the game / I'm in a different world / If I were a carpenter / What is a man / Walk away Renee / You keep running away / Yesterday's dreams / Just seven numbers.

Feb 72. (7"m) **BERNADETTE. / I GOT A FEELING / IT'S THE SAME OLD SONG** [23] [ ]

—— Final collaborations with The SUPREMES, came out (US Jan72 / UK Apr72) with DYNAMITE lp. Singles WITHOUT THE ONE YOU LOVE + REACH OUT AND TOUCH (SOMEBODY'S HAND) were issued May72 + Nov72 respectively.

May 72. (7") **I CAN'T QUIT YOUR LOVE. / HAPPY (IS A BUMPY ROAD)** [-] [ ]

Jun 72. (lp)(c) **NATURE PLANNED IT** [ ] [50] May 72
– I am your man / (It's the way) Nature planned it / I'll never change / She's an understanding woman / I can't quit your love / Walk with me, talk with me, darling / Medley: Hey man – We got to get you a woman / You got to forget him darling / If you let me / Happy (is a bumpy road) / How will I forget you.

Jul 72. (7") **WALK WITH ME, TALK WITH ME DARLING. / L.A. (MY TOWN)** [32] [ ]

Sep 72. (7") **(IT'S THE WAY) NATURE PLANNED IT. / I'LL NEVER CHANGE** [-] [53]

Sep 72. (7") **I'LL TURN TO STONE. / LOVE FEELS LIKE FIRE** [ ] [ ]

Probe Dunhill

Nov 72. (7") **KEEPER OF THE CASTLE. / JUBILEE WITH SOUL** [18] [10]

Nov 72. (lp)(c) **KEEPER OF THE CASTLE** [ ] [33]
– Keeper of the castle / Ain't no woman / Put a little love away / Turn on the light of your love / When tonight meets tomorrow / Love music / Remember what I told you to forget / Love makes you human / Dreaming / The good Lord knows / Jubilee with soul / Keeper of the castle (reprise) *(re-iss.Oct74 on 'A.B.C.') (re-iss.Jan76 on 'M.F.P.')*

Feb 73. (7") **(I THINK I MUST BE) DREAMING. / THE GOOD LORD KNOWS** [ ] [ ]

Feb 73. (7") **AIN'T NO WOMAN (LIKE THE ONE I'VE GOT). / THE GOOD LORD KNOWS** [-] [4]

Jul 73. (7") **ARE YOU MAN ENOUGH?. / PEACE OF MIND** [ ] [15]

—— (above from the film soundtrack SHAFT IN AFRICA, issued on 'Probe-ABC')

Oct 73. (7") **SWEET UNDERSTANDING LOVE. / MAIN STREET PEOPLE** [ ] [33]

Dec 73. (lp)(c) **MAIN STREET PEOPLE** [ ] [66] Sep 73
– Main street people intro / I just can't get you out of my mind / It won't be the first time / Sweet understanding love / Am I my brother's keeper / Are you man enough? / Whenever's there's blue / Too little, too late / Peace of mind / One woman man / Main street people. *(re-iss.Oct74 on 'A.B.C.')*

Feb 74. (7") **AM I MY BROTHER'S KEEPER. / I JUST CAN'T GET YOU OUT OF MY MIND** [ ] [62] B-side

Jun 74. (7") **ONE CHAIN DON'T MAKE A PRISON. / TURN ON THE LIGHT OF YOUR LOVE** [ ] [41]

Jul 74. (lp)(c) **MEETINGS OF THE MINDS** [ ] [ ] Apr 74
– One chain don't make no prison / Midnight flower / The well is dry / Love ain't easy to come by / No sad songs / Right on, brother / Tell me you love me / All my love / I found the spirit / Meeting the minds. *(re-iss.Oct74 on 'A.B.C.')*

Aug 74. (7") **MIDNIGHT FLOWER. / ALL MY LOVE** [-] [55]

A.B.C. A.B.C.

Oct 74. (7") **THE WELL IS DRY. / MIDNIGHT FLOWER** [ ] [-]

Oct 74. (lp)(c) **LIVE AND IN CONCERT (live)** [ ] [92]
– Intro and countdown / Are you man enough / Love ain't easy to come by / Medley / Love music / Reach out I'll be there / Standing in the shadow of love / Midnight flower / Baby i need your loving / Keeper of the castle / I am your man / Ain't no woman (like the one I've got) / One chain don't make no prison / I can't help myself (sugar pie honey bunch) (live)

Jun 75. (7") **SEVEN LONELY NIGHTS. / I CAN'T HOLD ON MUCH LONGER** [ ] [71]

Jul 75. (lp)(c) **NIGHT LIGHTS HARMONY** [ ] [ ] Jun 75
– Seven lonely nights / Is this the price / We all gotta stick together / I've got what you need / I can't hold on much longer / Drive me out of my mind / I'm glad you walked into my life / Let me know the truth.

Dec 75. (7") **WE ALL GOTTA STICK TOGETHER. / (IT WOULD ALMOST) DRIVE ME OUT OF MY MIND** [-] [97]

Sep 76. (7") **CATFISH. / LOOK AT ME BABY** [ ] [71]

Oct 76. (lp)(c) **CATFISH** [ ] [ ]
– Catfish / Feel free / You can't hold back on love / I know you like it / Strung out for your love / Love don't come easy / Disco daddy / Look at me baby.

Nov 76. (7") **FEEL FREE. / I KNOW YOU LIKE IT** [-] [ ]

Feb 77. (7") **STRUNG OUT FOR YOUR LOVE. / YOU CAN'T HOLD BACK ON LOVE** [-] [ ]

Nov 77. (7") **FOR YOUR LOVE. / YOU'LL NEVER A BETTER MAN** [ ] [-]

Nov 77. (lp)(c) **THE SHOW MUST GO ON** [ ] [ ]
– The show must go on / I can't live without you / Save it for a rainy day / Runnin' from your love / See the real me / Love is a joy / You'll never find a better man / Candy.

Jan 78. (7") **THE SHOW MUST GO ON. / RUNNIN' FROM YOUR LOVE** [-] [ ]

Oct 78. (7") **H.E.L.P. / INSIDE A BROKEN HEARTED MAN** [-] [ ]

Oct 78. (7") **PUT IT ON THE NEWS. / WINGS** [ ] [-]

Nov 78. (lp)(c) **AT THE TOP** [ ] [ ]
– H.E.L.P. / Bits and pieces / Seclusion / Put it on the news / This house / Just in time / Inside a broken hearted man / When your dreams take wings and fly.

Jan 79. (7") **JUST IN TIME. / THIS HOUSE** [-] [ ]

1980. (7") **I'M HERE AGAIN. /('A' instrumental)** [-] [ ]

Casablanca Casablanca

Sep 81. (7")(12") **WHEN SHE WAS MY GIRL. / SOMETHING TO REMEMBER** [3] [11]
(re-iss.Oct84)

Nov 81. (lp)(c) **TONIGHT!** [ ] [37] Sep 81
– When she was my girl / Don't walk away / Tonight / I'm gonna love you / Who's right, who's wrong / Let me set you free / Something to remember / From a distance / All I do / I'll never leave again. *(cd-iss. 1988)*

Nov 81. (7") **LET ME SET YOU FREE. / FROM A DISTANCE** [-] [ ]

Dec 81. (7")(12") **DON'T WALK AWAY. / I'LL NEVER EVER LEAVE AGAIN** [16] [ ]

Jan 82. (7") **TONIGHT I'M GONNA LOVE YOU ALL OVER. / I'LL NEVER EVER LEAVE AGAIN** [-] [-]
Feb 82. (7")(12") **TONIGHT I'M GONNA LOVE YOU ALL OVER. / FROM A DISTANCE** [43] [ ]
Apr 82. (7") **SAD HEARTS. / I BELIEVE IN YOU AND ME** [-] [ ]
—— Next 45 'BACK TO SCHOOL AGAIN' from the film 'Grease II' Jun82 on 'RSO', hit UK 62 & US No.71.
Jul 82. (7")(12") **SAD HEARTS. / I BELIEVE IN YOU AND ME** [ ] [84]
Aug 82. (lp)(c) **ONE MORE MOUNTAIN** [ ] [ ]
– Sad hearts / One more mountain to climb / Givin' it up / I believe in you and me / I'm the one / Keep on lightin' my fire / Nobody's gonna love you like I do / Dream on / Whatever it is.

Motown Motown
Oct 83. (7")(12") **I JUST CAN'T WALK AWAY. / HANG** [ ] [71]
Nov 83. (lp)(c) **BACK WHERE I BELONG** [ ] [ ]
– Make yourself right at home / I just can't walk away / Sail on / Back where I belong / What have we got to lose / The masquerade is over / Body and soul / Hang
Jan 84. (7") **MAKE YOURSELF RIGHT AT HOME. / SING A SONG OF YESTERDAY** [-] [ ]
Jun 85. (7") **SEXY WAYS. / BODY AND SOUL** [-] [ ]
Jul 85. (lp)(c) **MAGIC** [ ] [ ] Jun 85
– I can feel the magic / Don't tell me that it's over / Sexy ways / Easier said than done / Don't turn away / I'm ready for love / Again / Maybe tomorrow / Remember me.
Oct 85. (7") **I'M READY FOR LOVE. / DON'T TELL ME THAT IT'S OVER** [-] [ ]
Sep 86. (7") **HOT NIGHTS. / AGAIN** [-] [ ]
Oct 86. (lp)(c) **HOT NIGHTS** [ ] [ ]
– Hot nights / Red hot love / I believe in you and me / Let's jam / We got bus'ness / This is love / 80 up for you / Livin' it up too much / The four of us.

Arista Arista
Aug 88. (7") **INDESTRUCTABLE. / ARE YOU WITH ME** [55] [ ]
(12"+=)(cd-s+=) – ('A'version). *(re-iss.Feb89)*
Sep 88. (lp)(c)(cd) **INDESTRUCTABLE** [ ] [ ]
– Indestructable / Change of heart / If ever a love there was / The Sun ain't gonna shine / Next time / Loco in Acapulco / Are you with me / I'm only wounded / When you dance / Let's jam. *(re-iss.Jun91)*
Oct 88. (7") **LOVE IN ACAPULCO. / CHANGE OF HEART** [-] [ ]
Nov 88. (7") **LOCO IN ACAPULCO. / THE FOUR OF US** [9] [ ]
(12"+=)(cd-s+=) – ('A'body mix).
Feb 89. (7") **IF EVER A LOVE THERE WAS (w/ ARETHA FRANKLIN). / LET'S JAM** [-] [ ]
Jul 89. (7")(c-s) **THE SUN AIN'T GONNA SHINE (The Ben Liebrand Remix) / LOCO IN ACAPULCO** [ ] [ ]
(12"+=)(cd-s+=) – ?

– other compilations, etc. –

Feb 66. Tamla; (7"ep) **THE FOUR TOPS** [ ] [-]
– I can't help myself / Ask the lonely / Something about you.
Mar 67. Tamla; (7"ep) **FOUR TOPS HITS** [ ] [-]
– Reach out, I'll be there / Bernadette / Standing in the shadows of love / If I were a carpenter.
Note; All below releases were on 'Tamla Motown' unless mentioned.
Mar 73. (7") **SO DEEP WITHIN YOU. / HAPPY (IS A BUMPY ROAD)** [ ] [ ]
Jun 73. (7") **I CAN'T QUIT YOUR LOVE. / I AM YOUR MAN** [ ] [ ]
Oct 73. (d-lp)(c) **THE FOUR TOPS STORY** [35] [ ]
Oct 75. (7") **WALK AWAY RENEE. / YOU KEEP RUNNING AWAY** [ ] [ ]
Sep 76. (7") **REACH OUT, I'LL BE THERE. / STANDING IN THE SHADOWS OF LOVE** [ ] [ ]
Nov 76. (lp)(c) **SUPER HITS** [ ] [ ]
(re-iss.Oct81)
Sep 78. (7") **I CAN'T HELP MYSELF (SUGAR PIE, HONEY BUNCH). / IT'S THE SAME OLD SONG** [ ] [ ]
Sep 80. (7") **IF I WERE A CARPENTER. / 7 ROOMS OF GLOOM** [ ] [ ]
Sep 80. (7") **BERNADETTE. / IT'S ALL IN THE GAME** [ ] [ ]
Sep 80. (7") **STILL WATER (LOVE). / SIMPLE GAME** [ ] [ ]
Jan 82. (lp)(c) **THE BEST OF THE FOUR TOPS** [13] [ ]
Apr 82. (7") **BABY I NEED YOUR LOVING. / YESTERDAY'S DREAM** [ ] [ ]
Sep 82. (d-lp)(c) **ANTHOLOGY** [ ] [ ]
(cd-iss. Apr 89)
Jul 83. (c-ep) **FLIP HITS** [ ] [-]
– It's all in the game / Bernadeete / Standing in the shadows of love / If I were a carpenter.
Oct 84. (cd) **COMPACT COMMAND PERFORMANCE** [ ] [-]
Apr 85. (7")(12") **BERNADETTE. / IF I WERE A CARPENTER** [ ] [-]
Oct 86. (d-cd) **FOUR TOPS REACH OUT / STILL WATER RUN DEEP** [ ] [-]
Oct 86. (d-cd) **THE FOUR TOPS / THE FOUR TOPS SECOND ALBUM** [ ] [-]
May 88. (7") **REACH OUT I'LL BE THERE. / STANDING IN THE SHADOWS OF LOVE** [11] [ ]
(12"+=)(cd-s+=) – ('A'version) / ('A'instrumental).
Jan 79. M.F.P.; (lp) **IT'S ALL IN THE GAME** [ ] [-]
Jun 80. EMI-TV; (lp)(c) **20 GOLDEN GREATS** *(re-iss.Oct81)* [ ] [-]
Apr 82. A.B.C.; (lp)(c) **GREATEST HITS** [ ] [-]
Jun 82. Pickwick-Motown; (lp)(c) **THE FABULOUS FOUR TOPS** [ ] [-]
Oct 82. Pickwick-Motown; (lp)(c) **HITS OF GOLD** [ ] [-]
Jun 84. Calibre; (7")(12") **YOUR SONG. / I'M HERE AGAIN** [ ] [-]
Jan 91. Telstar; (cd)(c)(lp) **THEIR GREATEST HITS** [47] [-]
Jul 91. Knight; (cd)(c) **HEART AND SOUL** [ ] [-]
Jul 92. Castle; (cd) **THE COLLECTION** [ ] [-]
Jul 92. Raven-Topic; (cd) **SHAKE ME WAKE ME: 25 GREATEST HITS 1964-1973** [ ] [-]
Sep 92. Polygram; (cd)(c) **THE SINGLES COLLECTION** [11] [ ]
– Reach out I'll be there / Standing in the shadows of love / Bernadette / Walk away Renee / If i were a carpenter / Simple game / 7 Rooms of gloom / Loving you is sweeter than ever / You keep running away / Yesterday's dreams / I'm in a different world / What is a man / Loco in Acapulco / Indestructible / When she was my girl / It's all in the game / Still water (love) / I can't help myself / Do what you gotta do / Keeper of the castle / Don't walk away.
May 93. Spectrum; (cd)(c) **THE LOOK OF LOVE** [ ] [-]
Oct 93. Spectrum; (cd)(c) **WITH LOVE** [ ] [-]
Apr 94. Polygram TV; (cd)(c) **THE SINGLES COLLECTION** [ ] [-]
Apr 95. Motown; (cd) **MOTOWN'S GREATEST HITS** [ ] [ ]

John FOXX

Born: DENNIS LEIGH, Chorley, Lancashire, England. After leaving new wave oufit ULTRAVOX! who split in Mar'79, he concentrated on solo career. FOXX created new label 'MetalBeat' through 'Virgin', and released early 1980 debut 45 'UNDERPASS', which nearly broke UK Top 30. Its parent album 'METAMATIC', made the Top 30, as did his 2 early 80's follow-ups 'THE GARDEN' & 'THE GOLDEN SECTION'. • **Style:** Electro-rock mannequin, not too dissimilar to KRAFTWERK or GARY NUMAN. • **Songwriters:** Wrote all material. • **Trivia:** In the mid-80's, his book 'The Quiet Man', was published.

Recommended: ASSEMBLY (*7) / METAMATIC (*7).

JOHN FOXX – vocals, synthesizers, guitar, drum machine (ex-ULTRAVOX!) with **JOHN BARKER** – synth-drums / **JAKE DURANT** – bass / **ED CASE** – drums (on 2nd lp)

Virgin Virgin
Jan 80. (7") **UNDERPASS. / FILM 1** [31] [ ]
Jan 80. (lp)(c) **METAMATIC** [18] [ ]
– Plaza / He's a liquid / Underpass / Metal beat / No one driving / A new kind of man / Blurred girl / 030 / Tidal wave / Touch and go. *(re-iss.Mar84)(cd-iss.Apr93)*
Mar 80. (d7") **NO ONE DRIVING. / GLIMMER / / MR. NO. / THIS CITY** [32] [ ]
Jul 80. (7")(7"pic-d) **BURNING CAR. / 20th CENTURY** [35] [ ]
Oct 80. (7") **MILES AWAY. / A LONG TIME** [51] [ ]
—— **ROBIN SIMON** – guitar + **JO DWORNIAK** – bass repl. BARKER
Aug 81. (7") **EUROPE AFTER THE RAIN. / THIS JUNGLE** [40] [ ]
Sep 81. (lp)(c) **THE GARDEN** [24] [ ]
– Europe after the rain / Systems of romance / When I was a man and you were a woman / Dancing like a gun / Pater noster / Night suit / You were there / Fusion – Fission / Walk away / The garden. *(re-iss.Mar84) (cd-iss.Apr93)*
Oct 81. (7") **DANCING LIKE A GUN. / SWIMMER 2** [ ] [ ]
(12"+=) – Swimmer 1.
—— **PAUL WICKENS** (WIX) – drums, keyboards repl. DURANT
Jul 82. (7")(7"pic-d) **ENDLESSLY. / YOUNG MAN** [66] [ ]
(12"+=)/ /(d7"++=) – Dance with me. / / A kind of love.
Aug 83. (7") **YOUR DRESS. / WOMAN OF THE STAIRWAY** [61] [ ]
(12"+=)/ /(d7"+=) – The Garden. / / Lifting sky / Annexe.
Oct 83. (lp)(c) **THE GOLDEN SECTION** [27] [ ]
– My wild love / Someone / Your dress / Running across thin ice with tigers / Sitting at the edge of the world / Endlessly / Ghosts on water / Like a miracle / The hidden man / Twilight's last gleaming. *(c+=)–* Woman on the stairway / Young man / Dance with me / Wing and a wind / Lifting sky / Annexe. *(re-iss.Aug88)*
Oct 83. (7")(12")(7"sha-pic-d) **LIKE A MIRACLE. / WING AND A WIND** [ ] [ ]
Jun 85. (7")(12") **STARS ON FIRE. / WHAT KIND OF GIRL** [ ] [ ]
(free 7"w.a.)
Sep 85. (lp)(c) **IN MYSTERIOUS WAYS** [85] [ ]
– Stars on fire / Lose all sense of time / Shine on / Enter the angel / In mysterious ways / What kind of girl / This side of Paradise / Stepping softly / Enter the angel 2 / Morning glory. *(re-iss.Aug88) (cd-iss.Jul87)*
Sep 85. (7")(12") **ENTER THE ANGEL. / STAIRWAY** [ ] [ ]
—— FOXX retired from music biz.

– compilations etc. –

1988. Virgin; (cd) **ASSEMBLY** [ ] [-]
– A new kind of man / Underpass / Burning car / This city / Twilight's last gleaming / Ghosts on water / This jungle / Endlessly / Someone / Sitting at the edge of the world / In mysterious ways / Morning glory / Europe after the rain / Systems of romance / Walk away / When I was a man and you were a woman / Pater noster / The garden.

Peter FRAMPTON

Born: 22 Apr'50, Beckenham, Kent, England. After leaving HUMBLE PIE late '71, he signed solo deal with 'A&M'. His debut lp 'WINDS OF CHANGE', was supported by a US tour with headliners J.GEILS BAND, which helped lp hit Top 200. In 1973, his next project/album FRAMPTON'S CAMEL, faired little better, and it was decided to drop the CAMEL part, due to a band of same name. In 1974, he gained first US Top 30 lp with 'SOMETHIN'S HAPPENING', and followed it nicely with US Top 40 lp 'FRAMPTON'. In 1976, his live double-lp 'FRAMPTON COMES ALIVE' (recorded at Winterland, California), soon topped the US chart, becoming a 10 million seller in the process. It was aided by 3 smash hits, the best of which being 'SHOW ME THE WAY', which saw FRAMPTON trademarking his new Voicebox guitar sound. His 1977 studio follow-up 'I'M IN YOU', became an even higher success, and provided him with his second hit album in the UK. His 1979 effort 'WHERE I SHOULD BE', proved to be his last major success, as he all but faded commercially in the 80's. • **Style:** Talented guitarist, who established himself as the 'Golden boy of US mainstream AOR', although his curly locks and youthful face, had been teen idolized when with The HERD. • **Songwriters:** Self-penned numbers, except; JUMPING JACK FLASH (Rolling Stones) / SIGNED, SEALED, DELIVERED (I'M YOURS) (Stevie Wonder) / (I'M A) ROADRUNNER (Junior Walker) / FRIDAY ON MY MIND (Easybeats) / etc. • **Trivia:** Late in 1988, band WILL TO POWER hit US No.1 with a medley of his 'BABY I LOVE YOUR WAY' & LYNYRD SKYNYRD's 'Free Bird'.

Recommended: FRAMPTON COMES ALIVE (*6) / SHINE ON – A COLLECTION (*5)

PETER FRAMPTON – vocals, guitar (ex-HUMBLE PIE, ex-HERD) with **MIKE KELLIE** – drums (ex-SPOOKY TOOTH) / **RICK WILLS** – bass (ex-COCHISE) / & guests **BILLY PRESTON** – keyboards (solo artist) / **RINGO STARR** – drums, vox (solo artist) / **ANDY BOWN** – keyboards (ex-HERD) / **KLAUS VOORMAN** – keyboards (ex-MANFRED MANN)

A & M A & M

May 72. (7") **JUMPING JACK FLASH. / OH FOR ANOTHER DAY** [-] [ ]
May 72. (lp)(c) **WIND OF CHANGE** [ ] [ ]
– Fig tree bay / Wind of change / Lady lie right / Jumping Jack Flash / It's a plain shame / Oh for another day / All I want to be (is by your side) / The lodger / Hard / Alright.
Sep 72. (7") **IT'S A PLAIN SHAME. / OH FOR ANOTHER DAY** [ ] [ ]

—— FRAMPTON retained only WILLS and brought in **MICKEY GALLAGHER** – keyboards (ex-BELL & ARC) / **JOHN SIOMES** (b. USA) – drums (ex-MITCH RYDER)

May 73. (lp)(c) **FRAMPTON'S CAMEL** [ ] [ ]
– I got my eyes on you / All night long / Lines on my face / Which way the wind blows / I believe (when I fall in love with you it will be forever) / White sugar / Don't fade away / Just the time of year / Do you feel like we do.
(above lps & below 45s, credited to "FRAMPTON'S CAMEL")
May 73. (7") **ALL NIGHT LONG. / DON'T FADE AWAY** [ ] [ ]
Jul 73. (7") **WHICH WAY THE WIND BLOWS. / I BELIEVE (WHEN I FALL IN LOVE IT WILL BE FOREVER)** [-] [ ]

—— Disbanded, bringing in session people.

May 74. (lp)(c) **SOMETHIN'S HAPPENING** [ ] [25] Mar 74
– Doobie wah / Golden goose / Underhand / I wanna go to the sun / Baby (somethin's happening) / Waterfall / Magic Moon / Sail away.
May 74. (7") **BABY (SOMETHIN'S HAPPENING). / I WANNA GO TO THE SUN** [-] [ ]

—— **ANDY BOWN** – keyboards, bass returned to repl. GALLAGHER (to GLENCOE) and WILLS (to ROXY MUSIC)

Mar 75. (lp)(c) **FRAMPTON** [ ] [32]
– Day's dawning / Show me the way / One more time / The crying clown / Fanfare / Nowhere's too far (for my baby) / Nassau / Baby, I love your way / Apple of your eye / Penny for your thoughts / (I'll give you) Money.
Jun 75. (7") **SHOW ME THE WAY. / THE CRYING CLOWN** [ ] [ ]
Oct 75. (7") **(I'LL GIVE YOU) MONEY. / NOWHERE'S TOO FAR (FOR MY BABY)** [-] [ ]

—— Still with SIOMOS, also now w / **STANLEY SHELDON** – bass / **BOB MAYO** – keys

Apr 76. (d-lp)(c) **FRAMPTON COMES ALIVE! (live)** [6] [1] Jan 76
– Something's happening / Doobie wah / Show me the way / It's a plain shame / All I want to be (is by your side) / Wind of change / Baby, I love your way / I wanna go to the sun / Penny for your thoughts / (I'll give you) Money / Shine on / Jumping Jack Flash / Lines on my face / Do you feel like we do. *(re-iss.Feb85 as 'THE BEST OF FRAMPTON COMES ALIVE' on 'Hallmark') (cd-iss. 1988 =1 cd) (US pic-lp 1978)*
Apr 76. (7") **SHOW ME THE WAY (live). / SHINE ON (live)** [10] [6] Feb 76
Jun 76. (7") **BABY, I LOVE YOUR WAY (live). / IT'S A PLAIN SHAME (live)** [-] [ ]
Aug 76. (7") **BABY, I LOVE YOUR WAY (live). / (I'LL GIVE YOU) MONEY (live)** [43] [-]
Oct 76. (7") **DO YOU FEEL LIKE WE DO (live). / PENNY FOR YOUR THOUGHTS (live)** [39] [10] Sep 76
Jun 77. (lp)(c) **I'M IN YOU** [19] [2]
– I'm in you / (Putting my) Heart on the line / St.Thomas (don't you know how I feel) / Won't you be my friend / You don't have to worry / Tried to love / Rocky's hot club / (I'm a) Roadrunner / Signed, sealed, delivered (I'm yours).
Jul 77. (7") **I'M IN YOU. / ST.THOMAS (DON'T YOU KNOW HOW I FEEL)** [41] [2] May 77
Sep 77. (7") **SIGNED, SEALED, DELIVERED (I'M YOURS). / ROCKY'S HOT CLUB** [ ] [18] Aug 77
Dec 77. (7") **TRIED TO LOVE. / YOU DON'T HAVE TO WORRY** [-] [41]
May 79. (7") **I CAN'T STAND IT NO MORE. / WHERE SHOULD I BE** [-] [14]
Jun 79. (7") **I CAN'T STAND IT NO MORE. / MAY I BABY** [ ] [-]
Jun 79. (lp)(c) **WHERE I SHOULD BE** [ ] [19]
– I can't stand it no more / Got my feet back on the ground / Where I should be / Everything I need / May I baby / You don't know like I know / She don't reply / We've just begun / Take me by the hand / It's a sad affair.
Aug 79. (7") **SHE DON'T REPLY. / ST. THOMAS (DON'T YOU KNOW HOW I FEEL)** [-] [ ]
Jun 81. (lp)(c) **BREAKING ALL THE RULES** [ ] [43]
– Dig what I say / I don't wanna let you go / Rise up / Wasting the night away / Going to L.A. / You kill me / Friday on my mind / Lost a part of you / Breaking all the rules.
Aug 81. (7") **BREAKING ALL THE RULES. / NIGHT TOWN** [ ] [ ]
Nov 81. (7") **WASTING THE NIGHT AWAY. / YOU KILL ME** [-] [ ]
Aug 82. (7") **SLEEPWALK. / THEME FROM NIVRAM** [-] [ ]
Sep 82. (lp)(c) **THE ART OF CONTROL** [ ] [ ] Aug 82
– I read the news / Sleepwalk / Save me / Back to Eden / An eye for an eye / Don't think about me / Heart in the fire / Here comes Caroline / Barbara's vacation.

—— PETER now used guitar & synthesizers, etc. plus band **TONY LEVIN** – guitar / **STEVE FERRONE + OMAR HAKIM** – drums / **PETE SOLLEY** – piano / **RICHARD COTTLE** – keys / **RICHIE PUENTE** – percussion

Virgin Atlantic

Nov 85. (7") **LYING. / INTO VIEW** [-] [74]
Dec 85. (7")(12")(7"pic-d) **LYING. / YOU KNOW SO WELL** [ ] [-]
Jan 86. (lp)(c)(cd) **PREMONITION** [ ] [80]
– Stop / Hiding from a heartache / You know so well / Premonition / Lying / Moving a mountain / All eyes on you / Into view / Call of the wild.
Feb 86. (7") **ALL EYES ON YOU. / SO FAR AWAY** [-] [ ]
Apr 86. (7")(12") **ALL EYES ON YOU. / INTO VIEW** [ ] [-]
May 86. (7") **HIDING FROM A HEARTACHE. / INTO VIEW** [-] [ ]

—— He became guitarist for DAVID BOWIE in 1987. The following year he sessioned for KARLA BONOFF. He returned to solo work in 1989.

Atlantic Atlantic

Sep 89. (7") **HOLDING ON TO YOU. / GIVE ME A LITTLE LOVE THAT'S REAL** [-] [ ]
Oct 89. (lp)(c)(cd) **WHEN ALL THE PIECES FIT** [ ] [ ]
– More ways than one / Holding on to you / My heart goes out to you / Hold tight / People all over the world / Back to the start / Mind over matter / Now and again / Hard earned love / This time around.

—— His new back-up band now featured **DAVE MENIKETTI** – guitar (ex-Y & T) after signing to 'Geffen' (no releases)

Relativity Relativity

Apr 94. (cd)(c)(lp) **PETER FRAMPTON** [ ] [ ]
– Day in the Sun / You can be sure / It all comes down to you / You can't take that away / Young island / Off the hook / Waiting for your love / So hard to believe / Out of the blue / Shelter through the night / Changing all the time.

I.R.S. I.R.S.

Oct 95. (cd)(c) **FRAMPTON COMES ALIVE II (live)** [ ] [ ]
– (intro) / Day in the sun / Lying / For now / Most of all / You / Waiting for your love / I'm in you / Talk to me / Hang on to a dream / Can't take that away / More ways than one / Almost said goodbye / Off the hook. (cd w/ free live cd) – Show me the way / Baby I love your way / Lines on my face / Do you feel like we do.

– compilations, others –

Jun 79. Flyover; (lp) **THE SUPER DISC OF PETER FRAMPTON** [ ] [ ]
Oct 83. Old Gold; (7") **SHOW ME THE WAY. / BABY I LOVE YOUR WAY** [ ] [-]
Jun 84. Scoop; (7"ep)(c-ep) **6 TRACK HITS** [ ] [-]
– Show me the way / Baby, I love your way / Penny for your thoughts / I'm in you / Wind of change / Signed, sealed, delivered (I'm yours).
Dec 92. A&M; (d-cd) **SHINE ON – A COLLECTION** [ ] [ ]
– Wind of change / It's a plain shame / Jumping Jack Flash / All I want to be (is by your side) / The lodger / I got my eyes on you / All night long / Lines on my face / Don't fade away / I wanna go to the sun / Baby (somethin's happening) / Nowhere's too far (for my baby) / Nassau – Baby I love your way / The crying clown / Penny for your thoughts / (I'll give you) Money / Show me the way / Shine on / Do you feel like we do / I'm in you / (Putting my) Heart on the line / Signed sealed delivered (I'm yours) / I can't stand it no more / Breaking all the rules / Theme from Nivram / Lying / More ways than one / Holding on to you / The bigger they come / I won't let you down.
Jan 93. A&M; (cd) **SHOW ME THE WAY** [ ] [ ]
Mar 94. Spectrum; (cd)(c) **PETER FRAMPTON SHOWS THE WAY** [ ] [-]
Dec 95. Javelin; (cd) **LOVE TAKER** [ ] [-]

FRANK & WALTERS

Formed: Cork, Ireland ... 1990 by young brothers PAUL and NIALL LINEHAM, plus neighbour ASHLEY. Moved to Wimbledon and signed to 'Setanta'. Their 3rd ep now also on 'Go Discs!' was their initial break into the UK Top 50. • **Style:** Quirky alternative pop band. • **Songwriters:** Group except; FUNKY COLD MEDINA (Tone Loc) / I'M A BELIEVER (The Monkees) / LOVE IS IN THE AIR (John Paul Jones). • **Trivia:** Debut album produced by EDWYN COLLINS (ex-ORANGE JUICE).

Recommended: TRAINS, BOATS AND PLANES (*6).

PAUL LINEHAM – vocals, bass / **NIALL LINEHAM** – guitar / **ASHLEY KEATING** – drums

Setanta not issued

Aug 91. (12"ep) **THE FRANK AND WATERS EP** [ ] [-]
– Walter's trip / Frank's night / Michael / Never ending staircase.
Sep 91. (12"ep) **THE FRANK AND WATERS 2** [ ] [-]
– Fashion crisis hits New York / Rasputin / Daisy chain / Angela Gray. *(cd-ep+= EP1)*

Go! Discs Go Discs!

Mar 92. (7") **HAPPY BUSMAN. / THE WORLD CARRIES ON** [49] [ ]
(12"ep+=)(cd-ep+=) **EP 3** – Humphrey / If you're still waiting.
Sep 92. (7")(c-s) **THIS IS NOT A SONG. / DAVY CHASE** [46] [ ]
(12"+=)(cd-s+=) – Lawrence Olivier / Happy busman (live).
Oct 92. (cd)(c)(lp) **TRAINS, BOATS AND PLANES** [36] [ ]
– This is not a song / Walter's trip / Trainspotters / After all / Happy busman / Fashion crisis hits New York / Daisy chain / John and Sue / Bake us a song / Time / High is low.
Nov 92. (7")(c-s) **AFTER ALL. / FUNKY COLD MEDINA** [11] [ ]
(cd-s+=) – The day before the world ended / The turquoise gardens.
(cd-s+=) – Love is in the air / I'm a believer.
Apr 93. (7")(c-s) **FASHION CRISIS HITS NEW YORK. / TIME (R.T.E.session)** [42] [ ]
(cd-s+=) – Never ending staircase / Frank's right.
(cd-s) – ('A'side) / ('A'original) / Rasputin / Daisy chain / Angela Gray

FRANKIE GOES TO HOLLYWOOD

Formed: Liverpool, England ... Aug'80, initially as HOLLYCAUST by

HOLLY JOHNSON, who had issued 2 solo singles 'YANKEE ROSE' & 'HOBO JOE', after being part of BIG IN JAPAN. Taking name from a headline concerning singer FRANKIE VAUGHAN going into the movies, they embarked on TV exposure late 1982. After a session on the David Jensen Radio 1 show, they were included on the Channel 4 TV pop programme, demoing 'RELAX'. This led to 'ZTT' (Zang Tumb Tumm) label, run by PAUL MORLEY and TREVOR HORN (ex-BUGGLES) signing them Autumn 1983. With HORN on clever production, the song 'RELAX', soon climbed to the top in the UK, helped by another Radio 1 DJ Mike Read, getting it banned for its risque lyrics. In Jun'84, with RELAX still in the chart, the follow-up 'TWO TRIBES', went straight to No.1, and gave a new lease of life to RELAX, which re-ran up to No.2, while TWO TRIBES was still at the top. Their debut double-lp in Oct'84 'WELCOME TO THE PLEASURE DOME', also hit peak position, as did their 3rd consecutive No.1 single 'THE POWER OF LOVE'. A feat only previously achieved by another Merseyside group GERRY & THE PACEMAKERS. Their 4th 45 in 1985, spoiled the run, when it stalled at No.2. The group returned late Summer 1986 with Top 5 single 'RAGE HARD', but with a poor review of their Top 5 album 'LIVERPOOL', they faded commercially into decline. HOLLY JOHNSON was back with a solo contract on 'M.C.A.', and had 2 UK Top 5 hits 'LOVE TRAIN' & 'AMERICANOS', which previewed his No.1 album 'BLAST'. • **Style:** Well-produced power-disco rock outfit, whose controversial gay M&S sex themes, were provided by leather clad HOLLY and boyfriend/dancer PAUL RUTHERFORD. • **Songwriters:** All group compositions except; FERRY ACROSS THE MERSEY (Gerry & The Pacemakers) / BORN TO RUN (Bruce Springsteen) / WAR (Edwin Starr) / SUFFRAGETTE CITY (David Bowie) / GET IT ON (T.Rex) / SAN JOSE (Bacharach-David). HOLLY solo covered; LOVE ME TENDER (Elvis Presley). ACROSS THE UNIVERSE was not The BEATLES original. • **Trivia:** The 'TWO TRIBES' video, which contained Ronald Reagan & Chernenko lookalikes, fighting in a ring, was directed by GODLEY & CREME. In mid-1990, HOLLY was asked by friend RICHARD O'BRIEN, to act as FRANK 'N' FURTER in the 'Rocky Horror Picture Show'.

Recommended: WELCOME TO THE PLEASURE DOME (*7).

HOLLY JOHNSON (b. WILLIAM JOHNSON, 9 Feb'60, Khartoum, Sudan) – vocals (ex-solo artist, ex-BIG IN JAPAN) / **PAUL RUTHERFORD** (b. 8 Dec'59) – vocals (ex-SPITFIRE BOYS) / **BRIAN NASH** (b.20 Mar'63) – guitar repl. GED O'TOOLE / **MARK O'TOOLE** (b. 6 Jan'64) – bass / **PETER GILL** (b. 8 Mar'64) – drums

ZTT-Island | Island

Oct 83. (7")(7"pic-d) **RELAX. / ONE SEPTEMBER MORNING** [1] [67] Mar 84
(12")(12"pic-d) – ('A'version) / Ferry across the Mersey.
(c-ep) – "Relax's Greatest Bits" – (various mixes).

Jun 84. (7")(7"pic-d) **TWO TRIBES. / ONE FEBRUARY MORNING** [1] [43] Oct 84
(12")(12"pic-d) – ('A'version) / War (hide yourself).
(12"pic-d) – (all 3 tracks above)
(c-ep) – "Two Tribes (Keep The Peace)" – (various mixes).

Oct 84. (d-lp)(c)(cd)(d-pic-lp) **WELCOME TO THE PLEASURE DOME** [1] [33]
– Well . . . / The world is my oyster / Snatch of fury / Welcome to the pleasure dome / Relax / War / Two tribes / Ferry / Born to run / San Jose / Wish the lads were here (inc. 'Ballad of 32') / Black night white light / The only star in Heaven / The power of love / Bang . . . *(re-iss.cd+c May94 & Feb95)*

Nov 84. (7")(7"pic-d) **THE POWER OF LOVE. / THE WORLD IS MY OYSTER** [1] [ ]
(12"+=)(c-s+=)(12"pic-d+=) – Trapped and scrapped / Holier than thou.
(12"ep+=) – Pleasurefix / Starfix.

Mar 85. (7")(7"sha-pic-d) **WELCOME TO THE PLEASURE DOME. / HAPPY HI / GET IT ON** [2] [48]
(12"++=) – Relax (International).
(12"+=)(12"sha-pic-d+=) – Born to run (live).

Aug 86. (7") **RAGE HARD. / (DON'T LOSE WHAT'S LEFT) OF YOUR LITTLE MIND** [4] [ ]
(12"+=//+12"+=) – Suffragette City/ / Roadhouse blues.
(cd-s+=) – (above 2 tracks)

Sep 86. (lp)(c)(cd) **LIVERPOOL** [5] [88]
– Warriors of the wasteland / Rage hard / Kill the pain / Maximum joy / Watching the wildlife / Lunar bay / For Heaven's sake / Is anybody out there?. *(re-iss. 1989 on 'Island') (re-iss.cd+c May94)*

Nov 86. (7") **WARRIORS OF THE WASTELAND. / WARRIORS (instrumental)** [19] [ ]
(12"+=)(c-s+=)(cd-s+=) – Warriors (lots of different mixes).

Feb 87. (7") **WATCHING THE WILDLIFE. / THE WAVES** [28] [ ]
(12"+=) – Wildlife (Bit 3 & 4).
(c-s+=)(cd-s+=) – (various mixes, etc).

— They split after legal contractual problems. RUTHERFORD went solo,

– compilations, etc. –

Sep 93. Z.T.T.-Island; (7")(c-s) **RELAX. / ('A'mix)** [5] [ ]
(12"+=)(cd-s+=) – ('A'mixes).

Oct 93. Z.T.T.-Island; (cd)(c)(lp) **BANG! . . . THE GREATEST HITS OF . . .** [4] [ ]
– Relax / Two tribes / War / Ferry / Warriors of the wasteland / For Heaven's sake / The world is my oyster / Welcome to the Pleasure dome / Watching the wildlife / Born to run / Rage hard / The power of love / Bang . . . *(re-iss.cd+c Jun94)*

Nov 93. Z.T.T.-Island; (7")(c-s) **WELCOME TO THE PLEASURE DOME. / ('A'mix)** [18] [ ]
(12"+=)(cd-s+=) – ('A'mixes).

Dec 93. Z.T.T.-Island; (7")(c-s) **THE POWER OF LOVE. / ('A'mix)** [10] [ ]
(cd-s+=) – Rage hard (original DJ mix) / Holier than thou.

Feb 94. Z.T.T.-Island; (7")(c-s) **TWO TRIBES (Fluke's minimix). / ('A'mix)** [16] [ ]
(12"+=)(cd-s+=) – ('A'mixes).

May 94. Z.T.T.-Island; (cd)(c)(lp) **RELOAD** – THE WHOLE 12 [ ] [ ]

In Spring of '93, HOLLY revealed he had HIV positive (AIDS).

HOLLY JOHNSON

had earlier returned to a solo career.

M.C.A. | M.C.A.

Jan 89. (7")(c-s) **LOVE TRAIN. / MURDER IN PARADISE** [4] [ ]
(12"+=)(cd-s+=) – ('A'mix).

Mar 89. (7")(c-s) **AMERICANOS. / ('A'dub version)** [4] [ ]
(12"+=)(cd-s+=) – ('A' liberty mix).

Apr 89. (lp)(c)(cd) **BLAST** [1] [ ]
– Atomic city / Heaven's here / Americanos / Deep in love / S.U.C.C.E.S.S. / Love train / Got it made / Love will come / Perfume / Feel good.

Jun 89. (7")(c-s) **ATOMIC CITY. / BEAT THE SYSTEM** [18] [ ]
(12"+=)(cd-s+=) – ('A'extended).

Sep 89. (7")(c-s)(7"pic-d) **HEAVEN'S HERE. / HALLELUJAH** [62] [ ]
(12"+=)(cd-s+=) – ('A'version).

Jul 90. (cd)(c)(lp) **HALLELUJAH, THE REMIX ALBUM** (BLAST remixed) [ ] [-]

Nov 90. (7")(12")(c-s) **WHERE HAS THE LOVE GONE? / PERFUME** [73] [ ]
(cd-s+=) – ('A'version).

Mar 91. (7")(c-s) **ACROSS THE UNIVERSE. / FUNKY PARADISE** [ ] [ ]
(12"+=)(cd-s+=) – ('A'-Space a-go-go mix).

May 91. (cd)(c)(lp) **DREAMS THAT MONEY CAN'T BUY** [ ] [ ]
– Across the universe / When the party's over / The people want to dance / I need your love / Boyfriend '65 / Where has love gone? / Penny arcade / Do it for love / You're a hit / The great love story.

Aug 91. (7")(c-s) **PEOPLE WANT TO DANCE. / ('A'-Apollo 440 mix)** [ ] [ ]
(12"+=)(cd-s+=) – Love train (anxious big beat version).

Club Tool | not issued

Sep 94. (12"ep)(cd-ep) **LEGENDARY CHILDREN (ALL OF THEM QUEER). / (4-'A'mixes)** [ ] [-]

HOLLY

early solo

Eric's | not issued

Dec 79. (7"m) **YANKEE ROSE. / TREASURE ISLAND / DESPERATE DAN** [ ] [-]

1980. (7") **HOBO JOE. / STARS OF THE BARS** [ ] [-]

Aretha FRANKLIN

Born: 25 Mar'42, Memphis, Tennessee, USA. She was one of 6 children raised by her well-to-do preacher father Rev.C.L.FRANKLIN after they moved to Detroit, Michegan. In the early 50's, she was taught singing by family friends Mahalia Jackson and Clara Ward, who influenced her initial career. Heartened by SAM COOKE, she herself moved to New York and found manager Joe King. In 1960 she signed to 'Columbia' and released 45 'TODAY I SING THE BLUES'. After a minor hit, she attained her first US Top 40 entry in 1961 with standard 'ROCK-A-BYE YOUR BABY WITH A DIXIE MELODY'. She continued to break the Hot 100 many times, but things really took off, when she signed late 1966 to 'Atlantic'. Her veteran producer Jerry Wexler, began to motivate a new powerful side to her that previous producer Mitch Miller didn't see. It paid off, and in 1967 she had 5 US Top 10 albums and a No.1 classic 45 'RESPECT'. Her albums also went gold, making her the top star of this period. She went on to have hit after hit, lasting well into the 90's. The Lady of Soul was now The Queen of Soul. • **Style:** Regarded as the greatest female singer of all-time. Her vocal range and power, could only be matched through the years by say; TINA TURNER. ARETHA was the first lady of soul, whose gospel roots gave her self confidence and belief, even when difficult times in life prevailed. She married three times from 1962. Her present husband since 1978 is actor Glynn Turman. • **Songwriters:** Although ARETHA wrote many songs herself, her greatest success came with 'Atlantic' covers:- NATURAL WOMAN (Carole King) / CHAIN OF FOOLS + SEE SAW (Don Covay) / YOU SEND ME (Sam Cooke) / SATISFACTION (Rolling Stones) / I SAY A LITTLE PRAYER (Dionne Warwick) / THE WEIGHT (Band) / TRACKS OF MY TEARS (Miracles) / GENTLE ON MY MIND (John Hartford) / ELEANOR RIGBY + LET IT BE (Beatles) / SON OF A PREACHER MAN (Dusty Springfield) / BRIDGE OVER TROUBLED WATER (Simon & Garfunkel) / DON'T PLAY THAT SONG + SPANSH HARLEM (Ben E.King) / WHOLLY HOLY (Marvin Gaye) / YOU'RE ALL I NEED TO GET BY + AIN'T NOTHING LIKE THE REAL THING (Marvin Gaye & Tammi Terrell) / ANGEL (Jimi Hendrix) / UNTIL YOU COME BACK TO ME (Stevie Wonder) / WHEN YOU GET RIGHT DOWN TO IT (Ronnie Dyson) / WHAT A FOOL BELIEVES (Doobie Brothers) / EVERYDAY PEOPLE (Staple Singles) / etc. • **Trivia:** On her 1969 recordings, DUANE ALLMAN played slide guitar. She had been produced by many greats including QUINCY JONES (1973) / CURTIS MAYFIELD (1976) / LAMONT-DOZIER (1977) / ARIF MARDIN (1980) / LUTHER VANDROSS (1982-83) / NARADA MICHAEL WALDEN (1985-87). (see also discography for many duets). In 1980, she appeared as a waitress in the film 'The Blues Brothers'.

Recommended: 30 GREATEST HITS (*7)

ARETHA FRANKLIN – vocals(with session people)

not issued Chedar

1960. (7") **NEVER GROW OLD. / YOU GROW CLOSER** [-] [ ]
1960. (7") **PRECIOUS LORD. / (part 2)** [-] [ ]

Fontana Columbia

Oct 60. (lp) **THE GREAT ARETHA FRANKLIN** [ ] [ ]
– Won't be long / Over the rainbow / Love is the only thing / Sweet lover / All night long / Who needs you / Right now / Are you sure / Maybe I'm a fool / It ain't necessarily so / (Blue) By myself / Today I sing the blues
Feb 61. (7") **WON'T BE LONG. / RIGHT NOW** [-] [76]
Jul 61. (7") **MAYBE I'M A FOOL. / ARE YOU SURE** [-] [ ]
Oct 61. (7") **ROCK-A-BYE YOUR BABY WITH A DIXIE MELODY. / OPERATION HEARTBREAK** [ ] [37]
Jan 62. (7") **LOVE IS THE ONLY THING. / TODAY I SING THE BLUES** [ ] [ ] Oct 60
(re-iss. US-1970)
Jan 62. (lp) **ARETHA** [ ] [ ]
– Won't be long / Over the rainbow / Love is the only thing / Sweet lover / All night long / Who needs you? / Right now / Are you sure / Maybe I'm a fool / It ain't necessarily so / Blue by myself / Today I sing the blues. *(re-iss.Jan84 on 'Cameo-CBS')*

C.B.S. Columbia

Jan 62. (7") **I SURRENDER, DEAR. / ROUGH RIDER** [-] [87]
[94]
1961. (lp) **THE ELECTRIFYING ARETHA FRANKLIN** [-] [ ]
– You made me love you / I told you so / Rockabye your baby with a Dixie melody / Nobody like you / Exactly like you / It's so heartbreakin' / Rough lover / Blue holiday / Just for you / That lucky old Sun / I surrender dear / Ac-cent-tchu-ate the positive.
Jun 62. (7") **DON'T CRY BABY. / WITHOUT THE ONE YOU LOVE** [-] [92]
Sep 62. (7") **TRY A LITTLE TENDERNESS. / JUST FOR A THRILL** [-] [100]
Nov 62. (lp) **THE TENDER, THE MOVING, THE SWINGING ARETHA FRANKLIN** [-] [69]
– Don't cry baby / Try a little tenderness / I apologize / Without the one you love / Look for the silver lining / I'm sitting on top of the world / Just for a thrill / God bless the child / I'm wandering / How deep is the ocean / I don't know you anymore / Lover come back to me.
Dec 62. (7") **TROUBLE IN MIND. / GOD BLESS THE CHILD** [-] [86]
Jan 63. (lp) **LAUGHING (ON THE OUTSIDE)** [-] [ ]
– Skylark / For all we know / Make someone happy / I wonder / Solitude / Laughing on the outside / Say it isn't so / Until the real thing comes along / If ever I would leave you / Where are you / Mr.Ugly / I wanna be around.
1963. (7") **SAY IT ISN'T SO. / HERE'S WHERE I CAME IN** [-] [ ]
1963. (7") **SKYLARK. / YOU'VE GOT HER** [-] [ ]
1963. (7") **JOHNNY. / KISSIN' BY THE MISTLETOE** [-] [ ]
1964. (7") **SOULVILLE. / EVIL GAL BLUES** [-] [ ]
Sep 64. (7") **RUNNIN' OUT OF FOOLS. / IT'S JUST A MATTER OF TIME** [-] [57]
Oct 64. (lp) **UNFORGETTABLE: A TRIBUTE TO DINAH WASHINGTON** [-] [ ]
– Unforgettable / Cold cold heart / What a difference a day made / Drinking again / Evil gal blues / Nobody knows the way I feel this morning / Don't say you're sorry again / This bitter Earth / If I should lose you / Soulville. *(cd-iss.Jun95)*
Nov 64. (7") **WINTER WONDERLAND. / THE CHRISTMAS SONG** [-] [ ]
Dec 64. (lp) **RUNNIN' OUT OF FOOLS** [-] [84]
– Mockingbird / How glad I am / Walk on by / My guy / Every little bit hurts / Shoop shoop song / You'll lose a good thing / I can't wait until I see my baby's face / It's just a matter of time / Runnin' out of fools / Two sides of love / One room Paradise.
Mar 65. (7") **CAN'T YOU JUST SEE ME. / LITTLE MISS RAGGEDY ANNE** [ ] [96] Jan 65
May 65. (7") **I CAN'T WAIT UNTIL I SEE MY BABY'S FACE. / ONE STEP AHEAD** [-] [ ]
Nov 65. (lp) **YEAH!!!** [ ] [ ] Jul 65
– This could be the start of something / Once in a lifetime / Misty / More / There is no greater love / Muddy water / If I had a hammer / Impossible / Today I love everybody / Without the one you love / Trouble in mind / Love for sale.
Jul 66. (7") **SWEET BITTER LOVE. / I'M LOSING YOU** [-] [ ]
Aug 66. (lp) **SOUL SISTER** [ ] [ ]
– Until you were gone / You made me love you / Follow your heart / Ol' man river / Sweet bitter love / Mother's love / Swanee / I'm losing you / Take a look / Can't you just see me / Cry like a baby.
1966. (7") **THERE IS NO GREATER LOVE. / YOU MADE ME LOVE YOU** [-] [ ]
1966. (7") **HANDS OFF. / TIGHTEN UP YOUR TIE, BUTTON UP YOUR JACKET** [-] [ ]
1967. (7") **UNTIL YOU WERE GONE. / SWANEE** [-] [ ]

Atlantic Atlantic

Apr 67. (7") **I NEVER LOVED A MAN (THE WAY I LOVE YOU). / DO RIGHT WOMAN, DO RIGHT MAN** [ ] [9] Mar 67
Apr 67. (7") **RESPECT. / DR.FEELGOOD** [-] [1]
May 67. (7") **RESPECT. / SAVE ME** [10] [-]
Jul 67. (lp) **I NEVER LOVED A MAN THE WAY I LOVE YOU** [36] [2] Apr 67
– Respect / Drown in my own tears / I never loved a man (the way I loved you) / Soul serenade / Don't let me lose This dream / Baby, baby, baby / Dr Feelgood / Good times / Do right woman – do right man / Save me / A change is gonna come *(re-iss.1972) (cd-iss.Jun93)*
Aug 67. (7") **BABY I LOVE YOU. / GOING DOWN SLOW** [39] [4] Jul 67
Sep 67. (7") **A NATURAL WOMAN (YOU MAKE ME FEEL LIKE). / BABY BABY BABY** [-] [8]
Oct 67. (lp) **ARETHA ARRIVES** [ ] [5] Aug 67
– Satisfaction / You are my sunshine / Never let me go / 96 tears / Prove it / Night life / That's life / I wonder / Ain't nobody (gonna turn me around) / Going down slow / Baby, I love you. *(re-iss,1972) (cd-iss.Aug93 on 'Rhino')*
Oct 67. (7") **(YOU MAKE ME FEEL LIKE A) NATURAL WOMAN. / NEVER LET ME GO** [ ] [-]
Nov 67. (7") **CHAINS OF FOOLS. / PROVE IT** [-] [2]
Dec 67. (7") **CHAINS OF FOOLS. / SATISFACTION** [37] [-]
Mar 68. (7") **(SWEET SWEET BABY) SINCE YOU'VE BEEN GONE. / AIN'T NO WAY** [47] [5]

[16] Feb 68
Mar 68. (lp) **ARETHA: LADY SOUL** [25] [2] Feb 68
– Chain of fools / Money won't change You / People get ready / Niki Hoeky / (You make me feel like) A natural woman / Since you've been gone (sweet sweet baby) / Good to me as I am to you / Come back baby / Groovin' / Ain't no way. *(re-iss.Jun88, cd-iss.Sep89) (cd-iss.Jun93)*
May 68. (7") **THINK. / YOU SEND ME** [26] [7]
[56]
Jul 68. (7") **I SAY A LITTLE PRAYER. / SEE-SAW** [4] [-]
Aug 68. (7") **THE HOUSE THAT JACK BUILT. / I SAY A LITTLE PRAYER** [-] [6]
[10]
Sep 68. (7") **THE HOUSE THAT JACK BUILT. / DON'T LET ME LOSE THIS DREAM** [ ] [-]
Sep 68. (lp) **ARETHA NOW** [6] [3] Jul 68
– Think / I say a little prayer / See saw / Night time is the right time / You send me / You're a sweet sweet man / I take what I want / Hello sunshine / A change / I can't see myself leaving you *(cd-iss.Aug93 on 'Rhino')*
Nov 68. (7") **SEE SAW. / MY SONG** [-] [14]
[31]
Dec 68. (lp) **LIVE AT THE PARIS OLYMPIA (live)** [ ] [13] Nov 68
– (I can't get no) Satisfaction / Don't let me lose this dream / Soul serenade / Night life / Baby I love you / Groovin' / Natural woman / Come back baby / Dr.Feelgood / Since you've been gone / I never loved a man (the way I love you) / Chain of fools / Respect. *(US title 'ARETHA IN PARIS') (re-iss.cd Dec94 on 'Rhino-Atlantic')*
Mar 69. (7") **THE WEIGHT. / THE TRACKS OF MY TEARS** [ ] [19]
[71] Feb 69
Mar 69. (lp) **SOUL '69** [ ] [15] Feb 69
– Ramblin' / Today I sing the blues / River's invitation / Pitiful / Crazy he calls me / BrIng it on home to me / Tracks of my tears / If you gotta make a fool of somebody / Gentle on my mind / So long / I'll never be free / Elusive butterfly *(cd-iss.Feb94 on 'Rhino-Atlantic')*
Apr 69. (7") **I CAN'T SEE MYSELF LEAVING YOU. / GENTLE ON MY MIND** [-] [28]
[76]
Aug 69. (7") **SHARE YOUR LOVE WITH ME. / PLEDGING MY LOVE / THE CLOCK** [ ] [13] Jul 69
Nov 69. (7") **ELEANOR RIGBY. / IT AIN'T FAIR** [ ] [17] Oct69
Mar 70. (7") **CALL ME. / SON OF A PREACHER MAN** [ ] [13] Feb 70
Apr 70. (lp) **THIS GIRL'S IN LOVE WITH YOU** [ ] [17] Feb70
– Son of a preacher man / Share your love with me / The dark end of the street / Let it be / Eleanor Rigby / This girl's in love with you / It ain't fair / The weight / Call me / Sit down and cry *(cd-iss.Feb94 on 'Rhino-Atlantic')*
May 70. (7") **LET IT BE. / MY SONG** [ ] [-]
May 70. (7") **SPIRIT IN THE DARK. / THE THRILL IS GONE** [-] [23]

—— Her new band comprised **KING CURTIS** – saxophone / **CORNELL DUPREE** – guitar / **RICHARD TEE** – piano / **JERRY JEMMOTT** – bass / **BERNARD PURDIE** – drums

Aug 70. (7") **DON'T PLAY THAT SONG. / THE THRILL IS GONE** [13] [11]
Sep 70. (lp) **DON'T PLAY THIS SONG** [ ] [25]
– Don't play that song / The thrill is gone / Pullin' / You and me / Honest I do / Spirit in the dark / When the battle is over / One way ticket / Try Matty's / That's all I want from you / Oh no, not my baby / When I sing the blues. *(US title 'SPIRIT IN THE DARK') (cd-iss.Feb94 on 'Rhino-Atlantic')*
Oct 70. (7") **LET IT BE. / DON'T PLAY THAT SONG** [-] [ ]
Dec 70. (7") **OH NO NOT MY BABY. / YOU AND ME** [ ] [-]
Dec 70. (7") **BORDER SONG (HOLY MOSES). / YOU AND ME** [-] [37]
Feb 71. (7") **YOU'RE ALL I NEED TO GET BY. / PULLIN'** [-] [19]
Mar 71. (7") **YOU'RE ALL I NEED TO GET BY. / BORDER SONG** [ ] [-]
May 71. (7") **BRIDGE OVER TROUBLED WATER. / A BRAND NEW ME** [ ] [6] Apr 71
Jul 71. (lp)(c) **LIVE AT FILLMORE WEST (live)** [ ] [7] May 71
– Respect / Love the one you're with / Bridge over troubled water / Eleanor Rigby / Make it with you / Don't play that song / Dr.Feelgood / Spirit in the dark / Spirit in the dark (reprise with RAY CHARLES) / Reach out and touch (somebody's hand). *(cd-iss.Feb94 on 'Rhino-Atlantic')*
Jul 71. (7"m) **I SAY A LITTLE PAYER (live). / THINK (live) / (I CAN'T GET NO) SATISFACTION (live)** [ ] [ ]
Aug 71. (7") **A BRAND NEW ME. / SPIRIT IN THE DARK** [ ] [-]

—— On 13 Aug'71, her legendary sax player and soloist KING CURTIS was stabbed to death on the street. She and her father sang and gave sermon at funeral. She attended another funeral 6 months later of her friend/**mentor Mahalia Jackson.**

Sep 71. (7") **SPANISH HARLEM. / LEAN ON ME** [14] [2] Jul71
Oct 71. (7") **ROCK STEADY. / OH ME OH MY (I'M A FOOL FOR YOU BABY)** [-] [9]
[73]
Mar 72. (7") **DAYDREAMING. / I'VE BEEN LOVING TOU TOO LONG** [ ] [5]
Mar 72. (lp)(c) **YOUNG, GIFTED AND BLACK** [ ] [11] Feb 72
– Oh me oh my (i'm a fool for you baby) / Day dreaming / Rock steady / Young, gifted and black / All the king's horses / A brand new me / April fools / I've been loving you too long / First snow in Kokomo / The long and winding road / Didn't I (blow your mind this time) / Border song *(cd-iss.Feb94 on 'Rhino-Atlantic')*
May 72. (7") **ALL THE KING'S HORSES. / APRIL FOOLS** [-] [26]
Aug 72. (7") **WHOLY HOLY. / GIVE YOURSELF TO JESUS** [-] [81]
Sep 72. (7") **ALL THE KING'S HORSES. / ROCK STEADY** [ ] [ ]
Sep 72. (d-lp)(c) **AMAZING GRACE (live)** [ ] [7] Jun 72
– Mary don't you weep / *Medley / Precious Lord, Take my hand / You've got a friend / Old landmark / Give yourself to Jesus / How I got over / What a friend we have in Jesus / Amazing grace– Precious memories / Climbing higher mountains / Remarks by Reverend C L Franklin / God will take care of you / Wholy holy / You'll never walk alone / Never grow old *(re-iss.Nov87)(cd-iss.Aug93)*
Mar 73. (7") **MASTER OF EYES (THE DEEPNESS OF YOUR EYES). / MOODY'S MOOD FOR LOVE** [ ] [33] Feb 73
Aug 73. (7") **ANGEL. / SISTER FROM TEXAS** [37] [20] Jul73
Aug 73. (lp)(c) **HEY NOW HEY (THE OTHER SIDE OF THE SKY)** [ ] [30] Jul 73
– Hey now hey / Somewhere / So well when you're well / Angel / Sister from Texas / Mister Spain / That's the way I feel about cha / Moody's mood / Just right tonight.

(*re-iss.cd Dec94 on 'Rhino-Atlantic'*)

Jan 74. (7") **UNTIL YOU COME BACK TO ME (THAT'S WHAT I'M GONNA DO). / IF YOU DON'T THINK** 26 | 3 Nov 73

Apr 74. (lp)(c) **LET ME INTO YOUR LIFE** | 14 Mar 74
– Let me in your life / Every natural thing / Ain't nothing like the real thing / I'm in love / Until you come back to me (that's what I'm gonna do) / The masquerade is over / With pen in hand / Oh baby / Eight days on the road / If you don't think / A song for you. (*re-iss.cd Dec94 on 'Rhino-Atlantic'*)

Jun 74. (7") **I'M IN LOVE. / OH BABY** | 19 Apr 74

Aug 74. (7") **AIN'T NOTHING LIKE THE REAL THING. / EIGHT DAYS A WEEK** - | 47

Jan 75. (7") **WITHOUT LOVE. / DON'T GO BREAKING MY HEART** | 45 Nov 74

Feb 75. (lp)(c) **WITH EVERYTHING I FEEL IN ME** | 57 Jan 75
– Without love / Don't go breaking my heart / When you get right down to it / You'll never get to Heaven / With everything I feel in me / I love every little thing about you / Sing it again – say it again / All of these things / You move me.

Mar 75. (7") **WHEN YOU GET RIGHT DOWN TO IT. / SING IT AGAIN – SAY IT AGAIN**

Oct 75. (7") **MR. D.J. (5 FOR THE D.J.). / AS LONG AS YOU ARE THERE** | 53 Sep 75

Dec 75. (7") **YOU. / WITHOUT YOU**

Dec 75. (lp)(c) **YOU** | 83 Nov 75
– Mr D.J. / It only happens / I'm not strong enough to love you again / Walk softly / You make my life / Without you / The sha-la bandit / You / You got all the aces / As long as you are there.

Jun 76. (7") **SOMETHING HE CAN FEEL. / LOVING YOU BABY** | 28

Jun 76. (lp)(c) **SPARKLE (Soundtrack)** | 18
– Sparkle / Giving him something he can feel / Hooked on your love / Look into your heart / I get high / Jump / Loving you baby / Rock with me.

Sep 76. (7") **JUMP. / HOOKED ON YOUR LOVE** - | 72

Jan 77. (7") **LOOK INTO YOUR HEART. / ROCK WITH ME** - | 82

May 77. (7") **BREAK IT TO ME GENTLY. / MEADOWS OF SPRINGTIME** | 85

Jun 77. (lp)(c) **SWEET PASSION** | 49
– Break it to me gently / When I think about you / What I did for love / No one could ever love you more / Tender touch / Touch me up / Sunshine will never be the same / Meadows of Springtime / Mumbles / I've got the music in me / Passion.

Sep 77. (7") **WHEN I THINK ABOUT YOU. / TOUCH ME**

Jun 78. (lp)(c) **ALMIGHTY FIRE** | 63 May 78
– Almighty fire (woman of the future) / Lady day / More than just a joy / Keep on loving you / I needed you baby / Close to you / No matter who you love / This you can believe / I'm your speed.

Jun 78. (7") **ALMIGHTY FIRE. / I'M YOUR SPEED** - |

Nov 78. (7") **THIS YOU CAN BELIEVE. / MORE THAN JUST A JOY** - |

Oct 79. (7") **LADIES ONLY. / WHAT IF I SHOULD EVER NEED YOU**

Oct 79. (lp)(c) **LA DIVA**
– Ladies only / It's gonna get a bit better / What if I should ever need you / Honey I need your love / I was made for you / Only star / Reasons why / You brought me back to life / Half a love / The feeling.

Jan 80. (7") **HALF A LOVE. / ONLY STAR** - |

Arista | Arista

Oct 80. (7")(12") **WHAT A FOOL BELIEVES. / SCHOOLDAYS** 46 |

Oct 80. (lp)(c) **ARETHA** | 47
– Come to me / I can't turn you loose / United together / Take me with you / Whatever it is / What a fool believes / Together / Love me forever / Schooldays. (*re-iss.Jan84 + May88, cd-iss.Oct86*)

Mar 81. (7")(12") **UNITED TOGETHER. / I CAN'T TURN YOU LOOSE** | 56 Dec 80

May 81. (7") **COME TO ME. / SCHOOL DAYS** - | 84

Aug 81. (7")(12") **LOVE ALL THE HURT AWAY. ("ARETHA FRANKLIN & GEORGE BENSON") / HOLD ON I'M COMING** 49 | 46

Sep 81. (lp)(c) **LOVE ALL THE HURT AWAY** | 36
– Hold on I'm coming / You can't always get what you want / It's my turn / Living in the streets / Love all the hurt away / There's a star for everyone / Truth and honesty / Search on / Whole lot of me / Kind of man (*cd-iss.1988*)

Feb 82. (7")(12") **HOLD ON I'M COMING. / KIND OF MAN**

Aug 82. (7")(12") **JUMP TO IT. / JUST MY DAYDREAM** 42 | 24

Aug 82. (lp)(c) **JUMP TO IT** | 23
– Love me right / 16 she don't want your love / This is for real / (It's just) Your love / I wanna make it up to you / It's your thing / Just my day dream. (*re-iss.Mar84*) (*re-iss.+cd.May88*)

Jan 83. (7")(12") **LOVE ME RIGHT. / (IT'S JUST) YOUR LOVE**

Jul 83. (7")(12") **GET IT RIGHT. / JUMP TO IT** 74 | 61

Jul 83. (lp)(c) **GET IT RIGHT** | 36
– Get it right / Pretender / Every girl (wants my guy) / When you love me like that / I wish it would rain / Better friends than lovers / I got your love / Giving in.

In Jul'85, while attending a civil rights campaign, her father C.L. is shot and went into a coma. He never recovered fully and died in Jul'87.

Jul 85. (7") **FREEWAY OF LOVE. / UNTIL YOU SAY LOVE ME** 68 | 3 Jun 85
(12"+=) – Jump to it.
(c-s++=) – Get it right. (*7"/12"re-iss.Apr86, hit UK No.51*)

(Oct85) Duets with EURYTHMICS on her 'SISTERS ARE DOIN' IT FOR THEMSELVES'. It hit UK No.9 + US No.18.

Nov 85. (lp)(c)(cd) **WHO'S ZOOMIN' WHO** 49 | 13 Jul 85
– Who's zoomin' who / Freeway of love / Another night / Sweet bitter love / Sisters are doin' it for themselves / Until you say love me / Push / Ain't nobody ever loved you / Integrity. (*re-iss.+cd.Jul88*)

Nov 85. (7") **WHO'S ZOOMIN' WHO. / SWEET BITTER LOVE** 11 | 7 Sep 85
(12"+=) – ('A'dub version) / ('A'acapella mix).

Feb 86. (7")(12") **ANOTHER NIGHT. / KIND OF MAN** 54 | 22

Aug 86. (7") **AIN'T NOBODY EVER LOVED YOU. / INTEGRITY**
(12"+=) – ('A'dub mix).

Oct 86. (lp)(c)(cd) **ARETHA FRANKLIN** 51 | 32
– Jimmy Lee / I knew you were waiting (for me) / Do you still remember / Jumpin' Jack Flash / Rock-a-lott / An angel cries / He'll come along / If you need my love tonight / Look to the rainbow. (*re-iss.cd-Nov93 on 'Entertainers'*)

Oct 86. (7") **JUMPIN' JACK FLASH. / INTEGRITY** 58 | 21 Sep 86
(12"+=) – Who's zoomin' who / Sweet bitter love.

She hits No.1 UK/US with GEORGE MICHAEL duet 'I KNEW YOU WERE WAITING (FOR ME)', This was released 'Epic'UK / 'Arista'US.

Feb 87. (7") **JIMMY LEE. / AN ANGEL CRIES**
(12"+=)(cd-s+=) – ('A'dub version) / Aretha megamix.

Jun 87. (7") **ROCK-A-LOTT. / LOOK TO THE RAINBOW** | 82
(12") – ('A' side) / ('A' dub) / ('A' cappella mix)

Oct 87. (7") **IF YOU NEED MY LOVE TONIGHT. / HE'LL COME ALONG** - |

Nov 87. (lp)(c)(cd) **ONE LORD, ONE FAITH, ONE BAPTISM**
– Walking in the light / Prayer invitation by Cecil Franklin / Introduction by Rev.Jesse Jackson / Jesus hears every prayer / Surely God is able / The Lord's prayer / Oh happy day / We need prayer / Speech by Rev,Jesse Jackson / Ave Maria / Introduction by Rev.Jasper Williams / Higher ground / Prayer by Rev.Donald Person / I've been in the storm too long / Waking up ready to go.

Feb 88. (7")(12") **OH HAPPY DAY. / THE LORD'S PRAYER**

—— (above featured MAVIS STAPLES)

Apr 89. (7")(c-s)(7"pic-d) **THROUGH THE STORM. ("ARETHA FRANKLIN & ELTON JOHN") / COME TO ME** 41 |
(12"+=)(cd-s+=) – Oh happy day.

May 89. (lp)(c)(cd) **THROUGH THE STORM** 46 | 55
– Through the storm / Gimme your love / He's the boy / It ain't never gonna be / Think / Mercy / It isn't, it wasn't, it ain't never gonna be / If ever a love there was.

Sep 89. (7")(c-s) **IT ISN'T, IT WASN'T, IT AIN'T NEVER GONNA BE. / THINK '89** 29 |
(US b-side='A' version w/ FOUR TOPS)
(12"+=) – ('A'extended remix).
(cd-s++=) – ('A'hip hop remix).

(above featured WHITNEY HOUSTON) (below featured JAMES BROWN)

Nov 89. (7") **GIMME YOUR LOVE. / HE'S THE BOY**
(12"+=)(cd-s+=) – ('A' parts 1 & 2 versions).

Jul 91. (7")(cd-s) **EVERYDAY PEOPLE. / YOU CAN'T TAKE ME FOR GRANTED** 69 |
(12") – ('A'side) / ('A'people remix) / ('A'people dub).
(cd-s+=) – ('A'remixed).

Aug 91. (cd)(c)(lp) **WHAT YOU SEE IS WHAT YOU SWEAT**
– Everyday people / Everchanging times (w/MICHAEL McDONALD / What you see is what you sweat / Mary goes round / I dreamed a dream / Someone' else's eyes / Doctor's orders / You can't take me for granted / What did you give / Everyday people (remix). (*re-iss.cd Feb94*)

Sep 91. (c-s) **SOMEONE ELSE'S EYES. / WHAT DID YOU GIVE** - |

Nov 91. (c-s) **WHAT YOU SEE IS WHAT YOU SWEAT. /** - |

Feb 92. (c-s) **YOU CAN'T TAKE ME FOR GRANTED. / EVERCHANGING TIMES** - |

Jan 94. (12")(c-s)(cd-s) **A DEEPER LOVE. / ('A'mixes)** 5 | 63
(cd-s+=) – (2 other mixes).

Mar 94. (cd)(c) **GREATEST HITS 1980-1994** (compilation) 27 | 85
– Freeway of love / I knew you were waiting (for me) (w/ GEORGE MICHAEL) / Jump to it / Willing to forgive / Doctor's orders / United together / Who's zommin' who / A deeper love / Honey / Get it right / Another night / Ever changing times / Jimmy Lee / (You make me fee like) A natural woman / I dreamed a dream / Jumpin' Jack Flash.

Jun 94. (c-s)(12")(cd-s) **WILLING TO FORGIVE. / JUMP TO IT (mixes)** 17 | 26

– compilations, others, etc. –

1967. Checker; (lp) **SONGS OF FAITH**

Jan 87. Chess; (lp)(c) **NEVER GROW OLD (w / Rev.FRANKLIN)** | -

Note all releases on 'CBS' were issued on US counterpart 'Columbia'.

1967. C.B.S.; (7") **CRY LIKE A BABY. / SWANEE**

1967. C.B.S.; (lp) **QUEEN OF SOUL**

1967. Columbia; (7") **LEE CROSS. / UNTIL YOU WERE GONE** - |

Aug 67. Columbia; (7") **TAKE A LOOK. / FOLLOW YOUR HEART** - | 56

1967. C.B.S.; (lp) **TAKE IT LIKE YOU GIVE IT**

Dec 67. Columbia; (7") **MOCKINGBIRD. / A MOTHER'S LOVE** - | 94

Feb 68. Columbia; (7") **SOULVILLE. / EVIL GAL BLUES** - | 83

1967. C.B.S.; (7") **LEE CROSS. / TAKE A LOOK**

1967. C.B.S.; (lp) **LEE CROSS** | -

1967. C.B.S.; (lp) **TAKE A LOOK**

Jun 67. C.B.S.; (lp) **GREATEST HITS: ARETHA FRANKLIN 1960-65** | 94
(*re-iss.+c.Apr87*)

1968. C.B.S.; (lp) **GREATEST HITS VOL.2**

1968. Columbia; (lp) **SOFT & BEAUTIFUL** - |

1969. Columbia; (7") **TONIGHT I SING THE BLUES. / CAN'T YOU JUST SEE ME** - |

1969. Columbia; (7") **FRIENDLY PERSUASION. / JIM** - |

1969. Columbia; (lp) **TODAY I SING THE BLUES** - |

Apr 83. C.B.S.; (d-lp)(c) **THE LEGENDARY QUEEN OF SOUL**

Jun 85. C.B.S.; (d-lp)(c) **THE ELECTRIFYING ARETHA FRANKLIN / SOUL SISTER**

1968. Atlantic; (lp) **THE BEST OF ARETHA FRANKLIN** - |
(*re-iss.+c Jun84, cd-iss.1986*)

Jul 69. Atlantic; (lp) **ARETHA'S GOLD**
(*re-iss.1972)(cd-iss.Aug93*)

1970. Atlantic; (lp) **I SAY A PRAYER** | -

Sep 71. Atlantic; (lp)(c) **ARETHA'S GREATEST HITS** | 19
(*re-iss.1982)(cd-iss.Aug93*)

1973. Atlantic; (lp)(c) **THE COLLECTION**

1975. Atlantic; (d-lp) **TWO ORIGINALS OF ARETHA FRANKLIN**

Dec 76. Atlantic; (lp)(c) **TEN YEARS OF GOLD**

1977. Atlantic; (d-lp)(c) **ARETHA'S MOST BEAUTIFUL SONGS** | -

1978. Atlantic; (lp)(c) **STAR COLLECTION VOL.1**

1978. Atlantic; (lp)(c) **STAR COLLECTION VOL.2**

Apr 80. Atlantic; (7")(12") **THINK. / RESPECT**

Apr 84. Atlantic; (7") **I SAY A LITTLE PRAYER. / ROCK STEADY**

CHAIN OF FOOLS
I SAY A LITTLE PRAYER

May 86. Atlantic; (12") **(YOU MAKE ME FEEL LIKE A) NATURAL WOMAN. / DO RIGHT WOMAN, DO RIGHT MAN / NEVER LOVED A MAN (THE WAY I LOVE YOU)** [ ] [ ]
Jun 87. Atlantic; (7") **RESPECT. / DO RIGHT WOMAN, DO RIGHT MAN** [ ] [ ]
(12"+=) – Rock steady.
Jul 89. Atlantic; (7") **RESPECT. / DO RIGHT WOMAN – DO RIGHT MAN** [ ] [ ]
May 93. Atlantic; (cd) **ARETHA'S JAZZ** [ ] [ ]
Jun 93. Atlantic; (d-cd) **30 GREATEST HITS** [ ] [ ]
1973. Embassy-CBS; (lp)(c) **FIRST 12 SIDES** [ ] [ ]
May 86. Stylus; (cd)(c)(lp) **THE FIRST LADY OF SOUL** [89] [-]
Jul 81. Old Gold; (7") **I SAY A LITTLE PRAYER. / RESPECT** [ ] [-]
1988. Old Gold; (12") **JUMP TO IT. / GET IT RIGHT** [ ] [-]
Apr 89. Old Gold; (12") **IT'S JUST YOUR LOVE. / LOVE ME RIGHT** [ ] [-]
Sep 86. Castle; (d-lp)(c)(cd) **THE COLLECTION VOL.1 & 2** [ ] [-]
(re-iss.Jul87)
Jul 87. WEA; (cd) **20 GREATEST HITS** [ ] [ ]
– I never loved a man (the way I loved you) / Respect / Do right woman – do right man / Dr Feelgood / (You make me feel like) a natural woman / Chain of fools / Save me / The house that Jack built / Think / I say a little prayer / See saw / Day dreaming / Call me / Don't play that song / You're all I need to get by / I'm in love / Spanish Harlem / Rock steady / Angel / Until you come back to me (that's what I'm gonna do).
Dec 87. Blue Moon; (c)(cd) **SOUL SENSATION (w/ PERCY SLEDGE)** [ ] [ ]
May 88. Streetlife; (lp)(c)(cd) **SO SWELL** [ ] [-]
Mar 90. Collector's; (cd) **THE GREAT ARETHA FRANKLIN** [ ] [-]
Mar 90. East West; (7") **THINK. / (b-by Blues Brothers)** [31] [ ]
(re-iss.Jul91)
Nov 93. Legacy; (d-cd) **JAZZ TO SOUL** [ ] [-]
Apr 94. That's Soul; (cd) **RESPECT** [ ] [-]
Jul 94. Charly; (cd) **GOSPEL ROOTS** [ ] [-]
Oct 94. Atlantic; (cd)(c) **QUEEN OF SOUL – THE VERY BEST OF** [23] [ ]

FRANTIC ELEVATORS (see under ⇒ SIMPLY RED)

FREE

Formed: London, England ... Spring 1968, by KOSSOFF, KIRKE, RODGERS and FRASER. They were spotted at their first gig by white blues artist ALEXIS KORNER, who named them FREE, and introduced them to Chris Blackwell of 'Island'. They signed to label, and released 'TONS OF SOBS', by the end of year. In 1969, after supporting a US tour of BLIND FAITH, they broke UK Top lists with self-titled lp. In mid-1970, they stormed the charts with classic 'ALL RIGHT NOW', which hit both UK & US Top 5's. Its full version was available on UK Top3 / US Top 20 album 'FIRE AND WATER', which was followed by disappointing 'HIGHWAY' & 'FREE LIVE!', before their split May'71. After 9 months of other projects, noteably lp 'KOSSOFF, KIRKE, TETSU & RABBIT', they re-formed original line-up early '72, They struck back with Top 20 hit 'LITTLE BIT OF LOVE', taken from parent Top 10 album 'FREE AT LAST'. After another UK Top 10 hit 45 ('WISHING WELL') & album ('HEARTBREAKER'), they decided to announce split mid-73. • **Style:** Heavy-blues outfit, who came out of the shadow of CREAM, and gained own reputation for hard-edged rock'n'blues. Their basic riffs, were transported powerfully and sometimes melancholy by frontman RODGERS. • **Songwriters:** Group compositions, except some blues standards. Covered THE HUNTER (Albert King). • **Trivia:** Early in 1991, after being used on a chewing gum UK TV ad, 'ALL RIGHT NOW', hit the Top 10, as does compilation cd.

Recommended: THE BEST OF FREE – ALL RIGHT NOW (1991 compilation cd).

PAUL RODGERS (b.12 Dec'49, Middlesbrough, England) – vocals (ex-BROWN SUGAR) / **PAUL KOSSOFF** (b.14 Sep'50, Hampstead, London) – guitar (ex-BLACK CAT BONES) / **SIMON KIRKE** (b.28 Jul'49, Shrewsbury, England) – drums (ex-BLACK CAT BONES) / **ANDY FRASER** (b. 7 Aug'52, Shropshire, England) – bass (ex-JOHN MAYALL'S BLUESBREAKERS)

Island / A & M

Nov 68. (lp) **TONS OF SOBS** [ ] [ ] Aug 69
– Over the green hills (part 1) / Worry / Walk in my shadow / Wild Indian woman / Goin' down slow / I'm a mover / The hunter / Moonshine / Sweet tooth / Over the green hills (part 2). *(cd-iss.Jun88)*
Mar 69. (7") **I'M A MOVER. / WORRY** [-] [ ]
Mar 69. (7") **BROAD DAYLIGHT. / THE WORM** [ ] [ ]
Jul 69. (7") **I'LL BE CREEPIN'. / SUGAR FOR MR. MORRISON** [ ] [-]
Aug 69. (7") **I'LL BE CREEPIN'. / MOUTHFUL OF GRASS** [-] [ ]
Oct 69. (lp)(c) **FREE** [22] [ ]
– I'll be creepin' / Songs of yesterday / Lying in the sunshine / Trouble on double time / Mouthful of grass / Woman / Free me / Broad daylight / Mourning sad morning. *(cd-iss.Jun88)*
May 70. (7") **ALL RIGHT NOW. / MOUTHFUL OF GRASS** [2] [4]
(re-iss.Jul73 hit UK No.15)
Jun 70. (lp)(c) **FIRE AND WATER** [2] [17] Aug 70
– Oh I wept / Remember / Heavy load / Fire and water / Mr.Big / Don't say you love me / All right now. *(re-iss.+cd.Sep86, cd-iss.Apr90) (re-iss.lp Jan94 + May94)*
Nov 70. (7") **THE STEALER. / LYING IN THE SUNSHINE** [ ] [-]
Nov 70. (7") **THE STEALER. / BROAD DAYLIGHT** [-] [49]
Dec 70. (lp)(c) **HIGHWAY** [41] [ ] Feb 71
– The highway song / The stealer / On my way / Be my friend / Sunny day / Ride on pony / Love you so / Bodie / Soon I will be gone. *(cd-iss.Jun88)*
Jan 71. (7") **THE HIGHWAY SONG. / LOVE YOU SO** [-] [ ]
Mar 71. (7") **I'LL BE CREEPIN'. / MR. BIG** [-] [ ]
Apr 71. (7") **MY BROTHER JAKE. / ONLY MY SOUL** [4] [ ]
Jun 71. (lp)(c) **FREE LIVE! (live)** [4] [89] Aug 71
– All right now / I'm a mover / Be my friend / Fire and water / Ride on pony / Mr. Big / The hunter / Get where I belong (studio). *(cd-iss.Jun88)*

— They had already split May71. FRASER formed TOBY. RODGERS formed PEACE.

KOSSOFF, KIRKE, TETSU & RABBIT

were formed by the other two plus **TETSU YAMAUCHI** (b.21 Oct'47, Fukuoka, Japan)- bass / **JOHN 'RABBIT' BUNDRICK** – keyboards, vocals / and guest **B.J. COLE** – steel guitar

Nov 71. (lp) **KOSSOFF, KIRKE, TETSU & RABBIT** [ ] [ ]
– Blue grass / Sammy's alright / Just for the box / Colours / Hold on / Yellow house / Dying fire / Fool's life / Anna / I'm on the run. *(cd-iss.Aug 91) (re-iss.cd May95 on 'Repertoire')*

FREE

re-formed originals Feb72 (**RODGERS, KOSSOFF, FRASER** and **KIRKE**)

May 72. (7") **LITTLE BIT OF LOVE. / SAIL ON** [13] [ ]
Jun 72. (lp)(c) **FREE AT LAST** [9] [69]
– Catch a train / Soldier boy / Magic ship / Sail on / Travelin' man / Little bit of love / Guardian of the universe / Child / Goodbye. *(cd-iss.Jun88 & Feb90)*

— **TETSU YAMAUCHI** – bass(see above) repl. FRASER who joined SHARKS added **JOHN 'RABBIT' BUNDRICK** – keyboards (see above) **RODGERS** – also guitar

Dec 72. (7") **WISHING WELL. / LET ME SHOW YOU** [7] [ ]
Jan 73. (lp)(c) **HEARTBREAKER** [9] [47]
– Wishing well / Come together in the morning / Travellin' in style / Heartbreaker / Muddy water / Common mortal man / Easy on my soul / Seven angels. *(cd-iss.Jun88 & Feb90)*
Mar 73. (7") **TRAVELLIN' IN STYLE. / EASY ON MY SOUL** [ ] [ ]

— **WENDELL RICHARDSON** – guitar of OSIBISA, on UK & US tour early '73) repl. KOSSOFF who formed BACK STREET CRAWLER. He died in his sleep 19 Mar'76, after years of drug abuse. FREE split early '73. RABBIT went solo before joining (KOSSOFF's) CRAWLER. TETSU joined The FACES. RODGERS and KIRKE formed BAD COMPANY.

– compilations, etc. –

Island / A & M

Mar 74. Island/ US= A&M; (d-lp)(c) **THE FREE STORY** [2] [ ]
Apr 75. A&M; (lp)(c) **THE BEST OF FREE** [-] [ ]
Nov 76. Island; (lp)(c) **FREE AND EASY, ROUGH AND READY** [ ] [ ]
Nov 76. Island/ US= A&M; (7") **THE HUNTER. / WORRY** [ ] [ ]
Feb 78. Island/ US= A&M; (7"ep) **THE FREE EP** [11] [ ]
– All right now / My brother Jake / Wishing well. *(re-iss.Oct82 as 12"pic-d, hit 57)*
Oct 82. Island/ US= A&M; (lp)(c) **COMPLETELY FREE** [ ] [ ]
May 85. Island; (7")(12") **WISHING WELL. / WOMAN** [ ] [ ]
Feb 91. Island; (7")(c-s) **ALL RIGHT NOW. / I'M A MOVER** [8] [ ]
(12"+=)(cd-s+=) – Get where I belong.
Feb 91. Island; (cd)(c)(lp) **ALL RIGHT NOW – THE BEST OF FREE** [9] [ ]
– Wishing well / All right now / Be my friend / Fire and water / Travellin' in style / The hunter / Sail on / My brother Jake / Little bit of love / Come together in the morning / Mr.Big / The stealer / Travelling man / Don't say you love me.
Apr 91. Island; (7")(c-s) **MY BROTHER JAKE (remix). / WISHING WELL (remix)** [ ] [ ]
(12"+=)(cd-s+=) – The stealer (extended) / Only my soul (extended).

PAUL KOSSOFF

with all of FREE as guests; plus **TREVOR BURTON** – bass / **ALAN WHITE** – drums

Island / Island

Dec 73. (lp)(c) **BACK STREET CRAWLER** [ ] [ ]
– Tuesday morning / I'm ready / Time away / Molten gold / Back street crawler. *(re-iss.Apr87, cd-iss.Feb90) (cd-iss.Jul92 & May95 on 'Repertoire')*

BACK STREET CRAWLER

KOSSOFF – lead guitar with **TERRY WILSON-SLESSER** – vocals / **TERRY WILSON** – bass / **TONY BRAUNAGEL** – drums / **MIKE MONTGOMERY** – keyboards / plus **PETER VAN DER PUIJE** – sax / **EDDIE QUANSAH** – horns / **GEORGE LEE LARNYOH** – flute, saxes

Atlantic / Atco

Aug 75. (lp)(c) **THE BAND PLAYS ON** [ ] [ ]
– Who do women / New York, New York stealing my way / Survivor / It's a long way down to the top / All the girls are crazy / Jason blue / Train song / Rock & roll junkie / The band plays on.

— **GEOFF WHITEHORN** – guitar repl. wind section

May 76. (lp)(c) **2ND STREET** [ ] [ ]
– Selfish lover / Blue soul / Stop doing what you're doing / Raging river / Some kind of happy / Sweet beauty / Just for you / On your life / Leaves the wind.

— Tragedy had already struck when on 19th March '76 KOSSOFF died in his sleep, suffering from drug abuse.

— The rest carried on as CRAWLER and released 4 singles as well as 2 albums on 'Epic'; 'CRAWLER' (1977) & 'SNAKE, RATTLE & ROLL' (1978).

– compilations, etc –

Oct 77. D.J.M.; (d-lp) **KOSS** (1974 /75) [ ] [ ]
(re-iss.Aug83 on 'Street Tunes', cd-iss.Jul87)
May 83. Street Tunes; (lp) **THE HUNTER** (1969-75) [ ] [-]
Aug 83. Strret Tunes; (lp) **LEAVES IN THE WIND** (1975 /76) [ ] [-]
Sep 83. Street Tunes; (lp) **CROYDON** – JUNE 15th 1975 (live) [ ] [-]

(cd-iss.May95 on 'Repertoire')

Nov 83. Street Tunes; (c) **MR.BIG** | | - |
Apr 86. Island; (lp)(c) **BLUE SOUL** | | |
May 94. Island; (cd) **MOLTEN GOLD** | | - |

Ace FREHLEY (see under ⇒ KISS)

FREUR (see under ⇒ UNDERWORLD)

Glenn FREY (see under ⇒ EAGLES)

FRIDA (see under ⇒ ABBA)

FRIJID PINK

Formed: Detroit, Michegan, USA . . .early 1967 by school mates KELLY GREEN, GARY RAY THOMPSON, RICHARD STEVERS, LARRY ZELANKA (keyboards) and TOM HARRIS (bass). The latter two were replaced a year later by THOMAS BEAUDRY. In 1969, they signed to 'Parrot' where their 3rd 45 'HOUSE OF THE RISING SUN' hit US Top 10. After it became a massive success in Britain & Germany, their career took a sharp decline. In 1972, producers VINNY TESTA + CYLDE STEVENS were to bring in new group to no avail. • **Style:** Very loud psychedelic rock outfit. • **Songwriters:** Group except HOUSE OF THE RISING SUN (hit; Animals)/ HEARTBREAK HOTEL (hit; Elvis Presley).

Recommended: FRIJID PINK (*7)

KELLY GREEN – vocals / **GARY RAY THOMPSON** – guitar / **THOMAS BEAUDRY** – bass / **RICHARD STEVERS** – drums

Deram | Parrot

1969. (7") **TELL ME WHY. / CRYING SHAME** | - | |
1969. (7") **GOD GAVE ME YOU. / DRIVIN' BLUES** | - | |
Feb 70. (7") **HOUSE OF THE RISING SUN. / DRIVIN' BLUES** | 4 | 7 |
Mar 70. (lp) **FRIJID PINK** | | 11 | Jan70
– God gave me you / Crying shame / I'm on my way / Drivin' blues / Tell me why / End of the line / House of the rising sun / I want to be your lover / Boozin' blues. *(cd-iss.1990's on 'Repertoire'; +=)*– Heartbreak hotel / Music for the people.
Jul 70. (7") **SING A SONG OF FREEDOM. / END OF THE LINE** | | 55 |
Nov 70. (lp) **DEFROSTED** | | | Oct70
– Black lace / Sing a song for freedom / I'll never be lonely / Bye bye blues / Pain in my heart / Sloony / I'm movin' / I have't got the time.
Dec 70. (7") **HEARTBREAK HOTEL. / BYE BYE BLUES** | | 72 |
Apr 71. (7") **MUSIC FOR THE PEOPLE. / SLOONY** | | |
Jun 71. (7") **WE'RE GONNA GET THERE. / SHORTY KNIFE** | | |
Dec 71. (7") **LOST SON. / I LOVE HER** | | |

—— **STEVENS** was virtually left to recruit members; **JON WEARING** – vocals/ **LARRY ZELANKA** – piano, organ/ **CRAIG WEBB** – guitar/ TOM HARRIS – bass

not issued | Lion

Nov 72. (7") **EARTH OMEN. / LAZY DAY** | - | |
Jan 73. (lp) **EARTH OMEN** | - | |
– Miss Evil / Sailor / Earth omen / Lazy day / Train woman / Eternal dream / New horizon / Rainbow rider / Mr.Blood. *(cd-iss.Jan95 on 'Repertoire')*
1973. (7") **GO NOW. / LAZY DAY** | - | |
1974. (7") **SHADY LADY. / BIG BETTY** | - | |

not issued | Fantasy

1975. (lp) **ALL PINK INSIDE** | - | |

Split around the mid-70's.

re – issues, etc.

Sep 85. Old Gold; (7") **HOUSE OF THE RISING SUN. / (other artist)** | | - |

Robert FRIPP (see under ⇒ KING CRIMSON)

Edgar FROESE (see uner ⇒ TANGERINE DREAM)

FRONT 242

Formed: Belguim . . . 1981 by DANIEL B., etc (see below). After years in the wilderness of indie-dance rock, they finaly broke through in the early 90's, having just turned down the film soundtrack of 'BLADERUNNER II'. • **Style:** Pioneers of the anarcho techno-beat scene, that later emerged in the late 80's, their sound was a fusion of JOY DIVISION and TEST DEPT. DANIEL described them as "electronic body music". • **Songwriters:** DANIEL and PATRICK. • **Trivia:** JEAN-LUC and RICHARD were also part of REVOLTING COCKS with AL JOURGENSEN of MINISTRY.

Recommended: BACK CATALOGUE (*6)

DANIEL B. PROTHESE – keyboards / **RICHARD K. 23** – vocals, drum programmes / **JEAN-LUC DE MEYER** – vocals, drum machine / **PATRICK CODENYS** – keyboards

New Dance | not issued

Nov 81. (7") **PRINCIPLES. / BODY TO BODY** | | - |
May 82. (7") **U-MEN. / ETHICS** | | - |
(12"of above 4 tracks; issued Jan86, cd-ep Oct88)

Himalaya | not issued

1983. (12"ep) **ENDLESS RIDDANCE** | | - |
– Take one / Controversy / Between / Sample D. *(re-iss.+cd-ep.Aug88 on 'R.R.E.')*
1984. (7")(12") **NO SHUFFLE. / BODY TO BODY** | | - |

—— DANIEL B. had now departed in 1984.

Another Side | not iss.

Apr 85. (lp) **NO COMMENT** | | - |
– Commando (mix) / S.Fr. no menklatura (pt.1 & 2) / Deceit / Lonely day / No shuffle / Special forces (demo). *(re-iss.Jan87 on 'Mask', cd-iss.Sep93) (cd-iss.Jun92 on 'Red Rhino Europe')*(below iss.Europe on 'Operation Twilight')

Mask | not issued

May 86. (12"ep) **POLITICS OF PRESSURE** | | - |
– Commando (remix) / No shuffle / Don't crash / Funkahdafi.
Dec 86. (lp) **GEOGRAPHY** | | - |
– Operating tracks / With your cries / Art & strategy / Geography II / U-men / Dialogues / Least inkling / G.V.D.T. / Geography I / Black, white blues / Kinetics / Kampfbereit. *(iss.1983 in Belguim; cd-iss.Sep93 on 'Mask') (cd-iss.Jun92 on 'R.R.E.')*

R.R.E. | S.P.V.

Nov 86. (7")(ext-12") **INTERCEPTION: QUITE UNUSUAL. / AGGRESIVA** | | - |
(cd-s Aug88)
Jan 87. (cd) **BACK CATALOGUE** (compilation 1982-85) | | - |
(re-iss.cd.Jun92, with extra tracks)
Jun 87. (lp)(cd) **OFFICIAL VERSION** | | - |
– What you have is what you get / Re-run / Television station / Aggressive due / Masterhits 1 & 2 / Slaughter / Quite unusual / Red team / Aggressive angst. (cd+=) – (2 extended mixes). *(cd re-iss.Jun92, with 4 extra)*
Nov 87. (12"ep) **MASTERHIT (pt.1 masterblaster mix). / MASTERHIT (pt.2 hypno mix) / MASTERHIT (pt.3 lp edited version)** | | - |
(above single issued on 'Waxtrax', re-iss.+cd-ep Jan90 on 'Red Rhino . . . ')
Sep 88. (7")(12") **HEADHUNTER (V1.0). / WELCOME TO PARADISE (V1.0)** | | - |
(cd-s+=) – Headhunter (V2.0).
Oct 88. (lp)(cd) **FRONT BY FRONT** | | - |
– Until death (do us part) / Circling overland / Im rhythmus bleiben / Felines / First in – first out / Blend the strengths / Headhunter V 3.0 / Work 01 / Terminal state. *(cd re-iss.Jun92, with 6 extra)*
Mar 89. (7") **NEVER STOP (V1.1). / WORK 242** | | - |
(3"cd-s+=)(12"+=) – Never stop (V1.0) / Work 242 N.off is N.off / Agony (until death).

—— RICHARD was now only live performer.

R.R.E. | Epic

Oct 90. (7") **TRAGEDY FOR YOU. / ('A'short version)** | | - |
(12")(cd-s) – ('A'side) / ('A'long version) / ('A'slow-mo mix).
(12")(cd-s) – ('A'neurodancer mix) / ('A'instrumental) / Trigger 3.
Jan 91. (cd)(c)(lp) **TYRANNY FOR YOU** | 49 | 95 |
– Sacrifice / Rhythm of time / Moldavia / Trigger 2 (anatomy of a shot) / Gripped by fear / Tragedy for you / The untold / Neurobashing / Leitmotiv 136 / Soul manager.
Mar 91. (12")(cd-s) **MIXED BY FEAR. / ?** | | |
1991. (12") **RHYTHM OF TIME (Anti-G mix) / ('A'-Victor The Cleaner mix)** | - | |
Apr 93. (cd-s) **RELIGION (7"mix) / RELIGION (pussy whipped mix) / RELIGION (the Prodigy bass under siege mix) / RELIGION (bitch slapper mix) / RELIGION (the Pridigy trance U down mix)** | 46 | |
(12")(cd-s) – Crapage (never hurry a Murray mix) / Crapage (the turd mix) / Religion (lovelace a go-go mix). *(cd re-iss.Dec93)*
May 93. (cd)(c)(lp) **06: 21: 03: 11 UP EVIL** | 44 | |
– Crapage / Waste / Skin / Motion / Religion / Stratoscape / Hymn / Fuel / Melt / Flag / Mutilate.
(cd+=) – (S)Crapage / Religion (pussy whipped mix).
Sep 93. (cd)(c)(lp) **05: 22: 09: 12 OFF** | 46 | |
– Animal – Cage / Animal – Gate / Animal – Guide / Modern angel / Junkdrome / Serial killers don't kill their girlfriend / Skin – Fur coat / Genecide / Crushed / Offend / Animal – Zoo / Serial killers don't kill their boyfriend / Happiness – More angels / Crushed – Obscene / Melt – Again / Speed angels.
Nov 93. (m-cd) **ANGELS VERSUS ANIMALS** (re-workings) | | |
– Animal (radio) / Angel (wipe out) / Serial killers don't kill their dog either / Modern angel (KMFDM remix) / Animal (extended) / Break me / Der verfluchte engel / L'ange modern / Born to breathe.
Nov 93. (12")(cd-s) **ANIMAL. / ('A'version)** | | |

P.I.A.S.

Nov 94. (cd)(c)(lp) **LIVE CODE 6413356-424225** | | - |
– Der verfluchte engel / Motion / Masterhit / Flag / Tragedy for you / Im rhythmus bleiben / Skin / Headhunter / Welcome to Paradise / Crapage / Soul manager / Punish your machine / Religion.

– compilations, others, etc. –

Dec 92. Guzzi; (cd) **LIVE TARGET (live)** | | - |

FUGAZI

Formed: Washington DC, USA . . . 1988 by IAN MacKAYE who had the previous year issued EMBRACE lp. He had even earlier been part of MINOR THREAT, who unleashed hardcore ditties for own label 'Dischord'. Now in FUGAZI, he shared vocal duties with GUY PICCOTTO, ex-leader of RITES OF SPRING and INSURRECTION. Late in 1985 also for 'Dischord', the former issued lp 'SPRING' and a year later 7"ep 'ALL THROUGH A LIFE'. In Oct'88, INSURRECTION released their self-titled show for 'Peaceville'. FUGAZI's five album slog was rewarded in 1993, when 'IN ON THE KILLTAKER' broke the UK Top 30. • **Style:** Hard-core punk /metal similar to NOMEANSNO. • **Songwriters:** MacKAYE most. MINOR THREAT covered

12XU (Wire). • **Trivia:** HENRY ROLLINS (ex-BLACK FLAG) produced them early on. IAN MacKAYE produced the early '89 BEEFEATER single 'House Burning Down'.

Recommended: IN ON THE KILLTAKER (*7)

MINOR THREAT

IAN MacKAYE – vocals / **LYLE PRESLAR** – guitar / **BRIAN BAKER** – bass / **JEFF NELSON** – drums

not issued Dischord

1983. (lp)(c) **OUT OF STEP** [-] [ ]
– Betray / It follows / Think again / Look back and laugh / Sob story / No reason / Little friend / Out of step / Stand up / 12XU.

1984. (lp)(c) **MINOR THREAT** [-] [ ]
– Filler / I don't wanna hear it / Seeing red / Straight edge / Small man, big mouth / Screaming at a wall / Bottled violence / Minor threat / In my eyes / Out of step (with the world) / Guilty of being white / Steppin' stone.

Aug 85. (7"ep/?tracks) **SALAD DAYS / GOOD GUYS. / STUMPED / CASHING IN** [-] [ ]

Mar 90. (cd) **COMPLETE DISCOGRAPHY** (compilation / also rel.UK) [ ] [ ]

FUGAZI

IAN MacKAYE – vocals, guitar (ex-MINOR THREAT, ex-TEEN IDES, ex-EMBRACE) / **GUY PICCIOTTO** – vocals (ex-INSURRECTION, ex-RITES OF SPRING, ex-ONE LAST WISH)

Dischord Dischord

Jan 89. (lp)(c) **FUGAZI** [ ] [-]
– Waiting room / Bulldog front / Bad mouth / Burning / Give me the cure / Suggestion / Glue man.

Jul 89. (lp)(c) **MARGIN WALKER** [ ] [-]
– Margin walker / And the same / Burning too / Provisional / Lockdown / Promises. *(cd of both above '13 SONGS' Oct89)*

— Below single on US 'Sub Pop'.

Jan 90. (7")(7"green) **JOE £1. / BREAK IN / SONG £1** [ ] [ ]

Mar 90. (cd)(c)(lp) **REPEATER** [ ] [-]
– Turnover / Repeater / Brendan £1 / Merchandise / Blueprint / Sieve-fisted grind / Greed / Two beats off / Styrofoam / Reprovisional / Shut the door. (cd+=) – Song £1 / Joe £1 / Break-in.

Aug 91. (cd)(c)(lp) **STEADY DIET OF NOTHING** [63] [ ]
– Exit only / Reclamation / Nice new outfits / Stacks / Latin roots / Steady diet / Long division / Runaway return / Polish / Dear justice letter / K.Y.E.O.

Jun 93. (m-cd)(m-c)(m-lp) **IN ON THE KILLTAKER** [24] [ ]
– Facet squared / Public witness program / Returning the screw / Smallpox champion / Rend it / 23 beats off / Sweet and low / Cassavetes / Great cop / Walken's syndrome / Instrument / Last chance for a slow dance.

May 95. (cd)(lp) **RED MEDICINE** [ ] [ ]
– Do you like me / Bed for the scraping / Latest disgrace / Birthday pony / Forensic scene / Combination lock / Fell, destroyed / By you / Version / Target / Back to base / Downed city / Long distance runner.

FUGS

Formed: Greenwich Village, New York, USA ... 1964 by poets/satirists SANDERS, WEAVER and KUPFERBERG. After beginning life at the local McDougall Theatre, they built up reputation leading them to fit crude poetic works into songs. In 1965, they signed to jazz label 'ESP', and unleashed first album which contained the political theme 'KILL FOR PEACE', the drug orientated 'NEW AMPHETAMINE SHRIEK', and the sex-angled 'COCA COLA DOUCHE'. Not surprisingly, they were shunned by respectable US citizens, although they mellowed somewhat with next lp 'FUGS'. After a few more offensive productions, they signed to 'Reprise' in 1967, and might have scored a hit 45 with 'OUT DEMONS OUT', but it remained unreleased. • **Trivia:** This song was later a UK hit for The EDGAR BROUGHTON BAND. • **Style:** Outrageous underground rock outfit, who transformed WILLIAM BLAKE poems into pieces of avant-garde rock, lying somewhere between VELVET UNDERGROUND and satirist LENNY BRUCE. They turned from beatniks to hippies and helped found new pacifist anit-war movements around New York. • **Songwriters:** SANDERS or KUPFERBERG words and FUGS music.

Recommended: VIRGIN FUGS (*6).

ED SANDERS (b.Kansas) – vocals, guitar / **TULI KUPFERBERG** – vocals, percussion / **KEN WEAVER** (b.Texas) – drums, vocals / **PETER STAMPFEL** – guitar, banjo, vocals / **STEVE WEBER** – guitar (both ex-HOLY MODAL ROUNDERS) / **VINNY LEARY** – guitar, bass / **JOHN ANDERSON** – bass / **PETE KEARNEY** – guitar

not issued Broadside

Jan 65. (lp) **THE VIRGIN FUGS** [-] [ ]
– We're the fugs / New amphetamine shriek / Saran wrap / The ten commandments / Hallucination horrors / I command the house of the Devil / C.I.A. man / Coco Cola douche / My bed is getting crowded / Coca rocka / I saw the best of my generation rot. *(re-iss.1967 on 'ESP', UK-iss.1969 on 'Fontana')*

not issued E.S.P.

Oct 65. (lp) **THE FUGS FIRST ALBUM** [-] [ ]
– Slum Goddess / Ah, sunflower weary of time / Supergirl / Swineburne stomp / I couldn't get high / How sweet I roamed from field to field / Seize the day / My baby done left me / Boobs a lot / Nothing. *(hit US Top 200 Oct'66) (UK-iss.1969 on 'Fontana') (cd-iss.Jun93 on 'Big Beat')*

— WEBER left to re-join The HOLY MODAL ROUNDERS with STAMPFEL, and was repl. by **LEE CRABTREE** – piano + PETE KEARNEY – guitar (ANDERSON also missing)

Jun 66. (lp) **THE FUGS** [-] [95]
– Frenzy / I want to know / Skin flowers / Group grope / Coming down / Dirty old man / I kill for peace / Morning, morning / Doin' all right / Virgin forest. *(UK issue 1970 as 'FUGS II' on 'Fontana') (cd-iss.Sep 93 on 'Ace')*

Dec 66. (7") **FRENZY. / I WANT TO KNOW** [-] [ ]

— **SANDERS, KUPFERBERG & WEAVER** recruit new members **CHARLIE LARKEY** – drums / **KEN PINE** – guitar, vocals / **DANNY KORTCHMAR** – guitar

Transatla. Reprise

Jan 68. (lp) **TENDERNESS JUNCTION** [ ] [ ]
– Turn on, tune in, drop out / Knock knock / The garden is open / Wet dream / Hare Krishna / Exorcising the Devil spirits from the Pentagon / War song / Dover beach / Fingers of the Sun / Aphrodite mass: Litany of the street grope genuflection at the temple . . . – Petals in the sea – Sappho's hymn to Aphrodite – Homage to throb thrills. *(re-iss.Jan89 on 'Edsel')*

— added **BOB MASON** – 2nd drummer

Sep 68. (lp) **IT CRAWLED INTO MY HAND, HONEST** [ ] [ ]
– Crystal liason / Ramases II is dead, my love / Burial waltz / Wide wide river / Life is strange / Johnny Pissoff meets the red angel – Marijuana – Leprechaun – When the mode of the music changes – Whimpers from the jello – Divine toe (part 1) – We're both dead now, Alice – Life is funny – Grope need (part 1) – Tuli, visited by the ghost of Plotinus / More grope need (Grope need part 2) – Robinson Crusoe – Claude Pelieu and J.J.Lebel discuss the early Verlaine bread crust fragments – The national Haiku contest – The divine toe (part 2) – Irene.

Sep 68. (7") **CRYSTAL LIASON. / WHEN THE MODE OF THE MUSIC CHANGES** [ ] [ ]

— **DAN HAMBURG** – guitar repl. DANNY

Reprise Reprise

Nov 69. (lp) **THE BELLE OF AVENUE A** [ ] [ ]
– Bum's song / Dust devil / Chicago / Four minutes to twelve / Mr.Mack / The belle of Avenue A / Queen of the Nile / Flower children / Yodeling yippie / Children of the dream.

— **CARL LYNCH** – guitar repl. DAN added **HOWARD JOHNSON** – tuba / **JULIUS WATKINS** – horns / **RICHARD TEE** – organ

1970. (lp)(c) **GOLDEN FILTH ALIVE AT HTE FILLMORE EAST (live '68)** [ ] [ ]
– Slum goddess / CCD / How sweet I roamed / I couldn't get high / Saran wrap / I want to know / Homemade / Nothing / Supergirl. *(re-iss.Feb87 on 'Edsel')*

— Disbanded early 1970. LARKEY later married and played bass for CAROLE KING. In 1984, **SANDERS + KUPFERBERG** re-formed the **FUGS** w/ **STEVE TAYLOR** – vocals, guitar / **COBY BATY** – vocals, drums, percussion / **VINNIE LEARY** – guitar / **MARK KRAMER** – bass, keyboards (SHOCKABILLY)

New Rose FRANCE S.P.V.

Apr 85. (lp) **REFUSE TO BE BURNT-OUT (live in the 80's)** [ ] [-]
– The five feet / If you were to be President / Nova slum goddess / Nicaragua / Fingers of the sun / Wide wide river / How sweet I roamed / Refuse to be burnt-out / Country punk / C.I.A. man / Ban the bomb / Keeping the issues alive. *(cd-iss.Mar95 on 'Big Beat')*

— Now without **KRAMER** who joined BUTTHOLE SURFERS then BONGWATER.

Mar 86. (lp)(c) **NO MORE SLAVERY** [ ] [-]

— **SANDERS, KUPFERBERG, TAYLOR, BATY,** plus **SCOTT PETITO** – bass, guitar, synth / **MARILYN GRISPELL** – piano, synth / **LARRY BRODY + ANNE JACOBSON + LESLIE RITTER** – vocals.

Jun 87. (d-lp) **STAR PEACE (A MUSICAL DRAMA IN 3 ACTS)** [ ] [-]
– Act 1, Scene 1: Mr. President, this is the greatest hour – Dazzle the sky – The wagon trains – This evil empire – Go for it – La traison des journalists – the prayer / Hymn to America / Act 1, Scene 2: Rose petals veiled in smoke – the President's in my pocket / Act 1, Scene 3: Technology is going to act us free – There's a dim bulb burning – The pax coel: America / Slapping leather in strange, strange skies – The great spasm – the battle in the sky – I see Lois / Act 2, Scene 1: Da Vinci once thought of a secret weapon – A nuke free world – I believe in destiny / Act 2, Scene 2: The threat, the threat – How much do you really know about those whom you hate – the metastasis – The peer jeer – He was such a scientist / Act 2, Scene 3: Protest and survive – World wide green – Till the wormwood fell from the sky no more / Act 3, Scene 1: The rapture song – The sharing mind – Talking in nuke tongue – The list from Plymouth rock / Act 3, Scene 3: Liberty not war – The secret agenda / Act 3, Scene 3: She must die – The terrible things / Act 3, Scene 4: A death in the mountains – Oh the pain – Do not mourn for me.

– compilations, others, etc. –

Jun 75. E.S.P.; (lp) **FUGS 4, ROUNDERS SCORE** (out-takes some with HOLY MODAL ROUNDERS) [-] [ ]

Jun 94. Ace; (cd) **LIVE FROM THE 60's (live)** [ ] [-]

Oct 95. Big Beat; (cd) **THE REAL WOODSTOCK FESTIVAL (live)** [ ] [-]

TULI KUPFERBERG

not issued E.S.P.

1967. (lp)(gold-lp) **NO DEPOSIT, NO RETURN** [-] [ ]
– Pubol / Social studies / The hidden dissuaders lifetime guarentee / The art science / Want ads 1 / Rangoon / Rambler purina lanoflo / The hyperemiator / The sap glove / The bunny mother / Auto-da-fe / Fields matrimonial service / Want ads 2 / Howard Johnsons army / No deposit, no return.

Shimmy Disc Shimmy Disc

1989. (lp)(cd) **TULI AND FRIENDS** [-] [ ]

— In the 80's KUPFERBERG became director of the 'Revolting Theater' New York, after earlier surviving a jump off of Brooklyn Bridge.

ED SANDERS

not issued Reprise

1971. (lp) **SANDERS' TRUCKSTOP** [-] [ ]

– Jimmy Joe / The hippybilly boy / The maple court tragedy / Heartbreak crash pad / Banshee / The plaster song / The illiad / Breadtray mountain / The A.B.M. machine / They're cuttin' my coffin at the sawmill / Homesick blues / Pindar's revenge.

not issued E.S.P.

1972. (lp) **BEER CANS ON THE MOON** [-] [ ]

— ED SANDERS retired from music scene, but became underground writer, also managing to write a best-seller (The Family) about the Charles Manson case.

FUN BOY THREE (see under ⇒ HALL, Terry)

FUN-DA-MENTAL

Formed: Bradford, England ... mid-'91 by boss of 'Nation' records AKI NAWAZ (who had been drummer for SOUTHERN DEATH CULT alongside IAN ASTBURY, before leaving him to form GETTING THE FEAR). He recruited fellow Asians BAD-SHA LALLAMAN, GOLDFINGER and DJ OBEYO. Contributed an anti-SALMAN RUSHDIE song and video 'RIGHTEOUS PREACHER' to a Yorkshire TV programme 'Rhythm & Raag'. Needless to say, this was banned. • **Style:** Multi-ethnic Muslim militant rappers described as The Asian PUBLIC ENEMY or even the Pakistani PISTOLS. • **Songwriters: AKI / QURESHI / MATHARU.** • **Trivia:** Were credited on POP WILL EAT ITSELF's 'Ich Bin Auslander'. **Note:** Not to be confused with other band of same name who released disco single 'Somebody Tells Me' for 'Sticky' label.

Recommended: SEIZE THE TIME (*8)

PROPA GHANDI (AKI NAWAZ) – vocals (ex-SOUTHERN DEATH CULT, ex-GETTING THE FEAR) / **BAD-SHA LALLAMAN (QURESHI)** – vocals / **MAN THAROO GOLDFINGER** (b. INDER MATHARU) – vocals / **OBEYO** – DJ

Nation Beggar's

1992. (12") **RIGHTEOUS PREACHER. / JANAAM – THE MESSAGE / JANAAM DUB MESSAGE II** [ ] [ ]

Oct 92. (12") **GHANDI'S REVENGE. / AZAAN – THE CALLING / ('A'mix)** [ ] [ ]

Feb 93. (12") **WRATH OF THE BLACKMAN. / SISTER INDIA** [ ] [ ]

Nov 93. (12"ep)(cd-ep) **COUNTRYMAN / TRIBAL REVOLUTION. / COUNTRYMAN (Deliverance mix) / TRIBAL REVOLUTION (Black Buffalo mix)** [ ] [ ]
(c-ep+=)(cd-ep+=) – (2-'A'mixes) / ('B'mix).

— GOLDFINGER and LALLAMAN departed taking OBEYO with them. Legal wrangles ensued with AKI and new member BLACKA D (DAVE WATTS). They surprisingly lost out to the other three and were later to form DET-RA-MENTAL. Replaced by **QUERSHI + MATHARU**

May 94. (12"ep)(cd-ep) **DOG TRIBE / ('A'mix). / ('A'dub) / ('A'instrumental)** [ ] [ ]

Jun 94. (cd)(c)(d-lp) **SEIZE THE TIME** [74] [ ]
– Dog tribe / Seize the time / Mera Mazab / President Propa Ghandi / No more fear / Dollars or sense / Mother India / MMr.Bubbleman / English breakfast / Belfast solution? / Fatherland / New world order / White / Gold burger / Back to basix.

Aug 94. (12"ep)(cd-ep) **MOTHER INDIA. / ('A'mixes)** [ ] [ ]

Oct 94. (12") **WHITE GOLD BURGER. / ('A'-liberation time tolerance mix) / ('A'victory mix)** [ ] [ ]
(cd-s+=) – ('A'-Personal exploration of ignorance and hate mix).

Jul 95. (cd)(c)(lp) **WITH INTENT TO PERVERSE THE CAUSE OF JUSTICE** [ ] [ ]
–

Nov 95. (12"ep)(cd-ep) **MOTHER INDIA / SPIRIT OF THE TIGER (Moody Boyz remix) / SABRES AT DAWN (Sabres Of Paradise remix) / THE JUDGEMENT (remix)** [ ] [ ]

— above featured SUBI SHAH

FUNKADELIC (see under ⇒ CLINTON, George)

FUTURE SOUND OF LONDON

Formed: London, England ... 1991 by HUMANOID techno Manchester dance duo GARY COCKBAIN & BRIAN DOUGANS. They had a UK Top 20 hit late in 1988 with 'STAKKER HUMANOID'. Spawned other projects SEMI REAL, YAGE, METROPOLIS + ART SCIENCE TECHNOLOGY before 'Virgin' signed the duo as FUTURE SOUND OF LONDON in '92. • **Style:** Modern ambient conceptual soundscapes of gothic beauty, reminiscent of early TANGERINE DREAM. Could be dubbed The PREHISTORIC SOUND OF GERMANY? • **Songwriters:** DOUGANS / COCKBAIN except FLAK; co-written w / ROBERT FRIPP plus WILLIAMS / GROSSART / THOMPSON / NIGHTINGALE. OMNIPRESENCE co-wriiten with KLAUS SCHULZE. • **Trivia:** Augmented on NOMAD's single 'Your Love Has Lifted Me', SYLVIAN-FRIPP's album 'Darshan' and APOLLO 440's 'Liquid Cool'.

Recommended: ACCELERATOR (*7) / LIFEFORMS (*8)

HUMANOID

GARRY COCKBAIN (b. Bedford, England) – keyboards / **BRIAN DOUGANS** (b.Scotland) – keyboards

Westside not issued

Oct 88. (7") **STAKKER HUMANOID. / (part 2)** [6] [-]
(12"+=) – ('A'-open mix).
(re-iss.12"+cd-ep 8 mixes Jul92 on 'Jumpin' & Pumpin'', hit No.40)

— (note 7"+c-s+cd-s; original part 2 was repl. by 'A'-Smart Systems remix).

Apr 89. (7")(12") **SLAM. / BASS INVADERS** [54] [-]
(12"+=)(cd-s+=) – ('A'dub mix) / ('A'hip house version).

Aug 89. (7") **TONIGHT. / ?** [ ] [-]
(12"+=)(cd-s+=) –

Oct 89. (lp)(c)(cd) **GLOBAL** [ ] [ ]
–

Apr 90. (12"ep) **THE DEEP (3 mixes). / CRY BABY** [ ] [-]

The duo then formed SMART SYSTEMS, before re-grouping as . . .

FUTURE SOUND OF LONDON

same line-up as above.

Jumpin' & Pumpin' not issued

Feb 92. (12"ep) **PAPUA NEW GUINEA (Dali mix) / ('A'dumb child of a Q mix) / ('A'-Qube mix)** [22] [ ]
(12"ep)(c-ep)(cd-ep) – (the remixes by Andy Weatherall & Graham Massey). *(re-iss.May95)*

Jun 92. (cd)(c) **ACCELERATOR** [75] [ ]
– Expander / Stolen documents / While others cry / Calcium / It's not my problem / Papau New Guinea / Moscow / 1 in 8 / Pulse state / Central industrial. *(re-iss.Aug94)*

— above featured **BASIL CLARKE** – vocals (ex-YARGO)

1992. (12"ep) **EXPANDER (remix). / MOSCOW (remix) / CENTRAL INDUSTRIAL (remix)** [ ] [ ]
(cd-ep+=) – ('A'radio remix). *(re-iss Jul94, hit 72)*

AMORPHOUS ANDROGYNOUS

Virgin Virgin

Jun 93. (cd)(lp) **TALES OF EPHIDRINA** [ ] [ ]
– Swab / Mountain goat / In mind / Ephidrina / Auto pimp / Pod room / Fat cat.

Aug 93. (12"ep)(cd-ep) **ENVIRONMENTS** [ ] [ ]

FUTURE SOUND OF LONDON

Virgin Virgin

Oct 93. (12")(c-s) **CASCADE. / ('A'-parts 2-5)** [ ] [ ]
(cd-s+=) – ('A'-short form mix).

May 94. (d-cd)(c)(d-lp) **LIFEFORMS** [6] [ ]
– Cascade / Ill flower / Flak / Bird wings / Dead skin cells / Lifeforms / Eggshell / Among myselves / / Domain / Spineless jelly / Interstat / Vertical pig / Cerebral / Life form ends / Vit / Omnipresence / Room 208 / Elaborate burn / Little brother.

Aug 94. (7") **LIFEFORMS. / ('A'alternative mix)** [14] [ ]
(12"+=)(c-s+=)(cd-s+=) – ('A'-paths 1-7).

— (above featured LIZ FRASER (of COCTEAU TWINS) on vocals)

Dec 94. (cd)(c)(d-lp) **I.S.D.N.** [62] [ ]
– Just a f***in' idiot / Far out son of lung and the ramblings of a madman / Appendage / Slider / Smokin' Japanese babe / You're creeping me out / Eyes-pop-skin-explodes-everybody's dead / It's my mind that works / Dirty shadows / Tired of bugs / Egypt / Are they fighting us? / Hot knives. *(re-iss Jun95 with 3 new remixed tracks, hit No.44)*

— (In 1994, they were also at time abbreviated to F.S.O.L.)

May 95. (12"ep)(c-ep)(cd-ep) **FAR OUT SON OF LUNG AND THE RAMBLINGS OF A MADMAN. /** [22] [ ]
– Ramblings of a madman / Snake hips / Smokin' Japanese babe / Amoeba.

Peter GABRIEL

Born: 13 May'50, Cobham, Surrey, England. After 8 years as leader of GENESIS, he left in May'75 to go solo, although he didn't venture into the studio for over a year. Early in '77, he released first solo album, which was produced by Bob Ezrin, and this hit UK Top 10. A cut from it 'SOLISBURY HILL', also made Top 20, but its follow-up 'MODERN LOVE' failed. In Summer of '78, he issued second Top 10 album, also titled 'PETER GABRIEL', but produced by ROBERT FRIPP (ex-KING CRIMSON). In 1980, he had a Top 10 single 'GAMES WITHOUT FRONTIERS', which previewed No.1 third album, produced by Steve Lillywhite. He continued as a major artist throughout the 80's and early 90's. • **Style:** Adventurous rock performer, whose enigmatic personality always shined through into music. He experimentated with African rhythms, pop/rock music and more recently film soundtracks (i.e. 'BIRDY' & 'PASSION – MUSIC FOR THE LAST TEMPTATION OF CHRIST'). • **Songwriters:** Self-composed except; STRAWBERRY FIELDS FOREVER (Beatles) / SUZANNE (Leonard Cohen). • **Trivia:** In 1982, he co-wrote & produced 'Animals Have More Fun' for JIMMY PURSEY (ex-SHAM 69). Early in 1987, he won 'Best Video Award' for his revolutionary 'claymation' video single 'SLEDGEHAMMER'. He has also guested for ROBBIE ROBERTSON (1987 album) & JONI MITCHELL (1991 album).

Recommended: SHAKIN' THE TREE: SIXTEEN GOLDEN GREATS (*9).

PETER GABRIEL – vocals, keyboards (ex-GENESIS, ex-GARDEN WALL) with **TONY LEVIN** – bass / **STEVE HUNTER** – guitar / **LARRY FAST** – keyboards / **JIMMY MAELEN** – percussion / **ALAN SCHWARTZBERG** – drums / **ROBERT FRIPP** – guitar

Charisma | Atco

Feb 77. (lp)(c) **PETER GABRIEL** [7] [38]
– Moribund the burgermeister / Solisbury Hill / Modern love / Excuse me / Humdrum / Slowburn / Waiting for the big one / Down the Dolce Vita / Here comes the flood. *(cd-iss.May83 + re-iss.+cd.Aug88)*

Mar 77. (7") **SOLISBURY HILL. / MORIBUND THE BURGERMEISTER** [13] [68]

Jun 77. (7") **MODERN LOVE. / SLOWBURN** [ ] [ ]

— now with **FRIPP,** plus **JERRY MAROTTA** – drums / **ROY BITTAN** – piano / **SID McGINNIS** – guitar / **BAYETE** – keyboards

May 78. (7") **D.I.Y.. / PERSPECTIVE** [ ] [-]
(12") – ('A'remix) / Mother of violence / Me and my teddy bear.

Charisma | Atlantic

Jun 78. (lp)(c) **PETER GABRIEL** [10] [45]
– On the air / D.I.Y. / Mother of violence / A wonderful day in a one-way world / White shadow / Indigo / Animal magic / Exposure / Flotsam and jetsam / Perspective / Home sweet home. *(re-iss.Mar84) (cd-iss.May87)*

Jun 78. (7") **D.I.Y. / MOTHER OF VIOLENCE** [-] [ ]

Charisma | Mercury

Feb 80. (7"m) **GAMES WITHOUT FRONTIERS. / THE START / I DON'T REMEMBER** [4] [48] Aug 80

May 80. (7") **NO SELF CONTROL. / LEAD A NORMAL LIFE** [33] [ ]

— now with **FRIPP, LEVIN + MAROTTA** plus guests **PHIL COLLINS** – drums / **KATE BUSH + PAUL WELLER** – vocals

May 80. (lp)(c) **PETER GABRIEL** [1] [22]
– Intruder / No self control / Start / I don't remember / Family snapshot / And through the wire / Not one of us / Lead a normal life / Biko. *(re-iss.Sep83) (cd-iss.May87)*

Aug 80. (7")(12") **BIKO. / SHOSHOLOZA / JETZ KOMMT DIE FLUT** [38] [ ]

— guests on next incl. **DAVID LORD** – synthesizers, co-producer / **JOHN ELLIS** – guitar / + some of last line-up

Charisma | Geffen

Sep 82. (lp)(c) **PETER GABRIEL** [6] [28]
– The rhythm of the heat / San Jacinto / I have the touch / The family and the fishing net / Shock the monkey / Lay your hands on me / Wallflower / Kiss of life. *(US title 'SECURITY'; and on a sticker) (re-iss.Sep83) (cd-iss.1986)*

Sep 82. (7")(12") **SHOCK THE MONKEY. / SOFT DOG** [58] [29]
(7"pic-d) – ('A'side) / ('B'instrumental).

Dec 82. (7") **I HAVE THE TOUCH. / ACROSS THE RIVER** [ ] [ ]

Jun 83. (d-lp)(c) **PETER GABRIEL PLAYS LIVE (live)** [8] [44]
– The rhythm of the heat / I have the touch / Not one of us / Family snapshot / D.I.Y. / The family and the fishing net / Intruder / I go swimming / San Jacinto / Solisbury Hill / No self control / I don't remember / Shock the monkey / Humdrum / On the air / Biko. *(re-iss.Jun83) (cd-iss.Jun85 + 1988; omits 4 tracks).*

Jun 83. (7") **I DON'T REMEMBER (live). / SOLISBURY HILL (live)** [62] [ ]
(12"+=) – Kiss of life (live). (free-12"w/ 12") – GAMES WITHOUT FRONTIERS (live). / SCHNAPPSCHUSS

Virgin | Geffen

Nov 83. (7") **SOLISBURY HILL (live). / I GO SWIMMING (live)** [-] [84]

May 84. (7") **WALK THROUGH THE FIRE. / THE RACE** [69] [ ]
(12"+=) – I have the touch (remix).

Mar 85. (lp)(c)(cd) **BIRDY – MUSIC FROM THE FILM (soundtrack)** [51] [ ]
– At night / Floating dogs / Quiet and alone / Close up / Slow water / Dressing the wound / Birdy's flight / Slow marimbas / The heat / Sketchpad with trumpet and voice / Under lock and key / Powerhouse at the foot of the mountain. *(re-iss.Apr90)*

— with **MAROTTA, LEVIN** plus **DANIEL LANOIS** – guitar, co-producer / **MANU KATCHE** – percussion / **YOUSSOU N'DOUR + KATE BUSH** – guest vocals / **STEWART COPELAND** – drums /**etc.**

Apr 86. (7") **SLEDGEHAMMER. / JOHN HAS A HEADACHE** [4] [1]
('A'dance-12"+=) – I have the touch ('85 remix).
(12"++=)(c-s++=) – Biko.
(12"+=) – Don't break this rhythm. *(US; b-side)*

May 86. (lp)(c)(cd) **SO** [1] [2]
– Red rain / Sledgehammer / Don't give up / That voice again / In your eyes / Mercy street / Big time / We do what we're told. (cd+=) – This is the picture (excellent birds).

Sep 86. (7") **IN YOUR EYES. / ('A'-Special mix)** [-] [26]
(re-iss.Jun89 on 'WTG' US, reached 41)

Oct 86. (7") **DON'T GIVE UP. (by "PETER GABRIEL & KATE BUSH") / IN YOUR EYES** [9] [-]

Jan 87. (7") **BIG TIME. / WE DO WHAT WE'RE TOLD** [-] [8]

Mar 87. (7") **BIG TIME. / CURTAINS** [13] [-]
(12"+=) – ('A'extended).
(c-s) – ('A'extended) / ('B'side) / Across the river / No self control. *(re-iss.3"cd-s.1989)*

Mar 87. (7") **DON'T GIVE UP ("PETER GABRIEL & KATE BUSH"). / CURTAINS** [-] [72]

Jun 87. (7") **RED RAIN. / GAGA** [46] [ ]
(12"+=)(c-s+=) – Walk through the fire.

Jan 88. (7")(12")(c-s) **BIKO (live). / NO MORE APARTEID** [49] [-]
(cd-s+=) – I have the touch ('85 remix).

— In May 89, PETER ws credited with YOUSSOU N'DOUR on minor hit single 'SHAKIN THE TREE'.

Real World | Geffen

Jun 89. (d-lp)(c)(cd) **PASSION (Soundtrack film 'The Last Temptation Of Christ')** [29] [60]
– The feeling begins / Gethsemane / Of these, hope / Lazarus raised / Of these, hope – reprise / In doubt / A different drum / Zaar / Troubled / Open* / Before night falls / With this love / Sandstorm / Stigmata** / Passion / With this love – choir / Wall of breath / The promise of shadows / Disturbed / It is accomplished / Bread and wine. *(*= with SHANKAR) (**= with MAHMOUD TABRIZI ZADEH)*

Sep 92. (7")(c-s) **DIGGING IN THE DIRT. / QUIET STEAM** [24] [52]
(cd-s+=)/ /(cd-s++=) – ('A'instrumental). / / Bashi-bazouk.

Oct 92. (cd)(c)(lp) **US** [2] [2]
– Come talk to me / Love to be loved / Blood of Eden / Steam / Digging in the dirt / Fourteen black paintings / Kiss that frog / Secret world.

Jan 93. (7")(c-s) **STEAM. / ('A'-Carter . . . mix)** [10] [32] Nov 92
(cd-s) – ('A' mix) / Games without frontiers (mix) / (2 'A' extended + dub mix or Games (other mix)

Mar 93. (7")(c-s) **BLOOD OF EDEN. / MERCY STREET** [43] [ ]
(cd-s+=) – ('A'-special mix)
(cd-s+=) – Sledgehammer.

Sep 93. (7")(c-s) **KISS THAT FROG. / ('A' mindblender mix)** [46] [ ]
(cd-s+=) – Digging in the dirt.
(cd-s+=) – Across the river / Shaking the tree (Bottrill remix).

— Below single, another from 'Philadelphia' film on 'Epic' records.

Jun 94. (7")(c-s) **LOVE TOWN. / LOVE TO BE LOVED** [49] [ ]
(cd-s+=) – Different drum.

— live with **TONY LEVIN** – bass, vocals / **DAVID RHODES** – guitar, vocals / **MANU KATCHE** – drums / **PAULA COLE** – vocals / **JEAN CLAUDE NAIMRO** – keyboards, vocals / **RAVI SHANKAR** – violin, vocals / **LEVON MINASSIAN** – doudouk

Aug 94. (c-s) **SECRET WORLD (live). / COME TALK TO ME** [39] [ ]
(cd-ep) – ('A'live) / Red rain (live) / San Jacinto (live) / Mercy Street (live).

Sep 94. (d-cd)(d-c) **SECRET WORLD LIVE (live)** [10] [23]
– Come talk to me / Steam / Across the river / Slow marimbas / Shaking the tree / Red rain / Blood of Eden / Kiss that frog / Washing of the water / Solisbury Hill / Digging in the dirt / Sledgehammer / Secret world / Don't give up / In your eyes.

– compilations, etc. –

1988. Virgin; (3"cd-ep) **SOLISBURY HILL / MORIBUND THE BURGERMEISTER / SOLISBURY HILL (live)** [ ] [ ]
(re-iss.Apr90)

Oct 90. Virgin; (3xcd-box) **PETER GABRIEL 1 / 2 / 3** [ ] [ ]

Nov 90. Virgin/ US= Geffen; (cd)(c)(lp) **SHAKING THE TREE – SIXTEEN GOLDEN GREATS** [11] [48]
– Solisbury Hill / I don't remember / Sledgehammer / Family snapshot / Mercy Street / Shaking the tree / Don't give up / Here comes the flood / Games without frontiers / Shock the monkey / Big time / Biko.
(cd+c+=) – San Juanito / Red rain / I have the touch / Zaar.

Dec 90. Virgin; (7")(c-s) **SOLISBURY HILL. / SHAKING THE TREE (by "PETER GABRIEL & YOUSSOU N'DOUR")** [57] [ ]
(12"+=)(cd-s+=) – Games without frontiers.

Mar 83. Charisma; (d-c) **PETER GABRIEL 1 / PETER GABRIEL 2** [ ] [-]
Jan 83. Old Gold; (7") **SOLISBURY HILL. / GAMES WITHOUT FRONTIERS** [ ] [-]

GADGETS (see under ⇒ THE THE)

GALAXIE 500

Formed: New York City, USA . . . early 80's by DEAN WAREHAM, NAOMI YANG and DAMON KRUKOWSKI. In the late 80's, after completing an lp, they signed to UK indie label 'Rough Trade', for whom they released album 'ON FIRE'. • **Style:** College fast-guitar based band. • **Songwriters:** Group, except a RUTLES cover!, plus LISTEN THE SNOW IS FALLING (Yoko Ono) / HERE SHE COMES NOW (Velvet Underground) / CEREMONY (New Order) / ISN'T IT A PITY (George Harrison). • **Trivia:** KRAMER of The Butthole Surfers was their 1990 producer.

Recommended: ON FIRE (*6)

MICHAEL DEAN WAREHAM (b. 1 Aug'63, Wellington, New Zealand) – vox, guitar / **NAOMI YANG** (b.15 Sep'64) – bass, vocals / **DAMON KRUKOWSKI** (b. 6 Sep'63) – drums, percussion

Shimmy Disc / Aurora

Aug 89. (lp)(cd) **TODAY** [ ] [ ] Oct88
– Flowers / Pictures / Parking lot / Don't let our youth go to waste / Temperature's rising / Oblivious / It's getting late / Instrumental / Tugboat. (cd+=) – King of Spain / Crazy.

Sep 89. (12")(cd-s) **FOURTH OF JULY. / HERE SHE COMES NOW** [ ] [ ]
(re-iss.Sep90 on 'Rough Trade')

Rough Trade / R.Trade

Oct 89. (lp)(c)(cd) **ON FIRE** [ ] [ ]
– Blue thunder / Tell me / Snowstorm / Strange / When will you come home / Decomposing trees / Another day / Leave the planet / Plastic bird / Isn't it a pity.

Feb 90. (7") **CEREMONY. / BLUE THUNDER** [ ] [ ]
(12"+=)(cd-s+=) – Cold night / Victory garden.

— (below 45 on 'Caff')

mid90. (7"ltd) **RAIN. / DON'T LET OUR YOUTH GO TO WASTE** [ ] [-]

Oct 90. (cd)(c)(lp) **THIS IS OUR MUSIC** [ ] [ ]
– Fourth of July / Hearing voices / Spook / Summertime / Way up high / Listen, the snow is falling / Sorry / Melt away / King of Spain, part two.

— In Spring '91, DEAN WAREHAM departed to work on solo project and guest for MERCURY REV. The other two became PIERRE ETOILE and went in studio with Boston musicians.

DEAN WAREHAM

w / **JIMMY CHAMBERS** – (guest) drums (of MERCURY REV) / **JUSTIN HAREWOOD** – bass (ex-CHILLS) / **BYRON GUTHRIE** – drums (ex-ULTRA VIVID SCENE)

Mint Tea-Jungle / Tea?

Feb 92. (12"ep)(cd-ep) **ANAESTHESIA. / I CAN'T WAIT / TOMATO PEOPLE** [ ] [ ]

LUNA 2

DEAN WAREHAM with **JUSTIN HARWOOD** (of The CHILLS) / **STANLEY DEMESKI** (of The FEELIES)

Elektra / Elektra

Aug 92. (cd)(c) **LUNAPARK** [ ] [ ]
– Slide / Anaesthesia / Slash your tyres / Crazy people / Time / Smile / I can't wait / Hey sister / I want everything / Time to quit / Goodbye / We're both confused.

Mar 94. (cd)(c) **BEWITCHED** [ ] [ ]
– California (all the way) / Tiger Lily / Friendly advice / Bewitched / This time around / Great Jones Street / Going home / Into the fold / I know you tried / Sleeping pill.

Beggar's B / Beggar's B

Apr 95. (12"ep)(cd-ep) **BONNIE AND CLYDE EP** [ ] [ ]
– Bonnie and Clyde / Chinatown / Thank you for sending me an angel.

above w/ guest LAETITIA SADLER – vocals (of STEREOLAB)

Aug 95. (cd)(c)(lp) **PENTHOUSE** [ ] [ ]
– Chinatown / Sideshow by the seashore / Moon palace / Double feature / 23 minutes in Brussels / Lost in space / Rhythm king / Kalanazoo / Hedgehog / Freakin' and peakin' / Bonnie and Clyde (The Clyde Barrow version).

Nov 95. (7") HEDGEHOG. / 23 MINUTES IN BRUSSELS [ ] [ ]
(cd-s+=) – No regrets / Happy New Year.

PIERRE ETOILE

DAMON KRUKOWSKI / NAOMI YANG

Rough Trade / Rough Trade

Jul 91. (12"ep)(cd-ep) **IN THE SUN. / 1969 / THIS CAR CLIMBED MT. WASHINGTON** [ ] [ ]

DAMON & NAOMI

Shimmy Disc / Shimmy Disc

Nov 92. (cd)(c)(lp) **MORE SAD HITS** [ ] [ ]
– E.T.A. / Little red record co. / Information age / Laika / This car climbed Mt.Washington / Astrafiammante / Boston's daily temperature / (Scene change) / Sir Thomas and Sir Robert / Once more / This changing world / Memories.

Rory GALLAGHER

Born: 2 Mar'49, Ballyshannon, Donegal, Ireland. After playing in various school bands in Cork, he formed The FONTANA SHOWBAND, who soon became The IMPACT. In 1965, they secured residencies in Hamburg, mostly playing CHUCK BERRY songs. In 1966, he formed TASTE with NORMAN DAMERY and ERIC KITTERINGHAM, but they departed 2 years later, and were replaced by CHARLIE McCRACKEN and JOHN WILSON. After a debut lp failed to breakthrough, they hit UK Top20 in 1970 with 'ON THE BOARDS'. However they soon disbanded and GALLAGHER went solo. His first lp was self-titled, and made UK Top40 lists. He progressed the following year, when 'LIVE IN EUROPE' lp hit Top 10. He and his always accomplished sidekicks, scored a few more successes, and persevered with rock industry into the 90's. • **Style:** The gentle man of rock and blues, described as the people's guitarist, due to his unconformist rock star look (i.e. lumberjack shirt, jeans and ruffled hair). Renowned for his heavy bouts of seroius drinking. His inspirations stemmed from B.B. KING, FREDDIE KING, ALBERT KING, etc. • **Songwriters:** GALLAGHER penned many new blues numbers, incorporating past standards; SUGAR MAMA + DON'T START ME TALKING (Sonny Boy Williamson) / I'M MOVING ON (Hank Snow) / I TAKE WHAT I WANT (Hayes-Porter-Hedges) / ALL AROUND MAN (Davenport) / OUT ON THE WESTERN PLAINS (Leadbelly) / RIDE ON RED, RIDE ON (Levy-Glover-Reid) / I WONDER WHO (. . . Boyle) / AS THE CROW FLIES (Josh White) / JUST A LITTLE BIT (Dexter Gordon) / MESSING WITH THE KID (Julie London) / PISTOL SLAPPER BLUES (. . . Allen) / etc. • **Trivia:** VINCENT CRANE of ATOMIC ROOSTER guested on RORY's debut lp in '71. GALLAGHER also sessioned on albums by MUDDY WATERS (London Sessions) / JERRY LEE LEWIS (London Sessions) / LONNIE DONEGAN (Putting On The Style) / etc.

Recommended: THE BEST OF RORY GALLAGHER & TASTE (*6) / IRISH TOUR '74 (*7)

TASTE

RORY GALLAGHER – vocals, guitar / **CHARLIE McCRACKEN** (b.26 Jun'48) – bass repl. ERIC KITTERINGHAM / **JOHN WILSON** (b. 3 Dec'47) – drums (ex-THEM) repl. NORMAN DAMERY

Major Minor / not issued

Apr 68. (7") **BLISTER ON THE MOON. / BORN ON THE WRONG SIDE OF TIME** [ ] [-]
(re-iss.Jul70)

Polydor / Atco

Mar 69. (7") **BORN ON THE WRONG SIDE OF TIME. / SAME OLD STORY** [ ] [-]

Apr 69. (lp) **TASTE** [ ] [ ]
– Blister on the moon / Leaving blues / Sugar mama / Hail / Born on the wrong side of time / Dual carriageway of pain / Same old story / Hail / Catfish / I'm moving on. *(re-iss.'79) (cd-iss.Aug92)*

Jan 70. (lp) **ON THE BOARDS** [18] [ ]
– What's going on / Railway & gun / It's happened before, it'll happen again / If the day was any longer / Morning sun / Eat my words / On the boards / If I don't sing I'll cry / See here / I'll remember. *(cd-iss.Apr94)*

Feb 71. (lp) **LIVE TASTE (live)** [ ] [-]
– Sugar mama / Gamblin' blues / I feel so good (Pt.1 & 2) / Catfish / Same old story. *(cd-iss.Apr94)*

— GALLAGHER went solo. The other two formed STUD. McCRACKEN also joined SPENCER DAVIS GROUP

RORY GALLAGHER

solo – vocals, guitar with **GERRY MacAVOY** – bass (ex-DEEP JOY) / **WILGAR CAMPBELL** – drums (ex-METHOD)

Polydor / Atlantic

May 71. (lp)(c) **RORY GALLAGHER** [32] [ ]
– Laundromat / Just the smile / I fall apart / Wave myself goodbye / Hands up / Sinner boy / For the last time / It's you / I'm not surprised / Can't believe it's true. *(re-iss.'79 on 'Chrysalis')*

Jan 71. (7"m) **IT'S YOU. / JUST THE SMILE / SINNER BOY** [ ] [ ]

Nov 71. (lp)(c) **DEUCE** [39] [ ]
– Used to be / I'm not awake yet / Don't know where I'm going / Maybe I will / Whole lot of people / In your town / Out of my mind / Should've learn't my lesson / There's a light / Crest of a wave. *(re-iss.'79 on 'Chrysalis')*

Polydor / Polydor

May 72. (lp)(c) **LIVE! IN EUROPE (live)** [9] [ ]
– Messin' with the kid / Laundromat / I could've had religion / Pistol slapper blues / Going to my home town / Bullfrog blues / In your town. *(re-iss.'79 on 'Chrysalis')*

— **ROD DE'ATH** – drums (ex-KILLING FLOOR) repl. CAMPBELL / added **LOU MARTIN** – keyboards, mandolin (ex-KILLING FLOOR)

Feb 73. (lp)(c) **BLUEPRINT** [12] [ ]
– Walk on hot coals / Daughter of the Everglades / Banker's blues / Hands off / Race the breeze / The seventh son of a seventh son / Unmilitary two-step / If I had a reason. *(re-iss.'79 on 'Chrysalis') (cd-iss.Jan94)*

Aug 73. (lp)(c) **TATTOO** [32] [ ]
– Tattoo'd lady / Cradle rock / 20:20 vision / They don't make them like you anymore / Livin' like a trucker / Sleep on a clothes-line / A million miles away / Admit it. *(re-iss.'79 on 'Chrysalis') (cd-iss.Jan94)*

Jul 74. (d-lp)(c) **IRISH TOUR '74 (live)** [36] [ ]
– Cradle rock / I wonder who (who's gonn be your sweet man) / Tattoo'd lady / Too much alcohol / As the crow flies / A million miles away / Walk on hot coals / Who's that coming / Back on my (stompin' ground) / Just a little bit. *(re-iss.'79 on 'Chrysalis') (re-iss.+d-cd May88 on 'Demon')*

Chrysalis Chrysalis

Oct 75. (lp)(c) **AGAINST THE GRAIN**
– Let me in / Cross me off your list / Ain't too good / Souped up Ford / Bought and sold / I take what I want / Lost at sea / All around man / Out on the western plain / At the bottom. *(re-iss.+cd.May91 on 'Castle')*

Nov 75. (7") **SOUPED UP FORD. / I TAKE WHAT I WANT**

Oct 76. (lp)(c) **CALLING CARD** 32
– Do you read me / Country mile / Moonchild / Calling card / I'll admit you're gone / Secret agent / Jacknife beat / Edged in blue / Barley and grape rag. *(re-iss.+cd Jun91 on 'Essential') (cd re-iss.Mar94)*

— **TED McKENNA** – drums (ex-SENSATIONAL ALEX HARVEY BAND) repl.DE'ATH and MARTIN (to RAMROD)

Oct 76. (lp)(c) **PHOTO FINISH**
– Shin kicker / Brute force and ignorance / Cruise on out / Cloak and dagger / Overnight bag / Shadow play / The Mississippi sheiks / The last of the indepenents / Fuel to the fire.

Jan 79. (7"m) **SHADOW PLAY. / SOUPED UP FORD / BRUTE FORCE AND IGNORANCE**

Aug 79. (7")(7"colrd) **PHILBY. / HELLCAT / COUNTRY MILE**

Sep 79. (lp)(c) **TOP PRIORITY** 56
– Follow me / Philby / Wayward child / Keychain / At the depot / Bad penny / Just hit town / Off the handle / Public enemy No.1. *(re-iss.+cd May88 on 'Demon')*

Aug 80. (7")(7"colrd) **WAYWARD CHILD (live). / KEYCHAIN**

Sep 80. (lp)(c) **STAGE STRUCK (live)** 40
– Shin kicker / Wayward child / Brute force and ignorance / Moonchild / Follow me / Bought and sold / The last of the independents / Shadow play.

1980. (7") **HELLCAT. / NOTHIN' BUT THE DEVIL**

— (May81) **GALLAGHER** with **McAVOY** brought in **BRENDAN O'NEILL** – drums repl. McKENNA who joined GREG LAKE BAND then MSG

Apr 82. (lp)(c) **JINX** 68
– Signals / The Devil made me do it / Double vision / Easy come, easy go / Big guns / Jinxed / Bourbon / Ride on Red, ride on / Loose talk. *(re-iss.+cd May88 on 'Demon')*

Jun 82. (7") **BIG GUNS. / THE DEVIL MADE ME DO IT**

1983. (10"ep) **SHADOWPLAY / BRUTE FORCE AND IGNORANCE. / MOONCHILD / SOUPED UP FORD** -

Capo-Demon Intercord

Jul 87. (lp)(c)(cd) **DEFENDER** -
– Kickback city / Loanshark blues / Continental O.P. / I ain't no saint / Failsafe day / Road to Hell / Doing time / Smear campaign / Don't start me talkin' / Seven days. *(c+cd+=) – (below free 7") (free-7".w/a) –* **SEEMS TO ME. / NO PEACE FOR THE WICKED**

— guests **MARK FELTHAM** – harmonica / **LOU MARTIN** – piano / **JOHN EARL** – saxes. / **GERAINT WATKINS** – accordion / **JOHN COOKE** – keyboards / **RAY BEAVIS** – tenor sax. / **DICK HANSON** – trumpet.

Jun 90. (cd)(c)(lp) **FRESH EVIDENCE**
– 'Kid' gloves / The king of Zydeco (to: Clifton Chenier) / Middle name / Alexis / Empire state express / Ghost blues / Heaven's gate / The loop / Walkin' wounded / Slumming angel. *(re-iss.cd Oct92 on 'Essential')*

— On the 14th June 1995, RORY died after complications from a liver transplant operation.

– compilations etc. –

1974. Emerald/ US= Gem; (c) **IN THE BEGINNING (VOCAL AND GUITAR)** (rec.'67)

Aug 72. Polydor; (lp) **LIVE AT THE ISLE OF WIGHT (live)** 41 -
(cd-iss.Aug92)

Feb 75. Polydor; (lp)(c) **SINNER . . . AND SAINT** (1971 material) -

1977. Polydor; (lp) **TASTE** -

Oct 82. Polydor; (7"ep)(12"ep) **BLISTER ON THE MOON / SUGAR MAMA / CATFISH / ON THE BOARD** -

Feb 76. Polydor; (lp)(c) **THE STORY SO FAR**

Feb 88. Razor; (cd) **THE BEST OF RORY GALLAGHER & TASTE** -
– Blister on the Moon / Hail / Born on the wrong side of time / Dual carriageway pain / Same old story / On the boards / See here / I'll remember / Sugar mama (live) / Sinner boy (live) / I feel so good (live) / Catfish / I'm movin' on / What's going on / Ralway and gun / Morning Sun / Eat my words.

May 89. Castle; (d-lp)(cd) **LIVE! IN EUROPE / STAGE STRUCK** -

Jul 89. Castle; (d-lp)(cd) **TATTOO / BLUEPRINT** -

1991. Demon; (4xcd-box) **RORY GALLAGHER** -
– IRISH TOUR '74 / DEFENDER / TOP PRIORITY / JINX

Jun 92. Demon; (cd)(c)(lp) **EDGED IN BLUE** -

Nov 92. Essential; (3xcd-box) **G-MEN: BOOTLEG SERIES VOLUME ONE** -

GALLIANO

Formed: South London, England . . . late 80's by ROB GALLAGHER (GALLIANO) and friends CONSTANTINE and SPRY. Their early gigs were augmented by former STYLE COUNCIL musicians MICK TALBOT (who also became their producer) and STEVE WHITE. They soon were picked up by Giles Peterson's 'Talkin' Loud' label, who released debut single 'WELCOME TO THE STORY' late 1990. • **Style:** Hippy jazz-soul with rap and influenced by The LAST POETS. • **Songwriters:** GALLAGHER-ROBERTSON-WEIR except LONG TIME GONE (Crosby, Stills & Nash). • **Trivia:** They also featured on QUIET BOYS single 'Let The Good Times Roll'.

Recommended: A JOYFUL NOISE UNTO THE CREATOR (*6) / THE PLOT THICKENS (*7)

ROB GALLAGHER – vocals / **BROTHER CONSTANTINE** (b. WEIR) – vocals / **BROTHER SPRY** (CRISPIN ROBERTSON) – piano with many on session incl. TALBOT & WHITE

Talkin Loud Talkin' Loud

Nov 90. (7") **WELCOME TO THE STORY. / MOTHER NATURE**
(cd-s+=) – ('A'peace mix) / ('A'dub mix).
(12") – (3 'A'mixes).

Feb 91. (7") **NOTHING HAS CHANGED. / ('A'mix)**
(12"+=)(cd-s+=) – Little ghetto boy (remix) / Cheesy little cheese (instrumental).

Mar 91. (cd)(c)(lp) **IN PURSUIT OF THE 13th NOTE**
– Leg in the sea of history / Welcome to the story / Coming on strong / Sweet you like your favourite gears / Cemetary of drums / Five sons of the mother / Storm clouds gather / Nothing has changed / 57th minute of the 23rd hour / Power and glory / Stoned again / Reviewing the situation / Little ghetto boy. (c+=) – Me my mike my lyrics / Love bomb.
(cd++=) – Power and glory (live jazz mix) / Welcome to the story (summer breeze mix).

May 91. (7") **POWER AND GLORY (livin' mix). / ('A'-G-Funk edit)**
(12") – ('A'side) / ('A'-dirty claw Mick Talbot instrumental remix) / Stoned again.
(cd-s) – (all 4 tracks).

Oct 91. (7") **JUS' REACH. / ('A'-Easy nuh star mix)**
(12"+=)(cd-s+=) – ('A'instrumental).
(12") – (4-'A'mixes).

— added **SNAITH** – keyboards + 5th member **STEVE** – dancer

May 92. (7")(cd-s) **SKUNK FUNK (Marco Nelson mix). / ('A'-Andy Weatherall mix)** 41
(12") – ('A'cabin fever mix) / ('A'dub mix) / ('A'soldier mix).

Jun 92. (cd)(c) **A JOYFUL NOISE UNTO THE CREATOR** 28
– Grounation (part 1) / Jus' reach / Skunk funk / Earth boots / Phantom / Jazz? / New world order / So much confusion / Totally together / Golden flower / Prince of peace / Grounation (part 2).

— above featured vocalists – **CARLEEN ANDERSON, VALERIE ETIENNE + OMAR**

Jul 92. (12")(cd-s) **PRINCE OF PEACE. / TALES OF THE G / GOLDEN FLOWER (featuring OMAR)** 47

Sep 92. (12")(cd-s) **JUS' REACH RECYCLED. / HUNGRY LIKE A BABY / FROM THE NORTH, THE SOUTH, THE EAST AND THE WEST** 66
(cd-ep; live) – Jus' reach / Skunk funk / New world order / Vibe anthem.

— (now full-time) **VALERIE ETIENNE** – vocals repl. CONSTANTINE

May 94. (12")(c-s)(cd-s) **LONG TIME GONE (extended & palm skin productions remix) / WHAT COLOUR OUR FLAG (parts 1 & 2)** 15
(12"+=//cd-s++=) – Rivers. / / Scratching.
(cd-s+=) – Bloodlines.

May 94. (cd)(c) **THE PLOT THICKENS** 7
– Was this the time / Blood lines / Rise and fall / Twyford Down / What colour our flag (part 1) / Cold wind / Long time gone / Believe / Do you hear / Travels the road / Better all the time / Little one.

Jul 94. (c-s) **TWYFORD DOWN. / KOH PHAN GHAN** 37
(cd-s+=) – The homecoming.
(12") – (3-'A'mixes) / The return.
(cd-s) – (5-'A'mixes).

Dec 94. (cd)(d-lp) **A THICKER PLOT – THE REMIXES** -

GAMMA (see under ⇒ MONTROSE)

GANG OF FOUR

Formed: Leeds, England . . . 1977 by journalist ANDY GILL, JON KING, DAVE ALLEN and HUGO BURNHAM. After releasing debut EP 'DAMAGED GOODS' for Bob Last's 'Fast' label, they signed to 'EMI' late '78. Their debut 45 for the label 'AT HOME HE'S A TOURIST', hit Top60 and should have reached higher, but for a BBC ban, due to use of 'Rubbers' (i.e. contraceptives) in the lyrics. In Autumn '79, their debut album 'ENTERTAINMENT' hit the Top50, but they failed to maintain future chart status, although releasing some fine material. • **Style:** Energy fuelled alternative rock outfit, with political stance, rifled with staccato guitar sound reminiscent of DR.FEELGOOD. They shifted into dance and Philly sound, aided by female backing singers. • **Songwriters:** Penned by KING / ALLEN / GILL, until ALLEN departed to form SHRIEKBACK. Covered SOUL REBEL (Bob Marley). • **Trivia:** I LOVE A MAN IN UNIFORM was destined to give them a deserved hit, but for BBC blacklist, due to 1982 Falklands Conflict.

Recommended: A BRIEF HISTORY OF THE 20TH CENTURY (*8).

JON KING – vocals, melodica / **ANDY GILL** – guitar / **DAVE ALLEN** – bass / **HUGO BURNHAM** – drums

Fast not issued

Oct 78. (7"m) **DAMAGED GOODS. / LOVE LIKE ANTHRAX / ARMALITE RIFLE** -

E.M.I. Warners

Mar 79. (7") **AT HOME HE'S A TOURIST. / IT'S HER FACTORY** 58

Sep 79. (lp)(c) **ENTERTAINMENT** 45
– Ether / Natural's not in it / Not great men / Damaged goods / Return the gift / Guns before butter / I found that essence rare / Glass / Contract / At home he's a tourist / 5-45 / Anthrax. *(re-iss.1985) (cd-iss.Feb 95)*

Apr 80. (7") **OUTSIDE THE TRAINS DON'T RUN ON TIME. / HE'D SEND IN THE ARMY**

Mar 81. (7")(12") **WHAT WE ALL WANT. / HISTORY'S BUNK** -

Mar 81. (lp)(c) **SOLID GOLD** 52
– Paralysed / What we all want / If I could keep it for myself / Outside the trains don't run on time / Why theory? / Cheeseburger / The republic / In the ditch / A hole in the wallet / He'd send in the army.

May 81. (7")(12") **CHEESEBURGER. / PARALYSED** -

— (tour) **BUSTA CHERRY JONES** – bass (ex-SHARKS) repl. ALLEN (to SHRIEKBACK)

Jul 81. (7")(12") **TO HELL WITH POVERTY. / CAPITAL (IT FAILS US NOW)** [ ] [ ]

Feb 82. (m-lp) **ANOTHER DAY, ANOTHER DOLLAR** [-] [ ]
– To hell with poverty / What we all want / Cheeseburger / Capital (it fails us now) / History's bunk!

— **SARA LEE** – bass, vocals (ex-JANE AIRE, ex-ROBERT FRIPP) repl. BUSTA

Apr 82. (7")(12") **I LOVE A MAN IN A UNIFORM. / WORLD AT FAULT** [65] [-]

May 82. (lp)(c) **SONGS OF THE FREE** [61] [ ]
– Call me up / I love a man in a uniform / Muscle for brains / It is not enough / Life, it's a shame / I will be a good boy / History of the world / We live as we dream, alone / Of the instant.

Jun 82. (7") **CALL ME UP. / I WILL BE A GOOD BOY** [ ] [-]

Jul 82. (7") **I LOVE A MAN IN A UNIFORM. / I WILL A GOOD BOY** [-] [ ]
(12"+=) – ('A'extended).

— (**KING, GILL** and **BURNHAM** were joined by) **JON ASTROP / CHUCK KIRKPATRICK** and **JOHN SOMBATERO** – bass repl. SARA / added backing singers **ALFA ANDERSON** and **BRENDA WHITE**

Aug 83. (7")(12") **IS IT LOVE. / MAN WITH A GOOD CAR** [ ] [-]

Sep 83. (lp)(c) **HARD** [ ] [ ]
– Is it love / I fled / Silver lining / Woman town / A man with a good car / It don't matter / Arabic / A piece of my heart / Independence.

Sep 83. (7") **IS IT LOVE. / ARABIC** [-] [ ]

Nov 83. (7") **SILVER LINING. / INDEPENDENCE** [ ] [ ]

— **STEVE GOULDING** – drums (ex-RUMOUR) repl. BURNHAM who joined ILLUSTRATED MAN

Mercury / not issued

Oct 84. (12"m) **I WILL BE A GOOD BOY (live). / IS IT LOVE (live) / CALL ME UP (live)** [ ] [-]

Nov 84. (lp)(c) **AT THE PALACE (live)** [ ] [-]
– We live as we dream, alone / History is not made by great men / Silver lining / The history of the world / I love a man in uniform / Paralysed / Is it love / Damaged goods / At home he's a tourist / To hell with poverty. *(c+=)* – I will be a good boy / Call me up.

— (split mid-84) **JON** later formed KING BUTCHER

ANDY GILL

finally went solo.

Survival / not issued

Aug 87. (12") **DISPOSSESSION. / GENUINE** [ ] [-]
(12"+=) – ('A'version).

GANG OF FOUR

reformed 1990 (**JON KING & ALAN GILL**) added **HIROMI + STAN LOUBIERES**

Scarlett / not issued

Jun 90. (7") **MONEY TALKS (The Money mix). / USE THE COLOUR FROM THE TUBE** [ ] [-]
(12") – ('A'side) / ('A'dub version).
(cd-s) – ('A'extended) / (above 3 tracks)

Polydor / Polydor

Apr 91. (cd) **MALL** [-] [ ]
– Cadillac / Hotel favorites / Satellite / FMUSA / Don't fix what ain't broke / Impossible / Money talks / Soul rebel / Hiromi and Stan talk / Color from the tube / Hey yeah / Everybody wants to come / World falls apart

Aug 91. (12") **CADILLAC. / MOTEL FAVOURITES** [ ] [-]

— Disbanded again when record label dropped them. GILL then supplied the soundtrack in 1992 for the Labour Party's unsuccessful general election campaign. Re-formed again in 1994.

— **GILL + KING + STEVE MONTI** (ex-CURVE) + **PHIL BUTCHER** (ex-IGGY POP)

When! / not issued

Aug 95. (7")(c-s) **TATTOO. / BANNED WORDS / COP GOES HOME** [ ] [-]
(12"+=)(cd-s+=) – Tattoo (quiet guy mix).

Sep 95. (cd) **SHRINKWRAPPED** [ ] [-]
– Tattoo / Sleepwalker / I parade myself / Unburden / Better him than me / Something 99 / Showtime, valentine / Unburden, unbound / The dark side / I absolve you / Shrinkwrapped.

– compilations etc. –

Oct 86. Strange Fruit; (12"ep) **THE PEEL SESSIONS** (16.1.89) [ ] [-]
– I found that essence rare / Return the gift / 5-45 / At home he's a tourist. *(c-ep.issJun87)*

May 90. Strange Fruit; (cd)(c)(lp) **THE PEEL SESSIONS (1979-81)** [ ] [-]

Nov 90. E.M.I.; (cd)(c)(lp) **A BRIEF HISTORY OF THE 20th CENTURY** [ ] [-]
– At home he's a tourist / Damaged goods / Natural's not in it / Not great men / Anthrax / Return the gift / It's her factory / What we all want (live) / Paralysed / A hole in the wallet / Cheeseburger / To hell with poverty / Capital (it fails us now) / Call me up / I will be a good boy / History of the world / I love a man in a uniform / Is it love / Woman town / We live as we dream, alone. (c+cd.+=) – (4 tracks)

Jan 91. E.M.I.; (7")(c-s) **TO HELL WITH POVERTY (remix). / ('A'original version.)** [ ] [-]
(12"+=) – ('A'the louded remix) / ('A'other mix).
(d7"+=)(cd-ep+=) – Cheeseburger (live) / Call me up.

GARBAGE

Formed: Wisconsin, USA . . .1994 by DUKE ERIKSON, STEVE MARKER and BUTCH VIG. The latter had found fame in production work for greats like NIRVANA, SONIC YOUTH, SMASHING PUMPKINS, NINE INCH NAILS and U2, before coming across Edinburgh born SHIRLEY MANSON fronting ANGEL FISH on MTV. They contributed the track 'Vow' on a 'Volume' various compilation and this ended up as their limited edition debut 45 in 1995. By that years' summer, they had signed to Geffen's 'Almo' (UK 'Mushroom') records, which helped them break into UK Top 50 with 'SUBHUMAN'. • **Style:** Grungeful but melodic alternative rock outfit. • **Songwriters:** Group, except a CLASH 'Train In Vain' sample on 'STUPID GIRL'.

Recommended: GARBAGE (*8)

SHIRLEY MANSON – vocals, guitar (ex-GOODBYE MR MACKENZIE) / **STEVE MARKER** – guitar, samples, loops / DUKE ERIKSON – guitar, keyboards, bass / **BUTCH VIG** – drums, loops, efx

Discordant / Geffen

Mar 95. (7") **VOW. / VOW (TORN APART)** [ ] [97] Jun95

Mushroom / Geffen

Aug 95. (7") **SUBHUMAN. / £1 CRUSH** [50] [ ]
(cd-s+=) – Vow.

Sep 95. (7")(c-s)(cd-s) **ONLY HAPPY WHEN IT RAINS. / GIRL DON'T COME / SLEEP** [29] [ ]

Oct 95. (cd)(c)(d-lp)(boxed-7") **GARBAGE** [12] [ ]
– Supervixen / Queer / Only happy when it rains / As Heaven is wide / Not my idea / Stroke of luck / Vow / Stupid girl / Dog new tricks / My lover's box / Fix me now / Milk.

Nov 95. (7") **QUEER. / QUEER (Adrian Sherwood remix)** [13] [ ]
(silver-cd-s+=) – Trip my wire / ('A'-Martin Gore, Paul Freeguard and Jones remix).
(cd-s) – ('A'side) / Butterfly collector / ('A'-Rabbit in the Moon remix) / ('A'-Danny Saber remix).

Jerry GARCIA (see under ⇒ GRATEFUL DEAD)

Art GARFUNKEL (see under ⇒ SIMON & GARFUNKEL)

Marvin GAYE

Born: 2 Apr'39, Washington D.C., USA, son of an apostolic minister. In 1957, after being discharged from the army, he joined doo-wop outfit The MARQUEES. They released 2 singles (HEY LITTLE SCHOOL GIRL; produced by Bo Diddley, + BABY YOU'RE THE ONLY ONE) for label the 'Okeh'. The following year, HARVEY FUQUA invited them to become his new MOONGLOWS, and after moving to 'Chess' land Chicago, they issued ALMOST GROWN and MAMA LOOCIE singles. In 1960, GAYE moved to Detroit. FUQUA, who went with him to become solo artist, helped arrange for GAYE to play session drums on 45's by The MIRACLES. In 1961, after more work as backing singer for The MARVELETTES, he signed as a solo artist to 'Tamla Motown', and married the boss's younger sister ANNA GORDY. His success was almost immediate in 1963, when STUBBORN KIND OF FELLOW / HITCH HIKE / PRIDE AND JOY and CAN I GET A WITNESS gave him US Top 50 status. The following year although still mainly a credible solo artist, Berry Gordy teamed him up with MARY WELLS, and later KIM WESTON, to duet on more hits. The latter gave them another hit in 1967 with 'IT TAKES TWO'. This partnership was dissolved mid-67, when GAYE found Philadelphia born singer TAMMI TERRELL. They yielded a three-year run of hits on both sides of the Atlantic, but sadly to the obvious dismay of Marvin, TAMMI died of a brain tumour in March 1970, aged only 24. The previous year, Marvin had had his biggest hit to date when I HEARD IT THROUGH THE GRAPEVINE hit No.1 US + UK. Now a major star, MARVIN went on enjoy greater accolades in the 70's. • **Miscellaneous:** On 1st April 1984, MARVIN was shot dead by his father, after a violent argument about impending suicide talk and father's objection to Marvin's lifestyle. His father was given 5 year jail term for manslaughter. • **Style:** Superior soul/ballad artist of the 60's, who the following decade progressed into deeper conceptual releases, noteable WHAT'S GOING ON and the steamy LET'S GET IT ON. His second marriage to JANE HUNTER broke-up in 1977, which led to sparse recorded work and semi-hiatus, due to more financial tax problems, etc. His drug use (cocaine), gave him serious paranoia problems, but after a new contract deal in 1981 which gave money back to the I.R.S., he signed for 'Columbia-CBS'. Living in London and Belgium, he recorded a brilliant comeback 1982 album MIDNIGHT LOVE, which heralded his most sensuous song to date, SEXUAL HEALING. • **Songwriters:** MARVIN penned most of songs, except during periods in the 60's, when 'Motown' brought in their writers HOLLAND-DOZIER-HOLLAND. He also covered . . . GRAPEVINE (Whitfield-Strong) / ABRAHAM, MARTIN AND JOHN (c.Dick Holler). MARVIN's songs have been recorded by many international stars including PAUL YOUNG (Wherever I Lay My Hat) / ROBERT PALMER (Mercy Mercy Me) / CYNDI LAUPER (What's Going On) / etc.

Recommended: GREATEST HITS (*8) / WHAT'S GOING ON (*10) / LET'S GET IT ON (*8) / MIDNIGHT LOVE (*7).

MARVIN GAYE – vocals, drums, etc. (ex-MOONGLOWS, etc.) With Motown session people.

not issued / Tamla Motown

May 61. (lp) **THE SOULFUL MOODS OF MARVIN GAYE** [-] [ ]
– The masquerade is over / Love for sale / My funny valentine / Let your conscience be your guide / etc.

May 61. (7") **LET YOUR CONSCIENCE BE YOUR GUIDE. / NEVER LET YOU GO (SHA LA BOP)** [-] [ ]

1962. (7") **I'M YOURS, YOU'RE MINE. / SANDMAN** [-] [ ]

1962. (7") **TAKING MY TIME. / SOLDIER'S PLEA** [-] [ ]

Nov 62. (lp) **THAT STUBBORN KINDA FELLA** [-] [ ]

– That stubborn kinda fella / Pride and joy / Hitch hike / Get my hands on some lovin' / Soldier's plea / I'm yours, you're mine / Wherever I lay my hat (that's my home) / Taking my time / It hurt me too / Hello there angel.

Dec 62. (7") **HITCH HIKE. / HELLO THERE ANGEL** [-] [30]

Oriole Tamla

Feb 63. (7") **STUBBORN KIND OF FELLOW. / IT HURT ME TOO** [ ] [46] Jul 62

Jul 63. (7") **PRIDE AND JOY. / ONE OF THESE DAYS** [ ] [10] Apr 63

Jul 63. (lp) **LIVE ON STAGE (live)** [-] [ ]

– Stubborn kind of fellow / Hitchhike / One of these days / Days of wine and roses / You are my sunshine / etc.

Stateside Tamla

Nov 63. (7") **CAN I GET A WITNESS. / I'M CRAZY 'BOUT MY BABY** [ ] [22] [77]

1964. (lp) **WHEN I'M ALONE I CRY** [-] [ ]

– You've changed / I was telling her about you / I wonder / I'll be around / Because of you / I don't know why / I've grown accustomed to her face / When your lover has gone / When I'm alone I cry / If my heart could sing.

Apr 64. (7") **YOU'RE A WONDERFUL ONE. / WHEN I'M ALONE I CRY** [ ] [15] Feb 64

— Apr64, saw MARVIN duet with MARY WELLS on hit single ONCE UPON A TIME and album TOGETHER. (see further below and for further collaborations/ dueted with **KIM WESTON** and **TAMMI TERRELL.**

Aug 64. (7") **TRY IT BABY. / IF MY HEART COULD SING** [ ] [15] May 64

Sep 64. (7") **BABY DON'T YOU DO IT. / WALK ON THE WILD SIDE** [-] [27]

Nov 64. (lp) **MARVIN GAYE** [ ] [-]

– (7 tracks from studio '63 lp & 5 early '64 tracks).

Nov 64. (7") **HOW SWEET IT IS TO BE LOVED BY YOU. / FOREVER** [49] [6]

Tamla Motown Tamla

Apr 65. (lp) **HOW SWEET IT IS TO BE LOVED BY YOU** [ ] [ ] Feb 65

– How sweet it is to be loved by you / Try it baby / Baby don't you do it / You're a wonderful one / Now that you've won me / Me and my lonely room / Stepping closer to your heart / No good without you / One of these days / Need your lovin' (want you back) / Forever. *(US-tracks slightly diff.)*

Apr 65. (7") **I'LL BE DOGGONE. / YOU'VE BEEN A LONG TIME COMING** [ ] [8] Feb 65

Aug 65. (7") **PRETTY LITTLE BABY. / NOW THAT YOU'VE WON ME** [ ] [25] Jun 65

Sep 65. (lp) **HELLO BROADWAY** [ ] [ ]

– Walk on the wild side / What kind of fool am I / Party's over / Days of wine and roses / People / My way / On the street where you live / Hello Dolly / Hello Broadway / My kind of town / This is the life.

Nov 65. (7") **AIN'T THAT PECULIAR. / SHE'S GOT TO BE REAL** [ ] [8] Sep 65

Feb 66. (lp) **A TRIBUTE TO GREAT NAT KING COLE** [ ] [ ]

– Nature boy / Ramblin' Rose / Too young / Pretend / Straighten up and fly right / Mona Lisa / Unforgettable / To the ends of the Earth / Sweet Lorraine / It's only a paper Moon / Send for me / Calypso blues. *(cd-iss.Jul82) (cd-iss.1992)*

Mar 66. (7") **ONE MORE HEARTACHE. / WHEN I HAD YOUR LOVE** [ ] [29] Feb 66

Jun 66. (7") **TAKE THIS HEART OF MINE. / NEED YOUR LOVIN' (WANT YOU BACK)** [ ] [44] May 66

Sep 66. (7") **LITTLE DARLING (I NEED YOU). / HEY DIDDLE DIDDLE** [50] [47] Aug 66

Aug 67. (7") **YOUR UNCHANGING LOVE. / I'LL TAKE CARE OF YOU** [ ] [33] Jul 67

Jan 68. (7") **YOU. / CHANGE WHAT YOU CAN** [ ] [34]

Nov 68. (7") **CHAINED. / AT LAST (I FOUND A LOVE)** [ ] [32]

Nov 68. (7") **I HEARD IT THROUGH THE GRAPEVINE. / YOU'RE WHAT'S HAPPENING (IN THE WORLD TODAY)** [-] [1]

Jan 69. (lp) **I HEARD IT THROUGHT THE GRAPEVINE** (US-title 'IN THE GROOVE') [ ] [63] Oct68

– You / Tear it on down / Chained / I heard it through the grapevine / At last (I found a love) / Some kind of wonderful / Loving you is sweeter than ever / Change what you can / It's love I need / Every now and then / You're what's happening (in the world today) / There goes my baby

Feb 69. (7") **I HEARD IT THROUGH THE GRAPEVINE. / NEED SOMEBODY** [1] [-]

Jul 69. (7") **TOO BUSY THINKING ABOUT MY BABY. / WHEREVER I LAY MY HAT** [5] [4] Apr 69

(re-iss.Oct81 on 'Motown')

Nov 69. (lp)(c) **M.P.G.** [ ] [33] Jun 69

– Too busy thinking about my baby / This magic moment / I got to get to California / That's the way love is / The end of our road / Seek and you shall find / It's a bitter pill to swallow / Only a lonely man would know / Try my true love / Memories / More than a heart can stand / It don't take too much to keep me. *(re-iss.Jul82) (cd-iss.Aug93)*

Nov 69. (7") **THAT'S THE WAY LOVE IS. / GONNA KEEP TRYIN' TILL I WIN YOUR LOVE** [ ] [7] Aug 69

Jan 70. (7") **HOW CAN I FORGET. / GONNA GIVE HER ALL THE LOVE I'VE GOT** [-] [41] [67]

Apr 70. (lp) **THAT'S THE WAY LOVE IS** [ ] [ ] Oct 69

– Gonna give her all the love i've got / Yesterday / Groovin' / I wish it would rain / That's the way love is / How can I forget / Abraham, Martin and John / Gonna keep on tryin' till I win your love / No time for tears / Cloud nine / Don't you miss me a little bit baby / So long. *(cd-iss.Apr91 & Aug93)*

Apr 70. (7") **ABRAHAM, MARTIN AND JOHN. / HOW CAN I FORGET** [9] [-]

Jun 70. (7") **THE END OF OUR ROAD. / ME AND MY LONELY ROOM** [-] [40]

Jun 71. (7") **WHAT'S GOING ON. / GOD IS LOVE** [ ] [2] Feb 71

(re-iss.Mar83 on 'Motown')

Oct 71. (lp)(c) **WHAT'S GOING ON** [ ] [6] Jun 71

– What's going on / What's happening brother / Flyin' high (in the friendly sky) / Save the children / God is love / Mercy mercy me (the ecology) / Right on / Wholy holy / Inner city blues (make me wanna holler). *(re-iss.+cd.Apr88)*

Nov 71. (7") **SAVE THE CHILDREN. / LITTLE DARLING** [41] [ ]

Feb 72. (7") **MERCY MERCY ME. / SAD TOMORROWS** [ ] [4] Jul 71

May 72. (7") **INNER CITY BLUES (MAKE ME WANNA HOLLER). / WHOLY HOLY** [ ] [9] Oct 71

May 72. (7") **YOU'RE THE MAN. / (part 2)** [-] [50]

Feb 73. (lp)(c) **TROUBLE MAN** [ ] [14] Dec 72

– Main theme from "Trouble Man" / "T" plays it cool / Poor Abbey Walsh / The break-in (police shoot big) / Cleo's apartment / Trouble man / Theme from "Trouble Man" / "T" stands for trouble / Life is a gamble / Deep in it / Don't mess with Mister "T" / There goes Mister "T". *(re-iss.Jul82) (cd-iss.Apr93)*

Mar 73. (7") **TROUBLE MAN. / DON'T MESS WITH MISTER "T"** [ ] [7] Dec 72

Aug 73. (7") **LET'S GET IT ON. / I WISH IT WOULD RAIN** [31] [1] Jul 73

Nov 73. (lp)(c) **LET'S GET IT ON** [39] [2] Sep 73

– Let's get it on / Please don't stay (once you go away) / If I should die tonight / Keep gettin' it on / Come get to this / Distant lover / You sure love to ball / Just to keep you satisfied. *(re-iss.Mar82 & Apr84 on 'Motown')(re-iss.+cd.Apr88) (cd-iss.Jul92)*

Around this time MARVIN teams up with DIANA ROSS, on album DIANA AND MARVIN. Many hits were lifted from it including YOU ARE EVERYTHING.

Jan 74. (7") **COME GET TO THIS. / DISTANT LOVER** [ ] [21] Nov 73

Jan 74. (7") **YOU SURE LOVE TO BALL. / JUST TO KEEP YOU SATISFIED** [-] [50]

Sep 74. (lp)(c) **MARVIN GAYE LIVE! (live)** [ ] [8] Jul 74

– (the beginning: introduction & overture) / Trouble man – Inner city blues – Distant lover / Jan / Fossil medley: I'll be doggone – Try it baby – Can I get a witness – Subborn kind of fellow – How sweet it is to be loved by you / Now: Let's get it on – What's going on. *(re-iss.Mar82) (cd-iss.Feb88)(re-iss.Mar87 on 'Hallmark') (cd-iss.Sep 93 on 'Stardust')*

Sep 74. (7") **DISTANT LOVER. / TROUBLE MAN** [-] [28]

Apr 76. (7") **I WANT YOU. / I WANT YOU (instrumental)** [ ] [15]

May 76. (lp)(c) **I WANT YOU** [22] [4] Mar 76

– I want you / Come live with me angel / After the dance (instrumental) / Feel all my love inside / I wanna be where you are / I want you / All the way around / Since I had you / Soon I'll be loving you again / I want you (intro jam) / After the dance. *(re-iss.Oct81 & 1986 on 'Motown') (cd-iss.Mar90)*

Aug 76. (7") **AFTER THE DANCE. / FEEL ALL MY LOVE INSIDE** [ ] [74]

Motown Motown

Apr 77. (7") **GOT TO GIVE IT UP (part 1). / GOT TO GIVE IT UP (part 2)** [7] [1]

— next d-lp, * – duets with FLORENCE LYLES

May 77. (d-lp)(c) **LIVE AT THE LONDON PALLADIUM (live)** [ ] [3] Mar 77

– (intro theme) / All the way around / Since I had you / Come get to this / Let's get it on / Trouble man / Ain't peculiar / You're a wonderful one / Stubborn kind of fellow / Pride and joy / Little darling (I need you) / I heard it through the grapevine / Hitch hike / You / Too busy thinking about my baby / How sweet it is to be loved by you / Inner city blues (make me wanna holler) / God is love / What's going on / Save the children / You're all I need to get by * / Ain't nothing like the real thing * / Your precious love * / It takes two * / Ain't no mountain high enough * / Distant lover / (closing theme) / Got to give it up. *(re-iss.Aug86) (cd-iss.Mar87 & May89) (d-cd-iss.Sep 93 on 'Stardust')*

Jan 79. (d-lp)(c) **HERE, MY DEAR** [ ] [26]

– Here, my dear / I met a little girl / When did you stop loving me, when did I stop loving you / Anger / Is that enough / Everybody needs love / Time to get it together / Sparrow / Anna's song / When did you stop loving me, when did I stop loving you (instrumental) / A funky space reincarnation / You can leave, but it's going to cost you / Falling in love again / When did you stop loving me, when did I stop loving you (reprise). *(re-iss.Oct81) (re-iss.cd Nov93)*

Feb 79. (7") **A FUNKY SPACE REINCARNATION (part 1). / (part 2)** [ ] [ ]

(12"+=) – ('A'disco).

Around this a collaboration with SMOKEY ROBINSON, DIANA ROSS and STEVE WONDER gave them a minor hit single 'POPS WE LOVE YOU'.

Nov 79. (7") **EGO TRIPPING OUT. / ('A' instrumental)** [ ] [ ]

(12") – ('A'side) / What's going on / What's happening brother.

Feb 81. (lp)(c) **IN OUR LIFETIME** [48] [ ]

– Praise / Life is for learning / Love party / Funk me / Far cry / Love me now or love me later / Heavy love affair / In our lifetime.

Feb 81. (7")(12") **PRAISE. / FUNK ME** [ ] [ ]

Oct 81. (7")(12") **HEAVY LOVE AFFAIR. / FAR CRY** [ ] [ ]

— MARVIN now plays mostly all instruments

C.B.S. Columbia

Oct 82. (lp)(c) **MIDNIGHT LOVE** [10] [7]

– Midnight lady / Sexual healing / Rockin' after midnight / 'Til tomorrow / Turn on some music / Third world girl / Joy / My love is waiting. *(re-iss.Apr86)*

Oct 82. (7")(12") **SEXUAL HEALING. / ('A'instrumental)** [4] [3]

Nov 82. (7") **ROCKIN' AFTER MIDNIGHT. / 'TIL TOMORROW** [-] [ ]

Jan 83. (7")(12") **MY LOVE IS WAITING. / ROCKIN' AFTER MIDNIGHT** [34] [ ]

Jan 83. (7") **JOY. / ('A' instrumental)** [-] [ ]

Feb 83. (7") **STAR SPANGLED BANNER. / TURN ON SOME MUSIC** [-] [ ]

Mar 83. (7") **JOY. / TURN ON SOME MUSIC** [ ] [-]

— On the 1st April 1984, MARVIN was shot dead by his overtly religious father.

May 85. (7")(12") **SANCTIFIED LADY. / ('A'instrumental)** [51] [41]

(d7"+=) – Sexual healing / Rockin' after midnight.

Jun 85. (lp)(c) **DREAM OF A LIFETIME** (2 new & rec.70's) [46] [41]

– Sanctified lady / Savage in the sack / Masochistic beauty / It's madness / Ain't it funny (how things turn around) / Symphony / Life's opera / Dream of a lifetime. *(cd-iss.Jun91 on 'Pickwick') (cd-iss.Jun94 on 'Sony Collectors')*

Jul 85. (7") **IT'S MADNESS. / AIN'T IT FUNNY (HOW THINGS TURN AROUND)** [ ] [ ]

(12"+=) – Joy.

Dec 85. (lp)(c) **ROMANTICALLY YOURS** [ ] [ ]

– More / Why did I choose you? / Maria / The shadow of your smile / Fly me to the Moon (in other words) / I won't cry anymore / Just like / Walkin' in the rain /

	I live for you / Stranger in my life / Happy go lucky. *(cd-iss.Jul89 on 'Pickwick') (re-iss.cd Oct93 on 'Sony Europe') (cd-iss.Jun94 on 'Sony Collectors')*			
Jan 86.	(7") **JUST LIKE. / MORE**	-		
Jun 86.	(7") **THE WORLD IS RATED X. / LONELY LOVER**		-	
	(12"+=) – ('A'instrumental).			
Jun 86.	(7") **THE WORLD IS RATED X. / NO GREATER LOVE**	-		

– compilations etc. –

Note all below on 'Tamla Motown' until mentioned.

Mar 64.	(lp) **GREATEST HITS**	-	72	
Oct 66.	(lp) **THE MOODS OF MARVIN GAYE**			Jul 66
Mar 67.	(7"ep) **MARVIN GAYE**			
Mar 67.	(7"ep) **ORIGINALS FROM MARVIN GAYE**			
Sep 67.	(lp) **GREATEST HITS VOL. 2**	-		
Feb 68.	(lp) **MARVIN GAYE'S GREATEST HITS**	40		
Aug 70.	(lp) **MARVIN GAYE'S GREATEST HITS**	60		
Feb 72.	(lp)(c) **THE HITS OF MARVIN GAYE** *(re-iss.Oct81. on 'Motown')*			
Jun 74.	(d-lp)(c) **ANTHOLOGY** *(d-cd-iss.Oct86)(d-cd-iss.Apr93)*		61	
Nov 74.	(7") **I HEARD IT THROUGH THE GRAPEVINE. / CHAINED**			
Sep 76.	(7") **I HEARD IT THROUGH THE GRAPEVINE. / (b-side by The Supremes/Temptations**			
Nov 76.	(lp)(c) **THE BEST OF MARVIN GAYE** *(re-iss.Oct81)*	56		
Feb 80.	(7") **ABRAHAM, MARTIN & JOHN. / 'Ben' by Michael Jackson**			
Oct 80.	(lp)(c) **EARLY YEARS 1961-1964**			
Oct 83.	(lp)(c) **EVERY MOTOWN HIT OF MARVIN GAYE**	-	80	
Nov 83.	(7") **WHAT'S GOING ON. / I HEARD IT THROUGH THE GRAPEVINE**			
	(12"+=) – Wherever I lay my hat.			
May 84.	(lp)(c) **I HEARD IT THROUGH THE GRAPEVINE** *(cd-iss.Nov86 & Jun89)*			
May 84.	(cd) **15 GREATEST HITS**			
Apr 85.	(7") **GOT TO GIVE IT UP (Pt.1). / HOW SWEET IT IS**			
	(12"+=) – ('A'version-Pt.2).			
Apr 86.	(7") **I HEARD IT THROUGH THE GRAPEVINE. / CAN I GET A WITNESS**	8		
	(ext.12"+c-s) – ('A'side) / That's the way love is / You're a wonderful one.			
Jun 86.	(lp)(c) **MOTOWN REMEMBERS MARVIN GAYE**			Apr 86
Jul 86.	(cd) **THE VERY BEST OF MARVIN GAYE**			
Oct 86.	(d-cd) **THAT STUBBORN KINDA FELLA / HOW SWEET IT IS**			
Nov 86.	(d-cd) **WHAT'S GOING ON / LET'S GET IT ON**			
Feb 87.	(d-cd) **TROUBLE MAN / M.P.G.**			
Mar 87.	(cd) **20 GREATEST COMPACT COMMAND PERFOR-MANCES VOL. 2**			
Apr 88.	(7") **AIN'T THAT PECULIAR. / I'LL BE DOGGONE**			
Jul 88.	(d-lp)(c)(cd) **MUSICAL TESTAMENT 1964-1984**			
Sep 88.	(lp)(c)(cd) **18 GREATEST HITS** *(re-iss.Feb92 as 'MOTOWN'S GREATEST HITS' + 2 tracks)*			
Jan 88.	Old Gold; (7") **(SEXUAL) HEALING. / MY LOVE IS WAITING** *(re-iss.12"-Aug88)*			
Sep 73.	M.F.P.; (lp) **HOW SWEET IT IS** *(re-iss.Jan79)*		-	
Jun 82.	Pickwick; (lp)(c) **THE MAGIC OF MARVIN GAYE**		-	
Nov 83.	Telstar; (lp)(c) **GREATEST HITS**	13	-	
	– I heard it through the grapevine / Let's get it on / Too busy thinking about my baby / How sweet it is to be loved by you / You're all I need to get by / Got to give it up / You are everything / Midnight lady / Sexual healing / What's going on / Abraham, Martin & John / It takes two / Stop, look, listen (to your heart) / My love is waiting / The onion song / Wherever I lay my hat.			
Nov 88.	Telstar; (lp)(c)(cd) **LOVE SONGS (others by SMOKEY ROBINSON)**	69	-	
Oct 90.	Telstar; (cd)(c)(lp) **LOVE SONGS**	39	-	
Oct 92.	Columbia; (cd) **MIDNIGHT LADY / DREAM OF A LIFETIME**			
Oct 94.	Columbia; (3xcd-box) **DREAM OF A LIFETIME / ROMANTICALLY YOURS / MIDNIGHT LOVE**			
May 93.	Spectrum; (cd)(c) **NIGHT LIFE**		-	
Dec 93.	Star; (cd) **DISTANT LOVER**		-	
Jan 94.	Magnum; (cd) **FOR THE VERY LAST TIME**		-	
Mar 94.	Polygram TV; (cd)(c) **THE VERY BEST OF MARVIN GAYE**	3	-	
May 94.	Motown; (7")(c-s) **LUCKY LUCKY ME. / ('A'extended)**	67		
	(12"+=)(cd-s+=) – ('A'instrumental mix) / ('A'jazz mix) / ('A'ragga vibe mix).			
May 94.	Motown; (cd) **IN OUR LIFETIME**			
Jun 94.	Motown; (4xcd-box) **THE CLASSIC COLLECTION**			
Apr 95.	Prestige; (cd)(c) **IN CONCERT**		-	
Apr 95.	Top Masters; (cd) **THE BEST OF ...**		-	
May 95.	Motown; (4xcd-box) **THE MASTER 1961-1984**			
Jul 95.	Wisepack; (cd) **MARVIN GAYE LIVE**		-	
Nov 95.	Motown; (3xcd-box) **HOW SWEET IT IS / TRIBUTE TO NAT KING COLE / MPG**			

duetsdid

MARVIN GAYE and MARY WELLS

		Stateside	Tamla	
Jul 64.	(7") **ONCE UPON A TIME. / WHAT'S THE MATTER WITH YOU BABY**	50	19	
			17	Apr 64
Oct 64.	(lp) **TOGETHER**		42	May 64
	– Once upon a time / What's the matter with you baby / Deed I do / Until I met you / After the lights go down low / Together / Squeeze me / For sentimental reasons / You came a long way from St.Louis / Late late show.			

MARVIN GAYE and KIM WESTON

		Stateside	Tamla	
Dec 64.	(7") **WHAT GOOD AM I WITHOUT YOU. / I WANT YOU AROUND**		61	Oct 64
		Tamla Motown	Tamla	
Jan 67.	(7") **IT TAKES TWO. / IT'S GOT TO BE A MIRACLE**	16	14	
May 67.	(lp) **TAKE TWO**			
	– It takes two / I love you, yes I do / Baby I need your loving / It's got to be a miracle / Baby say yes / What good am I without you / Till there was you / Love fell on me / Secret love / I want you 'round / Heaven sent you I know / When.			

MARVIN GAYE and TAMMI TERRELL

		Tamla Motown	Tamla	
Jun 67.	(7") **AIN'T NO MOUNTAIN HIGH ENOUGH. / GIVE A LITTLE LOVE**		19	May 67
Sep 67.	(7") **YOUR PRECIOUS LOVE. / HOLD ME OH MY DARLING**		5	
Dec 67.	(7") **IF I COULD BUILD MY WHOLE WORLD AROUND YOU. / IF THIS WORLD WERE MINE**	41	10	
			68	
Jan 68.	(lp) **UNITED**		69	Oct 67
	– Ain't no mountain high enough / Hold me oh my darling / You got wht it takes / If I could build my whole world around you / Somethin' stupid / Your precious love / Two can have a party / Little ole boy, little ole girl / Give a little love / If this world were mine / Sad wedding / Oh how I'd miss you. *(re-iss.+c Mar82 on 'Motown') (re-iss.+cd.Feb88)*			
Apr 68.	(7") **AIN'T NOTHING LIKE THE REAL THING. / LITTLE OLE BOY LITTLE OLE GIRL**	34	8	
Jul 68.	(7") **YOU'RE ALL I NEED TO GET BY. / TWO CAN HAVE A PARTY**	19	7	
Oct 68.	(7") **KEEP ON LOVING ME HONEY. / YOU AIN'T LIVIN' TIL YOU'RE LOVIN'**	-	28	
Nov 68.	(lp) **YOU'RE ALL I NEED**		60	Sep 68
	– Ain't nothing like the real thing / Keep on loving me honey / You're all I need to get by / Baby don'tcha worry / Give in you can't win / You ain't livin' till you're lovin' / That's how it is (since you've been gone) / I'll never stop loving you / When love comes knockin' at my heart / Memory chest / I can't help but love you. *(UK-iss. cd+c. May 91) (cd-iss.Sep93)*			
Jan 69.	(7") **YOU AIN'T LIVIN' TILL YOU'RE LOVIN'. / OH HOW I MISS YOU**	21		
May 69.	(7") **GOOD LOVIN' AIN'T EASY TO COME BY. / SATISFIED FEELIN'**	26	30	Jan 69
Nov 69.	(7") **THE ONION SONG. / I CAN'T BELIEVE YOU LOVE ME**	9	-	
Nov 69.	(7") **WHAT YOU GAVE ME. / HOW YOU GONNA KEEP IT (AFTER YOU GET IT)**	-	49	
Feb 70.	(lp) **EASY**			Oct 69
	– Good lovin' ain't easy to come by / California soul / Love wake me up this morning / This poor heart of mine / I'm your puppet / Onion song / What you gave me / Baby I need your loving / I can't believe you love me / How you gonna keep it / More, more, more / Satisfied feeling. *(re-iss.+c.Sep86)*			
Apr 70.	(7") **THE ONION SONG. / CALIFORNIA SOUL**	-	50	

— At 23, TAMMI died 16 Mar'70 from a brain tumor, after collapsing Autumn '69. A few exploitation releases were forthcoming.

Aug 70.	Tamla Motown; (lp)(c) **GREATEST HITS** *(re-iss.Sep86, re-iss.Jul82)*			
Apr 85.	Tamla Motown; (7")(12") **THE ONION SONG. / YOU AIN'T LIVIN' TIL YOU'RE LOVIN'**			
Mar 74.	M.F.P.; (lp)(c) **THE ONION SONG**		-	

– more duet compilations –

Nov 69.	Tamla Motown; (lp)(c) **MARVIN GAYE & HIS GIRLS** *(re-iss.Feb83 on 'Motown', cd-iss.Oct87)*		
Jan 86.	Tamla Motown; (cd) **MARVIN GAYE & HIS WOMEN**		

J. GEILS BAND

Formed: Boston, Massachusetts, USA ... 1967, initially as The J.GEILS BLUES BAND, by GEILS and KLEIN, who soon recruited WOLF, DICK and BLADD. In 1970, after turning down an offer of Woodstock Festival the year previous, they signed to 'Atlantic'. Their eponymous debut early in '71 was well-received by critics, but sold only moderately. After a year though, they had first of many Top 40 US hits with 'LOOKING FOR A LOVE'. Ten years later, they were at the top with both single 'CENTERFOLD' and album 'FREEZE FRAME'. • **Style:** High-energy R&B outfit, who branched into more mainstream rock-pop with each release. • **Songwriters:** JUSTMAN contributed most. alongside GEILS and WOLK, etc. Covered; IT AIN'T WHAT YOU DO . . . (Juke Joint Jimmy) / FIRST I LOOK AT THE PURSE (Smokey Robinson) / HOMEWORK (Otis Rush) / SERVES YOU RIGHT TO SUFFER (John Lee Hooker) / LOOKING FOR A LOVE (Bobby Womack) / etc. • **Trivia:** On 7 Aug'74, WOLF married actress Faye Dunaway, but they were to later divorce.

Recommended: FLASHBACK – THE BEST OF J.GEILS BAND (*6)

PETER WOLF (b.PETER BLANKFIELD, 7 Mar'46, New York City, USA) – vocals / **J. GEILS** (b.JEROME, 20 Feb'46, New York City) – guitar / **DANNY KLEIN** (b.13 May'46,

Worcester, Massachusetts, USA) – bass / **MAGIC DICK** (b.RICHARD SALWITZ, 13 May'45, New London, Connect..) – harmonica / **STEPHEN JO BLADD** (b.13 Jul'45, Boston) – drums, vocals / **SETH JUSTMAN** (b.27 Jan'51, Washington DC) – keyboards, vocals

Atlantic Atlantic

Feb 71. (lp)(c) **J.GEILS BAND** [ ] [ ] Jan 71
– Wait / Ice breaker (for the big "M") / Cruisin' for a love / Hard drivin' man / Serves you right to suffer / Homework / First I look at the purse / What's your hurry / On borrowed time / Pack fair and square / Sno-cone. *(re-iss.Jul89 on 'Edsel')*
Feb 71. (7") **WAIT. / CRUISIN' FOR A LOVE** [-] [ ]
Oct 71. (7") **I DON'T NEED YOU NO MORE. / DEAD PRESIDENTS** [-] [ ]
Jan 72. (lp)(c) **THE MORNING AFTER** [ ] [64] Oct 71
– I don't need you no more / Whammer Jammer / So sharp / The usual place / Gotta have your love / Looking for a love / Gonna find me a new love / Cry one more time / Floyd's hotel / It ain't what you do (it's how you do it!).
Feb 72. (7") **LOOKING FOR A LOVE. / WHAMMER JAMMER** [ ] [33] Dec 71
Oct 72. (lp)(c) **LIVE – FULL HOUSE (live)** [ ] [54]
– First I look at the purse / Homework / Pack fair and square / Whammer jammer / Hard drivin' man / Serves you right to suffer / Cruisin' for a love / Looking for a love.
Oct 72. (7") **HARD DRIVIN' MAN (live). / WHAMMER JAMMER (live)** [ ] [ ]
Apr 73. (lp)(c) **BLOODSHOT** [ ] [10]
– (Ain't nothin' but a) House party / Make up your mind / Back to get ya / Struttin' with my baby / Don't try to hide it / Southside shuffle / Hold your loving / Start all over again / Give it to me.
May 73. (7") **GIVE IT TO ME. / HOLD YOUR LOVING** [ ] [30] Mar 73
Aug 73. (7") **MAKE UP YOUR MIND. / SOUTHSIDE SHUFFLE** [-] [98]
Jan 74. (lp)(c) **LADIES INVITED** [ ] [51] Nov 73
– Did you no wrong / I can't go on / Lay your good thing down / That's why I'm thinking of you / No doubt about it / The lady makes demands / My baby don't love me / Diddyboppin' / Take a chance / Chimes. *(cd-iss.Feb95 on 'Warners')*
Jan 74. (7") **DID YOU NO WRONG. / THAT'S WHY I'M THINKING OF YOU** [-] [ ]
Nov 74. (7") **MUST OF GOT LOST. / FUNKY JUDGE** [ ] [12]
Nov 74. (lp)(c) **NIGHTMARES ... AND OTHER TALES FROM THE VINYL JUNGLE** [ ] [26] Oct 74
– Detroit breakdown / Givin' it all up / Must of got lost / Look me in the eye / Nightmares / Stoop down 39 / I'll be coming home / Funky judge / Gettin' out.
Jan 75. (7") **GETTIN' OUT. / GIVIN' IT ALL UP** [-] [ ]
Jan 75. (7") **GETTIN' OUT. / FUNKY JUDGE** [ ] [-]
Mar 75. (7") **GIVIN' IT ALL UP. / LOOK ME IN THE EYES** [ ] [-]
Oct 75. (lp)(c) **HOTLINE** [ ] [36] Sep 75
– Love-itis / Easy way out / Think it over / Be careful / Jealous love / Mean love / Orange driver / Believe in me / Fancy footwork.
Oct 75. (7") **LOVE-ITIS. / THINK IT OVER** [-] [ ]
May 76. (7") **WHERE DID OUR LOVE GO. / WHAT'S YOUR HURRY** [ ] [68] Apr 76
Jun 76. (d-lp)(c) **LIVE – BLOW YOUR FACE OUT (live)** [ ] [40] May 76
– Southside shuffle / Back to get ya / Shoot your shot / Must of got lost / Where did our love go / Hard drivin' man / Love-itis / (Ain't nothin' but a) House party / So sharp / Detroit breakdown / Chimes / Sno-cone / Wait / Raise your hand / Start all over / Give it to me.
Oct 76. (7") **(AIN'T NOTHIN' BUT A) HOUSE PARTY (live). / GIVE IT TO ME (live)** [-] [ ]
Feb 77. (7") **PEANUT BUTTER. / MAGIC'S MOOD** [-] [ ]
Jul 77. (lp)(c) **MONKEY ISLAND (as "J. GEILS")** [ ] [51]
– Surrender / You're the only one / I do / Somebody / I'm falling / Monkey Island / I'm not rough / So good / Wreckage.
Jul 77. (7") **YOU'RE THE ONLY ONE. / WRECKAGE** [-] [83]
Sep 77. (7") **SURRENDER. / MONKEY ISLAND (part 1)** [-] [ ]

E.M.I. America E.M.I. America

Nov 78. (7") **ONE LAST KISS. / REVENGE** [-] [35]
Jan 79. (lp)(c) **SANCTUARY** [ ] [49] Dec 78
– I could hurt you / One last kiss / Take it back / Sanctuary / Teresa / Wild man / I can't believe you / I don't hang around much anymore / Jus' can't stop me. *(cd-iss.May95 on 'BGO')*
Apr 79. (7") **ONE LAST KISS. / I CAN'T BELIEVE YOU** [74] [-]
Jun 79. (7") **TAKE IT BACK. / I CAN'T BELIEVE YOU** [ ] [67] Mar 79
Aug 79. (7") **WILD MAN. / JUS' CAN'T STOP ME** [-] [ ]
—— MAGIC now added saxophone. (might have been earlier)
Feb 80. (lp)(c) **LOVE STINKS** [ ] [18]
– Just can't wait / Come back / Takin' you down / Night time / No anchovies, please / Love stinks / Tryin' not to think about it / Desire (please don't turn away) / Till the walls come tumblin' down. *(cd-iss.Dec94 on 'B.G.O.')*
Feb 80. (7") **COME BACK. / TAKIN' YOU DOWN** [ ] [32]
May 80. (7")(7"pic-d) **LOVE STINKS. / TILL THE WALLS COME TUMBLIN' DOWN** [ ] [38] Apr 80
Jul 80. (7") **JUST CAN'T WAIT. / NO ANCHOVIES, PLEASE** [-] [78]
Nov 81. (7") **CENTERFOLD. / RAGE IN THE CAGE** [-] [1]
Jan 82. (7") **CENTERFOLD. / FLAMETHROWER** [3] [-]
Jan 82. (lp)(c) **FREEZE-FRAME** [12] [1] Nov 81
– Freeze-frame / Rage in the cage / Centerfold / Do you remember when / Insane, insane again / Flamethrower / River blindness / Angel in blue / Piss on the wall. *(cd-iss.Mar 84) (cd-iss.Aug93 on 'B.G.O.')*
Feb 82. (7") **FREEZE-FRAME. / FLAMETHROWER** [-] [4]
Apr 82. (7")(7"pic-d) **FREEZE-FRAME. / RAGE IN THE CAGE** [27] [-]
May 82. (7") **ANGEL IN BLUE. / RAGE IN THE CAGE** [-] [40]
Jun 82. (7") **ANGEL IN BLUE. / RIVER BLINDNESS** [55] [-]
Dec 82. (lp)(c) **SHOWTIME! (live)** [ ] [23]
– Jus' can't stop me / Just can't wait / Till the walls come tumblin' down / Sanctuary / I'm falling / Love rap / Love stinks / Stoop down 39 / I do / Centerfold / Land of a thousand dances. *(cd-iss.Dec95 on 'BGO')*
Mar 83. (7") **I DO (live). / SANCTUARY (live)** [ ] [24] Nov 82
Feb 83. (7") **LAND OF A THOUSAND DANCES (live). / JUS' CAN'T STOP ME (live)** [-] [60]
—— Trimmed to a quintet, when WOLF left for semi-successful solo career.
Oct 84. (7") **CONCEALED WEAPONS. / TELL 'EM JONESY** [-] [63]
Dec 84. (lp)(c) **YOU'RE GETTIN' EVEN WHILE I'M GETTIN' ODD** [ ] [80] Nov 84
– Concealed weapons / Heavy petting / Wasted youth / Eenie meenie minie moe / Tell me Jonesy / You're gettin' even while I'm gettin' old / The bite from inside / Californicating / I will carry you home.
Apr 85. (7") **OO-EE-DIDDLEY-BOP!. / ?** [-] [ ]
Jul 85. (7") **FRIGHT NIGHT. / ?** [-] [91]
—— (above from the film of same name)

– compilations, others, etc. –

Jul 79. Atlantic; (lp)(c) **THE BEST OF THE J.GEILS BAND** [ ] [ ]
(cd-iss.May93)
Apr 87. EMI America; (lp)(c)(cd) **FLASHBACK – (THE BEST OF J.GEILS)** [ ] [ ]
– Love stinks / Freeze frame / Flamethrower / Just can't wait / I do / Centerfold / Come back / Wild man / One last kiss / Land of a 1000 dances.

MAGIC DICK & J. GEILS

Rounder Rounder

Oct 94. (cd)(c) **BLUESTIME** [ ] [ ]

Bob GELDOF (see under ⇒ BOOMTOWN RATS)

GENE

Formed: London, England . . . summer 1993 by MARTIN and 3 ex-members of SPIN. Debutted with 'FOR THE DEAD' in the Spring of '94. They and their label 'Costermonger' were then picked up by 'Polydor', who issued Top 60 single 'BE MY LIGHT . . . '. Broke through big time in '95, when the 'OLYMPIAN' album went Top 10 UK. • **Style:** Influenced by The SMITHS or The STONES. • **Songwriters:** Group penned except DON'T LET ME DOWN (Beatles).

Recommended: OLYMPIAN (*7)

MARTIN ROSSITER (b.Cardiff, Wales) – vocals, keyboards / **STEVE MASON** – guitars / **KEVIN MILES** – bass / **MATT JAMES** – drums, percussion

Coster-monger not issued

Apr 94. (7") **FOR THE DEAD. / CHILD'S BODY** [ ] [-]

Costermonger-Polydor Polydor

Aug 94. (7")(c-s) **BE MY LIGHT, BE MY GUIDE. / THIS IS NOT A CRIME** [54] [-]
(cd-s+=) – I can't help myself.
Oct 94. (7")(c-s)(cd-s) **SLEEP WELL TONIGHT. / SICK, SOBER AND SORRY / HER FIFTEEN YEARS** [36] [-]
Feb 95. (cd-s) **HAUNTED BY YOU / HOW MUCH FOR LOVE** [32] [ ]
(7"+=)(c-s+=)(cd-s+=) – Do you want to hear it from me.
Mar 95. (cd)(c)(lp) **OLYMPIAN** [8] [ ]
– Haunted by you / Your love, it lies / Truth, rest your head / A car that sped / Left-handed / London, can you wait? / To the city / Still can't find he phone / Sleep well tonight / Olympian / We'll find our own way.
Jun 95. (7") **BE MY LIGHT, BE MY GUIDE. / I CAN'T HELP MYSELF** [ ] [ ]
(above on 'Sub Pop' UK & feat. on 'HELTER SHELTER' box-set)
Jul 95. (cd-s) **OLYMPIAN / I CAN'T DECIDE IF SHE REALLY LOVES ME** [18] [ ]
(7"+=)(c-s+=)(cd-s+=) – To see the lights / Don't let me down.
(cd-s++=) – Don't let me down.

GENE LOVES JEZEBEL

Formed: Porthcawl, Wales . . . 1981 by identical twins JAY and MICHAEL ASTON. After a move to London and a support tour with The HIGSONS, they signed to 'Situation 2' label. Their 1982 debut release 'SHAVING MY NECK', scored an independent hit, although they had to wait 4 years for first UK Top 40 album 'DISCOVER'. Around the same time, they toured America with near fruitful results. • **Style:** Glamourous experimental gothic-rock outfit, influenced by tribal punk-rock and MARC BOLAN. • **Songwriters:** Group compositions. • **Trivia:** Produced by JOHN BRAID in 1985, until JOHN LECKIE took over.

Recommended: PROMISE (*6) / DISCOVER (*5).

MICHAEL ASTON (b. 4 May'61) – vocals / **JAY ASTON** (b.JOHN) – guitar, vox / **STEVE MARSHALL** – bass / **DICK HAWKINS** – drums

Situation 2 not issued

May 82. (7") **SHAVING MY NECK. / SUN AND INSANITY** [ ] [-]
(12"+=) – Machismo / Glad to be alive.
—— guests were **STEVE GOULDING** – saxophone / **JOHN MURPHY** – drums (ex-SPK, ex-ASSOCIATES)
Apr 83. (7") **SCREAMING (FOR EMMALENE). / SO YOUNG (HEAVE HARD HEAVE HO)** [ ] [-]
(12"+=) – No voodoo dollies.
On tour they used **JULIENNE REGAN – bass (future ALL ABOUT EVE) / ALBIO DE LUCA** – guitar (future FURYO)
Jul 83. (7") **BRUISES. / PUNCH DRUNK** [ ] [-]
(12"+=) – Brando bruises.

Oct 83. (lp)(c) **PROMISE** [ ] [-]
– Screaming (for Emmalene) / Bread from Heaven / Wraps and arms / Upstairs / Psychological problems / Scheming / Influenza / Punch drunk. *(re-iss.+cd.1988)*

Mar 84. (7") **INFLUENZA (RELAPSE). / WALKING IN THE PARK** [ ] [-]
(12"+=) – Stephen.

May 84. (7") **SHAME (WHOLE HEART BOWL). / THIN THINGS** [ ] [-]
(12"+=) – Gorgeous.

— The **ASTON's** brought in **PETER RIZZO** – bass repl. MARSHALL / **MARCUS GILVEAR** – drums (ex-KLAXON 5) repl. HAWKINS who joined SKELETAL FAMILY. / added **I.C. HUDSON** – guitar (who had joined on earlier tours)

May 85. (7") **COW. / ONE SOMEONE** [ ] [-]
(12") – ('A'extended) / Weep for her (cow).

Jun 85. (lp)(c) **IMMIGRANT** [ ] [-]
– Worth waiting for / Shame / Stephen / The rhino plasty / Cow / Cole Porter / Always a flame / The immigrant / Deep south whale. *(cd-iss.Jan88)*

— **JAMES STEVENSON** – guitar (ex-CHELSEA, ex-GENERATION X) repl. HUDSON

Nov 85. (7") **DESIRE. / FLAME (Steve Harley mix)** [ ] [ ]
(12"+=) – The immigrant.

Beggar's B. Geffen

Mar 86. (7") **THE SWEETEST THING. / PSYCHO II** [75] [ ]
(12"+=) – Sweetest Jezebel.

Jun 86. (7") **HEARTACHE. / BEYOND DOUBT** [71] [ ]
(12"+=) – Heartache I / Deli babies.

Jul 86. (lp)(c)(cd) **DISCOVER** [32] [ ]
– Heartache / Over the rooftops / Kick / White horse / Wait and see / Desire / Beyond doubt / The sweetest thing / Maid of Sker / Brand new moon. *(free-lp w/a)* **GLAD TO BE ALIVE (live)** – Upstairs / Over the rooftops / The rhino plasty / Worth waiting for / Cow / The immigrant / Brittle punches / Pop tarantula.

Oct 86. (7") **DESIRE (COME AND GET IT). / SAPPHIRE SCAVENGER** [ ] [ ]
(12"+=) – New horizons / Message.
(c-s+=) – ('A'-US mix) / Message.

— **CHRIS BELL** – drums (ex-SPEAR OF DESTINY, ex-THOMPSON TWINS, ex-SPECIMEN) repl. GILVEAR (he went to the States)

Aug 87. (d7")(d12") **THE MOTION OF LOVE. / A FRESH SLICE / BUGG'S BRUISES / VAGABOND (A NEW ADVENTURE)** [56] [-]

Oct 87. (lp)(c)(cd) **THE HOUSE OF DOLLS** [81] [ ]
– Gorgeous / The motion of love / Set me free / Suspicion / Every door / 20 killer hurts / Treasure / Message / Drowning crazy / Up there.

Nov 87. (7") **GORGEOUS. / SOMEONE ON THE 6TH FLOOR (AT THE JEZEBEL PALACE)** [68] [ ]
(12"+=)(cd-s+=) – Suspicion / Motion of love / (Jezebel mixes).

Jan 88. (7") **THE MOTION OF LOVE. / BUGG'S BRUISES** [-] [87]

Apr 88. (7") **SUSPICION. / DROWNING CRAZY** [-] [ ]

— (mid'89) **JAY** now sole survivor, when twin emigrated to the US. He brought in **RISINGHAM & RIZZO.**

Jun 90. (7") **JEALOUS. / LAST YEAR** [ ] [68]
(12"+=)(cd-s+=) – While you were there.

Jul 90. (cd)(c)(lp) **KISS OF LIFE** [ ] [ ]
– Jealous / It'll end in tears / Kiss of life / Why can't I / Syzygy / Walk away / Tangled up in you / Two shadows / Evening star / I die for you.

Dec 90. (12"ep)(cd-ep) **TANGLED UP IN YOU** [ ] [ ]
– Tangled up in you / Suspicion / Heartache / Stephen.

— line-up; **JAY ASHTON / RIZZO / STEVENSON + ROBERT ADAM**

Savage-Arista Savage-Arista

May 93. (7")(c-s) **JOSEPHINA. / TOMORROW COLOURS** [ ] [ ]
(cd-s+=) – ('A'extended).

Jun 93. (cd)(c) **HEAVENLY BODIES** [ ] [ ]
– American dreamer / Wild horse / Josephina / Any anxious colour / Break the chain / Down in a lonely place / Sweet sweet rain / Rosary / Heavenly bodies / Voice in the dark.

— Split for a while when JAMES STEVENSON was poached by The CULT.

— re-formed yet again with **ASHTON / STEVENSON + RIZZO**

Pink Gun not issued

Nov 95. (d-cd)(d-c) **IN THE AFTERGLOW (live)** [ ] [-]
– Gorgeous / Sweetest thing / Buggs bruises / Coal porter / Set me free / Suspicion / Over the rooftops / Stephen / Every door / Heartache / The motion of love / 20 killer hurts / Desire / American dreamer / Sweet sweet rain / Suspicion / Wild horse / Any anxious colour / Why can't I / Kiss of life / Evening star / 20 killer hurts / Jealous / Josephina / Always a flame / Desire.

GENERATION X

Formed: London, England . . . late 1976 by BILLY IDOL and TONY JAMES, whom had cut their teeth in embryonic CHELSEA group. After a few gigs at The ROXY in London, they were snapped up to 'Chrysalis' in 1977. Their debut 45 'YOUR GENERATION', gave them first entry into UK Top40, and an appearance on Top Of The Pops. • **Style:** Anthem riled punk-rock pop, fronted by the energetic lip curling blonde frontman BILLY IDOL. • **Songwriters:** IDOL-JAMES penned except; GIMME SOME TRUTH (John Lennon) / SHAKIN' ALL OVER (Johnny Kidd & The Pirates). • **Trivia:** IAN HUNTER (ex-MOTT THE HOOPLE) produced 1979 album 'VALLEY OF THE DOLLS', and took over from earlier producer MARTIN RUSHENT.

Recommended: PERFECT HITS (*7).

BILLY IDOL (b. WILLIAM BROAD, 30 Nov'55, Middlesex, England) – vocals (ex-CHELSEA, ex-INFANTS) / **BOB 'Derwood' ANDREWS** – guitar / **TONY JAMES** – bass, vocals (ex-CHELSEA, ex-INFANTS) / **MARK LAFF** – drums (ex-SUBWAY SECT) repl. JOHN TOWE (ex-CHELSEA, ex-INFANTS) who joined ALTERNATIVE TV then ADVERTS, etc

Chrysalis Chrysalis

Sep 77. (7") **YOUR GENERATION. / DAY BY DAY** [36] [ ]

Dec 77. (7") **WILD YOUTH. / WILD DUB / (ltd. mispress=) NO NO NO** [ ] [ ]

Mar 78. (7") **READY STEADY GO. / NO NO NO** [47] [ ]

Mar 78. (lp)(c) **GENERATION X** [29] [ ]
– From the heart / One hundred punks / Listen / Ready steady go / Kleenex / Promises promises / Day by day / The invisible man / Kiss me deadly / Too personal / Youth, youth, youth. *(cd-iss.1986) (re-iss.cd Mar94)*

Jan 79. (7")(7"red)(7"pink)(7"orange)(7"yellow) **KING ROCKER. / GIMME SOME TRUTH** [11] [ ]

Jan 79. (lp)(c) **VALLEY OF THE DOLLS** [51] [ ]
– Running with the boss sound / Night of the Cadillacs / Paradise west / Friday's angels / King rocker / Valley of the dolls / English dream / Love like fire / Paradise west / The prime of Kenny Silvers. *(cd-iss.1986)*

Mar 79. (7")(7"brown) **VALLEY OF THE DOLLS. / SHAKIN' ALL OVER** [23] [ ]

Jun 79. (7")(7"pink) **FRIDAY'S ANGELS. / TRYING FOR KICKS / THIS HEAT** [62] [ ]

— **TERRY CHIMES** – drums (ex-CLASH, ex-COWBOYS INTERNATIONAL) repl. LAFF / **JAMES STEPHENSON** – guitar (ex-CHELSEA) repl. 'DERWOOD' (later to WESTWORLD) (above 2 now with **IDOL** and **T. JAMES**)

GEN X

Chrysalis Chrysalis

Sep 80. (7") **DANCING WITH MYSELF. / UGLY RASH** [62] [ ]
(12"+=) – Loopy dub / What do you want

Jan 81. (lp)(c) **KISS ME DEADLY** [ ] [ ]
– Dancing with myself / Untouchables / Happy people / Heaven's inside / Triumph / Revenge / Stars look down / What do you want / Oh mother.

Jan 81. (7"ep)(12"ep)(7"clear-ep) **DANCING WITH MYSELF / UNTOUCHABLES / KING ROCKER / ROCK ON.** [60] [ ]

— Band split early '81. BILLY IDOL went solo. CHIMES rejoined The CLASH, TONY JAMES later formed SIGUE SIGUE SPUTNIK. STEPHENSON later joined GENE LOVES JEZEBEL, then The CULT.

– compilations etc. –

Nov 85. Chrysalis; (lp)(c) **THE BEST OF GENERATION X** [ ] [ ]

Oct 91. Chrysalis; (cd)(c)(lp) **PERFECT HITS (1975-81)** [ ] [ ]
– Dancing with myself / Your generation / Ready steady go / The untouchables / Day by day / Wild youth / Wild dub / One hundred punks / King rocker / Kiss me deadly / Gimme some truth / New order / English dream / Triumph / Youth, youth, youth.

Feb 87. Old Gold; (7") **KING ROCKER. / VALLEY OF THE DOLLS** [ ] [-]

Jun 87. M.B.C.; (lp) **THE ORIGINAL GENERATION X** [ ] [-]

Jun 87. M.B.C.; (lp) **GENERATION X LIVE (live)** [ ] [-]

GENESIS

Formed: Godalming, Surrey, England . . . early 1967 by Charterhouse public school boys PETER GABRIEL and TONY BANKS, both ex-The GARDEN WALL. They teamed up with former members of The ANON; MICHAEL RUTHERFORD, ANTHONY PHILLIPS and CHRIS STEWART. Still at school, they signed to 'Decca', having sent demos to solo artist and producer JONATHAN KING. Their first 2 singles flopped, as did 1969 lp 'FROM GENESIS TO REVELATION', which sold only around 500 copies. Early in 1970, they were seen live by TONY STRATTON-SMITH, who became their manager after signing them to his 'Charisma' label. Their lp 'TRESPASS' failed to breakthrough, although it contained live favourite and edited 45 'THE KNIFE'. After its release, they found new members PHIL COLLINS and STEVE HACKETT, who replaced recent additions JOHN MAYHEW and ANTHONY PHILLIPS. Late in '71, they unleashed 'NURSERY CRYME', which featured another 2 gems 'THE MUSICAL BOX' & 'THE RETURN OF THE GIANT HOGWEED'. It was also the brief debut on lead vox for COLLINS, who sang on the track 'FOR ABSENT FRIENDS'. A year later with many gigs behind them, they had first taste of chart success, when 'FOXTROT' hit the UK Top 20. This contained the excellent concept piece 'SUPPER'S READY', which lasted all of 23 minutes. In 1973, a live album of their best work so far, hit the Top 10, as did their studio follow-up 'SELLING ENGLAND BY THE POUND'. This enclosed another beaut 'THE BATTLE OF EPPING FOREST', plus another COLLINS sung song 'MORE FOOL ME'. Lifted from it was a near Top20 hit 45 'I KNOW WHAT I LIKE (IN YOUR WARDROBE)'. Late in 1974, they again made Top 10, with concept double album 'THE LAMB LIES DOWN ON BROADWAY', which was first US Top 50 entry and part of worldwide live show. Shortly after last concert in May'75, GABRIEL left for a solo career, and COLLINS stepped in for vocal duties. Surprisingly this did not harm commercial appeal of group, when they returned in 1976 with Top 3 album 'A TRICK OF THE TAIL'. His drum-stool was filled for live gigs by experienced BILL BRUFORD, then CHESTER THOMPSON, who appeared on 1977 double album 'SECONDS OUT'. This was also the last album to feature STEVE HACKETT, who also left for lucrative solo venture. In 1978, their next album, appropriately titled ' . . . AND THEN THERE WERE THREE' (COLLINS, BANKS & RUTHERFORD), hit No.3 and also climbed into US Top 20. The 80's became even more fruitful for the band, hitting top spot in the UK with each album release. They also amassed a number of hit singles on both sides of the Atlantic. During this era, PHIL COLLINS (who had sidelined drumming attributes, in own BRAND X group) scored a number of easier-listening hit singles and albums. He also re-launched his acting career (as a teenager, he was 'The Artful Dodger' in West End production of 'Oliver'), starring on TV series 'Miami Vice' and films 'RISKY BUSINESS', 'BUSTER' & 'HOOK'. He had also sessioned for over 100 groups/artists, including ENO, JOHN CALE and ARGENT. His later production work included; FRIDA (Abba) / ADAM & THE ANTS, HOWARD JONES and ERIC CLAPTON to name but a few. TONY BANKS also released solo work, as did MIKE RUTHERFORD, who also chose a pop outlet in MIKE + THE MECHANICS. • **Style:** Early GENESIS moved through pop/rock like MOODY BLUES sound, to progressive theatrical act, fronted by the bizarre extrovert PETER GABRIEL. After his untimely departure, group were not too dissimilar, although in recent years, they have mellowed with age. Although many PHIL COLLINS' pop fans might disagree, their best work definitely sprouted from the 70's. Ask any old MARILLION fan, especially their one-time singer FISH. PHIL COLLINS is undoubtably the most well-liked and respected of all great drummers, and showed why, when helping youngsters on recent teaching courses. • **Songwriters:** GABRIEL lyrics and group compositions. From 1978, the trio collaborated on all work. PHIL COLLINS covered; YOU CAN'T HURRY LOVE (Supremes) / SEPARATE LIVES (Stephen Bishop) / TWO HEARTS (co-with Lamont Dozier) / GROOVY KIND OF LOVE (Mindbenders) / ALWAYS (Irving Berlin) and a few more. MIKE + THE MECHANICS covered YOU'VE REALLY GOT A HOLD ON ME (Smokey Robinson & The Miracles) / I BELIEVE (WHEN I FALL IN LOVE IT WILL BE FOREVER) (Stevie Wonder & Syreeta). • **Miscellaneous:** COLLINS divorced wife in '78, and married Jill Taverman on 4 Aug'84. He guested on 1985 'LIVE AID' concert and played drums behind LED ZEPPELIN re-union of ROBERT PLANT and JIMMY PAGE.

Recommended: NURSERY CRYME (*8) / TRESPASS (*5) / FOXTROT (*9) / GENESIS LIVE (*6) / SELLING ENGLAND BY THE POUND (*8) / THE LAMB LIES DOWN ON BROADWAY (*7) / A TRICK OF THE TAIL (*6) / WIND & WUTHERING (*6) / . . . AND THEN THERE WERE THREE (*6) / DUKE (*6) / INVISIBLE TOUCH (*5).

PETER GABRIEL (b.13 May'50, London, England) – vocals / **TONY BANKS** (b.27 Mar'51, East Heathly, Sussex, England) – keyboards, vocals / **ANTHONY PHILLIPS** – guitar, vocals / **MICHAEL RUTHERFORD** (b. 2 Oct'50, Guildford, Surrey, England) – bass, guitar / **CHRIS STEWART** – drums

Decca / Parrot

Feb 68. (7") **THE SILENT SUN. / THAT'S ME** [ ] [ ]
May 68. (7") **A WINTER'S TALE. / ONE-EYED HOUND** [ ] [-]

—— **JOHN SILVER** – drums repl. CHRIS

Mar 69. (lp) **FROM GENESIS TO REVELATION** [ ] [ ]
– Where the sour turns to sweet / In the beginning / Fireside song / The serpent / Am I very wrong? / In the wilderness / The conqueror / In hiding / One day / Window / In limbo / The silent sun / A place to call my own. *(re-iss.'74 as 'IN THE BEGINNING') (re-iss.cd+c Oct93 on 'Music Club')*

Jun 69. (7") **WHERE THE SOUR TURNS TO SWEET. / IN HIDING** [ ] [-]

—— (Jul69) **JOHN MAYHEW** – drums repl. JOHN SILVER

Charisma / Impulse

Oct 70. (lp)(c) **TRESPASS** [ ] [ ]
– Looking for someone / White mountain / Visions of angels / Stagnation / Dusk / The knife. *(re-iss.Mar84, hit 98) (re-iss.Mar86, cd-iss.Jun88) (re-iss.'74 in US on 'A.B.C.') (cd re-iss.Aug94 on 'Virgin')*

Jun 71. (7") **THE KNIFE (Pt.1). / THE KNIFE (Pt.2)** [ ] [-]

—— (Dec70) **GABRIEL, BANKS and RUTHERFORD** recruit new members **PHIL COLLINS** (b.31 Jan'51, Chiswick, London, England) – drums, vocals (ex-FLAMING YOUTH) repl. MAYHEW / **STEVE HACKETT** (b.12 Feb'50, London) – guitar (ex-QUIET WORLD) repl. ANTHONY PHILLIPS who went solo

Charisma / Charisma

Nov 71. (lp)(c) **NURSERY CRYME** [ ] [ ]
– The musical box / For absent friends / The fountain of Salmacis / Seven stones / Harold the barrel / Harlequin / The return of the giant hogweed. *(hit UK No.39 May74) (re-iss.Mar84 on 'Virgin', hit 68) (cd-iss.Sep85) (cd re-iss.Aug94 on 'Virgin')*

May 72. (7") **HAPPY THE MAN. / SEVEN STONES** [ ] [ ]
Oct 72. (lp)(c) **FOXTROT** [12] [ ]
– Get 'em out by Friday / Time-table / Watcher of the skies / Can-utility and the coastliners / Horizon / Supper's ready; (i) Lover's leap, (ii) The guaranteed eternal sanctuary man, (iii) Ikhaton and Itsacon and their band of merry men, (iv) How dare I be so beautiful, (v) Willow farm, (vi) Apocalypse in 9/8 co-starring the delicious talents of Gabble Ratchet, (vii) As sure as eggs is eggs (aching men's feets). *(re-iss.Sep83 on 'Virgin') (cd-iss.Jul86) (cd re-iss.Aug94 on 'Virgin')*

Feb 73. (7") **WATCHER OF THE SKIES. / WILLOW FARM** [-] [ ]
Jul 73. (lp)(c) **GENESIS LIVE (live)** [9] [ ]
– Watcher of the skies / Get 'em out by Friday / The return of the giant hogweed / The musical box / The knife. *(re-iss.Frb86 on 'Virgin') (cd-iss.Jul87) (cd re-iss.Aug94 on 'Virgin')*

Oct 73. (lp)(c) **SELLING ENGLAND BY THE POUND** [3] [70]
– Dancing in the moonlight knight / I know what I like (in your wardrobe) / Firth of fifth / More fool me / The battle of Epping Forest / After the ordeal / The cinema show / Aisle of plenty. *(re-iss.Oct86 on 'Virgin') (cd-iss.Feb86) (cd re-iss.Aug94 on 'Virgin')*

Mar 74. (7") **I KNOW WHAT I LIKE (IN YOUR WARDROBE). / TWILIGHT ALEHOUSE** [21] [ ]

Charisma / Atco

Nov 74. (d-lp)(d-c) **THE LAMB LIES DOWN ON BROADWAY** [10] [41]
– The lamb lies down on Broadway / Fly on a windshield / Broadway melody of 1974 / Cuckoo cocoon / In the cage / The grand parade of lifeless packaging / Back in N.Y.C. / Hairless heart / Counting out time / Carpet crawlers / The chamber of 32 doors / / Lilywhite Lilith / The waiting room / Anyway / Here comes the supernatural anaesthetist / The lamia / Silent sorrow in empty boats / The colony of Slippermen (The arrival – A visit to the doktor – Raven) / Ravine / The light dies down on Broadway / Riding the scree / it. *(re-iss.Sep83 on 'Virgin') (d-cd-iss.Feb86) (cd re-iss.Aug94 on 'Virgin')*

Nov 74. (7") **COUNTING OUT TIME. / RIDING THE SCREE** [ ] [-]
1974. (7") **THE LAMB LIES DOWN ON BROADWAY. / COUNTING OUT TIME** [-] [ ]
Apr 75. (7") **CARPET CRAWLERS. / THE WAITING ROOM (evil jam)** [ ] [-]

—— Now just a quartet when PETER GABRIEL left to go solo.

Feb 76. (lp)(c) **A TRICK OF THE TAIL** [3] [31]
– Dance on a volcano / Entangled / Squonk / Mad mad Moon / Robbery, assault and battery / Ripples / A trick of the tail / Los endos. *(re-iss.+cd.Sep83 on 'Virgin') (cd re-iss.Oct94)*

Mar 76. (7") **A TRICK OF THE TAIL. / RIPPLES** [ ] [-]
Mar 76. (7") **RIPPLES. / ENTANGLED** [-] [ ]
Jan 77. (lp)(c) **WIND AND WUTHERING** [7] [26]
– Eleventh Earl of Mar / One for the vine / Your own special way / Wot gorilla? / All in a mouse's night / Blood on the rooftops / Unquiet slumbers for the sleepers . . .In that quiet Earth / Afterglow. *(re-iss.Sep83 on 'Virgin') (re-iss.Apr90) (cd-iss.Apr86) (cd re-iss.Oct94)*

Feb 77. (7") **YOUR OWN SPECIAL WAY. / IT'S YOURSELF** [43] [-]
Feb 77. (7") **YOUR OWN SPECIAL WAY. / . . .IN THAT QUIET EARTH** [-] [62]
May 77. (7"ep) **SPOT THE PIGEON** [14] [ ]
– Match of the day / Inside and out / Pigeons. *(cd-ep iss.1988 on 'Virgin')*

—— added **BILL BRUFORD** – drums (ex-YES, ex-KING CRIMSON) **CHESTER THOMPSON** – drums (ex-FRANK ZAPPA) they were both used on live album below, with CHESTER augmenting on tours.

Oct 77. (d-lp)(d-c) **SECONDS OUT (live)** [4] [47]
– Squonk / Carpet crawlers / Robbery, assault and battery / Afterglow / Firth of fifth / I know what I like (in your wardrobe) / The lamb lies down on Broadway / The musical box / Supper's ready / The cinema show / Dance on a volcano / Los endos. *(re-iss.Sep83 on 'Virgin', d-cd.iss.Nov85) (cd re-iss.Oct94)*

—— (Jun77) Now a trio of **COLLINS, BANKS & RUTHERFORD** when STEVE HACKETT continued solo career.

Charisma / Atlantic

Mar 78. (7") **FOLLOW YOU FOLLOW ME. / BALLAD OF BIG** [7] [-]
Mar 78. (7") **FOLLOW YOU FOLLOW ME. / INSIDE AND OUT** [-] [23]
Apr 78. (lp)(c) **. . .AND THEN THERE WERE THREE** [3] [14]
– Down and out / Undertow / Ballad of big / Snowbound / Burning rope / Deep in the motherlode / Many too many / Scene from a night's dream / Say it's alright Joe / The lady lies / Follow you follow me. *(re-iss.Sep83 on 'Virgin') (cd-iss.mid'83) (c+cd.re-iss.Aug91) (cd re-iss.Oct94)*

Jun 78. (7") **MANY TOO MANY. / THE DAY THE LIGHT WENT OUT IN VANCOUVER** [43] [ ]
Jul 78. (7") **SCENE FROM A NIGHT'S DREAM. / DEEP IN THE MOTHERLODE** [-] [ ]
Mar 80. (7") **TURN IT ON AGAIN. / BEHIND THE LINES (part 2)** [8] [-]
Mar 80. (lp)(c) **DUKE** [1] [11]
– Behind the lines / Duchess / Guide vocal / Man of our time / Misunderstanding / Heathaze / Turn it on again / Alone tonight / Cul-de-sac / Please don't ask / Duke's end / Duke's travels. *(re-iss.Sep83 on 'Virgin') (cd-iss.Apr85) (c+cd-re-iss.Mar91) (cd re-iss.Oct94)*

May 80. (7") **DUCHESS. / OPEN DOOR** [46] [ ]
May 80. (7") **MISUNDERSTANDING. / BEHIND THE LINES** [-] [14]
Sep 80. (7") **TURN IT ON AGAIN. / EVIDENCE OF AUTUMN** [-] [58]
Sep 80. (7") **MISUNDERSTANDING. / EVIDENCE OF AUTUMN** [42] [-]
Aug 81. (7") **ABACAB. / ANOTHER RECORD** [9] [-]
Sep 81. (lp)(c) **ABACAB** [1] [7]
– Abacab / No reply at all / Me and Sarah Jane / Kep it dark / Dodo / Lurker / Who dunnit? / Man on the corner / Like it or not / Another record. *(cd-iss.Sep83 & Apr85) (c+cd.re-iss.Mar91) (cd re-iss.Oct94)*

Oct 81. (7") **KEEP IT DARK. / NAMINANU** [33] [-]
(12"+=) – Abacab (long version).
Oct 81. (7") **NO REPLY AT ALL. / HEAVEN LOVE MY LIFE** [-] [29]
Jan 82. (7") **ABACAB. / WHO DUNNIT?** [-] [26]
May 82. (7") **PAPERLATE. / YOU MIGHT RECALL** [-] [32]
Mar 82. (7") **MAN IN THE CORNER. / SUBMARINE** [41] [40]
May 82. (7"ep)**3" X 3"** [10] [-]
– Paperlate / You might recall / Me and Virgil.
Jun 82. (d-lp)(c) **THREE SIDES LIVE (live except ***)** [2] [10]
– Turn it on again / Dodo / Abacab / Behind the lines / Duchess / Me and Sarah Jane / Follow you follow me / Misunderstanding / In the cage / Afterglow / One for the vine * / Fountain of Salmacis * / Watcher of the skies * / It * / Paperlate *** / You might recall *** / Me and Virgil *** / Evidence of Autumn *** / Open door *** / You might recall II ***. *(cd-iss.Apr85 & 1988) (US-cd.repl.* w/ The cinema show + The colony of Slippermen) (cd re-iss.Oct94)*

Virgin / Atco

Aug 83. (7")(12") **MAMA. / IT'S GONNA GET BETTER** [4] [73]
(cd-ep.iss.Jun88 with extended versions)
Oct 83. (lp)(c)(cd) **GENESIS** [1] [9]
– Mama / That's all / Home by the sea / Second home by the sea / Illegal alien / Taking it all too hard / Just a job to do / Silver rainbow / It's gonna get better. *(re-iss.Jul87)*

Nov 83. (7") **THAT'S ALL. / TAKING IT ALL TOO HARD** [16] [-]
(12"+=) – Firth of fifth (live).
Nov 83. (7") **THAT'S ALL. / SECOND HOME BY THE SEA** [-] [6]
Feb 84. (7")(7"sha-pic-d) **ILLEGAL ALIEN. / TURN IT ON AGAIN (live)** [46] [44]
(12"+=) – ('A'extended).
Jun 84. (7") **TAKING IT ALL TOO HARD. / SILVER RAINBOW** [-] [50]
May 86. (7")(7"clear) **INVISIBLE TOUCH. / THE LAST DOMINO** [15] [1]
(12"+=) – ('A'extended).
Jun 86. (lp)(c)(cd) **INVISIBLE TOUCH** [1] [3]
– Invisible touch / Tonight, tonight, tonight / Land of confusion / In too deep / Anything she does / Domino:- In the glow of the night – The last domino / Throwing it all away / The Brazilian. *(pic-lp+cd.Dec88)*

Aug 86. (7")(12") **IN TOO DEEP. / DO THE NEUROTIC** 19 –

Aug 86. (7") **THROWING IT ALL AWAY. / DO THE NEUROTIC** – 4

Nov 86. (7") **LAND OF CONFUSION. / FEED FIRE WITH THE FIRE** 16 4 Oct 86
(12"+=)/ /(cd-s++=) – Do the neurotic. / / ('A'extended).

Mar 87. (7")(12") **TONIGHT, TONIGHT, TONIGHT. / IN THE GLOW OF THE NIGHT** 3 Feb 87
(12"+=)(cd-s+=) – Paperlate / ('A'remix).

Apr 87. (7") **IN TOO DEEP. / I'D RATHER BE WITH YOU** – 3

Jun 87. (7") **THROWING IT ALL AWAY. / I'D RATHER BE WITH YOU** –
(12"+=)(c-s+=) – Invisible touch (live).

Oct 91. (7")(c-s) **NO SON OF MINE. / LIVING FOREVER** 6 13
(12"+=)(c-s+=)(cd-s+=) – Invisible touch (live).

Nov 91. (cd)(c)(d-lp) **WE CAN'T DANCE** 1 4
– No son of mine / Jesus he knows me / Driving the last spike / I can't dance / Never a time / Dreaming while you sleep / Tell me why / Living forever / Hold on my heart / Way of the world / Since I lost you / Fading lights.

Jan 92. (7")(c-s) **I CAN'T DANCE. / ON THE SHORELINE** 7 7
(cd-s+=) – In too deep (live) / That's all (live).
(cd-s+=) – ('A'sex mix).

Apr 92. (7")(c-s) **HOLD ON MY HEART. / WAY OF THE WORLD** 16 12
(cd-s+=)/ /(cd-s+=) – Your own special way./ / Home by the sea.

Jul 92. (7")(c-s) **JESUS HE KNOWS ME. / HEARTS OF FIRE** 20 23
(cd-s+=)/ /(cd-s+=) – I can't dance (mix)./ / Land of confusion.

Nov 92. (cd)(c)(d-lp) **THE WAY WE WALK VOLUME 1: THE SHORTS (live)** 3 35
– Land of confusion / No son of mine / Jesus he knows me / Throwing it all away / I can't dance / Mama / Hold on my heart / That's all / In too deep / Tonight, tonight, tonight / Invisible touch.

Nov 92. (7")(c-s) **INVISIBLE TOUCH (live). / ABACAB** 7 –
(cd-s+=) – The Brazilian.

Nov 92. (c-s) **NEVER A TIME. / ?** – 21

Jan 93. (cd)(c)(lp) **LIVE / THE WAY WE WALK VOLUME 2: THE LONGS (live)** 1
– Old medley: Dance on a volcano – Lamb lies down on Broadway – The musical box – Firth of fifth – I know what I like . . . / Driving the fast spike / Domino: part I – In the glow of the night, part II – The last domino / Home by the sea – Second home by the sea / Drum duet.

Feb 93. (7")(c-s) **TELL ME WHY. / DREAMING WHILE YOU SLEEP** 40
(cd-s+=) – Tonight, tonight, tonight.

– compilations etc. –

May 74. Charisma; (d-lp-box) **TRESPASS / NURSERY CRYME** –

May 74. Charisma; (d-lp-box) **FOXTROT / SELLING ENGLAND..** –

Mar 83. Charisma; (d-c) **FOXTROT / TRESPASS** –

May 76. Decca; (lp)(c) **ROCK ROOTS** (debut +early 45's) –

1976. Buddah; (d-lp) **THE BEST – GENESIS** (early) –

Mar 87. London; (cd) **AND THE WORLD WAS** (early) –

Oct 87. Razor; (lp)(c)(cd) **THE SOUR TURNS TO SWEET** –
(re-iss.Jul91)

Jun 88. Old Gold; (7") **FOLLOW YOU FOLLOW ME. / A TRICK OF THE TAIL** –

Jun 88. Old Gold; (7") **I KNOW WHAT I LIKE (IN YOUR WARDROBE). / COUNTING OUT TIME** –

Nov 90. Virgin; (pic-cd-box) **GENESIS CD COLLECTORS EDITION**
– (TRESPASS / NURSERY CRYME / FOXTROT)

— **PHIL COLLINS** with **BRAND X** (alongside **ROBIN LUMLEY** – keyboards / **JOHN GOODSALL** – bass / **PERCY JONES** – bass / **MORRIS PERT** – percussion / **etc.)** albums **UNORTHODOX BEHAVOIR** (Jun76) / **MOROCCAN ROLL** (Apr77 hit UK No.37) / **LIVESTOCK** (Nov77) / **MASQUES** (1978) / **PRODUCT** (Sep79) / **DO THEY HURT?** (May80) / **IS THERE ANYTHING ABOUT** (Sep82, without Phil) . (all re-iss.on cd)

— Compilation cd Dec92 **'THE PLOT THINS – A HISTORY OF BRAND X'** on 'Virgin'.

PHIL COLLINS

Virgin Atlantic

Jan 81. (7") **IN THE AIR TONIGHT. / THE ROOF IS LEAKING** 2 19 May 81

Feb 81. (lp)(c) **FACE VALUE** 1 7
– In the air tonight / This must be love / Behind the lines / The roof is leaking / Droned / Hand in hand / I missed again / You know what I mean / I'm not moving / If leaving me is easy / Tomorrow never knows / Thunder and lightning. *(cd-iss.Jun88)*

Mar 81. (7")(12") **I MISSED AGAIN. / I'M NOT MOVING** 14 19

May 81. (7") **IF LEAVING ME IS EASY. / DRAWING BOARD** 17

Oct 82. (7")(7"pic-d) **THRU THESE WALLS. / DO YOU KNOW, DO YOU CARE** 56

Nov 82. (lp)(c) **HELLO I MUST BE GOING!** 2 8
– I don't care anymore / I cannot believe it's true / Like China / Do you know, do you care? / You can't hurry love / It don't matter to me / Thru these walls / Don't let him steal your love away / The west side / Why can't it wait 'til morning. *(cd-iss.Jun88) (re-iss.Jun91 hit UK No.48)*

Nov 82. (7")(7"pic-d) **YOU CAN'T HURRY LOVE. / I CANNOT BELIEVE IT'S TRUE** 1 –
(12"+=) – Oddball.

Nov 82. (7") **YOU CAN'T HURRY LOVE. / DO YOU KNOW, DO YOU CARE** – 10

Mar 83. (7") **DON'T LET HIM STEAL YOUR HEART AWAY. / THUNDER AND LIGHTNING** 45
(12") – ('A'side) / And so to F.

Feb 83. (7") **I DON'T CARE ANYMORE. / THE WEST SIDE** – 39

May 83. (7") **WHY CAN'T IT WAIT 'TIL MORNING. / LIKE CHINA** –

May 83. (7") **I CANNOT BELIEVE IT'S TRUE. / THRU THESE WALLS** – 79

Feb 84. (7") **AGAINST ALL ODDS. / (b-side by Larry Carlton)** – 1

Mar 84. (7")(7"pic-d) **AGAINST ALL ODDS (TAKE A LOOK AT ME NOW). / MAKING A BIG MISTAKE ('B' side by MIKE RUTHERFORD)** 2 –

(above from the film of the same name)

1984. (7") **WALK THROUGH THE FIRE. / MAKING A BIG MISTAKE** –

Jan 85. (7") **SUSSUDIO. / THE MAN WITH THE HORN** 12 1 Apr 85
(12"+=)(12"sha-pic-d+=) – ('A'extended).

Feb 85. (lp)(c)(cd) **NO JACKET REQUIRED** 1 1
– Sussudio / Only you know and I know / Long long way to go / Don't want to know / One more night / Don't lose my number / Who said I would / Doesn't anybody stay together anymore? / Inside out / Take me home. (cd+=) – We said hello, goodbye.

Feb 85. (7") **ONE MORE NIGHT. / THE MAN WITH THE HORN** – 1

Mar85 saw him duet with **PHIL BAILEY (ex-EARTH, WIND & FIRE)** on single **EASY LOVER** which hit UK No.1 & US No.2 (Nov84)

Apr 85. (7")(12")(7"pic-d) **ONE MORE NIGHT. / I LIKE THE WAY** 4 –

Apr 85. (7") **SUSSIDIO. / I LIKE THE WAY** – 1

Jul 85. (7") **TAKE ME HOME. / WE SAID HELLO, GOODBYE** 19 –
(12"+=) – ('A'extended).
(d7"+=) – Against all odds / Making a big mistake.

Jul 85. (7") **DON'T LOSE MY NUMBER. / WE SAID HELLO GOODBYE** – 4

Oct 85. (7") **SEPARATE LIVES ("PHIL COLLINS & MARILYN MARTIN"). / I DON'T WANNA KNOW** – 1

Nov 85. (7")(12")(7"white)(7"-2-interlocking pic-discs) **SEPARATE LIVES. (by "PHIL COLLINS & MARILYN MARTIN") / ONLY YOU KNOW AND I KNOW** 4 –

Mar 86. (7") **TAKE ME HOME. / ONLY YOU AND I KNOW** – 7

Aug 88. (7")(12") **A GROOVY KIND OF LOVE. / BIG NOISE** 1 1
(cd-s+=) – Will you still be waiting.

— (above & below singles were from the film 'BUSTER', in which he starred and contributed some tracks to soundtrack released Sep88)

Nov 88. (7") **TWO HEARTS. / THE ROBBERY (excerpt)** 6 1
(12"+=)(cd-s+=) – ('B'extended).

Nov 89. (7")(12") **ANOTHER DAY IN PARADISE. / HEAT ON THE STREET** 2 1
(c-s+=)(cd-s+=) – Saturday night and Sunday morning.

Nov 89. (lp)(c)(cd) **... BUT SERIOUSLY** 1 1
– Hang in long enough / That's just the way it is / Do you remember? / Something happened on the way to Heaven / Colours / I wish it would rain down / Another day in Paradise / Heat on the street / All of my life / Saturday night and Sunday morning / Father to son / Find a way to my heart.

Jan 90. (7") **I WISH IT WOULD RAIN DOWN. / HOMELESS (ANOTHER DAY IN PARADISE) (demo)** 7 –
(12"+=)(cd-s+=) – You've been in love (that little bit too long). (US; b-side)

Jan 90. (7") **I WISH IT WOULD RAIN DOWN. / YOU'VE BEEN IN LOVE** – 3

Apr 90. (7") **DO YOU REMEMBER. / I WISH IT WOULD RAIN DOWN** – 4

Apr 90. (7")(c-s) **SOMETHING HAPPENED ON THE WAY TO HEAVEN. / I WISH IT WOULD RAIN DOWN (live)** 15 –
(12"+=)(cd-s+=) – ('A'remix).

Jul 90. (7")(c-s) **THAT'S JUST THE WAY IT IS. / BROADWAY CHORUS (SOMETHING HAPPENED ON THE WAY TO HEAVEN)** 26
(12"+=)(cd-s+=) – In the air tonight (extended).

Aug 90. (7") **SOMETHING HAPPENED ON THE WAY TO HEAVEN. / LIONEL** – 4

Sep 90. (7")(c-s) **HANG IN LONG ENOUGH. / AROUND THE WORLD IN 80 PRESETS** 34 –
(cd-s+=) – ('A'dub) / That's how I feel.
(cd-s+=) – ('A'-12"mix).
(12") – ('A'side) / ('A'dub) / ('A'-12"mix).

Nov 90. (c-s) **HANG IN LONG ENOUGH. / SEPARATE LIVES** – 23

— live with **LELAND SKLAR** – bass / **CHESTER THOMPSON** – drums / **DARYL STUERMER** – guitar / **BRAD COLE** – keyboards / **BRIDGETTE BRYANT, ARNOLD McCULLER and FRED WHITE** – backing vocals. plus **DON MYRICK** – alto sax / **LUI LUI** – trombone / **RAHMLEE MICHAEL DAVIS** – trumpet / **HARRY KIM** – trumpet.

Nov 90. (cd)(c)(lp) **SERIOUS HITS LIVE! (live)** 2 11
– Something happened on the way to Heaven / Against all odds (take a look at me now) / Who said I would / One more night / Don't lose my number / Another day in Paradise / Do you remember / Separate lives / In the air tonight / You can't hurry love / Two hearts / Sussidio / Groovy kind of love / Easy lover / Take me home.

Nov 90. (7")(c-s) **DO YOU REMEMBER (live). / AGAINST THE ODDS (live)** 57 –
(12"+=) – Doesn't anyone stay together anymore (live).
(cd-s++=) – The roof is leaking.

Feb 91. (c-s) **WHO SAID I WOULD (live). / ?** – 73

In May 93, PAUL was credited on DAVID CROSBY'S Top 50 hit 'Hero'.

Oct 93. (7")(c-s) **BOTH SIDES OF THE STORY. / ALWAYS** 7 25
(cd-s+=) Both sides of the demo.
(cd-s++=) Rad Dudeski.

Nov 93. (cd)(c)(lp) **BOTH SIDES** 1 13
– Both sides of the story / Can't turn back the years / Everyday / I've forgotten everything / We're sons of our fathers / Can't find my way / Survivors / We fly so close / There's a place for us / We wait and wonder / Please come out tonight

Jan 94. (7")(c-s) **EVERYDAY. / DON'T CALL ME ASHLEY** 15 24
(cd-s+=) – ('A'demo).
(cd-s+=) – Doesn't anybody stay together anymore (live).

Apr 94. (7")(c-s) **WE WAIT AND WE WONDER. / HERO** 45
(cd-s+=) – For a friend.
(cd-s) – ('A'side) / Take me with you / Stevie's blues – There's a place for us (instrumental).

– his compilations, others, etc. –

Jan 88. Virgin; (cd)(US-lp)(US-cd) **12 INCHERS**
– (12" remixed extended versions of 6 hits)

Jun 88. Vigin; (7") **IN THE AIR TONIGHT ('88 remix). / I MISSED AGAIN** 4

(12"+=)(cd-s+=) – ('A'extended).

TONY BANKS

Charisma Charisma

Oct 79. (7") **FOR A WHILE. / FROM THE UNDERTOW**
Oct 79. (lp)(c) **A CURIOUS FEELING** 21
– From the undertow / Lucky me / The lie / After the lie / A curious feeling / Forever morning / You / Somebody else's dream / The waters of Lethe / For a while / In the dark. *(re-iss.Oct86) (cd-iss.1988)*
Jul 80. (7") **FOR A WHILE. / A CURIOUS FEELING**
Apr 83. (7")(12") **THIS IS LOVE. / CHARM**

— May83, he released single and film soundtrack THE WICKED LADY on 'Atlantic'

Jun 83. (lp)(c) **THE FUGUTIVE** 50
– This is love / Man of spells / And the wheels keep turning / Say you'll never leave me / Thirty three's / By you / At the edge of night / Charm / Moving under.
Aug 83. (7")**AND THE WHEELS KEEP TURNING. / K.2.**
(12"+=) – Sometime never.
Sep 85. (7"ep) **'TONY BANKS' (with JIM DIAMOND and TOYAH)**
– Red wing (instrumental) / You call this victory / Line of symmetry.
Oct 86. (7") **SHORT CUT TO NOWHERE. (by "FISH & TONY BANKS") / SMILIN JACK CASEY**
(12"+=) – K.2.
Jul 87. (cd) **SOUNDTRACKS ('Quicksilver' // 'Lorca And The Outlaws')**
– Short cut to nowhere / Smilin' Jack Casey / Quicksilver suite: Rebirth – Gypsy – Final chase // You call this victory / Lion of symmetry / Redwing suite: Redwing – Lorca – Kid and Detective Droid – Lift off – Death of Abby. *(lp/c.Nov89)*

BANKSTATEMENT

TONY BANKS with friends, etc.

Virgin Atlantic

Jul 89. (7") **THROWBACK. / THURSDAY THE 12th**
(12"+=) – This is love.
Aug 89. (lp)(c)(cd) **BANKSTATEMENT**
– Throwback / I'll be waiting / Queen of darkness / That night / Raincloud / he border / Big man / A house needs a roof / The more I hide it. *(cd+=)* – Diamonds aren't so bad / Thursday the 12th.
Oct 89. (7") **I'LL BE WAITING. / DIAMONDS AREN'T SO BAD**
(12"+=)(cd-s+=) – And the wheels keep turning.

TONY BANKS

solo, with guest vocals **ANDY TAYLOR, FISH, JAYNEY KLIMEK**

May 91. (7")(c-s) **I WANNA CHANGE THE SCORE. / HERO FOR AN HOUR** 50
(12"+=) – Big man (BANKSTATEMENT).
(cd-s++=) – The waters of Lethe.
Jun 91. (cd)(c)(lp) **STILL**
– Red day on blue street / Angel face / The gift / Still it takes me by surprise / Hero for an hour / I wanna change the score / Water out of wine / Another murder of a day / Back to back / The final curtain.

MIKE RUTHERFORD

Charisma Passport

Jan 80. (7") **WORKING IN LINE. / COMPRESSION** – –
Feb 80. (lp)(c) **SMALLCREEP'S DAY** 13
– Smallcreep's day: Between the tick and the tock – Working in line – After hours – Cats and rats in the neighbourhood – Smallcreep alone – Out into the daylight – At the end of the day / Moonshine / Time and time again / Romani / Every road / Overnight job. *(re-iss.Oct86) (cd-iss.Jun89)*
Mar 80. (7") **WORKING IN LINE. / MOONSHINE** –
Jul 80. (7") **TIME AND TIME AGAIN. / AT THE END OF THE DAY** –

W.E.A. Atlantic

Aug 82. (7") **HALFWAY THERE. / A DAY TO REMEMBER** Nov 82
Aug 82. (7") **A DAY TO REMEMBER. / MAXINE** –
Sep 82. (lp)(c) **ACTING VERY STRANGE** 23
– Acting very strange / A day to remember / Maxine / Halfway there / Who's fooling who / Couldn't get arrested / I don't wanna know / Hideaway.
Oct 82. (7")(12") **ACTING VERY STRANGE. / COULDN'T GET ARRESTED** –
Jan 83. (7") **HIDEAWAY. / CALYPSO** –

MIKE + THE MECHANICS

RUTHERFORD with **PAUL CARRACK** – vocals, keyboards (ex-ACE, ex-SQUEEZE, ex-Solo artist) / **PAUL YOUNG** – vocals (ex-SAD CAFE) / **PETER VAN HOOKE** – drums / **ADRIAN LEE** – keys

WEA Atlantic

Oct 85. (lp)(c) **MIKE + THE MECHANICS** 78 26
– Silent running (on dangerous ground) / All I need is a miracle / Par Avion / Hanging by a thread / I get the feeling / Take the reins / You are the one / A call to arms / Taken in. *(cd-iss.Jul86)*
Nov 85. (7") **SILENT RUNNING (ON DANGEROUS GROUND). / PAR AVION** – 6
Feb 86. (7") **SILENT RUNNING (ON DANGEROUS GROUND). / I GET THE FEELING** 21 –
(12"+=) – Too far gone.
May 86. (7")(12") **ALL I NEED IS A MIRACLE. / YOU ARE THE ONE** 53 5 Mar 86
(12"+=) – A call to arms.
Jun 86. (7") **TAKEN IN. / A CALL TO ARMS** – 32

— added **TIM RENWICK** – guitar (ex-SUTHERLAND BROTHERS & QUIVER, etc.)

Nov 88. (7")(12") **NOBODY'S PERFECT. / NOBODY KNOWS** 63
(cd-s+=) – All I need is a miracle.
Nov 88. (lp)(c)(cd) **THE LIVING YEARS** 2 13
– Nobody's perfect / The living years / Seeing is believing / Nobody knows / Poor boy down / Blame / Don't / Black and blue / Beautiful day / Why me?.
Feb 89. (7") **THE LIVING YEARS. / TOO MANY FRIENDS** 2 1 Jan 89
(12"+=)(cd-s+=) – I get the feeling (live).
Apr 89. (7") **NOBODY KNOWS. / WHY ME?**
(12"+=)(cd-s+=)(c-s+=) – The living years / ('A'edit).
Apr 89. (c-s) **SEEING IS BELIEVING. /** – 62
Mar 91. (7")(12")(c-s)(cd-s) **WORD OF MOUTH. / LET'S PRETEND IT DIDN'T HAPPEN** 13 78
(cd-s+=) – Taken in (live).
Apr 91. (cd)(c)(lp) **WORD OF MOUTH** 11
– Get up / Word of mouth / A time and place / Yesterday, today, tomorrow / The way you look at me / Everybody gets a second chance / Stop baby / My crime of passion / Let's pretend it didn't happen / Before (the next heartache falls).
May 91. (7")(c-s) **A TIME AND A PLACE. / GET UP** 58
(12"+=)(cd-s+=) – I think I've got the message.
(cd-s) – ('A'side) (++=) – My crime of passion (acoustic).
Sep 91. (7")(c-s) **STOP BABY. / GET UP**
(cd-s+=) – Before the heartache falls.
Feb 92. (7")(c-s) **EVERYBODY GETS A SECOND CHANCE. / THE WAY YOU LOOK AT ME** 56
(cd-s+=) – At the end of the day (MIKE RUTHERFORD).

— now without RENWICK, who was repl. by guests **B.A. ROBERTSON / GARY WALLIS / WIX + CLEM CLEMPSON**

Feb 95. (7")(c-s) **OVER MY SHOULDER. / SOMETHING TO BELIEVE IN** 12
(cd-s+=) – Always the last to know.
(cd-s+=) – Word of mouth / ('A'version).
Mar 95. (cd)(c) **BEGGAR ON A BEACH OF GOLD** 9
– Beggar on a beach of gold / Another cup of coffee / You've really got a hold on me / Mea culpa / Over my shoulder / Someone always hates someone / The ghost of sex and you / Web of lies / Plain & simple / Something to believe in / A house of many rooms / I believe (when I fall in love it will be forever) / Going going . . .home.
Jun 95. (c-s)(cd-s) **BEGGAR ON A BEACH OF GOLD / HELP ME / NOBODY TOLD ME** 33
(cd-s) – ('A'side) / Boys at the front / Little boy / ('A'acoustic).
Aug 95. (c-s) **ANOTHER CUP OF COFFEE / YOU NEVER CHANGE** 65
(cd-s+=) – You don't know what love is.
(cd-s) – ('A'side) / Everyday hurts / How long.

GENIUS / GZA (see under ⇒ WU-TANG CLAN)

GENTLE GIANT

Formed: Portsmouth, England . . . 1966 as SIMON DUPREE & THE BIG SOUND, by SHULMAN brothers DEREK, RAY and PHIL. Early in '67, they had UK Top 50 hit with 'I SEE THE LIGHT'. By the end of the year, 'KITES' gave them a Top 10 smash, but they soon opted out of pop market. In late '69, the three brothers with 3 new recruits, re-launched themselves as GENTLE GIANT, and took new direction. Late in 1970, they appeared on 'Vertigo' with debut eponymous lp, which gained renewed support from stalward Radio 1 DJ Alan 'Fluff' Freeman. Their 4th lp 'OCTOPUS' late '72, although not a major success in Britain, became hit in North America. They might have progressed there, but for Columbia's decision not to release next project 'IN A GLASS HOUSE'. They persevered until 1980, and when they split RAY found fame as producer for 'O. L. Indian' records. DEREK moved to New York to become A&R executive, and signed CINDERELLA, KINGDOM COME and The DAN REED NETWORK. • **Style:** Graduated from psychedelic & pop-ish SIMON DUPREE . . . , to cult experimental and progressive 70's band, led by contemporaries like KING CRIMSON, YES and JETHRO TULL. • **Songwriters:** MINNEAR and the SHULMANS collaborated on most recordings. SIMON DUPREE covered; DAY TIME, NIGHT TIME (Mike Hugg). • **Trivia:** MINNEAR had graduated from Royal Academy Of Music in the late 60's.

Recommended: GIANT STEPS . . . THE FIRST FIVE YEARS (*6) / FREE HAND (*6).

SIMON DUPREE & THE BIG SOUND

DEREK SHULMAN (b. 2 Feb'47, Glasgow, Scotland) – vocals / **RAY SCHULMAN** (b. 8 Dec'49, Portsmouth, England) – lead guitar / **PHIL SCHULMAN** (b.27 Aug'37, Glasgow) – saxophone, trumpet / **ERIC HINE** – keyboards / **PETE O'FLAHERTY** – bass / **TONY RANSLEY** – drums

Parlophone Tower

Dec 66. (7") **I SEE THE LIGHT. / IT IS FINISHED** 45
Feb 67. (7") **RESERVATIONS. / YOU NEED A MAN**
May 67. (7") **DAY TIME, NIGHT TIME. / I'VE SEEN IT ALL BEFORE**
Aug 67. (lp) **WITHOUT RESERVATIONS** 39
– Medley: 60 minutes of your love – A lot of love / Love / Get off my Bach / There's a little playhouse / Day time, night time / I see the light / What is soul / Teacher, teacher / Amen / Who cares / Reservations.
Oct 67. (7") **KITES. / LIKE THE SUN LIKE THE FIRE** 9
Mar 68. (7") **FOR WHOM THE BELL TOLLS. / SLEEP** 43
May 68. (7") **PART OF MY PAST. / THIS STORY NEVER ENDS**
Sep 68. (7") **THINKING ABOUT MY LIFE. / VELVET AND LACE**
Nov 68. (7") **WE ARE THE MOLES Pt.1. (as "The MOLES") / Pt.2** –
Feb 69. (7") **BROKEN HEARTED PIRATES. / SHE GAVE ME THE SUN** –

— **GERRY KENWORTHY** – repl. HINE

Nov 69. (7") **THE EAGLE FLIES TONIGHT. / GIVE IT ALL BACK** [ ] [-]

— Split late '69. The SHULMAN's formed GENTLE GIANT while the others left the business.

- compilations etc. -

1978. E.M.I.; (7"ep) **SIMON DUPREE & THE BIG SOUND** [ ] [-]
– Kites / For whom the bells toll / Reservations / I see the light.

Mar 82. See For Miles; (lp) **AMEN** (w/ rare singles) [ ] [-]
(re-iss.Dec86 as 'KITES')

Mar 87. Old Gold; (7") **KITES. / (b-side by other artist)** [ ] [-]

GENTLE GIANT

DEREK SHULMAN – vocals, bass, saxophone / **RAY SHULMAN** – guitar, bass, violin, keyboards, drums / **PHIL SHULMAN** – saxophone, trumpet / **KERRY MINNEAR** (b.2 Apr'48, Salisbury, England) – keyboards, vocals (ex-RUST) / **GARY GREEN** (b.20 Nov'50, Stroud Green, England) – guitar, vocals / **MARTIN SMITH** – drums (ex-MOJOS)

Vertigo Vertigo

Nov 70. (lp)(c) **GENTLE GIANT** [ ] [ ]
– Giant / Funny ways / Alucard / Isn't it quiet and cold / Nothing at all / Why not? / The Queen. *(cd-iss.Aug89 on 'Line') (cd-iss.Nov94 on 'Repertoire')*

Aug 71. (lp)(c) **ACQUIRING THE TASTE** [ ] [ ]
– Pantagruel's nativity / Edge of twilight / The house, the street, the room / Acquiring the taste / Wreck / The Moon is down / Black cat / Plain truth. *(cd-iss.Oct89 on 'Line')*

— **MALCOLM MORTIMER** – drums repl. MARTIN

Vertigo Columbia

Jul 72. (lp)(c) **THREE FRIENDS** [ ] [ ]
– (prologue) / Schooldays / Working all day / Peel the paint / Mister Class and quality? / Three friends. *(cd-iss.Oct89)*

— **JOHN WEATHERS** (b.Wales) – drums (ex-GRAHAM BOND Band, ex-EYES OF BLUE, ex-ANCIENT GREASE, ex-PETE BROWN, etc.) repl. MALCOLM

Dec 72. (lp)(c) **OCTOPUS** [ ] [ ]
– The advent of Panurge / Raconteur troubadour / A cry for everyone / Knots / The boys in the band / Dog's life / Knots / Think of me with kindness / River. *(cd-iss.Oct89 on 'Line') (cd-iss.Nov94 on 'Repertoire')*

— now quintet of **DEREK, RAY, KERRY, GARY + JOHN** when PHIL left.

W.W.A. Capitol

Dec 73. (lp)(c) **IN A GLASS HOUSE** [ ] [-]
– The runaway / An inmate's lullaby / Way of life / A reunion / Experience / In a glass house / Index. *(cd-iss.Dec92 on 'R.F.G.')*

Jan 74. (7") **IN A GLASS HOUSE. / AN INMATE'S LULLABY** [ ] [-]

Vertigo Capitol

Oct 74. (lp)(c) **THE POWER AND THE GLORY** [ ] [78]
– Proclamation / So sincere / Aspirations / Playing the game / Cogs in cogs / No god's a man / The face / Valedictory. *(cd-iss.Dec92 on 'R.F.G.')*

Nov 74. (7") **THE POWER AND THE GLORY. / PLAYING THE GAME** [ ] [-]

Chrysalis Capitol

Aug 75. (lp)(c) **FREE HAND** [ ] [48]
– Just the same / On reflection / Free hand / Time to kill / His last voyage / Talybont / Mobile. *(cd-iss.Jul94 on 'Terrapin Truckin'')*

Apr 76. (lp)(c) **INTERVIEW** [ ] [ ]
– Interview / Give it back / Design / Another show / Empty city / Timing / I lost my head. *(cd-iss.Jul94 on 'Terrapin Truckin') (cd-iss.Oct95 on 'One Way')*

Jan 77. (d-lp)(d-c) **PLAYING THE FOOL - LIVE (live)** [ ] [89]
– Just the same / Proclamation / On reflection / Excerpts from Octopus (Boys in the band, etc) / Funny ways / In a glass house / So sincere / Free hand / Sweet Georgia Brown (breakdown in Brussels) / Peel the paint / I lost my head. *(re-iss.+cd.May89 on 'Essential')*

Aug 77. (lp)(c) **THE MISSING PIECE** [ ] [81]
– Two weeks in Spain / I'm turning around / Betcha thought we couldn't do it / Who do you think you are? / Mountain time / As old as you're young / Memories of old days / Winning / For nobody. *(cd-iss.Jul94 on 'Terrapin Truckin'')*

Aug 77. (7") **I'M TURNING AROUND. / JUST THE SAME (live)** [ ] [-]
Sep 77. (7") **I'M TURNING AROUND. / COGS IN COGS** [-] [ ]
Oct 77. (7") **TWO WEEKS IN SPAIN. / FREE HAND** [ ] [ ]
Sep 78. (7") **THANK YOU. / SPOOKY BOOGIE** [ ] [ ]
Sep 78. (lp)(c) **GIANT FOR A DAY** [ ] [ ]
– Words from the wise / Thank you / Giant for a day / Spooky boogie / Take me / Little brown bag / Friends / No stranger / It's only goodbye / Rock climber. *(cd-iss.Jul94 on 'Terrapin Truckin'')*

Jan 79. (7") **WORDS FROM THE WISE. / NO STRANGER** [ ] [-]
Jan 79. (7") **WORDS FROM THE WISE. / SPOOKY BOOGIE** [-] [ ]

Chrysalis Columbia

Aug 80. (lp)(c) **CIVILIAN** [ ] [ ]
– Convenience / All through the night / Shadows on the street / Number one / Underground / I'm a camera / Inside out / It's not imagination. *(cd-iss.Jul94 on 'Terrapin Truckin'')*

— Split around '80. RAY SHULMAN went into production. WEATHERS joined MAN.

- compilations, others, etc. -

Nov 75. Vertigo/ US= Columbia; (d-lp)(d-c) **GIANT STEPS . . . (THE FIRST FIVE YEARS) 1970-75** [ ] [ ]
– Giant / Alucard / Nothing at all / Plain truth / Prologue / A cry for everyone / Why not / Peel the paint / Mister Class and quality? / River / The face / The runaway / Power and the glory / Playing the game / In a glass house.

Oct 77. Vertigo; (d-lp)(d-c) **PRETENTIOUS (FOR THE SAKE OF IT)** [ ] [ ]
Aug 81. Vertigo Dutch import; (lp) **GREATEST HITS** [-] [-]
Dec 94. Windsong; (cd) **IN CONCERT (live)** [ ] [-]

Lowell GEORGE (see under ⇒ LITTLE FEAT)

GEORGIA SATELLITES

Formed: Atlanta, Georgia, USA . . . 1980 by DAN BAIRD, etc. After a well-received debut 'KEEP THE FAITH' in 1985 on independent US label 'Making Waves', they signed to 'Elektra'. Early in 1987, they hit US Top 5 with both single 'KEEP YOUR HANDS TO YOURSELF' and self-titled album. • **Style:** Hard basic R&B outfit. • **Songwriters:** All BAIRD compositions except; HIPPY HIPPY SHAKE (Swinging Blue Jeans) / GAMES PEOPLE PLAY (Joe South) / I'M WAITING FOR THE MAN (Velvet Underground) / EVERY PICTURE TELLS A STORY (Rod Stewart) / ALMOST SATURDAY NIGHT – ROCKIN' ALL OVER THE WORLD (John Fogerty).

Recommended: LET IT ROCK (BEST OF GEORGIA SATELLITES) (*6)

DAN BAIRD (b. 12 Dec '53, San Diego, Californiia) – vocals, guitar / **RICK RICHARDS** – guitar, vocals / **RICK PRICE** – bass / **MAURO MAGELLAN** – drums

Making Waves Making Waves

Mar 85. (lp)(c) **KEEP THE FAITH** [ ] [ ]
– Tell my fortune / Red light / Six years gone / Keep your hands to yourself / Crazy / The race is on. *(c-iss.Jul87)*

Elektra Elektra

Nov 86. (lp)(c)(cd) **GEORGIA SATELLITES** [52] [5] Oct 86
– Keep your hands to yourself / Railroad steel / Battleship chains / Red light / The myth of love / Can't stand the pain / Golden light / Over and over / Nights of mystery / Every picture tells a story. *(re-iss.cd+c Mar93 on 'Pickwick') (re-iss.cd/c Sep95 on 'Warners')*

Jan 87. (7") **KEEP YOUR HANDS TO YOURSELF. / CAN'T STAND THE PAIN** [69] [2] Dec 86
(12"+=) – Nights of mystery / I'm waiting for the man. *(re-iss.Aug87)*

Mar 87. (7") **BATTLESHIP CHAINS. / GOLDEN LIGHT** [-] [86]
Apr 87. (7")(12") **BATTLESHIP CHAINS (remix). / HARD LUCK BOY** [44] [-]
Jun 88. (7") **OPEN ALL NIGHT. / DUNK 'N' DIME** [-] [ ]
Jun 88. (lp)(c)(cd) **OPEN ALL NIGHT** [39] [77]
– Open all night / Sheila / Whole lotta shakin' / Cool inside / Don't pass me by / My baby / Mon cheri / Down and down / Dunk 'n' dine / Baby so fine / Hand to mouth.

Jan 89. (7") **HIPPY HIPPY SHAKE (from film 'Cocktail'). / HAND TO MOUTH** [63] [45] Oct 88
(12"+=) – Powerful stuff.

May 89. (7") **SHEILA. / HIPPY HIPPY SHAKE** [ ] [ ]
(12"+=) – Battleship chains (live) / Railroad steel (live).

Oct 89. (7") **ANOTHER CHANCE. / SADDLE UP** [-] [ ]
Oct 89. (7") **ANOTHER CHANCE. / OPEN ALL NIGHT** [ ] [-]
(12"+=) – Saddle up / That woman.

Oct 89. (lp)(c)(cd) **IN THE LAND OF SALVATION AND SIN** [ ] [ ]
– I dunno / Bottle o'tears / All over but the cryin' / Shake that thing / Six years gone / Games people play / Another chance / Bring down the hammer / Slaughterhouse / Stellazine blues / Days gone by / Sweet blue midnight / Crazy / Dan takes five.

Mar 90. (7") **ANOTHER CHANCE. / OPEN ALL NIGHT** [ ] [ ]
(12")(cd-s) – ('A'side) / Saddle up / That woman.

— Disbanded Feb92,

- compilations, etc. -

Jan 93. Elektra; (cd)(c) **LET IT ROCK (BEST OF GEORGIA SATELLITES)** [ ] [ ]

DAN BAIRD

Def Amer. Def Amer.

Nov 92. (cd)(c)(lp) **LOVE SONGS FOR THE HARD OF HEARING** [ ] [ ]
– The one I am / Julie and Lucky / I love you period / Look at what you started / Seriously gone / Pick up the knife / Knocked up / Baby talk / Lost highway / Dixie beauxderaunt.

Feb 93. (7")(c-s) **I LOVE YOU PERIOD. / LOST HIGHWAY** [ ] [26] Nov 92
(cd-s+=) – Rocket in my pocket.

GERRY & THE PACEMAKERS

Formed: Liverpool, England . . . 1959 by GERRY MARSDEN, his brother FREDDIE, LES CHADWICK and ARTHUR MACK. They originally called themselves The MARS BARS, until 1960, when the confectionary chocolate makers of the same name insisted they change it. Late in 1960 MACK left, to be soon replaced by LES MAGUIRE, who went with band to tour Germany. They were then spotted by BEATLES manager Brian Epstein, who gave them contract and set up deal with 'Columbia' late '62. Their debut 45 'HOW DO YOU DO IT?' (rejected by BEATLES), soon hit UK No.1, and was followed by 2 more chart toppers in 1963 'I LIKE IT' & 'YOU'LL NEVER WALK ALONE'. This record-breaking feat stood for 21 years, when it was equalled by other Merseyside popsters FRANKIE GOES TO HOLLYWOOD (who also covered their 'FERRY ACROSS THE MERSEY' as a B-side to 'Relax'). In 1964, they were part of the British invasion into American charts, hitting Top20 there many times. When flower-power scene came about in '66, the group all but faded into obscurity. • **Style:** 60's beat/pop combo, fronted by cocky frontman GERRY MARSDEN. • **Songwriters:** GERRY penned most, except covers; HOW DO YOU DO IT + I LIKE IT (Mitch Murray) / YOU'LL NEVER WALK ALONE (Rodgers-Hammerstein) / I'LL BE THERE (Bobby

Darin) / WALK HAND IN HAND (?) / etc. • **Trivia:** YOU'LL NEVER WALK ALONE was adopted by Liverpool Football Club as their crowd anthem.

Recommended: THE BEST OF THE E.M.I. YEARS (*5).

GERRY MARSDEN (b.24 Sep'42) – vocals, lead guitar / **LES CHADWICK** (b.JOHN LESLIE CHADWICK, 11 May'43) – bass / **FREDDIE MARSDEN** (b.23 Oct'40) – drums / **LES MAGUIRE** (b.27 Dec'41, Wallasey, England) – piano, saxophone (ex-UNDERTAKERS) repl. ARTHUR MACK

Columbia Laurie

Mar 63. (7") **HOW DO YOU DO IT?. / AWAY FROM YOU** [1] [ ] Apr 63
May 63. (7") **I LIKE IT. / IT'S HAPPENED TO ME** [1] [ ] Sep 63
Oct 63. (7") **YOU'LL NEVER WALK ALONE. / IT'S ALRIGHT** [1] [ ] Dec 63
Oct 63. (lp) **HOW DO YOU LIKE IT?** [2] [-]
– A shot of rhythm and blues / Jambalaya / Where have you been / Here's hoping / Pretend / Maybellene / You'll never walk alone / The wrong yo yo / You're the reason / Chills / You can't fool me / Don't you ever / Summertime / Slow down *(re-iss.Sep89 on 'B.G.O.') (cd-iss.Aug94 on 'Repertoire')*
Jan 64. (7") **I'M THE ONE. / YOU'VE GOT WHAT I LIKE** [2] [82] Feb 64
Apr 64. (7") **DON'T LET THE SUN CATCH YOU CRYING. / SHOW ME THAT YOU CARE** [6] [-]
May 64. (7") **DON'T LET THE SUN CATCH YOU CRYING. / AWAY FROM YOU** [-] [4]
Jul 64. (lp) **DON'T LET THE SUN CATCH YOU CRYING** [-] [29]
– Don't let the Sun catch you crying / I'm the one / Away from you / Jambalaya / Maybellene / You'll never walk alone / How do you do it / You're the reason / Don't you ever / Summertime / Slow down / Show me that you care.
Jul 64. (7") **HOW DO YOU DO IT. / YOU'LL NEVER WALK ALONE** [-] [9]
Aug 64. (7") **IT'S GONNA BE ALRIGHT. / IT'S JUST BECAUSE** [24] [23] Apr 65
Oct 64. (7") **I LIKE IT. / JAMBALAYA** [-] [17]
Dec 64. (7") **FERRY ACROSS THE MERSEY. / YOU YOU YOU** [8] [-]
Dec 64. (7") **I'LL BE THERE. / YOU YOU YOU** [-] [14]
Jan 65. (lp) **FERRY ACROSS THE MERSEY (live Film Soundtrack)** [19] [13] Feb 65
– How do you do it / Ferry across the Mersey / It's still rock & roll to me / I'm the one / Unchained melody / Roll over Beethoven / Imagine / Running man / Just the way you are (note 3 songs not by them) (on 'United Art' US) *(re-iss.+c.Apr86 on 'Showcase') (cd-iss.Aug94 on 'Repertoire')*
Feb 65. (7") **FERRY ACROSS THE MERSEY. / PRETEND** [-] [6]
Mar 65. (7") **I'LL BE THERE. / BABY YOU'RE SO GOOD TO ME** [15] [-]
May 65. (7") **IT'S GONNA BE ALRIGHT. / SKINNY MINNIE** [-] [ ]
Feb 65. (lp) **I'LL BE THERE** [-] [ ]
– I'll be there / What'd I say / Rip it up / You win again / You you you / Now I'm alone / My babe / Reelin' and rockin' / I count the tears / Whole lotta shakin' goin' on / It'll be me / Skinny Minnie.
Aug 65. (7") **GIVE ALL YOUR LOVE TO ME. / YOU'RE THE REASON** [-] [68]
Nov 65. (7") **WALK HAND IN HAND. / DREAMS** [29] [ ]
Feb 66. (7") **LA LA LA. / WITHOUT YOU** [ ] [90]
May 66. (7") **LOOKING FOR MY LIFE. / BRIGHT GREEN PLEASURE MACHINE** [-] [ ]
Sep 66. (7") **GIRL ON A SWING. / FOOL TO MYSELF** [ ] [28]

— Disbanded Oct'66.

GERRY MARSDEN

C.B.S. Columbia?

Jun 67. (7") **PLEASE LET THEM BE. / I'M NOT BLUE** [ ] [ ]
1967. (7") **GILBERT GREEN. / WHAT MAKES ME LOVE YOU** [ ] [ ]

— In 1968, GERRY landed leading role in stage play 'Charlie Girl'.

Jun 68. (7") **LIVERPOOL. ("GERRY MARSDEN & DEREK NIMMO") / CHARLIE GIRL** [ ] [-]

— Returned to sporadic solo work in 1969.

1969. Nems; (7") **EVERY LITTLE MINUTE. / IN DAYS OF OLD** [ ] [-]
May 71. Decca; (7") **I'VE GOT MY UKELELE. / WHAT A DAY** [ ] [-]
1972. Phoenix; (7") **AMOCREDO. / ('A'version)** [ ] [-]

GERRY MARSDEN & THE PACEMAKERS

(with new line-up)

Apr 74. D.J.M.; (7") **REMEMBER. / THERE'S STILL TIME** [ ] [-]

GERRY MARSDEN

went solo again.

D.J.M. not issued

Aug 74. (7") **THEY DON'T MAKE DAYS LIKE THAT. / CAN'T YOU HEAR THE SONG** [ ] [-]
Apr 75. (7") **YOUR SONG. / DAYS I SPENT WITH YOU** [ ] [-]
Sep 76. (7") **MY HOMETOWN. / LOVELY LADY** [ ] [-]

— GERRY semi-retired from biz, until his vocal contribution May85 on Disaster Fund (Bradford F.C. fire) No.1 re-indition of YOU'LL NEVER WALK ALONE by 'The CROWD'. The band are still regulars on the cabaret circuit.

– (GERRY & THE PACEMAKERS) compilations, etc. –

Jun 63. Columbia; (7"ep) **HOW DO YOU DO IT?** [34] [-]
– (see 1st 2 singles 'A'&'B')
Dec 63. Columbia; (7"ep) **YOU'LL NEVER WALK ALONE** [ ] [-]
Feb 64. Columbia; (7"ep) **I'M THE ONE** [ ] [-]
May 64. Columbia; (7"ep) **DON'T LET THE SUN CATCH YOU CRYING** [ ] [-]
Dec 64. Columbia; (7"ep) **IT'S GONNA BE ALRIGHT** [ ] [-]
Nov 64. Laurie; (lp) **GERRY & THE PACEMAKERS' SECOND ALBUM** [-] [ ]
– I like it / A shot of rhythm and blues / Where have you been / Here's hoping / Pretend / The wrong yo-yo / Chills / You can't fool me / It happened to me / It's all right / Slow down / Jambalaya.
Feb 65. Columbia; (7"ep) **GERRY IN CALIFORNIA (live)** [ ] [-]
Mar 65. Columbia; (7"ep) **(HITS FROM) FERRY ACROSS THE MERSEY** [ ] [-]
May 65. Laurie; (lp) **GERRY AND THE PACEMAKERS' GREATEST HITS** [-] [44]
Jun 65. Columbia; (7"ep) **RIP IT UP** [ ] [-]
Nov 73. E.M.I.; (7"m) **HOW DO YOU DO IT?. / I LIKE IT / YOU'LL NEVER WALK ALONE** [ ] [-]
(re-iss.Jun77)
Oct 77. E.M.I.; (lp)(c) **THE BEST OF GERRY & THE PACEMAKERS** [ ] [-]
Nov 77. E.M.I.; (7"m) **I LIKE IT. / HOW DO YOU DO IT? / CHILLS** [ ] [-]
May 84. E.M.I.; (7") **I LIKE IT. / HOW DO YOU DO IT?** [ ] [-]
Jan 86. E.M.I.; (lp)(c) **HIT SINGLES ALBUM** [ ] [ ]
(cd-iss.May87 as 'THE SINGLES PLUS')
Jun 92. E.M.I.; (cd) **THE BEST OF THE EMI YEARS** [ ] [-]
– How do you do it / Maybelline / I like it / Chills / Pretend / Jambalaya / You're the reason / Hello little girl / You'll never walk alone / A shot of rhythm and blues / Sow down / It's all right / I'm the one / Don't let the Sun catch you crying / You've got what I like / It's just because / You you you / It's gonna be all right / Ferry across the Mersey / I'll wait for you / Halelujah I love her so / Reelin' & rockin' / Why oh why / Baby you're so good to me / Walk hand in hand / Dreams / Give all your love to me / I'll be there / La la la / Fool to myself / Girl on a swing.
1982. Creole; (7") **FERRY ACROSS THE MERSEY. / YOU'LL NEVER WALK ALONE** [ ] [-]
Dec 82. Deb; (7") **UNCHAINED MELODY. / GIRL WHAT YOU DOIN'** [ ] [-]
1983. Deb; (7") **OH MY LOVE. / IF** [ ] [-]
Dec 83. Deb; (lp) **THE 20th ANNIVERSARY ALBUM** [ ] [-]
Oct 83. Old Gold; (7") **YOU'LL NEVER WALK ALONE. / HOW DO YOU DO IT?** [ ] [-]
Oct 83. Old Gold; (7") **FERRY ACROSS THE MERSEY. / DON'T LET THE SUN CATCH YOU CRYING** [ ] [-]
Jun 92. Old Gold; (cd-s) **HOW DO YOU DO IT / I LIKE IT / I'M THE ONE** [ ] [-]
Jul 92. Old Gold; (cd-s) **YOU'LL NEVER WALK ALONE. / FERRY ACROSS THE MERSEY** [ ] [-]
(re-iss.Nov95)
Jun 84. S.M.P.; (7"m) **FERRY ACROSS THE MERSEY. / HOW DO YOU DO IT? / I'M THE ONE** [ ] [-]
1984. M.F.P.; (lp)(c) **THE VERY BEST OF GERRY & THE PACEMAKERS** [ ] [-]
Apr 93. M.F.P.; (cd) **THE VERY BEST OF – 20 SUPERB TRACKS** [ ] [-]
Jun 87. See For Miles; (lp)(c) **THE EP COLLECTION** [ ] [-]
(cd-iss.Sep89 & May95)
May 93. Royal Collection; (cd)(c) **THE BEST OF GERRY & THE PACEMAKERS** [ ] [-]
Dec 94. D Sharp; (cd)(c) **50 NON STOP PARTY HITS** [ ] [-]
Feb 95. B.A.M.; (cd) **PEARLS OF THE PAST** [ ] [-]

G-FORCE (see under ⇒ MOORE, Gary)

Barry / Maurice / Robin GIBB (see under ⇒ BEE GEES)

GILBERT & LEWIS (see under ⇒ WIRE)

GILES, GILES & FRIPP (see under ⇒ KING CRIMSON)

Andy GILL (see under ⇒ GANG OF FOUR)

GILLAN (see under ⇒ DEEP PURPLE)

David GILMOUR (see under ⇒ PINK FLOYD)

GIN BLOSSOMS

Formed: Tempe, Arizona, USA . . . early 90's by (see below). In 1992, they signed to 'A&M', who issued debut 'NEW MISERABLE EXPERIENCE'. Although slow to get off the mark, it soon shot into Stateside Top 30, helped by 2 memorable major hit singles in 1993; 'HEY JEALOUSY' and 'FOUND OUT ABOUT YOU'. However tragedy struck when 32 year-old DOUG HOPKINS committed suicide on 5 Dec'93. • **Style:** Country-orientated rock outfit similiar to of course The BYRDS or The EAGLES. • **Songwriters:** Mostly HOPKINS or VALENZUELA / WILSON; except CHRISTINE SIXTEEN (Kiss). • **Trivia:** Produced by JOHN HAMPTON (ex-Replacements).

Recommended: NEW MISERABLE EXPERIENCE (*5)

ROBIN WILSON – vocals, acoustic guitar / **JESSE VALENZUELA** – guitar, vocals / **DOUG HOPKINS** – guitars / **BILL LEEN** – bass / **PHILLIP RHODES** – drums, percussion

A&M A&M

Nov 92. (cd)(c) **NEW MISERABLE EXPERIENCE** [ ] [30]
– Lost horizons / Hey jealousy / Mrs. Rita / Until I fall away / Hold me down / Cajun song / Hands are tied / Found out about you / Allison Road / 29 / Pieces of the night / Cheatin'. *(re-iss.Sep93 on 'Fontana', hit UK No.53 early '94) (re-iss.May94)*

Fontana A&M

Aug 93. (c-ep)(cd-ep) **HEY JEALOUSY / KELI RICHARDS / COLD RIVER DICK / KRISTINE IRENE** [ ] [25] Jul93

Oct 93. (12"colrd)(c-s)(cd-s) **MRS.RITA. / SOUL DEEP / HEART AWAY**

Jan 94. (7"ep)(c-ep) **HEY JEALOUSY / COLD RIVER DICK. / KRISTINE IRENE / KELI RICHARDS** 24 -
(cd-ep) – ('A'side) / Cajun song / Just south of nowhere / Angels tonight.
(9"ep) – ('A' side) / Keli Richards / Cajun song.

— **SCOTT JOHNSON** – guitars repl. HOPKINS who killed himself 5 Dec'93

Apr 94. (7")(c-s) **FOUND OUT ABOUT YOU. / HEY JEALOUSY (live)** 40 25 Nov93
(cd-s+=) – Hands are tied (live) / 29 (live) / Fulsome Prison (live).
(cd-s+=) – Hold me down (live) / Mrs.Rita (live).

Greg GINN / GONE (see under ⇒ BLACK FLAG)

GIRLSCHOOL

Formed: South London, England . . . Mar'78 by ex-PAINTED LADY members KIM McAULIFFE and ENID WILLIAMS. After debut indie 45 'TAKE IT ALL AWAY' for 'City', they moved to 'Bronze' late '79, and were snapped up by MOTORHEAD's manager Doug Smith. Later that year, they sprang into UK Top 30 album charts with debut 'DEMOLITION'. They peaked the following year, with the help of MOTORHEAD on Top 5 EP 'ST.VALENTINE'S DAY MASSACRE'. • **Style:** All-girl heavy-metal rock/pop band, influenced by glam-rock and punk-ish RUNAWAYS. • **Songwriters:** McAULIFFE and JOHNSON penned most, and used covers; RACE WITH THE DEVIL (Gun / Adrian Gurvitz) / PLEASE DON'T TOUCH (Johnny Kidd) / 20th CENTURY BOY (T.Rex) / TUSH (ZZ Top) / I'M THE LEADER OF THE PACK (Gary Glitter) / FOX ON THE RUN (Sweet) / C'MON LET'S GO (McCoys) / LIVE WITH ME (Rolling Stones). • **Trivia:** DENISE was the sister of DAVE DUFORT; drummer of ANGELWITCH.

Recommended: THE COLLECTION (*5).

KIM McAULIFFE – vocals, guitar / **KELLY JOHNSON** – lead guitar, vocals / **ENID WILLIAMS** – bass, vocals / **DENISE DUFORT** – drums

City / not issued

Nov 79. (7") **TAKE IT ALL AWAY. / IT COULD BE BETTER** -
(re-iss.Sep81)

Bronze / Stiff

Jan 80. (7") **EMERGENCY. / FURNITURE FIRE**

May 80. (7") **NOTHING TO LOSE. / BABY DOLL**

Jun 80. (lp)(c) **DEMOLITION** 28
– Demolition boys / Not for sale / Race with the Devil / Take it all away / Nothing to lose / Breakdown / Midnight ride / Emergency / Baby doll / Deadline.

Jul 80. (7") **RACE WITH THE DEVIL. / TAKE IT ALL AWAY** 49

Nov 80. (7") **YEAH RIGHT. / THE HUNTER**

Feb 81. (7"ep) **ST. VALENTINE'S DAY MASSACRE** 5
– (as "HEADGIRL" with MOTORHEAD)
– Please don't touch / Emergency / Bomber.

Apr 81. (7") **HIT AND RUN. / TONIGHT** 32
(12"+=) – Tush.

Apr 81. (lp)(c) **HIT AND RUN** 5
– C'mon let's go / The hunter / Victim / Kick it down / Following the crowd / Tush / Hit and run / Watch your step / Back to start / Yeah right / Future flash.

Jul 81. (7") **C'MON LET'S GO. / TONIGHT** 42
(12"+=) – Demolition boys.

— **GIL WESTON** – bass, vocals (ex-KILLJOYS) repl. ENID who joined FRAMED

Mar 82. (7") **WILDLIFE. / DON'T CALL IT LOVE** 58
(7"ep+=) – Don't stop.

Jun 82. (lp)(c) **SCREAMING BLUE MURDER** 27
– Screaming blue murder / Live with me / Take it from me / Wildlife / It turns your head around / Don't call it love / Hell razor / When your blood runs cold / You got me / Flesh and blood.

Aug 83. (7"m) **1-2-3-4 ROCK AND ROLL. / TUSH / DON'T CALL IT LOVE**
(12"+=) – Emergency.

Oct 83. (lp)(c) **PLAY DIRTY** 66
– Going under / High and dry / Play dirty / 20th century boy / Breaking all the rules / Burning in the heat / Surrender / Rock me shock me / Running for cover / Breakout.

Oct 83. (7") **20th CENTURY BOY. / BREAKING ALL THE RULES**
(12"+=) – Like it like that.

Jan 84. (7")(12") **BURNING IN THE NIGHT. / SURRENDER**

— added **JACKIE BONIMEAD** – vocals, guitar (ex-SHE) / **CHRIS BONACCI** – guitar (ex-SHE) repl. KELLY

not issued / Mercury

1985. (lp)(c) **RUNNING WILD** -
– Let me go / Running wild / Do you love me? / Something for nothing / Are you ready? / Nowhere to run / I want you back / Nasty nasty / Love is a lie / Can't you see.

G.W.R. / ?

May 86. (7")(12") **I'M THE LEADER OF THE GANG (I AM).(w / GARY GLITTER) / ?**

— Trimmed when BODIMEAD departed

1986. (lp)(c) **NIGHTMARE AT MAPLE CROSS**
– All day and all of the night / Play with fire / Danger sign / Never too late / Tiger feet / Back for more / Let's go crazy / You got me (under your skin) / Let's break out / Turn it up.

Oct 88. (lp)(c)(cd) **TAKE A BITE**
– Action / Girls on top / Fox on the run / Tear it up / Love at first bite / Up all night / Don't walk away / Head over heels / This time / Too hot to handle. *(re-iss.Nov92 on 'Dojo')*

— re-formed 1992 with **KIM, CRIS, DENISE & JACKIE CARRERA** – bass

– compilations, others, etc. –

Apr 86. Raw Power; (lp)(c) **RACE WITH THE DEVIL** -

Sep 89. Raw Power; (lp)(c)(cd) **CHEERS YOU LOT** -

Jul 91. Dojo Lama; (cd) **DEMOLITION / HIT AND RUN** -

Jan 92. Dojo Lama; (cd) **SCREAMING BLUE MURDER / PLAY DIRTY** -

Jan 92. Castle; (cd)(lp) **THE COLLECTION** -
– 1-2-3-4 rock'n'roll / Furniture fire / Take it all away / Kick it down / Midnight ride / Race with the Devil / Play dirty / Yeah right / Emergency / Breakout / Victim / Flesh and blood / Tush / Don't stop / Future flash / Rock me shock me / Screaming blue murder / Wild life / Bomber / Nothing to lose / Live with me / Like it like that / Tonight / Take it from me.

Apr 94. Sequel; (cd) **FROM THE VAULTS** -

Jul 94. Success; (cd)(c) **C'MON LET'S GO** -

Nov 95. Communique; (cd) **LIVE (live)** -

Gary GLITTER

Born: PAUL GADD, 8 May'40, Banbury, Oxfordshire, England. His musical career was launched in the late 50's, when film producer and manager Robert Hartford Davis, secured a deal with 'Decca'. His first 45 'ALONE IN THE NIGHT', under name of PAUL RAVEN flopped, but he found success in the Middle East, with 2nd 45 'WALK ON BOY'. After another unlucky miss in '61, he all but disappeared from studio sessions, until 1968, when MIKE LEANDER invited him to sing one of his songs 'MUSICAL MAN' as PAUL MONDAY. More singles followed, mostly under pseudonyms, before he joined the cast of 'JESUS CHRIST SUPERSTAR' in 1970. In 1972, he resurfaced as GARY GLITTER, and smashed the charts for the first time with 'ROCK'N'ROLL PART 2'. Between early '73 and late '74, he chalked up 7 UK Top 3 hits, including three No.1's: 'I'M THE LEADER OF THE PACK', 'I LOVE YOU LOVE ME LOVE' & 'ALWAYS YOURS'. He faded from the limelight from then on, but sparodically returned into the charts, aided by his always faithful fan club. • **Style:** Foot-stompin' glam-rock phenomenom, who brightened up pop music world in the 70's. His platform heels and glitter fashion accessories, became part of teenage attire during this pre-punk era. • **Songwriters:** GLITTER penned, except many covers including; TOWER OF STRENGTH (Bacharach-Hilliard) / HERE COMES THE SUN (Beatles) / STAND (Sly & The Family Stone) / PAPA OOM MOW MOW (Rivingtons) / • **Trivia:** His GLITTER BAND (without him), also scored a run of 7 consecutive UK hits, including biggest early 1975 No.2 'GOODBYE MY LOVE'.

Recommended: MANY HAPPY RETURNS – GARY GLITTER THE HITS (*5).

PAUL RAVEN

Decca / not issued

Jan 60. (7") **ALONE IN THE NIGHT. / TOO PROUD** -

Parlophone / not issued

Aug 61. (7") **WALK ON BOY. / ALL GROWN UP** -

Nov 61. (7") **TOWER OF STRENGTH. / LIVIN' THE BLUES** -

— (Unluckily FRANKIE VAUGHAN'S version of above hits No.1, and he was dropped by label. He briefly joined MIKE LEANDER ORCHESTRA, but soon became vocalist for (soon-to-be-called) The BOSTONS. The next half-decade saw them tour Germany, etc, but with no record contract. In 1968, through LEANDER, he signed to

M.C.A. / not issued

Jun 68. (7") **MUSICAL MAN.(as "PAUL MONDAY") / WAIT FOR ME** -

Aug 68. (7") **SOUL THING. / WE'LL GO WHERE THE WORLD CAN'T FIND US** -

Sep 69. (7") **WE ARE LIVING IN ONE PLACE.(by "RUBBER BUCKET") / TAKE ME AWAY** -

Oct 69. (7") **HERE COMES THE SUN. / MUSICAL MAN (as "PAUL MONDAY")** -

— Later in the year, he appears on Soundtrack lp 'JESUS CHRIST SUPERSTAR'.

Jun 70. (7") **STAND. / SOUL THING** -

GARY GLITTER

backed by **The GLITTER BAND**

Bell / Bell

Mar 72. (7") **ROCK'N'ROLL (Part 1). / ROCK'N'ROLL (Part 2)** 2 7 Jul 72

Sep 72. (7") **I DIDN'T KNOW I LOVE YOU (TILL I SAW YOU ROCK'N'ROLL). / HARD ON ME** 4 35 Nov 72

Oct 72. (lp)(c) **GLITTER** 8
– Rock and roll (part 1) / Baby please don't go / The wanderer / I don't know I loved you / Ain't that a shame / School day / Rock on Donna / The famous instigator / The clapping song / Shakey Sue / Rock and roll (part 2).

Jan 73. (7") **DO YOU WANNA TOUCH ME (OH YEAH). / I WOULD IF I COULD** 2

Mar 73. (7") **HELLO HELLO, I'M BACK AGAIN. / I.O.U.** 2

Jun 73. (lp)(c) **TOUCH ME** 2
– Hello hello I'm back again / Sidewalk sinner / Didn't I do it right / Lonely boy / Hold on to what you got / I.O.U. / Do you wanna touch me / Come on, come in, get on / Happy birthday / Hard on me / To know you is to love you / Money honey.

Jul 73. (7") **I'M THE LEADER OF THE GANG (I AM). / JUST FANCY THAT** 1

Nov 73. (7") **I LOVE YOU LOVE ME LOVE. / HANDS UP! IT'S A STICK UP** 1

Mar 74. (7") **REMEMBER ME THIS WAY. / IT'S NOT A LOT** 3

Jun 74. (7") **ALWAYS YOURS. / I'M RIGHT, YOU'RE WRONG, I WIN** 1

Jun 74. (lp)(c) **REMEMBER ME THIS WAY (live)** [5] [ ]
– I'm the leader of the gang (I am) / Sidewalk sinner / Baby please don't go / Do you wanna touch me / The wanderer / Rock and roll (parts 1 & 2) / Hello hello, I'm back again / I didn't know I loved you (till I saw you rock'n'roll) / I love you love me love / Remember me this way.

Nov 74. (7") **OH YES! YOU'RE BEAUTIFUL. / THANK YOU BABY FOR MYSELF** [2] [ ]

Apr 75. (7") **LOVE LIKE YOU AND ME. / I'LL CARRY YOUR PICTURE EVERYWHERE** [10] [ ]

Jun 75. (7") **DOING ALRIGHT WITH THE BOYS. / GOOD FOR NO GOOD** [6] [ ]

Oct 75. (lp)(c) **G.G.** [ ] [ ]
– Too late to put it down / Satan's daughters / Easy evil / Baby I love your way / Papa oom mow mow / Finder's keepers / Basic lady / Cupid / I'll carry your picture / Personality.

Nov 75. (7") **PAPA OOM MOW MOW. / SHE CAT, ALLEY CAT** [38] [ ]

Mar 76. (7") **YOU BELONG TO ME. / ROCK'N'ROLL (Part 1)** [40] [ ]

Arista not issued

Jan 77. (7") **IT TAKES ALL NIGHT LONG. / (Part 2)** [25] [-]

Jun 77. (7") **A LITTLE BOOGIE WOOGIE IN THE BACK OF MY MIND. / LAY IT ON ME** [31] [-]

Sep 77. (7") **OH WHAT A FOOL I'VE BEEN. / 365 DAYS** [ ] [-]

Dec 77. (7") **I DARE YOU TO LAY ONE ON ME. / HOOKED ON HOLLYWOOD** [ ] [-]

Jan 78. (lp)(c) **SILVER STAR** [ ] [-]
– You belong to me / Haven't I seen you somewhere before / I dare you to lay one on me / Roll of the dice / etc.

G.T.O. not issued

Apr 79. (7")(12") **SUPERHEROES. / SLEEPING BEAUTY** [ ] [-]

Eagle not issued

Nov 80. (7") **WHATCHA MOMMA DON'T SEE (YOUR MOMMA DON'T KNOW). / I'M NOT JUST ANOTHER PRETTY FACE** [ ] [-]

Jul 81. (7") **WHEN I'M ON, I'M ON. / WILD HORSES** [ ] [-]

— (He guested on BEF's (HEAVEN 17) album MUSIC OF QUALITY . . .)

Bell not issued

Sep 81. (7") **AND SHE KISSED ME. / I LOVE YOU LOVE ME LOVE** [39] [-]

Nov 81. (7")(12") **ALL THAT GLITTERS (segued hits medley). / REACH FOR THE SKY** [48] [-]

Aug 82. (7") **BE MY BABY. / IS THIS WHAT DREAMS ARE MADE OF** [ ] [-]

Arista not issued

Jun 84. (7")(7"pic-d) **DANCE ME UP. / TOO YOUNG TO DANCE** [25] [-]
(12"+=) – All that glitters.

Sep 84. (7")(12")(7"mirror-pic-d) **SHOUT SHOUT SHOUT. / HAIR OF THE DOG** [ ] [-]

Nov 84. (lp)(c)(cd) **BOYS WILL BE BOYS** [ ] [-]
– Crash crash / Let's get sexy / Dance me up / When I'm on, I'm on / Another rock'n'roll Christmas / Shout shout shout / If you want me / Hair of the dog / Boys will be boys.

Nov 84. (7")(12")(7"sha-pic-d) **ANOTHER ROCK'N'ROLL CHRISTMAS. / ('A'instrumental)** [7] [-]
(re-iss.Nov85)

Apr 85. (7")(7"pic-d) **LOVE COMES. / BOYS WILL BE BOYS** [ ] [-]
(12"+=) – ('A'extended) / Megastarmix (hits medley).

— Retired from recording, but still managed some live work, due to increasing revival of 'glam-pop'. In 1988, he featured on TIMELORDS (KLF's) No.1 (DOCTORIN' THE TARDIS) a near re-indition of ROCK'N'ROLL.

E.M.I. not issued

Oct 92. (7")(c-s) **AND THE LEADER ROCKS ON – Medley:- I'M THE LEADER OF THE GANG – COME ON, COME IN, GET ON – ROCK ON – I DIDN'T KNOW I LOVE YOU – DIDN'T I DO IT RIGHT – DO YOU WANNA TOUCH ME – HELLO HELLO, I'M BACK AGAIN – I'M THE LEADER OF THE GANG (I AM). / LET'S GO PARTY** [58] [-]
(12"+=) – ('A'extended).

Nov 92. (cd)(c)(d-lp) **MANY HAPPY RETURNS – GARY GLITTER THE HITS** – (compilation) [35] [-]
Rock and roll (part 1) / Rock and roll (part 2) / I didn't know I loved you (till I saw you rock and roll) / Ready to rock / Rock on / Doin' alright with the boys / I'm the leader of the gang (I am) / The wanderer / Do you wanna touch me (oh yeah) / Hello, hello, I'm back again / I love you love me love / You belong to me / If it takes all night long / Oh yes, you're beautiful / Love like you and me / Little boogie woogie in the back of my mind / Dance me up / Through the years / Remember me this way / And the leader rocks on / Another rock and roll Christmas / Always yours.
(re-is,cd+c Dec93 on 'Fame')

Nov 92. (7")(c-s) **THROUGH THE YEARS. / ANOTHER ROCK AND ROLL CHRISTMAS** [49] [-]
(12")(cd-s) – ('A'side) / Rock & roll (part 1 & 2).

Carlton not issued

Nov 95. (cd-ep) **BY PUBLIC DEMAND EP** [50] [-]
– Hello, hello, I'm back again (again!) /

– more compilations, etc. –

Sep 75. M.F.P.; (lp)(c) **ALWAYS YOURS** [ ] [-]
(re-iss.Apr86 on 'Dojo')

Mar 76. Bell; (lp)(c) **GREATEST HITS** [33] [ ]

Oct 76. Bell; (7"ep) **GARY GLITTER (EP)** [ ] [ ]
– I'm the leader of the gang (I am) / Rock and roll (Part 2) / Hello hello I'm back again / Do you wanna touch me (oh yeah). *(re-iss.Sep80 on 'GTO')*

Feb 77. Hallmark; (lp)(c) **I LOVE YOU LOVE** [ ] [-]

Mar 77. G.T.O.; (lp)(c) **GARY GLITTER'S GOLDEN GREATS** [ ] [-]

Aug 77. G.T.O.; (7") **BABY PLEASE DON'T GO. / THE WANDERER** [ ] [-]

Sep 80. G.T.O.; (7"ep) **GARY GLITTER EP** [57] [-]

Nov 80. G.T.O.; (lp)(c) **THE LEADER** [ ] [-]
(re-iss.Nov83)

Sep 83. Scoop; (7"ep)(c-ep) **6 TRACK HITS** [ ] [-]
– Rock'n'roll (Part 2) / Always yours / I'm the leader of the gang (I am) / I didn't know I loved you (till I saw you rock'n'roll) / Remember me this way / I love you love me love.

Mar 85. A.P.K.; (lp)(c) **ALIVE AND KICKING (live)** [ ] [-]

Apr 85. Illuminated; (7")(12") **ROCK'N'ROLL. / NOT JUST A PRETTY FACE** [ ] [-]

Jul 86. Illuminated; (12"ep) **LIVE ROCK'N'ROLL (live 3 track)** [ ] [-]

Aug 87. Object; (cd) **GARY GLITTER – COLLECTION** [ ] [-]

Nov 87. Telstar; (lp)(c)(cd) **C'MON C'MON – THE GARY GLITTER PARTY ALBUM** [ ] [-]

Dec 87. Stiff; (7") **ROCK'N'ROLL (Part 3). / ROCK'N'ROLL (Part 4)** [ ] [-]
(12") – ('A'side) / ('A'-Part 5) / ('A'-Part 6 instrumental).

Jan 89. Old Gold; (7") **ROCK'N'ROLL (Part 2). / I DIDN'T KNOW I LOVED YOU (TILL I SAW YOU ROCK'N'ROLL)** [ ] [-]
(12"+=//+cd-s+=) – Rock'n'roll (Part 1)./ / Do you wanna touch me . . .

Apr 89. Old Gold; (7") **OH YES! YOU'RE BEAUTIFUL. / REMEMBER ME THIS WAY** [ ] [-]

Mar 90. Old Gold; (7") **I LOVE YOU LOVE ME LOVE. / I'M THE LEADER OF THE GANG** [ ] [-]

Nov 89. Castle; (lp)(c)(cd) **GARY GLITTER'S GANGSHOW** [ ] [-]

Dec 89. Castle; (7")(12") **MEGA GLITTER ROCK-A-LIVE (medley). /** [ ] [-]

Apr 91. Pickwick; (cd)(c) **BACK AGAIN – THEIR VERY BEST** [ ] [-]
– (some tracks by GLITTER BAND)

Feb 93. Pickwick; (cd) **THE BEST OF GARY GLITTER** [ ] [-]

GLOVE (see under ⇒ SIOUXSIE AND THE BANSHEES)

Roger GLOVER (see under ⇒ DEEP PURPLE)

GO-BETWEENS

Formed: Brisbane, Australia . . . 1978 by FORSTER and McLENNAN. After two local Australian singles, they moved to Britain in 1980 to record one 45 for Scottish label 'Postcard'. Soon settled in London, after signing to top indie label 'Rough Trade'. They had already in 1982 released debut lp 'SEND ME A LULLABY', which was followed a year later by 'BEFORE HOLLYWOOD'. The rest of the 80's, was spent adding new members, and trying to penetrate unwielding charts. • **Style:** Described early on as an antipodean TALKING HEADS, although their inspiration stemmed from BOB DYLAN or The VELVET UNDERGROUND. Their well-balanced romantic sound, was always nicely blended with heavy subject material. • **Songwriters:** All compositions by FORSTER and McLENNAN, with LINDY MORRISON contributing some. McLENNAN covered BALLAD OF EASY RIDER (Byrds). • **Trivia:** In 1991, FORSTER and McLENNAN did support slot to LLOYD COLE on a Toronto gig, which prompted GO-BETWEENS reformation rumours.

Recommended: THE GO-BETWEENS 1979-1990 (*9) / WATERSHED (*7; E. W. McLENNAN).

GRANT McLENNAN (b.12 Feb'58) – vocals, lead guitar, bass / **ROB FORSTER** (b.29 Jun'57) – guitar, vocals / **DENNIS CANTWELL** – drums

Abel not issued

Oct 78. (7") **LEE REMICK. / KAREN** [-] [-] Aussie

— added **TIM MUSTAFA** – drums + **MALCOLM KELLY** – organ to repl. CANTWELL

Oct 79. (7") **PEOPLE SAY. / DON'T LET HIM COME BACK** [-] [-]
(above 2 first released UK as 12"ep Nov86 on 'Situation 2')

— **LINDY MORRISON** (b. 2 Nov'51) – drums (ex-ZERO) repl. TIM + MALCOLM

Postcard not issued

Nov 80. (7") **I NEED TWO HEADS. / STOP BEFORE YOU SAY IT** [ ] [-]

Missing L. not issued

Jul 81. (7") **YOUR TURN, MY TURN. / WORLD WEARY** [-] [-] Aussie

Rough Trade not issued

Jun 82. (lp) **SEND ME A LULLABY** [ ] [-]
– Your turn, my turn / One thing can hold us / Eight pictures / People know / The girls have moved / Midnight to neon / Ride / Caress / All about strength / Hold your horses / It could be anyone / Arrow in a bow. *(released Australia Nov81 on 'Missing Link')*

Jul 82. (7") **BY CHANCE. / HAMMER THE HAMMER** [ ] [-]

— added **ROBERT VICKERS** (b.25 Nov'59) – bass

Feb 83. (7") **CATTLE AND CANE. / HEAVEN SAYS** [ ] [ ]

Sep 83. (lp)(c) **BEFORE HOLLYWOOD** [ ] [-]
– A bad debt follows you / Two steps step out / Before Hollywood / Dusty in here / Ask / Cattle and cane / By chance / As long as that / On my block / That way.

Oct 83. (7") **MAN O' SAND TO GIRL O' SEA. / THIS GIRL BLACK GIRL** [ ] [-]

Sire Sire

Jul 84. (7") **PART COMPANY. / JUST A KING IN MIRRORS** [ ] [-]
(12"+=) – Newton told me.

Sep 84. (lp)(c) **SPRING HILL FAIR** [ ] [-]
– Bachelor kisses / Five words / The old way out / You've never lived / Part company / Slow slow music / Draining the pool for you / River of money / Unkind and unwise / Man o' sand girl o' sea.

Sep 84. (7") **BACHELOR KISSES. / RARE BREED** [ ] [-]
(12"+=) – Unkind and unwise (instrumental).

Beggar's B Beggar's B

Feb 86. (7") **SPRING RAIN. / LIFE AT HAND** [ ] [-]
(12"+=) – Little Joe.

Mar 86. (lp)(c)(cd) **LIBERTY BELLE AND THE BLACK DIAMOND EXPRESS** [ ] [ ]

– Spring rain / The ghost and the black hat / The wrong road / To reach me / Twin layers of lightning / In the core of the flame / Head full of steam / Palm Sunday (on board the S.S.Within) / Apology accepted. *(re-iss.+cd.Feb89)*

May 86. (7") **HEAD FULL OF STEAM. / DON'T LET HIM COME BACK** [ ] [-]
(12"+=) – The wrong road.

— added **AMANDA BROWN** (b.17 Nov'65) – keyboards, violin, guitar, oboe

Feb 87. (7") **RIGHT HERE. / WHEN PEOPLE ARE DEAD** [ ] [-]
(12"+=) – Don't call me gone.
(d7"++=) – A little romance (live).

May 87. (7") **CUT IT OUT. / TIME IN DESERT** [ ] [-]
(12"+=) – Doo wop in 'A'.

Jun 87. (lp)(c)(cd) **TALLULAH** [91] [ ]
– Right here / You tell me / Someone else's wife / I just get caught out / Cut it out / The house that Jack Kerouac built / Bye bye pride / Spirit of a vampyre / The Clarke sisters / Hope then strife. *(re-iss.+cd.Feb90)*

Aug 87. (7") **BYE BYE PRIDE. / THE HOUSE THAT JACK KEROUAC BUILT** [ ] [-]

— **JOHN WILSTEED** (b.13 Feb'57) – bass repl. VICKERS

Beggar's B / Capitol

Jul 88. (7") **STREETS OF YOUR TOWN. / WAIT UNTIL JUNE** [ ] [ ]
(12"+=) – Casanova's last words.
(cd-s++=) – Spring rain / Right here.

Aug 88. (lp)(c)(cd) **16 LOVERS LANE** [81] [ ]
– Love goes on / Quiet heart / Love is a sign / You can't say no forever / The Devil's eye / Streets of your town / Clouds / Was there anything I could do? / I'm alright / Dive for your memory.

Oct 88. (7") **WAS THERE ANYTHING I COULD DO. / ROCK'N'ROLL FRIEND** [ ] [-]
(12"+=) – Mexican postcard.
(cd-s++=) – Bye bye pride.

— Split 31 Dec'89. FORSTER and McLENNAN went solo. The latter also being part of JACK FROST with STEVE KILBEY of The CHURCH. AMANDA formed CLEOPATRA WONG.

– compilations, others, etc. –

Mar 90. Beggar's Banquet; (cd)(c)(d-lp) **THE GO-BETWEENS 1979-1990** [ ] [ ]
– Hammer the hammer / I need two heads / Cattle and cane / When people are dead / Man o' sand to girl o' sea / Bachelor kisses / People say / Draining the pool for you / World weary / Spring rain / Rock and roll friend / Dusty in here / The Clarke sisters / Right here / Second-hand furniture / Bye bye pride / This girl, black girl / The house that Jack Kerouac built / Don't call me gone / Streets of our own town / Love is a sign / You won't find it again. *(c+=)(d-lp+=)* – Karen / 8 pictures / The sound of rain / The wrong road / Mexican postcard.

Oct 89. Strange Fruit; (12"ep)(cd-ep) **THE PEEL SESSIONS** [ ] [-]
– The power that I have now / Second hand furniture / Fire woods / Rare breed.

Feb 85. Missing Link Australia; (lp) **VERY QUICK ON THE EYE BRISBANE 1981 (demo)** [-] [-]

1985. Pacific-Jem; (lp)(c) **METAL AND SHELLS** [-] [ ]

TUFF MONKS

(original GO-BETWEENS + BIRTHDAY PARTY members)

Oct 83. Au Go-Go Australia; (7") **AFTER THE FIREWORKS. / AFTER, AFTER THE FIREWORKS** [-] [-]

ROBERT FORSTER

(solo, with MICK HARVEY – producer)

Beggar's B. / Beggar's B.

Sep 90. (7") **BABY STONES. / ?** [ ] [-]
(12"+=)(cd-s+=) – ?

Oct 90. (cd)(c)(lp) **DANGER IN THE PAST** [ ] [ ]
– Baby stones / The river people / Leave here satisfied / Heart out to tender / Is this what you call change / Dear black dream / Danger in the past / I've been looking for somebody / Justice.

Apr 93. (cd)(c) **CALLING FROM A COUNTRY PHONE** [ ] [ ]
– Atlanta lie low / 121 / The circle / Falling star / I want to be quiet / Cats life / Girl to a world / Drop / Beyond their law / Forever & time. *(re-iss.cd Sep95)*

— with **JOHN KEANE** – guitars, banjos, keyboards, bass, etc / **JOEL MORRIS** – drums / **STEVE VENZ** – bass / **ANDY CARLSON** – guitars, mandolin / **TIM WHITE & BILL HOLMES** – porga & piano / **DWIGHT MANNING** – oboe / **SYD STRAW** – backing vocals

Jul 94. (cd-ep) **25-41 / 3 a.m. / FREDDIE FENDER / DANGER IN THE PAST (live)** [ ] [ ]

Aug 94. (cd)(c) **I HAD A NEW YORK GIRLFRIEND** [ ] [ ]
– Nature's way / Broken hearted people / Echo beach / Tell me that it isn't true / 2541 / Anytime / Locked away / Look out loves comes tomorrow / Alone / Bird / Frisco depot / 3 a.m. *(re-iss.cd Sep95)*

— FORSTER covered; NATURE'S WAY (Spirit) / BROKEN HEARTED PEOPLE (. . .Clarke) / ECHO BEACH (Martha & The Muffins) / TELL ME THAT IT ISN'T TRUE (Bob Dylan) / 2541 (Bob Mould) / ANYTIME (. . .Nelson) / LOCKED AWAY (Richards-Jordan) / LOOK OUT HERE COMES TOMORROW (Neil Diamond) / ALONE (Kelly-Steinberg) / BIRD (. . .Hansoms) / FRISCO DEPOT (. . .Newbury) / 3 A.M. (Anderson-Todd).

G.W. McLENNAN

Beggar's B. / Beggar's B.

Mar 91. (12"ep)(cd-ep) **WHEN WORD GET AROUND / BLACK MULE / SHE'S SO STRANGE / THE MAN WHO DIED IN RAPTURE** [ ] [ ]

May 91. (7") **EASY COME EASY GO. / MAKING IT RIGHT FOR HER** [ ] [-]
(12"+=)(cd-s+=) – Stones for you.

Jun 91. (cd)(c)(lp) **WATERSHED** [ ] [ ]
– When word get around / Haven't I been a fool / Haunted house / Stones for you / Easy come easy go / Black mule / Rory the weeks back on / You can't have everything / Sally's revolution / Broadway bride / Just get that straight / Dream about tomorrow.

Jan 93. (cd-ep) **FINGERS / WHOSE SIDE ARE YOU ON / WHAT WENT WRONG** [ ] [ ]

Feb 93. (cd-ep) **LIGHTING FIRES / DARK SIDE OF TOWN / IF I SHOULD FALL BEHIND** [ ] [ ]

Mar 93. (cd)(c) **FIREBOY** [ ] [ ]
– Lighting fires / Surround me / One million miles from here / The dark side of town / Things will change / The pawnbroker / Whose side are you on? / Fingers / Signs of life / The day my eyes Came back / Bathe (in the water) / When I close my eyes / Riddle in the rain. *(re-iss.cd Sep95)*

Aug 94. (cd-ep) **DON'T YOU CRY / COMING UP FOR AIR / GIRL IN A BERET / PUT YOU DOWN / NO PEACE IN THE PALACE / THAT'S THAT** [ ] [ ]

Nov 94. (d-cd)(c) **HORSEBREAKER STAR** [ ] [ ]
– Simone & Perry / Ice in Heaven / What went wrong / Race day rag / Don't you cry for me no more / Put you down / Late afternoon in early August / Coming up for air / Ballad of Easy Rider / Open invitation / Open my eyes / From my lips / / Dropping you / Hot water / Keep my word / Do your own thing / That's that / If I was a girl / Head over heels / Girl in a beret / All her songs / No peace in the palace / I'll call you wild / Horsebreaker star. *(re-iss.d-cd Sep95)*

Jun 95. (cd-ep) **SIMONE & PERRY / DON'T YOU CRY FOR ME NO MORE / BALLAD OF EASY RIDER / WHAT WENT WRONG (original)** [ ] [ ]

GODFATHERS

Formed: London, England . . . 1983 as The SID PRESLEY EXPERIENCE by the COYNE brothers PETER and CHRIS, plus DEL BARTLE and KEVIN MOONEY. When they split early '85, the brothers lost out on court battle to retain group name, so they chose The GODFATHERS. In 1987, after releases on own 'Corporate Image' label, they signed to 'Epic'. Their second album for the label 'MORE SONGS ABOUT LOVE AND HATE', finally broke them into UK Top50. • **Style:** Punk-ish R&B rock group with hard-like 'Kray Twin' image. • **Songwriters:** COYNE brothers, except; SUN ARISE (Rolf Harris) / COLD TURKEY (John Lennon) / BLITZKRIEG BOP (Ramones) / HOW DOES IT FEEL TO FEEL (Creation). • **Trivia:** In '84, The SID PRESLEY EXPERIENCE toured with BILLY BRAGG on 'Jobs For Youth' venues.

Recommended: HIT BY HIT (1986 compilation m-lp) / BIRTH, SCHOOL, WORK, DEATH (1988 cd).

SID PRESLEY EXPERIENCE

PETER COYNE – vocals / **DEL BARTLE** – guitar / **CHRIS COYNE** – bass / **KEVIN MOONEY** – drums

I.D. / not issued

May 84. (7")(12") **HUP TWO THREE FOUR. / PUBLIC ENEMY NO.1** [ ] [-]

S.P.E. / not issued

Dec 84. (7")(12") **COLD TURKEY. / FIREWATER / 'F' FOR FAKE** [ ] [-]

— Split early '85. DEL and KEVIN formed The UNHOLY TRINITY

The GODFATHERS

were formed by the **COYNE** brothers **PETER** and **CHRIS** with **MIKE GIBSON** – guitar / **KRIS DOLLIMORE** – guitar / **GEORGE MAZUR** – drums

Corporate Image / not issued

Oct 85. (7") **LONELY MAN. / I WANT YOU** [ ] [-]
(12"ep+=) – CAPO DI TUTTI (above 2 +) / Sticks and stones.

Apr 86. (12") **THIS DAMN NATION. / CAN'T LEAVE HER ALONE / JOHN BARRY** [ ] [-]

Sep 86. (7") **I WANT EVERYTHING. / SUN ARISE** [ ] [-]
(12"+=) – Unsatisfied.

Nov 86. (m-lp) **HIT BY HIT** [ ] [-]
– Lonely man / I want you / Sticks and stones / This damn nation / Can't leave her alone / John Barry / I want everything / Sun arise / Unsatisfied / Cold turkey. *(c+cd-iss.Dec87)*

Feb 87. (7") **LOVE IS DEAD. / ANGELA** [ ] [-]
(12"+=) – ('A' mix) / Gone to Texas.

Epic / Epic

Sep 87. (7")(7"pic-d) **BIRTH, SCHOOL, WORK, DEATH. / IF I ONLY HAD TIME** [ ] [ ]
(12"+=) – ('A'mix).

Feb 88. (lp)(c)(cd) **BIRTH, SCHOOL, WORK, DEATH** [80] [91]
– Birth, school, work, death / If I only had time / Tell me why / It's so hard / 'Cause I said so / Strangest boy / Obsession / S.T.B. / Just like you / Love is dead / When am I coming down.

Jul 88. (7") **'CAUSE I SAID SO. / WHEN AM I COMING DOWN** [ ] [ ]
(12"+=)(d7"+=) – I can only give you everything / Cold turkey.

Nov 88. (7")(7"pic-d) **LOVE IS DEAD. / THESE DAYS ARE OVER (live)** [ ] [ ]
(12"+=)(cd-s+=) – ('A' original version) / I'm satisfied (live).

Apr 89. (7")(7"pic-d) **SHE GIVES ME LOVE. / WALKING THROUGH JOHNNY CASH BLUES** [ ] [ ]
(12"+=)(cd-s+=) – Just because you're paranoid doesn't mean to say they're not out to get you.

May 89. (lp)(c)(cd) **MORE SONGS ABOUT LOVE AND HATE** [49] [ ]
– She gives me love / These days are over / How low is low? / Party girl / This is your life / I'm lost and then I'm found / I don't believe in you / Life has passed us

by / Another you / Walking talking Johnny Cash blues / Halfway paralysed.

— **CHRIS BURROWS** – guitar, vocals repl. DOLLIMORE

Feb 90. (7") **I'M LOST AND THEN I'M FOUND. / WALKING TALKING JOHNNY CASH BLUES** [ ] [ ]
(12")(cd-s) – ('A'side) / Still alone / She gives me love / Birth school work death (extended).
(10"+=) – How low is low? / Blitzkreig bop.

Feb 91. (7")(c-s) **UNREAL WORLD. / SOMETHING GOOD ABOUT YOU** [ ] [ ]
(12"+=)(cd-s+=) – This is your life (live) / This damn nation (live).

Mar 91. (cd)(c)(lp) **UNREAL WORLD** [ ] [ ]
– Unreal world / Don't let me down / King of misery / Believe in yourself / I'll never forget what's his name / How does it feel to feel / Drag me down again / Something good about you / I love what's happening to me / This is war.

Corporate Image — not issued

Jun 92. (cd)(c)(lp) **DOPE, RO**'N'ROLL AND FU**ING IN THE STREETS (live)** [ ] [-]
– Birth, school, work, death / She gives me love / Unreal world / I don't believe in you / Drag me down again / When am I coming down / Obsession / I love what's hapening to me / If I only had time / Lonely man / Don't let me down / I want everything / 'Cause I said so / This damn nation / This is war / Cold turkey.

— They had already split earlier in the year.

Intercord — not issued

Oct 93. (cd) **ORANGE** [ ] [-]
–

– compilations etc. –

Feb 89. Strange Fruit; (12"ep)(cd-ep) **THE EVENING SHOW SESSIONS** [ ] [-]
– I want you / If I only had time / I want everything / I'm satisfied.

GODLEY & CREME (see under ⇒ 10cc)

GO-GO'S

Formed: Los Angeles, California, USA . . . May'78, firstly as The MISFITS, by CARLISLE, CAFFEY and WIEDLIN. After one-off 45 in 1980 for UK semi-major label 'Stiff', they signed to Miles Copeland's 'IRS'. In 1981, they had first entry into US Top 20 with 'OUR LIPS ARE SEALED', which was lifted from No.1 album 'BEAUTY AND THE BEAT'. They continued to achieve chart status until their 1985 split. The following year, CARLISLE paved out a successful solo career, especially in Britain, where she peaked at the top in 1992 with hits album 'BEST OF . . . '. • **Style:** All-girl new wave romance'n'roll pop outfit. In the latter half of the 80's, BELINDA CARLISLE chose visual smoochy pop songs to boost fruitful solo career. • **Songwriters:** WIEDLIN or CARLISLE, and when the latter went solo, her songs were nearly all written by producer RICK NOWELS and ELLEN SHIPLEY. In 1992, she collaborated on some with new producer RICHARD FELDMAN. Others writers; I GET WEAK + WORLD WITHOUT YOU (Dianne Warren) / SUMMER RAIN (Seidman-Vidal) / I FEEL FREE (Cream) / THE AIR YOU BREATHE (Weiss-White). • **Trivia:** The GO-GO's briefly re-formed in 1990, for a naked but discreet anti-fur campaign.

Recommended: GREATEST (*6) / BEST OF BELINDA CARLISLE (*4)

BELINDA CARLISLE (b.17 Aug'58, Hollywood, USA) – vocals (ex-The GERMS) / **CHARLOTTE CAFFEY** (b.21 Oct'53, Santa Monica, USA) – lead guitar, vocals / **JANE WIEDLIN** (b.20 May'58, Oconomowoc, Wisconsin) – rhythm guitar, vocals / **MARGOT OLAVERRA** – bass / **GINA SHOCK** (b.31 Aug'57, Baltimore, USA) – drums (ex-EDDIE MASSEY & HER EGGS) repl. ELISA BELLO.

Stiff — not issued

May 80. (7") **WE GOT THE BEAT. / HOW MUCH MORE** [ ] [-]

— **KATHY VALENTINE** (b. 7 Jan'59, Austin, Texas) – bass (ex-TEXTONES) repl. MARGOT.

I.R.S. — I.R.S.

Jul 81. (7"pink) **OUR LIPS ARE SEALED. / SURFING AND SPYING** [ ] [20]

Aug 81. (lp)(c) **BEAUTY AND THE BEAT** [ ] [1] Jul 81
– Our lips are sealed / This town / How much more / Fading fast / We got the beat / Tonite / Skidmarks on my heart / Lust to love / Automatic / You can't walk in your sleep (if you can't sleep) / Can't stop the world. *(cd-iss.1988)*

Nov 81. (7")(7"pic-d) **WE GOT THE BEAT. / SKIDMARKS ON MY HEART** [ ] [-]

Jan 82. (7") **WE GOT THE BEAT. / CAN'T STOP THE WORLD** [-] [2]

Feb 82. (7")(7"pic-d) **AUTOMATIC. / TONITE** [ ] [-]

Apr 82. (7") **OUR LIPS ARE SEALED. / WE GOT THE BEAT** [47] [-]

Aug 82. (7") **VACATION. / BEATNIK BEACH** [ ] [8] Jul 82

Aug 82. (lp)(c) **VACATION** [75] [8]
– Vacation / This old feeling / He's so strange / Girl of 100 lists / It's everything but partytime / Get up and go / Beatnik beach / I think it's me / The way you dance / We don't get along / Worlds away / Cool jerk.

Sep 82. (7") **GET UP AND GO. / SPEEDING** [-] [50]

Nov 82. (7") **GIRL OF 100 LISTS. / I THINK IT'S ME** [ ] [-]

Dec 82. (7") **IT'S EVERYTHING BUT PARTYTIME. / THIS OLD FEELING** [-] [ ]

Nov 83. (7") **BELONG TO ME. / DON'T YOU LOVE ME** [ ] [ ]

Apr 84. (7") **HEAD OVER HEELS. / GOOD FOR GONE** [ ] [11] Mar 84

May 84. (lp)(c) **TALK SHOW** [ ] [18] Apr 84
– Turn to you / You thought / Capture the light / I'm the only one / Mercenary / I'm with you / Yes or no / Head over heels / Forget that day / Beneath the blue sky. *(cd-iss.1988)*

Jun 84. (7") **TURN TO YOU. / I'M WITH YOU** [-] [32]

Sep 84. (7") **YES OR NO. / MERCENARY** [-] [84]

— **PAULA JEAN BROWN** – rhythm guitar repl. JANE WIEDLIN who went solo. They disbanded May 1985 when CAFFEY and CARLISLE left.

BELINDA CARLISLE

went solo, taking with her **CHARLOTTE CAFFEY**

I.R.S. — I.R.S.

Jun 86. (7") **MAD ABOUT YOU. / I NEVER WANTED A RICH MAN** [ ] [3] May 86
(12"+=) – ('A'extended). *(re-iss.+3" cd-s Jan88) (re-iss Jul88 hit UK 67)*

Jul 86. (lp)(c) **BELINDA** [ ] [13]
– Mad about you / I need a disguise / Since you've gone / I feel the magic / I never wanted a rich man / Band of gold / Gotta get to you / From the heart / Shot in the dark / Stuff and nonsense. *(cd-iss.1988 & Jan90 on 'MCA')*

Sep 86. (7") **I FEEL THE MAGIC. / FROM THE HEART** [-] [82]

Virgin — M.C.A.

Nov 87. (7") **HEAVEN IS A PLACE ON EARTH. / WE CAN CHANGE** [1] [1] Sep 87
(12"+=)/ /(cd-s+=) – ('A'version)./ / ('A'-acappella version).

Dec 87. (lp)(c)(cd) **HEAVEN ON EARTH** [4] [13] Oct 87
– Heaven is a place on Earth / Circle in the sand / I feel free / Should I let you in? / World without you / I get weak / We can change / Fool for love / Nobody owns me / Love never dies . . . *(cd+pic-cd-iss.Nov88) (re-iss.Jan91 No.46.*

Feb 88. (7") **I GET WEAK. / SHOULD I LET YOU IN** [10] [2] Jan 88
(12"+=)(c-s+=)(pic-cd-s+=) – ('A'extended mix).

Apr 88. (7") **CIRCLE IN THE SAND. / WE CAN CHANGE** [-] [7]

Apr 88. (7") **CIRCLE IN THE SAND. / ('A'-seaside mix)** [4] [-]
(12"+=)(12"pic-d+) – ('A'-beach mix).
(c-s+=)(cd-s+=) – ('A'-sandblast mix).

Jul 88. (c-s) **I FEEL FREE. / SHOULD I LET YOU IN** [-] [88]

Aug 88. (7") **WORLD WITHOUT YOU (remix). / NOBODY OWES ME** [34] [ ]
(12"+=) – ('A' mix).
(cd-s) – ('A'side) / ('A' pana-mix) / ('A' mix).

Nov 88. (7") **LOVE NEVER DIES. / I FEEL FREE (live)** [54] [ ]
(12"+=) – Heaven is a place on Earth (live).
(cd-s++=) – Circle in the sand (live).

Sep 89. (7")(c-s) **LEAVE A LIGHT ON. / SHADES OF MICAELANGELO** [4] [11]
(12"+=) – ('A'extended version).
(cd-s++=) – ('A'other version).

Oct 89. (lp)(c)(cd) **RUNAWAY HORSES** [4] [37]
– Leave a light on / Runaway horses / Vision of you / Summer rain / La Luna / (We want) The same thing / Deep deep ocean / Valentine / Whatever it takes / Shades of Michaelangelo. *(re-iss Jan91 hit No.6).*

Nov 89. (7")(c-s) **LA LUNA. / WHATEVER IT TAKES** [38] [ ]
(12"+=) – ('A'extended mix).
(3"cd-s) – ('A'side) / ('A'dub version).

Dec 89. (7") **SUMMER RAIN. / SHADES OF MICHAELANGELO** [-] [30]

Mar 90. (7")(c-s) **RUNAWAY HORSES. / HEAVEN IS A PLACE ON EARTH (live)** [40] [ ]
(12"+=)(3"cd-s+=) – Circle in the sand (mix).

May 90. (7")(c-s) **VISION OF YOU. / LEAVE A LIGHT ON (mix)** [41] [ ]
(12"+=)(cd-s+=) – I feel free (extended).

Oct 90. (7")(c-s) **(WE WANT) THE SAME THING (summer remix). / SHADES OF MICHAELANGELO** [6] [ ]
(12"+=) – Heaven is a place on Earth / I get weak.
(pic-cd+=) – Circle in the sand.

Dec 90. (7")(c-s) **SUMMER RAIN. / LEAVE A LIGHT ON (mix)** [23] [-]
(12") – ('A'side) / ('A'mix).
(cd-s) – ('A'side) / ('A'extra mix).

Apr 91. (7")(c-s) **VISION OF YOU (remix '91). / LEAVE A LIGHT ON (mix)** [ ] [ ]
(12"+=)(cd-s+=) – I feel free (extended mix).
(12"pic-d) – ('A'side) / Heaven is a place on Earth

Sep 91. (7")(c-s) **LIVE YOUR LIFE BE FREE. / LONELINESS GAME** [12] [ ]
(12"pic-d+=)(cd-s+=) – ('A'club version).

Oct 91. (cd)(c)(lp) **LIVE YOUR LIFE BE FREE** [7] [ ]
– Live your life be free / Do you feel like I feel? / Half the world / You came out of nowhere / You're nothing without me / I plead insanity / Emotional highway / Little black book / Love revolution / World of love / Loneliness game.

Nov 91. (7")(7"pic-d) **DO YOU FEEL LIKE I FEEL. / WORLD OF LOVE** [29] [73]
(12"+=) – ('A'dance version).
(cd-s++=) – Live your life be free (dance instrumental).

Jan 92. (7")(c-s) **HALF A WORLD. / ONLY A DREAM** [35] [ ]
(cd-s+=) – Live your life be free (original).
(cd-s) – ('A'side) / Vision of you ('91 remix) / Circle in the sand / Love never dies.

Aug 92. (7")(c-s) **LITTLE BLACK BOOK. / ONLY A DREAM** [28] [ ]
(cd-s+=) – The air you breathe.
(cd-s+=) – ('A'mix) / ('A'house mix).

Sep 92. (cd)(c)(lp) **THE BEST OF BELINDA CARLISLE VOLUME 1** [1] [ ]
– (compilation) – Heaven is a place on Earth / (We want) The same thing / Circle in the sand / Leave a light on / Little black book / Summer rain / Vision of you / Live your life be free / I get weak / La Luna / I plead insanity / World without you / Do you feel like I feel? / Half the world / Runaway horses.

— with writers **CAFFEY** + brothers **THOMAS + RICHARD**, plus **JEFFREY McDONALD & STEVEN McDONALD** / and a host of musicians

Sep 93. (7")(c-s) **BIG SCARY ANIMAL. / WINDOWS OF THE WORLD** [12] [ ]
(cd-s+=) – Change (demo) / Too much water (demo).

Oct 93. (cd)(c)(lp) **REAL** [9] [ ]
– Goodbye day / Big scary animal / Too much water / Lay down your arms / Where love hides / One with you / Wrap my arms / Tell me / Windows of the world / Here comes my baby.

Nov 93. (7")(c-s) **LAY DOWN YOUR ARMS. / TELL ME** [27] [ ]

(cd-s+=) – Wrap my arms (demo).
(cd-s++=) Here comes my baby (demo).

GO-GO'S

had briefly re-united in 1990 and late in '94.

A&M A&M

Jan 91. (12") **COOL JERK. / WE GOT THE BEAT** 60

Feb 91. (cd)(c)(lp) **GO-GO'S GREATEST** (compilation) Nov 90
– Our lips are sealed / Cool jerk / We got the beat / Head over heels / Get up and go / Vacation / Beatnik beach / You thought / I'm the only one / This town / Lust to love / Mercenary / How much more / Turn to you. *(re-iss.cd Mar93 on 'A&M')*

Feb 95. E.M.I.; (7")(c-s) **THE WHOLE WORLD LOST ITS HEAD./ OUR LIPS ARE SEALED** 29
(cd-s+=) – Automatic / Lust to love.

Mar 95. E.M.I.; (cd)(c) **RETURN TO THE VALLEY OF THE GO-GO'S** (compilation) 52
– Living at the Canterbury – Party pose / Fashion seekers (live) / He's so strange / London boys (live) / Beatnik beach (live) / Cool jerk / We got the beat / Our lips are sealed / Surfing and spying / Vacation / Speeding / Good for gone / Head over heels / Can't stop the world (live) / Mercenary (acoustic) / Good girl / Beautiful / The whole world lost its head.

GOLDEN EARRING

Formed: Holland ... 1961 as The TORNADOS by GERRITSEN and KOOYMANS. In 1964, they had Dutch Top 10 single with 'PLEASE GO', which was followed by a string of others. In 1972, after a support tour to friends The WHO, they signed to Kit Lambert & Chris Stamp's 'Track'. The next year, they crossed over to UK, and made breakthrough into UK charts with classic 45 'RADAR LOVE'. But for a surprise US hit in '82 'TWILIGHT ZONE', they did little to emulate first promise. • **Style:** Initially a quasi-bubblegum psychedelic group, until late 60's move towards hard & heavy-rock, complimented by distinctive vox of HAY. • **Songwriters:** KOOYMANS, GERRITSEN and HAY. • **Trivia:** Early member JAAP EGGERMONT, went on to become man behind the fruitful 80's pop STARSOUND medleys.

Recommended: THE BEST OF GOLDEN EARRING (*7).

GEORGE KOOYMANS (b.11 Mar'48) – vocals, guitar / **RINUS GERRITSEN** – bass, keyboards / **FRANS KRASSENBURG** – vocals / **PETER DE PONDE** – guitar / **JOAP EGGERMONT** – drums

not issued Polydor

1964. (7") **PLEASE GO. / ?** - - Dutch

1966. (lp) **JUST EARRINGS (as "GOLDEN EARRINGS")** - - Dutch
– Nobody but you / I hate saying these words / She may be / Holy witness / No need to worry / Please go / Sticks and stones / I am a fool / Don't stay away / Lonely everyday / When people talk / Now I have.

— Trim slightly when PETER departed.

1967. (lp) **WINTER-HARVEST** - - Dutch
– Another man in town / Smoking cigarettes / In my house / Don't wanna lose that girl / Impecable / Tears and lies / There will be a tomorrow / You've got the intention to hurt me / You break my heart / Baby don't make me nervous / Call me / Happy and young together / Lionel the mission.

1968. (lp) **MIRACLE MIRROR** - - Dutch
– Truth about Arthur / Circus will be in town in time / Crystal heaven / Sam & Sue / I've just lost somebody / Mr.Fortune's wife / Who cares / Born a second time / Magnificent magistral / Nothing can change this world of mine / Gipsy rhapsody.

(Still signed to 'Polydor' in Holland)

— (1967) **KOOYMANS & GERRITSON** brought in **BARRY HAY** (b.16 Aug'48) – vocals, flute, saxophone / **SIEB WARNER** – drums repl. JOAP (He re-emerged in medley outfit STARSOUND)

Major Minor Atlantic

Mar 69. (7") **JUST A LITTLE BIT OF PEACE IN MY HEART. / REMEMBER MY FRIEND**

Aug 69. (7") **IT'S ALRIGHT BUT IT COULD BE BETTER. / WHERE WILL I BE** -

Jan 70. (lp) **EIGHT MILES HIGH**
– Landing / Song of a Devil's servant / One huge road / Everyday's torture / Eight miles high. *(cd-iss.Mar88)*

1970. (7") **INCREDIBLE MISS BROWN. / COMING HOME TO YOU** -

Feb 70. (7") **ANOTHER 45 MILES. / I CAN'T GET HOLD OF HER**

1970. (7") **EIGHT MILES HIGH. / ONE HUGE ROAD** -

— **CESAR ZUIDERWIJK** – drums / **ELLCO GELLING** – guitar / **BERTUS BORGERS** – sax repl. WARNER

Polydor Polydor

1970. (7") **THAT DAY. / WORDS I NEED** -

1970. (lp) **GOLDEN EARRING**
– Yellow and blue / The loner / This is the time of the year / As long as the wind blows / The wall of dolls / Back home / See see / I'm going to send my pigeons to the sky / Big tree blue sea.

1970. (7") **BACK HOME. / THIS IS THE TIME OF THE YEAR** -

— now without GELLING + BORGERS

1971. (lp) **SING MY SONG**
– Song of a Devil's servant / Angelina / High in the sky / The sad story of Sam Stone / Murdock 9-6182 / God bless the day / I'm a-runnin' / Just a little bit of peace in my heart / Remember my friend / My baby Ruby / I sing my song / The grand piano.

1971. (lp) **SEVEN TEARS**
– Silver ships / The road / Swallowed her name / Hope / Don't worry / She flies on strange wings / This is the other side of fire / You're better off free.

1972. (lp) **TOGETHER**
– All day watcher / Avalanche of love / Cruising Southern Germany / Brother wind / Buddy Joe / Jangalene / From Heaven to Hell / Thousand feet below.

Track Track

1973. (lp)(c) **HEARRING EARRING** (comp.last 2 lp's) -
– Jangeline / All day watcher / She flies on strange wings / Avalanche of love / Silver ships / Brother wind / Hope / Thousand feet below.

Nov 73. (7") **RADAR LOVE. / JUST LIKE VINCE TAYLOR** 7 13 May 74
(re-iss.Mar86 on 'Old Gold')

Dec 73. (lp)(c) **MOONTAN** 24 12 Apr 74
– Candy's going bad / Are you receiving me / Radar love / Big tree, blue sea / Just like Vince Taylor / The vanilla queen.

May 74. (7") **INSTANT POETRY. / FROM HEAVEN, FROM HELL**

Nov 74. (7") **CANDY'S GOING BAD. / SHE FLIES ON STRANGE WINGS** 91 Oct 74

Track M.C.A.

Mar 75. (7") **KILL ME, CE SOIR. / LUCKY NUMBERS**

Apr 75. (lp)(c) **SWITCH**
– (intro) / Plus minus absurdio / Love is a rodeo / Switch / Kill me, ce soir / Tons of times / Daddy's gonna save my soul / Troubles and hassles / Lonesome D.J.

Jun 75. (7") **SWITCH. / LONESOME D.J.** -

Polydor M.C.A.

Jan 76. (7") **SLEEPWALKIN'. / BABYLON**

Mar 76. (lp)(c) **TO THE HILT** Feb 76
– Why me / Facedancer / To the hilt / Nomad / Sleep walkin' / Latin lightnin' / Violins.

Feb 77. (7") **BOMBAY. / FADED JEANS**

Mar 77. (lp)(c) **CONTRABAND** -
– Bombay / Sueleen (Sweden) / Con man / Mad love's comin' / Fightin' windmills / Faded jeans / Time's up.

May 77. (lp)(c) **MAD LOVE** -
– I need love / Sueleen (Sweden) / Mad love's comin' / Bombay / Fightin' windmills / Con man / Time's up.

Sep 77. (lp)(c) **GOLDEN EARRING LIVE (live)**
– Candy's going bad / She flies on strange wings / Mad love's comin' / Eight miles high / The vanilla queen / To the hilt / Fightin' windmills / Con man / Radar love / Just like Vince Taylor.

Sep 77. (7") **RADAR LOVE (live). / JUST LIKE VINCE TAYLOR (live)** 44

Jan 79. (lp)(c) **GRAB IT FOR A SECOND**
– Movin' down life / Against the grain / Grab it for a second / Cell 29 / Roxanne / Leather / Temptin' / U-turn time. *(US-title 'NO PROMISES')*

1980. (lp)(c) **PRISONER OF THE NIGHT**
– Long blond animal / No for an answer / My town / Prisoner of the night / I don't wanna be nobody else / Cut 'em down to size / Will & Mercy / Come in Outerspace / Going crazy again. *(US-title 'LONG BLOND ANIMAL')*

Sep 81. (d-lp)(c) **2ND LIVE (live)**
– Don't stop the show / My town / No for an answer / Heartbeat / Save your skin / I don't wanna be nobody else / Long blond animal / Prisoner of the night / Weekend love / Sleepwalkin' / I do rock'n'roll / Slow down / Buddy Joe / Back home.

Mercury 21 Records

Jan 83. (7")(12") **TWILIGHT ZONE. / KING DARK** 10 Nov 82

Feb 83. (lp)(c) **CUT** 24 Nov 82
– The Devil made me do it / Future / Baby dynamite / Last of the Mohicans / Lost and found / Twilight zone / Chargin' up my batteries / Secrets.

Apr 83. (7") **THE DEVIL MADE ME DO IT. / CHARGIN' UP MY BATTERIES** - 79

Jul 84. (7") **CLEAR NIGHT MOONLIGHT. / FIST IN LOVE** -

Carrere 21 Records

Apr 84. (7")(12") **WHEN THE LADY SMILES. / ORWELL'S YEAR** 76 Mar 84

Apr 84. (lp)(c) **N.E.W.S.** Mar 84
– Clear night moonlight / When the lady smiles / Enough is enough / Fist in love / N.E.W.S. / I'll make it all up to you / Mission impossible / It's over now. *(cd-iss.1988)*

21 Records 21 Records

Feb 85. (lp)(c) **SOMETHING HEAVY GOING DOWN – LIVE FROM THE TWILIGHT ZONE (live)** Nov84
– Long blond animal / Twilight zone / When the lady smiles / Future / Something heavy going down / Enough is enough / Mission impossible / Clear night moonlight.

Jun 86. (lp)(c) **THE HOLE**
– They dance / Quiet eyes / Save the best for later / Have a heart / Love in motion / Jane Jane / Jump and run / Why do I / Shout in the dark.

Jun 86. (7") **QUIET EYES. / LOVE IN MOTION** -

Nov 86. (7") **WHY DO I. / LOVE IN MOTION** -

BARRY HAY

(solo)

Ring 21 Records

Dec 87. (lp)(c) **VICTORY OF BAD TASTE**
– Draggin' the line / I'd lie to you for your love / Jezebel / My favourite spot / Firewater / Did you really mean it / She's here / Girl / Going blind.

GOLDEN EARRING

reformed in the late 80's, with **HAY, GERRITSEN, KOOYMANS + ZUIDERWIJK**

Ring Jaws-MCA

Apr 89. (lp)(c)(cd) **KEEPER OF THE FLAME**
– Can do that / Too much woman / One word / Keeper of the flame / Turn the world around / Circles / My prayer, my shadow / Distant love.

Apr 89. (7") **MY PRAYER, MY SHADOW. / ?**

— (same line-up for over 20 years)

Columbia Columbia

Aug 91. (cd)(c)(lp) **BLOODY BUCHANEERS**
– Making love to yourself / Temporary madness / When love turns to pain / Joe / Planet blue / Going to the run / Bloody buchaneers / One shot away from Paradise / In a bad mood / Pourin' my heart out again.

Jun 95. (cd)(c) **FACE IT**
– Angel / Hold me now / Liquid soul / Minute by minute / Johnny make believe / Space ship / The unforgettable dream / I can't do without your kiss / Freedom don't

last forever / Maximum make up / Legalize telepathy.

- compilations, others, etc. -

Oct 76. Polydor; (lp)(c) **GOLDEN EARRING** [ ] [-]
(re-iss.Sep83 on 'Track')
Nov 80. Polydor; (d-lp)(c) **GREATEST HITS** [ ] [ ]
May 88. Arcane; (d-cd) **THE VERY BEST OF GOLDEN EARRING VOLUME 1 & 2** [ ] [-]
Mar 90. Old Gold; (7") **RADAR LOVE. / TWILIGHT ZONE** [ ] [-]
1991. M.C.A.; (cd)(c) **THE CONTINUING STORY OF RADAR LOVE** [-] [ ]
Jul 92. Connoisseur; (cd) **THE BEST OF GOLDEN EARRING** [ ] [-]
– Radar love / She flies on strange wings / Kill me / Mission impossible / Vanilla queen / Sleepwalkin' / Long blonde animal / Weekend love / When the lady smiles / Quiet eyes / Twilight zone / Turn the world around / Eight miles high.

GOLDIE

Born: 1966, Manchester, England. Lived in Miami in the late 80's, where he built up skills of graffiti artistry. Soon after he moved back to Britain to collaborate with Mancunian (A GUY CALLED) GERALD (famous for his 'Voodoo Ray' 45). They collaborated on single 'ENERGY'. / 'THE RENO'. After a few singles with his METALHEADZ outfit, GOLDIE made impact in 1995 when his 'TIMELESS' album hit UK Top 10 (a favourite of the NME). • **Style:** A hybrid of ambient jazz jungle beats and inner-city symphonies of bassy dub sounds. Obtained the GOLDIE motif, due to his gold designer molars. • **Songwriters:** Himself. Collaborated in 1994/5 with MEL GAYNOR (of-SIMPLE MINDS).
Recommended: TIMELESS (*9)

GOLDIE (b.1967) – vocals (with METALHEADZ)

Reinforced / not issued

1992. (12"ep) **KILLERMUFFIN EP** [ ] [-]
1993. (12"ep)(c-ep)(cd-ep) **TERMINATOR (original) / KEMISTRY / KNOWLEDGE / SINISTER** [ ] [-]
1993. (12"ep) ENFORCERS / [ ] [-]

ffrr / London

Nov 94. (12")(c-s)(cd-s) **INNER CITY LIFE / ('A'mixes)** [49] [ ]
(12") – ('A'mixes; Roni Size / Nookie remix).
(above as GOLDIE PRESENTS METALHEADS)
Mar 95. (c-s)(cd-s) **TIMELESS / INNER CITY LIFE** [ ] [ ]
Jul 95. (d-cd)(d-c)(d-lp) **TIMELESS** [7] [ ]
– Timeless / Saint Angel / State of mind / This is a bad / Sea of tears / Jah the seventh / State of rage (sensual V.I.P. mix) / Still life / Angel / Adrift / Kemistry / You & me. (d-lp+=) (2 other mixes).
Aug 95. (12")(c-s) **ANGEL. / SAINT ANGEL / YOU AND ME (THE BEAUTY - THE BEAST)** [41] [ ]
(cd-s+=) – Angel (Peshay back from Narm mix).
Nov 95. (c-s) **INNER CITY LIFE / ('A'-Peshay mix)** [39] [ ]
(cd-s+=) – Kemistry (Doc Scott mix).
(cd-s) – ('A'radio mix) / ('A'extended) / ('A'-4 Hero part 1 mix) / ('A'-Roni Size instrumental).

GOLLIWOGS (see under ⇒ CREEDENCE CLEARWATER REVIVAL)

GONG

Formed: Paris, France . . . 1968 by Australian DAEVID ALLEN who had lived in England since 1961. Gigged in Paris where he and future GONG members set up home, having been refused re-entry into UK. Recorded 2 albums under his own name, but by 1971 they had become GONG, recording debut CAMEMBERT ELECTRIQUE for French label 'Byg'. After appearing at hippy festival 'Glastonbury', they moved to Richard Branson's 'Virgin' records in 1973. STEVE HILLAGE was now a member and became forefront when ALLEN left to go solo. Splintered reformations of outfit, led to their near obscurity by the late 70's. • **Style:** Space-metal rock, exhuming unconventional psychedelia and weird experimentation. By the 70's, they or simply PIERRE MOERLEN had drifted unashamedly into jazz-rock. • **Songwriters:** DAEVID or GILLI and band, until HILLAGE then MOERLEN, etc took over. MOERLEN covered JIN GO LA BA (Olatunji; Santana hit). • **Trivia:** Played on one side of double live lp 'GREASY TRUCKERS' circa '72. Their CAMEMBERT ELECTRIQUE album was issued in UK 1974 for 49p. Sold well enough for chart placing but barred for being too cheap. Days of hype, eh!. KEVIN AYERS joined mid'71 to early '72, before returning to solo work.

Recommended: THE FLYING TEAPOT (*7)

DAEVID ALLEN – guitar, vocals (ex-SOFT MACHINE) / **GILLI SMYTH** – whispered vocals / **DIDIER MALHERBE** – sax, flute / **RACHID HOUARI** – drums, tabla / **DIETER GEWISSLER** – contrabass / **CARL FREEMAN** – contrabass / **BARE PHILLIPS** – contrabass / **BURTON GREEN** – piano, piano harp / **TASMIN SMYTH** (Gilli's daughter) – vocals

Byg / not issued

Feb 70. (lp) **MAGICK BROTHER, MYSTIC SISTER** [-] [-] France
– Mystick sister, Magick brother / Glad to say to say / Rational anthem / Chainstore chant – Pretty Miss Titty / Fable of a Fredfish – Hope you feel o.k.? / Ego / Gong song / Princess dreaming / 5 & 20 schoolgirls / Cos you got green hair. *(UK-iss.Nov77 on 'Charly', cd-iss.Nov86)*

— with **PIP PYLE, CHRISTIAN TRITSCH + ROBERT WYATT**

1971. (lp) **BANANA MOON** (by "DAEVID ALLEN") [-] [-]
– Time of our life / Memories / All I want is out of here / Fred the fish / White rock blues and cabin code / Stoned innocent / Frankenstein, and his adventures in the land of Flip / I am a bowl. *(UK-iss.Jul75 on 'Caroline') (re-iss.May79 on 'Charly') (cd-iss.May90)*

— **CHRISTIAN TRITSCH** – bass / **GERRY FIELDS** – violin / **DANIEL LALOU** – multi horns, percussion repl. **FREEMAN, GREEN, PHILLIPS** and **T. SMYTH**

1970. (7") **EST-CE-QUE JE SUIS./ HIP HIPNOTIZE YOU** [-] [-]
1971. (lp) **CAMEMBERT ELECTRIQUE** [-] [-]
– Radio gnome / You can't kill me / I've bin stone before / Mister long shanks: O mother – I am your fantasy / Dynamite: I am your animal / Wet cheese delirium / Squeezing sponges over policemen's heads / Fohat digs holes in space / Tried so hard / Tropical fish: Selene / Gnome the second. *(UK-iss.Jun74 on 'Caroline') (re-iss.+c.1982 on 'Charly') (cd-iss.Mar86 & Mar90 on 'Decal') (cd-iss.Nov94 on 'Gas') (re-iss.Sep95 on 'Spalax')*
Jan 71. (lp) **CONTINENTAL CIRCUS (Soundtrack on 'Phillips')** [ ] [-]
– Blues for Findlay / Continental circus world / What do you want / Blues for Findlay (instrumental).

— **LAURIE ALLEN** – drums repl. PYLE who joined HATFIELD + THE NORTH / added **FRANCIS MOZE** – bass (ex-MAGMA)

— Disbanded early '72 after Glastonbury Fayre, but re-formed by end of year. Added **STEVE HILLAGE** – guitar (ex-KEVIN AYERS, ex-KHAN, ex-URIEL) / **TIM BLAKE** – synthesizers

Virgin / Virgin

May 73. (lp) **THE FLYING TEAPOT** [ ] [-]
– Radio gnome invisible / The flying teapot / The pot head pixies / The octave doctors and the crystal machine / Zero to hero and the witch's spell / Witch's song / I am your pussy. *(re-iss.Mar84) (re-iss.Jan81 & 1985 on 'Charly') (cd-iss.Sep95 on 'Spalax')*

— Although DAEVID and GILLI moved to Majorca, Spain, they returned mid 1973. / **PIERRE MOERLEN** – drums repl. LAURIE / **MIKE HOWLETT** (b.Fiji) – bass, vocals repl. MOZE

Dec 73. (lp)(c) **ANGEL'S EGG** [ ] [ ]
– Other side of the sky / Sold to the highest Buddha / Castles in the clouds / Prostitute poem / Givin' my luv to you / Selene / Flute salad / Oily way / Outer temple – Inner temple / Percolations / Love is how you make it / I never glid before / Eat the phone book code. *(re-iss.Mar84) (re-iss.Aug82 on 'Charly' cd-iss.Jun90) (cd-iss.Apr91 on 'Decal' +=)*– Ooby-Stooby doomsday or The D-Day DJs got the DDT blues.

— **MIQUETTE GIRAUDY** – keyboards repl. GILLI

Oct 74. (lp)(c) **YOU** [ ] [ ]
– Thoughts for nought / A.P.H.P.'s advice / Magick mother invocation / Master builder / A sprinkling of clouds / Perfect mystery / The isle of everywhere / You never blow your trip forever. *(re-iss.Mar84) (re-iss.Aug82 on 'Charly') (cd-iss.Aug91 on 'Decal')*

— Virtually break-up, when DAEVID and GILLI move to Spain again. In May'76, DAEVID continued solo career and re-formed GONG in the late 80's. Meanwhile back in 1975, after he recorded solo FISH RISING album, STEVE HILLAGE also became solo artist using most of GONG!.

GONG

re-formed with only one original **DIDIER MALHERBE.** He recruited **JORGE PINCHEVSKY** – violin / **MIQUETTE GIRAUDY** – keyboards / **MIKE HOWLETT** – drums / **MIREILLE BAUER** – percussion, xylophone, etc. / **PATRICE LEMOINE** – keyboards
(note that HOWLETT went on to become producer of A FLOCK OF SEAGULLS, etc)

Feb 76. (lp)(c) **SHAMAL** [ ] [ ]
– Wingful of eyes / Chandra / Bambooji / Cat in Clark's shoes / Mandrake / Shamal. *(re-iss.Mar84)*

— **PIERRE MOERLEN** returned to repl. BRIAN DAVISON (ex-REFUGEE) who had toured with them in 1976 after BILL BRUFORD left to join GENESIS, ZAPPA, etc. / **ALLAN HOLDSWORTH** – guitar (ex-SOFT MACHINE, etc) / **FRANCIS MOZE** – bass returned / **BENOIT MOERLEN** – keyboards / **MINO CINELOU** – percussion / **DIDIER & MIREILLE** also

Feb 77. (lp)(c) **GAZEUSE!** (US title '**EXPRESSO**') [ ] [ ]
– Expresso / Night illusion / Percolations part 1 & 2 / Shadows of Mireille. *(re-iss.Mar84)*

— Disbanded again Spring 1977 (aargghh!!!). Left behind retrospective below (all line-ups).

Aug 77. (d-lp)(c) **LIVE! ETC. (live)** [ ] [-]
– You can't kill me / Zero the hero and the witches spell / Flying teapot / Dynamite: I am your animal / 6/8 (coit) / Est ce que je suis / Ooby Scooby doomsday or the D-day DJ's got the DDT blues / Radio gnome invisible / Oily way / Outer temple – Inner temple / Where have all the flowers gone / Isle of everywhere / Get it inner / Master builder / Flying teapot. *(cd-iss.Jun90)*

— **PIERRE MOERLEN** retained group name with **HOLDSWORTH, BENOIT MOERLEN, BAUER** (on next lp only), plus **DARYL WAY** – violin (ex-CURVED AIR) / **HANNY ROWE** – bass / **FRANCOISE CHAUSSE** – percussion / **BON LOZANGA** – percussion

Feb 78. (lp)(c) **EXPRESSO II** [ ] [-]
– Heavy tune / Golden dilemma / Sleepy / Soli / Burning / Three blind mice. *(re-iss.1986, cd-iss.1989)*

PIERRE MOERLEN'S GONG

Arista / Arista

Feb 79. (lp)(c) **DOWNWIND** [ ] [ ]
– Aeroplane / Crooscurrents / Downwind / Jin go la ba / What you know / Emotions / Xtasea. *(re-iss.+cdJul91 on 'Great Expectations')*
Oct 79. (lp)(c) **TIME IS THE KEY** [ ] [ ]
– And na greine / Earthrise / Supermarket / Faerie steps / An American in England / The organ grinder / Sugar street / The bender / Arabesque intro / Esnuria two / Time is the key. *(re-iss.+cd.Nov90 on 'Great Expectations')*
Jul 80. (lp)(c) **PIERRE MOERLEN'S GONG (live)** [ ] [-]
– Downwind / Mandrake / Golden dilemma / Soli / Drum solo / Esnurio / Cross-currents. *(re-iss.+cd.Nov90 on 'Great Expectations')*

(feat. **MIKE OLDFIELD – guitar**)

— **BRIAN HOLLOWAY** – guitar repl. HOLDSWORTH (to various groups)

1981. (lp)(c) **LEAVE IT OPEN** – DUTCH
– Leave it open / How much better it has become / I woke up this morning felt like playing the guitar / It's about time / Stok stok stok sto-gak / Adrien.

Arc – not issued

1986. (lp) **BREAKTHROUGH** – – Dutch
– Breakthrough / Spaceship disco / Rock in seven / Six 8 / Poitou / Children's dreams / Portrait / The road out / Romantic punk / Far east.

Line – not issued

1988. (lp) **SECOND WIND** –

– compilations, others –

Apr 89. Demi Monde; (lp)(cd) **THE MYSTERY AND THE HISTORY OF THE PLANET GONG** (some GONG material) –
Nov 95. Nectar; (cd) **THE BEST OF GONG** –
Dec 95. Spalax; (3xcd-box) **THE RADIO GNOME TRILOGY** –
Dec 95. Strange Fruit; (cd) **PRE MODERNIST WIRELESS ON RADIO** –

DAEVID ALLEN & EUTERPE

DAEVID + PEPSI MILAN – guitar, mandolin / **ANA CAMPS** – vocals / **TONI PASCUAL** – synths, keyboards / **TONI ARES** – bass / **TONI FREE FERNANDEZ** – guitar / with GONG guests; **MIKE HOWLETT** – bass / **PIERRE MOERLEN** – percussion

Virgin – not issued

May 76. (lp) **GOOD MORNING!** –
– Children of the new world / Good morning! / Spirit / Song of satisfaction / Have you seen my friend / French garden / Wise man in your heart / She doesn't she. *(cd-iss.Jun90 +=)* – Eutorpe gratitude piece.

DAEVID ALLEN

DAEVID + PEPSI + JUAN BIBLIONI – guitar / **SAM GOPAL** – percussion, synthesizers / **VICTOR PERAINO** – synth, keyboards / **MARIANNE OBERASCHER** – harp

Affinity – not issued

Nov 77. (lp) **NOW IS THE HAPPIEST TIME OF YOUR LIFE** –
– Flamenco zero / Why do we treat ourselves like we do / Tally & Orlando / Meet the cockpit pixie / See you on the moontower / Poet for sale / Crocodile nonsense poem / Only make love if you want to / I am / Deya goddess. *(cd-iss.Nov90 on 'Decal') (re-iss.cd Dec95 on 'Spalax')*

PLANET GONG

DAEVID ALLEN + HERE AND NOW (London musicians); **GILLIE SMYTH** – vocals / **PROF. S.SHARPSTRINGS** – guitar, vocals / **KEITH MISSILE** – bass / **KIF KIF LE BATTEUR** – drums / **GAVIN DA BLITZ** – synthesizers / **SUZA DA BLOOZ + ANNI WOMBAT** – vocals

Affinity – not issued

Feb 78. (7") **OPIUM FOR THE PEOPLE. / POET FOR SALE** –

Charly – not issued

1978. (10") **OPIUM FOR THE PEOPLE. / STONED INNOCENT FRANKENSTEIN** –
Apr 78. (lp) **LIVE FLOATING ANARCHY 77 (live)** –
– Psychological overture / Floating anarchy / Stoned innocent Frankenstein / New age transformation / Try no more sages / Opium for the people / Allez Ali Baba blacksheep have you any bullshit – Mama mya mantram. *(cd-iss.1990 on 'Decal') (re-iss.cd Dec95 on 'Spalax')*

DAEVID ALLEN

with **PEPSI + CHRIS CUTLER** – percussion / **GEORGE BISHOP** – sax, clarinet/ **ANGEL ADUANO** – banjo / **BRIAN DAMAGE** – drums / **RONALD WALTHERN** – pipes

Charly – not issued

May 79. (lp) **N'EXISTE PAS!** –
– Professor Sharpstrings says / The freedom of the city in a suitable box / The say the say / Something tells me / H's a fine air for fliss / But it's really not real / Because barroom philoshers / 333 / No other than the mother is my song / Theme from hashish to ashes / The turkeybirds breakfast / Rajneesh with thanks / No God will not go on or the wrong way to be right / O man you.

NEW YORK GONG

DAEVID ALLEN + MATERIAL; BILL LASWELL – bass / **MICHAEL BEINHORN** – synthesizers / **DON DAVIS** – alto sax / **FRED MAHER** – drums / **CLIFF CULTRERI** – guitar / + **BILL BACON** – drums / **MARK KRAMER** – organ / **GARY WINDO** – tenor sax

Charly – not issued

Jan 80. (7") **MUCH TOO OLD. / I AM A FREUD** –
Apr 80. (lp) **ABOUT TIME** –
– Preface / Much too old / Black September / Materialism / Strong woman / I am a freud / O my photograph / Jungle windo(w) / Hours gone. *(cd-iss.1990 on 'Decal')*
1980. (10"ep) **JUNGLE WINDO(W). / MUCH TOO OLD / MATERIALISM** –

DAEVID ALLEN

HARRY WILLIAMSON – bass, sax repl.DAVIS, WINDO + KRAMER

Charly – not issued

1981. (lp) **DIVIDED ALIEN PLAYBAX '80** –
– When / Well / Bell / Boon / Dab / Gray / Rude / Disguise / Pearls / Bodygas / Froghello / Fastfather / Smile. *(cd-iss.Dec 95 on 'Spalax')*
May 83. (12"ep) **ALIEN IN NEW YORK** –
– Bananareggae / Are you ready / Oo lala / Side windo.

with **MARK KRAMER** – piano / **ELIZABETH MIDDLETON** – piano, vocals / **W.S. BURROUGHS**

Shanghai – not issued

Nov 82. (lp) **THE DEATH OF ROCK AND OTHER ENTRANCES** –
– Death of rock / Poet for sale / Tally's birthday song / You never existed at all / Afraid. *(cd-iss.Jan93 on 'Voiceprint')*

He returned to Australia and teamed up with DAVID TOLLEY

Aug 86. (m-lp) **DON'T STOP** (as "The EX") –
– Do / Eat / Work / Dinosaur / What they say.

— Next as The INVISIBLE OPERA COMPANY OF TIBET

Invisible – not issued

1987. (7") **TRIAL BY HEADLINE. / TRIAL BY HEADLINE** – – Aussie

Demi Monde – not issued

Oct 89. (lp)(cd) **THE OWL AND THE TREE** –
– The owly song / I am my own lover / I am a tree / Lament for the future of the forest / Hands / Unseen alley / La dee Madri. (1 side by MOTHER GONG; Gilli's outfit)

GONG MAISON

DAEVID + GRAHAM CLARKE – violin / **DIDIER MALHERBE / KEITH MISSILE** – bass

Demi Monde – not issued

Dec 89. (cd)(lp) **GONG MAISON** –
– Flying teacup / 1989 / Titti-caca / Tatlas Logorythique / Negotiate / We circle around. (cd+=) – (1 track).

Code 90 – not issued

Mar 93. (cd) **LIVE ON TV 1990 (live)** –
– Planetary introduction / You can't kill me / I've bin stoned before – Long Shanks – Omotha / Radio gnome invisible / Pot-head pixies / Voix lactee / Outer vision / Inner vision / Gorbachev cocktail – I am your animal / Flying teacup / I am you.

— In 1991, their touring line-up of GONG MAISON was **DAEVID ALLEN, DIDIER MALHERBE, GRAHAM CLARKE** – violin, SHYAMAL MAITRA + KEITH THE BASS

Gas – not issued

Oct 92. (cd)(lp) **SHAPESHIFTER**
– Flying teacup / 1989 / Titti-caca / Tatlas Logorythique / Negotiate / We circle around.
Sep 95. (d-cd) **25th BIRTHDAY PARTY – OCTOBER 8-9, 1994, THE FORUM (GONG live)** –
– Thom intro / Floating into a birthday gig / You can't kill me / adio gnome 25 / I am your pussy / ot head pixies / Never glid before / Eat that phonebook / Gnomic address / Flute salad / Oily way.
Sep 95. (m-cd) **HOW TO NUKE THE EIFFEL TOWER (GONG GLOBAL FAMILY)** –
– Away away (South Pacific version) / Away away (twelve selves version) / Nuclear megawaste / Chernobyl rain.

Daevid ALLEN

Demi Monde – not issued

Feb 90. (cd)(lp) **AUSTRALIA AQUARIA / SHE** –
– Gaia / Peaceful warrior / Australia aquaria / She / Isis is calling / Slave queen / Voice of Om / Voice of Om dub. *(re-iss.cd Feb91 on 'Voiceprint' +=)* – Don't stop.

Amp – not issued

1990. (cd) **STROKING THE TAIL OF THE BIRD (w/ HARRY WILLIAMSON & GILLI SMYTH)** –
– (pt.1) / (pt.2).

Voiceprint – not issued

Feb 91. (cd) **THE SEVEN DRONES** –
– C drone (muladhara) / D drone (swadhishthana) / E drone (manipura) / F drone (anahata) / G drone (visuddha) / A drone (njna) / B drone (sahaiara) / Hello me.

Next by DAEVID ALLEN & THE MAGICK BROTHERS; GRAHAM CLARK + MARK ROBSON

1992. (cd) **LIVE AT THE WITCHWOOD 1991 (live)** –
– Wise man in your heart / etc.

— Late in 1992, DAEVID was credited on MARK KRAMER (ex-SHOCKABILLY) 'Shimmy Disc' US cd/lp 'WHO'S AFRAID')

Voiceprint – not issued

1992. (cd) **INVISIBLE OPERA COMPANY OF TIBET** –
1993. (cd) **TWELVE SELVES** –
Feb 94. (m-cd) **VOICEPRINT RADIO SESSION** –

GILLI SMYTH

with **DAEVID ALLEN – producer, guitar, vocals/ DIDIER MALHERBE – sax, flute/ PIP PYLE – drums/ PEPSI MILAN – guitar/ VERA BLUM – violin/ TONY PASCUAL – keyboards** etc

Charly – not issued

Jun 78. (lp) **MOTHER** –
– I am a fool / Back to the womb / Mother / Shakti Yoni / Next time ragtime / Time of the goddess / Taliesin / Keep the children free / Prostitute poem (street version) / O.k. man / This is your world.

MOTHER GONG

GILLI + HARRY WILLIAMSON – guitar/ etc.

Charly – not issued

Nov 79. (lp) **FAIRY TALES** –
– Wassilissa: Three riders / The Baba Yaga's collage / The forbidden room / Time machine / Flying / Wassilissa returns home / Through the machine again / The Baba Yaga / The three tongues: The shoemaker's son / Land of dogs / The frog / An Irish inn in Rome / The arena / Turtles / Birds / The feast / The Pied Piper: Hamelin / Rats amok / An angry crowd / Rat-rock / A thousand guilders / Children / Magic land.

settled line-up; **GILLI, HARRY, DIDIER / + GUY EVANS** – drums (ex-VAN DER GRAAF) / **DAYNE CRANENBURG** – bass / **YAN EMERIC** – slide guitar / **HUGH HOPPER** – bass

Butt – not issued

Jan 81. (lp) **ROBOT WOMAN** –

– Disco at the end of the world / Womans place / Robot woman / Machine song / The sea / Listen . . . / Searching the airwaves / Billi Bunker's blues / Military procession / Customs man / Red alert / Stars / Australia.

— **DAVE SAWYER** – percussion repl.EMERIC + HOPPER

Shanghai | not issued

Sep 82. (lp) **ROBOT WOMAN II** [ ] [-]
– Suggestive station / This train / I wanna be with you / The moving walkway / The upwardly mobile song / Tigers or elephants / Mirror / You can touch the sky / 1999 / Crazy town / Angry song / Looking for / Leotards.

Dec 86. (lp) **ROBOT WOMAN III** [ ] [-]
– It's you and me baby / Faces of woman / Desire / War / Children's song / Lady's song / Woman of streams / I'm sorry / Men cry / Solutions / Magenta part one.

— **GILLI + HARRY + ROBERT CALVERT** – sax (ex-CATAPILLA)

Mothermusic | not issued

1992. (cd) **LIVE 1991** [-] [-] Aussie

GILLI SMYTH

Voiceprint | not issued

1993. (cd) **SHE MADE THE WORLD – MAGENTA** [ ] [-]
1993. (cd) **EVERY WITCHES WAY** [ ] [-]

Demi Monde | not issued

Feb 94. (cd) **WILD CHILD** [ ] [-]

— In France, DIDIER MALHERBE issued 1979 lp 'BLOOM' (Sonopresse) and 1980 single 'DANSEKORLA. / BONG' (Sonopresse). In 1987 'Cryonic' of France released 'FATON BLOOM'. In 1990 'Mantra' issued 'FETISH'. Sep92; 'Tangram' issued 'ZEFF'.

GOODBYE MR. MACKENZIE

Formed: Bathgate, Scotland . . . 1985 by MARTIN METCALFE et all, who soon uprooted to Edinburgh. In 1986, they signed to Eliott Davis's (WET WET WET manager) 'Precious' label, but their debut 'THE RATTLER', had to wait over 2 years and a change of label 'Capitol', to make UK Top 40. This projected long-awaited debut album 'GOOD DEEDS AND DIRTY RAGS', into Top 30 in Spring 1989. • **Style:** Intelligent and creative alternative-rock outfit, fronted by BRUCE SPRINGSTEEN and NEIL DIAMOND sounding METCALFE. • **Songwriters:** All written by METCALFE-KELLY, except AMSTERDAM (Jaques Brel) / GREEN GREEN GRASS OF HOME (Engelbert Humperdink) / HEROES (David Bowie) / CANDY SAYS (Velvet Underground) / FRIDAY'S CHILD (Lee Hazlewood) / THE WAY I WALK (J.Scott). • **Trivia:** MARTIN refused to pay poll tax (community charge) early in 1990.

Recommended: GOOD DEEDS AND DIRTY RAGS (*7).

MARTIN METCALFE – vocals, guitar / **SHIRLEY MANSON** – vocals, keyboards / **JIMMY ANDERSON** – guitar / **RONA SCOBIE** – keyboards, vocals / **FINLAY WILSON** – bass / (DEREK) **KELLY** – drums

Precious | not issued

Sep 86. (7") **THE RATTLER. / CANDLESTICK PARK** [ ] [-]
(12"+=) – The end.

Mack | not issued

Oct 87. (12"ltd) **FACE TO FACE. / SECRETS. / GOOD DEEDS** [ ] [-]

— (above proceeds went to Rape Crisis Charity)

— **BIG JOHN DUNCAN** – guitar (ex-EXPLOITED, ex-BLOOD UNCLES) repl. ANDERSON

Capitol | Capitol

Jul 88. (7") **GOODBYE MR. MACKENZIE. / GREEN TURN RED** [62] [ ]
(12"+=)(cd-s+=) – Knockin' on Joe.
Nov 88. (7") **OPEN YOUR ARMS. / SECRETS** [ ] [ ]
(12"+=)(cd-s+=)(12"pic-d+=) – Amsterdam / Pleasure search.
Feb 89. (7") **THE RATTLER. / HERE COMES DEACON BRODIE** [37] [ ]
(12"+=)(cd-s+=)(12"pic-d+=) – Calton Hill / Drunken sailor.
Apr 89. (lp)(c) **GOOD DEEDS AND DIRTY RAGS** [26] [ ]
– Open your arms / Wake it up / His master's voice / Goodwill city / Candlestick park / Goodbye Mr. Mackenzie / The rattler / Dust / You generous thing you / Good deeds. *(cd+=)* – Amsterdam / Calton Hill / Secrets / Knockin' on Joe.
Jul 89. (7")(c-s) **GOODWILL CITY. / I'M SICK OF YOU** [49] [ ]
(12"+=)(cd-s+=) – What's got into you / Insidious thing.
Oct 89. (lp)(c)(cd) **FISH HEADS AND TAILS** (live & rare) [ ] [ ]
– Amsterdam / Somewhere in China / Face to face / Knockin' on Joe / Sick of you / Green turn red / Pleasure search / Strangle your animal / Mystery train / Here comes Deacon Brodie.
Apr 90. (7")(c-s) **LOVE CHILD. / HEROES** [52] [ ]
(12"+=) – ('A'extended mix).
(cd-s++=) – You generous thing you / Goodwill city.
(12"+=) – The rattler (live).
Jun 90. (7")(c-s) **BLACKER THAN BLACK. / THE GREEN GREEN GRASS OF HOME** [61] [ ]
(12"+=)(12"pic-d+=) – ('A'extended) / Mad cow disease.
(cd-s++=) – H.M.V.

Radioactive-MCA | M.C.A.

Feb 91. (7")(c-s) **NOW WE ARE MARRIED. / FRIDAY'S CHILD** [ ] [ ]
(12"+=) – Candlestick Park II.
(12"++=)(cd-s++=) – Candy says.
Mar 91. (cd)(c)(lp) **HAMMER AND TONGS** [61] [ ]
– Blacker than black / Bold John Barleycorn / Diamonds / The burning / Now we are married / Sick baby / Down to the minimum / She's strong / Love child / Tongue-tied.

— (album was scheduled for release 1990 but dropped by 'Capitol')

May 91. (cd-ep) **THE RATTLER / OPEN YOUR ARMS / DOWN TO THE MINIMUM / FRIDAY'S CHILD / GOODBYE MR MACKENZIE** [-] [ ]

Blokshok | not issued

Apr 93. (12"ep)(cd-ep) **GOODWILL CITY LIVE E.P. (live)** [ ] [-]
– Goodwill city / Mystery train / Open your arms / Working on the shoe-fly.
May 93. (cd)(lp) **LIVE: ON THE DAY OF STORMS (live)** [ ] [-]
– Goodwill city / Blacker than black / Face to face / Diamonds / Pleasure search / Sick baby / Goodbye Mr. Mackenzie / Dust / HMV / Tongue tied / The rattler / What's got into you / Working on the shoe-fly.
Sep 93. (12"ep)(cd-ep) **HARD** [ ] [-]
– *(re-iss.Dec95)*
Nov 93. (cd)(lp) **"FIVE"** [ ] [-]
– Hard / Bam bam / The grip / Jim's killer / Niagara / Touch the bullseye / The day of storms / Yelloueze / Bugdive / Normal boy / Hands of the receiver / Titanic.

— **METCALFE / WILSON / KELLY + DUNCAN** (vox on track 1)

Oct 94. (12"ep)(cd-ep) **THE WAY I WALK / SUPERMAN. / SICK BABY '94) / YOU WILL** [ ] [-]
Jul 95. (cd) **JEZEBEL** [ ] [-]

GOOD MISSIONARIES (see under ⇒ ALTERNATIVE TV)

Miles GOODWYN (see under ⇒ APRIL WINE)

Martin L. GORE (see under ⇒ DEPECHE MODE)

Robert GORL (see under ⇒ D.A.F.)

Graham GOULDMAN (see under ⇒ 10cc)

GRADUATE (see under ⇒ TEARS FOR FEARS)

GRAND FUNK RAILROAD

Formed: Michegan, USA . . . 1964 as TERRY KNIGHT & THE PACK, who quickly scored US Top 50 hit 'I (WHO HAVE NOTHING)'. KNIGHT became manager in 1969, after FARNER and BREWER became GRAND FUNK RAILROAD. They signed to 'Capitol', after appearing at Atlanta Pop Festival in mid'69, and hit immediately with Top 30 lp 'ON TIME', which featured hit 45 'TIME MACHINE'. In Mar'72 after several more hits, they fired KNIGHT and brought in new manager John Eastman (brother-in-law of PAUL McCARTNEY). They continued to be big attraction until they split in 1976. • **Style:** Loud heavy-metal outfit, who broke BEATLES' box-office records in 1971 after selling out New York's Shea Stadium. • **Songwriters:** Group compositions except: THE LOCOMOTION (Little Eva) / WE'VE GOTTA GET OUT OF THIS PLACE (Animals) / GIMME SHELTER (Rolling Stones) / etc. • **Trivia:** TODD RUNDGREN produced their 1973 album 'WE'RE AN AMERICAN BAND'.

Recommended: THE COLLECTION (*6).

TERRY KNIGHT & THE PACK

TERRY KNIGHT (b. RICHARD KNAPP) – vocals / **MARK FARNER** (b. 29 Sep'48) – vocals, bass (guitar from 1969) / **DONALD BREWER** (b. 3 Sep'48) – drums (ex-JAZZ MASTERS)

not iss. | A & M

1965. (7") **YOU LIE. / THE KIDS WILL BE THE SAME** [-] [ ]

Cameo Parkway | Lucky 11

1966. (7") **I'VE BEEN TOLD. / HOW MUCH MORE** [-] [ ]
1966. (7") **YOU'RE A BETTER MAN THAN I. / I GOT LOVE** [-] [ ]
1966. (7") **LOVIN' KIND. / LADY JANE** [-] [ ]
1966. (7") **WHAT'S ON YOUR MIND. / A CHANGE ON THE WAY** [-] [ ]
Nov 66. (lp) **TERRY KNIGHT & THE PACK** [-] [ ]
– Numbers / What's on your mind / Where do you go / You're a better man than I / Lovin' kind / The shut-in / Got love / A change on the way / Lady Jane / Sleep talkin' / I've been told / I (who have nothing).
Jan 67. (7") **I (WHO HAVE NOTHING). / NUMBERS** [ ] [46]
Apr 67. (7") **THIS PRECIOUS TIME. / LOVE, LOVE, LOVE, LOVE, LOVE** [-] [ ]
Jul 67. (7") **ONE MONKEY DON'T STOP NO SHOW. /** [-] [ ]

MARK FARNER & DON BREWER

not issued | Lucky 11

1968. (7") **WE GOTTA HAVE LOVE. / DOES IT MATTER TO YOU GIRL** [-] [ ]

GRAND FUNK RAILROAD

KNIGHT became their manager. Added **MEL SCHACHER** (b. 3 Apr'51) – bass (ex-? AND THE MYSTERIANS)

Capitol | Capitol

Sep 69. (7") **TIME MACHINE. / HIGH ON A HORSE** [-] [48]
Sep 69. (lp) **ON TIME** [ ] [27]
– Are you ready / Anybody's answer / Time machine / High on a horse / T.N.U.C. / Into the sun / Heartbreaker / Call yourself a man / Can't be too long / Ups and down.
Nov 69. (7") **MR. LIMOUSINE DRIVER. / HIGH FALOOTIN' WOMAN** [-] [97]
Jan 70. (lp)(c) **GRAND FUNK** [ ] [11]
– Got this thing on the move / Please don't worry / High falootin' woman / Mr.

Limousine driver / In need / Winter and my soul / Paranoid / Inside looking out.
Mar 70. (7") **HEARTBREAKER. / PLEASE DON'T WORRY** [ ] [72] Jan 70
Jun 70. (7") **NOTHING IS THE SAME. / SIN'S A GOOD MAN'S BROTHER** [-] [ ]
Jul 70. (lp)(c) **CLOSER TO HOME** [ ] [6]
– Sin's a good man's brother / Aimless lady / Nothing is the same / Mean mistreater / Get it together / I don't have to sing the blues / Hooked on love / I'm your captain.
Oct 70. (7") **CLOSER TO HOME. / AIMLESS LADY** [ ] [22] Aug 70
Dec 70. (7") **MEAN MISTREATER. / MARK SAYS ALRIGHT** [-] [47]
Jan 71. (d-lp)(c) **LIVE ALBUM (live)** [ ] [5] Nov 70
– (introduction) / Are you ready / Paranoid / In need / Heartbreaker / Inside looking out / Words of wisdom / Meam mistreater / Mark says alright / T.N.U.C. / Into the sun.
Jan 71. (7") **INSIDE LOOKING OUT. / PARANOID** [40] [ ]
Apr 71. (7") **FEELIN' ALRIGHT. / I WANT FREEDOM** [ ] [54]
Apr 71. (lp)(c) **SURVIVAL** [ ] [6]
– Country road / All you've got is money / Comfort me / Feelin' alright / I want freedom / I can feel him in the morning / Gimme shelter.
Jul 71. (7") **GIMME SHELTER. / I CAN FEEL HIM IN THE MORNING** [-] [61]
Sep 71. (7") **GIMME SHELTER. / COUNTRY ROAD** [ ] [ ] Aug 71
Dec 71. (7") **PEOPLE, LET'S STOP THE WAT. / SAVE THE LAND** [ ] [ ]
Jan 72. (lp)(c) **E PLURIBUS FUNK** [ ] [5] Nov 71
– Footstompin' music / People, let's stop the war / Upsetter / I come tumblin' / Save the land / No lies / Loneliness.
Mar 72. (7") **FOOTSTOMPIN' MUSIC. / I COME TUMBLIN'** [ ] [29] Jan 72
May 72. (7") **UPSETTER. / NO LIES** [ ] [73] Apr 72
Nov 72. (7") **ROCK'N'ROLL SOUL. / FLIGHT OF THE PHOENIX** [ ] [29] Sep 72
Jan 73. (lp)(c) **PHOENIX** [ ] [7] Oct 72
– Flight of the Phoenix / Trying to get away / Someone / She got to move me / Rain keeps falling / I just gotta know / So I won't have to die / Freedom is for children / Gotta find me a better dog / Rock & roll soul.

GRAND FUNK

Aug 73. (7")(7"US-pic-d) **WE'RE AN AMERICAN BAND. / CREEPIN'** [ ] [1] Jul 73
Aug 73. (lp)(c) **WE'RE AN AMERICAN BAND** [ ] [2]
– We're an American band / Stop / Lookin' back / Creepin' / Black lycurice / The railroad / Ain't got nobody / Walk like a man / Loneliest rider.
Nov 73. (7") **WALK LIKE A MAN. / RAILROAD** [ ] [19]
added **CRAIG FROST – keyboards**
May 74. (7") **THE LOCOMOTION. / DESTITUTE & LOSIN'** [ ] [1] Mar 74
Jun 74. (lp)(c) **SHININ' ON** [ ] [5] Mar 74
– Shinin' on / To get back in / The locomotion / Carry me through / Please me / Mr.Pretty boy / Gettin' over you / Little Johnny Hooker.
Jul 74. (7") **SHININ' ON. / MR.PRETTY BOY** [ ] [11]
—— reverted back to trio.
Dec 74. (lp)(c) **ALL THE GIRLS IN THE WORLD BEWARE!!!** [ ] [10]
– Responsibility / Runnin' life / Look at granny run run / Memories / All the girls in the world beware / Wild / Good and evil / Bad time / Some kind of wonderful.
Feb 75. (7") **SOME KIND OF WONDERFUL. / WILD** [ ] [3] Dec74
Mar 75. (7") **BAD TIME. / GOOD AND EVIL** [ ] [4]

GRAND FUNK RAILROAD

Dec 75. (d-lp)(c) **CAUGHT IN THE ACT (live)** [ ] [21] Sep75
– Footstompin' music / Rock'n'roll soul / Closer to home / Some kind of wonderful / Heartbreaker / Shinin' on / The locomotion / Black licorice / The railroad / We're an American band / T.N.U.C. / Inside looking out / Gimme shelter.
Dec 75. (7") **TAKE ME. / GENEVIEVE** [-] [53]
Mar 76. (7") **SALLY. / LOVE IS DYIN'** [-] [69]
Apr 76. (lp)(c) **BORN TO DIE** [ ] [47] Jan 76
– Born to die / Duss / Sally / I fell for your love / Talk to the people / Take me / Genevieve / Love is dying / Politician / Good things.
EMI Inter. M.C.A.
Aug 76. (7") **CAN YOU DO IT. / 1976** [ ] [45]
Aug 76. (lp)(c) **GOOD SINGIN' GOOD PLAYIN'** [ ] [52]
– Just couldn't wait / Can you do it / Pass it around / Don't let 'em take your gun / Miss my baby / Big buns / Out to get you / Crossfire / 1976 / Release your love / Goin' for the pastor.
Jan 77. (7") **PASS IT AROUND. / DON'T LET 'EM TAKE YOUR GUN** [ ] [-]
Jan 77. (7") **JUST COULDN'T WAIT. / OUT TO GET YOU** [-] [ ]
—— Disbanded when the rest formed FLINT.

MARK FARNER BAND

went solo. **FARNER** was joined by **DENNIS BELLINGER** – bass / **ANDY NEWMARK** – drums
Atlantic Atlantic
Nov 77. (7") **YOU AND ME BABY. / SECOND CHANCE TO DANCE** [-] [ ]
Jan 78. (lp)(c) **MARK FARNER** [ ] [ ]
– Dear Miss Lucy / Street fight / Easy breezes / Social disaster / He let me love / You and me baby / Second chance to dance / Lorraine / Lady luck / Ban the man.
Nov 78. (7") **WHEN A MAN LOVES A WOMAN. / IF IT TOOK ALL DAY** [-] [ ]
Jan 79. (lp)(c) **NO FRILLS** [-] [ ]
Feb 79. (7") **JUST ONE LOOK. / CRYSTAL EYES** [-] [ ]

GRAND FUNK

re-formed with **FARNER, BREWER & DENNIS BELLINGER** – bass, vocals.(FROST had joined BOB SEGER.)
Full Moon Full Moon
Nov 81. (7") **Y-O-U. / TESTIFY** [-] [ ]
Jan 82. (lp)(c) **GRAND FUNK LIVES** [ ] [ ] Oct 81
– Good times / Queen bee / Testify / Can't be with you tonight / No reason why / We gotta get out of this place / Y.O.U. / Stuck in the middle / Greed of man / Wait for me.
Feb 82. (7") **STUCK IN THE MIDDLE. / NO REASON WHY** [-] [ ]
Jan 83. (lp)(c) **WHAT'S FUNK?** [ ] [ ]
– Rock'n'roll American style / Nowhere to run / Innocent / Still waitin' / Borderline / El Salvador / It's a man's world / I'm so true / Don't lie to me / Life in Outer Space.
—— Disbanded again after appearing on 'Heavy Metal' soundtrack. BREWER joined BOB SEGER'S SILVER BULLET BAND. FARNER went solo again in 1988 releasing album 'JUST ANOTHER INJUSTICE' for 'Frontline'.

– compilations, others, etc. –

May 72. Capitol; (d-lp)(c) **MARK, DON & MEL 1969-1971** [ ] [17]
Oct 72. Capitol; (lp)(c) **MARK, DON AND TERRY 1966-67** [-] [ ]
Nov 76. Capitol; (lp)(c) **GRAND FUNK HITS** [-] [ ]
Apr 91. Capitol; (cd)(lp) **CAPITOL COLLECTORS** [ ] [ ]
– Time machine / Heartbreaker / Inside looking out / Medley / Closer to home / I'm your captain / Mean mistreater / Feelin' alright / Gimme shelter / Footstompin' music / Rock & roll soul / We're an American band / Walk like a man / The Locomotion / Shinin' on / Some kind of wonderful / Bad time.
Sep 91. Rhino; (cd) **MORE OF THE BEST**
Jun 92. Castle; (cd)(c) **THE COLLECTION** [ ] [-]
– The locomotion / Gimme shelter / Inside looking out / Closer to home / I'm your captain / We're an American band / Into the Sun / Loneliness / Paranoid / Walk like a man / Shinin' on / Creepin' / Sally.

GRANDMASTER FLASH

Formed: The Bronx, New York, USA, 1977, by ex-DJ; JOSEPH SADLER (i.e. GRANDMASTER FLASH). After a number of 45's under various pseudonyms, he formed The FURIOUS FIVE in the early 80's, and signed to 'Sugarhill' scoring alternative US dancefloor hit with 'BIRTHDAY PARTY'. In '82, they had UK Top 10 hit with superb 'THE MESSAGE'. In the mid-80's, FLASH and MEL MELLE were involved in legal wrangles over use of group name, which resulted in JOSEPH being allowed to retain GRANDMASTER FLASH title. • **Style:** Streetwise political rap act with scratching, break-dancing, influenced by Jamaican KOOL HERC. • **Songwriters:** All written by FLASH and MELLE (VAUGHAN), except loads of sampling and covers; WE WILL ROCK YOU (Queen) / WHO'S THAT LADY (Isley Brothers) / etc. • **Trivia:** The groups' KID CREOLE was not same as solo artist.

Recommended: THE MESSAGE (*8) / THE GREATEST HITS (*7).

GRANDMASTER FLASH & THE FURIOUS FIVE

GRANDMASTER FLASH (b.JOSEPH SADDLER, 1 Jan '58) – vocals / **MELLE MEL** (b.MELVIN GLOVER) – rapper / **COWBOY** – rapper / **KID CREOLE** – rapper / added **DUKE BOOTEE** (b.ED FLETCHER) – rapper / and **RAHEIM** – rapper repl. KURTIS BLOW who went solo
not issued Enjoy
1979. (7") **SUPERRAPPIN'. / ('A' instrumental)** [-] [ ]
not issued Brass
1979. (7") **WE RAP MORE MELLOW. ("The YOUNGER GENERATION") / ('A' instrumental)** [-] [ ]
—— added **SCORPIO** – electronics
Sugarhill Sugarhill
Apr 81. (7") **BIRTHDAY PARTY. / ('A' instrumental)** [ ] [ ]
Jul 81. (7") **FREEDOM. / ('A' instrumental)** [-] [ ]
Dec 81. (12") **THE ADVENTURES OF GRANDMASTER FLASH ON THE WHEELS OF STEEL. / THE BIRTHDAY PARTY** [ ] [ ] Oct81
Dec 81. (7") **FLASH TO THE BEAT. / ('A' instrumental)** [-] [ ]
(originally issued 1979 on 'Bozo Meko')
Mar 82 (7")(12") **IT'S NASTY (GENIUS OF LOVE). / BIRTHDAY PARTY** [ ] [ ]
May 82. (7") **THE MESSAGE. / THE MESSAGE (part 2)** [8] [62] Sep 82
Oct 82. (lp)(c) **THE MESSAGE** [77] [53]
– She's fresh / It's nasty (genius of love) / Scorpio / It's a shame / Dreamin' / You are / The message / Adventures of Grandmaster Flash on the wheels of steel.
Dec 82. (7")(12") **SCORPIO. / IT'S A SHAME** [ ] [ ]

MELLE MEL & DUKE BOOTEE

Jan 83. (7") **MESSAGE II (SURVIVAL). / ('A'instrumental)** [74] [ ]

The FURIOUS FIVE

May 83. (7")(12")**NEW YORK, NEW YORK. / ('A' instrumental)** [ ] [ ]

GRANDMASTER FLASH, CHILLI-T & STEVIE G

Eclipse Eclipse
Jun 83. (7") **ROCK THE MESSAGE. / ('A' instrumental)** [ ] [ ]
Feb 84. (7") **KING OF THE STREETS. / ('A' instrumental)** [-] [ ]

GRANDMASTER FLASH & MELLE MEL

Sugarhill Sugarhill
Nov 83. (7")(12") **WHITE LINES (DON'T DON'T DO IT). / ('A' version)** [7] [ ]
(12"+=) – White lines (New York remix) / ('A'original) / ('A'-US mix). *(re-iss.Nov84 as 'CONTINUOUS WHITE LINES') (re-iss.Jun87 on 'Blatant')*
—— GRANDMASTER FLASH, MELLE MEL & THE FURIOUS FIVE split Nov83.

FLASH and MEL split two ways, and went to court to use full group name. MEL adopted

GRANDMASTER MELLE MEL & THE FURIOUS FIVE

taking with him **SCORPIO** and **COWBOY**. He recruited new members **LEWIS GLOVER** (MEL's brother) / **TOMMY GUN CHEV / LES DE LA CRUZ**

Sugarhill Sugarhill

1984. (7")(12") **JESSE. / ('A' instrumental)**

—— (below from the film 'Beat Street' on 'Atlantic')

Jun 84. (7") **BEAT STREET BREAKDOWN. / (Pt.2)** 42 86
(12"+=) – Internationally known.

Jun 84. (lp)(c) **GREATEST MESSAGES** (compilation) 41
– The message / Survival (The message II) / Freedom / Flash to the beat / Jesse / White lines (don't do it) / New York New York / Internationally known / Birthday party / Adventures on the wheels of steel / Scorpio / It's nasty (genius of love).

Sep 84. (7")(12") **WE DON'T WORK FOR FREE. / ('A'instrumental)** 45

Oct 84. (lp)(c) **WORK PARTY** 45
– Rustler's convention / Yesterday / At the party / The truth / White lines (new UK master mix) / We don't work for free / World war III / Can't keep running away / The new adventures of Grandmaster.

Nov 84. (7") **STEP OFF (part 1). / STEP OFF (part 2)** 8
(12"+=) – The message.
(12"+=) – Continuous white lines.

Mar 85. (7") **PUMP ME UP. / ('A' instrumental)** 45
(12"+=)(12"pic-d+=) – ('A'version).

May 85. (lp)(c) **STEPPING OFF** (compilation) -
– Pump me up / Step off / The message / We don't work for free / White lines (don't do it) / Jesse / Survival (the message II) / The megaMelle mix.

Jul 85. (7") **WORLD WAR III. / THE TRUTH**
(12"+=) – Step off / The message (version).

Nov 85. (7") **VICE (from 'Miami Vice' TV). / KING OF THE STREET**

GRANDMASTER FLASH

went solo, taking **RAHEIM** and **KID CREOLE** plus new people **LEVON, BROADWAY** and **LARRY LOVE**

Elektra Elektra

Feb 85. (7") **SIGN OF THE TIMES. / LARRY'S DANCE THEME** 72
(12"+=) – ('A' instrumental).

Feb 85. (lp)(c) **THEY SAID IT COULDN'T BE DONE** 95
– Girls love the way he spins / The joint is jumpin' / Rock the house / Jailbait / Sign of the times / Larry's dance theme / Who's that lady / Alternative groove / Paradise.

May 85. (7") **GIRLS LOVE THE WAY HE SPINS. / WHO'S THAT LADY**
(12"+=) – Larry's dance theme. (US; b-side)

Jul 85. (7") **WHO'S THAT LADY. / ALTERNATIVE GROOVE** -

Apr 86. (lp)(c) **THE SOURCE**
– Street scene / Style (Peter Gunn theme) / Ms. Thang / P.L.U. (Peace, Love and Unity) / Throwin' down / Behind closed doors / Larry's dance theme (part 2) / Lies / Fastest man alive / Freelance.

May 86. (7") **STYLE (PETER GUNN THEME). / ('A' instrumental)**
(12"+=) – ('A' remix).

Jul 86. (7") **LIES. / BEHIND CLOSED DOORS** -

Mar 87. (7") **ALL WRAPPED UP. / KID NAMED FLASH** -

Mar 87. (7")(12") **U KNOW WHAT TIME IT IS?. / BUS DIS (WOO)** -

Mar 87. (lp)(c)(cd) **BA-DOP-BOOM-BANG**
– Ain't we funkin' now / U know what time it is? / Underarms / Kid named Flash / Get yours / Then jeans / We will rock you / All wrapped up / Tear the roof off / Big black caddy / House that rocked / Bus dis / I am somebody / Ain't we funkin' now (reprise).

GRANDMASTER FLASH & THE FURIOUS FIVE

(originals re-formed for 'Elektra')

Feb 88. (7") **GOLD. / BACK IN THE OLD DAYS OF HIP HOP**
(12"+=) – ('A'acappella) / ('A'acappella dub).

Mar 88. (lp)(c) **ON THE STRENGTH**
– Gold / Cold in effect / Yo baby / On the strength / The king / Fly girl / Magic carpet ride / Leave here / This is where you got it from / The boy is dope. *(cd+=)* – Back in the old days of hip-hop.

May 88. (7") **COLD IN EFFECT. / FLY GIRL** -

Jul 88. (7") **ON THE STRENGTH. / MAGIC CARPET RIDE** -

– compilations etc. –

1988. Special Edition; (3"cd-ep) **THE ADVENTURES OF GRANDMASTER FLASH ON THE WHEELS OF STEEL. / THE MESSAGE / IT'S NASTY (GENIUS OF LOVE)**

1988. Special Edition; (12"cd) **WHITE LINES (DON'T DON'T DO IT). / JESSE / THE MESSAGE II**

Nov 89. Old Gold; (12") **THE MESSAGE. / THE ADVENTURES ON THE WHEELS OF STEEL** -

Jul 90. Castle; (7") **WHITE LINES (DON'T DON'T DO IT) (freestyle Ben Legrand mix). / (Part 2)** -

May 92. Sequel; (cd) **THE GREATEST HITS** -
– White lines (don't do it) / Step off / Pump me up / Jesse / Beat Street / Vice / Freedom / Birthday party / Flash to the beat / It's nasty (genius of love) / The message / Scorpio / Survival (Message II) / New York, New York.

Dec 93. W.G.A.F.; (12")(c-s)(cd-s) **WHITE LINES (DON'T DO IT) (D & S 7" Remix) / HEY HEY (D & S 7" Remix)** 59 -

Mar 94. W.G.A.F.; (12")(cd-s) **THE MESSAGE. / ('A'remixes)** -

Aug 95. Old Gold; (cd-s) **WHITE LINES (DON'T DO IT) / PUMP ME UP** -

Sep 95. Old Gold; (cd-s) **THE MESSAGE / SURVIVAL (MESSAGE II)** -

Eddy GRANT

Born: EDMOND MONTAGUE GRANT, 5 Mar'48, Plaisance, Guyana. Moved to London with parents in 1960, and learned trumpet before taking up piano and guitar. In 1965, he formed school group who rehearsed for a year, before emerging as The EQUALS. They had many hits, including 1968 UK No.1 and re-issued 'BABY COME BACK'. In 1972 due to illness, he left The EQUALS although he stayed on as producer. He also produced other reggae-styled groups including The PIONEERS, and founded own Guyana-based label 'Ice', which soon moved base to London, after release of 1977 debut lp 'MESSAGE MAN'. In 1979, Ice was eaten up by 'Ensign', who issued 'LIVING ON THE FRONT LINE', a near return to UK Top 10 for EDDY. He continued to crack the charts at regular intervals until the late 80's. • **Style:** The EQUALS were a bubblegum/R&B group headed by mainman EDDY, who branched out into funky/reggae/dance artist in the late 70's. • **Songwriters:** EDDY penned all. • **Trivia:** American group ROCKER'S REVENGE hit UK Top 5 in 1982 with his 'WALKING ON SUNSHINE'. Two years previous, The CLASH covered The EQUALS' 'POLICE ON MY BACK' on their 'Sandinista!' triple.

Recommended: WALKING ON SUNSHINE (VERY BEST OF EDDY GRANT) (*5)

EQUALS

EDDY GRANT – vocals, guitar, piano / with **PAT LLOYD** (b.17 Mar'48, London) – vocals, bass / **DERV GORDON** (b.twin 29 Jun'48, Jamaica) – vocals / **LINCOLN GORDON** (b.twin 29 Jun'48, Jamaica) – rhythm guitar / **JOHN HALL** (b.25 Oct'47, London) – drums

President Laurie

Sep 66. (7") **I WON'T BE THERE. / FIRE** -
(re-iss.1968 as exploitation)

Around this time EDDY recorded 'CLUB SKA' album under different pseudonyms, thus giving impression of compilation.

Dec 66. (7") **HOLD ME CLOSER. / BABY COME BACK** -

—— (above 'B' side became big hit in Northern Europe on 'Ariola', see on)

Nov 67. (lp) **UNEQUALLED EQUALS** 10 -
– Giddy-up-a-ding-dong / Can't find a girl to love me / I get so excited / Ding-dong / My life ain't easy / Hey baby, it's time you got going / I won't be there / You lied just to save your name / To the church / Fire / I'm a poor man / Can't you hear that melody. *(charted due to budget price and radio promo..)*

President R.C.A.

Feb 68. (7") **I GET SO EXCITED. / SKIES ABOVE** 44

Mar 68. (lp) **EQUALS EXPLOSION** 32
– Giddy-up-a-ding-dong / Another sad and lonely night / I've got to have a little / Granny, granny / Police on my back / Give love a try / You got too many boyfriends / Teardrops / Let her dance / Leaving you is hard to do / You'd better tell her / She reminds me of Spring in the winter.

Apr 68. (7") **BABY COME BACK. / HOLD ME CLOSER** 1 32 Sep 68

(actually a re-issue flipped over) *(re-iss.Jul79 on 'Old Gold')*

Jun 68. (7") **GIVE LOVE A TRY. / ANOTHER SAD AND LONELY HEART**

Aug 68. (7") **LAUREL AND HARDY. / THE GUY WHO MADE HER A STAR** 35

Aug 68. (lp) **SENSATIONAL EQUALS**
– I get so excited / Is it right / Reincarnation / Cinderella / Look what you've done to my daughter / The guy who made her a star / Soul groovin' / Laurel and Hardy / I don't want you to know / The skies above / Butterfly red white and blue / Good time are gone forever.

Nov 68. (7") **SOFTLY SOFTLY. / LONELY RITA** 48

Nov 68. lp) **EQUALS SUPREME**
– Softly, softly / Christine / I'm gonna dance all night / Just you and me / Baby don't cry / Sunday morning / Green light / Lonely Rita / All I wanna do is love you / Love potion / Be my baby tonight / Ooh that kiss.

Mar 69. (7") **MICHAEL AND THE SLIPPER TREE. / HONEY GUM** 24

Jul 69. (7") **VIVA BOBBY JOE. / I CAN'T LET YOU GO** 6
(re-iss.1979 on 'Old Gold')

Aug 69. lp) **EQUALS STRIKE AGAIN**
– Viva Bobby Joe / Ain't got nothing to give you / Let's go to the moon / Bang bang goodbye / My little schoolgirl / Mary Jane / Michael and the slipper tree / A room of doom / Instant love / After the lights go down / No love can be sweeter / Honey gum.

Dec 69. (7") **RUB-A-DUB-DUB. / AFTER THE LIGHTS GO DOWN** 34

Feb 70. lp) **AT THE TOP**
– I can see / But you don't know / Every step I made / Help me Simone / Natural girl / Big man show your strength / Rub a dub dub / Happy birthday girl / Apache creek / Watching the girls / Gigolo Sam / Mandy Dandy / Soul brother Clifford.

Dec 70. (7") **BLACK SKIN BLUE-EYED BOYS. / HAPPY BIRTHDAY GIRL** 9
(re-iss.1979 on 'Old Gold')

—— In 1972 due to illness, EDDY GRANT left The EQUALS, becoming their producer. He was replaced by **JIMMY HAYNES** – vocals, guitar

Mar 72. (7") **STAND UP AND BE COUNTED. / WHAT WOULD YOU DO TO SURVIVE** -

—— **DAVE MARTIN** – vocals, guitar repl. HAYNES

Nov 73. (7") **DIVERSION. / HERE TODAY, GONE TOMORROW** -

Nov 73. (lp)(c) **EQUALS ROCK (AROUND THE CLOCK) VOL 1** -
– Diversion / Put some rock and roll in your soul / Cooga Booga / Shotgun Sally / Friday night / Honey bee / Lucille / Sea cruise / Long tall Sally / Johnny B. Goode / Shout shout (knock yourself out) / Rock around the clock.

—— **NEIL McBAIN** – drums repl. HALL

May 75. (7") **GEORGETOWN GIRL. / WE'VE GOT IT ALL WORKED OUT** -

Jun 76. (7") **KWANA SUNSHINE GIRL. / SOUL MOTHER** -

Mercury not issued

Jul 76. (7") **FUNKY LIKE A TRAIN. / IF YOU DIDN'T KNOW ME** -

Aug 76. (lp)(c) **BORN YA** -

– Born ya / Funky like a train / If you didn't miss me / Ire Harry / Irma la douce / Kaywana sunshine girl / Neighbour neighbour / People like me and you / Soul mother / Stone cold cat / Superman.

Jun 77. (7") **IRMA LA DOUCE. / AR'E HAPPY** | | -

—— The EQUALS still recorded several more singles, but when EDDY GRANT built up own studio and label 'Ice', these were put to the background.

EDDY GRANT

solo on all vocals, instruments.

(note: His eponymous first album was released in Nov75 on 'Torpedo' Guyana. A single NOBODY GOT TIME also issued there).

Ice | not issued

Nov 77. (lp) **MESSAGE MAN** | | -
– Curfew / It's our time / Cockney black / Jamaican child / Get down Soweto / Hello Africa / Race hate / Neighbour, neighbour / Hello Africa (reprise).

Dec 77. (7")(12") **HELLO AFRICA. / NEIGHBOUR, NEIGHBOUR** | | -

May 78. (7") **JAMAICAN CHILD. / ?** | | -

Sep 78. (7") **SAY I LOVE YOU. / (version)** | | -

Ice-Ensign | Epic

Apr 79. (7")(12") **LIVING ON THE FRONT LINE. / THE FRONTLINE SYMPHONY** | 11 |

Jul 79. (lp)(c) **WALKING ON SUNSHINE** | |
– Walking on sunshine / Living on the front line / The frontline symphony / My love, my love / Just imagine I'm loving you / Say I love you / We are. *(re-iss.Feb83)*

Sep 79. (7") **WALKING ON SUNSHINE. / SUNSHINE JAM** | | -

Nov 79. (7") **GRANDMA. / MY LOVE, MY LOVE** | | -

Apr 80. (7")(12") **MY TURN TO LOVE YOU. / USE IT OR LOSE IT** | | -

May 80. (lp)(c) **LOVE IN EXILE** | | -
– My turn to love you / Feel the rhythm / Use it or lose it / Nobody's time / Preachin' genocide / Exiled / Everybody dance.

Nov 80. (7")(12") **DO YOU FEEL MY LOVE. / SYMPHONY FOR MICHAEL OPUS 2** | 8 |

Apr 81. (7")(12") **CAN'T GET ENOUGH OF YOU. / NEIGHBOUR, NEIGHBOUR** | 13 | -

May 81. (lp)(c) **CAN'T GET ENOUGH** | 39 | -
– Do you feel my love / Time to let go / That is why / I love to truck / Can't get enough of you / Give yourself to me / I love you, yes I love you / Kill 'em with kindness / California style. *(re-iss.May83 on 'Ice')*

Jul 81. (7")(12") **I LOVE YOU, YES I LOVE YOU. / IT'S OUR TIME** | 37 | -

Nov 81. (7")(12") **TIME TO LET GO. / CALIFORNIA STYLE** | | -

Dec 81. (d-lp)(d-c) **LIVE AT NOTTING HILL (live)** | | -
– Say I love you / Jamaican child / Neighbour, neighbour / Cockney black / Curfew / My turn to love you / Hello Africa (rap) / Hello Africa / Walking on sunshine / Living on the frontline. *(re-iss.Dec84)*

EDDY moved to Barbados, Caribbean.

Ice (again) | Portrait

Sep 82. (7")(12") **I DON'T WANNA DANCE. / ('A'version)** | 1 | 53 Aug 83

Nov 82. (lp)(c) **KILLER ON THE RAMPAGE** | 7 | 10 Apr 83
– Electric avenue / I don't wanna dance / It's all in you / War party / Too young to fall / Another revoutionary / Funky rock'n'roll / Drop baby drop / Killer on the rampage.

Jan 83. (7")(12") **ELECTRIC AVENUE. / WALKING ON SUNSHINE** | 2 | 2 Apr 83

Apr 83. (7")(12") **WAR PARTY (remix). / SAY I LOVE YOU** | 42 |

Nov 83. (7")(12") **TILL I CAN'T TAKE LOVE NO MORE. / CALIFORNIA STYLE** | 42 |

May 84. (7")(12") **ROMANCING THE STONE. / MY TURN TO LOVE YOU** | 52 | 26

—— (above 'A' was to have been used for film of same name, but never used)

Jul 84. (lp)(c) **GOING FOR BROKE** | | 64
– Romancing the stone / Boys in the street / Come on let me love you / Till I can't take love no more / Political bassa bassa / Telepathy / Only Heaven knows / Ire Harry / Rock you good / Blue wave.

Oct 84. (7")(12") **BOYS IN THE STREET. / TIME TO LET GO** | |

Feb 85. (7")(12") **BABY COME BACK. / POLITICAL BASSA BASSA** | |

Jul 86. (7")(12") **DANCE PARTY. / ROCK YOU GOOD** | | -

Aug 86. (lp)(c)(cd) **BORN TUFF** | |
– Dance party / Next time around / Come along to my place / Melody of the night / Born tuff / Blood money / Village life / Funny little groove / In L.A. / She's standing at the corner / Water.

Ice – Parlophone | Capitol

Feb 88. (7") **GIMME HOPE JO'ANNA. / SAY HELLO TO FIDEL** | 7 |
(12"+=) – Living on the Front Line (live).

Apr 88. (lp)(c)(cd) **FILE UNDER ROCK** | |
– Harmless piece of fun / Don't talk to strangers / Hostile country / Win or lose / Gimme hope Jo'Anna / Another riot / Say hello to Fidel / Chuck (is the king) / Long as I'm wanted by you / Put a hold on it. *(re-iss.Aug89 on 'Fame')*

Blue Wave | Enigma

Apr 88. (7") **HARMLESS PIECE OF FUN. / BLOOD MONEY** | | -
(12"+=) – Born tuff / Who's leaving who?.
(cd-s+=) – Electric Avenue.

Jun 88. (7") **PUT A HOLD ON IT. / ('A'New York mix)** | |
(12"+=)(cd-s+=) – ('A'New York club mix) / Gimme hope Jo'Anna (Spanish).

May 89. (7") **WALKING ON SUNSHINE. / CALIFORNIA STYLE** | 63 | -
(12"+=)(cd-s+=) – ('A'original mix).

Jun 89. (lp)(c)(cd) **WALKING ON SUNSHINE (THE VERY BEST OF EDDY GRANT)** (compilation) | 20 |
– I don't wanna dance / Gimme hope Jo'anna / Electric Avenue / Living on the frontline / Do you feel my love / Till I can't take love no more / Walking on sunshine / Baby come back / Romancing the stone / Can't get enough of you / Harmless piece of fun / Put a hold on it. *(re-iss.c+cd.Sep91 on 'E.M.I.')*

Aug 89. (7") **BABY COME BACK. / DANCE PARTY** | | -
(12"+=)(cd-s+=) – ('A'remix).

Nov 90. (7") **RESTLESS WORLD. / SWEAT ON THE ROAD** | |
(12"+=)(cd-s+=) – ('A'version) / Wild cat.

Ice | Enigma

Jan 92. (7") **PACO AND RAMONE. / EULOGY FOR A LIVING MAN** | |
(cd-s+=)/ /(12") – (2 other mixes)./ / (3 mixes only).

Mar 92. (cd)(c)(lp) **PAINTINGS OF THE SOUL** | |
– Paco & Ramone / Nerumah / Welcome to La Tigre / Kidada / The youth tom tom / You just found my weakness / Leadbelly / Eulogy for a living man / I walk alone tonight / Barefoot soldier / Through the night / Talk about love.

Apr 92. (12") **WELCOME TO LA TIGRE. / KIDADA** | |
(cd-s) – ('A'side) / Electric avenue / I don't wanna dance / Hello Africa.

– compilations, others –

Mar 83. Mercury; (7") **DO YOU FEEL MY LOVE. / LIVING ON THE FRONTLINE** | 47 |

May 83. Ice-RCA; (c-ep) **CASSETTE EP** | | -
– Living on the front line / Do you feel my love / I don't wanna dance / Walking on sunshine.

Oct 84. K-Tel; (lp)(c) **ALL THE HITS: THE KILLER AT HIS BEST** | 23 | -

– compilations, others (EQUALS) – selective

1973. Joy; (lp) **BEST OF THE EQUALS** | | -

Jul 82. Old Gold; (7") **VIVA BOBBY JOE. / BLACK SKINNED BLUE-EYED BOYS** | | -

Sep 83. Scoop; (7"ep)(c-ep) **6 TRACK HITS** | | -

Nov 84. Astan; (lp)(c) **20 GREATEST HITS** | | -

May 88. Premier; (lp)(c)(cd) **GREATEST HITS** | | -

Aug 93. See For Miles; (cd) **THE VERY BEST OF THE EQUALS** | | -

Jul 94. Success; (cd)(c) **BABY COME BACK** | | -

Nov 94. Ice; (d-cd) **FIRST AMONG EQUALS** – THE GREATEST HITS | | -

GRANT LEE BUFFALO

Formed: North Hollywood, California, USA . . . 1992 by namesake GRANT LEE PHILLIPS. Released their debut 'FUZZY' the next year to deserved critical acclaim, although it was 1994's that broke them into commercial success. • **Style:** Hard-edged country rock, with a similiarity to The WATERBOYS. • **Songwriters:** PHILLIPS penned except covers BURNING LOVE (hit; Elvis Presley). • **Trivia:** Their debut was a favourite of MICHAEL STIPE (R.E.M.).

Recommended: FUZZY (*8) / MIGHTY JOE MOON (*7)

GRANT LEE PHILLIPS – vocals, guitars / **PAUL KIMBLE** – bass, piano, vocals, producer / **JOEY PETERS** – drums, percussion

Slash-London | Slash

Jun 93. (cd)(c)(lp) **FUZZY** | 74 |
– The shining hour / Jupiter and teardrop / Fuzzy / Wish you well / The hook / Soft wolf tread / Stars n' stripes / Dixie drug store / America snoring / Grace / You just have to be crazy.

Aug 93. (7")(c-s)(cd-s) **AMERICA SNORING. / WISH YOU WELL** | |
(12"+=)(cd-s+=) – The hook / Burning love.

Sep 93. (7")(c-s) **FUZZY. / STARS & STRIPES** | |
(12"+=)(cd-s+=) – Dixie drugstore (ju ju mix) / I will take him.

Nov 93. (12"ep)(cd-ep) **BUFFALONDON EP** | |
– Jupiter and teardrop / Wish you well / Soft wolf tread / The shining hour.

Sep 94. (cd)(c)(lp) **MIGHTY JOE MOON** | 24 |
– Lone star song / Mockingbirds / It's the life / Sing along / Mighty Joe Moon / Demon called Deception / Lady Godiva and me / Drag / Last days of Tecumseh / Happiness / Honey don't think / Side by side / Rock of ages.

Oct 94. (cd-ep) **MOCKINGBIRDS / ORPHEUS. / GOODNIGHT JOHN DEE** | |
(12"ep+=) – (first 3 tracks) / Let go of my hand.
(cd-ep) – (first track) / Let go of my hand / We're coming down.

GRATEFUL DEAD

Formed: San Francisco, California, USA . . . 1965 by JERRY GARCIA, who had spent 9 months of 1959 in the army, before finding ROBERT HUNTER and forming The THUNDER MOUNTAIN TUB THUMPERS. JERRY went onto make demos in 1963 as duo JERRY & SARAH GARCIA. As The WARLOCKS in 1965 (GARCIA, WEIR, PIGPEN, LESH and KREUTZMANN), became friends with 'One Flew Over The Cuckoo's Nest' author KEN KESEY, who introduced them to L.S.D. in his commune. By the end of '65, they had become GRATEFUL DEAD and toured California alongside JEFFERSON AIRPLANE. In 1966, they issued one-off 45 'DON'T EASE ME IN' for 'Fantasy' off-shoot label 'Scorpio', which led to 'Warners' giving them break early '67. Their eponymous debut soon broke the US Top 75, although they had to wait another 3 years for breakthrough into US Top 30 with 'WORKINGMAN'S DEAD'. In 1992, they were still survivors loved by most Americans and some other countries, even Britain. Sadly, JERRY GARCIA died on the 9th August 1995 of a heart attack after his arteries clogged up. • **Style:** Psychedelic hippie band who did concerts averaging 3 hours, and who verged on experimental harmonising country-tinged rock. • **Songwriters:** Most by HUNTER-GARCIA or WEIR, LESH and some by others, including JOHN BARLOW. Covered; GOOD MORNING LITTLE SCHOOLGIRL (Don & Bob) / NEW MINGLEWOOD BLUES + SAMSON AND DELILAH (trad.) / JOHNNY B.GOODE (Chuck Berry) / NOT FADE AWAY (Buddy Holly) / ME AND BOBBY McGEE (Kris Kristofferson) / BIG BOSS MAN

DARK STAR
JERRY GARCIA

(Bo Diddley) / DANCING IN THE STREET (Martha & The Vandellas) / STAGGER LEE (Lloyd Price) / LITTLE RED ROOSTER (Willie Dixon) / DEAR MR.FANTASY (Traffic) / WALKIN' BLUES (Robert Johnson) / NEXT TIME YOU SEE ME (Junior Parker) / etc. • **Trivia:** An edited 'DARK STAR', was used as theme in the US 70's series of 'Twilight Zone'.

Recommended: LIVE DEAD (*6) / WORKINGMAN'S DEAD (*6) WHAT A LONG STRANGE TRIP IT'S BEEN (*8).

JERRY GARCIA (b. JEROME JOHN GARCIA, 1 Aug'42) – vocals, lead guitar / **BOB WEIR** (b. ROBERT HALL, 6 Oct'47) – rhythm guitar / **RON 'PIGPEN' McKERNAN** (b. 8 Sep'45) – keyboards, vocals, mouth harp / **PHIL LESH** (b. PHILIP CHAPMAN, 15 Mar'40, Berkeley, Calif.,USA) – bass / **BILL KREUTZMANN** (b. 7 Apr'46, Palo Alto, Calif.) – drums (DAN MORGAN left before recording)

not issued Scorpio

Jun 66. (7") **DON'T EASE ME IN. / STEALIN'** [-] [ ]

Warners Warners

Feb 67. (7") **THE GOLDEN ROAD (TO UNLIMITED DEVOTION). / CREAM PUFF WAR** [-] [ ]

Dec 67. (lp) **THE GRATEFUL DEAD** [ ] [73] Feb 67
– The golden road (to unlimited devotion) / Cold rain and snow / Good morning little schoolgirl / Beat it on down / Sitting on top of the world / Cream puff war / Morning dew / New, new Minglewood blues / Viola Lee blues. *(re-iss.Mar87 on 'Edsel') (cd-iss.Jul88 on 'Atlantic') (cd-iss.Feb93) (re-iss.cd Oct95)*

— added **TOM CONSTANTEN** – keyboards / **MICKEY HART** – percussion and returning lyricist **ROBERT HUNTER**

Oct 68. (7") **BORN CROSS-EYED. / DARK STAR** [ ] [ ]

Nov 68. (lp) **ANTHEM OF THE SUN** [ ] [87] Aug 68
– That's it for other one:- Cryptical envelopment – Quadlibet for tender feet – The faster we go, the rounder we get – We leave the castle / New potato caboose / Born cross-eyed / Alligator / Caution (do not stop on the tracks). *(re-iss.Jul71) (c+cd-iss.1989 on 'WEA')*

Oct 69. (lp) **AOXOMOXOA** [ ] [73] Jun 69
– St. Stephen / Dupree's diamond blues / Rosemary / Doin' the rag / Mountains of the Moon / China cat sunflower / What's become of the baby / Cosmic Charlie. *(re-iss.Jul71 & Jan77) (c+cd-iss.1989 on 'WEA')*

Oct 69. (7") **DUPREE'S DIAMOND BLUES. / COSMIC CHARLIE** [-] [ ]

Feb 70. (d-lp) **LIVE / DEAD (live in the studio)** [ ] [64] Dec 69
– Dark star / Death don't have no mercy / Feedback / And we bid you goodnight / St. Stephen / The eleven / Turn on your love light. *(re-iss.Jul71)*

— **DAVID NELSON** – accoustic guitar repl. CONSTANTEN / added guest **JOHN DAWSON** – guitar, vocals (on some)

— above pairing also formed off-shoot band The NEW RIDERS OF THE PURPLE SAGE, who initially toured as support to DEAD, with GARCIA in their ranks.

Sep 70. (lp) **WORKINGMAN'S DEAD** [ ] [27] Jun 70
– Uncle John's band / High time / Dire wolf / New speedway boogie / Cumberland blues / Black Peter / Easy wind / Casey Jones. *(re-iss.Jul71) (re-iss.+cd.1989)*

Aug 70. (7") **UNCLE JOHN'S BAND. / NEW SPEEDWAY BOOGIE** [ ] [69]

— added guest **DAVID TORBERT** – bass (1)

Dec 70. (lp)(c) **AMERICAN BEAUTY** [ ] [30]
– Box of rain / Friend of the Devil / Sugar magnolia / Operator / Candyman / Ripple / Brokedown palace / Till the morning comes / Attics of my life / Truckin'. *(re-iss.Jul71 & Jan77) (c+cd-iss.1989 on 'WEA')*

Jan 71. (7") **TRUCKIN'. / RIPPLE** [-] [64]

— Now **GARCIA, WEIR, LESH, KREUTZMANN** and **'PIGPEN'** with new members **MERL SAUNDERS** – keyboards (repl. PIGPEN for a while when he was ill) all guests had departed, incl. HART and NELSON.

Oct 71. (d-lp) **GRATEFUL DEAD** (SKULL-FUCK & ROSES) (live) [ ] [25]
– Bertha / Mama tried / Big railroad blues / Playing in the band / The other one / Me & my uncle / Big boss man / Me & Bobby McGhee / Johnny B. Goode / Wharf rat / Not fade away / Goin' down road feeling bad. *(cd-iss.1988)*

Jan 72. (7") **JOHNNY B. GOODE. / SO FINE (by 'Elvin Bishop')** [-] [ ]

Apr 72. (7") **ONE MORE SATURDAY NIGHT. (by "GRATEFUL DEAD with BOBBY ACE" (aka BOB WEIR) / CASSIDY** (U.S.) / **BERTHA** (U.K.) [ ] [ ]

— added on tour **KEITH GODCHAUX** (b.14 Jul'48) – keyboards (ex-DAVE MASON band) and **DONNA GODCHAUX** – vocals (They both repl. SAUNDERS)

Dec 72. (t-lp) **EUROPE '72 (live)** [ ] [24] Nov 72
– Cumberland blues / He's gone / One more Saturday night / Jack Straw / You win again / China cat sunflower / I know you rider / Brown-eyed woman / Hurts me too / Ramble on Rose / Sugar magnolia / Mr. Charlie / Tennessee Jed / Truckin' / (epilog) / (prelude) / (Walk me out in the) Morning dew. *(cd-iss.Oct95)*

Dec 72. (7") **SUGAR MAGNOLIA (live). / MR. CHARLIE (live)** [-] [91]

— Now just basic 4 of **GARCIA, WEIR, LESH, KREUTZMANN** and both **GODCHAUX'S.** ('PIGPEN' sadly died 8 May'73 after a long and threatening bout of illness) note that ROBERT HUNTER was still writing their lyrics, next 2 albums also included ten or more session people.

Warners Grateful D

Jul 73. (lp)(c) **WAKE OF THE FLOOD** [ ] [18] Oct 73
– Mississippi half-step uptown toodeloo / Let me sing your blues away / Row Jimmy / Stella blue / Here comes sunshine / Eyes of the world / Weather Report suite (part 1; Prelude – part 2; Let it grow). *(re-iss.Apr89) (cd-iss.Feb90)*

Nov 73. (7") **LET ME SING YOUR BLUES AWAY. / HERE COMES SUNSHINE** [ ] [ ]

Jan 74. (7") **EYES OF THE WORLD. / WEATHER REPORT SUITE (part 1; PRELUDE)** [-] [ ]

Jul 74. (lp)(c) **FROM THE MARS HOTEL** [47] [16]
– Scarlet begonias / Ship of fools / Pride of Cucamonga / Loose Lucy / U.S. blues / Unbroken chain / China doll / Money money. *(re-iss.+cd.Mar89)*

Aug 74. (7") **U.S. BLUES. / LOOSE LUCY** [-] [ ]

— added the returning **MICKEY HART** – percussion

United Art Grateful D

Oct 75. (lp)(c) **BLUES FOR ALLAH** [45] [12] Sep 75
– Help on the way / Slipknot / Franklin's tower / King Solomon's marbles / Stronger than dirt or milkin' the turkey / The music never stopped / Crazy fingers / Sage & spirit / Blues for Allah / Sand castles & glass camels / Unusual occurances in the desert. *(re-iss.+cd.Mar89) (cd-iss.Feb90)*

Oct 75. (7") **THE MUSIC NEVER STOPPED. / HELP IS ON THE WAY** [-] [81]

Jun 76. (d-lp)(c) **STEAL YOUR FACE (live)** [42] [56]
– The promised land / Cold rain and snow / Around and around / Stella blue / Mississippi half-step uptown toodeloo / Ship of fools / Beat it down the line / Big river / Black-throated wind / U.S. blues / El Paso / Sugaree / It must have been the roses / Casey Jones. *(re-iss.+cd.Mar89) (cd-iss.Feb90)*

Arista Arista

Aug 77. (lp)(c) **TERRAPIN STATION** [ ] [28]
– Estimated prophet / Samson and Delilah / Passenger / Dancing in the street / Sunrise / Terrapin station. *(re-iss.Jan87) (cd-iss.1988 on 'Ariola')*

Oct 77. (12") **DANCING IN THE STREET. / TERRAPIN STATION** [ ] [ ]

Feb 78. (7") **PASSENGER. / TERRAPIN STATION** [-] [ ]

Dec 78. (lp)(c) **SHAKEDOWN STREET** [ ] [41]
– Good lovin' / France / Shakedown street / Serangetti / Fire on the mountain / I need a miracle / From the heart of me / Stagger Lee / New, new Minglewood blues / If I had the world to give. *(cd-iss.Jun91)*

Dec 78. (7") **GOOD LOVIN'. / STAGGER LEE** [ ] [ ]

Mar 79. (7") **SHAKEDOWN STREET. / FRANCE** [-] [ ]

— **BRENT MYDLAND** (b. 1953) – keyboards repl. both GODCHAUX'S (KEITH was killed in car crash 23 Jul'80)

May 80. (lp)(c) **GO TO HEAVEN** [ ] [23]
– Far from home / Althea / Feel like a stranger / Alabama getaway / Don't ease me in / Easy to love you / Lost sailor / Saint of circumstance.

Jun 80. (7") **ALABAMA GETAWAY. / FAR FROM ME** [-] [68]

Jan 81. (7") **DON'T EASE ME IN. / FAR FROM ME** [-] [ ]

Apr 81. (d-lp)(d-c) **RECKONING (live)** (all line-ups) [ ] [43]
– Dire wolf / The race is on / Oh babe it ain't no lie / It must have been the roses / Dark hollow / China doll / Been all around the world / Monkey and the engineer / Jack-a-roe / Deep Elam blues / Cassidy / To lay me down / Rosalie McFall / On the road again / Bird song / Ripple.

Sep 81. (d-lp)(d-c) **DEAD SET (live)** [ ] [29]
– Samson and Delilah / Friend of the Devil / New, new Minglewood blues / Deal / Candyman / Little red rooster / Loser / Passenger / Feel like a stranger / Franklin's tower / Fire on the mountain / Rhythm devils / Greatest story ever told / Brokedown palace.

Sep 87. (7")(12")(7"pic-d) **TOUCH OF GREY. / MY BROTHER ESAU** [ ] [9] Jul 87

Oct 87. (lp)(c)(cd) **IN THE DARK** [57] [6] Jul 87
– Touch of grey / Hell in a bucket / When push comes to shove / West L.A. fadeaway / Tons of steel / Throwing stones / Black muddy river.

Nov 87. (7") **THROWING STONES. / ('A'version)** [-] [ ]

— Late '87, they recorded live album 'DYLAN AND THE DEAD' with BOB DYLAN, which was released early 1989, and hit US No.37.

Nov 89. (lp)(c)(cd) **BUILT TO LAST** [ ] [27]
– Foolish heart / Just a little light / Built to last / Blow away / Standing on the Moon / Victim or the crime / We can run / Picasso moon / I will take you home.

Nov 89. (7") **FOOLISH HEART. / WE CAN RUN** [-] [ ]

Oct 90. (d-cd)(d-c)(t-lp) **WITHOUT A NET (live)** [ ] [43]
– Feel like a stranger / Mississippi half-step uptown toodeloo / Walkin' blues / Althea / Cassidy / Let it grow / China cat sunflower – I know you rider / Looks like rain / Eyes of the world / Victim or the crime / Help on the way – Slipknot! – Franklin's tower / Bird song / One more Saturday night / Dear Mr. Fantasy.

— BRETT MYDLAND died 26 Jul'90 of a drug overdose. Replaced by **VINCE WELNICK** – keyboards (ex-TUBES, ex-TODD RUNDGREN)

– compilations etc. –

Below releases on 'Polydor' issued on 'Sunflower' US.

Nov 70. Polydor; (lp) **VINTAGE DEAD (live '66)** [ ] [ ] Oct 71

Jul 71. Polydor; (lp) **HISTORIC DEAD (rare '66)** [ ] [ ] Jun 71

Sep 73. Warners/ US= Grateful Dead; (lp) **HISTORY OF THE DEAD - BEAR'S CHOICE (live rarities)** [ ] [60] Jul 73

Mar 74. Warners/ US= Grateful Dead; (lp)(c) **SKELETONS FROM THE CLOSET** [ ] [75]
(re-iss.+cd.Oct86 on 'Thunderbolt')

Feb 77. United Artists/ US= Grateful Dead; (d-lp)(d-c) **WAKE OF THE FLOOD / FROM MARS HOTEL** [ ] [ ]

Feb 78. Warners/ US= Grateful Dead; (d-lp)(d-c) **WHAT A LONG STRANGE TRIP IT'S BEEN: THE BEST OF GRATEFUL DEAD** [ ] [ ] Nov 77
– New, new Minglewood blues / Cosmic Charlie / Truckin' / Black Peter / Born cross-eyed / Ripple / Doin' that rag / Dark star / High time / New speedway boogie / St. Stephen / Jack Straw / Me & my uncle / Tennessee Jed / Cumberland blues / Playing in the band / Brown-eyed woman / Ramble on Rose.

— All below on 'Grateful Dead' records, unless otherwise mentioned.

Jun 91. (d-cd)(d-c)(t-lp) **ONE FROM THE VAULT** (live 13 Aug'75, Great American Music Hall, San Francisco) [ ] [ ] May 91
– (introduction) / Help on the way / Franklin's tower / Music never stopped / It must have been the roses / Eyes of the world – drums / King Solomon's marbles / Around and around / Sugaree / Big river / Crazy fingers – drums / The other one / Sage and spirit / Goin' down the road feeling bad / U.S. blues / Blues for Allah.

Jan 92. (cd) **INFRARED ROSES (live)** [ ] [ ]
– Crowd sculpture / Parallelogram / Little Nemo in Lightland / Riverside rhapsody / Post-modern highrise table top stomp / Infrared roses / Silver apples of the Moon / Speaking in swords / Magnesium night light / Sparrow hawk row / River of nine sorrows / Apollo at the Ritz.

Aug 92. (d-cd) **TWO FROM THE VAULT** (live 23/24 Aug'68, Shrine Auditorium, L.A.) [ ] [ ] May 92
– Good morning little schoolgirl / Dark star / St. Stephen / The eleven / Death don't have no mercy / The other one / New potato caboose / Turn on your lovelight / Morning dew.

Dec 93. Grateful Dead; (d-cd) **DICK'S PICK** [ ] [ ]
– Here comes sunshine / Big river / Mississippi half-step uptown toodeloo / Weather report suite (Prelude – part 1, Let it grow – part 2) / Big railroad blues / Playing in the band / He's gone / Truckin' / Nobody's fault but mine / Jam / The other one / Jam / Stella blue / Around and around.

Jan 94. Dare International; (cd)(c) **RISEN FROM THE VAULTS**
Jun 95. Grateful Dead; (cd) **DICK'S PICKS VOLUME 2**
– ark star / Jam / Sugar magnolia / St. Stephen / Not fade away / Going down the road feeling bad / Not fade away.
Oct 95. Grateful Dead; (d-cd)(d-c) **HUNDRED YEAR HALL** (live 26th April 1972, Jahrhundert Halle, Frankfurt) 26
– Bertha / Me & my uncle / The next time you see me / China cat sunflower / I know you rider / Jack Straw / Big railroad blues / Playing in the band / Turn on your love light / Going down the road feeling bad / One more Saturday night / Truckin' / Cryptical envelopment / Comes a time / Sugar magnolia.

JERRY GARCIA

solo used session men from the DEAD plus others

C.B.S. Douglas
Jul 71. (lp) **HOOTEROLL (by "JERRY GARCIA & HOWARD WALES")**
– South side strut / A trip to what next / Up from the desert / DC-502 / One a.m. approach / Uncle Martin's / Da bird song. *(cd-iss.Oct87 & Jun92 on 'Rykodisc')*
(below also by duo above)
Jan 72. (7") **SOUTH SIDE STRUT. / UNCLE MARTIN'S** -
Warners Warners
Jan 72. (lp)(c) **GARCIA** (aka 'THE WHEEL') 35
– Deal / Bird song / Sugaree / Loser / Late for supper / Spiderdawg / Eep hour / To lay me down / An odd little place / The wheel. *(re-iss.+c+cd.Feb89 on 'Grateful Dead')*
1973. (7") **SUGAREE. / EEP HOUR** -
1973. (7") **THE WHEEL. / DEAL** -
not issued Fantasy
1973. (lp) **LIVE AT THE KEYSTONE (live)** -
Round Round
Jun 74. (lp) **GARCIA (II)** 49
– Let it rock / When the hunter gets captured by the game / That's what love will make us do / Russian lullabye / Turn on the bright lights / He ain't give you none / What goes around / Let's spend the night together / Mississippi moon / Midnight town. *(re-iss.+c+cd.Apr89 as 'COMPLIMENTS OF . . . ')*
Jul 74. (7") **LET IT ROCK. / MIDNIGHT TOWN** -
— OLD & IN THE WAY:- **GARCIA, DAVID GRISMAN, PETER ROWAN, JOHN KAHN, VASSAR CLEMENTS**
Mar 75. (lp) **OLD AND IN THE WAY** -
– Pig in a pen / Midnight moonlight / Old and in the way / Knockin' on your door / The hobo song / Panama red / Wild horses / Kissimmee kid / White dove / Land of the Navajo. *(re-iss. Feb 85 on 'Sugarhill')*
United Art Round
Feb 76. (lp) **REFLECTIONS** 42
– Might as well / Mission in the rain / They love each other / I'll take a melody / It must have been the roses / Tore up over you / Catfish John / Comes a time. *(re-iss.+cd.Feb89 on 'Grateful Dead')*
Arista Arista
Apr 78. (lp)(c) **CAT UNDER THE STARS (as "JERRY GARCIA BAND")**
– Rubin and Cherise / Love in the afternoon / Palm Sunday / Cats under the stars / Rhapsody in red / Rain / Down home / Gomorrah.
Nov 82. (lp)(c) **RUN FOR THE ROSES**
– Run for the roses / I saw her standing there / Without love / Midnight getaway / Leave the little girl alone / Valerie / Knockin' on Heaven's door.
Grateful D Grateful D
Mar 89. (lp)(c)(cd) **ALMOST ACOUSTIC ("JERRY GARCIA ACOUSTIC BAND")**
– Swing low, sweet chariot / Deep Elam blues / Blue yodel £9 (standing on the corner) / Spike driver blues / I've been all around this world / I'm here to get my baby out of jail / I'm troubled / Oh, the wind and the rain / The girl at the Crossroads bar / Oh babe it ain't no lie / Casey Jones / Diamond Joe / Gone home / Ripple.
— with **JOHN KAHN** – bass / **DAVID KEMPER** – drums / **MARVIN SEALS** – keyboards / and backing vocalists **JACKIE LA BRANCH** and **GLORIA JONES**
Sep 91. (cd)(c)(lp) **JERRY GARCIA BAND (live)** 97
– The way you do the things you do / Waiting for a miracle / Simple twist of fate / Get out of my life / My sister and brothers / I shall be released / Dear Prudence / Deal / Stop that train / Senor (tales of Yankee power) / Evangeline / The night they drove old Dixie down / Don't let go / That lucky old Sun / Tangled up in blue.

BOB WEIR

solo, with DEAD session men

Warners Warners
Jun 72. (lp) **ACE**
– The greatest story ever told / Black-throated wind / Walk in the sunshine / Playing in the band / Looks like rain / Mexicali blues / One more Saturday night / Cassidy. *(re-iss.+c+cd.Apr89 on 'Grateful Dead')*

KINGFISH

with **BOB WEIR** and **DAVE TORBERT** plus DEAD and other sessioners

United Art Grateful Dead
Apr 76. (lp) **KINGFISH** 50 Mar 76
– Lazy lightnin' / Supplication / Wild northland / Asia minor / Home to Dixie / Jump for joy / Goodbye yer honor / Big iron / This time / Hypnotize / Bye and bye. *(re-iss.+cd.Nov89 on 'Grateful Dead') (cd-iss.Jun93)*
United Art Jet
Jun 77. (lp) **LIVE 'N' KICKIN'** (live, BOB appears rarely) May 77
– Goodbye yer honor / Juke / Mule skinner blues / I hear you knockin' / Hypnotize / Jump for joy / Overnight bag / Jump back / Shake and fingerpop / Around and around. *(re-iss.Feb79 on 'Jet')*
Nov 77. (7") **GOODBYE YER HONOR. / JUMP FOR JOY / I HEAR YOU KNOCKIN'**
— BOB left KINGFISH before they released another album 'TRIDENT' in '78 on 'Jet' US.

BOB WEIR

continued solo career as well as returning to the DEAD

Arista Arista
1977. (7") **I'LL BE DOGGONE. / SHADE OF GREY** -
Feb 78. (7") **BOMBS AWAY. / EASY TO SLIP** -
Apr 78. (lp)(c) **HEAVEN HELP THE FOOL** 69 Feb 78
– Easy to slip / I'll be doggone / Wrong way / Heaven help the fool / Shade of grey / This time forever / Salt Lake City / Bombs away.
— **"BOBBY & THE MIDNITES"BOB WEIR** – vocals, guitar / **BILLY COBHAM** – drums, vocals / **BOBBY COCHRAN** – guitar / **ALPHONSO JOHNSON** – bass / **BRENT MYLAND** – keyboards / **MATTHEW KELLY** – harmonica
1981. (lp)(c) **BOBBY AND THE MIDNITES** -
– Book of rules / Me without you / Josephine / Fly away / Carry me / Festival.
— **DAVE GARLAND** – keyboards, synths + **KENNY GRADNEY** – bass, vocals repl. JOHNSON, MYLAND + JOHNSON
C.B.S. Columbia
Dec 84. (lp)(c) **WHERE THE BEAT MEETS THE STREET**
– (I want to live in) America / Where the beat meets the street / She's gonna win your heart / Ain't that peculiar / Lifeguard / Rock in the 80's / Lifeline / Falling / Thunder and lightning / Gloria Monday.

SEASTONES

PHIL LESH with **NED LAGIN**, plus DEAD session men and others

not issued Round
1975. (lp) **SEASTONES** -

MICKEY HART

Warners Warners
Oct 72. (lp)(c) **ROLLING THUNDER**
– Rolling thunder – Shoestone invocation / The main ten (playing in the band) / Fletcher Carnaby / The chase (progress) / Blind John / Young man / Deep wide and frequent / Pump song / Granma's cookies / Hangin' on. *(re-iss.Mar89 on 'Grateful Dead')*
1974. (7") **BLIND JOHN. / THE PUMP SONG** -
Celestial.. not issued
1983. (lp) **YAMANTAKA** - - Germ'y
– Yamantaka (parts 1-7) / The revolving mask of Yamantaka.
Rykodisc Rykodisc
1989. (lp)(cd) **DAFOS (w/ AIRTO + PURIN)**
– Dry sands of the desert / Ice of the north / Reunion (1, 2, 3) / Saudacao popular / Psychopomp / Subterranean caves of Kronos / The gates of Dafos / Passage. *(re-iss.Nov 94)*
1990. (lp)(cd) **MUSIC TO BE BORN BY**
– Music to be born by.
Mar 91. (cd) **AT THE EDGE**
Nov 94. (cd) **PLANET DRUM**

DIGA RHYTHM BAND

MICKEY HART – drums, plus 10 percussionists

United Art Grateful D
1976. (lp) **DIGA**
– Razooli / Happiness is drumming / Tal Mala / Sweet sixteen / Magnificent sevens. *(cd+c-iss.1992 on 'Rykodisc')*

RHYTHM DEVILS

with HART, LESH and KREUTZMANN plus more percussionist

not issued Passport
1980. (lp) **RHYTHM DEVILS PLAY RIVER MUSIC** -
– Compound / Trenches / Street gang / The beast / Steps / Tar / Lance / Cave / Napalm for breakfast / Hell's bells. *(re-iss.+c Mar 89 on 'Rykodisc')*

ROBERT HUNTER

solo with numerous session people incl. GRATEFUL DEAD folk

not issued Round
1974. (lp) **TALES OF THE GREAT RUM RUNNERS** -
– Lady simplicity / That train / Dry dusty road / I heard you singing / Rum runners / Children's lament / Maybe she's a bluebird / Boys in the barroom / It must have been the roses / Arizona lightning / Standing at your door / Mad / Keys to the rain. *(re-iss.+cd.May89 on 'Grateful Dead')*
1974. (7") **RUM RUNNERS. / IT MUST HAVE BEEN THE ROSES** -
1975. (lp) **TIGER ROSE** -
– Tiger rose / One thing to try / Rose of Sharon / Wild Bill / Dance a hole / Cruel white water / Over the hills / Last flash of rock'n'roll / Yellow Moon / Ariel. *(re-iss.+cd.May89 on 'Grateful Dead')*
Dark Star Dark Star
1981. (lp) **JACK O'ROSES**
– Box of rain / Book of Daniel / Friend of the Devil / etc.
Relix Relix
1982. (lp) **PROMONTORY RIDER** (74-75 rare material) -
1984. (lp)(cd) **AMAGAMALIN STREET**
– Roseanne / Amagamalin Street / Gypsy parlor ight / Rambling ghost / Ithaca / Don't be deceived / Taking Maggie home / Out of the city / Better bad luck / Streetwise / Where did you go / 13 roses. *(re-iss. 1990+Jun 93)*
Aug 86. (lp) **ROCK COLUMBIA**
– Eva / End of the road / I never see you / Aim at the heart / Kick it on down / What'll you raise? / Who, baby who? / Rock Columbia. *(cd-iss.Jun93)*
Mar 89. (lp) **LIBERTY** 1987
– Liberty / Cry down the years / Bone alley / Black shamrock / The song goes on / Do deny / Worried song / Come and get it / When a man loves a woman.
Rykodisc Rykodisc
Jan 94. (cd) **SENTINEL**
Mar 94. (cd) **A BOX OF RAIN**

KEITH & DONNA

with GARCIA plus more sessioners

not issued / Relix

1975. (lp) **KEITH AND DONNA GODCHAUX** [-] [ ]
– River deep, mountain high / Sweet baby / Woman make you / When you start to move / Showboat / My love for you / Farewell Jack / Who was John / Every song I sing.

— also 'SAMPLER FOR DEAD HEADS' m-lp's featuring various solo material.

GREAT WHITE

Formed: Los Angeles, California, USA ... as DANTE FOX in 1981. Mid 1982 they became GREAT WHITE, obviously named after a shark. After many years of constant touring, they finally made US Top 30 with 1987 'Capitol' album 'ONCE BITTEN'. • **Style:** Bluesy but typical US hard-rock act, with visual aspect their forte. • **Songwriters:** Group compositions with fan/manager ALAN NIVEN contributing. Covered; IMMIGRANT SONG + ROCK AND ROLL (Led Zeppelin) / GIMME SOME LOVIN' (Spencer Davis Group) / BITCH + IT'S ONLY ROCK'N'ROLL (Rolling Stones) / ONCE BITTEN TWICE SHY (Ian Hunter) / I DON'T NEED NO DOCTOR (Ashford & Simpson) / BABY'S ON FIRE (Eno) / MONEY (Barrett Strong) / etc. • **Trivia:** DAN DOKKEN produced their 1982 debut mini-lp 'OUT OF THE NIGHT'. MARK KENDALL married long-time girlfriend Sharon Schsol.

Recommended: ONCE BITTEN ... (*5)

JACK RUSSELL – vocals / **MARK KENDALL** (b.29 Apr'59) – lead guitar / **LORNE BLACK** – bass / **GARY HOLLAND** – drums other **ALAN NIVEN** – percussion, co-writer

not issued / Aegian

1982. (m-lp) **OUT OF THE NIGHT** [-] [ ]
– Out of the night / Last time / On your knees / No way / Dead end. *(re-iss.'90 as 'ON YOUR KNEES – THE FIRST LP' on 'Enigma')*

EMI Inter. / EMI Amer..

Mar 84. (lp)(c) **STICK IT** (UK-title 'GREAT WHITE') [ ] [ ]
– Out of the night / Stick it / Substitute / Bad boys / On your knees / Streetkiller / No better than hell / Hold on / Dead end / Nightmares.

Apr 84. (7") **SUBSTITUTE. / NO BETTER THAN HELL** [ ] [ ]
(12"+=) – Bad boys.

Apr 86. (7"ep) **FACE THE DAY. / HARD AND COLD / NO WAY** [-] [ ]

Capitol / Capitol

Sep 86. (m-lp) **SHOT IN THE DARK** [-] [82] Aug 86
– She shakes me / What do you do / Face the day / Gimme some lovin' / Shot in the dark / Is anybody there / Run away / Waiting for love.

— **TONY MONTANA** – bass repl. LORNE / **AUDIE DESBROW** – drums repl. GARY, / added **MICHAEL LARDIE** – keyboards, guitar (later became producer)

Jan 87. (7") **FACE THE DAY. / RED HOUSE** [ ] [ ]
(12"+=) – ('A' version).

Aug 87. (7") **ROCK ME. / THIS FAST ROAD** [ ] [60]
(12"+=) – Immigrant / Rock and roll.

Nov 87. (lp)(c) **ONCE BITTEN** [ ] [23] Jul 87
– Lady red light / Gonna getcha / Rock me / All over now / Mistreater / Never change heart / Fast road / On the edge / Save my love. *(cd-iss.Apr90) (re-iss.cd Jun95 on 'Connoisseur')*

Jan 88. (c-s)(cd-s) **SAVE YOUR LOVE. / ALL OVER NOW** [-] [57]

Jul 89. (7") **ONCE BITTEN TWICE SHY. / WASTED ROCK RANGER** [ ] [5] May 89
(12"+=)(12"pic-d+=)(cd-s+=) – Slow ride.

Sep 89. (7") **THE ANGEL SONG. /** [-] [30]

Nov 89. (7")(7"pic-d) **HEART THE HUNTER. / ALL OVER NOW** [ ] [ ]
(12"+=)(cd-s+=) – She shakes me.

Dec 89. (lp)(c)(cd) **TWICE SHY** [ ] [9] Apr 89
– Move it / Heart the hunter / Hiway nights / The angel song / Mista bone / Baby's on fire / House of broken love / She only / Once bitten twice shy / Bitches and other women medley:- Bitch – It's only rock'n'roll – Woman / Wasted rock ranger. *(UK-iss.has 2 += tracks + free live lp)* **LIVE AT THE MARQUEE** – Shot in the dark / What do you do / Gonna getcha / Money / All over now / Is anybody there / Face the day / Rock me.

Feb 90. (7")(7"pic-d) **HOUSE OF BROKEN LOVE. / BITCHES AND OTHER WOMEN (Medley:- BITCH / IT'S ONLY ROCK'N'ROLL / WOMAN)** [44] [83]
(12"+=)(cd-s+=) – Red house (live).

Aug 90. (cd)(c)(lp) **LIVE IN LONDON (live)** [ ] [ ]
– Move it / Heart the hunter / On your knees / House of broken love / Face the day / All over now / Once bitten twice shy.

Feb 91. (7")(c-s) **CONGO SQUARE. / SOUTH BAY CITIES** [62] [ ]
(12"+=)(cd-s+=)(12"pic-d+=) – ('A'version) / House of broken love (live).

Mar 91. (cd)(c)(lp) **HOOKED** [43] [18]
– Call it rock'n'roll / The original Queen of Sheba / Cold hearted lovin' / Can't shake it / Lovin' kind / Heartbreaker / South Bay cities / Desert Moon / Afterglow (of your love).

Aug 91. (7")(c-s) **CALL IT ROCK'N'ROLL. / HEART THE HUNTER** [67] [53] Feb 91
(12"+=)(cd-s+=)(12"pic-d+=) – Train to nowhere.

— now without MONTANA, and employing **DAVE SPITZ** – guitar (ex-WHITE LION)

Nov 92. (cd)(c)(lp) **PSYCHO CITY** [ ] [ ] Oct 92
– Psycho city / Step on you / Old Rose hotel / Maybe someday / Big goodbye / Doctor me / I want you / Never trust a pretty face / Love is a lie / Get on home.

Nov 93. (cd)(c) **THE BEST OF GREAT WHITE** (compilation) [ ] [ ]
– Step on you / All over now / Save your love / House of broken love / Big goodbye / Rock me / Face the day (blues mix) / Old Rose motel / Once bitten twice shy / Afterglow.

not issued / Zoo

May 94. (cd)(c) **SAIL AWAY** [-] [ ]

– others, etc. –

Jul 88. Capitol/ US= Enigma; (lp)(c)(cd) **RECOVERY: ALIVE (live)** [ ] [99]
– (live side from 1983 & jam side from early 1986).

Al GREEN

Born: AL GREENE, 13 Apr'46, Forrest City, Arkansas, USA. In 1959, AL formed own gospel group with brothers ROBERT, WALTER and WILLIAM. By the mid-60's he initiated another singing group The CREATIONS, with PALMER JAMES, GENE MASON and CURTIS ROGERS. They had promising local following, with minor successes on 'Zodiac' label. Early in 1968, AL GREENE & THE SOUL MATES broke into the 50, with first single BACK UP TRAIN. Later that year, he dropped the E from his surname and went solo, signing to Willie Mitchell's 'Hi' records. After a few flops, he charted in 1971, with single TIRED OF BEING ALONE. This was succeeded in the 70's, by 5 consecutive US Top10 hits, starting with the classic LET'S STAY TOGETHER, which resided at No.1 for a week. His career was nearly ended abruptly on 25 Oct'74, when his kamikaze girlfriend Mary Woodson, attacked him in his shower with red-hot grits. She then shot herself with his gun, and AL was taken to hospital with second degree burns. • **Style:** Soul singer of immense quality and creativity, but after his move into Christianity and pure gospel music in 1975, his work lacked earlier sparkle. He became pastor/minister for local Memphis church and virtually stopped touring to compensate his new lifestyle. In 1988, he was back again at his best, duetting with ANNIE LENNOX on the hit single PUT A LITTLE LOVE IN YOUR HEART. • **Songwriters:** AL wrote most of material, except covers I WANT TO HOLD YOUR HAND + GET BACK (Beatles) / CAN'T GET NEXT TO YOU (Temptations) / etc. His songs have been re-done by many including TAKE ME TO THE RIVER (Talking Heads) / L.O.V.E. (Orange Juice) / LET'S STAY TOGETHER (Tina Turner) / HERE I AM (UB40) / etc. • **Trivia:** On 13 Feb'78, L.A. declared this the 'Al Green Day'.

Recommended: THE SUPREME AL GREEN: THE GREATEST HITS (*8)

AL GREENE & THE SOUL MATES

AL GREEN – vocals with **CURTIS ROGERS** and **PALMER JONES**

Stateside / Bell

Jan 68. (7") **BACK UP TRAIN. / DON'T LEAVE ME** [ ] [41] Oct 67

Ace of Clubs / Hot Line

Feb 68. (7") **DON'T HURT ME NO MORE. / GET YOURSELF TOGETHER** [ ] [ ]

1968. (lp) **BACK UP TRAIN** [ ] [ ]
– Back up train / Hot wire / Stop and check myself / Let me help you / I'm reaching out / Don't hurt me no more / Lovers hideaway / Don't leave me / What's it all about / I'll be good to you / Guilty / That's all it takes (lady) / Get yourself together.

1968. (7") **LOVER'S HIDEAWAY** [-] [ ]

AL GREEN

– vocals now using 'Hi' records house band **THE MEMPHIS HORNS** who were **WAYNE JACKSON** – trumpet / **JAMES MITCHELL** – baritone sax. / **ANDREW LOVE** – tenor sax. / **JACK HALE** – trombone / **ED LOGAN** – tenor sax. / plus **LEROY HODGES** – bass / **MABON HODGES** – guitar. / **CHARLES HUGHES** – organ and **HOWARD GRIMES** – drums who repl. AL JACKSON who joined BOOKER T.

London / Hi

1969. (7") **I WANT TO HOLD YOUR HAND. / WHAT AM I TO DO WITH MYSELF** [-] [ ]

1969. (7") **ONE WOMAN. / TOMORROW'S DREAM** [-] [ ]

1969. (lp) **GREEN IS BLUES** [-] [ ]
– One woman / Talk to me / My girl / I stand accused / Gotta find a new world / What am I gonna do with myself / Tomorrow's dream / What am I gonna do with myself / Get back baby / Get back / Summertime. *(UK-iss.Apr86 on 'Hi') (hit 19 US chart Jan73)*

Feb 70. (7") **YOU SAY IT. / GOTTA FIND A NEW WORLD** [ ] [ ]

Apr 70. (7") **RIGHT NOW RIGHT NOW. / ALL BECAUSE I'M A FOOLISH ONE** [-] [ ]

Jan 71. (7") **I CAN'T GET NEXT TO YOU. / RIDE SALLY RIDE** [ ] [60] Nov 70

Apr 71. (7") **DRIVIN' WHEEL. / TRUE LOVE** [-] [ ]

Jul 71. (7") **TIRED OF BEING ALONE. / GET BACK BABY** [-] [11]

Aug 71. (7") **TIRED OF BEING ALONE. / RIGHT NOW RIGHT NOW** [4] [-]

Nov 71. (lp)(c) **AL GREEN GETS NEXT TO YOU** [ ] [58] Aug 71
– I can't get next to you / Are you lonely for me baby / God is standing by / Tired of being alone / I'm a ram / Drivin' wheel / Light my fire / You say it / Right now right now / All because. *(re-iss.Apr86 on 'Hi')*

Dec 71. (7") **LET'S STAY TOGETHER. / TOMORROW'S DREAM** [7] [1] Nov 71

Mar 72. (lp)(c) **LET'S STAY TOGETHER** [ ] [8] Feb 72
– Let's stay together / La-la for you / So you're leaving / What is this feeling / Old time lovin' / I've never found a girl / How can you mend a broken heart / Judy / It ain't no fun to me. *(re-iss.Apr85 on 'Hi')*

Mar 72. (7") **LOOK WHAT YOU DONE FOR ME. / LA-LA FOR YOU** [-] [4]

May 72. (7") **LOOK WHAT YOU DONE FOR ME. / I'VE NEVER FOUND A GIRL** [44] [-]

Jul 72. (7") **I'M STILL IN LOVE WITH YOU. / OLD TIME LOVIN'** [35] [3] Jun 72

Oct 72. (7") **YOU OUGHT TO BE WITH ME. / WHAT IS THIS FEELING** [ ] [3]

Dec 72. (lp)(c) **I'M STILL IN LOVE WITH YOU** [ ] [4] Oct 72
– I'm still in love with you / I'm glad you're mine / Love and happiness / What a wonderful thing love is / Simply beautiful / Oh, pretty woman / For the good times /

Look what you done for me / One of these good old days. *(re-iss.Apr85 on 'Hi')*

Feb 73. (7") **CALL ME (COME BACK HOME). / WHAT A WONDERFUL THING LOVE IS** [ ] [10]

Apr 73. (7") **LOVE AND HAPPINESS. / SO YOU'RE LEAVING** [ ] [ ]

Jul 73. (7") **HERE I AM (COME AND TAKE ME). / I'M GLAD YOU'RE MINE** [ ] [10] Jun 73

Nov 73. (lp)(c) **CALL ME** [ ] [10] May 73
– Call me (come back home) / Have you been making out o.k. / Stand up / I'm so lonesome I could cry / Your love is like the morning sun / Here I am (come and take me) / You ought to be with me / Jesus is waiting. *(re-iss.Jul85 on 'Hi')*

Jan 74. (7") **LIVIN' FOR YOU. / IT AIN'T NO FUN TO ME** [ ] [19] Dec 73

Apr 74. (lp)(c) **LIVIN' FOR YOU** [ ] [24] Dec 73
– Livin' for you / Home again / Free at last / Let's get married / So good to be here / My sweet sixteen / Unchained melody / My God is real / Beware. *(re-iss.Nov85 on 'Hi')*

Apr 74. (7") **LET'S GET MARRIED. / SO GOOD TO BE HERE** [ ] [32] Mar 74

Oct 74. (7") **SHA-LA-LA (MAKE ME HAPPY). / SCHOOL DAYS** [20] [7] Sep 74

Dec 74. (lp)(c) **AL GREEN EXPLORES YOUR MIND** [ ] [15] Nov 74
– Sha-la-la (make me happy) / Take me to the river / God blessed our love / The city / One nite stand / Stay with me forever / Hangin' on / School days. *(re-iss.Sep86 on 'Hi')*

Feb 75. (7") **L-O-V-E. (LOVE). / I WISH YOU WERE HERE WITH ME** [24] [13]

Jul 75. (7") **OH ME, OH MY (DREAMS IN MY ARMS). / STRONG AS DEATH (SWEET AS LIFE)** [ ] [48]

Oct 75. (lp)(c) **AL GREEN IS LOVE** [ ] [28] Sep 75
– L.O.V.E. (love) / Rhymes / The love sermon / There is love / Could I be the one / Love ritual / I didn't know / Oh me, oh my (dreams in my heart) / I wish you were here. *(re-iss.Jul86 on Hi')*

Nov 75. (7") **FULL OF FIRE. / COULD I BE THE ONE** [ ] [28]

Mar 76. (lp)(c) **FULL OF FIRE** [ ] [59]
– Glory glory / That's the way it is / Always / There's no way / I'd fly away / Full of fire / Together again / Soon as I get home / Let it shine. *(re-iss.Sep86 on 'Hi')*

May 76. (7") **LET IT SHINE. / THERE'S NO WAY** [ ] [ ]

Oct 76. (7") **KEEP ME CRYIN'. / THERE IS LOVE** [ ] [37]

Dec 76. (lp)(c) **HAVE A GOOD TIME** [ ] [93] Nov 76
– Keep on cryin' / Smile a little bit more / I tried to tell myself / Something / The truth marches on / Have a good time / Nothing takes the place of you / Happy / Hold on forever. *(re-iss.Jul86 on 'Hi')*

Apr 77. (7") **I TRIED TO TELL MYSELF. / SOMETHING** [-] [ ]

May 77. (7"ep) **I TRIED TO TELL MYSELF / SOMETHING. / WHAT AM I GONNA DO WITH MYSELF / SUMMERTIME** [ ] [-]

Nov 77. (7") **LOVE AND HAPPINESS. / GLORY GLORY** [-] [ ]

Jan 78. (lp)(c) **TRUTH 'N' TIME** [-] [ ]
– Blow me down / Lo and behold / Wait here / To sir with love / Truth 'n' time / King of all / Say a little prayer / Happy days.

— AL GREEN completely changed his backing musicians recruiting **JAMES BASS** – guitar / **RUEBEN FAIRFAX** – bass / **JOHNNY TONEY** – drums / **FRED JORDAN** – trumpet / **BUDDY JARRETT** – alto sax. / **RON ECHOLS** – baritone sax.

Cream / Hi

Jan 78. (7") **BELLE. / CHARIOTS OF FIRE** [-] [83]

Aug 78. (7") **FEELS LIKE SUMMER. / I FEEL GOOD** [-] [ ]

Nov 78. (7") **TO SIR WITH LOVE. / WAIT HERE** [-] [ ]

Aug 79. (7") **BELLE. / TO SIR WITH LOVE** [ ] [-]

Sep 79. (lp)(c) **THE BELLE ALBUM** [ ] [ ] Dec 77
– Belle / Loving you / Feels like summer / Georgia boy / I feel good / Chariots of fire / All in all / Dream. *(re-iss.Apr86 on 'Hi')*

Jul 81. (d-lp)(d-c) **TOKYO LIVE (live)** [ ] [ ]
– L.O.V.E. (love) / Tired of being alone / Let's stay together / How can you mend a broken heart / All n all / Belle / Sha-la-la (make me happy) / Let's get married / God blessed our love / You ought to be with me / For the good times / Dream / I feel good / Love and happiness. *(re-iss.Aug87) (re-iss.Mar90)*

— The Rev. now used mainly session people and gospel backing singers.

Hi / Hi

Feb 82. (lp)(c) **HIGHER PLANE** [ ] [ ]
– Where love rules / Amazing Grace / His name is Jesus / Battle hymn of the republic / Higher plane / People get ready / By my side / Amazing grace / The spirit might come – on and on. *(re-iss.Nov85 on 'Hi')*

Nov 82. (lp)(c) **PRECIOUS LORD** [ ] [ ]
– Glory to his name / Rock of ages / In the garden / Hallelujah (I just want to praise the Lord) / Precious Lord / What a friend we have in Jesus / The old rugged cross / Morningstar / How great thou art. *(re-iss.Jul85 on 'Hi')*

Feb 85. (lp)(c) **TRUST IN GOD** [ ] [ ]
– Don't it make you wanna go home / Trust in God / Holy Spirit / Up the ladder to the roof / Ain't no mountain high enough / No not one / Lean on me / Never met anybody like you / Trust in God (reprise) / All we need is a little more love.

Feb 85. (7") **NEVER MET NOBODY LIKE YOU. / HIGHER PLANE** [ ] [ ]

A & M / A & M

Nov 85. (7") **GOING AWAY. / BUILDING UP** [-] [ ]

Nov 85. (lp)(c) **GOING AWAY** [ ] [ ]
– Going away / True love / He is the light / I feel like going on / Be with me Jesus / You brought the sunshine / Power / Building up / Nearer my God to thee.

Jan 86. (7") **TRUE LOVE. / YOU BROUGHT THE SUNSHINE** [ ] [-]
(12"+=) – Going away.

Jan 86. (7") **TRUE LOVE. / HE IS THE LIGHT** [-] [ ]

Feb 87. (7") **EVERYTHING'S GONNA BE ALRIGHT. / SO REAL TO ME** [-] [ ]

Apr 87. (lp)(c) **SOLE SURVIVOR** [ ] [ ]
– Everything's gonna be alright / Jesus will fix it / You know and I know / Yield not to temptation / So real to me / Sole survivor / You've got a friend / He ain't heavy / 23rd psalm.

Jun 87. (7") **YOU KNOW AND I KNOW. / TRUE LOVE** [-] [ ]

Sep 87. (7") **SOLE SURVIVOR. / JESUS WILL FIX IT** [-] [ ]

Nov 88. (7") **PUT A LITTLE LOVE IN YOUR HEART. (by "ANNIE LENNOX & AL GREEN") / A GREAT BIG PIECE OF LOVE** [28] [9]

Jun 89. (7") **AS LONG AS WE'RE TOGETHER. / BLESSED** [ ] [ ]
(12"+=) – ('A'other mix).

Jun 89. (lp)(c)(cd) **I GET JOY** [ ] [ ]
– You're everything to me / All my praise / The end is near / Mighty clouds of joy / I get joy / As long as we're together / Praise him / Blessed / Tryin' to do the best I can / Tryin' to get over you.

— He provided the vocals on ARTHUR BAKER + BACKSTREET DISCIPLES Oct89 single THE MESSAGE IS LOVE.

— Co-writes w / **DAVID STEELE** (ex-BEAT). **ANDY COX** also appears and is co-producer. The song 'DON'T LOOK BACK' was written by SMOKEY ROBINSON, and featured CURTIS STIGERS. JOE ROBERTS + A.GLASS wrote 'Fountain of Love'. LOVE IN MOTION was a cover, as was his single below, which was penned by S.SWIRSKY.

R.C.A. / R.C.A.

Sep 93. (7")(c-s) **LOVE IS A BEAUTIFUL THING. / ('A'mix)** [56] [ ]
(12"+=)(cd-s+=) – ('A'mixes).

Sep 93. (cd)(c)(lp) **DON'T LOOK BACK** [ ] [ ]
– Best love / Love is a beautiful thing / Waiting on you / What does it take / Keep on pushing love / You are my everything / One love / People in the world (Keep on lovin' you) / Give it everything / Your love (is more than I ever hoped for) / Fountain of love / Don't look back / Love in motion.

Mar 94. (7")(c-s) **KEEP ON PUSHING LOVE. / ('A'mix)** [ ] [ ]
(12"+=)(cd-s+=) – ('A'mix).

— In May 94, AL did duet 'Funny How Time Slips Away' with LYLE LOVETT on 'Geffen'. Originally a 1962 hit for JIMMY ELLEDGE.

Jul 94. (c-s) **WAITING ON YOU. / ('A'mix)** [ ] [ ]
(12"+=)(cd-s+=) – (2-'A'mixes).

– compilations etc. –

Mar 75. London/ US= Hi; (lp)(c) **AL GREEN'S GREATEST HITS** [18] [17] Mar 75
(re-iss.+cd.Jul86 on 'Hi')

Jan 80. Cream; (lp)(c) **THE CREAM OF AL GREEN** [ ] [ ]

Jan 80. Cream; (7") **TIRED OF BEING ALONE. / HOW CAN YOU MEND A BROKEN HEART** [ ] [ ]

1984. Cream; (7") **TIRED OF BEING ALONE. / LET'S STAY TOGETHER** [ ] [ ]
(12"+=) – How can you mend a broken heart.

Jul 86. Hi; (lp) **WHITE CHRISTMAS** [ ] [ ]
(re-iss.Nov87 on 'Demon') (cd-iss.Nov95)

Jul 77. Hi; (lp)(c) **TAKE ME TO THE RIVER – GREATEST HITS VOL.2** [ ] [ ]
(re-iss.+cd.Oct87)

Sep 85. Hi; (7") **LET'S STAY TOGETHER. / I'M STILL IN LOVE WITH YOU** [ ] [ ]
(12"+=) – You ought to be with me.

Jul 86. Hi; (lp)(c) **THE BEST OF AL GREEN** [ ] [ ]

Nov 88. Hi; (7") **LET'S STAY TOGETHER. / I'M STILL IN LOVE WITH YOU** [ ] [ ]

1991. Hi; (cd)(c)(lp) **COVER ME GREEN** [ ] [ ]

Jun 90. Hi-Demon; (lp) **YOU SAY IT** [ ] [-]

Sep 91. Hi-Demon; (cd) **HAVE A GOOD TIME / THE BELLE ALBUM** [ ] [-]

Jul 92. Hi-Demon; (cd) **THE SUPREME AL GREEN: THE GREATEST HITS** [ ] [-]
– Tired of being alone / I can't get next to you / Let's stay together / How can you mend a broken heart / Love & happiness / I'm still in love with you / Simply beautiful / What a wonderful thing love is / Call me (come back home) / My God is real / Let's get married / Sha-la-la (make me happy) / Take me to the river / Love ritual / L-O-V-E / I didn't know / Full of fire / Belle.

Jul 93. Hi-Demon; (cd) **THE FLIPSIDE OF AL GREEN** [ ] [ ]

Oct 81. P.R.T.; (d-lp)(d-c) **SPOTLIGHT ON . . .** [ ] [ ]

May 81. Myrrh; (lp) **THE LORD WILL MAKE A WAY** [-] [ ]
– Highway to heaven / Pass me not / The Lord will make a way / Too close / None but the righteous / I have a friend above all others / Saved / In the holy name of Jesus.

Sep 72. Bell; (lp) **AL GREEN** (rec.w / SOUL MATES) [-] [ ]

Sep 72. Bell; (7") **GUILTY. / LET ME HELP YOU** [-] [69]

Jan 73. Bell; (7") **HOT WIRE. / DON'T LEAVE ME** [-] [71]

Mar 89. Memphis; (lp)(c)(cd) **LOVE RITUAL (1968-76)** [ ] [ ]

Sep 88. K-Tel; (lp)(c)(cd) **HI LIFE – THE BEST OF AL GREEN** [34] [-]

Nov 92. Beechwood; (cd) **AL** [41] [-]

Dec 94. Hi; (cd) **CHRISTMAS CHEERS (w / ACE CANNON)** [ ] [ ]

Peter GREEN

Born: 29 Oct'46, Bethnal Green, London, England. Early in 1966, he joined PETER B'S LOONERS (aka with PETER BARDENS; future CAMEL), who cut one 'Columbia' 45 'IF YOU WANNA BE HAPPY' / 'JODRELL BLUES', before evolving into SHOTGUN EXPRESS in May'66. They included ROD STEWART on vocals, but GREEN departed in Jul'66, when he was asked to replace ERIC CLAPTON in JOHN MAYALL's BLUESBREAKERS. GREEN appeared on 'A Hard Road' album, but he left in summer 1967 with MICK FLEETWOOD to form FLEETWOOD MAC. They gained much credibility in the blues field, before he set out on solo career, after writing the haunting hit 'THE GREEN MANALISHI'. He also became heavily religious and gave all MAC royalties to certain charities. After shunning press attention, etc., he released solo debut lp 'END OF THE GAME' late '70, but this lack-lustre effort gained little support from critics or buying public. He then opted out of public eye again, gave away his guitar and grew his fingernails. He took up various jobs (i.e. grave-digger, hospital porter, etc.), but little was heard of his low-key activities until . . . Early in 1977, he was committed to a mental hospital, after returning an unwanted royalty cheque with rifle in hand, to his accountant. (No doubt subtlely wanting to re-form SHOTGUN EXPRESS). In 1978, he signed a new solo contract with 'PVK', and hit UK Top 40 with 2 following albums 'IN THE SKIES' (1979) & 'LITTLE DREAMER' (1980). • **Style:** Outstanding guitarist and songwriter, who sadly hit mental troubles throughout solo career. His bluesy solo output was at times filled with early roots, although never classic. • **Songwriters:** Self-penned bar; BORN UNDER A BAD SIGN (Cream) / etc. • **Trivia:** In Feb'71, GREEN helped out and returned briefly to FLEETWOOD MAC on their US tour, after JEREMY SPENCER also went religious.

Recommended: PETER GREEN BACKTRACKIN' (*6).

PETER GREEN solo – guitar, vocals (ex-FLEETWOOD MAC, ex-JOHN MAYALL) with **ZOOT MONEY** – piano / **NICK BUCK** – keyboards / **ALEX DMOCHOWSKI** – bass **GODFREY MacLEAN** – drums

Reprise Reprise

Nov 70. (lp)(c) **THE END OF THE GAME**
– Bottoms up / Timeless time / Descending scales / Burnt foot / Hidden depths / The end of the game.

Jun 71. (7") **HEAVY HEART. / NO WAY OUT**

Jan 72. (7") **BEAST OF BURDEN.("PETER GREEN & NIGEL WATSON") / UGANDA WOMAN**

—— Between 1971-78 PETER concentrated on religious activities, and after a time recovering in a mental hospital in 1977, he was gladly making a come-back with **SNOWY WHITE** – guitar / **PETER BARDENS** – keyboards / **KUMA HARADA** – bass and **REG ISADORE** – drums (all mainly on following album) (first 45 below quickly withdrawn)

P.V.K. Sail

Jun 78. (7") **THE APOSTLE. / TRIBAL DANCE** [ ] [-]

May 79. (lp)(c)(green-lp) **IN THE SKIES** [32] [-]
– In the skies / Slaybo day / A fool no more / Tribal dance / Seven stars / Funky chunk / Just for you / Proud Pinto / Apostle. *(cd-iss.1988)*

Jun 79. (7") **IN THE SKIES. / PROUD PINTO**

—— Continued to work with noted session people, too numerous to mention

Apr 80. (lp)(c) **LITTLE DREAMER** [34] [ ] Oct 80
– Loser two times / Momma don'tcha cry / Born under a bad sign / I could not ask for more / Baby when the sun goes down / Walkin the road / One woman love / Cryin' won't bring you back / Little dreamer.

Apr 80. (7") **WALKIN' THE ROAD. / WOMAN DON'T**

Jun 80. (7") **LOSER TWO TIMES. / MOMMA DON'TCHA CRY** [ ] [-]

—— (above 45 also quickly withdrawn)

Mar 81. (lp)(c) **WATCHA GONNA DO** [ ] [-]
– Gotta see her tonight / Promised land / Bullet in the sky / Give me back my freedom / Last train to San Antone / To break your heart / Bizzy Lizzy / Lost my love / Like a hot tomato / Head against the wall. *(cd-iss.Feb93 on 'Rhino')*

Mar 81. (7") **GIVE ME BACK MY FREEDOM. / LOST MY LOVE**

Jul 81. (7") **PROMISED LAND. / BIZZY LIZZY** [ ] [-]

Headline not issued

Jun 82. (lp) **WHITE SKY** [ ] [-]
– Time for me to go / Shining star / The clown / White sky (love that evil woman) / It's gotta be me / Born on the wild side / Fallin' apart / Indian lover / Just another guy. *(cd-iss.Nov92)*

Nov 83. (lp) **KOLORS** [ ] [-]
– What am I doing here / Bad bad feelings / Big boy now / Black woman / Bandit / Same old blues / Liquor and you / Gotta do it with me / Funky jam. *(cd-iss.Nov92)*

—— Virtually retired from the biz.

– compilations etc. –

Nov 81. Creole; (lp) **BLUE GUITAR** [ ] [-]

Jan 88. Creole; (lp)(c)(cd) **LEGEND** [ ] [-]
(cd+=) – (includes 'WHITE SKY' lp). *(re-iss.+cd Feb93)*

Jun 92. Creole; (cd)(c)(lp) **LAST TRAIN** [ ] [-]

Feb 86. Homestead; (lp) **COME ON DOWN** [ ] [-]

Aug 87. Mainline; (lp)(cd) **A CASE FOR THE BLUES** [ ] [-]

Jan 90. Backtrackin'; (cd)(c)(d-lp) **PETER GREEN** [ ] [-]
– In the skies / A fool no more / Tribal dance / Just for you / Born on the wild side / Proud Pinto / Shining star / Slaybo day / Indian lover / Carry my love / Corner of my mind / Cryin' won't bring you back / Little dreamer / Momma don'tcha cry / Baby when the Sun goes down / Born under a bad sign / Walkin' the road / Loser two times / What am I doing here / Big boy now / Time for me to go now / It's gonna be me / You won't see me anymore / Bad bad feeling.

Apr 91. Red Lightnin'; (cd) **TWO GREENS MAKE A BLUES**

—— (above by "PETER GREEN, MICK GREEN & The ENEMY WITHIN")

China

Jun 94. (cd) **ROCK'N'ROLL DISEASE – THE BEST OF ...**

GREEN DAY

Formed: Rodeo, nr. Berkeley, California, USA ... early 90's out of The SWEET CHILDREN by BILLY JOE and MIKE. When TRE COOL replaced BILLY JOE's sister ANA on drums, they became GREEN DAY. Their debut lp '39/ SMOOTH' was recorded in under 24 hours. Their third album 'DOOKIE' (their first for 'Reprise') was a surprise US smash in 1994 due to college /MTV favourite 'BASKET CASE'. • **Style:** Retro punk-rock for Americans (& now Brits!) who missed out on BUZZCOCKS, DICKIES, RAMONES, and even earlier 60's pop outfit MONKEES. • **Songwriters:** Lyrics; BILLY JOE, group songs except TIRED OF WAITING FOR YOU (Kinks). DIRNT guested on The SCREAMING WEASEL album 'How to Make Enemies And Irritate People'. BILLIE JOE was also a member of PINHEAD GUNPOWDER who released an album 'Jump Salty' plus a few EP's, also for 'Lookout'.

Recommended: DOOKIE (*8)

BILLY JOE ARMSTRONG (b.1972) – vocals, guitar / **MIKE PRITCHARD** (b.1972) – bass, vocals / **TRE COOL** (b.1972) – drums

not issued Lookout

1989. (7"ep) **1000 HOURS EP** [-] [ ]
– 1000 hours / Dry ice / Only of you / The one I want.

1990. (7"ep) **SLAPPY EP** [-] [ ]
– Paper lanterns / Why do you want him? / 409 in your coffeemaker / Knowledge.

1990. (lp) **39/ SMOOTH** [-] [ ]
– At the library / Don't leave me / I was there / Disappearing boy / Green day / Going to Pasalacgua / 16 / Road to exceptance / Rest / The judge's daughter / Paper lanterns / Why do you want him? / 409 in your coffeemaker / Knowledge / 1000 hours / Dry ice / Only of you / The one I want / I want to be alone. *(re-iss.+cd.Nov91) (UK-iss.Sep94 as '1,039/ SMOOTHED OUT SLAPPY HOURS' on 'Lookout')*

Dec 91. (lp) **KERPLUNK!** [-] [ ]
– 2000 light years away / One for the razorbacks / Welcome to Paradise / Christie Road / Private ale / Dominated love slave / One of my lies / 80 / Android / No one knows / Who wrote Holden Caulfield? / Words I might have ate. *(UK-iss.+cd.Sep94, on 'Lookout')* (cd+=) Sweet children / Best thing in town / Strangeland / My generation. (by SWEET CHILDREN and released US 1990 on 'Skene')

Reprise Reprise

Feb 94. (cd)(c) **DOOKIE** [ ] [2]
– Burnout / Having a blast / Chump / Longview / Welcome to Paradise / Pulling teeth / Basket case / She / Sassafras roots / When I come around / Coming clean / Emenius sleepus / In the end / F.O.D. (cd+=) (hidden track). *(re-iss.Jun94 + Nov94 on green-lp, hit UK No.35/ early '95 hit 13)*

Jun 94. (7")(c-s) **LONGVIEW. / ON THE WAGON**
(10")(cd-s) – ('A'side) / Going to Pasalaqua / F.O.D. (live) / Christy Road (live).

Aug 94. (7"green)(c-s) **BASKET CASE. / TIRED OF WAITING FOR YOU** [55] [ ]
(cd-s+=) – On the wagon / 409 in your coffeemaker.

Oct 94. (12"green)(c-s)(cd-s) **WELCOME TO PARADISE. / CHUMP (live) / EMENIUS SLEEPUS** [20] [ ]

Jan 95. (7"green)(c-s) **BASKET CASE. / 2,000 LIGHT YEARS AWAY (live)** [7] [ ]
(cd-s+=) – Burnout (live) / Longview (live).

Mar 95. (7")(c-s) **LONGVIEW. / WELCOME TO PARADISE (live)** [30] [ ]
(cd-s+=) – One of my lies (live).

May 95. (7"pic-d)(c-s) **WHEN I COME AROUND. / SHE (live)** [27] [ ]
(cd-s+=) – Coming clean (live).

Sep 95. (7"red)(c-s) **GEEK STINK BREATH. / I WANNA BE ON T.V.** [16] [ ]
(cd-s+=) – Don't wanna fall in love.

Oct 95. (cd)(c)(lp) **INSOMNIAC** [8] [2]
– Armatage Shanks / Brat / Stuck with me / Geek stink breath / No pride / Bab's Uvula who? / 86 / Panic song / Stuart and the Ave. / Brain stew / Jaded / Westbound sign / Tight wad hill / Walking contradiction.

Dec 95. (c-s) **STUCK WITH ME / WHEN I COME AROUND (live)** [24] [ ]
(cd-s+=) – Jaded (live).
(cd-s) – ('A'side) / Dominated love slave (live) / Chump (live).

Dave GREENFIELD & J. J. BURNEL (see under ⇒ STRANGLERS)

GREEN ON RED

Formed: Phoenix, Arizona, USA ... 1981 by DAN STUART and CHRIS CACAVAS. After spells on some US indies, namely 'Slash' & 'Zippo', they signed to major 'Mercury' in 1985. Were always on the verge of a commercial breakthrough, but were dogged by label failures, etc. • **Style:** West coast/country guitar sound, that was inspired by Nashville-era BYRDS or early NEIL YOUNG. They were always clumped alongside new wave country re-actifiers RAIN PARADE, DREAM SYNDICATE and LONG RYDERS. • **Songwriters:** DAN was main contributer, until CHUCK PROPHET replaced sacked members late '87 and became co-writer. Covered; AIN'T IT FUNNY NOW (Willie Nelson) / KNOCKIN' ON HEAVEN'S DOOR (Bob Dylan) / SMOKESTACK LIGHTNIN' (Howlin' Wolf) / RAINY DAYS AND MONDAYS (Carpenters). • **Trivia:** Their 1989 album 'HERE COMES THE SNAKES', was to have been issued Aug'88 by soon-to-be bust 'Red Rhino' records. AL KOOPER produced + featured on 1991 album 'SCAPEGOATS'.

Recommended: GAS FOOD LODGING (*8) / GRAVITY TALKS (*7) / GREEN ON RED (*6) / THE BEST OF GREEN ON RED (*7)

DAN STUART – vocals, guitar / **CHRIS CACAVAS** – keyboards / **JACK WATERSON** – bass / **ALEX MacNICOL** – drums

not issued Private

1981. (12"ep) **TWO BIBLES** [-] [ ]
– Green on red / etc.

not issued Down There

1982. (m-lp) **GREEN ON RED (UNTITLED)** [-] [ ]
– Death and angels / Hair and skin / Black night / Illustrated crawling / Aspirin / Lost world / Apartment 6. *(UK-issJun85 on 'Demon')*

Slash Slash

Aug 84. (lp) **GRAVITY TALKS** [ ] [ ] 1983
– Gravity talks / Old chief / 5 easy pieces / Deliverance / Over my head / Snake bite / Blue parade / That's what you're here for / Brave generation / Abigail's ghost / Cheap wine / Narcolepsy. *(re-iss.+c.Jan87 on 'London')*

—— added **CHUCK W. PROPHET** – steel guitar, vocals

Zippo Zippo

May 85. (lp)(c) **GAS, FOOD, LODGING**
– That's what dreams / Black river / Hair of the dog / This I know / Fading away / Easy way out / Sixteen ways / The drifter / Sea of Cortez / We shall overcome. *(cd-iss.1990 on 'Enigma')*

—— **KEITH MITCHELL** – percussion repl. ALEX

Mercury Mercury

Oct 85. (m-lp)(c) **NO FREE LUNCH** 99
– Time ain't nothing / Honest man / Ballad of Guy Fawkes / No free lunch / Funny how time slips away / Jimmy boy / Keep on moving. *(c+=)* – Smokestack lightnin'.

Nov 85. (7") **TIME AIN'T NOTHING. / NO FREE LUNCH**

Feb 87. (7") **CLARKSVILLE. / NO DRINKIN'**
(12"+=) – Broken.

Mar 87. (lp)(c)(cd) **THE KILLER INSIDE ME**
– Clarksville / Mighty gun / Jamie / Whispering wind / Ghost hand / Sorry Naomi / No man's land / Track you down (his master's voice) / Born to fight / We ain't feee / The killer inside me. *(cd+=)* – NO FREE LUNCH (m-lp)

Jun 87. (7") **BORN TO FIGHT. / DON'T SHINE YOUR LIGHT ON ME**
(12") – ('A'extended) / While the widow weeps.

— Disbanded late 1987, DAN and CHUCK reformed and brought in new sessioners.

China China

Apr 89. (7") **KEITH CAN'T READ. / VAYA CON DIOS / THAT'S THE WAY THE WORLD GOES ROUND**
(12") – (first 2 tracks) / Tenderloin.

Apr 89. (lp)(c)(cd) **HERE COME THE SNAKES**
– Keith can't read / Rock and roll disease / Morning blue / Zombie for love / Broken radio / Change / Tenderloin / Way back home / We had it all / D.T. blues.

Aug 89. (10"lp)(c) **LIVE AT THE TOWN & COUNTRY CLUB (live)**
– 16 ways / Change / DT blues / Fading away / Morning blue / Are you sure Hank done it this way / Zombie for love / Hair of the dog. *(c+=)* – Rock'n'roll disease / We had it all. *(ltd.lp- 3,000 / c- 2,000)*

— duo now with **RENE COMAN** – upright bass, bass / **MIKE FINNEGAN** – keyboards / **DAVID KEMPER** – drums, percussion / plus **BERNIE LEADON** – mandolin, acoustic guitar (4) / **PAT DONALDSON** – bass (4) / **SPOONER OLDHAM** – piano (3)

Oct 89. (7") **THIS TIME AROUND. / FADING AWAY (live)**
(12"+=)(cd-s+=) – 16 ways (live).

Nov 89. (lp)(c)(cd) **THIS TIME AROUND**
– This time around / Cool million / Rev. Luther / Good patient woman / You couldn't get arrested / The quarter / Foot / Hold the line / Pills and booze / We're all waiting. *(free-7"w.a.)* **MORNING BLUE / ROCK'N'ROLL DISEASE. / (interview)**

Dec 89. (7") **YOU COULDN'T GET ARRESTED. / BROKEN RADIO**
(12")(cd-s) – ('A'extended) / Hair of the dog.

— DAN and CHUCK recruit **MICHAEL RHODES** – bass / **DAREN HESS** – drums

Mar 91. (7") **LITTLE THINGS. / CHERRY KIND**
(12"+=)(cd-s+=) – Sun goes down / Waiting for love.

Mar 91. (cd)(c)(lp) **SCAPEGOATS**
– A guy like me / Little things in life / Two lovers (waitin' to die) / Gold in the graveyard / Hector's out / Shed a tear (for the lonesome) / Blowfly / Sun goes down / Where the rooster crows / Baby loves her gun.

Jun 91. (7") **TWO LOVERS (WAITIN' TO DIE). / KEITH CAN'T READ**

Sep 91. (cd)(c)(lp) **THE BEST OF GREEN ON RED** (compilation)
– Time ain't nothing / Born to fight / Hair of the dog / Keith can't read / Morning blue / This time around / Little things in life / You couldn't get arrested / That's what dreams / Zombie for love / Baby loves her gun.

— added **J.D.FOSTER**

Oct 92. (cd)(c)(lp) **TOO MUCH FUN**
– She's all mine / Frozen in my headlights / Love is insane / Too much fun / The getaway / I owe you one / Man needs woman / Sweetest thing / Thing or two / Hands and knees / Wait and see / Rainy days and Mondays.

– compilations, others, etc. –

Sep 91. Music Club/ US= Rhino; (cd) **THE LITTLE THINGS IN LIFE**

Nov 92. Mau Mau; (cd) **GAS FOOD LODGING / GREEN ON RED** -

Jun 94. China; (cd) **ROCK'N'ROLL DISEASE – THE BEST OF . . .**

DAN STUART also had appeared on album below.

DANNY & DUSTY

DUSTY being **STEVE WYNN of DREAM SYNDICATE.** Augmented by **LONG RYDERS – SYD GRIFFIN, TOM STEVENS** and **STEVE McCARTHY** plus **DENNIS DUCK** of **DREAM SYNDICATE** and **CHRIS CACAVAS** of **GREEN ON RED.**

Nov 85. Zippo; (lp) **THE LOST WEEKEND**
– Down to the bone / The word is out / Song for the dreamers / Miracle mile / Baby, we all gotta go down / The king of the losers / Send me a postcard / Knockin' on Heaven's door.

— DAN was also guest on two of NAKED PREY albums. CHRIS guested on the GIANT SAND album 'VALLEY OF RAIN' in Mar'86. In Sep'90, CHUCK PROPHET issued solo album 'BROTHER ALDO' for 'Fire'. In 1993 for 'China', he issued 'BALINESE DANCER' foolowed by in '95; 'FEAST OF HEARTS'. Meanwhile CACAVAS on 'Normal' released 'PALE BLONDE HELL' (1994) & 'NEW IMPROVED PAIN' (1995).

DAN STUART

Normal Normal

Jul 94. (cd) **RETRONEUVO ("AL PERRY & DAN STUART")**
– Daddy's girl / Hermit of Jerome / I could run / Little slant 6 / Sick and tired / Better than I did / Mamcita / Eyes of a fool / Empty chair / Lone wolf.

Jul 95. (cd) **CANO'WORMS**
– Panhandler / Home after dark / La pasionara / Who needs more / What a day / Expat blues / Waterfall / In Madrid / Filipina stripped / Can't get through / The greatest.

GREEN RIVER (see under ⇒ PEARL JAM)

GREENSLADE

Formed: London, England . . . late '72 by former COLOSSEUM members DAVE GREENSLADE and TONY REEVES. After 2 well-received albums in '73, they made UK Top 40 lists with third lp 'SPYGLASS GUEST'. Disbanded after the advent of punk rock, with DAVE continuing to score TV themes. • **Style:** Keyboard orientated outfit, with progressive leanings similiar to CAMEL or CARAVAN. • **Songwriters:** DAVE scored most.

Recommended: TIME AND TIDE (*6)

DAVE GREENSLADE – keyboards, vibes (ex-COLOSSEUM, ex-CHRIS FARLOWE, etc) / **DAVE LAWSON** – vocals, keyboards, clarinet, flute / **TONY REEVES** – bass (ex-COLOSSEUM) / **ANDREW McCULLOCH** – drums

Warners Mercury

1973. (lp)(c) **GREENSLADE**
– Feathered friends / An English western / Drowning man / Temple song / Melange / What are you doin' to me / Sun dance.

1973. (7") **TEMPLE SONG. / AN ENGLISH WESTERN** -

1973. (lp)(c) **BEDSIDE MANNERS ARE EXTRA**
– Bedside manners are extra / Pilgrim's progress / Time to dream / Drum folk / Sunkissed you're not / Chalkhill.

— added **DAVE CLEMPSON** – guitar (ex-HUMBLE PIE, ex-COLOSSEUM) / **GRAHAM SMITH** – violin (ex-STRING DRIVEN THING, etc.)

Aug 74. (lp)(c) **SPYGLASS GUEST** 34
– Spirit of the dance / Little red fry-up / Rainbow / Siam see saw / Joie de vivre / Red light / Melancholy race / Theme for an imaginary western.

— **MARTIN BRILEY** – bass repl. REEVES who joined CURVED AIR

Apr 75. (lp)(c) **TIME AND TIDE**
– Animal farm / Newsworth / Time / Tide / Catalan / The flattery stakes / Waltz for a fallen idol / The ass's ears / Doldrums / Gangsters.

Jul 75. (7") **CATALAN. / ANIMAL FARM**

Sep 76. (7") **GANGSTERS. / RUBBER FACE, LONELY EYES** -

— Disbanded early 1976.

DAVE GREENSLADE

went solo.

Warners Warners?

Nov 76. (lp)(c) **CACTUS CHOIR**
– Pedro's party / Gettysburg / Swings and roundabouts / Time takes my time / Cactus choir / Forever and ever / Country dance – finale.

— DAVE re-formed GREENSLADE early '77 with **TONY REEVES** – bass / **MICK RODGERS** – vocals, guitar / **JON HISEMAN** – drums (ex-COLOSSEUM) before DAVE went solo again.

E.M.I. not issued

Nov 79. (d-lp) **THE PENTATEUCH OF THE COSMOGONY** -
– Introit / Moondance / Bel tempest / Glass / Three brides / Birds bats and dragonflies / Nursery hymn / The minstrel / Fresco – Kahrinn / Bascarole / Dryland / Forest kingdom / Vivat Regina / Scream but not heard / Mischief – War / Lament for the sea / Miasma generator / Exile / Jubilate / The tiger and the dove. *(re-iss.1994)*

Nov 79. (7") **THE PENTATEUCH. / MISCHIEF – WAR**

— DAVE did no further recordings, and went into further TV work).

Virgin not issued

Apr 94. (cd)(c) **FROM THE DISCWORLD** -
– A-Tuin the turtle / Octane the colour of magic / The luggage / The shades of Ankhmorpork / Wyrd sisters / The unseen university – The librarian / Death / A wizard's staff has a knob on the end / Dryads / Pyramids / Smell gods / Stick and bucket dance / The one horseman and three pedestrians of the apocalypse / Hollywood dreams.

Glenn GREGORY & Claudia BRUCKEN (see under ⇒HEAVEN 17)

GRID

Formed: based London, England . . . Spring 1990, by DAVE BALL, and University graduate RICHARD NORRIS, after meeting in Ibiza about 9 months earlier. They signed to 'East West', and issued Top 60 breakthrough 'FLOATATION'. Both had already signed to 'WEA' in 1988, writings ads for Wow-Ball, T.S.B. and Shell-Oil. Also remixed some tracks for ART OF NOISE, SOFT CELL (remixes obviously), ERASURE, HAPPY MONDAYS, JESUS LOVES YOU, WORLD OF TWIST and The BHUNDU BOYS. • **Style:** Ambient club dance outfit like KRAFTWERK and CAN fused with soul, but influenced by PINK FLOYD's 'Dark Side Of The Moon' era. • **Songwriters:** The duo penned all. • **Trivia:** NORRIS was a former employee at 'Bam Caruso' record label. The GRID guested on comedian VIC REEVES (& MORTIMER)'s version of 'Abide With Me'.

Recommended: EVOLVER (*7)

DAVE BALL – keyboards, synthesizers (ex-SOFT CELL) / **RICHARD NORRIS** – DJ, vocals, keyboards, synthesizers, guitar (ex-PSYCHIC TV) with **SACHA REBECCA SOUTER** – vocals / **COBALT STARGAZER** (of ZODIAC MINDWARP) / **JULIAN STRINGLE** – clarinet / **ANDY MURRAY** – slide guitar / **GUY BARKER** – trumpet / etc

East West East West

Jun 90. (7")(c-s)(12")(cd-s) **FLOATATION (Andrew Weatherall remix). / ('A'-Richard Norris mix)** 60

Sep 90. (7")(c-s)(cd-s) **A BEAT CALLED LOVE. / ('A'original studio)** 64
(12"+=) – Floatation (Olimax and DJ Shapps remix).
(cd-s) – ('A'side) / ('A'club mix) / ('A'dub mix).

Oct 90. (cd)(c)(lp) **ELECTRIC HEAD**
– One giant step / Interference / Are you receiving / Islamatron / The traffic / Driving instructor / A beat called love / The first stroke / Central locking / Intergalactica / Beautiful & profound / This must be Heaven / Machine delay / Doctor Celine /

Typical Waterloo sunset / Strange electric Sun / Floatation. (cd+c+=) – Virtual.

— In Nov 90, they remix STEX (a soul trio, which featured JOHNNY MARR), on their single 'Still Feel The Rain'. A month later, they and TIMOTHY LEARY (yes! that 60's hippy who sanctioned the drug culture 'Tune In, Tune On, Drop Out') issued white label 12" 'ORIGINS OF DANCE'.

Virgin Virgin

Sep 91. (12")(cd-s) **BOOM! (freestyle mix). / ('A'-707 mix) / Bonus BOOM! beats**

Jul 92. (12")(c-s)(cd-s) **FIGURE OF EIGHT. / ('A'mixes)** 50
(12") – ('A'remixes by Todd Terry).

Sep 92. (12")(cd-s) **HEARTBEAT. / BOOM! (space cadet mix)** 72

— next feat. guests **ROBERT FRIPP** – guitar / **COBALT STARGAZER + ZOD** (of ZODIAC MINDWARP) / **RUN RA / DIETER MEIER** – keyboards (of YELLO) / **P.P. ARNOLD** – vocals

Oct 92. (cd)(c)(lp) **FOUR FIVE SIX**
– Face the Sun / Ice machine / Crystal clear / Aquarium / Instrument / Heartbeat / Oh six one / Figure of eight / Boom! / Leave your body / Fire engine red.

Mar 93. (12") **CRYSTAL CLEAR. / ('A'mix)** 27
(c-s+=)(cd-s+=) – (4 more 'A'mixes).

DeCon-struction DeCon-struction?

Oct 93. (7")(c-s) **TEXAS COWBOYS. / RISE** 21
(12"+=)//(cd-s++=) – ('A'mix). / / Cheerleader song.

May 94. (c-s) **SWAMP THING. / ('A'mix)** 3
(12"+=)//(cd-s++=) – ('A'mix). / / ('A'other mix).

Sep 94. (12")(c-s)(cd-s) **ROLLERCOASTER. / ('A'-Justin Robertson mix) / ('A'-Global Communication mix)** 19

Sep 94. (cd)(c)(lp) **EVOLVER** 14
– Wake up / Rollercoaster / Swamp thing / Throb / Rise / Shades of sleep / Higher peaks / Texas cowboys / Spin cycle / Golden dawn.

Nov 94. (c-s) **TEXAS COWBOYS. / ('A'mix)** 17
(12"+=) – (2 more 'A'mixes).
(cd-s++=) – (2 more 'A'mixes; now 6 in total).

Sep 95. (c-s) **DIABLO / ('A'-Acapulco mix)** 32
(12") – ('A'side) / ('A'-Atomic bidet mix) / ('A'-Devil rides out mix) / ('A'-Devil dubs out mix).
(cd-s) – (all 5 mixes).

Sep 95. (cd)(c)(d-lp) **MUSIC FOR DANCING** (remixes) 67
– Floatation (the subsonic Grid mix) / Crystal clear (456 mix) / Boom! (freestyle mix) / Figure of 8 (tribal trance mix) / Rollercoaster (nemesis mix) / Texas cowboys (ricochet mix) / Swamp thing (southern comfort mix) / Crystal clear (prankster prophet mix) / Figure of 8 (Todd's master dub) / Diablo (the Devil rides out mix) / Rollercoaster (the yellow submarine re-take).

Nanci GRIFFITH

Born: 6 Jul'53, Seguin, Texas, USA. Singing from a very age, she struck a deal with local 'BF' label, whom she recorded 'THERE'S A LIGHT BEYOND THESE WOODS' for in 1978. She majored at University of Texas, before she returned to another studio for 1982 follow-up 'POET IN MY WINDOW'. Came to the limelight in 1986, when her LOVE AT THE FIVE AND DIME was US country smash for KATHY METTEA. Her songs FLY BY NIGHT + DADDY SAID were soon covered by country star LYN ANDERSON. • **Style:** Storyteller and folkabilly poet with cute country vox and girl-next-door beauty. The heir-apparant to queen of country EMMYLOU HARRIS. • **Songwriters:** Self-penned except some w /PAT ALGER and covers; ONCE IN A VERY BLUE MOON + LONE STAR STATE OF MIND (Pat Alger /Gene Levine /Fred Koller) / DEADWOOD, SOUTH DAKOTA (Eric Taylor) / ROSEVILLE FAIR (Bill Staines) / FROM A DISTANCE + HEAVEN (Julie Gold) / NEVER MIND (Harlan Howard) / BALLAD OF ROBIN WINTERSMITH (Richard Dobson) / LET IT SHINE ON ME (P.Kennerly) / SING ONE FOR SISTER (R.E.Keen, Jr.) / NICKEL DREAMS (M.McAnally-D.Lowery) / THE SUN, MOON, AND STARS (Vince Bell) / SAN DIEGO SERENADE (Tom Waits). OTHER VOICES, OTHER ROOMS covers album; ACROSS THE GREAT DIVIDE (Kate Wolf) / WOMAN OF THE PHOENIX (Vince Bell) / TECUMSEH VALLEY (Townes Van Zandt) / THREE FLIGHTS UP (Frank Christian) / BOOTS OF SPANISH LEATHER (Bob Dylan) / SPEED OF THE SOUND OF LONELINESS (John Prine) / FROM CLARE TO HERE (Ralph McTell) / CAN'T HELP BUT WONDER WHERE I'M BOUND (Tom Paxton) / DO RE MI (Woody Guthrie) / THIS OLD TOWN (Janis Ian) / COMIN' DOWN IN THE RAIN (Buddy Mondlock) / TEN DEGREES AND GETTING OLD (Gordon Lightfoot) / MORNING SONG FOR SALLY (Jerry Jeff Walker) / NIGHT RIDER'S LAMENT (Michael Burton) / ARE YOU TIRED OF ME DARLING (G.P.Cook & Ralph Roland) / TURN AROUND (Harry Belafonte) / WIMOWEH (c.Paul Campbell). etc. • **Trivia:** She appeared on a CHIEFTAINS Celebration album.

Recommended: THE BEST OF . . . (*8) / ONE FAIR SUMMER EVENING (*7)

NANCI GRIFFITH – vocals, acoustic guitar

not issued B.F.Deal

Feb 78. (lp) **THERE'S A LIGHT BEYOND THESE WOODS** -
– I remember Joe / Alabama soft spoken blues / Michael's song / Song for remembered heroes / West Texas sun / There's a light beyond these woods / Dollar matinee / Montana backroads / John Philipp Griffith. *(US re-iss.1982 on 'Featherbed', re-iss.+c+cd Aug87 on 'Philo') (UK-iss.+c+cd Jul89 on 'MCA')*

not issued Featherbed

May 82. (lp) **POET IN MY WINDOW** -
– Marilyn Monroe – Neon and waltzes / Heart of a miner / Julie Ann / You can't go home again / October reasons / Wheels / Workin' in corners / Trouble with roses / Tonight I think I'm gonna go downtown / Poet in my window. *(re-iss.+c+cd Aug87 on 'Philo') (UK-iss Jul89 on 'MCA')*

not issued Philo

Jul 85. (7") **ONCE IN A VERY BLUE MOON. / ?** -

Dec 85. (lp) **ONCE IN A VERY BLUE MOON** -
– Ghost in the music / Love is a hard waltz / Mary & Omie / Roseville fair / Friend out in the madness / Time alone / I'm not drivin' these wheels / Spin on a red brick floor / Ballad of Richard Wintersmith / If I were a woman you wanted. *(UK-iss.+c+cd Jul89 on 'MCA')*

Nov 86. (7") **LOVE AT THE FIVE AND DIME. / ?** -

Dec 86. (lp)(c) **THE LAST OF TRUE BELIEVERS** -
– The last of the true believers / Love at the Five & Dime / St. Olav's gate / More than a whisper / Banks of the Pontchatrain / Looking for the time / Goin' gone / One of these days / Love's found a shoulder / Fly by night / The wing and the wheel. *(UK-iss.+cd Jun88 on 'Rounder')*

M.C.A. M.C.A.

Apr 87. (7") **LONE STAR STATE OF MIND. / THERE'S A LIGHT BEOND THE WOODS (MARY MARGARET)**

Apr 87. (lp)(c)(cd) **LONE STAR STATE OF MIND**
– Lone star state of mind / Cold hearts – closed minds / From a distance / Beacon Street / Nickel dreams / Sing one for sister / Ford Econoline / Trouble in the fields / Love in a memory / Let it shine on me / There's a light beyond these woods (Mary Margaret).

Jun 87. (7") **LOVE IN A MEMORY. / TROUBLE IN THE FIELDS** -

Jul 87. (7") **FROM A DISTANCE. / SING ONE FOR SISTER**
(cd-s) – ('A'side) / De Lejos / Gulf Coast highway.

Nov 87. (7"ep) **COLD HEARTS**
– Cold hearts, closed minds / Ford Econoline / Lone star state of mind.

Feb 88. (7") **OUTBOUND PLANE. / SO LONG AGO**
(12"+=) – Trouble in the fields.

Mar 88. (lp)(c)(cd) **LITTLE LOVE AFFAIRS** 78
– Anyone can be somebody's fool / I knew love / Never mind / Love wore a halo (back before the war) / So long ago / Gulf Coast highway / Little love affairs / I wish it would rain / Outbound plane / I would change my life / Sweet dreams will come.

Mar 88. (7") **I KNEW LOVE. / SO LONG AGO** -

Apr 88. (7") **I KNEW LOVE. / NEVER MIND** -
(12"+=) – Lone star state of mind.

Sep 88. (7") **ANYONE CAN BE SOMEBODY'S FOOL. / LOVE WORE A HALO (BACK BEFORE THE WAR)** -

Sep 88. (7") **FROM A DISTANCE. / LOVE WORE A HALO (BACK BEFORE THE WAR)** -
(cd-s+=) – There's a light beyond these woods (Mary Margaret).

— with musicians **JAMES HOOKER** – keyboards / **DENNY BIXBY** – bass

Nov 88. (lp)(c)(cd) **ONE FAIR SUMMER EVENING (live)**
– Once in a very blue moon / Looking for the time (workin' girl) / Deadwood, South Dakota / More than a whisper / I would bring you Ireland / Roseville fair / Workin' in corners / Trouble in the fields / The wing and the wheel / From a distance / Love at the Five & Dime / Spin on a red brick floor.

Jun 89. (7") **IT'S A HARD LIFE WHEREVER YOU GO. / FROM A DISTANCE** -

Jul 89. (7") **IT'S A HARD LIFE WHEREVER YOU GO. / GULF COAST HIGHWAY** -
(12"+=)(cd-s+=) – If wishes were changes.

Sep 89. (lp)(c)(cd) **STORMS** 38 99
– I don't wanna talk about love / Drive-in movies and dashboard lights / You made this love a teardrop / Brave companion of the road / Storms / It's a hard life wherever you go / If wishes were changes / Listen to the radio / Leaving the harbor / Radio Fragile.

Sep 89. (7") **I DON'T WANT TO TALK ABOUT LOVE. / DRIVE-IN MOVIES AND DASHBOARD LIGHTS** -

Sep 89. (7") **I DON'T WANT TO TALK ABOUT LOVE. / SPIN ON A RED BRICK FLOOR** -

Nov 89. (7") **YOU MADE THIS LOVE A TEARDROP. / MORE THAN A WHISPER**
(12"+cd+=) – Little love affairs.

Sep 91. (7")(c-s) **LATE NIGHT GRANDE HOTEL. / IT'S JUST ANOTHER MORNING HERE**
(12"+=)(c-s+=)/ /(cd-s++=) – Wooden heart. / / From a distance.

Sep 91. (cd)(c)(lp) **LATE NIGHT GRANDE HOTEL** 40
– It's just another morning here / Late night Grande Hotel / It's too late / Fields of summer / Heaven / The power lines / Hometown streets / Down'n'outer / One blade shy of a sharp edge / The Sun, Moon, and stars / San Diego serenade. *(re-iss.cd Oct95)*

Nov 91. (7")(c-s) **HEAVEN. / DOWN'N'OUTER**
(12"+=) – Tumble and fall.
(cd-s+=) – Love at the Five And Dime (live).

Feb 93. (c-s) **SPEED OF THE SOUND OF LONELINESS. / FROM CLARE TO HERE**
(cd-s+=) – Boots of Spanish leather.

Feb 93. (cd)(c) **OTHER VOICES, OTHER ROOMS** 18 54
– Across the great divide / Woman of the Phoenix / Tecumseh Valley / Three flights up / Boots of Spanish leather / Speed of the sound of loneliness / From Clare to here / Can't help but wonder where I'm bound / Do re mi / This old town / Comin' down in the rain / Ten degrees and getting colder / Morning song to Sally / Night rider's lament / Are you tired of me darling / Turn around / Wimoweh.

May 93. (c-s) **FROM CLARE TO HERE. / CRADLE OF THE INTERSTATE**
(cd-s+=) – De Lejos (From A Distance) (Spanish version) / ('A'extended).

Nov 93. (cd)(c) **THE BEST OF NANCI GRIFFITH** (compilation) 27
– Trouble in the fields / From a distance / Speed of the sound of loneliness / Love at the five and dime / Listen to the radio / Gulf Coast highway / I wish it would rain / Ford Econoline / If wishes were changes / The wing and the wheel / Late night Grande hotel / From Clare to here / It's just another morning here / Trouble and fall / There's a light beyond these woods (Mary Margaret) / Outbound plane / Lone star state of mind / It's a hard life wherever you go / The road to Aberdeen.

M.C.A. Elektra

Sep 94. (cd)(c) **THE FLYER** 20 48
– The flyer / Nobody's angel / Say it isn't so / Southbound train / These days in an open book / Time of inconvenience / Don't forget about me / Always will / Going back to Georgia / Talk to me while I'm listening / Fragile / On Grafton Street / Anything you need but me / Goodnight to a mother's dream / This heart.

Sep 94. (c-s) **ON GRAFTON STREET. / THIS HEART**
(cd-s+=) – These days in an open book.

– compilations, etc. –

1992. M.C.A.; (cd)(c) **INTRODUCING NANCI GRIFFITH**

GRIN (see under ⇒ LOFGREN, Nils)

Clare GROGAN (see under ⇒ ALTERED IMAGES)

GROUNDHOGS

Formed: New Cross, London, England . . . 1963 by TONY McPHEE, who named them after a JOHN LEE HOOKER track. In 1964, they signed with Mickie Most's Anglo-American agency, and soon had debut 45 'SHAKE IT' issued on 'Interphon'. Around the same time, they recorded a live lp 'LIVE AT THE AU-GO CLUB, NEW YORK', with hero HOOKER. They returned to England in 1965, but split Mar'66, only to re-form/split and re-form again in 1968. Just prior to this, McPHEE had teamed up with JOHN DUMMER BLUES BAND, who released 2 singles for 'Mercury'. However with advice from Andrew Lauder of 'United Art', a new GROUNDHOGS was born and a real debut 'SCRATCHING THE SURFACE' was unleashed. In the early 70's, they scored with 2 UK Top 10 lp's 'THANK CHRIST FOR THE BOMB' (which caused controversy while praising nuclear deterrence) and 'SPLIT' (which they always seemed to do, from then on). • **Style:** Chicago-based white blues outfit influenced by HOOKER, MEMPHIS SLIM and MUDDY WATERS. In the early 70's they diversified between heavy blues with some synths being incorporated into tight sound, which was panned by critics. • **Songwriters:** McPHEE penned except; EARLY IN THE MORNING (Sonny Boy Williamson) / STILL A FOOL (Muddy Waters) / etc. • **Trivia:** TONY McPHEE appeared on JOHN DUMMER BAND releases between 1968-69. Around the same time he guested on BIG JOE WILLIAMS recordings. GROUNDHOGS appeared on Top Of The Pops doing 'CHERRY RED' 22 Apr'71.

Recommended: DOCUMENT SERIES PRESENTS . . . THE GROUNDHOGS (*8) / THANK CHRIST FOR THE BOMB (*8) / SPLIT (*7).

TONY McPHEE (b.22 Mar'44, Lincolnshire, England) – guitar, vocals, keyboards / **JOHN CRUIKSHANK** – vocals, mouth harp / **PETE CRUIKSHANK** (b. 2 Jul'45) – bass / **DAVID BOORMAN** – drums / on session **TOM PARKER** – piano repl. BOB HALL

not issued Interphon

Jan 65. (7") **SHAKE IT. / ROCK ME** [-]

JOHN LEE'S GROUNDHOGS

HOOKER – solo blues guitarist **TERRY SLADE** – drums repl. BOORMAN added 3-piece brass section

Planet Planet

Jan 66. (7") **I'LL NEVER FALL IN LOVE AGAIN. / OVER YOU BABY**

— TONY McPHEE joined The TRUTH for a short stint before sessioning for CHAMPION JACK DUPREE on his '66 single 'Get Your Head Happy'

T.S. McPHEE

– solo with **PETE CRUIKSHANK / BOB HALL /** and **VAUGHN REES** – drums / **NEIL SLAVEN** – guitar

Purdah not issued

Aug 66. (7") **SOMEONE TO LOVE ME. / AIN'T GONNA CRY NO MORE**

— This band also backed JO-ANN KELLY. In summer McPHEE formed HERBAL MIXTURE around the same time he joined JOHN DUMMER BLUES BAND on 2 '66 singles.

GROUNDHOGS

re-formed (**TONY McPHEE** and **PETE CRUIKSHANK**) recruited **STEVE RYE** – vocals, mouth harp / **KEN PUSTELNIK** – drums

Liberty World Pac.

Nov 68. (lp) **SCRATCHING THE SURFACE (live)**
– Man trouble / Married men / Early in the morning / Come back baby / You don't love me / Rocking chair / Walkin' blues / No more daggin' / Still a fool. *(re-iss.+cd.Sep88 on 'B.G.O.' +=)* – Oh death / Gasoline / Rock me / Don't pass the hat around.

Dec 68. (7") **YOU DON'T LOVE ME. / STILL A FOOL**

— trimmed to a trio when RYE left due to illness

Liberty Imperial

Jul 69. (lp) **BLUES OBITUARY**
– B.B.D. / Daze of the weak / Times / Mistreated / Expressman / Natchez burning / Light was the day. *(re-iss.'87 on 'B.G.O.')*

Aug 69. (7") **B.D.D. / GASOLINE ('B'side by 'TONY McPHEE')**

Liberty Liberty

May 70. (lp)(c) **THANK CHRIST FOR THE BOMB** [9]
– Strange town / Darkness is no friend / Soldier / Thank Christ for the bomb / Ship on the ocean / Garden / Status people / Rich man, poor man / Eccentric man. *(re-iss.'72 on 'Sunset', re-iss.May86 on 'Fame/EMI') (re-iss.+cd.1989 on 'B.G.O.')*

1970. (7") **ECCENTRIC MAN. / STATUS PEOPLE** [-]

1970. (7") **SHIP ON THE OCEAN. / SOLDIER** [-]

Liberty United Art

Mar 71. (lp)(c) **SPLIT** [5]
– Split (parts 1-4) / Cherry red / A year in the life / Junkman / Groundhog. *(re-iss.Aug80 on 'EMI')*

United Art United Art

Mar 72. (lp)(c) **WHO WILL SAVE THE WORLD? THE MIGHTY GROUNDHOGS**
– Earth is not room enough / Wages of peace / Body in mind / Music is the food of thought / Bog roll blues / Death of the sun / Amazing Grace / The grey maze. *(re-iss.1989 on 'B.G.O.', cd-iss.Apr91 & Jun92)*

— **CLIVE BROOKS** – drums (ex-EGG) repl. PUSTELNIK

Oct 72. (lp)(c) **HOGWASH**
– I love Miss Ogyny / You had a lesson / The ringmaster / 3744 James Road / Sad is the hunter / S'one song / Earth shanty / Mr. Hooker, Sir John. *(re-iss.Apr89 on 'B.G.O.', cd-iss.May91)*

T.S. McPHEE

W.W.A. W.W.A.

Oct 73. (lp)(c) **THE TWO SIDES OF TONY (T.S.) McPHEE** [-]
– Three times seven / All my money, alimoney / Morning's eyes / Dog me, bitch / Take it out / The hurt. *(cd-iss.Dec92 on 'Castle')*

GROUNDHOGS

continue with the above line up

Nov 73. (7") **SAD GO ROUND. / OVER BLUE**

Jun 74. (lp)(c) **SOLID** [31]
– Light my light / Free from all alarm / Sins of the father / Sad go round / Corn cob / Plea sing – plea song / Snow storm / Joker's grave.

Aug 74. (7") **PLEA SING – PLEA SONG. / DOG ME BITCH (by 'TONY McPHEE')**

— **McPHEE** brought back **PETE CRUIKSHANK** – rhythm guitar, / plus new members **DAVE WELLBELOVE** – guitar / **MARTIN KENT** – bass / **MICK COOK** – drums

United Art United Art

Feb 76. (lp)(c) **CROSSCUT SAW**
– Crosscut saw / Promiscuity / Boogie with us / Fulfilment / Live a little lady / Three way split / Mean mistreater / Eleventh hour.

Mar 76. (7") **LIVE A LITTLE LADY. / BOOGIE WITH US**

— **RICK ADAMS** – rhythm guitar repl. PETE

Oct 76. (lp)(c) **BLACK DIAMOND**
– Body talk / Fantasy partner / Live right / Country blues / Your love keeps me alive / Friendzy / Pastoral future / Black diamond.

Oct 76. (7") **PASTORAL FUTURE. / LIVE RIGHT**

— They split '77. **McPHEE** formed **TERRAPLANE,** with **ALAN FISH** – bass / **WILGUR CAMPBELL** – drums They appeared on album CHECKIN' IT OUT by 'BILLY BOY ARNOLD'. (1979 split) **TONY** formed TURBO ('79-'83) with **CLIVE BROOKS** – drums / **PAUL RAVEN.**

TONY McPHEE BAND

with **MICK MIRTON** – drums / **STEVE TOWNER** – bass

T.S. not issued

May 83. (7") **TIME OF ACTION. / BORN TO BE WITH YOU** [-]

GROUNDHOGS

McPHEE with **ALAN FISH** – bass / **MICK MIRTON** – drums

Landslide not issued

May 85. (lp) **RAZOR'S EDGE**
– Razor's edge / I confess / Born to be with you / One more chance / The protector / Superseded / Moving fast, standing still / I want you to love me. *(re-iss.late '89 on 'Conquest')*

— (Early'86) **DAVE THOMPSON** – bass repl. FISH who joined DUMPY'S RUSTY NUTS / **KEN PUSTELNIK** – drums returned to repl. MIRTON who joined DUMPY'S RUSTY NUTS. They gigged several times and appeared on Radio 2's 'Rhythm and Blues'.

— **DAVE ANDERSON** – bass (ex-AMON DUUL II, ex-HAWKWIND) repl. THOMPSON / **MIKE JONES** – drums repl. PUSTELNIK

Demi Monde not issued

May 87. (lp) **BACK AGAINST THE WALL** [-]
– Back against the wall / Not to submission / Blue boar blues / Waiting in shadows / Ain't no slaver / Stick to your guns / In the meantime / 54156. *(cd-iss.Jul87 on 'Magnum')*

— ANDERSON re-formed AMON DUUL II, taking with him McPHEE as guest

TONY McPHEE and the GROUNDHOGS

recorded album below

Demi Monde not issued

Apr 88. (d-lp)(cd) **HOGS ON THE ROAD (live)** [-]
– Express man / Strange town / Eccentric man / 3744 James Road / I want you to love me / Split (part IV) / Soldier / Back against the wall / Garden / Split / Waiting in shadows / Light my light / Me and the Devil / Mistreated / Groundhogs blues / Cherry red.

H.T.D. not issued

Aug 89. (lp)(c)(cd) **NO SURRENDER** [-]
– Razor's edge / 3744 James Road / Superseeded / Light my light / One more chance / Garden / Split pt.2 / Eccentric man / Strange town / Cherry red.

Feb 93. (cd) **FOOLISH PRIDE** [-]
– Foolish pride / Every minute / Devil you know / Masqueradin' / Time after time / On the run / Took me by surprise / Whatever it takes / Been there done that / I'm gonna win.

Dec 94. (cd) **SLIDE T.S. SLIDE (T. S. McPHEE)** [-]

– compilations etc. –

Sep 74. U.A.; (d-lp) **THE BEST OF THE GROUNDHOGS 1969-1972**
(re-iss.Mar88 on 'B.G.O.') (cd-iss.May90 on 'EMI')
Apr 84. Psycho; (d-lp) **HOGGIN' THE STAGE** -
(with free 7")
May 86. Raw Power; (d-lp)(c) **MOVING FAST, STANDING STILL** -
(re-iss. of 'RAZOR'S EDGE' & 'THE TWO SIDES OF T.S. McPHEE', incl. 4 extra 'Immediate' 45's)
Jun 92. B.G.O.; (cd) **CROSSCUT SAW / BLACK DIAMOND** -
Dec 92. Document; (cd)(c) **DOCUMENT SERIES PRESENTS . . . THE GROUNDHOGS** -
– Still a fool / Walking blues / Mistreated / Express man / Eccentric man / Status people / Cherry red / Split (part IV) / Wages of peace / Amazing Grace / Love you Miss Ogyny / Earth shanty / Live a little lady / Boogie with us / Pastoral future / Live right.
Jul 93. H.T.D.; (d-cd) **GROUNDHOG NIGHT – GROUNDHOGS LIVE (live)** -
Sep 94. Windsong; (cd) **BBC RADIO 1 LIVE IN CONCERT** -

TONY McPHEE

also released solo work.
1968. Liberty; (lp) **ME AND THE DEVIL**
(contributed some tracks to this compilation)
1969. Liberty; (lp) **I ASKED FOR WATER, SHE GAVE ME GASOLINE**
— Next credited with **JO-ANN KELLY**
1971. Sunset; (lp) **SAME THING ON THEIR MINDS**

G.T.R. (see under ⇒ HACKETT, Steve)

GUESS WHO

Formed: Winnipeg, Canada . . . as AL & THE SILVERTONES in 1959 by CHAD ALLAN. After a few singles with CHAD as credited leader, they became The GUESS WHO? in 1965, and had US Top 30 success with 45 'SHAKIN' ALL OVER'. CHAD ALLAN soon quit to go to university, and group established themselves once again with BURTON CUMMINGS at the helm. In 1970, another stalward RANDY BACHMAN departed after hefty touring bout, and soon formed BACHMAN-TURNER OVERDRIVE. • **Style:** Powerful hard-rocking outfit, with CUMMINGS vox very similiar to JIM MORRISON. • **Songwriters:** Most by BACHMAN or CUMMINGS, until former's departure. Covered; SHAKIN' ALL OVER (Johnny Kidd & The Pirates) / etc. • **Trivia:** Jack Richardson produced all albums from 1969 onwards. In 1970, they were guests at the Whitehouse for President Nixon.

Recommended: GREATEST HITS OF THE GUESS WHO (*6)

CHAD ALLAN & THE REFLECTIONS

CHAD ALLAN (b.ALLAN KOBEL) – vocals, guitar / **BOB ASHLEY** – piano / **RANDY BACHMAN** (b.27 Sep'43) – guitar / **JIM KALE** (b.11 Aug'43) – bass / **GARY PETERSON** (b.26 May'45) – drums

not issued QualityCAN
Mar 63. (7") **TRIBUTE TO BUDDY HOLLY. / ?** -
— (Above initially released in 1962 'Canadian-American' label)
Dec 63. (7") **SHY GUY. / ?** -

CHAD ALLAN & THE ORIGINAL REFLECTIONS

Jun 64. (7") **A SHOT OF RHYTHM & BLUES. / ?** -

CHAD ALLAN & THE EXPRESSIONS

due to their label 'Quality' doing silly publicity stunt, they were credited on following 45 as

GUESS WHO?

Pye Inter . . . Scepter
May 65. (7") **SHAKIN' ALL OVER. / TILL WE KISSED** - 22
Jul 65. (lp) **SHAKIN' ALL OVER (by "GUESS WHO? CHAD ALLAN & THE EXPRESSIONS")** -
– Shakin' all over / Seven long years / And she's mine / Clock in the wall / Baby's birthday / I want you to love me / I'd rather be alone / I've been away / Turn around and walk away. *(US re-iss.1968 under name "GUESS WHO")*
— **BURTON CUMMINGS** (b.31 Dec'47) – vocals, keyboards repl. ASHLEY

GUESS WHO

name adopted as their own.
1965. (7") **HEY HO, WHAT YOU DO TO ME. / GOODNIGHT, GOODNIGHT** -
1965. (7") **HURTING EACH OTHER. / BABY'S BIRTHDAY** -
1966. (7") **BABY FEELIN'. / BELIEVE IN ME** -
1966. (7") **CLOCK ON THE WALL. / ONE DAY** -
— A quartet, when ALLAN departed. (He was briefly subbed by BRUCE DECKER)
King Amy
Oct 66. (7") **SHE'S ALL MINE. / ALL RIGHT** -
Dec 66. (7") **HIS GIRL. / IT'S MY PRIDE** 45
Fontana Quality
May 67. (7") **THIS TIME LONG AGO. / THERE'S NO GETTING AWAY FROM YOU**
Sep 67. (7") **MISS FELICITY GREY. / FLYING ON THE GROUND IS WRONG**
— In 1968, ALLAN returned, but he left as they signed to 'Nimbus 6' in Canada.
R.C.A. R.C.A.
Apr 69. (7") **THESE EYES. / LIGHTFOOT** 6
May 69. (lp) **WHEATFIELD SOUL** 45
– These eyes / Pink wine sparkles in the glass / I found her in a star / Friends of mine / When you touch me / A Wednesday in your garden / Lightfoot / Love and a yellow rose / Maple fudge / We're coming to dinner.
Jul 69. (7") **LAUGHING. / UNDUN** 10 22
Oct 69. (7") **FRIENDS OF MINE. / (part 2)** -
Nov 69. (lp) **CANNED WHEAT PACKED BY THE GUESS WHO** 91 Sep 69
– No time / Minstrel boy / Laughing / Undun / 6 a.m. or nearer / Old Joe / Of a dropping pin / Key fair warning.
Feb 70. (7") **NO TIME. / PROPER STRANGER** 5 Dec 69
Feb 70. (lp)(c) **AMERICAN WOMAN** 9
– American woman / No time / Talisman / No sugar tonight / New Mother Nature / 969 (the oldies man) / When friends fall out / 8:15 / Proper stranger / Humpty's blues / American woman – epilogue.
Mar 70. (7") **AMERICAN WOMAN. / NO SUGAR TONIGHT** 19 1
— **CUMMINGS, PETERSON & KALE** brought in newcomers **KURT WINTER** – guitar (ex-BROTHER) + **GREG LESKIW** – guitar (ex-WILD RICE) repl. RANDY BACHMAN who formed BRAVE BELT, later BACHMAN-TURNER OVERDRIVE.
Jul 70. (7") **HAND ME DOWN WORLD. / RUNNIN' DOWN THE STREET** 17
Oct 70. (7") **SHARE THE LAND. / BUS RIDER** 10
Jan 71. (lp)(c) **SHARE THE LAND** 14 Oct 70
– Bus rider / Do you miss me darlin' / Hand me down world / Moan for you Joe / Share the land / Hang on to your life / Coming down off the money bag – Song of the dog / Three more days.
Mar 71. (7") **HANG ON TO YOUR LIFE. / DO YOU MISS ME DARLIN'** 43 Jan 71
Jun 71. (7") **ALBERT FLASHER. / BROKEN** 29 55 Apr 71
(re-iss.Mar73)
Aug 71. (7") **RAIN DANCE. / ONE DIVIDED** - 19
Sep 71. (lp)(c) **SO LONG, BANNATYNE** 52 Aug 71
– Rain dance / She might have been a nice girl / Goin' a little crazy / Fiddlin' / Pain train / One divided / Grey day / Life in the bloodstream / One man army / Sour suite / So long, Bannatyne.
Nov 71. (7") **SOUR SUITE. / LIFE IN THE BLOODSTREAM** - 50
Mar 72. (7") **HEARTBROKEN BOPPER. / ARRIVEDERCI GIRL** - 47
Mar 72. (lp)(c) **ROCKIN'** 79
– Heartbroken bopper / Get your ribbons on / Smoke big factory / Arrivederci girl / Guns, guns, guns / Running bear / Back to the city / Your Nashville sneakers / Herbert's a loser / Sea of love – Heaven only moved once yesterday / Don't you want me.
May 72. (7") **GUNS, GUNS, GUNS. / HEAVEN ONLY MOVED ONCE YESTERDAY** -
— **DON McDOUGALL** – guitar repl. LESKIW who formed MOOD JGA JGA
Sep 72. (7") **RUNNIN' BACK TO SASKATOON. / NEW MOTHER NATURE** -
Sep 72. (lp)(c) **LIVE AT THE PARAMOUNT (live at Seattle)** 39 Aug 72
– Albert Fletcher / New Mother Nature / Glace Bay blues / American woman / Runnin' back to Saskatoon / Pain train / Truckin' off across the sky.
— **BILL WALLACE** – bass (ex-BROTHER) repl. KALE who formed own band
Feb 73. (lp)(c) **ARTIFICIAL PARADISE** Jan 73
– Bye bye baby / Samantha's living room / Rock and roller steam / Follow your daughter home / Those showbiz shoes / All hashed out / Orly / Lost and found town / Hamba gahle-usalang gahle / The watcher.
Feb 73. (7") **THE WATCHER. / ORLY** -
Apr 73. (7") **FOLLOW YOUR DAUGHTER HOME. / BYE BYE BABY** Jan 73
May 73. (7") **GLAMOUR BOY. / LIE DOWN** -
Aug 73. (lp)(c) **£10** Jan 73
– Take it off my shoulders / Musicione / Miss Frizzy / Glamour boy / Self pity / Lie down / Cardboard empire / Just let me sing.
Apr 74. (7") **STAR BABY. / MUSICIONE** 39 Feb 74
May 74. (lp)(c) **ROAD FOOD** 60
– Star baby / Attila's blues / Straight out / Don't you want me / One way road to Hell / Clap for the Wolfman / Pleasin' for a reason / Road food / Ballad of the last five years.
Jul 74. (7") **CLAP FOR THE WOLFMAN. / ROAD FOOD** 6
— **DOMENIC TROIANO** – guitar (ex-JAMES GANG) repl. WINTER and McDOUGALL
Feb 75. (7") **DANCIN' FOOL. / SEEMS LIKE I CAN'T LIVE WITHOUT YOU** 28 Nov 74
Feb 75. (lp)(c) **FLAVOURS** 48 Jan 75
– Dancin' fool / Hoe down time / Nobody knows his name / Diggin' yourself / Seems like I can't live without you / Dirty eye / Loves me like a brother / Long gone.
May 75. (7") **HOE DOWN TIME. / LOVES ME LIKE A BROTHER** -
Aug 75. (lp)(c) **POWER IN THE MUSIC** 87 Jul 75
– Down and out woman / Women / When the band was singin' "Shakin' All Over" / Dreams / Rich world – poor world / Shopping bag lady / Coors for Sunday / Rosanne / Power in the music.
Aug 75. (7") **DREAMS. / ROSANNE** -
Nov 75. (7") **WHEN THE BAND WAS SINGIN' "SHAKIN' ALL OVER". / WOMEN** -
— Disbanded Autumn 1975. TROIANO went solo and PETERSON formed DELPHIA.

BURTON CUMMINGS

went solo.

Portrait | Portrait

Oct 76. (7") **STAND TALL. / ?** [-] [10]

Dec 76. (lp)(c) **BURTON CUMMINGS** [ ] [30] Nov 76
– I'm scared / Your back yard / Nothing rhymed / That's enough / Is it really right / Stand tall / Niki hokey / Sugartime flashback joys / Burch magic / You ain't seen nothin' yet

Apr 77. (7") **I'M SCARED. / SUGARTIME FLASHBACK JOYS** [ ] [61]

Jun 77. (7") **NEVER HAD A LADY BEFORE. / TIMELESS LOVE** [-] [ ]

Sep 77. (7") **MY OWN WAY TO ROCK. / SONG FOR HIM** [ ] [74]

Sep 77. (lp)(c) **MY OWN WAY TO ROCK** [ ] [51] Jul 77
– Never had a lady before / Come on by / Try to find another man / Gotta find another way / My own way to rock / Charlemagne / Timeless love / Framed / A song for him.

Jul 78. (7") **BREAK IT TO THEM GENTLY. / ROLL WITH THE PUNCHES** [-] [85]

Sep 78. (7") **WHEN A MAN LOVES A WOMAN. / ROLL WITH THE PUNCHES** [ ] [ ]

Sep 78. (lp)(c) **DREAM OF A CHILD** [ ] [ ]
– Break it to them gently / Hold on I'm coming / I will play a rhapsody / Wait by the water / When a man loves a woman / Shiny stockings / Guns guns guns / Takes a fool to love a fool / Meaning so much / It all comes together / Roll with the punches / Dream of a child.

Nov 78. (7") **I WILL PLAY A RHAPSODY. / TAKES A FOOL TO LOVE A FOOL** [-] [ ]

1980. (7") **STAND TALL. / TAKES A FOOL TO LOVE A FOOL** [-] [ ]

not issued | Alfa

Oct 81. (7") **YOU SAVED MY SOUL. / ?** [-] [37]

Oct 81. (lp)(c) **SWEET SWEET** [-] [ ]
– You saved my soul / Real good / Mother keep your daughters in / Something old, something new / Nothin' wrong with the road / Gettin' my daddy's car / Bad news / Someone to lean on / Sweet sweet / Firefly.

— CUMMINGS later guested on famine Various 1985 under NORTHERN LIGHTS.

GUESS WHO

had already re-formed in 1978 without CUMMINGS. Line-up **CHAD ALLAN** – vocals / **JIM KALE** – bass / **DON McDOUGALL** – guitar / plus **DAVID INGLIS** – guitar / **VINCE MASTERS** – drums / **DAVIS PARASZ** – horns

not issued | Elektra

1978. (7") **TRULY GOOD SONG. / EVERY DAY'S A LOVELY DAY** [-] [ ]

not issued | Hilltak

Jan 79. (lp)(c) **ALL THIS FOR A SONG** [-] [ ]
– C'mon little mama / That's the moment / It's getting pretty bad / Raisin' hell on the prairies / Moon wave maker / Taxman / Sharin' love / Sweet young thing / All this for a song / Plastic Paradise.

Jan 79. (7") **C'MON LITTLE MAMA. / MOON WAVE MAKER** [-] [ ]

Apr 79. (7") **SWEET YOUNG THING. / IT'S GETTING PRETTY BAD** [-] [ ]

— Disbanded again, soon after above release.

— The late 60's line-up reformed (**CUMMINGS, BACHMAN, KALE + PETERSON**)

not issued | Ready

1984. (lp) **TOGETHER AGAIN (live)** [-] [ ]
– What's gonna happen to the kids / Let's watch the Sun go down / No time / Those eyes / Creepin' peepin' baby blues / C'mon and dance / Undun / Love grows / No sugar tonight – New mother nature / American woman.

– compilations, others, etc. –

Apr 71. R.C.A.; (lp)(c) **THE BEST OF THE GUESS WHO** [ ] [12]
– These eyes / Laughing / Undun / No time / American woman / No sugar tonight / New Mother Nature / Hand me down world / Bus rider / Share the land / Do you miss me darlin' / Hang on to your life.

Jan 74. R.C.A.; (lp)(c) **THE BEST OF THE GUESS WHO, VOLUME II** [ ] [ ]

1976. R.C.A.; (lp) **THE WAY THEY WERE** [-] [ ]

May 77. R.C.A.; (lp)(c) **GREATEST HITS OF THE GUESS WHO** [ ] [ ] Apr 77
– These eyes / Laughing / Undun / No time / American woman / Hand me down world / Stay baby / Clap for the Wolfman / Dancin' fool / Glamour boy / Albert Flasher / When the band was singing "Shaking All Over".

1977. R.C.A.; (7") **SILVERBIRD. / RUNNIN' DOWN THE STREET** [-] [ ]

1987. Old Gold; (7") **AMERICAN WOMAN. / (other artist)** [ ] [-]

1973. Pride; (lp) **HISTORY OF THE GUESS WHO** [-] [ ]

1974. Trip; (d-lp) **BORN IN CANADA (1965-68)** [-] [ ]

GULLIVER (see under ⇒ HALL, Daryl)

GUN

Formed: Glasgow, Scotland . . . 1986 by BABY STAFFORD and MARK RANKIN. Were originally called HAIRSPRAY TO HEAVEN then PHOBIA, before opting simply for GUN. Late 1987, they signed to 'A&M', and soon made UK Top 50 lists with debut 1989 album 'TAKING ON THE WORLD'. • **Style:** Hard'n'heavy rock act, influenced by AEROSMITH or BON JOVI. • **Songwriters:** RANKIN-GIZZI-GIZZI except; LET'S GO CRAZY (Prince) / DON'T BELIEVE A WORD (Thin Lizzy) / WORD UP (Cameo) / CHILDREN OF THE REVOLUTION (T.Rex) / SUFFRAGETTE CITY (David Bowie) / PANIC (Smiths) / KILLING IN THE NAME (Rage Against The Machine) / SO LONELY (Police) / ARE YOU GONNA GO MY WAY (Lenny Kravitz). • **Trivia:** SHARLEEN SPITERI of TEXAS guested on their debut album.

Recommended: TAKING ON THE WORLD (*7).

MARK RANKIN – vocals / **BABY STAFFORD** – guitar / **GUILIANO GIZZI** – guitar / **DANTE GIZZI** – bass / **SCOTT SHIELDS** – drums

A & M | A & M

May 89. (lp)(c)(cd) **TAKING ON THE WORLD** [44] [ ]
– Better days / The feeling within / Inside out / Shame on you / Money (everybody loves her) / Taking on the world / Shame / Can't get any lower / Something to believe in / Girls in love / I will be waiting. *(re-iss.cd Mar95)*

Jun 89. (7") **BETTER DAYS. / WHEN YOU LOVE SOMEBODY** [33] [ ]
(12"+=)(cd-s+=) – Coming home.

Aug 89. (7") **MONEY (EVERYBODY LOVES HER). / PRIME TIME** [73] [ ]
(12"+=)(cd-s+=) – Dance.

Oct 89. (7")(c-s)(7"pic-d) **INSIDE OUT. / BACK TO WHERE WE STARTED** [57] [ ]
(12"+=)(cd-s+=) – Where do we go?

Jan 90. (7") **TAKING ON THE WORLD. / DON'T BELIEVE A WORD** [50] [ ]
(12"+=)(cd-s+=) – Better days (extended).

Jun 90. (7")(c-s) **SHAME ON YOU. / BETTER DAYS (live)** [33] [ ]
(12"+=)(cd-s+=) – Money (everybody loves her).

— **ALEX DICKSON** – guitar repl. BABY STAFFORD

Mar 92. (7")(c-s) **STEAL YOUR FIRE. / DON'T BLAME ME** [24] [ ]
(12"+=)(cd-s+=) – Burning down the house / Reach out for love.

Apr 92. (7")(c-s) **HIGHER GROUND. / RUN** [48] [ ]
(12"+=)(pic-cd-s+=) – One desire.

Apr 92. (cd)(c)(lp) **GALLUS** [14] [ ]
– Steal your fire / Money to burn / Long road / Welcome to the real world / Higher ground / Borrowed time / Freedom / Won't break down / Reach out for love / Watching the world go by. *(re-iss.cd/c Mar95)*

Jun 92. (7")(c-s) **WELCOME TO THE REAL WORLD. / STEAL YOUR FIRE (live)** [43] [ ]
(12"pic-d+=) – Standing in your shadow.
(cd-s+=) – Better days / Shame on you (acoustic).

— **MARK KERR** – drums repl. SHIELDS + DICKSON

Jul 94. (12")(c-s) **WORD UP. / ('A'mixes)** [8] [ ]
(cd-s) – ('A'side) / Stay forever / The man I used to be / Stranger.

Aug 94. (cd)(c)(lp) **SWAGGER** [5] [ ]
– Stand in line / Find my way / Word up / Don't say it's over / The only one / Something worthwhile / Seems like I'm losing you / Crying over you / One reason / Vicious heart.

Sep 94. (7")(c-s) **DON'T SAY IT'S OVER. / MONEY** [19] [ ]
(cd-s) – ('A'side) / Steal your fire / Better days / Shame on you.

Feb 95. (c-s) **THE ONLY ONE / WORD UP (mix) / WORD UP (Tinman remix)** [29] [ ]
(12"+=) – Inside out – So lonely.
(cd-s++=) – Time.
(cd-s) – ('A'side) / Killing in the name / Panic / Are you gonna go my way.

Apr 95. (cd-ep) **SOMETHING WORTHWHILE / SUFFRAGETTE CITY / CHILDREN OF THE REVOLUTION / WORD UP** [39] [ ]
(cd-ep) – ('A'side) / One reason / ('A'-Mac attack mix) / ('A'-Priory mix).
(12"pic-d-ep) – ('A'side) / ('A'-Mac attack mix) / ('A'-King Dong mix) / ('A'-Breakdown mix).

GUN CLUB

Formed: Los Angeles, California, USA . . . 1980 by ex 'Splash' magazine editor JEFFREY LEE PIERCE and KID CONGO. They changed name from CREEPING DEATH, at the request of KEITH MORRIS of CIRCLE JERKS. In 1981, they unearthed debut lp 'FIRE OF LOVE', which was issued by own 'Ruby' label, and produced by CHRIS D. (Of FLEASHEATERS). It saw light in UK on 'Beggar's B.', and promted CHRIS STEIN's (Blondie) label 'Animal' label to sign them in '82. A couple of promising lp's followed, but after PIERCE's solo jaunt and group reformation in the mid-80's, they drifted to UK indie scene. In '87, they signed to soon-to-be defunct 'Red Rhino', and regained credibility with ROBIN GUTHRIE (Cocteau Twins) who produced album 'MOTHER JUNO'. • **Style:** Bluesy punk rock, in the mould of contemporaries The CRAMPS. • **Trivia:** The howling J.L.PIERCE was once head of the BLONDIE fan club, thus his association with STEIN. • **Songwriters:** PIERCE except; PREACHIN' THE BLUES + COOL DRINK OF WATER (Robert Johnson) / RUN THROUGH THE JUNGLE (Creedence Clearwater Revival) / etc.

Recommended: FIRE OF LOVE (*7) / MIAMI (*6) / MOTHER JUNO (*6)

JEFFREY LEE PIERCE – vocals, guitar / **WARD DOTSON** – lead guitar repl. KID CONGO POWERS who joined The CRAMPS / **ROB RITTER** – bass / **TERRY GRAHAM** – drums (ex-BAGS)

Beggar's B. | Ruby

May 82. (lp)(c) **FIRE OF LOVE** [ ] [ ] Dec 81
– Goodbye Johnny / Preachin' the blues / Jack on fire / She's like heroin to me / Ghost on the highway / Black train / Sex beat / Free spirit / Promise me / Cool drink of water / For the love of Ivy. *(re-iss.blue-lp Jan86 on 'New Rose')*

Jul 82. (7") **SEX BEAT. / GHOST ON THE HIGHWAY** [ ] [ ]

Chrysalis | Animal

Aug 82. (7") **WALKING WITH THE BEAST. / FIRE OF LOVE** [ ] [ ]

Sep 82. (lp)(c) **MIAMI** [ ] [ ]
– A devil in the woods / Carry home / Run through the jungle / Brothers and sisters / Texas serenade / Watermelon man / Like calling up thunder / Bad Indian / Fire of love / John Hardy / Sleeping in Blood city / Mother of Earth.

— **KID CONGO POWERS** (b.BRIAN TRISTIAN) – guitar returned to repl. RITTER + DOTSON (latter formed PONTIAC BROTHERS)

Feb 84. A.B.C.; (lp)(c) **THE BIRTH, THE DEATH, THE GHOST (live 1983)** [ ] [-]
– Bo Diddley's a gunslinger / Railroad Bill / Seven miles with the Devil / Preachin'

the blues / Goodbye Johnny / Black train / Walking with the beast / Bad mood / Not that much / Going down the red river / Willie Brown / Field Holler / Sex beat.

— **PIERCE** recruited new members

JIM DUCKWORTH – lead guitar (ex-TAV FALCO'S PANTHER BURNS) repl. KID CONGO who later formed FUR BIBLE / **DEE POP** – drum (ex-BUSH TETRAS) repl. TERRY GRAHAM

Apr 83. (7") **DEATH PARTY. / HOUSE OF HIGHLAND AVENUE / THE LIE**
(12+=) – Light of the world / Come back Jim.

— added **PATRICIA MORRISON** – bass

Jun 84. (lp)(c) **THE LAS VEGAS STORY**
– The Las Vegas story / Walking with the beast / Eternally is here / The stranger in our town / My dreams / The creator was a master plan / My man's gone now / Bad America / Moonlight hotel / Give up the Sun.

— Split late 1984. PATRICIA joined FUR BIBLE and later went to SISTERS OF MERCY

JEFFREY LEE PIERCE

went solo with **MURRAY MITCHELL** – guitar / **JOHN McKENZIE** – bass / **ANDY ANDERSON** – drums

Statik | not issued

Apr 85. (lp)(c) **WILDWEED** | -
– Love and desperation / Sex killer / Cleopatra dreams on / From temptation to you / Sensitivity / Hey Juana / Love Circus / Wildweed / From temptation to you / The midnight promise. *(cd-iss Jun 89 +=)* – The Fertility Goddess / Portrait of an artist in Hell / Love & Desperation (long) / Chris and Maggie meet Blind Willie McTell at . . .

— **PIERCE** brought in **HIROMI** – guitar / **DEAN DENNIS** – bass / **NICK SANDERSON** – drums (both ex-CLOCKDVA)

Aug 85. (7") **LOVE AND DESPERATION. / THE FERTILITY GODDESS** | -
(12"+=) – Portrait of an artist in Hell.

Nov 85. (12"ep) **FLAMINGO (part 1 & 2). / GET AWAY / FIRE / NO MORE FIRE / LOVE AND DESPERATION** | -

GUN CLUB

were reformed by **PIERCE, KID CONGO** and **SANDERSON plus ROMI MORI** – bass

Red Rhino | Solid

Oct 87. (lp)(c)(cd) **MOTHER JUNO**
– Breaking hands / Araby / Hearts / My cousin Kim / Port of souls / Bill Bailey / Thunderhead / Lupita screams / Yellow eyes.

Mar 88. (12"m) **BREAKING HANDS. / CRABDANCE / NO-BODY'S CITY** | -

— split again, KID CONGO went solo, but last line-up soon reformed.

Fire | Solid

Sep 90. (12"ep)(cd-ep) **THE GREAT DIVIDE. / CRABDANCE / ST JOHN'S DIVINE (part 2)** | -

Oct 90. (cd)(c)(lp) **PASTORAL HIDE AND SEEK**
– Humanesque / The straits of love and hate / Emily's changed / I hear your heart singing / St.John's divine / The great divide / Another country's young / Flowing / Temptation and I.

New Rose | Solid

Oct 91. (cd)(d-lp) **DIVINITY (3 live / 4 studio)** | - France
– Sorrow knows / Richard Speck / Keys to the kingdom / Black hole / Yellow eyes (live) / Hearts (live) / Fire of love (live). (cd+=) – St.John's divine

– compilations etc. –

Oct 84. Lolita; (lp) **SEX BEAT '81 (live)** - |
Jul 85. Dojo; (lp) **TWO SIDES OF THE BEAST** | -
(re-iss.Apr86)
Nov 85. Eva; (lp) **LOVE SUPREME (live '82)** - |
Dec 85. Roadrunner; (lp) **DANCE KALINDA BOOM (live)** - | -
May 89. New Rose; (cd-ep) **SEX BEAT / FOR THE LOVE OF IVY / BLACK TRAIN** - | -
Aug 92 Triple X; (cd) **IN EXILE**
1992 Solid; (cd) **AHMED'S WILD DREAM (live)**

JEFFREY LEE PIERCE

May 92. Solid; (cd) **RAMBLIN' JEFFREY LEE & CYPRESS GROVE WITH WILLIE LOVE**
– Goin' down / Pony blues / Future blues / Long long gone / Bad luck and trouble / Alabama blues / Good times / Stranger in my heart / Go tell the mountain / Moanin' in the moonlight / Hardtime / Killin' floor blues

GUNS N' ROSES

Formed: Los Angeles, California, USA . . . early 1985 by AXL ROSE, IZZY STRADLIN and moonlighting L.A.GUNS member TRACII GUNS, who was soon to return to said outfit. The new GUNS N' ROSES were soon found by SLASH, DUFF and STEVE, who begin 'hell' tour of the US. In the summer of '86, they unleashed debut recording, a 7"ep entitled 'LIVE ?!*' LIKE A SUICIDE', which quickly sold its limited 10,000 copies. It was soon issued by 'Geffen', who had just recently signed them. After failing with debut single 'IT'S SO EASY' in Jul'87, they released debut album 'APPETITE FOR DE-STRUCTION', which caused controversy due to its robot/rape sleeve cover. With constant tours between US and UK going great, it made steady progress on its way to US No.1 a year later! (it made UK No.5 a year after that!). This was aided by a US chart topping hit single 'SWEET CHILD O' MINE'. Hit singles taken from the album, continued to roll out, and they finally released official long-playing follow up in Sep'91. It came out as 2 double-lp's 'USE YOUR ILLUSION I' & 'USE YOUR ILLUSION II', which contained over 2 hours of new material. • **Style:** Raw heavy-metal rock, that exploded with menacing power, through the bleeding, always feeling vox of AXL, and the razor-sharp guitar-licks of SLASH. They balanced this with an acoustic ballad side, that diversed away from AXL's acidic voice, which was slated by his offendees; the blacks and gays. The group have always maintained their love of drink and drugs throughout turbulent and at times violent career. • **Songwriters:** All written by AXL except; MAMA KIN (Aerosmith) / NICE BOYS DON'T PLAY ROCK'N'ROLL (Rose Tattoo) / WHOLE LOTTA ROSIE (Ac-Dc) / KNOCKIN' ON HEAVEN'S DOOR (Bob Dylan) / LIVE AND LET DIE (Paul McCartney & Wings). Punk covers album; SINCE I DON'T HAVE YOU (Skyliners) / NEW ROSE (Damned) / DOWN ON THE FARM (UK Subs) / HUMAN BEING (New York Dolls) / RAW POWER (Iggy & The Stooges) / AIN'T IT FUN (Dead Boys) / BUICK MAKANE (T.Rex) / HAIR OF THE DOG (Nazareth) / ATTITUDE (Misfits) / BLACK LEATHER (Sex Pistols) / YOU CAN'T PUT YOUR ARMS AROUND A MEMORY (Johnny Thunders) / I DON'T CARE ABOUT YOU (Fear) / WHAT'S YOUR GAME! (Charles Manson, yes that one!). McKAGAN covered CRACKED ACTOR (David Bowie) • **Trivia:** On 28 Apr'90, AXL was married to ERIN, daughter of DON EVERLY (Brothers), but a couple of months later, they counterfiled for divorce. BAILEY was AXL's step-father's surname, and he found out real surname ROSE in the 80's.

Recommended: APPETITE FOR DESTRUCTION (*8) / G'N'R LIES (*5) / USE YOUR ILLUSION I (*7) / USE YOUR ILLUSION II (*6).

W. AXL ROSE (b. WILLIAM BAILEY, 6 Feb'62, Lafayette, Indiana, USA) – vocals / **SLASH** (b. SAUL HUDSON, 23 Jul'65, Stoke-On-Trent, England) – lead guitar / **IZZY STRADLIN** (b.JEFFREY ISBELL, 8 Apr'62) – guitar / **DUFF McKAGAN** (b. MICHAEL, 5 Feb'64, Seattle) – bass / **STEVE ADLER** (b.22 Jan'65, Ohio) – drums repl. ROB to L.A. GUNS again.

not issued | Uzi Suicide

Aug 86. (7"ep) **LIVE ?!*' LIKE A SUICIDE** - |
– Mama kin / Reckless life / Move to the city / Nice boys (don't play rock'n'roll). *(US re-iss.Jan87 on 'Geffen')*

Geffen | Geffen

Jun 87. (7") **IT'S SO EASY. / MR. BROWNSTONE**
(12"+=)(12"pic-d+=) – Shadow of your love / Move to the city.

Aug 87. (lp)(c)(cd) **APPETITE FOR DESTRUCTION** 68 | 1
– Welcome to the jungle / It's so easy / Nightrain / Out ta get me / Mr. Brownstone / Paradise city / My Michelle / Think about you / Sweet child o' mine / You're crazy / Anything goes / Rocket queen. *(peaked UK-No.5 in 1989) (re-iss.Nov90) (re-iss.cd/c Oct95)*

Sep 87. (7") **WELCOME TO THE JUNGLE. / WHOLE LOTTA ROSIE (live)** 67 |
(12"+=)(12"pic-d+=) – It's so easy (live) / Knockin' on Heaven's door (live).

Aug 88. (7") **SWEET CHILD O' MINE. / OUT TA GET ME** 24 | 1 Jun 88
(12"+=) – Rocket queen.

Oct 88. (7") **WELCOME TO THE JUNGLE. / NIGHTRAIN** 24 | 7
(12"+=)(12"pic-d+=) – You're crazy. *(re-iss.Apr89)*

Dec 88. (lp)(c)(cd) **G'N'R LIES (live)** 22 | 2
– Reckless life / Nice boys (don't play rock'n'roll) / Move to the city / Mama kin / Patience / I used to love her / You're crazy / One in a million. *(re-iss.Nov90) (re-iss.cd/c Oct95)*

Mar 89. (7")(7"sha-clear)(7"white pic-d) **PARADISE CITY. / I USED TO LOVE HER** 6 | 5 Jan 89
(12"+=) – Anything goes.
(c-s+=)(cd-s+=) – Sweet child o'mine.

May 89. (7")(12") **SWEET CHILD O'MINE. / OUT TO GET ME (live)** 6 | -
(3"cd-s+=) – Whole lotta Rosie (live) / It's so easy (live).

Jun 89. (7")(c-s) **PATIENCE. / ROCKET QUEEN** 10 | 4 Apr89
(12"+=)(3"cd-s+=) – (Axl Rose interview).

Aug 89. (7")(c-s)(7"sha-pic-d) **NIGHTTRAIN. / RECKLESS LIFE** 17 | Jul 89
(12"+=)(cd-s+=) – Knockin' on Heaven's door (live '87).

— (Aug90) **MATT SORUM** – drums (ex-CULT) repl. ADAM MARPLES (ex-SEA HAGS) who repl. ADLER due to bouts of drunkeness.

Jul 91. (7")(12")(c-s)(cd-s)(12"clear-pic-d) **YOU COULD BE MINE. / CIVIL WAR** 3 | 29

Sep 91. (cd)(c)(d-lp) **USE YOUR ILLUSION I** 2 | 2
– Right next door to Hell / Dust'n'bones / Live and let die / Don't cry (original) / Perfect crime / You ain't the first / Bad obsession / Back off bitch / Double talkin' jive / November rain / The garden / Garden of Eden / Don't damn me / Bad apples / Dead horse / Coma.

Sep 91. (cd)(c)(d-lp) **USE YOUR ILLUSION II** 1 | 1
– Civil war / 14 years / Yesterdays / Knockin' on Heaven's door / Get in the ring / Shotgun blues / Breakdown / Pretty tied up / Locomotive / So fine / Estranged / You could be mine / Don't cry (alt.lyrics) / My world.

Sep 91. (7") **DON'T CRY (original). / DON'T CRY (alt.lyrics)** 8 | 10
(12"+=)(cd-s+=) – ('A'demo).

Dec 91. (7")(12")(c-s) **LIVE AND LET DIE. / ('A' live)** 5 | 33
(cd-s+=) – Shadow of your love.

— (Sep91) **DAVID NAVARRO** – guitar (of JANE'S ADDICTION) repl. IZZY who walked out on tour. **GILBY CLARKE** – guitar finally repl. IZZY who went solo

Feb 92. (7")(c-s) **NOVEMBER RAIN. / SWEET CHILD O'MINE (live)** 4 | 3 Jun 92
(12"+=)(pic-cd-s+=) – Patience.

May 92. (7")(12")(c-s)(cd-s) **KNOCKIN' ON HEAVEN'S DOOR (live '92 at Freddie Mercury tribute). / ('A'studio)** 2 |

Oct 92. (7")(c-s) **YESTERDAYS. / NOVEMBER RAIN** 8 |
(12"pic-d+=) – ('A'live version) / Knockin' on Heaven's door (live 87)

May 93. (cd-ep) **CIVIL WAR EP** 11 |
– Civil war / Garden of Eden / Dead horse / (interview with Slash).

SLASH
BORN TO BE AMERICAN

Nov 93. (c-s) **AIN'T IT FUN. / DOWN ON THE FARM** [9] [ ]
(cd-s+=) – Attitude.

Nov 93. (cd)(c)(lp) **THE SPAGHETTI INCIDENT** [2] [4]
– Since I don't have you / New rose / Down on the farm / Human being / Raw power / Ain't it fun / Buick Makane / Hair of the dog / Attitude / Black leather / You can't put your arms around a memory / I don't care about you / What's your game!.

May 94. (7"colrd)(c-s) **SINCE I DON'T HAVE YOU. / YOU CAN'T PUT YOUR ARMS AROUND A MEMORY** [10] [69]
(cd-s+=) – Human being.
(cd-s) – ('A'side) / Sweet child o' mine / Estranged.

—— **PAUL HUGE** – guitar repl. GILBY who was sacked and had already went solo

Jan 95. (7") **SYMPATHY FOR THE DEVIL. / LIVE AND LET DIE** [9] [55]
(7")(c-s)(cd-s) – ('A'side) / Escape to Paris.

SLASH'S SNAKEPIT

—— with **MATT + GILBY/ + ERIC DOVER** – vocals (ex-JELLYFISH)/ **MIKE INEZ** – bass (of ALICE IN CHAINS)

Geffen Geffen

Feb 95. (cd)(c)(lp) **IT'S FIVE O'CLOCK SOMEWHERE** [15] [70]
– Neither can I / Dime store rock / Beggars and hangers-on / Good to be alive / What do you want to be / Monkey chow / Soma city ward / Jizz da pit / Lower / Take it away / Doin' fine / Be the ball / I hate everybody (but you) / Back and forth again.

DUFF McKAGAN

DUFF McKAGAN – vocals, guitar (ex-GUNS N' ROSES) with **TED ANDREADIS + DIZZY REED** – keyboards / **WEST ARKEEN** – lead guitar (co-wrote 'Man In The Meadow') / plus other guests **SLASH** – lead guitar / **MATT SORUM** – drums (co-wrote 'F@*ked Up Beyond Belief'), **GILBY CLARKE** – guitars (co-wrote '10 Years'), **JOIE MASTROKALOS** – b.vocals (co-wrote 'Just Not There'), **DOC NEWMAN** – vocals (+ co-wrote 'F@*k You'), **SNAKE, SEBASTIAN BACH, LENNY KRAVITZ + JEFF BECK**

Geffen Geffen

Oct 93. (cd)(c)(lp) **BELIEVE IN ME** [27] [ ]
– Believe in me / I love you / Man in the meadow / (F@*ked up) Beyond belief / Could it be U / Just not there / Punk rock song / The majority / 10 years / Swamp song / Trouble / F@*k you / Lonely tonite.

Nov 93. (cd-s) **BELIEVE IN ME. / BAMBI / CRACKED ACTOR** [ ] [ ]

GILBY CLARKE

Virgin America Virgin

Jul 94. (cd)(c) **PAWNSHOP GUITARS** [39] [ ]
– Cure me . . .or kill me . . . / Black / Tijuana jail / Skin and bones / Johanna's chopper / Let's get lost / Pawn shop guitar / Dead flowers / Jail guitar doors / Hunting dogs / Shut up.

—— Covered: DEAD FLOWERS (Rolling Stones) / JAIL GUITAR DOORS (Clash).

Arlo GUTHRIE

Born: 10 Jul'47, Coney Island, New York, USA. Son of legendary folk singer WOODY GUTHRIE, who bought him his first electric guitar. Went to school in Stockbridge, Massachusetts, where he sang his fathers' songs. In the mid-60's, he met school librarian ALICE, and they opened a restaurant, named as his debut lp late 1967. This renovated old church, became a meeting place for mainly middle-class hippies, who were radically against US involvement in Vietnam. He had earlier been refused induction into the army, due to a petty criminal charge. With help from his father's agent & friend Harold Leventhal, he gained tour work (i.e, Newport Festival), which helped debut lp reach US Top 20. Prior to its success, his dad WOODY died on 3 Oct'67, of a long-lasting Huntingdon's chorea disease. Although ARLO released many more albums, he never quite matched earlier promise. In 1970, an Arthur Penn film of 'ALICE'S RESTAURANT', was made, with ARLO playing himself. A year previous, after playing Woodstock, he bought a 250-acre farm where he settled with wife-to-be Jackie Hyde. • **Style:** Political but satirical folk-singer, in the mould of early BOB DYLAN. In 1974, ARLO wrote an attack on President Nixon 'PRESIDENTIAL RAG'. • **Songwriters:** Self-penned except; CITY OF NEW ORLEANS (Steve Goodman) / DON'T THINK TWICE, IT'S ALRIGHT + PERCY'S SONG + WHEN THE SHIP COMES IN (Bob Dylan) / 1913 MASSACRE (Woody Guthrie) / LIGHTNIN' BAR BLUES + SOMEBODY TURNED ON THE LIGHT (Hoyt Axton) / WHEN I GET TO THE BORDER (Richard Thompson) / etc. • **Trivia:** In 1977, he became a Catholic and appeared on 'The Muppet Show', as well as touring alongside JOE COCKER and JOHN SEBASTIAN on a 'Woodstock' reunion European tour.

Recommended: ALICE'S RESTAURANT (*7) / HOBO'S LULLABY (*6) / THE BEST OF ARLO GUTHRIE (*6).

ARLO GUTHRIE – vocals, guitar(with session people)

Reprise Reprise

Dec 67. (lp) **ALICE'S RESTAURANT** [ ] [17] Nov 67
– Alice's restaurant massacre / Chilling of the evening / Ring-a-round-rosy rag / Now and then / I'm going home / The motorcycle song / Highway in the wind. *(re-iss.'72) (US re-iss.Jul87)*

Mar 68. (7") **THE MOTORCYCLE SONG. / NOW AND THEN** [ ] [ ]

Oct 68. (lp) **ARLO (live)** [ ] [100]
– The motorcycle song / Wouldn't you believe it / Try me one more time / John looked down / Meditation / Standing at the threshold / The pause of Mr. Claus. *(re-iss.'72)*

Oct 69. (lp) **RUNNING DOWN THE ROAD** [ ] [54]
– Running down the road / Oklahoma hills / Every hand in the land / Living in the country / Wheel of fortune / Creole belle / Coming in to Los Angeles / Oh, in the morning / Stealin' / My front pages. *(re-iss.'72)*

Dec 69. (lp) **WASHINGTON COUNTY** [ ] [33]
– (introduction) / Fence post blues / Gabriel's mother's hiway ballad £16 blues / Washington County / Valley to pray / Lay down little doggies / I could be singing / If you would just drop by / Percy's song / I want to be around. *(re-iss.'72)*

Jan 70. (7") **ALICE'S ROCK'N'ROLL RESTAURANT. / COMING IN TO LOS ANGELES** [ ] [97]

May 70. (7") **GABRIEL'S MOTHER'S HIWAY BALLAD £16 BLUES. / VALLEY TO PRAY** [–] [ ]

1971. (7") **THE BALLAD OF TRICKY FRED. / SHACKLES AND CHAINS** [ ] [ ]

Jul 72. (7") **UKELELE LADY. / WHEN THE SHIP COMES IN** [ ] [–]

Jun 72. (lp) **HOBO'S LULLABY** [ ] [52]
– Anytime / City of New Orleans / Lightning bar blues / Shackles and chains / 1913 massacre / Somebody turned on the light / Ukelele lady / When the ship comes in / Mapleview (20%) rag / Days are short / Hobo's lullabye.

Sep 72. (7") **CITY OF NEW ORLEANS. / DAYS ARE SHORT** [ ] [18] Jul 72

Nov 72. (7") **UKELELE LADY. / COOPER'S LAMENT** [–] [ ]

Feb 73. (7") **LOVESICK BLUES. / FARREL O'GALA** [ ] [–]

Apr 73. (7") **GYPSY DAVE. / WEEK ON THE RAG** [–] [ ]

Apr 73. (lp)(c) **LAST OF THE BROOKLYN COWBOYS** [ ] [87]
– Farrell O'Gara / Gypsy Davy / This troubled mind of mine / Week of the rag / Miss the Mississippi and you / Lovesick blues / Uncle Jeff / Gates of Eden / Last train / Cowboy's song / Sailor's bonnett / Cooper's lament / Ramblin' round. *(re-iss.Aug77 +quad)*

Aug 74. (7") **PRESIDENTIAL RAG. / NOSTALGIA RAG** [ ] [ ]

Jul 74. (lp)(c) **ARLO GUTHRIE** [ ] [ ] Jun 74
– Won't be long / Presidential rag / Deportee (plane wreck at Los Gatos) / Children of Abraham / Nostalgia rag / When the cactus is in bloom / Me and my goose / Bling blang / Go down Moses / Hard times / Last to leave.

May 75. (d-lp) **TOGETHER IN CONCERT (live "with PETE SEEGER")** [ ] [ ]
– Way out there / Yodelling / Roving gambler / Declaration of independence / Don't think twice, it's alright / Get up and go / City of New Orleans / Estradio Chile / Guantanamera / On a Monday / Presidential rag / Walkin' down the line / Well may the world go / Henry my son / Mother, the queen of my heart / Deportee (plane wreck at Los Gatos) / Joe Hill / May there always be sunshine / Three rules of discipline and the eight rules of attention / Stealin' / Golden vanity / Lonesome valley / Quite early morning / Sweet Rosyanne.

Sep 76. (lp)(c) **AMIGO** [ ] [ ]
– Guabi, Guabi / Darkest hour / Massachusetts / Victor Jara / Patriot's dream / Grocery blues / Walking song / My love / Manzanillo Bay / Ocean crossing / Connection.

Sep 76. (7") **PATRIOT'S DREAM. / OCEAN CROSSING** [–] [ ]

Nov 76. (7") **GUABI, GUABI. / GROCERY BLUES** [–] [ ]

Mar 77. (7") **MASSACHUSETTS. / MY LOVE** [–] [ ]

Feb 78. (lp)(c) **THE BEST OF ARLO GUTHRIE** (compilation) [ ] [ ]
– Alice's restaurant massacre / Gabriel's mother's hiway ballad £16 blues / Cooper's lament / The motorcycle song / Coming in to Los Angeles / Last train / City of New Orleans / Darkest hour / Last to leave. *(re-iss.1984) (cd-iss.Feb93)*

Warners Warners

1978. (lp) **ONE NIGHT (live: - w / SHENANDOAH)** [–] [ ]
– One nite / I've just seen a face / Tennessee stud / Anytime / Little beggar man / Buffalo skinners / St.Louis tickle / The story of Reuben Clamzo and his strange daughter / In the hey of A / Strangest dream.

Jul 79. (lp)(c) **OUTLASTING THE BLUES (w/ SHENANDOAH)** [ ] [ ]
– Weddding song / Epilogue / Sailing down this golden river / Evangelina / Prologue / Which side / World away from me / Telephone / Carry me over / Drowning man / Underground.

Nov 79. (7") **WEDDING SONG. / PROLOGUE** [–] [ ]

Jul 81. (lp)(c) **POWER OF LOVE** [ ] [ ] Jun 81
– Power of love / Oklahoma nights / If I could only touch your life / Waimanalo blues / Living like a legend / Give it all you got / When I get to the border / Jamaica farewell / Slow boat / Garden song.

Aug 81. (7") **IF I COULD ONLY TOUCH YOUR LIFE. / SLOW BOAT** [–] [ ]

Feb 82. (7") **POWER OF LOVE. / OKLAHOMA NIGHTS** [–] [ ]

1982 (d-lp) **PRECIOUS FRIEND (live:- w/ SHENANDOAH and PETE SEEGER)** [–] [ ]
– Wabash cannonball / Circles / Hills of Glenshee / Ocean crossing / Celery-time / Run, come see Jerusalem / Sailin' up, sailin' down / How can I keep from singing / Old time religion / Pretty Boy Floyd / Ladies auxiliary / Please don't talk about me / When I'm gone / Precious friend you will be there / Do re mi / Tarantella / The neutron bomb / I'm changing my name to Chrysler / St.Louis tickle / Wimoweh / Will the circle be unbroken? / Garden song / Kisses sweeter than wine / Raggedy raggedy / In dead earnest / If I had a hammer / Amazing Grace.

– compilations, others, etc. –

Mar 70. United Artists; (lp)(c) **ALICE'S RESTAURANT (Soundtrack)** [44] [63] Oct 69
– Travelin' music / Alice's restaurant massacre – 1 / The let down / Songs to aging children (by TIGGER OUTLAW) / Amazing Grace (by The GARRY SHERMAN CHORUS) / Trip to the city / Alice's restaurant massacre – 2 / Crash pad improvs / You're a fink (by AL SCHACKMAN) / Harps and marriage.

—— Also contributed to various albums including 'Woodstock'

Buddy GUY

Born: GEORGE GUY, 30 Jul'36, Lettsworth, Louisiana. In his early teens he taught himself to play on a homemade guitar. Moved to Chicago in 1957, where he recorded with MAGIC SAM on 'Cobra' records. He also cut his own solo single, before becoming a house musician for 'Chess'. In 1962 while working with JUNIOR WELLS, he had an R&B Top 20 hit with 'STONE CRAZY'. He then signed to 'Vanguard' records and worked with OTIS RUSH and also JUNIOR WELLS again (BUDDY as 'Friendly Chap') on his 1966 solo lp 'Voodoo Man'. After signing to 'Atlantic' in the late 60's, he appeared in films 'The Blues Is Alive And Well In Chicago' (1970), 'Chicago Blues' (1970) and 'Out Of The Blacks And Into The Blues' (1972). Then recorded an lp with JUNIOR WELLS for 'Blind Pig' records; 'DRINKIN' TNT 'N' SMOKIN' DYNAMITE' which also featured BILL WYMAN then of The ROLLING STONES. In the early 80's he could be heard 'JSP' records, where he made 5 albums and a couple with brother PHIL. His career was resurrected in the early 90's (as was JOHN LEE HOOKER's), when he signed to UK label 'Silvertone', who had just had a showdown with newcomers The STONE ROSES. BUDDY's first and second albums for them (see below) both hit UK Top 50, and even secured his first Top 200 placings in his homeland. • **Style:** Blues legend and showman of respectable and lasting quality. • **Songwriters:** Writes own material and covers many incl. I GO CRAZY (James Brown) / FEELS LIKE RAIN (John Hiatt) / SHE'S NINETEEN YEARS OLD (Muddy Waters) / SOME KIND OF WONDERFUL (Jimmy Ellison) / SUFFERIN' MIND (Guitar Slim; aka E.Jones) / CHANGE IN THE WEATHER (John Fogerty) / MARY ANN (Junior Wells) / TROUBLE MAN (Marvin Gaye) / COUNTRY MAN (Ray Charles). • **Trivia:** DR.JOHN (MAC REBBENACK) also appeared on the 1972 'Atlantic' records lp with co-credit to JUNIOR WELLS.

Recommended: STONE CRAZY (*7) / DAMN RIGHT, I GOT THE BLUES (*8)

BUDDY GUY – vocals, guitar w / **OTIS RUSH** – guitar / **WILLIE DIXON** – bass / **ODIE PAYNE** – drums / **HAROLD ASHBY + McKINLEY EASTON** – saxes

not issued Artistic

1958. (7") **TRY TO QUIT YOU BABY. / SIT AND CRY (THE BLUES)** –
1959. (7") **THIS IS THE END. / YOU SURE CAN'T DO** –

Chess Chess

May 60. (7") **I GOT MY EYES ON YOU. / FIRST TIME I MET THE BLUES** –
Jul 60. (7") **SLOP AROUND. / BROKEN HEARTED BLUES** –
Feb 61. (7") **LET ME LOVE YOU BABY. / TEN YEARS AGO** –
Feb 62. (7") **STONE CRAZY. / SKIPPIN' (SCRAPIN')** –
Nov 62. (7") **WHEN MY LEFT EYE JUMPS. / THE TREASURE UNTOLD** –
May 63. (7") **HARD BUT IT'S FAIR. / NO LIE** –
Jul 64. (7") **MY TIME AFTER AWHILE. / I DIG YOUR WIG** –
1964. (7") **LET ME LOVE YOU BABY. / TEN YEARS AGO** –
Jul 65. (7") **LEAVE MY GIRL ALONE. / CRAZY LOVER (CRAZY MUSIC)** –

Also appeared / credited on JUNIOR WELLS lp's in 1966 / 68 'IT'S MY LIFE BABY' & 'COMING AT YOU'.

Oct 66. (7") **MY MOTHER. / MOTHER-IN-LAW BLUES** –
Aug 67. (7") **I SUFFER WITH THE BLUES. / KEEP IT TO YOURSELF** –
Nov 67. (7") **SHE SUITS ME TO A TEE (I DIDN'T KNOW MY MOTHER). / BUDDY'S GROOVE** –

—— now w / **OTIS SPANN** – piano / **WAYNE BENNETT** – guitar / **LONNIE TAYLOR** – drums / **JACK MEYERS** – bass / **A.C.REED, BOBBY FIELDS + DONALD HANKINS** – saxes

Fontana Vanguard

Jan 68. (7") **MARY HAD A LITTLE LAMB. / SWEET LITTLE ANGEL**

Vanguard Vanguard

Feb 68. (lp) **A MAN AND THE BLUES**
– I can't quit the blues / Money / Thousand miles from nowhere / Mary had a little lamb / Just playing my axe / Sweet little angel / Worry is all that I can do / Jam on a Monday morning / A man and the blues.

1968. (lp) **THIS IS BUDDY GUY**
– I got my eyes on you / Things I used to do / Fever / Knock on wood / I had a dream last night / 24 hours of the day / You were wrong / I'm not the best.

1968. (7") **FEVER. / I'M NOT THE BEST** –

Chess Chess

1969. (lp) **I LEFT MY BLUES IN SAN FRANCISCO**
– Keep it to myself / Crazy love / I suffer with the blues / When my left eye jumps / Buddy's groove / Goin' home / She suits me to tee / Leave my girl alone / Too many ways / Mother-in-law blues / Every girl I see. *(cd-iss.Feb90 + Apr92)*

Harvest Blue Thumb

1970. (lp) **BUDDY AND THE JUNIORS** (BUDDY GUY / JUNIOR MANCE / JUNIOR WELLS) –
– Talkin' 'bout women obviously / Motif is just a riff / Buddy's blues / Hoochie coochie man / Five long years / Rock me mama / Ain't no need.

—— now also w / **ERIC CLAPTON** (DEREK & THE DOMINOES) / **A.C.REED / J.GEILS BAND**

Atlantic Atlantic

1972. (lp)(c) **BUDDY GUY & JUNIOR WELLS PLAYS THE BLUES**
– A man of many words / My baby, she left me / Come on in this house / Have mercy baby / T-bone shuffle / A poor man's plea / Messin' with the kid / This old fool / I don't know / Bad bad whiskey / Honeydripper. *(cd-iss.Mar93)*

Aug 72. (7") **HONEYDRIPPER. / MAN OF MANY WORDS**
(above also credited DR> JOHN & ERIC CLAPTON)

—— now w / **REED / FREEBO / PHILIP GUY** – guitar / **MARK JORDAN** – keyboards / etc.

Vanguard Vanguard

1973. (lp) **HOLD THAT PLANE**
– Watermelon man / Hold that plane / I'm ready / My time after a while / You don't love me / Come see about me / Hello San Francisco. *(re-iss.+cd+c Jul89 on 'Start') (re-iss.cd Oct95 on 'Vanguard')*

—— now w / **P.GUY + WILLIAM McDONALD** – guitar / **GENE PICKETT** – keyboards / **NICK CHARLES** – bass / **MERLE PERKINS** – drums

J.S.P. J.S.P.

Jan 82. (lp) **THE DOLLAR DONE FELL (live at The Checkerboard 1979)**
– Buddy's blues (parts 1 & 2) / I've got a right to love my woman / Tell me what's inside of you (2 versions) / Done gone over you / The things I used to do / You don't know how I feel / The dollar done fell / Don't answer the door. *(cd-iss.Sep86 as 'LIVE AT THE CHECKERBOARD LOUNGE, CHICAGO 1979')*

Mar 82. (lp) **BREAKING OUT** 1981
– I didn't know my mother had a son like me / Have you ever been lonesome / She winked her eye / Boogie family style / Break out all over you / You called me in my dream / Me and my guitar / You can make it if you try. *(cd-iss.Jul88 on 'J.S.P.')*

—— **DOUG WILLIAMS** – guitar / **MIKE MORRISON** – bass / **RAY ALLISON** – drums repl. everyone except the GUY's

Oct 82. (lp) **D.J. PLAY MY BLUES** Apr82
– Dedication to the late T-Bone Walker / Good news / Blues at my baby's house / She suits me to a T / D.J. play my blues / Just teasin' / All your love. *(cd-iss.Jun87 w / other tracks)*

—— In 1982, BUDDY also featured on PHIL GUY's 'J.S.P.' lp's 'THE RED HOT BLUES' and 'BAD LUCK BOY' (Aug83).

Feb 85. (lp) **TEN BLUE FINGERS**
– Girl you're nice and clean / Garbage man blues / Tell me what's inside of you / You can make it if you really try / Have you ever been lonesome / She winked her eye.

Silvertone Silvertone

Jun 91. (cd)(c)(lp) **DAMN RIGHT, I'VE GOT THE BLUES** 43
– Damn right, I've got the blues / Mustang Sally / Too broke to spend the night / Wanna get with U / Black night / Five long years / Let me love you baby / Early in the morning / Rememberin' Stevie / There is something on your mind / Where is the next one coming from.

Sep 91. (7") **MUSTANG SALLY. ("JEFF BECK & BUDDY GUY") / TROUBLE DON'T LAST**
(cd-s+=) – ('A'version).

Jul 92. (7")(c-s) **WHERE IS THE NEXT ONE COMING FROM?. / MUSTANG SALLY**
(cd-s+=) – Let me love you baby.

—— now w / **IAN McLAGAN** – keyboards / **BILL PAYNE** – piano / **JOHNNY LEE SCHELL + JOHN PORTER** – guitar / **GREG RZAB** – bass / **RICHIE HAYWARD** – drums / **MARTY GREBB** – piano, horns

Feb 93. (cd-s) **I GO CRAZY /**
May 93. (cd)(c)(lp) **FEELS LIKE RAIN** 36 Apr93
– She's a superstar / I go crazy / Feels like rain / She's nineteen years old / Some kind of wonderful / Sufferin' mind / Change in the weather / I could cry / Mary Ann / Trouble man / Country man.

Jun 93. (7")(c-s) **SOME KIND OF WONDERFUL. / TOO BROKE TO SPEND THE NIGHT**
(cd-s+=) – I go crazy. ('A'side featured PAUL RODGERS)

Nov 94. (cd)(c)(lp) **SLIPPIN' IN**
– I smell trouble / Please don't drive me away / 7 to 11 / Shame, shame, shame / Love her with a feeling / Little dab-a-doo / Someone else's slippin' in / Trouble blues / A man of many words / Don't tell me 'bout the blues / Cities need help.

– compilations, others –

Apr 78. Vanguard; (lp)(c) **HOT AND COOL**
– I got my eyes on you / The things I used to do / (You give me) Fever / 24 hours of the day / I had a dream last night / Hold that plane / A man and the blues / Sweet little angel / Worry, worry.

Sep 79. Blues Ball; (lp) **GOT TO USE YOUR HOUSE** –
Sep 82. Red Lightnin'; (lp) **IN THE BEGINNING** (with JUNIOR WELLS) –
(re-iss.Jul84 as 'DRINKIN' T.N.T. 'N' SMOKIN' DYNAMITE' on 'Sonet', cd-iss.Aug88) (re-iss.cd Apr94 on 'Sequel') (US-iss.1988 on 'Blind Pig')

Sep 83. Blue Moon; (lp) **THE ORIGINAL BLUES BROTHERS** – LIVE (w / J.WELLS) –
(cd-iss.Feb89)

Apr 83. Chess/ US= Sugarhill; (lp) **BUDDY GUY**
Mar 92. M.C.A.; (d-cd)(d-c) **THE COMPLETE CHESS STUDIO RECORDINGS**
Oct 86. Charly; (lp) **I WAS WALKING THROUGH THE WOODS** (early 60's) –
Jan 87. Charly; (lp)(c) **CHESS MASTERS**
Apr 92. Charly; (cd)(c) **THE TREASURE UNTOLD** –
Nov 92. Charly; (cd)(c) **I CRY AND SING THE BLUES: MASTER-WORKS VOL.27** –
1988. Vogue; (cd) **BUDDY GUY ON CHESS VOL.1**
Oct 88. Vogue; (d-lp) **THE CHICAGO GOLDEN YEARS** –
Sep 88. Sonet/ US= Alligator; (lp)(cd) **STONE CRAZY**
(re-iss.cd+c May93)

Mar 89. Flyright; (lp) **I AIN'T GOT NO MONEY (w / BLUE CHARLIE + JOE JOHNSON)** –
Jan 90. Black & Blue/ US= Alligator; (cd) **BLUES GIANT**
Mar 93. Black & Blue/ US= Alligator; (cd)(c) **ALONE & ACOUSTIC (w / JUNIOR WELLS)** May93
1992. Blues Encore; (cd) **FIRST TIME I MET THE BLUES** –
Jun 93. Roots; (cd) **AMERICAN BANDSTAND** –
Jan 94. Vanguard; (cd-box) **MAN & BLUES / THIS IS BUDDY GUY / HOLD THAT PLANE** –
Jan 95. JSP; (cd) **D.J. PLAY MY BLUES** –
Sep 95. JSP; (cd) **LIVE AT THE CHECKBOARD LOUNGE** –

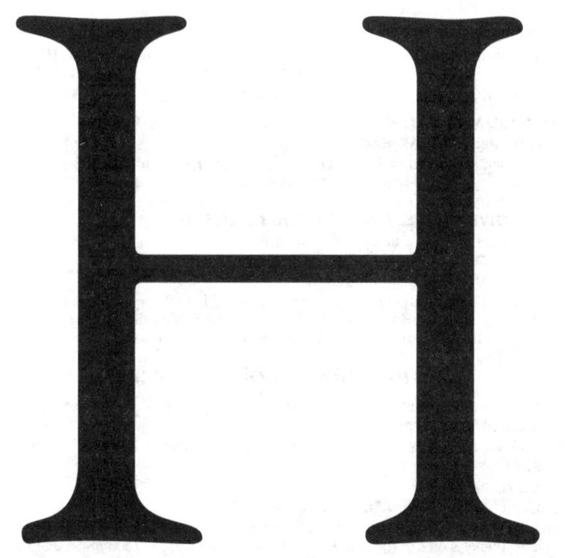

Steve HACKETT

Born: 12 Feb'50, London, England. In the late 60's, he formed QUIET WORLD, who made one 1970 lp 'THE ROAD' for 'Dawn' records. By the end of the year, he became guitarist of GENESIS. He featured on albums from 'NURSERY CRYME' (1971) to 'SECONDS OUT' (1977), before leaving to continue a solo career. In 1975, he had released first solo album 'VOYAGE OF THE ACOLYTE', which reached UK Top 30 lists. In 1978, he issued follow-up 'PLEASE DON'T TOUCH', which also broke into Top 40. He continued to hit album charts, until he signed a new deal with 'Lambourghini', which released late 1983 album 'BAY OF KINGS'. In 1986, he glowed again with supergroup G.T.R., who also featured STEVE HOWE of YES. Covered: BORN IN CHICAGO (N.Gravenites) / THE STUMBLE (King-Thompson) / BLUES WITH A FEELING (. . .Jacobs). • **Style:** Superb guitarist and concept album maker, with classical rock feel. • **Songwriters:** Self-penned all.

Recommended: VOYAGE OF THE ACOLYTE (*8) / DEFECTOR (*7) / SPECTRAL MORNINGS (*6) / CURED (*6).

STEVE HACKETT – guitar, vocals, keyboards (ex-GENESIS, ex-QUIET WORLD) with **JOHN HACKETT** – flute, keyboards / **JOHN ACOCK** – keyboards / **SALLY OLDFIELD** – vocals / **NIGEL WARREN GREEN** – cello / **ROBIN MILLER** – wind / guests **MICHAEL RUTHERFORD, JOHN GUSTAFSON + PERCY JONES** – all bass / **PHIL COLLINS** – drums, vocals

Charisma Chrysalis

Oct 75. (lp)(c) **VOYAGE OF THE ACOLYTE** [26] [ ]
– Ace of wands / Hands of the priestess (part I) / A tower struck down / Hands of the priestess (part II) / The hermit / Star of Sirius / The lovers / Shadow of the Hierophant. *(re-iss.+cd.Oct86)*

— STEVE left GENESIS (deciding on full-time career). Retained only his brother JOHN and friend JOHN ACOCK. Guest vocalists were **RICHIE HAVENS, RANDY CRAWFORD** and **STEVE WALSH**, also **CHESTER THOMPSON** – drums, percussion / **JAMES BRADLEY** – percussion / **PHIL EHART** – percussion / **TOM FOWLER** – bass / **DAVE LEBOLT** – keyboards / **GRAHAM SMITH** – violin.

Apr 78. (lp)(c) **PLEASE DON'T TOUCH** [38] [ ]
– Narnia / Carry on up the vicarage / Racing in A / Kim / How can I / Hoping love will last / Land of a thousand autumns / Please don't touch / The voice of Necam / Icarus ascending. *(re-iss.Sep83)*

May 78. (7") **HOW CAN I. / KIM** [ ] [-]

Oct 78. (7") **NARNIA. / PLEASE DON'T TOUCH** [ ] [ ]

— Steve and brother with **PETER HICKS** – vocals / **DICK CADBURY** – bass / **NICK MAGNUS** – keyboards / **JOHN SHEARER** – drums

May 79. (lp) **SPECTRAL MORNINGS** [22] [ ]
– Every day / The virgin and the gypsy / The red flower of Tachai blooms everywhere / Clocks – the angel of Mons / The ballad of the decomposing man / Lost time in Cordoba / Tigermoth / Spectral mornings. *(re-iss.Sep83) (re-iss.+cd.Aug88 on 'Virgin')*

Jun 79. (7") **EVERY DAY. / LOST TIME IN CORDOBA** [ ] [ ]

Sep 79. (7") **CLOCKS – THE ANGELS OF MONS. / ACOUSTIC SET** [ ] [ ]
(12"+=) – Tigermoth.

Charisma Charisma

Mar 80. (7") **THE SHOW. / HERCULES UNCHAINED** [ ] [ ]

Jun 80. (lp)(c) **DEFECTOR** [9] [ ]
– The Steppes / Time to get out / Slogans / Leaving / Two vamps as guests / Jacuzzi / Hammer in the sand / The toast / The show / Sentimental institution. *(re-iss.Mar83) (cd-iss.Apr89 on 'Virgin')*

Aug 80. (7") **SENTIMENTAL INSTITUTION. / THE TOAST** [ ] [ ]

— added **KIM POOR** – vocals / **BIMBO ACOCK** – sax

Charisma Epic

Aug 81. (7") **HOPE I DON'T WAKE. / TALES OF THE RIVERBANK** [ ] [-]

Aug 81. (lp)(c) **CURED** [15] [ ]
– Hope I don't wake / Picture postcard / Can't let go / The air-conditioned nightmare / Funny feeling / A cradle of swans / Overnight sleeper / Turn back time. *(re-iss.Mar84) (cd-iss.Apr89 on 'Virgin')*

Oct 81. (7") **PICTURE POSTCARD. / THEME FROM SECOND CHANCE** [ ] [ ]

Nov 81. (7") **HOPE I DON'T WAKE. / A CRADLE OF SWANS** [-] [ ]

— **CHRIS LAWRENCE** – bass / **NIGEL WARREN GREEN** – cello / returned **IAN MOSLEY** – drums

Apr 83. (7") **CELL 151. / TIME LAPSE AT MILTON KEYNES** [66] [ ]
(12"+=) – Air conditioned nightmare.
(free ltd-12" w/a **CLOCKS – THE ANGEL OF MONS / ACOUSTIC SET / TIGERMOTH**

Apr 83. (lp)(c) **HIGHLY STRUNG** [16] [ ]
– Camino royale / Cell 151 / Always somewhere else / Walking through walls / Give it away / Weightless / India rubber man / Hackett to pieces. *(re-iss.Aug88) (cd-iss.Apr89 on 'Virgin') (cd-iss.Mar94 on 'Virgin')*

— **STEVE HACKETT** now totally solo on guitars

Lambourghini

Nov 83. (lp)(c) **BAY OF KINGS** [70] [ ]
– Bay of kings / The journey / Kim / Marigold / St.Elmo's fire / Petropolis / Second chance / Cast adrift / Horizons / Black light / The barren land / Calamaria. *(re-iss.+cd Jun89 on 'Start') (re-iss.cd Jun94 on 'Permanent')*

— now with **NICK MAGNUS + FERNAND MOURA** – keyboards / **IAN MOSLEY** – drums / **KIM POOR** – vocals / **RONALDO DIAMANTE** – bass / etc

Aug 84. (7") **A DOLL THAT'S MADE IN JAPAN. / ('A' instrumental)** [ ] [-]
(12"+=) – Just the boss.

Sep 84. (lp)(c)(cd) **TILL WE HAVE FACES** [54] [-]
– Duel / Matilda Smith-Williams' home for the aged / Let me count the ways / A doll that's made in Japan / Myopia / What's my name / The Rio connection / Taking the easy way out / When you wish upon a star. *(re-iss.+cd.Oct89 on 'Start') (re-iss.cd Jun94 on 'Permanent')*

G.T.R.

were formed by **STEVE HACKETT** – guitar / **STEVE HOWE** – guitar (YES) / **MAX BACON** – vocals (ex-NIGHTWING, ex-BRONZ) / **PHIL SPALDING** – bass / **JONATHAN MOVER** – drums (ex-MARILLION, ex-S.O.S.)

Arista Arista

May 86. (7") **WHEN THE HEART RULES THE MIND. / REACH OUT (NEVER SAY NO)** [ ] [14]
(12"+=) – Sketches in the sun / Hackett to bits.

Jul 86. (lp)(c)(cd) **G.T.R.** [41] [11]
– When the heart rules the mind / The hunter / Here I wait / Sketches in the sun / Jeckyl and Hyde / You can still get through / Reach out (never say no) / Toe the line / Hackett to bits / Imagining. *(re-iss.Apr88)*

Aug 86. (7") **THE HUNTER. / SKETCHES IN THE SUN** [-] [85]
(12") – ('A'side) / Hackett to bits.

STEVE HACKETT

returned to solo work, retaining **JOHN HACKETT** – flute, and bringing in **FUDGE SMITH** – drums / **JULIAN COLBECK** – keyboard, bass.

Start not issued

Apr 88. (lp)(c)(cd) **MOMENTUM** [ ] [-]
– Cavalcanti / The sleeping sea / Portrait of a Brazilian lady / When the bells break / A bed, a chair & a guitar / Concert for Munich / Last rites of innocence / Troubled spirit / Variations on theme by Chopin / Pierrot / Momentum. *(re-iss.cd Jun94 on 'Permanent')*

Virgin Virgin

Dec 92. (cd)(c) **THE UNAUTHORISED BIOGRAPHY** (compilation) [ ] [ ]
– Narnia / Hackett to pieces / Don't fall away from me / Spectral mornings / The steppes / The virgin and the gypsy / The air-conditioned nightmare / Cell 151 / Slogans / Icarus ascending / Prayers and dreams / Star of Sirius / Hammer in the sand / Ace of wands / Hoping love will last. (with 2 new songs; Players and dreams / Don't fall away from me)

Permanent not issued

May 93. (cd)(c) **GUITAR NOIR** [ ] [-]
– Take these pearls / Dark as the grave / Paint your picture / There are many sides to the night / Like an arrow / Walking away from rainbows / Sierra quemada / Lost in your eyes / Little America / In the heart of the city / Vampyre with a healthy appetite / Tristesse.

Jun 94. (cd) **TIME LAPSE** [ ] [-]

— now w / **SINCLAIR / DEGENHARDT / COLBECK**(co-writer some)

Virgin Virgin

Oct 94. (cd)(c) **BLUES WITH A FEELING** [ ] [ ]
– Born in Chicago / The stumble / Love of another kind / Way down south / A blue part of town / Footloose / Tombstone roller / Blues with a feeling / Big Dallas sky / The 13th floor / So many roads / Solid ground.

– compilations, etc. –

Mar 83. Charisma; (d-c) **VOYAGE OF THE ACOLYTE / PLEASE DON'T TOUCH** [ ] [-]

Tony HADLEY (see under ⇒ SPANDAU BALLET)

Sammy HAGAR

Born: 13 Oct'47, Monterey, California, USA. After giving up first band the JUSTICE BROTHERS, he joined MONTROSE in 1973. After their late 1974 album 'PAPER MONEY', HAGAR was replaced with other vocalist BOB JAMES. HAGAR soon signed solo deal with 'Capitol', and released 1976 debut album 'NINE ON A TEN SCALE'. He struggled to break through commercially, until 1979's triumphant US Top 40 album 'DANGER ZONE'. He became top star, during the first half of the 80's, and became lead singer with VAN HALEN in 1985, replacing DAVID LEE ROTH. • **Style:** Heavy-metal rocker, with tremendous vocal range and image to match. • **Songwriters:** HAGAR except; THE DOCK OF A BAY (Otis Redding) / A WHITER SHADE OF PALE (Procol Harum). • **Trivia:** BETTE MIDLER covered his 'KEEP ON ROCKIN'', in the film 'The Rose'.

Recommended: THE BEST OF SAMMY HAGAR (*6)

SAMMY HAGAR – vocals (ex-MONTROSE) / with **GARY PIHL** – guitar / **BILL CHURCH** – bass (ex-MONTROSE) / **ALAN FITZGERALD** – keyboards / plus session drummers, etc.

Capitol Capitol

May 76. (lp)(c) **NINE ON A TEN SCALE** [ ] [ ]
– Keep on rockin' / Urban guerilla / Flamingos fly / China / Silver lights / All American / Confession / Please come back / Young girl blues / Rock'n'roll week-end. *(re-iss.May80 on 'Greenlight') (re-iss.May83 on 'Fame') (cd-iss. May93 on 'B.G.O.')*

Jun 76. (7") **FLAMINGOS FLY. / URBAN GUERILLA** [ ] [ ]

— **SCOTT MATTHEWS** – drums (new)

Mar 77. (lp)(c)(red-lp) **SAMMY HAGAR** [ ] [ ]
– Red / Catch the wind / Cruisin' and boozin' / Free money / Rock'n'roll weekend / Fillmore shuffle / Hungry / The pits / Love has found me / Little star / Eclipse. *(re-iss.Jun81)*

Mar 77. (7") **CATCH THE WIND. / ROCK'N'ROLL WEEKEND** [ ] [-]

Mar 77. (7") **CATCH THE WIND. / RED** [-] [ ]

— **DENNY CARMASSI** – drums repl. SCOTT / added **DAVID LEWARK** – guitar

Jan 78. (7") **YOU MAKE ME CRAZY. / RECKLESS** [ ] [62] Dec 77

Jan 78. (lp)(c) **MUSICAL CHAIRS** [ ] [100]
– Turn up the music / It's gonna be alright / You make me crazy / Reckless / Try (try to fall in love) / Don't stop me now / Straight from the hip kid / Hey boys / Someone out there / Crack in the world. *(re-iss.Jun81 on 'Greenlight') (cd-iss.May94 on 'BGO')*

May 78. (7") **TURN UP THE MUSIC. / STRAIGHT FROM THE HIP KID** [ ] [ ]

May 78. (7") **SOMEONE OUT THERE. / I'VE DONE EVERYTHING FOR YOU** [-] [ ]

— **GARY PIHL** – guitar repl. LEWARK

Sep 78. (lp)(c) **ALL NIGHT LONG (live)** [ ] [89] Aug 78
– Red / Rock'n'roll weekend / Make it last – Reckless / Turn up the music / I've done everything for you / Young girl blues / Bad motor scooter. *(re-iss.UK Mar80 as 'LOUD & CLEAR', hit No.12) (cd-iss.ec92 on 'BGO')*

Sep 78. (7") **I'VE DONE EVERYTHING FOR YOU (live). / BAD MOTOR SCOOTER (live)** [ ] [-]

Jun 79. (7") **(SITTIN' ON) THE DOCK OF THE BAY. / I'VE DONE EVERYTHING FOR YOU** [ ] [65] Apr 79

— **CHUCK RUFF** – drums repl. DENNY / **NEAL SCHON** – guitar (of JOURNEY) repl. FITZGERALD

Sep 79. (7") **PLAIN JANE. / WOUNDED IN LOVE** [ ] [77]

Sep 79. (lp)(c) **STREET MACHINE** [38] [71]
– Growing pains / Child to man / Trans am (highway wonderland) / Feels like love / Plain Jane / Never say die / This planet's on fire (burn to hell) / Wounded in love / Falling in love.
(re-iss.Jun86 & May87 on 'Revolver') (cd-iss.Dec92 on 'B.G.O.')

Nov 79. (7") **GROWING PAINS. / STRAIGHT TO THE TOP** [-] [ ]

Nov 79. (7") **THIS PLANET'S ON FIRE (BURN IN HELL). / SPACE STATION No.5** [52] [ ]

Jan 80. (7") **I'VE DONE EVERYTHING FOR YOU. / RED** [36] [ ]

— added **GEOFF WORKMAN** – keyboards

May 80. (lp)(c) **DANGER ZONE** [25] [85]
– Love or money / 20th century man / Miles from boredom / Mommy says, daddy says / In the night / The iceman / Bad reputation / Heartbeat / Run for your life / Danger zone. *(cd-iss.Jul95 on 'BGO')*

May 80. (7") **HEARTBEAT. / LOVE OR MONEY** [67] [-]

May 80. (7") **HEARTBEAT. / MILES FROM BOREDOM** [-] [ ]

— **DAVID LAUSER** – drums repl. CHUCK

Epic Epic

Sep 81. (7")(12") **HEAVY METAL. / SATISFIED** [ ] [ ]
(above from film 'Heavy Metal')

Geffen Geffen

Dec 81. (7")(7"pic-d) **PIECE OF MY HEART. / BABY'S ON FIRE** [67] [-]

Jan 82. (lp)(c) **STANDING HAMPTON** [84] [28]
– There's only one way to rock / Baby's on fire / Can't get loose / I'll fall in love again / Heavy metal / Baby it's you / Surrender / Inside looking in / Sweet hitchhiker / Piece of my heart. *(re-iss.Sep86)*

Dec 81. (7") **I'LL FALL IN LOVE AGAIN. / SATISFIED** [-] [43]

Jan 82. (7") **I'LL FALL IN LOVE AGAIN (from the film 'Vision Quest'). / ('B'side by "Journey")** [ ] [43]
(above was also issued on 'B'side of CRAZY FOR YOU by 'Madonna' Jun85 hit)

May 82. (7") **PIECE OF MY HEART. / SWEET HITCHHIKER** [-] [ ]

Dec 82. (lp)(c) **THREE LOCK BOX** [ ] [17]
– Three lock box / Remote love / Remember the heroes / Your love is driving me crazy / In the room / Rise of the animal / I wouldn't change a thing / Growing up / Never give up / I don't need love.

Dec 82. (7") **YOUR LOVE IS DRIVING ME CRAZY. / I DON'T NEED LOVE** [ ] [13]

Mar 83. (7") **NEVER GIVE UP. / FAST TIMES AT RIDGEMONT HIGH** [-] [46]

— **SCHON** – guitar / **AARONSON** – bass / **SHRIEVE** – drums

May 84. (lp)(c) **THROUGH THE FIRE (by "HAGAR, SCHON, AARONSON & SHRIEVE")** [92] [42] Mar 84
– Top of the rock / Missing you / Animation / Valley of the kings / Giza / A whiter shade of pale / Hot and dirty / He will understand / My home town.

May 84. (7") **WHITER SHADE OF PALE. ('HAGAR, SHON, AARONSON, SHRIEVE') / HOT AND DIRTY** [-] [ ]

— added to 1982 line-up **JESSE HARMS** – keyboards, vocals

Aug 84. (7") **TWO SIDES OF LOVE. / BURNING DOWN THE CITY** [ ] [38]

Sep 84. (7") **I CAN'T DRIVE 55. / PICK IN THE DIRT** [-] [26]

Sep 84. (lp)(c) **VOA (Voice Of America)** [ ] [32] Aug 84
– I can't drive / Swept away / Rock is in my blood / Two sides of love / Pick in the dirt / VOA / Don't make me wait / Burnin' down the city. *(re-iss.+cd.Sep86)*

— It was around this time he replaced DAVE LEE ROTH in VAN HALEN. Early '87 HAGAR released 'WINNER TAKES ALL' on 'Columbia', hit US 54. The B-side was by GIORGIO MORODER and from the film 'Vision Quest'.

— **EDWARD VAN HALEN** – bass, vocals repl. CHURCH + PIHL

Jul 87. (lp)(c)(cd) **SAMMY HAGAR** [86] [14]
– When the hammer falls / Hands and knees / Give to live / Boy's night out / Returning home / Standin' at the same old crossroads / Privacy / Back into you / Eagles fly / What you gonna say now. *(some w/free conversation disc)*

Aug 87. (7") **GIVE TO LIVE. / WHEN THE HAMMER FALLS** [ ] [23] Jun 87
(12"+=) – Standing at the same old crossroads.

Oct 87. (7") **EAGLES FLY. / HANDS AND KNEES** [-] [82]

Mar 94. (cd)(c) **UNBOXED** (compilation) [ ] [51]
– High hopes / Buying my way into Heaven / I'll fall in love again / There's only one way to rock / Heavy metal / Eagles fly / Baby's on fire / Three lock box / Two sides of love / I can't drive / Give to live / I don't need to love.

– compilations, others, etc. –

1979. Capitol; (7"m) **TURN UP THE MUSIC. / RED / BAD MOTOR SCOOTER** [ ] [ ]

Oct 82. Capitol; (lp)(c) **RED ALERT – DIAL NINE (THE VERY BEST OF SAMMY HAGAR)** [ ] [ ]
(cd-iss.Apr93)

Jan 83. Capitol; (lp)(c) **REMATCH (some live)** [-] [ ]
– Trans am (highway wonderland) / Love or money / Plain Jane / 20th century man / This planet's on fire (burn in Hell) / In the night / Danger zone / Space Station No.5.

Apr 87. C.B.S./ US= Columbia; (7") **THE WINNER TAKES IT ALL. / THE FIGHT** [ ] [54] Feb 87

Jan 87. Geffen; (lp)(c) **LOOKING BACK** [ ] [ ]

Aug 89. Warners; (lp)(c)(cd) **THE BEST OF SAMMY HAGAR** [ ] [ ]
– Red / (Sittin' on the) dock of the bay / I've done everything for you / Rock'n'roll weekend / Cruisin' and boozin' / Turn up the music / Reckless / Trans am (highway wonderland) / Love or money / This planet's on fire (burn in Hell) / Plain Jane / Bad reputation / Bad motor scooter / You make me crazy.

Nov 94. Connoisseur; (cd) **THE ANTHOLOGY** [ ] [-]

Paul HAIG (see under ⇒ JOSEF K)

Bill HALEY

Born: WILLIAM HALEY, 6 Jul'25, Highland Park, Detroit, USA. After leaving school in Pennsylvania, BILL became travelling musician and yodeller for country bands The DOWN HOMERS and then The RANGE DRIFTERS. In 1948, he set-off to be a DJ for local W-PWA in Chester, also airing recordings by himself and new outfit The FOUR ACES. He discontinued them in the early 50's, recruiting new backers The SADDLEMEN whose reputation rapidly grew. In 1952, he signed to 'Essex' and issued ICY HEART. / ROCK THE JOINT, but this was only a minor seller. He renamed outfit BILL HALEY & HIS COMETS, and they soon had first US Top20 hit with CRAZY MAN CRAZY. In 1954, he shifted stables to 'Decca'. They issued 'THIRTEEN WOMAN' as a single, but this flopped. On the flip side ROCK AROUND THE CLOCK began to gain airplay from some up and coming radio stations. Their next single SHAKE, RATTLE AND ROLL was a Transatlantic Top 20 hit, reaching US No.12 and UK No.4. ROCK AROUND THE CLOCK was re-issued by public demand, and eventually hit No.1 on both sides of the Atlantic. It was undenyably the birth of popular rock'n'roll, with the youth culture transforming virtually overnight. Parents hated it as their off-spring bopped/danced uninhibitively around local dancehalls. HALEY was now giving legendary performances up and down the States. More hits pursued, but they dried up in the late 50's, when rock'n'roll was now an image industry for fresh faced youngsters (i.e.ELVIS and CLIFF). On 9 Feb'81, after a past year in and out of hospital with a brain tumor, he died of a heart attack at his home in Harlingen, Texas. • **Style:** The 50's, saw him move from hillbilly & rockabilly to rock'n'roll. Always clean-cut and well-dressed, which disappointed initial UK following looking for a thin unmarried rebellious figurehead to portray new sound. In the 70's, he still gave revival concerts, which enabled ROCK AROUND THE CLOCK to often re-chart. • **Songwriters:** HALEY adapted songs from obscure originals, writing many himself. Covered ROCK THE JOINT (Jimmy Preston) / ROCKET 88 (hit. Jackie Brenston) / RIP IT UP (Little Richard) / WHEN THE SAINTS GO MARCHING IN (trad.) / ROCKIN' THROUGH THE RYE (Scot.trad) / etc. • **Trivia:** On the 5th Feb'57, he landed on British soil (Southampton), to rapturous crowds mobbing him until his departure to London hotel.

Recommended: THE VERY BEST OF BILL HALEY & HIS COMETS (*7)

BILL HALEY and the FOUR ACES OF WESTERN SWING

BILL HALEY – vocals, guitar with unknown backers. (all 78 rpm, 'til Feb60)(45 rpm, from 1951)

not iss. Cowboy

1948. (7") **TOO MANY PARTIES, TOO MANY PALS. / FOUR LEAF CLOVER BLUES** [-] [ ]

1948. (7") **CANDY KISSES. / TENNESSEE BORDER** [-] [ ]

JOHNNY CLIFTON & HIS STRING BAND

not issued / Center

1949. (7") **STAND UP AND BE COUNTED. / LOVELESS BLUES** – /

BILL HALEY WITH RENO BROWNE & HER BUCCKAROOS

Cowboy

1950 7") **MY SWEET LITTLE GIRL FROM NEVADA / MY PALOMINO AND I** – /

BILL HALEY and his SADDLEMEN

with **JOHNNY GRANDE** – piano / **BILLY WILLIAMSON** – steel guitar

not issued / Keystone

1950. (7") **DEAL ME A HAND (I PLAY THE GAME ANYWAY). / TEN GALLON STETSON (WITH A HOLE IN THE CROWN)** – /
1950. (7") **SUSAN VAN DUSAN. / I'M NOT TO BLAME** – /

(below was backing for **LOU GRAHAM**

not issued / Atlantic

1950. (7") **WHY DO I CRY OVER YOU. / I'M GONNA DRY EVERY TEAR WITH A KISS** – /

not iss. / Holiday

1951. (7") **ROCKET 88. / TEARSTAINS ON MY HEART** – /
(UK-iss.Feb81 on 'Thumbs Up')
1951. (7") **GREEN TREE BOOGIE. / DOWN DEEP IN MY HEART** – /
1951. (7") **I'M CRYING. / PRETTY BABY** – /
Nov 51. (7") **A YEAR AGO THIS CHRISTMAS. / I DON'T WANT TO ALONE THIS CHRISTMAS** – /
1952. (7") **JUKEBOX CANNONBALL. / SUNDOWN BOOGIE** – /

not issued / Essex

1952. (7") **ICY HEART. / ROCK THE JOINT** – /
1952. (7") **ROCKING CHAIR ON THE MOON. / DANCE WITH THE DOLLY (WITH A HOLE IN HER STOCKING)** – /

BILL HALEY and his COMETS

with **GRANDE + WILLIAMSON** plus **DANNY SEDRONE** – lead guitar / **MARSHALL PINGATORE** – up.bass / **DICK RICHARDS** – drums / **JOEY D'AMBROSIA** – tenor sax.

not issued / Essex

1952. (7") **STOP BEATIN' ROUND THE MULBURRY BUSH. / REAL ROCK DRIVE** – /

London / Essex

Aug 53. (7") **CRAZY MAN CRAZY. / WHATCHA GONNA DO** / Feb 53
Nov 53. (7") **PAT-A-CAKE. / FRACTURED** / Apr 53
1953. (7") **LIVE IT UP. / FAREWELL, SO LONG, GOODBYE** – /
1953. (7") **I'LL BE THERE. / TEN LITTLE INDIANS** – /
1953. (7") **STRAIGHT JACKET. / CHATTANOOGA CHOO-CHOO** – /
1954. (7") **SUNDOWN BOOGIE. / JUKEBOX CANNONBALL** – /
1954. (7") **ROCKET 88. / GREEN TREE BOOGIE** – /

— **BILLY GUSACK** – session drums (only 1)

Brunswick / Decca

Sep 54. (7") **ROCK AROUND THE CLOCK. / THIRTEEN WOMEN** / May 54
(re-dist.UK Dec54 hit No.17, Oct55 hit No.1, Sep56 hit No.5, stayed Top 30 until early next year) (re-dist.US Apr55, after 'Blackboard Jungle' film appearance, hit No.1, stayed in Top 50 for 1/2 a year)

— **FRANNY BEECHER** – lead guitar repl. CEDRONE who died of heart attack / **RUDY POMPILLI** – saxophone / **AL POMPILLI** – bass / **RALPH JONES** – drums repl. others

Nov 54. (7") **SHAKE RATTLE AND ROLL. / ABC BOOGIE** 4 / 12 Jul 54
Jan 55. (7") **DIM DIM THE LIGHTS (I WANT SOME ATMOSPHERE). / HAPPY BABY** / 11 Nov 54
Mar 55. (7") **MAMBO ROCK. / BIRTH OF THE BOOGIE** 14 / 18 Feb 55, 17
Jul 55. (7") **RAZZLE DAZZLE. / TWO HOUND DOGS** / 15
(UK re-dist.Sep56, hit No.13)
Nov 55. (7") **ROCK-A-BEATIN' BOOGIE. / BURN THAT CANDLE** 4 / 9, 23
Feb 56. (7") **SEE YOU LATER ALLIGATOR. / THE PAPER BOY** 7 / 6 Jan 56
(re-dist.UK Sep56, hit No.12)
May 56. (7") **THE SAINTS ROCK'N'ROLL. / R.O.C.K.** 5 / 18 Mar 56, 16
Jun 56. (lp) **ROCK AROUND THE CLOCK** / 12 Jan 56
(virtually a compilation, didn't chart UK, due to no lp chart until Nov58)
– Rock around the clock / Shake rattle and roll / ABC boogie / (You hit the wrong note) Billy goat / Thirteen women (and only one man in town) / Tonight's the night / Razzle dazzle / Two hound dogs / Dim dim the lights / Happy baby / Birth of the boogie / Rockin' rollin' Rover / Mambo rock / Hide and seek / Burn that candle / Rock-a-beatin' boogie. *(re-iss.1961 on 'Ace Of Hearts', re-iss.May68, hit UK No.34) (re-iss.Jan71 on 'Coral') (re-iss.Sep81 on 'M.C.A.')*
Aug 56. (7") **ROCKIN' THROUGH THE RYE. / HOT DOG BUDDY BUDDY** 3 / 78, 60
Nov 56. (7") **RIP IT UP. / TEENAGER'S MOTHER (ARE YOU RIGHT?)** 4 / 25, 68 Aug 56
Nov 56. (lp) **ROCK'N'ROLL STAGE SHOW** (hit singles chart=) 30 / 18 Sep 56
– Calling all comets / Rockin' through the rye / A rocking little tune / Hide and seek / Hey then there now / Goofin' around / Hook line and sinker / Rudy's rock / Choo choo ch'boogie / Blue comet blues / Hot dog buddy buddy / Tonight's the night. *(re-iss.Aug83 on 'Charly')*
Nov 56. (7") **RUDY'S ROCK. / BLUE COMET BLUES** 26 / 34
Dec 56. (7") **DON'T KNOCK THE ROCK. / CHOO CHOO CH'BOOGIE** – / 45
Feb 57. (7") **DON'T KNOCK THE ROCK. / CALLING ALL COMETS** 7 / –
Feb 57. (7") **HOOK, LINE AND SINKER. / GOOFIN' AROUND** / –
Mar 57. (7") **FORTY CUPS OF COFFEE. / HOOK LINE AND SINKER** – / 70
Apr 57. (7") **FORTY CUPS OF COFFEE. / CHOO CHOO CH'BOOGIE** / –

— **FRANKIE SCOTT** – saxophone repl. RUDY (He was to die 5 Feb'76)

Jul 57. (7") **(YOU HIT THE WRONG NOTE) BILLY GOAT. / ROCKIN' ROLLIN' ROVER** /
Oct 57. (7") **MISS YOU. / THE DIPSY DOODLE** /
Dec 57. (lp) **ROCKIN' THE OLDIES** /
– The dipsy doodle / You can't stop me from dreamin' / (I'll be with you) In apple blossom time / Moon over Miami / Is it true what they say about Dixie / Carolina in the morning / Miss you / Please don't talk about me when I'm gone / Ain't misbehavin' (I'm savin' my love for you) / One sweet letter from you / I'm gonna sit right down and write myself a letter / Somebody else is taking my place. *(re-iss.Oct62 on 'Ace Of Hearts')*
Feb 58. (7") **MARY MARY LOU. / IT'S A SIN** /
Apr 58. (7") **SKINNY MINNIE. / HOW MANY** / 22
Aug 58. (7") **LEAN JEAN. / DON'T NOBODY MOVE** / 67
Nov 58. (lp) **ROCKING THE JOINT** /
– Rock the joint / Rockin' chair on the Moon / Farewell – So long – Goodbye / Real rock drive / Fractured / Stop beatin' around the mulberry bush / Crazy man, crazy / Pat-a-cake / Live it up / Watcha gonna do / I'll be true to you / Dance with a dolly (with a hole in her stockin').
Nov 58. (7") **WHOA MABEL. / CHIQUITA LINDA** /
1959. (7") **CORRINE, CORRINA. / B.B.BETTY** – /
Mar 59. (7") **I GOT A WOMAN. / CHARMAINE** /
Jun 59. (lp) **BILL HALEY'S CHICKS** /
– Whoa Mabel / Ida, sweet as apple cider / Eloise / Dinah / Skinny Minnie / Mary, Mary Lou / Sweet Sue – Just you / B.B.Betty / Charmaine / Corrine Corrina / Marie / Lean Jean. *(re-iss.1960) (re-iss.Jan64 on 'Ace Of Hearts')*
1959. (7") **WHERE'D YOU GO LAST NIGHT. / (NOW AND THEN THERE'S) A FOOL SUCH AS I** – /
Aug 59. (7") **SHAKY. / CALEDONIA** /
Jan 60. (7") **JOEY'S SONG. / LOOK-A-THERE, AIN'T SHE PRETTY** / 46 Sep 59
Feb 60. (7") **SKOKIAAN. / PUERTO RICAN JUGGLER** / 70 Dec 59
1960. (7") **(PUT ANOTHER NICKEL IN) MUSIC, MUSIC, MUSIC!. / STRICTLY INSTRUMENTAL** – /
Apr 60. (lp) **STRICTLY INSTRUMENTAL** /
– Joey's song / (Put another nickel in) Music, music, music / Mack the knife / In a little Spanish town ('twas on a night like this) / Two shadows / Shaky / Strictly instrumental / Skokiaan (South African song) / Puerto Rican peddlar / Drowsy waters / Chiquita Linda (un poquito de tu amor) / The catwalk.
1960. (7") **CORRINE, CORRINA. / THE GREEN DOOR** – /

Warner Bros. / Warners

May 60. (7") **CANDY KISSES. / TAMIAMI** – /
1960. (7") **CHUCK SAFARI. / HAWK** – /
1960. (7") **SO RIGHT TONIGHT. / LET THE GOOD TIMES ROLL, CREOLE** – /
Nov 60. (lp) **HALEY'S JUKE BOX** /
– Sing the blues / Candy kisses / No letter today / This is the thanks I get / Bouquet of roses / There's a new Moon over my shoulder / Cold, cold heart / Wild side of life / Any time / Afraid / I don't hurt anymore.
1960. (7") **FLIP, FLOP AND FLY. / HONKY TONK** – /

London / Gone

Dec 61. (7") **SPANISH TWIST. / MY KIND OF WOMAN** /
1962. (7") **RIVIERA. / WAR PAINT** – /

not issued / Orfeon

1962. (7") **FLORIDA TWIST. / NEGRA CONSENTIDA** – / – Mexico
1962. (7") **PURE DE PAPAS. / ANOCHE** – / –

not issued / Logo

1962. (7") **YAKETY SAX. / BOOTS RANDOLPH – BOOTS BLUES** – /

Columbia / Columbia

Oct 62. (lp) **TWISTIN' KNIGHTS AT THE ROUND TABLE** /
– Lullaby of Birdland twist / Twist Marie / One two three twist / Down by the riverside twist / Queen of the twisters / Caravan twist / I want a little girl / Whistlin' and walkin' twist / Florida twist / Eight more miles to Louisville. *(re-iss.May81 on 'P.R.T.')*

Stateside / Newtown

Jun 63. (7") **TENOR MAN. / UP GOES MY LOVE** /
1963. (7") **MIDNIGHT IN WASHINGTON. / WHITE PARAKEET** – /
1963. (7") **DANCE AROUND THE CLOCK. / WHAT CAN I SAY AFTER I SAY I'M SORRY** – /
1963. (7") **TANDY. / YOU CALL EVERYBODY DARLING** – /

Brunswick / Decca

Aug 64. (7") **HAPPY BABY. / BIRTH OF THE BOOGIE** / –
Oct 64. (7") **GREEN DOOR. / (YEAH!) SHE'S EVIL** / –

not issued / Apt

1965. (7") **BURN THAT CANDLE. / STOP, LOOK AND LISTEN** – /
1965. (7") **HALEY A GO-GO. / TONGUE TIED TONY** – /

not issued / United Art

1969. (7") **THAT'S HOW I GOT TO MEMPHIS. / AIN'T LOVE FUNNY, HA! HA! HA!** – /

not issued / Kama Sutra

1970. (7") **ROCK AROUND THE CLOCK. / FRAMED** – /

Sonet / Janus

1971. (lp)(c) **ROCK AROUND THE COUNTRY** / –
– Dance around the clock / Games people play / A little piece at a time / I wouldn't have missed it for the world / Bony Moronie / There's a new Moon over my shoulder / Me and Bobby McGee / How many / Who'll stop the rain / Pink eyed pussycat / Travelin' band / No letter today. *(re-iss.Jun74 on 'Hallmark')*
1972. (7") **A LITTLE PIECE AT A TIME. / TRAVELIN' BAND** – /

Sonet / Speciality

May 73. (7") **ME AND BOBBY McGEE. / I WOULDN'T HAVE MISSED IT FOR THE WORLD** / –
1973. (lp)(c) **JUST ROCK AND ROLL MUSIC** /

– I'm walkin' / High-heel sneakers / Blue suede shoes / Tossin' and turnin' / Flip, flop and fly / Whole lotta shakin' goin' on / CC rider / Lawdy Miss Clawdy / Bring it on home to me / Personality / Crazy man crazy / Rock'n'roll music.

1974. (lp) **LIVE IN SWEDEN (live)** -
Jun 74. (7") **CRAZY MAN CRAZY (live). / LAWDY MISS CLAWDY (live)** -

Atlantic Atlantic

Jun 74. (lp)(c) **LIVE IN LONDON '74 (live)**
– Shake, rattle & roll / Rudy's rock / Rip it up / Spanish eyes / Razzle dazzle / Rock-a-beatin' boogie / Caravan / See you later alligator / Saints rock and roll / Rock around the clock / Rock the joint.

— HALEY became ill, leading him into retirement. Although in England, he had given final appearance at Royal Variety Show, Nov79. In 1980, now at age 55, he was diagnosed with brain tumor. On 9 Feb'81 he died of a heart attack.

– compilations, others, etc. –

1953. Transworld; (7") **YES INDEED. / REAL ROCK DRIVE** -
Jun 55. Brunswick; (7"ep) **DIM DIM THE LIGHTS** -
Jun 56. Brunswick; (7"ep) **ROCK AND ROLL** -
Jun 56. Brunswick; (7"ep) **ROCK AROUND THE CLOCK** -
Dec 56. Brunswick; (7"ep) **ROCK'N'ROLL STAGE SHOW (PART 1)** -
Dec 56. Brunswick; (7"ep) **ROCK'N'ROLL STAGE SHOW (PART 2)** -
Dec 56. Brunswick; (7"ep) **ROCK'N'ROLL STAGE SHOW (PART 3)** -
Feb 58. Brunswick; (7"ep) **ROCKING THE OLDIES (PART 1)** -
Feb 58. Brunswick; (7"ep) **ROCKING THE OLDIES (PART 2)** -
Feb 58. Brunswick; (7"ep) **ROCKING THE OLDIES (PART 3)** -
Apr 59. Brunswick; (7"ep) **ROCKING AROUND THE WORLD** -
Jul 59. Brunswick; (7"ep) **BILL HALEY AND HIS COMETS** -
Jun 55. London; (7") **GREEN TREE BOOGIE. / SUNDOWN BOOGIE** -
Aug 55. London; (10"lp) **LIVE IT UP**
Aug 55. London; (7") **FAREWELL, SO LONG, GOODBYE. / I'LL BE TRUE** -
Oct 55. London; (7") **TEN LITTLE INDIANS. / ROCKING CHAIR ON THE MOON** -
Dec 55. London; (7"ep) **ROCK AND ROLL** -
Feb 56. London; (7"ep) **LIVE IT UP (PART ONE)** -
Feb 56. London; (7"ep) **LIVE IT UP (PART TWO)** -
Oct 56. London; (7"ep) **LIVE IT UP (PART THREE)** -
Feb 57. Decca; (7") **ROCK THE JOINT. / HOW MANY** - -
Feb 57. London; (7") **ROCK THE JOINT. / YES INDEED** 20 -
Mar 57. London; (lp) **ROCK THE JOINT** ('Essex' work)
(re-iss.May64 on 'Golden Guinea') (re-iss.1966 on 'Marble Arch') (re-iss.10".May79 on 'Rollercoaster', 12"re-iss.1985, cd-iss.Nov89)
Nov 56. Melodisc; (7") **I'M GONNA DRY EVERY LITTLE TEAR WITH A KISS. / WHY DO I CRY OVER YOU** -
Jun 60. Warners; (7"ep) **HALEY AND HIS COMETS** -
May 61. Warners; (7"ep) **HALEY'S JUKEBOX** -
Aug 64. Warners; (7") **ROCK AROUND THE CLOCK. / LOVE LETTERS IN THE SAND** -
Oct 64. Warners; (7"ep) **BILL HALEY VOLUME 1** -
Nov 64. Warners; (7"ep) **BILL HALEY VOLUME 2** -
Jun 81. Warners; (lp)(c) **ROCK'N'ROLL FOREVER**
1961. Ksey; (7") **ABC BOOGIE. / (other artist)** -
1965. Xtra/ US= Essex; (lp) **BILL HALEY AND THE COMETS**
(re-iss.1970 on 'Valient')
1967. Ember; (7") **REAL LIVE ROCK AND ROLL** -
Jun 68. Ember; (lp) **KING OF ROCK'N'ROLL** -
Jan 69. Ember; (lp) **MR. ROCK'N'ROLL** -
Apr 68. Pye; (7") **CRAZY MAN CRAZY. / LAWDY MISS CLAWDY** -
Mar 68. M.C.A.; (7") **ROCK AROUND THE CLOCK. / SHAKE RATTLE AND ROLL** 20
May 68. M.C.A.; (lp) **RIP IT UP**
Mar 74. M.C.A.; (7") **ROCK AROUND THE CLOCK. / RIP IT UP** 12 39
(re-iss.Feb81)
Jun 74. M.C.A.; (lp)(c) **GOLDEN HITS**
Jun 74. M.C.A.; (7") **SEE YOU LATER ALLIGATOR. / RUDY'S ROCK**
Nov 76. M.C.A.; (7"m) **SHAKE RATTLE AND ROLL. / RAZZLE DAZZLE / ROCK-A-BEATIN' BOOGIE**
Jul 78. M.C.A.; (lp)(c) **ARMCHAIR ROCK'N'ROLL**
Sep 78. M.C.A.; (7"ep)(10"ep) **THE SAINTS ROCK'N'ROLL** -
(7"re-iss.Feb81)
Apr 81. M.C.A.; (7") **HALEY'S GOLDEN MEDLEY. / ABC BOOGIE** 50
May 81. M.C.A.; (d-lp)(c) **A TRIBUTE TO BILL HALEY**
(re-iss.Jun83)
Feb 85. M.C.A.; (cd) **GREATEST HITS**
Jul 85. M.C.A.; (lp)(c) **GOLDEN GREATS**
Sep 85. M.C.A.; (cd) **FROM THE ORIGINAL MASTER TAPES**
Jun 70. Hallmark; (lp)(c) **ROCK AROUND THE CLOCK** -
(re-iss.Feb83 on 'Spot')
Sep 70. Hallmark; (lp)(c) **ON STAGE (live)** -
Sep 72. Hallmark; (lp) **GOLDEN KING OF ROCK** -
Mar 87. Hallmark; (lp)(c) **THE ORIGINAL HITS '54-'57** -
(cd-iss.Mar90 on 'Pickwick')
Mar 76. Pickwick; (d-lp) **THE BILL HALEY COLLECTION** -
Feb 79. Bulldog; (lp) **20 GOLDEN PIECES OF BILL HALEY** -
(cd-iss.Vov89 as 'GOLDEN CD COLLECTION')
May 79. Rollercoaster; (7") **ROCK THE JOINT. / FRACTURED** -
(re-iss.1984)
May 79. Rollercoaster; (lp) **GOLDEN COUNTRY ORIGINS** -
Feb 80. Rollercoaster; (7"ep) **REAL ROCK DRIVE** -
Nov 84. Rollercoaster; (lp) **HILLBILLY HALEY** -
Oct 76. Sonet; (lp) **R.O.C.K.** -
Aug 79. Sonet; (7")(12") **HAIL HAIL ROCK'N'ROLL. / LET THE GOOD TIMES ROLL** -
(7"re-iss.Feb81)
Nov 79. Sonet; (7") **EVERYONE CAN ROCK AND ROLL. / I NEED THE MUSIC** -
(re-iss.Feb81)
Jun 80. Sonet; (lp) **EVERYONE CAN ROCK AND ROLL** -
Feb 81. Sonet; (7") **GOD BLESS ROCK AND ROLL. / SO RIGHT TONIGHT** -
Jul 82. Old Gold; (7") **ROCK AROUND THE CLOCK. / THIRTEEN WOMEN** -
(re-iss.Jul88)
Jul 82. Old Gold; (7") **SHAKE RATTLE AND ROLL. / SEE YOU LATER ALLIGATOR** -
Jul 90. Old Gold; (12"ep) **ROCK-A-BEATIN' BOOGIE / RAZZLE DAZZLE. / BURN THAT CANDLE / DIM DIM THE LIGHTS** -
Jul 82. Revival; (7") **RUDY'S ROCK. / ABC BOOGIE** -
Sep 82. Bear Family; (5xlp-box) **ROCK ROLLIN' BILL HALEY** -
(UK-iss.Sep84 on 'Rollercoaster')
Sep 83. Scoop; (7"ep)(c-ep) **SIX-TRACK HITS** -
– Whole lotta shakin' goin' on / Rock around the clock / Shake rattle and roll / Kansas City / Me and Bobby McGee / Rip it up.
1984. Charly; (d-lp) **MR.ROCK'N'ROLL / THE ESSENTIAL BILL HALEY** -
Jan 85. Topline; (lp) **BOOGIE WITH BILL HALEY** -
Jul 85. Buddah; (lp) **BILL HALEY'S ROCK'N'ROLL SCRAPBOOK** -
(cd-iss.Apr90 on 'Sequel')
Oct 87. M.F.P.; (lp)(c) **BILL HALEY & HIS COMETS** -
1988. Connoisseur; (d-lp) **GREATEST HITS** -
1988. Connoisseur; (d-lp) **RIP IT UP ROCK'N'ROLL** -
Jul 92. Music Club; (cd) **THE VERY BEST OF BILL HALEY & HIS COMETS** -
– Rock around the clock / Shake, rattle and roll / See you later alligator / The saints rock and roll / Rock-a beatin' boogie / Rockin' thru the rye / Rip it up / Don't knock the rock / Mambo rock / Rudy's rock / Razzle dazzle / Skinny Minnie / R.O.C.K. / Thirteen women / ABC boogie / Birth of the boogie / Forty cups of coffee / Two hound dogs / Burn that candle / Calling all Comets.
Oct 93. See For Miles; (cd) **THE EP COLLECTION** -
Jul 94. Rollercoaster; (7"ep) **REAL ROCK DRIVE / LIVE IT UP. / DANCE WITH A DOLLY / ROCKING CHAIR ON THE MOON** -
Aug 94. Dynamite; (cd) **BILL HALEY** -
Feb 95. More Music; (cd)(c) **ROCK AROUND THE CLOCK** -
Mar 95. Laserlight; (cd) **BILL HALEY & HIS COMETS** -
Sep 95. Hallmark; (cd)(c) **CRAZY MAN CRAZY** -

Terry HALL

Born: 19 Mar '59, Coventry, England. Ex-SPECIALS frontman TERRY HALL, broke away with other SPECIALS; NEVILLE STAPLES and LYNVAL GOULDING to form FUN BOY THREE. Still contracted to 'Chrysalis', they issued debut UK Top 20 single 'THE LUNATICS HAVE TAKEN OVER THE ASYLUM'. Early the next year, they teamed up with new all-girl trio BANANARAMA, to have a UK Top 5 hit with 30's standard 'IT AIN'T WHAT YOU DO IT'S THE WAY THAT YOU DO IT'. It was soon trailed by a Top 10 eponymous album, and 4 more Top 20 singles. After the release of a DAVID BYRNE (Talking Heads) produced Top 10 album in 1983, they soon split 2 ways. TERRY HALL formed The COLOUR FIELD, who continued sporadically to make entries into Top 50. • **Style:** FUN BOY THREE were a racially mixed politically motivated trio, who broke from ska-pop to intelligent pop with Afro-rhythm beat. The COLOUR FIELD became noted for smoother romance'n'roll tunes. • **Songwriters:** HALL/group penned except; SUMMERTIME (Gershwin). 'OUR LIPS ARE SEALED' was composed by HALL and GO-GO's singer BELINDA CARLISLE. The COLOUR FIELD covered; RUNNING AWAY (Sly & The Family Stone) / SHE (Charles Aznavour) / LOVE WILL KEEP US TOGETHER (Neil Sedaka) / THREE COOL CATS (Leiber-Stoller) / GOD ONLY KNOWS (Beach Boys) / THIS GUY'S IN LOVE WITH YOU (Herb Alpert). • **Trivia:** The COLOUR FIELD's 'THINKING OF YOU' single featured the dual vox of KATRINA PHILLIPS, who later joined GHOST DANCE.

Recommended: THE COLLECTION (*7; all TERRY HALL's work)

FUN BOY THREE

TERRY HALL – vocals (ex-SPECIALS) / **NEVILLE STAPLES** – vocals, percussion (ex-SPECIALS) / **LYNVAL GOULDING** – guitar (ex-SPECIALS)

Chrysalis Chrysalis

Oct 81. (7")(12") **THE LUNATICS (HAVE TAKEN OVER THE ASYLUM). / FAITH, HOPE & CHARITY** 20
Jan 82. (7")(12") **T'AIN'T WHAT YOU DO (IT'S THE WAY THAT YOU DO IT). (by "FUN BOY THREE & BANANARAMA") / THE FUNRAMA THEME** 4

now with **NICKY HOLLAND** – keyboards / JUNE MILES-KINGSTON – drums

Mar 82. (lp)(c) **THE FUN BOY THREE** 7
– Sanctuary / Way on down / The lunatics have taken over the asylum / Life in general / Faith, hope and charity / Funrama 2 / Best of luck mate / T'ain't what you do (it's the way that you do it) / The telephone always rings / I don't believe it / Alone. *(re-iss.Nov84 on 'Fame')*

— Mar82 teamed up with BANANARAMA again on 45, 'REALLY SAYING SOMETHING'.

May 82. (7")(12")(7"pic-d-2) **THE TELEPHONE ALWAYS RINGS. / THE ALIBI** 17
Jul 82. (7")(12")(7"pic-d) **SUMMERTIME. / SUMMER OF '82** 18

— with **BOTHAN PETERS** – bass / **INGRID SCHROEDER** – vocals / **DICK CUTHILL** – coronet / **CAROLINE LEVELLE** – cello / **ANNIE WHITEHEAD** – trombone / **GERALDO D'ARBUY** – perc.

Dec 82. (7")(12") **THE MORE I SEE (THE LESS I BELIEVE). / ?** 68

Jan 83. (7")(12")(7"pic-d) **THE TUNNEL OF LOVE. / THE LUNACY LEGACY** 10

Feb 83. (lp)(c) **WAITING** 14
– The tunnel of love / Our lips are sealed / The pressure of life (takes weight off the body) / Things we do / Well fancy that! / Murder she said / The more I see (the less I believe) / Going home / We're having all the fun / The farm yard connection.

Apr 83. (7")(12") **OUR LIPS ARE SEALED. / ('A'instrumental)** 7
(d7"+=) – We're having all the fun / Going home.

— (split mid'83) **NEVILLE AND LYNVAL to SUNDAY BEST.**

– compilations, etc. –

Jun 84. Chrysalis; (lp)(c) **THE BEST OF THE FUN BOY THREE**
– T'ain't what you do (it's the way that you do it) / Really saying something / Summertime / The lunatics (have taken over the asylum) / The more I see (the less I believe) / The telephone always rings / Our lips are sealed / The tunnel of love / We're having all the fun / The farm yard connection / The pressure of life (takes weight off the body).

Jan 88. Old Gold; (12") **OUR LIPS ARE SEALED. / THE TUNNEL OF LOVE / THE LUNATICS (HAVE TAKEN OVER THE ASYLUM)** -

May 94. Connoisseur; (cd) **THE SINGLES (FUN BOY THREE / COLOUR FIELD)** -

Jun 94. Windsong; (cd) **LIVE ON THE TEST (live)** -

COLOUR FIELD

TERRY HALL – vocals / **KARL SHALE** – bass / **TOBY LYONS** – guitar, keyboards (ex-SWINGING CATS) / guest drummer ?

Chrysalis Chrysalis

Jan 84. (7") **THE COLOUR FIELD. / SORRY** 43
(12"+=) – ('A' special mix).

— added guest **PETE DE FREITAS** – drums (of ECHO & THE BUNNYMEN)

Jul 84. (7") **TAKE. / PUSHING UP THE DAISIES** 70
(12"+=) Windmills of your mind.

— added **PAUL BURGESS** – drums

Jan 85. (7") **THINKING OF YOU. / MY WILD FLAME** 12
(12"+=) – ('A'instrumental).
(d7"++=) – Little things.

Apr 85. (lp)(c) **VIRGINS AND PHILISTINES** 12
– Thinking of you / Faint hearts / Castles in the air / Take / Cruel circus / Hammond song / Virgins and Philistines / Armchair theatre / Yours sincerely / Sorry.

Apr 85. (7") **CASTLES IN THE AIR. / LOVE STRINGS** 51
(12") – ('A'side) / ('A'extended) / Your love was smashing.
(d7") – ('A'side) / I can't get enough of you baby / ('A'instrumental mix) / Your love was smashing.

— **GARY DWYER** – drums (ex-TEARDROP EXPLODES) repl. BURGESS

Jan 86. (7")(12") **THINGS COULD BE SO BEAUTIFUL. / FROSTY MORNINGS**
(12"+=) – Pushing up the daisies (live) / Yours sincerely (live).

Feb 87. (7") **RUNNING AWAY. / DIGGING IT DEEP**
(12"+=)/ /(12"+=) – ('A'long version). / / ('A'vocal mix).

Mar 87. (lp)(c)(cd) **DECEPTION** 95
– Badlands / Running away / From dawn to distraction / Confession / Miss Texas 1967 / She / Heart of America / She / Digging it deep / Monkey in winter / Goodbye Sun valley.

Jul 87. (7") **SHE. / MONKEY IN WINTER**
(12"+=) – ('A' remix).

— disbanded 1987.

TERRY, BLAIR & ANOUCHKA

(TERRY HALL, BLAIR BOOTH & ANOUCHKA GROOCE)(BLAIR also co-wrote songs)

Oct 89. (7")(c-s) **MISSING. / HAPPY FAMILIES** 75
(12"+=)(cd-s+=) – Beautiful people.

Jan 90. (7")(c-s) **ULTRA MODERN NURSERY RHYMES. / HUSH HUSH BALLOO**
(12"+=)(cd-s+=) – Love will keep us together.

Feb 90. (cd)(c)(lp) **ULTRA MODERN NURSERY RHYMES**
– Ultra modern nursery rhyme / Missing / Fishbones and scaredy cats / Lucky in luv' / Day like today / Sweet September sacrifice / Beautiful people / Three cool cats / Happy families / Just go.

— In 1992, TERRY HALL partnered DAVE STEWART's (ex-EURYTHMICS) VEGAS.

VEGAS

(aka **DAVE STEWART & TERRY HALL** ex-COLOUR FIELD)(same label)

Sep 92. (7")(c-s) **POSSESSED. / THE DAY IT RAINED FOREVER** 32
(cd-s+=) – Lying in bed barefoot.
(cd-s+=) – Infectious.

Oct 92. (cd)(c)(lp) **VEGAS**
– Possessed / Walk into the wind / She's alright / Take me for what I am / The trouble with lovers / Nothing alas alack / The thought of you / Anthem / Wise guy / The day it rained forever / She.

Nov 92. (7")(c-s) **SHE. / ('A'disco version)** 43
(12") – ('A'rapino brothers mix) / ('A'extended disco).
(cd-s+=) – Tip of my tongue / If you kill my cat, I'll kill your dog.

Mar 93. (7")(c-s) **WALK INTO THE WIND. / WISE GUY**
(cd-s+=) – Truth is stranger than fiction / Art blind.

TERRY HALL

with **CRAIG GANNON** – guitar (ex-SMITHS, ex-AZTEC CAMERA, etc) / **LES PATTINSON** – bass (ex-ECHO & THE BUNNYMEN) / **CHRIS SHARROCK** – drums (ex-ICICLE WORKS)

Anxious Anxious

Aug 94. (c-ep)(cd-ep) **FOREVER J / FOREVER J (Pulp mix) / SUBURBAN CEMETRY / GUESS IT'S NOT A GREAT DAY TO BE ME** 67

Sep 94. (cd)(c) **HOME**
– Forever J / Grief disguised as joy / First attack of love / I don't got you / No no no / I drew a lemon / Moon on your dress / What's wrong with me / You / Sense. *(re-iss.Nov95)*

Nov 94. (7")(c-s) **SENSE / GOD ONLY KNOWS** 54
(12"+=)(cd-s+=) – This guy's in love with you.

— below with DAMON ALBARN (co-writer A), TRICKY and IAN BROUDIE.

Oct 95. (c-ep)(cd-ep) **RAINBOWS e.p.** 62
– Chasing a rainbow (with AMON ALBARN) / Ghost town (live with TRICKY) / Thinking of you (live) / Our lips are sealed (live).
(cd-s) – (first 2 tracks) / Mistakes (with IAN BROUDIE) / See no evil (live).

– compilations –

Oct 92. Chrysalis; (cd)(c) **THE COLLECTION** (TERRY HALL)
– (best material SPECIALS / FUN BOY THREE / COLOUR FIELD / TERRY, BLAIR, etc.)

HALF NELSON (see under ⇒ SPARKS)

Daryl HALL & John OATES

Formed: Philadelphia, USA ... 1972 by the duo, who signed to 'Atlantic', due to their work with band GULLIVER. They had originally met in 1967, while attending local Temple University. HALL had classical training as a boy, and progressed to doo-wop groups while also featuring on a single recorded by future producer KENNY GAMBLE & THE ROMEOS. He then sessioned for many including THE TEMPTONES and SMOKEY ROBINSON, before forming GULLIVER with TIM MOORE, TOM SELLERS and JIM HELMER. They released 1 self-titled lp in 1969 for 'Elektra', before being joined by OATES. They broke up before OATES could provide them with any songs. The duos debut lp 'WHOLE OATS', was produced by Arif Mardin, and was followed in 1974 by 'ABANDONED LUNCHEONETTE'. After moving to New York, the album hit US Top 40, helped by their Top 60 single 'SHE'S GONE'. Their 3rd album 'WAR BABIES' produced by TODD RUNDGREN, failed to provoke much interest and the duo were dropped by Atlantic. They then signed to 'RCA' in 1975, and issued eponymous 4th album, which eventually climbed into US Top 20 in 1976. It contained their first entry into US Top 5 'SARA SMILE', which provoked last label to re-issue 'SHE'S GONE' to hit US Top 10 and UK Top 50. Early in 1977, they made first of 6 US chart toppers with 'RICH GIRL'. • **Style:** White soul-rock / R&B duo, with one excursion into heavier field in '74's 'WAR BABIES'. • **Songwriters:** HALL-OATES except; YOU'VE LOST THAT LOVIN' FEELIN' (Righteous Brothers) / THE WAY YOU DO THE THINGS YOU DO – MY GIRL (Temptations) / CAN'T HELP FALLING IN LOVE (Elvis Presley) / LOVE TRAIN (O'JAYS) / etc. They co-wrote some songs with SARA and JANNA ALLEN. HALL covered; WRITTEN IN STONE (J.Allen-S.Dubin-K.Savigar) / ME AND MRS.JONES (Billy Paul).
• **Trivia:** ROBERT FRIPP (of KING CRIMSON) produced HALL's solo outing 'SACRED SONGS'.

Recommended: THE BEST OF HALL & OATES – LOOKING BACK (*6).

DARYL HALL (b.DARYL HOHL, 11 Oct'48, Pottstown, Philadelphia) – vocals, keys (ex-TEMPTONES, ex-solo artist, ex-CELLAR DOR, ex-EXECUTIVE SUITE, ex-GULLIVER) / **JOHN OATES** (b. 7 Apr'49, New York, USA) – vocals, guitar (ex-MASTERS) with various personnel session players.

Atlantic Atlantic

Sep 72. (7") **GOODNIGHT AND GOOD MORNING. / ALL OUR LOVE (as "WHOLE OATS")** -

Nov 72. (lp)(c) **WHOLE OATS** -
– I'm sorry / All our love / Georgie / Fall in Philadelphia / Water wheel / Lazy man / Good night & good morning / They needed each other / Southeast city window / Thank you for . . . / Lily (are you happy). *(UK-iss.Sep76) (cd-iss.Feb93)*

Nov 72. (7") **I'M SORRY. / LILY (ARE YOU HAPPY)** -

Jan 74. (lp)(c) **ABANDONED LUNCHEONETTE**
– I'm just a kid / Laughing boy / She's gone / Las Vegas turnaround / Had I known you better then / Lady rain / When the morning comes / Abandoned luncheonette / Everytime I look at you. *(US re-iss.Oct76, hit No.33) (cd-iss.Jun93)*

Jan 74. (7") **LAS VEGAS TURNAROUND. / I'M JUST A KID**

Feb 74. (7") **SHE'S GONE. / I'M JUST A KID** - 60
(re-iss. US Jul'76, hit No.7)

Jul 74. (7") **WHEN THE MORNING COMES. / LADY RAIN**

Sep 74. (7") **SHE'S GONE. / ABANDONED LUNCHEONETTE** -

Nov 74. (lp)(c) **WAR BABIES** 86 Oct 74
– Can't stop the music (he played it much too long) / Is it a star / Beanie G and the rose tattoo / You're much too soon / 70's scenario / War baby son of Zorro / I'm watching you (a mutant romance) / Better watch your back / Screaming through December / Johnny Gone and the "C" eaters.

Nov 74. (7") **CAN'T STOP THE MUSIC (HE PLAYED IT MUCH TOO LONG). / 70'S SCENARIO** -

R.C.A. R.C.A.

Sep 75. (lp)(c) **DARYL HALL & JOHN OATES** 56 17

– Camelia / Sara smile / Alone too long / Out of me, out of you / Nothing at all / Gino (the manager) / (You know) It doesn't matter anymore / Ennui on the mountain / Grounds for separation / Soldering. *(re-iss.Apr80)*

Sep 75. (7") **CAMELIA. / ENNUI ON THE MOUNTAIN** □ □
Nov 75. (7") **ALONE TOO LONG. / NOTHING AT ALL** - □
Jan 76. (7") **SARA SMILE. / SOLDERING** □ 4
May 76. (7") **GINO (THE MANAGER). / SOLDERING** □ -
Sep 76. (lp)(c) **BIGGER THAN BOTH OF US** 25 13 Aug 76
– Back together again / Rich girl / Crazy eyes / Do what you want, be what you are / Kerry / London luck and love / Room to breathe / You'll never learn / Falling.
Nov 76. (7") **DO WHAT YOU WANT, BE WHAT YOU ARE. / YOU'LL NEVER LEARN** □ 39 Oct 76
Nov 76. (7") **RICH GIRL. / YOU'LL NEVER LEARN** □ -
Late in '76 DARYL duetted with RUTH COPELAND on single 'Heaven'.
Jan 77. (7") **RICH GIRL. / LONDON LUCK & LOVE** - 1
May 77. (7") **BACK TOGETHER AGAIN. / ROOM TO BREATHE** - 28
May 77. (7") **BACK TOGETHER AGAIN. / ENNUI ON THE MOUNTAIN** □ -
Oct 77. (lp)(c) **BEAUTY ON A BACK STREET** 40 30 Sep77
– Don't change / Why do lovers (break each other's heart?) / You must be good for something / The emptyness / Love hurts (love heals) / Bigger than both of us / Bad habits and infections / Winged bull / The girl who used to be. *(re-iss.Jul84)*
Oct 77. (7") **WHY DO LOVERS (BREAK EACH OTHER'S HEART?). / THE GIRL WHO USED TO BE** □ 73
Jan 78. (7") **DON'T CHANGE. / THE EMPTYNESS** - □

— **CHARLES DE CHANT** – saxophone, keyboards, perc. repl. TOM SCOTT / **KENNY PASSARELLI** – bass repl. LEE SKLAR & SCOTT EDWARDS / **ROGER POPE** – drums repl. JEFF PORCARO / **CALEB QUAYE** – lead guitar / **DAVID KENT** – keyboards repl. other sessioners.

Jun 78. (lp)(c) **LIVE TIME (live)** □ 42 May 78
– Rich girl / The emptyness / Do what you want, be what you are / I'm just a kid / Sara smile / Abandoned luncheonette / Room to breathe. *(re-iss.Jun83)*
Aug 78. (7") **IT'S A LAUGH. / SERIOUS MATTER** - 20
Sep 78. (7") **THE LAST TIME. / SERIOUS MATTER** □ -
Sep 78. (lp)(c) **ALONG THE RED LEDGE** □ 27
– It's a laugh / Melody for a memory / The last time / I don't wanna lose you / Have I been away too long / Alley katz / Don't blame it on love / Serious matter / Pleasure beach / August day. *(re-iss.Jun83)*
Jan 79. (7") **I DON'T WANNA LOSE YOU. / AUGUST DAY** □ 42 Dec 78

— They retained **DECHANT, PASSARELLI** (on next only), and brought in **TOM 'T-Bone' WOLK** – bass, synthe / **G.E.SMITH** – guitar / **MICKEY CURRY** – drums

Nov 79. (7") **PORTABLE RADIO. / NUMBER ONE** □ -
Nov 79. (lp)(c) **X-STATIC** □ 33 Oct 79
– The woman comes and goes / Wait for me / Portable radio / All you want is Heaven / Who said the world was fair / Running from Paradise / Number one / Bebop – Drop / Hallofon / Intravino.
May 80. (7") **WAIT FOR ME. / NO BRAIN NO PAIN** - 18 Oct 79
May 80. (7") **WHO SAID THE WORLD WAS FAIR. / ALL YOU WANT IS HEAVEN** - □
Jun 80. (7") **RUNNING FROM PARADISE. / BEBOP – DROP** 41 -
Jul 80. (7") **HOW DOES IT FEEL TO BE BACK. / UNITED STATE** - 30
Aug 80. (lp)(c) **VOICES** □ 17
– How does it feel to be back / Big kids / United state / Hard to be in love with you / Kiss on my list / Gotta lotta nerve (perfect perfect) / You've lost that lovin' feelin' / You make my dreams / Everytime you go away / Africa / Diddy doo wop (I hear the voices). *(re-iss.Sep81) (re-iss.+cd.Oct87)*
Sep 80. (7") **YOU'VE LOST THAT LOVIN' FEELIN' / DIDDY DOO WOP (I HEAR THE VOICES)** - 12
Sep 80. (7") **YOU'VE LOST THAT LOVIN' FEELIN'. / UNITED STATE** 55 -
Nov 80. (7") **KISS ON MY LIST. / AFRICA** 33 1 Jan 81
Jun 81. (7") **YOU MAKE MY DREAMS. / GOTTA LOTTA NERVE (PERFECT PERFECT)** □ 5 Apr 81
Sep 81. (7")(12") **PRIVATE EYES. / TELL ME WHAT YOU WANT** □ 1 Aug 81
(UK re-iss.Mar82, hit No.32)
Sep 81. (lp)(c) **PRIVATE EYES** 8 5
– Private eyes / Looking for a good gun / I can't go for that (no can do) / Mama a mano / Did it in a minute / Head above water / Tell me what you want / Friday let me down / Ungaurded minute / Your imagination / Some men. *(re-iss.1984) (re-iss.+cd.Oct87)*
Jan 82. (7")(12") **I CAN'T GO FOR THAT (NO CAN DO). / UNGUARDED MINUTE** 8 1 Nov 81
Mar 82. (7") **DID IT IN A MINUTE. / HEAD ABOVE WATER** - 9
Jun 82. (7")(12") **YOUR IMAGINATION. / SARA SMILE** - 33
Oct 82. (7")(12") **MANEATER. / DELAYED REACTION** 6 1
Oct 82. (lp)(c) **H2O** 24 3
– Maneater / Crime pays / One on one / Art of heartbreak / Open all night / Family man / Italian girls / Guessing games / Delayed reaction / At tension / Go solo. *(re-iss.+cd.Oct87)*
Jan 83. (7")(12") **ONE ON ONE. / ART OF HEARTBREAK** 63 7
(US 12") – ('A'club) / I can't go for that (no can do) (extended).
Apr 83. (7") **FAMILY MAN. / CRIME PAYS** 15 6
(7"+=)(12"+=) – Open All Night. *(US B-side)*
Sep 83. (7") **SAY IT ISN'T SO. / KISS ON MY LIST** - 2
Oct 83. (7")(12") **SAY IT ISN'T SO. / DID IT IN A MINUTE** 69 -
Oct 83. (lp)(c)(cd) **ROCK'N SOUL, PART 1** (compilation) 16 7
– Sara smile / She's gone / Rich girl / Kiss on my list / You make my dreams / Private eyes / I can't go for that (no can do) / Maneater / One on one / Wait for me (live) / Adult education / Say it isn't so.
Feb 84. (7") **ADULT EDUCATION. / MANEATER** - 8
Feb 84. (7") **ADULT EDUCATION. / SAY IT ISN'T SO** 63 -
(12"+=) – I can't go for that (no can do).
Oct 84. (7")(12") **OUT OF TOUCH. / COLD DARK AND YESTERDAY** 48 1 Sep 84
Oct 84. (lp)(c)(cd) **BIG BAM BOOM** 28 5
– Going thru the motions / Cold dark and yesterday / All American girl / Possession obsession / Dance on your knees / Out of touch / Method of modern love / Bank on your love / Some things are better left unsaid
Jan 85. (7")(12") **METHOD OF MODERN LOVE. / BANK ON YOUR LOVE** 21 5 Dec 84
(d7"+=) – I can't go for that (live) / Maneater (live).
Mar 85. (7") **SOME THINGS ARE BETTER LEFT UNSAID. / ALL AMERICAN GIRL** - 18
May 85. (7") **OUT OF TOUCH (remix). / DANCE ON YOUR KNEES** 62 -
(12"+=) – Everytime you go away.
May 85. (7") **POSSESSION OBSESSION. / DANCE ON YOUR KNEES** - 30
Sep 85. (7")(12") **A NITE AT THE APOLLO LIVE! (live medley: – THE WAY YOU DO THE THINGS YOU DO – MY GIRL). / ADULT EDUCATION** 58 20 Aug 85

— (above and below credited DAVID RUFFIN & EDDIE KENDRICKS; ex-Temptations)

Sep 85. (lp)(c)(cd) **LIVE AT THE APOLLO (WITH DAVID RUFFIN & EDDIE KENDRICKS)** 32 21
– Get ready – Ain't too proud to beg – The way you do the things you do – My girl / When something is wrong with my baby / Everytime you go away / I can't go for that (no can do) / One by one / Possession obsession / Adult education. *(cd-iss.Sep93)*

In 1986 split for a while, HALL made solo album. See further below.

Arista Arista
Apr 88. (7")(12") **EVERYTHING YOUR HEART DESIRES. / REAL LOVE** □ 3
Jun 88. (lp)(c)(cd) **OOH YEAH!** 52 24 May 88
– Downtown life / Everything your heart desires / I'm in pieces / Missed opportunity / Talking all night / Rockability / Rocket to God / Soul love / ReaLove / Keep on pushin' love.
Jul 88. (7") **MISSED OPPORTUNITY. / SOUL LOVE** - 29
Sep 88. (7") **DOWNTOWN LIFE. / ('A'urban mix)** - 31
Sep 90. (7") **SO CLOSE. / ('A'unplugged)** 69 11
(cd-s+=) – She's gone (live) / Can't help falling in love.
Nov 90. (cd)(c)(lp) **CHANGE OF SEASON** 44 61 Oct 90
– So close / Starting all over again / Sometimes a mind changes / Change of season / I ain't gonna take it this time / Everywhere I look / Give it up (old habits) / Don't hold back your love / Halfway there / Only love / Heavy rain / So close – unplugged.
Dec 90. (c-s) **DON'T HOLD BACK YOUR LOVE. / CHANGE OF SEASON** - 41
Jan 91. (7")(c-s) **EVERYWHERE I LOOK. / I CAN'T GO FOR THAT (NO CAN DO) (remix)** 74 -
(12"+=)(cd-s+=) – Sometimes a mind changes.
Oct 91. (cd)(c)(lp) **LOOKING BACK – THE BEST OF DARYL HALL & JOHN OATES** (compilation) 9 □
– She's gone / Sara smile / Rich girl / You've lost that lovin' feelin' / Kiss on my list / Every time you go away / Private eyes / I can't go for that (no can do) / Maneater / One on one / Family man / Adult education / Out of touch / Method of modern love / Starting all over again. *(cd+)(c+=)* – Back together again / So close / Everything your heart desires.

– compilations, others –

Sep 76. Atlantic; (7"ep) **SHE'S GONE / WAR BABY SON OF ZORRO / LAZY MAN** 42 -
Jan 77. Atlantic; (7") **LAS VEGAS TURNAROUND. / HAD I KNOWN YOU BETTER THEN** □ □
Feb 77. Atlantic; (lp)(c) **NO GOODBYES** □ 92
Apr 77. Atlantic; (7") **IT'S UNCANNY. / BEANIE G. & THE ROSE TATTOO** □ -
Jun 77. Atlantic; (7") **IT'S UNCANNY. / LILY (ARE YOU HAPPY)** - 80
Jul 81. Atlantic; (7") **SHE'S GONE. / WHEN THE MORNING COMES** □ □
Apr 77. Chelsea; (lp)(c) **PAST TIMES BEHIND** (71-72) □ □
1977. Chelsea; (7") **THE REASON WAY (with GULLIVER) / IF THAT'S WHAT MAKES YOU HAPPY (Hall & Oates)** □ -
May 82. RCA Gold; (7") **KISS ON MY LIST. / RUNNING FROM PARADISE** □ -
May 83. R.C.A.; (c-ep) **CASSETTE EP** □ -
– I can't go for that (no can do) / Maneater / Private eyes / Kiss on my list.
Jun 84. Magnum Force; (lp) **THE PROVIDER** □ -
Oct 85. Thunderbolt; (lp)(c) **REALLY SMOKIN'** □ -
Apr 86. Showcase; (lp)(c) **THE EARLY YEARS** □ -
Nov 86. Old Gold; (7") **MANEATER. / I CAN'T GO FOR THAT (NO CAN DO)** □ -
Oct 92. Old Gold; (cd-ep) **I CAN'T GO FOR THAT (NO CAN DO) / PRIVATE EYES / KISS IS ON MY LIST** □ -
Oct 92. Old Gold; (cd-ep) **MANEATER / FAMILY MAN / METHOD OF MODERN LOVE** □ -
Nov 86. Meteor; (lp)(c)(cd) **20 CLASSIC TRACKS** □ -
1988. Big Time; (lp)(c)(cd) **FIRST SESSIONS** □ -
Feb 94. Javelin; (cd)(c) **SPOTLIGHT ON HALL & OATES** □ -
Sep 94. Prestige; (cd) **A LOT OF CHANGES COMIN'** □ -
Feb 95. B.A.M.; (cd) **PEARLS OF THE PAST** □ -
Oct 95. R.C.A.; (cd) **ROCK'N'SOUL PART 2 (GREATEST HITS)** □ -

DARYL HALL

not issued Parallex
1968. (7") **A LONELY GIRL / VICKY, VICKY** - □
not issued Amy
1968. (7") **THE PRINCESS & THE SOLDIER./ (Part 2)** □ □
R.C.A. R.C.A.
Apr 80. (lp)(c) **SACRED SONGS** (rec.1977) □ 58
– Sacred songs / Something in 4/4 time / Babs and Babs / Urban landscape / NYNCY / The farther away (I am) / Why was it so easy / Don't leave me alone with her / Survive / Without tears. *(re-iss.Jul84)*
Apr 80. (7") **SACRED SONGS. / SOMETHING IN 4-4 TIME** - □
Jul 86. (7")(12") **DREAMTIME. / LET IT OUT** 28 5

Aug 86. (lp)(c)(cd) **THREE HEARTS IN THE HAPPY ENDING MACHINE** 26 29
– Dreamtime / Only a vision / I wasn't born yesterday / Someone like you / Next stop / For you / Foolish pride / Right as rain / Let it out / What's going to happen to us. *(re-iss.May88)*
Oct 86. (7") **FOOLISH PRIDE. / WHAT'S GOING TO HAPPEN TO US** - 33
Nov 86. (7") **I WASN'T BORN YESTERDAY. / WHAT'S GONNA HAPPEN TO US**
(12"+=) – Dreamtime.
Jan 87. (7") **SOMEONE LIKE YOU. / ('A' sax solo version)** - 57

—— writes with **PETER LORD MORELAND** – keyboards / **V. JEFFREY SMITH** – synth.bass / **ALAN GORRIE** – bass / other musicians **TOMMY EYRE** – keyboards / **MEL WESSON** – programming / **TREVOR MURRELL** – drums / **BOB BITSAND** – bass / **MYLES BOULD** – percussion

Epic Epic
Sep 93. (7")(c-s) **I'M IN A PHILLY MOOD (Edit) / MONEY CHANGES EVERYTHING** 59 82
(cd-s+=) – I've finally seen the light.
(cd-s) – ('A'side) / Love T.K.O. (live) / Me and Mrs.Jones (live).
(re-iss.Mar94 hit UK 52)
Oct 93. (cd)(c)(lp) **SOUL ALONE** 57
– Power of seduction / This time / Love revelation / I'm in a Philly mood / Borderline / Stop loving me, stop loving you / Help me find a way to your heart / Send me / Wildfire / Money changes everything / Written in stone. *(re-dist. Jan94)*
Jan 94. (c-s) **STOP LOVING ME, STOP LOVING YOU. / MONEY CHANGES EVERYTHING** 30
(12"+=)(cd-s+=) – (4 more 'A'mixes).
May 94. (7")(c-s) **HELP ME FIND A WAY TO YOUR HEART. / POWER OF SEDUCTION** 70
(cd-s+=) – Stop loving me, stop loving you (live) / I'm in a Philly mood (live).

—— Below on 'Mercury' & the theme from USA soccer World Cup Finals.
Jun 94. (7"pic-d)(c-s)(cd-s) **GLORYLAND. ("DARYL HALL & SOUNDS OF BLACKNESS") / ('A'mixes)** 36
Aug 94. (c-s) **WILDFIRE. / THIS TIME**
(cd-s+=) – ('A'extended).

—— DARYL surfaced again when credited in May95 on DUSTY SPRINGFIELD's UK Top50 hit single 'WHEREVER WOULD I BE'.

GULLIVER

with **DARYL HALL**

Elektra Elektra
1969. (7") **EVERY DAY'S A LOVELY DAY / ANGELINA** -
1970. (lp) **GULLIVER**
– Everyday's a lovely day / I'm really smokin' / Christine / Rose come home / Enough – Over the mountain / Angelina / Flogene / Lemon road / Seventy / Truly good song.
1970. (7") **A TRULY GOOD SONG. /EVERY DAY'S A LOVELY DAY**

Toni HALLIDAY (see under ⇒ CURVE)

Peter HAMMILL (see under ⇒ VAN DER GRAAF GENERATOR)

Herbie HANCOCK

Born: 12 Apr'40, Chicago, USA. While at Iowa college in the late 50's, he formed 17-piece band/ensemble to play local gigs. At the turn of the 60's, he was invited to play piano in DONALD BYRD's combo. In 1962, while a member of said group, HANCOCK issued debut solo lp 'TAKIN' OFF', which yielded surprise US Top75 hit 'WATERMELON MAN'. This was noted by another trumpeter MILES DAVIS, who quickly poached him to enrol in his quintet. He remained an integral asset for MILES' jazz outfit, until his departure in 1968. He had made several albums for 'Blue Note' during this period, but moved on to 'Warners' with his own sextet, releasing highly acclaimed lp 'MWANDISHI'. After signing to 'Columbia' in 1972, he issued 2 more albums before flitting to Los Angeles. The second of which HEADHUNTERS gave him his first break through into mainstream US pop charts. This provided him with a platform to diversify between the jazz and pop world. **Style & Songwriters:** Classically trained jazz-rock composer, who fused experimentally and commercially, all facets of modern jazz, soul-funk and pop. In the late 70's, he introduced a vocoder (voice synthe.) into his new-found electronic disco sound. He collaborated with others on most releases. • **Trivia:** HANCOCK also wrote scores for the films BLOW UP (1967) and DEATH WISH (1974). In the mid-70's, he converted to worship a form of Buddhism (Nicherin Shoshu).

Recommended: THE COLLECTION (*7)

HERBIE HANCOCK – keyboards, etc. (ex-DONALD BYRD Band) with **DEXTER GORDON** – tenor sax / **FREDDIE HUBBARD** – trumpet / **BUTCH WARREN** – bass / **BILLY HIGGINS** – drums

not issued Blue Note
1962. (lp) **TAKIN' OFF** -
– Watermelon man / Three bags full / Empty pockets / The maze / Driftin' / Alone and I. *(UK-iss.Sep84, cd-iss.May86)*
In 1963, he joined MILES DAVIS until 1968. Carried on solo career).

—— Now a septet. w/ **DONALD BYRD** – trumpet / **GRACKEN MONCUR** – trombone / **HANK MOBLEY** – tenor sax / **GRANT GREEN** – guitar / **CHUCK ISRAELS** – bass / **ANTHONY WILLIAMS** – drums
1963. (lp) **MY POINT OF VIEW** -
– Blind man, blind man / A tribute to someone / King Cobra / The pleasure is mine / And what if I don't. *(re-iss.Oct84, cd-iss.1986)*
1963. (7") **BLIND MAN, BLIND MAN. / (part 2)**

—— with **PAUL CHAMBER** – bass / **WILLIE BOBO** – percussion / **OSVALDO MARTINEZ** – percussion
1963. (lp) **INVENTIONS & DIMENSIONS** -
– Sucotash / Triangle / Jack rabbit / Mimoson / Jump ahead. *(UK-iss.Apr89 on 'Blue Note') (cd-iss.Sep91 on 'Liberty')*

—— now with **FREDDIE HUBBARD / RON CARTER** – bass / **TONY WILLIAMS** – drums
Jun 64. (lp) **EMPYREAN ISLES** -
– One finer snap / Oliloqui valley / Cantaloupe Island / The egg. *(re-iss.Oct85)*

—— added **GEORGE COLEMAN** – tenor sax
1965. (lp) **MAIDEN VOYAGE** -
– Maiden voyage / The eye of the hurricane / The little one / Survival of the fittest / Dolphin dance. *(re-iss.+cd.May85 & Mar95)*
May 67. on 'M.G.M.'; **BLOW-UP (soundtrack)**
– Blow up / The bed / Bring down the birds / Curiosity / Jane's theme / The kiss / Verushka (part I & II) / The thief / Thomas studies photos / Naked camera / Stroll on (by The YARDBIRDS).

—— with **RON CARTER** – bass / **MICKEY ROKER** – drums / **THAD JONES** – flugelhorn / **JERRY DODGION** – flute / **PETER PHILLIPS** – trombone
Mar 68. (lp) **SPEAK LIKE A CHILD** -
– Riot / Speak like a child / First trip / Toys / Goodbye to childhood / The sorcerer. *(re-iss.+cd.Jul85)*
1969. (lp) **THE PRISONER** -
– I have a dream / The prisoner / Firewater / He who lives in fear / Promise of the Sun. *(re-iss.+cd.Sep87)*

—— Set up new sextet **BERNIE MAUPIN** – reeds / **BUSTER WILLIAMS** – bass, perc. / **BILLY HART** – drums, perc. / **LEON NDUGU CHANCLER** – drums / **JULIAN PRIESTER** – trombone / **EDDIE HENDERSON** – trumpet

Warners Warners
1970. (lp) **FAT ALBERT ROTUNDA** -
– Wiggle-waggle / Fat mama / Tell me a bedtime story / Oh! oh! here he comes / Jessica / Fat Albert Rotunda / Lil' brother.
Feb 70. (7") **WIGGLE-WAGGLE. / FAT MAMA**
1971. (lp) **MWANDISHI**
– Ostinato (suite for Angela) / You'll know when you get there / Wondering spirit song.
Feb 71. (lp) **CROSSINGS**
– Sleeping giant (part 1-5) / Quasar / Water torture / Crossings.
Mar 72. (7") **WATER TORTURE. / CROSSINGS** -

C.B.S. Columbia
May 73. (lp)(c) **SEXTANT**
– Rain dance / Hidden shadows / Hornets.
Jan 74. (lp)(c) **HEAD HUNTERS** 13
– Chameleon / Watermelon man / Sly / Vein melter. *(re-iss.Mar81)*
Jan 74. (7") **WATERMELON MAN (edit). / SLY (edit)** -
Apr 74. (7") **CHAMELEON (edit). / VEIN METER (edit)** 42 Mar 74
Oct 74. (lp)(c) **THRUST** 13 Sep 74
– Spank-a-lee / Butterfly / Actual proof / Palm grease.
Feb 75. (7") **PALM GREASE. / BUTTERFLY** Nov 74
Feb 75. (7") **SPANK-A-LEE. / ACTUAL PROOF** -
1975. (lp) **DEATH WISH (Soundtrack)**
– Death wish / Joanna's theme / Do a thing / Paint her mouth / Rich country / Suite revenge: (a) Striking back – (b) Riverside Park – (c) The alley – (d) Last stop – (e) 8th Avenue Station – Ochoa knose – Party people – Fill your hand.
1975. (d-lp) **FLOOD (live in Japan)** -
– Introduction – Maiden voyage / Actual proof / Spank-a-Lee / Watermelon man / Butterfly / Chameleon / Hang up your hang ups.
Oct 75. (lp)(c) **MAN-CHILD** 21
– Hang up your hang ups / Sun touch / The traitor / Bubbles / Steppin' in it / Heartbeat.
Oct 75. (7") **HANG UP YOUR HANG UPS. / SUNTOUCH** -
Sep 76. (lp)(c) **SECRETS**
– Doin' it / People music / Cantalope Island / Spider / Gentle thoughts / Swamp rat / Sansho Shima.
Sep 76. (7") **DOIN' IT. / PEOPLE MUSIC** -

—— His quintet:- **WAYNE SHORTER, RON CARTER, TONY WILLIAMS, FRED HUBBARD**
May 77. (lp)(c) **V.S.O.P. (live Newport)** 79
– (piano introduction) / Maiden voyage / Nefertiti / (introduction of players) / The eye of the hurricane / Toys / (introductions) / You'll know when you get there / Hang up your hang ups / Spider.
Jun 77. (7") **SPIDER. / MAIDEN VOYAGE** -

—— HANCOCK now introduced his voice, incorporated into music.
Jul 78. (lp)(c) **SUNLIGHT** 27 58
– I thought it was you / Come running to me / Sunlight / No means yes / Good question.
Aug 78. (7") **I THOUGHT IT WAS YOU. / NO MEANS YES** 15
(re-iss.May82)
Oct 78. (7") **SUNLIGHT. / COME RUNNING TO ME** -
Jan 79. (7")(12") **YOU BET YOUR LOVE. / KNEE DEEP** 18
Feb 79. (lp)(c) **FEETS DON'T FAIL ME NOW** 28 38
– You bet your love / Trust me / Ready or not / Tell everybody / Honey from the jar / Knee deep. *(cd-iss.Sep85)(cd-iss.Oct93 on 'Sony Collectors')*
Apr 79. (7") **READY OR NOT. / TRUST ME** -
Apr 79. (7") **TELL EVERYBODY. / TRUST ME** -
(re-iss.Apr86)
Jun 79. (7") **TELL EVERYBODY. / HONEY FROM THE JAR** -
Jun 79. (d-lp)(c) **AN EVENING WITH HERBIE HANCOCK & CHICK COREA IN CONCERT (live)** 100 Mar 79
– Someday my Prince will come / Liza / Button up / February moment / Maiden voyage / La fiesta.
Dec 79. (7") **DOIN' IT. / HONEY FROM THE JAR** -
Apr 80. (7") **GO FOR IT. / TRUST ME** -

Apr 80. (7") **GO FOR IT. / MAKING LOVE** [ ] [-]
May 80. (lp)(c) **MONSTER** [ ] [94] Apr 80
– Saturday night / Stars in your eyes / Go for it / Don't hold it in / Making love / It all comes round.
May 80. (7") **STARS IN YOUR EYES. / GO FOR IT** [-] [ ]
Jun 80. (7") **STARS IN YOUR EYES. / GO FOR IT** [-] [ ]
Sep 80. (7") **GO FOR IT. / STARS IN YOUR EYES** [-] [ ]
Nov 80. (7") **MAKING LOVE. / IT ALL COMES ROUND** [-] [ ]
Nov 80. (lp)(c) **MR. HANDS** [ ] [ ]
– Spiralling prism / Calypso / Just around the corner / 4 a.m. / Shiftless shuffle / Textures.

— on next with **RAY PARKER JNR.** – guitar, drums / **GEORGE JOHNSON** – rhythm guitar / **ADRIAN BELEW** – lead guitar / **FREDDIE WASHINGTON & LOUIS JOHNSON** – bass / **JOHN ROBINSON & ALPHONSE MOUZON** – drums / guest vocalists **SYLVESTER / VICKI RANDLE / GAVIN CHRISTOPHER**

Oct 81. (lp)(c) **MAGIC WINDOWS** [ ] [ ]
– Magic number / Tonight's the night / Everybody's broke / Help yourself / Satisfied with love / The twilight clone.
Oct 81. (7") **EVERYBODY'S BROKE. / HELP YOURSELF** [-] [ ]
(12"+=) – Magic number.
Jan 82. (7") **MAGIC NUMBER. / HELP YOURSELF** [-] [ ]
Apr 82. (7")(12") **LITE ME UP. / SATISFIED WITH LOVE** [ ] [ ]
May 82. (lp)(c) **LITE ME UP** [ ] [ ]
– Lite me up / The bomb / Gettin' to the good part / Paradise / Can't hide your love / The fun tracks / Motor mouth / Give it all your heart. *(re-iss.Jun84)*
Jul 82. (7") **THE FUN TRACKS. / GIVE IT ALL YOUR HEART** [ ] [-]
Jul 82. (7") **THE FUN TRACKS. / GETTIN' TO THE GOOD PART** [-] [ ]
Jan 83. (7") **PARADISE. / THE FUN TRACKS** [-] [ ]

— with **RON CARTER** – bass / **TONY WILLIAMS** – drums / **WYNSTON MARSALIS** – trumpet

Jan 83. (d-lp)(c) **HERBIE HANCOCK QUARTET (live)** [ ] [ ]
– Well you needn't / 'Round midnight / Clearways / A quick sketch / The eye of the hurricane / Parade / The sorcerer / Pee Wee / I fall in love too easily. *(cd-iss.Dec 93 on 'Columbia')*
Jul 83. (7") **ROCKIT. / (part 2)** [-] [71]
Jul 83. (7")(12") **ROCKIT. / ROUGH** [8] [-]
Aug 83. (lp)(c) **FUTURE SHOCK** [27] [ ]
– Rockit / Future shock / TFS / Earthbeat / Autodrive / Rough. *(re-iss.Apr87)*
Sep 83. (7") **AUTODRIVE. / THE BOMB** [33] [ ]
(12"+=) – Chameleon. *(US B-side).*
Jan 84. (7") **FUTURE SHOCK. / EARTHBEAT** [54] [ ]
(12"+=) – Herbie Hancock megamix; Rockit – Autodrive – Future shock – TFS – Rough – Chameleon.

— with **WAYNE SHORTER** – lyricon / **HENRY KAISER + NICKY SKOPELITIS** – guitar / **BILL CASWELL** – bass, synth. / **WILL ALEXANDER + BOB STEVENS** – electronics / **JOHNNY ST CYR** – turntables / **ANTON FIER** – drums, percussion / **HAMID DRAKE + DANIEL PONCE + AIYB DIENE** – percussion / **JALI FODAY MUSA SUSO** – balafon / **BERNARD FOWLER + TOSHINORI KONDO** – vocals.

Jul 84. (7") **HARDROCK. / ('A'version)** [-] [ ]
Jul 84. (7") **HARDROCK. / TFS** [65] [ ]
(12"+=) – ('A'-US megamix).
Aug 84. (lp)(c)(cd) **SOUND-SYSTEM** [ ] [71]
– Hardrock / Metal beat / Karabali / Junkie / People are changing / Sound-system. *(c+=)* – (extra mixes).
Sep 84. (7")(ext-12") **METAL BEAT. / KARABALI** [-] [ ]

— (below w / FODAY MUSA SUSO)

May 85. (lp)(c) **VILLAGE LIFE** [ ] [ ]
– Moon – Light / Ndan Ndan Nyaria / Early warning / Kanatente.
1986. (lp)(c) **ROUND MIDNIGHT (Soundtrack)** [-] [ ]
– Round midnight / Body and soul / Berangeres nightmare / Fair weather / Una noche con Francis / The peacocks / How long has this been going on / Rhythm-a-ning / Still time / Minuit aux champs – Elysees / Chan's song (never said).
May 88. (7")(12") **VIBE ALIVE. / MAIDEN VOYAGE** [ ] [ ]
(cd-s+=) – ('A'extended) / ('A'bonus beats).
Jun 88. (lp)(c)(cd) **PERFECT MACHINE** [ ] [ ]
– Perfect machine / Obsession / Vibe alive / Beat wise / Maiden voyage – P bop / Chemical residue.
Sep 88. (7") **BEAT WISE. / CHEMICAL RESIDUE** [-] [ ]

— HERBIE featured on 'Yanarete' cd with MILTON NASCIMENTO early 1992.

Mercury Mercury
Jun 95. (cd)(c) **DIS IS DA DRUM** [ ] [ ]
– Call it '94 / Dis is da drum / Shooz / The melody (on the deuce by 44) / Mojuba / Butterfly / Juju / Hump / Come and see me / Rubber soul / Bo ba be ba.

– compilations, others, etc. –

1970. Blue Note; (lp) **THE BEST OF HERBIE HANCOCK** [-] [ ]
1975. Blue Note; (lp) **SUCOTASH** [-] [ ]
1975. Blue Note; (lp) **HANCOCK** [-] [ ]
Oct 74. Warners; (d-lp) **TREASURE CHEST** (rare 69-70) [-] [ ]
Jan 80. CBS/ US= Columbia; (lp)(c) **GREATEST HITS** [ ] [ ]
Nov 84. CBS/ US= Columbia; (lp)(c) **THE BEST OF HERBIE HANCOCK** [ ] [ ]
Apr 81. MPS Jazz; (lp) **BY ALL MEANS ("& ALPHONSE MOUZON")** [ ] [ ]
Nov 84. Chase; (lp)(c)(cd) **HOT AND HEAVY** [ ] [ ]
(re-iss.Apr86 on 'Premier/Star Jazz')
Sep 85. Old Gold; (7") **YOU BET YOUR LOVE / I THOUGHT IT WAS YOU** [ ] [-]
Feb 86. (+=) – Rock it.
1991. Castle; (cd)(c) **THE COLLECTION** [ ] [-]
– Chameleon / Watermelon man / Maiden voyage / I thought it was you / No means yes / You bet your love / Tell everybody / Lite me up / Rockit / Auto drive / Hardrock / Round midnight.
Jul 91. Jazz Collection; (cd) **HOT PIANO** [ ] [-]
Jul 94. Blue Note; (cd) **CANTALOUPE ISLAND** [ ] [-]
Nov 94. Jazz Door; (cd) **LIVE IN NEW YORK (TRIO live)** [ ] [-]
Nov 94. Warners; (d-cd) **MWANDISHI – THE COMPLETE WARNER BROS. RECORDINGS** [ ] [ ]
Nov 95. Blue Note; (3xcd-box) **TAKIN' OFF / INVENTIONS & DIMENSIONS / EMPRYEAN ISLES** [ ] [-]

HANOI ROCKS

Formed: Helsinki, Finland . . . 1980 by ANDY McCOY and MICHAEL MONROE. After releasing a few lp's for 'Joanna' records, and moving to Stockholm, Sweden in Oct'81, they came to London late '82 to sign for 'Lick'. They worked with DALE GRIFFIN and OVEREND WATTS (both ex-MOTT THE HOOPLE), and made UK Top 100 with album 'BACK TO MYSTERY CITY'. The following year, they gained contract for 'CBS' and scored with UK Top 30 album 'TWO STEPS FROM HEAVEN'. However, tragedy struck on 3rd Dec'84, when RAZZLE was killed in a car driven by VINCE NEIL of MOTLEY CRUE. They disbanded soon after, and evolved into CHERRY BOMBZ, although this did not include solo bound MICHAEL MONROE. • **Style:** Glam-rock metal influenced image wise by The NEW YORK DOLLS, The ROLLING STONES or The FACES. • **Songwriters:** All written by McCOY except covers; GOOD GOOD LOVING (Link Wray) / AIN'T WHAT YOU DO (Juke Joint Jimmy) / UP AROUND THE BEND + TRAVELLIN' BAND (Creedence Clearwater Revival) / MAGIC CARPET RIDE (Steppenwolf) / UNDER MY WHEELS (Alice Cooper) / WALKIN' WITH MY ANGEL (Goffin-King). • **Trivia:** They were also a big hit in Japan, where they were signed to 'Nippon-Phonogram'.

Recommended: THE BEST OF HANOI ROCKS (*6).

MICHAEL MONROE (b.MATTI FAGERHOLM) – vocals / **ANDY McCOY** (b.ANTTI HULKKO) – guitar (ex-BRIARD) repl. STEFAN PIESHACK / **NASTY SUICIDE** (b.JAN STENFORS) – guitar (ex-BRIARD) / **SAM YAFFA** (b.SAMI TAKAHAKI) – bass repl. PASI STI / **GYP CASINO** (b.JESPER SPORE) – drums repl. PEKI SENOLA

Joanna not issued
Nov 80. (7") **I WANT YOU. / KILL CITY KILLS** [-] [-] Fin
Feb 81. (lp) **BANGKOK SHOCKS SAIGON SHAKES** [-] [-] Fin
– Tragedy / Village girl / Stop cryin' / Don't ever leave me / Lost in the city / First timer / Cheyenne / 11th street kidz / Walking with my angel / Pretender. *(UK-iss.+c Aug83 on 'Lick')(US yellow-lp Oct89 on 'Uzi Suicide') (cd-iss.Feb95 on 'Essential')*
Feb 81. (7") **TRAGEDY. / CAFE AVENUE** [-] [-] Fin
Oct 81. (7") **DESPERADOES. / DEVIL WOMAN** [-] [-] Fin
Dec 81. (7") **DEAD BY XMAS. / NOTHING NEW** [-] [-] Fin
Feb 82. (lp) **ORIENTAL BEAT** [-] [-] Fin
– Motorvatin' / Don't follow me / Visitor / Teenangels outsiders / Sweet home suburbia / M.C. baby / No law or order / Oriental beat / Devil woman / Lightnin' bar blues / Fallen star. *(UK-iss.+c Aug83 on 'Lick') (re-iss.Dec86 on 'Bootleg-Jungle') (US red-lp Oct89 on 'Uzi Suicide') (cd-iss.Apr95 on 'Essential')*

— (Jun82) **RAZZLE** (b.NICHOLAS DINGLEY) – drums (ex-DARK) repl.GYP

Sep 82. (7") **LOVE'S AND INJECTION. / TAXI DRIVER** [-] [-] Fin
(12"+=) – Malibu beach / Problem child / In the year '79.
Lick not issued
May 83. (7")(7"pic-d) **MALIBU BEACH NIGHTMARE. / REBELS ON THE RUN** [ ] [-]
(12"+=) – Beer and a cigarette / Taxi driver. *(re-iss.Oct86)*
May 83. (lp)(c) **BACK TO MYSTERY CITY** [87] [-]
– Strange boys play weird openings / Malibu Beach nightmare / Mental beat / Tooting bee wreck / Until I get you / Sailing down the years / Lick summer love / Beating gets faster / Ice cream summer / Back to Mystery City. *(re-iss.Jul86) (white-lp Apr85) (US green-lp Oct89 on 'Uzi Suicide') (cd-iss.Feb95 on 'Essential')*
Aug 83. (7") **UNTIL I GET YOU. / TRAGEDY** [ ] [-]
(12"+=) – Oriental beat.
C.B.S. Columbia
Jun 84. (7") **UP AROUND THE BEND. / UNTIL I GET YOU** [61] [ ]
(12"+=) – Back to mystery city / Mental beat.
(d7"+=) – Under my wheels / The train kept a-rollin' / I feel alright.
Sep 84. (7") **UNDERWATER WORLD. / SHAKES** [ ] [ ]
(12"+=)(12"pic-d+=) – Magic carpet ride.
Oct 84. (lp)(c) **TWO STEPS FROM THE MOVE** [28] [ ]
– Up around the bend / High school / I can't get it / Underwater world / Don't you ever leave me / Million miles away / Boulevard of broken dreams / Boiler (me boiler 'n' me) / Futurama / Cutting corners.
Nov 84. (7") **DON'T YOU EVER LEAVE ME. / OIL AND GASOLINE** [ ] [ ]
(12"+=)(12"pic-d(3-D)+=) – Malibu Beach (calypso).

— (Feb85) **TERRY CHIMES** – drums (ex-CLASH, ex-GENERATION X, ex-COWBOYS INTERNATIONAL) repl. RAZZLE who was killed in a car crash 3 Dec'84. Later **RENE BERG** – guitar (ex-IDLE FLOWERS) repl. JAFFA

— Split Jun85. MICHAEL MONROE later went solo. RAZZLE, NASTY and YAFFA had also been part of KNOX's band FALLEN ANGELS

– compilations etc. –

Oct 82. Joanna; (lp) **SELF DESTRUCTION BLUES** [-] [-] Fin
-(UK-iss.+c.Aug83 on 'Lick') (US blue-lp Oct89 on 'Uzi Suicide') (cd-iss.Feb 95 on 'Essential)
Dec 85. Lick; (lp)(c) **THE BEST OF HANOI ROCKS** [ ] [-]
– Strange boys play weird openings / Malibu Beach / Loves an injection / Lost in the city / Until I get you / 11th Street kids / Motor vatin' / Don't follow me / Back to Mystery City / Taxi driver / Oriental beat / Don't never leave me (live) / Visitor / Tragedy (live) / Under my wheels (live). *(cd-iss.Nov88)*
Apr 85. Lick; (lp)(c) **ALL THOSE WASTED YEARS** [ ] [-]
(cd-iss.Apr95 on 'Essential')
Dec 90. Lick; (lp) **TRACKS FROM A BROKEN DREAM** [ ] [ ]
Mar 93. Lick; (cd) **LEAN ON ME** [ ] [-]
(cd-iss.Apr95 on 'Essential')

Apr 86. Raw Power; (lp)(c) **DEAD BY CHRISTMAS** [ ] [-]
(with free flexi 7")
Dec 86. Bootlick; (lp) **ROCK'N'ROLL DIVORCE** [ ] [-]

CHERRY BOMBZ

were formed by guitarist **ANDY McCOY** and **NASTY SUICIDE**, plus **ANITA MAHADERLAN** – vocals (ex-TOTO CEOLO, ex-PAN'S PEOPLE) / **DAVE TREGANNA** – bass (ex-SHAM 69, etc.) / **TERRY CHIMES** – drums (ex-CLASH, ex-GEN X, ex-COWBOYS INTERNATIONAL)

Lick P.V.C.

Feb 86. (12"ep) **HOT GIRLS IN LOVE / FELINE FEELING. / 100 DEGREES IN THE SHADE / OIL AND GASOLINE** [ ] [-]
May 86. (7") **HOUSE OF ECSTASY. / DECLARATION** [ ] [ ]
(12") – ('A'side) / Running (Back to your lover) / Countryfield inner city blues.

High Dragon not issued

Mar 87. (lp)(c)(cd) **COMING DOWN SLOW** [ ] [-]
– Intro / House of ecstasy / 100° in the shade / Pin up boy / Life's been hard / Oil and gasoline / Sweet pretending / Coming down slow / Good good loving / Hot girl's in love / Ain't what you do / Travellin' band.

— ANITA became a SKY TV presenter in '88. NASTY, CHIMES and TREGANNA formed WYLDE THINGS.

not issued P.V.C.

1987. (c) **100° IN THE SHADE** (compilation) [-] [ ]

HAPPY MONDAYS

Formed: Salford, Manchester, England . . . 1984 by brothers SHAUN and PAUL RYDER. In 1985 helped by A&R man and producer Mike Pickering, they signed contract with Tony Wilson's 'Factory' records, and issued debut 12" 'FORTY-FIVE'. Soon became darlings of NME and indie chart scene after release of first lp in 1987 'SQUIRREL AND G-MAN . . . '. In late '89, they scored first top 20 hit with 'HALLELUJAH'. The following year, they had 2 Top 5 hits 'STEP ON' & 'KINKY AFRO', which premiered Top 5 album 'PILLS 'N' THRILLS & BELLYACHES'. • **Style:** Inovators and pioneers of the Manchester rave scene, that created a new breed of danceable rock. SHAUN's at times hoarse vox, was squeeky but nonetheless effective. The drug scene was also part of SHAUN and BEZ's outgoing culture, as was appearing alongside naked female models in a 1991 issue of Penthouse'. • **Songwriters:** Group compositions except; DESMOND (Ob-la-di Ob-la-da; Beatles) / LAZYITIS (Ticket To Ride; Beatles) / STEP ON + TOKOLOSHE MAN (John Kongos) / KINKY AFRO (similar to 'Lady Marmalade'; LaBelle). • **Trivia:** Produced by JOHN CALE in 1987 and The TOM TOM CLUB duo in 1992.

Recommended: SQUIRREL AND G-MAN TWENTY FOUR HOUR PARTY . . . (*8) / BUMMED (*8) / PILLS N' THRILLS AND BELLYACHES (*9) / YES PLEASE (*6).

SHAUN RYDER (b.23 Aug'62) – vocals / **PAUL RYDER** (b.24 Apr'64) – bass / **MARK DAY** (b.29 Dec'61) – guitar / **PAUL DAVIS** (b. 7 Mar'66) – keyboards / **GARY 'GAZ' WHELAN** (b.12 Feb'66) – drums

Factory RoughTrade

Sep 85. (12"ep) **FORTY-FIVE EP** [ ] [-]
– Delightful / This feeling / Oasis.

— added **MARK 'Bez' BERRY** (b.18 Apr'64) – percussion, dancer

Jun 86. (7") **FREAKY DANCIN'. / THE EGG** [ ] [-]
(12") – ('A'extended) / ('A'live).
Mar 87. (12") **TART TART. / LITTLE MATCHSTICK OWEN'S RAP** [ ] [-]
Apr 87. (lp)(c) **SQUIRREL AND G-MAN TWENTY-FOUR HOUR PARTY PEOPLE PLASTIC FACE CARNT SMILE (WHITE OUT)** [ ] [-]
– Kuff dam / Tart tart / 'Enery / Russell / Olive oil / Weekends / Little matchstick Owen / Oasis / Desmond * / Cob 20. *(cd-iss.Mar90 +=) – Little matchstick Owen's rap. (re-iss.Sep87, re-iss.Nov88, * repl. by* '24 hour party people') (re-iss.cd/c Sep95 on 'London')
Oct 87. (7") **24 HOUR PARTY PEOPLE. / YAHOO** [ ] [-]
(12"+=) – ('A'extended) / Wah wah (think tank).
Nov 88. (7") **WROTE FOR LUCK. / BOOM** [ ] [-]
(cd-s+=) – ('A'dance mix) / ('A'club mix).
(12") – (all above 3 tracks minus 'Boom').
Nov 88. (lp)(c)(cd)(dat) **BUMMED** [ ] [-]
– Country song / Moving in with / Mad Cyril / Fat lady wrestlers / Performance / Brain dead / Wrote for luck / Bring a friend / Do it better / Lazyitis. *(reached 59 UK chart Jan90) (re-iss.cd/c Sep95 on 'London')*
May 89. (7")(12") **LAZYITIS (ONE ARMED BOXER). / MAD CYRIL (HELLO GIRLS)** [85] [-]

— (above featured 50's pop star KARL DENVER – backing vocals) *(re-iss.May90 hit No.46)*

1989. (7"clear)(12"clear) **MAD CYRIL. / DO IT BETTER** [-] [ ]
Sep 89. (7")(12") **WFL (Vince Clarke mix). / WFL (THINK ABOUT THE FUTURE** [68] [-]
(cd-s+=) – ('A'&'B'extended) / Lazyitits (the one armed boxer).
Nov 89. (7"ep)(12"ep) **RAVE ON MADCHESTER EP** [19] [-]
– Hallelujah / Holy ghost / Clap your hands / Rave on.
Nov 89. (7")(c-s) **HALLELUJAH (MacColl mix). / HALLELUJAH (in out mix)** [ ] [-]
(12"+=)(cd-s+=) – ('A'club mix) / Rave on (club mix).
(cd-ep)(m-lp) – (all the above)(+=) WFL (Think about the future).

— added guest **ROWETA** – backing vocals to repl. other guest KIRSTY MacCOLL

Factory Elektra

Mar 90. (7")(12") **STEP ON (stuff it in mix). / ('A'-one louder mix)** [5] [57] Jan 91
(c-s+=)(cd-s+=) – ('A'twistin' my melons mix).
Oct 90. (7")(12")(c-s) **KINKY AFRO. / KINKY AFRO (live)** [5] [ ]
(cd-s+=) – ('A'radio edit).
Nov 90. (cd)(c)(lp) **PILLS'N THRILLS AND BELLYACHES** [4] [89]
– Kinky Afro / God's cop / Donovan / Grandbag's funeral / Loose fit / Dennis & Lois / Bob's your uncle / Step on / Holiday / Harmony. *(re-iss.cd/c Sep95 on 'London')*
Feb 91. (7")(12")(c-s) **LOOSE FIT (edit). / BOB'S YOUR UNCLE (edit)** [17] [ ]
(cd-s+=) – Kinky Afro (Euro mix).
Sep 91. (cd)(c)(d-lp) **LIVE (live BABY BIG HEAD Bootleg album)** [21] [ ]
– Hallelujah / Donovan / Kinky Afro / Clap your hands / Loose fit / Holiday / Rave on / E / Tokoloshe man / Dennis and Lois / God's cop / Step on / W.F.L. *(d-lp+=)(c+=)* – Bob's your uncle. *(re-iss.cd/c Sep95 on 'London')*
Nov 91. (12") **JUDGE FUDGE. / TOKOLOSHE MAN** [24] [ ]
(cd-s+=) – ('A'version).
Sep 92. (7")(c-s) **STINKIN' THINKIN'. / ('A'boys own mix)** [31] [ ]
(12"+=)(cd-s+=) – ('A'-Terry Farley mix) / Baby bighead.
Oct 92. (cd)(c)(lp) **. . . YES PLEASE!** [14] [ ]
– Stinkin' thinkin' / Monkey in the family / Sunshine & love / Dustman / Angel / Cut 'em loose Bruce / Theme from Netto / Love child / Total Ringo / Cowboy Dave. *(re-iss.cd/c Sep95 on 'London')*
Nov 92. (7")(c-s) **SUNSHINE & LOVE. / STAYING ALIVE (mix) / 24 HOUR PARTY PEOPLE (remix)** [62] [ ]
(12"+=)(cd-s+=) – ('A'dance mix).

— They disbanded early '93, with SHAUN and other two briefly forming The MONDAYS, which evolved into BLACK GRAPE.

– compilations, others, etc. –

May 90. Strange Fruit; (12"ep)(c-ep)(cd-ep) **THE PEEL SESSIONS (1989)** [ ] [-]
– Tart tart / Mad Cyril / Do it better. *(cd-ep re-iss.Feb92)*
Nov 91. Strange Fruit; (cd-ep) **THE PEEL SESSIONS (1986)** [ ] [-]
– Freaky dancin' / Kuff dam / Olive Oil / Cob 20.
Oct 95. London; (cd)(c) **LOADS** [41] [ ]
– Step on / W.F.L. / Kinky Afro / Hallelujah – MacColl mix / Mad Cyril / Lazyitis / Tokoloshe man / Loose fit / Bob's yer uncle / Judge fudge / Stinkin' thinkin' / Sunshine & love / Angel / Tart tart / Kuff dam / 24 hour party people. (some cd's w/free cd+=) **LOADS MORE** – Lazyitis (one armed boxer mix) / W.F.L. (Perfecto mix) / Bob's yer uncle (Perfecto mix) / Loose fit (Perfecto mix) / Hallelujah (Deadstock mix) / Freaky dancing / Delightful.

Tim HARDIN

Born: EUGENE, 23 Dec'41, Oregon, U.S.A., a descendant of JOHN WESLEY HARDIN. Moved to Cambridge, Massachusetts in 1961, after being discharged from the US Marines. Made an appearance at the Newport Folk Festival in 1966, which resulted in his signature for 'Verve'. His eponymous debut, contained the much covered 'REASON TO BELIEVE', later a hit for ROD STEWART. In fact from then on, it seemed everything other artists touched from his repertoire turned to gold (i.e. IF I WERE A CARPENTER for The FOUR TOPS, BOBBY DARIN, etc / BLACK SHEEP BOY for SCOTT WALKER and HANG ON TO A DREAM a track for The NICE!). His aplomb was also said to have inspired his rejuvenated new friend BOB DYLAN for his 1968 effort 'John Wesley Harding'. In the 70's after making a number of unsuccessful albums, he was groomed for the role of WOODY GUTHRIE in the biography 'Bound For Glory'. This didn't unfold and he later died of drug abuse on 29 Dec'80 in L.A. • **Style:** Folk artist of immense quality, who chose to chill out away from unyielding music scene and live off songwriting royalties. • **Songwriters:** Penned mostly everything himself except; HOUSE OF THE RISING SUN (trad) / BO DIDDLEY (Bo Diddley). • **Trivia:** His 1969 album 'SUITE FOR SUSAN MOORE AND DAMIEN' was dedicated to his wife and son. Resided in London 1974, where he set up a disastrous folk-club duo with TIM ROSE.

Recommended: THE BEST OF TIM HARDIN (*6)

TIM HARDIN – vocals, guitar, piano

Verve Verve F . . .

Oct 66. (7") **HANG ON TO A DREAM. / IT'LL NEVER HAPPEN AGAIN** [-] [ ]
Dec 66. (lp) **TIM HARDIN 1** [ ] [ ]
– Don't make promises / Green rocky road / Smugglin' man / How long / While you're on your way / It'll never happen again / Reason to believe / Never too far / Part of the wind / Ain't gonna do without / Misty roses / How can we hang on to a dream. *(cd-iss.Sep92 on 'Line')*
Dec 66. (7") **HANG ON TO A DREAM. / REASON TO BELIEVE** [-] [-]
Feb 67. (7") **DON'T MAKE PROMISES. / MISTY ROSES** [-] [ ]
May 67. (7") **HANG ON TO A DREAM. / MISTY ROSES** [-] [ ]
Sep 67. (7") **NEVER TOO FAR. / GREEN ROCKY ROAD** [-] [ ]
Sep 67. (lp) **TIM HARDIN 2** [ ] [ ]
– If I were a carpenter / Red balloon / Black sheep boy / Lady came from Baltimore / Baby close its eyes / You upset the grace of living when you lie / Speak like a child / See where you are and get out / It's hard to believe in love for long / Tribute to Hank Williams. *(cd-iss.Sep92 on 'Line')*
Nov 67. (7") **BLACK SHEEP BOY. / MISTY ROSES** [-] [ ]
Nov 67. (7") **THE LADY FROM BALTIMORE. / BLACK SHEEP BOY** [ ] [-]
Jun 68. (7") **TRIBUTE TO HANK WILLIAMS. / YOU UPSET THE GRACE OF LIVING** [-] [ ]
Jun 68. (lp) **TIM HARDIN 3 – LIVE IN CONCERT (live)** [ ] [ ]
– Lady came from Baltimore / Reason to believe / You upset the grace of living when you lie / Misty roses / Black sheep boy / Lenny's tune / Don't make promises / Danville dame / If I were a carpenter / Red balloon / Tribute to Hank Williams /

Smugglin' man. *(cd-iss.Sep92 on 'Line')*

Jul 68. (7") **DON'T MAKE PROMISES. / SMUGGLIN' MAN** [] [-]

Apr 69. (7") **SMUGGLIN' AMN. / REASON TO BELIEVE** [-] []

May 69. (lp) **TIM HARDIN IV** [] []
– Airmobile / Whiskey whiskey / Seventh son / How long / Danville dame / Ain't gonna do without (part 1 & 2) / House of the rising son / Bo Diddley / I can't slow down / Hello baby. *(cd-iss.Sep92 on 'Line')*

C.B.S. Columbia

May 69. (lp) **SUITE FOR SUSAN MOORE AND DAMION – WE ARE – ONE, ONE, ALL IN ONE** [] [] Apr69
– First love song / Everything good become more true / Question of birth / Once-touched by flame / Last sweet moments / Magician / Loneliness she knows / The country I'm living in / One, one, the perfect sum / Susan.

May 69. (7") **ONE-TOUCHED BY FLAME. / QUESTION OF BIRTH** [-] []

Sep 69. (7") **A SIMPLE SONG OF FREEDOM. / QUESTION OF BIRTH** [] []

Aug 71. (lp) **BIRD ON A WIRE** [] [] Jul71
– Bird on the wire / Moonshiner / Southern butterfly / A satisfied mind / Soft summer breeze / Hoboin' / Georgia on my mind / Andre Johray / If I knew / Love hymn.

Aug 71. (7") **BIRD ON THE WIRE. / SOFT SUMMER BREEZE** [-] []

Jan 73. (lp)(c) **PAINTED HEAD** [] []
– You can't judge a book by the cover / Midnight caller / Yankee lady / Lonesome valley / Sweet lady / Do the do / Perfection / Till we meet again / I'll be home / Nobody knows you when you're down and out.

Jan 73. (7") **DO THE DO. / SWEET LADY** [] []

G.M. Antilles

Jan 74. (lp)(c) **NINE** [] []
– Shiloh town / Never too far / Rags & old iron / Look our love over / Person to person / Darling girl / Blues on my ceiling / Is there no rest for the weary / Fire and rain / While you're on your way / Judge and jury. *(cd-iss.Apr92 on 'See For Miles')*

— Resided in the UK from 1974. He died in L.A. of drug abuse in 29 Dec'80.

– compilations, etc. –

Apr 68. Atlantic/ US= Atco; (lp) **THIS IS TIM HARDIN** (rec.1962) [] [] Sep67
– I can slow down / Blues on the ceilin' / I'm your hoochie coochie man / Stagger Lee / I've been working on the railroad / House of the rising Sun / Fast freight / Cocaine Bill / You got to have more than one woman / Danville dame. *(re-iss.Jul89 on 'Edsel')*

1970. Atco; (7") **REASON TO BELIEVE. / SMUGGLIN' MAN** [-] []

1970. Verve; (lp)(c) **THE BEST OF TIM HARDIN** [] []
(re-iss.1974)

1971. Verve; (7") **IF I WERE A CARPENTER. / HANG ON TO A DREAM** [] []

1974. Verve; (d-lp) **TIM HARDIN I & II** [] []

1981. Columbia; (lp) **THE SHOCK OF GRACE** [-] []

Feb 82. Polydor; (lp) **TIM HARDIN MEMORIAL ALBUM** [] []

May 88. Polydor; (lp)(cd) **REASON TO BELIEVE** [] []

May 82. Kamera; (lp) **HOMECOMING CONCERT** [] [-]
(cd-iss.1989 & Aug94 on 'Line')

HARDLINE (see under ⇒ JOURNEY)

Morten HARKET (see under ⇒ A-HA)

Steve HARLEY (see under ⇒ COCKNEY REBEL)

Charlie HARPER (see under ⇒ UK SUBS)

Roy HARPER

Born: 12 Jun'41, Manchester, England. Raised by his father, after his mother died in childbirth. His step-mother was a Jehovah's Witness, leading to him to become anti-religious. As a young teenager, he played in a skiffle group with his brother DAVID, but at 15 after leaving school, he joined the R.A.F. He soon feigned madness to escape further service. Roy then underwent ECT treatment at the mental hospital, and was later institutionalized in Lancaster Moor, then in jail for a year in Walton, Liverpool. In 1964, after busking around Europe, he moved to London and gained solo residency at LES COUSINS Soho folk club. In 1966, he was signed to Peter Richards's 'Strike' records, who issued debut lp 'THE SOPHISTICATED BEGGAR'. It captured and encompassed all of his best poems, while only using simple revox machine as backing. The next year, he signed to 'CBS', and issued second flop 45, which preceeded lp 'COME OUT FIGHTING, GENGHIS SMITH'. This featured an 11-minute track 'CIRCLE'. In the summer of '68, he played free concerts at London's Hyde Park, which brought him new underground audience. In 1969 he released 'Liberty' lp 'FOLKJOKEOPUS', which also featured another lengthy 15-minute track 'McGOOGHAN'S BLUES'. He then signed to 'Harvest' early in 1970, and released 4th lp 'FLAT, BAROQUE AND BESERK', which had featured uncredited The NICE on track 'HELL'S ANGEL'. Roy then embarked on a US tour, but after arriving there drunk and jet-lagged he was arrested for abusive behavior. He slept on West Coast beaches, while playing many gigs. In 1971, he released highly regarded 'STORMCOCK' set, which hosted DAVID BEDFORD on orchestration and friend JIMMY PAGE (of LED ZEPPELIN) on first of many guitar sessions for him. PAGE had already written an ode to ROY, on LED ZEPPELIN'S 1971 song 'Hats Off To Harper'. In 1972, he acted in the film 'Made' alongside Carol White. Most of the music from the film, appeared in his next project 'LIFEMASK', which was written as his last will and testament, during a near fatal recurring blood disorder disease. On 14 Feb'74, he released appropriately titled 'VALENTINE', which gave him first entry into UK album chart. It was premiered at a concert on Valentine's Day at London's Rainbow theatre, with backing from PAGE, BEDFORD, KEITH MOON and JOHN BONHAM. Later in 1974, he formed band TRIGGER (with BILL BRUFORD – drums / CHRIS SPEDDING – guitar & DAVE COCHRAN – bass), and supported PINK FLOYD at Knebworth concert. In 1975, he sang lead vox on PINK FLOYD's 'Have A Cigar', from the album 'Wish You Were Here'. They had already guested on his next album 'HQ', which like its 1977 follow-up 'BULLINAMINGVASE', hit UK Top 40. In between this, he had briefly stayed in the States. In 1982 with MARK THOMPSON, he set up 'Public' records, who issued a return to form 'WORK OF HEART' lp. Early in 1985, he scored his last UK Top 50 album with JIMMY PAGE collaboration 'WHATEVER HAPPENED TO JUGULA'. • **Style:** Cult blues and folk rock artist, with attitude showing melancholy or aggressive lyrics. • **Songwriters:** Self-penned all. • **Trivia:** PAUL and LINDA McCARTNEY guested on his 'ONE OF THOSE DAYS IN ENGLAND', and KATE BUSH on 'THE UNKNOWN SOLDIER'. Around the same time in 1980, he appeared on her hit 45 'Breathing'.

Recommended: THE SOPHISTICATED BEGGAR (*8) / STORMCOCK (*8) / HQ (*7) / BULLINAMINGVASE (*7) / WORK OF HEART (*6) / ROY HARPER 1970-75 (*6)

ROY HARPER – vocals, guitar (see above for famous session people)

Strike not issued

Mar 66. (7") **TAKE ME IN YOUR EYES. / PRETTY BABY** [] []

Dec 66. (lp) **THE SOPHISTICATED BEGGAR** [] [-]
– China girl / Goldfish / Sophisticated beggar / My friend / Big fat silver aeroplane / Blackpool / Legend / Girlie / October the twelfth / Black clouds / Mr. Station master / Forever / Committed.. *(re-iss.Aug70 & '72 as 'RETURN OF THE SOPHISTICATED BEGGAR' on 'Youngblood' and 'Birth' respectively) (re-iss.+cd.Jan89 on 'Sundown') (re-iss.cd Oct94 on 'Science Friction')*

C.B.S. Columbia

Oct 67. (7") **MIDSPRING DITHERING. / ZENGEM** [] [-]

Jan 68. (lp) **COME OUT FIGHTING GENGHIS SMITH** [] [-]
– Freak street / You don't need money / Ageing raver / In a beautiful rambling mess / All you need is / What you have / Circle / Highgate Cemetary / Come out fighting Genghis Smith / Zaney Janey / Ballad of songwriter / Midspring dithering / Zenjem / It's tomorrow and today is yesterday / Francesca / She's the one / Nobody's got any money in the summer. *(re-iss.Jun77 as 'THE EARLY YEARS' on 'CBS-Embassy') (re-iss.+cd.Sep91 on 'Awareness') (re-iss.cd Nov94 on 'Science Friction')*

Apr 68. (7") **LIFE GOES BY. / NOBODY'S GOT ANY MONEY IN THE SUMMER** [] []

Liberty World Pac.

Apr 69. (lp) **FOLKJOKEOPUS** [] []
– Sergeant Sunshine / She's the one / In the time of water / Composer of life / One for all / Exercising some control / McGoohan's blues / Manana. *(re-iss.Sep77 on 'Sunset', re-iss.Aug86 & Nov88 on 'Awareness', cd-iss.Oct89) (cd-iss.Oct94 on 'Science Friction')*

Harvest not issued

Jun 70. (lp)(c) **FLAT BAROQUE AND BESERK** [] [-] 1978
– Don't you grieve / I hate the white man / Feelin' all the Saturday / How does it feel / Goodbye / Another day / Davey / East of the sun / Tom Tiddler's ground / Francesca / Song of the ages / Hell's angels. *(re-iss.Jul85)*

May 71. (lp)(c) **STORMCOCK** [] [-] 1978
– Hors d'oeuvres / The same old rock / One man rock and roll band / Me and my woman. *(re-iss.Oct85 on 'Awareness') (re-iss.cd Oct94 on 'Science Friction')*

Oct 72. (7") **BANK OF THE DEAD. / LITTLE LADY** [] [-]

Feb 73. (lp)(c) **LIFEMASK** (music from film soundtrack 'MADE') [] [-] 1978
– Highway blues / All Ireland / Little lady / Bank of the dead / South Africa / The Lord's prayer: Poem – Modal song (part 1-4) – Front song – Middle song – End song – Front song (reprise). *(re-iss.Apr87 on 'Awareness' + 4 tracks) (cd-iss.Sep94 on 'Science Friction')*

Feb 74. (7") **(DON'T YOU THINK WE'RE) FOREVER. / MALE CHAUVINIST PIG BLUES** [] [-]

Feb 74. (lp)(c) **VALENTINE** [27] [-] 1978
– Forbidden fruit / Male chauvinist pig blues / I'll see you again / Twelve hours of sunset / Acapulco gold / Commune / Magic woman / Che / North country / (Don't you think we're) Forever. *(re-iss.+cd.Apr89 on 'Awareness', with extra tracks) (re-iss.cd Nov94 on 'Science Friction')* (cd+=) – (below single) / Too many movies.

Oct 74. (7") **HOME (live). / HOME (studio)** [] [-] '78

Nov 74. (d-lp)(d-c) **FLASHES FROM THE ARCHIVES OF OBLIVION (live)** [] [-] 1978
– Home / Commune / Don't you grieve / Twelve hours of sunset / Kangaroo blues / All Ireland / Me and my woman / South Africa / Interference / Highway blues / One man rock and roll band / Another day / M.C.P. blues / Too many movies / Home (studio version) *(re-iss.+cd.Apr89 on 'Awareness') (cd-iss.Sep94 on 'Science Friction')*

Harvest Chrysalis

May 75. (lp)(c) **HQ** [31] [] Feb 76
– The game (part I-V) / The spirit lives / Grown-ups are just silly children / Referendum / Forget-me-not / Hallucinating light / When an old cricketer leaves the crease / Referendum. (US title 'WHEN AN OLD CRICKETER LEAVES THE CREASE') *(cd-iss.Aug95 on 'Science Friction')*

May 75. (7") **WHEN AN OLD CRICKETER LEAVES THE CREASE. / HALLUCINATING LIGHT (live)** [] []

Oct 75. (7"m) **GROWN-UPS ARE JUST SILLY CHILDREN. / REFERENDUM / LEGEND** [] [-]

Feb 77. (lp)(c) **BULLINAMINGVASE** [25] []
– One of those days in England / These last days / Cherishing the lonesome / Naked flame / Watford Gap * / One of those days in England (parts 2-10). *(free 7"w/a)* REFERENDUM / ANOTHER DAY (live). / TOM TIDDLER'S GROUND (live) *(lp re-iss.Mar77, track * repl.by* 'Breakfast in bed') *(re-iss.Apr87)*

Mar 77. (7") **ONE OF THOSE DAYS IN ENGLAND. / WATFORD GAP** [] [-]

Nov 77. (7") **SAIL AWAY. / CHERISHING THE LONESOME (with "BLACK SHEEP")** [] [-]

Mar 80. (7") **PLAYING GAMES. / FIRST THING IN THE MORNING** [] [-]

Jun 80. (lp)(c) **THE UNKNOWN SOLDIER** [ ] [-]
– Playing games / I'm in love with you / The flycatcher / You / Old faces / Short and sweet / First thing in the morning / The unknown soldier / Ten years ago / True story.

Jun 80. (7") **SHORT AND SWEET. / WATER SPORTS / THE UNKNOWN SOLDIER** [ ] [ ]

Public — not issued

Oct 82. (7") **NO ONE EVER GETS OUT ALIVE. / CASUALITY (live)** [ ] [-]

Nov 82. (lp)(c) **WORK OF HEART** [ ] [-]
– Drawn to the flames / Jack of hearts / I am a child / Woman / I still care / Work of heart; (i) No one ever gets out alive – (ii) Two lovers in the Moon – (iii) We are the people – (iv) All us children (so sadly far apart) – (v) We are the people (reprise) – (vi) No one ever gets out alive (finale). *(re-iss.Nov86 on 'Awareness', with ltd 2 free 7". later copies had 1 free 7")(cd-iss.Oct89)*

Mar 83. (7") **I STILL CARE. / GOODBYE LADYBIRD** [ ] [ ]

Hardup — not issued

1984. (lp)(c) **BORN IN CAPTIVITY** (demos) (ltd. 880 copies) [ ] [-]
– Stan / Drawn to the flames / Come to bed eyes / No woman is safe / I am a child / Elizabeth / Work of heart; (i) No one ever gets out alive – (ii) Two lovers on the Moon – (iii) We are the people – (iv) All us children (so sadly far apart) – (v) We are the people (reprise) – (vi) No one ever gets out alive (finale). *(re-iss.Jul85 on 'Awareness')*

ROY HARPER and JIMMY PAGE

with **JIMMY PAGE** – guitar (ex-LED ZEPPELIN)

Beggar's B. — Beggar's B.

Feb 85. (lp)(c) **WHATEVER HAPPENED TO JUGULA** [44] [ ]
– Nineteen forty-eightish / Hangman / Elizabeth / Advertisement / Bad speech / Hope / Twentieth century man. *(re-iss.+cd Aug88)*

Mar 85. (12") **ELIZABETH. / ADVERTISEMENT / I HATE THE WHITE MAN (live)** [ ] [ ]

ROY HARPER

Harvest — not issued

Jun 86. (lp)(c) **IN BETWEEN EVERY LINE (live)** [ ] [ ]
– One of those days in England / Short and sweet / True story / Referendum / Highway blues / One man rock and roll band / The game / Hangman. *(re-iss.cd Nov94 on 'Science Friction')*

E.M.I. — issued?

Mar 88. (7") **LAUGHING INSIDE. / ('A'acoustic version)** [ ] [ ]

Mar 88. (lp)(c) **DESCENDENTS OF SMITH** [ ] [ ]
– Laughing inside / Garden of uranium / Still life / Pinches of salt / Desert island / Government surplus / Surplus liquorice / Liquorice alltime / Maile lei / Same shoes / Descendents of Smith. *(cd+=)* – Laughing inside (rough and ready version). (cd-iss.Sep94 as 'GARDEN OF URANIUM' on 'Science Friction')

Awareness — not issued

May 90. (cd)(c)(lp) **ONCE** [ ] [-]
– Once / Once in the middle of nowhere / Nowhere to run to / Black cloud of Islam / If / Winds of change / Berliners / Sleeping at the wheel / For longer than it takes / Ghost dance. (re-iss.cd Oct94 on 'Science Friction')

Nov 90. (cd)(c)(lp) **BURN THE WORLD** [ ] [-]
– Burn the world (studio) / Burn the world (live). *(re-iss.cd Oct94 on 'Science Friction')*

Nov 92. (cd)(c)(lp) **DEATH OR GLORY** [ ] [-]
(re-iss.cd Dec94 on 'Science Friction')

Griffin — not issued

Aug 95. (cd) **UNHINGED** [ ] [-]
–

– compilations etc. –

May 78. Harvest; (7") **WHEN AN OLD CRICKETER LEAVES THE CREASE. / HOME (studio)** [ ] [ ]

May 78. Harvest; (lp)(c) **ROY HARPER 1970-75** [ ] [ ]
– Don't you grieve / I hate the white man / Tom Tiddler's ground / Me and my woman / Little lady / South Africa / Forbidden fruit / I'll see you again / Commune / Another day / When an old cricketer leaves the crease / Home.

Dec 88. Awareness; (lp)(c)(cd) **LOONY ON THE BUS** (rare) [ ] [-]

Nov 94. Awareness; (cd) **BORN IN CAPTIVITY / WORK OF HEART** [ ] [-]
(re-iss.cd Nov94 on 'Science Friction')

Dec 94. Awareness; (cd) **COMMERCIAL BREAKS** (rec.1979) [ ] [-]
(re-iss.cd Dec94 on 'Science Friction')

Dec 94. Awareness; (cd) **AN INTRODUCTION TO ROY HARPER** [ ] [-]
(re-iss.Feb95 on 'Science Friction')

Emmylou HARRIS

Born: 2 Apr'47, Birmingham, Alabama, USA. She later moved to Washington, where she played East Coast dates and released a 1969 album 'GLIDING BIRD' for 'Jubilee' label. In the early 70's, she played several Nashville gigs, but drifted back with baby Hallie to Washington, when her marriage broke up. She was seen in clubs by GRAM PARSONS (of FLYING BURRITO BROTHERS), who invited her to augment on his 1972 solo work 'G.P.'. On his next year's 'GREVIOUS ANGEL', she virtually shared vocal duties, and featured on his tour outings, until his untimely death in Sep'73. In 1975, she stayed with 'Reprise' records, who released her comeback solo album 'PIECES OF THE SKY'. After this, she provided harmonies for BOB DYLAN's classic album 'DESIRE', which hit big at the same time as her cross-Atlantic Top 30 follow-up album 'ELITE HOTEL'. She then married her producer BRIAN AHERN on 9 Jan'77, and soon had second Top 30 album 'LUXURY LINER'. Although she eventually disappeared from commercial limelight throughout the 80's (except for a US Top Ten 1987 collaboration album with DOLLY PARTON and LINDA RONSTADT), she continued to be prolific recording artist. • **Style:** Clear harmonious country rock star, blending bluegrass, rather than contemporaries redneck attitude. • **Songwriters:** Writes some herself, collaborates with others, except covers I'LL BE YOUR BABY TONIGHT (Bob Dylan) / THE PRICE YOU PAY + MY FATHER'S HOUSE + BORN TO RUN + TOUGHER THAN THE REST (Bruce Springsteen) / YOU NEVER CAN TELL (Chuck Berry) / THE BOXER (Simon & Garfunkel) / MISTER SANDMAN (Chordettes) / TO DADDY (Dolly Parton) / BURN THAT CANDLE (Bill Haley) / TWO MORE BOTTLES OF WINE (Delbert McClinton) / PLEDGING MY LOVE (Johnny Ace) / DIAMONDS ARE A GIRL'S BEST FRIEND (Jule Styne) / WILD MONTANA SKIES (duet w / JOHN DENVER) / HERE, THERE AND EVERYWHERE + FOR NO ONE (Beatles) / NO REGRETS (Tom Rush) / ICY BLUE HEART (John Hiatt) / LOVE IS (Kate McGarrigle) / WHEELS OF LOVE (Marjy Plant) / SAVE THE LAST DANCE FOR ME (Drifters) / JAMBALAYA (Hank Williams) / BAD MOON RISING + LODI (Creedence Clearwater Revival) / ROSE OF CIMARRON (Poco) / HOT BURRITO + SLEEPLESS NIGHTS (Gram Parsons) / BRAND NEW DANCE (Paul Kennerley) / SWEET DREAMS OF YOU (Kennerley-David) / BETTER OFF WITHOUT YOU (Chapman-Walker-Brown) / NEVER BE ANYONE ELSE BUT YOU (Baker Knight) / RED RED ROSE (David Mallett) / GUITAR TOWN (Steve Earle) / ROLLIN' AND RAMBLIN' (Williams-Williams-Clark) / EASY FOR YOU TO SAY (Routh-Sharp) / IN HIS WORLD (Kostas-Reynolds) / ABRAHAM, MARTIN & JOHN (hit; Marvin Gaye) / SCOTLAND (. . . Monroe) / CATTLE CALL (Buck Owens) / THANKS TO YOU (Jesse Winchester) / BALLAD OF A RUNNING HORSE (Leonard Cohen) / etc. • **Trivia:** In 1980, she won a Grammy for her country lp 'BLUE KENTUCKY GIRL'.

Recommended: ELITE HOTEL (*8) / LUXURY LINER (*6) / QUARTER MOON IN A TEN CENT TOWN (*7) / PIECES OF THE SKY (*7)

EMMYLOU HARRIS – vocals, acoustic guitar with session people

not issued — Jubilee

1969. (lp) **GLIDING BIRD** [-] [ ]
– I'll be your baby tonight / Fugue for the fox / I saw the light / Clocks / Black gypsy / Gliding bird / Everybody's talkin' / Bobbie's gone / I'll never fall in love again / Waltz of the magic man. *(UK-iss.Jul78 on 'Pye' as THE LEGENDARY GLIDING BIRD) (re-iss.Apr79 on 'Flyover')*

1969. (7") **I'LL BE YOUR BABY TONIGHT. / I'LL NEVER FALL IN LOVE AGAIN** [-] [ ]

1969. (7") **FUGUE FOR THE FOX. / PADDY** [-] [ ]

She then went solo, augmented soon by The HOT BAND:- **JAMES BURTON** – guitar / **GLEN D.HARDIN** – piano / **EMORY GORDY** – bass / **RODNEY CROMWELL** – rhythm guitar, vocals / **HANK DE VITO** – pedal steel guitar / **JOHN WARE** – drums

Reprise — Reprise

Apr 75. (lp)(c) **PIECES OF THE SKY** [ ] [45] Mar 75
– Bluebird wine / Too far gone / If I could only win your love / Boulder to Birmingham / Before believing / Bottle let me down / Sleepless nights / Coat of many colours / For no one / Queen of the silver dollar. *(cd-iss.Nov93)*

May 75. (7") **BOULDER TO BIRMINGHAM. / TOO FAR GONE** [-] [ ]

Jun 75. (7") **BOULDER TO BIRMINGHAM. / QUEEN OF THE SILVER DOLLAR** [ ] [-]

Nov 75. (7") **IF I COULD ONLY WIN YOUR LOVE. / QUEEN OF THE SILVER DOLLAR** [ ] [58] Aug 75

Jan 76. (7") **LIGHT OF THE STABLE. / BLUEBIRD WINE** [ ] [ ]

Jan 76. (lp)(c) **ELITE HOTEL** [17] [25]
– Amarillo / Together again / Feelin' single – seeing double / Sin city / One of these days / Till I gain control again / Here, there and everywhere / Ooh Las Vegas / Sweet dreams / Jambalaya / Satan's jewel crown / Wheels. *(re-iss.May89 on 'Edsel')*

Feb 76. (7") **HERE, THERE AND EVERYWHERE. / AMARILLO** [30] [-]

Mar 76. (7") **HERE, THERE AND EVERYWHERE. / TOGETHER AGAIN** [-] [65]

May 76. (7") **TOGETHER AGAIN. / WHEELS** [ ] [-]

Jul 76. (7") **ONE OF THESE DAYS. / TILL I GAIN CONTROL AGAIN** [-] [ ]

Sep 76. (7") **AMARILLO. / SWEET DREAMS** [-] [ ]

Nov 76. (7") **LIGHT OF THE STABLE. / BOULDER TO BIRMINGHAM** [-] [ ]

—— **ALBERT LEE** – guitar (ex-Solo artist) repl. BURTON (returned to ELVIS)

Warners — Warners

Jan 77. (lp)(c) **LUXURY LINER** [17] [21]
– Luxury liner / Pancho & Lefty / Making believe / You're supposed to be feeling good / I'll be your San Antone rose / (You never can tell) C'est la vie / When I stop dreaming / Hello stranger / She / Tulsa queen. *(cd-iss.1989)*

Feb 77. (7") **(YOU NEVER CAN TELL) C'EST LA VIE. / HELLO STRANGER** [ ] [-]

Feb 77. (7") **(YOU NEVER CAN TELL) C'EST LA VIE. / YOU'RE SUPPOSED TO BE FEELING GOOD** [-] [ ]

May 77. (7") **MAKING BELIEVE. / I'LL BE YOUR SAN ANTONE ROSE** [-] [ ]

Jan 78. (lp)(c) **QUARTER MOON IN A TEN CENT TOWN** [40] [29]
– Easy from now on / Two more bottles of wine / To daddy / My songbird / Leavin' Louisiana in the broad daylight / Defying gravity / I ain't livin' long like this / One paper kid / Green rolling hills / Burn that candle. *(cd-iss.1989)*

Feb 78. (7") **TO DADDY. / TULSA QUEEN** [ ] [ ]

Apr 78. (7") **I AIN'T LIVIN' LONG LIKE THIS. / TWO MORE BOTTLES OF WINE** [-] [ ]

Apr 78. (7") **I AIN'T LIVIN' LONG LIKE THIS. / ONE PAPER KID** [ ] [-]

Jun 78. (7") **EVEN FROM NOW ON. / YOU'RE SUPPOSED TO BE FEELING GOOD** [-] [ ]

May 79. (7") **SAVE THE LAST DANCE FOR ME. / EVEN COWGIRLS GET THE BLUES** [-] [ ]

Jun 79. (lp)(c) **BLUE KENTUCKY GIRL** [ ] [43] May 79
– Sister's coming home / Beneath still waters / Rough and rocky / Hickory wind /

Date	Release	UK	US
	Save the last dance for me / Sorrow in the wind / They'll never take his love from me / Everytime you leave / Blue Kentucky girl / Even cowgirls get the blues.		
Jul 79.	(7") **BLUE KENTUCKY GIRL. / LEAVIN' LOUISIANA IN THE BROAD DAYLIGHT**	-	
Oct 79.	(7") **BENEATH STILL WATERS. / TILL I GAIN CONTROL AGAIN**	-	
Nov 79.	(lp)(c) **LIGHT OF THE STABLE (THE CHRISTMAS ALBUM)** (festive)		Nov80
Nov 79.	(7") **THE FIRST NOEL. / SILENT NIGHT**		
May 80.	(7") **GREEN PASTURES. / WAYFARING STRANGERS**	-	
May 80.	(lp)(c) **ROSES IN THE SNOW**		26
	– Roses in the snow / Wayfaring stranger / Green pastures / The boxer / Darkest hour just before dawn / I'll go stepping too / You're learning / Jordan / Miss the Mississippi / Gold watch and chain.		
Jul 80.	(7") **THAT LOVIN' YOU FEELIN' AGAIN. / (b-side by Craig Hindley)**		55 Jun 80
	(above from the film 'Roadie' and credited w / **ROY ORBISON**)		
Jul 80.	(7") **THE BOXER. / PRECIOUS LOVE**	-	
Nov 80.	(7") **BEAUTIFUL STAR OF BETHLEHEM. / LITTLE DRUMMER BOY**	-	
Dec 80.	(7") **LIGHT OF THE STABLE. / LITTLE DRUMMER BOY**	-	
Feb 81.	(7") **MISTER SANDMAN. / FOOLS THIN AIR**	-	37
Feb 81.	(7") **MISTER SANDMAN. / ASHES BY NOW**	-	-
Feb 81.	(lp)(c) **EVANGELINE**	53	22
	– I don't have to crawl / How high the Moon / Spanish Johnny / Bad Moon rising / Evangeline / Hot burrito £2 / Millworker / Oh Atlanta / Mister Sandman / Ashes by now.		
May 81.	(7") **COLORS OF YOUR HEART. / I DIDN'T HAVE TO CRAWL**	-	
May 81.	(7") **BAD MOON RISING. / I DON'T HAVE TO CRAWL**		-
Nov 81.	(7") **MAMA HELP. / TENNESSEE ROSE**	-	
Nov 81.	(lp)(c) **CIMARRON**		46
	– Rose of cimarron / Spanish is a loving tongue / If I needed you / Another lonesome morning / The last cheater's waltz / Born to run / The price you pay / Son of a rotten gambler / Tennessee waltz / Tennessee rose.		
Feb 82.	(7") **BORN TO RUN. / COLORS OF YOUR HEART**	-	
Feb 82.	(7") **BORN TO RUN. / ASHES BY NOW**		-
Nov 82.	(lp)(c) **LAST DATE (live)**		65
	– I'm moving on / It's not love (but it's not bad) / So sad (to watch good love go so bad) / Grevious angel / Restless / Racing in the streets / Long may you run / Well sweep out the ashes (in the morning) / Juanita / Devil in disguise / (Lost his love) On our last date / Buckaroo / Love's gonna live here.		
Nov 82.	(7") **(LOST HIS LOVE) ON OUR LAST DATE. / ANOTHER POT O' TEA**	-	
Feb 83.	(7") **I'M MOVIN' ON (live). / MAYBE TONIGHT**	-	
Apr 83.	(7") **SO SAD (TO WATCH GOOD LOVE GO BAD) (live). / AMARILLO (live)**	-	
Oct 83.	(7") **DRIVIN' WHEEL. / GOOD NEWS**	-	
Oct 83.	(lp)(c)(cd) **WHITE SHOES**		
	– Drivin' wheel / Pledging my love / In my dreams / White shoes / On the radio / It's only rock'n'roll / Diamonds are a girl's best friend / Good news / Baby, better start turnin' 'em down / Like an old fashioned waltz.		
Jan 84.	(7") **LIKE AN OLD FASHIONED WALTZ. / IN MY DREAMS**	-	
May 84.	(7") **PLEDGING MY LOVE. / BABY, BETTER START TURNIN' 'EM DOWN**	-	
May 84.	(7") **ON THE RADIO. / GOOD NEWS**		-
Nov 84.	(7") **SOMEONE LIKE YOU. / LIGHT OF THE STABLE**	-	
Feb 85.	(7") **WHITE LINE. / LONG TALL SALLY ROSE**	-	
Feb 85.	(lp)(c)(cd) **THE BALLAD OF SALLY ROSE**		
	– The ballad of Sally Rose / Rhythm guitar / I think I love him – (instrumental; You are my flower) – Heart to heart / Woman walk the line / Bad news / Timberline / Long tall Sally Rose / White line / Diamond in my crown / The sweetheart of the rodeo / K-S-O-S (instrumental medley; Ring of fire – Wildwood flower – Six days on the road) – Sweet chariot.		
May 85.	(7") **DIAMOND IN MY CROWN. / RHYTHM GUITAR**	-	
Aug 85.	(7") **TIMBERLINE. / SWEET CHARIOT**	-	
Mar 87.	(7") **I HAD MY HEART SET ON YOU. / YOUR LONG JOURNEY**	-	
Apr 87.	(lp)(c)(cd) **THIRTEEN**		Mar 87
	– Mystery train / You're free to go / Sweetheart of the pines / Just someone in the know / My father's house / Lacassine special / Today I started loving you again / When I was yours / I had my heart set on you / Your long journey.		
Jun 87.	(7") **TODAY I STARTED LOVING YOU AGAIN. / WHEN I WAS YOURS**	-	
Jul 87.	(lp)(c)(cd) **ANGEL BAND**	-	
	– Where could I go to the Lord / Angel band / If I be lifted up / Precious memories / Bright morning stars / When he calls / We shall rise / Drifting too far / Who will sing for me / Someday my ship will sail / The other side of your life / When they ring those golden bells.		
Aug 87.	(7") **SOMEDAY MY SHIP WILL SAIL. / WHEN HE CALLS**	-	
		Reprise	Reprise
Feb 89.	(7") **HEARTBREAK HILL. / ICY BLUE HEART**	-	
Feb 89.	(lp)(c)(cd) **BLUEBIRD**		
	– Heaven only knows / You've been on my mind / Icy blue heart / Love is / No regrets / Lonely street / Heartbreak hill / I still miss someone / A river for him / If you were a bluebird.		
May 89.	(7") **HEAVEN ONLY KNOWS. / A RIVER FOR HIM**	-	
Aug 89.	(7") **I STILL MISS SOMEONE. / NO REGRETS**	-	
Nov 90.	(cd)(c)(lp) **BRAND NEW DANCE**		
	– Wheels of love / Tougher than the rest / In his world / Sweet dreams of you / Easy for you to say / Rollin' and ramblin' (the death of Hank Williams) / Better off without you / Never be anyone else but you / Brand new dance / Red red rose. *(re-iss.cd Feb95)*		
1991.	(7") **GULF COAST HIGHWAY (w/ WILLIE NELSON). / EVANGELINE**	-	
1991.	(7") **RED RED ROSE. / NEVER BE ANYONE ELSE BUT YOU**	-	
Jan 92.	(cd)(c)(d-lp) **AT THE RYMAN (live "with The NASHVILLE RAMBLERS")**		
	– Guitar town / Halk as much / Cattle call / Guess things happen that way / Hard times / Mansion on the hill / Scotland / Montana cowboy / Like strangers / Lodi / Calling my children home / If I could be there / Walls of time / Get up John / Medley:- It's a hard life wherever you go / Smoke along the track. *(re-iss.cd Feb95)*		
Apr 94.	(cd-s) **HIGH POWERED LOVE. / BALLAD OF A RUNAWAY HORSE**		
May 94.	(cd)(c)(lp) **COWGIRLS PRAYER**		
	– A ways to go / The night / High powered love / You don't know me / Prayer in open D / Cresent city / Lovin' you again / Jerusalem tomorrow / Thanks to you / I hear a call / Ballad of a running horse.		
Sep 94.	(c-s)(cd-s) **YOU DON'T KNOW ME. / A WAYS TO GO**		
		Grapevine	Asylum
Oct 95.	(cd)(c)(lp) **WRECKING BALL**	46	94
	– Where will I be / Goodbye / All my tears / Wrecking ball / Goin' back to Harlan / Deeper well / Every grain of sand / Sweet old world / May this be love / Orphan girl / Blackhawk / Waltz across Texas tonight.		

– compilations, others –

Date	Release	UK	US
Nov 78.	Warners; (lp)(c) **PROFILE – THE BEST OF EMMYLOU HARRIS**		81
	– One of these days / Sweet dreams / To daddy / You never can tell (C'est la vie) / Making believe / Easy from now on / Together again / If I could only win your love / Too far gone / Two more bottles of wine / From Boulder to Birmingham / Hello stranger. *(cd-iss.Jul84)*		
Nov 78.	Warners; (7") **TOO FAR GONE. / TULSA QUEEN**	-	
Mar 80.	Warners; (7") **(YOU NEVER CAN TELL) C'EST LA VIE. / BOULDER TO BIRMIMGHAM**	-	
Oct 82.	Warners; (d-c) **ELITE HOTEL / LUXURY LINER**		-
Oct 84.	Warners; (lp)(c) **PROFILE II – THE BEST OF EMMYLOU HARRIS**	-	
Oct 88.	Warners; (cd)(c)(lp) **DUETS**		
	(re-iss.Jul90 on 'Reprise') (cd-iss Nov 93).		
Nov 94.	Warners; (cd)(c) **SONGS OF THE WEST**		
Mar 80.	K-Tel; (lp)(c) **HER BEST SONGS**	36	-
Nov 83.	Magnum Force; (lp) **LIVE (live w/ GRAM PARSONS)**		-
Jul 93.	Magnum Force; (cd) **NASHVILLE COUNTRY DUETS (with CARL JACKSON)**		-

DOLLY PARTON, LINDA RONSTADT, EMMYLOU HARRIS

Date	Release	UK	US
		Warners	Warners
Mar 87.	(lp)(c)(cd) **TRIO**	60	6
	– The pain of lovin' you / Making plans / To know him is to love him / Hobo's meditation / Wildflowers / Telling me lies / My dear companion / These memories of you / I've had enough / Rosewood casket. *(cd+=)(c+=)* – Farther along. *(re-iss.cd Feb95)*		
Apr 87.	(7") **TO KNOW HIM IS TO LOVE HIM. / FARTHER ALONG**		
Jun 87.	(7") **TELLING ME LIES. / ROSEWOOD CASKET**	-	
Sep 87.	(7") **THOSE MEMORIES OF YOU. / MY DEAR COMPANION**	-	
Nov 87.	(7") **WILDFLOWERS. / HOBO'S MEDITATION**	-	

George HARRISON

Born: 25 Feb'43, Wavertree, Liverpool, England. In late 1968, he was the first BEATLE to release a solo lp 'WONDERWALL MUSIC', but it flopped in UK. He soon released on own 'Zapple' label, another instrumental lp 'ELECTRONIC SOUND', which used moog synthesizer for first time. When the BEATLES officially split in 1969, he took solo activities more seriously, bringing in famous session people to augment 1970 triple album 'ALL THINGS MUST PASS'. It hit No.1 in the US and was quickly followed by cross-Atlantic chart topping 45 'MY SWEET LORD'. The song was claimed by Bright Tunes (owners of songwriter Ronnie Mack's estate) that it plagiarised their CHIFFONS song 'HE'S SO FINE'. 5 years later, the court gave 6-figure royalties to the plaintiffs. In 1972, he released another triple, this time live album 'CONCERT FOR BANGLA DESH'. After another successful album 'LIVING IN THE MATERIAL WORLD', he formed own label 'Dark Horse' in 1974. It soon issued his own releases, as well as new signings RAVI SHANKAR and SPLINTER. He continued to be major star, all but hiccup flop 1982 album 'GONE TROPPO'. He returned in 1987 with Top 10 album 'CLOUD NINE', with him also joining the ranks of veteran supergroup TRAVELING WILBURYS. • **Style:** Multi-talented rock-pop star, with eastern Indian leanings. • **Songwriters:** Self-penned except; I'D HAVE YOU ANYTIME + IF NOT FOR YOU (co-written with Bob Dylan) / BYE BYE LOVE (Everly Brothers) / I DON'T WANT TO DO IT (Bob Dylan) / GOT MY MIND SET ON YOU (James Ray) / ROLL OVER BEETHOVEN (Chuck Berry) / etc. • **Miscellaneous:** He and his wife PATTI were divorced in Jun'77, after her much publicised affair with ERIC CLAPTON. From 1979, he founded own 'Homemade' film productions, which released 80's movies 'Life Of Brian', 'The Long Good Friday', 'Time Bandits', 'The Missionary', 'Mona Lisa', 'A Private Function', 'Water', and 'Shanghai Surprise'.

Recommended: ALL THINGS MUST PASS (*8) / THE BEST OF GEORGE

HARRISON (*7) / THE BEST OF DARK HORSE 1976-89 (*6)

GEORGE HARRISON – instruments (no vocals) (of-BEATLES)

Apple Apple

Nov 68. (lp) **WONDERWALL MUSIC (Soundtrack)** [ ] [49]
– Microbes / Red lady too / Tabla and Pavajak / In the park / Drilling a hole / Guru Vandana / Greasy legs / Ski-ing / Gat Kirwani / Dream scene / Party Seacombe / Love scene / Crying / Cowboy music / Fantasy sequins / On the bed / Glass box / Wonderwall to be here / Singing om. *(cd-iss.Jun92)*

— **GEORGE** – moog synthesizer (no vocals)

Zapple Zapple

May 69. (lp) **ELECTRONIC SOUND** [ ] [ ]
– Under the Mersey wall / No time or space.

— He became in-house 'Apple' producer, before gigging with DELANEY & BONNIE late 1969. The BEATLES break-up, and he went solo again with vocals, etc. with **DEREK & THE DOMINOES** (Eric Clapton and his band) / **BADFINGER** / **BILLY PRESTON** – keyboards / **RINGO STARR, GINGER BAKER** – drums / etc.

Apple Apple

Nov 70. (t-lp) **ALL THINGS MUST PASS** [4] [1]
– I'd have you anytime / My sweet Lord / Wah-wah / Isn't it a pity / What is life / If not for you / Behind that locked door / Let it down / Run of the mill / Beware of darkness / Apple scruffs / Ballad of Frankie Crisp (let it roll) / Awaiting on you all / All things must pass / I dig love / Art of dying / Isn't it a pity / Hear me Lord / Out of the blue / It's Johnny's birthday / Plug me in / I remember Jeep / Thanks for the pepperoni. *(d-cd.iss.May87 on 'E.M.I.')*

Nov 70. (7") **MY SWEET LORD. / ISN'T IT A PITY** [-] [1]

Jan 71. (7") **MY SWEET LORD. / WHAT IS LIFE** [1] [-]
(re-iss.Nov76)

Feb 71. (7") **WHAT IS LIFE. / APPLE SCRUFFS** [-] [10]

Jul 71. (7") **BANGLA-DESH. / DEEP BLUE** [10] [23]

In Jan72, He with other artists released live triple album CONCERT FOR BANGLA-DESH which hit UK No.1 & US No.2. (d-cd-iss.Aug91)

— **GEORGE** now with various session people

May 73. (7") **GIVE ME LOVE (GIVE ME PEACE ON EARTH). / MISS O'DELL** [8] [1]

Jun 73. (lp)(c) **LIVING IN THE MATERIAL WORLD** [2] [1]
– Give me love (give me peace on earth) / Sue me, sue you blues / The light that has lighted the world / Don't let me wait too long / Who can see it / Living in the material world / The Lord loves the one (that loves the Lord) / Be here now / Try some buy some / The day the world gets 'round / That is all. *(cd-iss.Jan92 on 'E.M.I.')*

Dec 74. (7") **DING DONG; DING DONG. / I DON'T CARE ANYMORE** [38] [36] Jan 75

Dec 74. (lp)(c) **DARK HORSE** [ ] [4]
– Hari's on tour (express) / Simply shady / So sad / Bye bye love / Maya love / Ding dong; ding dong / Dark horse / Far East man / Is it he (Jai Sri Krishna). *(re-iss.Dec80 on 'M.f.P.') (cd-iss.Jan92 on 'E.M.I.')*

Feb 75. (7") **DARK HORSE. / HARI'S ON TOUR (EXPRESS)** [ ] [15] Nov 74

Sep 75. (7") **YOU. / WORLD OF STONE** [38] [20]

Oct 75. (lp)(c) **EXTRA TEXTURE (READ ALL ABOUT IT)** [16] [8]
– The answer's at the end / This guitar (can't keep from crying) / You / Ooh baby (you know that I love you) / World of stone / A bit more of you / Can't stop thinking about you / Tired of midnight blue / Grey cloudy lies / His name is legs (ladies & gentlemen). *(cd-iss.Jan92 on 'E.M.I.')*

Feb 76. (7") **THIS GUITAR (CAN'T KEEP FROM CRYING). / MAYA LOVE** [ ] [ ]

Oct 76. (lp)(c) **THE BEST OF GEORGE HARRISON** [ ] [31]
– Something (BEATLES) / If I needed someone (BEATLES) / Here comes the sun (BEATLES) / Taxman (BEATLES) / Think for yourself (BEATLES) / While my guitar gently weeps (BEATLES) / For you blue (BEATLES) / My sweet Lord / Give me love (give me peace on Earth) / You / Bangla-Desh / Dark horse / What is life. *(re-iss.Oct81 on 'MFP') (cd-iss.May87 on 'Parlophone')*

Dark Horse Dark Horse

Nov 76. (7") **THIS SONG. / LEARNING HOW TO LOVE YOU** [ ] [25]

Nov 76. (lp)(c) **THIRTY-THREE AND A THIRD** [35] [11]
– Woman don't you cry for me / Dear one / Beautiful girl / This song / See yourself / It's what you value / True love / Pure Smokey / Crackerbox palace / Learning how to love you. *(cd-iss.Jan92 on 'E.M.I.')*

Jan 77. (7") **CRACKERBOX PALACE. / LEARNING HOW TO LOVE YOU** [-] [19]

Feb 77. (7") **TRUE LOVE. / PURE SMOKEY** [ ] [-]

Jun 77. (7") **IT'S WHAT YOU VALUE. / WOMAN DON'T YOU CRY FOR ME** [ ] [-]

Feb 79. (7") **BLOW AWAY. / SOFT-HEARTED HANA** [-] [16]

Feb 79. (7") **BLOW AWAY. / SOFT TOUCH** [51] [-]

Feb 79. (lp)(c) **GEORGE HARRISON** [39] [14]
– Love comes to everyone / Not guilty / Here comes the moon / Soft- hearted Hana / Blow away / Faster / Your love is forever / Dark sweet lady / Soft touch / If you believe. *(cd-iss.Jan92 on 'E.M.I.')*

Apr 79. (7") **LOVE COMES TO EVERYONE. / SOFT-HEARTED HANA** [ ] [-]

Apr 79. (7") **LOVE COMES TO EVERYONE. / SOFT TOUCH** [-] [ ]

Jul 79. (7")(7"pic-d) **FASTER. / YOUR LOVE IS FOREVER** [ ] [ ]

May 81. (7") **ALL THOSE YEARS AGO. / WRITING'S ON THE WALL** [13] [2]

Jun 81. (lp)(c) **SOMEWHERE IN ENGLAND** [13] [11]
– Blood from a clone / Unconsciousness rules / Life itself / All those years ago / Batlimore oriole / Teardrops / That which I have lost / Writing's on the wall / Hong Kong blues / Save the world. *(re-iss.Jul88) (cd-iss.Jan92 on 'E.M.I.')*

Jul 81. (7") **TEARDROPS. / SAVE THE WORLD** [ ] [ ]

Oct 82. (7") **WAKE UP MY LOVE. / GREECE** [ ] [53]

Nov 82. (lp)(c) **GONE TROPPO** [ ] [ ]
– Wake up my love / That's the way it goes / I really love you / Greece / Gone troppo / Mystical one / Unknown delight / Baby don't run away / Dream away / Circles. *(re-iss.Jul88) (cd-iss.Jan92 on 'E.M.I.')*

Jan 83. (7") **I REALLY LOVE YOU. / CIRCLES** [-] [ ]

— Took long time off from solo career to establish his film production work. Returned after nearly five years with new session people.

Sep 87. (lp)(c)(cd) **CLOUD NINE** [10] [8] Nov 87
– Cloud 9 / That's what it takes / Fish on the sand / Just for today / This is love / When we was fab / Devil's radio / Someplace else / Wreck of the Hesperus / Breath away from Heaven / Got my mind set on you.

Oct 87. (7") **GOT MY MIND SET ON YOU. / LAY HIS HEAD** [2] [1]
(12"+=)(12"pic-d+=) – ('A'extended).

Feb 88. (7") **WHEN WE WAS FAB. / ZIGZAG** [25] [23]
(12"+=)(12"pic-d+=)(3"cd-s+=) – That's the way it goes (remix) / ('A'mix).

Jun 88. (7") **THIS IS LOVE. / BREATH AWAY FROM HEAVEN** [55] [ ]
(12"+=) – All those wasted years ago.
(3"cd-s++=) – Hong Kong blues.

— Later in 1988, HARRISON teamed up with BOB DYLAN, ROY ORBISON, JEFF LYNNE and TOM PETTY in The TRAVELLING WILBURYS. He also continued solo work below.

Oct 89. (lp)(c)(cd) **THE BEST OF DARK HORSE (1976-1989)** (compilation) [ ] [ ]
– Poor little girl / Blow away / That's the way it goes / Cockamamie business / Wake up my love / Life itself / Got my mind set on you / Here comes the Moon / Gone troppo / When we was fab / Love comes to everyone / All those years ago / Cheer down. *(c+cd+=)* – Crackerbox Palace.

Nov 89. (7")(c-s) **CHEER DOWN. / POOR LITTLE GIRL** [ ] [-]
(12"+=)(cd-s+=) – Crackerbox palace.

Jul 92. (cd)(c)(d-lp) **LIVE IN JAPAN (live with ERIC CLAPTON AND BAND)** [ ] [ ]
– I want to tell you / Old brown shoe / Taxman / Give me love (give me peace on Earth) / If I needed someone / Something / What is life / Dark horse / Piggies / Got my mind set on you / Cloud nine / Here comes the Sun / My sweet Lord / All those years ago / Cheer down / Devil's radio / Isn't it a pity / While my guitar gently weeps / Roll over Beethoven.

– compilations etc. –

Oct 82. Dark Horse; (d-c) **THIRTY-THREE AND A THIRD / GEORGE HARRISON** [ ] [ ]

Jerry HARRISON (see under ⇒ TALKING HEADS)

Deborah / Debbie HARRY (see under ⇒ BLONDIE)

HARRY CREWS (see under ⇒ LUNCH, Lydia)

Grant HART (see under ⇒ HUSKER DU)

Mickey HART (see under ⇒ GRATEFUL DEAD)

Tim HART (see under ⇒ STEELEYE SPAN)

Alex HARVEY

Born: 5 Feb'35, The Gorbals, Glasgow, Scotland. After loads of jobs from the early 50's, he played in various skiffle groups. After winning a local talent contest in 1956, he was dubbed 'The TOMMY STEELE Of Scotland'. In 1959, his BIG SOUL BAND backed touring American stars EDDIE COCHRAN and GENE VINCENT. They soon made their way to Germany, where they played many gigs and soon signed to 'Polydor'. They recorded a few lp's, and several 45's (some solo), before he joined the crew of the 'Hair' musical in London's West End. In 1972, he returned to Scotland and found TEAR GAS, who were just about to disband after 2 poorly received lp's. They became The SENSATIONAL ALEX HARVEY BAND, and released, after nationwide tours and signature for 'Vertigo', their debut album 'FRAMED'. Late in '73, he issued the near excellent 'NEXT . . . ', and should have scored with edited cut and fan favourite 'THE FAITH HEALER'. In Oct'74, they secured first UK Top 20 album with 'THE IMPOSSIBLE DREAM', which was followed by a Top 10 album in 1975, and a marvellous Top 10 single rendition of 'DELILAH'. They peaked for another year, but found it difficult to maintain success, with advent of punk. Sadly no longer in the limelight, ALEX died of a heart attack in Belguim on 4th Feb'82. • **Style:** HARVEY's solo R&B roots, were abandoned in the 70's, for more theatrical and comic book rock'n'roll. His buchaneer attitude and attire, was a visionary plus, only matched by his clown-like guitarist ZAL CLEMINSON. • **Songwriters:** Most by himsef and HUGH McKENNA, with additions from either ZAL or D.BATCHELOR. Covered; FRAMED (Leiber-Stoller) / I JUST WANT TO MAKE LOVE TO YOU (Willie Dixon) / NEXT (Jacques Brel) / GIDDY-UP-A-DING-DONG (Freddie Bell & The Bellboys) / THE IMPOSSIBLE DREAM (?) / RIVER OF LOVE (?) / TOMORROW BELONGS TO ME (German national anthem) / DELILAH (hit; Tom Jones) / CHEEK TO CHEEK (Irving Berlin) / LOVE STORY (Jethro Tull) / CRAZY HORSES (Osmonds) / SCHOOL'S OUT (Alice Cooper) / RUNAWAY (Del Shannon) / GOODNIGHT IRENE (Leadbelly) / SHAKIN' ALL OVER (Johnny Kidd) / etc. • **Trivia:** His 'LOCH NESS' lp, released unusually on 'K-Tel', featured only interviews from sightings of the monster.

Recommended: THE COLLECTION (*8). / NEXT . . . (*9)

ALEX HARVEY & HIS SOUL BAND

ALEX – vocals / **RICKY BARNES** – saxophone, vocals / **ISOBEL BOND** – vocals / **GIBSON KEMP** – drums / **IAN HINDS** – organ / **BILL PATRICK** – guitar

Polydor not issued

Jan 64. (7") **I JUST WANNA MAKE LOVE TO YOU. / LET THE GOOD TIMES ROLL** [ ] [-]

Mar 64. (lp) **ALEX HARVEY AND HIS SOUL BAND (live)** -
– Framed / I ain't worrying baby / Backwater blues / Let the good times roll / Going home / I've got my mojo working / Teensville U.S.A. / New Orleans / Bo Diddley is a gunslinger / When I grow too old to rock / Evil hearted man / I just wanna make love to you / The blind man / Reeling and rocking. *(re-iss.Oct87 Germany)*

Jun 64. (7") **GOT MY MOJO WORKING. / I AIN'T WORRIED BABY** -

— ALEX HARVEY brought in new soul band, (his brother **LES HARVEY** – guitar / **BOBBY THOMPSON** – bass / **GILSON KEMP** – drums)

Jul 65. (7") **AIN'T THAT JUST TOO BAD. / MY KIND OF LOVE** -
Nov 65. (lp) **THE BLUES** -
– Trouble in mind / Honey bee / I learned about woman / Danger zone / The riddle song / Waltzing Matilda / The blues / The big rock candy mountain / The Michegan massacre / No peace / Nobody knows you when you're down and out / St.James infirmary / Strange fruit / Kisses sweeter than wine / Good God almighty.

ALEX HARVEY

solo with session musicians.

Fontana not iss.

Sep 65. (7") **AGENT O-O-SOUL. / GO AWAY BABY** -
Nov 66. (7") **WORK SONG. / I CAN'T DO WITHOUT YOUR LOVE** -

— HARVEY now backed by **GIANT MOTH:- JIM CONDRON** – guitar, bass / **MOX** – flute / **GEORGE BUTLER** – drums

Decca not issued

Jul 67. (7") **THE SUNDAY SONG. / HORIZONS** -
Sep 67. (7") **MAYBE SOMEDAY. / CURTAINS FOR MY BABY** -

— with band ROCK WORKSHOP which incl. brother LES and loads of others.

Fontana not issued

Oct 69. (lp) **ROMAN WALL BLUES** -
– Midnight Moses / Hello L.A., bye bye Birmingham / Broken hearted fairytale / Donna / Roman wall blues / Jumping Jack Flash / Hammer song / Let my bluebird sing / Maxine / Down at Bart's place / Candy.

Nov 69. (7") **MIDNIGHT MOSES. / ROMAN WALL BLUES** -

— ALEX then formed his trio (**IAN ELLIS** – bass, ex-CLOUDS, **DAVE DUFORT** – drums) This was broken up after the death, by stage electrocution, of his brother LES, who had been part of STONE THE CROWS since '69 (Aug72) **ALEX** recruited a whole band

— **TEAR GAS** who had already made two albums – Nov70 'PIGGY GO BETTER' on 'Famous', without the McKENNA brothers. Aug71. 'TEAR GAS' on 'Regal Zono.', with all the members below of –

The SENSATIONAL ALEX HARVEY BAND

(ALEX – vocals, guitar) / **ZAL CLEMINSON** (b. 4 May'49) – guitar, vocals / **CHRIS GLEN** (b. 6 Nov'50) – bass / **HUGH McKENNA** (b.28 Nov'49) – keyboards / **TED McKENNA** (b.10 Mar'50) – drums

Vertigo Vertigo

Oct 72. (7") **JUNGLE JENNY. / BUFF'S BAR BLUES** -
Dec 72. (lp)(c) **FRAMED**
– Framed / Hammer song / Midnight Moses / Isobel Goudie (part 1 – My lady of the night, part 2 – Coitus interruptus, part 3 – The virgin and the hunter) / Buff's bar blues / I just want to make love to you / Hole in her stocking / There's no lights on the Christmas tree, mother, they're burning big Louie tonight / St. Anthony. *(re-iss.Mar79 on 'Mountain', re-iss.+cd '84 on 'Samurai', cd-iss+=)* – Smouldering / Chase it into the night.

Dec 72. (7") **THERE'S NO LIGHTS ON THE CHRISTMAS TREE, MOTHER, THEY'RE BURNING BIG LOUIE TONIGHT. / HARP** -
Nov 73. (lp)(c) **NEXT . . .**
– Swampsnake / Gang bang / The faith healer / Giddy up a ding dong / Next / Vambo marble eye / The last of the teenage idols (part I-III). *(re-iss.Mar79 on 'Mountain', re-iss.Mar82 on 'Fame', cd-iss.Jul86 on 'Samurai')*

Feb 74. (7") **THE FAITH HEALER (edit). / ST. ANTHONY** -
Feb 74. (7") **SWAMPSNAKE. / GANG BANG** - -
Aug 74. (7") **SERGEANT FURY. / GANG BANG** -
Sep 74. (7") **SERGEANT FURY. / TOMAHAWK KID** - -
Sep 74. (lp)(c) **THE IMPOSSIBLE DREAM** 16
– The hot city symphony; (part 1 – Vambo, part 2 – Man in the Jar) / River of love / Long hair music / Sergeant Fury / Weights made of lead / Money honey – The impossible dream / Tomahawk kid / Anthem. *(re-iss.Mar79 on 'Mountain', re-iss.+cd Jul86 on 'Samurai')*

Nov 74. (7") **ANTHEM. / ('A'version)** -
Apr 75. (lp)(c) **TOMORROW BELONGS TO ME** 9
– Action strasse / Snake bite / Soul in chains / The tale of the giant stoneater / Ribs and balls / Give my compliments to the chef / Sharks teeth / Ribs and balls / Shake that thing / Tomorrow belongs to me / To be continued . . . *(re-iss.+cd Jul86 on 'Samurai', cd-iss+=)* – Big boy / Pick it up and kick it.

Vertigo Atlantic

Jul 75. (7") **DELILAH (live). / SOUL IN CHAINS (live)** 7
Sep 75. (lp)(c) **THE SENSATIONAL ALEX HARVEY BAND "LIVE" (live)** 14 100
– Fanfare (justly, skillfully, magnanimously) / The faith healer / Tomahawk kid / Vambo / Give my compliments to the chef / Delilah / Framed. *(re-iss.+cd Jul86 on 'Samurai', cd-iss+=)* – I wanna have you back / Jungle Jenny / Runaway / Love story / School's Out. *(re-iss.Apr86 on 'Sahara', re-iss.Oct86 on 'Fame')*

Vertigo Vertigo

Nov 75. (7") **GAMBLIN' BAR ROOM BLUES. / SHAKE THAT THING** 38 -
Mar 76. (7") **RUNAWAY. / SNAKE BITE** -
Mar 76. (lp)(c) **PENTHOUSE TAPES** 14
– I wanna have you back / Jungle Jenny / Runaway / Love story / School's out / Goodnight Irene / Say you're mine / Gamblin' bar room blues / Crazy horses / Cheek to cheek. *(re-iss.Mar79 on 'Mountain', re-iss.Nov84 on 'Sahara', re-iss.+cd Jul86 on 'Samurai')*

Mountain Mountain

May 76. (7") **BOSTON TEA PARTY. / SULTAN'S CHOICE** 13
Jul 76. (lp)(c) **SAHB STORIES** 11
– Boston Tea Party / Sultan's choice / $25 for a massage / Dogs of war / Dance to your daddy / Amos Moses / Jungle rub out / Sirocco.

Aug 76. (7") **AMOS MOSES. / SATCHEL AND THE SCALP HUNTER**

SAHB WITHOUT ALEX

all 4 members without ALEX HARVEY (HUGH – vocals)

Jan 77. (lp)(c) **FOURPLAY**
– Smouldering / Chase it into the night / Shake your way to Heaven / Outer boogie / Big boy / Pick it up and kick it / Love you for a lifetime / Too much American pie. *(re-iss.Nov84 on 'Sahara')*

Jan 77. (7") **PICK IT UP AND KICK IT. / SMOULDERING** -

— **ALEX HARVEY** released in Apr 77 solo narrative lp PRESENTS THE LOCH NESS MONSTER on 'K-Tel'.

The SENSATIONAL ALEX HARVEY BAND

reformed **HARVEY, CLEMINSON, T.McKENNA and GLEN** recruited **TOMMY EYRE** – keyboards repl. HUGH

Mountain Mountain

Aug 77. (7") **MRS. BLACKHOUSE. / ENGINE ROOM BOOGIE** -
Mar 78. (lp)(c) **ROCK DRILL**
– The rock drill suite: Rock drill – The dolphins – Rock and roll – King Kong / Booids / Who murdered sex / Nightmare city / Water beastie / Mrs. Blackhouse. *(re-iss.Nov84 on 'Sahara')*

— (had already split late '77) CHRIS and TED joined ZAL in his own named band. ZAL later joined NAZARETH. TED later joined RORY GALLAGHER and then GREG LAKE BAND. TED and CHRIS later joined MICHAEL SCHENKER GROUP.

ALEX HARVEY BAND

with **TOMMY EYRE** – keyboards / **MATTHEW CANG** – guitar / **GORDON SELLAR** – bass / **SIMON CHATTERTON** – drums

R.C.A. not issued

Oct 79. (7") **SHAKIN' ALL OVER. / WAKE UP DAVIS** -
Nov 79. (lp)(c) **THE MAFIA STOLE MY GUITAR** -
– Don's delight / Back in the depot / Wait for me mama / The Mafia stole my guitar / Shakin' all over / The whalers (thar she blows) / Oh Sparticus / Just a gigolo / I ain't got nobody. *(re-iss.+cd.Sep91 on 'Demon')*

May 80. (7") **BIG TREE SMALL AXE. / THE WHALERS (THAR SHE BLOWS)** -

ALEX HARVEY died of a heart attack 4th Feb'82 while in Belguim.

- his posthumous releases -

Nov 83. Power Supply; (7") **THE POET AND I. /**
Nov 83. Power Supply; (lp)(c) **SOLDIER ON THE WALL** -

- other SAHB compilations, etc. -

May 77. Vertigo; (lp)(c) **BIG HITS AND CLOSE SHAVES**
(re-iss.Apr79 on 'Mountain')

Nov 92. Vertigo; (cd)(c) **ALL SENSATIONS** -
Jun 77. Vertigo; (7") **CHEEK TO CHEEK. / JUNGLE JENNY** -
Jul 80. Mountain; (lp)(c) **COLLECTOR'S ITEMS** -
Jul 80. Mountain; (7"m) **DELILAH (live). / BOSTON TEA PARTY / THE FAITH HEALER** -
Aug 82. R.C.A.; (d-lp)(d-c) **THE BEST OF THE SENSATIONAL ALEX HARVEY BAND**
– Next / Framed / The faith healer / Tomahawk kid / The hot city symphony; part 1 – Vambo, part 2 – Man in the jar / Sergeant Fury / The tale of the giant stoneater / Action strasse / Delilah / Weights made of lead / Boston Tea Party / Anthem / Runaway / Crazy horses / Big tree small axe / The Mafia stole my guitar / Gang bang / Tomorrow belongs to me. *(re-iss.May84)*

Nov 85. Sahara; (lp) **LEGEND** -
(cd-iss.1986 on 'Samurai')

Jan 86. Sahara; (c) **ANTHOLOGY** -
Apr 86. Aura; (c) **DOCUMENT** -
Sep 86. Castle; (d-lp)(cd) **THE COLLECTION** -
– $25 for a massage / The tale of the giant stoneater / Action strasse / Gang bang / Next / Give my compliments to the chef / Framed / Tomorrow belongs to me / Dance to your daddy / Sgt.Fury / Sultan's choice / Delilah (live) / Soul in chains / The faith healer / Boston tea party / Vambo (part 1) / Dogs of war / There's no lights on the Christmas tree mother, they're burning big Louie tonight / Giddy up a ding dong.

Jul 87. K-Tel; (lp)(c)(cd) **THE BEST OF THE SENSATIONAL ALEX HARVEY BAND** -
– Delilah / The faith healer / Framed / Sergeant Fury / Jungle rub out / Love story / School's out / Boston Tea Party / Gamblin' bar room blues / Next / The man in the jar / Snake bite / Give my compliments to the chef / Cheek to cheek.

Sep 87. Start; (lp)(c)(cd) **PORTRAIT** -
Feb 91. Music Club; (cd)(c) **THE BEST OF S.A.H.B.** -
Oct 91. Windsong; (lp) **LIVE IN CONCERT (live)** -
Nov 94. Windsong; (cd) **LIVE ON THE TEST** -
Jul 94. Success; (cd)(c) **THE BEST OF THE SENSATIONAL ALEX HARVEY BAND** -
Sep 94. Spectrum; (cd)(c) **DELILAH** -

PJ HARVEY

Formed: Yeovil, England . . . 1991 by POLLY JEAN HARVEY, who had just left Bristol-based covers band The AUTOMATIC DILAMINI. They made 3

singles; 'THE CRAZY SUPPER EP', 'I DON'T KNOW YOU BUT . . .' & 'ME AND MY CONSCIENCE', plus album 'THE D IS FOR DRUM' (on 'Idea') during 1986 + 87. PJ HARVEY soon became top self-financed indie band, which led to a near Top 10 success in 1992 with debut Steve Albini (ex-BIG BLACK) produced album 'DRY' (as was next). • **Style:** Uncompromising feminist rock act, led by sculptor POLLY. • **Songwriters:** POLLY, and covers; HIGHWAY 61 (Bob Dylan) / DADDY (Willie Dixon). • **Trivia:** POLLY guested for GRAPE on their 'Baby In A Plastic Bag' single, and also for The FAMILY CAT.

Recommended: DRY (*9) / RID OF ME (*8) / TO BRING YOU MY LOVE (*9)

POLLY HARVEY – vocals, guitar / **STEPHEN VAUGHAN** – bass / **ROB ELLIS** – drums, vocals

Too Pure / not issued

Oct 91. (12")(cd-s) **DRESS. / WATER / DRY** [ ] [-]
(re-iss.Mar92)

Feb 92. (12"ep)(cd-ep) **SHEELA-NA-GIG. / HAIR / JOE** [69] [-]

Mar 92. (cd)(c)(lp) **DRY** [11] [ ]
– Oh my lover / O Stella / Dress / Victory / Happy and bleeding / Sheela-na-gig / Hair / Joe / Plants and rags / Fountain water, (w/ free demos cd + lp)

Island / Island

Apr 93. (7"ep)(12"ep)(c-ep)(cd-ep) **50 FT. QUEENIE. / REELING / MAN SIZED (demo)** [27] [ ]

Apr 93. (cd)(c)(lp) **RID OF ME** [3] [ ]
– Rid of me / Missed / Legs / Rub till it bleeds / Hook / Man-size sextet / Highway '61 revisited / 50ft. Queenie / Yuri-G / Man-size / Dry / Me-Jane / Snake / Ecstasy

Jul 93. (12"ep)(cd-ep) **MAN-SIZE. / WANG DANG DOODLE / DADDY** [42] [ ]

— drummer ROB ELLIS departed after above.

Oct 93. (cd)(c)(lp) **4-TRACK DEMOS (demos)** [19] [ ]
– Rid of me / Legs / Reeling / Snake / Hook / 50ft Queenie / Driving / Ecstasy / Hardly wait / Rub 'til it bleeds / Easy / M-bike / Yuri-G / Goodnight.

Feb 95. (7"ep)(12"ep)(cd-ep) **DOWN BY THE WATER. / LYING IN THE SUN / SOMEBODY'S DOWN, SOMEBODY'S NAME** [38] [ ]

Feb 95. (cd)(c)(lp) **TO BRING YOU MY LOVE** [12] [40]
– To bring you my love / Meet ze monsta / Working for the man / C'mon Billy / Teclo / Long snake moan / Down by the water / I think I'm a mother / Send his love to me / The dancer. *(re-iss.d-cd Dec95 w/ extra B-sides)*

Jul 95. (12") **C'MON BILLY. / DARLING BE THERE / MANIAC** [29] [ ]
(cd-s+=) – One time too many.

Oct 95. (7"pic-d)(cd-s) **SEND HIS LOVE TO ME / HOOK (live) / WATER (live)** [34] [ ]
(cd-s) – Longtime coming (evening session version) / Harder.

Annie HASLAM (see under ⇒ RENAISSANCE)

HATER (see under ⇒ SOUNDGARDEN)

Juliana HATFIELD

Born: 1967, Boston, Massachusetts, USA. Formed the JULIANA HATFIELD THREE in 1993, out of The BLAKE BABIES and one solo album. This trio, were soon signed to 'Mammoth' where they issued two well-received early 90's albums 'EARWIG' and 'SUNBURN'. In 1992, JULIANA had a spell with friends The LEMONHEADS, before she went solo and formed her own named band. 1993's album 'BECOME WHAT YOU ARE', should have gave her deserved commercial break through. • **Style:** While The BLAKE BABIES were often compared to other Bostonians BUFFALO TOM or The LEMONHEADS, HATFIELD was more soft-grunge that sounded like a hard-edged GO-GO's. • **Songwriters:** HATFIELD. BLAKE BABIES covered TEMPTATION (Grass Roots) / SEVERED LIPS (Dinosaur Jr.). • **Trivia:** From 1987-1989, JULIANA was the girlfriend of EVAN DANDO.

Recommended: BECOME WHAT YOU ARE (*7) / EARWIG (*6; BLAKE BABIES).

BLAKE BABIES

JULIANA HATFIELD (b.1967) – vocals, guitar / **JOHN STROM** – guitar (of-LEMONHEADS) / **FREDA LOVE BONER** – drums

Utility / Chewbud

1988. (m-lp) **NICELY, NICELY** [-] [ ]
– Wipe it up / Her / Tom & Bob / A sweet burger lp / Bye / Let them eat chewy granola bars / Julius fast body / Better'n'you / Swill and the cocaine sluts. *(UK-iss.cd-s+c-s Oct94 on 'Mammoth')*

— added **EVAN DANDO** – bass, vocals (of-LEMONHEADS)

Jul 89. (m-lp)(cd) **SLOW LEARNER** [ ] [ ]
– Lament / Grateful / Your way or the highway / Take your head off my shoulder / Rain / From here to Burma / Putta my head. *(re-iss.cd,c,lp Mar93 as 'BLAKE BABIES')*

— now without DANDO who returned to The LEMONHEADS as drummer!

Mammoth / Mammoth

Mar 90. (lp) **EARWIG** [-] [ ]
– Cesspool / Dead and gone / Grateful you / You don't give up / Your way on the highway / Rain / Lament / Alright / Loose / Take your head off my shoulder / From here to Burma / Don't suck my breath / Outta my head / Steamy Gregg / Not just a wish. *(cd-iss.Oct94)*

Dec 90. (lp) **SUNBURN** [-] [ ]
– I'm not your mother / Out there / Star / Look away / Sanctify / Girl in a box / Train / I'll take anything / Watch me now I'm calling / Gimme some mirth / Kiss and make up / A million years. *(UK-iss.Mar92, cd-iss.Oct94)*

Feb 92. (m-lp) **ROSY JACK WORLD** [ ] [ ]
– Rosy Jack world / Temptation eyes / Downtime / Take me / Nirvana *(re-iss.cd Oct94)*

— HATFIELD joined The LEMONHEADS on mid-92 album 'IT'S A SHAME ABOUT RAY', before forming The JULIANA HATFIELD three. STROHM and BONER had already formed ANTENNA, who released for same label 'SWAY' album mid-92 and eponymous album Mar93.

– compilations, etc. –

Oct 93. Mammoth; (cd)(c)(lp) **INNOCENCE AND EXPERIENCE** [ ] [ ]
– Wipe it up / Rain / Boiled potato / Lament / Cesspool / You don't give up / Star / Sanctify / Out there / Girl in a box / I'm not your mother / Temptation eyes / Downtime / Over and over. *(re-iss.cd Oct94) (MR 0058-2)*

JULIANA HATFIELD

Mammoth / Mammoth

Jul 92. (12"ep)(cd-ep) **EVERYBODY LOVES ME BUT YOU. / NIRVANA / TAMARA** [ ] [ ]

Aug 92. (cd)(c)(lp) **HEY BABE** [ ] [ ]
– Everybody loves me but you / Lost and saved / I see you / The lights / Nirvana / Forever baby / Ugly / No outlet / Quit / Get off your knees / No answer.

— guested on above **EVAN DANDO** – guitars, vocals (of LEMONHEADS)

Nov 92. (12"ep)(cd-ep) **I SEE YOU / UGLY RIDER. / HERE COMES THE PAIN / FEED ME** [ ] [ ]

JULIANA HATFIELD three

JULIANA HATFIELD – vocals, guitar / **DEAN FISHER** – bass / **TODD PHILIPS** – drums

— guests **PETER HOLSAPPLE** – keyboards (ex-dB's) / **DENNY FONGHEISER** – percussion ('Mammoth' now taken over by the majors)

East West / Atco

Jul 93. (cd)(c) **BECOME WHAT YOU ARE** [44] [ ]
– Supermodel / My sister / This is the sound / For the birds / Mabel / A dame with a rod / Addicted / Feelin' Massachusetts / Spin the bottle / President Garfield / Little pieces / I got no idols.

Sep 93. (7")(c-s) **MY SISTER. / PUT IT AWAY** [71] [ ]
(10"+=)(cd-s+=) – A dame with rod / Ruthless.

Nov 93. (7")(c-s) **FOR THE BIRDS. / HELLO, MY NAME IS BABY** [ ] [ ]
(10"+=)(cd-s+=) – I got no idols (piano version) / Batwing.

Aug 94. (10"ep)(c-ep)(cd-ep) **SPIN THE BOTTLE. / MY DARLING / NIRVANA (live at Triple J) / MY SISTER (acoustic)** [ ] [97]

— (above on 'RCA' US and from the film 'Reality Bites')

Mar 95. (10"ep)(cd-ep)(c-ep) **UNIVERSAL HEART-BEAT / WHERE WOULD I BE WITHOUT YOU. / YARDSAILING / GIRL IN OLD BLUE VOLVO DISOWNS SELF** [65] [84]

Mar 95. (cd)(c) **ONLY EVERYTHING** [59] [ ]
– What a life / Fleur de lys / Universal heart-beat / Dumb fun / Live on tomorrow / Dying proof / Bottles and flowers / Outsider / Ok Ok / Congratulations / Hang down from Heaven / My darling / Simplicity is beautiful / You blues.

— In August '95, JULIANA suffered a nervous breakdown.

Richie HAVENS

Born: 21 Jan'41, Brooklyn, New York, USA and raised as the oldest of nine children in the New York ghetto area of Bedford-Stuyvesant. After inclinations of following in his pianist father's footsteps had left him due to lack of money, he began to busk the street-corners as a young teenager. He also formed The McCREA GOSPEL SINGERS, before he opted for a short move along to Greenwich Village, where he painted portraits of tourists to earn a living. It was now the early 60's and the folk revival was taking a hold of the area to the extent everybody (now even RICHIE) was picking up their guitar again. His unorthodox technique (tuning with an E-chord) helped him quickly adapt and characterise his own style, which he still maintains today. In 1965 having gained notoriety around the underground 'Village' scene, he was picked up by 'Douglas' records, who quickly shifted out copies of his debut lp 'THE RICHIE HAVENS ALBUM'. It was followed by another, before 'Verve' took over and set free his 'MIXED BAG' album, which contained a remarkable cover of 'ELEANOR RIGBY'. In 1968, he played a benefit gig for dust-bowl folk hero idol WOODY GUTHRIE, who had died the year previous. In August of 1969 he opened for the Woodstock Festival, which overnight made him into a star. One song from it 'FREEDOM', became his anthem and the American people's anthem delivered from the ashes of hippy psychedelia, to a hopeful early 70's generation that never quite disappeared. This showed itself to be the case in the Spring of 1971, when he resurrected into the US Top 20, a GEORGE HARRISON written BEATLES song 'HERE COMES THE SUN'. • **Style:** Black folk /soul singer & guitarist (see above). • **Songwriters:** Self-penned except; CHAIN GANG (Sam Cooke) / OXFORD TOWN + BOOTS OF SPANISH LEATHER + JUST LIKE A WOMAN + SAD EYED LADY + IF NOT FOR YOU + LAY LADY LAY + ALL ALONG THE WATCH-TOWER + THE TIMES THEY ARE-A CHANGIN' + IT'S ALL OVER NOW, BABY BLUE + LICENSE TO KILL (Bob Dylan) / C.C. RIDER (hit; Chuck Willis) / ELEANOR RIGBY + STRAWBERRY FIELDS FOREVER + LADY MADONNA + SHE'S LEAVING HOME + WITH A LITTLE HELP FROM MY FRIENDS + ROCKY RACCOON + HERE COMES THE SUN + IN MY LIFE + THE LONG AND WINDING ROAD + LET IT BE (Beatles) /

WEAR YOUR LOVE LIKE HEAVEN (Donovan) / FIRE AND RAIN (James Taylor) / TOMMY (Who) / TEACH YOUR CHILDREN (Crosby, Stills, Nash & Young) / GOD BLESS THE CHILD (Billie Holiday) / TUPELO HONEY (Van Morrison) / WHERE HAVE ALL THE FLOWERS GONE (hit; Kingston Trio) / THE LONER (Neil Young) / BAND ON THE RUN (Paul McCartney) / IMAGINE + WORKING CLASS HERO (John Lennon) / MY SWEET LORD (George Harrison) / DO IT AGAIN (Steely Dan) / LONG TRAIN RUNNING (Doobie Brothers) / I'M NOT IN LOVE (10 cc) / OL' 55 (Tom Waits) / WE'VE GOT TONIGHT (Bob Seger) / LIVES IN THE BALANCE (Jackson Browne) / THEY DANCE ALONE (Sting) / THE HAWK (Kris Kristopherson) / HOW THE NIGHTS CAN FLY (Bob Lind) / MY FATHER'S SHOES (Eberhardt) / COMING BACK TO ME (Marty Balin) / etc. • **Miscellaneous:** In 1972, he also took part in the stage production of The Who's 'Tommy'. RICHIE was heard of again in 1994, when he sued 'Time-Warner' for using his opening Woodstock footage for a new version of the film soundtrack.

Recommended: RICHIE HAVENS ON STAGE (*8) /

RICHIE HAVENS – vocals, guitar

Transatla. / Douglas

1965. (lp) **A RICHIE HAVENS RECORD** [-] [ ]
– I'm gonna make you glad / It hurts me / Chain gang / Drown in my own tears / I'm on my way / Baby, I'm leavin' / Nora's dove / Daddy roll 'em / The bag I'm in. *(UK-iss.1967)*

1966. (lp) **ELECTRIC HAVENS** [ ] [ ]
– Oxford Town / 900 miles from home / I'm a stranger here / My own way / Boots of Spanish leather / C.C. rider / 3:10 to Yuma / Shadow town. *(re-dist.US Nov68)*

— added **PAUL HARRIS** – piano, organ / **PAUL WILLIAMS + HOWARD COLLINS** – guitar / **HARVEY BROOKS** – bass / **BILL LA VORGNA** – drums / **JOE PRICE** – tabla

Verve / Verve Folkways

Feb 67. (lp) **MIXED BAG** [ ] [ ]
– High flyin' bird / I can't make it anymore / Morning morning / Adam / Follow / Three day eternity / Sandy / Handsome Johnny / San Francisco Bay blues / Just like a woman / Eleanor Rigby. *(re-dist.US Jul68)(US re-iss.Nov70 on 'MGM') (cd-iss.May88 + Jul94 on 'Polydor')*

Mar 67. (7") **I CAN'T MAKE IT ANYMORE. / MORNING MORNING** [-] [ ]

Jun 67. (7") **I'VE GOTTA GO. / MORNING MORNING** [-] [ ]

— **DANIEL BEN ZEBULON + DON McDONALD + SKIP PROKOP** – drums / **WARREN BERNHARDT** – keyboards / **JEREMY STEIG** – flute / **ADRIAN GULLEY** – guitar / **EDDIE GOMEZ + DON PAYNE** – bass / **JOHN BLAIR** – violin repl. everyone except WILLIAMS

Feb 68. (lp) **SOMETHING ELSE AGAIN** [ ] [ ]
– No opportunity necessary, no experience needed / Inside of him / The klan / Don't listen to me / Sugarplums / From the prison / New city / Run, shaker life / Maggie's farm / Something else again.

Jan 69. (7") **NO OPPORTUNITY NECESSARY, NO EXPERIENCE NEEDED. / THREE DAY ETERNITY** [ ] [ ]

— **ERIC OXENDINE** – bass repl. GOMEZ + PAYNE / (added others on session)

May 69. (d-lp) **RICHIE P.HAVENS, 1983** (some live) [ ] [80] Jan 69
– Stop pulling and pushing me / For Haven's sake / Strawberry fields forever / What more can I say John? / I pity the poor immigrant / Lady Madonna / Priests / Indian rope man / Cautiously / Just above my hobby horse's head / She's leaving home / Putting out the vibration, and hoping it comes home / The parable of Ramon / With a little help from my friends / Wear your love like Heaven / Run shaker life / Do you feel good?.

May 69. (7") **INDIAN ROPE MAN. / JUST ABOVE MY HOBBY HORSES HEAD** [-] [ ]

May 69. (7") **LADY MADONNA. / INDIAN ROPE MAN** [ ] [-]

Verve F... / Stormy Forest

Jul 69. (7") **ROCKY RACCOON. / STOP PULLING AND PUSHING ME** [ ] [ ]

Sep 69. (7") **THERE'S A HOLE IN THE FUTURE. / MINSTREL FROM GAULT** [ ] [ ]

Oct 69. (7") **HANDSOME JOHNNY. / SANDIE** [ ] [ ]

Polydor / Stormy Forest

Jan 70. (lp) **STONEHENGE** [ ] [ ]
– Open our eyes / Minstrel from Gault / It could be the first day / Ring around the Moon / Baby blue / There's a hole in the future / I started a joke / Prayer / Tiny little blues / Shouldn't all the world be dancing.

1970. (7") **GIVE ALL MY LOVE AWAY. / NOBODY KNOWS** [-] [ ]

Jan 71. (lp)(c) **ALARM CLOCK** [ ] [29]
– Here comes the Sun / To give all your love away / Younger men grow older / Girls don't run away / End of the seasons / Some will wait / Patient lady / Missing train / Alarm clock.

Apr 71. (7") **HERE COMES THE SUN. / YOUNGER MEN GET OLDER** [-] [16]

Apr 71. (7") **HERE COMES THE SUN. / SOME WILL WAIT** [ ] [-]

Jul 71. (7") **MISSING TRAIN. / I'VE GOT TO GET TO KNOW MYSELF** [-] [ ]

Jan 72. (lp)(c) **THE GREAT BLIND DEGREE** [ ] [ ] Nov71
– What about me / Fire and rain / Tommy / In these flames / Think about the children / Fathers & sons / Teach your children / What have we done.

1972. (7") **THINK ABOUT THE CHILDREN. / FIRE AND RAIN** [-] [ ]

1972. (7") **WHAT ABOUT ME. / FIRE AND RAIN** [ ] [-]

HAVENS still with **WILLIAMS + ZEBULON** live BBC, London, 19 Oct'71.

Sep 72. (d-lp) **RICHIE HAVENS ON STAGE (live)** [ ] [55]
– From the prison / Younger men grow older / God bless the child / High flying bird / Tupelo honey / Just like a woman / Handsome Johnny / Where have all the flowers gone / Rocky raccoon / Teach the children / Minstrel from Gault / Freedom.

Oct 72. (7") **I'VE GOT TO GET TO KNOW MYSELF (live). / WHERE YOU GONNA RUN TO (live)** [-] [ ]

1973. (7") **FREEDOM. / HANDSOME JOHNNY** [ ] [ ]

— added **OXENDINE / JERRY FRIEDMAN** – guitar / **ERIC WEISBERG** – steel guitar / etc.

Jul 73. (lp)(c) **PORTFOLIO** [ ] [ ] Jun73
– It was a very good year / Dreaming my life away / 23 days in September / I know I won't be there / I don't need nobody / Woman / What's goin' on / Tightrope / Mama loves you.

1973. (7") **IT WAS A VERY GOOD YEAR. / I KNOW I WON'T BE THERE** [-] [ ]

1973. (7") **TIGHTROPE. / WOMAN** [-] [ ]

1973. (7") **TIGHTROPE. / IT WAS A VERY GOOD YEAR** [ ] [-]

Jan 75. (lp)(c) **MIXED BAG II** [ ] [ ] Oct 74
– Ooh child / Headkeeper / Wandering Angus / Sad eyed lady (of the lowlands) / Someone suite / Band on the run / The loner / The makings of you / The Indian prayer.

— now with numerous session including **HERMAN ERNST** – drums / **DARRYL JOHNSON** – guitar / + (on first) **BOOKER T. & THE MG's**

A & M / A & M

Sep 76. (7") **WE CAN'T HIDE IT ANYMORE. / DREAMING AS ONE** [-] [ ]

Nov 76. (lp)(c) **THE END OF THE BEGINNING** [ ] [ ] Sep76
– I'm not in love / We can't hide it anymore / Dreaming as one / You can close your eyes / I was educated by myself / Daughter of the night / If not for you / Do it again / Wild night / Long train running.

Nov 76. (7") **I'M NOT IN LOVE. / DREAMING AS ONE** [ ] [ ]

Mar 77. (7") **YOU CAN CLOSE YOUR EYES. / WE CAN'T HIDE IT ANYMORE** [-] [ ]

Oct 77. (lp)(c) **MIRAGE** [ ] [ ] Apr77
– Live it up (one time) / Shadows of the past / I don't complain / Touch the sky / Billy John / We all wanna boogie / Avalon / Aviation man / Nobody left to crown / The end.

Jan 78. (7") **WE ALL WANNA BOOGIE. / NOBODY LEFT TO CROWN** [-] [ ]

— Around mid-78, RICHIE guested on STEVE HACKETT's single 'How Can I.' Later that year, he wrote and apeared in film 'Greased Lightning'. He now employed totally new session men incl. on next **JEFF BAXTER + RICHARD TEE**

Elektra / Elektra

Mar 80. (lp)(c) **CONNECTIONS** [ ] [ ] Nov79
– Mama we're gonna dance / Every night / You send me / We've got tonight / Ol' 55 / Going back to my roots / Dreams / She touched my heart / Fire down below / Here's a song.

Mar 80. (7") **THE GIRL, THE GOLD WATCH AND EVERYTHING. / TWO HEARTS IN PERFECT TIME** [-] [ ]

Connexion / not issued

Jun 83. (lp) **COMMON GROUND** [ ] [-]
– Death at an early age / Gay cavalier / Lay ye down boys / This is the hour / Stand up / Dear John / Leave well enough alone / Moonlight rain / Things must change.

Jun 83. (7") **DEATH AT AN EARLY AGE. / MOONLIGHT RAIN** [ ] [ ]

Start / Intercord

Sep 87. (lp)(c)(cd) **SIMPLE THINGS** [-] [ ]
– Drivin' / Simple things / Songwriter / Passin' by / Wake up and dream / I don't wanna know / Shouldn't we all be having a good time / Arrow through me / Runner in the night.

— In Jul 93, HAVENS and FRANSCESCO BRUNO (jazz artist) released single 'THE WORLD IS SO SMALL' from the 'Prestige' album 'EL LUGAR (THE PLACE)'.

Essential / Garden

Jun 94. (cd)(c) **CUTS TO THE CHASE** [ ] [ ]
– Lives in the balance / They dance alone / My father's shoes / Darkness, darkness / The hawk / Young boy / The times they are a-changin' / Fade to blue medley: Intro – Old love / How the nights can fly / Comin' back to me / Don't pass it up / At a glance.

– compilations, etc. –

Apr 69. Big T; (7") **OXFORD TOWN. / MY OWN WAY** [ ] [-]

Jul 71. Polydor; (lp) **A STATE OF MIND** [ ] [-]

Mar 76. Polydor; (lp) **RICHIE HAVENS** [ ] [-]

1986. Rykodisc; (cd)(c)(lp) **SINGS DYLAN & THE BEATLES** [-] [ ]

HAWKWIND

Formed: London, England . . . mid-69 as GROUP X, by ex-FAMOUS CURE members DAVE BROCK and MICK SLATTERY, who were joined by NIK TURNER, TERRY OLLIS, DIK MIK and JOHN HARRISON. They soon became HAWKWIND ZOO, but SLATTERY opted out, for gypsy lifestyle in Ireland, after they signed to 'United Art' late '69. Now as HAWKWIND and after many free concerts (mostly at open-air festivals) they released eponymous debut late summer 1970. With a few personnel changes (which always seemed to be always part of story), they unleashed second album 'IN SEARCH OF SPACE', which gave them initial entry into UK Top 20. The following summer (1972), they smashed the Top 3 with classic 45 'SILVER MACHINE'. It had previously featured on a live 'GREASY TRUCKERS' PARTY' lp, which had them on 1 side only, and a various artists 'GLASTONBURY FAYRE' album. The success of the single, secured them Top 20 placings, on all 4 of their future lp's for 'UA'. In 1976, they signed to 'Charisma', and still found many friends in the buying public. They were still going strong in 1992, but with only DAVE BROCK, the sole originator surviving in a trio with ALAN DAVEY and RICHARD CHADWICK. • **Style:** Drug-loving commune hippies, who mixed heavy psychedelia with electronic space rock music. • **Songwriters:** Mostly by BROCK or CALVERT until latter's departure. ALAN DAVEY finally replaced his writing assets. Other various personnel over the years, also took part in writing. Psi-fi writer MICHAEL MOORCOCK provided them with some words and vox, during mid-70's. • **Trivia:** They formed own 'Flicknife' records to accomodate legion of 'Hawkfans' (their ever-wanting loyal fan club).

Recommended: IN SEARCH OF SPACE (*8) / SPACE RITUAL (*8) / WARRIOR ON THE EDGE OF TIME (*6) / STASIS – THE U.A. YEARS 1971-1975 (*7)

DAVE BROCK – vocals, guitar / **NIK TURNER** – vocals, saxophone / **HUW-LLOYD LANGTON** – guitar repl. MICK SLATTERY (Oct69, when as HAWKWIND ZOO) **JOHN HARRISON** – bass / **TERRY OLLIS** – drums / **DIK MIK** (b. S.McMANUS) – electronics engineer, synthesizers

Liberty United A..

Jul 70. (7") **HURRY ON SUNDOWN. / MIRROR OF ILLUSION**

Aug 70. (lp)(c) **HAWKWIND**
– Hurry on sundown / The reason is / Be yourself / Paranoia (part 1 & 2) / Seeing it as you really are / Mirror of illusion. *(re-iss.Sep75 on 'Sunset') (re-iss.Feb84 on 'E.M.I.' hit 75) (re-iss.Feb80 as 'ROCKFILE') (cd-iss.Feb94 on 'Repertoire')*

— (Sep70) **THOMAS CRIMBLE** – bass repl. JOHN HARRISON / **DEL DETTMAR** – synthesizer repl. LANGTON (partway through next album)

— (May71) **DAVE ANDERSON** – bass (ex-AMON DUUL II) repl. CRIMBLE On stage they also added on vocals **BOB CALVERT** (b.South Africa) – poet, vocals, **MICHAEL MOORCOCK** – sci-fi writer and **STACIA** – exotic dancer

United Art United Art

Oct 71. (lp)(c) **IN SEARCH OF SPACE** 18
– You shouldn't do that / You know you're only dreaming / Master of the universe / We took the wrong step years ago / Adjust me / Children of the sun. *(re-iss.Jan81 on 'Liberty') (re-iss.Jun85 on 'Liberty-EMI') (cd-iss.May89 & Dec95 on 'Fame')*

— (Sep71) **LEMMY** – bass, vocals repl. ANDERSON

— (Jan72) **SIMON KING** – drums (ex-OPAL BUTTERFLY) repl. OLLIS (group now **KING, LEMMY, BROCK, TURNER, DIK MIK, DETTMAR, CALVERT, STACIA** and p/t **MOORCOCK**)

Jun 72. (7") **SILVER MACHINE. / SEVEN BY SEVEN** 3
(re-iss.'76) (Oct78 reached No.34) (re-iss.+12"+7"pic-d.Dec82 hit 67)

Nov 72. (lp)(c) **DOREMI FASOL LATIDO** 14
– Brainstorm / Space is deep / Down through the night / One change / Lord of light / Time we left this world today / The watcher. *(re-iss.1979)(re-iss.Jun85 on 'Liberty-EMI') (US cd-iss.Jul91 on 'One Way')*

May 73. (d-lp)(d-c) **SPACE RITUAL – RECORDED LIVE IN LIVERPOOL AND LONDON (live)** 9
– Earth calling / Born to go / Down through the night / The awakening / Lord of light / The black corridor / Space is deep / Electronic No.1 / Orgone accumulator / Upside down / 10 seconds of forever / Brainstorm / 7 by 7 / Sonic attack / Time we left this world today / Master of the universe / Welcome to the future. *(re-iss.1979)*

Aug 73. (7") **URBAN GUERILLA. / BRAINBOX POLLUTION** 39

— Now a trim sex/septet when DIK MIK and CALVERT departed. The latter going solo. (Apr74) **SIMON HOUSE** – keyboards, synthesizers, violin (ex-THIRD EAR BAND, ex-HIGH TIDE) repl. DETTMAR who emigrated to Canada

Aug 74. (7") **PSYCHEDELIC WARLORDS (DISAPPEAR IN SMOKE). / IT'S SO EASY**

Sep 74. (lp)(c) **HALL OF THE MOUNTAIN GRILL** 16
– Psychedelic warlords (disappear in smoke) / Wind of change / D-rider / Web weaver / You'd better believe it / Hall of the mountain grill / Lost Johnnie / Wind of change / Goat willow / Paradox. *(re-iss.Jan81 on 'Liberty') (re-iss.Jun85 on 'Liberty-EMI') (re-iss.Sep85 on 'Fame', cd-iss.May89 & Dec95)*

— added **ALAN POWELL** – 2nd drums (ex-STACKRIDGE, ex-CHICKEN SHACK, etc)

Charisma Atco

Mar 75. (7") **KINGS OF SPEED. / MOTORHEAD**

May 75. (lp)(c) **WARRIOR ON THE EDGE OF TIME** 13
– Assault and battery – part one / The golden void – part two / The wizard blew his horn / Opa-Loka / The demented man / Magnu / Standing at the edge / Spiral galaxy 28948 / Warriors / Dying seas / Kings of speed. *(re-iss.1979)(re-iss.Jan81 + Jun85 on 'Liberty-EMI')*

— **PAUL RUDOLPH** – bass (ex-PINK FAIRIES) repl. LEMMY who formed MOTORHEAD **BOB CALVERT** – vocals returned, STACIA the dancer left to get married. **CALVERT** and **RUDOLPH** now with **BROCK, TURNER, KING, HOUSE** and **POWELL**. note also that MOORCOCK left to form his DEEP FIX

Charisma Charisma

Jul 76. (7") **KERB CRAWLER. / HONKY DORKY** -

Aug 76. (lp)(c) **ASTOUNDING SOUNDS AND AMAZING MUSIC** 33 -
– Reefer madness / Steppenwolf / City of lagoons / The aubergine that ate Rangoon / Kerb crawler / Kadu flyer / Chronoglide skyway. *(re-iss.1983)(cd-iss.Apr89 on 'Virgin')*

Jan 77. (7") **BACK ON THE STREETS. / THE DREAM OF ISIS**

— **ADRIAN SHAW** – bass TURNER who formed SPHINX then INNER CITY BLUES

Jun 77. (lp)(c) **QUARK, STRANGENESS AND CHARM** 30 -
– Spirit of the age / Damnation alley / Fable of a failed race / Quark, strangeness and charm / Hassan I Sah Ba / The forge of Vulcan / Days of the underground / Iron dream. *(re-iss.Oct86) (cd-iss.Apr89)*

Jul 77. (7") **QUARK, STRANGENESS AND CHARM. / THE FORGE OF VULCAN** -

— **PAUL HAYLES** – keyboards repl. HOUSE who joined DAVID BOWIE on tour

HAWKLORDS

BROCK and **CALVERT** recruiting new members **STEVE SWINDELLS** – keyboards (ex-STRING DRIVEN THING, ex-PILOT) / **HARVEY BAINBRIDGE** – bass / **MARTIN GRIFFIN** – drums

Oct 78. (lp)(c) **25 YEARS ON** 48 -
– Psi-power / Free fall / Automotion / 25 years / Flying doctor / The only ones / The dead dreams of the cold war kid / The age of the micro man. *(re-iss.Aug82) (cd-iss.Apr89 on 'Virgin')*

Oct 78. (7") **PSI-POWER. / DEATH TRAP** -

Dec 78. (7") **PSI-POWER. / ('A'extended)** - -

HAWKWIND

recorded '78 by **BROCK, TURNER, SHAW, KING** and **HAYLES**

Mar 79. (7") **25 YEARS ON. / PXR 5**
(12"grey+=) – Only the dead dreams of the cold war kid.

May 79. (lp)(c) **PXR 5** 59
– Death trap / Jack of shadows / Uncle Sam's on Mars / Infinity / Life form / Robot / High rise / PXR 5. *(re-iss.Mar84) (cd-iss.Apr89 on 'Virgin')*

— **HAWKWIND** in 1979 were **SIMON KING** – drums returned from QUASAR, to repl. GRIFFITHS in Dec78 (CALVERT left to go solo). **TIM BLAKE** – keyboards (ex-GONG)repl. SWINDELLS who went solo, added **HUW-LLOYD LANGTON** – guitar who returned from QUASAR, band now – **BROCK, LANGTON, BAINBRIDGE, KING** and **BLAKE**

Bronze not issued

Jul 80. (lp)(c) **LIVE 1979 (live)** 15
– Shot down in the night / Motorway city / Spirit of the age / Brainstorm / Lighthouse / Master of the universe / Silver machine.

Jul 80. (7") **SHOT DOWN IN THE NIGHT (live). / URBAN GUERILLA (live)** 59 -

— **GINGER BAKER** – drums (ex-CREAM, ex-BLIND FAITH, ex-AIRFORCE etc) repl. KING who teamed up with SWINDELLS

Nov 80. (7") **WHO'S GONNA WIN THE WAR. / NUCLEAR TOYS**

Nov 80. (blue-lp)(c) **LEVITATION** 21
– Levitation / Motorway city / Psychosis / World of tiers / Prelude / Who's gonna win the war / Space chase / The 5th second forever / Dust of time. *(re-iss.+cdJul87 on 'Castle')*

— **MARTIN GRIFFIN** – drums returned to repl. BAKER / **KEITH HALE** – keyboards repl. BLAKE

R.C.A. not issued

Oct 81. (7") **ANGELS OF DEATH. / TRANS-DIMENSIONAL** -

Oct 81. (lp)(c) **SONIC ATTACK** 19 -
– Sonic attack / Rocky paths / Psychosonia / Virgin of the world / Angels of death / Living on the edge / Coded language / Disintigration / Streets of fear / Lost chances.

May 82. (lp)(c) **CHURCH OF HAWKWIND** 26 -
– Angel voices / Nuclear drive / Star cannibal / The phenomena of luminosity / Fall of Earth city / The church / The joker at the gate / Some people never die / Light specific data / Experiment with destiny / The last Messiah / Looking in the future. *(cd-iss.Jun94 on 'Dojo')*

— **NIK TURNER** – vocals, saxophone returned to repl. HALE

Aug 82. (7") **SILVER MACHINE (remix). / PSYCHEDELIC WARLORDS (remix)** -

Oct 82. (lp)(c) **CHOOSE YOUR MASQUES** 29 -
– Choose your masques / Dream worker / Arrival in Utopia / Silver machine / Void city / Solitary mind games / Fahrenheit 451 / The scan / Waiting for tomorrow.

Flicknife not issued

Oct 83. (lp)(c) **ZONES** (live, with other 80's line-ups) 57 -
– Zones / Dangerous vision / Running through the back brain / The island / Motorway city / Utopia 84 / Society alliance / Sonic attack / Dream worker / Brainstorm. *(re-iss.Mar84 on pic-lp)*

Oct 83. (7") **MOTORWAY CITY (live). / MASTER OF THE UNIVERSE (live)** -

Jan 84. (7") **NIGHT OF THE HAWKS. / GREEN FINNED DEMON** -
(12"ep) **THE EARTH RITUAL PREVIEW** (+=) – Dream dancers / Dragons + fables.

Nov 84. (lp)(c) **THIS IS HAWKWIND, DO NOT PANIC** -
– Psi power / Levitation / Circles / Space chase / Death trap / Angels of death / Shot down in the night / Stonehenge decoded / Watching the grass grow.

— **ALAN DAVEY** – bass, vocals repl. BAINBRIDGE and TURNER / **CLIVE DEAMER** – drums repl. GRIFFIN

Nov 85. (lp)(c)(cd) **CHRONICLE OF THE BLACK SWORD** 65 -
– Song of the swords / Shade gate / Sea king / Pulsing cavern / Elric the enchanter / Needle gun / Zarozinia / Demise / Sleep of a thousand tears / Chaos army / Horn of destiny. *(cd-iss.w / 3 extra tracks)*

Nov 85. (7") **NEEDLE GUN. / ARIOCH** -
(12"+=) – Song of the swords.

Mar 86. (7") **ZAROZINIA. / ASSAULT AND BATTERY** -
(12"+=) – Sleep of a thousand tears.

— **HAWKWIND** are now **BROCK**, as DR. HASBEEN – vocals, guitar, keys, synthesizers, **LANGTON, DAVEY, BAINBRIDGE** now vocals, keyboards, synthesizer and **DANNY THOMPSON** – drums, percussion, vocals

G.W.R. Roadrunner

May 88. (lp)(c)(cd) **THE XENON CODEX** 79 1989
– The war I survived / Wastelands of sleep / Neon skyline / Lost chronicles / Tides / Heads / Mutation zone / E.M.C. / Sword of the east / Good evening. *(US-iss. on pic-d)*

— **BROCK, BAINBRIDGE, DAVEY** plus **SIMON HOUSE, RICHARD CHADWICK & BRIDGETT WISHART**

Oct 90. (cd)(c)(lp) **SPACE BANDITS** 70 -
– Images / Black elk speaks / Wings / Out of the shadows / Realms / Ship of dreams / TV suicide.

Essential not issued

May 92. (cd)(c)(d-lp) **ELECTRIC TEEPEE** 53 -
– L.S.D. / Blue shift / Death of war / The secret agent / Garden pests / Space dust / Snake dance / Mask of the morning / Rites of Netherworld / Don't understand / Sadness runs deep / Right to decide / Going to Hawaii / Electric teepee. *(re-iss Jul95 on 'Dojo')*

Oct 93. (cd)(c)(lp) **IT'S THE BUSINESS OF THE FUTURE TO BE DANGEROUS** 75
– It's the business of the future to be dangerous / Space is their (Palestine) / Tibet is not China (pt.1 & 2) / Let barking dogs lie / Wave upon wave / Letting in the past / The camera that could lie / 3 or 4 erections during the course of the night / Technotropic zone exists / Give me shelter / Avante.

Emergency not issued

Sep 94. (12"ep)(cd-ep) **QUARK, STRANGENESS & CHARM / UNCLE SAM'S ON MARS / BLACK SUN** -

Sep 94. (cd)(c)(d-lp) **THE BUSINESS TRIP** -

– Altair / Quark strangeness and charm / LSD / The camera that would lie / Green finned demon / Do that / The day a wall came down / Berlin axis / Void of golden light / Right stuff / Wastelands / The dream goes on / Right to decide / The dream has ended / The future / Terra mystica.

Sep 95. (12"ep)(cd-ep) **AREA S.4.** -
– Alien / Sputnik Stan / Medley: Death trap – Wastelands of sleep – Dream has . . . .

Oct 95. (cd)(lp) **ALIEN 4** -
– Abducted / Alien (I am) / Reject your human touch / Blue skin / Beam me up / Vega / Xenonorph / Journey / Sputnik Stan / Kapal / Festivals / Deah trap / Wastelands / Are you losing your mind.

– compilations, etc. –

1973. United Artists; (d7") **HURRY ON SUNDOWN. / MASTER OF THE UNIVERSE/ / SILVER MACHINE. / ORGONE ACCUMULATOR** -

Apr 76. United Artists; (lp)(c) **ROADHAWKS (live in the 70's)** 34
– Hurry on sundown / Paranoia / You shouldn't do that / Silver machine / Urban guerilla / Space is deep / Wind of change / The golden void. *(re-iss.Apr84 on 'Fame')*

Feb 77. United Artists; (lp)(c) **MASTERS OF THE UNIVERSE**
(re-iss.May82 on 'Fame', re-iss.+cd Jun87 & Dec95) (re-iss.+cd.1991 on 'Marble Arch') (re-iss.cd+c Jul94 on 'Success')

Sep 80. Charisma; (lp)(c) **REPEAT PERFORMANCE** -

Mar 83. Charisma; (d-c) **QUARK, STRANGENESS & CHARM / PXR 5** -
(re-iss.'88)

May 81. Flicknife; (12"ep) **HURRY ON SUNDOWN. / KINGS OF SPEED / SWEET MISTRESS OF PAIN** -
(re-iss.Dec83)

Jul 81. Flicknife; (7")(12") **MOTORHEAD. / VALIUM TEN** -
(re-iss.12" Oct82)

Nov 81. Flicknife; (12") **OVER THE TOP. / FREEFALL / DEATH TRAP (by "SONIC ASSASSINS")** -

Mar 82. Flicknife; (lp)(c) **FRIENDS & RELATIONS** (1/2 live '77-78, 1/2 studio '82) -
(re-iss.Nov83) (re-iss.cd+c Nov94 on 'Emporio')

Jun 82. Flicknife; (7") **WHO'S GONNA WIN THE WAR. / TIME OFF (as "HAWKLORDS")** -

Feb 83. Flicknife; (7") **HURRY ON SUNDOWN. / LORD OF THE HORNETS / DODGEM DUKE** -

1983. Flicknife; (lp) **TWICE UPON A TIME: HAWKWIND FRIENDS AND RELATIONS VOL.2** -

Jun 84. Flicknife; (10"m-lp) **INDEPENDENTS DAY** -
(re-iss.Nov88 on 'Thunderbolt')

Feb 85. Flicknife; (lp)(c) **HAWKWIND, FRIENDS AND RELATIONS VOL.3** -
(c-iss.with VOL.1 on reverse / other c-iss.with VOL.2 on reverse)

Jul 86. Flicknife; (7") **MOTORHEAD. / HURRY ON SUNDOWN** -

Nov 86. Flicknife; (lp)(c) **INDEPENDENTS DAY VOL.2** -

Apr 87. Flicknife; (lp)(c) **CUT AND INTAKES** -
(cd+=) – (2 extra tracks).

Oct 87. Flicknife; (3xbox-pic-lp's/+lp) **OFFICIAL PICTURE LOGBOOK** -
– ('STONEHENGE' / 'BLACK SWORD' / 'OUT & INTAKE' / '(interview)' lp *(cd-iss.Nov94 on 'Dojo')*)

Nov 88. Flicknife; (cd) **ZONES / STONEHENGE** -

Dec 88. Flicknife; (d-lp)(c)(cd) **THE TRAVELLERS AND TRUST** -

Jul 83. Illuminated; (d-lp) **TEXT OF FESTIVAL (live '70-72)** -
(1-lp re-iss.Feb85 as 'IN THE BEGINNING') (re-iss.Dec88 on 'Thunderbolt',cd-iss.first 3 sides)

Nov 84. A.P.K.; (d-lp)(d-c) **SPACE RITUAL 2 (live)** -
(cd-iss.1987)

Jul 85. Demi Monde; (lp) **HAWKWIND '73** -
(cd-iss.'87 on 'Castle')

Feb 85. Demi Monde; (lp) **BRING ME THE HEAD OF YURI GAGARIN** (live '73 Empire Pool) -
(cd-iss.Nov92)

Jul 85. Dojo; (lp) **70-73** -

May 85. Mausoleum; (lp) **UTOPIA 84** -

Nov 85. Mausleum; (lp) **WELCOME TO THE FUTURE** -

Nov 85. Obsession; (lp) **RIDICULE** -
(re-iss.of disc 2 of 'SPACE RITUAL') (re-iss.1990)

Samurai not issued

Nov 85. Samurai; (lp) **ANTHOLOGY – HAWKWIND VOL.1** -
(cd+=) – Silver machine. *(re-iss.pic-lp.Nov86 as 'APPROVED HISTORY OF . . . ')(re-iss.Apr90 as 'ACID DAZE 1' on 'Receiver')*

Mar 86. Samurai; (lp)(c)(cd) **ANTHOLOGY – HAWKWIND VOL. 2** -
(cd-iss.1986 extra 4 tracks) (re-iss.Apr90 as 'ACID DAZE 2' on 'Receiver')

May 86. Samurai; (7")(7"sha-pic-d) **SILVER MACHINE. / MAGNU** -
(12"+=) – Angels of death.

Jul 86. Samurai; (lp) **ANTHOLOGY – HAWKWIND VOL.3** -
(re-iss.Apr90 as 'ACID DAZE 3' on 'Receiver')

Jul 86. Hawkfan; (lp) **HAWKFAN 12** -

Sep 86. Castle; (d-lp)(d-c) **THE COLLECTION (PTS.1 & 2)** -
(cd-iss.Dec86 omits some tracks

Dec 88. Castle; (d-lp)(d-cd) **LEVITATION / HAWKWIND LIVE** -

Jun 87. R.C.A.; (lp)(c) **ANGELS OF DEATH** -

Sep 87. Start; (lp)(c)(cd) **BRITISH TRIBAL MUSIC** -

Dec 87. Thunderbolt; (lp)(c)(cd) **EARLY DAZE THE BEST OF . . .** -

Sep 88. Vigin; (cd) **SPIRIT OF THE AGE** -
(re-iss.+c.Oct91 on 'Elite')(re-iss cd, Sep 93)

May 89. Powerhouse; (lp)(c)(cd) **NIGHT OF THE HAWKS** -
(cd-iss. has 3 extra tracks)

Mar 89. Avanti; (cd) **IRONSTRIKE** -

May 89. Legacy; (lp) **LIVE CHRONICLES** -

1990. Action Replay; (cd)(c) **BEST AND THE REST OF HAWKWIND** -

Mar 90. Receiver; (2xcd-box)(3xlp-box) **ACID DAZE (re-issue)** -
(3 VOLUMES re-iss.cd Jul93)

Dec 90. Receiver; (12"blue-ep) **THE EARLY YEARS LIVE** -
– Silver machine / Spirit of the age / Urban guerilla / Born to go.

May 90. E.M.I.; (cd)(c)(lp) **STASIS, THE U.A. YEARS 1971-1975** -
– Urban guerilla / Psychedelic warlords (disappear in smoke) / Brainbox pollution / 7 by 7 / Paradox / Silver machine / You'd better believe it / Lord of light / The black corridor (live) / Space is deep (live) / You shouldn't do that (live). *(re-iss.cd Dec95 on 'Fame')*

1990. Capitol; (c) **METAL CLASSICS 2: BEST OF HAWKWIND** -

1990. Knight; (cd)(c) **NIGHT RIDING** -

Jun 91. G.W.R.; (cd)(c)(lp) **PALACE SPRINGS** -
– (remixed tracks from 'WARRIORS . . . ' & 'XENON . . .)

Oct 91. Windsong; (cd)(c) **BBC RADIO 1 LIVE IN CONCERT (live)** -

Feb 92. Raw Fruit; (cd) **FRIDAY ROCK SHOW SESSIONS (live '86)** -

May 92. Essential; (3xcd-box) **ANTHOLOGY (re-issue)** -

Jun 92. Anagram; (cd)(c)(lp) **MIGHTY HAWKWIND CLASSICS 1980-1985** -

Jun 93. Real; (12"ep)(c-ep)(cd-ep) **SPIRIT OF THE AGE (The Solstice remixes)** -

Nov 93. Real; (12"ep)(cd-ep) **DECIDE YOUR FUTURE. / ?** -

Mar 94. Charly; (cd) **IN THE BEGINNING** -

Mar 94. Emergency Broadcast; (lp) **UNDISCLOSED FILES** -

Apr 94. Cleopatra; (cd) **LORD OF LIGHT** -

Apr 94. Cleopatra; (cd) **PSYCHEDELIC WARLORDS** -

Dec 94. Cyclops; (cd) **CALIFORNIA BRAINSTORM** -

Feb 95. Emergency Broadcast; (cd) **UNDISCLOSED FILES – ADDENDUM** -

Mar 95. Anagram; (cd) **THE RARITIES . . .** -

May 95. Spectrum; (cd) **SILVER MACHINE** -

Oct 95. Anagram; (cd) **INDEPENDENTS DAY VOLUMES 1 & 2** -

DAVE BROCK

Hawkfan not issued

Jun 83. (7") **ZONES / PROCESSED (as "DR.TECHNICAL & THE MACHINES")** -

Flicknife not issued

Sep 83. (7")(7"pic-d) **SOCIAL ALLIANCE. / RAPING ROBOTS IN THE STREET** -

Apr 86. (lp) **EARTHED TO THE GROUND** -
– Earth to the ground / Assassination / Green finned demon / Spirits / Sweet obsession / Oscillations / Machine dreams / Now is the winter of our discontent / On the case.

Apr 88. (lp)(c) **AGENT OF CHAOS ("DAVE BROCK & HIS AGENTS OF CHAOS")** -
– High tech cities / A day in the office / Hades deep / Words of a song / Heads / Nocturn / Wastelands of sleep / Empty dreams / Into the realms / Mountain in the sky. *(cd-iss.May89, with 1984 album minus 2 tracks)*

Emergency not issued

Jul 95. (cd) **STRANGE TRIPS AND PIPE DREAMS** -
– Hearing aid test / White zone / UFO line / Space / Pipe dream / Self / Something's going on / Bosnia / Parasites are here on Earth / Gateway / It's never too late / La forge / Encounters.

HUW LLOYD-LANGTON GROUP

Flicknife not issued

Jul 83. (7") **WIND OF CHANGE. / OUTSIDE THE LAW** -

Dec 83. (lp) **OUTSIDE THE LAW** -
– Outside the law / Five to four / Talk to you / Rocky paths / Space chase / Waiting for tomorrow / Mark of gain / Psychedelic warlords. (incl. 2 'Hawkwind' tracks). (free 7" w/a) – WORKING TIME. / I SEE YOU

Ultra Noise not issued

Jul 84. (12") **DREAMS THAT FADE AWAY. / OUTSIDE THE LAW** -

Mar 85. (lp) **NIGHT AIR** -

Gas not issued

Apr 86. (lp) **LIKE AN ARROW . . . (THROUGH THE HEART)** -

G W.R. not issued

Aug 88. (lp)(c) **TIME SPACE AND LLG** -

He released other album in 1991 'ELEGY', after departure from HAWKWIND. In 1994 he issued 'RIVER RUN' for 'Allegro' records.

ROBERT CALVERT

United Art United Art

May 74. (lp) **CAPTAIN LOCKHEED AND THE STARFIGHTERS**
– Franz Joseph Strauss / The aerospace inferno / Aircraft salesman / The widow maker / Test pilots / The right stuff / Board meeting / The song of the gremlin / Ground crew / Hero with a wing / Ground control to pilot / Ejection / Interview / I resign / The song of the gremlin (part 2) / Bier garten / Catch a falling starfighter (the gremlin). *(re-iss.+cd Jan87 on 'B.G.O.')*

Jun 74. (7") **CATCH A FALLING STARFIGHTER (THE GREMLIN). / EJECTION**

—— (above as "CAPTAIN LOCKHEED & THE STARFIGHTERS")

Sep 75. (lp) **LUCKY LIEF AND THE LONGSHIPS**
– Ship of fools / The lay of the surfers / Brave new world / Voyaging to inland / The making of Midgare / Moonshine in the mountains / Magical potion / Stormchant of the Skraelings / Volstead o vodeo do / Phase locked lopp / Ragna rock. *(cd-iss.Jan89 on 'BGO')*

Flicknife not issued

1981. (7") **LORD OF THE HORNETS. / THE GREENFLY & THE ROSE** -

A-side not issued

Sep 81. (m-lp) **HYPE (THE SONGS OF TOM MAHLER)** -
– Over my head / Ambitious / It's the same / Hanging out on the seafront / Sensitive / Evil rock / We like to be frightened / Teen ballad of Deano / Flight 105 / The

luminous green glow of the dials of the dashboard (at night) / Greenfly and the rose / Lord of the hornets. *(cd-iss.Dec89 on 'See For Miles')*

Flicknife — not issued

Sep 84. (m-lp) **FREQ** [ ] [-]
– Ned Ludd / Acid rain / All the machines are quiet / Picket line / The cool courage of the bomb squad / Work song. *(cd-iss.Jun92 as 'FREQ REVISITED', with 2 extra) – Lord of the hornets / The greenfly and the rose.*

Apr 86. (lp) **TEST TUBE CONCEIVED** [ ] [-]
– Telekinesis / I hear voices / Fanfare for the perfect race / On line / Save them from the scientists / Fly on the wall / Thanks to the scientists / ? / In vitro / Breed / The rah rah band. *(cd-iss.Aug87 on 'Cd Label')*

On 14 Aug'88, ROBERT CALVERT died of a heart attack.

– (CALVERT) posthumous, etc. –

Clear — not issued

Aug 89. (lp) **ROBERT CALVERT AT THE QUEEN ELIZABETH HALL (live)** [ ] [-]
(re-iss.cd May93 on 'B.G.O.')

B.G.O — not issued

Oct 92. (cd) **BLUEPRINTS FROM THE CELLAR** [ ] [-]

MICHAEL MOORCOCK

(whilst a member of HAWKWIND)

United Art — United Art

May 75. (lp) **NEW WORLD'S FAIR** [ ] [ ]
(cd-iss.Jun95 on 'Dojo')

MICHAEL MOORCOCK & DEEP FIX

Flicknife — not issued

Dec 80. (7") **DODGEM DUDE. / STARCRUSHER** [ ] [-]
1982. (7"ltd.) **THE BROTHEL OF ROSENSTRASSE. / TIME CENTRE** [ ] [-]

He and label 'Cyborg' released in May92 a cass 'BROTHEL IN ROSENSTRASSE'.

NIK TURNER

("SPHYNX")with **TIM BLAKE & MIQUETTE GIRAUDY** – synthesizers / **MORRIS PERT & ALAN POWELL** – percussion / **MIKE HOWLETT** – bass / **STEVE HILLAGE** – guitar

Charisma — not issued

Jun 78. (lp) **XITINTODAY** [ ] [-]
– The awakening / Pyramid spell / Tha hall of double truth / Anabus Thoth / Horos, Isis & Nepthys.

— ("INNER CITY UNIT") with **MICK STUPP** – drums / **BAZ MAGENTO** – bass / **DEAD FRED** – keyboards, vocals **TREN THOMAS** – guitar, vocals

Riddle — not issued

Oct 79. (7") **SOLITARY ASHTRAY. / SO TRY AS ID** [ ] [-]
1980. (lp) **PASS OUT (THE 360° PSYCHO DELERIA SOUND)** [ ] [-]
(cd-iss.Feb90 on 'Oldhitz', w/2 extra)
Jul 80. (7") **PARADISE BEACH. / AMYL NITRATE** [ ] [-]

— **DON FERARI** – drums repl. STUPP / **RAY BURNS** (CAPTAIN SENSIBLE) – guitar repl. BAZ added **BILL BOSTON** – horns / **MAX WALL** – vocals

Avatar — not issued

May 81. (lp) **THE MAXIMUM EFFECT** [ ] [-]
Sep 81. (7"red) **BEER, BACCY, BINGO, BENIDORM. / IN THE MOOD (NUDE)** [ ] [-]
Feb 82. (7") **BONES OF ELVIS. / SID'S SONG** [ ] [-]

Flicknife — not issued

Jul 82. (lp)(c) **PUNKADELIA** [ ] [-]
– Watching the grass grow / Space invaders / God disco / Disco tango / Polythene / Cars eat with autoface / Gas money / Blue mine haggard robot / Alright on the flight / Bildeborg.

— (not sure about this line-up)

Demi Monde — not issued

Dec 84. (lp) **NEW ANATOMY** [ ] [-]
– Young girls / Convoy / Beyond the stars / Help shark / Hectic electric / Birdland / Lonesome train / Forbidden planet / Stop the city / Doctor Strange / Wild hunt. *(cd-iss.Mar93 on 'Thunderb.')*

Flicknife — not issued

Sep 85. (lp) **THE PRESIDENT'S TAPES** [ ] [-]

Jettisound — not issued

Oct 85. (m-lp) **BLOOD AND BONES** [ ] [-]
– Blood and bones / Little black egg / Paint your windows white / Help sharks.

— TURNER later issued 'PROPHETS OF TIME' in 1994 for 'Cleopatra'.

NIK TURNER / ROBERT CALVERT

Pompadour — not issued

1982. (lp) **ERSATZ** [ ] [-]

STEVE SWINDELLS

(80's with SIMON KING, HUW-LLOYD LANGTON, and NIC POTTER

R.C.A. — not issued

1974. (lp) **MESSAGES** [ ] [ ]
– Miles away again / Energy crisis / The Earl's Court case / Living in sin / I don't like eating meat / Shake up your soul / Surrender / I can't see where the light switch is / Messages from Heaven.

Atco — not issued

Oct 80. (7") **SHOT DOWN IN THE NIGHT. / IT'S ONLY ONE NIGHT IN YOUR LIFE** [ ] [-]
Oct 80. (lp) **FRESH BLOOD** [ ] [-]
– Turn it on, turn it off / Fresh blood / I feel alive / Is it over now / Low life Joe / Bitter and twisted / I don't wait on the stairs / Down on Love street / Figures of authority / Shot down in the night.
Dec 80. (7") **TURN IT ON, TURN IT OFF. / LOW LIFE JOE** [ ] [-]

TIM BLAKE

— also had solo releases, mainly in France 1977 + 1978. CRYSTAL MACHINE lp + BLAKE'S NEW JERUSALEM lp on 'Egg' records. The later was issued UK Nov78 on 'Barclay Towers'. The cds were given light there in 1992 on 'Mantra' label. He issued 'MAGICK' cd in US 1991 on 'Voiceprint'.

ALAN DAVEY

Hawkfan — not issued

Oct 87. (d7") **THE ELF EP** [ ] [-]
– Solar jug / Cosmic dawn / Chinese whispers / Ode to a brass assassin / The switch (don't touch).

Barry HAY (see under ⇒ GOLDEN EARRING)

Colin James HAY (see under ⇒ MEN AT WORK)

Pete HAYCOCK (see under ⇒ CLIMAX BLUES BAND)

Isaac HAYES

Born: 20 Aug'42, Covington, Tennessee, USA. As a teenager he moved to Memphis, where he learned to play sax and piano. He was soon invited to session for the 'Stax' label. The following year, he formed writing partnership with DAVID PORTER, who went on to pen for 'Stax' artists OTIS REDDING, SAM & DAVE, EDDIE FLOYD, etc. After a dismal debut lp in 1968, his next 'HOT BUTTERED SOUL' gave him a US Top10 placing, gaining wide respect from critics for his venture into extended classics (noteably the 18-min.+ 'BY THE TIME I GET TO PHOENIX'). Late '71, his 'THEME FROM SHAFT' gave him international smash hit, reaching peak spot in the US. It's full version which won an Oscar, was from the (black detective) No.1 film soundtrack. After a couple more excursions into film scores, he left 'Enterprise-Stax', due to squabbles over non-payments. In 1975 he signed to 'A.B.C.', but after mediocre album sales and declaring bankruptcy in '77, he shifted to 'Polydor'. In the 80's, he became more interested in film acting, with sparse trips back into the studio. • **Style:** Sophisticated and sensuous soul singer, who breathed and orchestrated new life into black music. His sexy? macho (bare-chested) aura, made him dub himself The BLACK MOSES. He diversified into a more disco-orientated sound when he formed The ISAAC HAYES MOVEMENT in the mid-70's. He introduced soul-rap into his early work, years ahead of its commerciality in the late 70's. • **Songwriters:** HAYES wrote own work alongside covers; WALK ON BY (hit. Dionne Warwick) / BY THE TIME I GET TO PHOENIX (hit. Glen Campbell) / I STAND ACCUSED (Jerry Butler) / THE LOOK OF LOVE (Lesley Gore ;hit?) / NEVER CAN SAY GOODBYE (Jackson 5) / YOU'VE LOST THAT LOVIN' FEELIN' (Righteous Brothers) / LET'S STAY TOGETHER (Al Green) / HEY GIRL (Freddie Scott) / FRAGILE (Sting) / LET'S GO OUT TONIGHT (Blue Nile) / etc. • **Trivia:** When HAYES was Stax writer with PORTER, he co-wrote SOUL MAN and others for SAM & DAVE.

Recommended: ISAAC'S MOODS – THE BEST OF ISAAC HAYES (*8) / HOT BUTTERED SOUL (*9) / THE BEST OF SHAFT (*7) / BRANDED (*7)

ISAAC HAYES – vocals, keyboards, etc. with Stax session men **DUCK DUNN and AL JACKSON**

Stax — Enterprise

1968. (lp) **PRESENTING ISAAC HAYES** [ ] [ ]
– Precious, precious / When I fall in love / I just want to make love to me / Rock me baby / Going to Chicago blues / Misty / You don't know like I know.
– (re-iss.as 'IN THE BEGINNING' Mar72 on 'Atlantic')
1968. (7") **GOING TO CHICAGO BLUES. / PRECIOUS PRECIOUS** [-] [ ]
Oct 69. (lp) **HOT BUTTERED SOUL** [ ] [8] Jul 69
– Walk on by / Hyperbollesyllaciscesquelalymistc / One woman / By the time I get to Phoenix. *(re-iss.Aug74 + Aug81 + Nov87) (cd-iss.Jun91 on 'Stax-Ace')*
Sep 69. (7") **BY THE TIME I GET TO PHOENIX. / WALK ON BY** [ ] [37] Aug 69 [30]
Nov 69. (7") **THE MISTLETOE AND ME. / WINTER SNOW** [-] [ ]
May 70. (lp) **THE ISAAC HAYES MOVEMENT** [ ] [8] Apr 70
– I stand accused / One big unhappy family / I just don't know what to do with myself / Something. *(re-iss.Aug74) (re-iss.+cd.Feb90)*
Aug 70. (7") **I STAND ACCUSED. / I JUST DON'T KNOW WHAT TO DO WITH MYSELF** [ ] [42] Jul 70
(re-iss.US 1975)(other 45's from early to mid'70's were also re-iss.)
Dec 70. (lp) **TO BE CONTINUED** [ ] [11] Nov 70
– (monologue) / Ike's rap 1 / Our day will come / The look of love / Ike's mood – You've lost that lovin' feelin' / Runnin' out of fools. *(re-iss.Aug74 + Oct81) (cd-iss.Feb91 on 'Stax-Ace')*
Feb 71. (7") **THE LOOK OF LOVE. / IKE'S MOOD** [ ] [79]
May 71. (7") **NEVER CAN SAY GOODBYE. / I CAN'T HELP IT IF I'M STILL IN LOVE** [ ] [22]
Sep 71. (7") **YOU'VE LOST THAT LOVIN' FEELIN'. / OUR DAY WILL COME** [ ] [-]
Nov 71. (7") **THEME FROM SHAFT. / CAFE REGIO'S** [4] [1] Oct 71
Dec 71. (d-lp)(c) **SHAFT (Soundtrack)** [17] [1] Aug 71

– Theme from Shaft * / Bumpy's lament / Walk from Regio's / Ellie's love theme / Shaft's cab ride / Cafe Regio's / Early Sunday morning / Be yourself / A friend's place / Soulsville * / No name bar / Bumpy's blues / Shaft strikes again / Do your thing * / (the end theme). *(tracks *= have vocals)*

(above has background vocals by **HOT BUTTERED + SOUL**)

Feb 72. (d-lp)(c) **BLACK MOSES** 38 10 Dec 71
– Never can say goodbye / (They long to be) Close to you / Nothing takes the place of you / Man's temptation / Part time love / Ike's rap – A brand new me / Going in circles / Gonna give you up / Ike's rap 2 – Help me love / Need to belong / Good love / Ike's rap 3 – Your love is so doggone good / For the good times / I'll never fall in love again. *(re-iss.Aug74) (re-iss.+cd.Sep90 on 'Stax-Ace')*

Mar 72. (7") **DO YOUR THING. / ELLIE'S LOVE THEME** 30 Feb 72
Apr 72. (7") **LET'S STAY TOGETHER. / AIN'T THAT LOVING YOU (FOR MORE REASONS THAN ONE)** -
Apr 72. (7") **LET'S STAY TOGETHER. / SOULSVILLE** - 48
May 72. (7") **AIN'T THAT LOVING YOU (FOR MORE REASONS THAN ONE). ("ISAAC HAYES & DAVID PORTER") / BABY I'M A WANT YOU** -
Nov 72. (7") **THEME FROM THE MEN. / TYPE THANG** 38 Oct 72
(above was from US TV cop series 'The Men')
Jun 73. (d-lp)(c) **LIVE AT SAHARA TAHOE (live)** 14 May 73
– Theme from Shaft / The come on / Light my fire / Ike's rap / Never can say goodbye / Windows of the world / The look of love / Ellie's love theme / Use me / Do your thing / Theme from The Men / It's too late / Rock me baby / Stormy Monday blues / Type thang / The first time ever I saw your face / Ike's rap VI / Ain't no sunshine / Feelin' alright. *(re-iss.Aug74 + Nov86, cd-iss.Oct92)*
Nov 73. (lp)(c) **JOY** 16 Oct 73
– Joy / I love you that's all / A man will be a man / The feeling keeps on coming / I'm gonna make it (without you). *(re-iss.Aug74, cd-iss.Jun92)*
Nov 73. (7") **I DON'T WANT TO BE RIGHT. / ROLLING DOWN A MOUNTAINSIDE**
Dec 73. (7") **JOY (pt.1). / JOY (pt.2)** 30
May 74. (7") **WONDERFUL. / SOMEONE MADE YOU FOR ME** - 71
Jun 74. (lp)(c) **TOUGH GUYS (Soundtrack)**
– (title theme) / Randolph & Dearborn / The red rooster / Joe Bell / Hung up on my baby / Kidnapped / Run Fay run / Buns o'plenty / (the end theme).
Aug 74. (7") **TRUCK TURNER. / HUNG UP ON MY BABY**
Aug 74. (d-lp)(c) **TRUCK TURNER (Soundtrack)** Jul74
– Truck Turner / House of beauty / Blue's crib / Driving in the Sun / You're in my arms again / Give it to me / Drinking / Insurance company / Breakthrough / Now we're one / The duke / Dorinda's party / Pursuit of the pimpmobile / We need each other girl / A house full of girls / Hospital shootout / (end theme).

A.B.C. H.B.S.

Jun 75. (lp)(c) **CHOCOLATE CHIP** 18
– That loving feeling / Body language / Chocolate chip / Chocolate chip (instrumental) / I want to make love to you so bad / Come live with me / I can't turn around.
Jul 75. (7") **CHOCOLATE CHIP. / ('A'version)** 92
Dec 75. (lp)(c) **DISCO CONNECTION (by "ISAAC HAYES MOVEMENT")** - 85
– The first day of forever / St. Thomas Square / Vykkii / Disco connection / Disco shuffle / Choppers / After five / Aruba.
Feb 76. (7") **DISCO CONNECTION. / ST.THOMAS SQUARE** 10
(12"of above re-iss.Aug77)
Feb 76. (lp)(c) **GROOVE A THON** 45
– Groove-a-thon / Your loving is much too strong / Rock me easy baby / We've got a whole lot of love / Wish you were here / Make a little love to me.
Jun 76. (7") **ROCK ME EASY BABY. / ('A'instrumental)**
Aug 76. (lp)(c) **JUICY FRUIT (DISCO FREAK)** Jul 76
– Juicy fruit (disco freak) / Let's don't ever blow our thing / The storm is over / Music to make love by / Thank you love / Lady of the night / Love me or lose me.
Aug 76. (7") **JUICY FRUIT (DISCO FREAK). / (pt.2)**
Feb 77. (d-lp)(c) **A MAN AND A WOMAN ("ISAAC HAYES & DIONNE WARWICK")** 49
– Unity / Just don't know what to do with myself / Walk on by / My love / The way I want to touch you – Have you never been mellow – Love will keep us together – I love music – This will be (an everlasting love) – That's the way I like it – Get down tonight / By the time I get to Phoenix / I say a little prayer / Then came you / Feelings / My eyes adored you / Body language / Can't hide love / Come love with me / Once you hit the road / Chocolate chip.

not issued Stax

1977. (7") **FEEL LIKE MAKIN' LOVE. / (part 2)** -

Polydor Polydor

Jan 78. (lp)(c) **NEW HORIZON** 78 Dec 77
– Stranger in Paradise / Moonlight lovin' / Don't take your love away / Out of the ghetto / It's heaven to me.
Jan 78. (7") **OUT OF THE GHETTO. / IT'S HEAVEN TO ME** -
May 78. (7") **MOONLIGHT LOVIN'. / IT'S HEAVEN TO ME** -
Dec 78. (lp)(c) **FOR THE SAKE OF LOVE** 75 Nov 78
– Just the way you are / Believe in me / If we ever needed peace / Shaft II / Zeke the freak / Don't let me be lonely tonight.
Jan 79. (7")(12") **ZEKE THE FREAK. / IF WE EVER NEEDED PEACE**
Mar 79. (7") **JUST THE WAY YOU ARE. / (part 2)** -
(Later '79, he was credited with MILLIE JACKSON on 'Royal Rappin's' album, which hit US No.80)

—— Also issued 2 US singles with her on 'Polydor'; DO YOU WANNA MAKE LOVE / I CHANGED MY MIND / + YOU NEVER CROSS MY MIND / FEELS LIKE THE FIRST TIME

Nov 79. (lp)(c) **DON'T LET GO** 39 Sep 79
– Don't let go / What does it take / Few more kisses to go / Fever / Someone who will take the place of you.
Dec 79. (7")(12") **DON'T LET GO. / YOU CAN'T HOLD YOUR WOMAN** 18 Oct 79
Feb 80. (7") **FEW MORE KISSES TO GO. / WHAT DOES IT TAKE** -
May 80. (lp)(c) **AND ONCE AGAIN** 59
– It's all in the game / Ike's rap VII – This time I'll be sweeter / I ain't ever / Wherever you are / Love has been good to us.
Jun 80. (7") **I AIN'T EVER. / LOVE HAS BEEN GOOD TO US**
Sep 80. (7") **IT'S ALL IN THE GAME. / WHEREVER YOU ARE** -
Sep 81. (7") **I'M GONNA MAKE ME LOVE YOU. / I'M SO PROUD** -
Sep 81. (lp)(c) **LIFETIME THING**
– I'm gonna make you love me / Three times a lady / Fugitive / Summer / I'm so proud / Lifetime thing.
Nov 81. (7") **LIFETIME THING. / FUGITIVE** -

—— Took time out to concentrate on spiraling acting career. He had previously acted in own soundtrack films, 'Truck Turner', etc. He also appeared in 'The Rockford Files' with DIONNE WARWICK in 1977. In 1981, he plays a baddie (what else!) in the film 'Escape From New York'. In 85-86, he cameod in TV for series 'The A-Team' + 'Hunter'.

(Returned in '86, plays everything)

C.B.S. Columbia

Dec 86. (7") **HEY GIRL. / IKE'S RAP VIII**
(12"+=) – Hey Fred (you need a sunbed).
Dec 86. (lp)(c) **U-TURN**
– If you want my lovin' (do me right) / Flash backs / You turn me on / Ike's rap VIII – Hey girl / Doesn't rain in London / Can't take my eyes off you / Thing for you / Thank God for love.
Mar 87. (7") **THING FOR YOU. / THANK GOD FOR LOVE** -
Jun 87. (7") **IF YOU WANT MY LOVIN' (DO ME RIGHT). / (part 2)** -
Jul 88. (lp)(c) **LOVE ATTACK** -
– Love attack / Let me be your everything / Showdown / Eye of the storm / Accused rap / I stand accused '88 / She's got a way / Foreplay rap / Love won't let me wait.
Jul 88. (7") **SHOWDOWN. / (part 2)** -
Dec 88. (7") **LET ME BE YOUR EVERYTHING. / CURIOUS** -

—— He once again appears in films (i.e. 'Counter Force' + 'The Sofia Conspiracy').

PointBlank Virgin

May 95. (cd)(c)(lp) **BRANDED**
– Ike's plea / Life's mood / Fragile / Life's mood II / Summer in the city / Let me love you / I'll do anything (to turn you on) / Thanks to the fool / Branded / Soulsville / Hyperbolicsyllabicesquedalymistic.
Jun 95. (c-s)(12") **FRAGILE. / FRAGILE / BIRTH OF SHAFT**
(cd-s+=) – Let's go out tonight.

– compilations, others, etc. –

Below 'Stax' releases were issued on 'Enterprise' US.

Sep 75. Stax; (lp)(c) **THE BEST OF ISAAC HAYES**
Oct 75. Stax; (7") **GOOD LOVE 6-9969. / I'M GONNA HAVE TO TELL HER**
Nov 75. Stax; (lp)(c) **USE ME**
1977. Stax; (lp)(c)**MEMPHIS MOVEMENT**
1978. Stax; (lp)(c) **HOT BED** (rarities)
(cd-iss.Aug94)
1977. Stax; (7") **THEME FROM SHAFT. / DO YOUR THING**
Nov 77. Stax; (7") **THEME FROM SHAFT. / I DON'T WANT TO BE RIGHT**
Apr 78. Stax; (lp)(c) **THE ISAAC HAYES CHRONICLES**
Jan 80. Stax; (lp)(c) **LIGHT MY FIRE**
Nov 80. Stax; (d-lp)(c) **HIS GREATEST HITS**
Oct 81. Stax; (lp)(c) **THE BEST OF SHAFT**
(re-iss.Jun86)
Mar 82. Stax; (7") **THEME FROM SHAFT. / IF LOVING YOU IS WRONG** -
Apr 88. Stax; (lp)(c)(cd) **ISAAC'S MOODS – THE BEST OF ISAAC HAYES**
– Ike's mood / Soulsville / Joy (part 1) / If loving you is wrong I don't want to be right / Never can say goodbye / The theme from Shaft / Ike's rap VI / A brand new me / Do your thing / Walk on by / I stand accused. (cd+=) – Ike's rap I / Hyperbolic-syllabic-sesquedaly-mystic / Ike's rap III / Ike's rap II.
Aug 93. Stax; (d-cd) **TOUGH GUYS / TRUCK TURNER**
Mar 76. Golden Hour; (lp)(c) **THE GOLDEN HOUR OF . . .** -
Sep 85. Old Gold; (7") **THEME FROM SHAFT. / NEVER CAN SAY GOODBYE** -
May 89. Southbound; (7") **THEME FROM SHAFT. / THEME FROM THE MEN**
(12"+=) – Theme from The Men / Type thang.
(cd-s++=) – Walk on by.
Mar 95. Connoisseur; (cd) **THE COLLECTION** -

Justin HAYWARD (see under ⇒ MOODY BLUES)

Jowe HEAD (see under ⇒ SWELL MAPS)

Jeff HEALEY

Born: 1966, Toronto, Canada. Blind since one due to cancer, he learned guitar at age 3 and began playing live gigs as a teenager. Late '87, he and his band of 2 years (JOE ROCKMAN and TOM STEPHEN), signed to 'Arista' and soon issued top selling album 'SEE THE LIGHT'. From it, he gained a Top 5 US single 'ANGEL EYES', which surprisingly failed in the UK. • **Style:** Blues guitarist, who because of disability, sat on chair while playing unusual technique, although ROCKMAN did guide him on to standing exhilarating finales. HEALEY conjured images of past greats B.B.KING, ROBIN TROWER or JIMI HENDRIX. • **Songwriters:** All penned by HEALEY group except; ROADHOUSE BLUES (Doors) / BLUE JEAN BOP (ZZ Top) / WHILE MY GUITAR GENTLY WEEPS (George Harrison; Beatles) / ANGEL EYES +

CONFIDENCE MAN + LET IT ALL GO (John Hiatt) / I THINK I LOVE YOU TOO MUCH (Mark Knopfler) / HOW CAN A MAN BE STRONG (Steve Cropper & Jimmy Scott) / HOW MUCH (Greg Sutton & Danny Tate) / WHEN THE NIGHT (Bob Dylan) / LEAVE THE LIGHT ON (Lynch-Sharp) / LOST IN YOUR EYES (Tom Petty) / IT COULD ALL GET BLOWN AWAY (Gerry Goffin) / HEART OF AN ANGEL (. . . Holmes) / BABY'S LOOKING HOT (. . . Toll) / HOUSE THAT LOVE BUILT (Marscio-Marscio) / DOWN IN THE ALLEY (Elvis Presley) / SHAPES OF THINGS (Yardbirds) / FREEDOM + ANGEL (Jimi Hendrix) / YER BLUES (Beatles) / STOP BREAKIN' DOWN (Robert Johnson) / EVIL + I'M READY (Willie Dixon) / STUCK IN THE MIDDLE WITH YOU (Stealer's Wheel) / I GOT A LINE ON YOU (Spirit) / RUN THROUGH THE JUNGLE (John Fogerty) / AS THE YEARS GO PASSING BY (. . .Malone) / BADGE (Cream) / COMMUNICATION BREAKDOWN (Led Zeppelin) / ME & MY CRAZY SELF (Glover-Nathan). • **Trivia:** They did cameo in the 1988 film 'Roadhouse'.

Recommended: SEE THE LIGHT (*6).

JEFF HEALEY BAND

JEFF HEALEY – vocals, lead guitar / **JOE ROCKMAN** – bass / **TOM STEPHEN** – drums

Arista / Arista

Nov 88. (lp)(c)(cd) **SEE THE LIGHT** [58] [22] Oct 88
– Confidence man / My little girl / River of no return / Don't let your chance go by / Angel eyes / Nice problem to have / Someday, someday / I need to be loved / Blue jean blues / That's what they say / Hideaway / See the light. *(re-iss.cd Oct95)*

Nov 88. (7") **CONFIDENCE MAN. / THAT'S WHAT THEY SAY** [ ] [ ]
(12"+=)(cd-s+=) – See the light.

Mar 89. (7") **ANGEL EYES. / DON'T LET YOUR CHANCE GO BY** [ ] [5]
(12"+=)(10"+=)(cd-s+=) – See the light (live) / That's what they say.

Jul 89. (7") **MOOCHIE COOCHIE MAN. / RAISIN' HEAVEN & HELL TONIGHT (by Patrick Swayze)** [-] [ ]

Nov 89. (7") **WHEN THE NIGHT COMES FALLING FROM THE SKY. / ANGEL EYES** [ ] [ ]
(12"+=)(cd-s+=) – Roadhouse blues.

— Next w/ guests **GEORGE HARRISON, JOHN HIATT, MARK KNOPFLER**, etc.

Jun 90. (cd)(c)(lp) **HELL TO PAY** [18] [27]
– Full circle / I think I love you too much / I can't get my hands on you / How long can a man be strong / Let it all go / Hell to pay / While my guitar gently weeps / Something to hold on to / How much / Highway of dreams / Life beyond the sky.

Jul 90. (7") **FULL CIRCLE. / HOW LONG CAN A MAN BE STRONG** [-] [ ]

Nov 92. (cd)(c)(lp) **FEEL THIS** [72] [ ]
– Cruel little number / Leave the light on / Baby's looking hot / Lost in your eyes / House that love built / Evil and here to stay / My kinda lover / It could all get blown away / You're coming home / If you can't feel anything else / Heart of an angel / Live and love / Joined at the heart / Dreams of love. *(re-iss.cd Oct95)*

Nov 92. (c-s) **CRUEL LITTLE NUMBER /** [-] [ ]

Mar 95. (cd)(c) **COVER TO COVER** [50] [ ]
– Shapes of things / Freedom / Yer blues / Stop breakin' down / Angel / Evil / Stuck in the middle with you / I got a line on you / Run through the jungle / As the years go passing by / I'm ready / Badge / Communication breakdown / Me & my crazy self.

Apr 95. (c-s) **STUCK IN THE MIDDLE WITH YOU / BADGE** [ ] [ ]
(cd-s+=) – For what it's worth.

HEART

Formed: Vancouver, Canada . . . 1975 by sisters ANN and NANCY WILSON, who had evolved from Seattle groups The ARMY and WHITE HEART. In these line-ups were brothers ROGER and MIKE FISHER, the respective boyfriends of ANN and NANCY. The latter had arrived from solo-folk scene to replace MIKE, who became sound engineer, with group moving to Vancouver to avoid his draft papers. They were signed to local 'Mushroom' label by owner Shelley Siegal, and issued well-received debut lp 'DREAMBOAT ANNIE'. It gained a US release in Jun'76, and soon shot into Top 10, assisted by a couple of Top 50 hits, including Top 10'er 'CRAZY ON YOU'. They returned to Seattle late '76, and signed a new deal with 'CBS-Portrait', but Mushroom sued them for breach of contract. The new label issued 2nd album 'LITTLE QUEEN' in mid-77, and this also made Top 10. In 1978, a Seattle judge gave right to Mushroom to issue their out-takes album 'MAGAZINE', but allowed group to re-record it. Despite all this aggro, the album surprised most, even the band, by hitting Top 20. Later in 1978, their 4th album 'DOG AND BUTTERFLY' was another Top 20 success, although groups' love matches were now all but over. They continued the 80's as top act, peaking with 1985 US No.1 'THESE DREAMS'. • **Style:** Hard / soft-rock act, similiar to JEFFERSON STARSHIP or (mid-70's) FLEETWOOD MAC, but with visual aspect from glamourous WILSON's. • **Songwriters:** ANN WILSON or group wrote most except; TELL IT LIKE IT IS (Aaron Neville) / I'M DOWN (Beatles) / LONG TALL SALLY (Little Richard) / UNCHAINED MELODY (hit; Righteous Brothers) / I'VE GOT THE MUSIC IN ME (Kiki Dee) / THESE DREAMS (Martin Page & Bernie Taupin) / ALONE (Billy Steinberg & Tom Kelly) / ALL I WANNA DO IS MAKE LOVE TO YOU (Mutt Lange) / etc. • **Trivia:** In 1967, ANN WILSON AND THE DAYBREAKS issued a couple of singles on 'Topaz'; STANDIN' WATCHIN' YOU. / WONDER HOW I MANAGED and THROUGH EYES AND GLASS. / I'M GONNA DRINK MY HURT AWAY.

Recommended: DREAMBOAT ANNIE (*7) / LITTLE QUEEN (*6) / HEART (*6) / BAD ANIMALS (*5).

ANN WILSON (b.19 Jun'51, San Diego, California, USA) – vocals, flute / **NANCY WILSON** (b.16 Mar'54, San Francisco, California) – guitar, vocals / **ROGER FISHER** – guitar / **STEVE FOSSEN** – bass with session keyboard player and drummer

Arista / Mushroom

Sep 76. (7") **CRAZY ON YOU. / DREAMBOAT ANNIE** [-] [35]

Oct 76. (7") **MAGIC MAN. / HOW DEEP IT GOES** [ ] [9] Jul 76

Oct 76. (lp)(c)(US-pic-lp) **DREAMBOAT ANNIE** [36] [7] Apr 76
– Magic man / Dreamboat Annie (fantasy child) / Crazy on you / Soul of the sea / Dreamboat Annie / White lightning and wine (love me like music) / I'll be your song / Sing child / How deep it goes / Dreamboat Annie (reprise). *(re-iss.+cd Oct87 on 'Capitol')*

Feb 77. (7") **CRAZY ON YOU. / SOUL OF THE SEA** [ ] [-]
(re-iss.US Jan 78, hit US No.62)

Apr 77. (7") **DREAMBOAT ANNIE. / SING CHILD** [ ] [42] Dec 76

— added **HOWARD LEESE** – keyboards, guitar (he appeared as guest on debut album) / **MICHAEL DEROSIER** – drums

Portrait / Portrait

Jul 77. (lp)(c) **LITTLE QUEEN** [34] [9] May 77
– Barracuda / Love alive / Sylvan song / Dream of the archer / Kick it out / Little queen / Treat me well / Say hello / Cry to me / Go on cry. *(re-iss.Aug86, re-iss.+cd.May87) (cd-iss.Sep93 on 'Sony Collectors')*

Aug 77. (7") **BARRACUDA. / CRY TO ME** [ ] [11] May 77

Oct 77. (7") **KICK IT OUT. / LOVE ALIVE** [ ] [-]

Nov 77. (7") **LITTLE QUEEN. / TREAT ME WELL** [ ] [62]

Jan 78. (7") **KICK IT OUT. / GO ON CRY** [-] [79]

(The following few releases on 'Arista' UK & 'Mushroom' US were contractual)

Arista / Mushroom

Sep 77. (7") **HEARTLESS. / JUST THE WINE** [-] [24]

Apr 78. (lp)(c)(US-pic-lp) **MAGAZINE** [ ] [17]
– Heartless / Devil delight / Just the wine / Without you / Magazine / Here song / Mother Earth blues / I've got the music in me (live). *(re-iss.+cd Oct87 on 'Capitol')*

May 78. (7") **HEARTLESS (version II). / HERE SONG** [-] [-]

May 78. (7") **WITHOUT YOU. / HERE SONG** [-] [ ]

Jul 78. (7") **MAGAZINE. / DEVIL DELIGHT** [-] [ ]

Aug 78. (7") **MAGAZINE. / JUST THE WINE** [ ] [-]

Portrait / Portrait

Oct 78. (7") **STRAIGHT ON. / LIGHTER TOUCH** [ ] [15] Sep 78

Jan 79. (lp)(c) **DOG & BUTTERFLY** [ ] [17] Oct 78
– Cook with fire / High time / Hijinx / Straight on / Lighter touch / Dog & butterfly / Nada one / Mistral wind. *(re-iss.Aug86, re-iss.+cd May87)*

Mar 79. (7") **DOG & BUTTERFLY. / MISTRAL WIND** [-] [34]

— Now a quartet when Nancy's boyfriend ROGER FISHER left the band

Epic / Epic

Mar 80. (7") **EVEN IT UP. / PILOT** [ ] [34] Feb 80

Mar 80. (lp)(c) **BEBE LE STRANGE** [ ] [5]
– Bebe le strange / Down on me / Silver wheels / Break / Rockin' heaven down / Even it up / Strange night / Raised on you / Pilot / Sweet darlin'. *(re-iss.+cd '88) (re-iss.cd+c May93 on 'Sony Collectors')* **LITTLE QUEEN** *(cd-iss.Sep93 on 'Sony Collectors')*

May 80. (7") **DOWN ON ME. / RAISED ON YOU** [-] [ ]

Jul 80. (7") **BEBE LE STRANGE. / SILVER WHEELS** [-] [ ]

Nov 80. (7") **TELL IT LIKE IT IS. / STRANGE EUPHORIA** [-] [8]

Jan 81. (7") **TELL IT LIKE IT IS. / BARRACUDA (live)** [ ] [-]

Mar 81. (lp)(c)(US-d-lp) **GREATEST HITS / LIVE** (half comp / half live) [ ] [13] Nov 80
– Tell it like it is / Barracuda / Straight on / Dog & butterfly / Even it up / Bebe le strange / Sweet darlin' / I'm down – Long tall Sally – Unchained melody / Rock and roll. *(re-iss.+cd Dec88)*

Mar 81. (7") **UNCHAINED MELODY (live). / MISTRAL WIND** [-] [83]

Jun 82. (7") **THIS MAN IS MINE. / AMERICA** [ ] [33] May 82

Jun 82. (lp)(c) **PRIVATE AUDITION** [77] [25]
– City's burning / Bright light girl / Perfect stranger / Private audition / Angels / This man is mine / The situation / Hey darlin' darlin' / One word / Fast times / America. *(re-iss.+cd Feb88) (re-iss.cd May94)*

Sep 82. (7") **PRIVATE AUDITION. / BRIGHT LIGHT GIRL** [-] [ ]

— **MARK ANDES** – bass (ex-SPIRIT, ex-JO JO GUNNE, ex-FIREFALL) repl. FOSSEN **DENNY CARMASSI** – drums (ex-MONTROSE, ex-SAMMY HAGAR, ex-GAMMA) repl. DEROSIER who formed ORION THE HUNTER

Aug 83. (7") **HOW CAN I REFUSE. / JOHNNY MOON** [-] [ ]

Sep 83. (lp)(c) **PASSIONWORKS** [ ] [39]
– How can I refuse / Blue guitar / Johnny Moon / Sleep alone / Together now / Allies / (Beat by) Jealousy / Heavy heart / Love mistake / Language of love / Ambush. *(re-iss.+cd Feb88)*

Sep 83. (12"m) **HOW CAN I REFUSE. / BARRACUDA / LITTLE QUEEN** [ ] [-]

Oct 83. (7") **ALLIES. / TOGETHER NOW** [-] [83]

— While HEART looked for new contract ANN WILSON teamed up in '84 with MIKE RENO of LOVERBOY on 7" ALMOST PARADISE from the film 'Footloose'.

Capitol / Capitol

Jul 85. (7") **WHAT ABOUT LOVE?. / HEART OF DARKNESS** [ ] [10] May 85

Oct 85. (lp)(c)(cd) **HEART** [50] [1] Jul 85
– If looks could kill / What about love? / Never / These dreams / The wolf / All eyes / Nobody home / Nothin' at all / What he don't know / Shell shock. *(re-iss.cd Sep94)*

Oct 85. (7") **NEVER (remix). / SHELL SHOCK** [ ] [4] Sep 85
(12"+=) – ('A'extended).

Mar 86. (7") **THESE DREAMS. / IF LOOKS COULD KILL (live)** [62] [1] Jan 86
(12"+=) – Shell shock. *(US B-side)*
(d7"+=) – What about love? / Heart of darkness.

May 86. (7")(7"sha-pic-d) **NOTHIN' AT ALL (remix). / THE WOLF** [ ] [1] Apr 86
(12"+=) – ('A'extended).

Jul 86. (7") **IF LOOKS COULD KILL. / WHAT HE DON'T KNOW** [-] [54]

May 87. (7") **ALONE. / BARRACUDA** [3] [1]
(12"+=)(c-s+=) – Magic man (live).

May 87. (lp)(c)(cd) **BAD ANIMALS** [7] [5]

– Who will you run to / Alone / There's the girl / I want you so bad / Wait for the answer / Bad animals / You ain't so tough / Strangers of the heart / Easy target / RSVP. *(re-iss.cd Jul94)*

Aug 79. (7") **WHO WILL YOU RUN TO. / MAGIC MAN** [-] [ ]

Sep 87. (7")(7"pic-d) **WHO WILL YOU RUN TO. / NOBODY HOME** [30] [-]
(12"+=) – These dreams.
(cd-s++=) – ('A'rock mix).

Nov 87. (7") **THERE'S THE GIRL (remix). / BAD ANIMALS** [34] [12]
(12"+=) – ('A'extended).
(c-s+=)(cd-s++=) – Alone.

Jan 88. (7")(7"pic-d) **NEVER. / THESE DREAMS** [8] [-]
(12"+=) – ('A'extended) / ('B'version).
(cd-s+=) – Heart of darkness / If looks could kill (live).
(12"+=) – ('B'extended) / ('B'instrumental).

Feb 88. (7") **I WANT YOU SO BAD. / EASY TARGET** [-] [49]

May 88. (7")(7"pic-d) **WHAT ABOUT LOVE. / SHELL SHOCK** [14] [-]
(12"+=) – ('A'extended).
(cd-s+=) – Crazy on you / Dreamboat Annie.

Oct 88. (7") **NOTHIN' AT ALL (remix). / I'VE GOT THE MUSIC IN ME (live)** [38] [-]
(12"+=)(12"pic-d+=) – I want you so bad (extended version).
(cd-s++=) – Nothin' at all (extended remix).

Feb 89. (7") **SURRENDER TO ME. ("ANN WILSON & ROBIN ZANDER" of Cheap Trick). / TEQUILA DREAMS** [ ] [6]
(12"+=)(cd-s+=) – (other artist).

Dec 89. (7") **HERE IS CHRISTMAS. /** [-] [ ]

Mar 90. (7")(c-s) **ALL I WANNA DO IS MAKE LOVE TO YOU. / CALL OF THE WILD** [8] [2]
(12"+=)(12"clear+=)(12"pic-d+=)(cd-s+=) Cruel tears.

Apr 90. (cd)(c)(lp) **BRIGADE** [2] [3]
– Wild child / All I wanna do is make love to you / Secret / Tall, dark handsome stranger / I didn't want to need you / The night / Fallen from grace / Under the sky / Cruel nights / Stranded / Call of the wild / I want your world to turn / I love you. *(re-iss.cd+c Mar94)*

Jul 90. (7") **I DIDN'T WANT TO NEED YOU. / THE NIGHT** [47] [23] Jun 90
(12"+=)(c-s+=)(cd-s+=)(12"pic-d+=) – The will to love.

Nov 90. (7")(c-s) **STRANDED. / UNDER THE SKY** [60] [13] Sep 90
(12"+=)(cd-s+=)(12"pic-d+=) – I'll never stop loving you.

Feb 91. (7")(c-s) **SECRET. / I LOVE YOU** [ ] [ ]
(12"+=)(cd-s+=) – How can I refuse (live).

Sep 91. (cd)(c)(lp) **ROCK THE HOUSE (live)** [45] [ ]
– Wild child / Fallen from grace / Call of the wild / How can I refuse / Shell shock / Love alive / Under the sky / The night / Tall, dark, handsome stranger / If looks could kill / Who will you run to / You're the voice / The way back machine / Barracuda.

Sep 91. (7")(c-s) **YOU'RE THE VOICE (live). / CALL OF THE WILD (live)** [56] [ ]
(10"colrd+=)(cd-s+=) – Barracuda (live).

— In 1992, the WILSONS were in splinter groups FAUK HAUK and the LOVEMONGERS. The latter (which also included SUE ENNIS + FRANK COX) released a self-titled cd-ep on 'Capitol' w/tracks – Battle for evermore / Love of the common amn / Papa was a rollin' stone / Crazy on you

Nov 93. (7"pic-d)(c-s) **WILL YOU BE THERE (IN THE MORNING). / THESE DREAMS (live)** [19] [39]
(cd-s) – ('A'side) / What about love? / Risin' suspicion / Who will you run to.

Nov 93. (cd)(c) **DESIRE WALKS ON** [32] [48]
– Desire / Black on black II / Back to Avalon / The woman in me / Rage / In walks the night / My crazy head / Ring them bells / Will you be there (in the morning) / Voodoo doll / Anything is possible / Avalon (reprise) / Desire walks on (UK+=) / La mujer que hay en mi / Te quedaras (en la manana).

Mar 94. (cd-s) **BACK TO AVALON / WILL YOU BE THERE (IN THE MORNING) / ALL I WANNA DO IS MAKE LOVE TO YOU** [ ] [ ]

Aug 95. (cd)(c) **THE ROAD HOME** [-] [87]

- compilations etc. -

Sep 87. Epic; (d-lp)(c) **HEART (THE BEST OF . . .)** [ ] [ ]

1991. Epic; (d-cd) **DOG & BUTTERFLY / LITTLE QUEEN** [ ] [-]

Nov 88. Capitol; (box-lp)(box-cd) **WITH LOVE FROM HEART (HEART & BAD ANIMALS)** [ ] [-]
(re-iss.box-cd.1990 as HEART BOX SET)

May 94. Columbia; (cd)(c) **GREATEST HITS** [ ] [ ]

ANN WILSON

solo from the film 'The Golden Child'

Jan 87. (7 + 12") **THE BEST MAN IN THE WORLD. / ('A' instrumental)** [-] [ ]

HEARTBREAKERS

Formed: New York, USA . . . mid 1975 by ex-NEW YORK DOLLS members JOHNNY THUNDERS and JERRY NOLAN. They re-united with manager MALCOLM McLAREN late 1976, and he brought them to London to support SEX PISTOLS on their 'Anarchy' tour. The HEARTBREAKERS soon signed to UK label 'Track', which issued debut 45 'CHINESE ROCKS'. In Sep'77, they released lp 'L.A.M.F.' (New York street slang for Like A Mother F***** .', and although it suffered from bad production, it still managed a UK Top 60 placing. Later that year, they were deported from England and they split after NOLAN departed. JOHNNY THUNDERS went solo in 1978, although he re-formed them a year later. In the 80's, he released a few lp's for UK label 'Jungle', but never got out of cult legend mould. Sadly on 23rd April 1991, THUNDERS died in drug-related circumstances in New Orleans. • **Style:** Garage punk-rock / new wave outfit disgarding drag clothing for safety-pins and likened to SEX PISTOLS. • **Songwriters:** Group members LURE & NOLAN or THUNDERS. He co-wrote 'HURT ME' lp with ex-HEARTBREAKER; RICHARD HELL. Covered; CAN'T KEEP MY EYES OFF YOU (Andy Williams) / DO YOU LOVE ME (Brian Poole & The Tremeloes) / DOWNTOWN (Petula Clark) / LIKE A ROLLING STONE (Bob Dylan) / CRAWFISH (Elvis Presley) / QUE SERA SERA (hit; Doris Day). COPY CATS was a complete covers album. • **Trivia:** In 1978, THUNDERS teamed up with SID VICIOUS of The SEX PISTOLS in the ill-fated tour band LIVING DEAD.

Recommended: L.A.M.F. – REVISITED (*7)

JOHNNY THUNDERS (b.JOHN ANTHONY GENZALE, 15 Jul'52) – vocals, guitar / **JERRY NOLAN** – drums (both ex-NEW YORK DOLLS) / **WALTER LURE** – guitar, vocals / **BILLY WRATH** – bass, vocals repl. RICHARD HELL who formed his own group

Track / not issued

May 77. (7")(12") **CHINESE ROCKS. / BORN TO LOSE** [ ] [-]

Sep 77. (lp)(c) **L.A.M.F.** [55] [-]
– Born to lose / Baby talk / All by myself / I wanna be loved / It's not enough / Get off the phone / Chinese rocks / Pirate love / One track mind / I love you / Goin' steady / Let go. *(re-iss.May85 as 'L.A.M.F. – REVISITED' on 'Jungle') (pic-lp + pink-lp May84 +cd.)*

Nov 77. (7") **ONE TRACK MIND. / CAN'T KEEP MY EYES OFF YOU (live) / DO YOU LOVE ME (live)** [ ] [-]

Mar 78. (7") **IT'S NOT ENOUGH. / LET GO** [ ] [-]

— Split early '78. JERRY joined SNATCH. BILLY and WALTER returned to New York.

JOHNNY THUNDERS

— stayed in London and went solo, using session people

Real-W.E.A. / not issued

May 78. (7") **DEAD OR ALIVE. / DOWNTOWN** [ ] [-]

Sep 78. (7")(12")(12"pink)(12"blue) **YOU CAN'T PUT YOUR ARMS ROUND A MEMORY. / HURTIN'** [ ] [-]

Oct 78. (lp)(c) **SO ALONE** [ ] [-]
– Pipeline / You can't put your arms around a memory / Great big kiss / Ask me no questions / Leave me alone / Daddy rolling stone / London boys / Untouchable / Subway train / Downtown. *(re-iss.+cd.Jul92 & Feb95 on 'Warners')*

(above album featured PETER PERRETT (The Only Ones) / PHIL LYNOTT (Thin Lizzy) / CHRISSIE HYNDE (Pretenders) / PAUL COOK + STEVE JONES (Professionals)

JOHNNY THUNDERS & THE HEARTBREAKERS

— re-formed '79, with **WALTER, BILLY** and **STYX** – drums

Beggar's B. / not issued

Jul 79. (7") **GET OFF THE PHONE (live). / I WANT TO BE LOVED (live)** [ ] [-]

Sep 79. (lp)(c) **LIVE AT MAX'S KANSAS CITY (live)** [ ] [-]
– (intro) / Milk me / Chinese rocks / Get off the phone / London / Take a chance / One track mind / All by myself / Let go / I love you / Can't keep my eyes on you / I wanna be loved / Do you love me. *(cd-iss.Dec95 on 'ROIR USA')*

— Split again '79. In 1980, THUNDERS joined WAYNE KRAMER'S GANG WAR.

JOHNNY THUNDERS

went solo again with **WALTER LURE** – guitar / **BILLY ROGERS** – drums

New Rose / not issued

Dec 82. (7") **IN COLD BLOOD / ('A'live)** [-] [-] France

Jan 83. (d-lp) **IN COLD BLOOD** (some live) [-] [-] France
– In cold blood / Just another girl / Green onions / Diary of a lover / Look at my eyes / Live: (intro) / Just another girl / Too much junkie business / Sad vacation / Louie Louie / Gloria / Treat me like a nigger / Do you love me / Green onions / 10 commandments. *(re-iss.+cd.Apr91) (re-iss.cd Jun95 on 'Dojo')*

Jan 84. (7") **HURT ME. / IT'S NOT ENOUGH / LIKE A ROLLING STONE** [ ] [-]

Jan 84. (lp) **HURT ME** [ ] [-]
– So alone / It ain't me babe / Eve of destruction / You can't put your arms round a memory / You're so strange / I'm a boy in a girl / Lonely planet boy / Sad vacation / Hurt me / Diary of a lover / Ask me no questions. *(cd-iss.1990) (re-iss.cd Jul95 on 'Dojo')*

Jungle / not issued

Oct 85. (7") **CRAWFISH. / TIE ME UP (LOVE KNOT)** [ ] [-]
(12"+=) – ('A'bayou mix). *(re-iss.+7"pic-d.Apr87) (w/ PATTI PALLADIN – vocals (ex-SNATCH, FLYING LIZARDS)*

Dec 85. (lp)(c)(pic-lp) **QUE SERA, SERA** [ ] [-]
– Short lives / M.I.A. / I only wrote this song for you / Little bit of whore / Cool operator / Blame it on mom / Tie me up / Alone in a crowd / Billy boy / Endless party. *(cd-iss.1990) (cd-iss.Dec94)*

Jun 87. (12"m) **QUE SERA SERA. / SHORT LIVES / I ONLY WROTE THIS SONG FOR YOU** [ ] [-]

May 88. (7") **SHE WANTS TO MAMBO. / UPTOWN** [ ] [ ]
(12"+=) – Love is strange.

Jun 88. (lp)(c)(cd) **YEAH, YEAH, I'M A COPY CAT** [ ] [-]
– Can't seem to make you mine / Baby it's you / She wants to mambo / Treat her right / Uptown to Harlem / Crawfish / Alligator wine / Two time loser / Love is strange / (I was) Born to cry / He cried (she cried) / Let me entertain you (part 1 & 2).

Jan 89. (7") **(I WAS) BORN TO CRY. / TREAT HER RIGHT** [ ] [-]
(12"+=) – Can't seem to make her mine.

— THUNDERS died on 23 Apr'91 aged 38. He left 3 children from his first marriage plus another 3 year old daughter Jamie. He had lived in Sweden with girlfriend

Suzanne. JERRY NOLAN died on 14 Jan'92 of a stroke after a bout of pneumonia and meningitis, aged 45. Original drummer BILLY MURCIA also died in the 90's.

– compilations etc. –

May 81. Jungle; (lp) **D.T.K. – LIVE (live)** [ ] [-]
(pic-lp May88)
May 83. Jungle; (7"ep) **VINTAGE '77** [ ] [-]
– Let go / Chinese rocks / Born to lose.
Mar 84. Jungle; (7")(12")(7"pic-d) **GET OFF THE PHONE. / ALL BY MYSELF** [ ] [-]
May 85. Jungle; (7"ep)(12"ep) **CHINESE ROCKS / BORN TO LOSE / ONE TRACK MIND / I WANNA BE LOVED** [ ] [-]
May 88. Jungle; (box-lp) **ALBUM COLLECTION** [ ] [-]
Feb 90. Jungle; (cd)(lp) **BOOTLEGGIN' THE BOOTLEGGERS** [ ] [ ]
1983. R.O.I.R.; (c) **TOO MUCH JUNKIE BUSINESS** [-] [ ]
(cd-iss.Feb95 on 'ROIR Europe')
Feb 87. R.O.I.R.; (c) **STATIONS OF THE CROSS** [-] [ ]
(re-iss.cd Jul94 on 'Receiver') (cd-iss.Feb95 on 'ROIR Europe')
Jun 84. A.B.C.; (lp) **LIVE AT THE LYCEUM BALLROOM 1984 (live)** [ ] [-]
Feb 85. Twins; (7") **BORN TO LOSE. / IT'S NOT ENOUGH** [ ] [-]
Jun 91. Receiver; (cd)(lp) **LIVE AT THE LYCEUM (live)** [ ] [-]
Jan 92. Fan Club; (cd) **LIVE AT MOTHERS (live)** [ ] [-]
Oct 92. Fan Club; (cd)(c)(lp) **HAVE FAITH (solo)** [ ] [-]
Dec 93. Anagram; (cd) **CHINESE ROCKS – THE ULTIMATE LIVE COLLECTION (live)** [ ] [-]
Sep 94. Skydog; (cd) **VIVE LE REVOLUTION** – LIVE PARIS, 1977 (live JOHNNY THUNDERS & THE HEARTBREAKERS) [ ] [-]
Dec 94. Essential; (cd)(c) **LIVE IN JAPAN (live JOHNNY THUNDERS)** [ ] [-]
Dec 94. Jungle; (cd)(c) **D.T.K. / L.A.M.F.** [ ] [-]
(re-iss.cd Aug94 on 'Receiver')

HEAVEN 17

Formed: Sheffield, England ... Oct'80 by departing HUMAN LEAGUE members IAN CRAIG-MARSH and MARTYN WARE. They also founded B.E.F., and recruited former photographer GLENN GREGORY. Still signed to 'Virgin', they reached UK Top 50 with March '81 debut '(WE DON'T NEED THIS) FASCIST GROOVE THANG'. Their first album 'PENTHOUSE AND PAVEMENT' hit the Top 20, and was followed by more successes, until a barren period in the mid-80's. • **Style:** Electronic dance/funk rock outfit, with powerful vox supplied by smart-dressed GREGORY. • **Songwriters:** WARE & CRAIG-MARSH through a computer-synth. Their 1981-82 off-shoot project B.E.F. covered; ANYONE WHO HAD A HEART (Cilla Black) / WITCHITA LINEMAN (Glen Campbell) / BALL OF CONFUSION (Temptations) / IT'S OVER (Roy Orbison) / YOU KEEP ME HANGIN' ON (Diana Ross & The Supremes) / THE SECRET LIFE OF ARABIA (David Bowie) / THERE'S A GHOST IN MY HOUSE (R.Dean Taylor) / THESE BOOTS WERE MADE FOR WALKING (Nancy Sinatra) / PERFECT DAY (Lou Reed) / SUSPICIOUS MINDS (Elvis Presley). As disaster fund group The HILLSBOROUGH CREW, they covered in 1986; MOVE ON UP (Curtis Mayfield). • **Trivia:** Named themselves after a group in the controversial film 'Clockwork Orange'.

Recommended: PENTHOUSE AND PAVEMENT (*8) / HIGHER AND HIGHER – THE BEST OF ... (*7)

GLENN GREGORY (b.16 May'58) – vocals / **MARTYN WARE** (b.19 May'56) – synthesizers (ex-HUMAN LEAGUE) / **IAN CRAIG-MARSH** (b.11 Nov'56) – synthesizers (ex-HUMAN LEAGUE)

Virgin | Arista

Mar 81. (7")(12") **(WE DON'T NEED THIS) FASCIST GROOVE THANG. / THE DECLINE OF THE WEST** [45] [ ]
May 81. (7")(12") **I'M YOUR MONEY. / – ARE EVERYTHING** [ ] [ ]
Jul 81. (7")(12") **PLAY TO WIN. / PLAY** [46] [ ]
Sep 81. (lp)(c) **PENTHOUSE AND PAVEMENT** [14] [ ]
– (We don't need this) Fascist groove thang / Penthouse and pavement / Play to win / Soul warfare / Geisha boys and temple girls / Let's all make a bomb / The height of the fighting / Song with no name / We're going to live for a very long time. *(re-iss.Apr86) (cd-iss.Jul87)*
below 45 featured guests **JOHN WILSON** – bass / **JOSIE JONES** – vocals
Oct 81. (7")(12") **PENTHOUSE AND PAVEMENT. / ('A'instrumental)** [57] [ ]
Feb 82. (12")(7") **THE HEIGHT OF THE FIGHTING (HE-LA-HO). / HONEYMOON IN NEW YORK** [ ] [ ]
Oct 82. (7")(12") **LET ME GO. / ('A' instrumental)** [41] [-]
Feb 83. (7") **LET ME GO. / I'M YOUR MONEY** [-] [74]
(next single featured **CAROLE KENYON** – dual vocals)
Apr 83. (7")(12")(7"pic-d) **TEMPTATION. / WE LIVE SO FAST** [2] [ ]
May 83. (7")(12") **WE LIVE SO FAST. / BEST KEPT SECRET** [-] [ ]
May 83. (lp)(c)(cd) **THE LUXURY GAP** [4] [72]
– Crushed by the wheels of industry / Who'll stop the rain / Let me go / Key to the world / Temptation / Come live with me / Lady Ice and Mr. Hex / We live so fast / The best kept secret. *(cd-iss.Jul87)*
Jun 83. (7") **COME LIVE WITH ME. / LET'S ALL MAKE A BOMB** [5] [ ]
(12"+=) – Song with no name.
Sep 83. (7") **CRUSHED BY THE WHEELS OF INDUSTRY. / ('A' instrumental)** [17] [ ]
(12"+=) – ('A'dance version).
Aug 84. (7") **SUNSET NOW. / COUNTERFORCE** [24] [ ]
(12"+=) – Flame down / Counterforce II.
Sep 84. (lp)(c) **HOW MEN ARE** [12] [ ]
– Five minutes to midnight / Sunset now / This is mine / The fuse / Shane is on the rocks / The skin I'm in / Flame down / Reputation / . . . (And that's no lie). *(re-iss.+cd Jul87) (re-iss.cd Mar94)*
Oct 84. (7") **THIS IS MINE. / THE SKIN I'M IN** [23] [ ]
(12"+=) – That's mine (mixes).
Jan 85. (7")(12") **... (AND THAT'S NO LIE). / THE FUSE** [52] [ ]
(d7"+=) – ('A'&'B'versions).
next featured **JIMMY RUFFIN** – dual vocals (ex-60's soul singer)

Virgin | Virgin

Apr 86. (7") **THE FOOLISH THING TO DO. / MY SENSITIVITY** [ ] [ ]
(12"+=) – ('A' version).
Oct 86. (7") **CONTENDERS. / DIARY OF A CONTENDER** [ ] [ ]
(d12"+=) – ('A' extended dance)./ Penthouse and pavement.
Nov 86. (lp)(c)(cd) **PLEASURE ONE** [78] [ ]
– Contenders / Trouble / Somebody / If I were you / Low society / Look at me / Move out / Free.
Jan 87. (7") **TROUBLE. / (BIG) TROUBLE** [51] [ ]
(12"+=) – ('A' club version).
(d7"+=) – Move out / Contenders (US version).
Aug 88. (7") **THE BALLAD OF GO-GO BROWN. / I SET YOU FREE** [ ] [ ]
(12"+=)/ /(cd-s+=) – ('A' version)./ / Slow all over.
Sep 88. (lp)(c) **TEDDY BEAR, DUKE AND PSYCHO** [ ] [ ]
– Big square people / Don't stop for no one / Snake and two people / Can you hear me? / The ballad of Go-go Brown / Dangerous / I set you free / Train of love and motion / Responsibility. *(cd+=)* – Foolish thing to do / East seven days. *(cd++=)* – Work / Giving up / Slow all over.
Oct 88. (7") **TRAIN OF LOVE AND MOTION. / WORK** [ ] [ ]
(12"+=)(3"cd-s+=) – ('A'extended) / Giving up.

— Disbanded by the late 80's.

– compilations etc. –

Mar 83. Arista; (lp)(c) **HEAVEN 17** [-] [68]
Jul 86. Virgin; (cd)(d-c) **ENDLESS** [70] [ ]
(comp. of 12" mixes, d-c 17 mins extra)
Jun 88. Virgin; (cd-ep) **TEMPTATION. / WHO'LL STOP THE RAIN / WE LIVE SO FAST** [ ] [ ]
1988. Virgin; (3"cd-ep) **(WE DON'T NEED THIS) FASCIST GROOVE THANG. / I'M YOUR MONEY / THE HEIGHT OF THE FIGHTING / THE DECLINE OF THE WEST** [ ] [ ]
Nov 92. Virgin; (7")(c-s) **TEMPTATION (Brothers in rhythm remix). / ('A' mix)** [4] [ ]
(12"+=)(cd-s+=) – ('A' mixes)
Feb 93. Virgin; (7")(c-s) **(WE DON'T NEED THIS) FASCIST GROOVE THANG (Rapino Edit) / 'A' (Democratic Edit)** [40] [ ]
(cd-s+=) – ('A' mixes).
Mar 93. Virgin; (cd)(c)(lp) **HIGHER AND HIGHER – THE BEST OF HEAVEN 17** [31] [ ]
– Temptation (brothers in rhythm remix) / (We don't need this) Fascist groove thang (rapido edit) / Let me go / Come live with me / This is mine / I'm your money / play to win / (And that's no lie) / Contenders / we live so fast / Sunset now / Trouble / Height of the fighting (he-la-hu) / Penthouse and pavement / Crushed by the wheels of industry / (We don't need this) Fascist groove thang (original) / Temptation (original).
Mar 93. Virgin; (7")(c-s) **PENTHOUSE AND PAVEMENT. / ('A'mix)** [54] [ ]
(12"+=)(cd-s+=) – ('A'mixes).
Dec 93. V.I.P.; (cd)(c) **THE BEST OF HEAVEN 17** [ ] [-]
Nov 88. Old Gold; (7") **TEMPTATION. / COME LIVE WITH ME** [ ] [-]
Feb 89. Old Gold; (7") **LET ME GO. / PLAY TO WIN** [ ] [-]
May 95. Virgin-VIP; (cd)(c) **THE BEST OF HEAVEN 17** [ ] [-]

B.E.F.

(aka The BRITISH ELECTRIC FOUNDATION)(**IAN** and **MARTIN** with guest vocalists inc. **GARY GLITTER, PAUL JONES** etc.)

B.E.F. | not issued

Mar 81. (c) **MUSIC FOR STOWAWAYS** [ ] [ ]

Virgin | Arista

Nov 81. (lp) **MUSIC OF QUALITY AND DISTINCTION** [25] [ ]
– Anyone who had a heart / It's over / Ball and confusion / You keep me hangin' on / The secret life of Arabia / There's a ghost in my house / These boots are mad for walking / Perfect day / Suspicious minds / Wichita lineman.
Apr 82. (7") **ANYONE WHO HAD A HEART (by 'SANDIE SHAW'). / Pt.2** [ ] [ ]
Apr 82. (7") **THESE BOOTS ARE MADE FOR WALKING (by 'PAULA YATES'). / Pt.2** [ ] [ ]
May 82. (7") **IT'S OVER (by 'BILLY McKENZIE'). / Pt.2** [ ] [ ]
May 82. (7") **BALL OF CONFUSION (by 'TINA TURNER'). / Pt.2** [ ] [ ]

The HILLSBROUGH CREW

(aka HEAVEN 17)(tribute to Sheffield Wednesday F.C.)
Dec 86. Virgin; (7")(12") **STEEL CITY. / MOVE ON UP** [ ] [ ]

GLENN GREGORY & CLAUDIA BRUCKEN

(BRUCKEN – vocals, of PROPAGANDA)

Z.T.T. | Island

Aug 85. (7") **WHEN YOUR HEART RUNS OUT OF TIME. / ('A'drumless vers.)** [ ] [ ]
(12"+=) – ('A'extended) / (voices of) / Forever (what the Hell).

B.E.F.

with guests singers (see below)

10-Virgin Arista

Jul 91. (7")(c-s) **FAMILY AFFAIR. / ('A'instr.)** [37] [ ]
(cd-s+=) – ('A'party plan mix).

Sep 91. (cd)(c)(lp) **MUSIC OF QUALITY AND DISTINCTION VOLUME 2** [ ] [ ]
– (CHAKA KHAN) – Sunday we'll all be free / (LALAH HATHAWAY) – Family affair / (RICHARD DARBYSHIRE) – Early in the morning / (BILLY MacKENZIE) – Free / (TERENCE TRENT D'ARBY) – It's alright ma, I'm only bleeding / (TASHAN) – I want you / (MAVIS STAPLES) – A song for you / (BILLY PRESTON) – Try a little tenderness / (GREEN GARTSIDE) – I don't know why I love you / (TINA TURNER) – A change is gonna come / (GHIDA DE PALMA) – Feel like makin' love.

Richard HELL (& The VOID-OIDS)

Born: RICHARD MYERS, 2 Oct'49, Lexington, Kentucky, USA. He was raised in Wilmington, Delaware, but moved to New York in the late 60's, to write poetry and experiment with drugs. In 1971, he formed The NEON BOYS with TOM VERLAINE, and they evolved into TELEVISION by 1973. He was sacked 2 years later, but he quickly found other new wave band The HEARTBREAKERS. In 1976, he formed the VOID-OIDS and issued debut EP for 'Ork' (Stiff UK) label. The next year 'Sire' signed them up, and issued new version of 'BLANK GENERATION', from same titled album. After a quiet year in '78, he came back on 'Radar', with NICK LOWE produced 45 'THE KID WITH THE REPLACEABLE HEAD'. His work in the 80's was curtailed by drug problems, with only 1 lp 'DESTINY STREET' being released in '82. In 1992, he made a surprise comeback when he teamed up with SONIC YOUTH members in spin-off DIM STARS. • **Style:** New wave punk, not to disimilar to TELEVISION or LOU REED. Claimed to have been first to have punk mop head & ripped T-shirts. • **Songwriters:** HELL penned all, co-writing 'LOVE COMES IN SPURTS' with VERLAINE. DIM STARS covered RIP OFF (Marc Bolan) / NATCHEZ BURNING (Johnny Burnette). • **Trivia:** He also wrote a column for East Village Eye in the 80's. His biography 'Artifact: Notebooks from Hell' was issued by Hanuman in 1990.

Recommended: BLANK GENERATION (*7).

RICHARD HELL & THE VOID-OIDS

RICHARD HELL – vocals, bass / **ROBERT QUINE** (b.30 Dec'42, Akron, Ohio) – guitar, vocals / **IVAN JULIAN** (b.26 Jun'55, Washington) – guitar, vocals / **MARC BELL** – drums (ex-WAYNE COUNTY & THE ELECTRIC CHAIRS)

Stiff Ork

Nov 76. (7"ep) **(I COULD LIVE WITH YOU IN) ANOTHER WORLD. / YOU GOTTA LOSE / (I BELONG TO THE) BLANK GENERATION** [ ] [ ]

Sire Sire

Sep 77. (7") **BLANK GENERATION. / LOVE COMES IN SPURTS** [ ] [ ]
(12") – ('A'side) / Liars beware / Who says.

Sep 77. (lp)(c) **BLANK GENERATION** [ ] [ ]
– Love comes in spurts / Liars beware / New pleasure / Betrayal takes two / Down at the rock and roll club / Who says / Blank generation / Walking on the water / The plan / Another world. *(re-iss.Jun90)*

— **FRED MAURO** – drums repl. BELL who joined RAMONES / added **JERRY ANTONIUS** – keyboards, vocals

Radar not issued

Jan 79. (7") **THE KID WITH THE REPLACEABLE HEAD. / I'M YOUR MAN** [ ] [ ]

— **HELL** and **JULIAN** recruited **FRED MAHER** – drums repl. MAURO / **NAUX** (b.29 Jul'51, San Jose, Calif.) – guitar repl. QUINE to LYDIA LUNCH

Red Star Red Star

May 82. (lp) **DESTINY STREET** [ ] [ ]
– The kid with the replaceable head / You gotta move / Going going gone / Lowest common dominator / Downtown at dawn / Time / I can only give you everything / Ignore that door / Staring in her eyes / Destiny street. *(cd-iss.Sep93 & Mar95 on 'Danceteria')*

— Split 1982, RICHARD HELL starred in the film 'Smithereens'. MAHER joined SCRITTI POLITTI. In 1986, he made brief cameo in the film 'Desperately Seeking Susan' as Madonna's boyfriend.

RICHARD HELL

(solo) **with THURSTON MOORE + DON FLEMING** – guitar (of GUMBALL)

White label White label

Feb 92. (7")(cd-s) **THE NIGHT IS COMING ON. / BABY HUEY (BABY DO YOU WANNA DANCE?) / FRANK SINATRA** [ ] [ ]

DIM STARS

RICHARD HELL + DON FLEMING with **THURSTON MOORE + STEVE SHELLEY** (both of SONIC YOUTH)

Paperhouse Paperhouse

Apr 92. (12"ep)(cd-ep) **THE PLUG / DIM STAR THEME. / CHRISTIAN RAP ATTACK / YOU GOTTA LOSE** [ ] [-]

Jun 92. (cd)(c)(lp) **DIM STARS** [ ] [ ]
– She wants to die / All my witches come true / Memo to Marty / Monkey / Natchez burning / Stop breakin' down / Baby Huey (do you wanna dance?) / The night is coming on / Downtown at dawn / Try this / Stray cat generation / Rip off.

RICHARD HELL

Codex Codex

Apr 95. (cd) **GO NOW** (spoken word) [ ] [ ]

– compilations etc. –

1985. R.O.I.R.; (c) **R.I.P. (live)** [-] [ ]
(UK-iss.+cd.Jun90 on 'Danceteria')

Apr 90. R.O.I.R.; (c) **FOXHUNT** [ ] [ ]

May 95. Overground; (cd)(lp) **GO NOW** [ ] [ ]

HELLIONS (see under ⇒ MASON, Dave)

HELLOWEEN

Formed: Hamburg, Germany . . . 1982 by quartet below. In 1984, they signed to German label 'Noise International' and soon released eponymous 1985 debut lp. They finally broke through in 1988, when concept album 'KEEPER OF THE SEVEN KEYS PART 2' made UK Top 30. • **Style:** Heavy speed thrash-metal similiar to METALLICA or IRON MAIDEN. • **Songwriters:** Group compositions except BLUE SUEDE SHOES (Carl Perkins). • **Trivia:** In 1986, they employed new manager Rod Smallwood.

Recommended: KEEPER OF THE SEVEN KEYS PART 2 (*7).

MICHAEL WEIKATH – vocals, guitar / **KAI HANSEN** – guitar / **MARKUS GROBKOFF** – bass / **INGO SCHWICHTENBERG** – drums

Noise Int. R.C.A.

1985. (m-lp) **HELLOWEEN** [-] [-] Germ'y
– Starlight / Murderer / Warrior / Victim of fate / Cry for freedom. *(re-iss.May87, UK-iss.+cd Oct89) (cd-iss.Dec87)*

Dec 85. (lp) **WALLS OF JERICO** [-] [-] Germ'y
– Walls of Jericho / Ride the sky / Reptile / Guardians / Phantoms of death / Metal invaders / Gorgar / Heavy metal (is the law) / How many tears. *(UK-iss.+c+cd Oct89)*

— added **MICHAEL KISKE** – vocals

May 87. (m-lp) **KEEPER OF THE SEVEN KEYS – PART I** [-] [ ]
– Initiation / I'm alive / A little time / Twilight of the gods / A tale that wasn't right / Future world / Halloween / Follow the sign. *(UK-iss.+c+cd Oct89 +pic-lp)*

Noise Int. R.C.A.

Sep 87. (12")(12"pic-d) **FUTURE WORLD. / STARLIGHT / A LITTLE TIME** [ ] [-]

Sep 87. (m-lp) **JUDAS** [-] [ ]
– Judas / Ride the sky / Guardians / Victim of fate (live) / Cry for freedom (live) *. *(UK-iss.as 12" Sep89 on 'Noise International' omits *)*

Aug 88. (7") **DR. STEIN. / SAVAGE** [57] [-]
(12"+=)(12"pic-d+=)(3"cd-s+=) – Livin' ain't no crime / Victim of fate.

Sep 88. (lp)(c)(cd) **KEEPER OF THE SEVEN KEYS – PART II** [24] [ ]
– Invitation / Eagle fly free / You always walk alone / Rise and fall / Dr. Stein / We got the right / March of time / I want out / Keeper of the seven keys. *(pic-lp.Oct89)*

Oct 88. (7") **I WANT OUT. / DON'T RUN FOR COVER** [69] [-]
(12"pic-d+=)(cd-s+=) – Save us.

— added **JORN ELLERBROOK** – keyboards

E.M.I. R.C.A.

Apr 89. (lp)(c)(cd) **LIVE IN THE UK (live)** [26] [-]
– A little time / Dr. Stein / Future world / Rise and fall / We got the right / I want out / How many tears. (US title 'I WANT OUT – LIVE')

— (Feb89) **ROLAND GRAPOW** – guitar repl. HANSEN who joined GAMMA RAY

Feb 91. (7")(c-s) **KIDS OF THE CENTURY. / BLUE SUEDE SHOES** [56] [ ]
(12"+=)(cd-s+=) – Shit and lobster.
(10"++=)(12"++=) – (interview).

Mar 91. (cd)(c)(lp) **PINK BUBBLES GO APE** [41] [ ]
– Pink bubbles go ape / Kids of the century / Back on the streets / Number one / Heavy metal hamsters / Going home / Someone's crying / Mankind / I'm doin' fine – Crazy man / The chance / Your turn.

Jun 93. (cd)(c)(lp) **CHAMELEON** [ ] [ ]
– First time / When the sinner / I don't wanna cry no more / Crazy cat / Giants / Windmill / Revolution now / San Francisco (be sure to wear flowers in your hair) / In the night / Music / Step out of Hell / I believe / Longing. *(re-iss.cd+c Dec94 on 'Fame')*

Raw Power Rykodisc?

Aug 94. (cd)(c)(lp) **MASTER OF RINGS** [ ] [ ]
– Irritation / Sole survivor / Where the rain grows / Why? / Mr. Ego / Perfect gentlemen / The game is on / Secret alibi / Take me home / In the middle of a heartbeat / Still we go / Invitation. *(re-iss.cd Apr95)*

– compilations, others, etc. –

Aug 91. Noise; (cd)(c)(lp) **THE BEST, THE REST, THE RARE** [ ] [ ]
– I want out / Dr. Stein / Future world / Judas / Walls of Jericho / Ride the sky / Helloween / Livin' ain't no crime / Save us / Victim of fate / Savage / Don't run for cover / Keeper of the seven keys (w/free 12") **HELLOWEEN. / KEEPER OF THE SEVEN SEAS** (both over 13 minutes).

Jan 94. Noise; (cd) **KEEPER OF THE SEVEN KEYS – THE WHOLE STORY** [ ] [ ]

HELMET

Formed: New York, USA – based . . . 1989 by jazz-trained guitarist PAGE HAMILTON, who had briefly played for BAND OF SUSANS. He completed his line-up around 1990, when BOGDAN, MENGELE and STAINER were added. After a one-off release for US 'A. Reptile', they signed for 'East

West', who released debut album 'STRAP IT ON' late in 1990. Made massive impact in 1994, when 'BETTY' album hit cross-Atlantic Top 50. • **Style:** Unconventional non-image anti-fuss hard-core metal outfit, channeling HENRY ROLLINS-like aggression with avant-garde jazz. Influences from BLACK SABBATH to BLACK FLAG. • **Songwriters:** HAMILTON / some w /BOGDAN. • **Trivia:** STEVE ALBINI produced their 1992 effort. In 1994, recorded 'MILQUETOAST' for 'The Crow' film soundtrack.

Recommended: MEANTIME (*7).

PAGE HAMILTON (b.Oregon) – vocals, guitar / **PETER MENGELE** – guitar / **HENRY BOGDAN** – bass / **JOHN STAINER** (b.Australia) – drums

		Am-phetamine	Am-phetamine
1990.	(7") **BORN ANNOYING. /**	-	
Nov 91.	(cd)(c)(m-lp) **STRAP IT ON** – Repetition / Rude / Bad mood / Sinatra / FBLA / Blacktop / Distracted / Make room / Murder. *(re-iss.Jul93 on 'East West')(re-iss.cd Feb95 on 'Interscope')*		
		East West	Interscope
Jun 92.	(7") **IN THE MEANTIME. /** (12"+=)(cd-s+=) –		
Jun 92.	(cd)(c)(lp) **MEANTIME** – In the meantime / Iron head / Give it / Unsung / Turned out / He feels bad / Better / You borrowed / FBLA II / Role model.		68
Nov 92.	(7") **UNSUNG. / FBLA (live)** (cd-s+=) – FBLA II (live). (12") – ('A'side) / Better (live) / Bad mood (live) / Distracted (live).		

— **ROB ECHEVERRA** – guitar repl. MENGELE

		Interscope	Interscope
Jun 94.	(7")(12")(c-s) **BISCUITS FOR SMUT. / MILQUETOAST** (cd-s+=) – Flushings.		
Jun 94.	(cd)(c) **BETTY** – Wilma's rainbow / I know / Biscuits for smut / Milquetoast / Tie / Rollo / Street crab / Clean / Vaccination / Beautiful love / Speechless / The silver Hawaiian / Overrated / Sam Hell.	38	45
Nov 94.	(7"ep)(12"ep)(cd-ep) **WILMA'S RAINBOW EP (live)** – Wilma's rainbow / Sinatra / FBLA II / TIC / Just another victim / In the meantime.		

compilations, etc

Apr 95.	Amphetamine Reptile; (cd)(c)(lp) **BORN ANNOYING**		

Jimi HENDRIX EXPERIENCE

Born: JOHNNY ALLEN HENDRIX, 27 Nov'42, Seattle, Washington, USA. Raised by part Cherokee Indian mother and black father, who at 3 changed his forenames to JAMES MARSHALL and bought him first guitar in the summer of '58. Due to him being left-handed, he turned it upside down and reversed the strings. JIMI soon taught himself by listening to blues and rock'n'roll artists such as ROBERT JOHNSON, MUDDY WATERS, B.B. KING and CHUCK BERRY. In the early 60's, he enlisted in the paratroopers, thus avoided draft into US army. He was discharged for medical reasons in 1962, when he was injured during jump. Two years later, he moved to New York and backed acts LITTLE RICHARD, The ISLEY BROTHERS, IKE & TINA TURNER. He soon struck up partnership with soul singer CURTIS KNIGHT, while also obtaining contract with Ed Chalpin. He is said to have written 'The Ballad Of Jimi' in 1965, after JIMI told him he would die in 1970!. Early in 1966, JIMMY JAMES & THE BLUE FLAMES were born. With JIMI's reputation now spreading, he was seen by ex-ANIMALS bassman CHAS CHANDLER, who invited him to London. After auditions, they found a rhythm section of NOEL REDDING and MITCH MITCHELL, and smashed their way into UK Top 10 early '67 with 'Polydor' one-off 45 'HEY JOE'. Chandler then set up deal with Kit Lambert's new 'Track' label, and The JIMI HENDRIX EXPERIENCE exploded into place. Their first Hendrix-penned 45 'PURPLE HAZE', made UK Top 3, as did scintillating debut lp 'ARE YOU EXPERIENCED?' after their 3rd Top 10 single 'THE WIND CRIES MARY'. He was duly booked on the Monterey International Pop Festival bill, where he played a resounding version of 'WILD THING'. The next month of July, saw an weird support US tour with The MONKEES, leaving him and teenybop audiences baffled, but no doubt entertained for 7 nights. After another classic UK hit 'THE BURNING OF THE MIDNIGHT LAMP', he released 2nd lp 'AXIS: BOLD AS LOVE', which made Top 5 early '68, and was first to chart and hit Top 3 in his home U.S.A. In Autumn of '68, he revived and transformed BOB DYLAN's 'ALL ALONG THE WATCHTOWER', which broke into US Top 20 and UK 5. It was trailed by a superb UK Top 10 double-lp 'ELECTRIC LADYLAND', which went No.1 in US, and featured the now famous controversial naked women sleeve, which some shops sold in a brown cover!. In 1969, he was busted for drugs, which led to the split of his band who played together for last time on 29 June at Denver Pop Festival. REDDING had already FAT MATTRESS, but MITCHELL returned with other musicians BILLY COX and LARRY LEE. They played the Woodstock Festival 17-18 August '69, with excellent version of 'STAR SPANGLED BANNER' going down into folklore of rock music. To end the year, he was found not guilty of an earlier charge of heroin and marijuana possession. At the same time, he formed all-black outfit BAND OF GYPSYS, with COX and drummer BUDDY MILES. They released live lp 'BAND OF GYPSYS' in May'70 recorded at FILLMORE EAST, New Year's Eve/Day 1969/70. This hit Top 5 in the States, and due to court action, he paid ex-manager Ed Chalpin $1m in compensation and percentage of royalties. Tragically after a few more open-air festival concerts and some bad drugs trips, he died in London on 18th Sep'70. He was said to have left a phoned message to Chandler saying "I need help bad, man". The official cause of death, was an inhalation of vomit, due to barbituate intoxication, which led to coroner decided of an open verdict. • **Style:** Wild man of rock'n'roll, his well-crafted blues poems were always fused with "out of this world" guitar-virtuoso, never seen before or since!. His gentlemanly vox, was always climaxed in concert, with heavy lead guitar complete with teeth-playing, feedback and setting fire to his Stratocaster. He virtually re-invented the electric guitar and still to many rock music buffs, the greatest axegrinder of all-time. Who knows what he might have become and progressed onto, but for drug abuse and death. • **Songwriters:** HENDRIX except other covers; HEY JOE (William Roberts) / JOHNNY B.GOODE (Chuck Berry) / GLORIA (Them) / SGT. PEPPER (Beatles) / HANG ON SLOOPY (McCoys) / TUTTI FRUTTI + LUCILLE (LIttle Richard) / BO DIDDLEY (Bo Diddley) / PETER GUNN (Henry Mancini) / HOOCHIE COOCHIE MAN (Muddy Waters) / BLUE SUEDE SHOES (Carl Perkins) / etc. • **Trivia:** In Jan'69, he and band play live tribute of CREAM's 'Sunshine Of Your Love' on The LULU Show, much to annoyance of TV controllers.

Recommended: ARE YOU EXPERIENCED? (*10) / AXIS: AS BOLD AS LOVE (*9) / ELECTRIC LADYLAND (*10) / BAND OF GYPSYS (*8) / THE CRY OF LOVE (*7) / THE ULTIMATE EXPERIENCE (compilation *10)

JIMI HENDRIX – vocals, lead guitar (ex-CURTIS KNIGHT) with **NOEL REDDING** (b.DAVID REDDING, 25 Dec'45, Folkstone, Kent, England) – bass / **MITCH MITCHELL** (b.JOHN MITCHELL, 9 Jun'47, Ealing, London, England) – drums

		Polydor	Reprise
Dec 66.	(7") **HEY JOE. / STONE FREE (credited "JIMI HENDRIX")** *(re-iss.Jul84 on 'Old Gold')*	6	-
		Track	Reprise
Mar 67.	(7") **PURPLE HAZE. / 51ST ANNIVERSARY**	3	-
Mar 67.	(7") **HEY JOE. / 51st ANNIVERSARY**	-	
May 67.	(7") **THE WIND CRIES MARY. / HIGHWAY CHILE**	6	-
May 67.	(lp) **ARE YOU EXPERIENCED** – Foxy lady / Manic depression / Red house / Can you see me / Love or confusion / I don't live today / May this be love / Fire / Third stone from the sun / Remember / Are you experienced. *(re-iss.+c Nov70, re-iss.Nov81+Sep85 on 'Polydor' re+cd Jun91)(re-iss.cd+c Oct93)*	2	5 Aug 67
Aug 67.	(7") **PURPLE HAZE. / THE WIND CRIES MARY**	-	65
Aug 67.	(7") **BURNING OF THE MIDNIGHT LAMP. / THE STARS THAT PLAY WITH LAUGHING SAM'S DICE**	18	-
Dec 67.	(7") **FOXY LADY. / HEY JOE**	-	67
Dec 67.	(lp) **AXIS: BOLD AS LOVE** – Experience / Up from the skies / Spanish castle magic / Wait until tomorrow / Ain't no telling / Little wing / If six was nine / You've got me floating / Castles made of sand / She's so fine / One rainy wish / Little Miss Lover / Bold as love. *(re-iss.+c Nov70, re-iss Aug83, cd-iss.1987, re-iss.+cd Jul91 on 'Polydor')(re-iss.cd+c Oct93)*	5	3 Feb 68
Feb 68.	(7") **UP FROM THE SKIES. / ONE RAINY WISH**	-	82
May 68.	(7") **FOXY LADY. / PURPLE HAZE**	-	

— Jimi now brought in sessions **AL KOOPER** and **STEVE WINWOOD** – keyboards plus **JACK CASADY** – bass / **BUDDY MILES** – drums / (to repl.MITCHELL and REDDING)

Sep 68.	(7") **ALL ALONG THE WATCHTOWER. / CROSSTOWN TRAFFIC**	-	20
Oct 68.	(7") **ALL ALONG THE WATCHTOWER. / LONG HOT SUMMER NIGHT**	5	-
Nov 68.	(d-lp) **ELECTRIC LADYLAND** – And the gods made love / (Have you ever been to) Electric Ladyland / Crosstown traffic / Voodoo chile / Rainy day, dream away / 1983 (a merman I should turn to be) / Moon, turn the tide . . .gently gently away / Little Miss Strange / Long hot summer night / Come on / Gypsy eyes / The burning of the midnight lamp / Still raining still dreaming / House burning down / All along the watchtower / Voodoo chile (slight return). *(re-iss.'69, re-iss.+d-c Jun73, re-iss.+d-cd Jan84 on 'Polydor', cd-iss.Jul91) (re-iss.cd+c Oct93)*	6	1 Oct 68
Apr 69.	(7") **CROSSTOWN TRAFFIC. / GYPSY EYES**	37	52

JIMI HENDRIX

retained only **BUDDY MILES** and recruited **BILLY COX** – bass to repl. others

		Track	Capitol
Apr 70.	(7") **STEPPING STONE. / IZABELLA**	-	
Jun 70.	(lp)(c) **BAND OF GYPSYS (live)** – Who knows / Machine gun / Changes / Power to love / Message of love / We gotta live together. *(re-iss.Jun73, re-iss.Aug83 on 'Polydor', re-iss.+cd May88) (cd-iss.Dec89, re-iss.+cd Jul91)*	6	5 Apr 70

— On 18th Sep'70 HENDRIX died of a drug overdose.

– compilations etc. –

Feb 68.	London/ US= Capitol; (lp) **GET THAT FEELING (live 1964, with 'CURTIS KNIGHT' as above)**	39	75
Nov 68.	London/ US= Capitol; (lp) **STRANGE THINGS** *(re-iss.Apr86 on 'Showcase')*		

Note; All below 'Track' releases were issued on 'Reprise' US.

Sep 67.	Track; (7") **HOW WOULD YOU FEEL. / YOU DON'T WANT ME**		
Apr 68.	Track; (lp) **SMASH HITS** – Purple haze / Fire / The wind cries Mary / Can you see me / 51st anniversary / Hey Joe / Stone free / The stars that play with laughing Sam's dice / Manic depression / Highway chile / The burning of the midnight lamp / Foxy lady. *(re-iss.Jun73, re-iss.Aug83 on 'Polydor', cd-iss.Feb85)*	4	6 Jul 69
Oct 69.	Track; (7") **(LET ME LIGHT YOUR) FIRE. / BURNING OF THE MIDNIGHT LAMP**		

'Really, I'm just an actor – the only difference between me and those cats in Hollywood is that I write my own script.' Jimi H.

May 70. Track; (lp) **BACKTRACK:4 (shared with The WHO)**
May 70. Track; (lp) **BACKTRACK:8 (shared with The WHO**

– posthumous albums / singles (some exploitation), etc. –

Oct 70. London/ US= Capitol; (7") **THE BALLAD OF JIMI. / GLOOMY MONDAY (with 'CURTIS KNIGHT')**
Sep 70. Track; (lp)(c) **MONTEREY INTERNATIONAL POP FESTIVAL (live soundtrack)** [-] [16]
Oct 70. Track; (7"m) **VOODOO CHILE (SLIGHT RETURN). / HEY JOE / ALL ALONG THE WATCHTOWER** [1] [-]
Mar 71. Track; (lp)(c) **THE CRY OF LOVE** [2] [3]
– Freedom / Drifting / Ezy rider / Night bird flying / My friend / Straight ahead / Astro man / Angel / In from the storm / Belly button window. *(re-iss.Jun73 & Sep85, cd-iss.Mar89, re-+cd.Jul91 on 'Polydor')(re-iss.cd+c Mar93)*
Apr 71. Track; (7") **NIGHT BIRD FLYING. / FREEDOM** [ ] [-]
Apr 71. Reprise; (7") **FREEDOM. / ANGEL** [-] [59]
Oct 71. Reprise; (7") **DOLLY DAGGER. / STAR SPANGLED BANNER** [-] [74]
Oct 71. Track; (7"ep) **GYPSY EYES. / REMEMBER / PURPLE HAZE / STONE FREE** [35] [ ]
Note; All below releases on 'Polydor' were issued on 'Reprise' US.
Nov 71. Polydor; (lp)(c) **JIMI HENDRIX AT THE ISLE OF WIGHT (live)** [17] [ ]
– Midnight lightning / Foxy lady / Lover man / Freedom / All along the watchtower / In from the storm. *(re-iss.Apr84, re+cd.Mar89 & Jul91) (re-iss.cd+c Mar93)*
Jan 72. Polydor; (lp)(c) **HENDRIX IN THE WEST (live)** [7] [12]
– Johnny B.Goode / Lover man / Blue suede shoes / Voodoo chile (slight return) / The queen / Sergeant Pepper's lonely hearts club band / Little wing / Red house.
Jan 72. Reprise; (7") **JOHNNY BE GOODE. / LOVERMAN** [-] [ ]
Feb 72. Polydor; (7") **JOHNNY B. GOODE. / LITTLE WING** [35] [-]
May 72. Reprise; (7") **LITTLE WING. / THE WIND CRIES MARY** [-] [ ]
Nov 72. Polydor; (lp)(c) **WAR HEROES** [23] [48]
– Bleeding heart / Highway chile / Tax free / Peter Gunn / Catastrophe / Stepping stone / Midnight / 3 little bears / Beginning / Izabella. *(re-iss.Aug83 on 'Polydor') (cd-iss.Mar89, & re-iss.+cd.Jul91) (re-iss.cd+c Mar93)*
Oct 73. Polydor; (d-lp)(c) **ARE YOU EXPERIENCED / AXIS: BOLD AS LOVE**

Feb 74. Polydor; (lp)(c) **LOOSE ENDS** [ ] [-]
– Come down hard on me / Blue suede shoes / Jam 292 / The stars that play with laughing Sam's dice / Drifter's escape / Hoochie koochie man / (Have you ever been to) Electric Ladyland. *(cd-iss.Mar89)*
Mar 75. Polydor; (lp) **JIMI HENDRIX 'Flashback'** [35] [ ]
Sep 75. Polydor; (lp)(c) **CRASH LANDING** [35] [5] Mar 75
– Message to love / Somewhere over the rainbow / Crash landing / Coming down hard on me / Peace in Mississippi / With the power / Stone free again / Captain Coconut. *(re-iss.Mar85) (cd-iss.Mar89) (re-+cd.Jun91)(re-iss.cd+c Mar93)*
Nov 75. Polydor; (lp)(c) **MIDNIGHT LIGHTNING** [46] [43]
– Trashman / Midnight lightning / Hear my train a-coming / Gypsy boy / Blue suede shoes / Machine gun / Once I had a woman / Beginnings. *(re-iss.+cd.Mar89)*
Oct 76. Polydor; (lp) **JIMI HENDRIX VOL.2 'Flashback'**
Jul 78. Polydor; (d-lp)(d-c) **THE ESSENTIAL JIMI HENDRIX**
(with free one-sided 33rpm 7" **GLORIA.**
Jun 80. Polydor; (lp)(c) **NINE TO THE UNIVERSE**
Jun 80. Polydor; (lp)(c) **STONE FREE**
(re-iss.Nov83)
Sep 80. Polydor; (7") **VOODOO CHILE. / GLORIA**
Sep 80. Polydor; (6x7"-box) **6 SINGLES BOXED (1st 6)**
Sep 80. Polydor; (12xlp) **10th ANNIVERSARY BOXED SET**
Jan 81. Polydor; (lp)(c) **ESSENTIAL JIMI HENDRIX VOLUME 2** Aug 79
Nov 81. Polydor; (12"ep) **ALL ALONG THE WATCHTOWER. / FOXY LADY / PURPLE HAZE / MANIC DEPRESSION**
Jun 82. Polydor; (lp)(c) **VOODOO CHILE**
(re-iss.Nov83)
Sep 82. Polydor; (12"ep) **VOODOO CHILE. / GIPSY EYES / HEY JOE / 3RD STONE FROM THE SUN**
Feb 83. Polydor; (d-lp)(c) **SINGLES ALBUM** [77] [ ]
Jun 83. Polydor; (d-c) **CRASH LANDING / MIDNIGHT LIGHTNING**
Nov 84. Polydor; (lp)(c)(cd) **KISS THE SKY**
(re-iss.+cd.Jun91)(re-iss.cd+c Mar93)
Feb 86. Polydor; (lp)(c)(cd) **JIMI PLAYS MONTEREY (live)**
(re-iss.+cd.Jun91) (re-iss.cd+c Mar93)
Jul 87. Polydor; (lp)(c)(cd) **LIVE AT WINTERLAND (live)**
(re-iss.+cd.Jun91)(re-iss.cd+c Mar93)
Jan 89. Polydor; (7") **PURPLE HAZE. / 51ST ANNIVERSARY**
(12"+=) – All along the watchtower.
(cd-s+=) – Hey Joe.
1989. Polydor; (4xcd-box) **BOXED SET**
– ARE YOU EXPERIENCED? / WAR HEROES / IN THE WEST / BAND OF GYPSIES
Mar 90. Polydor; (7") **CROSSTOWN TRAFFIC. / PURPLE HAZE** [61] [ ]
(12"+=) – All along the watchtower.
(cd-s++=) – Hey Joe.
1990. Polydor; (cd) **THE JIMI HENDRIX EXPERIENCE**
Oct 90. Polydor; (cd)(c)(lp) **CORNERSTONES (1967-1970, FOUR YEARS THAT CHANGED THE MUSIC)** [5] [ ]
– Hey Joe / Foxy lady / Purple haze / The wind cries Mary / Have you ever been to

(Electric Ladyland) / Crosstown traffic / All along the watchtower / Voodoo chile (slight return) / Star spangled banner / Stepping stone / Room full of mirrors / Ezy rider / Freedom / Drifting / In from the storm / Angel. *(cd+c+=)* Fire (live) / Stone free (live).

Oct 90. Polydor; (7"m) **ALL ALONG THE WATCHTOWER. / VOODOO CHILE / HEY JOE** 52
(12"+=)(c-s+=) – Crosstown traffic.

Feb 91. Polydor; (4xcd-box) **SESSIONS BOX – ARE YOU EXPERIENCED? / AXIS: BOLD AS LOVE / ELECTRIC LADYLAND / CRY OF LOVE**

Mar 91. Polydor; (4xcd-box) **FOOTLIGHTS**
– JIMI PLAYS MONTEREY / ISLE OF WIGHT / BAND OF GYPSIES / LIVE AT WINTERLAND

Feb 92. Polydor; (4xcd-box) **STAGES (live)**
– (Stockholm 5 Sep'67 / Paris 29 Jan'68 / San Diego 24 May'69 / Atlanta 4 Jul'70)

Jul 93. Polydor; (cd)(c) **THE ULTIMATE EXPERIENCE** 28 72
– All along the watchtower / Purple haze / Hey Joe / The wind cries Mary / Angel / Voodoo chile (slight return) / Foxy lady / Burning of the midnight lamp / Highway chile / Crosstown traffic / Castles made of sand / Long hot summer night / Red house / Manic depression / Gypsy eyes / Little wing / Fire / Wait until tomorrow / Star spangled banner (live) / Wild thing (live). *(re-iss.Sep95)*

Nov 92. Polygram; (cd) **THE ULTIMATE COLLECTION** 25

Feb 94. I.T.M.; (cd) **PURPLE HAZE IN WOODSTOCK (live)**

Apr 94. Pulsar; (3xcd) **GREATEST HITS** -

Apr 94. Polydor/ US= M.C.A.; (cd)(c) **BLUES** 10 45

Aug 94. Polydor/ US= M.C.A.; (cd)(c) **WOODSTOCK (live)** 32 37

May 94. Ramble Tamble; (cd) **LIVE AT THE 'SCENE' CLUB N.Y., N.Y. (live)** -

Aug 94. Charly; (cd) **BEFORE THE EXPERIENCE** -

Oct 94. Charly; (cd) **THE EARLY YEARS** -

Oct 70. R.C.A.; (7") **NO SUCH ANIMAL (Pt.1). / (Pt.2) (with 'CURTIS KNIGHT')**

Apr 71. Saga; (lp)(c) **JIMI HENDRIX**

1972. Saga; (lp) **JIMI HENDRIX AT HIS BEST VOL.1**

1972. Saga; (lp) **JIMI HENDRIX AT HIS BEST VOL.2**

1972. Saga; (lp) **JIMI HENDRIX AT HIS BEST VOL.3**

Apr 71. Hallmark; (lp) **THE ETERNAL FIRE OF JIMI HENDRIX (with 'CURTIS KNIGHT')**

1973. Hallmark; (lp) **THE WILD ONE (with 'CURTIS KNIGHT')** -

Aug 71. Ember; (lp)(c) **EXPERIENCE** 9 -
– (opening jam) / Room full of mirrors / C-blues / Smashing of amps.
(re-iss.Sep79 on 'Bulldog', cd-iss.Jan87) (cd-iss.Mar95 on 'Nectar')

1972. Ember; (lp)(c) **MORE EXPERIENCE** -
(re-iss.Sep79 & Jul82 on 'Bulldog')

Sep 73. Ember; (lp) **LOOKING BACK WITH JIMI HENDRIX**

Oct 73. Ember; (lp) **IN THE BEGINNING**
(re-iss.'84 on 'Premier')

1974. Ember; (lp) **FRIENDS FROM THE BEGINNING (with 'LITTLE RICHARD')**

(re-iss.Jan77)

Nov 71. Reprise; (lp)(c) **RAINBOW BRIDGE (soundtrack)** 16 15 Oct 71
– Dolly dagger / Earth blues / Pali gap / Room full of mirrors / Star spangled banner / Look over yonder / Hear my train a-comin' / Hey baby. *(cd-iss.Mar87)*

Jun 73. Reprise; (7") **HEAR MY TRAIN A-COMIN'. / ROCK ME BABY**

Jul 73. Reprise; (d-lp)(c) **SOUNDTRACK RECORDINGS FROM THE FILM 'JIMI'** 37

Jun 82. Reprise; (7") **FIRE. / LITTLE WING** -

1972. M.F.P.; (lp) **WHAT'D I SAY** -

Sep 84. M.F.P.; (lp) **THE BIRTH OF SUCCESS** -

Nov 72. Enterprise; (lp) **RARE HENDRIX**

Dec 72. Enterprise; (lp) **JIMI HENDRIX IN SESSION**

1973. Enterprise; (lp) **HENDRIX '66**

1973. Boulevard; (lp) **JIMI HENDRIX 1964** -

Nov 75. D.J.M.; (lp)(c) **FOR REAL**
(re-iss.Feb82 on 'Audio Fidelity')

Aug 79. Bulldog/ US= Douglas; (lp) **GOLDEN PIECES OF JIMI HENDRIX**
(re-iss.Dec82)

Sep 79. Bulldog/ US= Douglas; (lp) **MORE ESSENTIAL**

Nov 80. Red Lightnin'; (lp) **WOKE UP THIS MORNING AND FOUND MYSELF DEAD** -
(cd-iss.Nov86) (pic-lp.Oct88)

Jun 81. Audio Fidelity; (lp)(c) **COSMIC TURNAROUND** -

Oct 81. Audio Fidelity; (4xlp) **THE GENIUS OF HENDRIX** -

Mar 82. Audio Fidelity; (lp) **HIGH, LIVE AND DIRTY** -

Oct 84. Audio Fidelity; (c) **JIMI HENDRIX VOL.1** -

Oct 84. Audio Fidelity; (c) **JIMI HENDRIX VOL.2** -

Oct 84. Audio Fidelity; (c) **JIMI HENDRIX VOL.3** -

Nov 81. Phoenix; (lp) **FREE SPIRIT**
(re-iss.Jun87 on 'Thunderb.')

Sep 82. Phoenix; (lp) **MOODS** -

Sep 82. Phoenix; (lp) **ROOTS OF HENDRIX** -

Aug 82. C.B.S./ US= Eprise; (d-lp)(c) **THE JIMI HENDRIX CONCERTS (live)** 16 79
– Fire / I don't live today / Red house / Stone free / Are you experienced? / Little wing / Voodoo chile (slight return) / Bleeding heart / Hey Joe / Wild thing / Hear

my train a-comin'. *(re-iss.Sep84) (re-iss.+cd.Aug89 on 'Media Motion')*

Aug 82. C.B.S.; (7")(12") **FIRE (live). / ARE YOU EXPERIENCED (live)**

Oct 82. Dakota; (lp)(c) **THE BEST OF JIMI HENDRIX** -

Nov 83. Contour; (lp) **THE JIMI HENDRIX ALBUM** -

Jul 84. Old Gold; (7") **PURPLE HAZE. / THE WIND CRIES MARY** -

Jul 84. Old Gold; (7") **VOODOO CHILE (SLIGHT RETURN). / BURNING OF THE MIDNIGHT LAMP** -

Jul 84. Old Gold; (7") **ALL ALONG THE WATCHTOWER. / FOXY LADY** -

Jul 85. Topline; (lp)(c) **GANGSTER OF LOVE** -

Apr 86. Arcade; (lp)(c) **THE LEGEND** -
(re-iss.Dec88)

May 86. Sierra; (lp)(c) **REPLAY OF JIMI HENDRIX** -

Aug 86. Fame-EMI; (lp)(c) **JOHNNY B. GOODE** -

May 87. E.M.I.; (cd) **THE BEST OF JIMI HENDRIX** -

May 88. Big Time; (cd) **16 GREAT CLASSICS** -

Jun 88. Thunderbolt; (cd) **VOICES IN THE WIND** -

Apr 90. Thunderbolt; (cd)(c)(lp) **NIGHT LIFE** -

Nov 88. Strange Fruit; (12"ep) **THE PEEL SESSIONS**
– Radio One theme / Day tripper / Wait until tomorrow / Hear my train a'comin' / Spanish castle magic.

Feb 89. Castle/ US= Rykodisc; (d-lp)(c)(cd) **THE RADIO ONE SESSIONS** 30
– Stone free / Radio one theme / Day tripper / Killing floor / Love or confusion / Catfish blues / Drivin' south / Wait until tomorrow / Hear my train a-comin' / Hound dog / Fire / Hoochie coochie man / Purple haze / Spanish castle magic / Hey Joe / Foxy lady / The burning of the midnight lamp.

Nov 89. Castle/ US= Rykodisc; (lp)(c)(cd) **LIVE AND UNRELEASED – THE RADIO SHOWS**

Feb 89. Koine; (cd) **JAM SESSIONS** -

Jan 90. Zeta; (cd) **THE LAST EXPERIENCE CONCERT (live)** -

Dec 90. Discussion; (pic-lp) **WELL I STAND NEXT TO A MOUNTAIN** -

Feb 91. Action Replay; (lp) **THE BEST & THE REST OF . . .** -

Dec 91. U.F.O.; (cd)(lp) **IN 1967 (free w/booklet)**

Nov 92. East West; (7")(c-s) **THE WIND CRIES MARY. / FIRE**
(12"+=)(cd-s+=) – Foxy lady / May this be love

Dec 92. Univibes; (cd) **CALLING LONG DISTANCE**

Apr 93. Deja Vu; (cd)(c) **THE GOLD COLLECTION** -
(re-iss.Jun95)

Apr 93. Pulsar; (cd) **HIS FINAL LIVE PERFORMANCE (live)** -

Sep 93. I.T.M.; (cd) **JIMI HENDRIX AT THE MONTEREY POP FESTIVAL, 1967 (live)**

Dec 93. Entertainers; (cd) **FIRE** -

Jan 95. Collection; (cd) **THE COLLECTION** -

Mar 95. Top Masters; (cd) **THE EARLY JIMI HENDRIX** -

Apr 95. Muskateer; (cd)(c) **LIVE IN NEW YORK** -

Apr 95. Polydor; (cd)(c) **VOODOO SOUP** 66
– The new rising sun / Belly button window / Stepping stone / Freedom / Angel / Room full of mirrors / Midnight / Night bird flying / Drifting / Ezy rider / Pali gap / Mesage to love / Peace in Mississippi / In from the storm.

May 95. Thunderbolt; (cd) **NIGHT LIFE** -

Jun 95. Receiver; (cd) **SUNSHINE OF YOUR LOVE** -

Aug 95. Voiceprint; (cd) **SUPERSESSION** -

Sep 95. Strawberry; (cd) **THE LAST EXPERIENCE** -

Nov 95. The Collection; (cd) **GREATEST HITS** -

Ken HENSLEY (see under ⇒ URIAH HEEP)

Mike HERON (see under ⇒ INCREDIBLE STRING BAND)

Kirsten HERSH (see under ⇒ THROWING MUSES)

HE SAID (see under ⇒ WIRE)

HEX (see under ⇒ CHURCH)

John HIATT

Born: 1952, Indianapolis, Indiana, USA. He became a staff songwriter for a Nashville publishing house, where he had songs covered by THREE DOG NIGHT + CONWAY TWITTY (Heavy Tears; which was a country No.1). He then was given the opportunity (he now wishes he wasn't) to record 2 demo-like albums for producer NORMAN PUTNAM, which saw light of day in the mid-70's. In 1978 he was given another chance by 'MCA', who delivered the critically acclaimed 'SLUG LINE' & 'TWO BIT MONSTERS'. His songs were now being used by the likes of RICK NELSON, DAVE EDMUNDS, MARIA MULDAUR and film soundtracks! 'American Gigolo' and 'Cruising'. Around this healthy early 80's period, he struck up a friendship with RY COODER and played on 2 of his albums 'Borderline' & 'The Slide Area', during a tour. In 1982 he moved to 'Geffen', where he released TONY VISCONTI produced album 'ALL OF A SUDDEN'. In the mid-80's, he found another English friend in NICK LOWE, whom he swapped guest spots on both their albums from that time. In 1987 now for 'A&M', he had his first solo chart appearance with near 100 breaker album 'BRING THE FAMILY', which included LOWE, COODER and JIM KELTNER, who were all later to become (in 1992) supertroubs LITTLE VILLAGE. • **Style:** Much lawded country-tinged rock singer, who ventured into new heavy and funky territory on 1986's 'WARMING UP TO THE ICE-AGE'. Well at least on one track; The Detroit Spinners cover:- LIVING A LITTLE, LAUGHING A LITTLE (a duet with other English friend ELVIS COSTELLO). • **Songwriters:** Sel-penned numbers except several covers. • **Trivia:** He guested on albums by RY COODER and LOS LOBOS. His 1982 album was produced by TONY VISCONTI.

Recommended: Y'ALL CAUGHT (*6) / WARMING UP TO THE ICE AGE (*7)

JOHN HIATT – vocals, guitar with many on session incl. **SHANE KEISTER** – keyboards

not issued Epic

1973. (7") **BOULEVARD AIN'T SO BAD. / WE MAKE SPIRIT** -

1974. (lp) **HANGIN' AROUND THE OBSERVATORY** -
– Maybe baby, say you do / Whistles in my ears / Sure as I'm sittin' here / Rose / Hangin' around the observatory / Full Moon / Wild-eyed gypsies / It's alright with me / Little blue song for you / Ocean. *(cd-iss.Jun94 on 'Sony Europe')*

1974. (7") **SURE AS I'M SITTIN' HERE. / OCEAN** -

1974. (7") **FULL MOON. / HANGIN' ROUND THE OBSERVATORY** -

1975. (7") **MOTORBOAT TO HEAVEN. / DOWN HOME (KEEP ON FALLIN')** -

1975. (lp) **OVERCOATS** -
– One more time / Smiling in the rain / I'm tired of your stuff / Distance / Down home / Overcoats / I want your love inside of me / I killed an ant with my guitar / Motorboat to Heaven / The lady of the night. *(cd-iss.Jun94 on 'Sony Europe')*

M.C.A. M.C.A.

Jun 79. (7") **SHARON'S GOT A DRUGSTORE. / RADIO GIRL** -

Aug 79. (lp)(c) **SLUG LINE**
– You used to kiss the girls / The negroes were dancing / Slug line / Madonna road / (No more) Dancin' in the street / Long night / The night that Kenny died / Radio girl / You're my love interest / Take off your uniform / Sharon's got a drugstore / Washable ink.

Aug 79. (7") **SLUG LINE. / MADONNA ROAD** -

—— now w / **SHANE KEISTER** – keyboards / **HOWARD EPSTEIN** – bass / **DARYL VERDUSCO** – drums

May 80. (7") **I SPY (FOR THE F.B.I.). / IT HASN'T HAPPENED YET** -

Aug 80. (7") **I SPY (FOR THE F.B.I.). / GOOD GIRL, BAD WORLD** -

Oct 80. (lp)(c) **TWO BIT MONSTERS**
– Back to normal / Down in front / I spy (for the F.B.I.) / Pink bedroom / Good girl, bad world / Face the nation / Cop party / Back to the war / It hasn't happened yet / String pull job / New numbers.

Oct 80. (7") **BACK TO THE WAR. /**

Feb 81. (7") **BACK TO NORMAL. / STRING PULL JOB**

—— **JESSE HARMS** – keyboards + **JAMES ROLLESTON** – bass repl. KEISTER + EPSTEIN

Apr 82. (7") **LOOK FOR LOVE. / TAKE TIME TO KNOW HER** -

Geffen Geffen

Apr 82. (lp)(c) **ALL OF A SUDDEN**
– I look for love / The secret life / Overnight story / Forever yours / Some fun now / The walking dead / I could use an angel / Getting excited / Doll hospital / Something happens / Marianne / My edge of the razor.

—— now w / **MARTIN BELMONT** – guitar / **PAUL CARRACK** – keyboards / **NICK LOWE** – bass, vocals / **SCOTT MATTHEWS** – drums, bass, sax, guitar / **BOBBY IRWIN** – drums

Feb 84. (7") **SHE LOVES THE JERK. / LOVE LIKE BLOOD**

Apr 84. (lp)(c) **RIDING WITH THE KING**
– I don't even try / Death by misadventure / Girl on a string / Lovers will / She loves the jerk / Say it with flowers / Riding with the king / You may already be a winner / Love like blood / Love that harms / Book lovers / Falling up. *(re-iss.cd May91 + Apr92)*

—— now w / **RANDY McCORMICK** – keyboards / **JESSE BOYCE** – bass / **LARRIE LONDON** – drums

Jan 85. (7") **SHE SAID THE SAME THINGS TO ME. / SHE LOVES THE JERK / SOMETHING HAPPENS**

May 85. (7") **LIVING A LITTLE, LAUGHING A LITTLE. / I'M A REAL MAN**
(12"+=) – When we ran / Everybody's girl.

Apr 86. (7") **THIS IS YOUR DAY. / SNAKE CHARMER** -
(above was issued US on 'Atlantic')

Sep 86. (lp)(c)(cd) **WARMING UP TO THE ICE AGE**
– The usual / Crush / When we ran / She said the same things to me / Living a little, laughing a little / Zero house / Warming up to the ice age / I'm a real man / Number one honest game / I got a gun. *(re-iss.cd May91 + Apr92)*

—— now w / **RY COODER** – guitar, vocals / **NICK LOWE** – bass, vocals / **JIM KELTNER** – drums

Demon A & M

May 87. (7") **THANK YOU GIRL. / MY GIRL** -

May 87. (lp)(c)(cd) **BRING THE FAMILY**
– Memphis in the meantime / Alone in the dark / A thing called love / Lipstick sunset / Have a little faith in me / Thank you girl / Tip of my tongue / Your dad did / Stood up / Learning how to love you.

Jul 87. (7") **THANK YOU GIRL. / LIPSTICK SUNSET** -

Oct 87. (7") **HAVE A LITTLE FAITH IN ME. / THANK YOU GIRL** -

—— now w / **BERNIE LEADON** – guitar, mandolin, banjo / **DAVID RANSON** – bass / **SONNY LANDRETH** – steel guitar / **KEN BLEVINS** – drums / **JAMES HOOKER** – organ

A & M A & M

Aug 88. (7") **SLOW TURNING. / YOUR DAD DID (live)** -

Aug 88. (lp)(c)(cd) **SLOW TURNING** 98
– Drive south / Trudy and Dave / Tennessee plates / Icy blue heart / Sometime other than now / Georgia Rae / Ride along / Slow turning / It'll come to you / Is anybody there? / Paper thin / Feels like rain.

Oct 88. (7") **SLOW TURNING. / IS ANYBODY THERE?** -
(12"+=) – Already love.

Feb 89. (7") **TENNESSEE PLATES. / GEORGIA RAE (live)**
(12"+=) – Thank you girl (live).

Jun 90. (cd)(c)(lp) **STOLEN MOMENTS** 72 61

– A real fine love / Seven little Indians / Child of the wild blue yonder / Back of my mind / Stolen moments / Bring back your love to me / The rest of the dream / Thirty years of tears / Rock back Billy / Listening to old voices / Through your hands / One kiss. *(re-iss.May95)*

Jul 90. (7") **A REAL FINE LOVE. / JUST ENOUGH ASLAND CITY**
(12"+=)(cd-s+=) – Feels like rain.

— In 1992, he joined LITTLE VILLAGE with NICK LOWE, JIM KELTNER + RY COODER.solo (vocals, guitar, piano, organ) again w / **MATT WALLACE** – guitar / **MICHAEL WARD** – lead guitar / **JOHN PIERCE** – bass / **BRIAN MacLEOD** – drums, percussion / **RAVI OLI** – electric sitar

Sep 93. (cd)(c) **PERFECTLY GOOD GUITAR** 67 47
– Something wild / Straight outta time / Perfectly good guitar / Buffalo River home / Angel / Blue telescope / Cross my fingers / Old habits / The wreck of the Barbie Ferrari / When you hold me tight / Permanent hurt / Loving a hurricane / I'll never get over you.

Oct 93. (7")(c-s) **ANGEL. / LITTLE GOODNIGHT**
(cd-s+=) – Drive south / I'll never get over you.

Dec 94. (cd)(c) **HIATT COMES ALIVE AT THE BUDOKAN (live)**

Capitol Capitol

Oct 95. (c-s) **CRY LOVE / THE OTHER SIDE / TWENTY ONE**
(cd-s+=) – Your love is my rent.

Nov 95. (cd)(c) **WALK ON** 74 48
– Cry love / You must go / Walk on / Good as she could be / The river knows your name / Native son / Dust down a country road / Ethylene / I can't wait / Shedding the document / Wrote it down and burned it / Your love is my rest / Friend of mine / Mile high.

– compilations, etc. –

Sep 89. Geffen; (lp)(c)(cd) **Y'ALL CAUGHT?**
– The crush / She said the same things to me / Love like blood / Slug line / She loves the jerk / My edge of the razor / Pink bedroom / It hasn't happened yet / Radio girl / I look for love / Washable ink / Riding with the King / When we ran.

Jul 93. B.G.O.; (cd) **SLUG LINE / TWO BIT MONSTERS** -

HIGH

Formed: Manchester, England ... 1990 by ANDY COUZENS and CHRIS GOODWIN. Quickly gained contract on 'London', but flopped with debut 45 'BOX SET GO', although when re-issued early '91, it made Top 30. Their early promise, failed to impress buying public in '92, when 2nd album 'HYPE' failed. • **Style:** Melodic and psychedelic rave outfit, too near the sound of The LA's, STONE ROSES or even The BYRDS. • **Songwriters:** Group penned.

Recommended: SOMEWHERE SOON (*6).

JOHN MATTHEWS (b.23 Sep'67, Torquay, Devon, England) – vocals / **ANDY COUZENS** (b.15 Jul'65) – guitar (ex-STONE ROSES, ex-BUZZCOCKS FOC) / **SIMON DAVY** (b.24 Jan'67) – bass / **CHRIS GOODWIN** (b.10 Aug'65) – drums (ex-BUZZCOCKS FOC, ex-INSPIRAL CARPETS)

London London

Jun 90. (7")(c-s) **BOX SET GO. / P.W.A.** -
(12"+=)(cd-s+=) – ('B'instrumental).

Aug 90. (7") **UP AND DOWN. / MAKE IT HAPPEN** 53
(12"+=)(cd-s+=) – ('A'Bombay mix).

Oct 90. (7")(c-s) **TAKE YOUR TIME. / ('A'Bombay mix-live)** 56
(12"+=)(cd-s+=) – ('A'extended).
(12"+=) – Box set go / A minor turn.

Oct 90. (cd)(c)(lp) **SOMEWHERE SOON** 59
– Box set go / Take your time / This is my world / Rather be Marsane / So I can see / A minor turn / Dreams of Dinesh / Up and down / P.W.A. / Somewhere soon.

Jan 91. (7") **BOX SET GO. / P.W.A.** 28
(12")(cd-s) – ('A'side) / ('A'original) / Up & down / This is my world.

Mar 91. (7")(c-s) **MORE ... / 4.30 / MAKE IT HAPPEN** 67
(12"+=)(cd-s+=) – Blue tourist.
(10"+=) – More madness.

Aug 92. (7") **BETTER LEFT UNTOLD. / HICKORY SMOKE**
(12"+=)(cd-s+=) – Joustabout.

Sep 92. (cd)(c)(lp) **HYPE**
– Better left untold / The healer / Sweet liberty / This is your life / Let nothing come between us / Goodbye girl / Keep on coming / Slowly happens here / Can I be / Lost and found.

Feb 93. (12"ep)(cd-ep) **SWEET LIBERTY. / THIS IS YOUR LIFE / BETTER LEFT UNTOLD**

Steve HILLAGE

Born: 2 Aug'51, London, England. While at school he joined URIEL for six months early 1968. They became EGG after his departure to university, and made 2 albums in the early 70's. One of them, 'ARACHEZ' issued on 'Evoluton', is now worth over £200. In Spring 1971 he formed KHAN, and after one album in 1972, he played live with KEVIN AYERS BAND. In 1973, HILLAGE joined and then became leader of GONG, until his departure to a solo career in 1975 with girlfriend MIQUETTE GIRAUDY. Sticking with Richard Branson's 'Virgin' records, he gained semi-success with albums throughout the 70's. • **Style:** Experimental quasi-psychedelia that leant on the extreme avant-garde, mixed with sense of rock feel. • **Songwriters:** Himself, except NOT FADE AWAY (Buddy Holly) / HURDY GURDY MAN (Donovan) / IT'S ALL TOO MUCH + GETTING BETTER (Beatles). In SYSTEM & he co-writes w/ GIRAUDY. • **Trivia:** TODD RUNDGREN produced 2nd lp 'L'.

Recommended: LIVE HERALD (*7) / SYSTEM 7 (*6) / FISH RISING (*6)

KHAN

STEVE HILLAGE – guitar, vocals (ex-GONG, ex-URIEL, ex-KHAN) / **DICK HENNINGHAM** – organ (ex-ARTHUR BROWN) / **NICK GREENWODD** – bass (ex-ARTHUR BROWN) / **ERIC PEACHEY** – drums

Deram P.V.C.

May 72. (lp) **SPACE SHANTY** - 1978
– Space shanty / Stranded effervescent psychonovelty No.5 / Mixed up man of the mountains / Driving to Amsterdam / Stargazers / Hollow stone escape of the space pirates. *(re-iss.Feb77) (cd-iss 1991 on 'Mantra' FRANCE)*

— **DAVE STEWART** – organ (ex-EGG, ex-URIEL) repl. HENNINGHAM / **NIGEL SMITH** – bass repl. GREENWOOD. (DAVE moved to HATFIELD + THE NORTH) Late 1972, HILLAGE joined KEVIN AYERS Band on tour. In 1973, he joined GONG making 3 lp's **FLYING TEAPOT** (1973), **ANGEL'S EYES** (1973), **YOU** (1974). He guested for EGG on their Nov74 album 'THE CIVIL SURFACE'.

STEVE HILLAGE

went solo with some GONG members.

Virgin Atlantic

Apr 75. (lp)(c) **FISH RISING** 33
– Solar musick suite:- (i) Sun song – (ii) Canterbury sunrise – (iii) Hiram afterglid meets the Dervish – (iv) Sun song (reprise) / Fish / Meditation of the snake / The salmon song:- (i) Salmon pool – (ii) Solomon's Atlantis – (iii) Swimming with the salmon – (iv) King of the fishes / Afterglid:- (i) Sun moon surfing – (ii) Great wave and the boat of Hermes – (iii) The silver ladder – (iv) Astral meadows – (v) The Lafta yoga song – (vi) Gliding – (vii) Golden vibe – the outglid. *(re-iss.Mar84) (cd-iss.Jun87)*

— Next used TODD RUNDGREN'S UTOPIA as backing with others.

Sep 76. (lp)(c) **L** 10
– Hurdy gurdy man / Hurdy gurdy glissando / Electrick gypsies / Om nama Shivaya / Luna musick suite / It's all too much. *(re-iss.Mar84) (cd-iss.Jun87)*

Oct 76. (7") **IT'S ALL TOO MUCH. / SHIMMER**

Feb 77. (7") **HURDY GURDY MAN. / OM NAMA SHIVAYA**

Sep 77. (lp)(c) **MOTIVATION RADIO** 28
– Mellow dawn / Motivation / Light in the sky / Radio / Wait one moment / Saucer surfing / Searching for the spark / Ovtave doctors / Not fade away (glide forever). *(re-iss.Mar84) (cd-iss.Jun88)*

Dec 77. (7") **NOT FADE AWAY (GLIDE FOREVER). / SAUCER SURFING**

Apr 78. (lp)(c)(green-lp) **GREEN** 30 -
– Sea nature / Ether ships / Musick of the trees / Palm trees (love guitar) / Unidentified (flying being) / U.F.O. over Paris / Leyliness to Glassdom / Crystal city / Activation meditation / The glorious om riff. *(re-iss.Mar84) (cd-iss.Jun90)*

May 78. (7") **GETTING BETTER. / PALM TREES (LOVE GUITAR)**

Feb 79. (d-lp)(c) **LIVE HERALD (live)** 54 -
– The salmon song / The Dervish riff / Castle in the clouds / Hurdy gurdy man / Light in the sky / Searching for the spark / Electrick gypsies / Radiom / Lunar musick suite / Meditation of the dragon / It's all too much / The golden vibe / Talking to the sun / 1988 aktivator / New age synthesis (unzipping the zype) / Healing feeling. *(cd-iss.Jun90, omits side 4)*

Apr 79. (lp)(c)(clear-lp) **RAINBOW DOME MUSICK** 52 -
– Garden of Paradise / Four ever rainbow. *(re-iss black vinyl 1984)*

Sep 79. (lp)(c) **OPEN** 71 -
– Day after day / Getting in tune / Open / Definite activity / Don't dither, do it / The fire inside / Earthrise. *(re-iss.Mar84) (cd-iss.Jun90 as "OPEN FEATURING STUDIO HERALD")*

Nov 79. (7") **DON'T DITHER, DO IT. / GETTING IN TUNE**

— Took time off for sessions, etc., until his return in 1982

Jan 83. (7")(12") **KAMIKAZE EYES. / BEFORE THE WORLD WAS MADE**

Feb 83. (lp)(c) **FOR TO NEXT** 48 -
– These uncharted lands / Kamikaze eyes / Alone / Anthems for the blind / Bright future / Frame by frame / Waiting / Glory. *(free instrumental-lp w/a 'AND NOT OR')* – Before the storm / Red Admiral / Serotonin / And not or / Knights templar / Still golden. *(re-iss.Aug88) (cd-iss.Jul90 with free album) (cd-iss.Mar94)*

Apr 83. (7") **ALONE. / FRAME BY FRAME** -
(12"+=) – Timelines.

— HILLAGE went more into production for SIMPLE MINDS, ROBYN HITCHCOCK, etc. In the 90's, he guested with ALEX PATERSON in The ORB and founded own ambient group SYSTEM 7.

– compilations, others, etc. –

1979. Virgin; (12"pic-ep) **SIX PACK** -
The salmon song / It's all too much / The golden vibe / Not fade away / Elektric gypsies / Radio.

1983 Aura; (lp) **AURA** -

Aug 92. Windsong; (cd) **BBC RADIO 1 LIVE IN CONCERT (live)** -

SYSTEM 7

STEVE HILLAGE – guitar / **with ALEX PATERSON** (Orb) / **YOUTH** / **DERRICK MAY** / **STEVE WADDINGTON** (Beloved) / **PAUL OAKENFIELD** / **MICK McNEIL** (ex-Simple Minds) / **MIQUETTE GIRAUDY** (ex-Gong) / **OLU ROWE** – vocals / **ZOE THRASH** (Orb) / **ANDY FALCONER** (engineer)

10-Virgin Virgin

Nov 90. (12"clear) **SUNBURST. / MIRACLE**

— now w/ **ANIFF COUSINS** (Chapter and the Verse) / + **MONDAY MICHIRU** – vocals

Sep 91. (cd)(c)(d-lp) **SYSTEM 7**
– Sunburst / Freedom fighters / Habibi / Altitude / Bon humeur / Fractal liaison / Dog / Thunderdog / Listen / Strange quotations / Miracle / Over and out

Oct 91. (12")(cd-s) **HABIBI. / MIRACLE**

Feb 92. (7")(12")(c-s)(cd-s) **FREEDOM FIGHTERS** (Robin Hancock mixes)

(12"clear+=)(pic-cd-s) ('A' version)
Jun 92. (cd)(c) **ALTITUDES** (8 mixes)

		Big Life	Big Life
Feb 93.	12") **7:7 EXPANSION**	39	

(12"ep)(cd-ep) – ('A' extended) / ('B' extended)

Feb 93. (cd)(c)(lp) **777** — 30
– 7:7 expansion / A cool dry place / Desir (ghost mix) / On the seventh night / Sinbad / Ship of the desert / Fay deau deau.
Jul 93. (12"ep)(cd-ep) **SINBAD. / QUEST**
Oct 94. (12"ep) **SIRENES. / ('A'-Marshall Jefferson mix) / ('A'-Laurent Garnier mix) / Coltrane (water mix)**
(cd-ep+=) – Alpha wave / Gliding in two-tone curves (water edit).
Oct 94. (cd)(c)(lp) **POINT 3: THE FIRE ALBUM**
– Sirenes / Alpha wave (water edit) / Mysterious traveler / Coltrane (remix) / Radiate / Overview / Gliding on duo-tone curves / Jupiter! / Dr.Livingstone I pressume / Batukau.
Oct 94. (cd)(c) **POINT 3: THE WATER ALBUM**
–
Apr 95. (12"ep)(cd-ep) **ALPHA WAVE (lastikman acid house mix). / ('A'-Alpha mix) / ('A'-That sound mix)**

Chris HILLMAN (see under ⇒ BYRDS)

HINDU LOVE GODS (see under ⇒ R.E.M.)

Jon HISEMAN (see under ⇒ COLOSSEUM)

Robyn HITCHCOCK (see under ⇒ SOFT BOYS)

Susanna HOFFS (see under ⇒ BANGLES)

HOLE

Formed: Los Angeles, USA ... late 1989 by COURTNEY LOVE and 6 foot 4 inch guitarist and Capitol records employee ERIC ERLANDSON. COURTNEY had played alongside JENIFER FINCH (L7) and KAT BJELLAND (Babes In Toyland), in a band called SUGAR BABY DOLL. Took their name HOLE from a line in Euripides' Medea. Placed an ad in local paper 'Flipside', and found a bassist and drummer. In Spring 1990, they released 'RAT BASTARD' EP, before moving to the Seattle area. Early the next year, 'Sub Pop' issued 'DICKNAIL' EP, before signing to 'Geffen', much to the dismay of MADONNA, who wanted her for 'Maverick'. Around the same time, her relationship with NIRVANA's KURT COBAIN, was being highlighted by music press. She had secretly married him in February '92, and soon gave birth to his child in August '92. 1993 saw their debut album 'PRETTY ON THE INSIDE' (produced by KIM GORDON and DON FLEMING) hit lower chart regions, and was voted album of the year by New York's Village Voice magazine. In Spring 1994, she celebrated a UK Top 20 album, but this was overshadowed by the untimely suicide of KURT on 8th April. She was to hold a memorial on the 10th, and hailing everyone there to call him an asshole. More press coverage followed, and more so on 16th June, when their new bassist KRISTIN PFAFF was found dead in her bath. It was believed to be an accidental drug related death. • **Style:** Grunge-rock fronted by wild child COURTNEY. Similiarities to BABES IN TOYLAND, LYDIA LUNCH or SONIC YOUTH (co-produced 1991 by KIM GORDON and DON FLEMING) • **Songwriters:** Group; except STAR BELLY which sampled DREAMS (Fleetwood Mac) + INTO THE BLACK (Neil Young). Covered; DO IT CLEAN (Echo & The Bunnymen) / CREDIT IN THE STRAIGHT WORLD (Young Marble Giants) / HUNGRY LIKE THE WOLF (Duran Duran) / SEASON OF THE WITCH (Donovan) / HE HIT ME (IT FELT LIKE A KISS) (hit; Crystals). 'I THINK THAT I WOULD DIE' was co-written w / KAT BJELLAND (Babes In Toyland). • **Miscellaneous:** After stints as an actress and a stripper, COURTNEY had a brief stint in FAITH NO MORE. In 1993, COURTNEY sued her doctor for allegedly disclosing her pregnancy details to the press.

Note: Not to be confused with band who released in the late 80's; OTHER TONGUES, OTHER FLESH (lp) and DYSKINSIA (12") both on 'Eyes Media'.

Recommended: PRETTY ON THE INSIDE (*8) / LIVE THROUGH THIS (*10).

COURTNEY LOVE – vocals, guitars / **ERIC ERLANDSON** – guitars / **JILL EMERY** – bass, vocals / **CAROLINE RUE** – drums

		not issued	Sympathy . . .
Apr 90.	(ep) **RETARD GIRL** – Rat bastard /	-	
		not issued	Sub Pop
Apr 91.	(7"grey)(7"green)(7"purple)(7"blue) **DICKNAIL. / BURNBLACK**	-	
		City Slang	Caroline
Aug 91.	(12"ep)(cd-ep) **TEENAGE WHORE. / DROWN SODA / BURN AND BLACK**		
Oct 91.	(cd)(c)(lp) **PRETTY ON THE INSIDE** – Teenage whore / Babydoll / Garbadge man / Sassy / Goodsister – bad sister / Mrs. Jones / Berry / Loaded / Star belly / Pretty on the inside / Clouds. *(re-iss.Sep95)*	59	

— **LESLEY** – bass repl. JILL / **PATTY SCHEMEL** – drums repl. CAROLINE

		City Slang	D.G.C.
Apr 93.	(7")(12")(c-s) **BEAUTIFUL SON. / 20 YEARS AT THE DAKOTA / OLD AGE** (cd-s+=) – Pale blue eyes (live).	54	-

— **KRISTEN PFAFF** – bass, piano, vocals repl. LESLEY

Mar 94.	(7"pink) **MISS WORLD. / ROCK STAR (alternate mix)** (cd-s+=) – Do it clean (live).	64	
Apr 94.	(cd)(c)(lp) **LIVE THROUGH THIS** – Violet / Miss World / Plump / Asking for it / Jennifer's body / Doll parts / Credit in the straight world / Softer, softest / She walks on me / I think that I would die / Gutless / Rock star. *(re-iss.cd/c Apr95)*	13	52

— KRISTEN was found dead in her bath 16th June 1994. COURTNEY, ERIC + PATTI continued and later recruited **MELISSA AUF DER MAUR** – bass

Apr 95.	(7") **DOLL PARTS. / THE VOID** (cd-s+=) – Hungry like the wolf. (cd-s) – ('A'side) / Credit in the straight world (live) / Plump (live) / I think that I would die (live).	16	58 Dec94
Jul 95.	(7"colrd)(c-s) **VIOLET. / HE HIT ME (IT FELT LIKE A KISS)** (cd-s+=) – Old age / Who's porno you burn (black). (7") – ('A'side) / Old age.	17	

— Back in the news again, COURTNEY was fined for assaulting BIKINI KILL's KATHLEEN HANNA.

HOLLIES

Formed: Manchester, England ... 1961 by ALLAN CLARKE and GRAHAM NASH, who quickly found DON RATHBONE and ERIC HAYCOCK.

In 1963, they signed to EMI's 'Parlophone' label, and added a 5th member TONY HICKS. Their debut 45 '(AIN'T THAT) JUST LIKE ME', made the UK Top 30, and was pursued by 'SEARCHIN'', their first of 21 consecutive Top 20 hits until 1971's 'LITTLE WILLY' failed to register. In Aug'71, CLARKE left for the first time, but returned in mid-73, when his Swedish replacement MICHAEL RICKFORS, failed to impress buying public. They immediately reinstated themselves, when a Top 30 hit, was followed by near No.1 smash 'THE AIR THAT I BREATHE'. Although future hits were few and far between, they plugged on throughout the 70's & 80's. • **Style:** Pop industry beat group, who went into near cabaret in 1968. They regained credibility late 1969 with 'HE AIN'T HEAVY' single. In the 70's, they opted for more country rock & pop feel. • **Songwriters:** CLARKE-HICKS-NASH, until latter's departure to CROSBY, STILLS & NASH. HOLLIES covered; (AIN'T THAT) JUST LIKE ME + SEARCHIN' (Coasters) / STAY (Maurice Williams & The Zodiacs) / JUST ONE LOOK (Doris Troy) / YES I WILL (Goffin-Titelman) / I'M ALIVE (Clint Ballard Jr.) / LOOK THROUGH ANY WINDOW + BUS STOP (Graham Gouldman) / IF I NEEDED SOMEONE (George Harrison; Beatles) / I CAN'T LET GO + THE BABY (Chip Taylor) / SORRY SUZANNE (T.MacAuley & G.Stephens) / GASOLINE ALLEY BRED (T.MacAuley-R.Cook-R.Greenaway) / WHEN THE SHIP COMES IN (Bob Dylan) / JESUS WAS A CROSSMAKER (Judee Sill) / SANDY (Bruce Springsteen) / STOP IN THE NAME OF LOVE (Supremes) / SOLDIER'S SONG (Mike Batt) / CARRIE (John Miles) / STAND BY ME (Ben E.King) / SHINE SILENTLY (Nils Lofgren) / etc. Also cover albums 'HOLLIES SING (Bob) DYLAN' and 'BUDDY HOLLY'. KENNY LYNCH collaborated on several with HICKS on 1971's 'DISTANT LIGHT'. • **Trivia:** In 1988 after exposure on Miller lite UK TV ad, the 1969 hit 'HE AIN'T HEAVY, HE'S MY BROTHER' re-charted, hitting No.1.

Recommended: THE AIR THAT I BREATHE (THE BEST OF THE HOLLIES) (*6).

ALLAN CLARKE (b. 5 Apr'42, Salford, Manchester, England) – vocals / **TONY HICKS** (b.16 Dec'43, Nelson, Lancashire, England) – lead guitar / **GRAHAM NASH** (b. 2 Feb'42, Blackpool, England) – guitar / **ERIC HAYDOCK** (b. 3 Feb'43) – bass / **DON RATHBONE** – drums

Parlophone Liberty

May 63. (7") **(AIN'T THAT) JUST LIKE ME. / HEY WHAT'S WRONG WITH ME** [25] [-]
Aug 63. (7") **SEARCHIN'. / WHOLE WORLD OVER** [12] [-]

— **BOBBY ELLIOTT** (b. 8 Dec'42, Burnley) – drums (ex-SHANE FENTON & THE FENTONES) repl. RATHBONE (still on next single b-side and album track – *)

Nov 63. (7") **STAY. / NOW'S THE TIME** [8] [ ] Mar 64
Jan 64. (lp) **STAY WITH THE HOLLIES** [2] [ ]
– Little lover * / Memphis / Talkin' 'bout you / It's only make believe / Rockin' Robin / Mr. Moonlight / You better move on / Watcha gonna do 'bout it / What king of girl are you / Candy man / What kind of boy. *(re-iss.Oct87 on 'B.G.O.', cd-iss.Oct88)*

Parlophone Imperial

Feb 64. (7") **JUST ONE LOOK. / KEEP OFF THAT FRIEND OF MINE** [2] [98] Apr 64
(US-iss.Sep67 reached 44)
May 64. (7") **HERE I GO AGAIN. / BABY THAT'S ALL** [4] [-]
Jul 64. (7") **HERE I GO AGAIN. / LUCILLE** [-] [ ]
Sep 64. (7") **WE'RE THROUGH. / COME ON BACK** [7] [ ] Oct 64
Nov 64. (lp) **IN THE HOLLIES STYLE** [ ] [-]
– The time for love / Don't you know / You'll be mine / It's in her kiss / Come on home / Set me free / Too much monkey business / I thought of you last night / Nitty gritty; something's got a hold of me. *(US title – 'BEAT GROUP') (UK re-iss.+cd.Mar88 on 'B.G.O.')*
Jan 65. (7") **(I'LL BE TRUE TO YOU) YES I WILL. / NOBODY** [9] [-]
May 65. (7") **I'M ALIVE. / YOU KNOW HE DID** [1] [-]
Aug 65. (7") **LOOK THROUGH ANY WINDOW. / SO LONELY** [4] [32] Nov 65
Sep 65. (lp) **THE HOLLIES** [8] [ ] Mid'66
– Put yourself in my place / When I come home to you / That's my desire / Mickey's monkey / Very last day / Down the line / Lawdy Miss Clawdy / You must believe me / Too many people / Fortune teller / I've been wrong. *(re-iss.Nov69 as 'REFLECTION' on 'Regal Star.') (re-iss.Jul88 on 'BGO')(cd-iss.Apr91 on 'BGO')*
Dec 65. (7") **IF I NEEDED SOMEONE. / I'VE GOT A WAY OF MY OWN** [20] [-]
Jan 66. (lp) **HEAR! HERE!** [-] [ ]
– I'm alive / Very last day / You must believe me / Put yourself in my place / Down the line / That's my desire / Look through any window / Lawdy Miss Clawdy / When I come home to you / Lonely / I've been wrong / Too many people.
Feb 66. (7") **I CAN'T LET GO. / I'VE GOT A WAY OF MY OWN** [2] [42] Mar 66
Jun 66. (lp) **WOULD YOU BELIEVE** [16] [75] Sep 66
– Stewball / Take your time / Don't you even care / Oriental sadness / I take what I want / Hard hard year / Fifi the flea / That's how strong my love is / I am a rock / Sweet little sixteen. *(US title – 'BUS STOP') (UK re-iss.Oct88 on 'B.G.O.', cd-iss.Apr91)*

— **BERNIE CALVERT** – bass repl. HAYDOCK who formed HAYDOCK'S ROADHOUSE **JOHN PAUL JONES** – bass sessioned on the next b-side. (Later to LED ZEPPELIN)

Jun 66. (7") **BUS STOP. / DON'T RUN AND HIDE** [5] [5] Jul 66
Oct 66. (7") **STOP! STOP! STOP!. / IT'S YOU** [2] [7]
Oct 66. (lp) **FOR CERTAIN BECAUSE** [23] [91]
– Don't even think about changing / Peculiar situation / Tell me to my face / Suspicious look in your eyes / Pay you back with interest / Clown / It's you / Crusader / What's wrong with the way I live / What went wrong / High classed. *(re-iss.Apr88 on 'BGO', cd-iss.Dec89) (re-iss.Dec71 as 'STOP, STOP, STOP', the US title, on 'Regal Star.')*
Feb 67. (7") **ON A CAROUSEL. / ALL THE WORLD IS LOVE** [4] [11] Mar 67
May 67. (7") **PAY YOU BACK WITH INTEREST. / WHAT'CHA GONNA DO ABOUT IT** [-] [28]

— Between 22 Feb'67 and 16 Jan68 used session drummer **DOUGIE WRIGHT** to repl. ELLIOT who had taken ill, also **CLEM CATTINI** guested

Parlophone Epic

May 67. (7") **CARRIE-ANNE. / SIGNS THAT WILL NEVER CHANGE** [3] [9] Jun 67
Jun 67. (lp) **EVOLUTION** [13] [43]
– When your light's turned on / Have you ever loved somebody / Lullaby to Tim / The games we play / Leave me / Rain on the window / Then the heartaches begin / Ye olde coffee shoppe / You need love / Stop right there / Water on the brain / Heading for a fall. *(re-iss.Feb72 as 'HOLLIES' on 'MFP') (re-iss.+c Aug78) (re-iss.+cd.1989)* (cd-iss Jun93)
Sep 67. (7") **KING MIDAS IN REVERSE. / EVERYTHING IS SUNSHINE** [18] [-]
Sep 67. (7") **KING MIDAS IN REVERSE. / WATER ON THE BRAIN** [-] [51]
Oct 67. (lp) **BUTTERFLY** [ ] [-]
– Try it / Wish you a wish / Step inside / Pegasus the flying horse / Dear Eloise / Away away away / Elevated observations / Would you believe / Butterfly / Maker / Charlie and Fred. *(re-iss.Aug78) (cd-iss.1989 on 'BGO')*
Dec 67. (7") **DEAR ELOISE. / WHEN YOUR LIGHTS TURNED ON** [-] [50]
Mar 68. (7") **JENNIFER ECCLES. / TRY IT** [-] [40]
Mar 68. (7") **JENNIFER ECCLES. / OPEN UP YOUR EYES** [11] [-]
Jun 68. (7") **DO THE BEST YOU CAN. / ELEVATED OBSERVATIONS** [-] [93]
Sep 68. (7") **LISTEN TO ME. / EVERYTHING IS SUNSHINE** [-] [ ]
Sep 68. (7") **LISTEN TO ME. / DO THE BEST YOU CAN** [11] [-]

— **TERRY SYLVESTER** – vocals, guitar (ex-SWINGING BLUE JEANS) repl. NASH who joined CROSBY, STILLS & NASH. **ELLIOT** also returned

Feb 69. (7") **SORRY SUZANNE. / NOT THAT WAY AY ALL** [3] [56]
May 69. (lp) **HOLLIES SING DYLAN** [3] [ ]
– Blowin' in the wind / I shall be released/ / This wheel's on fire / Mighty Quinn / The times they are a-changin' / I want you / Quit your lowdown ways / Just like a woman / When the ship comes in / My back pages / I'll be your baby tonight / tonight / All I really want to do. *(re-iss.Oct87 on 'MFP')*
Sep 69. (7") **HE AIN'T HEAVY, HE'S MY BROTHER. / 'COS YOU LIKE TO LOVE ME** [3] [7] Dec 69
(re-iss.Aug82)
Nov 69. (lp) **HOLLIES SING HOLLIES** [ ] [32]
– Do you believe in love / Please sign your letters / Please let me please / Goodbye tomorrow / My life is over with you / Soldier's dilemma / Marigold; Gloria swansong / You love 'cos you like it / Why didn't you believe / Look at life / Don't give up easily / Reflections of a time gone past. (US-title HE AIN'T HEAVY, HE'S MY BROTHER) (US version replaced Marigold . . . with He ain't heavy, he's my brother)
Apr 70. (7") **I CAN'T TELL THE BOTTOM FROM THE TOP. / MAD PROFESSOR BLYTHE** [7] [82]
Sep 70. (7") **GASOLINE ALLEY BRED. / DANDELION WINE** [14] [ ]
Nov 70. (lp)(c) **CONFESSIONS OF THE MIND** [30] [ ]
– I want to shout / Lady please / Separated / Confessions of a mind / Little girl / Survival of the fittest / Isn't it nice / Perfect lady housewife / Too young to be married / Frightened lady / Man without a heart. *(re-iss.Aug78, US title 'MOVING FINGER') (re-iss.+cd.Apr91 on 'B.G.O.')*
Jan 71. (7") **SURVIVAL OF THE FITTEST. / MAN WITHOUT A HEART** [-] [ ]
May 71. (7") **LITTLE WILLY. / ROW THE BOAT TOGETHER** [ ] [ ]
Jun 71. (lp)(c) **DISTANT LIGHT** [ ] [21] Jul 71
– Long cool woman (in a black dress) / You know the score / Pull down the blind / Promised land / What a life I've led / Cable car / Hold on / To do with love / Look what we got / Long dark road / Don't let a little thing like love. *(re-iss.+cd.Jul91 on 'B.G.O.')*
Jan 72. (7") **LONG COOL WOMAN (IN A BLACK DRESS). / CABLE CAR** [ ] [-]
Jun 72. (7") **LONG COOL WOMAN (IN A BLACK DRESS). / LOOK WHAT WE'VE GOT** [-] [2]
Nov 72. (7") **LONG DARK ROAD. / INDIAN GIRL** [-] [26]

— (Aug71) **MICHAEL RICKFORS** – vocals (ex-BAMBOO) repl. CLARKE who went solo

Polydor Epic

Feb 72. (7") **THE BABY. / OH GRANNY** [26] [ ]
Nov 72. (7") **MAGIC WOMAN TOUCH. / INDIAN GIRL** [ ] [60]
Nov 72. (lp)(c) **ROMANY** [ ] [84]
– Touch / Romany / Blue in the morning / Jesus was a crossmaker / Down river / Magic woman touch / Lizzy and the rainman / Slow down / Delaware Taggart and the outlaw boys / Won't we feel good that morning / Words sdon't come easy / Courage of your convictions.
Feb 73. (7") **JESUS WAS A CROSSMAKER. / I HAD A DREAM** [-] [ ]
Apr 73. (7") **SLOW DOWN. / WON'T WE FEEL GOOD** [-] [ ]

not issued Polydor

Apr 73. (lp) **OUT ON THE ROAD (studio)** [-] [-] GERM
– Don't leave the child alone / They don't realise I'm down / Transatlantic westbound jet / Nearer to you / Slow down go down / Pick up the pieces / The last wind / Mr. Heartbreaker / A better place / Out on the road / I was born a man / I had a dream.

— (Jul73) **ALLAN CLARKE** – vocals returned to repl. RICKFORS (CLARKE now joining others HICKS, SYLVESTER, CALVERT and ELLIOTT)

Oct 73. (7") **THE DAY THAT CURLY BILLY SHOT CRAZY SAM McGHEE. / BORN A MAN** [24] [ ]
Jan 74. (7") **THE AIR THAT I BREATHE. / NO MORE RIDERS** [2] [6] Apr 74
Mar 74. (lp)(c) **THE HOLLIES** [38] [28] May 74
– Out on the road / Pick up the pieces again / It's a shame, it's a game / Transatlantic westbound jet / Don't let me down / Falling calling / Rubber Lucy / Down on the run / Love makes the world go round.
May 74. (7") **SON OF A ROTTEN GAMBLER. / LAY TO THE MUSIC** [ ] [-]
May 74. (7") **DON'T LET ME DOWN. / LAY INTO THE MUSIC** [-] [ ]
Nov 74. (7") **I'M DOWN. / HELLO LADY GOODBYE** [ ] [-]
Feb 75. (lp)(c) **ANOTHER NIGHT** [ ] [ ]
– Give me time / Lonely hobo lullaby / You gave me life / Lucy / Sandy (4th of July, Asbury Park) / Look out Johnny (there's a monkey on your back) / Another night / Second-hand hang-ups / Time machine jive.

May 75. (7") **SANDY (4TH OF JULY ASBURY PARK). / SECOND-HAND HANG-UPS** [ ] [85] Apr 75
)re-iss.Apr 76)
Jun 75. (7") **ANOTHER NIGHT. / TIME MACHINE JIVE** [-] [71]
Aug 75. (7") **I'M DOWN. / LOOK OUT JOHNNY (THERE'S A MONKEY ON YOUR BACK)** [-] [ ]

—— **ROD ARGENT** – moog, piano (on next album track – *)

Jan 76. (lp)(c) **WRITE ON** [ ] [ ]
– Stranger / Narida / My island / Sweet country calling / Write on / Crocodile woman (she bites) / Star * / Love is the thing / There's always goodbye / I won't move over.
Feb 76. (7") **WRITE ON. / CROCODILE WOMAN (SHE BITES)** [-] [ ]
Feb 76. (7") **BOULDER TO BIRMINGHAM. / CROCODILE WOMAN (SHE BITES)** [ ] [-]
Apr 76. (7") **STAR. / LOVE IS THE THING** [ ] [-]
Sep 76. (7") **DADDY DON'T MIND. / C'MON** [ ] [-]
Oct 76. (7") **WIGGLE THAT WOTSIT. / CORRINE** [ ] [-]
Dec 76. (lp)(c) **RUSSIAN ROULETTE** [ ] [ ]
– My love / Russian roulette / Be with you / Lady of the night / Louise / 48 hour people / Thanks for the memories / Wiggle that wotsit / Draggin' my heels.
Dec 76. (7") **DRAGGIN' MY HEELS. / I WON'T MOVE OVER** [-] [ ]
Mar 77. (lp)(c) **HOLLIES LIVE HITS** [4] [ ]
– I can't let go / Just one look / I can't tell the bottom from the top / Another night / Bust stop / Sandy / Star / My island / I'm down / Stop, stop, stop / Long cool woman (in a black dress) / Carrie-Anne / The air that I breathe / Too young to be married / He ain't heavy, he's my brother.
May 77. (7") **HELLO TO ROMANCE. / 48 HOUR PAROLE** [ ] [-]
Jul 77. (7") **AMNESTY. / CROSSFIRE** [ ] [-]
Mar 78. (lp)(c) **A CRAZY STEAL** [ ] [ ]
– Let it pour / Burn out / Amnesty / Caracas / What am I gonna do / Feet on the ground / Writing on the wall / Clown service.
Apr 78. (7") **BURN OUT. / WRITING ON THE WALL** [-] [ ]
Mar 79. (7") **SOMETHING TO LIVE FOR. / SONG OF THE SUN** [ ] [-]
(12"+=) – The air that I breathe.
Mar 79. (lp)(c) **FIVE THREE ONE – DOUBLE SEVEN O FOUR** [ ] [ ]
– When I'm yours / Satellite three / Something to live for / Maybe it's dawn / Song of the sun / Stormy waters / Boys in the band / It's in every one of us / Say it ain't so / Harlequin.
Mar 80. (7") **SOLDIER'S SONG. / DRAGGIN' MY HEELS** [58] [-]
Sep 80. (7") **HEARTBEAT. / TAKE YOUR TIME** [ ] [-]
Oct 80. (lp)(c) **BUDDY HOLLY** [ ] [ ]
– Take your time / Wishing / Peggy Sue / Heartbeat / Love's made a fool of you / That'll be the day / Think it over / Tell me how / Maybe baby / I'm gonna love you too / What to do / It doesn't matter / Peggy Sue got married / Midnight shift / Everyday.

—— trimmed to a trio of CLARKE, HICKS and ELLIOTT when CALVERT and SYLVESTER left. Latter teamed with JAMES GRIFFIN (ex-BREAD) (next single b-side with **ALAN JONES** – bass)

Nov 81. (7") **TAKE MY LOVE AND RUN. / DRIVER** [ ] [ ]

—— added returning **GRAHAM NASH** – vocals, guitar

WEA | Atlantic

Jul 83. (7") **STOP! IN THE NAME OF LOVE. / MUSICAL PICTURES** [ ] [29] May 83
Jul 83. (lp)(c) **WHAT GOES AROUND** [ ] [90]
– Something ain't right / Casualty / Say you'll be mine / If the lights go out / Stop! In the name of love / I got what I want / Just one look / Someone else's eyes / Having a good time / Let her go down.
Aug 83. (7") **SOMEONE ELSE'S EYES. / IF THE LIGHTS GO OUT** [-] [ ]
Oct 83. (7") **CASUALTY. / IF THE LIGHTS GO OUT** [-] [ ]

—— basic trio of **CLARKE, HICKS** and **ELLIOTT** plus **ALAN COATES** – harmonies / **STEVE STROUD** – bass / **DENNIS HAYNES** – keyboards

Columbia | Columbia

May 85. (7") **TOO MANY HEARTS GET BROKEN. / YOU'RE ALL WOMAN** [ ] [ ]
(12"+=) – Laughter turns to tears.
Jan 87. (7") **THIS IS IT. / YOU GAVE ME STRENGTH** [ ] [ ]
(12"+=) – You're all woman.
Mar 87. (7") **REUNION OF THE HEART. / TOO MANY HEARTS GET BROKEN** [ ] [ ]
(12"+=) – Holliedaze (medley).

—— **RAY STILES** – bass (ex-MUD) repl. STROUD

Coconut G'MANY | not issued

Jan 88. (7") **STAND BY ME. / FOR WHAT IT'S WORTH** [-] [-]
Jun 88. (7") **SHINE SILENTLY. / YOUR EYES** [-] [-]

E.M.I. | Capitol

Feb 89. (7") **FIND ME A FAMILY. / NO RULES** [ ] [-]
Mar 93. (7")(c-s) **THE WOMAN I LOVE. / PURPLE RAIN (live)** [42] [ ]
(cd-s+=) – The air that I breathe / (Ain't) That just like me.
Mar 93. (cd)(c)(lp) **THE AIR THAT I BREATHE (THE BEST OF THE HOLLIES)** (compilation) [15] [ ]
– The air that I breathe / Bus stop / Just one look / Yes I will / Look through any window / He ain't heavy, he's my brother / I can't let go / We're through / Searchin' / Stay / I'm alive / If I needed someone / Here I go again / Stop stop stop / On a carousel / Carrie Ann / King Midas in reverse / Jennifer Eccles / Listen to me / Sorry Suzanne / I can't tell the bottom from the top / Gasoline alley bred / Hey Willy / The day that Curly Billy shot down Crazy Sam McGee / The woman I love.

– other compilations etc. –

Note; All 'Parlophone' releases were issued on 'Imperial' in the US.

Aug 68. Parlophone; (lp) **HOLLIES' GREATEST HITS** [1] [11]
(US version different)
1968. Parlophone; (7") **RUNNING THROUGH THE NIGHT** [-] [ ]
1968. Parlophone; (7") **IF I NEED SOMEONE. / I'LL BE TRUE TO YOU (YES I WILL)** [-] [ ]
Nov 72. Parlophone; (lp)(c) **THE HOLLIES GREATEST HITS VOL.2** [ ] [ ]
Aug 78. Parlophone; (lp)(c) **THE OTHER SIDE OF THE HOLLIES** [ ] [ ]
Aug 78. Parlophone; (lp)(c) **THE BEST OF THE HOLLIES EP's** [ ] [ ]
(re-iss.Mar81 on 'EMI')
Oct 74. M.F.P.; (lp) **I CAN'T LET GO** [ ] [-]
Sep 80. M.F.P.; (lp)(c) **LONG COOL WOMAN IN A BLACK DRESS** [ ] [-]
Apr 90. M.F.P.; (cd)(c)(lp) **THE LOVE SONGS** [ ] [-]
Sep 75. E.M.I.; (7") **LONG COOL WOMAN IN A BLACK DRESS. / CARRIE ANNE** [ ] [ ]
Nov 75. E.M.I.; (lp)(c) **THE HISTORY OF THE HOLLIES** [ ] [ ]
Jun 78. E.M.I.; (7") **LOOK THROUGH ANY WINDOW. / I'M ALIVE / JUST ONE LOOK** [ ] [ ]
Jul 78. E.M.I.; (lp)(c) **20 GOLDEN GREATS** [2] [ ]
– The air that I breathe / Carrie Anne / Bus stop / Listen to me / Look through any window / I can't let go / Long cool woman in a black dress / Here I go again / I can't tell the bottom from the top / I'm alive / Yes I will / Stay / Sorry Suzanne / Gasoline alley bred / We're through / Jennifer Eccles / Stop! stop! stop! / On a carousel / Just one look / He ain't heavy, he's my brother.
(cd-iss.Mar87 & Jan89)
Aug 81. E.M.I.; (7") **HOLLIEDAZE (MEDLEY). / HOLLIEPOPS** [28] [ ]
Aug 88. E.M.I.; (7") **HE AIN'T HEAVY, HE'S MY BROTHER. / CARRIE** [1] [ ]
(12"+=)(cd-s+=) – The air that I breathe.
Sep 88. E.M.I.; (d-lp)(d-c)(d-cd) **ALL THE HITS AND MORE** [51] [ ]
Nov 88. E.M.I.; (lp)(c)(cd) **RARITIES** [ ] [-]
Nov 88. E.M.I.; (7") **THE AIR THAT I BREATHE. /** [60] [ ]
(12"+=) –
Oct 83. Old Gold; (7") **HE AIN'T HEAVY, HE'S MY BROTHER. / BUS STOP** [ ] [-]
Jun 92. Old Gold; (cd-s) **HE AIN'T HEAVY, HE'S MY BROTHER / CARRIE ANN / ON A CAROUSEL** [ ] [-]
Jul 92. Old Gold; (cd-s) **I'M ALIVE / JUST ONE LOOK** [ ] [-]
Mar 84. EMI Gold; (7") **JUST ONE LOOK. / HERE I GO AGAIN** [ ] [-]
Feb 86. See For Miles; (lp) **NOT THE HITS AGAIN** [ ] [-]
(cd-iss.May89)
Sep 87. See For Miles; (lp)(c) **THE EP COLLECTION** [ ] [-]
(cd-iss.1989 & Apr95)
Sep 87. Hour Of Pleasure; (c) **AN HOUR OF THE HOLLIES** [ ] [-]
May 88. C.F.P.; (cd) **HOLLIES** [ ] [-]
May 94. B.R.Music; (cd) **THE AIR THAT I BREATHE** [ ] [-]
Feb 95. EMI; (4xcd-box) **FOUR HOLLIES ORIGINALS** [ ] [-]
Nov 95. Old Gold; (cd-s) **HE AIN'T HEAVY, HE'S MY BROTHER / CARRIE ANNE** [ ] [-]

ALLAN CLARKE

R.C.A. | Epic

Apr 72. (7") **YOU'RE LOSING ME. / COWARD BY NAME** [ ] [-]
Apr 72. (lp)(c) **MY NAME IS 'AROLD** [ ] [ ]
– Ruby / Mary Skeffington / Baby it's alright with me / Moonshine whiskey / Nature's way of saying goodbye / You're losing me / Let us pray / Patchwork quilts / Walpurgis night / Bring on your smile.
Jul 72. (7") **RUBY. / BABY IT'S ALRIGHT WITH ME** [-] [ ]

E.M.I. | issued?

May 73. (7") **WHO?. / I LOOKED INTO YOUR EYES** [ ] [ ]
Jul 73. (lp)(c) **HEADROOM** [ ] [ ]
– Complete controllable man / People of that kind / Fishin' / Who / Drift away / Shift lovin' lady / I look in your eyes / Give us a song / Would you believe (revisited).
Mar 74. (7") **SIDESHOW. / DON'T LET ME DOWN AGAIN** [ ] [ ]
Aug 74. (lp)(c) **ALLAN CLARKE** [ ] [ ]
– Don't let me down again / Can't get on / I'll be home / I wanna sail into your life / Side show / If I were the priest / New Americans / Love, love, love / Send me some lovin'.
Oct 75. (7") **BORN TO RUN. / WHY DON'T YOU CALL** [ ] [ ]

E.M.I. | Asylum

Jun 76. (7") **LIVING IN LOVE. / PEOPLE OF THAT KIND** [ ] [-]
Jul 76. (7") **IF YOU THINK YOU KNOW HOW TO LOVE ME. / LIGHT A LIGHT** [-] [ ]
Jul 76. (lp)(c) **I'VE GOT TIME** [ ] [ ]
– Blinded by the light / Light a light / We've got time / Stand by me / The long way / Hallelujah freedom / I think you know how to love me / If you walked away / Sunrise / Living in love / Finale.

Polydor | Atlantic

Jan 78. (7") **(I WILL BE YOUR) SHADOW IN THE STREET. / THE PASSENGER** [-] [ ]
Jan 78. (7") **I DON'T KNOW I'M BEAT. / THE PASSENGER** [-] [-]
Mar 78. (7") **MAN WHO MANUFACTURED DREAMS. / I WASN'T BORN YESTERDAY** [-] [ ]
May 78. (7") **WHO'S GOIN' OUT THE BACK DOOR. / I'M BETTING MY LIFE ON YOU** [-] [ ]
May 78. (7") **I'M BETTING MY LIFE ON YOU. / I WASN'T BORN YESTERDAY** [ ] [-]
May 78. (lp)(c) **I WASN'T BORN YESTERDAY** [ ] [ ]
– I'm betting my life on you / Who's goin' out the back door? / (I will be your) shadow in the street / I wasn't born yesterday / New blood / Hope / Man who manufactures dreams / No prisoner taken / Light of my smiles / Off the record. *(re-iss.Jun79 on 'Aura') (cd-iss.Oct93 on 'Repertoire')*

Elektra | Curb

1979. (lp)(c) **LEGENDARY HEROES** [ ] [ ]
– Slipstream / The only ones / Walls / Brandenberg plaza / The survivor / Driving the doomsday cars / Baby blue / Sanctuary / Imagination's child / Legendary heroes.
1979. (7") **SLIPSTREAM. / IMAGINATION'S CHILD** [-] [ ]
1979. (7") **THE ONLY ONES. / DRIVING THE DOMESDAY CARS** [-] [ ]

Aura | Atlantic

Jun 79. (7"m) **SHADOW IN THE STREET. / NO PRISONERS TAKEN / LIGHT BRIGADE** [ ] [-]
Sep 79. (7") **I WASN'T BORN YESTERDAY. / NEW BLOOD** [ ] [-]
Oct 80. (7") **THE ONLY ONE. / THE SURVIVOR** [ ] [-]
Nov 80. (lp)(c) **THE ONLY ONE** [ ] [-]

– (as last album) *(cd-iss.Nov93 on 'Repertoire')*

Jan 81. (7") **WALLS. / BABY BLUE** | | -

Forever	not issued

1982. (7") **SOMEONE ELSE WILL. / CASTLES IN THE WIND** | | -

– compilations, others, etc. –

1981. Aura; (lp) **THE BEST OF ALLAN CLARKE** | | -
Nov 81. Aura; (7") **BORN TO RUN. / IF I WERE A PRIEST** | | -
Mar 82. Aura; (7") **SHADOW IN THE STREET. / IF YOU WALKED AWAY** | | -
May 93. M.F.P.; (cd)(c) **SINGLES A'S & B'S 1970-1979** | | -

Buddy HOLLY

Born: CHARLES HARDIN HOLLEY, 7 Sep'36, Lubbock, Texas, USA. In the late 40's, he formed C&W duo with school mate BOB MONTGOMERY. In 1953-54, as BUDDY & BOB, they became regulars on a Saturday afternoon TV show, and soon put together a number of demos (later issued as HOLLY IN THE HILLS). They had added bassman LARRY WELBORN, with drummer JERRY ALLISON joining in 1955. After a gig supporting BILL HALEY & HIS COMETS, and through agent Eddie Crandall, BUDDY HOLLY was signed up by 'Decca' early 1956. Rejected MONTGOMERY, went on to become successful producer, etc. HOLLY formed backing band The THREE TUNES. He retained JERRY and recruited SONNY CURTIS on guitar plus DON GUESS – bass. After 2 flop singles, he and JERRY left record company and went to New Mexico to find producer NORMAN PETTY, who was soon to become their manager. Early 1957, BUDDY and JERRY were joined by NIKI SULLIVAN (rhythm guitar) and JOE B.MAUDLIN (bass). They became The CRICKETS, whose debut THAT'LL BE THE DAY, soon sold a million, hitting No.1 on both sides of the Atlantic. As a solo artist, with CRICKETS backing, BUDDY set up deal with 'Coral' who released his second hit PEGGY SUE. Over the next year, he dually released group hits (OH BOY / MAYBE BABY + THINK IT OVER) with his own solo classics (LISTEN TO ME / RAVE ON + EARLY IN THE MORNING). He and The CRICKETS split in August '58, after BUDDY married Maria Elena Santiago and moved to New York. His new single without them (HEARTBEAT), only reached No.82 in the States, but scraped into the UK 30. This was certainly a transitional period, but things looked brighter early the next year, as BUDDY headed a Winter package tour of the States. Tragically on the morning of 3 Feb'59, after a gig, 22 year-old BUDDY HOLLY and other stars, RICHIE VALENS and BIG BOPPER were killed in a chartered plane crash. His first postumous release (written by PAUL ANKA), IT DOESN'T MATTER ANYMORE gave him a UK No.1 and US Top 20 hit. • **Style:** Talented bespectacled genius, ahead of his time, and whose death came too early. Drifted through rock'n'roll, creating vocal manner of his own. • **Songwriters:** HOLLY wrote most himself, except EARLY IN THE MORNING + NOW WE'RE ONE (Bobby Darin) / BABY I DON'T CARE (Elvis Presley) / etc. His songs were later covered by Rolling Stones (NOT FADE AWAY) / Mud (OH BOY) / Showaddywaddy (HEARTBEAT) / Leo Sayer (RAINING IN MY HEART). • **Trivia:** In Sep'58, HOLLY produces his new bass player's (WAYLON JENNINGS) debut single 'JOLE BLON'.

Recommended: 20 GOLDEN GREATS (*8)

BUDDY HOLLY – vocals, guitar (backed by The **CRICKETS** ⇒) (all 78 + 45 rpm up to May60)

Brunswick	Decca

Jul 56. (7") **BLUE DAYS BLACK NIGHTS. / LOVE ME** | | | Apr 56
Dec 56. (7") **MODERN DON JUAN. / YOU ARE MY ONE DESIRE** | - | |

(with The CRICKETS ⇒ , he hit No.1 (May57-US / Sep57-UK) with the single **THAT'LL BE THE DAY. / I'M LOOKING FOR SOMEONE TO LOVE**

Coral	Coral

Jun 57. (7") **WORDS OF LOVE. / MAILMAN BRING ME NO MORE BLUES** | - | |
Nov 57. (7") **PEGGY SUE. / EVERYDAY** | 6 | 3 | Sep 57
(re-iss.Jul82 on 'Old Gold')

— (with The CRICKETS ⇒ again, he hit US No.10 (Nov57) / UK No.3 (Dec57) with single **OH BOY. / NOT FADE AWAY.**

— An album **THE CHIRPING CRICKETS** was issued Nov57-US / Mar58-UK. Another single **MAYBE BABY. / TELL ME HOW** hit US No.17 (Feb58) / UK No.4 (Mar58).

Mar 58. (7") **LISTEN TO ME. / I'M GONNA LOVE YOU TOO** | 16 | |
Jun 58. (7") **RAVE ON. / TAKE YOUR TIME** | 5 | 37 | Apr 58
Jul 58. (lp) **BUDDY HOLLY** | | | Mar 58
– I'm gonna love you too / Peggy Sue / Look at me / Listen to me / Valley of tears / Ready Teddy / Everyday / Mailman, bring me no more blues / Words of love / Baby I don't care / Rave on / Little baby. *(re-iss.Jul75) (re-iss.Mar83 + Nov86 on 'M.C.A.', cd-iss.Nov92 on 'Sequel') (re-iss.Jul68 as 'LISTEN TO ME' on 'MCA', re-iss.Feb74; all UK)*

(with The CRICKETS ⇒ again, he hit US No.27 (Jun58) / UK No.11 (Jul58) with single **THINK IT OVER. / FOOL'S PARADISE**

Aug 58. (7") **EARLY IN THE MORNING. / NOW WE'RE ONE** | - | 32 | Jul 58

— (with The CRICKETS ⇒ again, he was heard on their last single collaboration **IT'S SO EASY. / LONESOME TEARS** (which didn't chart US-Sep58 / UK-Oct58)

He had now left The CRICKETS to hop away on their own Oct'58.

Nov 58. (7") **HEARTBEAT. / WELL ALL RIGHT** | 30 | 82 |
Feb 59. (7") **IT DOESN'T MATTER ANYMORE. / RAINING IN MY HEART** | 1 | 13 |
| | 88 | Jan 59
(re-iss.Apr83 on 'Old Gold')

— On 3 Feb'59, BUDDY was killed in a plane crash alongside other pop stars RICHIE VALENS and BIG BOPPER.

– past early recording releases –

— (with back-up from The **THREE TUNES** aka **SONNY CURTIS** – guitar / **DON GUESS** – bass / **JERRY ALLISON** – drums

Sep 57. Decca; (7") **ROCK AROUND WITH OLLIE VEE. / THAT'LL BE THE DAY** | - | |
Nov 57. Decca; (7"ep) **THAT'LL BE THE DAY** | - | |
– That'll be the day / Ting-a-ling / Blue days, black nights / You are my one desire.
Jan 58. Decca; (7") **LOVE ME. / YOU ARE MY ONE DESIRE** | - | |
Apr 58. Decca; (lp) **THAT'LL BE THE DAY** | - | |
(UK-iss.Oct61 on 'Ace Of Hearts', hit No.5) (US re-iss.Mar67 as 'THE GREAT BUDDY HOLLY' on 'Vocalion') (UK re-iss.Dec69 + Feb74 on 'Coral')
Jun 58. Decca; (7") **GIRLS ON MY MIND. / TING-A-LING** | - | |
Sep 58. Coral; (7"ep) **BUDDY HOLLY** | | - |
– Listen to me / Peggy Sue / Everyday / I'm gonna love you too.
Dec 58. Coral; (7"ep) **RAVE ON** | | - |
– Rave on / Take your time / Early in the morning / Now we're one.
Jan 59. Coral; (7"ep) **HEARTBEAT** | | - |
– Heartbeat / Well all right / Baby I don't care / Little baby.

– postumous compilations, others, etc. –

Jul 59. Brunswick; (7") **MIDNIGHT SHIFT. / ROCK AROUND WITH OLLIE VEE** | 26 | - |
Jul 59. Brunswick; (7"ep) **BUDDY HOLLY NO.1** | | - |
– You are my one desire / Blue days, black nights / Ting-a-ling / Modern Don Juan.
Jul 59. Brunswick; (7"ep) **THE LATE GREAT BUDDY HOLLY** | | - |
– Look at me / Ready Teddy / Mailman, bring me no more blues / Little baby.

(some below featured CRICKETS' songs)

Apr 59. Coral; (lp) **THE BUDDY HOLLY STORY** | 2 | 11 | Mar 59
(UK re-iss.Jul68 as 'RAVE ON' on 'M.C.A.', re-iss.Feb74, also iss.Aug75 on 'M.F.P.')
Jun 59. Coral; (7"ep) **THE BUDDY HOLLY STORY** | | | Mar 59
– Early in the morning / Heartbeat / Raining in my heart / It doesn't matter anymore.
Aug 59. Coral; (7") **PEGGY SUE GOT MARRIED. / CRYING, WAITING, HOPING** | 13 | | Jul 59
Mar 60. Coral; (7") **HEARTBEAT. / EVERYDAY** | 30 | - |
May 60. Coral; (7") **TRUE LOVE WAYS. / MOONDREAMS** | 25 | - |
Jun 60. Coral; (7") **TRUE LOVE WAYS. / THAT MAKES IT TOUGH** | - | - |
Oct 60. Coral; (7") **LEARNING THE GAME. / THAT MAKES IT TOUGH** | 36 | - |
Oct 60. Coral; (lp) **THE BUDDY HOLLY STORY VOL.2** | 7 | | Mar60
(UK re-iss.Jul68 as 'TRUE LOVE WAYS' on 'M.C.A.', re-iss.Feb74)
Jan 61. Coral; (7") **WHAT TO DO. / THAT'S WHAT THEY SAY** | 34 | - |
Jun 61. Coral; (7") **BABY I DON'T CARE. / VALLEY OF TEARS** | 12 | - |
Nov 61. Coral; (7") **LOOK AT ME. / MAILMAN BRING ME NO MORE BLUES** | | - |
Feb 62. Coral; (7") **LISTEN TO ME. / WORDS OF LOVE** | 48 | - |
Jun 62. Coral; (7"ep) **PEGGY SUE GOT MARRIED** | - | |
– Peggy Sue got married / Crying, waiting, hoping / Learning the game / That makes it tough.
Jun 62. Coral; (7"ep) **BROWN-EYED HANDSOME MAN** | - | |
– Brown-eyed handsome man / Bo Diddley / Wishing / True love ways.
Sep 62. Coral; (7") **REMINISCING. / WAIT TILL THE SUN SHINES NELLIE** | 17 | | Aug 62
Mar 63. Coral; (7") **BROWN-EYED HANDSOME MAN. / SLIPPIN' & SLIDIN'** | 3 | - |

(below album was dubbed in 1962 with musicians The FIREBALLS)

Apr 63. Coral; (lp) **REMINISCING** | 2 | 40 | Feb 63
– Reminiscing / Slippin' and slidin' / Bo Diddley / Wait till the Sun shines, Nellie / Baby, won't you come out tonight / Brown-eyed handsome man / Because I love you / It's not my fault / I'm gonna set my foot down / Changing all those changes / Rock-a-bye-rock. *(UK re-iss.Nov86 on 'M.C.A.') (UK re-iss.Jul68 as 'BROWN-EYED HANDSOME MAN' on 'M.C.A.', re-iss.Feb74) (re-iss.Feb89) (cd-iss.Nov92 on 'Castle')*
Apr 63. Coral; (7") **BO DIDDLEY. / TRUE LOVE WAYS** | - | |
May 63. Coral; (7") **BO DIDDLEY. / IT'S NOT MY FAULT** | 4 | - |
Jul 63. Coral; (7") **BROWN-EYED HANDSOME MAN. / WISHING** | - | - |
Aug 63. Coral; (7") **WISHING. / BECAUSE I LOVE YOU** | 10 | - |
Dec 63. Coral; (7") **WHAT TO DO. / UMM OH YEAH (DEAREST)** | 27 | - |
Jan 64. Coral; (7") **ROCK AROUND WITH OLLIE VEE. / I'M GONNA LOVE YOU TOO** | - | |
Apr 64. Coral; (7") **MAYBE BABY. / NOT FADE AWAY** | - | |
Apr 64. Coral; (7") **YOU'VE GOT LOVE. ("BUDDY HOLLY & THE CRICKETS") / AN EMPTY CUP** | 40 | - |
Jun 64. Coral; (lp) **SHOWCASE** | 3 | | May 64
(UK re-iss.Nov86 & Feb89 on 'M.C.A.') (UK re-iss.Jul68 as 'HE'S THE ONE' on 'M.C.A.') (cd-iss Apr 93 on 'Castle')
Sep 64. Coral; (7") **LOVE'S MADE A FOOL OF YOU. / YOU'RE THE ONE** | 39 | - |
Sep 64. Coral; (7"ep) **BUDDY BY REQUEST** | | - |
– Brown-eyed handsome man / Bo Diddley / Umm..oh yeah (dearest) / Slippin' and slidin'.
Sep 64. Coral; (7"ep) **THAT TEX-MEX SOUND** | | - |
– I'm gonna set my foot down / It's not my fault / Rip it up / Baby won't you come out tonight.
Oct 64. Coral; (7"ep) **WISHING** | | - |
– Wishing / Reminiscing / Valley of tears / Learning the game.
Nov 64. Coral; (7"ep) **SHOWCASE VOL.1** | | - |
– Honky tonk / Gone / You're the one / Guess I was just a fool.
Nov 64. Coral; (7"ep) **SHOWCASE VOL.2** | | - |

– Blue suede shoes / Come back baby / Shake rattle and roll / Love's made a fool of you.
Jan 65. Coral; (7"ep) **BUDDY HOLLY SINGS** [ ] [-]
– Peggy Sue got married / Crying, waiting, hoping / What to do / That makes it tough.
Mar 65. Coral; (7") **WHAT TO DO. / SLIPPIN' AND SLIDIN'** [-] [ ]
Jun 65. Coral; (lp) **HOLLY IN THE HILLS** (1954 demos) [13] [ ] Jan 65
(some lp's have track 'Reminiscing' instead of 'Wishing') *(UK re-iss.Jul86 as 'WISHING' on 'M.C.A.')*
Apr 66. Coral; (d-lp) **THE BEST OF BUDDY HOLLY** [-] [ ]
May 66. Coral; (7") **MAYBE BABY. / THAT'S MY DESIRE** [ ] [-]
May 70. Coral; (lp)(c) **BUDDY HOLLY'S GREATEST HITS VOL.2** [ ] [ ]
May 70. Coral; (lp)(c) **BUDDY HOLLY'S GREATEST HITS VOL.3** [ ] [ ]
Sep 71. Coral; (lp)(c) **REMEMBER BUDDY HOLLY** [ ] [ ]
(re-iss.Feb74)
Feb 74. Coral; (lp)(c) **GREATEST HITS** [ ] [ ]
(re-iss.Jul75, w / 2 extra tracks, hit UK No.42) (UK re-iss.Sep81 + Sep84 on 'M.C.A.')
Feb 74. Coral; (lp)(c) **GREATEST HITS VOL.2** [ ] [ ]
Oct 74. Coral; (d-lp)(d-c) **LEGEND** [ ] [ ]
(re-iss.Mar82 on 'MCA-Coral') (re-iss.+cd.Feb89)
Nov 75. Coral; (lp)(c) **THE NASHVILLE SESSIONS** [ ] [ ]
(UK re-iss.Mar83 + Nov86 on 'M.C.A.')
Nov 77. Coral; (lp)(c) **WESTERN AND BOP ("& BOB MONTGOMERY")** [ ] [ ]
Mar 79. Coral; (6xlp-box)(6xc-box) **THE COMPLETE BUDDY HOLLY** [ ] [ ]
(re-iss.Aug86 on 'M.C.A.')
Note; All releases on 'M.C.A.' were issued on 'Coral' US until '78.
Mar 68. M.C.A.; (7") **PEGGY SUE. / RAVE ON** [32] [-]
Jul 68. M.C.A.; (7") **RAVE ON. / EARLY IN THE MORNING** [-] [ ]
Jan 69. M.C.A.; (7") **LOVE IS STRANGE. / YOU'RE THE ONE** [ ] [ ] Mar 69
Mar 69. M.C.A.; (lp) **GIANT** [13] [ ] Jan 69
(re-iss.Feb74 + Nov86)
May 69. M.C.A.; (7") **IT DOESN'T MATTER ANYMORE. / MAYBE BABY** [ ] [-]
Mar 70. M.C.A.; (7") **RAVE ON. / UMM OH YEAH (DEAREST)** [ ] [-]
May 73. M.C.A.; (7"m) **THAT'LL BE THE DAY. / WELL ALL RIGHT / EVERYDAY** [ ] [-]
Feb 74. M.C.A.; (7"m) **IT DOESN'T MATTER ANYMORE. / TRUE LOVE WAYS / BROWN-EYED HANDSOME MAN** [ ] [-]
Aug 75. M.C.A.; (7") **OH BOY!. / EVERYDAY** [ ] [-]
(above + below singles were credited to "BUDDY HOLLY & THE CRICKETS")
Sep 76. M.C.A.; (7"ep) **MAYBE BABY / THINK IT OVER. / THAT'LL BE THE DAY / IT'S SO EASY** [ ] [-]
Sep 76. M.C.A.; (7"ep) **PEGGY SUE / RAVE ON. / ROCK AROUND WITH OLLIE VEE / MIDNIGHT SHIFT** [ ] [-]
Sep 76. M.C.A.; (7"ep) **TRUE LOVE WAYS / MOONDREAMS. / IT DOESN'T MATTER ANYMORE / RAINING IN MY HEART** [ ] [-]
(re-iss.Aug81)
Jan 78. M.C.A.; (7") **WISHING. / LOVE'S MADE A FOOL OF YOU** [ ] [ ]
Mar 78. M.C.A.; (lp)(c) **20 GOLDEN GREATS** [1] [55]
– That'll be the day / Peggy Sue / Words of love / Everyday / Not fade away / Oh! boy / Maybe baby / Listen to me / Heartbeat / Think it over / It doesn't matter anymore / It's so easy / Well all right / Rave on / Raining in my heart / True love ways / Peggy Sue got married / Bo Diddley / Brown-eyed handsome man / Wishing. *(re-iss.Jun79) (cd-iss.Feb89)(re-iss.cd+c Aug93)*
1978. M.C.A.; (7") **IT DOESN'T MATTER ANYMORE. / PEGGY SUE** [ ] [-]
Aug 81. M.C.A.; (lp)(c) **LOVE SONGS** [ ] [ ]
Mar 83. M.C.A.; (lp)(c) **FOR THE FIRST TIME ANYWHERE** [ ] [ ]
(cd-iss.Sep87)
Sep 84. M.C.A.; (d-c) **GREATEST HITS / LOVE SONGS** [ ] [-]
Jul 85. M.C.A.; (lp)(c) **GOLDEN GREATS** [ ] [-]
(below are a boxed-set of 10 singles)
Aug 85. M.C.A.; (7") **THAT'LL BE THE DAY. / ROCK ME MY BABY** [ ] [ ]
Aug 85. M.C.A.; (7") **PEGGY SUE. / EVERYDAY** [ ] [ ]
Aug 85. M.C.A.; (7") **OH BOY. / NOT FADE AWAY** [ ] [ ]
Aug 85. M.C.A.; (7") **MAYBE BABY. / TELL ME NOW** [ ] [ ]
Aug 85. M.C.A.; (7") **RAVE ON. / READY TEDDY** [ ] [ ]
Aug 85. M.C.A.; (7") **THINK IT OVER. / IT'S SO EASY** [ ] [ ]
Aug 85. M.C.A.; (7") **IT DOESN'T MATTER ANYMORE. / RAINING IN MY HEART** [ ] [ ]
Aug 85. M.C.A.; (7") **TRUE LOVE WAYS. / WORDS OF LOVE** [ ] [ ]
Aug 85. M.C.A.; (7") **REMINISCING. / BABY I DON'T CARE** [ ] [ ]
Aug 85. M.C.A.; (7") **BROWN-EYED HANDSOME MAN. / BO DIDDLEY** [ ] [ ]
Oct 85. M.C.A.; (cd) **FROM THE ORIGINAL MASTER TAPES** [ ] [ ]
Aug 86. M.C.A.; (7") **THAT'LL BE THE DAY. / I'M LOOKING FOR SOMEONE TO LOVE** [ ] [-]
(12"+=) – It doesn't matter anymore / Raining in my heart.
Aug 86. M.C.A.; (7"box) **THAT'LL BE THE DAY. / ROCK ME BABY / PEGGY SUE** [ ] [-]
Jun 88. M.C.A.; (cd) **THE GREAT BUDDY HOLLY** [-] [ ]
Nov 88. M.C.A.; (7") **TRUE LOVE WAYS. / RAINING IN MY HEART** [65] [-]
(12"+=)(cd-s+=) – ?
Sep 89. M.C.A.; (7") **OH BOY. / NOT FADE AWAY** [ ] [-]
(10"+cd-s+=) – ?
Sep 89. M.C.A.; (lp-box)(c-box)(cd-box) **THE BUDDY HOLLY BOX SET** [ ] [ ]
Jun 67. Ace Of Hearts/ US= Coral; (lp) **BUDDY HOLLY'S GREATEST HITS** [9] [ ]
(UK re-iss.Nov69, re-iss.Aug71; hit No.32, on 'Coral')

Nov 75. World; (5xlp-box) **THE BUDDY HOLLY STORY** [ ] [-]
Aug 80. M&S; (lp)(c) **HEARTBEAT** [ ] [-]
Sep 80. Pickwick; (lp)(c) **BUDDY HOLLY** [ ] [-]
Mar 90. Pickwick; (cd)(c)(lp) **MOONDREAMS** [ ] [-]
Dec 92. Pickwick; (cd-box) **SPECIAL LIMITED EDITION** [ ] [-]
Sep 93. Pickwick; (cd)(c) **THE BEST OF BUDDY HOLLY** [ ] [-]
Oct 80. M.F.P.; (lp)(c) **ROCK WITH BUDDY HOLLY** [ ] [-]
Aug 82. M.F.P.; (lp)(c) **20 LOVE SONGS** [ ] [-]
Oct 87. M.F.P.; (lp)(c) **ROCK'N'ROLL GREATS** [ ] [-]
Sep 86. Hallmark; (lp)(c) **THE BEST OF BUDDY HOLLY** [ ] [-]
Oct 87. Hallmark; (lp)(c) **THE LEGENDARY BUDDY HOLLY** [ ] [-]
Apr 83. Old Gold; (7") **RAVE ON. / TRUE LOVE WAYS** [ ] [-]
May 89. Old Gold; (cd-ep) **THAT'LL BE THE DAY / OH BOY / MAYBE BABY** [ ] [-]
Nov 84. Astan; (lp)(c) **23 ALL TIME GREATEST HITS** [ ] [-]
May 85. Charly; (d-lp) **BUDDY HOLLY ROCKS** [ ] [-]
1983. Cambra; (d-c) **BUDDY HOLLY** [ ] [-]
May 84. Cambra; (d-lp)(d-c) **ROCK AROUND WITH BUDDY HOLLY & THE CRICKETS** [ ] [-]
(re-iss.Sep86)
Sep 86. Rollercoaster; (lp)(c) **SOMETHING SPECIAL FROM BUDDY HOLLY** [ ] [ ]
Oct 87. Rollercoaster; (7"ep) **GOOD ROCKIN' TONIGHT / RIP IT UP. / AIN'T GOT NO HOME / HOLLY HOP** [ ] [ ]
Oct 87. Castle; (d-lp)(c)(cd) **BUDDY HOLLY: THE COLLECTION** [ ] [-]
Feb 89. Telstar; (lp)(c)(cd) **TRUE LOVE WAYS** [8] [-]
May 88. Arcade; (cd) **VERY BEST OF BUDDY HOLLY** [ ] [-]
May 94. M.C.A.; (cd)(c) **THAT'LL BE THE DAY / BUDDY HOLLY** [ ] [ ]
Oct 94. Music Club; (cd)(c) **COVER TO COVER (w / CRICKETS)** [ ] [-]
Dec 94. Pickwick; (3xcd-box) **A SPECIAL COLLECTION** [ ] [-]
May 95. Pickwick; (cd)(c) **THE BEST OF BUDDY HOLLY** [ ] [-]
May 95. Pickwick; (cd)(c) **THE LEGENDARY BUDDY HOLLY** [ ] [-]
May 95. Pickwick; (3xcd) **A SPECIAL COLLECTION** [ ] [-]
May 95. Pickwick; (cd)(c **MOONDREAMS** [ ] [-]

HONEYDRIPPERS (see under ⇒ LED ZEPPELIN)

HOOK (see under ⇒ LEAVES)

John Lee HOOKER

Born: 22 August 1917, Clarksdale, Mississippi, USA. Lied about age, adding 3 years to get into the army. Moved to Memphis in the 30's and was soon augmenting bluesman ROBERT NIGHTHAWK. In 1943, he uprooted again, this time to Detroit, where it took five years for 'Modern' records to notice and sign him. His debut 'BOOGIE CHILLUN', eventually sold a million copies. To avoid contractual legalities from said label, he recorded scores of 78's, under pseudonyms JOHNNY WILLIAMS, TEXAS SLIM, DELTA JOHN, JOHNNY LEE, JOHN LEE BOOKER, etc. This type of recording, was curbed when he signed to Chicago label 'Vee Jay' in 1955. For the next decade, his prolific work included DIMPLES (a 1956 recording that hit UK charts in 1964) and BOOM BOOM (re-recorded smash UK hit in 1992 when aged 75). In 1991, after decades of dogged work but no commercial luck, he finally broke through with UK Top3 album MR.LUCKY. • **Style:** Blues giant, who helped create new electric blues sound, which pioneered elements of R&B, folk and new jazz. • **Songwriters:** Penned own material which was later covered by contemporaries The ANIMALS (mid-60's) / and CANNED HEAT (late 60's). Covered many including; SUGAR MAMA (Sonny Boy Williamson) / etc. • **Trivia:** On 11th April '61, at Gerde's Folk City hall in New York, HOOKER introduced BOB DYLAN as his opening singer.

Recommended: THE BEST OF JOHN LEE HOOKER (*7) / THE BLUES (*7) / CONCERT AT NEWPORT (*6) / THE HEALER (*10) / MR. LUCKY (*7).

JOHN LEE HOOKER – vocals, electric guitar

not issued — Modern
Jan 49. (78) **BOOGIE CHILLEN (BOOGIE CHILDREN). / SALLY MAE (THERE'S A DAY COMIN' BABY)** [-] [ ]
— now with **JAMES WATKINS** – piano / **CURTIS FOSTER** – drums
not issued — King
Mar 49. (78) **BLACK MAN BLUES. (as "TEXAS SLIM") / STOMP BOOGIE (FLUB)** [-] [ ]
— now w/ **ANDREW DUNHAM** – guitar / **EDDIE BURNS** – harmonica
— Released many US 78's over the next several years (some with pseudonyms)
— next as – DELTA JOHN- on 'Regent' records
1949. (78) **HELPLESS BLUES. / GOIN' MAD BLUES** [-] [ ]
— next as – BIRMINGHAM SAM & HIS MAGIC GUITAR- on 'Savoy' records
1949. (78) **LOW DOWN MIDNITE BOOGIE. / LANDING BLUES** [-] [ ]
— next 3 as – JOHN LEE HOOKER- on 'Modern'
1949. (78) **HOBO BLUES. / HOOGIE BOOGIE** [-] [ ]
1949. (78) **WEEPING WILLOW (BOOGIE). / WHISTLIN' AND MOANIN' BLUES (HUMMIN' THE BLUES)** [-] [ ]
1949. (78) **CRAWLING KING SNAKE. / DRIFTING FROM DOOR TO DOOR** [-] [ ]
— next as – JOHNNY WILLIAMS- on 'Prize'
1949. (78) **MISS ROSIE MAE. / HIGHWAY BLUES** [-] [ ]
— next 6 as – JOHN LEE HOOKER- on 'Sensation'

Mar 50. (78) **MISS SADIE MAE. / BURNIN' HELL** [-] [ ]
Apr 50. (78) **CANAL STREET BLUES. / HUCKLE UP BABY** [-] [ ]
May 50. (78) **GOIN' ON HIGHWAY 51 (GOIN' DOWN HIGHWAY 51). / LET YOUR DADDY RIDE (SLOW DOWN YOUR CHATTER BABY)** [-] [ ]
Jun 50. (78) **MY BABY'S GOT SOMETHIN'. / DECORATION DAY BLUES (LORD TAKETH MY BABY AWAY)** [-] [ ]
Jul 50. (78) **BOOGIE CHILLEN 2 (I GOTTA BE COMIN' BACK). / MISS ELOISE (MISS ELOISE, MISS ELOISE)** [-] [ ]
Aug 50. (78 – JOHN LEE COOKER-) **MOANING BLUES. / STOMP BOOGIE (FLUB)** [-] [ ]

—— next as – THE BOOGIE MAN- on 'Acorn'
1949. (78) **DO THE BOOGIE. / MORNING BLUES** [-] [ ]

—— next 3 as – JOHN LEE BOOKER- on 'Chance'
1949. (78) **MISS LORRAINE. / TALKIN' BOOGIE** [-] [ ]
1949. (78) **GRAVEYARD BLUES. / I LOVE TO BOOGIE** [-] [ ]
1949. (78 – JOHN L.BOOKER-) **609 BOOGIE. / ROAD TROUBLE** [-] [ ]

—— next 6 as – TEXAS SLIM- on 'King'
1950. (78) **THE NUMBERS. / DEVIL'S JUMP** [-] [ ]
1950. (78) **I'M GONNA KILL THAT WOMAN. / NIGHTMARE BLUES** [-] [ ]
1950. (78) **HEART TROUBLE BLUES. / SLIM'S STOMP (instrumental)** [-] [ ]
1950. (78) **DON'T GO BABY. / WANDERING BLUES** [-] [ ]
Oct 50. (78) **LATE LAST NIGHT. / DON'T YOU REMEMBER ME** [-] [ ]
Nov 50. (78) **MOANING BLUES. / THINKING BLUES** [-] [ ]

—— next 5 as – JOHN LEE HOOKER- 4 on 'Modern' / then 1 on 'Regal'
Apr 50. (78) **PLAYIN' THE RACES (DREAM A NUMBER). /** [-] [ ]
May 50. (78) **NO FRIEND AROUND (T.B.'S KILLIN' ME). / WEDNESDAY EVENING (SHE LEFT ME – ON MY BENDED KNEE)** [-] [ ]
Jun 50. (78) **GIMME YOUR PHONE NUMBER (IT'S A CRIME AND A SHAME). / ROCK'N'ROLL (I CRIED THE WHOLE NIGHT LONG)** [-] [ ]
Jul 50. (78) **ONE MORE TIME (LET'S TALK IT OVER). / LET YOUR DADDY RIDE** [-] [ ]
1950. (78) **NEVER SATISFIED (JUST LIKE A WOMAN). / NOTORIETY WOMAN (NO PLACE TO STAY)** [-] [ ]

—— next as – JOHN LEE BOOKER- on 'Gone /Chess'
1950. (78) **MAD MAN BLUES. / BOOGIE NOW (HEY BOOGIE)** [-] [ ]

—— next as – JOHN LEE HOOKER- on 'Modern'
1950. (78) **QUEEN BEE. / JOHN L'S HOUSE RENT BOOGIE (OUT THE DOOR I WENT)** [-] [ ]

—— next 4 as – JOHNNY WILLIAMS- 2 on 'Staff' / 2 on 'Gotham'
1950. (78) **HOUSE RENT BOOGIE. / WANDERING BLUES** [-] [ ]
1950. (78) **PRISON BOUND. / BUMBLE BEE BLUES** [-] [ ]
1951. (78) **REAL GONE GAL. / QUESTIONNAIRE BLUES** [-] [ ]
1951. (78) **LITTLE BOY BLUE. / MY DADDY WAS A JOCKEY** [-] [ ]

—— next as – JOHN LEE- on 'Gotham'
1951. (78) **CATFISH. / MEAN OLD TRAIN** [-] [ ]

—— next 3 as – JOHN LEE BOOKER- on 'Chess'
Jun 51. (78) **LEAVE MY WIFE ALONE. / RAMBLIN' BY MYSELF** [-] [ ]
Jul 51. (78) **GROUND HOG BLUES. / LOUISE** [-] [ ]
(above also issued Jan 52 as – JOHN L.HOOKER- on 'Modern')
Aug 51. (78) **HIGH PRICED WOMAN. / UNION STATION BLUES** [-] [ ]

—— next 5 as – JOHN LEE HOOKER- 4 on 'Modern' / then 1 on 'Chess'
Sep 51. (78) **(FOUR) WOMEN IN MY LIFE. / TEASE ME BABY (TEASE YOUR DADDY)** [-] [ ]
Nov 51. (78) **I'M IN THE MOOD. / HOW CAN YOU DO IT** [-] [ ]
Dec 51. (78) **TURN OVER A NEW LEAF. / ANYBODY SEEN MY BABY (JOHNNY SAYS COME BACK)** [-] [ ]
Feb 52. (78) **ROCK ME MAMA (GOOD ROCKIN' MAMA). / COLD CHILLS (ALL OVER ME)** [-] [ ]
Jul 52. (78) **WALKIN' THE BOOGIE. / SUGAR MAMA** [-] [ ]

—— next 2 as – JOHN LEE HOOKER & "LITTLE" EDDIE KIRKLAND- on 'Modern'
Sep 52. (78) **IT HURTS ME SO. / I GOT EYES FOR YOU** [-] [ ]
Nov 52. (78) **KEY TO THE HIGHWAY. / BLUEBIRD BLUES** [-] [ ]

—— next 3 as – JOHN LEE HOOKER- 2 on 'Modern' / 1 on 'Chess'
Feb 53. (78) **IT'S BEEN A LONG TIME BABY. / ROCK HOUSE BOOGIE** [-] [ ]
Apr 53. (78) **RIDE 'TIL I DIE. / IT'S STORMIN' AND RAININ'** [-] [ ]
Jun 53. (78) **IT'S MY OWN FAULT (BABY, I PROVE MY LOVE TO YOU). / WOMEN AND MONEY** [-] [ ]

—— next 4 as – JOHNNY LEE HOOKER- 1 on 'JVB' / then 3 on 'Modern'
1953. (78) **BOOGIE RAMBLER. / NO MORE DOGGIN'** [-] [ ]
Jul 53. (78) **PLEASE TAKE ME BACK. / LOVE MONEY CAN'T BUY** [-] [ ]
Aug 53. (78) **NEED SOMEBODY. / TOO MUCH BOOGIE** [-] [ ]
Sep 53. (78) **I WONDER (LITTLE DARLING). / JUMP ME (ONE MORE TIME)** [-] [ ]

—— next 3 as – JOHN LEE BOOKER- on 'DeLuxe' / then 2 on 'Rockin'
Sep 53. (78) **BLUE MONDAY (I AIN'T GOT NOBODY). / LOVIN' GUITAR MAN** [-] [ ]
Oct 53. (78) **MY BABY DON'T LOVE YOU. / REAL REAL GONE** [-] [ ]
Dec 53. (78 – JOHNNY LEE-) **I'M A BOOGIE MAN. / I CAME TO SEE MY BABY** [-] [ ]
Oct 53. (78) **BLUE MONDAY (I AIN'T GOT NOBODY). / LOVIN' GUITAR MAN** [-] [ ]
Nov 53. (78) **STUTTERIN' BLUES. / POURING DOWN RAIN (WOBBLIN' BABY)** [-] [ ]

—— next 9 as – JOHN LEE HOOKER- 2 on 'Chart' / then 7 on 'Modern'
1954. (78) **GOIN' SOUTH. / WOBBLIN' BABY** [-] [ ]
1954. (78) **BLUE MONDAY (I AIN'T GOT NOBODY). / MISBELIEVING BABY (MY BABY PUT YOU DOWN)** [-] [ ]
1954. (78) **DOWN CHILD. / GOTTA BOOGIE (GONNA BOOGIE)** [-] [ ]
1954. (78) **LET'S TALK IT OVER. / I TRIED HARD** [-] [ ]
1954. (78) **BAD BOY. / COOL LITTLE CAR** [-] [ ]
1954. (78) **SHAKE, HOLLER AND RUN. / HALF A STRANGER** [-] [ ]
1955. (78) **TAXI DRIVER. / YOU RECEIVE ME** [-] [ ]
1955. (78) **HUG AND SQUEEZE (YOU). / THE SYNDICATOR (SYNDICATE)** [-] [ ]
1955. (78) **LOOKIN' FOR A WOMAN. / I'M READY** [-] [ ]

—— from now on as – JOHN LEE HOOKER- on 'Vee Jay'
Dec 55. (7") **MAMBO CHILLUN. / TIME IS MARCHING** [-] [ ]
Apr 56. (7") **TROUBLE BLUES. / EVERY NIGHT** [-] [ ]
Jun 56. (7") **DIMPLES. / BABY LEE** [-] [ ]
Sep 56. (7") **I'M SO WORRIED BABY. / THE ROAD IS SO ROUGH** [-] [ ]
Apr 57. (7") **I'M SO EXCITED. / I SEE YOU WHEN YOU'RE WEAK** [-] [ ]
Aug 57. (7") **LITTLE WHEEL. / ROSIE MAE** [-] [ ]
Sep 57. (7") **YOU CAN LEAD ME BABY. / UNFRIENDLY WOMAN** [-] [ ]
Jul 58. (7") **I LOVE YOU HONEY. / YOU'VE TAKEN MY WOMAN** [-] [ ]
Feb 59. (7") **I'M IN THE MOOD. / MAUDIE** [-] [ ]
Apr 59. (7") **BOOGIE CHILLUN. / TENNESSEE BLUES** [-] [ ]
Jun 59. (7") **CRAWLIN' KINGSNAKE. / HOBO BLUES** [-] [ ]

Riverside | Battle

1959. (lp) **THE FOLK BLUES OF . . .** [ ] [ ]
– Black snake / How long blues / Wobblin' baby / She's long, she's tall, she weeps like a willow tree / Pea-vine special / Tupelo blues / I'm prison bound / I rowed a little boat / Water boy / Church bell tone / Bundle up and go / Good mornin' lil' school girl / Behind the plow.
1960. (lp) **THAT'S MY STORY** [-] [ ]
– I need some money / I'm wanderin' / Democrat man / I want to talk about you / Gonna use my rod / Wednesday evening blues / No more doggin' / One of these days, I'll believe I'll go back home / You're leavin' me baby / That's my story / Black snake / How long blues / Wobblin' baby / She's long, she's tall, she weeps like . . . / Peavine special / Tupelo blues / I rowed a little boat / Water boy / Church bell tone / Bundle up and go. *(UK-iss.Nov88 on 'Ace')*

not issued | Fortune

1959. (7") **609 BOOGIE. / (MISS SADIE MAE) CURL MY BABY'S HAIR** [-] [ ]
1960. (7") **CRY BABY. / LOVE YOU BABY** [-] [ ]
1960. (7") **CRAZY ABOUT THAT WALK. / WE'RE ALL GOD'S CHILLUN** [-] [ ]

not issued | Hi-Q / Elmor

1959. (7") **BIG FINE WOMAN. / BLUES FOR CHRISTMAS** [-] [ ]
1960. (7") **BALLAD TO ABRAHAM LINCOLN (HE GOT ASSASSINATED). / MOJO HAND (RISIN' SUN)** [-] [ ]
1960. (7") **I LOST MY JOB (TELL YOU A STORY). / DEEP DOWN IN MY HEART (HOW LONG CAN THIS GO ON)** [-] [ ]
1960. (7") **SHAKE IT UP (JOHNNY LEE & THE THING). / (I) LOST MY JOB (TELL YOU A STORY)** [-] [ ]

Stateside | Vee Jay

Apr 60. (7") **SOLID SENDER. / NO SHOES** [-] [ ]
Jul 60. (7") **TUPELO (BACKWATER BLUES). / DUSTY ROAD** [-] [ ]
Feb 61. (7") **I'M MAD AGAIN. / I'M GOING UPSTAIRS** [-] [ ]
Apr 61. (7") **WANT AD BLUES. / TAKE ME AS I AM** [-] [ ]
Feb 62. (7") **BOOM BOOM. / DRUG STORE WOMAN** [-] [60]
Apr 62. (7") **SHE'S MINE (KEEP YOUR HANDS TO YOURSELF). / A NEW LEAF** [-] [ ]
1962. (lp) **FOLKLORE OF JOHN LEE HOOKER** [ ] [ ]
– Tupelo / I'm mad again / I'm going upstairs / Wanted blues / Five years long / I like to see you walk / The hobo / Hard headed woman / Wednesday evening blues / Take me as I am / My first wife left me / You're looking good tonight. *(re-iss.1974 on 'Joy')*
Nov 62. (7") **FRISCO BLUES. / TAKE A LOOK AT YOURSELF** [-] [ ]
1963. (7") **I'M LEAVING. / BIRMINGHAM BLUES** [-] [ ]
1963. (7") **DON'T LOOK BACK. / SEND ME YOUR PILLOW** [-] [ ]
1963. (lp) **THE BIG SOUL OF . . .** [ ] [-]
– Frisco blues / Take a look at yourself / Send me your pillow / She shot me down / I love her / Old time shimmy / You know I love you / Big soul / Good rocking mama / Onions / No one told me. *(re-iss.1969 + 1974 on 'Joy')*
Jul 63. (7") **BOOM BOOM. / FRISCO BLUES** [ ] [60] May 62
May 64. (7") **DIMPLES. / I'M LEAVING** [23] [ ]
1964. (lp) **PREACHING THE BLUES** [-] [ ]
Sep 64. (7") **I LOVE YOU HONEY. / SEND ME YOUR PILLOW** [ ] [ ]
1964. (lp) **I WANT TO SHOUT THE BLUES** [ ] [ ]
– I'm leaving / Love is a burning thing / Birmingham blues / I want to shout / Don't look back / I want to hug you / Poor me / I want to ramble / Half a stranger / My grinding mill / Bottle up and go / One way ticket.
1964. (7") **YOUR BABE AIN'T SWEET LIKE MINE. / BIG LEGS, TIGHT SHIRT** [-] [ ]
1964. (7") **IT SERVES ME RIGHT (TO SUFFER). / FLOWERS ON THE HOUR** [-] [ ]
1964. (7") **SHAKE IT BABY. / LET'S MAKE IT BABY** [ ] [ ]
Some older singles were given light mid-60's

Pye Int. | Chess

Aug 64. (7") **HIGH PRICED WOMAN. / SUGAR MAMA** [ ] [ ]
Nov 64. (7"ep) **LOVE BLUES** [ ] [ ]

Sue | not issued

Jun 65. (7") **I'M IN THE MOOD. / BOOGIE CHILLUN'** [ ] [-]

Fontana | not issued

Nov 65. (lp) **BLUE** (rec. 1960) [ ] [-]

not issued Impulse
Jan 66. (7") **BOTTLE UP AND GO. / MONEY** [-] [ ]
Planet Planet
Feb 66. (7"as JOHN LEE'S GROUNDHOGS) **I'LL NEVER FALL IN LOVE AGAIN. / OVER YOU BABY** [-] [ ]
May 66. (7") **MAI LEE. / DON'T BE MESSING WITH MY BREAD** [ ] [ ]
Chess Chess
Aug 66. (7") **LET'S GO OUT TONIGHT. / I'M IN THE MOOD** [ ] [ ]
Jan 67. (lp) **REAL FOLK BLUES** [ ] [ ]
– Let's go out tonight / Please lovin' man / Stella Mae / I put my trust in you / I'm in the mood / You know, I know / I'll never trust your love again / One bourbon, one Scotch, one beer / The waterfront. *(cd-iss.Feb90 on 'M.C.A.')*
H.M.V. Impulse
1968. (lp) **IT SERVES YOU RIGHT TO SUFFER** [ ] [ ] Feb 66
– Sugar mama / Declaration day / Money (that's what I want) / It serves you right to suffer / Shake it baby / Country boy / Bottle up and go / You're wrong. *(re-iss.1977 on 'Impulse') (re-iss,Feb84 on 'Jasmine')*
H.M.V. Bluesway
1968. (lp) **LIVE AT THE CAFE AU GO-GO (live)** [ ] [ ] Jul 66
– I'm bad like Jesse James / She's long, she's tall / When my first wife left me / Heartaches and misery / One bourbon, on scotch and one beer / I don't want no trouble / I'll never get out of these blues alive / Seven days. *(re-iss.1973 on 'Bluesway') (re-iss.+c+cd.Oct88 on 'B.G.O.')*
Jan 68. (7") **WANT AD BLUES. / THE MOTOR CITY IS BURNING** [-] [ ]
Mar 68. (7") **CRY BEFORE I GO. / MR. LUCKY** [-] [ ]
Stateside Bluesway
1968. (lp) **URBAN BLUES** [ ] [ ]
– Cry before I go / Boom boom / Backbiters & syndicaters / Mr.Lucky / I can't stand to leave you / My own blues / Think twice before you go / I'm standing in line / Hot water springs (pt.1 & 2) / Wand ad blues *(re-iss.+cd.Oct91 on 'B.G.O.')*
Jun 68. (7") **THINK TWICE BEFORE YOU GO. / BACKBITERS AND SYNDICATER** [-] [ ]
Probe Bluesway
1969. (lp) **IF YOU MISS 'IM . . . I GET 'IM** [ ] [ ]
– Hookers (if you miss 'im . . .I got 'im) / Baby I love you / Lonesome mood / Bang bang bang / If you take care of me, I'll take care of you / Baby, be strong / I wanna be your puppy / I don't care when you go / Have mercy on my soul.

— next with **PRETTY PURDIE** – drums / **ERNIE HAYES** – mouth harp

Feb 69. (7") **MEAN MEAN WOMAN. / I DON'T WANNA GO TO VIETNAM** [-] [ ]
1969. (lp) **SIMPLY THE TRUTH** [ ] [-]
– I don't wanna go to Vietnam / I wanna boogaloo / Tantalizing with the blues / I'm just a drifter / Mini skirts / Mean mean woman / One room country shack. *(re-iss.+cd.Feb89 on 'B.G.O.')*
1968. (lp) **BURNIN'** [-] [ ]
– Boom boom / Process / Lost a good girl / A new leaf / Blues before sunrise / Let's make it / I got a letter / Thelma / Drug store woman / Keep you hands to yourself / What do you say. *(re-iss.1974 on 'Joy') (re-iss.+c.May87 on 'Topline')*
Joy Vee-Jay
1968. (lp) **I'M JOHN LEE HOOKER** [ ] [ ]
1969. (lp) **TRAVELIN'** [ ] [ ]
– No shoes / I wanna walk / Canal Street blues / Keep on / I'm a stranger / Whiskey and wimmen / Solid sender / Sunny land / Goin' to California / I can't believe / I'll know tonight / Dusty road. *(re-iss.1974)*
1969. (lp) **CONCERT AT NEWPORT (live 24 Jun'60)** [-] [ ]
– I can't quit you now blues / Stop baby don't hold me that way / Tupelo / Bus station blues / Freight train be my friend / Boom boom boom Talk that talk baby / Sometime baby you make me feel so bad / You've got to walk by yourself / Let's make it / The mighty fire
1969. (lp) **IN PERSON** [-] [ ]
– I'm leaving Love is a burning thing / Birmingham blues / I want to shout / Don't look back / I want to hug youu / Poor me / I want to ramble / Half a stranger / My grinding mill / Bottle up and go / One way ticket.

In 1970, he recorded dual live album 'HOOKER'N'HEAT' with CANNED HEAT.

Probe A.B.C.
May 71. (7") **KICK HIT 4 HIT KIX U. / DOIN' THE SHOUT** [-] [ ]
May 71. (d-lp) **ENDLESS BOOGIE** [ ] [ ] Mar 71
– (I got) A good 'un / Pots on, gas on high / Kick hit 4 hit kix u / I don't need no stream heart / We might as well call it through . . . / Sittin' in my dark room / Endless boogie parts 27 & 28.

— next with **ROBERT HOOKER** – organ / **LUTHER TUCKER** – guitar / **ELVIN BISHOP + DON 'Sugarcane' HARRIS** – piano / **CHARLIE MUSSELWHITE** – harmonica / **VAN MORRISON**

Apr 72. (lp) **NEVER GET OUT OF THESE BLUES ALIVE** [ ] [ ] Mar 72
– Bumblebee bumblebee / Hit the road / Country boy / Boogee with the Hook / If you take care of me (I'll take care of you) / I've got a go / T.B. sheets / Letter to my baby / Never get out of these blues alive / Baby I love you / Lonesome road. *(cd-iss.Feb90 & Jan91 on 'See For Miles', 4 extra tracks)*
Apr 72. (7") **BOOGIE WITH THE HOOK. / NEVER GET OUT OF THESE BLUES ALIVE** [-] [ ]
Dec 72. (lp) **LIVE AT SOLEDAD PRISON (live)** [-] [ ]
– Super lover / I'm your crosscut saw / What's the matter baby Lucille / Boogie everywhere I go / Serve me right to suffer / Bang bang bang bang.
1973. (lp) **BORN IN MISSISSIPPI, RAISED UP IN TENNESSEE** [-] [ ]
– Born in Mississippi, raised up in Tennessee / How many more years you gonna dog me 'round / Going down ./ Younger stud / King of the world / Tell me you love me.
A.B.C. A.B.C.
Nov 74. (lp) **FREE BEER & CHICKEN** [ ] [ ]
– Make it funky / Five long years / 713 blues / 714 blues / One bourbon one Scotch one beer / Homework / Bluebird / Sittin' on top of the world / (You'l never amount to anything if you don't go to) College (a fortuitous concatenation of events (a) I know how to rock, (b) Nothin' but the best, (c) The scratch. *(re-iss.+cd.Oct91 on 'B.G.O.')*
not issued Tomato
Mar 79. (d-lp) **THE CREAM (live 1978)** [-] [ ] 1977
– Hey hey / Rock steady / Tupelo / You know it ain't right / She's gone / T.B. sheets / Sugar mama / One room country shack / Drug store woman / I want you to roll me / Bar room drinking / Little girl / Louise / When my first wife left me* / Boogie on*. *(re-iss.+c+cd.Jan88 on 'Charly', cd-omits*)(re-iss. cd Jun93)*

In 1980, he cameos with loads of other stars, in the film 'BLUES BROTHERS'.

Silvertone Chameleon
Oct 89. (lp)(c)(cd) **THE HEALER** [63] [62]
– The healer / I'm in the mood / Baby Lee / Cuttin' out / Think twice before you go / Saly Mae / That's alright / Rockin' chair / My dream / No substitute.
Jan 90. (7")(12") **THE HEALER. / ROCKIN' CHAIR** [ ] [ ]
(cd-s+=) – No substitute. ('A' feat. CARLOS SANTANA)
May 90. (7") **I'M IN THE MOOD. ("JOHN LEE HOOKER & BONNIE RAITT") / MY DREAM** [ ] [ ]
(cd-s+=) – ('A'version) / That's alright. *(re-iss.Nov92)*
Oct 90. (7")(c-s) **BABY LEE. / CUTTIN' OUT** [ ] [-]

— with **STEVE EHERMAN** – bass / **SCOTT MATTHEWS** – drums + loads on sessions **C.SANTANA / A.COLLINS / R.CRAY / V.MORRISON / K.RICHARDS / BOOKER T. / R.COODER / etc.**

Silvertone Charisma
Aug 91. (cd)(c)(lp) **MR.LUCKY** [3] [ ]
– I want to hug you / Mr.Lucky / Backstabbers / This is hip / I cover the waterfront / Highway 13 / Stripped me naked / Susie / Crawlin' Kingsnake / Father was a jockey.
Aug 91. (7") **MR.LUCKY. / ?** [ ] [ ]
(12"+=)(cd-s+=) – ?
Pointblank Pointblank
Oct 92. (7")(c-s) **BOOM BOOM. / HOMEWORK** [16] [ ]
(cd-s+=) – The blues will never die / Thought I heard.
(cd-s) – ('A'version) / Thought I heard.
Nov 92. (cd)(c)(lp) **BOOM BOOM** (new rec.old tunes) [15] [ ]
– Boom boom / I'm bad like Jesse James / Same old blues again / Sugar mama / Trick bag (shoppin' for my tombstone) / Boogie at Russian Hill / Hittin' the bottle again / Bottle up and go / Thought I heard / I ain't gonna suffer no more. *(re-iss.cd+c Oct93)*
Jan 93. (7")(c-s) **BOOGIE AT RUSSIAN HILL. / THE BLUES WILL NEVER DIE** [53] [ ]
(cd-s+=) – I'm bad like Jesse James / Driftin' blues (w/ JOHN HAMMOND).

— In May'93, he teamed up with VAN MORRISON on UK No.31 hit 'GLORIA'.

— with **ROY ROGERS** – slide guitar/ **CHARLES BROWN** – piano/ **DANNY CARON** – guitar/ **RUTH DAVIS + JIM GYETT** – bass/ **GAYLORD BIRCH + BOWEN BROWN** – drums/ guests **CARLOS SANTANA + CHESTER THOMPSON** (track 1)/ **VAN MORRISON + BOOKER T** (track 4)

Feb 95. (7")(c-s) **CHILL OUT (THINGS GONNA CHANGE). / TUPELO** [45] [ ]
(cd-s+=) – Boom boom.
(cd-s+=) – Up and down / Thought I heard.
Feb 95. (cd)(c)(lp) **CHILL OUT** [23] [ ]
– Chill out (things gonna change) / Deep blue sea / Kiddio / Medley: Serves me right to suffer – Syndicator / One bourbon, one scotch, one beer / Tupelo / Woman on my mind / Annie Mae / Too young / Talkin' the blues / If you've never been in love / We'll meet again.

– more compilations, etc. –

1964. Ember; (lp) **SINGS THE BLUES** [ ] [-]
Jul 64. Pye Int./ US= Chess; (lp) **HOUSE OF THE BLUES** (50's recordings) [ ] [ ] 1960
(UK re-iss.Jan67 on 'Marble Arch', hit No.34) (re-iss.Oct87 on 'Chess') (cd-iss.Dec86 on 'Vogue')
Apr 82. Chess; (lp) **CHESS MASTERS** [-] [ ]
1969. Joy/ US= Vee Jay; (lp) **THE BEST OF JOHN LEE HOOKER** [ ] [ ]
(re-iss.1974 on 'Crescendo', cd,d-c,d-lp re-iss.Jan89)
1969. Polydor/ US= Riverside; (lp) **TUPELO BLUES** [ ] [ ]
1970. Stax; (lp) **THAT'S WHERE IT'S AT (rec. '61)** [ ] [ ]
– Teachin' the blues / Goin' to Louisiana / I need you / My love comes down for you / Please don't go / I just don't know / Slow and easy / Two white horses / So bad / Grinder man.
1970. Stax; (7") **SLOW AND EASY. / GRINDER MAN** [-] [ ]
1971. Fantasy; (d-lp) **BOOGIE CHILLUN (live 1962)** [-] [ ]
(UK-iss.+cd.May86 as 'MAMBO CHILLUN' on 'Charly')
1977. Fantasy; (lp) **BLACK SNAKE** [-] [ ]
1971. United Artists; (lp) **COAST TO COAST** [ ] [-]
1972. Atlantic/ US= Atco; (lp)(c) **DETROIT SPECIAL** [ ] [ ]
Mar 75. Atlantic/ US= Atco; (lp)(c) **DON'T TURN ME FROM YOUR DOOR** [ ] [ ]
1973. Greenbottle; (lp) **JOHNNY LEE VOL.1** [-] [ ]
(re-iss.May81 on 'Cadet-Ace')
1973. Checker/ US= Chess; (lp) **MADMEN BLUES** [ ] [ ]
1971. Speciality; (lp) **ALONE (rec. 48-51)** [-] [ ] 1967
(UK-iss.1981 on 'London') (US re-iss.+cd.Mar90 on 'Tomato')(re-iss.d-cd Oct93)
1973. Sonet; (lp) **HOOKER, HOPKINS & HOGE** [ ] [-]
(re-iss.1974)
Feb 77. D.J.M.; (d-lp) **DIMPLES** [ ] [-]
1972. New World; (lp) **JOHN LEE HOOKER** [ ] [-]
1973. Polydor; (lp) **SLIM'S STOMP** [ ] [-]
1975. Code; (lp) **BLACK RHYTHM & BLUES** [-] [ ]
(UK iss. Nov 84 on 'Festival')
Jan 76. Code; (lp) **L'ADVENTURE DU JAZZ** [-] [ ]
Sep 79. Jewel; (lp) **I FEEL GOOD** [ ] [-]
Oct 79. Gusto; (d-lp) **MOANIN' AND STONY BLUES** [ ] [-]
Aug 79. Charly; (lp) **NO FRIEND AROUND** [ ] [-]
(re-iss.Sep82 on 'Red Lightnin'; cd-iss.Apr95)
Jul 80. Charly; (7"m) **DIMPLES. / BOOM BOOM / ONIONS** [ ] [-]
1980. Charly; (lp) **THIS IS HIP** [ ] [-]
(re-iss.Jan85)
Mar 81. Charly; (lp) **EVERYBODY ROCKIN'** [ ] [-]
Nov 81. Charly; (lp) **MOANING THE BLUES** [ ] [-]
Jul 84. Charly; (lp) **SOLID SENDER** [ ] [-]
Feb 87. Charly; (cd) **HOUSE RENT BOOGIE** [ ] [-]
Oct 88. Charly; (lp)(cd) **THE BLUESWAY SESSIONS** [ ] [-]
Mar 89. Charly; (cd) **LET'S MAKE IT** [ ] [-]
Feb 93. Charly; (cd) **BLUES FOR BIG TOWN** [ ] [-]
Feb 93. Charly; (cd) **THE VEE-JAY YEARS 1955-1964** [ ] [-]
1981. Ace; (7") **SHAKE, HOLLER & RUN. / ?** [ ] [-]

1992. Ace; (cd) **GRAVEYARD BLUES.** [ ] [-]
May 93. Ace; (cd) **THE LEGENDARY MODERN RECORDINGS 1948-1954** [ ] [-]
Jul 93. Ace; (cd) **EVERYBODY'S BLUES** [ ] [-]
Apr 81. Muse; (lp) **SITTIN' HERE THINKIN'** [-] [ ] 1979
(re-iss.Jul83 on 'Happy Bird')
Apr 91. Muse; (cd) **SAD AND LONESOME** [ ] [ ]
1983. M.C.A.; (lp) **LONESOME MOOD** [-] [ ]
May 82. M.C.A.; (lp)(c) **TANTALIZING WITH THE BLUES** [ ] [ ]
Aug 91. M.C.A.; (cd) **INTRODUCING . . .** [ ] [ ]
Oct 91. M.C.A.; (cd)(c)(lp) **THE COMPLETE CHESS FOLK BLUES SESSIONS** [ ] [ ]
May 93. M.C.A.; (cd)(c) **THE BEST OF JOHN LEE HOOKER 1965-1974** [ ] [ ]

Below was issued in US as 'BLUES BEFORE SUNRISE' in 1976 of early work.
Jul 84. Bulldog; (lp) **DO THE BOOGIE** [ ] [ ]
(original title re-iss.1986) (US re-iss.Nov84 on 'Astan')
Aug 85. Deja Vu; (lp)(c) **THE COLLECTION: 20 BLUES GREATS** [ ] [-]
(cd-iss.Jun88)
Apr 93. Deja Vu; (cd)(c) **THE GOLD COLLECTION** [ ] [-]
Nov 87. Krazy Kat; (lp) **DETROIT BLUES (1950-51)** [ ] [-]
May 88. Blues City; (lp)(c)(cd) **GREATEST HITS** [ ] [-]
May 88. Tomato; (lp)(c)(cd) **LIVE (live)** [-] [ ]
Jun 88. Rhino; (lp) **INFINITE BOOGIE** [-] [ ]
Aug 89. Instant; (lp)(c)(cd) **THE BOOGIE MAN** [ ] [-]
Feb 90. Demon; (lp)(cd) **THE DETROIT LION** [ ] [-]
(re-iss.cd Oct93)
Apr 91. Magnum Force; (cd)(c) **NUTHIN' BUT THE BLUES** [ ] [-]
May 91. Music Club; (cd) **THE BEST OF JOHN LEE HOOKER** [ ] [-]
– Boom boom / Shake it baby (original) / The right time / Dimples / Boogie chillun / Mambo chillun / Wheel and deal / I'm so excited / Trouble blues / Everybody's rockin' / Unfriendly woman / Time is marchin' / I see you when you're weak / I'm in the mood / Will the circle be unbroken / This is hip / Hobo blues / Solid sender.
Jun 91. Mainstream; (cd) **HALF A STRANGER** [ ] [-]
Jun 93. Mainstream; (cd) **BOOM BOOM** [ ] [-]
Jun 93. Mainstream; (cd) **I'M IN THE MOOD** [ ] [-]
Jul 93. Mainstream; (cd) **SHAKE IT BABY** [ ] [-]
Mar 93. O.B.C.; (cd) **BURNING HELL** [ ] [-]
Apr 93. Sixteen; (cd) **16 GREATEST HITS** [ ] [-]
Mar 94. Ace; (cd) **ORIGINAL FOLK BLUES OF JOHN LEE HOOKER** [ ] [-]
Apr 94. Just A Memory; (cd) **THE RISING SUN COLLECTION** [ ] [-]
May 94. Laserlight; (cd)(c) **BOOM BOOM** [ ] [-]
Jul 94. See For MIles; (cd) **THE EP COLLECTION . . .PLUS** [ ] [-]
May 94. Charly; (cd) **TWO ON ONE** (w / MUDDY WATERS) [ ] [-]
Aug 94. Charly; (cd) **WHISKEY & WIMMEN** [ ] [-]
(re-iss.Aug95 on 'Imp')
Dec 94. Marble Arch; (cd)(c) **THE BOSS** [ ] [-]
Feb 95. Castle; (cd) **THE COLLECTION** [ ] [-]
Apr 95. Charly; (4xcd-box+book) **THE BOOGIE MAN** [ ] [-]
Jul 95. Charly; (d-cd) **THE VERY BEST OF JOHN LEE HOOKER** [ ] [-]
Sep 95. Best; (cd) **JOHN LEE HOOKER** [ ] [-]
Nov 95. The Collection; (3xcd-box) **THE COLLECTION** [ ] [-]
Dec 95. Opal; (cd) **CRAWLING KINGSNAKE 1948-52** [ ] [-]

Stix HOOPER (see under ⇒ CRUSADERS)

HOOTIE & THE BLOWFISH

Formed: South Carolina, USA . . .1993 by DARIUS, etc (see below). Their debut single 'HOLD MY HAND' stormed America, as did multi-million selling No.1 album 'CRACKED REAR VIEW'. In Britain, they were lauded by the likes of TV/radio presenter Danny Baker, which I suppose helped gain growing reputation on Virgin FM safe rock music station. • **Style:** Corporate melodic MTV adult-orientated rock, with similiar vox references of African-American DARIUS, to BRAD ROBERTS (Crash Test Dummies) or EDDIE VEDDER (Pearl Jam). • **Songwriters:** Group? • **Trivia:** DAVID CROSBY guested backing vox on the song 'HOLD MY HAND'.

Recommended CRACKED REAR VIEW (*7)

DARIUS RUCKER – vocals, acoustic guitar, percussion / **MARK BRYAN** – guitars, vocals, etc / **DEAN FELBER** – bass, clavinet, vocals / **JIM 'SONI' SONEFELD** – drums, vocals, piano, etc.

Atlantic Atlantic
Feb 95. (c-s) **HOLD MY HAND / I GO BLIND** [50] [10] Sep94
(cd-s+=) – Running from an angel.
Mar 95. (cd)(c) **CRACKED REAR VIEW** [12] [1] Jun94
– Hannah Jane / Hold my hand / Let her cry / Only wanna be with you / Running from an angel / I'm goin' home / Drowning / Time / Look away / Not even the trees / Goodbye.
May 95. (c-s) **LET HER CRY / FINE LINE** [75] [9]
(cd-s+=) – Hannah Jane (live) / Where were you.
(cd-s) – ('A'side) / Goodbye (live) / The ballad of John and Yoko (live) / Hold my hand (live).
Aug 95. (c-s) **ONLY WANNA BE WITH YOU / USE ME (live)** [ ] [6] Jul95
(cd-s) – ('A'live).
Nov 95. (c-s)(cd-s) **TIME /** [-] [27]

Peter HOPE & Richard H. KIRK (see under ⇒ CABARET VOLTAIRE)

Bruce HORNSBY

Born: 23 Nov'54, Williamsburg, Virginia, USA. In 1978, after studying music at Miami University and Boston's Berklee School Of Music, he formed The BRUCE HORNSBY BAND with older brother BOBBY and drummer JOHN MOLO. In 1980, on the advice of singer MICHAEL McDONALD, he moved to Los Angeles, where he and his brother wrote pop tunes for 20th Cent Publishing. 2 years later, he became friends with HUEY LEWIS, who was breaking big in the US, and who wanted to cover BRUCE's song on 'Sports' album. In 1983, BRUCE joined SHEENA EASTON's backing tour band, but continued to send demos to the majors. In 1985, he formed BRUCE HORNSBY & THE RANGE who soon signed to 'RCA'. A year later, he hit US Top 75 with 'EVERY LITTLE KISS', but by end of year he was at No.1 with 'THE WAY IT IS'. This also made UK Top 20 earlier, as did it's same-titled album, which went on to hit US Top 3. In 1987, a remixed 'EVERY LITTLE KISS' hit US Top 20, hot on the heels of another Top 5 smash 'MANDOLIN RAIN'. He/they continued to chart constantly as HORNSBY, looked for other outlets to show off his talents. He and brother JOHN had earlier written 'JACOB'S LADDER', which hit US No.1 for HUEY LEWIS & THE NEWS, and he guested on 'Sirius' album by CLANNAD. In 1989, he co-wrote and produced album 'End Of The Innocence' with DON HENLEY. In Sep'90, he filled in on the GRATEFUL DEAD tour for the recently deceased BRETT MYLAND. • **Style:** Soothing US AOR-pop balladeer. • **Songwriters:** He and brother JOHN penned most of material. • **Trivia:** He played accordion on albums by KIM CARNES (View From The House) / PATTI AUSTIN (The Real Me) & HUEY LEWIS (Small World).

Recommended: THE WAY IT IS (*6).

BRUCE HORNSBY & THE RANGE

BRUCE HORNSBY – vocals, keyboards, accordion (ex-SHEENA EASTON Band) / **DAVID MANSFIELD** – violin, mandolin, guitar / **GEORGE MARINELLI** – guitar, vocals / **JOE PUERTA** – bass, vocals / **JOHN MOLO** – drums

R.C.A. R.C.A.
Jul 86. (7") **THE WAY IT IS. / THE RED PLAINS** [15] [1] Sep 86
(12"+=) – The wild frontier.
Sep 86. (7") **EVERY LITTLE KISS. / THE RIVER RUNS LOW** [ ] [72] Jul 86
(12"+=) – The way it is (instrumental).
(re-iss.US May 87 hit No. 14)
Jan 87. (lp)(c)(cd) **THE WAY IT IS** [16] [3] Jun 86
– On the western skyline / Every little kiss / Mandolin rain / The long race / The way it is / Down the road tonight / The wild frontier / The river runs low / The red plains.
Feb 87. (7") **MANDOLIN RAIN. / THE RED PLAINS (live)** [70] [4] Jan 87
(12"+=) – Every little kiss (instrumental).
(cd-s+=) – The way it is (live).

—— **PETER HARRIS** – guitar, etc. repl. MANSFIELD
Apr 88. (lp)(c)(cd) **SCENES FROM THE SOUTHSIDE** [15] [5]
– The show goes on / The old playground / Defenders of the flag / Jacob's ladder / Till the dreaming's done / Look out any window / The valley road / I will walk with you / The road not taken.
May 88. (7") **THE VALLEY ROAD. / THE LONG RACE (live)** [44] [5] Apr 88
(12"+=)(cd-s+=) – Mandolin rain (live).
Jul 88. (7") **LOOK OUT ANY WINDOW. / THE WAY IT IS** [-] [35]
Jul 88. (7") **LOOK OUT ANY WINDOW. / ON THE WESTERN SKYLINE** [ ] [-]
(12"+=)(cd-s+=) – Mandolin rain.
Nov 88. (7") **DEFENDERS OF THE FLAG. / ON THE WESTERN SKYLINE** [-] [ ]
Nov 88. (7") **DEFENDERS OF THE FLAG. / LOOK OUT ANY WINDOW** [ ] [ ]
(12"+=)/ /(cd-s+=) – ('B' live)./ / ('A'live).

—— trimmed to quartet, when PETER HARRIS departed.
Jun 90. (cd)(c)(lp) **A NIGHT ON THE TOWN** [23] [20]
– A night on the town / Carry the water / Fire on the cross / Barren ground / Stranded on easy street / Stander on the mountain / Lost soul / Another day / Special night / These arms of mine.
Jul 90. (7") **ACROSS THE RIVER. / FIRE ON THE CROSS** [ ] [18] Jun 90
(12"+=)(cd-s+=) – Mandolin rain (live).
Oct 90 (c-s)(cd-s) **LOST SOUL / STANDER ON THE MOUNTAIN** [-] [84]

—— above featured SHAWN COLVIN on vocals
Jan 91. (12") **ANOTHER DAY / CARRY THE WATER / BARREN GROUND** [-] [ ]

Bruce HORNSBY

(solo) with **JIMMY HASLIP** – bass / **JOHN MOLO** – drums. Plus session people **PAT METHENY** – guitar / **BRANDFORD MARSALIS** – saxophone / **JOHN BIGHAM** – guitar / **PHIL COLLINS** – percussion, b.vocals / **WILL ROSS** – rhythm guitar / **JERRY GARCIA** – guitar / **BUD POWELL** – piano / **BONNIE RAITT** – vocals / **GLENN WILSON** – horns/ etc.

RCA-BMG RCA-BMG
Apr 93. (cd)(c)(lp) **HARBOR LIGHTS** [32] [46]
– Harbor lights / Talk of the town / Long tall cool one / China doll / Fields of gray / Rainbow's Cadillac / Passing through / The tide will rise / What a time / Pastures of plenty.
Oct 93. (c-s)(cd-s) **FIELDS OF GRAY. /** [-] [69]

—— with **JERRY CARCIA + PAT METHENY** – guitar / **DEBBIE HENRY** – vocals / **J.T. THOMAS** – organ / **JOHN MOLO** – drums / **JOHN D'EARTH** – trumpet / **BOBBY READ** – saxophone
Aug 95. (cd)(c) **HOT HOUSE** [ ] [68]
– Spider fingers / White wheeled Limousine / Walk in the Sun / The changes / The tango king / Big rumble / Country doctor / The longest night / Hot house ball / Swing

street / Cruise control.
Aug 95. (c-s)(cd-s) **WALK IN THE SUN /** - 54

HORSLIPS

Formed: Dublin, Ireland . . . 1970 out of THE CREATURES by CHARLES O'CONNOR, etc (see below). After a hit single in Ireland 'JOHNNY'S WEDDING', they decided to go pro on St.Patrick's Day, 17th Mar'72. After another homeland hit 'GREEN GRAVEL', they formed own independent label 'Oats', although many majors came knocking. Early in 1973, after using The ROLLING STONES mobile unit to record themselves, they unleashed debut lp 'HAPPY TO MEET . . . '. This became fastest selling album in Ireland for some time to come, and was soon distributed in Britain by 'RCA'. During a STEELEYE SPAN support tour, they issued mythical concept album 'THE TAIN', which hosted a one that got away 'DEARG DOOM'. After a few more releases on the mainland, they succumbed to 'D.J.M.' label, who provided them with first and only UK Top 40 lp 'BOOK OF INVASIONS' in 1977. Failed to match critically or commercially previous product, thus their split. • **Style:** Traditional folk-rock band, weaving a fusion of medieval sound lying between the instrumentation of The CHIEFTAINS and early THIN LIZZY. • **Songwriters:** Group merged trad. tunes with own compositions. • **Trivia:** Off-shoot group The HOST made an lp 'TRYAL' about the 19th century witch hunts.

Recommended: HORSLIPS STORY – STRAIGHT FROM THE HORSE'S MOUTH (*6)

CHARLES O'CONNOR – vocals, mandolin, fiddle, concertina / **JOHN FEAN** – guitar, vocals, banjo, flute repl. G.GUIEST who repl. DECLAN SINNOTT / **BARRY DEVLIN** – bass, vocals / **JIM LOCKHART** – keyboards, flute, pipes / **EAMON CARR** – drums, percussion

Irish / not issued

Feb 72. (7") **JOHNNY'S WEDDING. /** -
Jan 73. (7") **GRAVEL GREEN. / FAIRY KING** -
(above issued in Ireland Jul72)

Oats / Atco

Jan 73. (lp)(c) **HAPPY TO MEET . . . SORRY TO PART**
– Happy to meet / Hall of mirrors / Clergy's lamentation / An bratach ban / The shamrock shore / Flower among them all / Bim istigh ag ol / Furniture / Ace and deuce / Dance to your daddy / The high reel / Scalloway rip off / The musical priest / Sorry to part. *(re-iss.1979 on 'D.J.M.') (cd-iss.1989 on 'Oats') (cd-iss.Jan95 on 'Outlet')*
Jul 73. (7") **THE HIGH REEL. / FURNITURE**
Oct 73. (7") **DEARG DOOM. / THE SHAMROCK SHORE**
Nov 73. (lp)(c) **THE TAIN**
– Sentanta / Meave's court / Charolais march / You can't fool the beast / Dearg doom / Ferdials song / Gae bolga / Cu Chulainn's lament / Faster than the hound / Silver spear / More than you can chew / The Morrigan's dream / Time to kill. *(cd-iss.May89 & Jan95 on 'Outlet')*
Apr 74. (7") **MORE THAN YOU CAN CHEW. / FASTER THAN THE HOUND** -

Oats-RCA / R.C.A.

Aug 74. (7") **NIGHT TOWN BOY. / WE BRING THE SUMMER WITH US**
Sep 74. (lp)(c) **DANCEHALL SWEETHEARTS**
– Night town boy / The blind can't lead the blind / Stars / We bring the summer with us / Sunburst / Mad Pat / Blind man / King of the fairies / Lonely hearts / The best years of my life. *(cd-iss.1989 on 'I&B') (cd-iss.Jan95 on 'Outlet')*
Feb 75. (7") **KING OF THE FAIRIES. / SUNBURST**
Feb 75. (lp)(c) **THE UNFORTUNATE CUP OF TEA**
– (If that's what you want) That's what you get / Ring-a-rosey / Flirting in the shadows / Self defence / High volume love / The unfortunate cup of tea / Turn your face to the wall / The snakes' farewell to the Emerald Isle / Everything will be alright. *(re-iss.1989 on 'I&B') (cd-iss.Jan95 on 'Outlet')*
May 75. (7") **THAT'S WHAT YOU GET. / SNAKES FAREWELL TO THE EMERALD ISLE** -

Oats IRE / not issued

Nov 75. (lp) **DRIVE THE COLD WINTER AWAY** -
– Rug muire mac do hai (Mary bore a son to God) / Sir Festus Burke-Carolan's frolic / Do'n oiche ud I umbeithil (That night in Bethlehem) / The piper in the meadow straying / Drive the cold winter away / Thompson's / Cottage in the groove / Ny kirree fo nahgtey (The sheep 'neath the snow) / Crabs in the skillet / Denis O'Connor / The snow that melts the soonest / Lullaby / The snow and the frost are all over / Paddy Fahey's / When a man's in love. *(cd-iss.1989 on 'I&B') (cd-iss.Jan95 on 'Outlet')*
May 76. (lp) **HORSLIPS LIVE (live)** -
(cd-iss.Jan95 on 'Outlet')
Aug 76. (7") **DAYBREAK. /** -

D.J.M. / D.J.M.

Dec 76. (lp)(c) **THE BOOK OF INVASIONS – A CELTIC SYMPHONY** 39
– 1st movement – geantrai:- Daybreak / March into trouble / Trouble (with a capital T) / The power and the glory / The rocks remain / Dusk / Sword of light / Dark / 2nd movement – Goltrai:- Warm sweet breath of love / Fantasia (my lagan love) / King of morning, Queen of day / 3rd movement – suantrai:- Sideways to the Sun / Drive the cold winter away / Ride to Hell. *(re-iss.Apr82) (cd-iss.1989 on 'I&B') (cd-iss.Jan95 on 'Outlet')*
Mar 77. (7") **WARM SWEET BREATH OF LOVE. / KING OF MORNING, QUEEN OF DAY**
Jul 77. (7") **THE POWER AND THE GLORY. / SIR FESTUS BURKE** -
Aug 77. (7") **TROUBLE (WITH A CAPITAL T). /** -
Nov 77. (7") **NEW YORK WAKES. / GHOSTS** -
Nov 77. (lp)(c) **ALIENS** 98
– Before the storm / The wrath of the rain / Speed the plough / Sure the boy was green / Come summer / Stowaway / New York wakes / Exiles / Second avenue / Ghosts / A lifetime to pay. *(re-iss.Apr82) (re-iss.+cd.1989 on 'I&B') (cd-iss.Jan95 on 'Outlet')*
Feb 78. (7") **EXILES. / SURE THE BOY WAS GREEN** -
May 78. (7") **SPEED THE PLOUGH. / BRIDGE FROM HEART TO HEART** -
Feb 79. (7") **THE MAN WHO BUILT AMERICA. / LONG WEEKEND** -
Feb 79. (lp)(c) **THE MAN WHO BUILT AMERICA**
– Loneliness / Tonight (you're with me) / I'll be waiting / If it takes all night / Green star liner / The man who built America / Homesick / Long weekend / Letters from home / Long time again. *(re-iss.Apr82) (cd-iss.Aug87 & Jan95 on 'Outlet')*
Jun 79. (7")(10"green-sha-d) **LONELINESS. / HOMESICK** -

Mercury / Mercury

Jan 80. (lp)(c) **SHORT STORIES / TALL TALES**
– Guests of the nation / Law on the run / Unapproved road / Ricochet man / Back in my arms / Summer's most wanted girl / Amazing offer / Rescue me / The life you save / Soap opera. *(cd-iss.Jan95 on 'Outlet')*
Mar 80. (7") **RESCUE ME. / SOAP OPERA** -

Oats / Mercury

Dec 80. (lp)(c) **THE BELFAST GIGS (live)**
– Trouble (with a capital T) / The man who built America / Warm sweet breath of love / The power and the glory / Blindman / Shakin' all over / King of the fairies / Guests of the nation / Dearg doom. *(re-iss.Jan85) (cd-iss.May89) (cd-iss.Jan95 on 'Outlet')*
Dec 80. (7") **SHAKIN' ALL OVER (live). /** -
— Disband early in early 80's.

– compilations, others –

Jan 78. Oats; (lp) **TRACKS FROM THE VAULTS** -
(cd-iss.Jan95 on 'Outlet')
Aug 82. Oats; (lp)(c) **THE BEST OF HORSLIPS** -
(cd-iss.1989 on 'I&B')
Jan 85. Oats; (lp) **HORSLIPS HISTORY** -
Aug 84. Stoic; (lp)(c) **THE FOLK COLLECTION** -
Apr 89. Outlet; (lp)(c)(cd) **HORSLIPS STORY – STRAIGHT FROM THE HORSE'S MOUTH** -
– The high reel / Night town boy / Flower among them all / Dearg doom / Faster than the hounds / The best years of my life / The man who built America / Guests of the nation / Daybreak / Everything will be alright / Power and the glory / Sword of light / Warm sweet breath of love / Speed the plough / Trouble (with a capital T) / The Shamrock shore / The king of the fairies / High volume love / An bratach ban / The silver spear. *(cd-iss.Jan95)*
Jan 95. Outlet; (cd) **TRADITIONAL IRISH FOLK** -
Jan 95. Outlet; (cd) **GUESTS OF THE NATION** -
Above 2 might have been issued earlier in Ireland.

The HOST

were formed by **O'CONNOR, FEAN, CARR** plus **PETER KEAN** – keys / **CHRIS PAGE** – bass

Aura / not issued

1984. (lp) **TRYAL** -
Jan 85. (7") **WALK ON LOVE. / STRANGE DISEASE** -

HOTHOUSE FLOWERS

Formed: Christchurch, Dublin, Ireland . . . 1985 by Gaels LIAM O'MAONLAI and other 4 (see below). After a 1987 one-off 45 on BONO's 'Mother' label, they moved to 'London' records. In 1988, the re-issued 'DON'T GO' scored a near UK Top 10 hit, which preceeded No.2 album 'PEOPLE'. • **Style:** Trad.rock outfit likened to VAN MORRISON or The WATERBOYS. • **Songwriters:** Mostly band compositions except; HARD RAIN (Bob Dylan) / CARRICK FERGUS + BRIGHT SIDE OF THE ROAD (Van Morrison) / I CAN SEE CLEARLY NOW (Johnny Nash) / KANSAS CITY (Leiber-Stoller) / BETTER DAYS AHEAD (Gil Scott-Heron) / etc. • **Trivia:** In mid-87, they contributed 5 songs to film soundtrack of 'The Courier'.

Recommended: PEOPLE (*7).

LIAM O'MAONLAI – vocals / **FIACHNA O'BRAONAIN** – guitar / **LEO BARNES** – saxophone / **PETER O'TOOLE** – bass / **JERRY FEHILY** – drums

Mother / not issued

May 87. (7") **LOVE DON'T WORK THIS WAY. / FREEDOM** -
('A'extended-12"+=) – Seeline woman.

London / London

Nov 87. (7") **DON'T GO. / BETTER AND BETTER**
(12"+=) – Big fat heart.
(10"+=) – Don't go (acoustic) / Lonely lane.
Mar 88. (7") **FEET ON THE GROUND. / HARD RAIN**
(12"+=) – Strange feeling.
Apr 88. (7") **DON'T GO (remix). / SAVED** 11
(12"+=) – Hydromat.
(cd-s+=) – Feet on the ground / Lonely lane (live).
May 88. (lp)(c)(cd) **PEOPLE** 2 88
– I'm sorry / Don't go / Forgiven / It'll be easier in the morning / Hallelujah Jordan / If you go / The older we get / Yes I was / Love don't work this way / Ballad of Katie / Feet on the ground. *(cd+=)* – Lonely lane / Saved.
Jul 88. (7") **I'M SORRY. / MOUNTAINS** 53
(12"+=) – Seeline woman.
(cd-s+=) – Don't go (acoustic-live).
Sep 88. (7") **EASIER IN THE MORNING. / CARRICK FERGUS**
(12"+=) – Feet on the ground (live).
(cd-s+=) – Better and better.

FFRR-London / London

May 90. (7") **GIVE IT UP. / IF YOU'RE HAPPY** 30

(c-s+=)(cd-s+=)/ /(12"+=)(cd-s+=) – If you go./ / Bean phaidini.
Jun 90. (cd)(c)(lp) **HOME** 5
– Hardstone city / Give it up / Christchurch bells / Sweet Marie / Giving it all away / Shut up and listen / I can see clearly now / Movies / Eyes wide open / Water / Home / Trying to get through / Dance to the storm / Seoladh na nGamhna.
Jul 90. (7")(c-s) **I CAN SEE CLEARLY NOW. / KANSAS CITY** 23
(12"+=) – Better days ahead.
(cd-s++=) – Strange feelin'.
Oct 90. (7")(c-s) **MOVIES. / SWEET MARIE** 68
(12"+=) – Don't go (live).
(cd-s++=) – Give it up.
(12") – ('A'side) / She moves through the fair / Dance to the storm / Hydromat.
Feb 93. (7")(c-s) **AN EMOTIONAL TIME. / THE SEASONS WHEELS** 38
(cd-s+=) – Help us make our peace / Song of Equador.
(cd-s) – ('A'side) / Air from the hills / Banished misfortune / Let the rhythm take you home.
Mar 93. (cd)(c)(lp) **SONGS FROM THE RAIN** 7
– This is it (your soul) / One tongue / An emotional time / Be good / Good for you / Isn't it amazing / Thing of beauty / Your nature / Spirit of the land / Gypsy fair / Stand beside me.
Apr 93. (7")(c-s) **ONE TONGUE. / CARRY ON** 45
(pic-cd-s+=) – Thank you for believing / The rebel.
(cd-s) – ('A'side) / Same song / Wish you everything / The rain.
Jun 93. (7")(c-s) **ISN'T IT AMAZING. / LET HIM KNOW** 46
(cd-s) – ('A'side) / Fi do mhamo I / Of the people / The well.
Nov 93. (c-s)(cd-s) **THIS IS IT (YOUR SOUL) / SWEET MARIE / GIVE IT UP** 67
(cd-s+=) – ('A'side) / Suspicious minds / Forever young / Come together.

HOTLEGS (see under ⇒ 10cc)

HOT TUNA

Formed: San Francisco, California, USA . . . 1969 by JORMA KAUKONEN and JACK CASADY as an off-shoot to their JEFFERSON AIRPLANE. They originally called themselves HOT SHIT (in reference to dope, rather than excrement), but thought better when record company 'RCA', wanted to issue an eponymous lp in 1970. By this time, they had added mouth-harpist WILL SCARLET, and other 2 (see below). The album scraped into US Top 30, but was their only fruits of an 8 year campaign, that involved many other JEFFERSON renegades. • **Style:** Originally a jamming acoustic-folk duo, who branched out into electric sets after debuts appearance. Critical back-lash over KAUKONEN's seemingly lack of effort, dogged outfit throughout. • **Songwriters:** KAUKONEN and CASADY except a few covers. • **Trivia:** CASADY produced KAUKONEN's first solo outing in 1974 'QUAH'.

Recommended: FINAL VINYL (*6)

JORMA KAUKONEN (b.23 Dec'40, Washington DC) – vocals, lead guitar / **JACK CASADY** (b.13 Apr'44, Washington) – bass (both of JEFFERSON AIRPLANE) / **WILL SCARLETT** – mouth harp with **JOEY COVINGTON** – drums (new of JEFFERSON AIRPLANE) / **PAUL ZIEGLER** – guitar

R.C.A. R.C.A.
Aug 70. (lp) **HOT TUNA** 30 Jul 70
– Hesitation blues / How long blues / Uncle Sam blues / Don't you leave me here / Death don't have no mercy / Know you rider / Search my heart / Winin' boy blues / New song (for the morning) / Mann's fate. *(cd-iss Jul91 on 'Edsel')*

— **PAPA JOHN CREACH** (b.28 May 1917, Beaver Falls, Pennsylvania) – violin (new of JEFFERSON AIRPLANE) repl. ZIEGLER / **SAMMY PIAZZA** – drums repl. COVINGTON who also left JEFFERSON AIRPLANE (Apr72) and joined BLACK KANGAROO and later his own FAT FANDANGO.

Oct 71. (lp) **FIRST PULL UP, THEN PULL DOWN (live)** - Jun 71
– John's other / Candy man / Been so long / Want you to know / Keep your lamps trimmed and burning / Never happen no more / Come back baby.

— **RICHARD TALBOTT** – guitar, vocals repl. WILL

Grunt Grunt
Apr 72. (lp) **BURGERS** 68 Mar 72
– True religion / Highway song / 99 blues / Sea child / Keep on truckin' / Water song / Ode for Billy Dean / Let us get together right down here / Sunny day strut. *(re-iss Jul84 on 'R.C.A.')*
Apr 72. (7") **KEEP ON TRUCKIN'. / WATER SONG**

— **KAUKONEN** and **CASADY** had now (Aug72) departed from JEFFERSON AIRPLANE. The HOT TUNA trio was completed by **SAMMY PIAZZA** – drums. (PAPA went solo)

Feb 74. (lp) **THE PHOSPHORESCENT RAT**
– I see the light / Letter to the North Star / Easy now / Corners without exits / Day to day out the window blues / In the kingdom / Living just for you / Seaweed strut / Solilquy for 2 / Sally, where'd you get your liquor from.

— **BOB STEELER** – drums repl. SAMMY

Jul 75. (lp)(c) **AMERICA'S CHOICE** 75 May 75
– Sleep song / Funky £7 / Invitation / Walkin' blues / Hit single £1 / Serpent of dreams / I don't wanna go / Great divide: revisited.

— added **JOHN SHERMAN** – guitar / also **NICK BUCK** – keyboards, synths

Aug 75. (7") **HOT JELLYROLL BLUES. / SURPHASE TEN SION** -
Oct 75. (lp)(c) **YELLOW FEVER** 97
– Baby what you want me to do / Hot jelly roll blues / Free rein / Sunrise dance with the Devil / Song for the fire maiden / Bar room crystal ball / Half-time saturation / Surphase tension.
Sep 76. (7") **IT'S SO EASY. / I CAN'T BE SATISFIED**
Nov 76. (lp)(c) **HOPPKORV**
– Santa Claus retreat / Watch the north wind rise / It's so easy / Bowlegged woman, knock kneed man / Drivin' around / I wish you would / I can't be satisfied / Talking 'bout you / Extrication love song / Song from the stainless cymbal.
Mar 78. (d-lp)(c) **DOUBLE DOSE (live)** 92
– Winin' boy blues / Keep your lamps trimmed and burning / Embryonic journey / Killing time in the crystal city / I wish you would / Genesis / Extraction love song / Talking 'bout you / Funky £7 / Serpent of dreams / Bowlegged woman, knock kneed man / I see the light / Watch the north wind rise / Sunrise dance with the Devil / I can't be satisfied. *(cd-iss.Dec94 on 'Demon')*

— Broke-up early 1978. CASADY and BUCK formed S.V.T. in 1980 (NO REGRETS lp)

– compilations, others. –

Feb 80. Grunt; (lp)(c) **FINAL VINYL**
– Hesitation blues / Candy man / Ja da / Water song / Day to day out the window blues / Easy now / Funky No.7 / Hot jelly roll blues / Song from the stainless cymbal / I wish you would.
1985. Relix; (lp) **HISTORIC (live electric)** -
(cd-iss.Jun93)
Aug 86. Relix; (lp)(US-pic-lp) **SPLASHDOWN (live acoustic '75)** Oct 84

JORMA KAUKONEN

with sessioners.

R.C.A. Grunt
Feb 75. (lp) **QUAH** -
– Genesis / I'll be all right / Song for the North star / I'll let you know before I leave / Flying clouds / Another man done gone / I am the light of this world / Police dog blues / Blue prelude / Sweet Hawaiian sunshine / Hamar promenade.
Jan 80. (lp)(c) **JORMA** Oct79
– Straight ahead / Roads and roads / Valley of tears / Song for the high mountain / Wolves and lambs / Too long out, too long in / Requiem for an angel / Vampire woman / Da-ga-da-ga.

— (next with backing group VITAL PARTS)

1980. (lp)(c) **BARBEQUE KING** -
– Runnin' with fast crowd / Man for all seasons / Starting over again / Milkcow blues boogie / Roads and roads / Love is strange / To hate is to stay young / Rockabilly shuffle / Snout psalm / Barbeque king.

not issued Relix
Apr 85. (lp) **MAGIC** -
– Walkin' blues / Winnin' boy blues / I'll be alright some day / Embryonic journey / Candyman / Roads and roads / Good shepherd / Man's fate.
Aug 86. (lp) **TOO HOT TO HANDLE** -
– Broken highway / Too many years / Radical sleep / Killing time in the crystal city / Ice age / Waking blues / Death don't have no mercy / Too hot to handle.

KBC BAND

(aka **JORMA KAUKONEN, MARTY BALIN, JACK CASADY**)

Arista Arista
Feb 87. (lp)(c)(cd) **KBC BAND** 75 Nov 86
– Mariel / It's not you, it's not me / Hold me / America / No more heartaches / Wrecking crew / When love comes / Dream motorcycle / Sayonara.
Feb 87. (7")(12") **IT'S NOT YOU, IT'S NOT ME. / DREAM MOTORCYCLE** -
Feb 87. (7") **WRECKING CREW. / AMERICA** -
Apr 87. (7") **MARIEL. / HOLD ME** -

HOURGLASS (see under ⇒ ALLMAN BROTHERS BAND)

HOUSEMARTINS

Formed: Hull, England ... late 1983 by PAUL HEATON and STAN CULLIMORE. After local gigs, many of them for political causes (i.e.the miners & CND), they signed in '85 to Andy McDonald's new 'Go! Discs' label. With HUGH WHITAKER replacing LANG, their debut 45 'FLAG DAY' was released, but this flopped. In 1986, NORMAN COOK replaced KEY, and they made UK Top 60 with 'SHEEP'. Hot on its heels, was Top 3 single 'HAPPY HOUR' (complete with plasticine/animated video), and parent debut album 'LONDON 0 HULL 4'. By the end of the year, they had Christmas No.1 with acappella 'CARAVAN OF LOVE'. • **Style:** Like MADNESS or The UNDERTONES, fun pop – rock with meaning and lyrical intelligence. • **Songwriters:** Penned by HEATON-CULLIMORE except covers; HE AIN'T HEAVY, HE'S MY BROTHER (Hollies) / CARAVAN OF LOVE (Isley Jasper Isley). • **Trivia:** LONDON 0 HULL 4, stemmed from group's promotional hometown pride. They often described themselves as Hull's 4th best group. Who were better? RED GUITARS, EVERYTHING BUT THE GIRL and GARGOYLES?

Recommended: NOW THAT'S WHAT I CALL QUITE GOOD (*7).

PAUL HEATON (b. 9 May'62) – vocals / **STAN CULLIMORE** (b.IAN, 6 Apr'62) – guitar, vocals / **TED KEY** – bass / **HUGH WHITAKER** – drums repl. CHRIS LANG

Go! Discs Elektra
Oct 85. (7") **FLAG DAY. / STAND AT EASE** -
(12"+=) – Coaltrain to Hatfield Main.

— **NORMAN COOK** (b.QUENTIN COOK, 31 Jul'63) – bass repl. TED KEY who formed GARGOYLES

Mar 86. (7")(7"pic-d) **SHEEP. / DROP DOWN DEAD** 54 -
(12"+=) – I'll be your shelter / Anxious / People get ready.
(d7"+=)(d12"+=) – Flag day / Stand at ease.
May 86. (7")(7"sha-pic-d) **HAPPY HOUR. / THE MIGHTY SHIP** 3 Sep 86
(12"+=) – Sitting on a fence / He ain't heavy, he's my brother.
Jun 86. (lp)(c)(cd) **LONDON 0 HULL 4** 3 Feb 87

– Happy hour / Get up off your knees / Flag day / Anxious / Reverends revenge / Sitting on a fence / Sheep / Over there / Think for a minute / We're not deep / Lean on me / Freedom. *(c+=)* – I'll be your shelter (just like a shelter) / (other 'B'sides) *(re-iss.cd+c.Oct92)*

Sep 86. (7")(7"sha-pic-d) **THINK FOR A MINUTE. / WHO NEEDS THE LIMELIGHT** [18] [ ]
(12"+=) – I smell winter / Joy joy joy / Rap around the clock.
(d7"+=) Sheep / Drop down dead.

Nov 86. (7")(7"sha-pic-d) **CARAVAN OF LOVE. / WHEN I FIRST MET JESUS** [1] [ ]
(12"+=) – We shall not be moved / So much in love / Heaven help us.
(d7"+=) – Flag day / Stand at ease.

Feb 87. (7") **FLAG DAY. / THE MIGHTY SHIP** [-] [ ]

— **DAVE HEMMINGHAM** – drums repl. WHITAKER who joined GARGOYLES full-time

May 87. (7") **FIVE GET OVER EXCITED. / REBEL WITHOUT THE AIRPLAY** [11] [ ]
(12"+=)(c-s+=) – So glad / Hopelessly devoted to them.

Aug 87. (7") **ME AND THE FARMER. / I BIT MY LIP** [15] [ ]
(12"+=)(c-s+=) – Step outside / He will find you out.

Sep 87. (lp)(c)(cd) **THE PEOPLE WHO GRINNED THEMSELVES TO DEATH** [9] [ ] Jan 88
– The people who grinned themselves to death / I can't put my finger on it / The light is always green / The world's on fire / Pirate aggro / We're not coming back / Me and the farmer / Johannesburg / Bow down / You better be doubtful / Build. *(re-iss.cd+c.Oct92)*

Nov 87. (7") **BUILD. / PARIS IN FLAMES** [15] [ ]
(10"+=)(12"+=)(c-s+=)(cd-s+=) – Forwards and backwards / The light is always green.

Apr 88. (7") **THERE'S ALWAYS SOMETHING THERE TO REMIND ME. / GET UP OFF YOUR KNEES (live)** [35] [ ]
(12"+=)(cd-s+=) – Johannesburg (live) / Five get over excited (live).

Apr 88. (d-lp)(c)(cd) **NOW THAT'S WHAT I CALL QUITE GOOD** (compilation) [8] [ ]
– I smell winter / Bow down / Think for a minute / There is always something there to remind me / The mighty ship / Sheep / I'll be your shelter (just like a shelter) / Five get over excited / Everybody's the same / Build / Step outside / Flag day / Happy hour / You've got a friend / He ain't heavy, he's my brother / Freedom / The people who grinned themselves to death / Caravan of love / The light is always green / We're not deep / Me and the farmer / Lean on me.

— They had already decide to split up Jan88. NORMAN COOK went solo. HEATON and HEMINGWAY formed The BEAUTIFUL SOUTH.

– compilations etc. –

Dec 86. Go! Discs; (7"-box) **CHRISTMAS SINGLES BOX** [84] [-]

HOUSE OF LOVE

Formed: Camberwell, London, England ... 1986 by CHADWICK, BICKERS, GROOTIZEN and HEUKAMP. They quickly signed to Alan McGee's 'Creation' label, and unleashed classic debut 'SHINE ON', which became a John Peel favourite throughout 1987. The following year, they issued 2 more beauties 'CHRISTINE' & 'DESTROY THE HEART', which after a superb debut album, led to a contract on 'Fontana'. In 1989, they had first of several hits 'NEVER', which was pursued in the early 90's by UK Top 10 album 'FONTANA'. • **Style:** Inspired by 60's outfits VELVET UNDERGROUND, LOVE and The BYRDS. Progressed with similarities to the ONLY ONES, through 80's psychedelia and new breed rock. • **Songwriters:** CHADWICK penned except; I CAN'T STAND IT (Velvet Underground) / PINK FROST (Chills) / IT'S ALL TOO MUCH (Beatles) / STRANGE BREW (Cream) / ROCK YOUR BABY (George McCrae). • **Trivia:** Debut album was produced by PAT COLLIER (ex-Vibrators) and STEVE NUNN.

Recommended: THE HOUSE OF LOVE (*8) / FONTANA (*7).

GUY CHADWICK – vocals, guitar (ex-KINGDOMS) / **TERRY BICKERS** – guitar (ex-COLENSO PARADE) / **ANDREA HEUKAMP** (b.Germany) – guitar, vocals / **CHRIS GROOTHIZEN** (b.New Zealand) – bass / **PETE EVANS** – drums

Creation / Relativity

May 87. (12"m) **SHINE ON. / LOVE / FLOW** [ ] [-]

Sep 87. (12"m) **REAL ANIMAL. / PLASTIC / NOTHING TO ME** [ ] [-]

— Now a quartet when ANDREA returned to Germany

Apr 88. (7") **CHRISTINE. / LONELINESS IS A GUN** [ ] [-]
(12"+=) – The hill.

May 88. (lp)(c)(cd) **THE HOUSE OF LOVE** [ ] [ ]
– Christine / Hope / Road / Sulphur / Man to child / Salome / Love in a car / Happy / Fisherman's tale / Touch me. *(re-iss.cd+c Aug94)*

Aug 88. (7") **DESTROY THE HEART. / BLIND** [ ] [ ]
(12"+=) – Mr. Jo.

Fontana / Fontana

Apr 89.. (7") **NEVER. / SOFT AS FIRE** [41] [ ]
(12"+=)(cd-s+=) – Safe.

Nov 89. (7")(c-s) **I DON'T KNOW WHY I LOVE YOU. / SECRETS** [41] [ ]
(12"+=) – I can't stand it. (repl. on some 12") – The spy.
(cd-s++=) – Clothes. (above on some 7"b-side, repl. by) – Love II.

— **SIMON WALKER** – guitar (of DAVE HOWARD SINGERS) repl. BICKERS

Jan 90. (7") **SHINE ON (remix). / ALLERGY** [20] [ ]
(12"+=)(c-s+=) – Scratched inside.
(12"+=) – Rosalyn.
(cd-s+=) – Rough.

Feb 90. (cd)(c)(lp) **FONTANA** [8] [ ]
– Hannah / Shine on / Beatles and the Stones / Shake and crawl / Hedonist / I don't know why I love you / Never / Somebody's got to love you / In a room / Blind / 32nd floor / Se dest.

Mar 90. (7") **BEATLES AND THE STONES. / LOVE IV** [36] [ ]
(12"+=) – Phone.
(12"+=) – Cut the fool down.
(cd-s+=) – Marble.
(cd-s+=) – Phone (extended).
(12"+=)(cd-s+=) – Glorify me./ / Soft as fire.
(7"ltd.) – ('A'side) / Love IV / Love V.

Nov 90. (cd)(c)(lp) **SPY IN THE HOUSE OF LOVE** (rare material, etc.) [49] [ ]
– Safe / Marble / D song '89 / Scratched inside / Phone (full version) / Cut the fool down / Ray / Love II / Baby teen / Love III / Soft as fire / Love IV / No fire / Love V. *(re-iss.cd Aug94)*

— (Sep90) added returning **ANDREA HEUKAMP** – guitar, vocals

Oct 91. (7")(c-s) **THE GIRL WITH THE LONELIEST EYES. / PURPLE KILLER ROSE** [58] [ ]
(12"+=)(cd-s+=) – Tea in the Sun / Pink frost.

Apr 92. (7"ep) **FEEL / IT'S ALL TOO MUCH** [45] [ ]
(10"+=) – Let's talk about you / Strange brew.
(cd-s++=) – Real animal.

— During recording of following album, SIMON left. He was succeeded by album guests **ANDREA HEUKAMP** – guitar, vox / **WARNE LIVESEY** – guitar, keyboards, etc. / **CAROL KENYON** – vocals / **PANDIT DENESH** – tablas

Jun 92. (7") **YOU DON'T UNDERSTAND. / SWEET ANATOMY** [46] [ ]
(10"+=)(cd-s+=) – Kiss the mountain / Third generation liquid song.
(cd-s+=) – Destroy the heart / Blind / Mr.Jo.

Jul 92. (cd)(c)(lp) **BABE RAINBOW** [34] [ ]
– You don't understand / Crush me / Crue / High in your face / Fade away / Feel / The girl with the loneliest eyes / Burn down the world / Philly Phile / Yer eyes. *(re-iss.cd Aug94)*

Nov 92. (7") **CRUSH ME. / LOVE ME** [67] [ ]
(10"+=) – Last edition of love / Skin 2 phase 2.
(cd-s) – ('A'side) / Christine / Ladies is a gun / The hitch.

Jun 93. (cd)(c)(lp) **AUDIENCE WITH THE MIND** [38] [ ]
– Sweet Anatomy / Audience With The Mind / Haloes / Erosion / Call Me / Shining On / Portrait In Atlanta / Corridors / Hollow / All Night Long / Into The Tunnel / You've Got To Feel *(re-iss.cd+c Aug94)*

HOUSE OF PAIN

Formed: Woodland Hills, Los Angeles, California, USA ... 1991 by solo artist EVERLAST, DANNY BOY and LETHAL DJ. By late 1992, their sexist words 'JUMP AROUND', were being sprayed on both sides of the Atlantic. • **Style:** Shamrock-touting hip hoppers, with degradation to women, their forte. Besides this, their screeching gangsta sound, went a long way to establish them as top rap act of the early 90's. • **Songwriters:** Group penned, and partly produced by DJ MUGGS (Cypress Hill). Sampled HARLEM SHUFFLE (Bob Earl) / I COME TO YOU BABY (John Lee Hooker) • **Trivia:** DANNY BOY's preoccupation with his Irish ancestry, made him mark his body with a 'Sinn Fein' tattoo, although he admitted to being more influenced by actor Mickey Rourke, than the Irish political party.

Recommended: HOUSE OF PAIN (*7).

EVERLAST

w/**ICE-T** – vox / **BILAL BASHIR** – keyboards / **CLARENCE METHENY** – synth. / **JOHN BREYER** – guitar / **MIKE GREG** – sax

Warners / Warners

1989. (12") **SYNDICATION. / BUSTIN' LOOSE** [-] [ ]

Feb 90. (cd)(c)(lp) **FOREVER EVERLAST** [ ] [ ]
– Syndicate soldier / Speak no evil / Syndication (remix) / What is this? / The rhythm / I got the knack / On the edge / Fuck everyone / Goodbye / Pass it on / Never missin' a beat.

Mar 90. (12") **SYNDICATE SOLDIER. / NEVER MISSIN' A BEAT** [-] [ ]

Jun 90. (c-s) **PAY THE PRICE. / I GOT THE KNACK** [-] [ ]

HOUSE OF PAIN

ERIC "EVERLAST" SCHRODY– vocals / **"DANNY BOY" O'CONNER** – vocals / **LEOR "DJ LETHAL" DiMANT** (b.Latvia) – turntable

X.L. / Tommy Boy

Sep 92. (12")(cd-s) **JUMP AROUND (Master Mix) / HOUSE OF PAIN ANTHEM (Master Mix)** [32] [3] Jun 92

Nov 92. (cd)(c)(lp) **HOUSE OF PAIN** [73] [14] Aug 92
– Salutations / Jump around / Put your head out / Top o' the morning to ya / House and the rising sun / Shamrocks and shenanigans (boom shalock lock boom) / House of pain anthem / Danny boy, Danny boy / Guess who's back / Put on your shit kickers / Come and get some of this / Life goes on / One for the road / Feel it / All my love

Nov 92. (12")(cd-s) **SHAMROCKS AND SHENANIGANS (BOOM SHALOCK LOCK BOOM)** [ ] [65]

Ruffness / Ruffness

May 93. (12")(c-s)(cd-s) **JUMP AROUND (remix). / TOP O' THE MORNING TO YA (remix) / (other mixes of 'A'+'B')** [8] [ ]

May 93. (c-s) **WHO'S THE MAN. /** [-] [96]

Oct 93. (12")(c-s)(cd-s) **SHAMROCKS & SHENANIGANS. / WHO'S THE MAN** [23] [ ]

— EVERLAST was jailed at home for 3 months in Feb'94, for earlier carrying a weapon. 'IT AIN'T A CRIME' sampled UNDER THE BRIDGE (Red Hot Chili Peppers).

Jul 94. (12")(c-s)(cd-s) **ON POINT (The Beatminerz mix). / ('A'-DJ Lethal mix)** [19] [85]

Jul 94. (cd)(c)(d-lp) **SAME AS IT EVER WAS** [8] [12]

– Back from the dead / I'm a swing it / All that / On point / Runnin' up on ya / Over the shit / Word is bond / Keep it comin' / Interlude / Same as it ever was / It ain't a crime / Where I'm from / Still got a lotta love / Who's the man / On point (lethal dose remix).

Oct 94. (12")(c-s)(cd-s) **IT AIN'T A CRIME (madhouse remix). / LEGEND** [37] [ ]
(cd-s) – ('A'side) / Word is bond (Diamond D + Darkman remixes).

Jun 95. (12")(cd-s) **OVER THERE (I DON'T CARE). / JUMP AROUND (mastermix)** [20] [ ]
(cd-s+=) – Shamrocks and shenanigans / Top o' the morning to ya.
(cd-s) – ('A'side) / Runnin' up on ya (versions incl. House of Pain vs. Kerbdog).

Steve HOWE (see under ⇒ YES)

HOWLIN' WOLF

Born: CHESTER ARTHUR BURNETT, 10 June 1910, West Point, Mississippi, USA. In 1948 he moved to Memphis, where he soon was spotted by IKE TURNER, who signed him to 'Modern' records. In the early 50's, his label squabbled with 'Chess' who duly issued initial releases MOANING AT MIDNIGHT and THE WOLF. In 1964, with blues now burgeoning in the UK, he hit UK Top 50 with 1955 recording SMOKESTACK LIGHTNIN'. It was soon covered by major beat groups YARDBIRDS and MANFRED MANN. In 1972, he came to England to record THE LONDON SESSIONS. Many stars (ROLLING STONES, ERIC CLAPTON, STEVE WINWOOD & RINGO STARR, etc.), paid tribute to him by guesting on album. His comeback was short-lived, as ill-health and heart attacks dogged him until his death from kidney failure on 10 Jan'76. • **Style & Songwriters:** Like J.L.HOOKER, a blues legend who made impact enough for rock/pop artists to cover his material. SPOONFUL (Cream) / I AIN'T SUPERSTITIOUS (Savoy Brown) + (Jeff Beck) / THE (LITTLE) RED ROOSTER (Rolling Stones) / BACK DOOR MAN (Doors) / HOW MANY MORE YEARS? (Little Feat) / KILLIN' FLOOR (Electric Flag) / etc. His large (300 lb.) frame and suggestive gruff vocals, were not obvious when he issued the self-despised, 1969 psychedelia lp 'THE HOWLIN' WOLF ALBUM'. • **Trivia & Style:** In the 40's, he was taught guitar by bluesman CHARLEY PATTON. His nickname 'The Wolf' was given to him by family, with 'Howlin'' added by a local radio station in 1949, who parodied his singing.

Recommended: THE COLLECTION: 20 BLUES GREATS (*8)

HOWLIN' WOLF – vocals, guitar with **HUBERT SUMLIN + WILLIE JOHNSON** – guitar / **WILLIE STEZZ** – drums / **IKE TURNER** – piano

not issued / R.P.M.

Oct 51. (78) **MOANIN' AT MIDNIGHT. / RIDIN' IN THE MOONLIGHT** [-] [ ]
Nov 51. (78) **CRYING AT DAYBREAK. / PASSING BY BLUES** [-] [ ]
Dec 51. (78) **MY BABY STOLE OFF. / I WANT YOUR PICTURE** [-] [ ]

not issued / Chess

Dec 51 (78) **MOANING AT MIDNIGHT. / HOW MANY MORE YEARS** [-] [ ]
Feb 52. (78) **THE WOLF IS AT YOUR DOOR (HOWLIN' FOR MY BABY). / HOWLIN' WOLF BOOGIE** [-] [ ]
Mar 52. (78) **GETTING OLD AND GREY. / MR.HIGHWAY MAN** [-] [ ]
Jun 52. (78) **SADDLE MY PONY. / WORRIED ALL THE TIME** [-] [ ]
Nov 52. (78) **OH! RED. / MY LAST AFFAIR** [-] [ ]
Feb 53. (78) **ALL NIGHT BOOGIE (ALL NIGHT LONG). / I LOVE MY BABY** [-] [ ]

— now w / **WILLIE DIXON** – bass / **OTIS SPANN** – piano / **LEE COOPER** – guitar / **FRED BELOW** – drums

May 54. (78) **ROCKING DADDY. / NO PLACE TO GO (YOU GONNA WRECK MY LIFE)** [-] [ ]
Jul 54. (78) **BABY HOW LONG. / EVIL IS GOING ON** [-] [ ]
Dec 54. (78) **I'LL BE AROUND. / FORTY FOUR** [-] [ ]
May 55. (78) **WHO WILL BE NEXT. / I HAVE A LITTLE GIRL** [-] [ ]
Jul 55. (78) **COME TO ME BABY. / DON'T MESS WITH MY BABY** [-] [ ]

— now w / **HOSEA LEE KENNARD** – piano / **HUBERT SUMLIN + WILLIE JOHNSON** – guitar / **EARL PHILLIPS** – drums

Mar 56. (78) **SMOKESTACK LIGHTNIN'. / YOU CAN'T BE BEAT** [-] [ ]
Sep 56. (78) **I ASKED FOR WATER (SHE GAVE ME GASOLINE). / SO GLAD** [-] [ ]
Mar 57. (78) **GOING BACK HOME. / MY LIFE** [-] [ ]
Jul 57. (78) **NATURE. / SOMEBODY IN MY HOME** [-] [ ]
Feb 58. (78) **SITTIN' ON TOP OF THE WORLD. / POOR BOY** [-] [ ]
May 58. (78) **MOANIN' FOR MY BABY (MIDNIGHT BLUES). / I DIDN'T KNOW** [-] [ ]
Oct 58. (78) **I'M LEAVING YOU. / CHANGE MY WAY** [-] [ ]
Nov 58. (78) **I BETTER GO NOW. / HOWLIN' BLUES** [-] [ ]

— added **WILLIE DIXON** – bass / **OTIS SPANN** – piano / **EARL PHILLIPS** – drums

London / Chess

1958. (7"ep) **RHYTHM & BLUES WITH HOWLIN' WOLF** [ ] [-]
– Smokestack lightnin' / You can't be beat / Don't mess with me baby / Come to me baby.

— now used various personnel

Aug 59. (7") **MR.AIRPLANE MAN. / I'VE BEEN ABUSED** [-] [ ]
Nov 59. (7") **THE NATCHEZ BURNING. / YOU GONNA WRECK MY LIFE** [-] [ ]
Mar 60. (7") **WHO'S BEEN TALKING. / TELL ME** [-] [ ]
Jul 60. (7") **HOWLIN' FOR MY BABY. / SPOONFUL** [-] [ ]
Nov 60. (7") **WANG-DANG-DOODLE. / BACK DOOR MAN** [-] [ ]

Pye Int. / Chess

Sep 61. (7") **LITTLE BABY. / DOWN IN THE BOTTOM** [-] [ ]
Nov 61. (7") **THE RED ROOSTER. / SHAKE FOR ME** [-] [ ]
Feb 62. (7") **GOING DOWN SLOW. / YOU'LL BE MINE** [-] [ ]
Nov 62. (7") **MAMA'S BABY. / DO THE DO** [-] [ ]
Sep 63. (7") **THREE HUNDRED POUNDS OF JOY. / BUILT FOR COMFORT** [-] [ ]
Apr 63. (7") **JUST LIKE I TREAT YOU. / I AIN'T SUPERSTITIOUS** [ ] [ ] Apr 62
Nov 63. (7"ep) **SMOKESTACK LIGHTNIN'** [ ] [-]
– Smokestack lighnin' / Howling for my baby / Going down slow / You'll be mine.
May 64. (7") **SMOKESTACK LIGHTNIN'. / GOING DOWN SLOW** [42] [-]
(re-iss.Jul85 on 'Chess')
Oct 64. (7"ep) **TELL ME** [ ] [-]
– Tell me / Who's been talking / Shake for me / Back door man.
Oct 64. (7") **LITTLE BABY. / TAIL DRAGGER** [ ] [-]
Dec 64. (7") **LOVE ME DARLING. / MY COUNTRY SUGAR MAMA** [ ] [ ]

Chess / Chess

Feb 65. (lp) **MOANIN' IN THE MOONLIGHT** (compilation '50s) [ ] [ ]
– Moanin' in the moonlight / How many more years / Smokestack lightnin' / Baby how long / No place to go / Evil / I'm leading you / Moanin' for my baby / I ask for water / Forty-four / Somebody in my home. *(re-iss.Jan67 on 'Marble A.') (re-iss.+c.Apr87 on 'Charly')*
Apr 65. (7") **KILLING FLOOR. / LOUISE** [ ] [ ]
1965. (lp) **POOR BOY** [ ] [-]
– Cause Of It All / The Killing Floor / Little Red Rooster / Built For Comfort / Commit A Crime / Do The Do / Highway 49 / Worried About You / Poor Boy / Wang Dang Doodle.
Jun 65. (7") **OOH BABY. / TELL ME WHAT I'VE DONE** [ ] [ ]
Aug 65. (7") **I WALKED FROM DALLAS / DON'T LAUGH AT ME** [-] [ ]
1966. (lp) **REAL FOLK BLUES** [-] [ ]
– Killing floor / Lousie / Poor boy / Sittin' on top of the world / Nature / My country / Sugar mama / Tail draggerr / 300 lb. of joy / Natchez burning / Built for comfort / Ooh baby, hold me / Tell me what I've done. *(UK-iss.cd.Feb90 on 'MCA')*
Jun 66. (7") **NEW CRAWLIN' KING SNAKE. / MY MIND IS RAMBLIN'** [-] [ ]
1966. (7"ep) **REAL FOLK BLUES VOLUME 1** [ ] [ ]
– Three hundred pounds of joy / My country sugar mama / Oh baby hold me / Louise.
1967. (lp) **MORE REAL FOLK BLUES** (compilation 1952-56) [-] [ ]
Aug 67. (7") **I HAD A DREAM. / POP IT TO ME** [-] [ ]
May 68. (lp) **SUPER SUPER BLUES BAND ("& MUDDY WATERS & BO DIDDLEY)** [ ] [ ]
– Long distance call / Goin' down slow / You don't love me / I'm a man / Who do you love / The red rooster / Diddley daddy / I just want to make love to you.

Chess / Cadet

Feb 69. (7") **EVIL. / TAIL DRAGGER** [ ] [ ]
Apr 69. (lp) **THE NEW ALBUM** [ ] [ ]
– Spoonful / Tail dragger / Smokestack lightning / Moanin' at midnight / Built for comfort / The red rooster / Evil / Down in the bottom / Three hundred pounds of joy / Back door man.

Chess / Chess

Aug 69. (7") **MARY SUE. / HARD LUCK** [-] [ ]

Syndicate / Syndicate

May 70. (lp) **GOING BACK HOME** (compilation 1948-58) [ ] [ ]
– Saddle my pony / Worried all the time / Howlin' Wolf boogie / The Wolf is at your door / On red / My last affair / Mr.Highway man / Gettin' old and grey / Come to me baby / Don't mess with me baby / So glad / My life / Going back home / I don't know / Howlin' blues / I better go now. *(re-iss.Sep82)*
Jun 70. (lp) **WE THREE KINGS ("& MUDDY WATERS & LITTLE WALTER)** [ ] [ ]
– She's into something / Take the bitter with the sweet / Real way back / I'm your doctor / Tiger in your tank / Meanest woman / Lonesome road blues / Five long years / Twenty-four hours / I don't play / Just you fool / Change your money / I've been abused. *(re-iss.Sep82)*
Nov 70. (7") **IF I WERE A BIRD. / JUST AS LONG** [-] [ ]
Feb 71. (7") **DO THE DO. / THE RED ROOSTER** [-] [ ]
1971. (lp) **MESSAGE TO THE YOUNG** [-] [ ]
– If I were a bird / I smell a rat / Miss James / Message to the young / She's looking good / Just as long / Romance without finance / Turn me on.

(Below lp, feat. **BILL WYMAN & CHARLIE WATTS** (of The ROLLING STONES) / **ERIC CLAPTON** – guitar / **STEVE WINWOOD** – keyboards / **RINGO STARR** – drums)

Rolling Stones / Chess

Sep 71. (lp)(c) **THE LONDON HOWLIN' WOLF SESSIONS** [ ] [79] Aug 71
– I ain't superstitious / Poor boy / The red rooster / Worried about my baby / Do the do / Built for comfort / Sittin' on top of the world / Highway 49 / What a woman / Who's been talkin' / Rockin' daddy / Wang dang doodle. *(re-iss.Apr82) (re-iss.Dec85 on 'Charly', cd-iss.Jan91)*
1972. (lp) **LIVE & COOKIN' AT ALICES REVISITED (live)** [-] [ ]
– When I laid down I was troubled / I don't know / Mean mistreater / I had a dream / Call me The Wolf / Don't laugh at me / Just passing by / Sitting on top of the world.
1973. (lp) **THE BACK DOOR WOLF** [-] [ ]
– Movin' / Coon on the Moon / Speak now woman / Trying to fight you / Stop using me / Leave here walking / The back door wolf / You turn slick on me / Watergate blues / Can't stay here. *(UK-iss.+c.1989)*
1972. (d-lp) **AKA CHESTER BURNETT** (compilation 1951-65) [-] [ ]
1974. (lp) **LONDON REVISITED** [-] [ ]
– (cd+c-iss. Jul93 on 'Charly')

Earlier in the 70's, he suffered two heart attacks and a car crash in which he acrued kidney damage. After a concert at Chicago Amphitheater Nov'75 with B.B.KING, BOBBY BLAND and LITTLE MILTON, he was re-hospitalized and died there 10 Jan'76, following brain surgery.

– more compilations, etc. –

1966. Ember/ US= United; (lp) **BIG CITY BLUES** (rec. 1950) [-] [ ]
1965. Chess; (lp) **HOWLIN' WOLF** [-] [ ]
1974. Chess; (lp) **EVIL** (rec. 1951-59) [-] [ ]
1977. Chess; (lp) **CHANGIN' MY WAY** [-] [ ]
1977. Chess; (lp) **BLUES MASTERS** [ ] [-]

Jun 81. Chess; (d-lp) **CHESS MASTERS** [ ] [ ]
Apr 82. Chess; (d-lp) **CHESS MASTERS VOL.2** [ ] [ ]
May 83. Chess; (d-lp) **CHESS MASTERS VOL.3** [ ] [ ]
Dec 88. Chess; (lp)(c)(cd) **CHESS MASTERS VOL.4 – MOANIN' AND HOWLIN'** [ ] [ ]
Jun 76. Charly; (lp) **SAM'S BLUES (w / LITTLE MILTON)** [ ] [-]
1977. Charly; (lp) **LEGENDARY SUN PERFORMERS** [ ] [-]
Aug 86. Charly; (lp)(c) **HIS GREATEST HITS VOL.1** [ ] [-]
Jan 87. Charly; (lp)(c) **OFF THE RECORD – THE ROCKINGHAM ALBUM** [ ] [-]
Apr 87. Charly; (cd) **HOWLIN' FOR MY BABY** [ ] [-]
Nov 89. Charly; (lp-box)(c-box)(cd-box) **THE HOWLIN' WOLF BOX SET** [ ] [-]
Feb 93. Charly; (cd) **KILLING FLOOR** [ ] [-]
Jul 93. Charly; (7xcd-box) **THE COMPLETE RECORDINGS 1951-1969** [ ] [-]
Aug 81. Blues Ball; (lp) **HEART LIKE A RAILROAD STEEL** [-] [ ]
Aug 81. Blues Ball; (lp) **CAN'T PUT ME OUT** [-] [ ]
May 82. Ace-Chiswick; (lp) **RIDIN' IN THE MOONLIGHT** [ ] [-]
Jan 92. Ace; (cd) **HOWLIN' WOLF RIDES AGAIN** [ ] [-]
Apr 84. Blue Moon; (lp) **I AM THE WOLF** [ ] [-]
Nov 84. Blue Moon; (lp) **ALL NIGHT BOOGIE** [ ] [-]
Nov 84. Astan; (lp)(c) **GOLDEN CLASSICS** [ ] [-]
Nov 85. Deja Vu; (lp)(c) **COLLECTION: 20 BLUES GREATS** [ ] [-]
– Little red rooster / My baby walked off / Killing floor / My country sugar mama / My life / Going back home / Louise / Highway 49 / Hold on to your money / Built for comfort / Ain't superstitious / My last affair / Dorothy Mae / Commit a crime / Moanin' at midnight / Wang dang doodle / Ridin' in the moonlight / Everybody's in the mood / The wolf is at your door / I better go now. *(cd-iss.Aug87)*
Apr 93. Deja Vu; (cd)(c) **THE GOLD COLLECTION** [ ] [-]
1988. Joker; (lp)(c) **RED ROOSTER** [ ] [-]
(cd-iss.Aug95 on 'Imp')
1988. Sundown; (lp) **LIVE IN EUROPE – 1964 (live)** [ ] [ ]
Apr 89. Rounder; (lp) **CADILLAC DADDY (Memphis rec.)** [-] [ ]
Apr 89. Bear Family; (cd) **MEMPHIS DAYS (THE DEFINITIVE COLLECTION, VOL.1)** [ ] [-]
Jan 91. Bear Family; (cd) **MEMPHIS DAYS (THE DEFINITIVE COLLECTION, VOL.2)** [ ] [-]
1989. Wolf; (lp) **LIVE IN CHICAGO '75 (live)** [ ] [-]
Jul 91. Fan Club; (cd) **LIVE IN CAMBRIDGE MA., 1966 (live)** [ ] [-]
Jan 92. Fan Club; (d-cd) **THE WOLF IS AT YOUR DOOR** [ ] [-]
Feb 93. Roots; (cd)(c) **GOING DOWN SLOW VOLUME 4** [ ] [-]
Feb 93. Roots; (cd)(c) **THE WOLF IS AT YOUR DOOR VOLUME 3** [ ] [-]
Mar 93. Roots; (5xcd-box) **GOING DOWN SLOW** [ ] [-]
May 94. Charly; (cd) **SPOONFUL** [ ] [-]
May 94. M.C.A.; (c-s)(cd-s) **SMOKESTACK LIGHTNIN'. / ?** [ ] [-]
Jun 94. M.C.A.; (cd) **THE GENUINE ARTICLE** [ ] [-]
Jul 95. Charly; (d-cd) **THE VERY BEST OF HOWLIN' WOLF** [ ] [-]

HUANG CHUNG (see under ⇒ WANG CHUNG)

HUE AND CRY

Formed: Coatbridge, Scotland . . . 1985 by brothers PAT and GREG KANE. They were both in local band WINNING LOSERS, until they formed own UNITY EXPRESS, before it evolved into HUE AND CRY. After releasing debut 45 on own 'Stampede' records, they signed to Virgin subsidiary 'Circa', issuing flop follow-up 'I REFUSE' in Spring '86. Their next vinyl outing 'LABOUR OF LOVE', secured them a Top 10 hit, as they went from STRENGTH TO STRENGTH in 1987. • **Style:** Smooth laid back American influenced sound, highlighting PAT's soulful vox and thought provoking lyrics. • **Songwriters:** GREG wrote music, and they also covered:- THE MAN WITH THE CHILD IN HIS EYES (Kate Bush) / IT WAS A VERY GOOD YEAR (. . . Drake) / SHIPBUILDING (Elvis Costello & Clive Langer) / A CHANGE IS GONNA COME (Sam Cooke) / SIGNED, SEALED, DELIVERED + HE'S MISSTRA KNOW IT ALL + THAT GIRL + DO I DO + VISION + TILL YOU COME BACK TO ME (Stevie Wonder) / MOTHER GLASGOW (. . . Marra) / ROUND MIDNIGHT (Davis-Monk-Hancock) / DO NOTHING (Duke Ellington) / SEND IN THE CLOWNS (Steven Sondheim) / JUTE MILL SONG (M.Brooksbank) / MARTHA (Tom Waits) / SWEET HEART OF JESUS (trad.). • **Trivia:** In the late 80's, PAT was appointed rector at Glasgow University, a job made for his political Labour Party views.

Recommended: LABOUR OF LOVE – THE BEST OF . . . (*7).

PATRICK KANE (b.1964) – vocals / **GREGORY KANE** – keyboards, drum prog. with **NIGEL CLARK** – guitar / **JAME FINNIGAN** – bass / **TONY McCRACKEN** – drums

Stampede / not issued

Feb 86. (12"m) **HERE COMES EVERYBODY. / FROM FIRST TO LAST / THE SUCCESS OF MONETARISM** [ ] [-]

Circa / Virgin

May 86. (7")(12") **I REFUSE. / JOE AND JOSEPHINE** [ ] [-]
(c-s+=) – Shipbuilding / Dangerous wreck / Tempted.
Dec 86. (7") **LABOUR OF LOVE. / WIDESCREEN** [6] [ ] May 88
(10"+=)/ /(c-s+=) – I refuse./ / Goodbye to me.
(12"+=) – I refuse / Goodbye to me.
Sep 87. (7") **STRENGTH TO STRENGTH. / DANGEROUS WRECK** [46] [ ]
(12"+=)(c-s+=) – Seen it all / ('A'extended version).
Oct 87. (lp)(c)(cd) **SEDUCED AND ABANDONED** [22] [ ]
– Strength to strength / History city / Goodbye to me / Human touch / Labour of love / I refuse / Something warmer * / Alligator man / Love is the master / Just one word / Truth. *(cd+= *)*
Jan 88. (7") **I REFUSE. / INDIFFERENCE** [47] [ ]
(c-s+=) – Just one word (live).
(12"+=) – Kiss / Something warmer.
(cd-s+=) – History city (live) / Labour of love (Superbad version).

— with loads of session men, **WILL LEE** – bass / **TOMMY SMITH** – saxophone / **etc**

Oct 88. (7") **ORDINARY ANGEL. / I AM JOHN'S HEART** [42] [ ]
(12"+=) – Hymn to hands / ('A' version).
(cd-s++=) – Spending you.
(10"+=) – He won't smile / Remote.
Oct 88. (lp)(c)(cd) **REMOTE** [10] [ ]
– Ordinary angel / Looking for Linda / Guy on the wall / Violently (your words hit me) / Dollar William / The only thing (more powerful than the boss) / Where we wish to remain / Sweet invisibility / Three foot blasts of fire / Remote. *(c+cd+=)* – Family of eyes / Under neon.
Jan 89. (7") **LOOKING FOR LINDA. / HE WON'T SMILE** [15] [ ]
(12"+=) – Under neon.
(cd-s+=) – Remote.
Apr 89. (7") **VIOLENTLY (YOUR WORDS HIT ME). / THE MAN WITH THE CHILD IN HIS EYES** [21] [ ]
(7"ep+=)(12"ep+=)(cd-ep+=) – Calamity John / Rolling home.
Sep 89. (7")(c-s) **SWEET INVISIBILITY. / GREENOCK TIME** [55] [ ]
(12"+=)(cd-s+=) – ('A'side) / (2 other 'A'mixes).
Dec 89. (7")(c-s) **PEACEFUL FACE. / MOTHER GLASGOW** [ ] [ ]
(10"+=)(12"+=)(cd-s+=) – A change is gonna come.
Dec 89. (d-lp)(d-cd) **REMOTE / BITTER SUITE** [ ] [ ]
– BITTER SUITE – Mother Glasgow / The man with the child in his eyes / Shipbuilding / Rolling home / Peaceful face / Widescreen / O God head hid / Looking for Linda / Remote / It was a very good year / Round midnight / Truth.

— with **NIGEL CLARK** – guitar / **EWAN VERNAL** – bass / **MARK FORSHAW** – drums / **CALUM MALCOLM** – keyboards plus other guests **EDDI READER** / **BRIAN McFIE**

May 91. (7")(c-s) **MY SALT HEART. / WHITE COLLAR** [47] [ ]
(12"+=) – Poets day.
(cd-s) – ('A'side) / Poets day / ('A'acappella) / Signed, sealed, delivered (I'm yours) / He's mistra know it all.
Aug 91. (7"ep)(12"ep)(c-ep)(cd-ep) **LONG TERM LOVERS OF PAIN** [48] [ ]
– Long term lovers of pain / Heart of Saturday night / Rememberance and gold / Stars crash down.
Sep 91. (cd)(c)(lp) **STARS CRASH DOWN** [10] [ ]
– My salt heart / Life as text / She makes a sound / Making strange / Remembrance and gold / Long term lovers of pain / Stars crash down / Vera drives / Woman in time / Late in the day.

— The brothers added **NEIL WEIR** – trumpet + **GRAHAM WEIR** – trombone (ex-OMD) / **BOBBY HENRY + BRIAN McFIE** – guitar

Fidelity / not issued

Jun 92. (7")(c-s) **PROFOUNDLY YOURS. / NEW STATE (republic of love mix)** [74] [ ]
(cd-s+=) – Pawn of the weekend.
Aug 92. (cd)(c)(lp) **TRUTH AND LOVE** [33] [ ]
– New state / Profoundly yours / Because you are nothing / Everyday chains / Mr.Bell is calling / Inbetween / That girl / Forgotten wars / Bitter bitter / Start here / Whirlwind.

Permanent / not issued

Jul 94. (c-ep)(cd-ep) **JUST SAY YOU LOVE ME / WRONG QUESTION, RIGHT ANSWER / SHE'S NOT THERE MARTHA** [ ] [ ]
Aug 94. (cd)(c) **SHOWTIME** [ ] [ ]
– Just say you love me / Tinsel show / Bring me home / Wrong question right answer / He said, she said / Cynical / Perfect lie / Hannah and James / Shadow of a man / St. Christopher / Bright young thing.
Sep 94. (c-s) **CYNICAL. / ('A'mix)** [ ] [ ]
(cd-s+=) – Vision / Do I do.
Nov 95. (cd)(c) **PIANO & VOICE** [ ] [-]
– Till you come back to me / Do nothing / Send in the clowns / Jute mill song / She makes a sound (live) / Human touch / Sweet heart of Jesus / Martha / Mary Mary / I am John's heart / Violently (live).

– compilations, etc –

Mar 93. Circa; (7")(c-s) **LABOUR OF LOVE ('A' urban mix)** [25] [ ]
(12"+=)(cd-s+=) – ('A' other remixes 2)
Mar 93. Circa; (cd)(c)(lp) **LABOUR OF LOVE – THE BEST OF HUE AND CRY** [27] [ ]
– Labour of love / I refuse / Sweet invisibility / Looking for Linda / My salt heart / Violently (your words hit me) / Strength to strength / Ordinary angel / Long term lovers of pain / She makes a sound / Widescreen / Stars crash down / Peaceful face (live) / The man with the child in his eyes (live) / Truth.
May 95. Virgin-VIP; (cd)(c) **THE BEST OF HUE AND CRY** [ ] [-]

Alan HULL (see under ⇒ LINDISFARNE)

HUMAN LEAGUE

Formed: Sheffield, England . . . Autumn 1977 by computer operators MARTYN WARE and IAN CRAIG-MARSH. As The FUTURE, with vocalist ADI NEWTON, they recruited former hospital porter PHIL OAKEY, who soon replaced ADI (later to CLOCKDVA). Now as HUMAN LEAGUE, the trio recorded demo, which was accepted by Edinburgh-based indie 'Fast', run by Bob Last. Their debut 45 'BEING BOILED', became NME single of the week in mid-78. They added ADRIAN WRIGHT on visuals and synths, and after a dire instrumental EP 'THE DIGNITY OF LABOUR', they signed to 'Virgin' in Apr'79. Their first 45 for the label 'I DON'T DEPEND ON YOU', was credited to The MEN, but their credibility was restored later that year, when 'EMPIRE STATE HUMAN', nearly gave them hit. This was duly followed by a debut album 'REPRODUCTION', which failed to produce early promise. In Spring 1980, they went into UK Top 60 with double 7"EP 'HOLIDAY '80', and Top 20 with album 'TRAVELOGUE'. In Oct'80, OAKEY and

WRIGHT brought in teenage girls JOANNE and SUZANNE to replace WARE and CRAIG-MARSH who left to form HEAVEN 17. 12 months later, with new additions IAN BURDEN and JO CALLIS, they were at No.1 with both 'DARE' album, and 'DON'T YOU WANT ME' single, which also peaked at the top in the States. They continued to score on both sides of the Atlantic throughout the next decade. • **Style:** Initially an experimental industrial outfit, who manufactured themselves into top synth-pop group of the 80's. OAKEY's hair was always a main feature, as it was very long, only on one side!. • **Songwriters:** WARE and CRAIG-MARSH before their departure, and OAKEY and WRIGHT on all since early 80's. The 90's, featured OAKEY composing alongside new member NEIL SUTTON. Covered:- YOU'VE LOST THAT LOVIN' FEELIN' (Righteous Brothers) / ROCK'N'ROLL (Gary Glitter) / NIGHTCLUBBIN' (Iggy Pop) / ONLY AFTER DARK (Mick Ronson). • **Trivia:** MARTIN RUSHENT was their main producer, although JIMMY JAM & TERRY LEWIS worked with them in '86.

Recommended: GREATEST HITS (*8) / DARE (*8).

PHIL OAKEY (b. 2 Oct'55) – vocals / **IAN CRAIG-MARSH** (b.19 Nov'56) – synthesizers / **MARTYN WARE** (b.19 May'56) – synthesizers

Fast / not issued

Jun 78. (7") **BEING BOILED. / CIRCUS OF DEATH** [ ] [-]
(re-iss.Jan82 reached No.6 UK)

— added **ADRIAN WRIGHT** (b.30 Dec'56) – synthesizers, visuals

Apr 79. (12"ep) **THE DIGNITY OF LABOUR** [ ] [-]
– (part 1 / part 2 / part 3 / part 4) *(contains free flexi)*

Virgin / A & M

Jul 79. (12") **I DON'T DEPEND ON YOU. ("The MEN") / CRUEL** [ ] [-]
Sep 79. (7") **EMPIRE STATE HUMAN. / INTRODUCING** [ ] [-]
Oct 79. (lp)(c) **REPRODUCTION** [ ] [-]
– Almost medieval / Circus of death / The path of least resistance / Blind youth / The word before last / Empire state human / Morale / You've lost that lovin' feelin' / Austerity / Girl one / Zero as a limit. *(re-iss.+cd.1987)*
Apr 80. (7") **HOLIDAY '80** [56] [-]
– Rock'n'roll / Being boiled / Nightclubbing / Dancevision. *(re-iss.Nov81 as 12"ep += Marianne. reached No.46)*
May 80. (lp)(c) **TRAVELOGUE** [16] [-]
– The black hit of space / Only after dark / Life kills / Dreams of leaving / Toyota city / Crow and a baby / The touchables / Gordon's Gin / Being boiled / WXJL tonight. *(re-iss.+cd.1987)*
Jun 80. (7") **ONLY AFTER DARK. / TOYOTA CITY** [62] [ ]
(free 7" w/) – EMPIRE STATE HUMAN. / INTRODUCING

— **JO CATHERALL** (b.18 Sep'62) **& SUSANNE SULLEY** (b.22 Mar'63) – b.vocals repl. WARE and MARSH who formed HEAVEN 17. also added **IAN BURDEN** (b.24 Dec'57) – bass, synthesizers

Feb 81. (7") **BOYS AND GIRLS. / TOM BAKER** [48] [ ]
Apr 81. (7") **THE SOUND OF THE CROWD.(as "HUMAN LEAGUE RED") / ('A' instrumental)** [12] [ ]
(12"+=) – Tom Baker / Boys and girls / Dancevision.

— added **JO CALLIS** – guitar (ex-REZILLOS, ex-BOOTS FOR DANCING, ex-SHAKE)

Jul 81. (7") **LOVE ACTION (I BELIEVE IN LOVE). / HARD TIMES** [3] [ ] Apr 82
(12"+=) – ('A'&'B'instrumental). (with free 7"flexi) *(cd-ep.iss.Jun88, – the 4 12"tracks)*
Oct 81. (7") **OPEN YOUR HEART.(as "HUMAN LEGUE BLUE") / NON-STOP** [6] [ ]
(12"+=) – ('A'&'B'instrumental).
Oct 81. (lp)(c)(pic-lp) **DARE** [1] [3] Feb 82
– Things that dreams are made of / Open your heart / The sound of the crowd / Darkness / Do or die / Get Carter / I am the law / Seconds / Love action (I believe in love) / Don't you want me. *(cd-iss.1987)*
Nov 81. (7")(12") **DON'T YOU WANT ME. ("HUMAN LEAGUE 100") / SECONDS** [1] [1] Feb 82
Jul 82. (lp)(c) **LOVE AND DANCING ("LEAGUE UNLIMITED ORCHESTRA")** [6] [ ]
– (instrumental versions of "DARE" except) / Get Carter / Darkness.
Aug 82. (7") **THINGS THAT DREAMS ARE MADE OF. / ('A' instrumental)** [-] [ ]
Oct 82. (7") **DON'T YOU WANT ME ("LEAGUE UNLIMITED ORCHESTRA"). / (part 2)** [-] [ ]
Nov 82. (7")(12")(7"pic-d) **MIRROR MAN. / YOU REMIND ME OF GOLD** [2] [-]
Apr 83. (7")(12") **(KEEP FEELING) FASCINATION. / TOTAL PANIC** [2] [8] May 83
Jul 83. (m-lp) **FASCINATION** (import, recent hits). [-] [22]
Sep 83. (7") **MIRROR MAN. / NON-STOP** [-] [30]
Apr 84. (7")(12") **THE LEBANON. / THIRTEEN** [11] [64] Jul 84
May 84. (lp)(c)(cd) **HYSTERIA** [3] [62]
– I'm coming back / I love you too much / Rock me again and again and again and again and again and again / Louise / The Lebanon / Betrayed / The sign / So hurt / Life on your own / Don't you know I want you. *(cd-re-iss.Jul87) (re-iss.cd Mar94)*
Jun 84. (7")(12") **LIFE ON YOUR OWN. / THE WORLD TONIGHT** [16] [-]
Aug 84. (7") **DON'T YOU KNOW I WANT TO. / THIRTEEN** [-] [-]
Oct 84. (7") **LOUISE. / THE WORLD TONIGHT** [-] [-]
Nov 84. (7")(12")(7"pic-d) **LOUISE. / THE SIGN** [13] [-]

— Trimmed down to main trio of **PHIL, SUSANNE, JOANNE** plus **ADRIAN / JIM RUSSELL** – synthesizer repl. BURDEN and CALLIS

Aug 86. (7") **HUMAN. / ('A'instrumental)** [8] [1]
(12"+=) – ('A'extended) / ('A'acapella).
Sep 86. (lp)(c)(cd) **CRASH** [7] [24]
– Money / Swang / Human / Jam / Are you ever coming back? / I need your loving / Party / Love on the run / The real thing / Love is all that matters.
Nov 86. (7")(12") **I NEED YOUR LOVING. / ('A'version)** [72] [-]
Nov 86. (7") **I NEED YOUR LOVING. / ARE YOU EVER COMING BACK** [-] [44]
Jan 87. (7") **LOVE IS ALL THAT MATTERS. / ('A' instrumental)** [-] [ ]
Apr 87. (7") **ARE YOU EVER COMING BACK. / JAM** [-] [ ]
Oct 88. (7") **LOVE IS ALL THAT MATTERS. / I LOVE YOU TOO MUCH** [41] [ ]
(12"+=)(cd-s+=) – ('A'dub version).
Nov 88. (lp)(c)(cd) **GREATEST HITS** (compilation) [3] [ ]
– Mirror man / (Keep feeling) Fascination / The sound of the crowd / The Lebanon / Human / Together in electric dreams (PHIL OAKEY & GIORGIO MORODER) / Don't you want me? / Being boiled (re-boiled) / Love action (I believe in love) / Louise / Open your heart / Love is all that matters / Life on your own. *(re-iss.cd/c Nov95)*

— The basic trio, added **RUSSELL BENNETT** – guitar / **NEIL SUTTON** – keyboards

Aug 90. (7")(US-c-s) **HEART LIKE A WHEEL. / REBOUND** [29] [32] Sep 90
(12"+=)(cd-s+=) – ('A'extended).
(cd-s++=) – A doorway (dub mix).
Sep 90. (cd)(c)(lp) **ROMANTIC?** [24] [ ]
– Kiss the future / A doorway / Heart like a wheel / Men are dreamers / Mister Moon and Mister Sun / Soundtrack to a generation / Rebound / The stars are going out / Let's get together again / Get it right this time.
Nov 90. (7")(c-s) **SOUNDTRACK TO A GENERATION. / ('A'instrumental)** [ ] [ ]
(12"+=) – ('A'acappella version).
(cd-s++=) – ('A'dub version).

East West / East West

Dec 94. (c-s) **TELL ME WHEN. / ('A'mix)** [6] [31] Mar95
(cd-s+=) – Kimi ni mune kyun / The bus to Crookes.
(12")(cd-s) – ('A'side) / ('A'-Overworld mix) / ('A'-Red Jerry mix) / ('A'-strictly blind dub mix).
Jan 95. (cd)(c) **OCTOPUS** [6] [ ]
– Tell me when / These are the days / One man in my heart / Words / Filling up with Heaven / House full of nothing / John Cleese; is he funny? / Never again / Cruel young lover.
Mar 95. (c-s)(cd-s) **ONE MAN IN MY HEART / THESE ARE THE DAYS (Ba ba mix)** [13] [ ]
(cd-s+=) – These are the days (sonic radiation) / ('A'version).
(12") – ('B'side) / ('B'-Symphone Ba Ba mix) / ('B'instrumental) / ('A'-T.O.E.C. unplugged).
Jun 95. (c-s)(cd-s) **FILLING UP WITH HEAVEN / JOHN CLEESE, IS HE FUNNY?** [36] [ ]
(cd-s) – ('A'side) / ('A'-Hardfloor mix) / ('A'-Neil McLellen mix).
Oct 95. (c-s) **DON'T YOU WANT ME (remix) / ('A'-Snap remix) / (2-'A'-Red Jerry mix)** [16] [ ]
(12") – ('A'-Snap remix extended) / ('A'-Red Jerry remix extended).
(cd-s) – (all 6-'A'versions).

– compilations, etc. –

Oct 90. Virgin; (cd-box) **DARE / HYSTERIA / CRASH** [ ] [ ]

PHIL OAKEY & GIORGIO MORODER

– synthesizers

Virgin / A & M

Sep 84. (7")(7"pic-d) **TOGETHER IN ELECTRIC DREAMS. / ('A'instrumental)** [3] [ ]
(12"+=) – ('A'extended).
Jun 85. (7")(12") **GOODBYE BAD TIMES. /('A' version)** [44] [ ]
Jul 85. (lp)(c)(cd) **CHROME** [52] [ ]
– Goodbye bad times / Together in electric dreams / Valerie / Why must the show go on / Be me lover now / Shake it up / Brand new lover / In transit / Now. *(cd-re-iss.Jun88)*
Aug 85. (7")(12") **BE MY LOVER NOW. / ('A' instrumental)** [ ] [ ]

HUMANOID

(see under ⇒ FUTURE SOUND OF LONDON)

HUMBLE PIE

Formed: Essex, England . . . Spring 1969 as a mini-supergroup by STEVE MARRIOTT and PETER FRAMPTON. They signed to Andrew Loog Oldman's 'Immediate' label, and hit UK Top 5 with first single 'NATURAL BORN BUGIE', after a venture into Top 40 with album 'AS SAFE AS YESTERDAY'. After follow-up flopped and when the label liquidated, they re-surfaced on 'A&M', but found no friends with 1970's self-titled lp. By late 1971, they returned to chart action, with double live-lp 'PERFORMANCE – ROCKIN' AT THE FILLMORE', which also gave them initial entry into US Top 30. With MARRIOTT now at the helm, FRAMPTON departed for lucrative solo career. • **Style:** Hard rockin' outfit, who shifted into heavier course in 1972, and then soul-rock from then on, leading to MARRIOTT's panning by critics. • **Songwriters:** All took a shot at writing, with MARRIOTT the main contributor. Covered; C'MON EVERYBODY + HALLELUJAH I LOVE HER SO (Eddie Cochran) / ROADRUNNER (Junior Walker) / HONKY TONK WOMAN (Rolling Stones) / I WALK ON GUILDED SPLINTERS (Dr.John) / ROCK'N'ROLL MUSIC (Chuck Berry) / ALL SHOOK UP (Elvis Presley) / etc. • **Trivia:** Would have gone under in 1970, but for American lawyer DEE ANTHONY, who became their manager.

Recommended: THE HUMBLE PIE COLLECTION (*6).

STEVE MARRIOTT (b.30 Jan'47, London) – vocals, guitar (ex-SMALL FACES) / **PETER FRAMPTON** (b.22 Apr'50, Kent, England) – vocals, guitar (ex-HERD) / **GREG RIDLEY** (b.23 Oct'47) – bass (ex-SPOOKY TOOTH) / **JERRY SHIRLEY** (b. 4 Feb'52) – drums (ex-LITTLE WOMEN)

Immediate Immediate

Jul 69. (lp) **AS SAFE AS YESTERDAY** 32
– Desperation / Stick shift / Buttermilk boy / Growing closer / As safe as yesterday / Bang? / Alabama '69 / I'll go alone / A nifty little number like you / What you will. *(cd-iss.Dec92 on 'Repertoire' +=)* – Natural born bugie / Wrist job.

Sep 69. (7") **NATURAL BORN BUGIE. / WRIST JOB** 4
(re-iss.Feb83)

Oct 69. (7") **NATURAL BORN BUGIE. / I'LL GO ALONE** -

Dec 69. (lp) **TOWN AND COUNTRY**
– Take me back / The sad bag of shaky Jake / The light of love / Cold lady / Down home again / Ollie Ollie / Every mother's son / Heartbeat / Only you can say / Silver tongue / Home and away. *(cd-iss.Dec92 on 'Repertoire' +=)* – Greg's song / 79th Street blues.

A&M A&M

Jul 70. (lp)(c) **HUMBLE PIE**
– Live with me / Only a roach / One eyed trouser-snake rumba / Earth and water song / I'm ready / Theme from Skint (see you later liquidator) / Red light mamma / Red hot / Sucking on the sweet vine.

Mar 71. (lp)(c) **ROCK ON**
– Shine on / Sour grain / 79th and sunset / Stone cold fever / Rollin' stone / A song for Jenny / The light / Big George / Strange days / Red neck jump.

Sep 71. (7") **I DON'T NEED NO DOCTOR. / SONG FOR JENNY** - 73

Nov 71. (d-lp)(d-c) **PERFORMANCE – ROCKIN' THE FILLMORE (live)** 32 21
– Four day creep / I'm ready / Stone cold fever / I walk on guilded splinters / Rollin' stone / Hallelujah (I love her so) / I don't need no doctor. *(re-iss.1974)*

— **DAVE CLEMPSON** – guitar (ex-COLOSSEUM) repl. FRAMPTON who went solo

Mar 72. (lp)(c) **SMOKIN'** 28 6
– Hot'n'nasty / The fixer / You're so good to me / C'mon everybody / Old time feelin' / 30 days in the hole / (I'm a) Road runner / Roadrunner "G" jam / I wonder who / Sweet peace and time.

Apr 72. (7") **HOT'N'NASTY. / YOU"RE SO GOOD FOR ME** - 52

Sep 73. (7") **30 DAYS IN THE HOLE. / SWEET PEACE AND TIME** -

— now augmented by all-girl backing trio The BLACKBERRIES (**CLYDIE KING / BILLIE BARNUM + VANETTA FIELDS**)

Jan 73. (7") **BLACK COFFEE. / SAY NO MORE**

Apr 73. (d-lp)(d-c) **EAT IT** (1-side live) 34 13 Mar 73
– Get down to it / Good booze and bad women / Is it for love / Drugstore cowboy / Black coffee / I believe to my soul / Shut up and don't interrupt me / That's how strong my love is / Say no more / Oh, Bella (all that's hers) / Summer song / Beckton dumps / Up our sleeve / Honky tonk woman / (I'm a) Road runner.

Jun 73. (7") **GET DOWN TO IT. / HONKY TONK WOMAN (live)**

Oct 73. (7") **OH LA DE DA. / THE OUTCROWD**

Feb 74. (lp)(c) **THUNDERBOX** 52
– Thunderbox / Groovin' with Jesus / I can't stand the rain / Anna / No way / Rally with Ali / Don't worry, be happy / Ninety-nine pounds / Every single day / No money down / Drift away / Oh la-de-da.

May 74. (7") **NINETY-NINE POUNDS. / RALLY WITH ALI** -

Feb 75. (lp)(c) **STREET RATS** 100
– Street rat / Rock'n'roll music / We can work it out / Scored out / Road hog / Rain / Funky to the bone / Let me be your lovemaker / Countryman / Stomp / Drive my car / Queens and nuns.

Mar 75. (7") **ROCK'N'ROLL MUSIC. / SCORED OUT** -

Jul 75. (7") **ROCK'N'ROLL MUSIC. / ROAD HOG** -

— Disband Spring 1975. JERRY SHIRLEY formed NATURAL GAS, and the others joined

STEVE MARRIOTT ALL-STARS

which also included **DAMON BUTCHER** – keys / **IAN WALLACE** – drums (ex-KING CRIMSON) / **MICKEY FINN** – guitar (ex-T.REX)

A&M A&M

May 76. (lp)(c) **MARRIOTT**
– Star in my life / Are you lonely for me baby / You don't know me / Late night lady / Early evening light / East side struttin' / Lookin' for love / Help me through the day / Midnight rock'n'rollin' / Wam bam thank you ma'am.

Jun 76. (7") **STAR IN MY LIFE. / MIDNIGHT ROCK'N'ROLLIN'** -

Jun 76. (7") **STAR IN MY LIFE. / EAST SIDE STRUTTIN'** -

— CLEMPSON and BUTCHER joined ROUGH DIAMOND. WALLACE toured with BOB DYLAN. MICKEY FINN joined PHIL MAY'S FALLEN ANGELS. MARRIOTT re-formed The SMALL FACES

HUMBLE PIE

also re-formed in 1979, with **STEVE MARRIOTT** – vocals, guitar / **JERRY SHIRLEY** – drums / **BOBBY TENCH** – guitar (ex-STREETWALKERS, ex-JEFF BECK) / **ANTHONY JONES** – bass

Jet Atco

Apr 80. (lp)(c) **ON TO VICTORY** 60
– Fool for a pretty face (hurt by love) / You soppy pratt / Get it in the end / Infatuation / Further down the road / My lover's prayer / Take it from here / Baby don't do it.

Apr 80. (7") **FOOL FOR A PRETTY FACE (HURT BY LOVE). / YOU SOPPY PRATT** 52

Jun 81. (lp)(c) **GO FOR THE THROAT** May 81
– All shook up / Chip away / Driver / Go for the throat / Keep it on the island / Lottie and the charcoal queen / Restless blood / Teenage anxiety / Tin soldier.

— Finally call it a day 1981.

– compilations, others –

Sep 72. A&M; (d-lp) **LOST AND FOUND** (1st-2 lp's) - 37

1988. A&M; (cd) **THE BEST OF HUMBLE PIE**

Jul 76. Immediate; (lp)(c) **BACK HOME AGAIN** -

Jan 78. Immediate; (lp)(c) **HUMBLE PIE'S GREATEST HITS** -

Sep 85. Old Gold; (7") **NATURAL BORN BUGIE. / (other artist)** -

Nov 85. Castle; (d-lp)(c)(cd) **THE COLLECTION** -
– Bang? / Natural born bugie / I'll go alone / Buttermilk boy / Desperation / Nifty little number like you / Wrist job / Stick shift / Growing closer / As safe as yesterday / Heartbeat / Down home again / Take me back / Only you can see / Silver tongue / Every mother's son / The sad bag of Shaky Jake / Cold lady / Home and away / Light of love. *(cd-iss.Apr94)*

Feb 95. Band Of Joy; (cd) **NATURAL BORN BOOGIE** -

May 95. A&M; (cd) **PIECE OF THE PIE** -

Nov 95. Charly; (d-cd) **THE IMMEDIATE YEARS** -

STEVE MARRIOTT

went solo again.

Aura not issued

Jan 85 (7") **WHATCHA GONNA DO ABOUT IT. / ALL SHOOK UP** -

Steve MARRIOTT's PACKET OF THREE

Aura not issued

Apr 86. (lp)(c) **PACKET OF THREE** -
– What'cha gonna do about it / Bad moon rising / All shook up / The fixer / All or nothing / Five long years / I don't need no doctor.

— STEVE MARRIOT died 20 Apr'91, after accidentally setting his Essex cottage on fire with a lighted cigarette.

– (STEVE MARRIOTT) compilations, others –

Sep 89. Trax; (lp)(c)(cd) **30 SECONDS TO MIDNIGHT** -
(re-iss.cd. Apr93 on 'Castle')

Nov 91. Mau Mau; (lp)(cd) **DINGWALLS 6.7.84 (live)** -

Feb 92. Maste- Elastic Cat; (cd) **SCRUBBERS** (rec.1974, **STEVE MARRIOTT / TIM HINKLEY / GREG RIDLEY)** -

Ian HUNTER

Born: 3 Jun'46, Shrewsbury, England. After years playing in clubs in Hamburg, Germany, he joined AT LAST THE 1958 ROCK & ROLL SHOW, who released one-off 45 for 'CBS' in 1967 'I CAN'T DRIVE' / 'WORKIN' ON THE RAILROAD'. The next year, he wrote 1 or 2 songs for CHARLIE WOLFE demos, which went unissued until 'Nems' gave them light in mid-70's:- 'STAY STAY STAY' / 'HOME'. After answering an ad in music press, he successfully auditioned in Jun'69 for lead singer in MOTT THE HOOPLE. For the next 5 years, they became one of Britain's best rock acts, until HUNTER decided to opt for solo career in 1975. His debut 45 'ONCE BITTEN TWICE SHY', took off where THE HOOPLE left off, and made UK Top 20. With help from stalward supporter and guitarist MICK RONSON, he continued to surface either in England or New York, with credible material. They had already toured supporting each other's solo projects, as the HUNTER-RONSON BAND. • **Style:** Shady (dark-spectacled) rock'n'roll hero/icon, whose curly looks were also part of image. • **Songwriters:** HUNTER and some with RONSON. Covered; WHO DO YOU LOVE (Bo Diddley) / etc. • **Trivia:** In 1978, HUNTER produced the GENERATION X album 'Valley Of The Dolls'.

Recommended: THE VERY BEST OF IAN HUNTER (*6).

IAN HUNTER – vox, guitar (ex-MOTT THE HOOPLE, ex-AT LAST THE 1958 . . .) with **MICK RONSON** – guitar, vocals (ex-MOTT THE HOOPLE, ex-DAVID BOWIE, Solo artist) / **PETE ARNESEN** – keyboards / **JEFF APPLEBY** – bass / **DENNIS ELLIOTT** – drums

C.B.S. Columbia

Mar 75. (7") **ONCE BITTEN TWICE SHY. / 3,000 MILES FROM HERE** 14

Apr 75. (lp)(c) **IAN HUNTER** 21 50
– Once bitten twice shy / Who do you love / Lounge lizard / Boy / 3,000 miles from here / The truth, the whole truth, nuthin' but the truth / It ain't easy when you fall / Shades off / I get so excited. *(re-iss.cd Sep94 on 'Rewind')*

Jul 75. (7") **WHO DO YOU LOVE. / BOY**

— HUNTER with RONSON, brought in mainly session people including **AYNSLEY DUNBAR** – drums / **CORNELL DUPREEE** – guitar / **JACO PASTORUS** – bass / **CHRIS STAINTON** – keyboards / guests **BRIAN MAY + FREDDIE MERCURY** – vocals (QUEEN) All replaced PETE and JEFF who went into sessions + DENNIS who joined FOREIGNER

May 76. (7") **ALL AMERICAN ALIEN BOY. / RAPE**

May 76. (lp)(c) **ALL AMERICAN ALIEN BOY** 29
– Letter to Brittania from the Union Jack / All American alien boy / Irene Wilde / Restless youth / Rape / You nearly did me in / Apathy 83 / God (take 1).

Aug 76. (7") **YOU NEARLY DID ME IN. / LETTER FROM BRITANNIA TO THE UNION JACK**

— HUNTER formed tour band OVERNIGHT ANGELS:- **EARL SLICK** – guitar (ex-BOWIE) / **PETER OXENDALE** – keyboards / **BOB RAWLINSON** – bass / **CURLY SMITH** – drums MICK RONSON joined BOB DYLAN's Rolling Thunder Tour mid-76.

May 77. (7") **JUSTICE OF THE PEACE. / THE BALLAD OF LITTLE STAR**

May 77. (lp)(c) **OVERNIGHT ANGELS**
– Golden opportunity / Shallow crystals / Overnight angels / Broadway / Justice of the peace / Silver dime / Wild 'n' free / The ballad of little star / To love a woman. *(re-iss.cd Jun94 on 'Sony Europe')*

Jul 78. (7") **ENGLAND ROCKS. / WILD 'N' FREE**

— now with **RONSON** plus **ROY BITTAN** – keyboards / **MAX WEINBERG** – drums / **GEORGE YOUNG + LEW DELGATTO** – sax / **GARY TALLENT** – bass / **ELLEN FOLEY** – vocals

Chrysalis Chrysalis

Apr 79. (7")(7"white) **WHEN THE DAYLIGHT COMES. / LIFE AFTER DEATH**

May 79. (lp)(c) **YOU'RE NEVER ALONE WITH SCHIZOPHRENIC** 49 35 Apr 79

– Just another night / Wild east / Cleveland rocks / When the daylight comes / Ships / Life after death / Standin' in my light / Bastard / The outsider. *(re-iss.cd Mar94)*

Jul 79. (7") **SHIPS. / WILD EAST**

Aug 79. (7") **JUST ANOTHER NIGHT. / ?** [-] [68]

Oct 79. (7") **CLEVELAND ROCKS. / BASTARD**

— **MARTIN BRILEY** – bass repl. TALLENT / **ERIC PARKER** – drums repl. WEINBERG / **GEORGE MEYER + TOM MANDEL** – keyboards repl. BITTAN also to BRUCE SPRINGSTEEN / **TOMMY MORRONGIELLO** – guitar, bass repl. YOUNG + DELGATTO

Apr 80. (d-lp)(c) **WELCOME TO THE CLUB (live)** [61] [69]
– F.B.I. / Once bitten twice shy / Angelline / Laugh at me / All the way from Memphis / I wish I was your mother / Irene Wilde / Just another night / Cleveland rocks / Standin' in my light / Bastard / Walkin' with a mountain / Rock'n'roll queen / All the young dudes / Slaughter on Tenth Avenue / We gotta get out of here / Silver needles / Man o' war / Sons and daughters. *(re-iss.cd May94)*

Jun 80. (d7") **WE GOTTA GET OUT OF HERE (Medley)./ / SONS AND DAUGHTERS. / ONE OF THE BOYS**

— virtualy same band except featured guests **TODD RUNDGREN** – vocals, bass / **MICK JONES** – guitar / **TOPPER HEADON** – drums (both of CLASH) / **TYMON DOGG** – violin

Aug 81. (7") **LISA LIKES ROCK'N'ROLL. / NOISES**

Aug 81. (lp)(c) **SHORT BACK 'N' SIDES** [79] [62]
– Central Park 'n' West / Lisa likes rock'n'roll / I need your love / Old records never die / Noises / Rain / Gun control / Theatre of the absurd / Leave me alone / Keep on burning. *(re-iss.cd + extra tracks May94)*

— now with **RONSON + ROBBIE ALTER + JIMMY RIP** – guitar / **MARK CLARKE + DAN HARTMAN** – bass / **MANDAL / JEFF BOVA + BOB MAYO** – keyboards / **CLARENCE CLEMONS + LOU CORTLEZZI** – sax / **HILLY MICHAELS** – drums

C.B.S. Columbia

Jul 83. (7") **ALL THE GOOD ONES ARE TAKEN. / DEATH AND GLORY BOYS**

Aug 83. (lp)(c) **ALL THE GOOD ONES ARE TAKEN**
– All the good ones are taken / Every step of the way / Fun / Speechless / Death 'n' glory boys / Somethin's goin' on / That girl is rock'n'roll / Captain Void 'n' the video jets / Seeing double / All the good ones are taken (reprise). *(re-iss.cd Jun94 on 'Sony Europe')*

Oct 83. (7") **SOMETHIN'S GOIN' ON. / ALL THE GOOD ONES ARE TAKEN** [-]

Oct 83. (7") **SEEING DOUBLE. / THAT GIRL IS ROCK'N'ROLL** [-]

— HUNTER retired from public eye until late '89 he and RONSON re-formed the

HUNTER-RONSON

band, with **PAT KILBRIDE** – bass / **MICKEY CURRY** – drums / **TOMMY MANDEL** – keyboards

Mercury Mercury

Jan 90. (cd)(c)(lp) **YUI ORTA** [ ] [ ] Oct 89
– American music / The loner / Women's intuition / Tell it like it is / Livin' in a heart / Big time / Cool / Beg a little love / Following in your footsteps * / Sons 'n' lovers / Pain * / How much more can I take * / Sweet dreamer. *(c/cd+= *)*

Feb 90. (7")(c-s) **AMERICAN MUSIC. / TELL IT LIKE IT IS**
(12"+=)(cd-s+=) – Sweet dreamer.

– (IAN HUNTER) compilations, etc. –

Feb 80. C.B.S.; (lp)(c) **SHADES OF IAN HUNTER – THE BALLAD OF IAN HUNTER & MOTT THE HOOPLE**

Apr 91. C.B.S.; (cd)(c)(lp) **THE VERY BEST OF IAN HUNTER**

Jul 91. Castle; (cd)(c) **THE COLLECTION** [-]
(Includes tracks by MOTT THE HOOPLE)

Oct 95. Windsong; (cd) **BBC 1 LIVE IN CONCERT** [-]

Robert HUNTER (see under ⇒ GRATEFUL DEAD)

HUSKER DU

Formed: Minneapolis, USA ... 1978 by MOULD, HART and NORTON. In 1980-82, they issued a few 45's and a live lp 'LAND SPEED RECORD', which was on own label 'New Alliance'. After another lp on 'Reflex' in 1983, they shifted to BLACK FLAG's US indie label 'SST', and unleashed mini-lp 'METAL CIRCUS'. Three classic lp's 'ZEN ARCADE', 'NEW DAY RISING' & 'FLIP YOUR WIG' (1st was double) appeared between Autumn '84 & '85, before they were snapped up by 'Warners'. After 2 uncompromising sets 'CANDY APPLE GREY' & 'WAREHOUSE' in 1986, they argued and split up the next year. Solo projects by MOULD and HART appeared, but commercial success arrived in 1992, when BOB MOULD's band "SUGAR" signed to 'Creation' and made UK Top 10. • **Style:** Innovators of hardcore speed-metal, which in the mid-80's, became integrated with 2 or 3 minute rock gems. SUGAR were energy and melody fused together somewhere between NIRVANA and PIXIES. • **Songwriters:** MOULD-HART compositions except; SUNSHINE SUPERMAN (Donovan) / TICKET TO RIDE + SHE'S A WOMAN + HELTER SKELTER (Beatles) / EIGHT MILES HIGH (Byrds). NOVA MOB covered I JUST WANT TO MAKE LOVE TO YOU (Willie Dixon) / SHEENA IS A PUNK ROCKER (Ramones). Solo GRANT HART covered SIGNED D.C. (Love). • **Trivia:** HUSKER DU means; DO YOU REMEMBER in Swedish.

Recommended: NEW DAY RISING (*8) / FLIP YOUR WIG (*9) / ZEN ARCADE (*8) / CANDY APPLE GREY (*7) / WAREHOUSE (*7)

BOB MOULD (b.Lake Placid) – vocals, guitar, keyboards, percussion / **GRANT HART** – drums, keyboards, percussion, vocals / **GREG NORTON** – bass

not issued Reflex

1980. (7") **STATUES. / AMUSEMENT (live)** [-]

not issued New Allia..

Aug 81. (lp) **LAND SPEED RECORD (live)** [-]
– All tensed up / Don't try to call / I'm not interested / Big sky / Guns at my school / Push the button / Gilligan's Island / MTC / Don't have a life / Bricklayer / Tired of doing things / You're naive / Strange week / Do the bee / Ultracore / Let's go die / Data control. *(UK import mid-82 on 'Alternative Tentacles') (UK rel.Nov88 on 'S.S.T.' & re-iss.cd/c/lp Oct95)*

1982. (7"m) **IN A FREE LAND. / WHAT DO I WANT? / M.I.C.** [-]

not issued Reflex

Jul 83. (lp) **EVERYTHING FALLS APART** [-]
– From the gut / Blah, blah, blah / Punch drunk / Bricklayer / Afraid of being wrong / Sunshine Superman / Signals from above / Everything falls apart / Wheels / Obnoxious / Gravity. *(cd-iss. May93 with extra tracks)*

S.S.T. S.S.T.

Dec 83. (m-lp) **METAL CIRCUS**
– Real world / Deadly skies / It's not funny anymore / Diane / First of the last calls / Lifeline / Out on a limb.

Apr 84. (7"colrd) **EIGHT MILES HIGH. / MASOCHISM WORLD**
(iss.cd-s.Dec88)

Sep 84. (d-lp) **ZEN ARCADE**
– Something I learned today / Broken home, broken heart / Never talking to you again / Chartered trips / Dreams reoccurring / Indecision time / Hare Krishna / Beyond the threshold / Pride / I'll never forget you / The biggest lie / What's going on / Masochism world / Standing by the sea / Somewhere / One step at a time / Pink turns to blue / Newest industry / Monday will never be the same / Whatever / The tooth fairy and the princess / Turn on the news / Reoccurring dreams. *(cd-iss.Oct87) (re-iss.cd/c/d-lp Oct95)*

Feb 85. (lp) **NEW DAY RISING**
– New day rising / Girl who lives on Heaven Hill / I apologize / Folklore / If I told you / Celebrated summer / Perfect example / Terms of psychic warfare / 59 times the pain / Powerline / Books about UFO's / I don't know what you're talking about / How to skin a cat / Watcha drinkin' / Plans I make. *(cd-iss.Oct87) (re-iss.cd/c/lp Oct95)*

Aug 85. (7") **MAKE NO SENSE AT ALL. / LOVE IS ALL AROUND (MARY'S THEME)**

Oct 85. (lp) **FLIP YOUR WIG**
– Flip your wig / Every everything / Makes no sense at all / Hate paper doll / Green eyes / Divide and conquer / Games / Find me / The baby song / Flexible flyer / Private plane / Keep hanging on / The wit and the wisdom / Don't know yet. *(cd-iss.Oct87) (re-iss.cd/c/lp Oct95)*

Warners Warners

Feb 86. (7") **DON'T WANT TO KNOW IF YOU ARE LONELY. / ALL WORK NO PLAY**
(12"+=) – Helter skelter (live).

Mar 86. (lp)(c) **CANDY APPLE GREY**
– Crystal / Don't want to know if you are lonely / I don't know for sure / Sorry somehow / Too far down / Hardly getting over it / Dead set on destruction / Eiffel Tower high / No promises have I made / All this I've done for you.

Sep 86. (7") **SORRY SOMEHOW. / ALL THIS I'VE DONE FOR YOU**
(d7+=)(12"+=) – Flexible flyer / Celebrated summer.

Jan 87. (7")(12") **COULD YOU BE THE ONE. / EVERYTIME**

Jan 87. (d-lp)(d-c) **WAREHOUSE: SONGS & STORIES** [72]
– These important years / Charity, chastity, prudence and hope / Standing in the rain / Back from somewhere / Ice cold ice / You're a soldier / Could you be the one? / Too much spice / Friend, you've got to fall / Visionary / She floated away / Bed of nails / Tell you why tomorrow / It's not peculiar / Actual condition / No reservations / Turn it around / She's a woman (and now he is a man) / Up in the air / You can live at home.

Jun 87. (7")(12") **ICE COLD ICE. / GOTTA LETTA**

– compilations –

May 94. Warners; (cd)(c) **THE LIVING END (live)**
– New day rising / Heaven Hill / Standing in the rain / Back from somewhere / Ice cold ice / Everytime / Friend you're gonna fall / She floated away / From the gut / Target / It's not funny anymore / Hardly getting over it / Terms of psychic warfare / Powertime / Books about UFO's / Divide and conquer / Keep hangin' on / Celebrated summer / Now that you know me / Ain't no water in the well / What's goin' on / Data control / In a free land / Sheena is a punk rocker.

— Disbanded in 1987 after manager DAVID SAVOY Jr. committed suicide. GRANT HART went solo in '89, as did BOB MOULD. In 1992 he formed SUGAR.

GRANT HART

S.S.T. S.S.T.

Nov 89. (lp,cd) **INTOLERANCE**
– All of my senses / Now that you know me / The main / Roller risk / Fanfare in D major (come, come) / You're the victim / 2541 / Anything / She can see the angels coming / Reprise.

May 90. (12"ep)(cd-ep) **ALL OF MY SENSES. / THE MAIN (edit) / SIGNED D.C.**

World Ser. World Ser.

Dec 95. (cd) **ECCE HOMO**
–

NOVA MOB

(GRANT HART) & his group:- **TOM MERKL** – bass / **MICHAEL CRECO** – drums

Rough Trade Rough Trade

Feb 91. (cd)(c)(lp) **THE LAST DAYS OF POMPEII**
– Introduction / Woton / Getaway (gateway) in time / Admiral of the sea (79 a.d. version) / Wernher Von Braun / Space jazz / Where you grave land (next time you fall off of yo) / Over my head / Admiral of the sea / Persuaded / Lavender and grey / Medley:- The last days of Pompeii / Benediction.

Feb 91. (12"ep)(cd-ep) **ADMIRAL OF THE SEA (first avenue mix) / ('A' milk off mix) / THE LAST DAYS OF POMPEII (mix) / GETAWAY IN TIME (instrumental) / I JUST WANT TO MAKE LOVE TO YOU (live)**

— **MARK RELISH** – drums repl. CRECO

		Southern	Big Shoe
Jul 92.	(cd-ep) **SHOT YOUR WAY TO FREEDOM / BALLAD NO. 19 / OH! TO BEHOLD / CHILDREN IN THE STREET**	☐	☐

— **HART** with **CHRIS HENSLER** – guitar / **TOM MERKL** – bass / **STEVE SUTHERLAND** – drums

		World Service	World Service
May 94.	(cd)(lp) **NOVA MOB**	☐	☐

– Shoot your way to freedom / Puzzles / Buddy / See and feel and know / Little Miss Information / I won't be there anymore / Please don't ask / The sins of their sons / Beyond a reasonable doubt / I was afraid – Coda.

Sep 94.	(cd-ep) **OLD EMPIRE / PLEASE DON'T ASK / LITTLE MISS INFORMATION / BEYOND A REASONABLE DOUBT**	☐	☐

Janis IAN

Born: JANIS EDDY FINK, 7 May'51, New York, USA. While attending Manhattan High School of Music & Art, she had her first song 'HAIR OF SPUN GOLD' published by Broadside magazine. In 1965, while singing at The Village Gate, she signed as a songwriter to 'Elektra' records, but was soon dropped when she wanted to sing herself!. Early in 1966, after her family moved from New Jersey to New York, she secured another contract, this time with 'MGM'. Her debut 45 'SOCIETY'S CHILD', released while she was still 15, broke into US chart, and finally reached Top 20 in 1967. Her eponymous debut lp at the same time, also made Top 30, but she failed to establish herself, and moved to Philadelphia. In 1971, she uprooted again, this time to California after she married, and 'Capitol' issued 'PRESENT COMPANY'. In 1974, she re-surfaced on 'Columbia' records, and hit minor chart placing with 'STARS' album. The next year, her comeback was complete when 45 'AT SEVENTEEN' hit Top 3. This won her a Grammy and was taken from US No.1 album 'BETWEEN THE LINES'. By the end of the 70's, she was again suffering commercial failure. • **Style:** Melancholy singer of the folk college circuit, who turned into classy jazzy contemporary lyricist of the mid-70's. • **Songwriters:** Writes her own material. • **Trivia:** Her song JESSE was covered by ROBERTA FLACK and JOAN BAEZ.

Recommended: THE BEST OF JANIS IAN (*6).

JANIS IAN – vocals, guitar, piano with session people

Verve-MGM | Verve Folkways

Oct 66. (7") **SOCIETY'S CHILD (BABY I'VE BEEN THINKING). / LETTER TO JOHN** [ ] [ ]
(re-iss.May67, hit US No.14)

Jun 67. (lp) **JANIS IAN** [ ] [29]
– Society's child (baby I've been thinking) / Too old to go 'way little girl / Hair of spun gold / Then tangles of my mind / I'll give you a stone if you throw it (changing tymes) / Pro-girl / Younger generation blues / New Christ cardiac hero / Lover be kindly / Mrs. McKenzie / Janey's blues. *(re-iss.+c.Jun82)*

Oct 67. (7") **YOUNGER GENERATION BLUES. / I'LL GIVE YOU A STONE IF YOU THROW IT (CHANGING TYMES)** [-] [ ]

Jan 68. (lp) **FOR ALL THE SEASONS OF YOUR MIND** [ ] [ ] Dec 67
– A song for all the seasons of your mind / And I did ma / Honey d'ya think? / Bahimsa / Queen Merka & me / There are times / Lonely one / Sunflakes fall, snowrays call / Evening star / Shady acres / Insanity comes quietly to the structured mind.

Nov 68. (7") **SUNFLAKES FALL, SNOWRAYS CALL. / INSANITY COMES QUIETLY TO THE STRUCTURED MIND** [ ] [ ]

Jan 69. (7") **A SONG FOR ALL THE SEASONS OF YOUR MIND. / LONELY ONE** [-] [ ]

Feb 69. (lp) **THE SECRET LIFE OF J. EDDY FINK** [ ] [ ]
– Everybody knows / Mistaken identity / Friends again / 42nd St. psycho blues / She's made of porcelain / Sweet misery / When I was a child / What do you think of the dead / Look to the rain / Son of love / Baby's blue.

Mar 69. (7") **FRIENDS AGAIN. / LADIES OF THE NIGHT** [-] [ ]

Jul 69. (7") **EVERYBODY KNOWS. / JANEY'S BLUES** [-] [ ]

Nov 69. (7") **CALLING YOUR NAME. / MONTH OF MAY** [-] [ ]

Nov 69. (lp) **WHO REALLY CARES** [ ] [ ]
– Time on my hands / Snowbird / Love you more than yesterday / Orphan of the wind / Sea and sand / Galveston / Do you remember / Month of May / Calling your name.

Capitol | Capitol

Feb 71. (lp)(c) **PRESENT COMPANY** [ ] [ ]
– The seaside / Present company / See my Grammy ride / Here in Spain / On the train / He's a rainbow / Weary lady / Nature's at peace / See the river / Let it run free / Alabama / Liberty / My land / Hello Jerry / Can you reach me / The sunlight. *(re-iss.Apr76)*

Feb 71. (7") **HE'S A RAINBOW. / HERE IN SPAIN** [-] [ ]

May 71. (7") **HE'S A RAINBOW. / SEE MY GRAMMY RIDE** [ ] [-]

C.B.S. | Columbia

May 74. (7") **JESSE. / THE MAN YOU ARE IN ME** [-] [ ]

Jun 74. (lp)(c) **STARS** [ ] [83] May 74
– Stars / The man you are in me / Sweet sympathy / Page nine / Thankyous / Dance with me / Without you / Jesse / You've got me on a string / Applause. *(re-iss.Jun81) (re-iss.cd/c Aug95 on 'Grapevine')*

Jul 74. (7") **WITHOUT YOU. / YOU'VE GOT ME ON A STRING** [ ] [-]

May 75. (7") **WHEN THE PARTY'S OVER. / BRIGHT LIGHTS AND PROMISES** [-] [ ]

Jul 75. (7") **AT SEVENTEEN. / STARS** [ ] [3] Jun 75

Aug 75. (lp)(c) **BETWEEN THE LINES** [ ] [1] Mar 75
– When the party's over / At seventeen / From me to you / Brights lights and promises / In the winter / Water colors / Between the lines / The come on / Light a light / Tea or symphony / Lover's lullaby. *(re-iss.cd/c Aug95 on 'Grapevine')*

Oct 75. (7") **IN THE WINTER. / THANKYOUSE** [-] [ ]

Nov 75. (7") **IN THE WINTER. / WHEN THE PARTY'S OVER** [ ] [-]

Feb 76. (lp)(c) **AFTERTONES** [ ] [12] Jan 76
– Aftertones / I would like to dance / Love is blind / Roses / Belle of the blues / Goodbye to morning / Boy I really tied one on / This must be wrong / Don't cry, old man / Hymn. *(re-iss.Mar81) (re-iss.cd/c Aug95 on 'Grapevine')*

Mar 76. (7") **BOY I REALLY TIED ONE ON. / AFTERTONES** [ ] [ ]

May 76. (7") **I WOULD LIKE TO DANCE. / GOODBYE TO MORNING** [-] [ ]

Sep 76. (7") **LOVE IS BLIND. / ROSES** [-] [ ]

Jan 77. (7") **MIRACLE ROW. / TAKE IT TO THE SKY** [-] [ ]

Mar 77. (lp)(c) **MIRACLE ROW** [ ] [45] Jan 77
– Party lights / I want to make you love me / Sunset of your life / Take to the sky / Candlelight / Let me be lonely / Slow dance romance / Will you dance? / I'll cry tonight / Miracle row – Maria. *(re-iss.cd/c Aug95 on 'Grapevine')*

May 77. (7") **CANDLELIGHT. / I WANT TO MAKE YOU LOVE ME** [-] [ ]

Sep 78. (7") **THAT GRAND ILLUSION. / HOPPER PAINTING** [-] [ ]

Sep 78. (lp)(c) **JANIS IAN** [ ] [ ]
– That grand illusion / Some people / Tonight will last forever / Hotels & one-night stands / Do you wanna dance? / Silly habits / The bridge / My mama's house / Streetlife serenaders / I need to live alone again / Hopper painting. *(re-iss.cd/c Aug95 on 'Grapevine')*

Dec 78. (7") **DO YOU WANNA DANCE?. / THE BRIDGE** [-] [ ]

Apr 79. (7") **TONIGHT WILL LAST FOREVER. / HERE COMES THE NIGHT** [-] [ ]

Oct 79. (7") **FLY TOO HIGH. / NIGHT RAINS** [44] [ ]

Oct 79. (lp)(c) **NIGHT RAINS** [ ] [ ]
– The other side of the sun / Fly too high / Memories / Night rains / Here comes the night / Day by day / Have mercy love / Lay low / Photographs / Jenny (Iowa sunrise). *(re-iss.Mar83) (re-iss.cd/c Aug95 on 'Grapevine')*

Jan 80. (7") **HAVE MERCY LOVE. / JENNY (IOWA SUNRISE)** [ ] [-]

May 80. (7") **THE OTHER SIDE OF THE SUN. / PHOTOGRAPHS** [44] [-]

Jul 80. (7") **THE OTHER SIDE OF THE SUN. / MEMORIES** [-] [ ]

Nov 80. (7") **HERE COMES THE NIGHT. / MEMORIES** [ ] [-]

Mar 81. (7") **UNDER THE COVERS. / SUGAR MOUNTAIN** [-] [71]

Jun 81. (7") **UNDER THE COVERS. / PASSION PLAY** [ ] [-]

Jul 81. (lp)(c) **RESTLESS EYES** [ ] [ ]
– Under the covers / I remember yesterday / I believe I'm myself again / Restless eyes / Get ready to roll / Passion play / Down and away / Bigger than real / Dear Billy / Sugar mountain. *(re-iss.cd/c Aug95 on 'Grapevine')*

Oct 81. (7") **I REMEMBER YESTERDAY. / RESTLESS EYES** [ ] [ ]

— Retired from studio work 1981. She guested on a MEL TORME album in 1982 and continued to appear live throughout the 80's. In 1991, she wrote 'Some People's Lives', which became a hit for BETTE MIDLER. That year she also made an appearance at the Cambridge Folk Festival. JANIS returned in 1993.

Sony | Sony

Jun 93. (cd) **BREAKING SILENCE** [ ] [ ]
– All roads to the river / Ride me like a wave / Tattoo / Guess you had to be there / What about the love? / His hands / Walking on sacred ground / This train still runs / Through the years / This house / Some people's lives / Breaking silence.

Grapevine | Asylum?

May 95. (cd)(c)(lp) **REVENGE** [ ] [ ]
– Ready for the war / Take no prisoners / Tenderness / No one else like you / Davy / When the silence falls / Take me walking in the rain / Berlin / Stolen fire / Ruby / The mission / When angels cry.

Jul 95. (c-s)(cd-s) **TENDERNESS / TAKE NO PRISONERS / WHEN ANGELS CRY** [ ] [ ]

– compilations, others, etc. –

1975. Polydor; (7") **SOCIETY'S CHILD (BABY I'VE BEEN THINKING) . / I'LL GIVE YOU A STONE IF YOU THROW IT (CHANGING TYMES)** [-] [ ]

Dec 80. C.B.S.; (lp)(c) **THE BEST OF JANIS IAN** [ ] [ ]
– At seventeen / Have mercy love / Aftertones / When the party's over / In the winter / Stars / Fly too high / The other side of the sun / Without you / Here comes the night / Jesse (Iowa sunrise) / The bridge / Between the lines / Miracle row / Maria.

Aug 83. C.B.S.; (d-c) **STARS / NIGHT RAINS** [ ] [ ]

Jun 95. Nightracks; (cd) **LIVE ON THE TEST (live)** [ ] [-]

Sep 95. Polydor; (cd) **SOCIETY'S CHILD – THE VERVE YEARS** [ ] [ ]

ICE CUBE

Born: OSHEA JACKSON, Jun'69, Crenshaw, Los Angeles, USA. Was a former leader of group N.W.A. (NIGGERS WITH ATTITUDE), who hit US Top 40 with album 'STRAIGHT OUTA COMPTON'. Departed from them due to verbal confrontations with himself and Jewish manager Jerry Hellen. ICE CUBE debutted in summer of 1990, with the politicised 'AMERIKKKA'S MOST WANTED'. By December '92, 'THE PREDATOR' had bolted straight in at No.1. • **Style:** Idealogical black rapper, with overtly sexist lyrics. Controversial for being anti-white power, anti-police, anti-media, anti-poverty, etc, etc. • **Songwriters:** Co-writes with SADLER or JINX. Sample The ISLEYS, JAMES BROWN, STEELY DAN and MICHAEL JACKSON, OHIO PLAYERS, PUBLIC ENEMY, DAS EFX, MOMENTS + GRANDMASTER FLASH. • **Trivia:** Starred and contributed to soundtracks for the films 'Boyz'n'the hood' and 'Trespass' (circa early 90's). In 1991, he co-wrote with JAMES BROWN and produced female hardcore rapper YO-YO on their 'East-West' debut US hit single 'You can't Play With My World'.

Recommended: AMERIKKKA'S MOST WANTED (*8) / THE PREDATOR (*7) / DEATH CERTIFICATE (*7)

ICE CUBE – vocals (with LENCH MOB)

4th & Broad. | Priority

May 90. (7") **AMERIKKKA'S MOST WANTED. / ONCE UPON A TIME IN THE PROJECTS** [ ] [ ]
(12"+=)(cd-s+=) – ('A'&'B' instrumentals)

Jun 90. (cd)(c)(lp) **AMERIKKKA'S MOST WANTED** [48] [19] May 90
– Better off dead / The nigga ya love to hate / Amerikkka's most wanted / What they hittin' foe? / You can't fade me / JD's gaffilin' / Once upon a time in the projects / Turn off the radio / Endangered species (tales from the darkside) / A gangsta's fairytale / I'm only out for one thing / Get off my Dick and tell yo bitch to come here / The drive-by / Rollin' with the Lench Mob / Who's the Mack? / It's a man's world / The bomb.

Mar 91. (cd)(c)(m-lp) **KILL AT WILL** (above remixes) [66] [34] Dec 90
– Endangered species (tales from the darkside) / Jackin' for beats / Get off my Dick and tell yo bitch to come here / The product / Dead Homiez / JD's gaffilin (part 2) / I gotta say what up!!!.

Oct 91. (cd)(c)(lp) **DEATH CERTIFICATE** [ ] [2]
– The funeral / The wrong nigga to fuck wit / My summer vacation / Steady mobbin' / Robin Lench / Givin' up the nappy dug out / Look who's burnin' / A bird in the hand / Man's best friend / Alive on arrival / Death / The birth / I wanna kill Sam / Horny lil' devil / True to the game / Color blind / Doing dumb shit / Us. *(cd+=) –* No Vaseline / Black Korea.

Dec 91. (7")(cd-s) **STEADY MOBBIN?. / US** [ ] [ ]
(12"+=)(cd-s+=) – Dead Homrez / Endangered species (tales from the dark side) (remix).

Nov 92. (12")(cd-s) **WICKED. / WE HAD TO TEAR THIS MOTHAFUCKA UP / THE WRONG NIGGA TO FUCK WIT / ('A'instrumental)** [ ] [55]
(cd-s+=) – ('A'&'B' instrumental). *(re-iss.Sep93, hit UK 62)*

Nov 92. (cd)(c)(lp) **THE PREDATOR** [73] [1]
– (the first day of school intro) / When will they shoot? / (I'm scared) / Wicked / Now I gotta wet 'cha / The predator / It was a good day / We had to tear this mothafucka up / **** 'em / Dirty Mack / Don't trust 'em / Gangsta's fairytale 2 / Check yo self / Who's got the camera? / Integration / Say hi to the bad guy.

Mar 93. (c-s) **IT WAS A GOOD DAY. / AIN'T GONNA TAKE MY LIFE** [27] [15]
(12"+=)(cd-s+=) – ('A'&'B' instrumentals).

Jul 93. (c-s) **CHECK YO SELF. ("ICE CUBE feat. DAS EFX") / IT WAS A GOOD DAY (radio mix)** [36] [20]
(12"+=)(cd-s+=) – 24 with an L / ('A'version).
(cd-s+=) – It was a good day (instrumental) / Who got the camera.

Dec 93. (cd)(c)(lp) **LETHAL INJECTION** [52] [5]
– The shot / Really doe / Ghetto bird / You know how we do it / Cave bitch / Bop gun (one nation) / What can I do? / Lil ass gee / Make it ruff, make it smooth / Down for whatever / Enemy / When I get to heaven

Dec 93. (12") **REALLY DOE. / MY SKIN IS MY SKIN** [66] [54]
(cd-s+=) – ('A'&'B'mixes).

Mar 94. (7")(c-s) **YOU KNOW HOW WE DO IT. / 2 N THE MORNING** [41] [30]
(12"+=)(cd-s+=) – ('A'instrumental). *(re-entered UK No.46 Dec94)*

Aug 94. (7")(c-s) **BOP GUN (ONE NATION). / DOWN FOR WHATEVER** [22] [23]
(12"+=)(cd-s+=) – ('A'-MYR mix) / Ghetto bird (Dr.Jam's mix).

— Above single features GEORGE CLINTON (ex-PARLIAMENT), with snippets from his FUNKADELIC song 'One Nation Under A Groove'.

Dec 94. (cd)(c)(d-lp) **BOOTLEGS AND B-SIDES** (compilation) [ ] [19]
– Robin Hood (cause it ain't all good) / What can I do (remix) / 24 with an L / You know how we do it (remix) / 2 n the morning / Check yo self (remix) / You don't want to fuck with these (unreleased '93 shit) / Lil piss gee (eerie gumbo mix) / My skin is my sin / It was a good day (remix) / D'voidofpopniggafied – megamix.

Dec 94. (12")(c-s)(cd-s) **YOU KNOW HOW WE DO IT (remix). / D'VOIDOFPOPNIGGAFIED (megamix)** [ ] [ ]
(cd-s+=) – 2 n the morning (mixes).

ICEHOUSE

Formed: Sydney, Australia … early 1980 as The FLOWERS, by IVA DAVIES (former member of The ABC NATIONAL TRAINING ORCHESTRA OF AUSTRALIA) and JOHN LLOYD (from New Zealand?). After a few releases for homeland 'Regular' records, they took their debut lp's title ICEHOUSE as new group name, due to a Scots band FLOWERS objecting. After it made Top 10 alongside its single out-takes, they signed to 'Chrysalis' early in '81, and re-cut debut album for UK/US market. With IVA now controlling band identity, he brought in various personnel and had early 1983 UK Top 20 hit with 'HEY LITTLE GIRL'. They struggled to maintain chart stability, until single 1988 when 'CRAZY', gave them a cross-Atlantic Top 40 hit. • **Style:** Cool modernist rock outfit, similiar to JAPAN or ROXY MUSIC. • **Songwriters:** DAVIS penned all, except COLD TURKEY (John Lennon). • **Trivia:** Late in '83, DAVIS wrote soundtrack for the Aussie film 'Razorback'. He and KRETCHMER wrote 'BOXES' ballet for the Sydney Opera House late '85.

Recommended: GREAT SOUTHERN LANDS (*6).

FLOWERS

IVA DAVIES (b.22 May'55) – vocals, guitar / **ANTHONY SMITH** – keyboards repl. MICHAEL HOSTE / **KEITH WELSH** – bass / **JOHN LLOYD** – drums

Regular AUSTRALIA | not issued

May 80. (7") **CAN'T HELP MYSELF. /** [-] [-]

Aug 80. (7") **WE CAN GET TOGETHER. /** [-] [-]

Sep 80. (lp) **ICEHOUSE** [-] [-]
– (see below lp for tracks).

ICEHOUSE

Chrysalis | Chrysalis

Jun 81. (lp)(c) **ICEHOUSE** [ ] [82]
– Icehouse / Can't help myself / Sister / Walls / Sons / We can get together / Boulevard / Fatman / Skin / Not my kind.

Jun 81. (7") **WE CAN GET TOGETHER. / PARADISE LOST** [ ] [62]
(12"+=) – Send somebody.

Sep 81. (7") **CAN'T HELP MYSELF. / FAT MAN** [ ] [ ]
(12"+=) – ('A'club 2 mixes).

— **IVA DAVIES** alone, was now ICEHOUSE the group. (IVA used session people)

Nov 81. (7") **LOVE IN MOTION. /** [-] [ ]

Jan 82. (7") **ICEHOUSE. / ALL THE WAY** [ ] [ ]
(12"+=) – Cold turkey.

May 82. (lp)(c) **PRIMITIVE MAN** [ ] [ ] Oct 82
– Uniform / Street cafe / Hey little girl / Trojan blue / Glam / Great southern land / Love in motion / Mysterious thing / One by one / Goodnight Mr. Matthews.

May 82. (7") **GREAT SOUTHERN LAND. / ?** [-] [ ]

— IVA brought in the returning **JOHN LLOYD** – drums / **MICHAEL HOSTE** – keyboards / plus **ANDY QUNTA** – keyboards, vocals / and **ROBERT KRETSCHMER** – guitar,vocals / **GUY PRATT** – bass (ex-KILLING JOKE)

Dec 82. (7")(7"pic-d)(7"colrd) **HEY LITTLE GIRL. / MYSTERIOUS THING** [17] [ ]
(12"+=) – ('A' disco mix) / Can't help myself (US mix).

Feb 83. (lp)(c) **LOVE IN MOTION** [64] [ ]
– (remixed PRIMITIVE MAN album). *(cd-iss.Jan86)*

Apr 83. (7")(7"pic-d) **STREET CAFE. / WALLS** [62] [ ]
(12"+=)(c-s+=) – Over the line.

Jun 83. (7")(12") **UNIFORM. / GREAT SOUTHERN LAND** [ ] [ ]
(d7"+=) – Can't help myself / We can be together (live).

Apr 84. (7")(12") **TAKING THE TOWN. / JAVA** [ ] [ ]

May 84. (lp)(c) **SIDEWALK** [ ] [ ]
– Take the town / This time / Someone like you / Don't believe any more / Stay close Tonight. *(cd-iss.Oct84)*

Jun 84. (7") **DON'T BELIEVE ANYMORE. / DANCE ON** [ ] [ ]
(12"+=) – The mountain.

— **STEPHEN MORGAN** – bass, vocals repl. PRATT who joined PINK FLOYD / **PAUL WHEELER** – drums, percussion repl. JOHN LLOYD / **SIMON LLOYD** – horns, keyboards, vocals repl. HOSTE.

Mar 86. (lp)(c) **MEASURE FOR MEASURE** [ ] [55]
– No promises / Cross the border / Spanish gold / The flame / Paradise / Regular boys / Mr. Big.

May 86. (7") **NO PROMISES. / THE PERFECT CRIME** [72] [79]
(12"+=) – ('A' dance mix).

Aug 86. (7") **PARADISE. / BABY YOU'RE SO STRANGE** [ ] [ ]
(12"+=) – Hey little girl.

Jul 87. (7") **CRAZY. / COMPLETELY GONE** [74] [ ]
(12"+=) – Hey little girl.
(cd-s++=) – ('A' mix). *(reached No.38-UK and No.14-US Jan88)*

Sep 87. (lp)(c)(cd) **MAN OF COLOURS** [93] [43]
– Crazy / Electric blue / My possession / Heartbreak kid / Man of colours / The kingdom / Nothing too serious / Girl in the room / Anybody's war / Sunrise.

Apr 88. (7") **ELECTRIC BLUE. / OVER MY HEAD** [53] [7]
(12"+=) – ('A' dub mix) (ST.edit).
(cd-s+=) – ('A' instrumental) / Crazy (manic mix).

Jun 88. (7") **MY OBSESSION. /** [-] [88]

— Trimmed slightly when QUNTA left

Dec 89. (7") **TOUCH THE FIRE. / THE LAST OUT** [ ] [84] Oct 89
(12"+=)(cd-s+=) – Hey little girl.

Feb 90. (cd)(c)(lp) **GREAT SOUTHERN LANDS** (compilation) [ ] [ ]
– Crazy / Cross the border / Street cafe / Don't believe anymore / No promises (dance mix) / Touch the fire / Jimmy Dean / Hey little girl / Great Southern land / Electric blue. *(re-iss cd+c Mar93)*

— Trimmed slightly when QUNTA departed. They disbanded soon after.

ICE-T

Born: TRACEY MARROW, 1958, Newark, New Jersey, USA. Moved to South Central L.A. and took the name from the black exploitation writer ICEBERG SLIM. His first record 'THE COLDEST RAPPER' appeared in 1983, but this led to his contract being retained by WILLIE STRONG. In 1991, he starred as a cop in the film 'New Jack City'. He had earlier formed own label 'Rhyme Syndicate' in 1988, which was soon distributed by 'Sire'. • **Style:** Extreme and aggressive pro-black, anti-establishment rapper, who branched into hard – core rock for his 1992 project BODY COUNT, with co-writer ERNIE C. Also liked to show off near-naked wife Darlene to promote sales. • **Songwriters:** ICE-T except; BACK IN BLACK (Ac-Dc). • **Trivia:** Clashed with President George Bush & Colonel Oliver North, over his controversial hard-talking single 'COP KILLER'.

Recommended: BODY COUNT (*6) / O. G. ORIGINAL GANGSTER (*8).

ICE-T – vocals / w/**AFRIKA ISLAM** – synthesizers

		Rhyme Synd.	Sire	Rhyme Synd.	Sire
Jul 87.	(12") **MAKE IT FUNKY. / SEX**				
Jul 87.	(lp)(c)(cd) **RHYME PAYS**			93	

– (intro) / Rhyme pays / 6 'n the mornin' / Make it funky / Somebody gotta do it (pimpin' ain't easy) / 409 / I love ladies / Sex / Pain / Squeeze the trigger.

Nov 87.	(12") **SOMEBODY GOT DO IT (PIMPIN' AIN'T EASY). / OUR MOST REQUESTED RECORD**		
Jun 88.	(12")(c-s) **COLORS. / SQUEEZE THE TRIGGER**	-	10
Sep 88.	(lp)(c)(cd) **POWER**		35

– (intro) / Power / Drama / Heartbeat / The syndicate / Radio suckers / I'm your pusher / Personal / High rollers / Girls L.G.B.N.A.F. / Grand larceny / Soul on ice / (outro).

Nov 88.	(7") **I'M YOUR PUSHER. / GIRLS L.G.B.N.A.F.**	-	

(12"+=) – ('A'instrumental) / ('A'acappella) / ('B'instrumental) / ('B'acappella).

Mar 89.	(7") **HIGH ROLLERS. / THE HUNTED CHILD**	63	

(12"+=) – Power.

Sep 89.	(7") **LETHAL WEAPON. / HEARTBEAT (remix)**		

(12"+=)(cd-s+=) – ('A'instrumental).

Oct 89.	(lp)(c)(cd) **THE ICEBERG: FREEDOM OF SPEECH . . . JUST WATCH WHAT YOU SAY**	42	37

– (intro) / Shut up, be happy / The iceberg / Lethal weapon / You played yourself / Peel their caps back / The girl tried to kill me / Black'n'decker / Hit the deck / This one's for me / The hunted child / What ya wanna do? / Freedom of speech / My word is bond. *(re-iss.cd Feb95)*

— Guested on CURTIS MAYFIELD's re-make of classic 'Superfly'.

Feb 90.	(7") **YOU PLAYED YOURSELF. / MY WORD IS BOND**	64	

(12"+=) – Freedom of speech (with HENDRIX sample) *(US b-side)*

Apr 90.	(c-s) **WHAT DO YOU WANNA DO? / THE GIRL TRIED TO KILL ME**	-	
1990.	(7")(12")(cd-s) **NEW JACK HUSTLER (NINO'S THEME) (Master Radio Version) / NEW JACK HUSTLER (NINO'S THEME) (Instrumental)**		67

(above US label 'Giant')

May 91.	(7") **O.G. ORIGINAL GANGSTER. / BITCHES 2**		

(12"+=)(cd-s+=) – Mind over matter / Midnight.

May 91.	(cd)(c)(lp) **O.G. ORIGINAL GANGSTER**	38	5

– Home of the bodybag / First impression / Ziplock / Mic contract / Mind over matter / New Jack hustler / Ed / Bitches 2 (incl. sample:- Dr. Funkenstein) / Straight up nigga / O.G. Original Gangster / The house / Evil E – what about sex? / Fly by / Midnight / Fried chicken / M.V.P.'s / Lifestyles of the rich and infamous / Body count / Prepared to die / Escape from the killing fields / Street killer / Pulse of the rhyme / The tower / Ya should killed me last year. *(re-iss.cd Feb95)*

BODY COUNT

ICE-T with **ERNIE C and D-ROC** – guitar / **MOOSEMAN** – bass / **BEATMASTER 'V'** – drums

		Sire	Sire
Jan 92.	(12")(cd-s) **COP KILLER. / (withdrawn)**	-	
Mar 92.	(cd)(c)(lp) **BODY COUNT**		26

– Smoked pork / Body Count's in the house / New sports / Body count / A statistic / Bowels of the Devil / The real problem / KKK bitch / C note / Voodoo / The winner loses / There goes the neighborhood / Oprah / Evil Dick / Body Count anthem / Momma's gotta die tonight / Freedom of speech.

Jun 92.	(12") **THERE GOES THE NEIGHBORHOOD. / KKK BITCH**		
Sep 94.	(cd)(c)(red-lp) **BORN DEAD**	15	74

– Body M-F Count / Masters of revenge / Killin' floor / Necessary evil / Drive by / Last breath / Hey Joe / Shallow graves / Surviving the game / Who are you / Sweet lobotomy / Born dead.

Sep 94.	(c-s) **BORN DEAD. / BODY COUNT'S IN THE HOUSE (live)**	28	

(12"pic-d+=) – ('A'live).
(cd-s+=) – Body M-F Count (live) / On with the Body Count (live).

Dec 94.	(etched-10"pic-d) **NECESSARY EVIL / NECESSARY EVIL (live) / BOWELS OF THE DEVIL (live)**	45	

(cd-s) – ('A'side) / Body Count anthem (live) / Drive by (live) / There goes the neighborhood (live).

— In Dec 94, ICE-T was credited with WHITFIELD CRANE (Ugly Kid Joe) on MOTORHEAD single 'Born To Raise Hell', hit UK No.47

ICE-T

		Sire	Sire
Mar 93.	(cd)(c)(lp) **HOME INVASION**	15	14

– Warning / It's on / Ice MFT / Home invasion / G style / Addicted to danger / Question and answer / Watch the ice break / Race war / That's how I'm livin' / I ain't new ta this / Pimp behind the wheels (DJ Evil E the great) / Gotta lotta love / Hit the fan / Depths of Hell (featuring DADDY NITRO) / 99 problems (featuring BROTHER MARQUIS) / Funky Gripsta / Message to the soldier / Ain't a damn thing changed

Apr 93.	(12"ep)(c-ep)(cd-ep) **I AIN'T NEW TA THIS. / MIXED UP / MIXED UP (instrumental)**	62	
Dec 93.	(12"ep)(c-ep)(cd-ep) **THAT'S HOW I'M LIVIN'. / COLOURS – RICOCHET – NEW JACK HUSTLER (film excerpts)**	21	
Mar 94.	(c-s)(12")(cd-s) **GOTTA LOTTA LOVE. / ('A'mixes) / excerpt from book 'The Ice Opinion (who gives a f***)'**	24	

(cd-s) – ('A'mix) / Addicted to danger / G style / Racewar (remixes).

– compilations, etc. –

May 93.	Warners; (cd)(c)(lp) **THE CLASSICS COLLECTION**		
Apr 94.	Warners; (cd)(d-lp) **HOME INVASION / THE LAST TEMPTATION OF ICE**		

ICICLE WORKS

Formed: Liverpool, England . . . 1980 by IAN McNABB, CHRIS LAYHE and CHRIS SHARROCK. After initial cassingle on 'Probe' & a 45 on indie 'Troll Kitchen' label in 1982, they signed to 'Beggar's B.' the next year. Their 3rd single 'LOVE IS A WONDERFUL COLOUR' soon gave them a UK Top 20 entry, and was followed by a re-issue of 'BIRDS FLY (WHISPER TO A SCREAM)', which also broke into US Top 40. Their eponymous debut album also cracked the 40 there, having already made No.24 in UK. They continued to score with some quality releases, until their signature with 'Epic', led to a slide in their popularity and their split. • **Style:** Power-rock outfit, fronted by McNABB (complete with attached microphone gadget) sounding SCOTT WALKER-ish early on and loved by college circuit. • **Songwriters:** Mostly McNABB compositions except; SEA SONG (Robert Wyatt) / NATURE'S WAY (Spirit) / COLD TURKEY (John Lennon) / INTO THE MYSTIC (Van Morrison) / YOU AIN'T SEEN NOTHIN' YET (Bachman-Turner Overdrive) / SHOULD I STAY OR SHOULD I GO (Clash) / MR SOUL + FOR WHAT IT'S WORTH (Buffalo Springfield) / ROCK'N'ROLL (Led Zeppelin) / PRIVATE REVOLUTION (World Party) / ROADHOUSE BLUES (Doors). McNABB covered CAROLINE NO (Brian Wilson) / UNKNOWN LEGEND (Neil Young). • **Trivia:** In Aug'85, an off-shoot MELTING POT, were supposed to have had a single 'IT MAKES NO DIFFERENCE' issued.

Recommended: THE BEST OF THE ICICLE WORKS (*8) / HEAD LIKE A ROCK (*8; IAN McNABB).

(ROBERT) **IAN McNABB** (b. 3 Nov'62) – vocals, guitar, keyboards / **CHRIS LAYHE** – bass, keyboards, vocals / **CHRIS SHARROCK** – drums, percussion

		Probe	not issued
1981.	(c-ep) **ASCENDING**		-
		Troll Kitchen	not issued

Oct 82. (7"m) **NIRVANA. / LOVE HUNT / SIROCCO** [ ] [-]

Situation 2 not issued

Jun 83. (7") **BIRDS FLY (WHISPER TO A SCREAM). / REVERIE GIRL** [ ] [-]
(12"+=) – Gun boys.

Beggar's B. Arista

Oct 83. (7")(7"pic-d) **LOVE IS A WONDERFUL COLOUR. / WATERLINE** [15] [ ]
(12"+=)(12"pic-d+=) – In the dance The Shamen led.
(d7"++=) – The Devil on horseback.

Mar 84. (7")(12") **BIRDS FLY (WHISPER TO A SCREAM). / IN THE CAULDRON OF LOVE** [53] [-]
(12"+=) – Scarecrow / Ragweed campaign.

Mar 84. (lp)(c) **THE ICICLE WORKS** [24] [40]
– Chop the tree / Love is a wonderful colour / Reaping the rich harvest / As the dragonfly flies / Lover's day / In the cauldron of love / Out of season / A factory in the desert / Birds fly (whisper to a scream) / Nirvana. *(re-iss.+cd Jul88) (cd-iss Jul86)*

Mar 84. (7") **BIRDS FLY (WHISPER TO A SCREAM). / IN THE DANCE THE SHAMEN LED** [-] [37]

Sep 84. (7") **HOLLOW HORSE. / THE AETHIEST** [ ] [ ]
(12"+=) – Nirvana (live).
(12"+=) – ('A'remix).

May 85. (7") **ALL THE DAUGHTERS (OF HER FATHER'S HOUSE). / A POCKETFUL OF NOTHING** [ ] [ ]
(12"+=) – Mr. Soul.

Jul 85. (7") **SEVEN HORSES. / SLINGSHOT** [ ] [ ]
(12") – ('A'-US version) / – Beggar's legacy.
(d7"++=) – Goin' back.

Sep 85. (lp)(c) **THE SMALL PRICE OF A BICYCLE** [55] [ ]
– Hollow horse / Perambulator / Seven horses / Rapids / Windfall / Assumed sundown / Saint's sojourn / All the daughter's (of her father's horse) / Book of reason / Conscience of kings. *(re-iss.+cd Jan89)*

Oct 85. (7") **WHEN IT ALL COMES DOWN. / LET'S GO DOWN TO THE RIVER** [ ] [ ]
(12"+=) – Cold turkey.

Jun 86. (7") **UNDERSTANDING JANE. / I NEVER SAW MY HOMETOWN TILL I WENT ROUND THE WORLD** [52] [ ]
(d7"+=) – Hollow horses (live) / You ain't seen nothin' yet (live).
(12"+=) – Into the mystic.
(c-s+=) – Seven horses (live) / Perambulator (live) / Rapids (live).

Sep 86. (7")(c-s) **WHO DO YOU WANT FOR LOVE. / UNDERSTANDING JANE (live)** [54] [ ]
(d7"+=) – John Jeffrey Muir shopkeeper / Impossibly three lovers.
(12"+=) – Should I stay or should I go / Roadhouse blues.

Dec 86. (12"ep) **UP HERE IN THE NORTH OF ENGLAND. / SEA SONG / NATURE'S WAY / IT MAKES NO DIFFERENCE** [ ] [ ]
(issued on 'Situation 2' UK-only)

Jan 87. (7") **EVANGELINE. / EVERYBODY LOVE TO PLAY THE FOOL** [53] [ ]
(12"+=) – Waiting in the wings.

Mar 87. (lp)(c) **IF YOU WANT TO DEFEAT YOUR ENEMY SING HIS SONG** [28] [ ]
– Hope springs eternal / Travelling chest / Sweet Thursday / Up here in the north of England / Who do you want for your love / When you were mine / Evangeline / Truck driver's lament / Understanding Jane / Walking with a mountain. *(c+=)* – Everybody loves to play the fool. *(cd++=)* – Don't let it rain on my parade / I never saw my hometown till went round the world / Into the mystic.

Nov 87. (7") **HIGH TIME. / BROKEN HEARTED FOOL** [ ] [ ]
(12"+=) – Private revolution (live) / Travelling light (live).

Feb 88. (7") **THE KISS OFF. / SURE THING** [ ] [ ]
(12"ep+=)(c-ep+=)(cd-ep+=) – THE NUMB EP – High time / Whipping boy.

Apr 88. (7"m) **LITTLE GIRL LOST. / TIN CAN / HOT PROPHET GOSPEL** [59] [ ]
(12"+=)(pic-cd-s+=) – One time.

May 88. (lp)(c)(cd) **BLIND** [40] [ ]
– (intro) Shit creek / Little girl lost / Starry blue-eyed wonder / One true love / Blind / Two two three / What do you want me to do? / Stood before Saint Peter / The kiss off / Here comes trouble / Walk a while with me.

Jun 88. (7") **HERE COMES TROUBLE. / STARRY BLUE-EYED WONDER** [ ] [ ]
(12"+=) – Rock'n'roll (live) / For what it's worth (live).

—— **ZAK STARKEY** (son of RINGO) – drums repl. LAYHE SHARROCK who joined WILD SWANS+The LA'S / added **DAVE GREEN** – keyboards / **ROY CORKHILL** – bass (both ex-BLACK) /

—— (1989) **IAN and ROY** brought in **DAVE BALDWIN** – keyboards / **MARK REVELL** – guitar, vocals / **PAUL BURGESS** – drums

Epic Epic

Mar 90. (7")(12") **MOTORCYCLE RIDER. / TURN ANY CORNER** [73] [ ]
(cd-s+=) – Victoria's ghost.

May 90. (cd)(c)(lp) **PERMANENT DAMAGE** [ ] [ ]
– I still want you / Motorcycle rider / Melanie still hurts / Hope street rag / I think I'm gonna be OK / Baby don't burn / What she did to my mind / One good eye / Permanent damage / Woman on my mind / Looks like rain / Dumb angel.

May 90. (7") **MELANIE STILL HURTS. / WHEN THE CRYING'S DONE** [ ] [ ]
(12"+=) – Mickey's blue.
(7"ep++=)(cd-ep++=) – I dreamt I was a beautiful woman.

Jul 90. (7")(c-s) **I STILL WANT YOU. / I WANT THE GIRL** [ ] [ ]
(10"+=)(12"+=)(cd-s+=) – It's gonna rain forever / Sweet disposition.

—— McNABB joined the WILD SWANS briefly.

– compilations, etc. –

Feb 86. Beggar's Banquet; (m-lp)(c) **SEVEN SINGLES DEEP** [52] [ ]
(re-iss.+cd Sep88, cd+=6 extra tracks)

Aug 92. Beggar's Banquet; (cd)(c) **THE BEST OF THE ICICLE WORKS** [60] [ ]
– Hollow horse (long version) / Love is a wonderful colour / Birds fly (whisper to a scream) / Understanding Jane ('92 version) / Shit creek / High time (acoustic) / Who do you want for your love? / Evangeline / Little girl lost / When it all comes down ('92 version) / Starry blue eyed wonder / Out of season / The kiss off / Up here in the North of England / Firepower / Blind. *(re-iss.cd Sep95)*

Aug 92. Beggar's Banquet; (7") **UNDERSTANDING JANE '92. / LITTLE GIRL LOST** [ ] [ ]
(12"+=) – When it all comes down '92 / Firepower.
(cd-s+=) – Solid ground / Like weather.

Nov 88. Nighttracks; (12"ep) **THE EVENING SHOW SESSIONS (14.11.82)** [ ] [ ]
– Birds fly (whisper to a scream) / Lover's day / Love hunt / As the dragonfly flies.

Jan 90. Strange Fruit; (7") **LOVE IS A WONDERFUL COLOUR. / BIRDS FLY (WHISPER TO A SCREAM)** [ ] [-]

Mar 94. Windsong; (cd) **BBC RADIO 1 LIVE IN CONCERT (live)** [ ] [-]

IAN McNABB

Way Cool not issued

Jun 91. (12"ep) **GREAT DREAMS OF HEAVEN / UNKNOWN LEGEND. / I'M GAME / CAROLINE NO** [ ] [-]

This Way Up not issued

Jan 93. (7") **IF LOVE WAS LIKE GUITARS. / TRAMS IN AMSTERDAM** [67] [-]
(12"+=)(cd-s+=) – Great dreams of Heaven

Jan 93. (cd)(c)(lp) **TRUTH AND BEAUTY** [51] [-]
– (I go) My own way / These are the days / Great dreams of Heaven / Truth and beauty / I'm game / If love was like guitars / Story of my life / That's why I believe / Trip with me / Make love to you / Presence of the one. *(re-iss.cd/c Apr95)*

Mar 93. (7")(c-s) **GREAT DREAMS OF HEAVEN. / UNKNOWN LEGEND** [ ] [ ]
(12"+=)(cd-s+=) – I'm game / Caroline no.

Sep 93. (10"ep)(cd-ep) **(I GO) MY OWN WAY / PLAY THE HAND THEY DEAL YOU / IF MY DADDY COULD SEE ME NOW / FOR YOU, ANGEL** [ ] [ ]

—— with **RALPH MOLINA + BILLY TALBOT** (of NEIL YOUNG's CRAZY HORSE) **+ MIKE 'TONE' HAMILTON** (of SMITHEREENS)

Jun 94. (12")(cd-s) **YOU MUST BE PREPARED TO DREAM. / THAT'S WHY THE DARKNESS EXISTS** [54] [ ]
(cd-s+=) – Sometimes I think about you / Woo yer.
(cd-s+=) – Love is a wonderful colour / When it all comes down (both acoustic).

Jul 94. (cd)(c) **HEAD LIKE A ROCK** [29] [ ]
– Fire inside my soul / You must be prepared to dream / Child inside a father / Still got the fever / Potency / Go into the light / As a life goes by / Sad strange solitary Catholic mystic / This time is forever / May you always.

Aug 94. (c-s) **GO INTO THE LIGHT. / TIME YOU WERE IN LOVE** [ ] [ ]
(12"+=)(cd-s+=) – For you angel.
(cd-s) – ('A'side) / I stood before St.Peter / Rock.

Billy IDOL

Born: WILLIAM BROAD, 30 Nov'55, Stanmore, Middlesex, England. After 4 years, fronting punk-pop band GENERATION X, he went solo in 1981 and moved to New York, where he met manager Bill Aucoin and producer Keith Forsey. He also enlisted American guitarist STEVE STEVENS and others to augment his first album 'DON'T STOP', which didn't receive a UK release. In 1982, he scored first US Top 30 hit with 'HOT IN THE CITY' single, which featured on eponymous Top 50 second album. After hit album 'REBEL YELL' in 1984, he became major star on both sides of the big lake. • **Style:** Hard-driving sexual rocker, whose lip sneer was reminiscent of CLIFF, and who was loved by teeny boppers to heavy-metal fans. • **Songwriters:** IDOL & STEVENS collaborated until 1990 when he wrote with WERNER. Covered; MONY MONY (Tommy James & The Shondells) / SHAKIN' ALL OVER (Johnny Kidd & The Pirates) / L.A. WOMAN (Doors) / HEROIN (Velvet Underground) / MOTHER DAWN (McBrook – Youth). • **Trivia:** BILLY drove a Harley-Davison motorbike, which he loved to drive around the States. This was scuppered slightly on 6 Feb'90, when he suffered a broken leg and wrist in a crash. In mid 1988, his girlfriend Perry Lister, gave birth to his son.

Recommended: IDOL SONGS – 11 OF THE BEST (*7).

BILLY IDOL – vocals (ex-GENERATION X) with **STEVE STEVENS** – guitar / **PHIL FEIT** – bass / **STEVE MISSAL** – drums

Chrysalis Chrysalis

Sep 81. (7") **MONY MONY. / BABY TALK** [ ] [71] m-lp
(12"+=) – Dancing with myself / Untouchables. *(US-title 'DON'T STOP')*

Jul 82. (lp)(c) **BILLY IDOL** [ ] [45]
– Come on, come on / White wedding (part 1 & 2) / Hot in the city / Dead on arrival / Nobody's business / Love calling / Hole in the wall / Shooting stars / It's so cruel / Congo man. *(cd-iss.1986) (re-iss.cd+c Jul94)*

Aug 82. (7")(12")(7"pic-d) **HOT IN THE CITY. / DEAD ON ARRIVAL** [58] [23] Jul 82

Oct 82. (7")(12") **WHITE WEDDING. / HOLE IN THE WALL** [ ] [ ]

Sep 83. (7")(7"clear) **WHITE WEDDING. / HOT IN THE CITY** [ ] [36] May 83
(12"+=) – Love calling / Dancing with myself.

Jan 84. (lp)(c) **REBEL YELL** [36] [6] Nov 83
– Rebel yell / Daytime drama / Eyes without a face / Blue highway / Flesh for fantasy / Catch my fall / Crank call / (Do not) Stand in the shadows / The dead next door. *(re-iss.+cd Jan86) (re-iss.cd Mar94)*

Feb 84. (7")(7"square pic-d) **REBEL YELL. / CRANK CALL** [62] [46] Jan 84
(12"+=)(d7"+=) – White wedding.

Jun 84. (7") **EYES WITHOUT A FACE. / THE DEAD NEXT DOOR** [18] [4] May 84
(12"+=)(d7"+=)(12"pic-d+=) – Dancing with myself / Rebel yell.

Sep 84. (7") **FLESH FOR FANTASY. / BLUE HIGHWAY** [54] [29] Aug 84

(12"+=)(12"pic-d+=) – ('A'version).
Nov 84. (7") **CATCH MY FALL. /** [-] [50]
Jun 85. (7")(7"white) **WHITE WEDDING. / FLESH FOR FANTASY** [6] [-]
(12")(12"white)(12"pic-d)(7"clear) – ('A'shotgun mix) / ('A'mega-mix)
Sep 85. (7")(7"pic-d) **REBEL YELL. / (DO NOT) STAND IN THE SHADOWS (live)** [6] [ ]
(12"+=)(12"pic-d+=) – Blue highway.
Sep 86. (7")(7"colrd) **TO BE A LOVER. / ALL SUMMER SINGLE** [22] [6]
(12"+=)(12"pic-d+=) – ('A'version).
(d7"+=) – Mega-Idol-mix / White wedding.
Oct 86. (lp)(c)(cd) **WHIPLASH SMILE** [8] [6]
– Worlds forgotten boy / To be a lover / Soul standing by / Sweet sixteen / Man for all seasons / Don't need a gun / Beyond belief / Fatal charm / All summer single / One night, one chance. *(re-iss.cd+c. Mar93)*
Feb 87. (7")(7"colrd) **DON'T NEED A GUN. / FATAL CHARM** [26] [37] Jan 87
(12"+=)(12"pic-d+=) – ('A'version).
May 87. (7") **SWEET 16. / BEYOND BELIEF** [17] [20] Apr 87
(12"+=)(12"pic-d+=) – Rebel yell.
Sep 87. (7") **MONY MONY (live). / SHAKIN' ALL OVER (live)** [7] [1]
(12"+=) – ('A'version).

— now with **MARK YOUNGER-SMITH** – guitar, bass / **KEITH FORSEY** – drums, producer **VITO** and **PHIL SOUSSAN** – bass / **ARTHUR BARROW** – keyboards / **MIKE BAIRD** – drums

Apr 90. (7")(c-s) **CRADLE OF LOVE. / 311 MAN** [34] [2]
(cd-s+=) – ('A'extended) / Rob the cradle of love.
(12") – (as above) (except 7" b-side).
Apr 90. (cd)(c)(lp) **CHARMED LIFE** [15] [11]
– The loveless / Pumping on steel / Prodigal blues / L.A. woman / Trouble with the sweet stuff / Cradle of love / Mark of Caine / Endless sleep / Love unchained / The right way / License to thrill.
Jul 90. (7")(c-s) **L.A. WOMAN. / LICENSE TO THRILL** [70] [52]
(12"+=)(cd-s+=) – Love child.
Dec 90. (7")(c-s) **PRODIGAL BLUES. / MARK OF CAINE** [47] [ ]
(12"+=)(cd-s+=) – Flesh for fantasy.

— **IDOL** retained co-writer **YOUNGER-SMITH** + recruited **ROBIN HANCOCK** – keyboards, producer / **DOUG WIMBUSH** – bass / **JAMIE MAMOBERAC** – organ / **TAL BERGHAN** – drums

Jun 93. (7")(12") **SHOCK TO THE SYSTEM. / HEROIN (overloads mix) / HEROIN (durge trance dub)** [30] [ ]
(cd-s) – ('A'side) / Heroin (original) / Rebel yell.
(cd-s) – ('A'side) / Heroin (smack attack) / White wedding.
Jun 93. (cd)(c)(lp) **CYBERPUNK** [20] [48]
– Wasteland / Shock to the system / Tomorrow people / Adam in chains / Neuromancer / Power junkie / Love labours on / Heroin / Shangrila / Concrete kingdom / Venus / Then the night comes / Mother Dawn.
Sep 93. (7")(c-s) **ADAM IN CHAINS. / SHOCK TO THE SYSTEM** [ ] [ ]
(cd-s) – ('A'side) / Venus / Eyes without a face.

Fox-Arista Arista
Sep 94. (7")(c-s)(cd-s) **SPEED. / REBEL YELL (acoustic)** [47] [ ]

– compilations etc. –

Jul 85. Chrysalis; (lp)(c) **VITAL IDOL** (remixes) [7] [10] Oct 87
– White wedding (part 1 & 2) / Dancing with myself / Flesh for fantasy / Catch my fall / Mony Mony / Love calling (dub) / Hot in the city. *(cd-iss.1986)*
Jan 88. Chrysalis; (7") **HOT IN THE CITY. / CATCH MY FALL (remix)** [13] [48] Dec 87
(12"+=) – Soul standing by.
(cd-s++=) – Mony Mony.
Jun 88. Chrysalis; (lp)(c)(cd) **IDOL SONGS – 11 OF THE BEST** [2] [ ]
– Rebel yell / Hot in the city / White wedding / Eyes without a face / Catch my fall / Mony mony / To be a lover / Sweet sixteen / Flesh for fantasy / Don't need a gun / Dancing with myself.
Aug 88. Chrysalis; (7") **CATCH MY FALL. / ALL SUMMER SINGLE** [63] [-]
(12"+=)(cd-s+=) – ?

John ILLSLEY (see under ⇒ DIRE STRAITS)

IMPRESSIONS

Formed: Chicago, Illinois, USA ... 1957, stemmed from Tennessee doo-wop quintet The ROOSTERS who enlisted mainmen JERRY BUTLER and CURTIS MAYFIELD. After two flops for local Chicago labels, they signed to 'Vee Jay' in Spring 1958. They became The IMPRESSIONS and with JERRY BUTLER credited on debut, made US No.11 with first single 'FOR YOUR PRECIOUS LOVE'. BUTLER then left to branch out on own fruitful solo career. After spell as BUTLER's guitarist, CURTIS then re-formed The IMPRESSIONS. In 1961 they relocated to New York and signed for 'ABC-Paramount'. They quickly scraped into the Top 20, with GYPSY WOMAN. From 1963 onwards, as trio of MAYFIELD, SAM GOODEN and FRED CASH, they had first of string of hits with IT'S ALRIGHT. CURTIS left them for solo career in 1970, and although he stayed on as writer/producer, and retained them on his label 'Curtom', they never quite re-activated earlier triumphs. • **Style:** Tamla Motown-influenced singing group, who moved from ballad type soul to the disco scene by the mid-70's. • **Songwriters:** After BUTLER's abrupt departure in 1959, MAYFIELD took the role of chief writer. • **Trivia:** Their 1968 hit single WE'RE A WINNER received radio censorship, due to its black political lyrics.

Recommended: THE DEFINITIVE IMPRESSIONS (*7)

JERRY BUTLER (b. 8 Dec'39, Sunflower, Missouri, USA) – lead vocals / **ARTHUR BROOKS + RICHARD BROOKS** (b.Chattannooga, Tennessee, USA) – vocals / **SAM GOODEN** (b. 2 Sep'39, Chattanooga) – vocals / **CURTIS MAYFIELD** (b. 3 Jun'42, Chicago, Illinois, USA) – guitar, vocals

The ROOSTERS

not issued Bandera
1957. (7") **SHORTY'S GOT TO GO. / LISTEN TO ME** [-] [ ]
not issued Swirl
1957. (7") **I NEED YOUR LOVE. / DON'T LEAVE ME** [-] [ ]

JERRY BUTLER & The IMPRESSIONS

London Abner
Sep 58. (7") **FOR YOUR PRECIOUS LOVE. / SWEET WAS THE WINE** [ ] [11] May 58
1958. (7") **COME BACK MY LOVE. / LOVE ME** [-] [ ]
1959. (7") **THE GIFT OF LOVE. / AT THE COUNTRY FAIR** [-] [ ]
1959. (7") **LOVELY ONE. / SENORITA I LOVE YOU** [-] [ ]
1959. (7") **THAT YOU LOVE ME. / A NEW LOVE** [-] [ ]

— Break-up, when JERRY BUTLER left to go solo in 1959. Although CURTIS remained in The new IMPRESSIONS as lead vox, he also augmented JERRY BUTLER. **FRED CASH** (b. 8 Oct'40, Chattanooga) – vocals (ex-ROOSTERS) repl. BUTLER

IMPRESSIONS

H.M.V. ABC-Para..
Dec 61. (7") **GYPSY WOMAN. / AS LONG AS YOU LOVE ME** [ ] [20] Oct 61
Jan 62. (7") **GROW CLOSER TOGETHER. / CAN'T YOU SEE** [-] [99]
Jun 62. (7") **LITTLE YOUNG LOVER. / NEVER LET ME GO** [-] [96]
Oct 62. (7") **YOU'VE COME HOME / MINSTREL AND QUEEN** [-] [ ]
Mar 63. (7") **I'M THE ONE WHO LOVES YOU. / I NEED YOUR LOVE** [ ] [73] Jan 63

— Trim to a trio (**MAYFIELD** – falsetto / **GOODEN** – bass / **CASH** – tenor)

Apr 63. (7") **SAD, SAD GIRL AND BOY. / TWIST AND LIMBO** [-] [84]
Aug 63. (lp) **THE IMPRESSIONS** [-] [43]
– It's all right / Gypsy woman / Grow closer together / Little young lover / You've come home / Never let me go / Minstrel and queen / I need your love / I'm the one who loves you / Sad, sad girl and boy / As long as you love me / Twist and limbo. *(re-iss.Oct83 on 'Kent')*
Nov 63. (7") **IT'S ALL RIGHT. / YOU'LL WANT ME BACK** [ ] [4] Sep 63
Feb 64. (7") **TALKING ABOUT MY BABY. / NEVER TOO MUCH LOVE** [ ] [12] Jan 64
Mar 64. (7") **GIRL YOU DON'T KNOW ME. / A WOMAN WHO LOVES ME** [-] [ ]
May 64. (7") **I'M SO PROUD. / I MADE A MISTAKE** [ ] [14] Apr 64
Jul 64. (lp) **THE NEVER-ENDING IMPRESSIONS** [ ] [52] Mar 64
– Sister love / Little boy blue / Satin doll / Girl don't you know me / I gotta keep on moving / You always hurt the one you love / That's what love will do / I'm so proud / September song / Lemon tree / Ten to one / A woman who loves me. *(re-iss.Oct83 on 'Kent')*
Jul 64. (7") **KEEP ON PUSHING. / I LOVE YOU (YEAH)** [ ] [10] Jun 64
Aug 64. (lp) **KEEP ON PUSHING** [-] [8]
– Keep on pushing / I've been trying / I ain't supposed to / Dedicate my song to you / Long long winter / Somebody help me / Amen / I think Heaven / Talking about my baby / Don't let it hide / I love you (yeah) / I made a mistake. *(re-iss.Oct83 on 'Kent')*
Oct 64. (7") **YOU MUST BELIEVE ME. / SEE THE REAL ME** [ ] [15] Sep 64
Mar 65. (7") **PEOPLE GET READY. / I'VE BEEN TRYING** [ ] [14] Feb 65
Mar 65. (lp) **PEOPLE GET READY** [-] [23]
– Woman's got soul / Emotions / Sometimes I wonder / We're in love / Just another dance / Can't work no longer / People get ready / I've found that I've lost / Hard to believe / See the real me / Get up and move / You must believe me. *(re-iss.Oct83 on 'Kent')*
Jun 65. (7") **WOMAN'S GOT SOUL. / GET UP AND MOVE** [ ] [29] Apr 65
Jul 65. (7") **A MEETING OVER YONDER. / I FOUND THAT I'VE LOST** [ ] [48] Jun 65
Oct 65. (7") **I NEED YOU. / NEVER COULD YOU BE** [-] [64] Aug 65
Oct 65. (7") **JUST ONE KISS FROM YOU. / TWILIGHT TIME** [-] [76] Sep 65
Oct 65. (lp) **ONE BY ONE** [-] [ ] Sep 65
– Twilight time / I wanna be around / Nature boy / Just one kiss from you / I want to be with you / Answer me, my love / It's not unusual / Without a song / Falling in love with you / My prayer / Mona Lisa / Lonely man.
Nov 65. (7") **AMEN. / LONG LONG WINTER** [ ] [7] Nov 64
Dec 65. (lp) **BIG SIXTEEN (compilation)** [ ] [-]
– Gypsy woman / Talking about my baby / I'm so proud / Keep on pushing / Never let go / It's all right / People get ready / Woman's got soul / You must believe me / Sad, sad girl and boy / I'm the one who loves you / Minstrel and queen / Grow closer together / Amen / Meeting over yonder / I need. *(re-iss.Feb75 on 'ABC')*
Dec 65. (7") **YOU'VE BEEN CHEATIN'. / MAN OH MAN** [-] [33]
Jan 66. (7") **YOU'VE BEEN CHEATIN'. / JUST ONE KISS FROM YOU** [ ] [ ]
Mar 66. (7") **SINCE I LOST THE ONE I LOVE. / FALLING IN LOVE WITH YOU** [ ] [90] Feb 66
May 66. (7") **TOO SLOW. / NO ONE ELSE** [ ] [91] Apr 66
Jul 66. (lp) **RIDIN' HIGH** [ ] [ ] Mar 66
– Ridin' high / I'm a telling you / No one else / Gotta get away / I need to belong to someone / Right on time / I need a love / Too slow / Man's temptation / That's what mama say / Let it be me
Aug 66. (7") **CAN'T SATISFY. / THIS MUST END** [ ] [65]
May 67. (7") **YOU'VE GOT ME RUNNIN'. / IT'S HARD TO BELIEVE** [-] [ ]
Mar 67. (7") **YOU ALWAYS HURT ME. / LITTLE GIRL** [ ] [96]
Sep 67. (lp) **THE FABULOUS IMPRESSIONS** [ ] [ ] Jul 67
– You always hurt me / It's all over / Little girl / Hundred pounds of clay / Love's a-comin' / You ought to be in Heaven / I can't stay away from you / Aware of love /

Isle of sirens / I'm still waitin' / She don't love me.

Sep 67. (7") **I CAN'T STAY AWAY FROM YOU. / YOU OUGHT TO BE IN HEAVEN** [-] [80]

Stateside ABC-Para..

Dec 67. (7") **WE'RE A WINNER. / IT'S ALL OVER** [-] [ ]
Jan 68. (7") **WE'RE A WINNER. / YOU'VE GOT ME RUNNIN'** [ ] [ ]
Apr 68. (7") **WE'RE ROLLING ON. / (part 2)** [-] [59]
Jul 68. (lp) **WE'RE A WINNER** [ ] [35] Feb 68

– We're a winner / Moonlight shadows / Let me tell the world / I'm getting ready / Nothing can stop me / No one to love / Little Brown boy / I loved and I lost / Romancing to the folk / Up up and away.

Jul 68. (7") **I LOVED AND I LOST. / UP UP AND AWAY** [-] [61]

Buddah Curtom

Oct 68. (7") **FOOL FOR YOU. / I'M LOVING NOTHING** [ ] [22] Sep 68
Dec 68. (7") **THIS IS MY COUNTRY. / MY WOMAN'S LOVE** [-] [25]
Feb 69. (7") **YOU WANT SOMEBODY ELSE. / MY DECEIVING HEART** [-] [ ]
Mar 69. (lp) **THIS IS MY COUNTRY** [ ] [ ] Dec 68

– Fool for you / They don't know / Gone away / So unusual / I'm loving nothing / Loves happening / This is my country / You want somebody else / Stay close to me / My woman love.

Apr 69. (7") **SEVEN YEARS. / THE GIRL I FIND** [-] [84]
Aug 69. (7") **CHOICE OF COLORS. / MIGHTY MIGHTY SPADE AND WHITEY** [ ] [21] Jun 69
Oct 69. (7") **SAY YOU LOVE ME. / YOU'LL ALWAYS BE MINE** [-] [58]

Polydor Curtom

Mar 70. (7") **AMEN (1970). / WHEREVER SHE LEADETH ME** [-] [ ]
Jun 70. (7") **CHECK OUT YOUR MIND. / CAN'T YOU SEE** [ ] [28] May 70
Aug 70. (lp) **YOUNG MOD'S FORGOTTEN STORY** [ ] [ ] May 69

– The young mod's forgotten story / Choice of colours / The girl I find / Wherever he leadeth me / My decieving heart / Seven years / Love's miracle / Jealous man / Soulful love / Mighty, mighty (Spade & Whitey).

Oct 70. (7") **(BABY) TURN ON TO ME. / SOULFUL LOVE** [ ] [56]
Nov 70. (lp) **AMEN** [ ] [-]

– Gipsy woman / Keep on pushin' / I'm so proud / Say you love me / I've been tryin' / Amen / Choice of colours / Fool for you / Wherever she leadeth me / Mighty mighty spade and Whitey / Gone away / This is my country.

Feb 71. (lp) **CHECK OUT YOUR MIND** [ ] [ ] 1970

– Check out your mind / Can't you see / You're really something / Sadie / Do you want to win / You'll always be mine / Only you / Turn on to me / Madam Mary / We must be in love / Say you love me.

— Earlier in 1970, CURTIS MAYFIELD had moved on to a solo career. He also continued to write and produce for The IMPRESSIONS. Replaced by **LEROY HUTTON**

Apr 71. (7") **AIN'T GOT TIME. / I'M SO PROUD** [ ] [53] Feb 71
Jul 71. (7") **LOVE ME. / I NEED TO BELONG TO SOMEONE** [-] [94]
Aug 71. (7") **LOVE ME. / DO YOU WANNA WIN** [ ] [-]
Oct 71. (7") **INNER CITY BLUES. / WE MUST BE IN LOVE** [-] [ ]
Oct 71. (7") **INNER CITY BLUES. / AMEN / KEEP ON PUSHING** [ ] [ ]

— (above 3 singles, featured some vocals w / **CURTIS).**

May 72. (7") **OUR LOVE GOES ON AND ON. / THIS LOVE'S FOR REAL** [ ] [ ]
Jun 72. (lp)(c) **TIMES HAVE CHANGED** [ ] [ ] Apr 72

– Stop the war / Potent love / Times have changed / Inner city blues / This love for real / I need to belong to someone / Our love goes on and on / Love me.

1973. (7") **PREACHER MAN. / TIMES HAVE CHANGED** [-] [ ]
Jul 73. (7") **THIN LINE. / I'M LOVING YOU** [ ] [ ]
1973. (lp)(c) **PREACHER MAN** [-] [ ]

– What it is / Preacher man / Simple message / Find the way / Thin line / Color us all gray (I'm lost) / I'm loving you.

— **REGGIE TORIAN + RALPH JOHNSON** – vocals repl. HUTTON who went solo

Buddah-Pye Curtom

Feb 74. (7") **IF IT'S IN YOU TO DO WRONG. / TIMES HAVE CHANGED** [-] [ ]
Aug 74. (7") **FINALLY GOT MYSELF TOGETHER (I'M A CHANGED MAN). / I'LL ALWAYS BE THERE** [ ] [17] Apr 74
Sep 74. (lp)(c) **FINALLY GOT MYSELF TOGETHER** [ ] [ ] Jul 74

– If it's in you to do wrong / I'm a changed man (finally got myself together) / I'll always be here / Miracle woman / We go back a ways / Guess what I've got / Try me / Don't forget what I told you.

Curtom-WEA Curtom

1974. (7") **SOMETING'S MIGHTY, MIGHTY WRONG. / THREE THE HARD WAY** [-] [ ]
Jun 75. (7") **SOONER OR LATER. / MIRACLE WOMAN** [ ] [68]
Aug 75. (lp)(c) **FIRST IMPRESSIONS** [ ] [ ]

– Sooner or later / Same thing it took / Old before my time / First impressions / Groove / I'm so glad / How high is high / Why must a love song be a sad song. *(re-iss.Aug79 on 'R.S.O.')*

Sep 75. (7") **SAME THING IT TOOK. / I'M SO GLAD** [-] [75]
Nov 75. (7") **FIRST IMPRESSIONS. / OLD BEFORE MY TIME** [16] [-]
Nov 75. (7") **FIRST IMPRESSIONS. / LOVING POWER** [-] [ ]
Mar 76. (lp)(c) **LOVING POWER** [ ] [ ]

– Loving power / Sunshine / I can't wait to see you / If you have to ask / You can't be wrong / I wish I'd stayed in bed / Keep on trying. *(re-iss.Aug79 on 'R.S.O.')*

May 76. (7") **I WISH I'D STAYED IN BED. / I'M SO GLAD** [ ] [-]
May 76. (7") **I WISH I'D STAYED IN BED. / SUNSHINE** [-] [ ]

— **NATE EVANS** – vocals repl. JOHNSON who formed own MYSTIQUE

not issued Cotillion

1976. (7") **THIS TIME. / I'M A FOOL FOR LOVE** [-] [ ]
1976. (lp) **IT'S ABOUT TIME** [-] [ ]

– In the palm of my hands / You'll never find / Same old heartaches / I need you / This time / Stardust / I'm a fool for love / What might have been.

1976. (7") **SILENT NIGHT. / I SAW MOMMY KISSING SANTA CLAUS** [-] [ ]
1977. (7") **STARDUST. / YOU'LL NEVER FIND** [-] [ ]

— Dissolve for a while until they sign for

1977. (7") **CAN'T GET ALONG. / YOU'RE SO RIGHT FOR ME** [-] [ ]

not iss. Rob-in Hood

1978. (7") **BELIEVE IN ME. / A LONG TIME AGO** [-] [ ]
1978. (7") **YOUNG LOVER. / DON'T SEND ME AWAY** [-] [ ]
1978. (7") **LOVER'S LANE. / LET ME KNOW** [-] [ ]
1979. (7") **ALL THROUGH THE NIGHT. / MEANWHILE BACK IN MY HEART** [-] [ ]

20th Cent 20th Cent

1979. (lp)(c) **COME TO MY PARTY** [-] [ ]

– Come to my party / All I want to do is make love to you / This can't be real sorry / Whole lot of good good lovin' / I could never make you stay / Maybe I'm mistaken.

1979. (7") **SORRY. / ALL I WANT TO DO IS MAKE LOVE TO YOU** [-] [ ]
1979. (7") **MAYBE I'M MISTAKEN. / ALL I WANT TO DO IS MAKE LOVE TO YOU** [-] [ ]
1981. (7") **FOR YOUR PRECIOUS LOVE. / YOU'RE MINE** [-] [ ]
1981. (7") **FAN THE FIRE. / LOVE LOVE LOVE** [-] [ ]
Aug 81. (7")(12") **FAN THE FIRE. / FOR YOUR PRECIOUS LOVE** [ ] [ ]
Sep 81. (lp)(c) **FAN THE FIRE** [ ] [ ]

– Fan the fire / I don't wanna lose your love / Love love love / You're mine / I surrender / Take everything / I don't mind / For your precious love.

not iss. Port

1981. (7") **LISTEN. / SHORTY'S GOT TO GO** [-] [ ]

M.C.A. M.C.A.

1982. (lp)(c) **IN THE HEAT OF THE NIGHT** [ ] [ ]
1982. (7") **CAN'T WAIT 'TIL TOMORROW. / LOVE WORKIN' ON ME** [-] [ ]

— Although JERRY BUTLER and CURTIS MAYFIELD re-joined for reunion tour, they broke-up in 1983.

– compilations, others, etc. –

Mar 65. ABC Paramount; (lp) **THE IMPRESSIONS' GREATEST HITS** [-] [79]
Jun 65. H.M.V.; (7"ep) **IT'S ALL RIGHT** [ ] [-]
Sep 66. H.M.V.; (7"ep) **SOULFULLY** [ ] [-]
Sep 68. ABC Paramount; (lp) **THE BEST OF THE IMPRESSIONS** [-] [ ]
Nov 68. ABC Paramount; (7") **DON'T CRY MY LOVE. / SOMETIMES I WONDER** [-] [71]
Feb 69. ABC Paramount; (7") **JUST BEFORE SUNRISE. / EAST OF JAVA** [-] [ ]
Aug 68. Joy; (lp) **FOR YOUR PRECIOUS LOVE** [ ] [-]

— (w / **JERRY BUTLER**) (re-iss.Nov76 on 'DJM') (re-iss.Dec81 on 'Charly')

Feb 69. Stateside; (7") **CAN'T SATISFY. / YOU'VE BEEN CHEATIN'** [ ] [-]
Jul 69. Stateside; (lp) **BIG SIXTEEN VOLUME 2** [ ] [-]

— (Below 2 credited CURTIS MAYFIELD)

Mar 73. Probe; (7") **PEOPLE GET READY. / WE'RE ROLLING ON** [ ] [-]
Jul 73. Probe; (lp)(c) **CURTIS MAYFIELD: HIS EARLY YEARS WITH THE IMPRESSIONS** [ ] [ ]
Mar 71. A.B.C.; (lp) **16 GREATEST HITS** [-] [ ]
Oct 76. A.B.C.; (7") **YOU'VE BEEN CHEATIN'. / AMEN** [ ] [-]
Nov 76. A.B.C.; (lp)(c) **ORIGINALS** [ ] [ ]
Feb 77. Sire; (d-lp)(c) **THE VINTAGE YEARS** [-] [ ]

— (Next featured/credited JERRY BUTLER)

1979. J.S.P.; (7"m) **SHORTY'S GOT TO GO. / PRETTY BETTY / LISTEN** [ ] [-]
Nov 83. Charly; (lp) **RIGHT ON TIME** [ ] [-]
Aug 87. Topline; (lp)(c) **YOUR PRECIOUS LOVE** [ ] [-]
Oct 89. Kent; (cd) **THE DEFINITIVE IMPRESSIONS** [ ] [ ]

– Gypsy woman / Grow closer together / Little young lover / Minstrel and Queen / I'm the one who loves you / Sad, sad girl and boy / It's all right / Talking about my baby / I'm so proud / Keep on pushing / I've been trying / Girl you don't know me / I made a mistake / You must believe me / Amen / People get ready / Woman's got soul / Meeting over yonder / I need you / Just one kiss from you / You've been cheatin' / Since I lost the one I love / I can't satisfy / You always hurt me / I can't stay away from you / We're a winner / We're rolling on / I loved and I lost.

Oct 89. Curtom; (lp)(c)(cd) **LASTING IMPRESSIONS** [ ] [ ]
Jun 94. Pickwick; (cd)(c) **ALL THE BEST (feat. CURTIS MAYFIELD)** [ ] [-]

IN-BETWEENS (see under ⇒ SLADE)

INCREDIBLE STRING BAND

Formed: Glasgow, Scotland ... early 1966 by ROBIN WILLIAMSON, CLIVE PALMER and MIKE HERON. From the early 60's, WILLIAMSON had played London gigs alongside BERT JANSCH (future PENTANGLE), before he returned to Glasgow. In April 1961, he formed a duo with Englishman PALMER, but they found it difficult to establish themselves, until 1965 when PALMER set up the 'Incredible' folk club in Sauchiehall Street. That same year, the pair performed at the Edinburgh Folk Festival, and caught the eye of Nathan Joseph of 'Transatlantic' records, who recorded them for the concert's Various Artists compilation. After their folk club was shut down by the police, they became a trio, adding MIKE HERON to become The INCREDIBLE STRING BAND. After months tracking them down, American producer JOE BOYD finally found them and duly gave them contract on 'Elektra'. He also took them to London, where they recorded eponymous debut lp, issued Summer '66. With a well-received debut under their belt, PALMER departed for Afghanistan, but when he returned he did not re-join duo, who were now broke but under the management of BOYD. After ROB-

IN returned from Morocco, the duo, augmented by some friends, played an 'Elektra' records package alongside TOM PAXTON and JUDY COLLINS, at The Royal Albert Hall. It helped promote their second lp '5,000 SPIRITS OR THE LAYERS OF THE ONION', which made UK Top 30 in 1967. In Spring 1968, they crashed into UK Top 5 with lp 'THE HANGMAN'S BEAUTIFUL DAUGHTER', and toured America, augmented by new additions; girlfriends LICORICE and ROSE. At the end of the year, they issued 2 single lp's as a double 'WEE TAM' & 'THE BIG HUGE', but this brilliant but confusing package, failed to sell. Over the next 2 years, they released 3 UK Top 40 lp's, but after a move to 'Island' in 1971, they soon faded from commercial limelight. • **Style:** Underground psychedelic folk outfit, who skilfully blended charming and witty lyrics, with ethnic multi-instrumentation. During the early 70's, their self-indulgent eclectic baroque sound on 'I LOOKED UP', and their near pantomine of 'U', spoiled for many their past credentials. • **Songwriters:** WILLIAMSON or HERON penned. • **Trivia:** MIKE HERON went onto write a hit for MANFRED MANN'S EARTH BAND; 'Don't Kill It Carol'.

Recommended: 5,000 SPIRITS (*7) / THE HANGMAN'S BEAUTIFUL DAUGHTER (*7) / WEE TAM & THE BIG HUGE (*8) / SEASONS THEY CHANGE – THE BEST OF THE INCREDIBLE STRING BAND (*8).

ROBIN WILLIAMSON (b.24 Nov'43, Edinburgh, Scotland) – vocals, guitars, etc. / **CLIVE PALMER** (b. England) – guitar, banjo, vocals / **MIKE HERON** (b.12 Dec'42) – vocals, rhythm guitar, sitar, etc.

Elektra Elektra

Jun 66. (lp) **THE INCREDIBLE STRING BAND** [ ] [ ]
– Maybe someday / October song / When the music starts to play / Schaeffer's jig / Womankind / The tree / Whistle tune / Dandelion blues / How happy am I / Empty pocket blues / Smoke shovelling song / Can't keep me here / Good as gone / Footsteps of the heron / Niggertown / Everything's fine right now. *(re-iss.Jul68 reached No.34) (cd-iss. Jul93)*

— Now a duo when PALMER went to Afghanistan. He later formed FAMOUS JUG BAND added **CHRISTINA 'LICORICE' McKENNA** – some vocals, organ (a guest on below) plus guests **DANNY THOMPSON** – double bass (of PENTANGLE) / **JOHN HOPKINS** – piano

Jul 67. (lp) **THE 5,000 SPIRITS OR THE LAYERS OF THE ONION** [26] [ ]
– Chinese white / No sleep blues / Painting box / The Mad Hatter's song / Little cloud / The eyes of fate / Blues for the muse / The hedgehog's song / First girl I loved / You know that you could be / My name is death / Gently tender / Way back in the 1960's. *(re-iss.'68, re-iss.Jan73, re-iss.'76) (cd-iss.1992)*

Mar 68. (7") **PAINTING BOX. / NO SLEEP BLUES** [ ] [ ]

Mar 68. (lp) **THE HANGMAN'S BEAUTIFUL DAUGHTER** [5] [ ] Jun68
– Koeeoaddi there / The minotaur's song / Witches hat / A very cellular song / Mercy I cry city / Waltz of the new Moon / The water song / Three is a green crown / Swift as the wind / Nightfall. *(re-iss.Jan73, re-iss.'76) (cd-iss.1992)*

— **MIKE, ROBIN** and his girlfriend **LICORICE** introduced MIKE'S girlfriend **ROSE SIMPSON** – some vocals, bass, percussion, violin

Oct 68. (d-lp) **WEE TAM & THE BIG HUGE** [ ] [ ]
(re-iss.Jan73, re-iss.'76) (cd-iss.Dec94 on 'Hannibal')

Oct 68. (lp) **WEE TAM** [ ] [ ] Mar69
– Job's tears / Puppies / Beyond the see / The yellow snake / Log cabin home in the sky / You get brighter / The half-remarkable question / Air / Ducks on a pond. *(cd-iss.1992 on 'WEA Int.')*

Oct 68. (lp) **THE BIG HUGE** [ ] [ ] Mar69
– Maya / Greatest friend / The son of Noah's brother / Lordly nightshade / The mountain of God / Cousin caterpillar / The iron stone / Douglas Traherne Harding / The circle is unbroken. *(cd-iss.1992 on 'WEA Int.') (cd-iss.Jul93)*

— LICORICE was now a full-time member

Oct 69. (7") **BIG TED. / ALL WRIT DOWN** [ ] [ ]

Nov 69. (lp)(c) **CHANGING HORSES** [30] [ ]
– Big Ted / White bird / Dust be diamonds / Sleepers, awake! / Mr. & Mrs. / Creation. *(cd-iss. Jul93) (cd-iss.Dec94 on 'Hannibal')*

— added guest **DAVE MATTACKS** – drums of FAIRPORT CONVENTION

Apr 70. (lp)(c) **I LOOKED UP** [30] [ ] Jul70
– Black Jack Davy / The letter / Pictures in a mirror / This moment / When you find out who you are / Fair as you. *(cd-iss.Dec94 on 'Hannibal')*

Apr 70. (7") **THIS MOMENT. / BLACK JACK DAVY** [ ] [ ]

— augmented by **JANET SHANKMAN** – b.vocals (ROBIN married her Dec70) **PETE GRANT** – banjo / **GREG HART** – sitar (of STONE MONKEY) plus guest **MALCOLM LE MAISTRE** – keyboards, bass (of EXPLODING GALAXY)

Oct 70. (d-lp) **"U"** [34] [ ] Jan71
– El wool suite / The juggler's song / Time / Bad Sadie Lee / Queen of love / Partial belated overture / Light in the time of darkness – Glad to see you / Walking along with you / Hirem pawn Itof – Fairies' hornpipe / Bridge theme / Bridge song / Astral plane theme / Invocation / Robot blues / Puppet song / Cutting the strings / I know you / Rainbow. *(re-iss.Jan73)*

— Back to basic duo of **ROBIN + MIKE** plus **LICORICE + ROSE**

Island Reprise

Apr 71. (lp)(c) **BE GLAD FOR THE SONG HAS NO ENDING** [ ] [ ]
– Come with me / All writ down / Vishangro / See all the people / Waiting for you / (Be glad for) The song has no ending.

— **MALCOLM LE MAISTRE** – keyboards, bass, vocals returned to repl. ROSE

Oct 71. (lp)(c) **LIQUID ACROBAT AS REGARDS THE AIR** [46] [ ] Feb72
– Talking of the end / Dear old battlefield / Cosmic boy / Worlds they rise and fall / Evloution rag / Painted chariot / Adam and Eve / Red hair / Here till here is there / Tree / Jigs: Eyes like leaves – Sunday is my wedding day – Drops of whiskey – Grumbling old men / Darling Belle. *(cd+c-iss.Aug91)*

— added **GERARD DOTT** – clarinet, saxophone (he played on HERON's 1972 solo album) and guest on one **STUART GORDON** – viola

Oct 72. (lp)(c) **EARTHSPAN** [ ] [ ]
– My father was a lighthouse keeper / Antoine / Restless night / Sunday song / Black Jack David / Banks of sweet Italy / The actor / Moon hang low / The sailor and the dancer / Seagull. *(cd-iss. Dec 92 on 'Demon')*

Nov 72. (7") **BLACK JACK DAVID. / MOON HANG LOW** [ ] [ ]

— **STAN LEE** – bass repl. LICORICE who joined WOODY WOODMANSEY Band **JACK INGRAM** – drums (added to ROBIN, MIKE, MALCOLM, GERARD and STAN)

Feb 73. (7") **AT THE LIGHTHOUSE DANCE. / JIGS** [ ] [ ]

Feb 73. (lp)(c) **NO RUINOUS FEUD** [ ] [ ]
– Explorer / Down before Cathy / Saturday maybe / Jigs / Old Bouccaneer / At the lighthouse dance / Second fiddle / Circus girl / Turquoise blue / My blue tears / Weather the storm / Little girl.

— **GRAHAM FORBES** – electric guitar (ex-POWERHOUSE) repl. GERARD / **JOHN GILSTON** – drums repl. INGRAM

Mar 74. (lp)(c) **HARD ROPE & SILKEN TWINE** [ ] [ ]
– Maker of islands / Cold February / Glancing love / Dreams of no return / Dumb Kate / Ithkos. *(cd-iss. 1993 on 'Edsel')*

– compilations etc. –

Mar 71. Elektra/ US= Reprise; (lp)(c) **RELICS OF THE INCREDIBLE STRING BAND** [ ] [ ]

Nov 76. Island/ US= Reprise; (d-lp) **SEASONS THEY CHANGE – BEST OF THE INCREDIBLE STRING BAND** [ ] [ ]
– Black Jack David / Blues for the muse / Nightfall / Puppies / Cold days of February / Worlds they rise and fall / Chinese white / Empty pocket blues / When the music starts to play / Saturday maybe / Red hair / The circle is unbroken / First girl I loved / Cosmic boy / Darling Belle / My father was a lighthouse keeper / Queen Juanita and her fisherman lover.

Jan 92. Band Of Joy; (cd) **ON AIR (live)** [ ] [ ]

MIKE HERON

solo incl. members of **FAIRPORT CONVENTION** plus **GERARD DOTT**

Island Elektra

Apr 71. (7") **CALL ME DIAMOND. / LADY WONDER** [ ] [-]

Apr 71. (lp)(c) **SMILING MEN WITH BAD REPUTATIONS** [ ] [ ]
– Call me Diamond / Flowers of the forest / Audrey / Brindaban / Feast of Stephen / Spirit beautiful / Warm heart pastry / No turning back / Beautiful stranger. *(c+cd-iss.Aug91)*

May 71. (7") **CALL ME DIAMOND. / BRINDABAN** [-] [ ]

ROBIN WILLIAMSON

with guest **DAVID CAMPBELL** – viola

Island/Help Reprise

Apr 72. (lp)(c) **MYRRH** [ ] [ ]
– Strings in the earth and air / Rends moi-demain / The dancing of the Lord of Weir / Will we open the Heaven's / Through the horned clouds / Sandy islands / Cold harbour / Dark eyed lady / Dark dance / I see us all get home. *(re-iss.'74)*

— After ISB folded, both went their own separate ways.

MIKE HERON'S REPUTATION

Neighbourhood Neighborhood

1975. (lp)(c) **MIKE HERON'S REPUTATION** [ ] [ ]
– Down on my knees / Easy Street / Evie / Residential boy / Without love / Born to gone / Angels in disguise / Wine of his song / Meanwhile the rain / One of the finest / Singing the dolphin.

1975. (7") **EVIE. / DOWN ON MY KNEES, AFTER MEMPHIS** [ ] [ ]

HERON

Bronze not issued

May 77. (7") **DO IT YOURSELF (DESERT SONG). / DON'T KILL IT CAROL** [ ] [ ]

May 77. (lp)(c) **DIAMOND OF DREAMS** [ ] [ ]
– Are you going to hear the music / Don't kill it Carol / Do it yourself (desert song) / Redbone / Turn up your love light / Draw back the veil / Stranded in Iowa / Diamond of dreams / Baby goodnight.

MIKE HERON

Zoom not issued

Aug 78. (7") **SOLD ON YOUR LOVE. / PORTLAND BLUES** [ ] [ ]

not issued Casablanca

1980. (lp)(c) **MIKE HERON** [-] [ ]

– compilations etc. –

Jan 88. Glenrow; (lp)(c) **THE GLENROW TAPES** [ ] [-]
(cd-iss.Jun93 on 'Voiceprint')

Jan 88. Glenrow; (lp)(c) **THE GLENROW TAPES VOL.2** [ ] [-]

Jan 88. Glenrow; (lp)(c) **THE GLENROW TAPES VOL.3** [ ] [-]

ROBIN WILLIAMSON with his MERRY MEN

with **CHRIS CASWELL** – wind / **SYLVIA WOODS** – harp / **JERRY McMILLAN** – strings / **PETE GRANT** – dobro, banjo / **DIRK DALTON + STU BROTMAN** – bass / **LOUIS KILLEN** – concertina

not issued Flying Fish

1977. (lp) **JOURNEY'S END** [-] [ ]
– Border tango / The tune I hear so well / Red eye blues / Tomorrow / Mystic times / Lullaby for a rainy day / Wrap city phapsody / The Maharajah of Magador / The bells / Voices of the Barbary Coast / Out on the water. *(re-iss.Mar89)(cd-iss.Jun93 on 'Edsel')*

Criminal Flying Fish

1978. (lp) **AMERICAN STONEHENGE** [ ] [ ]

– Port London early / Pacheco / Keepsake / Zoo blues / These islands green / The man in the van / Sands in the glass / Her scattered gold / When evening shadows fall / Rab's last woollen testament. *(re-iss.Mar89 on 'Flying Fish') (cd-iss.Jul94 on 'Demon')*

Jun 79. (lp) **A GLINT AT THE KINDLING** [ ] [ ]
– The road the gypsies go / Me and the mad girl / Lough Foyle / The woodcutter's song / By weary well / Boyhood of Henry Morgan the Pooka / Five denials on Merlin's grave / The poacher's song / Song of Mabon. *(re-iss.+c Jun86 on 'Awareness') (US-iss. Mar89 on 'Flying Fish') (cd-iss.1994 w/ 'SELECTED WRITINGS' on 'Claddagh')*

Aug 86. Awareness; (lp) **SONGS AND MUSIC 1977** (compilation) [ ] [-]
(re-iss.+c Apr87)

ROBIN WILLIAMSON

Claddagh FlyingFish

1981. (lp) **SONGS OF LOVE & PARTING** [ ] [ ]
– Verses in Stewart Street / For Mr. Thomas / Fare thee well Sweet Mally / Return no more / Tarry wool / For three of us / Sigil / Flower of the briar / The forming of Blodeuwedd / Gwydion's dream / Verses at Balwearie tower / A night at Ardpatrick / The parting glass. *(re-iss.Sep84) (cd-iss.1995 w/ 'FIVE BARDIC MYSTERIES')*

1983. (lp) **MUSIC FOR THE MABINOGI** [ ] [ ]
(US-iss.Jun88 as 'SONGS FOR THE MABINOGI')

Nov 84. (lp) **LEGACY OF THE SCOTTISH HARPERS** [ ] [ ]

1986. (lp) **LEGACY OF THE SCOTTISH HARPERS VOL.2** [ ] [ ]

Plant Life FlyingFish

Sep 87. (lp)(c) **WINTER'S TURNING** [ ] [ ]

1988. (lp)(c)(cd) **THE TEN OF SONGS** [ ] [ ]

below are; spoken word with some instrumentation
(mainly mail order on 'Claddagh' Ireland)

1981. (c) **THE FISHERMAN'S SON AND THE GRUGACH OF TRICK** [-] [-]

1982. (c) **PRINCE DOUGIE AND THE SWAN MAIDEN** [-] [-]

1982. (c) **RORY MOR AND THE GRUGACH GAIR** [-] [-]

1983. (c) **FIVE HUMOROUS TALES OF SCOTLAND** [-] [-]

1984. (c) **SELECTED WRITINGS** [-] [-]
– The fair / The fair dance / Edinburgh / Lammas.

1984. (c) **FIVE HUMOUROUS TALES OF SCOTLAND AND IRELAND** [-] [-]

Feb 85. Towerbell; (lp)(c) **THE DRAGON HAS TWO TONGUES** [ ] [-]
(TV film soundtrack)
(re-iss.Aug87 on 'TER')

1985. (c) **FIVE CELTIC TALES OF ENLIGHTENMENT** [-] [-]

1985. (c) **FIVE BARDIC TALES** [-] [-]
– The spolis of Annwn / The battle of the trees / The dialogue of the two sages / The voyage of the Bran, son of Febal / Three Celtic nature poems.

1985. (c) **FIVE LEGENDARY HISTORIES OF BRITAIN** [-] [-]

1985. (c) **FIVE CELTIC TALES OF PRODIGIES AND MARVELS** [-] [-]

1985. (c) **FIVE TALES OF ENCHANTMENT** [-] [-]

1987. (lp)(c) **SONGS FOR CHILDREN OF ALL AGES** [ ] [-]

1991. (cd)(c) **MUSIC FOR THE NEWBORN** [ ] [-]

INDIGO GIRLS

Formed: Decatur, Georgia, USA . . . 1986 by AMY RAY and EMILY SALIERS. Signed the dotted line 'Epic' in '87 and scored near US Top 20 album with eponymous second album, which featured R.E.M. and HOT-HOUSE FLOWERS. • **Style:** Folksy apple-pie college duo, similiar to British outfits EVERYTHING BUT THE GIRL or FAIRGROUND ATTRACTION, although obvously a litter deeper lyrically. • **Songwriters:** Either AMY or EMILY. • **Trivia:** 'CLOSER TO FINE' featured mandolin & backing vox by PETER O'TOOLE! of HOTHOUSE FLOWERS. In Sep'91, they participated with ELTON JOHN and many others on an AIDS charity walk, which raised over half a million dollars. Their 2nd & 3rd albums were produced by SCOTT LITT (of R.E.M. fame). PETER COLLINS took over the controls in 1992, and this album featured guest spots for DAVID CROSBY, JACKSON BROWNE & The ROCHES.

Recommended: INDIGO GIRLS (*6) / SWAMP OPHELIA (*6)

AMY RAY – vocals, guitars / **EMILY SALIERS** – vocals, acoustic guitar

not issued Columbia

1987. (lp)(c) **STRANGE FIRE** [-] [ ]
– Strange fire / Crazy game / Left me a fool / I don't wanna know / Hey Jesus / Get together / Walk away / Make it easier / You left it up to me / Land of Canaan. *(US re-iss.Nov89 on 'Epic')*

—— now with **JAY DEE DAUGHERTY** – drums (ex-HOTHOUSE FLOWERS, ex-WATERBOYS, etc.) / **JOHN KEANE** – guitar, bass / **JOHN VAN TONGEREN** – keyboards / **KASIM SULTAN + DEDE VOGT** – bass / **PAULINHO DA COSTA** – percussion / **JAI WINDING** – piano

Epic Epic

Jun 89. (7") **CLOSER TO FINE. / COLD AS ICE** [-] [ ]

Jun 89. (7") **CLOSER TO FINE. / HISTORY OF US** [ ] [-]
(12"+=) – American tune / Mona Lisas and mad hatters.
(cd-s+=) – Center stage. *(re-iss.Oct89)*

Jul 89. (lp)(c)(cd) **INDIGO GIRLS** [ ] [22] Apr89
– Closer to fine / Secure yourself / Kid fears / Prince of darkness / Blood and fire / Tried to be true / Love's recovery / Land of Canaan / Center stage / History of us.

Sep 89. (7") **LAND OF CANAAN. / NEVER STOP** [-] [ ]

Feb 90. (7") **GET TOGETHER. / FINLANDIA** [-] [ ]

—— now w / **DAUGHERTY / PETER BUCK** (of R.E.M.) / **SARA LEE** – bass (ex-GANG OF FOUR) / **MARY CHAPIN CARPENTER / KENNY ARONOFF / BENMONT TENCH / JIM KELTNER / PETER HOLSAPPLE / JOHN JENNINGS / DA COSTA / CHRIS McGUIRE / CRAIG EDWARDS** / etc.

Oct 90. (c-s) **HAMMER AND NAIL. / WELCOME (live)** [-] [ ]

Nov 90. (cd)(c)(lp) **NOMADS, INDIANS, SAINTS** [ ] [43] Oct90
– Hammer and nail / Welcome me / World falls / Southland in the springtime / 1,2,3 / Keeper of my heart / Watershed / Hand me downs / You and me of the 10,000 wars / Pushing the needle too far / The girl with the weight of the world in her hands.

1991. (cd) **BACK ON THE BUS (live)** [-] [ ]

—— now w / **SARA LEE** – bass / **BUDGIE** – drums (of SIOUXSIE & THE BANSHEES) / **LISA GERMANO** – fiddle / **JERRY MAROTTA** – drums / **MARTIN McCARRICK** – cello / **DONAL LUNNY** – bouziki, bodhran / **JENNINGS** – guitar / **WINDING** – piano

Jun 92. (cd)(c) **RITES OF PASSAGE** [ ] [21] May92
– Three hits / Galileo / Ghost / Joking / Jonas & Ezekial / Love will come to you / Romeo & Juliet / Virginia Woolf / Chicken man / Airplane / Nashville / Let it be me / Cedar tree.

Aug 92. (c-s)(cd-s) **GALILEO / GHOST / JOKING / LOVE WILL COME TO YOU / JONAS & EZEKIAL** [-] [89]

Oct 92. (7")(c-s) **GALILEO. / KID FEARS** [ ] [-]
(cd-s) – ('A'side) / Closer to fine / Tried to be true / Hammer and nail.

—— Augmented by **SARA LEE** – bass (ex-GANG OF FOUR, etc.) / **JERRY MAROTTA** – drums / **JAMES HALL** – trumpet / **DANNY THOMPSON** – acoustic bass / **LISA GERMANO** – violin / **JOHN PAINTER** – flugel horn / **JANE SCARPANTONI** – cello / **MICHAEL LORANT** – drums, b.vocals

May 94. (cd-ep) **LEAST COMPLICATED / DEAD MAN'S HILL / MYSTERY / KID FEARS** [ ] [ ]

May 94. (cd)(c)(lp) **SWAMP OPHELIA** [66] [9]
– Fugitive / Least complicated / Language or the kiss / Reunion / Power of two / Touch me fall / The wood song / Mystery / Dead man's hill / Fare thee well / This train revised.

Jun 95. (c-ep)(cd-ep) **CLOSER TO FINE / ROCKIN' IN THE FREE WORLD** [ ] [ ]
(cd-s+=) – Dead man's hill (acoustic) / Mystery (acoustic).
(cd-s) – ('A'side) / Kid fears / All along the watchtower (live) / Let me a fool (live).

Jul 95. (cd)(c) **4.5 THE BEST OF THE INDIGO GIRLS** (compilation) [43] [ ]
– Joking / Hammer and nail / Kid fears / Galileo / Tried to be true / Power of love / Pushing the needle tto far / Reunion / Closer to fine / Three hits / Least complicated / Touch me fall / Love's recovery / Land of Canaan / Ghost.

Oct 95. (cd)(c) **1200 CURFEWS (live)** [-] [40]

INSPIRAL CARPETS

Formed: Manchester, England . . . 1980 initially as The FURS, by schoolboy GRAHAM LAMBERT. He was joined in the mid-80's by STEPHEN HOLT, TONY WELSH and CHRIS GOODWIN. In 1986, as The INSPIRAL CARPETS, they replaced GOODWIN and WELSH, with CRAIG GILL, DAVE SWIFT and CLINT BOON. Early in '87, they recorded a version of 'GARAGE' for a 7" flexi-disc given free with 'Debris' magazine. After gigs supporting the WEDDING PRESENT, JAMES, STONES ROSES and The SHAMEN, they issued official debut 'PLANE CRASH EP in mid-'88 for indie 'Playtime' records. Early in 1989, they set up own 'Cow' label, after their distributers 'Red Rhino' went bust. At the same time, HOLT and SWIFT left to form The RAINKINGS, and were replaced by HINGLEY and WALSH. After a late 1988 recording 'TRAIN SURFING EP' was issued, they issued 808 STATE produced 'JOE' single/EP. Late 1989, they had first UK Top 50 entry with 'MOVE', which led to Daniel Miller of 'Mute' records giving them & 'Cow' a record deal. In April 1990, they broke into UK Top 20 with single 'THIS IS HOW IT FEELS', which aided their debut album 'LIFE' to reach Top 3. • **Style:** Heavy organ-orientated alternative-pop group, who lay somewhere between The DOORS and The FALL. • **Songwriters:** Group penned except; 96 TEARS (? & The Mysterians) / GIMME SHELTER (Rolling Stones) / TAINTED LOVE (Soft Cell) / PARANOID (Black Sabbath). • **Trivia:** To promote debut album, they employed the services of the Milk Marketing Board who ran a TV ad on their bottles. Early 1990, they penned 'THE 8.15 FROM MANCHESTER' (theme) from children's Saturday morning TV show.

Recommended: LIFE (*8) / THE BEAST INSIDE (*7).

GRAHAM LAMBERT – guitar / **STEPHEN HOLT** – vocals / **DAVE SWIFT** – bass repl. TONY WELSH / **CRAIG GILL** – drums repl. CHRIS GOODWIN who joined ASIA FIELDS (later BUZZCOCKS F.O.C. and The HIGH) / added **CLINT BOON** – organ, vocals

Playtime not issued

Jul 88. (7"ltd.) **KEEP THE CIRCLE AROUND. / THEME FROM COW** [ ] [-]
(12"ep+=) **PLANE CRASH EP** – Seeds of doubt / Garage full of flowers / 96 tears.

Cow not issued

Mar 89. (12"ep) **TRAIN SURFING** [ ] [-]
– Butterfly / Causeway / You can't take the truth / Greek wedding song.

—— **TOM HINGLEY** – vocals (ex-TOO MUCH TEXAS) repl. HOLT who formed RAINKINGS **MARTIN WALSH** – bass (ex-NEXT STEP) repl. SWIFT who formed RAINKINGS

May 89. (12"ep) **JOE. / COMMERCIAL MIX / DIRECTING TRAFFIK / COMMERCIAL RAIN** [ ] [-]

Aug 89. (7") **FIND OUT WHY. / SO FAR** [ ] [-]
(12"+=)(cd-s+=) – Plane crash (live).

Oct 89. (7") **MOVE. / OUT OF TIME** [49] [-]
(12"+=)(cd-s+=) – Move in.

Cow-Mute Sire

Mar 90. (7") **THIS IS HOW IT FEELS. / TUNE FOR A FAMILY** [14] [ ]
(12") – ('A'-Rob mix) / ('B'drum mix)
(cd-s) – ('A'radio mix) / Seeds of doubt.
(c-s) – ('A'radio mix) / Whiskey.

Apr 90. (cd)(c)(lp) **LIFE** [2] [ ]
– Real thing / Song for a family / This is how it feels / Directing traffik / Besides me / Many happy returns / Memories of you / She comes in the fall / Monkey on my

back / Sun don't shine / Inside my head / Move * / Sackville. *(cd+= *) (US++=)* – Commercial rain / Weakness / Biggest mountain / I'll keep it in mind.

Jun 90. (7") **SHE COMES IN THE FALL. / SACKVILLE** [27] [ ]
(12"+=)(cd-s+=) – Continental reign (version).
(12"+=) – ('A'acapella version).

Nov 90. (7"ep)(12"ep) **ISLAND HEAD** [21] [ ]
– Biggest mountain / I'll keep it in mind / Weakness / Gold to . . .
(cd-ep+=) – Mountain sequence.

Mar 91. (7") **CARAVAN. / SKIDOO** [30] [ ]
(7")(12") – ('A'side) / ('B'possession mix)
(cd-s) – ('A'what noise rethink mix) / ('B'side)

Apr 91. (cd)(c)(lp) **THE BEAST INSIDE** [5] [ ]
– Caravan / Please be cruel / Born yesterday / Sleep well tonight / Grip / Beast inside / Niagara / Mermaid / Further away / Dreams are all we have.

Jun 91. (7")(c-s) **PLEASE BE CRUEL. / THE WIND IS CALLING YOUR NAME** [50] [ ]
(12"+=)(cd-s+=) – St.Kilda (version).

Feb 92. (7")(c-s) **DRAGGING ME DOWN. / I KNOW I'M LOSING YOU** [12] [ ]
(12"+=)(cd-s+=) – (2 other 'A'mixes).

May 92. (7") **TWO WORLDS COLLIDE. / BOOMERANG** [32] [ ]
(12"+=)(cd-s+=) – ('A'-Mike Pickering remix).

Sep 92. (7") **GENERATIONS. / ('A'remix)** [28] [ ]
(cd-s) – ('A'side) / She comes in the fall / Move / Directing traffik (all live).
(cd-s) – ('A'side) / Joe / Commercial rain / Butterfly (all live).

Oct 92. (cd)(c)(lp) **REVENGE OF THE GOLDFISH** [17] [ ]
– Generations / Saviour / Bitches brew / Smoking her clothes / Fire / Here comes the flood / Dragging me down / A little disappeared / Two worlds collide / Mystery / Rain song / Irresistable force.

Nov 92. (12"ep)(c-ep) **BITCHES BREW / TAINTED LOVE. / BITCHES BREW (Fortran 5 remix) / IRRESISTABLE FORCE (Fortran 5 mix)** [36] [ ]
(cd-ep+=) – Mermaid / Born yesterday / Sleep well tonight (all live).
(cd-ep+=) – Dragging me down / Smoking her clothes / Fire (all live).

Have now parted company with 'Cow' co-founder/manager Anthony Boggiano.

May 93. (7")(c-s) **HOW IT SHOULD BE. / IT'S ONLY A PAPER MOON** [49] [ ]
(12"+=)(cd-s+=) – I'm alive.

Jan 94. (7")(c-s) **SATURN 5. / PARTY IN THE SKY** [20] [ ]
(cd-s+=)(12"+=) – ('A'mixes).
(cd-s) – ('A'side) / Well of seven heads / Two cows / Going down.

Feb 94. (7")(c-s) **I WANT YOU. / I WANT YOU (feat. MARK E.SMITH)** [18] [ ]
(cd-s+=) – We can do everything / Inside of you.
(cd-s) – ('A'side) / Dragging me down / Party in the sky / Plutoman.

Mar 94. (cd)(c)(lp) **DEVIL HOPPING** [10] [ ]
– I want you / Party in the sky / Plutoman / Uniform / Lovegrove / Just Wednesday / Saturn 5 / All of this and more / The way the light falls / Half way there / Cobra / I don't want to go blind. *(w / free ltd-cd of 'BBC SESSIONS' or free ltd.red-10"lp)*

Apr 94. (7")(c-s)(cd-s) **UNIFORM. / PARANOID** [51] [ ]
(cd-s) – ('A'side) / Paranoid (Collapsed Lung mix).

Aug 95. (7"m) **JOE (acoustic). / SEEDS OF DOUBT / WHISKEY** [37] [ ]
(7"m) – Joe (live) / Sackville (live) / Saviour (live).
(cd-s) – ('A'side) / I want you / I'll keep it in mind / Tainted love.

Sep 95. (cd)(c)(d-lp) **THE SINGLES** (compilation) [17] [ ]
– Joe / Find out why / Move / This is how it feels / (extended) / She comes in the fall / Commercial reign / Sackville / Biggest mountain / Weakness / Caravan / Please be cruel / Dragging me down / Two worlds collide / Generations / Bitches brew / How it should be / Saturn 5 / I want you / Uniform.

— Had already been dropped from the 'Mute' roster late in 1994.

– compilations, etc. –

May 89. Cow; (c) **DEMO CASSETTE (ltd. edition)** [ ] [-]
– Keep the circle around / Seeds of doubt / Joe / Causeway / 26 / Inside my head / Sun don't shine / Theme from Cow / 96 tears / Butterfly / Garage full of flowers. *(rec.Dec87)*

Jul89. Strange Fruit; (12"ep)(cd-ep) **THE PEEL SESSIONS** [ ] [-]
– Out of time / Directing traffic / Keep the circle around / Gimme shelter.

Aug92. Strange Fruit; (cd)(10"lp) **PEEL SESSIONS** [ ] [-]

— also released import 7"colrd/12"colrd/pic-cd-s, GIMME SHELTER

INTERNATIONAL SUBMARINE BAND (see under ⇒ PARSONS, Gram)

INXS

Formed: Sydney, Australia . . . 1977 as The FARRISS BROTHERS by TIM, ANDREW and JON, plus MICHAEL HUTCHENCE, KIRK PENGILLY and GARRY BEERS. After briefly moving to Perth in 1978, they returned the next year as INXS, and with a contract on 'Deluxe' through 'RCA'. They released 2 albums and several singles in the early 80's, before moving to 'WEA' Australia in '82. Their 3rd album 'SHABOOH SHOOBAH' became another Australian success, and led to a contract on 'Atco' in the US, where it made the Top 50. Early in 1983, they also signed to 'Mercury' in the UK, but debut 45 'DON'T CHANGE' flopped. With progress from 1985's 'LISTEN LIKE THIEVES' album, they became massive outfit late in 1987, with cross-Atlantic Top 10 album 'KICK'. Taken from it, were 4 US Top 10 singles including No.1 'NEED YOU TONIGHT', which also made No.2 a year later in UK. • **Style:** Sophisticated and complex rock-pop outfit, fronted by JIM MORRISON like HUTCHENCE, who was once boyfriend of Aussie pop star KYLIE MINOGUE. • **Songwriters:** Most by ANDREW FARRISS and HUTCHENCE, except some B-sides by TIM. Covered; THE LOVED ONE (The Loved One). • **Trivia:** In 1987, idol HUTCHENCE starred as a drug crazed punk in the Australian film 'Dogs In Space'. Two years later he appeared in 'Frankenstein Unbound'.

Recommended: INXS – THE GREATEST HITS (*8).

MICHAEL HUTCHENCE (b.12 Jan'60, Lain Cove, Sydney, Australia) – vocals / **ANDREW FARRISS** (b.27 Mar'59) – keyboards, guitar / **TIM FARRISS** (b.16 Aug'57) – guitar / **KIRK PENGILLY** (b. 4 Jul'58) – saxophone, guitar, vocals / **GARRY BEERS** (b.22 Jun'57) – bass, vocals / **JON FARRISS** (b.18 Aug'61) – drums

not issued / Deluxe

May 80. (7") **SIMPLE SIMON. / WE ARE ALL VEGETABLES** [-] [-] Aussie

Oct 80. (7") **JUST KEEP WALKING. / SCRATCH** [-] [-] Aussie
(UK-rel.Sep81 on 'RCA')

Oct 80. (lp) **INXS** [-] [-] Aussie
– On a bus / Doctor / Just keep walking / Learn to smile / Jumping in vain / Roller skating / Body language / Newsreel babies / Wishy washy. *(UK-iss.May89/Jul90 on 'Vertigo') (US-iss.Aug84 on 'Atco')*

not issued / Deluxe-RCA

Feb 81. (7") **THE LOVED ONE.** [-] [-] Aussie

1981. (7") **STAY YOUNG.** [-] [-] Aussie

1981. (7") **NIGHT OF REBELLION.** [-] [-] Aussie

Nov 81. (lp) **UNDERNEATH THE COLOURS** [-] [-] Aussie
– Stay young / Horizons / Big go-go / Underneath the colours / Fair weather ahead / Night of rebellion / What would you do / Follow / Barbarian / Just to learn again. *(UK-iss.Mar82 on 'RCA') (re-iss.+c.Jul89 on 'Vertigo')*

not issued / R.C.A.

1982. (7") **THE ORIGINAL SIN.** [-] [-] Aussie

not issued / Atco

Oct 82. (lp) **SHABOOH SHABOOH** [-] [46]
– The one thing / To look at you / Spy of love / Soul mistake / Here comes / Black and white / Golden playpen / Jan's song / Old world new world / Don't change. *(UK-iss.Jun87) (cd-iss.May90 on 'Mercury')*

1983. (7") **DON'T CHANGE. / GO WEST** [-] [-] Aussie

— from now on UK + US releases only, with US labels, etc. mentioned

Mercury / Atco

Mar 83. (7") **THE ONE THING. / PHANTOM OF THE OPERA** [-] [30]

Jun 83. (7") **DON'T CHANGE. / LONG IN TOOTH** [-] [80]

Jun 83. (7") **DON'T CHANGE. / YOU NEVER USED TO CRY** [ ] [ ]
(12"+=) – Golden playpen.

1983. (m-lp) **DEKADANCE** [-] [ ]
– Black and white / Here comes / The one thing / To look at you

Sep 83. (7") **THE ONE THING. / THE SAX THING** [ ] [-]
(12") – ('A'side) / Black and white.
(12") – ('A'side) (++=) – Here comes II.

Oct 83. (7") **TO LOOK AT YOU. / THE SAX THING** [-] [ ]

Feb 84. (7") **ORIGINAL SIN. / JAN'S SONG (live)** [ ] [-]
(12"+=) – To look at you (live) / ('A'extended version).

Apr 84. (7") **ORIGINAL SIN. / STAY YOUNG** [-] [58]

May 84. (lp)(c)(cd) **THE SWING** [ ] [52]
– Original sin / Melting in the sun / I send a message / Dancing on the jetty / The swing / Johnson's aeroplane / Love is (what I say) / Face the change / Burn for you / All the voices.

Philips / Atco

May 84. (7") **I SEND A MESSAGE. / MECHANICAL** [ ] [77] Jul 84
(12"+=) – ('A'longer version)

Oct 84. (7") **BURN FOR YOU. / JOHNSON'S AEROPLANE** [-] [ ]

Mercury / Atlantic

Nov 85. (lp)(c)(cd) **LISTEN LIKE THIEVES** [48] [11]
– What you need / Listen like thieves / Kiss the dirt (falling down the mountain) / Shine like it does / Good and bad times / Biting bullets / This time / Three sisters / Same direction / One x one / Red red sun. *(ltd. copies of the above cont. THE SWING album) (re-iss.cd/c Apr95)*

Feb 86. (7") **THIS TIME. / ORIGINAL SIN (ext.)** [ ] [81] Nov 85
(12"+d7"+=) – Burn for you / Dancing on the jetty.

Apr 86. (7") **WHAT YOU NEED. / SWEET AS SIN** [51] [5] Jan 86
(12"+=) – ('A' live) / The one thing.
(d12"++=) – Don't change / Johnson's aeroplane.
(c-s+=) – ('B' + 2 alt. versions) / This time / I'm over you.

Jun 86. (7")(7"sha-pic-d) **LISTEN LIKE THIEVES. / BEGOTTEN** [46] [54] May 86
(d7"+=) – One x one / Xs verbage.
(12"+=) – ('A' instrumental) / ('A' extended).

Aug 86. (7") **KISS THE DIRT (FALLING DOWN THE MOUNTAIN). / 6 KNOTS / THE ONE THING (live)** [54] [ ]
(12"+=) – Spy of love.
(d7"+=) – This time / Original sin.

Sep 87. (7") **NEED YOU TONIGHT. / I'M COMING (HOME)** [58] [1] Oct 87
(12"+=)(cd-s+=) – Mediate.

Nov 87. (lp)(c)(cd) **KICK** [9] [3]
– Guns in the sky / New sensation / Devil inside / Need you tonight / Mediate / The loved one / Wild life / Never tear us apart / Mystify / Kick / Calling all nations / Tiny daggers. *(pic-lp Dec88) (re-iss.Jul91 hit UK No.50)*

Nov 87. (7")(7"pic-d) **NEW SENSATION. / DO WOT YOU DO** [25] [-]
(12"+=) – Love is (what I say).
(12"+=)(c-s+=)(cd-s+=) – Same direction.

Feb 88. (7") **DEVIL INSIDE. / ON THE ROCKS** [47] [2]
(12"+=) – Devil inside (extended).
(cd-s+=) – What you need.
(10"+=) – Dancing on the jetty / Shine like it does.

May 88. (7") **NEW SENSATION. / GUNS IN THE SKY (kooka-burra mix)** [-] [ ]

Jun 88. (7")(12") **NEVER TEAR US APART. / GUNS IN THE SKY (remix)** [24] [-]
(12"+=) – Burn for you / One world new world.
(cd-s+=) – Different world / This time.
(10"white+=) – Need you tonight / Listen like thieves.

Aug 88. (7") **NEVER TEAR US APART. / DIFFERENT WORLD** [-] [7]

Oct 88. (7") **NEED YOU TONIGHT. / MOVE ON** [2] [-]

(12"+=) – New sensation.
(12"+=) – Kiss the dirt / ('A' remix).
(cd-s+=) – Original sin / Don't change.

Mar 89. (7") **MYSTIFY. / DEVIL INSIDE** [14] [ ]
(12"+=) – Never tear us apart (live) / Shine like it does (live).
(cd-s+=) – Listen like thieves / What you need (remix).

Sep 90. (7") **SUICIDE BLONDE. / EVERYBODY WANTS U TONIGHT** [11] [9]
(12"+=)(cd-s+=) – ('A'milk mix).

Sep 90. (cd)(c)(lp) **X** [2] [5]
– Suicide blonde / Disappear / The stairs / Faith in each other / By my side / Lately / Who pays the price / Know the difference / Bitter tears / On my way / Hear that sound. *(re-iss.cd/c Apr95)*

Nov 90. (7") **DISAPPEAR. / MIDDLE EAST** [21] [8]
(12"+=)(cd-s+=) – What you need (Cold Cut force mix).
(12") – ('A'side) / Need you tonight (mix) / New sensation.

Mar 91. (7")(c-s) **BY MY SIDE. / THE OTHER SIDE** [42] [-]
(12"+=)(cd-s+=) – Faith in each other (live).
(cd-s++=) – Disappear (mix).

Jul 91. (7") **BITTER TEARS. / SOOTHE ME** [30] [46] Apr 91
(12"+=) – Disappear (mix) / ('A'tears are bitter mix) / ('A'other mix).
(cd-s+=) – Original sin / Listen like thieves (extended remixes).

Oct 91. (7")(12")(cd-ep) **SHINING STAR** [27] [ ]
– Shining star / Send a message (live) / Faith in each other (live) / Bitter tears (live).

Nov 91. (cd)(c)(lp) **LIVE BABY LIVE (live)** [8] [72]
– New sensation / Mystify / Never tear us apart / Need you tonight / Suicide blonde / By my side / Mediate / Hear that sound / The stairs / What you need / Shining star (studio).

Jul 92. (7")(12")(c-s)(cd-s)(7"pic-d) **HEAVEN SENT. / IT AIN'T EASY** [31] [-]

Aug 92. (c-s) **NOT ENOUGH TIME / ?.** [-] [28]

Aug 92. (cd)(c)(lp) **WELCOME TO WHEREVER YOU ARE** [1] [16]
– Questions / Heaven sent / Communication / Taste it / Not enough time / All around / Baby don't cry / Beautiful girl / Wishing well / Back on line / Strange desire / Men and women. *(re-iss.cd/c Apr95)*

Sep 92. (7")(c-s) **BABY DON'T CRY. / (Part 2)** [20] [ ]
(cd-s+=) – Ptar speaks / Question 8 (instrumental) / ('A'acappella mix).

Nov 92. (7")(c-s) **TASTE IT. / LIGHT THE PLANET** [21] [ ]
(cd-s+=) – Youth / Not enough time (mix).

Feb 93. (7")(c-s) **BEAUTIFUL GIRL. / IN MY LIVING ROOM / ASHTAR SPEAKS** [23] [46]
(cd-s) – ('A'side) / Strange desire.
(cd-s) – ('A'side) / Underneath my colours / Wishing well.

Oct 93. (7"-c-s) **THE GIFT. / BORN TO BE WILD** [11] [ ]
(cd-s) – ('A'side) / ('A'mix) / Heaven sent (live).

Nov 93. (cd)(c)(lp) **FULL MOON, DIRTY HEARTS** [3] [53]
– Days of rust / The gift / Make your peace / Time / I'm only looking / Please (you've got that . . .) / Full moon, dirty hearts / Freedom deep / Kill the pain / Cut your roses down / The messenger / Viking juice

Dec 93. (12")(c-s) **PLEASE (YOU GOT THAT . . .). ("INXS & RAY CHARLES") / ('A'mixes)** [50] [ ]
(cd-s) – ('A'side) / Freedom deep / Communication (live) / Taste it (live).

Oct 94. (7"red)(c-s) **THE STRANGEST PARTY (THESE ARE THE TIMES). / WISHING WELL** [15] [ ]
(cd-s+=) – ('A'mix) / Sing something.
(cd-s) – ('A'side) / Need you tonight (remix) / I'm only looking (remix).

Nov 94. (cd)(c)(lp) **INXS – THE GREATEST HITS** (compilation) [3] [ ]
– Mystify / Suicide blonde / Taste it / The strangest party (these are the times) / Need you tonight / Original sin / Heaven sent / Disappear / Never tear us apart / The gift / Devil inside / Beautiful girl / Deliver me / New sensation / What you need / Listen like thieves / Bitter tears / Baby don't cry.

– some other AUSTRALIA only releases –

Oct 83. WEA; (7")(12") **ORIGINAL SIN. / IN VAIN / JUST KEEP WALKING** [-] [-]
1984. WEA; (7")(12") **BURN FOR YOU. /** [-] [-]
1984. WEA; (7")(12") **DANCING ON THE JETTY. /** [-] [-]
MICHAEL HUTCHENCE also released below single
1987. WEA; (7") **ROOMS FOR THE MEMORY. / GOLFCOURSE** [-] [-]

MAX Q

(HUTCHENCE with **IAN 'OLLIE' OLSEN** duo named after his dog!)

Mercury Atlantic

Sep 89. (7") **WAY OF THE WORLD. / ZERO 2-0** [ ] [ ]
(12"+=)(c-s+=)(cd-s+=) – Ghost of the year.

Oct 89. (lp)(c)(cd) **MAX Q** [69] [ ]
– Sometimes / Way of the world / Ghost of the year / Everything / Zero 2-0 / Soul engine / Buckethead / Monday night by satellite / Tight / Ot-ven-rot.

Feb 90. (7")(c-s) **SOMETIMES. / LOVE MAN** [53] [-]
(12"+=) – ('A'instrumental).
(12"+=)(cd-s+=) – ('A'-land of Oz mix) / ('A'rock home mix).

Feb 90. (7") **SOMETIMES. / GHOST OF THE YEAR** [-] [ ]

JIMMY BARNES & INXS

Atlantic Atlantic

Jun 87. (7") **GOOD TIMES. / LAY DOWN THE LAW** [ ] [47]
(UK-iss.7"/12"/cd-s Jan91, hit No.18)

IRON BUTTERFLY

Formed: San Diego, California, USA . . . 1966 by DOUG INGLE, RON BUSHY, DANNY WEIS, JERRY PENROD and DARRYL DeLOACH. They soon moved to Los Angeles and after being spotted at the Whiskey A-Go-Go, they signed to Atlantic subsidiary label 'Atco'. Early 1968, they issued 'HEAVY' lp, which broke into the US Top 100. In the summer of '68, WEIS and PENROD departed, and were succeeded by DORMAN and BRAUN. This line-up completed another 1968 lp 'IN-A-GADDA-DA-VIDA' (aka 'The Garden of Life'), and this classic hit US Top 5 going on to sell over 3 million copies. Taken from it, the edited title track (from lp version of 17-minutes) made No.30. With the album still riding high in the charts, their 1969 'BALL' lp, cracked the Top 3, but after 2 more Top 20 entries in 1970, they fell away from favour. • **Style:** Progressive heavy-metal outfit, keyboard orientated, until the inclusion of twin guitarists PINERA and REINHARDT. • **Songwriters:** INGLE and BUSHY were main contributors, until addition then departure of BRAUN and DORMAN. • **Trivia:** In 1968, 2 tracks 'OSSESSION' & 'UNCONSCIOUS POWER' were used on the film soundtrack of 'The Savage Seven'.

Recommended: IN-A-GADDA-DA-VIDA (*9) / LIGHT AND HEAVY – THE BEST OF . . . (*7)

DOUG INGLE (b. 9 Sep'46, Omaha, Nebraska, USA) – keyboards, vocals / **JERRY PENROD** – guitar / **DANNY WEIS** – guitar (both ex-DAVID ACKLES band) / **RON BUSHY** (b.23 Sep'45, Washington DC) – drums, vocals / **DARRYL DeLOACH** – bass, vocals

Atlantic Atco

Feb 68. (lp) **HEAVY** [ ] [78]
– Possession / Unconscious power / Get out of my life,woman / Gentle as it may seem / You can't win / So-lo / Look for the sun / Fields of sun / Stamped ideas / Iron butterfly theme. *(cd-iss.1992 on 'Repertoire' +=)*– I can't help but deceive you little girl / To be alone.

Jun 68. (7") **POSSESSION. / UNCONSCIOUS POWER** [ ] [ ] May68

— **ERIK BRAUN** (b.11 Aug'50, Boston, Massachusetts, USA) – lead guitar, vocals repl. WEIS and PENROD who formed RHINOCEROS / **LEE DORMAN** (b.19 Sep'45, St.Louis, Missouri) – bass, multi repl. DeLOACH

Jul 68. (lp) **IN-A-GADDA-DA-VIDA** [ ] [4]
– Most anything you want / Flowers and beads / My mirage / Termination / Are you happy / In-a-gadda-da-vida. *(re-iss.1974) (cd-iss Jul87) (cd-iss Jun93) (re-iss.cd deluxe version Nov95 on 'Rhino')*

Sep 68. (7") **IN-A-GADDA-DA-VIDA (edit). / TERMINATION** [ ] [-]
Sep 68. (7") **IN-A-GADDA-DA-VIDA (edit). / IRON BUTTERFLY THEME** [-] [30] Aug 68

Feb 69. (lp) **BALL** [ ] [3]
– In the time of our lives / Soul experience / Lonely boy / Real fright / In the crowds / It must be love / Her favourite style / Filled with fear / Belda-beast.

Mar 69. (7") **SOUL EXPERIENCE. / IN THE CROWDS** [ ] [75] Feb 69
Jul 69. (7") **IN THE TIME OF OUR LIVES. / IT MUST BE LOVE** [-] [96]
Nov 69. (7") **I CAN'T HELP BUT DECEIVE YOU LITTLE GIRL. / TO BE ALONE** [-] [ ]

Apr 70. (lp) **IRON BUTTERFLY LIVE (live)** [ ] [20]
– In the time of our lives / Filled with fear / Soul experience / You can't win / Are you happy / In-a-gadda-da-vida. *(re-iss.1982)*

— **INGLE, BUSHY and DORMAN** recruited new members **MIKE PINERA** (b.29 Sep'48, Tampa Bay, Florida) – guitar, vocals (ex-BLUES IMAGE) repl. BRAUN who later formed FLINTWHISTLE / added **LARRY REINHARDT** (b. 7 Jul'48, Florida) – guitar

Oct 70. (7") **EASY RIDER (LET THE WIND PAY THE WAY). / SOLDIER IN OUR TOWN** [-] [66]

Jan 71. (lp) **METAMORPHOSIS** [ ] [16] Aug70
– Free flight / New day / Shady lady / Best years of our lives / Slower than guns / Stone believer / Soldier in our town / Easy rider (let the wind pay the way) / Butterfly bleu. *(cd-iss.Jun92 on 'Repertoire')*

Feb 71. (7") **STONE BELIEVER. / SILLY SALLY** [-] [ ]

— Disbanded Spring '71, with DORMAN and REINHARDT forming CAPTAIN BEYOND. PINERA formed RAMATAM before later joining ALICE COOPER (1981-82). Re-formed 1974, as 4-piece with **BUSHY, BRAUN** and newcomers **HOWARD REITZES** (b.22 Mar'51, Southgate, California) – keyboards, vocals / **PHIL KRAMER** (b.12 Jul'52, Youngtown, Ohio) – bass, vocals

M.C.A. M.C.A.

Feb 75. (lp)(c) **SCORCHING BEAUTY** [ ] [ ]
– 1975 overture / Hard miseree / High on a mountain top / Am I down / People of the world / Searchin' circles / Pearly Gates / Lonely hearts / Before you go. *(cd-iss.Jun95 on 'Repertoire')*

Feb 75. (7") **SEARCHIN' CIRCLES. / PEARLY GATES** [-] [ ]

— **BILL DeMARTINES** – keyboards repl. REITZES

Dec 75. (lp)(c) **SUN AND STEEL** [ ] [ ]
– Sun and steel / Lightnin' / Beyond the Milky Way / Free / Scion / Get it out / I'm right, I'm wrong / Watch the world goin' by / Scorching beauty. *(cd-iss.Mar95 on 'Edsel')*

Jan 76. (7") **BEYOND THE MILKY WAY. / GET IT OUT** [ ] [ ]

— Broke up again in 1976, BUSHY formed JUICY GROOVE.

— In May'89, IRON BUTTERFLY reformed w/**DORMAN, BRAUN, REINHARDT** and new men **STEVE FELDMANN** – vocals / **DEREK HILLARD** – keyboards / **KENNY SUAREZ** – drums

– compilations, others, etc. –

Jan 72. Atlantic/ US= Atco; (lp) **EVOLUTION – THE BEST OF IRON BUTTERFLY** [ ] [ ] Dec 71
– Iron Butterfly theme / Possession / Unconscious power / Flowers and beads / Termination / In-a-gadda-da-vida / Soul experience / Stone believer / Belda-beast / Easy rider (let the wind pay the way) / Slower than guns.

1975. Atco; (lp) **STAR COLLECTION** [-] [ ]
Oct 75. Atlantic/ US= Atco; (d-lp) **TWO ORIGINALS OF . . .** [ ] [ ]
– (BALL / METAMORPHISIS)

May 93. Rhino; (cd) **LIGHT AND HEAVY: THE BEST OF IRON BUTTERFLY** [ ] [ ]

IRONHORSE (see under ⇒ BACHMAN-TURNER OVERDRIVE)

IRON MAIDEN

Formed: Leytonstone, East London, England . . . mid 1976 by DI'ANNO, MURRAY, HARRIS and SAMPSON, who first gigged around mid-'77. In 1978, they recorded demo EP 'THE SOUNDHOUSE TAPES', which got to the ears of DJ Neal Kay, who set them on a 'Heavy Metal Crusade' tour at London's Music Machine. Late in 1979, they signed to 'EMI', and had first of personnel changes (see below). Their debut single 'RUNNING FREE', hit the shops and UK Top 40 early 1980, and was followed by a self-titled debut album, which made Top 5. They had further chart triumphs, but surpassed everything before, when in 1982 they recruited Sheffield vocalist BRUCE DICKINSON. He added his power to give them first Top 10 single 'RUN TO THE HILLS' & first No.1 album 'THE NUMBER OF THE BEAST'. They went from strength to strength and scored a run of 7 UK Top 3 albums, and 17 UK Top 30 singles. Not only this, but like metal rivals DEF LEPPARD, they had stormed America. • **Style:** Instigated from early 1980 tag 'The New Wave Of British Heavy Metal', although their identity spurred from occult lyrics. Sounded not far removed from 70's heavies URIAH HEEP. • **Songwriters:** All mostly HARRIS and group. In the 90's, HARRIS or DICKINSON + GERS. Covered; COMMUNICATION BREAKDOWN (Led Zeppelin) / KILL ME, CE SOIR (Golden Earring) / SPACE STATION No.5 (Montrose). DICKINSON solo re-hashed; ALL THE YOUNG DUDES (hit; Mott The Hoople). • **Trivia:** Derek Riggs became the groups' artistic designer and created 'EDDIE', an evil skeleton comic-strip character, who appeared on album sleeves, poster bills & theatrical stage shows. Banned in Chile for being interpreted as 'devils and satanists'.

Recommended: LIVE AFTER DEATH (*8) / FEAR OF THE DARK (*8) / NO PRAYER FOR THE DYING (*7) / SEVENTH SON OF A SEVENTH SON (*7).

PAUL DI'ANNO (b.17 May'59, Chingford, Essex, England) – vocals / **DAVE MURRAY** (b.23 Dec'58) – guitar / **STEVE HARRIS** (b.12 Mar'57) – bass, vocals / **DOUG SAMPSON** – drums

Rock Hard | not issued

Jan 79. (7"ep) **THE SOUNDHOUSE TAPES** [ ] [-]
– Invasion / Iron Maiden / Prowler.

—— (Nov79) **CLIVE BURR** (b. 8 Mar'57) – drums repl. SAMPSON / **DENNIS STRATTON** (b. 9 Nov'54) – guitar repl. TONY PARSONS (brief stay)

E.M.I. | Harvest

Feb 80. (7") **RUNNING FREE. / BURNING AMBITION** [34] [ ]
Apr 80. (lp)(c) **IRON MAIDEN** [4] [ ]
– Prowler / Remember tomorrow / Running free / Phantom of the opera / Transylvania / Strange world / Charlotte the harlot / Iron maiden. *(re-iss.May85 on 'Fame' hit 71, cd-iss.Oct87) (re-iss.cd Jul94)*
May 80. (7"m) **SANCTUARY. / DRIFTER / I'VE GOT THE FIRE (live)** [29] [ ]
Oct 80. (7") **WOMEN IN UNIFORM. / INVASION** [35] [ ]
(12"+=) – Phantom of the opera (live).

—— **ADRIAN SMITH** (b.27 Feb'57) – guitar (ex-URCHIN) repl. STRATTON who formed LIONHEART

Feb 81. (lp)(c) **KILLERS** [12] [78]
– The ides of march / Wrathchild / Murders of the Rue Morgue / Another life / Ghenghis Khan / Innocent exile / Kllers / Prodigal son / Purgatory / Drifter. *(re-iss.May85 & cd-iss.Oct87 on 'Fame') (re-iss.cd Jul94)*
Mar 81. (7")(c-s)(7"clear)(7"red) **TWILIGHT ZONE. / WRATH CHILD** [31] [ ]
Jun 81. (7") **PURGATORY. / GHENGIS KHAN** [52] [ ]
Sep 81. (7"ep)(12"ep) **MAIDEN JAPAN** [43] [89] m-lp
– Remember tomorrow / Killers / Running free / Innocent exile.

—— **BRUCE DICKINSON** (b. 7 Aug'58, Sheffield, England) – vocals (ex-SAMSON) repl. DI'ANNO who formed LONE WOLF

Feb 82. (7")(7"pic-d) **RUN TO THE HILLS. / TOTAL ECLIPSE** [7] [ ]
Mar 82. (lp)(c) **THE NUMBER OF THE BEAST** [1] [33]
– Invaders / Children of the damned / The prisoner / 22 Acacia Avenue / The number of the beast / Run to the hills / Gangland / Hallowed be thy name. *(re-iss.May87) (also on pic-lp) (cd-iss.Jan87 & Apr88 on 'Fame') (re-iss.cd Jul94)*
Apr 82. (7")(7"red) **THE NUMBER OF THE BEAST. / REMEMBER TOMORROW** [18] [ ]

—— now **HARRIS, MURRAY, DICKINSON** and **SMITH** were joined by **NICKO McBAIN** (b. MICHAEL, 5 Jun'54) – drums (ex-PAT TRAVERS, ex-TRUST, ex-STREETWALKERS) repl. BURR who joined STRATUS

E.M.I. | Capitol

Apr 83. (7")(12"pic-d) **FLIGHT OF ICARUS. / I'VE GOT THE FIRE** [11] [ ]
May 83. (lp)(c) **PIECE OF MIND** [3] [14]
– Where eagles dare / Revelation / Flight of Icarus / Die with your boots on / The trooper / Still life / Quest for fire / Sun and steel / To tame a land. *(cd-iss.Dec86 & Jun91) (re-iss.cd Jul94)*
Jun 83. (7")(7"sha-pic-d) **THE TROOPER. / CROSS-EYED MARY** [12] [-]
Aug 84. (7") **2 MINUTES TO MIDNIGHT. / RAINBOW'S GOLD** [11] [-]
(12"pic-d+=) – Mission from 'Arry.
Sep 84. (lp)(c)(cd) **POWERSLAVE** [2] [21]
– Aces high / 2 minutes to midnight / Losfer words (big 'orra) / Flash of the blade / The duellists / Back in the village / Powerslave / Rime of the ancient mariner. *(also on pic-lp) (re-iss.Jun91) (re-iss.cd Jul94)*
Oct 84. (7") **ACES HIGH. / KING OF TWILIGHT** [20] [-]
(12"+=)(12"pic-d+=) – The number of the beast (live).
Sep 85. (7") **RUNNING FREE (live). / SANCTUARY (live)** [19] [-]
(12"+=)(12"pic-d+=) – Murders in the Rue Morgue (live).
Oct 85. (d-lp)(c)(cd) **LIVE AFTER DEATH (live)** [2] [19]
– Aces high / 2 minutes to midnight / The trooper / Revelations / Flight of Icarus / The rime of the ancient mariner / Powerslave / The number of the beast / Hallowed be thy name / Iron maiden / Run to the hills / Running free. (d-lp+c+=) Wrathchild / 22 Acacia Avenue / Children of the damned / Die with your boots on / Phantom of the opera. *(re-iss.Jun91) (re-iss.cd Jul94)*
Nov 85. (7") **RUN TO THE HILLS (live). / PHANTOM OF THE OPERA (live)** [26] [-]
(12"+=)(12"pic-d+=) – Losfer words (The big 'Orra) (live).
Aug 86. (7")(7"sha-pic-d) **WASTED YEARS. / REACH OUT** [18] [-]
(12"+=) – The sheriff of Huddersfield.
Sep 86. (lp)(c)(cd) **SOMEWHERE IN TIME** [3] [11]
– Caught somewhere in time / Wasted years / Sea of madness / Heaven can wait / The loneliness of the long distance runner / Stranger in a strange land / Deja-vu / Alexander the Great. *(re-iss.Jun91) (re-iss.cd Jul94)*
Nov 86. (7") **STRANGER IN A STRANGE LAND. / THAT GIRL** [22] [-]
(12"+=)(12"pic-d+=) – Juanita.
Mar 88. (7")(7"sha-pic-d) **CAN I PLAY WITH MADNESS. / BLACK BART BLUES** [3] [ ]
(12"+=)(cd-s+=) – Massacre.
Apr 88. (lp)(c)(cd) **SEVENTH SON OF A SEVENTH SON** [1] [12]
– Moonchild / Infinite dreams / Can I play with madness / The evil that men do / Seventh son of a seventh son / The prophecy / The clairvoyant / Only the good die young. *(also on pic-lp) (re-iss.Jun91) (re-iss.cd Jul94)*
Aug 88. (7")(7"sha-pic-d) **THE EVIL THAT MEN DO. / PROWLER '88** [5] [ ]
(12"+=)(cd-s+=) – Charlotte the harlot '88.
Nov 88. (7")(7"clear)(7"sha-pic-d) **THE CLAIRVOYANT (live). / THE PRISONER (live)** [6] [ ]
(12"+=)(cd-s+=)(12"pic-d+=) – Heaven can wait (live).
Nov 89. (7")(7"sha-pic-d) **INFINITE DREAMS (live). / KILLERS (live)** [6] [ ]
(12"+=)(c-s+=)(cd-s+=)(12"etched+=) – Still life (live).

—— (Feb90) **JANICK GERS** – guitar (ex-GILLAN, ex-WHITE SPIRIT, etc.) repl. SMITH who formed A.S.A.P.

Sep 90. (7")(c-s) **HOLY SMOKE. / ALL IN YOUR MIND** [3] [ ]
(12"+=)(cd-s+=)(12"pic-d+=) – Kill me ce soir.
Oct 90. (cd)(c)(lp) **NO PRAYER FOR THE DYING** [2] [17]
– Tailgunner / Holy smoke / No prayer for the dying / Public enemy number one / Fake warning / The assassin / Run silent run deep / Hooks in you / Bring your daughter . . . to the slaughter / Mother Russia. *(re-iss.cd Jul94)*
Dec 90. (7")(c-s)(7"pic-d) **BRING YOUR DAUGHTER . . . TO THE SLAUGHTER. / I'M A MOVER** [1] [ ]
(12"+=)(cd-s+=)(12"pic-d+=) – Communication breakdown.

—— In Summer 1991, HARRIS and McBAIN back up tennis stars McENROE & CASH on their version of LED ZEPPELIN'S 'Rock And Roll'. In Mar'92, BRUCE DICKINSON was to feature on single with Rowan Atkinson's comic character 'MR.BEAN & SMEAR CAMPAIGN' on a version of an Alice Cooper song '(I Want To Be) Elected'.

Apr 92. (7") **BE QUICK OR BE DEAD. / NODDING DONKEY BLUES** [2] [ ]
(12"+=)(cd-s+=)(12"pic-d+=) – Space station No.5.
May 92. (cd)(c)(lp) **FEAR OF THE DARK** [1] [12]
– Be quick or be dead / From here to eternity / Afraid to shoot strangers / Fear is the key / Childhood's end / Wasting love / The fugitive / Chains of misery / The apparition / Judas be my guide / Weekend warrior / Fear of the dark. *(re-iss.cd Jul94)*
Jul 92. (7") **FROM HERE TO ETERNITY. / ROLL OVER VELLA** [21] [ ]
(12"+=)(cd-s+=) – No prayer for the dying.
Mar 93. (7")(7"sha-pic-d) **FEAR OF THE DARK (live). / TAILGUNNER (live)** [8] [ ]
(cd-s) – ('A'side) / Hooks in you (live) / Bring your daughter . . . to the slaughter (live).
Mar 93. (cd)(c)(lp) **A REAL LIVE ONE (live)** [3] [ ]
– Be quick or be dead / From here to eternity / Can I play with madness / Wasting love / Tailgunner / The evil that men do / Afraid to shoot strangers / Bring your daughter . . .to the slaughter / Heaven can wait / The clairvoyant / Fear of the dark.

—— DICKINSON had already announced he had departed from group to go solo in'94.

Oct 93. (7"red) **HALLOWED BE THY NAME (live). / WRATHCHILD (live)** [9] [ ]
(12"pic-d+=)(cd-s+=) – The trooper (live) / Wasted years (live).
Oct 93. (cd)(c)(lp) **A REAL DEAD ONE (live)** [12] [ ]
– The number of the beast / The trooper / Prowler / Transylvania / Remember tomorrow / Where eagles dare / Sanctuary / Running free / 2 minutes to midnight / Iron Maiden / Hallowed be thy name.
Nov 93. (cd)(c)(lp) **LIVE AT DONINGTON 1992 (live)** [23] [ ]
– Be quick or be dead / The number of the beast / Wrathchild / From here to eternity / Can I play with madness / Wasting love / Tailgunner / The evil that men do / Afraid to shoot strangers.

—— **BLAZE BAILEY** – vocals (ex-WOLFSBANE) finally repl.DICKINSON

Sep 95. (c-s) **MAN ON THE EDGE / THE EDGE OF DARKNESS** [10] [ ]
(12"pic-d+=) – I live my way.
(cd-s+=) – Judgement day / (Blaze Bailey interview part 1).
(cd-s+=) – Justice of the peace / (Blaze Bailey interview part 2).
Oct 95. (cd)(c)(clear-d-lp) **THE X FACTOR** [9] [ ]
– Sign of the cross / Lord of the flies / Man on the edge / Fortunes of war / Look for the truth / The aftermath / Judgement of Heaven / Blood on the world's hands / The edge of darkness / 2 a.m. / The unbeliever.

– compilations, others, etc. –

Feb 90. E.M.I.; (d12")(cd-ep) **RUNNING FREE / BURNING AMBITION / SANCTUARY / DRIFTER (live) / I'VE GOT THE FIRE (live) / Listen with Nicko (part 1)** [10] [ ]
Feb 90. E.M.I.; (d12")(cd-ep) **WOMEN IN UNIFORM / INVASION / PHANTOM OF THE OPERA / TWILIGHT ZONE / WRATHCHILD / Listen with Nicko (part 2)** [10] [ ]
Feb 90. E.M.I.; (d12")(cd-ep) **PURGATORY / GENGHIS KHAN / RUNNING FREE / REMEMBER TOMORROW / KILLERS / INNOCENT EXILE / Listen with Nicko (part 3)** [5] [ ]

Mar 90. E.M.I.; (d12")(cd-ep) **RUN TO THE HILLS / TOTAL ECLIPSE / THE NUMBER OF THE BEAST / REMEMBER TOMORROW (live) / Listen with Nicko (part 4)** [3] [ ]
Mar 90. E.M.I.; (d12")(cd-ep) **FLIGHT OF ICARUS / I'VE GOT THE FIRE / THE TROOPER / CROSS-EYED MARY / Listen with Nicko (part 5)** [7] [ ]
Mar 90. E.M.I.; (d12")(cd-ep) **2 MINUTES TO MIDNIGHT / RAINBOW'S GOLD / MISSION FROM 'ARRY / ACES HIGH / KING OF TWILIGHT / THE NUMBER OF THE BEAST (live) / Listen with Nicko (part 6)** [11] [ ]
Apr 90. E.M.I.; (d12")(cd-ep) **RUNNING FREE / MURDERS OF THE RUE MORGUE / RUN TO THE HILLS / PHANTOM OF THE OPERA / LOSFER WORDS (THE BIG 'ORRA) / Listen with Nicko (part 7)** [9] [ ]
Apr 90. E.M.I.; (d12")(cd-ep) **WASTED YEARS / REACH OUT / THE SHERIFF OF HUDDERSFIELD / STRANGER IN A STRANGE LAND / THAT GIRL / JUANITA / Listen with Nicko (part 8)** [9] [ ]
Apr 90. E.M.I.; (d12")(cd-ep) **CAN I PLAY WITH MADNESS / BLACK BART BLUES / MASSACRE / THE EVIL THAT MEN DO / PROWLER '88 / CHARLOTTE THE HARLOT '88 / Listen with Nicko (part 9)** [10] [ ]
Apr 90. E.M.I.; (d12")(cd-ep) **THE CLAIRVOYANT (live) / THE PRISONER (live) / HEAVEN CAN WAIT (live) / INFINITE DREAMS (live) / KILLERS (live) / STILL LIFE (live) / Listen with Nicko (part 10)** [11] [ ]
— (all 10 releases above, basically hit peak number before crashing out of 50)
Aug 94. E.M.I.; (cd)(cd-vid) **MAIDEN ENGLAND (live)** [ ] [-]

NICKO McBRAIN

E.M.I. ?
Jul 91. (7") **RHYTHM OF THE BEAST. / BEEHIVE BOOGIE** [ ] [-]
(7"pic-d) – ('A'extended) / (McBrain damage interview).

Chris ISAAK

Born: 26 Jun'56, Stockton, California, USA. In 1984, after graduating with a degree in English & Communications, he formed own rockabilly outfit SILVERTONE, who became his backers from then on. They were found by Erik Jacobsen, who became manager and producer of album 'SILVERTONE' in 1985. His next 2 albums in '87 & '89 were also well-received and made the US Top 200. After many film-makers had used his music on movies such as 'Blue Velvet' & 'Wild At Heart', he signed new contract with 'Reprise' US and 'London' UK. In late 1990, he hit cross-Atlantic Top 10 with single 'WICKED GAME', which re-actified 1989 album 'HEART SHAPED WORLD' into US Top 10. He had already had a big hit in France with 'BLUE HOTEL'. This finally made the UK Top 20, when issued early 1991. • **Style:** Influenced by ELVIS PRESLEY, although sounding ROY ORBISON. • **Songwriters:** Self-penned except SOLITARY MAN (Neil Diamond). • **Trivia:** CHRIS has also played bit parts in movies 'Married To The Mob' & 'The Silence Of The Lambs'. In 1987, he appeared for the first time on Channel 4 TV's 'The Last Resort' which was hosted by fan Jonathan Ross.

Recommended: WICKED GAME (*6).

CHRIS ISAAK – vocals, guitar with back-up from SILVERTONE who feature **JAMES CALVIN WILSEY** – lead guitar / **ROWLAND SALLEY** – bass, vocals / **KENNEY DALE JOHNSON** – drums, vocals

Warners Warners
Mar 85. (lp)(c) **SILVERTONE** [-] [ ]
– Dancin' / Talk to me / Livin' for your lover / Back on your side / Voodoo / Funeral in the rain.
Apr 85. (7") **DANCIN'. / HAPPINESS** [-] [ ]
Jul 85. (7") **TALK TO ME. / LIVIN' FOR YOUR LOVER** [-] [ ]
Oct 85. (7") **GONE RIDIN' (theme from 'American Flyer'). / TEARS** [-] [ ]
Apr 87. (lp)(c)(cd) **CHRIS ISAAK** [-] [ ]
– You owe me some kind of love / Heart full of soul / Blue hotel / Lie to me / Fade away / Wild love / This love will last / You took my heart / Cryin' / Lovers game / Waiting for the rain to fall.
Jul 89. (lp)(c)(cd) **HEART SHAPED WORLD** [-] [7]
– Heart shaped world / I'm not waiting / Don't make me dream about you / Kings of the highway / Wicked game / Blue Spanish sky / Wrong to love you / Forever young / Nothing's changed / In the heart of the jungle / Diddley daddy. *(re-dist.Jan91, hit US No.7)*

London Reprise
Nov 90. (7")(c-s) **WICKED GAME. / COOL CAT WALK** [10] [6]
(12"+=)(cd-s+=) – Dark Spanish symphony / Blue Hawaiian music.

WEA Inter. Reprise
Jan 91. (cd)(c)(lp) **WICKED GAME** (compilation) [3] [-]
Wicked game / You owe me some kind of love / Blue Spanish sky / Heart shaped world / Funeral in the rain / Blue hotel / Dancin' / Nothing's changed / Voodoo / Lie to me / Wicked game (instrumental).
Jan 91. (7") **BLUE HOTEL. / WICKED GAME** [17] [ ]
(12"+=)(cd-s+=) – Wrong to love you.
Mar 91. (7")(c-s) **DANCIN'. / NOTHING'S CHANGED** [ ] [ ]
(12"+=)(cd-s+=) – Wild love.
Sep 91. (7") **BLUE SPANISH SKY. / WICKED GAME (instrumental)** [ ] [ ]
(12")(cd-s) – ('A'side) / Don't make me dream about you / The lovely ones / Lovers game.
Mar 93. (7")(c-s) **CAN'T DO A THING (TO STOP ME). / BLUE HOTEL** [36] [ ]
(cd-s) – ('A'side) / Tears / Blue Spanish sky / Lonely with a broken heart.
(cd-s) – ('A'side) / Talk to me / Gone ridin' / Waiting for the rain to fall.
Apr 93. (cd)(c)(lp) **SAN FRANCISCO DAYS** [12] [35]
– San Francisco days / Beautiful homes / Round 'n' round / Two hearts / Can't do a thing (to stop me) / Except the new girl / Waiting / Move along / I want your love / 5:15 / Lonely with a broken heart / Solitary man.
Jul 93. (7")(12")(c-s)(cd-s) **SAN FRANCISCO DAYS. / 5:15** [62] [ ]
Sep 93. (7")(c-s) **SOLITARY MAN. / WICKED GAME** [ ] [ ]
(cd-s+=) – Lie to me / Lovers game.
— SILVERTONE band; **MARK GOLDENBERG / GREGG ARREGUIN / FRANK MARTIN / JASON MORGAN / JEFF WATSON / STEPHEN BISHOP / DAVID GRISMAN / DAVID GRISSOM / BRUCE KAPHAN**
May 95. (c-s) **SOMEBODY'S CRYING / CHANGE YOUR MIND** [ ] [45]
(cd-s+=) – Little white cloud that lied. *(re-iss.Oct95)*
May 95. (cd)(c) **FOREVER BLUE** [27] [31]
– Baby did a bad bad thing / Somebody's crying / Graduation day / Go walking down there / Don't leave me on my own / Things go wrong / Forever blue / There she goes / Goin' nohere / Changed your mind / Shadows in a mirror / I believe / The end of everything.

ISLEY BROTHERS

Formed: Cincinatti, Ohio, USA ... 1957 by trio of brothers RONALD, RUDOLPH and O'KELLY. In the mid-50's, they had originally toured as a quartet with brother VERNON, until he was killed in a bicycle accident. After a number of independent singles, they signed to 'R.C.A.' in 1959. Their second 45 for the label 'SHOUT', cracked the US Top50 but eventually shifted over a million copies. It also enabled the brothers to move the family to Teaneck, New Jersey. After briefly signing for 'Atlantic', they joined 'Wand' in 1962, where they scored again with Top20 hit 'TWIST AND SHOUT' (later a US hit for The BEATLES). They failed to emulate previous successes, after switching to labels 'United Art', 'T-Neck' (their own label) and 'Atlantic' (again!). Luck changed early in 1966, when 'Tamla Motown' took them in, giving them US No.12 hit 'THIS OLD HEART OF MINE'. After two years there, they re-actified 'T-Neck' records, and immediately smashed American charts with 'IT'S YOUR THING'. Later in 1969, they added younger brothers ERNIE and MARVIN, plus cousin CHRIS JASPER on instruments. This was to be major turning point in their career, peaking in the mid-70's, when semi-classic albums '3+3', 'LIVE IT UP', 'THE HEAT IS ON' & 'HARVEST FOR THE WORLD', all gave them massive commercial glory. • **Style:** A typical classy soul outfit in the 60's, that progressed into heavier sound the following decade. This full sound, was already working for the likes of The TEMPTATIONS and The CHAMBERS BROTHERS. From 1977 onwards, they moved into the disco market, resurrecting their soulful roots throughout the 80's. • **Songwriters:** On 'Atlantic' in '61, their producers LEIBER & STOLLER provided them with little fortune. The following year, producer BERT BERNS wrote RIGHT NOW and hit TWIST AND SHOUT. In 1966 with 'Tamla Motown', they were presented hits by HOLLAND-DOZIER-HOLLAND. In 1969, their move to own 'T-Neck' records, provided them with confidence to write own material. In this time they also covered LOVE THE ONE YOU'RE WITH (Stephen Stills) / LAY LADY LAY (Bob Dylan) / SPLII THE WINE (War) / COLD BOLOGNA (Bill Withers) / FIRE AND RAIN (James Taylor) / MACHINE GUN (Jimi Hendrix) / OHIO (Neil Young) / SUMMER BREEZE (Seals & Croft) / IT'S TOO LATE + BROTHER, BROTHER, BROTHER (Carole King) / etc. • **Trivia:** In 1964, a 21 year-old member of their stage group, featured on their single 'TESTIFY'. His name was JIMI HENDRIX.

Recommended: ISLEY BROTHERS STORY VOL.1 (THE ROCK'N'ROLL YEARS 1959-68) / ISLEY BROTHERS STORY VOL.2 (THE T-NECK YEARS 1969-1985) (both *8).

RONALD ISLEY (b.21 May'41) – lead vocals / **RUDOLPH ISLEY** (b. 1 Apr'39) – vocal / **O'KELLY ISLEY** (b.25 Dec'37) – vocals

not issued Teenage
1957. (7") **THE COW JUMPED OVER THE MOON. / ANGELS CRIED** [-] [ ]

not issued Mark-X
1957. (7") **ROCKIN' McDONALD. / DON'T BE JEALOUS** [-] [ ]

not issued Gone
1958. (7") **EVERYBODY'S GONNA ROCK'N'ROLL. / I WANNA KNOW** [-] [ ]
1958. (7") **THE DRAG. / THE LOVE** [-] [ ]

not issued Cindy
1958. (7") **THIS IS THE END. / DON'T BE JEALOUS** [-] [ ]

R.C.A. R.C.A.
1959. (7") **TURN TO ME. / I'M GONNA KNOCK ON YOUR DOOR** [-] [ ]
Oct 59. (7") **SHOUT. / SHOUT (Pt.2)** [ ] [47] Sep 59
(re-iss.US Mar 62, hit No.94)
Jun 60. (lp) **SHOUT!** [ ] [ ] Oct 59
– Shout! (part 1 & 2) / Tell me who / How deep is the ocean (part 1 & 2) / Respectable (parts 1 & 2) / Say you love me / Open up your heart / He's got the whole world in his hands / Without a song / Yes indeed / Ring a ling a ling / That lucky old Sun / When the saints go marching in / Gypsy love song / St.Louis blues / Rock around the clock / Turn to me / Not one minute more / I'm gonna knock on your door. *(re-iss.Nov70) (cd-iss.on 'Bear Family' extra tracks)*
Feb 60. (7") **RESPECTABLE. / WITHOUT A SONG** [-] [ ]
Feb 60. (7") **RESPECTABLE. / I'M GONNA KNOCK ON YOUR DOOR** [ ] [-]
May 60. (7") **HE'S GOT THE WHOLE WORLD IN HIS HANDS. / HOW DEEP IS THE OCEAN** [ ] [ ]

Aug 60. (7") **GYPSY LOVE SONG. / OPEN UP YOUR HEART** | - | |
Nov 60. (7") **TELL ME WHO. / SAY YOU LOVE ME TOO** | | |

not issued | Atlantic

1961. (7") **TELL ME HOW TO SHIMMY. / JEEPERS CREEPERS** | - | |
1961. (7") **SHINE ON HARVEST MOON. / STANDING ON THE DANCE FLOOR** | - | |
1961. (7") **WRITE TO ME / YOUR OLD LADY** | - | |
1961. (7") **FOOL FOR YOU. / JUST ONE MORE TIME** | - | |

Oriole | Wand

Feb 62. (7") **RIGHT NOW. / THE SNAKE** | - | |
Jun 62. (7") **TWIST AND SHOUT. / SPANISH TWIST** | | 17 | May 62
('B' as "I.B. SPECIAL") *(UK-iss.Jul63 on 'Stateside', reached No.42)*
Oct 62. (7") **TWISTING WITH LINDA. / YOU BETTER COME HOME** | | 54 | Sep 62
Oct 62. (lp) **TWIST AND SHOUT** | | 61 |
– Twist and shout / Don't you feel / Hold on baby / Time after time / Twisting with Linda / I say love / Right now / Spanish twist / The drag / Don't be jealous / This is the end / Rockin' McDonald. *(UK-iss.Feb76 on 'DJM', c-iss.Oct82 on 'Orchid')*
Aug 63. (7") **NOBODY BUT ME. / I'M LAUGHING TO KEEP FROM CRYING** | | |
1963. (7") **HOLD ON BABY. / I SAY LOVE** | - | |

United Art | United Art

Oct 63. (7") **TANGO. / SHE'S GONE** | | |
1963. (7") **SURF AND SHOUT. / WHAT'CHA GONNA DO** | - | |
1964. (7") **YOU'LL NEVER LEAVE HIM. / PLEASE, PLEASE, PLEASE** | | |
Apr 64. (7") **WHO'S THAT LADY. / MY LITTLE GIRL** | - | |
Apr 64. (7") **SHAKE IT WITH ME BABY. / STAGGER LEE** | | - |
May 64. (lp) **THE FAMOUS ISLEY BROTHERS – TWISTING AND SHOUTING** | | |
– Surf and shout / Please please please / Do the twist / She's the one / Tango / What'cha gonna do / Stagger Lee / You'll never leave him / Let's go, let's go, let's go / Shake it with me baby / She's gone / Long tall Sally.

Atlantic | T-Neck

May 64. (7") **TESTIFY. / (part 2)** | - | |

Atlantic | Atlantic

Oct 64. (7") **THE LAST GIRL. / LOOKING FOR A LOVE** | | |
1965. (7") **SIMON SAYS. / WILD AS A TIGER** | - | |
1965. (7") **MOVE OVER AND LET ME DANCE. / HAVE YOU EVER BEEN DISAPPOINTED** | - | |

Tamla Motown | Tamla

Mar 66. (7") **THIS OLD HEART OF MINE (IS WEAK FOR YOU). / THERE'S NO LOVE LEFT** | 47 | 12 | Jan 66
(re-act.Oct68 reached No.3) (re-iss Jan 75)
Oct 66. (lp)**THIS OLD HEART OF MINE (IS WEAK FOR YOU).** | | | Jun 66
– Nowhere to run / Stop in the name of love / This old heart of mine (is weak for you) / Take some time out for love / I guess I'll always love you / Baby don't you do it / Who could ever doubt my love / Put yourself in my place / Just ain't enough love / I hear a symphony / There's no love left / Seek and you shall find. *(re-iss.+c-Jul81, re-iss.Dec68 reached No.23)*
Jun 66. (7") **TAKE SOME TIME OUT FOR LOVE. / WHO COULD EVER DOUBT MY LOVE** | | 66 | May 66
(re-iss.Nov69 – different cat. no.)
Aug 66. (7") **I GUESS I'LL ALWAYS LOVE YOU. / I HEAR A SYMPHONY** | 45 | 61 | Jul 66
1967. (lp) **TAMLA MOTOWN PRESENTS . . . THE ISLEY BROTHERS** | - | |
– . *(UK-iss.Mar73 on 'MFP')*
May 67. (7") **GOT TO HAVE YOU BACK. / JUST AIN'T ENOUGH LOVE** | | 93 |
Jan 68. (7") **ONE TOO MANY HEARTACHES. / THAT'S THE WAY LOVE IS** | - | |
Feb 68. (lp) **SOUL ON THE ROCKS** | | |
– Got to have you back / That's the way love is / Whispers (gettin' louder) / Tell it's just a rumour baby / One too many heartaches / It's out of the question / Why when love is gone / Save me from the misery / Little Miss Sweetness / Good things / Catching up on time / Behind a painted smile.
Apr 68. (7") **TAKE ME IN YOUR ARMS (ROCK ME A LITTLE WHILE). / WHY WHEN LOVE IS GONE** | | |
1968. (7") **BEHIND A PAINTED SMILE. / ALL BECAUSE I LOVE YOU** | - | |
1968. (7") **TAKE SOME TIME OUT FOR LOVE. / JUST AIN'T ENOUGH LOVE** | - | |

Major Minor | T-Neck

Jun 69. (7") **IT'S YOUR THING. / DON'T GIVE IT AWAY** | | 2 | Feb 69
Jul 69. (lp) **IT'S OUR THING** | | 22 | Apr 69
– This old heart of mine (is weak for you) / Who could ever doubt my love / I guess I'll always love you / That's the way love is / One too many heartaches / Why when love is gone / Just ain't enough love / Got to have you back / There's no love left / I hear a symphony / Take me in your arms (rock me for a while) / Take some time out for love.
Sep 69. (7") **I TURNED YOU ON. / I KNOW WHO YOU BEEN SOCKING IT TO** | | 23 | May 69
Aug 69. (7") **BLACK BERRIES. / (part 2)** | - | 79 |
1969. (7") **TURN ON, TUNE IN, DROP OUT. / (part 2)** | - | |

—— RONNIE, RUDOLPH and O'KELLY (who was now just KELLY) with brass section added **ERNIE ISLEY** – guitar, drums (later EVERETT COLLINS – drums) / **MARVIN ISLEY** – bass, percussion / **CHRIS JASPER** – keyboards

Stateside | T-Neck

Dec 69. (7") **BLESS YOUR HEART. / GIVE THE WOMEN WHAT THEY WANT** | - | |
Feb 70. (7") **WAS IT GOOD TO YOU. / I GOT TO GET MYSELF TOGETHER** | | 83 | Oct 69
Feb 70. (7") **KEEP ON DOIN'. / SAVE ME** | - | 75 |
Apr 70. (7") **IF HE CAN, YOU CAN. / HOLDIN' ON** | - | |
Jun 70. (lp) **THE BROTHERS: ISLEY** | | | Oct 69
– Black berries / Vacuum cleaner / I turned you on / Was it good to you / She's my girl / Get down off the train / Gotta get myself together / Feel like the world / Holdin' on.
Jul 70. (7") **GIRLS WILL BE GIRLS, BOYS WILL BE BOYS. / GET DOWN OFF THE TRAIN** | - | 75 |
Sep 70. (7") **GET INTO SOMETHING. / (part 2)** | - | 89 |
Sep 70. (lp) **LIVE AT THE YANKEE STADIUM (live)** | - | | Oct 69
– . *(shared with The Edwin Hawkins Singers + Brooklyn Bridge)*
Dec 70. (7") **FREEDOM. / I NEED YOU SO** | - | 72 |
May 71. (7") **WARPATH. / I GOT TO FIND ME ONE** | | |
Oct 71. (7") **LOVE THE ONE YOU'RE WITH. / HE'S GOT YOUR LOVE** | | 18 | Jun 71
Sep 71. (7") **SPILL THE WINE. / TAKE INVENTORY** | - | 49 |
Sep 71. (lp) **GIVIN' IT BACK** (all covers) | - | 71 |
– Fire and rain / Ohio machine gun / Lay lady lay / etc.
Dec 71. (7") **LAY LADY LAY. / VACUUM CLEANER** | - | 71 |
Mar 72. (7") **LAY AWAY. / FEEL LIKE THE WORLD** | - | 54 |
Jul 72. (lp) **BROTHER, BROTHER, BROTHER** | - | 29 | Jun 72
– Brother, brother / Put a little love in your heart / Sweet seasons / Keep on walkin' / Work to do / Pop that thang / Lay away / It's too late / Love put me on the corner.
Jun 72. (7") **POP THAT THANG. / I GOT TO FIND ME ONE** | - | 24 |
Oct 72. (7") **WORK TO DO. / BEAUTIFUL** | - | 51 |
Mar 73. (lp) **ISLEY BROTHERS LIVE (live)** | - | |
– Work to do / It's too late / It's your thing / Pop that thang / Love the one you're with / Lay lady lay / Lay away / Ohio / Machine gun. *(cd-iss Sep93)*
May 73. (7") **IT'S TOO LATE. / NOTHING TO DO BUT TODAY** | - | |

Epic | T-Neck

Aug 73. (7") **THAT LADY. / THAT LADY (part 2)** | 14 | 6 | Jul 73
Nov 73. (lp)(c) **3 + 3** | | | Sep 73
– That lady / Don't let me be lonely tonight / If you were there / You walk your way / Listen to the music / What it comes down to / Sunshine (go away today) / Summer breeze / The highways of my life. *(re-iss.Mar81 on 'Embassy-CBS') (cd-iss.Apr94 on 'Sony')*
Nov 73. (7") **WHAT IT COMES DOWN TO. / HIGHWAYS OF MY LIFE** | - | 55 |
Dec 73. (7") **THE HIGHWAYS OF MY LIFE. / DON'T LET ME BE LONELY TONIGHT** | 25 | - |
Apr 74. (7") **SUMMER BREEZE. / SUMMER BREEZE (part 2)** | 16 | 60 | Mar 74
Aug 74. (7") **LIVE IT UP. / LIVE IT UP (part 2)** | | 52 | Jul 74
Sep 74. (lp)(c) **LIVE IT UP** | | 14 |
– Live it up / Brown eyed girl / Need a little taste of love / Lover's eye / Midnight sky / Hello it's me / Ain't I been good to you.
Nov 74. (7") **NEED A LITTLE TASTE OF LOVE. / IF YOU WERE THERE** | | - |
Feb 75. (7") **MIDNIGHT SKY. / MIDNIGHT SKY (part 2)** | | 73 | Nov 74
Jul 75. (7") **FIGHT THE POWER. / FIGHT THE POWER (part 2)** | | 4 | Jun 75
Jul 75. (lp)(c) **THE HEAT IS ON** | | 1 | Jun 75
– Fight the power / Hope you feel better love / For the love of you / Sensuality / Make me say it again girl.
Jan 76. (7") **FOR THE LOVE OF YOU. / YOU WALK YOUR WAY** | | 22 | Nov 75
Jun 76. (7") **HARVEST FOR THE WORLD. / LET ME DOWN EASY** | 10 | - |
Jun 76. (lp)(c) **HARVEST FOR THE WORLD** | 50 | 9 | May 76
– Harvest for the world (prelude) / Harvest for the world / People of today / Who loves you better / Let me down easy / (At your best) You are love / So you wanna stay down / You still feel the need. *(re-iss.Jun85)(cd-iss.Oct93 on 'Sony Europe')*
Aug 76. (7") **HARVEST FOR THE WORLD. / (part 2)** | - | 63 |
Sep 76. (7") **WHO LOVES YOU BETTER. / WHO LOVES YOU BETTER (Pt.2)** | | 47 | May 76
Apr 77. (lp)(c) **GO FOR YOU GUNS** | 46 | 6 |
– Livin' in the life / Go for your guns / Voyage to Atlantis / Footsteps in the dark (Pts.1 & 2) / Tell me when you need it again (Pts.1 & 2) / The pride (Pts.1 & 2). *(re-iss.cd+c May93 on 'Sony Collectors')*
May 77. (7") **THE PRIDE. / THE PRIDE (part 2)** | | 63 |
Jul 77. (7") **VOYAGE TO ATLANTIS. / TELL ME WHEN YOU NEED IT AGAIN** | | - |
Apr 78. (7") **TAKE ME TO THE NEXT PHASE. / LIVIN' IN THE LIFE** | | - |
Apr 78. (7") **LIVIN' IN MY LIFE. / GO FOR YOUR GUNS** | - | 40 |
Apr 78. (lp)(c) **SHOWDOWN** | 46 | 4 |
– Showdown (Pt.1 & 2) / Groovin' with you / Ain't givin' up no love / Rockin' with fire (Pt.1 & 2) / Take me to the next phase (Pt.1 & 2) / Coolin' me out (Pt.1 & 2) / Fun and games / Love fever (Pt.1 & 2).
May 78. (7") **SO YOU WANNA STAY DOWN. / VOYAGE TO ATLANTIS** | - | |
Jun 78. (7") **TAKE ME TO THE NEXT PHASE. / TELL ME WHEN YOU NEED IT AGAIN** | - | |
Jul 78. (7") **GROOVE WITH YOU. / FOOTSTEPS IN THE DARK** | | |
Jul 79. (d-lp)(d-c) **WINNER TAKES ALL** | | 14 |
– I wanna be with you / Liquid love / Winner takes all / Life in the city / It's a disco night (rock don't stop) / Let's fall in love / (Can't you see) What you do to me / How lucky I am / You're the key to my heart / You're beside me / Love comes and goes / Let me into your life / Go for what you know / Mind over matter.
Aug 79. (7") **LIFE IN THE CITY. / LIFE IN THE CITY (part 2)** | | |
Oct 79. (7") **IT'S A DISCO NIGHT (ROCK DON'T STOP). / AIN'T GIVIN' UP ON LOVE** | 14 | 90 |
Jan 80. (7") **WINNER TAKES ALL. / FUN AND GAMES** | | |
Apr 80. (lp)(c) **GO ALL THE WAY** | | 8 |
– Go all the way / Say you will / Pass it on / The belly dancer / Here we go again / Don't say goodnight (it's time for love). *(cd-iss.Oct93 on 'Sony Europe')*
Jun 80. (7") **DON'T SAY GOODNIGHT (IT'S TIME FOR LOVE). / (part 2)** | | 39 | Apr 80
. (7") | - | |
Apr 81. (7") **TONIGHT IS THE NIGHT (IF I HAD YOU). / WHO SAID** | | - |
Apr 81. (lp)(c) **GRAND SLAM** | | 28 | Mar 81
– Tonight is the night (if I had you) / Hurry up and wait / I once had your love (and I can't let go) / Young girls / Party night / Don't let go / Who said.

Apr 81. (7") **HURRY UP AND WAIT. / ('A' instrumental)** [-] [58]
Jul 81. (7") **I ONCE HAD YOUR LOVE (AND CAN'T LET GO). / ('A' instrumental)** [-] [ ]
Nov 81. (7") **INSIDE YOU. / (part 2)** [-] [ ]
Nov 81. (7") **INSIDE YOU. / LOVE ZONE** [ ] [-]
Nov 81. (lp)(c) **INSIDE YOU** [ ] [45] Oct 81
– Inside you (Pt.1 & 2) / Baby hold on / First love / Welcome into my heart / Don't hold back your love (Pt.1 & 2) / Love merry-go-round / Love zone.
Jan 82. (7") **WELCOME INTO MY HEART. / PARTY NIGHT** [-] [ ]
Sep 82. (7") **THE REAL DEAL. / ('A'instrumental)** [-] [ ]
Sep 82. (lp)(c) **THE REAL DEAL** [ ] [87] Aug 82
– The real deal (Pt.1 & 2) / Are you with me / I'll do it all for you / Stone cold lover / It's alright with me / All in my lover's eyes / Under the influence.
Nov 82. (7") **IT'S ALRIGHT WITH ME. / ('A'instrumental)** [-] [ ]
Feb 83. (7") **ALL IN MY LOVER'S EYES. / I'LL DO IT ALL FOR YOU** [-] [ ]
Jun 83. (lp)(c) **BETWEEN THE SHEETS** [ ] [19] May 83
– Choosey lover / Touch me / I need your body / Let's make love tonight / Between the sheets / Ballad for the fallen soldier / Slow down children / Way out love / Gettin' over you / Rock you.
Jun 83. (7") **BETWEEN THE SHEETS. / (part 2)** [-] [ ]
Jun 83. (7")(12") **BETWEEN THE SHEETS. / THAT LADY** [52] [-]
Aug 83. (7")(12") **CHOOSEY LOVER. / CHOOSEY LOVER (part 2)** [ ] [ ]
Nov 83. (7") **LETS MAKE LOVE TONIGHT. / ('A'instrumental)** [-] [ ]

—— Reverted to original trio when others formed ISLEY, JASPER, ISLEY

Warners Warners

Nov 85. (7") **COLDER ARE MY NIGHTS. / BREAK THIS CHAIN** [-] [ ]
Dec 85. (7")(12") **COLDER ARE MY NIGHTS. / ('A'instrumental)** [ ] [ ]
Dec 85. (lp)(c) **MASTERPIECE** [ ] [ ]
– May I / My best was good enough / If leaving me is easy / You never know when you're gonna fall in love / Stay gold / Colder are my nights / Come to me / Release your love / The most beautiful girl.
Mar 86. (7") **MAY I. / ('A'instrumental)** [-] [ ]

—— Now a duo of RONNIE and RUDOLF, when KELLY died of a heart attack 31 Mar 86.

Warners Paisley P.

Jun 87. (7") **SMOOTH SAILIN' TONIGHT. / (part 2)** [-] [ ]
Jul 87. (lp)(c)(cd) **SMOOTH SAILIN'** [ ] [64] Jun 87
– Everything is alright / Pick it out / It takes a good woman / Send a message / Smooth sailin' tonight / Somebody I used to know / Come my way / I wish.
Sep 87. (7") **COME MY WAY. / (part 2)** [-] [ ]
Nov 87. (7") **I WISH. / ('A'instrumental)** [-] [ ]
Feb 88. (7") **IT TAKES A GOOD WOMAN. / (part 2)** [-] [ ]
Jun 89. (7") **SPEND THE NIGHT (CE SOIR). / ('A'instrumental)** [-] [ ]
Jul 89. (lp)(c)(cd) **SPEND THE NIGHT** [ ] [89]
– Spend the night (ce soir) / You'll never walk alone / One of a kind / Real woman / Come together / If you ever need somebody / Baby come back home / One of a kind (reprise).
Oct 89. (7") **YOU'LL NEVER WALK ALONE. / ONE OF A KIND** [-] [ ]
Nov 89. (7") **ONE OF A KIND. / YOU'LL NEVER WALK ALONE** [-] [ ]
Feb 90. (7") **IF YOU EVER NEED SOMEBODY. / ONE OF A KIND** [-] [ ]
May 90. (c-s) **COME TOGETHER /** [-] [ ]

In Mar 90, RONALD ISLEY backed ROD STEWART on their US Top10 version of THIS OLD HEART OF MINE. Rod of course, had made UK No.4 with it, in Dec75.

Jun 92. (cd)(c) **TRACKS OF LIFE** [-] [ ]
– Turn on the demon / Bedroom eyes / Morning love / Sensitive lover / Searching for a miracle / No axe to grind / Brazilian wedding song (setembro) / Dedicate this song / Got my licks in / I'll be there 4 u / Koolin' out / Lost in your love / Red hot.

– compilations, etc. –

Jun 64. R.C.A.; (7"ep) **THE ISLEY BROTHERS** [ ] [ ]
Aug 79. R.C.A.; (7") **SHOUT. / RESPECTABLE** [ ] [ ]
Apr 80. R.C.A.; (12"ep) **SHOUT / RESPECTABLE / RESPECTABLE (version) / TELL ME WHO** [ ] [ ]

Note; All below on 'Tamla Motown' until otherwise mentioned.

Jan 69. (7") **I GUESS I'LL ALWAYS LOVE YOU. / IT'S OUT OF THE QUESTION** [11] [ ]
Apr 69. (7") **BEHIND A PAINTED SMILE. / ONE TOO MANY HEARTACHES** [5] [ ]
Aug 69. (7") **PUT YOURSELF IN MY PLACE. / LITTLE MISS SWEETNESS** [13] [ ]
Sep 69. (lp) **BEHIND A PAINTED SMILE** [ ] [ ]
Oct 73. (7") **TELL ME IT'S JUST A RUMOUR BABY. / SAVE ME FROM THIS MISERY** [ ] [ ]
Dec 73. (lp) **THE ISLEY'S GREATEST HITS** [-] [ ]
Feb 76. (lp)(c) **SUPER HITS** [ ] [ ]
(re-iss.Oct81)
Sep 76. (7") **THIS OLD HEART OF MINE. / BEHIND A PAINTED SMILE** [ ] [ ]
(re-iss.Jun83)
May 83. (7") **I GUESS I'LL ALWAYS LOVE YOU. /** [ ] [ ]
Jul 83. (c-ep) **FLIP HITS** [ ] [ ]
– This old heart of mine / I guess I'll always love you / Behind a painted smile / Put yourself in my place.
Feb 87. (lp)(c)(cd) **GREATEST MOTOWN HITS** [ ] [ ]

Epic Epic

Mar 77. (7") **THAT LADY. / SUMMER BREEZE** [ ] [ ]
(re-iss.Apr83 on 'Old Gold')
Oct 77. (lp)(c) **FOREVER GOLD** [ ] [58]
(re-iss.Aug84)
Jan 79. (d-lp)(d-c) **TIMELESS** [ ] [ ]
May 82. (7") **HARVEST FOR THE WORLD. / HIGHWAYS OF MY LIFE** [ ] [ ]
(re-iss.Apr83 on 'Old Gold')
Jul 84. (7") **HARVEST FOR THE WORLD. / SUMMER BREEZE** [ ] [ ]
Nov 88. (7") **HARVEST FOR THE WORLD. / SUMMER BREEZE** [ ] [ ]
(12"+=) – Who loves you better (parts 1 & 2).

Jun 84. (lp)(c) **GREATEST HITS: ISLEY BROTHERS VOL.1** [ ] [ ]
Oct 94. (cd) **THE BEST** [ ] [ ]
1970. T-Neck; (lp) **IN THE BEGINNING: WITH JIMI HENDRIX** [-] [ ]
Jul 68. Hallmark; (lp) **THE ISLEY BROTHERS** [ ] [-]
(re-iss.Feb82 on 'Regal Starline')
Feb 69. Marble Arch; (lp) **TAKE SOME TIME OUT FOR THE ISLEY BROTHERS** [ ] [-]
Oct 70. Regal Starline; (lp)(c) **THE ISLEY BROTHERS' GREATEST HITS** [ ] [-]
Feb 76. D.J.M.; (7") **TWIST AND SHOUT. / TIME AFTER TIME** [ ] [-]
Feb 82. Orchid; (c) **TWIST AND SHOUT** [ ] [-]
Apr 83. Bulldog; (lp)(c) **20 GOLDEN PIECES OF THE ISLEY BROTHERS** [ ] [-]
Sep 83. Scoop; (7"ep)(c-ep) **6 TRACK HITS** [ ] [-]
– Listen to the music / Brown eyed girl / Harvest for the world / Under the influence / You still feel the need / Don' let me be lonely tonight.
1986. Stateside; (lp)(c) **LET'S GO** [ ] [-]
Mar 88. Telstar; (lp)(c)(cd) **GREATEST HITS** [41] [-]
Dec 88. Bear Family; (cd) **SHOUT** [ ] [-]
Mar 89. Blatant; (lp) **THE SOUND OF SOUL** [ ] [-]
Apr 90. Ace; (cd) **TWIST AND SHOUT WITH RUDOLPH, RONALD AND O'KELLY** [ ] [-]
May 91. Rhino; (d-cd) **ISLEY BROTHERS STORY VOL 1: ROCK'N'SOUL YEARS 1959-68** [ ] [ ]
May 91. Rhino; (d-cd) **ISLEY BROTHERS STORY VOL.2: THE T-NECK YEARS 1969-85** [ ] [ ]
Apr 91. E.M.I.; (cd) **THE COMPLETE U.A. SESSIONS** [ ] [ ]
Feb 95. B.A.M.; (cd) **PEARLS OF THE PAST** [ ] [-]
Jun 95. Epic; (cd) **BEAUTIFUL BALLADS** [ ] [-]
Jun 95. Epic; (cd) **FUNKY FAMILY** [ ] [-]

IT BITES

Formed: Wyndham, Cumbria, England . . . 1982 by DUNNERY, DALTON, NOLAN and BECK, although they split in 1984, when DUNNERY moved to a squat in Peckham, London. He was soon joined by the others, who after a gig, met A&R man Martin Mayhead, who secured them a deal with 'Virgin' in 1985. After a tour supporting GO WEST, they issued debut 45 'ALL IN RED', but this flopped. Their next in Jun'86 'CALLING ALL THE HEROES', became a UK Top 10 smash, and was quickly followed by a Top 40 lp 'THE BIG LAD IN THE WINDMILL'. They scored with minor hits from then on, but surprised many critics by having 2 further Top 50 albums. • **Style:** A unique blend of GENESIS/YES type progressive, keyboard orientated rock, which although slightly pop at the outset, became more adventurous and self-indulgent from 1988. • **Songwriters:** DUNNERY lyrics / group compositions, with no cover versions. • **Trivia:** STEVE HILLAGE produced 1988 single 'MIDNIGHT', and ROGER DEAN (former lp sleeve artist for YES, etc) designed their 1989 album 'EAT ME IN ST.LOUIS'. Around the same time it was recorded, DUNNERY was called on by his heroes, to guest on their ANDERSON, BRUFORD, WAKEMAN & HOWE (aka YES) album. Not to be outdone, NOLAN featured on TONY BANKS' 'Bankstatement' album.

Recommended: ONCE AROUND THE WORLD (*6) / EAT ME IN ST.LOUIS (*7)

FRANCIS DUNNERY – vocals, guitar / **JOHN BECK** – keyboards / **RICHARD NOLAN** – bass / **ROBERT DALTON** – drums

Virgin Geffen

Mar86. (7") **ALL IN RED. / HEARTBREAKER** [ ] [ ]
(12"+=) – ('A' extended).
Jun 86. (7")(7"pic-d) **CALLING ALL THE HEROES. / STRANGE BUT TRUE** [6] [ ]
(12"+=) – ('A' extended).
(d7"+=) – All in red / Heartbreaker.
Jul 86. (lp)(c)(cd) **THE BIG LAD IN THE WINDMILL** [35] [ ]
– I got you eating out of my hand / All in red / Whole new world / Screaming on the beaches / Wanna shout / Turn me loose / Cold, tired and hungry / Calling all the heroes / You'll never go the Heaven / The big lad in the windmill.
Sep 86. (7") **WHOLE NEW WORLD. / BLACK DECEMBER** [54] [ ]
(12"+=) – Calling all the heroes (live).
(d7"++=) – Screaming on the beaches (live).
Nov 86. (7") **WHOLE NEW WORLD. / STRANGE BUT TRUE** [-] [ ]
May 87. (7") **OLD MAN AND THE ANGEL. / CASTLES** [72] [ ]
(12"+=) – ('A'extended) / ('B'extended).
(cd-s+=) – Calling all the heroes (extended).
Feb 88. (7") **KISS LIKE JUDAS. / STARING AT THE WHITEWASH** [ ] [ ]
(12"+=)(cd-s+=) – ('A'extended).
Mar 88. (lp)(c)(cd) **ONCE AROUND THE WORLD** [43] [ ]
– Midnight / Kiss like Judas / Yellow Christian / Rose Marie / Black December / Old man and the angel / Plastic dreamer / Once around the world. *(cd+=)* – Hunting the whale.
Apr 88. (small square disc-7") **MIDNIGHT. / YOU'LL NEVER GO TO HEAVEN (live)** [ ] [ ]
(12"+=)(cd-s+=) – ('A'extended).
Apr 89. (7")(7"sha-pic-d) **STILL TOO YOUNG TO REMEMBER. / VAMPIRES** [66] [ ]
(12"+=)(3"cd-s+=) – ('A'extended).
Jun 89. (lp)(c) **EAT ME IN ST. LOUIS** [40] [ ]
– Positively animal / Underneath your pillow / Let us all go / Still too young to remember / Murder of the Planet Earth / People of America / Sister Sarah / Leaving without you. *(cd+=)* – Till the end of time / Charlie. *(ltd. 3" cd-ep w/a)*– HAVING A GOOD DAY / REPRISE / BULLET IN THE BARREL
Jul 89. (7") **SISTER SARAH. / BULLET IN THE BARREL** [ ] [ ]
(12"+=)(12"pic-d+=) – The woman is an addict.

(3"cd-s++=) – Heartbreaker.

Oct 89. (7") **UNDERNEATH YOUR PILLOW. / STILL TOO YOUNG TO REMEMBER (live)** ☐ ☐
(10"pic-d+=)(3"cd-s+=) – ('A' live version).

Feb 90. (7") **STILL TOO YOUNG TO REMEMBER (remix). / HAVING A GOOD DAY** 60 ☐
(12"+=) – ('A'extended).
(cd-s++=) – I'll meet you in Spring.

— (Nov90) **LEE KNOTT** – vocals (ex-INNOCENCE LOST) repl. DUNNERY (now solo). / added **JOHN BECK** – now guitar

Aug 91. (cd)(c)(d-lp) **THANKYOU AND GOODNIGHT (live)** 59 ☐
– Kiss like Judas / All in red / Underneath your pillow / Murder of the Planet Earth / Ice melts (into water) / Yellow Christian / You'll never go to Heaven / Calling all the heroes / Screaming on the boards / Still too young to remember.

— Had already disbanded, but re-formed as SISTER SARAH, then NAVAJO KISS.

compilations, etc. –

Mar 95. Virgin; (cd) **CALLING ALL THE HEROES – THE BEST OF IT BITES** ☐ -

FRANCIS DUNNERY

Atlantic Atlantic

Jul 94. (c-ep)(cd-ep) **AMERICAN LIFE IN THE SUMMERTIME / NEW VIBRATION / LIVING IN THE PAST** ☐ ☐

Aug 94. (cd)(c) **FEARLESS** ☐ ☐
– American life in the summertime / Homegrown / Fade away / Climbing up the love tree / What's he gonna say / Feel like kissing you again / King of the blues / Everyone's a star / Couldn't find a reason / New vibration / Good life. *(re-iss.Jan95)*

Oct 94. (cd-s) **WHAT'S HE GONNA SAY? / LET'S END IT NOW (acoustic) / WHAT THE WORLD NEEDS NOW (acoustic)** ☐ ☐
(c-s+cd-s) – ('A'side) / American life in the summertime (acoustic) / Homegrown (acoustic).

IT'S A BEAUTIFUL DAY

Formed: San Francisco, California, USA . . .mid 1967, by classically endowed DAVID LaFLAMME. Released eponymous debut on local"Sound" label in 1968, before "Columbia" took over reigns. In 1969-70, it hit US & UK Top 50, and shelled inside, the classic track/single "WHITE BIRD". In summer of 1970, they followed this with another cross-Atlantic Top 50 lp "MARRYING MAIDEN", but they lost momentum by late '71. • **Style:** West-coast art-rock outfit, similiar to JEFFERSON AIRPLANE, but who relied on classically trained violin virtuoso of LaFLAMME. • **Songwriters:** LaFLAMME contributed most. • **Trivia:** Most of their guests on 1971 lp "CHOICE QUALITY STUFF", went on to join SANTANA.

Recommended: IT'S A BEAUTIFUL DAY (*8)/ MARRYING MAIDEN (*7).

DAVID LaFLAMME (b. 5 Apr'41, Salt Lake City, Utah, USA) – electric violin / **PATTIE SANTOS** (b.16 Nov'49) – vocals / **BILL GREGORY** – guitar / **MITCHELL HOLMAN** – bass / **VAL FUENTES** (b.25 Nov'47) – drums. Plus guest (wife) **LINDA LaFLAMME** – keyboards, co-composer

C.B.S. Columbia

May 69. (lp) **IT'S A BEAUTIFUL DAY** 58 47
– White bird / Hot summer day / Wasted union blues / Girl nothing eyes / Bombay calling / Bulgaria / Time is. *(hit UK chart May70) (re-iss.Sep79)*

Aug 69. (7") **WHITE BIRD. / WASTED UNION BLUES** ☐ ☐

Feb 70. (7") **SOAPSTONE MOUNTAIN. / GOOD LOVIN'** - ☐

Apr 70. (7") **SOAPSTONE MOUNTAIN. / DO YOU REMEMBER THE SUN** ☐ -

Jul 70. (lp)(c) **MARRYING MAIDEN** 45 28
– Don and Dewey / The dolphins / Essence of now / Hoedown / Soapstone mountain / Waiting for the song / Let a woman flow / It comes right down to you / Good lovin' / Galileo / Do you remember the sun. *(re-iss.+c.Apr82)*

Nov 70. (7") **BABY BE WISE. / EASY WOMAN** - ☐

— **HAL WAGENET** – guitar repl. GREGORY / **TOM FOWLER** – bass repl. JOHN NICHOLAS who had repl. HOLMAN / added **FRED WEBB** – keyboards

Dec 71. (lp)(c) **CHOICE QUALITY STUFF / ANYTIME** ☐ ☐
– Creed of love / Bye bye baby / The Grand Camel Suite / No word for glad / Lady love / Words / Place of dreams / Oranges & apples / Anytime / Bitter wine / Misery love / Company.

Jan 72. (7") **ANYTIME. / APPLE AND ORANGES** - ☐

Dec 72. (lp)(c) **AT CARNEGIE HALL (live)** ☐ ☐
– Give your woman what she wants / A hot summer day / Angels and animals / Bombay calling / Going to another party / Good lovin' / The Grand Camel suite / White bird.

Feb 73. (7") **WHITE BIRD (live). / WASTED UNION BLUES (live)** - ☐

— **BUD COCKRELL – bass** repl. FOWLER who later joined FRANK ZAPPA

Apr 73. (lp)(c) **. . .TODAY** ☐ ☐
– Ain't that lovin' you baby / Child / Down on the bayou / Watching you watching me / Mississippi Delta / Ridin' thumb / Time / Lie to me / Burning low / Creator.

Apr 73. (7") **AIN'T THAT LOVIN' YOU BABY. / TIME** ☐ ☐

Feb 74. (lp)(c) **1,001 NIGHTS (live)** ☐ ☐
– White bird / Ain't that lovin' you baby / Ridin' thumb / Bombay calling / A hot summer day / Soapstone mountain / The dolphins / Don and Dewey / Bye bye baby / Hoedown. *(re-iss.+c.Mar82)*

— Break-up 1974. BUD joined PABLO CRUISE around mid'73.

DAVID LaFLAMME

eventually went solo + **MITCHELL FROOM** – keyboards / **JAMES RALSTON** – guitar / **DOUG KILMER** – bass / **PETER MILO** – drums / **DOMINIQUE DELACROIX** – vocals

Amherst Amherst

Dec 76. (lp) **WHITE BIRD** ☐ ☐
– White bird / Hot summer day / Swept away / Easy woman / This man / Baby be wise / Spirit of America.

Dec 76. (7") **WHITE BIRD./ SPIRIT OF AMERICA** - 89

1978. (lp) **INSIDE OUT** ☐ ☐
– Who's gonna love me? / My life / Nightsong / Forever and a day / Somewhere down the road / Where flamingos fly / Need somebody / The day you went away / Can't wait until tomorrow. *(cd-iss.w/ other lp Sep95 on 'Edsel')*

— DAVID retired from music scene the same year.

IVEYS (see under ⇒ BADFINGER)

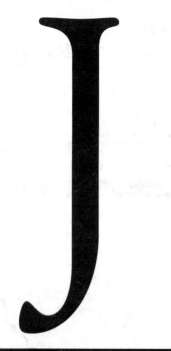

David J (see under ⇒ BAUHAUS)

JACK FROST (see under ⇒ CHURCH)

JACK OFFICERS (see under ⇒ BUTTHOLE SURFERS)

Joe JACKSON

Born: 11 Aug'54, Burton-On-Trent, Staffordshire, England. Raised from a very early age in Gosport, near Portsmouth. He left school with top grade music honour and enrolled at The Royal College Of Music in 1973. After a spell in JOHNNY DANKWORTH's NATIONAL YOUTH JAZZ ORCHESTRA, he joined pub rock outfit ARMS & LEGS. They released 3 flop singles for 'MAM' between 1976-1977, before he quit. In 1977, he became musical director for 'Opportunity Knocks' (TV talent show, hosted by Hughie Green) winners COFFEE AND CREAM. The next year, he moved away from the cabaret scene and to London, to record own demo tape, which 'A&M''s David Kershenbaum approved of. He also produced first solo attempt, 'IS SHE REALLY GOING OUT WITH HIM?', but it took a re-issue of this 45 in Summer 1979 to break him into UK + US charts. Although he had several more UK hits, his appeal came mainly in the albums market. • **Style:** Progressed from ELVIS COSTELLO-like comparisons to a more sophisticated rock-pop, which incorporated many styles, including jazz, Latin-salsa and ballads. In 1982, he moved to New York, USA, after the bust-up of his marriage. • **Songwriters:** Self-penned, except his second jazz LOUIS JORDAN inspired album JUMPIN' JIVE, which contained covers of 40's & 50's CAB CALLOWAY / GLENN MILLER. JOE also went on to cover OH WELL (Fleetwood Mac) / MAKING PLANS FOR NIGEL (Xtc). • **Trivia:** He also produced The KEYS in '81, and reggae outfits RASSES and The TOASTERS.

Recommended: STEPPIN' OUT – THE VERY BEST OF JOE JACKSON (*6)

ARMS AND LEGS

JOE JACKSON – piano, violin, vocals, harmonica / **MARK ANDREWS** – vocals / **GRAHAM MABY** – bass

		M.A.M.	not issued
Apr 76.	(7") **JANICE. / SHE'LL SURPRISE YOU**		-
Aug 76.	(7") **HEAT OF THE NIGHT. / GOOD TIMES**		-
Feb 77.	(7") **IS THERE ANYMORE WINE. / SHE'LL SURPRISE YOU**		-

JOE JACKSON

solo – lead vocals, piano with backing band **GRAHAM MABY** – bass / **GARY SANFORD** – guitar / **DAVE HOUGHTON** – drums

		A & M	A & M
Sep 78.	(7") **IS SHE REALLY GOING OUT WITH HIM?. / YOU GOT THE FEVER**		-
Jan 79.	(lp)(c) **LOOK SHARP!**	40	20
	– One more time / Sunday papers / Is she really going out with him? / Happy loving couples / Throw it away / Baby stick around / Look sharp! / (Do the) Instant mash / Pretty girls / Got the time. *(re-iss.Aug79 on white-lp re-iss.Mar82, re-iss.Jul85 on 'Hallmark') (cd-iss.Nov84 & re-iss.1988)*		
Feb 79.	(7") **SUNDAY PAPERS. / LOOK SHARP!**		-
May 79.	(7") **IS SHE REALLY GOING OUT WITH HIM? / (DO THE) INSTANT MASH**	-	21
May79.	(7"white)(10"white) **ONE MORE TIME. / DON'T ASK ME**		-
Jul 79.	(7") **IS SHE REALLY GOING OUT WITH HIM?. / YOU GOT THE FEVER**	13	-
Aug 79.	(7") **IT'S DIFFERENT FOR GIRLS. / COME ON**	-	
Oct 79.	(7") **I'M THE MAN. / COME ON (live)**		
Oct 79.	(lp)(c)(5x7"box) **I'M THE MAN**	12	22
	– On your radio / Geraldine and John / Kinda kute / It's different for girls / I'm the man / The band wore blue shirts / Don't wanna be like that / Amateur hour / Get that girl / Friday. *(re-iss.+cd.1988)*		
Dec 79.	(7") **IT'S DIFFERENT FOR GIRLS. / FRIDAY**	5	-
Mar 80.	(7") **KINDA KUTE. / GERALDINE AND JOHN**		-

JOE JACKSON BAND

Jun 80.	(7")(12") **THE HARDER THEY COME. / OUT OF STYLE / TILT**		-
Oct 80.	(7") **MAD AT YOU. / ENOUGH IS NOT ENOUGH**		-
Oct 80.	(lp)(c) **BEAT CRAZY**	42	41
	– Beat crazy / One to one / In every dream home (a nightmare) / The evil eye / Mad at you / Crime don't pay / Someone up there / Battleground / Biology / Pretty boys / Fit. *(cd-iss.1988) (re-iss.c. Jan93)*		
Nov 80.	(7") **ONE TO ONE. / ENOUGH IS NOT ENOUGH**	-	
Jan 81.	(7") **BEAT CRAZY. / IS SHE REALLY GOING OUT WITH HIM?**		
Mar 81.	(7") **ONE TO ONE. / SOMEONE UP THERE**		

JOE JACKSON'S JUMPIN' JIVE

JOE retained **GRAHAM MABY** plus **PETE THOMAS** – sax / **RAUOL OLIVERA** – trumpet / **DAVE BITELI** – wind instr. NICK WELDON – piano / **LARRY TOLFREE** – drums / **NICK WELDON** – piano

Jun 81.	(7") **JUMPIN' JIVE. / KNOCK ME A KISS**	43	
Jun 81.	(lp)(c) **JOE JACKSON'S JUMPIN' JIVE**	14	42
	– Jumpin' with symphony Sid / Jack, you're dead / Is you or is you ain't my baby / We the cats will help ya / San Francisco fan / Five guys named Moe / Jumpin' jive / You run your mouth (and I'll run my business) / What's the use of getting sober (when you're gonna get drunk again) / You're my meat / Tuxedo junction / How long must I wait for you. *(cd-iss.1988) (re-iss.cd+c May93 on 'Spectrum')*		
Aug 81.	(7") **JACK, YOU'RE DEAD. / FIVE GUYS NAMED MOE**		

JOE JACKSON

SUE HADJOPOULOS – percussion, vocals, flute, etc. repl. WELDON + horns

Jun 82.	(7")(7"pic-d) **REAL MEN. / CHINATOWN**		
Jun 82.	(lp)(c) **NIGHT AND DAY**	3	4
	– Another world / Chinatown / T.V. age / Target / Steppin' out / Breaking us in two / Cancer / Real men / A slow song. *(cd-iss.1983)*		
Aug 82.	(7") **BREAKING US IN TWO. / EL BLANCO**		-
Aug 82.	(7") **STEPPIN' OUT. / CHINATOWN**	-	6
Oct 82.	(7")(12") **STEPPIN' OUT. / ANOTHER WORLD**	6	-
Jan 83.	(7") **BREAKING US IN TWO. / TARGET**	-	18
Feb 83.	(7") **BREAKING US IN TWO. / EL BLANCO**	59	-
	(12"+=) – T.V. age.		
May 83.	(7") **A SLOW SONG. / REAL MEN**		
Jul 83.	(7") **ANOTHER WORLD. / ORTO MUNDO**	-	

— added **JOY ASKEW** – synthesizers

Aug 83.	(7") **COSMOPOLITAN. / BREAKDOWN**		
Sep 83.	(lp)(c) **MIKE'S MURDER (soundtrack)**		64
	– Cosmopolitan / 1-2-3-go (this town's a fairground) / Laundromat Monday / Memphis / Moonlight / Zemeo / Breakdown / Moonlight theme.		
Nov 83.	(7") **MEMPHIS. / BREAKDOWN**	-	85

— retained only **MABY** and brought in **GARY BURKE** – drums / **VINNIE ZUMMO** – guitar / **ED ROYNESDAL** – keyboards, violin / **TONY AIELLO** – sax, flute / **MICHAEL MORREALE** – wind

Mar 84.	(lp)(c) **BODY AND SOUL**	14	20
	– The verdict / Cha cha loco / Not here, not now / You can't get what you want ('till you know what you want) / Go for it / Loisaida / Be my number two / Heart of ice. *(cd-iss.Oct84)*		
Apr 84.	(7")(12") **HAPPY ENDING. / LOISAIDA**	58	57 Jul 84
Jun 84.	(7")(12") **BE MY NUMBER TWO. / HEART OF ICE**	70	
	(7") – ('A'side) / Is she really going out with him?		
Sep 84.	(7") **YOU CAN'T GET WHAT YOU WANT ('TILL YOU KNOW WHAT YOU WANT). / CHA CHA LOCO**		15 Apr 84
	(12"+=) – ('A' dub version).		

— **RICK FORD** – bass, guitar, vox repl. MABY, AIELLO, ROYNESDAL + MORREALE

Mar 86.	(d-lp)(c)(cd) **BIG WORLD (live)**	41	34
	– Wild west / Right and wrong / (It's a) Big world / Precious time / Tonight and forever / Shanghai sky / Fifty dollar love affair / We can't live together / Forty years / Survival / Soul kiss / The jet-set / Tango Atlantico / Hometown / Man in the street. *(not 4-sided d-lp, but 3-sided)*		
Apr 86.	(7") **RIGHT OR WRONG. / BREAKING US IN TWO (live)**		
	(12"+=) – I'm the man (live).		
Jun 86.	(7")(12") **HOME TOWN. / TANGO ATLANTICO**		
Apr 87.	(lp)(c)(cd) **WILL POWER**		
	– No Pasaran / Solitude / Will power / Nocturne / Symphony in one movement.		
May 87.	(7") **WILL POWER. / NOCTURNE**		-
Apr 88.	(7")(12") **JUMPIN' JIVE (live). / MEMPHIS (live)**	-	
May 88.	(d-lp)(c)(cd) **LIVE 1980/86 (live)**	66	91
	– One to one / I'm the man / Beat crazy / Is she really going out with him? / Cancer / Don't wanna be like that / On your radio / Fools in love / Cancer / Is she really going out with him? (acappella version) / Look sharp! / Sunday papers / Real men / Is she really going out with him? (acoustic) / Memphis / A slow song / Be my number two / Breaking us in two / It's different for girls / You can't get what you want ('till you know what you want) / Jumpin' jive / Steppin' out.		
Jun 88.	(7") **LOOK SHARP (live). / MEMPHIS (live**	-	
Aug 88.	(7") **(HE'S A) SHAPE IN A DRAPE. / SPEEDWAY**		

(12"+=) – Sometime in Chicago.

Nov 88. (lp)(c)(cd) **TUCKER – A MAN AND HIS DREAMS (Soundtrack)** [ ] [ ]
– Captain of industry / Car of tomorrow / No chance blues / (He's a) Shape in a drape / Factory / Vera / It pays to advertise / Tiger rag / Showtime in Chicago / Loan bank loan blues / Speedway / Marilee / Hangin' in Howard Hughes' hangar / The toast of the town / Abe's blues / The trial / Freedom swing / Rhythm delivery.

— Now with 10-piece line-up, **MABY, ZUMMO, BURKE, ASKEW, AIELLO, FORD, ROYNESDAL, HADJOPOULOS + TOM TEELEY** – guitar / **ANTHONY COX** – bass

Apr 89. (lp)(c)(cd) **BLAZE OF GLORY** [36] [61]
– Tomorrow's child / Me and you (against the world) / Down to London / Sentimental thing / Acropolis now / Blaze of glory / Rant and rave / Nineteen forever / The best I can do / Evil empire / Discipline / The uman touch.

May 89. (7") **NINETEEN FOREVER. / ACROPOLIS NOW (instrumental)** [ ] [ ]
(cd-s+=) – ('A'extended).

Oct 89. (7")(12") **DOWN TO LONDON. / YOU CAN'T GET WHAT YOU WANT (TIL YOU KNOW WHAT YOU WANT)** [ ] [ ]
(cd-s+=) – Sunday papers.

Aug 90. (7")(c-s) re-issue **STEPPIN' OUT. / SENTIMENTAL THING** [ ] [ ]
(cd-s+=) – It's a big worth.

Sep 90. (cd)(c)(lp) **STEPPIN' OUT – THE VERY BEST OF JOE JACKSON** (compilation) [7] [ ]
– Is she really going out with him? / Fools in love / I'm the man / It's different for girls / Beat crazy / Jumpin' jive / Breaking us in two / Steppin' out / Slow song (live) / You can't get what you want ('till you know what you want) / Be my number two / Right and wrong / Home town / Down to London / Nineteen forever.

Virgin | Virgin

Apr 91. (7") **STRANGER THAN FICTION. / DROWNING** [ ] [ ]
(12"+=)(cd-s+=) – Different for girls (acoustic).

May 91. (cd)(c)(lp) **LAUGHTER AND LUST** [41] [ ]
– Obvious song / Goin' downtown / Stranger than fiction / Oh well / Jamie G / Hit single / It's all too much / When you're not around / The other me / Trying to cry / My house / The old songs / Drowning.

Oct 94. (cd)(c) **NIGHT MUSIC** [ ] [ ]
– Nocturne No.1 / Flying nocturne No.2 / Ever after / The man who wrote Danny Boy / Nocturne No.3 / Lullaby / Only the future / Nocturne No.4 / Sea of secrets.

– compilations, others, etc. –

Oct 93. A&M; (cd) **NIGHT AND DAY / LOOK SHARP** [ ] [-]

Michael JACKSON (& The JACKSONS)

Born: 29 Aug'58, Gary, Indiana, USA. Joined his JACKSON FAMILY group in 1964 when they became The JACKSON 5. In 1966, they won a New York talent contest at the famous Apollo Theater. After a couple of years on the road, they were touted by 'Motown' stars GLADYS KNIGHT and DIANA ROSS. After a local single on 'Steeltown' in 1968, they finally signed contract with 'Motown'. Label owner Berry Gordy moved the whole family to Hollywood, California. In 1970, their debut 'I WANT YOU BACK', gave them their first of 4 consecutive US No.1's. Late the following year, MICHAEL launched own solo career and hit US + UK Top5 with debut 'GOT TO BE THERE'. By the end of 1972, he was top of the US charts with 'BEN', a song about a pet rat!. At this time, MICHAEL combined both solo and JACKSON 5 work, and continued to do so throughout his career. Although The JACKSON 5, were still competing high in the charts, MICHAEL had definitely his worse period during the mid-70's. It was then the group and MICHAEL decided to break (tight 2.7% royalties) contract with 'Motown', and enrol with 'Epic-CBS'. In 1977, now as The JACKSONS, they resurrected past glories when they had string of hits, including first UK No.1 'SHOW YOU THE WAY TO GO'. Meanwhile MICHAEL, had started film work as the scarecrow (type-casting!) on the musical 'The Wiz'. He met up with its producer QUINCY JONES, who worked with him on all his future solo material. In 1979, their first collaboration, yielded the OFF THE WALL album. Lifted from it were 2 US No.1's 'DON'T STOP TIL YOU GET ENOUGH' & 'ROCK WITH YOU'. He allowed three years to slip by, before he discharged the multi-40 million selling album 'THRILLER'. Needless to say, this got him back to the top slot both commercially and critically. Its title track was best known for its award winning mild-horror video-epic. In 1987, 'BAD' his third 'Epic' album in 10 years, was released. This was also a massive seller, and featured no less than a record 5 US No.1's (see further below). On the back of this, his film autobiography 'MOONWALK' was released, but this received mediocre reviews. In March 1991, MICHAEL signed a multi-media billion dollar deal with 'Sony'. To end this lucritive year, he released a 4th 'Epic' album 'DANGEROUS', which rewarded him with yet another No.1. • **Style:** Creative singer/dancer, at first apeing himself on JAMES BROWN + STEVIE WONDER. His dance routines (The Moonwalk, etc.) were always brilliant, but off-stage his antics were always shrouded with mystery. He came across to many as a shy, gentle but lonely human being, that the music industry could not manipulate. His reclusive lifestyle (lives in mansion with exotic animals) and behaviour (nose jobs, pigmenting his dark skin), made the public always wonder, WHO IS IT? His family group The JACKSONS (5) were mainly a Motown groomed teenybop group, although they moved into disco-orientated, easy listening market. • **Songwriters:** When with Motown, it is said they weren't allowed to use own material. They virtually all branched out on their own solo ventures. JACKSON 5 singles covered NEVER CAN SAY GOODBYE (Clifton Davis) / LITTLE BITTY PRETTY ONE (Thurston Moore) / DOCTOR MY EYES (Jackson Browne) / FOREVER CAME TODAY (Supremes) / etc. The JACKSONS:- BLAME IT ON THE BOOGIE (Mick Jackson; no relation). MICHAEL covered ROCKIN' ROBIN (Bobby Day) / AIN'T NO SUNSHINE (Bill Withers) / GIRLFRIEND (Paul McCartney; who he also had 2 Top3 duets with) / COME TOGETHER (Beatles; who he bought from all rights to their recordings). • **Miscellaneous:** Their father JOE, was the family's tour driver and had once played guitar for The FALCONS. In the late 80's, he was at the centre of a controversial allegation by daughter/singer LaTOYA, who alleged in a book and on US TV, that she was beaten as a child by him. This divided the family into either defending their father or saying nothing. LaTOYA, of course had recently shocked them all by baring herself in the centre spread of Playboy magazine.

Recommended: THRILLER (*8)(pop*10) / BAD (*7)(pop*9) / OFF THE WALL (*6)(pop*8) / DANGEROUS (*6) / ANTHOLOGY (*5) / HIStory (*7)

JACKSON 5

MICHAEL JACKSON – lead vocals / **JACKIE JACKSON** (b.SIGMUND, 4 May'51) – vocals / **TITO JACKSON** (b.TORIANO, 15 Oct'53) – vocals / **JERMAINE JACKSON** (b.11 Dec'54) – vocals / **MARLON JACKSON** (b.12 Mar'57) – vocals

not issued | Steeltown

1968. (7") **BIG BOY. / YOU'VE CHANGED** [-] [ ]

1969. (7") **SOME GIRLS WANT ME FOR THEIR LOVE. / YOU DON'T HAVE TO BE 21 TO FALL IN LOVE** [-] [ ]
(re-iss. 1980s, US, on 'Dynamo')

Tamla Motown | Motown

Jan 70. (7") **I WANT YOU BACK. / WHO'S LOVING YOU** [2] [1] Nov 69
(re-iss.Oct81)

Mar 70. (7") **ABC. / IT'S ALL IN THE GAME** [-] [1]

Apr 70. (lp)(c) **DIANA ROSS PRESENTS THE JACKSON 5** [16] [5] Jan 70
– Zip-a-dee doo-dah / Nobody / I want you back / Can you remember / Standing in the shadows of love / You've changed / My Cherie amour / Who's loving you / Chained / I'm losing you / Stand / Born to save you. *(re-iss.Aug81)*

May 70. (7") **ABC. / THE YOUNG FOLKS** [8] [-]

Jul 70. (7") **THE LOVE YOU SAVE. / I FOUND THAT GIRL** [7] [1] May 70

Aug 70. (lp)(c) **ABC** [22] [4] May 70
– The love you save / One more chance / ABC / Come round here (I'm the one you need) / Don't know why I love you / Never had a dream come true / True love can be beautiful / La la means I love you / I'll bet you / I found that girl / The young folks. *(re-iss.Jun82)*

Nov 70. (7") **I'LL BE THERE. / ONE MORE CHANCE** [4] [1] Sep 70

Dec 70. (7") **SANTA CLAUS IS COMING TO TOWN. / CHRISTMAS WON'T BE THE SAME THIS YEAR** [-] [ ]

Dec 70. (lp)(c) **THE JACKSON 5 CHRISTMAS ALBUM** [ ] [ ]
(festive material, that hit US Xmas special chart at No.1) *(cd-iss.Nov94 on 'Spectrum')*

Feb 71. (lp)(c) **THE THIRD ALBUM** [ ] [4] Sep 70
– I'll be there / Ready or not here I come / Oh how happy / Bridge over troubled water / Can I see you in the morning / Goin' back to Indiana / How funky is your chicken / Mama's pearl / Reach in / The love I saw in you was just a mirage / Darling dear. *(re-iss.Mar82)(re-iss.cd Sep93)*

Apr 71. (7") **MAMA'S PEARL. / DARLING DEAR** [25] [2] Jan 71

Jun 71. (7") **NEVER CAN SAY GOODBYE. / SHE'S GOOD** [33] [2] Mar 71

Jul 71. (7") **MAYBE TOMORROW. / I WILL FIND A WAY** [-] [20]

Oct 71. (lp)(c) **MAYBE TOMORROW** [ ] [11] Apr 71
– Maybe tomorrow / She's good / Never can say goodbye / The wall / Petals / 16 Candles / (We've got) blue skies / My little baby / It's great to be here / Honey chile / I will find a way *(re-iss.cd Aug93)*

Oct 71. (lp)(c) **GOIN' BACK TO INDIANA (TV Soundtrack)** [-] [16]
– (contained live hits from TV show)

Mar 72. (7") **SUGAR DADDY. / I'M SO HAPPY** [ ] [10] Dec71

Sep 72. (lp)(c) **THE JACKSON 5 GREATEST HITS** [26] [12] Jan 72
– (compilation of hits, so far) *(re-iss. Mar 82, re-iss.+cd. Feb 88)*

MICHAEL JACKSON

started solo career as well on same label.

Jan 72. (7") **GOT TO BE THERE. / MARIA (YOU WERE THE ONLY ONE)** [5] [4] Oct 71

May 72. (7") **ROCKIN' ROBIN. / LOVE IS HERE AND NOW YOU'RE GONE** [3] [2] Mar 72

May 72. (lp)(c) **GOT TO BE THERE** [37] [14] Feb 72
– Ain't no sunshine / I wanna be where you are / Girl don't take your love from me / In our small way / Got to be there / Rockin' robin / Wings of my love / Maria (you were the only one) / Love is here and now / You're gone / You've got a friend. *(re-iss.Aug81 & May84) (cd-iss.Jun89)(re-iss.cd Aug93)*

May 72. (7") **I WANNA BE WHERE YOU ARE. / WE GOT A GOOD THING GOIN'** [-] [16]

Jul 72. (7") **AIN'T NO SUNSHINE. / I WANNA BE WHERE YOU ARE** [8] [-]
(re-iss.Oct81)

Nov 72. (7") **BEN. / YOU CAN CRY ON MY SHOULDER** [7] [1] Aug 72
(re-iss.Oct81)

Dec 72. (lp)(c) **BEN** [17] [5] Sep 72
– Ben / Greatest show on Earth / People make the world go round / We've got a good thing going / Everybody's fool / My girl / What goes around comes around / In our small way / Shoo-be-doo-be-doo-da-day / You can cry on my shoulder. *(re-iss.Oct81 + May84) (cd-iss.Feb90)(re-iss.cd Sep93)*

May 73. (7") **WITH A CHILD'S HEART. / MORNING GLOW** [-] [50]

Jul 73. (lp)(c) **MUSIC AND ME** [ ] [92] Apr 73
– With a child's heart / Up again / All the things you are / Happy / Too young /

Doggin' around / Johnny Raven / Euphoria / Morning glow / Music and me. *(re-iss.Nov84) (re-iss.cd/c May93 on 'Spectrum')*

Jul 73. (7") **MORNING GLOW. / MY GIRL** [ ] [ ]
May 74. (7") **MUSIC AND ME. / JOHNNY RAVEN** [ ] [ ]
Feb 75. (7") **WE'RE ALMOST THERE. / TAKE ME BACK** [-] [54]
Mar 75. (lp)(c) **FOREVER MICHAEL** [ ] [ ]
– We're almost there / Take me back / One day in your life / Cinderella stay awhile / We've got forever / Just a little bit of you / You are there / Dapper Dan / Dear Michael / I'll come home to you. *(re-iss.Jun83 + Jun88) (cd-iss.Mar90)*
Apr 75. (7") **ONE DAY IN YOUR LIFE. / WITH A CHILD'S HEART** [ ] [-]
Oct 75. (7") **JUST A LITTLE BIT OF YOU. / DEAR MICHAEL** [ ] [23] Jun 75
Oct 75. (lp)(c) **THE BEST OF MICHAEL JACKSON** [ ] [ ]
(compilation of solo work) *(re-iss.Mar80 + May84) (Jul81 saw it hit UK No.11)*

JACKSON 5

MICHAEL had continued with them at the helm simultaneously.

Apr 72. (7") **LITTLE BIT PRETTY ONE. / IF I HAVE TO MOVE A MOUNTAIN** [-] [13]
Sep 72. (7") **LITTLE BITTY PRETTY ONE. / MAYBE TOMORROW** [ ] [-]
Oct 72. (lp)(c) **LOOKIN' THROUGH THE WINDOWS** [16] [7] Jun 72
– Ain't nothing like the real thing / Lookin' through the windows / Don't let your baby catch you / To know / Doctor my eyes / Little bitty pretty one / E-ne-me-ne-mi-ne-moe / I'll have to move a mountain / Don't want to see you tomorrow / Children of the light / I can only give you love. *(re-iss.Feb83)*
Oct 72. (7") **LOOKIN' THROUGH THE WINDOWS. / LOVE SONG** [9] [16] Jul 72
Nov 72. (7") **CORNER OF THE SKY. / ?** [-] [18]
Dec 72. (7"m) **SANTA CLAUS IS COMING TO TOWN. / SOMEDAY AT CHRISTMAS / CHRISTMAS WON'T BE THE SAME THIS YEAR** [43] [-]
Feb 73. (7") **DOCTOR MY EYES. / MY LITTLE BABY** [9] [-]
Mar 73. (7") **HALLELUJAH DAY. / YOU MAKE ME WHAT I AM** [-] [16]
May 73. (7") **HALLELUJAH DAY. / TO KNOW** [20] [-]
Jul 73. (lp)(c) **SKYWRITER** [ ] [44] Apr 73
– Skywriter / Hallelujah day / Boogie man / Touch / Corner of the sky / I can't quit your love / Uppermost / World of sunshine / Ooh, I'd love to be with you / You made me what I am. *(re-iss.Nov84)(re-iss.cd Aug93)*
Aug 73. (7") **SKYWRITER. / AIN'T NOTHING LIKE THE REAL THING** [25] [-]
Nov 73. (7") **GET IT TOGETHER. / TOUCH** [ ] [28] Sep 73
Nov 73. (lp)(c) **GET IT TOGETHER** [ ] [100]
– Dancing machine / Get it together / Don't say goodbye again / Reflections / Hum along and dance / Mama I gotta brand new thing (don't say no) / It's too late to change the time / You need love like I do (don't you).
Apr 74. (7") **THE BOOGIE MAN. / DON'T LET YOUR BABY CATCH YOU** [ ] [ ]
Jun 74. (7") **DANCING MACHINE. / IT'S TOO LATE TO CHANGE THE TIME** [ ] [2] Mar 74
Nov 74. (lp)(c) **DANCING MACHINE** [ ] [16] Oct 74
– Dancing machine / I am love / Whatever you got, I want / She's a rhythm child / The life of the party / What you don't know / If I don't love you this way / It all begins and ends with love / The mirrors of my mind.
Nov 74. (7") **WHATEVER YOU GOT, I WANT. / I CAN'T QUIT YOUR LOVE** [-] [38]
Nov 74. (7") **WHATEVER YOU GOT, I WANT. / THE LIFE OF THE PARTY** [ ] [-]
Mar 75. (7") **I AM LOVE. / (Part 2)** [ ] [15] Feb 75
Jun 75. (7") **FOREVER CAME TODAY. / ALL I DO IS THINK OF YOU** [-] [60]
Jul 75. (lp)(c) **MOVING VIOLATION** [ ] [36]
– Forever came today / Moving violation / (You were made) Especially for me / Honey love / Body language (do the love dance) / All I do is think of you / Breezy / Call of the wild / Time explosion.
Sep 75. (7") **FOREVER CAME TODAY. / I CAN'T QUIT YOUR LOVE** [ ] [-]

JACKSONS

RANDY JACKSON (b.29 Oct'62) – vocals repl. JERMAINE who is having own solo career. Temporarily added sisters **LaTOYA** (b.29 May'56) – vocals / **REBBIE** (b.MAUREEN, 29 May'50) – vocals. In 1976, another sister **JANET** also appeared on tours.

Epic Epic

Oct 76. (7") **ENJOY YOURSELF. / STYLE OF LIFE** [ ] [6]
(UK re-iss.Feb77, hit No.42)
Feb 77. (lp)(c) **THE JACKSONS** [54] [36] Dec 76
– Enjoy yourself / Think happy / Good times / Keep on dancing / Blues away / Show you the way to go / Living together / Strength of one man / Dreamer / Style of life. *(also on pic-lp US) (re-iss.cd Jun94 on 'Sony')*
May 77. (7") **SHOW YOU THE WAY TO GO. / BLUES WAYS** [1] [28] Apr 77
Jul 77. (7") **DREAMER. / GOOD TIMES** [22] [-]
Oct 77. (7") **GOIN' PLACES. / DO WHAT YOU WANNA** [26] [52]
Oct 77. (lp)(c) **GOIN' PLACES** [45] [63]
– Music's takin' over / Goin' places / Different kind of lady / Even though you're gone / Jump for joy / Heaven knows I love you girl / Man of war / Do you wanna / Find me a girl. *(also iss.pic-lp US) (re-iss.cd Jun94 on 'Sony')*
Jan 78. (7") **FIND ME A GIRL. / DIFFERENT KIND OF LADY** [-] [ ]
Jan 78. (7") **EVEN THOUGH YOU'RE GONE. / DIFFERENT KIND OF LADY** [31] [-]
Apr 78. (7") **MUSIC'S TAKING OVER. / MAN OF WAR** [ ] [-]
Sep 78. (7") **BLAME IT ON THE BOOGIE. / DO WHAT YOU WANNA** [8] [-]
Oct 78. (7") **BLAME IT ON THE BOOGIE. / EASE ON DOWN THE ROAD** [-] [54]
Dec 78. (7") **DESTINY. / THAT'S WHAT YOU GET** [39] [-]
(12"+=) – Blame it on the boogie.
Apr 79. (lp)(c) **DESTINY** [33] [11] Dec 78
– Blame it on the boogie / Push me away / Things I do for you / Shake your body (down to the ground) / Destiny / Bless his soul / All night dancin' / That's what you get. *(re-iss.1984)*
Mar 79. (7")(12") **SHAKE YOUR BODY (DOWN TO THE GROUND). / ALL NIGHT DANCIN'** [4] [-]
Mar 79. (7") **SHAKE YOUR BODY (DOWN TO THE GROUND). / THAT'S WHAT YOU GET** [-] [7]

MICHAEL JACKSON

solo again. In Oct78, he duetted with DIANA ROSS ⇒ on 'MCA' Top 50 US/UK single 'EASE ON DOWN THE ROAD'. (re-iss.May84)

Epic Epic

May 79. (7")(12")(7"pic-d) **YOU CAN'T WIN. / (Pt.2)** [ ] [81] Feb 79
Aug 79. (7") **DON'T STOP 'TIL YOU GET ENOUGH. / I CAN'T HELP IT** [3] [1]
Aug 79. (lp)(c) **OFF THE WALL** [5] [3]
– Don't stop 'til you get enough / Rock with you / Working day and night / Get on the floor / Off the wall / Girlfriend / She's out of my life / I can't help it / It's the falling in love / Burn this disco out. *(re-dist.1980 w / free 7" YOU CAN'T WIN) (re-iss.Nov86) (cd-iss.1983 & Dec95) (re-iss.Aug92, hit UK No.48)*
Oct 79. (7") **ROCK WITH YOU. / WORKING DAY AND NIGHT** [-] [1]
Nov 79. (7") **OFF THE WALL. / WORKING DAY AND NIGHT** [7] [-]
Feb 80. (7") **OFF THE WALL. / GET ON THE FLOOR** [-] [10]
(re-iss.Apr82)
Feb 80. (7")(12") **ROCK WITH YOU. / GET ON THE FLOOR** [7] [-]
(re-iss.Apr82)
Apr 80. (7") **SHE'S OUT OF MY LIFE. / PUSH ME AWAY (By "JACKSONS")** [3] [-]
Apr 80. (7") **SHE'S OUT OF MY LIFE. / GET ON THE FLOOR** [-] [10]
Jul 80. (7") **GIRLFRIEND. / BLESS HIS SOUL (By "JACKSONS")** [41] [ ]

JACKSONS

returned to the fold.

Oct 80. (7") **LOVELY ONE. / BLESS HIS SOUL** [-] [12]

Epic Epic

Oct 80. (7") **LOVELY ONE. / THINGS I DO FOR YOU** [29] [-]
Oct 80. (lp)(c) **TRIUMPH** [13] [10]
– Can you feel it / Lovely one / Your ways / Everybody / Heartbreak hotel / Time waits for no one / Walk right now / Give it up / Wondering who.
Dec 80. (7") **HEARTBREAK HOTEL. / THINGS I DO FOR YOU** [-] [22]
Dec 80. (7") **HEARTBREAK HOTEL. / DIFFERENT KIND OF LADY** [44] [-]
Feb 81. (7") **CAN YOU FEEL IT. / EVERYBODY** [-] [77]
Feb 81. (7") **CAN YOU FEEL IT. / WONDERING WHO** [6] [-]
Jun 81. (7") **WALK RIGHT NOW. / YOUR WAYS** [7] [73]
Sep 81. (7") **TIME WAITS FOR NO ONE. / GIVE IT UP** [ ] [-]
Nov 81. (7") **THE THINGS I DO FOR YOU (LIVE). / WORKING DAY AND NIGHT (live)** [-] [ ]
Nov 81. (d-lp)(d-c) **THE JACKSONS – LIVE! (live)** [53] [30]
– Opening: Can you feel it? Things I do for you / Off the wall / Ben / Heartbreak hotel / She's out of my life / Movie and rap medley (a) I want you back, (b) Never can say goodbye, (c) Got to be there / The love you save / I'll be there / Rock with you / Lovely one / Working day and night / Don't stop 'til you get enough / Shake your body (down to the ground).
Nov 81. (7") **THINGS I DO FOR YOU (live). / DON'T STOP 'TIL YOU GET ENOUGH (live)** [ ] [ ]

MICHAEL JACKSON

returned to solo work again.

Epic Epic

Nov 82. (7")(7"pic-d) **THE GIRL IS MINE. (by "MICHAEL JACKSON & PAUL McCARTNEY") / CAN'T GET OUT OF THE RAIN** [10] [2]
— (Nearly a year later, they had another hit SAY SAY SAY No.2 UK / No.1 US)
Dec 82. (lp)(c)(cd)(pic-lp) **THRILLER** [1] [1]
– Wanna be startin' something / Baby be mine / The girl is mine / Thriller / Beat it / Billie Jean / Human nature / P.Y.T. (Pretty Young Thing) / The lady in my life. *(pic-lp Jul83) (re-iss.Aug92 hit UK No.17)*
Jan 83. (7") **BILLIE JEAN. / CAN'T GET OUT OF THE RAIN** [-] [1]
Jan 83. (7") **BILLIE JEAN. / IT'S FALLING IN LOVE** [1] [-]
(12"+=) – ('A'extended).
Mar 83. (7") **BEAT IT. / GET ON THE FLOOR** [-] [1]
Mar 83. (7")(12") **BEAT IT. / BURN THIS DISCO OUT** [3] [-]
May 83. (7") **WANNA BE STARTIN' SOMETHING. / (part 2)** [-] [5]
May 83. (7") **WANNA BE STARTIN' SOMETHING. / ROCK WITH YOU (by "JACKSONS")** [8] [-]
(12"+=) – ('A'instrumental).
Jul 83. (7") **HUMAN NATURE. / BABY BE MINE** [-] [7]
Oct 83. (7") **P.Y.T. (PRETTY YOUNG THING). / WORKING DAY AND NIGHT** [-] [10]
Nov 83. (7")(12") **THRILLER. / THE THINGS I DO FOR YOU** [10] [-]
Jan 84. (7") **THRILLER. / CAN'T GET OUTTA THE RAIN** [-] [4]
Mar 84. (7") **P.Y.T. (PRETTY YOUNG THING). / HEARTBREAK HOTEL** [11] [-]
(12"+=) – Thriller (instrumental).

JACKSONS

now 6-piece when **JERMAINE** returned to join the 5 brothers.

Jun 84. (7")(12")(7"pic-d) **STATE OF SHOCK. / YOUR WAYS** [14] [3]
— (Above featured MICK JAGGER on dual vocals with MICHAEL)
Jul 84. (lp)(c) **VICTORY** [3] [4]
– Torture / Wait / One more chance / Be not always / State of shock / We can change the world / The hurt / Body. *(cd-iss.May87) (cd-iss.Dec94)*
Aug 84. (7") **TORTURE. / ('A'instrumental)** [26] [17]

(12"+=) – Show you the way to go / Blame it on the boogie.
Nov 84. (7")(12") **BODY. / ('A'instrumental)** [ ] [47]
Feb 85. (7") **WAIT. / SHE'S OUT OF MY LIFE** [ ] [ ]

MICHAEL JACKSON

Jul 87. (7")(12") **I JUST CAN'T STOP LOVING YOU. / BABY BE MINE** [1] [1]
—— (Above featured duet with SIEDAH GARRETT)
Sep 87. (7") **BAD. / I CAN'T HELP IT** [-] [1]
Sep 87. (7") **BAD. / ('A'instrumental)** [3] [-]
(12"+=) – ('A'accapella mix) / ('A'dub version).
(c-s+=) – ('A'extended).
Sep 87. (lp)(c)(cd) **BAD** [1] [1]
– Bad / The way you make me feel / Speed demon / Liberian girl / Just good friends / Another part of me / Man in the mirror / I just can't stop loving you / Dirty Diana / Smooth criminal. *(re-iss.Jul88 as 5x7"box) (re-iss.Aug92, hit UK No.14)*
Nov 87. (7") **THE WAY YOU MAKE ME FEEL. / ('A'instrumental)** [3] [1]
(12"+=) – ('A'dance mix) / ('A'dub mix).
(cd-s+=) – ('A'accapella mix).
Feb 88. (7") **MAN IN THE MIRROR. / ('A'instrumental)** [21] [1]
(12"+=)(cd-s+=) – ('A'mix).
(In Apr88, he did duet 'GET IT' with STEVIE WONDER ⇒ , which hit UK Top40 & US No.80.)
Jul 88. (7")(12") **DIRTY DIANA. / ('A'instrumental)** [4] [1]
(cd-s+=) – Bad (extended dance).
Sep 88. (7") **ANOTHER PART OF ME. / ('A'instrumental)** [15] [11]
(12"+=)(cd-s+=) – ('A'acappella) / ('A'radio).
Nov 88. (7") **SMOOTH CRIMINAL. / ('A'instrumental)** [8] [?]
(12"+=)(cd-s+=) – ('A'extended) / ('A'acappella) / ('A'dance dub).
(cd-s++=) – ('A'Arnie mix).

JACKSONS

Epic Epic
Apr 89. (7")(c-s) **NOTHIN' (THAT COMPARES 2 U). / HEART-BREAK HOTEL / ALRIGHT WITH ME** [ ] [77]
(12"+=)(cd-s+=) – ('A'choice dub extended).
Jun 89. (lp)(c)(cd) **2300 JACKSON STREET** [ ] [59]
– Art of madness / Nothin' (that compares 2 U) / Maria / Private affair / 2300 Jackson Street / Harley / She / Alright with me / Play it up / Midnight rendezvous / If you'd only believe.
Aug 89. (7")(c-s) **2300 JACKSON STREET. / WHEN I LOOK AT YOU** [ ] [ ]
(12"+=) – Please come back to me.
(cd-s++=) – ('A'lp version) / Keep her.

MICHAEL JACKSON

Epic Epic
Nov 91. (7") **BLACK OR WHITE. / ('A'instrumental)** [1] [1]
(12"+=) – Bad / Thriller.
(cd-s+=) – Smooth criminal.
(12"+=)(cd-s+=) – (4 other 'A'mixes, incl. 1 by C&C MUSIC FACTORY)
Dec 91. (cd)(c)(lp) **DANGEROUS** [1] [1]
– Jam / Why you wanna trip on me / In the closet / She drives me wild / Remember the time / Can't let her get away / Heal the world / Black or white / Who is it / Give in to me / Will you be there / Keep the faith / Gone too soon / Dangerous.
Feb 92. (7")(12")(c-s)(cd-s) **REMEMBER THE TIME. / COME TOGETHER** [3] [3]
Apr 92. (7")(c-s) **IN THE CLOSET. / ('A'mix)** [8] [6]
(12"+=)(cd-s+=) – (other 'A'mixes).
Jul 92. (7")(12")(c-s)(cd-s) **WHO IS IT. / ROCK WITH YOU (mix) / DON'T STOP 'TIL YOU GET ENOUGH (remix)** [10] [14] Apr 93
Sep 92. (7")(c-s) **JAM. / BEAT IT (Moby mix)** [13] [26] Jun 92
(12"+=)(cd-s+=) – Wanna be starting something.
Nov 92. (7")(c-s) **HEAL THE WORLD. / SHE DRIVES ME WILD / MAN IN THE MIRROR** [2] [27]
(12"+=)(cd-s+=) – Wanna be starting something / Don't stop till you get enough / Rock with you.
Feb 93. (7")(c-s) **GIVE IT TO ME. / DIRTY DIANA** [2] [-]
(cd-s+=) Beat it.
Jun 93. (7")(c-s)(cd-s) **WILL YOU BE THERE. / KEEP THE FAITH** [9] [7]
Dec 93. (7")(c-s) **GONE TOO SOON. / GONE TOO SOON (Instrumental)** [33] [ ]
(12"+=)(cd-s+=) – ('A' mixes).
—— Early in 1994, he reputedly paid off a sum of between $13m & $30m to 14 year-old Jordy Chandler and his family, who had accused him of sexual assault. It was decided by the police that they would take no further action (the US justice system strikes again!). This surely alienated some of his fans, and plummeted sales figures were reported. Only one! lowly album chart appearance on both sides of the Atlantic during 1994.
Jun 95. (c-s)(cd-s) **SCREAM. (with JANET JACKSON) / CHILD-HOOD** [3] [5]
(cd-s)(12") – ('A'album version) / ('A'-Pressurized dub pt.1 & 2) / ('A'-Naughty By Nature pretty-pella mix) / ('A'-N.B.N. acappella).
(12") – ('A'-classic club mix) / ('A'-David Morales R&B extended mix) / ('A'-Def radio mix). / ('A'-Naughty By Nature main mix) / ('A'-Naughty By Nature main mix no rap) / ('A'-Dave "Jam" Hall's extended urban remix). *(note the above 4th & 5th formats hit UK No.43)*
Jun 95. (d-cd)(d-c)(t-lp)(d-md) **HIStory – PAST, PRESENT AND FUTURE, BOOK 1** [1] [1]
– Billie Jean / The way you make me feel / Black or white / Rock with you / She's out of my life / Bad / I just can't stop loving you / Man in the mirror / Thriller / Beat it / The girl is mine / Remember the time / Don't stop 'til you get enough / Wanna be startin' somethin' / Heal the world. // Scream / hey don't care about us / Stranger in Moscow / This time around / Earth song / DS / Money / Come together / You are not alone / Childhood / Tabloid junkie / 2 bad / History / Little Susie / Smile.
Aug 95. (c-s) **YOU ARE NOT ALONE / SCREAM LOUDER (Flyte Tyme mix)** [1] [1]
(cd-s) – ('A'-Frankie Knuckles remix) / ('A'-Jon B remix).
(cd-s) – ('A'-R Kelly remix) / Rock with you (Masters At work remix) / Rock with you (Frankie Knuckles remix).
Nov 95. (c-s) **EARTH SONG / ('A'-Hani's extended radio experience)** [1] [ ]
(cd-s) – ('A'side) / ('A'-Hani's club experience) / Michael Jackson DMC megamix.
(cd-s) – ('A'side) / Wanna be startin' somethin' / ('A'-Brothers In Rhythm mix) / ('A'-Tommy D's main mix).

– (MICHAEL JACKSON) compilations, others –

Note; All below on 'Motown' unless stated.
Apr 80. (7") **BEN. / ('B'by MARVIN GAYE)** [ ] [ ]
(re-iss.Oct81)
Oct 80. (7") **GOT TO BE THERE. / ('B'by MARV JACKSON)** [ ] [ ]
(re-iss.Oct81)
Apr 81. (7") **ONE DAY IN YOUR LIFE. / TAKE ME BACK** [1] [55]
(re-iss.Oct81)
Jul 81. (lp)(c) **ONE DAY IN YOUR LIFE** [29] [ ]
– One day in your life / We're almost there / You're my best friend, my love / Don't say goodbye again / Take me back / It's too late to change the time / We've got a good thing going / You are there / Doggin' around / Dear Michael / Girl, don't take your love from me / I'll come home to you.
(re-iss.Mar85)
Jul 81. (7")(12") **WE'RE ALMOST THERE. / WE GOT A GOOD THING GOING** [46] [ ]
Jul 83. (7")(12")(7"pic-d) **HAPPY (LOVE THEME FROM 'LADY SINGS THE BLUES'). / WE'RE ALMOST THERE** [52] [ ]
Jul 83. (c-ep) **FLIPHITS** [ ] [-]
– One day in your life / Got to be there / Ben / Ain't no sunshine.
May 84. (7")(12") **FAREWELL MY SUMMER LOVE. / CALL ME** [7] [38]
Aug 84. (lp)(c) **FAREWELL MY SUMMER LOVE** [9] [46]
– Don't let it get you down / You've really got a hold on me / Melodie / Touch the one you love / Girl you're so together / Farewell my summer love / Call on me / Here I am / To make my father proud.
(re-iss.Jun88, cd-iss.Oct89)
Aug 84. (7") **GIRL YOU'RE SO TOGETHER. / TOUCH THE ONE YOU LOVE** [ ] [ ]
(12"+=) – Ben / Ain't no sunshine.
Nov 84. (lp)(c) **THE GREAT LOVE SONGS OF MICHAEL JACKSON** [ ] [ ]
May 86. (lp)(c) **LOOKING BACK TO YESTERDAY** [ ] [ ]
Apr 87. (d-cd) **MICHAEL JACKSON ANTHOLOGY** [ ] [ ]
– Got to be there / Rockin' Robin / Ain't no sunshine / Maria (you were the only one) / I wanna be where you are / Girl don't take your love from me / Love is here and now you're gone / Ben / People make the world go 'round / Shoo-be-doo-be-doo-da-day / With a child's heart / Everybody's somebody's fool / In our small way / All the things you are / You can cry on my shoulder / Maybe tomorrow / I'll be there / Never can say goodbye / It's too late to change the time / Dancing machine / When I come of age / Dear Michael / Music and me / You are there / One day in your life / Love's gone bad / That's what love is made of / Who's looking for a lover / Lonely teardrops / We're almost there / Take me back / Just a little bit of you / Melodie / I'll come home to you / If'n I was God / Happy / Don't let it get you down / Call on me / To make my father proud / Farewell my summer love. – (w / JACKSON 5 tracks) *(re-iss.d-cd Apr93)*
1987. (7") **25 MILES. / UP ON THE HOUSETOP** [-] [ ]
Feb 92. (cd)(c)(lp) **MOTOWN'S GREATEST HITS** [ ] [ ]
Apr 82. Epic; (7") **OFF THE WALL. / DON'T STOP 'TIL YOU GET ENOUGH** [ ] [ ]
Dec 82. Epic; (c-ep) **GREATEST ORIGINAL HITS** [ ] [-]
(re-iss.Mar83 as 7"ep)
Nov 83. Epic; (9x7"red-pack) **SINGLES PACK** [66] [ ]
(re-iss.Jul88)
Sep 86. Epic; (c-ep) **THE 12" TAPE** [ ] [ ]
– Billie Jean / Beat it / Wanna be startin' something / Thriller.
Jul 88. Epic; (singles pack) **SOUVENIR SINGLES PACK** [91] [-]
Jul 92. Epic; (4xpic-cd-ep's) **TOUR SOUVENIR PACK** [32] [ ]
– (3 tracks on each disc)
Jul 82. Pickwick; (lp)(c) **AIN'T NO SUNSHINE** [ ] [-]
(re-iss.Nov84 on 'Astan')
Jul 83. Telstar; (lp)(c)(cd) **18 GREATEST HITS (by MICHAEL JACKSON / JACKSON 5)** [1] [ ]
(re-iss.Jun88)
May 84. Motown; (cd) **COMPACT COMMAND PERFORMANCES: 18 GREATEST HITS** [ ] [ ]
(re-iss.Oct87)
Nov 86. Motown; (d-cd) **GOT TO BE THERE / BEN** [ ] [ ]
Oct 87. Telstar; (lp)(c)(cd) **LOVE SONGS (w / DIANA ROSS)** [15] [ ]
Nov 87. Stylus; (lp)(c)(cd) **THE MICHAEL JACKSON MIX** [27] [ ]
Nov 95. Motown; (3xcd-box) **FOREVER MICHAEL / MUSIC & ME / BEN** [ ] [-]

– (JACKSONS) compilations, others. –

Note; All on 'Motown' unless stated.
Apr 74. (7") **BOOGIE MAN. / DON'T LET YOUR BABY TOUCH YOU** [ ] [ ]
Dec 76. (lp)(c) **JOYFUL JUKEBOX MUSIC** [ ] [ ]
Jan 77. (d-lp)(d-c) **THE JACKSON 5 ANTHOLOGY** [ ] [84] Aug 76
(cd-iss.Jun87)(re-iss.d-cd. Apr93)
Mar 77. (lp)(c) **MOTOWN SPECIAL – JACKSON 5** [ ] [ ]
Aug 77. (7") **SKYWRITER. / I WANT YOU BACK / THE LOVE YOU SAVE** [ ] [ ]
Sep 79. (lp)(c) **20 GOLDEN GREATS** [ ] [ ]
(re-iss.Oct81 & Apr84)
Mar 82. (lp)(c) **GREATEST HITS** [ ] [ ]
Jul 83. (c-ep) **FLIP HITS** [ ] [-]

– I want you back / I'll be there / ABC / Lookin' through any window.
Nov 84. (lp)(c) **GREAT LOVE SONGS OF THE JACKSON 5** [ ] [ ]
Nov 86. (cd) **DIANA ROSS PRESENTS . . . / ABC** [ ] [ ]
Nov 87. (7") **I SAW MOMMY KISSING SANTA CLAUS / SANTA CLAUS IS COMING TO TOWN. / UP ON THE HOUSE TOP / FROSTY THE SNOWMAN** [ ] [-]
Feb 88. (lp)(c)(cd) **THE ORIGINAL SOUL OF . . .** [ ] [ ]
Apr 88. (7")(12") **I WANT YOU BACK ('88 remix – Stock Aitken Waterman). / NEVER CAN SAY GOODBYE** [8] [ ]
Jan 79. M.F.P.; (lp)(c) **ZIP-A-DEE-DOO-DAH** [ ] [-]
Aug 80. Epic; (7")(12") **SHAKE YOUR BODY (DOWN TO THE GROUND). / BLAME IT ON THE BOOGIE** [ ] [-]
1984. Epic; (d-c) **GOIN' PLACES / DESTINY** [ ] [ ]
Jul 84. Epic; (7") **SHOW YOU THE WAY TO GO. / BLAME IT ON THE BOOGIE** [ ] [ ]
Sep 82. Pickwick; (lp)(c) **THE JACKSON 5** [ ] [-]
Mar 90. S.D.E.G.; (cd)(c)(lp) **BEGINNING YEARS 1965-67** [ ] [ ]
Mar 90. S.D.E.G.; (cd)(c)(lp) **THE JACKSON 5 AND JOHNNY** [ ] [ ]
May 93. Spectrum; (cd)(c) **CHILDREN OF THE NIGHT ("JACKSON 5")** [ ] [-]
Sep 93. Stardust; (cd) **THE JACKSON 5 FEATURING MICHAEL JACKSON ("JACKSON 5")** [ ] [-]
Jul 95. Charly; (cd) **THE HISTORIC EARLY RECORDINGS** [ ] [-]
Jul 95. Wisepack; (cd) **SOUL LEGENDS** [ ] [-]
Jul 95. Motown; (4xcd-box) **SOULSATION** [ ] [-]
Nov 95. Motown; (3xcd-box) **MAYBE TOMORROW / SKYWRITER / THE THIRD ALBUM** [ ] [-]

— JERMAINE, JACKIE, LaTOYA and more successfully JANET, had own solo hits.

Ray JACKSON (see under ⇒ LINDISFARNE)

Mick JAGGER (see under ⇒ ROLLING STONES)

JAM

Formed: Woking, Surrey, England . . . late '73 by WELLER, FOXTON, BUCKLER and 4th member STEVE BROOKS – guitar. This quartet first gigged mid-74, and progressed in late 1976 to London's Marquee, 101 Club & Red Cow, but as a trio without BROOKS. Early in 1977 after many gigs, they were signed by A&R man Chris Parry to 'Polydor'. In Spring '77, their debut 'IN THE CITY' cracked the UK Top 40, and preceded by a month the Top 20 album of the same. They advanced greatly throughout the next 3 years, and had first of 4 UK No.1's early 1980 with 'GOING UNDERGROUND'. • **Style:** Mod revivalists, with power and energy of punk rock, but with mid-60's fashion (parkers, mohair suits, two-tone shoes & motor scooters). By 1982, their music had incorporated more of a soul sound, which led to WELLER taking off to form STYLE COUNCIL. • **Songwriters:** WELLER penned except; SWEET SOUL MUSIC (Arthur Conley) / BACK IN MY ARMS AGAIN (Holland-Dozier-Holland) / DAVID WATTS (Kinks) / MOVE ON UP (Curtis Mayfield). • **Trivia:** In Oct'81, WELLER started own record company 'Respond', and signed acts The QUESTIONS and TRACIE.

Recommended: SNAP (*10) / ALL MOD CONS (*8) / IN THE CITY (*5) / THIS IS THE MODERN WORLD (*5) / SETTING SONS (*7) / SOUND EFFECTS (*7) / THE GIFT (*6).

PAUL WELLER (b.JOHN WELLER, 25 May'58) – vocals, guitar / **BRUCE FOXTON** (b. 1 Sep'55) – bass, vocals / **RICK BUCKLER** (b.PAUL RICHARD BUCKLER, 6 Dec'55) – drums

Polydor Polydor

Apr 77. (7") **IN THE CITY. / TAKIN' MY LOVE** [40] [ ]
(re-iss.Apr80 hit No.40. re-iss.Jan83 hit No.47.)
May 77. (lp)(c) **IN THE CITY** [20] [ ]
– Art school I've changed my address / Slow down / I got by in time / Away from the numbers / Batman / In the city / Sounds from the street / Non stop dancing / Time for truth / Takin' my love / Bricks and mortar. *(re-iss.Aug83, hit 100) (re-iss.+cd.Jul90)*
Jul 77. (7") **ALL AROUND THE WORLD. / CARNABY STREET** [13] [-]
(re-iss.Apr80 hit No.43. re-iss.Jan83 hit No.38.)
Oct 77. (7"m) **THE MODERN WORLD. / SWEET SOUL MUSIC / BACK IN MY ARMS AGAIN / BRICKS AND MORTAR** [36] [-]
(re-iss.Apr80 hit No.52. re-iss.Jan83 hit No.51)
Nov 77. (lp)(c) **THIS IS THE MODERN WORLD** [22] [ ]
– The modern world / London traffic / Standards / Life from the window / The combine / Don't tell them you're sane / In the street today / London girl / I need you / Here comes the weekend / Tonight at noon / In the midnight hour. *(re-iss.Aug83) (re-iss.+cd.Jul90 & Sep95)*
Feb 78. (7") **I NEED YOU. / IN THE CITY** [-] [ ]
Mar 78. (7"m) **NEWS OF THE WORLD. / AUNTIES AND UNCLES / INNOCENT MAN** [27] [-]
(re-iss.Apr80 hit No.53) (re-iss.Jan83 hit No.39.)
Aug 78. (7") **DAVID WATTS. / 'A' BOMB IN WARDOUR STREET** [25] [-]
(re-iss.Apr80 hit No.54) (re-iss.Jan83 hit No.50)
Oct 78. (7") **DOWN IN THE TUBE-STATION AT MIDNIGHT. / SO BAD ABOUT US / THE NIGHT** [15] [-]
(re-iss.Apr80) (re-iss.Jan83 hit No.30)
Nov 78. (lp)(c) **ALL MOD CONS** [6] [ ]
– All mod cons / To be someone (didn't we have a nice time) / Mr. Clean / David Watts / English rose / In the crowd / Billy Hunt / It's too bad / Fly 3.18 / The place I love / 'A' bomb in Wardour Street / Down in the tube station at midnight. *(re-iss.Aug80) (re-iss.+cd.1989)*
Jan 79. (7") **DOWN IN THE TUBE STATION AT MIDNIGHT. / MR. CLEAN** [-] [ ]
Mar 79. (7") **STRANGE TOWN. / THE BUTTERFLY COLLECTOR** [15] [ ]
(re-iss.Apr80 hit No.44. (re-iss.Jan83 hit No.42.)
Aug 79. (7") **WHEN YOU'RE YOUNG. / SMITHERS-JONES** [17] [-]
(re-iss.Jan83 hit No.53)
Oct 79. (7") **THE ETON RIFLES. / SEE-SAW** [3] [-]
(re-iss.Jan83 hit No.54)
Nov 79. (lp)(c) **SETTING SONS** [4] [ ]
– Girl on the phone / Thick as thieves / Private hell / Little boy soldiers / Waste land / Burning sky / Smithers-Jones / Saturday's kids / The Eton rifles / Heat wave. *(re-iss.Aug83) (cd-iss.May88)*
Feb 80. (7") **GOING UNDERGROUND. / DREAMS OF CHILDREN** [1] [-]
(d7"+=) – The modern world / Away from the numbers / Tube-station. *(re-iss.Jan83 hit No.21.)*
Aug 80. (7") **START!. / LIZA RADLEY** [1] [-]
(re-iss.Jan83 hit 60)
Nov 80. (lp)(c) **SOUND AFFECTS** [2] [72]
– Pretty green / Monday / But I'm different now / Set the house ablaze / Start! / That's entertainment / Dreamtime / Man in the cornershop / Music for the last couple / Boy about town / Scrape away. *(re-iss.Aug83) (cd-iss.May88, re-iss.+cd.Apr90)*
Jan 81. (7") **THAT'S ENTERTAINMENT. / DOWN IN THE TUBE STATION AT MIDNIGHT** [21] [-]
(above 45, was actually issued on German import *'Metrognome') (re-iss.Jan83 on 'Polydor', hit 60)*
May 81. (7") **FUNERAL PYRE. / DISGUISES** [4] [ ]
(re-iss.Jan83)
Oct 81. (7") **ABSOLUTE BEGINNERS. / TALES FROM THE RIVERBANK** [4] [ ]
(re-iss.Jan83)
Dec 81. (m-lp) **THE JAM** [-] [ ]
– Absolute beginners / Funeral pyre / Liza Radley / Tales from the riverbank.
Feb 82. (7")(12") **TOWN CALLED MALICE. / PRECIOUS** [1] [ ]
(re-iss.Jan83 hit 73)
Mar 82. (lp)(c) **THE GIFT** [1] [82]
– Happy together / Ghosts / Precious / Just who is the 5 o'clock hero? / Trans-global express / Running on the spot / Circus / The planner's dream goes wrong / Carnation / Town called Malice / The gift. *re-iss.Aug83) (re-iss.+cd.Apr90)*
Jun 82. (7") **JUST WHO IS THE 5 O'CLOCK HERO?. / THE GREAT DEPRESSION** [6] [ ]
(12"+=) – War.
Sep 82. (7") **THE BITTEREST PILL. / PITY POOR ALFIE / FEVER** [2] [ ]
(US-iss. Nov 82 as 12"m-lp w/extra track)
Nov 82. (7") **BEAT SURRENDER. / SHOPPING** [1] [ ]
(d7"+=)(d12"+=) – Move on up / War / Stoned out of my mind.
(US-iss. Apr 83 as 12"m-lp)
Dec 82. (lp)(c) **DIG THE NEW BREED (live 77-82)** [2] [ ]
– In the city / All mod cons / To be someone / It's too bad / Start! / Big bird / Set the house ablaze / Ghosts / Standards / In the crowd / Going underground / Dreams of children / That's entertainment / Private hell. *(re-iss.Jun87) (re-iss.Jun90 & Sep95)*

— They split late '82. WELLER formed The STYLE COUNCIL. FOXTON went solo. BUCKLER formed TIME UK before both formed SHARP.

– compilations, etc. –

Sep 80. Polydor; (d-lp)(d-c) **IN THE CITY / THIS IS THE MODERN WORLD** [ ] [ ]
(cd-iss.Jan90)
Jan 83. Polydor; (d-lp)(d-c) **SOUND AFFECTS / THE GIFT** [ ] [ ]
Feb 83. Polydor; (d-lp)(d-c) **ALL MOD CONS / SETTING SONS** [ ] [ ]
Oct 83. Polydor; (d-lp)(d-c) **SNAP** [2] [ ]
– In the city / Away from the numbers / All around the world / The modern world / News of the world / Billy Hunt / English Rose / Mr. Clean / David Watts / 'A' bomb in Wardour Street / Down in the tube station at midnight / Strange town / The butterfly collector / When you're young / Smithers-Jones / Thick as thieves / The Eton rifles / Going underground / Dreams of children / That's entertainment / Start! / Man in the cornershop / Funeral pyre / Absolute beginners / Tales from the riverbank / Town called Malice / Precious / The bitterest pill (I ever had to swallow) / Beat surrender. *(d-lp.w / free 7"ep)* **LIVE AT WEMBLEY (live)**– The great depression / But I'm different now / Move on up / Get yourself together. *(cd-iss.Sep84 cd-omits 8 tracks).*
Jun 91. Polydor; (7")(c-s) **THAT'S ENTERTAINMENT. / DOWN IN THE TUBE-STATION AT MIDNIGHT (live)** [57] [-]
(12"+=)(cd-s+=) – Town called Malice (live).
Jul 91. Polydor; (cd)(c)(lp) **GREATEST HITS** [2] [ ]
Mar 92. Polydor; (7")(c-s) **THE DREAMS OF CHILDREN. / AWAY FROM THE NUMBERS (live)** [ ] [-]
(12"+=)(cd-s+=) – This is the modern world (live).
Apr 92. Polydor; (cd)(c)(lp) **EXTRAS** (available for Fan Club members) [-] [-]
Oct 93. Polydor; (cd)(c)(d-lp) **LIVE JAM (live)** [28] [ ]
– The modern world / Billy Hunt / Thick as thieves / Burning sky / Mr. Clean / Smithers-Jones / Little boy soldiers / The Eton Rifles / Away from the numbers / Down in the tube station at midnight / Strange town / When you're young / 'A' Bomb In Wardour Street / Pretty green / Boy about town / Man in the cornershop / David Watts / Funeral pyre / Move on up / Carnation / The butterfly collector / Precious / Town called Malice / Heatwave.
1989. Old Gold; (7") **BEAT SURRENDER. / THE BITTEREST PILL** [ ] [-]
Mar 90. Old Gold; (7") **TOWN CALLED MALICE. / ABSOLUTE BEGINNERS** [ ] [-]
Mar 90. Old Gold; (7") **GOING UNDERGROUND. / START!** [ ] [-]
Mar 90. Old Gold; (7") **THE ETON RIFLES. / DOWN IN THE TUBE-STATION AT MIDNIGHT** [ ] [-]
Sep 90. Strange Fruit; (12"ep)(cd-ep) **THE PEEL SESSIONS** [ ] [-]
– In the city / Art school / I've changed my address / The modern world.
Oct 92. Pickwick; (cd)(c) **WASTELAND** [ ] [-]
Sep 95. Polydor; (cd) **EXTRAS** [ ] [-]

Eton Rifles

JAMES

Formed: Manchester, England . . . 1982 by JIM GLENNIE, TIM BOOTH, LARRY GOTT and GAVAN WHELAN. In 1983 they signed to Tony Wilson's 'Factory' label, and issued debut 3-track 'JIMONE EP'. Soon loved by the music press, especially after their 2nd classic 45 'HYMN FROM A VILLAGE', topped the indie chart early in '85. They were soon snapped up by Seymour Stein's 'Sire', but financial difficulties after release of Lenny Kaye produced album 'STUTTER', led to them moving to WEA subsidiary 'Blanco Y Negro'. In 1990, after a change of personnel and a spell on 'Rough Trade', they had first Top 40 hit on 'Fontana' with 'HOW WAS IT FOR YOU?'. It was soon followed by a Top 20 album 'GOLD MOTHER', that when re-promoted early 1991 with No.2 hit 'SIT DOWN', also hit No.2. • **Style:** Sometimes erratic and unorthodox, intelligent rock band tinged with INCREDIBLE STRING BAND like folk, with the overtly accented TIM BOOTH their feature. • **Songwriters:** TIM BOOTH penned, except SUNDAY MORNING (Velvet Underground). • **Trivia:** In the 1990s, they were produced by BRIAN ENO, who also contributed musicianship.

Recommended: GOLD MOTHER (*8) / STUTTER (*6) / LAID (*7) / SEVEN (*8).

TIM BOOTH – vocals / **LARRY GOTT** (b.JAMES GOTT) – guitar / **JIM GLENNIE** – bass / **GAVAN WHELAN** – drums

		Factory	not issued
Sep 83.	(7") **JIMONE**		-
	– What's the world / Fire so close / Folklore.		
Feb 85.	(7") **JAMES II: HYMN FROM A VILLAGE. / IF THINGS WERE PERFECT**		-
Jun 85.	(12"ep) **VILLAGE FIRE**		-
	– (remixes of the above 5 tracks).		

		Sire	Warners
Feb 86.	(7") **CHAIN MAIL. / HUP STRINGS**		-
	(12"+=) – ('A' extended) / Uprising.		
Jun 86.	(lp)(c) **STUTTER**	68	-
	– Skullduggery / Scarecrow / So many ways / Just hip / Johnny Yen / Summer song / Really hard / Billy's shirts / Why so close / Withdrawn / Black hole. *(re-iss.+cd.Nov91)*		
Jul 86.	(7") **SO MANY WAYS. / WITHDRAWN**		-
	(12"+=) – Just hipper.		

		Blanco YN	Sire
Sep 87.	(7") **YAHO. / MOSQUITO**		-
	(12"+=) – New nature / Left out of her will.		
Mar 88.	(7") **WHAT FOR. / ISLAND SWING**		-
	(12"+=)(c-s+=) – Not there.		
May 88.	(lp)(c)(cd) **STRIP MINE**	90	
	– What for / Charlie Dance / Fairground / Are you ready / Yaho / Medieval / Not there / Riders / Vulture / Strip mining / Refrain. *(re-iss.Sep88) (re-iss.+cd.Jul91) (cd-iss.Feb95)*		

		Rough Trade	not issued
Mar 89.	(lp)(c)(cd) **ONE MAN CLAPPING (live in Bath)**		-
	– Chain mail / Sandman (hup strings) / Whoops / Riders / Why so close / Leaking / Johnny Yen / Scarecrow / Are you ready / Really hard / Burned / Stutter. *(cd+=)* – Yaho.		

— **DAVE BAIGNTON-POWER** – drums repl. WHELAN, / added **SAUL DAVIS** – violin, percussion, guitar / **MARK HUNTER** – keyboards

Jun 89.	(7") **SIT DOWN. / SKY IS FALLING**		-
	(12"+=)(cd-s+=) – Goin' away / Sound investment.		

— added **ANDY DIAGRAM** – trumpet (ex-PALE FOUNTAINS, ex-DIAGRAM BROS.)

Nov 89.	(7") **COME HOME. / PROMISED LAND**		-
	('A'ext-12"+=)(cd-s+=) – Slow right down.		

		Fontana	Mercury
May 90.	(7") **HOW WAS IT FOR YOU?. / WHOOPS (live)**	32	
	(12") – ('A'side) / Hymn from a village (live) / Lazy.		
	(cd-s) – ('A'side) / Hymn from a village (live) / Undertaker.		
	(12") – ('A'different mix) / Lazy / Undertaker.		
Jun 90.	(cd)(c)(lp) **GOLD MOTHER**	16	
	– Come home / Government walls / God only knows / You can tell how much suffering (on a face that's always smilimg) / How was it for you? / Crescendo / Hang on / Walking the ghost / Gold mother / Top of the world. *(re-iss.Apr91, hit No.2)* (tracks =repl. by) – Sit down / Lose control.		
Jul 90.	(7")(c-s) **COME HOME (flood mix). / DREAMING UP TOMORROW**	32	
	(12") – ('A'side) / Stutter (live) / Fire away.		
	(cd-s) – ('A'side) / Gold mother (remix) / Fire away.		
Nov 90.	(7")(c-s) **LOSE CONTROL. / SUNDAY MORNING**	38	
	(12"+=)(cd-s+=) – ('A'extended) / Out to get you.		
Mar 91.	(7")(c-s) **SIT DOWN. / ('A'live version)**	2	
	(12"+=)(cd-s+=) – Tonight.		
Nov 91.	(7")(c-s) **SOUND. / ALL MY SONS**	9	
	(12"+=)(cd-s+=) – ('A'full version) / Come home (Youth mix).		
Jan 92.	(7")(c-s) **BORN OF FRUSTRATION. / BE MY PRAYER**	13	
	(12"+=)(cd-s+=) – Sound (mix).		
Feb 92.	(cd)(c)(lp) **SEVEN**	2	
	– Born of frustration / Ring the bells / Sound / Bring a gun / Mother / Don't wait that long / Live a life of love / Heavens / Protect me / Seven. (cd/c+=) – Next lover.		
Mar 92.	(7")(c-s) **RING THE BELLS. / FIGHT**	37	
	(12"+=)(cd-s+=) – The skunk weed skank / Come home (live dub version).		
	(12"++=) – Once a friend.		
Jul 92.	(7"ep)(c-ep)(cd-ep) **SEVEN**	46	
	– Seven / Goalies ball / William Burroughs / Still alive.		
Sep 93.	(7")(c-s) **SOMETIMES. / AMERICA**	18	
	(12"+=)(cd-s+=) – Building a charge.		
Sep 93.	(cd)(c)(lp) **LAID**	3	64
	– Out to get you / Sometimes (Lester Piggott) / Dream thrum / One of the three / Say something / Five-o / P.S. / Everybody knows / Knuckle too far / Low, low / Laid / Lullaby / Skindiving. *(re-iss.Apr94)*		
Nov 93.	(7")(c-s) **LAID. / WAH WAH KITS**	25	61
	(cd-s+=) – The lake / Seconds away.		
	(cd-s) – ('A'live) / Five-O / Say something / Sometimes.		
Mar 94.	(c-s) **JAM J. / SAY SOMETHING**	24	
	(cd-s+=) – Assassin / ('B'new version).		
	(12") – ('A'side) / (James VS The Sabres Of Paradise – 33 mins of instrumental remix).		
Sep 94.	(cd)(c)(d-lp;ltd) **WAH WAH** (w / BRIAN ENO)	11	
	–		

Elmore JAMES

Born: 27 January 1918, Richland, Mississippi, USA. Self-taught on a home-made lard can instrument, he worked in sawmills and part-time in juke joints. He was to meet ROBERT JOHNSON in 1937 while at a local dance in the blues capital of Helena. This was to inspire him immensely, especially after JOHNSON's untimely death in the summer of 1938. He formed his own band in 1939, and tributed his mentor by adopting his 'CROSSROADS' and 'DUST MY BROOM'. He had also met RICE MILLER (SONNY BOY WILLIAMSON) around this time, but this was just prior to, and after he served his country in the US Navy 1943-45. After his service was over, he played on the infamous radio shows 'KING BISCUIT TIME' in 1947. He finally appeared on disc in 1951, when LILLIAN McMURRAY's 'Trumpet' label, issued some of SONNY BOY WILLIAMSON's cuts, with ELMORE on guitar. After these recordings SONNY convinced ELMO (as he was credited then) to record 'DUST MY BROOM', and this, the best ever version of the song, hit R&B Top 10 in 1952. It also featured SONNY on harmonica. ELMORE then signed to JOE BIHARI's 'Modern' label, and with IKE TURNER as engineer, they recorded a new version as 'I BELIEVE'. He moved to Chicago that year, and shared an apartment with SONNY and another giant HOWLIN' WOLF. His next recordings, mostly for Modern's 'Flair', were never even minor hits, but he slightly resurrected career with a new working of debut, now called 'DUST MY BLUES'. Early in 1956, after his heavy drinking was affecting his recording schedules, he was dropped by 'Flair'. He went into semi-retirement after a mild heart attack, caused him degree of reflection. Still with the blues bug, he returned to Chicago in 1957 and recorded for MEL LONDON's 'Mel' records. After backing from WAYNE BENNETT, EDDIE TAYLOR, WILLIE DIXON and FRED BELEW on these cuts, he was to suffer his second heart attack. At the end months of the 50's, he was tempted to return to club gigs, which were seen by 'Fire' records boss BOBBY ROBINSON. His first for the label was in 1960, when 'THE SKY IS CRYING' was another major R&B success. He also made another one-off disc for 'Chess' at this time, a thing that would be hard to emulate these days. The rest of the early 60's, saw him make another classic 'SHAKE YOUR MONEYMAKER', and return to studio in February 1963 to attempt a crossover hit 'PICKIN' THE BLUES'. On the 23th May that year, while on his fifth tiresome night at Chicago's Copa Cobana, he suffered his third heart attack. This time fatal, he died at his cousin's (HOMESICK JAMES) house the next day. **Legacy:** Due to it not being reported, his death went unnoticed in the UK, until that is in 1967, when the early FLEETWOOD MAC recorded DUST MY BROOM + SHAKE YOUR MONEYMAKER. More covers were to follow . . . **Blues style:** Singer /guitarist whose new modified techniques were influenced by another bluesmen ROBERT JOHNSON and KOKOMO ARNOLD. Was a fine exponent of these Delta blues and guitar riffs, which inspired future stars B.B.KING, SON SEALS, J.B. HUTTO, HOUND DOG TAYLOR, ROBERT LOCKWOOD, JIMI HENDRIX and FLEETWOOD MAC, to mention several. • **Miscellaneous:** He was credited on some releases with The /HIS BROOM DUSTERS. • **Songwriters:** Self-penned except DUST MY BROOM + STANDING AT THE CROSSROADS (Robert Johnson) / etc.

Recommended: LET'S CUT IT: THE VERY BEST OF ELMORE JAMES (*7)

ELMORE JAMES – vocals, guitar with **JOHNNY JONES** – piano / **J.T. BROWN** – tenor sax / **ODIE PAYNE** – drums / **RANSOM KNOWLING** – bass

		not issued	Trumpet
1952.	(78) **DUST MY BROOM. (by "ELMO JAMES") / Catfish Blues (by "BOBO THOMAS")**	-	
	(re-iss.1954 on 'Ace')		

		not issued	Modern
1953.	(78) **I BELIEVE. / I HELD MY BABY LAST NIGHT**	-	
1953.	(78) **BABY WHAT'S WRONG. / SINFUL WOMAN**	-	

		not issued	Checker
1953.	(78) **COUNTRY BOOGIE. / SHE JUST WON'T DO RIGHT**	-	

		not issued	Flair
1953.	(78) **HAWAIIAN BOOGIE. / EARLY IN THE MORNING**	-	
1953.	(78) **CAN'T STOP LOVIN'. / MAKE A LITTLE LOVE**	-	
1954.	(78) **SAXONY BOOGIE. / DUMB WOMAN BLUES**		
	(above single on 'Meteor')		
1954.	(78) **PLEASE FIND MY BABY. / STRANGE KINDA BABY**	-	
1954.	(78) **MAKE MY DREAMS COME TRUE. / HAND IN HAND**	-	
1954.	(78) **SHO'NUFF I DO. / 1839 BLUES**	-	

— now with new line-up **WILLARD McDANIEL** – piano / **CHUCK HAMILTON** – bass / **JESSE SAILES** – drums / **MAXWELL DAVIES** – tenor sax / **JAMES PARR** – trumpet / **JEWEL GRANT** – baritone sax

1955.	(78) **DARK AND DREARY. / ROCK MY BABY RIGHT**	-	
1955.	(78) **SAX SYMPHONY BOOGIE. / FLAMING BLUES**	-	

(above single on 'Meteor')
1955. (78) **SUNNY LAND. / STANDING AT THE CROSSROADS**
(re-iss.1964 on 'Kent')
1955. (78) **LATE HOURS AT MIDNIGHT. / THE WAY YOU TREAT ME**
1955. (78) **HAPPY HOME. / NO LOVE IN MY HEART**
1955. (78) **DUST MY BLUES. / I WAS A FOOL**
1955. (78) **BLUES BEFORE SUNRISE. / GOODBYE BABY**

not issued Modern

1956. (7") **LONG TALL WOMAN. / WILD ABOUT YOU**

— returned to his original line-up + added **HOMESICK JAMES** – guitar

not issued Mel-Chief

1957. (7") **THE TWELVE-YEAR OLD BOY. / COMING HOME**
1957. (7") **IT HURTS ME TOO. / ELMORE'S CONTRIBUTION TO JAZZ**
1957. (7") **CRY FOR ME BABY. / TAKE ME WHERE YOU GO**
(above also on 'S&M' and 'M-Pac')(re-iss.1966 on 'USA')
1958. (7") **KNOCKING AT YOUR DOOR. / CALLING ALL BLUES**

not issued Fire

1959. (7") **MAKE MY DREAMS COME TRUE. / BOBBY'S ROCK**
1959. (7") **DUST MY BLUES (I BELIEVE). / HAPPY HOME**
(above single iss.on 'Kent', re-iss.1963)(UK-iss.Oct64 with The BOOM BUSTERS on 'Sue' records)
1960. (7") **THE SKY IS CRYING. / HELD MY BABY LAST NIGHT**
1960. (7") **I CAN'T HOLD OUT. / THE SUN IS SHINING**
(above single on 'Chess')
1960. (7") **ROLLIN' AND TUMBLIN'. / I'M WORRIED**
1960. (7") **DONE SOMEBODY WRONG. / FINE LITTLE MAMA**
1961. (lp) **BLUES AFTER HOURS**
– Dust my blues / Sunnyland / Mean and evil / Dark and dreamy / Standing at the crossroads / Happy home / No love in my heart for you / Blues before sunrise / I was a fool / Goodbye baby. *(re-iss.1963 on 'Crown' + 1964 /1969 as 'THE ORIGINAL FOLK BLUES') (re-iss.1968 as 'ELMORE JAMES' on 'Kent') (re-iss.1969 as 'BLUES IN MY HEART, RHYTHM IN MY SOUL' on 'United' then 'Custom')*

— retained **HOMESICK JAMES** + recruited **SPRUCE JOHNSON** – guitar

1961. (7") **STRANGER BLUES. / ANNA LEE**
1961. (7") **LOOK ON YONDER WALL. / SHAKE YOUR MONEYMAKER**
(re-iss.1965 on 'Enjoy')

— His 1962 line-up were **JOHNNY ACEY** – piano / **RIFF RUFFIN** – guitar / **DANNY MOORE** – trumpet / **WILLIAMS** – drums

1963. (7") **PICKIN' THE BLUES. / IT HURTS ME TOO**

— ELMORE died of a heart attack on 23 May '63.

– postumous releases –

1965. Enjoy; (7") **MEAN MISTREATING MAMA (version). / BLEEDING**
1965. Enjoy; (7") **EVERYDAY I HAVE BLUES. / DUST MY BROOM**
Jul 65. Sue/ US= Enjoy; (7") **IT HURTS ME TOO. / (MY) BLEEDING HEART** 1964
Sep 65. Sue; (7") **CALLING THE BLUES. / KNOCKING AT YOUR DOOR**
(above 'A'side actually by 'JUNIOR WELLS & EARL HOOKER')
1966. Sue; (lp) **THE BEST OF ELMORE JAMES**
– Dust my blues / Fine little mama / The sky is crying / Shake your moneymaker / Anna Lee / I'm worried / Stranger blues / Rollin' and tumblin' / Look on yonder wall / Happy home / Bobby's rock / Held my baby last night / Done somebody wrong / Make my dreams come true. *(re-iss.1981 on 'Ace')*
Apr 66. Sue; (7") **I NEED YOU. / MEAN MISTREATING MAMA**
1967. Sue; (lp) **ELMORE JAMES MEMORIAL ALBUM**
– Standing at the crossroads / The twelve year old boy / One way out / It hurts me too (part 1) / Elmore's contribution to jazz / Take me where you go / I can't stop lovin' you / It hurts me too (part 2) / Dust my broom / Knocking at your door / Coming home / Pickin' the blues / Bleeding heart / Cry for me baby.
1965. Jewel; (7") **DUST MY BROOM. / ('b' by Arthur Crudup)**
1966. Jewel; (7") **MAKE A LITTLE LOVE (as "ELMER JAMES"). / ('b' by Bobo Thomas)**
1965. Kent; (lp) **ANTHOLOGY OF THE BLUES: THE LEGEND OF ELMORE JAMES**
(re-iss.1970 on 'United' / UK-iss.1970 on 'United Artists')
1966. Kent; (7") **SUNNYLAND. / GOODBYE BABY**
1966. Kent; (lp) **ANTHOLOGY OF THE BLUES: THE RESURRECTION OF ELMORE JAMES**
(re-iss.1970 on 'United')
1967. Kent; (7") **STRANGER BLUES (version). / ANNA LEE**
1968. Kent; (7") **I BELIEVE. / 1839 BLUES**
1968. Bell; (lp) **ELMORE JAMES**
1968. Bell; (lp) **SOMETHING INSIDE OF ME**
1968. Ember; (lp) **THE LATE FANTASTICALLY GREAT ELMORE JAMES**
Note; 5 releases on 'Sphere Sound'.
1969. (lp) **THE SKY IS CRYING**
1969. (7") **MY BLEEDING HEART. / ONE WAY OUT**
1969. (7") **I NEED YOU (BABY). / SHAKE YOUR MONEYMAKER**
1969. (7") **DUST MY BROOM. / ROLLIN' AND TUMBLIN'**
1969. (7") **SOMETHING INSIDE OF ME. / SHE DONE MOVED**
1969. (lp) **I NEED YOU**
1969. Fury; (7") **UP JUMPED ELMORE. / EVERYDAY I HAVE THE BLUES**
1969. Chess; (lp) **WHOSE MUDDY SHOES (w / some tracks by JOHN BRIM)**
(UK-iss.+cd 1989 on 'Chess')
1970. Blue Horizon; (lp) **TOUGH (w / 4 tracks by JOHN BRIM)**
1970. Blue Horizon; (d-lp) **TO KNOW A MAN**
1971. Trip; (lp) **THE HISTORY OF ELMORE JAMES VOL.1**
1972. Trip; (lp) **THE HISTORY OF ELMORE JAMES VOL.2**
1972. Upfront; (lp) **THE GREAT ELMORE JAMES**
1973. Polydor; (lp) **COTTON PATCH HOTFOOTS (other side by WALTER HORTON)**
1975. D.J.M.; (d-lp) **ALL THEM BLUES**
1977. Pickwick; (lp) **SCREAMIN' BLUES**
1978. Charly; (lp)(c) **ONE WAY OUT**
Mar 81. Charly; (lp) **GOT TO MOVE**
Apr 81. Charly; (7"m) **DONE SOMEBODY WRONG. / PICKIN' THE BLUES / DUST MY BROOM**
1984. Charly; (lp) **COME GO WITH ME**
(cd-iss.May89)
Dec 86. Charly; (cd) **SHAKE YOUR MONEYMAKER**
Dec 92. Charly; (4xcd-box) **KING OF THE SLIDE GUITAR**
Apr 83. Ace; (lp)(yellow-lp) **KING OF THE SLIDE GUITAR**
Aug 84. Ace; (lp) **THE ORIGINAL METEOR AND FLAIR SIDES**
Nov 86. Ace; (lp)(cd) **LET'S CUT IT: THE VERY BEST OF ELMORE JAMES**
(re-iss.Nov93)
Oct 93. Ace; (cd-box) **THE CLASSIC EARLY RECORDINGS (1951-1956)**
Nov 83. Blue Moon; (lp) **RED HOT BLUES**
Jan 85. Topline; (lp)(c) **DUST MY BROOM**
Nov 85. Deja Vu; (lp)(c) **20 BLUES GREATS**
(cd-iss.Jul88)
May 89. Deja Vu; (cd)(c) **THE ELMORE JAMES STORY**
Feb 86. Crown; (lp)(c) **KING OF THE BOTTLENECK BLUES**
Apr 86. Castle; (lp)(c) **PICKIN' THE BLUES**
May 88. Blues City; (lp)(c)(cd) **GREATEST HITS**
Jul 90. Instant; (d-cd) **DUST MY BROOM**
Apr 92. Blues Project; (cd)(lp) **STREET TALKIN'**
Jun 95. Ace; (cd) **THE BEST OF ELMORE JAMES – THE EARLY YEARS**
Nov 95. The Collection; (d-cd) **GREATEST HITS**

Etta JAMES

Born: JAMESETTA HAWKINS, 25 Jan'38, Los Angeles, California, USA; an illegitimate daughter of a black mother and a father of Italian extraction. She was initially raised by step-parents under the name of ROGERS, until they died and she returned to her real mother. Discovered by JOHNNY OTIS in 1954 while she sang in vocal group The CREOLETTES. OTIS soon nicknamed her PEACHES, after her lighter-than-brown complexion and red-ish hair. Their /her first recording for 'Modern' was 'THE WALLFLOWER', which was originally recorded as 'ROLL WITH ME BABY', but this was censored. This song was quickly snatched by white pop singer GEORGIA GIBBS, who took it to No.1 in the US charts, much to the annoyance of ETTA, OTIS and her group. It did however make Top 3 for her in the R&B charts, although she fell out with OTIS over the next decade, due to non-payment of royalties. Her second solo venture in 1955 'I HOPE YOU'RE SATISFIED', was first to feature duet with HARVEY FUQUA, with backing from musician MAXWELL DAVIS. In the early 60's, her contract was bought by 'Chess' subsidiary 'Argo' records, who quickly rushed out 'ALL I COULD DO WAS CRY', which was her first crossover into pop Top 40. Many hits followed but by the mid-60's it was clear her increasing drug habit (heroin) was taking over. In 1967 she recorded what was to become her greatest song 'I'D RATHER GO BLIND', which 2 years later was a massive UK hit for CHICKEN SHACK (who featured at the time CHRISTINE PERFECT (McVIE), later of FLEETWOOD MAC). In the 70's, she recorded sporadically, although her choice of standards didn't return her to her former glory. In the late 80's & 90's she was signed to 'Island' then 'Warners', who kept her name alive and hip-shakin'. • **Style:** Legendary and emotionally fuelled No.1 female R&B soul singer. • **Songwriters:** She co-wrote many and covered; BABY WHAT YOU WANT ME TO DO (Jimmy Reed) / NO PITY (Jackie Wilson) / STRANGE MAN (Dorothy Love Coates) / ONLY WOMEN BLEED (Alice Cooper) / PIECE OF MY HEART (Bert Berns) / TAKE IT TO THE LIMIT (Eagles) / 99 AND A HALF WON'T DO (Wilson Pickett) / etc. • **Trivia:** West Coast producer JERRY WEXLER worked on her return 1978 album (see below).

Recommended: HER GREATEST SIDES VOL.1 (*7)

ETTA JAMES – vocals, with session people

not issued Modern

Jan 55. (7") **WALLFLOWER (ROLL WITH ME HENRY). / HOLD ME SQUEEZE ME**

— above with The PEACHES / below now with The MAXWELL DAVIS ORCHESTRA

Apr 55. (7") **HEY HENRY. / BE MINE**
Jul 55. (7") **GOOD ROCKIN' DADDY. / DO SOMETHING CRAZY (CRAZY FEELING)**
Oct 55. (7") **W-O-M-A-N. / THAT'S ALL**
Jan 56. (7") **NUMBER ONE (MY ONE AND ONLY). / I'M A FOOL (HOW BIG A FOOL)**
Apr 56. (7") **SHORTIN' BREAD ROCK. / TEARS OF JOY**
Jul 56. (7") **FOOLS WE MORTAL BE. / TOUGH LOVER**

— now as ETTA "MISS PEACHES" JAMES

Oct 56. (7") **THEN I'LL CARE. / GOOD LOOKIN'** [-] [ ]
May 57. (7") **MARKET PLACE. / THE PICK UP** [-] [ ]
Apr 57. (7") **COME WHAT MAY. / BY THE LIGHT OF THE SILVERY MOON** [-] [ ]

not issued | Kent

Sep 57. (7") **SUNSHINE OF LOVE. / BABY BABY EVERY NIGHT** [-] [ ]
Feb 58. (7") **I HOPE YOU'RE SATISFIED. / IF IT AIN'T ONE THING** [-] [ ]
Jun 58. (7") **WALLFLOWER (TWIST WITH ME HENRY). / HEY HENRY (DOIN' FINE HENRY)** [-] [ ]
Oct 58. (7") **HOW BIG A FOOL. / GOOD ROCKIN' DADDY** [-] [ ]
Feb 59. (7") **GOOD ROCKIN' DADDY. / CRAZY FEELING** [-] [ ]

not issued | Crown

1958. (lp) **MISS ETTA JAMES** [-] [ ]
1959. (lp) **THE BEST OF ETTA JAMES** (compilation) [-] [ ]
1959. (lp) **TWIST WITH ETTA JAMES** [-] [ ]
1960. (lp) **ETTA JAMES** [-] [ ]

— (above 4 release dates were approx. & tracks feat. on 1, 2 or 3 of them) *(most re-issued on 'United' US)*

London | Argo

Apr 60. (7") **ALL I COULD DO WAS CRY. / GIRL OF MY DREAMS** [-] [33]
Jun 60. (7") **ALL I COULD DO WAS CRY. / TOUGH MARY** [ ] [-]
Sep 60. (7") **MY DEAREST DARLING. / TOUGH MARY** [-] [34]
Nov 60. (7") **MY DEAREST DARLING. / GIRL OF MY DREAMS** [ ] [-]

London | Chess

Sep 60. (7") **IF I CAN'T HAVE YOU. / MY HEART CRIES** [ ] [ ]
Dec 60. (7") **SPOONFUL. / IT'S A CRYING SHAME** [-] [ ]

— above 2 as – ETTA & HARVEY (HARVEY FUQUA of The MOONGLOWS) + others later

Pye Int. | Argo

Jan 61. (7") **AT LAST. / I JUST WANT TO MAKE LOVE TO YOU** [-] [47]
May 61. (7") **TRUST IN ME. / ANYTHING TO SAY YOU'RE MINE** [ ] [ ] Mar61
Aug 61. (lp) **AT LAST!** (UK-diff.5 tracks) [ ] [68]
– Something's got a hold on me / My dearest darling / At last / Fool that I am / Sunday kind of love / Pushover / All I could do was cry / Stop the wedding / Trust in me / Would it make any difference. *(UK-iss.Oct87 on 'Charly', cd-iss.Mar93) (re-iss.Jul90 on 'MCA', cd-iss.Nov91)*
Oct 61. (7") **FOOL THAT I AM. / DREAM** [ ] [50] Jun61
Aug 61. (7") **DON'T CRY, BABY. / A SUNDAY KIND OF LOVE** [-] [39]
Nov 61. (7") **IT'S TOO SOON TO KNOW. / SEVEN DAY FOOL** [-] [ ]
Jan 62. (lp) **THE SECOND TIME AROUND** [-] [ ]
– Plum nuts / I'll dry my tears / Seven day fool / In my diary / Dream / Don't cry baby / Fool that I am / One for my baby / It's too soon to know / Don't get around much more.
Apr 62. (7") **SOMETHING'S GOT A HOLD ON ME. / WAITING FOR CHARLIE TO COME HOME** [ ] [37] Feb62
1962. (lp) **ETTA JAMES** [-] [ ]
– Let me know / My heart cries / Spoonful / Nobody but you / You can count on me / My dear / Lover's mourn / Waiting for my Charlie to come home / Guess again.
Sep 62. (7") **STOP THE WEDDING. / STREET OF TEARS** [ ] [34] Aug62
Nov 62. (7") **FOOLS RUSH IN. / NEXT DOOR TO THE BLUES** [-] [ ]
Jan 63. (7") **WOULD IT MAKE ANY DIFFERENCE TO YOU. / HOW DO YOU TALK TO AN ANGEL** [-] [ ]
Feb 63. (lp) **ETTA JAMES SINGS FOR LOVERS** [-] [ ]
– Don't take your love from me / How do you speak to an angel / Fools rush in / Don't blame me / Someone to watch over me / Again / I want to be loved / It could happen to you / These foolish things / Prisoner of love.
Jun 63. (7") **PUSHOVER. / I CAN'T HOLD IT ANYMORE** [ ] [25] Apr63
Aug 63. (7") **PAY BACK. / BE HONEST WITH ME** [-] [ ]
Aug 63. (lp) **ETTA JAMES' TOP TEN** (compilation) [-] [ ]
– All I could do was cry / My dearest darling / A Sunday kind of love / At last / Fool that I am / Something's got a hold on me / Stop the wedding / Pushover / Would it make any difference to you.
Oct 63. (7") **TWO SIDES (TO EVERY STORY). / I WORRY ABOUT YOU** [-] [ ]
Jan 64. (7") **BABY WHAT YOU WANT ME TO DO. / WHAT I SAY** [-] [ ]

Chess | Argo

Jan 64. (lp) **ETTA JAMES ROCKS THE HOUSE (live)** [ ] [ ]
– Something's got a hold on me / Baby what you want me to do / What I say / Money / Seven day fool / Sweet little angel / Ooh poo pah doo / Woke up this morning.
Apr 64. (7") **LOVING YOU MORE EVERY DAY. / LOOK WHO'S BLUE** [-] [ ]
Jun 64. (7") **THAT MAN BELONGS BACK HERE WITH ME. / BREAKING POINT** [-] [ ]
Dec 64. (lp) **QUEEN OF SOUL** [-] [ ]
– Flight 101 / You better do right / I worry 'bout you / Lovin' you more every day / I wish someone would care / That man belongs back here with me / Breaking point / Somewhere out there / Mellow fellow / Bobby is his name.
Jan 65. (7") **MELLOW FELLOW. / BOBBY IS HIS NAME** [-] [ ]

Chess | Cadet

Dec 65. (7") **DO I MAKE MYSELF CLEAR. / SOMEWHERE DOWN THE LINE** [-] [ ]
Jan 66. (7") **ONLY TIME WILL TELL. / I'M SORRY FOR YOU** [ ] [ ]
Aug 66. (7") **IN THE BASEMENT** – PART 1. / PART 2 [-] [ ]

Singles from Dec 65 + Aug 66 were by – ETTA JAMES & SUGAR PIE DeSANTO –

Jan 67. (7") **I PREFER YOU. / I'M SO GLAD** [ ] [ ]
Feb 67. (lp) **CALL MY NAME** [-] [ ]
– Happiness / I prefer you / I'm so glad (I found love in you) / Nobody like you / That's all I want from you / It must be your love / Have faith in me / 842-3089 (Call my name) / Nobody loves me / Don't pick me for your fool / It's all right / You are my sunshine.
Apr 67. (7") **IT MUST ME YOUR LOVE. / DON'T PICK ME FOR YOUR FOOL** [-] [ ]
Jul 67. (7") **SECURITY. / I'M GONNA TAKE WHAT HE'S GOT** [ ] [-]
Sep 67. (7") **842-3089 (CALL MY NAME). / HAPPINESS** [-] [ ]
Nov 67. (7") **TELL MAMA. / I'D RATHER GO BLIND** [-] [23]
Feb 68. (7") **SECURITY. / IT MUST BE YOUR LOVE** [-] [35]
Mar 68. (lp) **TELL MAMA** [ ] [ ]
– Tell mama / I'd rather go blind / Love of my man / I'm gonna take what he's got / The same rope / Security / Steal away / My mother-in-law / Don't lose your good thing / It hurts me so much / Just a little bit. *(cd-iss.Oct88 on 'Charly') (re-iss.cd Feb90 + Apr92 on 'Chess-MCA')*
Jul 68. (7") **I GOT YOU BABE. / I WORSHIP THE GROUND YOU WALK ON** [ ] [ ]
Sep 68. (7") **YOU GOT IT. / FIRE** [ ] [ ]
Jan 69. (7") **ALMOST PERSUADED. / STEAL AWAY** [ ] [ ]
Aug 69. (7") **MISS PITIFUL. / BOBBY IS HIS NAME** [-] [ ]
Jan 70. (7") **WHAT FOOLS WE MORTALS BE. / TIGHTEN UP YOUR OWN THING** [-] [ ]
Jan 70. (lp) **ETTA JAMES SINGS FUNK** [-] [ ]
– Tighten up your own thing / Quick reaction and satisfaction / Nothing from nothing leaves nothing / Your replacement / Sound of love / What fools we mortals be / My man is together / Sweet memories / The man I love / Are my thoughts with you / When I stop dreaming.
Mar 70. (7") **SOUND OF LOVE. / WHEN I STOP DREAMING** [-] [ ]
Oct 70. (7") **LOSERS WEEPERS – PART 1. / WEEPERS** [-] [ ]
Nov 70. (lp) **LOSERS WEEPERS** [-] [ ]
– Losers weepers / I got it bad / For all we know / Someone / You're the fool / Ease away a little bit at a time / Take out some insurance / I think it's you / Hold back my tears / Look at the rain / Love of my man / Weepers.

Chess | Chess

1971. (7") **LOVE OF MY MAN. / NOTHING FROM NOTHING LEAVES NOTHING** [-] [ ]
1971. (7") **I THINK IT'S YOU. / TAKE OUT SOME INSURANCE** [-] [ ]
1971. (d-lp) **PEACHES** (compilation) [ ] [ ]
(re-iss.1989)
1972. (7"m) **TELL MAMA. / I'D RATHER GO BLIND / I FOUND A LOVE** [ ] [-]
1972. (7") **I FOUND A LOVE. / NOTHING FROM NOTHING LEAVES NOTHING** [-] [ ]
1972. (7") **TELL IT LIKE IT IS. / W.O.M.A.N.** [-] [ ]
1973. (7") **ALL THE WAY DOWN. / LAY BACK DADDY** [-] [ ]
1973. (lp) **ETTA JAMES** [-] [ ]
– All the way down / God's song / Only a fool / Down so low / Leave your hat on / Sail away / Yesterday's music / Lay back daddy / Just one more day.
1973. (7") **LEAVE YOUR HAT ON. / ONLY A FOOL** [-] [ ]
Aug 74. (7") **OUT ON THE STREET AGAIN. / COME A LITTLE CLOSER** [ ] [ ]
Aug 74. (lp) **COME A LITTLE CLOSER** [-] [ ]
– Power play / Feeling uneasy / St.Louis blues / Gonna have some fun tonight / Sooki sooki / Out on the street again / Mama told me / You give me what I want / Come a little closer / Let's burn down the cornfield. *(re-iss.May88 on 'Charly')*
1976. (7") **LOVIN' ARMS. / TAKE OUT SOME INSURANCE** [-] [ ]
1976. (7") **JUMP INTO LOVE. / I'VE BEEN A SICK FOOL** [-] [ ]
1976. (lp) **ETTA IS BETTA THAN EVVAH!** [-] [ ]

Warners | Warners

Jul 78. (7") **PIECE OF MY HEART. / LOVESICK BLUES** [ ] [ ]
Jul 78. (lp)(c) **DEEP IN THE NIGHT** [ ] [ ]
– Laying beside you / Piece of my heart / Only women bleed / Take it to the limit / Lovesick blues / Strange man / Sugar on the floor / Sweet touch of love / I'd rather go blind.
Sep 78. (7") **TAKE IT TO THE LIMIT. / STRANGE MAN** [ ] [ ]
Jan 79. (7") **SUGAR ON THE FLOOR. / LOVESICK BLUES** [-] [ ]

not issued | T-Electric-MCA

1980. (7") **MEAN MOTHER. / IT TAKES LOVE TO KEEP A WOMAN** [-] [ ]
1980. (lp) **CHANGES** [-] [ ]
– Mean mother / Donkey / Changes / Don't stop / Who's getting your love / Night by night / It takes love to keep a woman / Wheel of fire / Night people / With you in mind.

Late in '88 she was credited on DAVE STEWART'S (of EURYTHMICS) single 'My Head Is A City'.

Island | Epic

Mar 89. (lp)(c)(cd) **SEVEN YEAR ITCH** [ ] [ ]
– I got the will / Jump into fire / Shakey ground / Come to mama / Damn your eyes / Breakin' up somebody's home / The jealous kind / How strong is a woman / It ain't always what you do (it's who you let see you do it) / One night.
Sep 89. (7") **BABY WHAT YOU WANT ME TO DO. / MAX'S THEME (instrumental)** [-] [ ]
Apr 90. (cd)(c)(lp) **STICKIN' TO MY GUNS** [ ] [ ]
– (re-iss.cd Aug94)

W.E.A. | Warners

Oct 92. (cd)(c) **THE RIGHT TIME** [ ] [ ]
– I sing the blues / Love and happiness / Evening of love / Wet match / You're taking up another man's place / Give it up / Let it rock / 99 and a half (won't do) / You've got me / Night time is the right time / Down home blues.

Private | Private

Apr 94. (cd) **MYSTERY LADY** – THE SONGS OF BILLIE HOLIDAY [ ] [ ]
– Don't explain / You've changed / I don't stand a ghost of a chance (with you) / Embraceable you / How deep is the ocean / (I'm afraid) The masquerade is over / Body and soul / The very thought of you / Lover man (oh where can you be) / I'll be seeing you.

– compilations, etc. –

Feb 65. Sue; (7") **ROLL WITH ME HENRY. / GOOD ROCKIN' DADDY** [ ] [-]
1967. Ember; (lp) **SOUL OF ETTA JAMES** [ ] [-]
Dec 72. Chess; (lp)(c) **GOLDEN DECADE** [ ] [-]
Apr 83. Chess; (d-lp) **CHESS MASTERS** [ ] [-]
Jul 85. Chess; (7") **TELL MAMA. / SECURITY** [ ] [-]
Mar 74. Santa Ponsa; (7") **JUST ASK ME. / 99 WAYS** [ ] [-]
Apr 81. Ace; (10"lp) **GOOD ROCKIN' MAMA** [ ] [-]

Nov 83. Ace; (lp) **TUFF LOVER** [ ] [-]
Feb 85. Ace; (c) **GOOD ROCKIN' MAMA / TUFF LOVER** [ ] [-]
Jun 87. Ace; (lp) **R&B DYNAMITE** [ ] [-]
(cd-iss.Nov93)
Apr 94. Ace; (d-cd) **THE LATE SHOW (live w / EDDIE CLEANHEAD VINSON)** [ ] [-]
Feb 86. Crown; (lp)(c) **R&B QUEEN** [ ] [ ]
Nov 86. Fantasy; (lp)(c) **BLUES IN THE NIGHT (w / EDDIE CLEANHEAD VINSON)** [ ] [ ]
(cd-iss.Apr94 on 'Ace')
1987. Charly; (lp)(c) **HER GREATEST SIDES VOL.1** [ ] [-]
– Tell mama / Something's got a hold on me / Pushover / Only time will tell / Stop the wedding / Security / I'd rather go blind / Trust in me / Sunday kind of love / My dearest darling / At last / Waiting for Charlie to come home / All I could do was cry / Fool that I am.
Feb 94. Charly; (cd) **SOULFUL MISS PEACHES** [ ] [-]
Oct 88. Vogue; (d-lp) **CHICAGO GOLDEN YEARS** [ ] [ ]
Oct 88. Vogue; (cd) **ON CHESS** [ ] [ ]
Nov 90. Roots; (cd)(c) **TELL MAMA VOL.1** [ ] [-]
May 92. Roots; (cd) **SOMETHING'S GOT A HOLD ON ME VOL.2** [ ] [-]
1992. Sound Soultion; (cd)(c) **BACK IN THE BLUES** [ ] [-]
Oct 92. Jazz Archives; (cd) **LEGENDARY HITS** [ ] [-]
Sep 93. Disky; (cd) **THE GOSPEL SOUL OF ETTA JAMES** [ ] [-]
Apr 94. That's Soul; (cd) **MISS PEACHES SINGS THE SOUL** [ ] [-]
Aug 94. Tomato; (cd)(c) **LIVE (live)** [ ] [ ]

Wendy JAMES (see under ⇒ TRANSVISION VAMP)

JAMES GANG

Formed: Cleveland, Ohio, USA . . . 1967 by JIM FOX, TOM KRISS and GLENN SCHWARTZ. When the latter left to PACIFIC GAS & ELECTRIC, he was replaced by guitarist JOE WALSH. Late in '69, their debut lp 'YER ALBUM', broke into US Top 100, and was loved by The WHO's PETE TOWNSHEND, who invited them to support his group on a European tour. The following year, they hit singles chart with 'FUNK 49', taken from US Top 20 lp 'JAMES GANG RIDES AGAIN'. Two more chart albums followed, but without WALSH, who departed for solo career in '72, they failed with future products. • **Style:** Intelligent hard-rock group that went through 2 dynamic axemen JOE WALSH and TOMMY BOLIN. • **Songwriters:** WALSH – KRISS to WALSH-PETERS to group compositions. Covered; CAST YOUR FATE TO THE WIND (Guaraldi-Werber) / STOP (Ragavoy-Schean) / YOU'RE GONNA NEED ME (B.B. King) / LOST WOMAN (Yardbirds) / BLUEBIRD (Buffalo Springfield) / etc. • **Miscellaneous:** On 4 May'70, WALSH witnessed the killings of four students on the campus of his old university of Kent State, Ohio. He was later to campaign vigorously for a memorial.

Recommended: THE TRUE STORY OF THE JAMES GANG (*7)

JOE WALSH (b.20 Nov'47, New York, USA) – guitar, vocals repl. G.SCHWARTZ / **TOM KRISS** – bass, vocals / **JIM FOX** – drums, vocals

Stateside / Bluesway

Nov 69. (lp) **YER ALBUM** [ ] [83] Oct 69
– Take a look around / Funk £48 / Bluebird / Lost woman / Stone rap / Collage / I don't have the time / Wrapcity in English – Fred / Stop. *(re-iss.1989 on 'B.G.O.')*
Jan 70. (7") **FUNK £48. / COLLAGE** [ ] [ ] Aug 69
Jun 70. (7") **STOP. / TAKE A LOOK AROUND** [ ] [ ]

— **DALE PETERS** – bass, vocals repl. KRISS

Probe / A.B.C.

Aug 70. (7") **FUNK £49. / THANKS** [-] [59]
Oct 70. (lp)(c) **JAMES GANG RIDES AGAIN** [ ] [20] Jul 70
– Funk £49 / Asshtonpark / Woman / The bomber: (a) Closet queen – (b) Cast your fate to the wind / Tend my garden / Garden gate / There I go again / Thanks / Ashes the rain and I. *(re-iss.Oct74, US cd-iss.Jun88) (cd-iss.Sep91 on 'BGO')*
Apr 71. (7") **WALK AWAY. / YADIG?** [ ] [51]
Jul 71. (lp)(c) **THIRDS** [ ] [27] Apr 71
– Walk away / Yadig? / Things I could be / Dreamin' in the country / It's all the same / Midnight man / Again / White man – black man / Live my life again. *(cd-iss.Sep91 on 'BGO')*
Oct 71. (7") **MIDNIGHT MAN. / WHITE MAN – BLACK MAN** [-] [80]
Dec 71. (lp)(c) **JAMES GANG LIVE IN CONCERT (live)** [ ] [24] Sep 71
– Stop / You're gonna need me / Take a look around / Tend my garden / Ashes the rain and I / Walk away / Lost woman. *(cd-iss.Sep91 on 'BGO')*
Mar 72. (lp)(c) **STRAIGHT SHOOTER** [ ] [58]
– Madness / Kick back man / Get her back again / Looking for my lady / Getting old / I'll tell you why / Hairy hypochondriac / Let me come home / My door is open.
Apr 72. (7") **LOOKING FOR MY LADY. / HAIRY HYPOCHONDRIAC** [-] [ ]
Jul 72. (7") **KICK BACK MAN. / HAD ENOUGH** [-] [ ]

— **DOMENIC TROIANO** (b.Canada) – guitar, vocals repl. WALSH went solo / added **ROY KENNER** – vocals

Oct 72. (lp)(c) **PASSIN' THRU** [ ] [72]
– Ain't seen nothin' yet / One way street / Had enough / Up to yourself / Every day needs a hero / Run, run, run / Things I want to say to you / Out of control / Drifting girl.

Atlantic / Atco

Dec 73. (lp)(c) **BANG** [ ] [ ]
– Standing in the rain / The Devil is singing our song / Must be love / Alexis / Ride the wind / Got no time for trouble / Rather be alone with you / From another time / Mystery.
Nov 73. (7") **STANDING IN THE RAIN. / FROM ANOTHER TIME** [-] [ ]
Jan 74. (7") **MUST BE LOVE. / GOT NO TIME FOR TROUBLES** [ ] [54]

— **TOMMY BOLIN** – guitar (ex-ENERGY, ex-ZEPHYR) repl. TROIANO (to GUESS WHO)

Aug 74. (7") **CRUISIN' DOWN THE HIGHWAY. / MIAMI TWO-STEP** [-] [ ]
Sep 74. (lp)(c) **MIAMI** [ ] [97]
– Cruisin' down the highway / Do it / Wildfire / Sleepwalker / Miami two-step / Red skies / Spanish lover / Summer breezes / Head above the water.

— **PETERS** and **FOX** recruited **RICHARD SHACK** – guitar repl. KENNER **BUBBA KEITH** – vocals, guitar repl. BOLIN who joined DEEP PURPLE / added **DAVID BRIGGS** – keyboards

May 75. (7") **MERRY GO ROUND. / RED SATIN LOVER** [-] [ ]
May 75. (lp)(c) **NEWBORN** [ ] [ ]
– Merry-go-round / Gonna get by / Earthshaker / All I have / Watch it / Driftin' dreamer / Shoulda' seen your face / Come with me / Heartbreak Hotel / Red satin lover / Cold wind.

— **BOB WEBB** – vocals, guitar / **PHIL GIALLOMARDO** – keyboards, vocals / **FLACO PADRON** – percussion repl. BUBBA, RICHARD + DAVID

Feb 76. (7") **I NEED LOVE. / FEELIN' ALRIGHT** [-] [ ]
Feb 76. (lp) **JESSE COME HOME** [-] [ ]
– I need love / Another year / Feelin' alright / Pleasant song / Hollywood dream / Love hurts / Pick up the pizzas / Stealin' the show / When I was a sailor.

— Disbanded later in 1976.

– compilations, others –

Jan 73. Probe/ US= ABC; (lp)(c) **THE BEST OF THE JAMES GANG FEATURING JOE WALSH** [ ] [79]
– Walk away / Funk £49 / Midnight man / The bomber: (a) Closet queen – (b) Cast your fate to the wind / Yadig? / Take a look around / Funk £48 / Woman / Ashes the rain and I / Stop. *(re-iss.Oct74 & Oct81)*
Dec 73. ABC; (lp) **16 GREATEST HITS** [-] [ ]
Mar 87. See For Miles; (lp) **THE TRUE STORY OF THE JAMES GANG** [ ] [-]
(cd-iss.Mar93, with . . . PLUS tracks)
Jun 94. Pickwick; (cd)(c) **ALL THE BEST (JOE WALSH /JAMES GANG)** [ ] [-]
(re-iss.Jul95)

JAMIE WEDNESDAY (see under ⇒ CARTER THE UNSTOPPABLE SEX MACHINE)

JAMIROQUAI

Formed: Ealing, London based . . . from early 1991 by 22 year-old JAY K. After hitting minor placing with debut 'WHEN YOU GONNA LEARN?', they switched labels to 'Sony Soho Square', where they soon had Top 20 singles. Their debut album 'EMERGENCY ON PLANET EARTH', went straight to UK No.1, as they await to conquer America. • **Style:** Jazzy soulful dirty funk band, led by JAY K, whose green views and vox, was not too dissimilar to STEVIE WONDER. • **Songwriters:** JAY and TOBY are main contributers. • **Trivia:** Pronounced JAM-EAR-OH-KWAI, they took name from a tribe of American Indians.

Recommended: EMERGENCY ON PLANET EARTH (*9).

JAY K – vocals / **TOBY SMITH** – keyboards / **NICK VAN GELDER** – drums / **STUART ZENDER** – bass / plus **KOFI KARIKARI** – percussion / **MAURIZIO RAVALIO** – percussion / **GLENN NIGHTINGALE** + **SIMON BARTHOLOMEW** – guitars / **D-ZIRE** – DJ / **GARY BARNACLE** – sax, flute / **JOHN THIRKELL** – trumpet, flugel horn / **RICHARD EDWARDS** – trombone / etc

Acid Jazz / not iss.?

Oct 92. (12") **WHEN YOU GONNA LEARN?. / ('A'-Mark Nelson mix)** [52] [ ]
(re-iss. Feb93)

Sony / Epic

Mar 93. (12")(c-s)(cd-s) **TOO YOUNG TO DIE. / ('A'mixes)** [10] [ ]
Jun 93. (12")(c-s)(cd-s) **BLOW YOUR MIND (PART 1) / HOOKED UP** [12] [ ]
Jun 93. (cd)(c)(lp) **EMERGENCY ON PLANET EARTH** [1] [ ]
– When you gonna learn (digeridoo) / Too young to die / Hooked up / If I like it, I do it / Music of the mind / Emergency on Planet Earth / Whatever it is, I just can't stop / Blow your mind / Revolution 1993 / Didgin' out.
Aug 93. (12")(c-s)(cd-s) **EMERGENCY ON PLANET EARTH. / IF I LIKE IT, I DO IT (MTV acoustic) / REVOLUTION 1993 (demo)** [32] [ ]
Sep 93. (12")(c-s)(cd-s) **WHEN YOU GONNA LEARN (Didgeri-doo) / DIDGIN' OUT** [28] [ ]
Sep 94. (c-s) **SPACE COWBOY. / ('A'mix)** [17] [ ]
(12"+=)(cd-s+=) – Journey to Arnhem land / Kids.
Oct 94. (cd)(c)(d-lp) **THE RETURN OF THE SPACE COWBOY** [2] [ ]
– Just another story / Stillness in time / Half the man / Light years / Manifest destiny / The kids / Mr.Moon / Scam / Journey to Arnhemland / Morning glory / Space cowboy.
Nov 94. (c-s) **HALF THE MAN. / SPACE CLAV** [15] [ ]
(12"+=)(cd-s+=) – Emergency on Planet Earth (version).
(cd-s) – ('A'side) / Jamiroquai's Greatest Hits: When you gonna learn? / Too young to die / Blow your mind.
Feb 95. (c-s) **LIGHT YEARS / JOURNEY TO ARNHEMLAND (live)** [ ] [ ]
(ext.12"+=) – Light years (live).
(cd-d+=) – Scan / We gettin' down.
Jun 95. (c-s)(cd-s) **STILLNESS IN TIME / SPACE COWBOY (mix)** [9] [ ]
(12"+=)(cd-s+=) – Emergency on Planet Earth / Light years.

JANE'S ADDICTION

Formed: Los Angeles, California, USA . . . 1984 by Miami raised PENNY FARRELL. In 1988 after a self-financed eponymous debut on 'Triple XXX', they signed to 'Warner Bros.'. Their first product for them 'NOTHING'S SHOCKING', caused quite a stir, mainly due to its banned sleeve cover, depicting two naked females strapped to an electric chair. In 1990, their third album 'RITUAL DE LO HABITUAL', reached Top 40 on both sides of the Atlantic. • **Style:** Weird heavy rock outfit, who blend in ecletic folk & thrash. • **Songwriters:** Group penned, except SYMPATHY FOR THE DEVIL (Rolling Stones).

Recommended: RITUAL DE LO HABITUAL (*9) / NOTHING'S SHOCKING (*8) / PORNO FOR PYROS (*5).

PENNY FARRELL (b.BERNSTEIN, New York, USA) – vocals / **DAVE NAVARRO** – guitar / **ERIC A's** – bass / **STEPHEN PERKINS** – drums

not issued | Triple X

Aug 87. (lp) **JANE'S ADDICTION (live)** [-] [ ]
– Trip away / Whores / Pigs in Zen / 1% / I would for you / My time / Jane says / Rock'n'roll / Sympathy / Chip away. *(UK-iss.cd/c/lp.Dec90 on 'Warner Bros.') (re-iss.cd Aug95)*

Warners | Warners

Dec 88. (lp)(c)(cd) **NOTHING'S SHOCKING** [ ] [ ] Sep 88
– Up the beach / Ocean size / Had a dad / Ted, just admit it . . . / Standing in the shower . . .thinking / Summertime rolls / Mountain song / Idiots rule / Jane says / Thank you boys. *(cd+=)*– Pigs in Zen.

Mar 89. (7") **MOUNTAIN SONG. / STANDING IN THE SHOWER . . . THINKING** [-] [ ]

May 89. (12"ep) **THE SHOCKING EP** [ ] [ ]
– Mountain song / Jane says / Had a dad (live).

—— added guest **MORGAN** (a female) – violin

Aug 90. (cd)(c)(lp) **RITUAL DE LO HABITUAL** [37] [19]
– Stop / No one's leaving / Ain't no right / Obvious / Been caught stealing / Three days / Then she did . . . / Of course / Classic girl. *(re-iss.cd/c Feb95)*

Aug 90. (7")(c-s) **THREE DAYS. / (part 2)** [ ] [ ]
(12")(cd-s) – ('A'side) / I would for you (demo) / Jane says (demo).

Mar 91. (7") **BEEN CAUGHT STEALING. / HAD A DAD (demo)** [34] [ ]
(12"+=)(cd-s+=) – ('A'remix) / L.A. medley:- L.A. woman / Nausea / Lexicon devil.

May 91. (7")(c-s)(7"pic-d) **CLASSIC GIRL. / NO ONE'S LEAVING** [ ] [ ]
(12"+=)(cd-s+=) – Ain't no right.

—— Had already disbanded when FARRELL looked liked heading into film acting. NAVARRO had briefly filled in for IZZY STRADLIN in GUNS'N'ROSES.

PORNO FOR PYROS

FARRELL + PERKINS with **PETER DiSTEFANO** – guitar / **MARTIN LENBLE** – bass (ex-THELONLUS MONSTER) / **DJ SKATEMASTER TATE** – keys, samples

Warners | Warners

Apr 93. (cd)(c)(lp) **PORNO FOR PYROS** [13] [3]
– Sadness / Porno for pyros / Meija / Cursed female – cursed male / Pets / Badshit / Packin' / • 25 / Black girlfriend / Blood rag / Orgasm.

Jun 93. (7")(c-s) **PETS. / TONIGHT (from 'West Side Story')** [53] [67]
(12"pic-d+=)(cd-s+=) – Cursed female – cursed male (medley).

Bert JANSCH (see under ⇒ PENTANGLE)

JAPAN

Formed: Catford / Lewisham, London, England . . . mid-70's by DAVID SYLVIAN, his brother STEVE JANSEN, MICK KARN and RICHARD BARBIERI. In 1977, they added second guitarist ROB DEAN, and won a talent competition run by 'Ariola-Hansa', who duly signed them. In the Spring of '78, they released debut album 'ADOLESCENT SEX', which was followed 6 months later by 'OBSCURE ALTERNATIVES'. In 1979, they scored a hit in of all places Japan, with Giorgio Moroder produced single 'LIFE IN TOKYO'. Early in 1980, they had first UK chart placing with 'QUIET LIFE'. Later that year, they moved to 'Virgin', and released Top 50 John Punter produced album 'GENTLEMEN TAKE POLAROIDS'. The next year, after 3 Top 50 hits in UK, they had Top 20 classic album 'TIN DRUM'. Early in 1982, their haunting Top 5 single 'GHOSTS', scored at the same time that their old label re-issued 'EUROPEAN SON'. They split soon after, but exploitation releases filled the charts for the next 18 months. All the band went on to other projects, with DAVID SYLVIAN having the greatest success. After a 1982 collaboration with RYUICHI SAKAMOTO, he released debut solo album 'BRILLIANT TREES' in 1984, which made UK Top 5. • **Style:** Initially influenced by ROXY MUSIC, they turned to disco and later melancholy atmospheric alternative rock. • **Songwriters:** SYLVIAN lyrics / group compositions except; DON'T RAIN ON MY PARADE (Rogers-Hammerstein) / AIN'T THAT PECULIAR (Marvin Gaye) / I SECOND THAT EMOTION (Smokey Robinson) / ALL TOMORROW'S PARTIES (Velvet Underground). • **Trivia:** MICK KARN whose solo work was reminiscent of ENO or BILL NELSON, went on to work as a sculptor. His piece 'TRIBAL DAWN' was used on Channel 4's arty TV programme 'Altered States'.

Recommended: EXORCISING GHOSTS (*9) / ASSEMBLAGE (*7) / TIN DRUM (*9) / GENTLEMEN TAKE POLAROIDS (*7). BRILLIANT TREES (*8; DAVID SYLVIAN) / GONE TO EARTH (*6; DAVID SYLVIAN) / TITLES (*7; MICK KARN).

DAVID SYLVIAN (b. DAVID BATT, 23 Feb'58) – vocals, guitar, keyboards / **RICHARD BARBIERI** (b.30 Nov'57) – keyboards, synthesizers / **ROB DEAN** – guitar, mandolin / **MICK KARN** (b. ANTHONY MICHAELIDES, 24 Jul'58) – bass, saxophone / **STEVE JANSEN** (b. STEVE BATT, 1 Dec'59) – drums, percussion

Ariola | Ariola

Mar 78. (7") **DON'T RAIN ON MY PARADE. / STATELINE** [ ] [-]

Apr 78. (lp)(c) **ADOLESCENT SEX** [ ] [ ]
– Transmission / The unconventional / State line / Wish you were black / Performance / Lovers on Main Street / Don't rain on my parade / Suburban love / Adolescent sex / Communist China / Television. *(re-iss.Sep82) (re-iss.Sep84 on 'Fame') (cd-iss.1989 on 'Hansa')*

Aug 78. (7") **THE UNCONVENTIONAL. / ADOLESCENT SEX** [ ] [-]

Nov 78. (lp)(c) **OBSCURE ALTERNATIVES** [ ] [ ]
– Automatic gun / Rhodesia / Love is infectious / Sometimes I feel so low / Obscure alternatives / Deviation / Suburban Berlin / The tenant. *(re-iss.Sep82) (re-iss.Apr84 on 'Fame') (cd-iss.1989 on 'Hansa')*

Nov 78. (7")(7"blue) **SOMETIMES I FEEL SO LOW. / LOVE IS INFECTIOUS** [ ] [ ]

May 79. (7"red)(12"red) **LIFE IN TOKYO (part 1). / LIFE IN TOKYO (part 2)** [ ] [-]

Jul 79. (7") **LIFE IN TOKYO. / LOVE IS INFECTIOUS** [-] [ ]

Jan 80. (lp)(c) **QUIET LIFE** [53] [ ]
– Quiet life / Fall in love with me / Despair / In-vogue / Halloween / All tomorrow's parties / Alien / The other side of life. *(re-iss.Jul81) (re-iss.Sep82 on 'Fame') (cd-iss.1989 on 'Hansa')*

Feb 80. (7") **I SECOND THAT EMOTION. / QUIET LIFE** [ ] [-]

Virgin | Virgin

Oct 80. (7") **GENTLEMEN TAKE POLAROIDS. / THE EXPERIENCE OF SWIMMING** [60] [ ]
(d7"+=) – The width of a room / Burning bridges.

Oct 80. (lp)(c) **GENTLEMEN TAKE POLAROIDS** [45] [ ]
– Gentlemen take polaroids / Swing / Some kind of fool / My new career / Methods of dance / Ain't that peculiar / Night porter / Taking islands in Africa. *(re-iss.+cd.Apr85) (cd-re-iss.Jun88)*

—— Trimmed to quartet when ROB DEAN left, to later form ILLUSTRATED MAN

Apr 81. (7")(12") **THE ART OF PARTIES. / LIFE WITHOUT BUILDINGS** [48] [-]

Oct 81. (7")(12") **VISIONS OF CHINA. / TAKING ISLANDS IN AFRICA** [32] [-]

Nov 81. (lp)(c) **TIN DRUM** [12] [ ]
– The art of parties / Talking drum / Ghosts / Canton / Still life in mobile homes / Visions of China / Sons of pioneers / Cantonese boy. *(re-iss.+cd.Apr86)*

Jan 82. (7")(12") **GHOSTS. / THE ART OF PARTIES (version)** [5] [ ]

Feb 82. (7") **VISIONS OF CHINA. / CANTON** [-] [ ]

May 82. (d7")(12") **CANTONESE BOY. / BURNING BRIDGES // GENTLEMEN TAKE POLAROIDS / THE EXPERIENCE OF SWIMMING** [24] [ ]

—— They had earlier in the year quietly branched out into new projects. DAVID SYLVIAN went solo after a brief collaboration with RYUICHI SAKAMOTO. MICK KARN went solo, had one-off single with MIDGE URE, then went into sessions before forming DALI'S CAR with PETE MURPHY in '84. BARBERI and JANSEN produced Swedes LUSTAN LAKEJER. The pair formed their own duo (The DOLPHIN BROTHERS) before joining DAVID SYLVIAN again.

– compilations, exploitation releases etc. –

Apr 81. Hansa-Ariola; (7")(12") **LIFE IN TOKYO. / EUROPEAN SON** [ ] [ ]

Aug 81. Hansa-Ariola; (7")(12") **QUIET LIFE. / A FOREIGN PLACE / FALL IN LOVE WITH ME** [19] [ ]

Sep 81. Hansa-Ariola; (lp)(c) **ASSEMBLAGE** [26] [ ]
– Adolescent sex / State line / Communist China / Rhodesia / Suburban Berlin / Life in Tokyo / European son / All tomorrow's parties / Quiet life / I second that emotion. *(cassette includes 12" extended versions) (re-iss.lp/c.Sep85 on 'Fame')*

Jan 82. Hansa-Ariola; (7")(12") **EUROPEAN SONG. / ALIEN** [31] [ ]

Jun 82. Hansa-Ariola; (7")(12") **I SECOND THAT EMOTION. / HALLOWEEN** [9] [ ]

Sep 82. Hansa-Ariola; (7")(12") **LIFE IN TOKYO. / THEME** [28] [ ]

Feb 83. Hansa-Ariola; (7")(12") **ALL TOMORROW'S PARTIES. / IN VOGUE** [38] [ ]

Aug 83. Hansa-Ariola; (d-c) **ADOLESCENT SEX / OBSCURE ALTERNATIVES** [ ] [-]

Dec 89. Hansa-Ariola; (lp)(c)(cd) **A SOUVENIR FROM JAPAN** [ ] [-]

Nov 82. Virgin; (7") **NIGHT PORTER. / AIN'T THAT PECULIAR** [29] [ ]
(12"+=) – Methods of dance.

May 83. Virgin; (7") **CANTON (live). / VISIONS OF CHINA (live)** [42] [ ]

Jun 83. Virgin; (d-lp)(c) **OIL ON CANVAS (live)** [5] [ ]
– Oil on canvas / Sons of pioneers / Gentlemen take polaroids / Swing / Cantonese boy / Visions of china / Ghosts / Voices raised in welcome, hands held in prayer / Night porter / Still life in mobile homes / Methods of dance / Quiet life / The art of parties / Canton / Temple of dawn. *(cd-iss. Apr85)*

Nov 84. Virgin; (d-lp)(c)(cd) **EXORCISING GHOSTS** [45] [ ]
– Methods of dance / Swing / Gentlemen take polaroids / Quiet life / A foreign place * / Night porter / My new career / The other side of life / Visions of China / Sons of pioneers * / Talking drum / The art of parties / Taking islands in Africa / Voices raised in welcome, hands held in prayer / Life without buildings / Ghosts. *(cd-omits *)*

Dec 84 Virgin; (7")**VISIONS OF CHINA / TAKING ISLANDS IN AFRICA** [ ] [ ]
(12"+=) – Swing

Jun 88. Virgin; (3"cd-ep) **GHOSTS / THE ART OF PARTIES / VISIONS OF CHINA** [ ] [ ]

Nov 88. Virgin; (3"cd-ep) **GENTLEMEN TAKE POLAROIDS / CANTONESE BOY / METHODS OF DANCE** [ ] [ ]

Sep 87. Old Gold; (7") **I SECOND THAT EMOTION. / ALL TOMORROW'S PARTIES** [ ] [-]
(12"+=) – Life in Tokyo.

Nov 87. Old Gold; (7") **QUIET LIFE. / LIFE IN TOKYO** ☐ [-]
Nov 88. Old Gold; (7") **GHOSTS. / CANTONESE BOY** ☐ [-]
Nov 92. Old Gold; (cd-ep) **I SECOND THAT EMOTION / QUIET LIFE / LIFE IN TOKYO** ☐ [-]
Oct 91. Receiver; (cd)(c)(lp) **THE OTHER SIDE OF JAPAN** ☐ [-]

SYLVIAN/SAKAMOTO

DAVID SYLVIAN – vocals, instruments (ex-JAPAN) / **RYUICHI SAKAMOTO** – synthesizers (ex-YELLOW MAGIC ORCHESTRA)

Virgin Virgin
Jun 82. (7") **BAMBOO HOUSES. / BAMBOO MUSIC** [30] ☐
(12"+=) – ('A' & 'B' mixes).

DAVID SYLVIAN & RYUICHI SAKAMOTO

Jun 83. (7") **FORBIDDEN COLOURS. / THE SEED AND THE SOWER (by "RYUICHI SAKAMOTO")** [16] ☐
(12"+=) – Last regrets.
(from the the film soundtrack 'Merry Christmas Mr.Lawrence')

– compilations etc. –

Aug 88. Virgin; (3"cd-ep)(5"cd-ep) **FORBIDDEN COLOURS. / BAMBOO HOUSES / BAMBOO MUSIC** ☐ ☐

DAVID SYLVIAN

solo, – vocals, keyboards, guitar, percussion, with **RICHARD BARBIERI** and **STEVE JANSEN** (ex-JAPAN) / **RYUICHI SAKAMOTO** – synthesizers / **HOLGER CZUKAY** – tapes / **DANNY THOMPSON** – upright bass / **KENNY WHEELER** – horns

Virgin Virgin
May 84. (7")(12")(7"pic-d) **RED GUITAR. / FORBIDDEN COLOURS (version)** [17] ☐
Jun 84. (lp)(c)(cd) **BRILLIANT TREES** [4] ☐
– Pulling punches / The ink in the well / Nostalgia / Red guitar / Weathered wall / Backwaters / Brilliant trees. *(re-iss.Apr90)*
Aug 84. (7")(12") **THE INK IN THE WELL (remix). / WEATHERED WALL (instrumental)** [36] ☐
Oct 84. (7") **PULLING PUNCHES. / BACKWATERS (remix)** [56] ☐
(12"+=) – ('A'extended).

— now with **JOHN HASSELL** and **ROBERT FRIPP** – guitar / **HOLGER CZUKAY** – tapes / **KENNY WHEELER** – horns

Nov 85. (12"ep) **WORDS WITH THE SHAMEN** [72] ☐
– Part 1:-Ancient evening / Part 2:-Incantation / Part 3:-Awakening. *(re-iss.as c.Dec85.***ALCHEMY (AN INDEX OF POSSIBILITIES)**(c+=) – Preparations for a journey / Steel cathedrals.

— with **ROBERT FRIPP** and **BILL NELSON** – guitar / **PHIL PALMER** – accoustic guitar / **MEL COLLINS** – soprano sax. / **KENNY WHEELER** – flugel horn

Jul 86. (7")(7"square pic-d) **TAKING THE VEIL. / ANSWERED PRAYERS** [53] ☐
(12"+=) – Bird of prey vanishes into a bright blue sky.
Aug 86. (d-lp)(c)(cd) **GONE TO EARTH** [24] ☐
– Taking the veil / Laughter and forgetting / Before the bullfight / Gone to earth / Wave / River man / Silver moon / The healing place / Answered prayers * / Where the railroad meets the sea / The wooden cross * / Silver moon over sleeping steeples * / Campfire: Coyote country * / A bird of prey vanishes into a blue cloudless sky * / Sunlight seen through the towering trees * / Upon this Earth. *(cd-omits tracks *)*
Sep 86. (7") **SILVER MOON. / GONE TO EARTH** ☐ ☐
(12"+=) – Silver moon over sleeping steeples.

— DAVID was also credited on VIRGINIA ASTLEY's Feb87 'Some Small Hope'.

— now with **SAKAMOTO, PALMER, JANSEN** plus **DANNY CUMMINGS** – percussion / **DAVID TORN** – guitar / **DANNY THOMPSON** – d. bass / **MARK ISHAM** – trumpet

Oct 87. (lp)(c)(cd) **SECRETS OF THE BEEHIVE** [37] ☐
– September / The boy with the gun / Maria / Orpheus / The Devil's own / When poets dreamed of angels / Mother and child / Let the happiness in / Waterfront.
Oct 87. (7") **LET THE HAPPINESS IN. / BLUE OF MOON** [66] ☐
(12"+=) – Buoy (remix).
Apr 88. (7") **ORPHEUS. / THE DEVIL'S OWN** ☐ ☐
(12"+=) – Mother and child.

— His touring band **JANSEN, BARBIERI, TORN, ISHAM** plus **IAN MAIDMAN** – bass, percussion / **ROBBY ALEDO** – guitar

DAVID SYLVIAN & HOLGER CZUKAY

with **JAKI LIEBEZEIT** – drums (ex-CAN)

Venture-Virgin Venture
Mar 88. (lp)(c)(cd) **PLIGHT AND PREMONITION** [71] ☐
– Plight (the spiralling of winter ghosts) / Premonition (giant empty iron vessel).

— with **LIEBEZEIT, MICHAEL KAROLI** – guitar / **MARKUS STOCKHAUSEN** – flugel horn / **MICHI** – vocals

Sep 89. (lp)(c)(cd) **FLUX AND MUTABILITY** ☐ ☐
– Flux (a big, bright, colourful world) / Mutability ("a new beginning is in the offing").

DAVID SYLVIAN

Virgin Virgin
Nov 89. (7") **POP SONG. / A BRIEF CONVERSATION ENDING IN DIVORCE** ☐ ☐
(12"+=)/ /(cd-box-s+=) – ('A'remix). / / Stigma of childhood.
Nov 89. (5-cd-box) **WEATHERBOX** (all 3 solo albums + 1 extra). ☐ ☐

SYLVIAN-SAKAMOTO

with **INGRID CHAVEZ**

Virgin Virgin . . .
Jun 92. (7") **HEARTBEAT (TAINAI KAIKI II) RETURNING TO THE WOMB. / NUAGES** [58] ☐
(cd-s+=) – The lost emperor.
(cd-s)- ('A' side) / Forbidden colours / Heartbeat.

MICK KARN

– vocals, bass, keyboards, synthesizers (ex-JAPAN) with session

Virgin Virgin
Jun 82. (7")(12") **SENSITIVE. / THE SOUND OF WAVES** ☐ ☐
Nov 82. (lp)(c) **TITLES** [74] ☐
– Tribal dawn / Lost affections in a room / Passion in moisture / Weather the windmill / Saviour, are you with me / Trust me / Sensitive / Piper blue. *(re-iss.Aug88)*

— In Jun83, he teamed up with ULTRAVOX's MIDGE URE, on the single AFTER A FASHION which reached UK No.39. In 1984 KARN formed **DALI'S CAR** with **PETE MURPHY** (ex-BAUHAUS, see ⇒) and **PAUL VINCENT LAWFORD. MICK KARN** returned solo '86.

Virgin Virgin
Jan 87. (lp)(c)(cd) **DREAMS OF REASON PRODUCE MONSTERS** [89] ☐
– First impression / Language of ritual / Buoy / Land / The three fates / When love walks in / Dreams of reason / Answer.
Jan 87. (7") **BUOY. ("MICK KARN featuring DAVID SYLVIAN"). / DREAMS OF REASON** [63] ☐
(12"+=) – Language of ritual.

C.M.P. not issued
Oct 93. (cd) **BESTIAL CLUSTER** ☐ [-]
– Bestial cluster / Back in the beginning / Beard in the letterbox / The drowning dream / The sad velvet breath of Summer & Winter / Saday, Maday / Liver and lungs / Bones of mud.

— with **RICHARD BARBIERI** – keyboards / **STEVE JANSEN** – drums / **DAVID TORN** – guitar / **DAVID LIEBMAN** – soprano sax

May 95. (cd) **THE TOOTH MOTHER** ☐ [-]
– Thundergirl mutation / Plaster the magic tongue / Lodge of skins / Gossip's cup / Feat funk / The tooth mother / Little less hope / There was not anything but nothing.

JANSEN / BARBIERI

JANSEN – vocals, etc / **BARBIERI** – keyboards, etc

Pan-East not issued
Oct 86. (lp)(c)(cd) **WORLD IN A SMALL ROOM** ☐ [-]
(At same time JANSEN w/TAKAHASHI rel.7" STAY CLOSE. / BETSU-NI on 'Rime')

— The JAPAN duo now

The DOLPHIN BROTHERS

with **DAVID RHODES** – guitar / **DANNY THOMPSON** – ac. bass / **MATTHEW SELIGMAN + ROBERT BELL** – bass / **PHIL PALMER** – acoustic guitar / **MARTIN DITCHAM** – percussion

Virgin Virgin?
Jun 87. (7")(12") **SHINING. / MY WINTER** ☐ [-]
Jul 87. (lp)(c) **CATCH THE FALL** ☐ ☐
– Catch the fall / Shining / Second sight / Love that you need / Real life, real answers / Host to the holy / My winter / Pushing the river.
Aug 87. (7")(12") **SECOND SIGHT. / HOST TO THE HOLY** ☐ [-]

STEVE JANSEN & RICHARD BARBIERI

Venture Virgin
Sep 91. (cd) **STORIES ACROSS BORDERS** ☐ ☐
– Long tales, tall shadows / When things dream / Luman / The insomniac's bed / The night gives birth / Celebration 1988 remix (saw) / Nocturnal sightseeing / One more zombie.

Medium not issued
Oct 95. (cd) **STONE TO FLESH** ☐ [-]
– Mother London / Sleepers awake / Ringing the bell backwards: Siren – Drift / Swim there / Closer than "I" / Everything ends in darkness.

— JAPAN reformed quartet in 1990, but as . . .

RAIN TREE CROW

Virgin Virgin
Mar 91. (7")(c-s) **BLACK WATER. / RAIN TREE CROW / I DRINK TO FORGET** [62] ☐
(12") – (1st + 3rd track) / Red Earth (as summertime ends).
(cd-s) – (all above 4).
Apr 91. (cd)(c)(lp) **RAIN TREE CROW** [24] ☐
– Big wheels in Shanty town / Every colour you are / Rain tree crow / Red Earth (as summertime ends) / Rocket full of charge / Boat's for burning / New Moon Red Deer wallow / Black water / A reassuringly dull Sunday / Blackcrow hats shoe shine city.

DAVID SYLVIAN & ROBERT FRIPP

FRIPP – guitar (ex-KING CRIMSON & solo artist) / **TREY GUNN** – synthesizers, vocals, co-writer plus band **DAVID BOTTRILL** – synthesizers / **JERRY MAROTTA** – drums, percussion / **MARC ANDERSON** – percussion / **INGRID CHAVEZ** – backing vocals.

Virgin Virgin
Jul 93. (cd)(c)(lp) **THE FIRST DAY** [21] ☐
– God's monkey / Jean the birdman / Firepower / Brightness falls / 20th century dreaming (a shaman's song) / Darshan (the road to Graceland).
Aug 93. (c-ep)(cd-ep) **JEAN THE BIRDMAN / EARTHBOUND / STARBLIND / ENDGAME** [68] ☐
(cd-ep) – ('A'side) / Tallow moon / Dark water / Gone to Earth.

Dec 93. (cd)(c)(lp) **DARSHAN (mixes)**
Sep 94. (cd) **DAMAGE (live)**
– Damage / God's monkey / Brightness falls / Every colour you are / Firepower / Gone to Earth / 20th century dreaming (a shaman's song) / Wave / Riverman / Darshan (the road to Graceland) / Blinding light of Heaven / The first day.

JANSEN, BARBIERI, KARN

Medium / not issued

Mar 94. (cd) **BEGINNING TO MELT** | | -
– Beginning to melt / The wilderness / March of the innocents / Human agie / Shipwrecks / Ego dance / The orange asylum.
Oct 94. (cd) **SEED** | | -
– Beginning to melt / In the black of desire / The insect tribe / Prey.

Jean-Michel JARRE

Born: 24 Aug'48, Lyon, France. In the late 60's, having played lead guitar for a few rock bands, he enrolled at Pierre Schaeffer's Musical Research Group, studying ethnic music. His love of free-form conflicted with GMR, and he left to work in his own studio with new synthesizer. He released 3 lp's in France at the turn of the decade, but chose to write jingles for radio and TV, etc. In 1971 he had become youngest composer to appear at the Palais Garnier Opera House. In 1973, he composed soundtrack for film Les Granges Brulee'. In 1977 he was signed to 'Polydor', and issued 'OXYGENE', which was earlier released in France on 'Disques Motors'. The album soon rose to No.2 in the UK charts, helped by a surprise Top 5 single 'OXYGENE (part 4)'. Late in 1978, his next album 'EQUINOXE' hit No.11 and he continued to excel commercially throughout the 80's. • **Style:** Multi-layered electronic rock & pop musak, with concepts similiar to MIKE OLDFIELD, but without the instrumentation. • **Songwriters:** Wrote all material. • **Trivia:** He married actress Charlotte Rampling, after meeting her at 1976 Cannes film festival. In 1983, he released 1 copy of an lp 'MUSIC FOR SUPERMARKETS', and after auctioning it for around £10,000, destroyed the master disc. In Apr'86, he set another record, when playing live to over one million people at Houston, Texas. Two and a half years later, he appeared in front of 3 million people at Docklands, London, on 2 seperate nights, due to earlier Newham Council objection. HANK MARVIN guitarist of The SHADOWS, featured on 'LONDON KID' hit single, which was even played by him at the concert.

Recommended: OXYGENE (*7) / EQUINOXE (*6) / IMAGES – THE BEST OF JEAN-MICHEL JARRE (*6).

JEAN-MICHEL JARRE – synthesizers, keyboards

not issued / EMI-Pathe

1969. (lp) **LA CAGE** | - | - | France
1971. (lp) **EROS MACHINE** | - | -

not issued / Disques Motors

1972. (lp) **DESERTED PALACE** | - | - | France
1973. (7") **HYPNOSE. / DESERTED PALACE** | - | -

Polydor / Polydor

Jul 77. (lp)(c) **OXYGENE** | 2 | 78
– Oxygene (Parts 1 – 6). *(cd-iss.1983)*
Aug 77. (7") **OXYGENE (part 4). / OXYGENE (part 6)** | 4 |
Dec 78. (lp)(c) **EQUINOXE** | 11 |
– Equinoxe (Parts I – VIII). *(cd-iss.1983; re-iss.c Jan93)*
Dec 78. (7") **EQUINOXE (part V). / EQUINOXE (part I)** | 45 |
Jul 79. (7") **EQUINOXE (part IV remix). / EQUINOXE (part III)**
Jun 80. (7") **EQUINOXE (part VII) (live). / EQUINOXE (part VIII) (live)**
May 81. (lp)(c) **MAGNETIC FIELDS** | 6 | 98
– Magnetic fields (parts 1 – 5) / The last rumba. *(cd-iss.1983)(re-iss.c. Jan93)*
Jun 81. (7") **MAGNETIC FIELDS (part 2 remix). / MAGNETIC FIELDS (part 1 excerpt)**
Nov 81. (7") **MAGNETIC FIELDS (part 4 remix). / MAGNETIC FIELDS (part 1 excerpt)**

—— added **DOMINIQUE PERRIER + FREDERIC ROUSSEAU** – synthesizers / **ROGER RIZZITELLI** – percussion, drums

May 82. (d-lp)(d-c) **THE CONCERTS IN CHINA (live)** | 6 |
– The overture / Arpegiator / Equinoxe IV / Fishing junks at sunset / Band in the rain / Equinoxe VII / Laser harp / Orient express / Magnetic fields I, III & IV / Night in Shanghai / The last rumba / Magnetic fields II Souvenir of China. *(cd-iss.1983) (re-iss.c. Jan93)*
May 82. (7") **ORIENT EXPRESS. / FISHING JUNKS AT SUNSET**
Nov 84. (lp)(c)(cd) **ZOOLOOK** | 47 |
– Ethnicolour / Diva / Zoolook / Wooloomooloo / Zoolookologie / Blah-blah cafe / Ethnicolour II. *(cd+=)* – Zoolook (remix) / Zoolookologie (remix).

—— retained **FREDERIC** and recruited **ADRIAN BELEW + IRA SIEGEL** – guitar / **MARCUS MILLER** – bass / **YOGI HORTON** – drums, percussion / **LAURIE ANDERSON** – vocals

Nov 84. (7")(12") **ZOOLOOK (remix). / WOOLOOMOOLOO**
(re-iss.Jan85 as 12") (+=) – (extra effects) / ('A'extended).
Mar 85. (7") **ZOOLOOKOLOGIE. / ETHNICOLOUR**
(12"+=) – ('A'extended remixed).
(d7"+=) – Oxygene (part 4) / Oxygene (part 6).

—— w / **PERRIER / MICHEL GEISS** – synth / **JO HAMMER** – electro drums / **DAVID JARRE** – keyboards

Apr 86. (lp)(c)(cd) **RENDEZ-VOUZ** | 9 | 52
– First rendez-vous / Second rendez-vous (part I / II / III / IV) / Third rendez-vous / Fourth rendez-vous / Fifth rendez-vous (part I / II / III) / Last rendez-vous – Ron's piece.
Aug 86. (7") **FOURTH RENDEZ-VOUS. / FIRST RENDEZ-VOUS** | 65 |
(12") – ('A'side) / Rendez-vous (special + original mix) / Moon machine.

—— with **GEISS** – synthesizers / **FRANCIS LIMBERT** – keyboards, synth. / **PASCAL LEBOURG** – keyboards, synth. / **SYLVIAN DURAND** – keyboards, synthesizers / **PERRIER** – keys, synth (HOUSTON only) / **CHRISTINE DURAND** – soprano / **HAMMER** – drums / **KIRK WHALUM** – sax / **GUY DELACROIX** – bass (LYON only) / **DINO LUMBROSO** – percussion (LYON only) / also used choirs & orchestra, etc.

Jul 87. (lp)(c)(cd) **IN CONCERT – LYON / HOUSTON (live)** | 18 |
– Oxygene V / Ethnicolour / Magnetic fields I / Souvenir of China / Equinoxe 5 / Rendez-vous III / Rendez-vous II / Ron's piece / Rendez-vous IV.

—— with **DOMINIQUE, MICHAEL, JO** and **GUY,** plus guests **SYLVIAN** – synth / & **HANK MARVIN** – guitar (of SHADOWS) on track – *

Aug 88. (lp)(c)(cd) **REVOLUTIONS** | 3 |
– Industrial revolution: (overture – part 1 – part 2 – part 3) / London kid * / Revolutions / Tokyo kid / Computer weekend / September / The emigrant.
Oct 88. (7") **REVOLUTIONS. / INDUSTRIAL REVOLUTION 2** | 52 |
(12"+=) – ('A'extended).
(cd-s++=) – ('A'mix).
Dec 88. (7")(c-s) **LONDON KID. / INDUSTRIAL REVOLUTION 3** | 48 |
(12"+=)(cd-s+=) – Revolutions (remix).
Sep 89. (7") **OXYGENE IV (remix). / INDUSTRIAL REVOLUTION OVERTURE** | 65 |
(12"+=) – ('A'live version).
(cd-s++=) – September.
Oct 89. (lp)(c)(cd) **JARRE LIVE (live)** | 16 |
– Introduction (revolution) / Industrial revolution: (Overture – part I – part II – part III) / Magnetic fields II / Oxygene IV / Computer weekend / Revolutions / Rendez-vous IV / Rendez-vous II / The emigrant. *(cd+=)* – (2 extra).

—— Retained **PERRIER and GEISS,** plus introduced The **AMACO RENEGADES** – steel drums / guests **GUY DELACROIX** – bass / **CHRISTOPHE DESCHAMPS** – drums

Jun 90. (cd)(c)(lp) **WAITING FOR COSTEAU**
– Calypso / Calypso (pt.2) / Calypso (pt.3, finale side) / Waiting for Costeau. *(cd+=)* – (extra music).
May 93. (cd)(c)(lp) **CHRONOLOGIE** | 11 |
– (part.1 – part.4) / (part.5 – part.8).
Jun 93. (12")(c-s)(cd-s) **CHRONOLOGIE (part 4). / ('A'part)** | 55 |
(re-mixed re-iss.Oct93, hit 56)
May 94. (cd)(c)(lp) **CHRONOLOGIE VI**
– (slam mix) / (slam mix 2) / (main mix) / (alternative mix) / (original mix).
Oct 95. (cd) **JARREMIX** (dance mixes compilation) | | -

– compilations etc. –

1981. Polydor; (d-c) **OXYGENE / EQUINOXE** | | -
Oct 83. Polydor; (lp)(c) **THE ESSENTIAL JEAN-MICHEL JARRE** | 14 |
(cd-iss.Sep84)
Dec 87. Polydor; (3xcd-box) **CD BOX SET** (1st-3 lp's)
Oct 91. Polydor; (cd)(c)(lp) **IMAGES – THE BEST OF JEAN MICHEL JARRE** | 16 |
– Oxygene 4 / Equinoxe 5 / Magnetic fields 2 / Oxygene 2 / Computer weekend / Equinoxe 4 / Band in the rain / Rendez-vous 2 / London kid / Ethnicolor 1 / Orient express / Calypso 1 / Calypso 3 (fin de siecle) / Rendez-vous 4 / Moon machine / Eldorado / Globe trotter.
Jan 93. Polydor; (cd)(c)(lp) **MUSIK AUS ZEIT UND RAUM**
Feb 88. Old Gold; (7") **OXYGENE (part IV). / EQUINOXE (part 5)** | | -

JAYHAWKS

Formed: Minneapolis, Minnesota, USA ...1985 by MARK OLSON and GARY LOURIS. After a few low-key lp's, they were signed by George Drakoulias to Rick Rubin's 'Def American' label. Their 3rd album 'HOLLYWOOD TOWN HALL' finally broke them in a minor way, when it hit US Top 200 in 1993. • **Style:** Country/R&B-rock influenced by FLYING BURRITO BROTHERS or NEIL YOUNG to The BLACK CROWES. • **Songwriters:** OLSON-LOURIS except; REASON TO BELIEVE (Tim Hardin). • Trivia: OLSON and LOURIS can also be heard on sessions for MARIA McKEE, COUNTING CROWS and former stablemates SOUL ASYLUM.

Recommended: HOLLYWOOD TOWN HALL (*8) / TOMORROW THE GREEN GRASS (*6)

MARK OLSON – vocals, guitar, harmonica / **GARY LOURIS** – vocals, electric guitar / **KAREN GROTBERG** – keyboards / **MARC PERLMAN** – bass repl.KEN CALLAHAN

not issued / Bunkhouse

1986. (lp) **THE JAYHAWKS** | - |

not issued / Twin Tone

1989. (lp)(cd) **THE BLUE EARTH** | - |
– Two angels / She's not alone anymore / Will I be married / Dead end angel / Commonplace streets / Ain't no end / Five cups of coffee / The Baltimore sun / Red firecracker / Sioux City / I'm still dreaming, now I'm yours / Martin's song. *(UK-iss.Jul95)*

—— session **NICKY HOPKINS** – keyboards (ex-JEFF BECK GROUP, etc)

Def Amer.. / Def Amer..

Sep 92. (cd)(c)(lp) **HOLLYWOOD TOWN HALL**
– Waiting for the Sun / Crowded in the wings / Clouds / Two angels / Take me with you / Sister cry / Settled down like rain / Witghita / Nevada, California / Martin's song. *(re-iss.cd Apr95)*
Aug 93. (7")(c-s) **SETTLED DOWN LIKE RAIN. / SISTER CRY**
(cd-s+=) – Live medley: Settled down like rain – Martin's song.
Nov 93. (7")(c-s) **WAITING FOR THE SUN. / MARTIN'S SONG**
(cd-s+=) – Up above my head / Keith & Quentin.
(cd-s+=) – Reason to believe / Sister cry / Medley: Martin's song – Settled down like rain.
(cd-s) – ('A'side) / Up above my head.

— now on drums **DON HEFFINGTON** (studio) / **TIM O'REGAN** (tour)

Feb 95. (cd)(c) **TOMORROW THE GREEN GRASS** [41] [92]
– Blue / I'd run away / Miss Williams' guitar / Two hearts / Real light / Over my shoulder / Bad time / See him on the streets / Nothing left to borrow / Ann Jane / Pray for me / Red's song / Ten little kids.

Feb 95. (7")(c-s) **BLUE. / TOMORROW THE GREEN GRASS** [ ] [ ]
(cd-s+=) – Darling today.

Jun 95. (c-s) **BAD TIME / LAST CIGARETTE** [70] [ ]
(cd-s+=) – Get the load out / Sing me back home.

JAZZ CRUSADERS (see under ⇒ CRUSADERS)

JB's

Formed: early 70's by JAMES BROWN sidekick FRED WESLEY. However their splinter roots could be heard early in 1960, when drummer NAT KENDRICK & THE SWANS hit US No.84 with '(DO THE) MASHED POTATOES (part 1)'; (Dade 1804)/ UK 'Top Rank'; (JAR 351). Other non-hits pursued 'DISH RAG (part 1)'; (Dade 1808)/ 'HOT CHILI'./ 'SLOWDOWN'; (Dade 1812)/ 'WOBBLE WOBBLE (part 1)' (Dade 5003) & debut re-iss.; (Dade 5004). In the early 70's, they branched out on their ownsome and even scored with a few US chart hits. • **Style:** Super-funk mostly instrumental outfit. • **Songwriters:** JB's, all written and arranged by JAMES BROWN. WESLEY took over controls in 1973.

Recommended: GIVIN' UP FOOD FOR FUNK (*6)

FRED WESLEY – trombone / **BOOTSY COLLINS** – bass/ **MACEO PARKER**

Polydor / not issued

Mar 71. (7") **THESE ARE THE JB'S. / (part 2)** [ ] [ ]

Mojo / People

Jun 71. (7") **MY BROTHER. / (part 2)** [-] [ ]
Aug 71. (7") **GRUNT. / (part 2)** [ ] [-]
Jan 72. (7") **GIMME SOME MORE. / THE RABBIT GOT THE GUN** [ ] [67]
May 72. (7") **PASS THE PEAS. / HOT PANTS ROAD** [ ] [95]
Jun 72. (lp) **PASS THE PEAS** (US-title 'FOOD FOR THOUGHT') [ ] [ ]
– Pass the peas / Gimme some more / My brother / Wine spot / Hot pants road / Grunt / Blessed blackness / Escape-ism / King Heroin theme / These are the JB's.
Aug 72. (7") **GIVIN' UP FOOD FOR FUNK. / (part 2)** [ ] [ ]

FRED WESLEY & THE JB's

Polydor / People

Nov 72. (7") **JB SHOUT. / BACK STABBERS** [ ] [ ]
Jan 73. (7") **IF YOU DON'T GET IT THE FIRST TIME, BACK IT UP AND TRY AGAIN. / YOU CAN HAVE WATERGATE, JUST GIVE ME SOME BUCKS AND I'LL BE STRAIGHT** [-] [ ]
(US re-iss.1974)
Feb 73. (7") **WATERMELON MAN. / ALONE AGAIN** [-] [ ]
Apr 73. (7") **DIRTY HARRI. / SPORTIN' LIFE** [-] [ ]
May 73. (7") **DOING IT TO DEATH. / EVERYBODY GOT SOUL** [ ] [22]
Jul 73. (lp) **DOING IT TO DEATH** [ ] [77]
– Doing it to death (parts 1 & 2) / You can have Watergate just gimme some bucks and I'll be straight (x3) / More peas / La di da la di day / Sucker.
Jun 74. (lp) **DAMN RIGHT I'M SOMEBODY** [-] [ ]
– Damn right I'm somebody / Blow your mind / If you don't get it the first time, back up and try again, parrty / I'm payin' taxes, what am I buyin' / Same beat (part 1) / You sure love to ball / Make me what you want me to be / Going to get a thrill.
1974. (7") **SAME BEAT./ (part 2)** [-] [ ]
1975. (7") **DAMN RIGHT I'M SOMEBODY. / (part 2)** [-] [ ]
1975. (7") **ROCKIN' FUNKY WATERGATE. / (part 2)** [-] [ ]
1975. (lp) **BREAKIN' BREAD** [ ] [ ]
1975. (7") **LITTLE BOY BLACK. / ROCKIN' FUNKY WATERGATE (part 2)** [-] [ ]
1975. (7") **BREAKIN' BREAD. / FUNKY MUSIC IS MY STYLE** [-] [ ]
1975. (7") **RICE AND RIBS. / MAKING LOVE** [-] [ ]
1976. (7") **THANK YOU FOR LETTING ME BE MYSELF AND BE YOURS. / (part 2)** [-] [ ]
1976. (7") **(IT'S NOT THE EXPRESS) IT'S JB'S MONORAIL. / (part 2)** [-] [ ]

J.B.'s

1976. (lp) **HUSTLE WITH SPEED** [ ] [ ]
– (It's not the express) It's JB's monorail / Here we come, here we go, here we are / All aboard for the soul funky train / Transmographication / Thank you for letting me be myself and you be yours / Taurus, Aries and Leo / Things to do.
1976. (7") **THANK YOU FOR LETTING ME BE MYSELF AND BE YOURS. / (part 2)** [-] [ ]
1976. (7") **ALL ABOARD THE FUNKY SOUL TRAIN. / THANK YOU FOR LETTING ME BE MYSELF AND YOU BE YOURSELF** [-] [ ]
1976. (lp) **GIVIN' UP FOOD FOR FUNK – THE BEST OF THE JB's** (compilation) [ ] [ ]
– Gimme some more / Givin' up food for funk (part 1 & 2) / If you don't get it the first time, back it up and try again, parrty / Pass the peas / Same beat / Damn right I'm somebody / Doing it to death / Breakin' bread / Keep on bumpin' before you give out of gas / Parrty / J.B. shout.

FRED WESLEY

R.S.O. / R.S.O.

Oct80. (7")(12") **I MAKE MUSIC. / HOUSE PARTY** [ ] [ ]

MACEO & ALL THE KING'S MEN

with 7 others

Pye Int. / ???

Jan 72. (7") **GOT TO GET 'CHA. / (part 2)** [ ] [ ]

Polydor / Polydor

1972. (lp) **FUNKY MUSIC MACHINE** [ ] [ ]
– Funky music machine / I want to sing / Dreams / Feeling alright / Something / Born to wander / T.S.U. (aristocrat of bands) / For no one / Make it with you / Funky tale to tell.

MACEO & THE MACKS

MACEO PARKER – tenor sax (also of PARLIAMENT/ FUNKADELIC)

not issued / People

Aug 73. (7") **PARRTY (part 1). / (part 2)** [-] [71]

MACEO

1974. (7") **FUTURE SHOCK. / (part 2)** [-] [ ]
(re-iss.1976)
1974. (lp) **US** [ ] [ ]
– Soul power '74 / Parrty / Show and tell / Drowning in the sea of love / I can play (just for you and me) / Doing it to death / The soul of a black man.
1974. (7") **SOUL POWER '74. / (part 2)** [-] [ ]
1975. (7") **I CAN PLAY (JUST FOR YOU AND ME). / DOING IT TO DEATH** [-] [ ]
1975. (7") **SHOW AND TELL. / DROWNING IN THE SEA OF LOVE** [-] [ ]
1975. (7") **CROSS THE TRACK. / BOOGIE'N'TWIST** [-] [ ]

– exploitation release

Urban / Urban

Apr 87. (7") **CROSS THE TRACK. / (part 2)** [ ] [ ]
(12"+=) – Soul power.

JEFFERSON AIRPLANE

Formed: San Francisco, California, USA . . . early 1965 by MARTY BALIN and PAUL KANTNER. They recruited others and signed to 'RCA' late '65, releasing debut 45 'IT'S NO SECRET' which flopped. In Sep66, their first lp ' . . . TAKES OFF' was finally issued, although group went through major personnel changes. In came vocalist GRACE SLICK and SPENCER DRYDEN, who added extra needed power to second lp 'SURREALISTIC PILLOW'. In 1967 it soared up to No.3 in USA, and included 2 Top 10 singles 'SOMEBODY TO LOVE' & 'WHITE RABBIT' (the latter inspired by Lewis Carroll book 'Alice In Wonderland'). In Jul'68, the band bought headquarters at 2400 Fulton, San Franscisco and continued to score in the charts until their fragmentation in 1970. They had made an appearance in Aug'69, at the 'Woodstock' festival, with song 'VOLUNTEERS' being used in film. Live-in lovers SLICK and KANTNER produced daughter China in Jan71 and also released own lp in '71 'SUNFIGHTER'. A year earlier, KANTNER had formed initial aggregation of his JEFFERSON STARSHIP, releasing 'BLOWS AGAINST THE EMPIRE' lp. JEFFERSON AIRPLANE returned in 1971 without BALIN, but on own RCA distributed 'Grunt' label. Their album 'BARK' introduced a 54 year-old violinist PAPA JOHN CREACH to the fold, and nearly broke them back into US Top 10. In Mar'74, the group became JEFFERSON STARSHIP and soon added the returning MARTY BALIN for a US No.1 album 'RED OCTOPUS' in 1975, which included Top 3 single 'MIRACLES'. Remained in the limelight for the next 10 years, and when they changed name to STARSHIP (due to departure of KANTNER) in the mid-80's, they had 3 US top spots 'WE BUILT THIS CITY', 'SARA' & 'NOTHING'S GONNA STOP US NOW'. The latter, from the film 'Mannequin', also gave them a UK No.1 hit in 1987. • **Style:** Acid-rock blues & psychedelia outfit, whose drug-orientated epics were put aside in 1974 for AOR textures when JEFFERSON STARSHIP came to be. Confusion was rife in the late 80's, when STARSHIP were competing with re-formed JEFFERSON AIRPLANE. • **Songwriters:** KANTNER or BALIN, plus SLICK, who initially brought in 2 songs (first 2 Top 10's in 1967) written with husband at the time JERRY SLICK and brother-in-law DARBY SLICK.

Recommended: SURREALISTIC PILLOW (*8) / AFTER BATHING AT BAXTER'S (*7) / CROWN OF CREATION (*7) / VOLUNTEERS (*6) GREATEST HITS (TEN YEARS AND CHANGE 1979-1991) (STARSHIP *6).

MARTY BALIN (b.30 Jan'42, Cincinnati, Ohio, USA) – vocals, guitar (ex-solo) / **PAUL KANTNER** (b.12 Mar'42, San Francisco) – guitar, vocals / **JORMA KAUKONEN** (b.23 Dec'40, Washington DC) – lead guitar / **SIGNE TOLY ANDERSON** – vocals / **JACK CASADY** – bass repl. BOB HARVEY / **SKIP SPENCE** – drums (ex-QUICKSILVER MESSENGER SERVICE) repl. JERRY PELOQUIN

R.C.A. / R.C.A.

Feb 66. (7") **IT'S NO SECRET. / RUNNIN' ROUND THIS TABLE** [-] [ ]
1966. (7") **COME UP THE YEARS. / BLUES FROM AN AEROPLANE** [-] [ ]
Sep 66. (lp) **JEFFERSON AIRPLANE TAKES OFF** [-] [ ]
– Blues from an airplane / Let me in / It's no secret / Bringing me down / Tobacco road / Coming up the years / Run around / Let's get together / Don't slip away / Chauffeur blues / And I like it. *(UK rel.Oct71, re-iss.Jun74)*
1966. (7") **BRINGING ME DOWN. / LET ME IN** [-] [ ]

— **GRACE SLICK** (b.GRACE WING, 30 Oct'39, Chicago, Illinois) – vocals (ex-GREAT SOCIETY) repl. SIGNE who left to look after her baby / **SPENCER DRYDEN** (b. 7 Apr'38, New York) – drums (ex-PEANUT BUTTER CONSPIRACY, ex-ASHES) repl. SKIP who formed MOBY GRAPE

Dec 66. (7") **MY BEST FRIEND. / HOW DO YOU FEEL** [-] [ ]
Sep 67. (lp) **SURREALISTIC PILLOW** [ ] [3] Feb 67
– She has funny cars / Somebody to love / My best friend / Today / Comin' back to me / How do you feel / 3/5 mile in 10 seconds / D.C.B.A. – 25 / Embryonic journey / White rabbit / Plastic fantastic lover. *(UK-rel.differed tracks) (cd-iss.Sep84 & Oct87)*
May 67. (7") **SOMEBODY TO LOVE. / SHE HAS FUNNY CARS** [ ] [5] Feb 67
Sep 67. (7") **WHITE RABBIT. / PLASTIC FANTASTIC LOVER** [ ] [8] Jun 67
Nov 67. (7") **THE BALLAD OF YOU AND ME AND POONEIL. / TWO HEADS** [ ] [42] Sep 67
Jun 68. (lp) **AFTER BATHING AT BAXTER'S** [ ] [17] Dec 67
– (Streetmasse): / The ballad of you and me and Pooneil – A small package of value will come to you, shortly – Young girl Sunday blues / (The war is over): / Martha – Wild thyme / (Hymn to an older generation): / The last wall of the castle – Rejoyce / How sweet it is:- Watch her ride – Spare chaynge / Shizoforest love suite: Two heads – Won't you try – Saturday afternoon.
Jan 68. (7") **WATCH HER RIDE. / MARTHA** [-] [1] Dec 67
Jun 68. (7") **GREASY HEART. / SHARE A LITTLE JOKE** [ ] [98] Mar 68
Sep 68. (7") **IF YOU FEEL. / LIKE CHINA BREAKING** [ ] [-]
Oct 68. (7") **CROWN OF CREATION. / TRIAD** [-] [64]
Dec 68. (lp) **CROWN OF CREATION** [ ] [6] Sep 68
– Lather / In time / Triad / Star track / Share a little joke / Chushingura / If you feel / Crown of creation / Ice cream Phoenix / Greasy heart / The house at Pooh Corner. *(re-iss.Oct85) cd-iss.Jun88)*
Jun 69. (lp) **BLESS IT'S POINTED LITTLE HEAD (live)** [38] [17] Feb 69
– Clergy / 3/5 of a mile in 10 seconds / Somebody to love / Fat angel / Rock me baby / The other side of this life / It's no secret / Plastic fantastic lover / Turn out the lights / Bear melt.
1969. (7") **PLASTIC FANTASTIC LOVER (live). / THE OTHER SIDE OF THIS LIFE (live)** [-] [ ]
Feb 70. (lp) **VOLUNTEERS** [34] [13] Nov 69
– We can be together / Good shepherd / The farm / Hey Frederick / Turn my life down / Wooden ships / Eskimo blue day / A song for all seasons / Meadowlands / Volunteers. *(re-iss.Oct85)*
Mar 70. (7") **VOLUNTEERS. / WE CAN BE TOGETHER** [ ] [65] Nov 69

— **JOEY COVINGTON** – drums repl. DRYDEN who joined NEW RIDERS OF THE PURPLE SAGE (above new with **SLICK, CASADY, BALIN** and **KAUKONEN)** (note also DRYDEN played on below 'A' side)

Aug 70. (7") **MEXICO. / HAVE YOU SEEN THE SAUCERS?** [ ] [ ]

— At this time various mambers, mainly KAUKONEN and CASADY side lined HOT TUNA. PAUL KANTNER then recorded album with what was then p/t JEFFERSON STARSHIP (see further below and his late '71 co-credit with GRACE SLICK

— **PAPA JOHN CREACH** (b.28 May 1917, Beaver Falls, Pennsylvania) – violin (of HOT TUNA) finally repl. BALIN who left earlier.

Grunt Grunt

Oct 71. (lp)(c) **BARK** [42] [11] Sep 71
– When the Earth moves again / Feel so good / Crazy Miranda / Pretty as you feel / Wild turkey / Law man / Rock and roll island / Third week in Chelsea / Never argue with a German if you're tired or European song / Thunk / War movie. *(re-issJul84)*
Oct 71. (7") **PRETTY AS YOU FEEL. / WILD TURKEY** [ ] [60]

— **JOHN BARBATA** – drums (ex-CROSBY & NASH ex-TURTLES) repl. JOEY

Jun 72. (lp)(c) **LONG JOHN SILVER** [30] [20]
– Long John Silver / Aerie (gang of eagles) / Twilight double leader / Milk train / Son of Jesus / Easter? / Trial by fire / Alexander the medium / Eat starch mom.
Sep 72. (7") **LONG JOHN SILVER. / MILK TRAIN** [ ] [ ]
1972. (7") **TWILIGHT DOUBLE DEALER. / TRIAL BY FIRE** [-] [ ]

— **DAVID FREIBERG** – vocals (ex-QUICKSILVER MESSENGER SERVICE) (They made last album recorded between 71-72)

Apr 73. (lp)(c) **30 SECONDS OVER WINTERLAND (live)** [ ] [52]
– Have you seen the saucers / Feel so good / Crown of creation / When the Earth moves again / Milk train / Trial by fire / Twilight double leader. *(re-iss.Oct85)*

— Now non-recoding quintet of SLICK, KANTNER, FREIBERG, BARBATA and CREACH. CASADY and KAUKONEN made HOT TUNA their full-time band.

PAUL KANTNER & JEFFERSON STARSHIP

with JERRY GARCIA, DAVID CROSBY, GRAHAM NASH, MICKEY HART

R.C.A. Grunt

Apr 71. (lp) **(IT'S A FRESH WIND THAT) BLOWS AGAINST THE NORTH** [ ] [20] Nov 70
– Mau mau (Amerikon) / The baby tree / Let's go together / A child is coming / Sunrise / Hijack / Home / Have you seen the stars tonite / X-M / Starship.

PAUL KANTNER & GRACE SLICK

Grunt Grunt

Dec 71. (lp) **SUNFIGHTER** [ ] [89]
– Silver spoon / Diana (part 1) / Sunfighter / Titanic / Look at the wood / When I was a boy I watched the wolves / Million / China / Earth mother / Diana (part 2) / Universal Copernican mumbles / Holding together. *(re-iss.+cd.Apr89 on 'Essential')*

— KANTNER later released a US only album 'THE PLANET EARTH ROCK AND ROLL ORCHESTRA iss.Aug83. After leaving JEFFERSON STARSHIP he formed KBC with BALIN and CASADY. (ex-JEFFERSON members). They released a single and album early '83.

PAUL KANTNER, GRACE SLICK, DAVID FREIBERG

with guests **JORMA KAUKONEN** – guitar / **JACK CASADY** – bass / **CHAQUICO** – guitar / **JERRY GARCIA** ('Grateful Dead') / **DAVID CROSBY** ('Crosby, Stills & Nash')

Grunt Grunt

May 73. (lp) **BARON VON TOLBOOTH AND THE CHROME NUN** [ ] [ ]
– Ballad of the chrome nun / Fat / Flowers of the night / Walkin' / Your mind has left your body / Across the board / Harp tree lament / White boy (transcaucasian airmachine blues) / Fishman / Sketches of China.
Jun 73. (7") **BALLAD OF THE CHROME NUN. / SKETCHES OF CHINA** [-] [ ]

JEFFERSON STARSHIP

(new name re-formed)**SLICK, KANTNER, FREIBERG, CREACH** and **BARBATA** recruited **CRAIG CHAQUICO** (b.26 Sep'54) – guitar (ex-STEELWIND)repl. JORMA / **PETE SEARS** – bass, keyboards, vocals repl. PETER KAUKONEN who had repl. JACK

Grunt-RCA Grunt-RCA

Nov 74. (7") **RIDE THE TIGER. / DEVIL'S SON** [-] [84]
Dec 74. (lp) **DRAGONFLY** [ ] [11] Oct 74
– Ride the tiger / That's for sure / Be young you / Caroline / Devil's den / Come to life / All fly away / Hyperdrive.
1975. (7") **BE YOUNG YOU. / CAROLINE** [-] [ ]

— added the returning **MARTY BALIN** – vocals, guitar

Jul 75. (lp)(c) **RED OCTOPUS** [ ] [1]
– Fast buck Freddie / Miracles / Git fiddler / Al Garimasu (there is love) / Sweeter than honey / Play on love / Tumblin' / I want to see another world / Sandalphon / There will be love. *(re-iss.Feb81, re-iss.Oct84 on 'RCA Int.')(re-iss.Jun86 on 'Fame') (cd-iss.Oct87)*
Sep 75. (7") **MIRACLES. / AL GARIMASU (THERE IS LOVE)** [ ] [3] Aug 75
Nov 75. (7") **PLAY ON LOVE. / I WANT TO SEE ANOTHER WORLD** [-] [49]

— Trimmed to sextet when PAPA JOHN CREACH went solo. GRACE SLICK also left

Jul 76. (lp)(c) **SPITFIRE** [30] [3]
– Hot water / Big city / Switchblade / Cruisin' / Love lovely love / St. Charles / Dance with the dragon / St. Charles / With your love / Song to the sun / Ozymandias / Don't let it rain.
Aug 76. (7") **WITH YOUR LOVE. / SWITCHBLADE** [ ] [12] Jul 76
Nov 76. (7") **ST.CHARLES. / LOVE LOVELY LOVE** [-] [64]
Feb 78. (7") **COUNT ON ME. / SHOW YOURSELF** [ ] [8]
Mar 78. (lp)(c) **EARTH** [ ] [5]
– Love too good / Count on me / Take your time / Crazy feelin' / Skateboard / Fire / Show yourself / All nite long.
Jun 78. (7") **RUNAWAY. / HOT WATER** [ ] [12] May 78
Aug 78. (7") **CRAZY FEELIN' / LOVE TOO GOOD** [-] [54]
Nov 78. (7")(12") **LIGHT THE SKY ON FIRE. / HYPERDRIVE** [-] [66]

— **MICKEY THOMAS** – vocals (ex-ELVIN BISHOP) repl. BALIN who went solo / **AYNSLEY DUNBAR** – drums (ex-JOURNEY ex-KGB) repl. BARBATA (above 2 joining **KANTNER, FREIBERG, CHAQUICO** and **SEARS) / GRACE SLICK** also guested uncredited on the next album (she joined full-time Feb81.)

Jan 80. (7") **JANE. / FREEDOM AT POINT ZERO** [21] [14] Nov 79
Jan 80. (lp) **FREEDOM AT ZERO POINT** [22] [10] Nov 79
– Girl with hungry eyes / Freedom at Zero Point / Fadiing lady night / Lightning Rose / Things to come / Just the same / Rock music / Awakening / Jane. *(re-iss.Sep81 on 'RCA') (re-iss.Jun89, cd-iss.Feb90)*
Apr 80. (7") **GIRL WITH THE HUNGRY EYES. / JUST THE SAME** [ ] [55]
Jun 80. (7") **ROCK MUSIC. / LIGHTNING ROSE** [-] [ ]

R.C.A. Grunt

May 81. (7")(12") **FIND YOUR WAY BACK. / MODERN TIMES** [ ] [29] Apr 81
Jun 81. (lp) **MODERN TIMES** [ ] [26] Apr 81
– Find your way back / Stranger / Wild eyes / Save your love / Modern times / Mary / Free / Alien / Stairway to Cleveland. *(re-iss.Sep81)*
Jul 81. (7") **STRANGER. / FREE** [-] [48]
Oct 81. (7")(12") **SAVE YOUR LOVE. / WILD EYES** [-] [ ]
Oct 82. (7") **BE MY LADY. / OUT OF CONTROL** [-] [28]
Feb 83. (lp)(c) **WINDS OF CHANGE** [ ] [26] Oct 82
– Winds of change / Keep on dreamin' / Be my lady / I will stay / Out of control / Can't find love / Black widow / I came back from the jaws of the dragon / Quit wasting time. *(re-iss.+cd.Oct84)*
Jan 83. (7") **WINDS OF CHANGE. / BLACK WIDOW** [-] [38]
Apr 83. (7") **CAN'T FIND LOVE. / I WILL STAY** [-] [ ]

— **DON BALDWIN** – drums (ex-ELVIN BISHOP BAND) repl. DUNBAR

Jun 84. (7") **NO WAY OUT. / ROSE GOES TO YALE** [ ] [ ] May 84
(12"+=) – Be my lady.
Jun 84. (lp)(c)(cd) **NUCLEAR FURNITURE** [ ] [28]
– Layin' it on the line / No way out / Sorry me, sorry you / Live and let live / Connection / Nuclear furniture / Rose goes to Vale / Magician / Assassin / Shining in the moonlight / Showdown / Champion.
Sep 84 (7") **LAYIN' IT ON THE LINE. / SHOWDOWN** [-] [66]

STARSHIP

was the name they were allowed to use after KANTNER left. Now **GRACE SLICK, MICKEY THOMAS, CRAIG CHAQUICO, PETE SEARS** and **DON BALDWIN**

Oct 85. (7")(12") **WE BUILT THIS CITY. / PRIVATE ROOM** [12] [1] Sep 85
Nov 85. (lp)(c)(cd) **KNEE DEEP IN THE HOOPLA** [ ] [7] Oct 85
– We built this city / Sara / Tomorrow doesn't matter tonight / Rock myself to sleep / Desperate heart / Private room / Before I go / Hearts of the world (will understand) / Love rusts. *(re-iss.+cd.Sep89)*
Jan 86. (7") **SARA. / HEARTS OF THE WORLD (WILL UNDERSTAND)** [ ] [1] Dec 85
(12"+=) – Jane.
May 86. (7") **TOMORROW DOESN'T MATTER TONIGHT. / LOVE RUSTS** [ ] [26] Apr 86
(12"+=) – No way out / Laying it on the line.
Jun 86. (7")(12") **BEFORE I GO. / CUT YOU DOWN** [-] [68]

— now w/out SEARS

Mar 87. (7") **NOTHING'S GONNA STOP US NOW. / LAYING IT ON THE LINE** [1] [1] Jan 87

(12"+=) – We built this city / Tomorrow doesn't matter tonight.
Jul 87. (lp)(c)(cd) **NO PROTECTION** [26] [12]
– Beat patrol / Nothing's gonna stop us now / It's not over ('til it's over) / Girls like you / Wings of a lie / The children / I don't know why / Transatlantic / Babylon / Set the night to music.
Aug 87. (7") **IT'S NOT OVER ('TIL IT'S OVER). / BABYLON** [ ] [9] Jun 87
(12"+=) – Jane / Sara. *(also on US cass.)*
Nov 87. (7") **BEAT PATROL. / GIRLS LIKE YOU** [ ] [46] Sep 87
Feb 88. (7") **SET THE NIGHT TO MUSIC. / I DON'T KNOW WHY** [-] [ ]
(12"+=) – ('A' dub version) / ('A' instrumental).

— STARSHIP in the 90's were: – **MICKEY THOMAS, DONNY BALDWIN, CRAIG CHAQUICO** plus **MARK MORGAN** – keyboards / **BRETT BLOOMFIELD** – bass.

Feb 89. (7") **WILD AGAIN. / LAYIN' IT ON THE LINE** [ ] [73] Dec 88
(12"+=) – Tutti Frutti.
Sep 89. (7")(c-s) **IT'S NOT ENOUGH. / LOVE AMONG THE CANNIBALS** [ ] [12] Aug 89
(12"+=) – Wild again.
(cd-s++=) – Nothing's gonna stop us now.
Sep 89. (lp)(c)(cd) **LOVE AMONG THE CANNIBALS** [ ] [64] Aug 89
– The burn / It's not enough / Trouble in mind / I didn't mean to stay all night / Send a message / Love among the cannibals / We dream in colour / Healing waters / Blaze of love / I'll be there. *(cd+=)*– Wild again.
Nov 89. (7")(c-s) **I DIDN'T MEAN TO STAY ALL NIGHT. / ?** [-] [75]
Apr 91. (c-s)(cd-s) **GOOD HEART. /** [-] [81]
Aug 91. (cd)(c)(lp) **GREATEST HITS (TEN YEARS AND CHANGE 1979-1991)** (compilation) [ ] [-]
– Jane / Find your way back / Stranger / No way out / Layin' it on the line / Don't lose any sleep / We built this city / Sara / Nothing's gonna stop us now / It's not over ('til it's over) / It's not enough / Good heart. *(re-iss.cd Oct95)*

JEFFERSON AIRPLANE

were reformed with **SLICK, KANTNER, KAUKONEN, CASADY and BALIN.** Augmented by **KENNY ARONOFF** – drums / **PETER KAUKONEN and RANDY JACKSON** – guitar (ex-ZEBRA)

Epic Epic

Oct 89. (lp)(c)(cd) **JEFFERSON AIRPLANE** [ ] [85]
– Planes / Solidarity / Summer of love / The wheel / True love / Now is the time / Panda / Freedom / Ice age / Madeleine Street / Common market madrigal / Upfront blues / Too many years.
Oct 89. (7") **SUMMER OF LOVE. / PANDA** [-] [ ]
Jan 90. (7") **TRUE LOVE. /** [-] [ ]

JEFFERSON STARSHIP

Essential Rykodisc

Jul 95. (cd)(c) **DEEP SPACE – VIRGIN SKY** [ ] [ ]
– Shadowlands / Ganja of love / Dark ages / I'm on fire / Papa John / Women who fly / Gold / The light / Crown of creation / Count on me / Miracles / Intro to lawman / Lawman / Wooden ships / Somebody to love / White rabbit.

– (AIRPLANE) compilations, etc. –

Jun 70. RCA; (7") **WHITE RABBIT. / SOMEBODY TO LOVE** [ ] [ ]
Nov 70. RCA; (lp)(c) **THE WORST OF JEFFERSON AIRPLANE** [ ] [12]
(re-iss.Sep86 on 'Fame')
Dec 76. RCA; (d-lp) **FLIGHT LOG (1966-76 all work)** [ ] [37]
Apr 76. RCA; (7") **WHITE RABBIT. / SOMEBODY TO LOVE / CROWN OF CREATION** [ ] [ ]
(re-iss. as 12" Apr79 on 'RCA Gold') (re-iss.Nov86 on 'Old Gold')
Jul 80. RCA; (lp)(c) **THE BEST OF JEFFERSON AIRPLANE** [ ] [ ]
Aug 81. RCA; (d-lp) **ROCK GALAXY ('CROWN OF CREATION' & 'VOLUNTEERS')** [ ] [ ]
Jul 87 RCA; (d-lp)(c)(d-cd) **2400 FULTON STREET – AN ANTHOLOGY** [ ] [ ]
– It's no secret / Come up the years / My best friend / Somebody to love / Comin' back to me / Embryonic journey / She has funny cars / Plastic fantastic lover / Wild tyme / The ballad of you & me & Pooneil – A small package of value will come to you, shortly / White rabbit / Won't you try Saturday afternoon / Lather / We can be together / Crown of creation / Mexico / Wooden ships / Rejoyce / Volunteers / Pretty as you feel / Martha / Today / Third week in Chelsea. *(d-cd+=)*– Let's get together / Blues from an airplane / J.P.P. McStep B. Blues / Fat angel / Greasy heart / We can be together / Have you seen the saucers / Eat starch mom / Good shepherd / Eskimo blue day / The Levi commercials. *(re-iss.d-cd 1992)*
Nov 92. RCA; (3xcd-box) **JEFFERSON AIRPLANE LOVES YOU** [ ] [ ]
May 87. Ariola; (7") **WHITE RABBIT. / SOMEBODY TO LOVE** [ ] [ ]
(12"+=) – She has funny cars / Third week in Chelsea.
Oct 88. Castle; (d-lp)(c)(cd) **THE COLLECTION** [ ] [-]
(iss.US on cd Oct92)
May 90. Thunderbolt; (cd)(lp) **LIVE AT THE MONTEREY FESTIVAL (live)** [ ] [-]
Apr 74. Grunt; (lp) **EARLY FLIGHT (rare)** [ ] [ ]
Apr 93. Pulsar; (cd) **WOODSTOCK REVIVAL** [ ] [-]
Sep 93. Remember; (cd)(c) **WHITE RABBIT** [ ] [-]

– (STARSHIP) compilations etc. –

Mar 79. Grunt-RCA; (lp)(c) **GOLD** [ ] [20] Feb 79
(with free 7" **LIGHT THE SKY ON FIRE. / HYPERDRIVE)**
1979. Grunt-RCA; (7") **MIRACLES. / WITH YOUR LOVE** [-] [ ]
Nov 92. Old Gold; (cd-ep) **NOTHING'S GONNA STOP US NOW / WE BUILT THIS CITY / SARA** [ ] [-]

GRACE SLICK

solo, all featuring JEFFERSON's and session people

Grunt Grunt

Jan 74. (lp)(c) **MANHOLE** [ ] [ ]
– Jay / Theme from 'Manhole' / Come again? Toucan / It's only music / Better lying down / Epic (£38).

R.C.A. R.C.A.

May 80. (7") **SEASONS. / ANGEL OF NIGHT** [-] [ ]
May 80. (7") **DREAMS. / ANGEL OF NIGHT** [50] [-]
May 80. (lp)(c) **DREAMS** [28] [32]
– Dreams / El Diablo / Face to the wind / Angel of night / Seasons / Do it the hard way / Full Moon man / Let it go / Garden of man. *(re-iss.Sep81) (cd-iss.Sep91 on 'Great Expectations')*
Jul 80. (7")(12") **DREAMS. / DO IT THE HARD WAY** [-] [ ]
Feb 81. (7") **MISTREATER. / FULL MOON MAN** [ ] [ ]
Feb 81. (lp)(c) **WELCOME TO THE WRECKING BALL** [ ] [48]
– Wrecking ball / Mistreater / Shot in the dark / Round & round / Shooting star / Just a little love / Sea of love / Lines / Right kind / No more heroes. *(cd-iss.Sep91 on 'Great Expectations')*
Mar 84. (lp)(c) **SOFTWARE** [ ] [ ]
– Call it right call it wrong / Me and me / All the machines / Fox face / Through the window / It just won't stop / Habits / Rearrange my face / Bikini Atoll.
Mar 84. (7") **ALL THE MACHINES. / ('A'long version)** [-] [ ]
May 84. (7") **THROUGH THE WINDOWS. / HABITS** [-] [ ]

— In 1965, with GREAT SOCIETY, she released a single 'SOMEBODY TO LOVE'. / 'FREE ADVICE'; for 'North Beach' US. An album of these 1965/66 recordings was rel.Apr68 by 'Columbia'/'CBS' as 'CONSPICUOUS ONLY IN ITS ABSENCE'. Later in the year, another album 'HOW IT WAS' and single 'SALLY GO ROUND THE ROSES'. / 'DIDN'T THINK SO' were credited to GRACE SLICK & THE GREAT SOCIETY.

JELLYFISH

Formed: Pleasanton, San Francisco, California, USA . . . 1990 by STURMER and brothers CHRIS and ROGER. They were previously known as BEATNIK BEACH, before they signed to 'Charisma'. Their classic debut 45 'THE KING IS HALF UNDRESSED' made charts on both sides of the Atlantic in 1991, and was quickly pursued by acclaimed first album 'BELLYBUTTON'. • **Style:** 60's/70's influenced rock-pop group, similiar to BEACH BOYS or QUEEN in harmonies and BEATLES in kitsch complexity. • **Songwriters:** STURMER or most with MANNING, except; NO MATTER WHAT (Badfinger) / LET 'EM IN + JET (Paul McCartney & Wings). • **Trivia:** Their debut album was produced by Albhy Galuten, his first since 'Saturday Night Fever'!.

Recommended: BELLYBUTTON (*8).

ANDY STURMER – vocals, drums, keyboards / **JASON FALKNER** – guitar / **CHRIS MANNING** – bass / **ROGER MANNING** – keyboards, vocals

Charisma Charisma

Jan 91. (7")(c-s) **THE KING IS HALF UNDRESSED. / CALLING SARAH** [39] [ ]
(12"+=)(cd-s+=) – The man I used to be.
Feb 91. (cd)(c)(lp) **BELLYBUTTON** [ ] [ ] Nov 90
– The man I used to be / That is why / The king is half undressed / I wanna stay home / She still loves him / All I want is everything / Now she knows she's wrong / Bedspring kiss / Baby's coming back / Calling Sarah. (free 12"w / lp + on c+cd) – No matter what / Medley live:- Let 'em in – That is why / The king is half undressed (live) / Jet (live) / Now she knows she's wrong (live). *(re-iss.Feb92)*
Apr 91. (7")(c-s) **BABY'S COMING BACK. / ALL I WANT IS EVERYTHING (live)** [51] [62] Mar 91
(12"+=)(cd-s+=) – No matter what (live).
Jul 91. (7"ep) **THE SCARY-GO-ROUND EP** [49] [ ]
– Now she knows she's wrong / Bedspring kiss / She still loves him (live) / Baby's coming back (live).
(12"ep) – (1st-2 tracks) / The man I used to be (live) / Calling Sarah (live).
(cd-ep) – (1st-2 tracks) / Let 'em in – that is why (live) / The king is half undressed (live).
Oct 91. (7")(c-s) **I WANNA STAY HOME. / JET (live)** [59] [ ]
(10"+=)(cd-s+=) – Now she knows she's wrong (live).

— Now duo of **ANDY** and **ROGER**, after the departure of CHRIS and JASON.

— added **TIM SMITH** – bass, vocals / and guests guitarists – **LYLE WORKMAN + JON BRION /** additional bass – **T-BONE**

Apr 93. (7")(c-s) **THE GHOST AT NUMBER ONE. / ALL IS FORGIVEN** [43] [ ]
(cd-s+=) – Worthless heart / Ignorance is bliss.
(cd-s) – ('A'side) / Watchin' the rain / Family tree.
May 93. (cd)(c)(lp) **SPILT MILK** [21] [ ]
– Hush / Joining a fan club / Sabrina, paste & Plato / New mistake / The glutton of sympathy / The ghost at mumber one / Bye, bye, bye / All is forgiven / Russian hill / He's my best friend / Too much, too little, too late / Brighter day.
Jul 93. (7")(c-s) **NEW MISTAKE. / HE'S MY BEST FRIEND** [55] [ ]
(cd-s+=) – All is forgiven / Russian Hill (demos).
(cd-s) – ('A'side) / Sabrina, Paste & Patto (demo) / The man I used to be (demo) / Bedspring kiss (demo).

Bedspring kiss (demo).

JENNIFERS (see under ⇒ SUPERGRASS)

JESUS & MARY CHAIN

Formed: East Kilbride, Scotland . . . 1983, by brothers WILLIAM and JIM REID. After local Glasgow gigs, they moved to Fulham in London, having signed for Alan McGhee's independent 'Creation' label in May'84. Their debut SLAUGHTER JOE produced 45 'UPSIDE DOWN', soon topped indie charts which led to WEA subsidiary label 'Blanco Y Negro' snapping them up early 1985. They hit the UK Top 50 with next single 'NEVER UNDERSTAND', and they were soon antagonising new audiences, when crashing gear after 20 minutes on set. Riots ensued at nearly every major gig, and more controversy arrived when the next 45's B-side 'JESUS SUCKS', was boycotted by pressing plant. With new B-side, the single 'YOU TRIP ME UP', hit only No.55, but was soon followed by another Top 50 hit in October 'JUST LIKE HONEY'. A month later they unleashed their debut album 'PSYCHOCANDY', and although this just failed to breach the UK Top 30, it was regarded by many (NME critics especially) as the album of the year. They hit the Top 20 in 1986 with next 45 'SOME CANDY TALKING', and scored first Top 10 single & album in '87 with 'APRIL SKIES' and 'DARKLANDS' respectively. • **Style:** Initially a noisy post-punk outfit who screeched with feedback. Described as VELVET UNDERGROUND meeting The SEX PISTOLS, they soon mellowed at times into romantic garage type rock. • **Songwriters:** All written by JIM and WILLIAM except; VEGETABLE MAN (Syd Barrett) / SURFIN' USA (Beach Boys) / WHO DO YOU LOVE (Bo Diddley) / MY GIRL (Temptations) / MUSHROOM (Can) / GUITAR MAN (Jerry Lee Hubbard) / TOWER OF SONG (Leonard Cohen) / LITTLE RED ROOSTER (Willie Dixon) / (I CAN'T GET NO) SATISFACTION (Rolling Stones) / REVERBERATION (13th Floor Elevators) / GHOST OF A SMILE (Pogues) / ALPHABET CITY (Prince) / NEW KIND OF KICK (Cramps). • **Trivia:** Their 1986 single 'SOME CANDY TALKING' was banned by Radio 1 DJ Mike Smith, due to its drug references. The following year in the States, they were banned from a chart show due to their blasphemous name. Although yet not overwhelming, their success in the US, have made albums reach between 100 & 200. In 1989 they produced and featured on The SUGARCUBES '89 version of hit 'Birthday'.

Recommended: PSYCHOCANDY (*10) / DARKLANDS (*8) / AUTOMATIC (*7) / HONEY'S DEAD (*8) / BARBED WIRE KISSES (*7).

JIM REID (b.1961) – vox, guitar / **WILLIAM REID** (b.1958) – guitar, vox / **MURRAY DALGLISH** – drums (bass tom & snare) / **DOUGLAS HART** – bass

Creation | not issued

Nov 84. (7") **UPSIDE DOWN. / VEGETABLE MAN** [ ] [-]
(12"+=) – ('A' demo).

— **BOBBY GILLESPIE** – drums (ex-WAKE, of PRIMAL SCREAM) repl. DALGLISH who formed BABY'S GOT A GUN

Blanco YN | Reprise

Feb 85. (7") **NEVER UNDERSTAND. / SUCK** [47] [ ]
(12"+=) – Ambition.
Jun 85. (7") **YOU TRIP ME UP. / JUST OUT OF REACH** [55] [ ]
(12"+=) – Boyfriend's dead.
Oct 85. (7") **JUST LIKE HONEY. / HEAD** [45] [ ]
(12"+=) – Just like honey (demo) / Cracked.
(d7"+=) – ('A'demo) / Inside me.
Nov 85. (lp)(c) **PSYCHOCANDY** [31] [ ]
– Just like honey / The living end / Taste the floor / Hardest walk / Cut dead / In a hole / Taste of Cindy / Never understand / It's so hard / Inside me / Sowing seeds / My little underground / You trip me up / Something's wrong. *(cd-iss.Apr86 +=)–* Some candy talking.

— **JOHN LODER** – drums (on stage when BOBBY was unavailable)
Jul 86. (7") **SOME CANDY TALKING. / PSYCHO CANDY / HIT** [13] [ ]
(12"+=) – Taste of Cindy.
(d7"+=) – Cut dead / You trip me up / Some candy talking / Psycho candy (all four tracks accoustic versions).

— now basic trio of **JIM, WILLIAM** and **DOUGLAS** brought in **JOHN MOORE** – drums repl. GILLESPIE (who was busy with PRIMAL SCREAM) / **JAMES PINKER** – drums (ex-DEAD CAN DANCE) repl. MOORE now on guitar
Apr 87. (7") **APRIL SKIES. / KILL SURF CITY** [8] [ ]
(12"+=) – Who do you love.
(d7"+=) – Mushroom / Bo Diddley is Jesus.
Aug 87. (7") **HAPPY WHEN IT RAINS. / EVERYTHING IS ALRIGHT WHEN YOU'RE DOWN** [25] [ ]
(12"+=) – Happy place / F-Hole.
(10"+=) – ('A' version) / Shake.

— trimmed to basic duo of REID brothers.
Sep 87. (lp)(c)(cd) **DARKLANDS** [5] [ ]
– Darklands / Deep one perfect morning / Happy when it rains / Down on me / Nine million rainy days / April skies / Fall / Cherry came too / On the wall / About you. *(re-iss.cd Nov94)*
Oct 87. (7") **DARKLANDS. / RIDER / ON THE WALL (demo)** [33] [ ]
(12"+=) – Surfin' U.S.A.
(10"+=)(cd-s+=) – Here it comes again.

— **DAVE EVANS** – rhythm guitar repl. MOORE who formed EXPRESSWAY
Mar 88. (7") **SIDEWALKING. / TASTE OF CINDY (live)** [30] [ ]
(12"+=) – ('A' extended) / April skies (live).
(cd-s++=) – Chilled to the bone.
Apr 88. (lp)(c)(cd) **BARBED WIRE KISSES** (part compilation) [9] [ ]
– Kill Surf City / Head / Rider / Hit / Don't ever change / Just out of reach / Happy place / Psychocandy / Sidewalking / Who do you love / Surfin' USA / Everything's alright when you're down / Upside down / Taste of Cindy / Swing / On the wall. *(c+cd+=)–* Cracked / Here it comes again / Mushroom / Bo Diddley is Jesus.
Nov 88. (7") **KILL SURF CITY. / SURFIN' USA (summer mix)** [-] [ ]

— Basically REID brothers, HART and EVANS. (added **RICHARD THOMAS** – drums) / **BEN LURIE** – rhythm guitar repl. EVANS
Sep 89. (7") **BLUES FROM A GUN. / SHIMMER** [32] [-]
(10"+=) – Break me down / Penetration.
(12"+=)(c-s+=) – Penetration / Subway.
(3"cd-s+=) – Penetration / My girl
Oct 89. (lp)(c)(cd) **AUTOMATIC** [11] [ ]
– Here comes Alice / Coast to coast / Blues from a gun / Between planets / UV ray / Her way of praying / Head on / Take it / Halfway to crazy / Gimme hell.
Nov 89. (7") **HEAD ON. / IN THE BLACK** [57] [-]
(7") – ('A'side) / DEVIANT SLICE (or) I'M GLAD I NEVER
(12"+=)(cd-s+=) – Terminal beach.
Mar 90. (7") **HEAD ON. / PENETRATION** [-] [ ]
Aug 90. (7") **ROLLER COASTER. / SILVER BLADE** [46] [ ]
(12"+=) – Tower of song.
(7"ep++=)(cd-ep++=) – Low-life.

— Trimmed again, when THOMAS joined RENEGADE SOUNDWAVE on U.S.tour. HART became video director. The **REID** brothers and **BEN** recruited **MATTHEW PARKIN** – bass + **BARRY BLACKER** – drums (ex-STARLINGS)
Feb 92. (7") **REVERENCE. / HEAT** [10] [ ]
(12"+=)(cd-s+=) – ('A'radio remix) / Guitar man.
Mar 92. (cd)(c)(lp) **HONEY'S DEAD** [14] [ ]
– Reverence / Teenage lust / Far gone and out / Almost gold / Sugar Ray / Tumbledown / Catchfire / Good for my soul / Rollercoaster / I can't get enough / Sundown / Frequency.
Apr 92. (7") **FAR GONE AND OUT. / WHY'D DO YOU WANT ME** [23] [ ]
(12"+=)(cd-s+=) – Sometimes you just can't get enough.
Jun 92. (7") **ALMOST GOLD. / TEENAGE LUST (acoustic)** [41] [ ]
(12"+=) – Honey's dead.
(gold-cd-s+=) – Reverberation (doubt) / Don't come down.
Jun 93. (7"ep)(10"ep)(c-ep)(cd-ep) **SOUND OF SPEED EP** [30] [ ]
– Snakedriver / Something I can't have / White record release blues / Little red rooster.
Jul 93. (cd)(c)(lp) **THE SOUND OF SPEED** (part comp '88-'93) [15] [ ]
– Snakedriver / Reverence (radio mix) / Heat / Teenage lust (acoustic version) / Why'd you want me / Don't come down / Guitar man / Something I can't have / Sometimes / White record release blues / Shimmer / Penetration / My girl / Tower of song / Little red rooster / Break me down / Lowlife / Deviant slice / Reverberation / Sidewalking (extended version).

— next album feat. guest vox HOPE SANDOVAL (Mazzy Star) + SHANE McGOWAN.
Jul 94. (7") **SOMETIMES ALWAYS. / PERFECT CRIME** [22] [96]
(10"+=)(cd-s+=) – Little stars / Drop.
Aug 94. (cd)(c)(lp) **STONED AND DETRONED** [13] [98]
– Dirty water / Bullet lovers / Sometimes always / Come on / Between us / Hole / Never saw it coming / She / Wish I could / Save me / Till it shines / God help me / Girlfriend / Everybody I know / You've been a friend / These days / Feeling lucky.
Sep 94. (7")(c-s) **COME ON. / I'M IN WITH THE OUT-CROWD** [52] [ ]
(cd-s+=) – New York City / Taking it away.
(cd-s) – ('A'side) / Ghost of a smile / Alphabet city / New kind of kick.
Jun 95. (12"ep)(c-ep)(cd-ep) **I LOVE ROCK'N'ROLL / BLEED ME / 33 1/3 / LOST STAR** [61] [ ]

– compilations etc. –

Sep 91. Strange Fruit; (cd)(m-lp) **PEEL SESSIONS (1985-86)** [ ] [-]
Jun 94. Audioglobe; (cd+book) **LIVE (live)** [ ] [-]

ACID ANGELS

DOUGLAS HART, plus **JO HEAD** – vocals / **PHIL ERB** – computers / **PETER FOWLER** – videos

Product Inc. | not issued

Nov 88. (12") **SPEED SPEED ECSTACY. / TOP FUEL ELIMINATOR** [ ] [ ]

JESUS JONES

Formed: Bradford-Upon-Avon, Wiltshire, England . . . late 1986 as CAMOUFLAGE, by MIKE, GEN and AL. In Aug'88 after moving to Wathamstow, London, they became JESUS JONES. They were soon snapped up by David Balfe's 'Food' label, through 'EMI. Early in '89, they released Craig Leon produced debut single 'INFO-FREAKO', which hit Top 50. Their 2 follow-ups 'NEVER ENOUGH' and 'BRING IT ON DOWN', also both hit the Top 50, and premiered the UK Top 40 album 'LIQUIDIZER'. Further success came in the early 90's, when album 'DOUBT' hit UK No.1 and US Top 30, after their single 'RIGHT HERE, RIGHT NOW' was a surprise No.2 smash there in '91. • **Style:** Sampled danceable punk-ish pop rock outfit influenced by skateboards, early SHAMEN, etc. • **Songwriters:** MIKE EDWARDS penned except; I DON'T WANT THAT KIND OF LOVE (Crazyhead) / VOODOO CHILE (Jimi Hendrix Experience). • **Trivia:** The song 'NEVER ENOUGH' was inspired by Woody Allen's film 'Stardust Memories'.

Recommended: LIQUIDIZER (*7) / DOUBT (*7).

MIKE EDWARDS – vocals / **JERRY DE BORG** – guitar / **AL JAWORSKI** (b.ALAN DOUGHTY) – bass / **BARRY D.** (b.IAIN BAKER) – keyboards, samplers / **GEN** (b.SIMON MATTHEWS) – drums

Food-EMI S.B.K.

Feb 89. (7") **INFO-FREAKO. / BROKEN BONES** [42] [ ]
(12"+=)(cd-s+=) – Info sicko.
(12") – ('A'side) / Info-psycho.
Jun 89. (7")(c-s) **NEVER ENOUGH. / WHAT'S GOING ON** [42] [ ]
(12")(cd-s) – ('A'side) / – Enough – Never enough / It's the . . . ..that counts.
Sep 89. (7") **BRING IT ON DOWN. / CUT AND DRIED** [46] [ ]
(12"+=) – Info sicko.
(cd-s++=) – None of the answers / Beat it down.
Oct 89. (lp)(c)(cd) **LIQUIDIZER** [32] [ ]
– Move mountains / Never enough / The real world / All the answers / What's going on / Song 13 / Info-freako / Bring it on down / Too much to learn / What would you know? / Too much to learn / One for the money / Someone to blame.
Mar 90. (7")(c-s) **REAL REAL REAL. / DEAD PEOPLE'S LIVES** [19] [4] May 91
(12"+=)(cd-s+=) – ('A'-12"mix) / Info freako.
(12") – ('A'side) / (above 2).
Sep 90. (7")(c-s) **RIGHT HERE RIGHT NOW. / MOVE ME / DAMN GOOD AT THIS** [31] [ ]
(10"+=)(cd-s+=) – Are you satisfied.
(12") – ('A'side) / Are you satisfied / Move mountains (mix) / ('A'different mix).
Dec 90. (7")(c-s) **INTERNATIONAL BRIGHT YOUNG THING. / MARYLAND** [7] [ ]
(12"+=) – ('A'mix).
(12"pic-d) – ('A'side) / Need to know / I.B.Y.T.
(cd-s) – (all 4 tracks above).
Feb 91. (cd)(c)(lp) **DOUBT** [1] [25]
– Trust me / Who? where? why? / International bright young thing / I'm burning / Right here right now / Real real real / Welcome back Victoria / Two and two / Stripped / Blissed. *(re-iss.cd+c Mar94)*
Feb 91. (7")(c-s) **WHO? WHERE? WHEN? (crisis mix). / CARICATURE** [21] [ ]
(12"+=) – ('A'-12"mix).
(10"++=) – Kill today.
(cd-s+=) – ('A'versions).
Jul 91. (7")(c-s) **RIGHT HERE RIGHT NOW. / WELCOME BACK VICTORIA** [31] [2] Apr 91
(12"+=)(cd-s+=) – Info psycho / Broken bones.
Jan 93. (7") **THE DEVIL YOU KNOW. / PHOENIX** [10] [ ]
(12"+=)(cd-s+=) – What to know
Jan 93. (cd)(c)(lp) **PERVERSE** [6] [59]
– Zeroes and heroes / The Devil you know / Get a good thing / From love to war / Yellow brown / Magazine / The right decision / Your crusade / Don't believe it / Tongue tied / Spiral / Idiot stare.
Mar 93. (7")(c-s) **THE RIGHT DECISION. / STARTING FROM SCRATCH** [36] [ ]
(12"+=)(cd-s+=) – ('A'mixes).
Jun 93. (c-s) **ZEROES AND HEROES. / MACHINE DRUG / ZEROES AND HEROES (mixes)** [30] [ ]
(cd-s) – ('A'side) / Real real real (rhythm 2) / International bright young thing / Right here, right now.
(12") – ('A'side) / ('A'mixes).

– compilations, others, etc. –

Nov 89. Food; (7"ep) **FOOD CHRISTMAS** [ ] [-]
– I don't want that kind of love. (others by CRAZYHEAD / DIESEL PARK WEST)

JESUS LIZARD

Formed: Austin, Texas, USA . . . late 80's by DAVID YOW and DAVID SIMS, who had just folded SCRATCH ACID. They found Chicago-born DENNISON and McNEILLY, and set up more rampaging tours from US to UK. After a few albums for 'Touch & Go', they were approached by 'Atlantic' in 1991. They refused a lucrative money-spinning deal and opted to stay as a US indie band. Remarkably after worldly tours, they broke through early in 1993 with the help from NIRVANA on a joint single. • **Style:** Psychotic apocalyptic cabaret fronted by the BUTTHOLE SURFERS, BIRTHDAY PARTY and IGGY POP influenced DAVID YOW. He was renowned for taking off from stage into the crowd, and at times getting lost, although remarkably still managing to sing!. • **Songwriters:** Group except WHEELCHAIR EPIDEMIC (Dicks). • **Trivia:** JESUS LIZARD were produced by STEVE ALBINI (ex-BIG BLACK, RAPEMAN).

Recommended: LIAR (*7)

SCRATCH ACID

DAVID YOW – vocals, bass / **BRETT BRADFORD** – guitar, vocals / **DAVID WILLIAM SIMS** – bass, guitar / **REY WASHAM** – drums, piano

Fun-damental Rabid Cat

Apr 86. (lp) **SCRATCH ACID** [ ] [ ]
– Cannibal / Greatest gift / Monsters / Owners lament / She said / Mess / El spectro / Lay screaming.
Jul 86. (m-lp) **JUST KEEP EATING** [ ] [ ]
– Crazy Dan / Eyeball / Big bone lick / Unlike a beast / Damned for all time / Ain't that love / Holes / Albino slug / Spit a kiss / Amicus / Cheese plug.
Mar 87. (lp) **BESERKER** [ ] [ ]
– Mary had a little drug problem / For crying out loud / Moron's moron / Skin drips / Thing is bliss / Flying houses.

—— In 1988, YOW joined RAPEMAN alongside STEVE ALBINI (BIG BLACK). WESHAM joined TAD. One of the others formed The BIG BOYS.

– compilation –

Oct 91. Touch & Go; (cd)(lp) **THE GREATEST GIFT** [ ] [ ]

JESUS LIZARD

DAVID YOW – vocals / **DUANE DENISON** – guitar / **DAVID WILLIAM SIMS** – bass / **MAC McNEILLY** – drums

Touch & Go Touch & Go

1989. (m-lp) **PURE** [ ] [ ]
– Blockbuster / Bloody Mary / Rabid pigs / Starlet / Happy bunny goes fluff fluff along. *(re-iss Jul93)*
Feb 90. (7") **CHROME. / ?** [ ] [ ]
May 90. (cd)(c)(lp) **HEAD** [ ] [ ]
– One evening / S.D.B.J. / My own urine / If you had lips / 7 vs 8 / Pastoral / Waxeater / Good thing / Tight 'n shiny / Killer McHann. *(re-iss.+cd Jul93 incl. 'PURE')*
Nov 90. (7") **MOUTHBREAKER. / ?**
Jan 91. (cd)(lp) **GOAT** [ ] [ ]
– Then comes Dudley / Mouthbreaker / Nub / Monkey trick / Karpis / South mouth / Lady shoes / Rodeo in Joliet / Seasick. *(re-iss.Apr94)*

—— In Apr'91, YOW featured for PIGFACE super techno-punks on 'GUB' album.

May 92. (7") **WHEELCHAIR EPIDEMIC. / DANCING NAKED LADIES** [ ] [ ]
Oct 92. (cd)(c)(lp) **LIAR** [ ] [ ]
– Boilermaker / Gladiator / The art of self-defence / Slave ship / Puss / Whirl / Rope / Perk / Zachariah / Dancing naked ladies.
Feb 93. (7") **PUSS. / (b-side by NIRVANA)** [12] [ ]
Jun 93. (cd)(lp) **SHOW** [-] [ ]
(imported into UK Jul 94 on 'Collision')
Sep 93. (12")(cd-s) **LASH. /** [ ] [ ]
Nov 93. (12")(cd-s) **FLY ON THE WALL. / WHITE HOLE** [ ] [ ]
Aug 94. (cd)(c)(lp) **DOWN (live)** [64] [ ]
– Fly on the wall / Mistletoe / Countless backs of sad losers / Queen for a day / The associate / Destroy before reading / Low rider / 50 cents / American BB / Horse / Din / Elegy / The best parts.

JESUS LOVES YOU (see under ⇒ BOY GEORGE)

JET (see under ⇒ JOHN'S CHILDREN)

JETHRO TULL

Formed: London, England . . . late 1967 by Scots-born IAN ANDERSON and GLENN CORNICK, who had both been for 4 years in Blackpool band JOHN EVANS' SMASH, alongside school friends EVANS and JEFFREY HAMMOND-HAMMOND. IAN and GLENN brought in former McGREGORY'S ENGINE members MICK ABRAHAMS plus CLIVE BUNKER, and used an 18th Century name of an English agriculturist/inventor. It was often mistaken by the uninitiated, as the name of lead singer IAN ANDERSON. Early in 1968, through agents Terry Ellis & Chris Wright, 'MGM' issued debut single 'SUNSHINE DAY', but mistakenly they credited it to JETHRO TOE at the pressing plant. (It has since changed hands for over £50 at record fairs). On 29 Jun'68, after a residency at Marquee Club, they supported PINK FLOYD at a free rock concert at Hyde Park, London. Due to another enthusiastically received concert at Sunbury's Jazz & Blues Festival in August, they signed to 'Island'. By the end of the year, debut lp 'THIS WAS' cracked the UK Top 10, and even managed to make Top 75 in the US. Early in 1969, they played a few gigs with TONY IOMMI (future BLACK SABBATH) and DAVID O'LIST (of The NICE), to briefly deputize for the departing ABRAHAMS. In May '71 with new member MARTIN BARRE, they hit UK Top 3 with classic 'LIVING IN THE PAST' single, which was quickly followed by UK No.1 & US Top 20 album 'STAND UP'. They then signed to associate label 'Chrysalis', and scored 2 more UK Top 10 singles 'SWEET DREAM' & 'THE WITCHES PROMISE'. The group continued to burst into the UK & US, with nearly every album throughout the 70's, 80's & early 90's?. • **Style:** Initially blues orientated, they shifted into more progressive-rock field by the early 70's. ANDERSON's medieval vagrant-look and eccentric flute-playing, gave group its visual trademark. In 1972-73 their concept albums 'THICK AS A BRICK' & 'A PASSION PLAY', were originally panned by UK rock critics, although both survived this unfair onslaught, and both surprisingly hit No.1 in the States. • **Songwriters:** ANDERSON lyrics / group compositions, except BOUREE (J.S.Bach) / JOHN BARLEYCORN (trad.) / CAT'S SQUIRREL (Cream). • **Trivia:** ANDERSON still controls his trout-farming business in Northern Scotland. In 1974, he produced STEELEYE SPAN's 'Now We Are Six' album.

Recommended: AQUALUNG (*8) / A PASSION PLAY (*7) / LIVING IN THE PAST (*7) / THE VERY BEST OF JETHRO TULL (*8)

IAN ANDERSON (b.10 Aug'47, Edinburgh, Scotland) – vocals, flute / **GLENN CORNICK** (b.24 Apr'47, Barrow-in-Furness, England) – bass / **MICK ABRAHAMS** (b. 7 Apr'43, Luton) – guitar, vocals (ex-McGREGORY'S ENGINE) / **CLIVE BUNKER** (b.12 Dec'46) – drums (ex-McGREGORY'S ENGINE)

M.G.M. not issued

Mar 68. (7") **SUNSHINE DAY. / AEROPLANE (as "JETHRO TOE")** [ ] [-]

Island Reprise

Aug 68. (7") **SONG FOR JEFFREY. / ONE FOR JOHN GEE** [ ] [ ]
Oct 68. (lp)(c) **THIS WAS** [10] [62] Feb 69

– My Sunday feeling / Some day the sun won't shine for you / Beggar's farm / Move on alone / Serenade to a cuckoo / Dharma for one / It's breaking me up / Cat's squirrel / A song for Jeffrey / Round. *(re-iss.+c.Jan74) (cd-iss.1986)*

Dec 68. (7") **LOVE STORY. / A CHRISTMAS SONG** [29] [ ]
Mar 69. (7") **LOVE STORY. / A SONG FOR JEFFREY** [-] [ ]

— **MARTIN BARRIE** – guitar repl. MICK ABRAHAMS to BLODWYN PIG,

May 69. (7") **LIVING IN THE PAST. / DRIVING SONG** [3] [-]
Jul 69. (lp)(c) **STAND UP** [1] [20] Oct 69
– A new day yesterday / Jeffrey goes to Leicester Square / Bouree / Back to the family / Look into the sun / Nothing is easy / Fat man / We used to know / Reasons for waiting / For a thousand mothers. *(re-iss.Nov83 on 'Fame') (cd-iss.1986 & 1989)*

Chrysalis Reprise

Oct 69. (7") **SWEET DREAM. / SEVENTEEN** [9] [-]
Oct 69. (7") **SWEET DREAM. / REASONS FOR WAITING** [-] [ ]
Jan 70. (7") **THE WITCHES PROMISE. / TEACHER** [4] [ ]

— augmented by **JOHN EVANS** – keyboards (he later joined full-time)

Apr 70. (lp)(c) **BENEFIT** [3] [11]
– With you there to help me / Nothing to say / Alive and well and living in / Son / For Michael Collins, Jeffrey and me / To cry you a song / A time for everything / Inside / Play in time / Sossity; you're a woman. *(cd-iss.Jun87)*
May 70. (7") **INSIDE. / ALIVE AND WELL AND LIVING IN** [ ] [-]
Jul 70. (7") **INSIDE. / A TIME FOR EVERYTHING** [-] [ ]

— **JEFFREY HAMMOND-HAMMOND** – bass repl. CORNICK who formed WILD TURKEY

Mar 71. (lp)(c) **AQUALUNG** [4] [7] Apr 71
– Aqualung / Cross-eyed mary / Cheap day return / Mother goose / Wond'ring aloud / Up to me / My God / Hymn £43 / Slipstream / Locomotive breath / Wind-up. *(re-iss.Jan74, cd-iss.1988) (re-iss.cd Mar94)*
Jul 71. (7") **HYMN £43. / MOTHER GOOSE** [-] [91]

— **ANDERSON, BARRE, HAMMOND-HAMMOND** and **EVAN** were joined by **BARRIEMORE BARLOW** – drums (ex-JOHN EVANS' SMASH) who repl. BUNKER who joined BLODWYN PIG

Sep 71. (7"ep) **LIFE IS A LONG SONG. / UP THE POOL / DR. BOGENBROOM / FOR LATER / NURSIE** [11] [-]
Oct 71. (7") **LOCOMOTIVE BREATH. / WIND** [-] [ ]

Chrysalis Reprise

Mar 72. (lp)(c) **THICK AS A BRICK** [5] [1] May 72
– Thick as a brick (side 1) / Thick as a brick (side 2). *(re-iss.Jan74, cd-iss.1986) (cd-re-Apr89 on 'Mobile Fidelity')*
Apr 72. (7") **THICK AS A BRICK (edit £1). / HYMN £43** [-] [ ]

Chrysalis Chrysalis

Jul 72. (d-lp)(d-c) **LIVING IN THE PAST** (live / studio comp) [8] [3] Nov 72
– By kind permission of / Dharma for one / Wond'ring again / Locomotive breath / Life is a long song / Up the pool / Dr.Bogenbroom / For later / Nursie / A song for Jeffrey / Love story / Christmas song / Teacher / Living in the past / Driving song / Bouree / Sweet dream / Singing all day / Teacher / The witches promise / Inside / Just trying to be. *(cd-iss.Oct87) (re-iss.cd+c Mar94)*
Oct 72. (7") **LIVING IN THE PAST. / ?** [-] [11]
May 73. (7") **A PASSION PLAY (edit £8). / A PASSION PLAY (edit £6)** [-] [80]
Jul 73. (lp)(c) **A PASSION PLAY** [13] [1]
– A passion play (part 1; including 'The story of the hare who lost his spectacles' part 1)- /- (part 2) / A passion play (part 2). *(cd-iss.Jan89)*
Aug 73. (7") **A PASSION PLAY (edit £9). / A PASSION PLAY (edit £10)** [-] [ ]
Oct 74. (7") **BUNGLE IN THE JUNGLE. / BACK DOOR ANGEL** [ ] [12]
Oct 74. (lp)(c) **WAR CHILD** [14] [2]
– War child / Queen and country / Ladies / Back-door angels / Sea lion / Skating away on the thin ice of a new day / Bungle in the jungle / Only solitaire / The third hooray / Two fingers.
Jan 74. (7") **SKATING AWAY ON THE THIN ICE OF A NEW DAY. / SEA LION** [-] [ ]
Sep 75. (lp)(c) **MINSTREL IN THE GALLERY** [20] [7]
– Minstrel in the gallery / Cold wind to Valhalla / Black satin dancer / Requiem / One white duck / 0x10 = Nothing at all – Baker St. Muse (including Pig-me and the whore – Nice little tune – Crash barrier waltzer – Mother England reverie) / Grace. *(cd-iss.1986)*
Oct 75. (7") **MINSTREL IN THE GALLERY. / SUMMER DAY SANDS** [ ] [79]

— **JOHN GLASCOCK** – bass (ex-CHICKEN SHACK, ex-TOE FAT) repl. HAMMOND

Mar 76. (7") **TOO OLD TO ROCK'N'ROLL, TOO YOUNG TO DIE. / RAINBOW BLUES** [ ] [-]
Mar 76. (lp)(c) **TOO OLD TO ROCK'N'ROLL, TOO YOUNG TO DIE** [25] [14] May 76
– Quizz kid / Crazed institution / Salamander / Taxi grab / From a dead beat to an old greaser / Bad-eyed and loveless / Big dipper / Too old to rock'n'roll, too young to die / Pied piper / The chequered flag (dead or alive).
Apr 76. (7") **TOO OLD TO ROCK'N'ROLL, TOO YOUNG TO DIE. / BAD- EYED AND LOVELESS** [-] [ ]

— added **DAVID PALMER** – keyboards (He had been their past orchestrator)

Nov 76. (7"ep) **RING OUT, SOLSTICE BELLS. / MARCH THE MAD SCIENTIST / A CHRISTMAS SONG / PAN DANCE** [28] [-]
(re-iss.Dec79)
Jan 77. (7") **THE WHISTLER. / STRIP CARTOON** [ ] [59] Apr 77
Feb 77. (lp)(c) **SONGS FROM THE WOOD** [13] [8]
– Songs from the wood / Jack-in-the-green / Cup of wonder / Hunting girl / Ring out, solstice bells / Velvet green / The whistler / Pibroch (cap in hand) / Fire at midnight. *(cd-iss.1986)*
Apr 78. (7") **MOTHS. / LIFE IS A LONG SONG** [ ] [-]
Apr 78. (lp)(c) **HEAVY HORSES** [20] [19]
– . . .And the mouse police never sleeps / Acres wild / No lullaby / Moths / Journeyman / Rover / One brown mouse / Heavy horses / Weathercock. *(cd-iss.1986)*
Nov 78. (7")(7"white) **A STITCH IN TIME. / SWEET DREAM (live)** [ ] [-]
Nov 78. (d-lp)(c) **LIVE-BURSTING OUT** [17] [21] Oct 78
– No lullaby / Sweet dream / Skating away on the thin ice of a new day / Jack-in-the-green / One brown mouse / A new day yesterday / Flute solo improvisation – God rest ye merry gentlemen / Bouree / Songs from the wood / Thick as a brick / Hunting girl / Too old to rock'n'roll, too young to die / Conundrum / Cross-eyed Mary / Quatrain / Aqualung / Locomotive breath / The dambuster's march – medley. *(cd-iss.1990)*
Sep 79. (7") **NORTH SEA OIL. / ELEGY** [ ] [ ]
Sep 79. (lp)(c) **STORMWATCH** [27] [22]
– North Sea oil / Orion / Home / Dark ages / Warm sporran / Something's on the move / Old ghosts / Dun Ringill / Flying Dutchman / Elegy. *(cd-iss Jan89)*
Nov 79. (7"ep) **HOME / RING OUT, SOLSTICE BELLS. / WARM SPORRAN / KING HENRY'S MADRIGAL** [ ] [-]
Nov 79. (7") **HOME. / WARM SPORRAN** [-] [ ]

— ANDERSON for what was supposed to be a solo album retained **BARRE** / plus new **DAVE PEGG** – bass (ex-FAIRPORT CONVENTION) repl. GLASCOCK who died. / **EDDIE JOBSON** – keyboards (ex-ROXY MUSIC, ex-CURVED AIR, etc) repl. EVANS and PALMER who took up session work / **MARK CRANEY** – drums repl. BARLOW who went solo.

Aug 80. (lp)(c)**"A"** [25] [30] Sep 80
– Crossfire / Fylingdale flyer / Working John, working Joe / Black Sunday / Protect and survive / Batteries not included / 4.W.D. (low ratio) / The Pine Marten's jig / And further on.

— **PETER JOHN VITESSE** – keyboards repl. JOBSON who went solo / **GERRY CONWAY** – drums (ex-STEELEYE SPAN) repl. CRANEY

Apr 82. (lp)(c) **BROADSWORD AND THE BEAST** [27] [19] May 82
– Beastie / Clasp / Fallen on hard times / Flying colours / Slow marching band / Broadsword / Pussy willow / Watching me watching you / Seal driver / Cheerio.
May 82. (7")(7"pic-d) **BROADSWORD. / FALLEN ON HARD TIMES** [ ] [-]
May 82. (7") **PUSSY WILLOW. / FALLEN ON HARD TIMES** [-] [ ]

— **DOANNE PERRY** – drums repl. CONWAY

Sep 84. (lp)(c)(cd) **UNDER WRAPS** [18] [76]
– Lap of luxury / Under wraps I / European legacy / Later that same evening / Saboteur / Radio free Moscow / Nobody's car / Heat / Under wraps II / Paperazzi / Apogee. *(c+=)(cd+=)–* Automatic engineering / Astronomy / Tundra / General crossing.
Sep 84. (7") **LAP OF LUXURY. / ASTRONOMY** [70] [ ]
(d7"+=)(12"+=) – Tundra / Automatic engineering.
Jun 86. (7") **CORONIACH. / JACK FROST AND THE HOODED CROW** [ ] [ ]
(12"+=) – Living in the past.

— **ANDERSON, BARRE, PEGG** and **PERRY** recruited new member **MARTIN ALLCOCK** – keyboards (ex-FAIRPORT CONVENTION) repl. VITESSE

Sep 87. (lp)(c)(cd) **CREST OF A KNAVE** [19] [32]
– Steel monkey / Farm on the freeway / Jump start / Said she was a dancer / Dogs in midwinter * / Budapest / Mountain men / The waking edge * / Raising steam. *(cd+= *)*
Oct 87. (7")(7"pic-d) **STEEL MONKEY. / DOWN AT THE END OF YOUR ROAD** [ ] [ ]
(12"+=)(c-s+=) – Too many too / I'm your gun.
Dec 87. (7")(7"pic-d) **SAID SHE WAS A DANCER. / DOGS IN MIDWINTER** [55] [ ]
(12"+=) – The waking edge.
(cd-s+=) – Down at the end of your road / Too many too.
Aug 89. (lp)(c)(cd) **ROCK ISLAND** [18] [56]
– Kissing Willie / The rattlesnake trail / Ears of tin / Undressed to kill / Rock Island / Heavy water / Another Christmas song / The whalers dues / Big Riff and Mando / Strange avenues.
Aug 89. (c-s) **KISSING WILLIE. / EARS OF TIN** [-] [ ]
Nov 89. (7") **ANOTHER CHRISTMAS SONG. / SOLSTICE BELLS** [ ] [ ]
(12"+=) – Jack Frost.
(cd-s) – ('A'side) / – A Christmas song (live) / Cheap day return (live) / Mother goose (live) / Locomotive breath (live).

— **ANDY GIDLINGS** – keyboards (3) / **MATT PEGG** – bass (3) / etc. repl. ALLCOCK

Aug 91. (7")(c-s) **THIS IS NOT LOVE. / NIGHT IN THE WILDERNESS** [ ] [ ]
(12"+=)(cd-s+=) – Jump start (live).
Sep 91. (cd)(c)(lp) **CATFISH RISING** [27] [88]
– This is not love / Occasional demons / Rocks on the road / Thinking round corners / Still loving you tonight / Doctor to my disease / Like a tall thin gin / Sparrow on the schoolyard wall / Roll yer own / Goldtipped boots, black jacket and tie. (free 12"ep) **WHEN JESUS CAME TO PLAY. / SLEEPING WITH THE DOG / WHITE INNOCENCE**

— **DAVID MATTACKS** – drums, percussion, keyboards repl. PERRY and guests

Mar 92. (7") **ROCKS ON THE ROAD. / JACK-A-LYNN** [47] [ ]
(cd-s+=)/ /(cd-s++=) – Mother goose./ / Bouree.
(c-s+=)(cd-s+=) – Tall thin god / Fat man.
(12"pic-d+=) – Aqualung / Locomotive breath.
Sep 92. (cd)(c)(d-lp) **A LITTLE LIGHT MUSIC (live in Europe '92)** [34] [ ]
– Someday the Sun won't shine for you / Living in the past / Life is a long song / Under wraps / Rocks on the road / Nursie / Too old to rock and roll, too young to die / One white duck / A new day yesterday / John Barleycorn / Look into the Sun / A Christmas song / From a dead beat to an old greaser / This is not love / Bouree / Pussy willow / Locomotive breath.

— **PERRY** returned to repl.MATTACKS. Bass playing was provided by **DAVE PEGG / STEVE BAILEY**

Sep 95. (cd)(c) **ROOTS TO BRANCHES** [20] [ ]
– Roots to branches / Rare and precious chain / Out of the noise / This free will / Wounded, old and reacherous / Dangerous veils / Beside myself / Valley / At last, forever / Stuck in the August rain / Another Harry's bar.

– compilations, others, etc. –

Jan 76. Chrysalis; (7") **LIVING IN THE PAST. / REQUIEM** [ ] [ ]
Jan 76. Chrysalis; (lp)(c) **M.U. – THE BEST OF JETHRO TULL** [44] [13]
– Teacher / Aqualung / Thick as a brick (edit £1) / Bungle in the jungle / Locomotive breath / Fat man / Living in the past / A passion play (£8) / Skating away on the thin ice of a new day / Rainbow blues / Nothing is easy. *(re-iss.+cd.Dec85)*

Feb 76. Chrysalis; (7") **LOCOMOTIVE BREATH. /** [-] [62]
Nov 77. Chrysalis; (lp)(c) **REPEAT – THE BEST OF JETHRO TULL VOL.2** [ ] [94]
–'Minstrel in the gallery / Cross-eyed Mary / A new day yesterday / Bouree / Thick as a brick (edit £1) / War child / A passion play (edit £9) / To cry you a song / Too old to rock'n'roll, too young to die / Glory row. *(cd-iss.Apr86)*
Dec 82. Chrysalis; (d-c) **M.U. / REPEAT** [ ] [ ]
Oct 85. Chrysalis; (lp)(c)(cd) **ORIGINAL MASTERS** [63] [ ]
Jun 88. Chrysalis; (5xlp-box)(3xc-box)(3xcd-box) **20 YEARS OF JETHRO TULL** [78] [97]
– THE RADIO ARCHIVES:- A song for Jeffrey / Love story * / Fat man / Bouree / Stormy Monday blues * / A new day yesterday * / Cold wind to Valhalla / Minstrel in the gallery / Velvet green / Grace * / The clasp / / Pibroch (pee-break) – Black satin dancer (instrumental) * / Fallen on hard times // THE RARE TRACKS:- Jack Frost and the hooded crow / I'm your gun / Down at the end of your road / Coronach * / Summerday sands * / Too many too / March the mad scientist * / Pan dance / Strip cartoon / King Henry's madrigal / A stitch in time / 17 / One for John Gee / Aeroplane / Sunshine day // FLAWED GEMS:- Lick your fingers clean * / The Chateau Disaster Tapes: Scenario – Audition – No reheasal / Beltane / Crossword * / Saturation * / Jack-A-Lynn * / Motoreyes * / Blues instrumental (untitled) / Rhythm in gold // THE OTHER SIDES OF TULL:- Part of the machine * / Mayhem, maybe * / Overhang * / Kelpie * / Living in these hard times / Under wraps II * / Only solitaire / Cheap day return / Wond'ring aloud * / Dun Ringill * / Salamander / Moths / Nursie * / Life is a long song * / One white duck – 0x10 = Nothing at all // THE ESSENTIAL TULL:- Songs from the wood / Living in the past * / Teacher * / Aqualung * / Locomotive breath * / The witches promise * / Bungle in the jungle / Farm on the freeway / Thick as a brick / Sweet dream. *(re-iss.Aug88 as d-lp/d-c/d-cd; tracks *)*
Apr 93. Chrysalis; (4xcd-box) **25th ANNIVERSARY BOXED SET** [ ] [ ]
REMIXED (CLASSIC SONGS) / CARNEGIE HALL N.Y. (RECORDED LIVE NEW YORK CITY 1970) / THE BEACON'S BOTTOM (TAPES) / POT POURRI (LIVE ACROSS THE WORLD AND THROUGH THE YEARS)
May 93. Chrysalis; (7") **LIVING IN THE PAST. / HARD LINER** [32] [ ]
(12") – ('A'side) / ('A'mix).
(cd-s) – ('A'side) / Truck stop runner / Piece of cake / Man of principle.
(cd-s) – Living in the (slightly more recent) past / Silver river turning / Rosa on the factory floor / I don't want to be me.
May 93. Chrysalis; (d-cd)(d-c) **THE VERY BEST OF JETHRO TULL – THE ANNIVERSARY COLLECTION** [ ] [ ]
– A song for Jeffrey / Beggar's farm / A Christmas song / A new day yesterday / Bouree / Nothing is easy / Living in the past / To cry you a song / Teacher / Sweet dream / Cross-eyed Mary / Mother goose / Aqualung / Locomotive breath / Life is a long song / Thick as a brick (extract) / Skating away on the thin ice of a new day / Bungle in the jungle/ / Minstrel in the gallery / Too old to rock'n'roll / Songs from the wood / Jack in the green / The whistler / Heavy horses / Dun Ringill / Fylingdale flyer / Jack-a-Lynn / Pussy willow / Broadsword / Under wraps II / Steel monkey / Farm on the freeway / Jump start / Kissing Willie / This is not love.
Nov 93. Chrysalis; (d-cd) **NIGHTCAP – THE UNRELEASED MASTERS 1972-1991** [ ] [ ]
– CHATEAU D'ISASTER – First post / Animelee / Tiger Moon / Look at the animals / Law of the bungle part II / Left right / Solitaire / Critique oblique / Post last / Scenario / Audition / No rehearsal/ / UNRELEASED & RARE TRACKS – Paradise steakhouse / Sealion II / Piece of cake / Quartet / Silver river turning / Crew nights / The curse / Rosa on the factory floor / A small cigar / Man of principle / Commons brawl / No step / Drive on the young side of life / I don't want to be me / Broadford bazaar / Lights out / Truck stop runner / Hard liner.
Aug 87. Old Gold; (7") **LIVING IN THE PAST. / THE WITCHES' PROMISE** [ ] [-]
Jan 91. Raw Fruit; (cd)(c)(lp) **LIVE AT HAMMERSMITH 1984 (live)** [ ] [-]
Apr 95. Winsong; (cd) **IN CONCERT (live)** [ ] [-]

IAN ANDERSON

solo album augmented by **PETER JOHN VITESSE** – synth, keyboards

Chrysalis Chrysalis
Nov 83. (7") **FLY BY NIGHT. / END GAME** [ ] [ ]
Nov 83. (lp)(c) **WALK INTO LIGHT** [78] [ ]
– Fly by night / Made in England / Walk into light / Trains / End game / Black and white television / Toad in the hole / Looking for Eden / User-friendly / Different Germany.

Joan JETT

Born: 22 Sep'60, Philadelphia, Pennsylvania, USA. After 3 years in new wave all-girl outfit The RUNAWAYS, she went to London, where she cut tracks with ex-SEX PISTOLS men STEVE JONES and PAUL COOK. It was soon to appear on 'Cherry Red' records in the UK as 'AND NOW . . . THE RUNAWAYS'. Late in 1979, she signed solo deal with 'Ariola', and issued eponymous debut the year after. After its release, she formed JOAN JETT & THE BLACKHEARTS, who gained contract on 'Boardwalk-Epic' early '81. With renewed promotion and tours, the album now as 'BAD REPUTATION' just missed US Top 50. In Spring of '82, she/they broke through with US No.1 single 'I LOVE ROCK'N'ROLL', from the same titled US No.2 parent album. But for a few misses, she continued to be integral hitmaker of the 80's. • **Style:** Glam-rock metal, suitable for AOR and teenybop audiences. • **Songwriters:** Writes own material with some collaborations. Covered:- I CAN'T CONTROL MYSELF (Troggs) / BITS AND PIECES (Dave Clark Five) / I'M GONNA RUN AWAY FROM YOU (Tammi Lynn) / I LOVE ROCK'N'ROLL (Arrows) / CRIMSON AND CLOVER (Tommy James & The Shondells) / EVERYDAY PEOPLE (Sly & The Family Stone) / SHOUT (Isley Brothers) / WOOLY BULLY (Sam The Sham & The Pharoahs) / TOSSIN' AND TURNIN' (Searchers) / DO YOU WANNA TOUCH ME + I LOVE YOU LOVE ME LOVE (Gary Glitter) / TULANE (Chuck Berry) / LITTLE DRUMMER BOY (Harry Simone Chorale) / LIGHT OF DAY (Bruce Springsteen) / FUN FUN FUN (Beach Boys). THE HIT ALBUM was full of covers:- DIRTY DEEDS (Ac-Dc) / LOVE HURTS (Everly Brothers) / PRETTY VACANT (Sex Pistols) / TUSH (ZZ Top) / ROADRUNNER (Jonathan Richman) / HAVE YOU EVER SEEN THE RAIN (Creedence Clearwater Revival) / LOVE ME TWO TIMES (Doors) / CELLULOID HEROES (Kinks) / TIME HAS COME TODAY (Chamber Brothers). • **Trivia:** In 1987, she starred alongside Michael J.Fox in the film 'Light And Day', with her on theme song. In 1989, JOAN tried to sue Playboy magazine for publishing nude pics of a lookalike, but it was allegedly dropped when JOAN failed to turn up in court.

Recommended: I LOVE ROCK'N'ROLL (*5)

JOAN JETT – vocals, rhythm guitar (ex-RUNAWAYS) / with **RICKY BIRD** – lead guitar repl. ERIC AMBLE / **GARY RYAN** – bass / **LEE CRYSTAL** – drums (later to become The BLACKHEARTS)

Ariola not issued
Apr 80. (7") **MAKE BELIEVE. / CALL ME LIGHTNING** [ ] [-]
Jun 80. (lp) **JOAN JETT** [ ] [-]
– (Do you wanna) Touch me (oh yeah) / Make believe / You don't know what you've got / You don't own me / Too bad on your birthday / Bad reputation / Shout / Let me go / Doin' all right with the boys / Jezebel / Don't abuse me / Wooly bully.
Jun 80. (7") **YOU DON'T KNOW WHAT YOU GOT. / DON'T ABUSE ME** [ ] [-]
Aug 80. (7") **JEZEBEL. / BAD REPUTATION** [ ] [-]

JOAN JETT & THE BLACKHEARTS

(same line-up)

Epic Boardwalk
Mar 81. (lp)(c) **BAD REPUTATION** (debut remixed) [ ] [51]
– Bad reputation / Make believe / You don't know what you've got / You don't own me / Too bad on your birthday / Doing all right with the boys / Do you wanna touch me (oh yeah) / Let me go / Jezebel / Shout / Don't abuse me / Wooly bully.
Jan 82. (7") **I LOVE ROCK'N'ROLL. / YOU DON'T KNOW WHAT YOU GOT** [-] [1]
Mar 82. (7")(7"pic-d) **I LOVE ROCK'N'ROLL. / LOVE IS PAIN** [4] [-]
Mar 82. (lp)(c) **I LOVE ROCK'N'ROLL** [25] [2] Dec 81
– I love rock'n'roll / (I'm gonna) Run away / Bits and pieces / Love is pain / Nag / Crimson and clover / Victim of circumstance / Bits and pieces / Be straight / You're too possessive / Little drummer boy. *(pic-lp 1983)*
Jun 82. (7")(7"pic-d) **CRIMSON AND CLOVER. / OH WOE IS ME** [60] [7] Apr 82
Jul 82. (7") **DO YOU WANNA TOUCH ME (OH YEAH). / VICTIM OF CIRCUMSTANCE** [-] [20]
Aug 82. (7") **DO YOU WANNA TOUCH ME (OH YEAH). / JEZEBEL** [ ] [-]
Oct 82. (7") **YOU DON'T KNOW WHAT YOU'VE GOT. / (I'M GONNA) RUN AWAY** [ ] [ ]

Epic Blackheart
Jul 83. (7") **FAKE FRIENDS. / CONEY ISLAND WHITEFISH** [ ] [35]
(12"+=) – Nightime *(US; b-side)*.
Jul 83. (lp)(c) **ALBUM** [ ] [20]
– Fake friends / Handyman / Everyday people / A hundred feet away / Secret love / The French song / Tossin' and turnin' / Why can't we be happy / I love playin' with fire / Coney Island whitefish / Had enough. *(c+=)*– Star, star.
Sep 83. (7") **EVERYDAY PEOPLE. / WHY CAN'T WE BE HAPPY** [ ] [37]
May 84. (7") **I NEED SOMEONE. / TALKIN' 'BOUT MY BABY** [ ] [ ]
(12"+=) – The French song.
Oct 84. (7") **I LOVE YOU LOVE ME LOVE. / LONG TIME** [ ] [-]
(12"+=) – Bird dog.
Sep 84. (7") **I LOVE YOU LOVE ME LOVE. / TALKIN' 'BOUT MY BABY** [-] [ ]
Oct 84. (lp)(c) **GLORIOUS RESULTS OF A MISSPENT YOUTH** [ ] [67]
– Cherry bomb / I love you love me love / Frustrated / Hold me / Long time / Talkin' 'bout my baby / I need someone / Love like mine / New Orleans / Someday / Push and stomp / I got no answers.

—— (below 45 with others from film and soundtrack of same name)

Feb 87. (7") **LIGHT OF DAY. (as "The BARBUSTERS") / ROADRUNNER** [-] [33]

Polydor Blackheart
Jul 87. (7") **GOOD MUSIC. / FANTASY** [ ] [83] Oct 86
(12"+=) – Fun, fun, fun (with "The BEACH BOYS").
Sep 87. (lp)(c)(cd) **GOOD MUSIC** [ ] [ ]
– Good music / This means war / Roadrunner / If ya want my luv / Light of day / Black leather / Outlaw / Just lust / You got me floatin' / Fun, fun, fun / Contact.

—— Jan88, featured on 'B' side of BANGLES 45 from the film 'Less Than Zero'. The track SHE'S LOST YOU on 'Def Jam'.

—— retained **BIRD,** and recruited **TOMMY PRICE** – drums (ex-BILLY IDOL) / **CASMIN SULTAN** – bass (ex-TODD RUNDGREN / UTOPIA)

London Blackheart
Aug 88. (7") **I HATE MYSELF FOR LOVING YOU. / LOVE IS PAIN** [46] [8] Jun 88
(12"+=) – I can't control myself.
(cd-s++=) – ('A'live version).
Sep 88. (lp)(c)(cd) **UP YOUR ALLEY** [ ] [19] May 88
– I hate myself for loving you / Ridin' with James Dean / Little liar / Tulane / I wanna be your dog / I still dream about you / You want in I want out / Just like in the movies / Desire / Back it up / Play that song again.
Oct 88. (7") **LITTLE LIAR. / WHAT CAN I DO FOR YOU** [-] [19]

Chrysalis Blackheart
Jan 90. (c-s)(12") **DIRTY DEEDS. / LET IT BLEED** [-] [36]
Mar 90. (7")(c-s) **DIRTY DEEDS (DONE DIRT CHEAP). / PRETTY VACANT** [69] [-]
(12"+=)(cd-s+=)(12"pic-d+=) – ('A'extended).
Apr 90. (cd)(c)(lp) **THE HIT LIST** [ ] [36] Jan 90
– Dirty deeds (done dirt cheap) / Love hurts / Pretty vacant / Celluloid heroes / Tush / Time has come today / Up from the skies / Have you ever seen the rain? / Love me

two times / Roadrunner USA (1990 version).

Apr 90. (c-s) **LOVE HURTS. / HANDYMAN** [-] [ ]
Jul 90. (7") **LOVE HURTS. / UP FROM THE SKIES** [ ] [ ]
(12"+=)(cd-s+=) – Tush.

Silenz / Epic

Feb 92. (c-s) **DON'T SURRENDER. / ('A' version)** [-] [ ]
Apr 92. (cd-s) **TREADIN' WATER / WAIT FOR ME / MISUNDER-STOOD** [ ] [ ]
Apr 92. (cd)(c) **NOTORIOUS** [ ] [ ]
– Backlash / Ashes in the wind / The only good thing (you ever said was goodbye) / Lie to me / Don't surrender / Goodbye / Machismo / Treadin' water / I want you / Wait for me.

Reprise / Reprise

Feb 94. (7")(c-s) **I LOVE ROCK'N'ROLL. / ACTIVITY GRRRL** [75] [ ]
(cd-s+=) – Wayne's World theme.

Blackheart / Blackheart

Jun 94. (cd)(c) **YEAH, RIGHT** [ ] [ ]

Richard JOBSON (see under ⇒ SKIDS)

Billy JOEL

Born: WILLIAM MARTIN JOEL, 9 May'49, The Bronx, New York, USA. In 1965 he played piano in first group The ECHOES, having been a welter-weight boxing champ for local Hicksville, Long Island boys' club. In 1967 he joined The HASSLES who signed to 'United Art' and released 2 lp's, after initial SAM & DAVE cover version 45 'YOU GOT ME HUMMIN''. In 1969, JOEL became a rock critic for 'Changes' art-magazine and formed own hard-rock duo ATTILA with JON SMALL. They issued one 1970 album for 'Epic', before disbanding. JOEL then suffered bout of depression and entered Meadowbrook mental hospital, with psychiatric problems. In 1971 he was back in circulation to sign a solo contract with Family Productions' Artie Ripp (alledgedly known as 'Ripp-off' to his employees, due to his large percentage of artist royalties). JOEL's debut lp 'COLD SPRING HARBOR' was soon issued but, due to mixing fault, was pressed at the wrong speed!! Embarrass-ingly for JOEL, who had been well-received by live audiences, it hit shops without being corrected, and it made him sound slightly Chipmunk-ish. He moved to Los Angeles, and soon married ex-wife of JON SMALL; Elizabeth Weber. In 1973, he got deserved break with 'Columbia', after his 'CAPTAIN JACK' track was played on FM radio. The following year, his acclaimed 2nd lp 'PIANO MAN' made US Top 30, as did its title track. He went from strength to strenth from then on, becoming major US star during next 15 or so years. In 1989, he had his 3rd US No.1 with 'WE DIDN'T START THE FIRE', which was taken from top album 'STORM FRONT'. **Style & Songwriters:** Influenced in early teens by BEETHOVEN and The BEATLES, he went on to write own story-telling ballads or uptempo rock'n'roll numbers, which were similiar to The FOUR SEASONS or DION. Covered: BACK IN THE USSR (Beatles) / THE TIMES THEY ARE A CHANGIN' (Bob Dylan) / LIGHT AS THE BREEZE (Leonard Cohen) / and a few more. • **Trivia:** Divorced from his wife in Jul'82, he soon married supermodel and star of his 'UPTOWN GIRL' promo video; Christine Brinkley. In 1989, he fired his manager ex-brother-in-law Frank Weber, after an audit of the accounts showed nearly $100 million missing. The following year, JOEL was awarded $2 million by the courts, and a countersuit by Weber for $30 million was thrown out.

Recommended: THE STRANGER (*8) / GREATEST HITS VOLUMES 1&2 (*7)

The HASSLES

BILLY JOEL – piano / **JOHN DIZEK** – vocals / **RICHARD McKENNAR** – guitar / **HOWARD BLAUVELT** – bass / **JONATHAN SMALL** – drums

United Art / United Art

1968. (7") **YOU GOT ME HUMMIN'. / I'M THINKIN'** [ ] [ ]
1968. (7") **EVERY STEP I TAKE (EVERY MOVE I MAKE). / I HEAR VOICES** [-] [ ]

—— Released 2 lp's 'THE HASSLES' and 'HOUR OF THE WOLF' in US.

1968. (7") **4 O' CLOCK IN THE MORNING. / LET ME BRING YOU SUNSHINE** [-] [ ]
1969. (7") **NIGHT AFTER DAY. / COUNTRY BOY** [-] [ ]
1969. (7") **GREAT BALLS OF FIRE. / TRAVELIN' BAND** [-] [ ]

ATTILA

was formed by JOEL and SMALL.

not issued / Epic

1970. (lp) **ATTILA** [-] [ ]
– Wonder woman / California flash / Revenge is sweet / Amplifier fire: part 1 – Godzilla, part 2 – March of the Huns / Rollin' home / Tear this castle down / Holy Moses / Brain invasion. *(cd-iss.Apr93 on 'Sony Europe')*

BILLY JOEL

went solo, and many session people

Philips / Family

May 72. (7") **SHE'S GOT A WAY. / EVERYBODY LOVE YOU NOW** [ ] [ ]
Jun 72. (lp)(c) **COLD SPRING HARBOUR** [ ] [ ] Nov 71
– She's got a way / You can make me free / Everybody loves you now / Why Judy why / Falling of the rain / Turn around / You look so good to me / Tomorrow is today / Nocturne / Got to begin again. *(re-iss.& re-mixed Jan84 on 'CBS', hit 95 UK)*

Jan 73. (7") **TOMORROW IS TODAY. / EVERYBODY LOVES YOU NOW** [-] [ ]
Apr 74. (7") **THE BALLAD OF BILLY THE KID. / IF I ONLY HAD THE WORDS (TO TELL YOU)** [ ] [ ]

—— Stage band around this time were **DON EVANS** – guitar / **PAT McDONALD** – bass / **TOM WHITEHORSE** – steel guitar, banjo / **RHYS CLARK** – drums

C.B.S. / Columbia

Jun 74. (7") **WORSE COMES TO THE WORST. / SOMEWHERE ALONG THE LINE** [-] [80]
Aug 74. (7") **TRAVELIN' PRAYER. / AIN'T NO CRIME** [-] [77]
Apr 75. (lp)(c) **PIANO MAN** [ ] [27] Nov 73
– Travelin' prayer / Piano man / Ain't no crime / You're my home / The ballad of Billy The Kid / Worse comes to the worst / Stop in Nevada / If I only had the words (to tell you) / Somewhere along the line / Captain Jack. *(re-iss.Mar81, re-iss.Jun84, hit 98 UK) (cd-iss.Sep85 & Apr89) (also US iss.quad)*

—— (above should have been released May74 by 'Philips' but withdrawn)

Nov 74. (7") **THE ENTERTAINER. / THE MEXICAN CONNECTION** [-] [34]
Apr 75. (7") **PIANO MAN. / YOU'RE MY HOME** [ ] [25] Feb 74
Sep 75. (7") **IF I ONLY HAD THE WORDS (TO TELL YOU). / STOP IN NEVADA** [ ] [-]
Jul 75. (lp)(c) **STREETLIFE SERENADE** [ ] [35] Nov 74
– Streetlife serenader / Los Angelenos / The great suburban showdown / Root beer rag / Roberta / Last of the big time spenders / Weekend song / Souvenir / The Mexican connection. *(re-iss.Jul78, re-iss.Mar81) (cd-iss.Mar87) (re-iss.cd+c May94 on 'Columbia')*

—— band now incl. **NIGEL OLSSON + DEE MURRAY** (both ex-ELTON JOHN)

Jul 76. (lp)(c) **TURNSTILES** [ ] [ ] Jun 76
– Say goodbye to Hollywood / Summer, Highland falls / All you wanna do is dance / New York state of mind / James / Prelude / Angry young man / I've loved these days / Miami 2017 (seen the lights go on Broadway). *(re-iss.Nov81) (cd-iss.Mar87) (c+cd-iss.Nov89 on 'Pickwick') (re-iss.cd Sep93 'Sony Collectors')*

Jul 76. (7") **SUMMER, HIGHLAND FALLS. / JAMES** [-] [ ]
Oct 76. (7") **I'VE LOVED THESE DAYS. / SAY GOODBYE TO HOLLYWOOD** [-] [ ]
Nov 76. (7") **SAY GOODBYE TO HOLLYWOOD. / STOP IN NEVADA** *(re-iss.Feb77)* [ ] [ ]
Sep 77. (7") **MOVIN' OUT (ANTHONY'S SONG). / SHE'S ALWAYS A WOMAN** [-] [ ]
Dec 77. (lp)(c) **THE STRANGER** [25] [2] Oct 77
– Movin' out (Anthony's song) / The stranger / Just the way you are / Scenes from an Italian restaurant / Vienna / Only the good die young / She's always a woman / Get it right the first time / Everybody has a dream. *(re-iss.Nov80 & May87) (cd-iss.Dec85 & Jun89)*

Jan 78. (7") **JUST THE WAY YOU ARE. / GET IT RIGHT THE FIRST TIME** *(re-iss.May82)* [19] [3] Nov 77
Mar 78. (7") **MOVIN' OUT (ANTHONY'S SONG). / EVERYBODY HAS A DREAM** [-] [17]
Apr 78. (7") **SHE'S ALWAYS A WOMAN. / EVERYBODY HAS A DREAM** [ ] [-]
May 78. (7") **ONLY THE GOOD DIE YOUNG. / GET IT RIGHT THE FIRST TIME** [-] [24]
Jun 78. (7") **MOVIN' OUT (ANTHONY'S SONG). / VIENNA** [35] [-]
Aug 78. (7") **SHE'S ALWAYS A WOMAN. / VIENNA** [-] [17]
Nov 78. (lp)(c) **52nd STREET** [10] [1] Oct 78
– Big shot / Honesty / My life / Zanzibar / Stiletto / Rosalind's eyes / Half a mile away / Until the night / 52nd Street. *(re-iss.Nov85, cd-iss.Nov87) (re-iss.cd/c Mar93 + Feb95 on 'Columbia')*

Nov 78. (7") **MY LIFE. / 52nd STREET** [12] [3]
Feb 79. (7") **BIG SHOT. / ROOT BEER BAG** [-] [14]
Mar 79. (7") **UNTIL THE NIGHT. / ROOT BEER RAG** [50] [-]
Jun 79. (7") **HONESTY. / THE MEXICAN CONNECTION** [ ] [24] Apr 79
Feb 80. (7") **SOUVENIR. / ALL FOR LENYA** [-] [ ]
Mar 80. (lp)(c) **GLASS HOUSES** [9] [1]
– You may be right / Sometimes a fantasy / Don't ask me why / It's still rock'n'roll to me / All for Lenya / I don't want to be alone / Sleeping with the television on / C'Etait toi (you were the one) / Close to the borderline / Through the long night. *(re-iss.+cd.Nov86) (cd-iss.Mar91) (re-iss.cd+c May94 on 'Columbia')*

Mar 80. (7") **ALL FOR LEYNA. / CLOSE TO THE BORDERLINE** [40] [-]
Mar 80. (7") **YOU MAY BE RIGHT. / CLOSE TO THE BORDERLINE** [-] [7]
May 80. (7") **YOU MAY BE RIGHT. / THROUGH THE LONG NIGHT** [ ] [-]
Jul 80. (7") **IT'S STILL ROCK'N'ROLL TO ME. / THROUGH THE LONG NIGHT** [14] [1] May 80
Oct 80. (7") **DON'T ASK ME WHY. / C'ETAIT TOI (YOU WERE THE ONE)** [ ] [19] Aug 80
Oct 80. (7") **SOMETIMES A FANTASY. / ALL FOR LEYNA** [-] [36]
Jan 81. (7") **SOMETIMES A FANTASY. / SLEEPING WITH THE TELEVISION ON** [ ] [-]
Sep 81. (7") **SAY GOODBYE TO HOLLYWOOD (live). / SUMMER, HIGHLAND FALLS (live)** [ ] [17]
Sep 81. (lp)(c) **SONGS IN THE ATTIC (live)** [57] [8]
– Miami 2017 (seen the lights go out on Broadway) / Summer, Highland Falls / Streetlife serenader / Los Angelenos / She's got a way / Everybody loves you now / Say goodbye to Hollywood / Captain Jack / You're my home / The ballad of Billy The Kid / I've loved these days. *(re-iss.Nov83, cd-iss.May87 & Jun89) (re-iss.cd Jan94 on 'Sony Europe')*

Nov 81. (7") **YOU'RE MY HOME (live). / THE BALLAD OF BILLY THE KID (live)** [ ] [-]
Jan 82. (7") **SHE'S GOT A WAY (live). / THE BALLAD OF BILLY THE KID (live)** [ ] [23] Nov 81
Sep 82. (7") **PRESSURE. / LAURA** [ ] [20]
Sep 82. (lp)(c) **THE NYLON CURTAIN** [27] [7]
– Allentown / Laura / Pressure / Goodnight Saigon / She's right on time / A room on your own / Surprises / Scandinavian skies / Pressure / Where's the orchestra. *(cd-iss.Jan83) (lp re-iss.Mar88)*

Nov 82. (7") **ALLENTOWN. / ELVIS PRESLEY BOULEVARD** [ ] [17]
Feb 83. (7") **GOODNIGHT SAIGON. / WHERE'S THE ORCHESTRA** [ ] [-]
Feb 83. (7") **GOODNIGHT SAIGON. / A ROOM OF OUR OWN** [-] [56]
Aug 83. (7") **TELL HER ABOUT IT. / EASY MONEY** [ ] [1] Jul 83
Sep 83. (lp)(c) **AN INNOCENT MAN** [2] [4] Aug 83
– Easy money / An innocent man / The longest time / This night / Tell her about it / Uptown girl / Careless talk / Christie Lee / Leave a tender moment alone / Keeping the faith. *(cd-iss.Aug84)*
Oct 83. (7") **UPTOWN GIRL. / CARELESS TALK** [1] [3] Sep 83
(12"+=) – Just the way you are / It's still rock'n'roll to me.
Dec 83. (7") **TELL HER ABOUT IT. / EASY MONEY** [4] [-]
(12"+=) – You got me hummin' (live).
Dec 83. (7") **AN INNOCENT MAN. / I'LL CRY INSTEAD** [-] [10]
Feb 84. (7") **AN INNOCENT MAN. / YOU'RE MY HOME (live)** [8] [ ]
(12"+=) – She's always a woman / Until the night.
Apr 84. (7") **THE LONGEST TIME. / CHRISTIE LEE** [25] [14] Mar 84
(12"+=) – Captain Jack (live) / The ballad of Billy the kid (live).
Jun 84. (7") **LEAVE A TENDER MOMENT ALONE. / GOODNIGHT SAIGON** [29] [-]
(12"+=) – Movin' out (Anthony's song) / Big shot / You may be right.
Jul 84. (7") **LEAVE A TENDER MOMENT ALONE. / THIS NIGHT** [-] [27]
Nov 84. (7") **THIS NIGHT. / I'LL CRY INSTEAD (live)** [ ] [ ]
Jan 85. (7") **KEEPING THE FAITH. / SHE'S RIGHT ON TIME** [-] [18]

— featured on the 'USA for AFRICA' single 'WE ARE THE WORLD'.

Jun 85. (7") **YOU'RE ONLY HUMAN. / SURPRISES** [ ] [9]
(12"+=) – Keeping the faith / Scenes from an Italian restaurant.
Oct 85. (7") **THE NIGHT IS STILL YOUNG. / SUMMER, HIGHLAND FALLS** [ ] [34]
Jul 86. (7") **MODERN WOMAN. / SLEEPING WITH THE TELEVISION ON** [ ] [10] Jun 86
(d7"+=) – Uptown girl / All for love.
(12"+=) – The night is still young / You're only human.
Aug 86. (lp)(c)(cd) **THE BRIDGE** [38] [7]
– Running on ice / This is the time / A matter of trust / Modern woman / Baby grand (w/ RAY CHARLES) / Big man on Mulberry Street / Temptation / Code of silence (w/ CYNDI LAUPER) / Getting closer. *(re-iss.Oct89) (re-iss.cd+c Feb94 on 'Columbia')*
Sep 86. (7") **A MATTER OF TRUST. / GETTING CLOSER** [52] [10] Aug 86
(12"+=) – An innocent man / Tell her about it.
Nov 86. (7") **THIS IS THE TIME. / CODE OF SILENCE** [-] [18] Dec 86
Mar 87. (7") **BABY GRAND. / BIG MAN ON MULBERRY STREET** [-] [75]
Nov 87. (d-lp)(c)(cd) **KOHYEPT – LIVE IN LENINGRAD (live)** [92] [38]
– Odoya / Angry young man / Honesty / Goodnight Saigon / Stiletto / Big man on Mulberry Street / Baby grand / An innocent man / Allentown / A matter of trust / Only the good die young / Sometimes a fantasy / Uptown girl / Big shot / Back in the U.S.S.R. / The times they are a-changin'.
Nov 87. (7") **BACK IN THE U.S.S.R. (live). / BIG SHOT (live)** [ ] [ ]
(12"+=)(cd-s+=) – A matter of trust (live) / The times they are a-changin' (live).
Feb 88. (7") **THE TIMES THEY ARE A-CHANGIN' (live). / BACK IN THE U.S.S.R. (live)** [-] [ ]

— new band **MINDY JOSTIN** – rhythm guitar, violin, harp / **DAVID BROWN** – guitar / **MARK RIVIERA** – sax / **LIBERTY DeVITO** – drums / **SCHUYLER DEALE** – bass / **JEFF JACOBS** – synthesizers / **CRYSTAL TALIEFERO** – vocals, percussion

Sep 89. (7")(c-s) **WE DIDN'T START THE FIRE. / HOUSE OF BLUE LIGHT** [7] [1] Oct 89
(12"+=)(cd-s+=) – Just the way you are.
Oct 89. (lp)(c)(cd) **STORM FRONT** [5] [1]
– That's not her style / We didn't start the fire / The downeaster "Alexa" / I go to extremes / Shameless / Storm front / Leningrad / State of Grace / When in Rome / And so it goes.
Dec 89. (7")(c-s) **LENINGRAD. /** [53] [-]
(12"+=)(cd-s+=) –
Mar 90. (7")(c-s) **I GO TO EXTREMES. / WHEN IN ROME** [70] [6] Jan 90
(12"+=)(cd-s+=) – Uptown girl / All for Leyna.
(c-ep+=) – Prelude / Angry young man / Tell her about it / Leave a tender moment alone.
May 90. (7")(c-s) **DOWNCASTER ALEXA. / AND SO IT GOES / STREETLIFE SERENADE** [ ] [ ]
(12"+=) – I've loved these days / An innocent man.
(pic-cd-s+=) – Say goodbye to Hollywood / Allentown / Only the good die young.
Oct 90. (7"ep)(cd-ep) **THAT'S NOT HER STYLE / WE DIDN'T START THE FIRE / UNTIL THE NIGHT / JUST THE WAY YOU ARE** [ ] [ ] Jul 90
Sep 90. (c-s) **THAT'S NOT HER STYLE. / AND SO IT GOES** [-] [ ]
Oct 90. (c-s) **AND SO IT GOES. / THE DOWNEASTER ALEXA / SHAMELESS / STATES OF GRACE** [-] [37]
Jan 91. (c-s) **SHAMELESS. / STORM FRONT (live)** [-] [ ]

— (below from film 'Honeymoon In Las Vegas' on 'Epic records')

Aug 92. (7")(c-s) **ALL SHOOK UP. / ('b' side by Ricky Van Shelton)** [27] [92]
(cd-s+=) – other artist

other musicians; **DAN KORTCHMAR, TOMMY BYRNES, LESLIE WEST** – guitar / **T.H. STEVENS, LONNIE HILLER** – bass / **STEVE JORDAN, ZACHARY ALFORD, LIBERTY DeVITTO** – drums.

Jul 93. (7")(c-s) **THE RIVER OF DREAMS. / NO MAN'S LAND** [3] [3]
(cd-s+=) The great wall of China
Aug 93. (cd)(c)(lp) **RIVER OF DREAMS** [3] [1]
– No man's land / The great wall of China / Blonde over blue / A minor variation / Shades of grey / All about soul / Lullabye (goodnight, my angel) / The river of dreams / Two thousand years / Famous last words.
Oct 93. (c-s) **ALL ABOUT SOUL (Radio Edit) / YOU PICKED A REAL BAD TIME** [32] [29]
Feb 94. (7")(c-s) **NO MAN'S ISLAND. / SHADES OF GREY (live)** [50] [ ]
(cd-s+=) – ('A'mix).
Mar 94. (c-s)(cd-s) **LULLABY (GOODNIGHT MY ANGEL) /** [-] [77]

- compilations etc. -

Note; All 'CBS' releases were issued on US counterpart 'Columbia'.

Oct 79. CBS; (3-lp-box) **3-LP BOX SET** [ ] [ ]
– 'TURNSTILES' / 'THE STRANGER' / '52nd STREET'. *(re-iss.Oct80)*
Feb 83. CBS; (7"ep) **GREATEST ORIGINAL HITS** [ ] [ ]
– Just the way you are / Movin' out (Anthony's song) / My life / She's a woman. *(c-iss.Aug82)*
Jul 84. CBS; (7") **JUST THE WAY YOU ARE. / MY LIFE** [ ] [ ]
Jul 85. CBS; (d-lp)(c)(cd) **GREATEST HITS VOL.1 & VOL.2** [7] [6]
– Piano man / Say goodbye to Hollywood / New York state of mind / The stranger / Just the way you are / Movin' out (Anthony's song) / Only the good die young / She's always a woman / My life / Big shot / Honesty / You may be right / It's still rock and roll to me / Pressure / Allentown / Goodnight Saigon / Tell her about it / Uptown girl / The longest time / You're only human (second wind) / The night is still young.
Feb 86. CBS; (7") **SHE'S ALWAYS A WOMAN. / JUST THE WAY YOU ARE** [53] [-]
Jul 87. CBS; (d-lp) **THE STRANGER / AN INNOCENT MAN** [ ] [ ]
1988. CBS; (d-c) **PIANO MAN / STREETLIFE SERENADE** [ ] [ ]
Aug 88. CBS; (3"cd-ep) **IT'S STILL ROCK'N'ROLL TO ME. / JUST THE WAY YOU ARE** [-] [ ]
Nov 91. CBS; (4xcd)(4xc) **THE BILLY JOEL SOUVENIR** [ ] [ ]
– (GREATEST HITS VOL.1 & 2 / STORM FRONT / LIVE AT THE YANKEE STADIUM plus 50 minute interview)
Sep 92. Columbia; (d-cd) **THE BRIDGE / GLASS HOUSES** [ ] [ ]
Mar 93. Columbia; (d-cd) **AN INNOCENT MAN / THE STRANGER** [ ] [ ]
(re-iss.Feb95)
1980. Columbia; (7") **DOWN IN THE BOONDOCKS. / 21ST CENTURY MAN** [-] [ ]
Apr 86. Showcase; (lp)(c) **CALIFORNIA FLASH** [ ] [-]

David JOHANSEN (see under ⇒ NEW YORK DOLLS)

Elton JOHN

Born: REGINALD KENNETH DWIGHT, 25 Mar'47, Pinner, Middlesex, England. After learning piano at an early age, he attained scholarship from Royal Academy Of Music. In the early 60's, he joined BLUESOLOGY, and by 1965 wrote first 45 'COME BACK BABY' for 'Fontana'. They toured in the UK as back-up to American acts (i.e. MAJOR LANCE, The BLUE BELLES with PATTI LaBELLE, etc). Late in 1966, the band were joined by 5 others including singer LONG JOHN BALDRY, who virtually took over show, much to the dislike of the young REG DWIGHT. In 1967, he left BLUESOLOGY and auditioned for 'Liberty', but after failure he found other writer BERNIE TAUPIN (b.22 May'50, Lincolnshire). They wrote LONG JOHN BALDRY's 'B'side 'Lord You Made The Night Too Long', for his UK No.1 'Let The Heartaches Begin'. DWIGHT of course became ELTON JOHN, taking names from BLUESOLOGY members ELTON DEAN and LONG JOHN BALDRY. In 1968, ELTON and BERNIE joined the Dick James Music Publishing (later D.J.M.) stable, and earned around £10 a week each. With CALEB QUAYE (ex-BLUESOLOGY) on production, ELTON released debut solo single 'I'VE BEEN LOVING YOU TOO LONG' for 'Philips'. Early in '69, he gained needed airplay for 'LADY SAMANTHA', but when this failed, he tried to join KING CRIMSON, but to no avail. The pair now wrote a song for Eurovision song contest 'I CAN'T GO ON LIVING WITHOUT YOU', which was heard but rejected by LULU for eventual winner 'Boom Bang A Bang'. Early in 1969, ELTON signed to 'DJM', and flopped with both 45 'IT'S ME THAT YOU NEED' & lp 'EMPTY SKY'. To make ends meet, ELTON played on HOLLIES 'He Ain't Heavy . . . ' session, and worked for budget labels 'Pickwick' & 'MFP', on some pop covers. In 1970 after more HOLLIES sessions, he released 'BORDER SONG', which when picked up by 'Uni', broke into US Top 100. His eponymous 2nd lp that year hit Top 5 there, and resurrected in the UK made No.11 early 1971. This was mainly brought on by his first UK Top 10 hit 'YOUR SONG', which also peaked into US Top 10. An lp 'TUMBLEWEED CONNECTION' not containing the song, and released late 1970, was the first of many UK & US Top 10 lp's. In 1972, he scored a massive hit with 'ROCKET MAN', and after another summer hit 'HONKY CAT', he had first of 6 US No.1's with 'CROCODILE ROCK'. It took another 18 years for ELTON to clock up first UK solo top spot with 'SACRIFICE', although his duet with KIKI DEE on 'DON'T GO BREAKING MY HEART' made it in 1976. • **Style:** Flashy but talented showman, described early on as 'The Liberace of Rock'. His elaborate over-the-top costumes, and numerous spectacles, slightly detracted from his more serious ballads. In the late 80's, after his 3-year marriage to Renate Blauer had ended in divorce, he turned to alcohol and pills, but happily announced on TV, he was tee-total in 1992. • **Songwriters:** ELTON co-wrote with BERNIE TAUPIN on lyrics for most of career, although between mid-1978 & 1982, co-wrote with lyricist GARY OSBOURNE. ELTON also covered; MY BABY LEFT ME (?) / GET BACK + LUCY IN THE SKY WITH DIAMONDS + I SAW HER STANDING THERE (Beatles; on which ELTON did duet with JOHN LENNON) / PINBALL WIZARD (Who; from the film 'Tommy', in which he featured) / JOHNNY B.GOODE (Chuck Berry) / WHERE HAVE ALL THE GOOD TIMES GONE (Kinks) / I HEARD IT THROUGH THE GRAPEVINE (hit; Marvin Gaye) / I'M YOUR MAN (Leonard Cohen) / etc. • **Trivia:** He was chairman of Watford Football Club between Nov'73 to early 90's, and is still an honourary president. Early in 1986 after a long court battle, he and TAUPIN were given £5 million in back royalties from Dick James' publishers. In Oct'88, ELTON was awarded one million pounds damages after The Sun printed false and libelous stories concerning his sex life.

Recommended: GOODBYE YELLOW BRICK ROAD (*9) / DON'T SHOOT ME I'M ONLY THE PIANO PLAYER (*8) / ELTON JOHN (*8) / BLUE MOVES (*7) / THE VERY BEST OF ELTON JOHN (*8)

BLUESOLOGY

REG DWIGHT – vocals, piano / **STUART BROWN** – guitar, vocals / **REX BISHOP** – bass / **MICK INKPEN** – drums

Fontana / not issued

Jul 65. (7") **COME BACK BABY. / TIME'S GETTING TOUGHER THAN TOUGH** [ ] [-]
Feb 66. (7") **MR.FRANTIC. / EVERYDAT (I HAVE THE BLUES)** [ ] [-]

—— added **LONG JOHN BALDRY** – vocals / **CALEB QUAYE** – guitar / **ELTON DEAN** – sax / **PETE GAVIN, NEIL HUBBARD + MARK CHARIG** – wind

Polydor / not iss

Oct 67. (7") **SINCE I FOUND YOU BABY. / JUST A LITTLE BIT** [ ] [-]

ELTON JOHN

(solo) – vocals, piano with session people, incl.**NIGEL OLSSON** (note most of BLUESOLOGY later joined SOFT MACHINE)

Philips / Congress

Mar 68. (7") **I'VE BEEN LOVING YOU TOO LONG. / HERE'S TO THE NEXT TIME** [ ] [-]
Jan 69. (7") **LADY SAMANTHA. / ALL ACROSS THE HEAVENS** [ ] [-]
1969. (7") **LADY SAMANTHA. / IT'S ME THAT YOU NEED** [-] [ ]
1969. (7") **BORDER SONG. / BAD SIDE OF THE MOON** [-] [ ]

—— In 1969, ELTON was part of BREAD & BEER BAND, who issued 1 'Decca' single 'THE DICK BARTON THEME. / BREAKDOWN BLUES. (re-iss.1972)

D.J.M. / Uni

May 69. (7") **IT'S ME THAT YOU NEED. / JUST LIKE STRANGE RAIN** [ ] [-]
Jun 69. (lp) **EMPTY SKY** [ ] [-]
– Empty sky / Valhala / Western Ford gateway / Hymn 2000 / Lady what's tomorrow / Sails / The scaffold / Skyline pigeon / Gulliver – Hay chewed – Reprise. *(re-iss.Nov76, re-iss.May81, US-re-iss.Jan75 reached No.6) (re-iss.+cd.May87 & May95 on 'Rocket')*

—— now with band **NIGEL OLSSON** (b.10 Feb'49, Merseyside) – drums / **DEE MURRAY** (b.DAVID MURRAY OATES, 3 Apr'46, Southgate, London) – bass / **CALEB QUAYE** – guitar (ex-BLUESOLOGY)

Mar 70. (7") **BORDER SONG. / BAD SIDE OF THE MOON** [ ] [92] Jul 70
Apr 70. (lp)(c) **ELTON JOHN** [11] [4] Sep 70
– Your song / I need you to turn to / Take me to the pilot / No shoestrings on Louise / First episode at Heinton / Sixty years on / Border song / Greatest discovery / The cage / The king must die. *(re-iss.Nov76, re-iss.May81) (re-iss.+cd Apr87 & May95 on 'Rocket')*
Jun 70. (7") **ROCK AND ROLL MADONNA. / GREY SEAL** [ ] [-]
Oct 70. (lp)(c) **TUMBLEWEED CONNECTION** [6] [5] Jan 71
– Ballad of well-known gun / Come down in time / Country comfort / Son of your father / My father's gun / Where to now St. Peter / Love song / Amoreena / Talking old soldiers / Burn down the mission. *(re-iss.Nov76, re-iss.May81) (re-iss.+cd Apr87 & May95 on 'Rocket')*
Nov 70. (7") **YOUR SONG. / TAKE ME TO THE PILOT** [-] [8]
Jan 71. (7") **YOUR SONG. / INTO THE OLD MAN'S SHOES** [7] [-]
Apr 71. (7") **FRIENDS. / HONEY ROLL** [ ] [34] Mar 71
Apr 71. (lp)(c) **17.11.70 THE ELTON JOHN LIVE ALBUM** [20] [11] May 71
– Take me to the pilot / Honky tonk women / Sixty years on / Can I put you on / Bad side of the Moon / Burn down the mission: My baby left me – Get back. *(re-iss.Mar78 on 'Hallmark') (cd-iss.Sep95 on 'Rocket')*
Nov 71. (lp)(c) **MADMAN ACROSS THE WATER** [41] [8]
– Tiny dancer / Levon / Razor face / Madman across the water / Indian sunset / Holiday inn / Rotten Peaches / All the nasties / Goodbye. *(reached No.41 May72, re-iss.Nov76, re-iss.May81, re-iss.+cd Apr87 & Aug95 on 'Rocket')*
Dec 71. (7") **LEVON. / GOODBYE** [-] [24]
Feb 72. (7") **TINY DANCER. / RAZOR FACE** [-] [41]

—— **DAVEY JOHNSTONE** (b. 6 May'51, Edinburgh, Scotland) – guitar (ex-MAGNA CARTA) repl. QUAYE. Added **RAY COOPER** – percussion

Apr 72. (7"m) **ROCKET MAN. / HOLIDAY INN / GOODBYE** [2] [-]
May 72. (7") **ROCKET MAN. / SUZIE (DREAMS)** [-] [6]
May 72. (lp)(c) **HONKY CHATEAU** [2] [1] Jun 72
– Honky cat / Mellow / I think I'm going to kill myself / Susie (dramas) / Rocket man / Salvation / Slave / Amy / Mona Lisas and mad hatters / Hercules. *(re-iss.Nov76, re-iss.May81) (re-iss.Apr87 & Aug95 on 'Rocket')*
Aug 72. (7"m) **HONKY CAT. / LADY SAMANTHA / IT'S ME THAT YOU NEED** [31] [-]
Aug 72. (7") **HONKY CAT. / SLAVE** [-] [8]

D.J.M. / M.C.A.

Oct 72. (7") **CROCODILE ROCK. / ELDERBERRY WINE** [5] [1] Dec 72
Jan 73. (7") **DANIEL. / SKYLINE PIGEON** [4] [2] Apr 73
Feb 73. (lp)(c) **DON'T SHOOT ME I'M ONLY THE PIANO PLAYER** [1] [1]
– Daniel / Teacher I need you / Elderberry wine / Blues for my baby and me / Midnight creeper / Have mercy on the criminal / I'm going to be a teenage idol / Texan love song / Crocodile rock / High flying bird. *(re-iss.Nov76, re-iss.May81) (re-iss.+cd Apr87 & May95 on 'Rocket')*
Jun 73. (7"m) **SATURDAY NIGHT'S ALRIGHT FOR FIGHTING. / JACK RABBIT / WHEN YOU'RE READY (WE'LL GO STEADY AGAIN)** [7] [12] Jul 73
Sep 73. (7") **GOODBYE YELLOW BRICK ROAD. / SCREW YOU** [6] [-]
Oct 73. (7") **GOODBYE YELLOW BRICK ROAD. / YOUNG MAN'S BLUES** [-] [2]
Oct 73. (d-lp)(d-c) **GOODBYE YELLOW BRICK ROAD** [1] [1]
– Funeral for a friend / Love lies bleeding / Bennie and the jets / Candle in the wind / Goodbye yellow brick road / This song has no title / Grey seal / Jamaica jerk off / I've seen that movie too / Sweet painted lady / The ballad of Danny Bailey (1909-34) / Dirty little girl / All the girls love Alice / Your sister can't twist (but she can rock'n'roll) / Saturday night's alright for fighting / Roy Rogers / Social disease / Harmony. *(re-iss.Nov76) (re-iss.+cd.Nov87 & May95 on 'Rocket')*
Nov 73. (7") **STEP INTO CHRISTMAS. / HO! HO! HO! WHO'D BE A TURKEY AT CHRISTMAS** [24] [ ]
Feb 74. (7") **BENNY AND THE JETS. / HARMONY** [-] [1]
Feb 74. (7") **CANDLE IN THE WIND. / BENNIE AND THE JETS** [11] [-]
May 74. (7") **DON'T LET THE SUN GO DOWN ON ME. / SICK CITY** [16] [2] Jun 74
Jun 74. (lp)(c) **CARIBOU** [1] [1]
– The bitch is back / Pinky / Grimsby / Dixie Lily / Solar prestige a gammon / You're so static / I've seen the saucers / Stinker / Don't let the sun go down on me / Ticking. *(re-iss.Nov76 & May81) (re-iss.+cd.Nov87 & May95 on 'Rocket')*
Sep 74. (7") **THE BITCH IS BACK. / COLD HIGHWAY** [15] [4]
Nov 74. (7") **LUCY IN THE SKY WITH DIAMONDS. / ONE DAY AT A TIME** [10] [1]
Feb 75. (7") **PHILADELPHIA FREEDOM. (as "ELTON JOHN'S BAND") / I SAW HER STANDING THERE (w/ JOHN LENNON)** [12] [1]
May 75. (lp)(c) **CAPTAIN FANTASTIC AND THE BROWN DIRT COWBOY** [2] [1]
– Captain Fantastic and the brown dirt cowboy / Tower of Babel / Bitter fingers / Tell me when the whistle blows / Someone saved my life tonight / (Gotta get a) Meal ticket / Better off dead / Writing / We fall in love sometimes / Curtains. *(re-iss.Nov76, re-iss.pic-disc '78, re-iss.May81) (re-iss.+cd. Nov87 & Aug95 on 'Rocket')*
Jun 75. (7") **SOMEONE SAVED MY LIFE TONIGHT. / HOUSE OF CARDS** [22] [4]

—— ELTON now w/ others, after firing MURRAY and OLSSON (to BILLY JOEL)

Sep 75. (7") **ISLAND GIRL. / SUGAR ON THE FLOOR** [14] [1]
Nov 75. (lp)(c) **ROCK OF THE WESTIES** [5] [1]
– Medley: Yell help – Wednesday night – Ugly / Dan Dare (pilot of the future) / Island girl / Grow some funk of your own / I feel like a bullet (in the gun of Robert Ford) / Street kids / Hard luck story / Billy Bones and the white bird. *(re-iss.Nov76, re-iss.May81) (re-iss.+cd.Nov87 & Aug95 on 'Rocket')*
Jan 76. (7") **GROW SOME FUNK OF YOUR OWN. / I FEEL LIKE A BULLET (IN THE GUN OF ROBERT FORD)** [ ] [14]
Mar 76. (7") **PINBALL WIZARD. / HARMONY** [7] [-]
May 76. (lp)(c) **HERE AND THERE (live)** [6] [4]
– Skyline pigeon / Border song / Honky cat / Love song / Crocodile rock / Funeral for a friend / Love lies bleeding / Rocket man / Bennie and the jets / Take me to the pilot. *(re-iss.Nov76, re-iss.Sep78 as 'LONDON AND NEW YORK' on 'Hallmark') (cd-iss.Sep95)*

Rocket / M.C.A.

Jun 76. (7") **DON'T GO BREAKING MY HEART. ("ELTON JOHN & KIKI DEE") / SNOW QUEEN** [1] [1]
Oct 76. (d-lp)(c) **BLUE MOVES** [3] [3]
– Your starter for ... / Tonight / One horse town / Chameleon / Boogie pilgrim / Cage the songbird / Crazy water / Shoulder holster / Sorry seems to be the hardest word / Out of the blue / Between seventeen and twenty / The wide-eyed and laughing / Someone's final song / Where's the shoorah / If there's a God in Heaven (what's he waiting for) / Idol / Theme from a non-existant TV series / Bite your lip (get up and dance!). *(re-iss.Sep84) (cd-iss.Jun89)*
Oct 76. (7") **SORRY SEEMS TO BE THE HARDEST WORD. / SHOULDER HOLSTER** [11] [6]
Feb 77. (7") **BITE YOUR LIP (GET UP AND DANCE!). / CHAMELEON** [-] [28]
Feb 77. (7") **CRAZY WATER. / CHAMELEON** [27] [ ]
May 77. (7")(12") **BITE YOUR LIP (GET UP AND DANCE!). / CHICAGO** [28] [-]
Apr 78. (7") **EGO. / FLINTSTONE BOY** [34] [34]
Oct 78. (7") **PART-TIME LOVE. / I CRY AT NIGHT** [15] [22]
Oct 78. (lp)(c) **A SINGLE MAN** [8] [15]
– Shine on through / Return to Paradise / I don't care / Big dipper / Georgia / It ain't gonna be easy / Part-time love / Georgia / Shooting star / Madness / Reverie / Song for Guy. *(re-iss.+cd.Jun83)*
Dec 78. (7") **SONG FOR GUY. / LOVESICK** [4] [ ]
May 79. (7") **ARE YOU READY FOR LOVE (part 1). / (part 2)** [42] [51] (m-lp)
(12"+=) – Three way love affair / Mama can't buy you love.

Above was named in the US 'THE THOM BELL SESSIONS' recorded 1977.

Jun 79. (7") **MAMA CAN'T BUY YOU LOVE. / THREE WAY LOVE AFFAIR** [-] [9]
Sep 79. (7") **VICTIM OF LOVE. / STRANGERS** [ ] [31]
Oct 79. (lp)(c) **VICTIM OF LOVE** [41] [35]
– Johnny B. Goode / Warm love in a cold climate / Born bad / Thunder in the night / Spotlight / Street boogie / Born Bad / Victim of love. *(re-iss.Jul84)*
Dec 79. (7") **JOHNNY B. GOODE. / GEORGIA** [-] [ ]
Dec 79. (7")(12") **JOHNNY B. GOODE. / THUNDER IN THE NIGHT** [ ] [-]
May 80. (7") **LITTLE JEANNIE. / CONQUER THE SUN** [33] [3]
May 80. (lp)(c) **21 AT 33** [12] [13]
– Chasing the crown / Little Jeannie / Sartorial eloquence / Two rooms at the end of the world / White lady, white powder / Dear God / Never gonna fall in love again / Take me back / Give me the love. *(re-iss.+cd.Jul84) (cd-iss.Jun88)*
Aug 80. (7") **SARTORIAL ELOQUENCE. / WHITE MAN DANCER; CARTIER** [44] [39]
Nov 80. (7") **DEAR GOD. / TACTICS** [ ] [ ]
(d7") – Steal away child / Love so cold.

Rocket / Geffen

May 81. (7") **NOBODY WINS. / FOOLS IN FASHION** [42] [21]
May 81. (lp)(c) **THE FOX** [12] [21]
– Breaking down barriers / Heart in the right place / Just like Belgium / Nobody wins / Fascist faces / Carla etude / Fanfare / Chloe / Heels of the wind / Elton's song / The fox. *(re-iss.+cd.Jul84)*

Jul 81. (7") **JUST LIKE BELGIUM. / CAN'T GET OVER LOSING YOU** [ ] [-]

Jul 81. (7") **CHLOE. / TORTURED** [-] [34]

Mar 82. (7") **BLUE EYES. / HEY PAPA LEGBA** [8] [12] Jul 82

Apr 82. (lp)(c) **JUMP UP!** [13] [17]
– Dear John / Spiteful child / Ball and chain / Legal boys / I am your robot / Blue eyes / Empty garden /Princess / Where have all the good times gone? / All quiet on the western front. *(cd-iss.1983)*

May 82. (7")(7"pic-d) **EMPTY GARDEN. / TAKE ME DOWN TO THE OCEAN** [51] [13] Mar 82

Sep 82. (7") **PRINCESS. / THE RETREAT** [ ] [-]

Nov 82. (7") **ALL QUIET ON THE WESTERN FRONT. / WHERE HAVE ALL THE GOOD TIMES GONE?** [ ] [-]

Nov 82. (7") **BALL AND CHAIN. / WHERE HAVE ALL THE GOOD TIMES GONE?** [-] [ ]

Apr 83. (7") **I GUESS THAT'S WHY THEY CALL IT THE BLUES. / LORD CHOC ICE GOES MENTAL** [5] [-]

May 83. (7") **I'M STILL STANDING. / LOVE SO COLD** [-] [12]

Jun 83. (lp)(c)(cd) **TOO LOW FOR ZERO** [7] [25]
– Cold at Christmas / I'm still standing / Too low for zero / Religion / I guess that's why they call it the blues / Crystal / Kiss the bride / Whipping boy / Saint / One more arrow.

Jul 83. (7")(12")(7"sha-pic-d) **I'M STILL STANDING. / EARN WHILE YOU LEARN** [4] [-]

Aug 83. (7") **KISS THE BRIDE. / LORD CHOC ICE GOES MENTAL** [-] [25]

Oct 83. (7")(12") **KISS THE BRIDE. / DREAMBOAT** [20] [-]

Oct 83. (7") **I GUESS THAT'S WHY THEY CALL IT HTE BLUES. / THE RETREAT** [-] [4]
(d7"+=) – Ego / Song for Guy.

Dec 83. (7") **COLD AT CHRISTMAS. / CRYSTAL** [33] [ ]
(d7"+=) – Don't go breaking my heart / Snow queen.

May 84. (7")(12")(7"sha-pic-d) **SAD SONGS (SAY SO MUCH). / SIMPLE MAN** [7] [5]

Jun 84. (lp)(c)(cd) **BREAKING HEARTS** [2] [20]
– Restless / Slow down Georgie (she's poison) / Who wears these shoes? / Breaking hearts (ain't what it used to be) / Li'l fridgerator / Passengers / In neon / Burning bridges / Did he shoot her? / Sad songs (say so much).

Aug 84. (7")(12") **PASSENGERS (remix). / LONELY BOY** [5] [ ]

Sep 84. (7") **WHO WEARS THESE SHOES? / LONELY EYES** [-] [16]

Oct 84. (7") **WHO WEARS THESE SHOES? / TORTURED** [50] [-]
(12"+=) – I heard it through the grapevine.

Nov 84. (7") **IN NEON. / TACTICS** [-] [38]

Feb 85. (7") **BREAKING HEARTS (AIN'T WHAT IT USED TO BE). / IN NEON** [59] [38] Nov 84

Jun 85. (7") **ACT OF WAR (part 1). ("ELTON JOHN & MILLIE JACKSON") / (part 2)** [32] [ ]
(12"+=) – (part 3) / (part 4).

Sep 85. (7") **NIKITA. / THE MAN WHO NEVER DIED** [3] [-]
(12"+=)(d7"+=) – Sorry seems to be the hardest word (live) / I'm still standing (live).

Oct 85. (7") **WRAP HER UP. / THE MAN WHO NEVER DIED** [-] [ ]

Nov 85. (lp)(c)(cd) **ICE ON FIRE** [3] [48]
– Wrap her up / Satellite / Tell me what the papers say / Candy by the pound / Shoot down the Moon / This town / Cry to heaven / Soul glove / Nikita / Too young. *(c+=)(cd+=)*– Act of war (with MILLIE JACKSON).

Nov 85. (7")(7"sha-pic-d) **WRAP HER UP. / RESTLESS (live)** [12] [ ]
(12"+=) – ('A' extended).
(d12"+=) – Nikita / The man who never died.

Jan 86. (7") **NIKITA. / RESTLESS** [-] [7]

Feb 86. (7") **CRY TO HEAVEN. / CANDY BY THE POUND** [47] [ ]
(12"+=)/ /(d7"++=) – Rock'n'roll medley./ / Your song.

Sep 86. (7") **HEARTACHES ALL OVER THE WORLD. / HIGH-LANDER** [45] [55]
(12"+=) – ('A'version).
(d7"+=) – Passengers / I'm still standing.

Nov 86. (lp)(c)(cd) **LEATHER JACKETS** [24] [91]
– Leather jackets / Hoop of fire / Go it alone / Don't trust that woman / Gypsy heart / Slow rivers / Heartache all over the world / Angeline / Memory of love / Paris / I fall apart.

Nov 86. (7") **SLOW RIVERS. ("ELTON JOHN & CLIFF RICHARD") / BILLY AND THE KIDS** [44] [ ]
(12"+=) – Lord of the flies.
(c-s+=) – Nikita / Blue eyes / I guess that's why they call it the blues

Rocket M.C.A.

Jun 87. (7") **YOUR SONG (live). / DON'T LET THE SUN GO DOWN ON ME (live)** [ ] [ ]
(12"+=) – I need you to turn to / The greatest discovery.

Sep 87. (d-lp)(c)(cd) **LIVE IN AUSTRALIA (live)** [43] [24] Dec 87
– Sixty years on / I need you to turn to / The greatest discovery / Tonight / Sorry seems to be the hardest word / The king must die / Take me to the pilot / Tiny dancer / Have mercy on the criminal / Madman across the water / Candle in the wind / Burn down the mission / Your song / Don't let the Sun go down on me.

Dec 87. (7")(7"pic-d) **CANDLE IN THE WIND (live). / SORRY SEEMS TO BE THE HARDEST WORD (live)** [5] [6] Nov 87
(12"+=)(c-s+=)(cd-s+=) – Your song (live) / Don't let the sun go down on me (live).

Mar 88. (7") **TONIGHT. / TAKE ME TO THE PILOT** [-] [ ]

May 88. (7")(12") **I DON'T WANT TO GO ON WITH YOU LIKE THAT. / ROPE AROUND A FOOL** [30] [2] Jun 88
(12"+=)/ /(cd-s+=) – ('A'version)/ / ('A'-Shep Pettibone mix).

Jun 88. (lp)(c)(cd) **REG STRIKES BACK** [18] [16]
– Town of plenty / A word in Spanish / Mona Lisas and mad hatters (part 2) / I don't want to go on with you like that / Japanese hands / Goodbye Marlon Brando / The camera never lies / Heavy traffic / Poor cow / Since God invented girls.

Sep 88. (7") **TOWN OF PLENTY. / WHIPPING BOY** [74] [ ]
(12"+=) – My baby's a saint.
(cd-s++=) – I guess that's why they call it the blues.

Nov 88. (7") **A WORD IN SPANISH. / HEAVY TRAFFIC** [ ] [19] Sep88
(12"+=) – Live in Australia medley: Song for Guy – I guess that's why they call it the blues – Blue eyes.
(cd-s++=) – Daniel.

— In Apr89, he was credited on 'THROUGH THE STORM' UK No.41 / No.16 single with ARETHA FRANKLIN.

Aug 89. (7")(c-s) **HEALING HANDS. / DANCING IN THE END ZONE** [45] [13]
(12"+=)(cd-s+=) – ('A'version).

Sep 89. (lp)(c)(cd) **SLEEPING WITH THE PAST** [1] [23]
– Durban deep / Healing hands / Whispers / Club at the end of the street / Sleeping with the past / Stone's throw from hurtin' / Sacrifice / I never knew her name / Amazes me / Blue avenue. *(re-dist. May90, No.1)*.

Oct 89. (7")(c-s) **SACRIFICE. / LOVE IS A CANNIBAL** [55] [18] Jan 90
(12"+=)(cd-s+=) – Durban deep.

Apr 90. (7") **CLUB AT THEN END OF THE STREET. / SACRIFICE** [-] [28]

Jun 90. (7")(c-s) **SACRIFICE. / HEALING HANDS** [1] [-]
(12"+=)(cd-s+=) – Durban deep.

Aug 90. (7")(c-s) **CLUB AT THE END OF THE STREET. / WHISPERS** [47] [-]
(12"+=) – I don't wanna go on with you like that.
(cd-s+=) – Give peace a chance.

Oct 90. (7")(c-s) **YOU GOTTA LOVE SOMEONE. / MEDICINE MAN** [33] [43] Nov 90
(12"+=)(cd-s+=) – ('B'-Adamski version).

Nov 90. (7")(c-s) **EASIER TO WALK AWAY. / SWEAR I HEARD THE NIGHT TALKING** [63] [ ]
(12"+=)(cd-s+=) – Made for me.

— 45 year-old DEE MURRAY died of a heart attack, after suffering from cancer

May 92. (7")(c-s) **THE ONE. / SUIT OF WOLVES** [10] [9]
(cd-s+=) – Fat boys and ugly girls.

Jun 92. (cd)(c)(lp) **THE ONE** [2] [8]
– Simple life / The one / Sweat it out / Runaway train / Whitewash county / The North / When a woman doesn't want you / Emily / On dark street / Understanding women / The last song.

Jul 92. (7")(c-s) **RUNAWAY TRAIN. ("ELTON JOHN & ERIC CLAPTON") / UNDERSTANDING WOMEN** [31] [ ]
(cd-s+=) – Made for me.
(cd-s) – ('A'side) / Through the storm (with ARETHA FRANKLIN) / Don't let the Sun go down on me (with GEORGE MICHAEL) / Slow rivers (with CLIFF).

Oct 92. (7")(c-s) **THE LAST SONG. / THE MAN WHO NEVER DIED / SONG FOR GUY** [21] [23]
(cd-s) – ('A'side) / Are you ready / Three way love affair / Mama can't buy you love.

May 93. (7")(c-s) **SIMPLE LIFE. / THE LAST SONG** [44] [30] Feb 93
(cd-s+=) – The north.

Nov 93. (7")(c-s) **TRUE LOVE. ("ELTON JOHN & KIKI DEE") / THE SHOW MUST GO ON** [2] [56]
(cd-s+=) – Runaway train.
(cd-s) – ('A'side) / Wrap her up / That's what friends are for / Act of war.

Nov 93. (cd)(c)(d-lp) **DUETS** (w/ whoever in brackets) [5] [25]
– Teardrops (k.d.LANG) / When I think about love (I think about you) (P.M.DAWN) / The power (LITTLE RICHARD) / Shakey ground (DON HENLEY) / True love (KIKI DEE) / If you were me (CHRIS REA) / A woman's needs (TAMMY WYNETTE) / Don't let the Sun go down on me (GEORGE MICHAEL) / Old friend (NIK KERSHAW) / Go on and on (GLADYS KNIGHT) / Don't go breaking my heart (RuPAUL) / Ain't nothing like the real thing (MARCELLA DETROIT) / I'm your puppet (PAUL YOUNG) / Love letters (BONNIE RAITT) / Born to lose (LEONARD COHEN) / Duets for one (ELTON JOHN solo).

Feb 94. (7")(c-s) **DON'T GO BREAKING MY HEART. ("ELTON JOHN & RuPAUL") / DONNER POUR DONNER** [7] [92]
(cd-s+=) – A woman's needs.
(cd-s) – ('A'side) / ('A'mixes).

— In May 94, he & MARCELLA DETROIT (ex-SHAKESPEAR'S SISTER) hit UK No.24 with 'AIN'T NOTHIN' LIKE THE REAL THING'.

Jun 94. (7")(c-s) **CAN YOU FEEL THE LOVE TONIGHT?. / ('A'mix)** [14] [4] May94
(cd-s+=) – Hakuna Matata / Under the stars.

Sep 94. (c-s) **CIRCLE OF LIFE. / ('A'mix)** [11] [18]
(cd-s+=)(pic-cd-s+=) – I just can't wait to be king / This land.

— with **GUY BABYLON** – keyboards/ **BOB BIRCH** – bass/ **DAVEY JOHNSTONE** – guitar, mandolin, banjo/ **CHARLIE MORGAN** – drums/ **RAY COOPER** – percusion

Feb 95. (c-s) **BELIEVE / SORRY SEEMS TO BE THE HARDEST WORD (live)** [15] [13]
(cd-s+=) – Believe (live).
(cd-s) – ('A'side) / The one / The last song.

Mar 95. (cd)(c)(lp) **MADE IN ENGLAND** [3] [13]
– Believe / Made in England / House / Cold / Pain / Belfast / Latitude / Please / Man / Lies / Blessed.

May 95. (cd-s) **MADE IN ENGLAND / DANIEL (live)** [18] [52]
(c-s+=) – Can you feel the love tonight.
(cd-s+=) – Your song / Don't let the sun go down on me.
(cd-s) – ('A'side) / Whatever gets you thru the night / Lucy in the sky with diamonds / I saw her standing there.

Oct 95. (c-s)(cd-s) **BLESSED / LATITUDE** [ ] [34]
(cd-s) – ('A'side) / Made in England (mixes).
(cd-s) – ('A'side) / Honky cat (live) / Take me to the pilot (live) / The bitch is back (live).

Nov 95. (cd)(c) **LOVE SONGS** (compilation) [7] [ ]
– Sacrifice / Candle in the wind / I guess that's why they call it the blues / Don't let the sun go down on me (with GEORGE MICHAEL) / Sorry seems to be the hardest word / Blue eyes / Daniel / Nikita / Your song / The one / Someone saved my life tonight / True love (with KIKI DEE) / Can you feel the love tonight / Circle of life / Blessed / Please / Song for Guy.

– compilations, exploitation releases, etc. –

Apr 71. Paramount; (lp) **FRIENDS (soundtrack)** [ ] [36]
(re-iss. on 'Anchor')

Note; All 'DJM' releases were issued on 'MCA' in the US.

Nov 74. DJM; (lp)(c) **ELTON JOHN'S GREATEST HITS** [1] [1]
– Your song / Daniel / Honky cat / Goodbye yellow brick road / Saturday night's alright for fighting / Rocket man / Candle in the wind / Don't let the Sun go

down on me / Border song / Crocodile rock / The bitch is back / Lucy in the sky with diamonds / Sorry seems to be the hardest word / Don't go breaking my heart / Someone saved my life tonight / Philadelphia freedom / Island girl / Grow somw funk of your own / Benny & the jets / Pinball wizard. *(re-iss.Nov76) (cd-iss.Oct84)*

Sep 76. DJM; (7") **BENNIE AND THE JETS. / ROCK AND ROLL MADONNA** [37] [-]

May 77. DJM; (7"ep) **FOUR FROM FOUR EYES** [ ] [ ]
– Your song / Rocket man / Saturday night's alright for fighting / Whenever you're ready (we'll go steady again).

Sep 77. DJM; (lp)(c) **GREATEST HITS VOL.2** [6] [21]

Sep 78. DJM; (12"ep) **FUNERAL FOR A FRIEND; LOVE LIES BLEEDING / CURTAINS / WE ALL FALL IN LOVE SOMETIMES** [ ] [ ]
(re-iss.'88)

Sep 78. DJM; (12x7"-box) **THE ELTON JOHN SINGLES COLLECTION** [ ] [ ]
(also available separately as below)

Sep 78. DJM; (7") **LADY SAMANTHA. / SKYLINE PIGEON** [ ] [ ]

Sep 78. DJM; (7") **YOUR SONG. / BORDER SONG** [ ] [ ]

Sep 78. DJM; (7") **HONKY CAT. / SIXTY YEARS ON** [ ] [ ]

Sep 78. DJM; (7") **CROCODILE ROCK. / COUNTRY COMFORT** [ ] [ ]

Sep 78. DJM; (7") **ROCKET MAN. / DANIEL** [ ] [ ]

Sep 78. DJM; (7") **GOODBYE YELLOW BRICK ROAD. / SWEET PAINTED LADY** [ ] [ ]

Sep 78. DJM; (7") **DON'T LET THE SUN GO DOWN ON ME. / SOMEONE SAVED MY LIFE** [ ] [ ]

Sep 78. DJM; (7") **CANDLE IN THE WIND. / I FEEL LIKE A BULLET (. . .** [ ] [ ]

Sep 78. DJM; (7") **THE BITCH IS BACK. / GROW SOME FUNK OF YOUR OWN** [ ] [ ]

Sep 78. DJM; (7") **ISLAND GIRL. / SATURDAY NIGHT'S ALRIGHT FOR FIGHTING** [ ] [ ]

Sep 78. DJM; (7") **PHILADELPHIA FREEDOM. / BENNIE AND THE JETS** [ ] [ ]

Sep 78. DJM; (7") **PINBALL WIZARD. / BENNIE AND THE JETS** [ ] [ ]

Feb 79. Pickwick; (d-lp)(d-c) **THE ELTON JOHN LIVE COLLECTION** [ ] [ ]
(live albums Apr71 + May76) *(re-iss. Nov88 as 'THE COLLECTION')*

Aug 79. DJM; (5xlp-box) **ELTON JOHN** [ ] [ ]
(originally released in US contains 'EARLY YEARS', 'ELTON ROCKS', 'MOODS', 'SINGLES' & 'CLASSICS')

Oct 80. DJM; (lp)(c) **LADY SAMANTHA** (rare 'B's) [56] [ ]

Nov 80. DJM; (7") **HARMONY. / MONA LISA AND THE MAD HATTERS** [ ] [ ]

Mar 81. DJM; (7") **I SAW HER STANDING THERE. / WHATEVER GETS YOU THROUGH THE NIGHT / LUCY IN THE SKY WITH DIAMONDS (with JOHN LENNON)** [30] [ ]

1988. DJM; (d-c) **ROCK OF THE WESTIES / ELTON JOHN'S GREATEST HITS** [ ] [ ]

1988. DJM; (d-c) **EMPTY SKY / GREATEST HITS VOL.2** [ ] [ ]

1988. DJM; (d-c) **CAPTAIN FANTASTIC AND THE BROWN DIRT COWBOY / ELTON JOHN** [ ] [ ]

1988. DJM; (d-c) **DON'T SHOOT ME I'M ONLY THE PIANO PLAYER / TUMBLEWEED CONNECTION** [ ] [ ]

1988. DJM; (d-c) **GREATEST HITS / ROCK OF THE WESTIES** [ ] [ ]

1988. DJM; (7") **LUCY IN THE SKY WITH DIAMONDS. / ONE DAY AT A TIME** [ ] [ ]

1988. DJM; (7") **CANDLE IN THE WIND. / BENNIE AND THE JETS** [ ] [ ]

1988. DJM; (7") **YOUR SONG. / INTO THE OLD MAN'S SHOES** [ ] [ ]

Note; All 'Rocket' releases were issued on 'MCA' in the US.

Apr 77. Rocket; (7") **THE GOALDIGGER SONG. / (spoken)** [ ] [ ]

Mar 81. Rocket; (7") **DON'T GO BREAKING MY HEART. / SNOW QUEEN 7** [-] [ ]

Oct 90. Rocket; (cd)(c)(d-lp) **THE VERY BEST OF ELTON JOHN** [1] [ ]
– Your song / Rocket man / Crocodile rock / Daniel / Goodbye yellow brick road / Saturday night's alright for fighting / Candle in the wind / Don't let the Sun go down on me / Lucy in the sky with diamonds / Philadelphia freedom / Someone saved my life tonight / Don't go breaking my heart / Bennie and the jets / Sorry seems to be the hardest word / Song for Guy / Part time love / Blue eyes / I guess that's why they call it the blues / I'm still standing / Kiss the bride / Sad songs / Passengers / Nikita / Sacrifice / You gotta love someone. *(cd+c+=)* – Pinball wizard / The bitch is back / I don't wanna go on with you like that / Easier to walk away. *(re-iss.Nov91 hit UK No.29)*

Feb 91. Rocket; (7")(c-s) **DON'T LET THE SUN GO DOWN ON ME. / SONG FOR GUY** [ ] [ ]
(12"+=)(cd-s+=) – Sorry seems to be the hardest word.

Nov 91. MCA; (cd-box)(c-box) **TO BE CONTINUED . . .** [ ] [82]

Sep 87. Geffen; (cd)(c)(lp) **ELTON JOHN'S GREATEST HITS, VOLUME III, 1979-1987** [?] [84]

Jan 78. St.Michael; (lp) **CANDLE IN THE WIND (ltd)** [ ] [-]

Oct 80. K-Tel; (lp)(c) **THE VERY BEST OF ELTON JOHN** [24] [-]

Sep 81. Hallmark; (lp)(c) **THE ALBUM** [ ] [-]

Nov 82. T.V.; (lp)(c) **LOVE SONGS** [ ] [-]

Jun 83. Everest; (lp)(c) **THE NEW COLLECTION** [ ] [-]

Jun 83. Everest; (lp)(c) **THE NEW COLLECTION VOL.2** [ ] [-]

1983. Cambra; (d-c) **ELTON JOHN (hits)** [ ] [-]

May 84. Cambra; (d-c) **SEASONS . . . THE EARLY LOVE SONGS** [ ] [-]

Oct 84. DJM; (cd) **THE SUPERIOR SOUND OF . . .** [ ] [-]

Jun 88. Old Gold; (7") **DON'T GO BREAKING MY HEART. / I GOT THE MUSIC IN ME (Kiki Dee)** [ ] [-]

Feb 88. Old Gold; (7") **NIKITA. / I'M STILL STANDING** [ ] [-]

Jun 88. Old Gold; (7") **SONG FOR GUY. / BLUE EYES** [ ] [-]

1988. Starr; (cd) **BIGGEST** [ ] [-]

— below, a guest spot w/**KIKI DEE.**

Apr 81. Ariola; (7") **LOVING YOU IS SWEETER THAN EVER. / 24 HOURS** [ ] [ ]

May 87. CBS/ US= Epic; (7") **FLAMES OF PARADISE. / CALL ON ME** [ ] [36]

above JENNIFER RUSH & ELTON JOHN single

Mar 94. Spectrum; (cd)(c) **ROCK & ROLL MADONNA** [ ] [-]

Feb 95. D.J.; (cd-s) **UNITED WE STAND / NEANDERTHAL MAN** [ ] [-]

(above credited to REG DWIGHT) (early recordings)

Apr 95. RPM; (cd) **CHARTBUSTERS ARE GO** [ ] [-]

JOHNNY & THE SELF-ABUSERS (see under ⇒ SIMPLE MINDS)

JOHN'S CHILDREN

Formed: Leatherhead, Surrey, England . . . May'66 as SILENCE by ANDY ELLISON, GEOFF McCLELLAND, JOHN HEWLETT and CHRIS TOWNSON. In Sep'66, they became JOHN'S CHILDREN and signed record deal with 'Columbia', through manager Simon Napier-Bell. They issued 2 singles at the turn of '66, and nearly came to prominence in Mar'67, when MARC BOLAN arrived for 4 months, replacing McCLELLAND. Their third 45 'DESDEMONA' now on 'Track', became underground classic, but was banned from daytime airplay, due to lyrics 'lift up your skirt and fly'. When BOLAN left to start TYRANNOSAURUS REX (T.REX), band lost momentum. ELLISON went solo, and later returned in 1974 with JET. In 1977 he/they evolved into RADIO STARS, and scored UK Top 40 hit with 'NERVOUS WRECK'. • **Style:** R&B and YARDBIRDS influenced outfit, whose psychedlic power unfortunately only gave them cult notoriety. **Songwriters:** ELLISON wrote most. RADIO STARS covered DEAR PRUDENCE + NORWEGIAN WOOD (Beatles). • **Trivia:** Their early 1967 recorded lp 'ORGASM' was surprisingly issued in the US Sep70 on 'White Whale'.

Recommended: THE LEGENDARY ORGASM ALBUM (1982 lost 'ORGASM' lp)

ANDY ELLSION – vocals / **GEOFF McLELLAND** – guitar, vocals / **JOHN HEWLETT** – bass / **CHRIS TOWNSON** – drums

Columbia / not issued

Oct 66. (7") **THE LOVE I'D THOUGHT I'D FOUND. / STRANGE AFFAIR** [ ] [-]

Feb 67. (7") **JUST WHAT YOU WANT – JUST WHAT YOU'LL GET. / BUT SHE'S MINE** [ ] [-]

— **MARC BOLAN** – guitar, vocals (ex-solo artist) repl. McLELLAND

Track / not issued

May 67. (7") **DESDEMONA. / REMEMBER THOMAS A BECKETT** [ ] [-]

— **CHRIS COLVILLE** – drums repl. BOLAN who formed TYRANNOSAURUS REX **TOWNSON** switched to guitar (ELLISON and HEWLETT still remained)

Aug 67. (7") **COME AND PLAY WITH ME IN THE GARDEN. / SARA CRAZY CHILD** [ ] [-]

Oct 67. (7") **GO GO GIRL. / JAGGED TIME LAPSE** [ ] [-]

— They split Autumn '67. The original line-up did record an album '67 but due to its title 'ORGASM' it was not released for over 15 years.

May 82. Cherry Red; (lp) **THE LEGENDARY ORGASM ALBUM** [ ] [-]
– Smashed blocked (live & studio) / Just what you want, just what you'll get (live & studio) / Killer Ben / Jagged time lapse / Not the sort of girl / You're a nothing / Cold on me / Leave me alone / Let me know / Why do you lie / Strange affair / But she's mine.

Dec 90. Zinc Alloy; (m-lp) **PLAYING WITH THEMSELVES** [ ] [-]

May 91. Zinc Alloy; (m-lp) **PLAYING WITH THEMSELVES VOL.2** [ ] [-]

— Of compilations JOHN'S CHILDREN tracks appeared on BOLAN's BEGINNING OF DOVES album. After split drummer TOWNSON later joined The JOOK in '71, he later joined JET with ANDY.

ANDY ELLISON

had went straight into solo career in '67.

Track / not issued

Dec 67. (7") **BEEN A LONG TIME. / ARTHUR GREEN** [ ] [-]

Feb 68. (7") **YOU CAN'T DO THAT. / CASBAH** [ ] [-]

Apr 68. (7") **FOOL FROM UPPER EDEN. / ANOTHER LUCKY LIE** [ ] [-]

JET

ANDY ELLISON – vocals / **DAVID O'LIST** – guitar (ex-NICE, ex-ROXY MUSIC) / **PETER OXENDALE** – keyboards / **MARTIN GORDON** – bass / **CHRIS TOWNSON** – drums

C.B.S. / not issued

Mar 75. (lp)(c) **JET** [ ] [-]
– Start here / Brian damage / It would be good / Song for hymn / Nothing to do with us / Tittle-tattle / Fax n' info / My river / Diamonds are a girls best friend / Whangdepootenawah / Cover girl.

— **TREVOR WHITE** – guitar (ex-JOOK, ex-SPARKS) repl. OXENDALE who joined GLITTER BAND. **IAN McLEOD** – guitar repl. O'LIST who went into sessions

— After their split, they became

RADIO STARS

PAUL SIMON – drums (of NEO)repl. TOWNSON and WHITE

Chiswick / not issued

Apr 77. (7") **DIRTY PICTURES. / SAIL AWAY** [ ] [-]

— (Jul77) **STEVE PARRY** – drums repl. PAUL who joined COWBOYS INTERNA-

TIONAL

Aug 77. (7"ep) **STOP IT** [ ] [-]
– No Russians in Russia / Box 29 / Johnny Mekon / Sorry I'm tied up.

Oct 77. (7")(12") **NERVOUS WRECK. / HORRIBLE BREATH** [39] [-]

Dec 77. (lp) **SONGS FOR SWINGING LOVERS** [ ] [-]
– Good personality / Is it really necessary / Eric / The beast of Barnsley / Nervous wreck / Nothing happened today / Buy Chiswick records / Don't waste my time / Arthur is dead boring / Macaroni and mice / Nice girls / Talkin' 'bout you. *(free-7"w.a.)*– NO RUSSIANS IN RUSSIA. / DIRTY PICTURES

Apr 78. (7")(6") **FROM A RABBIT. / THE BEAST No.2** [ ] [-]

— **JAMIE CROMPTON** – drums (ex-NEW HEARTS) repl. MARTIN to BLUE MEANIES

Sep 78. (7") **RADIO STARS. / ACCOUNTANCY BLUES** [ ] [-]

Sep 78. (lp) **THE RADIO STARS HOLIDAY ALBUM** [ ] [-]
– Radio stars / Boy meets girl / Baffin Island / (I've got dem old) Sex in chains blues (again mama) / Sitting in the rain / The real me / Rock and roll for the time being / Norwegian wood / Get on a plane / I'm down / No Russians in Russia / It's all over / Goodnight.

— (tour after lp) **JOHN MACKIE** – drums (ex-STUKAS) repl. CROMPTON / added **TREVOR WHITE** – guitar (solo artist since JET)

Jan 79. (7") **THE REAL ME. / GOOD PERSONALITY** [ ] [-]

— (Feb79) **STEVE PARRY** – drums returned to repl. MACKIE and GORDON

— Disbanded but re-formed 1982 by **ELLISON,** etc

- others, etc. -

Moonlight / not issued

May 82. (7") **GOOD PERSONALITY. / TALKIN' 'BOUT YOU** [ ] [-]

May 82. (lp) **TWO MINUTES MR.SMITH** [ ] [-]

Snap / not issued

Sep 82. (7") **MY MOTHER SAID. / TWO MINUTES MR.SMITH** [ ] [-]

Oct 92. Chiswick; (cd) **SOMEWHERE THERE'S A PLACE FOR US** [ ] [-]

Holly JOHNSON (see under ⇒ FRANKIE GOES TO HOLLYWOOD)

Linton Kwesi JOHNSON

Born: 1952, Chapelton, Jamaica, West Indies. In 1963 he and his family moved to Brixton, London, where after leaving school, he studied sociology at Brixton Academy. In 1971, he got 2 books published, 'Voices Of The Living And The Dead' & 'Dread Beat And Blood'. The latter's poems were recorded for an EP in 1977 on 'Virgin' as POET & THE ROOTS. His gigs at that time were a mixture of verse and little accompaniment, mostly provided by DENNIS BOVELL. Late in 1978, he signed to Chris Blackwell's 'Island' records, and issued Spring next year debut album 'FORCES OF VICTORY'. This reached UK Top 75, as he toured country with fellow poet/ranter JOHN COOPER CLARKE. **Songwriters & Style:** Penned own words, with black social problems the main subject, which with reggae/dub backing, tried to hit establishment nerve. • **Trivia:** He often cut his own suits, as he was a tailor before he received honours degree for sociology.

Recommended: FORCES OF VICTORY (*8) / BASS CULTURE (*7).

POET & THE ROOTS

aka LINTON KWESI JOHNSON, plus DENNIS BOVELL of MATUMBI

Virgin / not issued

Dec 77. (7"ep)(12"ep) **DREAD BEAT AND BLOOD. / ALL WE DOIN' IS DEFENDING / ('A'dub version)** [ ] [-]

LINTON KWESI JOHNSON

solo poet/singer.

Island / Island

Apr 79. (lp)(c) **FORCES OF VICTORY** [66] [ ]
– Want fi go rave / It noh funny / Sonny's lettah (anti-sus poem) / Independant intavenshan / Fite dem back / Forces of viktry / Time come. *(re-iss.Oct86) (cd-iss.Sep91 on 'Mango')*

May 79. (7")(12") **WANT FI GO RAVE. / REALITY POEM** [ ] [-]

Sep 79. (7"ep) **SONNY'S LETTAH (ANTI-SUS POEM). / IRON BAR DUB / TEK CHANCE / FUNNY DUB** [ ] [-]

Jan 80. (7") **DI BLACK PETTY BOSSHWAH. / STRAIGHT TO MADRAY'S HEAD** [ ] [-]
(12"+=) – Action line / Action (dub).

Apr 80. (lp)(c) **BASS CULTURE** [46] [-]
– Bass culture / Street 66 / Reggae fi Peach / Di black petty booshwah / Inglan is a bitch / Loriane / Reggae sounds / Two sides of silence. *(cd-iss.Jan91)*

Nov 80. (lp) **L.K.J. IN DUB (dub versions)** [ ] [-]
– Victorious dub / Reality dub / Peach dub / Shocking dub / Iron bar dub / Bitch dub / Cultural dub / Brain smashing dub. *(cd+c.Sep91)*

Feb 84. (7") **DI EAGLE AN DI BEAR. / ?** [ ] [-]

Feb 84. (lp)(c) **MAKING HISTORY** [73] [-]
– Di eagle an' di bear / Wat about di workin' claas / Di great insoreckshan / Making history / Reggae fi Radni / Reggae fi Dada / New craas massahkah.

Rough Trade / not issued

Oct 84. (d-lp)(c) **LINTON KWESI JOHNSON IN CONCERT (live)** [ ] [-]
– Five nights of bleeding / Dread beat an' blood / Intro / All wi doin' is defendin' / It dread inna Inglan / Man free / Wnat fi goh rave / It noh funny / Forces of viktry / Independant intavenshan / Reggae fi Peach / Di black petty booshwah / New craas Massahkah / Reality poem / Wat about di workin' claas / Di great insohreckshan / Making history. *(re-iss.May88 on 'Shanachie') (cd-iss.Apr95 on 'LKJ')*

Sterns / not issued

1980s. (7") **HISTORY REPEATS ITSELF** [-] [ ]

LKJ / not issued

Jun 91. (cd)(c)(lp) **TINGS AN' TIMES** [ ] [-]
– Story / Sense outta nansense / Tings an' times / Mi revalueshanary fren / Di good life / Di anfinish revalueshan / Dubbing for life. *(re-iss.cd/lp Nov95)*

- compilations etc. -

Jul 81. Virgin; (lp) **DREAD BEAT'N'BLOOD** (1978 material) [ ] [-]
– Dread beat'n'blood / Five nights of bleeding / Down de road / Song of blood / It dread inna Inglan (for George Lindo) / Come wi goh dung deh / Man free (for Darcus Howe) / All wi doin' is defending. *(cd-iss.1988 on 'Heartbeat')*

May 85. Island; (lp)(c) **REGGAE GREATS** [ ] [-]
(re-iss.+cd.Apr88 & 1990)

Apr 95. LKJ; (cd) **LKJ IN DUB VOLUME 2** [ ] [-]

Matt JOHNSON (see under ⇒ THE THE)

JO JO GUNNE

Formed: Los Angeles, California, USA ... 1971 by ex-SPIRIT men; JAY FERGUSON and MARK ANDES. They signed to 'Asylum' and soon issued eponymous debut lp, which held inside a gem of a hit single 'RUN, RUN, RUN'. However they never fulfilled critical or commercial promise, and fell away, although JAY did score with a few solo single hits 1978-79. • **Style:** A fusion between CANNED HEAT and The EAGLES, they epitomized soft-rock boogie and nice image. • **Songwriters:** FERGUSON wrote most, and covered as solo artist; MEDICATED GOO (Traffic) / LET'S SPEND THE NIGHT TOGETHER (Rolling Stones) / DO IT AGAIN (Beach Boys?). • **Trivia:** 'RUN, RUN, RUN' was later covered by heavy girl-group GIRLSCHOOL.

Recommended: JO JO GUNNE (*5).

JAY FERGUSON (b.JOHN, 10 May'47, Burbank, USA) – vocals (ex-SPIRIT) **/ MATT ANDES** – guitar / **MARK ANDES** (b.19 Feb'48, Philadelphia, USA) – bass (ex-SPIRIT) / **CURLY SMITH** (b.31 Jan'52, Wolf Point, Montana, USA) – drums

Asylum / Asylum

Mar 72. (7") **RUN RUN RUN. / TAKE IT EASY** [6] [27]

Apr 72. (lp)(c) **JO JO GUNNE** [ ] [57] Feb 72
– Run run run / Shake that fat / Babylon / I make love / Barstow blues eyes / 99 days / Academy award / Take it easy / Flying home.

Jun 72. (7") **SHAKE THAT FAT. / I MAKE LOVE** [ ] [ ]

— **JIMMIE RANDALL** (b.14 Feb'49, Dallas, Texas, USA) – bass repl. MARK who returned to SPIRIT

Mar 73. (7") **READY FREDDY. / WAIT A LIFETIME** [ ] [ ]

Apr 73. (lp)(c) **BITE DOWN HARD** [ ] [75]
– Ready Freddy / Roll over me / Sixty minutes to go / Rock around the symbol / Broken down man / Special situations / Take me down easy / Wait a lifetime / Rhoda.

Sep 73. (7") **ROCK AROUND THE SYMBOL. / TAKE ME DOWN EASY** [ ] [ ]

Dec 73. (lp)(c) **JUMPIN' THE GUNNE** [ ] [ ]
– I wanna love you / To the island / Red meat / Getaway / Before you get your breakfast / At the spa / Monkey music / Couldn't love you better / High school drool / Neon city / Turn the boy loose.

Jan 74. (7") **I WANNA LOVE YOU. / NEON CITY** [ ] [ ]

— **CHRIS STAEHELY** (b.25 Jan'52, Austin) – guitar (ex-SPIRIT) repl. MATT who also became part of SPIRIT (another swop!)

Oct 74. (7") **WHERE IS THE SHOW?. / INTO MY LIFE** [-] [ ]

Oct 74. (7") **WHERE IS THE SHOW?. / SINGLE MAN** [ ] [-]

Nov 74. (lp)(c) **SO . . .WHERE'S THE SHOW?** [ ] [ ]
– Where is the show? / I'm your shoe / Single man / She said alright / S & M Blvd. / Falling angel / Big, busted bombshell from Bermuda / Into my life / Around the world.

Mar 75. (7") **I'M YOUR SHOE. / BIG, BUSTED BOMBSHELL FROM BERMUDA** [ ] [ ]

Jul 76. (7") **RUN RUN RUN. / SHAKE THAT FAT** [ ] [ ]

— Disbanded early '75. JAY sent solo.

JAY FERGUSON

with **JOE WALSH / JOE VITALE / JOEY MURCIA / GEORGE PERRY / JOE LALA**

Asylum / Asylum

Jun 76. (lp)(c) **ALL ALONE IN THE END ZONE** [ ] [ ]
– Snakes on the run / Turn it up / Medicated goo / Madam doctor / Hit and run / Cinnamon city / To the island / Everybody goes from here / Time and time again / All alone in the end zone.

Jul 76. (7") **MEDICATED GOO. / ALL ALONE IN THE END ZONE** [ ] [-]

Sep 76. (7") **SNAKES ON THE RUN. / TURN IT UP** [-] [ ]

— **ED BROWN + HAROLD COWART** – bass (+ others) repl.PERRY + LALA

Nov 77. (7") **THUNDER ISLAND. / LOVE IS COLD** [ ] [-]

Feb 78. (lp)(c) **THUNDER ISLAND** [ ] [72]
– Thunder Island / Soulin' / Happy birthday, baby / Losing control / Cozumel / Night shift / Babylon / Love is cold / Happy too! / Magic moment.

Mar 78. (7") **THUNDER ISLAND. / MAGIC MOMENT** [ ] [9] Dec 77

Jun 78. (7") **LOSING CONTROL. / HAPPY BIRTHDAY, BABY** [ ] [ ]

— retained VITALE

Apr 79. (lp)(c) **REAL LIFE AIN'T THIS WAY** [ ] [86]
– Shakedown cruise / No secrets / Real life ain't this way / Davey / Turn yourself in / Do it again / Paying time / Too late to save your heart / Let's spend the night together – Have you seen your mother, standing in the shadow? / City of angels.

May 79. (7") **SHAKEDOWN CRUISE. / CITY OF ANGELS** [ ] [31]
Aug 79. (7") **TOO LATE TO SAVE YOUR HEART. / PAYING TIME** [-] [ ]

— brought back WALSH

not issued Capitol

Sep 80. (lp)(c) **TERMS AND CONDITIONS** [-] [ ]
– Love at the red line / Modern girl / This is your life / The last laugh / Missing persons / You should know better than that / Local color / Hard enough being a man / My baby's eyes / The juggler.
Sep 80. (7") **MODERN GIRL. / MY BABY'S EYES** [-] [ ]
Feb 82. (7") **EMPTY SKY. / TONITE (FALLIN' FOR YA)** [-] [ ]
Apr 82. (lp)(c) **WHITE NOISE** [-] [ ]
– White noise / I'm down / I come alive / Inside out / Empty sky / Tonite (falin' for ya) / Baby come back / The heat of the night / Million $ / She's mine tonight.
Jul 82. (7") **I COME ALIVE. / INSIDE OUT** [-] [ ]

— JAY retired from music business?

JON & VANGELIS (see under ⇒ VANGELIS)

Grace JONES

Born: 19 May'52, Spanishtown, Jamaica, West Indies. As a teenager, she was raised in Syracuse, New York, but moved to Paris in the mid-70's, when she became top model, featuring on front covers of Vogue magazine, etc. Around this time she also married photographer Jean-Paul Goude, and had bit-part in the film 'Gordon's War'. Late in 1976, she was given solo contract by US label 'Beam Junction', and scored first Top 75 hit in 1977 with 'THAT'S THE TROUBLE'. In Oct'77, she signed to 'Island' and cut debut album 'PORTFOLIO', which nearly made US Top 100. In 1980 on UK Top 50 album 'WARM LEATHERETTE', she acquired the services of reggae/dub duo SLY & ROBBIE, and this was to mark change in commercial appeal. It was of course helped that year, by the publicity caused when she slapped about UK chat-show host Russell Harty live on his TV programme. In 1984-85 she re-actified acting career in the films 'Conan The Destroyer' (with Arnold Schwarzenegger) & 'View To A Kill' (with Roger Moore as James Bond). • **Miscellaneous:** In Aug'88, she claimed that airline officials dragged her and her 2 kids from their plane, after her boyfriend complained of the delay. Just over a year later, she was on trial for cocaine possession in her hometown of Kingston. • **Style:** A black 70's Euro-disco queen, who progressed in the early 80's into reggae-funk, that combined her deep manly monotone effectively. • **Songwriters:** She mainly provided lyrics, for backers SLY & ROBBIE, who wrote for her in the early 80's. In 1985 & 86, her songs were co-written with TREVOR HORN and BRUCE WOOLLEY respectively. She also covered many including; SEND IN THE CLOWNS (hit; Judy Collins) / WHAT I DID FOR LOVE (hit; Shirley Bassey) / DON'"T MESS WITH THE MESSER (Koko Taylor) / THE HUNTER GETS CAPTURED BY THE GAME (Marvelettes) / WARM LEATHERETTE (The Normal) / LOVE IS THE DRUG (Roxy Music) / PRIVATE LIFE (Pretenders) / SHE'S LOST CONTROL (Joy Division) / NIGHTCLUBBING (Iggy Pop-David Bowie) / DEMOLITION MAN (Police) / TYPICAL MALE (Consolidated) / SEX DRIVE (Sheep on Drugs).

Recommended: ISLAND LIFE – THE BEST OF GRACE JONES (*8).

GRACE JONES – vocals with various session people.

Polydor Beam Junc.

Mar 77. (7") **THAT'S THE TROUBLE. / SORRY** [ ] [71]
Jul 77. (7") **I NEED A MAN. / I NEED A MAN (Pt.2)** [ ] [ ]

Island Island

Dec 77. (7") **LA VIE EN ROSE. / I NEED A MAN** [ ] [ ]
Dec 77. (lp)(c) **PORTFOLIO** [ ] [ ] Oct 77
– Send in the clowns / What I did for love / Tomorrow / La vie en Rose / Sorry / That's the trouble / I need a man. *(re-iss.Feb87) (cd-iss.May89)*
Jul 78. (7") **DO OR DIE. / COMME UN OISEAU QUI S'ENVOLE** [ ] [ ] Nov 78
Jul 78. (lp)(c) **FAME** [ ] [97]
– Do or die / Pride / Fame / Autumn leaves / All on a summers night / Am I ever gonna fall in love in New York City / Below the belt. *(re-iss.cd+c Oct93 on 'Spectrum')*
Aug 79. (7")(12") **ON YOUR KNEES. / DON'T MESS WITH THE MESSER** [ ] [ ]
Sep 79. (lp)(c) **MUSE** [ ] [ ] Aug 79
– Sinning / Suffer / Repentance / Saved / Atlantic City gambler / I'll find my way to you / Don't mess with the messer / On your knees.

— now with **SLY & ROBBIE** – drums + bass / **BARRY REYNOLDS + MIKEY CHUNG** – guitar / **WALLY BADAROU** – keyboards / **UZZIAH THOMPSON** – percussion

Apr 80. (7")(12") **A ROLLING STONE. / SINNING** [ ] [ ]
May 80. (lp)(c) **WARM LEATHERETTE** [45] [ ]
– Warm leatherette / Private life / A rolling stone / Love is the drug / The hunter gets captured by the game / Bullshit / Breakdown / Pars. *(re-iss.Sep86) (re-iss.+cd Jun89)*
Jun 80. (7")(12") **PRIVATE LIFE. / SHE'S LOST CONTROL** [17] [ ]
Sep 80. (7") **THE HUNTER GETS CAPTURED BY THE GAME. / (part 2)** [ ] [-]
(12"+=) – Warm leatherette.
Feb 81. (7") **DEMOLITION MAN. / WARM LEATHERETTE** [ ] [ ]
(12") – ('A'side) / Bullshit.
May 81. (lp)(c) **NIGHTCLUBBING** [35] [32]
– Walking in the rain / Pull up to the bumper / Use me / Nightclubbing / Art groupie / I've seen that face before / Feel up / Demolition man / I've done it again. *(re-iss Jan87) (re-iss.+cd Jun89)*
May 81. (7") **PULL UP TO THE BUMPER. / FEEL UP** [53] [-]
May 81. (7") **PULL UP TO THE BUMPER. / BREAKDOWN** [-] [ ]
Jul 81. (7") **USE ME. / FEEL UP** [-] [ ]
Jul 81. (7") **I'VE SEEN THAT FACE BEFORE. / LIBERTANGO** [ ] [-]
Oct 81. (7") **WALKING IN THE RAIN. / PEANUT BUTTER** [ ] [-]
(12"+=) – Pull up to the bumper.
Oct 81. (7") **WALKING IN THE RAIN. / FEEL UP** [-] [ ]
Oct 82. (7")(12") **THE APPLE STRETCHING. / NIPPLE TO THE BOTTLE** [50] [ ]
Nov 82. (lp)(c) **LIVING MY LIFE** [15] [86]
– My Jamaican Guy / Nipple to the bottle / The apple stretching / Everybody hold still / Cry now, laugh later / Inspiration / Unlimited capacity for love. *(re-iss.Feb87) (re-iss.+cd Jun89) (also as pic-lp)*
Mar 83. (7")(12")(7"pic-d) **MY JAMAICAN GUY. / CRY NOW, LAUGH LATER** [56] [-]
Mar 83. (7") **CRY NOW, LAUGH LATER. / NIPPLE TO THE BOTTLE (dub)** [-] [ ]

— now with new producer **TREVOR HORN** (and new sessioners)

ZTT-Island Manhattan

Oct 85. (7")(7"pic-d) **SLAVE TO THE RHYTHM. / ('A'annihilate mix)** [12] [ ]
(12"+=)(12"pic-d+=) – Jones the rhythm.
Oct 85. (lp)(c)(cd) **SLAVE TO THE RHYTHM** [12] [73]
– Jones the rhythm / The fashion show / The frog and the princess / Operattack / Slave to the rhythm / The crossing (ooh the action) / Don't cry – it's only the rhythm / Ladies and gentlemen: Miss Grace Jones.

Manhattan Manhattan

Oct 86. (7") **I'M NOT PERFECT (BUT I'M PERFECT FOR YOU). / SCARY BUT FUN** [56] [ ]
(12"+=)(12"pic-d+=) – ('A' mix) / ('A' instrumental).
Nov 86. (lp)(c)(cd) **INSIDE STORY** [61] [81]
– I'm not perfect (but I'm perfect for you) / Hollywood liar / Chan hitchhikes to Shanghai / Victor should have been a jazz musician / Party girl / Crush / Barefoot in Beverley Hills / Scary but fun / White collar crime / Inside story.
Jan 87. (7") **CRUSH. / WHITE COLLAR CRIME** [-] [ ]
Mar 87. (7") **PARTY GIRL. / ('A' instrumental)** [-] [ ]
Mar 87. (7")(7"sha-pic-d) **PARTY GIRL (remix). / WHITE COLLAR CRIME** [ ] [ ]
(12"+=) – ('A'version).

Capitol Capitol

Oct 89. (7") **LOVE ON TOP OF LOVE. / KILLER KISSES / DREAM** [-] [ ]
Nov 89. (7") **LOVE ON TOP OF LOVE. / ON MY WAY** [ ] [-]
(12"+=) – ('A' garage mixes) / (other 'A' mixes).
(cd-s+=) – ('A'swing mix / dub mix / club mix).
Nov 89. (lp)(c)(cd) **BULLETPROOF HEART** [ ] [ ]
– Driving satisfaction / Kicked around / Love on top of love / Paper plan / Crack attack / Bulletproof heart / On my way / Dream ** / Seduction surrender / Someone to love / Don't cry freedom * / Amado mio. *(c/cd+= **)(cd+= *)*

— GRACE went bankrupt Apr'92, after her accountant ran off with some money.

Island Island

Nov 93. (12")(cd-s) **SEX DRIVE. / ('A'mixes) / TYPICAL MALE** [ ] [ ]

– compilations, others, etc. –

Dec 85. Island; (lp)(c)(cd) **ISLAND LIFE (THE BEST OF GRACE JONES)** [4] [ ]
– La vie en rose / I need a man / Do or die / Private life / Libertango / Love is the drug / Pull up to the bumper / Walking in the rain / My Jamaican guy / Slave to the rhythm. *(re-iss.Apr91)*
Dec 85. Island; (7")(7"pic-d) **PULL UP THE BUMPER. / LA VIE EN ROSE** [12] [ ]
(12"+=) – Feel up / ('A' mix)
(c-s+=) – Peanut butter / Nipple to the bottle
Feb 86. Island; (7")(7"pic-d) **LOVE IS THE DRUG. / LIVING MY LIFE** [35] [ ]
(12"+=)(12"pic-d+=) – The apple stretching.
May 86. Island; (7") **PRIVATE LIFE (groucho mix). / MY JAMAICAN GUY** [ ] [ ]
(12"+=) – Feel up (vocal) / She's lost control (again).
Apr 94. ZTT; (12")(c-s)(cd-s) **SLAVE TO THE RHYTHM. / ('A'mixes)** [28] [ ]
(cd-s+=) **('A'other mixes).**

Mick JONES (see under ⇒ FOREIGNER)

Rickie Lee JONES

Born: 8 Nov'54, Chicago, Illinois, USA. At age 15, she ran away from home, stealing a car with a friend in the process. She was later expelled from a number of schools in her new Olympia, Washington family home. In 1973, she went to Los Angeles, where she became a waitress while writing own songs. In 1977, she befriended TOM WAITS, and wrote 'CHUCK E'S IN LOVE' about another friend Chuck E.Weiss. In 1978, she signed to 'Warners', having had 'EASY MONEY' track recorded by LOWELL GEORGE on his debut album 'Thanks, I'll Eat Here'. In the summer of '79, her Lenny Waronker produced eponymous first album, hit Top 3 in US & Top 20 in Britain, after 'CHUCK E . . . ', cracked both Top 20's. Although she never emulated earlier promise, she still continued throughout the 80's, with 4 cross-Atlantic Top 50 albums. She had moved to New York in 1982, but returned to L.A. in early '84 with boyfriend. • **Style:** Narrative-singer with folky trad-rock leanings, which were compared to JONI MITCHELL. • **Songwriters:** Self-penned songs, also co-writing with PASCAL NABAT-MAYER in '89. She covered; WALK AWAY RENEE (Four Tops) / ANGEL WINGS (Tom Waits) / ON BROADWAY (Drifters) / DON'T LET THE SUN CATCH YOU CRYING (Gerry & The Pacemakers) / FRIDAY ON MY MIND (Easybeats). • **Trivia:** Late in 1978, she featured on the cover of TOM WAITS' album sleeve of 'Blue Valentine'.

Recommended: RICKIE LEE JONES (*7).

RICKIE LEE JONES – vocals, keyboard, guitar with session people

Warners Warners

Jun 79. (lp)(c) **RICKIE LEE JONES** 18 3 Apr 79
– Chuck E.'s in love / On Saturday afternoons in 1963 / Night train / Young blood / Easy money / Last chance Texaco / Danny's all star joint / Coolsville / Weasel and the white boys cool / Company / After hours (twelve bars past goodnight). *(cd-iss.1989)*

Jun 79. (7") **CHUCK E.'S IN LOVE. / ON SATURDAY AFTERNOONS IN 1963** 18 4 Apr 79

Aug 79. (7") **YOUNG BLOOD. / COOLSVILLE** 40 Jul 79

Oct 79. (7") **DANNY'S ALL-STAR JOINT. / LAST CHANCE TEXACO** -

Nov 79. (7") **DANNY'S ALL-STAR JOINT. / NIGHT TRAIN** -

Jan 80. (7") **EASY MONEY. / COMPANY** -

Jul 81. (lp)(c) **PIRATES** 37 5
– We belong together / Living it up / Skeletons / Woody and Dutch on the slow train to Peking / Pirates / Traces of the western slopes / Returns. *(cd-iss Jan86)*

Aug 81. (7") **A LUCKY GUY. / SKELETONS** - 64

Sep 81. (7") **WOODY AND DUTCH ON THE SLOW TRAIN TO PEKING. / SKELETONS** -

Oct 81. (7") **WE BELONG TOGETHER. / RETURNS** -

Jan 82. (7") **PIRATES. / SKELETONS** -

Jun 83. (10"m-lp)(c) **GIRL AT HER VOLCANO** 51 39
– Lush life / Walk away Renee / Hey, Bub / My funny valentine / Under the boardwalk / Rainbow sleeves / So long.

Aug 83. (7") **UNDER THE BOARDWALK. / SO LONG**

Oct 84. (lp)(c) **THE MAGAZINE** 40 44
– (prelude to gravity) / Gravity / Juke box fury / It must be love / Magazine / The real end / Deep space / Runaround / Rorschachs – Theme for the Pope – The unsigned painting – The weird beast. *(cd-iss.Mar86)*

Sep 84. (7") **THE REAL END. / WOODY AND DUTCH ON A SLOW TRAIN TO PEKING** - 83

Oct 84. (7")(12") **THE REAL END. / MAGAZINE** -

Apr 85. (7") **IT MUST BE LOVE. / MAGAZINE** -

Geffen Geffen

Sep 89. (lp)(c)(cd) **FLYING COWBOYS** 50 39
– The horses / Just my baby / Ghetto of my mind / Rodeo girl / Satellites / Ghost train / Flying cowboys / Don't let the sun catch you crying / Love is gonna bring us back alive / Away from the sky / Atlas' marker.

Sep 89. (7") **SATELLITES. / GHOST TRAIN**
(12"+=)(cd-s+=) – Friday on my mind.

Aug 91. (cd)(c)(lp) **POP POP**
– My one and only love / Spring can really hang you up the most / Hi-li hi-lo / Up from the skies / Second time around / Dat dere / I'll be seeing you / Bye bye blackbird / The ballad of the sad young men / I won't grow up / Love junkyard / Come back to me. *(re-iss.cd Oct95)*

—— with **JOHN LEFTWICH** – bass, cello, vocals / **LEO KOTTKE** – guitars, vocals / **SAL BERNARDI** – acoustic guitar, vocals / **JIM KELTNER** – drums / **BOBBY BRUCE** – violin / **BRAD DUTZ** – percussion / **DOUG LYONS** – French horn / + guest guitarists on 1 track each **DAVID HIDALGO, BRIAN SETZER, DEAN PARKS + DAVID BAERWALD**

Sep 93. (cd)(c)(lp) **TRAFFIC FROM PARADISE**
– Pink flamingos / Alter boy / Stewart's coat / Beat angels / Tigers / Rebel rebel / Jolie Jolie / Running from mercy / A stranger's car / The albatross.

Reprise Reprise

Oct 95. (cd)(c) **NAKED SONGS LIVE AND ACOUSTIC (live)**
– The horses / Weasel and the white boy's cool / Altar boy / It must be love / Young blood / The last chance TExaco / Skeletons / Magazine / Loving it up / We belong together / Coolsville / Flying cowboys / Stewart's coat / Chuck E's in love / Autumn leaves.

Janis JOPLIN

Born: 19 Jan'43, Port Arthur, Texas, USA. In the early 60's, she hitched to California and San Francisco, where she sang in WALLER CREEK BOYS trio alongside future 13th FLOOR ELEVATORS member R.POWELL ST.JOHN. In 1963, she sang alongside JORMA KAUKONEN (later JEFFERSON AIRPLANE) at local night spots. In 1966, after nearly giving up singing and her hippy drug life to marry, she returned to Texas, where she briefly rehearsed with 13th FLOOR ELEVATORS. That same year, she again ventured to San Francisco, but this time she joined BIG BROTHER & THE HOLDING COMPANY (see ⇒). They made 2 lp's, the second of which 'CHEAP THRILLS', stayed at US No.1 for 8 weeks. When they temporary folded late in '68, she went solo, although her alcohol and drug abuse was becoming more apparent. After 3 major concerts at London's Royal Albert Hall, Newport Festival and New Orleans pop festival, she unleashed 1969 solo debut 'I GOT DEM OL' KOSMIC BLUES AGAIN', which made US Top 5. In May'70, she formed her new backing group The FULL-TILT BOOGIE BAND, and they began working on an album in Autumn 1970. However before it was completed, on 4 Oct'70, JANIS was found dead at her Hollywood apartment. The coroner's verdict said it was due to an accidental overdose she took at a party. Early in 1971, her last recordings 'PEARL' were issued, and they topped the US charts for 9 weeks, and gave her first dent into UK Top 50. She also scored a US No.1 single with a great version of KRIS KRISTOFFERSON's 'ME AND BOBBY McGEE'. But for her death, she would probably have become greatest female singer of all-time. • **Style:** Powerful 3 octave vocalist, with the capacity to roust any standard or rock tune into her own. • **Songwriters:** She used many outside writers, including JERRY RAGAVOY, and covered; PIECE OF MY HEART (hit; Erma Franklin) / MAYBE (Chantells) / TO LOVE SOMEBODY (Bee Gees) / etc. • **Trivia:** In 1979, a film 'The Rose' was released based on her life, and featuring BETTE MIDLER in her role.

Recommended: JANIS JOPLIN'S GREATEST HITS (*8)

JANIS JOPLIN – vocals (ex-BIG BROTHER & THE HOLDING COMPANY) / **SAM ANDREW** – guitar (ex-BIG BROTHER & THE HOLDING COMPANY) / others in her KOZMIC BLUES BAND were **BRAD CAMPBELL** (aka KEITH CHERRY) – bass / **TERRY CLEMENTS** – saxophone / **RICHARD KERMODE** – organ repl. BILL KING (Feb69) / **LONNIE CASTILLE** – drums repl. ROY MARKOWITZ (Apr69) / **TERRY HENSLEY** – trumpet repl. MARCUS DOUBLEDAY (Apr69) / added **SNOOKY FLOWERS** – saxophone (Feb69)

—— (Jul69) **JOHN TILL** – guitar, vocals repl. SAM ANDREW / **MAURY BAKER** – drums repl. CASTILLE / **DAVE WOODWARD** – trumpet repl. GASCA who repl. HENSLEY

C.B.S. Columbia

Oct 69. (lp) **I GOT DEM OL' KOZMIC BLUES AGAIN MAMA!** 5
– Try (just a little bit harder) / Maybe / One good man / As good as you've been to this world / To love somebody / Kozmic blues / Little girl blue / Work me, Lord. *(re-iss.+c.1983) (cd-iss Jan91)*

Nov 69. (7") **KOZMIC BLUES. / LITTLE GIRL BLUE** 41

1970. (7") **TRY (JUST A LITTLE BIT HARDER). / ONE GOOD MAN** -

1970. (7") **MAYBE. / WORK ME, LORD** -

JANIS JOPLIN & THE FULL TILT BOOGIE BAND

She retained **CAMPBELL** and **TILL** / added **RICHARD BELL** – piano / **KEN PEARSON** – organ / **CLARK PIERSON** – drums/ On the 4th Oct70, JANIS died of a drug overdose. She had just recorded below lp

Jan 71. (lp)(c) **PEARL** 50 1
– Move over / Cry baby / A woman left lonely / Half Moon / Buried alive in the blues / My baby / Me and Bobby McGee / Mercedes Benz / Trust me / Get it while you can. *(contains 2 instrumentals. re-iss Jan84) (also as quad-lp) (cd-iss. Jan91)*

Jan 71. (7") **ME AND BOBBY McGEE. / HALF MOON** 1

May 71. (7") **CRY BABY. / MERCEDES BENZ** 42

Sep 71. (7") **GET IT WHILE YOU CAN. / MOVE OVER** - 78

– other posthumous JANIS JOPLIN releases –

Note; Below were issued on 'CBS' UK/ 'Columbia' US until stated.

Oct 71. (7"ep) **MOVE OVER. / TRY (JUST A LITTLE BIT HARDER) / PIECE OF MY HEART**

Jul 72. (d-lp)(c) **JANIS JOPLIN IN CONCERT (live)** 30 4 May 72
– Down on me / Bye, bye baby / All is loneliness / Piece of my heart / Road block / Flower in the sun / Summertime / Ego rock / Half moon / Kozmic blues / Move over / Try (just a little bit harder) / Get it while you can / Ball and chain. *(half with 'BIG BROTHER & etc..', half with 'FULL TILT')*

Jul 72. (7") **DOWN ON ME (live). / BYE, BYE BABY (live)** 91

Jul 73. (lp)(c) **JANIS JOPLIN'S GREATEST HITS** 37
– Piece of my heart / Summertime / Try (just a little bit harder) / Cry baby / Me and Bobby McGee / Down on me / Get it while you can / Bye, bye baby / Move over / Ball and chain. *(re-iss. +cd 1992 on 'Sony')*

May 75. (d-lp)(d-c) **JANIS (soundtrack)** 54
(includes rare 1963-65 material)

Mar 76. (7") **PIECE OF MY HEART. / KOZMIC BLUES** -

Jul 80. (d-lp)(d-c) **ANTHOLOGY**

Feb 82. (lp)(c) **FAREWELL SONG**

Nov 84. (d-c) **PEARL / CHEAP THRILLS**

(some of the above posthumous releases were recorded with 'BIG BROTHER & etc.')

Sep 92. Sony; (d-cd) **PEARL / I GOT DEM OL' KOZMIC BLUES AGAIN**

Sep 93. I.T.M.; (cd) **LIVE AT WOODSTOCK, 1969 (live)**

Jan 94. Legacy; (3xcd) **JANIS**

Dec 94. Columbia; (cd) **THE BEST**

Apr 95. Legacy; (cd) **18 ESSENTIAL SONGS** -

JOSEF K

Formed: Edinburgh, Scotland . . . 1979 by PAUL HAIG, etc (see below). After 1 single on own 'Absolute' label, they signed to Alan Horne's Glasgow label 'Postcard' in 1980. They released 4 well-received 45's and an lp before moving on to other projects in 1982. HAIG continued as a solo artist, but only gained limited notoriety. • **Style:** Heralded alongside stablemates ORANGE JUICE and AZTEC CAMERA as 'The Sound of Young Scotland', their jangly pop-rock singles were indie gems of the early 80's. • **Songwriters:** HAIG and group penned, except APPLEBUSH (Alice Cooper). • **Trivia:** Their withdrawn debut lp 'SORRY FOR LAUGHING' changes hands at collector's fairs for over £100.

Recommended: THE ONLY FUN IN TOWN (*6) / YOUNG AND STUPID (*8) / RHYTHM OF LIFE (*7; PAUL HAIG).

PAUL HAIG – vocals, guitar / **MALCOLM ROSS** (b.31 Jul'60) – guitar, keyboards / **DAVID WENDELL** – bass / **RONNIE TORRANCE** – drums

Absolute not issued

Dec 79. (7") **ROMANCE. / CHANCE MEETING** -

Postcard not issued

Aug 80. (7")(7"pic-d) **RADIO DRILL TIME. / CRAZY TO EXIST** -

Dec 80. (7") **IT'S KINDA FUNNY. / FINAL REQUEST** -

Feb 81. (7") **SORRY FOR LAUGHING. / REVELATION** -

May 81. (7") **CHANCE MEETING. / PICTURES (OF CINDY)** -

Jun 81. (lp) **THE ONLY FUN IN TOWN** -
– Fun 'n' frenzy / Revelation / Crazy to exist / It's kinda funny / The angle / Forever drone / Heart of song / 16 years / Citizens / Sorry for laughing. *(re-iss.cd.Sep90 on*

'P.I.A.S.' with lost album 'SORRY FOR LAUGHING')

		Operation Twilight	not issued
Feb 82.	(7") **MISSIONARY. / ONE ANGEL / SECOND ANGEL**		-

— Split early '82 TORRANCE joined BOOTS FOR DANCING, before teaming up with DAVID to form HAPPY FAMILY. MALCOLM joined ORANGE JUICE and later AZTEC CAMERA. In 1992, MALCOLM and DAVID formed MAGIC CLAN.

– compilations etc. –

Mar 87.	Supreme; (12") **HEAVEN SENT. / ENDLESS SOUL / RADIO DRILL TIME (demo)**		-
Jun 87.	Supreme; (lp) **YOUNG AND STUPID**		-

– Heart of song / Endless soul / Citizens / Variation of scene / It's kinda funny / Sorry for laughing / Chance meeting / Heaven sent / Drone / Sense of guilt / Revelation / Romance. *(re-iss.Mar89) (cd-iss.Sep90 on 'P.I.A.S.')*

PAUL HAIG

(solo) – vocals, guitar with various session people

		Operation Twilight	not issued
May 82.	(7") **RUNNING AWAY. / TIME**		-
		Crepescule	not issued
Sep 82.	(7") **CHANCE. / JUSTICE**		-
Dec 82.	(12") **BLUE FOR YOU. /**		-
		Crepescule-Island	not issued
Apr 83.	(7")(12") **HEAVEN SENT. / RUNNING AWAY, BACK HOME**		-
Jul 83.	(7")(12") **NEVER GIVE UP (PARTY, PARTY). / HEARTACHE**		-
Oct 83.	(lp)(c) **RHYTHM OF LIFE**	82	-

– Heaven sent / Never give up (party, party) / Adoration / In the world / Stolen love / Don't rush in / Blue for you / Justice / Work together.

Oct 83.	(7") **JUSTICE. / ON THE NIGHT OF DECISION**		-

(12"+=) – Justice '82.

Sep 84.	(7") **THE ONLY TRUTH. / GHOST RIDER**		-

(12"+=) – ('A' US remix).

— with **ALAN RANKINE** – lead guitar / **MIKE McCANN** – bass / **JAMES LOCK** – drums

		Operation Twilight	not issued
Sep 85.	(7") **HEAVEN HELP ME NOW. / WORLD RAW**		-

(12"+=) – ('A' version) / Chance.

Nov 85.	(lp)(c) **THE WARP OF PURE FUN**		-

– Silent motion / Heaven help me now / Love eternal / This dying flame / Sense of fun / Scare me / Big blue world / The only truth / One lifetime away / Love & war.

Feb 86.	(7")(12") **LOVE ETERNAL. /**		-
		Crepescule	not issued
Jan 88.	(lp)(cd) **EUROPEAN SUN**		-
Mar 88.	(12"ep) **TORCHOMATIC. / BEAT PROGRAMME / CHASE MANHATTAN / WHITE HOTEL / SONG FOR**		-

— with **ALAN RANKINE** – keyboards, guitar, co-producer / **JOHN TURNER** – piano.

		Circa	not issued
Mar 89.	(lp)(c)(cd) **CHAIN**		-

– Something good / True blue / Communication / Swinging for you / True of her life / Faithless / Times can change / Tune the vision / Sooner or later / Chained.

Jun 89.	(7") **SOMETHING GOOD. / OVER YOU**		-

(12"+=)(3"cd-s+=) – ('A' version) / Free to go.

Sep 90.	(7") **I BELIEVE IN YOU. / FLIGHT X**		-

(12"+=)(cd-s+=) – ?

Feb 91. (12") **FLIGHT X. / ('A'-DJ mix)** [ ] [-]

Les Tempes Modernes — not issued

Jan 92. (cd)(c)(lp) **CINEMATIQUE** [ ] [-]

Crepescule — not issued

May 93. (cd-ep) **SURRENDER / HEAVEN HELP YOU NOW ('93 remix) / COINCIDENCE VS FATE** [ ] [-]

Nov 93. (cd) **COINCIDENCE VS FATE** [ ] [-]
– I believe in you / Flight X / Born innocence / My kind / Si senorita / Right on line / Out of mind / Surrender / Stop and stare / The originator / 1959.

– compilations, etc. –

Jun 84. Operation Twilight; (m-lp) **RHYTHM OF LIFE** (5 remixes) [ ] [-]

Apr 85. Crepescule; (12"ep) **SWING '82** [ ] [-]
– All of you / Love me tender / + 2.

JOURNEY

Formed: San Francisco, California, USA . . . early 1973 originally as The GOLDEN GATE BRIDGE by NEAL SCHON, GEORGE TICKNER, ROSS VALORY and PRAIRIE PRINCE. Due to manager Walter Herbert auditioning through a radio station for a group name, they came up with JOURNEY. They added GREGG ROLIE and replaced TUBES-bound PRAIRIE PRINCE, with English-born AYNSLEY DUNBAR. Late in 1974, they gained contract on 'Columbia', and soon issued eponymous US Top 200 lp. Early in 1976 & 1977, they dented the Top 100 with albums 'LOOK INTO THE FUTURE' and 'NEXT'. In Oct'77, they brought in new voxist STEVE PERRY, who brought them much needed venom and a US Top 30 album 'INFINITY' in 1978. After a 1979 Top 20 album 'EVOLUTION', they soared in the 80's, to become one of America's top bands. • **Style:** They switched from jazz-rock in the mid-70's to pomp AOR in the late 70's & 80's. • **Songwriters:** SCHON-ROLIE penned most? • **Trivia:** They made their live debut on 31st Dec'73, in front of over 10,000 people at San Francisco's 'Wonderland' venue. A couple of JOURNEY tracks, featured on the 1980 & 1981 film soundtracks of 'Caddyshack' & 'Heavy Metal'.

Recommended: ESCAPE (*7) / THE BEST OF JOURNEY (*7).

NEAL SCHON (b.27 Feb'54, San Mateo) – lead guitar, vocals (ex-SANTANA) / **GREGG ROLIE** (b.1948) – vocals, keyboards (ex-SANTANA) / **GEORGE TICKNER** – guitar, vocals / **ROSS VALORY** (b. 2 Feb'49) – bass, vocals (ex-STEVE MILLER BAND) / **AYNSLEY DUNBAR** (b.1946, Liverpool, England) – drums (ex-FRANK ZAPPA, ex-JOHN MAYALL, ex-JEFF BECK) repl. PRAIRIE PRINCE who joined The TUBES.

C.B.S. — Columbia

Apr 75. (lp)(c) **JOURNEY** [ ] [ ]
– Of a lifetime / In the morning day / Kohoutek / To play some music / Topaz / In my lonely feeling – Conversations / Mystery mountain. *(cd-iss.Oct93 on 'Sony Collectors') (cd-iss.Oct94 on 'Rewind')*

Jun 75. (7") **TO PLAY SOME MUSIC. / TOPAZ** [-] [ ]

—— (Apr75) reverted to a quartet when TICKNER departed

Jan 76. (lp)(c) **LOOK INTO THE FUTURE** [ ] [100]
– On a Saturday nite / It's all too much / Anyway / She makes me (feel alright) / You're on your own / Look into the future / Midnight dreamer / I'm gonna leave you. *(re-iss.Mar82)*

Mar 76. (7") **ON A SATURDAY NIGHT. / TO PLAY SOME MUSIC** [-] [ ]

Jul 76. (7") **SHE MAKES ME (FEEL ALRIGHT). / IT'S ALL TOO MUCH** [-] [ ]

Feb 77. (7") **SPACEMAN. / NICKEL AND DIME** [-] [ ]

Feb 77. (lp)(c) **NEXT** [ ] [85]
– Spaceman / People / I would find you / Here we are / Hustler / Next / Nickel & dime / Karma.

—— (Jun77) added **ROBERT FLEISCHMAN** – lead vocals

—— (Oct77) **STEVE PERRY** (b.22 Jan'53) – lead vocals repl. FLEISCHMAN

May 78. (lp)(c) **INFINITY** [ ] [21] Feb 78
– Lights / Feeling that way / Anytime / La do da / Patiently / Wheel in the sky / Somethin' to hide / Winds of March / Can do / Opened the door. *(cd-iss.!)*

Apr 78. (7") **WHEEL IN THE SKY. / CAN DO** [-] [57]

Jun 78. (7") **ANYTIME. / CAN DO** [-] [83]

Aug 78. (7") **LIGHTS. / OPEN THE DOOR** [ ] [-]

Aug 78. (7") **LIGHTS. / SOMETHIN' TO HIDE** [-] [68]

—— (Nov78) **STEVE SMITH** – drums repl. DUNBAR who joined JEFFERSON STARSHIP (above now alongside SCHON, ROLIE, PERRY and VALORY)

Apr 79. (lp)(c) **EVOLUTION** [100] [20]
– Sweet and simple / Just the same way / Do you recall / City of angels / Lovin', touchin', squeezin' / Daydream / When you're alone (it ain't easy) / Lady luck / Too late / Lovin' you is easy / Majestic. *(re-iss.Jul83) (cd-iss.Oct93 on 'Sony Europe')*

Apr 79. (7") **JUST THE SAME WAY. / SOMETHIN' TO HIDE** [-] [58]

Sep 79. (7") **LOVIN', TOUCHIN', SQUEEZIN'. / DAYDREAM** [-] [16] Jul 79

Dec 79. (7") **TOO LATE. / DO YOU RECALL** [-] [70]

Feb 80. (7") **ANY WAY YOU WANT IT. / WHEN YOU'RE ALONE (IT AIN'T EASY)** [-] [23]

Mar 80. (lp)(c) **DEPARTURE** [ ] [8]
– Any way you want it / Walks like a lady / Someday soon / People and places / Precious time / Where were you / I'm cryin' / Line of fire / Departure / Good morning girl / Stay awhile / Homemade love. *(re-iss.Feb86) (cd-iss.Oct93 on 'Sony Europe')*

Sep 80. (7") **ANY WAY YOU WANT IT. / DO YOU RECALL** [ ] [-]

May 80. (7") **WALKS LIKE A LADY. / PEOPLE AND PLACES** [-] [ ]

Aug 80. (7") **GOOD MORNING GIRL. / STAY AWHILE** [-] [55]

Feb 81. (d-lp)(c) **CAPTURED (live)** [ ] [9]
– Majestic / Where were you / Just the same way / Line of fire / Lights / Stay awhile / Too late / Dixie highway / Feeling that way / Anytime / Do you recall / Walks like a lady / La do da / Lovin', touchin', squeezin' / Wheel in the sky / Any way you want it / The party's over (hopelessly in love). *(re-iss.+cd.Sep87)*

Mar 81. (7") **THE PARTY'S OVER (HOPELESSLY IN LOVE) (live). / WHEEL IN THE SKY (live)** [ ] [34] Feb 81

—— (Apr81) **JONATHAN CAIN** (b.26 Feb'50, Chicago, Illinois) – keyboards, guitar, vocals (ex-BABYS) repl. ROLIE who went solo, and later formed The STORM with VALORY and SMITH

Aug 81. (lp)(c) **ESCAPE** [32] [1]
– Don't stop believin' / Stone in love / Who's crying now / Keep on runnin' / Still they ride / Escape / Lay it down / Dead or alive / Mother, father / Open arms. *(re-iss.Feb88)*

Jul 81. (7") **WHO'S CRYING NOW. / MOTHER, FATHER** [-] [4]

Aug 81. (7")(12") **WHO'S CRYING NOW. / ESCAPE** [ ] [4] Jul 81

Dec 81. (7")(12")(12"pic-d) **DON'T STOP BELIEVIN'. / NATURAL THING** [62] [9] Oct 81

Apr 82. (7") **OPEN ARMS. / LITTLE GIRL** [ ] [2] Jan 82

May 82. (7") **STILL THEY RIDE. / RAZA DEL SOL** [-] [19]

Aug 82. (7") **WHO'S CRYING NOW. / DON'T STOP BELIEVIN'** [46] [-]
(12") – ('A'side) / THE JOURNEY STORY (14 best snips).

Oct 82. (7") **STONE IN LOVE. / ONLY SOLUTIONS** [ ] [ ]

Feb 83. (lp)(c) **FRONTIERS** [6] [2]
– Separate ways (worlds apart) / Send her my love / Chain reaction / After the fall / Faithfully / Edge of the blade / Troubled child / Back talk / Frontiers / Rubicon. *(re-iss.cd Jun94 on 'Sony Europe')*

Feb 83. (7")(12") **SEPARATE WAYS (WORLDS APART). / FRONTIERS** [ ] [8]

Apr 83. (7") **FAITHFULLY. / FRONTIERS** [-] [12]

Apr 83. (7") **FAITHFULLY. / EDGE OF THE BLADE** [ ] [-]

Jul 83. (7") **AFTER THE FALL. / OTHER SOLUTIONS** [-] [23]

Jul 83. (7") **AFTER THE FALL. / RUBICON** [ ] [-]
(12"+=) – Any way you want me / Don't stop believin'.

Sep 83. (7") **SEND HER MY LOVE. / CHAIN REACTION** [-] [ ]

—— (the band take on some solo projects, see further below)

Feb 85. (7") **ONLY THE YOUNG. / ('B' side by Sammy Hagar)** [ ] [9] Jan 85
(above songs from the film 'Vision Quest')

—— **PERRY, SCHON and CAIN** regrouped and added **RANDY JACKSON** – bass (ex-ZEBRA) / **LARRIE LONDIN** – drums

Apr 86. (7") **BE GOOD TO YOURSELF. / ONLY THE YOUNG** [ ] [9]
(12"+=) – Any way you want it / Stone in love.
(d7"+=) – After the fall / Rubicon.

May 86. (lp)(c)(cd) **RAISED ON RADIO** [22] [4]
– Girl can't help it / Positive touch / Suzanne / Be good to yourself / Once you love somebody / Happy to give / Raised on radio / I'll be alright without you / It could have been you / The eyes of a woman / Why can't this night go on forever. *(re-iss.cd+c.Apr91 on 'Columbia')*

Jul 86. (7") **SUZANNE. / ASK THE LONELY** [ ] [17] Jun 86
(12"+=) – Raised on radio.

—— (Aug86) **MIKE BAIRD** – drums repl. LONDIN

Oct 86. (7") **GIRL CAN'T HELP IT. / IT COULD HAVE BEEN YOU** [ ] [17] Aug 86

Jan 87. (7") **I'LL BE ALRIGHT WITHOUT YOU. / THE EYES OF A WOMAN** [ ] [14] Dec 86

Apr 87. (7") **WHY CAN'T THIS NIGHT GO ON FOREVER. / POSITIVE TOUCH** [-] [60]

—— split early '87. CAIN and VALORY joined MICHAEL BOLTON. SCHON joined BAD ENGLISH in '89, then HARDLINE in '92 with ROLIE and SMITH.

– compilations, others, etc. –

All below on 'CBS' were issued on 'Columbia' US.

Sep 80. CBS; (t-lp) **IN THE BEGINNING** (first 3 albums) [ ] [ ] Jan 80
(re-iss.Aug84)

Dec 82. CBS; (c-ep) **CASSETTE EP** [ ] [ ]
– Don't stop believing / Who's crying now / Open arms / Lovin' touchin' squeezin'.

Feb 83. CBS; (d-c) **INFINITY / NEXT** [ ] [ ]

Aug 87. CBS; (d-lp)(d-c) **FRONTIERS / ESCAPE** [ ] [ ]

Dec 88. CBS; (lp)(c)(cd) **GREATEST HITS** [ ] [10]
– Only the young / Don't stop believin' / Wheel in the sky / Faithfully / I'll be alright with you / Any way you want it / Ask the lonely / Who's crying now / Separate ways (worlds apart) / Lights / Lovin', touchin', squeezin' / Open arms / Girl can't help it / Send her my love / Be good to yourself.

Mar 92. Columbia; (cd)(c) **JOURNEY – THE BALLADS** [ ] [ ]

Dec 92. Columbia; (t-cd)(t-c) **TIME 3** [ ] [90]

Jan 93. Columbia; (c-s)(cd-s) **LIGHTS. /** [-] [74]

Jan 89. Old Gold; (7") **WHO'S CRYING NOW. / OPEN ARMS** [ ] [ ]
(12"+=)(cd-s+=) – Suzanne / Don't stop believing.

NEAL SCHON / JAN HAMMER

collaboration with HAMMER – keyboards (solo)

C.B.S. — Columbia

Nov 81. (lp)(c) **UNTOLD PASSION (instrumental)** [ ] [ ] Oct 81
– Wasting time / I'm talking to you / The ride / I'm down / Arc / It's alright / Hooked on love / On the beach / Untold passion.

Feb 83. (lp)(c) **HERE TO STAY** [ ] [ ]
– No more lies / Don't stay away / (You think you're) So hot / Turnaround / Self defence / Long time / Time again / Sticks and stones / Peace of mind / Covered by midnight.

—— **NEAL SCHON** collaborated next (May84) on album 'THROUGH THE FIRE' with **SAMMY HAGAR, KENNY AARONSON & MIKE SHRIEVE.**

STEVE PERRY

C.B.S. — Columbia

May 84. (7") **OH SHERRIE. / DON'T TELL ME WHY YOU'RE LEAVING** [ ] [3] Mar 84

May 84. (lp)(c) **STREET TALK** [ ] [12] Apr 84
– Oh Sherrie / I believe / Go away / Foolish heart / It's only love / She's mine / You should be happy / Running alone / Captured by the moment / Strung out.
Jul 84. (7") **SHE'S MINE. / YOU SHOULD BE HAPPY** [ ] [21] Jun 84
Sep 84. (7") **STRUNG OUT. /** [ ] [40]
Jan 85. (7") **FOOLISH HEART. / IT'S ONLY LOVE** [ ] [18] Nov 84

— STEVE PERRY released solo recordings between 88-89. In Aug94, 'Columbia' issued the album 'FOR THE LOVE OF STRANGE MEDICINE' hit UK 64.

The STORM

(**ROLIE** – vox, keys / **ROSS VALORY** – bass / **STEVE SMITH** – drums) with **KEVIN CHALFONT** – vocals (ex-707) / **JOSH RAMOS** – guitar (ex-LE MANS)

East West Interscope

Nov 91. (cd)(c)(lp) **THE STORM** [ ] [ ]
– You got me waiting / I've got a lot to learn about love / In the raw / You're gonna miss me / Call me / Show me the way / I want you back / Still loving you / Touch and go / Gimme love / Take me away / Can't live without your love.
Sep 91. (7")(c-s) **I'VE GOT A LOT TO LEARN ABOUT LOVE. / ?** [ ] [26]
(12"+=)(cd-s+=) – ?

HARDLINE

NEIL SCHON – lead guitar, vocals / **JOHNNY SCHON** – vocals / **JOEY GIOELLI** – guitar / **TODD JENSEN** – bass (ex-DAVID LEE ROTH) / **DEAN CASTRONOVO** – drums (ex-BAD ENGLISH)

M.C.A. M.C.A.

May 92. (cd)(c)(lp) **DOUBLE ECLIPSE** [ ] [ ]
– Life's a bitch / Doctor love / Red car / Change of heart / Everything / Taking me down / Hot Cheri / Bad taste / Can't find my way / I'll be there / 31-91 / In the hands of time.
Jun 92. (c-s) **CAN'T FIND MY WAY / HOT CHERIE / TAKIN' ME DOWN / I'LL BE THERE** [-] [ ]

JOY DIVISION

Formed: Salford, Manchester, England . . . mid'77 as The STIFF KITTENS, then WARSAW by IAN CURTIS, BERNARD ALBRECHT, PETER HOOK and STEPHEN MORRIS. By late '77 they became JOY DIVISION, and after an indie EP in 1978, signed to Tony Wilson's new 'Factory' records. They recorded a track 'AT A LATER DATE' for 10" 'Virgin' Various Artists lp 'Short Circuit: Live At The Electric Circus', before featuring on double compilation 'Factory' artists EP 'A Factory Sample', with tracks 'GLASS' & 'DIGITAL'. In mid'79, another 2 tracks 'AUTO-SUGGESTION' & 'FROM SAFETY TO WHERE', surfaced on 'Fast' records compilation EP 'Earcom 2'. Having earlier been given a longer termed contract by 'Factory' through manager Rob Gretton, they unleashed the excellent Martin Hannett produced lp 'UNKNOWN PLEASURES'. It's well documented the now rich and famous TONY WILSON (TV presenter), put his life savings of over £8,000 into band's lp expenses. It soon topped the indie charts, and was pursued by classic debut 45 'TRANSMISSION'. With a new lp in the can, and a free flexi-7" in the shops, IAN an epileptic suffered illness which cancelled several gigs. Tragically on the 18 May 1980, IAN CURTIS hanged himself after his depression caused by his recent marriage break-up. A month later, they were to have first UK Top 20 with superb 'LOVE WILL TEAR US APART'. It was soon followed by UK Top 10 lp 'CLOSER', which might have, who knows, made it in the States, where they were heading 3 days after IAN's death. With the remaining members becoming the massive NEW ORDER, many exploitation releases later hit chart. • **Style:** Alternative underground rock band, fronted by the manic, glossy-eyed IAN CURTIS, whose deep melancholy sound was reminiscent of JIM MORRISON but without the female fan adulation. • **Songwriters:** Group compositions except; SISTER RAY (Velvet Underground). • **Trivia:** Their name JOY DIVISION, was taken from Nazi concentration camp book 'House Of Dolls'. Obviously, they ran into a little media trouble, who unfairly branded them little Adolfs.

Recommended: UNKNOWN PLEASURES (*10) / CLOSER (*10) / SUBSTANCE (*9) / STILL (*8).

IAN CURTIS (b.1957, Macclesfield, England) – vocals / **BERNARD ALBRECHT** (b.BERNARD DICKEN, 4 Jan'56) – guitar, vocals / **PETER HOOK** (b.13 Feb'56) – bass / **STEPHEN MORRIS** (b.28 Oct'57, Macclesfield) – drums

Anony-mous not issued

Jun 78. (12"ep) **AN IDEAL FOR LIVING** [ ] [-]
– An ideal for living / Warsaw / Leaders of men / No love lost / Failures. *(7" on 'Enigma', re-iss.1985 as 'THE IDEAL BEGINNING')*

Factory not issued

Aug 79. (lp) **UNKNOWN PLEASURES** [ ] [-]
– Disorder / Day of the lords / Candidate / Insight / New dawn fades / She's lost control / Shadowplay / Wilderness / Interzone / I remember nothing. *(re-dist.Jul80, hit No.71) (re-iss.Jul82, c-iss.Nov84, cd-iss.Apr86)(re-iss.cd+lp Jul93 on 'Centredate')*
Oct 79. (7")(12") **TRANSMISSION. / NOVELTY** [ ] [-]
Apr 80. (free 7"flexi) **KOMAKINO. / INCUBATION** [-] [-]
Jun 80. (7") **LOVE WILL TEAR US APART. / THESE DAYS** [13] [-]
(12"+=) – ('A' version). *(re-iss.Oct83, hit UK No.19)*
Jul 80. (lp) **CLOSER** [6] [-]
– Heart and soul / 24 hours / The eternal / Decades / Atrocity exhibition / Isolation / Passover / Colony / Means to an end. *(re-iss.+c.Jul82) (cd-iss.Apr86) (re-iss.cd+c Jul93 on 'Centredate')*

— After another fit of depression, IAN CURTIS hanged himself 18th May 1980. The others became NEW ORDER ⇒ .

- compilations & other posthumous releases etc. -

Sep 80. Factory Benelux; (12") **ATMOSPHERE. / SHE'S LOST CONTROL** [ ] [-]
(above was first released Mar80 in France with 'B' side 'DEAD SOULS')
Apr 81. Factory; (7"flexi) **KOMAKINO. / INCUBATION / THEN AGAIN** [ ] [-]
Oct 81. Factory; (d-lp) **STILL (rare & live)** [5] [-]
– Exercise one / Ice age / The sound of music / Glass / The only mistake / Walked in line / The kill / Something must break / Dead souls / Sister Ray / Ceremony / Shadowplay / Means to an end / Passover / New dawn fades / Transmission / Disorder / Isolation / Decades / Digital. *(re-iss.+c.Dec86, cd-iss.Mar90) (re-iss.cd+c Jul93 on 'Centredate')*
Jun 88. Factory; (7") **ATMOSPHERE. / THE ONLY MISTAKE** [34] [-]
(12"+=) – The sound of music / Transmission.
(cd-s+=) – Love will tear us apart.
Jul 88. Factory; (lp)(c) **SUBSTANCE** (The best of..) [7] [ ]
– She's lost control / Dead souls / Atmosphere / Love will tear us apart / Warsaw / Leaders of men / Digital / Transmission / Auto-suggestion. (cd+=) – (7 extra tracks). *(re-iss.cd+c Jul93 on 'Centredate')*
Jun 95. London; (c-s) **LOVE WILL TEAR US APART (radio version) / ('A'-original version)** [19] [ ]
(12"+=)(cd-s+=) – These days / Transmission.
Jun 95. London; (cd)(c)(d-lp) **PERMANENT: JOY DIVISION 1995 (remixes)** [16] [ ]
– Love will tear us apart / Transmission / She's lost control / Shadow play / Day of the lords / Isolation / Passover / Heart and soul / 24 hours / These days / Novelty / Dead souls / The only mistake / Something must break / Atmosphere / Love will tear us apart (permanent mix).
Nov 86. Strange Fruit; (12"ep) **THE PEEL SESSIONS (31.1.79)** [ ] [-]
– Exercise one / Insight / She's lost control / Transmission. *(cd-ep.iss.Jul88)*
Sep 87. Strange Fruit; (12"ep)**THE PEEL SESSIONS 2 (26.11.79)** [ ] [-]
– Love will tear us apart / 24 hours / Colony / The sound of music. *(cd-ep.iss.Jul88)*
Sep 90. Strange Fruit; (cd)(lp) **THE PEEL SESSIONS** (above 2) [ ] [-]

JUDAS PRIEST

Formed: Birmingham, England . . . 1969 by KK DOWNING and IAN HILL. In 1971, they recruited singer ROB HALFORD and drummer JOHN HINCH. 3 years later, after a few hundred gigs behind them, they brought in other guitarist GLENN TIPTON and signed to 'Decca' off-shoot 'Gull'. They released in 1974, a Roger Bain produced lp 'ROCKA ROLLA', and surfaced again in '76 with the excellent 'SAD WINGS OF DESTINY'. After a resounding appearance at the Reading Festival, they signed to 'CBS' early '77, and soon had a UK Top 30 album 'SIN AFTER SIN', produced by ROGER GLOVER (ex-Deep Purple). In the 80's, they became worldwide success with Top 20 lp's on both sides of the lake. • **Style:** Demonic heavy-metal act, fronted by leather-clad HALFORD. • **Songwriters:** TIPTON, HALFORD & DOWNING on most, except covers; DIAMONDS AND RUST (Joan Baez) / BETTER BY YOU, BETTER BY ME (Spooky Tooth) / THE GREEN MANALISHI (Fleetwood Mac) / JOHNNY B.GOODE (Chuck Berry). • **Trivia:** Their name was taken from the DYLAN track 'Frankie Lee & Judas Priest'. • **Miscellaneous:** Late in 1985, two of their fans shot themselves while listening to a track off the 'STAINED CLASS' album. A year later, the parents of the boys, sued the group and 'CBS', saying the album had sublimal Satanic messages in the lyrics, forcing the boys to commit suicide. This fiasco finally got to court in Jul'90, when the judge ruled against the dead boys' parents, although he did fine 'CBS' a 5-figure sum for withholding master tapes!!?

Recommended: SAD WINGS OF DESTINY (*8) / SIN AFTER SIN (*7) / THE COLLECTION (*7). STAINED CLASS is recommended to anyone who can't easily get a gun, a bazooka, a tank or any tacticle nuclear weapon to harm themselves with.

ROB HALFORD (b.25 Aug'51) – vocals repl. ALAN ATKINS / **KK DOWNING** (b.KENNETH) – guitars / **GLENN TIPTON** (b.25 Oct'48) – guitar, vocals / **IAN HILL** – bass / **JOHN HINCH** – drums repl. JOHN ELLIS

Gull-Decca Janus

Aug 74. (7") **ROCKA ROLLA. / NEVER SATISFIED** [ ] [-]
Sep 74. (lp) **ROCKA ROLLA** [ ] [-]
– One for the road / Rocka rolla / Winter / Deep freeze / Winter retreat / Cheater / Never satisfied / Run of the mill / Dying to meet you / Caviar and meths. *(re-iss.Sep77) (re-iss.Nov85 on 'Fame') (cd-iss.Nov87 on 'Line') (US-release Oct82 on 'Visa') (cd-iss.Mar93 on 'Repertoire')*

— **ALAN MOORE** – drums (who had been 1971 member) returned to repl. HINCH

Mar 76. (7") **THE RIPPER. / ISLAND OF DOMINATION** [ ] [ ]
(re-iss.12".Aug80)
Apr 76. (lp)(c) **SAD WINGS OF DESTINY** [ ] [ ]
– Prelude / Tyrant / Genocide / Epitaph / Island of domination / Victim of changes / The ripper / Epitaph / Dreamer deceiver. *(re-iss.Sep77) (cd-iss.Nov87 on 'Line') (re-iss.cd May95 on 'Repertoire')*

— **SIMON PHILLIPS** – drums repl. MOORE

C.B.S. Columbia

Apr 77. (7") **DIAMONDS AND RUST. / DISSIDENT AGGRESSOR** [ ] [-]
Apr 77. (lp)(c) **SIN AFTER SIN** [23] [ ]
– Sinner / Diamonds and rust / Starbreaker / Last rose of summer / Let us prey / Call for the priest / Raw deal / Here come the tears / Dissident aggressor. *(re-iss.Mar81) (re-iss.cd.Nov93 on 'Sony Collectors')*

— **LES BINKS** – drums repl. PHILLIPS

Jan 78. (7") **BETTER BY YOU, BETTER BY ME. / INVADER** [ ] [-]
Feb 78. (lp)(c) **STAINED CLASS** [27] [ ]

– Exciter / White heat, red hot / Better by you, better by me / Stained class / Invader / Saints in Hell / Savage / Beyond the realms of death / Heroes end. *(re-iss.Nov81) (cd+c re-iss.May91 on 'Columbia')*

Sep 78. (7") **EVENING STAR. / STARBREAKER** [ ] [-]

Nov 78. (lp)(c) **KILLING MACHINE** (US-title 'HELL BENT FOR LEATHER') [32] [ ]

– Delivering the goods / Rock forever / Evening star / Hell bent for leather / Take on the world / Burnin' up / Killing machine / Running wild / Before the dawn / Evil fantasies. *(re-iss.red-lp.Sep82)*

Oct 78. (7") **BEFORE THE DAWN. / ROCK FOREVER** [ ] [ ]

Jan 79. (7") **TAKE ON THE WORLD. / STARBREAKER** [ ] [14]

(re-iss.May82)

Apr 79. (7") **EVENING STAR. / BEYOND THE REALMS OF DEATH** [53] [ ]

(12"+=)(12"clear+=) – The green Manalishi.

May 78. (7") **ROCK FOREVER. / THE GREEN MANAZISHI (WITH THE TWO-PRONGED CROWN)** [-] [ ]

Sep 79. (lp)(c) **UNLEASHED IN THE EAST (live)** [10] [70]

– Exciter / Running wild / Sinner / The ripper / The green manalishi (with the two-pronged crown) / Diamonds and rust / Victim of changes / Genocide / Tyrant. *(free 7"w.a.)* **ROCK FOREVER / HELL BENT FOR LEATHER. / BEYOND THE REALMS OF DEATH** *(cd-iss.1988) (re-iss.cd May94 on 'Columbia')*

Dec 79. (7") **DIAMONDS AND RUST (live). / STARBREAKER (live)** [-] [ ]

— **DAVE HOLLAND** – drums repl. BINKS

Mar 80. (7") **LIVING AFTER MIDNIGHT. / DELIVERING THE GOODS** [12] [ ]

Apr 80. (lp)(c) **BRITISH STEEL** [4] [34]

– Breaking the law / Rapid fire / Metal gods / Grinder / United / Living after midnight / You don't have to be old to be wise / The rage / Steeler. *(re-iss.+cd. Jan84) (re-iss.cd Jun94 on 'Sony')*

May 80. (7") **LIVING AFTER MIDNIGHT. / METAL GODS** [-] [-]

May 80. (7") **BREAKING THE LAW. / METAL GODS** [12] [ ]

Aug 80. (7") **UNITED. / GRINDER** [26] [ ]

(re-iss.Apr82)

Feb 81. (7") **DON'T GO. / SOLAR ANGELS** [51] [ ]

Feb 81. (7") **HEADING OUT TO THE HIGHWAY. / ROCK FOREVER** [-] [ ]

Feb 81. (lp)(c) **POINT OF ENTRY** [14] [39]

– Heading out to the highway / Don't go / Hot rockin' / Turning circles / Desert plains / Solar angels / You say yes / All the way / Troubleshooter / On the run.

Apr 81. (7") **HOT ROCKIN' / BREAKING THE LAW (live)** [60] [ ]

(12") – ('A'side) / Steeler / You don't have to be old to be wise.

Jul 82. (lp)(c) **SCREAMING FOR VENGEANCE** [11] [17]

– The hellion / Electric eye / Riding on the wind / Bloodstone / (Take these) Chains / Pain and pleasure / Screaming for vengeance / You've got another thing comin' / Fever / Devil's child. *(re-iss.Feb86)*

Aug 82. (7")(7"pic-d) **YOU'VE GOT ANOTHER THING COMIN'. / EXCITER (live)** [66] [-]

Oct 82. (7") **YOU'VE GOT ANOTHER THING COMIN'. / DIAMONDS AND RUST** [-] [67]

Oct 82. (7") **(TAKE THESE) CHAINS. / JUDAS PRIEST AUDIO FILE** [ ] [ ]

Jan 84. (7") **FREEWHEEL BURNING. / BREAKING THE LAW** [42] [-]

(12"+=) – You've got another thing comin'.

Jan 84. (lp)(c)(cd) **DEFENDERS OF THE FAITH** [19] [18]

– Freewheel burning / Jawbreaker / Rock hard ride free / The sentinel / Love bites / Eat me alive / Some heads are gonna roll / Night comes down / Heavy duty / Defenders of the faith.

Feb 84. (7") **SOME HEADS ARE GONNA ROLL. / BREAKING THE LAW (live)** [-] [-]

Mar 84. (7") **SOME HEADS ARE GONNA ROLL. / THE GREEN MANALISHI (WITH THE TWO-PRONGED CROWN)** [ ] [ ]

(12"+=) – Jailbreaker.

Apr 84. (7") **JAWBREAKER. / LOVE BITES** [-] [ ]

Apr 86. (lp)(c)(cd) **TURBO** [33] [17]

– Turbo lover / Locked in / Private property / Parental guidance / Rock you all around the world / Out in the cold / Wild night, hot and crazy days / Hot for love / Reckless. *(re-iss.Feb89)*

Apr 86. (7") **TURBO LOVER. / HOT FOR LOVE** [ ] [-]

May 86. (7") **LOCKED IN. / RECKLESS** [ ] [-]

('A'ext-12"+=) – Desert plains (live) / Freewheel burning (live).

May 86. (7") **LOCKED IN. / HOT FOR LOVE** [-] [ ]

Aug 86. (7") **TURBO LOVER. / RESTLESS** [-] [ ]

Nov 86. (7") **PARENTAL GUIDANCE. / ROCK YOU AROUND THE WORLD** [-] [ ]

Jun 87. (d-lp)(c)(cd) **PRIEST . . . LIVE (live)** [47] [38]

– Out in the cold / Heading out to the highway / Metal gods / Breaking the law / Love bites / Some heads are gonna roll / The sentinel / Private property / Rock you all around the world / Electric eye / Turbo lover / Freewheel burning / Parental guidance / Living after midnight / You've got another thing comin'.

Atlantic Columbia

Apr 88. (7") **JOHNNY B.GOODE. / ROCK AROUND THE WORLD** [64] [ ]

(12"+=) – Turbo lover.

May 88. (lp)(c)(cd) **RAM IT DOWN** [24] [31]

– Ram it down / Heavy metal / Love zone / Come and get it / Hard as iron / Blood red skies / I'm a rocker / Johnny B. Goode / Love you to death / Monsters of rock.

— **SCOTT TRAVIS** – drums (ex-RACER-X) repl. HOLLAND

C.B.S. Columbia

Sep 90. (7")(c-s) **PAINKILLER. / UNITED** [74] [ ]

(12"+=)(cd-s+=) – Better by you, better than me.

Sep 90. (cd)(c)(lp) **PAINKILLER** [24] [26]

– Painkiller / Hell patrol / All guns blazing / Leather rebel / Metal meltdown / Night crawler / Between the hammer and the anvil / A touch of evil / Battle hymn (instrumental) / One shot at glory.

Columbia Columbia

Mar 91. (7")(c-s)(7"sha-pic-d) **A TOUCH OF EVIL. / BETWEEN THE HAMMER AND THE ANVIL** [58] [ ]

(12"+=)(cd-s+=) – You've got another thing comin' (live).

— In Oct'92, HALFORD left after already forming FLIGHT in 1991.

Apr 93. (7")(c-s) **NIGHT CRAWLER (Edit) / BREAKING THE LAW** [63] [ ]

(cd-s+=) – Living After MIdnight

Apr 93. (d-cd)(d-c)(t-lp) **METAL WORKS '73-'93** (compilation) [37] [ ]

– The hellion / Electric eye / Victim of changes / Painkiller / Eat me alive / Devil's child / Dissident agrressor / Delivering the goods / Exciter / Breaking the law / Hell bent for leather / Blood red skies / Metal gods / Before the dawn / Turbo lover / Ram it down / Metal meltdown/ / Screaming for vengeance / You've got another thing comin' / Beyond the realms of death / Solar angels / Bloodstone / Desert plains / Wild nights, hot & crazy days / Heading out to the highway / Living after midnight / A touch of evil / The rage / Night comes down / Sinner / Freewheel burning / Night crawler.

– more compilations, others, etc. –

Feb 78. Gull; (lp)(pic-lp) **THE BEST OF JUDAS PRIEST** (early work) [ ] [-]

(cd-iss.May87, 2 extra tracks)

1979. Gull; (7") **THE RIPPER. / VICTIMS OF CHANGE** [ ] [-]

(12"+=) – Never satisfied.

Jun 83. Gull; (12"m) **TYRANT. / ROCKA ROLLA / GENOCIDE** [ ] [-]

Jan 83. CBS; (c-ep) **CASSETTE EP** [ ] [-]

– Breaking the law / Living after midnight / Take on the world / United.

Aug 83. CBS; (d-c) **SIN AFTER SIN / STAINED GLASS** [ ] [ ]

Sep 83. Scoop; (7"ep)(c-ep) **6 TRACK HITS** [ ] [-]

– Sinner / Exciter / Hell bent for leather / The ripper / Hot rockin' / The green manalishi.

Aug 86. Shanghai; (lp)(pic-lp) **JUDAS PRIEST** [ ] [-]

Feb 89. Old Gold; (7") **LIVING AFTER MIDNIGHT. / BREAKING THE LAW** [ ] [-]

May 89. Castle; (lp)(c)(cd) **THE COLLECTION** [ ] [-]

– (first two albums)

Mar 93. Columbia; (3xcd-box) **BRITISH STEEL / SCREAMING FOR VENGEANCE / STAINED GLASS** [ ] [ ]

Jul 95. Connoisseur; (cd) **HERO, HERO** [ ] [-]

JUICY LUCY (see under ⇒ MISUNDERSTOOD)

JUSTIFIED ANCIENTS OF MUMU (see under ⇒ KLF)

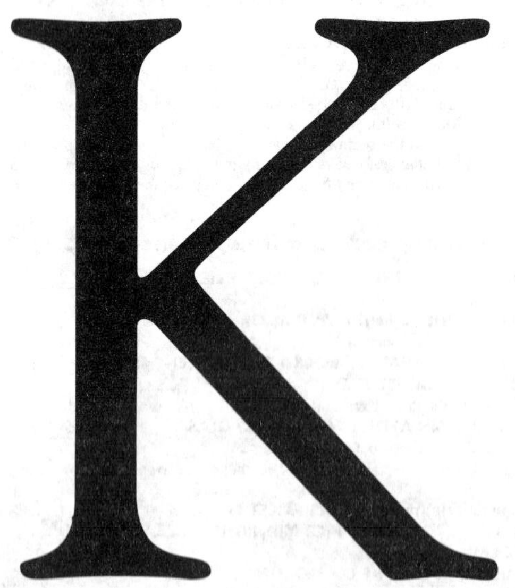

KALEIDOSCOPE (US)

Formed: California, USA ... 1963 by ex-RODENTS player DAVID LINDLEY etc. The RODENTS released 1 US 'Pequod' 45 'AND YOUR BIRD CAN SING'. / 'COME AND LIVE ME', before breaking up early 1966. LINDLEY soon found others (see below), and formed The BAGHDAD BLUES BAND, who quickly became KALEIDOSCOPE. Due to producer Barry Freidman (alias Frazier Mohawk), they signed to 'Epic' in the States and flopped commercially with everything but their minor hit lp in 1969 'INCREDIBLE KALEIDOSCOPE'. They had by this time, flitted to New York and had played 1969 Newport Folk Festival. • **Style:** Ecletic R&B outfit, with Eastern influences blending together acid-rock, cajun and new heavy blues for disappointing 'BERNICE' set. • **Songwriters:** LINDLEY and group, except MINNIE THE MOOCHER (Cab Calloway). • **Trivia:** Group backed LEONARD COHEN on his 1968 debut lp. In 1969 the group recorded 2 tracks 'Brother Mary' & 'Mickey's Tune' for the Various Artists film soundtrack 'Zabriskie Point'.

Recommended: BACON FROM MARS (*7) / A BEACON FROM MARS (*6) / SIDE TRIPS (*6).

DAVID LINDLEY (b.1944) – banjo, fiddle, guitar (ex-RODENTS, ex-MAD RAMBLERS) / **SOLOMON FELDTHOUSE** – vocals, guitar types, kazoo repl. JOHN WELSH – guitar / **CHRIS DARROW** – mandolin, bass (ex-DRY CITY PLAYERS) repl. RICK O'NEILL – bass / **CHARLES CHESTER CRILL** – harmonica, keyboards, fiddle repl. BRIAN MONSOUR (CRILL's aliases were CONNIE / **FENRUS EPP / MAX**(WELL) **BUDA / TEMPLETON PARCELY) / JOHN VIDICAN** – drums

not issued / Epic

Dec 66. (7") **PLEASE. / ELEVATOR MAN** [-] [ ]

Jun 67. (7") **WHY TRY. / LITTLE ORPHAN ANNIE** [-] [ ]

Jun 67. (lp) **SIDE TRIPS** [-] [ ]
– Egyptian gardens / If the night / Hesitation blues / Please / Keep your mind open / Pulsating dreams / Oh death / Come on in / Why try / Minnie the moocher. *(UK-rel.Jul88 on 'Edsel')*

Sep 67. (7") **I FOUND OUT. / RAMPE RAMPE** [-] [ ]

Jan 68. (lp) **A BEACON FROM MARS** [-] [ ]
– I found out / Greenwood sidee / Life will pass you by / Taxim / Baldheaded end of a broom / Louisiana man / You don't love me / Beacon from Mars. *(cd-iss.Feb91 on 'Edsel')*

— **STUART BROTMAN** – bass repl. DARROW who joined NITTY GRITTY DIRT BAND **PAUL LAGOS** – drums repl. JOHN VIDICAN

May 68. (7") **HELLO TROUBLE. / JUST A TASTE** [-] [ ]

Jun 69. (7") **KILLING FLOOR (alt. title TEMPE ARIZONA). / LIE TO ME** [-] [ ]

Jun 69. (lp) **INCREDIBLE KALEIDOSCOPE** [-] [ ]
– Lie to me / Let the good love flow / Tempe Arizona (or) Killing floor / Petite fleure / Banjo / Cuckoo / Seven-ate sweet. *(cd-iss.Feb91 on 'Edsel')*

— **ROB JOHNSON** – bass repl. BROTMAN

— added **JEFF KAPLAN** – guitar, vocals

credited to "AMERICAN KALEIDOSCOPE" in UK for next album. C.B.S. / Columbia

Mar 70. (lp) **BERNICE** [ ] [ ]
– Chocolate whale / Another lover / Sneakin' thru the ghetto / To know is not to be / Lulu Arfin nanny / Lie & hide / Ballad of Tommy Udo / Bernice / Soft ann easy / New blue ooze.

— **RICHARD APLAN** – fiddle repl. FELDTHOUSE and CRILL before they split late '70. DAVID LINDLEY worked with TERRY REID then sessions with WARREN ZEVON, MARIA MULDAUR, AMERICA, LINDA RONSTADT, RY COODER, etc. Below was a reunion album which featured DARROW, FELDTHOUSE, BROTMAN, CRILL as 'PARCELY + BUDA' and the heavily disguised DAVID LINDLEY as 'DePARIS LETANTE'

Island / Pacific ..

Jan 77. (lp) **WHEN SCOPES COLLIDE** [ ] [ ] Sep 76
– Ghost riders in the sky / Canun tune / Younever Cantell / Little Egypt / My love comes softly / Your love / Black and tan fantasy / Hard on the trail / Stu's balkan blues / Man of constant sorrow / It's long you're after / So long.

— DARROW and PARCEL (CRILL) teamed up forming The RANK STRANGERS, they released one eponymous US album in '77 on 'Pacific Arts'.

– compilations, etc. –

Oct 67. Okeh; (7") **NOBODY. / (b-side 'Larry Williams & Johnny 'Guitar' Watson')** [-] [ ]

Aug 83. Edsel; (lp) **BACON FROM MARS** (1967-69) [ ] [-]
– Egyptian gardens / If the night / Please / Keep your mind open / Pulsating dream / Oh death / Why try / I found out / Life will pass you by / Lie to me / Petite fleure / Banjo / Cuckoo / Nobody / Elevator man / Hello trouble. *(cd-iss.Aug93 as 'BLUES FROM BAGHDAD – THE VERY BEST OF KALEIDOSCOPE' +=)*– Rampe rampe / Greenwood sidee / Beacon from Mars / Seven-ate sweet.

Jun 84. Edsel; (lp) **RAMPE RAMPE** (rarities comp.) [ ] [-]

DAVID LINDLEY

solo, with **IAN WALLACE** – drums / **WILLIAM SMITH** – keyboards / **REGGIE McBRIDE** – bass / **GARTH HUDSON** – keyboards, **JORGE CALDERON** – bass, percussion / **BERNIE LARSEN** – guitar, percussion, vocals

Asylum / Asylum

May 81. (lp)(c) **EL RAYO-X** [ ] [83]
– She took off my Romeos / Bye bye love / Mercury blues / Quarter of a man / Ain't no way / Twist and shout / El rayo-x / Your old lady / Don't look back / Petit fleur / Tu-ber-cu-lucas and the sinus blues / Pay the man. *(re-iss.cd+c Mar93 on 'Pickwick', Sep95 on 'Warners')*

May 81. (7") **YOUR OLD LADY. / MERCURY BLUES** [ ] [ ]

Sep 81. (7") **BYE BYE LOVE. / PAY THE MAN** [-] [ ]

Nov 81. (7") **MERCURY BLUES. / EL RAYO-X** [-] [ ]

— **BOB GLAUB** – bass repl. McBRIDE

Oct 82. (lp)(c) **WIN THIS RECORD** [-] [ ]
– Premature / Talk to the lawyer / Look so good / Something's got a hold on me / Ram-a-lamb-a man / Rock it with I / Brother John / Make it on time / Turning point / Spodie. *(cd-iss.Nov93)*

Oct 84. (lp)(c) **EL RAYO LIVE (live)** [-] [-] Germ'y
– Wooly bully / Rag bag / Turning point / Talk to the lawyer / Spodie / Mercury blues.

WEA / WEA

Jul 85. (lp)(c) **MR.DAVE** [-] [ ]
– Pretty girls rule the world / Truly do / Look bad feel better / Hearts on fire / Walk to the sun / Hands like a man / Follow your heart / Hurts so bad / Alien invasion / Starting all over again.

Sep 85. (7") **PRETTY GIRLS RULE THE WORLD. / ALIEN INVASION** [ ] [ ]

Oct 88. (lp)(c) **VERY GREASY** (w/ EL RAYO X) [ ] [ ] Sep 88
– Gimme da' ting / I just can't work no longer / Do ya' wanna dance? / Talk about you / Papa was a rolling stone / Werewolves of London / Texas tango / Never knew her / Talkin' to the wino too / Tiki torches at twilight. *(re-iss.cd/c Dec94 & Sep95 on 'Warners')*

— (above contained lots of covers).

In May 92, CHRIS DARROW released a cd-album of 'A SOUTHERN CALIFORNIA' on 'Line'.

HENRY KAISER & DAVID LINDLEY

Shanachie / Shanachie

Nov 94. (cd)(c) **THE SUNNY NORTH: IN NORWAY** [ ] [ ]

KALEIDOSCOPE (UK)

Formed: West London, England ... 1964 initially as The SIDE KICKS by EDDIE PUMER, DAN BRIDGEMAN, PETER DALTREY and STEVE CLARK. They moved from being R&B influenced covers group and became The KEY. Early in 1967, with help of music publisher Dick Leahy (who became their producer), they signed to 'Fontana'. Their first single 'FLIGHT FROM ASHIYA' (complete with rare pic-sleeve) flopped, but was soon followed by cult late 1967 lp 'TANGERINE DREAM'. They became unlucky not to have a hit, although they built up strong underground following. • **Style:** Kaftan attired psychedelic rock-pop group, with dreamy collages of PINK FLOYD-ish material. After they became FAIRFIELD PARLOUR, they shifted into progressive-rock mould. • **Songwriters:** DALTREY-PUMER numbers. • **Trivia:** In 1970, FAIRFIELD PARLOUR worked on the film soundtrack of 'Eye Witness', starring Mark Lester. Radio 1 DJ and future TV comedy celebrity KENNY EVERETT was a noted fan of FAIRFIELD PARLOUR. The lp 'TANGERINE DREAM', has been known to change hands for over £100+. In fact anything from quartet, is known to be worth lots of dosh.

Recommended: TANGERINE DREAM (*7) / FAINTLY BLOWING (*6) / FROM HOME TO HOME (*6; FAIRFIELD PARLOUR).

EDDIE PUMER – guitar / **PETE DALTREY** – vocals, keyboards / **DAN BRIDGEMAN** – drums, percussion / **STEVE CLARKE** – bass, flute

Fontana / not issued

Sep 67. (7") **FLIGHT FROM ASHIYA. / HOLIDAYMAKER** [ ] [-]

Nov 67. (lp) **TANGERINE DREAM** [ ] [-]
– Kaleidoscope / Please excuse my face / Drive into yesterday / Mr. Small, the watch repairer man / Flight from Ashiya / The murder of Lewis Tollani / (Further reflections) In the room of percussion / Dear Nellie Goodrich / Holidaymaker / A lesson, perhaps / The sky children. *(re-iss.Mar87 on '5 Hours Back')*

Jan 68. (7") **A DREAM FOR JULIE. / PLEASE EXCUSE MY FACE** [ ] [-]

Sep 68. (7") **JENNY ARTICHOKE. / JUST HOW MUCH YOU ARE** [ ] [-]

Mar 69. (7") **DO IT AGAIN FOR JEFFREY. / POEM** [ ] [-]
Apr 69. (lp) **FAINTLY BLOWING** [ ] [-]
– Faintly blowing / Poem / Snapdragon / A story from Tom Bitz / (Love song) For Annie / If you so wish / Opinion / Bless the executioner / Black fjord / The feathered tiger / I'll kiss you once / Music. *(re-iss.Mar87 on '5 Hours Back')*
Jul 69. (7") **BALOON. / IF YOU SO WISH** [ ] [-]
Recorded "lost" album below in 1970.

Kalei-doscope not issued

Feb 91. (cd) **WHITE-FACED LADY** [ ] [-]
– Overture / Broken mirrors / Dear Elvis Presley . . . (angel's song) / Nursey, nursey / Small song – Heaven in the back row / Burning bright / The matchseller / The coronation of the fledgling / All hail to the hero / White faced lady / Freefall / Standing / The Indian head (diary song) / Song from Jon / Long way down / The locket / Picture with conversation / Angel (epitaph).

I LUV WIGHT

(same line-up)
1970. (7") **LET THE WORLD WASH IN. / MEDIAEVAL MASQUERADE** [ ] [-]

FAIRFIELD PARLOUR

(same line-up)

Vertigo not issued

1970. (7") **BORDEAUX ROSE. / CHALK ON THE WALL** [ ] [-]
1970. (lp) **FROM HOME TO HOME** [ ] [-]
– Aries / In my box / By your bedside / Soldier of the flesh / I will always feel the same / Free / Emily / Chalk on the wall / Glorious house of Arthur / Monkey / Sunny side circus / Drummer boy of Shiloh. *(re-iss.+cd.Jul91 on 'Repertoire' +=)*– Just another day / Caraminda / I am all the animals / Songs for you.
1970. (7"m) **JUST ANOTHER DAY / CARAMINDA. / I AM ALL THE ANIMALS / SONGS FOR YOU** [ ] [-]

Prism not issued

Apr 76. (7") **BORDEAUX ROSE. / BABY STAY FOR TONIGHT** [ ] [-]
— When they split late '70, only DAN cropped up as FREEN BEANS to make one-off single 'BLISTER BOOGIE'.

KANSAS

Formed: Topeka, Kansas, USA . . . 1970 initially as WHITE CLOVER, by LIVGREN, HOPE and EHART. They brought in other 3 (see below) and became KANSAS during 1972. Two years later after constant touring, they signed to 'Kirshner' and hit US Top 200 with self-titled lp. In 1977, they had classic near US Top 10 smash with 'CARRY ON WAYWARD SON', from the Jeff Glixman produced Top 5 album 'LEFTOVERTURE'. Became major attractions for the next decade, until 1988 album 'IN THE SPIRIT OF THINGS' failed to make Top 100. • **Style:** Progressive hard-rock act, with harmonies and sound similiar to BOSTON or STYX. • **Songwriters:** Mostly LIVGREN compositions. • **Trivia:** In 1977, STEVE WALSH guested vox on STEVE HACKETT album 'Please Don't Touch'.

Recommended: THE BEST OF KANSAS (*6)

STEVE WALSH (b.1951, St.Joseph) – vocals, keyboards, synthesizer / **KERRY LIVGREN** (b.18 Sep'49) – guitar, piano, synthesizer / **ROBBY STEINHARDT** (b.1951, Mississippi) – violin / **RICH WILLIAMS** (b.1951) – guitar / **DAVE HOPE** (b. 7 Oct'49) – bass / **PHIL EHART** (b.1951) – drums

Kirshner Kirshner

Nov 74. (7") **CAN I TELL YOU. / THE PILGRIMAGE** [-] [ ]
Feb 75. (7") **BRINGING IT ALL BACK. / LONELY WIND** [-] [ ]
Apr 75. (lp)(c) **KANSAS** [ ] [ ] Jun 74
– Can I tell you / Bringing it back / Lonely wind / Belexes / Journey from Mariabronn / The pilgrimage / Apercu / Death of Mother Nature suite. *(cd-iss.Oct93 on 'Sony Europe')*
Apr 75. (7") **SONG FOR AMERICA. / (part 2)** [-] [ ]
Aug 75. (lp)(c) **SONG FOR AMERICA** [ ] [57] Mar 75
– Down the road / Song for America / Lamplight symphony / Lonely street / The Devil game / Incomudro – hymn to the Atman.
Feb 76. (7") **IT TAKES A WOMAN'S LOVE (TO MAKE A MAN). / IT'S YOU** [-] [ ]
May 76. (lp)(c) **MASQUE** [ ] [70] Dec 75
– It takes a woman's love (to make a man) / Two cents worth / Icarus – borne on wings of steel / All the world / Child of innocence / It's you / Mysteries and mayhem / The pinnacle.
Dec 76. (lp)(c) **LEFTOVERTURE** [ ] [5] Nov 76
– Carry on wayward son / The wall / What's on my mind / Miracles out of nowhere / Opus insert / Questions of my childhood / Cheyenne anthem / Magnus opus: Father Padilla meets the gnat – Howling at the Moon – Man overboard – Industry on parade – Release the beavers – Gnat attack.
Jan 77. (7") **CARRY ON WAYWARD SON. / QUESTIONS OF MY CHILDHOOD** [-] [11]
May 77. (7") **WHAT'S ON MY MIND. / LONELY STREET** [-] [ ]
Nov 77. (lp)(c)(US-pic-lp) **POINT OF KNOW RETURN** [ ] [4] Oct 77
– Point of know return / Paradox / The spider / Portrait (he knew) / Closet chronicles / Lightning's hand / Dust in the wind / Sparks of the tempest / Nobody's home / Hopelessly human.
Dec 77. (7") **POINT OF KNOW RETURN. / CLOSET CHRONICLES** [ ] [28] Oct 77
Mar 78. (7") **DUST IN THE WIND. / PARADOX** [ ] [6] Jan78
Jun 78. (7") **CARRY ON WAYWARD SON. / QUESTIONS OF MY CHILDHOOD** [51] [-]
Jun 78. (7") **PORTRAIT (HE KNEW). / LIGHTNING'S HAND** [-] [64]
Dec 78. (d-lp)(c) **TWO FOR THE SHOW (live)** [ ] [32] Nov78
– Songs for America / Point of know return / Paradox / Icarus – borne on wings of steel / Portrait (he knew) / Carry on wayward son / Journey from Mariabronn / Dust in the wind / Lonely wind / Mysteries and mayhem / Lamplight symphony / The wall / Closet chronicles / Magnum opus: Father Padilla meets the gnat – Howling at the Moon – Man overboard – Industry on parade / Release the beavers – Gnat attack.
Jan 79. (7") **LONELY WIND. / SONG FOR AMERICA (live)** [-] [60]
Jun 79. (7") **PEOPLE OF THE SOUTH WIND. / STAY OUT OF TROUBLE** [ ] [23]
Jul 79. (lp)(c) **MONOLITH** [ ] [10] May 79
– On the other side / People of the south wind / Angels have fallen / How my soul cries out for you / A glimpse of home / Away from you / Stay out of trouble / Reason to be.
Sep 79. (7") **REASON TO BE. / HOW MY SOUL CRIES OUT FOR YOU** [-] [52]
Sep 80. (7") **HOLD ON. / DON'T OPEN YOUR EYES** [-] [40]
Oct 80. (lp)(c) **AUDIO-VISIONS** [ ] [26] Sep 80
– Relentless / Anything for you / Hold on / Loner / Curtain of iron / Got to rock on / Don't open your eyes / No one together / No room for a stranger / Back door.
Dec 80. (7") **GOT TO ROCK ON. / NO ROOM FOR A STRANGER** [-] [76]
— **JOHN ELEFANTE** (b.1958, New York, USA) – vocals, keyboards repl. WALSH who continued on recent solo work.
Jul 82. (7") **PLAY THE GAME TONIGHT. / PLAY ON** [ ] [17] May 82
Jul 82. (lp)(c) **VINYL CONFESSIONS** [ ] [16] Jun 82
– Play the game tonight / Right away / Fair exchange / Chasing shadows / Diamonds and pearls / Face it / Windows / Borderline / Play on / Crossfire.
Aug 82. (7") **RIGHT AWAY. / WINDOWS** [-] [73]
— now w/out STEINHARDT

Epic CBS Assoc.

Aug 83. (7") **FIGHT FIRE WITH FIRE. / INCIDENT ON A BRIDGE** [-] [58]
Sep 83. (lp)(c) **DRASTIC MEASURES** [ ] [41]
– Fight fire with fire / Everybody's my friend / Mainstream / Andi / Going through the motions / Get rich / Don't take your love away / End of the age / Incident on a bridge.
Sep 83. (7") **FIGHT FIRE WITH FIRE. / CARRY ON WAYWARD SON / DUST IN THE WIND** [ ] [-]
Nov 83. (7") **EVERYBODY'S MY FRIEND. / END OF THE AGE** [-] [ ]
— Disbanded late 1983. Re-formed 1986 but without LIVGREN, HOPE & ELEFANTE. Past members **EHART & WILLIAMS** brought back **STEVE WALSH.** They recruited **STEVE MORSE** – guitar (ex-DIXIE DREGS) / **BILLY GREER** – bass (ex-STREETS)

M.C.A. M.C.A.

Dec 86. (lp)(c)(cd) **POWER** [ ] [35] Nov 86
– Silhouettes in disguise / Power / All I wanted / Secret service / We're not alone anymore / Musicatto / Taking in the view / Three pretenders / Tomb 19 / Can't cry anymore.
Jan 87. (7")(12") **ALL I WANTED. / WE'RE NOT ALONE ANYMORE** [ ] [19] Oct 86
Feb 87. (7") **POWER. / TOMB 19** [-] [84]
Apr 87. (7") **CAN'T CRY ANYMORE. / THREE PRETENDERS** [-] [ ]
Oct 88. (lp)(c)(cd) **IN THE SPIRIT OF THINGS** [ ] [ ]
– Ghosts / One big sky / Inside of me / One man, one heart * / House on fire / Once in a lifetime * / Stand beside me / I counted on love * / The preacher / Rainmaker / T.O. Witcher * / Bells of Saint James. *(cd+= *)*
Nov 88. (7") **STAND BESIDE ME. / HOUSE ON FIRE** [-] [ ]
— In 1991, they added **DAVID RAGSDALE** – violin
— **WALSH / LIVGREN / EHART / RAGSDALE**
Jul 93. Now & Then; (cd) **LIVE AT THE WHISKY (live)** [ ] [ ]

Essential Rykodisc

Jul 95. (cd)(c) **FREAKS OF NATURE** [ ] [ ]
– I can fly / Desperate times / Hope once again / Black fathom four / Under the knife / Need / Freaks of nature / Cold grey morning / Peaceful and warm.

– compilations, others –

Sep 84. Epic/ US= CBS Assoc; (lp)(c) **THE BEST OF KANSAS** [ ] [ ]
– Carry on wayward son / The point of know return / Fight fire / No one together / Play the game tonight / The wall. *(cd-iss. Nov85)*
Jul 94. Legacy; (d-cd) **THE KANSAS BOXED SET** [ ] [ ]

STEVE WALSH

solo, with some KANSAS members.

not issued Kirshner

Mar 80. (lp) **SCHEMER-DREAMER** [-] [ ]
– Schemer-dreamer (that's all right) / Get too far / So many nights / You think you got it made / Every step of the way / Just how does it feel / Wait until tomorrow.
Mar 80. (7") **SCHEMER-DREAMER (THAT' ALL RIGHT). / JUST HOW DOES IT FEEL** [-] [ ]
Jun 80. (7") **EVERY STEP OF THE WAY. / YOU THINK YOU GOT IT MADE** [-] [ ]
After his KANSAS departure early '81, WALSH formed STREETS with **MIKE SLAMER** – guitar (ex-CITY BOY) / **BILLY GREER** – bass / **TIM GEHRT** – drums. Released 2 albums for 'Atlantic' between 1983 & 1985; STREETS & CRIMES IN MIND.

KERRY LIVGREN

solo, with KANSAS members.

not issued Kirshner

Oct 80. (lp) **SEEDS OF CHANGE** [-] [ ]
– Just one way / Mask of the great deceiver / How can you live / Whiskey seed / To live for the king / Down to the core / Ground zero.
Oct 80. (7") **MASK OF THE GREAT DECEIVER. / TO LIVE FOR THE KING** [-] [ ]
— After he left KANSAS in 1982, he made 4 more albums, mostly religious. He also formed Christian band AD in 1984.

Paul KANTER & Grace SLICK (see under ⇒ JEFFERSON AIRPLANE)

Mick KARN (see under ⇒ JAPAN)

Jorma KAUKONEN (see under ⇒ HOT TUNA)

John KAY (see under ⇒ STEPPENWOLF)

KBC BAND (see under ⇒ HOT TUNA)

K.G.B. (see under ⇒ ELECTRIC FLAG)

KHAN (see under ⇒ HILLAGE, Steve)

Chaka KHAN (see under ⇒ RUFUS)

Johnny KIDD / (& The PIRATES)

Born: FREDERICK HEATH, 23 Dec'39, Willesden, London, England. In 1956, with future PIRATE; ALAN CADDY in the ranks, he formed skiffle combo FREDDIE HEATH & THE NUTTERS. Early 1959, after toying with calling himself CAPTAIN KIDD, he became JOHNNY KIDD. Signing for 'H.M.V.', his vinyl debut, 'PLEASE DON'T TOUCH' (written w/manager Guy Robinson), hit UK Top30. He borrowed follow-up 'IF YOU WERE THE ONLY GIRL IN THE WORLD' from music hall, but this bombed. In 1960 with new approach in mind, he enlisted new back-up band The PIRATES to give him needed oompf. His 4th single for the label, 'SHAKIN' ALL OVER' went to UK No.1, but didn't quite give him deserved total stardom. Six years later (7 Oct'66), JOHNNY was killed when the touring group's van collided with a lorry on the M1. He was only 26, and would have certainly enjoyed a renewed acquaintance with success, as the advent of hard rock to come. • **Style:** Classic rock'n'roll R&B that a initiated a new generation of 60's & 70's!, guitar riff-laded basic rock. Their tongue-in-cheek Pirate stage gear, and 45's-only policy, didn't help the American public to take them seriously. • **Songwriters:** Although not prolific, JOHNNY wrote/co-wrote some fine gems. Also covered; YOU GOT WHAT IT TAKES (Marv Johnson) / LINDA LU (Ray Sharpe) / THE BIRDS AND THE BEES (Jewel Atkins) / I CAN TELL (Bo Diddley) / A SHOT OF RHYTHM AND BLUES (Arthur Alexander) / MY BABE (Little Walter) / ALWAYS AND EVER (Latin-American standard) / WHOLE LOTTA WOMAN (Marvin Rainwater) / etc. • **Trivia:** NICK SIMPER, later an early member of DEEP PURPLE, was also injured in the crash.

Recommended: CLASSIC AND RARE (*8)

JOHNNY KIDD – vocals (solo with session people)

H.M.V. — not issued

May 59. (7") **PLEASE DON'T TOUCH. / GROWL** — 25 — -

Dec 59. (7") **IF YOU WERE THE ONLY GIRL IN THE WORLD. / FEELIN'** — — -

JOHNNY KIDD & THE PIRATES

(still session men) His live line-up **ALAN CADDY** – guitar / **TONY DOHERTY** – rhythm guitar / **JOHNNY GORDON** – bass / **KEN McKAY** – drums / **MIKE WEST** and **TOM BROWN** – backing vocals

Feb 60. (7") **YOU GOT WHAT IT TAKES. / LONGIN' LIPS** — 25 — -

— **KIDD** retained only **CADDY** (JOE MORETTI – lead guitar on below 1 only) with **BRIAN GREGG** – bass (ex-BEAT BOYS) / **CLEM CATTINI** – drums (ex-BEAT BOYS)

H.M.V. — Capitol

Jun 60. (7") **SHAKIN' ALL OVER. / YES SIR, THAT'S MY BABY** — 1 —
(re-iss.Feb76 on 'EMI')

Sep 60. (7") **RESTLESS. / MAGIC OF LOVE** — 22 —

Mar 61. (7") **LINDA LU. / LET'S TALK ABOUT US** — 47 —

— KIDD now reverted to session men

Sep 61. (7") **PLEASE DON'T BRING ME DOWN. / SO WHAT** — —

— KIDD completely changed his PIRATES line-up; **JOHNNY PATTO** – guitar / **JOHNNY SPENCE** – bass / **FRANK FARLEY** – drums (all ex-CUDDLY DUDLEY) repl. ALAN, BRIAN + CLEM who all joined COLIN HICKS' Band

Jan 62. (7") **HURRY ON BACK TO LOVE. / I WANT THAT** — —

— **MICK GREEN** – guitar repl. PATTO

Nov 62. (7") **A SHOT OF RHYTHM AND BLUES. / I CAN TELL** — 48 — -

Jun 63. (7") **I'LL NEVER GET OVER YOU. / THEN I GOT EVERYTHING** — 4 — Oct 63

Nov 63. (7") **HUNGRY FOR LOVE. / ECSTACY** — 20 — -

Apr 64. (7") **ALWAYS AND EVER. / DOCTOR FEELGOOD** — 46 — -

— added **VIC COOPER** – organ

Jun 64. (7") **JEALOUS GIRL. / SHOP AROUND** — — -

— **JOHN WIEDER** – guitar (ex-TONY MEEHAN) repl. MICK to BILLY KRAMER

Oct 64. (7") **WHOLE LOTTA WOMAN. / YOUR CHEATIN' HEART** — — -

Feb 65. (7") **THE BIRDS AND THE BEES. / DON'T MAKE THE SAME MISTAKE AS I DID** — — -

May 65. (7") **SHAKIN' ALL OVER '65. / I GOTTA TRAVEL ON** — — -

— KIDD, SPENCE, FARLEY and COOPER recruited **JON MORSHEAD** – guitar repl. WIEDER who later joined ERIC BURDON

Apr 66. (7") **IT'S GOT TO BE YOU. / I HATE TO GET UP IN THE MORNING** — — -

— JOHNNY KIDD brought in completely new musicians **MICK STEWART** – guitar repl. MORSHEAD / **NICK SIMPER** – bass (ex-SIMON RAVEN CULT) repl. SPENCE / **ROGER TRUTH** – drums (ex-SIMON RAVEN CULT) repl. FARLEY / also **RAY SOAPER** – keyboards (left before recording below). First three that left became band The PIRATES.

— JOHNNY KIDD was killed in a car crash 7 Oct66. Below released posthumously

Nov 66. (7") **SEND FOR THAT GIRL. / THE FOOL** — — -

— without KIDD the new PIRATES continued until May67. SIMPER to DEEP PURPLE

- compilations etc. -

1960. H.M.V.; (7"ep) **PLEASE DON'T TOUCH** — — -
– Shakin' all over / Please don't touch / You got what it takes / Restless.

1964. H.M.V.; (7"ep) **I'LL NEVER GET OVER YOU** — — -
– I'll never get over you / A shot of rhythm and blues / Hungry for love / Then I got everything.

Jun 80. H.M.V.; (7") **SHAKIN' ALL OVER. / A SHOT OF RHYTHM AND BLUES** — — -

1971. EMI; (lp) **I'LL NEVER GET OVER YOU. / PLEASE DON'T TOUCH** — — -

Apr 78. EMI; (lp)(c) **THE BEST OF JOHNNY KIDD & THE PIRATES** — — -
– A shot of rhythm & blues / Shakin' all over / Longing lips / Restess / Growl / I want that / Linda Lu / You've got what it takes / Your cheatin' heart / I'll never get over you / Hungry for love / I can tell / Jealous girl / Shop around / Please don't touch / Always and ever. *(re-iss.Feb87)*

Aug 92. EMI; (d-cd)(d-c) **THE COMPLETE JOHNNY KIDD & THE PIRATES** — — -

1971. Starline; (lp) **SHAKIN' ALL OVER** — — -

Oct 83. Old Gold; (7") **SHAKIN' ALL OVER. / I'LL NEVER GET OVER YOU** — — -

May 87. See For Miles; (lp) **RARITIES** — — -
(re-iss.1987) (cd-iss.Oct89) (re-iss.cd+c Aug93)

Feb 90 See For Miles; (cd)(lp)**CLASSIC AND RARE** — — -
(re-iss. Aug93)

Jul 95. EMI; (cd) **THE VERY BEST OF JOHNNY KIDD & THE PIRATES** — — -

The PIRATES

(without KIDD one-off by **GREEN, SPENCE** and **FARLEY**)

H.M.V. — not issued

Jan 64. (7") **MY BABE. / CASTING MY SPELL** — — -

The PIRATES

between Apr-Jul66 (**SPENCE** – vocals, **MORSHEAD** and **FARLEY**)

Polydor — not issued

Jul 66. (7") **SHADES OF BLUE. / CAN'T UNDERSTAND** — — -

The PIRATES

re-formed late 1976. (**SPENCE** – vocals, **GREEN** and **FARLEY**)

Warners — Warners

Sep 77. (7") **SWEET LOVE. / DON'T MUNCHEN IT / YOU DON'T OWN ME** — —

Oct 77. (lp)(c) **OUT OF THEIR SKULLS** — 57 —
– Please don't touch / I can tell / Peter Gunn / Lonesome train / Shakin' all over / Milk cow blues / Drinkin' wine spondee-o-dee / Do the dog / Gibson Martin Fender / Don't Munchen it / That's the way you are / You don't own me.

Mar 78. (7") **ALL IN IT TOGETHER. / DR. FEELGOOD** — —

Apr 78. (lp)(c) **SKULL WARS** — —
– Long journey home / Dr. Feelgood / All in it together / Johnny B. Goode's good / Johnny B. Goode * / Talkin' about you * / I'm in love again * / Voodoo / Four to the bar / Honey hush * / Diggin' my potatoes / Shake hands with the Devil. *(4 tracks – * live)*

May 78. (7") **JOHNNY B. GOODE'S GOOD. / JOHNNY B. GOODE** — —

Sep 78. (7") **SHAKIN' ALL OVER. / SATURDAY NIGHT SHOOTOUT** — —

Cube — not issued

Sep 79. (7") **GOLDEN OLDIES. / MERCY PIRATES** — —

Sep 79. (lp)(c) **HAPPY BIRTHDAY ROCK'N'ROLL** — —

Nov 79. (7") **LADY, PUT THE LIGHT ON ME. / LEMONADE** — —

- compilations etc. -

May 81. Edsel; (lp) **A FISTFUL OF DUBLOONS** — — -
(re-iss.May89, cd-iss.Jul92)

Aug 82. Charly; (7"ep) **PETER GUNN** — — -
– Peter Gunn / Just another party / Something very strange / Cap in han.

Dec 88. Thunderbolt; (lp)(c) **STILL SHAKIN'** — — -

May 93. Thunderbolt; (cd) **LIVE IN JAPAN (live)** — — -

Mar 93. RPM; (cd) **DON'T MUNCHEN IT! - THE PIRATES LIVE IN EUROPE** — — -

Greg KIHN

Born: 1952, Baltimore, Maryland, USA. In 1974 he moved to Berkeley, California, where he signed to local indie label 'Beserkley'. After supplying labelmates JONATHAN RICHMAN and EARTHQUAKE, with backing vox on their recent 45's, he formed own band in 1975. Two lp's followed, and gathered interest, after the airplay for track 'FOR YOU' received. In '81, they broke through into US Top 20 with 45 'THE BREAKUP SONG', which was lifted from Top 40 album 'ROCKIHNROLL'. • **Style:** Folk-rock near new wave artist, who went mainstream in the 80's. • **Songwriters:** KIHN co-writes most with WRIGHT except; FOR YOU + RENDEZVOUS (Bruce Springsteen) / LOVE'S MADE A FOOL OF YOU (Buddy Holly) / I FALL TO PIECES (Patsy Cline) / ANOTHER GIRL, ANOTHER PLANET (Only Ones) / etc. • **Trivia:** All his Berkeley stuff, were produced by Matthew Kaufman.

Recommended: UNKIHNTROLLABLE (*5)

GREG KIHN – vocals, guitar w/band **STEVEN WRIGHT** – bass, vocals / **LARRY LYNCH** – drums, vocals. Guest on tour **ROBBIE DUNBAR** – guitar

Beserkley | Beserkley

1975. (lp) **GREG KIHN** [-] [ ]
– Don't expect to be right / Any other woman / Emily Davison / Try to fall in love / Kid from Louieville / Worse or better / He will break your heart / What goes on / Satisfied / Why don't you try me.

1976. (7") **WHAT GOES ON. / MY OTHER WOMAN** [-] [ ]

— added **DAVE CARPENDER** – guitar

Dec 76. (7") **FOR YOU. / MADISON AVENUE MAN** [-] [ ]
Nov 77. (7") **FOR YOU. / MOOD MOOD NUMBER** [ ] [-]
Dec 77. (lp) **GREG KIHN AGAIN** [ ] [ ] May 76
– Love's made a fool of you / Island / Last of me / Real big man / Politics / Hurt so bad for you / If you be my love / Madison Avenue / Untie my hands.

Jan 78. (7") **LOVE'S MADE A FOOL OF YOU. / SORRY** [-] [ ]
Sep 78. (7") **REMEMBER. / POLITICS** [-] [ ]
Jan 79. (7")(12") **REMEMBER. / SATISFIED** [ ] [-]
Mar 79. (lp)(c) **NEXT OF KIHN** [ ] [ ] Sep 78
– Cold hard cash / Museum / Chinatown / Sorry / Everybody else / Understander / Secret meetings.

GREG KIHN BAND

(Beserkley label was now licensed to 'Elektra' in the States).

May 79. (7")**MOULIN ROUGE. / GETTING AWAY WITH MURDER** [ ] [ ]
Aug 79. (lp)(c) **WITH THE NAKED EYE** [ ] [ ]
– Rendezvous / In the naked eye / Getting away with murder / Moulin Rouge / Beside myself / Roadrunner / Another lonely Saturday night / Can't have the highs (without the lows) / Fallen idol.

Aug 79. (7") **GETTING AWAY WITH MURDER. / BESIDE MYSELF** [-] [ ]
Jan 80. (7") **ROADRUNNER. / GETTING AWAY WITH MURDER** [-] [ ]
Apr 80. (lp)(c) **GLASS HOUSE ROCK** [ ] [ ]
– Castaway / Desire me / Anna Belle Lee / Things to come / Small change / The only dance there is is / The man who shot Liberty Valance / Serenade her / Night after night / For your love. *(UK-title 'POWERLINES')*

Nov 80. (7") **SERENADE HER. / I CAN'T STOP HURTING MYSELF** [-] [ ]

— added **GARY PHILLIPS** – keyboards, vocals (ex-EARTHQUAKE, ex-COPPERHEAD) (had guested in 1976)

Apr 81. (7") **SHEILA. /** [-] [ ]
Aug 81. (7") **THE BREAKUP SONG (THEY DON'T WRITE 'EM). / WHEN THE MUSIC STARTS** [ ] [15] Jun 81
Aug 81. (lp)(c) **ROCKIHNROLL** [ ] [32] Apr 81
– Valerie / The breakup song (they don't write 'em) / Womankind / Can't stop hurtin' myself / Trouble in Paradise / Sheila / Nothing's gonna change / The girl most likely / When the music starts / True confessions. *(cd-iss.Mar89)*

Oct 81. (7") **TRUE CONFESSIONS. / THE GIRL MOST LIKELY** [-] [ ]
Jan 82. (7") **EVERY LOVE SONG. / TROUBLE IN PARADISE** [-] [ ]
(US re-iss.Jul82, hit No.84)
May 82. (7") **HAPPY MAN. / TROUBLE IN PARADISE** [ ] [62] Apr 82
(re-iss.Aug83)
May 82. (lp)(c) **KIHNTINUED** [ ] [33] Apr 82
– Happy man / Every love song / Everyday – Saturday / Dedication / Tell me lies / Testify / Sound system / Seeing is believing / Higher and higher / Family. *(cd-iss.Mar89)*

— **GREG DOUGLAS** – guitar repl. CARPENDER

Mar 83. (7")(12") **JEOPARDY. / FASCINATION** [63] [2] Feb 83
May 83. (lp)(c) **KIHNSPIRACY** [ ] [15] Mar 83
– Jeopardy / Fascination / Tear that city down / Talkin' to myself / Can't love them all / I fall to pieces / Someday / Curious / How long / Love never fails. *(cd-iss.Jan84)*

May 83. (7") **LOVE NEVER FAILS. / TALKIN' TO MYSELF** [-] [59]
May 84. (lp)(c) **KIHNTAGIOUS** [ ] [ ]
– Reunited / Rock / Make up / Stand together / Confrontation music / One thing about love / Worst that could happen / Trouble with the girl / Cheri baby / Hard times / Work, work, work. *(cd-iss.Mar89)*

Jul 84. (7") **REUNITED. / WORK, WORK, WORK** [-] [ ]
Sep 84. (7") **STAND TOGETHER. / ROCK** [-] [ ]

GREG KIHN

solo again, but retaining **WRIGHT + DOUGLAS** and **PAT MOSCA** – keyboards / **TYLER ENG** – drums.

EMI America | EMI America

Mar 85. (7")(12") **LUCKY. / SAD SITUATION** [ ] [30]
Mar 85. (lp)(c) **CITIZEN KIHN** [ ] [51]
– I'm in love again / Go back / Lucky / Whenever / Piracy / Free country / They rock by night / Boys won't / Imitation love / Temper, temper / Good life.

— **JOE SATRIANI** – guitar (solo artist) repl. DOUGLAS

Mar 86. (lp)(c) **LOVE AND ROCK AND ROLL** [ ] [ ]
– Love and rock and roll / Little red book / Wild in love with you / Beat of the night / Another girl, another planet / Worst job I ever had / Privilege / Okay to cry / Paint you a picture / Pastures of green. *(cd-iss.Mar89)*

Mar 86. (7") **LOVE AND ROCK AND ROLL. /** [-] [92]

Demon | ???

Sep 94. (cd) **MUTINY** [ ] [ ]
– Blood red roses / Mutiny / Sittin' on top of the world / Anniversary of my broken heart / Joshua gone Barbados / Anastasia / I wish it would rain / Not fade away / Mona / Femme fatale / Shot in the dark / Subterranean homesick blues / Love of the land / Been on the job too long / Gwabi.

All covers above including; I WISH IT WOULD RAIN (Temptations) / FEMME FATALE (Velvet Underground) / SUBTERRANEAN HOMESICK BLUES (Bob Dylan) / MONA (Bo Diddley) / NOT FADE AWAY (Buddy Holly).

– compilations, others, etc. –

Oct 87. Beserkley; (7"m) **JEOPARDY. / ROADRUNNER / RE-UNITED** [ ] [-]
1989. Rhino; (lp)(cd) **UNKIHNTROLLABLE** [ ] [ ]

Steve KILBEY (see under ⇒ CHURCH)

KILBURN & THE HIGH ROADS (see under ⇒ DURY, Ian)

KILLING JOKE

Formed: London, England ... 1979 by JAZ COLEMAN and PAUL FERGUSON, who soon moved to Cheltenham. After supporting the likes of JOY DIVISION and The RUTS, they signed to 'Island-EG', and started own label 'Malicious Damage'. After a number of singles received airplay on John Peel show, they unleashed classic eponymous debut lp in Autumn of 1980. This dented the UK Top 40, and paved the way for future chart ventures. • **Style:** Mix a hybrid of angst punk-metal, experimental rock with occult lyrics, fronted by the extreme clown-faced showman JAZ. **Songwriters:** COLEMAN and group compositions. • **Trivia:** YOUTH's departure early in '82, was due to JAZ and GEORDIE's disappearance on tour in Iceland.

Recommended: KILLING JOKE (*9) / FIRE DANCES (*7) / LAUGH, I NEARLY BOUGHT ONE (*8) / WHAT'S THIS FOR (*6).

JAZ COLEMAN (b. Egypt) – vocals, keyboards / **GEORDIE** (WALKER) – guitar, synthesizers / **YOUTH** (b. MARTIN GLOVER, 27 Dec'60, Africa) – bass, vocals (ex-RAGE) / **PAUL FERGUSON** – drums

Malicious Damage | not issued

Oct 79. (10"m) **ARE YOU RECEIVING ME. / TURN TO RED / NERVOUS SYSTEM** [ ] [-]

Island | not issued

Nov 79. (7") **NERVOUS SYSTEM. / TURN TO RED** [ ] [-]
(12"+=) – Almost red / Are you receiving me.

Malicious Damage | not issued

Mar 80. (7") **WARDANCE. / PSYCHE** [ ] [-]

Malicious Damage-EG | not issued

Sep 80. (7") **REQUIEM. / CHANGE** [ ] [-]
(12"+=) – Requiem 434 / Change (version).
Oct 80. (lp)(c) **KILLING JOKE** [39] [-]
– Requiem / Wardance / Tomorrow's world / Bloodsport / The wait / Complications / S.O. 36 / Primitive. *(re-iss.+cd Jan87)*
May 81. (7") **FOLLOW THE LEADERS. / TENSION** [55] [-]
(10"+=)(12"+=) – ('A'dub).
Jun 81. (lp)(c) **WHAT'S THIS FOR ...!** [42] [-]
– The fall of Because / Tension / Unspeakable / Butcher / Follow the leaders / Madness / Who told you how? / Exit. *(re-iss.+cd Jan87)*

E.G. | Virgin

Mar 82. (7") **EMPIRE SONG. / BRILLIANT** [43] [-]

— **GUY PRATT** – bass repl. YOUTH who formed BRILLIANT

Apr 82. (lp)(c) **REVELATIONS** [12] [-]
– The hum / Empire song / We have joy / Chop-chop / The Pandys are coming / Chapter III / Have a nice day / Land of milk and honey / Good samaritan / Dregs. *(re-iss.+cd Jan87)*
Jun 82. (7") **CHOP-CHOP. / GOOD SAMARITAN** [ ] [-]
Oct 82. (7") **BIRDS OF A FEATHER. / FLOCK THE B-SIDE** [64] [-]
(12"+=) – Sun goes down.
Nov 82. (10"m-lp) **HA – KILLING JOKE LIVE (live)** [66] [-]
– Psyche / Sun goes down / The Pandys are coming / Take take take / Unspeakable / Wardance.

— **PAUL RAVEN** – bass (ex-NEON HEARTS) repl. PRATT who joined ICEHOUSE

Jun 83. (7") **LET'S ALL GO (TO THE FIRE DANCES). / DOMINATOR** [51] [-]
(12"+=) – The fall of Because (live).
Jul 83. (lp)(c) **FIRE DANCES** [29] [ ]
– The gathering / Fun and games / Rejuvenation / Frenzy / Harlequin / Feast of blaze / Song and dance / Dominator / Let's all go (to the fire dances) / Lust almighty. *(re-iss.+cd Jan87)*
Oct 83. (7") **ME OR YOU?. / WILFUL DAYS** [57] [-]
(10"+=)(12"+=) – Feast of blaze.
(d7"++=) – ('A'side again).
Mar 84. (7") **EIGHTIES. / ('A'-The coming mix)** [60] [-]
(12"+=) – ('A'dance mix).
Jun 84. (7") **A NEW DAY. / DANCE DAY** [56] [-]
(12"+=) – ('A'dub).
Jan 85. (7") **LOVE LIKE BLOOD. / BLUE FEATHER** [16] [-]
(12"+=) – ('A'instrumental).
(d7"+=) – ('A'-Gestalt mix).
Feb 85. (lp)(c) **NIGHT TIME** [11] [ ]
– Night time / Darkness before dawn / Love like blood / Kings and queens / Tabazan /

Multitudes / Europe / Eighties. *(re-iss.+cd Jan87)*

Mar 85. (7") **KINGS AND QUEENS. / THE MADDING CROWD** 58
(12"+=) – ('A'-Royal mix).
(12"+=) – ('A'-Knave mix).

Aug 86. (7") **ADORATIONS. / EXILE** 42 -
(12"+=) – Ecstacy.
(d7"++=) – ('A'instrumental).

Oct 86. (7") **SANITY. / GOODBYE TO THE VILLAGE** 70 -
(12"+=) – Victory.
(free c-s with-7"+=) – Wardance.

Nov 86. (lp)(c)(cd) **BRIGHTER THAN A THOUSAND SUNS** 54
– Adorations / Sanity / Chessboards / Twilight of the mortal / Love of the masses / A southern sky / Wintergardens / Rubicon. *(c+=)(cd+=)*– Goodbye to the village / Victory.

Apr 88. (7") **AMERICA. / JIHAD** -
(12"+=) – ('A'extended).
(cd-s+=) – Change.

Jun 88. (lp)(c)(cd) **OUTSIDE THE GATE** 92
– America / My love of this land / Stay one jump ahead / Unto the ends of the Earth / The calling / Obsession / Tiahuanaco / Outside the gate. *(cd+=)*– America (extended) / Stay one jump ahead (extended).

Jul 88. (7") **MY LOVE OF THIS LAND. / DARKNESS BEFORE DAWN** -
(12"+=) – Follow the leaders (dub) / Psyche.
(10"+=) – Follow the leaders (dub) / Sun goes down.

— **JAZ** and **GEORDIE** brought in new members **MARTIN ATKINS** – drums (ex-PUBLIC IMAGE LTD.) repl. FERGUSON / **TAFF** – bass repl. ANDY ROURKE (ex-SMITHS) who had repl. RAVEN. Early 1990, **JAZ COLEMAN** teamed up with **ANNE DUDLEY**(see; ART OF NOISE)

— **KILLING JOKE** reformed (**JAZ, GEORDIE, MARTIN & PAUL**)

Noise Int. Noise Int.

Nov 90. (cd)(c)(lp) **EXTREMITIES, DIRT AND VARIOUS REPRESSED EMOTIONS** -
– Money is not our god / Age of greed / Beautiful dead / Extremities / Inside the termite mound / Intravenus / Solitude / North of the border / Slipstream / Kalijuga struggle.

Jan 91. (12")(cd-s) **MONEY IS NOT OUR GOD. / NORTH OF THE BORDER** -

Invisible not issued

Jul 93. (d-lp) **THE COURTHOLD TALKS** -
– (spoken word with JAZ, GEORDIE & JAFF SCANTLEBURY on percussion)

Butterfly-Big Life

Mar 94. (10"ep)(cd-ep) **EXORCISM. / ('A'live) / ('A'-German mix) / WHITEOUT(ugly mix) / ANOTHER CULT GOES DOWN (mix) / ('A'-bictonic revenge mix)** -

Apr 94. (7"clear)(c-s) **MILLENNIUM. / ('A'-Cybersank remix)** 34
(12"+=)(cd-s+=) – ('A'-Drum Club remix) / ('A'Juno Reactor remix).

Jul 94. (12")(c-s)(cd-s) **PANDEMONIUM. / ('A'mix)** 28
(cd-s) – ('A'side) / Requiem (Kris Weston & Greg Hunter remix).

Jul 94. (cd)(c)(d-lp) **PANDEMONIUM** 16
– Pandemonium / Exorcism / Millenium / Communion / Black Moon / Labyrinth / Jana / Whiteout / Pleasures of the flesh / Mathematics of chaos.

— Re-united originals **JAZ COLEMAN / GEORDIE + YOUTH**

Jan 95. (cd-ep) **JANA (Youth remix) / JANA (Dragonfly mix) / LOVE LIKE BLOOD (live) / WHITEOUT** 54
(12"ep)(cd-ep+=) – Jana (live) / Wardance (live) / Exorcism (live) / Kings and queens (live).

– compilations, others, etc. –

Sep 92. Virgin; (12")(c-s) **CHANGE. / REQUIEM**
(cd-s) – ('A'spiral tribe mix). / ('B'trash Greg Hunter mix).
(cd-s) – ('A'-Youth mix). / ('B'-Youth mix).

Oct 92. (cd)(c)(lp) **LAUGH, I NEARLY BOUGHT ONE**
– Turn to red / Psyche / Requiem / Wardance / Follow the leaders / Unspeakable / Butcher / Exit / The hum / Empire song / Chop-chop / The Sun goes down / Eighties / Darkness before dawn / Love like blood / Wintergardens / Age of greed.

May 95. Virgin; (cd) **WILFUL DAYS** (remixes) -

Oct 95. Windsong; (cd) **BBC LIVE IN CONCERT (live)** -

Albert KING

Born: 25 April 1923, Indianola, Mississippi, USA. In the early 50's he took off to Chicago (home of the blues), where he and JIMMY REED sessioned for The SPANIELS (KING on drums!). In 1953, he recorded his debut single 'BAD LUCK BLUES' for 'Parrot' records. For six years he became inactive until he was picked up by St.Louis based label 'Bobbin'. Recordings were made around the early 60's, and these were soon leased to 'King' records, who issued lp 'THE BIG BLUES' in 1962. Three years later, he cut tracks for 'Coun-Tree', but his big break came in 1966, when 'Stax' (home of BOOKER T & THE M.G.'s) gave him contract. There he made his first real debut lp 'BORN UNDER A BAD SIGN' with house-band in 1967. It received many critical appraisals due to strong R&B tracks 'CROSSCUT SAW', 'LAUNDROMAT BLUES' & 'PERSONAL MANAGER'. After several more albums, he shifted in the mid-70's to the 'Utopia' stable run by GIORGIO GOMELSKY. There he made 3 albums starting with 'TRUCKLOAD OF LOVIN'', before he moved again, this time to 'Tomato'. In the 80's, he recorded sparsly due to ill-health. Sadly on 20th December 1992, he died at his home. • **Style:** Earthy raw blues giant (he weighed over 250 lb. and was 6 foot 4 inches), whose early inspiration was T-BONE WALKER, but who in his own right was the innovator for many of the 60's white rock /blues greats like PAUL BUTTERFIELD, FREE, GROUNDHOGS to name just a few. In 1973 /74 he drifted into more mainstream funk /rock, although there was always moments of his blues guitar work around. • **Songwriters:** Self-penned mainly. In 1969 he released an lp of ELVIS covers 'KING, DOES THE KING'S THINGS'. Also interpreted HONKY TONK WOMAN (Rolling Stones) / CORINA CORINA (Bob Dylan) / THE SKY IS CRYING (Elmore James) / I CAN'T STAND THE RAIN (Ann Peebles; hit) / FEEL THE NEED IN ME (Detroit Emeralds) / etc. • **Trivia:** Played left-handed, a custom-made v-shaped Gibson Flying Arrow guitar.

Recommended: I'LL PLAY THE BLUES FOR YOU – BEST OF.. (*7) / BORN UNDER A BAD SIGN (*8)

ALBERT KING – vox, guitar

not issued Parrot

1954. (7") **BAD LUCK BLUES. / BE ON YOUR MERRY WAY** -

not issued Bobbin

1958. (7") **WHY ARE YOU SO MEAN TO ME. / OOH-EE BABY** -

1959. (7") **THE TIME HAS COME. / NEED YOU BY MY SIDE** -

1959. (7") **BLUES AT SUNRISE. / LET'S HAVE A NATURAL BALL** -

1960. (7") **I WALKED ALL NIGHT LONG. / I'VE MADE NIGHTS BY MYSELF** -

1960. (7") **TRAVELIN' TO CALIFORNIA. / DYNAFLOW** -

(above + below singles also issued on 'King'.

1960. (7") **DON'T THROW YOUR LOVE ON ME SO STRONG. / THIS MORNING** -

1961. (7") **I GET EVIL. / WHAT CAN I DO TO CHANGE YOUR MIND** -

1962. (7") **GOT TO BE SOME CHANGES MADE. / I'LL DO ANYTHING YOU SAY** -

1962. (7") **OLD BLUE RIBBON. / I'VE HAD NIGHTS BY MYSELF** -

not issued King

1962. (lp) **THE BIG BLUES** -

1963. (7") **HAD YOU TOLD IT LIKE IT WAS. / THIS FUNNY FEELING** -

— now w / **STEVE CROPPER** – guitar / **DONALD 'Duck' DUNN** – bass / **AL JACKSON** – drums

Atlantic Stax

1966. (7") **LAUNDROMAT BLUES. / OVERALL JUNCTION** -

1966. (7") **PRETTY WOMAN (CAN'T MAKE YOU LOVE ME). / FUNK-SHUN** -

Feb 67. (lp) **BORN UNDER A BAD SIGN**
– Laundromat blues / Oh, pretty woman / Crosscut saw / Down don't bother me / Born under a bad sign / Personal manager / Kansas City / The very thought of you / The hunter / Almost lost my mind / As the years go passing by.

Feb 67. (7") **CROSSCUT SAW. / DOWN DON'T BOTHER ME**

Jul 67. (7") **BORN UNDER A BAD SIGN. / PERSONAL MANAGER**

Stax Stax

Feb 68. (7") **COLD FEET. / YOU SURE DRIVE A HARD BARGAIN** 67 Jan68

Jul 68. (7") **(I LOVE) LUCY. / YOU'RE GONNA NEED ME**

Nov 68. (lp) **LIVE WIRE / BLUES POWER**
– Watermelon man / Blues power / Night stomp / Blues at sunrise / Please love me / Lookout. *(US re-iss.1980, cd-iss.Nov88)*

Jan 69. (7") **BLUES POWER. / NIGHT STOMP** -

Jan 69. (lp) **KING, DOES THE KING'S THINGS** -
– Hound dog / That's all right / All shook up / Jailhouse rock / Heartbreak hotel / Don't be cruel / One night / Blue suede shoes / Love me tender. *(cd-iss.Nov92 as 'BLUES FOR ELVIS')*

May 69. (lp) **YEARS GONE BY**
– Wrapped up in love again / You don't love me / Cockroach / Killing floor / Lonely man / If the washing don't get you, the rinsing will / Drowning on dry land / Drowning on dry land (instrumental) / Heart fixing business / You threw your love on me too strong / The sky is crying. *(cd-iss.Apr92 on 'Ace'; extra tracks)*

Jun 69. (7") **DROWNING ON DRY LAND. / ('A'instrumental)** -

Jul 69. (lp) **JAMMED TOGETHER** -
– What'd I say / Tupelo / Opus de soul / Baby, what you want me to do / Big bird / Homer's theme / Trashy dog / Don't turn your heater down / Water / Knock on wood.

Aug 69. (7") **TUPELO. / (part 2)** -

Oct 69. (7") **WATER. / OPUS DE SOUL** -

(above 2 singles and album credited to "ALBERT KING, STEVE CROPPER & POP STAPLES")

Mar 70. (7") **COCKROACH. / WRAPPED UP IN LOVE AGAIN** -

1970. (7") **COLD SWEAT. / CAN'T YOU SEE WHAT YOU'RE DOING TO ME** -

— now w / **session people JESSE ED DAVIS, TIPPY ARMSTRONG, WAYNE PERKINS, MICHAEL TOLES** – guitar / **JOHN GALLIE, BARRY BECKETT** – keyboards / **DUNN, DAVID HOOD** – bass / **ROGER HAWKINS, JIM KELTNER** – drums / **SANDY KONIKOFF** – percussion

Jul 71. (7") **EVERYBODY WANTS TO GET TO HEAVEN. / LOVEJOY** -

Jul 71. (lp) **LOVEJOY**
– Honky tonk woman / Bay Area blues / Corina Corina / She caught the Katy & left me a mule to ride / For the love of a woman / Lovejoy / Everybody wants to get to Heaven / Going back to Luka / Like a road leading home.

Feb 72. (7") **ANGEL OF MERCY. / FUNKY LONDON** -

Sep 72. (7") **I'LL PLAY THE BLUES FOR YOU. / (part 2)** -

Oct 72. (lp) **I'LL PLAY THE BLUES FOR YOU** -
– I'll play the blues for you (parts 1 & 2) / Little brother / Breaking up somebody's home / High cost of loving / I'll be doggone / Answer to the laundromat blues / Don't burn down the bridge (cause you might wanna come back) / Angel of mercy.

Apr 73. (7") **BREAKING UP SOMEBODY'S HOME. / LITTLE BROTHER** 91 Feb73

Sep 73. (7") **PLAYIN' ON TIME. / HIGH COST OF LOVING** -

Nov 73. (7") **I WANNA GET FUNKY. / THAT'S WHAT THE BLUES IS ALL ABOUT** -

Dec 73. (lp) **I WANNA GET FUNKY**

– I wanna get funky / Playin' on me / Walkin' the back streets and cryin' / Till my back ain't got no bone / Flat tire / I can't hear nothing but the blues / Travelin' man / Crosscut saw / That's what the blues is all about.

Aug 74. (7") **FLAT TIRE. / I CAN HEAR NOTHING BUT THE BLUES**

Oct 74. (7") **CROSSCUT SAW. / DON'T BURN DOWN THE BRIDGES**

1975. (lp) **MONTREUX FESTIVAL (live)**

–

— now w / **BERT DE COTEAUX, JOE SAMPLE, JERRY PETERS** – keyboards / **CHUCK RAINEY, HENRY DAVIS** – bass / **WAH WAH WATSON, GREG POREE, BILL FENDER** – guitar / **JAMES GADSON** – drums / **KING ERRISON** – percussion / + backing vocalists: DEE IRVIN, MAXINE WILLARD, LANI GROVES, JULIA TILMAN, DENIECE WILLIAMS, JEANIE ARNOLD

Utopia-RCA Utopia

Mar 76. (lp)(c) **TRUCKLOAD OF LOVIN'**

– Cold women with warm hearts / Gonna make it somehow / Sensation, communication, together / I'm your mate / Truckload of lovin' / Hold hands with one another / Cadillac assembly line / Nobody wants a loser. *(re-iss.Aug88 on 'Charly')*

Apr 76. (7") **NOBODY WANTS A LOSER. / CADILLAC ASSEMBLY LINE**

Jun 76. (7') **GONNA MAKE IT SOMEHOW. / SENSATION, COMMUNICATION, TOGETHER**

— **MARVIN JENKING** – keyboards repl. PETERS / **JOE CLAYTON** – congas repl. ERRISON /

— **ROY GAINES + JAY GRAYDON** – guitar repl. WATSON + FENDER /

— **HAROLD MASON + PAUL HUMPHREY** – drums repl. GADSON / **ALEX BROWN** – vocals repl. JEANIE / **SCOTT EDWARDS + WILLIAM UPCHURCH** – bass repl. RAINEY /

— added **ERNIE FIELDS + HERMAN RILEY** – sax, flute / **BOB ZIMMITTI** – percussion / etc

Jan 77. (7") **GUITAR MAN. / RUB MY BACK**

Jan 77. (lp)(c) **ALBERT**

– Guitar man / I'm ready / Ain't nothing you can do / I don't care what my baby do / Change of pace / My babe / Running out of steam / Rub my back / (Ain't it) A real good sign. *(re-iss.Mar88 on 'Charly')*

Mar 77. (7") **AIN'T NOTHIN' YOU CAN DO. / I DON'T CARE WHAT MY BABY DO**

Mar 77. (d-lp) **ALBERT LIVE (live)**

– Watermelon man / Don't burn down the bridge / Blues at sunrise / That's what the blues is all about / Stormy Monday / Kansas city / I'm gonna call you as soon as the Sun goes down / Matchbox / Jam in a flat / As the years go passing by / Overall junction / I'll play the blues for you. *(re-iss.+c+cd Nov88 on 'Charly')*

not issued Tomato

1977. (lp)(c) **GREAT KING ALBERT**

– Love shock / You upset me baby / Chump chance / Let me rock you easy / Boot lace / Love mechanic / Call my job / Good time Charlie. *(UK-iss.+c+cd May88 on 'Tomato')*

— returned **DUNN, JACKSON + The MEMPHIS HORNS** to the fold, and recruited **BOBBY MANUEL, MICHAEL TOLES + VERNON BURCH** – guitar / **LESTER SNELL, MARVEL THOMAS + WINSTON STEWART** – keyboards / **WILLIE HALL** – drums / **EARL THOMAS** – bass

Stax Stax

1978. (lp)(c) **THE PINCH**

– The blues don't change / I'm doing fine / Nice to be nice / Oh, pretty woman / King of kings / Feel the need in me / Firing line / The pinch paid off (parts 1 & 2) / I can't stand the rain / Ain't it beautiful.

Dec 79. (7") **SANTA CLAUS WANTS SOME LOVIN'. / DON'T BURN DOWN THE BRIDGES**

Fantasy not issued

Nov 83. (lp)(c) **SAN FRANCISCO '83 (live)**

–

— now w / **ALLEN TOUSSAINT, ROBERT DABON + WARDELL QUEZERQUE** – piano / **GEORGE PORTER** – bass / **LEROY BREAUX, CHARLES WILLIAMS + JUNE GARDNER** – drums / **LEO NOCENTELLI** – guitar / **KENNETH WILLIAMS** – percussion

Charly Tomato

1984. (lp) **NEW ORLEANS HEAT**

– Get out of my life woman / Born under a bad sign / The feeling / We all wanna boogie / The very thought of you / I got the blues / I get evil / Angel of mercy / Flat time. *(re-iss.+cd Aug87)*

– compilations, etc. –

Nov 67. Polydor/ US= Stax; (lp) **TRAVELIN' TO CALIFORNIA**

– Travelin' to California / What can I do to change your mind / I get evil / Had I told you like it was / This morning / I walked all night long / Don't throw your love on me so strong / Let's have a natural ball / I've had nights by myself / This funny feeling / Ooh-lee baby / Dynaflow. *(re-iss.Jun88 on 'Bellaphon')*

Apr 69. Atlantic; (lp) **KING OF THE BLUES GUITAR**

– Cold feet / You're gonna need me / Born under a bad sign / (I love) Lucy / Crosscut saw / You sure drive a hard bargain / Oh, pretty woman / Overall junction / Funkshun / Laundromat blues / Personal manager.

1974. Chess; (lp) **DOOR BY DOOR** (w / OTIS RUSH; rec.1953 / 1960 /61)

(UK-iss.Oct88 on 'Vogue') (UK re-iss.+cd+c Sep90 on 'M.C.A.')

1986. Stax; (lp) **THE LOST SESSION** (rec.1971)

– She won't gimme no loving / Cold in hand / Stop lying / All the way down / Tell me what true love is / Down the road I go / Money lovin' women / Sun gone down (take 1) / Brand new razor / Sun gone down (take 2).

— above feat. **JOHN MAYALL** – producer, keyboards, harmonica, guitar / **ERNIE WATTS** – tenor sax / **RON SELICO** – drums / **LARRY TAYLOR** – bass / **LEE KING** – guitar / **CLIFF SOLOMON** – saxophones / **BLUE MITCHELL** – trumpet / **KEVIN** – keyboards

Mar 88. Stax; (lp)(c) **I'LL PLAY THE BLUES FOR YOU** – THE BEST OF . . .

– Born under a bad sign / Answer to the laundromat blues / You threw your love on me too strong / Crosscut saw / I'll play the blues for you (part 1) / Angel of mercy / Heart fixing business / Killing floor / The sky is crying / Going back to Luka / (I think I'm) Drowning on dry land (part 1) / That's what the blues is all about / Left hand woman (get right with me) / Driving wheel. *(cd-iss.Jan90 + Mar91)* (cd+=) – Firing line / Don't burn the bridge (cause you might wanna come back) / Can't you see what you're doing to me.

Nov 88. Stax; (lp) **BLUES AT SUNRISE**

(cd-iss.Sep92 on 'Demon' & Jun94 on 'Blues Encore')

May 91. Stax; (cd) **I'LL PLAY THE BLUES FOR YOU / LOVEJOY**

1979. Stax; (lp) **CHRONICLE (w / LITTLE MILTON on 1-side)**

Sep 90. Stax; (cd)(lp) **WEDNESDAY NIGHT IN SAN FRANCISCO (live)**

Oct 90. Stax; (cd)(lp) **THURSDAY NIGHT IN SAN FRANCISCO (live)**

Apr 84. Edsel; (lp) **LAUNDROMAT BLUES**

Apr 91. Essential; (cd)(c)(lp) **RED HOUSE**

Apr 93. Ace; (cd) **THE BLUES DON'T CHANGE** (rec.1973-74)

May 89. Charly; (cd) **VINTAGE BLUES (w / OTIS RUSH)**

Sep 92. Koch Int.; (cd) **THE BIG BLUES**

Oct 92. Tomato; (cd) **I'LL PLAY THE BLUES FOR YOU (w / JOHN LEE HOOKER)**

Aug 94. Tomato; (cd) **THE TOMATO YEARS**

Oct 95. Stax; (cd) **BLUES FOR YOU: THE BEST OF ALBERT KING**

Nov 95. Charly; (cd) **LIVE IN CANADA (live)**

B.B. KING

Born: RILEY KING, 16 Sep'25, Itta Bena, Mississippi, USA. In 1946, he moved to Memphis, where he gained spot on radio show. After being dubbed 'Blues Boy' (abbreviated to B.B.), he issued 1949 debut single 'MISS MARTHA KING', on local 'Bullet' label. The next year, BB was spotted by talent scout IKE TURNER, and was subsequently given deal with both 'Modern' & 'Kent' labels. His constant stage appearances helped him breakthrough in 1957 into US Hot 100. In the early 60's, he shifted to 'ABC-Paramount', and by '64, had US Top40 hit with 'ROCK ME BABY'. His most commercial period came between the late 60's and mid-'70's, when he notched up hit albums (his best were live) and a string of hit 45's, noteably: PAYING THE COST TO BE BOSS / THE THRILL IS GONE and GUESS WHO. • **Style:** Well-respected blues giant influenced by his cousin BUKKA WHITE. Crossed-over successfully to wider white audiences, due to blend of jazzy-R&B sound mixed with pure blues. • **Songwriters:** Writes own material originally with TAUBB. Covers; ? (John Lee Hooker) / LOVE ME TENDER (Elvis Presley) / ONE OF THOSE NIGHTS (Conway Twitty) / DON'T CHANGE ON ME (James Holiday & Edward Reeves) / LEGEND IN MY TIME (Don Gibson) / YOU'VE ALWAYS GOT THE BLUES + TIME IS A THIEF (Mickey Newbury) / NIGHTLIFE (Willie Nelson) / PLEASE SEND ME SOMEONE TO LOVE (Percy Mayfield) / YOU AND ME, ME AND YOU (Will Jennings) / SINCE I MET YOU BABY (Ivory Joe Hunter) / A WORLD I NEVER MADE (Doc Pomus & Dr.John) / YOU SHOOK ME (Willie Dixon) / PLAYIN' WITH MY FRIENDS (Robert Cray & T-Bone Walker) / YOU'RE THE BOSS (Lieber-Stoller) / etc. • **Trivia:** The LUCILLE album, was named after his personalized Gibson guitar. He gave it a cameo role, in the 1985 film 'Into The Night'. Two years later he appeared in the film 'Amazon Women On The Moon'.

Recommended: 20 BLUES GREATS (*8)

B.B. KING – vocals, guitar

not issued Bullet

1949. (78) **MISS MARTHA KING. / WHEN YOUR BABY PACKS UP AND GOES**

Note: All release dates in the 50's & 60's are approximate guesses, through working out dates / years of session recordings relating to catalogue numbers.

1949. (78) **GOT THE BLUES. / TAKE A SWING WITH ME**

not issued R.P.M.

Oct 50. (78) **MISTREATED WOMAN. / B.B.'S BOOGIE**

Jan 51. (78) **THE OTHER NIGHT BLUES. / WALKIN' AND CRYIN'**

B.B.KING & HIS ORCHESTRA

Mar 51. (78) **MY BABY'S GONE. / DON'T WANT A MAN LIKE ME**

Jun 51. (78) **SHE'S DYNAMITE. / B.B.'S BLUES**

Sep 51. (78) **SHE'S A MEAN WOMAN. / HARD WORKING WOMAN**

Dec 51. (78) **3 O'CLOCK BLUES. / THAT AIN'T THE WAY TO DO IT**

Mar 52. (78) **SHE DON'T MOVE ME NO MORE. / FINE LOOKING WOMAN**

May 52. (78) **MY OWN FAULT DARLIN'. / SHAKE IT UP AND GO**

Jul 52. (78) **SOME DAY SOME WHERE. / GOTTA FIND MY BABY**

Sep 52. (78) **YOU KNOW I LOVE YOU. / YOU DIDN'T WANT ME**

Nov 52. (78) **STORY FROM MY HEART AND SOUL. / BOOGIE WOOGIE WOMAN**

Jan 53. (78) **DON'T HAVE TO CRY (PAST DAY). / WOKE UP THIS MORNING (MY BABY WAS GONE)**

Mar 53. (78) **PLEASE LOVE ME. / HIGHWAY BOUND**

May 53. (78) **NEIGHBORHOOD AFFAIR. / PLEASE HURRY HOME**

Jul 53. (78) **WHY DID YOU LEAVE ME. / BLIND LOVE (WHO CAN YOUR GOOD MAN BE)**

Sep 53. (78) **PRAYING TO THE LORD. / PLEASE HELP ME**

B.B. "BLUES BOY" KING & HIS ORCHESTRA

(same label)

Nov 53. (78) **I LOVE YOU BABY. / THE WOMAN I LOVE** [-] [ ]
Jan 54. (78) **EVERYTHING I DO IS WRONG. / DON'T YOU WANT A MAN LIKE ME** [-] [ ]
Feb 54. (78) **WHEN MY HEART BEATS LIKE A HAMMER. / BYE! BYE! BABY** [-] [ ]
1954. (78) **YOU UPSET ME BABY. / WHOLE LOT OF LOVIN'** [-] [ ]
1955. (78) **EVERYDAY I HAVE THE BLUES. / SNEAKIN' AROUND** [-] [ ]
1955. (78) **JUMP WITH YOU BABY. / LONELY AND BLUE** [-] [ ]
1955. (78) **SHUT YOUR MOUTH. / I'M IN LOVE** [-] [ ]
1955. (78) **WHAT CAN I DO (JUST SING THE BLUES). / TEN LONG YEARS (I HAD A WOMAN)** [-] [ ]
Feb 56. (78) **I'M CRACKING UP OVER YOU. / RUBY LEE** [-] [ ]
Mar 56. (78) **SIXTEEN TONS. / CRYING WON'T HELP YOU** [-] [ ]
May 56. (78) **DID YOU EVER LOVE A WOMAN. / LET'S DO THE BOOGIE** [-] [ ]
Jun 56. (78) **DARK IS THE NIGHT. / (part 2)** [-] [ ]
Sep 56. (78) **SWEET LITTLE ANGEL. / BAD LUCK** [-] [ ]
Feb 57. (78) **ON MY WORD OF HONOUR. / BIM BAM** [-] [ ]
Apr 57. (78) **EARLY IN THE MORNING. / YOU DON'T KNOW** [-] [ ]
May 57. (78) **HOW DO I LOVE YOU. / YOU CAN'T FOOL MY HEART** [-] [ ]
Jun 57. (78) **I WANT TO GET MARRIED. / TROUBLES TROUBLES (TROUBLES)** [-] [ ]
Jul 57. (78) **BE CAREFUL WITH A FOOL. / (I'M GONNA) QUIT MY BABY** [-] [95]
Oct 57. (78) **I NEED YOU SO BAD. / I WONDER** [-] [85]
Dec 57. (78) **THE KEY TO MY KINGDOM. / MY HEART BELONGS TO YOU** [-] [ ]

not issued Kent (45's) Crown (lp's)

1958. (lp) **SINGING THE BLUES** (compilation) [-] [ ]
– 3 o'clock blues / You know I love you / Woke up this morning / Please love me / You upset me baby / Everyday I have the blues / Ten years long (I had a woman) / Did you ever love a woman / Crying won't help you / Sweet little angel / Bad luck.

1958. (lp) **THE BLUES** (compilation) [-] [ ]
– Boogie woogie woman / Don't have to cry (past day) / Don't you want a man like me / When my heart beats like a hammer / What can I do (just sing the blues) / Ruby Lee / Early in the morning / I want to get married / Troubles troubles / Why does everything happen to me.

Sep 58. (7") **WHY DOES EVERYTHING HAPPEN TO ME. / YOU KNOW I GO FOR IT** [-] [ ]
Nov 58. (7") **DON'T LOOK NOW, BUT I'VE GOT THE BLUES. / DAYS OF OLD** [-] [ ]
Feb 59. (7"-B.B.KING & THE VOCAL CHORDS-) **PLEASE ACCEPT MY LOVE. / YOU'VE BEEN AN ANGEL** [-] [ ]
1959. (lp) **WAILS** [-] [ ]
– Tomorrow is another day / We can't make it / I've got papers on you baby (do what I say) / Sweet thing / Treat me right (oh baby) / Time to say goodbye / I love you so / The woman I love / The fool (a fool too long) / Come by here

B.B. KING

(same label)

Aug 59. (7") **I AM. / WHY WORRY** [-] [ ]
Sep 59. (7") **COME BY HERE. / THE FOOL (A FOOL TOO LONG)** [-] [ ]
Oct 59. (7") **A LONELY LOVER'S PLEA. / THE WOMAN I LOVE** [-] [ ]
Nov 59. (7") **EVERYDAY I HAVE THE BLUES. / TIME TO SAY GOODBYE** [-] [ ]
(above 'A'side featured members of The COUNT BASIE BAND)
Dec 59. (7") **MEAN OLE FRISCO. / SUGAR MAMA** [-] [ ]
Jan 60. (7") **SWEET SIXTEEN. / (part 2)** [-] [ ]
Feb 60. (lp) **SWEET SIXTEEN (B.B.KING)** (compilation) [-] [ ]
– Sweet sixteen (parts 1 & 2) / Days old old / Be careful with a fool / (I'm gonna) Quit my baby / What can I do (just sing the blues) / Ten long years (I had a woman) / I was blind / Whole lotta lovin' / Someday baby.

Feb 60. (7") **(I'VE) GOT A RIGHT TO LOVE MY BABY. / MY OWN FAULT** [-] [ ]
Mar 60. (7") **CRYING WON'T HELP YOU. / PLEASE LOVE ME** [-] [ ]
Apr 60. (7") **BLIND LOVE (WHO CAN YOUR GOOD MAN BE). / YOU UPSET ME BABY** [-] [ ]
May 60. (7") **TEN LONG YEARS (I HAD A WOMAN). / EVERYDAY I HAVE THE BLUES** [-] [ ]
Jun 60. (7") **WOKE UP THIS MORNING (MY BABY WAS GONE). / SWEET LITTLE ANGEL** [-] [ ]
(above 4 singles were recorded between 1953-56)
Jul 60. (7") **GOOD MAN GONE BAD. / PARTIN' TIME** [-] [ ]
Aug 60. (lp) **KING OF THE BLUES** [-] [ ]
– (I've) Got a right to love my baby / Good man gone bad / Partin' time / Long nights (the feeling they call the blues) / I'll survive / What a way to go / Feel like a million / If I lost you / You're on top / I'm king. *(UK-iss.1976 on 'MfP')*

Sep 60. (7") **YOU DONE LOST YOUR GOOD THING NOW. / WALKING DR.BILL** [-] [ ]
Oct 60. (7") **THINGS ARE NOT THE SAME. / FISHIN' AFTER ME (CATFISH BLUES)** [-] [ ]
Nov 60. (7") **GET OUT OF HERE. / BAD LUCK SOUL** [-] [ ]
Jan 61. (lp) **MY KIND OF BLUES** [-] [ ]
– You done lost your good thing now / Walking Dr.Bill / Fishin' after me (catfish blues) / Hold that train / Understand / Someday baby / Mr.Pawnbroker / Driving wheel / My own fault (baby) / Please set a date.

Feb 61. (7") **HOLD THAT TRAIN. / UNDERSTAND** [-] [ ]
Jun 61. (7") **PEACE OF MIND. / SOMEDAY BABY** [-] [ ]
Jul 61. (lp) **MORE B.B.KING** [-] [ ]
– My reward / Don't cry anymore / You're breaking my heart / Blues for me (groovin' twist) / Just like a woman (rockin' twist) / Bad case of love / Bad luck soul / Get out of here / Shut your mouth.

Oct 61. (7") **BAD CASE OF LOVE. / YOU'RE BREAKING MY HEART** [-] [ ]
Nov 61. (lp) **TWIST WITH B.B.KING** (compilation recent & old) [-] [ ]
Feb 62. (lp) **EASY LISTENING BLUES** [-] [ ]
– Hully gully (twist) / Easy listening (blues) / Blues for me / Slow walk (slow burn) / Shoutin' the blues / Night long / Confessin' / Don't touch / Rambler / Walkin'.

Mar 62. (7") **HULLY GULLY (TWIST). / GONNA MISS YOU AROUND HERE** [-] [ ]
1962. (lp) **BLUES FOR ME** [-] [ ]
– Got 'em bad / I can't explain / You're gonna miss me / Troubles don't last / Strange things / Down hearted / So many days / I need you baby / The wrong road / The letter / You never know / Sundown / You won't listen.

H.M.V. ABC Para.

Apr 62. (7") **YOU ASK ME. / I'M GONNA SIT IN TILL YOU GIVE IN** [-] [ ]
Jun 62. (7") **BLUES AT MIDNIGHT. / MY BABY'S COMIN' HOME** [-] [ ]
Sep 62. (7") **SNEAKIN' AROUND. / CHAINS OF LOVE** [-] [ ]
Nov 62. (7") **TOMORROW NIGHT. / A MOTHER'S LOVE** [-] [ ]
1963. (lp) **MR.BLUES** [-] [ ]
– Young dreamers / By myself / Chains of love / A mother's love / Blues at midnight / Sneakin' around / On my word of honor / Tomorrow night / My baby's comin' home / Guess who / You ask me / I'm gonna sit in 'til you give in.

Mar 63. (7") **GUESS WHO. / BY MYSELF** [-] [ ]
Jun 63. (7") **YOUNG DREAMERS. / ON MY WORD OF HONOR** [-] [ ]
Oct 63. (7") **HOW DO I LOVE YOU. / SLOWLY LOSING MY MIND** [-] [ ]
Feb 64. (7") **HOW BLUE CAN YOU GET. / PLEASE ACCEPT MY LOVE** [-] [97]
May 64. (7") **HELP THE POOR. / I WOULDN'T HAVE IT ANY OTHER WAY** [-] [98]
Jul 64. (7") **THE HURT. / WHOLE LOTTA LOVIN'** [-] [ ]
Oct 64. (7") **NEVER TRUST A WOMAN. / WORRYIN' BLUES** [-] [90]
Dec 64. (7") **STOP LEADING ON ME. / PLEASE SEND ME SOMEONE TO LOVE** [-] [ ]
Feb 65. (7") **IT'S MY OWN FAULT. / EVERYDAY I HAVE THE BLUES** [-] [ ]
Apr 65. (7") **TIRED OF YOUR JIVE. / NIGHT OWL** [-] [ ]
Jun 65. (7") **ALL OVER AGAIN. / THE THINGS YOU PUT ME THROUGH** [-] [ ]
Jul 65. (lp) **LIVE AT THE REGAL (live in Chicago 1964)** [ ] [ ]
– Everyday (I have the blues) / Sweet little angel / It's my own fault / How blue can you get / Please love me / You upset me baby / Worry, worry / Woke up this mornin' / You done lost you good thing / Help the poor. *(re-iss.Sep 71 + 1978) (re-iss.Oct83 on 'Ace') (cd-iss.Dec94 on 'B.G.O.')*

Aug 65. (7") **I'D RATHER DRINK MUDDY WATER. / GOIN' TO CHICAGO BLUES** [-] [ ]
Mar 66. (lp) **CONFESSIN' THE BLUES** [ ] [ ]
– See see rider / Do you call that a buddy / Wee baby blues / I'd rather drink muddy water / In the dark / Confessin' the blues / Goin' to Chicago blues / I'm gonna move to the outskirts of town / World of trouble / How long blues / Cherry red / Please send me someone to love. *(re-iss.1977 on 'A.B.C.')*

Jun 66. (7") **TORMENTED. / YOU'RE STILL A SQUARE** [-] [ ]
Dec 66. (7") **DON'T ANSWER THE DOOR. / (part 2)** [ ] [72] Oct 66
Jan 67. (lp) **BLUES IS KING** [ ] [-]
– Waitin' on you / Gambler's blues / Tired of your jive / Night life / Buzz me / Don't answer the door / Blind love / I know what you're puttin' down / Baby get lost / Gonna keep on loving you. *(re-iss.1977 on 'ABC') (cd-iss.Jul92 on 'BGO', with extra track)*

1967. (7") **NIGHT LIFE. / WAITIN' ON YOU** [ ] [ ]

Stateside Bluesway

Jul 67. (lp) **BLUES ON TOP OF BLUES** [ ] [ ]
1967. (7") **THINK IT OVER. / MEET MY HAPPINESS** [-] [ ]
1967. (7") **I DON'T WANT YOU CUTTIN' YOUR HAIR. / THINK IT OVER** [ ] [-]
1967. (7") **WORRIED DREAM. / THAT'S WRONG LITTLE MAMA** [-] [ ]
1967. (7") **HEARTBREAKER. / RAINING IN MY HEART** [-] [ ]
1968. (7") **SWEET SIXTEEN. / (part 2)** [-] [ ]
May 68. (7") **PAYING THE COST TO BE THE BOSS. / HAVING MY SAY** [ ] [39] Feb 68
Jun 68. (7") **I'M GONNA DO WHAT THEY DO TO ME. / LOSING FAITH IN YOU** [-] [74]
– Heartbreaker / Losing faith in you / Dance with me / That's wrong little mama / Having my say / I'm not wanted anymore / Worried dream / Paying the cost to be the boss / Until I found you / I'm gonna do what they do to me / Raining in my heart / Now that you've lost me. *(re-iss.1977 on 'A.B.C.') (re-iss.+cd.1989 on 'B.G.O.')*

Sep 68. (7") **THE B.B. JONES. / YOU PUT IT ON ME** [ ] [98] [82]
Dec 68. (7") **DANCE WITH ME. / PLEASE SEND ME SOMEONE TO LOVE** [-] [ ]

—— (below feat. musicians **The MAXWELL DAVIS BAND**

Jan 69. (lp) **LUCILLE** [ ] [ ] Oct 68
– Lucille / You move me so / Country girl / No money no luck / I need your love / Rainin' all the time / I'm with you / Stop putting the hurt on me / Watch yourself *(re-iss.1977 on 'A.B.C.') (cd-iss.Feb89 on 'BGO')*

Feb 69. (7") **DON'T WASTE MY TIME. / GET MYSELF SOMEBODY** [ ] [ ]
Mar 69. (lp) **THE ELECTRIC B.B.KING** (compilation) [ ] [ ]
– Tired of your jive / Don't answer the door / B.B.Jones / All over again / Paying the cost to the boss / Think it over / I done got wise / Meet my happiness / Sweet sixteen / You put it on me / I don't want you cuttin' off your hair. *(re-iss.1977 on 'A.B.C.') (re-iss.+cd Jan89 on 'BGO')*

Apr 69. (7") **WHY I SING THE BLUES. / FRIENDS** [-] [61]
Jun 69. (7") **GET OFF MY BACK WOMAN. / I WANT YOU SO BAD** [-] [74]
Jun 69. (lp) **LIVE AND WELL (half live)** [ ] [56]

– Don't answer the door / Just a little love / My mood / Sweet little angel / Please accept my love / I want you so bad / Friends / Get off my back woman / Let's get down to business / Why I sing the blues. *(US cd-iss.Jun88 on 'M.C.A.') (cd-iss.Jul94 on 'B.G.O.')*

Sep 69. (7") **EVERYDAY I HAVE THE BLUES. / FIVE LONG YEARS** – | –

—— (above iss.UK on 'Blue Horizon')

Oct 69. (7") **JUST A LITTLE LOVE. / MY MOOD** – | 76

Feb 70. (7") **THE THRILL IS GONE. / YOU'RE MEAN** | 15 Jan 70

Feb 70. (lp) **COMPLETELY WELL** | 38 Dec 69

– The thrill is gone / So excited / No good / You're losing me / What happened / Confessin' the blues / Key to my kingdom / Crying won't help you now / You're mean. *(re-iss.1977 on 'A.B.C.') (cd-iss.Jul87 on 'M.C.A.')*

May 70. (7") **SO EXCITED. / CONFESSIN' THE BLUES** | 54 Mar 70

Probe | A.B.C.

Aug 70. (7") **HUMMINGBIRD. / ASK ME NO QUESTIONS** | 48 Jun 70

Oct 70. (7") **CHAINS AND THINGS. / KING'S SPECIAL** – | 45

Nov 70. (lp) **INDIANOLA MISSISSIPPI SEEDS** | 26 Oct 70

– Nobody loves me but my mother / You're still my woman / Ask me no questions / Until I'm dead and cold / King's special / Ain't gonna worry my life anymore / Chains and things / Go underground / Hummingbird. *(re-iss.1977) (re-iss.+c.May88 on 'Castle') (cd-iss.Apr95 on 'BGO')*

Feb 71. (7") **ASK ME NO QUESTIONS. / NOBODY LOVES ME BUT MY MOTHER** – | 40

Mar 71. (lp)(c) **LIVE IN COOK COUNTY JAIL (live)** | 25 Feb 71

– Every day I have the blues / How blues can you get / Worry, worry, worry / 3 o'clock blues / Darlin' you know I love you / Sweet sixteen / The thrill is gone / Please accept my love. *(re-iss.Oct87, US cd-iss.Jun88)*

Jun 71. (7") **HELP THE POOR. / LUCILLE'S GRANNY** – | 90

Aug 71. (7") **GHETTO WOMAN. / SEVEN MINUTES** – | 68

—— below feat. **RINGO STARR, DR.JOHN, ALEXIS KORNER + STEVE MARRIOTT**

Oct 71. (lp)(c) **B.B.KING IN LONDON** | 57

– Introduction / Every day I have the blues / Night life / Love the life I'm living / When it all comes down (I'll still be around) / I've got a right to give up livin' / Encore. *(re-iss.1977 on 'A.B.C.') (re-iss.Apr84 on 'M.C.A.') (cd-iss.Oct89 on 'BGO')*

Oct 71. (7") **AIN'T NOBODY HOME. / ALEXI'S BOOGIE** – | 46

Feb 72. (7") **SWEET SIXTEEN. / I'VE BEEN BLUE TOO LONG** – | 93

Feb 72. (lp)(c) **L.A. MIDNIGHT** | 53

– I got some help I don't need help / The poor / Can't you hear me talking to you / Midnight / Sweet sixteen / I believe (I've been blue too long) / Lucille's granny.

May 72. (7") **I GOT SOME HELP I DON'T NEED IT. / LUCILLE'S GRANNY** – | 92

Aug 72. (7") **GUESS WHO. / BETTER LOVIN' MAN** – | 62

Aug 72. (lp)(c) **GUESS WHO** | 65

– Summer in the city / Just can't please you / Any other way / You don't know nothin' about love / Found what I need / Neighborhood affair / It takes a young girl / Better lovin' man / Guess who / Shouldn't have left me / Five long years *(re-iss.+cd.May89 on 'B.G.O.')*

Oct 72. (7") **FIVE LONG YEARS. / SUMMER IN THE CITY** – |

Jul 73. (7") **TO KNOW YOU IS TO LOVE YOU. / I CAN'T LEAVE** | 38

Aug 73. (lp)(c) **TO KNOW YOU IS TO LOVE YOU** | 71

– I like to live the love / Respect yourself / Who are you / Love / I can't leave / To know you is to love you / Thank you for loving the blues / Oh to me. *(re-iss,Oct74 on 'A.B.C.')*

Jan 74. (7") **I LIKE TO LIVE THE LOVE. / LOVE** | 28

A.B.C. | A.B.C.

Aug 74. (7") **WHO ARE YOU. / OH TO ME** | 78 Jun 74

Aug 74. (lp)(c) **FRIENDS**

– Friends / I got them blues / Baby I'm yours / Up at 5 a.m. / Philadelphia / When everything else is gone / My song. *re-iss.1977) (re-iss.+cd.Sep91 on 'B.G.O.')*

Oct 74. (7") **PHILADELPHIA. / UP AT 5 P.M.** | 64

Nov 74. (d-lp)(c) **TOGETHER FOR THE FIRST TIME ... LIVE (live "with BOBBY BLAND")** | 43

– Introduction / 3 o'clock in the morning / It's my own fault baby / Driftin' blues / That's the way love is / I'm sorry / I'll take care of you / Don't cry no more / Don't want a soul hangin' around / Medley / Everybody wants to know why I sing the blues / Goin' down slow / I like to live the love. *(cd-iss.Sep89 on 'M.C.A.')*

(above originally issued UK 'Anchor' / US 'Dunhill')

Jan 75. (7") **FRIENDS. / MY SONG** – |

Sep 75. (7") **HAVE FAITH. / WHEN I'M WRONG** – |

Oct 75. (lp)(c) **LUCILLE TALKS BACK**

– Lucille talks back (copulation) / Breaking up somebody's home / Reconsider baby / Don't make me pay for his mistakes / When I'm wrong / I know the price / Have faith / Everybody lies a little.

Jul 76. (lp)(c) **TOGETHER AGAIN ... LIVE (live "with BOBBY BLAND")** | 73

– Let the good times roll / Strange things happen / Feel so bad / Mother-in-law blues / Mean old world / Everyday (I have the blues) / The thrill is gone / I ain't gonna be the first to cry.
(iss.on 'Impulse' UK/US as was below 2 singles w/ BOBBY BLAND)

1976. (7") **LET THE GOOD TIMES ROLL. / STRANGE HINGS HAPPEN** – |

1976. (7") **EVERYDAY (I HAVE THE BLUES). / THE THRILL IS GONE** – |

Feb 77. (lp)(c) **KINGSIZE**

– Confessin' the blues / Paying the cost to be the boss / Think it over / You move me so / Heartbreaker / I'm gonna do what they do to me / What happened / By myself / That's wrong little mama / How long, how long blues / I'm not wanted anymore / My baby's comin' home.

1977. (7") **I WONDER WHY. / SLOW AND EASY** – |

1977. (7") **LET ME MAKE YOU CRY A LITTLE LONGER. / NEVER MADE A MOVE TOO SOON** – |

Mar 78. (7") **I JUST CAN'T LEAVE YOUR LOVE ALONE. / ?**

Apr 78. (lp)(c) **MIDNIGHT BELIEVER**

– When it all comes down / Midnight believer / I just can't leave your love alone / Hold on (I feel our love is changing) / Never make a move too soon / A world full of strangers / Let me make you cry a little longer. *(re-iss.Jun84 on 'M.C.A.', cd-iss.May90)*

Jun 78. (7") **HOLD ON (I FEEL OUR LOVE IS CHANGING). / MIDNIGHT BELIEVER**

M.C.A. | M.C.A.

Aug 79. (7") **BETTER NOT LOOK DOWN. / HAPPY BIRTHDAY BLUES**

Aug 79. (lp)(c) **TAKE IT HOME** 60 |

– Better not look down / Same old story / Happy birthday blues / I've always been lonely / Second hand woman / Tonight I'm gonna make you a star / The beginning of the end / A story everybody knows / Take it home. *(re-iss.Feb84)*

Oct 79. (7") **TAKE IT HOME. / SAME OLD STORY**

Apr 80. (d-lp)(c) **NOW APPEARING AT OLE MISS (live)**

– B.B.King theme / Caledonia / Don't answer the door / You done lost your good thing now / I need love so bad / Nobody loves me but my mother / Hold on (I feel our love is changing) / I got some outside help (I don't really need) / Darlin' you know I love you / When I'm wrong / The thrill is gone / Never made a move too soon / Three o'clock in the morning / Rock me baby / Guess who / I just can't leave your love alone. *(re-iss.Oct81 + Feb86)*

May 80. (7") **CALEDONIA (live). / ROCK ME BABY (live)**

Feb 81. (7") **THERE MUST BE A BETTER WORLD SOMEWHERE. / YOU'RE GOING WITH ME** – |

Feb 81. (lp)(c) **THERE MUST BE A BETTER WORLD SOMEWHERE**

– Life ain't nothing but a party / Born again human / There must be a better world somewhere / The victim / More, more, more / You're going with me. *(re-iss.+cd.Sep91 on 'B.G.O.')*

Apr 82. (7") **LEGEND IN MY TIME. / LOVE ME TENDER**

Apr 82. (lp)(c) **LOVE ME TENDER**

– One of these nights / Love me tender / Don't change on me / (I'd be) A legend in my time / You've always got the blues / Please send me someone to love / You and me, me and you / Since I met you baby / Time is a thief / A world I never made.

Jun 82. (7") **ONE OF THESE NIGHTS. / SINCE I MET YOU BABY**

augmented The CRUSADERS and The Royal Philharmonic Orchestra on the 'Street Life' single.

Sep 82. (7") **LOVE ME TENDER. / THE WORD I NEVER MADE** – |

Jul 83. (7") **INFLATION BLUES. / SELL MY MONKEY** – |

Jul 83. (lp)(c) **BLUES'N'JAZZ** | Jun 83

– Inflation blues / Broken hearted / Sell my monkey / Heed my warning / Teardrops from my eyes / Rainbow riot / Darlin' you know I love you / I can't let you go. *(re-iss.Oct87)*

Jul 85. (7") **INTO THE NIGHT. / CENTURY CITY CHASE**

(12"+=) – Midnight believer.

Sep 85. (lp)(c) **SIX SILVER STRINGS**

– Sirings / Big boss man / In the midnight hour / Into the night / My Lucille / Memory lane / My guitar sings the blues / Double trouble. *(US cd-iss.Jun88)*

Sep 85. (7") **MY LUCILLE. / Keep It Light (by Thelma Houston)** – |

Nov 85. (7") **BIG BOSS MAN. / MY GUITAR SINGS THE BLUES** – |

Feb 86. (7") **SIX SILVER STRINGS. / MEMORY LANE** – |

Mar 87. (7") **STANDING ON THE EDGE OF LOVE. / DON'T TELL ME NOTHING**

(12"+=) – Let yourself in for it.

Sep 87. (7") **IN THE MIDNIGHT HOUR. / HEED MY WARNING**

Jan 89. (7") **GO ON. / LAY ANOTHER LOG ON THE FIRE** – |

Feb 89. (lp)(c)(cd) **KING OF THE BLUES 1989**

– (You've become a) Habit to me / Drowning in the sea of love / Can't get enough / Standing on the edge / Go on / Let's straighten it out / Change in your lovin' / Undercover man / Lay another log on the fire / Business with my baby tonight.

—— (Apr89), BB was credited on U2's UK Top10 hit 'WHEN LOVE COMES TO TOWN'.

Aug 89. (7") **AIN'T NOBODY HOME. / LAY ANOTHER LOG ON THE FIRE**

(12"+=)(cd-s+=) – Standing On The Edge

Oct 91. (cd)(c)(lp) **THERE IS ALWAYS ONE MORE TIME**

– I'm moving on / Back in L.A. / The blues come over me / Fool me once / The lowdown / Mean and evil / Something up my sleeve / Roll, roll, roll / There is always one more time.

Feb 92. (c-s) **THE BLUES COME OVER ME (wild & bluesy club mix) / ('A'-integrity mix)** – |

Jul 93. (cd)(c) **BLUES SUMMIT**

– Playin' with my friends / Since I met you baby / I pity the fool / You shook me / Something you got / There's something on your mind / Call it stormy Monday / You're the boss / We're gonna make it / Medley: I gotta move out of this neighborhood – Nobody loves me but my mother / Little by little / Everybody had the blues.

G.R.P. | G.R.P.

Nov 93. (cd-s) **MERRY CHRISTMAS BABY. ("B.B.KING / PHILIP BENT & TONY REMY / DIANE SCHUUR" / ?**

– compilations, others, etc. –

1959. Modern; (7") **CRYING WON'T HELP YOU. / PLEASE LOVE ME** – |

1959. Modern; (7") **WOKE UP THIS MORNING (MY BABY WAS GONE). / BAD CASE OF LOVE** – |

1960. Modern; (7") **EVERYDAY I HAVE THE BLUES. / TIME TO SAY GOODBYE** – |

1960. Modern; (7") **DID YOU EVER LOVE A WOMAN. / 3 O'CLOCK BLUES** – |

1960. Modern; (7") **YOU UPSET ME BABY. / WHEN MY HEART BEATS LIKE A HAMMER** – |

1961. Modern; (7") **TEN LONG YEARS (I HAD A WOMAN). / YOU KNOW I LOVE YOU** – |

1962. Modern; (7") **BLUES STAY AWAY. / EYESIGHT TO THE BLIND** – |

1962. Kent; (lp) **ROCK ME BABY** – |

– You know I love you / Bad case of love / You upset me baby / Rock me baby / Woke up this morning / 3 o'clock blues / When my heart beats like a hammer / Sweet sixteen / Ten long years / Sneakin' around / Every day I have the blues / Sweet little angel / Please love me. *(re-iss.Jun64 on 'United')*

1962. Kent; (lp) **LET ME LOVE YOU** – |

– You're gonna miss me / I'm gonna quit my baby / Come by here / Whole lotta lovin' / I've got a right to love my baby / I can't explain / Walking Dr. Bill / Hold that train / Let me love you / Driving wheel / Did you ever love a woman / Troubles don't last.

1963. Kent; (7") **MASHED POTATO TIME. / 3 O'CLOCK STOMP** [-] [ ]
1963. Kent; (7") **MASHING TO POPEYE. / TELL ME BABY** [-] [ ]
1963. Kent; (7") **WHEN MY HEART BEATS LIKE A HAMMER. / GOING DOWN SLOW** [-] [ ]
1963. Kent; (lp) **LIVE (live)** [-] [ ]
(also iss.US on 'United')
Nov 63. Kent; (7") **3 O'CLOCK BLUES. / YOUR LETTER** [-] [ ]
Dec 63. Kent; (7") **CHRISTMAS CELEBRATION. / EASY LISTENING (BLUES)** [-] [ ]
(re-iss.Nov64, hit US special Christmas Top 20)
Jan 64. Kent; (7") **DOWN NOW. / WHOLE LOTTA LOVIN'** [-] [ ]
Feb 64. Kent; (7") **THE ROAD I TRAVEL. / MY REWARD** [-] [ ]
Mar 64. Kent; (7") **THE LETTER. / YOU NEVER KNOW** [ ] [ ]
(above iss.UK Apr65 on 'Sue')
1964. Kent; (lp) **PURE SOUL** [-] [ ]
Apr 64. Kent; (7"-B.B. KING with The CHARIOTEERS-) **PRECIOUS LORD. / ARMY OF THE LORD** [-] [ ]
May 64. Kent; (7") **ROCK ME BABY. / I CAN'T LOSE** [ ] [34]
(also iss.US on 'Modern')

Note all below released on 'Kent'.

Jul 64. (7") **LET ME LOVE YOU. / YOU'RE GONNA MISS ME** [-] [ ]
Oct 64. (7") **BEAUTICIAN BLUES. / I CAN HEAR MY NAME** [-] [82]
Feb 65. (7") **THE WORST THING IN MY LIFE. / GOT 'EM BAD** [-] [ ]
Apr 64. (7") **PLEASE LOVE ME. / BABY LOOK AT YOU** [-] [ ]
Jun 65. (7") **BLUE SHADOWS. / AND LIKE THAT** [-] [97]
Aug 65. (7") **WHY DOES EVERYTHING HAPPEN TO ME. / JUST A DREAM** [-] [ ]
Nov 65. (7") **BROKEN PROMISE. / HAVE MERCY BABY** [-] [ ]
Mar 66. (7") **EYESIGHT TO THE BLIND. / JUST LIKE A WOMAN (ROCKIN' TWIST)** [-] [ ]
May 66. (7") **FIVE LONG YEARS. / LOVE HONOR AND BABY** [-] [ ]
Jun 66. (7") **AIN'T NOBODY'S BUSINESS. / I WONDER WHY** [-] [ ]
Aug 66. (7") **I STAY IN THE MOOD. / EARLY EVERY MORNING** [-] [ ]
Nov 66. (7") **BLUES STAY AWAY. / IT'S A MEAN WORLD** [-] [ ]
Dec 66. (lp) **THE JUNGLE** [-] [ ]
– The jungle / Eyesight to the blind / Ain't nobody's business / Five long years / Blue shadows / Worst thing in my life / Blues stay away / Beautician blues / I stay in the mood / I can hear my name / Got 'em bad / It's a mean world.
Mar 67. (7") **THE JUNGLE. / LONG GONE BABY** [-] [94]
1967. (7") **BAD BREAKS. / GROWING OLD** [-] [ ]
1967s. (lp) **BOSS OF THE BLUES** [-] [ ]
1967. (d-lp) **FROM THE BEGINNING** [-] [ ]
1967. (lp) **UNDERGROUND BLUES** [-] [ ]
1968. (lp) **THE INCREDIBLE SOUL OF B.B.KING** [-] [ ]
(UK-iss.Apr70 on 'Polydor')
1968. (7") **WHY DOES EVERYTHING HAPPEN TO ME. / WORRY WORRY** [-] [ ]
1968. (lp) **TURN ON WITH B.B. KING** [-] [ ]
1968. (lp) **GREATEST HITS VOL.1** [-] [ ]
Sep 68. Blue Horizon/ US= Kent; (7") **THE WOMAN I LOVE. / YOU PUT IT ON ME** [-] [94]
1969. (lp) **BETTER THAN EVER** [-] [ ]
1969. (lp) **DOING MY THING LORD** [-] [ ]
1969. (lp) **B.B. KING LIVE (live)** [-] [ ]
1969. (lp) **THE ORIGINAL SWEET SIXTEEN** [-] [ ]
1969. (7") **YOUR FOOL. / SHOUTING THE BLUES** [-] [ ]
1970. (lp) **ON STAGE LIVE (live)** [-] [ ]
1970. (lp) **THE SOUL OF B.B. KING** [-] [ ]
(most of lp's above were also iss.on 'United', above only also on 'Custom' & 'Festival')
Apr 71. (7") **THAT EVIL CHILD. / HELP THE POOR** [-] [97]
1967. Crown Ember; (lp) **R & B SOUL** [ ] [-]
1968. Blue Horizon; (lp) **THE B.B.KING STORY** [ ] [-]
1969. Blue Horizon; (lp) **THE B.B.KING STORY, CHAPTER TWO** [ ] [-]
(both above re-iss.US Jul88 on'Joker')
1971. Blue Horizon; (lp) **TAKE A SWING WITH ME** [ ] [-]
Sep 71. ABC; (lp) **LIVE AT THE REGAL live 1964)** [ ] [78]
Feb 73. ABC; (lp)(c) **THE BEST OF B.B.KING** [ ] [ ]
(re-iss.Oct74) (re-iss.Jan83 on 'Fame') (re-iss.+cd.1987 on 'Ace')
1976. ABC; (lp)(c) **B.B.KING ANTHOLOGY** [ ] [ ]
1977. ABC; (lp)(c) **CLASSICS REVISITED** [ ] [ ]
1977. ABC; (lp)(c) **MR.BLUES** [ ] [ ]
1973. Bluesway; (lp) **BACK IN THE ALLEY** [-] [ ]
Nov 87. MCA; (lp)(c) **INTRODUCING B.B.KING** [ ] [ ]
(cd-iss.Apr89)
Sep 90. MCA; (cd)(c)(lp) **LIVE AT SAN QUENTIN (live 1970)** [ ] [ ]
(re-iss.cd+c Sep94)
Nov 92. MCA; (4xcd-box)(4xc-box) **KING OF THE BLUES** [ ] [ ]
Aug 93. MCA; (cd)(c) **KING OF THE BLUES 1989** [ ] [ ]
1974. New World; (lp) **B.B.KING VOLUME 1** [ ] [-]
1974. New World; (lp) **B.B.KING VOLUME 2** [ ] [-]
May 81. Ace; (7") **BIM BAM. / SHAKE HOLLER AND RUN** [ ] [-]
Jan 85. Ace; (c) **THE BEST OF MEMPHIS MASTERS** [ ] [-]
Aug 86. Ace; (lp)(c)(cd) **SPOTLIGHT ON LUCILLE** [ ] [-]
Nov 86. Ace; (d-lp)(c) **COMPLETELY LIVE AND WELL** [ ] [-]
– (The 2 albums from 1969)
Jan 87. Ace; (lp)(c)(cd) **THE BEST OF B.B.KING VOLUME 2** [ ] [-]
Apr 87. Ace; (lp) **ONE NIGHTER BLUES** [ ] [-]
Aug 89. Ace; (lp)(cd) **LUCILLE HAD A BABY** [ ] [-]
Aug 91. Ace; (cd)(c) **THE FABULOUS B.B.KING** [ ] [-]
Jul 92. Ace; (cd) **MY SWEET LITTLE ANGEL** [ ] [-]
Nov 85. Deja Vu; (lp)(c) **20 BLUES GREATS** [ ] [-]
– Help the poor / Everyday I have the blues / Woke up this morning / Worry worry / Sweet little angel / How blue can you get / You upset me baby / It's my own fault / Please love me / She don't love me no more / Three o'clock blues / Fine looking woman / Blind love / You know I love you / Ten long years / Mistreated woman / Shake it up and go / Sweet sixteen / You done lost your good thing now / Outside help. *(cd-iss.Sep87)*
Apr 93. Sixteen; (cd)(c) **THE GOLD COLLECTION** [ ] [-]
Feb 86. Crown; (lp)(c) **AMBASSADOR OF THE BLUES** [ ] [ ]
Jan 87. Kingdom Jazz; (cd) **LIVE (w / PAT METHANY / DAVE BRUBECK / HEATH BROS.)** [ ] [-]
Aug 87. Blues Boy; (lp) **THE RAREST B.B.KING** [ ] [-]
Oct 89. Blue Moon; (lp)(cd) **B.B.'S BOOGIE** [ ] [-]
(cd-iss.Jan95 on 'Success')
Jun 91. G.R.P.; (cd)(c)(lp) **LIVE AT THE APOLLO (live)** [ ] [ ]
Mar 94. Nectar; (cd)(c) **HOW BLUE CAN YOU GET** [ ] [-]
Aug 94. Connoisseur; (cd) **GREATEST HITS 1951-1960** [ ] [-]
Nov 94. Pickwick; (cd)(c) **KING OF THE BLUES** [ ] [-]
Nov 94. Charly; (cd) **KANSAS CITY 1972 (live)** [ ] [-]
Feb 95. Castle; (cd) **THE COLLECTION** [ ] [-]
Jul 95. MCA; (cd) **LUCILLE / FRIENDS** [ ] [-]
Dec 95. Opal; (cd) **THE EARLY BLUES BOY YEARS VOLUME 1** [ ] [-]
Dec 95. Opal; (cd) **THE EARLY BLUES BOY YEARS VOLUME 2** [ ] [-]

Ben E. KING

Born: BENJAMIN EARL NELSON, 23 Sep'38, Henderson, North Carolina, USA. In 1947, his family moved to Harlem, New York, where he soon learned to sing in church choirs. In 1957-58, he joined doo-wop outfits The FOUR B's / The MOONGLOWS and then The CROWNS. In summer 1958, the latter became The new DRIFTERS, when manager (George Treadwell) fired originals. In 1959-60, BEN provided the main vox on their US Top20 hits; THERE GOES MY BABY / DANCE WITH ME / THIS MAGIC MOMENT / SAVE THE LAST DANCE FOR ME + I COUNT THE TEARS. His complaint of low wages, gave Treadwell reason to virtually fire him in May 1960. Early the next year, he had first 2 classic US Top10 hits with 'SPANISH HARLEM' & 'STAND BY ME'. The latter, regarded by many as his finest 3 minutes, eventually hit the UK No.1 spot early 1987, from film of same name. He struggled commercially between 1964-1974, but when re-signing for 'Atlantic' in '75, SUPERNATURAL THING gave him return to the US Top5. • **Style:** Legendary ballad performer whose solo career had hit both highs and lows during three decades. • **Songwriters:** In the early 60's, producers LEIBER & STOLLER were sometimes helped out by DOC POMUS and PHIL SPECTOR. BEN E. also proved to be worthy contributor throughout the 60's & 70's. • **Trivia:** In 1974, BEN E briefly gave cameo performance on GENESIS album 'The Lamb Lies Down on Broadway', providing vox for last 2 words, although he wasn't the Drifter that originally sang it!

Recommended: STAND BY ME (THE ULTIMATE COLLECTION) (*6)

BEN E. KING – vocals with session players

London / Atco

Oct 60. (7") **SHOW ME THE WAY. / BRACE YOURSELF** [-] [ ]
Dec 60. (7") **FIRST TASTE OF LOVE. / SPANISH HARLEM** [27] [53] [10]
Jun 61. (7") **STAND BY ME. / ON THE HORIZON** [27] [4] May61
Sep 61. (7") **AMOR, AMOR. / SOUVENIR OF MEXICO** [38] [18] Jul 61
Nov 61. (lp) **SPANISH HARLEM** [ ] [57] Jul 61
– Amor / Sway / Come closer to me / Perfidia / Granada / Sweet and gentle / Quizas, quizas (Perhaps, perhaps, perhaps) / Frenesi / Souvenir of Mexico / Besame mucho / Love me, love4 me / Spanish Harlem. *(UK re-iss.Jun67 on 'Atlantic', hit No.30)*
Nov 61. (7") **HERE COMES THE NIGHT. / YOUNG BOY BLUES** [ ] [81] [66] Oct 61
Mar 62. (7") **ECSTASY. / YES** [ ] [56] Feb 62
May 62. (7") **DON'T PLAY THAT SONG (YOU LIED). / THE HERMIT OF MISTY MOUNTAIN** [ ] [11] Apr 62
Aug 62. (7") **TOO BAD. / MY HEART CRIES FOR YOU** [ ] [88]
Oct 62. (lp) **DON'T PLAY THAT SONG** [ ] [ ]
– Don't play that song (you lied) / Ecstasy / On the horizon / Show me the way / Here comes the night / First taste of love / Stand by me / Yes / Young boy blues / The hermit of misty mountain / I promise love / Brace yourself
Nov 62. (7") **I'M STANDING BY. / WALKING IN THE FOOTSTEPS OF A FOOL** [ ] [ ]
Jan 63. (7") **TELL DADDY. / AUF WIEDERSEHEN** [-] [ ]
Mar 63. (7") **HOW CAN I FORGET. / GLORIA, GLORIA** [ ] [85]
Sep 63. (7") **I (WHO HAVE NOTHING). / THE BEGINNING OF TIME** [ ] [29] Jun 63
Dec 63. (7") **I COULD HAVE DANCED ALL NIGHT. / GYPSY** [ ] [72] Oct 63
Jan 64. (lp) **SONGS FOR SOULFUL LOVERS** [ ] [ ] 1963
– My heart cries for you / He will break your heart / Dream lover / Will you love me tomorrow / My foolish heart / Fever / Moon River / What a difference a day made / Because of you / at last / On the street where you live / It's all in the game
Jan 64. (7") **WHAT NOW MY LOVE. / GROOVIN'** [-] [ ]
Feb 64. (7") **AROUND THE CORNER. / GROOVIN'** [-] [-]
1964. (lp) **GREATEST HITS** – (compilation) [ ] [ ]
– Stand by me / Don't play that song (you lied) / Amor / Young boy blues / Goodnight my love / Spanish Harlem / How can i forget / It's all over / I (who have nothing) / Save the last dance for me / I Count the tears / This magic moment. *(re-iss.1973 on 'Atlantic') (re-iss.cd+c May93 on 'Prestige')*

Atlantic / Atco

Mar 64. (7") **THAT'S WHEN IT HURTS. / AROUND THE CORNER** [-] [63]
Jun 64. (7") **WHAT CAN A MAN DO. / SI SENOR** [-] [ ]
Oct 64. (7") **IT'S ALL OVER. / LET THE WATER RUN DOWN** [ ] [72] Sep 64
Jan 65. (7") **SEVEN LETTERS. / RIVER OF TEARS** [ ] [45] Dec 64
Jan 65. (lp) **SEVEN LETTERS** [-] [ ]

– Seven letters / River of tears / I'm standing by / Jamaica / Down home / Si senor / It's all over / Let the water run down / This is my dream / It's no good for me / In the middle of the night / Don't drive me away. *(UK-iss.1968)*

Apr 65. (7") **THE RECORD (BABY I LOVE YOU). / THE WAY YOU SHAKE IT** [ ] [84]
Jun 65. (7") **NOT NOW (I'LL TELL YOU WHEN). / SHE'S GONE AGAIN** [-] [ ]
Sep 65. (7") **CRY NO MORE. / NO PLACE TO HIDE** [ ] [ ]
Nov 65. (7") **GOODNIGHT MY LOVE, PLEASANT DREAMS. / I CAN'T BREAK THE NEWS TO MYSELF** [-] [ ]
Jan 66. (7") **GOODNIGHT MY LOVE, PLEASANT DREAMS. / TELL DADDY** [ ] [91]
May 66. (7") **SO MUCH LOVE. / DON'T DRIVE ME AWAY** [ ] [96]
Oct 66. (7") **I SWEAR BY THE STARS ABOVE. / GET IN A HURRY** [ ] [ ]
Jan 67. (7") **WHAT IS SOUL? / THEY DON'T GIVE MEDALS TO YESTERDAY'S HEROES** [ ] [ ]
Feb 67. (lp) **WHAT IS SOUL?** [ ] [ ]
– The record (baby I love you) / She's gone again / There's no place to hide / Cry no more / Goodnight my love / Katherine / I can't break the news to myself / I swear by stars above / Get in a hurry / They don't give medals to yesterday's heroes / Teeny weeny little bit / What is soul.
Apr 67. (7") **TEARS, TEARS, TEARS. / MAN WITHOUT A DREAM** [-] [93]
Jul 67. (7") **TEENY WEENIE LITTLE BIT. / KATHERINE** [-] [ ]
Oct 67. (7") **SHE KNOWS WHAT TO DO FOR ME. / DON'T TAKE YOUR SWEET LOVE AWAY** [-] [ ]
Jan 68. (7") **WE GOT A THING GOING ON ("BEN E. KING & DEE DEE SHARP"). / WHATCHA GONNA DO** [-] [ ]
Apr 68. (7") **DON'T TAKE YOUR LOVE FROM ME. / FORGIVE THIS FOOL** [ ] [ ]
Aug 68. (7") **IT'S AMAZING. / WHERE'S THE GIRL** [ ] [ ]
Feb 69. (7") **'TILL I CAN'T TAKE ANYMORE. / IT AIN'T FAIR** [ ] [ ]
May 69. (7") **WHEN YOU LOVE SOMEBODY. / HEY LITTLE ONE** [-] [ ]

— BEN had already moved into cabaret work.

Crewe Maxwell
1970. (7") **GOODBYE MY OLD GIRL. / I CAN'T TAKE IT LIKE A MAN** [ ] [ ]
1970. (lp) **ROUGH EDGES** [ ] [ ]
– She lets her hair down (early in the morning) / Little green apples / Wishing for tomorrow / If you've gotta make a fool of somebody / Come together / One man / In the midnight hour / Lay lady lay / Don't let me down / Tonight I'll be staying here with you.

C.B.S. Mandela
Feb 72. (7") **TAKE ME TO THE PILOT. / I GUESS IT'S GOODBYE** [ ] [ ]
Feb 72. (lp)(c) **THE BEGINNING OF IT ALL** [ ] [ ]
May 72. (7") **INTO THE MYSTIC. / WHITE MOON** [-] [ ]
Aug 72. (7") **SPREAD MYSELF AROUND. /** [-] [ ]

Atlantic Atlantic
Apr 75. (7") **SUPERNATURAL THING. / (part 2)** [ ] [5] Feb75
(re-iss.Jan77)
Apr 75. (lp)(c) **SUPERNATURAL** [ ] [39]
– Supernatural thing (part 1 & 2) / You're lovin' ain't good enough / Drop my heart off (on your way to the door) / Do it in the name of love / Happiness is where you find it / Do you wanna do a thing / Imagination / What do you want me to do.
Jul 75. (7") **DO IT IN THE NAME OF LOVE. / IMAGINATION** [ ] [60]
Nov 75. (7") **HAPPINESS IS WHERE YOU FIND IT. / DROP MY HEART OFF (ON YOUR WAY TO THE DOOR)** [ ] [ ]
Jan 76. (7") **I HAD A LOVE. / WE GOT LOVE** [ ] [ ]
Apr 76. (lp)(c) **I HAD A LOVE** [ ] [ ]
– I had a love / I betcha didn't know that / Smooth sailing / No danger ahead / Everybody plays the fool / Standing in the wings of heartache / We got love / Tower of strength / You're stepping on my heart.
May 76. (7") **I BETCHA DIDN'T KNOW THAT. / SMOOTH SAILING** [-] [ ]
Dec 76. (7") **SOMEBODY'S KNOCKING. / ONE MORE TIME** [-] [ ]
Apr 77. (7") **GOT IT UP FOR LOVE. / KEEPIN' IT TO MYSELF** [-] [ ]
(mid'77) BEN teamed up with AVERAGE WHITE BAND on album 'BENNY & US'.
Jan 79. (lp)(c) **LET ME LIVE IN YOUR LIFE** [ ] [ ]
– Fifty years / Tippin' / Spoiled / Wonder woman / Let me live in your life / I see the light / Fly away (to my wonderland) / Dark storm on the horizon / Family jewels / Sweet rhapsody / Fifty years . . . (US title 'RHAPSODY')
Feb 79. (7") **TIPPIN'. / I SEE THE LIGHT** [-] [ ]
Apr 79. (7") **SPOILED. / FLY AWAY TO MY WONDERLAND** [-] [ ]
Nov 79. (7") **MUSIC TRANCE. / AND THIS IS LOVE** [-] [ ]
May 80. (lp)(c) **MUSIC TRANCE** [ ] [ ]
– And this is love / Music trance / Touched by your love / You've only got one chance to be young / Hired gun / Work that body.
Jun 80. (7")(12") **YOU'VE ONLY GOT ONE CHANCE TO BE YOUNG. / MUSIC TRANCE** [ ] [ ]
May 81. (lp)(c) **STREET TOUGH** [ ] [ ]
– Street tough / Staying power / Souvenirs of love / Stay a while with me / Something to be loved / Made for each other / Why is the question / You made the difference to my life.
May 81. (7") **STREET TOUGH. / WHAT IS THE QUESTION** [-] [ ]
Oct 81. (7") **SOUVENIRS OF LOVE. / YOU MADE THE DIFFERENCE TO MY LIFE** [-] [ ]

— In 1982, he re-joined The DRIFTERS. By the late 80's, he had resurrected solo career after hitting No.1 w / 'STAND BY ME'.

Bold Reprieve ?
May 87. (7")(12") **SPREAD MYSELF AROUND. / DO IT NOW** [ ] [ ]
Syncopate ?
Jun 87. (7")(12") **DANCING IN THE NIGHT. / ('A'version)** [ ] [ ]
Manhattan Manhattan
Jun 87. (7")(12") **SAVE THE LAST DANCE FOR ME. / WHEEL OF LOVE** [69] [ ]
Nov 87. (7")(12") **LOVER'S QUESTION. / BECAUSE OF LAST NIGHT** [ ] [ ]

– compilations, others, etc. –

1963. London/ US= Atco; (7"ep) **HOW CAN I FORGET?** [ ] [-]
1964. London/ US= Atco; (7"ep) **I'M STANDING BY** [ ] [-]
Note; All below releases on 'Atlantic' UK/ 'Atco', US until stated.
1964. (7"ep) **WHAT NOW MY LOVE** [ ] [-]
Mar 67. (7") **SAVE THE LAST DANCE FOR ME (w / DRIFTERS). / STAND BY ME** [ ] [ ]
Apr 67. (7") **TEARS, TEARS, TEARS. / A MAN WITHOUT A DREAM** [ ] [ ]
Feb 68. (7") **SEVEN LETTERS. / GOODNIGHT MY LOVE** [ ] [ ]
Jul 71. (7") **IT'S AMAZING. / TEARS, TEARS, TEARS** [ ] [ ]
Sep 71. (7"ep) **SAVE THE LAST DANCE FOR ME – (w/Drifters)- UNDER THE BOARDWALK. / SPANISH HARLEM / STAND BY ME** [ ] [ ]
Jul 75. (lp)(c) **THE BEN E.KING STORY** [ ] [ ]
Apr 80. (7"ep) **WHAT IS SOUL? / STAND BY ME. / (2 by 'Percy Sledge')** [ ] [-]
Feb 87. (7") **STAND BY ME. / ('B' by 'Coasters')** [1] [9] Sep 86
(12"+=) – Music trance.
Mar 87. (lp)(c)(cd) **STAND BY ME (THE ULTIMATE COLLECTION)** [14] [ ]
– Stand by me / Save the last dance for me / I (who have nothing) / That's when it hurts / I could have danced all night / First taste of love / Dream lover / Moon river / Spanish Harlem / Amor / I count the tears / Don't play that song / This magic moment / Young boy blues / It's all in the game / Supernatural thing (pt.1).
– (above also featured DRIFTERS tracks) *(re-iss.cd Jun93 on 'Prestige')*
Apr 87. (7") **SPANISH HARLEM. / FIRST TASTE OF LOVE** [ ] [ ]
(12"+=) – Medley: Spanish Harlem – Stand by me – Don't play that song.
Jul 81. Old Gold; (7") **SPANISH HARLEM. / STAND BY ME** [ ] [-]
(re-iss.Mar90)
Jan 95. Collection; (cd) **THE COLLECTION** [ ] [-]
Feb 95. B.A.M.; (cd) **PEARLS OF THE PAST** [ ] [-]
Dec 95. Javelin; (cd) **THE LEGENDARY BEN E.KING** [ ] [-]

Carole KING

Born: CAROLE KLEIN, 9 Feb'40, Brooklyn, New York, USA. Taught early in childhood by mother to play piano and sing, she started to write songs, firstly with Paul Simon in 1958. She then met lyricist (and future husband) GERRY GOFFIN and began writing partnership for music publishers Don Kirshner and Al Nevin. Their first successes came in 1961, when 'WILL YOU STILL LOVE ME TOMORROW' (by The SHIRELLES) and 'TAKE GOOD CARE OF MY BABY' (by BOBBY VEE), both hit US top spot. The following year, 'THE LOCOMOTION' (by LITTLE EVA), gave them their 3rd No.1. Throughout the 60's, they also put together more massive sellers for other artists. Meanwhile Kirshner had persuaded CAROLE to release her solo version of 'IT MIGHT AS WELL RAIN UNTIL SEPTEMBER', which hit US Top30 & UK Top3! in Autumn '62. Four mild years elapsed 'till GOFFIN-KING had another major success with 'GO AWAY LITTLE GIRL' (a US No.1 by STEVE LAWRENCE). That year (1967), she formed own recording label 'Tomorrow', and signed new flower-power outfit The MYDDLE CLASS, where she met bass player and future second husband CHARLES LARKEY. In 1968, she formed her own band The CITY, which featured CHARLES and two others. In 1969, JAMES TAYLOR asked her to provide piano on his debut 'Apple' lp 'Sweet Baby James'. That year she also moved out to Los Angeles, where she soon completed her debut solo album for Lou Adler's 'Ode' records. Her second album 'TAPESTRY' in 1971, heralded a major comeback, and gave her her first massive selling US No.1. Lifted from it, the classic 'IT'S TOO LATE', also peaked at this position, as did JAMES TAYLOR's version of 'YOU'VE GOT A FRIEND'. Throughout the 70's, she became a highly regarded top-selling superstar. **Style & Songs:** Singer-songwriter of many AOR standards / ballads. Her nervous shyness on stage, was eventually overcome in 1972, when she successfully toured both sides of the Atlantic. On 1974's 'WRAP AROUND JOY', her lyricist was ex-STEELY DAN singer DAVID PALMER. • **Trivia:** Her daughter LOUISE GOFFIN has recently embarked on her own solo career.

Recommended: TAPESTRY (*8) / HER GREATEST HITS (*6)

CAROLE KING – vocals, piano (with session people)

not issued ABC-Para..
Jan 59. (7") **GOIN' WILD. / THE RIGHT GIRL** [-] [ ]
Mar 59. (7") **BABY SITTIN'. / UNDER THE STARS** [-] [ ]
not issued RCA Victor
May 59. (7") **QUEEN OF THE BEACH. / SHORT-MORT** [-] [ ]
not issued Alpine
Nov 59. (7") **OH! NEIL. / A VERY SPECIAL BOY** [-] [ ]

— She keeps on writing for others husband GERRY GOFFIN. After two and a half years she returned to solo work for . . .

London Dimension
Aug 62. (7") **IT MIGHT AS WELL RAIN UNTIL SEPTEMBER. / NOBODY'S PERFECT** [3] [22]
(first issued in US on 'Companion' records) *(re-iss.Sep72 reached No.43 UK, re-iss.Feb82 on 'Decca', re-iss.Oct83 on 'Old Gold')*
Nov 62. (7") **SCHOOL BELLS ARE RINGING. / I DIDN'T HAVE ANY** [-] [ ]
Apr 63. (7") **HE'S A BAD BOY. / WE GROW UP TOGETHER** [-] [94]

— Soon divorced her husband GERRY, although they still carried on writing.
Apr 66. (7") **SOME OF YOUR LOVIN'. / ROAD TO NOWHERE** [ ] [ ]

The CITY

CAROLE KING with **CHARLES LARKEY** – bass (of FUGS) / **DANNY 'KOOTCH' KORTCHMAR** – guitar / **JIM GORDON** – drums

A & M / Ode

Jan 69. (lp) **NOW THAT EVERYTHING'S BEEN SAID** [-] [ ]
– Snow queen / I wasn't born to follow / Now that everything's been said / Paradise alley / Man without a dream / Victim of circumstance / Why are you leaving / Lady / My sweet home / I don't believe it / That old sweet roll (hi-de-do) / All my time.

1969. (7") **PARADISE ALLEY. / SNOW QUEEN** [-] [ ]

1969. (7") **THAT OLD SWEET ROLL. / WHY ARE YOU LEAVING** [-] [ ]

CAROLE KING

solo, with session people

May 70. (lp)(c) **WRITER: CAROLE KING** [ ] [ ]
– Spaceship races / No easy way down / Child of mine / Goin' back / To love / What have you got to lose / Eventually / Raspberry jam / Can't you be real / I can't hear you no more / Sweet sweetheart / Up on the roof. *(re-promoted Apr71 hit US 84, re-iss.Feb79 on 'Epic')*

Mar 70. (7") **EVENTUALLY. / UP ON THE ROOF** [-] [ ]

— now again with regulars LARKEY and KORTCHMAR plus **RUSS KUNKEL** – drums and guest **JAMES TAYLOR** – guitar, backing vocals (solo artist)

Nov 70. (lp)(c) **TAPESTRY** [4] [1]
– I feel the earth move / So far away / It's too late / Home again / Beautiful / Way over yonder / You've got a friend / Where you lead / Will you still love me tomorrow / Smackwater Jack / Tapestry / (You make me feel like) A natural woman. *(re-iss.'77 & Aug84 on 'Epic', cd-iss.Jun89)*

Apr 71. (7") **IT'S TOO LATE. / I FEEL THE EARTH MOVE** [6] [1]

Jul 71. (7") **SO FAR AWAY. / SMACKWATER JACK** [ ] [14]

Dec 71. (lp)(c) **MUSIC** [18] [1]
– Brother, brother / Song of long ago / Brighter / Surely / Some kind of wonderful / It's going to take some time / Music / Sweet seasons / Carry your load / Growing away from me / Too much rain / Back to California. *(re-iss.1974 on 'A&M') (re-iss.Feb79 + 83 on 'Epic') (cd-iss.Jun91 on 'Pickwick')*

Mar 72. (7") **BROTHER, BROTHER. / IT'S GOING TO TAKE SOME TIME** [-] [ ]

Dec 71. (7") **SWEET SEASONS. / POCKET MONEY** [ ] [9]

Ode / Ode

Oct 72. (7") **BEEN TO CANAAN. / BITTER WITH THE SWEET** [ ] [24]

Nov 72. (lp)(c) **RHYMES AND REASONS** [40] [2] Oct 72
– Come down easy / My my she cries / Peace in the valley / Feeling sad tonight / The first day in August / Bitter with the sweet / Goodbye don't mean I'm gone / Stand behind me / Gotta get through another day / I think I can hear you / Ferguson Road / Been to Canaan. *(re-iss.'74 on 'A&M')*

Jun 73. (7") **YOU LIGHT UP MY LIFE. / BELIEVE IN HUMANITY** [ ] [28] [67]

Jul 73. (lp)(c) **FANTASY** [ ] [6] Jun 73
– Fantasy beginning / You've been around too long / Being at war with each other / Directions / That's how things go down / Weekdays / Haywood / A quiet place to live / Welfare symphony / You light up my life / Corazon / Believe in humanity / Fantasy end. *(cd-iss.Oct93 on 'Sony Collectors')*

Oct 73. (7") **CORAZON. / THAT'S HOW THINGS GO DOWN** [-] [37]

— added guest **TOM SCOTT** – saxophone

Jul 74. (7") **JAZZMAN. / YOU GO YOUR WAY, I'LL GO MINE** [ ] [2]

Oct 74. (lp)(c) **WRAP AROUND JOY** [ ] [1] Sep 74
– Nightingale / Change in mind, change of heart / Jazzman / You go your way, I'll go mine / You're something new / We are all in this together / Wrap around joy / You gentle me / My lovin' eyes / Sweet Adonis / A night this side of dying / The best is yet to come. *(cd-iss.May92 on 'Thunderbolt')*

Jan 75. (7") **NIGHTINGALE. / YOU'RE SOMETHING NEW** [ ] [9]

Mar 75. (lp)(c) **REALLY ROSIE** (children's TV) [-] [20]
– Really Rosie / One was Johnny / Alligators all around / Pierre / Screaming and yelling / The ballad of chicken soup / Chicken soup and rice / Ave. P / My simple humble neighborhood / The awful truth / Such suffer / Really Rosie. *(cd-iss.Sep93 on 'Sony Collectors')*

Jul 75. (7") **PIERRE. / CHICKEN SOUP WITH RICE** [-] [ ]

Mar 76. (7") **ONLY LOVE IS REAL. / WE'RE STILL HERE THINKIN' OF YOU** [-] [37] Jan 76

Jan 76. (lp)(c) **THOROUGHBRED** [ ] [3]
– So many ways / Daughter of light / High out of time / Only love is real / There's a space between us / I'd like to know you better / We all have to be alone / Ambrosia / Still here thinking of you / It's gonna work out fine. *(re-iss.Jul80 & '84 on 'Epic')*

Jul 76. (7") **HIGH OUT OF TIME. / I'D LIKE TO KNOW YOU BETTER** [ ] [76] May 76

— She now worked with backing band NAVARRO, which included new 3rd husband **RICK EVERS** – guitar

Capitol / Capitol

Jul 77. (7") **HARD ROCK CAFE. / TO KNOW THAT I LOVE YOU** [ ] [30]

Aug 77. (lp)(c) **SIMPLE THINGS** [ ] [17]
– Simple things / Hold on / In the name of love / Labyrinth / You're the one who knows / Hard rock cafe / Time alone / God only knows / To know that I love you / One.

Oct 77. (7") **HOLD ON. / SIMPLE THINGS** [-] [ ]

Nov 77. (7") **LABYRINTH. / SIMPLE THINGS** [ ] [-]

Apr 78. (lp)(c) **WELCOME HOME** [ ] [ ]
– Main Street Saturday night / Sunbird / Venusian diamond / Changes / Morning sun / Disco tech / Ways of love / Ride the music / Everybody's got the spirit / Welcome home.

Apr 78. (7") **MAIN STREET SATURDAY NIGHT. / CHANGES** [-] [ ]

Aug 78. (7") **MORNING SUN. / SUNBIRD** [-] [ ]

Aug 78. (7") **DISCO TECH. / VENUSIAN DIAMOND** [ ] [-]

— Her husband RICK died Mar78 of a drug overdose. She recorded next album with ex-JERRY JEFF WALKER's musicians.

Jul 79. (lp)(c) **TOUCH THE SKY** [ ] [ ] Jun 79
– Time gone by / Move lightly / Dreamlike I wander / Walk with me / Good mountain people / You still want her / Passing of the days / Crazy / Eagle / Seeing red.

Aug 79. (7") **MOVE LIGHTLY. / WHISKEY** [ ] [ ]

Oct 79. (7") **TIME GONE BY. / DREAMLIKE I WANDER** [-] [ ]

— ex-husband **LARKEY** returned on bass and **CHRISTOPHER CROSS** – guitar

Jun 80. (lp)(c) **PEARLS – SONGS OF GOFFIN AND KING** (new versions old songs) [ ] [44]
– Dancin' with tears in my eyes / Locomotion / One fine day / Hey girl / Snow queen / Chains / Oh no not my baby / Hi de ho / Wasn't born to follow / Goin' back.

Jun 80. (7") **ONE FINE DAY. / RULERS OF THE WORLD** [ ] [ ] May80

Aug 80. (7") **LOCOMOTION. / OH NO NOT MY BABY** [-] [ ]

Oct 80. (7") **CHAINS. / HEY GIRL** [-] [ ]

— Now with new session people

Atlantic / Atlantic

Mar 82. (lp)(c) **ONE TO ONE** [ ] [ ]
– One to one / It's a war / Lookin' out for number one / Life without love / Golden man / Read between the lines / Love is like (a boomerang) / Goat Annie / Someone you never met before / Little prince.

Mar 82. (7") **ONE TO ONE. /** [-] [45]

Apr 82. (7") **READ BETWEEN THE LINES. / GOLDEN MAN** [ ] [ ]

May 82. (7") **READ BETWEEN THE LINES. / LIFE WITHOUT LOVE** [-] [ ]

Jun 82. (7") **LITTLE PRINCE. / SOMEONE YOU NEVER MET BEFORE** [ ] [ ]

— **KUNKEL** and **KORTCHMAR** returned to line-up

Dec 83. (lp)(c)(cd) **SPEEDING TIME** [ ] [ ]
– Computer eyes / Small voice / Crying in the rain / Sacred heart of stone / Speeding time / Standin' on the border line / So ready for love / Chalis Borealis / Dancing / Alabaster lady.

Dec 83. (7") **CRYING IN THE RAIN. / A SACRED HEART OF STONE** [-] [ ]

Feb 84. (7") **SPEEDING TIME. /** [-] [ ]

In 1985, she and JOHN SEBASTIAN write songs for the "Care Bears" film

Capitol / Capitol

Apr 89. (7") **CITY STREETS. / I CAN'T STOP THINKING ABOUT YOU** [ ] [ ]
(12"+=)(cd-s+=) – Time heals all wounds *(US; b-side).*

Apr 89. (lp)(c)(cd) **CITY STREETS** [ ] [ ]
– City streets / Sweet life / Down to the darkness / Lovelight / I can't stop thinking about you / Legacy / Ain't that the way / Midnight flyer / Homeless heart / Someone who believes in you.

— (above featured ERIC CLAPTON – guitar / MAX WEINBERG – drums)

Jul 89. (7") **SOMEONE WHO BELIEVES IN YOU. / CITY STREETS** [-] [ ]

– compilations etc. –

Note; All below releases on 'Epic' were issued on 'Ode' US.

May 78. Epic; (lp)(c) **HER GREATEST HITS** [ ] [47] Mar 78
– Jazzman / So far away / Sweet seasons / I feel the Earth move / Brother, brother / Only love is real / It's too late / Nightingale / Smackwater Jack / Been to Canaan / Corazon / Believe in humility. *(re-iss.Jul83) (cd-iss.Mar87 on 'C.B.S.')*

Jun 79. Epic; (7") **IT'S TOO LATE. / YOU'VE GOT A FRIEND** [ ] [-]

Oct 83. Old Gold; (7") **IT MIGHT AS WELL RAIN UNTIL SEPTEMBER. / THE ROAD TO NOWHERE** [ ] [-]

Feb 94. Dino; (cd)(c) **IN CONCERT** – THE GREATEST HITS LIVE (live) [ ] [ ]

Above was recorded at LA's Amphitheater, with guest spots for CROSBY & NASH, plus SLASH of GUNS'N'ROSES playing guitar on 'The Locomotion'.

Jul 94. Connoisseur; (cd) **PEARLS / TIME GONE BY** [ ] [-]

Oct 94. Legacy-Epic; (d-cd)(d-c) **A NATURAL WOMAN** – THE ODE COLLECTION 1968-1976 [ ] [ ]

Freddie KING

Born: FREDERICK CHRISTIAN, 3 Sep'34, Gilmer, Texas, USA. Moved to Chicago after he left school and soon began playing at clubs jamming with the likes of WILLIE DIXON, MUDDY WATERS and MEMPHIS SLIM. Cut his first recording in 1956, but by 1960 he was part of 'King /Federal' stable. His debut for them 'HIDEAWAY' contained many R&B hits including the instrumental title track. The 60's saw more instrumentals stretched over many sides, which were curtailed gradually as his voice became more competant. Unusually while his lp's on 'King' records were being issued as FREDDIE, his 45's on 'Federal' were as FREDDY. KING's songs were being noticed by a new breed of up and coming blues artists, such as JOHN MAYALL, ERIC CLAPTON, PETER GREEN of FLEETWOOD MAC and STAN WEBB of CHICKEN SHACK, who recorded many of his numbers. In the late 60's, he shifted to 'Atlantic' records where he released a couple of KING CURTIS produced lp's (see below). In the early 70's he was recruited to LEON RUSSELL's 'Shelter', but by 1974 he signed to 'R.S.O.', where ERIC CLAPTON augmented on his album 'BURGLAR'. Tragically aged only 42, he died at his Dallas home of ulcers and heart failure. • **Style:** Prolific pure roots blues artist, who was inspiration to burgeoning mid-60's blues movement. • **Songwriters:** FREDDIE penned most and covered other standards. • **Trivia:** HIDEAWAY (his first real release) was about a Chicago Lounge Bar he slipped into when he was only a young teenager.

Recommended: 1934 TO 1976 (*7)

FREDDY KING – guitar with session people

not issued / El-Bee

1956. (7") **COUNTRY BOY. / THAT'S WHAT I THINK** [-] [ ]

— **FREDDIE KING** – vocals, guitar with **SONNY THOMPSON** – piano / **FREDDIE JORDAN** – guitar / **BILL WILLIS** – bass / **GENE REDD** – sax / **PHILIP PAUL** – drums not issued King (lps)/ Federal 45's

Nov 60. (lp) **HIDEAWAY**
– Hideaway / I'm tore down / Wash out / Have you ever loved a woman / Low tide / The stubble / See see baby / Side tracked / I love the woman / Remington ride. *(re-iss.1977 on 'Starday')*

Jan 61. (7") **YOU'VE GOT TO LOVE HER WITH A FEELING. / HAVE YOU EVER LOVED A WOMAN** - 93

Mar 61. (7") **HIDEAWAY. / I LOVE THE WOMAN** 29

— added **FRED JORDAN** – guitar

May 61. (7") **LONESONE WHISTLE BLUES. / IT'S TOO BAD (THINGS ARE GOING SO TOUGH)** - 88

Aug 61. (7") **SAN-HO-ZAY. / SEE SEE BABY** - 47

Aug 61. (lp) **FREDDIE KING SINGS** -
– You mean mean woman (how can your love be true) / Takin' care of business / Let me be (stay away from me) / It's too bad (things are going so tough) / If you believe (in what you do) / Lonesome whistle blues / I love the woman / Have you ever loved a woman / You know that you love me (but you never tell me so) / See see baby / You've got to love her with a feeling / I'm tore down. *(UK-iss.cd Jun 93)*

Oct 61. (7") **I'M TORE DOWN. / SEN-SA-SHUN (BUMBLE BEE STING)** -

Nov 61. (lp) **LET'S HIDEAWAY AND DANCEAWAY** -
– In the open / Out front / Heads up / Just pickin' / San-Ho-Zay / Wash out / The stumble / Side tracked / Onion rings (butterscotch) / Hide away / Sen-sa-shun (bumble bee sting) / Swooshy. *(UK-iss.cd Sep93)*

Dec 61. (7") **I HEAR JINGLE BELLS. / CHRISTMAS TEARS** -
(above re-iss.Dec64 flipped over & hit US Christmas Special No.12)

Jan 62. (7") **IF YOU BELIEVE (IN WHAT YOU DO). / HEADS UP** -

Feb 62. (lp) **GIRL BOY GIRL** -
– You can't hide / Do the president twist / (Let your love) Watch over me / It's easy child /

Mar 62. (7") **TAKIN' CARE OF BUSINESS. / THE STUMBLE** -

Apr 62. (7") **SITTIN' ON THE BOATDOCK. / SIDE TRACKED** -

May 62. (7") **YOUR LOVE KEEP A-WORKIN' ON ME. / DO THE PRESIDENT TWIST** -

Jul 62. (7") **WHAT ABOVE LOVE. / TEXAS OIL** -

Aug 62. (7") **COME ON. / JUST PICKIN'** -

Oct 62. (7") **YOU CAN'T HIDE. / (LET YOUR LOVE) WATCH OVER ME** -

Dec 62. (7") **IN THE OPEN. / I'M ON MY WAY TO ATLANTA** -

— FREDDY was then credited on LULA REED's 'Federal' 45 'IT'S EASY CHILD'.

Feb 63. (7") **THE BOSSA NOVA WATUSI TWIST (FREEWAY 75). / LOOK MA I'M CRYING** -

Mar 63. (lp) **BOSSA NOVA & BLUES** -
– The bossa nova watusi twist (Freeway 75) / Look ma I'm crying / Bossa nova blues / It hurts to be in love / The welfare (turns it back on you) / Is my baby mad with me / You're barkin' up the wrong tree / You walked in / Someday after a while (you'll be sorry) / Walk down the aisle (honey chile) / High rise (closed door) / (I'd love to) Make love to you / One hundred years.

Apr 63. (7") **(I'D LOVE TO) MAKE LOVE TO YOU. / ONE HUNDRED YEARS** -

May 63. (lp) **FREDDIE KING GOES SURFIN'** -
– In the open / Out front / Low tide (zoo surfin') / Remington ride / Swooshy /

Jul 63. (7") **STUFF MONKEY. / MONKEY DONKEY** -

Sep 64. (lp) **BONANZA OF INSTRUMENTALS** -
– Man hole / Fish fare / King-a-ling / Remington ride / Low tide (zoo surfin') / Surf monkey / The bossa nova watusi twist (freeway 75) / Funny bone / Cloud sailin' (don't move) / The sad nite owl / Nickel plated / Freddie's midnite dream. *(UK-iss.Nov84 + Nov88 +cd on 'Crosscut')*

Oct 63. (7") **MEET ME AT THE STATION. / KING-A-LING** -

Nov 63. (7") **SOMEDAY AFTER A WHILE (YOU'LL BE SORRY). / DRIVING SIDEWAYS** -

Dec 63. (7") **HIGH RISE (CLOSED DOOR). / SHE PUT THE WHAMMY ON ME** -

Feb 64. (7") **NOW I'VE GOT A WOMAN. / ONION RINGS (BUTTERSCOTCH)** -

Apr 64. (7") **YOU'RE BARKING UP THE WRONG TREE. / THE WELFARE (TURNS IT'S BACK ON YOU)** -

Jun 64. (7") **SOME OTHER DAY SOME OTHER TIME. / MAN HOLE** -

Jul 64. (7") **I LOVE YOU MORE EVERY DAY. / IF YOU HAVE IT** -

Sep 64. (7") **SHE'S THE ONE. / FULL TIME LOVE** -

Oct 64. (lp) **FREDDIE KING** -
– She's the king / She's the one / Some other day some other time / Teardrops on your letter / I love you more everyday / Monkey donkey / Now I've got a woman / If you have it / Come on.

Nov 64. (7") **OVER DRIVE (THE UNTOUCHABLE GLIDE). /** -

Sue not issued

Mar 65. (7") **DRIVING SIDEWAYS. / HIDE AWAY** -

— In the mid-60's, FREDDIE formed his own orchestra, although he returned to usual form in the late 60's with various label session men.

Atlantic Cotillion

1969. (lp) **FREDDIE KING IS A BLUES MASTER**
– Play it cool / That will never do / It's too late / She's gone / Blue shadows / Today I sing the blues / Get out of my life woman / Highway / Funky / Hot tomato / Wide open / Sweet thing / Let me down easy.

1969. (7") **PLAY IT COOL. / FUNKY**

1970. (lp) **MY FEELING FOR THE BLUES**
– Yonder wall / Stumble / I wonder why / Stormy Monday / I don't know / What'd I say / Ain't nobody's business what we do / You don't have to go / Woke up this morning / The things I used to do / My feeling for the blues.

— now w / **DON PRESTON** – guitar / **JOHN GALLIE + LEON RUSSELL** – keyboards / **CHUCK BLACKWELL** – drums / **DONALD 'Duck' DUNN** – bass

A & M Shelter

1971. (lp) **GETTING READY**
– Same old blues / Dust my broom / Worried life blues / Five long years / Key to the highway / Going down / Living on the highway / Walking by myself / Tore down / Palace of the King / Gimme some lovin' / Send someone to love.

1971. (7") **GOING DOWN. / I'M TORE DOWN** -

— added **JIM GORDON + AL JACKSON** – drums / **CARL RADLE** – bass

1972. (lp) **TEXAS CANNONBALL (live)**
– Lowdown in Lodi / Reconsider baby / Big legged woman / Me and my guitar / I'd rather be blind / Can't trust your neighbor / You was wrong / How many more years / Ain't no sunshine / The sky is crying. *(re-iss.May90 on 'Music Maniac') (cd-iss.Jul91 on 'Sequel')*

1972. (7") **ME AND MY GUITAR. / LOWDOWN IN LODI** -

1972. (7") **I'd RATHER BE BLIND. / AIN'T NO SUNSHINE** -

— **JIM KELTNER** – drums + **REV. PAT HENDERSON** – keyboards repl. GALLIE, GORDON, DUNN + JACKSON

Jul 73. (lp)(c) **WOMAN ACROSS THE WATER**
– Woman across the water / Hootchie cootchie man / Danger zone / Boogie man / Leave my woman alone / Just a little bit / Yonder wall / Help me through the day / I'm ready / Trouble in mind / You don't have to go. *(cd-iss.Feb93 on 'Sequel')*

Jul 73. (7") **WOMAN ACROSS THE WATER. / HELP ME THROUGH THE DAY**

— now w / many session people **STEVE FERRONE + JAMIE OLDAKER** – drums / **ROY DAVIES + PETE WINGFIELD** – keyboards / **DESLISLE HARPER + CARL RADLE** – bass / **CHRIS MERCER + BUD BEADLE + STEVE GREGORY** – sax / + guests **ERIC CLAPTON + BRIAN AUGER**

R.S.O. R.S.O.

1974. (lp)(c) **BURGLAR**
– Pack it up / My credit didn't go through / I got the same old blues / Only getting second best / Texas flyer / Pulp wood / She's a burglar / Sugar sweet / I had a dream / Let the good times roll. *(re-iss.Jul88 on 'Polydor') (cd-iss.Apr92 on 'B.G.O.')*

Oct 74. (7") **PACK IT UP. / SHAKE YOUR BOOTY**

Oct 74. (7") **TEXAS FLYER. / MY CREDIT DIDN'T GO THROUGH** -

1975. (lp)(c) **LARGER THAN LIFE**
– It's better go to have / You can run but you can't hide / Woke up this morning / It's your move / Boogie bump / Meet me in the morning / The things I used to do / Ain't that I don't love you / Have you ever loved a woman. *(re-iss.Jul88 on 'Polydor')*

Oct 75. (7") **BOOGIE BUMP. / IT'S YOUR MOVE**

— On 28 Dec'76, FREDDIE died in Dallas of a hepatitis related heart attack.

– compilations, etc. –

1977. R.S.O.; (lp)(c) **1934 TO 1976**
– Pack it up / Shake your bootie / T'ain't nobody's bizness if I do / Woman across the river / Sweet home Chicago / Sugar sweet / T.V. mama / Gambling woman blues / Farther on up the road. *(cd-iss.May88)*

Note; All below releases on 'Polydor' UK/ 'King' US.

Feb 65. (lp) **VOCALS & INSTRUMENTALS** -

1968. (7") **YOU'VE GOT ME LICKED. / GIRL FROM KOOKAMUNGA** -

1969. (7") **HIDEAWAY. / HAVE YOU EVER LOVED A WOMAN** -

1969. (lp) **KINGS OF RHYTHM & BLUES VOL.2** -

1972. (lp) **HIS EARLY YEARS VOL.1** -

1977. (lp)(c) **ORIGINAL HITS** -

1975. A&M/ US= Shelter; (lp)(c) **THE BEST OF FREDDIE KING**

Jun 75. A&M/ US= Shelter; (7") **GOING DOWN. / ME AND MY GUITAR**

1976. Island; (lp)(c) **THE REST OF FREDDIE KING** -

Oct 83. Crosscut; (lp)(c) **ROCKIN' THE BLUES LIVE (live 74-75)** -

Jul 85. Charly; (lp)(c) **TAKING CARE OF BUSINESS** -
(cd-iss.Oct86)

Oct 90. Charly; (cd) **TEXAS SENSATION** -

Aug 93. Ace; (cd) **BLUES GUITAR HERO: THE INFLUENTIAL EARLY SESSIONS** -

Feb 92. Magnum Force; (cd) **PALACE OF THE KING** -

Oct 93. Magnum Force; (cd) **LIVE AT LIBERTY HALL (live)** -

Apr 94. King Biscuit; (cd) **LIVE IN GERMANY (live)** -

Aug 95. Deja Vu; (cd) **MODERN TIMES** -

Nov 95. Charly; (cd) **LIVE** -

Dec 95. EMI; (cd) **KING OF THE BLUES**

Mark KING (see under ⇒ LEVEL 42)

KING CRIMSON

Formed: Bournemouth, England . . . summer 1967 by ROBERT FRIPP, plus brothers MIKE and PETE GILES, who formed soft-rock trio GILES, GILES & FRIPP. After signing to 'Deram' early in '68, and adding couple IAN McDONALD and JUDY DYBLE, they issued flop lp 'THE CHEERFUL INSANITY OF . . .' in Sep'68. With IAN now replacing PETE, the trio soon became KING CRIMSON, and added new vocalist GREG LAKE, who debuted at The Speakeasy on 9th Apr'69. 3 months later, they supported The ROLLING STONES at Hyde Park's free concert, which attracted 'Island' label. In Oct'69, they unleashed 'IN THE COURT OF THE CRIMSON KING', a masterful debut lp which made UK Top 5 and US Top 30. During the early 70's, they were in turmoil once more, when more group members departed, leaving FRIPP and lyricist and road manager PETE SINFIELD to work things out. Eventually with augmentation from session men and departees, they recorded 1970 follow-up lp 'IN THE WAKE OF POSEIDON'. An aggregation of KING CRIMSON members had earlier in March, played on 'Top Of The Pops' with weird 'CAT FOOD' 45. FRIPP and group went through more upheavals, but with astounding album successes, until they split late 1974. FRIPP had already been prolific session man for VAN DER GRAAF GENERATOR plus ENO. With the latter he was co-credited on 2 experimental budget lp's 'NO PUSSYFOOTIN'' (1973) & 'EVENING STAR' (1975). He then moved to New York and worked with PETER GABRIEL on his first 3 albums, BOWIE on 'Heroes' & BLONDIE. In 1979, FRIPP released debut solo album 'EXPOSURE', which featured many of said friends handling vocals (see below). The next year, his instrumental set 'GOD SAVE THE QUEEN / UNDER HEAVY MANNERS', was followed by his short-lived project/band LEAGUE OF GENTLEMEN. In 1981, he re-formed KING CRIMSON with BILL BRUFORD, ADRIAN BELEW & TONY LEVIN. They made 3 more fruitful albums, before they too left FRIPP to ponder solo pastures. Between 1982-84, FRIPP had collaborated on 2 albums 'I ADVANCE MASKED' & 'BEWITCHED', with ANDY SUMMERS (ex-POLICE). • **Style:** Progressive neo-classical rock outfit, whose initial MOODY BLUES' mellotron-sound was swopped for the distinctive self-indulgence master of guitar FRIPP. In the early 70's, they advanced with jazz-rock tinted fusion, and in the 80's a more modern, solid & basic approach with many directions. FRIPP solo often experimented with his electronics, which were dubbed in the early 80's as 'Frippertronics'. • **Songwriters:** FRIPP music, lyrics as said. BELEW collaborated in the 80's. • **Trivia:** In the mid-80's, FRIPP married singer / actress TOYAH WILLCOX, and even collaborated with her on an album 'THE LADY OR THE TIGER' (1987).

Recommended: IN THE COURT OF THE CRIMSON KING (*9) / IN THE WAKE OF POSEIDON (*6) / LIZARD (*6) / ISLANDS (*7) / LARK'S TONGUE'S IN ASPIC (*8) / RED (*8) / STARLESS & BIBLE BLACK (*8) / FRAME BY FRAME – THE CONCISE . . . (*9) / NETWORK (*7).

GILES, GILES & FRIPP

PETE GILES – bass / **MICHAEL GILES** (b.1942)– drums / **ROBERT FRIPP** (b. May'46, Wimbourne, Dorset, England)– guitar

Deram | not issued

Jun 68. (7") **ONE IN A MILLION. / NEWLY WEDS** [ ] [-]

— added **IAN McDONALD** (b.25 Jun'46, London) – keyboards / and guest **JUDY DYBLE** – vocals (ex-FAIRPORT CONVENTION) also featured as did KING CRIMSON lyricist **PETE SINFIELD**

Sep 68. (lp) **THE CHEERFUL INSANITY OF GILES, GILES & FRIPP** [ ] [-]
– The Saga of Rodney Toady / One in a million / Just George / Thursday morning / North meadow / Call tomorrow / Newly weds / Digging my lawn / Suite No.1 / Little children / The crukster / How do you know / The sun is shining / Brudite eyes / Elephant song. *(re-iss.Apr82)*

— IAN now on vocals (JUDY left to join TRADER HORNE)

Sep 68. (7") **THURSDAY MORNING. / ELEPHANT SONG** [ ] [-]

KING CRIMSON

ROBERT, IAN & MIKE recruited **GREG LAKE** (b.10 Nov'48) – vocals, bass (ex-GODS)

Island | Atlantic

Oct 69. (7") **THE COURT OF THE CRIMSON KING. / (Pt.2)** [ ] [80] Dec 69

Oct 69. (lp)(c) **IN THE COURT OF THE CRIMSON KING** [5] [28] Dec 69
– 21st century schizoid man (including: Mirrors) / I talk to the wind / Epitaph (including; March for no reason – Tomorrow and tomorrow / Moonchild (including: The dream – The illusion) / The court of the Crimson King (including; The return of the fire witch – (b) The dance of the puppets. *(re-iss.Mar77 on 'Polydor', cd-May83) (re-iss.+cd.Jan87 on 'EG')*

— **PETE GILES** – bass (ex-GILES, GILES & FRIPP) repl. IAN who with MIKE had formed McDONALD & GILES. IAN later formed FOREIGNER. MIKE appeared below. Added **KEITH TIPPET** – piano (other two were FRIPP & LAKE)

Mar 70. (7") **CAT FOOD. / GROON** [ ] [ ]

— added **MEL COLLINS** – saxophone (ex-CIRCUS) / plus guest on 1 track **GORDON HASKELL** – vocals

May 70. (lp)(c) **IN THE WAKE OF POSEIDON** [4] [31] Sep 70
– Peace – a beginning / Pictures of a city (including; 42nd at Treadmill) / Cadence and cascade / In the wake of Poseidon (including; Libra's theme) / Peace – a theme / Cat food / The Devil's triangle: Merday morn – Hand of Sceiron – Garden of worm / Peace – an end. *(re-iss.Mar77 on 'Polydor') (re-iss.+cd.Jan87 on 'EG')*

— **GORDON HASKELL** (now full-time) repl. GREG who formed EMERSON, LAKE & PALMER (earlier). FRIPP had also retained **MEL COLLINS. / ANDY McCULLOCH** – drums repl. MIKE

Dec 70. (lp)(c) **LIZARD** [30] [ ]
– Cirkus (including; Entry of the chameleons) / Indoor games / Happy family / Lady of the dancing water / Lizard suite: Prince Rupert awakes – Bolero-The peacock's tale – The battle of glass tears; (a) Dawn song – (b) Last skirmish – (c) Prince Rupert's lament / Big top. *(re-iss.Apr77 on 'Polydor') (re-iss.+cd.Jan87 on 'EG')*

— **BOZ BURRELL** – vocals, bass repl. HASKELL who went solo / **IAN WALLACE** – drums repl. McCULLOCH who joined GREENSLADE

Dec 71. (lp)(c) **ISLANDS** [30] [76]
– Formentera lady / The sailor's tale / Letters / (prelude) / Song of the gulls – Islands / Ladies of the road. *(re-iss.Apr77 on 'Polydor') (re-iss.+cd.Jan87 on 'EG')*

Island-Help | Antilees

Jun 72. (lp) **EARTHBOUND (live)** [ ] [ ]
– 21st century schizoid man / Peoria / The sailor's tale / Earthbound / Groon. *(re-iss.Oct77 on 'Polydor') (re-iss.Apr82 on 'EG')*

— FRIPP was sole survivor (lyricist PETE SINFIELD left early '72, to go into production for ROXY MUSIC's debut and be lyricist for Italiand P.F.M.) / **JOHN WETTON** – vocals, bass (ex-FAMILY) repl. BOZ who formed BAD COMPANY / **BILL BRUFORD** – drums (ex-YES) repl. WALLACE who joined STREETWALKERS / **DAVID CROSS** – violin, flute repl. COLLINS who later joined CAMEL + sessions / added **JAMIE MUIR** – percussion and new lyricist **RICHARD PALMER-JAMES**

Island | Atlantic

Mar 73. (lp)(c) **LARKS' TONGUES IN ASPIC** [20] [61]
– Larks' tongues in aspic (part one) / Book of Saturday / Exiles / Easy money / The talking drum / Larks' tongues in aspic (part two). *(re-iss.Apr77 on 'Polydor')(re-iss.+cd.Jan87 on 'EG')*

— Reverted to a quartet when JAMIE became a Tibetan monk

Feb 74. (7") **THE NIGHT WATCH. / THE GREAT DECEIVER** [ ] [ ]

Feb 74. (lp)(c) **STARLESS AND BIBLE BLACK** [28] [64]
– The great deceiver / Lament / We'll let you know / The night watch / Trio / The mincer / Starless and bible black / Trio / Fracture. *(re-iss.Apr77 on 'Polydor') (re-iss.+cd.Jan87 on 'EG')*

— now just basically a trio of FRIPP, WETTON and BRUFORD with old guests **MEL COLLINS, IAN McDONALD** and the departing **CROSS** augmenting on a track

Oct 74. (lp)(c) **RED** [45] [66]
– Red / Fallen angel / One more red nightmare / Providence / Starless. *(re-iss.Apr77 on 'Polydor') (re-iss.+cd.Jan87 on 'EG')*

— Split just before last album. Next live album was recorded with DAVID CROSS

Apr 75. (lp)(c) **U.S.A. (live)** [ ] [ ]
– Larks' tongues in aspic (part II) / Lament / Exiles / Asbury park / Easy money / 21st century schizoid man. *(re-iss.Dec79 on 'Polydor')*

— JOHN WETTON joined BRIAN FERRY, then URIAH HEEP and later ASIA etc. As above BILL BRUFORD went solo and formed UK, after GONG stints.

ROBERT FRIPP

solo adding keyboards and a number of friends **PETER GABRIEL, PETER HAMILL & DARYL HALL** on vox, plus **PHIL COLLINS, BARRY ANDREWS, TONY LEVIN & MICHAEL NARADA WALDEN** – other instruments

E.G. | Polydor

Apr 79. (lp)(c) **EXPOSURE** [71] [79]
– (prelude) / You burn me up I'm a cigarette / Breathless / Disengage / North star / Chicago / NY3 / Mary / Exposure / Haaaden two / Urban landscape / I may not have had enough of me but I've had enough of you / (first inaugural address to the J.A.C.E. Sherborne House) / Water music I / Here comes the flood / Water music II / Postscript. *(re-iss.Jul85 & Jan87)*

Mar 80. (lp)(c) **GOD SAVE THE QUEEN / UNDER HEAVY MANNERS (instrumental)** [ ] [ ]
– Under heavy manners / The zero of the signified / Red two scorer / God save the Queen / 1983. *(re-iss.Jan87)*

Apr 81. (lp) **LET THE POWER FALL (FRIPPERTRONICS)** [ ] [ ]
– 1984 / 1985 / 1986 / 1987 / 1988 / 1989. *(re-iss.+cd.Jan87)*

LEAGUE OF GENTLEMEN

FRIPP retained **BARRY ANDREWS** adding **SARA LEE** – bass (ex-JANE AIRE) / **JOHNNY TOOBAD** – drums

E. G. | Polydor

Dec 80. (7")**HEPTAPARAPARSHINOKH / MARRIAGEMUZIC** [ ] [-]

Mar 81. (lp)(c) **LEAGUE OF GENTLEMEN (instrumental)** [ ] [ ]
– Indiscreet / Inductive recurrance / Minor man / Heptaparaparshinokh / Dislocated / Pareto optimum 1 / Eye needles / Indiscreet II / Pareto optimum 2 / Cognitive dissonance / H.G. Wells / Trap / Ochre / Indiscreet III.

Mar 81. (7") **DISLOCATED. / 1984** [ ] [ ]

KING CRIMSON

FRIPP along with past member BRUFORD recruits newcomers **ADRIAN BELEW** – guitar, vocals (ex-TOM TOM CLUB) / **TONY LEVIN** – bass (ex-session man including PETER GABRIEL)

E.G. | Warners

Sep 81. (lp)(c) **DISCIPLINE** [41] [45]
– Elephant talk / Frame by frame / Matte Kudasai / Indiscipline / ThelaHun ginjeet / The sheltering sky / Discipline. *(re-iss.+cd.Jan87) (re-iss.Jun88)*

Nov 81. (7") **MATTE KUDASAI. / ELEPHANT TALK** [ ] [-]

Jun 82. (lp)(c) **BEAT** [39] [52]
– Neal and Jack and me / Heartbeat / Sartori in Tangier / Waiting man / Neurotica / Two hands / The howler / Requiem. *(cd-iss.Apr84) (re-iss.+cd.Jan87)*

Jun 82. (7") **HEARTBEAT. / REQUIEM (excerpt)** [ ] [ ]

Feb 84. (7") **SLEEPLESS. / NUAGES** [ ] [ ]
(12") – ('A'side) / ('A'instrumental & dance vesions).

Mar 84. (lp)(c)(cd) **THREE OF A PERFECT PAIR** [30] [58]
– Three of a perfect pair / Model man / Sleepless / Man with an open heart / Nuages (that which passes, passes like clouds) / Industry / Dig me / No warning / Lark's tongues in aspic (part three). *(re-iss.Jan87)*

— FRIPP disbanded KING CRIMSON project for a decade.

– compilations, others, etc. –

Feb 76. Island/ US= Atlantic; (d-lp)(c) **A YOUNG PERSON'S GUIDE TO KING CRIMSON** [ ] [ ]
– Epitaph (including; (a) March for no reason – (b) Tomorrow and tomorrow / Cadence and cascade / Ladies of the road / I talk to the wind / Red / Starless / The night watch / Book of Saturday / Peace – a beginning / Cat food / Groon / Coda from Larks' tongue's in aspic part 2 / Moonchild; (a) Mirrors – (b) The illusion / Trio / The court of the crimson king (including; (a) The return of the fire witch – (b) Dance of the puppets / 21st century schizoid man. *(re-iss.Mar77 on 'Polydor', cd-iss.1986 on 'E.G.')*

Feb 76. Island; (7") **21ST CENTURY SCHIZOID MAN. / EPITAPH** [ ] [ ]

Dec 80. Polydor; (d-lp) **IN THE COURT OF THE CRIMSON KING / LARKS' TONGUES IN ASPIC** [ ] [-]

Dec 86. E.G.; (cd)(d-lp)(d-c) **THE COMPACT KING CRIMSON** [ ] [ ]

Dec 89. E.G.; (3xlp)(3xc)(3xcd) **IN THE COURT OF THE CRIMSON KING / LARK'S TONGUES IN ASPIC / DISCIPLINE** [ ] [-]

(above 3 albums were packaged with other 'Island' artists)

Dec 91. Virgin; (cd) **FRAME BY FRAME: THE ESSENTIAL KING CRIMSON** [ ] [-]

Sep 93. Virgin; (cd)(c) **SLEEPLESS: THE CONCISE KING CRIMSON** [ ] [ ]
– 21st century schizoid man / Epitaph / In the court of the crimson king / Cat food /

Ladies of the road / Starless (abridged) / Red / Fallen angel / Elephant talk / Frame by frame / Matte Kudasai / Heartbeat / Three of a perfect pair / Sleepless.
Dec 93. Virgin; (3xcd-box) **IN THE COURT OF THE CRIMSON KING / IN THE WAKE OF POSEIDON / LIZARD** [ ] [-]

ROBERT FRIPP / LEAGUE OF GENTLEMEN

E.G. E.G.
1985. (lp)(c) **GOD SAVE THE KING** [ ] [ ]
– God save the King / Under heavy manners / Heptaparparshinokh / Inductive resonance / Cognitive dissonance / Dislocated / HG Wells / Eye needles / Trap.
Nov 86. (lp)(c)(cd) **ROBERT FRIPP AND THE LEAGUE OF CRAFTY GUITARISTS: LIVE! (live)** [ ] [ ]
– Guitar craft theme 1: Invocation / Tight muscle party at Love Beach / The chords that bind / Guitar craft theme 3: Eye of the needle / All or nothing II / Guitar craft theme 2: Aspiration / All or nothing I / Circulation / A fearful symmetry / The new world / Crafty march.

— Late 1988, FRIPP / FRIPP (TOYAH) toured augmented by **TREY GUNN** – stick bass / **PAUL BEAVIS** – percussion, drums

— In mid'93, ROBERT FRIPP collaborated with ex-JAPAN singer DAVID SYLVIAN on near UK Top 20 album 'THE FIRST DAY'.

— In Aug'94, FRIPP was part of FFWD alongside THOMAS FEHLYN, KRIS WESTON + Dr.ALEX PATTERSON of The ORB. In Sep'94, FRIPP again teamed up with DAVID SYLVIAN on album 'DAMAGE'.

KING CRIMSON

— **FRIPP / BRUFORD / BELEW / LEVIN / GUNN / MASTELOTTO**

Discipline Virgin
Dec 94. (cd)(c) **VROOOM** [ ] [ ]
– Vrooom / Sex, sleep, eat, drink, dream / Cage / Thrak / When I say stop, continue / One time.
Apr 95. (cd)(c) **THRAK** [58] [83]
– Vrooom / Coda: Marine 475 / Dinosaur / Walking on air / B'boom / Thrak / Inner garden I / People / Radio I / One time / Radio II / Inner garden II / Sex, sleep, eat, drink, dream / Vrooom vrooom / Vrooom vrooom coda.
Aug 95. (d-cd) **B'BOOM: OFFICIAL SOUNDTRACK – LIVE IN ARGENTINA (live** [ ] [-]
– Vrooom / Frame by frame / Sex, sleep, eat, drink, dream / Red / One time / B'boom / Thrak / Improv – Two sticks / Elephant talk / Indiscipline // Vrooom vrooom / Matte Kudesai / The talking drum / Lark's tongues in aspic (part 2) / Heartbeat / Sleepless / People / B'boom / Thrak.

ROBERT FRIPP

Discipline Virgin
Nov 94. (cd) **THE BRIDGE BETWEEN (w/ his STRING QUARTET)** [ ] [ ]
–
Feb 95. (cd) **1999 – SOUNDSCAPES – LIVE IN ARGENTINA (live)** [ ] [-]
– 1999 (part one) / 2000 / 2001 / Interlude / 2002.
Sep 95. (cd) **1995 SOUNDSCAPES – VOLUME TWO – LIVE IN CALIFORNIA (live)** [ ] [-]
– The cathedral of tears / First light / Midnight blue / Reflection 1 / Second light / A blessing of tears / Returning I / Returning II.
Oct 95. (cd) **INTERGALACTIC BOOGIE EXPRESS – LIVE IN EUROPE 1991** (live with The LEAGUE OF CRAFTY GUITARISTS) [ ] [-]
– A Connecticut Yankee in the court of King Arthur / Rhythm of the universe / Lark's hrak / Circulation 1 / Intergalactic boogie express / G force / Eye of the needle / Corrente / Driving force / Groove penetration / Flying home / Circulation II / Fireplace / Fragments of skylab / Asturias / Prelude circulation / Cheeseballs / Prelude in c minor / Wabash cannonball / Fractal Jazn / Ashesis.

– FRIPP compilations, etc. –

Jan 87. E.G.; (m-lp)(c) **NETWORK** [ ] [ ]
– North star / (i) Water music 1 (ii) Here comes the flood / God save the king / Under heavy manners.

KINGDOM COME

Formed: USA . . . 1987 by German born LENNY WOLF. They were soon signed worldwide to 'Polygram' by A&R man Derek Shulman (ex-GENTLE GIANT), issuing eponymous hit album in '88. • **Style:** Until 1989, they were regarded as heavy metal's answer to LED ZEPPELIN. They soon moved into DEF LEPPARD territory for their second album. • **Songwriters:** WOLFF-WOLF-STEIER collaborations, until 1991 WOLF-TATUM. Covered; WHO DO YOU LOVE (Bo Diddley). • **Trivia:** LENNY WOLF fronted on 2 albums 'Burns Like A Star' & 'Let Them Talk' for 'MCA' band STONE FURY in the mid-80's. MARTY WOLFF (no relation) was co-writer and manager.

Recommended: KINGDOM COME (*5).

LENNY WOLF – vocals (ex-STONE FURY) / **DANNY STAG** – lead guitar / **RICK STEIER** – rhythm guitar / **JOHNNY B.FRANK** – bass / **JAMES KOTTACK** – drums

Polydor Polydor
Mar 88. (7") **GET IT ON. / 17** [75] [69]
(12"+=)(cd-s+=)(12"pic-d+=) – Loving you.
Mar 88. (lp)(c)(cd) **KINGDOM COME** [43] [12]
– Living out of touch / Pushin' hard / What love can be / 17 / The shuffle / Get it on / Now "forever after" / Hideaway / Loving you / Shout it out.
Jul 88. (7") **WHAT LOVE CAN BE. / THE SHUFFLE** [ ] [ ]
(12"+=)(cd-s+=) – Helping hand.
Apr 89. (7")(7"clear) **DO YOU LIKE IT. / HIGHWAY 6** [73] [ ]
(12"+=)(12"pic-d+=) – Slow down.
(cd-s++=) – Get it on (the full version).
May 89. (lp)(c)(cd) **IN YOUR FACE** [25] [49]
– Do you like it / Who do you love / The wind / Gotta go (can't wage a war) / Highway 6 / Perfect "O" / Just like a wild rose / Overrated / Mean dirty Joe / Stargazer.
Sep 89. (7") **OVERRATED. / JUST LIKE A WILD ROSE** [ ] [ ]
(12"+=)(cd-s+=) – The perfect "O" (live).
(10"+=) – The wind (live).

— Split Aug'89, but WOLF reformed in '91 complete with **BLUES SARACENO** – guitar / **VOEN VAN BAAL** – keyboards / **JIMMY BRALOWER + STEVE BURKE** – drums

Jun 91. (cd)(c)(lp) **HANDS OF TIME** [ ] [ ]
– I've been trying / Should I / You'll never know / Both of us / Stay / Blood on the land / Shot down / You're not the only . . . I know / Do I belong / Can't deny / Hands of time.
Disbanded after above failed.

W.E.A. W.E.A.
Feb 94. (cd)(c)(lp) **BAD IMAGE** [ ] [ ]
– Passion departed / You're the one / Fake believer / Friends / Mad queen / Pardon the difference (but I like it) / Little wild thing / Can't resist / Talked too much / Glove of stone / Outsider.

KINGDOM COME (UK) (see under ⇒ BROWN, Arthur)

KINGFISH (see under ⇒ GRATEFUL DEAD)

KING L (see under ⇒ DANNY WILSON)

KINGMAKER

Formed: Hull, England . . . late 1990, by ex-TOMBSTONE GRAFFITI members LOZ and MILES. After a 45 on own 'Sacred Heart', they signed in 1991 to 'Scorch' through 'Chrysalis'. The following year, 'EAT YOURSELF WHOLE' became Top 20 hit. • **Style:** Alternative pop outfit, similiar to WONDER STUFF, likened to a mutilated NEIL YOUNG. • **Songwriters:** LOZ wrote lyrics except LADY MADONNA (Beatles). • **Trivia:** Produced by PAT COLLIER (ex-VIBRATORS).

Recommended: EAT YOURSELF WHOLE (*7). / SLEEPWALKING (*6) .

LOZ HARDY – vocals (ex-TOMBSTONE GRAFFITI) / **MILES HOWELL** – bass (ex-TOMBSTONE GRAFFITI, ex-RAIN) / **JOHN ANDREW** – drums

Sacred H. not issued
Jan 91. (12"ep) **CELEBRATED WORKING MAN / LITTLE MISS KINGMAKER. / FREEWHEELIN' / POCKETS OF ST.MALACHI** *(re-iss.Feb92)* [ ] [-]

Scorch-Chrysalis Chrysalis
Apr 91. (7")(c-s) **WHEN LUCY'S DOWN. / WHERE YOU STAND** [ ] [-]
(12"+=)(cd-s+=) – High as a kite / Join the human race.
Aug 91. (12"ep)(cd-ep) **TWO HEADED, YELLOW BELLIED HOLE DIGGER. / THIS TIME THIS TOWN THIS SEA. / WONDERFUL GARDEN / POCKETS OF ST.MALACHI (live)** [ ] [-]
Sep 91. (cd)(c)(lp) **EAT YOURSELF WHOLE** [69] [ ]
– Revelation / Really scrape the sky / Two headed, yellow bellied hole digger / Hard times / Loveless-defamed / When Lucy's down / Wave / Lady Shakespeare's bomb / Everything in life / High as a kite. *(re-iss.Feb92, hit No.29)*
Jan 92. (7"ep) **IDIOTS AT THE WHEEL** [30] [ ]
– Really scrape the sky / Every teenage suicide / Strip away.
(12"ep+=)(cd-ep+=) – Revelation (Bombay mix).
Mar 92. (7"ep)(12"ep)(c-ep)(cd-ep) **KILLJOY WAS HERE** [ ] [ ]
– Eat yourself whole / Highway's gate / Pyjama girl. *(withdrawn)*
May 92. (7")(c-s) **EAT YOURSELF WHOLE. / PJAMA GIRL** [15] [ ]
(12"+=)(cd-s+=) – Highway's gate.
Oct 92. (7"ep)(12"ep)(cd-ep) **ARMCHAIR ANARCHIST / EVERYTHING'S CHANGED (SINCE YOU'VE BEEN TO LONDON). / KISSING UNDER ANAESTHETIC** [ ] [ ]
Apr 93. (7"ep)(c-ep) **TEN YEARS ASLEEP. / BROADMOOR HOTEL / DON'T COME OVER / I'M IN LOVE** [15] [ ]
(cd-ep) – ('A'side) / Genuine liar / Lady Madonna / When Lucy's down (live).
(cd-ep) – ('A'side) / Shiver / High as a kite (live) / Hard times (live).
May 93. (cd)(c)(lp) **SLEEPWALKING** [15] [ ]
– Playground reality / Armchair anarchist / Queen Jane / Sad to see you go / Help yourself / Tomorrow's world / Ten years asleep / Honesty kills / Sequinned thug / Sleepwalking in the five o'clock shadow / Stay free / Pyromaniacs anonymous.
Jun 93. (7") **QUEEN JANE. / SICK AND ANGRY CHILDREN** [29] [ ]
(12"+=) – Flesh phobia / Sequinned thug ('92 version).
(cd-s) – ('A'side) / Your place / Electric Sue.
(cd-s) – ('A'side) / No way out / Sequinned thug ('92 version).
Oct 93. (cd-ep) **SATURDAY'S NOT WHAT IT USED TO BE / ARMCHAIR ANARCHIST (live) / HIGHWAY'S GATE (live) / FREEWHEELIN' (live)** [63] [ ]
(10") – (1st track) / Eat yourself whole (live) / Everything's changed (since you've . . .) (live) / Every teenage suicide (live).
Nov 93. (cd)(c)(m-lp) **TO HELL WITH HUMDRUM** (part compilation) [ ] [ ]
– Saturday's not what it used to be / Never too high to fall / Lies before kisses / Loose lips sink ships / Ten years asleep / Honesty kills / Sleepwalking (in the five o'clock shadow) / Queen Jane.
Apr 95. (c-s) **YOU AND I WILL NEVER SEE THINGS EYE TO EYE / BITCH OF A SON / YOU OF ALL PEOPLE** [33] [ ]
(cd-s) – ('A'side) / When Lucy's down / Queen Jane / Saturday's not what it used to be.
(cd-s) – ('A'side) / Friends in low places / S*T*A*R / Warm heart, cold feet.
Apr 95. (cd)(c) **IN THE BEST POSSIBLE TASTE** [ ] [ ]

– In the best possible taste (part 2) / You and I will never see things eye to eye / Hey, birdman / Frustrated gangster / Story of my life / Sometimes I think she takes me along just for the ride / One false move / Side by side / A fool like you / End of the line / In the best possible taste (part 1).

May 95. (7"pink) **IN THE BEST POSSIBLE TASTE (part 2). / AMATEUR'S LULLABY / IF YOU WERE MINE** [41] [ ]
(cd-s) – ('A'side) / Two headed yellow bellied hole digger / Sad to see you go / Never too high to fall.
(cd-s) – ('A'side) / Backroom boys / Another bad dose of home truths / Dissatisfaction guarenteed.

— Split October 1995.

KINGSMEN

Formed: Portland, Oregon, USDA . . . 1958 by schoolboys EASTON and ELY, who soon recruited MITCHELL, NORDBY and GALLUCCI. In May'63, after tours supporting PAUL REVERE & THE RAIDERS, they gained studio time and recorded debut 45 'LOUIE LOUIE'. This soon got issued on 'Jerden', and became a hit in Boston, before it was re-issued on 'Wand'. It soared to No.2 in the American charts, and became a classic standard for many future rock groups. At the time of its success, group went through turmoil, when EASTON took over leadership and vox of group, which led to his friend ELY departing. On US TV, EASTON was seen miming to ELY's raunchy vocals. **Style & Songwriters:** Mainly a cover versions garage rock group, who will best be remembered for 1 song 'LOUIE LOUIE'. Covers:- LOUIE LOUIE (Richard Berry) / MONEY (Barrett Strong) / LITTLE LATIN LUPE LU (Righteous Brothers) / KILLER JOE (Rocky Fellers) / etc. • **Trivia:** LOUIE LOUIE was banned in many States, including our one in Britain.

Recommended: LOUIE LOUIE – GREATEST HITS (*5).

LYNN EASTON – saxophone, vocals / **JACK ELY** – vocals, guitar / **MIKE MITCHELL** – lead guitar / **BOB NORDBY** – bass / **DON GALLUCCI** – organ

not issued / Jerden

Jun 63. (7") **LOUIE LOUIE. / HAUNTED CASTLE** [-] [ ]

Pye Inter. / Wand

Jan 64. (7") **LOUIE LOUIE. / HAUNTED CASTLE** [26] [2] Nov 63
(re-iss.US May66, hit No.97)

— (Aug63) **EASTON** took over vox from **ELY** who moves to drums! just before he departed / **GARY ABBOTT** – drums repl. ELY. **NORM SUNDHOLM** – bass repl. NORDBY

Jan 64. (lp) **LOUIE LOUIE: THE KINGSMEN IN PERSON (live Portland)** [-] [20]
– Louie Louie / The waiting / Mojo workout / Fever / Money / Bent scepter / Long tall Texan / You can't sit down / Twist & shout / J.A.J. / Night train / Mashed potatoes.

Mar 64. (7") **MONEY. / BENT SCEPTER** [-] [16]

— **BARRY CURTIS** – organ repl. **DON DICK PETERSON** – drums repl. GARY

Jul 64. (7") **LITTLE LATIN LUPE LU. / DAVID'S MOOD** [ ] [46]
Sep 64. (7") **DEATH OF AN ANGEL. / SEARCHING FOR LOVE** [ ] [42]
Feb 65. (7") **JOLLY GREEN GIANT. / LONG GREEN** [ ] [4] Jan 65
Feb 65. (lp) **THE KINGSMEN VOLUME 2** [ ] [15] Sep 64
– Kingsmen introduction / Little Latin Lupe Lu / Long green / Do you love me / New Orleans / Walking the dog / David's mood / Something's got a hold on me / Come on baby, let the good times roll / Ooh poo pah doo / Great balls of fire / Linda Lou / Earth of an angel.
Feb 65. (lp) **THE KINGSMEN VOL.3** [-] [22]
– Jolly green giant / Over you / That's cool, that's trash / Don't you just know it / I go crazy / La-do-dada / Long green / Mother-in-law / Shout / Searching for love / Tall cool one / Comin' home baby.
Jun 65. (7") **THE CLIMB. / WAITING** [ ] [65] May 65
Aug 65. (7") **ANNIE FANNY. / GIVE HER LOVIN'** [-] [47]
Aug 65. (7") **ANNIE FANNY. / SOMETHING'S GOT A HOLD ON ME** [ ] [-]
Feb 66. (7") **IT'S THE ONLY DOG. / (YOU GOT) GAMMA GOOCHE** [-] [ ]
Mar 66. (lp) **THE KINGSMEN ON CAMPUS (live)** [ ] [68] Oct 65
– Annie Fanny / Rosalie / A hard day's night / I like it like that / Stand by me / Little green thing / The climb / Sticks and stones / Peter Gunn / Some times / Shotgun / Genevieve.
Jun 66. (7") **KILLER JOE. / LITTLE GREEN THING** [ ] [77] Mar 66
Jun 66. (7") **THE KRUNCH. / THE CLIMB** [-] [ ]
Sep 66. (lp) **15 GREAT HITS** (compilation) [ ] [87] Aug 66
– Killer Joe / Good lovin' / Jenny take a ride / Ooh poo pah doo / Fever / Quarter to three / Poison Ivy / Satisfaction / Twist and shout / Money / Searchin' / Hang on Sloopy / Do you love me / Shout / New Orleans.
Sep 66. (7") **LITTLE SALLY TEASE. / MY WIFE CAN'T COOK** [-] [ ]
Nov 66. (7") **IF I NEEDED SOMEONE. / THE GRASS IS GREEN** [-] [ ]
Jan 67. (7") **DAYTIME SHADOWS. / TROUBLE** [-] [ ]

Wand / Wand

Jan 67. (lp) **UP AND AWAY** [ ] [ ]
– Trouble / If I needed someone / Grass is green / Tosin' and turnin' / Under my thumb / Wild thing / (I have found) Another girl / Daytime shadows / Shake a tailfeather / Children's caretaker / Land of a thousand dances / Mustang Sally / Little Sally tease / Hushabye.
Mar 67. (7") **THE WOLF OF MANHATTAN. / CHILDREN'S CARETAKER** [-] [ ]
May 67. (7") **DON'T SAY NO. / ANOTHER GIRL (I HAVE FOUND)** [-] [ ]
Jul 67. (7") **BO DIDDLEY BACH. / JUST BEFORE THE BREAK OF DAY** [-] [ ]
Sep 67. (7") **GET OUT OF MY LIFE WOMAN. / SINCE YOU'VE BEEN GONE** [-] [ ]
Nov 67. (7") **I GUESS I WAS DREAMIN'. / ON LOVE** [-] [ ]

— In 1967, EASTON left group and they dissolved.

– more compilations, etc. –

1964. Pye Int./ US= Wand; (7"ep) **THE KINGSMEN** [ ] [ ]
1965. Pye Int./ US= Wand; (7"ep) **MOJO WORKOUT** [ ] [ ]
1966. Pye Int./ US= Wand; (7"ep) **FEVER** [ ] [ ]
Apr 66. Pye Int./ US= Wand; (7") **LITTLE LATIN LUPE LU. / LOUIE LOUIE** [ ] [ ]
1969. Marble Arch; (lp) **THE KINGSMEN'S GREATEST HITS** [ ] [-]
1972. Scepter; (lp) **THE BEST OF THE KINGSMEN** [-] [ ]
(re-iss.Jan86 on 'Rhino', cd-iss.Sep91)
1980. Piccadilly; (lp) **A QUARTER TO THREE** [-] [ ]
1980. Piccadilly; (lp) **HOUSE PARTY** [-] [ ]
Jul 81. Old Gold; (7") **LOUIE LOUIE. / JOLLY GREEN GIANT** [ ] [-]
Jan 87. Decal; (lp) **LOUIE LOUIE – GREATEST HITS** [ ] [-]
– Louie Louie / Money (that's what I want) / Jolly green giant / Death of an angel / The climb / Get out of my life woman / Little Latin lupe lu / Killer Joe / Annie Fanny / Long green / Little Sally tease / Trouble / If I needed someone.

KINGS X

Formed: Springfield, Houston, Texas, USA . . . 1981, initially as The EDGE by PILNICK, TABOR and GASKELL. With help from manager Sam Taylor, they signed to US indie label 'Megaforce' in 1987. Their debut 'OUT OF THE SILENT PLANET', soon found friends in 'Atlantic', and was followed a year later by excellent chart album 'GRETCHEN GOES TO NEBRASKA'. • **Style:** Hard-rock trio with exceptional blues sound and tremendous near LEVEL 42 type harmonies. • **Songwriters:** Group penned. • **Trivia:** Below album titles' inspiration comes from English author C.S.Lewis.

Recommended: GRETCHEN GOES TO NEBRASKA (*8).

DOUG PINNICK (b.Chicago) – vocals, bass / **TY TABOR** (b.Mississippi) – guitar / **JERRY GASKILL** (b.New Jersey) – drums

Megaforce Atlantic / Megaforce Atlantic

Mar 88. (lp)(c)(cd) **OUT OF THE SILENT PLANET** [ ] [ ]
– In the new age / Goldilox / Power of love / Wonder / Sometimes / King / What is this? / Far, far away / Shot of love / Visions.
Jun 89. (lp)(c)(cd) **GRETCHEN GOES TO NEBRASKA** [52] [ ]
– Out of the silent planet / Over my head / Summerland / Everybody knows a little bit of something / The difference (in the garden of St.Anne's-On-the-Hill) / I'll never be the same / Mission / Fall on me / Pleiades / Don't believe it (it's easier said than done) / Send a message / The burning down. *(re-iss.cd Feb95)*
Mar 90. (7") **OVER MY HEAD. / SHOT OF LOVE** [ ] [ ]
(12"+=)(cd-s+=) – I'll never be the same.
May 90. (7") **SUMMERLAND. /** [-] [ ]
Oct 90. (cd)(c)(lp) **FAITH HOPE LOVE** [70] [85]
– We are finding who we are / It's love / I'll never get tired of you / Fine art of friendship / Mr. Wilson / Moonjaw / Six broken soldiers / I can't help it / Talk to you / Everywhere I go / We were born to be loved / Faith hope love / Legal kill.
Apr 91. (7")(c-s) **IT'S LOVE. / WE WERE BORN TO BE LOVED** [ ] [ ]
(12"+=)(cd-s+=) – Six broken soldiers.

— The track 'Junior's Gone Wild', appeared on the film 'Bill & Ted's Bogus Journey', & the b-side of ARGENT's 'God Gave Rock'n'roll To You II' single.

Mar 92. (cd)(c)(lp) **KINGS X** [46] [ ]
– World around me / Prisoner / The big picture / Lost in Germany / Chariot song / Ooh song / Not just for the dead / What I know about love / Black flag / Dream in my life / Silent wind.
Feb 94. (cd)(c)(lp) **DOGMAN** [49] [ ]
– Dogman / Shoes / Pretend / Flies and blue skies / Black the sky / Fool you / Don't care / Sunshine rain / Complain / Human behavior / Cigarettes / Go to Hell / Pillow / Manic depression.

KINKS

Formed: Muswell Hill, London, England . . . 1963 by brothers RAY and DAVE DAVIES, who found QUAIFE from The RAVENS. With help from managers Robert Wace and Grenville Collins, they met Larry Page who gave them name KINKS late '63. He also arranged demos, which were soon heard by American SHEL TALMY, who got them signed to 'Pye' early '64. Two singles flopped, but third 'YOU REALLY GOT ME' stormed into No.1 in the UK, and soon broke into US Top 10. A top selling eponymous lp followed, as did a series of Top 10 sixties singles, including two more UK No.1's 'TIRED OF WAITING FOR YOU' & 'SUNNY AFTERNOON'. After 2 big hits in 1970; 'LOLA' & 'APEMAN', they struggled on new label 'RCA', from then on. It was different in the States, where they progressed commercially again from 1975's 'SOAP OPERA' album. • **Style:** Fashionable R&B beat-pop outfit, whose teenage anthems, drifted more into concept theories by 1968. They developed into a more US mainstream rock act in the 80's, with RAY never quite forgetting his Englishness. • **Songwriters:** RAY DAVIES wrote all of work, except covers; TOO MUCH MONKEY BUSINESS (Chuck Berry) / GOT LOVE IF YOU WANT IT (Slim Harpo) / MILK COW BLUES (Elvis Presley) / etc. • **Trivia:** RAY produced 1969 lp 'Turtle Soup' for The TURTLES. He was married 12 Dec'64 to Rasa Dicpetri, but divorced later (see KINKS biography by Johnny Rogan). In 1981 he divorced second wife Yvonne. (RAY had for 3 years a relationship with CHRISSIE HYNDE of The PRETENDERS.) She gave him daughter Natalie on Feb'83, although they separated when she started dating JIM KERR (of SIMPLE MINDS). In 1986, RAY appeared in the film musical 'Absolute Beginners'.

Recommended: FACE TO FACE (*8) / VILLAGE GREEN PRESERVATION SOCIETY (*8) / THE ULTIMATE COLLECTION (*9) / COME DANCING WITH THE KINKS – THE BEST OF . . . 1977-1986 (*7).

RAY DAVIES (b.21 Jun'44) – vocals, guitar / **DAVE DAVIES** (b. 3 Feb'47) – guitar, vocals / **PETER QUAIFE** (b.31 Dec'43, Tavistock, Devon) – bass with session drummers

Pye Cameo

Mar 64. (7") **LONG TALL SHORTY. / I TOOK MY BABY HOME** [ ] [ ] Apr 64
(US re-iss.Nov64)
May 64. (7") **YOU STILL WANT ME. / YOU REALLY GOT ME** [ ] [-]

Pye Reprise

Aug 64. (7") **YOU REALLY GOT ME. / IT'S ALRIGHT** [1] [7] Sep 64

— **MICK AVORY** (b.15 Feb'44) – drums was now used although he joined 9 months previous.

Oct 64. (lp) **THE KINKS** (US-title 'YOU REALLY GOT ME') [3] [29] Dec64
– Beautiful Delilah / So mystifying / Just can't go to sleep / Long tall Shorty / You really got me / Cadillac / Bald headed woman / Revenge / Too much monkey business / Revenge / I've been driving on Bald mountain / Stop your sobbing / Got love if you want it. *(UK re-as.May80 on 'P.R.T.', c+cd.Oct87) (cd-iss.Dec89 on 'Castle')*
Oct 64. (7") **ALL DAY AND ALL OF THE NIGHT. / I GOTTA MOVE** [2] [7] Dec 64
(re-iss 7" pic-d Oct 84 on 'PRT') (re-iss 7" Jan 88)
Jan 65. (7") **TIRED OF WAITING FOR YOU. / COME ON NOW** [1] [6] Mar 65
Mar 65. (lp) **KINDA KINKS** [3] [60]
– Look for me baby / Got my feet on the ground / Nothin' in the world can stop me worryin' 'bout that girl / Naggin' woman / Wonder where my baby is tonight / Tired of waiting for you / Dancing in the street / Don't ever change / Come on now / So long / You shouldn't be sad / Something better beginning. *(re-iss.+c.May80 on 'P.R.T.', c+cd.Oct87) (cd-iss.Dec89 on 'Castle')*
Mar 65. (lp) **KINKS-SIZE** [-] [13]
– Tired of waiting for you / Louie Louie / I've got that feeling / Revenge / I gotta move / Things are getting better / I gotta go now / I'm a lover not a fighter / Come on now / All day and all of the night.
Mar 65. (7") **EVERYBODY'S GONNA BE HAPPY. / WHO'LL BE THE NEXT IN LINE** [11] [34] Aug65b
May 65. (7") **SET ME FREE. / I NEED YOU** [9] [23] Jun 65
Jul 65. (7") **SEE MY FRIEND. / NEVER MET A GIRL LIKE YOU BEFORE** [10] [ ]
Nov 65. (7") **TILL THE END OF THE DAY. / WHERE HAVE ALL THE GOOD TIMES GONE** [6] [50] Mar 66
Nov 65. (lp) **THE KINK KONTROVERSY** [9] [95] Apr 66
– Milk cow blues / Ring the bells / Gotta get the first plane home / When I see that girl of mine / Till the end of the day / The world keeps going round / I'm on the island / Where have all the good times gone / It's too late / What's in store for me / You can't win. *(re-iss.May80 on 'P.R.T.', c+cd.Oct87) (cd-iss.Dec89 on 'Castle')*
Dec 65. (lp) **KINKS KINKDOM** [-] [13]
– Well respected man / Such a shame / Wait 'til the summer comes along / Naggin' woman / Who'll be the next in line / Don't you fret / I need you / It's all right / Louie Louie.
Dec 65. (7") **A WELL RESPECTED MAN. / MILK COW BLUES** [-] [13]
Feb 66. (7") **DEDICATED FOLLOWER OF FASHION. / SITTING ON MY SOFA** [4] [36] May 66

— **JOHN DALTON** – bass deputised on tour for QUAIFE while injured

Jun 66. (7") **SUNNY AFTERNOON. / I'M NOT LIKE EVERYBODY ELSE** [1] [14] Aug 66

— **JOHN DALTON** sessioned on songs between 66-69, QUAIFE's photo on covers

Oct 66. (lp) **FACE TO FACE** [12] [ ]
– Party line / Rosy won't you please come home / Dandy / Too much on my mind / Session man / Rainy day in June / House in the country / Sunny afternoon / Holiday in Waikiki / Most exclusive residence for sale / Fancy / Little Miss Queen of Darkness / You're looking fine / I'll remember. *(re-iss.Jun80 on 'P.R.T.', c+cd. Oct87) (cd-iss.Dec89 on 'Castle')*
Nov 66. (7") **DEAD END STREET. / BIG BLACK SMOKE** [5] [73] Jan 67
May 67. (7") **WATERLOO SUNSET. / TWO SISTERS** [-] [ ]
May 67. (7") **WATERLOO SUNSET. / ACT NICE AND GENTLE** [2] [ ]
May 67. (lp) **LIVE AT KELVIN HALL (live in Glasgow)** (US-title 'THE LIVE KINKS') [ ] [ ]
– Till the end of the day / I'm on an island / You really got me / All day and all of the night / A well respected man / You're looking fine / Sunny afternoon / Dandy / Come on now / Milk cow blues – Batman theme – Tired of waiting for you. *(re-iss.Aug80 on 'P.R.T.', c+cd.Sep87) (cd-iss.Dec89 on 'Castle')*
Jun 67. (7") **MR. PLEASANT. / HARRY RAG** [-] [80]
Oct 67. (lp) **SOMETHING ELSE BY THE KINKS** [35] [ ]
– David Watts / Death of a clown / Two sisters / No return / Harry Rag / Tin soldier man / Situation vacant / Love me till the sun shines / Lazy old sun / Afternoon tea / Funny face / End of the season / Waterloo sunset. *(re-iss.Feb81 on 'P.R.T.', c+cd.Sep87) (cd-iss.Dec89 on 'Castle')*
Oct 67. (7") **AUTUMN ALMANAC. / MR. PLEASANT** [3] [ ]

— (above UK 'B'side was US 'A'side)

Apr 68. (7") **WONDERBOY. / POLLY** [37] [ ]
Jul 68. (7") **DAYS. / SHE'S GOT EVERYTHING** [12] [ ]
Jul 68. (lp) **THE KINKS ARE THE VILLAGE GREEN PRESERVATION SOCIETY** [ ] [ ]
– Village green preservation society / Do you remember Walter / Picture book / Johnny Thunder / The last of the steam powered trains / Big sky / Sitting by the riverside / Animal farm / Village green / Starstruck / Phenomenal cat / All my friends were there / Wicked Annabella / Monica / People take pictures of each other. *(re-iss.Feb81 on 'P.R.T.', re-iss.Nov85, cd-iss.Sep87)*
Apr 69. (7") **PLASTIC MAN. / KING KONG** [31] [ ]
Apr 69. (7") **STARSTRUCK. / PICTURE BOOK** [-] [ ]

— **JOHN DALTON** (b.21 May'43) – bass officially repl. QUAIFE

Jun 69. (7") **WALTER. / VILLAGE GREEN PRESERVATION SOCIETY** [-] [ ]
Jun 69. (7") **DRIVIN'. / MINDLESS CHILD OF MOTHERHOOD** [ ] [-]
Sep 69. (7") **SHANGRI-LA. / THIS MAN HE WEEPS TONIGHT** [ ] [-]
Oct 69. (lp) **ARTHUR (OR THE DECLINE AND FALL OF THE BRITISH EMPIRE** [ ] [ ]
– Victoria / Yes sir, no sir / Some mother's son / Brainwashed / Australia / Shangri-la / Mr. Churchill says / She bought a hat like Princess Marina / Young and innocent days / Nothing to say / Arthur. *(re-iss.1974) (re-iss.Oct87 on 'P.R.T.'+cd.) (cd-iss.Dec89 on 'Castle')*
Dec 69. (7") **VICTORIA. / MR. CHURCHILL SAYS** [33] [-]
Jan 70. (7") **VICTORIA. / BRAINWASHED** [-] [62]
Jun 70. (7") **LOLA. / BERKELEY MEWS** [2] [-]
Aug 70. (7") **LOLA. / MINDLESS CHILD OF MOTHERHOOD** [-] [9]
Nov 70. (lp)(c) **LOLA VERSUS POWERMAN & THE MONEYGOROUND, PART ONE** [ ] [35]
– The contenders / Strangers / Denmark Street / Get back in line / Lola / Top of the pops / The moneygoround / This time tomorrow / A long way from home / Rats / Apeman / Powerman / Got to be free. *(re-iss.Oct74 on 'Golden Hour')*
Nov 70. (7") **APEMAN. / RATS** [5] [45] Jan 71
Mar 71. (lp)(c) **(SOUNDTRACK FROM THE FILM) "PERCY"** [ ] [ ]
– God's children / Lola / The way love used to be / Completely / Running round town / Moments / Animals in the zoo / Just friends / Helga / Willesden Green / God's children – end.
Apr 71. (7"ep) **GOD'S CHILDREN. / THE WAY LOVE USED TO BE / DREAMS / MOMENTS** [ ] [-]
Qpr 71. (7") **GOD'S CHILDREN. / THE WAY LOVE USED TO BE** [-] [ ]

— added **JOHN GOSLING** – keyboards (he guested on 'LOLA' album), plus **LAURIE BROWN** – trumpet / **JOHN BEECHAM** – trombone / **ALAN HOLMES** – saxophone recruited from The MIKE COTTON SOUND. The three became full-time members '73, adding to **R. DAVIES, D. DAVIES, AVORY and DALTON**

R.C.A. R.C.A.

Nov 71. (lp)(c) **MUSWELL HILLBILLIES** [ ] [100]
– 20th century man / Acute schizophrenia paranoia blues / Holiday / Skin and bone / Alcohol / Complicated life / Here come the people in the grey / Have a cuppa tea / Holloway jail / Oklahoma U.S.A. / Uncle son / Muswell hillbilly.
May 72. (7") **SUPERSONIC ROCKET SHIP. / YOU DON'T KNOW MY NAME** [16] [ ]
Jun 72. (7") **20th CENTURY MAN. / SKIN AND BONE** [-] [ ]
Aug 72. (d-lp)(c) **EVERYBODY'S IN SHOWBIZ** [ ] [70]
– Here comes yet another day / Maximum consumption / Unreal reality / Hot potatoes / Sitting in my hotel / You don't know my name / Supersonic rocket ship / Look a little on the sunny side / Celluloid heroes / Motorway. *(live-lp)* **EVERYBODY'S A STAR (live)** – Top of the pops / Brainwashed / Mr. Wonderful / Acute schizophrenia paranoia blues / Holiday / Muswell Hillbilly / Alcohol / Banana boat song / Skin and bone / Baby face / Lola.
Nov 72. (7") **CELLULOID HEROES. / HOT POTATOES** [ ] [ ]
Jun 73. (7") **SCRAPHEAD CITY. / ONE OF THE SURVIVORS** [-] [ ]
Jun 73. (7") **SITTING IN THE MIDDAY SUN. / ONE OF THE SURVIVORS** [ ] [ ]
Sep 73. (7") **SWEET LADY GENEVIEVE. / SITTING IN MY HOTEL** [ ] [ ]
Dec 73. (d-lp)(c) **PRESERVATION ACT I** [ ] [ ]
– Morning song / Daylight / Sweet Lady Genevieve / There's a change in the weather / Where are they now / One of the survivors / Cricket / I am your man / Here comes Flash / Sitting in the midday Sun / Demolution.

— note: next 45 only contained **RAY & DAVE DAVIES**, before full 5 + 3 again

Apr 74. (7") **MIRROR OF LOVE. / CRICKET** [ ] [-]
Jun 74. (d-lp)(c) **PRESERVATION ACT II** [ ] [ ]
– (announcement) / Introduction to solution / When a solution comes / Money talks / (announcement) / Shepherds of the nation / Scum of the Earth / Secondhand car spiv / He's evil / Mirror of love / (announcement) / Nobody gives / Oh where oh where is love? / Flash's dream / Flash's confession / Nothing lasts forever / (announcement) / Artificial man / Scrapheap city / (announcement) / Salvation Road.
Jul 74. (7") **MIRROR OF LOVE. / HE'S EVIL** [-] [ ]
Oct 74. (7") **HOLIDAY ROMANCE. / SHEPHERDS OF THE NATION** [ ] [-]
Oct 74. (7") **PRESERVATION. / SALVATION** [-] [ ]
Apr 75. (7") **ORDINARY PEOPLE. / STAR MAKER** [-] [ ]
Apr 75. (7") **DUCKS ON THE WALL. / RUSH HOUR BLUES** [ ] [-]
May 75. (lp)(c) **SOAP OPERA** [ ] [51]
– Everybody's a star (starmaker) / Ordinary people / Rush hour blues / Nine to five / When work is over / Have another drink / Underneath the neon sign / Holiday romance / You make it all worth while / Ducks on the wall / Face in the crowd / You can't stop the music. *(re-iss.Jul84)*
May 75. (7") **YOU CAN'T STOP THE MUSIC. / HAVE ANOTHER DRINK** [ ] [-]
Nov 75. (lp)(c) **SCHOOLBOYS IN DISGRACE** [ ] [45]
– Schooldays / Jack the idiot dunce / Education / The first time we fall in love / I'm in disgrace / Headmaster / The hard way / The last assembly / No more looking back / (finale).
Nov 75 (7") **THE HARD WAY. / I'M IN DISGRACE** [-] [ ]
Jan 76. (7"m) **NO MORE LOOKING BACK. / JACK THE IDIOT DUNCE / THE HARD WAY** [ ] [-]

— Now down to basic 5-piece after the 3 brass section members departed

Arista Arista

Feb 77. (lp)(c) **SLEEPWALKER** [ ] [21]
– Life on the road / Mr. Big man / Sleepwalker / Brother / Juke box music / Sleepless night / Stormy sky / Full moon / Life goes on.
Mar 77. (7") **SLEEPWALKER. / FULL MOON** [ ] [48]
Jun 77. (7") **JUKE BOX MUSIC. / SLEEPLESS NIGHT** [ ] [-]
Jun 77. (7") **JUKE BOX MUSIC. / LIFE GOES ON** [-] [ ]

— **ANDY PYLE** – bass (ex-BLODWYN PIG, ex-SAVOY BROWN, etc) repl. DALTON

Dec 77. (7") **FATHER CHRISTMAS. / PRINCE OF THE PUNKS** [ ] [ ]
May 78. (lp)(c) **MISFITS** [ ] [40]
– Misfits / Hay fever / Live life / Rock'n'roll fantasy / In a foreign land / Permanent waves / Black Messiah / Out of the wardrobe / Trust your heart / Get up.
May 78. (7") **ROCK'N'ROLL FANTASY. / ARTIFICIAL LIGHT** [ ] [30] Jul 78
Jul 78. (7") **LIVE LIFE. / IN A FOREIGN LAND** [ ] [-]
Jul 78. (7") **LIVE LIFE. / BLACK MESSIAH** [-] [ ]
Sep 78. (7") **BLACK MESSIAH. / MISFITS** [ ] [-]

— RAY DAVIES, DAVE DAVIES and MICK AVORY recruited new members **GORDON EDWARDS** – keyboards (ex-PRETTY THINGS) repl. GOSLING (formed NETWORK) / **JIM RODFORD** – bass (ex-ARGENT, ex-PHOENIX) repl. PYLE (formed NETWORK)

Jan 79. (7")(12") **(WISH I COULD FLY LIKE) SUPERMAN. / LOW BUDGET** □ –

— **IAN GIBBON** – keyboards repl. EDWARDS

Apr 79. (7") **(WISH I COULD FLY LIKE) SUPERMAN. / PARTY LINE** – 41
Sep 79. (7") **MOVING PICTURES. / IN A SPACE** □ –
Sep 79. (lp)(c) **LOW BUDGET** □ 11 Jul 79
– Attitude / Catch me now I'm falling / Pressure / National health / (I wish I could fly like) Superman / Low budget / In a space / Little bit of emotion / Gallon of gas / Misery / Moving pictures. *(cd-iss.Apr88)*
Sep 79. (7") **GALLON OF GAS. / LOW BUDGET** – □
Nov 79. (7") **CATCH ME NOW I'M FALLING. / LOW BUDGET** – □
Nov 79. (7") **PRESSURE. / NATIONAL HEALTH** □ –
Jul 80. (d-lp)(c) **ONE FOR THE ROAD (live)** □ 14 Jun 80
– The hard way / Catch me now I'm falling / Where have all the good times gone / Lola / Pressure / All day and all of the night / 20th century man / Misfits / Prince of the punks / Stop your sobbing / Low budget / Attitude / (Wish I could fly like) Superman / National health / Till the end of the day / Celluloid heroes / You really got me / Victoria / David Watts.
Jul 80. (7"ep) **WHERE HAVE ALL THE GOOD TIMES GONE (live)** □ –
– Where have all the good times gone / Victoria / Attitude / David Watts.
Aug 80. (7") **LOLA (live). / CELLULOID HEROES (live)** – 81
Oct 80. (7") **YOU REALLY GOT ME (live). / ATTITUDE (live)** – □
Jun 81. (lp)(c) **GIVE THE PEOPLE WHAT THEY WANT** □ 15
– Around the dial / Give the people what they wnt / Killer's eyes / Predictable / Add it up / Destroyer / Yo-yo / Back to front / Art lover / A little bit of abuse / Better things.
Jun 81. (7") **BETTER THINGS. / MASSIVE REDUCTIONS** 46 –
(d7"+=) – Lola / David Watts.
Oct 81. (7")(7"pic-d) **PREDICTABLE. / BACK TO FRONT** □ □
Oct 81. (7") **DESTROYER. / BACK TO FRONT** – 85
Nov 81. (7") **BETTER THINGS. / YO-YO** – 92
Jun 83. (lp)(c) **STATE OF CONFUSION** □ 12
– State of confusion / Definite maybe / Labour of love / Come dancing / Property / Don't forget to dance / Young Conservatives / Heart of gold / Cliches of the world (B movie) / Bernadette. *(cd-iss.1988 on 'Ariola')*
Jul 83. (7")(12") **COME DANCING. / NOISE** 12 6 May 83
Aug 83. (7") **DON'T FORGET TO DANCE. / YOUNG CONSERVATIVES** – 29
Sep 83. (7")(12") **DON'T FORGET TO DANCE. / BERNADETTE** 58 –
Mar 84. (7") **STATE OF CONFUSION. / HEART OF GOLD** □ □
(12"+=) – 20th century man (live) / Lola (live).
Jul 84. (7") **GOOD DAY. / TOO HOT** □ □
(12"+=) – Superman / Don't forget to dance.
Nov 84. (lp)(c) **WORD OF MOUTH** □ 57
– Do it again / Word of mouth / Good day / Living on a thin line / Sold me out / Massive reductions / Guilty / Too hot / Missing persons / Summer's gone / Going solo. *(cd-iss.Jun88 on 'Ariola')*
Apr 85. (7") **DO IT AGAIN. / GUILTY** □ 41 Dec 84
(12"+=) – Summer's gone.
Apr 85. (7") **SUMMER'S GONE. / GOING SOLO** – □

— Returned to original line-up of **RAY, DAVE + MICK,** plus sessioners. (RODFORD and GIBBONS departed).

London M.C.A.

Nov 86. (7") **ROCK'N'ROLL CITIES. / WELCOME TO SLEAZY TOWN** – □
Nov 86. (lp)(c)(cd) **THINK VISUAL** □ 81
– Working at the factory / Lost and found / Repetition / Welcome to Sleazy Town / The video shop / Rock'n'roll cities / How are you / Think visual / Natural gift / Killing time / When you were a child.
Dec 86. (7") **HOW ARE YOU. / KILLING TIME** □ –
(12"+=) – Welcome to Sleazy town.
Mar 87. (7") **LOST AND FOUND. / KILLING TIME** □ □
(12"+=) – (Ray Davies interview).
May 87. (7") **HOW ARE YOU. / WORKING AT THE FACTORY** – □
Feb 88. (7") **THE ROAD. / ART LOVER** □ □
(12"+=) – Come dancing. / ('A' version).
May 88. (lp)(c)(cd) **THE ROAD (live / studio *)** □ □
– The road * / Destroyer / Apeman / Come dancing / Art lover / Cliches of the world (B-movie) / Living on a thin line / Lost and found / It * / Around the dial / Give the people what they want.
Feb 89. (7") **DOWN ALL THE DAYS (TILL 1992). / YOU REALLY GOT ME (live)** □ □
(12"+=)(cd-s+=) – Entertainment. *(re-dist.Sep89)*

— **BOB HENRIT** – drums repl. AVORY / added **MARK HALEY** – keyboards, vocals

Oct 89. (lp)(c)(cd) **UK JIVE**
– Aggravation / How do I get close / UK jive / Now and then / What are we doing / Entertainment / War is over / Down all the days (till 1992) / Loony balloon / Dear Margaret. *(c++)(cd+=)*– Bright lights / Perfect strangers. *(re-iss.Apr91)*
Feb 90. (7") **HOW DO I GET CLOSE. / DOWN ALL THE DAYS (TILL 1992)** □ □
(12"+=)(cd-s+=) – War is over. *(US 7" b-side)*

Columbia Columbia

Mar 93. (cd)(c) **PHOBIA**
– Opening / Wall of fire / Drift away / Still searching / Phobia / Only a dream / Don't / Babies / Over the edge / Surviving / It's alright (don't think about it) / The informer / Hatred (a duet) / Somebody stole my car / Close to the wire / Scattered. (cd+=) – Did ya.
Jul 93. (cd-s) **SCATTERED. / HATRED (A DUET) / DAYS** □ □
Nov 93. (7")(cd-s) **ONLY A DREAM (Radio Version) / SOMEBODY STOLE MY CAR / BABIES** □ □

Konk Konk

Oct 94. (cd)(c)(lp) **TO THE BONE (live)** □ □
– All day and all of the nigt / Apeman / Tired of waiting for you / See my friend / Death of a clown / Waterloo sunset / Muswell hillbillies / Better things / Don't forget to dance / Autumn almanac / Sunny afternoon / Dedicated follower of fashion / You really got me.
Oct 94. (cd-ep) **WATERLOO SUNSET E.P. (live)** □ □
– Waterloo sunset / You really got me / Elevator man / On the outside.

– compilations etc. –

Nov 64. Pye; (7"ep) **KINGSIZE SESSION** □ □
– I've gotta go now / I've got that feeling / Things are getting better / Louie Louie.
Jan 65. Pye; (7"ep) **KINGSIZE HITS** □ □
– You really got me / It's alright / All day and all of the night / I gotta move.
Sep 65. Pye; (7"ep) **KWYET KINKS** □ □
– Wait till the summer / Such a shame / A well respected man / Don't you fret.
Jul 66. Pye; (7"ep) **DEDICATED KINKS** □ □
– Dedicated follower of fashion / Till the end of the day / See my friend / Set me free.
Aug 66. Reprise; (lp) **THE KINKS GREATEST HITS** – 9
Apr 68. Pye; (7"ep) **SOMETHING ELSE** □ □
– David Watts / Two sisters / Lazy old Sun / Situation.
Feb 70. Pye/ US= Reprise; (d-lp)(c) **THE KINKS** □ □
Aug 71. Pye; (7"ep) **YOU REALLY GOT ME. / WONDERBOY / SET ME FREE / LONG TALL SALLY** □ □
Oct 71. Pye; (lp)(c) **THE GOLDEN HOUR OF THE KINKS** 21 □
(re-iss.Oct74) ((cd+c.Apr91 on 'Knight')
Apr 72. Reprise; (lp)(c) **THE KINKS KRONICLES** – 94
Feb 73. Reprise; (lp)(c) **THE GREAT LOST KINKS ALBUM** – □
Nov 73. Pye; (7") **WHERE HAVE ALL THE GOOD TIMES GONE. / LOLA** □ □
May 75. Pye; (7") **SUNNY AFTERNOON/. SITTING ON MY SOFA** □ □
May 77. Pye; (12"ep) **LOLA / SUNNY AFTERNOON. / WATERLOO SUNSET / DEDICATED FOLLOWER OF FASHION** □ –
Nov 77. Pye; (d-lp)(c) **THE KINKS FILE** □ –
Nov 78. Pye; (7"ep) **EP** □ –
– Long tall Shorty / I took my baby home / You still want me / You do something to me.
Apr 79. Pye; (7") **YOU REALLY GOT ME. / ALL DAY AND ALL OF THE NIGHT** □ □
(re-iss.Feb80) (re-iss Jun 84 on 'Old Gold')
Mar 80. Pye; (7") **DEDICATED FOLLOWER OF FASHION. / WATERLOO SUNSET** □ □
(re-iss.Mar82 on 'Old Gold')
Jun 80. Pye; (7"ep) **WATERLOO SUNSET / DAVID WATTS. / A WELL RESPECTED MAN / STOP YOUR SOBBIN'** □ –
1980. Pye; (d-lp)(d-c) **SPOTLIGHT ON THE KINKS** □ –
Oct 78. Pye-Ronco; (d-lp)(c) **THE KINKS 20 GOLDEN GREATS** 19 □
Jun 66. Marble Arch; (lp) **WELL RESPECTED KINKS** 5 □
Sep 67. Marble Arch; (lp) **SUNNY AFTERNOON** 9 □
Jun 76. RCA; (lp)(c) **CELLULOID HEROES – THE KINKS GREATEST** □ □
Jul 80. Pickwick; (lp)(c) **THE KINKS COLLECTION** □ –
Aug 89. Pickwick; (lp)(c)(cd) **THE BEST OF THE KINKS – 1964-66** □ –
Aug 91. Pickwick; (cd)(c) **THE BEST OF THE KINKS 1966-67** □ –
Jun 82. P.R.T.; (c) **100 MINUTES OF . . .** □ –
Feb 83. P.R.T.; (7") **SUNNY AFTERNOON. / TIRED OF WAITING FOR YOU** □ –
Apr 83. P.R.T.; (lp)(c) **SHAPE OF THINGS TO COME** □ –
Jul 83. P.R.T.; (lp)(c) **CANDY FROM MR. DANDY** □ –
Oct 83. P.R.T.; (lp)(c) **KINKS' GREATEST HITS – DEAD END STREET** 96 –
Oct 83. P.R.T.; (7")(7"pic-d) **YOU REALLY GOT ME. / MISTY WATER** 47 –
(12"pic-d+=) – All day and all of the night.
Oct 84. P.R.T.; (lp)(c)(cd) **THE KINKS GREATEST HITS** □ –
Nov 84. P.R.T.; (lp)(c) **KOLLECTABLES** □ –
Nov 84. P.R.T.; (lp)(c) **KOVERS** □ –
Nov 84. P.R.T.; (box-c) **THE KINKS BOX SET** □ –
Mar 86. P.R.T.; (7") **DEDICATED FOLLOWER OF FASHION. / AUTUMN ALMANAC** □ –
(re-iss. 7"pic-d. Mar 88)
Oct 87. P.R.T.; (lp)(c) **HIT SINGLES** □ –
Sep 87. P.R.T.; (d-lp)(c) **THE KINKS ARE WELL RESPECTED MEN** □ –
Mar 86. Old Gold; (7") **LOLA. / APEMAN** □ –
Mar 86. Old Gold; (7") **SUNNY AFTERNOON. / TIRED OF WAITING FOR YOU** □ –
(re-iss. Jul 87 on 7"pic-d 'PRT')
Nov 88. Old Gold; (cd-ep) **YOU REALLY GOT ME / ALL DAY AND ALL OF THE NIGHT / TIRED OF WAITING FOR YOU** □ –
Feb 89. Old Gold; (cd-ep) **WATERLOO SUNSET / SUNNY AFTERNOON / LOLA** □ –
Nov 85. Castle; (d-lp)(c) **THE COLLECTION** □ –
(cd-iss.1988 & Jul92 on 'BMG-RCA')
Sep 89. Castle; (lp)(c)(cd) **THE ULTIMATE COLLECTION** 35 –
– You really got me / All day and all of the night / Tired of waiting for you / Everybody's gonna be happy / Set me free / Till the end of the day / Dedicated follower of fashion / Sunny afternoon / Dead end street / Waterloo sunset / Autumn almanac / Wonder boy / Days / Plastic man / Victoria / Lola / Apeman / David Watts / Where have all the good times gone / Well respected man / I'm not like everybody else / End of the season / Death of a clown (DAVE DAVIES) / Suzannah's still alive (DAVE DAVIES).
Dec 85. Starblend; (d-lp)(c)(cd) **BACKTRACKIN' – THE DEFINITIVE COLLECTION** □ –
Apr 89. Legacy; (c)(cd) **C90 COLLECTOR** □ –
Sep 91. Rhino; (d-cd) **PRESERVATION (A PLAY IN TWO ACTS)** □ □
Feb 92. See For MIles; (cd)(c)(lp) **THE EP COLLECTION VOL.2** □ –
Sep 93. Polygram TV; (cd)(c) **THE DEFINITIVE COLLECTION – THE KINKS' GREATEST HITS** 18 □
Dec 93. Disky; (cd) **GOLD: GREATEST HITS** □ –
May 94. BR Music; (cd)(c) **GREATEST HITS** □ –
Jul 94. Success; (cd)(c) **YOU REALLY GOT ME** □ –
Aug 94. Spectrum; (cd)(c) **YOU REALLY GOT ME** □ –

Feb 95. Essential; (cd) **REMASTERED** [ ] [-]
Aug 95. Spectrum; (cd) **LOLA** [ ] [-]

DAVE DAVIES

Pye / Reprise

Jul 67. (7") **DEATH OF A CLOWN. / LOVE ME TILL THE SUN SHINES** [3] [ ]
Nov 67. (7") **SUSANNAH'S STILL ALIVE. / FUNNY FACE** [21] [ ]
Aug 68. (7") **LINCOLN COUNTY. / THERE IS NO LOVE WITHOUT LIFE** [ ] [ ]
Jan 69. (7") **HOLD MY HAND. / CREEPING JEAN** [ ] [ ]

R.C.A. / R.C.A.

Sep 80. (7") **IMAGINATION'S REAL. / WILD MAN** [-] [ ]
Sep 80. (lp)(c) **AFLI-3603 (UK) / PL-13603 (US)** [-] [42] Jul 80
– Where do you come from / Doing the best for you / Move over / Visionary dreamer / Nothin' more to lose / Imagination real / In you I believe / See the beast / Run / The world is changing hands.
Nov 80. (7") **DOING THE BEST FOR YOU. / NOTHING MORE TO LOSE** [-] [ ]
Dec 80. (7") **DOING THE BEST FOR YOU. / WILD MAN** [ ] [-]
Oct 81. (lp)(c) **GLAMOUR** [ ] [ ] Jul 81
– Is this the only way / Reveal yourself / World of our own / Two serious / Glamour / 7th channel / Body / Eastern eyes / Body.

Warners / Warners

Sep 83. (lp)(c) **CHOSEN PEOPLE** [ ] [ ] Aug 83
– Mean disposition / Love gets you / Take one more / True story / Danger zone / Tapes / Freedom lies / Fire burning / Cold winter / Matter of decision / Is it any wonder / Charity / Chosen people.
Sep 83. (7") **LOVE GETS YOU. / ONE NIGHT WITH YOU** [-] [ ]
Nov 83. (7") **MEAN DISPOSITION. / COLD WINTER** [-] [ ]

– DAVE DAVIES compilations etc. –

Apr 68. Pye; (7"ep) **DAVE DAVIES HITS** [ ] [ ]
Aug 82. Old Gold; (7") **DEATH OF A CLOWN. / SUZANNAH'S STILL ALIVE** [ ] [-]
Feb 88. P.R.T.; (lp)(c) **DAVE DAVIES – THE ALBUM THAT NEVER WAS** [ ] [-]
– (1960's singles)
Jul 92. Mau Mau; (cd) **DAVE DAVIES / GLAMOUR** [ ] [-]

RAY DAVIES

not issued / R.C.A.

1984. (lp) **RETURN TO WATERLOO** (withdrawn) [-] [ ]
(below from film 'Absolute Beginners')

Virgin / Virgin

May 86. (7")(12") **QUIET LIFE. / VOICES IN THE DARK** [ ] [ ]

KIPPINGTON LODGE (see under ⇒ BRINSLEY SCHWARZ)

Richard H. KIRK (see under ⇒ CABARET VOLTAIRE)

KISS

Formed: New York, USA ... late '71 by ex-WICKED LESTER members GENE SIMMONS and PAUL STANLEY, who recruited ACE FREHLEY and PETER CRISS. After a year of touring in '73, they signed to 'Casablanca', and hit US Top 100 with eponymous lp early '74. After another Top 100 success at the end of '74, they scored with first of many US Top 40 albums 'DRESSED TO KILL' in 1975. • **Style:** Heavy riffed glam-rockers, with explosive stage shows their forte. Their comic-book image and facial character make-up led to a legion of young fans copying them, that is, until they were 'UNMASKED' on album in 1980. Their following album, THE ELDER, was dismissed by loyal supporters, for having concept inclinations. For the rest of the 80's, they were back to early hard-rock anthems and ballads of sex and violence. KISS' favourite haunts have been Detroit and Japan, where they have amassed tremendous KISS army. • **Songwriters:** Most by STANLEY or SIMMONS, with some ballads by CRISS. Covered; THEN (S)HE KISSED ME (Crystals) / GOD GAVE ROCK'N'ROLL TO YOU (Argent). MICHAEL BOLTON co-wrote with STANLEY their minor hit ballad 'FOREVER'. GENE SIMMONS solo covered; WHEN YOU WISH UPON A STAR (Judy Garland). • **Trivia:** BOB EZRIN produced 'DESTROYER' & 'THE ELDER'. First live double and several studio lp's from EDDIE KRAMER. In 1977, Marvel Comics started a KISS feature series in their monthly mag. In 1984, SIMMONS starred as a villain in the film 'Runaway' alongside Tom Selleck. Two years later 'The Bat-Winged Vampire' featured in films 'Never Too Young To Die', 'Trick Or Treat' & 'Wanted Dead Or Alive'. In 1994, a tribute album 'KISS MY ASS' was released by 'Mercury'. It featured star cover versions by LENNY KRAVITZ, GARTH BROOKS, ANTHRAX, GIN BLOSSOMS, TOAD THE WET SPROCKET, SHANDI's ADDICTION, DINOSAUR JR. / EXTREME / LEMONHEADS / etc.

Recommended: ALIVE! (*8) / SMASHES, THRASHES AND HITS (*7).

GENE SIMMONS (b.GENE KLEIN, 25 Aug'50, Haifa, Israel) – vocals, bass / **PAUL STANLEY** (b.STANLEY EISEN, 20 Jan'50, Queens, NY) – guitar, vocals / **ACE FREHLEY** (b.PAUL FREHLEY, 22 Apr'51, The Bronx, NY) – lead guitar, vocals / **PETER CRISS** (b.PETER CRISSCOULA, 27 Dec'47, Brooklyn, NY) – drums, vocals.

Casablanca / Casablanca

Feb 74. (7") **NOTHIN' TO LOSE. / LOVE THEME FROM KISS** [ ] [-]
Feb 74. (lp) **KISS** [-] [87]
– Strutter / Nothin' to lose / Firehouse / Cold gin / Let me know / Kissin' time / Love theme from Kiss / Deuce / 100,000 years / Black diamond. *(UK-iss.Feb75, re-iss.May77 red vinyl, re-iss.+c Feb82, cd-iss Aug88)*
May 74. (7") **KISSIN' TIME. / NOTHIN' TO LOSE** [-] [83]
Aug 74. (7") **STRUTTER. / 100,000 YEARS** [-] [ ]
Nov 74. (lp) **HOTTER THAN HELL** [-] [100]
– Got to choose / Parasite / Goin' blind / Hotter than Hell / Let me go, rock'n roll / All the way / Watchin' you / Mainline / Comin' home / Strange ways. *(UK-iss.May77 red vinyl, re-iss.+c Feb82, re-iss.+cd Aug88)*
Jan 75. (7") **NOTHIN' TO LOSE. / LOVE THEME FROM KISS** [ ] [ ]
Mar 75. (7") **LET ME GO ROCK'N'ROLL. / HOTTER THAN HELL** [-] [ ]
Mar 75. (lp)(c) **DRESSED TO KILL** [ ] [32]
– Room service / Two timer / Ladies in waiting / Getaway / Rock bottom / C'mon and love me / Anything for my baby / She / Love her all I can / Rock and roll all nite. *(UK-iss.Aug75, re-iss.May77 red vinyl, re-iss.+c Feb82, re-iss.+cd Aug88)*
May 75. (7") **ROCK AND ROLL ALL NITE. / GETAWAY** [-] [68]
Jun 75. (7") **ROCK AND ROLL ALL NITE. / ANYTHING FOR MY BABY** [ ] [-]
Oct 75. (7") **C'MON AND LOVE ME. / GETAWAY** [-] [ ]
Oct 75. (d-lp)(d-c) **ALIVE! (live)** [49] [9]
– Deuce / Strutter / Got to choose / Hotter than Hell / Firehouse / Nothin' to lose / C'mon and love me / Parasite / She / Watchin' you / 100,000 years / Black diamond / Rock bottom / Cold gin / Rock and roll all nite / Let me go rock 'n roll. *(UK-iss.Jun76, re-iss.May77 red vinyl, re-iss.+c Sep84, re-iss.+cd May89)*
Dec 75. (7") **ROCK AND ROLL ALL NITE (live). / ('A' new studio mix)** [ ] [12] Nov 75
Apr 76. (7") **SHOUT IT OUT LOUD. / SWEET PAIN** [ ] [31] Mar 76
May 76. (lp)(c) **DESTROYER** [22] [11] Mar 76
– Detroit rock city / King of the night time world / God of thunder / Great expectations / Flaming youth / Sweet pain / Shout it out loud / Beth / Do you love me. *(re-iss.May77 red vinyl, re-iss.+c Feb82, re-iss.+cd May89)*
Jun 76. (7") **FLAMING YOUTH. / GOD OF THUNDER** [-] [74]
Aug 76. (7") **BETH. / DETROIT ROCK CITY** [-] [7]
Jul 76. (7") **BETH. / GOD OF THUNDER** [ ] [-]
Nov 76. (lp)(c) **ROCK AND ROLL OVER** [ ] [11]
– See you in your dreams / Love 'em and leave 'em / Hard luck woman / Makin' love / Take me / I want you / Calling Dr. Love / Baby driver / Ladies room / Mr. Speed. *(re-iss.Feb77 red vinyl, re-iss.Feb82, re-iss.+cd May89) (re-iss.cd Jan93 on 'Vertigo')*
Dec 76. (7") **HARD LUCK WOMAN. / MR. SPEED** [-] [15]
May 77. (7"m) **HARD LUCK WOMAN. / CALLING DR. LOVE / BETH** [ ] [-]
Jun 77. (7") **CALLING DR. LOVE. / TAKE ME** [ ] [16] Mar 77
Jun 77. (lp)(c) **LOVE GUN** [ ] [4]
– Love gun / Got love for sale / Tomorrow and tonight / Christine sixteen / Almost human / Plaster caster / Shock me / The she kised me / I stole your love / Hooligan. *(UK-iss red vinyl, re-iss.Feb82, re-iss.Jul84, cd-iss.Aug88 US) (cd-iss.Jan93 on 'Vertigo')*
Jul 77. (7") **CHRISTINE SIXTEEN. / SHOCK ME** [-] [25]
Aug 77. (7"m) **THEN SHE KISSED ME. / HOOLIGAN / FLAMING YOUTH** [ ] [-]
Sep 77. (7") **LOVE GUN. / HOOLIGAN** [-] [61]
Nov 77. (d-lp)(d-c) **KISS ALIVE II** [60] [7]
– Detroit rock city / King of the night time world / Ladies room / Makin' love / Love gun / Calling Dr. Love / Christine sixteen / Shock me / Hard luck woman / Tomorrow and tonight / I stole your love / Beth / God of thunder / I want you / Shout it loud / All American man / Rockin' in the U.S.A. / Larger than life / Rocket ride / Any way you want it. *(re-iss.Feb82, cd-iss.May89)*
Jan 78. (7") **SHOUT IT OUT LOUD (live). / NOTHIN' TO LOSE (live)** [-] [54]
Feb 78. (7") **ROCKET RIDE. / TOMORROW AND TONIGHT** [-] [39]
Mar 78. (7") **ROCKET RIDE. / LOVE GUN (live)** [ ] [-]
(12"+=) – Detroit rock city (live).

—— Took time to do solo projects (all on label below)

GENE SIMMONS

Casablanca / Casablanca

Sep 78. (lp) **GENE SIMMONS** [-] [22]
– Radioactive / Burning up with fever / See you tonite / Tunnel of love / True confessions / Living in sin / Always near you / Nowhere to hide / Man of 1,000 faces / Mr. Make Believe / See you in your dreams / When you wish upon a star. *(re-iss.'87 in +pic-lp Europe) (cd-iss.Nov91)*
Jan 79. (7") **RADIOACTIVE. / WHEN YOU WISH UPON A STAR** [41] [ ]

PAUL STANLEY

Sep 78. (lp) **PAUL STANLEY** [-] [40]
– Tonight you belong to me / Move on / Ain't quite right / Wouldn't you like to know / Take me away (together as one) / It's alright / Hold me touch me (think of me when we're apart) / Love in chains / Goodbye. *(re-iss.'87 +pic-lp in Europe) (cd-iss.Nov91)*
Feb 79. (7") **HOLD ME TOUCH ME. / GOODBYE** [ ] [ ]

ACE FREHLEY

Sep 78. (lp) **ACE FREHLEY** [-] [26]
– Rip it out / Speedin' back to my baby / Snowblind / Ozone / What's on your mind / New York groove / I'm in need of love / Wiped out / Fractured mirror. *(re-iss.+pic-lp 1987 in Europe) (cd-iss.Nov91)*
Nov 78. (7")(7"blue) **NEW YORK GROOVE. / SNOW BLIND** [ ] [13]

PETER CRISS

Sep 78. (lp) **PETER CRISS** [-] [43]

– I'm gonna love you / You matter to me / Tossin' and turnin' / Don't you let me down / That's the kind of sugar papa likes / Easy thing / Rock me, baby / Kiss the girl goodbye / Hooked on rock'n'roll / I can't stop the rain. *(re-iss.'87 +pic-lp in Europe) (cd-iss.Nov91) (re-iss.cd+red-lp+book Aug94 on 'Megarock')*

Dec 78. (7") **DON'T YOU LET ME DOWN. / HOOKED ON ROCK AND ROLL** [-] [ ]

Feb 79. (7") **HOOKED ON ROCK AND ROLL. / YOU MATTER TO ME** [ ] [ ]

KISS

returned to studio

Casablanca Casablanca

Jun 79. (7") **I WAS MADE FOR LOVIN' YOU. / HARD TIMES** [50] [11] May 79
(12") – ('A'side) / Charisma.

Jun 79. (lp)(c) **DYNASTY** [50] [9]
– Charisma / Dirty livin' / Hard times / I was made for lovin' you / Magic touch / Save your love / Sure know something / X-ray eyes / 2,000 man. *(re-iss.Oct83, cd-iss.'88 US import) (cd-iss.Jan93 on 'Vertigo')*

Aug 79. (7") **SURE KNOW SOMETHING. / DIRTY LIVIN'** [ ] [47]

Feb 80. (7"m) **2,000 MAN. / I WAS MADE FOR LOVIN' YOU / SURE KNOW SOMETHING** [ ] [-]

Mercury Casablanca

Jun 80. (7") **SHANDI. / SHE'S SO EUROPEAN** [-] [47]

Jun 80. (7") **TALK TO ME. / SHE'S SO EUROPEAN** [ ] [-]

Jun 80. (lp)(c) **KISS UNMASKED** [48] [35]
– Easy as it seems / Is that you? / Naked city / Shandi / She's so European / Talk to me / Tomorrow / Torpedo girl / Two sides of the coin / What makes the world go 'round / You're all that I want. *(cd-iss.Dec89)*

Aug 80. (7") **WHAT MAKES THE WORLD GO 'ROUND. / NAKED CITY** [ ] [-]

Aug 80. (7") **TOMORROW. / NAKED CITY** [-] [ ]

—— (May80) **ERIC CARR** (b.12 Jul'50) – drums, producer repl. CRISS who went solo (early 80's albums; OUT OF CONTROL / LET ME ROCK YOU)

Nov 81. (lp)(c) **MUSIC FROM THE ELDER** [51] [75]
– Just a boy / Odyssey / Only you / Under the rose / Darl light / A world without heroes / The oath / Mr. Blackwell / Escape from the island. *(cd-iss.Jun89) (cd-iss.Jun94 on 'Sony . . . ')*

Nov 81. (7") **A WORLD WITHOUT HEROES. / DARK LIGHT** [-] [56]

Jan 82. (7")(7"pic-d) **A WORLD WITHOUT HEROES. / MR. BLACKWELL** [55] [-]

—— **VINNIE VINCENT** (b.VINCENT CUSANO) – guitar repl. BOB KULICK who had repl. FREHLEY who formed own band.

Casablanca Casablanca

Oct 82. (7") **DANGER. / I LOVE IT LOUD** [-] [ ]

Oct 82. (7") **KILLER. / I LOVE IT LOUD** [ ] [-]
(12"+=) – I was made for lovin' you.

Oct 82. (lp)(c) **CREATURES OF THE NIGHT** [22] [45]
– Creatures of the night / Saint and sinner / Keep me comin' / Rock and roll Hell / Danger / I love it loud / I still love you / Killer / ar machine. *(re-iss.+cd Aug88) (re-iss.cd Jan93 on 'Vertigo')*

Mar 83. (7")(12") **CREATURES OF THE NIGHT. / ROCK AND ROLL ALL NIGHT (live)** [34] [-]
(12"+=) – War machine.

Vertigo Mercury

Oct 83. (7") **LICK IT UP. / DANCE ALL OVER YOUR FACE** [-] [66]

Oct 83. (7")(7"sha-pic-d) **LICK IT UP. / NOT FOR THE INNOCENT** [34] [-]
(12"+=) – I still love you.

Oct 83. (lp)(c) **LICK IT UP** [7] [24]
– Exciter / Not for the innocent / Lick it up / Young and wasted / Gimme more / All Hell's breakin' loose / A million to one / Fits like a glove / Dance all over your face / And on the 8th day. *(re-iss.+cd Dec89 on 'Mercury')*

Jan 84. (7") **ALL HELL'S BREAKIN' LOOSE. / YOUNG AND WASTED** [-] [ ]

—— **MARK** (NORTON) **ST.JOHN** – guitar repl. VINCENT who formed his INVASION

Sep 84. (7") **HEAVEN'S ON FIRE. / LONELY IS THE HUNTER** [43] [49]
(12"+=) – All Hell's breakin' loose.

Sep 84. (lp)(c) **ANIMALIZE** [11] [19]
– I've had enough (into the fire) / Heaven's on fire / Burn bitch burn / Get all you can take / Lonely is the hunter / Under the gun / Thrills in the night / While the city sleeps / Murder in high-heels. *(re-iss.+cd Dec89 on 'Mercury') (re-iss.cd Jan93)*

Nov 84. (7") **THRILLS IN THE NIGHT. / BURN BITCH BURN** [-] [ ]

—— **BRUCE KULICK** – guitar repl. MARK who became ill

Oct 85. (lp)(c)(cd) **ASYLUM** [12] [20]
– King of the mountain / Any way you slice it / Who wants to be lonely / Trial by fire / I'm alive / Love's a deadly weapon / Tears are falling / Secretly cruel / Radar for love / Uh! All night. *(re-iss.+cd Dec89 on 'Mercury') (re-iss.cd Jan93)*

Oct 85. (7") **TEARS ARE FALLING. / HEAVEN'S ON FIRE (live)** [57] [51]
(12"+=) – Any way you slice it (US b-side).

Sep 87. (7") **CRAZY CRAZY NIGHTS. / NO, NO, NO** [4] [65]
(12"+=) – Lick it up / Uh! All night.
(12"pic-d+=) – Heaven's on fire / Tears are falling.

Oct 87. (lp)(c)(cd) **CRAZY NIGHTS** [4] [18]
– Crazy crazy nights / I'll fight Hell to hold you / Bang bang you / No, no, no / Hell on high water / My way / When your walls come down / Reasons to live / Good girl gone bad / Turn on the night / Thief in the night. *(cd-iss.Feb91)*

Dec 87. (7") **REASON TO LIVE. / THIEF IN THE NIGHT** [33] [64]
(c-s+=) – Who wants to be lonely.
(12"++=) – Thrills in the night.
(12"pic-d++=) – Secretly cruel.
(cd-s+=) – Tears are falling / Crazy crazy nights.

Feb 88. (7") **TURN ON THE NIGHT. / HELL OR HIGH WATER** [41] [ ]
(12"+=)(12"pic-d+=) – King of the mountain / Any way you slice it.
(cd-s+=) – Heaven's on fire / I love it loud.

Oct 89. (7")(c-s)(7"red) **HIDE YOUR HEART. / BETRAYED** [59] [66]
(12"+=)(cd-s+=) – Boomerang.
(10"pic-d) – ('A'side) / Lick it up / Heaven's on fire.

Oct 89. (lp)(c)(cd) **HOT IN THE SHADE** [35] [29]
– Rise to it / Betrayed / Hide your heart / Prisoner of love / Read my body / Love's a slap in the face / Forever / Silver spoon / Cadillac dreams / King of hearts / The street giveth and the street taketh away / You love me to hate you / Somewhere between Heaven and Hell / Little Caesar / Boomerang.

Mar 90. (7") **FOREVER. / THE STREET GIVETH AND THE STREET TAKETH AWAY** [65] [8] Feb 90
(12"+=) – Deuce (demo) / Strutter (demo).
(12") – ('A'side) / All American man / Shandi / The Oath.
(cd-s) – ('A'side) / Creatures of the night / Lick it up / Heaven's on fire.

Jun 90. (7")(c-s) **RISE TO IT. / SILVER SPOON** [-] [81]

—— In May'91, ERIC CARR underwent open heart surgery. He was admitted to hospital again but they found malignant cancer growth. He died 24th Nov'91. In Jan'92, KISS hit UK No.4 with 'GOD GAVE ROCK'N'ROLL TO YOU II' from the film 'Bill & Ted's Bogus Journey'. On the same single issued on 'Interscope' were tracks by 'KINGS X' & 'SLAUGHTER'.

May 92. (7")(c-s) **UNHOLY. / GOD GAVE ROCK'N'ROLL TO YOU II** [26] [ ]
(12"+=)(cd-s+=)(12"pic-d+=) – Partners in crime / Deva / Strutter (demos).

May 92. (cd)(c)(lp) **REVENGE** [10] [6]
– Unholy / Take it off / Tough love / Spit / God gave rock'n'roll to you II / Domino / Heart of chrome / Thou shalt not / Every time I look at you / Paralysed / I just wanna / Carr jam 1981.

May 93. (cd)(c) **KISS ALIVE III (live)** [24] [9]
– Creatures of the night / Deuce / I just wanna / Unholy / Heaven's on fire / Watchin' you / Domino / I was made for lovin' you / I still love you / Rock'n'roll all nite / Lick it up (featuring BOBBY WOMACK) / Take it off / I love it loud / Detroit rock city / God gave rock'n'roll to you / Star spangled banner.

– compilations etc. –

Aug 76. Casablanca; (t-lp) **THE ORIGINALS** (first 3 albums) [ ] [ ]

May 78. Casablanca; (d-lp)(d-c) **DOUBLE PLATINUM** [ ] [24]
(re-iss.Feb82 & May85, cd-iss.Jun87)

Jun 78. Casablanca; (7") **ROCK AND ROLL ALL NITE. / C'MON AND LOVE ME** [ ] [-]

Jan 81. Casablanca; (lp) **THE BEST OF THE SOLO ALBUMS** [-] [ ]

Jun 82. Casablanca; (lp)(c) **KILLERS** [42] [-]

Nov 88. Mercury; (7") **LET'S PUT THE 'X'. / CALLING DR. LOVE** [-] [97]

Nov 88. Vertigo/ US= Mercury; (lp)(c)(cd) **SMASHES, THRASHES AND HITS** [62] [21]
– Let's put the X in sex / Crazy crazy nights / (You make me) Rock hard / Love gun / Detroit rock city / I love it loud / Deuce / Lick it up / Heaven's on fire / Strutter / Beth / Tears are falling / I was made for lovin' you / Rock and roll all nite / Shout it out loud.

Oct 88. Vertigo; (5"vid-cd) **CRAZY CRAZY NIGHTS. / NO, NO, NO / WHEN YOUR WALLS COME DOWN / THIEF IN THE NIGHT** [ ] [-]

1989. Mercury; (7") **BETH. / HARD LUCK WOMAN** [-] [ ]

1989. Mercury; (7") **ROCK AND ROLL ALL NITE. / I WAS MADE FOR LOVIN' YOU** [-] [ ]

Sep 89. Vertigo; (5"vid-cd) **LICK IT UP. / DANCE ALL OVER YOUR FACE / GIMME MORE / FITS LIKE A GLOVE** [ ] [-]

Sep 89. Vertigo; (5"vid-cd) **TEARS ARE FALLING. / ANY WAY YOU SLICE IT / WHO WANTS TO BE LONELY / SECRETLY CRUEL** [ ] [-]

—— (all lp's were released as pic-lp's in Europe).

KITCHENS OF DISTINCTION

Formed: Tooting Broadway, London, England . . . 1986 by trio (see below). After an indie 45, they moved to Derek Shulman's (ex-GENTLE GIANT) label 'O. L. Indian', where they hit UK Top 50 in 1991 with stunning album 'STRANGE FREE WORLD'. • **Style:** Dark enterprising melodic rock outfit, fronted by the openly homosexual PATRICK FITZGERALD. • **Songwriters:** Group compositions. • **Trivia:** Toured at times as The TOILETS OF DESTRUCTION alongside POPINJAYS.

Recommended: STRANGE FREE WORLD (*8) / LOVE IS HELL (*7) / THE DEATH OF COOL (*7).

PATRICK FITZGERALD (b. 7 Apr'64, Basle, Switzerland) – vocals / **JULIAN SWALES** (b.23 Mar'64, Gwent, Wales) – guitar / **DANIEL GOODWYN** (b.22 Jul'64, Salamanca, Spain) – drums (ex-AR KANE)

Goldrush not issued

Oct 87. (7") **ESCAPE. / THE LAST GASP DEATH SHUFFLE** [ ] [-]

One Little Indian Elektra

Oct 88. (12"ep) **THE PRIZE. / CONCEDE / INNOCENT** [ ] [-]

May 89. (12"ep) **THE THIRD TIME WE OPENED THE CAPSULE / 4 MEN. / INTO THE SEA / THE PRIZE (demo)** [ ] [-]

May 89. (lp)(c)(cd) **LOVE IS HELL** [ ] [-]
– In a cave / Time to groan / Shiver / Prize / The 3rd time we opened the capsule / Her last day in bed / Courage, mother / Mainly mornings / Hammer.

Oct 89. (12"ep) **ELEPHANTINE / MARGARET'S INJECTION. / THE 1000st FAULT / ANVIL DUB** [ ] [-]

Apr 90. (12"ep)(cd-ep) **QUICK AS RAINBOWS. / MAINLY MORNINGS (live) / IN A CAVE (live) / SHIVER** [ ] [-]

Feb 91. (12"ep)(cd-ep) **DRIVE THIS FAST / THESE DRINKERS. / ELEPHANTLY / THREE TO BEAM UP** [ ] [-]

Mar 91. (cd)(c)(lp) **STRANGE FREE WORLD** [45] [ ]
– Railwayed / Quick as rainbows / Hypnogogie / He holds her, he needs her / Polaroids / Gorgeous love / Aspray / Drive that fast / Within the days of passion / Under the sky, inside the sea.

May 92. (7") **BREATHING FEAR. / GOODBYE VOYAGER** [ ] [ ]

(12"+=)(cd-s+=) – Skin (instrumental) / Air shifting (instrumental).
(12"+=) – Smiling / When in Heaven.

Aug 92. (cd)(c)(lp) **THE DEATH OF COOL** 72
– What happens now / Four men / On Tooting Broadway Station / Breathing fear / One world gone / When in Heaven / Madas snow / Smiling / Blue pedal / Can't trust the waves.

Sep 92. (12"ep)(cd-ep) **WHEN IN HEAVEN / GLITTERY DUST. / DON'T COME BACK / SPACEDOLPHINS**

Sep 94. (12"+c-s+cd-s) **NOW IT'S TIME TO SAY GOODBYE. / JESUS NEVADA / WHITE HORSES / WHAT WE REALLY WANTED TO DO**

Sep 94. (cd)(c)(lp) **COWBOYS AND ALIENS**
– Sand on fire / Get over yourself / Thought he had everything / Cowboys and aliens / Come on now / Remember me? / One of these sometimes is now / Here comes the swans / Now it's time to say goodbye / Pierced / Prince of Mars.

KLF

Formed: KOPYRIGHT LIBERATION FRONT. Based; London, England . . . 1986 by BILL DRUMMOND and JIM CAUTY. BILL DRUMMOND had been the owner of 'Zoo' records, who signed up TEARDROP EXPLODES and ECHO & THE BUNNYMEN, with the latter being his first major managerial experience. Calling themselves JUSTIFIED ANCIENTS OF MU MU, the KLF issued a number of limited edition 45's, which sold well in the indie shops on their own label. In the summer of '88, they surprised many when hitting UK No.1 with TIMELORDS 'Dr.Who theme / Rock And Roll Part 2 – Gary Glitter theme'. They then spread their name as KLF, and soon mastered the charts with 1990 anthems 'WHAT TIME IS LOVE' and the answer '3 A.M. ETERNAL'. The latter hit UK No.1 early 1991, as did the album 'THE WHITE ROOM', as they stormed across America. • **Style:** Experimental dance power-rock samplers, both appealing to underground and pop fans alike. • **Songwriters:** Pen own material, with a host of lenders from ABBA, The BBC, GARY GLITTER, PETULA CLARK, BEATLES and STEVIE WONDER, to mention a few. • **Trivia:** Their 9th official release was a book entitled 'The Manuel Of How To Have A Number One The Easy Way'.

Recommended: SHAG TIMES (*6) / THE WHITE ROOM (*8).

JUSTIFIED ANCIENTS OF MU MU

(aka J.A.M.M.s) **KING BOY D** (aka BILL DRUMMOND) (b.WILLIAM BUTTERWORTH, 29 Apr'53, S.Africa, raised Clydebank, Scotland) – synths (ex-BIG IN JAPAN, ex-LORI & CHAMELEONS) / **ROCKMAN ROCK** (aka JIM CAUTY) (b.1957) – synthesizers (ex-BRILLIANT, etc.)

K.L.F. / not issued

May 87. (12") **ALL YOU NEED IS LOVE. / BABY, YOU'RE A RICH MAN**
(7"+=) – ('A' me ru con mix) (above ltd-5,000).

Jun 87. (lp) **1987 WHAT THE FUCK IS GOING ON**

Sep 87. (12") **WHITNEY JOINS THE JAMS. /** (1 sided) – SCOT

Nov 87. (12") **1987 – THE EDITS** (excerpts from above album) –

Dec 87. (12") **DOWNTOWN. / ('A'version)** –

Feb 88. (lp) **WHO KILLED THE JAMMS**
– The candy store / The candy man / Disaster fund collection / King boy's dream / The porpoise song / The Prestwich prophet's grin / Burn the bastards.

Mar 88. (12") **BURN THE BASTARDS. / BURN THE BEAT / THE PORPOISE SONG**

The TIMELORDS

KLF / TVT

May 88. (7")(7"sha-pic-d)**DOCTORIN' THE TARDIS. / ('A'version)** 1 / 66 Dec 88
(12"+=) – ('A'-with Gary Glitter).
(cd-s+=) – ('A'club version).

K.L.F.

Jun 88. (12")**WHAT TIME IS LOVE?. /** ('A'trance)
(re-iss.Jun89 – ('A' (primal remix)). / ('A' techno) / ('A' original)

Jul 89. (7") **KYLIE SAID TO JASON. / KYLIE SAID TRANCE**
(12"+=)(cd-s+=) – Madrugaral eternal.

Oct 89. (lp)(cd) **WHAT TIME IS LOVE?**
– What time is love? (original) / Relax your body / What time is love? (Italian) / Heartbeat / No limit (dance mix) / What time is love? (live at the Land of Oz).

Dec 89. (7") **LAST TRAIN FROM TRANCENTRAL./(withdrawn)**

— added **MAXINE HARVEY** – vocals

KLF / Arista

Jul 90. (12") **WHAT TIME IS LOVE? (live at Transcentral). / ('A' wonderful) or ('A' Technogat mix)** 5
(cd-s+=) – ('A'Trance mix).
(d-c-s) – (all 3 mixes above).

Aug 90. (12") **3 A.M. ETERNAL (live at SSL). / ETERNAL (GUNS OF MU MU)** 1 / 5 Jun 91
(cd-s+=)(d-c-s+=) – Break for love.

Mar 91. (cd)(c)(lp) **THE WHITE ROOM** 3 / 39
– What time is love? / Make it rain / 3 a.m. eternal (live at the S.S.L.) / Church of the KLF / Last train to Transcentral / Build a fire / The white room / No more tears / Justified and ancient.

Apr 91. (7") **LAST TRAIN TO TRANSCENTRAL. / THE IRON HORSE** 2

Oct 91. (c-s) **WHAT TIME IS LOVE? / BUILD A FIRE** – / 57
(12"+=) – Live from the Lost Continent.
(cd-s++=) – ('A' Pure trance version '89).

JUSTIFIED ANCIENTS OF MU MU

Oct 91. (7")(12")(c-s)**IT'S GRIM UP NORTH. / (part 2)** 10
(cd-s+=) – Jerusalem on the Moors.

Nov 91. (7") **JUSTIFIED AND ANCIENT (STAND BY THE JAMMS). / ('A' original version)** 2 / 11 Jan 92
(12"+=)(cd-s+=) – Let them eat ice-cream / Make mine a 99 / All bound for Mu Mu land (with MAXINE).

(above 'A'side credited THE FIRST LADY OF COUNTRY: MISS TAMMY WYNETTE)

Jan 92. (7")(c-s) **P.O. 3 A.M. ETERNAL / ('A'guns of MuMu mix)**
(12"+=)(cd-s+=) – ('A'diff.versions).

KLF

Feb 92. (7")(c-s)**AMERICA:- WHAT TIME IS LOVE?. / AMERICA NO MORE** 4
(12"+=)(cd-s+=) – (other 'A'mixes).

Discipline / not issued

Dec93. (12") **3 A.M. ETERNAL. ("EXTREME NOISE TERROR & KLF") / 3AM Eternal (Christmas Top Of The Pops 1991)** –

– compilations, etc. –

Jan 89. KLF; (d-lp)(cd) **SHAG TIMES**
– All you need is love / Don't take five (take what you want) / Whitney joins the JAMS / Downtown / Candyman / Burn the bastards / Doctorin' the tardis / 114 BPM / 90 BPM / 118 BPM / 125 BPM / 120 BPM / 118 BPM / 120 BPM (all releases, from all aliases)

Jan 90. KLF; (cd)(lp) **CHILL OUT** –

BILL DRUMMOND

Creation / not issued

Nov 86. (lp) **THE MANAGER**
– True to the trail / Ballad for a sex god / Julian Cope is dead / I want that girl / Going back / Queen of the south / I believe in rock'n'roll / Married man / I'm the king of joy / Son of a preacher man / Such a parcel of rogues in a nation. *(re-iss.+cd.Sep90)*

Mar 87. (12") **KING OF JOY. / THE MANAGER**

DISCO 2000

(aka DRUMMOND)

D2000 / not issued

Apr 88. (12") **I GOTTA CD. / I LOVE DISCO 2000** –

Apr 88. (12") **ONE LOVE NATION. / ('A'edit) / ('A'instrumental)** –

Jan 89. (7") **UPTIGHT (EVERYTHING'S ALRIGHT – edit). / MR.HOTTY LOVES YOU (edit)** –
(12") – ('A'discorama mix) / ('B'side)

— JIM CAUTY released eponymous album under **SPACE** banner mid-1990 on 'Space-Rough Trade'.

KNACK

Formed: Los Angeles, California ... mid-78 by ex-SKY (US) members FIEGER and AVERRE, plus former sessioners NILES and GARY. In early '79, they became large attractions on the live scene, thus gaining many record contract offers before opting for 'Capitol'. In the summer of '79, they issued 'MY SHARONA', which quickly sold a million and became a US No.1, also reaching Top 10 in UK. Its parent album 'GET THE KNACK', although not a seller in the UK, became another No.1 and multi-million success. In 1980, they had a few more semi-major triumphs before they virtually fizzled out the year after, only managing a Top 100 placing for album 'ROUND TRIP'. • **Style:** Dubbed power-pop beat group, similiar to pre-'Revolver' BEATLES. • **Songwriters:** Group penned. • **Trivia:** Their MIKE CHAPMAN produced debut lp, sold over 7 million copies in the States.

Recommended: GET THE KNACK (*5).

DOUG FIEGER (b.20 Aug'50.c, Detroit, Michegan) – vocals, guitar / **BERTON AVERRE** (b.13 Dec'50.c, Van Nuys, California) – guitar / **PRESTON NILES** (b. 2 May'50.c, New York) – bass / **BRUCE GARY** (b. 7 Apr'52, Burbank, California) – drums (ex-JACK BRUCE BAND)

Capitol / Capitol

Jun 79. (7") **MY SHARONA. / LET ME OUT** 6 / 1

Jul 79. (lp)(c) **GET THE KNACK** 65 / 1 Jun 79
– Let me out / Your number of your name / Oh Tara / (She's so) Selfish / Maybe tonight / Good girls don't / My Sharona / Heartbeat / Siamese twins (the monkey and me) / Lucinda / That's what little girls do / Frustrated. *(re-iss.Sep82 on 'Fame')*

Sep 79. (7") **GOOD GIRLS DON'T. / FRUSTRATED** 66 / 11 Aug 79

Feb 80. (7") **BABY TALKS DIRTY. / END OF THE GAME** 38

Feb 80. (lp)(c) **BUT THE LITTLE GIRLS UNDERSTAND** 15
– Baby talks dirty / I want ya / Tell me you're mine / Mr. Handleman / Can't put a price on love / Hold on tight and don't let go / The hard way / It's you / End of the game / The feeling I get / Rave up / How can love hurt so much.

Mar 80. (7") **IT'S YOU. / I WANT YA / RAVE UP** –

Apr 80. (7") **CAN'T PUT A PRICE ON LOVE. / RAVE UP** – / 62

Nov 81. (7") **PAY THE DEVIL (OOO, BABY, OOO). / LIL' CALS BIG MISTAKE** 67 Oct 81

Dec 81. (lp)(c) **ROUND TRIP** 93

– Radiating love / Soul kissin' / Africa / She likes the beat / Just wait and see / We are waiting / Boys are crazy / Sweet dreams / Lil' Cal's big mistake / Another lousy day in Paradise / Pay the Devil (ooo, baby, ooo) / Art war.

— Disbanded 1982, AVERRE, NILES and GARY formed The GAME. DOUG FIEGER formed TAKING CHANCES before guesting for WAS (NOT WAS) on 1983 lp 'Born To Laugh At Tornados'. **The KNACK** re-formed with **FIEGER, AVERRE & NILES. / BILLY WARD** – drums repl. GARY

Charisma Charisma

Mar 91. (cd)(c)(lp) **SERIOUS FUN**

— In Apr94, 'MY SHARONA' was re-issued & hit US No.91 by 'R.C.A.' for 'Reality Bites' film.

– compilations, etc. –

Apr 93. Capitol; (cd) **RETROSPECTIVE (THE BEST OF THE KNACK)**
– My Sharona / Your number or your name / One day at a time / The hard way / Good girls don't / (She's so) Selfish / Just wait and see / Baby talks dirty / We are waiting / I want love / Africa / Can't put a price.

Dec 94. B.G.O.; (cd) **GET THE KNACK / BUT THE LITTLE GIRLS UNDERSTAND** –

Terry KNIGHT & THE PACK (see under ⇒ GRAND FUNK RAILROAD)

Mark KNOPFLER (see under ⇒ DIRE STRAITS)

Al KOOPER

Born: 5 Feb'44, Brooklyn, New York, USA. After leaving school at 15, he formed his first pro-band The ROYAL TEENS, for whom he played guitar. They scored a minor US novelty hit with 'SHORT SHORTS', before he became noted session man for first half of the 60's. He also set up writing partnership with IRWIN LEVINE and BOBBY BRASS, penning hits for GARY LEWIS & THE PLAYBOYS ('This Diamond Ring'), GENE PITNEY ('I Must Be Seeing Things') and ROCKIN' BERRIES ('Water Is Over my Head'). In 1965, he was asked by producer TOM WILSON to sit in on a BOB DYLAN session, which led him to play organ to MIKE BLOOMFIELD's guitar. Their electric sound was noteably highlighted on DYLAN's 'Like A Rolling Stone' from the classic 'Highway 61 Revisited' album. The following year, he stayed for 'Blonde On Blonde', while sessioning for other folk stars TOM RUSH plus PETER, PAUL & MARY. That year (1966) saw him joined his first rock band BLUES PROJECT and stayed for 3 albums 'LIVE AT THE CAFE AU GO GO', 'PROJECTIONS' and 'LIVE AT THE TOWN HALL'. His departure in 1967, was due to his formation of R&B brass-laden hitmakers BLOOD, SWEAT & TEARS. However arguments over direction led him to depart after only one 1968 album 'CHILD IS FATHER TO THE MAN'. His next project was an inspiration from MOBY GRAPE's 'Grape Jam' and he decided to do the same on a collaboration with MIKE BLOOMFIELD (ex-ELECTRIC FLAG) and STEVE STILLS (ex-BUFFALO SPRINGFIELD). The resulting album 'SUPER SESSION' was a massive hit in the States, thus resulting in label 'Columbia' asking AL and MIKE to do another. Early in 1969, their live in the studio self-indulgent double-lp 'THE LIVE ADVENTURES OF MIKE BLOOMFIELD & AL KOOPER' was complete and this also made US Top 20 lists. Later in the year, KOOPER released his solo debut 'I STAND ALONE' but this failed to emulate predecessers. During these releases, KOOPER had kept up his session work for the likes of JIMI HENDRIX EXPERIENCE ('Electric Ladyland' lp) and The ROLLING STONES ('Let It Bleed' lp). For the next decade KOOPER continued as a solo artist, although session and production work for LYNYRD SKYNYRD, NILS LOFGREN and The TUBES took up most of his time. In the early 70's, he re-united for concerts with past group BLUES PROJECT and set up own label 'Sounds Of The South'. The early 80's saw him complete a new album 'CHAMPIONSHIP WRESTLING', superseding his involvement in ad hoc outfit SWEET MAGNOLIA. In 1991, he came out of semi-retirement in Nashville to produce GREEN ON RED's 'Scapegoats'. • **Style:** Accomplished blues musician, although his singing voice was questionable by critics of the day. • **Songwriters:** Self-penned some with others. He covered many classics including; 59th STREET BRIDGE SONG (Simon & Garfunkel) / DEAR MR. FANTASY (Traffic) / GREEN ONIONS (Booker T & The MG's) / BLUE MOON OF KENTUCKY (Bill Monroe) / BABY PLEASE DON'T GO (. . .Williams) / etc. **Trivia:** In the 80's, he also produced EDDIE & THE HOT RODS ('Fish & Chips') / LEO SAYER ('Here') / DAVID ESSEX ('Be-Bop The Future') and an album for JOHNNY VAN ZANDT.

• **Note:** For albums with MIKE BLOOMFIELD (see under ELECTRIC FLAG)

Recommended: AL'S BIG DEAL (*7)

AL KOOPER (solo) – vocals, keyboards, guitar with session people

Mercury Verve F..

Nov 65. (7") **PARCHMAN FARM. (as "ALAN KOOPER") / YOU'RE THE LOVING END** –

Became a session man for BOB DYLAN, etc.

1967. (7") **CHANGES. / PACK UP YOUR SORROWS** –

— Joined The BLUES PROJECT then BLOOD, SWEAT & TEARS before returning solo. Also see under ELECTRIC FLAG (albums with MIKE BLOOMFIELD)

C.B.S. Columbia

Mar 69. (lp) **I STAND ALONE** 54 Feb69
– Overture / I stand alone / Camille / One / Coloured rain / Soft landing on the Moon / I can love a woman / Blue Moon of Kentucky / Toe hold / Right now for you / Hey, Western Union man / Song and dance for the unborn, frightened child.

Apr 69. (7") **YOU NEVER KNOW WHO YOUR FRIENDS ARE. / SOFT LANDING ON THE MOON** Dec68

Jul 69. (7") **HEY, WESTERN UNION MAN. / I STAND ALONE**

1969. (lp) **YOU NEVER KNOW WHO YOUR FRIENDS ARE** Oct69
– Magic in my socks / Lucille / Too busy thinking about my baby / First time around / Loretta (Union turnpike eulogy) / Blues part IV / You never know who your friends are / The great American marriage – Nothing / I don't know why I love you / Mourning glory story / Anna Lee (what can I do for you) / Never gonna let you down.

— next with SHUGGIE OTIS – guitar / STU WOODS – bass / WELLS KELLY – drums

1970. (lp) **KOOPER SESSION – WITH SHUGGIE OTIS** Jan70
– Bury my body / Double or nothing / One room country shack / Lookin' for a home / The blues:- 12:15 Slow goonbash blues- Shuggie's old time dee-di-lee-di-leet-deet slide boogie- Shuggie's shuffle.

1970. (7") **BURY MY BODY. / ONE ROOM COUNTRY SHACK** –

— Reverted to numerous session people

1970. (d-lp) **EASY DOES IT** Sep70
– Brand new day (main theme from 'The Landlord') / I got a woman / Country road / I bought you the shoes (you're walking away with it) / Easy does it / Buckskin boy / Love theme from 'The Landlord' / Sad, sad sunshine / Let the Duchess no / She gets me where I live / A rose and a baby Ruth / Baby please don't go / God sheds his grace on thee.

1970. (7") **GOD SHEDS HIS GRACE ON THEE. / SHE GETS ME WHERE I LIVE** –

Mar 71. (7") **BRAND NEW DAY. / LOVE THEME FROM THE LANDLORD**

1971. (7") **I GOT A WOMAN. / EASY DOES IT** –

A few of above tracks appeared on 1971 'United Artists' UK film soundtrack of 'THE LANDLORD' (UAS 29120), which also featured STAPLE SINGERS and LORRAINE ELLISON.

1971. (lp) **NEW YORK CITY (YOU'RE A WOMAN)** Jun71
– New York City (you're a woman) / John The Baptist (Holy John) / Can you hear it now (500 miles) / The ballad of the hard rock kid / Going quietly mad / Medley: Oo wee baby, I love you- Love is a man's friend / Back on my feet / Come down in time / Dearest darling / Nightmare No.5 / The warning (someone's on the cross again).

Jul 71. (7") **JOHN THE BAPTIST. / BACK ON MY FEET**

1972. (lp) **A POSSIBLE PROJECTION OF THE FUTURE / CHILDHOOD'S END** Apr72
– Bended knees (please don't leave me now) / Possible projection of the future / Childhood's end / The man in me / Please tell me why / Love trap / The monkey time / Let your love shine / Swept for you baby.

1972. (7") **MONKEY TIME. / BENDED KNEES (PLEASE DON'T LEAVE ME NOW)**

1972. (7") **SAM STONE. / BE REAL** –

1973. (lp) **NAKED SONGS**
– Be real / As the tears go passing by / Jolie / Blend baby / Been and gone / Sam Stone / Peacock lady / Touch the hem of his garment / Where were you when I needed you / Unrequited.

1973. (7") **JOLIE. / BE REAL** –

1975. (d-lp) **AL'S BIG DEAL (UNCLAIMED FREIGHT)** (compilation)
– I can't quit her / I love you more than you'll ever know / My days are numbered / Without her / So much love- Underture / Albert's shuffle / Season of the witch / If dogs run free / The 59th Street Bridge song (fellin' groovy) / The weight / Bury my body / Jolie / I stand alone / Brand new day / Sam Stone / New York City (you're a woman) / I got a woman.

United Art United Art

Dec 76. (7") **HOLLYWOOD VAMPIRE. / THIS DIAMOND RING** –

Jan 77. (lp) **ACT LIKE NOTHING'S WRONG** Dec76
– Is we on the downbeat? / This diamond ring / She don't ever lose her groove / I forgot to be your lover / Missing you / Out of left field / (Please not) One more time / In my own sweet way / Turn my head towards home / A visit to the Rainbow bar & grill / Hollywood vampire.

C.B.S. Columbia

1982. (7") **TWO SIDES (TO EVERY SITUATION). (with VALERIE CARTER) / SNOWBLIND** –

1982. (lp) **CHAMPIONSHIP WRESTLING**
– I wish you would / Two sides / Wrestless with this / Lost control / I'd rather be an old man's sweetheart / The heart is a lonely hunter / Bandstand / Finders keepers / Snowblind.

— Returned into production work.

Peter KOPPES (see under ⇒ CHURCH)

Alexis KORNER

Born: 19 Apr'28, Paris, France. Raised by Austrian father and Greek / Turkish mother who settled in London, England during the mid-1930's. After being introduced to the music business in the late 40's, the next decade saw him playing stints with CHRIS BARBER's Jazz Band. He then combined together with CYRIL DAVIES in 1961, when they formed BLUES INCORPORATED. They initiated own club 'The Ealing Rhythm & Blues Club' in Mar'62, bringing in musicians, noteably CHARLIE WATTS (future ROLLING STONES drummer). Many other stars, passed through on their way to greater things (i.e. MICK JAGGER, ERIC BURDON, PAUL JONES and LONG JOHN BALDRY). Always anti-commercial, ALEXIS disassembled said band in '67, puzzling loyal fans when he moved into Children's TV with future PENTANGLE members; DANNY THOMPSON and TERRY COX. By the late 60's, he formed FREE AT LAST who managed to only surface on

German 'Metrognome' label. He encouraged a now famous young blues band to use name FREE. By 1968, he had toured Scandinavia with Danish singer and band PETER THORUP and The BEEFEATERS. On his return, he formed new outfit The NEW CHURCH which included PETER and his daughter SAPPHO. They managed a support slot on The ROLLING STONES' Hyde Park concert before splitting. In 1970, with THORUP still in tow, ALEXIS formed C.C.S. (Collective Consciousness Society), who were mainly sessioners directed by JOHN CAMERON and produced by MICKIE MOST. Their first single, a cover of Led Zeppelin's 'WHOLE LOTTA LOVE' shot into the UK charts hitting 13. This was his most lucrative period as more Top10 hits followed. Later in the seventies, he concentrated on solo work and moved into Radio 1 broadcasting. His voice was heard on many a TV ad, until he died of lung cancer on 1st January 1984. • **Style:** Moved from jazz to own blend of blues, jazz/R&B. In the 70's for CCS, his husky voice, gave simple tunes their identity. • **Songwriters:** KORNER and CYRIL DAVIES until 1962. For CCS he wrote with JOHN CAMERON. Many blues standards were covered on all work. Others incl. GET OFF MY CLOUD (Rolling Stones) / THE WASP (Doors) / YOU ARE MY SUNSHINE (Mitchell-Davis) / AIN'T THAT PECULIAR (Marvin Gaye) / SHAKIN' ALL OVER (Johnny Kidd). CCS covered SATISFACTION (Rolling Stones) / WADE IN THE WATER (Ramsey Lewis) / LIVING IN THE PAST (Jethro Tull) / BOOM BOOM (John Lee Hooker) / etc. • **Trivia:** WHOLE LOTTA LOVE was later used for 'Top Of The Pops' intro-theme.

Recommended: THE COLLECTION (*6)

ALEXIS KORNER SKIFFLE GROUP

Tempo / not issued

1957. (7") **COUNTY JAIL. / I AIN'T GONNA WORRY NO MORE** — -
1958. (7"ep) **I AIN'T GONNA WORRY NO MORE** — -
– I ain't gonna worry no more / County jail / Kid man / Easy rider.
1959. (7"ep) **ALEXIS KORNER BLUES INCORPORATED** — -
– Sail on / National defence blues / Go down, sunshine / Death letter.

— An album 'THE LEGENDARY CYRIL DAVIS WITH ALEXIS KORNER'S BREAKDOWN GROUP AND THE ROUNDHOUSE JUG FOUR' was issued in the early 60's by 'Folklore'.

ALEXIS KORNER / BLUES INCORPORATED

ALEXIS KORNER – guitar / **CYRIL DAVIES** – harmonica / **KEITH SCOTT** – piano / **ANDY HOOGENBOOM** – bass / **CHARLIE WATTS** – drums / **ART WOOD** – vox

Ace Of Clubs / not issued

1962. (lp) **R&B FROM THE MARQUEE (live)** — -
– Gotta move / Rain is such a lonesome sound / I got my brand on you / Spooky but nice / Keep your hands off / I wanna put a tiger in your tank / I got my mojo working / Finkles cafe / Hoochie coochie / Downtown / How long, how long blues / I thought that train whistle blew. *(re-iss.Feb84) (re-iss.+cd.Dec91 on 'Deram'; with other tracks, c-iss. Jul 93)*

— **KORNER** with new band **GINGER BAKER** – drums repl. WATTS (to STONES) / **JACK BRUCE** – bass repl. ANDY / **DICK HECKSTALL-SMITH** – tenor sax repl. DAVIES who formed own ALL STARS.

Parlophone / not issued

1964. (7") **I NEED YOUR LOVIN'. / PLEASE PLEASE PLEASE** — -
Feb 65. (7") **LITTLE BABY. / ROBERTA** — -

Ace Of Clubs / not issued

1965. (lp) **ALEXIS KORNER'S BLUES INCORPORATED** — -
– Woke up this morning / Skippin' / Herbie's tune / Stormy Monday / It's happening / Roberta Jones / Cabbage greens / Chicken shack / Haitian fight song. *(re-iss.Sep67 as 'BLUES INCORPORATED' on 'Polydor')*

Transatla. / not issued

1964. (lp) **RED HOT FROM ALEX** — -
– Woke up this morning / Skippin' / Herbie's tune / Stormy Monday / It's happening / Roberta Jones / Cabbage greens / Chicken shack / Haitian fight song.

Oriole / not issued

1964. (lp) **AT THE CAVERN (live)** — -
– Overdrive / Who babe / Every day I have the blues / Hoochie coochie man / Herbie's tune / Little bitty girl blues / Well alright, OK, you win / Kansas City.

Spot / not issued

1966. (lp) **SKY HIGH** — -
(cd-iss.Nov94 on 'Indigo')

ALEXIS KORNER

(solo)

Fontana / not issued

May 66. (7") **RIVER'S INVITATION. / EVERYDAY I HAVE THE BLUES** — -
Mar 67. (7") **ROSIE. / ROCK ME** — -
Mar 67. (lp) **I WONDER WHO** — -
– Watermelon man / Streamline train / Rock me / Come back / Going down slow / 2.19 blues / River's invitation / I wonder who? / Chicken shack back home / County jail blues / Roll 'em Pete / Betty & Dupree / See see rider. *(cd-iss.Jul92 on 'B.G.O.')*

Liberty / not issued

Jul 68. (lp) **A NEW GENERATION OF BLUES** — -
– Mary open the door / Little bitty girl / Baby don't you love me / Go down sunshine / Same for you / I'm tore down / In the evening / Something you got / New worried blues / What's that sound I hear / A flower *(re-iss.1971 as 'WHAT'S THAT SOUND I HEAR' on 'Sunset')*

FREE AT LAST

ALEXIS KORNER – vocals, guitar / **MARSHA HUNT** – vox / **VICTOR BRONX** – trumpet

Metrognome / not issued

1970 (lp) **BOTH SIDES (live / studio)** - - GERM
– Mighty mighty / Funky / Wild Injun woman / I see it / You don't miss your water till your well runs dry / Polly put the kettle on / Worried blues / The duo thing / Rosie.

The NEW CHURCH

were formed by ALEXIS, plus **PETER THORUP** – vocals / **SAPPHO KORNER** – vocals / **COLIN HODGKINSON** – bass/ etc.

Metrognome / not issued

1970. (lp) **THE NEW CHURCH** - - GERM
– (1969 & 1970 were iss.on 1 album?)

C.C.S.

ALEXIS – vocals, guitar / **THORUP** – vocals / **JOHN CAMERON** – piano / **HAROLD BECKETT** – trumpet / **IAN CARR** – drums / **HENRY LOWTHER** – trumpet / **HAROLD McNAIR** – wind / **JOHN MARSHALL** – trombone / **TONY FISHER** – trumpet / **HERBIE FLOWERS** – bass / **SPIKE HEATLEY** – bass / **ALAN PARKER** – guitar / **etc.**

R.A.K. / R.A.K.

Oct 70. (7") **WHOLE LOTTA LOVE. / BOOM BOOM** 13 58
(re-iss.Nov73)
Nov 70. (lp)(c) **C.C.S.**
– Boom boom / Satisfaction / Waiting song / Lookin' for fun / Whole lotta love / Living in the past / Sunrise / Dos Cantos / Wade in the water.
Feb 71. (7") **WALKIN'. / SALOME** 7 -
Aug 71. (7") **TAP TURNS ON THE WATER. / SAVE THE WORLD** 5
Feb 72. (7") **BROTHER. / MISTER WHAT YOU CAN'T HAVE** 25 -
Mar 72. (lp)(c) **C.C.S. 2** 23
– Brother / Black dog / I want you back / Running out of sky / Whole lotta rock'n'roll: School days – Lucille – Long tall Sally – Whole lotta love / Chaos / Can we ever get it back / This is my life / Misunderstood / Maggie's song / City.
Oct 72. (7") **SIXTEEN TONS. / THIS IS MY LIFE**
1973. (lp)(c) **THE BEST BAND IN THE LAND**
– The band played the boogie / Wild witch lady / Lola / Primitive love / Hundred highways / Shakin' all over / Memphis / Sunshine of your love / Our man in London / Cannibal sheep.
Jul 73. (7") **BAND PLAYED THE BOOGIE. / HANG IT ON ME** 36 -
Apr 74. (7") **HURRICANE COMING. / DRAGSTER** -
1974. (7") **SHAKIN' ALL OVER. / CANNIBAL SHEEP** -

— C.C.S. were no longer.

ALEXIS KORNER

also had simultaneous solo career.

R.A.K. / Warners

1971. (lp)(c) **ALEXIS** -
– Black woman / Frankie Diamond / Clay House Inn / Stump blues / You can make it like you want it to be gold / Saturday Sun / I don't know / Am I my brother's keeper / Stop playing games / That's all.
Dec 71. (d-lp) **BOOTLEG HIM (compilation?)** -
– She fooled me / I'm your hoochie coochie man / Yellow dog blues / I wonder who / Dee / Oh Lord, don't let 'em drop that atomic bomb on me / Rockin' / Honesty / I got a woman / Mighty mighty spade and whitey / Corina Corina / Operator / The love you save (may be your own) / Jesus is just alright / That's all

SNAPE

KORNER in 1972 with **THORUP** – vocals / **IAN WALLACE** – drums / **MEL COLLINS** – saxophone + **BOZ BURRELL** – bass (all 3 ex-KING CRIMSON)

Transatla. / Warners

1973. (lp) **ACCIDENTLY BORN IN NEW ORLEANS**
– Gospel ship / One scotch, one bourbon, one beer / Sweet sympathy / Rock me / Don't change on me / You got the power (to turn me on) / Lo and behold / Country shoes.

Brain / not issued

1974. (lp) **SNAPE LIVE IN GERMANY (live)** - - GERM
– Going down / Early in the morning / You got the power / Snape / Rock me baby / These kind of blues / The night time is the right time / Bottom of the sea / Cowhee baby.

ALEXIS KORNER

(solo)

Toadstool / not issued

1974. (lp) **MR.BLUES** - - Germ'y

— next feat. guests **KEITH RICHARD / PETER FRAMPTON / STEVE MARRIOTT / KOKOMO / NICKY HOPKINS / COLIN HODGKINSON** / etc.

C.B.S. / Columbia

Sep 75. (7") **GET OFF OF MY CLOUD. / STRANGE'N'DERANGED**
Sep 75. (lp)(c) **GET OFF OF MY CLOUD**
– I gotcha number / The wasp (Texas radio & the beat) / Robert Johnson / Tree top fever / You are my sunshine / Strange'n'deranged / Slow down / Song for Jimi / Ain't that peculiar / Get off of my cloud.
Jan 76. (7") **AIN'T THAT PECULIAR. / TREE TOP FEVER** -

Intercord / not issued

1978. (lp) **JUST EASY** - - GERM
– Roll me / If I never sing another song / Lend me some time / Everyday since you've been gone / Daytime song / The gambler / Angel band / The love you save.

Jeton / not issued

1979. (lp) **ME** - GERM
– Honky tonk woman / Louise / Hammer and nails / Santa Fe blues / How long blues / Roberta / Precious Lord / Honour the young man / And again / East St.Louis blues.

— In Mar'81, he guested on ROCKET 88 eponymous album on 'Atlantic'.

— On 1 Jan'84, ALEXIS died of lung cancer after recording below album.

Charisma not issued

May 84. (7") **BEIRUT. / MEAN FOOL** [ ] [-]
Jun 84. (lp)(c) **JUVENILE DELINQUENT** [ ] [-]
– Beirut / Mean fool / The sphinx / Get of my cloud / King BB / Juvenile delinquent.

– more compilations, etc. –

1969. Transatlantic; (lp) **ALEXIS KORNER'S ALL STAR BLUES INCORPORATED** [ ] [-]
May 81. Teldec; (lp)(c) **PROFILE** [ ] [-]
Jun 85. Thunderbolt; (lp)(cd) **TESTAMENT** [ ] [-]
Jan 87. Thunderbolt; (lp)(c) **HAMMER AND NAILS** [ ] [-]
Sep 86. Castle; (d-lp)(c)(cd) **THE COLLECTION: ALEXIS KORNER 1961-72** [ ] [-]
Sep 88. Castle; (d-lp)(c)(cd) **THE COLLECTION: ALEXIS KORNER** [ ] [-]
– Gospel ship / Captain America / The thief / Robert Johnson / Get off my cloud / Honky tonk women / Spoonful / Daytime song / Lend me some time / Hey pretty mama / Stump blues / I got my mojo working / Geneva / Wreck of the ole '97 / Casey Jones / High heel sneakers / King BB / Juvenile delinquent. *(re-iss.cd Apr94)*
Feb 88. CD Label; (cd) **LIVE IN PARIS (live) ("ALEXIS KORNER & COLIN HODGKINSON")** [ ] [-]
Dec 94. Music Club; (cd)(c) **THE BBC RADIO SESSIONS** [ ] [-]
Jan 95. Thunderbolt; (cd) **THE LOST ALBUM** [ ] [-]
Jun 77. RAK; (lp)(c) **C.C.S.; THE BEST OF C.C.S.** [ ] [-]
Jul 77. RAK; (7") **C.C.S.; BROTHER. / PRIMITIVE LOVE** [ ] [-]
May 84. EMI Gold; (7") **C.C.S.; WHOLE LOTTA LOVE. / WALKING** [ ] [-]
Aug 91. (cd)(c)(lp) **WHOLE LOTTA LOVE: THE BEST OF C.C.S.** [ ] [-]

Paul KOSSOFF (see under ⇒ FREE)

KRAFTWERK

Formed: Dusseldorf, Germany ... 1969 as ORGANISATION by RALF HUTTER, FLORIAN SCHNEIDER and 3 others (see below). After one Conrad Plank produced lp 'TONE FLOAT' for 'RCA' in 1970, the pair broke away to form KRAFTWERK (German for POWERPLANT), with KLAUS DINGER and THOMAS HOMANN. After one lp for 'Philips', RALF & FLORIAN became KRAFTWERK and released 1973 album of their names as title for #096Vertigo'. In 1974, they added KLAUS ROEDER & WOLFGANG FLUR, and issued their magnus-opus 'AUTOBAHN'. This UK & US Top 5 album contained a 22 minute title track, which edited into 3 minutes, also became hit. The next album 'RADIO ACTIVITY' (which was also now issued on own 'Kling Klang' label in Germany), disappointed most and failed to secure a Top 50 placing. In 1978, they were back in the UK Top 10 at least, with excellent return to form 'THE MAN MACHINE'. In the early 80's, they enjoyed another hit album 'COMPUTER WORLD', and a run of UK hit singles, one of which 'THE MODEL' (from 1978 lp) made top spot. Sparodic recording followed with only 1 album of new material being released in the next decade. • **Style:** Robotic electronic rock act, with minimalist synth-tunes at times being twidled by their dummies. Were more inspirational than contemporaries TANGERINE DREAM, and were a major influence to ULTRAVOX!, GARY NUMAN, DAVID BOWIE '77, JEAN-MICHEL JARRE, SIMPLE MINDS, OMD, etc. • **Songwriters:** RALF & FLORIAN. • **Trivia:** They have been sampled by many including AFRIKA BAMBAATAA in 1983 on single 'Planet Rock'.

Recommended: AUTOBAHN (*7) / RADIOACTIVITY (*4) / TRANS-EUROPE EXPRESS (*8) / THE MAN MACHINE (*8) / COMPUTER WORLD (*6)

ORGANISATION

RALF HUTTER (b.1946, Krefeld, Germany)– electric organ, strings / **FLORIAN SCHNEIDER-ESLEBEN** (b.1947, Dusseldorf)– flute, echo unit, strings / **BUTCH HAUF** – bass, percussion / **FRED MONICKS** – drums / **BASIL HAMMOND** – percussion, vocals

R.C.A. not issued

1970. (lp) **TONE FLOAT** [ ] [-] GERM
– Tone float / Milk float / Silver forest / Rhythm salad / Noitasinagro.

KRAFTWERK

HUTTER + SCHNEIDER with KLAUS DINGER – guitar, keyboards / **THOMAS HOMANN** – percussion

not issued Philips

1971. (lp) **KRAFTWERK (HIGHRAIL)** [-] [-] Germ'y
– Ruckzuck / Stratowargius / Megaherz / Vom Himmel hoch.

— **HUTTER** and **SCHNEIDER** trimmed to a duo. (DINGER and HOMANN formed NEU!)

1972. (lp) **KRAFTWERK II (VAR)** [-] [-] Germ'y
– Klingklang / Atem / Strom / Spule 4 / Wellenlange / Harmonika.

Vertigo Vertigo

1972. (d-lp) **KRAFTWERK** (2 German lp's combined) [ ] [-]
Nov 73. (lp)(c) **RALF AND FLORIAN** [ ] [ ] Sep 75
– Elektrisches roulette (Electric roulette) / Tongebirge (Mountain of sound) / Kristallo (Crystals) / Heimatklange (The bells of home) / Tanzmusik (Dance music) / Ananas symphonie (Pineapple symphony).

— added **KLAUS ROEDER** – violin, guitar / **WOLFGANG FLUR** – percussion

Nov 74. (lp)(c) **AUTOBAHN** [4] [5]
– Autobahn / Kometenmelodie 1 & 2 (Comet melody) / Mitternacht (Midnight) / Morgenspaziergang (Morning walk). *(re-iss.Mar82 & Jun85 on 'EMI' hit 61 UK, cd-iss.Jun87) (re-iss.Jun83)*
Feb 75. (7") **AUTOBAHN. / KOMETENMELODIE** [11] [-]
Feb 75. (7") **AUTOBAHN. / MORGENSPAZIERGANG** [-] [25]
Jul 75. (7") **KOMETENMELODIE. / MITTERNACHT** [-] [ ]
Jul 75. (7") **KOMETENMELODIE 2. / KRISTALLO** [ ] [-]

— Oct75, **KARL BARTOS** – percussion repl. ROEDER

Capitol Capitol

Nov 75. (lp)(c) **RADIO-ACTIVITY** [ ] [ ]
– Geiger counter / Radio-activity / Radioland / Airwaves / (intermission) / News / The voice of energy / Antenna / Radio stars / Uran / Transistor / Ohm sweet ohm. *(re-iss.Jun84 on 'Fame/Capitol') (re-iss.+cd.Jun87) (re-iss.cd Apr94 on 'Cleopatra') (cd-iss.Apr95 on 'EMI')*
Feb 76. (7") **RADIO-ACTIVITY. / ANTENNA** [ ] [ ]
Apr 77. (lp)(c) **TRANS-EUROPE EXPRESS** [ ] [ ]
– Europe endless / The hall of mirrors / Showroom dummies / Trans-Europe express / Metal on metal / Franz Schubert / Endless endless. *(reached No.49 Feb82, re-iss.'85, re-iss.Jun86 on 'Fame')(cd-iss.May87) (re-iss.cd Apr94 on 'Cleopatra')*
Apr 77. (7") **TRANS-EUROPE EXPRESS. / EUROPE ENDLESS** [ ] [-]
Jun 77. (7") **TRANS EUROPE EXPRESS. / FRANZ SCHUBERT** [-] [67]
Aug 77. (7") **SHOWROOM DUMMIES. / EUROPE EXPRESS** [ ] [ ]
May 78. (lp)(c) **THE MAN MACHINE** [9] [ ]
– The robots / Spacelab / Metropolis / The model / Neon lights / The man machine. *(re-iss.+cd.Jul88 on 'Fame') (re-iss.cd Apr94 on 'Cleopatra') (cd-iss.Apr95 on 'EMI')*
May 78. (7") **THE ROBOTS (edit). / SPACELAB** [ ] [ ]
Jun 78. (7") **NEON LIGHTS. / THE ROBOTS** [-] [ ]
Sep 78. (12"m) **SHOWROOM DUMMIES. / EUROPE ENDLESS / SPACELAB** [ ] [-]
Sep 78. (7"luminous)(12"luminous) **NEON LIGHTS. / TRANS-EUROPE EXPRESS / THE MODEL** [53] [ ]

E.M.I. Warners

Apr 81. (7")(12")(US-7"green) **POCKET CALCULATOR. / DENTAKU** [39] [ ]
(c-s) – ('A'extended version) / Numbers.
May 81. (lp)(c) **COMPUTER-WORLD** [15] [72]
– Pocket calculator / Numbers / Computer-world / Computer love / Home computer / It's more fun to compute. *(cd-iss.Apr95 on EMI')*
Jun 81. (7")(12") **COMPUTER LOVE. / THE MODEL** [36] [-]
(above double 'A'-side, flipped over Dec81 reached No.1.*(re-1983)*
Jun 81. (7") **COMPUTER LOVE. / NUMBERS** [-] [ ]
Feb 82. (7")(12") **SHOWROOM DUMMIES. / NUMBERS** [25] [ ]
Jul 83. (7") **TOUR DE FRANCE. / TOUR DE FRANCE (instrumental)** [22] [ ]
(12"+=)(c-s+=) – ('A'&'B' versions). *(re-iss.+ remixed 7+12" Aug84, reached No.24, 12" had all versions)*
Aug 83. (lp)(c) **TECHNO POP** (cancelled) [-] [-]
Oct 86. (7")(12") **MUSIQUE NON STOP. / MUSIQUE NON STOP (version)** [ ] [ ]
Nov 86. (lp)(c)(cd) **ELECTRIC CAFE** [58] [ ]
– Boom boom tschak / Techno pop / Musique non stop / The telephone call / Sex object / Techno pop / Electric cafe.
Feb 87. (7") **THE TELEPHONE CALL. / DER TELEFON ANRUF** [ ] [ ]
(12"+=) – Housephone.

— **FRITZ HIJBERT** repl. WOLFGANG FLUR

May 91. (7")(c-s) **THE ROBOTS (remixed). / ('A'version)** [20] [ ]
(12"+=)(cd-s+=) – Robotronix / ('A'version).
Jun 91. (cd)(c)(d-lp) **THE MIX** ('91 remixes) [15] [ ]
– The robots / Computer love / Pocket calculator / Dentaku / Autobahn / Radioactivity / Trans Europe express / Abzug / Metal on metal / Homecomputer / Musique non stop.
Oct 91. (7")(c-s) **RADIOACTIVITY (remix). / ('A'orbit remix)** [43] [ ]
(12"+=)(cd-s+=) – ('A'remixes extended).

— In Jul'91, BARTOS and FLUR formed own project ELEKTRIC.

– compilations, others, imports –

1975. Philips; (d-lp) **DOPPELALBUM** [-] [-]
Oct 75. Vertigo; (lp)(c) **EXCELLER 8** [ ] [-]
Oct 80. Vertigo Germany; (7") **AUTOBAHN. / ('B'by BEGGAR'S OPERA)** [-] [-]
Apr 81. Vertigo; (lp)(c) **ELEKTRO KINETIC** [ ] [ ]
May 81. Vertigo; (7") **KOMETENMELODIE 2. / VON HIMMEL HOCH** [ ] [ ]
1976. Fontana Germany; (lp) **POP LIONS** [-] [-]
May 84. Old Gold; (7") **THE MODEL. / COMPUTER LOVE** [ ] [-]

— (In the States, there was also comp.lp 'THE ROBOTS' on 'Capitol')

Apr 94. Cleopatra; (cd) **SHOWROOM DUMMIES** [ ] [-]
Apr 94. Cleopatra; (cd) **THE MODEL** [ ] [-]

Wayne KRAMER (see under ⇒ MC5)

Lenny KRAVITZ

Born: 26 May'64, New York, USA, son of a Russian Jew and black Bahamian actress. As a teenager, they moved to Los Angeles, where he joined local boys' choir and learned himself to play guitar and piano. In 1987, he formed own one-man band ROMEO BLUE, and married 'Cosby Show' actress Lisa Bonet in Nov'87. For the next 2 years, he recorded demos which were soon heard by Henry Hirsch, who recommended them to 'Virgin'. By the time they signed him, LENNY had divorced (1988) and befriended new circle of friends like SEAN LENNON and his mother YOKO ONO. In Oct'89, after many arguments with record company over use of production, etc., he finally released debut album and single 'LET LOVE RULE'. The album notched up sales of half a million copies in the US, and eventually reached Top 60 in the UK. In 1990, the title track became first Top 40 success in Britain, and tempted MADONNA into asking him and INGRID CHAVEZ to write her controversial 'Justify My Love' single. Later that year, he also appeared in Liverpool at YOKO ONO's tribute to her late husband JOHN LENNON. Early in '92, after a Top 10 album 'MAMA SAID', LENNY settled out of court royalties to INGRID CHAVEZ. • **Style:** Late 60's influenced heavy soul-rock artist, reminiscent of JIMI HENDRIX, CURTIS MAYFIELD and LED ZEPPELIN. His psychedelic-pop image, leant more from 80's star PRINCE, while definitely filling the gap in the 90's for the musically vacationing TERENCE TRENT D'ARBY. • **Songwriters:** Writes and plays in studio all instruments, and covers; COLD TURKEY + GIVE PEACE A CHANCE (John Lennon) / IF SIX WAS NINE (Jimi Hendrix / DEUCE (Kiss). • **Trivia:** SLASH of GUNS'N'ROSES played guitar on 2 tracks from 'MAMA SAID'.

Recommended: MAMA SAID (*8) / LET LOVE RULE (*7) / ARE YOU GONNA GO MY WAY (*7).

LENNY KRAVITZ – vocals, guitar, piano, bass, drums with a few on session / **HENRY HIRSCH** – keyboards / **KARL DENSON** – sax / +guests.

Virgin America | Virgin

Oct 89. (7") **LET LOVE RULE. / EMPTY HANDS** [ ] [89]
(12"+=)(cd-s+=) – Blues for Sister Someone / Flower child.

Nov 89. (lp)(c)(cd) **LET LOVE RULE** [56] [61] Jan 90
– Sitting on top of the world / Let love rule / Freedom train / My precious love / I build this garden for us / Fear / Does anybody out there even care / Mr. Cab driver / Rosemary / Be. (c+=)– Blues for Sister Someone / Flower child. (cd++=)– Empty hands. *(re-dist.May90.hit UK No.56)*

Jan 90. (7")(c-s) **I BUILD THIS GARDEN FOR US. / FLOWER CHILD** [81] [ ]
(12"+=)(cd-s+=) – Fear.

May 90. (7")(c-s) **MR. CAB DRIVER. / BLUES FOR SISTER SOMEONE (live) / DOES ANYBODY OUT THERE EVEN CARE (live)** [58] [ ]
(12"+=) – (first 2 tracks) / Rosemary (live).
(10"++=) – (first 2 tracks) / Let love rule (live).

Jul 90. (7")(c-s) **LET LOVE RULE. / COLD TURKEY (live)** [39] [ ]
(12"+=) – Flower child (live).
(cd-s+=) – My precious love (live).
(10") – ('A'side) / My precious love (live) / If six was nine (live).

Mar 91. (7")(c-s) **ALWAYS ON THE RUN. / ('A'instrumental)** [41] [ ]
(12"box+=) – Light skin girl from London.
(cd-s++=) – Butterfly.

Apr 91. (cd)(c)(lp) **MAMA SAID** [8] [39]
– Fields of joy / Always on the run / Stand by my woman / It ain't over 'til it's over / More than anything in this world / What goes around comes around / The difference is why / Stop draggin' around / Flowers for Zoe / Fields of joy (reprise) / All I ever wanted / When the morning turns to night / What the . . . . are we saying? / Butterfly.

May 91. (7")(c-s) **IT AIN'T OVER 'TIL IT'S OVER. / THE DIFFERENCE IS WHY** [11] [2]
(12"+=)(cd-s+=) – I'll be around.
(12"pic-d) – ('A'side) / (interview).

Sep 91. (7")(c-s) **STAND BY MY WOMAN. / FLOWERS FOR ZOE** [55] [76]
(12"+=) – Stop dragging around (live).
(cd-s+=) – What the . . . . are we saying / Always on the run (both live)

— with **CRAIG ROSS** – electric guitar (co-writes, some music) / **TONY BRETT** – bass / **MICHAEL HUNTER** – flugel horn

Feb 93. (7")(c-s) **ARE YOU GONNA GO MY WAY. / MY LOVE** [4] [ ]
(cd-s) – ('A' side) Always on the run / It ain't over 'til it's over / Let love rule.

Mar 93. (cd)(c)(lp) **ARE YOU GONNA GO MY WAY** [1] [12]
– Are you gonna go my way / Believe / Come on and love me / Heaven help / Just be a woman / Is there any love in your heart / Black girl / My love / Sugar / Sister / Eleutheria.

May 93. (7")(c-s) **BELIEVE. / FOR THE FIRST TIME** [30] [60]
(10"pic-d+=)(cd-s+=) – ('A'acoustic) / Sitar (acoustic).

Aug 93. (7")(c-s) **HEAVEN HELP. / ELEUTHERIA** [21] [-]
(cd-s+=) – Ascension / Brother.

Nov 93. (7"pic-d)(12") **IS THERE ANY LOVE IN YOUR HEART. / ALWAYS ON THE RUN (live)** [52] [ ]
(cd+=) – What goes around comes around (live) / Freedom train (live).

Mar 94. (c-s)(cd-s) **HEAVEN HELP. / SPINNING AROUND OVER YOU** [-] [80]

Aug 95. (7")(c-s) **ROCK AND ROLL IS DEAD. / ANOTHER LIFE** [22] [75]
(10"+=)(cd-s+=) – Confused / Is it me or is it you.

Sep 95. (cd)(c)(lp) **CIRCUS** [5] [10]
– Rock and roll is dead / Circus / Beyond the 7th sky / Tunnel vision / Can't get you off my mind / Magdalene / God is love / Thin ice / Don't go and put a bullet in your head / In my life today / The resurrection.

Dec 95. (c-s) **CIRCUS / ('A'acoustic)** [54] [ ]
(10"+=)(cd-s+=) – Tunnel vision (live) / Are you gonna go my way (live).

Sonja KRISTINA (see under ⇒ CURVED AIR)

KROKUS

Formed: Soluthurn, Switzerland ... 1974 by VON ROHR, VON ARB, KIEFER, NAEGELLI and STEADY. After releasing 2 lp's on a Swiss label, they signed to European outlet 'Philips', before changing to 'Ariola' late in '79. They soon moved to London, and after a well-received Reading Festival in Aug'80, their second album for the label 'HARDWARE', cracked the UK Top 50. Became worldly favourites for the next 3 years. • **Style:** Initially a symphonic rock outfit, who turned to heavy, high-speed metal, similiar to AC/DC from early 80's onwards. • **Songwriters:** Most by VON ARB / VON ROHR, except SCHOOL'S OUT (Alice Cooper) / BALLROOM BLITZ (Sweet). • **Trivia:** In 1981, MANNY and a roadie were kidnapped by a cab driver in Little Rock, Arkansas.

Recommended: METAL RENDEZ-VOUS (*7)

HENRY FRIEZ – vocals / **TOMMY KIEFER** – guitar, vocals / **FERNANDO VON ARB** – guitar, bass / **JUERG NAEGELLI** – keyboards, vocals / **CHRIS VON ROHR** – bass, vocals / **FREDDY STEADY** – drums

Schmoritz | not issued

1976. (lp) **KROKUS** [-] [-]

1977. (lp) **TO YOU ALL** [-] [-] Swiss

— **CHRIS** now lead vocals, percussion when HENRY left.

Philips | not issued

Oct 78. (lp) **PAINKILLER** [-] [-] Euro
– Killer / Werewolf / Rock ladies / Bad love / Get out of my mind / Rock me, rock you / Deadline / Susie / Pay it! / Bye by baby. *(imported Mar81) (re-iss.Aug82 as PAY IT IN METAL)*

— added **MARC STORACE** – vocals

Ariola | Ariola

Mar 80. (7") **BEDSIDE RADIO. / BACK SEAT ROCK'N'ROLL** [ ] [-]

May 80. (7") **HEATSTROKES. / SHY KID** [ ] [ ]

Jul 80. (lp)(c) **METAL RENDEZ-VOUS** [ ] [ ]
– Heat strokes / Bedside radio / Come on / Streamer / Shy kid / Tokyo nights / Lady double dealer / Fire, fire / No way / Back seat rock'n'roll. *(re-iss.Sep82) (cd-iss.Jun88 on 'Arista')*

Aug 80. (7") **TOKYO NIGHTS. / BEDSIDE RADIO** [ ] [-]
(12"+=) – Shy kid.

— now a quintet when NAEGELLI departed. (but retained on some studio work) .

Feb 81. (7"m) **ROCK CITY. / MR.69 / MAD RACKET** [ ] [-]

Feb 81. (lp)(c) **HARDWARE** [44] [ ]
– Celebration / Easy rocker / Smelly Nelly / Mr. 69 / She's got everything / Burning bones / Rock city / Winning man / Mad racket.

Apr 81. (7") **WINNING MAN. / MAD RACKET** [-] [ ]

— **RANDY MEIER** – guitar repl. KEIFER (He committed suicide 24 Dec'86)

Apr 81. (7"ep) **INDUSTRIAL STRENGTH** [62] [-]
– Bedside radio / Easy rocker / Celebration / Bye bye baby.

— **MARK KOEHLER** – guitar, vocals repl. MEIER who joined ASIA

Arista | Arista

Feb 82. (7") **BAD BOYS RAG DOLLS. / SAVE ME** [ ] [-]

Feb 82. (lp)(c) **ONE VICE AT A TIME** [28] [53]
– Long stick goes boom / Bad boys rag dolls / Playin' the outlaw / To the top / Down the drain / American woman / I'm on the run / Save me / Rock'n'roll.

Jun 82. (7") **SAVE ME. / LONG STICK GOES BOOM** [-] [ ]

Jul 82. (7") **AMERICAN WOMAN. / LONG STICK GOES BOOM** [ ] [ ] Aug 82

— **(STORACE, VON ARB, KOEHLER** and **VON ROHR)** recruited **STEVE PACE** – drums to repl. FREDDY

Apr 83. (lp)(c) **HEADHUNTER** [74] [25]
– Headhunter / Eat the rich / Screaming in the night / Ready to burn / Night wolf / Stayed awake all night / Stand and be counted / White din / Russian winter. *(re-iss.+cd.Apr88)*

May 83. (7") **SCREAMING IN THE NIGHT. / RUSSIAN WINTER** [-] [ ]

Sep 83. (7") **STAYED AWAKE ALL NIGHT / ('A'version)** [-] [ ]

— on tour **PATRICK MASON** – guitar repl. KOEHLER / **KOEHLER** returned on – bass repl. VON ROHR / **JEFF KLAVEN** – drums (ex-COBRA) repl. PACE

Aug 84. (7") **BALLROOM BLITZ. / READY TO ROCK** [ ] [ ]
(12"+=) – Out of control.

Aug 84. (lp)(c) **THE BLITZ** [ ] [31]
– Midnite maniac / Out of control / Boys nite out / Our love / Out to lunch / Ballroom blitz / Rock the nation / Hot stuff / Ready to rock. *(cd-iss.1988)*

Sep 84. (7") **MIDNITE MANIAC. / READY TO ROCK** [-] [71]

— now a 4-piece (**STORACE, VON ARB** and **KLAVEN** plus **ANDY TAMAS** – bass (ex-BLACK OAK ARKANSAS) repl. KOEHLER (reverted to guitar?)

— Late'85, **TOMMY KESSLER** – bass repl. TAMAS

Jun 86. (7") **SCHOOL'S OUT. / SCREAMING IN THE NIGHT** [-] [61]

Jun 86. (lp)(c) **CHANGE OF ADDRESS** [ ] [45] Apr 86
– Now (all through the night) / Hot shot city / School's out / Let this love begin / Burning up the night / Say goodbye / World on fire / Hard luck hero / Long way from home.

Feb 87. (lp)(c)(cd) **ALIVE AND SCREAMIN' (live)** [ ] [97] Oct 86
– Long stick goes boom / Eat the rich / Screaming in the night / Hot shot city / Midnite maniac / Bedside radio / Lay me down / Stayed awake all night / Headhunter.

Feb 87. (7") **LET THE LOVE BEGIN. / HOT SHOT CITY** [-] [ ]

Apr 87. (7") **SCREAMING IN THE NIGHT (live). / HEADHUNTER (Live)** [-] [ ]

— **CHRIS VON ROHR** – bass, vocals returned to repl. KESSLER. **DANI CRIVELLI** – drums (ex-KILLER) repl. KLAVEN

M.C.A. | M.C.A.

Mar 88. (lp)(c)(cd) **HEART ATTACK** [ ] [87]
– Everybody rocks / Wild love / Let it go / Winning man / Axx attack / Rock'n'roll tonight / Flyin' high / Shoot down the night / Bad, bad girl / Speed up.

Apr 88. (7") **LET IT GO. / WINNING MAN** [ ] [ ]
(12"+=) – Bourbon Street.

— **MANNY MAURER** – guitar repl. VON ARB and **SCOTT ALAN** – vocals repl. STORACE

1990. (cd)(c)(lp) **STAMPEDE** [ ] [ ]

It was no wonder they split with virtually no originals remaining.

Phonag | not issued

Jul 95. (cd) **TO ROCK OR NOT TO BE** [ ] [-]

KUKL (see under ⇒ BJORK)

Tuli KUPFERRBERG (see under ⇒ FUGS)

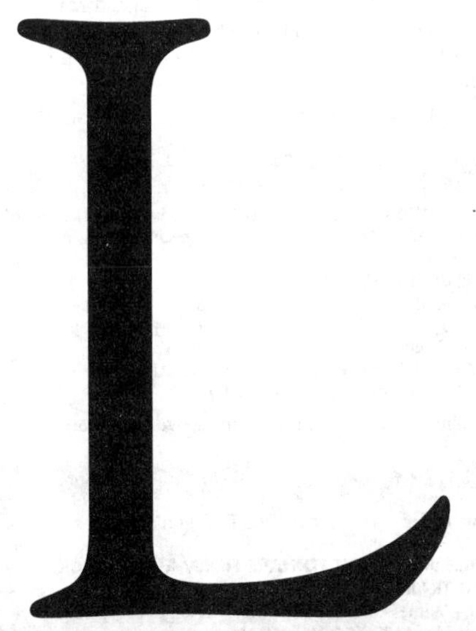

David LaFLAMME (see under ⇒ IT'S A BEAUTIFUL DAY)

L.A. GUNS

Formed: Los Angeles, California, USA . . . 1984, by TRACII GUNS and other brief GUNS N'ROSES and FASTER PUSSYCAT members. They soon found English-born LEWIS in 1987, and a worldwide 'Polygram' contract. Their eponymous debut early '88, showed them at their sleaziest best, and gave them Top 75 success. • **Style:** Glam/heavy rock outfit, that might have but for time, been what GUNS N'ROSES became. • **Songwriters:** LEWIS-GUNS penned, with HOLLYWOOD TEASE originally from LEWIS' time in other UK glam-rock act GIRL. In mid'91, original member PAUL BLACK won substantial royalties, after being uncredited on co-writing duties. • **Trivia:** In 1991, TRACII was also part of heavy supergroup CONTRABAND, who made self-titled lp.

Recommended: COCKED AND LOADED (*5).

PHILIP LEWIS – vocals (ex-GIRL) / **TRACII GUNS** – lead guitar (ex-GUNS'N'ROSES) / **MICK CRIPPS** – guitar / **KELLY NICKELS** – bass / **STEPHEN RILEY** – drums (ex-WASP) repl. BOB

Vertigo / Vertigo

Feb 88. (lp)(c)(cd) **L.A. GUNS** [73] [50]
– No mercy / Sex action / One more reason / The bitch is back / Electric gypsy / Nothing to lose / Hollywood tease / One way ticket / Shoot for thrills / Down in the city.

Sep 89. (lp)(c)(cd) **COCKED & LOADED** [45] [38] Jun 89
– Letting go / Rip and tear / Never enough / 17 crash / Give a little / The ballad of Jane / Wheels of fire / Slap in the face / Sleazy come easy go / Malaria / I'm addicted / Magdalaine / Showdown (riot on sunset). (cd+=) I wanna be your man

Apr 90. (c-s) **THE BALLAD OF JANE. / ?** [-] [33]

— RILEY left for a while with a heart condition in May90, but later returned

Mercury / Polydor

Jun 91. (cd)(c)(lp) **HOLLYWOOD VAMPIRES** [44] [42]
– Over the edge / Some lie 4 love / Kiss my love goodbye / Here it comes / Crystal eyes / Wild obsession / Dirty luv / My koo ka choo / It's over now / Snake eyes boogie / The ballad of Jayne / Big house.

Nov 91. (7") **SOME LIE 4 LOVE. / DIRTY LUV** [61] [ ]
(12")(12"pic-d) – ('A'side) / Slap in the face (live) / Electric gypsy (live).
(cd-s++=) – Malaria (live).
(10"pic-d) – ('A'side) / Rip and tear (live) / Sex action (live) / Bitch is back (live).

Dec 91. (7")(7"pic-d) **THE BALLAD OF JAYNE. / LIFE** [53] [ ]
(12") – ('A'side) / Kiss my love goodbye (live) / Some lie 4 love (live) / Over the edge (live).
(cd-s) – ('A'side) / Dirty luv (live) / My koo ka choo (live) / Over the edge (live).

Mar 92. (c-s)(cd-s) **IT'S OVER NOW. /** [-] [62]

— (Mar92) **BONES** – drums repl. RILEY

Polydor / Polydor

Apr 95. (cd)(c) **VICIOUS CIRCLE** [ ] [ ]
–

Greg LAKE (see under ⇒ EMERSON, LAKE & PALMER)

Robert LAMM (see under ⇒ CHICAGO)

Jerry LANDIS (see under ⇒ SIMON & GARFUNKEL)

Mark LANEGAN (see under ⇒ SCREAMING TREES)

k.d. LANG

Born: KATHRYN DAWN LANG, 2 Nov'61, Consort, Alberta, Canada. Her country roots, began in the early 80's when she took the part of Nashville starlet PATSY CLINE in a college musical. In 1981, she formed The RECLINES who signed for 'Bumstead' productions. After one 1984 album, she signed to 'Sire' records in 1986 and soon issued debut 'ANGEL WITH A LARIAT'. Her acclaimed 1992 work INGENUE, was soon to give her first Grammy award early in '93. • **Style:** Country ballad star of the 80's, who blended sweet melodies into her hard exterior. In 1992, the once ELVIS PRESLEY and EDITH PIAF admirer, admitted she was a lesbian, and changed her style to classy moody torch ballads, similar to EVERYTHING BUT THE GIRL fused with RITA COOLIDGE. • **Songwriters:** Collaborates with BEN MINK. Covered; CRAZY + I FALL TO PIECES (Patsy Cline) / LOCK, STOCK AND TEARDROPS (Roger Miller) / WESTERN STARS (Chris Isaak) / ROSE GARDEN (Lynn Anderson) / JOHNNY GET ANGRY (Carol Deene) / SO IN LOVE (Cole Porter) / THREE DAYS (Willie Nelson & Faron Young) / FULL MOON FULL OF LOVE (Jeannie Smith & Leroy Preston) / BIG BIG LOVE (Wynn Stewart) / WHAT'S NEW PUSSYCAT? (Bacharach-David) etc. • **Trivia:** Late in 1992, she allegedly began a relationship with tennis ace Martina Navratilova.

Recommended: INGENUE (*9).

k.d. LANG AND THE RECLINES

k.d. LANG – vocals, acoustic guitar with / **STEWART MacDOUGALL** – keyboards repl. MIKE CREBER + TED BOROWIECKI / **JOHN DYMOND** – bass repl. DENNIS MARCENKO + FARLEY SCOTT / **MICHEL POULIOT** – drums repl. DAVE BARNSON / **GORDIE MATTHEWS** – guitar (other early members **GARY KOLIGER** – slide guitar / **JAMIE KIDD** – organ)

not issued / Bumstead

1983. (7") **DAMNED OLD DOG. / FRIDAY DANCE PROMENADE** [-] [-] Canada

Feb 84. (lp) **A TRULY WESTERN EXPERIENCE** [-] [-] Canada
– Bopatena / Pine and stew / Up to me / Tickled pink / Hanky Panky / There you go / Busy being blue / Stop, look and listen / Hooked on junk.

— **k.d. LANG & The RECLINES,** with in 1986 **HAROLD BRADLEY** – bass / **JIMMY CAPPS** – rhythm guitar / **BUDDY HARMAN** – drums / **PETE WADE** – guitar / **HAL RUGG** – steel guitar / **HENRY STRZELECKI** – bass / **ROB HAJACOBS** – fiddle / **MARCUS 'Pig' ROBBINS** – piano / **TONY MIGLIORE** – piano / **BUDDY EMMONS** – steel / **BEN MINK** – violin

Sire / Sire

Feb 87. (lp)(c) **ANGEL WITH A LARIAT** [ ] [ ]
– Turn me around / High time for detour / Diet of strange places / Got the bull by the horns / Watch your step polka / Tune into my wave / Rose garden / Angel with a lariat / Pay dirt / Three cigarettes in an ashtray.

Apr 88. (7") **I'M DOWN TO MY LAST CIGARETTE. / WESTERN STARS** [-] [ ]

Apr 88. (lp)(c)(cd) **SHADOWLAND ("k.d.LANG")** [ ] [73]
– Western stars / Lock, stock and teardrops / Sugar moon / I wish I didn't love you so / Once again around the dancefloor / Black coffee / Shadowland / Don't let the stars get in your eyes / Tears don't care who cries them / I'm down to my last cigarette / Too busy, being blue / Honky tonk angel's medley: In the evening (when the Sun goes down) – You nearly lose your mind – Blues stay away from me.

Jun 88. (7") **LOCK, STOCK AND TEARDROPS. / DON'T LET THE STARS GET IN YOUR EYES** [-] [ ]

Jun 88. (7") **SUGAR MOON. / HONKY TONK ANGELS MEDLEY** [ ] [ ]
(12"+=) – I'm down to my last cigarette. (single as "k.d.LANG")

(below 'A'side featured in the soundtrack to 'Shag' film.

Nov 88. (7") **OUR DAY WILL COME. / THREE CIGARETTES IN AN ASHTRAY (live at the BBC)** [ ] [ ]
(12"+=) – Johnny get angry (live at the BBC).

— Jan'89, she duetted on ROY ORBISON's 'Crying', a B-side to 'You Got It'. The same song featured on his B-side to Mar89 single 'She's A Mystery To Me'. In Jul89, she again sang with the recently deceased ROY on 'Blue Bayou', which was a B-side to his 'California Blue'. The song had originally featured in the 1987 film 'Hiding Out'. In Jun'89, she guested on DION's album 'Yo Frankie'.

— Her band still included **MINK, POULIOT, DYMOND, MATTHEWS, CREBER** plus **GREG LEISZ** – steel guitar / **GRAHAM BOYLE** – perc. / **DAVID PILTCH** – fretless bass

May 89. (7") **WALLFLOWER WALTZ. / FULL MOON OF LOVE** [-] [-]

May 89. (lp)(c)(cd) **ABSOLUTE TORCH AND TWANG** [ ] [69]
– Luck in my eyes / Three days / Trail of broken hearts / Big boned gal / Didn't I / Wallflower waltz / Full Moon full of love / Pullin' back the reins / Big big love / It's me / Walkin' in and out of your arms / Nowhere to stand.

Nov 89. (7") **TRAIL OF BROKEN HEARTS. / THREE DAYS** [-] [ ]

— In Jul '90, she guested on WENDY & LISA's album 'Eroica'.

Oct 90. (7") **RIDIN' THE RAILS. / (track by Darlene Love)** [ ] [ ]

— (above single appeared on 'Warners' and the soundtrack to 'Dick Tracy') Late in 1991, she guested on JANE SIBERRY's song 'Calling All Angels'.

— She is now credited solo, but still retaining some or most of band.

Mar 92. (cd)(c)(lp) **INGENUE** [28] [44]
– Save me / The mind of love (where is your head Kathryn?) / Miss Chatelaine / Wash me clean / So it shall be / Still thrives this love / Season of hollow soul / Outside myself / Tears of love's recall / Constant craving. *(album will climb a year later, to UK No.3 + US No.18)*

May 92. (7")(c-s) **CONSTANT CRAVING. / BAREFOOT** [52] [38]
(12"+=)(cd-s+=) – Season of hollow soul. (US; b-side)

CRYING was re-iss. by 'Virgin' Aug92 as 'A'side and hit UK No.13. 2 months later it again featured as a 'B'side. This time on his 'Heartbreak Radio'.

Sep 92. (7")(c-s) **MISS CHATELAINE. / ('A'-St.Tropez edit)** [ ] [ ]
(cd-s+=) – Wash me clean / The mind of love.
(cd-s+=) – (2 'A'versions).

Feb 93. (7")(c-s) **CONSTANT CRAVING. / MISS CHATELAINE** 15 -
(cd-s+=) – Wash me clean (live) / The mind of love (live).
(cd-s) – ('A'side) / Big boned gal (live) / Outside myself (live).
Apr 93. (7")(c-s) **THE MIND OF LOVE (WHERE IS YOUR HEAD KATHRYN?). / THE MIND OF LOVE (live)** 72
(cd-s+=) – Pullin' back the reins.
(cd-s) – ('A'side) / Three cigarettes in a ashtray / Trail of broken hearts / Busy being blue.
Jun 93. (7")(c-s) **MISS CHATELAINE. / ('A'mix)** 68
(cd-s) – ('A'side) / ('A'-St.Tropez mix) / ('A'-Paris 92 mix).
Nov 93. (cd)(c) **EVEN COWGIRLS GET THE BLUES (Soundtrack)** 36 82
– Just keep me moving / Much finer place / Or was I / Hush sweet lover / Myth / Apogee / Virtual vortex / Lifted by love / Overture / Kundalini yoga waltz / In perfect dreams / Curious soul astray / Ride of Bonanza Jellybean / Don't be a lemming polka / Sweet little Cherokee / Cowgirl pride.
Dec 93. (7")(c-s) **JUST KEEP ME MOVING. / IN PERFECT DREAMS** 59
(12")(cd-s) – ('A'side) / ('A'wild planet mixes) / ('A'moving mixes).
Warners Warners
Sep 95. (c-s) **IF I WERE YOU / WHAT'S NEW PUSSYCAT** 53
(cd-s+=) – Get some.
Oct 95. (cd)(c) **ALL YOU CAN EAT** 7 37
– If I were you / Maybe / You're ok / Sexuality / Get some / Acquiesce / This / World of love / Infinite and unforeseen / I want it all.

Gerard LANGLEY & Ian KEARNEY (see under ⇒ BLUE AEROPLANES)

LARD (see under ⇒ DEAD KENNEDYS)

LA'S

Formed: Liverpool, England . . . 1986 by LEE MAVERS, etc. They signed to 'Go! Discs' in 1987, and released a single a year, until eponymous debut album in 1990. It scraped into the UK Top 30, helped by a new version of 'THERE SHE GOES' hitting Top 20. • **Style:** Influenced from 60's garage to The TROGGS or R.E.M. • **Songwriters:** LEE MAVERS penned. • **Trivia:** Steve Lilywhite produced them in 1990.

Recommended: THE LA'S (*8).

LEE MAVERS (b. 2 Aug'62) – vocals, guitar / **JOHN BYRNE** – guitar / **JOHN POWER** (b.14 Sep'67) – bass / **PAUL HEMMINGS** – guitar / **JOHN TIMSON** – drums

Go! Discs London
Oct 87. (7") **WAY OUT. / ENDLESS**
(12"+=) – Knock me down.
(12"++=) – Liberty ship (demo) / Freedom song (demo).

— **CHRIS SHARROCK** – drums (ex-ICICLE WORKS) repl. TIMSON

Nov 88. (7") **THERE SHE GOES. / COME IN COME OUT** 59
(12"+=)(cd-s+=) – Who knows / Man I'm only human.
(7"ep+=) – Who knows / Way out.
May 89. (7") **TIMELESS MELODY. / CLEAN PROPHET** 57
(12"+=)(cd-s+=) – Knock me down. *(re-iss.Sep90, hit 57)*
(10"+=) – All by myself / There she goes.

— **NEIL MAVERS** (b. 8 Jul'71) – drums repl. SHARROCK / **JAMES JOYCE** (b.23 Sep'70) – bass repl. POWER who formed The CAST / added **CAMMY** (b.PETER JAMES CAMELL, 30 Jun'67) – guitar (ex-MARSHMALLOW)

Oct 90. (cd)(c)(lp) **THE LA'S** 30
– Son of a gun / I can't stop / Timeless melody / Liberty ship / There she goes / Doledrum / Feelin' / Way out / I.O.U. / Freedom song / Failure / Looking glass.
Oct 90. (7")(c-s) **THERE SHE GOES (new version). / FREEDOM SONG** 13 49 Jun 91
(12"+=)(cd-s+=) – All by myself.
Feb 91. (7"ep)(c-ep) **FEELIN' 91 / I.O.U. / ('A'alternative) / DOLEDRUM** 43
(12"ep+=)(cd-ep+=) – Liberty ship. (repl. 3rd track above.)

Cyndi LAUPER

Born: CYNTHIA ANNE STEPHANIE LAUPER, 22 Jun'53, New York, USA. Raised by her mother in Italian district of Queens, NY, after her parents divorced. In 1974 after a spell hitch-hiking in Canada, she joined as lead singer of Long Island band DOC WEST. She soon quit to join FLYER, but left when she lost voice (nearly permanently). In 1979, she formed BLUE ANGEL with JOHN TURI, and they signed to 'Polydor'. They issued one self-titled album, but after its flop she was soon declared bankrupt. Around the same time, she met DAVID WOLFF, who became her boyfriend and manager in 1982. The next year he secured a solo deal for her with CBS subsidiary 'Portrait', and she released debut album 'SHE'S SO UNUSUAL' late '83. It climbed into US & UK Top 20, helped by the success of 4 consecutive US Top 5 hits, beginning with 'GIRLS JUST WANT TO HAVE FUN'. She continued to brighten up the charts during the rest of the 80's. • **Style:** Extroverted rebellious female, who has contributed some fine heart-rendering ballads as well as more up-tempo rock-pop tunes. Although she was often tempted to take elocution lessons, she has never lost her squeaky broad New York accent. • **Songwriters:** As said, with some collaborations. Covered; GIRLS JUST WANT TO HAVE FUN (Robert Hazard) / ALL THROUGH THE NIGHT + STEADY (Jules Shear) / TRUE COLORS (Kelly-Steinberg) / WHEN YOU WERE MINE (Prince) / WHAT'S GOIN' ON (Marvin Gaye) / IKO IKO (Dixie Cups) / CHANGE OF HEART (Essra Mohawk) / etc. • **Trivia:** Jazz legend MILES DAVIS instrumentally covered her US No.1 'TIME AFTER TIME'. In 1990, she guested on ROGER WATERS 'The Wall' concert in Berlin, having become a Christian the year before.

Recommended: TWELVE DEADLY CYNS AND THEN SOME (*7).

BLUE ANGEL

formed by **CYNDI LAUPER** – vocals / **JOHN TURI** – saxophone, keyboards / plus **ARTHUR NEILSON** – guitar / **LEE BROVITZ** – bass / **JOHN MORELLI** – drums

Polydor Polydor
Feb 81. (lp)(c) **BLUE ANGEL**
– Maybe he'll know / I have a love / Fade / Anna Blue / Cut out / Can't blame me / Late / Take a chance. / Just the other day / I'm gonna be strong / Lorraine / Everybody's got an angel.
Jan 81. (7") **I'M GONNA BE STRONG. / ANNA BLUE**
Mar 81. (7") **I HAD A LOVE. / CAN'T BLAME ME**

— They had already split by the time of the above UK releases.

CYNDI LAUPER

went solo, augmented at first by The HOOTERS group.

Portrait Portrait
Dec 83. (7") **GIRLS JUST WANT TO HAVE FUN. / RIGHT TRACK, WRONG TRAIN** 2 2
(12"+=) – Witness. (US-12"+=) Money changes everything.
Jan 84. (lp)(c)(pic-lp) **SHE'S SO UNUSUAL** 16 4 Dec 83
– Money changes everything / Girls just want to have fun / When you were mine / Time after time / She bop / All through the night / Witness / I'll kiss you / He's so unusual / Yeah yeah. *(re-iss.+cd.Feb89 on 'Epic')*
Mar 84. (7")(7"pic-d) **TIME AFTER TIME. / I'LL KISS YOU** 3 1
(12") – ('A'side) – Girls just want to have fun (extended) / Fun with V. Knutz (instrumental).
Aug 84. (7")(12")(7"pic-d) **SHE BOP. / WITNESS** 46 3 Jul84
Oct 84. (7")(12") **ALL THROUGH THE NIGHT. / WITNESS** 64 5 Sep 84
Dec 84. (7") **MONEY CHANGES EVERYTHING. / ('A' live)** - 27
Feb 85. (7") **MONEY CHANGES EVERYTHING. / HE'S SO UNUSUAL**
(12") – ('A'live version) / Extra fun (live).
(12"+=) – Yeah yeah / Girls just want to have fun.
Jun 85. (7") **THE GOONIES 'R' GOOD ENOUGH. / WHAT A THRILL** 10 May 85
(12"+=) – ('A'dub version). *(Above from the film 'The Goonies')*
Aug 86. (7") **TRUE COLOURS. / MONEY CHANGES EVERYTHING** 12 1
(12"+=) – Heading for the Moon. *(US; b-side)*
Aug 86. (lp)(c)(cd) **TRUE COLORS** 25 4
– Change of heart / Maybe he'll know / Boy blue / True colors / Calm inside the storm / What's going on / Iko Iko / The faraway nearby / 911 / One track mind. *(re-iss.Aug90)*
Dec 86. (7") **CHANGE OF HEART. / WHAT A THRILL** 67 3 Nov 86
(12"+=) – ('A'extended) / Heartbeats.
Feb 87. (7")(7"pic-d) **WHAT'S GOING ON. / ONE TRACK MIND** 57 12
(d7"+=) – Change of heart / What a thrill.
(12") – ('A'extended) / ('A'instrumental) / ('A'club).
Jul 87. (7") **BOY BLUE. / THE FARAWAY NEARBY** 71
(12"+=) – Time after time.

— Next from film 'Vibes'.

Epic Epic
Jul 88. (7") **HOLE IN MY HEART (ALL THE WAY TO CHINA). / BOY BLUE (live)** 54
Apr 89. (7")(c-s)(7"pic-d) **I DROVE ALL NIGHT. / MAYBE HE'LL KNOW** 7 6
(12"+=) – Boy blue (live).
(cd-s++=) – Girls just want to have fun.
(cd-s+=) – What's going on (club version) / Time after time.
Jun 89. (lp)(c)(cd) **A NIGHT TO REMEMBER** 9 37 May 89
– I drove all night / Primitive / My first night without you / Like a cat / Heading west / A night to remember / Unconditional love / Insecurious / Dancing like a stranger / I don't want to be your friend / Kindred spirit.
Jul 89. (7")(c-s) **MY FIRST NIGHT WITHOUT YOU. / UNABBREVIATED** 53 62
(12"+=)(cd-s+=) – True colours / All through the night.
(3"cd-s+=) – Iko Iko / When you were mine.
Nov 89. (7")(c-s) **HEADING WEST. / INSECURIOUS** 68
(12"+=)(12"pic-d+=)(cd-s+=) – She bop (live) / Money changes everything (live).

— In 1991, she starred in the film 'Off And Running'. Below was from the film 'Starmania' which changed title to 'Tycoon'.

May 92. (7") **THE WORLD IS STONE. / LEARN TO LEAVE ALONE** 15
(cd-s+=) – Time after time.
(cd-s+=) – What's going on.
Nov 93. (c-s) **THAT'S WHAT I THINK / THAT'S WHAT I THINK** 31
(12"+=)(cd-s+=) – ('A'-4mixes – 3 dub / 1 dub)
Nov 93. (cd)(c)(lp) **HATFUL OF STARS** 56
– That's what I think / Product of misery / Who let in the rain / Lies / Broken glass / Sally's pigeons / Feels like Christmas / Dear John / Like I used to / Someone like me / A part hate / Hatful of stars.
Jan 94. (7")(c-s) **WHO LET IN THE RAIN. / COLD** 32
(cd-s+=) – Like I used to.
(cd-s) – ('A'side) / Girls just want to have fun (remix) / That's what I think (deep mix) / Girls just want to have fun.
Aug 94. (cd)(c)(md) **TWELVE DEADLY CYNS . . . AND THEN SOME** (compilation) 2 81 Aug95
– I'm gonna be strong / Girls just want to have fun / Money changes everything / Time after time / She bop / All through the night / Change of heart / True colors / What's going on / I drove all night / The world is stone / Who let in the rain / That's what I think / Sally's pigeons / Hey now (girls just want to have fun) / Come on home.

Sep 94. (c-s) **(HEY NOW) GIRLS JUST WANT TO HAVE FUN. / ('A'mix)** 4 87 Aug95
(cd-s+=) – ('A'mixes).
Jan 95. (c-s) **I'M GONNA BE STRONG / A PART HATE** 37
(cd-s+=) – Product of misery.
(cd-s) – ('A'side) / Broken glass / Dear John.
Jul 95. (c-s) **COME ON HOME / HEY NOW (GIRLS JUST WANT TO HAVE FUN)** 39
(cd-s+=) – ('A'-Junior's soundfactory version) / ('A'-Techno mix).
(cd-s) – (6 different 'A'mixes; incl. Techno dub / Jungle box).

– compilations etc. –

Sep 86. Epic; (c) **THE 12" TAPE (12"mixes)**
– Girls just want to have fun / Time after time / She bop / All through the night / Money changes everything.
Oct 94. Columbia; (3xcd-box) **A NIGHT TO REMEMBER / SHE'S SO UNUSUAL / TRUE COLOURS**
Feb 95. Columbia; (d-cd) **SHE'S SO UNUSUAL / A NIGHT TO REMEMBER** -

LAW (see under ⇒ RODGERS, Paul)

LEAGUE OF GENTLEMEN (see under ⇒ KING CRIMSON)

Paul LEARY (see under ⇒ BUTTHOLE SURFERS)

LEAVES

Formed: Los Angeles, California, USA . . . 1964 out of college based frat-band The ROCKWELLS, by JIM PONS and BILL RINEHART. In 1965, they were awarded a residency at Sunset strip club, which led to TV appearances and a contract for 'Mira'. After 3 flops, they finally broke into US Top 40 in mid-'66, with a new version of 'HEY JOE'. This annoyed both The BYRDS and LOVE, who thought they'd stolen the traditional song. It received a UK release, but after its failure, it became a solitary issue. • **Style:** Folk-rock outfit in the mould of The BYRDS, although they incorporated psychedelia. • **Songwriters:** PONS + RINEHART penned, until latter's departure. Covered; YOU BETTER MOVE ON (Arthur Alexander) / LOVE MINUS ZERO + HE WAS A FRIEND OF MINE (Bob Dylan) / CODINE (Buffy Sainte-Marie) / TRY FOR THE SUN (Donovan) / etc. • **Trivia:** HEY JOE was later in '66, a bigger hit for JIMI HENDRIX.

Recommended: 1966 (*7).

JOHN BECK – vocals (added to quartet 1965) / **BILL RINEHART** – lead guitar / **ROBERT LEE REINER** – guitar / **JIM PONS** – bass / **TOM RAY** – drums repl. JIMMY KERN

Fontana Mira

Sep 65. (7") **TOO MANY PEOPLE. / LOVE MINUS ZERO** -
Nov 65. (7") **HEY JOE, WHERE YOU GONNA GO. / BE WITH YOU** -
Jan 66. (7") **YOU BETTER MOVE ON. / A DIFFERENT STORY** -

— **BOB ARLIN** – lead guitar (ex-CATALINAS) repl. RINEHART (to GENE CLARK)

Apr 66. (7") **HEY JOE. / GIRL FROM THE EAST (then) / MERRY GO ROUND** - 31
Jun 66. (7") **HEY JOE. / FUNNY LITTLE WORLD** -
Aug 66. (lp) **HEY JOE** - -
– Dr. Stone / Just a memory / Get out of my life woman / Girl from the East / He was a friend of mine / Hey Joe / Words / Back on the avenue / War of distortion / Tobacco Road / Goodbye, my lover / Too many people. *(re-iss.'67 on 'Surrey')*
Sep 66. (7") **TOO MANY PEOPLE. / GIRL FROM THE EAST** -
Nov 66. (7") **GET OUT MY LIFE WOMAN. / GIRL FROM THE EAST** -
Jan 67. (7") **YOU BETTER MOVE ON. / BE WITH YOU** -

— Now quartet of **BECK** (now guitar), **ARLIN, PONS and RAY**, when REINER left

not issued Capitol

1967. (7") **TWILIGHT SANCTUARY. / LEMON PRINCESS** -
1967. (lp) **ALL THE GOOD THAT'S HAPPENING** -
– Codine / Try for the sun / etc.

— Disbanded '67. PONS had left to join The TURTLES. He was later to join FRANK ZAPPA'S MOTHERS

– compilations, etc. –

May 85. Fan Club/ US= Panda; (lp) **THE LEAVES** 1982
1982. Panda; (7"pic-d) **HEY JOE. / (group interview)** - -
Feb 84. Line Germany; (7") **HEY JOE. /** - -
May 84. Fan Club; (lp) **1966**
(cd-iss.Apr91)

— **ARLIN** and **BECK** formed **The NEW LEAVES** with **BUDDY SKLAR** – bass / **CRAIG BOYD** – drums. Soon became trio when BECK left. Changed name to

The HOOK

ARLIN, SKLAR plus **DALE LOYALE** – drums / **DENNIS PROVISOR** – keyboards

Uni Uni

1970. (7") **SON OF FANTASY. / PLUG YOUR HEAD IN** -
1970. (7") **HOMES. / LOVE THEME IN E MINOR** -
1970. (lp) **THE HOOK WILL GRAB YOU** -
– Homes / Lookin' for you / You know I do / Turn your head / Son of fantasy / Dr.B and his friends / Plug your head in / Everything's groovy / Garbage man / Dimples.

— **CRAIG BOYD** – drums returned to repl. LOYALE and PROVISOR

1970. (7") **IN THE BEGINNING. / SHOW YOU THE WAY**
1971. (lp) **HOOKED** -

— Disbanded 1970.

LED ZEPPELIN

Formed: London, England . . . mid-68 out of The NEW YARDBIRDS by JIMMY PAGE, JOHN PAUL JONES and ROBERT PLANT. They soon found another former session man JOHN BONHAM, who arrived in time for live debut, 15 Oct'68 at Surrey University. They had chosen group name through KEITH MOON's often said phrase "going down like a lead zeppelin". With manager PETER GRANT at the helm, they secured a worldwide deal on 'Atlantic'. Early in 1969, they unleashed eponymous debut, which due to growing reputation, hit cross-Atlantic Top 10. Later in the year 'LED ZEPPELIN II' plants itself into both top spots, with a lifted cut 'WHOLE LOTTA LOVE' making US Top 5. As with all their US singles, it was thought better by Peter Grant not to issue any 45's in Britain, although they were readily available in import shops. They topped each chart with every album release, until the untimely death on 25 Sep'80 of JOHN BONHAM. In 1982, PAGE and PLANT went solo, but re-united in 1984 as The HONEYDRIPPERS. PLANT continued to be the more successful of the two, having mostly hit albums during the next decade. Sadly, PETER GRANT died of a heart attack on 21st Nov'95. • **Style:** Greatest heavy-metal band of all-time, who re-arranged the blues into own distinctive sound, based around PLANT's power-vox and PAGE's climatic guitar epics, that also showed a folkier acoustic side on some songs. • **Songwriters:** PAGE + PLANT wrote nearly all with some help from JONES and/or BONHAM. They also covered; I CAN'T QUIT YOU BABY (Otis Rush) / YOU SHOOK ME (Willie Dixon) / BRING IT ON HOME (Sonny Boy Williamson) / GALLOW'S POLE + HATS OFF TO HARPER (trad.) / etc. JIMMY PAGE covered; HUMMINGBIRD (B.B.King). The HONEYDRIPPERS;- SEA OF LOVE (Phil Phillips with the Twilights). ROBERT PLANT: LET'S HAVE A PARTY (Elvis Presley) / IF I WERE A CARPENTER (Robert Plant). • **Trivia:** SANDY DENNY featured on track 'BATTLE OF EVERMORE' from 1971's symbol album. The previous year, C.C.S. (aka. ALEXIS KORNER) had a Top 10 hit with 'WHOLE LOTTA LOVE'. In 1985, with PHIL COLLINS on drums, LED ZEPPELIN played LIVE AID. JOHN BONHAM's drumming son JASON formed his band BONHAM in the late 80's. Around the same time, a kitsch mickey-take outfit DREAD ZEPPELIN, hit the music scene, playing reggae versions of group's classics. In 1992, Australian 60's hitmaker and TV personality ROLF HARRIS charts, but destroys top college favourite 'STAIRWAY TO HEAVEN'. It was even worse than 1985's FAR CORPORATION version, which also hit UK Top 10. • **Early work:** As well as session work with many (THEM, etc.), JIMMY PAGE released solo single in Mar'65 'SHE JUST SATIFIES' / 'KEEP MOVIN'' for 'Fontana'. He had earlier played on 45's by NEIL CHRISTIAN & THE CRUSADERS, plus CARTER-LEWIS & THE SOUTHERNERS. JOHN PAUL JONES played in The TONY MEEHAN COMBO, before issuing solo 45 in Apr'64 'A FOGGY DAY IN VIETNAM' / 'BAJA', for 'Pye' label. ROBERT PLANT had been part of LISTEN, who released one single for 'CBS' in Nov'66; 'YOU'D BETTER RUN' / 'EVERYBODY'S GOTTA SAY'. He stayed with label for 2 solo releases in Mar'67; 'OUR SONG' / 'LAUGHIN' CRYIN' LAUGHIN'', & Jul'67 'LONG TIME COMIN'' / 'I'VE GOT A SECRET'. He then teamed up that year with BONHAM, to form Birmingham based group BAND OF JOY. All these rare singles now fetch upwards of £100.

Recommended: LED ZEPPELIN (*8) / LED ZEPPELIN II (*9) / LED ZEPPELIN III (*9) / UNTITLED (LED ZEPPELIN IV) (*9) / HOUSES OF THE HOLY (*8) / PHYSICAL GRAFFITI (*9) / PRESENCE (*6) / THE SONG REMAINS THE SAME (*7) / IN THROUGH THE OUT DOOR (*7) / REMASTERS (*10). ROBERT PLANT solo: PICTURES AT ELEVEN (*6) / PRINCIPLES OF MOMENT (*6) / MAGIC NIRVANA (*7) / FATE OF NATIONS (*6) / JIMMY PAGE solo: OUTRIDER (*6).

ROBERT PLANT (b.20 Aug'48, West Bromwich, England) – vocals (ex-LISTEN) / **JIMMY PAGE** (b. 9 Jan'44, Heston, England) – lead guitars (ex-YARDBIRDS) / **JOHN PAUL JONES** (b.JOHN BALDWIN, 3 Jun'46, Sidcup, Kent, England) – bass / **JOHN BONHAM** (b.31 May'48, Bromwich, England) – drums

Atlantic Atlantic

Mar 69. (lp)(c) **LED ZEPPELIN** 6 10 Feb 69
– Good times bad times / Babe I'm gonna leave you / You shook me / Dazed and confused / Your time is gonna come / Black mountain side / Communication breakdown / You shook me / I can't quit you baby / How many more times. *(cd-iss.Jan87) (re-iss.cd+c Jul94)*
Mar 69. (7") **GOOD TIMES BAD TIMES. / COMMUNICATION BREAKDOWN** - 80
Oct 69. (lp)(c) **LED ZEPPELIN II** 1 1
– Whole lotta love / What is and what should never be / The lemon song / Thank you / Heartbreaker / Livin' lovin' maid (she's just a woman) / Ramble on / Moby Dick / Bring it on home. *(cd-iss.Jan87) (re-iss.cd+c Jul94)*
Nov 69. (7") **WHOLE LOTTA LOVE. / LIVIN' LOVIN' MAID (SHE'S JUST A WOMAN)** - 4
65
Oct 70. (lp)(c) **LED ZEPPELIN III** 1 1
– Immigrant song / Friends / Celebration day / Since I've been loving you / Out on the tiles / Gallow's pole / Tangerine / That's the way / Bron-y-aur stomp / Hats off to (Roy) Harper. *(cd-iss.Jan87)*
Nov 70. (7") **IMMIGRANT SONG. / HEY HEY WHAT CAN I DO** - 16
Nov 71. (lp)(c) **(UNTITLED – 4 SYMBOLS)** 1 2

– Black dog / Rock and roll / The battle of Evermore / Stairway to Heaven / Misty mountain hop / Four sticks / Goin' to California / When the levee breaks. *(lilac-lp Nov78) (cd-iss.Jul83) (re-iss.cd+c Jul94)*

Dec 71. (7") **BLACK DOG. / MISTY MOUNTAIN HOP** [-] [15]
Mar 72. (7") **ROCK AND ROLL. / FOUR STICKS** [-] [47]
Apr 73. (lp)(c) **HOUSES OF THE HOLY** [1] [1]
– The song remains the same / The rain song / Over the hills and far away / The crunge / Dancing days / D'yer maker / No quarter / The ocean. *(cd-iss.Jan87) (re-iss.cd+c Jul94)*
Jun 73. (7") **OVER THE HILLS AND FAR AWAY. / DANCING DAYS** [-] [51]
Oct 73. (7") **D'YER MAKER. / THE CRUNGE** [-] [20]

Swan Song Swan Song

Mar 75. (d-lp)(d-c) **PHYSICAL GRAFFITI** [1] [1]
– Custard pie / The rover / In my time of dying / Houses of the holy / Trampled underfoot / Kashmir / In the light / Bron-y-aur / Down by the seaside / Ten years gone / Night flight / The wanton song / Boogie with Stu / Black country woman / Sick again. *(d-cd-iss.Jan87)*
Mar 75. (7") **TRAMPLED UNDERFOOT. / BLACK COUNTRY WOMAN** [-] [38]
Apr 76. (lp)(c) **PRESENCE** [1] [1]
– Achilles last stand / For your life / Royal Orleans / Nobody's fault but mine / Candy store rock / Hots for nowhere / Tea for one. *(cd-iss.Jun87)*
May 76. (7") **CANDY STORE ROCK. / ROYAL ORLEANS** [-] [ ]
Oct 76. (d-lp)(d-c) **THE SONG REMAINS THE SAME (live)** [1] [2]
– Rock and roll / Celebration day / The song remains the same / The rain song / Dazed and confused / No quarter / Stairway to Heaven / Moby Dick / Whole lotta love. *(d-cd-iss.Feb87)*

— Above was also a film from concerts at Madison Square Gardens in 1973. It featured some dream sequences / fantasies of each member.

Aug 79. (lp)(c) **IN THROUGH THE OUT DOOR** [1] [1]
– In the evening / South bound Saurez / Fool in the rain / Hot dog / Carouselambra / All my love / I'm gonna crawl. *(cd-iss.Jan87) (re-iss.cd+c Oct94 on 'Atlantic')*
Dec 79. (7") **FOOL IN THE RAIN. / HOT DOG** [-] [21]

— Disbanded when JOHN BONHAM died after a drinking session 25 Sep'80.

– compilations, others, etc. –

Nov 82. Swan Song; (lp)(c) **CODA (demos from 68-79)** [4] [6] Dec 82
– We're gonna groove / Poor Tom / I can't quit you baby / Walter's walk / Ozone baby / Darlene / Bonzo's Montreaux / Walter's walk / Wearing and tearing.
Oct 90. Swan Song; (4xcd)(4xc)(6xlp) **LED ZEPPELIN** [48] [18]
Nov 90. Swan Song; (d-cd)(d-c)(t-lp) **REMASTERS** [10] [47] Mar 92
– Communication breakdown / Babe I'm gonna leave you / Good times bad times / Dazed and confused / Whole lotta love / Heartbreaker / Ramble on / Immigrant song / Celebration day / Since I've been loving you / Black dog / Rock and roll / The battle of Evermore / Misty mountain hop / Stairway to Heaven / The song remains the same / The rain song / D'yer maker / No quarter / Houses of the holy / Kashmir / Trampled underfoot / Nobody's fault but mine / Achilles last stand / All my love / In the evening.
Sep 93. Atlantic; (10xcd-box) **LED ZEPPELIN BOXED SET II** [56] [87]
Oct 93. Atlantic; (d-cd)(d-c) **REMASTERS 2** [ ] [ ]

— JOHN PAUL JONES went on to become a top producer. In 1992, he contributed string arrangements to R.E.M.'s classic album 'Automatic For The People'. ROBERT PLANT went solo and teamed up with JIMMY PAGE in The HONEYDRIPPERS. PAGE also went solo and formed The FIRM.

In Aug 94; JOHN PAUL JONES turned up on an unusual collaboration (single 'Do You Take This Man') between himself and loud punk-opera diva DIAMANDA GALAS.

ROBERT PLANT

with **BOBBIE BLUNT** – guitar / **JEZZ WOODRUFFE** – keyboards / **PAUL MARTINEZ** – bass / **COZY POWELL** – drums / guest **PHIL COLLINS** – drums, perc.

Swan Song Swan Song

Jul 82. (lp)(c) **PICTURES AT ELEVEN** [2] [5]
– Burning down one side / Moonlight in Samosa / Pledge pin / Slow dancer / Worse that Detroit / Fat lip / Like I've been gone / Mystery title. *(cd-iss.1986)*
Sep 82. (7")(12") **BURNING DOWN ONE SIDE. / MOONLIGHT IN SAMOSA** [ ] [44]
Nov 82. (7") **PLEDGE PIN. /** [-] [74]

— **RITCHIE HAYWARD** – drums (ex-LITTLE FEAT) repl. COZY / added **BOB MAYO** – keyboards, guitar

W.E.A. Atlantic

Jul 83. (lp)(c) **THE PRINCIPLE OF MOMENTS** [7] [8]
– Other arms / In the mood / Messin' with the Mekon / Wreckless love / Thru with the two-step / Horizontal departure / Stranger here . . .than over there / Big log. *(cd-iss.1984)*
Jul 83. (7") **BIG LOG. / MESSIN' WITH THE MEKON** [11] [-]
(12"+=) – Stranger here . . . than over there.
Sep 83. (7") **BIG LOG. / FAR POSY** [-] [20]
Nov 83. (7") **IN THE MOOD. / HORIZONTAL DEPARTURE** [-] [39]
Jan 84. (7") **IN THE MOOD. / PLEDGE PIN (live)** [ ] [-]
(12"+=) – Horizontal departure.

Es Paranza Es Paranza

May 85. (7")(12") **PINK AND BLACK. / TROUBLE YOUR MONEY** [ ] [ ]
May 85. (7") **LITTLE BY LITTLE. / TROUBLE YOUR MONEY** [-] [36]
May 85. (lp)(c)(cd) **SHAKEN 'N' STIRRED** [19] [20]
– Hip to hoo / Kallalou Kallalou / Too loud / Trouble your money / Pink and black / Little by little / Doo doo a do do / Easily led / Sixes and sevens.
Jul 85. (7") **TOO LOUD. / KALLALOU KALLALOU** [-] [ ]
Aug 85. (7") **LITTLE BY LITTLE. / DOO DOO A DO DO** [ ] [-]
(12"+=) – Easily led.

— now with **DOUG BOYLE** – guitars / **PHIL SCRAGG** – bass / **PHIL JOHNSTONE** – keys, co-writer / **JIMMY PAGE** – guitar 2 / **CHRIS BLACKWELL** – drums, perc. / **MARIE PIERRE, TONI HALLIDAY and KIRSTY MacCOLL** – backing vocals

Jan 88. (7")(12") **HEAVEN KNOWS. / WALKING TOWARDS PARADISE** [33] [ ]
(cd-s+=) – Big log.
Feb 88. (lp)(c)(cd) **NOW AND ZEN** [10] [6]
– Heaven knows / Dance on my own / Tall cool one / The way I feel / Helen of Troy / Billy's revenge / Ship of fools / Why / White, clean and neat. *(cd+=)–* Walking towards Paradise.
Apr 88. (7")(12") **TALL COOL ONE. / WHITE, CLEAN AND NEAT** [ ] [25]
(cd-s+=) – ('A' extended version) / Little by little.
Aug 88. (7") **SHIP OF FOOLS. / HELEN OF TROY** [ ] [-]
(12"+=) – Heaven Knows (live).
(cd-s+=) – Dimples (live).
Aug 88. (7") **SHIP OF FOOLS. / BILLY'S REVENGE** [-] [84]

— **PAT THORPE** – drums repl. BLACKWELL who became ill.

— now with **BLACKWELL, CHARLIE JONES, JOHNSTONE and BOYLE**

Mar 90. (cd)(c)(lp) **MANIC NIRVANA** [15] [ ]
– Hurting kind (I've got my eyes on you) / Big love / S S S & Q / I cried / She said / Nirvana / The dye on the highway / Your ma said you cried in your sleep last night / Anniversary / Liars dance / Watching you.
Apr 90. (7")(c-s) **HURTING KIND (I'VE GOT MY EYES ON YOU). / OOMPAH (WATERY BINT)** [45] [46] Mar 90
(12"+=) – I cried / One love.
(cd-s+=) – Don't look back / One love.
Jun 90. (7")(c-s) **YOUR MA SAID YOU CRIED IN YOUR SLEEP LAST NIGHT. / SHE SAID** [ ] [ ]
(12")(cd-s) – ('A'side) / ('A'version) / One love.

— with **KEVIN SCOTT MACMICHAEL** – guitar / **PHIL JOHNSTONE** – electric piano / **CHARLIE JONES** – bass / **MICHAEL LEE** – drums / **CHRIS HUGHES** – drums, co-producer / plus guests **FRANCIS DUNNERY, MAIRE BRENNAN, NIGEL KENNEDY + RICHARD THOMPSON**

Es Paranza Es Paranza

Apr 93. (7")(c-s) **29 PALMS. / 21 YEARS** [21] [ ]
(cd-s+=) – Dark Moon.
(cd-s++=) – Whole lotta love (you need love).
May 93. (cd)(c)(lp) **FATE OF NATIONS** [6] [ ]
– Calling to you / Down to the sea / Come into my life / I believe / 29 palms / Memory song (hello, hello) / If I were a carpenter / Colours of a shade / Promised land / The greatest gift / Great spirit / Network news.
Jun 93. (7")(c-s) **I BELIEVE. / GREAT SPIRIT (acoustic mix)** [ ] [ ]
(cd-s+=) – Hey Jayne.
(12"pic-d++=) – Whole lotta love (you need love).
Aug 93. (c-s) **CALLING TO YOU. / NAKED IF I WANT TO** [ ] [ ]
(12"+=)(cd-s+=) – 8.05.
Dec 93. (7")(c-s) **IF I WERE A CARPENTER. / SHIP OF FOOLS (live)** [ ] [ ]
(cd-s) – ('A'side) / I believe (live) / Tall cool one (live).

JIMMY PAGE

solo with **CHRIS FARLOWE** – vocals / **DAVE LAWSON + DAVID SINCLAIR WHITTAKER + GORDON EDWARDS** – piano / **DAVE PATON** – bass / **DAVE MATTACKS** – drums

Swan Song Swan Song

Feb 82. (lp)(c) **DEATH WISH II (Soundtrack)** [40] [50]
– Who's to blame / The chase / City sirens / A jam sandwich / Of Carole's theme / The release / Hotelrats and photostats / A shadow in the sky / Jill's theme / Prelude / Big band, sax & violence / Hypnotizing ways (oh mamma).

— In 1985, PAGE collaborated with friend ROY HARPER on dual album 'WHATEVER HAPPENED TO JUGULA', which hit UK Top 50.

— now guest vocals – **JOHN MILES, ROBERT PLANT, CHRIS FARLOWE JASON BONHAM** – drums / **DURBAN LEVERDE** – bass / **FELIX KRISH, TONY FRANKLIN, BARRYMORE BARLOW** – drums

Geffen Geffen

Jun 88 (lp)(c)(cd) **OUTRIDER** [27] [26]
– Wasting my time / Wanna make love / The only one / Writes of winter / Hummingbird / Liquid mercury / Emerald eyes / Prison blues / Blues anthem (if I cannot have your love). *(re-cd+c.Aug91)*
Jun 88. (7") **WASTING MY TIME. / WRITES OF WINTER** [ ] [ ]

– other recordings, etc –

Jan 82. Charly; (lp) **JAM SESSION** (rec.1964 with SONNY BOY WILLIAMSON & BRIAN AUGER) [ ] [-]
– Don't send me no flowers / I see a man downstairs / She was so dumb / The goat / Walking / Little girl, how old are you / It's a bloody life / Getting out of town.

— below featured on session; **JOHN PAUL JONES / ALBERT LEE / NICKY HOPKINS + CLEM CATTINI**

Sep 84. Thunderbolt; (lp)(c)(cd) **NO INTRODUCTION NECCESSARY** [ ] [-]
– Lovin' up a storm / Everything I do is wrong / Think it over / Boll Weevil song / Livin' lovin' wreck / One long kiss / Dixie friend / Down the line / Fabulous / Breathless / Rave on / Lonely weekends / Burn up. *(re-iss.cd May93)*

— below from early 70's featuring; **JOHN BONHAM / JEFF BECK + NICKY HOPKINS**

May 85. Thunderbolt; (lp)(c)(cd) **SMOKE AND FIRE** [ ] [-]
– Wailing sounds / 'Cause I love you / Flashing lights / Gutty guitar / Would you believe / Smoke and fire / Thumping beat / Union Jack car / One for you baby / L-O-N-D-O-N / Brightest lights / Baby come back.

— below featured him in session with:- JET HARRIS & TONY MEEHAN / MICKIE MOST / DAVE BERRY / The FIRST GEAR / MICKEY FINN / solo / etc.

Jan 90. Archive; (cd)(lp) **JAMES PATRICK PAGE SESSION MAN VOLUME 1** [ ] [-]
Jul 90. Archive; (cd)(lp) **JAMES PATRICK PAGE SESSION MAN VOLUME 2** [ ] [-]
Aug 92. Sony; (cd)(c)(lp) **JIMMY'S BACK PAGES: THE EARLY YEARS** [ ] [ ]

HONEYDRIPPERS

ROBERT PLANT – vocals / **JIMMY PAGE** – guitar / **JEFF BECK** – guitar (also solo artist) / **NILE RODGERS** – producer, etc.

Es Paranza / Es Paranza

Oct 84. (7") **SEA OF LOVE. / I GET A THRILL** [-] [3]
Nov 84. (m-lp)(c) **VOLUME 1** [56] [4] Oct 84
– I get a thrill / Sea of love / I got a woman / Young boy blues / Rockin' at midnight. *(re-iss.cd Feb93)*
Jan 85. (7") **SEA OF LOVE. / ROCKIN' AT MIDNIGHT** [56] [-]
Mar 85. (7") **ROCKIN' AT MIDNIGHT. / YOUNG BOY BLUES** [-] [25]

THE FIRM

JIMMY PAGE – guitar / **PAUL RODGERS** – vocals (ex-FREE, ex-BAD COMPANY) / **TONY FRANKLIN** – bass, keys / **CHRIS SLADE** – drums (ex-MANFRED MANN'S EARTH BAND)

Atlantic / Atlantic

Feb 85. (lp)(c)(cd) **THE FIRM** [15] [17]
– Closer / Make or break / Someone to love / Radioactive / You've lost that lovin' feeling / Money can't buy satisfaction / Satisfaction guarenteed / Midnight moonlight.
Feb 85. (7")(7"sha-pic-d) **RADIOACTIVE. / TOGETHER** [ ] [28]
(12"+=) – City sirens / Live in peace.
Apr 85. (7") **SATISFACTION GUARENTEED. / CLOSER** [-] [73]
Apr 86. (lp)(c)(cd) **MEAN BUSINESS** [46] [22] Feb 86
– Fortune hunter / Cadillac / All the King's horses / Live in peace / Tear down the walls / Dreaming / Free to live / Spirit of love.
Apr 86. (7") **ALL THE KING'S HORSES. / FORTUNE HUNTER** [ ] [61]
Jun 86. (7") **LIVE IN PEACE. / FREE TO LIVE** [-] [ ]

— In 1993, JIMMY collaborated with DAVID COVERDALE to make one hit album 'COVERDALE • PAGE'.

JIMMY PAGE & ROBERT PLANT

with **CHARLIE JONES** – bass, percussion / **PORL THOMPSON** – guitar, banjo / **MICHAEL LEE** – drums, percussion / **NAJMA AKHTAR** – vocals / **JOE SUTHERLAND** – mandolin, bodhran / **NIGEL EASTON** – hurdy gurdy / **ED SHEARMUR** – hammond organ & orchestral arrangements for (large) English + Egyptian Ensemble + London Metropolitan Orchestra

Fontana / Fontana

Nov 94. (cd)(c)(d-lp) **NO QUARTER – UNLEDDED** [7] [4]
– Nobody's fault but mine / Thank you / No quarter / Friends / Yallah / City don't cry / Since I've been loving you / The battle of Evermore / Wonderful one / Wah wah / That's the way / Gallow's pole / Four sticks / Kashmir.
Dec 94. (cd-s) **GALLOW'S POLE / CITY DON'T CRY / THE RAIN SONG** [35] [ ]
(cd-s) – ('A'side) / Four sticks / What should never be.

Alvin LEE (see under ⇒ TEN YEARS AFTER)

Arthur LEE (see under ⇒ LOVE)

John LEES (see under ⇒ BARCLAY JAMES HARVEST)

LEFT BANKE

Formed: New York, USA ... early '66, by classically-trained MICHAEL BROWN. He had just written for one-off project CHRISTOPHER & THE CHAPS, who issued Feb 66 single 'IT'S ALRIGHT MA (I'M ONLY BLEE DING)' / 'THEY JUST DON'T CARE' for 'Philips'. He then assembled group with STEVE MARTIN, TOM FINN, JEFF WINFIELD and GEORGE CAMERON, in his father Harry's studio. Their first 45 'WALK AWAY RENEE', hit the US Top 5, and was quickly pursued by Top 20 smash 'PRETTY BALLERINA'. Group then split from MICHAEL, and he was left with group name, but only for a short while, as they returned later in '67. Without MICHAEL they failed to get anywhere, and folded a few years later. In 1973, BROWN briefly resurrected career, when his group STORIES hit US No.1 with version of 'BROTHER LOUIE'. • **Style:** Baroque'n'roll group, who fused heavy orchestration with bubblegum psychedelia. The STORIES were more rockier, although melody was always upfront. • **Songwriters:** BROWN contributed most to early LEFT BANKE, and used some outside writers in The STORIES. The latter covered; BROTHER LOUIE (Hot Chocolate) / etc. • **Trivia:** The FOUR TOPS had a massive hit in 1969 with their 'WALK AWAY RENEE'.

Recommended: AND FINALLY IT'S ... THE LEFT BANKE (*6).

MICHAEL BROWN (b.LOOKOFSKY, 25 Apr'49) – keyboards / **STEVE MARTIN** – vocals / **JEFF WINFIELD** – guitar / **TOM FINN** – bass (ex-MAGIC PLANETS) / **GEORGE CAMERON** – drums

Philips / Smash

Sep 66. (7") **WALK AWAY RENEE. / I HAVEN'T GOT THE NERVE** [ ] [5] Jul 66
Jan 67. (7") **PRETTY BALLERINA. / LAZY DAY** [ ] [15] Dec66

— **RICK BRAND** – guitar (ex-SPYDERS) repl. WINFIELD

Apr 67. (lp) **WALK AWAY RENEE ... PRETTY BALLERINA** [ ] [67] Mar 67
– Pretty ballerina / She may call you up tonight / Barterers and their wives / I've got something on my mind / Let go of you girl / Evening gown / Walk away renee / What do you know / Shadows breaking over my head / I haven't got the nerve / Lazy day *(US re-iss.1970 on 'Mercury')*

— **BROWN** split from rest of band, but retained name LEFT BANKE. The other 4 members disputed this and soon got radio stations to boycott following 45. Meanwhile BROWN had recruited **TOM FEHER** – vocals / **BERT SOMNER** – guitar / **+2**

Jun 67. (7") **IVY IVY. / AND SUDDENLY** [ ] [ ]

— (above was soon withdrawn, as others patch up dispute with BROWN)

Jun 67. (7") **SHE MAY CALL YOU UP TONIGHT. / BATTERERS AND THEIR WIVES** [-] [ ]
Oct 67. (7") **DESIREE. / I'VE GOT SOMETHING ON MY MIND** [ ] [98]

— More confusion, upset proceedings, as BROWN (to MONTAGE) and BRAND break. This left others (**FINN, MARTIN** and **CAMERON**) with what they wanted; LEFT BANKE.

Jun 68. (7") **DARK IS THE BARK. / MY FRIEND TODAY** [-] [ ]
Nov 68. (7") **GOODBYE HOLLY. / SING LITTLE BIRD SING** [-] [ ]
Feb 69. (7") **BRYANT HOTEL. / GIVE THE MAN A HAND** [-] [ ]
Mar 69. (lp) **THE LEFT BANKE TOO** [-] [ ]
– Goodbye Holly / There's gonna be a storm / Sing little bird sing / Nice to see you / Give the man a hand / Bryant Hotel / Desiree / Dark is the bark / In the morning light / My friend today.
1969. (7") **NICE TO SEE YOU. / THERE'S GONNA BE A STORM** [-] [ ]
Nov 69. (7") **MYRAH. / PEDESTAL** [-] [ ]

— Disbanded early 1970. STEVE MARTIN went solo recording one 45 for 'Buddah'

Mar 71. (7") **TWO BY TWO. / LOVE SONGS IN THE NIGHT** [-] [ ]

— Meanwhile, **MICHAEL BROWN** had formed

MONTAGE

in 1968 with **BOB STEURER** – vocals / **MIKE SMYTH** – guitar / **LANCE CORNELIUS** – bass / **VANCE CHAPMAN** – drums

not issued / Laurie

Mar 68. (7") **I SHALL CALL HER MARY. / AN AUDIENCE WITH MISS PRISCILLA GRAY** [-] [ ]
Jun 68. (7") **WAKE UP JIMMY. / TINSEL AND IVY** [-] [ ]
Jan 69. (lp) **MONTAGE** [-] [ ]
– She's alone / Grand pianist / Men are building sand / Desiree / The song is love / My love / I shall call her Mary / Tinsel & Ivy / An audience with Miss Priscilla Grey / Wake up Jimmy (something's happening outside). *(UK-iss.Jan87 on 'Bam Caruso')*

— Disbanded and **BROWN** later formed

STORIES

with **IAN LLOYD** – vocals / **STEVEN LOVE** – guitar / **BRIAN MALDEN** – drums

Polydor / Kama Sutra

May 72. (7") **I'M COMING HOME. / YOU TOLD ME** [-] [42]
Jun 72. (lp)(c) **STORIES** [-] [ ]
– Hello people / I'm coming home / Winter scenes / Step back / You told me / St.James / Kathleen / Take cover / Nice to have you here / High and low.
Jul 72. (7") **TOP OF THE CITY. / STEP BACK** [-] [ ]

Kama Sutra / Kama Sutra

Apr 73. (7") **DARLING. / TAKE COVER** [ ] [ ] Jan 73
Mar 73. (7") **LOVE'S IN MOTION. / CHANGES HAVE BEGUN** [-] [ ]
Mar 73. (lp)(c) **ABOUT US** [-] [ ]
– Brother Louie / Darling / Don't ever let me down / Love is in motion / Hey France / Please, please / Changes have begun / Circles / Believe me / Words / Top of the city / Down time blooze / What comes after. *(US re-iss.Aug73, hit No.29) (+= Brother Louie)*
May 73. (7") **BROTHER LOUIE. / WHAT COMES AFTER** [-] [1]
Sep 73. (7") **BROTHER LOUIE. / DARLING** [ ] [-]

— BROWN left to be replaced by **KENNY AARONSON** – bass / **KEN BISCHEL** – keyboards

Oct 73. (7") **MAMMY BLUE. / TRAVELLING UNDERGROUND** [-] [50]
1974. (lp)(c) **TRAVELLING UNDERGROUND** [-] [ ]
– Soft rain / Hard when you're so far away / If it feels good, do it / Mamy blue / Stories untold / I can't understand it / Earthbound / Freefall / Travelling underground
Mar 74. (7") **IF IT FEELS GOOD (by "IAN LLOYD & STORIES") / CIRCLES** [-] [ ]
Jun 74. (7") **ANOTHER LOVE. / LOVE IS IN MOTION** [-] [ ]

— When they finally split, IAN LLOYD went solo releasing albums IAN LLOYD (1976 'Polydor') / GOOSE BUMPS (1979 'Scotti Bros') / 3 WC (1980 'Scotti Bros')

MICHAEL BROWN

had released solo single meanwhile; 45 below (while in STORIES)

Dec 72. (7") **CIRCLES. / PREMONITION** [-] [ ]

The BECKIES

BROWN with **GARY HODGDEN** – drums / **MAYO JAMES McALLISTAIR** – lead guitar / **SCOTT THRUSTY** – bass

Sire / Sire

Mar 76. (lp) **BECKIES** [-] [ ]
– Midnight and you / Right by my side / Fran / Other side of town / Can't be alone / River song / On the morning that she came / One of these days / Run Jenny run.
Apr 76. (7") **CIRCLES. / TRY** [-] [ ]
Mar 77. (7") **RIVER BAYOU. / SONG CALLED LOVE** [-] [ ]
Mar 77. (7") **RIVER BAYOU. / RUN JENNY RUN** [ ] [-]

LEFT BANKE

re-formed in 1978, but without BROWN. Line-up was **MARTIN, FINN + CAMERON.**

not issued / Camerica

Sep 78. (7") **QUEEN OF PARADISE. / AND ONE DAY** [-] [ ]

— Disbanded after an album was recorded but was shelved, (see further below).

– compilations, others, etc. –

1970. Smash; (7") **WALK AWAY RENEE. / PRETTY BALLERINA** [-] [ ]
Feb 84. Bam Caruso; (lp) **AND SUDDENLY IT'S . . . THE LEFT BANKE** [ ] [-]
– Walk away Renee / There's gonna be a storm / Desiree / Myrah / Shadows breaking over my head / Let go of you girl / Sing little bird sing / I haven't got the nerve / Goodbye Holly / Dark is the bark / I've got something on my mind / Pretty ballerina / In the morning light / She may call you up tonight / My friend tonight / Batterers and their wives / Pedestal / Foggy waterfall. *(re-iss.Feb88, +=2 extra tracks) (cd-iss.Dec88 as 'AND FINALLY IT'S . . . THE LEFT BANKE')*
Feb 84. Bam Caruso; (7"ep) **WALK AWAY RENEE / EVENING GOWN. / BRYANT HOTEL / NICE TO SEE YOU** [ ] [-]
Mar 86. Bam Caruso; (lp) **VOICES CALLING** (1978 album) [ ] [-]
Mar 86. Bam Caruso; (7") **AND ONE DAY. / I CAN FLY** [ ] [-]
May 86. Bam Caruso; (m-lp) **WALK AWAY RENEE** [ ] [-]
Aug 85. Rhino; (lp)(c) **THE HISTORY OF THE LEFT BANKE** [-] [ ]
Aug 86. Rhino; (lp)(c) **STRANGERS ON A TRAIN** [-] [ ]
1988. See For Miles; (lp)(c)(cd) **WALK AWAY FROM THE LEFT BANKE (by "STORIES")** [ ] [-]
(cd+=) – (4 extra tracks).

LEFTFIELD

Formed: London, England . . . 1990 by ex-teacher of English NEIL BARNES and PAUL DALEY, whom also founded indie dance label 'Hard Hands' after first 2 singles. The first of these 'NOT FORGOTTEN', used sample /snippets from the film 'Mississippi Burning'. In the summer of 1993, they teamed up vocalist JOHN LYDON (of PUBLIC IMAGE LTD), to record with great secrecy their track 'OPEN UP' (LYDON chants 'Burn Hollywood Burn'). His record label 'Virgin' finally let them release it in November that year and it soon shot into UK Top 20, aided by its controversial video which coincidentally was released same time as the Californian fires. • **Style:** Dance orientated experimentalists, who broke new ground with each release. • **Songwriters:** The duo and samples. • **Trivia:** Their label 'Hard Hands' run by manager LISA HORRAN, also included acts VINYL BLAIR, DELTA LADY, DEE PATTEN and SCOTT HARRIS.

Recommended: LEFT-ISM (*8)

— **NEIL BARNES** – DJ, percussion, synthesizers / **PAUL DALEY** – samples (ex-A MAN CALLED ADAM)

Outer Rhythm / not issued
Mar 90. (12") **NOT FORGOTTEN. / PATELL'S ON THE CASE / ('A'version)** [ ] [-]

Rhythm King / not issued
Feb 91. (12")(cd-s) **MORE THAN I KNOW. / NOT FORGOTTEN** [ ] [-]

Hard Hands / Hard Hands
Aug 92. (12"ltd.) **RELEASE THE PRESSURE. / ('A'mixes)** [ ] [-]
Nov 92. (12"ltd.) **SONG OF LIFE. / ('A'mixes)** [59] [-]
Dec 92. (cd) **BACKLOG** (compilation of above) [ ] [-]
Below single credited to "LEFTFIELD / LYDON" (vocals= LYDON of PUBLIC IMAGE LTD.)
Nov 93. (7") **OPEN UP (radio edit). / ('A'instrumental)** [13] [ ]
(12"+=)(cd-s+=) – ('A'vocal 12" mix) / ('A'-Dervish overdrive mix) / ('A'-Andrew Weatherall mix) / ('A'-Dust Brothers mix).
Jan 95. (d-cd)(c)(d-lp)(3x12") **LEFT-ISM** [3] [ ]
– Release the pressure / Afro-left / Melt / Song of life ('95 remix) / Original / Black flute / Space shanty / Inspection (check one) / Storm 3000 / Half past dub *(3x12"only)* / Open up / 21st century poem.
below as "LEFTFIELD/ HALLIDAY" feat. TONI HALLIDAY – vocals (ex-CURVE)
Mar 95. (c-ep)(cd-ep) **ORIGINAL / ('A'live mix) / ('A'jam mix) / FILTER FISH** [18] [-]
(12"ep) – ('A'-Drift version) – repl.'A'live.
below featured DJUM DJUM
Jul 95. (12"ep)(c-ep)(cd-ep) **AFRO-LEFT EP** [22] [ ]
– Afro left / Afro ride / Afro sol / Afro central.

LEMONHEADS

Formed: Boston, Massachusetts, USA . . . 1983 by DANDO who had come from middle-class upbringing, but whose parents divorced when he was 12. In March 86, they were joined by another school-friend; jazz-bassist JESSE PORETZ. After releases on 'Taang!', they finally hit the big time in 1992 after earlier signing to 'Atlantic', and mellowing during a stay in Australia. • **Style:** Moved from hardcore rock outfit similiar to DINOSAUR JR, PIXIES, HUSKER DU, REPLACEMENTS to more jangly melodic zany rock. • **Songwriters:** DANDO is main pensmith, although DELLY or MADDOX were contributors early on. Covered; I AM A RABBIT (Proud Scum) / HEY JOE + AMAZING GRACE (trad.) / MOD LANG (Big Star) / LUKA (Suzanne Vega) / DIFFERENT DRUM (Michael Nesmith) / BRASS BUTTONS (Gram Parsons) / STRANGE (Patsy Cline) / YOUR HOME IS WHERE YOU ARE HAPPY (C. MANSON / PLASTER CASTER (Kiss) / SKULLS (Misfits) / GONNA GET ALONG WITHOUT YA NOW ('50s) / STEP BY STEP (New Kids On The Block) / FRANK MILLS (from 'Hair' musical) / KITCHEN (Hummingbirds) / MRS.ROBINSON (Simon & Garfunkel) / MISS OTIS REGRETS (Cole Porter). • **Trivia:** DANDO and JOHN STROHM appeared on BLAKE BABIES lp 'Slow Learners'.

Recommended: IT'S A SHAME ABOUT RAY (*8) / COME ON FEEL THE LEMONHEADS (*9) / LICK (*7).

EVAN DANDO – vocals, guitar + some drums / **JESSE PERETZ** – bass / **BEN DEILY** – guitar, + some drums.

not issued / Armory Arms/ Huh Bag
Jul. 86. (7"ep) **LAUGHING ALL THE WAY TO THE CLEANERS** [-] [ ]
– Glad I don't know / I like to / I am a rabbit / So I fucked up.

— added **DOUG TRACHTON** – drums

Jun 87. (lp)(c) **HATE YOUR FRIENDS** [-] [ ]
– I don't wanna / 394 / Nothing time / Second change / Sneakyville / Amazing Grace / Belt / Hate your friends / Don't tell yourself it's ok / Uhhh / Fed up / Rat velvet. *(UK-iss. May88 on 'World Service') (US-cd 1989+=)* – Glad I don't know / I like to / I am a rabbit / So I fucked up / Ever / Sad girl / Buried alive / Gotta stop. *(re-iss.cd Mar93 with 5 extra tracks including 'Laughing all the way. . .')*

— **EVAN,** on bass, also joined BLAKE BABIES in 1988, whose punk image wasn't suitable at the time, alongside girlfriend JULIANNA HATFIELD. **JOHN STROHM** – drums (ex-BLAKE BABIES) repl. DOUG.

World Service / Taang!
Sep 88. (lp)(c) **CREATOR** [ ] [ ]
– Burying ground / Sunday / Clang bang clang / Out / Your home is where you're happy / Falling / Die right now / Two weeks in another town / Plaster caster / Come to my window / Take her down / Postcard / Live without. *(US-cd 1989 +=)*– Luka (live) / Interview / Mallo cup. *(re-iss.Sep92 on 'Taang!', with 6 extra live tracks included) (re-iss.cd Mar93 with all re-issued tracks + 2 acoustic)*

— **COREY LOOG BRENNAN**– guitar (ex-BULLET LAVOLTA) repl. JOHN STROHM

Apr 89. (7"colrd) **LUKA / STRANGE / MAD** [ ] [-]
(re-iss. 7"/12"/cd-s Apr93)
Apr 89. (lp)(c)(cd) **LICK** [ ] [-]
– Mallo cup / Glad I don't know / 7 powers / A circle of one / Cazzo di ferro / Anyway / Luka / Come back D.A. / I am a rabbit / Sad girl / Ever. *(US-cd+=)* Strange / MAD. *(re-iss.cd Mar93 = Mad / Strange)*

— **MARK "BUDOLA"** – drums, toured until he checked out mid '89. (COREY also left to concentrate on his PhD.

Roughneck / Roughneck
Jun 90. (7") **DIFFERENT DRUM. / PAINT** [ ] [ ]
(12"+=)(cd-s+=) – Ride with me. *(re-iss.12"+cd-s.Feb93)*

Atlantic / Atlantic
Jun 90. (cd-ep) **FAVOURITE SPANISH DISHES EP** [-] [ ]
– Different drum / Paint / Ride with me / Skulls / Step by step.

— **DAVID RYAN** b. 20 Oct '64, Fort Wayne, Indiana – drums repl. DEILY

Aug 90. (cd)(c)(lp) **LOVEY** [-] [ ]
– Ballarat / Half the time / Year of the cat / Ride with me / Li'l seed / Stove / Come downstairs / Left for dead / Brass buttons / (The) Door. *(UK-iss. Oct91)(re-iss.cd,c,lp Nov93)*

— In Sep. 90, **DANDO** recruited **BEN DAUGHTY** – drums (ex-SQUIRREL BAIT) repl. RYAN / **BYRON HOAGLAND – bass** (ex-FANCY PANTS) repl. PERETZ.

Sep 91. (7") **GONNA GET ALONG WITHOUT YA NOW. / HALF THE TIME** [ ] [ ]
(12"ep+=) **PATIENCE AND PRUDENCE**: Stove (remix) / Step by step.

— **DANDO, RYAN + JULIANA HATFIELD** – bass, vocals (ex BLAKE BABIES)

Jul 92. (cd)(c)(lp) **IT'S A SHAME ABOUT RAY** [69] [68]
– Rockin' stroll / Confetti / Rudderless / My drug buddy / The turnpike down / Bit part / Alison's starting to happen / Hannah and Gaby / Kitchen / Ceiling fan in my spoon / Frank Mills. *(album will hit UK No.33 Jan'93) (re-iss.Feb95)*
Oct 92. (7")(c-s) **IT'S A SHAME ABOUT RAY. / SHAKEY GROUND** [70] [ ]
(10"+=)(cd-s+=) – Dawn can't decide / The turnpike down.
Nov 92. (7")(c-s) **MRS.ROBINSON. / BEING AROUND** [19] [ ]
(10"+=)(cd-s+=) – Divan / Into your arms.

— 1993 line-up: **DANDO, RYAN, NIC DALTON** (b. 6 Jun '66, Australia) although she did provide b.vox for 1993 releases. – bass HATFIELD formed own trio)

Jan 93. (7")(c-s) **CONFETTI (remix). / MY DRUG BUDDY** [44] [ ]
(10"+=)(cd-s+=) – Ride with me (live) / Confetti (acoustic).
Mar 93. (c-s) **IT'S A SHAME ABOUT RAY. / ALISON'S STARTING TO HAPPEN** [31] [ ]
(cd-s) – Different drum (Evan acoustic) / Stove (Evan acoustic).
(10"+=) Different drum (acoustic) / Rockin' stroll (live).
(cd-s) – ('A'side) / Confetti / Mallo cup / Rudderless (all 4 live).
Oct 93. (7")(c-s) **INTO YOUR ARMS. / MISS OTIS REGRETS** [14] [67]
(10"+=)(cd-s+=) – Little black egg / Learning the game.
Oct 93. (cd)(c)(lp) **COME ON FEEL THE LEMONHEADS** [5] [56]
– The great big no / Into your arms / It's about time / Down about it / Paid to smile / Big gay heart / Style / Rest assured / Dawn can't decide / I'll do it anyway / Rick James style / Being around / Favourite T / You can take it with you / The jello fund. *(lp+=)* Miss Otis regrets.
Nov 93. (7")(c-s) **IT'S ABOUT TIME. / RICK JAMES ACOUSTIC STYLE** [57] [ ]
(10"+=)(cd-s+=) – Big gay heart (demo) / Down about it (acoustic).
(above 'A' side was written about JULIANA. I'LL DO IT ANYWAY for BELINDA CARLISLE)
May 94. (10"ep)(c-ep)(cd-ep) **BIG GAY HEART. / DEEP BOTTOM COVE / HE'S ON THE BEACH / FAVORITE T (live in session)** [55] [ ]

— Offending lyrics to above 'A'side, were changed; with Stroke & Brick.

— DALTON departed Sep 94

— **MURPH** – drums (ex-DINOSAUR JR) repl.RYAN

– compilations, etc. –

1990. Taang!; (cd) **CREATE YOUR FRIENDS** –
– HATE YOUR FRIENDS / CREATOR / LAUGHING E.P.

LEMON INTERRUPT (see under ⇒ UNDERWORLD)

John LENNON

Born: 9 Oct'40, Liverpool, England. While still a member of The BEATLES late 1968, he teamed up with his new girlfriend at the time YOKO ONO, to issue controversial 'UNFINISHED MUSIC NO.1: TWO VIRGINS', which displayed a self-taken full-frontal photo of both on lp sleeve. This was sold in brown paper wrapping, to save embarrassment to customer and retailer!. During Spring next year, its follow-up 'UNFINISHED MUSIC NO.2: LIFE WITH THE LIONS', hit the shops and continued anti-commercial free-form, mainly recorded on small cassette. Now divorced from wife CYNTHIA, JOHN had already married YOKO on 20 Mar'69, and even changed by deed poll, his middle name from WINSTON to ONO. After the LENNONS completed an 8-day peace protest, while publicly lying/sitting in a hotel bed, they released PLASTIC ONO BAND's debut 45 'GIVE PEACE A CHANCE'. This gave JOHN his first non-BEATLES hit, when it rose to UK Top 3 and US Top 20. Later that year 'COLD TURKEY' (a drug withdrawal song), also gave him a Top 30 smash on both sides of the Atlantic. Late 1969, he unveiled 2 albums, one another avant-garde collaboration with YOKO; 'THE WEDDING ALBUM', and the other a more standard commercial product THE PLASTIC ONO BAND 'LIVE IN TORONTO 1969', which breached US Top 10. They also scored with another UK/US Top 5 hit 'INSTANT KARMA', which was produced by PHIL SPECTOR early 1970. In May that year, The BEATLES officially split just prior to another No.1 album 'LET IT BE'. JOHN then concentrated completely on solo career with The PLASTIC ONO BAND and returned to the chart with late 1970 album 'JOHN LENNON: PLASTIC ONO BAND', which was followed by another Top 20 anthem 'POWER TO THE PEOPLE'. On 3rd Sep'71, he went to New York to live with YOKO, and subsequently never returned to UK. A month later, his classic album 'IMAGINE', was a No.1 in both US & UK, with its US-only released title track hitting No.3. He failed in a bid to have US-only Christmas hit with 'HAPPY XMAS WAR IS OVER), although this reached Top 5 a year later in '72. During the next 3 years in which he released 3 albums, he fought to stay in the US, after being ordered by immigration authorities to leave. In this time, he also went through drinking bouts, while temporarily splitting from YOKO. On 9 Oct'75, YOKO gave birth to their first child (together) SEAN, and LENNON went into retirement to look after him in their Manhattan apartment. He left behind a charting greatest hits 'SHAVED FISH', and soon was to receive his green-card, allowing him to permanently reside in US. However, he returned to studio in 1980, with David Geffen offering to release an album on his label. In November, 'DOUBLE FANTASY' was unleashed, and this soon topped both album charts. There was also a return to the singles chart, when appropriately title '(JUST LIKE) STARTING OVER' made Top 10. Tragically on 8th December 1980, JOHN was shot 5 times by so-called fan/mental case Mark Chapman, outside the LENNON's apartment block. He died shortly afterwards at Roosevelt hospital. Not surprisingly his previous 45, climbed back up the charts and peaked at No.1, with also a re-issue of 'IMAGINE' following it there early 1981. His killer was sent to a mental institution for the rest of his life, and we can only ponder on what 40-year-old JOHN might have achieved in the 80's & 90's. • **Style:** Much revered genius, who attempted to alienate pop industry by non-conventional musics. A peaceful man, whose outbursts and human faults, seemed to be portrayed wickedly by media, especially in his BEATLES days. His love of YOKO was undoubtably his turning point, finding both himself and the world around him a happier place to life. His music with all its facets, showed a poetic beauty and untouched romance, although other songs exploded into frenetic rock anthems of anti-war and anti-government feelings. • **Songwriters:** LENNON, except covers album ROCK'N'ROLL which contained;- BE-BOP-A-LULA (Gene Vincent) / STAND BY ME (Ben E.King) / PEGGY SUE (Buddy Holly) / AIN'T THAT A SHAME (Fats Domino) / SWEET LITTLE SIXTEEN + YOU CAN'T CATCH ME (Chuck Berry) / BONY MORONIE (Larry Williams) / BRING IT HOME TO ME + SEND ME SOME LOVIN' (Sam Cooke) / JUST BECAUSE (Lloyd Price) / YA YA (Lee Dorsey) / RIP IT UP + SLIPPIN' AND SLIDIN' + READY TEDDY (Little Richard) / DO YOU WANT TO DANCE (Bobby Freeman). • **Trivia:** In 1967, JOHN acted in the film 'How I Won The War', and also appeared in many zany films with The BEATLES. In 1975, he co-wrote 'Fame' with DAVID BOWIE, which hit US No.1. His son from his first marriage JULIAN, is currently enjoying chart status, and SEAN has also began to sing at benefits, etc.

Recommended: IMAGINE (*8) / MIND GAMES (*7) / THE JOHN LENNON COLLECTION (*9).

JOHN LENNON & YOKO ONO

JOHN LENNON – vocals, guitar, etc. / **YOKO ONO** (b.18 Feb'33, Tokyo, Japan) – wind, vocals

Apple Apple

Nov 68. (lp) **UNFINISHED MUSIC NO.1: TWO VIRGINS**
– Section 1, 2, 3, 4, 5, 6 / Side 2. *(cd-iss.Jan93 on 'Rock Classics')*

Zapple Zapple

May 69. (lp) **UNFINISHED MUSIC NO.2: LIFE WITH THE LIONS (1/2 live)**
– Cambridge 1969 / No bed for Beatle John / Baby's heartbeat / Two minutes silence / Radio play.

The PLASTIC ONO BAND

Apple Apple

Jul 69. (7") **GIVE PEACE A CHANCE. / REMEMBER LOVE** 2 14
(re-iss.Jan81, reached UK No.33)

Oct 69. (7") **COLD TURKEY. / DON'T WORRY KYOKO** 14 30 Dec 69

—— JOHN and YOKO hired the following musicians **ERIC CLAPTON** – guitar (ex-YARDBIRDS, ex-CREAM, ex-BLUESBREAKERS) / **KLAUS VOORMAN** – bass (ex-MANFRED MANN) / **ALAN WHITE** – drums

Dec 69. (lp) **THE PLASTIC ONO BAND – LIVE PEACE IN TORONTO 1969 (live 13 Sep'69)** – 10 Jan 70
– Blue Suede shoes / Money (that's what I want) / Dizzy Miss Lizzy / Yer blues / Cold turkey / Give peace a chance / Don't worry Kyoko / John John (let's hope for peace).

Dec 69. (lp) **WEDDING ALBUM** (as "JOHN ONO LENNON & YOKO ONO LENNON")
– John and Yoko / Amsterdam.

LENNON / ONO & THE PLASTIC ONO BAND

Feb 70. (7") **INSTANT KARMA!. / WHO HAS SEEN THE WIND (Yoko Ono)** 5 3

JOHN LENNON & THE PLASTIC ONO BAND

The **LENNONs** retained only **KLAUS / RINGO STARR** – drums (ex-BEATLES) repl. WHITE who later joined YES

Dec 70. (lp)(c) **JOHN LENNON: PLASTIC ONO BAND** 11 6
– Mother / Hold on / I found out / Working class hero / Isolation / Remember / Love / Well well well / Look at me / God / My mummy's dead. *(re-iss.Jul84 on 'Fame', cd-iss.Dec94) (cd-iss.Apr88 on 'EMI')*

Dec 70. (7") **MOTHER. / WHY (Yoko Ono)** – 43

—— next single also credited with **YOKO ONO**

Mar 71. (7") **POWER TO THE PEOPLE. / OPEN YOUR BOX** 7 –

Mar 71. (7") **POWER TO THE PEOPLE. / TOUCH ME (Yoko Ono)** – 11

Oct 71. (lp)(c) **IMAGINE** 1 1 Sep 71
– Imagine / Crippled inside / Jealous guy / It's so hard / I don't want to be a soldier / Give me some truth / Oh my love / How do you sleep? / How? / Oh Yoko!. *(also on quad-lp Jun72) (cd-iss.May87 on 'Parlophone')*

Oct 71. (7") **IMAGINE. / IT'S SO HARD** – 3

May 72. (7") **WOMAN IS THE NIGGER OF THE WORLD. / SISTERS, OH SISTERS (Yoko Ono)** – 57

JOHN & YOKO / PLASTIC ONO BAND

with ELEPHANT'S MEMORY & FLUX / INVISIBLE STRINGS and lots of guests including **FRANK ZAPPA, ERIC CLAPTON,** etc.

Sep 72. (d-lp)(d-c) **SOMETIME IN NEW YORK CITY (live)** 11 48
– Woman is the nigger of the world / Sisters o sisters / Attica state / Born in a prison / New York City / Sunday bloody Sunday / The luck of the Irish / John Sinclair / Angela / We're all water / (w/ CAST OF THOUSANDS); Cold turkey / Don't worry Kyoko / (w/ The MOTHERS); Jamrag / Scumbag / Au. *(re-iss.Feb86 on 'Parlophone')*

—— Next single credited as **JOHN & YOKO / PLASTIC ONO BAND** with **The HARLEM COMMUNITY CHOIR**

Nov 72. (7")(7"green) **HAPPY XMAS (WAR IS OVER). / LISTEN THE SNOW IS FALLING** 4 – Nov 71
(re-iss.Dec74 reached No.48, re-iss.Dec80 – No.2, re-iss.Dec81 – No.28, re-iss.Dec82, hit 56)

JOHN LENNON

Nov 73. (7")**MIND GAMES. / MEAT CITY** 26 18

Nov 73. (lp)(c) **MIND GAMES ("JOHN LENNON & PLASTIC U.F.ONO BAND")** 13 9
– Mind games / Tight a $ / Aisumasen (I'm sorry) / One day (at a time) / Bring on the Lucie (Freeda people) / Nutopian international anthem / Intuition / Out of the blue / Only people / I know (I know) / You are here / Meat city. *(re-iss.Oct80 on 'MFP') (cd-iss.Aug87 on 'Parlophone')*

Oct 74. (7") **WHATEVER GETS YOU THRU THE NIGHT. (as "JOHN LENNON & THE PLASTIC ONO NUCLEAR BAND featuring ELTON JOHN") / BEEF JERKY** 36 1 Sep 74

Oct 74. (lp)(c) **WALLS AND BRIDGES** 6 1
– Going down on love / Whatever gets you thru the night / Old dirt road / What you got / Bless you / £9 dream / Surprise surprise (sweet bird of Paradise) / Steel and glass / Beef jerky / Nobody loves you (when you're down and out) / Ya-ya / Scared. *(re-iss.Jan85 on 'Parlophone', cd-iss.Jul87)*

Jan 75. (7") **£9 DREAM. / WHAT YOU GOT** 23 9

Feb 75. (lp)(c) **ROCK'N'ROLL** 6 6
– Be-bop-a-lula / Stand by me / Medley: Rip it up – Ready Teddy / You can't catch me / Ain't that a shame / Do you want to dance / Sweet little sixteen / Slippin' and slidin' / Peggy Sue / Medley: Bring it on home to me – Send me some lovin' / Ya ya / Just because. *(re-iss.Nov81 on 'MFP') (cd-iss.Jul87 on 'Parlophone')*

Apr 75. (7") **STAND BY ME. / MOVE OVER MS. L** 30 20 Mar 75
(re-iss.Apr81)

Oct 75. (7") **IMAGINE. / WORKING CLASS HERO** 6 –
(re-iss.Dec80 reached UK No.1)

Nov 75. (lp)(c) **SHAVED FISH** (compilation) 8 12
– Give peace a chance / Cold turkey / Instant karma / Power to the people / Mother /

Woman is the nigger of the world / Imagine / Whatever gets you thru the night / Mind games / £9 dream / Happy Xmas (war is over) / Give peace a chance (reprise). *(cd-iss May 87 on 'E.M.I.')*

— JOHN was also credited on a few singles by ELTON JOHN – Feb75 'I Saw Her Standing There' which was also realeased Mar81 with 2 other. In Jul71 a rare single 'GOD SAVE US'/'DO THE OZ' was released by him and Plastic Ono Band backing 'BILL ELLIOT AND THE ELASTIC OZ BAND'

JOHN LENNON & YOKO ONO

returned after a long break

Geffen Geffen

Oct 80. (7") **(JUST LIKE) STARTING OVER. / KISS KISS KISS (Yoko Ono)** [1] [1]

Nov 80. (lp)(c) **DOUBLE FANTASY** [1] [1]
– (Just like) Starting over / Every man has a woman who loves him (YOKO ONO) / Clean up time / Give me something (YOKO ONO) / I'm losing you / I'm moving on (YOKO ONO) / Beautiful boy (darling boy) / Watching the wheels / I'm your angel (YOKO ONO) / Dear Yoko / Beautiful boys (YOKO ONO) / Kiss kiss kiss (YOKO ONO) / Woman / Hard times are over (YOKO ONO). *(re-iss.+cd.Jan89 on 'Capitol')*

Jan 81. (7") **WOMAN. / BEAUTIFUL BOYS (Yoko Ono)** [1] [2]

Mar 81. (7") **WATCHING THE WHEELS. / I'M YOUR ANGEL (Yoko Ono)** [30] [10]

— His last two singles were released after his untimely murder 8 Dec80.

JOHN & YOKO

had recorded one more album prior to his death.

Polydor Polydor

Jan 84. (7") **NOBODY TOLD ME. / O SANITY** [6] [5]

Jan 84. (lp)(c)(cd)(pic-lp) **MILK AND HONEY** [3] [11]
– I'm stepping out / Sleepless night (YOKO ONO) / I don't wanna face it / Don't be scared (YOKO ONO) / Nobody told me / O'sanity (YOKO ONO) / Borrowed time / Your hands (YOKO ONO) / (Forgive me) My little flower princess / Let me count the ways (YOKO ONO) / Grow old with me / You're the one (YOKO ONO).

Dec 83. (lp)(c) **A HEART PLAY: UNFINISHED DIALOGUE** (interview with Playboy) [ ] [ ]

Mar 84. (7") **BORROWED TIME. / YOUR HANDS (Yoko Ono)** [32] [ ]
(12"+=) – Never say goodbye.

Jul 84. (7") **I'M STEPPING OUT. / SLEEPLESS NIGHT (Yoko Ono)** [ ] [55]
(12"+=) – Loneliness.

Nov 84. (7") **EVERY MAN HAS A WOMAN WHO LOVES HIM. / IT'S ALRIGHT** [ ] [ ]
(above from various compilation 'B'-side by his son SEAN ONO LENNON)

– posthumous exploitation releases etc. –

Jun 81. Apple; (8xlp-box) **JOHN LENNON (BOXED)** [ ] [ ]
(All lp's from LIVE PEACE – SHAVED FISH)
– Give peace a chance / Instant karma / Power to the people / Whatever gets you thru the night / 9 dream / Mind games / Love / Happy Xmas (war is over) / Imagine / Jealous guy / Stand by me / Starting over / Woman / I'm losing you / Beautiful boy, darling boy / Watching the wheel / Dear Yoko. (cd+=) – Move over Miss L. / Cold turkey.

Nov 82. EMI/ US= Geffen; (lp)(c) **THE JOHN LENNON COLLECTION** [1] [33]
(re-iss. Jun 85, cd-iss. Oct 89; 2 extra tracks)

Oct 90. EMI/ US= Geffen; (cd-box) **LENNON** [ ] [ ]

Note; Below 'Parlophone' UK /'Capitol' US, until stated.

Nov 82. (7") **LOVE. / GIVE ME SOME TRUTH** [41] [ ]

Nov 85. (7") **JEALOUS GUY / GOING DOWN ON LOVE** [65] [ ]
(12"+=) – Oh Yoko!

Feb 86. (lp)(c)(cd) **LIVE IN NEW YORK CITY (live)** [55] [41]

Nov 86. (lp)(c)(cd) **MENLOVE AVE.** (sessions 74-75) [ ] [ ]
– Here we go again / Rock'n'roll people / Angel baby / Since my baby left me / To know her is to love her / Steel and glass / Scared / Old dirt road / Nobody loves you (when you're down and out).

Aug 87. (cd) **LIVE JAM** (half of SOMETIME lp) [ ] [ ]

Oct 88. (lp)(c)(cd) **IMAGINE** (Music from the Motion Picture; with some songs by The BEATLES) [64] [31]
– Real love / Twist and shout / Help! / In my life / Strawberry fields forever / A day in the life / Revolution / The ballad of John & Yoko / Julia / Don't let me down / Give peace a chance / How? / Imagine (rehearsal / God / Mother / Stand by me / Jealous guy / Woman / Beautiful boy (darling boy) / (Just like) Starting over / Imagine.

Nov 88. (7")(7"pic-d) **IMAGINE. / JEALOUS GUY** [45] [80] B-side
(12"+=)(12"pic-d+=) – Happy Xmas (war is over).
(cd-s+=) – Give peace a chance.

Mar 84. Old Gold; (7") **GIVE PEACE A CHANCE. / COLD TURKEY** [ ] [-]

May 87. Antar; (7") **TWO MINUTES SILENCE. / TWO MINUTES SILENCE (dub!)** [ ] [ ]

Annie LENNOX (see under ⇒ EURYTHMICS)

Deke LEONARD (see under ⇒ MAN)

LEVEL 42

Formed: Isle Of Wight, England … late 1979 by MARK KING, MIKE LINDUP and The GOULD brothers. After releasing debut 45 'LOVE MEETING LOVE' on Andy Sojka's disco 'Elite' label, they moved to London and re-issued it later 1980 on 'Polydor'. In the Spring of '81, they had first UK Top 40 hit with 'LOVE GAMES', which later appeared on self-titled Top 20 debut album. Gradually progressed into a Top 10 band by 1983, when 'THE SUN GOES DOWN (LIVING IT UP)' preceded album 'STANDING IN THE LIGHT'. They peaked commercially in 1985, when UK Top 3 album 'WORLD MACHINE', also made Top 20 in the States. • **Style:** Started out as white jazz-funk instrumental outfit inspired by EARTH, WIND & FIRE. Branched out into a mainstream pop-funk band, fronted by smooth vox and virtuoso bassman MARK 'Thunderthumbs' KING. • **Songwriters:** All penned by KING-LINDUP. KING's solo lp contained a cover of; I FEEL FREE (Cream). • **Trivia:** The album 'A PHYSICAL PRESENCE' was produced by West African 5th member WALLY BADAROU.

Recommended: LEVEL BEST (*6).

MARK KING (b.20 Oct'58) – vocals, bass, etc. (ex-PETE COTTON BAND) / **MIKE LINDUP** (b.17 Mar'59) – keyboards, vocals / **BOON GOULD** (b. 4 Mar'55) – guitar / **PHIL GOULD** (b.28 Feb'57) – drums, percussion

Elite not issued

Apr 80. (7")(12") **LOVE MEETING LOVE. / INSTRUMENTAL LOVE** [ ] [-]
(re-iss.Aug80 on 'Polydor', hit 61)

Polydor Polydor

Nov 80. (7") **(FLYING ON THE) WINGS OF LOVE. / WINGS OF LOVE** [ ] [-]
(12") – ('A'-U.S.mix). / ('A'-U.K.dance mix)
(12") – ('A'-'81 remix). / Love meetong love

Mar 81. (7")('A'ext.-12") **LOVE GAMES. / "43"** [38] [-]

Aug 81. (7")('A'ext.-12") **TURN IT ON. / BEEZER ONE** [57] [-]

Aug 81. (lp)(c) **LEVEL 42** [20] [ ]
– Turn it on / "43" / Why are you leaving / Almost there / Love games / Heathrow / Dune tune / Starchild. *(cd-is Jul84)* (cd+=) – (extra remixes)

Oct 81. (7") **STARCHILD. / FOUNDATION AND EMPIRE PART 1** [47] [-]
('A'extended-12"+=) – ('B'-part 2).

Feb 82. (7") **STARCHILD. / TURN IT ON** [-] [ ]

Apr 82. (7")(12") **ARE YOU HEARING (WHAT I HEAR). / THE RETURN OF THE HANDSOME RUGGED MAN** [49] [ ]

Sep 82. (lp)(c) **THE PURSUIT OF ACCIDENTS** [17] [ ]
– Weave your spell / The pursuit of accidents / Last chance / Are you hearing (what I hear) / You can't blame Louie / Eyes waterfalling / Shapeshifter / The Chinese way. *(re-iss.+cd Jun90 +=)*– (extra remixes).

Sep 82. (7") **WEAVE YOUR SPELL. / LOVE GAMES (live)** [43] [ ]
(12"+=) – Dune tune (live).

Jan 83. (7")('A'ext.-12"yellow) **THE CHINESE WAY. / 88 (live)** [24] [ ]
(d12"+=) – Weave your spell (ext) / Dune tune (live) / Love games (live).

Polydor A&M

Apr 83. (7")(7"pic-d) **OUT OF SIGHT, OUT OF MIND. / YOU CAN'T BLAME LOUIE (live)** [41] [ ]
(12") – ('A'&'B'extended).

Jul 83. (7") **THE SUN GOES DOWN (LIVING IT UP). / CAN'T WALK YOU HOME** [10] [ ]
(free c-ep+=) – Love games / (excerpts from below lp).
(12"+=) – Love games (extended) / Forty two.

Aug 83. (lp)(c)(cd) **STANDING IN THE LIGHT** [9] [ ]
– Micro-kid / The sun goes down (living it up) / Out of sight, out of mind / Dance on heavy weather / A pharoah's dream (of endless time) / Standing in the light / I want eyes / People / The machine stops. *(re-iss.+cd Jun90)*

Oct 83. (7")(12") **MICRO-KID. / TURN IT ON (live)** [37] [ ]
(d12"+=) – The Chinese way (New York mix) / The Chinese way (dub).

Dec 83. (7")(12") **STANDING IN THE LIGHT. / LOVE MEETING LOVE** [ ] [ ]

Aug 84. (7") **THE SUN GOES DOWN (LIVING IT UP). / DANCE ON HEAVY WEATHER** [-] [ ]

Aug 84. (7")('A'-different-12") **HOT WATER. / STANDING IN THE LIGHT (remix)** [18] [ ] Jul 86

Sep 84. (lp)(c)(cd) **TRUE COLOURS** [14] [ ]
– The chant has begun / Kansas City milkman / Seven days / Hot water / A floating life / True believers / Kouyate / Hours by the window. *(c+=)*– (3 extra tracks). *(cd-iss.Nov89)*

Oct 84. (7") **THE CHANT HAS BEGUN. / ALMOST THERE** [41] [ ]
('A'power mix-12"+=) – The sun goes down (up front mix).
(7"ep+=) – Love games (US remix). *(free c-s w/7")*

Polydor Polydor

Jun 85. (7"ep)(12"ep) **FOLLOW ME. / MR. PINK / TURN IT UP / KANSAS CITY MILKMAN (live)** [ ] [ ]

Jun 85. (d-lp)(c)(cd) **A PHYSICAL PRESENCE (live)** [28] [ ]
– Almost there / Turn it on / Mr. Pink / Eyes waterfalling / Kansas city milkman / Follow me / Foundation and empire / The chant has begun / The Chinese way / The sun goes down (living it up) / Hot water / 88 *. *(not on cd *)*

Sep 85. (7")(12") **SOMETHING ABOUT YOU. / COUP D'ETAT** [6] [7] Feb 86
(10") – ('A'side) / The Chinese way / Follow me (live).
(extra-12"+=) – Hot water / The sun goes down.

Oct 85. (lp)(c)(cd) **WORLD MACHINE** [3] [18] Mar 86
– World machine / Physical pressence / Something about you / Leaving me now / I sleep on my heart / It's not the same for us / Good man in a storm / Coup d'etat / Lying still. *(c+=)(cd+=)*– Dream crazy. *(US-cd+=)*– Hot water / The chant has begun. *(re-iss.cd Jan93)*

Nov 85. (7")(10") **LEAVING ME NOW. / I SLEEP ON MY HEART (remix)** [15] [ ]
(12"+=) – ('A'version) / Dream crazy.
(d7"+=) – ('A'version) / Coup d'etat.

Apr 86. (7") **LESSONS IN LOVE. / HOT WATER (live)** [3] [12] Apr 87
(12"+=) – World machine.
(12") – ('A'side) / Something about you (US remix).

Jul 86. (7") **HOT WATER. /** [-] [87]

Feb 87. (7") **RUNNING IN THE FAMILY. / DREAM CRAZY** [6] [83] Jul 87
(12"+=) – ('A'extended version).
(d12"+=) – Running in the family / World machine (Shep Pettibone remix) / World machine (dub).

Apr 87. (7")(7"pic-d) **TO BE WITH YOU AGAIN. / MICRO KID (live)** [10] [ ]

(12"+=) – ('A' dub version).
(extra-12"+=) – Lessons in love.

— added guests **GARY BARNACLE** and **KRYS MACH** – saxophone

Jun 87. (lp)(c)(cd) **RUNNING IN THE FAMILY** [2] [23]
– Lessons in love / Children say / Running in the family / It's over / To be with you again / Two solitudes / Fashion fever / Sleepwalkers. *(c+=)(cd+=)–* Freedom somesay. *(re-iss.Oct87 as d-lp 'THE PLATINUM EDITION' w/ extra versions & tracks) (re-iss.Nov89 & Mar93)*

Aug 87. (7")(c-s) **IT'S OVER (remix). / PHYSICAL PRESENCE (live)** [10] [ ]
(12"+=) – ('A'instrumental).
(12"+=) – Running in the family (remix).

Dec 87. (7")(12")(7"pic-d) **CHILDREN SAY. / STARCHILD** [22] [ ]
(cd-s+=) – ('A'-Platinum Edition remix).
(c-s+=) – Something about you.

— Now down to a duo of **KING** and **LINDUP**, when PHIL and BOON departed, using session people, **ALAN MURPHY** – guitar / **DOMINIC MILLER** – guitar / **GARY HUSBAND** – drums. plus **WALLY BADAROU** – keys / **STEVE SIDWELL** – horns / **KRYS MACH** – sax

Aug 88. (7")(12") **HEAVEN IN MY HANDS. / GRESHAM BLUES** [12] [ ]
(cd-s+=) – ('A' extended mix).

Sep 88. (lp)(c)(cd) **STARING AT THE SUN** [2] [ ]
– Heaven in my hands / I don't know why / Take a look / Over there / Silence / Tracie / Staring at the sun / Two hearts collide / Man. *(re-iss.cd+c Mar93)*

Oct 88. (7") **TAKE A LOOK. / MAN** [32] [ ]
(12"+=)(cd-s+=) – ('A'extended version).

Jan 89. (7") **TRACIE. / THREE WORDS** [25] [ ]
(12"+=)(cd-s+=) – ('A'instrumental) / ('A'-US remix).

Oct 89. (7") **TAKE CARE OF YOURSELF. / SILENCE** [39] [ ]
(12"+=)(cd-s+=) – Man.

Nov 89. (lp)(c)(cd) **LEVEL BEST** (compilation) [5] [ ]
– Running in the family / The sun goes down (livin' it up) / Something about you / Tracie / Starchild / It's over / Hot water / Take care of yourself / Heaven in my hands / Children say / Love games / The Chinese way / Leaving me now / Lessons in love. *(c+=)(cd+=)–* Micro-kid / Take a look / To be with you again / The chant has begun.

— ALAN MURPHY tragically died of AIDS 19th Oct'89.

R.C.A. R.C.A.

Aug 91. (7")(c-s) **GUARENTEED. / ALL SHE WANTS** [17] [ ]
(12"+=) – ('A'-New Avengers mix).
(cd-s++=) – If you were mine.

Sep 91. (cd)(c)(lp) **GUARENTEED** [3] [ ]
– Guarenteed / Overtime / Her big baby / Seven years / Set me up / The ape / My father's shoes / A kinder eye / She can't help herself / If you were mine. *(re-iss.cd Apr95)*

Oct 91. (7") **OVERTIME. / SHE CAN'T HELP HERSELF** [62] [ ]
(12") – ('A'side) / (2 other 'A'mixes).
(cd-s) – ('A'side) / (2 other 'A'mixes) / All this great distance.

Apr 92. (7")(c-s) **MY FATHER'S SHOES. / AS YEARS GO BY** [55] [ ]
(cd-s+=) – Her big day / The Sun goes down (or an interview).

— **KING, LINDUP, GOULD, BADAROU + DANNY BLOOM** – guitars / **MILES BOULD** – percussion / **GARY BARNACLE** – sax / **JOHN THIRKELL, DEREK WATKINS + STUART BROOKS** – trumpet / **RICHARD EDWARDS** – trombone / **GAVIN WRIGHT** – strings

Feb 94. (cd-s) **FOREVER NOW / ALL OVER YOU (mixes)** [19] [ ]
(cd-s)(c-s)(12") – ('A'side) / Romance / Play me / Past lives.

Mar 94. (cd)(c) **FOREVER NOW** [8] [ ]
– Forever now / Model friend / Tired of waiting / All over you / Love in a peaceful world / Romance / Billy's gone / One in a million / The sunbed song / Talking in your sleep / Don't bother me. *(re-iss.cd Nov95 on 'Resurgence')*

Apr 94. (c-s) **ALL FOR YOU. / LEARN TO SAY NO** [26] [ ]
(12"+=)(cd-s+=) – ('A'mix).
(cd-s) – ('A'side) / The Sun goes down (living it up) / Lessons in love / Running in the family.

Jul 94. (12")(c-s) **LOVE IN A PEACEFUL WORLD. / THE BENDS** [31] [ ]
(cd-s+=) – Heart on the line.
(cd-s) – ('A'side) / Leaving me now / It's over / Take a look.

– compilations etc. –

Mar 82. Polydor; (lp)(c) **THE EARLY TAPES (JULY-AUGUST 1980)** [46] [ ]
– Sandstorm / Love meeting love / Theme to Margaret / Autumn / Paradise is free / Wings of love / Woman / Mr. Pink / 88.

Nov 91. Polydor; (9xcd-box) **1980-1989 COMPLETE (all)** [ ] [ ]

Jul 92. Polydor; (cd)(c)(lp) **THE REMIXES** [ ] [ ]
(re-iss.cd Apr95)

Oct 92. Old Gold; (12") **RUNNING IN THE FAMILY. / SOMETHING ABOUT YOU** [ ] [-]

May 93. Spectrum; (cd)(c) **ON A LEVEL** [ ] [-]

THUNDERTHUMBS AND THE TOETSENMAN

alias **KING** and **LINDUP**

Jul 82. Polydor; (7")(12") **FREEDOM. / FREEDOM A GO GO** [ ] [ ]

MARK KING

Polydor Polydor

Jun 84. (7")(12") **I FEEL FREE. / THERE IS A DOG** [ ] [ ]

Jul 84. (m-lp)(c) **INFLUENCES** [77] [ ]
– The essential / Clocks go forward / I feel free / Pictures on the wall / There is a dog.

MIKE LINDUP

Polydor Polydor

Aug 90. (7")(c-s) **THE SPIRIT IS FREE. / JUNG** [ ] [ ]
(12"+=)(cd-s+=) – ('A'extended).

Sep 90. (cd)(c)(lp) **CHANGES** [ ] [ ]
– Changes / Lovely day / Fallen angel / The spirit is free / Desire / West Coast man / Judgement day / Life will never be the same / Paixao (passion). *(re-iss.pic-cd Oct94 on 'Voiceprint')*

LEVELLERS

Formed: Brighton, England, early 1988, and after heavy touring and some indie singles, they released album for French label 'Musidisc'. In 1991, after signing to 'China', they made UK Top 20 with album 'LEVELLING THE LAND'. • **Style:** New-age group mixing hippie travellers folk with angst theme-rock. • **Songwriters:** Group compositions except; THE DEVIL WENT DOWN TO GEORGIA (Charlie Daniels Band) / TWO HOURS (McDermott). • **Trivia:** The FENCE had one single in May 87 on 'Flag'; FROZEN WATER. / EXIT.

Recommended: LEVELLING THE LAND (*8) / WEAPON CALLED THE WORD (*7) / LEVELLERS (*6).

MARK CHADWICK – vocals, guitar, banjo (ex-FENCE) / **JEREMY CUNNINGHAM** – bass, bazouki / **CHARLIE HEATHER** – drums / **JON SEVINK** – violin (ex-FENCE) / **ALAN MILES** – vocals, guitar, mandolin, harmonica.

H A G not issued

May 89. (12"ep) **CARRY ME** [ ] [-]
– Carry me / What's in the way / The lasy days of winter / England my home /

Oct 89. (12"ep) **OUTSIDE INSIDE. / HARD FIGHT / I HAVE NO ANSWERS / BARREL OF A GUN** [ ] [-]

Musidisc not issued

Apr 90. (7") **WORLD FREAK SHOW. / BARREL OF A GUN (acoustic)** [ ] [-]
(12"+=) What you know. *(re-iss Jan92)*

Apr 90. (cd)(c)(lp) **WEAPON CALLED THE WORD** [ ] [-]
– World freak show / Carry me / Outside-inside / Together all the way / Barrel of a gun / Three friends / I have no answers / No change / Blind faith / The ballad of Robbie Jones / England my home / What you know.

Oct 90. (7") **TOGETHER ALL THE WAY. / THREE FRIENDS (re-mix) (Arfa mix short version)** [ ] [-]
(12"+=) – Cardboard box city / Social security

— **SIMON FRIEND** – guitars, vocals repl. ALAN.

China Elektra

Sep 91. (7")(c-s) **ONE WAY. / HARD FIGHT (acoustic) / THE LAST DAYS OF WINTER** [51] [ ]
(12"+=)(cd-s+=) – ('A'mix) / The Devil went down to Georgia.

Oct 91. (cd)(c)(lp) **LEVELLING THE LAND** [14] [ ]
– One way / The game / The boatman / The liberty song / Far from home / Sell out / Another man's cause / The road / The riverflow / Battle of the beanfield. *(re-iss.Jun92 hit No.22)*

Nov 91. (7")(c-s) **FAR FROM HOME. / WORLD FREAK SHOW (live)** [71] [ ]
(12"+=)(cd-s+=) – Outside inside / The boatman / Three friends (all live).

May 92. (10"pic-d-ep)(12"ep)(c-ep)(cd-ep) **15 YEARS** [11] [ ]
– 15 years / Dance before the storm / River flow (live) / Plastic Jeezus.

(In May'93 'LEVELLING THE LAND' returned to finally hit UK No.40 by Sep 93)

Jun 93. (c-s) **BELARUSE. / SUBVERT (live) / BELARUSE RETURN** [12] [ ]
(12"+=)(cd-s+=) – Is this art.

Sep 93. (cd)(c)(lp) **LEVELLERS** [2] [ ]
– Warning / 100 years of solitude / The likes of you and I / Is this art? / Dirty Davey / This garden / Broken circles / Julie / The player / Belarose.

Oct 93. (7"pic-d)(c-s) **THIS GARDEN. / LIFE (acoustic)** [12] [ ]
(12"+=)(cd-s+=) – ('A'Marcus Dravs remix) / ('A'-Banco De Gaia remix).

May 94. (7"clear-ep)(c-ep)(10"pic-d-ep)(cd-ep) **THE JULIE EP** [17] [ ]
– Julie (new version) / English civil war / Warning (live) / 100 years of solitude / The lowlands of Holland.

Jul 95. (7"pic-d) **HOPE ST. / LEAVE THIS TOWN** [12] [ ]
(7"pic-d) – ('A'side) / Miles away.
(cd-s++=)(c-s++=) – Busking on Hope Street.

Aug 95. (cd)(c)(lp) **ZEITGEIST** [1] [ ]
– Hope St. / The fear / Exodus / Maid of the river / Saturday to Sunday / 4.am / Forgotten ground / Fantasy / P.C. Keen / Just the one / Haven't made it / Leave this town / Men-an-tol.

Oct 95. (7")(c-s)(cd-s) **FANTASY. / SARA'S BEACH / SEARCHLIGHTS (extended)** [16] [ ]

— (below featured JOE STRUMMER (ex-CLASH) on piano)

Dec 95. (7"ep)(c-ep)(cd-ep) **JUST THE ONE / A PROMISE. / YOUR 'OUSE / DRINKING FOR ENGLAND** [12] [ ]

– compilations, etc. –

Mar 93. China; (cd)(c)(lp) **SEE NOTHING, HEAR NOTHING, DO SOMETHING** (early) [ ] [ ]

LEVON & THE HAWKS (see under ⇒ BAND)

Huey LEWIS & THE NEWS

Formed: San Francisco, USA . . . Spring 1980 by ex-CLOVER cohorts HUEY LEWIS and SEAN HOPPER, with 4 other ex-West Coast session men (see below), who had all backed VAN MORRISON. Country-rockers CLOVER had issued a number of 45's and 2 albums 'UNAVAILABLE' & 'LOVE ON THE WIRE' for 'Vertigo', in the late 70's. They had also featured on ELVIS

COSTELLO's 1977 debut lp 'My Aim Is True'. In 1980, HUEY LEWIS & THE NEWS issued self-titled debut album for 'Chrysalis', but this failed to sell. In 1982, they borrowed a song 'DO YOU BELIEVE IN LOVE' from former CLOVER producer Robert John Lange, and this hit the US Top 10. Its parent album 'PICTURE THIS', also reached the Top 20, and was followed the next year by a multi-million selling No.1 'SPORTS'. They remained at the top of the tree for the next 8 years, supplying America with 3 No.1 singles 'THE POWER OF LOVE', 'STUCK WITH YOU' & 'JACOB'S LADDER'. • **Style:** Pure mainstream AOR/pop, with throaty effective vox by HUEY. • **Songwriters:** LEWIS penned except many covers; BUZZ BUZZ BUZZ (Hollywood Flames) / HEART AND SOUL (hit; Exile) / HOPE YOU LOVE ME LIKE YOU SAY YOU LOVE ME (Wet Willie) / TATTOO (Phil Lynott) / JACOB'S LADDER (Bruce & John Hornsby) / SHAKE RATTLE AND ROLL (Bill Haley) / BLUE MONDAY (Fats Domino) / SEARCHING FOR MY LOVE (R.Moore) / (SHE'S) SOME KIND OF WONDERFUL (J.Ellison) / BUT IT'S ALRIGHT (J.Jackson-P.Tubbs) / IF YOU GOTTA MAKE A FOOL OF SOMEBODY (R.Clark) / MOTHER IN LAW (Allen Toussaint) / LITTLE BITTY PRETTY ONE (R.Byrd) / GOOD MORNING LITTLE SCHOOLGIRL (Lightnin' Hopkins) / STAGGER LEE (Lloyd Price) / SHE SHOT A HOLE IN MY SOUL (M.Gayden-C.Neese) / SURELY I LOVE YOU (M.Oliver-J.Bracken) / YOU LEFT THE WATER RUNNING (R.Hall-D.Penn-O.Franck) / YOUR CASH AIN'T NOTHIN' BUT TRASH (C.Calhoun) / FUNCTION AT THE JUNCTION (F.Long-E.Holland) / BETTER TO HAVE AND NOT NEED (Don Covay) / GOING DOWN SLOW (J.Olden) / etc. • **Trivia:** In the mid-80's, LEWIS sues and gets out of court settlement from RAY PARKER JR., who admits to plagiarising HUEY's 'I WANT A NEW DRUG (CALLED LOVE)' on hit 'Ghostbusters'.

Recommended: THE HEART OF ROCK AND ROLL – THE BEST OF . . . (*5)

HUEY LEWIS (b.HUGH ANTHONY CREGG III, 5 Jul'50, New York) – vox, harmonica / **SEAN HOPPER** (b.31 Mar'53) – keyboards, vocals / **JOHNNY COLLA** (b. 2 Jul'52) – guitar, saxophone (ex-SLY STONE) / **CHRIS HAYES** (b.24 Nov'57) – guitar, vocals / **MARIO CIPOLLINA** (b.10 Nov'54) – bass (ex-RONNIE MONTROSE) / **BILL GIBSON** (b.13 Jul'51) – drums, percussion, vocals.

		UK: Mercury	US: Mercury
Apr 79.	(7") **EXODISCO. / KICKBACK** (as **"AMERICAN EXPRESS"**)		
		Chrysalis	**Chrysalis**
Jul 80.	(lp)(c) **HUEY LEWIS AND THE NEWS**		

– Some of my lies are true / Sooner or later / Don't make me do it / Stop trying / Now here's you / I want you / Don't ever tell me that you love me / Hearts / Troubles in Paradise / Who cares / If you really love me you'll let me go. *(cd-iss.1986)*

Feb 82.	(lp)(c) **PICTURE THIS**		13

– Change of heart / Tell me a little lie / Giving it all up for love / Hope you love me like you say you do / Workin' for a livin' / Do you believe in love / Is it me / Whatever happened to true love / The only one / Buzz buzz buzz. *(cd-iss.1988)*

Mar 82.	(7") **DO YOU BELIVE IN LOVE. / IS IT ME**		7 Feb 82
May 82.	(7") **HOPE YOU LOVE ME LIKE YOU SAY YOU DO. /**	-	36
Jun 82.	(7"ep)(7"pic-d-ep) **TATTOO**		-

– Giving it all up for love / Do you believe in love / Some of my lies are true.

Aug 82.	(7") **WORKIN' FOR A LIVIN'. /**	-	41
Sep 83.	(lp)(c) **SPORTS**		1

– The heart of rock'n'roll / Heart and soul / Bad is bad / I want a new drug (called love) / Walking on a thin line / Finally found a home / If this is it / You crack me up / Honky tonk blues. *(re-iss.+cd.Nov84) (re-iss.Sep85 hit UK No.23) (re-iss.cd. Apr89 on 'Mobile Fidelity') (re-iss.cd Mar94)*

Nov 83.	(7") **HEART AND SOUL. / YOU CRACK ME UP**		8 Sep 83
Mar 84.	(7") **I WANT A NEW DRUG (CALLED LOVE). / FINALLY FOUND A HOME**		6 Jan 84

(12"+=) – ('A' extended) / Heart and soul / Tattoo.

Apr 84.	(7") **THE HEART OF ROCK'N'ROLL. / WORKIN' FOR A LIVIN' (live)**	-	
Jun 84.	(7")(7"sha-pic-d) **THE HEART OF ROCK'N'ROLL. / DO YOU BELIEVE IN LOVE**		-

(12"+=)(12"pic-d+=) – I want a new drug (called love) / Heart and soul / Tattoo.

Sep 84.	(7") **IF THIS IS IT. / CHANGE OF HEART**	39	6 Jul 84

(12"+=) – I want a new drug (called love) / Heart and soul.
(d7"+=) – Walkin' on a thin line (live) / Workin' for a livin' (live).

Oct 84.	(7") **WALKING ON A THIN LINE. / ?**	-	18
Aug 85.	(7")(7"pic-d-US) **THE POWER OF LOVE. / BAD IS BAD**	11	1 Jun 85

(12"+=)(d7"+=) – I want a new drug (called love) (live) / It's all right (live).

Nov 85.	(7"ep)(12"ep) **HEART AND SOUL. / HOPE YOU LOVE ME LIKE YOU SAY YOU DO / HEART OF ROCK'N'ROLL / BUZZ BUZZ (live)**	61	-
Jan 86.	(7")(7"pic-d) **THE POWER OF LOVE. / DO YOU BELIEVE IN LOVE**	9	-

(12"+=) – Back in time.

Apr 86.	(7") **THE HEART OF ROCK'N'ROLL. / HOPE YOU LOVE ME LIKE YOU SAY YOU DO**	49	-

(d7"+=)('A'ext-12"+=)(12"pic-d+=) – Bad is bad / Tattoo (Giving it all up for you).

Aug 86.	(7") **STUCK WITH YOU. / DON'T EVER TELL ME**	12	1 Jul 86

(12"+=) – Heart of rock'n'roll (live) / Trouble in Paradise (live).

Sep 86.	(lp)(c)(cd) **FORE!**	8	1

– Jacob's ladder / Stuck with you / Whole lotta lovin' / Doing it all for my baby / Simple as that / Hip to be square / I know what I like / I never walk alone / The power of love / Forest for the tree / Naturally / Simple as that. *(re-iss.cd+c Jul94)*

Nov 86.	(7") **HIP TO BE SQUARE. / SOME OF MY LIES ARE TRUE**	41	3 Oct 86

(12"+=) – ('A' version).

Jan 87.	(7") **JACOB'S LADDER. / ?**	-	1
Mar 87.	(7") **SIMPLE AS THAT. / WALKING ON A THIN LINE**	47	-

(12"+=)(cd-s+=) – Do you believe in love / Bad is bad / Workin' for a living (live).
(d7"+=) – The power of love / Do you believe in love.

Mar 87.	(7") **I KNOW WHAT I LIKE. / ?**	-	9
Jul 87.	(7") **DOING IT ALL FOR MY BABY. / JACOB'S LADDER**		6

(12"+=) – I know what I like.

Oct 87.	(7") **BAD IS BAD. / GIVING IT ALL UP FOR LOVE**		

(12"+=) – Doing it all for my baby / Back in time.

Jul 88.	(7") **PERFECT WORLD. / SLAMMIN'**	48	3

(12"+=)(cd-s+=) – Workin' for a livin' (live).

Jul 88.	(lp)(c)(cd) **SMALL WORLD**		11

– Small world (part 1) / Old Antone's / Perfect world / Bobo tempo / Small world (part 2) / Walking with the kid / World to me / Better be true / Give me the keys (and I'll drive you crazy) / Slammin'.

Sep 88.	(7") **SMALL WORLD. / ?**	-	25
Nov 88.	(7") **WORLD TO ME. / IT'S ALL RIGHT**		

(12"+=)(cd-s+=) – Naturally.

Jan 89.	(7") **GIVE ME THE KEYS (AND I'LL DRIVE YOU CRAZY). / ?**	-	47
Feb 89.	(7") **WALKING WITH THE KID. / BAD IS BAD**		

(12"+=)(cd-s+=) – Back in time / I wanna new drug (called love).

		Chrysalis	E.M.I.
May 91.	(cd)(c)(lp) **HARD AT PLAY**	39	27

– Build me up / It hit me like a hammer / Attitude / He don't know / Couple of days off / That's not me / We should be making love / The best of me / Do you love me, or what? / Don't look back / Time ain't money. *(re-iss.cd+c Mar94)*

Jul 91.	(7")(c-s) **IT HIT ME LIKE A HAMMER. / DO YOU LOVE ME, OR WHAT?**		21

(12"+=)(cd-s+=) – ('A'sax version).

Sep 91.	(7")(c-s)(US-c-s) **COUPLE DAYS OFF. / TIME AIN'T MONEY**		11 Apr 91

(12"+=) – The heart of rock'n'roll.
(cd-s++=) – ('A'version).

Nov 92.	(cd)(c)(lp) **THE HEART OF ROCK AND ROLL: THE BEST OF HUEY LEWIS & THE NEWS** (compilation)	23	

– Power of love / Hip to be square / Do you believe in love / If this is it / Some of my lies are true / Workin' for a livin' (live) / Bad is bad / I want a new drug / The heart of rock & roll / Heart and soul / Jacob's ladder / Stuck with you / Trouble in Paradise / Walking on a thin line / Perfect world / Small world (part one) / Back in time.

		Elektra	Elektra
May 94.	(7")(c-s) **(SHE'S) SOME KIND OF WONDERFUL. / IT'S ALRIGHT**		44

(cd-s+=) – Good morning little schoolgirl / Going down slow.

May 94.	(cd)(c) **FOUR CHORDS AND SEVERAL YEARS AGO**		55

– Shake rattle and roll / Blue Monday / Searching for my love / (She's) Some kind of wonderful / But it's alright / If you gotta make a fool of somebody / Mother in law / Little bitty pretty one / Good morning little schoolgirl / Stagger Lee / She shot a hole in my soul / Surely I love you / You left the water running / Your cash ain't nothin' but trash / Function at the junction / Better to have and not need / Going down slow.

Aug 94.	(c-ep)(cd-ep) **BUT IT'S ALRIGHT / (SHE'S) SOME KIND OF WONDERFUL (live) / FLIP, FLOP & FLY (live) / BUT IT'S ALRIGHT (live)**		54

– others, etc. –

Aug 95.	Old Gold; (cd-s) **OWER OF LOVE / I WANT A NEW DRUG**		-
Nov 95.	Chrysalis; (3xcd-box) **HUEY LEWIS & THE NEWS / PICTURE THIS / SPORTS**		-

Jerry Lee LEWIS

Born: 29 Sep'35, Ferriday, Louisiana, USA. In 1949, when a teenager, his parents mortgaged their house to buy him a piano which he learnt in 2 weeks. In Feb'52, after being expelled from a religious school that taught music, he married a preacher's daughter. He soon deserted her and married another bigamously shotgun style. In the same month (Oct'53), he divorced his first wife, his second wife gave birth to Jerry Lee Jr. In 1956, LEWIS went to Memphis, Tennessee with his father and through perseverance, sets up recording time in Sam Phillips' 'Sun' studios. The following year, after his debut 'CRAZY ARMS' was banned from airplay, Judd Phillips managed to get him a couple of appearances on the Steve Allen Show. This exposure enabled his second single 'WHOLE LOTTA SHAKIN' GOIN' ON' to sell massively, hitting Top 3 in US Summer of '57. Later that year, he bigamously married again!, this time secretly to his 13 year-old second cousin Myra Gale Brown. Early the following year he had two enourmous worldwide hits with classics 'GREAT BALLS OF FIRE' & 'BREATHLESS'. Meanwhile, he divorced his second wife, and gained wrath of the US churches, when his past and present lifestyle was revealed. His UK arrival in May'58, caused uproar and near tour cancellation, after newspapers printed the scandal of him being married to a minor. Although JERRY LEE made a few more sparodic returns into the charts, his career was severely dented by this late 50's hysteria. In Feb'59, Myra gave birth to his second son Steve Allen, but by the early 60's, LEWIS was increasing his intake of alcohol and pills. On Apr'62, his son Steve Allen was drowned in a swimming pool accident. A year & a half later, coinciding with LEWIS' signature for new label 'Smash', Myra produced another child, this time a daughter Phoebe Allen. In the early 70's, Myra finally divorced him, claiming neglect, etc. It didn't stop him marrying a fourth time, but this time legally, late 1971. With career going through a resurrected state in 1973, his son and tour drummer Jerry Lee Jr. was killed in a motor accident. In '76, LEWIS was involved in 2 gun incidents, one injuring his bassman NORMAN OWENS and the other outside Gracelands (Elvis Presley's home), hours after being charged with drunk driving. He signed to 'Elektra' in 1978, but after 3 albums and a serious stomach ulcer operation in 1981, he sued them. In 1982, his estranged 4th wife Jaren Pate, drowned in a swimming pool. The following year, coming up for his 50th birthday, he married again, this time to a 25 year-old, Shawn

Michelle Stevens, who was to be tragically found dead in their home 2 months later. He was suspected of foul play, but nothing was proved and LEWIS went on to marry 6th wife Kerrie McCarver (aged 22). Early in 1987, she gave birth to a son Jerry Lee Lewis III. In 1989, his biopic film story appears, featuring re-recordings of his oldies, with his part being played by actor Dennis Quaid. • **Style:** Controversial rocker, who by the late 60's, had shifted into Country-pop. Always a showman, his wild piano playing at concerts gave him nickname 'The Killer'. • **Songwriters:** Wrote own material, except CRAZY ARMS (Ray Price) / WHOLE LOTTA SHAKIN' GOIN' ON (D.Williams & Sunny Dave) / YOU WIN AGAIN + SETTIN' THE WOODS ON FIRE (Hank Williams) / WHAT'D I SAY + HIT THE ROAD JACK (Ray Charles) / BREAK UP + I'LL MAKE IT ALL UP TO YOU (Charlie Rich) / SWEET LITTLE SIXTEEN + LITTLE QUEENIE (Chuck Berry) / GOOD GOLLY MISS MOLLY + LONG TALL SALLY (Little Richard) / ME AND BOBBY McGEE (Kris Kristofferson) / GREEN GREEN GRASS OF HOME (Curly Putnam) / CHANTILLY LACE (Big Bopper) / JACK DANIELS (Heads, Hands & Feet) / DRINKIN' WINE SPO- . . . (Stick McGhee) / RITA MAE (Bob Dylan) etc. • **Trivia:** His sister LINDA GAIL LEWIS also issued solo recordings between 1965 and 74. Another cousin of his, is the TV evangelist Jimmy Swaggart.

Recommended: THE BEST OF JERRY LEE LEWIS (*7)

JERRY LEE LEWIS – vocals, piano + sessions

Date	Release	London	Sun	
Dec 56.	(7") **CRAZY ARMS. / END OF THE ROAD**	-		
Jul 57.	(7") **WHOLE LOTTA SHAKIN' GOIN' ON. / IT'LL BE ME**	8	3	Jun 57
Nov 57.	(7") **GREAT BALLS OF FIRE. / YOU WIN AGAIN**	-	2 / 95	
Dec 57.	(7") **GREAT BALLS OF FIRE. / MEAN WOMAN BLUES**	1	-	
Feb 58.	(7") **YOU WIN AGAIN. / I'M FEELIN' SORRY**		-	
Apr 58.	(7") **BREATHLESS. / DOWN THE LINE**	8	7	Feb 58
Jun 58.	(7") **THE RETURN OF JERRY LEE. / LEWIS BOOGIE**	-		
Sep 58.	(7") **BREAK-UP. / I'LL MAKE IT ALL UP TO YOU**		52 / 85	Aug 58
Jan 59.	(lp) **JERRY LEE LEWIS**			Dec 57

– Don't be cruel / Goodnight Irene / Put me down / It all depends / Ubangi stomp Crazy arms / Jambalaya / Fools like me / High school confidential ./ Where the saints go marching in Matchbox / It'll be me. *(re-iss.May82 on 'Mercury') (cd-iss.Apr86 on 'Pickwick')*

Date	Release	London	Sun	
Jan 59.	(7") **HIGH SCHOOL CONFIDENTIAL. / FOOLS LIKE ME**	12	12	May 58
Apr 59.	(7") **LOVIN' UP A STORM. / BIG BLON' BABY**	28		
Sep 59.	(7") **LET'S TALK ABOUT US. / THE BALLAD OF BILLY JOE**			
Nov 59.	(7") **LITTLE QUEENIE. / I COULD NEVER BE ASHAMED OF YOU**			
Mar 60.	(7") **I'LL SAIL MY SHIP ALONE. / IT HURT ME SO**	-	93	Dec 58
May 60.	(7") **BABY, BABY, BYE, BYE. / OLD BLACK JOE**	47		
Oct 60.	(7") **JOHN HENRY. / HANG UP MY ROCK'N'ROLL SHOES**			
Dec 60.	(7") **WHEN I GET PAID. / LOVE MADE A FOOL OF ME**	-		
Apr 61.	(7") **WHAT'D I SAY. / LIVIN' LOVIN' WRECK**	10	30	
1961.	(lp) **JERRY LEE'S GREATEST**	-		

– (part compilation)

Date	Release	London	Sun	
Sep 61.	(7") **IT WON'T HAPPEN WITH ME. / COLD COLD HEART**			
Oct 61.	(7") **AS LONG AS I LIVE. / WHEN I GET PAID**		-	
Oct 61.	(7") **SAVE THE LAST DANCE FOR ME. / AS LONG AS I LIVE**	-		
Dec 61.	(7") **MONEY. / BONNIE B**	-		
Mar 62.	(7") **I'VE BEEN TWISTIN'. / RAMBLING ROSE**			
May 62.	(lp) **JERRY LEE LEWIS VOL.2**	14		

– Money As long as I live / Country music is here to stay / Frankie and Johnny / Home / Hello baby / Let's talk about us / What'd I say Breakup Great balls of fire / Cold, cold heart / Hello Josephine *(cd-iss.Apr86 on 'Pickwick')*

Date	Release	London	Sun	
Aug 62.	(7") **SWEET LITTLE SIXTEEN. / HOW'S MY EX TREATING YOU**	38	95	
Feb 63.	(7") **GOOD GOLLY MISS MOLLY. / I CAN'T TRUST ME (IN YOUR ARMS ANYMORE)**	31		Dec 62
May 63.	(7") **TEENAGE LETTER. ("& LINDA GAIL LEWIS") / SEASONS OF MY HEART**			Feb63

Date	Release	Philips	Smash	
1963.	(7") **HIT THE ROAD JACK. / PEN AND PAPER**	-		
Mar 64.	(7") **I'M ON FIRE. / BREAD AND BUTTER MAN**		98	
1964.	(7") **SHE WAS MY BABY. / THE HOLE HE SAID HE'D DIG FOR ME**	-		
Oct 64.	(7") **HI HEAL SNEAKERS. / YOU WENT BACK ON YOUR WORD**		91	
Dec 64.	(7") **WHOLE LOTTA SHAKIN' GOIN' ON (live). / BREATHLESS (live)**	-		
Feb 65.	(7") **GREAT BALLS OF FIRE (live). / HIGH SCHOOL CONFIDENTIAL (live)**	-		
Apr 65.	(7") **BABY HOLD ME CLOSE. / I BELIEVE IN YOU**			
May 65.	(lp) **THE GREATEST LIVE SHOW ON EARTH (live)**		71	Dec 64

– Jenny Jenny / Who will the next fool be / Memphis Tennessee / Hound dog / Mean woman blues / Hi-heel sneakers / No particular place to go / Together again / Long tall Sally / Whole lotta shakin' goin' on / Little Queenie (intro) / How's my ex treating you / Johnny B.Goode / Green, green grass of home / What'd I say (part 2) / You win again / I'll sail my ship alone / Cryin' time / Money / Roll over Beethoven.

Date	Release	Philips	Smash	
Jul 65.	(7") **ROCKIN' PNEUMONIA AND THE BOOGIE WOOGIE FLU. / THIS MUST BE THE PLACE**			
Jul 65.	(lp) **THE RETURN OF ROCK**			May 65

– I believe in you / Maybeline / Flip, flop and fly / Roll over Beethoven / Baby, hold me close / Herman the hermit / Don't let go / You went back on your word / Corrine, Corrina / Sexy ways / Johhny B.Goode / Got you on my mind.

Date	Release	Philips	Smash	
1965.	(7") **GREEN GREEN GRASS OF HOME. ("& LINDA GAIL LEWIS") / BABY, YOU'VE GOT WHAT IT TAKES**	-		
Jan 66.	(lp) **COUNTRY SONGS FOR CITY FOLKS**			

– Green green grass of home / Wolverton mountain Funny how time slips away North to Alaska / The wild side of life / Ray of fire / Detroit city / Crazy arms King of the road / Seasons of my heart.

Date	Release	Philips	Smash	
1966.	(7") **STICKS AND STONES. / WHAT A HECK OF A MESS**	-		
May 66.	(lp) **MEMPHIS BEAT**	-		

– Memphis beat / Mathilda / Darlin' wine spo-dee-o-dee / Hallelujah, I love her so / She thinks I still care / Just because / Sticks and stones / Whenever you're ready / Lincoln limousine / Big boss man / Too young / The urge.

Date	Release	Philips	Smash	
Oct 66.	(7") **MEMPHIS BEAT. / IF I HAD TO DO IT OVER**			
Jan 67.	(lp) **BY REQUEST – MORE GREATEST LIVE SHOW ON EARTH (live)**			

– Introduction / Little Queenie / How's my ex treating you / Johnny B.Goode / Green green grass of home / What'd I say / You win again / I'll sail my ship alone / Crying time / Money / Roll over Beethoven.

Date	Release	Philips	Smash	
Jul 67.	(7") **IT'S A HANG-UP BABY. / HOLDIN' ON**			

Date	Release	Mercury	Smash	
Mar 68.	(7") **ANOTHER TIME ANOTHER PLACE. / WALKING THE FLOOR OVER YOU**		97	
Jul 68.	(lp) **SOUL MY WAY**			

– Turn on your love light / It's a hang-up baby / Dream baby (how long must I dream / Just dropped in Wedding bells / He took it like a man / Hey baby / Treat her right / Holdin' on Shotgun man I bet you're gonna like it.

Date	Release	Mercury	Smash	
Aug 68.	(7") **WHAT MADE MILWAUKEE FAMOUS. / ALL THE GOOD IS GONE**		94	
1968.	(7") **SHE STILL COMES AROUND. / SLIPPIN' AROUND**	-		
Jan 69.	(lp) **ANOTHER PLACE ANOTHER TIME**			Jun 68

– What made Milwaukee famous Play me a song I can cry to / On the back row / Walking the floor over you All night long / I'm a lonesome fugitive Another place, another time / Break my mind / Before the next teardrop falls / All the good is gone / We live in two different worlds (w / Linda)

Date	Release	Mercury	Smash	
Mar 69.	(7") **TO MAKE LOVE SWEETER FOR YOU. / LET'S TALK ABOUT US**			Dec 68
May 69.	(lp) **SHE STILL COMES AROUND (TO LOVE WHAT'S LEFT OF ME)**			Feb 69

– To make love sweeter for you / Let's talk about us / I can't get over you / Out of my mind / Today I started loving you again / She still comes around (to love what's lkeft of me) / Louisiana man / Release me / Listen, they're playing my song / There stands the glass / Echoes.

Date	Release	Mercury	Smash	
May 69.	(7") **LONG TALL SALLY. / JENNY JENNY**		-	
1969.	(7") **DON'T LET ME CROSSOVER. / WE LIVE IN TWO DIFFERENT WORLDS**	-		
1969.	(7") **ONE HAS MY NAME. ("& LINDA GAIL LEWIS") / I CAN'T STOP LOVING YOU**	-		
Feb 70.	(lp) **TOGETHER ("& LINDA GAIL LEWIS")**			Nov 69

– Milwaukee here I come / Jackson / Don't take it out on me / Cryin' time / Sweet thing / Secret places / Don't let me cross over / Gotta travel on / We live in two different worlds / Earth up above / Roll over Beethoven.

Date	Release	Mercury	Smash	
1970.	(7") **SHE EVEN WOKE ME UP TO SAY GOODBYE. / ECHOES**	-		
Jun 70.	(lp) **SHE EVEN WOKE ME UP TO SAY GOODBYE**			Feb 70

– Once more with feeling / Working man blues / Waiting for a train / Brown eyed handsome man / My only claim to fame / Since I met you baby / She woke me up to say goodbye / Wine me up / When the grass grows over me / You went out of your way / Echoes.

Date	Release	Mercury	Smash	
1970.	(7") **ONCE MORE WITH FEELING. / YOU WENT OUT OF YOUR WAY**	-		
Nov 70.	(7") **I CAN'T HAVE A MERRY CHRISTMAS MARY (WITHOUT YOU). / IN LOVING MEMORIES**	-		
1971.	(7") **THERE MUST BE MORE TO LOVE THAN THIS. / HOME AWAY FROM HOME**	-		
Jun 71.	(lp) **THERE MUST BE MORE TO LOVE THAN THIS**			Jan 71

– There must be more to love than this / Bottles and barstools / Rueben James / I'd be talkin' / All the time / One more time / Sweet Georgia Brown / Woman, woman / I forget more than you'll ever know / Foolaid / Home away from home / Life's little ups and downs.

Date	Release	Mercury	Smash	
1971.	(7") **TOUCHING HOME. / WOMAN, WOMAN**	-		
Jul 71.	(lp) **TOUCHING HOME**	-		
1971.	(7") **WHEN HE WALKS ON YOU. / FOOLISH KIND OF MAN**	-		
Nov 71.	(lp) **WOULD YOU TAKE ANOTHER CHANCE ON ME**	-		
Jan 72.	(7") **ME AND BOBBY McGEE. / WOULD YOU TAKE ANOTHER CHANCE ON ME**		40	
Apr 72.	(7") **CHANTILLY LACE. / THINK ABOUT IT DARLIN'**	33	43	
1972.	(7") **LONELY WEEKENDS. / TURN ON YOUR LOVELIGHT**	-		
Jun 72.	(7") **TURN ON YOUR LOVELIGHT. / I'M WALKIN'**		95	
1972.	(7") **WHO'S GONNA PLAY THIS OLD PIANO.("& LINDA GAIL LEWIS") / NO HONKY TONKS IN HEAVEN**	-		
Mar 73.	(7") **DRINKIN' WINE SPO-DEE-O-DEE. / ROCK & ROLL MEDLEY**		41	
Apr 73.	(d-lp)(c) **THE SESSION**		37	Mar 73

– Johnny B.Goode / Trouble in mind / Early morning rain / No headstone on my grave / Pledgin' my love / Memphis / Drinkin' wine spo-dee o-dee / Music to the man / Bad Moon rising / Sea cruise / Sixty minute man / Moving on down the line / What'd I say / Medley: Good golly Miss Molly – Long tall Sally – Jenny . . . – Tutti frutti – Whole lotta shakin' goin' on. *(cd-iss.May85)*

— (above recorded with PETER FRAMPTON, ALBERT LEE, RORY GALLAGHER, ALVIN LEE)

Date	Release	Mercury	Smash	
1973.	(7") **NO MORE HANGING ON. / THE MERCY OF A LETTER**	-		
1973.	(7") **NO HEADSTONE ON MY GRAVE. / JACK DANIELS (OLD No.7)**	-		
Jul 73.	(lp)(c) **LIVE AT THE INTERNATIONAL, LAS VEGAS (live)**			Oct 70

– Mean woman blues / High school confidential / Money / Matchbox / What'd I say / What'd I say (pt.2) / Great balls of fire / Good golly Miss Molly / Lewis boogie / Your cheating heart / Hound dog / Long tall Sally / Whole lotta shakin' goin' on.

Sep 73. (7") **TAKING MY MUSIC TO THE MAN. / JACK DANIELS** [ ] [-]
1973. (7") **SOMETIMES A MEMORY AIN'T ENOUGH. / I NEED TO PRAY** [-] [ ]
1974. (7") **JUST A LITTLE BIT. / MEAT MAN** [-] [ ]
Mar 74. (lp)(c) **SOUTHERN ROOTS** [ ] [ ]
– Meat man / When a man loves a woman / Hold on I'm coming / Just a little bit / Born to be a loser / The haunted house / Blueberry hill The revolutionary man / Big blue diamond / That Old Bourbon Street church.
1974. (7") **TELL TALE SIGNS. / COLD, COLD MORNING LIGHT** [-] [ ]
1974. (7") **HE CAN'T FILL MY SHOES. / TOMORROW'S TAKING BABY AWAY** [-] [ ]
1974. (7") **I CAN STILL HEAR THE MUSIC IN THE RESTROOM. / REMEMBER ME I'M THE ONE WHO LOVES YOU** [-] [ ]
1975. (7") **BOOGIE WOOGIE COUNTRY MAN. / I'M STILL JEALOUS OF YOU** [-] [ ]
1975. (7") **A DAMN GOOD COUNTRY SONG. / WHEN I TAKE MY VACATION IN HEAVEN** [-] [ ]
Nov 75. (lp)(c) **I'M A ROCKER** [ ] [ ]
1976. (7") **DON'T BOOGIE WOOGIE. / THAT KIND OF FOOL** [-] [ ]
1976. (7") **LET'S PUT IT BACK TOGETHER AGAIN. / JERRY LEE'S ROCK'N' ROLL REVIVAL SHOW** [-] [ ]
1976. (7") **THE CLOSEST THING TO YOU. / YOU BELONG TO ME** [-] [ ]
1977. (7") **MIDDLE-AGE CRAZY. / GEORGIA ON MY MIND** [-] [ ]
1978. (7") **COME ON IN. / WHO'S SORRY NOW** [-] [ ]
1978. (7") **I'LL FIND IT WHERE I CAN. / DON'T LET THE STARS GET IN YOUR EYES** [-] [ ]
Nov 78. (d-lp)(c) **BACK TO BACK** [ ] [ ]
1979. (7") **I'M SO LONESOME I COULD CRY. / PICK ME UP ON THE WAY DOWN** [-] [ ]

Elektra Elektra

May 79. (7") **ROCKIN' MY LIFE AWAY. / I WISH I WAS EIGHTEEN AGAIN** [-] [ ]
May 79. (7") **DON'T LET GO. / I WISH I WAS EIGHTEEN AGAIN** [ ] [-]
Apr 79. (lp)(c) **JERRY LEE LEWIS** [-] [ ]
– Don't let go / Rita May / Every day I have to cry / I like it like that / Number one lovin' man / Rockin' my life away / Who will the next fool be (you've got) / Personality / I wish I was eighteen again / Rockin' little angel. *(re-iss.cd. Apr92 as 'ROCKIN' MY LIFE AWAY' on 'Warners')*
Aug 79. (7") **ROCKIN' MY LIFE AWAY. / RITA MAE** [-] [ ]
1979. (7") **WHO WILL THE NEXT FOOL BE?. / RITA MAE** [-] [ ]
Nov 79. (7") **EVERYDAY I HAVE TO CRY. / WHO WILL THE NEXT FOOL BE?** [ ] [-]
Feb 80. (7") **ROCKIN' JERRY LEE. / GOOD TIME CHARLIE'S GOT THE BLUES** [ ] [ ]
Apr 80. (7") **WHEN TWO WORLDS COLLIDE. / GOOD NEWS TRAVELS FAST** [-] [ ]
Apr 80. (lp)(c) **WHEN TWO WORLDS COLLIDE** [ ] [ ]
– Rockin' Jerry Lee / Who will buy the wine / Love game / Alabama jubilee / Goodtime Charlie's got the blues / When two worlds collide / Good news travels fast / I only want a buddy not a sweetheart / Honky tonk stuff / Toot toot Tootsie
1980. (7") **HONKY TONK STUFF. / ROCKIN' JERRY LEE** [-] [ ]
Jan 81. (7") **FOLSAM PRISON BLUES. / OVER THE RAINBOW** [-] [ ]
May 81. (lp)(c) **KILLER COUNTRY** [ ] [ ]
– Folsam prison blues / I'll do it all over again / Jukebox junkie / Too weak to fight / Late night lovin' man / Change places with me / Let me on / Thirty-nine and holding / Mama, this one's for you / Over the rainbow. *(re-iss.Feb87)*
May 81. (7") **THIRTY-NINE AND HOLDING. / CHANGE PLACES WITH ME** [-] [ ]
Aug 81. (7") **I'D DO IT ALL AGAIN. / WHO WILL BUY THE WINE** [-] [ ]

— On Apr'82, he was one of the stars alongside JOHNNY CASH & CARL PERKINS to feature on 'THE SURVIVORS' album, recorded in Germany 1981 for 'CBS-Columbia'.

M.C.A. M.C.A.

Jan 83. (7") **MY FINGERS DO THE TALKIN'. / FOREVER FORGIVING** [ ] [ ]
May 83. (lp)(c) **MY FINGERS DO THE TALKING** [ ] [ ]
– My fingers do the talkin' / She sure makes leaving look easy / Why you been gone so long / She sings Amazing Grace / Better not look down / Honky tonk rock and roll piano man / Come as you were / Circumstantial evidence / Forever forgiving / Honky tonk Heaven.
May 83. (7") **CIRCUMSTANTIAL EVIDENCE. / COME AS YOU WERE** [-] [ ]
Aug 83. (7") **SHE SINGS AMAZING GRACE. / WHY YOU BEEN GONE SO LONG** [-] [ ]
Jun 84. (7") **I AM WHAT I AM. / THAT WAS THE WAY IT WAS THEN** [-] [ ]
Jul 84. (lp)(c) **I AM WHAT I AM** [ ] [ ]
– I am what I am / Only you (and you alone) / Get out your big roll daddy / Have I got a song for you / Careless hands / Candy kisses / I'm looking over a four leaf clover / Send me the pillow that you dream on / Honky tonk heart / That was the way it was then. *(re-iss.May85) (re-iss.+cd.Aug89 on 'Instant')*

not issued Sire

Jun 90. (7") **IT WAS THE WHISKEY TALKIN' (NOT ME). / ('A'-rock 'n' roll version)** [-] [ ]

Warners Warners

Jun 95. (cd)(c) **YOUNG BLOOD** [ ] [ ]
–

- compilations, others, etc. -

1958. Sun; (7"ep) **GREAT BALLS OF FIRE** [-] [ ]
– Whole lotta shakin' goin' on / Mean woman blues / I'm feeling sorry / Turn around.
Nov 58. London/ US= Sun; (7"ep) **JERRY LEE LEWIS** [ ] [ ]
May 59. London/ US= Sun; (7"ep) **JERRY LEE LEWIS No.2** [ ] [ ]
May 59. London/ US= Sun; (7"ep) **JERRY LEE LEWIS No.3** [ ] [ ]
Nov 61. London; (7"ep) **JERRY LEE LEWIS No.4** [ ] [-]
Sep 62. London; (7"ep) **JERRY LEE LEWIS No.5** [ ] [-]
Mar 63. London; (7"ep) **JERRY LEE LEWIS No.6** [ ] [-]
Aug 63. London; (7"ep) **FOUR MORE FROM JERRY LEE LEWIS** [ ] [-]
Mar 64. London; (7") **LEWIS BOOGIE. / BONNIE B** [ ] [-]
Jul 65. London; (7") **I KNOW WHAT IT MEANS. / CARRY ME BACK TO OLD VIRGINIA** [ ] [ ]
Nov 65. London; (lp) **WHOLE LOTTA SHAKIN' GOIN' ON** [ ] [-]
(re-iss.+c.Oct74) (re-iss.10"lp.Jul82 on 'Charly') (re-iss.Jul86 on 'Sun')
Jun 67. London; (lp) **BREATHLESS** [ ] [-]
1960. Philips Int.; (7") **IN THE MOOD. (as "The HAWK") / I GET THE BLUES WHEN IT RAINS** [-] [ ]
Jun 64. Philips/ US= Smash; (lp) **GOLDEN HITS OF JERRY LEE LEWIS** [ ] [ ]
(re-iss.1976 on 'Mercury')
Apr 65. Philips; (lp) **LIVE AT THE STAR CLUB, HAMBURG (live w / NASHVILLE TEENS)** [ ] [-]
(re-iss.Feb80 on 'Mercury') (re-iss.Sep84)
Mar 67. Philips; (7"ep) **COUNTRY STYLE** [ ] [-]
Aug 87. Philips; (lp)(c) **THE VERY BEST OF JERRY LEE LEWIS** [ ] [-]
Oct 67. London/ US= Smash; (7") **TURN ON YOUR LOVELIGHT. / SHOTGUN MAN** [ ] [ ]
May 68. London/ US= Smash; (7") **WHAT'D I SAY. / I'VE BEEN TWISTING** [ ] [ ]
Apr 68. Mercury/ US= Smash; (7") **GREAT BALLS OF FIRE. / WHOLE LOTTA SHAKIN' GOIN' ON** [ ] [ ]
Sep 69. Mercury/ US= Smash; (lp) **I'M ON FIRE** [ ] [-]
Sep 69. Mercury/ US= Smash; (lp) **COUNTRY MUSIC HALL OF FAME HITS VOL.1** [ ] [ ] May 69
Sep 69. Mercury/ US= Smash; (lp) **COUNTRY MUSIC HALL OF FAME HITS VOL.2** [ ] [ ] May 69
(above re-iss.d-lp 'THE BEST OF . . . ' Apr81)
Sep 70. Mercury/ US= Smash; (lp)(c) **THE BEST OF JERRY LEE LEWIS** [ ] [ ]
Jun 72. Mercury; (lp)(c) **THE KILLER ROCKS ON** [ ] [ ] Apr 72
Oct 74. Mercury; (lp)(c) **FAN CLUB CHOICE** [ ] [-]
Feb 87. Mercury; (cd) **THE 30th ANNIVERSARY** [ ] [ ]
Nov 89. Mercury; (3xlp)(3xc)(3xcd) **THE KILLER: THE MERCURY YEARS 1963-1968, VOL.1 / 1969-1972, VOL.2 / 1973-1977, VOL.3** [ ] [ ]
Oct 68. Fontana; (lp) **GOT YOU ON MY MIND** [ ] [-]
Below releases on 'Sun International' until stated.
1969. (7") **INVITATION TO YOUR PARTY. / I COULD NEVER BE ASHAMED OF YOU** [-] [ ]
1969. (7") **ONE MINUTE PAST ETERNITY. / FRANKIE AND JOHNNY** [-] [ ]
1970. (7") **I CAN'T SEEM TO SAY GOODBYE. / GOODNIGHT IRENE** [-] [ ]
1970. (7") **WAITING FOR A TRAIN. / BIG LEGGED WOMAN** [-] [ ]
Oct 70. (7") **BREATHLESS. / GREAT BALLS OF FIRE** [ ] [ ]
Oct 70. (lp) **ORIGINAL GOLDEN HITS VOL.1** [ ] [ ] Sep 69
Jan 71. (lp) **ORIGINAL GOLDEN HITS VOL.2** [ ] [ ] Sep 69
Mar 71. (lp) **A TASTE OF COUNTRY** [ ] [ ]
Aug 71. (lp) **ROCKIN' RHYTHM AND BLUES** [ ] [ ]
Sep 71. (7"m) **GREAT BALLS OF FIRE. / WHOLE LOTTA SHAKIN' GOIN' ON / HIGH SCHOOL CONFIDENTIAL** [ ] [ ]
Oct 71. (lp) **THE GOLDEN CREAM OF THE COUNTRY** [ ] [ ]
Oct 71. (lp) **JOHNNY CASH AND JERRY LEE LEWIS SING HANK WILLIAMS** [ ] [ ]
Nov 71. (lp) **MONSTERS** [ ] [ ]
1971. (7") **LOVE ON BROADWAY. / MATCHBOX** [-] [ ]
1972. (7") **YOUR LOVIN' WAYS. / I CAN'T TRUST ME (IN YOUR ARMS)** [-] [ ]
Aug 72. (lp) **OLD TYME COUNTRY MUSIC** [ ] [ ]
Nov 72. (lp) **SUNDAY DOWN SOUTH (w / JOHNNY CASH)** [ ] [ ]
1973. (7") **I CAN'T TRUST ME (IN YOUR ARMS). / GOOD ROCKIN' TONIGHT** [-] [ ]
Apr 74. (d-lp) **ROCKIN' UP A STORM** [ ] [ ]
(re-iss.Feb87)
Jul 74. (lp) **ROCKIN' AND FREE** [ ] [ ]
1978. (7") **AM I TO BE THE ONE. / MATCHBOX** [-] [ ]
Jan 79. (lp) **DUETS** [ ] [ ]
1979. (7") **HELLO JOSEPHINE. / COLD COLD HEART** [-] [ ]
May 80. (lp) **TRIO PLUS (w / other 'Sun' artists)** [ ] [ ]
Jul 82. (10"lp) **THE PUMPIN' PIANO CAT** [-] [ ]
(re-iss.lp Jul86)
Jul 82. (10"lp) **THE WILD ONE AT THE HIGH SCHOOL HOP** [ ] [ ]
(re-iss.lp Aug86)
1983. (7"ep) **THE FABULOUS JERRY LEE LEWIS VOL.1** [ ] [-]
1983. (7"ep) **THE FABULOUS JERRY LEE LEWIS VOL.2** [ ] [-]
Sep 89. (8xcd-box) **THE SUN YEARS** [ ] [ ]
Nov 89. (lp) **KILLER'S BIRTHDAY CAKE** [ ] [ ]
Nov 89. (lp) **KILLER'S RHYTHM & BLUES** [ ] [ ]
1973. Hallmark; (lp)(c) **GREAT BALLS OF FIRE** [ ] [-]
(re-iss.10"lp Jul82 & lp Aug86 on 'Charly', re-as d-lp+cd.Jul89) (cd re-iss.Dec89 on 'Pickwick')
Apr 75. Hallmark; (lp)(c) **GOOD ROCKIN' TONIGHT** [ ] [-]
(re-iss.Feb80 on 'Sun')
Mar 76. Hallmark; (d-lp)(c) **THE JERRY LEE LEWIS COLLECTION** [ ] [-]

Note; All below on UK 'Charly' until stated.

Oct 75. (lp) **JERRY LEE LEWIS AND HIS PUMPING PIANO** [ ] [-]
Oct 75. (lp) **RARE JERRY LEE LEWIS VOL.1** [ ] [-]
Oct 75. (lp) **RARE JERRY LEE LEWIS VOL.2** [ ] [-]
Oct 76. (lp) **THE ORIGINAL JERRY LEE LEWIS** [ ] [-]
Dec 76. (7"ep) **LEWIS BOOGIE** [ ] [-]
Mar 77. (lp) **NUGGETS** [ ] [-]
Apr 77. (7") **OLD BLACK JOE. / THE RETURN OF JERRY LEE** [ ] [ ]
Aug 77. (7") **IN THE MOOD. / GREAT BALLS OF FIRE** [ ] [-]
Dec 77. (lp) **NUGGETS VOL.2** [ ] [-]
Aug 78. (7") **WHOLE LOTTA SHAKIN' GOIN' ON. / (other artist)** [ ] [-]
Oct 78. (lp) **THE ESSENTIAL JERRY LEE LEWIS** [ ] [-]
Dec 78. (7") **SAVE THE LAST DANCE FOR ME. / AM I TO BE THE ONE (by "JERRY LEE LEWIS & FRIEND")** [ ] [-]
Dec 78. (12") **BREATHLESS. / HIGH SCHOOL CONFIDENTIAL** [ ] [-]
Feb 79. (7") **MY GIRL JOSEPHINE. / WHAT'D I SAY** [ ] [-]
Feb 81. (lp) **JERRY LEE'S GREATEST** [ ] [ ]
Mar 86. (cd) **FERRIDAY FIREBALL** [ ] [-]
Apr 87. (cd) **RARE AND ROCKIN'** [ ] [-]
Mar 89. (cd-ep) **GREAT BALLS OF FIRE / HIGH SCHOOL CONFIDENTIAL / BREATHLESS / WHOLE LOTTA SHAKIN' GOIN' ON** [ ] [-]
Feb 93. (cd) **GOOD ROCKIN' TONITE** [ ] [-]
Mar 93. (11xcd-box) **THE SUN YEARS** [ ] [-]
Nov 78. Arcade; (d-lp) **SHAKIN' JERRY LEE** [ ] [-]
Jul 79. Hammer; (lp) **JERRY LEE LEWIS** [ ] [-]
Sep 79. Hammer; (7") **LONG TALL SALLY. / BREATHLESS** [ ] [-]
Jan 80. Bulldog; (7"ep) **JERRY LEE LEWIS** [ ] [-]
– Bonnie B / Baby baby bye bye / Down the line / I'm feeling sorry.
Feb 80. Bravo; (lp) **GOOD GOLLY MISS MOLLY** [ ] [-]
Apr 81. Old Gold; (7") **GREAT BALLS OF FIRE. / WHOLE LOTTA SHAKIN' GOIN' ON** [ ] [-]
Feb 89. Old Gold; (12"m) **GREAT BALLS OF FIRE / WHOLE LOTTA SHAKIN' GOIN' ON. / WHAT'D I SAY (part 1 & 2)** [ ] [-]
Sep 83. Scoop; (7"ep)(c-ep) **6 TRACK HITS** [ ] [-]
Nov 84. Topline; (lp)(c) **THE KILLER STRIKES** [ ] [-]
Feb 85. Cambra; (lp)(c) **JERRY LEE LEWIS** [ ] [-]
Mar 86. Pickwick; (d-lp)(c) **THE JERRY LEE LEWIS COLLECTION** [ ] [-]
Apr 88. Pickwick; (cd) **THE COUNTRY SOUND OF JERRY LEE LEWIS** [ ] [-]
Jul 86. Castle; (d-lp)(c) **THE COLLECTION** [ ] [-]
(cd-iss.Dec90)
Apr 87. Starblend; (lp)(c) **AT THE COUNTRY STORE** [ ] [-]
(cd-iss.Mar89)
Nov 87. Zu Jazz; (lp)(c) **KEEP YOUR HANDS OFF IT** [ ] [ ]
Oct 88. Zu Jazz; (lp)(c) **DON'T DROP IT** [ ] [ ]
Apr 89. Ocean; (lp)(c)(cd) **THE CLASSIC JERRY LEE LEWIS** [ ] [-]
May 89. Magnum Force; (cd) **LIVE IN ITALY (live)** [ ] [-]
Jul 89. Polydor; (lp)(c)(cd) **GREAT BALLS OF FIRE: ORIGINAL MOTION PICTURE SOUNDTRACK** [ ] [62]
Sep 89. Polydor; (7")(12") **GREAT BALLS OF FIRE. / BREATHLESS** [ ] [ ]
Feb 90. Instant; **(cd,c,lp) ROCKET** [ ] [ ]
Dec 90. See For Miles; (cd)(lp) **THE EP COLLECTION** [ ] [-]
Apr 91. Ace; (cd) **LIVE AT THE VAPORS CLUB (live)** [ ] [-]
Dec 91. Ace; (cd) **HONKY TONK ROCK'N'ROLL PIANO MAN** [ ] [-]
Apr 92. Ace; (cd) **PRETTY MUCH COUNTRY** [ ] [-]
Sep 91. Electrovert; (cd) **THE KILLERS' PRIVATE STASH** [ ] [-]
Feb 92. Tomato; (d-cd) **THE COMPLETE PALAMINO SESSIONS** [-] [ ]
Sep 92. Music Club; (cd)(c) **THE BEST OF JERRY LEE LEWIS** [ ] [-]
– Great balls of fire / Whole lotta shakin' goin' on / Drinkin' wine spo-dee-o-dee / Lewis boogie / Mean woan blues / You win again / Jailhouse rock / Lovin' up a storm / Pumpin' piano rock / High school confidential / Fools like me / Down the line / Breathless / Wild one / Milkshake mademoiselle / Pink pedal pushers / I could never be ashamed of you / In the mood / Let's talk about us / What'd I say.
Jun 93. Tomato; (d-cd) **THE COMPLETE PALOMINO CLUB RECORDINGS** [ ] [ ]
Aug 93. Tomato; (cd) **HEARTBREAKER** [ ] [ ]
Mar 94. Spectrum; (cd)(c) **CHANTILLY LACE** [ ] [-]
Mar 94. Charly; (cd)(c) **GREAT BALLS OF FIRE** [ ] [-]
May 94. Charly; (cd) **TWO ON ONE** (w / CARL PERKINS) [ ] [-]
Apr 94. See For Miles; (cd) **THE EP COLLECTION . . . PLUS: VOLUME 2** [ ] [-]
Jul 94. Success; (cd)(c) **GREATEST HITS LIVE** [ ] [-]
Jul 94. Success; (cd)(c) **GREAT BALLS OF FIRE** [ ] [-]
Aug 94. Legends In Music; (cd) **JERRY LEE LEWIS** [ ] [-]
Dec 94. Bear Family; (9xcd-box) **LOCUST YEARS & THE RETURN TO THE PROMISED LAND** [ ] [ ]
Feb 95. B.A.M.; (cd) **PEARLS OF THE PAST** [ ] [-]
Apr 95. Charly; (4xcd-box+book) **SUN CLASSICS** [ ] [-]
Apr 95. Wisepack; (d-cd) **THE ESSENTIAL COLLECTION** [ ] [-]
May 95. Pickwick; (cd)(c) **KILLER HITS! – THE ORIGINAL CLASSICS** [ ] [-]
Jul 95. Summit; (cd) **HIGH SCHOOL CONFIDENTIAL** [ ] [-]

Jaki LIEBZEIT (see under ⇒ CAN)

Gordon LIGHTFOOT

Born: 17 Nov'38, Orillia, Ontario, Canada. In the late 50's, he went to Westlake College, L.A., to study orchestration, but he returned to Toronto after a year to work as a jingle writer. He cut a few solo singles during the early 60's, and had a couple of his songs recorded by IAN & SYLVIA (TYSON). Others followed suit, prompting Albert Grossman to manage him and obtain deal with 'United Art' records in 1965. His first 45 for the label 'JUST LIKE TOM THUMB'S BLUES' flopped, although b-side 'RIBBON OF DARKNESS', became a C&W hit for MARTY ROBBINS. After a series of lp's for label, he switched to the 'Reprise' label in 1970, and started working with producer Lenny Waronker. In 1971 he hit US Top 5 with single 'IF YOU COULD READ MY MIND', which was lifted from lp 'SIT DOWN YOUNG STRANGER'. He continued to chart systematically throughout the 70's, peaking at US No.1 in 1974, with single & album 'SUNDOWN'. • **Style:** Deep folk-singer, whose DYLAN aspirations were forgotten when finding own identity in the 70's. Compared light-heartedly to his singing compatriot LEONARD COHEN, although he was certainly a little brighter in tone. • **Songwriters:** Prolific pensmith, who also included a few covers; ME AND BOBBY McGEE (Kris Kristofferson) / etc. Co-wrote 1986 effort with DAVID FOSTER. • **Trivia:** Folk-pop act PETER, PAUL & MARY had a US Top 30 hit early 1965 with his 'FOR LOVIN' ME'.

Recommended: THE BEST OF GORDON LIGHTFOOT (*6)

as The TWO TONES (GORDON LIGHTFOOT & TERRY WHELAN) he made debut 45 as

GORD LIGHTFOOT

Decca / Chateau

1962. (7") **(REMEMBER ME) I'M THE ONE. / DAISY DOO** [ ] [ ]

GORDIE LIGHTFOOT

Fontana / Chateau

1963. (7") **NEGOTIATIONS. / IT'S TOO LATE, HE WINS** [ ] [ ]
— (above 2 singles also iss. US on 'ABC Paramount' around 64-65)
1964. (7") **THE DAY BEFORE YESTERDAY. / TAKE CARE OF YOURSELF** [ ] [ ]
1964. (7") **I'LL MEET YOU IN MICHEGAN. / IS MY BABY BLUE TONIGHT** [-] [ ]

GORDON LIGHTFOOT

– vocals, guitar, piano with **DAVID REA + BRUCE LANGHORNE** – guitar / **BILL LEE** – bass

U.A. / U.A.

Oct 65. (7") **JUST LIKE TOM THUMB'S BLUES. / RIBBON OF DARKNESS** [ ] [ ]
Jan 66. (lp) **LIGHTFOOT** [ ] [ ]
– Rich man's spiritual / Long river / The way I feel / For lovin' me / The first time / Changes / Early morning rain / Steel rail blues / Sixteen miles / I'm not sayin' / Pride of man / Ribbon of darkness / Oh, Linda / Peaceful waters.
1966. (7") **FOR LOVIN' ME. / SPIN SPIN** [-] [ ]
— **RED SHEA** – guitar / **JOHN STOCKFISH** – bass
1967. (lp) **THE WAY I FEEL** [ ] [ ]
– Walls / If you got it / Softly / Crossroads / A minor ballad / Go-go round / Rosanna / Home from the forest / I'll be alright / Song for a winter's night / Canadian railroad trilogy / The way I feel. *(re-iss.1971 on 'Sunset') (cd-iss.Dec95 on 'BGO')*
1967. (7") **GO-GO ROUND. / I'LL BE ALRIGHT** [-] [ ]
1967. (7") **THE WAY I FEEL. / PEACEFUL WATERS** [-] [ ]
Apr 68. (7") **BLACK DAY IN JULY. / PUSSY WILLOWS, CAT TAILS** [ ] [ ]
May 68. (lp) **DID SHE MENTION MY NAME** [ ] [ ]
– The last time I saw her / Black day in July / May I / Magnificent outpouring / Does your mother know / The mountain and Maryann / Pussywillows cat tails / I want to hear it from you / Something very special / Boss man / Did she mention my name.
Mar 69. (7") **THE CIRCLE IS SMALL. / DOES YOUR MOTHER KNOW** [ ] [-]
Mar 69. (7") **BITTER GREEN. / DOES YOUR MOTHER KNOW** [-] [ ]
May 69. (7") **BITTER GREEN. / MAY I** [ ] [-]
1969. (lp) **BACK HERE ON EARTH** [-] [ ]
– Long way back home / Unsettled ways / Long thin dawn / Bitter green / The circle is small / Marie Christine / Cold hands from New York / Affair on 8th Avenue / Don't beat me down / The gypsy / If I could / Wherefor & why.
Sep 69. (7") **EARLY MORNING RAIN. / THE GYPSY** [ ] [ ]
(re-iss.1971)
Feb 70. (lp) **SUNDAY CONCERT (live)** [ ] [ ] Nov 69
– Canadian railroad trilogy / Cat-tails / Pussy willows / Boss man / Softly / Ballad of Yarmouth Castle / Bitter green / Apology / Medley: Ribbon of darkness / I'm not sayin' / The lost children / In a windowpane / Peaceful waters / Oh, Linda.
– *(cd-iss.Mar93 with extra studio tracks)*
— **RICK HAYNES** – bass repl. JOHN

Reprise / Reprise

Nov 70. (7") **ME AND BOBBY McGEE. / THE PONY MAN** [-] [ ]
Jan 71. (lp)(c) **SIT DOWN YOUNG STRANGER** [ ] [12] May 70
– Minstrel of the dawn / Me and Bobby McGee / Approaching Lavender / Saturday clothes / Cobweb and dust / Poor little Alison / Sit down young stranger / If you could read my mind / Baby it's alright / Your love's return / The pony man. *(re-titled in UK 'IF YOU COULD READ MY MIND' Jun71)(cd-iss.Feb93)*
May 71. (7") **IF YOU COULD READ MY MIND. / POOR LITTLE ALISON** [30] [5] Dec 70
Jun 71. (7") **TALKING IN YOUR SLEEP. / NOUS VIVONS ENSEMBLE** [-] [64]
— now w /diff. session people.
Jun 71. (lp)(c) **SUMMER SIDE OF LIFE** [ ] [38] May 71
– 10 degrees and getting colder / Miguel / Go my way / Summer side of life / Cotton Jenny / Talking in your sleep / Nous vivons ensemble / Same old loverman / Redwood Hill / Love and maple syrup / Cabaret.
Aug 71. (7") **SUMMER SIDE OF LIFE. / LOVE AND MAPLE SYRUP** [-] [98]
— the last 1970 personnel added **TERRY CLEMENTS** – guitar

Mar 72. (7") **BEAUTIFUL. / DON QUIXOTE** [-] [58]
Apr 72. (lp)(c) **DON QUIXOTE** [44] [42] Mar 72
– Don Quixote / Christian Island / Alberta bound / Looking at the rain / Ordinary man brave mountaineers / Ode to big blue second cup of coffee / Beautiful / On Susan's floor / The patriot's dream.
May 72. (7") **BEAUTIFUL. / CHRISTIAN ISLAND** [ ] [-]
Nov 72. (7") **THE SAME OLD OBSESSION. / YOU ARE WHAT I AM** [-] [ ]
Nov 72. (lp)(c) **OLD DAN'S RECORDS** [ ] [95]
– Old Dan's records / Farewell to Annabelle / That same old obsession / Lazy mornin' / You are what I am / Can't depend on love / My pony won't go / It's worth believin' / Mother of a miner's child / Hi way songs.
Jan 73. (7") **CAN'T DEPEND ON LOVE. / IT'S WORTH BELIEVIN'** [ ] [ ]

— brought back **JOHN STOCKFISH** – bass

May 74. (lp)(c) **SUNDOWN** [45] [1] Jan 74
– Sundown / Somewhere U.S.A. / High and dry / Seven Island suite / Circle of steel / Is there anyone home / The watchman's gone / Carefree highway / The list / Too late for prayin'. *(US re-iss.1980 on 'Mobile')(cd-iss.Feb93)*
May 74. (7") **SUNDOWN. / TOO LATE FOR PRAYIN'** [33] [1] Apr 74
Nov 74. (7") **CAREFREE HIGHWAY. / SEVEN ISLAND SUITE** [ ] [10] Aug 74
Mar 75. (lp)(c) **COLD ON THE SHOULDER** [ ] [10] Feb 75
– Rainy day people / Bells of the evening / Rainbow trout / Cold on the shoulder / A tree to weak to stand / All the lovely ladies / Fine as can be / Now and then / Slide on over / Bend with the water / Soul is the rock / Cherokee band.
Apr 75. (7") **RAINY DAY PEOPLE. / CHEROKEE BAND** [ ] [26] Mar 75

— live band now **RED SHEA + TERRY CLEMENTS** – guitar / **RICK HAYNES** – bass / **PEE WEE CHARLES** – steel guitar / **JIM GORDON** – (studio) drums

Dec 75. (d-lp)(c) **GORD'S GOLD** (remixed compilation) [ ] [34] Nov 75
– I'm not sayin' – Ribbon of darkness / Song for a winter's night / Canadian railroad trilogy / Softly / For lovin' me – Did she mention my name / Affair on 8th Avenue / Steel rail blues / Wherefore and why / Bitter green / Early morning rain / Minstrel of the dawn / Sundown / Beautiful / Summer side of life / Rainy day people / Cotton Jenny / Don Quixote / Circle of steel / Old Dan's records / If you could read my mind / Cold on the shoulder / Carefree highway.
Aug 76. (lp)(c) **SUMMERTIME DREAM** [ ] [12] Jun 76
– The wreck of the Edmund Fitzgerald / Race among the ruins / I'm not supposed to care / I'd do it again / Never too close / Protocol / The house you live in / Summertime dream / Spanish moss / Too many clues in the room.
Nov 76. (7") **THE WRECK OF THE EDMUND FITZGERALD. / THE HOUSE YOU LIVE IN** [40] [2] Aug 76
Feb 77. (7") **RACE AMONG THE RUINS. / PROTOCOL** [-] [65]

Warners Warners

Feb 78. (lp)(c) **ENDLESS WIRE** [ ] [22] Jan 78
– Endless wire / If there's a reason / Daylight Katy / The circle is small (I can see it in your eyes) / Sweet Guinevere / Hang dog hotel room / Dreamland / Songs of the minstrel / Sometime I don't mind / If children had wings.
Feb 78. (7") **THE CIRCLE IS SMALL (I CAN SEE IT IN YOUR EYES). / SWEET GUINEVERE** [ ] [33]
Jul 78. (7") **DAYLIGHT KATY. / HANG DOG HOTEL ROOM** [41] [ ]
Nov 78. (7") **DREAMLAND. / SONGS THE MINISTER SANG** [-] [ ]
Jun 80. (lp)(c) **DREAM STREET ROSE** [ ] [60] Apr 80
– Sea of tranquility / Ghosts of Cape Horn / Dream street Rose / On the high seas / Whisper my name / If you need me / Hey you / Make way for the lady / Mister rock of ages / Auctioneer.
Jun 80. (7") **DREAM STREET ROSE. / MAKE WAY FOR THE LADY** [ ] [ ]
Feb 82. (lp)(c) **SHADOWS** [ ] [87]
– 14 karat gold / In my fashion / Shadows / Blackberry wine / Heaven help the Devil / Thank you for the promises / Baby step back / All I'm after / Triangle / I'll do anything / She's not the same.
Apr 82. (7") **BABY STEP BACK. / THANK YOU FOR THE PROMISES** [ ] [50]
Jul 83. (lp)(c) **SALUTE** [ ] [ ]
– Salute (a lot more livin' to do) / Gotta get away / Whispers of the north / Someone to believe in / Romance / Knotty pine / Biscuit city / Without you / Tattoo / Broken dreams.
Sep 86. (7") **STAY LOOSE. / MORNING GLORY** [-] [ ]
Sep 86. (lp)(c) **EAST OF MIDNIGHT** [ ] [ ] Aug 86
– Stay loose / Morning glory / East of midnight / A lesson in love / Anything for love / Let it ride / Ecstasy made easy / You just gotta be / A passing ship / I'll tag along.
Nov 86. (7") **ECSTASY MADE EASY. / MORNING GLORY** [-] [ ]

— LIGHTFOOT's band now incl.**TERRY CLEMENTS** – guitar / **RICK HAYNES** – bass / **MIKE HEFFERNAN** – keyboards / **BARRY KEANE** – drums

Nov 88. (d-lp)(c)(cd) **GORD'S GOLD, VOLUME II** (remixed compilation) [ ] [ ]
– If it should please you / Endless wire / Hangdog hotel room / I'm not supposed to care / High and dry / The wreck of the Edmund Fitzgerald / The pony man / Race among the ruins / Christian Island / All the lovely ladies / Alberta bound / Cherokee band / Triangle / Shadows / Make way (for the lady) / Ghosts of Cape Horn / Baby step back / It's worth believin'.

– compilations, others, etc –

Sep 69. United Artists; (lp) **EARLY LIGHTFOOT** [-] [ ]
Jul 71. United Artists; (lp)(c) **CLASSIC LIGHTFOOT (THE BEST OF GORDON LIGHTFOOT, VOL.2)** [ ] [ ] Jun 71
Aug 74. United Artists; (d-lp)(c) **THE VERY BEST OF GORDON LIGHTFOOT VOL.I & II** [ ] [ ] Jul 74
1966. President; (7") **ADIOS ADIOS. / MY BABY IS BLUE TONIGHT** [ ] [ ]
1972. Reprise; (7"ep) **IF YOU COULD READ MY MIND / ME AND BOBBY McGEE. / SUMMER SIDE OF LIFE / TALKING IN YOUR SLEEP** [ ] [-]
1974. Reprise; (7"ep) **IF YOU COULD READ MY MIND / CHRISTIAN ISLAND. / ODE TO BIG BLUE SECOND CUP OF COFFEE / ME AND BOBBY McGEE** [ ] [-]
1975. Reprise; (d-lp) **TWO ORIGINALS OF . . .** [ ] [ ]
– (albums 'DON QUIXOTE' + 'SUMMER SIDE OF LIFE')
May 81. Reprise; (lp)(c) **THE BEST OF GORDON LIGHTFOOT** [ ] [ ]
– Early morning rain / The wreck of Edmund Fitzgerald / Carefree highway / Minstrel / Rainy day people / Sundown / Summer side of life / Cold on the shoulder / Endless wire / If you could read my mind / Canadian railroad trilogy / If there's a reason / Cotton Jenny / Song for the winters night / Daylight Katy / Old Dan's records / Me and Bobby McGee / The circle is small.
Nov 76. Sunset; (lp) **EARLY MORNING RAIN** [ ] [-]
1969. Warners; (7") **I'M NOT SAYIN'. / FOR LOVING ME** [ ] [ ]
Feb 92. Bear Family; (cd) **LIGHTFOOT! / THE WAY I FEEL** [ ] [ ]
Mar 93. Bear Family; (cd) **DID SHE MENTION MY NAME / BACK HERE ON EARTH** [ ] [ ]
Apr 93. B.G.O.; (cd) **EARLY LIGHTFOOT / SUNDAY CONCERT** [ ] [-]

LIGHTNING SEEDS

Formed: By IAN BROUDIE, 4 Aug'58, Liverpool, England. He had been an integral part of BIG IN JAPAN (Autumn 77-78), before joining The SECRETS and then London-based band ORIGINAL MIRRORS late '78. They cut one eponymous lp early 1980 for 'Mercury', but he left to go into production work. He was chosen by ECHO & THE BUNNYMEN, The WAH!, The FALL and ICICLE WORKS, amongst many to want his services. He helped form The CARE in 1983, with ex-WILD SWANS leader PAUL SIMPSON, but they disbanded after around a year and 3 singles. BROUDIE re-surfaced in 1989, when he and a few session people formed The LIGHTNING SEEDS. They signed to new label 'Ghetto', and immediately scored with debut 45 'PURE'. This and its parent album 'CLOUDCUCKOOLAND', surprised many by also making US lists in '91. • **Style:** One-man alternative rock-pop studio act, similiar to NEW ORDER, PET SHOP BOYS or FRAZIER CHORUS. • **Songwriters:** BROUDIE obviously, except SOMETHING IN THE AIR (Thunderclap Newman) / HANG ON TO A DREAM (Tim Hardin). LUCKY YOU + FEELING LAZY + MY BEST DAY were co-written & sung w / **TERRY HALL + IAN McNABB + ALISON MOYET respectively. The track OPEN GOALS sampled; LOOK KA PY PY (Meters). • Trivia:** The track 'PERSUASION' featured IAN McCULLOCH (ex-ECHO & THE BUNNYMEN). He has also produced NORTHSIDE, PRIMITIVES and TERRY HALL.

Recommended: CLOUDCUCKOOLAND (*7).

IAN BROUDIE – vocals, keyboards, guitar / with **PETER COYLE + PAUL SIMPSON** (ex-LOTUS EATERS + WILD SWANS)

Ghetto M.C.A.

Jun 89. (7")(c-s) **PURE. / FOOLS** [16] [31] Apr 90
(12"+=) – God help them.
(cd-s++=) – All I want.
Oct 89. (7") **JOY. / FRENZY** [ ] [ ]
(12"+=)(cd-s+=) – Control The Flame.
(US cd-ep+=) Hang on to a dream.
Jan 90. (cd)(c)(lp) **CLOUDCUCKOOLAND** [51] [46]
– All I want / Bound in a nutshell / Pure / Sweet dreams / The nearly man / Joy / Love explosion / Don't let go / Control the flame / The price / Fools / Frenzy. *(c+=)(cd+=)*– God help them.
Feb 90. (7") **SWEET DREAMS. /** (withdrawn) [ ] [ ]
Apr 90. (7")(c-s) **ALL I WANT. / PERSUASION** [ ] [ ]
(12"+=)(cd-s+=) – ('A'extended).

Virgin M.C.A.

Mar 92. (7")(c-s) **THE LIFE OF RILEY. / SOMETHING IN THE AIR** [28] [98]
(12"+=)(cd-s+=) – Marooned.
(US c-s) ('A' side) / excerpts: Blowing bubbles – Sense – A cool place.
Apr 92. (cd)(c)(lp) **SENSE** [53] [ ]
– Sense / The life of Riley / Blowing bubbles / Cool place / Where flowers fade / A smal slice of Heaven / Tingle tangle / Happy / Marooned / Tracking up, looking down.
May 92. (7")(c-s) **SENSE. / FLAMING SWORD** [31] [-]
(12"+=)(cd-s+=) – The life of Riley (remix) / Hang on to a dream.
Apr 92. (c-s) **SENSE. / TINGLE TANGLE** [-] [ ]
(cd-s) ('A' side) / The life of Riley / Flaming sword / Lucifer Sam.

— **BROUDIE** added **SIMON ROGERS** – instruments, co-producer / **CLIVE LAYTON** – Hammond organ / **MARINA VAN RODY** – vocals (Why Why Why). The live band **BROUDIE** – vocals, guitar / **w / ALI KANE** – keyboards / **MARTIN CAMPBELL** – bass / **CHRIS SHARROCK** – drums

Epic Epic

Aug 94. (c-s) **LUCKY YOU. / ('A'lunar mix)** [43] [ ]
(12")(cd-s) – ('A'hard luck mix) / ('A'lucky devil mix) / ('A'lunar cabaret mix).

— Above was co-written w / **TERRY HALL**. They are now best known for contributing football theme to Match of the Day's 'Goal Of The Month'. ALISON MOYET wrote a track for the next album.

Sep 94. (cd)(c)(lp) **JOLLIFICATION** [13] [ ]
– Perfect / Lucky you / Open goals / Change / Why why why / Marvellous / Feeling lazy / My best day / Punch & Judy / Telling tales.
Jan 95. (7")(c-s) **CHANGE. / SAY YOU WILL** [13] [ ]
(cd-s+=) – Dust.
(cd-s) – ('A'side) / The life of Riley (inst.) / Lucky you (live).
Apr 95. (c-s) **MARVELLOUS / LUCIFER SAM** [24] [ ]
(cd-s+=) – I met you.
(cd-s) – ('A'side) / ('A'mix) / All I want.
Jul 95. (c-s) **PERFECT / PERFECT (acoustic)** [18] [ ]
(cd-s+=) – Howl / Blowing bubbles (extended remix).
(cd-s) – ('A'side) / Change (live) / Flaming sword (live).
Oct 95. (c-s) **LUCKY YOU / LUCKY YOU (Lunar mix)** [15] [ ]
(cd-s) – ('A'side) / Life of Riley (live) / Pure (live) / Here today (live).

LINDISFARNE

Formed: Newcastle, England . . . 1967 as The DOWNTOWN FACTION by ALAN HULL, who was soon to release a solo credited single in 1969 'WE CAN SWING TOGETHER' / 'OBADIAH'S GRAVE' for 'Transatlantic'. That year, the band became LINDISFARNE, and gained some support on college circuit, which led to a contract on Tony Stratton-Smith's 'Charisma'. After 1970 debut, he sent them to Nashville producer Bob Johnston, who worked on their second lp 'FOG ON THE TYNE'. Released late '71, it soon shot up the next year to top placing, aided by 2 hit 45's 'MEET ME ON THE CORNER' & re-issued 'LADY ELEANOR'. By the end of 1973, they had split from ALAN HULL, after he went solo and they formed JACK THE LAD. After more personnel turmoil in the mid-70's, the originals re-formed in 1978, and enjoyed a brief return to chart form with single 'RUN FOR HOME', and album 'BACK AND FOURTH'. • **Style:** Good time folk-rock outfit, full of rich harmonies, which went mainstream in the late 70's, although they never lost Geordie roots. • **Songwriters:** HULL, JACKSON plus others contributed. • **Trivia:** In 1990, they returned to back Geordie football star GAZZA (PAUL GASCOINE) on his UK Top 3 interpretation of their tune 'FOG ON THE TYNE'.

Recommended: FOG ON THE TYNE (*8) / NICELY OUT OF TUNE (*7) / CAUGHT IN THE ACT (*7)

ALAN HULL (b.20 Feb'45) – vocals, guitar (ex-CHOSEN FEW, solo artist) / **RAY JACKSON** (b.12 Dec'48) – guitar, mandolin, mouth harp / **SIMON COWE** (b. 1 Apr'48) – guitar, mandolin / **ROD CLEMENTS** (b.17 Nov'47) – bass, violin, vocals / **ROY LAIDLAW** (b.28 May'48) – drums

Charisma Elektra

Sep 70. (7") **CLEAR WHITE LIGHT (part II). / KNACKER'S YARD BLUES** [ ] [-]

Nov 70. (lp)(c) **NICELY OUT OF TUNE** [ ] [ ]
– Lady Eleanor / Road to kingdom come / Winter song / Turn a deaf ear / Clear white light (part II) / We can swing together / Alan in the river with flowers / Down / The things I should have said / Jackhammer blues / Scarecrow song. *(re-dist. Jan 72, hit No.8) (re-iss.1974) (re-iss.Aug88 +cd+=)*– Knacker yard blues / Nothing but the marvellous is beautiful.

Jan 71. (7") **LADY ELEANOR. / NOTHING BUT THE MARVELLOUS IS BEAUTIFUL** [ ] [-]
(re-iss.May72, hit No.3)

Sep 71. (7") **LADY ELEANOR. / DOWN** [-] [ ]
(re-iss. US; Aug72, hit No. 82)

Oct 71. (lp)(c) **FOG ON THE TYNE** [1] [ ]
– Meet me on the corner / Alright on the night / Uncle Sam / Together forever / January song / Peter Brophy don't care / City song / Passing ghosts / Train in G major / Fog on the Tyne. *(re-iss.Jan74 & Sep83) (re-iss.Oct86) (cd-iss. 1988.& Feb91 +=)*– Scotch mist / No time to lose.

Feb 72. (7"m) **MEET ME ON THE CORNER. / SCOTCH MIST / NO TIME TO LOSE** [5] [-]

Mar 72. (7") **MEET ME ON THE CORNER. / FOG ON THE TYNE** [-] [ ]

Sep 72. (7") **ALL FALL DOWN. / WE CAN SWING TOGETHER (live)** [34] [ ]

Sep 72. (lp)(c) **DINGLY DELL** [5] [ ]
– All fall down / Plankton's lament / Bring down the government / Poor old Ireland / Don't ask me / Oh, no not again / Dingle regatta / Wake up little sister / Go back / Court in the act / Mandolin king / Dingly dell. *(re-iss. 1974) (cd-iss.1988 +=)*– We can swing together (live).

Dec 72. (7") **COURT IN THE ACT. / DON'T ASK ME** [ ] [ ]

Jul 73. (lp)(c) **LINDISFARNE LIVE (live)** [25] [-]
– No time to lose / Meet me on the corner / All right on the night / Train in G major / Fog on the Tyne / We can swing together / Jackhammer blues.

— COWE, CLEMENTS and LAIDLAW bailed out to form JACK THE LAD. Made 4 albums **JACK THE LAD** (1974) / **OLD STRAIGHT TRACK** (1974) / **ROUGH DIAMONDS** (1975) . **The 4th JACKPOT** (1976) on 'United Art' was without CLEMENTS, COWE or LAIDLAW.

ALAN HULL

went solo.

Charisma Warners

Jun 73. (7"m) **NUMBERS (TRAVELLING BAND). / DRINKING SONG / ONE OFF PAT** [ ] [-]

Jul 73. (lp)(c) **PIPEDREAM** [29] [ ]
– Breakfast / Monkey game / Country gentleman's wife / Just another sad song / Numbers (travelling band) / For the bairns / Drinking song / Song for a windmill / United States of mind / I hate to see you cry / Blue murder. *(cd-iss.Feb91 & Mar94 on 'Virgin')*

Sep 73. (7") **JUST ANOTHER SAD SONG. / WAITING** [ ] [-]

LINDISFARNE

reformed Autumn 1973. Same label. **HULL & JACKSON** brought in **CHARLIE HARCOURT** – lead guitar / **KENNY CRADDOCK** – keyboards / **TOMMY DUFFY** – bass / **PAUL NICHOLS** – drums

Dec 73. (lp)(c) **ROLL ON RUBY** [ ] [ ]
– Taking care of business / North Country boy / Steppenwolf / Nobody loves you anymore / When the war is over / Moonshine / Lazy / Roll on river / Tow the line / Goodbye.

Mar 74. (7") **TAKING CARE OF BUSINESS. / NORTH COUNTRY BOY** [ ] [ ]

Warners Asylum

Oct 74. (lp)(c) **HAPPY DAZE** [ ] [ ]
– Tonight / In year head / River / You put the laff on me / No need to tell me / I'm juiced / Up to lose / Dealer's choice / Nellie / The man down there / Gin and tonic all round / Tomorrow.

Jan 75. (7") **TONIGHT. / NO NEED TO TELL ME** [ ] [ ]

— Disbanded once more.

ALAN HULL

returned with own studio work.

Warners Warners

May 75. (7") **DAN THE PLAN. / ONE MORE BOTTLE OF WINE** [ ] [-]

May 75. (lp)(c) **SQUIRE** [ ] [ ]
– Squire / Dan the plan / Picture a little girl / Nuthin' shakin' / One more bottle of wine / Golden oldies / I'm sorry squire / Waiting / Bad side of town / Mr.Inbetween.

Aug 75. (7") **SQUIRE. / ONE MORE BOTTLE OF WINE** [ ] [-]

Dec 75. (7") **CRAZY WOMAN. / GOLDEN OLDIES** [ ] [-]

RAY JACKSON

also had brief solo excursion.

E.M.I. not issued

Aug 76. (7") **TAKE SOME TIME. / WORKING OUT** [ ] [-]

LINDISFARNE

re-formed originals from 1970.

Mercury Atco

May 78. (7") **RUN FOR HOME. / STICK TOGETHER** [10] [33] Sep 78

Jun 78. (lp)(c) **BACK AND FOURTH** [22] [ ]
– Juke box gypsy / Warm feeling / Woman / Only alone / Run for home / Kings X blues / Get wise / You and me / Marshall Riley's army / Angels at eleven / Make me want to stay. *(re-iss.Dec83, cd-iss.1991)*

Sep 78. (7") **JUKE BOX GYPSY. / WHEN IT GOES THE HARDEST** [56] [-]

Nov 78. (7") **BRAND NEW DAY. / WINTER SONG** [ ] [-]

Dec 78. (7") **WARM FEELING. / WOMAN** [-] [ ]

Dec 78. (d-lp)(c) **MAGIC IN THE AIR (live)** [ ] [-]
– Lady Eleanor / Road to kingdom come / Turn a deaf ear / January song / Court in the act / Meet me on the corner / Bye bye birdie / Train in G-major / Scarecrow song / Dingly dell / Scotch mist / No time to lose / Winter song / Uncle Sam / Wake up little sister / All fall down / We can swing together / Fog on the Tyne / Clear white light.

Feb 79. (7") **WARM FEELING. / CLEAR WHITE LIGHT (live)** [ ] [-]

Aug 79. (7") **EASY AND FREE. / WHEN FOREVER COMES ALONG** [ ] [ ]

Sep 79. (lp)(c) **THE NEWS** [ ] [-]
– Call of the wild / People say / 1983 / Log on your fire / Evening / Easy and free / Miracles / When Friday comes along / Dedicated hound / This has got to end / Good to be here.

Oct 79. (7") **CALL OF THE WILD. / DEDICATED HOUND** [ ] [-]

Subterranean not issued

Jun 80. (7") **FRIDAY GIRL. / 1983** [ ] [-]

Hangover not issued

Nov 81. (7") **I MUST STOP GOING TO PARTIES. / SEE HOW THEY RUN** [ ] [-]

L.M.P. not issued

Jun 82. (7") **SUNDERLAND BOYS. / CRUISING TO DISASTER** [ ] [-]

Sep 82. (7") **NIGHTS. / DOG RUFF** [ ] [-]

Oct 82. (lp)(c) **SLEEPLESS NIGHTS** [ ] [-]
– Nights / Start again / Cruising to disaster / Same way down / Winning the game / About you / Underland boys / Love is a pain / Do what I want / Never miss the water / I must stop going to parties / Stormy weather. *(cd-iss.May93 on 'Castle')*

Jan 83. (7") **DO WHAT I WANT. / SAME WAY DOWN** [ ] [-]

Sep 84. (lp)(c) **LINDISFARNTASTIC LIVE (live)** [ ] [-]

Nov 84. (lp)(c) **LINDISFARNTASTIC VOL.2 (live)** [ ] [-]

Jun 85. (7") **I REMEMBER THE LIGHTS (acappella version). / DAY OF THE JACKAL** [ ] [-]

Dec 85. (7"; at concerts) **CHRISTMAS EP (live)** [ ] [-]
– Warm feeling / Red square dance / Run for home / Nights (acappella version).

— **HULL + JACKSON** added **MARTY CRAGGS** – saxophone / + 4th member/producer **STEVE DAGGETT** – keyboards

River City not issued

Sep 86. (7"m) **SHINE ON. / HEROES / DANCE YOUR LIFE AWAY (Gogo mix)** [ ] [-]

Oct 86. (lp)(c)(cd) **DANCE YOUR LIFE AWAY** [ ] [-]
– Shine on / Love on the run / Heroes / All in the same boat / Dance your life away / Beautiful day / Broken doll / One hundred miles to Liverpool / Take your time / Song for a stranger. *(re-iss.cd May93 on 'Castle')*

Feb 87. (7") **LOVE ON THE RUN. / ONE HUNDRED MILES TO LIVERPOOL** [ ] [-]
(free 7"w.a.+=) – Save our ales. / Save our ales (sub mix).

Honeybee not issued

Dec 87. (7")(ext.-12") **PARTY DOLL. / Medley; C'MON EVERYBODY – DO YOU WANNA DANCE – TWIST AND SHOUT – DO YOU LOVE ME** [ ] [-]

Virgin not issued

Nov 88. (7") **LADY ELEANOR '88. / MEET ME ON THE CORNER** [ ] [-]
(12"+=)/ /(cd-s++=) – Lost in space./ / Reason to be.

Black Crow not issued

Nov 89. (lp)(cd) **AMIGOS** [ ] [-]
– One world / Everything changes / Working for the man / Roll on that day / You're the one / Wish you were here / Do it like this / Any way the wind blows / Strange affair / When the night comes down / Don't say goodnight / Another world. *(re-iss.May93 on 'Castle')*

— Next backing Geordie England footballer GAZZA (aka PAUL GASCOIGNE)

Best not issued

Nov 90. (7")(7"pic-d)(c-s) **FOG ON THE TYNE (REVISITED). ("GAZZA & LINDISFARNE") / ('A'instrumental)** [2] [-]

(12"+=)(cd-s+=) – ('A'extended).

— now without JACKSON; repl. by **KENNY CRADDOCK** – multi

		Essential	not issued
May 93.	(7")(12") **DAY OF THE JACKAL. / DEMONS** (cd-s+=) – So lonely / ('A'extended).		-
Jun 93.	(cd)(c) **ELVIS LIVES ON THE MOON** – Day of the jackal / Soho Square / Old peculiar feeling / Mother Russia / Demons / Don't leave me tonight / Elvis lives on the Moon / Keeping the rage / Heaven waits / Spoken like a man / Think.		-
Sep 94.	(cd-s) **WE CAN MAKE IT / WALK IN THE SEA (live)**		-
Sep 94.	(cd) **ON TAP: A BARREL FULL OF HITS** (compilation) – Run for home / Lady Eleanor / Meet me on the corner / We can make it / All fall down / Warm feeling / Winter song / Road to kingdom come / Fog on the tyne / Miracles / No time to lose / Running man / Elvis lives on the Moon / Juke box gypsy / Dance your life away / Evening / Roll on that day / Clear white light II.		-

— Tragically, ALAN HULL died of a heart attack 17th Nov'95.

– compilations, others –

1974.	Charisma; (7") **FOG ON THE TYNE. / MANDOLIN KING**		-
Oct 75.	Charisma; (lp)(c) **FINEST HOUR** *(re-iss.Sep83)*		-
Nov 75.	Charisma; (7") **LADY ELEANOR. / FOG ON THE TYNE**		-
May 81.	Charisma; (7") **CLEAR WHITE LIGHT. / THE TRAVELLER**		-
May 81.	Charisma; (lp)(c) **REPEAT PERFORMANCE: THE SINGLES ALBUM**		-
Mar 83.	Charisma; (d-c) **FOG ON THE TYNE / NICELY OUT OF TUNE**		-
Aug 77.	Hallmark; (lp)(c) **LADY ELEANOR**		-
Jul 82.	Old Gold; (7") **MEET ME ON THE CORNER. / LADY ELEANOR**		-
Oct 87.	Stylus; (d-lp)(d-c)(d-cd) **C'MON EVERYBODY**		-
Nov 88.	Strange Fruit; (12"ep)(cd-ep) **THE PEEL SESSION** (8.5.72) – Mandolin king / Poor old Ireland / Lady Eleanor / Road to kingdom come.		-
Sep 89.	VIP-Virgin; (cd) **THE BEST OF LINDISFARNE** *(re-iss.Dec93)*		-
Aug 92.	Castle; (cd) **CAUGHT IN THE ACT** – Moving house / Taxman / Lady Eleanor / Nights / Mr.Inbetween / Brand new day / Mystery play / Lover not a fighter / Day of the jackal / Stormy weather / I must stop going to parties / Marshall Riley's army / Warm feeling / Fog on the tyne / Run for home / Meet me on the corner / Clear white light.		-
Nov 92.	Virgin; (cd) **BURIED TREASURES VOLUME 1**		-
Nov 92.	Virgin; (cd) **BURIED TREASURES VOLUME 2**		-
Jun 93.	Code 90; (cd) **LIVE – 1990 (live)**		-
Oct 94.	Essential; (cd)(c) **ON TAP (THE VERY BEST OF . . .)**		-

ALAN HULL

more solo work.

		Rocket	not issued
Apr 79.	(7") **I WISH YOU WELL. / LOVE IS THE ANSWER**		-
May 79.	(lp)(c) **PHANTOMS** – Anywhere is everywhere / Corporation rock / Dancin' / I wish you well / Love is an alibi / Love is the answer / Madman and loonies / Make me want to stay / Somewhere out there / A walk in the sea.		-
Jul 79.	(7") **A WALK IN THE SEA. / CORPORATION ROCK**		-
		Black Crow	**not issued**
Oct 83.	(7") **MALVINAS MELODY. / ODE TO A TAXMAN**		-
Nov 83.	(lp) **ON THE OTHER SIDE** – *(c-iss.Jun88)*		-
Jun 88.	(lp) **ANOTHER LITTLE ADVENTURE**		-
		Mooncrest	**not issued**
Jul 94.	(cd) **BACK TO BASICS** – United states of mind / Poor old Ireland / All fall down / Lady Eleanor / Wintersong / Walk in the sea / Mother Russia / This heart of mine / Mister inbetween / January song / Breakfast / Day of the jackal / Oh no not again / Run for home / Fog on the Tyne.		-

RAY JACKSON

more solo.

		Mercury	not issued
Jan 80.	(7") **IN THE NIGHT. / WAITING FOR THE TIME**		-
Apr 80.	(7") **LITTLE TOWN FLIRT. / MAKE IT LAST**		-
May 80.	(lp)(c) **IN THE NIGHT** – Everything will turn out fine / Make it last / In the night / Another lovely day / Stick around Joe / Waiting for the time / Little town flirt / Tread on a good thing / You send me / Easy love / Solo again / In the midnight hour.		-

David LINDLEY (see under ⇒ KALEIDOSCOPE US)

Mark LINDSAY (see under ⇒ Paul REVERE)

Mike LINDUP (see under ⇒ LEVEL 42)

LITTLE ANGELS

Formed: Scarborough, England . . . May'87. In 1984, TOBY & MARK were in school band as ZEUS. Just over a year later, with BRUCE, they form MR.THRUD. To end 1985, they found JIM. They were spotted in Sep 86, by manager to be KEVIN NIXON. They changed group name in Feb'87. On 20 Nov'87, they appear on Channel 4's 'Famous For 15 Minutes'. They were briefly Mr.THRUD, with JEPSON, PLUNKETT, HOPPER and the DICKINSON brothers. They soon issued an EP on a label run by their managers, adding these tracks later in the year to 'TOO POSH TO MOSH' mini-lp. In 1988, they signed to 'Polydor', and supported YWNGIE MALMSTEEN and CINDERELLA on US and UK tours, before issuing single '90° IN THE SHADE'. Their first taste of major chart action, was provided early in 1990 when 'KICKIN' UP DUST' hit UK Top 50. This was soon bettered by Top 40 'RADICAL YOUR LOVER' and near Top 20 hit 'SHE'S A LITTLE ANGEL'. After early 1991 UK Top 20 album 'YOUNG GODS', everything turned to gold, with America beckoning them for greater heights. • **Style:** Heavy rock combo, blending aggressive and American acoustic sound, fronted by ROBERT PLANT lookalike JEPSON. • **Songwriters:** Mostly group compositions or JEPSON and collaborations with DESMOND CHILD or JIM VALLANCE in the early 90's. Covers:- TIE YOUR MOTHER DOWN (Queen) / BROKEN WINGS OF AN ANGEL (Hugh Cornwall) / FORTUNATE SON (Creedence Clearwater Revival) / RADICAL YOUR LOVER (co-with; Dan Reed) / BABYLON'S BURNING (Ruts) / OH WELL (Fleetwood Mac) / FUNK 49 (James Gang) / TIRED OF WAITING FOR YOU (Kinks) / WON'T GET FOOLED AGAIN (Who) / JAILHOUSE ROCK (Elvis Presley) / THE MIGHTY QUINN (Bob Dylan) / Feb 92 German single cover; FIRST CUT IS THE DEEPEST (Cat Stevens). • **Trivia:** Their 1991 work was produced by James 'Jimbo' Barton & Andy Julian Paul. In late '87, they featured on Channel 4 TV programe 'Famous For 15 Minutes'.

Recommended: LITTLE OF THE PAST (*7).

TOBY JEPSON – vocals, acoustic guitar / **BRUCE JOHN DICKINSON** – guitars, banjo / **JIMMY DICKINSON** – keyboards, vocals / **MARK PLUNKETT** – bass, vocals / **DAVE HOPPER** – drums

		Man-agement	not issued
Jul 87.	(12"ep) **THE '87 EP** – Bad or just no good / Better than the rest / Burning me / Reach for me.		-
		Powerstation	**not issued**
Nov 87.	(m-lp) **TOO POSH TO MOSH** – (1st EP tracks) / Too posh to mosh / No more whiskey / Down in the night. *(re-iss.cd,c,lp Jun94 on 'Essential', w / 3 extra '94 remix tracks 'Reach For Me', 'Bad Or Just No Good' & 'Burning Me' ; hit UK No.18)*		-

— **MICHAEL LEE** – drums, percussion (ex-HOLOSAIDE) repl. HOPPER

		Polydor	Polydor
Nov 88.	(7")(7"pic-d) **90° IN THE SHADE. / ENGLAND ROCKS (live)** (12"+=) – Big bad world.		
Feb 89.	(7") **SHE'S A LITTLE ANGEL. / BETTER THAN THE REST** (12"ep+=)(c-ep+=)(cd-ep+=) **THE BIG BAD EP** – Don't waste my time / Sex in cars.	74	
Sep 89.	(7") **DO YOU WANNA RIOT. / MOVE IN SLOW** (12"+=)(cd-s+=) – Some kind of alien (live). (10"++=) – Snatch (edited highlights of below lp).		
Nov 89.	(lp)(c)(cd) **DON'T PREY FOR ME** – Do you wanna riot / Kick hard / Big bad world / Kickin' up dust / Don't prey for me / Broken wings of an angel / Bitter and twisted / Promises / When I get out of here / No solution / She's a little angel. *(c+=)*– Pleasure pyre. *(cd+=)*– Radical your lover (version) / Broken wings of an angel (version). *(re-dist.Jun90)*		
Nov 89.	(7")(c-s) **DON'T PREY FOR ME. / RADICAL YOUR LOVER** (12"+=) – What do you want. (cd-s++=) – ('A'extended).		
Feb 90.	(7") **KICKIN' UP DUST. / ('A'live)** (12"+=) – Big bad world (Nashville version). (cd-s+=) – Pleasure pyre (live) / Kick hard (live). (12"pic-d+=) – When I get out of here (live) / Kick hard (live) / Sex in cars (live).	46	
Apr 90.	(7")(c-s) **RADICAL YOUR LOVER. / DON'T LOVE YOU NO MORE** (12"pic-d-ep+=)(12"ep+=)(cd-ep+=) **GET RADICAL EP** – ('A'adult remix) / Promises (live).	34	
Jul 90.	(7")(c-s) **SHE'S A LITTLE ANGEL. / DOWN ON MY KNEES** (12") – ('A'side) / ('A'-Voodoo mix). (12") – ('A'side) / ('A'-club) / When I get out of here. (other 7") – ('A'side) / Sex in cars (live).	21	
Jan 91.	(7")(c-s) **BONEYARD. / FORTUNATE SON** (12"+=) – ('A'mix). (12"++=) – Sweet love sedation. (12"pic-d+=) – Jump the gun / ('A'album mix).	33	
Feb 91.	(cd)(c)(lp) **YOUNG GODS** – Back door man / Boneyard / Young gods (stand up, stand up) / I ain't gonna cry / The wildside of life / Product of the working class / That's my kinda life / Juvenile offender / Love is a gun / Sweet love sedation / Smoke in my eyes / Natural born fighter / Feels like the world has come undone (featuring the angel's anthem). *(re-iss.cd Apr95)*	17	
Mar 91.	(7")(c-s) **PRODUCT OF THE WORKING CLASS. / REVIVAL** (12"+=) – Take it off. (cd-s++=) – Might like you better. (12"+=) – ('A'hot mix).	40	
May 91.	(7")(c-s) **YOUNG GODS. / GO AS YOU PLEASE** (cd-s+=) – Bad imitation. (12"+=) – Frantic.	34	
Jul 91.	(7") **I AIN'T GONNA CRY. / BABYLON'S BURNING** (12"+=) – Funk 49. (12"++=)(cd-s++=) – Oh well.	26	

— **MARK 'Rich' RICHARDSON** – drums repl. LEE

Nov 92.	(7")(c-s) **TOO MUCH TOO YOUNG. / THE FIRST CUT IS THE DEEPEST** (12"+=)(cd-s+=) – 90° In The Shade / Young Gods	22	
Jan 93.	(7") **WOMANKIND. / SCHIZOPHRENIA BLUES** (12"+=)(cd-s+=) – ?	12	

Jan 93. (cd)(c)(lp) **JAM** [1] [ ]
– The way that I live / Too much too young / Splendid isolation / Soapbox / S.T.W. / Don't confuse sex with love / Womankind / Eyes wide open / The colour of love / I was not wrong / Sail away / Tired of waiting for you (so tired) / S.T.W. (reprise), (with ltd.live cd+lp + extra tracks 1-side of c) **LIVE JAM**
– She's a little angel / Product of the working class (grooved & jammed) / I ain't gonna cry / Boneyard 1993 (featuring Big Dave Kemp) / Don't prey for me (extended version) / Won't get fooled again. *(re-iss.cd Apr95)*

Apr 93. (7")(c-s) **SOAPBOX (remix). / I GOT THE SHAKES** [33] [ ]
(cd-s+=) – Womankind (live) / Too much too young (live).
(cd-s) – ('A'side) / Young gods (live) / Jailhouse rock (live) / I ain't gonna cry (live).

Sep 93. (12")(c-s) **SAIL AWAY. / I AIN'T GONNA CRY (live) / SOAPBOX (live)** [45] [ ]
(cd-s) – ('A'side) / The mighty Quinn / This ain't the way it's supposed to be.

Sony Sony

Mar 94. (c-s)(12")(cd-s) **TEN MILES HIGH. / I WANNA BE LOVED BY YOU** [18] [ ]

Apr 94. (cd)(c)(lp) **LITTLE OF THE PAST** (compilation) [20] [ ]
– She's a little angel / Too much too young / Radical your lover / Womankind / Boneyard / Kickin' up dust / I ain't gonna cry / Sail away / Young gods / Ninety in the shade / Product of the working class / Soapbox / The first cut is the deepest / Ten miles high / I wanna be loved by you / Don't pray for me.

— now w/out **JIMMY + BRUCE DICKINSON**, who formed b.l.o.w.

LITTLE FEAT

Formed: Los Angeles, California, USA . . . late 1969, by ex-FRANK ZAPPA stalwarts LOWELL GEORGE and ROY ESTRADA, who found BILL PAYNE and RICHIE HAYWARD. They signed to 'Warners' in 1970, and finally issued acclaimed eponymous debut later that year. It featured guest appearances from RY COODER and SNEAKY PETE KLEINOW, and was produced by RUSS TITELMAN. In 1974 after 2 more well-received commercial flops, they hit big with US Top 40 album 'FEATS DON'T FAIL ME NOW'. For the rest of the decade, they scored on both sides of the Atlantic, until their split and the untimely death of LOWELL GEORGE on 29th Jun'79. • **Style:** Classy country funk & boogie band, who drifted into milder stuff by the late 70's & late 80's on their re-union. • **Songwriters:** GEORGE penned most, until 1977 when his contribution was minimum. Covered; HOW MANY MORE YEARS (Howlin' Wolf) / ON YOUR WAY DOWN (Allen Toussaint) / etc. LOWELL solo:- EASY MONEY (Rickie Lee Jones) / + a few more. • **Trivia:** Their name was given to them by JIMMY CARL BLACK of FRANK ZAPPA's MOTHERS OF INVENTION, who joked about LOWELL's shoe size. ROBERT PALMER was once touted as a 1973 replacement for LOWELL, until their reformation. LOWELL produced GRATEFUL DEAD on their 'Shakedown Street' album, and sessioned for ROBERT PALMER 'Sneaking Sally . . . ', VAN DYKE PARKS 'Discover America' and JOHN CALE 'Paris 1919'.

Recommended: SAILIN' SHOES (*8) / FEATS DON'T FAIL ME NOW (*8) / THE LAST RECORD ALBUM (*8) / AS TIME GOES BY – THE BEST OF . . . (*9)

LOWELL GEORGE (b.13 Apr'45) – vocals, guitar (ex-MOTHERS OF INVENTION/ZAPPA) / **ROY ESTRADA** (b. Santa Ana) – bass, vocals (ex-MOTHERS OF INVENTION/ZAPPA) / **BILL PAYNE** (b.12 Mar'49, Waco, Texas) – keys, vocals (ex-FRATERNITY OF MAN) / **RICHIE HAYWARD** – drums (ex-FRATERNITY OF MAN)

Warners Warners

May 70. (7") **STRAWBERRY FLATS. / HAMBURGER MIDNIGHT** [-] [ ]

Nov 70. (lp)(c) **LITTLE FEAT** [ ] [ ]
– Snakes on everything / Strawberry flats / Truck stop girl / Brides of Jesus / Willin' / Hamburger midnight; (a) Forty four blues, (b) How many more years / Crack in your door / I've been the one / Takin' my time / Crazy Captain Gunboat Willie. *(re-iss.Jan75)*

May 72. (lp)(c) **SAILIN' SHOES** [ ] [ ]
– Easy to slip / Cold cold cold / Trouble / Tripe face boogie / Willin' / Apolitical blues / Sailin' shoes / Teenage nervous breakdown / Got no shadows / Cat fever / Texas rose cafe. *(cd-iss.1988)*

— **KENNY GRADNEY** (b. New Orleans) – bass (ex-DELANEY AND BONNY) repl. ESTRADA who joined CAPTAIN BEEFHEART & HIS MAGIC BAND / added **PAUL BARRERE** (b. 3 Jul'48, Burbank, California) – guitar, vocals / **SAM CLAYTON** – congas / **BONNIE BRAMLETT** – guest vocals

Nov 72. (7") **DIXIE CHICKEN. / LAFAYETTE RAILROAD** [-] [ ]

Feb 73. (lp)(c) **DIXIE CHICKEN** [ ] [ ]
– Dixie chicken / Two trains / Roll um easy / On your way down / Kiss it off / Fool yourself / Walkin' all night / Fat man in the bathtub / Juliette / Lafayette railroad. *(cd-iss Jul88)*

— Band split for 6 months (Oct '73-May '74). BILL joined DOOBIE BROTHERS and others, mainly LOWELL went into sessions. The sextet re-formed May74

Jul 74. (7") **OH ATLANTA. / DOWN THE ROAD** [-] [ ]

Sep 74. (7") **SPANISH MOON. / DOWN THE ROAD** [-] [ ]

Sep 74. (lp)(c) **FEATS DON'T FAIL ME NOW** [ ] [36]
– Rock and roll doctor / Cold cold cold / Tripe face boogie / The fan / Oh Atlanta / Skin it back / Down the road / Spanish moon / Down the road / Feats don't fail me now. *(cd-iss Jan89)*

Nov 75. (lp)(c) **THE LAST RECORD ALBUM** [36] [36]
– Romance dance / All that you dream / Long distance love / Day or night / One love / Down below the borderline / Somebody's leavin' / Mercenary territory. *(cd-iss Jul88)*

Feb 76. (7") **LONG DISTANCE LOVE. / ROMANCE DANCE** [ ] [ ] Oct 75

Feb 76. (7") **ALL THAT YOU DREAM. / ONE LOVE** [-] [ ]

May 77. (lp)(c) **TIME LOVES A HERO** [8] [34]
– Time loves a hero / Hi roller / New elhi freight train / Old folks boogie / Red streamliner / Keepin' up with the Joneses / Rocket in my pocket / Missin' you / Day at the dog races. *(cd-iss Jul88)*

Jun 77. (7") **TIME LOVES A HERO. / SAILIN' SHOES** [-] [ ]

Jul 77. (7") **TIME LOVES A HERO. / ROCKET IN MY POCKET** [ ] [-]

Mar 78. (d-lp)(d-c) **WAITING FOR COLUMBUS (live)** [43] [18]
– Join the band / Fat man in the bathtub / All that you dream / Oh Atlanta / Old folks boogie / Time loves a hero / Day or night / Mercenary territory / Spanish moon / Dixie chicken / Tripe face boogie / Rocket in my pocket / Don't bogart that joint / Willin' / Apolitical blues / Sailin' shoes / Feats don't fail me now.

Jul 78. (7") **WILLIN' (live). / OH ATLANTA (live)** [-] [ ]

Oct 79. (lp)(c) **DOWN ON THE FARM** [46] [29]
– Down on the farm / Six feet of snow / Perfect imperfection / Kokomo / Be one now / Straight from the heart / Front page news / Wake up dreaming / Feel the groove. *(cd-iss Jul88)*

— The had by this time split (Apr79). BARRERE and CLAYTON joined NICOLETTE LARSON. BARRERE went solo '83 and released 'ON MY OWN TWO FEET'. The others went into sessions.

– compilations, etc. –

Feb 75. Warners; (7") **DIXIE CHICKEN. / OH ATLANTA** [ ] [ ]

Oct 75. Warners; (d-lp) **TWO ORIGINALS OF . . . (LITTLE FEAT / DIXIE CHICKEN)** [ ] [ ]

Aug 81. Warners; (d-lp)(d-c) **HOY-HOY!** (remixes of rare material) [76] [39]
– Rocket in my pocket / Rock and roll doctor / Skin it back / Easy to slip / Red streamliner / Lonesome whistle / Front page news / The fan / Forty-four blues / Teenage nervous breakdown (live) / Framed / Strawberry flats / Gringo / Over the edge / Two trains / China white / All that you dream / Feats don't fail me now.

Aug 81. Warners; (7") **EASY TO SLIP. / FRONT PAGE NEWS** [-] [ ]

Oct 81. Warners; (7") **GRINGO. / STRAWBERRY FLATS** [-] [ ]

Aug 86. Warners; (lp)(c)(cd) **THE BEST OF LITTLE FEAT – AS TIME GOES BY** [ ] [ ]
– Dixie chicken / Willin' / Rock and roll doctor / Trouble / Sailin' shoes / Spanish Moon / Feats don't fail me now / All that you dream / Long distance love / Mercenary territory / Old folks boogie / Twenty million dollars.

LOWELL GEORGE

– solo (vocals, guitar) with **FRED TACKETT** – guitar / **EDDIE ZIP** – keyboards,vocals / **PETER WASNER** – keyboards / **JERRY JUMONVILLE** – saxophone / **LEE THORNBERG** – trumpet / **MAXINE DIXON** – b. vocals / **ARMANDO COMPION** – bass / **DON HEFFINGTON** – drums

Warners Warners

Apr 79. (7") **WHAT DO YOU WANT THE GIRL TO DO. / 20 MILLION THINGS** [-] [ ]

Apr 79. (lp)(c) **THANKS, I'LL EAT IT HERE** [ ] [71]
– What do you want the girl to do / Honest man / Two trains / Can't stand the rain / Cheek to cheek / Easy money / 20 million things / Find a river / Himmler's ring.

Jul 79. (7") **CHEEK TO CHEEK. / HONEST MAN** [ ] [ ]

— Tragically LOWELL died 29th June '79 of a drug induced heart attack. He had gigged the night before.

LITTLE FEAT

re-formed 1988. (**ESTRADA, PAYNE, HAYWARD & FRED TACKETT**) plus **CRAIG FULLER** – vocals (ex-PURE PRAIRIE LEAGUE)

Warners Warners

Jul 88. (lp)(c)(cd) **LET IT ROLL** [ ] [36]
– Hate to lose your lovin' / One clear moment / Cajun girl / Hangin' on to the good times / Listen to your heart / Let it roll / Long time till I get over you / Business as usual / Changin' luck / Voices on the wind. *(re-iss.cd Feb95)*

Jul 88. (7") **HATE TO LOSE YOUR LOVIN'. / CAJUN GIRL** [-] [ ]

Sep 88. (7") **ONE CLEAR MOMENT. / CHANGIN' LUCK** [-] [ ]

Nov 88. (7") **LET IT ROLL. / ?** [ ] [ ]

Apr 90. (cd)(c)(lp) **REPRESENTING THE MAMBO** [ ] [45]
– Texas twister / Daily grind / Representing the mambo / Woman in love / Rad gumbo / Teenage warrior / That's her, she's mine / Feelin's all gone / Those feet'll steer ya wrong sometimes / The ingenue / Silver screen. *(re-iss.cd Feb95)*

— added **MARTIN KIBBEE** – bass (ex-FRATERNITY OF MAN) / **& SAM CLAYTON** – percussion

Morgan Creek Morgan Creek

Oct 91. (cd)(c)(lp) **SHAKE ME UP** [ ] [ ]
– Spider's blues (might need it sometime) / Shake me up / Things happen / Mojo haiku / Loved and lied to / Don't try so hard / Boom boy car / Fast & furious / Livin' on dreams / Clownin' / Down in flames.

Zoo Zoo

Jun 95. (cd)(c)(lp) **AIN'T HAD ENOUGH FUN** [ ] [ ]
– Drivin' blind / Blue jean blues / Cadillac hotel / Romance without finance / Big bang theory / Cajun rage / Heaven's where you find it / Borderline blues / All that you can stand / Rock and roll every night / Shakeytown / Ain't had enough fun / That's a pretty good love.

LITTLE RICHARD

Born: RICHARD WAYNE PENNIMAN, 5 Dec'35, Macon, Georgia, USA. Raised in large family by preacher parents who involved him with gospel singing. At age 16, he was given chance to record for 'RCA-Victor' by singer Billy Wright. After 4 flop singles there, he moved on to Don Robey's 'Peacock' label in 1953, where he sessioned for doo-wop group The TEMPO-TOPPERS. After fronting The JOHNNY OTIS ORCHESTRA in 1955, he signed solo deal with 'Speciality'. His first single for the label 'TUTTI FRUTTI', gave him his maiden entry into the US Top 20. In 1957, with exposure from the rock'n'roll movie 'The Girl Can't Help It', he also had 5 UK Top 20 smashes. Later that year he publicly denounced his 'evil' rock'n'roll music for that of gospel. In 1960, the now Rev.LITTLE RICHARD spent a couple of years under the production of QUINCY JONES. He never quite returned to earlier 50's success, but flitted between black gospel music and rock'n'roll revival tours in the next two decades. • **Style:** Eccentric clowning early pioneer of rock'n'roll, whose courageous dress sense, borrowed nothing from contemporary peers. • **Songwriters:** Penned own material except sound covers. His songs were later covered by other rock'n'roll artists and 60's beat bands. • **Trivia:** For a better insight to his work, read Charles White biographical book 'The Life And Times Of Little Richard'.

Recommended: 20 CLASSIC CUTS (*8)

LITTLE RICHARD – vocals, piano + sessions

Date	Release	UK	US
		not issued	RCA Victor
1952.	(7") **EVERY HOUR. / TAXI BLUES**	-	
1952.	(7") **GET RICH QUICK. / THINKIN' 'BOUT MY MOTHER**	-	
1952.	(7") **WHY DID YOU LEAVE. / AIN'T NOTHIN' HAPPENIN'**	-	
1953.	(7") **I BROUGHT IT ALL ON MYSELF. / PLEASE HAVE MERCY ON ME**	-	

The TEMPO-TOPPERS Featuring LITTLE RICHARD

Date	Release	UK	US
		not issued	Peacock
1953.	(7") **AIN'T THAT GOOD NEWS. / FOOL AT THE WHEEL**	-	
1954.	(7") **ALWAYS. / RICE, RED BEANS & TURNIP GREENS**	-	

—— On the same label, he joined The JOHNNY OTIS BAND in 1955. They released 2

Date	Release	UK	US
1955.	(7") **LITTLE RICHARD BOOGIE. / DIRECTLY FROM MY HEART TO YOU**	-	
1955.	(7") **MAYBE I'M RIGHT. / I LOVE MY BABY**	-	

LITTLE RICHARD

went solo again, backed by **RED TYLER** – saxophone / **LEE ALLEN** – saxophone / **FRANK FIELDS** – bass / **ERNEST McLEAN & JUSTIN ADAMS** – guitar / **EARL PALMER** – drums / plus pianists **HUEY SMITH, EDWARD FRANK, LITTLE BOOKER & SALVADOR DOUCHETTE.**

Date	Release	UK	US
		London	Speciality
Dec 55.	(7") **TUTTI FRUTTI. / I'M JUST A LONELY GUY**	-	17
Mar 56.	(7") **LONG TALL SALLY. / SLIPPIN' AND SLIDIN' (PEEPIN' AND HIDIN')**	-	6 33
Jul 56.	(7") **RIP IT UP. / READY TEDDY**	30	17 44
1956.	(7") **SHE'S GOT IT. / HEEBIE JEEBIES**	-	
Jan 57.	(7") **LONG TALL SALLY. / TUTTI FRUTTI**	3 29	-
Feb 57.	(7") **THE GIRL CAN'T HELP IT. / ALL AROUND THE WORLD**	-	49
Feb 57.	(7") **SHE'S GOT IT. / THE GIRL CAN'T HELP IT**	15 9	-
Jun 57.	(7") **LUCILLE. / SEND ME SOME LOVIN'**	10	21 54 Mar 57
Jul 57.	(lp) **HERE'S LITTLE RICHARD**		13
	– Tutti frutti / True fine mama / Ready Teddy / Baby / Slippin' and slidin' (peepin' and hidin') / Long tall Sally / Miss Ann / Oh why / Rip it up / Jenny, Jenny / She's got it / Can't believe you wanna leave. *(re-iss.Feb85 on 'Ace', cd-iss.Jun89)*		
Aug 57.	(7") **JENNY, JENNY. / MISS ANN**	11	14 56 Jun 57
Nov 57.	(7") **KEEP A KNOCKIN'. / CAN'T BELIEVE YOU WANNA LEAVE**	21	8 Sep 57
Feb 58.	(7") **GOOD GOLLY MISS MOLLY. / HEY HEY HEY HEY**	8	10
Jun 58.	(7") **OOH! MY SOUL. / TRUE FINE MAMA**	22	31 68
Dec 58.	(7") **BABY FACE. / I'LL NEVER YOU GO**	2	41 Sep58
1958.	(lp) **LITTLE RICHARD 2**		
	– Keep a knocking / Send me some lovin' / I'll never let you go / All around the world / By the light of the silvery Moon / Good golly Miss Molly / Baby face / Hey hey hey hey / Ooh my soul / Lucille / The girl can't help it. *(re-iss.Feb85 on 'Ace', cd-iss.Jul89)*		
Jan 59.	(7") **SHE KNOWS HOW TO ROCK. / EARLY ONE MORNING**		-
Mar 59.	(7") **BY THE LIGHT OF THE SILVERY MOON. / WONDERING**	-	
Mar 59.	(7") **BY THE LIGHT OF THE SILVERY MOON. / EARLY ONE MORNING**	17	-
May 59.	(7") **KANSAS CITY. / LONESOME AND BLUE**	26	95
1959.	(lp) **THE FABULOUS LITTLE RICHARD**		
	– Shake a hand / Chicken little baby / All night long / Most I can offer / Lonesome and blue / Wonderin' / Whole lotta shakin' goin' on / She knows how to rock / Kansas City / Directly from my heart / Maybe I'm right / Early one morning / I'm just a lonely girl. *(re-iss.Jul80 on 'Sonet') (re-iss.Feb85 on 'Ace', cd-iss.Aug89 & Sep91)*		
1959.	(7") **SHAKE A HAND. / ALL NIGHT LONG**	-	
1959.	(7") **WHOLE LOTTA SHAKIN' GOIN' ON. / MAYBE I'M RIGHT**	-	
Feb 60.	(7") **BABY. / I GOT IT**		Dec 59
1960.	(7") **DIRECTLY FROM MY HEART. / THE MOST I CAN OFFER**	-	
		Coral	Coral
1960.	(7") **NEED HIM. / MILKY WHITE WAY**		
		Mercury	Mercury
1961.	(7") **HE'S NOT JUST A SOLDIER. / JOY JOY JOY**		
1962.	(7") **DO YOU CARE. / RIDE ON KING JESUS**		
Sep 62.	(7") **HE GOT WHAT HE WANTED. / WHY DON'T YOU CHANGE YOUR WAYS**	38	
		London	Woodman
Apr 63.	(7") **CRYING IN THE CHAPEL. / HOLE IN THE WALL**		
	(re-dist.US 1963 on 'Atlantic')		
		London	Atlantic
Jul 63.	(7") **TRAVELLIN' SHOES. / IT IS NO SECRET**		
1964.	(lp) **COMING HOME**		
	– ust a closer walk with thee / Coming home / Search me Lord / I want Jesus to walk with me / Milky white way / Need him / Every time I feel the spirit / Does Jesus care / God is real / I'm trampin' / Jesus walked this lonesome valley / Precious Lord.		
		London	Speciality
Apr 64.	(7") **BAMA LAMA BAMA LOO. / ANNIE'S BACK**	-	82
May 64.	(7") **BAMA LAMA BAMA LOO. / KEEP A KNOCKIN'**	20	-
		Stateside	Vee-Jay
Sep 64.	(7") **WHOLE LOTTA SHAKIN' GOIN' ON. / GOODNIGHT IRENE**		
1964.	(7") **POOR BOY PAUL. / WONDERIN'**	-	
	(UK-iss.1976 on 'Speciality')		
		Stateside	20th Cent.
1964.	(lp) **LITTLE RICHARD SINGS GOSPEL**		
	– Every time I feel the spirit / I'm trampin' / Milky white way / Does Jesus care / Coming home / I know the Lord / I've just come from the fountain / God is real / Troubles of the world / Certainly Lord / Tell God my troubles / Precious Lord. *(re-iss.Jul82 on 'Bulldog')*		
		Mercury	Mercury
Jan 65.	(7") **PEACE IN THE VALLEY. / JOY JOY JOY**		
Jan 65.	(lp) **IT'S REAL**		
	– It's real / Joy, joy, joy / Do you care / The captain calls for you / In times like these / Do Lord, remember me / Ride on King Jesus / (There'll be) Peace in the valley (for me) / He's not just a soldier / My desire / He's my star / It takes everything to serve the Lord.		
		Fontana	Vee-Jay
Jan 65.	(7") **BLUEBERRY HILL. / CHERRY RED**		
Feb 65.	(lp) **LITTLE RICHARD IS BACK**		
	– A whole lotta shakin' goin' on / Going home tomorrow / Money honey / Only you ./ Hound dog / Goodnight Irene / Lawdy Miss Clawdy / Groovy little Suzy / Short Fat Fanny / Cherry red / Memories are made of this / Blueberry hill. *(re-iss Jul 68 on 'Joy')*		
Oct 65.	(7") **I DON'T KNOW WHAT YOU'VE GOT BUT IT'S GOT ME. / (Pt.2)**		92
		Sue	Vee-Jay
Feb 66.	(7") **WITHOUT LOVE. / DANCE WHAT YOU WANNA**		
Jul 66.	(7") **CROSS OVER. / IT AIN'T WHAT'CHA DO**		
		Stateside	Modern
May 66.	(7") **HOLY MACKERAL. / BABY DON'T YOU WANT A MAN LIKE ME**		
1966.	(7") **DO YOU FEEL IT. / (Part 2)**	-	
1966.	(7") **DIRECTLY FROM THE HEART. / I'M BACK**	-	
1966.	(7") **BABY WHAT YOU WANT ME TO DO. / (Part 2)**	-	
	(re-iss.Feb69 on 'Action')		
		issued?	Kent
1966.	(7") **IN THE NAME. / DON'T YOU KNOW I**	-	
		Columbia	Okeh
1966.	(7") **POOR DOG (WHO CAN'T WAG HIS TAIL). / WELL**		
1966.	(7") **I NEED LOVE. / THE COMMANDMENTS OF LOVE**		
Jan 67.	(7") **GET DOWN WITH IT. / ROSEMARY**		-
1967.	(7") **HURRY SUNDOWN. / I DON'T WANT TO DISCUSS IT**	-	
May 67.	(lp) **THE EXPLOSIVE LITTLE RICHARD**		
	– I don't want to discuss it / Land of a 1000 dances / Commandments of love / Money / Poor dog / I need love / Never gonna let you go / Don't deceive me / Function at the junction / Well.		
1967.	(7") **DON'T DECEIVE ME (PLEASE DON'T GO). / NEVER GONNA LET YOU GO**		-
Jul 67.	(7") **LITTLE BIT OF SOMETHING. / MONEY**		
Aug 67.	(lp) **LITTLE RICHARD'S GREATEST HITS (live)**		
	(re-iss Jul 68 on 'Joy')		
1967.	(7") **LUCILLE. / WHOLE LOTTA SHAKIN' GOIN' ON**	-	
		M.C.A.	Brunswick
Mar 68.	(7") **TRY SOME OF MINE. / SHE'S TOGETHER**		-
1968.	(7") **TEAR MY CLOTHES. / STINGY JENNY**		
1968.	(7") **SOUL TRAIN. / CAN I COUNT ON YOU**		
		Reprise	Reprise
Jun 70.	(7") **FREEDOM BLUES. / DEW DROP INN**		47
Aug 70.	(7") **GREENWOOD MISSISSIPPI. / I SAW HER STANDING THERE**		85
1970.	(lp) **THE RILL THING**		
	– Freedom blues / Greenwood, Mississippi / Two-time loser / Dew Drop Inn / Somebody saw you / Spreadin' Natta, what's the matter / The rill thing / Lovesick blues / I saw her standing there.		
1971.	(7") **SHAKE A HAND. / SOMEBODY SAW YOU**		
Nov 71.	(lp) **KING OF ROCK'N'ROLL**		
	– King of rock'n'roll / Joy to the world / Brown sugar / In the name / Dancing in the street / Midnight special / The way you do the things you do / Green power / I'm so lonesome I could die / Settin' the woods on fire / Born on the bayou. *(re-iss.+c+cdJul88 on 'Entertainers')*		
Dec 71.	(7") **SHAKE A HAND. / SOMEBODY SAW YOU**		
Feb 72.	(7") **MONEY RUNNER. / MONEY IS**		
1972.	(7") **MOCKINGBIRD SALLY. / ROCKIN' ROCKIN' BOOGIE**		
1972.	(lp) **THE SECOND COMING**		
	– Mockingbird Sally / It ain't what you do, it's the way that you do it / The saints / Nuki Suki / Rockin' rockin' boogie / Prophet of peace / Thomasine / Sanctified, satisfied toe-tapper.		

(Around this time teamed w / CANNED HEAT on lp 'ROCKIN' WITH THE KING')

Date	Release	UK	US
		Green Mountain	same?
1973.	(7") **IN THE MIDDLE OF THE NIGHT. / WHERE WILL I FIND A PLACE TO SLEEP THIS EVENING**		
		Reprise	Reprise
1974.	(7"ep) **ROCKIN' ROLLIN' BOOGIE / KING OF THE ROCK'N'ROLL / SAINTS / MOCKINGBIRD SALLY**		

Manticore Atlantic

1976. (7") **CALL MY NAME. / STEAL MISS LIZA** issued? Main-stream

1979. (lp) **GOD'S BEAUTIFUL CITY** -
1980. (7") **TRY TO HELP YOUR BROTHER. / (part 2)**

— Next from film 'Down And Out In Beverley Hills'

M.C.A. M.C.A.

Feb 86. (7") **GREAT GOSH A'MIGHTY (IT'S A MATTER OF TIME). / THE RIDE** 42
(12"+=) – Down and out in Beverley Hills.

W.E.A. Warners

Oct 86. (7")(12") **OPERATOR. / BIG HOUSE REUNION**
Oct 86. (lp)(c)(cd) **LIFETIME FRIEND**
– Great gosh a'mighty (it's a matter of time) / Operator / Somebody's comin' / Destruction / I found my way / The world can't do me / One ray of sunshine / Someone cares / Big house reunion.
Jan 87. (7") **SOMEBODY'S COMIN'. / ONE RAY OF SUNSHINE**

Atco Atco

Nov 87. (7"pic-d)(12"pic-d) **HAPPY ENDING (as "LITTLE RICHARD & BEACH BOYS".) / CALIFORNIA GIRLS**

Epic W.T.G.

Nov 88. (7") **TWINS. ("LITTLE RICHARD & PHILIP BAILEY" from film 'Twins') / ('A'instrumental)**
('A'ext-12"+=)(cd-s+=) – ('A'acappella) / ('A'dub version).

– compilations, others, etc. –

1962. Little Star; (7") **I'M IN LOVE AGAIN. / EVERYNIGHT ABOUT THIS TIME** -
1963. Little Star; (7") **THE VALLEY OF TEARS. / FREEDOM RIDE** -
1963. Little Star; (lp) **LITTLE RICHARD AND SISTER ROSETTA** -
Aug 65. Ember; (lp) **REALLY MOVING GOSPEL** -
1974. Ember; (lp) **FRIENDS FROM THE BEGINNING (with JIMI HENDRIX)** -
Mar 66. Fontana/ US= Vee Jay; (lp) **LITTLE RICHARD'S GREATEST HITS**
May 68. Fontana; (lp) **KING OF THE GOSPEL SINGERS** -
May 68. President; (7") **WHOLE LOTTA SHAKIN' GOIN' ON. / LAWDY MISS CLAWDY** -
May 68. London; (7") **GOOD GOLLY MISS MOLLY. / LUCILLE** -
1971. Speciality; (lp) **WELL ALL RIGHT** (rec.'59) - -
1973. Bell; (7") **GOOD GOLLY MISS MOLLY. / (pt.2)** - -
Oct 76. Sonet; (lp) **20 LITTLE RICHARD ORIGINAL HITS** -
Note; Below issued on 'Sonet' UK/ 'Speciality' US, until stated.
1976. (7") **TUTTI FRUTTI. / KEEP A KNOCKIN'**
1976. (7") **GOOD GOLLY MISS MOLLY. / ALL AROUND THE WORLD**
1976. (7") **LONG TALL SALLY. / HEEBIE GEEBIES**
1976. (7"ep) **I GOT IT / ROCK'N'ROLL IS HERE TO STAY. / KEEP A KNOCKIN' / BAMA LAMA BAMA LO** -
Jun 80. (lp) **HIS BIGGEST HITS** -
Jun 77. Creole; (7"m) **GOOD GOLLY MISS MOLLY. / RIP IT UP / BY THE LIGHT OF THE SILVERY MOON** 37 -
Oct 77. Creole; (lp) **LITTLE RICHARD – NOW** -
Sep 78. Creole; (7") **SEND ME SOME LOVIN' 1978. / KING SAX** -
1979. Creole; (7"m) **GOOD GOLLY MISS MOLLY. / BABY FACE / THE GIRL CAN'T HELP IT** -
(re-iss.Mar82 on 'Jukebox') (re-iss.Aug82)
Jul 77. Charly; (7") **LUCILLE. / GOOD GOLLY MISS MOLLY** -
1980. Charly; (lp) **GEORGIA PEACH** -
??. Charly; (lp) **DOLLARS, DOLLARS AND DOLLARS MORE** -
1983. Charly; (lp) **OOH! MY SOUL** -
Aug 86. Charly; (lp)(c) **ROCK'N'ROLL RESURRECTION** -
(cd-iss.Mar87)
Feb 93. Charly; (cd) **THE WILDEST** -
1981. Ace-Chiswick; (10"lp) **THE MODERN SIDES: LITTLE RICHARD** -
Dec 86. Ace; (lp)(c)(cd) **20 CLASSIC CUTS** -
– Long tall Sally / Ready Teddy / The girl can't help it / Rip it up / Miss Ann / She's got it / Lucille / Keep a knockin' / Good golly Miss Molly / Send me some lovin' / Hey-hey-hey-hey / Slippin' and slidin' / Tutti frutti / Heeby jeebies / Baby face / Jenny Jenny / By the light of the silvery Moon / Ooh! my soul / True fine mama / Bama lama bama loo. (cd+c+=) – Can't believe you leave / I'll never let you go.
Apr 87. Ace; (7"m) **TUTTI FRUTTI / SHE'S GOT IT / I'LL NEVER LET YOU GO** -
Oct 89. Ace; (lp-box)(c-box)(cd-box) **THE SPECIALITY SESSIONS** -
Feb 80. Bravo; (lp) **LUCILLE** -
(re-iss.+c.1984) (re-iss.1988 on 'Lifetime')
Jul 82. Bulldog; (lp)(c) **WHOLE LOTTA SHAKIN'** -
Oct 82. Edsel; (lp) **GET DOWN WITH IT** -
Aug 83. Cambra; (lp)(c) **LITTLE RICHARD** -
Jul 84. CBS/ US= Columbia; (lp)(c) **GREATEST HITS**
(cd-iss.1988 on 'Pickwick')
Nov 84. Topline; (lp)(c) **HE'S GOT IT** -
May 87. Topline; (cd) **RIP IT UP** -
Jan 85. Old Gold; (7") **GOOD GOLLY MISS MOLLY. / THE GIRL CAN'T HELP IT** -
Jan 85. Old Gold; (7") **TUTTI FRUTTI. / LONG TALL SALLY** -
Jan 85. Old Gold; (7") **LUCILLE. / BABY FACE** -
Oct 86. RCA; (lp)(c) **ROCKIN' AND RAVIN' ("LITTLE RICHARD with BOTTS BROWN & HIS BLOCKBUSTERS")**
Jan 87. Deja Vu; (lp)(c) **LITTLE RICHARD** -
Feb 87. Arena; (lp)(c) **16 ROCK AND ROLL CLASSICS** -
Mar 87. Sunjay; (lp) **EARLY STUDIO OUTTAKES** -
Apr 87. Delta; (cd) **TUTTI FRUTTI** -
May 87. Bescol; (cd) **16 GREATEST HITS** -
Sep 83. Magnum Force; (lp) **THE REAL THING** -
Nov 86. Magnum Force; (lp) **OOH MA SOUL!** -
Jun 87. Magnum Force; (7"ep) **I'M QUITTING SHOW BUSINESS** -
– I've just come from the mountain / Search me Lord / Coming home / I'm quitting show business.
Oct 87. Demand; (lp) **THE GREAT LITTLE RICHARD** -
Oct 87. Subway; (lp) **THE SESSIONS** -
May 88. Black Tulip; (lp)(c) **20 GREATEST HITS: LITTLE RICHARD** -
May 88. Rhino; (cd-ep) **LIL' BIT OF GOLD**
– Tutti frutti / Good Golly Miss Molly / Slippin' and slidin' / The girl can't help it.
1988. Joker; (lp) **AT HIS WILDEST VOL.1** -
1988. Joker; (lp) **AT HIS WILDEST VOL.2** -
1988. Joker; (lp) **AT HIS WILDEST VOL.3** -
1988. GNP Crescendo; (lp)(c) **BIG HITS** -
Jul 88. Entertainers; (lp)(c)(cd) **KING OF ROCK'N'ROLL** -
Dec 88. Sierra; (lp)(c) **REPLAY ON LITTLE RICHARD** -
Sep 86. Cstle; (lp)(c) **LONG TALL SALLY** -
(cd-iss.Dec87)
Jul 89. Castle; (lp)(c)(cd) **THE COLLECTION** -
Jul 89. Ocean; (lp)(c)(cd) **LITTLE RICHARD** -
Jul 89. Bear Family; (cd) **THE FORMATIVE YEARS 1951-1953** -
Aug 89. Instant; (lp)(c)(cd) **SLIPIN', SLIDIN' & SHAKIN'** -
Dec 91. Quality; (cd) **WILD AND WONDERFUL** -
Mar 93. See For Miles; (cd) **THE E.P. COLLECTION** -
Jun 93. Rhino; (cd) **NOW** -
Feb 94. Javelin; (cd)(c) **SPOTLIGHT ON LITTLE RICHARD** -
Jul 94. Success; (cd)(c) **GREATEST HITS** -
Aug 94. Dynamite; (cd) **LITTLE RICHARD** -
Feb 95. B.A.M.; (cd) **PEARLS OF THE PAST** -
Apr 95. Wisepack; (d-cd) **THE ESSENTIAL COLLECTION** -
Jun 95. Collection; (cd) **THE COLLECTION** -
Jul 95. Summit; (cd) **THE BEST OF LITTLE RICHARD** -

LITTLE VILLAGE (see under ⇒ LOWE, Nick)

LIVE

Formed: York, Pennsylvania, USA . . . early 90's by (see below). Signed to 'MCA' subsidiary 'Radioactive', where they unleashed debut album 'MENTAL JEWELRY'. • **Style:** Guitar-laden grunge-rock in the mould of PEARL JAM fused with GREEN ON RED. • **Songwriters:** Group penned. • **Trivia:** Produced by JERRY HARRISON (ex-Talking Heads).

Recommended: THROWING COPPER (*7)

ED KOWALCZYK – vocals / **CHAD TAYLOR** – guitar / **PATRICK DALHEIMER** – bass / **CHAD GRACEY** – drums

Radio-active Radio-active

Jan 92. (7") **PAIN LIES ON THE RIVERSIDE. / HEAVEN WORE A SKIRT** -
Apr 92. (cd)(c)(lp) **MENTAL JEWELRY** 73 Jan92
– Pain lies on the riverside / Operation spirit (the tyranny of tradition) / The beauty of Gray / Brothers unaware / Tired of me / Mirror song / Waterboy / Take my anthem / You are the world / Good pain / Mother Earth is a vicious crowd / 10,000 years (peace is now).
Apr 92. (cd-ep) **OPERATION SPIRIT (THE TYRANNY OF TRADITION) (live) / THE BEAUTY OF GRAY (live) / GOOD PAIN / LIES ON THE RIVERSIDE (live)** -
Jun 92. (7") **OPERATION SPIRIT. / HEAVEN WORE A SKIRT**
(12"+=)(cd-s+=) – Negation / Good pain.
Sep 94. (c-s)(cd-s) **SELLING THE DRAMA. / ('A'acoustic) / WHITE DISCUSSION** 43 Jun94
Oct 94. (cd)(c)(lp) **THROWING COPPER** 37 1 May94
– The dam at Otter Creek / Selling the drama / I alone / Iris / Lightning crashes / Top / All over you / S*** towne / T.B.D. / Stage / Waitress / Pillar of Davidson / White discussion.
Feb 95. (7"clear)(c-s) **I ALONE. / PAIN LIES ON THE RIVERSIDE** 48
(cd-s+=) – ('A'mix).
Jun 95. (c-s) **SELLING THE DRAMA / THE DAN AT OTTER CREEK** 30
(cd-s+=) – ('A'acoustic).
Sep 95. (c-s) **ALL OVER YOU / SHIT TOWNE** 48
(cd-s+=) – ('A'live at Glastonbury).
(cd-s) – ('A'side) / Waitress (live) / Iris (live at Glastonbury).

Kerry LIVGREN (see under ⇒ KANSAS)

LIVING COLOUR

Formed: New York, USA . . . 1984 by English-born VERNON REID and 2 others. In 1986, COREY GLOVER and WILL CALHOUN joined, with MUZZ being added in 1987. They guested on MICK JAGGER's 'Primitive Cool' album, which led him to produce a demo for them. Later that year, they obtained deal with 'Epic', and released 'VIVID' album in Spring '88. With a re-issue of single 'CULT OF PERSONALITY' hitting US Top 20 in 1989, it revived album to make Top 10. • **Style:** Politico outfit, described as black rock avengers, who brought back memories of HENDRIX, heavy psychedelia and deep soulful blues. • **Songwriters:** VERNON penned except; SHOULD I STAY OR SHOULD I GO (Clash) / FINAL SOLUTION (Pere Ubu) / MEMORIES CAN'T WAIT (Talking Heads) / BURNING OF THE MIDNIGHT LAMP (Jimi Hendrix) / TALKING LOUD AND SAYING NOTHING (James

Brown) / LOVE AND HAPPINESS (Al Green) / SUNSHINE OF YOUR LOVE (Cream). • **Trivia:** COREY played a smart-assed soldier in the Vietnam film 'Platoon'. REID also guested for KEITH RICHARDS on his album 'Talk Is Cheap'.

Recommended: VIVID (*7) / TIME'S UP (*7) / STAIN (*6).

COREY GLOVER – vocals / **VERNON REID** – guitar / **MUZZ SKILLINGS** – bass / **WILLIAM CALHOUN** – drums

Epic Epic

May 88. (7")(7"pic-d) **MIDDLE MAN. / DESPERATE PEOPLE** [ ] [ ]
(12"+=)(cd-s+=) – Funny vibe.

May 88. (lp)(c)(cd) **VIVID** [ ] [6]
– Cult of personality / I want to know / Middle man / Desperate people / Open letter (to a landlord) / Funny vibe / Memories can't wait / Broken hearts / Glamour boys / What's your favourite colour / Which way to America? *(US hit May89)*

Jul 88. (7")(7"pic-d) **GLAMOUR BOYS. / WHICH WAY TO AMERICA?** [ ] [ ]
(12"+=)(cd-s+=) – Middle man / Rap track (conversation with LIVING COLOUR)

Sep 88. (7")**CULT OF PERSONALITY. / OPEN LETTER (TO A LANDLORD)** [ ] [ ]
(12"+=)(cd-s+=) – Middle Man (live).

Dec 88. (7")**OPEN LETTER (TO A LANDLORD). / CULT OF PERSONALITY (live)** [ ] [82] Jul 89
(12"+=)(cd-s+=) – Talkin' 'bout a revolution (live). (US; b-side)

Mar 89. (7") **CULT OF PERSONALITY. / FUNNY VIBE** [-] [13]

Apr 89. (7") **CULT OF PERSONALITY. / SHOULD I STAY OR SHOULD I GO** [ ] [-]
(12"+=)(cd-s+=) – What's your favourite colour.

Oct 89. (7") **GLAMOUR BOYS (remix). / CULT OF PERSONALITY (live)** [ ] [31] Aug 89
(12"+=) – Memories can't wait.
(cd-s++=) – I want to know.
(d7"+=) – Middle man / Open letter (to a landlord).

Oct 89. (7") **FUNNY VIBE. / ('A' instrumental)** [-] [ ]

Aug 90. (7") **TYPE. / SHOULD I STAY OR SHOULD I GO** [-] [ ]

Aug 90. (7") **TYPE. / FINAL SOLUTION** [75] [-]
(12"+=)(cd-s+=) – Should I stay or should I go / Middle man (live).

Sep 90. (cd)(c)(lp) **TIME'S UP** [20] [13]
– Time's up / History lesson / Pride / Love rears its ugly head / New Jack theme / Someone like you / Elvis is dead / Type / Information overload / Undercover of darkness / Olozy I / Fight the fight / Tag team partners / Solace of you / This is the life. *(cd+=)*– Final solution (live) / Middle man (live) / Love rears its ugly head (soul power mix).

Jan 91. (7")(c-s)(7"sha-pic-d) **LOVE REARS IT'S UGLY HEAD. / ('A'soul power mix)** [12] [ ]
(12"+=) – Type (remix).
(cd-s+=)(pic-cd+=) – ('A'version) / Love and happiness.

May 91. (c-s)(cd-s) **SOLACE OF YOU / SOMEONE LIKE YOU** [-] [ ]

May 91. (7")(c-s) **SOLACE OF YOU. / NEW JACK THEME** [33] [-]
(12"+=) – Elvis is dead (mix).
(cd-s+=) – ('A'live) / Type (live) / Information overload (live) / Desperate people (live).

Jul 91. (7"ep)(12"ep)(cd-ep) **BURNING OF THE MIDNIGHT LAMP / MEMORIES CAN'T WAIT / TALKING LOUD AND SAYING NOTHING** [ ] [ ]

Aug 91. (cd) **BISCUITS (live)** [-] [ ]
– Burning of the midnight lamp / Memories can't wait (live) / Talking loud and saying nothing / Desperate people (live) / Money talks / Love and happiness.

Oct 91. (7")(7"pic-d) **THE CULT OF PERSONALITY. / LOVE REARS IT'S UGLY HEAD (live)** [67] [ ]
(12"+=) – ('A'live) / Pride (live).
(cd-s+=) – Talkin' loud and saying nothing / Burning of the midnight lamp.

—— MUZZ SKILLINGS departed Nov'91, and was replaced (Jun92) by **DOUG WIMBUSH** – bass (ex-TACKHEAD)

Feb 93. (7") **LEAVE IT ALONE. / 17 DAYS** [34] [ ]
(cd-s+=)(12"pic-d+=) – T.V. News / Hemp (Full Version)

Feb 93. (cd)(c)(lp) **STAIN** [19] [26]
– Go away / Ignorance is bliss / Leave it alone / B1 / Mind your own business / Auslander / Never satisfied / Nothingness / Postman / W.T.F.F. / This little pig / Hemp / Wal / T.V. news / Love rears its ugly head (live)

Apr 93. (7"pic-d) **AUSLANDER (Remix) / AUSLANDER (Dublander Mix)** [53] [ ]
(12"colrd+=)(pic-cd-s+=) – Auslander (Radio Days Mix) / New Jack theme.

May 93. (7"colrd) **NOTHINGLESS. / 17 DAYS** [ ] [ ]
(cd-s+=) – ('A'remix) / ('A'acoustic mix).

Aug 94. (c-ep) **SUNSHINE OF YOUR LOVE / AUSLANDER (overload mix) / ('A'-Adrian Sherwood & S.McDonald mix)** [ ] [ ]
(cd-ep) – (first 2 tracks) / ('A'remix) / Love rears its ugly head (extended).

—— They disbanded after poor sales early 1995.

Nov 95. (cd)(c) **PRIDE – THE GREATEST HITS** (compilation) [ ] [ ]
– Pride / Release the pressure / Sacred ground / Visions / Love rears it's ugly head (soul power remix) / These are happy times / Memories can't wait / Cult of personality / Funny vibe / WTFF / Glamour boys / Open letter (to a landlord) / Solace of you / Nothingless / Type / Time's up / What's your favourite colour? (theme song).

Richard LLOYD (see under ⇒ TELEVISION)

Huw LLOYD-LANGTON (see under ⇒ HAWKWIND)

Los LOBOS

Formed: Los Angeles, California, USA . . . 1974 by Spanish-Americans HIDALGO, PEREZ, ROSAS and LOZANO, who were all from LA's Chicano community. They named themselves Los LOBOS (The WOLVES), and performed regularly at local clubs and weddings, mainly doing chart covers. In 1978, they sold at gigs an official self-financed debut lp 'JUST ANOTHER BAND FROM L.A.'. In 1980 when supporting PUBLIC IMAGE LTD at a local concert, they were subjected to object throwing punk audience, who didn't appreciate acoustic set. 3 years later, they were given break by independent 'Slash' records, who released mini-lp 'AND A TIME TO DANCE', which was produced by T-BONE BURNETT and guest saxist/fan STEVE BERLIN. He in fact joined them early '84, after they won a Grammy. They started 1985 with a US Top 50 album 'HOW WILL THE WOLF SURVIVE?', which when licensed to 'London' in the UK made minor chart placing. In 1987, after another chart album 'BY THE LIGHT OF THE MOON', they contributed several songs to the 'LA BAMBA' film soundtrack, about 1959 star RITCHIE VALENS. In Aug'87, the title track hit the top spot in both US + UK, and helped project its soundtrack to become top box-office and album seller. A quick follow-up 'COME ON, LET'S GO' also cracked the singles charts, but group abandoned commercial leanings to return to Mexican roots. • **Style:** Chicano folk band, blending together Tex-Mex, soul and acoustic R&B, which was inspired by RY COODER, FLACO JIMINEZ and RITCHIE VALENS. • **Songwriters:** Group penned except; LA BAMBA + COME ON, LET'S GO (Ritchie Valens) / RIP IT UP (Little Richard) / CRYING, WAITING, HOPING (Buddy Holly) / and some trad. • **Trivia:** Country star WAYLON JENNINGS later covered 'HOW WILL THE WOLF SURVIVE'. HIDALGO and ROSAS featured on RY COODER's (Alamo Bay; 1985 lp), with the former guesting on albums (King Of America) by ELVIS COSTELLO and (Gracelands) by PAUL SIMON, with other members.

Recommended: JUST ANOTHER BAND FROM L.A. – THE BEST OF (*7).

DAVID HIDALGO – vocals, guitar, accordion / **CESAR ROSAS** – vocals, guitar / **CONRAD LOZANO** – bass, vocals, guitar / **LUIS PEREZ** – drums, guitar

not issued Los Lobos

1978. (lp) **JUST ANOTHER BAND FROM L.A.** [-] [ ]
– Volver, volver / El cuchipe / La foria de la flores / Sabrami / Bella Maria de mi alma / What's going on / Wrong man these / Blue moods / New Zanda.

Rough Trade Slash

Jan 84. (m-lp) **AND A TIME TO DANCE** [ ] [ ] 1983
– Let's say goodnight / Walking song / Anselma / Come on, let's go / How much can I do? / Why do you do / Ay te dejo en San Antonio. *(re-iss.+c Jan87)*

—— added **STEVE BERLIN** – saxophone, soprano vocals (ex-BLASTERS)

London-Slash Slash

Nov 84. (lp)(c) **HOW WILL THE WOLF SURVIVE?** [77] [47]
– Don't worry baby / A matter of time / Corrida £1 / Our last night / The breakdown / I got loaded / Serenata Nortena / Evageline / I got to let you know / Lil' king of everything / Evangeline / Will the wolf survive?. *(re-iss.+cd Jan87)*

Mar 85. (7")(12") **WILL THE WOLF SURVIVE?. / DON'T WORRY BABY** [57] [78]
(10"+=) – ('A'live).

Jan 87. (lp)(c)(cd) **BY THE LIGHT OF THE MOON** [77] [47]
– One time one night / Shakin' shakin' shakes / Is this all there is? / Prenda del Alma / All I wanted to do was dance / Set me free (Rosa Lee) / The hardest time / My boy's gone / River of fools / The mess we're in / Tears of God.

Feb 87. (7"m) **SET ME FREE (ROSA LEE). / SHAKIN' SHAKIN' SHAKES / PREUDEABELALAMA** [ ] [ ]
(12"+=) – Will the wolf survive?.

Mar 87. (7") **ONE TIME ONE NIGHT. / ALL I WANTED TO DO WAS DANCE** [-] [ ]

Apr 87. (7") **ONE TIME ONE NIGHT. / RIVER OF FOOLS** [ ] [-]
(12"+=) – Anselma / Don't worry baby.

Jul 87. (7")(c-s) **LA BAMBA. / CHARLENA** [1] [1]
(12"+=) – Rip it up.

Aug 87. (lp)(c) **LA BAMBA (soundtrack)** [24] [1]
– La Bamba / Come on, let's go / Ooh! my head / We belong together / Framed / Donna / Lonely teardrops (HOWARD HUNTSBERRY) / Crying, waiting, hoping (MARSHALL CRENSHAW) / Summertime blues (BRIAN SETZER) / Who do you love (BO DIDDLEY) / Charlena / Goodnight my love.

Sep 87. (7") **COME ON, LET'S GO. / OOH! MY HEAD** [18] [21]
(12"+=) – Crying, waiting, hoping (MARSHALL CRENSHAW).

Nov 87. (7") **DONNA. / FRAMED** [ ] [ ]
(12"+=)(10"+=) – Goodnight my love.

Oct 88. (lp)(c)(cd) **LA PISTOLA Y EL CORAZON** [ ] [ ]
– La Guacamaya / Las amarillas / Si yo quisiera / (Sonajas) Mananitas Michoacanas / Estoy sentado aqui / El gusto / Que nadie sepa mi sufrir / El Canelo / La pistola y el corazon.

—— guests **JIM KELTNER** – drums / **JOHN HIATT** – vocals / **ALEX ACUNA** – percussion

Sep 90. (cd)(c)(lp) **THE NEIGHBOURHOOD** [ ] [ ]
– Down on the riverbed / Emily / I walk alone / Angel dance / Little John of God / Deep dark hole / Georgia slop / I can't understand / The giving tree / Take my hand / Jenny's got a pony / Be still / The neighbourhood.

May 92. (cd)(c)(lp) **KIKO** [ ] [ ]
– Dream in blue / Wake up Dolores / Angels with dirty faces / That train don't stop here / Kiko and the lavender Moon / Saint behind the glass / Reva's house / When the circus comes / Arizona skies / Short side of nothing / Two Janes / Wicked rain / Whiskey trail / Just a man / Peace / Rio de Tenampa.

Sep 93. (cd)(c) **JUST ANOTHER BAND FROM L.A. THE BEST OF LOS LOBOS** (compilation) [ ] [ ]
– Volver, volver / El cuchipe / La feria de la flores / Saborami / Let's say goodnight / Anselma / Will the wolf survive? / A matter of time / I got to let you know / Don't worry baby / One time one night / Shakin' shakin' shakes / River of fools / Carabina 30-30 / Tears of God / Set me free (Rosa Lee) / Come on, let's go / La bamba / El gusto / Estoy sentado aqui / La pistola y el corazon / I wanna be like you (the monkey song) / Some day / Down on the riverbed / Be still / The neighbourhood / I can't understand / Angel dance / Bertha / Saint behind the glass / Angels with dirty faces / Wicked rain / Kiko and the lavender Moon / When the circus comes / Peace /

Bella Maria de mi alma / What's going on / Wrong man theme / Blue moonlight / Politician / New Zandu.

John LODGE (see under ⇒ MOODY BLUES)

Nils LOFGREN

Born: 21 Jun'51, Chicago, USA. Raised in Maryland, Washington DC with Italian/Swedish parents. In 1969, he formed PAUL DOWELL & THE DOLPHIN, but after two flop 45's, he broke them up to start GRIN. While building up their live reputation, he sessioned for NEIL YOUNG & CRAZY HORSE on 'After The Goldrush'. CRAZY HORSE also employed him the following year as part writer and session man on their brilliant eponymous debut. Meanwhile GRIN had signed to 'Spindizzy' who gained distribution from 'Columbia'. Their debut lp, issued late summer '71, only scraped the US Top 200, as did their follow-ups '1 + 1' and 'ALL OUT' (the latter added NILS' younger brother TOM). In 1973, they signed to 'A&M' but soon split after NILS joined NEIL YOUNG & CRAZY HORSE for tour work late '73. By Mar'74 he went solo again, re-signing for 'A&M'. By 1976, he and his solo band were reaching Top40 on both sides of the Atlantic. In 1984, after guesting on NEIL YOUNG's 'Trans' album, he joined BRUCE SPRINGSTEEN's E-STREET SHUFFLE. He continued to work parallel projects together, also fitting in a RINGO STARR ALL-STAR BAND tour in 1990. • **Style:** Highly praised cool-in-the shades rock guitarist, who progressed from cult youth following, to gain diserning adult audience. • **Songwriters:** Self-penned except covers; FOR YOUR LOVE (Yardbirds) / ANYTIME AT ALL (Beatles) / IT'S ALL OVER NOW (Valentinos) / etc. • **Trivia:** 'KEITH DON'T GO' was about 'Glimmer Twin' idol KEITH RICHARDS.

Recommended: THE BEST OF NILS LOFGREN – DON'T WALK (*7)

PAUL DOWELL & THE DOLPHIN

NILS LOFGREN – vocals, lead guitar, keyboards, / and **BOB GORDON** (b.1951, Oklahoma)– bass, vocals / unknown drummer

not issued / Sire

1969. (7") **THE LAST TIME I SAW YOU. / IT'S BETTER TO KNOW YOU** [-] [ ]

GRIN

(NILS + BOB)plus **BOB BERBERICH** (b.1949, Maryland)– drums (ex-REEKERS)

Epic / Spindizzy

Oct 70. (7") **WE ALL SUNG TOGETHER. / SEE WHAT A LOVE CAN DO** [ ] [ ]

Jun 71. (lp) **GRIN** [ ] [ ]
– Like rain / See what a love can do / Everybody's missin' the sun / 18 faced lover / Outlaw / We all sung together / If I were a song / Take you to the movies tonight / Direction / Pioneer Mary / Open wide / I had too much (Miss Dazi). *(re-iss.1975 on 'Spindizzy')*

Sep 71. (7") **EVERYBODY'S MISSIN' THE SUN. / 18 FACED LOVER** [ ] [ ]

Jan 72. (7") **WHITE LIES. / ?** [-] [75]

Jan 72. (lp) **1 + 1** [ ] [ ]
– White lies / Please don't hide / Slippery fingers / Moon tears / End unkind / Sometimes / Lost a number / Hi, hello home / Just a poem / Soft fun. *(re-iss.1975 on 'Spindizzy')*

—— added **TOM LOFGREN** – rhythm guitar

Mar 73. (lp)(c) **ALL OUT** [ ] [ ]
– That letter / Heavy Chevy / Don't be long / Love again / She ain't right / Love or else / Ain't love nice / Hard on fire / All out / Rusty gun. *(cd-iss.Oct94)*

Apr 73. (7") **AIN'T LOVE NICE. / LOVE OR ELSE** [ ] [ ]

A & M / A & M

Nov 73. (lp)(c) **GONE CRAZY** [ ] [ ]
– You're the weight / Boy and girl / What about me / One more time / True thrill / Beggar's day / Nightmare / Believe / Ain't for free. *(re-iss.Jan76)*

Feb 74. (7") **YOU'RE THE WEIGHT. / BEGGAR'S DAY** [-] [ ]

He joined NEIL YOUNG & CRAZY HORSE (Aug73-Mar74, on 'Tonight's The Night')

– (GRIN) compilations, others, etc. –

C.B.S. / Columbia

Jun 76. (d-lp) **GRIN FEATURING NILS LOFGREN** [ ] [ ]
– ('GRIN' & '1 + 1' albums)

Jun 76. (7") **SOFT FUN. / SLIPPERY FINGERS** [ ] [ ]

Oct 79. (lp)(c) **THE BEST OF NILS LOFGREN AND GRIN** [ ] [ ]
(re-iss.Feb86)

NILS LOFGREN

with **WORNELL JONES** – bass / **AYNSLEY DUNBAR** – drums

A & M / A & M

Apr 75. (lp)(c) **NILS LOFGREN** [ ] [ ] Mar 75
– Be good tonight / Back it up / One more Saturday night / If I say it, it's so / I don't want to know / Keith don't go (ode to the Glimmer twin) / Can't buy a break / Duty / The sun hasn't set on this boy yet / Rock and roll crook / Two by two / Goin' back.

Jun 75. (7") **BACK IT UP. / IF I SAY IT, IT'S SO** [ ] [ ]

1975. (7") **I DON'T WANT TO KNOW. / ONE MORE SATURDAY NIGHT** [ ] [ ]

Jan 76. (ltd.lp) **BACK IT UP** (live radio show) [ ] [ ]

—— added **TOM LOFGREN** – rhythm guitar, vocals (ex-GRIN)

Mar 76. (lp)(c) **CRY TOUGH** [8] [32]
– Cry tough / It's not a crime / Incidentally . . . it's over / For your love / Share a little / Mud in your eye / Can't get closer (WCGC) / You lit a fire / Jailbait. *(re-iss.Jul83 on 'Fame') (re-iss.1988)*

May 76. (7") **CRY TOUGH. / SHARE A LITTLE** [ ] [ ]

Aug 76. (7") **IT'S NOT A CRIME. / SHARE A LITTLE** [ ] [ ]

—— **ANDY NEWMARK** – drums repl. ZACK

—— added **PATRICK HENDERSON** – keyboards

Mar 77. (lp)(c) **I CAME TO DANCE** [30] [36]
– I came to dance / Rock me at home / Home is where your hurt is / Code of the road / Happy ending kids / Goin' south / To be a dreamer / Jealous gun / Happy.

May 77. (7") **I CAME TO DANCE. / CODE OF THE ROAD** [ ] [ ]

—— **DAVID PLATSHON** – drums repl. NEWMARK

Oct 77. (d-lp)(c) **NIGHT AFTER NIGHT (live)** [38] [44]
– Take you to the movies / Back it up / Keith don't go (ode to the Glimmer twin) / Like rain / Cry tough / It's not a crime / Goin' back / You're the weight / Beggars day / Moon tears / Code of the road / Rock and roll crook / Goin' south / Incidentally . . . it's over / I came to dance.

—— now used mainly session people except TOM (on next only)

Jun 79. (lp)(c) **NILS** [ ] [54]
– No mercy / I'll cry tomorrow / Baltimore / Shine silently / Steal away / Kool skool / A fool like me / I found her / You're so easy.

Jul 79. (7") **NO MERCY. / KOOL SKOOL** [-] [ ]

Jul 79. (7")(7"colrd) **SHINE SILENTLY. / KOOL SKOOL** [ ] [-]

Sep 79. (7") **SHINE SILENTLY. / BALTIMORE** [-] [ ]

Oct 79. (7") **NO MERCY. / A FOOL LIKE ME** [ ] [-]

Backstreet-MCA / Backstreet-MCA

Sep 81. (lp)(c) **NIGHTS FADE AWAY** [50] [99]
– Nights fade away / I go to pieces / Empty heart / Don't touch me / Dirty money / Sailor boy / Anytime at all / Ancient history / Streets again / In motion. *(re-iss.Feb84 on 'M.C.A.')*

Sep 81. (7") **NIGHT FADES AWAY. / ANCIENT HISTORY** [-] [ ]

Sep 81. (7") **NIGHTS FADE AWAY. / ANYTIME AT ALL** [ ] [-]

Nov 81. (7") **I GO TO PIECES. / ANCIENT HISTORY** [ ] [ ]

Aug 83. (lp)(c) **WONDERLAND** [ ] [ ]
– Across the tracks / Into the night / It's all over now / I wait for now / Daddy dream / Wonderland / Room without love / Confident girl / Lonesome ranger / Everybody wants / Deadline. *(re-iss.Jun87)*

Oct 83. (7") **ACROSS THE TRACKS. / DADDY DREAM** [ ] [ ]

—— Split his own band to join BRUCE SPRINGSTEEN & THE E-STREET SHUFFLE between 1984-1985. He returned to solo work, bringing back **NEWMARK + JONES** plus **TOMMY MANDELS + T. LAVITZ** – synthesizers

Towerbell / Columbia

May 85. (7") **SECRETS IN THE STREET. / FROM THE HEART** [53] [ ]
(12"+=) – ('A'extended).
(d7"+=) – Message / Little bit of time.

Jun 85. (lp)(c) **FLIP** [36] [ ]
– Flip ya flip / Secrets in the street / From the heart / Delivery night / King of the rock / Sweet midnight / New holes in old shoes / Dreams die hard / Big tears fall. *(cd-iss.Dec92 on 'Castle')*

Aug 85. (7") **FLIP YA FLIP. / NEW HOLES IN OLD SHOES** [ ] [-]
(12"+=) – ('A'extended).
(12"pic-d) – ('A'side) / Message (11 minute).

Aug 85. (7") **FLIP YA FLIP. / DELIVERY NIGHT** [-] [ ]

Nov 85. (7") **DELIVERY NIGHT. / DREAMS DIE HARD** [ ] [ ]
(12") – ('A'side) / Keith don't go (live).

Jan 86. (7") **SECRETS IN THE STREET. / FROM THE HEART** [ ] [-]
(d7"+=) – Message / Little bit of time.

—— Live band = **JONES, TOM LOFGREN, STEWART SMITH, JOHNNY 'BEE' BADANJEK**

Mar 86. (d-lp)(c) **CODE OF THE ROAD (live)** [86] [ ]
– Beggars day / Secrets in the street / Across the tracks / Delivery night / Cry tough / Dreams die hard / Believe / The sun hasn't set on this boy yet / Code of the road / Moon tears / Back it up / Like rain / Sweet midnight / No mercy / Anytime at all / New holes in old shoes / Keith don't go / Shine silently / I came to dance. *(cd-iss.Dec92 on 'Castle')*

Mar 86. (7") **ANYTIME AT ALL (live). / NEW HOLES IN OLD SHOES (live)** [ ] [ ]

—— He decided to re-join BRUCE SPRINGSTEEN, mainly for stage work. Returned in '91 with main band **SCOTT THURSTON** – keyboards / **ANDY NEWMARK** – drums / **KEVIN McCORMICK** – bass, keyboards, percussion / **+ LEVON HELM** – harmonica, vocals

Essential / Rykodisc

May 91. (cd)(c)(lp) **SILVER LINING** [61] [ ] Mar91
– Silver lining / Valentine / Walkin' nerve / Live each day / Sticks and stones / Trouble's back / Little bit of time / Bein' angry / Gun and run / Girl in motion.

Nov 92. (cd)(c)(lp) **CROOKED LINE** [ ] [ ]
– A child could tell / Blue skies / Misery / You / Shot at you / Crooked line / Walk on me / Someday / New kind of freedom / Just a little / Drunken driver / I'll fight for you.

Permanent / Rykodisc

Oct 94. (d-cd) **EVERY BREATH** (feat. LOU GRAMM) [ ] [ ]

—— next with **ANDY NEWMARK** – drums / **ROGER GREENAWALT** – bass, percussion, samples / **MICHAEL MATOUSEK** – production coordinator

Essential / Rykodisc

Oct 95. (cd)(c) **DAMAGED GOODS** [ ] [ ]
– Damaged goods / Only five minutes / Alone / Trip to Mars / Here for you / Black books / Setting Sun / Life / Heavy hats / In the room / Nothin's fallin' / Don't be late for yesterday.

– compilations, others, etc. –

Apr 82. A&M; (lp)(c) **A RHYTHM ROMANCE** [100] [ ]

Apr 82. A&M; (7") **SHINE SILENTLY. / KEITH DON'T GO (ODE TO THE GLIMMER TWIN)** [ ] [ ]

Jun 85. A&M; (7") **SHINE SILENTLY. / I CAME TO DANCE** (12"+=) – No mercy.

Jun 90. Connoisseur; (cd)(c)(d-lp) **THE BEST OF NILS LOFGREN – DON'T WALK . . . ROCK** [-]
– Moon tears (live) / Back it up / Keith don't go (ode to the Glimmer twin) / The sun hasn't set on this boy yet / Goin' back / Cry tough / Jailbait / Can't get closer (WCGC) / Mud in your eye / I came to dance / To be a dreamer / No mercy / Steal away / Baltimore / Shine silently / Secrets in the street / Flip ya flip / Delivery night / Anytime at all (live).

Jun 94. Windsong; (cd) **LIVE ON THE TEST (live)** [-]

May 95. Spectrum; (cd) **SHINE SILENTLY** [-]

Jul 95. Raven; cd) **SOFT FUN, TOUGH TEARS 1971-79** [-]

LOGGINS & MESSINA

Formed: California, USA . . . early 70's by experienced KENNY LOGGINS and JIM MESSINA. LOGGINS had been member of studio band GATOR CREEK, then SECOND HELPING before he joined the touring ELECTRIC PRUNES (for a week). Meanwhile MESSINA had left his surf band JIM MESSINA & THE JESTERS, to join BUFFALO SPRINGFIELD and then POCO. In 1971, LOGGINS wrote a number of songs for NITTY GRITTY DIRT BAND, one of which 'House At Pooh Corner', hit US Top 60. The duo came together when KENNY LOGGINS invited and eventually credited JIM MESSINA on their debut 'Columbia' label lp. In 1973, LOGGINS & MESSINA had first of many US Top 20 hits, when 'YOUR MAMA DON'T DANCE' made No.4. This was also later covered by ELVIS, and became a huge late 80's smash for POISON. • **Style:** Non brain-taxing lightweight pop-rock typically akin to US mainstream of the era. • **Songwriters:** Most by LOGGINS (some with MESSINA), plus covers of 50's & 60's songs on album 'SO FINE'. Covers:- I LIKE IT LIKE THAT (Chris Karrer) / A LOVER'S QUESTION (Clyde McPhatter) / SPLISH SPLASH (Bobby Darin). LOGGINS covered:- DOWN IN THE BOONDOCKS (Billy Joe Royal) / WHAT A FOOL BELIEVES (co-with Michael McDonald) / FOOTLOOSE (co-with Dean Pitchford) / etc. • **Trivia:** Their 'DANNY'S SONG' was a US Top 10 hit for ANNE MURRAY. In 1976, LOGGINS turned down an offer to play opposite BARBRA STREISAND in the re-make of 'A Star Is Born'. FLEETWOOD MAC lady STEVIE NICKS guested on their 1978 album 'NIGHTWATCH'.

Recommended: THE BEST OF FRIENDS (*5).

KENNY LOGGINS with JIM MESSINA

KENNY LOGGINS (b. 7 Jan'48, Everett, Washington, USA) – vocals, guitar / **JIM MESSINA** (b. 5 Dec'47, Maywood, California, USA) – guitar, vocals with session people, incl. **LARRY SIMS** – bass / **MEREL BREGANTE** – drums / **AL GARTH** – sax, fiddle / **JON CLARKE** – horns / **MICHAEL OMARTIAN** – keyboards / **MILT HOLLAND** – percussion

C.B.S. Columbia

Sep 71. (lp) **KENNY LOGGINS WITH JIM MESSINA SITTIN' IN** [ ] [70]
– Nobody but you / Danny's song / Vahevala / Trilogy:- Lovin' me – To make a woman feel wanted – Peace of mind / Back to Georgia / House at Pooh Corner / Listen to a country song / Same old wine / Rock'n'roll mood. *(cd-iss. 1986 on 'Mobile Fidelity')*

Mar 72. (7") **VAHEVALA. / SAME OLD WINE** [-] [84]

May 72. (7") **NOBODY BUT YOU. / DANNY'S SONG** [ ] [86]

Aug 72. (7") **HOUSE AT POOH CORNER. / PEACE OF MIND** [-] [ ]

LOGGINS & MESSINA

C.B.S. Columbia

Nov 72. (lp)(c) **LOGGINS & MESSINA** [ ] [16]
– Good friend / Whiskey / Your mama don't dance / Long tail cat / Golden ribbons / Thinking of you / Just before the news / Till the end meets / Holiday hotel / Lady of my heart / Angry eyes.

Nov 72. (7") **YOUR MAMA DON'T DANCE. / GOLDEN RIBBONS** [ ] [4]

Apr 73. (7") **THINKING OF YOU. / TILL THE END MEETS** [ ] [18] Mar 73

—— now w/out OMARTIAN

Feb 74. (lp)(c) **FULL SAIL** [ ] [10] Nov 73
– Lahaina / Travelin' blues / My music / A love song / You need a man / Coming to you / Watching the river run / Pathway to glory / Didn't know you when / Sailin' the wind. *(also on quad-lp)*

Feb 74. (7") **MY MUSIC. / A LOVE SONG** [ ] [16] Nov 73

Apr 74. (7") **WATCHING THE RIVER RUN. / TRAVELIN' BLUES** [ ] [71] Feb 74

Jun 74. (d-lp)(c) **ON STAGE (live)** [ ] [5] May 74
– House at Pooh Corner / Danny's song / You could break my heart / Lady of my heart / Long tail cat / Listen to a country song / Holiday hotel / Just before the news / Angry eyers / Golden ribbons / Another road / Vahevala / Back to Georgia / Trilogy: Lovin' me – To make a woman feel wanted – Peace of mind / Your mama don't dance / Nobody but you.

Jul 74. (7") **VAHEVALA (live). / SAME OLD WINE (live)** [ ] [ ]

Jan 75. (lp)(c) **MOTHER LODE** [ ] [8] May 74
– Growin' / Be free / Changes / Brighter days / Time to space / Lately my love / Move on / Get a hold / Keep me in mind / Fever dream.

Jan 75. (7") **CHANGES. / GET A HOLD** [-] [84]

Mar 75. (7") **GROWIN'. / LATELY MY LOVE** [ ] [-]

Mar 75. (7") **GROWIN'. / KEEP ME IN MIND** [-] [52]

—— added **RICHARD GREENE** – violin / **STEVE FORMAN** – percussion / **VINCE DENHAM + DON ROBERTS** – sax

Aug 75. (7") **I LIKE IT LIKE THAT. / ANGRY EYES** [ ] [84]

Oct 75. (lp)(c) **SO FINE** (50's/60's covers) [ ] [21] Sep75
– Oh, lonesome me / My baby left me / Wake up little Suzie / I'm movin' on / Hello Mary Lou / Hey good lookin' / Splish splash / A lover's question / You never can tell / I like it like that / So fine / Honky tonk (part 2).

Oct 75. (7") **A LOVER'S QUESTION. / ANGRY EYES** [-] [89]

Feb 76. (lp)(c) **NATIVE SONS** [ ] [16] Jan 76
– Sweet Marie / Pretty princess / My lady my love / When I was a child / Peacemaker / It's all right / Boogie man / Fox fire / Native son.

May 76. (7") **PEACEMAKER. / WHEN I WAS A CHILD** [ ] [ ] Feb 76

Sep 76. (7") **PRETTY PRINCESS. / NATIVE SON** [-] [ ]

—— The duo split amicably, each going into solo work (see further below)

– compilations, others, etc. –

Note; Below releases until mentioned on 'CBS' UK/ 'Columbia' US.

1975. (7") **MY MUSIC. / THINKING OF YOU** [ ] [-]

1975. (7") **YOUR MAMA DON'T DANCE. / PEACE OF MIND** [ ] [-]

Dec 76. (lp)(c) **THE BEST OF FRIENDS** [ ] [61]
(cd-iss.1988)

Dec 76. (7") **WATCHING THE RIVER RUN. / ANGRY EYES** [-] [ ]

Dec 77. (d-lp)(c) **FINALE (live '75-'76)** [ ] [83] Nov 77
– (introduction) / Travelin' blues / Medley: Danny's song – A love song – House at Pooh Corner / Thinking of you / Keep me in mind / Pretty princess / Brighter days / Be free / Peacemaker / Groovin' / Motel cowboy / Country medley: Listen to a country song – Oh lonesome me – I'm movin' on – Listen to a country song (reprise) / Oklahoma / Home of mine / Changes / You need a man / Lately my love / Rock'n'roll medley: My music – Splish splash – Boogie man.

Jul 80. (lp)(c) **THE BEST OF LOGGINS & MESSINA** [ ] [ ]
– Vehevala / Danny's song / Nobody but you / Whiskey / House at Pooh Corner / Angry eyes / Golden ribbons / My music / Brighter days / Watching the river run / Keep me in mind / Peacemaker / I'm movin' on / Till the end meets.

KENNY LOGGINS

had already gone solo. His backing band were **MIKE HAMILTON** – guitar / **BRIAN MANN** – keyboards / **VINCE DENHAM** – saxophone / **JON CLARKE** – wind / **GEORGE HAWKINS** – bass / **TRIS IMBODEN** – drums

C.B.S. Columbia

Jun 77. (lp)(c) **CELEBRATE ME HOME** [ ] [27] May 77
– Lady luck / If you be wise / I believe in love / Set it free / Why do people lie / Enter my dream / I've got the melody (deep in my heart) / Celebrate me home / Daddy's back / You don't know me.

Aug 77. (7") **I BELIEVE IN LOVE. / ENTER MY DREAM** [ ] [66] Jul 77

Nov 77. (7") **CELEBRATE ME HOME. / WHY DO PEOPLE LIE** [ ] [ ]

Jul 78. (lp)(c) **NIGHTWATCH** [ ] [7]
– Angelique / Wait a little while / Down 'n' dirty / What a fool believes / Nightwatch / Easy driver / Somebody knows / Whenever I call you "friend" / Down in the boondocks. *(re-iss.cd+c Jun93 on 'Sony Collectors')*

Sep 78. (7") **WHENEVER I CALL YOU "FRIEND". / ANGELIQUE** [ ] [5] Jul 78

Dec 78. (7") **EASY DRIVER. / SOMEBODY KNOWS** [ ] [ ]

Dec 79. (lp)(c) **KEEP THE FIRE** [ ] [16] Oct 79
– Mr. Night / Love has come of age / Who's right, who's wrong / Junkanoo holiday (fallin'-flyin') / Will it last / Give it half a chance / Keep the fire / Now and then / This is it.

Feb 80. (7") **THIS IS IT. / WILL IT LAST** [ ] [11] Oct 79

Apr 80. (7") **KEEP THE FIRE. / NOW AND THEN** [ ] [36] Feb 80

May 80. (7") **LOVE HAS COME OF AGE. / JUNKANOO HOLIDAY (FALLIN'- FLYIN')** [-] [ ]

Aug 80. (7") **I'M ALRIGHT. / LEAD THE WAY** [ ] [7] Jul 80

—— (above from the film 'Caddyshack', which LOGGINS contributed half the songs to the soundtrack album in 1980.)

Oct 80. (d-lp)(c) **KENNY LOGGINS: ALIVE (live)** [ ] [11] Sep 80
– I believe in love / Whenever I call you "friend" / Wait a little while / Why do people lie / What a fool believes / Junkanoo holiday (fallin'-flyin') / I'm alright / Celebrate me home / You don't know me / Now and then / All alone tonight / Here, there and everywhere / Angelique / Love has come of age / This is it / Down 'n' dirty / Easy driver / Keep the fire.

Feb 81. (7") **THIS IS IT (live). / I'M ALRIGHT (live)** [-] [ ]

Sep 82. (7") **DON'T FIGHT IT. ("KENNY LOGGINS & STEVE PERRY") / THE MORE WE TRY** [ ] [17] Aug 82

Nov 82. (lp)(c) **HIGH ADVENTURE** [ ] [13] Sep 82
– Don't fight it / Welcome to Heartlight / I gotta try / Swear your love / The more we try / Heart to heart / If it's not what you're lookin' for / It must be imagination / Only a miracle.

Nov 82. (7") **HEART TO HEART. / THE MORE WE TRY** [-] [15]

Jan 83. (7") **WELCOME TO HEARTLIGHT. / ONLY A MIRACLE** [-] [24]

Mar 83. (7") **WELCOME TO HEARTLIGHT. / THE MORE WE TRY** [ ] [-]

Apr 84. (7") **FOOTLOOSE. / SWEAR YOUR LOVE** [6] [1] Jan 84

—— (Above/below from film 'Footloose', feat. other artists, hit UK 7, US 1)

May 84. (7") **I'M FREE (HEAVEN HELPS THE MAN). / WELCOME TO HEARTLIGHT** [-] [22]

Jun 84. (7")(12") **I'M FREE (HEAVEN HELPS THE MAN). / I GOTTA TRY** [ ] [-]

Mar 85. (7") **VOX HUMANA. / LOVE WILL FOLLOW** [-] [29]

Apr 85. (7") **VOX HUMANA. / WELCOME TO HEARTLIGHT** [ ] [-]
(12"+=) – Love will follow.

Jun 85. (lp)(c) **VOX HUMANA** [ ] [41] Apr 85
– Vox humana / No lookin' back / Let there be love / I'll be there / I'm gonna do it right / Forever / At last / Loraine / Love will follow.

Jun 85. (7") **FOREVER. / AT LAST** [ ] [40] May 85

Sep 85. (7") **I'LL BE THERE. / NO LOOKIN' BACK** [-] [88]

Oct 86. (7") **DANGER ZONE. / I'M GONNA DO IT RIGHT** [45] [2] May 86
(12"+=) – Footloose / I'm free (Heaven helps the man).

—— (above/below 7"singles, from film 'Top Gun', which hit UK 4, US 1)

Dec 86. (7") **PLAYIN' WITH THE BOYS. / LOVE WILL FOLLOW** [ ] [60] Aug 86

Mar 87. (7") **MEET ME HALF WAY. / SEMI-FINAL** [-] [ ]

Aug 88. (lp)(c)(cd) **BACK TO AVALON** [ ] [69]
– Nobody's fool / I'm gonna miss you / Tell her / One woman / Back to Avalon /

She's dangerous / True confessions / Hope for the runaway / Isabella's eyes / Blue on blue / Meet me half way.

Aug 88. (7") **NOBODY'S FOOL. / I'M GONNA DO IT RIGHT** [ ] [8] Jul 88

— (Above used on the film soundtrack 'Caddyshack II')

Nov 88. (7") **I'M GONNA MISS YOU. / ISABELLA'S EYES** [ ] [82]
(ext-12"+=)(cd-s+=) – This is it / Love will follow.

Jan 89. (7") **TELL HER. / HOPE FOR THE RUNAWAY** [-] [76]

Columbia Columbia

Oct 91. (c-s)(cd-s) **CONVICTION OF THE HEART. /** [-] [65]

Jan 92. (7") **CODY'S SONG. / THE REAL THING** [-] [ ]

Jun 92. (cd)(c)(lp) **LEAP OF FAITH** [ ] [71] Sep 91
– Will of the wind / Leap of faith / The real thing / Convicyion of the heart / If you believe / I would do anything / Sweet reunion / Now or never / My father's house / Cody's song / Will of the wind (reprise) / Too early for the Sun.

Oct 93. (cd)(c) **OUTSIDE: FROM THE REDWOODS** (compilation) [ ] [60]
– Conviction of the heart / What a fool believes / Your mama don't dance / I would do anything / Now and then / Angry eyes / If you believe / Celebrate me home / Love will follow / Leap of faith / This is it / Footloose / I'm alright.

Jul 95. (cd)(c) **RETURN TO POOH CORNER** [ ] [65]
–

JIM MESSINA

also released solo albums **OASIS** (1979 'CBS') / **MESSINA** (1980 'Warners') / **ONE MORE MILE** (1983 'Warners') / others?

LONE JUSTICE (see under ⇒ McKEE, Maria)

Ray LONEY (see under ⇒ FLAMIN' GROOVIES)

LONG RYDERS

Formed: Paisley, Los Angeles, California, USA . . . Mar'82 initially as The UNCLAIMED by GRIFFINS, SOWDERS and McCARTHY. This aggregation made a – track ep for 'Moxie', which included tracks 'Time to Time' and 'Deposition Central'. As The LONG RYDERS, they issued debut '10-5-60', on own 'Jem' label, before moving to 'Zippo' in '84. Their follow-up 'NATIVE SONS', received critical acclaim, and woke up 'Island' records, who duly gave them contract the next year. Two promising albums followed between 1985 & 87, but as other contemporaries like R.E.M., GREEN ON RED and BANGLES were blossoming, they disbanded. GRIFFIN resurfaced in 1992 with The COAL PORTERS, whose product was released on GRIFFIN's own 'Prima' records. • **Style:** Countryfied rock outfit, similiar to BYRDS or FLYING BURRITO BROTHERS with idol GRAM PARSONS. • **Songwriters:** GRIFFIN-McCARTHY compositions, except YOU'RE GONNA MISS ME (13th Floor Elevators) / I SHALL BE RELEASED + MASTERS OF WAR (Bob Dylan) / DIRTY OLD TOWN (Ewan MacColl) / PRISONERS OF ROCK'N'ROLL (Neil Young) / ANARCHY IN THE UK (Sex Pistols) / PUBLIC IMAGE (P.I.L. w/ STEVE MACK of THAT PETROL EMOTION on vox). • **Trivia:** Will Birch produced them in 1985. SID, STEPHEN + TOM featured on 'Zippo' lp THE LOST WEEKEND by DANNY & DUSTY. They also guested on DREAM SYNDICATE album 'Medicine Show'.

Recommended: NATIVE SONS (*8) / STATE OF OUR UNION (*7).

SID GRIFFIN (b.Kentucky) – vocals, guitar (ex-The UNCLAIMED) / **STEPHEN McCARTHY** – (steel) guitar, vocals / **GREG SOWDERS** – drums / **DES BREWER** – bass repl. BARRY SKANK

not issued Jem

1983. (m-lp) **10-5-60** [-] [ ]
– Join my gang / I don't care what's right, I don't care what's wrong / 105-60 / And she rides / Born to believe in you. *(re-iss.Nov85 on 'Zippo'/'P.V.C.' +=)*– The trip.

— **TOM STEVENS** – drums repl. DON McCALL who had repl. DES BREWER

Zippo Zippo

Nov 84. (lp) **NATIVE SONS** [ ] [ ]
– Final wild sun / Still by / Ivory tower / Run Dusty run / (Sweet) Metal revenge / Fair game / Tell it to the judge on Sunday / Too close to the light / Wreck of the 809 / Never got to meet the man / I had a dream. *(cd-iss.Jan88 w/ last m-lp tracks).*

Apr 85. (7") **I HAD A DREAM. / TOO CLOSE TO THE LIGHT (Buckskin mix)** [ ] [ ]

Island Island

Sep 85. (7") **LOOKING FOR LEWIS & CLARK. / CHILD BRIDE** [59] [ ]
(d7"+=)(10"+=) – Southside of the story / If I were a bramble and you were a rose.

Oct 85. (lp)(c) **STATE OF OUR UNION** [66] [ ]
– Looking for Lewis & Clark / Lights of downtown / WDIA / Mason-Dixon line / Here comes that train again / Years long ago / Good times tomorrow, hard times today / Two kinds of love / You just can't ride the boxcars anymore / Capturing the flag / State of my union. *(cd-iss.late95! on 'Prima' +=)*– If I were a bramble and you were a rose / Southside of the story / Child bride / Christmas in New Zealand.

Jun 87. (lp)(c)(cd) **TWO FISTED TALES** [ ] [ ]
– Gunslinger man / I want you bad / A stitch in time / The light gets in the way / Prairie fire / Baby's in toyland / Long short story / Man of misery / Harriet Tubman's gonna carry me home / For the rest of my life / Spectacular fall. *(re-iss.cd late'95! on 'Prima' +=)*– Ring bells / Time keeps travelling / State of our union (live) / Baby we've all got to go down (live).

Jun 87. (7") **I WANT YOU BAD. / RING BELLS** [ ] [ ]
(12"+=) – State of our union.

— The split New Year '88. In spring '90, GRIFFIN formed The COAL PORTERS.

– compilations, others, etc. –

Jan 91. Overground; (cd) **METALLIC B.O.** (covers) [ ] [ ]
– You're gonna miss me / Route 66 / Brand new headache / Prisoners of rock'n'roll / Dirty old town / Billy Jean / Circle round the sun / Six days on the road / Anarchy in the U.K. / Masters of war / Sandwich man / Blues theme / P.I.L. theme / I shall be released. *(re-iss.Apr95 on 'Prima')*

COAL PORTERS

GRIFFIN w / **ST.JOHN + McGARVEY**

Rubber Rubber

Aug 92. (cd) **REBELS WITHOUT APPLAUSE** [ ] [ ]
– Roll Columbia roll / I tell her all the time / The light that shines within / Rhythm and blues angel / Stealin' horses / Sittin' in an isle of palms (live). *(UK-iss.+=)* – Stuck on an island / John F. Kennedy blues (live) / March of the tap-dancing rats.

Prima Prima

Sep 94. (cd) **THE LAND OF HOPE AND CROSBY** [ ] [ ]
– Imperial beach / Death like a valentine / She loved me / What am I doing? (in this thing called love) / How did we get this far? / You can see them there / Windy city / Playing dumb £1 / Everybody's fault but mine / What about tomorrow / All the colours of the world / The pipsqueaks theme.

Sep 95. (cd) **LOS LONDON** [ ] [ ]
– Me, here at the door / Crackin' at the seams / Chasing rainbows / A woman to love / Apple tree / It happened to me / Santa Mira / After it's broken / A Jacobite at heart / Someone's gonna love you too / Help me / Ain't no way I'll be your cowboy.

LOOP

Formed: Croydon, London, England . . . 1986 by ROB HAMPSON and JOHN WILLS. Issued own releases on 'Head' records, until indie 'Chapter 22', came along in '88. Spiralled upwards from indie to major charts, when 'FADE OUT' album nearly hit the 50. • **Style:** Alternative rave psychedelic rock outfit, similiar to SPACEMEN 3 or even MC5. • **Songwriters:** All penned by HAMPSON and group, except CINNAMON GIRL (Neil Young).

Recommended: ETERNAL – THE SINGLES (*7).

ROB 'Josh' HAMPSON – vocals, guitar / **JAMES** – guitar / **GLEN** – bass repl. PHILIP KING (ex-SERVANTS) / **JOHN WILLS** – drums (ex-SERVANTS)

Head not issued

Jan 87. (12"m) **16 DREAMS. / HEAD ON / BURNING WORLD** [ ] [-]

Jun 87. (7"pic-d) **SPINNING. / SPINNING (part 2)** [ ] [-]
(12") – ('A'side) / Deep hit / I'll take you there.

Nov 87. (lp)(cd) **HEAVEN'S END** [ ] [-]
– Soundhead / Straight to your heart / Forever / Heaven's end / Too real to feel / Fix to fall / Head on / Carry me / Rocket U.S.A. / Spinning / Brittle head girl. *(re-iss.1988 on 'Creation') (re-iss.cd/c/lp Mar94 on 'Reactor')*

— **NEIL McKAY** – bass repl. GLEN / **SCOTT DOWSON** – guitar repl. JAMES

Chapter 22 not issued

Apr 88. (7") **COLLISION. / CRAWLING HEART** [ ] [-]
(12"+=) – Thief of fire / Thief.

— Trimmed to trio, when NEIL departed

Dec 88. (12"m) **BLACK SUN. / CIRCLE GRAVE / MOTHER SKY** [ ] [-]

Jan 89. (2x12"lp)(c)(cd) **FADE OUT** [51] [-]
– Black sun / This is where you end / Fever knife / Torched / Fade out / Pulse / Vision strain / Got to get it over / Collision / Crawling heart / Thief of fire / Thief (motherfucker) / Mother sky.

Situation 2 not isssued

Nov 89. (7") **ARC-LITE (SONAR). / ARC-LITE (RADIATED)** [ ] [-]
(12"+=) – Sunburst.

Jan 90. (cd)(2x12"m-lp) **A GILDED ETERNITY** [39] [ ]
– Vapour / Afterglow / The nail will burn / Blood / Breathe into me / From centre to wave / Be here now. *(cd+=+free-7"w.a.)* **SHOT WITH A DIAMOND. / THE NAIL WILL BURN (BURNT OUT) / Arc-lite (sonar).** *(re-iss.cd Sep95)*

— Disbanded in 1990; WILLS founded HAIR & SKIN TRADING CO. (w/ McKay)

MAIN

were founded by **HAMPSON + DOWSON**

Situation 2 not issued

Nov 91. (12"ep) **HYDRA** [ ] [-]
– Flametracer / Time over (dub) / Suspension.

May 92. (12"ep) **CALM** [ ] [-]
(cd-ep+=) – Thirst.

— HAMPSON joined GODFLESH, when MAIN split, leaving below recordings.

Beggar's B.Beggar's B.

Jul 93. (cd)(m-lp) **DRY STONE FEED** [ ] [-]

Aug 93. (cd) **FIRMANENT (cloudscape). / CYPHER (Pentode) / HEAT REALM (shortwave) / SUSPENSION (hyaline) Code rays.** [ ] [ ]
(re-iss. 12"ep Oct 94 as 'LIGATURE').

Apr 94. (cd)(3x12"lp) **MOTION POOL** [ ] [ ]
– VII / Rail / Crater star / Core / Spectra decay / Rotary eclipse / Reformation / Heat realm / VIII / Liquid reflection.

Nov 94. (cd) **FIRMAMENT II** – (part IX, X) [ ] [-]

Jun 95. (cd-ep) **CORONA** – (part I & II) [ ] [-]

Aug 95. (cd-ep) **TERMINUS** – (part I, II & III) [ ] [-]

Sep 95. (cd-ep) **MASER** – (part I, II, III & IV) [ ] [-]

Nov 95. (cd-ep) **KAON** – (part I, II, III, IV & V) [ ] [-]

Dec 95. (cd-ep) **NEPER** – (part I, II & III) [ ] [-]

– (LOOP) compilations, others, etc. –

1988. Creation; (lp)(cd) **WORLD IN YOUR EYES** [ ] [-]
(re-iss.cd/c/lp Mar94 on 'Reactor')

Nov 89. Chapter 22; (lp)(c)(cd) **ETERNAL – THE SINGLES 1988** [ ] [-]
(all Chapter 22 singles)

May 91. Reactor; (cd)(c)(2x12"lp) **WOLF FLOW** (Peel sessions) □ -
(re-iss.cd/c/d-lp Mar94 on 'Reactor')
Nov 92. Reactor; (cd) **FADE OUT / BLACK SUN / COLLISION** □ -
(re-iss.cd/lp Mar94 on 'Reactor')
Mar 94. Reactor; (cd)(lp) **DUAL** □ -

Jon LORD (see under ⇒ DEEP PURPLE)

LOVE

Formed: Los Angeles, California, USA . . . early '65 originally as The GRASS ROOTS, by ARTHUR LEE and former BYRDS roadie BRYAN MacLEAN. When another band of that name made the US charts, they became LOVE, and soon signed to Jac Holzman's 'Elektra' records. In 1966, with their debut 45 'MY LITTLE RED BOOK' nearly hitting US Top 50, they also scored Top 60 eponymous lp. It was soon pursued by their first and only major hit '7 AND 7 IS', as group went through first of many personnel changes by end of the year. Early in 1967, they re-emerged with classic 'DA CAPO' lp, which contained a near 20 minute track 'REVELATION' alongside some other 3 minute beauts. The next year, they matched it with another gem 'FOREVER CHANGES', which contained 2 pieces of excellence 'ALONE AGAIN OR' & 'ANDMOREAGAIN', and which made the UK Top 30, but not the US Top 150! (These albums are still being sought out by cult collectors, despite receiving a cd re-issue in the late 80's.) In Aug'68, ARTHUR LEE sacked the rest of the group "cause they couldn't cut it", and recruited entire new line-up to make future lp's. Not surprisingly, LEE was left to pursue a solo career in 1972, although he resurrected another LOVE in 1974. After various other re-unions in the late 70's, LEE released a self-titled solo effort in 1981, before going AWOL again. Just recently in the early 90's with renewed LOVE interest, LEE re-formed group for a re-union album. • **Style:** Psychedelic & twee soulful R&B outfit, headed by the HENDRIX-like ARTHUR LEE, who shaped a soft melodic rock alongside more powerful electrifying songs. • **Songwriters:** ARTHUR LEE or BRYAN MacLEAN until latter's departure in 1967. Covered; HEY JOE (trad.) / MY LITTLE RED BOOK (Bacharach-David). • **Trivia:** In 1970, LEE was about to project idea BAND AID (not the charity), with STEVE WINWOOD and JIMI HENDRIX (but the latter died on Sep'70). In 1973, he recorded lp 'BLACK BEAUTY' for 'Buffalo' records, but this was shelved, although bootlegs did appear.

Recommended: DA CAPO (*8) / FOREVER CHANGES (*9).

ARTHUR LEE (b.1945, Memphis) – vocals, guitar (ex-LAG'S, ex-AMERICAN FOUR) / **BRYAN MacLEAN** (b.1947, Los Angeles) – guitar, vocals / **JOHN ECHOLS** (b.1945, Memphis) – lead guitar (ex-LAG'S) / **KEN FORSSI** (b.1943, Cleveland) – bass (ex-SURFARIS) / **ALBAN 'SNOOPY' PFISTERER** (b.1947, Switzerland) – drums repl. DON CONKA

London Elektra

Mar 66. (7") **MY LITTLE RED BOOK. / A MESSAGE TO PRETTY** - 52
Jun 66. (7") **HEY JOE. / MY LITTLE RED BOOK** - □
Sep 66. (7") **7 AND 7 IS. / No.14** □ 33 Aug 66

Elektra Elektra

Sep 66. (lp) **LOVE** □ 57 Jul 66
– My little red book / A message to Pretty / Softly to me / Emotions / Gazing / Signed D.C. / Mushroom clouds / Can't explain / My flash on you / No matter what you do / You I'll be following / Hey Joe / Coloured bells falling / And more. *(re-iss.+cJan72) (re-iss.Feb87 on 'Edsel') (cd-iss.Feb93 & Dec93)*

— added **MICHAEL STUART** – drums ('SNOOPY' now on keyboards), / and **TJAY CANTRELLI** – saxophone

Dec 66. (7") **SHE COMES IN COLOURS. / ORANGE SKIES** □ -
Feb 67. (lp) **DA CAPO** □ 80
– Stephanie knows who / Orange skies / Que vida / 7 and 7 is / The castle / She comes in colours / Revelation. *(re-iss.+cJan72) (re-iss.May81) (cd-iss.1989 on 'WEA')*
Mar 67. (7") **QUE VIDA (edit). / HEY JOE** - □
Sep 67. (7") **THE CASTLE. / SOFTLY TO ME** □ -

— Reverted to a quintet when 'SNOOPY' and TJAY left. (latter to DOMINIC TROIANO)

Jan 68. (7") **ALONE AGAIN OR. / A HOUSE IS NOT A MOTEL** - □
Jan 68. (7") **ALONE AGAIN OR. / BUMMER IN THE SUMMER** □ -
(re-iss.Sep70, hit US No.99)
Feb 68. (lp) **FOREVER CHANGES** 24 □ Jan 68
– Alone again or / A house is not a motel / The Daily planet / Andmoreagain / Old man / The red telephone / Between Clark and Hilldale / Live and let live / Good honor man / Everything like this / Bummer in the summer / You set the scene. *(re-iss.+cJan72) (re-iss.Jan84) (cd-iss.Jul88 on 'WEA')*
Mar 68. (7") **ANDMOREAGAIN. / THE DAILY PLANET** □ -

— ARTHUR LEE dismissed others and recruited new people below **JAY DONELLAN** (LEWIS) – guitar / **JIM HOBSON** – keyboards / **FRANK FAYAD** – bass / **GEORGE SURANOVICH** – drums

Sep 68. (7") **YOUR MIND AND WE BELONG TOGETHER. / LAUGHING STOCK** □ □

— Augmented by **PAUL MARTIN** and **GARY ROWLES** – guitar plus **DRACKEN THEAKER** – keyboards (ex-CRAZY WORLD OF ARTHUR BROWN)

Nov 69. (lp) **FOUR SAIL** □ □ Sep 69
– August / Your friend and mine – Neil's song / I'm with you / Good times / Singing cowboy / Dream / Robert Montgomery / Nothing / Talking in my sleep / Always see your face. *(re-iss.+cJan72) (re-iss.Nov87 on 'Thunderb.', cd-iss.Jun88)*
Mar 70. (7") **I'M WITH YOU. / ROBERT MONTGOMERY** □ -

Harvest Blue Thumb

May 70. (d-lp)(c) **OUT HERE** 29 □ Dec 69
– I'll pray for you / Abalony / Signed D.C. / Listen to my song / I'm down / Stand out / Discharged / Doggone / I still wonder / Love is more than words or better late than never / Nice to be / Car lights on in the day time blues / Run to the top / Willow willow / Instra-mental / You are something / Gather round. *(re-iss.Jul88 as 1-lp on 'Big Beat') (cd-iss.Jul90)*
May 70. (7") **I'LL PRAY FOR YOU (edit). / STAND OUT** - □
Nov 70. (7") **KEEP ON SHINING (edit). / THE EVERLASTING FIRST** □ □

— **GARY ROWLES** now full time , repl. JAY

Jan 71. (lp) **FALSE START** □ □ Dec 70
– The everlasting first / Flying / Gimi a little break / Stand out / Keep on shining / Anytime / Slick Dick / Love is coming / Feel daddy feel good / Ride that vibration. *(cd-iss.Sep91 & Jul92 on 'B.G.O.')*
Mar 71. (7") **STAND OUT. / DOGGONE** □ -

ARTHUR LEE with BAND AID

a solo venture retaining **FAYAD** and new men **CHARLES KARP** – guitar / **CRAIG TARWATER** – guitar / **CLARENCE McDONALD** – keyboards / **DON PONCHA** – drums / and guest **DAVID HULL** – extra bass

A & M A & M

Aug 72. (lp) **VINDICTIVE** □ □
– Sad song / You can save up to 50% / Love jumped through my window / Find somebody / He said she said / Everytime I look up / Everybody's gotta live / He knows a lot of good women / You want change for your re-run / Hamburger breath stinkfinger / Ol' morgue mouth / Busted feet.
Aug 72. (7") **EVERYBODY'S GOT TO LIVE. / LOVE JUMPED THROUGH MY WINDOW** - □
Nov 72. (7") **SAD SONG. / YOU WANT TO CHANGE FOR YOUR RE-RUN** - □

— ARTHUR re-formed

LOVE

recruiting **MELVIN WHITTINGTON** and **JOHN STERLING** – guitar / **SHERWOOD AKUNA** and **ROBERT ROZENO** – bass / **JOE BLOCKER** – drums

R.S.O. R.S.O.

Jan 75. (7") **TIME IS LIKE A RIVER. / YOU SAID YOU WOULD** □ □ Dec 74
Jan 75. (lp)(c) **REEL TO REAL** □ □
– Time is like a river / Stop the music / Who are you? / Good old fashioned love / Which witch is which / With a little energy / Singing cowboy / Be thankful for what you got / You said you would / Busted feet / Everybody's gotta live.
1975. (7") **YOU SAID YOU WOULD (edit). / GOOD OLD FASHIONED DREAM** - □

ARTHUR LEE

solo again, using loads of session people

Da Capo not issued

1977. (7"ep) **I DO WONDER / JUST US. / DO YOU KNOW THE SECRET? / HAPPY YOU** □ -

Beggar's B. Rhino

Jul 81. (lp) **ARTHUR LEE** □ -
– One / I do wonder / Just us / Happy you / Do you know the secret / One and one / Seven and seven is / Mr. Lee / Bend down / Stay away from evil / Many rivers to cross.

— LOVE re-formed in Autumn '91, with **ARTHUR LEE, DON CONKA, SHUGGIE OTIS** – guitar / **MELLAN WHITTINGTON** – guitar / **SHERWOOD AKUNA** – bass. Credited to

ARTHUR LEE

New Rose not issued

May 92. (cd)(lp) **ARTHUR LEE AND LOVE** □ □

– LOVE compilations etc. –

Aug 70. Elektra; (7") **ALONE AGAIN OR. / GOOD TIMES** - □
Jul 73. Elektra; (7") **ALONE AGAIN OR. / ANDMOREAGAIN** □ -
(re-iss.Apr84 on 'Edsel')
Dec 70. Elektra; (lp)(c) **LOVE REVISITED** □ □ Sep 70
(re-iss.+cJan72)
Feb 73. Elektra; (lp)(c) **LOVE MASTERS** □ □
– My little red book / Signed D.C. / Hey Joe / 7 and 7 is / Stephanie knows who / Orange skies / Que vida / The castle / She comes in colours / Laughing stock / Your mind / And we belong together / Old man / The Daily Planet / A house is not a motel / Andmoreagain / Alone again or.
Sep 76. Elektra; (7") **ALONE AGAIN OR. / THE CASTLE** □ □
1980. Rhino; (lp) **THE BEST OF LOVE** - □
1981. Rhino; (pic-lp) **LOVE LIVE (live)** - □
1986. Rhino; (lp) **GOLDEN ARCHIVE** - □
1982. M.C.A.; (lp)(c) **STUDIO / LIVE** - □

Mike LOVE / CELEBRATION (see under ⇒ BEACH BOYS)

LOVE SCULPTURE (see under ⇒ EDMUNDS, DAVE)

LOVE SPIT LOVE (see under ⇒ PSYCHEDELIC FURS)

LOVIN' SPOONFUL

Formed: Greenwich Village, New York, USA . . . early '65 by JOHN SEBASTIAN and ZAL YANOVSKY. They had been part of N.Y. folk scene during 63-64 and had played in bands The HALIFAX THREE and The MUGWUMPS, who featured DENNY DOHERTY and CASS ELLIOT (future MAMAS & THE PAPAS). With producer ERIK JACOBSEN, they secured a deal with 'Kama Sutra' label, and issued debut 45 'DO YOU BELIEVE IN MAGIC', which hit US Top 10. A string of Top 10 hits followed, including a 1966 US No.1 'SUMMER IN THE CITY'. They disintegrated in 1968, when SEBASTIAN departed for a place in 'Woodstock' and a Top 20 lp in 1970 'JOHN B.SEBASTIAN'. • **Style:** Drug-loving jug-band, who fused love and hippy anthems into light-weight pop/rock tunes. • **Songwriters:** SEBASTIAN (with some traditional arrangements of 30's songs) until his departure, when BUTLER was virtually going solo under LOVIN' SPOONFUL banner, although using pensmiths BONNER and GORDON. Covered; YOU BABY (Ronettes) / OTHER SIDE OF THIS LIFE (Fred Neil) / ALMOST GROWN (Chuck Berry) / SEARCHIN' (Coasters) / NEVER GOING BACK (John Stewart) / etc. • **Trivia:** In 1980, the original line-up re-formed to guest on PAUL SIMON's 'One Trick Pony'.

Recommended: THE COLLECTION (*7).

JOHN SEBASTIAN (b.17 Mar'44 New York) – vocals, guitar, harmonica, autoharp / **ZALMAN YANOVSKY** (b.19 Dec'44, Toronto, Canada) – guitar, vocals / **STEVE BOONE** (b.23 Sep'43, New Connecticut, USA) – bass, vocals / **JOE BUTLER** (b.16 Sep'43, Long Island, New York) – drums, vocals

Pye Inter / Kama Sutra

Oct 65. (7") **DO YOU BELIEVE IN MAGIC. / ON THE ROAD AGAIN** [ ] [9] Aug 65
Jan 66. (7") **YOU DIDN'T HAVE TO BE SO NICE. / MY GAL** [ ] [10] Nov 65
Mar 66. (lp) **DO YOU BELIEVE IN MAGIC** [ ] [32] Nov 65
– Do you believe in magic / Blues in the bottle / Sportin' life / My gal / You baby / Fishin' blues / Did you ever have to make up your mind / Wild about my lovin' / Other side of this life / Younger girl / On the road again / Night owl blues.
Apr 66. (7") **DAYDREAM. / NIGHT OWL BLUES** [2] [2] Feb 66
May 66. (7") **DID YOU EVER HAVE TO MAKE UP YOUR MIND. / DIDN'T WANT TO HAVE TO DO IT** [-] [2]
May 66. (lp) **DAYDREAM** [8] [10] Mar 66
– Daydream / There she is / It's not time now / Warm baby / Day blues / Let the boy rock and roll / Jug band music / Didn't want to have to do it / You didn't have to be so nice / Bald headed Lena / Butchie's tune / Big noise from Speonk. *(cd-iss.1990 on 'Castle')*

Kama Sutra / Kama Sutra

Jul 66. (7") **SUMMER IN THE CITY. / BALD HEADED LENA** [8] [1]
Oct 66. (lp) **WHAT'S UP, TIGER LILY (Soundtrack)** [-] [ ]
– (introduction to Flick) / POW / Gray prison blues / POW revisited / Unconscious minuet / Fishin' blues / Respoken / A cool million / Speakin' of spoken / Lookin' to spy / Phil's love theme / (end title).
Oct 66. (7") **RAIN ON THE ROOF. / POW** [-] [10]
Oct 66. (7") **RAIN ON THE ROOF. / WARM BABY** [ ] [-]
Dec 66. (lp) **HUMS OF THE LOVIN' SPOONFUL** [ ] [14] Nov66
– Sittin' here lovin' you / Bes' friends / Voodoo in the basement / Darlin' companion / Henry Thomas / Full measure / Rain on the roof / Coconut grove / Nashville cats / 4 eyes / Summer in the city. *(cd-iss.1990 on 'Castle')*
Dec 66. (7") **NASHVILLE CATS. / FULL MEASURE** [26] [8] [87]
Feb 67. (7") **DARLING BE HOME SOON. / DARLIN' COMPANION** [44] [15]
Mar 67. (lp) **THE BEST OF THE LOVIN' SPOONFUL** (compilation) [ ] [3]
– Do you believe in magic / Did you ever have to make up your mind / Butchie's tune / Jug band music / Night owl blues / You didn't have to be so nice / Daydream / Blues in the bottle / Didn't want to have to do it / Wild about my lovin' / Younger girl / Summer in the city. *(re-iss.Mar69 on 'Marble A.')*
Apr 67. (lp) **YOU'RE A BIG BOY NOW (Soundtrack)** [ ] [ ]
– You're a big boy now / Lonely (Amy's theme) / Wash her away / Kite chase / Try and be happy / Peep show percussion / Girl, beautiful girl / Darling be home soon / Dixieland big boy / Letter to Barbara / Barbara's theme / Miss Thing's thang / March / The finale.
Apr 67. (7") **SIX O'CLOCK. / YOU'RE A BIG BOY NOW** [-] [18]
May 67. (7") **SIX O'CLOCK. / THE FINALE** [ ] [-]
Jul 67. (7") **YOU'RE A BIG BOY NOW. / LONELY (AMY'S THEME)** [-] [ ]

—— **JERRY YESTER** – guitar, vocals (ex-MODERN FOLK QUARTET) repl. YANOVSKY who was ostracized by rest after reportedly being busted for drugs and incriminating others to avoid prosecution and deportation back to Canada.

Oct 67. (7") **SHE IS STILL A MYSTERY. / ONLY PRETTY, WHAT A PITY** [ ] [27]
Nov 67. (7") **MONEY. / CLOSE YOUR EYES** [ ] [48]
Mar 68. (lp) **EVERYTHING PLAYING** [ ] [ ] Jan 68
– She is still a mystery / Priscilla millionaira / Boredom / Six o'clock / Forever / Darling be home soon / Younger generation / Money / Old folks / Only pretty, what a pity / Try a little bit / Close your eyes.
May 68. (lp) **THE BEST OF THE LOVIN' SPOONFUL VOL. 2** (compilation) [ ] [ ]
– Money / She is still a mystery / Younger generation / Six o'clock / Darling be home soon / lovin' you / Boredom / Full measure / Nashville cats / Rain on the roof / Darlin' companion. *(re-iss.Mar69 on 'Marble A.')*

—— Now a trio (BUTLER now vocals) after SEBASTIAN left to go solo.

Oct 68. (7") **NEVER GOING BACK. / FOREVER** [ ] [73] Jul68
Oct 68. (7") **(TIL I) RUN WITH YOU. / REVELATION** [-] [ ]
Jan 69. (7") **ME ABOUT YOU. / AMAZING AIR** [-] [91]
Jun 69. (lp) **REVELATION: REVOLUTION '69** [ ] [ ] Mar 69
– Amazing air / Never going back / The prophet / Only yesterday / War games / (Til I) Run with you / Jug of wine / Revelation: revolution '69 / Me about you / Words.

—— (Above credited to "The LOVIN' SPOONFUL featuring JOE BUTLER") BUTLER was virtually solo, with BONNER & GORDON the main songwriters.

—— In 1969, BUTLER packed in group name. 20 years later BUTLER, BOONE, JERRY YESTER and brother JIM YESTER re-formed for US concerts.

– more compilations, others, etc. –

Jun 66. Kama Sutra; (7"ep) **DID YOU EVER HAVE TO MAKE UP YOUR MIND** [ ] [-]
Aug 66. Kama Sutra; (7"ep) **JUG BAND MUSIC** [ ] [-]
Oct 66. Kama Sutra; (7"ep) **SUMMER IN THE CITY** [ ] [-]
Feb 67. Kama Sutra; (7"ep) **DAY BLUES** [ ] [-]
Apr 67. Kama Sutra; (7"ep) **NASHVILLE CATS** [ ] [-]
Jun 67. Kama Sutra; (7"ep) **LOVIN' YOU** [ ] [-]
Oct 67. Kama Sutra; (7"ep) **SOMETHING IN THE NIGHT** [ ] [-]
Dec 68. Kama Sutra; (7") **SUMMER IN THE CITY. / DAYDREAM** [ ] [-]
(re-iss.Sep73) (re-iss.Jan83 on 'Flashback') (re-iss.1985 on 'WEA') (re-iss. Oct88 on 'Old Gold')
Jun 70. Kama Sutra; (7") **DARLING BE HOME SOON. / NEVER GOING BACK** [ ] [-]
Jun 71. Kama Sutra; (7"m) **SUMMER IN THE CITY. / DAYDREAM / DO YOU BELIEVE IN MAGIC?** [ ] [-]
Dec 71. Kama Sutra; (lp)(c) **ONCE UPON A TIME** [ ] [ ]
Jan 72. Kama Sutra; (lp)(c) **JOHN SEBASTIAN SONGBOOK** [ ] [-]
Oct 73. Kama Sutra (d-lp)(c) **GOLDEN SPOONFUL** [ ] [ ]
Aug 74. Kama Sutra; (lp)(c) **MORE GOLDEN SPOONFUL** [ ] [ ]
1974. Golden Hour; (lp)(c) **GOLDEN OF THE LOVIN' SPOONFUL** [ ] [-]
(cd-iss.1990 on 'Knight')
May 76. Golden Hour; (d-lp) **THE BEST OF THE LOVIN' SPOONFUL VOLS.1 & 2** [ ] [ ]
Jul 75. Pye; (7") **DAYDREAM. / YOU BABY** [ ] [-]
1977. Pye; (d-lp) **THE FILE SERIES** [ ] [-]
1977. Pye; (12"ep) **SUMMER IN THE CITY / NASHVILLE CATS. / DAYDREAM / DO YOU BELIEVE IN MAGIC** [ ] [-]
1978. Buddah; (7") **SUMMER IN THE CITY. / NASHVILLE CATS** [ ] [-]
Jul 85. Buddah; (lp)(c) **GREATEST HITS** [ ] [-]
Jun 80. Pye Flashback; (7"ep) **SUMMER SOUNDS** [ ] [-]
1983. Breakaway; (lp) **DISTANT ECHOES** [ ] [-]
Apr 83. P.R.T.; (10"lp) **BEST IN THE WEST** [ ] [-]
Apr 83. Old Gold; (7") **DAYDREAM. / DO YOU BELIEVE IN MAGIC** [ ] [-]
Jul 84. Old Gold; (7") **SUMMER IN THE CITY. / ('B'side by "Lemon Pipers")** [ ] [-]
Mar 84. Scoop; (7"ep)(c-ep) **6 TRACK HITS** [ ] [-]
1986. Edsel; (lp) **JUG BAND MUSIC** [ ] [-]
1987. Design; (c) **NASHVILLE CATS** [ ] [-]
May 88. See For Miles; (lp)(cd) **THE EP COLLECTION** [ ] [-]
1988. Castle; (d-lp)(d-c)(d-cd) **DO YOU BELIEVE IN MAGIC / EVERYTHING PLAYING** [ ] [-]
Aug 88. Castle; (d-lp)(c)(cd) **THE COLLECTION** [ ] [-]
– Do you believe in magic? / Did you ever have to make up your mind? / Younger girl / Jug band music / Didn't want to have to do it / Daydream / You're a big boy now / Wash her away / Girl beautiful girl (Barbara's theme) / Bespoken / Darling be home soon / Lookin' to spy / You didn't have to be so nice / Sittin' here lovin' you / Darlin' companion / Rain on the roof / Coconut grove / Summer in the city / She is still a mystery / Boredom / Six o'clock / Younger generation / Till I run with you / Never goin' back.
1988. Castle; (cd-ep) **THE LOVIN' SPOONFUL** [ ] [-]
Sep 89. Mainline; (lp)(c)(cd) **20 GREATEST HITS** [ ] [-]
1989. Success; (lp) **SUMMER IN THE CITY** [ ] [-]
(cd-iss.1990 on 'Movieplay')
1991. Sequel; (cd) **THE LOVIN' SPOONFUL GO TO THE MOVIES** [ ] [-]
Apr 93. Pulsar; (cd) **SUMMER IN THE CITY** [ ] [-]
Dec 93. Disky; (cd) **GOLD: GREATEST HITS** [ ] [-]
Jan 95. Spectrum; (cd) **SUMMER IN THE CITY** [ ] [-]
Sep 95. RCA; (cd-s) **SUMMER IN THE CITY /** [ ] [-]

—— A various compilation WHAT'S SHAKIN' featured 4 songs was released 1966 on 'Elektra'. re-iss.1988 on 'Edsel')

Nick LOWE

Born: 24 Mar'49, Woodchurch, Suffolk, England. He formed a school band SOUND 4 PLUS 1, with BRINSLEY SCHWARZ in 1963. They evolved into KIPPINGTON LODGE, and after a series of singles were re-launched in 1969 under BRINSLEY SCHWARZ banner. After fine reviews and critical attention, they disbanded in 1975 after several lp's. LOWE then released a couple of pop singles for 'United Art' in 1975-76 under psuedonyms; TARTAN HORDE (Bay City Rollers, We Love You / Rollers Theme) & DISCO BROTHERS (Let's Go To The Disco / Everybody Dance). Around the same period he was involved in more serious work (i.e. producing GRAHAM PARKER & THE RUMOUR). In 1976, he signed to Jake Riviera's new 'Stiff' label and issued their first 45 'SO IT GOES'. He released 2 more singles for the label, and also produced stablemates The DAMNED, WRECKLESS ERIC, ELVIS COSTELLO, etc. Early in '78, he went with Jake to 'Radar', and hit the UK charts with single 'I LOVE THE SOUND OF BREAKING GLASS' and album 'JESUS OF COOL'. In 1979, he scored with more hits, including UK + US Top 20 single 'CRUEL TO BE KIND'. In the early 80's, he joined DAVE EDMUNDS in ROCKPILE, but they folded after self-titled flop lp. He also married singer CARLENE CARTER (daughter of JOHNNY CASH), and continued to produce her, and others including PRETENDERS, PAUL CARRACK, FABULOUS THUNDERBIRDS, JOHN HIATT, etc. He still sold enough records to maintain a solo career, and in the early 90's initiated semi-supergroup LITTLE VILLAGE. • **Style:** Intelligent commercial 'new wave', with similarities to that of his production artists. • **Songwriters:** Self-penned except; PEACE, LOVE & UNDERSTANDING (Brinsley Schwarz) / HALF-WAY TO PARADISE (Billy Fury) / ENDLESS SLEEP (Joey Reynolds) / I KNEW THE BRIDE (Dave Edmunds) / etc. • **Trivia:** In 1981, he featured on IAN GOMM's (ex-BRINSLEY SCHWARZ) single 'I Like You But I Don't Love You'.

Recommended: BASHER: THE BEST OF NICK LOWE (*6).

NICK LOWE (solo) – vocals, bass, guitar (ex-BRINSLEY SCHWARZ) He was also a member of DAVE EDMUNDS' ROCKPILE group between Jul77-Feb81. His solo band included **EDMUNDS** – guitar and other ROCKPILE members **BILLY BREMNER** – guitar and **TERRY WILLIAMS** – drums (ex-MAN, etc.) used mainly on 2 albums below.

Stiff / not issued

Aug 76. (7") **SO IT GOES. / HEART OF THE CITY** [ ] [-]
May 77. (7"ep) **BOWI** [ ] [-]
– Born a woman / Shake that rat / Marie Provost / Endless sleep.
Oct 77. (7") **HALFWAY TO PARADISE. / I DON'T WANT THE NIGHT TO END** [ ] [-]

Radar / Columbia

Feb 78. (7") **I LOVE THE SOUND OF BREAKING GLASS. / THEY CALLED IT ROCK** [7] [-]
Feb 78. (lp)(c) **THE JESUS OF COOL** (US-title 'PURE POP FOR NOW PEOPLE') [22] [ ]
– Music for money / I love the sound of breaking glass / Little Hitler / Shake & pop / Tonight / So it goes / No reason / 36 inches high / Marie Provost / Netted by reality / Heart of the city. *(re-iss.+cd Oct88 on 'Demon')*
May 78. (7") **LITTLE HITLER. / CRUEL TO BE KIND** [ ] [-]
Jul 78. (7") **HEART OF THE CITY. / SO IT GOES** [-] [ ]
Sep 78. (7") **I LOVE THE SOUND OF BREAKING GLASS. / ENDLESS SLEEP** [-] [ ]
Nov 78. (7") **AMERICAN SQUIRM. / (WHAT'S SO FUNNY 'BOUT) PEACE, LOVE AND UNDERSTANDING** [ ] [-]
May 79. (7") **CRACKING UP. / BASING STREET** [34] [-]
Jun 79. (lp)(c) **LABOUR OF LUST** [43] [31]
– Cruel to be kind / Cracking up / Big kick, plain scrap / Born fighter / You make me / Skin deep / Switchboard Susan / Grey ribbon / Without love / Dose of you / Love so fine. *(re-iss.Apr90)*
Aug 79. (7") **CRUEL TO BE KIND. / ENDLESS GREY RIBBON** [12] [12] Jul 79
Dec 79. (7") **SWITCHBOARD SUSAN. / BASIN STREET** [-] [ ]

— After he split from ROCKPILE in Feb81 he formed his own band

NICK LOWE & THE CHAPS

(They became NOISE TO GO early '82) **MARTIN BELMONT** – guitar / **PAUL CARRACK** – keyboards / **BOBBY IRWIN** – drums

F-Beat / Columbia

Feb 82. (7") **BURNING. / ZULU KISS** [ ] [ ]
Feb 82. (lp)(c) **NICK THE KNIFE** [99] [50]
– Burning / Heart / Stick it where the sun don't shine / Queen of Sheba / My heart hurts / Couldn't love you (any more than I do) / Let me kiss ya / Too many teardrops / Ba doom / Raining raining / One's too many / Zulu kiss. *(re-iss.1986 on 'Demon', cd-iss.Apr90)*
Apr 82. (7") **MY HEART HURTS. / PET YOU AND HOLD YOU** [ ] [-]
(d7"+=) – Cracking up / (What's so funny 'bout) Peace, love and understanding.
Apr 82. (7") **MY HEART HURTS. / STICK IT WHERE THE SUN DON'T SHINE** [-] [ ]

— added **JAMES ELLER** – bass

Apr 83. (7") **RAGIN' EYES. / TANGUE-RAE** [ ] [ ]
(12"+=) – Cool reaction.
Jun 83. (lp)(c) **THE ABOMINABLE SHOWMAN** [ ] [ ]
– We want action / Ragin' eyes / Cool reaction / Time wounds all heels / Man of a fool / Tanque-Rae / Wish you were here / Chicken and feathers / Paid the price / Mess around with love / Saint beneath the paint / How do you talk to an angel.
Jun 83. (7") **HOW DO YOU TALK TO AN ANGEL / I WISH YOU WERE HERE** [-] [ ]

R.C.A. / R.C.A.

May 84. (7") **HALF A BOY AND HALF A MAN. / AWESOME** [53] [ ]
(12"+=) – Cruel to be kind.
May 84. (lp)(c) **NICK LOWE & HIS COWBOY OUTFIT** [ ] [ ]
– Half a boy and half a man / You'll never get me up / (in one of those) / Maureen / God's gift to women / The Gee and the Rick and the three card trick / (Hey big mouth) Stand up and say that / Awesome / Breakaway / Love like a glove / Live fast, love hard, die young / L.A.F.S.
Aug 84. (7") **L.A.F.S. / (HEY BIG MOUTH) STAND UP AND SAY THAT** [ ] [ ]
(12"+=) – Baby it's you.
Jul 85. (7") **I KNEW THE BRIDE (WHEN SHE USED TO ROCK'N'ROLL). / DARLIN' ANGEL EYES** [ ] [77] Nov 85
(12"+=) – Seven nights to rock.
Aug 85. (lp)(c) **THE ROSE OF ENGLAND** [ ] [ ]
– Darlin' angel eyes / She don't love nobody / 7 nights to rock / Long walk back / The rose of England / Lucky dog * / I knew the bride (when she used to rock'n'roll) / Indoor fireworks / (Hope to God) I'm right / I can be the one you love / Everyone * / Bobo ska diddle daddle. *(re-iss.+cd Dec88 on 'Demon', omits tracks *)*

Demon / Columbia

Jan 88. (7") **CRYING IN MY SLEEP. / LOVER'S JAMBOREE** [-] [ ]
Feb 88. (lp)(c)(cd) **PINKER AND PROUDER THAN PREVIOUS** [ ] [ ]
– (You're my) Wildest dream / Crying in my sleep / Big hair / Love gets strange / I got the love / Black Lincoln Continental / Cry it out / Lover's jambouree / Geisha girl / Wishing well / Big big love.

— now with **DAVE EDMUNDS, PAUL CARRACK, JIM KELTNER /** plus **BILL KIRCHEN** – electric guitar / **AUSTIN DE LONE** – piano, guitar / **RY COODER** – steel guitar

Reprise / Reprise

Apr 90. (7") **ALL MEN ARE LIARS. / GAI-GIN MAN** [ ] [ ]
(12"+=)(cd-s+=) – I love the sound of breaking glass / Cruel to be kind.
Apr 90. (cd)(c)(lp) **PARTY OF ONE** [ ] [ ]
– You got the look I like / (I want to build a) Jumbo ark / Gai-gin man / Who was that man? / What's shakin' on the hill / Shting-shtang / All men are liars / Rocky road / Refrigerator white / I don't know why you keep me on / Honeygun. *(re-iss.cd Nov95 with extra tracks)*

LITTLE VILLAGE

were another amalgamation of near superstars; **NICK LOWE** – vocals, bass / **RY COODER** – vocals, guitar / **JOHN HIATT** – vocals, guitar / **JIM KELTNER** – drums, percussion, guitar, composer.

Reprise / Reprise

Feb 92. (cd)(c)(lp) **LITTLE VILLAGE** [23] [66]
– Solar sex panel / The action / Inside job / Big love / Take another look / Do you want my job / Don't go away mad / Fool who knows / She runs hot / Don't think about her when you're trying to drive / Don't bug me when I'm working. *(re-iss.cd Feb95)*
Mar 92. (7")(c-s) **SOLAR SEX PANEL. / DO WITH ME WHAT YOU WANT TO DO** [ ] [ ]
(12"+=)(cd-s+=) – Haunted house.
May 92. (7")(c-s) **DON'T GO AWAY MAD. / BIG LOVE** [ ] [ ]
(12"+=)(cd-s+=) – Do with me what you want to do.

NICK LOWE

Nov 94. (cd-s) **TRUE LOVE TRAVELS ON A GRAVEL ROAD. / ?** [ ] [-]
Nov 94. (cd) **THE IMPOSSIBLE BIRD** [ ] [-]
– Soulful wind / The beast in me / True love travels on a gravel road / Trail of tears / Shelly my love / Where's my everything / 12-step program / Lover don't go / Drive-thru man / Withered on the vine / I live on a battlefield / 14 days / I'll be there.

– (NICK LOWE) compilations etc. –

1983. Magnum Force; (lp) **LIGHT UP THE DYNAMITE (with SHAKIN' STEVENS)** [ ] [-]
Sep 84. Demon; (lp)(c) **16 ALL-TIME LOWES** [ ] [ ]
– Born fighter / Marie Provost / American squirm / Skin deep / When I write the book / Little Hitler / Cruel to be kind / Heart of the city / Switchboard Susan / (I love the sound of) Breaking glass / Big kick plain scrap / Cracking up / Without love / Nutted by reality / So it goes / They called it rock. (cd) **20 ALL-TIME LOWES**
Mar 86. Demon; (lp)(c) **NICK'S NACK** [ ] [ ]
Aug 89. Demon; (d-lp)(c)(cd) **BASHER: THE BEST OF NICK LOWE** [ ] [ ]
Jun 91. Demon; (cd)(c)(lp) **THE WILDERNESS YEARS** [ ] [-]
– (rare material 1974-1977)

L7

Formed: Los Angeles, California, USA ... 1986 by SPARKS and GARDNER. Move east to Chicago to sign for the now-famous indie label 'Sub Pop' in 1989, after an eponymous album for 'Epitaph'. They cracked the charts in 1992, when on 'Slash' they hit with near Top 20 classic 'PRETEND WE'RE DEAD'. • **Style:** All-girl grunge metal outfit influenced by METALLICA or NIRVANA. • **Songwriters:** Group or SPARKS penned. • **Trivia:** In Nov92, DONITA caused controversy on UK TV pop programme 'The Word', after dropping her jeans on stage, revealing that she didn't wear knickers.

Recommended: BRICKS ARE HEAVY (*8).

DONITA SPARKS (b.Chicago) – vox, guitar / **SUZI GARDNER** – guitar, vocals / **JENNIFER FINCH** – bass, vocals repl. ? / **ANNE ANDERSON** (b.Chicago) – drums

Epitaph / Epitaph

Dec 88. (lp) **L7** [-] [ ]
– Bite the wax tadpole / Cat o' nine tails / Metal stampede / Let's rock / Uncle Bob / Snake handler / Runnin' from the law / Cool out / It's not you / I drink / Ms.45.

— **DEE PLAKAS** – drums repl. ANNE

not issued / Sub Pop

Jan 90. (7")(7"green) **SHOVE. / PACKIN' A ROD** [-] [ ]

Glitter... / Sub Pop

Nov 90. (12"ep)(12"purple-ep) **SMELL THE MAGIC** [ ] [ ] Aug 90
– Shove / Til the wheels fall off / Fast'n'frightening / (Right on) Thru / Deathwish / Broomstick. (cd-ep+=) – Packin' a rod / Just like me / American society.

Slash / London

Mar 92. (7")(c-s)(7"red) **PRETEND WE"RE DEAD. / SHIT LIST** [21] [ ]
(12"+=)(cd-s+=) – Lopsided head / Mr.Integrity.
Apr 92. (cd)(c)(lp) **BRICKS ARE HEAVY** [24] [ ]
– Wargasm / Scrap / Pretend we're dead / Diet pill / Everglade / Slide / One more thing / Mr.Integrity / Monster / Shit list / This ain't pleasure.
May 92. (7")(c-s)(7"colour) **EVERGLADE. / FREAK MAGNET** [27] [ ]
– (12"+=)(cd-s+=) – Scrap.
Sep 92. (7")(c-s) **MONSTER. / USED TO LOVE HIM** [33] [ ]
(12"+=)(cd-s+=) – Diet pill.
Nov 92. (7")(c-s) **PRETEND WE'RE DEAD. / FAST'N'FRIGHTENING (live)** [50] [ ]
(cd-s+=) – (Right on) Thru / Shove / Shit list / Diet pill.

— Band will appear as CAMEL LIPS group in the film 'SERIAL MOM'.

Jun 94. (7"colrd)(12"colrd) **ANDRES. / BOMB** [34] [ ]
(cd-s+=) – (KRXT radio interview).
Jul 94. (cd)(c)(lp) **HUNGRY FOR STINK** [26] [ ]
– Andres / Baggage / Can I run / The bomb / Questioning my sanity / Riding with a movie star / Stuck here again / Fuel my fire / Freak magnet / She has eyes / Shirley / Talk box.

Steve LUKATHER (see under ⇒ TOTO)

LUNA (see under ⇒ GALAXIE 500)

Lydia LUNCH

Born: Rochester, New York, USA. She became part of New York's 'No Wave' scene in 1976-78, when her band TEENAGE JESUS & THE JERKS exploded onto the scene with their screaching classic 'ORPHANS'. After disbanding them and her other band BEIRUT SLUMP in the late 70's, she embarked on a solo xareer, releasing 'Ze' label debut 'QUEEN OF SIAM'. Always an experimentalist, she tried out R&B and funk in her next project; 8-EYED SPY. In 1982, she unleashed her second solo lp '13:13' for 'Ruby'. Collaborations with The BIRTHDAY PARTY, ROWLAND HOWARD, EINSTURZENDE NEUBAUTEN, DIE HAUT and Danish band SORT SOL, took her abroad to Berlin, but she returned in 1984 with 'IN LIMBO' on CABARET VOLTAIRE's indie label 'DoubleVision'. The following year, she founded own 'Widowspeak' label and this issued her 'UNCENSORED' cassette. In between further solo work, she spent time in the studio with MICHAEL GIRA (Swans), SONIC YOUTH and collaborated with JIM FOETUS as STINKFIST, and KIM GORDON in late 80's splinter group HARRY CREWS. • **Style:** Provocative punk banshee, who confronted all the boundaries of outrageous experimental rock. Her sound has now been heard in 90's groups; BABES IN TOYLAND and HOLE. • **Songwriters:** Herself, except SPOOKY (Association) / DON'T FEAR THE REAPER (Blue Oyster Cult) / WHY DON'T WE DO IT IN THE ROAD (Beatles). • **Trivia:** She featured in a semi-porn film with JIM THIRLWELL (FOETUS).

Recommended: HYSTERIE (*7)

TEENAGE JESUS & THE JERKS

LYDIA LUNCH – vocals, guitar / **GORDON STEVENSON** – bass / **BRADLY FIELD** – drums

not issued — Migraine

Apr 78. (7") **ORPHANS. / LESS OF ME** [-] [ ]

not issued — Lust Unlust

Mar 79. (7") **BABY DOLL. / FREUD IN A FLOP / RACE MIXING** [-] [ ]

Disbanded when she formed . . .

BEIRUT SLUMP

LYDIA LUNCH – vocals, guitar / **ROBERT QUINE** – guitar / **PAT IRWIN** – sax / **GEORGE SCOTT** – bass

not issued — unknown

1979. (7") **TRY ME. / ?** [-] [ ]

LYDIA LUNCH

— went solo added piano & was backed by **ROBERT QUINE** – guitar / **PAT IRWIN** – guitar, keyboards / **JACK RUBY** – bass / **DOUGLAS BROWNE** – drums

Celluloid — Ze

Nov 80. (lp) **QUEEN OF SIAM** [ ] [ ]
– Mechanical flattery / Gloomy Sunday / Tied and twisted / Spooky / Los banditos / Atomic bongos / Lady Surface / A cruise to the Moon / Carnival fat man / Knives in the drain / Blood of tin. *(cd-iss.Jul91 on 'UFO') (re-iss.cd Aug95 on 'Triple X')*

8 EYED SPY

— were formed by **LUNCH / IRWIN + SCOTT** plus **JIM SCLAVUNOS** – sax / **MICHAEL PAUMGARDHEN** – drums

Fetish — Fetish

Nov 81. (m-lp) **8 EYED SPY** [ ] [ ]
– Lazy in love / etc.

May 82. (7") **DIDDY WAH DIDDY. / DEAD YOU ME B SIDE** [ ] [ ]

Had already disbanded, after SCOTT died late in 1981.

Lydia LUNCH

— went solo, but she first half shared an album with The BIRTHDAY PARTY, then a single with their guitarist ROWLAND S. HOWARD

4 a.d. — Ruby?

Feb 82. (lp) **THE AGONY & THE ECSTASY (other side 'Drunk On The Pope's Blood' by BIRTHDAY PARTY)** [ ] [ ]
– Afraid of your company / (2).

Sep 82. (12") **SOME VELVET MORNING. ("ROWLAND S.HOWARD & LYDIA LUNCH") / I FELL IN LOVE WITH A GHOST** [ ] [ ]

— now w / **DIX DENNEY** – guitar / **GREG WILLIAMS** – bass / **CLIFF MARTINEZ** – drums

Situation 2 — Ruby

Jun 82. (lp) **13:13** [ ] [ ]
– Stares to . . . / 3*3 / This side of nowhere / Snakepit breakdown / Dance of the dead children / Suicide ocean / Lock your door / Afraid of your company. *(cd-iss.Oct89 + Oct94 on 'Line')*

— Between 1982 + Aug83, she guested on 2 German 12"ep's on labels 'Ripoff' & 'Zensor' respectively. These were; **EINSTURZENDE NEUBAUTEN** – 'DURSTIGES TIER' the B-side of 'THIRSTY ANIMAL' + **DIE HAUT** – 'DER KARIBISCHE WESTERN'.

— Next with musicians **PAT PLACE** – guitar / **THURSTON MOORE** – bass + RICHARD EDSON – drums (of SONIC YOUTH) / **KRISTIAN HOFFMAN** – piano / **JIM SCLAVUNOS** – sax

DoubleVision — unknown

Sep 84. (m-lp; some red) **IN LIMBO** [ ] [ ]
– I wish . . . I wish / Friday afternoon / 1000 lies / Some boys / Still burning / What did you do. *(re-iss.1986 on 'Widowspeak', cd-iss.see DROWNING . . .)*

— Early in 1985, she was again credited on a 12", this time **SONIC YOUTH's** 'DEATH VALLEY '69, which was released on 'Blast First' UK 'Irredescence' US.

Rough Trade — Torso

Mar 85. (c) **THE UNCENSORED** [ ] [ ]
– Dear whores / Shotgun / Black Romeo / Daddy dearest. *(cd-see ORAL . . .)*

Widowspeak — Torso

Apr 85. (c-box;ltd) **THE INTIMATE DIARIES OF THE SEXUALLY INSANE** [ ] [ ]

Jun 85. (lp) **THE DROWNING OF LUCY HAMILTON** [ ] [ ]
(cd-iss.Jul90 as 'DROWNING IN LIMBO' w / 1984 album)

Oct 85. (10"ep) **HEART OF DARKNESS ("w / NO TREND")** [ ] [ ]

Jun 86. (d-lp) **HYSTERIE** (compilation of all material 1976-1986) [ ] [ ]
(cd-iss.1989)

Mar 88. (12"m) **THE CRUMB. (w / THURSTON MOORE) / DONE DUN / DEAD RIVER** [ ] [ ]

— next featured backing from **BIRTHDAY PARTY** + recorded 1983-84

Apr 88. (lp) **HONEYMOON IN RED (w/ ROWLAND S. HOWARD)** [ ] [ ]
– Done dun / Still burning / Fields of fire / Dead in the head / Some velvet morning / Come fall / So your heart / Dead river / Three kings.

Nov 88. (m-lp) **STINKFIST ("w / CLINT RUIN – JIM THIRLWELL")** [ ] [ ]
– Stinkfist / Meltdown oratorio (part 1,2,3) / Son of Stink. *(cd-iss.Feb89)* (cd+=) – THE CRUMB.

Sep 89. (lp) **ORAL FIXATION** (spoken word live in Detroit) [ ] [ ]
– Dear whores / Shotgun / Black Romeo / Daddy dearest / Oral fixation. *(cd/c-iss.Jul90 w/ THE UNCENSORED)*

HARRY CREWS

LYDIA LUNCH – vocals, guitar / **KIM GORDON** – bass (of SONIC YOUTH) / **SADIE MAE** – drums

Big Cat — Widowspeak

Apr 90. (cd)(lp) **NAKED IN GARDEN HILLS (live in Vienna; late 1988)** [ ] [ ]
– About the author / Distopia / Gospel singer / (She's in a) Bad mood / Bring me down / S.O.S. / Man hates a man / You're it / Knockout artist / Way out / Car / Orphans.

Lydia LUNCH

Big Cat — Widowspeak

Oct 91. (12"ep)(cd-ep) **("w / CLINT RUIN"): DON'T FEAR THE REAPER / CLINCH. / SERPENTINE / WHY DON'T WE DO IT IN THE ROAD** [ ] [ ]

Patho-logical — Patho-logical

May 91. (cd) **C.O.W. (CONSPIRACY OF WOMEN)** [ ] [ ]
– The right to revolt / The conspiracy of women.

UFO — not issued

Oct 91. (cd)(lp) **SHOTGUN WEDDING ("w / ROWLAND S.HOWARD")** [ ] [-]
(re-iss.cd Aug95 on 'Triple X') (d-cd Sep94 w /'TRANCE MUTATION' cd on 'Trident')

Clawfist — Clawfist

Feb 93. (7") **UNEARTHLY DELIGHTS. / BUSTED** [ ] [ ]

Rykodisc — Rykodisc

Nov 95. (cd) **RUDE HIEROGLPHICS (w/ EXENE CERVENKA)** [ ] [ ]
–

– compilations, etc –

Jul 93. Triple X; (3xcd-box) **CRIMES AGAINST NATURE** [ ] [ ]
– Crimes against nature / The beast / Unearthly delights / Cruel story of youth / Daddy dearest / Terminal distraction / Shock corridor / Oral fixation / The right to revolt / Conspiracy of women. *(re-iss.Aug95)*

LUSH

Formed: Camberwell, London, England . . . Oct'88 by girls MIKI and EMMA, plus lads STEVE and CHRIS. After supports slots to DARLING BUDS, etc, they signed to top independent label '4.a.d.' in 1989. Their first release 'SCAR', paved way for 1990 minor hits produced by Robin Guthrie (of COCTEAU TWINS). • **Style:** Alternative rock, both melodic and lazy in harmony, and not unlike The COCTEAUS or MY BLOODY VALENTINE. • **Songwriters:** MIKI and EMMA, except HEY HEY HELEN (Abba) / FALLIN' IN LOVE (Dennis Wilson) / OUTDOOR MINER (Wire) / LOVE AT FIRST SIGHT (Young Marble Giants). • **Trivia:** In 1990, they all posed topless although artisticly painted for an NME cover shot.

Recommended: SPOOKY (*8) / GALA (*7) / SPLIT (*6).

MIKI BERENYI – vocals, guitar / **EMMA ANDERSON** – guitar, vocals / **STEVE RIPPON** – bass / **CHRIS ACLAND** – drums

4 a.d. — Relativity

Oct 89. (m-lp)(c)(cd) **SCAR** [ ] [ ]
– Thoughtforms / Baby talk / Scarlet / Bitter / Second sight / Etheriel / Hey hey Helen / Scarlet.

Feb 90. (12"ep)(c-ep)(cd-ep) **MAD LOVE EP** [55] [ ]
– De luxe / Leaves me cold / Downer / Thoughtforms.

Oct 90. (7"ep)(c-ep)(cd-ep) **SWEETNESS AND LIGHT. / SUNBATHING / BREEZE** [47] [ ]

Dec 90. (cd)(c)(lp) **GALA** [ ] [ ]
– Sweetness and light / Sunbathing / Breeze / De luxe / Leaves me cold / Downer / Thoughtforms / Baby talk / Thoughtforms / Scarlet / Bitter / Second light / Etheriel / Hey hey Helen / Scarlet.

Sep 91. (7")(c-s) **NOTHING NATURAL. / GOD'S GIFT** [43] [ ]

(12"ep)(cd-ep) – 'BLACK SPRING EP'(+=) – Monochrome / Fallin' in love.

Dec 91. (10"ep)(12"ep)(c-ep)(cd-ep) **FOR LOVE / OUTDOOR MINER. / STARLUST / ASTRONAUT** [35] [ ]

— Although on above + below recording RIPPON had left Oct'91.

4ad 4ad-Reprise

Jan 92. (cd)(c)(lp) **[SPOOKY]** [7] [ ]
– Stray / Nothing natural / Tiny smiles / Covert / Ocean / For love / Superblast! / Untogether / Fantasy / Take / Laura / Monochrome.

— **RIPPON** was replaced by **PHIL KING** – bass (ex-SEE SEE RIDER, ex-APPLE BOUTIQUE, ex-FELT)

May 94. (7"ep)(12"ep)(cd-ep) **HYPOCRITE / LOVE AT FIRST SIGHT. / CAT'S CHORUS / UNDERTOW** [52] [ ]

May 94. (7"ep)(12"ep)(cd-ep) **THE DESIRE LINES / GIRL'S WORLD. / WHITE WOOD / LOVELIFE** [60] [ ]

Jun 94. (cd)(c)(lp) **SPLIT** [19] [ ]
– Light from a dead star / Kiss chase / Blackout / Hypocrite / Lovelife / Desire lines / The invisible man / Undertow / Never-never / Lit up / Stardust / When I die.

LUXURIA (see under ⇒ MAGAZINE)

Phil LYNOTT (see under ⇒ THIN LIZZY)

LYNYRD SKYNYRD

Formed: Jacksonville, Florida, USA . . . 1966 initially as MY BACKYARD, by RONNIE VAN ZANT, GARY ROSSINGTON, ALLEN COLLINS, BOB BURNS and bassist LARRY JUNSTROM. They quickly became The NOBLE FIVE, but abandoned this title when they chose ex-school gym coach LEONARD SKINNER's name. To avoid legal action, they became LYNYRD SKYNYRD and issued late 60's limited single 'NEED ALL MY FRIENDS' for local 'Shade Tree' label. After local tours and another single release in 1971, they signed to 'MCA', after turning down Phil Walden's 'Capricorn'. They finally released debut album 'PRONOUNCED LEH-NERD SKIN-HERD' late 1973, which was produced (as was their future 2), by the man who spotted them; AL KOOPER (ex-BLUES PROJECT). This made US Top 30, due to airplay for its DUANE ALLMAN epic tribute track 'FREE BIRD'. Late the following year, they had Top 10 US hit with 'SWEET HOME ALABAMA' (a slight at NEIL YOUNG), which was lifted from US Top 15 album 'SECOND HELPING'. Became major attractions at home and in Britain, and had just released 6th album 'STREET SURVIVORS', when tragedy struck. On 20th Oct'77 while in between gigs, their chartered plane ran out of fuel and crashed into a swamp in McComb, Mississippi. All on board were seriously injured, but VAN ZANT, STEVE and sister CASSIE GAINES, plus roadie DEAN KILPATRICK were killed. Immediately afterwards the cover-shot of lp 'STREET SURVIVORS' was withdrawn, as it had flames apparently sprouting from group's heads. The remaining 4 (ROSSINGTON, COLLINS, POWELL & WILKESON) re-grouped in 1979 with 3 new members, and became the near equally profitable ROSSINGTON-COLLINS BAND. In 1987, the surviving LYNYRD SKYNYRD members re-formed, although this had little commercial impact, even after release of 1991 album. • **Style:** Southern hard rock'n'boogie, triple-guitar playing outfit, inspired by The ALLMAN BROTHERS and FREE. • **Songwriters:** Bulk by VAN ZANT + COLLINS or VAN ZANT + GAINES after '75. When they re-formed in '87, ROSSINGTON, KING and the new VAN ZANDT contributed all. Covered; HONKY TONK NIGHT TIME MAN (Merle Haggard) / SAME OLD BLUES + CALL ME THE BREEZE (J.J. Cale) / CROSSROADS (Robert Johnson) / etc. • **Trivia:** RONNIE's little brother DONNIE formed simiiarly boogiefied • 38 SPECIAL.

Recommended: FREEBIRD – THE VERY BEST OF . . .(*8)

RONNIE VAN ZANT (b.15 Jan'49) – vocals / **GARY ROSSINGTON** – guitar / **ALLEN COLLINS** – guitar / **GREG WALKER** (or) **LEON WILKESON** – bass / **RICKY MEDLOCKE** (or) **BOB BURNS** – drums

not issued Shade Tree

1971. (7") **I'VE BEEN YOUR FOOL. / GOTTA GO** [-] [ ]
(UK iss. Oct82 on 'Me.')

— **ED KING** – bass (ex-STRAWBERRY ALARM CLOCK) repl. LEON & GREG / added **BILLY POWELL** – piano (RICKY MEDLOCKE had now formed BLACKFOOT, after contributing vox + drums on 2 tracks 'White Dove' & 'The Seasons')

M.C.A. M.C.A.

Nov 73. (7") **GIMME THREE STEPS. / MR. BANKER** [-] [ ]

Jan 74. (lp)(c) **PRONOUNCED LEH-NERD SKIN-NERD** [ ] [ ] Nov 73
– I ain't the one / Tuesday's gone / Gimme three steps / Simple man / Things goin' on / Tuesday's gone / Mississippi kid / oison whiskey / Free bird. *(re-iss.Jun84, cd-iss. Jul88) (was US hit No.27 in Feb75)*

— added returning **LEON WILKESON** – bass (ED KING now 3rd guitarist)

May 74. (7") **DON'T ASK ME NO QUESTIONS. / TAKE YOUR TIME** [ ] [ ] Jan 74

Oct 74. (lp)(c) **SECOND HELPING** [ ] [12] May 74
– Sweet home Alabama / I need you / Don't ask me questions / Workin' for MCA / The ballad of Curtis Loew / Swamp music / The needle and the spoon / Call me the breeze. *(re-iss.1983, cd-iss.Aug89) (re-iss.Oct87 on 'Fame')*

Oct 74. (7") **SWEET HOME ALABAMA. / TAKE YOUR TIME** [ ] [8] Jul 74

Nov 74. (7") **FREE BIRD (edit). / DOWN SOUTH JUKIN'** [-] [19]
(UK-iss Jan77)

— (Dec74) **ARTIMUS PYLE** – drums repl. BURNS

May 75. (lp)(c) **NUTHIN' FANCY** [43] [9] Apr 75
– Saturday night special / Cheatin' woman / Railroad song / I'm a country boy / On the hunt / Am I losin' / Made in the shade / Whiskey rock-a-roller. *(re-iss.1983, cd-iss.Aug87)*

Jul 75. (7") **SATURDAY NIGHT SPECIAL. / MADE IN THE SHADE** [ ] [27] May 75

— Reverted to six-piece, when ED KING departed. / Added backing vocalists **CASSIE GAINES, LESLIE HAWKINS & JO JO BILLINGSLEY**

Feb 76. (7") **DOUBLE TROUBLE. / ROLL GYPSY ROLL** [ ] [80]

Mar 76. (lp)(c) **GIMME BACK MY BULLETS** [34] [20] Feb 76
– Gimme back my bullets / Every mother's son / Trust / I got the same old blues / Double trouble / Roll gypsy roll / Searching / Cry for the bad man / All I can do is write about it. *(re-iss.Feb82)*

Jun 76. (7") **GIMME BACK MY BULLETS. / ALL I CAN DO IS WRITE ABOUT IT** [-] [ ]

— added **STEVE GAINES** – 3rd guitar (ex-SMOKEHOUSE)

Oct 76. (7") **TRAVELIN' MAN (live). / GIMME THREE STEPS (live)** [-] [ ]

Oct 76. (d-lp)(d-c) **ONE MORE FOR THE ROAD (live)** [17] [9] Sep 76
– Workin' for MCA / I ain't the one / Searching / Tuesday's gone / Saturday night special / Travelin' man / Whiskey rock-a-roller / Sweet home Alabama / Gimme three steps / Call me the breeze / T for Texas / The needle and the spoon / Crossroads / Free bird. *(US cd-iss. 1991 with edited applause)*

Dec 76. (7") **FREE BIRD (live). / SEARCHING (live)** [-] [38]

Oct 77. (lp)(c) **STREET SURVIVORS** [13] [5]
– What's your name / That smell / One more time / I know a little / You got that right / I never dreamed / Honky tonk night time man / Ain't no good life. *(re-iss.Jul82)*

— On 20th Oct'77, a few days after release of above album, the band's tour plane crashed. RONNIE VAN ZANT, STEVE & CASSIE GAINES plus roadie DEAN KILPATRICK were all killed. The remainder all suffered other injuries, but will recover. ARTIMUS went solo, the rest became ROSSINGTON-COLLINS BAND.

Jan 78. (7") **WHAT'S YOUR NAME. / I KNOW A LITTLE** [ ] [13] Dec 77

Mar 78. (7") **YOU GOT THAT RIGHT. / AIN'T NO GOOD LIFE** [-] [69]

ROSSINGTON-COLLINS BAND

formed 1979 by **GARY & ALLEN** with **BILLY POWELL** – keyboards / **LEON WILKESON** – bass / **DALE KRANTZ** – vocals / **BARRY HAREWOOD** – guitars, slide / **DEREK HASS** – drums, percussion

M.C.A. M.C.A.

Jul 80. (lp)(c) **ANYTIME, ANYPLACE, ANYWHERE** [ ] [13]
– Prime time / Three times as bad / Don't misunderstand me / Misery loves company / One good man / Opportunity / Getaway / Winners and losers / Sometimes you can put it out. *(re-iss.1983)*

Aug 80. (7") **DON'T MISUNDERSTAND ME. / WINNERS AND LOSERS** [ ] [55]

Oct 80. (7") **GETAWAY. / SOMETIMES YOU CAN PUT IT OUT** [-] [ ]

Oct 80. (7") **ONE GOOD MAN. / MISERY LOVES COMPANY** [ ] [-]

Jun 81. (7") **GOTTA GET IT STRAIGHT. / DON'T STOP ME NOW** [-] [ ]

Oct 81. (lp)(c) **THIS IS THE WAY** [ ] [24]
– Gotta get it straight / Teshawana / Gonna miss it when it's gone / Pine box / Fancy ideas / Don't stop me now / Seems like every day / I'm free today / Next phone call / Means nothing to you.

Oct 81. (7")(12") **TESHAWANA. / GONNA MISS IT WHEN IT'S GONE** [ ] [ ]

ROSSINGTON

with **GARY** & his wife **DALE** with **HASS** – drums / **JAY JOHNSON** – guitar / **TIM LINDSAY** – bass

Atlantic Atlantic

Nov 86. (lp)(c) **RETURNED TO THE SCENE OF THE CRIME** [-] [ ]
– Turn it up / Honest hearts / God luck to you / Wounded again / Waiting in the shadows / Dangerous love / Can you forget about my love / Returned to the scene of the crime / Are you leaving me / Path less chosen.

Nov 86. (7") **TURN IT UP. / PATH LESS CHOSEN** [-] [ ]

The ROSSINGTON BAND

with **TIM LINDSEY** – bass / **TIM SHARPTON** – keyboards / **RONNIE EADES** – sax / **MITCH RIGER** – drums

M.C.A. M.C.A.

Jul 88. (lp)(c)(cd) **LOVE YOUR MAN** [ ] [ ]
– Losin' control / Welcome me home / Call it love / Holdin' my own / Rock on / Love your man / Stay with me / Nowhere to run / Say it from the heart / I don't want to leave you.

ALLEN COLLINS BAND

with **COLLINS, HAREWOOD, POWELL, WILKESON, HESS,** plus **JIMMY DOUGHERTY** – vocals / **RANDALL HALL** – guitar

M.C.A. M.C.A.

1983. (lp)(c) **HERE THERE AND BACK** [-] [ ]
– Just trouble / One known soldier / Hangin' judge / Time after time / This ride's on me / Ready to move / Chapter one / Commitments / Everything you need.

— After spell in prison, POWELL joined Christian band VISION. Also in 1986, ALLEN COLLINS was involved in a car crash which killed his girlfriend, and paralized himself from the waist down. On the 23rd Jan'90 he died of pneumonia.

LYNYRD SKYNYRD

re-formed Autumn 1987, (ROSSINGTON, POWELL, PYLE, WILKESON, KING plus **DALE KRANTZ ROSSINGTON, RANDALL HALL** and **JOHNNY VAN ZANT.)**

M.C.A. M.C.A.

Apr 88. (d-lp)(c)(cd) **SOUTHERN BY THE GRACE OF GOD (live)** [ ] [68]
– (intro) / Workin' for MCA / That smell / I know a little / Comin' home / You got that right / What's your name / Gimme back my bullets / Swamp music / Call me the breeze / Dixie – Sweet home Alabama / Free bird.

— **LYNYRD SKYNYRD** re-formed again in 1991. **ROSSINGTON, KING** and **HALL** – guitars / **JOHNNY VAN ZANT** – vocals / **POWELL** – keyboards / **WILKESON** – bass / **PYLE** – percussion, drums / **CUSTER** – drums, percussion

Atlantic Atlantic

Jun 91. (cd)(c)(lp) **LYNYRD SKYNYRD 1991** [ ] [64]
– Smokestack lightning / Keeping the faith / Southern women / Pure & simple / I've seen enough / Backstreet crawler / Good thing / Money man / It's a killer / Mama (afraid to say goodbye) / End of the road. *(re-iss.cd Feb95)*

— extended members **JERRY JONES** – bass, guitar / **DALE KRANTZ-ROSSINGTON** – backing vocals repl. ARTIMUS PYLE

Mar 93. (cd)(c) **THE LAST REBEL** [ ] [64]
– Good lovin's hard to find / One thing / Can't take that away / Best things in life / The last rebel / Outta Hell in my Dodge / Kiss your freedom goodbye / South of Heaven / Love don't always come easy / Born to run. *(re-iss.cd Feb95)*

– compilations, others, etc. –

All 'MCA' unless stated.

Aug 76. (7"m) **FREE BIRD. / SWEET HOME ALABAMA / DOUBLE TROUBLE** [31] [-]
(re-iss.Dec79 hit No.43, re-iss.May82 hit No.21, re-iss.12" +12"pic-d. Dec83)

Oct 78. (lp)(c) **SKYNYRD'S FIRST AND LAST** (rec.1970-72) [50] [15] Sep 78
– Down south jukin' / Preacher's daughter / White dove / Was I right or wrong / Lend a helpin' hand / Wino / Comin' home / The seasons / Things goin' on. *(re-iss.Aug81)*

Oct 78. (7") **DOWN SOUTH JUKIN'. / WINO** [-] [ ]

Oct 78. (7"ep) **DOWN SOUTH JUKIN' / THAT SMELL. / LEND A HELPIN' HAND / CALL ME THE BREEZE** [ ] [-]

Jan 80. (d-lp)(d-c) **GOLD AND PLATINUM** [49] [12] Dec 79
– Down south jukin' / Saturday night special / Gimme three steps / What's your name / You got that right / Gimme back my bullets / Sweet home Alabama / Free bird / That smell / On the hunt / I ain't the one / Whiskey rock-a-roller / Simple man / I know a little / Tuesday's gone / Comin' home. *(re-iss Jul82)*

Apr 82. (d-c) **PRONOUNCED LEH-NERD SKIN-NERD / SECOND HELPING** [ ] [-]

Nov 82. (lp)(c) **THE BEST OF THE REST** [-] [ ]

Sep 86. (d-c)**NUTHIN' FANCY / GIVE ME BACK MY BULLETS** [ ] [ ]

1987. (7") **WHEN YOU GOT GOOD FRIENDS. / TRUCK DRIVIN' MAN** [-] [ ]

Nov 87. (lp)(c)(cd) **LEGEND (rare live)** [ ] [41] Oct 87
– Georgia peaches / When you got good friends / Sweet little Missy / Four walls of Ralford / Simple man / Truck drivin' man / One in the sun / Mr. Banker / Take your time.

Apr 89. (lp)(c)(cd) **SKYNYRD'S INNYRDS** [ ] [ ]

Feb 92. (3xcd)(3xc)(3xlp) **THE DEFINITIVE LYNYRD SKYNYRD COLLECTION** [ ] [ ]

Jul 84. Old Gold; (7") **FREE BIRD. / SWEET HOME ALABAMA** [ ] [-]
(re-iss.7"/12" Jan89 on 'M.C.A.')

Mar 87. Raw Power; (d-lp)(c) **ANTHOLOGY** [ ] [-]

Mar 94. Nectar; (cd)(c) **FREEBIRD – THE VERY BEST** [ ] [-]
– Saturday night special / Whiskey rock & roller / Workin' for MCA / I ain't the one / Sweet home Alabama / Ballad of Curtis Loew / Tuesday's gone / Gimme 3 steps / The needle & the spoon / Free bird / Call me the breeze / What's your name / Swamp music / Gimme back my bullets / That smell / You got that right.

Sep 94. MCA; (cd)(c) **STREET SURVIVORS / FIRST AND LAST** [ ] [ ]

Aug 95. Old Gold; (cd-s) **FREE BIRD / SWEET HOME ALABAMA** [ ] [-]

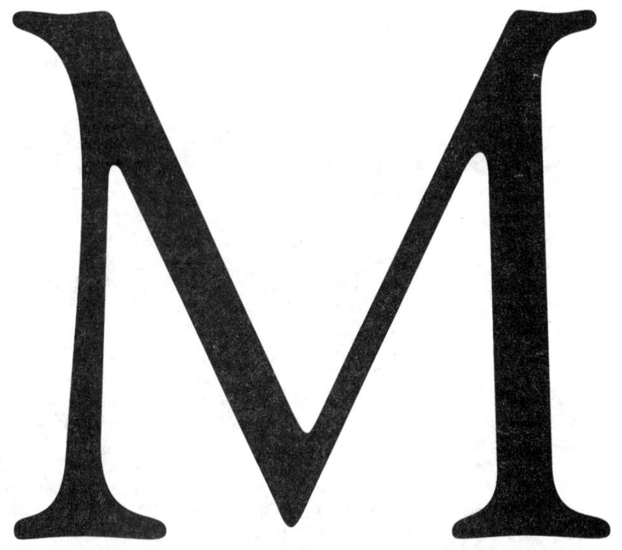

Kirsty MacCOLL

Born: 10 Oct'59, London, England, daughter of folk singer EWAN MacCOLL. After leaving punk outfit The DRUG ADDIX, (as MANDY DOUBT), she went solo in 1979 and signed to 'Stiff'. In 1980 she signed to 'Polydor' and hit the UK Top 20 with novelty-type 3rd single 'THERE'S A GUY WORKS DOWN THE CHIPSHOP SWEARS HE'S ELVIS'. A return to 'Stiff' in the mid-80's, heralded a return to the charts with Top 10 cover song 'A NEW ENGLAND'. She then worked and guested for The POGUES, before re-launching successful solo career in '89. • **Style:** C&W tinged pop star, who although varying in all pop's facets, blossomed into a more complete rock-pop star in the late 80's. • **Songwriters:** Writes / co-writes material. In 1990, she collaborated with MARK NEVIN (ex-FAIRGROUND ATTRACTION). She has covered many songs including; TEENAGER IN LOVE (Dion) / JUST ONE LOOK (Hollies) / TERRY (Twinkle) / A NEW ENGLAND (Billy Bragg) / YOU JUST HAVEN'T EARNED IT YET BABY (Smiths) / CLUBLAND (Elvis Costello) / DAYS (Kinks) / DON'T GO NEAR THE WATER (Ray Charles) / WALK RIGHT BACK (Everly Brothers) / PERFECT DAY (Lou Reed) / EL PASO (Marty Robbins). • **Trivia:** The DRUG ADDIX released one EP for 'Chiswick' in 1978; THE DRUG ADDIX MAKE A RECORD. Her brothers are NEIL of The BIBLE, and CALLUM of MacCOLL & SEEGER. She has been married to producer STEVE LILLYWHITE for several years now. Early in 1990, she guested on comedy programme 'French & Saunders'.

Recommended: ELECTRIC LANDLADY (*5) / KIRSTY MacCOLL (*5).

KIRSTY MacCOLL – vocals with various members of ROCKPILE

Stiff — not issued

Jun 79. (7")(7"pic-d) **THEY DON'T KNOW. / TURN MY MOTOR ON** [ ] [-]

Oct 79. (7") **YOU CAUGHT ME OUT. / BOYS** (withdrawn) [-] [-]

Polydor — Polydor

Feb 81. (7") **KEEP YOUR HANDS OFF MY BABY. / I DON'T NEED YOU** [ ] [-]

May 81. (7") **THERE'S A GUY WORKS DOWN THE CHIPSHOP SWEARS HE'S ELVIS. / HARD TO BELIEVE** [14] [-]

Jul 81. (7") **THERE'S A GUY WORKS DOWN THE CHIPSHOP SWEARS HE'S ELVIS. / OVER YOU** [-] [ ]

Jul 81. (lp)(c) **DESPERATE CHARACTER** [ ] [-]
– Clock goes round / See that girl / There's a guy works down the chipshop swears he's Elvis / Teenager in love / Mexican sofa / Until the night / Falling for faces / Just one look / The real ripper / Hard to believe / He thinks I still care / There's a guy works down the chipshop swears he's Elvis (country version).

Sep 81. (7") **SEE THAT GIRL. / OVER YOU** [ ] [-]

Nov 81. (7") **YOU STILL BELIEVE IN ME. / QUEEN OF THE HIGH TEAS** [ ] [-]

—— (Early 1983, she guested for MATCHBOX on single 'I Want Out').

North Of Watford — not issued

Aug 83. (7")(12") **BERLIN. / RHYTHM OF THE REAL THING** [ ] [-]

Stiff — not issued

Oct 83. (7")(12") **TERRY. / QUIETLY ALONE** [ ] [-]

—— (Early '84, she guested on SIMPLE MINDS hit '45 'Speed Your Love To Me').

Jan 85. (7")(7"pic-d) **A NEW ENGLAND. / PATRICK** [7] [ ]
(12"+=) – I'm going out with an 80 year old millionaire.

Jun 85. (7")(12") **HE'S ON THE BEACH. / PLEASE GO TO SLEEP** [ ] [ ]

—— In 1986-87, she guested on tours & in studio for The POGUES.

Virgin — Virgin

Feb 89. (7")(c-s) **FREE WORLD. / CLOSER TO GOD?** [43] [ ]
(12"+=) – You just haven't earned it yet, baby.
(3"cd-s++=) – La floret de mimosas.
(10"+=) – The end of a perfect day.

Apr 89. (lp)(c)(cd) **KITE** [34] [ ]
– Innocence / free world / Mother's ruin / Days / No victims / Fifteen minutes / Don't come the cowboy with me Sonny Jim / Tread lightly / What do pretty girls do? / Dancing in limbo / The end of a perfect day / You and me baby.

Jun 89. (7")(c-s)(3"cd-s) **DAYS. / HAPPY** [12] [ ]
(10"++=) – Still life / El Paso.
(cd-s+=) – Please help me, I'm falling / Still life.

Sep 89. (7")(c-s) **INNOCENCE. / CLUBLAND** [ ] [ ]
(10"+=) – Don't run awayfrom me.
(12"+=)(3"cd-s+=) – ('A'guilt mix) / ('A'guitar mix) / No victims (mix).

Mar 90. (7")(c-s) **DON'T COME THE COWBOY WITH ME SONNY JIM. / OTHER PEOPLES HEARTS** [ ] [ ]
(12"+=) – Complainte pourste Catherine.
(cd-s++=) – Am I right?

May 91. (7")(c-s) **WALKING DOWN MADISON. / ONE GOOD THING** [23] [ ]
(12"+=)(cd-s+=) – ('A' club mix) / ('A' ambient mix).
(cd-s) – ('A' side) / ('A' urban mix) / Days / Darling let's have another baby (duet w / BILLY BRAGG).

Jun 91. (cd)(c)(lp) **ELECTRIC LANDLADY** [17] [ ]
– Walking down Madison / All I ever wanted / Children of the revolution / Halloween / My affair / Lying down / He never mentioned love / We'll never pass this way again / The hardest word / Maybe it's imaginary / My way home / The one and only.

Jul 91. (7")(c-s) **MY AFFAIR. / ALL THE TEARS I CRIED** [68] [ ]
(cd-s+=) – Don't go near the water / ('A' olive groove mix).
(12") – ('A' Ladbroke mix) / ('A'bass sexy mix) / ('A'olive groove).

Oct 91. (7")(c-s) **ALL I EVER WANTED. / THERE'S A GUY WORKS DOWN THE CHIPSHOP SWEARS HE'S ELVIS (live)** [ ] [-]
(cd-s+=) – Walk right back (live) / A new England (live wIth BILLY BRAGG).
(12"+=) – What do pretty girls do? / Walk right back (live)

—— In 1991, she helped present BBC2's TV consumer programme 'Byline', and featured guest vox on WONDER STUFF's hit single 'Welcome To The Cheap Seats'.

Z.T.T. — I.R.S.

Dec 93. (7")(c-s) **ANGEL (Gregg Jackson edit) // (Jay's edit)** [ ] [ ]
(12"+=)(cd-s+=) – ('A'remix Apollo 440)/ ('A'remix Stuart Crichton).

—— with **MARK NEVIN** – guitars, co-writer (ex-FAIRGROUND ATTRACTION, ex-MORRISSEY) / **DAVID RUFFY** – drums (ex-AZTEC CAMERA) / **GARY TIBBS** – bass (ex-ADAM & THE ANTS) / **PETE GLENISTER** – guitars / **STEVE NIEVE** – keyboards / etc.

Feb 94. (cd)(c) **TITANIC DAYS** [46] [ ]
– You know it's you / Soho Square / Angel / Last days of Summer / Bad / Can't stop killing you / Titanic days / Don't go home / Big boy on a Saturday night / Just woke up / Tomorrow never comes.

Feb 95. (7")(c-s) **CAROLINE. / IRISH COUSIN** [58] [ ]
(cd-s+=) – New England / The butcher boy.
(cd-s) ('A'side) / El Paso / My affair (Ladbroke Grove mix).

Mar 95. (cd)(c) **GALORE** (compilation) [6] [ ]
– They don't know / A new England / There's a guy works down the chip shop swears he's Elvis / He's on the beach / Fairytale of New York (w/ POGUES) / Miss Otis regrets / Free world / Innocence / You just haven't earned it yet baby / Don't come the cowboy with me Sonny Jim / Walking down Madison / My affair / Angel / Titanic days / Can't stop killing you / Caroline / Perfect day.

Jun 95. (c-s) **PERFECT DAY ("KIRSTY MacCOLL & EVAN DANDO") / TERRY** [75] [ ]
(cd-s+=) – Tread lightly / He's on the beach.

Jul 95. (c-s) **DAYS / STILL LIFE (extended)** [42] [ ]
(cd-s+=) – Happy / Walking down Madison (club mix).

– other compilation –

Mar 85. Polydor; (lp)(c) **KIRSTY MacCOLL** [ ] [-]
– There's a guy works down the chipshop swears he's Elvis / See that girl / You still believe in me / Roman gardens / Man with no name / Annie / Keep your hands off my baby / Hard to believe / Berlin / Falling for faces / Clock goes round / Sleepless nights.

MACEO (PARKER) . . . (see under ⇒ JB'S)

Shane MacGOWAN & THE POPES

Formed: King's Cross area, London, England ... early 1994 by ex-NIPPLE ERECTORS (1978), ex-NIPS (1978-81) & ex-POGUES (1983-1991) frontman SHANE (b.25 Dec'57, Kent, England). Late in 1992, he teamed up with friend NICK CAVE on an interpretation of 'What A Wonderful World'. His new outfit were a hit immediately, after POGUEY-like uptempo single 'CHURCH OF THE HOLY SPOOK' broke the Top 75. • **Style:** Due to MacGOWAN's presence, they were gladly welcomed as the new POGUES in 1994, when the real POGUES were absent from recording studio. • **Songwriters:** MacGOWAN except HER FATHER DIDN'T LIKE ME ANYWAY (Gerry Rafferty) / CRACKLIN' ROSIE (Neil Diamond) / THE RISING OF THE MOON + NANCY WHISKEY (trad.). • **Trivia:** Actor JOHNNY DEPP played guitar on their Top Of The Pops debut. Their /his debut album also featured guest appearances from ex-POGUES; SPIDER and FINER, plus DUBLINERS musician /friend BARNEY McKENNA. 'VICTORIA' was written about his recent writer girlfriend VICTORIA CLARKE. MacGOWAN is still a reader & fan of writer JAMES JOYCE and Spanish poet LORCA.

Recommended: THE SNAKE (*8)

SHANE McGOWAN – vocals (ex-POGUES, ex-NIPS) / **PAUL McGUINNESS** – guitar / **BERNIE FRANCE** – bass / **DANNY POPE** – drums / **TOM NcMANAMON** – banjo

Z.T.T. Warners

Sep 94. (7")(c-s) **THE CHURCH OF THE HOLY SPOOK. / RAKE AT THE GATES OF HELL** 74
(cd-s+=) – King of the bop / Nancy Whiskey.

Oct 94. (c-s) **THAT WOMAN'S GOT ME DRINKING. / HER FATHER DIDN'T LIKE ME ANYWAY** 34
(12"+=)(cd-s+=) – Roddy McCorley / Minstrel boy.

Oct 94. (cd)(c)(lp) **THE SNAKE** 37
– The church of the holy spook / That woman's got me drinking / The song with no name / Aisling / I'll be your handbag / Her father didn't like me anyway / A Mexican funeral in Paris / The snake with the eyes of Garnet / Donegal express / Victoria / The rising of the Moon / Bring down the lamp. *(re-iss.cd/c Jun95)* – Haunted (with SINEAD O'CONNOR) / You're the one (with MAIRE BRENNAN) / Cracklin' Rosie / Bring down the . . .

Dec 94. (c-s) **THE SONG WITH NO NAME. / NANCY WHISKEY**
(12"+=)(cd-s+=) – Cracklin' Rosie.

Apr 95. (c-s) **HAUNTED. ("SHANE MacGOWAN & SINEAD O'CONNOR") / THE SONG WITH NO NAME** 30
(cd-s+=)(12"+=) – Bring down the . . . / Cracklin' Rosie.

Jun 95. (c-s) **YOU'RE THE ONE. ("SHANE MacGOWAN & MAIRE BRENNAN") / AISLING**
(cd-s) – Victoria.

MACHINE HEAD

Formed: Oakland, California, USA . . .mid '92 by (see below). In 1994, they unleashed what was to become one of Kerrang magazine favourite albums; 'BURN MY EYES'. • **Style:** Hard-metal similiar to BIOHAZARD or ANTHRAX. • **Songwriters:** Group except 1 by POISON IDEA and CRO-MAGS.

Recommended: BURN MY EYES (*8)

ROBB FLYNN – vocals, guitar (ex-VIOLENCE) / **LOGAN MADER** – guitar / **ADAM DUCE** – bass / **CHRIS KONTOS** – drums

Road-runner Road-runner

Aug 94. (cd)(c)(lp) **BURN MY EYES** 25
– Davidian / Old / A thousand lies / None but my own / The rage to overcome / Death church / A nation on fire / Blood for blood / I'm your god now / Real eyes, realize, real lies / Block.

Oct 94. (12") INFECTED. / PROTOPLAN
(re-iss.Jun95)

May 95. (10"pic-d-ep) **OLD / A NATION ON FIRE (demo) / REAL LIES – FUCK IT ALL (demo) / OLD (demo)** 43
(cd-ep) – ('A'side) / Davidian (live) / Hard times (live) / Death church (demo).
(cd-s) – ('A'side) / Death church (convent mix) / Old (eve of apocalypse mix) / The rage to overcome.

Aug 95. (10"pic-d) **DEATH CHURCH. / A NATION ON FIRE (demo)**
(cd-s+=) – Fuck it all (demo) / Old (demo).
(cd-s) – ('A'side) / Old (mix) / The rage to overcome (demo).

Andy MACKAY (see under ⇒ ROXY MUSIC)

Billy MacKENZIE (see under ⇒ ASSOCIATES)

MADDER ROSE

Formed: Greenwich Village, New York, USA . . . 1991 by LORSON and COTE. After a few well-received independent releases in 1993, they signed to 'Atlantic', who issued chart-making 'PANIC ON' in 1994. • **Style:** Melancholy alternative rock outfit for the 90's, with similarities to SUZANNE VEGA, BELLY or The SUNDAYS, although band influenced by VELVET UNDERGROUND or TELEVSION. • **Songwriters:** COTE or LORSON.

Recommended: BRING IT DOWN (*7) / PANIC ON (*8)

MARY LORSON – vocals, guitar, keyboards / **BILLY COTE** – guitars, bass, vibes / **MATT VERTA-RAY** – bass, rhythm guitar, slide guitar, organ, violin, vibes / **JOHNNY KICK** – drums, keyboards, vocals, vibes

not issued Rockville

Mar 93. (7"ep)(12"ep)(cd-ep) **MADDER ROSE E.P.** -

Seed Seed

May 93. (7"ep)(cd-ep) **BEAUTIFUL JOHN / BABY GETS HIGH. / LIGHTS GO DOWN / TAKE IT AWAY**

Jun 93. (cd)(c)(lp) **BRING IT DOWN**
– Beautiful John / While away / Bring it down / 20 foot red / Swim / Lay down low / Altar boy / Lights go down / (Living a) Daydream / Sugarsweet / Razor pilot / Waiting for engines / Pocket fulla medicine.

Oct 93. (7") **SWIM (remix). / LIKED YOU MORE (WHEN YOU WERE HIGH)**
(12"+=)/ / (cd-s++=) – Z. / / Amnesia.

Atlantic Atlantic

Mar 94. (7") **PANIC ON. / ONE ARMED BANDIT** 65
(10"+=)(cd-s+=) – Mad dog.

Mar 94. (cd)(c)(lp) **PANIC ON** 52
– Sleep, forever / Car song / Panic on / What Holly sees / Almost lost my mind / Drop a bomb / Ultra anxiety (teenage style) / Happy new year / Day in, day out / Margaret / Foolish ways / Black eye town / When you smile / Mad dog.

Jul 94. (7")(c-s) **CAR SONG. / JENNY TAKE A RIDE** 68
(10"+=)(cd-s+=) – The widow song / Holiday.

— **CHRIS GIAMMALVO** – bass repl. MATT

Apr 95. (7") **THE LOVE YOU SAVE. / DIANE**
(cd-s+=) – No avail / Ruler of my heart.

MADNESS

Formed: Camden, London, England . . . early '79, out of Kentish Town ska outfit The INVADERS, by MIKE BARSON, LEE THOMPSON and CHRIS FOREMAN. Now a 7-piece, they became friends with The SPECIAL AKA, signing one-off deal with JERRY DAMMERS' '2-Tone' label. They issued 'THE PRINCE' (a self-penned tribute to ska artist PRINCE BUSTER), and this gave them first of 19 consecutive UK Top 20 hits. In Oct'79 after a 2-Tone tour with The SPECIALS and The SELECTER, they signed to 'Stiff' records and unleashed No.2 hit album 'ONE STEP BEYOND', which was first product produced by CLIVE LANGER and ALAN WINSTANLEY. For the next 7 years, they became one of Britain's most popular groups, who even had time to conquer America in 1983. In 1984, they set up own 'Zarjazz' label, and signed FEARGAL SHARKEY who had first solo hit release 'Listen To Your Father'. • **Style:** White ska revivalists, whose humourous 'nutty boy' postures and sound, shifted in the 80's to intelligent fun-pop, made for video age. • **Songwriters:** Either McPHERSON-THOMPSON or BARSON or BEDFORD-FOREMAN. Covered; MADNESS (Prince Buster) / ONE STEP BEYOND (Cornell Campbell) / SWAN LAKE (Tchaikovski) / IT MUST BE LOVE (Labi Siffre) / THE SWEETEST GIRL (Scritti Politti) / THE HARDER THEY COME (Jimmy Cliff). SUGGS covered; I'M ONLY SLEEPING (Beatles) / CECILIA (Simon & Garfunkel). • **Trivia:** Early in 1982, SUGGS married singer and fellow 'Stiff' artist BETTE BRIGHT.

Recommended: ONE STEP BEYOND (*7) / DIVINE MADNESS (*9).

GRAHAM 'SUGGS' McPHERSON (b.13 Jan'61, Hastings, England) – vocals / **MIKE BARSON** (b.21 May'58) – keyboards / **CHRIS 'CHRISSIE BOY' FOREMAN** (b. 8 Aug'58) – guitar / **LEE 'KIX' THOMPSON** (b. 5 Oct'57) – saxophone, vocals / **MARK 'BEDDERS' BEDFORD** (b.24 Aug'61) – bass / **DAN 'WOODY' WOODGATE** (b.19 Oct'60) – drums repl. JOHN HASLER / **CHAS SMASH** (b.CATHAL SMYTH, 14 Jan'59) – horns, vocals, dancer

2-Tone not issued

Aug 79. (7")(12") **THE PRINCE. / MADNESS** 16 -
(re-iss.Feb87 on 'Old Gold')

Stiff Sire

Oct 79. (lp)(c) **ONE STEP BEYOND . . .** 2
– One step beyond / My girl / Night boat to Cairo / Believe me / Land of hope & glory / The prince / Tarzan's nuts / In the middle of the night / Bed and breakfast man / Razor blade alley / Swan Lake / Rockin' in Ab / Mummy's boy / Chipmunks are go. *(re-iss.Aug88 on 'Virgin', cd-iss.Apr90)*

Oct 79. (7") **ONE STEP BEYOND. / MISTAKES** 7
(12"+=) – Nutty theme.

Dec 79. (7") **MY GIRL. / STEPPING INTO LINE** 3
(12"+=) – In the rain. *(7" re-iss.Aug88 on 'Virgin')*

Mar 80. (7"ep) **WORK, REST AND PLAY** 6
– Night boat to Cairo / Deceives the eye / The young and the old / Don't quote me on that.

Sep 80. (7") **BAGGY TROUSERS. / THE BUSINESS** 3

Sep 80. (lp)(c) **ABSOLUTELY** 2
– Baggy trousers / Embarrassment / E.R.N.I.E. / Close escape / Not home today / On the beat Pete / Solid gone / Take it or leave it / Shadow of fear / Disappear / Overdone / In the rain / You said / Return of the Los Palmas 7. *(re-iss.Aug88 on 'Virgin', cd-iss.Nov89)*

Nov 80. (7") **EMBARRASSMENT. / CRYING SHAME** 4

Jan 81. (7") **RETURN OF THE LOS PALMAS 7. / THAT'S THE WAY TO DO IT** 7
(12"+=) – My girl (demo) / Swan Lake (live).

Apr 81. (7")(c-s) **GREY DAY. / MEMORIES** 4 -

Sep 81. (7") **SHUT UP. / A TOWN WITH NO NAME** 7 -
(12"+=) – Never ask twice.

Oct 81. (lp)(c) **7** 5 -
– Cardiac arrest / Shut up / Sign of the times / Missing you / Mrs. Hutchinson / Tomorrow's dream / Opium eaters / Grey day / Pac-amac / Promises promises / Benny bullfrog / When dawn arrives / The opium eaters / Aeroplane. *(re-iss.Aug88 on 'Virgin', cd-iss.Nov89)*

Stiff Geffen

Nov 81. (7")(12") **IT MUST BE LOVE. / SHADOW ON THE HOUSE** 4 -

Feb 82. (7")(12") **CARDIAC ARREST. / IN THE CITY** 14

May 82. (7")(7"pic-d) **HOUSE OF FUN. / DON'T LOOK BACK** 1
(7" re-iss.Aug88 on 'Virgin')

Jul 82. (7")(7"pic-d) **DRIVING IN MY CAR. / ANIMAL FARM** 4
(12"+=) – Riding on my bike. *(7" re-iss.Aug88 on 'Virgin')*

Oct 82. (7")(7"pic-d) **OUR HOUSE. / WALKING WITH MR. WHEEZE** 5 -
(12"+=) – ('A'extended). *(7" re-iss. Aug88 'Virgin')*

Nov 82. (lp)(c) **PRESENT THE RISE AND FALL** 10
– Rise and fall / Tomorrow's (just another day) / Blue skinned beast / Primrose hill / Mr. Speaker (gets the word) / Sunday morning / Our house / Tiptoes / New Delhi / That face / Calling cards / Are you coming (with me) / Madness (is all in the mind). *(re-iss.Aug88 on 'Virgin', cd-iss.Nov89)*

Feb 83. (7")(7"pic-d) **TOMORROW'S (JUST ANOTHER DAY). / MADNESS (IS ALL IN THE MIND)** 8
(12"+=) – Blue skinner beast / ('A'version w / ELVIS COSTELLO) *(7" re-iss.Aug88 on 'Virgin')*

Mar 83. (lp)(c) **MADNESS** - 41
– It must be love / Shut up / Rise and fall / Tomorrow's just another day / Primrose Hill / Madness (is all in the mind) / Grey day / House of fun / Blue skinned beast /

Cardiac arrest / Night boat to Cairo / Shadow of fear.
May 83. (7")(12") **OUR HOUSE. / CARDIAC ARREST** [-] [7]
Aug 83. (7") **IT MUST BE LOVE. / CALLING CARDS** [-] [33]
Aug 83. (7")(7"pic-d) **WINGS OF A DOVE. / BEHIND THE 8 BALL** [2] [ ]
(12"• =) – One's second thoughtlessness.
Oct 83. (7")(7"pic-d) **THE SUN AND THE RAIN. / FIREBALL XL5** [5] [-]
(12"+=) – My girl (live). *(7" re-iss. Aug88 on 'Virgin')*
Jan 84. (7") **THE SUN AND THE RAIN. / TIME FOR TEA** [-] [72]

— Trimmed to a 6-piece, when BARSON went to stay in Holland with Dutch wife.

Jan 84. (7")(7"pic-d) **MICHAEL CAINE. / IF YOU THINK THERE'S SOMETHING** [11] [ ]
(12"+=) – ('A'extended). *(7" re-iss.Aug88 on 'Virgin')*
Feb 84. (lp)(c)(pic-lp) **KEEP MOVING** [6] [ ]
– Keep moving / Michael Caine / Turning blue / One better day / March of the gherkins / Waltz into mischief * / Brand new beat / Victoria Gardens. *(re-iss. Aug88 on 'Virgin', cd-iss.Nov89) (US-iss.repl. * w/) – Wings of a dove (a celebratory song) / The sun and the rain / Prospects / Samantha.*
May 84. (7")(7"pic-d) **ONE BETTER DAY. / GUNS** [17] [ ]
(12"+=) – Victoria Gardens / Sarah. *(7"re-iss.Aug88 on 'Virgin')*

Zarjazz Virgin

Aug 85. (7") **YESTERDAY'S MEN. / ALL I KNEW** [18] [ ]
('A'ext-12") – ('A'demo).
(7"square-pic-d/incl.free-7") – ('A'harmonica mix) / It must be love (live).
Oct 85. (lp)(c)(cd) **MAD NOT MAD** [16] [ ]
– I'll compete / Yesterday's men / Uncle Sam / White heat / Mad not mad / Sweetest girl / Burning the boats / Tears you can't hide / Time / Coldest day. *(cd-iss.Jul87 & 1990)*
Oct 85. (7") **UNCLE SAM. / PLEASE DON'T GO** [21] [ ]
(12"+=) – ('A'demo).
(7"pic-d+=) – Infanity over Christmas.
Jan 86. (7")(one-sided-7"pic-d) **SWEETEST GIRL. / JENNIE (A PORTRAIT OF)** [35] [ ]
(12"+=) – ('A'dub).
(d7"+=) – Tears you can't hide / Call me.
Oct 86. (7")(7"square-pic-d) **WAITING FOR THE GHOST TRAIN. / MAYBE IN ANOTHER LIFE** [18] [ ]
(12"+=) – Seven Year Scratch.

— Had already split Sep86. BEDDERS and WOODY joined VOICE OF THE BEEHIVE. They had recently backed female duo STRAWBERRY SWITCHBLADE.

THE MADNESS

(**McPHERSON, THOMPSON, FOREMAN** and **SMYTH**) re-formed Feb'88, with slight change of name (allowed to add just THE), bringing in some session people.

Virgin Virgin

Mar 88. (7") **I PRONOUNCE YOU. / PATIENCE** [44] [ ]
(d7"+=)(12"+=)(cd-s+=) – 11th hour / 4BF.
May 88. (lp)(c)(cd) **THE MADNESS** [65] [ ]
– Nail down the days / What's that / I pronounce you / Oh / In wonder / Song in red / Nightmare nightmare / Thunder and lightning / Beat the bride / Gabriel's horn. *(cd+=)*– 11th Hour / 4BF / Be Good Boy / Flashings.
May 88. (7")(7"sha-pic-d) **WHAT'S THAT. / BE GOOD BOY.** [ ] [ ]
(7"sha-pic-d) – ('A'side) / Flashings.
(12"+=) – Flashings.

— Disbanded again in 1988. SUGGS became a TV presenter and the manager of The FARM, who he produced in 1985, and CHAS became A&R man for 'Go! Discs'. They were encouraged to re-unite for a one-off gig on 8 Aug'92 at Finsbury Park, after old hits re-charted (see further below).

MADNESS

(original line-up, see above)

Go! Discs London

Oct 92. (cd)(c)(lp) **MADSTOCK (live)** [22] [ ]
– One step beyond / The Prince / Embarrassment / My girl / The Sun and the rain / Grey day / It must be love / Shut up / Driving in my car / Bed and breakfast man / Close escape / Wings of a dove / Our house / Night boat to Cairo / Madness / House of fun / Baggy trousers / The harder they come.
Nov 92. (7")(c-s) **THE HARDER THEY COME. / TOMORROW'S JUST ANOTHER DAY / TAKE IT OR LEAVE IT (all live)** [44] [ ]
(cd-s+=) – Land of hope & glory.

– compilations, etc. –

Apr 82. Stiff/ US= Sire; (lp)(c) **COMPLETE MADNESS** [1] [ ]
– Embarrassment / Shut up / My girl / Baggy trousers / It must be love / The prince / Bed and breakfast man / Night boat to Cairo / One step beyond / House of fun / Cardiac arrest / Take it or leave it / Madness / The return of the Los Palmas 7 / In the city. *(cd-iss Jul 86)*
Nov 86. Zarjazz/ US= Virgin; (lp)(c)(cd) **UTTER MADNESS** [29] [ ]
– Our house / Driving in my car / Michael Caine / Wings of a dove / Yesterday's men / Tomorrow's (just another day) / I'll compete / Waiting for the ghost train / Uncle Sam / The sun and the rain / Sweetest girl / One better day / Victoria Gardens. *(cd+=)*– Seven Year Scratch (hit megamix). *(re-iss.Apr90 on 'Virgin')*
Dec 86. Strange Fruit; (12"ep) **THE PEEL SESSIONS (27.8.79.)** [ ] [ ]
– The prince / Bed and breakfast man / Land of hope & glory / Stepping into line. *(c-ep Jun87) (cd-ep Jul88)*
Nov 88. Old Gold; (7") **BAGGY TROUSERS. / EMBARRASSMENT** [ ] [ ]
Nov 88. Old Gold; (7") **IT MUST BE LOVE. / MY GIRL** [ ] [ ]
May 89. Virgin; (7") **IT MUST BE LOVE. / RETURN OF THE LOS PALMAS 7** [6] [ ]
Jan 92. Virgin; (7")(c-s) **IT MUST BE LOVE. / BED AND BREAKFAST MAN** [6] [ ]
(cd-s+=)(pic-cd-s+=) – Airplane / Don't quote me on that.
Feb 92. Virgin; (cd)(c)(d-lp) **DIVINE MADNESS** [1] [ ]
– The Prince / One step beyond / My girl / Night boat to Cairo / Baggy trousers / Embarrassment / The return of Los Palmas 7 / Grey day / Shut up / It must be love / Cardiac arrest / House of fun / Driving in my car / Our house / Tomorrow's just another day / Wings of a dove / the Sun and the rain / Michael Caine / One better day / Yesterday's men / Uncle Sam / (Waiting for the) Ghost train.
Apr 92. Virgin; (7")(c-s) **HOUSE OF FUN. / UN PASO ADELAINTE (ONE STEP BEYOND – Spanish version)** [40] [ ]
(12"+=)(cd-s+=) – Yesterday's men / Gabriel's horn (demo).
Aug 92. Virgin; (7")(c-s) **MY GIRL. / MADNESS** [27] [ ]
(cd-s) – ('A'side) / E.R.N.I.E. / Embarrassment / Tomorrow's dream.
Feb 93. Virgin; (7")(c-s) **NIGHT BOAT TO CAIRO. / ('A'mix)** [56] [ ]
(12"+=)(cd-s+=) – ('A'mixes).
Nov 93. Virgin; (3xcd-box) **THE BUSINESS – THE DEFINITIVE SINGLES COLLECTION** [ ] [ ]
Sep 90. Pickwick; (cd)(c)(lp) **IT'S . . . MADNESS** [ ] [-]
(re-iss.cd+c May94 on 'Virgin-VIP')
1991. Pickwick; (cd) **IT'S MADNESS . . . TOO** [ ] [-]
(re-iss.cd+c Oct94)

— In Oct'93, 'THE PRINCE' alongside other ska-revival bands on '2-TONE EP' hit UK No.30.

NUTTY BOYS

THOMPSON & FOREMAN with **SEAN FLOWERDEN, STEVE NIEVE, CHRIS SIMPSON** and **PASCAL GABRIEL.**

May 90. Streetlink; (cd)(c)(lp) **CRUNCH!** [ ] [-]
– Magic carpet / (Always) The innocent / Day dreamers / Complications / Pop my top / Whistle / Pipedream / For Elise / People / You get it. **CRUNCH! (NUTTY BOYS)** *(re-iss.cd+c Apr93 on 'Dojo')*

— The duo were now augmented by **EL TOMMO** – vocals / **SPIDER** – drums / **TAD** – bass / **DIAMOND LEG LEWIS** – piano / **DREAMBOAT STEVE** – saxophone / **CHRISSIE BOY** – guitar / **HONG KONG DAVE** – organ

Dec 92. Nil Satis; (7")(c-s) **IT'S OK, I'M A POLICEMAN. / FIGHT AMONGST YOURSELVES** [ ] [ ]
(cd-s+=) – Birthday girl / Saving for a rainy day.

The FINK BROTHERS

(SMYTH and McPHERSON)

Jan 85. Zarjazz; (7")(12")(7"square-pic-d) **MUTANTS IN MEGA CITY ONE. / MUTANT BLUES** [50] [ ]

— In 1985, MADNESS also appeared on a charity single with other ska-revivalists as STARVATION.

SUGGS

WEA WEA

Aug 95. (7")(c-s) **I'M ONLY SLEEPING. / OFF ON HOLIDAY** [7] [ ]
(cd-s+=) – Off on holiday (instrumental).
(cd-s+=) – Animal / When you came.
Oct 95. (7")(c-s) **CAMDEN TOWN. / BEDAZZLED** [14] [ ]
(cd-s+=) – ('A'-Chili pepper dub) / ('A'-Ragga in London mix).
Oct 95. (cd)(c) **THE LONE RANGER** [14] [ ]
– I'm only sleeping / Camden Town / Alcohol / 4 am / The tune / Cecilia / Haunted / Off on holiday / Green eyes / Fortune fish / She's gone.
Dec 95. (7")(c-s) **THE TUNE. / ALRIGHT** [33] [ ]
(cd-s+=) – Sleigh ride.

MADONNA

Born: MADONNA LOUISE CICCONE, 16 Aug'59, Rochester, Michegan, USA. After winning a scholarship at local university (where she also learned ballet), she headed for New York in 1977, where she became waitress and part-time model (nude photos were published in Playboy & Penthouse in 1985). In '79, she became disco dancer/singer for PATRICK 'Born To Be Alive' HERNANDEZ, but she left to form own ill-fated outfits the year after. To make ends meet (as they say), she appeared in a budget soft-porn film 'A Certain Sacrifice', which was later, without her consent, (1988) released on video. In 1982, after working with boyfriend STEVE BRAY on some solo material, she signed to 'Sire'. Her debut 45 'EVERYBODY', became US dance favourite, but she had to wait another year until 'HOLIDAY', gave her Top 20 hit on both sides of the Atlantic. It also prompted the re-issue of 2nd single 'LUCKY STAR', which made both Top 20's by Aug'84. By the end of the year, she was at No.1 with both single and album 'LIKE A VIRGIN'. She went on to become No.1 international female star, who was never out of the Top 10 or controversial headlines. • **Trivia:** Her 'real' acting career started in 1985, when she starred opposite Rosanna Arquette in the film 'Desperately Seeking Susan'. She went on to star in other films:- SHANGHAI SURPRISE (1986, with husband since 16 Aug'85; Sean Penn) / WHO'S THAT GIRL (1987, with Griffin Dunne) / BLOODHOUNDS ON BROADWAY (1989) / DICK TRACY (1990, alongside Warren Beatty, her recent beau after a stormy divorce from Penn) / A LEAGUE OF THEIR OWN (1992, with Geena Davis). She still plans to star in the role of Eva Peron in the film 'Evita', and has had the script since '88. That year she also opened on Broadway in the play 'Speed The Plow'. Her steamy videos have also caused uproar, especially with the church, due to her lewd sexual advances to a black priest in 1989 promo for 'LIKE A PRAYER', which also gained her $5 million sponsorship from Pepsi-cola. After a virtual topless MADONNA was glimpsed on in 'VOGUE', she surpassed all before with lustful 'JUSTIFY MY LOVE', which was banned by all except UK's late-night Channel 4 show 'The Word'. In 1992 to promote her forthcoming album, she released same-titled 'EROTICA', an expensive (£25) sexual story book, with explicit soft-porn poses of her and some model friends. • **Style:** Initially a self-motivated disco lip-synch pop artist, who progressed into adult-orientated and sleeze seductress, who exploits the expoliters. • **Trivia:** On a good note, MADONNA has also appeared and given money to AIDS benefits and charities, although this is never mentioned by the tabloids. • **Songwriters:** She collaborated on most material, the bulk with ex-boyfriend STEVE BRAY. Others & covers; PHYSICAL ATTRACTION (Reggie Lucas) / HOLIDAY (Jellybean Benitez) / LOVE DON'T LIVE HERE ANYMORE (Rose Royce; hit) / LIKE A VIRGIN (Tom Kelly & Billy Steinberg) / CRAZY FOR YOU (Jon Lind & John Bettis) / JUSTIFY MY LOVE (Lenny Kravitz & Ingrid Chavez) / FEVER (Peggy Lee) LOVE SONG (co-w / PRINCE) / BEDTIME STORY (Bjork).

Recommended: THE IMMACULATE COLLECTION (*9) / BEDTIME STORIES (*7).

MADONNA – vocals with session people, producers, etc.

Sire Sire

Dec 82. (7")(12") **EVERYBODY. / EVERYBODY (dub version)**
Sep 83. (7")(12") **LUCKY STAR. / I KNOW IT**
(re-iss.Mar84 UK+US) 14 4 Aug 84
Sep 83. (lp)(c) **MADONNA** 6 8
– Lucky star / Borderline / Burning up / I know it / Holiday / Think of me / Physical attraction / Everybody. *(re-iss.Sep85 as 'THE FIRST ALBUM')*
Nov 83. (7") **HOLIDAY. / THINK OF ME** 6 16 Oct 83
(12") – ('A'extra version). *(above re-iss.+12"pic-d. Jul85 reached UK-No.2)*
May 84. (7") **BORDERLINE (edit). / PHYSICAL ATTRACTION** 56 10 Mar 84
(12"+=)/ /(d7"+=) – ('A'dub version)./ / Holiday / Think of me. *(7"/12"/7"pic-d/7"sha-pic-d. re-iss.Jan86 hit UK No.2)*
Nov 84. (7")(7"pic-d) **LIKE A VIRGIN. / STAY** 3 1
(12") – ('A' US dance remix).
Nov 84. (lp)(c) **LIKE A VIRGIN** 1 1
– Material girl / Angel / Like a virgin / Over and over / Love don't live here anymore / Dress you up / Shoo-be-doo / Stay / Pretender. *(re-iss.pic-lp/cd.Aug85, cd+=)*– Into the groove.
Feb 85. (7")(12"dance) **MATERIAL GIRL. / PRETENDER** 3 2
(below single issued on 'Geffen' from the film 'Vision Quest')
Mar 85. (7") **CRAZY FOR YOU. /('B' by "Berlin")** - 1
Apr 85. (7") **ANGEL. / ('A'dance mix)** - 5
Jun 85. (7")(7"pic-d)(7"sha-pic-d) **CRAZY FOR YOU. / ('B' by "Sammy Hagar")** 2 -

—— (below from the film 'Desperately Seeking Susan')
Jul 85. (7")(7"pic-d)(7"sha-pic-d) **INTO THE GROOVE. / SHOO-BE-DOO** 1 -
(12"+=) – Everybody.
Aug 85. (7") **DRESS YOU UP. / SHOO-BE-DOO** - 5
Sep 85. (7")(7"pic-d)(7"sha-pic-d) **ANGEL. / BURNING UP** 5 -
(12") – ('A' 12"-extended dance mix).
(below single issued on 'Geffen' from the film 'Vision Quest')
Oct 85. (7") **GAMBLER. / ('B' by "Black'n'Blue")** 4 -
(12"+=) – ('A'instrumental). (US 'b'side INTO THE GROOVE)
Nov 85. (7")(7"pic-d)(7"sha-pic-d) **DRESS YOU UP. / I KNOW IT** 5 -
(12"+=) – ('A' dub mix)
Apr 86. (7") **LIVE TO TELL. / ('A'instrumental)** 2 1
(12"+=) – ('A'dub).
Jun 86. (7") **PAPA DON'T PREACH. / THE PRETENDER** - 1
Jun 86. (7") **PAPA DON'T PREACH. / AIN'T NO BIG DEAL** 1 -
(12"+=)(12"pic-d+=) – ('A'extended).
Jul 86. (lp)(c)(cd)(blue-lp) **TRUE BLUE** 1 1
– Papa don't preach / Open your heart / White heat / Live to tell / Where's the party / True blue / La Isla Bonita / Jimmy Jimmy / Love makes the world go round.
Sep 86. (7") **TRUE BLUE (remix). / HOLIDAY (lp version).** 1 -
(12")(12"pic-d) – ('A'extended version).
Sep 86. (7"blue) **TRUE BLUE. / AIN'T NO BIG DEAL** - 3
Dec 86. (7") **OPEN YOUR HEART. / WHITE HEAT** - 1
Dec 86. (7") **OPEN YOUR HEART. / LUCKY STAR** 4 -
(12"+=)(12"pic-d+=) – ('A'dub mix).
Mar 87. (7") **LA ISLA BONITA (remix). / ('A'instrumental)** 1 4
(12")(12"pic-d) – ('A'-12"extended version).
Jul 87. (7") **WHO'S THAT GIRL. / WHITE HEAT** 1 1
(12")(12"pic-d) – ('A'extended). / ('A'dub version).
(above 'A'side from the film 'Who's That Girl')(Various Artists Sound-track hit 4) 7 Aug 87
Sep 87. (7") **CAUSING A COMMOTION. / JIMMY JIMMY** 4 2
(12"+=)(12"pic-d+=) – ('A'-movie house mix).
Nov 87. (lp)(c)(cd) **U CAN DANCE** (remixes) 5 14
– Spotlight / Holiday / Everybody / Physical attraction / Over and over / Into the groove / Where's the party / Spotlight (dub) / Holiday (dub) / Into the groove (dub) / Over and over (dub). *(re-iss.cd/c Feb95)*
Dec 87. (7") **THE LOOK OF LOVE. / I KNOW IT** 9 -
(12"+=)(12"pic-d+=) – Love don't live here anymore.
Mar 89. (7") **LIKE A PRAYER. / ACT OF CONTRITION** 1 1
(12"pic-d+=) – ('A'club mix).
(c-s)(cd-s) – ('A'side) / ('A'extended) / ('A'club mix).
Mar 89. (lp)(c)(cd) **LIKE A PRAYER** 1 1
– Like a prayer / Express yourself / Love song / Till death us do part / Promise to try / Cherish / Dear Jessie / Oh father / Keep it together / Spanish eyes / Act of contrition.
May 89. (7")(c-s) **EXPRESS YOURSELF. / THE LOOK OF LOVE** 5 2
(12")(cd-s)(c-s)(12"pic-d) – ('A'side) / ('A'non-stop mix) / ('A'stop & go mix).
Aug 89. (7")(c-s) **CHERISH. / SUPERNATURAL** 3 2
(12"+=)(cd-s+=)(12"pic-d+=) – ('A'extended).
Nov 89. (7")(c-s)(7"pic-d) **DEAR JESSIE. / TILL DEATH US DO PART** 5 -
(12"+=)(cd-s+=)(pic-cd-s+=) – Holiday (12"mix).

Nov 89. (7")(c-s) **OH FATHER. / PRAY FOR SPANISH EYES** - 20
Jan 90. (7") **KEEP IT TOGETHER. / ('A' instrumental)** - 8
Mar 90. (7")(c-s)(7"pic-d) **VOGUE. / KEEP IT TOGETHER** 1 -
(12"+=)(cd-s+=) – ('A'dub mix).
(12"pic-d+=) – ('A'Bette Davis dub).
Apr 90. (7") **VOGUE. / ('A'-Bette Davis dub)** - 1
May 90. (cd)(c)(lp) **I'M BREATHLESS** (music inspired by the film 'Dick Tracy') 2 2
– He's a man / Sooner or later / Hanky panky / I'm going bananas / Cry baby / Something to remember / Back in business / More / What can you lose / Now I'm following you (pt.1 & 2) / Vogue.
Jul 90. (7")(c-s) **HANKY PANKY. / MORE** 2 10 Jun 90
(12"+=)(cd-s+=)(12"pic-d+=) – ('A'bare bottom mix).
Nov 90. (7")(c-s) **JUSTIFY MY LOVE. / EXPRESS YOURSELF** 2 1
(12"+=)(cd-s+=) – ('A'extended).
Nov 90. (cd)(c)(lp) **THE IMMACULATE COLLECTION** (compilation) 1 5
– Spotlight / Holiday / Everybody / Physical attraction / Over and over / Into the groove / Where's the party / Spotlight (dub) / Holiday (dub) / Into the groove (dub) / Over and over (dub).
Feb 91. (7"+7"sha-pic-d) **CRAZY FOR YOU (remix). / KEEP IT TOGETHER** 2 -
(12"+=)(c-s+=)(cd-s+=) – Into the groove.
Apr 91. (7")(c-s) **RESCUE ME (remix). / SPOTLIGHT (version)** 3 9 Feb 91
(cd-s+=) – ('A' Titanic mix).
May 91. (7")(c-s)(7"pic-d) **HOLIDAY. / TRUE BLUE** 5 -
(12") – ('A'side) / Where's the party / Everybody (remix).
(cd-s) – ('A'side) / Causin' a commotion / Who's that girl.

—— Below from her film 'A League Of Their Own'.
Jul 92. (7")(12")(c-s) **THIS USED TO BE MY PLAYGROUND. / (long version)** 3 1
(12"+=)(cd-s+=) – ('A'mixes).

Maverick-Sire Maverick-Sire

Oct 92. (7")(c-s)(7"pic-d) **EROTICA. / ('A' instrumental)** 3 3
(12"+=)(12"pic-d+=)(cd-s+=) – Erotica (radio edit)
Oct 92. (cd)(c)(lp)(pic-lp) **EROTICA** 2 2
– Erotica / Fever / Where life begins / Bye bye baby / Bad girl / Waiting / Deeper and deeper / Thief of hearts / Words / Rain / Why it's so hard / In this life / Did you do it / Secret garden.
Dec 92. (7")(c-s) **DEEPER AND DEEPER. / ('A'mix)** 6 13
(cd-s+=) – Deeper And Deeper (Edit) / Deeper And Deeper (Instrumental)
Feb 93. (7")(c-s) **BAD GIRL. / EROTICA (William Orbit mix)** 10 36
(12"+=)(cd-s+=) – ('A' club) / ('A' other mix).
Mar 93. (7"pic-d)(c-s) **FEVER. / ('A'remix)** 6
(12"+=)(cd-s+=) – ('A'mixes).
Jul 93. (7")(c-s) **RAIN. / OPEN YOUR HEART** 7 14
(12"pic-d+=)(cd-s+=) – Up down suite (dub).

—— her backing; **DALLAS AUSTIN** – drums, keyboards, co-writer / **TOMMY MARTIN** – guitar / **ME'SHELL NDEGEOCELLO + COLIN WOLFE** – bass / **MARCUS DeVRIES** – prog. / **BABYFACE** – synth, drum prog / etc.
Mar 94. (7")(c-s) **I'LL REMEMBER. / SECRET GARDEN** 7 2
(12")(cd-s) – ('A' Orbit + Guerilla Beach mixes) / Why is it so hard? (live).
Sep 94. (7"pic-d) **SECRET. / LET YOUR GUARD DOWN (rough mix edit)** 5 3
(12"+=) – ('A'instrumental) / ('A'other version).
(cd-s) – ('A'side) / ('A'-Junior mixes).
Oct 94. (cd)(c)(lp) **BEDTIME STORIES** 2 3
– Survival / Secret / I'd rather be your lover / Don't stop / Inside of me / Human nature / Forbidden love / Love tried to welcome me / Sanctuary / Bedtime story / Take a bow.
Dec 94. (7"pic-d)(c-s) **TAKE A BOW. / ('A'instrumental)** 17 1
(cd-s+=) – ('A'version).

—— Above single co-written w /BABYFACE as was 7th track. The singular title track was written by NELLEE HOOPER, BJORK & MARCUS DeVRIES. DAVE HALL co-wrote 5th, 6th & 8th track. Many samples included The ISLEYS (written) / AALIYAH / GAP BAND / GUTTERSNYPES / MAIN SOURCE / GRANT GREEN / HERBIE HANCOCK.
Feb 95. (c-s) **BEDTIME STORY / ('A'-Junior's mix)** 4 42 Apr95
(12")(cd-s) – ('A'side) / ('A'-Junior's wet dream mix) / ('A'-Junior's Dreamy drum dub) / ('A'-Orbital mix) / ('A'-Junior's sound factory mix).
(cd-s) – ('A'-Junior's mix) / Secret (Allstar mix) / Secret (Some Bizarre mixes).
Aug 95. (c-s) **HUMAN NATURE / ('A'-Chorus door slam mix)** 8 46 Jul95
(cd-s+=) – ('A'club mix) / ('A'-runway club mix) / I'm not your bitch.
(12") – (all above except 'A'side).
Oct 95. (c-s) **YOU'LL SEE / ('A'-instrumental)** 5 6
(cd-s+=) – Rain.
(cd-s) – ('A'side) / Secret (Junior Luscious club mix) / Sooner or later / Bad girl.
Nov 95. (cd)(c)(lp) **SOMETHING TO REMEMBER** 3 6
– I want you / I'll remember (theme from "With Honors") / Take a bow / You'll see / Crazy for you / This used to be my playground / Live to tell / Love don't live here anymore (remix) / Something to remember / Forbidden love / One more chance / Rain / Oh father / I want you (orchestral).
Dec 95. (c-s) **OH FATHER / LIVE TO TELL (live)** 16
(cd-s+=) – Why it's so hard (live).

– more compilations, exploitation releases, etc. –

Feb 87. Replay; (12") **WILD DANCING. / ('A'dance mix) (w / 'OTTO VON WERNHERR')** -
(re-iss.cd-s Sep93 & Apr95)
Apr 89. Replay; (12") **COSMIC CLUB (extended dance mix). / WE ARE THE GODS** -
(re-iss.cd-s Sep93)
May 89. Replay; (12") **TIME TO DANCE (extended). / (instrumental) / (radio mix)** -
Sep 89. Replay; (12") **ON THE STREET (edit). / (extended mix)** -
May 90. Replay; (12") **OH MY!!! (edit). / ('A'disco mix)** -

Aug 90. Replay; (cd) **THE BEST & THE REST OF MADONNA AND OTTO WERNKERR** [ ] [-]
Sep 90. Replay; (12") **SHAKE (extended). / ('A'mix) / ('A'instrumental)** [ ] [-]
Oct 89. Receiver; (lp)(c)(cd) **THE EARLY YEARS** [ ] [-]
1989. Receiver; (lp)(c)(cd) **IN THE BEGINNING (with 'OTTO WERNKERR')** [ ] [-]
Jul 91. Receiver; (cd)(c) **GIVE IT TO ME** [ ] [-]
Apr 92. Receiver; (7")(12"pic-d)(pic-cd-s) **SHINE A LIGHT. / ON THE GROUND / LITTLE BOY** [ ] [-]
Jul 93. Receiver; (cd)(c) **BEST OF THE REST VOLUME II** [ ] [-]
Jul 93. Receiver; (cd)(c) **THE BEST OF MADONNA** [ ] [-]

MAD SEASON (see under ⇒ ALICE IN CHAINS)

MAGAZINE

Formed: Manchester, England ... Spring 1977 by former BUZZCOCKS frontman HOWARD DEVOTO. After 6 months of rehearsals, they finally progressed to live gigs, and almost immediately signed to 'Virgin'. They commenced 1978 with a gem of a debut single 'SHOT BY BOTH SIDES', which pierced the UK Top 50. After a flop follow-up, they secured a Top 30 placing with classy first album 'REAL LIFE'. From then on, with radio airplay help from the John Peel show, they scored with 3 more studio Top 40 albums. • **Style:** Futuristic & progressive new-wave band, fronted by the incredibly intelligent and receeding DEVOTO. • **Songwriters:** DEVOTO penned all except; GOLDFINGER (John Barry) / THANK YOU (Sly & The Family Stone) / I LOVE YOU BIG DUMMY (Captain Beefheart). LUXURIA covered JEZEBEL (Marty Wilde) • **Trivia:** Some of the musicians, also featured on the VISAGE album of 1980.

Recommended: REAL LIFE (*9) / THE CORRECT USE OF SOAP (*8) / MAGIC, MURDER AND THE WEATHER (*6) / RAYS AND HAIL (*8).

HOWARD DEVOTO – vocals (ex-BUZZCOCKS) / **JOHN McGEOGH** – guitar / **BARRY ADAMSON** – bass / **MARTIN JACKSON** – drums / **BOB DICKINSON** – keyboards

— (BOB left before debut recording)

Virgin / not issued

Jan 78. (7") **SHOT BY BOTH SIDES. / MY MIND AIN'T SO OPEN** [41] [ ]
Apr 78. (7") **TOUCH AND GO. / GOLDFINGER** [ ] [ ]

— added **DAVE FORMULA** – keyboards

Jun 78. (lp)(c) **REAL LIFE** [29] [ ]
– Definitive gaze / My tulpa / Shot by both sides / Recoil / Burst / Motorcade / The great beautician in the sky / The light pours out of me / Parade. *(re-iss.Mar84) (cd-iss.1988)*

— **JOHN DOYLE** – drums repl. JACKSON (to CHAMELEONS, then SWING OUT SISTER)

Nov 78. (7") **GIVE ME EVERYTHING. / I LOVE YOU, YOU BIG DUMMY** [ ] [ ]
Feb 79. (7") **RHYTHM OF CRUELTY. / TV BABY** [ ] [ ]
Mar 79. (lp)(c) **SECONDHAND DAYLIGHT** [38] [ ]
– Feed the enemy / Rhythm of cruelty / Cut-out shapes / Talk to the body / I wanted your heart / The thin air / Back to nature / Believe that I understand / Permafrost. *(re-iss.+cd.Aug88)*
Feb 80. (7") **A SONG FROM UNDER THE FLOORBOARDS. / TWENTY YEARS AGO** [ ] [ ]
Mar 80. (7") **THANK YOU (FALETTINME BE MICE ELF AGIN). / THE BOOK** [ ] [ ]
Apr 80. (7") **UPSIDE DOWN. / THE LIGHT POURS OUT OF ME (live)** [ ] [ ]

Virgin / I.R.S.

May 80. (lp)(c) **THE CORRECT USE OF SOAP** [28] [ ]
– Because you're frightened / Model worker / I'm a party / You never knew me / Philadelphia / I want to burn again / Thank you (falettinme be mice elf agin) / Sweetheart contract / Stuck / A song from under the floorboards.
Jul 80. (d7)(12") **SWEETHEART CONTRACT. / FEED THE ENEMY (live)./ / TWENTY YEARS AGO. / SHOT BY BOTH SIDES (live)** [54] [ ]

— **ROBIN SIMON** – guitar (ex-ULTRAVOX) repl. McGEOGH who joined SIOUXSIE ... (above now alongside **DEVOTO, ADAMSON, FORMULA** and **DOYLE**).

Nov 80. (lp)(c) **PLAY (live at Melbourne Festival Hall)** [69] [ ]
– Give me everything / A song from under the floorboards / Permafrost / The light pours out of me / Model worker / Parade / Thank you (falettinme be mice elf agin) / Because you're frightened / Twenty years ago / Definitive gaze. *(re-iss.+cd.Aug88)*

— **BEN MANDELSON** – guitar (ex-AMAZORBLADES) repl. ROBIN.

May 81. (7") **ABOUT THE WEATHER. / IN THE DARK** [ ] [ ]
(12"+=) – The operative.
Jun 81. (lp)(c) **MAGIC, MURDER AND THE WEATHER** [39] [ ]
– About the weather / So lucky / The honeymoon killers / Vigilante / Come alive / The great man's secrets / This poison / Naked eye / Suburban Rhonda / The garden. *(re-iss.+cd.Aug88)*

— They split mid '81. DEVOTO went solo with help from FORMULA (see below). BEN MANDELSON joined The MEKONS, JOHN DOYLE later joined ARMOURY SHOW. BARRY ADAMSON joined PETE SHELLEY then later NICK CAVE & THE BAD SEEDS. FORMULA had also joined the group DESIGN FOR LIVING.

– compilations etc. –

May 82. Virgin; (lp)(c) **AFTER THE FACT** (best of) [ ] [-]
May 83. Virgin; (12"ep) **SHOT BY BOTH SIDES** [ ] [-]
– Shot by both sides / Goldfinger / Give me everything / Song from under the floorboards.
May 87. Virgin; (cd) **RAYS AND HAIL 1978-81** (best of) [ ] [ ]
– Shot by both sides / Definitive gaze / Motorcade / The light pours out of me / Feed the enemy / Rhythm of cruelty / Back to nature / Permafrost / Because you're frightened / You never knew me / A song from under the floorboards / I want to burn again / About the weather / Parade. *(re-iss.cd Jul93)*
Jul 90. Virgin; (cd) **SCREE** (rarities 76-81) [ ] [-]
Aug 93. Windsong; (cd) **BBC RADIO 1 LIVE IN CONCERT** [ ] [-]

HOWARD DEVOTO

went solo, with **DAVE FORMULA** – keyboards / **PAT AHORN** – drums / **ALAN ST. CLAIR** – guitar / **NEIL PYZER** – keyboards,synth / **MARTIN HEATH** – bass

Virgin / I.R.S.

Jun 83. (7")(12") **RAINY SEASON. / RAIN FOREST** [ ] [-]
Aug 83. (lp)(c) **JERKY VERSIONS OF THE DREAM** [57] [ ]
– Cold imagination / Topless / Rainy season / I admire you / Way out of shape / Some will pay (for what others pay to avoid) / Waiting for a train / Out of shape with me / Taking over Heaven / Seeing is believing. *(re-iss.Aug88)*
Aug 83. (7")(12") **COLD IMAGINATION. / OUT OF SHAPE WITH ME** [ ] [ ]

— PYZER and ST.CLAIR joined SPEAR OF DESTINY. HEATH and AHORN joined DAVE HOWARD SINGERS, DEVOTO guested for B.SZAJNER a French electronic wizard. He then took 4 years off before his new venture . . .

LUXURIA

DEVOTO with **NOKO** (b.Liverpool) – guitar, co-composer

Beggar's B. / Beggar's B.

Jan 88. (7") **REDNECK. / SHE'S YOUR LOVER NOW pt.1** [ ] [ ]
(12"+=) – She's your lover now (pt.2).
Feb 88. (lp)(c)(cd) **THE UNANSWERABLE LUST** [ ] [ ]
– Redneck / Flesh / Public highway / Pound / Lady 21 / Celebrity / Rubbish / Mile / Luxuria.
May 88. (7") **PUBLIC HIGHWAY (Short cut) / SICKLY THUG AND I** [ ] [ ]
(12"+=) – Luxuria (The wilderness mix).
Mar 90. (7"ep)(12"ep)(cd-ep) **THE BEAST BOX IS DREAMING / BEAST BOX / USELESS LOVE** [ ] [ ]
Apr 90. (cd)(c)(lp) **BEAST BOX** [ ] [ ]
– The beast box is dreaming / Stupid blood / Against the past / Our curious leader / We keep on getting there / Ticket / Animal in the mirror / Dirty beating heart / Smoking mirror / I've been expecting you / Karezza / Beast box / Jezebel.
May 90. (7") **JEZEBEL. / SMOKING MIRROR (instrumental)** [ ] [ ]
(12"+=) – Sickly thug and I.
(cd-s++=) – Luxuria (live).

MAGICK (see under ⇒ BOND, Graham)

MAGNUM

Formed: Birmingham, England . . . 1973 by CATLEY and CLARKIN. After initially backing US stars like DEL SHANNON, and playing mostly covers, they came to life in 1978, when 'Jet' records took over. They had of course issued an uncharacteristic Searchers cover pop single 'SWEETS FOR MY SWEET', which featured DAVE MORGAN on vox, way back in '75. With new 1978 pomp-rock approach, they unleashed debut album 'KINGDOM OF MADNESS', which broke into UK Top 60. Their album chart status progressed further with each release, culminating in 1988 with UK Top 5 'WINGS OF HEAVEN'. • **Style:** Heavy pomp-metal rock, which was fused with orchestration and a classical side, in flautest RICHARD BAILEY. • **Songwriters:** CLARKIN compositions, plus 1990 collaborations with RUSS BALLARD and JIM VALLANCE. • **Trivia:** Producers were; in 1979 LEO LYONS (ex-TEN YEARS AFTER) / 1982; JEFF GLIXMAN / 1986 by ROGER TAYLOR (of QUEEN).

Recommended: CHAPTER AND VERSE (*6).

BOB CATLEY – vocals / **TONY CLARKIN** – guitar / **RICHARD BAILEY** – keyboards, flute / **DAVE MORGAN** – bass, vox / **KEX GORIN** – drums

C.B.S. / not issued

Feb 75. (7") **SWEETS FOR MY SWEET. / MOVIN' ON** [ ] [-]

— **COLIN 'Wally' LOWE** – bass, vocals repl. MORGAN

Jet / Jet

Jul 78. (7") **KINGDOM OF MADNESS. / IN THE BEGINNING** [ ] [ ]
Aug 78. (lp)(c) **KINGDOM OF MADNESS** [58] [ ]
– In the beginning / Baby rock me / Universe / Kingdom of madness / All that is real / The bringer / Invasion / Lord of chaos / All come together. *(re-iss.+cd.Mar87 on 'Castle') (re-iss.lp/c/cd/pic-lp.Feb89 on 'FM-Revolver')*
Sep 78. (7") **INVASION. / UNIVERSE** [ ] [ ]
May 79. (7") **UNIVERSE. / BABY ROCK ME** [-] [ ]
Sep 79. (7") **CHANGES. / LONESOME STAR** [ ] [ ]
Oct 79. (lp)(c) **MAGNUM II** [ ] [ ]
– Great adventure / Changes / The battle / If I could live forever / Reborn / So cold the night / Foolish heart / Stayin' alive / Firebird / All of my life. *(re-iss.+cd.Mar87 on 'Castle') (re-iss.lp/c/cd/pic-lp. Feb89 on 'FM-Revolver')*
Nov 79. (7") **FOOLISH HEART. / BABY ROCK ME** [ ] [-]
Mar 80. (7") **ALL OF MY LIFE (live). / GREAT ADVENTURE (live)** [47] [ ]
(d7"+=) – Invasion (live) / Kingdom of madness (live).
Apr 80. (lp)(c) **MARAUDER (live)** [34] [ ]
– If I could live forever / The battle / Foolish heart / In the beginning / Reborn / Changes / So cold the night / Lord of chaos. *(re-iss.+cd.Mar87 on 'Castle')*

— **MARK STANWAY** (b.27 Jul'54) – keyboards repl. BAILEY

1980. (7") **CHANGES (live remix). / EVERYBODY NEEDS**
Feb 82. (7") **LIGHTS BURNED OUT. / LONG DAYS BLACK NIGHTS**
Mar 82. (lp)(c)(pic-lp) **CHASE THE DRAGON** 17
– Soldier of the line / On the edge of the world / The spirit / Sacred hour / Walking the straight line / We all play the game / The teacher / The lights burned out. *(re-iss.Jun88 on 'FM-Revolver') (cd-iss.Jan87)*
Sep 82. (7") **BACK TO EARTH (live). / HOLD BACK YOUR LOVE (live)**
(d7"+=) – Soldier of the line (live) / Sacred Hour (live).
May 83. (lp)(c) **THE ELEVENTH HOUR** 38
– The prize / Breakdown / The great disaster / Vicious companions / So far away / Hit and run / One night of passion / The word / Young and precious souls / The road to Paradise. *(re-iss.+cd.Jun88 on 'FM-Revolver') (cd-iss.Jan87)*

— **JIM SIMPSON** – drums (ex-BLOOMSBURY SET) repl. GORIN / **EDDIE GEORGE** – keyboards repl. STANWAY who also joined ROBIN GEORGE

— **MARK STANWAY** – keyboards returned GRAND SLAM, to repl. EDDIE

FM-Revolver / not issued

Mar 85. (7") **JUST LIKE AN ARROW. / TWO HEARTS**
(12"+=) – The word.
May 85. (lp)(c)(cd)(pic-lp) **ON A STORYTELLER'S NIGHT** 24
– How far Jerusalem / Just like an arrow / Storyteller's night / Before first light / Les morts dansant / Endless love / Two hearts / Steal your heart / All Englands eyes / The last dance. *(re-iss.cd May 90 + Jul 93)*
May 85. (7")(12") **STORYTELLER'S NIGHT. / BEFORE FIRST LIGHT**

— **CATLEY, CLARKIN, STANWAY** and **LOWE** recruited new member **MICKEY BARKER** – drums to repl. SIMPSON.

Polydor / Polydor

Jul 86. (7") **LONELY NIGHT. / LES MORT DANSANT (live)** 70
(12") – ('A'extended) / Hold Back Your Love (live).
(d7"+=) – All England's Eyes (live) / Hit And Run (live).
Oct 86. (7") **MIDNIGHT. / BACK STREET KID**
(12"+=) – ('A'version).
(12"pic-d) – ('A'version) / Kingdom of madness (live).
Oct 86. (lp)(c)(cd)(pic-lp) **VIGILANTE** 24
– Lonely night / Need a lot of love / Sometime love / Midnight (you won't be sleeping) / Red on the highway / Holy rider / When the world comes down / Vigilante / Back street kid.
Feb 87. (7") **WHEN THE WORLD COMES DOWN. / VIGILANTE**
(12"+=)(cd-s+=) – ('A'extended).
Mar 88. (7") **DAYS OF NO TRUST. / MAYBE TONIGHT** 32
('A'ext-12"+=) – The spirit (live) / Two hearts (live) / How far Jerusalem (live).
(cd-s+=) – ('A'extended) / How far Jerusalem (live).
(12"white-ltd.) – ('A'side) / The spirit (live) / Two hearts (live).
Apr 88. (lp)(c)(cd) **WINGS OF HEAVEN** 5
– Days of no trust / Wild swan / Start talking love / One step away / It must have been love / Different worlds / Pray for the day / Don't wake the lion (too old to die young). *(pic-lp.Dec88 +=)* – C'est La Vie. *(re-is.cd Apr95)*
Apr 88. (7") **START TALKING LOVE. / C'EST LA VIE** 22
(12"+=)(12"red+=) – Back to Earth (live) / Storyteller's night (live).
(cd-s+=) – Back to Earth (live) / Sacred hour (live).
(7"sha-pic-d) – ('A'side) / Days of no trust.
Jun 88. (7") **MUST HAVE BEEN LOVE. / CRYING TIME** 33
(12"+=)(12"blue+=) – Lonely night (live) / Just like an arrow (live).
(cd-s+=) – Lonely night (live) / Lights burned out (live).
Jun 90. (7")(c-s) **ROCKIN' CHAIR. / MAMA** 27
(12"+=)(cd-s+=) – Where do you run to.
Jul 90. (cd)(c)(lp) **GOODNIGHT L.A.** 9
– Rockin' chair / Mama / Only a memory / Reckless man / Matter of survival / What kind of love is this / Heartbroke & busted / Shoot / No way out / Cry for you / Born to be king.
Aug 90. (7") **HEARTBROKE AND BUSTED. / HANGING TREE** 49
(12"+=)(cd-s+=) – Cry for you.
Aug 91. (cd)(c)(d-lp) **THE SPIRIT (live)** 50
– Introduction / Vigilante / Days of no trust / Mama / Need a lot of love / Pray for the day / Les morts dansants / Reckless man / How far Jerusalem / The spirit / On a storyteller's night / Rocking chair / Kingdom of madness / Sacred hour / When the world comes down.

M.F.N. / Megaforce

Sep 92. (7")(12") **ONLY IN AMERICA. / SLEEPWALKING / JUST A LITTLE BIT / CAUGHT IN LOVE**
Oct 92. (cd)(c)(lp) **SLEEPWALKING** 27 -
– Stormy weather / Too much to ask / You're the one / The flood / Broken wheel / Just one more heartbreak / Every woman, every man / Only in America / Sleepwalking / Prayer for a stranger / The long ride.

E.M.I. / Capitol

Jun 94. (cd)(c) **ROCK ART** 57
– We all need to be loved / Hard hearted woman / Back in your arms again / Rock heavy / The tall ships / Tell tale eyes / Love's a stranger / Hush a bye baby / Just this side of Heaven / I will decide myself / On Christmas day.

– compilations, etc. –

Apr 86. Raw Power; (d-lp)(cd) **ANTHOLOGY** -
– In the beginning / Lord of chaos / Kingdom of madness / The bringer / Greta adventures / Firebird / Foolish heart / Stayin' alive / If I could live forever / Reborn (live) / Changes (live) / Walking the straight line / We all play the game / The spirit / The prise / Vicious companions / The word / Hit and run / So far away.
Oct 86. Jet; (lp)(c) **VINTAGE MAGNUM** -
Apr 93. Jet; (cd)(c)(lp) **ARCHIVE** -
Nov 93. Jet; (cd)(c)(lp) **KEEPING THE NITE LITE BURNING** -
Nov 87. FM-Revolver; (lp)(c)(cd)(pic-lp) **MIRADOR** -
Feb 88. Castle; (d-lp)(d-cd) **VINTAGE MAGNUM / THE ELEVENTH HOUR** -
1988. Castle; (3"cd-ep) **THE LIGHTS BURNED OUT / IF I COULD LIVE FOREVER / SACRED HOUR** -
Jul 88. Knight; (c)(cd)(lp) **NIGHTRIDING** -
May 89. Receiver; (lp)(c)(cd) **INVASION / MAGNUM LIVE (live)** -
(w/free+=) – (interview disc).
May 93. Polydor; (cd)(c) **CHAPTER & VERSE (THE VERY BEST OF MAGNUM)** -
– Rockin' chair / Vigilante / C'est la vie / Heartbroke & busted / On a storyteller's night (live) / Start talking love / Mama / Lonely nights / Crying time / Midnight (remix) / It must have been love / Days of no trust / Don't wake the lion / Just like an arrow / No way out / When the world comes down. *(re-iss.cd Apr95)*
Jun 93. Optima; (cd)(c) **CAPTURED LIVE (live)** -
Jun 94. Jet; (cd) **UNCORKED (THE BEST OF MAGNUM)** -
May 95. Spectrum; (cd) **FIREBIRD** -
Sep 95. Emporio; (cd)(c) **VINTAGE MAGNUM – ELECTRIC AND ACOUSTIC** -

Taj MAHAL

Born: HENRY FREDERICKS, 17 May'40, New York City, USA. From Caribbean stock, he became influenced by the work of MARCUS GARVEY and HAILE SELASSIE. He studied animal husbandry at the University of Massachusetts, before moving to California, where he formed The RISING SONS with RY COODER and JESSE ED DAVIS. They augmented him on his 'Columbia' solo debut, which was hailed by critics. Became popular too with the people, when 2 albums 'THE NATCH'L BLUES' and 'GIANT STEP ...', made the US Top 200 in 1969. In the 70's, he wrote scores for films 'SOUNDER' and 'BROTHERS', and even managed to act in the movie 'THE MAN WHO BROKE A 1,000 CHAINS'. • **Style:** New breed of late 60's cosmic electric bluesmen. • **Songwriters:** Self-penned except those plucked from blues archives from the likes of ROBERT JOHNSON, BLIND WILLIE McTELL, ELMORE JAMES, WILLIE JOHNSON, etc. • **Trivia:** AL KOOPER appeared on second album, which was produced by DAVID RUBINSON until 1972 when he himself took over. That years' UK soundtrack lp featured LIGHTNIN' HOPKINS on one track 'Needed Time'.

Recommended: TAJ MAHAL (*8) / THE NATCH'L BLUES (*7)

TAJ MAHAL – vocals, steel guitar, harmonica / **JESSE EDWIN DAVIS** – guitar, keyboards / **GARY GILMORE** – bass / **CHARLES "CHUCK" BLACKWELL** – drums

Direction / Columbia

1967. (7") **SHIMMY LIKE SISTER KATE. / LET THE GOOD TIMES ROLL** -
Feb 68. (lp) **TAJ MAHAL** Oct67
– Leaving trunk / Statesboro blues / Checkin' up on my baby / Everybody's got to change sometime / EZ rider / Dust my broom / Diving duck blues / The celebrated walkin' blues. *(re-iss.Dec85 lp/c on 'Edsel')*
Feb 68. (7") **EE ZEE RIDER. / LEAVING TRUNK** -
Apr 68. (7") **EVERYBODY'S GOT TO CHANGE. / STATESBORO BLUES**
Jan 69. (7") **GOING UP TO THE COUNTRY, PAINT MY MAILBOX BLUE. / YOU DON'T MISS YOUR WATER ('TIL YOUR WELL RUNS DRY)** -
Mar 69. (lp) **THE NATCH'L BLUES** Feb69
– Good morning Miss Brown / Corinna / I ain't gonna let nobody steal my jellyroll / Going up to the country, paint my mailbox blue / Done changed my way of living / She caught the Katy and left me a mule to ride / The cuckoo / You don't miss your water ('til your well runs dry) / Ain't that a lot of love. *(re-iss.May87 on 'Edsel')*
Mar 69. (7") **EE ZEE RIDER. / YOU DON'T MISS YOUR WATER ('TIL YOUR WELL RUNS DRY)** -
1969. (7") **AIN'T THAT A LOT OF LOVE. / CORINA** -
Dec 69. (d-lp) **GIANT STEP / DE OLE FOLKS AT HOME** 85 Oct69
– Ain't gwine whistle Dixie (anymo') / Take a giant step / Give your woman what she wants / Good morning little school girl / You're gonna need somebody on your bond / Six days on the road / Farther on down the road (you'll accompany me) / Keep your hands off her / Bacon fat / Linin' track / Country blues / Wild ox moan / Light rain blues / A little soulful / Candy man / Cluck old hen / Colored aristocracy / Blind boy rag / Stagger Lee / Cajun tune / Fishing blues / Annie's lover. *(re-iss.Apr88 d-lp/cd on 'Edsel')*
Nov 69. (7") **SIX DAYS ON THE ROAD. / LIGHT RAIN BLUES** -
Feb 70. (7") **DIVING DUCK BLUES. / FISHING BLUES** -
Apr 70. (7") **GIVE YOUR WOMAN WHAT SHE WANTS. / FARTHER DOWN THE ROAD** -
May 70. (7") **AIN'T GWINE WHISTLE DIXIE (ANYMO'). / (part 2)** -

— now with **BILL RICH** – bass / **JOHN HALL** – guitar / **GREG THOMAS** – drums / **BOB STEWART + HOWARD JOHNSON + JOSEPH DALEY + EARLE McINTYRE** – tubas trombones, flugelhorns / **KWASI DZIDZOURNU** – percussion

C.B.S. / Columbia

1971. (d-lp) **THE REAL THING (live)** 84 Jun71
– Fishing blues / Ain't gwine to whistle Dixie (anymo') / Sweet Mama Janisse / Going up to the country, paint my mailbox blue / Big kneed gal / You're going to need somebody on your bond / Tom and Sally Drake / Diving duck blues / John, ain't it hard / You ain't no street walker mama, honey but I do love the way you strut your stuff.

— **JAMES CHARLES OTEY** – drums / **HOSHAL WRIGHT + DAVID COLMAN** – guitar / **JOHN SIMON** – piano / **ANDY NARELL** – steel drums repl.THOMAS + HALL

1972. (lp) **HAPPY JUST TO BE LIKE I AM** Jan72
– Happy just to be like I am / Stealin' / Oh Susanna / Eighteen hammers / Tomorrow may not be your day / Chevrolet / West Indian revelation / Black spirit boogie.
1972. (7") **OH SUSANNA. / CHEVROLET** -

— now featured only **JOHNSON** – tuba / **POINTER SISTERS** – back-up vox (2)

1972. (lp) **RECYCLING THE BLUES & OTHER RELATED STUFF (1 side live)** Oct72
– (introduction) – Kalimba / Bound to love me some / Ricochet / A free song (rise up children let the Devil out of your soul) / Corinna – (close) / Cakewalk into town / Texas woman blues / Sweet home Chicago / Gitano Negro.
1972. (lp) **SOUNDER (Soundtrack)** -

– Needed time / Sounder chase a coon / Needed time (hummin' and pickin') / Morning work – N' meat's on the stove / I'm running and I'm hapy / Speedball / Goin' to the country – Critters in the woods / Motherless children (hummin') / Jailhouse blues / Just workin' / Harriet's dance song / Two spirits reunited / David runs again / Curiosity blues / Someday be a change / Horseshoes / Cheraw / David's dream / Needed time (guitar) / Needed time (banjo and hand-clapping).

Dec 73. (lp) **OOOH SO GOOD 'N BLUES** — Nov73
– Buck dancer's choice / Little red hen / Mama don't you know / Frankie and Albert / Railroad Bill / Dust my broom / Built for comfort / Teacup's jazzy blues tune.

Jan 74. (7") **BUCK DANCER'S CHOICE. / LITTLE RED HEN** -

Apr 74. (7") **BUILT FOR COMFORT. / TEACUP'S JAZZY BLUES TUNE** -

— now with **HOSHAL / BILL / KWASI / + MERL SAUNDERS** – organ / **ASTON BARRETT** – piano / **RUDY COSTA** – saxes / **KESTER SMITH** – percussion / + vocalist **CAROLE FREDERICKS**

1974. (lp) **MO' ROOTS** — Oct74
– Johnny too bad / Blackjack Davey / Big mama / Cajun waltz / Slave driver / Why did you have to desert me? / Desperate lover / Clara (St.Kitts woman).

1975. (7") **WHY DID YOU HAVE TO DESERT ME?. / CAJUN WALTZ** -

1975. (7") **SLAVE DRIVE. / CAJUN WALTZ** -

— **EARL WIRE LINDO** – keyboards / **LARRY McDONALD** – percussion / **RAY FITZPATRICK** – bass repl.SAUNDERS + BARRETT

1975. (lp) **MUSIC KEEPS ME TOGETHER** — Oct75
– Music keeps me together / When I feel the sea beneath my soul / Dear ladies / Aristocracy / Further on down the road / Roll, turn, spin / West Indian revelation / My ancestors / Brown-eyed handsome man / Why? . . .and we repeat why? . . .and we repeat!.

1975. (7") **WHY? . . .AND WE REPEAT WHY? . . .AND WE REPEAT!. /** -

1976. (lp) **SATISFIED 'N TICKLED TOO**
– Satisfied 'n tickled too / New E-Z rider blues / Black man, brown man / Baby love / Ain't nobody's business / Misty morning ride / Easy to love / Old time song – Old time love / We tune.

1976. (7") **AIN'T NOBODY'S BUSINESS. / EAST TO LOVE** -

Jun 76. (7") **BLACK MAN, BROWN MAN. / NEW E-Z RIDER BLUES** — -

— added various people from now on session

Warners Warners

1977. (lp) **MUSIC FUH YA' (MUSICA PARA TU)** — Jan77
– You got it / Freight train / Baby, you're my destiny / Sailin' into Walker's Cay / Truck driver's two-step / The four Mills Brothers / Honey babe / Curry.

1978. (lp) **BROTHERS** -

1979. (lp) **EVOLUTION – THE MOST RECENT** -
– Sing a happy song / Queen bee / Lowdown showdown / The most recent (evolution of Muthafusticus Modern Usticus) / Why you do me this way? / Salsa de Laventille / The big blues / Highnite / Southbound with the hammer down.

1979. (7") **SING A HAPPY SONG. / SOUTHBOUND WITH THE HAMMER DOWN** -

Magnet Crystal C.

1980. (lp)(c) **TAJ MAHAL & THE INTERNATIONAL RHYTHM BAND – LIVE AND DIRECT (live)** — Nov79
– And who / Jorge Ben / Take a giant step / Airplay / L-O-V-E, love / Little brown dog. *(re-dist.1983)*

Jul 80. (7") **TAKE A GIANT STEP. / JORGE BEN**

— with numerous session people

Sonet Alligator?

Jan 87. (lp)(cd=1988) **TAJ**
– Everybody is somebody / Paradise / Do I love her / Light of the Pacific / Deed I do / Soothin' / Pillow talk / Local local girl / Kauai kalypso / French letter.

Mar 87. (7") **EVERYBODY IS SOMEBODY. / FRENCH LETTER**
(12"+=) – Deed I do.

Aug 87. (7") **SOOTHIN'./ KAUAI KALYPSO**
(12"+=) – Local local girl.

Essential Rykodisc

Feb 90. (cd)(c) **BIG BLUES (live At Ronnie Scott's)** — -
– Big blues / Mail box blues / Stagger Lee / Come on in my kitchen / Local local girl / Soothin' / Fishing blues / Statesboro' blues / Everybody is somebody. *(re-iss.cd 1990's on 'Castle Classics')*

compilations, etc

1976. Columbia; (lp) **ANTHOLOGY VOL.1 1966-76** -

Jul 80. CBS; (lp)(c) **GOING HOME** — -
– Statesboro blues / Dust my broom / You don't miss your water (till your well runs dry) / Good morning Miss Brown / Six days on the road / Sweet home Chicago / Little red hen / Frankie and albert / Johnny too bad / New E-Z rider blues / Blackjack Davey / Satisfied 'n tickled too / Brown-eyed handsome man / Clara.

1987. Castle; (d-lp)(d-c)(cd) **THE COLLECTION** — -
– Fishing blues / Leaving trunk / Six days on the road / Dust my broom / Going up to the country, paint my mailbox blue / Candy man / Stagger Lee / Diving duck blues / Clara (St.Kitts woman) / Statesboro blues / A lot of love / Take a giant step / Further down the road / Little red hen / Ee zee rider / Texas woman blues / A free song / Oh mama, don't you know / Railroad Bill / Everybody's gotta change sometime.

MAHAVISHNU ORCHESTRA (see under ⇒ McLAUGHLIN, John)

MAHOGANY RUSH

Formed: Montreal, Canada . . .September 1970 by FRANK MARINO, who while recovering drug abuse in a hospital, claimed he was visited by an apparition of the recently deceased JIMI HENDRIX!. He recruited for his trio; PAUL HARWOOD and JIM AYOUB, to form his own 'experience'. After his 1973 debut 'MAXOOM', he and MAHOGANY RUSH hit Top 100 with album 'CHILD OF THE NOVELTY'. • **Style:** As said very similiar to JIMI HENDRIX EXPERIENCE, although by his IV'th album, he had acquired own innovative heavy metal techniques. • **Songwriters:** MARINO except; PURPLE HAZE (Jimi Hendrix)/ ALL ALONG THE WATCHTOWER (Bob Dylan)/ JOHNNY B.GOODE (Chuck Berry)/ I'M A KING BEE (Slim Harpo)/ NORWEGIAN WOOD (Beatles)/ MONA (Bo Diddley)/ etc.

Recommended: FRANK MARINO & MAHOGANY RUSH LIVE (*7)

FRANK MARINO – vocals, lead guitar / **PAUL HARWOOD** – bass / **JIM AYOUB** – drums

not issued Nine

1973. (lp) **MAXOOM** -
– Maxoom / Buddy / Magic man / Funky woman / Madness / All in your mind / Blues / Boardwalk lady / Back on home / The new beginning. *(US re-iss.Feb75 on '20th Century')*

Aug 74. (lp) **CHILD OF THE NOVELTY** - 74
– Look outside / Thru the Milky Way / Talking 'bout a feelin' / Child of the novelty / Makin' my wave / A new rock and roll / Changing / Plastic man / Guit war / Chains of (s)pace. *(cd-iss.1990 on 'Repertoire')*

Sep 74. (7") **CHILD OF THE NOVELTY. / A NEW ROCK AND ROLL** -

Jun 75. (lp) **STRANGE UNIVERSE** - 84
– Tales of the Spanish warrior / The king who stole (. . .the universe) / Satisfy your soul / Land of 1000 nights / Moonlight lady / Dancing lady / Once again / Tryin' anyway / Dear music / Strange universe.

Jul 75. (7") **SATISFY YOUR SOUL. / BUDDY** -

C.B.S. Columbia

Dec 76. (lp) **MAHOGANY RUSH IV** — May76
– I'm going away / Man at the back door / The answer / Jive baby / It's begun to rain / Dragonfly / Little sexy Annie / Moonwalk / IV . . .(the emperor).

FRANK MARINO & MAHOGANY RUSH

(same label)

Jul 77. (lp) **WORLD ANTHEM** — May77
– Requiem for a sinner / Hey, little lover / Broken heart blues / In my ways / World anthem / Look at me / Lady / Try for freedom.

Mar 78. (lp) **FRANK MARINO & MAHOGANY RUSH LIVE (live)**
– (introduction) / The answer / Dragonfly / I'm a king bee – Back door man – Who do ya love / A new rock and roll / Johnny B.Goode / Talkin' 'bout a feeling – Electric reflections of war / World anthem / Purple haze.

May 79. (lp) **TALES OF THE UNEXPECTED (half studio/ half live)**
– Sister change / All along the watchtower / Norwegian wood (this bird has flown) / Tales of the unexpected / Down, down, down / Door of illusion / Woman / Bottom of the barrel.

Jun 79. (7") **ALL ALONG THE WATCHTOWER. / DOWN, DOWN, DOWN** -

— brother **VINCE MARINO** contributed guitar to below.

Apr 80. (lp) **WHAT'S NEXT** — 88 Mar80
– You got livin' / Finish line / Rock me baby / Something's comin' our way / Roadhouse blues / Loved by you / Rock'n'roll hall of fame / Mona.

May 80. (7") **YOU GOT LIVIN'. / WORLD ANTHEM**

FRANK MARINO

solo but with same 2 man backing **HARWOOD + AYOUB** (on same label)

Aug 81. (lp) **THE POWER OF ROCK & ROLL**
– The power of rock & roll / Play my music / Stay with me / Runnin' wild / Crazy Miss Daisy / Go strange / Young man / Ain't dead yet.

Sep 82. (lp) **JUGGERNAUT** — Aug82
– Strange dreams / Midnight highway / Stories of a hero / Free / Maybe it's time / Ditch queen / For your love / Juggernaut.

— now without AYOUB replaced by **TIM BIERY**

S.P.V. Grudge

Aug 87. (cd) **FULL CIRCLE**
– Breakin' away / Imagine / When love is lost / Razor's edge / Hang on / Full circle / Long ago / Had enough / Genesis.

FRANK MARINO & MAHOGANY RUSH

with **VINCE MARINO** – guitar, vocals / **PAUL HARWOOD** – bass / **TIM BIERY** – drums / **CLAUDIO PESAVENTO** – keyboards

Maze Maze

May 89. (d-lp)(cd) **DOUBLE LIVE (live)**
– You got livin' / Midnite highway / Free / Poppy / Roadhouse blues / Who do ya love / Guitar prelude / Electric reflections revisited / Sky symphony to a little town / Rock'n'roll hall of fame / Juggernaut / Strange dreams.

MAIN (see under ⇒ LOOP)

Stephen MALLINDER (see under ⇒ CABARET VOLTAIRE)

MAMAS AND THE PAPAS

Formed: St.Thomas, Virgin Islands, USA . . . 1964 as The NEW JOURNEYMAN by DENNY DOHERTY, and 2 JOURNEYMEN; JOHN PHILLIPS and MICHELLE GILLIAM. They soon brought in CASS ELLIOT and relocated to California, where they became The MAMAS & THE PAPAS, taking title from Hell's Angels' name for their girlfriends. They were introduced by BARRY McGUIRE, to producer and owner of 'Dunhill' records Lou Adler. He contracted them initially as backing singers for McGUIRE's 1965 lp 'Precious

Time', which included PHILLIPS' 'CALIFORNIA DREAMIN''. The following year, this became their debut 45, hitting Top 5 in the US. Their follow-up 'MONDAY MONDAY' reached No.1, and 3 in the UK, foreshadowed by a succession of hits, halted by the break-up of group in '68. This was due to the eventual marriage split of JOHN and MICHELLE. All subsequently took off on solo ventures, and often re-united for one-off concerts, etc. Tragically on 29 Jul'74, MAMA CASS ELLIOT died of a heart attack, while choking on food. • **Style:** Harmony orientated folk-pop hippy quartet fronted by overweight MAMA CASS, but who were dogged by drug busts and alleged record company rip-offs. • **Songwriters:** PHILLIPS penned most. Covered; DANCING IN THE STREET (Martha & The Vandellas) / DEDICATED TO THE ONE I LOVE (Shireles) / DO YOU WANNA DANCE (Bobby Freeman) / I CALL YOUR NAME (Beatles) / etc. In 1967, PHILLIPS wrote No.1 smash 'SAN FRANCISCO' for late 80's PAPA-to-be SCOTT McKENZIE. 20 years later JOHN co-wrote US No.1 'Kokomo' with The BEACH BOYS. • **Trivia:** On 31 Oct'70, MICHELLE now divorced from JOHN, married cult actor DENNIS HOPPER, but only for a week.

Recommended: CREEQUE ALLEY: HISTORY OF . . . (*7)

JOHN PHILLIPS (b.30 Aug'35, Parris Island, S.Carolina) – vocals / **CASS ELLIOT** (b.ELLEN NAOMI COHEN, 19 Sep'41, Baltimore, Maryland) – vocals / **MICHELLE GILLIAM** (b.HOLLY MICHELLE GILLIAM, 4 Jun'45, Long Beach, California) – vocals (ex-JOURNEYMEN, with PHILLIPS) (ELLIOT ex-MUGWUMPS with DOHERTY) / **DENNY DOHERTY** (b.29 Nov'41, Halifax, Nova Scotia, Canada) – vocals

R.C.A. | Dunhill

Jan 66. (7") **CALIFORNIA DREAMIN'. / SOMEBODY GROOVY** [23] [4] Dec 65

May 66. (7") **MONDAY MONDAY. / GOT A FEELIN'** [3] [1] Apr 66

Jun 66. (lp) **IF YOU CAN BELIEVE YOUR EYES AND EARS** [3] [1] Feb 66
(UK-title **'THE MAMAS AND THE PAPAS'**)
– Do you wanna dance / Go where you wanna go / California dreamin' / Spanish harlem / Somebody groovy / Hey girl / You baby / In crowd / Monday, Monday / Straight shooter / Got a feelin' / I call your name. *(cd-iss.1990 on 'MCA')*

Jul 66. (7") **I SAW HER AGAIN. / EVEN IF I COULD** [11] [5] Jun 66

— **JILL GIBSON** – vocals repl. MICHELLE for a while

Oct 66. (7") **LOOK THRU ANY WINDOW. / ONCE THERE WAS A TIME I THOUGHT** [ ] [24]

— **MICHELLE** returned when she reconciled with husband JOHN

Jan 67. (lp) **THE MAMAS AND THE PAPAS** [24] [4] Sep 66
(UK-title **('CASS, JOHN, MICHELLE, DENNY')**
– No salt on her tail / Trip, stumble and fall / Dancing bear / Words of love / My heart stood still / Dancing in the steet / I saw her again / Strange young girl / I can't wait / Even if I could / That kind of girl / Once was a time I thought.

Jan 67. (7") **WORDS OF LOVE. / DANCING IN THE STREET** [47] [5] / [75] Nov 66

Mar 67. (7") **DEDICATED TO THE ONE I LOVE. / FREE ADVICE** [2] [2] Feb 67

Apr 67. (7") **CREEQUE ALLEY. / NO SALT IN HER TAIL** [-] [5]

Jun 67. (lp) **THE MAMAS AND THE PAPAS DELIVER** [4] [2] Mar 67
– Dedicated to the one I love / My girl / Creeque Alley / Sing for your supper / Twist and shout / Free advice / Look through any window / Boys and girls together / String man / Frustration / Did you ever want to cry / John's music box.

Jul 67. (7") **CREEQUE ALLEY. / DID YOU EVER WANT TO CRY** [9] [-]

Sep 67. (7") **12:30 (YOUNG GIRLS ARE COMING TO THE CANYON). / STRAIGHT SHOOTER** [ ] [20] Aug 67

Dec 67. (7") **GLAD TO BE UNHAPPY. / HEY GIRL** [ ] [26] Oct 67

Dec 67. (lp) **FAREWELL TO THE FIRST GOLDEN ERA** [ ] [5] Oct 67
– Dedicated to the one I love / Go where you wanna go / Words of love / Look through any window / Dancing in the street / Monday Monday / Creeque Alley / Got a feelin' / Twelve-thirty (young girls are coming to the canyon) / I call your name / I saw her again last night / California dreamin'.
– (compilation)

Dec 67. (7") **DANCING BEAR. / JOHN'S MUSIC BOX** [-] [51]

Jun 68. (7") **SAFE IN MY GARDEN. / TOO LATE** [ ] [53] May 68

Sep 68. (lp) **. . . PRESENTING THE PAPAS AND THE MAMAS** [ ] [15] May 68
– Dream a little dream of me / Gemini child / Ivy / Mansions / Meditation mama (transcendental woman travels) / Midnight voyage / Nothing's too good for my little girl / Rooms / Safe in my garden / The right somebody to love / Too late / Twelve thirty.

Sep 68. (7") **FOR THE LOVE OF IVY. / STRANGE YOUNG GIRLS** [ ] [81]

— (Jul68) Disbanded, when JOHN and MICHELLE broke up. JOHN PHILLIPS later went solo, as did DENNY and MICHELLE.

– other compilations, etc. –

1966. Stateside; (7"ep) **IF YOU CAN BELIEVE YOUR EYES AND EARS** [-] [ ]

Dec 68. Stateside/ US= Dunhill; (lp) **GOLDEN ERA, VOL.2** [ ] [53] Sep 68

Dec 68. Dunhill; (7") **DO YOU WANNA DANCE. / MY GIRL** [-] [76]

Feb 69. Stateside; (7") **YOU BABY. / MY GIRL** [ ] [-]

Apr 69. Stateside; (lp) **HITS OF GOLD** [7] [-]
(re-iss.+c.Oct74 + Aug81 on 'ABC')

Sep 69. Dunhill; (lp) **16 OF THEIR GREATEST HITS** [-] [61]

Sep 70. Stateside/ US= Dunhill; (7") **GO WHERE YOU WANNA GO. / NO SALT ON HER TAIL** [ ] [-]

MAMA CASS

had already gone solo.

R.C.A. | Dunhill

Aug 68. (7") **DREAM A LITTLE DREAM OF ME (live). / MIDNIGHT VOYAGE** [11] [12] Jul 68

(above also credited with The MAMAS AND THE PAPAS)

Stateside | Dunhill

Nov 68. (7") **CALIFORNIA EARTHQUAKE. / TALKIN' TO YOUR TOOTHBRUSH** [ ] [67] Oct 68

Dec 68. (lp) **DREAM A LITTLE DREAM** [ ] [87] Oct 68
– Dream a little dream of me / California earthquake / The room nobody lives in / Talkin' to your toothbrush / Blues for breakfast / You know who I am / Rubber band / Long time loving you / Jane, the insane dog lady / What was I thinking of / Burn your hatred / Sweet believer.

Feb 69. (7") **MOVE IN A LITTLE BIT CLOSER. / ALL FOR ME** [-] [58]

Mar 69. (7") **MOVE IN A LITTLE BIT CLOSER. / I CAN DREAM, CAN'T I** [ ] [-]

Jul 69. (7") **IT'S GETTING BETTER. / WHO'S TO BLAME** [8] [30] May 69

Nov 69. (lp) **BUBBLEGUM, LEMONADE AND . . . SOMETHING FOR MAMA** [ ] [91] Jun 69
– Blow me a kiss / It's getting better / Easy come, easy go / I can dream, can't I / Welcome to the world / Lady Love / He's a runner / Move in a little closer, baby / When I just wear my smile / Who's to blame / Sour grapes.
– (US re-iss.Nov69 as 'MAKE YOUR OWN KIND OF MUSIC', with extra title track)

MAMA CASS ELLIOT

Nov 69. (7") **MAKE YOUR OWN KIND OF MUSIC. / LADY LOVE** [ ] [36] Oct 69

Mar 70. (7") **NEW WORLD COMING. / BLOW ME A KISS** [ ] [42] Jan 70

Mar 70. (7") **SOMETHING TO MAKE YOU HAPPY. / NEXT TO YOU** [-] [ ]

Sep 70. (7") **A SONG THAT NEVER COMES. / I CAN DREAM, CAN'T I** [ ] [99] Jul 70

Mar 71. (lp)(c) **MAMA'S BIG ONES** (compilation) [ ] [ ]
– Dream a little dream of me / Make your own kind of music / It's getting better / Easy come, easy go / Words of love / Move in a little closer, baby / Song that never comes / One way ticket / Ain't nobody else like you / Don't let the good life pass you by / The good times are coming / New world coming.
(re-iss.Oct74 on 'ABC') (re-iss.Oct76 on 'MFP')

— Late 1970-early 1971, MAMA CASS teamed up with DAVE MASON on some releases.

MAMAS AND THE PAPAS

re-united.

Probe | Dunhill

Nov 71. (lp)(c) **PEOPLE LIKE US** [ ] [84] Oct 71
– Dream a little dream of me / Make your own kind of music / It's getting better / Easy come, easy go / Words of love / Move in a little closer, baby / Song that never comes / One way ticket / Ain't nobody else like you / Don't let the good life pass you by / The good times are coming / New world coming.
– (re-iss.Oct74 on 'ABC') (re-iss.Nov76 on 'MFP')

Jan 72. (7") **STEP OUT. / SHOOTING STAR** [-] [81]

Feb 72. (7") **SHOOTING STAR. / NO DOUGH** [ ] [-]

— Break-up, once again for final time. All try-out solo careers.

CASS ELLIOT

went solo again.

R.C.A. | R.C.A.

1972. (7") **BABY I'M YOURS. / CHERRIES JUBILEE** [ ] [ ]

1972. (lp)(c) **CASS ELLIOT** [ ] [ ]
– Introduction – Dream a little dream of me / Extraordinary / I think a lot about you / Don't call me Mama anymore / My love / I'm coming to the best part of my life / The torchsong medley: I came here to sing a torchsong – I got a right to sing the blues – I've got it bad and that ain't good – Mean to me – Why was a born – I came here to sing a torchsong (reprise) / The night before / I like what I like / I'll be seeing you / Closing – I don't call me Mama anymore (reprise).

1972. (7") **THAT SONG. / WHEN IT DOESN'T WORK OUT** [-] [ ]

1972. (7") **DISNEY GIRLS (1957). / BREAK ANOTHER HEART** [-] [ ]

1973. (7") **DOES ANYBODY LOVE YOU. / THE ROAD IS NO PLACE FOR A LADY** [-] [ ]

1973. (lp)(c) **THE ROAD IS NO PLACE FOR A LADY** [ ] [ ]

1973. (7") **LISTEN TO THE WORLD. / I THINK A LOT ABOUT YOU** [-] [ ]

Jul 74. (7") **IF YOU'RE GONNA BREAK ANOTHER HEART. / DON'T CALL ME MAMA ANYMORE** [ ] [-]

Jul 74. (lp)(c) **DON'T CALL ME MAMA ANYMORE** [ ] [ ]
– Introduction – Dream a little dream of me / Extraordinary / I think a lot about you / Don't call me Mama anymore / My love / I'm coming to the best part of my life / The torchsong medley: I came here to sing a torchsong – I got a right to sing the blues – I've got it bad and that ain't good – Mean to me – Why was a born – I came here to sing a torchsong (reprise) / The night before / I like what I like / I'll be seeing you / Closing – I don't call me Mama anymore (reprise).

— On 29th Jul'74, CASS ELLIOT died of a heart attack, caused by choking.

– more (MAMAS & PAPAS) compilations, etc. –

Note; Below releases on 'Probe' UK/ 'Dunhill' US unless mentioned.

Oct 70. (d-lp) **A GATHERING OF FLOWERS** [ ] [ ]

1971. (lp) **MONTEREY INTERNATIONAL POP FESTIVAL (live)** [-] [ ]

Jun 72. (7") **CALIFORNIA DREAMIN'. / DEDICATED TO THE ONE I LOVE** [ ] [-]

May 73. (d-lp)(c) **20 GOLDEN HITS** [ ] [ ] Feb 73
(re-iss.Oct74 on 'ABC') (re-iss.Oct80 on 'MFP') (re-iss.Mar82 on 'MCA')

Sep 73. (7") **MONDAY MONDAY. / CREEQUE ALLEY** [ ] [-]
(re-iss.Sep76 on 'ABC')

Jan 74. M.F.P.; (lp)(c) **MONDAY MONDAY** [ ] [-]

Sep 74. M.F.P.; (lp)(c) **CALIFORNIA DREAMING** [ ] [-]
(re-iss.Apr79 on 'Marks & Spencer')

May 77. Arcade; (lp)(c) **THE BEST OF THE MAMAS AND THE PAPAS** [6] [-]

1972. M.C.A.; (7"ep) **PEOPLE LIKE US** [-] [ ]

1976. M.C.A.; (lp)(c) **THE ABC COLLECTION: GREATEST HITS** [-] [ ]

Jun 80. M.C.A.; (7"ep) **MONDAY MONDA / CALIFORNIA DREAMIN'. / CREEQUE ALLEY / I SAW HER AGAIN** [ ] [-]

Jul 85. M.C.A.; (lp)(c) **GOLDEN GREATS** [ ] [-]

(cd-iss.Dec88)

May 91. M.C.A.; (d-cd) **CREEQUE ALLEY: THE HISTORY OF THE MAMAS & PAPAS**
– Wild women / Winken', blinkin' and nod / I'll remember tonight / I don't wanna know / This precious time / (John Phillips dialogue) / California dreamin' / Go where you wanna go / Monday, Monday / You baby / Do you wanna dance / I call your name / Spanish harlem / Straight shooter / Got a feelin' / I saw her again last night / Look through my window / Words of love / Dancing in the street / (Mama Cass dialogue) / Once was a time I thought / No salt in her tail / Trip, stumble and fall / Dancing bear / Dedicated to the one I love / Creeque Alley / My girl / Twist and shout / I call your name / Twelve thirty (young girls are coming to the canyon) / Glad to be unhappy / For the love of Ivy / Safe in my garden / Midnight voyage / Dream a little dream of me / California earthquake / It's getting better / Mississippi / Watcha gonna do / (Mama Cass dialogue) / Step out / The achin' kind.

Jul 82. Old Gold; (7") **DEDICATED TO THE ONE I LOVE. / CREEQUE ALLEY** [ ] [-]
Jul 82. Old Gold; (7") **CALIFORNIA DREAMIN'. / MONDAY MONDAY** [ ] [-]
Jun 88. Old Gold; (7") **IT'S GETTING BETTER ("MAMA CASS"). / DREAM A LITTLE DREAM OF ME** [ ] [-]
1987. Castle; (d-lp) **THE COLLECTION** [ ] [-]
Mar 88. Platinum; (lp)(c) **THE VERY BEST OF THE MAMAS & THE PAPAS** [ ] [-]
Jun 88. Connoisseur; (d-lp)(c)(cd) **ELLIOT, PHILLIPS, GILLIAM, DOHERTY** [ ] [-]
Jul 89. Object; (cd) **THE MAMAS & THE PAPAS (live)** [ ] [-]
Jun 92. See For Miles; (cd) **THE EP COLLECTION** [ ] [-]
Nov 93. Double Platinum; (d-cd) **ALL TIME GREATEST HITS** [ ] [-]
Jul 94. Success; (cd)(c) **GREATEST HITS LIVE (Live)** [ ] [-]
Dec 94. Polygram TV; (cd)(c) **CALIFORNIA DREAMING – THE VERY BEST OF THE MAMAS & THE PAPAS** [14] [-]

JOHN PHILLIPS

Stateside / Dunhill

May 70. (7") **MISSISSIPPI. / APRIL ANNE** [ ] [32] Apr 70
Jun 70. (lp) **JOHN PHILLIPS: (THE WOLFKING OF L.A.)** [ ] [ ] May 70
– April Anne / Topanga Canyon / Malibu people / Someone's sleeping / Drum / Captain – The mermaid / Let it bleed, Genevieve / Down the beach / Mississippi / Holland tunnel. *(re-iss.Oct88 as 'THE WOLFKING OF L.A.' on 'Decal')*

not issued / Columbia

1975. (7") **REVOLUTION ON VACATION. / CUP OF TEA** [-] [ ]

— DENNY DOHERTY and MICHELLE PHILLIPS also released solo recordings around the mid 70's. MICHELLE appeared in the TV films 'Dillinger' & 'Valentino' 1977. Early in 1982, the remaining members plus SPANKY McFARLANE (ex-SPANKY & OUR GANG) reformed The MAMAS & THE PAPAS, but only revived 60's circuit. MICHELLE had also been replaced by MacKENZIE PHILLIPS, daughter of JOHN.

MAN

Formed: Merthyr Tydfil, nr. Swansea, Wales . . . 1964 as The BYSTANDERS by MICKY JONES, CLIVE JOHN, RAY WILLIAMS and JEFFREY JONES. They released many 45's during a 4-year period, one of them '98• 6' hitting Top 50 early '67. The following year, they amalgamated with other Welsh group The DREAM, and found singer / guitarist DEKE LEONARD. Signed to 'Pye' and released debut lp 'REVELATION' in 1969, but they had to wait a few years and numerous personnel changes, before fruits of labour were appreciated. This was in the mid-70's, when albums 'BACK INTO THE FUTURE', 'RHINOS WHINOS AND LUNATICS' & 'MAXIMUM DARKNESS', all enjoyed a wee run in UK Top 30. • **Style:** West Coast sounding rock, so identifiably similar to drug loving QUICKSILVER MESSENGER SERVICE, that one of their members JOHN CIPPOLINA joined MAN in '75. Their psychedelically fused harmonies were often entwined with jam-like over-indulgent pieces that either pierced or missed ear altogether. • **Songwriters:** Group penned from the 70's, except covers; CODINE (Buffy Sainte-Marie) / I'M GONNA LEAVE YOU (Quicksilver Messenger Service) / LET THE GOOD TIMES ROLL (Shirley & Lee) / etc. • **Trivia:** Also featured on live Various Artists albums GREASY TRUCKERS PARTY VOL.1 and CHRISTMAS AT THE PATTI, both on 'United Art' 1972 + 1973.

Recommended: PERFECT TIMING (THE U.A. YEARS 1970-75) (*8) MAXIMUM DARKNESS (*7) / DO YOU LIKE IT HERE NOW (*7)

THE BYSTANDERS

VIC OAKLEY – vocals / **MICKY JONES** – guitar, vocals / **CLIVE JOHN** – keyboards, vocals / **RAY 'TAFF' WILLIAMS** – bass (ex-EYES OF BLUE) / **JEFFREY JONES** – drums

Pylot / not issued

1965. (7") **THAT'S THE END. / THIS TIME** [ ] [-]

Piccadilly / not issued

Jun 66. (7") **(YOU'RE GONNA) HURT YOURSELF. / HAVE I OFFENDED THE GIRL** [ ] [-]
Oct 66. (7") **MY LOVE – COME HOME. / IF YOU WALK AWAY** [ ] [-]
Dec 66. (7") **98.6. / STUBBORN KIND OF FELLOW** [45] [-]
May 67. (7") **ROYAL BLUE SUMMER SUNSHINE DAY. / MAKE UP YOUR MIND** [ ] [-]
Jul 67. (7") **PATTERN PEOPLE. / GREEN GRASS** [ ] [-]

Pye / not issued

Feb 68. (7") **WHEN JEZAMINE GOES. / CAVE OF CLEAR LIGHT** [ ] [-]
Apr 68. (7") **THIS WORLD IS MY WORLD. / PAINTING THE TIME** [ ] [-]

— (disbanded 1968)

MAN

were formed by **DEKE LEONARD** – guitar, vocals (ex-The DREAM) / **MICKY JONES** – vocals, guitar / plus **CLIVE, RAY** and **JEFFREY.**

Pye / Philips

Jan 69. (7") **SUDDEN LIFE. / LOVE** [ ] [-]
Jan 69. (lp) **REVELATION** (US-title 'MANPOWER') [ ] [ ]
– And in the beginning . . . / Sudden life / Empty room / Puella! Puella! (woman! woman!) / Love / Erotica / Blind man / And castles rise in children's eyes / Don't just stand there (come in out of the rain) / The missing pieces / The future hides it's face. *(re-iss.+cd.Oct89. on 'See For Miles')*

Dawn / Philips

Sep 69. (lp) **2 ozs. OF PLASTIC WITH A HOLE IN THE MIDDLE** [ ] [ ]
– (prelude) – The storm / It is as it might be / Spunk box / My name is Jesus Smith / Parchment and candles / Brother Arnold's red and white striped tent. *(re-iss.+cd.Oct89. on 'See For Miles')*

— **MARTIN ACE** – bass (ex-The DREAM) repl. RAY who joined The BIG SLEEP / **TERRY WILLIAMS** – drums (ex-The DREAM) repl. JEFFREY

Liberty / United A..

Oct 70. (lp) **MAN** [ ] [ ]
– Romain / Country girl / Would the Christians wait five minutes? the lions are having a draw / Daughter of the fireplace / The alchemist. *(re-iss.Feb76.as 'MAN 1970' on 'Sunset')*

Mar 71. (7") **DAUGHTER OF THE FIREPLACE. / COUNTRY GIRL** [ ] [ ]

United A. / United A..

Nov 71. (lp) **DO YOU LIKE IT HERE NOW, ARE YOU SETTLING IN?** [ ] [ ]
– Angel easy / All good clean fun / We're only children / Many are called but few get up / Manillo / Love your life. *(re-iss. Aug80. on 'Liberty')*

— Now a quartet when CLIVE joined PORWITH, PRITCHARD & THE NEUTRONS.

Sep 72. (lp) **LIVE AT THE PADGET ROOMS, PENARTH (live)** [ ] [ ]
– Many are called, but few get up / Daughter of the fireplace / "H" / Samuel.

— **MICKY and TERRY** plus the returning **CLIVE** – guitar / recruited **PHIL RYAN** – keyboards (ex-EYES OF BLUE) repl. DEKE who went solo. / **MICHAEL 'WILL' YOUATT** – bass (ex-ANCIENT GREASE) repl. MARTIN.

Oct 72. (lp) **BE GOOD TO YOURSELF AT LEAST ONCE A DAY** [ ] [ ]
– C'mon / Keep on crinting / Bananas / Life on the road. *(re-iss.May88. on 'B.G.O.', cd-iss.Feb92)*

— **ALAN 'TWEKE' LEWIS** – keyboards (ex-WILD TURKEY) repl. RYAN (in studio).

Sep 73. (d-lp)(c) **BACK INTO THE FUTURE** (half live / half studio). [23] [ ]
– A night in dad's bag / Just for you / Back into the future / Don't go away / Ain't their fight / Never say nups to Nepalese / Sospan fack (featuring The Gwalia male choir) / C'mon / Jam up jelly tight. *(cd-iss.Dec93 on 'B.G.O.' +=)*– Oh no, not again (spunk rock '73).

Sep 73. (7") **DON'T GO AWAY. / BACK TO THE FUTURE** [-] [ ]

— **MICKY & TERRY** added the returning **DEKE LEONARD** – guitar, vocals / **MALCOLM MORLEY** – keyboards (ex-HELP YOURSELF) repl. WILL (to NEUTRONS) / **KEN WHALEY** – bass (ex-HELP YOURSELF, ex-BEES MAKE HONEY) repl. CLIVE and TWEKE

May 74. (lp)(c) **RHINOS, WINOS AND LUNATICS** [24] [ ]
– Taking the easy way out again / The thunder and lightning kid / California silks and satins / Four day Louise / Intro / Kerosene / Scotch corner / Exit. *(cd-iss.Nov93 on 'B.G.O.')*

Jul 74. (7") **TAKING THE EASY WAY OUT AGAIN. / CALIFORNIA SILKS AND SATINS** [ ] [ ]

— Trimmed to a quartet when MALCOLM departed.

Oct 74. (7") **DAY AND NIGHT. / HARD WAY TO LIVE (live)** [ ] [ ]
Nov 74. (lp)(c) **SLOW MOTION** [ ] [ ]
– Hard way to die / Grasshopper / Rock & roll you out / You don't like us / Bedtime bone / One more chance / Rainbow eyes / Day and night. *(cd-iss.Nov93 on 'B.G.O.')*

Nov 74. (7") **DAY AND NIGHT. / RAINBOW EYES** [-] [ ]

— **MARTIN ACE** – bass returned to replace KEN who joined TYLA GANG. added American **JOHN CIPPOLINA** – guitar (ex-QUICKSILVER MESSENGER SERVICE)

Sep 75. (lp)(c) **MAXIMUM DARKNESS (live)** [25] [ ]
– Codine / 7171-551 / Babe I'm gonna leave you / Many are called, but few get up / Bananas. *(re-iss.Mar89 on 'B.G.O.', cd-iss.Feb92)*

— **PHIL RYAN** – keyboards returned to replace CIPPOLINA / **JOHN McKENZIE** – bass (of GLOBAL VILLAGE TRUCKING CO.) repl. MARTIN ACE who joined The MOTORS.

M.C.A. / M.C.A.

Mar 76. (lp)(c) **THE WELSH CONNECTION** [40] [ ]
– The ride and the view / Out of your head / Love can find a way / The Welsh connection / Something is happening / Cartoon / Born with a future.

Mar 76. (7") **OUT OF YOUR HEAD. / I'M A LOVE TAKER** [ ] [ ]

— (disbanded Spring '76)

Nov 77. (lp)(c) **ALL'S WELL THAT ENDS WELL (live farewell gigs)** [ ] [ ]
– Let the good times roll / The Welsh connection / The ride and the view / A hard way to live / Born with a future / Spunk Rock / Romain.

— TERRY WILLIAMS continued in DAVE EDMUNDS' ROCKPILE, before joining The MOTORS and later DIRE STRAITS. PHIL RYAN joined PETE BROWN Band.

DEKE LEONARD

solo career, with **ICEBERG** group. With at times MAN members **MICKY JONES, MARTIN ACE, KEN WHALEY** and **TERRY WILLIAMS.** Plus others incl. **TOMMY RILEY** – drums, etc.

United A / United A

Feb 73. (7") **DIAMOND ROAD. / CIRCLES AND SQUARES** [ ] [ ]
Jul 73. (lp) **ICEBERG** [ ] [ ]
– Razor blade and rattlesnake / I just can't win / Lisa / Nothing is happening /

Looking for a man / A hard way to live / Broken ovation / Jesse / Ten thousand takers / The ghost of Musket flat / Jesse / Crosby (second class citizen blues) / 7171 551. *(re-iss.Dec80 on 'Liberty') (cd-iss.Nov95 on 'BGO' w/next album)*

Sep 73. (7") **A HARD WAY TO LIVE. / THE ACHING IS SO SWEET** [ ] [-]

Oct 73. (7") **A HARD WAY TO LIVE. / JESSE (live)** [-] [ ]

Mar 74. (lp) **KAMIKAZE** [50] [ ]
– Cool summer rain / Jayhawk special / Sharpened claws / Taking the easy way out / The black gates of death / Stacia / Broken glass and limejuice / April the third / Louisiana hoedown / In search of Sarah and twenty-six horses / The Devil's gloves.

Apr 74. (7") **LOUISIANA HOEDOWN. / SHE'S A CAR** [ ] [ ]

Feb 79. (7") **MAP OF INDIA. / LADY IN THE BLUE TUXEDO** [ ] [-]

Mar 81. (lp)(c) **BEFORE YOUR VERY EYES** [ ] [-]
– Someone is calling / Fools like me / Marlene / Oh / When am I coming back / Get off the line / Hiding in the darkness / Big hunk of love / I feel like a pill / The world exploded in my face / What am I gonna do when the money runs out / Bad luck.

Liberty not issued

Jun 81. (7") **BIG HUNK OF LOVE. / MARLENE** [ ] [-]

MAN

reformed briefly 1983. **MICKY JONES, DEKE LEONARD, MARTIN ACE** plus **JOHN WEATHERS** – drums (ex-EYES OF BLUE, ex-GENTLE GIANT)

Picasso not issued

Dec 83. (lp)(c) **FRIDAY THE 13th (live Marquee, May '83)** [ ] [ ]
– C'mon / Talk about a morning / Kerosene / A hard way to die / Back into the future / The ride and the view / Romain. *(cd-iss.Aug93 on 'Great Expectations')*

Omox-ROR. not issued

1984. (7") **WHAT A NIGHT. / THE LAST BIRTHDAY PARTY** [-] [-] GERM

— (1987 reformed again but only to do gigs) **TERRY WILLIAMS** – drums had returned to replace WEATHERS.

Road Goes not issued

Feb 93. (cd)(c) **THE TWANG DYNASTY** [ ] [-]
– A feather on the scales of justice / Mad on her / Jumpin' like a kangaroo / The chimes at midnight / Circumstances / The price / Women / The Chinese cut / Out of the darkness / Fast and dangerous / The wings of Mercury.

Hypertens. not issued

May 95. (cd) **CALL DOWN THE MOON** [ ] [-]
– Call down the Moon / If I were you / Dream away / Blackout / The man with x-ray eyes / Heaven and Hell / The girl is trouble / Drivin' around / Burn my workin' clothes.

– compilations, others –

Oct 73. Pye; (lp)(c) **GOLDEN HOUR OF MAN** [ ] [-]

Nov 76. United Artists; (7"ep) **BANANAS. / BANANAS (pt.2)** [ ] [-]

Nov 86. Latymer; (lp) **GREEN FLY** [ ] [-]

Aug 90. See For Miles; (cd)(lp) **BIRTH OF MAN** ("BYSTANDERS" material) [ ] [-]

Feb 91. Worldwide; (cd) **LIVE AT THE RAINBOW 1972 (live)** [ ] [-]

Jun 91. E.M.I.; (cd)(c)(lp) **PERFECT TIMING (THE U.A. YEARS: 1970-1975)** [ ] [-]
(cd/c.iss.+=) – (3 extra tracks).

Mar 93. Raw Fruit; (cd) **LIVE AT READING '83 (live)** [ ] [-]

Oct 93. Windsong; (cd) **BBC RADIO 1 LIVE IN CONCERT** (live shared with DEKE LEONARD'S ICEBERG) [ ] [-]

MANIC STREET PREACHERS

Formed: Blackwood, Gwent, South Wales . . . 1988 by JAMES DEAN BRADFIELD and cousin SEAN MOORE. They quickly found former school friends RICHEY and NICKY, and set about recording self-financed debut 45 'SUICIDE ALLEY'. After another indie 45 in 1990, they signed to 'Heavenly', where they had 2 minor UK hits. In summer of '91, after being snapped up by 'Columbia', they had first entry into the Top 40 with 'STAY BEAUTIFUL'. Darlings of the music press, they soon had Top 20 debut double lp 'GENERATION TERRORISTS' early '92. • **Style:** Talented heavy/punk outfit, taking influences from The CLASH, The ALARM or GUNS'N'ROSES. • **Songwriters:** NICKY + RICHEY lyrics, SEAN & JAMES music. Covered; IT'S SO EASY (Guns'n'Roses) / UNDER MY WHEELS (Alice Cooper) / SUICIDE IS PAINLESS (Theme from 'Mash') / CHARLES WINDSOR (McCarthy) / THE DROWNERS (Suede) / STAY WITH ME (Faces) / WROTE FOR LUCK (Happy Mondays) / RAINDROPS KEEP FALLING ON MY HEAD (Bacharach-David). • **Trivia:** LITTLE BABY NOTHING featured porn star Traci Lords on guest vocals.

Recommended: GENERATION TERRORISTS (*8) / GOLD AGAINST THE SOUL (*9) / THE HOLY BIBLE (*8).

JAMES DEAN BRADFIELD (b.21 Feb'69) – vocals, guitar / **RICHEY EDWARDS** (b.27 Dec'69) – rhythm guitar / **NICKY WIRE** (b.JONES) – bass / **SEAN MOORE** (b.30 Jul'70) – drums

S.B.S. not issued

Aug 89. (7") **SUICIDE ALLEY. / TENNESSEE (I FEEL SO LOW)** [ ] [-]

Damaged Goods not issued

Jun 90. (12"ep) **NEW ART RIOT** [ ] [-]
– New art riot / Stip it down / Last exit on yesterday / Teenage 20-20. *(re-iss.12"pink/cd-ep.Dec91) (re-iss.12"/cd-ep Jul93)*

Heavenly not issued

Jan 91. (12"ep)(cd-ep) **MOTOWN JUNK. / SORROW 16 / WE HER MAJESTY'S PRISONERS** [92] [-]

May 91. (7") **YOU LOVE US. / SPECTATORS OF SUICIDE** [62] [-]
(12"+=)(cd-s+=) – Starlover / Strip it down (live).

Columbia Columbia

Jul 91. (7") **STAY BEAUTIFUL. / R.P. McMURPHY** [40] [ ]
(12"+=)(cd-s+=) – Soul contamination.
(US-cd-ep+=) – Motown junk / Sorrow 16 / Star lover.

Nov 91. (7") **LOVE'S SWEET EXILE. / REPEAT** [26] [ ]
(12"+=)(cd-s+=) – Democracy coma.
(12"ltd.++=) – Stay beautiful (live).

Jan 92. (7") **YOU LOVE US. / A VISION OF DEAD DESIRE** [16] [ ]
(12"+=) – It's so easy.
(cd-s++=) – We want majesty's prisoners.

Feb 92. (cd)(d-c)(d-lp)(pic-d-lp) **GENERATION TERRORISTS** [13] [ ]
– Slash'n'burn / Nat West-Barclays-Midland-Lloyds / Born to end / Motorcycle emptiness / You love us / Love's sweet exile / Little baby nothing / Repeat (stars and stripes) / Tennessee / Another invented disease / Stay beautiful / So dead / Repeat (UK) / Spectators of suicide / Damn dog / Crucifix kiss / Methadone pretty / Condemned to rock'n'roll.

Mar 92. (7")(c-s) **SLASH'N'BURN. / AIN'T GOING DOWN** [20] [ ]
(12"+=) – Motown junk.
(cd-s++=) – ('A'version).

Jun 92. (7")(c-s) **MOTORCYCLE EMPTINESS. / BORED OUT OF MY MIND** [17] [ ]
(12"pic-d+=) – Under my wheels.
(cd-s++=) – Crucifix kiss (live).

Sep 92. (7")(cd-s) **SUICIDE IS PAINLESS (Mash mix). / ('b'side by 'Fatima Mansions' – Everything I Do (I Do It For You)** [7] [ ]

Nov 92. (7") **LITTLE BABY NOTHING. / SUICIDE ALLEY** [29] [ ]
(12"+=)(cd-s+=) – Yankee drawl / Never want again.

Jun 93. (c-s) **FROM DESPAIR TO WHERE. / HIBERNATION** [25] [ ]
(12"+=) – Spectators of suicide (Heavenly version).
(cd-s+=) – Star lover (Heavenly version).

Jun 93. (cd)(c)(lp) **GOLD AGAINST THE SOUL** [8] [ ]
– Sleepflower / From despair to where / La tristesse durera (scream to a sigh) / Yourself / Life becoming a landslide / Drug drug druggy / Roses in the hospital / Nostalgic pushead / Symphony of tourette / God against the soul.

Jul 93. (7")(c-s) **LA TRISTESSE DURERA (SCREAM TO A SIGH). / PATRICK BATEMAN** [22] [ ]
(12"+=) – Repeat (live) / Tennessee.
(cd-s+=) – What's my name (live) / Slash'n'burn (live).

Sep 93. (7")(c-s) **ROSE'S IN THE HOSPITAL. / US AGAINST YOU / DONKEY** [15] [ ]
(cd-s+=) – Wrote for luck.
(12") – ('A'side) / (5-'A' mixes).

Jan 94. (c-s) **LIFE BECOMING A LANDSLIDE EP** [36] [ ]
– Landslide / Comfort comes.
(12"+=) – Are mothers saints.
(cd-s++=) – Charles Windsor.

Jun 94. (7")(c-s)(10")(cd-s) **FASTER. / P.C.P.** [16] [ ]

Aug 94. (10")(c-s) **REVOL. / TOO COLD HERE** [22] [ ]
(cd-s+=) – You love us (original Heavenly version) / Love's sweet exile (live).
(cd-s) – ('A'side) / (3 live at Glastonbury tracks).

— RICHEY booked himself into a health clinic, after wasting himself down to 5 stone.

Aug 94. (cd)(c)(pic-lp) **THE HOLY BIBLE** [6] [ ]
– Yes / Ifwhiteamericatoldthetruthforonedayit'sworldwouldfallapart / Of walking abortion / She is suffering / Archives of pain / Revol / 4st 7lb / Mausoleum / Faster / This is yesterday / Die in the summertime / The intense humming of evil / P.C.P.

Oct 94. (10")(c-s) **SHE IS SUFFERING. / LOVE TORN US UNDER (acoustic)** [25] [ ]
(cd-s+=) – The drowners / Stay with me (both live w/ BERNARD BUTLER).
(cd-s) – ('A'side) / La tristesse durera (scream to a sigh) / Faster (Dust Brothers remixes).

— RICHEY was now fully recuperated . . . but on 1st Feb '95, he went AWOL again after walking out of London's Embassy Hotel at 7 that morning. Two weeks later, his car was found abandoned and after police frog search the Severn, it was believed he might be dead. By the end of 1995, with RICHEY still missing, the group carried on as a trio.

— Meantime, BRADFIELD produced the debut of hits to be NORTHERN UPROAR.

Aimee MANN

Born: Boston, Massachusetts, USA. From 1984-89, she fronted local pop-rock group 'TIL TUESDAY, who had large US hit with 'VOICES CARRY'. They disbanded due to corporate record label pressures. She returned in 1993, with a debut solo release, that was lawded by many especially fan ELVIS COSTELLO. • **Style:** Her eclectic pop was quite close to PRETENDERS. • **Songwriters:** JULES SHEAR wrote for 'TIL TUESDAY, AIMEE co-wrote her solo album with ELVIS COSTELLO. Five years previous, he had guested on 'TIL TUESDAY's final album. • **Trivia:** 'TIL TUESDAY were produced by RHETT DAVIES apart from debut which was MIKE THORNE. In 1987, she guested on RUSH's hit single 'Time Stand Still'.

Recommended: WHATEVER (*7) / I'M WITH STUPID (*6)

'TIL TUESDAY

AIMEE MANN – vocals, bass / **ROBERT HOLMES** – guitar, vocals / **JOEY PESCE** – synthesizers, piano, vocals / **MICHAEL HAUSMANN** – drums, percussion

Epic Epic

Apr 85. (7") **VOICES CARRY. / ARE YOU SERIOUS** [ ] [8]

Jun 85. (lp)(c) **VOICES CARRY** [ ] [19] Apr85
– Love in a vacuum / Looking over my shoulder / I could get used to this / No more crying / Voices carry / Winning the war / You know the rest / Maybe Monday / Don't watch me bleed / Sleep. *(cd-iss.1988)*

Aug 85. (7") **LOOKING OVER MY SHOULDER. / DON'T WATCH ME BLEED** [-] [61]
Oct 85. (7") **LOVE IN A VACUUM. / NO MORE CRYING** [-] [ ]
Jan 87. (lp)(c)(cd) **WELCOME HOME** [ ] [49] Oct86
– What about love / Coming up close / On Sunday / Will she just fall down / David denies / Lover's day / Have mercy / Sleeping and walking / Angels never call / No one is watching you now.
Feb 87. (7") **WHAT ABOUT LOVE. / WILL SHE JUST FALL DOWN** [ ] [26] Sep86
– ('A'extended-12"+=) – Voices carry.
Apr 87. (7") **COMING UP CLOSE. / ANGELS NEVER CALL** [-] [59]

—— **MICHAEL MONTES** – keyboards / + sessioners **MARCUS MILLER** – bass / **HAERYUNG SHIN** – violin / **PETER ABRAMS** – French horn / **MIKE DENNEEN** – keyboards repl. PESCE

Jan 89. (7") **(BELIEVED YOU WERE) LUCKY. / LIMITS TO LOVE** [ ] [95]
(12"+=)(cd-s+=) – Voices carry / What about love.
Mar 89. (lp)(c)(cd) **EVERYTHING'S DIFFERENT NOW** [ ] [ ] Nov88
– Everything's different now / R.I.P. in Heaven / Why must I / J for Jules / (Believed you were) Lucky / Limits to love / Long gone (buddy) / The other end (of the telescope) / Crash and burn / How can you give up.
Jul 89. (7") **R. I. P. IN HEAVEN. / HOW CAN YOU GIVE UP** [-] [ ]

—— Disbanded after above album.

AIMEE MANN

solo with **DAVE GREGORY** – guitar (of XTC)

Imago Imago

Aug 93. (7")(c-s) **I SHOULD'VE KNOWN. / JIMMY HOFFA JOKES** [55] [ ]
(cd-s+=) – Jacob Marley's chains.
Sep 93. (cd)(c)(lp) **WHATEVER** [39] [ ]
– I should've known / Fifty years after the fair / 4th of July / Could've been anyone / Put me on top / Stupid thing / Say anything / Jacob Marley's chain / Mr. Harris / I could hurt you now / I know there's a word / I've had it / Way back when.
Nov 93. (7")(c-s) **STUPID THING. / I'VE HAD IT** [47] [ ]
(cd-s) – ('A'side) / Baby blue / Telescope / Say anything.
(cd-s) – ('A'side) / Put me on top / 4th of July / I should've known (all live).
Feb 94. (7")(c-s) **I SHOULD'VE KNOWN. / TRUTH ON MY SIDE** [45] [ ]
(cd-s+=) – Fifty years after the fair / Put on some speed.
(10") – ('A'side) / 4th July / Stupid thing / The other end (of the telescope).

—— with **JON BRION** – guitars, drums, co-writer (some) / **JOHN SANDS – drums / guests BERNARD BUTLER** (co-writer SUGARCOATED) / **GLENN TILBROOK + CHRIS DIFFORD / JULIANA HATFIELD / MICHAEL PENN**

Geffen Geffen

Jan 95. (c-s)(cd-s) **THAT'S JUST WHAT YOU ARE /** [-] [93]
Nov 95. (cd)(c) **I'M WITH STUPID** [51] [ ]
– Long shot / Choice in the matter / Sugarcoated / You could make a killing / Superball / Amateur / All over now / Par for the course / You're with stupid now / That's just what you are / Frankenstein / Ray / It's not safe.

Manfred MANN

Formed: as MANFRED MANN, the group, London, England . . . late '62, initially as The MANN-HUGG BLUES BAND, by namesake MANFRED MANN and MIKE HUGG. They recruited DAVE RICHMOND, PAUL JONES and MIKE VICKERS, and played local gigs which attracted EMI's subsidiary label 'HMV' to sign them. Early 1964 after 2 flops, they had first chart success, with UK Top 5 single '5-4-3-2-1'. They continued to storm charts throughout the 60's, and hit UK top spot 3 times with 'DOO WAH DIDDY DIDDY', 'PRETTY FLAMINGO' & 'THE MIGHTY QUINN'. In 1969, MANN and HUGG wrote commercial jingles for Michelen and Ski yogurt, before forming MANFRED MANN CHAPTER THREE. They made a couple of lp's for 'Vertigo', but soon reverted to original name in '71. The following year, they re-emerged without HUGG, in the more adventurous MANFRED MANN'S EARTH BAND. They struggled initially, although they had 3 fine UK Top 10 singles in the 70's 'JOYBRINGER', 'BLINDED BY THE LIGHT' & 'DAVY'S ON THE ROAD AGAIN'. Continued to surface during the 80's, and had a Top 30 US single 'THE RUNNER'. • **Style:** R&B pop group, excelled by JONES' harmonica playing until '66. In the 70's, the EARTH BAND were a more heavier synth-band, although they did not disregard hit-making cover versions. • **Songwriters:** MANN-HUGG until latter's departure in '71. Covered; DOO WAH DIDDY DIDDY (Exciters) / SHA LA LA (Shirelles) / OH NO NOT MY BABY (Goffin-King) / SMOKESTACK LIGHTNING (Howlin' Wolf) / MY LITTLE RED BOOK (Bacharach-David) / WITH GOD ON OUR SIDE + IF YOU GOTTA GO, GO NOW + JUST LIKE A WOMAN + THE MIGHTY QUINN + PLEASE, MRS.HENRY + others (Bob Dylan) / SWEET PEA (Tommy Roe) / SO LONG DAD + LIVING WITHOUT YOU (Randy Newman) / MY NAME IS JACK (John Simon) / etc. His EARTH BAND covered JOYBRINGER (adapt. Gustav Holst 'The Planets') / FATHER OF DAY, FATHER OF NIGHT + YOU, ANGEL YOU (Bob Dylan) / SPIRIT IN THE NIGHT + BLINDED BY THE LIGHT + FOR YOU (Bruce Springsteen) / DON'T KILL IT CAROL (Mike Heron) / REDEPTION SONG (Bob Marley) / DO ANYTHING YOU WANNA DO (Eddie & The Hot Rods) / GOING UNDERGROUND (Jam) / BANQUET (Joni Mitchell) / etc. • **Trivia:** MIKE HUGG wrote 'SHAPES OF THINGS' in 1966 for fellow R&B hitmakers The YARDBIRDS. MANFRED guested Moog synthsizer on URIAH HEEP's 1971 album 'Look At Yourself'. 'GLORIFIED MAGNIFIED' track was used for the theme to Radio 1's 'Sound Of The 70's'.

Recommended: AGES OF MANN (22 CLASSICS OF THE 60s) (*8) / 20 YEARS OF MANFRED MANN'S EARTH BAND (*6).

MANFRED MANN (b.MICHAEL LUBOWITZ, 21 Oct'40, Johannesburg, S.Africa) – keys / **PAUL JONES** (b.PAUL POND, 24 Feb'42, Portsmouth, England) – vocals, harmonica / **MIKE VICKERS** (b.18 Apr'41, Southampton, England) – guitar / **DAVE RICHMOND** – bass / **MIKE HUGG** (b.11 Aug'42, Andover, England) – drums

H.M.V. Prestige

Jul 63. (7") **WHY SHOULD WE NOT. / BROTHER JACK** [ ] [-]
Oct 63. (7") **COCK-A-HOOP. / NOW YOU'RE NEEDING ME** [ ] [-]

—— **TOM McGUINESS** (b. 2 Dec'41, Wimbledon, London, England) – bass (ex-ROOSTERS) repl. RICHMOND

Jan 64. (7") **5-4-3-2-1. / WITHOUT YOU** [5] [ ] Mar 64

H.M.V. Ascot

Apr 64. (7") **HUBBLE BUBBLE TOIL AND TROUBLE. / I'M YOUR KINGPIN** [11] [ ]
Jul 64. (7") **DOO WAH DIDDY DIDDY. / WHAT YOU GONNA DO** [1] [1] Aug 64
(re-iss.Oct82)
Sep 64. (lp) **THE FIVE FACES OF MANFRED MANN** [3] [ ] Feb 65
– Smokestack lightning / Don't ask me what I say / It's gonna work out fine / Sack of wool / What you gonna do / I'm your kingpin / Hoochie coochie / Down the road apiece / I've got my mojo working / Mr. Analles / Untie me / Bring it to Jerome / Without you / You've got to take it.
Oct 64. (7") **SHA LA LA. / JOHN HARDY** [3] [12] Nov 64
Nov 64. (lp) **MANFRED MANN ALBUM** [-] [35]
– (singles compilation)
– (* tracks I'm your kingpin , Mr.Anello & You've got to take it were repl. by Do wah diddy diddy on US version)
Jan 65. (7") **COME TOMORROW. / WHAT DID I DO WRONG** [4] [50] Feb 65
Apr 65. (7") **OH NO NOT MY BABY. / WHAT AM I DOING WRONG** [11] [ ]
Apr 65. (7") **POISON IVY. / I CAN'T BELIEVE WHAT YOU SAY** [-] [ ]
Jun 65. (7") **MY LITTLE BOOK. / WHAT AM I DOING WRONG** [-] [-]
Jul 65. (lp) **MY LITTLE RED BOOK OF WINNERS** [-] [ ]
– My little red book / Oh no, not my baby / What am I to do / One in the middle / You gave me somebody to love / You're for me / Poison Ivy / Without you / Brother Jack / Love like yours / I can't believe what you say / With God on your side.
Sep 65. (7") **IF YOU GOTTA GO, GO NOW. / STAY AROUND** [2] [-]
Sep 65. (lp) **MANN MADE** [7] [ ]
– Since I don't have you / You're for me / Look away / L.S.D. / The abominable snowman / Watch your step / The way you do the things you do / Stormy Monday blues / Hi lili hi lo / I really do believe / Bear Hugg / You don't know me / I'll make it up to you. *(re-iss.Nov69 on 'Starline')*
Oct 65. (7") **IF YOU GOTTA GO, GO NOW. / THE ONE IN THE MIDDLE** [-] [ ]
Jan 66. (7") **HI LILI, HI LO. / SHE NEEDS COMPANY** [-] [ ]

—— (PETE BURFORD and DAVID HYDE deputised for VICKERS on tour until) / **JACK BRUCE** – bass (ex-JOHN MAYALL, ex-GRAHAM BOND) repl. VICKERS added / **LYN DOBSON** – saxophone / **HENRY LOWTHER** – trumpet (McGUINESS now guitar)

H.M.V. United Art

Apr 66. (7") **PRETTY FLAMINGO. / YOU'RE STANDING BY** [1] [29] Jul 66

—— **MANN, HUGG** and **McGUINESS** added new members **MIKE D'ABO** (b. 1 Mar'44, England) – vocals (ex-BAND OF ANGELS) repl. JONES who went solo, etc. / **KLAUS VOORMAN** (b.29 Apr'42, Berlin, W.Germany) – bass repl. JACK BRUCE who formed CREAM.

Jun 66. (7") **YOU GAVE ME SOMEBODY TO LOVE. / POISON IVY** [36] [ ]

Fontana United Art.

Jul 66. (7") **JUST LIKE A WOMAN. / I WANNA BE RIGHT** [10] [-]
Oct 66. (7") **SEMI-DETACHED SUBURBAN MR. JAMES. / MORNING AFTER THE PARTY** [2] [ ]
Oct 66. (lp) **AS IS** (US title 'PRETTY FLAMINGO') [22] [ ]
– Trouble and tea/ A now and then thing / Each other's company / Box office draw / Dealer dealer / Morning after the party / Another kind of music / As long as I have lovin' / Autumn leaves / Superstitious guy / You're my girl / Just like a woman.
Mar 67. (7") **HA HA SAID THE CLOWN. / FEELING SO GOOD** [4] [ ]
May 67. (7") **SWEET PEA. / ONE WAY** [36] [ ]
Sep 67. (7") **SO LONG DAD. / FUNNIEST GIG** [ ] [ ]
Jan 68. (lp) **UP THE JUNCTION (Soundtrack)** [ ] [-]
– Up the junction (vocal) / Sing songs of love / Walking around up the junction (instrumental) / Love theme (instrumental) / Up the junction (vocal & instrumental) / Just for me / Love theme (instrumental) / Sheila's dance / Belgravia / Wailing horn / I need your love / Up the junction (vocal). *(re-iss.1970)*

Fontana Mercury

Jan 68. (7") **THE MIGHTY QUINN. / BY REQUEST EDWIN GARVEY** [1] [10]
Mar 68. (7") **UP THE JUNCTION. / SLEEPY HOLLOW** [ ] [ ]
Jun 68. (lp) **MIGHTY GARVEY** (US 'THE MIGHTY QUINN') [ ] [ ]
– Happy families / No better no worse / Each and every day / Country dancing / It's so easy falling / Happy families / Mighty Quinn / Big Betty / The vicar's daughter / Every day another hair turns grey / Cubist town / Ha! ha! said the clown / Harry the one-man band / Happy families.
Jun 68. (7") **MY NAME IS JACK. / THERE IS A MAN** [8] [ ]
Dec 68. (7") **FOX ON THE RUN. / TOO MANY PEOPLE** [5] [97]
May 69. (7") **RAGAMUFFIN MAN. / A 'B' SIDE** [8] [ ]

—— split mid 69. TOM formed McGUINESS FLINT. D'ABO went solo, and VOORMAN joined The PLASTIC ONO BAND (see JOHN LENNON)

MANFRED MANN CHAPTER THREE

MANFRED retained **MIKE HUGG now** – vocals, electric piano. Recruited **BRIAN HUGG** – guitar / **STEVE YORK** – bass plus session singers, drummers and wind section.

Vertigo Polydor

Nov 69. (lp) **MANFRED MANN CHAPTER THREE** [ ] [ ]
– Travelling lady / Snakeskin garter / Konekuf / Sometimes / Devil woman / Time / One way glass / Mister you're a better man than I / Ain't it sad / A study in

inaccuracy / Where am I going. *(cd-iss.Feb94 on 'Cohesion')*

Mar 70. (7") **SNAKESKIN GARTER. / SOMETIMES** [-] [ ]

— on session **CHRIS SLADE** – drums (alongside others)

Sep 70. (7") **HAPPY BEING ME. / DEVIL WOMAN** [ ] [ ]

Oct 70. (lp) **CHAPTER THREE, VOLUME TWO** [ ] [-]

– Lady Ace / I ain't laughing / Poor sad Sue / Jump before you think / It's good to be alive / Happy being me / Virginia. *(cd-iss.Feb94 on 'Cohesion')*

MANFRED MANN'S EARTH BAND

His new band now featured **CHRIS SLADE** – drums (now a full time member) / **MICK ROGERS** – vocals, guitar repl. MIKE HUGG / **COLIN PATTENDEN** – bass repl. STEVE YORK and BRIAN HUGG

Philips Polydor

Jun 71. (7") **LIVING WITHOUT YOU. / TRIBUTE** [ ] [69] Jan 72

Sep 71. (7") **PLEASE MRS. HENRY. / PRAYER** [ ] [ ]

Feb 72. (lp) **MANFRED MANN'S EARTH BAND** [ ] [ ]

– California coastline / Captain Bobby Stout / Sloth / Living without you / Tribute / Please Mrs. Henry / Jump sturdy / Prayer / Part time man / I'm up and leaving. *(re-iss.Apr77 & 1981 on 'Bronze') (cd-iss.Jan91 on 'Cohesion')*

Mar 72. (7") **PART TIME MAN. / I'M UP AND LEAVING** [-] [ ]

Sep 72. (lp) **GLORIFIED MAGNIFIED** [ ] [ ]

– Meat / Look around / One way glass / I'm gonna have you all / Down home / Our friend George / Ashes to the wind / It's all over now, baby blue / Glorified magnified. *(re-iss.Apr77 & 1981 on 'Bronze') (cd-iss.Dec93 on 'Cohesion')*

Nov 72. (7") **MEAT. / GLORIFIED MAGNIFIED** [ ] [ ]

Feb 73. (7") **IT'S ALL OVER NOW, BABY BLUE. / ASHES TO THE WIND** [-] [ ]

Vertigo Polydor

Apr 73. (7") **GET YOUR ROCKS OFF ("EARTH BAND"). / SADJOY** [ ] [-]

Jun 73. (lp) **MESSIN'** (US-title 'GET YOUR ROCKS OFF') [ ] [ ]

– Buddah / Messin' / Cloudy eyes / Get your rocks off / Sadjoy / Black and blue / Mardi Gras day. *(re-iss.Apr77 & 1981 on 'Bronze') (cd-iss.Jan91 on 'Cohesion')*

Jun 73. (7") **MARDI GRAS DAY. / SADJOY** [-] [ ]

Aug 73. (7") **GET YOUR ROCKS OFF. / ASHES TO THE WIND** [-] [ ]

Aug 73. (7") **JOYBRINGER. / CAN'T EAT MEAT** [9] [ ]

Sep 73. (7") **JOYBRINGER. / CLOUDY EYES** [-] [ ]

Bronze Polydor

Nov 73. (lp)(c) **SOLAR FIRE** [ ] [96]

– Father of night, in the beginning / Pluto the dog / Solar fire / Saturn (Mercury) / Earth the circle (pts.1 & 2). *(re-iss.Apr77 & 1981) (re-iss.Nov87 on 'Legacy') (cd-iss.Jan91 on 'Cohesion')*

Mar 74. (7") **FATHER OF DAY, FATHER OF NIGHT. / SOLAR FIRE 2** [ ] [ ]

Bronze Warners

Oct 74. (7") **BE NOT TOO HARD. / EARTH HYMN (part 2a)** [ ] [ ]

Oct 74. (lp)(c) **THE GOOD EARTH** [ ] [ ]

– Give me the good earth / Launching place / I'll be gone / Earth hymn (pts.1 & 2) / Sky high / Be not too hard. *(re-iss.Apr77 + 1981) (cd-iss.Dec93 on 'Cohesion')*

Jul 75. (7") **SPIRITS IN THE NIGHT. / AS ABOVE SO BELOW (part 2)** [ ] [97] Mar 76

Aug 75. (lp)(c) **NIGHTINGALES AND BOMBERS** [ ] [ ]

– Spirits in the night / Countdown / Time is right / Crossfade / Visionary mountains / Nightingales and bombers / Fat Nelly / As above so below. *(re-iss.Apr77 + 1981) (cd-iss.Jan91 on 'Cohesion')*

— **CHRIS THOMPSON** – vocals repl. ROGERS who later formed AVIATOR / added **DAVE FLETT** – guitar

Aug 76. (7") **BLINDED BY THE LIGHT. / STARBIRD No.2** [6] [1]

Aug 76. (lp)(c) **THE ROARING SILENCE** [10] [10]

– Blinded by the light / Singing the dolphin through / Waiter, there's a yawn in my ear / The road to Babylon / This side of Paradise / Starbird / Questions. *(re-iss.Apr77 + 1981) (re-iss.Nov87 on 'Legacy') (cd-iss.Jan91 on 'Cohesion')*

Nov 76. (7") **QUESTIONS. / WAITER, THERE'S A YAWN IN MY EAR No.2** [ ] [-]

Dec 76. (7") **QUESTIONS. / SPIRITS IN THE NIGHT** [-] [ ]

— **PAT KING** – bass (ex-SHANGHAI, etc.) repl. PATTENDEN (to TERRA NOVA)

Nov 77. (7") **CALIFORNIA. / CHICAGO INSTITUTE** [ ] [-]

Feb 78. (lp)(c) **WATCH** [33] [83]

– Circles / Drowning on dry land / Fish soup / California / Chicago institute / Davy's on the road again / Martha's madman / The mighty Quinn. *(re-iss.1981) (re-iss.Nov87 on 'Legacy') (cd-iss.Jan91 on 'Cohesion')*

Mar 78. (7") **THE MIGHTY QUINN. / TINY** [ ] [-]

Apr 78. (7") **DAVY'S ON THE ROAD AGAIN. / BOUILLABAISE** [6] [ ] Sep 78

Jul 78. (7") **CALIFORNIA. / BOUILLABAISE** [-] [ ]

— After a short split, MANN reformed band retaining **THOMPSON + KING / STEVE WALLER** – guitar (ex-GONZALES) repl. FLETT / **GEOFF BRITTON** – drums (ex-EAST OF EDEN, ex-WINGS, ex-ROUGH DIAMOND, ex-CHAMPION) repl. CHRIS SLADE who joined URIAH HEEP. He later joined The FIRM (see; LED ZEPPELIN.)

Feb 79. (7") **YOU ANGEL YOU. / OUT IN THE DISTANCE** [54] [-]

Mar 79. (lp)(c) **ANGEL STATION** [30] [ ]

– Don't kill it Carol / You angel you / Hollywood town / Belle of the Earth / Platform end / Angels at my gate / You are I am / Waiting for the rain / Resurrection. *(re-iss.1981) (re-iss.Nov87 on 'Legacy') (cd-iss.Jan91 on 'Cohesion')*

May 79. (7") **YOU ANGEL YOU. / BELLE OF THE EARTH** [-] [58]

Jun 79. (7")(7"pic-d) **DON'T KILL IT CAROL. / BLINDED BY THE LIGHT** [45] [ ]

— **JOHN LINGWOOD** – drums repl. BRITTON who became ill. / guests included **PETER MARSH, WILLY FINLAYSON.** (vocals – **CHRIS THOMPSON**)

Oct 80. (lp)(c) **CHANCE** [ ] [87]

– Lies (through the 80's) / On the run / For you / Adolescent dream / Fritz the blank / Stranded / This is your heart / No guarentee / Heart on the street. *(re-iss.1981) (cd-iss.Jan91 on 'Cohesion')*

Nov 80. (7") **LIES (THROUGH THE 80'S). / ADOLESCENT DREAM** [ ] [ ] Jun 81

Jan 81. (7") **FOR YOU. / A FOOL I AM** [ ] [ ]

— **MATT IRVING** – bass (ex-DREAM POLICE, ex-BABYS, ex-LONGDANCER) repl. KING

Nov 81. (7") **I (WHO HAVE NOTHING). / MAN IN JAM** [ ] [-]

Bronze Arista

Feb 82. (7")(12") **EYES OF NOSTRADAMUS. / HOLIDAY'S END** [ ] [-]

Jun 82. (7")(12") **REDEMPTION SONG (NO KWAZULU). / WARDREAM** [ ] [-]

Nov 82. (7") **TRIBAL STATISTICS. / WHERE DO THEY SEND THEM** [ ] [-]

Jan 83. (lp)(c) **SOMEWHERE IN AFRIKA** [87] [40] Mar 84

– Tribal statistics / Eyes of Nostradamus / Third world service / Demolition man / Brothers and sisters of Azania:- (a) Afrika suite – (b) Brothers and sisters of Afrika – (c) To ban Tustan – (d) Koze Kobenini (how long must we wait?) / Lalela / Redemption song (no Kwazulu) / Somewhere in Afrika. *(re-iss.Nov87 on 'Legacy') (cd-iss.Jan91 on 'Cohesion')*

Jan 83. (7") **DEMOLITION MAN. / IT'S STILL THE SAME** [ ] [-]

Feb 84. (7") **DAVY'S ON THE ROAD AGAIN (live). / THE MIGHTY QUINN (live)** [ ] [-]

(12"+=) – Don't kill it Carol (live).

Feb 84. (lp)(c) **BUDAPEST (live)** [ ] [ ]

– Spirits in the night / Demolition man / For you / Davy's on the road again / Lies (through the 80's) / Blinded by the light / Redemption song (no Kwazulu) / The mighty Quinn. *(cd-iss.Jan91 on 'Cohesion')*

— **MICK RODGERS** – vocals, guitar returned to repl. WALLER (MANN, THOMPSON, LINGWOOD) also still in band. (IRVING left to join LORDS OF THE NEW CHURCH. He later joined PAUL YOUNG band).

Jan 84. (7") **(THE) RUNNER. / NO TRANSKEI** [ ] [-]

(12"+=) – Lies (through the 80's).

Jan 84. (7") **(THE) RUNNER. / WHERE DO THEY SEND THEM** [-] [22]

JUn 84. (7") **REBEL. / FIGURES ON A PAGE** [-] [ ]

10-Virgin Virgin

Mar 86. (7")(12") **DO ANYTHING YOU WANNA DO. / CROSSFIRE** [ ] [ ]

May 86. (7")(12") **GOING UNDERGROUND. / I SHALL BE RESCUED** [ ] [ ]

Jun 86. (lp)(c)(cd) **CRIMINAL TANGO** [ ] [ ]

– Going underground / Who are the mystery kids / Banquet / Killer on the loose / Do anything you wanna do / Rescue / You got me through the heart / Hey bulldog / Crossfire.

— **MAGGIE RYDER** – vocals repl. CHRIS THOMPSON who went solo (guests incl.**FRANK MEAD** – saxophone / **DENNY NEWMAN** – bass, vocals on 1)

Oct 87. (7")(12") **GERONIMO'S CADILLAC. / TWO FRIENDS** [ ] [ ]

Nov 87. (lp)(c)(cd) **MASQUE** [ ] [ ]

– Joybringer (from 'Jupiter') / Billies orno bounce (including Billies bounce) / What you give is what you get (start) / Rivers run dry / Planets schmanets / Geronimo's Cadillac / Sister Billies bounce (including Sister Sadie & Billies bounce) / Telegram to Monica / A couple of mates (from 'Mars' & 'Saturn') / Neptune *Icebringer) / The hymn (from 'Jupiter') / We're going wrong.

– compilations, others, etc. –

Jun 77. Bronze/ US= Warners; (7") **SPIRITS IN THE NIGHT. / ROAD TO BABYLON** [ ] [40]

Jul 77. Vertigo/ US= Warners; (lp)(c) **MANFRED MANN'S EARTH BAND 1971-73** [ ] [ ]

Oct 90. Cohesion; (7") **DAVY'S ON THE ROAD AGAIN. / BLINDED BY THE LIGHT** [ ] [-]

Jan 91. Cohesion; (cd) **20 YEARS OF MANFRED MANN'S EARTH BAND 1971-1991** [ ] [-]

– Blinded by the light / California / Joybringer / Tribal statistics / Somewhere in Africa / Davy's on the road again / You angel you / The runner / Questions / The mighty Quinn / Angels at the gate / For you / Demolition man.

Nov 92. (10xcd-box)(10xlp-box) **MANFRED MANN'S EARTH BAND** [ ] [ ]

– (albums from 1972-1986) (free-12"+=) – ?

– (MANFRED MANN) compilations etc. –

H.M.V. Ascot

Apr 64. H.M.V.; (7"ep) **MANFRED MANN'S COCK-A-HOOP WITH 5-4-3-2-1** [ ] [-]

– Cock-a-hoop / 5-4-3-2-1 / Why should we not / Without you.

Dec 64. H.M.V.; (7"ep) **GROOVING WITH MANFRED MANN** [ ] [-]

– Do wah diddy diddy / etc.

Jul 65. H.M.V.; (7"ep) **ONE IN THE MIDDLE** [6] [-]

– With God on our side / Watermelon man / What am I to do / One in the middle.

Sep 65. H.M.V.; (7"ep) **NO LIVING WITHOUT YOU** [ ] [-]

– Let's go and get stoned / I put a spell on you / Tired of trying / (1).

Apr 66. H.M.V.; (7"ep) **MACHINES** [ ] [-]

– She needs company / Machines / Tennessee waltz / When will I be loved.

Jun 66. H.M.V.; (7"ep) **INSTRUMENTAL ASYLUM** [ ] [-]

Sep 66. H.M.V./ US= Ascot; (lp) **MANN MADE HITS** [11] [ ]

Oct 66. H.M.V.; (7"ep) **AS WAS** [ ] [-]

Dec 66. H.M.V.; (lp) **SOUL OF MANN** (instrumentals) [40] [ ]

(re-iss.Jul86 on 'See For Miles')

Jan 67. Ascot; (7") **MY LITTLE RED BOOK. / I CAN'T BELIEVE WHAT YOU SAY** [-] [ ]

Aug 83. E.M.I.; (d-lp)(c) **THE FIVE FACES OF MANFRED MANN / MANN MADE** [ ] [-]

Dec 66. Fontana; (7"ep) **INSTRUMENTAL ASSASSINATION** [ ] [-]

– Wild thing / With a girl like you / Sunny / Get away.

Mar 68. Fontana; (lp) **WHAT A MANN** [ ] [-]

1988. Fontana; (lp) **HIT RECORDS 1966-69** [ ] [-]

Nov 71. Philips; (lp) **THIS IS MANFRED MANN** [ ] [-]

Jul 77. Philips; (7"ep) **HA! HA! SAID THE CLOWN / THE MIGHTY QUINN. / SEMI-DETACHED SUBURBAN MR.JAMES / A 'B' SIDE** [ ] [-]

1971. M.F.P.; (lp) **GREATEST HITS OF MANFRED MANN** [ ] [-]

Dec 93. M.F.P.; (cd)(c) **THE BEST OF MANFRED MANN 1964-1966** [ ] [-]

Jul 76. Sonic; (lp) **MANNERISMS** [ ] [-]
Jul 77. Nutt-EMI; (lp)(c) **THE BEST OF MANFRED MANN** [ ] [-]
Aug 77. E.M.I.; (7") **PRETTY FLAMINGO. / THE ONE IN THE MIDDLE / GOT MY MOJO WORKING** [ ] [-]
Sep 79. E.M.I.; (d-lp)(c) **SEMI-DETACHED SUBURBAN** [9] [-]
– Do wah diidy diddy / 5-4-3-2-1 / Sha la la / Hubble bubble, toil and trouble / Hi lili hi lo / One in the middle / Got my mojo working / With God on our side / Come tomorrow / If you gotta go, go now / Pretty flamingo / Semi-detached suburban Mr.James / There's no living without your loving / Just like a woman / Oh no not my baby / Ha ha said the clown / My name is Jack / Fox on the run / Ragamuffin man / Mighty Quinn.
Feb 86. E.M.I.; (lp)(c) **THE SINGLES ALBUM** [ ] [-]
(cd-iss. 1987 as 'THE SINGLES PLUS', cont.+ tracks)
Jun 93. E.M.I.; (cd) **THE BEST OF THE EMI YEARS** [ ] [ ]
May 82. E.M.I.; (lp)(c) **THE R&B YEARS** [ ] [-]
(re-iss.Nov86)
Jun 89. E.M.I.; (lp)(cd) **THE EP COLLECTION** [ ] [-]
(re-iss.cd Nov94)
Jun 82. Old Gold; (7") **THE MIGHTY QUINN. / BY REQUEST EDWIN GARVEY** [ ] [-]
Oct 82. Old Gold; (7") **PRETTY FLAMINGO. / 5-4-3-2-1** [ ] [-]
(above flipped over + re-iss.May84 on 'EMI')
Apr 87. Old Gold; (7") **PRETTY FLAMINGO. / COME TOMORROW** [ ] [-]
Sep 92. Old Gold; (cd-ep) **PRETTY FLAMINGO / IF YOU GOTTA GO, GO NOW / COME TOMORROW** [ ] [-]
Jul 90. Castle; (cd)(d-lp) **THE COLLECTION** [ ] [-]
Jan 93. Polygram TV; (cd)(c)(lp) **AGES OF MANN (22 CLASSICS OF THE 60's)** [23] [-]
(re-iss.cd/c Sep95)
Aug 94. Arcade; (cd)(c) **THE VERY BEST OF MANFRED MANN'S EARTH BAND** [69] [-]

Phil MANZANERA / 801 (see under ⇒ ROXY MUSIC)

MARILLION

Formed: Aylesbury, Buckinghamshire, England . . . late '78 initially as SILMARILLION by MICK POINTER and DOUG IRVINE. They took name from J.R.Tolkien novel, but soon shortened it to MARILLION a year later. By this time, they had added STEVE ROTHERY and BRIAN JELLIMAN. After IRVINE departed in late '80, they found Scotsman FISH and also DIZ MINNITT. In Nov'81 & Mar'82 they (FISH, POINTER & ROTHERY) secured last steady members Irishman MARK KELLY plus PETE TREWAVAS, and built up even larger following. In the summer of '82, they were finally snapped up by 'EMI', who issued 'MARKET SQUARE HEROES', which dented UK Top 60. Surprisingly they were voted early in '83, the best newcomer in Sounds magazine. Around the same time, they hit the Top 40 with single 'HE KNOWS, YOU KNOW', from parent debut Top 10 album 'SCRIPT FOR A JESTER'S TEAR'. They continued the rest of the 80's, with more hit 45's and Top 10 studio albums, one of which 'MISPLACED CHILDHOOD' hit UK No.1. • **Style:** Until the arrival of FISH, their early gigs were instrumental. Their progressive keyboard-orientated sound, was heavily influenced by GENESIS, and fulfilled vocally by PETER GABRIEL (Genesis) soundalike FISH. • **Songwriters:** FISH words, group compositions. In 1989, HOGARTH (a virtual PETER GABRIEL clone; sound and looks!) took over FISH mantle. Covered; SYMPATHY (Rare Bird). • **Trivia:** Their first 2 albums were produced by Nick Tauber, the 4th by Chris Kimsey. Their fan club 'The Web' was initiated in 1981, and included Radio 1 DJ Tommy Vance.

Recommended: SCRIPT FOR A JESTER'S TEAR (*7) / FUGAZI (*7) / MISPLACED CHILDHOOD (*6) / A SINGLES COLLECTION 1982-1992 (*8)

FISH (b.DEREK WILLIAM DICK, 25 Apr'58, Dalkeith, Scotland) – vocals / **MARK KELLY** (b. 9 Apr'61, Dublin, Eire) – keyboards repl. BRIAN JELLIMAN / **MICK POINTER** (b.22 Jul'56) – drums / **STEVE ROTHERY** (b.25 Nov'59) – guitar / **PETER TREWAVAS** (b.15 Jan'59) – bass repl. DOUG IRVINE

E.M.I. Capitol

Oct 82. (7") **MARKET SQUARE HEROES. / THREE BOATS DOWN FROM THE CANDY** [60] [-]
(12"+=)(12"pic-d+=) – Grendel. *(12" re-iss.Apr83, hit 53)*
Jan 83. (7")(12") **HE KNOWS, YOU KNOW. / CHARTING THE SINGLE** [35] [-]
Mar 83. (lp)(c) **SCRIPT FOR A JESTER'S TEAR** [7] [ ]
– Script for a jester's tear / He knows, you know / The web / Garden party / Chelsea Monday / Forgotten sons. *(pic-lp Jun84) (cd-iss.Feb87) (re-iss.May90 on 'Fame')*
Jun 83. (7")(7"sha-pic-d) **GARDEN PARTY. / MARGARET** [16] [-]
(12"+=) – Charting the single (live).

—— **ANDY WARD** – drums (ex-CAMEL) replaced POINTER / **IAN MOSLEY** (b.16 Jun'53) – drums (ex-STEVE HACKETT, ex-CURVED AIR) repl. WARD

Jan 84. (7")(12")(12"pic-d) **PUNCH AND JUDY. / MARKET SQUARE HEROES / THREE BOATS DOWN FROM THE CANDY** [29] [-]
Mar 84. (lp)(c)(cd)(pic-lp) **FUGAZI** [5] [ ]
– Assassing / Punch and Judy / Jigsaw / Emerald lies / She chameleon / Incubus / Fugazi. *(re-iss.+cd.May88 on 'Fame')*
Apr 84. (7") **ASSASSING. / CINDERELLA SEARCH** [22] [-]
(12"+=)(12"pic-d+=) – ('A'&'B'extended).
Nov 84. (m-lp)(c)(cd) **REAL TO REEL (live)** [8] [ ]
– Assassing / Incubus / Cinderella search / Forgotten sons / Garden party / Market square heroes. *(c/cd+=)– Emerald lies. (re-iss.Nov85 on 'Fame', cd-re-iss.Oct87)*
May 85. (7")(7"pic-d) **KAYLEIGH. / LADY NINJA** [2] [-]
(12"+=)(12"pic-d+=) – ('A'&'B'extended).
Jun 85. (lp)(c)(cd)(pic-lp) **MISPLACED CHILDHOOD** [1] [47]
– The pseudo silk kimono / Kayleigh / Lavender / Bitter suite – Heart of Lothian / Waterhole (expresso bongo) / Lords of the backstage / Blind curve / Childhood's end? / White feather. *(re-iss.1991 on 'Fame')*
Jun 85. (7") **KAYLEIGH. / HEART OF LOTHIAN** [-] [74]
Aug 85. (7") **LAVENDER. / FREAKS** [5] [ ]
(12"+=)(12"pic-d+=) – ('A'version).
Nov 85. (7") **HEART OF LOTHIAN. / CHELSEA MONDAY (live)** [29] [-]
(12"+=)(12"pic-d+=) – ('A'version).

In early 1986, FISH teamed up with TONY BANKS (GENESIS) on a single.

Dec 85. (7") **HEART OF LOTHIAN. / LADY NINJA** [-] [ ]
May 87. (7") **INCOMMUNICADO. / GOING UNDER** [6] [ ]
(12"+=)(cd-s+=) – ('A'version).
Jun 87. (lp)(c)(cd)(pic-lp) **CLUTCHING AT STRAWS** [2] [ ]
– Hotel hobbies / Warm wet circles / That time of the night (the short straw) / Going under * / Just for the record / White Russian / Incommunicado / Torch song / Slainte Mhath / Sugar mice / The last straw. *(cd+= *) (re-iss.1989)*
Jul 87. (7")(7"pic-d) **SUGAR MICE. / TUX ON** [22] [ ]
(12"+=)(12"pic-d+=) – ('A'version).
Oct 87. (7") **WARM WET CIRCLES. / WHITE RUSSIAN (live)** [22] [ ]
(cd-s+=) – Incommunicado (live).
(12"++=)(12"pic-d++=) – Up On Top Of A Rainbow.
Nov 88. (d-lp)(c)(d-cd) **THE THIEVING MAGPIE (live)** [25] [ ]
– (intro) / La gazza ladra / Slainte mhath / He knows, you know / Chelsea Monday / Freaks / Jigsaw / Punch and Judy / Sugar mice / Fugazi / Script for a jester's tear / Incommunicado / White Russian / Misplaced childhood part 1:- Pseudo silk kimono – Kayleigh – Lavender – Bitter suite – Heart of Lothian. *(d-cd+=)–* Misplaced childhood part 2:- Waterhole (expresso bongo) – Lords of the backstage – Blind curve – Childhood's end? – White feather.
Nov 88. (7")(7"pic-d) **FREAKS (live). / KAYLEIGH (live)** [24] [ ]
(12"+=)(cd-s+=) – Childhood's end (live) / White feather (live).

—— **STEVE HOGARTH** – vocals (ex-HOW WE LIVE, ex-EUROPEANS, ex-LAST CALL) finally repl. FISH. (He left to go solo Sep'88).

Aug 89. (7") **HOOKS IN YOU. / AFTER ME** [30] [ ]
(12"+=)(c-s+=)(cd-s+=)(12"pic-d+=) – ('A'meaty mix).
Sep 89. (lp)(c)(cd) **SEASON'S END** [7] [ ]
– King of sunset town / Easter / The uninvited guest / Season's end / Holloway girl / Berlin / After me / Hooks in you / The space. (c+cd+=) – After me.
Nov 89. (7")(7"pic-d) **THE UNINVITED GUEST. / THE BELL IN THE SEA** [53] [ ]
(12"+=)(c-s+=)(cd-s+=) – ('A'version).
Mar 90. (7")(c-s)(7"pic-d) **EASTER. / THE RELEASE** [34] [ ]
(12"+=)(cd-s+=) – ('A'version) / The uninvited guest.
Jun 91. (7")(c-s) **COVER MY EYES (PAIN AND HEAVEN). / HOW CAN IT HURT** [34] [ ]
(12"+=)(cd-s+=) – The party.
Jul 91. (cd)(c)(lp) **HOLIDAYS IN EDEN** [7] [ ]
– Splintered heart / Cover my eyes (pain and Heaven) / The party / No one can / Holidays in Eden / Dry land / Waiting to happen / This town / The rakes progress / 100 nights.
Jul 91. (7")(c-s)(7"box) **NO ONE CAN. / A COLLECTION** [33] [ ]
(cd-s+=) – Splintered heart (live).
Sep 91. (7") **DRY LAND. / HOLLOWAY GIRL / AFTER ME** [34] [ ]
(12"+=) – Substitute.
(10"+=) – Waiting to happen.
(10"clear+=)(cd-s+=) – Easter / Sugar mice.
(12"pic-d+=) – King of Sunset town.
May 92. (7") **SYMPATHY. / KAYLEIGH (live)** [17] [ ]
(12"pic-d+=)(cd-s+=) – Dry land (live).
(cd-s+=) – Walk on water.
Jun 92. (cd)(c)(lp) **A SINGLES COLLECTION 1982-1992** (compilation) [27] [ ]
– Cover my eyes (pain & Heaven) / Kayleigh / Easter / Warm wet circles / Uninvited guest / Assassing / Hooks in you / Garden party / No one can / Incommunicado / Dry land / Lavender / I will walk on water / Sympathy.
Jul 92. (7")(c-s) **NO ONE CAN. / A COLLECTION** [26] [ ]
(cd-s+=) – Splintered heart.
Feb 94. (cd)(c)(lp) **BRAVE** [10] [ ]
– Bridge / Living with the big lie / Runaway / Goodbye to all that (i) Wave (ii) Mad (iii) The opium den (iv) The slide (v) Standing in the swing / Hard as love / The hollow man / Alone again in the lap of luxury (i) Now wash your hands / Paper lies / Brave / The great escape (i) The last of you (ii) Fallin' from the Moon / Made again.
Mar 94. (7")(c-s) **THE HOLLOW MAN. / BRAVE** [30] [ ]
(cd-s+=) – Marouatte jam.
(cd-s) – ('A'side) / The last of you – Falling from the Moon (the great escape) / Winter trees.
Apr 94. (c-s) **ALONE AGAIN IN THE LAP OF LUXURY. / LIVING WITH THE BIG LIE (live)** [53] [ ]
(12"+=) – The space (live).
(cd-s+=) – River (live) / Bridge (live).
(cd-s) – ('A'side) / Cover my eyes / Slainte Mhath / Uninvited guest (all live).
Jun 95. (c-s)(cd-s) **BEAUTIFUL / AFRAID OF SUNRISE / ICON** [29] [ ]
(cd-s) – ('A'side) / Live forever / Great escape (demo) / Hard as love (demo).
Jun 95. (cd)(c)(lp) **AFRAID OF SUNLIGHT** [16] [ ]
– Gazpacho / Cannibal surf babe / Beautiful / Afraid of sunrise / Out of this world / Afraid of sunlight / Beyond you / King.

– other compilations etc. –

Jan 88. EMI; (cd)(lp) **B SIDES THEMSELVES (rare flips)** [64] [ ]
Dec 85. Capitol; (m-lp) **BRIEF ENCOUNTER (live & 'B'sides)** [-] [ ]
Nov 95. EMI; (3xcd-box) **SCRIFT FOR A JESTER'S TEAR / FUGAZI / MISPLACED CHILDHOOD** [ ] [-]

Frank MARINO (see under ⇒ MAHOGANY RUSH)

MARK FOUR (see under ⇒ CREATION)

Bob MARLEY

Born: ROBERT NESTA MARLEY, 2 Feb'45, Rhoden Hall, St.Ann's, Jamaica, the son of an English sailor/captain and a Jamaican woman. In the early 60's, like most other Jamaicans (except older calypso fans), he became influenced by ska, and went to Leslie Kong's studio to record 'JUDGE NOT'. In 1964, after another solo 45, he formed The WAILIN' WAILERS, alongside PETER TOSH, BUNNY WAILER LIVINGSTONE, JUNIOR BRAITHWAITE and BEVERLEY KELSO. Their first 45 'SIMMER DOWN', sold well in homeland, promting Chris Blackwell to take note. On 10 Feb'66, he married RITA, and left for America to visit his mother. The following year, he was back in Jamaica to set up own 'Wailin' Soul' label with JOHNNY NASH. BOB re-united with The WAILERS again, and they issued numerous 45's during this period, which gained export to Britain. They became Rastafarians in 1969, and teamed up with 'Tuff Gong' producer LEE 'Scratch' PERRY, who issued WAILERS debut lp 'SOUL REBEL' in 1970. In 1972, after JOHNNY NASH had taken 'STIR IT UP' into UK Top 20, The WAILERS signed to Blackwell's 'Island' label. Two lp's were issued in '73 'CATCH A FIRE' & 'BURNIN'', before TOSH and BUNNY WAILER decided on own solo careers. In 1975, BOB MARLEY & THE (new) WAILERS released exceptional 'NATTY DREAD', which contained studio version of live smash hit 'NO WOMAN NO CRY'. MARLEY then enjoyed commercial worldwide superstar status for the next 5 years until his untimely death from lung cancer and brain tumor on 11 May'81. He had survived an attempt on his life on 6 Dec'76, when gunmen broke into his Kingston home, shooting and injuring him, his wife and manager Don Taylor. • **Style:** Rastafarian reggae giant, who drifted through ska and soul in the 60's, before finding and helping pioneer accessible roots reggae in the 70's. • **Songwriters:** Self-penned with other WAILERS until their departure in '74. • **Trivia:** On 6 Aug'81, a Sunsplash Reggae Festival was dedicated to BOB and was attended by over 20,000 fans, as well as his children The MELODY MAKERS. • **Miscellaneous:** On 17 Apr'87, ex-WAILER; CARLTON BARRETT is shot dead outside his Kingston home. The following month, the remaining WAILERS oust RITA as executor of MARLEY's will, calling for an investigation to his estate. On 11 Sep'87, PETER TOSH was murdered by burglers to his home.

Recommended: CATCH A FIRE (*9) / BURNIN' (*9) / NATTY DREAD (*8) / RASTAMAN VIBRATIONS (*7) / EXODUS (*9) / KAYA (*7) / UPRISING (*7) / LEGEND (*10)

ROBERT MARLEY

Island / not issued

Dec 62. (7") **JUDGE NOT (UNLESS YOU JUDGE YOURSELF). / DO YOU STILL LOVE ME?**
1963. (7") **ONE CUP OF COFFEE. /('B'by "Ernest Ranglin")**

The WAILERS

were formed by **MARLEY** (-vocals, +later guitar) plus **PETER TOSH** (b.WINSTON HUBERT McINTOSH, 19 Oct'44) – vocals, +later guitar / **BUNNY LIVINGSTONE** (b.NEVILLE O'RILEY, 10 Apr'47) – vocals, percussion / **JUNIOR BRAITHWAITE** – vocals / **BEVERLEY KELSO** – vocals / plus occasionally **RITA MARLEY** (b.ALPHARITA CONSTANTIA ANDERSON) – backing vocals / Instruments by SOUL BROTHERS then SKATELITES

Ska Beat / not issued

Jan 65. (7") **SIMMER DOWN. ("WAILIN' WAILERS") / I DON'T NEED YOUR LOVE**

— Released in Jamaica earlier, UK in batches?

Island / not issued

Mar 65. (7") **IT HURTS TO BE ALONE. / MR.TALKATIVE**
Apr 65. (7") **PLAYBOY. / YOUR LOVE**

— added **CHERRY SMITH** – backing vocals

May 65. (7") **HOOT NANNY ROLL.(by "Peter Tosh") / DO YOU REMEMBER (by "BOB MARLEY")**
May 65. (7") **HOOLIGAN. / MAGA DOG**
Jun 65. (7") **SHAME AND SCANDAL. (by "PETER TOSH & THE WAILERS") / THE JERK**
Jun 65. (7") **DON'T EVER LEAVE ME. / DONNA**
Dec 65. (7") **WHAT'S NEW PUSSYCAT. / WHERE WILL I FIND**
Mar 66. (7") **JUMBIE JAMBOUREE. /('B'by "Skatelites")**
Apr 66. (7") **PUT IT ON (FEEL THE SPIRIT). / LOVE WON'T BE MINE**
Aug 65. (7") **LONESOME FEELINGS. / THERE SHE GOES**
1965. (7") **I MADE A MISTAKE. /('B'by "SOUL BROTHERS")**

— (above 'A'side probaby by The "WAILIN' RUDEBOYS")

1966. (7") **LOVE AND AFFECTION. / TEENAGER IN LOVE**
1966. (7") **AND I LOVE HER. / DO IT RIGHT**
1966. (7") **LONESOME TRACK. / SINNER MAN**

— (below might be without MARLEY)

Rio / not issued

1966. (7") **DANCING SHOES. / DON'T LOOK BACK**

— MARLEY left Feb'66, to marry RITA but soon returned. CHERRY also left. LIVINGSTONE was imprisoned in 1966.

Doctor Bird / not issued

1966. (7") **RUDE BOY. /('B' by "Roland Al & The Soul Brothers")**
1966. (7") **GOOD GOOD RUDIE. /('B' by "City Slickers")**
Nov 66. (7") **RASTA PUT IT ON. /('B' by "Roland Al & The Soul Brothers")**
(re-iss.Apr67 on 'Island')

— (below iss.JAMAICA on 'Rocksteady')

1967. (7") **NICE TIME. / HYPOCRITE**

— (below 2 without MARLEY)

Island / not issued

Nov 66. (7") **HE WHO FEELS IT KNOWS IT. / SUNDAY MORNING**
Dec 66. (7") **LET HIM GO (RUDE BOY GOT BAIL). / SINNER MAN**
Apr 67. (7") **I NEED YOU. /('B' by "Ken Boothe")**

— Now a trio of **MARLEY, TOSH & BUNNY.** (KELSO and BRAITHWAITE departed)

Apr 67. (7") **BEND DOWN LOW. / FREEDOM TOWN**
Apr 67. (7") **I AM THE TOUGHEST. ("Peter Tosh & The Wailers") /('B' by "Marcia Griffiths")**

Studio One / not issued

1967. (7") **I STAND PREDOMINANT. / ('B' by 'Norma Fraser')**

Trojan / not issued

Oct 68. (7") **STIR IT UP. / THIS TRAIN**

Bamboo / not issued

1970. (7") **JAILHOUSE. /('B' by "JOHN HOLT")**

Escort / not issued

1970. (7") **RUN FOR COVER. / TO THE RESCUE**

BOB MARLEY & THE WAILERS

added **ASTON BARRETT** (b.22 Nov'46, KIngston, Jamaica) – bass / **CARLTON BARRETT** (b.17 Dec'50, Kingston) – drums

Upsetter / Shelter

1970. (7") **MY CUP. / SON OF THUNDER (by "LEE PERRY & THE WAILERS")**
1970. (7") **VERSION OF CUP.(by "WAILERS") /('B' by "Upsetters")**
Dec 70. (7") **DUPPY CONQUEROR. /('B'by "UPSETTERS")**
Jan 71. (7") **MR.BROWN. /('B'by "Upsetters")**
Feb 71. (7") **KAYA. / ('A'version by "Upsetters")**
Feb 71. (7") **SMALL AXE. / ALL IN ONE**
1971. (7") **DREAMLAND ("WAILERS"). /('B'by "Upsetters")**
1971. (7") **MORE AXE. /('B'by "Upsetters")**
1971. (7") **PICTURE ON THE WALL.(by "Ras Dawkins & The Wailers") /('B'by "Upsetters")**

Trojan / not issued

Sep 70. (7") **SOUL SHAKEDOWN PARTY. /('B'by "Beverley All-Stars")**
Dec 70. (lp) **SOUL REBEL**
– There she goes / Put it on / How many times / Mellow mood / Changes are / Hammer / Tell me / Touch me / Treat you right / Soul rebel. *(re-iss.+c.Sep81 on 'New Cross') (re-iss.Jun84 on 'Blue Moon') (re-iss.Apr90 on 'Action Replay') (cd-iss.Jan90 on 'Receiver')*

Jackpot / not issued

1971. (7") **MR.CHATTERBOX. / WALK THROUGH THE WORLD**

Punch / not issued

1971. (7") **MORE AXE. /('B'by "Dave Berber")**
1971. (7") **DOWN DRESSER ("WAILERS"). /('B'by "Junior Byles")**
1972. (7") **SCREW FACE. / FACE MAN**

Bullet / not issued

1971. (7") **SOULTOWN. / LET THE SUN SHINE ON ME**
1971. (7") **LICK SAMBA. / SAMBA**

Summit / not issued

1971. (7") **STOP THE TRAIN. / CAUTION**
1971. (7") **FREEDOM TRAIN. / ?**

Green Door / Tuff Gong

1971. (7") **LIVELY UP YOURSELF. /('B'by "Tommy McCook")** JAMAI
Nov 71. (7") **TRENCHTOWN ROCK. / GROOVING KINGDOM**
1972. (7") **GUAVA JELLY. / REDDER THAN RED**

— (below was 1968 demo)

C.B.S. / not issued

May 72. (7") **REGGAE ON BROADWAY. / OH LORD I GOT TO GET THERE**

Trojan / not issued

Sep 72. (7") **KEEP ON MOVING. / AFRICAN HERBSMAN**
1972. (lp) **AFRICAN HERBSMAN**
– Lively up yourself / Small axe / Duppy conqueror / African herbsman / Trenchtown rock / Keep on moving / Fussing and fighting / Stand alone / All in one / Don't rock the boat / Put it on / Sun is shining / Kaya / Riding high / 400 years / Brain washing. *(re-iss.+c.1981 & Jul84) (re-iss.Nov83 on 'Fame') (cd-iss. Jun88) (cd-iss.Mar94 on 'Trojan')*

The WAILERS

Blue Mountain / Island

Jan 73. (7") **BABY WE'VE GOT A DATE (ROCK IT BABY). / STOP THAT TRAIN**

Island / Island

Apr 73. (lp)(c) **CATCH A FIRE**
– Concrete jungle / Slave driver / 400 years / Stop that train / Baby we've got a date (rock it baby) / Stir it up / Kinky reggae / No more trouble / Midnight ravers. *(re-iss.Oct86) (re-iss.+cd.Jun90 on 'Tuff Gong')*
Jun 73. (7") **CONCRETE JUNGLE. / REINCARNATION SOUL**
Jul 73. (7") **CONCRETE JUNGLE. / NO MORE TROUBLE**

Sep 73. (7") **GET UP, STAND UP. / SLAVE DRIVER** □ □
Nov 73. (lp)(c) **BURNIN'** □ □
– Get up, stand up / Hallelujah time / I shot the sheriff / Burnin' and lootin' / Put it on / Small axe / Pass it on / Duppy conqueror / One foundation / Rastaman chant. *(re-iss.Mar87) (re-iss.+cd.Jun90 on 'Tuff Gong')*
Feb 74. (7") **I SHOT THE SHERIFF. / PUT IT ON** - □

— added **The I-THREES** (female backers **JUDY MOWAT, MARCIA GRIFFITHS**, and **RITA**). They replaced PETER TOSH and BUNNY WAILER who both went solo.

BOB MARLEY & THE WAILERS

MARLEY, ASTON and **BARRETT** added **EARL LINDO** – keyboards / **BERNARD HARVEY** – keyboards / **AL ANDERSON** – guitar.
May 75. (lp)(c) **NATTY DREAD** (in Oct75 hit) 43 92
– Lively up yourself / No woman no cry / Them belly full (but we hungry) / Rebel music (3 o'clock road block) / So jah seh / Natty dread / Bend down low / Talkin' blues / Revolution. *(re-iss.May87) (re-iss.+cd.Jun90 on 'Tuff Gong')*
Jun 75. (7") **NATTY DREAD. / SO JAH SEH** □ -
Jun 75. (7") **LIVELY UP YOURSELF. / SO JAH SEH** - □

— **TYRONE DOWNIE** – keyboards repl. HARVEY / **ALVIN 'SHECO' PATTERSON** – percussion repl. LINDO / added **JULIAN 'JUNIOR' MURVIN** – guitar

Aug 75. (7") **NO WOMAN NO CRY (live). / KINKY REGGAE** 22 □
Dec 75. (lp)(c) **LIVE! (live)** 38 90
– Trenchtown rock / Burnin' and lootin' / Them belly full (but we hungry) / Lively up yourself / No woman no cry / I shot the sheriff / Get up, stand up. *(re-iss.Jul81 + Sep86.as 'LIVE AT THE LYCEUM', cd-iss.Jan87) (re-iss.cd+c.Nov90 on 'Tuff Gong')*
Jan 76. (7") **JAH LIVE. / CONCRETE JUNGLE (live)** □ □
Apr 76. (7") **JOHNNY WAS (WOMAN HANG HER HEAD AND CRY). / CRY TO ME** □ □
Apr 76. (lp)(c) **RASTAMAN VIBRATION** 15 8
– Positive vibration / Roots, rock, reggae / Johnny was / Cry to me / Want more / Crazy baldhead / Who the cap fit / Night shift / War / Rat race. *(re-iss.+cd.Apr87) (re-iss.cd+c.Nov90 on 'Tuff Gong')*
Jun 76. (7") **ROOTS ROCK REGGAE. / STIR IT UP** □ -
Jun 76. (7") **ROOTS ROCK REGGAE. / CRY TO ME** - 51
Nov 76. (7") **WHO THE CAP FITS** - □
May 77. (lp)(c) **EXODUS** 8 20 Jun 77
– Natural mystic / So much things to say / Guiltiness / The heathen / Exodus / Jamming / Waiting in vain / Turn your lights down low / Three little birds / One love – People get ready. *(re-iss.+cd.Mar87) (re-iss.cd+c.Nov90 on 'Tuff Gong')*
Jun 77. (7") **EXODUS. / EXODUS (dub)** 14 □
Aug 77. (7") **WAITING IN VAIN. / ROOTS** 27 □
Dec 77. (7") **JAMMING. / PUNKY REGGAE PARTY** 9 □

— added the returning **EARL 'WIRE' LINDO** – keyboards

Feb 78. (7") **IS THIS LOVE. / CRISIS (version)** 9 □
(re-iss.as 12"-Jun81)
Mar 78. (lp)(c) **KAYA** 4 50
– Easy shanking / Kaya / The sun is shining / Is this love / Satisfy my soul / She's gone / Misty morning / Crisis / Running away / Time will tell. *(re-iss.+cd.Feb87) (re-iss.cd+c.Nov90 on 'Tuff Gong')*
May 78. (7") **SATISFY MY SOUL. / SMILE JAMAICA** 21 □
Dec 78. (d-lp)(c) **BABYLON BY BUS (live)** 40 □
– Positive vibration / Punky reggae party / Exodus / Stir it up / Rat race / Concrete jungle / Kinky reggae / Lively up yourself / Rebel music (3 o'clock road block) / War / No more trouble / Is this love / The heathen / Jamming. *(re-iss.+cd.Feb87) (re-iss.cd+c.Nov90 on 'Tuff Gong')*
Jan 79. (7") **STIR IT UP (live). / RAT RACE (live)** □ -
(12") – ('A'side) / War (live) / No more trouble (live).
Jul 79. (7") **WAKE UP AND LIVE. / (part 2)** - □
Sep 79. (7") **SO MUCH TROUBLE IN THE WORLD. / ('A'instrumental)** 56 □
Oct 79. (lp)(c) **SURVIVAL** 20 70
– Wake up and live / Top rankin' / Ambush in the night / Babylon system / Survival / Ride Natty ride / One drop / So much trouble in the world / Zimbabwe / Africa unite. *(re-iss.+cd.Mar87) (re-iss.cd+c.Nov90 on 'Tuff Gong')*
Nov 79. (7") **ONE DROP. / KAYA** - □
Nov 79. (7") **SURVIVAL. / WAKE UP AND LIVE** □ -
Mar 80. (7") **ZIMBABWE. / SURVIVAL** □ -
(12") – ('A'side) / Africa unite / Wake up and live.
May 80. (7") **COULD YOU BE LOVED. / ONE DROP** 5 □
(12"+=) – Ride natty ride. *(US; b-side)*
Jun 80. (lp)(c) **UPRISING** 6 45
– Coming in from the cold / Real situation / Bad card / We and them / Work / Zion train / Pimper's paradise / Could you be loved / Forever loving Jah / Redemption song. *(cd-iss.Feb87) (re-iss.cd+c.Nov90 on 'Tuff Gong')*
Aug 80. (7") **THREE LITTLE BIRDS. / EVERY NEED GOT AN EGO FEED** 17 □
Oct 80. (7")(12") **REDEMPTION SONG. / ('A'band version)** □ □

— In Oct'80, BOB MARLEY was diagnosed with lung cancer. He died on 11 May'81.

– compilations, others, etc. –

1974. Trojan; (7") **SOUL SHAKEDOWN PARTY. / CAUTION** □ -
Jul 74. Trojan; (lp)(c) **RASTA REVOLUTION** □ -
(re-iss.1981 + Jul84) (cd-iss.Jun88) (re-iss.Jul85 on 'Fame') (cd-iss.Mar94)
Aug 74. Trojan; (7") **MR.BROWN. / ('A'version)** □ -
1976. Trojan; (7") **MR.BROWN. / TRENCHTOWN ROCK** □ -
Jun 81. Trojan; (7") **THANK YOU LORD. / WISDOM** □ -
Oct 83. Trojan; (7") **SOUL SHAKEDOWN PARTY. / CAUTION** □ -
('A'-disco 12") – Keep on skanking.
Jan 84. Trojan; (lp)(c) **IN THE BEGINNING** □ -
(cd-iss.Jun88) (cd-iss.Mar94 on 'Trojan')
Jun 88. Trojan; (d-lp)(d-c)(d-cd) **SOUL REVOLUTION 1 & 2** □ -
(d-cd+d-c Mar94 on 'Trojan')
Jun 89. Trojan; (cd) **SOUL REVOLUTION / RHYTHM ALBUM** □ -
May 91. Trojan; (cd-box)(lp-box) **IN MEMORIAM** □ -
Jul 77. Epic; (lp)(c) **BIRTH OF A LEGEND VOL.1 (featuring PETER TOSH)** □ -
(re-iss.Jun80 + Nov81) (cd-iss.Jun91 on 'Pickwick')
Sep 77. Embassy; (lp)(c) **EARLY MUSIC** □ -
(re-iss.Nov81 on 'C.B.S.')
Oct 79. Hammer; (lp)(c) **BOB MARLEY & THE WAILERS** □ -
Oct 79. Psycho; (lp)(c) **IN THE BEGINNING** □ -
(re-iss.Jul84, cd-iss.Jun88 on 'Trojan')
Mar 81. Hallmark; (lp)(c) **BOB MARLEY & THE WAILERS WITH PETER TOSH** □ -
(re-iss.1981 on 'SS International')
1981. Accord; (lp) **JAMAICAN STORM** □ -
Sep 81. Warners/ US= Cotillion; (lp)(c) **CHANCES ARE** □ □
Sep 81. Warners/ US= Cotillion; (7")(12") **REGGAE ON BROADWAY. / GONNA GET YOU** □ □
Nov 81. Warners/ US= Cotillion; (7") **CHANCES ARE. /** - □
Jun 81. Island; (12") **NO WOMAN NO CRY (live). / JAMMING** 8 □
Mar 82. Island; (7") **NATURAL MYSTIC. / CARRY ON BEYOND** □ -
1982. Island; (9xlp-box) **BOB MARLEY - THE BOXED SET** □ -
1982. Island; (lp)(c) **COUNTRYMAN (Soundtrack,** w/8 MARLEY songs**)** □ -
Apr 83. Island; (7")(12") **BUFFALO SOLDIER. / BUFFALO (dub)** 4 □
May 83. Island; (lp)(c) **CONFRONTATION** 5 55
– Chant down Babylon / Buffalo soldier / Jump Nyabinghi / Mix up, mix up / Give thanks and praises / Blackman redemption / Trenchtown / Stiff neked fools / I know / Rastaman live up!. *(re-iss.Mar87) (cd-iss.1988 on 'Mango') (re-iss.cd+c Jun90 on 'Tuff Gong')*
Apr 84. Island; (7") **ONE LOVE. / PEOPLE GET READY** 5 □
(12"+=)(12"pic-d+=) – Keep on moving / So much trouble.
May 84. Island; (lp)(c) **LEGEND** 1 54
– Is this love / Jamming / No woman no cry / Stir it up / Get up, stand up / Satisfy my soul / I shot the sheriff / One love / People get ready / Buffalo soldier / Exodus / Redemption song / Could you be loved / Want more. *(cd-iss.Aug85) (cd re-iss.May91 on 'Tuff Gong' hit UK No.11, Mar92 No.18 / Jul92 No.25)*
Jun 84. Island; (7") **WAITING IN VAIN. / BLACK MAN REDEMPTION** 31 □
(12"+=) – Marley mix-up.
Aug 84. Island; (7") **IS THIS LOVE. / BLACK MAN REDEPTION** - □
Nov 84. Island; (7")(7"pic-d) **COULD YOU BE LOVED. / NO WOMAN NO CRY** 71 □
(12"+=) – Jamming / Coming in from the cold.
Apr 85. Island; (lp)(c) **REGGAE GREATS** □ -
Jun 85. Island; (7")(12")(c-s) **THREE LITTLE BIRDS. / ('A'dub version)** □ -
Jun 86. Island; (lp)(c)(cd) **REBEL MUSIC** 54 □
(re-iss.cd+c.Jun90 on 'Tuff Gong')
Oct 83. C.B.S.; (d-c) **BIRTH OF A LEGEND / EARLY MUSIC** □ -
May 84. Breakaway; (lp)(c)(pic-lp) **THE ESSENTIAL** □ -
Jun 84. Happy Bird; (d-lp)(c) **25 GREATEST HITS** □ -
Nov 84. Topline; (lp)(c) **MELLOW MOOD** □ -
(cd-iss.Apr87)
Dec 84. Premier; (lp) **ONE LOVE** □ -
(cd-iss.1987, c-iss.1988, lp re-iss.Feb90 on 'Pickwick')
Feb 87. Premier; (lp)(c) **LIVELY UP YOURSELF** □ -
(cd-iss.Jun93 on 'Prestige')
Feb 85. Sierra; (lp)(c) **REPLAY ON BOB MARLEY** □ -
Feb 85. Cambra; (d-lp)(d-c) **ETERNAL** □ -
Aug 85. Daddy Kool; (12") **RAINBOW COUNTRY. /('B'by "PABLO & THE UPSETTERS")** □ -
Jan 86. Daddy Kool; (12") **NATURAL MYSTIC. / ('A'version)** □ -
Apr 86. Showcase; (lp)(c) **PUT IT ON** □ -
Apr 86. Castle; (d-lp)(c) **THE COLLECTION** □ -
(cd-iss.1988)
Nov 86. Blue Moon; (lp)(c) **ROOTS** *(cd-iss.1988)* □ -
Dec 88. Blue Moon; (cd) **ROOTS VOL.2** □ -
Jan 89. Blue Moon; (lp)(cd) **ONE LOVE / ROOTS VOL.2** □ -
Feb 87. Konnexion; (lp) **THE LEE PERRY SESSIONS** □ -
May 88. Streetlife; (lp)(c)(cd) **GREATEST HITS** □ -
Sep 88. Pickwick; (cd-ep) **REACTION / I GOTTA KEEP ON MOVING / PUT IT ON** □ -
Feb 87. Arena; (lp)(c) **THE CLASSIC YEARS** □ -
Nov 88. Arena; (cd-ep) **CLASSIC (w / TOOTS)** □ -
Jul 87. Intertape; (cd) **BOB MARLEY** □ -
May 88. Black Tulip; (lp)(c) **20 GREATEST HITS** □ -
1990. Connoisseur; (lp)(c)(cd) **THE BEST OF BOB MARLEY (1968-72)** □ -
Mar 91. Tuff Gong; (cd)(c)(lp) **TALKIN' BLUES** □ -
– (radio sessions 1973 + interviews 1975)
May 91. Tuff Gong; (7")(c-s) **ONE LOVE - PEOPLE GET READY. / SO MUCH TROUBLE IN THE WORLD** 42 -
(12"+=)(cd-s+=) **('A'extended) / Keep on moving.**
Sep 92. Tuff Gong; (7")(c-s) **IRON ZION LION ('74 track). / COULD YOU BE LOVED** 5 □
(12")(cd-s) – ('A'side) / Smile Jamaica / Three little birds.
Sep 92. Tuff Gong; (4xcd-box)(4xc-box) **SONGS OF FREEDOM** 10 86
– (discovered demos, by wife Rita)
(re-iss.May93 as 8-lp box)
Nov 92. Tuff Gong; (7")(c-s) **WHY SHOULD I (Bone Remix Edit). / (Kindread Spirit Edit)** 42 □
(cd-s+=) – Exodus (rebel the remix)

Apr 91. Rohit; (cd)(c)(lp) **ALL THE HITS** [ ] [-]
Aug 91. Entity; (cd)(c) **SAGA** [ ] [-]
Sep 91. Music Coll..; (cd)(c) **THE VERY BEST OF THE EARLY YEARS 1968-74** [ ] [-]
Feb 93. Charly; (cd) **TREAT HER RIGHT** [ ] [-]
Nov 93. Charly; (cd) **THE LEE PERRY SESSIONS** [ ] [-]
Nov 93. Charly; (cd) **RIDING HIGH** [ ] [-]
Mar 94. Charly; (cd) **RAINBOW COUNTRY** [ ] [-]
Sep 93. Trojan; (4xlp-box) **THE EARLY YEARS 1969-1973** [ ] [-]
Mar 94. Trojan; (cd)(c) **IN MEMORIAM** [ ] [-]
Sep 93. Laserlight; (d-cd) **BOB MARLEY** [ ] [-]
Feb 94. Studio One; (lp) **THE WAILING WAILERS ("WAILERS")** [ ] [-]
Jun 94. Sony; (cd) **THE BIRTH OF A LEGEND (with PETER TOSH)** [ ] [-]
Jul 94. Success; (cd)(c) **KEEP ON MOVING** [ ] [-]
Jul 94. Success; (cd)(c) **SOUL REBEL** [ ] [-]
Jul 94. Success; (cd)(c) **DON'T ROCK MY BOAT** [ ] [-]
Jul 94. Success; (cd)(c) **SOUL SHAKEDOWN PARTY** [ ] [-]
Jan 95. Reggae Best; (cd) **SOUL CAPTIVE** [ ] [-]
Feb 95. More Music; (cd) **POWER** [ ] [-]
Feb 95. B.A.M.; (cd) **PEARLS OF THE PAST** [ ] [-]
Feb 95. B.A.M.; (cd) **PEARLS OF THE PAST VOLUME 2** [ ] [-]
May 95. Tuff Gong; (c-s) **KEEP ON MOVING. / PIMPER'S PARADISE** [17] [ ]
(12+=)(cd-s+=) – ('A'mixes).
May 95. Tuff Gong; (cd)(c)(lp) **NATURAL MYSTIC** [5] [67]
May 95. Heartbeat; (cd)(c) **SIMMER DOWN AT STUDIO ONE** [ ] [-]
May 95. Heartbeat; (cd)(c) **THE WAILING WAILERS AT STUDIO ONE** [ ] [-]
Jul 95. A&A; (cd) **LEGEND IN SAX** [ ] [-]
Aug 95. Sony Europe; (cd) **GOLD COLLECTION** [ ] [-]
Dec 95. Columbia; (cd)(c) **EARLY COLLECTION** [ ] [-]

— His son ZIGGY MARLEY (real name DAVID) & The MELODY MAKERS (other sons & daughters; STEPHEN, CEDELLA and SHARON) signed to EMI USA in 1986 and released album 'KEY WORLD'. In 1988, with producers TOM TOM CLUB (TINA WEXMOUTH and CHRIS FRANTZ of TALKING HEADS), they signed to 'Virgin' and had US No.23 hit album 'CONSCIOUS PARTY'. A single from it 'TOMORROW PEOPLE' made no.39 there mid-'88. A year later, the album 'ONE BRIGHT DAY' gave them last US chart appearance, hitting No.26.

Steve MARRIOTT (see under ⇒ HUMBLE PIE)

Gerry MARSDEN (see under ⇒ GERRY & THE PACEMAKERS)

MARSHALL TUCKER BAND

Formed: South Carolina, USA ... 1971 by DOUG GRAY and the CALDWELL brothers. The previous two years, they had emerged out of The TOY FACTORY, with TOY also from The RANTS, before he enlisted in the US Marines. In 1973, after support slot to The ALLMANS, they signed to their 'Capricorn' label, hitting US Top 30 with eponymous debut. They enjoyed many successes, until the untimely death of joint-leader TOMMY CALDWELL in Apr'80. • **Style:** Southern country rock boogie outfit, in the mould of The ALLMANS, LYNYRD SKYNYRD or WET WILLIE. • **Songwriters:** TOY contributed most, with a few covers. • **Trivia:** In 1976, WAYLON JENNINGS had country hit with their 'CAN'T YOU SEE'. In 1977, they played at the White House for newly elected president Jimmy Carter.

Recommended: THE BEST OF THE MARSHALL TUCKER BAND (*5).

DOUG GRAY – vocals, percussion (ex-TOY FACTORY) / **TOY CALDWELL** (b.1948) – lead guitar, steel guitar, vocals (ex-TOY FACTORY) / **TOMMY CALDWELL** (b.1950, Spartenburg, S.Carolina) – bass, vocals / **GEORGE McCORKLE** – rhythm guitar (ex-RANTS) / **PAUL RIDDLE** – drums / **JERRY EUBANKS** – saxophone, flute, etc. (ex-TOY FACTORY)

Capricorn Capricorn

Aug 73. (7") **CAN'T YOU SEE. / SEE YOU LATER, I'M GONE** [-] [ ]
Nov 73. (lp)(c) **THE MARSHALL TUCKER BAND** [ ] [29] Jul 73
– Take the highway / Can't you see / Losing you / Hillbilly band / See you later, I'm gone / Ramblin' / My Jesus told me so / Ab's song. *(cd-iss.Oct93 on 'Repertoire')*
Nov 73. (7") **TAKE THE HIGHWAY. / MY JESUS TOLD ME SO** [-] [ ]
Apr 74. (7") **BLUE RIDGE MOUNTAIN SKY. / ANOTHER CRUEL LOVE** [-] [ ]
Nov 74. (lp)(c) **A NEW LIFE** [ ] [37] Mar 74
– A new life / Southern woman / Blue ridge mountain sky / Too stubborn / Another cruel love / You ain't foolin' me / 24 hours at a time / Fly eagle fly.
Apr 75. (d-lp)(c) **WHERE WE ALL BELONG (pt.live)** [ ] [ ] Dec 74
– This ol' cowboy / Low down ways / In my own way / How can I slow down / Where a country boy belongs / Now she's gone / Try one more time / Ramblin' / 24 hours at a time / Everyday (I have the blues) / Take the highway.
Apr 75. (7") **THIS OL' COWBOY. / TRY ONE MORE TIME** [-] [78]
Nov 75. (lp)(c) **SEARCHIN' FOR A RAINBOW** [ ] [15] Sep 75
– Fire on the mountain / Searchin' for a rainbow / Walkin' and talkin' / Virginia / Bob away my blues / Keeps me from all wrong / Bound and determined / Can't you see. *(cd-iss.Nov93 on 'Repertoire')*
Nov 75. (7") **FIRE ON THE MOUNTAIN. / BOB AWAY MY BLUES** [-] [38] Oct 75
Jan 76. (7") **SEARCHIN' FOR A RAINBOW. / WALKIN' AND TALKIN'** [-] [ ]
Jul 76. (7") **LONG HARD RIDE. / WINDY CITY BLUES** [-] [ ]
Aug 76. (lp)(c) **LONG HARD RIDE** [ ] [32] Jun 76
– Long hard ride / Property line / Am I the kind of man / Walkin' the streets alone / Windy city blues / Holding on to you / You say you love me / You don't live forever. *(cd-iss.Mar94 on 'Repertoire')*
Nov 76. (7") **YOU SAY YOU LOVE ME. / WALKIN' THE STREETS ALONE** [ ] [ ]
Jan 77. (7") **LONG HARD RIDE. / AM I THE KIND OF MAN** [ ] [ ]
Apr 77. (7") **HEARD IT IN A LOVE SONG. / LIFE IN A SONG** [ ] [14] Mar 77
Apr 77. (lp)(c) **CAROLINA DREAMS** [ ] [23] Feb 77
– Fly like an eagle / Heard it in a love song / I should have never started lovin' you / Life in a song / Desert skies / Never trust a stranger / Tell it to the Devil.
Jun 77. (7") **CAN'T YOU SEE. / FLY LIKE AN EAGLE** [-] [ ]
Jun 78. (7") **DREAM LOVER. / CHANGE IS GONNA COME** [-] [ ]
Jul 78. (lp)(c) **TOGETHER FOREVER** [ ] [22] May 78
– I'll be loving you / Love is a mystery / Singing rhymes / Dream lover / Everybody needs somebody / Change is gonna come / Asking too much of you.
Sep 78. (7") **I'LL BE LOVING YOU. / EVERYBODY NEEDS SOMEBODY** [-] [ ]

Warners Warners

Jun 79. (lp)(c) **RUNNING LIKE THE WIND** [ ] [30] May 79
– Running like the wind / Last of the singing cowboys / Answer to love / Unto these hills / Melody Ann / My best friend / Pass it on.
Jun 79. (7") **LAST OF THE SINGING COWBOYS. / PASS IT ON** [-] [42]
Nov 79. (7") **RUNNING LIKE THE WIND. /** [-] [ ]
Mar 80. (lp)(c) **TENTH** [ ] [32]
– It takes time / Without you / See you one more time / Disillusioned / Cattle drive / Gospel singin' man / Save my soul / Sing my blues / Jimi / Foolish dreaming.
Apr 80. (7") **IT TAKES TIME. / JIMI** [-] [ ]
Aug 80. (7") **WITHOUT YOU. / DISILLUSIONED** [-] [ ]

— **FRANKLIN WILKIE** – bass repl. TOMMY who died 28 Apr'80 in a car crash.

Mar 81. (7") **THIS TIME I BELIEVE. / TELL THE BLUES TO TAKE OFF THE NIGHT** [-] [ ]
Mar 81. (lp)(c) **DEDICATED** [-] [ ]
– Rumors are raging / Tonight's the night / Love some / Silverado / Something's missing in my life / This time I believe / Tell the blues to take off the night / Special someone / The time has come / Ride in peace.
Jul 81. (7") **THE TIME HAS COME. / LOVE SOME** [-] [ ]
Jun 82. (7") **MR. PRESIDENT. / SEA, DREAMS AND FAIRY TALES** [-] [ ]
Jun 82. (lp)(c) **TUCKERIZED** [-] [ ]
– Reachin' for a little bit more / If you think you're hurtin' me / Even a fool would let go / Sea, dreams & fairy tales / Anyway the wind blows rider / Mr.President / Heartbroke / Unforgiven / Sweet Elaine / Ace high love.
Sep 82, (7") **REACHIN' FOR A LITLE BIT MORE. / SWEET ELAINE** [-] [ ]

— **RONNIE GODFREY** – piano, vocals repl. GEORGE

1983. (7") **8:05. / A PLACE I'VE NEVER BEEN** [-] [ ]
1983. (lp)(c) **JUST US** [-] [ ]
– 8:05 / Stay a step behind / Time don't pass by here / Testify / Long Island lady / A place I've never been / Wait for you / When love begins to fade / Paradise.

— **McCORKLE** returned to repl. RONNIE

Jan 84. (lp)(c) **GREETINGS FROM SOUTH CAROLINA** [-] [ ]
– Carolina sunset / Good ole hurtin' song / If I could only have my way / I may be easy but you make it hard / Closer to Jesus / Blood red eagle / Shot down where you stand / Feel a drunk comin' on / Bags half packed / Rollin' river.
Feb 84. (7") **I MAY BE EASY BUT YOU MAKE IT HARD. / SHOT DOWN WHERE YOU STAND** [-] [ ]

— Disbanded around 1984.

— **GRAY + EUBANKS** re-formed band with **RUSTY MILNER** – guitar / **BOBBY OGDIN** – keyboards / **JAMES STROUD** – drums / **BOB WRAY** – bass / **KENNY MIMS + BRENT ROWAN** – guitar

not issued Mercury

1989. (lp)(c)(cd) **STILL HOLDIN' ON** [-] [ ]
– Dancin' shoes / Keeping the love alive / Once you get the feel of it / Still holdin' on / Dangerous road / Hangin' out in smokey places / I'm glad it's gone / Why did you lie / The same old Moon / Why didn't I think of that.

– compilations, others, etc. –

Sep 79. Capricorn; (lp)(c) **THE BEST OF MARSHALL TUCKER BAND** [ ] [ ]
– Can't you see / Fire on the mountain / Another cruel love / Searchin' for a rainbow / Long hard ride / 24 hours at a time / Heard it in a love song / Take the highway / Walkin' the streets alone. (US-title 'GREATEST HITS')
Apr 93. Movieplay Gold; (cd) **FIRE ON THE MOUNTAIN** [ ] [-]
Apr 93. Movieplay Gold; (cd) **HEARD IT IN A LOVE SONG** [ ] [-]
May 94. Laserlight; (cd)(c) **FINEST SOUTHERN ROCK** [ ] [-]

MARTHA & THE VANDELLAS

Formed: Detroit, Michegan, USA ... 1960 as The DEL-PHIS by MARTHA REEVES, and high school pals ROSALIND ASHFORD and ANNETTE STERLING. They released a 45 for 'Checkmate' records, but this flopped. In 1962, after being promoted from working to singing in the 'Tamla Motown' stable, MARTHA and the girls backed up MARVIN GAYE on his debut hits STUBBORN KIND OF FELLOW and HITCH HIKE. Then as MARTHA & THE VANDELLAS, they were given own contract by 'Gordy' (Tamla), but first 45 failed. However in 1963, they broke through with US Top30 hit COME AND GET THESE MEMORIES. Soon became competition for other girl groups of this era (i.e.SUPREMES / CHIFFONS / RONETTES / etc.). Their peak undeniably came in '64, when DANCING IN THE STREET nearly gave them what would have been their only US No.1. 21 years later, JAGGER + BOWIE were to compensate them (and deceased co-writer GAYE), when with the help of LIVE AID, it hit top slot in the UK. • **Style:** Dance-orientated soul, that highlighted the superb production work of the Motown industry. • **Songwriters:** Trio penned alongside label writers HOLLAND-DOZIER-HOLLAND. Covered THEN HE KISSED ME (Crystals) / MY BOYFRIEND'S BACK (Angels) / IF I HAD A HAMMER (Trini Lopez) / MOCKINGBIRD (Inez Foxx) / etc. • **Trivia:** In 1989, REEVES, STERLING and ASHFORD re-united for UK gigs.

Recommended: COMPACT COMMAND PERFORMANCES – 24 GREATEST HITS (*6)

MARTHA REEVES (b.18 Jul'41, Alabama) – lead vocals / **ROSALIND ASHFORD** (b. 2 Sep'43) – vocals / **ANNETTE STERLING** – vocals

Date	Release		
		Oriole	Gordy
Sep 62.	(7") **I'LL HAVE TO LET HIM GO. / MY BABY WON'T COME BACK**		
Mar 63.	(7") **COME AND GET THESE MEMORIES. / JEALOUS LOVER**		29
		Stateside	Gordy
Jun 63.	(lp) **COME AND GET THESE MEMORIES** – Come and get these memories / Can't get used to losing you / Moments to remember / This is when I need you most / love like ours (don't come knocking every day) / Tears on my pillow / To think you would hurt me / Old love (let's try it again) / There he is (at my door) / I'll have to let him go / Give him up / Jealous lover / Old love (let's try it again).	–	
Oct 63.	(7") **HEAT WAVE. / A LOVE LIKE OURS**		4 Aug 63
Nov 63.	(lp) **HEAT WAVE** – Heat wave / The he kissed me / Hey there lonely boy / More / Dance shoes / If I had a hammer / Hell stranger / Just one look / Wait till my Bobby gets home / My boyfriend's back / Mockingbird / Quicksand. *(UK-iss.Mar65 on 'Tamla Motown') (re-iss.+c.Oct81)*	–	
Jan 64.	(7") **QUICKSAND. / DARLING I HUM YOUR SONG**		8 Nov 63

—— **BETTY KELLY** (b.16 Sep'44) – vocals repl. STERLING

Date	Release		
Apr 64.	(7") **LIVE WIRE. / OLD LOVE (LET'S TRY IT AGAIN)**		42 Feb 64
Jun 64.	(7") **IN MY LONELY ROOM. / A TEAR FOR THE GIRL**		44 Apr 64
Oct 64.	(7") **DANCING IN THE STREET. / THERE HE IS (AT MY DOOR)**	28	2 Aug 64
Jan 65.	(7") **WILD ONE. / DANCING SLOW**		34 Dec 64
		Tamla Motown	Gordy
Mar 65.	(7") **NOWHERE TO RUN. / MOTORING**	26	8 Feb 65
Aug 65.	(7") **YOU'VE BEEN IN LOVE TOO LONG. / LOVE (MAKES ME DO FOOLISH THINGS)**		36 / 70
Sep 65.	(lp) **DANCE PARTY** – Dancing in the street / Dancing slow / Wild one / Nowhere to run / Nobody'll care / There he is (at my door) / Mobile Lil the dancing witch / Dance party / Motoring / The jerk / Mickey's monkey / Hitch hike.		Apr 65
Feb 66.	(7") **MY BABY LOVES ME. / NEVER LEAVE YOUR BABY'S SIDE**		22 Jan 66
May 66.	(7") **WHAT AM I GONNA DO WITHOUT YOUR LOVE?. / GO AHEAD AND LAUGH**		71
Jun 66.	(lp) **GREATEST HITS** (compilation) – My baby loves me / Come and get these memories / Heatwave / Dancing in the street / Quicksand / Live wire / You've been in love too long / In my lonely room / Love (makes me do foolish things) / A love like yours / Nowhere to run / Wild one. *(re-iss.+c.Mar82) (cd-iss. Aug 88)*		50
Nov 66.	(7") **I'M READY FOR LOVE. / HE DOESN'T LOVE HER ANYMORE**	29	9 Oct 66
Jan 67.	(lp) **WATCHOUT!** – I'm ready for love / One way out / Jimmy Mack / Let this day be / Keep it up / Happiness is guarenteed / I'll follow you / No more tear stained make-up / Go ahead and laugh / What am I going to do without your love / Tell me I'll never be alone / He don't live here anymore.		
Mar 67.	(7") **JIMMY MACK. / THIRD FINGER, LEFT HAND** *(re-entered UK chart Aug70, again hit No.21) (re-iss.Mar80)*	21	10 Feb 67
Aug 67.	(7") **LOVE BUG LEAVE MY HEART ALONE. / ONE WAY OUT**		25
Sep 67.	(lp) **MARTHA & THE VANDELLAS LIVE! (live)** – Introduction – I'm ready for love / Love bug leave my heart alone / For once in my life / Love is like a heatwave / Nowhere to run / My baby loves me / I found a love / Jimmy Mack / You've been in love too long / Love (makes me do foolish things) / Do right woman / Respect / Medley: Dancing in the street – I can't help myself (sugar pie, honey bunch) – Sweet soul music – Uptight (everything's alright).		

MARTHA REEVES & THE VANDELLAS

Date	Release		
Jan 68.	(7") **HONEY CHILE. / SHOW ME THE WAY**	30	11 Nov 67

—— **LOIS REEVES** (MARTHA's younger sister) – vocals (ex-ORLONS) repl. BETTY

Date	Release		
Apr 68.	(7") **I PROMISE TO WAIT, MY LOVE. / FORGET ME NOT**		62 / 93
May 68.	(lp) **RIDIN' HIGH** – I promise to wait my love / Honey chile / (There's) Always something there to remind me / Leave it in the hands of love / Love bug leave my heart alone / I'm in love (and I know it) / To sir, with love / Forget me not / (We've got) Honey love / I say a little prayer / Without you / Show me the way.		
Aug 68.	(7") **I CAN'T DANCE TO THAT MUSIC YOU'RE PLAYIN'. / I TRIED**		42
Oct 68.	(7") **SWEET DARLIN'. / WITHOUT YOU**	–	80

—— Early to Spring 1969, UK re-issues of DANCING IN THE STREET and NOWHERE TO RUN hit Nos.4 and 42 respectively. At the same time, MARTHA suffered breakdown.

Date	Release		
Apr 69.	(7") **(WE'VE GOT) HONEY LOVE. / I'M IN LOVE AND I KNOW IT)**	–	56
Feb 70.	(lp) **SUGAR N' SPICE** – Taking my love (and leaving me) / Shoe leather expressway / You're the loser now / I'm a winner / What now my love / Soul appeal / Loneliness is a lonely feelin' / I love the man / It ain't like that / / I can't get along without you / Heartless / I hope that you have better luck than I did.		
Oct 70.	(7") **I'VE GOTTA LET YOU GO. / YOU'RE THE LOVER NOW**	–	93

—— (1971) **SANDRA TILLEY** – vocals (ex-VELVELETTES) repl. ASHFORD

Date	Release		
Jan 71.	(7") **FORGET ME NOT (remix). / I GOTTA LET YOU GO**	11	–
Oct 71.	(7") **BLESS YOU. / HOP I DON'T GET MY HEART BROKEN**	33	53
Feb 72.	(7") **YOUR LOVE MAKES IT ALL WORTHWHILE. / IN AND OUT OF MY LIFE**	–	
Mar 72.	(lp) **BLACK MAGIC** – No one there / Your love makes it worthwhile / Something / Benjamin / Tear it on down / The best years of my life I've been givin' you / Bless you / I want you back / In and out of my life / Anyone who had a heart / Hope I don't get my heart broke.		
May 72.	(7") **I WANT YOU BACK. / TEAR IT ALL DOWN**	–	
Nov 72.	(7") **BABY DON'T LEAVE ME. / I WON'T BE THE FOOL I'VE BEEN AGAIN**	–	

—— Break-up on 1st Dec'72, after farewell concert. LOIS joined QUIET ELEGANCE

MARTHA REEVES

went solo after initially providing songs with JJ JOHNSON on the 1973 Film Soundtrack 'WILLIE DYNAMITE' for 'M.C.A'.

Date	Release		
		Tamla Motown	Gordy
Feb 73.	(7") **NO ONE THERE. / THE BEST YEARS OF MY LIFE**		
		M.C.A.	M.C.A.
Mar 74.	(7") **POWER OF LOVE. / STAND BY ME**		76
Jul 74.	(lp) **POWER OF LOVE** – Wild night / You've got me for company / Fascimile / Ain't that peculiar / Dixie highway / Power of love / My man (you changed my tune) / Sweet misery / I've got to use my imagination / Storm in my soul / Many rivers to cross.		Feb 74
Jul 74.	(7") **WILD NIGHT. / MY MAN (YOU CHANGED MY TUNE)**		–
Jul 74.	(7") **WILD NIGHT. / STAND BY ME**	–	
Oct 74.	(7") **MY MAN (YOU CHANGED MY TUNE). / FACSIMILIE**	–	
May 75.	(7") **I'VE GOT TO USE MY IMAGINATION. / YOU'VE GOT ME FOR COMPANY**	–	
		Arista	Arista
Oct 76.	(7") **LOVE BLIND. / THIS TIME I'LL BE SWEETER**	–	
Dec 76.	(7") **YOUR LOVE KEEPS LIFTING ME HIGHER AND HIGHER. / NOW THAT WE FOUND LOVE**		
Dec 76.	(lp)(c) **THE REST OF MY LIFE** – This time I'll be sweeter / Love blind / Second chance / Love strong enough to move mountains / (Your love keeps lifting me) Higher and higher / Now that we found love.		
Feb 77.	(7") **THE REST OF MY LIFE. / THANK YOU**	–	
May 77.	(7") **YOU'VE LOST THAT LOVIN' FELIN'. / NOW THAT WE FOUND LOVE**	–	

On 1st Jul'78, MARTHA & THE VANDELLAS re-united for benefit for actor Will Geer. MARTHA will retire from music business.

Date	Release		
		Fantasy	Fantasy
Jul 78.	(7") **YOU'RE LIKE SUNSHINE. / LOVE DON'T COME NO STRONGER**	–	
Jul 78.	(lp)(c) **WE MEET AGAIN** – Free again / You're like sunshine / I feel like magic / One line from every love song / Love don't come no stronger / What are you doing the rest of your life / Dedicated to your woman / Special to me.		
Nov 78.	(7") **DANCING IN THE STREETS (SKATING IN THE STREETS). / WHEN YOU CAME**	–	
Feb 79.	(7") **THAT'S WHAT I WANT. / REALLY LIKE YOUR RAP**	–	

– more compilations, etc. –

Note; below releases on 'Tamla Motown' UK/ 'Gordy' US, until mention

Date	Release		
Jan 69.	(7") **DANCING IN THE STREET. / QUICKSAND**	4	–
Mar 69.	(7") **NOWHERE TO RUN. / LIVE WIRE**	42	–
1973.	(lp)(c) **GREATEST HITS VOL.2**		
Sep 76.	(7") **DANCING IN THE STREET. / JIMMY MACK**		
Jun 77.	(lp)(c) **ANTHOLOGY** *(re-iss.Sep82)*		
Jan 80.	(7") **DANCING IN THE STREET. / HEAT WAVE** *(re-iss.Oct81 & Jun83)*		
Feb 83.	(7") **FORGET ME NOT. / I'M READY FOR LOVE**		
May 83.	(c-ep) **FLIP HITS** – Dancing in the street / Forget me not / Jimmy Mack / I'm ready for love.		–
Mar 87.	(cd) **COMPACT COMMAND PERFORMANCES – 24 GREATEST HITS** – Come and get these memories / (Love is like a) Heat wave / A love like yours (don't come knocking everyday) / Quicksand / Live wire / In my lonely room / Dancing in the street / Wild one / Motoring / Nowhere to run / You've been in love too long / Love (makes me do foolish things) / My baby loves me / I'm ready for love / Jimmy Mack / Third finger left hand / Love bug / Leave my heart alone / Honey chile / I promise to wait my love / I can't dance to that music you're playin' / Sweet darlin' / (We've got) Honey love / I gotta let you go / Bless you. *(re-iss.Nov92)*		
Jul 93.	(7")(c-s) **DANCING IN THE STREET. / I CAN'T DANCE TO THE MUSIC YOU'RE PLAYIN'** (cd-s+=) – My baby loves me / Motoring.		
Aug 93.	(cd)(c) **DANCING IN THE STREETS – THE GREATEST HITS**		
Mar 87.	Creole; (7") **JIMMY MACK. / DANCING IN THE STREET** (12"+=) – Medley / My guy.		–
Nov 88.	A&M; (7") **NOWHERE TO RUN. /('B'by 'James Brown')**	52	
Jul 94.	Success; (cd)(c) **DANCING IN THE STREET (MARTHA REEVES)**		–
Apr 92.	Motor City; (12") **ANGEL IN DISGUISE. / ?**		–
Apr 95.	Motown; (cd) **DANCING IN THE STREETS – THE GREATEST HITS**		

John MARTYN

Born: 28 Jun'48, Glasgow, Scotland. Learned guitar techniques from folk singer HAMISH IMLACH, moved to London in 1967 after being first white solo artist to get deal with Chris Blackwell's 'Island' label. He released 2 solo lp's in 1968, before he married Coventry girl BEVERLEY KUTNER. The pair became a duo in 1969 and issued 2 lp's 'STORMBRINGER' & 'THE ROAD TO RUIN' the following year. He returned to solo work in 1971, after BEVERLEY gave birth to their second child in 1971. His 70's work drew a large cult following which gave him fruitful commercial 1981 UK Top 30 album 'GLORIOUS FOOL' (a political assault on newly elected US president Ronald Reagan). He had already signed to 'Warners', where he secured another UK Top 30 album in '82 with 'WELL KEPT SECRET'. • **Style:** Bearded acoustic folk singer, who delved into easy jazz in 1971. MARTYN improvised his deliberate slurred deep vox, into its own identity, even instrumentation. His manner was as laid back as slowhand ERIC CLAPTON or even cool as LOWELL GEORGE (Little Feat). • **Songwriters:** Self-penned except; COCAINE BLUES (trad.) / I'D RATHER BE THE DEVIL (Skip James) / JOHNNY TOO BAD (Slickers) / TIGHT CONNECTION TO MY HEART (Bob Dylan) / NEVER LET ME GO (Joe Scott) / etc. • **Trivia:** He has also guested on albums by CLAIRE HAMMILL, BURNING SPEAR and BACK STREET CRAWLER, to mention but a few. ERIC CLAPTON has recorded 'MAY YOU NEVER' on his 'Slowhand' album.

Recommended: BLESS THE WEATHER (*7) / SOLID AIR (*8) / SO FAR SO GOOD (*7) / COOL TIDE (*6).

JOHN MARTYN – vocals, acoustic guitar

Island Warners

Feb 68. (lp) **LONDON CONVERSATION** [ ] [-]
– Fairy tale lullaby / Sandy grey / London conversation / Ballad of an elder woman / Cocaine blues / Run honey run / Back to stay / Rolling home / Who's grown up now / Golden girl / This time / Don't think twice. *(re-iss.cd+c.Aug91)*

— added **HAROLD McNAIR** – flute / **PAUL WHEELER** – guitar / **DAVE MOSES** – bass

Dec 68. (lp) **THE TUMBLER** [ ] [-]
– Sing a song of summer / The river / Goin' down to Memphis / The gardeners / A day at the sea / Fishin' blues / Dusty / Hello train / Winding boy / Fly on home / Knuckledy crunch and slipp ledee slee song / Seven black roses.

JOHN & BEVERLEY MARTYN

(as BEVERLEY, she recorded solo 45's) **BEVERLEY** nee KUTNER – vocals, with + **LEVON HELM** – drums (The BAND) / **PAUL HARRIS** – piano / **HARVEY BROOKS** – bass / **BIUX MUNDI** + **HERBIE LOVELL** – drums

Jan 70. (7") **JOHN THE BAPTIST. / THE OCEAN** [ ] [-]
Feb 70. (lp) **STORMBRINGER** [ ] [ ]
– Go out and get it / Can't get the one I want / Stormbringer / Sweet honesty / Woodstock / John the baptist / The ocean / Traffic light lady / Tomorrow time / Would you believe me. *(re-iss.cd+c.Aug91)*

Apr 70. (7") **GO OUT AND GET IT. / CAN'T GET THE ONE I WANT** [-] [ ]

— with **DANNY THOMPSON** – bass (of PENTANGLE) / **WELLS KELLY** – drums, bass + **PAUL HARRIS**

Nov 70. (lp) **THE ROAD TO RUIN** [ ] [ ]
– Primrose hill / Parcels / Auntie aviator / New day / Give us a ring / Sorry to be so long / Tree garden / Say what you can / The road to ruin. *(cd-iss.Mar93)*

JOHN MARTYN

went solo again, with **DANNY THOMPSON** – double bass / **RICHARD THOMPSON** – guitar (solo artist) / **TONY REEVES** – (of COLOSSEUM) / **IAN WHITEMAN** and **ROGER POWELL** (of MIGHTY BABY)

Island Island

Nov 71. (lp)(c) **BLESS THE WEATHER** [ ] [ ]
– Go easy / Bless the weather / Sugar lump / Walk to the water / Just now / Head and heart / Let the good times come / Back down the river / Glistening Glyndebourne / Singing in the rain. *(re-iss.cd+c.Aug91)*

— retained **DANNY, RICHARD** and brought in **JOHN 'RABBIT' BUNDRICK** – keyboards / **DAVE PEGG** – bass / **DAVE MATTACKS** – drums / and **SPEEDY** (NEEMOI ACQUAYE) – congas / (all of FAIRPORT CONVENTION).

Nov 72. (7") **MAY YOU NEVER. / JUST NOW** [ ] [-]
Feb 73. (lp)(c) **SOLID AIR** [ ] [ ]
– Over the hill / Don't want to know / I'd rather be with the Devil / Go down easy / Dreams by the sea / May you never / The man in the station / Easy blues / Solid air. *(re-iss.+cd. Nov86.)*

Mar 73. (7") **MAY YOU NEVER. / DON'T WANT TO KNOW ABOUT EVIL** [-] [ ]

— retained **DANNY,** and brought in **BOBBY KEYES** and **REMI KABAKA** plus **STEVE WINWOOD** and **CHRIS WOOD** (both of TRAFFIC)

Oct 73. (lp)(c) **INSIDE OUT** [ ] [ ]
– Fine lines / Eibhli ghail ghiuin ni chearbhaill / Ain't no saint / Outside in / The glory of love / Look in / Beverley / Make no mistake / Ways to cry / So much in love with you. *(cd-iss.Apr94)*

— with **DANNY THOMPSON / JOHN STEVENS** – drums / **PAUL KOSSOFF** – guitar (ex-FREE) and guests **BEVERLEY MARTYN** – vocals

Jan 75. (lp)(c) **SUNDAY'S CHILD** [ ] [-]
– One day without you / Lay it all down / Root love / My baby girl / Sunday's child / Spencer the rover / Clutches / The message / Satisfied mind / You can discover / Call me crazy. *(cd-iss.Mar93)*

Sep 75. (lp) **LIVE AT LEEDS (live)** (ltd. 10,000 mail-order) [ ] [-]
– Outside in / Solid air / Make no mistake / Bless the weather / The man in the station / I'd rather be the Devil. *(re-iss.Jun87 on 'Cacophony') (cd-iss.May92 on 'Awareness' & Jul95 on 'Hypertension')*

Feb 77. (7") **OVER THE HILL. / HEAD AND HEART** [ ] [-]

— with guests **STEVE WINWOOD** – keyboards / **MORRIS PERT** – percussion.

Nov 77. (lp)(c) **ONE WORLD** [54] [-]
– Couldn't love you more / Certain surprise / Dancing / Small hours / Dealer / One world / Smiling stranger / Big Muff. *(re-iss.+cd Sep86).*

Jan 78. (7") **DANCING. / DEALER (version)** [ ] [-]

— with **PHIL COLLINS** – drums,vocals / **JOHN GIBLIN** – bass (both of BRAND X) / **TOMMY EYRE** – keyboards (GREASE BAND) / **DAVE LAWSON** – keyboards (ex-GREENSLADE).

Island Atlantic

Oct 80. (lp)(c) **GRACE AND DANGER** [54] [ ]
– Some people are crazy / Grace and danger / Lookin' on / Johnny too bad / Sweet little mystery/ Hurt in your heart / Baby please come home / Save some for me / Our love. *(cd-iss.May87)*

Oct 80. (7") **JOHNNY TOO BAD. / ('A'instrumental) / (or) /('A'version)** [ ] [ ]
Mar 81. (12") **JOHNNY TOO BAD (ext. dub version) / BIG MUFF (ext.mix)** [ ] [ ]
May 81. (7") **SWEET LITTLE MYSTERY. / JOHNNY TOO BAD** [ ] [ ]

— with **PHIL COLLINS** – drums, vocals, producer / **ALAN THOMSON** – bass / **MAX MIDDLETON** – keyboards / **DANNY CUMMINGS** – perc. / **DICK CUTHELL** – horns 2.

WEA Duke

Aug 81. (7") **PLEASE FALL IN LOVE WITH ME. / DON'T YOU GO** [ ] [ ]
Sep 81. (lp)(c) **GLORIOUS FOOL** [25] [ ]
– Couldn't love you more / Amsterdam / Hold on my heart / Perfect hustler / Hearts and keys / Glorious fool / Never say never / Oascanel (get back home) / Didn't do that / Please fall in love with me / Don't you go.

Feb 82. (7") **COULDN'T LOVE YOU MORE. /** [-] [ ]

— with **DANNY** and **ALAN** plus **JEFFREY ALLEN** – drums / **JIM PRIME** – keyboards / **MEL COLLINS** – sax / **MARTIN DROVER** – trumpet / **LEE KOSMIN** and **STEVE LANGE** – harmony.

Aug 82. (lp)(c) **WELL KEPT SECRET** [20] [ ]
– Could've been me / You might need a man / Hung up / Gun money / Never let me go / Love up / Changes her mind / Hiss on the tape / Back with a vengeance / Livin' alone.

Sep 82. (7") **HISS ON THE TAPE. / LIVIN' ALONE** [ ] [ ]
Nov 82. (7") **GUN MONEY (US remix). / HISS ON THE TAPE (live)** [ ] [ ]

— touring line-up **ALAN THOMSON** – bass / **JEFFREY ALLEN** – drums / **DANNY CUMMINGS** – percussion / **RONNIE LEAHY** – keyboards.

Body Swerve not issued

Nov 83. (lp)(c) **PHILENTHROPY (live)** [ ] [-]
– Sunday's child / Don't want to know / Johnnie too bad / Make no mistake / Root love / Lookin' on / Hung up / Smiling stranger. *(re-iss.+cd. Mar86 on 'Dojo')*

— **MARTYN** retained **JIM** and **ALAN** plus **BARRY REYNOLDS** add. guitar / **JACK WALDMAN** – keyboards / **ROBIN RANKIN** – keyboards / **JAMES HOOKER** – keyboards / **STEVEN STANLEY** – linn drums / **ANDY LYDEN** – linn drums / **UZZIAH 'STICKY' THOMPSON** – percussion / **COLIN TULLY** – saxophone / harmony by **MORWENNE LAIDLAW, TERRY NELSON** and **LORNA BROOKS**.

Island Island

Oct 84. (7") **OVER THE RAINBOW. / ROPE SOUL'D** [ ] [ ]
Nov 84. (lp)(c) **SAPPHIRE** [57] [ ]
– Sapphire / Over the rainbow / You know / Watching her eyes / Fisherman's dream / Acid rain / Mad dog days / Climb the walls / Coming in on time / Rope soul'd. *(cd-iss.Mar93)*

— **with ALAN THOMSON** – fretless bass / **DANNY CUMMINGS** – percussion / **COLIN TULLY and FOSTER PATTERSON** – keyboards, vocals.

Feb 86. (lp)(c)(cd) **PIECE BY PIECE** [28] [ ]
– Nightline / Lonely love / Angeline / One step too far / Piece by piece / Serendipity / Who believes in angels / Love of mine / John Wayne. *(cd+=)*– Tight connection to my heart / Solid air / One world / May you never.

Feb 86. (7") **ANGELINE. / TIGHT CONNECTION TO MY HEART** [ ] [ ]
(12"+=) – May you never / Certain surprise / One day without you.
(cd-ep+=) – May you never / Solid air / Glistening Glydebourne.

May 86. (7") **LONELY LOVE. / SWEET LITTLE MYSTERY (live)** [ ] [ ]
(12"+=) – Fisherman's Dream (live).

— **DAVID BALL** – bass repl. THOMPSON / added **ARRAN ABMUN** – drums + **JEFF CASTLE** – keyboards

Oct 87. (lp)(c)(cd) **FOUNDATIONS (live)** [ ] [ ]
– Mad dog days / Angeline / The apprentice / May you never / Deny this love / Send me one line / John Wayne / Johnny too bad / Over the rainbow.

Permanent not issued

Mar 90. (cd)(c)(lp) **THE APPRENTICE** [ ] [-]
– Live on love / Look at that gun / Send me one line / Hold me / The apprentice / The river / Income town / Deny this love / UPO / Patterns in the rain. (cd+=) – The moment.

Aug 90. (7") **DENY THIS LOVE (remix). / THE APPRENTICE (live)** [ ] [-]
(cd-s+=) – ('A'-lp version).

Nov 91. (cd)(c)(lp) **COOLTIDE** [ ] [ ]
– Hole in the rain / Annie says / Jack the lad / Number nine / The cure / Same difference / Father Time / Call me / Cooltide.

Apr 92. (7")(c-s) **JACK THE LAD. / ?** [ ] [-]
(cd-s+=) – ?

Sep 92. (7")(c-s) **SWEET LITTLE MYSTERY. / ?** [ ] [ ]
(cd-s+=) – ?

Oct 92. (cd)(c)(lp) **COULDN'T LOVE YOU MORE** [65] [ ]
– Lonely love / Couldn't love you more / Sweet little mystery / Head & heart / Could've been me / One day without you / Over the hill / Fine lines / May you never / One world / Way's to cry / Angeline / Man in the station / Solid air / Never let me go.

Dec 92. (7")(c-s) **LONELY LOVE. / ?** [ ] [ ]
(cd-s+=) – ?

— with on next album **SPENCER COZENS** or **CHRIS CAMERON** – keyboards / **GERRY CONWAY** or **WAYNE STEWART** – drums / **ALAN THOMPSON** or **JOHN GIBLIN** –

bass / **MILES BOULD** or **MARK WALKER** – percussion / **DAVE GILMOUR** or **ALAN DARBY** or **BILL RUPERT** – guitar / **ANDY SHEPHERD** or **GERRY UNDERWOOD** – sax / **FRED NELSON** – piano / **LEVON HELM** – guest / and of course **PHIL COLLINS** – b.vocals, etc.

Jul 93. (cd)(c) **NO LITTLE BOY** (old songs re-worked) [ ] [-]
– Solid air / Ways to cry / Could've been me / I don't wanna know / Just now / One day without you / Sweet little mystery / Pascanel / Sunday's child / Head and heart / Fine lines / Bless the weather / Man in the station / One world / Rock salt and nails / Hole in the rain.

Jul 95. (d-cd)(d-c) **LIVE AT THE SHAW THEATRE (live)** [ ] [-]

– compilations, etc. –

Mar 77. Island; (lp)(c) **SO FAR SO GOOD** [ ] [-]
– May you never / Bless the weather / Head and heart / Over the hill / Spencer the rover / Glistening Glyndebourne / Solid air / One day without you / I'd rather be the Devil.

Oct 82. Island; (lp)(c) **THE ELECTRIC JOHN MARTYN** [ ] [ ]
(cd-iss.Apr88)

Jun 94. Island; (d-cd) **SWEET LITTLE MYSTERIES – THE ISLAND ANTHOLOGY** [ ] [ ]

May 92. Windsong; (cd) **BBC RADIO 1 LIVE IN CONCERT (live)** [ ] [-]

Richard MARX

Born: 16 Sep'63, Chicago, Illinois, USA. in 1982, he sent demo tape to LIONEL RICHIE, who invited him to cut backing vocals for his 1983 'Can't Slow Down' album. The next year, he collaborated with KENNY ROGERS on his single 'CRAZY', having previously jointly worked on 'WHAT ABOUT ME' (a US Top 20 hit for ROGERS, KIM CARNES & JAMES INGRAM). After more contributions to other artists, he signed solo deal in 1986 through BOBBY COLOMBY (ex-BLOOD, SWEAT & TEARS) with 'EMI Manhattan'. In Sep'87, his debut single 'DON'T MEAN NOTHING', hits US Top 3, as did his next 'SHOULD'VE KNOWN BETTER'. These were also lifted from his first US No.1 self-titled parent album. For the next half decade, he became one of America's top selling stars. • **Style:** AOR artist with smooth vox and youthful looks. • **Songwriters:** Self-penned numbers & co-wrote some of third album with FEE WAYBILL (ex-TUBES), who he had produced in 1988. His other productions were RANDY MEISNER, VIXEN and POCO. • **Trivia:** He married actress/singer Cynthia Rhodes on 8 Jan'89.

Recommended: RICHARD MARX (*5) / RUSH STREET (*6).

RICHARD MARX – vocals, piano with guest on debut album **JOE WALSH** – guitar / **PRAIRIE PRINCE** – drums / **JOHN PIERCE** – bass / **MICHAEL LANDALL** – guitar / **FEE WAYBILL** – vocals / **PAULINKO DA COSTA** – percussion / etc.

Manhattan Manhattan

Jun 87. (7")(12") **DON'T MEAN NOTHING. / THE FLAME OF LOVE** [ ] [3]
(cd-s+=) – Should've known better / Endless summer nights (edit).

Aug 87. (lp)(c) **RICHARD MARX** [68] [8] Jun 87
– Should've known better / Don't mean nothing / Endless summer nights / Lonely heart / Hold on to the nights / Have mercy / Remember Manhattan / The flame of love / Rhythm of life / Heaven only knows. *(cd-iss.Apr88)(re-iss.Oct91 on 'Capitol')*

Oct 87. (7") **SHOULD'VE KNOWN BETTER. / RHYTHM OF LIFE** [50] [3] Sep 87
(12"+=) – ('A'radio mix).
(cd-s++=) – Have mercy (live).

Apr 88. (7")(7"pic-d) **ENDLESS SUMMER NIGHTS. / HAVE MERCY (live)** [50] [2] Jan 88
(12"+=) – Should've known better (extended).
(cd-s+=) – Rhythm of life.

Jun 88. (7") **HOLD ON TO THE NIGHTS. / LONELY HEART** [ ] [1] May 88
(12"+=) – ('A'live).

Apr 89. (7") **SATISFIED. / SHOULD'VE KNOWN BETTER** [52] [1]
(12"+=)(cd-s+=) – (2 'A'versions).

May 89. (lp)(c)(cd) **REPEAT OFFENDER** [8] [1]
– Nothin' you can do about it / Satisfied / Angelia / Too late to say goodbye / Right here waiting / Heart on the line / Real world / If you don't want my love / Wait for the sunrise / Children of the night. *(cd+=)*– That was Lulu. *(re-iss.Oct91 on 'Capitol')*

Aug 89. (7") **RIGHT HERE WAITING. / HOLD ON TO THE NIGHT (live)** [2] [1] Jul 89
(12"+=) – That was Lulu (live).
(c-s+=)(cd-s+=) – Wild life.

Oct 89. (7") **ANGELIA. / RIGHT HERE WAITING (edit)** [45] [4]
(12"+=)(c-s+=) – ('A'version).
(cd-s+=) – Don't mean nothing (live).

Feb 90. (7")(c-s) **TOO LATE TO SAY GOODBYE. / SATISFIED (live)** [38] [12] Jan 90
(12"+=) – ('A'version).
(cd-s++=) – Endless summer nights.

May 90. (7")(c-s) **CHILDREN OF THE NIGHT. / RIGHT HERE WAITING (live)** [54] [13] Apr 90
(12"+=) – Real world (live).
(cd-s++=) – Too late to say goodbye (live).

Aug 90. (7") **ENDLESS SUMMER NIGHTS. / HOLD ON TO THE NIGHT** [60] [-]
(12"+=) – Nothing you can do about it (live).
(cd-s+=) – Real world (live).

—— now w/ **STEVE LUKATHER** – guitar / **JEFF PORCARO** – drums / etc.

Capitol Capitol

Oct 91. (7") **KEEP COMING BACK. / I GET NO SLEEP** [-] [ ]

Oct 91. (7")(c-s) **KEEP COMING BACK. / SUPERSTAR** [55] [-]
(12") – ('A'side) / ('A'quiet storm mix).
(cd-s) – ('A'side) / (3 mixes incl. Spanish + AOR).

Nov 91. (cd)(c)(lp) **RUSH STREET** [60] [35]
– Playing with fire / Love unemotional / Keep coming back / Take this heart / Hazard / Hands in your pocket / Calling you / Superstar / Streets of pain / I get no sleep / Big boy now / Chains around my heart / Your world. *(After 'HAZARD' single hit the UK Top 3, the album made No.7)*

May 92. (7")(c-s) **HAZARD. / KEEP COMING BACK** [3] [9] Feb 92
(cd-s+=) – Thunder and lightning / Endless summer nights.
(cd-s) – ('A'side) / Right here waiting / Too late to say goodbye / Edge of a broken heart.

Aug 92. (7")(c-s) **TAKE THIS HEART. / HAZARD** [13] [20] Jun 92
(cd-s+=) – Ride with the idol / Love emotional.
(cd-s) – ('A'side) / Take it to the limit (live) / That was Lulu (live) / Rhythm of life (live).

Nov 92. (7")(c-s) **CHAINS AROUND MY HEART. / YOUR WORLD** [29] [44] Oct 92
(cd-s+=) – Should've known better / Living in the real world.
(cd-s) – ('A'side) / I can't help falling in love with you (acoustic) / Angelina / Wildlife.

Dave MASON

Born: 10 May'46, Worcester, England. In the early 60's, he played with instrumental group The JAGUARS, before forming The HELLIONS, alongside JIM CAPALDI, POLI PALMER and LUTHER GROSVENOR. They released 3 singles in the mid-60's, before becoming REVOLUTION, which did not include MASON (he became roadie for The SPENCER DAVIS GROUP). In Apr'67, MASON re-united with CAPALDI, when they plus STEVE WINWOOD and CHRIS WOOD formed TRAFFIC. MASON penned their UK Top 3 hit 'HOLE IN MY SHOE', and some tracks for debut 'MR.FANTASY' album, before departing for first time in Dec'67. After production work on FAMILY's debut lp 'Music In A Doll's House', he re-joined TRAFFIC in May'68. He contributed a few more tracks to their eponymous hit 2nd album in Oct'68, before again departing to form WOODEN FROG. Around the same time, he cut a solo 45 for 'Island', and sessioned for JIMI HENDRIX and The ROLLING STONES. In 1969, he toured with DELANEY & BONNIE & FRIENDS (aka ERIC CLAPTON / DEREK & THE DOMINOES), and appeared on their 1970 hit lp 'On Tour'. Earlier that year, he signed a new solo deal with 'Blue Thumb', and released a few 45's, before issuing US hit debut lp 'ALONE TOGETHER' (in multi-coloured vinyl). That year, he also recorded an album with MAMA CASS ELLIOT. before returning to TRAFFIC briefly (again!) and fruitful solo work. • **Style:** Erratic but accomplished guitarist/singer, who was dogged commercially by record company troubles until 'Columbia' came along in '73. • **Songwriters:** Prolific pensmith, although he also covered; BRING IT ON HOME TO ME (Sam Cooke) / GIMME SOME LOVIN' (Spencer Davis Group) / CRYING, WAITING & HOPING (Buddy Holly) / ALL ALONG THE WATCHTOWER (Bob Dylan) / WILL YOU LOVE ME TOMORROW (Shirelles) / TWO GUITAR LOVERS (Maureen Gray) / etc. • **Trivia:** MANHATTAN TRANSFER, GRAHAM NASH and DAVID CROSBY guested on his 1975 album 'SPLIT COCONUT'.

Recommended: ALONE TOGETHER (*7) / GREATEST HITS (*7)

HELLIONS

DAVE MASON – vocals, guitar / **POLI PALMER** – keyboards / **LUTHER GROSVENOR** – bass / **JIM CAPALDI** – drums

Piccadilly not issued

Oct 64. (7") **DAYDREAMING OF YOU. / SHADES OF BLUE** [ ] [-]

May 65. (7") **TOMORROW NEVER COMES. / DREAM CHILD** [ ] [-]

Sep 65. (7") **A LITTLE LOVIN'. / THINK IT OVER** [ ] [-]

—— Evolved into REVOLUTION in 1966, but without MASON and CAPALDI who joined TRAFFIC in Apr'67. POLI later joined FAMILY, and LUTHER who was in V.I.P.'s (aka SPOOKY TOOTH) later joined MOTT THE HOOPLE (as ARIEL BENDER).

DAVE MASON

(solo) – vocals, guitar (ex-TRAFFIC)with sessioners

Island not issued

Feb 68. (7") **JUST FOR YOU. / LITTLE WOMAN** [ ] [-]

—— Used musicians from DEREK & THE DOMINOES (aka ERIC CLAPTON band)

Harvest Blue Thumb

Apr 70. (7") **WORLD IN CHANGES. / CAN'T STOP WORRYING, CAN'T STOP LOVING** [ ] [ ]

Aug 70. (7") **ONLY YOU KNOW AND I KNOW. / SAD AND DEEP AS YOU** [ ] [42] Jul 70
(re-iss. US 1977)

Nov 70. (7") **SATIN RED AND BLACK VELVET WOMAN. / SHOULDN'T HAVE TOOK MORE THAN YOU GAVE** [-] [97]

Dec 70. (lp)(marble-lp) **ALONE TOGETHER** [ ] [22] Jul70
– Only you know and I know / Can't stop worrying, can't stop loving / Waitin' on you / Shouldn't have took more than you gave / World in changes / Sad and deep as you / Just a song / Look at you look at me. *(re-iss.1973 on 'ABC') (cd-iss. Dec 88 on 'M.C.A.')*

Jan 71. (7") **WAITIN' ON YOU. / JUST A SONG** [-] [ ]

DAVE MASON and MAMA CASS

DAVE with **MAMA CASS ELLIOT** (ex-MAMAS & THE PAPAS) – vocals, with backing from **PAUL HARRIS** – keyboards, strings / **BRYAN GARO** – bass / **RUSS KUNKEL** – drums, percussion

Probe / Dunhill

Nov 70. (7") **GOOD TIMES ARE COMING. / WELCOME TO THE WORLD**

Feb 71. (7") **TOO MUCH TRUTH, TOO MUCH LOVE. / WALK TO THE POINT**

Probe / Blue Thumb

Mar 71. (lp)(c) **DAVE MASON AND MAMA CASS** — 49
– Work to the point / On and on / To be free / Here we go again / Pleasing you / Sit and wonder / Something to make you happy / Too much truth, too much love / Next to you / Glittering facade.

Mar 71. (7") **SOMETHING TO MAKE YOU HAPPY. / NEXT TO YOU**

—— DAVE rejoined TRAFFIC for live album WELCOME TO THE CANTEEN in 1971.

DAVE MASON

went solo again with **MARK JORDAN** – keyboards / **LONNIE TURNER** – bass / **DR. RICK JAEGER** – drums / **FELIX FALCON** (aka FLACO) – congas, percussion

Island / Blue Thumb

Apr 72. (lp)(c) **HEADKEEPER** (half live) — 51 Feb 72
– To be free / In my mind / Here we go again / A heartache, a shadow /, a lifetime / Headkeeper / Pearly queen / Just a song / World in changes / Can't stop worrying, can't stop lovin' / Feelin' alright?.

Apr 72. (7") **A HEARTACHE, A SHADOW, A LIFETIME. / CAN'T STOP WORRYING, CAN'T STOP LOVIN' (live)** -

Jul 72. (7") **TO BE FREE. / PEARLY QUEEN** -

May 73. (lp)(c) **DAVE MASON IS ALIVE! (live)** - — Apr 72
– Walks to the point / Shouldn't have took more than you gave / Look at you look at me / Only you and I know / Sad and deep as you / Just a song / Feelin' alright?

C.B.S. / Columbia

Jan 74. (7") **BABY . . . PLEASE. / SIDE-TRACKED** -

Jan 74. (lp)(c) **IT'S LIKE YOU NEVER LEFT** — 50 Dec73
– Baby . . . please / Every woman / If you've got love / Maybe / Headkeeper / Misty morning stranger / Silent partner / Side tracked / The lonely one / It's like you never left.

Apr 74. (7") **THE LONELY ONE. / MISTY MORNING STRANGER**

—— **JIM KREUGER** – guitar repl. TURNER

Nov 74. (lp)(c) **DAVE MASON** — 25 Oct 74
– Show me some affection / Get ahold on love / Every woman / It can't make any difference to me / All along the watchtower / Bring it on home to me / Harmony & melody / Relation ships / You can't take it when you go. *(cd-iss.Nov95 on 'One Way')*

Nov 74. (7") **BRING IT ON HOME TO ME. / HARMONY & MELODY** -

May 75. (7") **SHOW ME SOME AFFECTION. / GET A HOLD ON LOVE** -

—— retained KREUGER + JAEGER. New **GERALD JOHNSON** – bass / **JAY WINDING** – keys

Sep 75. (7") **YOU CAN'T LOSE IT. / YOU CAN'T TAKE IT WHEN YOU GO** — -

Oct 75. (lp)(c) **SPLIT COCONUT** — 27
– Split coconut / Crying, waiting & hoping / You can't lose it / She's a friend / Save your love / Give me a reason why / Two guitar lovers / Sweet music / Long lost friend. *(cd-iss.Oct95 on 'One Way')*

Oct 75. (7") **SPLIT COCONUT. / LONG LOST FRIEND** -

Jan 76. (7") **CRYING, WAITING & HOPING. / SAVE YOUR LOVE** — -

—— His live band 1976 were; **JIM KRUEGER** – guitar / **JAI WINDING** – keyboards / **GERALD JOHNSON** – bass / **RICK JAEGER** – drums

Dec 76. (d-lp)(c) **CERTIFIED LIVE (live)** — 78 Nov 76
– Feelin' alright / Pearly queen / Show me some affection / All along the watchtower / Take it to the limit / Give me a reason why / Sad and deep as you / Every woman / World in changes / Goin' down slow / Look at you, look at me / Only you know and I know / Bring it on home to me / Gimme some lovin'. *(cd-iss.Sep95 on 'One Way')*

Dec 76. (7") **ALL ALONG THE WATCHTOWER (live). / SAD AND DEEP AS YOU (live)** -

Mar 77. (7") **ALL ALONG THE WATCHTOWER (live). / EVERY WOMAN (live)** — -

May 77. (lp)(c) **LET IT FLOW** — 37 Apr 77
– So high (rock me baby and roll me away) / We just disagree / Mystic traveller / Spend your life with me / Takin' the time to find / Let it go, let it flow / It's alright / Seasons / You just have to wait now / What do we got here?.

Jun 77. (7") **SO HIGH (ROCK ME BABY AND ROLL ME AWAY). / YOU JUST HAVE TO WAIT NOW** — 89 May 77

Sep 77. (7") **TIGERS WILL SURVIVE. / TIMES** -

Nov 77. (7") **WE JUST DISAGREE. / MYSTIC TRAVELLER** — 12 Sep 77

Jan 78. (7") **LET IT GO, LET IT FLOW. / TAKIN' THE TIME TO FIND** - 45

Jun 78. (7") **WILL YOU STILL LOVE ME TOMORROW. / MYSTIC TRAVELLER** — 39

Jul 78. (lp)(c) **MARIPOSA DE ORO** (Spanish for 'Gold Butterfly') — 41 Jun 78
– Don't it make you wonder / Searchin' (for a feeling) / All gotta go sometime / Warm desire / A warm and tender love / Will you still love me tomorrow / Shake your love / Bird in the wind / So good to be home / The words.

Oct 78. (7") **DON'T IT MAKE YOU WONDER. / WARM DESIRE**

Jul 80. (7") **SAVE ME. / TRYING TO GET BACK TO YOU** — 71

Aug 80. (lp)(c) **OLD CREST ON A NEW WAVE** — 74 Jun 80
– Paralyzed / You're a friend of mine / I'm missing you / Talk to me / Gotta be on my way / Save me / Life is a ladder / Tryin' to get back to you / Get it right / Old crest on a new wave.

Polydor / Polydor

1982. (7") **FIVE CIRCLES. / 909**

—— Retired from music business except an 'MCA' single in 1987 with PHOEBE SNOW; 'DREAMS I DREAM. / FIGHTING FOR LOVE. In 1994, he joined FLEETWOOD MAC for the 1995 album 'TIME'.

– compilations, others, etc. –

1972. Island/ US= Blue Thumb; (d-lp) **SCRAPBOOK** – (all of his work 1967-1971)

1977. Blue Thumb; (lp)(c) **THE BEST OF DAVE MASON** -
(iss. in UK + US Apr75 as 'DAVE MASON AT HIS BEST' 1 song diff.)

Feb 82. Blue Thumb; (lp)(c) **THE VERY BEST OF DAVE MASON** — Nov79
– Only you know and I know / Pearly queen / Just a song / World in changes / Sad and deep as you / Shouldn't have took more than you gave / Can't stop worrying, can't stop loving / Headkeeper / Waitin' on you / Feelin' alright *(cd-iss.Jun88 on 'MCA')*

Jul 81. CBS/ US= Columbia; (lp)(c) **THE BEST OF DAVE MASON**

1988. CBS/ US= Columbia; (cd) **GREATEST HITS**

May 91. Elite; (cd)(c) **SHOW ME SOME AFFECTION** — -
(re-iss.Sep93)

Nick MASON (see under ⇒ PINK FLOYD)

MASSIVE ATTACK

Formed: Bristol, England . . . 1988 by 3-D, MUSHROOM and DADDY G. Founded own label 'Wild Bunch', which was snapped up by Virgin subsidiary 'Circa' late in 1990. Their second single 'UNFINISHED SYMPATHY' although suffering undignified name change (to MASSIVE) due to Gulf War. This was quickly followed up by what was quickly to become a classic album 'BLUE LINES', which made UK Top 20 lists. • **Style:** Classical dance /hip hop & dub reggae trio revered by music press and public alike. • **Songwriters:** Group except; BE THANKFUL FOR WHAT YOU'VE GOT (William DeVaughn) / LIGHT MY FIRE (Doors). Sampled JAMES BROWN, PIECES OF A DREAM, YOUNG HOLT TRIO. • **Trivia:** Remixed PETER GABRIEL, LES NEGRESSES VERTES.

Recommended: BLUE LINES (*10) / PROTECTION (*9) / NO PROTECTION (*8; MASSIVE ATTACK V MAD PROFESSOR)

3d (b. DEL NAJA) – vocals / **MUSHROOM** (b. A.VOWLES) – keyboards / **DADDY G.** (b. MARSHALL) – keyboards

Warners / Warners

Jul 88. (12") **ANY LOVE. / ('A'mix)**

—— w / **SHARA NELSON** – vocals / **NELLEE HOOPER** – programmer / arranger

Wild Bunch-Circa / Virgin

Nov 90. (7")(c-s) **DAYDREAMING. / ('A'instrumental)**
(12"+=)(cd-s+=) – Any love (2).
(12") – ('A'-luv it mix) / ('A'-Brixton bass mix) / ('A'-luv it dub).

Feb 91. (7")(c-s) **UNFINISHED SYMPATHY. / ('A'-Nellee Hooper mix)** 13
(12")(cd-s) – ('A'side) / ('A'-Paul Oakenfold mix) / ('A'-P.O. instrumental) / ('A'instrumental).

—— (above single as "MASSIVE") Below also featured **HORACE ANDY** – vox

Apr 91. (cd)(c)(2x12"lp) **BLUE LINES** 13
– Safe from harm / One love / Blue lines / Be thankful for what you've got / Five man army / Unfinished sympathy / Daydreaming / Lately / Hymn of the big wheel.

May 91. (7") **SAFE FROM HARM. / ('A'version)** 25
(cd-s+=) – ('A'-Perfecto mix).
(12") – ('A'-Perfecto mix) / ('A'dub mix) / ('A'instrumental).

Feb 92. (7"ep)(12"ep)(cd-ep) **MASSIVE ATTACK** 27
– Hymn of the big wheel / Home of the whale / Be thankful / Any love.

—— now w / **TRACEY THORN** (Everything But The Girl) **/ NICOLETTE / TRICKY + HORACE ANDY** – vocals. **CRAIG ARMSTRONG** – piano / **CHESTER KAMEN** – guitar / **ROB MERRIL** – drums

Sep 94. (cd)(c)(lp) **PROTECTION** 4
– Protection / Karmacoma / Three / Weather storm / Spying glass / Better things / Eurochild / Sly / Heat miser / Light my fire (live).

Oct 94. (c-ep)(cd-ep) **SLY / ('A'mix by UNDERDOG) / ('A'-Mad Professor mix) / ('A'-Tim Simenon mix)** 24
(12"ep+=)(cd-ep+=) – (extra 'A'mix).

Jan 95. (7") **PROTECTION. ("MASSIVE ATTACK with TRACEY THORN") / ('A'-J.Sw!ft mix)** 14
(cd-s+=) – ('A'-Radiation for the nation mix).
(c-s++=) – ('A'-Eno mix).
(12"+++=) – ('A'-Mad Professor mix).
(cd-s) – ('A'-Underdog dust mix) / Three (Don T's house of fortune mix).

Feb 95. (cd)(c)(lp) **NO PROTECTION** ("MASSIVE ATTACK v MAD PROFESSOR")
– Radiation ruling the nation (Protection) / Bumper ball dub (Karmacoma) / Trinity dub (Three) / Cool monsoon (Weather storm) / Eternal feedback ((Sly) / Moving dub (Better things) / I spy (Spying glass) / Backward sucking (Heat miser).

Mar 95. (12"ep) **KARMACOMA. / ('A'-Napoli trip mix) / ('A'-Unkle mix) / BLACKSMITH - DAYDREAMING** 28
(cd-ep+=) – ('A'-Portishead experience mix) / ('A'-Bumper ball mix).
(c-ep++=)(cd-ep++=) – ('A'-Portishead mix).

MATCHING HOLE (see under ⇒Robert Wyatt)

MATERIAL

Formed: New York, USA ... 1979 by BILL LASWELL, MICHAEL BEINHORN, FRED MAHER, CLIFF CULTRERI and DON DAVIS. All had been recently part of DAEVID ALLEN's (NEW YORK) GONG who issued one album 'About Time'. MATERIAL's debut outing 'TEMPORARY MUSIC 1' highlighted a stark contrast from late 70's rock. Each individual continued to moonlight, especially LASWELL who in the 80's was a much in demand session man and producer. When MATERIAL separated for the first time in '83, he also went solo starting with 'BASELINES' in '84. He had sidelined with GOLDEN PALOMINOS and LAST EXIT during the mid-80's. The former of these (which were mainly collaborations with ANTON FIER and ARTO LINDSAY), also included BEINHORN and future MATERIAL member NICKY SKOPELITIS. They released a number of albums; GOLDEN PALOMINOS (1984), VISIONS OF EXCESS (1985) / BLAST OF SILENCE (1987) / A DEAD HORSE (1989) / DRINK WITH PASSION (1991). LAST EXIT (aka LASWELL / SONNY SHARROCK / RONALD SHANNON JACKSON + PETER BROTZMANN) released several for German label 'Enemy', before moving to 'Venture' in 1988 with 'IRON PATH'. LASWELL's production work (often sessioned too) was virtually a who's who of 80's rock; HERBIE HANCOCK co-(Future Shock + Sound-System + Village Life + Perfect Machine) / NONA HENDRYX (Nona + The Art Of Defense) / LAURIE ANDERSON co-(Mister Heartbreak) / MICK JAGGER co-(She's The Boss) / LAST POETS (Oh My People) / SLY & ROBBIE (Language Barrier + Rhythm Killers) / YOKO ONO (Star Peace) / PUBLIC IMAGE LTD. co-(Album) / GINGER BAKER (Horses And Trees) / RYUICHI SAKAMOTO co-(Neo Geo) / IGGY POP (Instinct) / AFRIKA BAMBAATAA co-(The Light) / WHITE ZOMBIE (Make Them Die Slowly) / RAMONES co-(Brain Drain) / SWANS co-(Burning The World). Of course there were others such as other moonlights with MASSACRE in 1981, SHANGO in 1983 and CURLEW in 1983. He even had time to fit in a guest spot for DAVID BYRNE & BRIAN ENO's 'My Life In The Bush Of Ghosts'. • **Style:** Avant-garde dubstrumentals, willing to expand musical inspirations and directions to any field of rock and Afro-rock. • **Songwriters:** LASWELL and group except COSMIC FLOP (George Clinton) / MELLOW MOOD (Bob Marley). • **Trivia:** Produced by GIORGIO GOMELSKY on debut, then with MARTIN BISI in the early 80's. WHITNEY HOUSTON was guest vocalist on 1983 album 'ONE DOWN'.

Recommended: ONE DOWN (*7) / THE THIRD POWER (*8) / BASELINES (*7; BILL LASWELL)

BILL LASWELL – bass / **MICHAEL BEINHORN** – keyboards, synthesizers / **FRED MAHER** – drums (ex-RICHARD HELL) / **CLIFF CULTRERI** – guitar / **DON DAVIS** – alto sax

not issued — Red

1979. (12"ep) **TEMPORARY MUSIC 1**
– O.A.O. / On sadism / White man / Process motion.

— now without CULTRERI + DAVIS who were repl. by **RONNIE DRAYTON** – guitar

Fresh — Red

Aug 81. (m-lp) **TEMPORARY MUSIC TWO**
– Reduction / Heritage / Discourse / Slow murder / A.O.A. / White man / Secret life.

Ze-Island — Island

May 81. (7") **BUSTIN' OUT. ("MATERIAL & NONA HENDRYX") / OVER AND OVER**
(12"+=) – ('A'long version).

— added **FRED FRITH** – guitar, violin, vibes / **SONNY SHARROCK** – guitar / **HENRY THREADGILL** – alto sax / **GEORGE LEWIS** – trombone / **OLU DARA** – trumpet / **CHARLES K. NOYES** – drums, percussion / **BILLY BANG** – violin

Nov 81. (lp) **MEMORY SERVES**
– Memory serves / Disappearing / Upriver / Metal test / Conform to the rhythm / Unauthorized / Square dance / Silent land.

— now without MAHER who joined LOU REED

Red — Ze

Mar 82. (7")(12") **CIGURI. / DETATCHED**

— **LASWELL, BEINHORN, FRITH + DRAYTON + NICKY SKOPOLITES** – guitar / **DANIEL PONCE** – bongos / **YOGI HORTON + J.T.LEWIS** – drums / **NICKY MARRERO** – percussion

Sep 82. (7") **I'M THE ONE. /** [-]

Elektra — Elektra

Mar 83. (lp) **ONE DOWN**
– Take a chance / I'm the one / Time out / Let me have it all / Come down / Holding on / Memories / Don't lose control.

— Disbanded while all concentrated on solo and session work.

BILL LASWELL

with **MICHAEL BEINHORN** – synthesizers, tapes / **FRED FRITH** – guitar, violin / **MARTIN BISI** – drums, percussion / **RALPH CARNEY** – sax / **RONALD SHANNON JACKSON + PHILIP WILSON** – drums / **DAVID MOSS** – vocals, steel drums / etc.

Rough Trade — Recommended

May 84. (lp) **BASELINES**
– Activate / Work song / Hindsight / Uprising / Barricade / Upright man / Moving target / Lowlands / Conservations.

1984. (12") **WORK SONG. / ?**

— BILL then recorded in 1985 with JOHN ZORN + METLABLE SNAPS on 2 German albums 'Points Blank' & 'Metable Snaps'.

— now w / **SKOPELITIS / SHANKAR / PONCE + AIYB DIENG + ZAKIR HUSSAIN** – percussion

Venture — Venture

Mar 88. (lp)(c)(cd) **HEAR NO EVIL**
– Lost roads / Bullet hole memory / Illinois Central / Assassin / Stations of the cross / Kingdom come.

MATERIAL

re-formed with **LASWELL / SKOPELITIS / DIENG / SLY DUNBAR** – drums / **JEFF BOVA** – keyboards / **SHANKAR + SIMON SHAHEEN** – violin / + guest vocalists

Venture — Venture

Jul 89. (lp)(c)(cd) **SEVEN SOULS**
– Ineffect / Seven souls / Soul killer / The western lands / Deliver / Equation / The end of words.

— Producer & co-writer **BILL LASWELL** now with musicians **SLY DUNBAR** – drums, drum programing / **ROBBIE SHAKESPEARE** – bass / **JEFF BOVA** – synthesizers / **BERNIE WORRELL** – piano, organ / **NICKY SKOPELITIS** – guitar, fairlight / **JUNGLE BROTHERS** (BABY BAM + MIKE G.) + **JALALUDDIN MANSUR NURUDDIN** (of The Last Poets) + **SHABBA RANKS + GARY MUDBONE COOPER + JENNY PETERS** – vocals / **BOOTSY COLLINS + GARY SHIDER** – vocals, guitar / **HERBIE HANCOCK** – piano / **MICHAEL HAMPTON** – guitar / **HENRY THREADGILL** – flute / **AIYB DIENG** – percussion. Horn section: **FRED WESLEY, MACEO PARKER + PEE WEE ELLIS.** Brass section: **OLU DARA, JOE DALY, RICHARD HARPER, MARCUS ROJAS + JOEL BRANDON.** + a string section

Axiom — Axiom

Jul 91. (cd)(c)(lp) **THE THIRD POWER**
– Reality / Playin' with fire / Cosmic slop / E-pluribus-unum / Drive-by / Power of soul (black chant) / Mellow mood / Glory.

1991. (12")(cd-s) **REALITY. (w/ SHABBA RANKS) / ('A'mix)**
(re-iss.Aug93)

Jul 93. (12")(cd-s) **MANTRA. / ('A'mixes)**

— **SLY DUNBAR, BOOTSY COLLINS, BERNIE WORRELL, BILL LASWELL + WILLIAM BURROUGHS**

Feb 94. (cd)(lp) **HALLUCINATION ENGINE**
– Black light / Mantra / Ruins / Eternal drift / Words of advice / Cucumber slumber / Hidden garden: Naima.

BILL LASWELL

Stone Heights — ???

Jun 94. (d-cd) **DIVINATION – LIGHT IN EXTENSION**
– Divination / Seven Heavens / Errata / Delta / Tian Zhen / Agrippa / Godspeed / Ain soph sour / Najm-ai-din / Dead slow / Baraka / Silent fields / Evil eye / Dream light / Journeys / Last words of Hassan I Sabbath.

Axiom — Axiom

Aug 95. (d-cd)(d-c) **AXIOM FUNK – FUNKCRONIMICON**

— In Oct95, LASWELL was credited on MJ HARRIS cd 'SOMNIFIC FLUX' for 'Sentrax'.

– MATERIAL compilations –

Mar 85. Celluloid; (lp) **THE BEST OF BILL LASWELL** (MATERIAL + FRIENDS)

Jun 86. Jungle; (d-lp) **SECRET LIFE 1979-81** [-]
(re-iss.+cd Aug91)

Mar 94. D.I.W.; (cd) **LIVE FROM SOUNDSCAPE (live)** [-]

Ian MATTHEWS

Born: IAN MATTHEW McDONALD, '46, Lincolnshire, England. In 1966 he joined London-based outfit PYRAMID, who released 1 flop 45 for 'Deram'. Late 1967, MATTHEWS joined FAIRPORT CONVENTION, but after supplying dual vocals on two 1969 lp's 'WHAT WE DID ON OUR HOLIDAYS' & 'UNHALFBRICKING', he departed to form MATTHEWS SOUTHERN COMFORT. He signed to 'Uni' in 1969, and recorded eponymous lp, prior to 1970's UK No.1 smash 'WOODSTOCK' (written by JONI MITCHELL). In 1971, he signed a solo deal with 'Vertigo', but further success eluded him until 1978, when the single 'SHAKE IT' hit the US Top 20. He was then involved in a legal wrangle for over half a million dollars, from his US label 'Mushroom'. • **Style:** Folk & country-based singer. • **Songwriters:** Self-penned, except other covers; DA DOO RON RON (Crystals) / DO RIGHT WOMAN (Aretha Franklin) / BROWN EYED GIRL (Van Morrison) / TELL ME WHY (Neil Young) / GIVE ME AN INCH (Robert Palmer) / etc. • **Trivia:** MIKE NESMITH (ex-MONKEES and Solo artist) produced 73's 'VALLEY HI'.

Recommended: THE BEST OF MATTHEWS SOUTHERN COMFORT (*6).

PYRAMID

Deram — not issued

Jan 67. (7") **SUMMER OF LAST YEAR. / SUMMER EVENING** [-]

— After a period (Nov67-Jan69) in FAIRPORT CONVENTION, he formed

MATTHEWS SOUTHERN COMFORT

IAN MATTHEWS – vocals, guitar / **GORDON HUNTLEY** – pedal steel guitar / **CARL BARNWELL** – guitar, vocals / **MARK GRIFFITHS** – lead guitar / **ANDY LEIGH** – bass / **RAY DUFFY** – drums

Uni — Decca

Nov 69. (7") **COLORADO SPRINGS ETERNAL. / THE STRUGGLE** [-]

Jan 70. (lp) **MATTHEWS SOUTHERN COMFORT** [-]
– Colorado Springs eternal / A commercial proposition / The castle far / Please be

my friend / What we say / Dream song / Fly pigeon fly / The watch / Sweet bread / Thoughts for a friend / I've lost you / Once upon a lifetime. *(re-iss.+c.1974 on 'MCA')*

May 70. (7") **THE BALLAD OF OBRAY RAMSAY. / PARTING** [-] [-]
Jul 90. (7") **COLORADO SPRINGS ETERNAL. / THE WATCH** [-] [ ]
Jul 70. (lp) **SECOND SPRING** [52] [ ]
– Ballad of Obray Ramsay / Moses in the sunshine / Jinkson Johnson / Tale of the trail / Blood red roses / Even as / D'Arch Farrow / Something in the way she moves / Southern comfort. *(re-iss.+c.1974 on 'MCA')*
Sep 70. (7") **WOODSTOCK. / SCION** [1] [-]
M.C.A. Decca
Dec 70. (lp) **LATER THAT SAME YEAR** [ ] [72]
– To love / And me / Tell me why / Jonah / My lady / And when she smiles (she makes the sun shine) / Mare, take me home / Sylvie / The brand new Tennessee waltz / For Melanie / Road to Ronderlin. *(re-iss.+c.1974)*
Mar 71. (7") **WOODSTOCK. / THE BALLAD OF OBRAY RAMSAY** [-] [22]
Jul 71. (7") **MARE, TAKE ME HOME. / BRAND NEW TENNESSEE WALTZ** [-] [96]
Oct 71. (7") **TELL ME WHY. / TO LOVE** [-] [98]

IAN MATTHEWS

went solo from SOUTHERN COMFORT. They released 3 more albums 1971-1972 on Harvest, Columbia; 'FROG CITY', 'SOUTHERN COMFORT' & 'STIR DON'T SHAKE'. MATTHEWS brought in session people **ANDY ROBERTS** – guitar / **TIM RENWICK** – guitar / **GERRY CONWAY** – drums / etc.

Vertigo Vertigo
Jan 71. (lp) **IF YOU SAW THRO' MY EYES** [ ] [ ]
– Desert Inn / Hearts / Never ending / Reno, Nevada / Litle known / Hinge / Southern wind / It came without warning / You couldn't lose / Morgan the pirate / If you saw thro' my eyes. *(cd-iss w/next lp; iss. Mar 93)*
Jan 71. (7") **HEARTS. / IF YOU SAW THRO' MY EYES** [ ] [ ]
May 71. (7") **DESERT INN. / RENO, NEVADA** [-] [ ]
Jan 72. (7") **DA DOO RON RON (WHEN HE WALKED ME HOME). / NEVER AGAIN** [-] [96]
Feb 72. (lp) **TIGERS WILL SURVIVE** [ ] [ ]
– Never again / Close the door lightly when you go / House unamerican blues activity dream / Morning song / The only dancer / Tigers will survive / Midnight on the water / Right before my eyes / Da doo ron ron (when he walked me home) / Hope you know / Please be my friend.
Mar 72. (7") **DA DOO RON RON (WHEN HE WALKED ME HOME). / HOUSE OF UNAMERICAN BLUES** [-] [ ]
Mar 72. (7") **DEVIL IN DISGUISE. / IF YOU SAW THRO' MY EYES** [ ] [-]
Jun 72. (7") **TIGERS WILL SURVIVE. / HOPE YOU KNOW** [-] [ ]

— Recorded solo lp 'JOURNEY FROM GOSPEL OAK', which was later issued Aug74 on 'Mooncrest' (re-issued Dec79 on 'Boulevard', re-iss.+cd.Mar91). A single from this period was also issued Jun74 'MET HER ON A PLANE'. / 'KNOWING THE GAME'. Also on 'Mooncrest' label was Mar77 single 'BRIDE 1945'. / 'SING ME BACK HOME'.

PLAINSONG

MATTHEWS with **ROB RONGA** – bass, vocals / **ANDY ROBERTS** – guitar, vocals / **DAVE RICHARDS** – keyboards, vocals

Elektra Elektra
Sep 72. (lp) **IN SEARCH OF AMELIA EARHART** [ ] [ ]
– For the second time / Yo yo man / Louise / Call the tune / Diesel on my tail / Amelia Earhart's last flight / I'll fly away / True story of Amelia Earhart / Ever the guiding light / Side roads / Raider.
Nov 72. (7") **YO YO MAN. /** [-] [ ]

— They disbanded after recording shelved lp 'PLAINSONG II'. ANDY ROBERTS went solo and issued a few lp's.

IAN MATTHEWS

(solo again, having moved to California, USA)(same label) with **TOM MOONEY** – drums (ex-NAZZ) / **MICHAEL CURTIS** – guitar / **RICK CURTIS** – guitar (both ex-CRAZY HORSE)

Elektra Elektra
Sep 73. (lp) **VALLEY HI** [ ] [ ]
– Keep on sailing / Old man at the mill / Shady lies / These days / Leaving alone / 7 Bridges Road / Save your sorrows / What are you waiting for / Propinquity / Blue blue day.
Oct 73. (7") **THESE DAYS. / SAME OLD MAN** [-] [ ]
Jan 74. (7") **7 BRIDGES ROAD. / YOU FELL THROUGH MY MIND** [-] [ ]

— toured the States as IAN MATTHEWS & ANOTHER FINE MESS with **TOMMY NUNES** – guitar / **BILLY GRAHAM** – bass / **JOHN WARE** – drums / **JOEL TEPP** – harmonica

Jun 74. (lp) **SOME DAYS YOU EAT THE BEAR, SOME DAYS THE BEAR EATS YOU** [ ] [ ]
– I don't want to talk abouit it / A wailing goodbye / Keep on sailing / Tried so hard / The poor ditching boy / Do I still figure in your life / Home / Biloxi / The fault.
Jun 74. (7") **DIRTY WORK. / WAILING GOODBYE** [ ] [ ]
Jan 76. (7") **I DON'T WANT TO TALK ABOUT IT. / KEEP ON SAILING** [ ] [ ]

— now with **DON WHALEY** – bass, vocals / **TRIS IMBODEN** – drums / **JAY LACY** – guitar / **DAVID BRIGGS + STEVE WOOD** – keyboards

C.B.S. Columbia
May 76. (7") **BROWN-EYED GIRL. / STEAM BOAT** [ ] [ ]
May 76. (lp)(c) **GO FOR BROKE** [ ] [ ]
– Darkness, darkness / I'll be gone / Brown-eyed girl / Rhythm of the west / Groovin' / Lonely hunter / Steam boat / A fool like you / Just one look / When the morning comes.
Aug 76. (7") **A FOOL LIKE YOU. / I'LL BE GONE** [ ] [ ]

— **CHARLIE HARWOOD** – keyboards, vocals repl. BRIGGS + WOOD / **STEVEN HOOKS** – sax repl. loads of sessioners

May 77. (lp)(c) **HIT AND RUN** [ ] [ ]
– The frame / One day without you / Times / I will not fade away / Tigers will survive / Just one look / Help to guide me (I need your help) / Shuffle / Hit and run.

— now w / new band **PHIL PALMER + BRYN HAWORTH** – guitar / **PETE WINGFIELD** – keyboards / **RICK KEMP** – bass / **JIM RUSSELL** – drums

Rockburgh Mushroom
Oct 78. (7") **MAN IN THE STATION. / SLIP AWAY** [ ] [ ]
Dec 78. (lp)(c) **STEALIN' HOME** [ ] [80] Aug 78
– Gimme an inch girl / Don't hang up your dancing shoes / King of the night / Man in the station / Let there be blues / Carefully taught / Stealin' home / Shake it / Yank and Mary / Slip away / Sail my soul.
Nov 78. (7") **SHAKE IT. / STEALIN' HOME** [-] [13]
Dec 78. (7") **KING OF THE NIGHT. / LET THERE BE BLUES** [ ] [-]
Feb 79. (7") **SHAKE IT. / SAIL MY SOUL** [ ] [-]
Mar 79. (7") **GIMME AN INCH GIRL. / STEALIN' HOME** [ ] [-]
Mar 79. (7") **GIMME AN INCH GIRL. / LET THERE BE BLUES** [-] [67]
May 79. (7") **SLIP AWAY. / DON'T HANG UP YOUR DANCING SHOES** [-] [ ]

— retained **RUSSELL** and recruited **MARK GRIFFITHS** – bass, guitar, vocals / **ROB METZGER** – guitar / **MICK WEAVER** – keyboards / **CRAIG BUHLER** – sax

Sep 79. (lp)(c) **SIAMESE FRIENDS** [ ] [ ]
– You don't see me / Survival / Heatwave / Home somewhere / Crying in the night / The baby she's on the street / Hearts on the line / Anna / Lies / Runaway.
Nov 79. (7") **HEATWAVE. / YOU DON'T SEE ME** [ ] [-]
Jan 80. (7") **CRYING IN THE NIGHT. / LIVE** [ ] [-]
Jan 80. (7") **ANNA. / YOU DON'T SEE ME** [-] [ ]

— **WYNDER K. FROG** – keyboards / **DAVE WINTOUR** – bass / **BOB HENRIT** – drums repl. WEAVER, BUHLER + RUSSELL

Rockburgh R.S.O.
Jun 80. (lp)(c) **SPOT OF INTERFERENCE** [ ] [ ]
– I survived the 70's / She may call you up tonight / I can't fade away / The hurt / Driftwood from disaster / Why am I? / No time at all / For the lonely hunter / See me / Civilisation / What do I do?. *(re-iss.Jun86 on 'Sundown')*
Jun 80. (7") **SHE MAY CALL YOU UP TONIGHT. / SEE ME** [ ] [ ]

— **MATTHEWS** moved to Seattle, Washington, and teamed up with **DAVID SURKAMP** (ex-PAVLOV'S DOG) to form

HI-FI

with **BRUCE HAZEN** – guitar / **GARY SHELTON** – bass, vocals / **BOB BAILEY** – drums

Apr 82. Butt; (12"ep) **DEMONSTRATION RECORD** [ ] [-]
– Savage / Heart of mine / I can't fade away / 9 o' clock / Man in a station
Jul 83. Shanghai; (lp) **MOODS FOR MALLARDS** [ ] [ ]
– Walk away / Blue shirt / Holding out for rain / Throw a line / Knocking on your door / Desire / Time after time / Alcohol / When you were mine. *(UK-iss.Aug86)*

IAN MATTHEWS

WYNDER K.FROG – keyboards / **DAVE WINTOUR** – bass / **BOB HENRIT** – drums repl. WEAVER, BUHLER + RUSSELL

1983. (lp) **SHOOK** [-] [ ]
– Shorting out / Views (dance goes on) / Wild places / Indiscreet / Wish / Driver / Tomorrow falls on Saturday / Fear strikes out / Over under sideways down / Room service. *(cd-iss.1989 on 'Line')*

In 1986, he briefly re-united with FAIRPORT CONVENTION for some gigs.

— new band:- **MARK HALLMAN** – guitar, vocals / **VAN DYKE PARKS** – piano / **PATRICK O'HEARN** – guitar, synth / **RAY NEOPOLITAN** – bass / **ELIZA GILKYSON** – vocals

Windham H. Windham H.
Apr 88. (lp)(c)(cd) **WALKING A CHANGING LINE** [ ] [ ]
– Dream sequence / Standing still / Except for a tear / Following every finger / Alive alone / On squirrel hill / Shadows break / This fabrication / Lovers by rote / Only a motion / Why fight.

IAIN MATTHEWS

GoldCastle GoldCastle
1990. (cd)(c)(lp) **PURE AND CROOKED** [ ] [ ]
– Like dominoes / Mercy Street / A hardly innocent mind / New shirt / Bridge of Cherokee / Busby's babes / Rains of '62 / Say no more / Perfect timing / Out of my range / This town's no lady. *(cd-iss Jan95 on 'Watermelon')*
1991. (cd) **NIGHTS IN MANHATTAN - LIVE (live)** [-] [ ]
1992. (cd) **ORPHANS AND OUTCASTS VOLUME 1** [-] [ ]
Water-melon GoldCastle
Sep 94. (cd) **THE DARK RIDE** [ ] [ ]
– I drove / Girl with the clouds in her eyes / Ballad of Gruene Hall / Tigers will survive (part II) / The breath of life / Save her love / For better or worse / Davey's stung / Morning glory / In London / This is it / Rooted to the spot.

– compilations, others, etc. –

Oct 75. M.C.A.; (lp)(c) **THE BEST OF MATTHEWS SOUTHERN COMFORT** [ ] [ ]
(re-iss.Feb82)
Aug 89. M.C.A.; (7") **WOODSTOCK. / ?** [ ] [ ]
(12"+=)(cd-s+=) – ?
Mar 80. Rockburgh/ US= Mushroom; (d-lp) **DISCREET REPEAT** [ ] [ ]
(re-iss Jan89 on 'Temple')
Mar 80. (7"m) **DA DOO RON RON (WHEN HE WALKED ME HOME). / SHAKE IT / GIMME AN INCH GIRL** [ ] [ ]
Jul 82. Old Gold; (7") **WOODSTOCK. / ('b' by 'Three Dog Bight')** [ ] [-]
(re-iss Jul88)
Mar 87. See For Miles; (d-lp)(c) **MATTHEWS SOUTHERN COMFORT MEET SOUTHERN COMFORT** [ ] [-]

Nov 93. Elektra; (cd) **THE SOUL OF MANY PLACES** [ ] [ ]
May 94. Band Of Joy; (cd) **SCION (MATTHEWS SOUTHERN COMFORT)** [ ] [-]

PLAINSONG

re-formed by **MATTHEWS + ANDY ROBERTS** for 1992 Cambridge Folk Festival

German / not issued

1993. (cd) **DARK SIDE OF THE ROOM** [ ] [-]

below is a compilation from PLAINSONG

1995. Band Of Joy; (cd) **CERTIFIED UNRELEASED / BBC SESSIONS 1972** [ ] [-]

MAX Q (see under ⇒ INXS)

Brian MAY (see under ⇒ QUEEN)

Phil MAY & The FALLEN ANGELS (see under ⇒ PRETTY THINGS)

John MAYALL

Born: 29 Nov'33, Macclesfield, Cheshire, England. Early in 1963 after forming Manchester based outfit The BLUES SYNDICATE, he moved to London on the suggestion of ALEXIS KORNER. There he founded The BLUESBREAKERS, with ever-changing personnel including stalwart JOHN McVIE. They signed to 'Decca' Spring '64, and released 1 single 'CRAWLING UP A HILL', before MAYALL recruited HUGHIE FLINT and ROGER DEAN to replace MARTIN HART and BERNIE WATSON. This quartet lasted a year and issued (live at Klook's Kleek) debut lp 'JOHN MAYALL PLAYS JOHN MAYALL', and a single. In Apr'65, they substituted DEAN, with ex-YARDBIRDS guitar hero ERIC CLAPTON, and issued 2 more 45's. After some of group (CLAPTON and McVIE) took a vacation, they were back late '65, doing one-nighters and to record in the Spring of '66 the legendary 'BLUESBREAKERS' lp. Released in July and crediting JOHN MAYALL WITH ERIC CLAPTON, it soon raced into UK Top 10. At the same time CLAPTON quit to form CREAM, and was replaced by PETER GREEN. In Sep' 66, AYNSLEY DUNBAR moved in, after FLINT was ousted. This new line-up also hit Top 10 with lp 'A HARD ROAD' early '67, before drummer MICK FLEETWOOD joined. When all 3 of his band (FLEETWOOD, McVIE & GREEN) got together as FLEETWOOD MAC in Sep'67, MAYALL recruited entire new line-up on yet another Top 10 lp 'CRUSADE'. MAYALL continued to change personnel, although it didn't affect album chart appearances until late 1971's 'MEMORIES'. In his ranks between 1967-1971, were future stars KEEF HARTLEY (solo), MICK TAYLOR (Rolling Stones), CHRIS MERCER (Juicy Lucy), ANDY FRASER (Free) / DICK HECKSTALL-SMITH, TONY REEVES & JON HISEMAN (Colosseum), COLIN ALLEN & STEVE THOMPSON (Stone The Crows). • **Style:** Raw blues bandleader who developed with time into jazz & roots blues outfit. • **Songwriters:** Self-penned alongside covers; MY BABY IS SWEETER (Willie Dixon) / DOUBLE TROUBLE (Otis Rush) / ALL YOUR LOVE (Dixon-Rush) / BERNARD JENKINS (Eric Clapton) / + DOUBLE CROSS (w/ Clapton) / DUST MY BLUES (Elmore James) / THE SUPERNATURAL (Peter Green) / SO MANY ROADS (. . . Paul) / LOOKING BACK (Johnny Guitar Watson) / ALL MY LIFE (. . . Robinson) / RIPIN' ON THE L & N (Barley Hampton) / IT HURTS ME TOO (. . . London) / OH, PRETTY WOMAN (Big Joe Williams) / MAN OF STONE (. . . Kirkland) / NIGHT TRAIN (?) / LUCILLE (Little Richard) / PARCHMAN FARM (Jerry Allison) / STEPPIN' OUT (. . . Bracken) / etc. • **Trivia:** Another great young guitarist WALTER TROUT became member in 1984, and subsequently departed for his own solo career in the late 80's.

Recommended: THE COLLECTION (*7) / BLUESBREAKERS (*8).

BLUESBREAKERS

JOHN MAYALL – vocals, keyboards, harmonica, guitar(ex-BLUES SYNDICATE) / **BERNIE WATSON** – guitar repl. JOHN GILBEY who had repl. SAMMY PROSSER / **JOHN McVIE** – bass repl. PETE BURFORD who had repl. RICKY BROWN / **MARTIN HART** – drums repl. PETER WARD who had repl. KEITH ROBERTSON (note previous drummers early 1963 =BRIAN MYALL after SAM STONE.)

JOHN MAYALL'S BLUESBREAKERS

Decca / not issued

Apr 64. (7") **CRAWLING UP A HILL. / MR.JAMES** [ ] [-]

— MAYALL retained only McVIE, and recruited **ROGER DEAN** – guitar replaced WATSON **HUGHIE FLINT** – drums (ex-BLUES SYNDICATE) repl. HART

Feb 65. (7") **CROCODILE WALK. / BLUES CITY SHAKEDOWN** [ ] [-]
Mar 65. (lp) **JOHN MAYALL PLAYS JOHN MAYALL (live at Klook's Kleek)** [ ] [-]
– Crawling up a hill / I wanna teach you everything / When I'm gone / I need your love / The hoot owl / R&B time; Night train – Lucille / Crocodile walk / What's the matter with you / Doreen / Runaway / Heartache / Chicago line. *(cd-iss. Jun 88 on 'London')*

— **ERIC CLAPTON** – guitar, vocals (ex-YARDBIRDS) repl. DEAN

Immediate / Immediate

Oct 65. (7") **I'M YOUR WITCHDOCTOR. / TELEPHONE BLUES** [ ] [ ]

— (a month earlier CLAPTON departed to join The GONADS.) (he was repl. by ?) **JACK BRUCE** – bass (ex-GRAHAM BOND ORGANISATION) repl. McVIE

— MAYALL's band were now FLINT, McVIE and CLAPTON again. (BRUCE joined MANFRED MANN)

Decca / London

Jul 66. (lp) **BLUESBREAKERS (as "JOHN MAYALL WITH ERIC CLAPTON")** [6] [ ]
– All your love / Hideaway / Little girl / Another man / Double crossin' time / What'd I say / Key to love / Parchman farm / Have you heard / Ramblin' on my mind; (a) Steppin' out – (b) It ain't right. *(re-iss.1983) (cd-iss.Feb89)*

Sep 66. (7") **KEY TO LOVE. / PARCHMAN FARM** [ ] [ ]
Nov 66. (7") **ALL YOUR LOVE. / HIDEAWAY** [-] [ ]

— (Jul66) **PETER GREEN** – guitar(on above b-side) repl. CLAPTON who formed CREAM

— (Sep66) **AYNSLEY DUNBAR** – drums (ex-MOJOS) repl. FLINT who later formed McGUINNESS FLINT

Oct 66. (7") **LOOKING BACK. / SO MANY ROADS** [ ] [-]
Oct 66. (7") **SITTING IN THE RAIN. / OUT OF REACH** [ ] [ ]
Feb 67. (lp) **A HARD ROAD** [10] [ ]
– A hard road / It's over / You don't love me / The stumble / Another kinda love / Hit the highway / Leaping Christine / Dust my blues / There's always work / The same way / The super natural / Top of the hill / Someday after a while (you'll be sorry) / Living alone.

Mar 67. (7") **CURLY. / RUBBER DUCK** [ ] [ ]
(above credited to **"The BLUESBREAKERS"**)

— next ep was a collaboration with PAUL B of BUTTERFIELD BLUES BAND.

Apr 67. (7"ep) **JOHN MAYALL'S BLUESBREAKERS WITH PAUL BUTTERFIELD** [ ] [ ]

— **MICK FLEETWOOD** – drums repl. MICKEY WALLER who had repl. DUNBAR (to JEFF BECK GROUP) (others still in band MAYALL, GREEN and McVIE.)

Apr 67. (7") **DOUBLE TROUBLE. / IT HURTS ME TOO** [ ] [ ]

— added **TERRY EDMONDS** – rhythm guitar(for Jun67 only before he joined FERRIS WHEEL) / **MICK TAYLOR** – guitar, vocals (ex-GODS) repl. PETER who formed FLEETWOOD MAC / **KEEF HARTLEY** – drums (ex-ARTWOODS) repl. MICK who formed FLEETWOOD MAC / added **CHRIS MERCER** and **RIP KANT** – saxophones

Sep 67. (lp) **CRUSADE** [8] [ ]
– Oh pretty woman / Stand back baby / My time after a while / Snowy wood / Man of stone / Tears in my eyes / Driving sideways / The death of J.B. Lenoir / I can't quit you baby / Streamline / Me and my woman / Checkin' up on my baby.

— **MAYALL** retained **TAYLOR, HARTLEY** and **MERCER,** bringing in **PAUL WILLIAMS** – bass (ex-ZOOT MONEY) repl. McVIE who also joined FLEETWOOD MAC / **DICK HECKSTALL-SMITH** – saxophone (ex-GRAHAM BOND) repl. KANT / added **HENRY LOWTHER** – trumpet

Sep 67. (7") **SUSPICIONS (part 1). / SUSPICIONS (part 2)** [ ] [-]
Sep 67. (7") **SUSPICIONS. / OH PRETTY WOMAN** [-] [ ]

— **KEITH TILLMAN** – bass repl. WILLIAMS

Dec 67. (7") **JENNY. / PICTURES ON THE WALL** [ ] [ ]
Jan 68. (lp) **DIARY OF A BAND** (live interviews & chat) [27] [ ] Feb 70
– Blood on the night / (chat; Edmonton cooks Ferry Inn) / I can't quit you baby / (Keef Hartley interview x2) / Anzio Annie / (John Mayall interview x2) / Snowy wood / The lesson / My own fault / God save the queen.

Jan 68. (lp) **DIARY OF A BAND (Volume 2)** (live interviews & chat) [28] [ ] May 71
– (Gimme some lovin') / The train / Crying shame / (chat); local boy makes good / Help me / Blues in Bb / Soul of a short fat man. *(US title 'JOHN MAYALL LIVE IN EUROPE')*

Feb 68. (7") **BROKEN WINGS. / SONNY BOY BLUE** [-] [ ]

— **TONY REEVES** – bass repl. ANDY FRASER (to FREE) who had repl. TILLMAN / **JON HISEMAN** – drums (ex-GRAHAM BOND, ex-GEORGIE FAME) repl. HARTLEY (to solo)

Jun 68. (lp) **BARE WIRES (JOHN MAYALL'S BLUESBREAKERS)** [3] [59]
– Where did I belong / I start walking / Open up a new door / Fire / I know now / Look in the mirror / I'm a stranger / Hartley quits / No reply / Killing time / She's too young / Sandy. *(cd-iss. Jun 88 on 'London')*

Jun 68. (7") **NO REPLY. / SHE'S TOO YOUNG** [ ] [ ]

— **MAYALL** only retained **MICK TAYLOR / COLIN ALLEN** – drums (ex-ZOOT MONEY) repl. HISEMAN who formed COLOSSEUM / **STEVE THOMPSON** – bass repl. REEVES. (he & HECKSTALL-SMITH also formed above) (also note MERCER left going into sessions and LOWTHER joined KEEF HARLEY BAND)

Nov 68. (7") **THE BEAR. / 2401** [ ] [ ]
Dec 68. (lp) **BLUES FROM LAUREL CANYON** [33] [68]
– Vacation / Walking on sunset / Laurel Canyon home / 2401 / Ready to ride / Medicine man / Somebody's acting like a child / The bear / Miss James / First time alone / Long gone midnight / Fly tomorrow. *(cd-iss.Dec89)*

Dec 68. (7") **WALKING ON SUNSET. / LIVING ALONE** [-] [ ]

JOHN MAYALL

(his new band played without a drummer) **DUSTER BENNETT** – guitar, vocals repl. TAYLOR who joined ROLLING STONES / **JON MARK** – guitar / **JOHNNY ALMOND** – saxophone repl. ALLEN who joined STONE THE CROWS / (after below lp **ALEX DMOCHOWSKI** – bass repl. THOMPSON who joined STONE THE CROWS)

Polydor / Polydor

Oct 69. (lp) **THE TURNING POINT (live 1969)** [11] [32] Sep 69
– The laws must change / Saw mill Gulch road / I'm gonna fight for you J.B. / So hard to share / California / Thoughts about Roxanne / California / Room to move. *(re-iss.May82) (cd-iss.1992 on 'BGO')*

Oct 69. (7") **DON'T WASTE MY TIME. / DON'T PICK A FLOWER** [ ] [81]
Jan 70. (7") **ROOM TO MOVE. / SAW MILL GULCH ROAD** [-] [ ]

— **LARRY TAYLOR** – bass deputised for the ill THOMPSON. (DMOCHOWSKI tour)

Mar 70. (lp) **EMPTY ROOMS** [9] [33]

– Don't waste my time / Plan your revolution / Don't pick a flower / Something new / People cling together / Waiting for the right time / Thinking of my woman / Counting the days / When I go / Many miles apart / To a princess / Lying in my bed. *(re-iss.Aug74)*

May 70. (7") **THINKING OF MY WOMAN. / PLAN YOUR REVOLUTION** [ ] [-]

— MAYALL's completely new band of US musicians **HARVEY MANDEL** – guitar (ex-CANNED HEAT) repl. MARK who formed MARK-ALMOND / **DON 'SUGURCANE' HARRIS** – vocals (ex-FRANK ZAPPA) repl. ALMOND (as above) / **LARRY TAYLOR** – bass finally repl. DMOCHOWSKI

Dec 70. (lp)(c) **U.S.A. UNION** [50] [22] Oct 70
– Nature's disappearing / You must be crazy / Night flyer / Off the road / Possessive emotions / Where did my legs go / Took the car / Crying / My pretty girl / Deep blue sea.

Jan 71. (7") **NATURE'S DISAPPEARING. / MY PRETTY GIRL** [-] [ ]

— Next reunified MAYALL with nearly all old BLUESBREAKERS + new US musicians

Jun 71. (d-lp) **BACK TO THE ROOTS** [31] [52] Apr 71
– Prisons on the road / My children / Accidental suicide / Groupie girl / Blue fox / Home again / Television eye / Marriage madness / Looking at tomorrow / Dream with me / Full speed ahead / Mr. Censor man / Force of nature / Boogie Albert / Goodbye December / Unanswered questions / Devil's tricks / Travelling.

— MAYALL retained only LARRY TAYLOR and recruited **JERRY McGEE** – guitar (ex-VENTURES) to replace MANDEL (who formed own band) and HARRIS

Nov 71. (lp)(c) **MEMORIES** [ ] [ ]
– Memories / Wish I knew a woman / Back from Korea / Home in a tree / Seperate ways / The fighting line / Grandad / The city / Nobody cares / Play the harp.

Feb 72. (7") **NOBODY CARES. / PLAY THE HARP** [-] [ ]

— **MAYALL** and **TAYLOR** brought in a drummer! – **RON SELICO / plus FREDDY ROBINSON** – guitar to repl. McGEE / added **BLUE MITCHELL** – trumpet / **CLIFFORD SOLOMON** – saxophone

May 72. (lp)(c) **JAZZ BLUES FUSION (live)** [ ] [64]
– Country road / Mess around / Good time boogie / Change your ways / Dry throat / Exercise in c-major for harmonica, bass and shufflers / Got to be this way. *(re-iss.1974)*

— **VICTOR GASKIN** – bass repl. LARRY / **KEEF HARTLEY** – drums returned to repl. RON

— added on next **CHARLES OWEN** – flute / **FRED JACKSON + ERNIE WATTS** – saxophones

Jan 73. (lp)(c) **MOVING ON** [ ] [ ] Oct 72
– (a brief introduction by Bill Cosby) / Worried mind / Keep our country green / Christmas 71 / Things go wrong / Do it / Moving on / Red sky / Reasons / High pressure living.

Jan 73. (7") **MOVING ON. / KEEP OUR COUNTRY GREEN** [-] [ ]

Nov 73. (d-lp) **TEN YEARS ARE GONE** [ ] [ ] Nov 73
– Ten years are gone / Driving till the break of day / Drifting / Better pass you by / California campground / Undecided / Good looking stranger / I still care / Don't hang me up / (introduction) / Sitting here thinking / Harmonica free form / Burning Sun / Dark of the night.

Nov 74. (7") **GASOLINE BLUES. / BRAND NEW BAND** [-] [ ]

Dec 74. (lp)(c) **THE LATEST EDITION** [ ] [ ]
– Gasoline blues / Perfect peace / Going to take my time / Deep down feelings / Troubled times / The pusher man / One of the few / Love song / Little kitchen / A crazy game.

Feb 75. (7") **LET ME GIVE. / PASSING THROUGH** [-] [ ]

— MAYALL brought back **LARRY TAYLOR** and **SUGERCANE HARRIS** plus new members **DEE McKINNIE** – vocals / **RICK VITO** – guitar / **JAY SPELL** – keyboards / **SOKO / RICHARDSON** – drums

A.B.C. / Blue Thumb

Mar 75. (lp)(c) **NEW YEAR, NEW BAND, NEW COMPANY** [ ] [ ]
– Sitting on the outside / Can't get home / Step in the sun / To match the wind / Sweet Scorpio / Driving on / Taxman blues / So much to do / My train time / Respectively yours.

Apr 75. (7") **STEP IN THE SUN. / AL GOLDSTEIN BLUES** [-] [ ]

— **MAYALL** now totally solo.

Nov 75. (lp)(c) **TIME EXPIRED, NOTICE TO APPEAR** [ ] [ ]
– Lil boogie in the afternoon / Mess of love / That love / The boy most likely to succeed / Who's next who's now / Hail to the man who lives alone / There will be a way / Just knowing you is a pleasure / A hard day's night / Oldtime blues.

— His following albums feature session musicians.

Apr 76. (lp)(c) **A BANQUET OF BLUES** [ ] [ ]
– Sunshine / You can't put me down / I got somebody / Turn me loose / Seven days too long / Table top girl / Lady / Fantasyland.

Apr 77. (lp)(c) **LOTS OF PEOPLE** (live) [ ] [ ]
– (spoken introduction by Red Holloway) / Changes in the wind / Burning down / Play the harp / A helping hand / I got to get down with you / He's a travelling man / Seperate ways / Room to move.

— now with **JAMES QUILL SMITH** – vocals, guitar / **STEVE THOMPSON** – bass / **SOKO RICHARDSON** – drums / and a brass section

Feb 78. (lp)(c) **A HARD CORE PACKAGE** [-] [ ]
– Rock and roll hobo / Do I please you / Disconnected line / An old sweet picture / The last time / Make up your mind / Arizona bound / Now and then / Goodnight dreams / Give me a chance.

— now with loads of session people.

D.J.M. / D.J.M.

May 79. (lp)(c) **BOTTOM LINE** [ ] [ ]
– Bottom line / Dreamboat / Desert flower / I'm gonna do it / Revival / Game of love / Celebration / Come with me.

Jul 79. (7") **BOTTOM LINE. / DREAMBOAT** [ ] [ ]

Dec 79. (lp)(c) **NO MORE INTERVIEWS** [ ] [ ]
– Hard going up / A bigger slice of pie / Falling / Take me home tonight / Sweet honey bee / Stars in the night / Consideration / Gypsy lady / Wild new lover.

— now with **SMITH, RICHARDSON + KEVIN McCORMICK** – bass / **MAGGIE PARKER** – vox

May 81. (lp)(c) **ROAD SHOW BLUES** [ ] [ ]
– Why worry / Road show / Mama talk to your daughter / A big man / Lost and gone / Mexico City / John Lee boogie / Reaching for a mountain / Baby what you want me to do. *(re-iss.+cd Jun88 on 'Thunderbolt')*

Jun 81. (7") **JOHN LEE BOOGIE. / WHY WORRY. / MAMA TALK TO YOUR DAUGHTER** [ ] [ ]

— **MAYALL'S** new line-up featured **COCO MONTAYA + WALTER TROUT** – guitar / **BOBY HAYES** – bass / **JOE YUELE** – drums

P.R.T. / GNP Cres..

May 86. (lp)(c) **BEHIND THE IRON CURTAIN** (rec.1984) [ ] [ ] 1985
– Somebody's acting like a child / Rolling with the blues / The laws must change / Parchman farm / Have you heard / Fly tomorrow / Steppin' out. *(cd-iss.Dec95 on 'GNP Crescendo')*

— After couple of years out of the studio he returned Spring '87. with famous guests **MICK TAYLOR, JOHN McVIE,** etc.

Charly / Entente

Dec 88. (lp)(c) **CHICAGO LINE** [ ] [ ]
– Chicago line / Gimme one more day / One life to live / The last time / Dream about the blues / Fascination lover / Cold blooded woman / The dirty dozen / Tears came rollin' down / Life in the jungle.

Island / Island

Jun 90. (lp)(c)(cd) **A SENSE OF PLACE** [ ] [ ]
– I want to go / Congo square / Send me down to Vicksburg / Without her / Sensitive kind / Jacksboro highway / Let's work together / I can't complain / Black cat moon / Sugarcane / All my life. *(re-iss.cd Mar93)*
(above contained a number of covers)

Silvertone / Silvertone

Apr 93. (cd)(c)(lp) **WAKE UP CALL** [61] [ ]
– Mail order mystics / Maydell / I could cry / Wake up call / Loaded dice / Undercover agent for the blues / Light the fuse / Anything I can see / Nature's disappearing / I'm a sucker for love / Not at home / Ain't that lovin' you baby.

– compilations, exploitation, etc. –

Aug 66. Purdah; (7") **LONELY HEARTS. / BERNARD JENKINS** [ ] [-]
Jun 67. Ace Of Hearts; (lp) **RAW BLUES** [ ] [-]
Nov 67. Ace Of Clubs; (lp) **THE BLUES ALONE** (nearly all instruments himself) [24] [-]
– Brand new start / Please don't tell / Down the line / Sonny Boy blow / Marsha's mood / No more tears / Catch that train / Cancelling out / Harp man / Brown sugar / Broken wings / Don't kick me. *(cd-iss. Jun 88 on 'London')*
Aug 69. Decca/ US= London; (lp) **LOOKING BACK** [14] [79]
– Mr.James / Blues city shakedown / They call it stormy Monday / So many roads / Looking back / Sitting in the rain / It hurts me too / Double trouble / Suspicions (part 2) / Jenny / Picture on the wall. *(cd-iss. Jan 89 on 'London')*
Jan 70. Decca; (lp)(c) **THE WORLD OF JOHN MAYALL** [ ] [-]
Feb 70. Decca/ US= London; (lp) **THE DIARY OF A BAND (live 1967)** [ ] [93]
Apr 71. Decca; (lp)(c) **THE WORLD OF JOHN MAYALL VOL.2** [ ] [-]
1978. Decca; (lp)(c) **BLUES ROOTS** [ ] [-]
Oct 78. Decca; (7") **CROCODILE WALK. / SITTING IN THE RAIN** [ ] [-]
Apr 83. Decca; (lp)(c) **PRIMAL SOLOS** [ ] [-]
(cd-iss.Feb89)
Oct 83. Decca;; (lp)(c) **THE JOHN MAYALL STORY VOL.1** [ ] [-]
Oct 83. Decca; (lp)(c) **THE JOHN MAYALL STORY VOL.2** [ ] [-]
Aug 84. Decca; (d-c) **STORMY MONDAY** [ ] [-]
Oct 71. London; (lp)(c) **THRU THE YEARS** [-] [ ]
(cd-iss.Jan91 on 'Deram')
Feb 73. London; (d-lp) **DOWN THE LINE** [-] [ ]
– (60's demos & 'JOHN MAYALL PLAYS JOHN MAYALL' lp)
Oct 71. Polydor; (lp)(c) **BEYOND THE TURNING POINT** [ ] [-]
Apr 76. Polydor; (lp)(c) **JOHN MAYALL** [ ] [-]
Nov 80. Polydor; (lp)(c) **GREATEST HITS** [ ] [ ]
Apr 84. Polydor; (lp)(c) **ROOM TO MOVE** [ ] [ ]
(re-iss.cd Mar93)
Feb 82. M.C.A.; (lp)(c) **LAST OF THE BRITISH BLUES** [ ] [-]
Apr 86. Castle; (d-lp)(c)(cd) **THE COLLECTION** [ ] [-]
– Key to love / Hideaway / Ramblin' on my mind / All your love / They call it stormy Monday / Hoochie coochie man / Crocodile walk (1st version) / Crawling up a hill / Marsha's mood / Sonny Boy blow / Looking back / A hard road / The supernatural / You don't love me / Leaping Christine / Suspicions (part 2) / Picture on the wall / The death of J.B. / Lenoir / Sandy / The bear / Walking the sunset / Fly tomorrow.
Apr 86. Charly; (lp) **SOME OF MY BEST FRIENDS ARE BLUES** [ ] [-]
1992. Charly; (cd)(c) **LIFE IN THE JUNGLE** (rec. '84) [ ] [-]
Jun 88. Knight; (c) **NIGHTRIDING** [ ] [-]
Jun 91. Elite; (cd)(c) **WAITING FOR THE RIGHT TIME** [ ] [-]
Apr 93. Pulsar; (cd) **A BIG MAN** [ ] [-]
Jul 93. Deram; (cd) **LONDON BLUES 1964-1969** [ ] [-]
Jul 94. Success; (cd)(c) **WHY WORRY** [ ] [-]
Sep 94. Spectrum; (cd)(c) **STORMY MONDAY** [ ] [-]

Curtis MAYFIELD

Born: 3 Jun'42, Chicago, USA. Goes went in 1970, after 13 years a major part of The IMPRESSIONS ⇒ . Having formed his own 'Curtom' label two years previous, his debut solo release 'CURTIS', gave him US Top 20 status. From it, edited versions of '(DON'T WORRY) IF THERE'S A HELL . . . ' & 'MOVE ON UP' broke him into the US & UK Pop 30 respectively. After a live double album consisting of solo and Impressions songs, he issued third Top 40 album 'ROOTS' late '71. He was then commissioned to score 'Shaft' inspired 'SUPERFLY' film soundtrack, and this gave him his first and only No.1. It also contained two US Top 10 hits, including the superb title track. By the mid-70's though, his worked failed to appeal to mass audiences. • **Style:** Exponent of hard black political soul music in the early 70's. He transferred his creativity to number of soundtracks and heavy disco themes in the mid-late 70's. This included production work for GLADYS KNIGHT & THE PIPS / The STAPLE SINGERS and ARETHA FRANKLIN. • **Songwriters:** Writes own material, except TONIGHT'S THE NIGHT (Neil Young) / etc. • **Trivia:** His 1973 US TV special 'CURTIS IN CHICAGO' featured guest appearances by past and present IMPRESSIONS' members JERRY BUTLER and GENE CHANDLER.

Recommended: SUPERFLY (*9) / A MAN LIKE CURTIS – THE BEST OF (*8)

CURTIS MAYFIELD – vocals, guitar, keyboards + live band

Buddah / Curtom

Nov 70. (7") **(DON'T WORRY) IF THERE'S A HELL BELOW WE'RE ALL GOING TO GO. / THE MAKINGS OF YOU** [ ] [29]

Feb 71. (lp)(c) **CURTIS** [ ] [19] Oct 70
– (Don't worry) If there's a Hell below we're all going to go / The other side of town / The makings of you / We the people who are darker than blue / Move on up / Miss Black America / Wild and free / Give it up. *(re-iss.Oct74) (re-iss.Jun76 on 'Curtom') (cd-iss.Nov93 on 'Movieplay Gold')*

May 71. (7") **GIVE IT UP. / BEAUTIFUL BROTHER OF MINE** [-] [ ]

Jun 71. (7"m) **MOVE ON UP. / GIVE IT UP / BEAUTIFUL BROTHER OF MINE** [12] [-]

Aug 71. (d-lp) **CURTIS – LIVE (live)** [ ] [21] May 71
– Mighty mighty (spade and Whitey) / I plan to stay a believer / We're a winner (rap) / We've only just begun / Check out your mind / People get ready / Stare and stare / Gypsy woman / The makings of you / We the people who are darker than blue / (Don't worry) If there's a Hell below we're all going to go / Stone junkie. *(re-iss.Oct74) (re-iss.Jun76 on 'Curtom')*

Sep 71. (7") **MIGHTY MIGHTY (SPADE AND WHITEY) (live). /** [-] [ ]

Nov 71. (7") **WE GOT TO HAVE PEACE. / PEOPLE GET READY** [ ] [-]

Dec 71. (7") **GET DOWN. / WE'RE A WINNER** [-] [69]

Jan 72. (lp)(c) **ROOTS** [ ] [40] Nov 71
– Get down / Keep on keeping on / Underground / We got to have peace / Beautiful brother of mine / Now you're gone / Love to keep you in my mind. *(re-iss.Oct74) (re-iss.Jun76 on 'Curtom') (cd-iss.Nov93 on 'Movieplay Gold')*

Feb 72. (7") **WE GOT TO HAVE PEACE. / WE'RE A WINNER** [-] [ ]

Apr 72. (7") **BEAUTIFUL BROTHER OF MINE. / LOVE TO KEEP YOU IN MY MIND** [-] [ ]

May 72. (7") **KEEP ON KEEPING ON. / STONE JUNKIE** [ ] [-]

JUn 72. (7") **MOVE ON UP. / UNDERGROUND** [-] [ ]

Sep 72. (7") **FREDDIE'S DEAD. / UNDERGROUND** [ ] [4] Aug 72

Nov 72. (lp)(c) **SUPERFLY (Soundtrack)** [26] [1] Aug 72
– Little child runnin' wild / Freddie's dead / Give me your love / No thing on me (cocaine song) / Superfly / Pusherman / Junkie chase / Eddie you should know / Think. *(re-iss.Nov74) (re-iss.Aug79 on 'RSO') (re-iss.+cd.Jun88 on 'Ichiban') (cd-iss.Nov93 on 'Movieplay Gold')*

Nov 72. (7") **SUPERFLY. / UNDERGROUND** [-] [8]

Feb 73. (7") **SUPERFLY. / GIVE ME YOUR LOVE** [ ] [-]

Jul 73. (7") **FUTURE SHOCK. / THE OTHER SIDE OF TOWN** [-] [39]

Sep 73. (lp)(c) **BACK TO THE WORLD** [ ] [16] Jun 73
– Back to the world / Future shock / Right on for the darkness / If I were only a child again / Can't say nothin' / Keep on trippin' / Future song (love of a good woman, love of a good man). *(re-iss.Oct74) (re-iss.Jun76 on 'Curtom') (cd-iss.Nov93 on 'Movieplay Gold')*

Oct 73. (7") **BACK TO THE WORLD. / OTHER SIDE OF TOWN** [ ] [ ]

Oct 73. (7") **IF I WERE ONLY A CHILD AGAIN. / THINK** [-] [71]

Jan 74. (7") **CAN'T SAY NOTHIN'. / FUTURE SHOCK** [-] [88]

Mar 74. (lp)(c) **CURTIS IN CHICAGO (TV Soundtrack)** [ ] [ ] Nov 73
– Superfly / For your precious love / I'm so proud / Once in my life (IMPRESSIONS) / Preacher man (IMPRESSIONS) / Duke of Earl (GENE CHANDLER) / Love oh love (LEROY HUTSON) / Amen. *(cd-iss.Oct94 on 'Charly')*

Aug 74. (lp)(c) **SWEET EXORCIST** [ ] [39] May 74
– Ain't got time / Sweet exorcist / To be invisible / Power to the people / Kung Fu / Suffer / Make me believe in you. *(re-iss.Aug76 on 'Curtom') (cd-iss.Oct94 on 'Charly')*

Aug 74. (7") **KUNG FU. / RIGHT ON FOR THE DARKNESS** [ ] [40] Jun 74

Oct 74. (7") **SWEET EXORCIST. / SUFFER** [-] [ ]

Jan 75. (lp)(c) **GOT TO FIND A WAY** [ ] [76] Nov 74
– Love me (right in the pocket) / So you don't love me / A prayer / Mother's son / Cannot find a way / Ain't no love lost. *(cd-iss.Oct94 on 'Charly')*

Mar 75. (7") **MOTHER'S SON. / LOVE ME RIGHT IN THE POCKET** [ ] [ ]

Jun 75. (7") **STASH THAT BUTT, SUCKER. / ZANZIBAR** [-] [ ]

(above single issued on 'Columbia')

—— His band from this period onwards **GARY THOMPSON** – guitar / **RICH TUFO** – keyboards / **LUCKY SCOTT** – bass / **QUINTON JOSEPH** – drums

Aug 75. (lp)(c) **THERE'S NO PLACE LIKE AMERICA TODAY** [ ] [ ] Jun 75
– Billy Jack / When seasons change / So in love / Jesus / Blue Monday people / Hard times / Love to the people.

Sep 75. (7") **SO IN LOVE. / HARD TIMES** [-] [67]

Jul 76. (7") **ONLY YOU BABE. / LOVE TO THE PEOPLE** [-] [ ]

Jul 76. (lp)(c) **GIVE, GET, TAKE AND HAVE** [ ] [ ]
– In your arms again / This love is sweet / P.S. I love you / Party night / Get a little bit (give, get, take and have) / Soul music / Only you babe / Mr. Welfare you.

Sep 76. (7") **PARTY NIGHT. / P.S. I LOVE YOU** [-] [ ]

Curtom / Curtom

Mar 77. (7") **SHOW ME LOVE. / JUST WANT TO BE WITH YOU** [-] [ ]

Mar 77. (lp)(c) **NEVER SAY YOU CAN'T SURVIVE** [ ] [ ]
– Show me love / Just want to be with you / When we're alone / Never say you can't survive / I'm gonna win your love / All night long / When you used to be mine / Sparkle. *(cd-iss.Oct94 on 'Charly')*

Nov 77. (7") **DO DO WAP IS STRONG IN HERE. / NEED SOMEONE TO LOVE** [-] [ ]

Feb 78. (lp)(c) **SHORT EYES (Soundtrack)** [ ] [ ] Nov 77
– Do do wap is strong in here / Back against the wall / Need someone to love / A heavy dupe / Short eyes / Break it down / Another fool in love / Father confessor.

Jul 78. (7") **YOU ARE, YOU ARE. / GET A LITLE BIT (GIVE, GET, TAKE AND HAVE)** [-] [ ]

Sep 78. (7") **DO IT ALL NIGHT. / PARTY PARTY** [-] [ ]

Oct 78. (lp)(c) **DO IT ALL NIGHT** [-] [ ]
– Do it all night / No goodbyes / Party party / Keeps me loving you / In love, in love, in love / You are, you are. *(cd-iss.Oct94 on 'Charly')*

Nov 78. (12") **NO GOODBYES. / PARTY PARTY** [65] [-]

Dec 78. (7") **IN LOVE, IN LOVE, IN LOVE. / KEEPS ME LOVING YOU** [-] [ ]

—— With various session people

R.S.O. / R.S.O.

Mar 79. (7") **THIS YEAR. / ('A'instrumental)** [ ] [ ]

Sep 79. (lp)(c) **HEARTBEAT** [ ] [42] Aug 79
– Tell me, tell me (how ya like to be loved) / What is my woman for? / Between you baby and me / Victory / Over the hump / You better stop / You're so good to me / Heartbeat.

—— Next single & album credited vocalist LINDA CLIFFORD.

Aug 79. (7") **BETWEEN YOU BABY AND ME. / YOU'RE SO GOOD TO ME** [ ] [ ]

Jun 80. (lp)(c) **THE RIGHT COMBINATION** [ ] [ ]
– Rock to your socks / The right combination / I'm so proud / Ain't no love lost / It's lovin' time / Love's sweet sensation / Between you baby and me.

Sep 80. (lp)(c) **SOMETHING TO BELIEVE IN** [ ] [ ] Jul 80
– Something to believe in / Love me love me now / Never let me go / Tripping out / People never give up / It's alright / Never stop loving me. *(re-iss.+cd.Oct89 on 'Curtom')*

Oct 80. (7") **IT'S ALRIGHT. / SUPERFLY** [ ] [-]

not issued / Boardwalk

1981. (lp) **LOVE IS THE PLACE** [-] [ ]
– She don't let nobody (but me) / Toot an' toot an' toot / Baby doll / Love is the place / Just ease my mind / You mean everything to me / You get all my love / Come free your people.

1981. (7") **SHE DON'T LET NOBODY (BUT ME). / YOU GET ALL MY LOVE** [-] [ ]

1981. (7") **COME FREE YOUR PEOPLE. / TOOT AN' TOOT AN' TOOT** [-] [ ]

Epic / Boardwalk

Oct 82. (7") **HEY BABY (GIVE IT ALL TO ME). / SUMMER HOT** [-] [ ]

Mar 83. (lp)(c) **HONESTY** [ ] [ ] Oct 82
– Hey baby (give it all to me) / Still within your heart / Dirty laundry / Nobody but you / If you need me / What you gawn do? / Summer hot.

Mar 83. (7") **DIRTY LAUNDRY. / NOBODY BUT YOU** [-] [ ]

not issued / C.R.C.

Sep 85. (lp)(c) **WE COME IN PEACE WITH A MESSAGE OF LOVE** [-] [ ]
– *(UK-iss.cd/c/lp.Feb91 on 'Curtom')*

98.6 / 98.6

Nov 86. (7")(12") **BABY IT'S YOU. / BREAKIN' IN THE STREETS** [ ] [ ]

—— (In mid'87 he was credited on BLOW MONKEYS single 'Celebrate The Day'.)

Capitol / Capitol

1987. (lp)(c) **LIVE IN LOS ANGELES (live)** [ ] [ ]
– *(withdrawn?)*

Ichiban / Ichiban

Jun 88. (lp)(c)(cd) **LIVE IN EUROPE (live)** [ ] [ ]
– (intro) / Freddie's dead / We gotta have peace / People get ready / Move on up / Back to the world / Gypsy woman / Pusher man / We've only just begun / When seasons change / (Don't worry) If there's a Hell below we're all going to go.

Jul 88. (12") **MOVE ON UP (live). / LITTLE CHILD RUNNIN' WILD (live)** [ ] [ ]

Curtom / Arista

May 89. (7") **HE'S A FLY GUY. (w/ FISHBONE) / ('A'instrumental)** [-] [ ]

May 89. (7") **I MO GIT U SUCKA. / HE'S A FLY GUY** [ ] [ ]
(12"+=)(cd-s+=) – ('A'extended).

Feb 90. (7")(12") **HOMELESS. / PEOPLE NEVER GIVE UP** [ ] [ ]

Mar 90. (cd)(c)(lp) **TAKE IT TO THE STREET** [ ] [ ]
– Homeless / Got to be real / Do be down / Who was that lady / On and on / He's a fly guy / Don't push / I mo git u sucka.

Jun 90. (7") **DO BE DOWN. / GOT TO BE REAL** [ ] [ ]
(12"+=) – ('A'extended) / ('A'radio version).

—— On 13 Aug'90, he suffered broken neck and head injuries after he was struck by stage lighting, etc. He was temporary paralysed during this time.

Next single features rapper ICE-T.

Capitol / Capitol

Sep 90. (7") **SUPERFLY 1990. / SUPERFLY 1990 (Fly edit mix)** [48] [ ]
(12"+=)(cd-s+=) – ('A'diff.mix).

– compilations, others, etc. –

Nov 74. Buddah/ US= Curtom; (lp)(c) **MOVE ON UP – THE BEST OF CURTIS MAYFIELD** [ ] [ ]

Nov 74. Buddah/ US= Curtom; (7") **MOVE ON UP. / GIVE IT UP** [ ] [ ]

Jan 83. P.R.T.; (7") **MOVE ON UP. /('B'by 'Melba Moore')** [ ] [-]

Feb 90. Essential; (cd)(c)(lp) **PEOPLE GET READY (live At Ronnie Scott's)** [ ] [-]

Nov 92. Music Collection; (cd) **A MAN LIKE CURTIS – THE BEST OF . . .** [ ] [-]
– Move on up / Superfly / (Don't worry) If there's a Hell below we're all gonna go / You are, you are / Give me your love / Never stop loving me / Tripping out / Soul music / This year / Ain't no love lost / Pusherman / Freddie's dead / Do do wop is strong in here / Hard times / In your arms again (shake it) / So in love.

Sep 93. Traditional Line; (cd) **HARD TIMES** [ ] [-]

Jan 94. Windsong; (cd) **BBC RADIO 1 LIVE IN CONCERT** [ ] [-]

Mar 94. Charly; (cd) **GET DOWN TO THE FUNKY GROOVE** [ ] [-]

Aug 94. Charly; (cd) **GROOVE ON UP** [ ] [-]

Nov 94. Charly; (cd) **TRIPPING OUT** [ ] [-]

Apr 94. Movieplay Gold; (cd) **LIVE! (live)** [ ] [-]

May 94. Laserlight; (cd)(c) **CURTIS MAYFIELD** [ ] [-]

— CURTIS also collaborated on other Film Soundtracks. 'CLAUDINE' in Aug74 with GLADYS KNIGHT & THE PIPS, 'LET'S DO IT AGAIN' in Sep76 with STAPLE SINGERS and 'SPARKLE' Oct76 with ARETHA FRANKLIN.

MAZZY STAR

Formed: Santa Monica, Los Angeles, California, USA . . . .early 90's by duo DAVID ROBACK and HOPE SANDOVAL. In 1993, their second album 'SO TONIGHT . . . ' cracked the US Top 50, and paved the way for hit single 'FADE INTO YOU'. • **Style:** Part acoustic psychedelic /folky rock outfit, with dreamy soft-VELVETS side. • **Songwriters:** SANDOVAL / ROBACK except; BLUE FLOWER (Slapp Happy) / I'M GONNA BAKE MY BISCUIT (McCoy) / I'M SAILIN' (Lawler) / FIVE STRING SERENADE (. . . Lee) / GIVE YOU MY LOVIN' (. . . Gomez). • **Trivia:** HOPE SANDOVAL guested on The JESUS & MARY CHAIN's 1994 single 'SOMETIMES ALWAYS'.

Recommended: SO TONIGHT THAT I MIGHT SEE (*8) / SHE HANGS BRIGHTLY (*8)

HOPE SANDOVAL – vocals, guitar / **DAVID ROBACK** – guitar (ex-RAIN PARADE, ex-RAINY DAY, ex-OPAL) /

Rough Trade Rough Trade

Apr 90. (cd)(c)(lp) **SHE HANGS BRIGHTLY** [ ] [ ]
– Halah / Blue flower / Ride it on / She hangs brightly / I'm sailin' / Give you my lovin' / Be my angel / Taste of blood / Ghost highway / Free / Before I sleep. *(re-iss.May93 + Sep94 on 'Capitol')*

Capitol Capitol

Oct 93. (cd)(c)(lp) **SO TONIGHT THAT I MIGHT SEE** [68] [36]
– Fade into you / Bells ring / Mary of silence / Five string serenade / Blue light / She's my baby / Unreflected / Wasted / Into dust / So tonight that I might see. *(re-iss.Jun94)*

Aug 94. (cd-s) **FADE INTO YOU / BLUE FLOWER / I'M GONNA BAKE MY BISCUIT** [48] [44]
(10") – ('A'side) / Five string serenade / Under my car / Bells ring (acoustic).

— The track 'TELL ME NOW' featured in the film 'Batman Forever' and the was on B-side of U2's 'Hold Me, Kiss Me, Kill Me!'.

McALMONT & BUTLER

Formed: Croydon, London, England . . .early 1995, by ex-THIEVES singer DAVID McALMONT and ex-SUEDE guitarist BERNARD BUTLER. McALMONT was raised by his mother in Norfolk until when he was 11, divorced she to him and his sister Guyana. He returned to London in 1993 and soon joined he HIEVES, who split after completing one unreleased album. His eponymous debut album was quickly issued by Virgin subsidiary 'Hut', after debut solo single 'EITHER'. • **Style:** Black and open homosexual McALMONT (he of the Danny La Rue influence), was described as Britain's answer to TERENCE TRENT D'ARBY. Although many likened him to AL GREEN or even LIZ FRASER of The COCTEAU TWINS!. • **Songwriters:** Partnership except YOU'LL LOSE A GOOD THING (Ozen-Meaux).

Recommended: THE SOUND OF McALMONT & BUTLER (*7)

McALMONT

DAVID McALMONT – vocals (with BERNARD, etc.)

Hut Hut

Dec 94. (7") **EITHER. / YOU MADE ME** [ ] [ ]
(12"+=)(cd-s+=) – As if I'd known (live) / Either (mix).

Jan 95 (cd(c)(lp) **McALMONT** [ ] [ ]
– Either / Not wiser / Unworthy / Misunderstood / Is it raining? / Conversation / He loves you / Worn away / It's always this way / My grey boy / They hide.

On the 19th June '95, he made available for one day a cdep 'SATURDAY (GAY PRIDE EP). The tracks were:- Saturday / Fort James / My grey boy.

McALMONT & BUTLER

Hut Hut

May 95. (c-s) **YES / DON'T CALL IT SOUL** [8] [ ]
(cd-s+=) – How about you?.
(cd-s) – ('A'side) / What's the excuse this time? / Disappointment.

Oct 95. (c-s) **YOU DO / TONIGHT** [17] [ ]
(cd-s+=) – You'll lose a good thing.
(cd-s) – The debitor / Although.

Nov 95. (cd)(c)(lp) **THE SOUND OF McALMONT & BUTLER** [33] [ ]
– Yes / What's the excuse this time? / The right thing / Although / Don't call it soul / Disappointment / The debitor / How about you? / Tonight / You'll lose a good thing / You do.

McAULEY-SCHENKER GROUP
(see under ⇒ SCHENKER, Michael)

Nicko McBRAIN (see under ⇒ IRON MAIDEN)
(see under ⇒ IRON MAIDEN)

Dan McCAFFERTY (see under ⇒ NAZARETH)

Paul McCARTNEY

Born: JAMES PAUL McCARTNEY, 18 Jun'42, Liverpool, England. Major part of The BEATLES in the 60's, he and JOHN LENNON were easily the greatest contemporary writing partnership of the 20th Cent. They officially split on 11 Apr'70, having just prior to issuing last recordings 'LET IT BE', (which was also name of docu-film, telling the last days of the fab four). Released 3 weeks earlier was McCARTNEY's first solo outing 'McCARTNEY', which included backing from wife LINDA (married 12 Mar'69). It topped the American charts, but was held off UK No.1 by SIMON & GARFUNKEL's 'Bridge Over Troubled Water'. The next year, he hit cross-Atlantic Top 5 with debut 45 'ANOTHER DAY', and then took unusual step of co-billing wife LINDA on subsequent album 'RAM'. This reversed chart positions of its predecessor, and encased US-only 45 'UNCLE ALBERT – ADMIRAL HALSEY', which hit No.1. Later in '71, he launched WINGS, which included LINDA, DENNY LAINE and DENNY SEIWELL. They hit critical low, with 'WILDLIFE' lp, which was followed by controversial and radio banned hit single 'GIVE IRELAND BACK TO THE IRISH'. Annoyed at its ban, WINGS then put music to nursery rhyme 'MARY HAD A LITTLE LAMB', which made UK Top 10 although losing much credibility. The McCARTNEYs then underwent a series of drug busts, and another this time silly BBC ban on next hit 'HI HI HI'. In Spring '73, PAUL McCARTNEY & WINGS hit US top with single 'MY LOVE', and album 'RED ROSE SPEEDWAY'. In 1974, they/he surpassed all before when album 'BAND ON THE RUN' hit the top and sold over 6 million copies during its 2 year plus stay in both UK & US charts. In 1975 wings continued to soar, until PAUL McCARTNEY reverted to even more fruitful solo career late '79. In 1977, they had massive selling UK No.1 for 9 weeks 'MULL OF KINTYRE', and he with STEVIE WONDER called for racial harmony in 1982, with cross-Atlantic No.1 'EBONY & IVORY'. • **Style:** Evergreen pop-rock superstar, talented singer & multi-instrumentalist with ability to write clever love songs, etc. with ease. • **Songwriters:** 99% by PAUL, except some with group. Covered; MONY MONY (Tommy James & The Shandells) / GO NOW (Moody Blues) / RUDOLPH THE RED-NOSED REINDEER (Christmas trad.) / KANSAS CITY (Wilbert Harrison) / MATCHBOX (Carl Perkins) / TWENTY FLIGHT ROCK (Eddie Cochran) / LAWDY MISS CLAWDY + IT'S NOW OR NEVER + BLUE MOON OF KENTUCKY (Elvis Presley) / BE-BOP – A-LULA (Gene Vincent) / BACK ON MY FEET (co-with Elvis Costello) / HI-HEEL SNEAKERS (Tommy Tucker) / GIVE PEACE A CHANCE (John Lennon) / AIN'T THAT A SHAME (Fats Domino) / etc., and many past BEATLES songs live. • **Trivia:** The 'BAND ON THE RUN' album sleeve featured the group being caught escaping alongside celebrities; Michael Parkinson, Kenny Lynch, James Coburn, Clement Freud, Christopher Lee & John Conteh.

Recommended: BAND ON THE RUN (*8) / ALL THE BEST (*7) / McCARTNEY (*6) / RAM (*7) / WILD LIFE (*5) / RED ROSE SPEEDWAY (*5)

PAUL McCARTNEY

– vocals, bass, guitar, keyboards, drums (ex-BEATLES) with **LINDA McCARTNEY** (b. LINDA EASTMAN, 24 Sep'42, Scarsdale, New York, USA) – backing vocals

Apple Apple

Apr 70. (lp)(c) **McCARTNEY** [2] [1]
– The lovely Linda / That would be something / Valentine day / Every night / Hot as sun / Glasses / Junk / Man we was lonely / Momma miss America / Teddy boy / Singalong junk / Maybe I'm amazed / Kreen-Akrove. *(re-iss.+cd.May84 on 'Fame') (re-iss.cd+c Jun93)*

Feb 71. (7") **ANOTHER DAY. / OH WOMAN OH WHY** [2] [5]

PAUL AND LINDA McCARTNEY

PAUL – vocals, guitar, bass / **LINDA** – keyboards, backing vocals, percussion / added **DENNY SEIWELL** – drums, vocals (plus various session people)

May 71. (lp)(c) **RAM** [1] [2]
– Too many people / Three legs / Ram on / Dear boy / Uncle Albert – Admiral Halsey / Smile away / Heart of the country / Monkberry moon delight / Eat at home / Long-haired lady / Ram on / The back seat of my car. *(re-iss.Jan85 on 'Parlophone') (re-iss.cd+c Jun93)*

Aug 71. (7") **THE BACK SEAT OF MY CAR. / HEART OF THE COUNTRY** [39] [-]

Aug 71. (7") **UNCLE ALBERT – ADMIRAL HALSEY. / TOO MANY PEOPLE** [-] [1]

WINGS

was the group the above trio formed; adding **DENNY LAINE** – guitar, vocals (ex-MOODY BLUES, ex-UGLYS, ex-BALLS, etc.)

Dec 71. (lp)(c) **WILD LIFE** [8] [10]
– Mumbo / Bip bop / Love is strange / Wild life / Some people never know / I am your singer / Tomorrow / Dear friend. *(re-iss.+cd.Apr84 on 'Fame', cd+=)* – Mary had a little lamb / Little woman love / Oh woman, oh why. *(re-iss.cd+c Jun93)*

— added **HENRY McCULLOCH** – guitar, vocals (ex-JOE COCKER, etc.)

Feb 72. (7") **GIVE IRELAND BACK TO THE IRISH. / ('A'version)** [16] [21] Mar 72

May 72. (7") **MARY HAD A LITTLE LAMB. / LITTLE WOMAN LOVE** [9] [28] Jun 72

Dec 72. (7") **C MOON. / HI HI HI** [5] [10]
(above flipped over in the States)

PAUL McCARTNEY AND WINGS

Mar 73. (7") **MY LOVE. / THE MESS (live)** 9 1 Apr 73

May 73. (lp)(c) **RED ROSE SPEEDWAY** 5 1

– Big barn bed / My love / Get on the right thing / One more kiss / Little lamb dragonfly / Single pigeon / When the night / Hold me tight – Lazy dynamite – Hands of love – Power cut / Loup (1st Indian on the Moon). *(re-iss.+cd Jan85 on 'Parlophone', cd+=)*– The mess (live) / I lie around / Country dreamer. *(re-iss. +cd ct 87 on 'Fame') (re-iss.cd+c Jun93)*

Jun 73. (7") **LIVE AND LET DIE. (as "WINGS") / I LIE AROUND** 9 2 Jul 73

— **PAUL & LINDA** plus **DENNY LAINE.** (McCULLOCH went solo, SEIWELL to sessions)

Oct 73. (7") **HELEN WHEELS. / COUNTRY DREAMER** 12 10 Nov 73

Dec 73. (lp)(c) **BAND ON THE RUN** 1 1

– Band on the run / Jet / Bluebird / Mrs. Vanderbilt / Let me roll it / Mamunia / No words / Picasso's last words (drink to me) / Nineteen hundred and eighty-five. *(re-iss.+cd Jan85 on 'Parlophone', cd+=)*– Helen wheels. *(re-iss.cd+c Jun93) (US-pic-lp 1978)*

Feb 74. (7") **JET. / LET ME ROLL IT** 7 7

Apr 74. (7") **BAND ON THE RUN. / 1985** - 1

Jun 74. (7") **BAND ON THE RUN. / ZOO GANG** 3 -

— added **JIMMY McCULLOCH** (b. 4 Jun'53) – guitar, vocals (ex-THUNDERCLAP NEWMAN, ex-STONE THE CROWS) + **GEOFF BRITTON** – drums (ex-EAST OF EDEN)

Nov 74. (7") **JUNIOR'S FARM. / SALLY G** 16 3 / 17

WINGS

JOE ENGLISH (b. Rochester, New York) – drums (ex-JAM FACTORY) repl. BRITTON who joined CHAMPION

Capitol Capitol

May 75. (7") **LISTEN TO WHAT THE MAN SAID. / LOVE IN SONG** 6 1

Jun 75. (lp)(c) **VENUS AND MARS** 1 1

– Venus and Mars rock show / Love in song / You gave me the answer / Magneto and Titanium man / Letting go / Venus and Mars (reprise) / Spirits of ancient Egypt / Medicine jar / Call me back again / Listen to what the man said / Treat her gently – lonely old people / Crossroads theme. *(re-iss.+cd.1985 on 'Parlophone')* (cd+=) – Zoogang / My carnival / Lunch box – odd socks. *(re-iss.+cd Nov 88 on 'Fame') (re-iss.cd+c Jun93)*

Sep 75. (7") **LETTING GO. / YOU GAVE ME THE ANSWER** 41 39

Nov 75. (7") **VENUS AND MARS ROCK SHOW. / MAGNETO AND TITANIUM MAN** 12

E.M.I. Capitol

Apr 76. (lp)(c) **WINGS AT THE SPEED OF SOUND** 2 1

– Let 'em in / The note you never wrote / She's my baby / Beware my love / Wino junko / Silly love songs / Cook of the house / Time to hide / Must do something about it / San Ferry Anne / Warm and beautiful. *(re-iss 1985, cd-iss Jul89 on 'Parlophone') (re-iss.+cd.Oct89 on 'Fame') (re-iss.cd+c Jun93)*

May 76. (7") **SILLY LOVE SONGS. / COOK OF THE HOUSE** 2 1 Apr 76

Jul 76. (7") **LET 'EM IN. / BEWARE MY LOVE** 2 3

Jan 77. (t-lp)(d-c) **WINGS OVER AMERICA (live)** 8 1 Dec 76

– Venus and Mars rock show / Jet / Let me roll it / Spirits of ancient Egypt / Medicine jar / Maybe I'm amazed / Call me back again / Lady Madonna / The long and winding road / Live and let die / Picasso's last words (drink to me) / Richard Cory / Bluebird / I've just seen a face / Yesterday / You gave me the answer / Magnet and Titanium man / Go now / My love / Listen to what the man said / Let 'em in / Time to hide / Silly love songs / Beware my love / Letting go / Band on the run / Hi hi hi / Soily. *(d-cd-iss. May 87)*

Feb 77. (7") **MAYBE I'M AMAZED (live). / SOILY (live)** 28 10

— cut to trio of **PAUL, LINDA** and **DENNY** when JIMMY joined SMALL FACES, and JOE joined SEA LEVEL (ex-ALLMANS).

Capitol Capitol

Nov 77. (7")(7"blue) **MULL OF KINTYRE. / GIRLS SCHOOL** 1 33

(Above flipped over in the States)

— added **STEVE HOLLY** – drums (on session but joined f/t Jul'78)

Parlophone Capitol

Mar 78. (7") **WITH A LITTLE LUCK. / CUFF LINK: BACKWARDS TRAVELLER** 5 1

Apr 78. (lp)(c) **LONDON TOWN** 4 2

– London town / Cafe on the Left Bank / I'm carrying / Backwards traveller – Cuff link / Children children / Girlfriend / I've had enough / With a little luck / Famous groupies / Deliver your children / Name and address / Don't let it bring you down / Morse Moose and the Grey Goose. *(re-iss.1985) (re-iss.+cd.Aug89 on 'Fame') (re-iss.cd+c Jun93)*

Jun 78. (7") **I'VE HAD ENOUGH. / DELIVER YOUR CHILDREN** 42 25

Aug 78. (7") **LONDON TOWN. / I'M CARRYING** 60 39

Nov 78. (lp)(c) **WINGS GREATEST** 5 29

– Another day / Silly love songs / Live and let die / Junior's farm / With a little luck / Band on the run / Uncle Albert – Admiral Halsey / Hi hi hi / Let 'em in / My love / Mull of Kintyre. *(re-iss.+cd.1985) (re-iss.cd+c Aug93)*

— added **LAURENCE JUBER** – guitar, vocals

Parlophone Columbia

Mar 79. (7")(12") **GOODNIGHT TONIGHT. / DAYTIME NIGHTIME SUFFERING** 5 5

Jun 79. (7") **OLD SIAM, SIR. / SPIN IT ON** 35 -

Jun 79. (7") **GETTING CLOSER. / SPIN IT ON** - 20

Jun 79. (lp)(c) **BACK TO THE EGG** 6 8

– Reception / Getting closer / We're open tonight / Spin it on / Again and again and again / Old Siam, sir / Arrow through me / Rockestra theme / To you / After the ball – Million miles / Winter rose – Love awake / The broadcast / So glad to see you here / Baby's request. *(US promo pic-lp became worth $1,000) (re-iss.+cd Jul 89) (re-iss.cd+c Aug93)*

Aug 79. (7") **GETTING CLOSER. / BABY'S REQUEST** 60 -

Sep 79. (7") **ARROW THROUGH ME. / OLD SIAM, SIR** - 29

PAUL McCARTNEY

went solo, augmented by LINDA plus session people

Parlophone Columbia

Nov 79. (7") **WONDERFUL CHRISTMASTIME. / RUDOLPH THE RED-NOSED REINDEER** 6

(re-iss. Nov '83 US)

Apr 80. (7") **COMING UP. / COMING UP (live) / LUNCH BOX – ODD SOX** 2 1

May 80. (lp)(c) **McCARTNEY II** 1 3

– Coming up / Temporary secretary / On the way / Waterfalls / Nobody knows / Front parlour / Summer's day song / Frozen Jap / Bogey music / Darkroom / One of these days. *(re-iss.+cd.Sep87 on 'Fame' cd+=)*– Secret friend / Check my machine. *(re-iss.cd+c Aug93)*

Jun 80. (7") **WATERFALLS. / CHECK MY MACHINE** 9

Sep 80. (12") **TEMPORARY SECRETARY. / SECRET FRIEND**

Apr 82. (7") **EBONY AND IVORY.(as "PAUL McCARTNEY & STEVIE WONDER") / RAINCLOUDS** 1 1

(12"+=) – ('A'solo version).

Apr 82. (lp)(c) **TUG OF WAR** 1 1

– Tug of war / Take it away / Somebody who cares / What's that you're doing? / Here today / Ballroom dancing / The pound is sinking / Wanderlust / Get it / Be what you see / Dress me up as a robber / Ebony and ivory. *(cd-iss.1985) (re-iss.+cd.Nov88 on 'Fame') (re-iss.cd+c Aug93)*

Jun 82. (12"m) **TAKE IT AWAY. / I'LL GIVE YOU A RING / DRESS ME UP AS A ROBBER** 15 10

Sep 82. (7") **TUG OF WAR. / GET IT** 53 53

— (In Oct82, duetted w /MICHAEL JACKSON on duet 'THE GIRL IS MINE' Top 10)

Oct 83. (7") **SAY SAY SAY. (as "PAUL McCARTNEY & MICHAEL JACKSON") / ODE TO KOALA BEAR** 2 1

(12"+=) – ('A' instrumental).

Nov 83. (lp)(c)(cd) **PIPES OF PEACE** 4 15

– Pipes of peace / Say say say / The other me / Keep under cover / So bad / The man / Sweetest little show / Average person / Hey hey / Tug of peace / Through our love. *(re-iss.cd+c Aug93)*

Dec 83. (7") **PIPES OF PEACE. / SO BAD** 1

(flipped over US May'84, hit No. 23)

Sep 84. (7") **NO MORE LONELY NIGHTS. / ('A' extended)** 2 6

(12"+=)(12"pic-d+=) – Silly love songs.

Oct 84. (d-lp)(c)(cd) **GIVE MY REGARDS TO BROAD STREET – ORIGINAL SOUND TRACK** 1 21

– No more lonely nights (ballad) / Good day sunshine / Corridor music / Yesterday / Here, there and everywhere / Wanderlust / Ballroom dancing / Silly love songs (reprise) / Not such a bad boy / No values / No more lonely nights (reprise) / For no one / Eleanor Rigby – Eleanor's dream / The long and winding road / No more lonely nights (play out version). *(re-iss.cd+c Aug93)*

Nov 84. (7")(7"pic-d) **WE ALL STAND TOGETHER.(as "PAUL McCARTNEY & THE FROG CHORUS") / ('A' humming version)** 3

(re-iss.Dec85 reached No.34 UK)

Parlophone Capitol

Nov 85. (7")(7"pic-d) **SPIES LIKE US. / MY CARNIVAL** 16 7

(12"+=)(12"pic-d+=) – ('A' party mix).

Jul 86. (7") **PRESS. / IT'S NOT TRUE** 25 21

(12"+=) – Hanglide. / ('A' dub).

(10"++=) – ('A'version).

Sep 86. (lp)(c)(cd) **PRESS TO PLAY** 8 30

– Stranglehold / Good times coming – Feel the sun / Talk more talk / Footprints / Only love remains / Press / Pretty little head / Move over busker / Angry / However absurd. *(cd+=)*– Write away / It's not true / Tough on a tightrope. *(re-iss.cd+c Aug93)*

Oct 86. (7") **PRETTY LITTLE HEAD. / WRITE AWAY** -

(12"+c-s+=) – Angry.

Nov 86. (7") **STRANGLEHOLD. / ANGRY (remix)** - 81

Dec 86. (7")(12") **ONLY LOVE REMAINS. / TOUGH ON A TIGHTROPE** 34

Nov 87. (7") **ONCE UPON A LONG AGO. / BACK ON MY FEET** 10

(12"+=) – Midnight special / Don't get around much anymore.

(12"extra+=) – Lawdy Miss Clawdy / Kansas City.

(cd-s+=) – Don't get around much anymore / Kansas City.

Nov 87. (lp)(c)(cd) **ALL THE BEST** (compilation) 2 62

– Coming up / Ebony and ivory (w/ STEVIE WONDER) / Listen to what the man said / No more lonely nights / Silly love songs / Let 'em in / C Moon / Pipes of peace / Live and let die / Another day / Maybe I'm amazed / Goodnight tonight / Once upon a long time ago / Say say say / With a little luck / My love / We all stand together / Mull of Kintyre / Jet / Band on the run. *(US slightly different tracks)*

— now with **LINDA / WIX** (PAUL WICKENS) – keyboards / **CHRIS WHITTEN** – drums / **ROBBIE McINTOSH** – guitar / **HAMISH STUART** – guitar, bass (ex-AVERAGE WHITE BAND)

May 89. (7") **MY BRAVE FACE. / FLYING TO MY HOME** 18 25

(12"+=)(c-s+=)(cd-s+=) – I'm gonna be a wheel someday / Ain't that a shame.

Jun 89. (lp)(c)(cd) **FLOWERS IN THE DIRT** 1 21

– My brave face / Rough ride / You want her too / Distractions / We got married / Put it there / Figure of eight / This one / Don't be careless love / That day is done / How many people / Motor of love. *(cd+=)*– Ou est le soleil. *(re-iss.lp,cd.Nov89, as 'FLOWERS . . . WORLD TOUR PACK', w/free 7" PARTY PARTY free 3" cd-s.w/cd version) (re-iss.cd+c Aug93)*

Jul 89. (7")(c-s) **THIS ONE. / THE FIRST STONE** 18 94

(12"+=)(cd-s+=) – I wanna cry / I'm in love again.

Nov 89. (7")(c-s) **FIGURE OF EIGHT. / OU EST LE SOLEIL** 42 92

(12"+=) – ('B'dub mix).

(3"cd-s+=) – Rough ride.

(12") – ('A'side) / This one (club mix).

(cd-s) – ('A'side) / Long and winding road / Loveliest thing.

Feb 90. (7")(c-s) **PUT IT THERE. / MAMA'S LITTLE GIRL** 32

(12"+=)(cd-s+=) – Same time next year.

Oct 90. (7")(c-s) **BIRTHDAY (live). / GOOD DAY SUNSHINE (live)** 29

(12"+=)(cd-s+=) – P.S. I love you (live) / Let 'em in (live).
Nov 90. (d-cd)(d-c)(t-lp) **TRIPPING THE LIVE FANTASTIC (live)** 17 26
– Figure of eight / Jet / Rough ride / Got to get you into my life / Band on the run / Birthday / Ebony and ivory / we got married / Inner city madness / Maybe I'm amazed / The long and winding road / Cracking up / Fool on the hill / Sgt. Pepper's lonely hearts club band / Can't buy me love / Matchbox / Put it there / Together / Things we said today / Eleanor Rigby / This one / My brave face / I saw her standing there / Back in the USSR / Twenty flight rock / Coming up / Sally / Let it be / Ain't that a shame / Live and let die / If I were not upon the stage / Hey Jude / Yesterday / Get back / Golden slumbers – Carry that weight – The end / Don't let the Sun catch you crying.
Dec 90. (7") **ALL MY TRIALS (live). / C MOON (live)** 35 ☐
(12"+=) – Mull of Kintyre / Put it there.
(cd-s+=) – Live medley:- Strawberry fields forever / Help / Give peace a chance.

—— **BLAIR CUNNINGHAM** – drums (ex-LLOYD COLE) repl. WHITTEN

Jun 91. (cd)(c)(lp) **UNPLUGGED – THE OFFICIAL BOOTLEG** 7 14
– Be-bop-a-lula / I lost my little girl / Here there and everywhere / Blue Moon of Kentucky / We can work it out / San Francisco Bay blues / I've just seen a face / Every night / She's a woman / Hi-heel sneakers / And I love her / That would be something / Blackbird / Ain't no sunshine / Good rockin' tonight / Singing the blues / Junk. *(re-cd+c.Aug91 as 'CHOBA B CCCP', hit UK 63) (re-iss.Sep94)*?? same
Jan 93. (7")(c-s) **HOPE OF DELIVERANCE. / DELIVERANCE (dub)** 18 83
(12")(cd-s) – ('A'side) / Big boys bickering / Long leather coat / Kicked around no more.
Feb 93. (cd)(c)(lp) **OFF THE GROUND** 5 17
– Off the ground / Looking for changes / Hope of deliverance / Mistress and maid / I owe it all to you / Biker like an icon / Peace in the neighbourhood / Golden Earth girl / The lovers that never were / Get out of my way / Winedark open sea / C'mon people.
Feb 93. (7")(c-s) **C'MON PEOPLE. / I CAN'T IMAGINE** 41 ☐
(cd-s+=) – Down to the river / Keep coming back to love.
(cd-s) – ('A'side) / Deliverance / Deliverance (dub).
Nov 93. (cd)(c)(lp) **PAUL IS LIVE! (live)** 34 78
– Drive my car / Let me roll it / Looking for changes / Peace in the neighbourhood / All my loving / Robbie's bit / Good rocking tonight / We can work it out / Hope of deliverance / Michelle / Biker like an icon / Here there and everywhere / My love / Magical mystery tour / C'mon people / Lady Madonna / Paperback writer / Penny Lane / Live and let die / Kansas City / Welcome to Soundcheck / Hotel in Benidorm / I wanna be your man / A fine day.

– compilations, etc. –

Feb 81. EMI/ US= Capitol; (lp)(c) **McCARTNEY INTERVIEW** 34 ☐

– under an alias (various connections) –

The **COUNTRY HAMS** featuring PAUL's brother MIKE McGEAR (ex-SCAFFOLD)
Oct 74. E.M.I.; (7") **WALKING IN THE PARK WITH ELOISE. / BRIDGE OVER THE RIVER SUITE** ☐ ☐

—— **PERCY 'THRILLS' THRILLINGTON**

Apr 77. E.M.I.; (7") **UNCLE ALBERT, ADMIRAL HALSEY. / EAST AT HOME** ☐ ☐

—— next by **SUZI AND THE RED STRIPES** LINDA McCARTNEY's band.

Aug 79. A&M/ US= Epic; (7")(7"yellow) **SEASIDE WOMAN. / B SIDE TO SEASIDE** ☐ 59 Jun 77
(re-iss.+12" Jul80)

—— PAUL had also guested on numerous singles and albums. DENNY LAINE has also had solo career, but with no commercial success.

David McCOMB & Adam PETERS (see under ⇒ TRIFFIDS)

McCOYS (see under ⇒ DERRINGER, Rick)

Ian McCULLOCH (see under ⇒ ECHO & THE BUNNYMEN)

Country Joe McDONALD (& THE FISH)

Born: 1 Jan'42, El Monte, California, USA. In the early 60's, JOE joined the navy, but left after his service period was over. In 1964, he befriended BLAIR HARDIMAN and issued dual work 'THE GOODBYE BLUES', before forming COUNTRY JOE & THE FISH the next year. They cut a few EP's for local 'RAG BABY' magazine, and through its editor Ed Denson, signed a recording contract with folk label 'Vanguard'. In the summer of '67, after a much heralded Monterey Pop Festival outing, their debut lp 'ELECTRIC MUSIC FOR THE MIND AND BODY' breached US Top 40. After 5 more lp's, McDONALD ventured solo, but to no great commercial degree. • **Style:** Urban folk-country star, whose satrical politico-drugs and anti-war themes, induced many to identify with his anarchic outfit in the 60's. In 1970, he was convicted and fined $500 for obscenity and inciting anti-social crowd behaviour, after chanting 'Gimme A F.*.*.*.' This 'Fish Cheer' had been part of his and crowd repertoire from mid-60's. • **Songwriters:** Self-penned anthems. • **Trivia:** In 1971, he joined actors JANE FONDA and DONALD SUTHERLAND, in a 'Free The Army' revue. In 1976, he campaigned to 'SAVE THE WHALES', and even wrote a single of that title.

Recommended: THE COLLECTED COUNTRY JOE & THE FISH (*7).

COUNTRY JOE and BLAIR HARDMAN

not issued unknown
1964. (lp) **THE GOODBYE BLUES** - ☐
– (ltd.10 copies, re-1968, 200 copies)

COUNTRY JOE & THE FISH

JOE McDONALD – vocals, guitar / **BARRY 'THE FISH' MELTON** (b.1947, Brooklyn, New York) – guitar, vocals / **CARL SHRAGER** – washboard / **BILL STEEL** – bass / **MIKE BEARDSLEE** – harp, vocals.

not issued Rag Baby
Oct 65. (7"ep) **COUNTRY JOE & THE FISH** - ☐
– I-feel-like-I'm-fixin'-to-die rag / Superbird. PETER KRUG: Fire in the city / Johnny's gone to war.

—— **McDONALD + MELTON** introduced **BRUCE BARTHOL** – bass / **DAVID COHEN** – electric guitar / **PAUL ARMSTRONG** – harp / **JOHN FRANCIS GUNNING** – drums.

Jun 66. (7"ep) **RAG BABY** - ☐
– Bass strings / Section 43 / (Thing called) Love.

—— **MARK RYAN** repl. BRUCE

Fontana Vanguard
Jul 67. (7") **NOT SO SWEET MARTHA LORRAINE. / THE MASKED MARAUDER** - 95
Oct 67. (lp) **ELECTRIC MUSIC FOR THE MIND AND BODY** ☐ 39 Apr 67
– Flying high / Not so sweet Martha Lorraine / Death sound blues / Porpoise mouth / Section 43 / Superbird / Sad and lonely times / Love / Bass strings / The masked marauder / Grace. *(re-iss. Mar69 & Feb72 on 'Vanguard') (cd-iss.Oct95)*
Nov 67. (7") **NOT SO SWEET MARTHA LORRAINE. / LOVE** ☐ -
Nov 67. (7") **JANIS. / (part 2)** - ☐
Jan 68. (7") **WHO AM I. / THURSDAY** - ☐
Mar 68. (lp) **I-FEEL-LIKE-I'M-FIXIN'-TO-DIE** ☐ 67 Nov 67
– (the fish cheer) / I-feel-like-I'm-fixin'-to-die rag / Who am I / Pat's song / Rock coast blues / Magoo / Janis / Thought dream / Thursday / Eastern jam / Colors for Susan. *(re-iss. Mar69 & Feb72 on 'Vanguard') (cd-iss.Oct95)*

Vanguard Vanguard
Jul 68. (7") **ROCK AND SOUL. / (part 2)** - ☐
Nov 68. (lp) **TOGETHER** ☐ 23 Jul 68.
– Rock and soul music / Susan / Mojo navigator / Bright suburban Mr. & Mrs. Clean machine / Good guys – bad guys cheer / The streets of your town / The fish moan / The Harlem song / Waltzing in the moonlight / Away bounce my bubbles / Cetacean / An untitled protest. *(cd-iss.Oct95)*

—— **JOE** and **BARRY** recruited new members **MARK KAPNER** – keyboards to replace COHEN (He joined BLUES PROJECT). **PETER ALBIN** – bass (ex-BIG BROTHER & THE HOLDING COMPANY) / **DAVID GETZ** – drums (ex-BIG BROTHER & THE HOLDING COMPANY) repl. others.

Jun 69. (7") **HERE I GO AGAIN. / BABY YOU'RE DRIVING ME CRAZY** - ☐
Sep 69. (lp) **HERE WE GO AGAIN** ☐ ☐ Jun 69
– Here I go again / Donovan's reef / It's nice to have love / Baby, you're driving me crazy / Crystal blues / For no reason / I'll survive / Maria / My girl / Doctor of electricity.
Oct 69. (7") **HERE I GO AGAIN. / IT'S SO NICE TO HAVE LOVE** ☐ -

—— **DOUG METZNER** – bass repl. ALBIN / **GREG DEWEY** – drums (ex-MAD RIVER) repl. GETZ who went solo.

Jun 70. (7") **I FEEL LIKE I'M FIXIN' TO DIE. / JANIS** - ☐
Jun 70. (7") **I FEEL LIKE I'M FIXIN' TO DIE. / MARIA** ☐ -
Oct 70. (lp) **C.J. FISH** ☐ ☐ Apr 70
– Sing sing sing / She's a bird / Mara / Hang on / The baby song / Hey Bobby / Silver and gold / Rocking 'round the world / The love machine / The return of sweet Lorraine / Hand of man. *(re-iss. Feb72.)*

—— They split Autumn 1970 leaving behind

– compilations –

Mar 70. Vanguard; (lp) **COUNTRY JOE & THE FISH / GREATEST HITS** ☐ 74 Dec 69
Nov 73. Vanguard; (d-lp) **THE LIFE AND TIMES OF COUNTRY JOE AND THE FISH FROM HAIGHT-ASTBURY TO WOODSTOCK** ☐ ☐ Oct 71

COUNTRY JOE McDONALD

had solo releases between 69-71. with **HAROLD BRADLEY** – guitar, bass / **RAY EDENTON** – guitar / **GRADY MARTIN** – guitar / **NORMAN PUTMAN** – bass / **BUDDY HARMON** – drums / **HARGUS 'PIG' ROBBINS** – percussion

Vanguard Vanguard
Apr 70 (lp) **THINKING OF WOODY** ☐ ☐ Dec 69
– Pastures of plenty / Talkin' dust bowl / Blowing down that old dusty road / So long it's been good to know yuh / Tom Joad / The sinking of Rueben James / Roll on Columbia / Pretty Boy Floyd / When the curfew blows / This land is your land. *(re-iss. Feb72.)*
Jan 71 (lp) **TONIGHT I'M SINGING JUST FOR YOU** ☐ ☐ Mar 70.
– Ring of fire / Tennessee stud / Heartaches by the number / Tiger by the tail / Crazy arms / You've done me wrong / All of me belongs to you / Oklahoma hills / Tonight I'm singing just for you / Friend, lover, woman, wife / Six days on the road. *(re-iss.Feb72.)*

—— His solo releases now post-FISH, were augmented by some UK session men.

Jan 71. (7") **HOLD ON IT'S COMING. / PLAYING WITH FIRE** - ☐
Sep 71. (lp) **HOLD ON IT'S COMING** ☐ ☐ Apr 71
– Hold on it's coming / Air Algiers / Only love is worth this pain / Playing with fire / Travelling / Joe's blues / Mr.Big pig / Balancing on the edge of time / Jamila / Hold on it's coming No.2.
Sep 71. (7") **HOLD ON IT'S COMING. / (part 2)** ☐ -

—— with **ANNA RIZZO** – vocals / **GREG DEEY** – drums / **NACKO DEWEY** – harp / **JOHN REWIND** – electric guitar / **VIC SMITH** – bass

1971 (7"ep)**COUNTRY JOE McDONALD & EROOTNA** -
– Kiss my ass / Tricky Dicky / Free some day.

(above was issued in he States on his 'Rag Baby' label.

Jan 72. (lp) **WAR WAR WAR** Aug 71
– The call / Forward / Young fellow, my lad / he man from Aphabaska / The munition maker / he twins / Jean Desprez / ar widow / The march of the dead.

1972. (7") **HANG ON. / HAND OF MAN** -

Jul 72. (lp) **INCREDIBLE! LIVE! COUNTRY JOE!** Feb 72.
– Entertainment is my business / Sweet Marie / Kiss my ass / Living in the future in a plastic dome / Walk in Santiago / Tricky Dicky / You know what I mean / Fly so high / Deep down in our hearts / Free some day / I'm on the road again.

COUNTRY JOE

formed his ALL-STAR BAND with **PETER ALBIN** – bass / **DAVID GETZ** – drums / **TUCKI BAILEY** – saxophone / **DOROTHY MOSCOWITZ** – vocals, piano (ex-UNITED STATES OF AMERICA) / **PHIL MARSH** – guitar repl. BARRY MELTON / **ANNA RIZZO** – drums repl. SALLY HENDERSON – vocals / **SEBASTIAN NICHOLSON** – congas repl. **SUSAN LYDON** – vocals

Vanguard Vanguard

Apr 73. (7") **FANTASY. / I SEE A ROCKET** -

Aug 73. (lp) **PARIS SESSIONS**
– Fantasy / Movieola / I'm so tired / Moving / I don't know why / Zombies in a house of madness / Sexist pig / Colorado Town / Coulene Anne / St.Tropez.

Oct 73. (7") **FANTASY. / HOLD ON IT'S COMING** -

—— **GINNY WHITTAKER** – drums repl. GETZ, BAILEY, MARSH and NICHOLSON.

—— (Feb74) **COUNTRY JOE** toured as duo with BARRY MELTON. Still solo below.

Nov 74. (7") **DR. HIP. / SATISFACTORY** -

Apr 75. (lp) **COUNTRY JOE** Dec 74
– Dr. Hip / Old Joe Corey / Making money in Chile / You messed over me / Memories / Chile / Pleasin' / Jesse James / Satisfactory / It's finally over.

Apr 75. (7") **JESSE JAMES. / CHILE** -

COUNTRY JOE McDONALD

also augmented by ENERGY CRISIS (below)**PHIL MARSH** – guitar / **BRUCE BARTHOL** – bass / **JOHN BLAKELEY** – guitar / **PETER MILIO** – drums / **TED ASHFORD** – keyboards

Fantasy Fantasy

Oct 75. (lp) **PARADISE WITH AN OCEAN VIEW**
– Tear down the walls / Holy roller / Lost my connection / The limit / Save the whales / Oh! Jamaica / Lonely on the road / Tricks / Breakfast for two.

Jan 76. (7") **BREAKFAST FOR TWO. / LOST MY CONNECTION** 92 Nov 75

Apr 76. (7") **SAVE THE WHALES. / OH! JAMAICA**

Aug 76. (lp) **LOVE IS A FIRE**
– It won't burn / You're the song / In love naturally / Oh no / Baby baby / True love at last / Who's gonna fry your eggs / Colortone / I need you (this and that) / Love is a fire.

Oct 76. (7") **I NEED YOU. / LOVE IS A FIRE** -

Oct 76. (7") **IN LOVE NATURALLY. / LOVE IS A FIRE** -

—— next solo albums used BARRY MELTON and session people.

Apr 77. (lp) **GOODBYE BLUES**
– Copiapo / Thought dreams / Goodbye blues / Let's go ridin' in the car / Blood on the ice / Primitive people / TV blues / Dark clouds / Little blue whale / Wilderness trail.

Oct 77. (7") **LA DI DA. / RING OF FIRE** -

May 78. (lp) **ROCK'N'ROLL MUSIC FROM PLANET EARTH** Feb 78
– Coyote / Bring back the sixties man / Sunshine through my window / Rock & roll again / Dark ship / Y.O.U. / Southern cross / Space patrol / U.F.O. / Get it together.

Mar 78. (7") **COYOTE. / SOUTHERN CROSS** -

Jul 78. (7") **SUNSHINE THROUGH MY WINDOW. / BRING BACK THE 60'S MAN** -

—— (Sep78) **COUNTRY JOE** reformed THE FISH, with **BARRY MELTON** – guitar, vocals / **PETER ALBIN** – bass / **BOB FLURIE** – guitar / **HAROLD ACEVES** – drums.

—— continued solo work.

Nov 79. (7") **DOO WOP OH. / COYOTE** -

Dec 79. (lp) **LEISURE SUITE**
– Private parts / Take this time out / Doo-wop-oh / Hard work no play / La di da / Sure cure for the blues / Reaching for the stars.

Dec 79. (7") **TAKE THIS TIME OUT. / PRIVATE PARTS** -

Rag Baby Rag Baby

Aug 81. (lp) **ON MY OWN** (totally solo)
– Standing at the crossroads / Calamity Jane / Give some love, get some back / C-O-U-N-T-R-Y / The Halloween tree / Slide trombone blues / Your last few records just didn't make it / Power plant blues / A Vietnam veteran still alive / Yankee doodle / Darlin' Dan.

—— now with ever-changing personnel.

Jun 82. (d-lp) **INTO THE FRAY (live)** -
– Kiss my ass / Quiet days in Clichy / Sexist pig / Here I go again / Breakfast for two / Love is a fire / Picks and lasers / Coyote / Hold on it's coming / Entertainment is my business / Holy roller / Not so sweet Martha Lorraine / Janis / Get it all together / A Vietnam veteran still alive / Breakfast for two / Fixin'-to-die-rag / Save the whales / Ring of fire.

Oct 83. (lp) **CHILDS PLAY** -
– Not in a Chinese restaurant / Power plant blues / Picks and lasers / Ice pack / One more good year of good times / Vietnam never again / America my home / Star Yeck: Voyage of the good ship Undersize / Mi Corazon.

Feb 85. (lp) **PEACE ON EARTH** -
– Live in peace / Sunshine / Let it rain / You can get it if you really want / War hero / Feeling better / The girl next door / Darlin' man (the rocket man) / Pledging my love / Garden of Eden / Space lovin' / Peace on Earth.

1986. (d-lp) **VIETNAM EXPERIENCE** -
– I-feel-like-I'm-fixin'-to-die rag / Foreign policy blues / Agent Orange song / The girl next door (combat nurse) / Kiss my arse / Secret agent / Vietnam veteran still alive / Vietnam never again / Mourning blues / Welcome home / Vietnam requiem – part 1:- The beginning, part 2:- The end.

—— Returned in 1990 to recording studio.

not issued Rykodisc

Jan 91. (cd) **SUPERSTITIOUS BLUES** -

Line Rykodisc

Jan 95. (cd) **CARRY ON**

– compilations, etc. (with the FISH *) –

Jul 76. Vanguard; (d-lp) **THE ESSENTIAL COUNTRY JOE McDONALD**

Mar 77. Golden Hour-Pye; (lp)(c) **THE GOLDEN HOUR OF COUNTRY JOE McDONALD** -

Jun 76. Fantasy; (lp) **REUNION** (live '67-'69 line-up)

Jul 81. Rag Baby; (lp) **COLLECTOR'S ITEMS – THE FIRST THREE EP'S** *
(cd-iss. 1992 on 'Sequel')

Aug 83. Animus; (lp) **ANIMAL TRACKS**

Sep 83. Animus; (7") **BLOOD ON THE TRACKS. / (no b-side)**

—— (also appeared on Various Artists compilations WOODSTOCK, QUIET DAY IN CLICHY, CELEBRATION – BIG SUE FESTIVAL (live), A TRIBUTE TO WOODY GUTHRIE, ZACHARIAH (Soundtrack).

Jun 91. Pickwick; (cd) **COLLECTED COUNTRY JOE & THE FISH** * -
– Superbird / Bass strings / Section 43 / Flying high / Not so sweet Martha Lorraine / Death sound blues / Porpoise mouth / Sad and lonely times / The fish cheer – I-feel-like-I'm-fixin'-to-die rag / Rock coast blues / Janis / Eastern jam / Good guys – bad guys cheer / Rock and roll music / An unlimited protest / Here I go again / Maria, my own / Crystal blues / Rockin' round the world.

1992 Big Beat; (cd) **CLASSICS** -

Michael McDONALD

Born: 2 Sep'52, St.Louis, Missouri, USA. In 1970, he signed to 'RCA' and issued debut 45 'GOD KNOWS I LOVE MY BABY', but an lp was shelved after its flop. After a spell as a session man for DAVID CASSIDY, etc, he gained contract to 'Bell', and released 4 more 1972 flops. He then spent 1974 as part of STEELY DAN, before in 1975 replacing TOM JOHNSTON in The DOOBIE BROTHERS. McDONALD soon added his songwriting skills to group, and scored first No.1 late in 1978 with 'WHAT A FOOL BELIEVES'. In 1982, the DOOBIE's split, and he soon signed a new solo deal with 'Warners'. In the Autumn his single 'I KEEP FORGETTIN'' and its parent Ted Templeman produced album 'IF THATS WHAT IT TAKES', both made US Top 10. Continued to make his mark throughout the rest of the 80's. • **Style:** Grey bearded AOR artist with dusky vox. • **Songwriters:** self-penned except; MIDNIGHT RIDER (Allman Brothers) / HEY GIRL (Gofin-King) / I WANT YOU (Paul Buchanan / Blue Nile). etc?. • **Trivia:** He has contributed to songs by friends CHRISTOPHER CROSS, KENNY LOGGINS and AMY HOLLAND.

Recommended: SWEET FREEDOM – THE BEST OF . . . (*6).

MIKE McDONALD

not issued R.C.A.

1970. (7") **GOD KNOWS I LOVE MY BABY. / I YOU WON'T, I WILL** -

not issued Bell

Apr 72. (7") **DEAR ME. / I THINK I LOVE YOU** -

Jul 72. (7") **WHEN I'M HOME. / GOOD OLD TIME LOVE SONG** -

Nov 72. (7") **DRIVIN' WHEEL. /** -

Jan 73. (7") **WHERE DO I GO FROM HERE. /** -

—— In Mar'74, he joined STEELY DAN. In Apr'75, he became part of The DOOBIE BROTHERS until their demise early 1982. Two years previous (Jan80) he duetted on single 'LET ME GO, LOVE' with NICOLETTE LARSON. It hit US No.35.

MICHAEL McDONALD

not issued Arista

Mar 82. (lp) **THAT WAS THEN – THE EARLY RECORDINGS OF MICHAEL McDONALD** (compilation) -

—— He then embarked on new solo career. Augmented by **ROBBEN FORD** – guitar / **WILLIE WEEKS** – bass / **JEFF PORCARO** – drums / **PAULINHO DA COSTA** – percussion / etc.

Warners Warners

Aug 82. (lp)(c) **IF THAT'S WHAT IT TAKES** 6
– Playin' by the rules / I keep forgettin' (every time you're near) / Love lies / I gotta try / I can let you go now / That's why / If that's what it takes / No such luck / Losin' end / Believe in it. *(cd-iss.1988)*

Sep 82. (7") **I KEEP FORGETTIN' (EVERY TIME YOU'RE NEAR). / LOSIN' END** 4 Aug 82
(UK re-iss.Jun86, hit No.43)

Jan 83. (7") **I GOTTA TRY. / BELIEVE IN IT** 44 Nov 82

Mar 83. (7") **PLAYIN' BY THE RULES. / BELIEVE IN IT** -

—— Dec83, he duets on single 'YAH MO B THERE' with JAMES INGRAM. It hit UK No.44 + US No.19, re-iss.& re-mixed UK Dec84, hit No.12.

Aug 85. (lp)(c) **NO LOOKIN' BACK** 45
– No lookin' back / Bad times / (I'll be your) Angel / By heart / Any foolish thing / Our love / (I hang) On your every word / Lost in the parade / Don't let me down.

Sep 85. (7") **NO LOOKIN' BACK. / DON'T LET ME DOWN** 34 Jul 85
(12"+=) – I gotta try. *(re-iss.Oct86)*

Nov 85. (7") **LOST IN THE PARADE. / BY HEART** -

Nov 85. (7") **OUR LOVE. / DON'T LET ME DOWN** -
(12"+=) – Bad times. *(re-iss.Apr87)*

In Apr'86, he duetted with PATTI LaBELLE on her UK No.2/US No.1 hit single 'ON MY OWN'. This was issued on 'MCA' as was his following solo single.

Aug 86. (7")(12") **SWEET FREEDOM. / THE FREEDOM LIGHTS** 12 7 Jun 86

Nov 86. (7") **OUR LOVE (theme from 'No Mercy'). / DON'T LET ME DOWN** -

— Later in the year, he made appearances for DAVID PACK (ex-AMBROSIA) 'I Can't Let Go', and TOTO's 'I'll Be Over You'.

Nov 86. (lp)(c)(cd) **SWEET FREEDOM – THE BEST OF MICHAEL McDONALD** (compilation) 6 -

– Sweet freedom / I'll be your angel / Yah mo b there (w / JAMES INGRAM) / I gotta try / I keep forgettin' (every time you're near) / Our love / On my own (w/ PATTI LaBELLE) / No lookin' back / Any foolish thing / That's why / What a fool believes (by The DOOBIE BROTHERS) / I can let go now.

— Mar'88, he is credited on single 'Love Has No Colour' with The WINIANS. This gospel song, like the JAMES INGRAM 45 before was issued on 'Qwest'.

— His next solo outing, was augmented by sessions + **MICHAEL LANDAU** – guitar / **ABRAHAM LABOREI** – bass / **JEFF PORCARO** – drums

Reprise Reprise

Mar 90. (cd)(c)(lp) **TAKE IT TO HEART** 35

– All we got / Get the word started / Love can break your heart / Take it to heart / Tear it up / Lonely talk / Searchin' for understanding / Homeboy / No amount of reason / One step away / You show me.

May 90. (c-s) **TAKE IT TO HEART. / PLAIN OF JARS** - 98

— with **JEFF BOVA** – keyboards / **JIMMY BRALOWER** – drum prog. / **MANU KATCHE** – drums / **PINO PALLADINO** – bass / **PAUL JACKSON JR.** – guitar / **LENNY CASTRO** – congas/ etc.

Aug 93. (cd)(c) **BLINK OF AN EYE**

– I stand for you / East of Eden / More to us than that / I want you / No more prayin' / Matters of the heart / Hey girl / What makes a man hold on / Blink of an eye / Everlasting / For a child.

Sep 93. (7")(c-s) **I STAND FOR YOU. / ('A'mix)**

(cd-s+=) – ('A'mixes).

— In Jun 94, his 'I KEEP FORGETTIN'' was used on backing on WARREN G and NATE DOGG's massive hit single 'Regulate'.

MC5

Formed: Detroit, Michegan, USA ... 1965 by TYNER, SMITH and KRAMER. After 2 limited singles releases, MC5 (MOTOR CITY FIVE) signed contract with 'Elektra' mid'68, helped by local DJ John Sinclair. Their controversial lp 'KICK OUT THE JAMS' (live late Oct'68) hit the shops on May'69. Its original uncensored version contained the line 'Kick Out The Jams, Motherfuckers!', with the offending word later supplanted with new ' ... Brothers And Sisters' on later copies. It had by this time dented the US Top 30, although they moved to 'Atlantic' in 1970 for another excellent lp 'BACK IN THE USA'. John Sinclair was sentenced to 10 years in the early 70's for a minor dope charge, but served only 2 of them after appeal. • **Style:** Pioneering political punk-rock activists, who competed with STOOGES. **Songwriters:** Group compositions, except; I CAN ONLY GIVE YOU EVERYTHING (Them) / TUTTI FRUTTI (Little Richard). • **Trivia:** JON LANDAU (now manager of SPRINGSTEEN), produced their 2nd lp.

Recommended: KICK OUT THE JAMS (*9) / BACK IN THE USA (*8).

ROB TYNER – vocals, harmonica / **WAYNE KRAMER** (b.30 Apr'48, Detroit, USA) – guitar, vocals, keyboards / **FRED 'SONIC' SMITH** – guitar / **MICHAEL DAVIS** – bass / **DENNIS THOMPSON** – drums

not issued A.M.G.

1966. (7") **I CAN ONLY GIVE YOU EVERYTHING. / I JUST DON'T KNOW** -

not issued A2.

Mar 68. (7") **LOOKING AT YOU. / BORDERLINE** -

— added 6th member **Brother J.C.CRAWFORD** – rapper / narrative

Elektra Elektra

May 69. (7") **KICK OUT THE JAMS. / MOTOR CITY IS BURNING** 82 Mar 69

May 69. (lp) **KICK OUT THE JAMS** 30 Mar 69

– Ramblin' rose / Kick out the jams / Come together / Rocker reducer No.62 / Borderline / Motor city is burning / I want you right now / Starship. *(re-iss.May77.) (re-iss.+cd.Nov91) (re-iss.cd+c Mar93 on 'Pickwick') (re-iss.cd/c Sep95 on 'Warners')*

1969. (7") **RAMBLIN' ROSE. / BORDERLINE** -

Atlantic Atlantic

Oct 70. (7") **TONIGHT. / LOOKING AT YOU** -

Nov 70. (lp)(c) **BACK IN THE U.S.A.** Feb 70

– Tutti frutti / Tonight / Teenage list / Looking at you / Let me try / High school / Call me animal / The American ruse / Shakin' Street / The human being lawnmower / Back in the U.S.A. *(cd-iss.May93 on 'Rhino-Atlantic')*

1970. (7") **SHAKIN' STREET. / THE AMERICAN RUSE** -

Oct 71. (lp)(c) **HIGH TIME**

– Sister Anne / Baby won't ya / Miss X / Gotta keep movin' / Future – Now / Poison / Over nnd over / Skunk (sonically speaking). *(cd-iss.May93 on 'Rhino-Atlantic')*

— (split early '72 when DAVIS departed) THOMPSON, SMITH and DAVIS formed short-lived ASCENSION. FRED SMITH married PATTI SMITH and later formed SONIC'S RENDEZVOUS BAND. TYNER was credited on HOT RODS single, late'77. (see ⇒ EDDIE & THE HOT RODS.

– compilations, etc. –

1969. A.M.G.; (7") **I CAN ONLY GIVE YOU EVERYTHING. / ONE OF THE GUYS** -

Jul 83. R.O.I.R.; (c) **BABES IN ARMS** -

(cd-iss.Apr90 & Dec92 on 'Danceteria')

Nov 94. Alive; (cd)(10"lp) **POWER TRIP**

May 94. Receiver; (cd) **BACK TO COME** -

Nov 94. Receiver; (cd) **LOOKING AT YOU** -

Feb 95. Alive; (10"lp) **AMERICAN RUSE** -

Feb 95. Skydog; (cd) **THUNDER EXPRESS – ONE DAY IN THE STUDIO** -

Mar 95. Alive; (10"lp) **ICE PICK SLIM** -

Sep 95. Alive; (10"lp) **LOOKING AT YOU** -

WAYNE KRAMER

went solo after spending 5 years in prison for cocaine dealing.

Stiff-Chiswick not issued

Oct 77. (7") **RAMBLIN' ROSE. / GET SOME** -

Radar not issued

1979. (7") **THE HARDER THEY COME. / EAST SIDE GIRL** -

not issued Pure&Easy

1983. (7") **NEGATIVE GIRLS. / STREET WARFARE** -

WAYNE KRAMER'S GANG WAR

were formed in 1980 with **JOHNNY THUNDERS** – vocals

Zodiac not issued

1987. (7"ep) **GANG WAR (live at Max's May 1980)** -

— Their self-titled lp was issued by same label in May 1990. WAYNE joined the DEVIANTS in 1984 for their album HUMAN GARBAGE.

WAYNE KRAMER'S DEATH TONGUE

not issued Curio

1987. (7") **SPIKE HEELS. / ?** -

Apr 92. (cd) **DEATH TONGUE**

— (WAYNE played late 80's with DAS DAMEN and G.G. ALLIN)

In Sep'91, ROB TYNER was found dead after suffering heart attack. He was 46.

WAYNE KRAMER

Epitaph Epitaph

Dec 94. (cd)(c)(lp) **THE HARD STUFF**

Roger McGUINN (see under ⇒ BYRDS)

Maria McKEE

Born: 17 Aug'64, Los Angeles, California, USA. In 1984, she formed LONE JUSTICE with four guys (see below) and soon signed to 'Geffen'. Their eponymous debut in 1985 received rave reviews and sold well in UK for a Top 50 place, helped by song 'WAYS TO BE WICKED' co-penned with TOM PETTY. In 1986, she recruited entire new line-up for 'SHELTER' album, but this was their last. Previous to this release, FEARGAL SHARKEY (ex-UNDERTONES), had hit UK No.1 with her song 'A GOOD HEART', which prompted her to think solo. By 1989, her first solo outing was complete, although ex-LONE JUSTICE players also appeared. It dented the UK Top 50 again, but by the next year, she was at No.1 with 'SHOW ME HEAVEN', from the 'Days Of Thunder' film soundtrack. • **Style:** Mixes her girl-next-door beauty and sweet high vox, with country accented gospel rock. • **Songwriters:** Writes own work (debut co-with ETZIONI), and covered; SWEET JANE (Velvet Underground) / HAS HE GOT A FRIEND FOR ME (Richard Thompson) / WICHITA LINEMAN (Jim Webb). NOBODY'S CHILD was co-written w/ ROBBIE ROBERTSON (ex-BAND). • **Trivia:** She is the younger sister of BRYAN McLEAN of 60's rock band LOVE.

Recommended: MARIA McKEE (*5) / LONE JUSTICE (*7).

LONE JUSTICE

MARIA McKEE – vocals / **RYAN HEDGECOCK** – guitar / **TONY GILKYSON** – guitar / **MARVIN ETZIONI** – bass / **DON HEFFINGTON** – drums

Geffen Geffen

Apr 85. (7") **WAYS TO BE WICKED. / CACTUS ROSE** 71

(12"+=) – You are the light.

Jun 85. (lp)(c) **LONE JUSTICE** 49 56 May 85

– East of Eden / After the flood / Ways to be wicked / Don't toss us away / Working late / Sweet, sweet baby (I'm falling) / Pass it on / Wait 'til we get home / Soap, soup and salvation / You are the light. *(re-iss. Apr86 & Mar91)*

Aug 85. (7") **SWEET, SWEET BABY (I'M FALLING). / PASS IT ON** -

(12"+=) – Go 'way little boy.

Aug 85. (7") **SWEET, SWEET BABY (I'M FALLING). / DON'T TOSS US AWAY** -

— **MARIA McKEE** brought in entire new band, **SHANE FONTAYNE** – guitar (ex-STEVE FORBERT) who repl. HEDGECOCK / **BRUCE BRODY** – guitar (ex-PATTI SMITH) who repl. GILYKSON / **GREG SUTTON** – bass who repl. ETZIONI / **RUDY RICHMAN** – drums who repl. HEFFINGTON.

Oct 86. (7") **SHELTER. / CAN'T LOOK BACK** 49

(12"+=) – Belfry. (US; b-side)

Nov 86. (lp)(c)(cd) **SHELTER** 84

– I found love / Shelter / Reflected (on my side) / Beacon / Wheels / Belfry / Dreams come true (stand up and take it) / The gift / Inspiration / Dixie storms. *(re-iss.Mar91)*

Feb 87. (7") **I FOUND LOVE. / IF YOU DON'T LIKE THE RAIN** [45]
(12"+=)(12"pic-d+=) – ('A'extended).
(d7"+=) – Sweet Jane (live) / Don't toss us away (live).

MARIA McKEE

went solo, taking with her **FONTAYNE** and **BRODY** plus session people.

Jun 89. (lp)(c)(cd) **MARIA McKEE** [49]
– I've forgotten what it was in you (that put the need in me) / To miss someone / Am I the only one (who's ever felt this way?) / Nobody's child / Panic beach / Can't pull the wool (over the little lamb's eyes) / More than a heart can hold / This property is condemned / Breathe / Has he got a friend for me? / Drinkin' in my Sunday dress. *(re-iss.Mar91) (re-iss.cd Mar93)*

Jan 90. (7")(c-s) **TO MISS SOMEONE. / PANIC BEACH** Nov 90
(12"+=)(cd-s+=) – Drinkin' in my Sunday dress.

(below from 'Days Of Thunder' film on 'Epic'.

Aug 90. (7") **SHOW ME HEAVEN. / ('Car Building' by "HANS ZIMMER")** [1]
(12"+=)(cd-s+=) – (track by "APOLLO SMILE").

Jan 91. (7")(c-s) **BREATHE. / PANIC BEACH** [59]
(12"+=)(cd-s+=) – Drinkin' in my Sunday dress.

Jul 92. (7")(c-s) **SWEETEST CHILD. (as "MARIA McKEE & YOUTH") / ('A'acappella remix)** [45]
(12"+=)(cd-s+=) – ('A'trans tribal ritual stomp mix).

May 93. (c-s) **I'M GONNA SOOTHE YOU. / WHY WASN'T I MORE GRATEFUL (WHEN LIFE WAS SWEET)** [35]
(cd-s+=) – This thing (don't lead to Heaven).
(cd-s) – ('A'side) / If love was a red dress (hang me in rags) / Show me Heaven (acoustic demo).

Jun 93. (cd)(c)(lp) **YOU GOTTA SIN TO GET SAVED** [26]
– I'm gonna soothe you / My lonely sad eyes / My girlhood among the outlaws / One only / I forgive you / I can't make it alone / Precious time / The way young lovers do / Why wasn't I more grateful (when life was sweet) / You gotta sin to be saved. *(re-iss.cd Oct95)*

Aug 93. (c-s) **I CAN'T MAKE IT ALONE. / MY GIRLHOOD AMONG THE OUTLAWS** [74]
(cd-s+=) – I'm gonna soothe you / Wichita lineman (both acoustic).
(cd-s+=) – I wish I was your mother.

– (LONE JUSTICE) compilation, etc. –

Dec 93. Windsong; (cd) **BBC RADIO 1 LIVE IN CONCERT (live)**

John McLAUGHLIN / MAHAVISHNU ORCHESTRA

Born: 4 Jan'42, Yorkshire, England. Although he learned piano and violin at an early age, it was the guitar that he took up as a teenager. In the mid 60's, he joined GRAHAM BOND ORGANISATION then BRIAN AUGER TRINITY. His debut solo outing EXTRAPOLATION in '69, paved the way for more session work, helping him gain virtuosity accolade and near legendary status. During the turn of the decade, he featured in TONY WILLIAMS' LIFETIME and MILES DAVIS' jazz-rock outings. After 2 early 70's solo lp's, he formed the MAHAVISHNU ORCHESTRA, an exceptional group who also contained JAN HAMMER. They peaked in 1973, when album 'BIRDS OF FIRE' made the US Top 20, although he broke from all commercial rock roots with advent of SHAKTI in 1976. • **Style:** Seminal jazz-fusion artist with dazzling rock credentials, who branched out into spiritual Eastern acoustic vein by mid-70's. • **Songwriters:** McLAUGHLIN compositions except BLUES IN GREEN (Miles Davis) / PASHA'S LOVE (Gurtu – band member 1990) / etc. • **Trivia:** Since the late 60's, JOHN has been a practising vegetarian and convert to Sri Chimnoy. He still meditates and practises Yoga.

Recommended: THE BEST OF THE MAHAVISHNU ORCHESTRA (*7)

JOHN McLAUGHLIN

solo with **JOHN SURMAN** – saxophone / **BRIAN ODGERS** – bass / **TONY OXLEY** – drums

Marmalade Polydor

1969. (lp) **EXTRAPOLATION** Oct 72
– Extrapolation / It's funny / Argen's bag / Pete the poet / This is for us to share / Spectrum / Binky's beam / Really you know / Two for two / Peace piece. *(re-iss.1974 + Aug81 on 'Polydor')*

— He was then credited on album 'THINGS WE LIKE' with JACK BRUCE, JON HISEMAN & DICK HECKSTAL-SMITH. McLAUGHLIN then went to America to join (TONY WILLIAM'S) LIFETIME, playing on 2 lp's 'EMERGENCY' + 'TURN IT OVER'. Around the same time MILES DAVIS gave him work on his 'BITCHES' BREW' + 'IN A SILENT WAY'. Returned to solo work once more. Augmented by **BUDDY MILES** – drums / **JERRY GOODMAN** – violin (ex-FLOCK) / **BILLY RICH** – bass / **LARRY YOUNG** (aka KHALID YASIN) – keyboards

Barclay FRANCE C.B.S.

1970. (lp) **DEVOTION** [-] [-] 1972
– Devotion / Dragon song / Marbles / Siren / Don't let the dragon eat your mother / Purpose of when. *(re-iss.Jul87 on 'C.B.S.')*

— **BILLY COBHAM** – drums, percussion (ex-MILES DAVIS) repl. BUDDY MILES

Douglas Columbia

1971. (lp)(c) **MY GOAL'S BEYOND (as "JOHN MAHAVISHNU McLAUGHLIN")**
– Peace one / Peace two / Goodbye pork-pie hat / Something spiritual / Hearts and flowers / Philip Lane / Waltz for Bill Evans / Follow your heart / Song for my mother / Blue is green. *(re-iss.Mar82 on 'Elektra')*

Dawn not issued

1972. (lp) **WHERE FORTUNES SMILES** [-]
– Glancing backwards (for Junior) / Earth bound hearts / Where fortune smiles / New place, old place / Hope. *(cd-iss.Sep93 on 'B.G.O.') (cd-iss.Jul93)*

MAHAVISHNU ORCHESTRA

JOHN McLAUGHLIN with **COBHAM + GOODMAN** and adding **RICK LAIRD** – bass / **JAN HAMMER** – keyboards

C.B.S. Columbia

Jan 72. (lp)(c) **THE INNER MOUNTING FLAME** [89]
– Meeting of the Spirits / Dawn / The noonward race / A lotus on Irish streams / Vital transformation / You know you know / The dance of Maya / Awakening. *(re-iss.1976)*

Feb 73. (lp)(c) **BIRDS OF FIRE** [20] [15]
– Birds of fire / Miles beyond (Miles Davis) / Celestial terrestrial commuters / Sapphire bullets of pure love / Thousand Island park / Hope / One word / Sanctuary / Open country joy / Resolution. *(re-iss.Mar83, cd-iss.Nov83)(also issued on quad-lp) (cd re-iss.Jun92 on 'Columbia')*

May 73. (7") **OPEN COUNTRY BOY. / CELESTIAL COMMUTERS** [-]

— Mid'73, released collaboration Top 20 album 'LOVE DEVOTION SURRENDER' with CARLOS SANTANA. (see: SANTANA ⇒)

Jan 74. (lp)(c) **BETWEEN NOTHINGNESS & ETERNITY (live)** [41] Dec 73
– Trilogy / The sunlit path – La mere de la mer – Tomorrow's story not the same / Sister Andrea / Dream. *(cd-iss.1988) (re-iss.Dec88 on 'B.G.O.', cd-iss.Dec91)*

— (Jan74) McLAUGHLIN disbanded group, COBHAM went solo as did JAN HAMMER. Recruited new people **JEAN LUC-PONTY** – electric violin (ex-Solo, ex-ZAPPA) / **MICHAEL NARADA WALDEN** – drums / **GAYLE MORAN** – keyboards, vocals / **RALPHE ARMSTRONG** – bass / **STEVE FRANKOVITCH** – brass / **BOB KNAPP** – reeds / plus **PHILIP HIRSCHI** – cello / **MARSHA WESTBROOK** – viola / **CAROL SHIRE** – violin / **STEVE KINDLER** – violin also credited The LONDON SYMPHONY ORCHESTRA conducted by MICHAEL TILSON-THOMAS

Jun 74. (lp)(c) **APOCALYPSE** [43] May 74
– Power of love / Vision of a naked sword / Smile of the beyond / Wings of Karma / Hymn to him.

Jan 75. (lp)(c) **VISIONS OF THE EMERALD BEYOND** [68]
– Eternity's breath (part 1 & 2) / Lila's dance / Can't stand your funk / Pastoral / Faith / Cosmic strut / If I could see / Be happy / Earth ship / Pegasus / Opus 1 / On the way home to Earth.

Feb 75. (7") **CAN'T STAND YOUR FUNK. / ETERNITY'S BREATH (part 1)**

— Retained **WALDEN, PONTY, ARMSTRONG.** New **STU GOLDBERG** – keyboards

Feb 76. (lp)(c) **INNER WORLDS**
– All in the family / Miles out / In my life / Gita / Morning calls / The way of the pilgrim / River of my heart / Planetary citizen / Louis feet / Inner worlds (parts 1 & 2). *(re-iss.1987) (cd-iss.Nov94 on 'Columbia')*

SHAKTI with JOHN McLAUGHLIN

(**SHAKTI** = **LEVI SHANKAR** – violin / **TH VINYAKRAM** – percussion, vocals / **ZAKIR HUSSAIN** – percussion)

Jun 76. (lp)(c) **SHAKTI** (live)
– Joy / Lotus feet / What need have I for this? – What need have I for that? / I am dancing at the feet of my Lord / All bliss – All bliss.

Mar 77. (lp)(c) **A HANDFUL OF BEAUTY**
– La danse du bonheur / Lady L / India / Kriti / Isis / Two sisters.

Dec 77. (lp)(c) **NATURAL ELEMENTS**
– Mind ecology / Face to face / Come on baby dance with me / The daffodil and the eagle / Happiness is being together / Bridge of sighs / Get down and strut / Peace of mind.

JOHNNY McLAUGHLIN

went solo again, using past band members, etc.

May 78. (lp)(c) **ELECTRIC GUITARIST**
– New York on my mind / Friendship / Every tear from your eye / Do you hear the voices that you left behind / Are you the one? are you the one? / Phenomenon: Compulsion / My foolish heart.

— Next album he was backed by **The ONE TRUTH BAND** who were **SHANKER** – violin / **ANTHONY ALLEN SMITH** – drums / **STU GOLDBERG** – keyboards

May 79. (lp)(c) **ELECTRIC DREAMS** Apr 79
– Guardian angels / Miles Davis / Electric dreams, electric sighs / Desire and the comforter / Love and understanding / Singing Earth / The dark prince / The unknown dissident.

Jun 81. (lp)(c) **FRIDAY NIGHT IN SAN FRANCISCO (live) (by "JOHN, McLAUGHLIN, AL DiMEOLA, PACO DE LUCIA")** [97] May 81
– Mediterranean sundance – Rio Ancho / Short tales of the Black Forest / Frevo resgado / Fantasia suite / Guardian angels.

Warners Warners

Jan 82. (lp)(c) **BELO HORIZONTE** Dec 81
– Belo horizonte / La baleine / Very early / One melody / Stardust on your sleeve / Waltz for Katia / Zamfir / Manita's d'aro (for Paco De Lucia).

1982. (lp)(c) **MUSIC SPOKEN HERE** [-]
– Aspan / Blues for L.W. / The translators / Honky-tonk Heaven / Viene Clare Ando / David / Negative ions / Briese de coeur / Loro.

DiMEOLA, McLAUGHLIN, DE LUCIA

AL DiMEOLA – guitar (ex-CHICK COREA, etc) / **PACO DE LUCIA** – guitar

Mercury Columbia

Jun 83. (lp)(c) **PASSION, GRACE & FIRE**
– Aspen / Orient blue / Chiquito / Sichia / David / Passion, grace & fire.

JOHN McLAUGHLIN

solo with **MITCHELL FORMAN** – keyboards / **BILL EVANS** – saxophone / **JONAS HELLBORG** – bass / **DANNY GOTTLIEB** – drums

WEA WEA

Jan 85. (lp)(c) **MAHAVISHNU**
– Radio activity / Nostalgia / Nightriders / East side west side / Clarendon hills / Jazz / The unbeliever / Pacific express / When blue turns gold.

Polygram Intercord

Jul 87. (lp)(c)(cd) **ADVENTURES IN RADIOLAND**
– The wait / Just ideas / Jozy / Half man, half cookie / Florianapolis / Gotta dance / The wall will fall / Reincarnation / Mitch match / 20th century limited.

JOHN McLAUGHLIN TRIO

with **KAI ECKHARDT** – bass / **TRILOK GURTU** – percussion

J.M.T. J.M.T.

Apr 90. (cd)(c)(lp) **LIVE AT THE ROYAL FESTIVAL HALL (live)**
– Blue in green / Medley: Just ideas – Jozy / Florianapolis / Pasha's love / Mother tongues. *(c+=)(cd+=)*– Blues for L.W.

JOHN McLAUGHLIN

solo with **LONDON SYMPHONY ORCHESTRA & MICHAEL TILSON THOMAS / KATIA LABEQUE** – piano

C.B.S. Columbia

1990. (cd)(c) **CONCERTO FOR GUITAR & ORCHESTRA 'THE MEDITERRANEAN' / / DUOS FOR GUITAR & PIANO**
– (I)- Rhythmic / (II)- Slow & sad / (III)- Animato / Briese de coeur / Montana / Two sisters / Until such time / Zakir.

—— now with **JOEY DeFRANCESCO** – organ/ **ELVIN JONES** – drums

Verve Verve

Jun 95. (cd) **AFTER THE RAIN**
– Take the Coltrane / My favorite things / Sing me softly of the blues / Encuentros / Naima / Tones for Elvin Jones / Crescent / Afro blue / After the rain.

– his compilations, others, etc. –

Oct 75. Polydor; (d-lp) **IN RETROSPECT**
1976. Polydor; (lp)(c) **THE BEST OF THE MAHAVISHNU ORCHESTRA**
– A love supreme / New York on my mind / The dark prince / La danse du bonheur / Friendship / Face to face / The unknown dissident / Lotus feet. *(re-iss.Jun80)*
Jan 81. CBS; (lp)(c) **THE BEST OF JOHN McLAUGHLIN**

Don McLEAN

Born: 2 Oct'45, New Rochelle, New York, USA. Having been a club singer from 1963, he acquired a residency at Lena's bar in 1968, and was dubbed 'The Hudson River Troubadour'. The following year, he was invited to join PETE SEEGER on his expedition tour of the Hudson river. This 6-week journey involved over 25 concerts at various riverside destinations, and made people aware of the river's industrial pollution. In 1970, McLEAN's efforts were finally rewarded, when 'Mediarts' released debut lp 'TAPESTRY'. The next year, 'AMERICAN PIE' (an 8+minute epic 45 & put into 2 parts), was issued on 'United Art'. It raced to the top of US charts, as did its parent album of the same name. It was quickly pursued by his second UK hit 'VINCENT' (about painter Van Gogh), which although only making No.12 in US, hit UK No.1 early '72. These 2 songs became something of an albatross around his neck for the remaining 70's, although in 1980 he returned to the top of UK charts with 'CRYING'. • **Style:** Talented socially aware balladeer, whose narrative soft-pastel toned love songs became trademark. Moved into C&W scene throughout the 80's. • **Songwriters:** As said, except covers; KILLING ME SOFTLY WITH HIS SONG (Fox-Gimbel) / EVERYDAY (Buddy Holly) / CRYING IN THE CHAPEL (Elvis Presley) / MULE SKINNER BLUES (Fendermen) / SUNSHINE LIFE FOR ME (George Harrison) / FOOLS PARADISE (Linsley – Petty – LeGlaire) / GOING FOR THE GOLD (C.Bowder – J.W. Ryles) / MOUNTAINS OF MOURNE (P. French – H. Collinson) / CRYING (Roy Orbison) / SINCE I DON'T HAVE YOU (Skyliners) / LOVE HURTS (Everly Brothers) / etc. Albums 'PLAYIN' FAVOURITES', 'LOVE TRACKS' & 'FOR THE MEMORIES VOLUMES 1 & 2' were collections of unoriginals. • **Trivia:** AND I LOVE YOU SO became UK Top 3 hit for pop crooner PERRY COMO in '41.

Recommended: THE VERY BEST OF DON McLEAN (*7).

DON McLEAN – vocals, guitar (with session people)

not issued Mediarts

Feb 71. (lp) **TAPESTRY** –
– Castles in the air / General store / Magdalene lane / Tapestry / Respectable / Orphans of wealth / Three flights up / And I love you so / Bad girl / Circus song / No reason for your dreams. *(US re-dist. Feb 72) (UK-iss.Jun72 on 'United Artists', hit No.16) (re-iss.Sep84 on 'Fame') (cd-iss.Jul94 on 'B.G.O.')*

United Art United Art

Sep 71. (7") **AND I LOVE YOU SO. / CASTLES IN THE AIR** –
Nov 71. (7") **AMERICAN PIE. / EMPTY CHAIRS** – 1
Jan 72. (7") **AMERICAN PIE (part 1). / (part 2)** 2 –
(re-iss.Jan84 + Sep86)
Feb 72. (lp)(c) **AMERICAN PIE** 3 1 Nov 71
– American pie (parts 1 & 2) / Till tomorrow / Vincent / Crossroads / Winterwood / Empty chairs / Everybody loves me, baby / Sister Fatima / The grave / Babylon. *(re-iss.May81 on 'Greenlight') (re-iss.May82 on 'Fame', cd-iss.May88)*

Apr 72. (7") **VINCENT. / CASTLES IN THE AIR** 1 12 Mar72
Jan 73. (7") **DREIDEL. / BRONCO BILL'S LAMENT** 21
Jan 73. (lp)(c) **DON McLEAN** 23 Dec 72
– If we try / Narcisissma / Dreidel / Bronco Bill's lament / Birthday song / The pride parade / The more you pay / Falling through time / On the Amazon / Oh my what a shame.
Mar 73. (7") **EVERYDAY. / THE MORE YOU PAY** 38 –
Mar 73. (7") **IF WE TRY. / THE MORE YOU PAY** – 58
Oct 73. (7"m) **MOUNTAINS O' MOURNE. / MEDLEY (BILL CHEETHAM – OLD JOE CLARK)** –
Nov 73. (lp)(c) **PLAYIN' FAVOURITES** 42
– Sittin' on top of the world / Living with the blues / Mountains O'mourne / Fool's paradise / Love o love / Medley:- (Bill Cheetham – Old Joe Clark) / Ancient history / Over the mountains / Lovesick blues / New mule skinner blues / Happy trails. *(cd-iss.Jun95 on 'BGO')*
Mar 74. (7") **FOOL'S PARADISE. / HAPPY TRAILS** –
Jun 74. (7") **NEW MULE SKINNER BLUES. / SITTIN' ON TOP OF THE WORLD** –
Nov 74. (lp)(c) **HOMELESS BROTHER**
– Winter has me in its grip / La la love you / Homeless brother / Sunshine life for me (sail away Raymond) / The legend of Andrew McCrew / Wonderful baby / We have lived / Great big man / Tangled (like a spider in her hair) / Crying in the chapel / Did you know. *(cd-iss.Nov94 on 'B.G.O.')*
Apr 75. (7") **HOMELESS BROTHER. / LA LA I LOVE YOU** –
Jun 75. (7") **WONDERFUL BABY. / BIRTHDAY SONG** – 93
Jun 75. (7") **WONDERFUL BABY. / HOMELESS BROTHER** –
Sep 76. (d-lp)(c) **SOLO (live)**
– Magdalene lane / Masters of war / Wonderful baby / Where were you bany / Empty chairs / Geordie's lost his penker / Babylon / And I love you so / MacTavish is dead / Cripple creek / New mule skinner blues / Great big man / Bronco Bill's lament / Happy trails / Circus song / Birthday song / On the Amazon / American pie / Over the waterfall / Arkansas traveller / Homeless brother / Castles in the air / Three flights up / Lovesick blues / Winter has me in its grip / The legend of Andrew McCrew / Dreidel / Vincent / Till tomorrow. *(d-cd-iss.Nov95 on 'BGO')*

EMI Int. Arista

Sep 77. (7") **PRIME TIME. / THE STATUE** –
Nov 77. (lp)(c) **PRIME TIME** Jun 77
– Prime time / The statue / Jump / Redwing / The wrong thing to do / The pattern is broken / When love begins / Colour TV blues / Building my body / Down the road / Sally Ann / When one good thing goes bad / South of the border (down Mexico way).
Nov 77. (7") **PRIME TIME. / REDWING** –
Jan 78. (7") **WHEN LOVE BEGINS. / COLOUR TV BLUES**

EMI Int. Millennium

Feb 79. (7") **IT DOESN'T MATTER ANYMORE. / IF WE TRY**
Mar 79. (lp)(c) **CHAIN LIGHTNING**
– Words and music / Crying / It's just the sun / Lotta lovin' / Your cheating heart / Wonderful night / It doesn't matter anymore / Since I don't have you / Genesis (in the beginning) / It's a beautiful life. *(UK re-dist.May80 hit No. 19, US re-iss. Feb 81 hit No.28)*
Apr 79. (7") **WORDS AND MUSIC. / YOUR CHEATING HEART**
Mar 80. (7") **CRYING. / GENESIS (IN THE BEGINNING)** 1 5 Jan 81
Jul 80. (7") **SINCE I DON'T HAVE YOU. / IT'S A BEAUTIFUL LIFE** –
Apr 81. (7") **SINCE I DON'T HAVE YOU. / YOUR CHEATING HEART** – 23
Jul 81. (7") **IT'S JUST THE SUN. / WORDS AND MUSIC** – 83
Jan 82. (7") **CASTLES IN THE AIR. / CRAZY EYES** 47 36 Oct 81
Jan 82. (lp)(c) **BELIEVERS** Nov 81
– Castles in the air / Love hurts / Jerusalem / Crazy eyes / Love letters / Sea cruise / I tune the world out / Isn't it strange / Left for dead on the road of love / Believers / Sea man.
Nov 82. (7") **JERUSALEM. / LEFT FOR DEAD ON THE ROAD OF LOVE** –
Nov 82. (7") **THE VERY THOUGHT OF YOU. / LEFT FOR DEAD ON THE ROAD OF LOVE** –
Feb 83. (d-lp)(d-c) **DOMINION (live)** Nov 82
– It's just the sun / Building my body / Wonderful baby / The very thought of you / Fool's paradise / You're so square (baby I don't care) / You have lived / The statue / Prime time / American pie / Left for dead on the road of love / Believers / Sea man / It's a beautiful life / Chain lightning / Crazy eyes / La la I love you / Dream lover / Crying / Vincent.
Apr 87. (7") **HE'S GOT YOU. / ?**
Apr 87. (lp)(c)(cd) **DON McLEAN'S GREATEST HITS – THEN AND NOW**
– He's got you / American pie / To have and to hold / Castles in the air / But she loves me / Superman's ghost / Vincent / And I love you so / Crying / Don't burn the bridge.

Capitol Capitol

Dec 87. (7") **YOU CAN'T BLAME THE TRAIN. / PERFECT LOVE** –
Jun 88. (7") **LOVE IN THE HEART. / EVERY DAY'S A MIRACLE** –
Sep 88. (7") **IT'S NOT YOUR FAULT. / EVENTUALLY** –
Nov 89. (lp)(c)(cd) **FOR THE MEMORIES**
– Don't / Crazy / Travelin' man / You don't know me / Sittin' in the balcony / Wonderful world / I can't help it / Maybe baby / White sports coat / If I only had a match / But beautiful / Over the weekend / Someone to watch over me / Somebody loves me / Count your blessings / It had to be you / Not a moment too soon / Change partners / Nobody knows you when you're down and out / Stardust.

– compilations, others, etc. –

1974. U.A.; (7") **VINCENT. / DREIDEL** –
1974. U.A.; (7") **AMERICAN PIE. / (part 2)** –
Jun 78. U.A.; (7") **AND I LOVE YOU SO. / VINCENT** –
Aug 80. U.A.; (lp)(c) **THE BEST OF DON McLEAN** 4
Sep 88. M.F.P.; (lp)(c) **LOVE TRACKS** –
Oct 89. Goldcastle; (lp)(c)(cd) **AND I LOVE YOU SO**
1990. Goldcastle; (cd)(c)(lp) **GREATEST HITS LIVE! (live 1980)**
Nov 91. E.M.I.; (cd)(c)(lp) **THE BEST OF DON McLEAN**
– American pie / Castles in the air (1981 version) / Dreidel / Winterwood / Everyday /

Sister Fatima / Empty chairs / The birthday song / Wonderful baby / La la I love you / Vincent / Crossroads / And I love you so / Fool's Paradise / If we try / Mountains of Mourne / The grave / Respectable / Going for the gold / Crying. (cd+=) – Bronco Bill's lament / Oh my what a shame / If we try / Babylon / Love in my heart.

Aug 91. Liberty; (7")(c-s) **AMERICAN PIE. / VINCENT** ☐ ☐
(cd-s+=) – Castles in the air.

G. W. McLENNAN (see under ⇒ GO-BETWEENS)

Ian McNABB (see under ⇒ ICICLE WORKS)

Tony McPHEE (see under ⇒ GROUNDHOGS)

MC REN (see under ⇒ N.W.A.)

Christine McVIE (see under ⇒ FLEETWOOD MAC)

MEAT LOAF

Born: MARVIN LEE ADAY, 27 Sep'48, Dallas, Texas, USA. In 1966 he moved to Los Angeles and formed psychedelic-rock outfit POPCORN BLIZZARD, who opened for The WHO, AMBOY DUKES and The STOOGES, before disbanding early 1969. That year, he successfully auditioned for the 'Hair' musical, where he met female soul singer STONEY. In 1970, they made a self-titled lp together for 'Rare Earth', but he soon re-joined 'Hair' tour in Cleveland. Later in '72, he took the role of Buddha in the musical 'Rainbow'. Early in '74, he starred in JIM STEINMAN's Broadway musical 'More Than You Deserve'. The following year, he acted/sang in Richard O'Brien's Broadway musical 'The ROCKY HORROR PICTURE SHOW', which was soon made into a film with MEAT LOAF taking his part of EDDIE. He and STEINMAN went on to tour with comedy show 'National Lampoon', with MEAT LOAF playing the part of a priest in 'Rockabye Hamlet'. Also in 1976, he sang on TED NUGENT's 'Free For All' album. Early in 1977, he got together again with STEINMAN in New York, to start work on 'NEVERLAND' project. They signed to 'RCA', but moved stables after it was clear the label didn't want producer TODD RUNDGREN. Later in '77, MEAT LOAF and crew switched to 'Cleveland International', and gained promotion from 'Epic'. Late in 1977, they unleashed the project as 'BAT OUT OF HELL', and with heavy tours, it made US Top 20, also hitting UK Top 10. For the next 8 years, it featured on chart, selling millions in the process. In the late 70's, MEAT LOAF went through throat problems, but starred the following year in film 'Roadie', alongside DEBBIE HARRY & BLONDIE. In 1981, impatient with waiting on MEAT LOAF's recovery, STEINMAN released 'BAD FOR GOOD' album which was intended for ML. The long-awaited follow-up 'DEAD RINGER FOR LOVE' was issued 4 months later, and although it hit UK No.1, it only managed to scrape into US Top 50. For the rest of the 80's, MEAT LOAF's activities lay mainly in Britain, where he soon became widely known celebrity. In 1993, he was back at the top again on both sides of the Atlantic, with 'BAT OUT OF HELL II'. This re-united him with STEINMAN, and provided him with first multi-selling No.1 'I WOULD DO ANYTHING FOR YOU (BUT I WOULDN'T DO THAT)'. • **Style:** 20-stone anthemic rocker, whose large vox range on 'BAT OUT OF HELL', is or should be part of everybody's collection. • **Songwriters:** JIM STEINMAN wrote everything, until he went solo after 1981 work. MEATLOAF then co-wrote w/ PAUL CHRISTIE + others in 1983. P. JACOBS + S. DURKEE took the bulk of the load in 1984 + STEINMAN was 'BACK INTO HELL' for 1993's 'BAT OUT OF HELL II'. Veteran pensmith DIANE WARREN took up most of the work for his mid-90's album. Covered; MARTHA (Tom Waits) / OH WHAT A BEAUTIFUL MORNING (Rogers-Hammerstein) / WHERE ANGELS SING (Davis) / WHATEVER HAPPENED TO SATURDAY NIGHT (O'Brien). • **Trivia:** His nickname MEAT LOAF, was given to him after he trod on the toes of his school coach. In 1967, POPCORN BLIZZARD issued 7" ONCE UPON A TIME. / HERO on 'Magenta'.

Recommended: BAT OUT OF HELL (*9) / HITS OUT OF HELL (*7).

STONEY AND MEAT LOAF

STONEY – vocals,(who later joined BOB SEGER).

		Rare Earth	Rare Earth
Apr 71.	(7") **WHAT YOU SEE IS WHAT YOU GET. / LADY OF MINE**	-	
Jun 71.	(7") **IT TAKES ALL KINDS OF PEOPLE. / THE WAY YOU DO THE THINGS YOU DO**		-
May 71.	(7") **WHAT YOU SEE IS WHAT YOU GET. / THE WAY YOU DO THE THINGS YOU DO**	-	71
Oct 71.	(lp) **FEATURING STONEY AND MEAT LOAF**	-	

– Jimmy Bell / She waits by the window / It takes all kind of people / Stone heart / Who is the leader of the people / What you see is what you get / Kiss me again / Sunshine (where's Heaven) / Jessica White / Lady be mine / Everything under the sun. *(re-iss. as 'FEATURING STONEY AND MEAT LOAF', Mar79 on 'Prodigal') (re-iss.1986 on 'Motown') (UK-iss. Oct 72)*

— Returned to feature in the musical 'Hair' (plus see above biography).

MEAT LOAF

		Ode	Ode
1973.	(7") **CLAP YOUR HANDS AND STAMP YOUR FEET. / STAND BY ME** (not released until 75)		
		not iss.	R.S.O.
1974	(7") **MORE THAN YOU DESERVE / PRESENCE OF THE LORD**	-	

— **MEAT LOAF** – vocals / **JIM STEINMAN** – composer, keyboards, percussion / **TODD RUNDGREN** – multi- / **ROY BITTAN** – piano, keyboards / **MAX WEINBERG** – drums / **KASIM SULTAN** – bass / **ROGER POWELL** – synth. / **ELLEN FOLEY + RORY DODD** – back.vox

		Epic	Cleveland-Epic
Jan 78.	(lp)(c) **BAT OUT OF HELL**	9	14 Oct 77

– Bat out of Hell / You took the words right out of my mouth / Heaven can wait / All reved up with no place to go / Two out of three ain't bad / Paradise by the dashboard light:- Let me sleep on it – I'll be praying for the end of time / For crying out loud. *(cd-iss.1983) (pic-lp 1978) (re-iss.Jul91, hit UK No.14, re-entered Jan92, peaked again at No.24-Jul92) (returned to hit UK No.19 Autumn 1993)*

Apr 78.	(7") **YOU TOOK THE WORDS RIGHT OUT OF MY MOUTH. / FOR CRYING OUT LOUD**	33	39 Nov 78
Jul 78.	(7") **TWO OUT OF THREE AIN'T BAD. / FOR CRYING OUT LOUD**	32	11 Mar 78
Sep 78.	(7") **PARADISE BY THE DASHBOARD LIGHT. / ALL REVED UP WITH NO PLACE TO GO**		39 Mar 78
Jan 79.	(ext-7"red)(ext-12"red) **BAT OUT OF HELL. / HEAVEN CAN WAIT** *(re-iss.Apr81)*	15	

— MEAT LOAF now brought in many session people, including **CHER** on title track.

Sep 81.	(lp)(c)(pic-lp) **DEAD RINGER**	1	45

– Peel out / I'm gonna love her for both of us / More than you deserve / I'll kill you if you don't come back / Read 'em and weep / Nocturnal pleasure / Dead ringer for love / Everything is permitted. *(re-iss.Nov85) (cd-iss.Nov87)*

Sep 81.	(7") **I'M GONNA LOVE HER FOR BOTH OF US. / EVERYTHING IS PERMITTED**	62	84
Nov 81.	(7")(7"pic-d) **DEAD RINGER FOR LOVE. / MORE THAN YOU DESERVE** *(re-iss.Aug88)*	5	
Mar 82.	(7") **READ 'EM AND WEEP. / EVERYTHING IS PERMITTED** (12"+=) – (interview disc).		
1982.	(12"ep-clear) **MEAT LOAF IN EUROPE '82 (live)**		-

– Two out of three ain't bad / You took the words . . . / I'm gonna love you. / Dead ringer for love.

May 83.	(lp)(c) **MIDNIGHT AT THE LOST AND FOUND**	7	

– Razor's edge / Midnight at the lost and found / Wolf at your door / Keep driving / The promised land / You never can be too sure about the girl / Priscilla / Don't you look at me like that / If you really want to / Fallen angel. *(cd-iss.Jan87)*

May 83.	(7")(7"pic-d) **IF YOU REALLY WANT TO. / KEEP DRIVING** (12"+=)(12"pic-d+=) – Lost love.	59	
Jul 83.	(7")(7"pic-d) **RAZOR'S EDGE. / YOU NEVER CAN BE TOO SURE ABOUT THE GIRL** (12"+=) Don't look at me like that		
Sep 83.	(7") **MIDNIGHT AT THE LOST AND FOUND. / FALLEN ANGEL** (d7"+=)(12"+=)(12"pic-d+=) – Bat out of Hell (live) / Dead ringer for love (live).	17	
Jan 84.	(7") **RAZOR'S EDGE. / PARADISE BY THE DASHBOARD LIGHT** (12"+=) – Read 'em and weep.	41	
		Arista	R.C.A.
Sep 84.	(7")(7"sha-pic-d) **MODERN GIRL. / TAKE A NUMBER** (12"+=)(12"pic-d+=) – ('A'extended).	17	
Nov 84.	(lp)(c)(cd) **BAD ATTITUDE**	8	74

– Bad attitude / Modern girl / Nowhere fast / Surf's up / Piece of the action / Jumpin' the gun / Cheatin' in your dreams / Don't leave your mark on me / Sailor to a siren. *(re-iss.May86 on 'Fame') (cd re-iss.Jun88)*

Nov 84.	(7")(7"sha-pic-d) **NOWHERE FAST. / CLAP YOUR HANDS** (ext-12"+=) – Stand by me. (d7"+=) – Bat out of Hell (live) / Modern Girl (US mix). (d12") – (all 5 tracks)	67	
Mar 85.	(7")(7"sha-pic-d) **PIECE OF THE ACTION. / SAILOR TO A SIREN** (12"+=) – Bad attitude.	47	
Aug 86.	(7")(7"sha-pic-d) **ROCK'N'ROLL MERCENARIES. / REVOLUTIONS PER MINUTE** (12"+=)(12"sha-pic-d+=) – ('A'extended). ('A'featured JOHN PARR)	31	
Sep 86.	(lp)(c)(cd) **BLIND BEFORE I STOP**	28	

– Execution day / Rock'n'roll mercenaries / Getting away with murder / One more kiss / Night of the soft parade / Blind before I stop / Burning down / Standing on the outside / Masculine / Man and a woman / Special girl / Rock'n'roll hero.

Nov 86.	(7")(7"sha-pic-d) **GETTING AWAY WITH MURDER. / ROCK'N'ROLL HERO** (12"+=) – Scot free (remix).		
Feb 87.	(7")(12") **BLIND BEFORE I STOP. / EXECUTION DAY** (12"+=) – Dead ringer for love / Paradise by the dashboard light (live).		
Apr 87.	(7") **SPECIAL GIRL. / ONE MORE KISS** (12"+=)(cd-s+=) – Dead ringer for love (live) / Paradise by the dashboard light (live).		
Oct 87.	(7") **BAT OUT OF HELL (live). / MAN AND A WOMAN** (12"+=) – ('A'full version).		
Nov 87.	(lp)(c)(cd) **LIVE AT WEMBLEY (live)**	60	

– Blind before I stop / Rock'n'roll mercenaries / You took the words right out of mouth / Midnight at the lost and found / Modern girl / Paradise by the dashboard light / Two out of three ain't bad / Bat out of Hell. *(cd+=)*– Masculine / Rock'n'roll medley: Johnny B. Goode – Slow down – Jailhouse rock – Blue suede shoes.

— MEAT LOAF became more involved with the media / television interviews, etc. Revitalised interest in 'ROCKY HORROR PICTURE SHOW' also brought him renewed limelight which enabled his past solo work to hit charts.

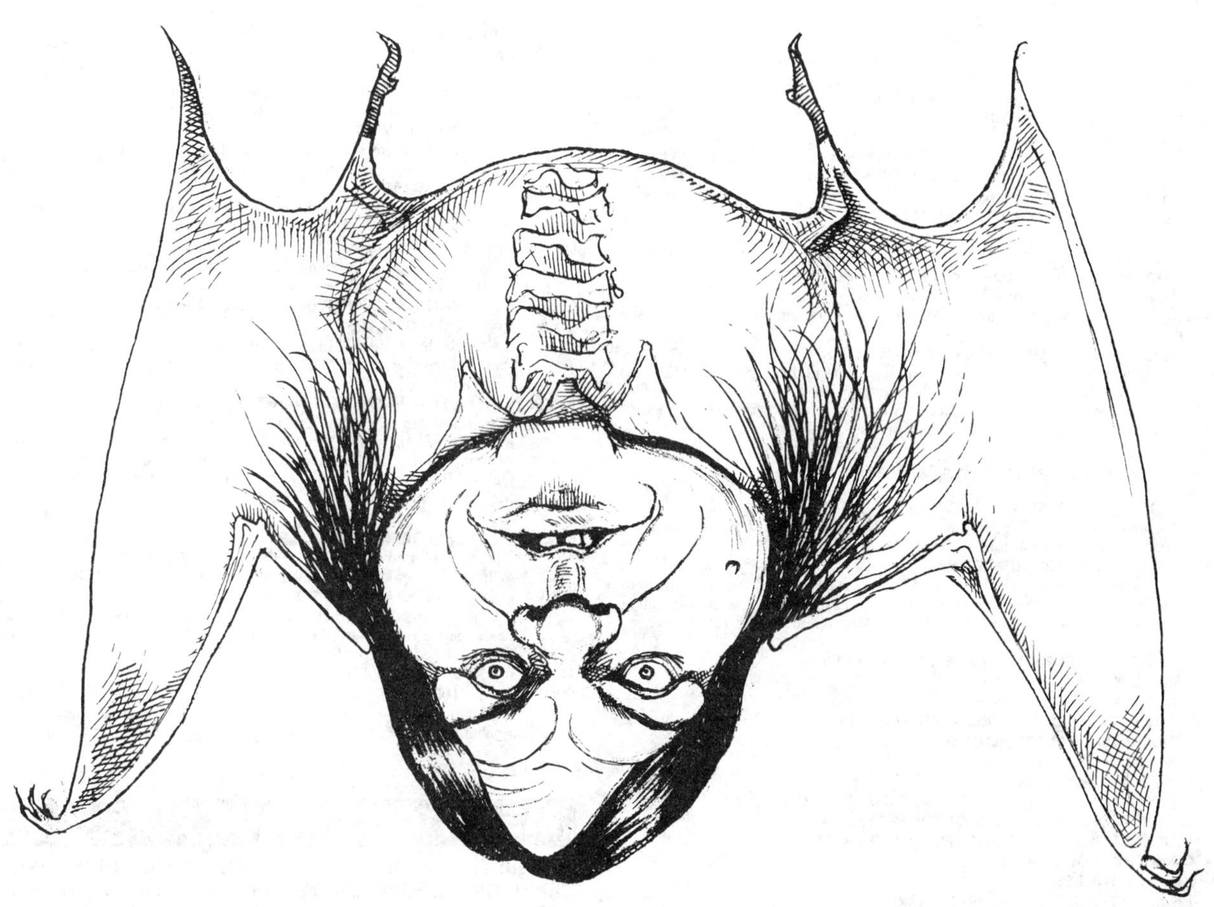

— **MRS LOUD** – female vocal / **ROY BITTAN & BILL PAYNE** – piano / **TIM PIERCE & EDDIE MARTINEZ** – guitar / **KENNY ARONOFF & RICK MAROTTA & BRIAN MEAGHER & JIMMY BRALOWER** – drums / **STEVE BUSLOWE** – bass / **PAT THRALL** – guitar solo / **LENNY PICKETT** – sax / **JEFF BOVA** – synth. & prog. / **etc.**

Virgin | M.C.A.

Sep 93. (cd)(c)(lp) **BAT OUT OF HELL II: BACK INTO HELL** [1] [1]
– I'd do anything for love (but I won't do that) / Life is a lemon and I want my money back / Rock and roll dreams come through / It just won't quit / Out of the frying pan (and into the fire) / Objects in the rear view mirror may appear closer than they are / Wasted youth / Everything louder than everything else / Good girls go to heaven (bad girls go everywhere) / Back into Hell / Lost boys and golden girls. *(ltd.pic-lp Dec93) (re-iss.Nov95)*

Oct 93. (7")(c-s) **I'D DO ANYTHING FOR LOVE (BUT I WON'T DO THAT). / BACK INTO HELL** [1] [1] Sep 93
(cd-s+=) – Everything louder than everything else.
(cd-s) – ('A'side) / You took the words right out of my mouth (live NYC) / Bat out of hell (live NYC).

Feb 94. (7"pic-d)(c-s) **ROCK'N'ROLL DREAMS COME THROUGH. / WASTED YOUTH** [11] [13] Jan94
(cd-s+=) – I'd do anything for love (but I won't do that) (live).
(cd-s) – ('A'side) / Heaven can wait (live) / Paradise by the dashboard light (live).

Apr 94. (7")(c-s)(cd-s) **OBJECTS IN THE REAR VIEW MIRROR MAY APPEAR CLOSER THAN YOU THINK. / ROCK AND ROLL DREAMS COME THROUGH (live)** [26] [38]
(cd-s+=) – All revved up (live) / Two out of three ain't bad (live).

Oct 95. (7")(c-s) **I'D LIE FOR YOU (AND THAT'S THE TRUTH). / I'D DO ANYTHING FOR LOVE (BUT I WON'T DO THAT)** [2] [13]
(cd-s+=) – Whatever happened to Saturday night.
(cd-s) – ('A'-Fountain Head mix) / Oh, what a beautiful mornin' / Runnin' for the red light (I gotta life).

Oct 95. (cd)(c)(d-lp) **WELCOME TO THE NEIGHBOURHOOD** [3] [17] Nov95
– When the rubber meets the road / I'd lie for you (and that's the truth) / Original sin / 45 seconds of ecstacy / Runnin' for the red light (I gotta life) / Fiesta de las Almas Perdidas / Left in the dark / Not a dry eye in the house / Amnesty is granted / If this is the last kiss (let's make it last all night) / Martha / Where angels sing.

– compilations, others, etc. –

Aug 82. Epic; (c-ep) **GREATEST ORIGINAL HITS** [ ] [-]
– Bat out of Hell / Read 'em and weep / Dead ringer for love / I'm gonna love her for both of us. *(7"ep iss.Mar83, re-iss.Sep86)*

Jan 85. Epic; (lp)(c)(cd) **HITS OUT OF HELL** [2] [ ]
– Bat out of Hell / Read 'em and weep / Midnight at the lost and found / Two out of three ain't bad / Dead ringer for love / Modern girl / I'm gonna love her for both of us / You took the words right out of my mouth (hot summer night) / Razor's edge / Paradise by the dashboard light.

Jun 91. Epic; (7")(c-s) **DEAD RINGER FOR LOVE. / HEAVEN CAN WAIT** [53] [ ]
(12"+=)(cd-s+=) – Bat out of Hell.

Oct 91. Epic; (7") **TWO OUT OF THREE AIN'T BAD. / I'M GONNA LOVE HER FOR BOTH OF US** [69] [ ]
(12"+=)(cd-s+=) – Midnight at the lost and found. *(re-iss.Jun92)*

Mar 93. Epic; (cd)(c) **THE 12" MIXES** [ ] [ ]

Dec 93. Epic; (12"pic-d-ep)(c-ep)(pic-cd-ep) **BAT OUT OF HELL / READ 'EM AND WEEP. / OUT OF THE FRYING PAN (AND INTO THE FIRE) / ROCK AND ROLL DREAMS COME THROUGH (Jim Steinman)** [8] [ ]

Oct 94. Epic; (cd) **THE BEST** [ ] [ ]

Oct 94. Epic; (cd) **THE BEST (w/ BONNIE TYLER)** [ ] [ ]

Feb 86. Old Gold; (7") **BAT OUT OF HELL. / DEAD RINGER FOR LOVE** [ ] [-]
(re-iss.Jan88)

Feb 89. Old Gold; (7") **YOU TOOK THE WORDS RIGHT OUT OF MY MOUTH. / MIDNIGHT AT THE LOST AND FOUND** [ ] [-]

Nov 89. Arista; (lp)(c) **PRIME CUTS** [ ] [ ]

Nov 89. Telstar; (lp)(c)(cd) **HEAVEN AND HELL** [ ] [-]
(above was shared album with BONNIE TYLER on 1 side)
(re-iss.cd-c.May93 & Dec95 on 'Columbia')

May 94. Pickwick; (cd)(c) **ROCK'N'ROLL HERO** [ ] [-]
(re-iss.Jul95)

Oct 94. Pure Music; (cd)(c)(lp) **ALIVE IN HELL (live)** [33] [ ]
– (tracks on 'LIVE AT WEMBLEY' album) + (studio tracks;-) Piece of the action / Bad attitude / Surf's up.

Feb 95. Epic; (d-cd) **DEAD RINGER / MIDNIGHT AT THE LOST AND FOUND** [ ] [-]

Apr 95. Arista; (cd) **BLIND BEFORE I STOP / BAD ATTITUDE** [ ] [-]

MEAT PUPPETS

Formed: Tempe, Phoenix, Arizona, USA . . . 1980 by brothers CURT and CRIS KIRKWOOD. They were soon snapped up by rising US indie label 'SST' in 1981, after a debut on own label. 13 years later, they had finally made headway (well at least in America) with Top 75 album 'TOO HIGH TO DIE'. • **Style:** Mystical psychedelia short-fusing hardcore punk rock and the country-boy slurr of CRIS. • **Songwriters:** Most by CURT, some with CRIS or DERRICK. Covered TUMBLIN' TUMBLEWEEDS (Bob Nolan). • **Trivia:** On 18 Nov'93, CURT & CRIS guested with NIRVANA's on an unplugged MTV spot. The tracks they performed were 'PLATEAU', 'OH ME' & 'LAKE OF FIRE'.

Recommended: UP ON THE SUN (*8) / MONSTERS (*9) / TOO HIGH TO DIE (*7) / FORBIDDEN PLACES (*6)

CURT KIRKWOOD – guitar, vocals / **CRIS KIRKWOOD** – vocals, bass, rhythm guitar / **DERRICK BOSTROM** – drums

not issued | World Invitation

Sep 81. (7"ep) **IN A CAR / BIG HOUSE. / DOLFIN FIELD / OUT IN THE GARDINER / FOREIGN LAWNS** [-] [ ]
(cd-ep iss.Nov88 on 'S.S.T.')

S.S.T. | S.S.T.

Jan 82. (lp) **MEAT PUPPETS I** [-] [ ]
– Reward / Love offering / Blue green god / Walking boss / Melons rising / Saturday morning / Our friends / Tumblin' tumbleweeds / Milo, Sarghum and maize / Meat puppets / Playing dead / Litterbox / Electromud / The goldmine. *(re-iss.+cd+c early 90's)*

Apr 84. (lp) **MEAT PUPPETS II** [ ] [ ]
– Split myself in two / Magic toy missing / Lost plateau / Aurora Borealis / We are here / Climbing / New gods / Oh, me / Lake on fire / I'm a mindless idiot / The whistling song. *(re-iss.+cd+c early 90's)*

Apr 85. (lp) **UP ON THE SUN** [ ] [ ]
– Up on the Sun / Maiden's milk / Away / Animal kingdom / Hot pink / Swimming ground / Bucket head / Too real / Enchanted pork fist / Seal whales / Two rivers / Creator. *(cd-iss.Sep87, and re-iss.+cd+c early 90's)*

Aug 86. (m-lp) **OUT MY WAY** [ ] [ ]
– She's hot / Out my way / Other kinds of love / Not swimming ground / Mountain line / Good golly Miss Molly. *(re-iss.+cd+c.Sep87)*

Apr 87. (lp)(c)(cd) **MIRAGE** [ ] [ ]
– Get on down / Love your children forever / Liquery / Confusion fog / Look at the rain / I am a machine / Quit it / Beauty / etc.****

Oct 87. (lp)(c)(cd) **HEUVOS** [ ] [ ]
– Paradise / Look at the rain / Bad love / Sexy music / Crazy / Fruit / Automatic mojo / Dry rain / I can't be counted on at all.

Oct 87. (12") **I CAN'T BE COUNTED ON AT ALL. / PARADISE** [ ] [ ]

Oct 89. (lp)(c)(cd) **MONSTERS** [ ] [ ]
– Attacked by monsters / Light / Meltdown / In love / The void / Touchdown king / Party till the world obeys / Flight of the fire weasel / Strings on your heart / Like being alive.

Nov 90. (cd)(d-lp) **NO STRINGS ATTACHED** (compilation) [ ] [ ]
– Big house / In a car / Tumblin' tumbleweeds / Reward / The whistling song / New gods / Lost / Lake of fire / Split myself in two / Up on the Sun / Swimming ground / Maiden's milk / Bucket head / Out my way / Confusion fog / I am a machine / Quit it / Beauty / Look at the rain / I can't be counted on at all / Automatic mojo / Meltdown / Like being alive / Attacked by monsters.

London | London

Nov 91. (cd)(c)(lp) **FORBIDDEN PLACES** [ ] [ ]
– Sam / Nail it down / This day / Open wide / Another Moon / That's how it goes / Whirlpool / Popskull / No longer gone / Forbidden places / Six gallon pie.

Mar 94. (cd)(c)(lp) **TOO HIGH TO DIE** [ ] [62]
– Violet eyes / Never to be found / We don't exist / Severed goddess head / Flaming heart / Shine / Backwater / Roof with a hole / Station / Things / Why / Evil love / Comin' down / Lake of fire.

Jul 94. (c-s)(cd-s) **BACKWATER. / ?** [ ] [47]

Oct 95. (cd)(c) **NO JOKE!** [ ] [ ]
– Scum / Nothing / Head / Taste of the sun / Vampires / Predator / Poison arrow / Eyeball / For free / Cobbler / Inflamable / Sweet ammonia / Chemical garden.

MEGA CITY FOUR

Formed: Farnborough, England . . . early 1987 by CHRIS JONES and ex-CAPRICORN members GERRY BRYANT and brothers WIZ and DANNY BROWN. After a number of local indie hits mostly for 'Decoy', they signed to 'Big Life' Jun'91. Hit the UK Top 50 in 1992, when 'SEBASTAPOL RD.' album made No.41. • **Style:** Uptempo melodic punk combo, similar to BUZZCOCKS and friends The SENSELESS THINGS. • **Songwriters:** WIZ. Covered; DON'T WAN'T TO KNOW IF YOU ARE LONELY (Husker Du). • **Trivia:** Took their name from a comic book hero Judge Dredd.

Recommended: TRANZOPHOBIA (*8) / SEBASTAPOL RD (*7) / WHO CARES WINS (*7).

DARREN 'WIZ' BROWN – vocals, guitar / **DANNY BROWN** – guitar / **GERRY BRYANT** – bass / **CHRIS JONES** – drums (ex-EXIT EAST) repl. MARTIN

Primitive | not issued

Mar 88. (7"ltd.) **MILES APART. / RUNNING IN DARKNESS** [ ] [-]
(re-iss.Jun88 on 'Mega City')

Decoy | not issued

Nov 88. (7") **DISTANT RELATIVES. / CLEAR BLUE SKY** [ ] [-]

Feb 89. (7") **LESS THAN SENSELESS. / DANCING DAYS ARE OVER** [ ] [-]

May 89. (lp)(cd) **TRANZOPHOBIA** [67] [-]
– Start / Pride and prejudice / Severe attack of the truth / Paper tiger / January / Twenty one again / On another planet / Things I never said / New years day / Occupation / Alternative arrangements / Promise / What you've got / Stupid way to die.

Oct 89. (7") **AWKWARD KID. / CRADLE** [ ] [-]

Mar 90. (7"ep)(12"ep) **FINISH / SEVERANCE. / THANX / SQUARE THROUGH A CIRCLE** [ ] [-]

Sep 90. (cd)(c)(lp) **WHO CARES WINS** [ ] [-]
– Who cares? / Static interference / Rose coloured / Grudge / Me not you / Messenger / Violet / Rail / Mistook / Open / Revolution / No such place as home / Storms to come / Balance.

Big Life | Chrysalis

Sep 91. (7"ep)(12"ep)(cd-ep)(7"green-ep) **WORDS THAT SAY / UNTOUCHABLE. / LIPSCAY / MANSION** [66] [-]
(re-iss 12"ep/cd-ep Aug93)

Jan 92. (7"red-ep)(12"ep)(cd-ep) **STOP / DESERT. / BACK TO ZERO / OVERLAP** [36] [ ]
(live-7"ep) – Stop / Revolution / Who cares / Finish.
(re-iss. 7"ep/12"ep/cd-ep Aug93)

Feb 92. (cd)(c)(lp) **SEBASTOPOL RD** [41] [ ]
– Ticket collector / Scared of cats / Callous / Peripheral / Anne Bancroft / Prague / Clown / Props / What's up / Vague / Stop / Wasting my breath. *(re-iss.Sep93)*

May 92. (7")(12")(cd-s) **SHIVERING SAND. / EVERYBODY LOVES YOU / DISTURBED** [35] [ ]
(live-7"ep) – Shivering sand / Words that say / Callous / Don't want to know if you are lonely. *(re-iss.7"ep/12"ep/cd-ep Aug93)*
Nov 92. (cd)(c)(lp) **INSPIRINGLY TITLED (THE LIVE ALBUM) (live)** [ ] [ ]
– Who cares / Finish / Thanx / Shivering sand / Props / Messenger / Stop / Revolution / Words that say / Callous / Lipscar / Peripheral / Clown / Open / What've you've got / Don't want to know if you are lonely. *(re-iss.Sep93)*
Apr 93. (7"ep)(10"ep)(c-ep)(cd-ep) **IRON SKY. / ON THE EDGE / SOMETIMES** [48] [ ]
May 93. (cd)(c)(lp) **MAGIC BULLETS** [57] [ ]
– Perfect circle / Drown / Rain man / Toys / Iron sky / So / Enemy skies / Wallflower / President / Shadow / Underdog / Greener / Speck.
Jul 93. (7")(c-s) **WALLFLOWER. / INAMORATA** [69] [ ]
(12"+=)(cd-s+=)(cd-s+=) – Wilderness.

Fire / not issued

Sep 95. (cd-s) **SKIDDING / STAY DEAD / LAZERGAZE** [ ] [ ]
Nov 95. (7") **SUPERSTAR. / CHRYSANTH** [ ] [ ]

– compilations, others, etc. –

Apr 91. Decoy; (cd)(c)(lp) **TERRIBLY SORRY BOB** (all singles 1987-Mar90) [ ] [-]
Nov 93. Strange Fruit; (cd) **THE PEEL SESSIONS** [ ] [-]

MEGADETH

Formed: San Franscisco, California, USA . . . 1983 by ex-METALLICA guitarist DAVE MUSTAINE alongside DAVE ELLEFSON, POLAND and SAMUELSON. They were given deal with 'Combat' records, who issued in 1985 their debut lp 'KILLING IS MY BUSINESS . . . AND BUSINESS IS GOOD'. They were soon snapped up by 'Capitol', who issued their next album 'PEACE SELLS . . . BUT WHO'S BUYING' late 1986. They commercially progressed with each release, culminating with 1992 US & UK Top 5 album 'COUNTDOWN TO EXTINCTION'. • **Style:** Aggressive thrash speed-metal outfit lying somewhere between heavy & punk-rock. • **Songwriters:** MUSTAINE penned most except; THESE BOOTS ARE MADE FOR WALKING (hit; Nancy Sinatra) / ANARCHY IN THE UK; which featured STEVE JONES (Sex Pistols) / NO MORE MR.NICE GUY (Alice Cooper). • **Trivia:** Wildman MUSTAINE went into seclusion after heroin abuse in the late 80's.

Recommended: KILLING IS MY BUSINESS . . . AND BUSINESS IS GOOD (*8) / RUST IN PEACE (*7) / COUNTDOWN TO EXTINCTION (*6).

DAVE MUSTAINE – vocals, lead guitar (ex-METALLICA) / **CHRIS POLAND** – guitar / **DAVE ELLEFSON** (b.12 Nov'64) – bass / **GAR SAMUELSON** – drums

M.F.N. / Combat

Jun 85. (lp)(c) **KILLING IS MY BUSINESS . . . AND BUSINESS IS GOOD** [ ] [ ]
– Last rites / Killing in my business . . .and business is good / The skull beneath the skin / Boots / Rattlehead / Chosen ones / Looking down the cross / Mechanix. *(re-iss as d-lp May88, cd-iss.Aug87)*

— POLAND was replaced by MIKE ALBERT (ex-KING CRIMSON) briefly until his return.

Capitol / Capitol

Nov 86. (lp)(c)(cd) **PEACE SELLS . . . BUT WHO'S BUYING?** [ ] [76]
– Wake up dead / The conjuring / Peace sells / Devils island / Good mourning – Black Friday / Bad omen / I ain't superstitious / My last words. *(cd-iss.Sep88, also on pic-d) (re-iss.cd+c Jul94 on 'Capitol')*
Nov 87. (7")(7"pic-d) **WAKE UP DEAD. / BLACK FRIDAY (live)** [65] [ ]
(12"+=) – Devil's island (live).

— **CHUCK BEHLER** – drums replaced SAMUELSON / **JEFF YOUNG**– guitar repl. JAY REYNOLDS who had briefly repl. POLAND.

Feb 88. (7")(7"pic-d) **ANARCHY IN THE U.K.. / LIAR** [45] [ ]
(12"+=) – 502.
Mar 88. (lp)(c)(cd)(pic-lp) **SO FAR . . . SO GOOD . . . SO WHAT!** [18] [28] Jan 88
– Into the lungs of Hell / Set the world afire / Anarchy in the U.K. / Mary Jane / 502 / In my darkest hour / Liar / Hook in mouth.
May 88. (7")(7"pic-d) **MARY JANE. / HOOK IN MOUTH** [46] [ ]
(12"+=) – My last words.

— Late '88, YOUNG joined BROKEN SILENCE and BEHLER joined BLACK & WHITE.

Nov 89. (7")(c-s)(7"pic-d) **NO MORE MR. NICE GUY. / DIFFERENT BREED** [13] [ ]
(12"+=)(cd-s+=) – Demon bell (the ballad of Horace Pinker).

— (Mar90) **MUSTAINE + ELLEFSON** bring in new members **MARTY FRIEDMAN** – guitar (ex-CACOPHONY) / **NICK MENZA** – drums

Sep 90. (7")(c-s) **HOLY WARS . . . THE PUNISHMENT DUE. / LUCRETIA** [24] [ ]
(12"+=)(cd-s+=) – Information
Oct 90. (cd)(c)(lp) **RUST IN PEACE** [8] [23]
– Holy wars . . . the punishment due / Hangar 18 / Take no prisoners / Five magics / Poison was the cure / Lucretia / Tornado of souls / Dawn patrol / Rust in peace . . . Polaris. *(re-iss.cd+c Sep94)*
Mar 91. (7")(7"sha-pic-d) **HANGAR 18. / THE CONJURING (live)** [26] [ ]
(cd-s+=) – ('A'live) / Hook in mouth (live).
Jun 92. (7") **SYMPHONY OF DESTRUCTION. / PEACE SELLS (live)** [15] [71] Oct 92
(12"+=)(cd-s+=) – God to Hell / Breakpoint.
(7"pic-d) – ('A'side) / In my darkest hour (live).
Jul 92. (cd)(c)(lp) **COUNTDOWN TO EXTINCTION** [5] [2]
– Skin o' my teeth / Symphony of destruction / Architecture of aggression / Foreclosure of a dream / Sweating bullets / This was my life / Countdown to extinction / High speed dirt / Psychotron / Captive honour / Ashes in your mouth.
Oct 92. (7")(c-s)(7"pic-d) **SKIN O' MY TEETH. / HOLY WARS . . . THE PUNISHMENT DUE (General Norman Schwarzkopf)** [13] [ ]
(cd-s+=) – ('A'version) / Lucretia.
(10"+=) – High speed drill / (Dave Mustaine interview).
Mar 93. (7")(c-s) **SWEATING BULLETS. / ASHES IN YOUR MOUTH (live)** [26] [ ]
(12")(cd-s) – ('A'side) / Countdown to extinction (live '92) / Symphony of destruction (gristle mix) / Symphony of destruction (live).
Oct 94. (cd)(c)(blue-lp) **YOUTHANASIA** [6] [4]
– Reckoning day / Train of consequences / Addicted to chaos / A tout le monde / Elysian fields / The killing road / Blood of heroes / Family tree / Youthanasia / I thought I knew it all / Black curtains / Victory. *(re-iss.Aug95 cd/c w/ free album; HIDDEN TREASURES, hit UK No.28 + US No.90)*
Dec 94. (7")(12") **TRAIN OF CONSEQUENCES. / CROWN OF WORMS** [22] [ ]
(12"+=) – Holy wars . . . the punishment due (live).
(cd-s) – ('A'side) / Peace sells . . . but who's buying (live) / Anarchy in the UK (live).

Dieter MEIER (see under ⇒ YELLO)

Melle MEL (see under ⇒ GRANDMASTER FLASH)

MELANIE

Born: MELANIE SAFKA, 3 Feb'47, Astoria, Long Island, New York, USA, out of Ukrainian-Italian parents. In 1966, she went to audition for a bit part in a play, but was shown into the wrong office. It was being used as a music publisher's room, but she was asked to sing and play her guitar. Fortunately, they liked her and invited her back to sign for their 'Columbia' records. They brought in producer PETER SCHEKERYK, who soon became her husband, giving her 3 children and making her a star. After 2 orchestra-laden 45's, she signed to 'Buddah' late in 1968. Her first album 'BORN TO BE', hit the shops in May'69, and through it she was invited to play 'Woodstock' festival in August '69. In 1970, The SEEKERS had a US hit with her 'WHAT HAVE THEY DONE TO MY SONG, MA?'. She also had a double 'A'-sided Top 10 UK hit with 'RUBY TUESDAY'. They were both from parent Top 5 album 'CANDLES IN THE RAIN'. Three more successful albums followed, the last of which 'GATHER ME', featured US No.1 / UK No.4 hit 'BRAND NEW KEY'. This appeared on her newly formed 'Neighborhood' label, which she had initiated with husband PETER. Her commerciality slightly dwindled for the rest of the 70's, although she was always highly regarded. • **Style:** A child-like and coy vocalist who was inspired by LOTTE LENYA and EDITH PIAF. • **Songwriters:** Writes her own except; RUBY TUESDAY + JIGSAW PUZZLE + WILD HORSES (Rolling Stones) / MR.TAMBOURINE MAN + SIGN ON THE WINDOW + LAY LADY LAY (Bob Dylan) / CAROLINA ON MY MIND (James Taylor) / LOVER'S CROSS (Jim Croce) / PRETTY BOY FLOYD (Woody Guthrie) / I THINK IT'S GOING TO RAIN TODAY (Randy Newman) / WILL YOU LOVE ME TOMORROW (Goffin-King) / CHORDS OF FAME (Phil Ochs) / MY FATHER (Judy Collins) / YOU CAN'T HURRY LOVE (Supremes) / etc. • **Trivia:** Her Neighborhood label also, signed folky MIKE HERON'S REPUTATION (ex-INCREDIBLE STRING BAND) in 1973.

Recommended: THE BEST OF MELANIE (*7)

MELANIE – vocals, acoustic guitar

not issued / Columbia

1967. (7") **BEAUTIFUL PEOPLE. / GOD'S ONLY DAUGHTER** [-] [ ]
1968. (7") **GARDEN IN THE CITY. / (WHY) DIDN'T MY MOTHER TELL ME?** [-] [ ]

Buddah / Buddah

Dec 68. (7") **MR.TAMBOURINE MAN. / CHRISTOPHER ROBIN** [ ] [-]
Feb 69. (7") **BOBO'S PARTY. / I'M BACK IN TOWN** [ ] [ ]
May 69. (lp) **BORN TO BE** [ ] [ ] Jan 69
– In the hour / I'm back in town / Bobo's party / Mr. Tambourine man / Momma momma / I really loved Harold / Animal crackers / Christopher Robin (is saying his prayer) / Close to it all / Merry Christmas. *(re-packaged late '69 as "MY FIRST ALBUM") (UK-re-iss.Aug74 +c.) (cd-iss.Jul92 on 'C5')*
Sep 69. (7") **BEAUTIFUL PEOPLE. / ANY GUY** [-] [ ]
Sep 69. (7") **BEAUTIFUL PEOPLE. / UPTOWN DOWN** [ ] [-]
Dec 69. (lp) **AFFECTIONATELY MELANIE** [ ] [ ] Nov 69
– I'm back in town / Tuning my guitar / Soul sister Annie / Any guy / Uptown down again / Beautiful people / Johnny boy / Baby guitar / Deep down low / For my father / Take me home. *(re-iss.Aug74 +c.) (cd-iss.Nov93 on 'Sequel')*
Feb 70. (7") **TAKE ME HOME. /** [-] [ ]
Apr 70. (7") **LAY DOWN (CANDLES IN THE RAIN). / ANIMAL CRACKERS** [-] [6]
Aug 70. (7") **RUBY TUESDAY. / WHAT HAVE THEY DONE TO MY SONG MA?** [9] [-]
(above single was flipped over Jan71 with above 'B' reaching No.39 in UK)
Sep 70. (lp)(c) **CANDLES IN THE RAIN** [5] [17] May 70
– The good guys / Lovin' baby girl / Ruby Tuesday / Leftover wine / Lay down (candles in the rain) / Carolina in my mind / Citiest people / What have they done to my song ma. *(re-iss.UK-Aug74 diff.order tracks +=)– Alexander Beetle. (cd-iss.Jan88 on 'Rock Machine' + Jul91 on 'Razor')*
Nov 70. (7") **PEACE WILL COME (ACCORDING TO PLAN). / CLOSE TO IT ALL** [ ] [ ] Aug 70
Nov 70. (7") **RUBY TUESDAY. / MERRY CHRISTMAS** [-] [52]

— with **RONALD FRAGIPANE** – keyboards / etc, & onwards with sessioners

Nov 70. (lp)(c) **LEFTOVER WINE (live Carnagie Hall)** [22] [33] Sep 70

– Close to it all / Uptown and down / Momma momma / The saddest thing / Beautiful people / Animal crackers / I don't eat animals / Happy birthday / Tuning my guitar / Psychotherapy / Leftover wine / Peace will come (according to plan). *(re-iss.Aug74 +c)*

Dec 70. (lp) **ALL THE RIGHT NOISES (Soundtrack)** [ ] [ ]
– (basically orchestrated versions of her earlier songs).

Feb 71. (7") **STOP! I DON'T WANNA HEAR IT ANYMORE. / BEAUTIFUL PEOPLE** [ ] [-]

Feb 71. (7") **THE GOOD BOOK. / WE DON'T KNOW WHERE WE'RE GOING** [-] [ ]

May 71. (lp)(c) **THE GOOD BOOK** [9] [80] Feb 71
– The good book / Babe rainbow / Sign on the window / The saddest thing / Nickel song / Isn't it a pity / My father / Chords of fame / You can go fishin' / Birthday of the sun / The prize / Babe rainbow. *(cd-iss.Mar93 on 'C5')*

May 71. (7") **THE NICKEL SONG. / THE GOOD BOOK** [ ] [-]

Buddah | Neighborhood

Nov 71. (7") **BRAND NEW KEY. / SOME SAY (I GOT DEVIL)** [4] [1] Oct 71

Dec 71. (lp)(c) **GATHER ME** [14] [15] Nov 71
– Little bit of me / Some day I'll be a farmer / Ring around the Moon / Steppin' / Brand new key / Ring around the Moon / shine the living light (chant) – Ring the living bell – Shine the living light (chant reprise) / Railroad / Kansas / Some say (I got the Devil) / Center of the circle / What wondrous love / Baby day / Tell me why. *(re-iss.Aug74)*

Mar 72. (7") **RING THE LIVING BELL. / RAILROAD** [ ] [31] Jan 72

JUl 72. (7") **SOMEDAY I'LL BE A FARMER. / STEPPIN'** [-] [ ]

Jul 72. (7") **SOMEDAY I'LL BE A FARMER. / LAY LADY LAY** [ ] [-]

Neighbour. | Neighbor..

Oct 72. (7") **TOGETHER ALONE. / CENTER OF THE CIRCLE** [-] [86]

Oct 72. (7") **TOGETHER ALONE. / SUMMER WEAVING** [ ] [-]

Nov 72. (lp)(c) **STONEGROUND WORDS** [ ] [70]
– Together alone / Between the road signs / Summer weaving / My rainbow race / Do you believe / I am not a poet (night song) / Stoneground words / Song of the south (based on a theme from song of the north, adapted from the original) / Maybe I was (a golf ball) / Here I am. *(re-iss.Jan75)*

Jan 73. (7") **DO YOU BELIEVE?. / STONEGROUND WORDS** [ ] [ ]

Feb 73. (7") **BITTER BAD / DO YOU BELIEVE?** [ ] [36]

Jun 73. (7") **SEEDS. / SOME SAY (I GOT THE DEVIL)** [ ] [ ]

Jul 73. (d-lp) **AT CARNEGIE HALL (live)** [ ] [ ] May 73
– Baby guitar / Lay your hands / Across the six strings / Pretty Boy Floyd / Someday I'll be a farmer / Baby rainbow / It's me again / Any guy / Brand new key / Some day / Bitter sad / Psycho therapy / Together alone / Beautiful people / Hearing the news / Seasons to change / Peace will come (according to plan) / My rainbow race / Poet / Ring the living bell – Shine the living light / The actress.

Nov 73. (7") **WILL YOU STILL LOVE ME TOMORROW?. / HERE I AM** [37] [82]

Mar 74. (7") **LOVE TO LOSE AGAIN. / PINE AND FEATHER** [ ] [ ]

May 74. (7") **LOVER'S CROSS. / HOLDING OUT** [ ] [ ]

May 74. (lp)(c) **MADRUGADA** [ ] [-]
– Love to lose again / Lover's cross / Pretty Boy Floyd / Wild horses / Think it's going to rain today / Maybe not for a lifetime / Holding out / I am being guided / The actress / Pine and feather. *(re-iss.Jan75 on 'Anchor')*

Jan 75. (7") **YOU'RE NOT A BAD GHOST, JUST AN OLD SONG. / EYES OF A MAN** [-] [ ]

Feb 75. (7") **YOU'RE NOT A BAD GHOST, JUST AN OLD SONG. / MONOGAUELA RIVER** [ ] [-]

Feb 75. (lp)(c) **AS I SEE IT NOW** [ ] [ ]
– Yankee man / You're not a bad ghost / Just an old song / Record machine / Eyes of man / Stars up there / Don't think twice, it's alright / Sweet misery / Monongahela River / Yes sir, that's my baby / Autumn lady / Chart song / As I see it now.

Apr 75. (7") **YES SIR, THAT'S MY BABY. / RECORD MACHINE** [ ] [-]

Jun 75. (7") **SWEET MISERY. / RECORD MACHINE** [-] [ ]

Sep 75. (7") **YOU CAN'T HURRY LOVE – MAMA SAID. / THE SUN AND THE MOON** [ ] [-]

Oct 75. (lp)(c) **SUNSET AND OTHER BEGINNINGS** [ ] [ ]
– Perceive it / Almost like being in love / Loving my children / You can't hurry love – Mama said / People are just getting ready / Ol' man river / I got my mojo working / Where's the band / Dream seller (meet me on the corner) / What do I keep / Sandman / The Sun and the Moon / Afraid of the dark.

Nov 75. (7") **ALMOST LIKE BEING IN LOVE. / BEAUTIFUL PEOPLE (live)** [ ] [-]

not issued | Atlantic

1976. (lp) **PHOTOGRAPH** [-] [ ]
– Cyclone / If I needed you / The letter / Groundhog day / Nickel song / Photograph / I'm so blue / Secret of the darkness (I believe) / Save me / Raindance / Friends & co.

Jan 77. (7") **CYCLONE. / IF I NEEDED YOU** [-] [ ]

R.C.A. | Midsong

Sep 78. (7") **I'D RATHER LEAVE WHILE I'M IN LOVE. / RECORD PEOPLE** [-] [ ]

Sep 78. (lp)(c) **PHONOGENIC – NOT JUST A PRETTY FACE** [ ] [ ]
– Knock on wood / Bon apetite / Spanky / Runnin' after love / We can work it out / I'd rather leave while I'm in love / Let it be me / Yankee man / Record people / California dreamin'.

Nov 78. (7") **KNOCK ON WOOD. / RECORD PEOPLE** [-] [ ]

R.C.A. | Tomato

Aug 79. (7") **RUNNIN' AFTER LOVE. / HOLDIN' OUT** [-] [ ]

Aug 79. (d-lp)(c) **BALLROOM STREETS (live)** [ ] [ ]
– Runnin' after love / Holdin' out / Cyclone / Beautiful sadness / Do you believe? / Nickel song / Any guy / What have they done to my song, ma? / I believe / Poet / Save me / Together alone / Ruby Tuesday / Buckle down / Miranda / Brand new key / Groundhog day / Friends and company.

R.C.A. | R.C.A.

Apr 82. (7") **DETROIT OR BUFFALO. / IMAGINARY HEROES** [-] [ ]

Apr 82. (7") **DETROIT OR BUFFALO. / ROADBURN** [ ] [-]

Aug 82. (lp)(c) **ARABESQUE** [ ] [ ]
– Detroit or Buffalo / It don't matter now / Anyway that you want me / Roadburn / Fooling yourself / Too late / Standing on the other side / Love you to loathe me / When you're dead and gone / Imaginary heroes / Chances.

Aug 82. (7") **DETROIT OR BUFFALO. / WHEN YOU'RE DEAD AND GONE** [-] [ ]

Neigh-bourhood | Neighborhood

Sep 83. (7")(7"pic-d) **EVERY BREATH OF THE WAY. / LOVERS LULLABY** [70] [ ]
(12"+=) – Put a hat on your head.

Nov 83. (lp)(c) **SEVENTH WAVE** [ ] [ ]
– Every breath of the way / Apathy / Dance to the music / Lovers lullaby / If you go your way / Son of a rotten gambler / Lonesome eyes / The nickel song / Refrain from music, music, music / Lovin' the boy next door / Lay down Sally / Didn't you ever love somebody / What do I keep.

Nov 83. (7") **DIDN'T YOU EVER LOVE SOMEBODY. / DANCE TO THE MUSIC** [ ] [ ]

not issued | Amherst

1985. (7") **WHO'S BEEN SLEEPING IN MY BED. / MAYBE I'M LONELY** [-] [ ]

1985. (lp) **AM I REAL OR WHAT** [-] [ ]
– Who's been sleeping in my bed / Maybe I'm lonely / Private parts / Cut the cord / Am I real to you / Crack seeks the edge / Abuse / Every breath of the way / Some buddy love.

F.F.T. | Relativity

Mar 89. (7") **RUBY TUESDAY ('89 version). / SHOW YOU** [ ] [-]
(12"+=)(cd-s+=) – Rock'n'roll heart.

Apr 89. (lp)(c) **COWABONGA – NEVER TURN YOUR BACK ON A WAVE** [ ] [ ]
– Ruby Tuesday / Racing heart / Show you / To be a star / What have they done to the rain / On a lamb from a cow / Another lie / Window pain / Lovin' / Prematurely gay / Chosen few / The boy next door.

Hypertens. | Rykodisc?

Feb 95. (cd) **SILENCE IS KING** [ ] [-]
– Estate sale / Silence is king / I will get over / In my rock'n'roll heart / A hard rain's a-gonna fall / Gone with the wind / Detroit or Buffalo / Fallen angel / Wear it like a flag / Undertow / Some day I'll be an old record.

– compilations, etc. –

Oct 71. Buddah; (7"m) **ALEXANDER BEETLE. / CHRISTOPHER ROBIN. / ANIMAL CRACKERS** [ ] [ ]

Nov 71. Buddah; (7") **THE NICKEL SONG. / WHAT HAVE THEY DONE TO MY SONG, MA** [-] [35]

Mar 72. Buddah; (lp)(c) **GARDEN IN THE CITY** [19] [ ] Dec 71
– Garden in the city / Love in my mind / We don't where we're going / Lay lady lay / Jigsaw puzzle / Don't you wait by the water / Stop I don't want to hear it anymore / Somebody loves me / People in the front row. *(re-iss. Aug 74)*

Sep 72. Buddah; (d-lp) **THE FOUR SIDES OF MELANIE** [23] [ ] Mar 72
– Somebody loves me / Beautiful people / In the hour / I really loved Harold / Johnny boy / Any guy / I'm back in town / What have they done to my song, ma / Lay down / Peace will come (according to plan) / Good book / The nickel song / Babe rainbow / Mr.Tambourine man / Carolina on my mind / Ruby Tuesday / Sign in the window / Lay lady lay / Christopher Robin / Animal crackers / I don't eat animals / Psychotherapy / Leftover wine. *(re-iss.Aug74)*

Oct 72. Buddah; (7") **JOHNNY BOY. / I'M BACK IN TOWN** [-] [ ]

Apr 73. Buddah; (7") **THE NICKEL SONG. / CLOSE TO IT ALL** [ ] [ ]

May 73. Buddah; (lp)(c) **THE VERY BEST OF MELANIE** [ ] [ ]
(re-iss.Aug74)

Dec 73. Buddah; (lp)(c) **PLEASE LOVE ME** [ ] [ ]

1976. Buddah; (lp) **BEST OF MELANIE** [ ] [ ]
(re-iss.Jul85)

Jun 77. Buddah-Pye; (12"ep) **LAY DOWN. / BRAND NEW KEY. / RUBY TUESDAY. / WHAT HAVE THEY DONE TO MY SONG, MA?** [ ] [ ]

Oct 73. Lyntone; (7"flexi) **A GIFT FROM HONEY** [ ] [ ]
– I am not a poet / Song of the south / Brand new key (live) / Seeds.

Apr 75. A.B.C.; (lp)(c) **FROM THE BEGINNING** [ ] [ ]

Feb 77. Pye; (lp)(c) **GOLDEN HOUR OF MELANIE** [ ] [ ]

Oct 82. P.R.T.; (d-lp) **SPOTLIGHT ON . . .** [ ] [ ]

Jan 83. Flashback-Pye; (7") **BRAND NEW KEY. / RUBY TUESDAY** [ ] [ ]

Jun 88. Castle; (d-lp)(c)(cd) **THE COLLECTION** [ ] [ ]

Jul 88. Knight; (lp)(c) **EASY RIDING** [ ] [ ]

Dec 88. B.R.Music; (lp)(c)(cd) **VERY BEST OF MELANIE** [ ] [ ]

Oct 89. Mainline; (lp)(c)(cd) **20 GREATEST HITS** [ ] [-]

Mar 91. Music Club; (cd)(c) **THE BEST OF MELANIE** [ ] [-]
– Ruby Tuesday / Brand new key / Animal crackers / Mr.Tambourine man / Baby day / Beautiful people / Save the night / Lay down (candles in the rain) / Close to it all / What have they done to my song ma / Lay lady lay / Some day I'll be a farmer / Good book / Peace will come according to my plan / Gardens in the city / Nickel song / Pebbles in the sand / Tell me why.

Jul 92. Sequel; (cd) **THE BEST OF THE REST OF MELANIE: THE BUDDAH YEARS** [ ] [-]

May 93. Royal Collection; (cd)(c) **LOOK WHAT THEY'VE DONE** [ ] [-]

Dec 93. Disky; (cd) **GOLD: GREATEST HITS** [ ] [-]

Feb 94. Hypertension; (d-cd) **SILVER ANNIVERSARY** [ ] [ ]

John (Cougar) MELLENCAMP

Born: 7 Oct '51, Seymour, Indiana, USA. After graduating from high school, where he played in 2 bands; CREPE SOUL and SNAKEPIT BANANA BARN. He left home in 1970 and moved to Valonia, where he married Priscilla. In the early 70's, he formed glam-rock outfit TRASH, alongside LARRY CRANE. In the mid 70's, he graduated from university, but separated from wife and child. At the same time he made a demo, and sent it to Tony DeFries, who gave him a deal with MainMan productions & 'MCA' records. In 1976 as JOHN COUGAR, his debut lp 'CHESTNUT STREET INCIDENT' was issued, but after parting with management, he moved to Bloomington. After another lp, 'THE KID INSIDE', he shifted to ROD STEWART's 'Riva' records, who released UK-only lp 'A BIOGRAPHY'. Most of the tracks re-surfaced the next year in lp 'JOHN COUGAR', which also included his first US top 30 entry 'I NEED A LOVER'. In the early 80's, he scored more hits, but surpassed all before when 45's 'HURTS SO GOOD' & 'JACK AND DIANE', hit US No.2 & 1 respectively. They were the main feature on his 1982 No.1 album 'AMERICAN FOOL', which also cracked the 40 in UK. For the rest of the 80's, all his lp's went US Top 10, and mostly all 45's went Top 10 or 20. • **Style:** SPRINGSTEEN sounding rocker, who finally broke away from tag, after the brilliant 1989 lp 'BIG DADDY'. • **Songwriters:** Penned most himself, with collaborations mainly stemming from CRANE. Covered; KICKS (Paul Revere & The Raiders) / JAILHOUSE ROCK (Elvis Presley) / OH PRETTY WOMAN (Roy Orbison) / DO YOU BELIEVE IN MAGIC (Lovin' Spoonful) / UNDER THE BOARDWALK (Drifters) / etc. • **Trivia:** Due to his height, he produced under the alias of The LITTLE BASTARD. His work in this field has included; MITCH RYDER (Never Kick A Sleeping Dog) / BLASTERS (Hard Line) / WILD NIGHT (Van Morrison). STEVE CROPPER (ex-BOOKER T. & THE MG'S) produced his 1980 lp 'NOTHING MATTERS AND WHAT IF IT DID'. In 1988, he became a grandfather, when his 18 year-old daughter Michelle had a baby. In 1990, he starred in the film 'Falling from Grace'.

Recommended: AMERICAN FOOL (*6) / SCARECROW (*7) / THE LONESOME JUBILEE (*7) / BIG DADDY (*8).

JOHN COUGAR

– vocals, guitar

not issued M.C.A.

1976. (lp) **CHESTNUT STREET INCIDENT** [-] [ ]
– American dream / Oh pretty woman / Jailhouse rock / Dream killin' town / Supergirl / Chestnut street revisited / Good girls / Do you believe in magic / Twentieth century fox / Sad lady. *(UK-rel.Oct84 on 'Mainman') (re-iss.lp,c,cd.Apr86 on 'Castle')*

— his band **TIGER FORCE** were **LARRY CRANE** – guitars / **TOM WINCE** – keys / **DAVID PARMAN** – bass, guitar, violin, percussion / **TERENCE SALSA** – drums, perc. / **WAYNE HALL** – saxophone, flute, percussion

1977. (lp)(c) **THE KID INSIDE** [-] [ ]
– Kid inside / Take what you want / Cheap shot / Side-walks and street lights / R.Gang / American son / Gearhead / Young genocides / Too young to live / Survive. *(UK-iss.May86 on 'Castle', cd-iss. Nov 86)*

not issued Gulcher

1977. (7"ep) **U.S. MALE** [-] [ ]
– 2000 a.d. / Lou-ser / Hot man / Kicks.

Riva Riva

Mar 78. (7") **I NEED A LOVER. / BORN RECKLESS** [ ] [-]
Mar 78. (lp)(c) **A BIOGRAPHY** [ ] [-]
– Born reckless / Factory / Night slumming / Taxi dancer / I need a lover / Alley of the angels / High "C" Cherie / Where the side walk ends / Let them run your lives / Goodnight.
Jun 78. (7") **FACTORY. / ALLEY OF THE ANGELS** [ ] [-]
Jun 79. (7")(7"pic-d) **MIAMI. / DO YOU THINK THAT'S FAIR** [ ] [-]
Jul 79. (lp)(c) **JOHN COUGAR** [ ] [64]
– A little night dancin' / Small Paradise / Great mid-west / Miami / Take home pay / Sugar Marie / Welcome to Chinatown / Pray for me / Do you think that's fair / Taxi dancer. *(re-iss.Jun88 on 'Mercury', cd-iss.Jan86)*
Sep 79. (7") **I NEED A LOVER. / ELCOME TO CHINATOWN** [-] [28]
Oct 79. (7") **TAXI DANCER. / SMALL PARADISE** [-] [ ]
Feb 80. (7") **SMALL PARADISE. / SUGAR MARIE** [-] [87]
Apr 80. (7") **PRAY FOR ME. / A LITTLE NIGHT DANCIN'** [-] [ ]
Sep 80. (7") **THIS TIME. / DON'T UNDERSTAND ME** [ ] [27]
Jan 81. (7") **AIN'T EVEN DONE WITH THE NIGHT. / MAKE ME FEEL** [-] [17]
Feb 81. (lp)(c) **NOTHIN' MATTERS, & WHAT IF IT DID?** [ ] [37] Sep 80
– Hot night in a cold town / Ain't even done with the night / Don't understand me / This time / Make me feel / To M.G. (wherever she may be) / Tonight / Wild angel / Cheap shot. *(cd-iss.Jan87)*
Feb 81. (7") **HOT NIGHT IN A COLD TOWN. / TONIGHT** [ ] [-]
May 81. (7") **AIN'T EVEN DONE WITH THE NIGHT. / TO M.G. WHEREVER SHE MAY BE** [ ] [-]

— his live band consisted of **LARRY CRANE** – guitar, vocals / **MIKE WANCHIC** – guitar, vocals / **TOBY MYERS** – bass, vocals / **KENNY ARONOFF** – drums, vocals

May 82. (7") **HURTS SO GOOD. / CLOSE ENOUGH** [ ] [2] Apr 82
Jul 82. (7") **JACK & DIANE. / CAN YOU TAKE IT** [-] [1]
Nov 82. (lp)(c) **AMERICAN FOOL** [37] [1] May 82
– Hurts so good / Jack & Diane / Hand to hold on to / Danger list / Can you take it / Thundering hearts / China girl / Close enough / Weakest moments. *(re-iss.Sep85 on 'Mercury', cd-iss.Jan85 + 1988)*
Sep 82. (7") **JACK & DIANE. / DANGER LIST** [25] [-]
(12"+=) – Need a lover.
Nov 82. (7") **HAND TO HOLD ON TO. / SMALL PARADISE** [-] [3]
Jan 83. (7")(12")(7"pic-d) **HAND TO HOLD ON TO. / HURTS SO GOOD** [ ] [-]

JOHN COUGAR MELLENCAMP

Nov 83. (7")(12") **CRUMBLIN' DOWN. / GOLDEN GATES** [ ] [9] Oct 83
Dec 83. (7") **PINK HOUSES. / SERIOUS BUSINESS** [-] [8]
Feb 84. (lp)(c)(cd) **UH-HUH!** [92] [9] Oct 83
– Crumblin' down / Pink houses / Authority song / Warmer place to sleep / Jackie O / Play guitar / Serious business / Lovin' mother fo ya / Golden Gates.
Feb 84. (7") **AUTHORITY SONG. / HURTS SO GOOD** [ ] [ ]
(12"+=) – Thundering hearts.
Mar 84. (7") **AUTHORITY SONG. / PINK HOUSES (acoustic)** [-] [15]
Jun 84. (7") **PINK HOUSES. / WARMER PLACE TO SLEEP** [ ] [-]

— added **JOHN CASCELLA** – keyboards plus others on session

Oct 85. (7")(12") **LONELY OL' NIGHT. / JACK & DIANE** [ ] [6] Aug 85
Nov 85. (lp)(c)(cd) **SCARECROW** [ ] [2] Sep 85
– Rain on the scarecrow / Grandma's theme / Small town / Minutes to memories / Lonely ol' night / The face of the nation / Justice and independence / Between a laugh and a tear / Rumbleseat / You've got to stand for somethin' / R.O.C.K. in the U.S.A. *(c+=)(cd+=)–* The kind of fella I am.
Jan 86. (7")(12") **SMALL TOWN. / SMALL TOWN (acoustic)** [53] [6] Oct 85
(d7"+=) – Hurt so good / The kinda fella I am.
(d12"+=) – Pink houses / Small town (acoustic).
Apr 86. (7")(12") **R.O.C.K. IN THE U.S.A. / UNDER THE BOARDWALK** [67] [2] Jan 86
Apr 86. (7") **RAIN ON THE SCARECROW. / ?** [-] [21]
Jun 86. (7") **RUMBLESEAT. / ?** [-] [28]

— added **LISA GERMANO** – violin / **PAT PETERSON** – backing vocals, percussion.

Mercury Mercury

Sep 87. (7")(12") **PAPER IN FIRE. / NEVER TO OLD** [ ] [9] Aug 87
Sep 87. (lp)(c)(cd) **THE LONESOME JUBILEE** [31] [6]
– Paper in fire / Down and out in paradise / Check it out / Real life / Cherry bomb / We are the people / Empty hands / Hard times for an honest man / Hot dogs and hamburgers / Rooty toot toot.
Nov 87. (7") **CHERRY BOMB. / SHAMA LAMA DING DONG** [ ] [8] Oct87
(12"+=) – Under the boardwalk.
(cd-s++=) – Pretty ballerina.
Feb 88. (7") **CHECK IT OUT. / WE ARE THE PEOPLE** [ ] [14]
(12"+=) – Shama lama ding dong / Pretty ballerina.
(cd-s+=) – Check it out (live) / Pink houses (acoustic).
Jul 88. (7") **ROOTY TOOT TOOT. / CHECK IT OUT (live)** [ ] [61] May 88
(12"+=) – Pretty ballerina.
(cd-s+=) – Like home (acoustic).
Apr 89. (7")(12") **RAVE ON. / (other track by LITTLE RICHARD)** [-] [ ]

— (above from the film 'Cocktail' on 'Elektra' label)

— added **CRYSTAL TALIEFERO** – backing vocals, percussion

May 89. (lp)(c)(cd) **BIG DADDY** [25] [7]
– Big daddy of them all / To live / Martha say / Theo and weird Henry / Jackie Brown / Pop singer / Void in my heart / Mansions in Heaven / Sometimes a great notion / Country gentlemen / J.M.'s question. *(cd+=)–* Let it all hang out.
Jun 89. (7") **POP SINGER. / JM'S QUESTION** [ ] [15] Apr 89
(12"+=) – Like a rolling stone (live).
(cd-s++=) – Check it out (live).
Jul 89. (7") **JACKIE BROWN. / ?** [-] [48]

JOHN MELLENCAMP

Sep 91. (7") **GET A LEG UP. / WHENEVER WE WANTED** [ ] [14]
(12"+=)(cd-s+=) – Seventh son.
Oct 91. (cd)(c)(lp) **WHENEVER WE WANTED** [39] [17]
– Love and happiness / Now more than ever / I ain't ever satisfied / Get a leg up / Crazy ones / Last chance / They're so tough / Melting pot / Whenever we wanted / Again tonight. *(re-iss.cd Apr95)*
Jan 92. (7")(c-s) **LOVE AND HAPPINESS. / ('A'-LA rock dance mix)** [ ] [ ]
(12"+=)/ /(cd-s++=) – ('A'mix)./ / ('A'other mix).
Feb 92. (c-s) **AGAIN TONIGHT. / ?** [-] [36]
Apr 92. (7")(c-s) **NOW MORE THAN EVER. / LONELY OLD NIGHT** [ ] [ ]
(cd-s+=) – Small town / Pink houses.
(cd-s) – ('A'side) / Jack and Diane / Check it out / Martha say (all live).

— Mid'92, MELLENCAMP suffered nervous exhaustion and cancelled gigs when his bassist MYERS severed a big toe in a boating accident. On 14th Nov '92, also saw his keyboard player JOHN CASCELLA die. He was only 35, but still played on half of next album. He was replaced by **MALCOLM BURN** – organ, guitar, harmonica, synth.

— **DAVID GRISSOM** – guitars, mandolin, bass repl. CRANE

Sep 93. (cd)(c) **HUMAN WHEELS** [37] [7]
– When Jesus left Birmingham / Junior / Human Wheels / Beige to beige / Case 795 (the family) / Suzanne and the jewels / Sweet evening breeze / What if I came knocking / French shoes / To the river.
Oct 93. (c-s) **HUMAN WHEELS. / ?** [-] [48]

— now w / **WANCHIC, MYERS, ARONOFF, ME'SHELL NDEGECELLO** (bass, vocals), **GERMANO, PETERSON + ANDY YORK** – guitar

Jun 94. (cd)(c) **DANCE NAKED** [ ] [13]
– Dance naked / Brothers / When Margaret comes to town / Wild night / L.U.V. / Another sunny day 12 /25 / Too much to think about / The big jack / The breakout.
Aug 94. (7"white)(c-s) **WILD NIGHT. (w/ ME'SHELL NDEGEOCELLO) / HURTS SO GOOD** [34] [3] Jun94
(cd-s) – ('A'side) / Dance naked (live) / When Jesus left Birmingham / Small town (acoustic).
(cd-s) – ('A'side) / Jack and Diane / Pink houses / Rock in the U.S.A. (a salute to the 60's).

— Above 'A' shared vocal duties with MADONNA's 'Maverick' protegee ME'SHELL.

Nov 94. (c-s)(cd-s) **DANCE NAKED. / ?** [-] [41]

– compilations, etc. (JOHN COUGAR) –

Mar 86. Castle; (lp)(c)(cd) **THE COLLECTION** (early) [ ] [-]

MEN AT WORK

Formed: Melbourne, Australia ... 1979 by STRYKERT and Scots-born HAY, who added his former La Troube university mates SPEISER and HAM, plus REES. In the early 80's, they became resident band at Richmond,

Melbourne pub; The Cricketer's Arms, where A&R man Peter Karpin saw them. Through his persistence they signed to 'CBS-Epic', and had 1982 debut Aussie No.1 with 'WHO CAN IT BE NOW?'. After a US tour supporting FLEETWOOD MAC, it hit top spot there, and heralded massive selling worldwide No.1 album 'BUSINESS AS USUAL'. At the start of '83, they had simultaneous UK + US top slot with 45 'DOWN UNDER'. However, after another Top 10 album 'CARGO' in 1983, they slid into medium sales and soon folded mid-85. • **Style:** Described as the 'Antipodean answer to The POLICE', blending together AOR with white reggae rhythm. • **Songwriters:** Mostly by HAY with STRYKERT, and some by HAM. • **Trivia:** Debut lp was produced by American PETER McIAN.

Recommended: BUSINESS AS USUAL (*5)

COLIN JAMES HAY (b.29 Jun'58, Scotland) – vocals, rhythm guitar / **RON STRYKERT** (b.18 Aug'57) – guitar / **GREG HAM** (b.27 Sep'53) – saxophone, keyboards, flute / **JOHN REES** (b.18 Aug'57) – bass, vocals / **JERRY SPEISER** – drums

		Epic	Columbia
Jun 82.	(lp)(c) **BUSINESS AS USUAL**	1	1
	– Who can it be now? / I can see it in your eyes / Down under / Underground / Helpless automation / People just love to play with words / Be good Johnny / Touching the untouchables / Catch a star / Down by the sea. *(UK-re-dist.+cd.Jan83) (re-iss.+cd.May87) (cd-iss.May94)*		
Jul 82.	(7") **WHO CAN IT BE NOW?. / ANYONE FOR TENNIS**	45	1
Nov 82.	(7")(7"sha-pic-d) **DOWN UNDER. / CRAZY**	1	1
Mar 83.	(7") **OVERKILL. / TILL THE MONEY RUNS OUT**	21	3
Apr 83.	(lp)(c)(cd) **CARGO**	8	3
	– Dr. Jeckyll and Mr. Jive / Overkill / Settle down my boy / Upstairs in my house / No sign of yesterday / It's a mistake / High wire / Blue for you / I like to / No restrictions. *(re-iss.Apr86) (cd-iss.Nov93 on 'Sony Collectors')*		
Jun 83.	(7")(12")(7"pic-d) **IT'S A MISTAKE. / SHINTARO**	33	6
	(US-12"+=) – Who can it be now?.		
Sep 83.	(7") **DR. JECKYLL AND MR. JIVE. / I'D LIKE TO (live)**	-	28
Sep 83.	(7") **DR. JECKYLL AND MR. JIVE. / NO RESTRICTIONS**	31	-
	(12"+=)(d7"+=) – Be good Johnny / Down under.		
Feb 84.	(7") **SETTLE DOWN MY BOY. / UPSTAIRS AT MY HOUSE**		
	(d7+=)(12"+=) – Who can it be now? / Be good Johnny.		

— session players **JEREMY ALSOP** – bass / **MARK KENNEDY** – drums, percussion repl. REES and SPEISER

May 85.	(7")(12") **EVERYTHING I NEED. / SAIL TO YOU**		47
Aug 85.	(7")(12") **MARIA. / SNAKES AND LADDERS**		
Sep 85.	(lp)(c)(cd) **TWO HEARTS**		50 Jun 85
	– Man with two hearts / Giving up / Everything I need / Sail to you / Children on parade / Maria / Stay at home / Hard luck story / Snakes and ladders / Still life.		
Oct 85.	(7") **HARD LUCK STORY. / SNAKES AND LADDERS**	-	

— The sole survivor **HAY** with **ALSOP** plus **JAMES BLACK** – guitar (ex-MONDO ROCK) / **COLIN BAYLEY** – keyboards (ex-MI SEX) / **CHAD WACKERMAN** – drums toured in Asia late '85, but soon disbanded.

COLIN JAMES HAY

with session people plus **ALSOP**

		Epic	Columbia
Jan 87.	(7") **HOLD ME. / HOME SWEET HOME**		
	(12"+=) – ('A'version).		
Feb 87.	(lp)(c)(cd) **LOOKING FOR JACK**		
	– Hold me / Can I hold you / Looking for Jack / Master of crime / These are our finest days / Nature of the beast / Puerto Rico / Ways of the world / I don't need you anymore / Circles erratica / Fisherman's friend.		
May 87.	(7")(12") **CAN I HOLD YOU. / NATURE OF THE BEAST**		
Sep 87.	(7") **LOOKING FOR JACK. / THESE ARE OUR FINEST DAYS**	-	

COLIN HAY BAND

w/ **GERRY HALE** – viola, vocals, guitar / **PAUL GADSBY** – bass, vocals / **ROBERT DILLON** – percussion, vocals

		M.C.A.	M.C.A.
Feb 90.	(cd)(c)(lp) **WAYFARING SONS**		
	– Wayfaring song / Into my life / Storm in my heart / Dream on (in the night) / Not so lonely / Don't drink the water / Help me / Dreamtime in Glasgow / Back in my loving arms / Ya (rest in peace).		
Apr 90.	(7")(c-s) **INTO MY LIFE. / IF YOU WANT IT**		
	(12"+=)(cd-s+=) – Wayfaring Sons.		

MENSWEAR

Formed: Camden, London, England . . .1994 by quintet below. In 1995, they scored first of 3 major UK hits with WIRE sounding 'DAYDREAMER'. • **Style:** WIRE meets mods, although BLUR and a punky MONKEES come to mind. • **Songwriters:** Group penned. • **Trivia:** CHRIS GENTRY is the boyfriend of DONNA from ELASTICA.

Recommended: NUISANCE (*7)

JOHNNY DEAN – vocals / **CHRIS GENTRY** – guitar / **SIMON WHITE** – guitar / **STUART BLACK** – bass / **MATT EVERETT** – drums

		Laurel	not issued
Dec 94.	(7") **DAYDREAMER. / I'LL MANAGE SOMEHOW**		-
Apr 95.	(7")(cd-s) **I'LL MANAGE SOMEHOW. / SECOND HAND**	49	-
Jun 95.	(7")(c-s) **DAYDREAMER. / GENTLEMAN JIM**	14	
	(cd-s+=) – Around you again.		
Sep 95.	(7")(c-s) **STARDUST. / DAYDREAMER (dub dreamer)**	16	
	(cd-s+=) – Back in the bar / Satellite.		
Oct 95.	(cd)(c)(lp) **NUISANCE**	11	
	– 125 West 3rd Street / I'll manage somehow / Sleeping in / Little Miss Pinpoint eyes / Daydreamer / Hollywood girl / Being brave / Around you again / The one / Stardust / Piece of me.		
Nov 95.	(7")(c-s) **SLEEPING IN. / SUNDAY DRIVER**	24	
	(cd-s+=) – Now is the hour / 26 years.		

MEN THEY COULDN'T HANG

Formed: London, England . . . 1983 by former buskers SWILL, etc (see below). In 1984, they signed to ELVIS COSTELLO's 'Imp' and issued debut 45 'GREEN FIELDS OF FRANCE', which made No.3 in John Peel's Radio One Festive 50. In 1986 after their UK Top 100 debut album 'NIGHT OF A 1,000 CANDLES', they were given contract by 'MCA'. This progressed them further, and they finally made it into the Top 40 in 1989 with 'Silvertone' album 'SILVERTOWN'. • **Style:** Hard-edged political anthem-folk rock outfit, in similar vein to POGUES. The connection being that HASLER, was once in same group The NIPPLE ERECTORS with SHANE McGOWAN. • **Songwriters:** SIMMONDS lyrics / group compositions (some just SWILL). Covered; GREEN FIELDS OF FRANCE (Eric Bogle) / DONALD WHERE'S YOUR TROOSERS? (hit; Andy Stewart) / RAWHIDE (Link Wary) / MAN IN THE CORNER SHOP (Paul Weller) / GOODBYE T'JANE (Slade) / etc. • **Trivia:** GREENBACK DOLLAR was produced by NICK LOWE.

Recommended: FIVE GLORIOUS YEARS (*7) / NIGHT OF 1,000 CANDLES (*8) / HOW GREEN IS MY VALLEY (*6)

PHIL SWILL (b.ODGERS) – vocals, accoustic guitar, tin whistle, melodia / **PAUL SIMMONDS** – guitar, vocals, mandolin, keyboards / **STEPHAN CUSH** (b.Wales) – guitar, vocals / **SHANNE HASLER** – bass (ex-NIPPLE ERECTORS, ex-NIPS) / **JON** – drums, percussion

		Imp-Demon	not issued
Oct 84.	(7") **THE GREEN FIELDS OF FRANCE. / ('A'version)**		-
	(12"+=) – Hush little baby.		
Jun 85.	(7") **IRONMASTERS. / DONALD WHERE'S YOUR TROOSERS?**		-
	(12"+=) – Rawhide.		
		Demon	**not issued**
Jul 85.	(lp)(c) **NIGHT OF A 1,000 CANDLES**	91	-
	– The day after / Jack Dandy / A night to remember / Johnny comes home / The green fields of France (no man's land) / Ironmasters / Hush little baby / Walkin' talkin' / Kingdom come / Scarlet ribbons. *(cd-iss.1988)*		
Nov 85.	(7") **GREENBACK DOLLAR. / A NIGHT TO REMEMBER**		
	(12"+=) – The bells.		
		M.C.A.	**M.C.A.**
Jun 86.	(7") **GOLD RUSH. / GHOSTS OF CABLE STREET**		
	(12"+=) – Walkin' talkin'.		
Oct 86.	(7") **SHIRT OF BLUE. / JOHNNY COME HOME**		
	(12"+=) – Whisky in me giro / Scarlet ribbons.		
Oct 86.	(lp)(c) **HOW GREEN IS MY VALLEY**	68	
	– Gold strike / Gold rush / Ghosts of Cable Street / Dancing on the pier / The bells / Wishing well / Going back to Coventry / Shirt of blue / Rabid underdog / Tiny soldiers / The parade / Parted from you. *(cd-iss.1990)*		
Mar 87.	(7")(12") **GHOSTS OF CABLE STREET. / DREAM MACHINE**		
	(c-s+=) – Liverpool lullaby.		

— **RICKY** – bass repl. SHANNE

		Magnet	not issued
Oct 87.	(7")(7"pic-d) **ISLAND IN THE RAIN. / COUNTRY SONG**		-
	(7"ep+=)(12"ep+=) – Silver dagger / Restless highway.		
Mar 88.	(7") **THE COLOURS. / RORY'S GRAVE**	61	-
	(12"+=) – Big iron.		
	(cd-s++=) – ('A'-full remix).		
Mar 88.	(lp)(c)(cd) **WAITING FOR BONAPARTE**	41	-
	– The crest / Smugglers / Dover lights / Bounty hunter / Island in the rain / The colours / Midnight train / Father's wrong / Life of a small fry / Mary's present. *(cd+=)–* The crest (12"version). *(c+=)–* Silver dagger / Restless highway / Country song.		
Jun 88.	(7")(12") **THE CREST. / TIME AT THE BAR**		-
	(cd-s+=) – Goodbye t'Jane / Ironmasters.		

— added p/t **NICKY MUIR** – keyboards, accordion

		Silvertone	not issued
Feb 89.	(7") **RAIN, STEAM AND SPEED. / SHIRT OF BLUE**		-
	(12"+=) – Scarlet ribbons.		
	(cd-s++=) – Iron masters.		
Apr 89.	(lp)(c)(cd) **SILVERTOWN**	39	-
	– Rosettes / A place in the sun / Home fires / Diamonds, gold & fur / Company town / Lobotomy gets 'em home / Blackfriar's bridge / Rain, steam and speed / Down all the days / Hellfire and damnation / Homefires / El vaquero. *(cd+=)–* A map of Morocco / Rain, steam and speed (12"mix).		
May 89.	(7") **A PLACE IN THE SUN. / A MAP OF MOROCCO**		-
	(12"+=) – Scarlet ribbons.		
	(cd-s++=) – The day after (live).		
Dec 89.	(7") **A MAP OF MOROCCO. / ROSETTES / THE DAY THE CLOCK WENT BACK**		-
	(12"+=) – Rosettes (live).		
	(cd-s++=) – The iron men of rap (features "ATTILA THE STOCKBROKER")		
Jul 90.	(7") **GREAT EXPECTATIONS. / MARGARET PIE**		-
	(12"+=)(cd-s+=) – Green fields of France. *(re-iss.1992)*		
Aug 90.	(cd)(c)(lp) **THE DOMINO CLUB**	53	-
	– The lion and the unicorn / Great expectations / The family man / Handy man / Kingdom of the blind / Grave rosting in gig harbour / Industrial town / You're the one / Australia / Dog eyes, owl meat, man-chops / Billy Morgan / On the razzle.		

— Disbanded Feb'91 after farewell gigs.

Fun After All / not issued

May 91. (cd)(c)(lp) **ALIVE, ALIVE-O** (live 8th Feb'91) [ ] [-]
– The crest / Billy Morgan / You're the one / Home fires / Going back to Coventry / The colours / Ironmasters / Lobotomy, gets 'em home / Man in the corner shop / Australia / Night to remember / Scarlet ribbons.

– compilations, others, etc. –

Aug 88. Strange Fruit; (12"ep) **THE EVENING SHOW SESSIONS (15.6.86)** [ ] [-]
– Dancing on the pier / Ghosts of Cable Street / Going back to Coventry / Tiny tin soldiers.
Apr 90. Silvertone; (cd)(c)(lp) **FIVE GLORIOUS YEARS** [ ] [-]

Natalie MERCHANT (see under ⇒ 10,000 MANIACS)

Freddie MERCURY (see under ⇒ QUEEN)

MERCURY REV

Formed: Buffalo, New York, USA . . . early 90's as a sextet (see below). Made quick headway, and after Reading Festival August 1991, they re-issued nearly forgotten debut album 'YERSELF IS STEAM'. Soon were snapped up by 'Beggar's B.' in 1992 /93, and unleashed UK Top 50 album 'BOLES'. • **Style:** Freaky BUTTHOLE SURFERS / DINOSAUR JR like guitar-angst rock outfit. • **Songwriters:** Group penned, except IF YOU WANT ME TO STAY (Sly Stone). • **Trivia:** ALAN VEGA (ex-Suicide) appeared on their 1994 single 'EVERLASTING ARM'.

Recommended: YERSELF IS STEAM (*9) / BOLES (*7)

JONATHAN DONAHUE – vocals, guitar / **DAVID BAKER** – vocals / **SEAN GRASSHOPPER** – guitar / **DAVID FRIDMANN** – bass / **JIMMY CHAMBERS** – drums / **SUZANNE** – flute

Mint Films / Mint Films

Feb 91. (m-cd)(m-lp) **YERSELF IS STEAM** [ ] [ ]
– Space patrol / Oh . . . it's out there / Mom is coming over. *(re-iss.Sep91)*
Nov 91. (12"ep)(cd-ep) **CAR WASH HAIR** [ ] [ ]
– Lego my ego / Shhh-peaceful-very sleepy rivers (live) / If you want me to stay (demo) / Blood on the moon (demo).

Rough Trade / Rough Trade

Apr 92. (7") **IF YOU WANT ME TO STAY. / THE LEFT-HANDED RAYGUN OF PAUL SHARITS** [ ] [ ]

Beggar's B. / Columbia

Nov 92. (12")(cd-s) **CHASING A BEE. / CONEY ISLAND CYCLONE** [ ] [ ]
Nov 92. (cd)(c)(d-lp) **LEGO MY EGO** [ ] [ ]
– Chasing a bee / Syrine mouth / Coney Island cyclone / Blue and black / Sweet oddysee of a commercial t' th' center of yer heart / Frittering / Continuous tracks and thunder under a mother's smile / Very sleepy rivers. *(re-iss.Mar93)*
Mar 93. (10")(cd-s) **THE HUM IS COMING FROM HER. / SO THERE (with ROBERT CREELY)** [ ] [ ]
May 93. (7") **SOMETHING FOR JOEY. / THREE SPIDER'S EGGS (Live)** [ ] [ ]
(12"+=) – Suzanne peels out.
(cd-s++=) – Noise. *(re-iss.Jul93)*
Jun 93. (cd)(c)(lp) **BOLES** [43] [ ]
– Meth of a rockette's kick / Trickle down / Bronx cheer / Boys peel out / Downs are feminine balloons / Something for Joey / Snorry mouth / Hi-speed boats / Continuous drunks and blunders / Girlfren.
Jun 94. (12"white)(cd-s) **EVERLASTING ARM. / DEAD MAN** [ ] [ ]
—— Have now disbanded (late '94) leaving below . . .
May 95. (cd)(c)(pic-lp) **SEE YOU ON THE OTHER SIDE** [ ] [ ]
– Empire state (Sun house in excelsis) / Young man's stride / Sudden ray of hope / Everlasting arm / Racing the tide / Close encounters of the third grade / A kiss from an old flame (a trip to the Moon) / Peaceful night.

METALLICA

Formed: Norvale, California, USA . . . 1981 by ULRICH and HETFIELD. The former had earlier emigrated from Denmark, and enjoyed drumming on UK tour for English group DIAMOND HEAD. After recruiting shifting personnel, they moved to New Jersey early in '83, where they signed to John Zazula's 'Megaforce' label. Their debut lp 'KILL 'EM ALL', gained a licence deal with UK label 'Music For Nations'. Their 2nd lp 'RIDE THE LIGHTNING', was the last for US label, and they soon moved to 'Elektra'. In 1986, they broke into major chart territory with album 'MASTER OF PUPPETS', and by 1991 had a cross-Atlantic No.1 with self-titled masterpiece. This contained no less than 5 hit singles, all of them gems. • **Style:** New breed of high-speed heavy metal, influenced initially by BLACK SABBATH and MOTORHEAD, but progressing into a more WISHBONE ASH sound, with bouts of thrash. • **Songwriters:** ULRICH-HETFIELD, bar; BLITZKREIG (Blitzkreig) / AM I EVIL + HELPLESS + THE PRINCE (Diamond Head) / CRASH COURSE IN BRAIN SURGERY + BREADFAN (Budgie) / THE SMALL HOURS (Holocaust) / STONE COLD CRAZY (Queen). • **Miscellaneous:** In Spring'92, they paid tribute to the late FREDDIE MERCURY, when appearing at his AIDS benefit concert at Wembley.

Recommended: METALLICA (*10) / . . . AND JUSTICE FOR ALL (*7) / MASTER OF PUPPETS (*8) / RIDE THE LIGHTNING (*8) / KILL 'EM ALL (*7).

JAMES HETFIELD (b. 3 Aug'63) – vocals, rhythm guitar (ex-OBSESSION, etc) / **LARS ULRICH** (b.26 Dec'63, Copenhagen, Denmark) – drums / with **LLOYD GRAND** – guitar

not issued / Bootleg.US

Dec 81. (7") **LET IT LOOSE. / KILLING TIME** [-] [ ]
—— (Jan82) **DAVE MUSTAINE** – lead guitar, co-writer / **RON McGOVNEY** – bass repl. GRAND (JEF WARNER also played guitar in 1982)
—— (early '83) **KIRK HAMMETT** (b.18 Nov'62) – lead guitar (ex-EXODUS) repl. MUSTAINE who was fired due to drunkeness. He was soon to form rivals MEGADETH.
—— **CLIFF BURTON** (b.10 Feb'62) – bass (ex-TRAUMA) replaced McGOVNEY

M.F.N. / Megaforce

Jul 83. (lp)(c) **KILL 'EM ALL** [ ] [ ]
– Hit the lights / The four horsemen / Motorbreath / Jump in the fire / (Anesthesia) Pulling teeth / Whiplash / Phantom Lord / No remorse / Seek and destroy / Metal militia. *(re-iss.Aug86 on pic-lp) (cd-iss.Apr87) (re-iss.Nov89 on 'Vertigo')*
Jan 84. (12")(12"red) **JUMP IN THE FIRE. / SEEK AND DESTROY (live). / PHANTOM LORD** [ ] [ ]
(re-iss.Mar86 on 7"sha-pic-d) (re-iss.+cd+c.Feb90, with other EP below)
Jul 84. (lp)(c) **RIDE THE LIGHTNING** [87] [ ]
– Fight fire with fire / Ride the lightning / For whom the bell tolls Fade to black / Trapped under ice / Escape / Creeping death / The call of Ktulu. *(re-iss.Sep86 on cd+pic-d) (US.re-iss.Oct84 on 'Elektra' hit 100) (re-iss.Nov89 on 'Vertigo')*

M.F.N. / Elektra

Nov 84. (12")(12"pic-d) **CREEPING DEATH. / AM I EVIL. / BLITZKRIEG** [ ] [ ]
(above re-iss.Jan87 in gold + blue vinyl) (re-iss.+cd+c.Feb90, w/Mar86)
Mar 86. (lp)(c)(cd) **MASTER OF PUPPETS** [41] [29]
– Battery / Master of puppets / The thing that should not be / Welcome home (sanitarium) / Disposable heroes / Leper messiah / Orion / Damage Inc. *(also iss.Dec87 as d-lp,pic-d) (re-iss.Nov89 on 'Vertigo')*
—— **JASON NEWSTEAD** (b. 4 Mar'63) – bass (ex-FLOTSAM AND JETSAM) repl. CLIFF who was killed in tour bus crash 27 Sep'86

Vertigo / Elektra

Aug 87. (12"ep) **$5.98 EP – GARAGE DAYS REVISITED** [27] [28]
– Helpless / The small hours / Crash course in brain surgery / Last caress / Green hell. *(US version incl. 'The Wait' and was also m-lp) (re-iss.+cd.May90)*
Sep 88. (7") **EYE OF THE BEHOLDER. / BREAD FAN** [-] [ ]
Sep 88. (7")(12") **HARVESTER OF SORROW. / BREADFAN. / THE PRINCE** [20] [ ]
Oct 88. (d-lp)(c)(cd) **. . .AND JUSTICE FOR ALL** [4] [6] Sep 88
– Blackened / . . .And justice for all / Eye of the beholder / One / The shortest straw / Harvester of sorrow / The frayed ends of sanity / To live is to die / Dyers eve.
Feb 89. (7")(3"cd-s) **ONE. / THE PRINCE** [-] [35]
Mar 89. (7") **ONE. / SEEK AND DESTROY (live)** [13] [-] Feb 89
(12"+=) – Creeping death (live) / For whom the bell tolls (live).
(10"+=)(cd-s+=) – Welcome home (sanitarium).
Jul 91. (7")(7"pic-d) **ENTER SANDMAN. / STONE COLD CRAZY** [5] [16]
(12"+=)(cd-s+=) – Holier than thou.
Aug 91. (cd)(c)(d-lp) **METALLICA** [1] [1]
– Enter sandman / Sad but true / Holier than thou / The unforgiven / Wherever I may roam / Don't tread on me / Through the never / Nothing else matters / Of wolf and man / The god that failed / My friend of misery / The struggle within.
Nov 91. (7")(7"pic-d) **THE UNFORGIVEN. / KILLING TIME** [15] [35]
(12"+=)(cd-s+=) – ('A'demo) / So what.
Apr 92. (7")(7"pic-d) **NOTHING ELSE MATTERS. / ENTER SANDMAN (live)** [6] [34] Oct 92
(12"+=)(cd-s+=) – Harvester of sorrow (live) / ('A'demo).
(cd-s+=) – Stone cold crazy (live).
(cd-s+=) – Sad but true (live).
—— On tour **JOHN MARSHALL (of METAL CHURCH)** repl. injured (burnt) HETFIELD
Oct 92. (7")(7"pic-d) **WHEREVER I MAY ROAM. / FADE TO BLACK (live)** [25] [82] Jul 92
(12"+=) – ('A'demo).
(12")(cd-s) – ('A'side) / Medley (live) / ('A'demo).
Feb 93. (7") **SAD BUT TRUE. / NOTHING ELSE MATTERS** [20] [98]
(12"+=)(cd-s+=) – Creeping death (live) / Sad but true (demo).
(cd-s+=) – Sad but true (live).
Dec 93. (cd)(c) **LIVE SHIT: BINGE & PURGE (live)** [54] [26]
– *(also issued d-cd + 3 videos + book)*

– compilations, others, etc. –

May 90. Vertigo; (6x12"box) **THE GOOD, THE BAD & THE LIVE** [56] [-]
Aug 87. Megaforce; (7"ep) **WHIPLASH EP** [-] [ ]

METERS (see under ⇒ NEVILLE BROTHERS)

Pat METHENY

Born: 12 Aug'54, Lee Summit, Kansas City, USA. Former member of GARY BURTON band from 1974, he ventured solo in 1975 recording debut 'BRIGHT SIZE LIFE' for 'E.C.M.'. In 1979, his 4th instrumental album 'NEW CHAUTAUQUA', was a huge success making the US Top 50 lists. Became one of the most popular jazz figures of the next decade and a half. In between, he and group collaborated with DAVID BOWIE on Top 20 single 'THIS IS NOT AMERICA'. • **Style:** Instrumental virtuoso & AOR/Latin jazz-rock guitarist, augmented by accomplished ever-faithful band of musicians including pianist LYLE MAYS. • **Songwriters:** Self-penned with some collaborations. Covered; LONELY WOMAN (Horace Silver) / REJOICING (Ornette Coleman) / etc. • **Trivia:** Produced by MANFRED EICHER until 1986.

Recommended: TRAVELS (*9) / OFFRAMP (*8) / AMERICAN GARAGE (*7) / STILL LIFE (TALKING) (*7)

PAT METHENY – guitar with **JACO PASTORIUS** – bass / **BOB MOSES** – drums

E.C.M. E.C.M.

Apr 76. (lp) **BRIGHT SIZE LIFE** ☐ ☐ Feb76
– Bright size life / Sirabhorn / Unity village / Missouri uncompromised / Mid western nights dream / Omaha celebration / Round trip / Broadway blues. *(cd-iss.Dec86)*

PAT METHENY GROUP

now with **LYLE MAYS** (b.27 Nov'53, Wausaukee, Wisconsin) – piano / **EBERHARD WEBER** – bass / **DAN GOTTLIEB** – drums

May 77. (lp) **WATERCOLOURS** ☐ ☐ Feb 77
– Watercolours / Icefire / Oasis / Lakes / River Quay / Florida greeting song / Legend of the fountain / Sea song. *(re-iss.Nov88) (cd-iss.Feb86)*

— **MARK EGAN** – bass repl.WEBER

Jul 78. (lp) **PAT METHENY GROUP** ☐ ☐
– San Lorenzo / Phase dance / Jaco / Aprilwind / April joy / Lone Jack. *(cd-iss.Aug88)*

May 79. (lp) **NEW CHAUTAUQUA** (solo) ☐ 44 Apr79
– New Chautauqua / Country poem / Longago child – Fallen star / Hermitage / Sueno con Mexico / Daybreak. *(cd-iss.Aug85; 825 471-2)*

Jan 80. (lp)(c) **AMERICAN GARAGE** ☐ 53 Nov79
– (Cross the) Heartland / Airstream / The search / American garage / The epic. *(cd-iss.Dec85)*

PAT METHENY

with **CHARLIE HADEN** – bass / **JACK DE JOHNETTE** – drums / **DEWEY REDMAN + MIKE BRECKER** – tenor saxophones – (on same label; E.C.M.)

Dec 80. (d-lp)(d-c) **80/81** ☐ 89 Oct80
– Two folk songs / 80/81 / The bat / Turn around / Open / Pretty scattered / Every day / Goin' ahead. *(cd-iss.Sep84; 815 579-2)*

PAT METHENY & LYLE MAYS

with also **NANA VASCONCELOS** – drums, vocals, percussion (on same label)

Jun 81. (lp) **AS FALLS WICHITA, SO FALLS WICHITA FALLS** ☐ 50
– As falls Wichita, so falls Wichita Falls / Ozark / September fiftheenth / It's for you / Estupenda graca. *(cd/c-iss.Jul85)*

PAT METHENY GROUP

with **MAYS, GOTTLIEB, VASCONCELOS / + STEVE RODBY** – bass

May 82. (lp)(c) **OFFRAMP** ☐ 50
– Barcarolle / Are you going with me? / Au lait / Eighteen / Offramp / James / The bat (part II). *(cd-iss.Sep84)*

Jun 82. (7") **ARE YOU GOING WITH ME. / AU LAIT** ☐ ☐

May 83. (d-lp) **TRAVELS (live)** ☐ 62
– Are you going with me? / The fields, the sky / Goodbye / Phase dance / Straight on red / Farmer's trust / Extradition / Goin' ahead / As falls Wichita, so falls Wichita Falls / Travels / Song for Bilbao / San Lorenzo. *(cd-iss.Aug86)*

May84. (lp)(cd) **REJOICING** (solo) ☐ ☐
– Lonely woman / Tears inside / Humpty Dumpty / Blues for Pat / Rejoicing / Story from a stranger / The calling / Waiting for an answer.

— above w/ musicians **CHARLIE HADEN** – bass / **BILLY HIGGINS** – drums

— **METHENY, LYLE + RODBY** added **PEDRO AZNAR** – guitar, etc / **PAUL WERTICO** – drums

Nov 84. (lp)(cd) **FIRST CIRCLE** ☐ 91 Oct84
– Forward march / Yolanda, you learn / The first circle / If I could / Tell it all / End of the game / Mas Alla (beyond) / Praise.

EMI Amer.. EMI Amer..

Jan 85. (7")(12") **THIS IS NOT AMERICA. ("DAVID BOWIE/ PAT METHENY GROUP")/ ('A'instrumental)** 14 32

Mar 85. (lp) **THE FALCON & THE SNOWMAN (Soundtrack)** ☐ 54
– Psalm 121 – Flight of the falcon / Daulton Lee / Chris / The Falcon / This is not America / Extent of the lie / The level of deception / Capture / Epilogue (psalm 121).

Geffen Geffen

May 86. (lp)(c)(cd) **SONG X** ("ORNETTE COLEMAN/ PAT METHENY") ☐ ☐
– Song X / Mob job / Endangered species / Video games / Kathelin Gray / Trigonometry / Song X duo / Long time no see.

— above with **HADEN, DE JOHNETTE + ORNETTE & DENARDO COLEMAN** – sax & drums

— below now with **LYLE, RODBY, WERTICO + ARMANDO MARCAL** – percussion, vocals / **MARK LEDFORD + DAVID BLAMIRES** – vocals

Aug 87. (lp)(c)(cd) **STILL LIFE (TALKING)** ☐ 86
– Minuano (six eight) / So may it secretly begin / Last train home / (It's just) Talk / Third wind / Distance / In her family.

— **PEDRO AZNAR** – vocals, guitar, vibes, percussion – returned to repl.MARK + DAVID

Jul 89. (lp)(c)(cd) **LETTER FROM HOME** ☐ 66
– Have you heard / Every summer night / Better days ahead / Spring ain't here / 45-8 / 5-5-7 / Beat 70 / Dream of the return / Are we there yet / Vidala / Slip away / Letter from home.

PAT METHENY

solo with **DAVE HOLLAND** – bass / **ROY HAYNES** – drums – (same label)

Jul 90. (cd)(c)(lp) **QUESTION AND ANSWER** ☐ ☐
– Solar / Question and answer / H & H / Never too far away / Law years / Change of heart / All the things you are / Old folks / Three flights up.

— now with **MAYS, RODBY, VASCONCELOS, WERTICO, HADEN, MARCAL/ + STEVE FERRONE** – drums / **WILL LEE** – bass / **GIL GOLDSTEIN** – piano + London Orchestra conducted by JEREMY LUBBOCK + feat. string musicians

Jul 92. (cd)(c) **SECRET STORY** ☐ ☐
– Above the treetops / Facing west / Cathedral in a suitcase / Finding and believing / The longest summer / Sunlight / Rain river / Always and forever / As a flower blossoms (I am running to you) / Antonia / The truth will always be / Tell her you saw me / Not to be forgotten (our final hour).

Jan 95. (cd)(c) **WE LIVE HERE** ☐ 83
– Here to stay / And then I knew / The girls next door / To the end of the world / We live here / Episdom Zazure / Something to remind you / Red sky / Stranger in town.

more compilations, others

Nov 83. ECM; (lp) **WORKS** ☐ ☐
– Sueno con Mexico / (Cross the) Heartland / Travels / James / It's for you / Every day (I think of you) / Goin' ahead. *(re-iss.lp/cd Jun89)*

Jan 85. Kingdom Come; (lp)(c)(cd) **LIVE IN CONCERT (live with HEATH BROTHERS, DAVE BRUBECK 4, B.B.KING)** ☐ -
– Introduction / Move to the groove / Lover man / Blue rondo / Ol' Bill Basie / The thrill is gone / Guess who / Pay the cost to be the boss.

Jun 89. ECM; (lp)(cd) **WORKS II** ☐ ☐
– Uniquity road / Unity village / Open / Story from a stranger / Oasis / Sirabhorn / Farmer's trust.

Jul 89. Cleo; (cd) **PAT METHENY** ☐ -

METHOD MAN (see under ⇒ WU-TANG CLAN)

MG'S (see under ⇒ BOOKER T. & THE MG'S)

George MICHAEL

Born: GEORGIOS PANAYIOTOU, 25 Jun'63, Finchley, Middlesex, England. Met and befriended ANDREW RIDGELEY (b.26 Jan'63, Windlesham, Surrey, England) at Bushey Meads comprehensive school. In '79, they left to form ska-band The EXECUTIVE with DAVID AUSTIN, ANDREW LEAVER and RIDGELEY's brother PAUL. In 1981 GEORGE formed duo WHAM! with RIDGELEY, after frustrating bout of meaningless jobs and dole queues. Early the next year, they sent home-made demos to many record companies. Mark Dean of new 'Innervision', gave them contract through 'CBS'. In the summer of '82, their debut 'WHAM! RAP', failed to score, but follow-up 'YOUNG GUNS (GO FOR IT)', was their first of many Top 3 hits. Early in 1984, they broke out of financially restrictive deal with Dean, to join the ranks of 'Epic'. Until their amicable split in '86, they enjoyed many worldwide No.1's. GEORGE, who had already held 2 solo No.1 spots while in duo; 'CARELESS WHISPER' & 'A DIFFERENT CORNER', decided to go own way, after an early 1987 No.1 duet 'I KNEW YOU WERE WAITING (FOR ME)' with ARETHA FRANKLIN. His first post-WHAM hit in Jun'87 'I WANT YOUR SEX', caused much controversy with its raunchy subject matter and video, giving BBC excuse to ban it. It still went Top 3 on both sides of the Atlantic, and paved the way for massive selling 'FAITH' single follow-up and album. • **Style:** WHAM were mainly groomed for teenybop dance audience, with solo GEORGE moving away to more credible romantic and soulful pop. • **Songwriters:** All material by GEORGE, even most in WHAM. Covered; I BELIEVE WHEN I FALL IN LOVE IT WILL BE FOREVER (Stevie Wonder). • **Trivia:** GEORGE was another artist to feature greatly on the BAND AID single 'Do They Know It's Christmas', and sang duet 'DON'T LET THE SUN GO DOWN ON ME' with its writer ELTON JOHN at Wembley's 13 Jul'85 LIVE AID concert.

Recommended: FAITH (*8) / LISTEN WITHOUT PREJUDICE VOL.1 (*7).

WHAM!

GEORGE MICHAEL – vocals, bass / **ANDREW RIDGELEY** – guitar, keyboards

Innervision Columbia

Jun 82. (7")(12") **WHAM RAP (ENJOY WHAT YOU DO). / WHAM RAP! (unsocial mix)** ☐ ☐ Feb 83
(re-activated Jan83 hit UK-No.8)

Sep 82. (7")(12") **YOUNG GUNS (GO FOR IT). / GOIN' FOR IT** 3 -

May 83. (7")(12")(7"pic-d) **BAD BOYS. / ('A'instrumental)** 2 60 Aug 83

Jul 83. (lp)(c) **FANTASTIC** (US as "WHAM U.K.") 1 83
– Bad boys / A ray of sunshine / Love machine / Wham rap (enjoy what you do) / Club Tropicana / Nothing looks the same in the light / Come on / Young guns (go for it). *(cd-iss.Jan84, re-iss.lp Mar88 +cd.on 'Epic') (c/cd-iss.+= extra instrumental).*

Jul 83. (7")(7"pic-d) **CLUB TROPICANA. / BLUE (ARMED WITH LOVE)** 4 -
(12"+=) – ('A'instrumental).

Nov 83. (7") **CLUB FANTASTIC MEGAMIX. / A RAY OF SUNSHINE (instrumental)** 15 -
(12"+=) – Come on / Love machine.

Epic Columbia

May 84. (7") **WAKE ME UP BEFORE YOU GO-GO. / ('A'instrumental)** 1 1 Sep 84

— next by **GEORGE MICHAEL** (solo) (in US still credited to **WHAM featuring GEORGE MICHAEL**)

Jul 84. (7")(7"sha-pic-d) **CARELESS WHISPER. / ('A'instrumental)** 1 1 Dec 84

Oct 84. (7")(7"sha-pic-d) **FREEDOM. / ('A'instrumental)** 1 -
(12"+=) – ('A'extended).

Nov 84. (lp)(c)(cd) **MAKE IT BIG** 1 1

– Wake me up befor you go-go / Everything she wants / Heartbeat / Like a baby / Freedom / If you were there / Credit card baby / Careless whisper. *(re-iss.Oct89) (iss.in US also on pic-lp*

Dec 84. (7")(12") **LAST CHRISTMAS. / EVERYTHING SHE WANTS** 2 –
Feb 85. (7") **EVERYTHING SHE WANTS. / LIKE A BABY** – 1
Jul 85. (7") **FREEDOM. / HEARTBEAT** – 3

— (In Jun'85, He dueted with ELTON JOHN for LIVE AID on his song 'DON'T LET THE SUN GO DOWN ON ME'). Also from same source Nov85, 'WRAP HER UP' again w / ELTON JOHN was issued as 45 and hit UK No.12, US No.20.

Nov 85. (7") **I'M YOUR MAN. / DO IT RIGHT (instr.)** 1 20
(12"+=)(12"pic-d+=) – ('A'acapella version).
Dec 85. (7") **LAST CHRISTMAS. / BLUE (ARMED WITH LOVE) (live)** 6 –
(12"+=) – Everything she wants.

GEORGE MICHAEL

Mar 86. (7")(12") **A DIFFERENT CORNER. / ('A'instrumental)** 1 7

WHAM!

Jun 86. (7") **THE EDGE OF HEAVEN. / WHERE DID YOUR HEART GO?** 1 –
(d7"+=)(12"+=) – Battlestations / Wham rap '86.
Jun 86. (7") **THE EDGE OF HEAVEN. / BLUE (live)** – 10
(12"+=) – Where did your heart go? / Battlestations / Wham rap '86 / A different corner.
Oct 86. (7") **WHERE DID YOUR HEART GO?. / WHAM RAP '86** – 50

— (WHAM by this time had already split)

Oct 86. (d-lp)(c)(cd) **THE FINAL** (live, their last concert) 1 –
– Wham! rap (enjoy what you do) / Young guns (go for it!) / Bad boys / Club Tropicana / Wake me up before you go-go / Careless whisper / Freedom / Last Christmas (pudding mix) / Everything she wants (remix) / I'm your man / A different corner / Battlestations / Where did your heart go? / The edge of Heaven. *(also iss.on 2 gold-lp's)*

– others, compilations, etc. (UK) –

Sep 86. Epic; (12")(c-s) **THE 12" TAPE** –
– Wham rap / Careless . . . / Freedom / Everything . . . / I'm your . . .
Dec 86. Epic; (7") **LAST CHRISTMAS. / WHERE DID YOUR HEART GO** –
(12"+=) – ('A'&'B'extended).

ARETHA FRANKLIN & GEORGE MICHAEL

Epic / Arista – Columbia

Jan 87. (7")(12") **I KNEW YOU WERE WAITING (FOR ME). / ('A'instrumental)** 1 3

GEORGE MICHAEL

went solo as did ANDREW RIDGELEY

Epic / Columbia

Jun 87. (7")(12") **I WANT YOUR SEX. / ('A'instrumental)** 3 2
(c-s+=)(cd-s+=) – Rhythm 1 – Lust / Rhythm 2 – Brass in love / Rhythm 3 – A last request.
Oct 87. (7")(c-s)(7"sha-pic-d) **FAITH. / ('A'instrumental)** 2 1
(12"+=) – Hard day (mix) / Hand to mouth. (US; b-side)
(cd-s+=) – Hard day (mix) / Rhythm 3 – A last request.
Nov 87. (lp)(c)(cd) **FAITH** 1 1
– Faith / Father figure / I want your sex (part 1 & 2) / One more try / Hard day / Hand to mouth / Look at your hands / Monkey / Kissing a fool. *(re-iss.Sep90, hit UK 40)*
Dec 87. (7") **FATHER FIGURE. / LOVE'S IN NEED OF LOVE TODAY** 11 1
(12"+=)(12"pic-d+=)(3"cd-s+=) – ('A'instrumental).
Apr 88. (7")(12")(pic-cd-s) **ONE MORE TRY. / LOOK AT YOUR HANDS** 8 1
Jul 88. (7") **MONKEY. / MONKEY (acapella)** 13 1
(12"+=)(cd-s+=) – ('A'extended versions).
Nov 88. (7") **KISSING A FOOL. / ('A'instrumental)** 18 5 Oct 88
(12"+=)(cd-s+=) – Rhythm 3 – A last request.
Aug 90. (7")(c-s) **PRAYING FOR TIME. / IF YOU WERE MY WOMAN** 6 1
(12"+=)(cd-s+=) – Waiting (reprise).
Aug 90. (cd)(c)(lp) **LISTEN WITHOUT PREJUDICE VOL.1** 1 2
– Praying for time / Freedom '90 / They won't go when I go / Something to save / Cowboys and angels / Waiting for that day / Mother's pride / Head the pain / Soul free / Waiting (reprise).
Oct 90. (7")(12") **WAITING FOR THAT DAY. / FANTASY** 23 –
(cd-s+=) – Kissing a fool / Father figure.
Dec 90. (7")(c-s) **FREEDOM '90. / FREEDOM (mix)** 28 8 Oct 90
(12"+=)(cd-s+=) – Mother's pride.
Jan 91. (c-s) **MOTHER'S PRIDE. / WAITING FOR THAT DAY** – 46
27
Feb 91. (7")(c-s) **HEAL THE PAIN. / SOUL FREE** 31
(12"+=)(cd-s+=) – Hand to mouth.
Mar 91. (7")(12")(c-s)(cd-s) **COWBOYS AND ANGELS. / SOMETHING TO SAVE** 45
Nov 91. (7")(c-s) **DON'T LET THE SUN GO DOWN ON ME. ("GEORGE MICHAEL & ELTON JOHN") / I BELIEVE (WHEN I FALL IN LOVE IT WILL BE FOREVER)** 1 1
(12"+=) – Last Christmas.
(cd-s+=) – If you were my woman / Fantasy.
Jun 92. (7")(12")(c-s)(cd-s) **TOO FUNKY. / CRAZY MAN DANCE** 4 10

— In Nov'92, GEORGE sued 'Sony' for $50m. He is under contract until 2003. The outcome expected in 1994. In Apr93, he teamed up with QUEEN on UK No.1 + US No.46 'FIVE LIVE EP'.

MICRODISNEY

Formed: Cork, Ireland . . . 1982 by CATHAL COUGHLIN and SEAN O'HAGAN. After 2 local 45's for 'Kabuki', they moved to London in 1984 and signed for major indie 'Rough Trade'. Their first lp 'EVERYBODY IS FANTASTIC', made them several friends in the music press, and raced into independent charts that year. In 1987, on 'Virgin', they had brief liason in UK Top 60 with single 'TOWN TO TOWN', but by '88 all was over, and CATHAL set up his FATIMA MANSIONS. • **Style:** Hard-edged thought-provoking rock, fronted by the green man of rock and JIM MORRISON (Doors) lookalike; CATHAL COUGHLIN. • **Songwriters:** CATHAL pens most with SEAN O'HAGAN. FATIMA MANSIONS: covered STIGMATA (Ministry) / LONG ABOUT NOW (Scott Walker) / THE GREAT VALERIO (Richard Thompson) / PAPER THIN HOTEL (Leonard Cohen) / SHINY HAPPY PEOPLE (R.E.M.). • **Trivia:** In '92, CATHAL teamed up with co-median SEAN HUGHES in BUBONIQUE.

Recommended: BIG SLEEPING HOUSE . . .FINEST MOMENTS (*8) / 82-84: WE HATE YOU SOUTH AFRICAN BASTARDS (*7)

CATHAL COUGHLAN – vocals, keyboards / **SEAN O'HAGAN** – guitar, vocals, harmonica / **MICK LYNCH** – bass, vocals / **ROB MacKAHEY** – drums

Kabuki / not issued

Sep 82. (7") **HELICOPTER OF THE HOLY GHOST. / HELLO RASCALS** –
May 83. (7") **FICTION LAND. / PINK SKINNED MAN** –

— **ED FLESH** – bass repl. LYNCH who formed STUMP / **TOM FENNER** – drums, percussion repl. MacKAHEY who formed STUMP

Rough Trade / not issued

May 84. (lp) **EVERBODY IS FANTASTIC** –
– Idea / A few kisses / Escalator in the rain / Dolly / Dreaming drains / I'll be a gentleman / Moon / Sun / Sleepless /Come on over and cry / This liberal love / Before famine / Everybody is dead.
Jun 84. (7") **DOLLY. / THIS LIBERAL LOVE** –
(12"+=) – Everbody Is Dead / Dear Rosemary.
Mar 85. (12"ep) **IN THE WORLD** –
– In the world / Loftholdingswood / Teddy dogs / 464.
Sep 85. (7") **BIRTHDAY GIRL. / HARMONY TUNES** –
(12"+=) – Money for the trams.
Oct 85. (lp) **THE CLOCK COMES DOWN THE STAIRS** –
– Horse overboard / Birthday girl / Past / Humane / Begging bowl / And / Are you happy / Genius / Begging Bowl / A friend with a big mouth / Goodbye it's 1987 / And.

— **STEVE PREGNANT** – bass repl. ED / added **JAMES COMPTON** – keyboards (now with **COUGHLAN, O'HAGAN, FENNER**)

Virgin / Virgin

Jan 87. (7") **TOWN TO TOWN. / LITTLE TOWN IN IRELAND** 55 –
(12"+=) – Genius / Bullwhip road.
(d7") – 'PEEL SESSIONS' EP: Begging bowl / Loftholdingswood / Horse overboard.
Jan 87. (lp)(c)(cd) **CROOKED MILE**
– Town to town / Angels / Our children / Mrs. Simpson / Hey hey Sam / Give me all your clothes / Armadillo man / Bullwhip road / And he descended into Hell / Rack / Big sleeping house / People just want to dream.

— **CRAZY JOHNNY NANCY** – bass repl. STEVE

Oct 87. (7") **SINGER'S HAMPSTEAD HOME. / SHE ONLY GAVE INTO ANGER** –
(12"+=) – Brother Olaf.
Feb 88. (7") **GALE FORCE WIND. / I CAN'T SAY NO** –
(c-s+=) – Irish nationl anthem / Say no I can't.
(12+=) – ('A'-2 versions).
(cd-s+=) – ('A'-1 version) / Town to town.
Mar 88. (lp)(c)(cd) **39 MINUTES**
– Singer's Hampstead home / High and dry / Send Herman home / Ambulance for one / Soul boy / Back to the old town / United colours / Gale force wind / Herr direktor / Bluerings.

— (split around Spring '88). SEAN O'HAGAN formed the TWILIGHT before going solo in 1989. CATHAL formed FATIMA MANSIONS.

– compilations, others, etc. –

Oct 84. Rough Trade; (m-lp) **82-84: WE HATE YOU SOUTH AFRICAN BASTARDS!** –
– Helicopter of the holy ghost / Michael Murphy / Love your enemies / Fiction land / Pink skinned man / Patrick Moore says you can't sleep here / Hello rascals / Pretoria quickstep.
Dec 89. Strange Fruit; (lp)(c)(cd) **DOUBLE PEEL SESSIONS** –
Nov 94. Strange Fruit; (cd) **THE PEEL SESSIONS ALBUM** –
Mar 95. Virgin; (cd) **BIG SLEEPING HOUSE . . .FINEST MOMENTS** –

MIDNIGHT FLYER (see under ⇒ STONE THE CROWS)

MIDNIGHT OIL

Formed: Sydney, Australia . . . 1976, by ex-FARM members MOGONIE, HIRST and ROTSEY, who found law student PETER GARRETT. After many releases on homeland 'Powderworks', they signed in 1981 to 'CBS-Columbia'.

They finally cracked charts outside Australiasia, when in 1988 'BEDS ARE BURNING' made US 17 & UK Top 50. It was re-issued a year later in Britain, making Top 10. • **Style:** Politically aware rock-pop outfit, fronted by bald GARRETT, a campaigner for Aboriginal rights and member of The Nuclear Disarmament Party since 1984. GARRETT was also a Christian Socialist and gained his law degree in 1977. • **Songwriters:** MOGINIE-GARRETT-HIRST written (perm any 2 of 3). Covered; WHARF RAT (Grateful Dead). • **Trivia:** The BLUE SKY MINING album was about victims of blue asbestos cancer, which killed thousands of immigrant workers of Western Australia.

Recommended: BLUE SKY MINING (*7).

PETER GARRETT – vocals / **JAMES MOGINIE** – guitar, keyboards / **MARTIN POTSEY** – guitar / **DWAYNE 'Bones' HILLMAN** (b.New Zealand) – bass, vocals (ex-SWINGERS) / **ROB HIRST** – drums, vocals

Powderworks not issued

1978. (lp) **MIDNIGHT OIL** – – AUST
– Powderworks / Head over heels / Dust / Used and abused / Surfing with a spoon / Run with you / Nothing lost . . . nothing gained. *(re-iss.cd+c Feb94 on 'Columbia')*

1979. (7") **RUN BY NIGHT. / ?** – –

— **ANDREW JAMES** – bass, vocals repl. HILLMAN

1979. (lp) **HEAD INJURIES** – –
– Cold cold change / Section 5 (bus to Bondi) / Naked flame / Bad on the borderline / Koal spirit / No reaction / Stand in line / Profiteers / Is it now?. *(cd+c.UK-iss.Apr91 on 'Columbia')*

Nov 80. (12"ep) **BIRD NOISES** – –
– No time for games / Knife's edge / Wedding cake Island / I'm the cure.

1981. (lp) **PLACE WITHOUT A POSTCARD** – –
– Don't wanna be the one / Brave faces / Armistice day / Someone else to blame / Basement flat / Written in the heart / Burnie / Quinella holiday / Loves on sale / If Ned Kelly was king / Lucky country. *(UK-iss.cd+c.Apr91 on 'Columbia')*

C.B.S. Columbia

May 83. (7") **U.S. FORCES. / OUTSIDE WORLD** –
(12"+=) – Some kids / Knife edge.

Jun 83. (lp)(c) **10,9,8,7,6,5,4,3,2,1**
– Outside world / Only the strong / Short memory / Read about it / Scream in blue / U.S. Forces / Power and the passion / Maralinga / Tin legs and tin mines / Somebody's trying to tell me something. *(cd-iss.Jun88 on 'Collector's Choice') (re-iss.cd+c Mar93 on 'Columbia')*

Jul 83. (7")(12") **POWER AND THE PASSION. / GLITCH BABY**

Sep 83. (7") **TIN LEGS AND TIN MINES. / POWER AND THE PASSION** –

Feb 84. (7") **OUTSIDE WORLD. / READ ABOUT IT** –

Jul 85. (7") **BEST OF BOTH WORLDS. / KOSCRUSKO**
(12"+=) – Power and the passion.

Jul 85. (lp)(c) **RED SAILS IN THE SUNSET**
– When the generals talk / Best of both worlds / Sleep / Minutes to midnight / Jimmy Sharman's boxers / Bakerman / Who can stand in the way / Kosciusko / Helps me helps you / Harrisburg / Bells and horns in the back of beyond / Shipyards of New Zealand. *(cd-iss.Jun88 on 'Collector's Choice')*

Sep 85. (7") **WHEN THE GENERALS TALK. / WHO CAN STAND IN THE WAY**

— **PETER GIFFORD** – bass repl. ANDREW JAMES

Mar 86. (7") **BEDS ARE BURNING. / GUN BARREL HIGHWAY** 48 17
(12"+=) – Hercules / Power and the passion. *(re-iss.Feb89 hit UK No.6)*

Apr 88. (lp)(c)(cd) **DIESEL AND DUST** 19 21 Feb 88
– Beds are burning / Put down that weapon / Dreamworld / Whoah / Arctic world / Warakurna / Dead heart / Whoah / Bullroarer / Sell my soul / Sometimes. *(re-dist. Apr89 hit UK 19)*

Jun 88. (7")(c-s) **DEAD HEART. / KOSCIUSKO** 68 53
(12"+=)(cd-s+=) – Whoah / ('A'extended) / Beds are burning (mix).
(7"ep+=) – Blossom and blood / Pictures. *(re-iss.Jun89 hit 62 UK)*

Nov 88. (7") **PROGRESS. / DREAMWORLD** –
(cd-s+=) – SPECIES DECEASES – Hercules / Blossom and blood / Pictures.

Feb 90. (7")(c-s) **BLUE SKY MINE. / WEDDING CAKE ISLAND** 66 47
(12"+=)(cd-s+=) – Beds are burning.

Mar 90. (cd)(c)(lp) **BLUE SKY MINING** 28 20
– Blue sky mine / Stars of Warburton / Forgotten years / Bedlam bridge / Mountains of Burma / King of the mountain / River runs red / Shakers and movers / One country / Antartica. *(re-iss.cd+c Sep93 on 'Columbia')*

May 90. (7")(c-s) **FORGOTTEN YEARS. / YOU MAY NOT BE RELEASED**
(12"+=)(cd-s+=) – Shakers and movers / Don't wanna be the one.

Columbia Columbia

May 92. (7")(c-s) **SOMETIMES (live '89). / USED AND ABUSED (live)**
(cd-s+=) – Written in my heart (live).
(cd-s) – ('A'side) / No reaction (live) / Wharf rat.

Jun 92. (cd)(c)(lp) **SCREAM IN BLUE (live '82-'90)**
– Scream in blue / Read about it / Dreamworld / Brave faces / Only the strong / Stars of Warburton / Progress / Beds are burning / Sell my soul / Sometimes / Hercules / Powderworks.

Mar 93. (12")(cd-s) **TRUGANINI. / BEDS ARE BURNING / READ ABOUT IT / STARS OF WARBURTON** 29

Apr 93. (cd)(c)(lp) **EARTH AND SUN AND MOON** 27 49
– Feeding frenzy / My country / Renaissance man / Earth and Sun and Moon / Trugnanini / Bushfire / Drums of Heaven / Outbreak of love / In the valley / Tell me the truth / Now or never land.

May 93. (c-s)(cd-s) **MY COUNTRY (Radio Version). / GLITCH BABY GLITCH** 66

Nov 93. (7") **IN THE VALLEY. / SHIPS OF FREEDOM / MY COUNTRY (live)** 60
(12"+=)(cd-s+=) – Blue sky mine (live).

– compilations –

Oct 94. Columbia; (3xcd-box) **DIESEL AND DUST / HEAD INJURIES / MIDNIGHT OIL**

MIGHTY WAH! (see under ⇒ WAH!)

MIKE + THE MECHANICS (see under ⇒ GENESIS)

Buddy MILES

Born: GEORGE MILES, 5 Sep'46, Omaha, USA. Was lead singer in late 50's doo-wop act The FIDELITY'S before taking up drums. In 1963/64 he joined the DICK CLARK REVUE, before playing alongside WILSON PICKETT two years later. Became a member of ELECTRIC FLAG in 1967, who were led at that time by MICHAEL BLOOMFIELD. In 1969, he formed BUDDY MILES EXPRESS, who were produced on their 2nd outing, by JIMI HENDRIX leader of BUDDY's moonlight oufit The BAND OF GYPSYS. In the early 70's, he had a run of successful albums, noteably his live collaboration with CARLOS SANTANA in summer of '72. • **Style:** Session rock/soul drummer, who fused both these sounds, blending together the blues of JIMI HENDRIX, the funk/soul of JAMES BROWN and the brass of BLOOD, SWEAT & TEARS. • **Songwriters:** MILES except DREAMS (Allman Brothers Band)/ WHOLESALE LOVE (Otis Redding)/ SUNSHINE OF YOUR LOVE (Cream)/ • **Trivia:** Became voice of The CALIFORNIA RAISINS TV ad of 1987.

Recommended: EXPRESSWAY TO YOUR SKULL (*7) / THEM CHANGES (*6)

BUDDY MILES EXPRESS

BUDDY MILES – vocals, drums / **JIM McCARTY** – guitar (ex-MITCH RYDER) / **HERBIE RICH** – organ / **BILLY RICH** – bass / **TERRY CLEMENTS + VIRGIL GONSALVES + BILL McPHERSON** – saxes / **MARCUS DOUBLEDAY** – trumpet / **RON WOODS** – drums

Mercury Mercury

Nov 68. (7") **MEMPHIS TRAIN. / (part 2)** –

Feb 69. (lp) **EXPRESSWAY TO YOUR SKULL** Aug 68
– Memphis train / Let your lovelight shine / Don't mess with Cupid / Funky mule / You're the one / Wrap it up / Spot the wall.

— retained only **McCARTY** + recruited **DUANE HITCHINGS** – keyboards / **BOBBY ROCK + TOBIE WYNN + JAMES TATUM** – saxes / **TOM HALL + PETER CARTER** – trumpet

Jun 69. (7") **MISS LADY. / '69 FREEDOM SPECIAL**

Aug 69. (7") **MEMPHIS TRAIN. / MY CHANT** – 100

Nov 69. (lp) **ELECTRIC CHURCH** Jun69
– Cigarettes and coffee / Miss Lady / '69 Freedom special / Destructive love / Texas / My chant / Wrap it up.

BUDDY MILES

with **ANDREW LEWIS** – keyboards / **MARLO HENDERSON + CHARLIE KARP** – guitar, vocals / **DAVE HULL** – bass, vocals / **FRED ALLEN** – percussion / etc.

Apr 70. (7") **THEM CHANGES. ("BUDDY MILES & THE FREEDOM EXPRESS") / YOUR FEELING IS MINE** – 81
(US re-iss.Jul71; hit No.62) (UK-iss.Jan71)

Jul 70. (lp) **THEM CHANGES** 35 Jun70
– Them changes / I still love you, anyway / Heart's delight / Dreams / Down by the river / Memphis train / Paul B. Allen, Omaha, Nebraska / Your feeling is mine.

Jul 70. (7") **DOWN BY THE RIVER. / HEART'S DELIGHT** – 68

Oct 70. (7") **DREAMS. / YOUR FEELING IS MINE** – 86

Feb 71. (lp) **WE GOT TO LIVE TOGETHER** 53 Nov70
– Runaway child (little Miss Nothin') / Walking down the highway / Easy greasy / We got to live together / Take it off him and put it on me.

Dec 70. (7") **WE GOT TO LIVE TOGETHER. / (part 2)** – 86

Feb 71. (7") **RUNAWAY CHILD (LITTLE MISS NOTHIN'). /** –

— added **HANK REDD** – tenor sax / **STEMSEY HUNTER** – alto sax / **MIKE FUGATE** – trombone

Jun 71. (lp) **A MESSAGE TO THE PEOPLE** 60 Apr71
– Joe Tex / The way I feel tonight / Place over there / Segment / Don't keep me wondering / Midnight rider / Sudden stop / Wholesale love / That's the way life is.

May 71. (7") **WHOLESALE LOVE. / THAT'S THE WAY LIFE IS** 71

Jul 71. (7") **WAY I FEEL TONIGHT . / THEM CHANGES** –

— **DONNIE BECK** – organ / **BOB HOGINS** – trombone, organ / **ZOM HALL** – trumpet – repl.LEWIS, HENDERSON + ALLEN

1971. (d-lp) **BUDDY MILES LIVE (live)** 50 Sep71
– (introduction) / Joe Tex / Take it off him and put it on me / Down by the river / Wrap it up / Place over there / The segment / Them changes / We got to live together.

1972. (7") **GIVE AWAY NONE OF MY LOVE. / TAKE IT OFF HIM AND PUT IT ON ME**

1972. (7") **LIFE IS WHAT YOU MAKE IT. / (part 2)** –

— In mid '72, BUDDY MILES teamed up with CARLOS SANTANA for live US Top 10 lp for 'Columbia'. Also single 'THEM CHANGES' was revived by duo. He briefly became part of The ELECTRIC FLAG re-union in 73/74.

BUDDY MILES BAND

with **ADRIAN (CURTIS) GURVITZ** – guitar, vocals / **RON JOHNSON** – bass / **ROBERT HOGGINS** – organ / **RICHARD APLANALP** – sax / **BILLY SPRAGUE + DAVID DHALSTON** – wind

C.B.S. Columbia

1973. (lp) **CHAPTER VII** Mar73
– L.A. resurrection / Life is what you make it (part 1) / Elvira / Hear no evil / Love affair / Life is what you make it (part 2) / Visions / Crossfire / There was a time.

1973. (7") **HEAR NO EVIL. / ELVIRA** –

BUDDY MILES EXPRESS

with **STEVE BUSFIELD** – guitar / **ROLAND ROBINSON** – bass / **DONNY BECK** – keyboards / **PETER WALKER + BILL ATWOOD** – trumpet / **PAT O'HARA** – sax / **RINGO LEWIS** – congas

Jan 74. (lp) **BOOGER BEAR** [ ] [ ]
– Booger bear / Thinking of you / You really got love / United Nation's stomp / Crazy love / You are everything / Louie's blues.

Jan 74. *7") **THINKING OF YOU. / CRAZY LOVE** [-] [ ]

— complete new line-ups

Nov 74. (lp) **ALL THE FACES** [ ] [ ]
– Pull yourself together / We got love / All the faces / I'm just a kiss away / It's only the good times / Got to find Ms.Right / Pain / Kiss and run / Wants and needs (the Earth song) / Baby don't stop (sit on the rock).

Dec 74. (7") **PAIN. / WE GET LOVE** [-] [ ]

Mar 75. (7") **PULL YOURSELF TOGETHER. / I'M JUST A KISS AWAY** [-] [ ]

BUDDY MILES

Casablanca Casablanca

Sep 75. (lp) **MORE MILES PER GALLON** [ ] [68] Aug75
– Rockin' and rollin' on the streets of Hollywood / Do it to me / Blues city / Nasty disposition / No time for sorrow / Nichols Canyon funk / Livin' in the right space / You don't have a kind word to say / My last words of love.

Sep 75. (7") **ROCKIN' AND ROLLIN' ON THE STREETS OF HOLLYWOOD. / LIVIN' IN THE RIGHT SPACE** [-] [84]

Dec 75. (7") **NASTY DISPOSITION. / DO IT TO ME** [-] [ ]

Oct 76. (lp) **BICENTENNIAL GATHERING OF THE TRIBES** [-] [ ]
– Now's the time / Where you gonna run to lady / Inflation / I've got to be me / Grecian lady / Won't you be my friend / Searchin' / Reuben "The Hurricane" / Wake me shake me.

Nov 76. (7") **REUBEN "THE HURRICANE". / WHERE YOU GONNA RUN TO LADY** [-] [ ]

BUDDY MILES REGIMENT

with a plethera of musicians incl. **J.P.CERVONI** – guitar / **JIMMY CALHOUN** – bass / **ALTON HARRIS** – drums / **JOHN MURRAY + L.D.DIXON** – keyboards / **DON HARRIS** – violin

Atlantic not issued

Sep 81. (d-lp) **SNEAK ATTACK (live/studio)** [ ] [-]
– Latin rock fusion / Can you hold me / Sunshine of your love / I've made up my mind / Working hard every day / Colossus / Let's make it together / Jazz fusion / Hold her tight / Duet in the wind / For your precious wind.

Frankie MILLER

Born: 1950, Glasgow, Scotland. After playing in a series of pub bands during the 60's, he moved to London mid-71 to join JUDE, alongside ROBIN TROWER – guitar / JIM DEWAR – bass / CLIVE BUNKER – drums. They broke up early '72, after TROWER went solo, taking with him DEWAR. MILLER signed solo contract for 'Chrysalis' in 1973, and issued debut album 'ONCE IN A BLUE DREAM'. He peaked commercially in 1977-78, when 2 singles 'BE GOOD TO YOURSELF' & 'DARLIN', hit UK Top 30. • **Style:** Gravel-voxed bluesman turned pop-rock star, inspired by JOE COCKER, WILSON PICKETT or OTIS REDDING. • **Songwriters:** Writes most himself, except several covers. • **Trivia:** In 1979, he began acting career in Peter McDougall's TV play 'Just A Boy's Game', and sang theme 'Playin' The Game'. **Note:-** There was also a FRANKIE MILLER from the States, who had albums on 'Starday'.

Recommended: THE VERY BEST OF FRANKIE MILLER (*6)

FRANKIE MILLER – vocals (ex-JUDE) with ex-members of BRINSLEY SCHWARZ (aka NICK LOWE – bass / **BOB ANDREWS** – keyboards / **BRINSLEY SCHWARZ** – guitar / **BILLY RANKIN** – drums)

Chrysalis Chrysalis

Jan 73. (lp)(c) **ONCE IN A BLUE MOON** [ ] [ ]
– You don't need to laugh (to be happy) / I can't change it / Candlelight sonata in f major / Ann Eliza Jane / It's all over / In no resistance / After all (I live my life) / Just like Tom Thumb's blues / Mail box / I'm ready.

— Brought in number of session men to repl. last band.

Jan 74. (lp)(c) **HIGHLIFE** [ ] [ ]
– Highlife / Play something sweet (brickyard blues) / Trouble / A fool / Little angel / With you in mind / The devil gun / I'll take a melody / Just a song / Shoorah / I'm falling in love again. *(cd-iss.Mar94)*

FRANKIE MILLER BAND

with **HENRY McCULLOCH** – guitar / **MICK WEAVER** – keyboards / **CHRISSIE STEWART** – bass / **STU PERRY** – drums

Sep 75. (7") **A FOOL IN LOVE. / I KNOW WHY THE SUN DON'T SHINE** [ ] [ ]
(re-iss.May76)

Sep 75. (lp)(c) **THE ROCK** [ ] [ ]
– A fool in love / The heartbreak / The rock / I know why the Sun don't shine / Hand on the lever / Ain't got no money / All my love to you / I'm old enough / Bridgeton / Drunken nights in the city.

Jul 76. (7") **THE ROCK. / THE HEARTBREAK** [ ] [ ]

Oct 76. (7") **LOVING YOU IS SWEETER THAN EVER. / I'M OLD ENOUGH** [ ] [ ]

May 77. (7") **BE GOOD TO YOURSELF. / ?** [27] [ ]

FRANKIE MILLER'S FULL HOUSE

with **RAY MINHINNIT** – guitar / **JAMES HALL** – keyboards / **CHARLIE HARRISON** – bass / **GRAHAM DEACON** – drums

Jun 77. (lp)(c) **FULL HOUSE** [ ] [ ]
– Be good to yourself / The doodle song / Jealous guy / Searching / Love letters / Take good care of yourself / Down the Honky Tonk / The love of mine / Let the candlelight shine / (I'll never) Live in vain.

Jun 77. (7") **THE DOODLE SONG. / (I'LL NEVER) LIVE IN VAIN** [-] [71]

Aug 77. (7") **LOVE LETTERS. / LET THE CANDLELIGHT SHINE** [ ] [ ]

Nov 77. (7"ep) **ALVERIC'S ELFLAND JOURNEY** [ ] [ ]
– Jealous guy / A fool in love / Brickyard blues / Sail away.

— went solo again, augmented by **PAUL CARRACK** – keys / **RAY RUSSELL** – guitar / **MARTIN DROVER** – trumpet / **CHRIS MERCER** – saxophone / **B.J.WILSON** – drums

Apr 78. (lp)(c) **DOUBLE TROUBLE** [ ] [ ]
– Have you seen me lately Joan / Double heart trouble / The train / You'll be in my mind / Good time love / Love waves / (I can't) Breakaway / Stubborn kind of fellow / Love is all around / Goodnight sweetheart.

Jun 78. (7")(7"colrd) **STUBBORN KIND OF FELLOW. / GOOD TIME LOVE** [ ] [ ]

FRANKIE MILLER

FRANKIE only retained **CARRACK,** and brought in **CHRIS HALL** – keyboards / **TIM RENWICK + STEVE SIMPSON + TERRY BRITTON** – guitar / **RON ASPERY** – horns / **TEX COMER + DAVE WINTOUR** – bass / **CHRIS SLADE + FRAN BYRNE** – drums

Oct 78. (7") **DARLIN'. / DRUNKEN NIGHTS IN THE CITY** [6] [ ]
(re-iss.Nov81)

Jan 79. (7") **WHEN I'M AWAY FROM YOU. / AIN'T GOT NO MONEY** [42] [ ]

Jan 79. (lp)(c) **FALLING IN LOVE . . . PERFECT FIT** [ ] [ ]
– When I'm away from you / Is this love / If I can love somebody / Darlin' / And it's your love / A woman to love / Falling in love with you / Everytime a teardrop falls / Pappa don't know / Good to see you.

— His backing band were now **REGGIE YOUNG + BOBBY THOMPSON** – guitar / **JOE OSBOURNE** – bass / **LARRY LONDIN** – drums

Jun 80. (7") **SO YOUNG, SO YOUNG. / TEARS** [ ] [ ]

Jul 80. (lp)(c) **EASY MONEY** [ ] [ ]
– Easy money / The woman in you / Why don't you spend the night / So young so young / Forget about me / Heartbreak radio / Cheap . . .thrills / No chance / Gimme love / Tears.

Jul 80. (7") **WHY DON'T YOU SPEND THE NIGHT. / HEART-BREAK RADIO** [ ] [ ]

— now with **BARRY BECKETT** – keyboards, producer / **DAVID HOOD** – bass / **ROGER HAWKINS** – drums / **CHRIS SPEDDING** – guitar

not iss. Good Foot

Jul 81. (7") **STANDING ON THE OTHER SIDE. / FIRE IN THE FURNACE** [-] [ ]

Capitol Capitol

Jun 82. (7") **TO DREAM THE DREAM. / DON'T STOP** [ ] [62]

Jun 82. (lp)(c) **STANDING ON THE EDGE** [ ] [ ]
– Danger danger / Standing on the edge / Zap zap / To dream the dream / Don't stop / Angels with dirty faces / Firin' line / Jealousy / It's all coming down tonight / On my way.

Aug 82. (7") **ANGELS WITH DIRTY FACES. / JEALOUSY** [ ] [-]

Sep 82. (7") **DANGER DANGER. / ON MY WAY** [-] [ ]

— brought in **BRIAN ROBERTSON** – lead guitar / **CHRISSIE STEWART** – bass / **SIMON KIRKE** – drums (ex-BAD COMPANY)

Vertigo not issued

Mar 86. (7") **I'D LIE TO YOU FOR LOVE. / DANCING IN THE RAIN** [ ] [-]

Apr 86. (lp)(c)(cd) **DANCING IN THE RAIN** [ ] [-]
– I'd lie to you for love / Do it till we drop / That's how long my love is / How many tears can you hide / Dancing in the rain / Shakey ground / The boys and girls are doing it / Game of love / Gladly go blind / You're a puzzle I can't put down.

— FRANKIE concentrated more on acting in the mid 80's. Through a TV advert for Tennent's lager, an old song 'CALEDONIA' gave him a hit in the 90's.

M.C.S. ???

Mar 92. (7")(c-s)(cd-s) **CALEDONIA. / I'LL NEVER BE THAT YOUNG AGAIN** [45] [ ]

— In the past year (1994) FRANKIE has suffered serious ill health.

- compilations, others, etc. -

Feb 87. Old Gold; (7") **DARLIN'. / BE GOOD TO YOURSELF** [ ] [-]

Mar 94. Chrysalis; (cd)(c) **THE VERY BEST OF FRANKIE MILLER** [ ] [-]

Apr 94. Windsong; (cd) **BBC RADIO 1 LIVE IN CONCERT (live)** [ ] [-]

Steve MILLER

Born: 5 Oct'43, Milwaukee, Wisconsin, USA, but raised in Dallas, Texas. After forming school band The MARKSMAN COMBO with BOZ SCAGGS, he played for bluesman JIMMY REED at a 1957 gig. In the early 60's, he and SCAGGS joined The ARDELLS, who with BEN SIDRAN became The FABULOUS NIGHT TRAIN. In 1964, after a brief spell in Denmark, he moved to Chicago, where he sessioned for MUDDY WATERS, HOWLIN' WOLF and PAUL BUTTERFIELD. The next year, he partnered BARRY GOLDBERG in group The WORLD WAR III BAND, who issued one-off 45 'THE MOTHER SONG' as The GOLDBERG-MILLER BAND. Late in 1966, he moved to San Francisco and formed The MILLER BAND with JAMES 'Curly' COOKE, LONNIE TURNER and TIM DAVIS. In Spring of '67, they added JIM PETERMAN, and replaced COOKE with BOZ. After a

June appearance at The Monterey Pop Festival, they soon signed to 'Capitol' records. Early in 1968, they recorded 3 songs for the 'Revolution' film soundtrack, which hit shops late '69. In Apr'68, their debut lp 'CHILDREN OF THE FUTURE' was issued and made No.134 on the US charts. Its mild success, was overshadowed by the follow-up 'SAILOR', which gave them first of many entries into US Top 30. In 1973, after a lean couple of years, they hit US No.1 with 45 'THE JOKER'. Although it became a classic in the UK, it failed to chart. That is until 1990, when it hit No.1 after it was given fresh exposure on Levi jeans TV ad. • **Style:** The gangster of love & rock moved from progressive electronic music in the late 60's, which shaped into harmonious laid back rock by '73. In 1987-88, he chose a fusion of blues-jazz covers on his 2 albums. • **Songwriters:** MILLER and band SIDRAN compositions, except covers on 87 & 88 albums. • **Trivia:** On '69 song 'MY DARK HOUR', PAUL McCARTNEY played bass under psuedonym MARK RAMON.

Recommended: THE BEST OF STEVE MILLER BAND 1968-1973 (*8) / FLY LIKE AN EAGLE (*8) / ABRACADABRA (*6).

GOLDBERG / MILLER BLUES BAND

BARRY GOLDBERG – keyboards / **STEVE MILLER** – guitar, vocals

		not issued	Epic
1965.	(7") **THE MOTHER SONG. / MORE THAN SOUL**	-	

— Late 1966, the MILLER BAND evolved into

The STEVE MILLER BAND

STEVE MILLER – vocals, guitar / **LONNIE TURNER** – bass, vocals / **BOZ SCAGGS** – guitar / **JIM PETERMAN** – organ, vocals / **TIM DAVIS** – drums

		Capitol	Capitol
Apr 68.	(7") **SITTING IN CIRCLES. / ROLL WITH IT**		
Sep 68.	(lp) **CHILDREN OF THE FUTURE**		Apr 68

– Children of the future / Pushed me to it / You've got the power / In my first mind / The beauty of time is that it's snowing / Baby calling me home / Steppin' stone / Roll with it / Junior saw it happen / Fanny Mae / Key to the highway.

Oct 68. (7") **LIVING IN THE U.S.A. / QUICKSILVER GIRL** — [ ] [94]
Jan 69. (lp) **SAILOR** — [ ] [24] Oct 68
– Song for our ancestors / Dear Mary / My friend / Living in the U.S.A. / Quicksilver girls / Lucky man / Gangster of love / You're so fine / Overdrive / Dime-a-dance romance. *(re-iss.Nov83 on 'Fame', +cd.Apr91)*

— Trim to a trio of **MILLER, TURNER** and **DAVIS** with session men. (PETERMAN left just after SCAGGS who went solo) **BEN SIDRAN** – keyboards (joined briefly)

— (Mar69) **NICKY HOPKINS** – keyboards (ex-JEFF BECK GROUP) repl. SIDRAN

Sep 69. (lp) **BRAVE NEW WORLD** — [ ] [22] Jun 69
– Brave new world / Space cowboy / Got love 'cause you need it / It's a midnight dream / Can't you hear daddy's heartbeat / Celebration song / Seasons / Kow kow calculator / My dark hour. *(re-iss.Feb84 on 'EMI')*
Jul 69. (7") **MY DARK HOUR. / SONG FOR OUR ANCESTORS** — [ ] [ ]
Nov 69. (7") **LITTLE GIRL. / DON'T LET NOBODY TURN YOU AROUND** — [ ] [ ]
Mar 70. (lp) **YOUR SAVING GRACE** — [ ] [38] Nov 69
– Little girl / Just a passin' fancy in a midnight dream / Don't let nobody turn you around / Baby's house / Motherless children / The last wombat in Mecca / Feel so glad / Your saving grace. *(cd-iss.May91 on 'E.M.I.')*

— **BOBBY WINKLEMAN** – bass, vocals repl. TURNER and HOPKINS who joined QUICKSILVER MESSENGER SERVICE

Nov 70. (lp)(c) **NUMBER 5** — [ ] [23] Jul 70
– Good morning / I love you / Going to the country / Hot chili / Tokin's / Going to Mexico / Steve Miller's midnight tango / Industrial military complex hex / Jackson-Kent blues / Never kill another man.
Sep 70. (7") **GOING TO THE COUNTRY. / NEVER KILL ANOTHER MAN** — [ ] [69] Aug 70
Dec 70. (7") **GOING TO MEXICO. / STEVE MILLER'S MIDNIGHT TANGO** — [-] [ ]

— **STEVE MILLER** recruited entire new band **ROSS VALORY** – bass, vocals repl. WINKLEMAN / **JACK KING** – drums, vocals repl. DAVIS who went solo

Sep 71. (7") **ROCK LOVE. / LET ME SERVE YOU** — [-] [ ]
Nov 71. (lp)(c) **ROCK LOVE** — [ ] [ ] Oct 71
– The gangster is back / Blues without blame / Love shock / Let me serve you / Rock love / Harbour lights / Deliverance.

— **GERALD JOHNSON** – bass, vocals repl. VALORY who later joined JOURNEY / added **DICKY THOMPSON** – keyboards / **ROGER ALAN CLARK** – 2nd drummer

May 72. (lp)(c) **RECALL THE BEGINNING . . . A JOURNEY FROM EDEN** — [ ] [ ] Mar 72
– Welcome / Enter Maurice / High on you mama / Heal your heart / The sun is going down / Somebody somewhere help me / Love's riddle / Fandango / Nothing lasts / Journey from Eden.
May 72. (7") **FANDANGO. / LOVE'S RIDDLE** — [-] [ ]

— (Mar72) **JOHN KING** – drums repl. JACK and ROGER / **LONNIE TURNER** – bass, vocals returned to repl. JOHNSON who joined BOZ SCAGGS

Oct 73. (7") **THE JOKER. / SOMETHING TO BELIEVE IN** — [ ] [1]
Oct 73. (lp)(c) **THE JOKER** — [ ] [2]
– Sugar babe / Mary Lou / Loving cup / Shu ba da du ma ma / Your cash ain't nothin' but trash / The joker / Lovin' cup / Come on into my kitchen / Evil / Something to believe in. *(re-iss.Oct80) (re-iss.Jan83 on 'EMI')*
Feb 74. (7") **YOUR CASH AIN'T NOTHIN' BUT TRASH. / EVIL** — [-] [51]

— (May74) **STEVE MILLER** retired for a while, when THOMPSON and KING departed.

— (Jul75) **MILLER** retained **TURNER** and recruited for Knebworth festival **LES DUDEK** – guitar, vocals / **DOUG CLIFFORD** – drums (ex-CREEDENCE CLEARWATER REVIVAL)

— (1976) **GARY MALLABER** – drums repl. CLIFFORD and DUDEK

		Mercury	Capitol
May 76.	(7") **TAKE THE MONEY AND RUN. / SWEET MARIE**		11
May 76.	(lp)(c) **FLY LIKE AN EAGLE**	11	3

– (Space intro) / Fly like an eagle / Wild mountain honey / Serenade / Dance, dance, dance / Mercury blues / Take the money and run / Rock'n'me / You send me / Blue odyssey / Sweet Maree / The window. *(re-iss.Nov84)*

Aug 76. (7") **ROCK'N'ME. / LIVING IN THE U.S.A.** — [-] [1]
Aug 76. (7") **FLY LIKE AN EAGLE. / MERCURY BLUES** — [-] [-]
Oct 76. (7") **ROCK'N'ME. / THE WINDOW** — [11] [-]
Nov 76. (7") **FLY LIKE AN EAGLE. / LOVIN' CUP** — [-] [2]
Jan 77. (7") **SERENADE. / DANCE DANCE DANCE** — [ ] [-]

— (Oct76) added **DAVID DENNY** – guitar, vocals (ex-TERRY & THE PIRATES) / **BYRON ALLRED** – keyboards / **NORTON BUFFALO** – harmonica, vocals

Apr 77. (7") **JET AIRLINER. / BABES IN THE WOOD** — [ ] [8]
May 77. (lp)(c) **BOOK OF DREAMS** — [12] [2]
– Threshold / Jet airliner / Winter time / Swingtown / True fine love / Wish upon a star / Jungle love / Electro lux imbroglio / Sacrifice / The stake / My own space / Babes in the wood. *(re-iss.Jan85)*
Sep 77. (7") **JUNGLE LOVE. / WISH UPON A STAR** — [ ] [23] Aug 77
Jan 78. (7") **SWINGTOWN. / WINTER TIME** — [ ] [17] Oct 77

— trimmed to a quintet of **MILLER, MALLABER, ALLRED, DOUGLAS** and **BUFFALO**

Oct 81. (lp)(c) **CIRCLE OF LOVE** — [ ] [26]
– Heart like a wheel / Get on home / Baby wanna dance / Cricle of love / Macho city.
Oct 81. (7") **HEART LIKE A WHEEL. / TRUE FINE LOVE** — [-] [24]
Nov 81. (7") **HEART LIKE A WHEEL. / JET AIRLINER / THRESHOLD** — [ ] [-]
Jan 82. (7") **CIRCLE OF LOVE. / (part 2)** — [-] [55]
Feb 82. (7") **MACHO CITY. / FLY LIKE AN EAGLE** — [ ] [-]

— **KENNY LEWIS** – guitar / **JOHN MASSARO** – guitar both repl. DOUGLAS

May 82. (7") **ABRACADABRA. / GIVE IT UP** — [-] [1]
Jun 82. (7") **ABRACADABRA. / NEVER SAY NO** — [2] [-]
(re-iss.Oct84)
Jun 82. (lp)(c) **ABRACADABRA** — [10] [3]
– Keeps me wondering why / Abracadabra / Something special / Give it up / Never say no / Things I told you / Young girl's heart / Goodbye love / Cool magic / While I'm waiting. *(cd-iss.Jan83)*
Aug 82. (7") **KEEPS ME WONDERING WHY. / GET ON HOME** — [52] [ ]
(12"+=) – Abracadabra.
Oct 82. (7") **GIVE IT UP. / ROCK'N'ME** — [ ] [-]
Oct 82. (7") **COOL MAGIC. / YOUNG GIRL'S HEART** — [-] [57]
Dec 82. (7") **GIVE IT UP. / HEART LIKE A WHEEL** — [-] [60]
Mar 83. (7") **LIVING IN THE U.S.A. (live). / BUFFALO SERENADE** — [-] [ ]
Apr 83. (lp)(c) **THE STEVE MILLER BAND LIVE! (live)** — [79] [ ]
– Gangster of love / Rock'n'me / Living in the U.S.A. / Fly like an eagle / Jungle love / The joker / Mercury blues / Take the money and run / Abracadabra / Jet airliner. *(cd-iss.1988)* (cd+=) – Buffalo serenade.
Apr 83. (7") **TAKE THE MONEY AND RUN (live). / THE JOKER (live)** — [ ] [ ]
(12"+=) – Buffalo serenade (live).

— Now without MASSARO

Oct 84. (7") **SHANGRI-LA. / CIRCLE OF LOVE** — [ ] [57]
(12"+=) – Abracadabra.
Nov 84. (lp)(c)(cd) **ITALIAN X-RAYS** — [ ] [ ]
– Radio 1 / Italian x-rays / Daybreak / Shangri-la / Who do you love / Harmony of the spheres 1 / Radio 2 / Bongo bongo / Out of the night / Golden opportunity / The Hollywood dream / One in a million / Harmony of the spheres 2.
Jan 85. (7") **BONGO BONGO. / GET ON HOME** — [ ] [84]
Mar 85. (7") **ITALIAN X-RAYS. / WHO DO YOU LOVE** — [-] [ ]

— **MILLER** with **MALLABER** and **BUFFALO** bring back **LES DUDEK** – guitar

		Capitol	Capitol
Jan 87.	(lp)(c)(cd) **LIVING IN THE 20TH CENTURY**		65 Nov 86

– Nobody but you baby / I want to make the world turn around / Slinky / Living in the 20th century / Maelstrom / I wanna be loved / My babe / Big boss man / Caress me baby / Ain't that lovin' you baby / Behind the barn.

Mar 87. (7")(12") **I WANT TO MAKE THE WORLD TURN AROUND. / SLINKY** — [ ] [97] Nov 86
Apr 87. (7") **NOBODY BUT YOU BABY. / MAELSTROM** — [-] [ ]
Jun 87. (7") **I WANNA BE LOVED. / (part 2)** — [-] [ ]

STEVE MILLER

solo with **BEN SIDRAN** – keyboards / **BILLY PATERSON** – bass / **GORDY KNUDTSON** – drums

Sep 88. (7")(12") **YA YA. / FILTHY McNASTY** — [ ] [ ]
Sep 88. (lp)(c)(cd) **BORN 2 B BLUE** — [ ] [ ]
– Zip-a-dee-doo-dah / Ya ya / God bless the child / Filthy McNasty / Born to be blue / Mary Ann / Just a little bit / When Sunny gets blue / Willow weep for me / Red top.

		Polydor	Sailor
Jul 93.	(cd)(c) **WIDE RIVER**		85

– Wide river / Midnight train / Blue eyes / Lost in your eyes / Perfect world / Horse and rider / Circle of ir / Conversation / Cry cry cyr / Stranger blues / Walks like a lady / All your love (I miss loving).

Jul 93. (c-s)(cd-s) **WIDE RIVER. /** — [-] [64]
Aug 93. (7")(c-s) **WIDE RIVER. / STRANGER BLUES** — [ ] [ ]

– compilations, etc. –

Feb 72. Capitol; (7"ep) **MY DARK HOUR. / SONG FOR OUR ANCESTORS / THE GANGSTER IS BACK** — [ ] [ ]
Mar 73. Capitol; (lp)(c) **ANTHOLOGY** — [ ] [56] Nov 72
1973. Capitol; (d-lp) **CHILDREN OF THE FUTURE / LIVING IN THE U.S.A.** — [ ] [ ]
Jun 74. Capitol; (7") **LIVING IN THE U.S.A. / KOW KOW CALQULATOR** — [ ] [49] May 74
Mar 77. Capitol; (lp)(c) **THE BEST OF THE STEVE MILLER BAND 1968-73** — [ ] [ ]

– Living in the U.S.A. / I love you / Don't let nobody turn you around / Seasons / Shu ba da du ma ma ma / Kow kow calculator / The joker / Going to the country / My dark hour / Your saving grace / Celebration song / Space cowboy. *(re-iss May 82 on 'Fame') (re-iss. Aug 86 on 'E.M.I.') (re-iss.+cd.Sep90, hit UK No.34)* (cd+= 4 extra).

Jan 83. Capitol; (7") **THE JOKER. / MY DARK HOUR. / LIVING IN THE U.S.A.** [ ] [ ]
Aug 90. Capitol; (7")(c-s) **THE JOKER. / DON'T LET NOBODY TURN YOU AROUND** [1] [ ]
(12"+=) – Shu ba da du ma ma ma.
(cd-s++=) – Living in the U.S.A.
Oct 75. Capitol Vine; (lp)(c) **THE LEGEND** [ ] [-]
Oct 78. Capitol; (7") **THE JOKER. / THE STAKE** [ ] [ ]
Nov 78. Capitol; (lp)(c) **GREATEST HITS 1974-78** [ ] [18]
(re-iss.May88) (cd-iss. 1983)
May 87. Mercury; (lp)(c)(cd) **GREATEST HITS – A DECADE OF AMERICAN MUSIC (1976-1986)** [ ] [ ]

MINISTRY

Formed: Chicago, Illinois, USA . . . 1981 by ex-SPECIAL EFFECT member AL JOURGENSEN. He formed own 'Wax Trax' label, and issued debut 12" COLD LIFE in 1982. Ten years later, MINISTRY were deservedly in both US & UK Top 40 with 'PSALM 69' album. • **Style:** Experimental heavy electronic outfit run by JOURGENSEN. The REVOLTING COCKS were described as 'disco for psychopaths'. • **Songwriters:** REVOLTING COCKS covered LET'S GET PHYSICAL (Olivia Newton John) / DO YA THINK I'M SEXY? (Rod Stewart) / SUPERNAUT (1000 Komo DJs). • **Trivia:** JOURGENSEN was also a member of LARD, with DEAD KENNEDYS leader JELLO BIAFRA. Early '91, The REVOLTING COCKS shocked many when they performed on stage with 2 naked go-go dancers.

Recommended: PSALM 69: HOW TO SUCCEED AND HOW TO SUCK EGGS (*7)

AL JOURGENSEN – keyboards, guitar, synthesizers, vocals

Situation 2 / Wax Trax
Mar 82. (12"m) **COLD LIFE. / I'M FALLING / COLD LIFE (dub) / PRIMENTAL** [ ] [ ]

—— AL used musicians on next lp; **SHAY JONES** – vocals / **WALTER TURBETT** – guitar / **JOHN DAVIS** – keyboards / **ROBERT ROBERTS** – keyboards / **STEPHEN GEORGE** – drums / **MARTIN SORENSEN** – bass

Arista / Arista
Apr 83. (7") **REVENGE (YOU DID IT AGAIN). / SHE'S GOT A CAUSE** [-] [ ]
Jun 83. (7") **I WANTED TO TELL HER. / A WALK IN THE PARK** [ ] [ ]
(12"+=) – ('A'tongue tied mix).
Sep 83. (7")(12") **WORK FOR LOVE. / FOR LOVE (instrumental)** [ ] [ ]
Sep83. (lp)(c) **WORK FOR LOVE** (US title 'WITH SYMPATHY') [ ] [96] Jun 83
– Work for love / Do the Etawa / I wanted to tell her / Say you're sorry / Here we go / Effigy / Revenge / She's got a cause / Should have known better. *(cd-iss.1989 as 'WITH SYMPATHY'; the original US title, += 'What He Say')*
Nov 83. (7") **REVENGE (YOU DID IT AGAIN). / EFFIGY** [ ] [-]
(12"+=) – Work for love.

—— now basically AL solo.

Wax Trax / Wax Trax
Oct 85. (12") **NATURE OF LOVE. / ('A'cruelty mix)** [ ] [ ]

Sire / Sire
Apr 86. (lp)(c)(cd) **TWITCH** [ ] [ ]
– Just like you / We believe / All day remix / The angel / Over the shoulder / My possession / Where you at now? / Crash and burn / Twitch (version II). *(cd+=)–* Over the shoulder (mix) / Isle Of Man.

—— added partner **PAUL BARKER** – instruments (ex-FRONT 242)

1987. (lp)(c) **IN CASE YOU DIDN'T FEEL LIKE SHOWING UP (live)** [-] [ ]
– The missing / deity / So what / Burning inside / Seed / Stigmata. *(re-iss.cd Dec92)*
Jan 89. (lp)(c)(cd) **THE LAND OF RAPE AND HONEY** [ ] [ ] Nov 88
– Stigmata / The missing / Deity / Golden dawn / Destruction / The land of rape and honey / You know what you are / Flashback / Abortive. *(cd+=)–* Hizbollah / I prefer. *(re-iss.cd Dec92)*
Feb 90. (cd)(c)(lp) **THE MIND IS A TERRIBLE THING TO TASTE** [ ] [ ] Dec 89
– Thieves / Burning inside / Never believe / Cannibal song / Breathe / So what / Test / Faith collapsing / Dream song. *(re-iss.cd Dec92)*

—— next with guest **GIBBY HAYNES** (of BUTTHOLE SURFERS)

Apr 92. (7") **JESUS BUILT MY HOTROD. / TV SONG** [ ] [ ]
(12"+=)(cd-s+=) – ('A'red line-white line version).
Jul 92. (cd)(c)(10"lp) **PSALM 69: HOW TO SUCCEED AND HOW TO SUCK EGGS** [33] [27]
– N.W.O. / Just one fix / TV II / hero / Jesus built my hot rod / Scarecrow / Psalm 69 / Corrosion / Grace.
Jul 92. (7") **N.W.O. / F***ED (non lp version)** [49] [ ]
(12"+=)(cd-s+=) – ('A'extended dance mix).

W.E.A. / W.E.A.
Dec 95. (c-s) **THE FALL / RELOAD** [53] [ ]
(cd-s+=) – TV III.

– compilation, others, etc. –

1985. Hot Trax; (lp) **12" INCH SINGLES 1981-1984** [-] [ ]

REVOLTING COCKS

AL's studio outfit, with FRONT 242 members; LUC and RICHARD 23. The latter was soon replaced CHRIS CONNELLY of FINI TRIBE.

Beauty &.. / Wax Trax
Feb 86. (12"m) **NO DEVOTION. / ATTACK SHIPS / ON FIRE** [ ] [ ]

Wax Trax / Wax Trax
Feb 87. (12") **YOU OFTEN FORGET. / ?** [ ] [ ]

—— AL with VAN ACKER + JONCKHEERE

1988. (lp)(cd) **BIG SEXY LAND** [ ] [ ]
– 38 / We shall change the world / Attack ships on fire / Big sexy land / Union carbide / TV mind / No devotion / Union carbide (Bhopal version). *(re-iss.Mar92 on 'Devotion')*
Jun 88. (d-lp,cd) **YOU GODAMNED SON OF A BITCH** (live + 2 studio) [ ] [ ]
– You Goddamned son of a bitch / Cattle grid / We shall cleanse the world / 38 / In the neck / You often forget / TV mind / Union carbide / Attack ships on fire / No devotion. *(re-iss.May92 on 'Devotion')*
Mar 89. (12") **STAINLESS STEEL PROVIDERS. / AT THE TOP** [ ] [ ]

—— **AL + PHIL** were also part of JELLO BIAFRA'S (Dead Kennedys) group LARD.

AL now with **BARKER, VAN ACKER, RIEFLIN + CONNELLY** – vocals.

May 90. (cd)(c)(lp) **BEERS, STEERS AND QUEERS** [ ] [ ]
– Beers, steers and queers / (Let's get) Physical / In the neck / Get down / Stainless steel providers / Can't sit still / Something wonderful / Razor's edge. *(cd+=)–* (Let's talk) Physical. *(re-iss.Feb92 on 'Devotion')*
May 90. (12") **(LET'S GET) PHYSICAL. / (LET'S TALK) PHYSICAL** [ ] [ ]

—— now without RIEFLIN

Apr 91. (12"ep)(cd-ep) **SUPERNAUT / BY "1000 HOMO DJ'S" / HEY ASSHOLE / APATHY / BETTER WAYS** [ ] [ ]
Sep 93. (12")(cd-s) **DA YA THINK I'M SEXY? / SERGIO GUITAR / WRONG (sexy mix)** [61] [ ]
Sep 93. (cd)(c)(lp) **LINGER FICKEN' GOOD . . . AND OTHER BARNYARD ODDITIES** [39] [ ]
– Gila copter / Creep / Mr.Lucky / Crackin' up / Sergio / Da ya think I'm sexy? / The rockabye / Butcher flower's woman / Dirt / Linger ficken' good . . . and other barnyard oddities.
Jun 94. (12")(cd-s) **CRACKIN' UP. / ('A'-amylnitrate mix) / GUACOPTER (version 2)** [ ] [-]

LEAD INTO GOLD

AL + PAUL with **WILD BILL RIEFLIN** This was BARKER's main outlet.

Devotion / Devotion
1992. (lp)(c) **AGE OF REASON** [ ] [ ]
– Age of reason / Unreason / Snake oil / A giant on Earth / Faster than light / Lunatic-genius / Sweet thirteen / Fell from Heaven.

MINK DE VILLE

Formed: San Francisco, California, USA . . . 1974 by WILLY DeVILLE, who had lived in London for a few years in the early 70's. After becoming hits on the New York scene, they were snapped up by 'Capitol' early '77. Their debut 45 'SPANISH STROLL', gave them a surprise break into UK charts, although it barely got noticed at home. Debut album 'CABARETTA' gained fine reviews, but did not chart, like all their future releases. • **Style:** Hispanic accented WILLY DeVILLE, owed a lot to LOU REED, and the new wave movement for only hit. He later branched out into more mainstream AOR, which was tinged with cajun rock in the early 80's. • **Songwriters:** WILLY penned most of material, except MIXED UP, SHOOK UP (Patti & The Emblems)/ HEY JOE (hit; Jimi Hendrix). • **Trivia:** Their debut was produced by JACK NITZSCHE. They also contributed tracks to the Al Pacino film soundtrack of 'Cruisin''.

Recommended: SAVOIR FAYRE (*5)

WILLY DE VILLE (b.27 Aug'53, New York City) – vocals, guitar, mouth harp RUBEN SIGUENZA – bass / **THOMAS 'MANFRED' ALLEN** – drums / **BOBBY LEONARDS** – keyboards / **LOUIS X.ERLANGER** – guitar, vocals

Capitol / Capitol
Jun 77. (7") **SPANISH STROLL. / MIXED UP, SHOOK UP** [-] [ ]
Jun 77. (7")(12") **SPANISH STROLL. / GUNSLINGER** [20] [-]
Jun 77. (lp)(c) **CABARETTA (US title 'MINK DE VILLE')** [ ] [ ]
– Venus of Avenue D / Little girl / One way street / Mixed up, shook up girl / Gunslinger / Can't do without it / Cadillac walk / Spanish stroll / She's so tough / Party girls. *(re-iss.Feb87 on 'Razor') (cd-iss.Mar93 on 'Secret')*
Sep 77. (7") **LITTLE GIRL. / SHE'S SO TOUGH** [ ] [-]
Nov 77. (7") **CADILLAC WALK. / CAN'T DO WITHOUT IT** [ ] [-]
Dec 77. (7") **CADILLAC GIRL. / LITTLE GIRL** [-] [-]
May 78. (7") **JUST YOUR FRIEND. / ONE WAY STREET** [ ] [-]
Jun 78. (7") **GUARDIAN ANGEL. / EASY SLIDER** [-] [ ]
Jul 78. (lp)(c) **RETURN TO MAGENTA** [ ] [ ] Jun 78
– Guardian angel / Soul twist / "A" train lady / Rolene / Desperate days / Just your friends / Steady drivin' man / Easy slider / I broke that promise / Confidence to kill. *(cd-iss.May93 on 'Wrote Music')*
Aug 78. (7") **SOUL TWIST. / ROLENE** [ ] [-]

—— **WILLY** retained **ERLANGER** and brought in new men **RICK BORGIA** – guitar / **KENNY MARGOLIS** – keyboards / **JERRY SCHEFF** – bass / **RON TUTT** – drums

Apr 80. (7") **THIS MUST BE THE NIGHT. / MIXED UP, SHOOK UP GIRL** [ ] [-]
(12"+=) – Lipstick traces.
Apr 80. (lp)(c) **THE CHAT BLEU** [ ] [ ]
– This must be the night / Savoir faire / That world outside / Slow drain / You just keep holding on / Lipstick traces / Bad boy / Mazurka / Just to walk that little girl home / Heaven stood still. *(cd-iss.May93 on 'Wrote Music')*
Jun 80. (7") **LIPSTICK TRACES. / JUST TO WALK THAT LITTLE GIRL HOME** [-] [ ]

— Disbanded Spring 1980.

WILLY DE VILLE

C.B.S. Columbia

Sep 80. (7") **HEAT OF THE MOMENT. / PULLIN' MY STRING**

MINK DE VILLE

re-grouped in 1981. **WILLY, RICK + KENNY** recruited **JOEY VASTA** – bass / **TOMMY PRICE** – drums

Atlantic Atlantic

Oct 81. (7") **YOU BETTER MOVE ON. / SHE WAS MINE**

Oct 81. (lp)(c) **COUP DE GRACE**
– Just give me one good reason / Help me to make it / Maybe tomorrow / Teardrops must fall / You better move on / Love and emotion / So in love are we / Love me like you did before / She was made in Heaven / End of the line.

Jan 82. (7") **MAYBE TOMORROW. / SO IN LOVE ARE WE** -

— (unsure of line-ups stayed the same, etc.)

Jan 84. (lp)(c) **WHERE THE ANGELS FEAR TO TREAD**
– Each word's a beat of my heart / River of tears / Demasiado / corazon (Too much heart) / Lilly's daddy's Cadillac / Around the corner / Pick up the pieces / Love's got a hold on me / Keep your monkey away from my door / Are you lonely tonight / The moonlight let me down.

Apr 84. (7") **EACH WORD'S A BEAT OF MY HEART. / RIVER OF TEARS** 89 Feb 84
(12"+=) – Harlem nocturne / Maybe tomorrow.

Apr 84. (7") **PICK UP THE PIECES. /** -

— now with complete new personnel of session people.

Jun 85. (7") **IN THE HEART OF THE CITY. / PRIDE AND JOY** -
(12"+=) – Italian shoes (New York mix).

Jun 85. (lp)(c)(cd) **SPORTIN' LIFE**
– In the heart of the city / I must be dreaming / Italian shoes / Slip away / When you walk my way / A woman's touch / Easy street / Little by little / There's no living (without your loving) / Something beautiful is dying.

Oct 85. (7") **I MUST BE DREAMING. / IN THE HEART OF THE CITY**
(12"+=) – ('A'mix).

— Split late '85.

– compilations, etc. –

Nov 81. Capitol; (lp)(c) **SAVOIR FAIRE**
– This must be the night / "A" train lady / Spanish stroll / Cadillac walk / Soul twist / Just your friends / Mixed up, shook up girl / Gunslinger / One way street / Mazurka / I broke that promise / Just to walk that little girl home.

Jul 84. EMI Gold; (7") **SPANISH STROLL. / CADILLAC WALK** -

Nov 95. EMI; (3xcd-box) **CABERETTA / RETURN TO MAGENTA / LE CHAT BLEU**

WILLY DE VILLE

continued solo.

Polydor A&M

Nov 87. (7") **ASSASSIN OF LOVE. / I CALL YOUR NAME** -

Nov 87. (7") **MIRACLE. / I CALL YOUR NAME** -
(12"+=) – Stand by me.
(c-s+=)(cd-s+=) – Could you would you.

Jan 88. (lp)(c)(cd) **MIRACLE**
– (Due to) Gun control / Could you would you / Heart & soul / Assassin of love / Spanish Jack / Miracle / Angel eyes / Nightfalls / Southern politician / Storybook love. *(cd-iss.Dec94 on 'Raven')*

Feb 88. (7") **ASSASSIN OF LOVE. / SPANISH JACK** -
(12"+=) – Spanish stroll (live) / Desperate ways (live).

WILLY was credited with MARK KNOPFLER (Dire Straits) on 'Storybook Love', (circa Mar88).

New Rose Sky Ranch

1990. (cd) **VICTORY MIXTURE**
– Hello my lover / It do me good / Key to my heart / Beating like a tom-tom / Every dog has its day / Big blue diamonds / Teasin' you / Ruler of my heart / Who shot the la-la / Junker's blues. *(UK re-iss.Mar95)*

F.N.A.C. F.N.A.C.

1992. (cd)(c) **BACKSTREETS OF DESIRE**

1992. (cd-s) **HEY JOE /**

Apr 94. (cd) **LIVE (live)**

East West WEA

Nov 95. (c-s) **STILL / WHEN YOU'RE AWAY FROM ME**
(cd-s+=) – Still (I love you still).

MINOR THREAT (see under ⇒ FUGAZI)

MINUTEMEN

Formed: San Pedro, California, USA . . . 1979 originally as The REACTIONARIES, by BOON, WATT and TONCHE. They featured on Various Artists US lp's on indie labels 'Radio Tokyo', 'New Alliance' and 'Posh Boy', before signing for 'S.S.T.' home base of BLACK FLAG and MEAT PUPPETS. For 5 years they committed many songs to vinyl before having to disband late in 1985, due to the untimely death of D.BOON. The next year the remaining two MIKE WATT and GEORGE HURLEY re-formed as fIREHOSE alongside guitarist ED CRAWFORD. This trio debutted with album 'RAGIN' FULL ON' in 1987 and still for 'S.S.T.'. After an acclaimed 1989 third album 'FROMOHIO', they shifted to 'Columbia', where they scored minor hit albums in the early 90's. • **Style:** Hardcore punk outfit, named so due to their early songs only lasting a minute. fIREHOSE were a more melodic rock trio. • **Songwriters:** Covered HAVE YOU EVER SEEN THE RAIN (Creedence Clearwater Revival). fIREHOSE covered WALKING THE COW (Daniel Johnston). • **Trivia:** MIKE WATT also recorded with DOS alongside KIRA ROESSIER, who released 'New Alliance' cd /lp 'UNO CO DOS' in August 1991.

Recommended: BALLOT RESULTS (*7) / fROMOHIO (*8; fIREHOSE)

D.BOON (b.DENNIS DALE) – vocals, guitar / **MIKE WATT** – bass (of DOS) / **GEORGE HURLEY** – drums repl. FRANK TONCHE

not issued Thermador

1979. (7") **BEANSPILL. /** -

S.S.T. S.S.T.

Dec 80. (12"ep) **PARANOID TIME** -
– Untitled song for Latin America / political song for Michael Jackson to song / Validation / the maze / Definitions / Fascist / Joe McCarthy's ghost. *(UK-iss.Mar83, cd-ep iss.Nov88)*

Nov 81. (m-lp) **THE PUNCH LINE** (18 songs) -

Feb 83. (lp) **WHAT MAKES A MAN START FIRES** -
– Split red / The archer / etc.
(re-iss.+c+cd Aug91 + May93)

1983. (m-lp) **BUZZ OR HOWL UNDER THE INFLUENCE OF HEAT** -

Oct 84. (d-lp) **DOUBLE NICKELS ON THE DIME**
(cd-iss.Oct87)

Jun 85. (12"ep) **PROJECT: MERSH**
– The red and the black / Have you ever seen the rain / etc.

— Tragedy struck on the 22nd Dec'85, when D.BOON was killed in a car crash.

Jan 86. (lp) **3 WAY TIE (FOR LAST)**
– The price of Paradise / Lost / The big stick / Political nightmare / Courage / Have you ever seen the rain? / The red and the black / Spoken word piece / No one / Stories / What is it? / Ack ack ack / Just another soldier / Situations at hand / Hittin' the bong / Bermuda. *(cd-iss.Aug87)*

— Broke-up early 1986. WATT guested for CICCONE YOUTH (aka SONIC YOUTH).

– compilations, etc. –

Apr 85. Homestead; (7"ep) **TOUR SPIEL (live)**

Dec 86. S.S.T.; (cd)(d-lp) **BALLOT RESULTS**
– Little man with a black gun in his hand / Political song for Michael Jackson to sing / I felt like a gringo / Jesus and tequila / Courage / King of the hill / Bermuda / No one / Mr.Robot's holy orders / Ack ack ack / History lesson (part two) / This ain't no picnic / The cheerleaders / Time / Cut / Split red / Shit you hear at parties / Hell (second take) / Tour-spiel / Take our test / The punch line / Search / Bob Dylan wrote propaganda songs / Badges / Tension / If Reagan played disco / No! no! no! to draft and war – Joe McCarthy ghost. *(re-iss.May93)*

1987. S.S.T.; (cd) **POST-MERSH, VOL.I** -
– PUNCH LINE ep / WHAT MAKES A MAN START FIRES lp *(re-iss.May93)*

1987. S.S.T.; (cd) **POST-MERSH, VOL.II** -
– BUZZ OR HOWL UNDER THE INFLUENCE OF HEAT lp / PROJECT: MERSH ep *(re-iss.May93)*

Nov 88. S.S.T.; (cd) **FAT**

May 89. S.S.T.; (cd) **POST-MERSH VOL.III**

May 93. S.S.T.; (cd)(lp) **POLITICS OF TIME** -

Sep 87. New Alliance; (7"ep) **JOY / BLACK SHEEP. / MORE JOY**
(re-iss.10"colrd Feb90 on 'S.S.T.')

fIREHOSE

MIKE WATT – bass (also of **CRIMONY**, with **PAUL ROESSLER** – keyboards) / **GEORGE HURLEY** – drums / **ED CRAWFORD** – vocals, guitar (of COLUMBUS)

S.S.T. S.S.T.

Apr 87. (lp)(c) **RAGIN' fULL ON**
– Caroma / Mutiny / Perfect pairs / Chemical wires / Choose and memory / Relating dudes to jazz? / Another theory shot to shit on your . . . / Under the influence of the Meat Puppets / Locked in / Brave captain.

Mar 88. (lp)(c)(cd) **If'N**
– Sometimes / Hear me / Honey, please / Backroads / From one cums one / Making the freeway / Anger / For the singer of R.E.M. / Operation solitaire / Windmilling / Me & you, remembering / In memory of Elizabeth Cotton / Soon / Thunder child.

Jun 88. (12"ep) **SOMETIMES. / RHYMIN' SPILIN' / SHE PAINTS PICTURES**
(re-iss.cd-ep Aug93, last track repl. by 'For The Singer Of R.E.M.')

Mar 89. (lp)(c)(cd) **fROMOHIO**
– In my mind / Whisperin' while hollerin' / Mas cojones / What gets heard / Fiddle of the eighties / Time with you / If'n / Understanding / The softest hammer / Vastapol / Let the drummer have some / Liberty for our friend / Some things / Not that shit George.

Columbia Columbia

Oct 91. (cd)(c)(lp) **fLYIN' THE fLANNEL**
– Down with the bass / Up Finnegan's ladder / Can't believe / Walking the cow / Flyin' the flannel / Epoxy for example / O'er the town of Pedro / Too long / The first class / Anti-misogyny manoever / Toolin' song for Dave Alvin / Tienan man dream again / Lost colors / Towin' the line / Losers, boozers and heroes.

Mar 93. (cd)(c)(lp) **MR. MACHINERY OPERATOR**
– Formal introduction / Blaze / Herded into pools / Witness / Number seven / Powerful hankerin' / Rocket sled-fuel tank / Quicksand / Disciples of the 3-way / More famous quotes / Sincerely / Hell-hole / 4.29.92 / The cliffs thrown down.

MIKE WATT

Columbia Columbia

Mar 95. (cd)(c) **MIKE WATT: BALL-HOG OR TUGBOAT?**
– Big train / Against the 70's / Drove up from Pedro / Piss-bottle man / Chinese

firedrill / Song for Madonna to sing / Tuff gnarl / Sexual military dynamics / Max and Wells / E-ticket ride / Forever – one reporter's opinion / Song for Igor / Tell 'em boy! / Sidemouse advice / Heartbeat / Maggot brain / Coincidence is either hit or miss.

MIRACLES

Formed: Detroit, Michegan, USA ... 1957 by 15 year-old SMOKEY ROBINSON and school friends. They are spotted by Berry Gordy Jr., and after a couple of singles on local labels they signed to Gordy's new label 'Tamla' in 1960. The first-ever release on the label 'WAY OVER THERE' flopped, but by early 1961 they were at No.2 with 'SHOP AROUND'. By late 1961, Berry gave SMOKEY the job of company vice-president, as he did donate most of the material for the label. The MIRACLES continued to progress commercially and credibly in the 60's, with SMOKEY ROBINSON awarded front billing in 1967. Hits continued to roll off the procession line, including 2 more classic Top 10 hits 'I SECOND THAT EMOTION' & 'TEARS OF A CLOWN'. In Summer of 1972, SMOKEY departed for solo career, and they found WILLIAM GRIFFIN to replace him. They never emulated their earlier success, although they re-activated cross-Atlantic chart status when LOVE MACHINE hit the top in America. **Style & Songwriters:** Soul/R&B outfit, who relied on SMOKEY's falsetto vox and prolific songwriting abilities to pull them through. However the group, did collaborate with SMOKEY from 1965 onwards, and had to obviously pen own work when he left. Like The IMPRESSIONS in the mid-70's (whose leader CURTIS MAYFIELD similarly left), they moved into disco market. The MIRACLES covered several including; ABRAHAM, MARTIN & JOHN (c.Dick Holler). • **Trivia:** SMOKEY and CLAUDETTE married on the 7 Nov'59, and had two children appropriately named Berry and Tamla.

Recommended: COMPACT COMMAND PERFORMANCES (*7)

SMOKEY ROBINSON (b.WILLIAM, 19 Feb'40) – lead vocals / **RONNIE WHITE** (b. 5 Apr'39) – vocals / **BOBBY ROGERS** (b.19 Feb'40) – vocals / **CLAUDETTE ROGERS** (b.1942) – vocals / **PETE MOORE** (b.19 Nov'39) – vocals / **MARVIN TARPLIN** – guitar, musical director

not issued — Fury

1958. (7") **I LOVE YOU SO. / YOUR LOVE (IS ALL I NEED)** [-] [ ]

not issued — End

1958. (7") **GOT A JOB. / MY MAMA DONE TOLD ME** [-] [ ]

1959. (7") **I CRY. / MONEY** [-] [ ]

not issued — Chess

Sep 59. (7") **BAD GIRL. / I LOVE YOU BABY** [-] [93]

Jan 60. (7") **I NEED A CHANGE. / ALL I WANT** [-] [ ]

London — Tamla

Mar 60. (7"by "RON & BILL") **DON'T SAY BYE BYE. / IT** [-] [ ]
(originally issued 1958 on 'Argo')

Jun 60. (7") **WAY OVER THERE. / DEPEND ON ME** [-] [ ]

Feb 61. (7") **SHOP AROUND. / WHO'S LOVIN' YOU** [ ] [2] Dec 60

Feb 61. (lp) **HI, WE'RE THE MIRACLES** (debut US lp) [ ] [ ]
– Who's lovin' you / Depend on me / Heart like mine / Shop around / Won't you take me back / 'Cause I love you / Your love / After all / Way over there / Money / Don't leave me. *(UK-iss Jul 63 on 'Oriole')*

Apr 61. (7") **AIN'T IT BABY. / THE ONLY ONE I LOVE** [ ] [49] Mar 61

Jul 61. (7") **MIGHTY GOOD LOVIN'. / BROKEN HEARTED** [-] [51]

Oct 61. (7") **EVERYBODY'S GOTTA PAY SOME DUES. / I CAN'T BELIEVE** [-] [52]

Nov 61. (lp) **COOKIN' WITH THE MIRACLES** [-] [ ]
– Embraceable you / Everybody's gotta pay some dues / Mama / You never miss a good thing / That's the way I feel / Ain't it baby / Determination / Broken hearted / Only one I love / I can't believe.

Fontana — Tamla

Mar 62. (7") **WHAT'S SO GOOD ABOUT GOODBYE. / I'VE BEEN SO GOOD TO YOU** [ ] [35] Dec 61

May 62. (7") **I'LL TRY SOMETHING NEW. / YOU NEVER MISS A GOOD THING** [-] [39]
– I'll try something new / Speak low / What's so good about goodbye / I've got you under my skin / On the street where you live / Love that can never be / If your mother only knew / I've been good to you / He don't care about me / This I swear, I promise.

Jun 62. (lp) **I'LL TRY SOMETHING NEW** [-] [ ]

Sep 62. (7") **WAY OVER THERE. / IF YOUR MOTHER ONLY KNEW** [-] [94]

Dec 62. (lp) **CHRISTMAS WITH THE MIRACLES** [-] [ ]
– (festive material)

—— In 1963, SMOKEY married stage member CLAUDETTE sister of BOBBY. She will retire the following year to bring up family.

Oriole — Tamla

Jan 63. (7") **YOU'VE REALLY GOT A HOLD ON ME. / HAPPY LANDING** [ ] [8] Nov 62

Mar 63. (7") **A LOVE SHE CAN COUNT ON. / I CAN TAKE A HINT** [-] [31]

Sep 63. (7") **MICKEY'S MONKEY. / WHATEVER MAKES YOU HAPPY** [ ] [8] Jul 63

Oct 63. (lp) **THE MIRACLES ON STAGE (live)** [-] [ ]
– Mighty good lovin' / A love she can count on / Happy landing / I've been good to you / What's so good about goodbye / You've really got a hold on me / Way over there.

Dec 63. (lp) **DOIN' MICKEY'S MONKEY** [-] [ ]
– Mickey's monkey / Dance what you wanna / The Wah-Watusi / The twist / Dancin' holiday / Land of a 1000 dances / I gotta dance to keep from crying / The monkey time / The groovey thing / Twist and shout / Do you love me.

Stateside — Tamla

Feb 64. (7") **I GOTTA DANCE TO KEEP FROM CRYING. / SUCH IS LOVE, SUCH IS LIFE** [ ] [35] Nov 63

Apr 64. (7") **(YOU CAN'T LET THE BOY OVERPOWER) THE MAN IN YOU. / HEARTBREAK ROAD** [ ] [59] Jan 64

Aug 64. (7") **I LIKE IT LIKE THAT. / YOU'RE SO FINE AND SWEET** [ ] [27] Jun 64

Nov 64. (lp) **THE FABULOUS MIRACLES** [ ] [ ] Jun 63
– The man in you / Such is love, such is life / I can take a hint / Heartbreak Road / Your love / He don't care about me / Speak low / I've been good to you / If your mother only knew / Won't you take me back / A love that can never be / On the street where you live.

Nov 64. (7") **THAT'S WHAT LOVE IS MADE OF. / WOULD I LOVE YOU** [ ] [35] Sep 64

Jan 65. (7") **COME ON DO THE JERK. / BABY DON'T YOU GO** [ ] [50] Nov 64

Tamla Motown — Tamla

Mar 65. (7") **OOH BABY BABY. / ALL THAT'S GOOD** [ ] [16]

Apr 65. (lp) **I LIKE IT LIKE THAT** [ ] [ ] Oct 64

Jul 65. (7") **THE TRACKS OF MY TEARS. / A FORK IN THE ROAD** [ ] [16] Jun 65

Nov 65. (7") **MY GIRL HAS GONE. / SINCE YOU WON MY HEART** [ ] [14] Sep 65

Feb 66. (7") **GOING TO A GO-GO. / CHOOSEY BEGGAR** [44] [11] Dec 65

Feb 66. (lp) **GOING TO A GO-GO** [ ] [8] Nov 65
– The tracks of my tears / Going to a go-go / Ooh baby baby / My girl has gone / In case you need love / Choosey beggar / Since you won my heart / From head to toe / All that's good / My baby changes like the weather / Let me have some / A fork in the road.

Jul 66. (d-lp) **GREATEST HITS FROM THE BEGINNING** [ ] [21] Apr 65
– (compilation) *(US-title 'GREATEST HITS FROM THE BEGINNING')*
– Get a job / I cry / Mama done told me / (I need some) Money / Bad girl / I love your baby / I need a change / All I want is you / (You can) Depend on me / Who's loving you / That's what love is made of / Mickey's monkey / I gotta dance to keep from crying / You've really got a hold on me / I like it like that / A love she can count on / Shop around / Way over there / I've been good to you / Would I love you / I'll try something new / What's so good about goodbye.

Jul 66. (7") **WHOLE LOT OF SHAKIN' IN MY HEART (SINCE I MET YOU). / OH BE MY LOVE** [ ] [46] May 66

Dec 66. (7") **(COME ROUND HERE) I'M THE ONE YOU NEED. / SAVE ME** [45] [17] Oct 66

Feb 67. (lp) **AWAY WE A GO-GO** [ ] [41] Dec 66
– Whole lot of shakin' in my heart (since I met you) / You don't have to say you love me / Save me / (Come 'round here) I'm the one you need / Oh be my love / etc.

SMOKEY ROBINSON & THE MIRACLES

Tamla Motown — Tamla

Feb 67. (7") **THE LOVE I SAW IN YOU WAS JUST A MIRAGE. / COME SPY WITH ME** [-] [20]

Mar 67. (7") **THE LOVE I SAW IN YOU WAS JUST A MIRAGE. / SWEPT FOR YOU BABY** [ ] [-]

Jun 67. (7") **MORE LOVE. / SWEPT FOR YOU BABY** [-] [23]

Jul 67. (7") **MORE LOVE. / COME SPY WITH ME** [ ] [-]

Nov 67. (7") **I SECOND THAT EMOTION. / YOU MUST BE LOVE** [27] [4] Oct 67

Feb 68. (lp) **MAKE IT HAPPEN** [ ] [28] Oct 67
– Soulful shack / Love I saw in you was just a mirage / My love for you / I'm on the outside looking in / Don't think it's me / My love is your love (forever) / More love / After you put back the pieces / It's a good feeling / You must be love / Dancing's alright / Tears of a clown. *(US re-iss. Dec70 as 'TEARS OF A CLOWN')*

Mar 68. (7") **IF YOU CAN WANT. / WHEN THE WORDS FROM YOUR HEART GET CAUGHT UP IN YOUR THROAT** [50] [11] Feb 68

Jun 68. (lp) **GREATEST HITS, VOL.2** (compilation) [ ] [7] Feb 68
– Going to a go go / The tracks of my tears / I second that emotion / Ooo baby baby / My girl has gone / Come on do the jerk / Whole lot of shakin' in my heart (since I met you) / The love I saw in you was just a mirage / (Come 'round here) I'm the one you need / More love / Choosey beggar / Save me. *(re-iss.+cJul73)*

Jun 68. (7") **YESTER LOVE. / MUCH BETTER OFF** [ ] [31] May 68

Oct 68. (7") **SPECIAL OCCASION. / GIVE HER UP** [ ] [26] Aug 68

Jan 69. (lp) **SPECIAL OCCASION** [ ] [42] Oct 68
– Yester love / If you can wait / Special occasion / Everybody needs love / Just losing you / Give her up / I heard it through the grapevine / Yesterday / Your mother's only daughter / Much better off / You only build me up to tear me down.

Feb 69. (7") **BABY, BABY DON'T CRY. / YOUR MOTHER'S ONLY DAUGHTER** [ ] [8] Jan 69

Apr 69. (7") **THE TRACKS OF MY TEARS. / COME ON DO THE JERK** [9] [-]

May 69. (lp) **LIVE! (live)** [ ] [71] Feb 69
– Once in a lifetime / You and the night and the music / I second that emotion / The tracks of my tears / Poinciana / Up, up and away / Theme from 'Valley of the Dolls' / Yester love / Walk on by / Yesterday / If you can wait / Mickey's monkey / Ooh baby baby / Going to a go-go

Jul 69. (7") **DOGGONE RIGHT. / HERE I GO AGAIN** [-] [33] [37]

Jul 69. (7") **ABRAHAM, MARTIN AND JOHN. / MUCH BETTER OFF** [-] [33]

Dec 69. (7") **POINT IT OUT. / DARLING DEAR** [-] [37] [100]

Feb 70. (lp) **TIME OUT FOR SMOKEY ROBINSON AND THE MIRACLES** [ ] [25] Aug 69

Feb 70. (7") **WHO'S GONNA TAKE THE BLAME. / I GOTA THING FOR YOU** [-] [ ]

Jul 70. (lp) **FOUR IN BLUE** [ ] [78] Dec 69
– You send me (with your good lovin') / Dreams, dreams / Tomorrow is another day / Hey Jude / California soul / A legend in his own time / You've lost that lovin' feelin' / We can make it if we can / When nobody cares / Don't say you love me / Wish I knew / My world is empty without you.

May 70. (lp) **WHAT LOVE HAS JOINED TOGETHER** [-] [97]
– What love has joined together / My cherie amour / If this world were mine / You've

made me so very happy / This guy's in love with you / And I love her.

Jul 70. (7") **THE TEARS OF A CLOWN. / YOU MUST BE LOVE** 1 -

Oct 70. (7") **THE TEARS OF A CLOWN. / PROMISE ME** - 1 46

Oct 70. (lp) **A POCKETFUL OF MIRACLES** - 56

Jan 71. (7") **(COME ROUND HERE) I'M THE ONE YOU NEED. / WE CAN MAKE IT, WE CAN** 13 -

Feb 71. (lp) **SMOKEY ROBINSON & THE MIRACLES**

May 71. (7") **I DON'T BLAME YOU AT ALL. / THAT GIRL** 11 18 Mar 71

Jun 71. (7") **CRAZY 'BOUT THE LA LA LA. / OH BABY BABY I LOVE YOU** - 56

Sep 71. (lp) **ONE DOZEN ROSES** - 92

Nov 71. (7") **SATISFACTION. / FLOWER GIRL** - 49

Apr 72. (7") **CRAZY 'BOUT THE LA LA LA. / MY GIRL HAS GONE** -

Jun 72. (7") **WE'VE COME TOO FAR TO END IT NOW. / WHEN SUNDOWN COMES** - 46

Jul 72. (lp) **FLYING HIGH TOGETHER** - 46

– I can't stand to see you cry / Love story / We've come too far to end it now / Flying high together / With you love came / It will be alright / Oh girl / You ain't livin' you're lovin' / We had a love so strong / Got to be there / Betcha by golly wow.

Dec 72. (7") **I CAN'T STAND TO SEE YOU CRY. / WITH YOUR LOVE CAME** - 45

— In Jul'72, SMOKEY ROBINSON had already left to concentrate on solo career.

The MIRACLES

replaced him with **WILLIAM GRIFFIN** – vocals

Tamla Motown Tamla

Oct 73. (lp)(c) **RENAISSANCE** May 73

– What is a heart good for / If you're ever in the neighbourhood / I wanna be with you / Wigs and lashes / Don't let it end (til you let it begin) / I love you secretly / I don't need no reason / Nowhere to go / I didn't realise the show was over.

Mar 74. (7") **DON'T LET IT END (TIL YOU LET IT BEGIN). / I WANNA BE WITH YOU** 56 Jul 73

Aug 74. (7") **DO IT BABY. / WIGS AND LASHES** 13

Dec 74. (lp)(c) **DO IT BABY** 41 Sep 74

– Do it baby / Up again / Where are you going to my love / What is a heart good for / You are love / Give me just another day / We feel the same / Calling out your name / A foolish thing to say / Can't get ready for losing you.

Dec 74. (7") **DON'T CHA LOVE IT. / UP AGAIN** - 78

Feb 75. (7") **WHERE ARE YOU GOING TO MY LOVE. / UP AGAIN** -

Sep 75. (7") **YOU ARE LOVE. / GEMINI** -

Nov 75. (7") **LOVE MACHINE (part 1). / LOVE MACHINE (part 2)** 3 1 Oct 75

Nov 75. (lp)(c) **CITY OF ANGELS** 33 Oct 75

– Overture / City of angels / Free press / Ain't nobody straight in L.A. / Night life / Love machine / My name is Michael / Poor Charlotte / Waldo Roderick / Dehammersmith / Smog.

Feb 76. (7") **NIGHT LIFE. / SMOG** -

Feb 76. (7") **NIGHT LIFE. / THE MIRACLE WORKERS: OVERTURE** -

Apr 76. (lp)(c) **LOVE MACHINE** 96

– Love machine / Don't cha love it / Keep on keepin' on (doin' what you do) / Sweet sweet lovin' / Got me goin' (again) / You are love / Gemini / Take it all / Broken-hearted girl, broken-hearted boy / A little piece of Heaven / Gonna tell the world (wedding song).

(Above was issued in US Feb 75 as 'DON'T CHA LOVE IT')

Oct 76. (lp)(c) **THE POWER OF MUSIC**

– The power of music / Love to make love / Can I pretend / Let the children play (overture) / gossip / Let the children play / Street of love / You need a miracle.

C.B.S. Columbia

Jan 77. (7") **SPY FOR BROTHERHOOD. / THE BIRD MUST FLY AWAY**

Feb 77. (lp)(c) **LOVE CRAZY**

– Love crazy – introductory / Love crazy – overture / Too young / Spy for brotherhood / A better way to live / Women (make the world go round) / The bird must fly away / I can touch the sky.

Jun 77. (7") **WOMEN (MAKE THE WORLD GO ROUND). / I CAN TOUCH THE SKY**

Jul 78. (lp)(c) **MIRACLES** -

– I can't stand it / Love doctor / The magic of your eyes (Laura's eyes) / Freeway / Hot dance / Mean machine / Sad rain / Reach for the sky.

Jul 78. (7") **MEAN MACHINE. / THE MAGIC OF YOUR EYES (LAURA'S EYES)** -

— Disbanded around 1978.

– (SMOKEY ROBINSON & THE MIRACLES) – -compilations, others, etc.-

Note; All released on 'Tamla Motown' UK + US until mentioned

Apr 73. (d-lp)(c) **1957-1972** (live) 75 Dec 72

Apr 73. (7"m) **GOING TO A GO-GO. / WHOLE LOT OF SHAKING IN MY HEART (SINCE I MET YOU) / YESTER LOVE** -

Mar 74. (t-lp) **ANTHOLOGY** 97

(re-iss.+c.Sep82, cd-iss.Jun87 & Apr89)

Sep 76. (7") **THE TEARS OF A CLOWN. / THE TRACKS OF MY TEARS** 34 -

Sep 80. (7") **(COME ROUND HERE) I'M THE ONE YOU NEED. / I SECOND THAT EMOTION** -

Aug 81. (lp)(c) **THE TEARS OF A CLOWN** (rec.1967) -

(re-iss.+cd.Aug88)

May 83. (c-ep) **SMOKEY ROBINSON & THE MIRACLES** -

– The tears of a clown / (Come round here) I'm the one you need / The tracks of my tears / Don't blame you at all.

Jun 83. (7") **THE TEARS OF A CLOWN. / THE TRACKS OF MY TEARS** -

May 87. (7") **THE TRACKS OF MY TEARS. / I SECOND THAT EMOTION** -

(12"+=) – Going to a go-go / Shop around.

Oct 87. (cd) **COMPACT COMMAND PERFORMANCES (18 GREATEST HITS)**

– Shop around / You've really got a hold on me / I'll try something new / You can depend on me / Mickey's monkey / Tracks of my tears / Going to a go-go / I second that emotion / If you can wait / Baby, baby don't cry / Doggone right / Tears of a clown / I don't blame you at all / Baby come close / Baby that's backatcha / Quiet storm / Cruisin' / Being with you (last 3 SMOKEY ROBINSON solo).

Sep 73. MFP; (lp)(c) **I HEARD IT THROUGH THE GRAPEVINE** -

Jan 79. MFP; (lp)(c) **THE TEARS OF A CLOWN** -

May 93. Spectrum; (cd)(c) **TEARS OF A CLOWN (SMOKEY ROBINSON & THE MIRACLES)** -

Nov 94. Spectrum; (cd)(c) **CHRISTMAS WITH THE MIRACLES** -

MISFITS (see under ⇒ DANZIG)

MISSION

Formed: Leeds, England . . . late 1985 by ex-SISTERS OF MERCY members WAYNE HUSSEY and CRAIG ADAMS. Originally planned to be The SISTERHOOD, and did some gigs, until ANDREW ELDRITCH wanted group name for himself. To save fuss, they became The MISSION, and signed to indie 'Chapter 22' on Mar'86. 2 months later, their debut single 'SERPENT'S KISS', breached the Top 75, with a Summer follow-up 'GARDEN OF DELIGHT' scraping the 50. To end the Summer, they signed to major 'Mercury', and cracked the Top 30 with 'STAY WITH ME', and parent debut Top 20 album 'GOD'S OWN MEDICINE'. Continued consecutive string of hit UK albums and singles, although their last of '92 'SHADES OF GREEN', only just managed to make No.49. • **Style:** Goth supergroup, fusing a mixture of acoustic and hard-rock deep metal. • **Songwriters:** HUSSEY penned, except LIKE A HURRICANE (Neil Young) / DANCING BAREFOOT (Patti Smith) / SHELTER FROM THE STORM (Bob Dylan) / OVER THE HILLS AND FAR AWAY (Led Zeppelin) / LOVE (John Lennon) / ATOMIC (Blondie). • **Trivia:** Were called The MISSION U.K. for the States. JOHN PAUL JONES (ex-LED ZEPPELIN) produced 2nd album 'CHILDREN'. In 1991, HUSSEY was ushered off James Whale's late night TV show, for being drunk and abusive to its ever-polite presenter!!

Recommended: SUM AND SUBSTANCE (*8)

WAYNE HUSSEY (b.26 May'59, Bristol, England) – vocals, guitar (ex-SISTERS OF MERCY, ex-DEAD OR ALIVE, ex-HAMBI & THE DANCE, ex-WALKIE TALKIES) / **CRAIG ADAMS** – bass (ex-SISTERS OF MERCY, ex-EXPELAIRES) / **SIMON HINKLER** – guitar (ex-ARTERY) / **MICK BROWN** – drums (ex-RED LORRY YELLOW LORRY)

Chapter 22 not issued

May 86. (7") **SERPENT'S KISS. / WAKE (R.S.V.)** 70 -

(12"+=) – Naked and savage.

Jul 86. (7") **GARDEN OF DELIGHT. / LIKE A HURICANE** 50 -

(12"+=) – Over the hills and far away / The crystal ocean.

(12"+=) – Dancing barefoot / The crystal ocean.

Mercury Mercury

Oct 86. (7") **STAY WITH ME. / BLOOD BROTHER** 30

(12"+=) – Islands in a stream.

Nov 86. (lp)(c)(cd) **GODS OWN MEDICINE** 14

– Wasteland / Bridges burning / Garden of delight (hereafter) / Stay with me / Blood brother * / Let sleeping dogs lie / Sacrilege / Dance on glass / And the dance goes on / Severina / Love me to death / Island in a stream *. *(c+= *)(cd+= *)*

Jan 87. (7") **WASTELAND. / SHELTER FROM THE STORM** 11

(12"+=) – Dancing barefoot (live).

(12"+=) – 1969 / Wake (both live).

(d7") – 1969 (live) / Serpent's kiss (live).

Mar 87. (7") **SEVERINA. / TOMORROW NEVER KNOWS** 25

(12"+=) – Wishing well.

— **PETE TURNER** – bass took over on tour while ADAMS recovered from illness **CRAIG ADAMS** was soon back after a 4 month lay-off.

Jan 88. (7")(12") **TOWER OF STRENGTH. / FABIENNE / BREATHE (vocal)** 12

(12"+=)(c-s+=)(cd-s+=) – Dream on / Breathe (instrumental; repl. vocal=)

Mar 88. (lp)(c)(cd) **CHILDREN** 2

– Beyond the pale / A wing and a prayer / Fabienne * / Heaven on Earth / Tower of strength / Kingdom come / Breathe / Child's play / Shamera kye / Black mountain mist / Dream on * / Heat / Hymn (for America). *(c+=)(cd+=)*

Jul 88. (7") **BEYOND THE PALE. / TADEUSZ (1912-1988)** 32

(12"+=) – For ever more.

(cd-s+=) – Tower of strength (reprise).

(12"+=)(cd-s+=) – Love me to death (reprise).

Nov 88. (7") **KINGDOM COME. / CHILD'S PLAY (live)**

(12"+=) – The crystal ocean.

(12"++=)(cd-s++=) – Garden of delight (live).

(all formats on above single withdrawn)

Jan 90. (7")(c-s) **BUTTERFLY ON A WHEEL. / THE GRIP OF DISEASE** 12

(12"+=)(cd-s+=) – ('A'magni-octopus) / Kingdom come (forever and again).

Feb 90. (cd)(c)(lp) **CARVED IN SAND** 7

– Amelia / Into the blue / Butterfly on a wheel / Sea of love / Deliverance / Grapes of wrath / Belief / Paradise (will shine like the Moon) / Hungry as the hunter / Lovely.

Mar 90. (7")(c-s) **DELIVERANCE. / MR.PLEASANT** 27

(10"+=)(12"+=)(cd-s+=)(pic-cd-s+=) – Heaven sends us.

May 90. (7")(c-s) **INTO THE BLUE. / BIRD OF PARADISE** 32

(12"+=)(cd-s+=) – Divided we fall.

— **DAVID WOLFENDEN** – guitar (ex-RED LORRY YELLOW LORRY) repl.

HINKLER.

— (Oct90) added **ETCH** – guitar (ex-GHOST DANCE)

Oct 90. (cd)(c)(lp) **GRAINS OF SAND** (out-takes) 28
– Hands across the ocean / The grip of disease / Divided we fall / Mercenary / Mr.Pleasant / Kingdom come (forever and again) / Heaven sends you / Sweet smile of a mystery / Love / Bird of passage.
(c+cd+=) – (2 extra acoustic tracks)

Nov 90. (7")(c-s) **HANDS ACROSS THE OCEAN. / AMELIA / LOVE** 28
(12"+=) – Amelia (live) / Tower of strength (mix) / Mercenary.
(cd-s+=) – Amelia (live) / Stay with me / Mercenary.

Vertigo Mercury

Apr 92. (7")(c-s) **NEVER AGAIN. / BEAUTIFUL CHAOS** 34
(12"+=)(cd-s+=) – ('A'-F1 mix) / ('A'-Zero G mix.

Jun 92. (cd)(c)(lp) **MASQUE** 23
– Never again / Shades of green (part II) / Even you may shine / Trail of scarlet / Spider and the fly / She conjures me wings / Sticks and stones / Like a child again / Who will love me tomorrow? / You make me breathe / From one Jesus to another / Until there's another sunrise. *(re-is.cd/c Aug94)*

Jun 92. (7")(c-s) **LIKE A CHILD AGAIN (remix). / ALL TANGLED UP IN YOU** 30
(12"+=)(cd-s+=) – ('A'-Mark Saunders remix) / Hush a bye baby (child again) (Joe Gibbs remix).

Oct 92. (7")(c-s) **SHADES OF GREEN. / YOU MAKE ME BREATHE** 49
(cd-s) – ('A'side) / Sticks and stones / Trail of scarlet / Spider and the fly.
(etched-12"+=) – ('A'mix).

— (Nov92) **MARK THWAITE** – guitar (ex-SPEAR OF DESTINY) repl. HINKLER + ADAMS. Note:- **RIC SAUNDERS** – violin (of FAIRPORT CONVENTION) on last lp.

Jan 94. (7") **TOWER OF STRENGTH (Youth remix). / WASTELAND** 33
(12"+=) – Serpent's kiss.
(cd-s) – ('A'mixes) / ('A'-East India Cairo mix) / Deliverance.

Feb 94. (cd)(c)(d-lp) **SUM AND SUBSTANCE** (compilation) 49
– Never again / Hands across the ocean / Shades of green / Like a child again / Into the blue / Deliverance / Tower of strength / Butterfly on a wheel / Kingdom come / Beyond the pale / Severina / Stay with me / Wasteland / Garden of delight / Like a hurricane / Serpent's kiss / Sour puss / Afterglow.

Mar 94. (7") **AFTERGLOW. / SOUR-PUSS** 53
(cd-s+=) – Cold as ice / Valentine.

Equator not issued

Oct 94. (7"ep)(12"ep)(c-ep)(cd-ep) **MISSION 1 EP**
– Raising Cain / Sway / Neverland.

Jan 95. (7"ep)(10"ep)(cd-ep) **SWOON / WHERE / WASTING AWAY / ('A'-Resurrection mix)** 73

Feb 95. (cd)(c) **NEVERLAND** 58
– Raising Cain / Sway / Lose myself / Swoon / Afterglow (reprise) / Stars don't shine without you / Celebration / Cry like a baby / Heaven knows / Swim with the dolphins / Neverland / Daddy's going to Heaven now.

– compilations, others, etc. –

Jun 87. Chapter 22; (lp)(c) **THE FIRST CHAPTER** 35 -
(contains all 'Chapter 22' material)

Jul 94. Nighttracks; (cd)(lp) **SALAD DAZE** -

MISUNDERSTOOD

Formed: Riverside, California, USA ... 1965. After 1 US independent 45, they moved to London and signed to 'Fontana' in 1966. John Ravenscroft (aka JOHN PEEL) became manager?. When JUICY LUCY came about in 1970, they scored UK Top 20 smash with 'WHO DO YOU LOVE'. • **Style:** Guitar-based psychedelic rock outfit. • **Songwriters:** Group compositions except; I'M NOT TALKING (Yardbirds) / LITTLE RED ROOSTER (Willie Dixon) / etc. JUICY LUCY covered; WHO DO YOU LOVE (Bo Diddley) / etc.

Recommended: BEFORE THE DREAM FADED (*8) / THE BEST OF JUICY LUCY (*5)

RICK BROWN – vocals / **GREG TREADWAY** – guitar / **GLENN ROSS CAMPBELL** – steel guitar / **STEVE WHITING** – bass / **RICK MOE** – drums

not iss. Blues Sound

1966. (7") **YOU DON'T HAVE TO GO. /** -

— **GUY EVANS** – drums repl. MOE **TONY HILL** – guitar (ex-ANSWER) repl. TREADWAY

Fontana Fontana

Dec 66. (7") **I CAN TAKE YOU TO THE SUN. / WHO DO YOU LOVE**

— Disbanded when BROWN was drafted into US army. In 1969, **GLENN ROSS** reformed a new line-up (on same label), completed by **STEVE HOARD** – vocals / **NEIL HUBBARD** – guitar (ex-GRAHAM BOND ORGANISATION, ex-GREASY BAND) / **CHRIS MERCER** – saxophone, keyboards (ex-JOHN MAYALL'S BLUESBREAKERS) / **NIC POTTER** – bass / **GUY EVANS** – drums (EVANS joined VAN DER GRAAF . . .) **TONY HILL** later joined HIGH TIDE.

1969. (7") **CHILDREN OF THE SUN. / I UNSEEN**

May 69. (7") **(YOU'RE) TUFF ENOUGH. / LITTLE RED ROOSTER**

Jul 69. (7") **NEVER HAD A GIRL (LIKE YOU BEFORE). / GOLDEN GLASS**

— above as "The MISUNDERSTOOD featuring GLENN 'Fernando' CAMPBELL"

— Group evolved into JUICY LUCY, except POTTER who joined VAN DER GRAAF . . .

– compilations, others, etc. –

May 81. Cherry Red; (7"m) **CHILDREN OF THE SUN. / WHO DO YOU LOVE / I'LL TAKE YOU TO THE SUN** -

Apr 82. Cherry Red; (lp) **BEFORE THE DREAM FADED** -
– COLOR OF THEIR SOUND:- Children of the Sun / My mind / Who do you love? / I unseen / Find a hidden door / I can take you to the sun / BLUE DAY IN RIVERSIDE:- I'm not talkin' / I need your love / You don't have to go / I cried my eyes out / Like I do. *(cd-iss.May92)*

Jun 84. Cherry Red; (12"m) **GOLDEN GLASS. / SHAKE YOUR MONEY MAKER / I'M NOT TALKING** -

Aug 84. Time Stood Still; (lp) **GOLDEN GLASS** -
– Never had a girl (like you before) / Golden glass / I don't want to discuss it (you're my girl) / Little red rooster / (You're) Tuff enough / Flamingo music / Freedom / Keep on running / I'm cruisin'.

JUICY LUCY

were formed by **RAY OWEN** – vocals / **PETE DOBSON** – drums / **NEIL HUBBARD** – guitar / **GLENN ROSS CAMPBELL** – steel guitar, mandolin / **CHRIS MERCER** – saxophone, keys / **KEITH ELLIS** – bass (ex-VAN DER GRAAF GENERATOR)

Vertigo Atco

Jan 70. (lp) **JUICY LUCY** 41
– Mississippi woman / Who do you love? / She's mine / She's young / Just one time / Chicago North-Western / Train / Nadine / Are you satisfied?. *(re-iss.Dec75 on 'Bronze')*

Feb 70. (7") **WHO DO YOU LOVE?. / WALKING DOWN THE HIGHWAY** 14

— **PAUL WILLIAMS** – vocals, keyboards repl. OWEN / **ROD COOMBES** – drums repl. DOBSON / **MICK MOODY** – guitar repl. HUBBARD

Oct 70. (7") **PRETTY WOMAN. / I AM A THIEF** 44

Nov 70. (lp) **LIE BACK AND ENJOY IT** 53
– Thinking of my life / Built for comfort / Pretty woman / Whisky in my jar / Hello L.A. bye bye Birmingham / Changed my mind / That woman's got something / Willie the wimp / Lie back and enjoy it. (cd+=) – Walking down the highway / I'm a thief. *(cd-iss.Jan94 on 'Repertoire')*

— **JIM LEVERTON** – bass repl. ELLIS

Bronze Atco

1971. (lp) **GET A WHIFF A THIS**
– Mr.Skin / Midnight Sun / Midnight rider / Harvest / Mr. A. Jones / Sunday morning / Big Lil / Jessica / Future days. *(cd-iss.Jan94 on 'Repertoire')*

— JEAN ROUSSELL – keyboards (was added soon after above). The last JUICY LUCY line-up with JEAN, were **PAUL WILLIAMS, MICK MOODY,** plus newcomers **ANDY PYLE** – bass (ex-SAVOY BROWN, ex-BLODWYN PIG) who repl. JIM to HEMLOCK / **RON BERG** – drums repl. COOMBES to STEALER'S WHEEL (CAMPBELL and MERCER also left to surface later in other bands)

1972. (7") **IT AIN'T EASY. / PROMISED LAND**

1972. (lp) **PIECES** -
– Promised land / Cuckoo / All my life / It ain't easy / Suicide pilot / Why can't it happen to me / Dead flowers in the mirror / Prospector man / How can a poor man stand these times and live.

— Broke up after CHRIS STEWART repl. PYLE who joined SAVOY BROWN with RON BERG. MICK MOODY was later to join WHITESNAKE. PAUL WILLIAMS joined TEMPEST.

– compilations, others, etc. –

1973. Bronze; (lp)(c) **THE BEST OF JUICY LUCY** -
– Who do you love / Midnight rider / Pretty woman / That woman's got something / Jessica / Willie the wimp – Lie back and enjoy it / Changed my mind / Changed my sign / Just one time / I'm a thief / Built for comfort / Mr.Skin / Mr.A.Jones. (cd+=) – Future days / Chicago North Western / Hello L.A. bye bye Birmingham / Thinking of my life. *(re-iss.+cd.Mar90 on 'Castle') (cd-iss.+= 4 extra)*

Mar 81. Bronze; (7") **WHO DO YOU LOVE. / CHICAGO NORTH WOMAN** -

Jan 95. H.T.D.; (cd) **HERE SHE COME NOW** -

May 95. Spectrum; (cd) **PRETTY WOMAN** -

Jun 95. BGO; (cd) **JUICY LUCY / LIE BACK AND ENJOY IT** -

Joni MITCHELL

Born: ROBERTA JOAN ANDERSON, 7 Nov'43, Fort McLeod, Alberta, Canada. In 1964 she performed at the Mariposa Folk Festival in Ontario, and married CHUCK MITCHELL in Jun'65, but after they relocated to Detroit the next year, they divorced. She retained surname and moved to New York, where her songs were gradually recorded by others, mainly JUDY COLLINS('BOTH SIDES NOW' & 'MICHAEL FROM MOUNTAINS') and TOM RUSH('THE CIRCLE GAME'). Her self-titled DAVID CROSBY produced debut lp, came out in Summer of '68, and managed to only scrape into US Top 200. In August 1969 on the advice of David Geffen, she pulled out of WOODSTOCK free festival, and instead wrote classic song of that name. It was later a US hit for CROSBY, STILLS, NASH & YOUNG, and also a UK No.1 for MATTHEWS' SOUTHERN COMFORT. Her 2nd solo lp 'CLOUDS' broke through into US Top 40, after her non-appearance, and was her second of many classic albums of the 70's. Her '79 album 'MINGUS' was dedicated to jazz legend CHARLIE MINGUS, who she had recently worked with, but who died of Lou Gegrig's disease on 5 Jan'79. • **Style:** Undoubtedly the greatest female singer/songwriter of all-time. She eased her romantically inclined moods, through folk, jazz and sophisticated rock, and was / is the inspiration for many female rock-pop acts. • **Songwriters:** All self-penned except; TWISTED (Annie Ross) / WHY DO FOOLS FALL IN LOVE (Frankie Lymon) / BABY I DON'T CARE (hit; Elvis Presley) / SLOUCHING TOWARDS BETHLEHEM (poem; W.B.Yeats). • **Trivia:** Her excellent paintings, were mostly always featured as the album cover.

Recommended: JONI MITCHELL (*7) / CLOUDS (*7) / LADIES OF THE CANYON (*9) / BLUE (*7) / FOR THE ROSES (*7) / COURT AND SPARK (*7) / HEJIRA (*10) / THE HISSING OF SUMMER LAWNS (*7) / CHALK MARK IN A RAINSTORM (*7).

JONI MITCHELL – vocals, acoustic guitar, piano with **STEPHEN STILLS** – bass /

Reprise Reprise

Jun 68. (lp) **JONI MITCHELL** [ ] [ ] Mar 68
– I CAME TO THE CITY:- I had a king / Michael from the mountains / Night in the city / Marcie / Nathan la Freneer / OUT OF THE CITY AND DOWN TO THE SEASIDE:- Sisotowbell Lane / The dawntreader / The pirate of penance / Song to a seagull / Cactus tree. *(cd-iss.1987)*

Jul 68. (7") **NIGHT IN THE CITY. / I HAD A KING** [ ] [-]

Aug 69. (7") **CHELSEA MORNING. / BOTH SIDES NOW** [ ] [-]
(iss. US Jun '72)

Oct 69. (lp) **CLOUDS** [ ] [31] May 69
– Tin angel / Chelsea morning / I don't know where I stand / That song about the Midway / Roses blue / The gallery / I think I understand / Songs to ageing children come / The fiddle and the drum / Both sides now. *(re-iss.c+cd.1989 on 'WEA')*

— next guests **MILT HOLLAND** – percussion / **TERESSA ADAMS** – cello / **JIM HORN** – baritone sax / **PAUL HORN** – clarinet, flute

May 70. (lp)(c) **LADIES OF THE CANYON** [8] [27] Apr 70
– Morning Morgantown / For free / Conversation / Ladies of the canyon / Willy / The arrangement / Rainy night house / The priest / Blue boy / Big yellow taxi / Woodstock / The circle game. *(cd-iss.Jul88)*

Jun 70. (7") **BIG YELLOW TAXI. / WOODSTOCK** [11] [67]

— with **STILLS + JAMES TAYLOR** – guitar / **SNEAKY PETE KLEINOW** – steel guitar / **RUSS KUNKEL** – drums / etc.

Jul 71. (lp)(c) **BLUE** [3] [15] Jun 71
– All I want / My old man / Little green / Carey / Blue / California / This flight tonight / River / A case of you / The last time I saw Richard. *(cd-iss.Jan87)*

Aug 71. (7") **CAREY. / THIS FLIGHT TONIGHT** [-] [93]

Aug 71. (7") **CAREY. / MY OLD MAN** [ ] [-]

Apr 72. (7") **CALIFORNIA. / A CASE OF YOU** [ ] [ ] Oct 71

Jul 72. (7") **CAREY. / BIG YELLOW TAXI** [-] [ ]

— Her band now **STILLS + NASH** (her recent boyfriend) + **KUNKEL / WILTON FELDER / JAMES BURTON** – guitar / **TOM SCOTT** – wind

Asylum Asylum

Nov 72. (7") **YOU TURN ME ON, I'M A RADIO. / URGE FOR GOING** [ ] [25]

Dec 72. (lp)(c) **FOR THE ROSES** [ ] [11] Nov 72
– Banquet / Cold blue steel and sweet fire / Barangrill / Lesson in survival / Let the wind carry me / For the roses / See you sometime / Electricity / You turn me on, I'm a radio / Blonde in the bleachers / Woman of heart and mind / Judgement of the Moon and stars (Ludwig's tune). *(cd-iss.Dec87 on 'WEA')*

Mar 73. (7") **COLD BLUE STEEL AND SWEET FIRE. / BLONDE IN THE BLEACHERS** [ ] [-]

— Retained **TOM SCOTT's L.A.EXPRESS** with new boyfriend **JOHN GUERIN** – drums / **WILTON FELDER** – bass / **LARRY CARLTON** – guitar / **CHUCK FINDLEY** – trumpet / **JOE SAMPLE** – keyboards / **ROBBIE ROBERTSON** – guitar

Jan 74. (7") **RAISED ON ROBBERY. / COURT AND SPARK** [ ] [65] Dec 73

Mar 74. (lp)(c) **COURT AND SPARK** [14] [2] Feb 74
– Court and spark / Help me / Free man in Paris / People's parties / The same situation / Car on a hill / Down to you / Just like this train / People's parties / Raised on robbery / Trouble child. *(re-iss.Jun76) (cd-iss.May83)*

Mar 74. (7") **HELP ME. / JUST LIKE THIS TRAIN** [-] [7]

Jul 74. (7") **FREE MAN IN PARIS. / PEOPLE'S PARTIES** [-] [ ]

Oct 74. (7") **FREE MAN IN PARIS. / CAR ON A HILL** [ ] [-]

Jan 75. (7") **BIG YELLOW TAXI (live). / RAINY NIGHT HOUSE (live)** [ ] [24] Dec 74

Jan 75. (d-lp)(c) **MILES OF AISLES** [34] [2] Nov 74
– You turn me on, I'm a radio / Big yellow taxi / Rainy night house / Woodstock / Cactus tree / Cold blue steel and sweet fire / Woman of heart and mind / A case of you / The circle game / People's parties / All I want / Real good for free / Both sides now / Carey / The last time I saw Richard / Jericho / Love or money. *(cd-iss.1989, omits some dialogue)*

— (above also with **TOM SCOTT & THE L.A.EXPRESS;- SCOTT / GUERIN** plus **ROBBEN FORD** – guitar / **LARRY NASH** – piano / **MAX BENNETT** – bass

Nov 75. (lp)(c) **THE HISSING OF SUMMER LAWNS** [14] [4]
– In France they kiss on Main Street / The jungle line / Edith and the kingpin / Don't interrupt the sorrow / Shades of Scarlett conquering The hissing of summer lawns / The boho dance / Harry's house – Centerpiece / Sweet bird / Shadows and light. *(cd-iss.Nov87 on 'WEA')*

Mar 76. (7") **IN FRANCE THEY KISS ON MAIN STREET. / BOHO DANCE** [ ] [66] Feb 76

Nov 76. (lp)(c) **HEJIRA** [11] [13]
– Coyote / Amelia / Furry sings the blues / A strange boy / Hejira / Song for Sharon / Black crow / Blue motel room / Refuge of the roads. *(cd-iss.Oct87 on 'WEA')*

Feb 77. (7") **COYOTE. / BLUE MOTEL ROOM** [ ] [ ]

— now with **JACO PASTORIUS** – bass / **GLENN FREY** – vocals / **WAYNE SHORTER** – sax / **J.D.SOUTHER + CHAKA KHAN** – both backing vocals

Dec 77. (d-lp)(d-c) **DON JUAN'S RECKLESS DAUGHTER** [20] [25]
– Overture – Cotton Avenue / Talk to me / Jericho / Paprika plains / Otis and Marlena / The tenth world / Dreamland / Don Juan's reckless daughter / Off night backstreet / The silky veils of Ardor. *(cd-iss.1988)*

Feb 78. (7") **OFF NIGHT BACKSTREET. / JERICHO** [ ] [-]

Feb 78. (7") **JERICHO. / DREAMLAND** [-] [ ]

— now with **STANLEY CLARKE** – bass / **GERRY MULLIGAN** – / **JOHN McLAUGHLIN** – guitar / **JAN HAMMER** – keyboards

Jun 79. (7") **THE DRY CLEANER FROM DES MOINES. / GOD MUST BE A BOOGIE MAN** [ ] [ ]

Jul 79. (lp)(c) **MINGUS** [24] [17] Jun 79
– Happy birthday 1975 (rap) / God must be a boogie man / Funeral (rap) / A chair in the sky / The wolf that lives in Lindsey / I's a muggin' (rap) / Sweet sucker dance / Coin in the pocket (rap) / Lucky (rap) / Goodbye pork pie hat.

— now with **PAT METHENY** – lead guitar / **JACO PASTORIUS** – bass / **LYLE MAYS** – keys / **DON ALIAS** – drums / **MICHAEL BRECKER** – saxophone

Sep 80. (d-lp)(c) **SHADOWS AND LIGHT (live)** [63] [38]
– (introduction) / In France they kiss on Main Street / Edith and the kingpin / Coyote / Goodbye pork pie hat / The dry cleaner from Des Moines / Amelia / Pat's solo / Hejira / Black crow / Don's solo / Dreamland / Free man in Paris / (band introduction) / Furry sings the blues / Why do fools fall in love? / Shadows and light / God must be a boogie man / Woodstock.

Oct 80. (7") **WHY DO FOOLS FALL IN LOVE? (live). / BLACK CROW (live)** [ ] [ ]

— **LARRY KLEIN** – bass (she marries him Nov'82) / **LARRY WILLIAMS** – keyboards / **LARRY CARLTON / JOHN GUERIN / VICTOR FELDMAN /** etc.

Geffen Geffen

Nov 82. (7") **(YOU'RE SO SQUARE) BABY I DON'T CARE. / LOVE** [ ] [47]

Nov 82. (lp)(c) **WILD THINGS RUN FAST** [32] [25]
– Chinese cafe – Unchained melody / Wild things run fast / Ladies man / Moon at the window / Solid love / Be cool / (You're so square) Baby, I don't care / You dream flat tyres / Man to man / Underneath the streetlight / Love. *(cd-iss.Jul88)*

Feb 83. (7") **BE COOL. / UNDERNEATH THE STREETLIGHT** [-] [ ]

Feb 83. (7") **CHINESE CAFE. / LADIES MAN** [ ] [-]

Nov 85. (7") **GOOD FRIENDS. / SMOKIN' (EMPTY TRY ANOTHER)** [ ] [85]

— Above feat. guest duet **MICHAEL McDONALD**

— now with co-producer **THOMAS DOLBY** – synthesizers / etc.

Nov 85. (lp)(c) **DOG EAT DOG** [57] [63]
– Good friends / Fiction / Three great stimulants / Tax free / Smokin' (empty, try another) / Dog eat dog / Shiny toys / Ethiopia / Impossible dreamer / Lucky girl. *(re-iss.Oct87) (cd-iss.May86) (re-iss.cd+c Mar93)*

Apr 86. (7")(12") **SHINY TOYS. / THREE GREAT STIMULANTS** [ ] [ ]

— guests **THOMAS DOLBY, TOM PETTY, WILLIE NELSON, DON HENLEY, WENDY & LISA, BILLY IDOL, PETER GABRIEL, etc. KLEIN** co-produced, as was next

Mar 88. (lp)(c)(cd) **CHALK MARK IN A RAIN STORM** [26] [45]
– My secret place / Number one / Lakota / The tea leaf prophecy / Dancing clown / The beat of black wings / Snakes and ladders / The recurring dream / The bird that whistles. *(re-iss.Jan91) (re-iss.cd+c Mar93)*

Apr 88. (7") **MY SECRET PLACE. / LAKOTA** [-] [ ]

May 88. (7") **MY SECRET PLACE. / NUMBER ONE** [ ] [-]
(12"+=) – Chinese cafe / Good friends.

('A'featured **PETER GABRIEL**)

— retained **KLEIN** with band **VINNIE COLAIUTA** – drums / **ALEX ACUNA** – percussion / **WAYNE SHORTER** – saxophone / **BILL DILLON + MICHAEL LANDAU** – guitars

Mar 91. (cd)(c)(lp) **NIGHT RIDE HOME** [25] [41]
– Night ride home / Passion play (when all the slaves are free) / Cherokee Louise / The windfall (everything for nothing) / Slouching towards Bethlehem / Come in from the cold / Nothing can be done / The only joy in town / Ray's dad's cadillac / Two grey rooms.

Jul 91. (7") **COME IN FROM THE COLD. / RAY'S DAD'S CADILLAC** [ ] [ ]
(cd-s+=)(pic-cd-s+=) – ('A'extended).

Warners Warners

Oct 94. (cd)(c) **TURBULENT INDIGO** [53] [47]
– Sunny Sunday / Sex kills / The Magdalene laundries / Turbulent indigo / How do you stop / Last chance lost / Not to blame / Borderline / Yvette in English / The sire of sorrow (Job's sad song).

Nov 94. (c-s)(cd-s) **HOW DO YOU STOP / THE SIRE OF SORROW / MOON AT THE WINDOW** [ ] [ ]

– compilations, others, etc. –

May 74. Reprise; (7"ep) **CAREY / BOTH SIDES NOW. / BIG YELLOW TAXI / WOODSTOCK** [ ] [-]

Oct 82. Reprise; (d-c) **CLOUDS / BLUE** [ ] [-]

Jul 76. Asylum; (7") **YOU TURN ME ON, I'M A RADIO. / FREE MAN IN PARIS** [ ] [-]

Nov 83. Asylum; (d-c) **FOR THE ROSES / COURT AND SPARK** [ ] [-]

MOBY

Born: RICHARD MELVILLE HALL, 1967, New York, USA. After being raised by his middle-class mother, he joined hardcore outfit The VATICAN COMMANDOES, which led to him having a brief stint in similiar FLIPPER. He didn't record anything with them and moved back to New York to become a DJ, making hardcore techno/dance records under the guise of BRAINSTORM and UHF3, etc. Became mixer for The PET SHOP BOYS, ERASURE and MICHAEL JACKSON, before and during his return into solo work in the early 90's. • **Style:** As said. • **Songwriters:** Himself / samples including 'Twin Peaks' on 'GO'. Covered NEW DAWN FADES (Joy Division). • **Trivia:** In 1992 he remixed JAM & SPOON's club smash 'STELLA', which had sampled his 'GO'. He also provided vox for RECOIL's 1992 album 'Bloodline'. MOBY also remixed B-52's, ESKIMOS AND EGYPT, LFO, FORTRAN 5, ORBITAL, ENO, PET SHOP BOYS + The OTHER TWO.

Recommended: THE STORY SO FAR (*6) / EVERYTHING IS WRONG (*7)

MOBY – vocals, keyboards, etc.

Outer Rhythm / not issued

Jul 91. (12")(cd-s) **GO (analog mix). / ('A'night time mix)/ ('A'soundtrack mix)** [10] [ ]
(12") – ('A'side) / ('A'video aux w/ LYNCH & BADALAMENTI) / ('A'rain forest mix).
(cd-s) – ('A'side) / ('A'low spirit mix) / ('A'woodtick mix).

Mute Elektra?

Jun 93. (c-s) **I FEEL IT. / THOUSAND** [38] [ ]
(12")(cd-s) – (3-'A'mixes).

Aug 93. (cd)(c)(lp) **THE STORY SO FAR** (rel.on 'Equator')
Ah ah / I feel it / Everything / Help me to believe / Go (woodtick mix) / Yeah / Drop a beat (the new version) / Thousand / Slight return / Go (sublimal mix unedited version) / Stream. (cd+=) Mercy.

Sep 93. (c-s) **MOVE (YOU MAKE ME FEEL SO GOOD)./ ('A'disco threat mix)** 21
(12")(cd-s) – ('A'side) / ('A'subversion) / ('A'xtra mix) / ('A'-MK-Blades mix).
(cd-s) – ('A'side) / All that I need is to be loved / Unloved symphony / Rainfalls and the sky shudders.
(12") – (last track repl.by;) Morning dove.

Oct 93. (cd)(c)(lp) **AMBIENT** (rel.on 'Equator')
– My beautiful blue sky / Heaven / Tongues / J Breas / Myopia / House of blue leaves / Bad days / Piano & string / Sound / Dog / 80 / Lean on me.

Nov 93. (12") **ALL THAT I NEED IS TO BE LOVED. / (3 other 'A'mixes)** -

May 94. (c-s) **HYMN – THIS IS MY DREAM (extended). / ALL THAT I NEED IS TO BE LOVED (H.O.S. mix)** 31
(cd-s+=) – ('A'-European edit) / ('A'-Laurent Garnier mix).
(12") – ('A'extended) / ('A'-Laurent Garnier mix) / ('A'-Upriver mix)/ ('A'-Dirty hypo mix).
(cd-s) – Hymn (alternate quiet version 33 mins).

Sep 94. (c-s) **GO (woodtick mix). / ('A'-Low spirit mix)**
(12"+=) – ('A'-Voodoo chile mix).
(12"+=) – ('A'-Appathoski mix) / ('A'-Amphemetix mix).
(cd-s+=) – ('A'-Delirium mix).

Oct 94. (c-s) **FEELING SO REAL. / NEW DAWN FADES** 30
(cd-s+=) – ('A'-Unashamed ecstatic piano mix) / ('A'-Old skool mix).
(cd-s) – ('A'-Westbam remix) / ('A'-Ray Keith remix) / ('A'dub mix) / Everytime you touch me (remix parts).
(12") – ('A'side) / (4-'A'versions from cd's above).

Feb 95. (c-s) **EVERYTIME YOU TOUCH ME / THE BLUE LIGHT OF THE UNDERWATER SUN** 28
(cd-s+=) – ('A'-Beatmasters mix) / ('A'-competition winner; Jude Sebastian mix) / ('A'Freestyle mix).
(cd-s++=) – ('A'-Uplifting mix).
(12") – ('A'-Sound Factory mix) / ('A'-SF dub) / ('A'-Follow me mix) / ('A'-Tribal mix).

Mar 95. (cd)(c)(d-lp) **EVERYTHING IS WRONG** 21
– Hymn / Feeling so real / All that I need is to be loved / Let's go free / Everytime you touch me / Bring back my happiness / What love? / First cool hive / Into the blue / Anthem / Everything is wrong / God moving over the face of the waters / When it's cold I'd like to die. (cd w/free cd) Underwater (43.11 mins).

Jun 95. (c-s) **INTO THE BLUE / ('A'-Shining mix)** 34
(cd-s+=) – ('A'-Summer night mix) / ('A'-Beastmasters mix).
(12")(cd-s) – (other various mixes).
(12")(cd-s) – ('A'-Beastmasters mix) / ('A'-Jnr Vasquez mix) / ('A'-Phil Kelsey mix) / ('A'-Jon Spencer Blues mix).

MOBY GRAPE

Formed: San Franscisco, California, USA ... Sep'66 by former drummer of JEFFERSON AIRPLANE, turned guitarist SKIP SPENCE. He with manager instigator / manager MATTHEW KATZ, plus LEWIS and MOSELEY, brought in MILLER and STEVENSON, and signed to 'Columbia', where they launched debut 10 track eponymous lp, alongside 5 simultaneously issued A & B side 45's on May'67. The album went US Top 30, but 'Omaha' was their biggest 7", but with only a Top 100 placing. Their Top 20 follow-up in '68 'WOW', was complete with another gimmick sale point, in its free 'GRAPE JAM' lp. Early the next year, SPENCE left due to drug problems, and group went through various degrees of turmoil (see further below). • **Style:** Excellent live exponents of psychedelic West-coast rock and hype. • **Songwriters:** Group penned. • **Trivia:** Watch out for a track on the 'WOW' original lp, which plays ' 78 rpm, not now on most new record players.

Recommended: MOBY GRAPE (*8) / WOW (*6).

ALEXANDER 'SKIP' SPENCE (b.18 Apr'46, Canada) – vocals, guitar (ex-JEFFERSON AIRPLANE) / **PETER LEWIS** (b.15 Jul'45) – guitar, vocals (ex-CORNELLS) / **JERRY MILLER** (b.10 Jul'43) – guitar, vocals (ex-FRANTICS) / **BOB MOSELEY** (b. 4 Dec'42) – bass (ex-MISFITS) / **DON STEVENSON** (b.15 Oct'42) – drums (ex-FRANTICS) repl. KENT DUNBAR

C.B.S. Columbia

Mar 67. (7") **CHANGES. / FALL ON YOU** -
Mar 67. (7") **SITTING ON THE WINDOW. / INDIFFERENCE** -
Mar 67. (7") **8:05. / MISTER BLUES** -
Mar 67. (7") **OMAHA. / HEY GRANDMA** - 88
Mar 67. (7") **COME IN THE MORNIG. / HEY GRANDMA** -
(above 5 singles released simultaneously)

Jun 67. (lp) **MOBY GRAPE** 24
– Hey grandma / Mr. Blues / Fall on you / 8:05 / Come in the morning / Omaha / Naked, if I want to / Someday / Ain't no use / Sitting by the window / Changes / Lazy me / Indifference. *(re-iss.Sep84 on 'Edsel', cd-iss.Apr89)*

Jul 68. (lp) **WOW** 20 Apr 68
– Murder in my heart for the judge / Bitter wind / Can't be so bad / Three-four / The place and the time / Motorcycle Irene / Rose coloured eyes / Funky-tunk / Miller's blues / He / Just like Gene Autrey, a foxtrot / Naked, if I want to. (US +free live-lp) **GRAPE JAM** – Never / Boysenberry jam / Black currant jam / Marmalade / The lake.

— above featured AL KOOPER & MIKE BLOOMFIELD.

Jul 68. (7") **CAN'T BE SO BAD. / MURDER IN MY HEART FOR THE JUDGE** -
Jul 68. (7") **CAN'T BE SO BAD. / BITTER WIND** -

— SPENCE became drug addict, and left, going into hospital for 6 months. He went solo later in 1969, releasing OAR album (see further below).

Feb 69. (lp) **MOBY GRAPE '69**
– Ooh mama ooh / Ain't that a shame / I am not willing / It's a beautiful day today / Hoochie / Trucking man / If you can't learn from my mistakes / Captain Nemo / What's to choose / Going nowhere / Seeing. *(re-iss.Aug76)*

Feb 69. (7") **TRUCKING MAN. / IF YOU CAN'T LEARN FROM MY MISTAKES** -
Feb 69. (7") **TRUCKING MAN. / OOH MAMA OOH** -
Jun 69. (7") **OOH MAMA OOH. / IT'S SO BEAUTIFUL TODAY** -

— session man **BOB MOORE** – bass repl. MOSLEY who joined the US marines.

Sep 69. (lp) **TRULY FINE CITIZEN**
– Changes, circles spinning / Looper / Truly fine citizen / Beautiful is beautiful / Love song / Right before my eyes / Open up your heart / Now I know high / Treat me bad / Tongue-tied / Love song (part 2).

— MOBY GRAPE had already split Spring 1969. For nearly 2 years, MILLER and STEVENSON joined The RHYTHM DUKES. Original quintet re-formed with newcomer **GORDON STEVENS** – viola, mandolin

Reprise Reprise

Sep 71. (lp)(c) **20 GRANITE CREEK**
– Gypsy wedding / I'm the kind of man that baby you can trust / About time / Goin' down to Texas / Road to the Sun / Apocalypse / Chinese song / Roadhouse blues / Ode to the man at the end of the bar / Wild oats moan / Horse out in the rain. *(re-iss.+May86 on 'Edsel')*

Sep 71. (7") **GYPSY WEDDING. / APOCAYPSE** -
Nov 71. (7") **GOIN' DOWN TO TEXAS. / ABOUT TIME** -
Jul 72. (7") **GONE FISHING. / GYPSY WEDDING** -

— In the early 70's, their manager Matthew Katz had put together a fake **MOBY GRAPE** with **FRANK RECARD** – vocals, guitar / **TOMMY SPURLOCK** – guitar / **DANNY TIMMS** – keyboards / **BOB NEWKIRK** – drums. BOB MOSLEY had gone solo Mar'72 releasing eponymous album on 'Warner Bros.'. The real MOBY GRAPE re-formed late 1973-Spring'75 with **LEWIS, MILLER, MOSLEY,** plus **JEFF BLACKBURN** – guitar + JOHN CRAVIOTTA – drums. With no new record deal, they broke again and **LEWIS, MILLER, CRAVIOTTA** and **MICHAEL BEAN** – guitar (ex-HP LOVECRAFT) formed **FINE WINE**. They issued one eponymous album in Germany mid'75. With NEIL YOUNG; MOSLEY, CRAVIOTTA and BLACKBURN formed the shortly defunct DUCKS (mid'77).

— **MOBY GRAPE** re-formed again, this time with **SKIP SPENCE** returning with **MILLER + LEWIS**, plus newboys **CORNELIUS BUMPUS** – keyboards / **CHRISTIAN POWELL** – bass / **JOHN OXENDINE** – drums

not issued Escape

Apr 78. (lp) **LIVE GRAPE (live)** -
– The last horizon / Here I sit / Honk tonk / Cuttin' in / Must be goin' now dear / Your rider / Up in the air / Set me down easy / Love you so much / You got everything I need. *(UK-iss.Jun87 on 'Line')*

— Finally let go around the late 70's. They reformed mid 1990 as The LEGENDARY GRAPE.

– compilations, others, etc. –

Jun 74. Columbia; (lp)(c) **GREAT GRAPE**
Jun 76. Columbia; (lp) **THE BEST OF MOBY GRAPE** -
Feb 85. Edsel; (lp) **MURDER IN MY HEART** (2nd-4th lp's) -
– Murder in my heart for the judge / He / Can't be so bad / Motorcycle Irene / Three-four / Rose coloured eyes / Bitter wind / I am not willing / It's a beautiful day today / If you can't learn from my mistakes / What's to choose / Seeing / Changes, circles spinning / Right before my eyes.
Nov 93. Legacy; (d-cd) **VINTAGE / THE VERY BEST OF** -

ALEXANDER SPENCE

solo (all instruments)

not issued Columbia

Oct 69. (lp) **OAR** -
– Little hands / Cripple creek / Diana / Margaret – Tiger rug / Weighted down (the prison song) / War in peace / Broken heart / All come to meet her / Book of Moses / Dixie peach promenade / Lawrence of Euphoria / Grey / Afro. *(UK-iss. Sep88 on 'Edsel')*

MOCK TURTLES

Formed: Manchester, England ... late 1986 by COOGAN. Earlier in 1985, as JUDGE HAPPINESS they had won a Manchester Bands competition and released one single. After becoming The MOCK TURTLES they were signed to indie label 'Imaginary' by Alan Duffy. Struggled for a while, until their breakthrough in 1991 with CAN U DIG IT? for 'Siren' records. • **Style:** Jangly 60's type psychedelia, influenced by BYRDS to BE-BOP DELUXE or even The MONKEES. • **Songwriters:** COOGAN wrote all, except covers PALE BLUE EYES (Velvet Underground) / ARE YOU EXPERIENCED? (Jimi Hendrix) / NO GOOD TRYING (Syd Barrett) / THE WILLOW SONG (from the film 'The Wicker Man'). • **Trivia:** MARTIN GLYN MURRAY is an actor and appeared in the TV soap 'Families'.

Recommended: 87-90 (*8) / TURTLE SOUP (*7)

JUDGE HAPPINESS

MARTIN COOGAN – vocals, guitar / **KRZYSZTOF KORAB** – keyboards / **STEVE GREEN** – bass / **STEVE COWAN** – drums

Mynah not issued

1985. (7") **HEY JUDGE. / PIG IN PINK** -

MOCK TURTLES

added **MARTIN GLYN MURRAY** – guitar

Imaginary / not issued

Jun 87. (12"ep) **POMONA** [ ] [-]
– John O'War / Bathing in blue / Mary's garden / Watching the waning moon.

May 89. (12"m) **WICKER MAN / THE WILLOW SONG. / ANOTHER JESUS WALKS ON WATER / FIONNUALA** [ ] [-]

— **ANDREW STEPHENSON** – bass, viola, violin repl. GREEN

Nov 89. (12"m) **AND THEN SHE SMILES. / CALM BEFORE THE STORM / SHANGRI-LA** [ ] [-]

— **JOANNE GENT** – keyboards repl. KORAB

Apr 90. (12")(cd-s) **LAY ME DOWN. / CAN U DIG IT?** [ ] [-]

May 90. (cd)(lp) **TURTLE SOUP** [ ] [-]
– Kathy come home / Head run wild / Lay me down / Another Jesus walks on water / Oh Helen how? / How does it feel? / And then she smiles / The willow song / Mary's garden / Can you dig it? / Wicker man. *(re-dist.May91, hit No.54)*

Oct 90. (7") **MAGIC BOOMERANG. / TAKE YOUR TIME** [ ] [-]
(12"+=)(cd-s+=) – ('A'version).

Mar 91. (cd)(c)(lp) **87-90** (rare singles + demo for the label) [ ] [-]

Siren / Virgin

Mar 91. (7")(c-s) **CAN U DIG IT. / LOSE YOURSELF** [18] [ ]
(12"+=)(cd-s+=) – Lay me down (live) / ('A' yeah version).

Jun 91. (7") **AND THEN SHE SMILES. / ANOTHER JESUS WALKS ON WATER (live)** [44] [ ]
(12"+=)(cd-s+=) – How does it feel (live).

Jul 91. (cd)(c)(lp) **TWO SIDES** [33] [ ]
– Strings and flowers / And then she smiles / Shine on me / Baby and the stars / Words of wisdom / Pearls for my girl / Brush of a butterfly's wing / Can u dig it? / You move me / Deep down / Why must I share this air with foolish men?

Sep 91. (7")(c-s) **STRINGS AND FLOWERS. / SHE TOLD ME** [ ] [ ]
(12"+=) – ('A' Steve Proctor mix).
(cd-s++=) – Deep down (remix).

— Re-formed in the mid-90's as UGLI.

MODERN LOVERS (see under ⇒ RICHMAN, Jonathan)

MOIST

Formed: Canada . . . 1993 by DAVID USHER, etc (see below). Late in 1994, they exploded onto the music scene with MTV-loved 'SILVER' album, which easily surpassed that award, when selling over a quarter a million copies worldwide. • **Style:** Mix hard LED ZEPPELIN-esque rock with R.E.M. harmonies and stadium U2-like sound. • **Songwriters:** USHER and group.

Recommended: SILVER (*6)

DAVID USHER – vocals/ **MARK MAKOWY** – guitar / **KEVIN YOUNG** – keyboards / **JEFF PEARCE** – bass, vocals / **PAUL WILCOX** – drums

Chrysalis / Chrysalis

Nov 94. (c-s) **PUSH / MACHINE PUNCH THROUGH** [ ] [ ]
(cd-s+=) – Morphine.

Nov 94. (cd)(c) **SILVER** [35] [ ]
– Push / Believe me / Kill for you / Silver / Freaky be beautiful / Break her down / Into everything / Picture Elvis / Machine punch through / This shrieking love / Low low low.

Feb 95. (c-s) **SILVER / BREAK HER DOWN** [50] [ ]
(12"clear+=) – Kid conductor.
(cd-s+=) – See touch feel.

Apr 95. (12") **FREAKY BE BEAUTIFUL. / KILL FOR YOU** [47] [ ]
(c-s+=) – Push (acoustic).
(cd-s++=) – Picture Elvis (acoustic).

Aug 95. (7"purple)(c-s) **PUSH. / MISS YOU** [20] [ ]
(cd-s) – ('A'side) / Machine punch through / This shrieking love / Low low low.
(cd-s) – ('A'side) / ('A'-Youth mix) / ('A'-other mix).

MOLLY HATCHET

Formed: Jacksonville, Florida, USA . . . 1971 by HLUBECK and HOLLAND. Took years to find major label 'Epic' in 1976. By that time BANNER THOMAS in '73, BRUCE CRUMP in '75, DANNY JOE BROWN and DUANE ROLAND had completed line-up. • **Style:** Heavy metal Southern boogie much in the mould of LYNYRD SKYNYRD or ZZ TOP. • **Songwriters:** Group compositions except LONG TALL SALLY (Little Richard) / I AIN'T GOT YOU (Yardbirds; b-side) / LET THE GOOD TIMES ROLL (Shirley & Lee) / HIDE YOUR HEART (Kiss). • **Trivia:** The group name was taken from a 17th century Salem woman who chopped off her lover's head.

Recommended: DOUBLE TROUBLE (*5)

DANNY JOE BROWN (b.1951) – vocals (ex-RUM CREEK) / **STEVE HOLLAND** (b.1954, Dotham, Alabama) – lead guitar (ex-ICE) / **DAVE HLUBECK** (b.1952) – guitar / **DUANE ROLAND** (b. 3 Dec'52, Jefferson) – guitar / **BANNER THOMAS** – bass / **BRUCE CRUMP** – drums

Epic / Epic

Nov 78. (7") **DREAMS I'LL NEVER SEE. / THE CREEPER** [-] [ ]

May 79. (lp)(c) **MOLLY HATCHET** [ ] [64] Oct 78
– Bounty hunter / Gator country / Big apple / The creeper / The price you pay / Dreams I'll never see / I'll be running / Cheatin' woman / Trust your old friend. *(cd-iss.Jul93 on 'Sony Europe')*

Aug 79. (7") **JUKIN' CITY. / GUNSMOKE** [-] [ ]

Oct 79. (lp)(c) **FLIRTIN' WITH DISASTER** [ ] [19] Sep 79
– Whiskey man / It's all over now / One man's pleasure / Jukin' City / Boogie no more / Flirtin' with disaster / Good rockin' / Gunsmoke / Long time / Let the good times roll. *(also iss.US pic-lp) (cd-iss.Jul93 on 'Sony Europe')*

Oct 79. (7") **IT'S ALL OVER NOW. / GOOD ROCKIN'** [-] [ ]

Feb 80. (7") **FLIRTIN' WITH DISASTER. / GUNSMOKE** [ ] [42] Dec 79

May 80. (7") **BOOGIE NO MORE. / BOUNTY HUNTER** [ ] [ ]
(12"+=) – Flirtin' with disaster.

— **JIMMY FARRAR** – vocals repl. DANNY JOE who released solo album summer '81

Sep 80. (7") **BEATIN' THE ODS. / FEW AND FAR BETWEEN** [-] [ ]

Oct 80. (lp)(c) **BEATIN' THE ODDS** [ ] [25] Sep 80
– Beatin' the odds / Penthouse pauper / Far and few between / Dead and gone / The rambler / Double talker / Poison pen / Sailor / Get her back.

Mar 81. (7") **THE RAMBLER. / GET HER BACK** [-] [91]

Dec 81. (lp)(c) **TAKE NO PRISONERS** [ ] [36]
– Bloody reunion / Respect me in the morning / Long tall Sally / Loss of control / All mine / Lady luck / Power play / Don't mess around / Don't leave me lonely / Dead giveaway.

Jan 82. (7") **POWER PLAY. / BLOODY REUNION** [-] [96]

Apr 82. (7") **LOSS OF CONTROL. / LADY LUCK** [-] [ ]

Oct 82. (7") **DREAMS I'LL NEVER SEE. / FLIRTIN' WITH DISASTER** [-] [ ]

— **DANNY JOE BROWN** – vocals returned to repl. FARRAR / **B.B. QUEEN** (b.BARRY BORDEN) – drums (ex-MOTHER'S FINEST) repl. CRUMP / added **JIMMY GALVIN** – keyboards / **RIFF WEST** (b. 3 Apr'50, Ortando, Florida) – bass repl. THOMAS

Mar 83. (lp)(c) **NO GUTS . . .NO GLORY** [ ] [59]
– Fall of the peacemakers / Under the gun / On the prowl / Both sides / Ain't even close / What's it gonna take / What does it matter / Kinda like love / Sweet Dixie. *(re-iss.Feb86)*

Apr 83. (7") **SWEET DIXIE. / KINDA LIKE LOVE** [-] [ ]

— **BRUCE CRUMP** – drums returned to repl. QUEEN who joined ILLUSION

Jan 85. (lp)(c) **THE DEED IS DONE** [ ] [ ] Nov 84
– Satisfied man / Backstabber / She does she does / (intro piece) / Stone in your heart / Man on the run / Good smoke and whiskey / Heartbreak radio / I ain't got you / Straight shooter / Song for the children. *(cd-iss.Oct93 on 'Sony Collectors')*

Jan 85. (7")(12") **SATISFIED MAN. / STRAIGHT SHOOTER** [ ] [81] Oct84

Mar 85. (7") **MAN ON THE RUN. / STONE IN YOUR HEART** [-] [ ]

Jan 86. (d-lp)(d-c) **DOUBLE TROUBLE LIVE (live)** [94] [ ] Dec 85
– Whiskey man / Bounty hunter / Gator country / Flirtin' with disaster / Stone in your heart / Satisfied / Bloody reunion / Boogie no more / Walk on the side of angels / Walk with you / Dreams I'll never see / Edge of sundown / Fall of the peacemakers / Beatin' the odds.

— Disbanded when BROWN suffered diabetic problems. Re-formed again in '88.

— **BOBBY INGRAM** – guitar, vocals repl. HLUBEK

Capitol / Capitol

1989. (lp)(c)(cd) **LIGHTNING STRIKES TWICE** [ ] [ ]
– Take Miss Lucy home / There goes the neighborhood / No room on the crew / Find somebody new / The big payback / I can't be watching you / Goodbye to love / Hide your heart / What's the story, old glory / Heart of my soul.

– compilations, others, etc. –

Dec 90. Epic; (cd)(c)(lp) **GREATEST HITS** [ ] [ ]

MONKEES

Formed: The brainchild of Hollywood TV producers BOB RAFELSON and BERT SCHNEIDER in 1965, who wanted to make a US sit-com based around BEATLES' film 'A Hard Day's Night'. On Sep'65, they ran a wanted ad for 4 boys aged between 17-21. Out of over 400, they picked DAVY JONES, MICKEY DOLENZ, MIKE NESMITH & PETER TORK, signing them to 'Colpix' label. All had fairly noted previous experience (see below), and were sent for acting and grooming lessons early '66. After failure on songwriting front, BOB & BERT brought in pensmiths TOMMY BOYCE and BOBBY HART who also became producers, on appointment from 'Screen Gems' top man Don Kirshner. Other writers were brought in, mainly NEIL DIAMOND, GERRY GOFFIN & CAROLE KING, NEIL SEDAKA plus BARRY MANN & CYNTHIA WEIL. On 12 Sep'66, "The MONKEES" TV show premiered on NBC, and although not an overnight success, became a teenage favourite. A month later, their debut 45 'LAST TRAIN TO CLARKSVILLE' was released and it soon climbed to US No.1. Their follow-up 'I'M A BELIEVER' (penned by NEIL DIAMOND), also hit the top, and with show now on BBC TV, it soared to No.1 in Britain. Another DIAMOND composition 'A LITTLE BIT ME, A LITTLE BIT YOU', made both Top 3's in Mar'67, with two of their lp's, having earlier both hit cross-Atlantic peak spots. They carried on with more shows and massive hits, until the late 60's, when their series had been axed. They had by this time gone into movies, and made box-office disaster 'HEAD' with writers BOB RAFELSON and JACK NICHOLSON (yes that one!). • **Style:** Like The BEATLES, a pop phenomenon, whose bubblegum-psychedelia records have long-since become both cult & sing-a-long standards. • **Songwriters:** As said, until NESMITH took more of a controlling hand in the late 60's. They also covered; DAYDREAM BELIEVER (John Sebastian) / D.W.WASHBURN (Leiber-Stoller) / etc. • **Trivia:** In 1967, their 'RANDY SCOUSE GIT' (taken from character Alf Garnett 'Til Death Us Do Part' UK TV sit-com) was banned by the BBC, and later given 'ALTERNATIVE TITLE' motif. That year they recorded last TV series with guests FRANK ZAPPA and TIM BUCKLEY.

Recommended: HEY HEY IT'S THE MONKEES – GREATEST HITS (*7)

DAVY JONES (b.30 Dec'46, Manchester, England) – vocals, rhythm guitar (ex-apprentice jockey, actor UK TV 'Coronation Street' & 'Z Cars' / solo artist) / **MICKEY DOLENZ**

(b.GEORGE MICHAEL DOLENZ JR., 8 Mar'45, L.A., California, USA) – drums, vocals (child actor 'Circus Boy' as Corky, 'Peyton Place', etc.) / **MIKE NESMITH** (b.ROBERT MICHAEL NESMITH, 30 Dec'42, Houston, Texas, USA) – guitar, vocals (ex-folk solo act as MICHAEL BLESSING on 'Colpix' label) / **PETER TORK** (b.PETER THORKELSON, 13 Feb'44, Washington DC, USA) – bass, vocals (ex-AU GO GO SINGERS with RICHIE FURAY / recommended by STEPHEN STILLS)
Session men on discs were; JAMES BURTON, GLEN CAMPBELL, LEON RUSSELL, HAL BLAINE + DAVID GATES.

R.C.A. / Colgems

Oct 66. (7") **LAST TRAIN TO CLARKSVILLE. / TAKE A GIANT STEP** [ ] [1] Sep 66
— (late Jan67 – debut single hit UK No.23)
Dec 66. (7") **I'M A BELIEVER. / I'M NOT YOUR STEPPING STONE** [1] [1] [20]
Jan 67. (lp) **THE MONKEES** [1] [1] Oct 66
– Theme from The Monkees / Saturday's child / I wanna be free / Tomorrow's gonna be another day / Papa Gene's blues / Take a giant step / Last train to Clarksville / This just doesn't seem to be my day / Let's dance on / I'll be true to you / Sweet young thing / Gonna buy me a dog. *(cd-iss.Apr88 on 'Arista') (re-iss.+cd Aug'86 on 'Rhino', hit US No.92) (cd-iss.Dec94 on 'Rhino')*
Mar 67. (7") **A LITTLE BIT OF ME, A LITTLE BIT OF YOU. / THE GIRL I KNEW SOMEWHERE** [3] [2] [39]
Apr 67. (lp) **MORE OF THE MONKEES** [1] [1] Feb 67
– When love comes knockin' (at your door) / She / Mary, Mary / Hold on girl / Your Auntie Grizelda / (I'm not you) Steppin' stone / Look out (here comes tomorrow) / The kind of girl I could love / The day we fell in love / Sometime in the morning / Laugh / I'm a believer. *(cd-iss.Jun88 on 'Arista') (re-iss.+cd Aug'86 on 'Rhino', hit US 96) (cd-iss.Dec94 on 'Rhino')*
Jun 67. (7") **ALTERNATIVE TITLE ('Randy Scouse Git'). / FORGET THAT GIRL** [2] [-]
Jul 67. (lp) **HEADQUARTERS** [2] [1] Jun 67
– You told me / I'll spend my life with you / Forget that girl / Band 6 / You just may be the one / Shades of grey / I can't get her off my mind / For Pete's sake / Mr. Webster / Sunny girlfriend / Zilch / No time / Early morning blues and greens / Randy Scouse git. *(US re-iss.+cd Aug'86 on 'Rhino') (cd-iss.Feb95 on 'WEA Int.')*
Jul 67. (7") **PLEASANT VALLEY SUNDAY. / WORDS** [11] [3] [11]
Nov 67. (7") **DAYDREAM BELIEVER. / GOING DOWN** [5] [1]
Jan 68. (lp) **PISCES, AQUARIUS, CAPRICORN AND JONES LTD.** [5] [1] Nov 67
– Salesman / She hangs out / The door into summer / Love is only sleeping / Cuddly toy / Words / Hard to believe / What am I doing hangin' round? / Peter Percival Patterson's pet pig Porky / Pleasant Valley Sunday / Daily nightly / Don't call on me / Star collector. *(cd-iss.Feb95 on 'WEA Int.')*
Mar 68. (7") **VALLERI. / TAPIOCA TUNDRA** [12] [3] [34]
May 68. (lp) **THE BIRDS, THE BEES & THE MONKEES** [ ] [3]
– Dream world / Auntie's municipal court / We were made for each other / Tapioca tundra / Daydream believer / Writing wrongs / I'll be back on my feet / The poster / P.O.box 9847 / Magnolia Simms / Valleri / Zor and Zam. *(US re-iss.+cd Aug'86 on 'Rhino') (cd-iss.Dec94 on 'Rhino')*
Jun 68. (7") **D.W.WASHBURN. / IT'S NICE TO BE WITH YOU** [17] [19] [51]
Sep 68. (7") **PORPOISE SONG. / AS WE GO ALONG** [-] [62]
— now down to trio when TORK departed. (he still appeared on below s/track)
Mar 69. (7") **TEARDROP CITY. / A MAN WITHOUT A DREAM** [46] [56] Feb 69
May 69. (lp) **INSTANT REPLAY** [ ] [32] Feb 69
– Through the looking glass / Don't listen to Linda / I won't be the same without her / Me without you / Just a game / Don't wait for me / You and I / While I cry / Teardrop city / The girl I left behind me / Man without a dream / Shorty Blackwell. *(cd-iss.Feb95 on 'WEA Int.')*
Jun 69. (7") **SOMEDAY MAN. / LISTEN TO THE BAND** [47] [81] [63]
Aug 69. (7") **DADDY'S SONG. / THE PORPOISE SONG** [ ] [ ]
Sep 69. (lp) **HEAD (Soundtrack)** [ ] [45] Dec 68
– Opening ceremony / Porpoise song / Ditty Diego-war chant / Circle sky / Supplicio / Can you dig it / Gravy / Superstitious / As we go along / Dandruff / Daddy's song / Poll / Long title: Do I have to do this all over again / Swami-plus strings. *(cd-iss.Sep93 on 'Lightning') (cd-iss.Dec94 on 'Rhino')*
Sep 69. (7") **GOOD CLEAN FUN. / MOMMY AND DADDY** [ ] [82]
Oct 69. (lp) **THE MONKEES PRESENT . . .** [-] [100]
– Little girl / Good clean fun / If I knew / Bye bye baby bye bye / Never tell a woman yes / Looking for the good times / Ladies Aid Society / Listen to the band / French song / Mommy and daddy / Oklahoma backroom dancer / Pillow time. *(cd-iss.Dec94 on 'Rhino')*
— now down to **JONES + DOLENZ** duo when NESMITH left to go solo.
Jun 70. (7") **OH MY MY. / LOVE YOU BETTER** [ ] [98]
1970. (lp) **CHANGES** [-] [ ]
– Oh my my / Ticket on a ferry ride / You're so good to me / It's got to be love / Acapulco sun / 99 pounds / Tell me love / Do you feel it too / I love you better / All alone in the dark / Midnight train / I never thought it peculiar. *(US re-iss+cd Aug 86 on 'Rhino') (cd-iss.Dec94 on 'Rhino')*

DOLENZ AND JONES

not issued / Bell

Apr 71. (7") **DO IT IN THE NAME OF LOVE. / LADY JANE** [-] [ ]
— After short solo careers DOLENZ and JONES reformed

DOLENZ, JONES, BOYCE & HART

recruited new members **TOMMY BOYCE** – guitar, (past and present co-songwriter) **BOBBY HART** – bass, (past and present co-songwriter)

not issued / Capitol

Apr 76. (lp) **DOLENZ, JONES, BOYCE AND HART** [-] [ ]
1976. (7") **I REMEMBER THE FEELING. / YOU AND I** [-] [ ]
1976. (7") **I LOVE YOU (AND I'M GLAD I SAID IT). / SAVIN' MY LOVE FOR YOU** [-] [ ]

DOLENZ AND JONES

M.C.A. / M.C.A.

Jan 78. (lp) **THE POINT (Soundtrack)** [ ] [ ]
1978. (7") **LIFE LINE. / IT'S A JUNGLE OUT THERE. / GOTTA GET UP** [ ] [ ]
— They finally split shortly after The Point. DOLENZ went into children's TV productions noteably writing 'Metal Mickey'. In 1985 The MONKEES reformed with DOLENZ, JONES and TORK and session people.

Arista / Arista

Oct 86. (7") **THAT WAS THEN, THIS IS NOW. / THEME FROM THE MONKEES** [68] [20] Jul 86
(12"+=) – Pleasant valley Sunday / Last train to Clarksville.
Oct 86. (lp)(c)(cd) **THEN & NOW . . . THE BEST OF THE MONKEES** [ ] [21] Jul 86
(w/ 3 new)
– Then and now / Tripwire / Theme from The Monkees / Last train to Clarksville / Take a giant step / I'm a believer / I'm not your stepping stone / A little bit me, a little you / Anytime, anyplace, anywhere / That was then, this is now / The girl I knew somewhere / Pleasant valley Sunday / What am I doing hangin' 'round / Daydream believer / Valeri / Kicks.
Oct 86. (7") **DAYDREAM BELIEVER. / RANDY SCOUSE GIT** [-] [79]

Rhino / Rhino

Aug 87. (7") **HEART AND SOUL. / M.G.B.G.T.** [ ] [87]
Aug 87. (lp) **POOL IT!** [ ] [72]
– Heart and soul / (I'd go the) Whole wide world / Long way home / Secret heart / Gettin' in / (I'll) Love you forever / Every step of the way / Don't bring me down / Midnight / She's movin' in with Rico / Since you went away / Counting on you. *(cd-iss.Nov95)*
Nov 87. (7") **EVERY STEP OF THE WAY. / I LOVE YOU FOREVER** [-] [ ]

– other compilations, etc. –

Jun 69. Colgems; (lp) **GREATEST HITS** [-] [89]
1971. Colgems; (lp) **GOLDEN HITS** [-] [ ]
1972. Colgems; (lp) **BARREL FULL OF MONKEES** [-] [ ]
1973. Laurie H..; (d-lp) **THE MONKEES** [-] [ ]
1974. Bell; (lp) **RE-FOCUS** [-] [ ]
May 74. Bell; (7") **I'M A BELIEVER. / MONKEES THEME** [ ] [ ]
Sep 74. M.F.P.; (lp)(c) **THE MONKEES** [ ] [-]
Jun 81. M.F.P.; (lp)(c) **THE BEST OF THE MONKEES** [ ] [-]
Aug 76. Arista; (lp)(c) **THE MONKEES' GREATEST HITS** [-] [58]
Feb 80. Arista; (7"ep) **THE MONKEES** [33] [ ]
– Daydream believer / Last train to Clarksville / I'm a believer / A little bit me, a little bit you.
Jun 81. Arista; (7"ep) **THE MONKEES VOL.2** [ ] [ ]
– I'm not your stepping stone / Pleasant valley Sunday / Alternative title (Randy Scouse git) / What am I doing.
Jun 81. Arista; (lp)(c) **THE MONKEES** [99] [ ]
Aug 82. Arista; (7"ep) **I'M A BELIEVER / DON'T LISTEN TO LINDA / LAST TRAIN TO CLARKSVILLE / THEME FROM THE MONKEES** [ ] [ ]
Mar 89. Arista; (7"ep) **HEY HEY IT'S THE MONKEES** [62] [ ]
– Daydream believer / A little bit me, a little bit you / Theme from The Monkees.
Apr 89. Arista; (7"ep) **EP 2** [ ] [ ]
– Last train to Clarksville / I'm a believer / Pleasant valley Sunday.
Jul 82. Old Gold; (7") **DAYDREAM BELIEVER. / LAST TRAIN TO CLARKSVILLE** [ ] [-]
Oct 82. Ronco; (lp)(c) **20 GOLDEN GREATS** [ ] [-]
Jun 84. Scoop; (7"ep)(c-ep) **6 TRACK HITS** [ ] [-]
– I'm a believer / Valleri / Alternative title (Randy Scouse git) / Somebody . . . / A little bit you, a little bit me / Pleasant valley Sunday.
Jul 84. Rhino; (lp) **MONKEE FLIPS** [-] [ ]
1984. Rhino; (lp)(pic-lp) **MONKEE BUSINESS** [-] [ ]
Oct 87. Rhino; (lp) **MISSING LINKS(rare)** [-] [ ]
Oct 87. Rhino; (lp)(c)(cd) **LIVE 1967 (live)** [-] [ ]
Nov 84. Platinum; (lp)(c) **THE MONKEES' GREATEST HITS** [ ] [-]
Oct 87. Missing Link; (lp)(c)(cd) **THAT WAS THEN . . .** [ ] [-]
Apr 89. K-Tel; (lp)(c)(cd) **HEY HEY IT'S THE MONKEES – GREATEST HITS** [12] [-]
– Theme from The Monkees / Pleasant valley Sunday / The girl I knew somewhere / D.W. Washburn / Last train to Clarksville / A little bit me, a little bit you / teardrop city / Some day man / What am I doing hangin' 'round / Daydream believer / I'm not your stepping stone / Alternative title (randy scouse git) / Words / I'm a believer / Listen to the band / Valeri / Tapioca tundra / That was then, this is now.
Apr 94. Movieplay Gold; (cd)(c) **GREATEST HITS** [ ] [-]

MICKEY DOLENZ

A & M / A & M

Jun 83. (7") **TOMORROW. / FAT SAM** [ ] [ ]

MONOCHROME SET

Formed: London, England . . . early 1978 by BID, LESTER and ANDY WARREN, all out of The B-SIDES, who changed their name to ADAM & THE ANTS!, although WARREN stayed with them until 1979. Signed to 'Rough Trade' in 1978, and released 3 excellent singles during 1979. Early in 1980, they moved to Virgin subsidiary 'DinDisc', where their debut album 'STRANGE BOUTIQUE' nearly dented the UK Top 60. They released a few more albums, although they split not for the first time in 1983. Eleven years on, BID, LESTER and ANDY were still going strong after releasing a new 1994 'Cherry Red' album 'MISERIE'. • **Style:** Quirky eclectic rock /pop, featuring the vox of BID (the alternative JAKE THACKARY). • **Songwriters:**

Most by BID.

Recommended: VOLUME, BRILLIANCE, CONTRAST (*7)

BID (b. J.BIVOUAC – ???) – vocals, guitar / **LESTER SQUARE** – lead guitar, vocals (ex-ADAM & THE ANTS, ex-B-SIDES) / **JEREMY HARRINGTON** – bass, percussion (ex-GLORIA MUNDI and MEAN STREET) repl. SIMON CROFT who had replaced CHARLIE / **J.D. HANEY** – drums (ex-ART ATTACKS) / plus 5th member **TONY POTTS** – visuals

Rough Trade I.R.S.

Dec 78. (7") **ALPHAVILLE. / HE'S FRANK (SLIGHT RETURN)** [ ] [-]
Apr 79. (7") **EINE SYMPHONIE DES GRAUENS. / LESTER LEAPS IN** [ ] [-]
Sep 79. (7") **THE MONOCHROME SET (I PRESSUME). / MR.BIZARRO** [ ] [-]

Disques Bleu not issued

Dec 79. (7") **HE'S FRANK. / SILICON CARNE / FALLOUT (all live)** [-] [-] France

— **ANDY WARREN** – bass (ex-ADAM & THE ANTS, ex-B SIDES) repl. JEREMY

Dindisc not issued

Apr 80. (7") **STRANGE BOUTIQUE. / SURFING S.W.12** [ ] [-]
Apr 80. (lp)(c) **STRANGE BOUTIQUE** [62] [-]
– The Monochrome Set (I pressume) / Expresso / The Puertol Rican fence climber / Martians go home / Love goes down the drain / Ici les enfants / The ecetera stroll / Goodbye Joe / Strange boutique / The lighter side of dating / Tomorrow will be too long. *(re-iss.Mar84 on 'Virgin')*
Jun 80. (7") **405 LINES. / GOODBYE JOE** [ ] [-]
Oct 80. (7") **APOCALYPSO. / FIASCO BONGO** [ ] [-]
Oct 80. (lp)(c) **LOVE ZOMBIES** [ ] [-]
– Apocalypso / Adesta fiedes / Love zombies / 405 lines / Kama Sutra / B.I.D. spells Bid / R.S.V.P. / The man with the black moustache / In love, cancer? / The weird, wild and wonderful world of Tony Potts. *(re-iss.Mar84 on 'Virgin')*

Pre-Charisma not issued

Jul 81. (7") **TEN DON'TS FOR HONEYMOONERS. / STRAITS OF MALACCA** [ ] [-]

— **LEXINGTON CRANE** – drums repl. HANEY

Cherry Red not issued

Jul 82. (7") **THE MATING GAME. / J.D.H.A.N.E.Y.** [ ] [-]
Aug 82. (lp) **ELIGIBLE BACHELORS** [ ] [-]
– The jet-set junta / The mating game / Cloud 10 / The ruling class / The great barrier reef / I'll cry instead / Fun for all the family / The Devil rides out / On the 13th day / March of the eligible bachelors. *(re-iss.+cd May91)*

— **CARRIE BOOTH** – keyboards (ex-THOMPSON TWINS) repl. LESTER who went solo

— **MORRIS WINDSOR** – drums (ex-SOFT BOYS) repl. LEXINGTON

Oct 82. (7") **CAST A LONG SHADOW. / THE BRIDGE** [ ] [-]
May 83. (7") **THE JET-SET JUNTA. / LOVE GOES DOWN THE DRAIN / NOISE** [ ] [-]
May 83. (lp) **VOLUME! BRILLIANCE! CONTRAST!** (compilation) [ ] [-]
– Eine symphonie des grauens / The jet-set junta / Love zombies / Silicon Carne / The ruling class / Viva death row / The man with the black moustache / He's Frank (slight return) / Fun for all the family / Lester leaps in / Ici les enfants / Fat fun / Alphaville / Avanti. *(cd-iss.May91 + Jul93)*

— **BID + WARREN** recruited **NICK WESOLOWSKI** – drums repl. WINDSOR

— **FOZ** (b. JAMES FOSTER) – guitar repl. CARRIE (to The SING MARKET)

Blanco Y Negro not issued

Jan 85. (7") **JACOB'S LADDER. / ANDIANO** [ ] [-]
(12"+=) – La boom boom / Sailor beware / Starry nowhere.
May 85. (7")(12") **WALLFLOWER. / BIG BEN BONGO** [ ] [-]
Jun 85. (lp)(c) **THE LOST WEEKEND** [ ] [-]
– Wallflower / Sugar plum / Take Foz / Starry nowhere / Jacob's ladder / Cargo / Don't touch / Letter from Viola / The twitch / Cowboy country / La boom boom.

— Disbanded after above album.

BID

El not issued

Jun 86. (7") **REACH FOR YOUR GUN. / SWEET CHARIOTS** [ ] [-]
(12"+=) – Love.

RAJ QUARTET

were formed by **BID**

El not issued

Mar 87. (12"ep) **WHOOPS: WHAT A PALAVER / INVOCATION OF TOTH. / RAZBOYNIKA / THE MANEATER OF SURREY GREEN** [ ] [-]

Split, and BID went onto join KING OF LUXEMBOURG in '86-87, or did he?

MONOCHROME SET

re-formed 4-piece late 1989 with **BID, LESTER, WARREN** plus **ORSON PRESENCE** – guitar, keyboards

Vinyl Japan not issued

Sep 90. (cd)(lp) **DANTE'S CASINO** [ ] [-]

Honey-moon not issued

Nov 91. (12")(cd-s) **KILLING DAVE. / HOUSE OF GOD (live) / SWEET DEATH** [ ] [-]
Nov 91. (cd)(c)(lp) **JACK** [ ] [-]
– Big wheel / Jack / Blood act / Sweet death / Cerebella / Killing Dave / Jane / Black are the flowers / Yo Mo fo / Ground zero. *(re-iss.Nov93)*

Cherry Red not issued

Mar 93. (cd)(lp) **CHARADE** [ ] [-]
– Prelude / Forever young / Clover / Snowgirl / White garden / Her pain / Little noises / Crystal chamber / Girl / Oh Angie / Talking about you / No time for girls / Christine / Tilt.
Mar 93. (cd-s) **FOREVER YOUNG. / HURTING YOU / LITTLE NOISES** [ ] [-]
May 94. (cd) **MISERIE** [ ] [-]
– Milk and honey / Pauper / Dr.Robinson / Achilees / Leather jacket / Bed / Handsome / The ethereal one / UFO / Intergrate me / Twang 'em high.
Sep 95. (cd-ep) **I LOVE LAMBETH / KISSY KISSY / ALL OVER / CLOSING TIME** [ ] [ ]

– compilations, etc. –

Jun 86. El; (lp) **FIN! (live)** [ ] [-]
Aug 88. El; (lp)(cd) **WESTMINSTER AFFAIR – BANDE ORIGINALE DU FILM (as 'Les MONOCHROME SET")** [ ] [-]
(cd-iss.3 extra tracks; re-cd Nov93)
Jun 87. Virgin; (cd) **COLOUR TRANSMISSION** [ ] [-]
Apr 92. Richmond; (cd) **WHAT A WHOPPER!** [ ] [-]
Oct 92. Richmond; (cd) **THE GOOD LIFE** [ ] [-]
May 93. Code 90; (cd) **LIVE (live)** [ ] [-]
Mar 95. Virgin; (cd) **TOMORROW WILL BE TOO LONG . . .FINEST MOMENTS** [ ] [-]
Mar 95. Cherry Red; (cd) **BLACK & WHITE MINSTRELS – 1975-1979** [ ] [-]

MONSTER MAGNET

Formed: New Jersey, USA . . .1989 by DAVID WYNDORF and co. Non-stop touring of the USA and Europe paid off, when they were awarded a support to SOUNDGARDEN in 1993. This tempted SOUNDGARDEN's stable 'A&M' to sign them, with the result the fine 'SUPERJUDGE' album. • **Style:** Retro-rock fusing HAWKWIND-like space-age psychedelia with guitar-based heavy rock. • **Songwriters:** WYNDORF except BRAINSTORM (Hawkwind).

Recommended: SPINE OF GOD (*8)

DAVE WYNDORF – vocals / **JOHN McBAIN** – guitar / **JOE CALENDRA** – bass / **JON KLEINMAN** – drums

Glitterhouse Primo Scree

1991. (cd) **MONSTER MAGNET** [-] [ ]
1991. (cd) **TAB** [-] [ ]
1992. (cd) **SPINE OF GOD** [-] [ ]

— **ED MUNDELL** – guitar repl.McBAIN

A&M A&M

Apr 93. (cd)(c)(lp) **SUPERJUDGE** [ ] [ ]
– Cyclops revolution / Twin Earth / Superjudge / Cage around the sun / Elephant bell / Dinosaur vacume / Evil / Stadium / Face down / Brainstorm / Black balloon.
May 93. (12")(cd-s) **EVIL** [ ] [ ]
May 95. (7") **TWIN EARTH. / NOD SCENE** [67] [ ]
(12"+=)(cd-s+=) – Medicine.
Mar 95. (7"sha-pic-d) **NEGASONIC TEENAGE WARHEAD. / BLOW 'EM OFF** [49] [ ]
(cd-s+=) – Murder (live) / Superjudge live).
(cd-s) – ('A'side) / Eclipse this / Third alternative / Look into your orb for a warning.
Mar 95. (cd)(c)(lp) **DOPES TO INFINITY** [51] [ ]
– Dopes to infinity / Megasonic teenage warhead / Look to your orb for the warning / All friends and kingdom come / Ego, the living planet / Blow 'em off / Third alternative / I control, I fly / King of Mars / Dead Christmas / Theme from "Masterburner" / Vertigo.
Apr 95. (7"pic-d)(c-s) **DOPES TO INFINITY. / I'M FIVE YEARS AHEAD OF MY TIME** [58] [ ]
(cd-s+=) – Looking to the orb for a warning.
(cd-s+=) – Dinosaur vacume / Theme from "Masterburner".

MONTROSE

Formed: California, USA . . . Autumn '73 by RONNIE with SAMMY HAGAR, BILL CHURCH and DENNY CARMASSI. Through past multi-session work, they were signed to 'Warner Bros.', and by Spring '74, had unleashed excellent Ted Templeman produced eponymous lp. After 2 more albums, they dissolved in 1976, with RONNIE releasing solo album 'OPEN FIRE', before forming GAMMA in 1979. They released 3 albums in 4 years, until RONNIE moved on to solo pastures again in the mid-80's. • **Style:** Their loud, abrasive sound, was a prototype for all 80's heavy-metal bands. RONNIE went on to become well-respected axeman of the hard-rock genre. • **Songwriters:** MONTROSE-HAGAR, until latter's departure. Covered; CONNECTION (Rolling Stones). RONNIE later covered STAY WITH ME BABY (Walker Brothers). • **Trivia:** RONNIE first sessioned on BEAVER & KRAUSE's 'Gandharva' lp.

Recommended: MONTROSE (*8) / MEAN (*5).

RONNIE MONTROSE (b.Colorado, USA) – guitar (ex-VAN MORRISON, ex-EDGAR WINTER) / **SAMMY HAGAR** (b.13 Oct'47, Monterey, California) – vocals / **BILL CHURCH** – bass (ex-VAN MORRISON sessions) / **DENNY CARMASSI** – drums

Warners Warners

Mar 74. (lp)(c) **MONTROSE** [43] [ ]
– One thing on my mind / Good rockin' tonight / Bad motor scooter / Rock the

nation / Space station No.5 / I don't want it / Make it last / Rock candy. *(cd-iss.Nov93)*
Mar 74. (7") **SPACE STATION NO.5. / MAKE IT EASY** -
Apr 74. (7") **BAD MOTOR SCOOTER. / ONE THING ON MY MIND** -
Jul 74. (7") **ROCK THE NATION. / ONE THING ON MY MIND** Jan 74

—— **ALAN FITZGERALD** – bass repl. BILL who later joined SAMMY HAGAR Band
Sep 74. (7") **PAPER MONEY. / THE DREAMER** -
Nov 74. (lp)(c) **PAPER MONEY** 65
– Underground / Connection / The dreamer / Starliner / I got the fire / Spaceage sacrifice / We're going home / Paper money.
Nov 74. (7") **WE'RE GOING HOME. / CONNECTION** -

—— **BOB JAMES** – vocals repl. HAGAR who went solo / added **JIM ALCIVER** – keyboards
Sep 75. (7") **CLOWN WOMAN. / MATRIARCH** -
Oct 75. (lp)(c) **WARNER BROS. PRESENTS MONTROSE!** 79
– Matriarch / All I need / Twenty fight rock / Whaler / Dancin' feet / O lucky man / One and a half / Clown woman / Black train.

—— **RANDY JO HOBBS** – bass repl. FITZGERALD who also joined SAMMY HAGAR Band
Sep 76. (7") **MUSIC MAN. / TUFT-SIEGE** -
Nov 76. (lp)(c) **JUMP ON IT** Sep 76
– Let's go / What are you waitin' for / Tuft-sedge / Music man / Jump on it / Rich man / Crazy for you / Merry-go-round. *(cd-iss.Nov93)*
Nov 76. (7") **LET'S GO. /** -

—— Disbanded in 1977, CARMASSI joined SAMMY HAGAR.

– compilations, others, etc. –

Both below on 'Heavy Metal' UK.
Jun 80. (7") **BAD MOTOR SCOOTER. / I DON'T WANT IT** -
Jun 80. (7") **SPACE STATION No.5. / GOOD ROCKIN' TONIGHT** -

RONNIE MONTROSE

went solo, augmented by **ALCIVAR, FITZGERALD** plus **RICK SCHLOSSER** – drums / and guest **EDGAR WINTER** – keyboards

Elektra Warners
Jan 78. (lp)(c) **OPEN FIRE** 98
– Openers / Mandolinia / Town without pity / Leo rising / Heads up / Rocky road / My little mystery / No beginning no end.
Jan 78. (7") **TOWN WITHOUT PITY. / NO BEGINNING NO END** -

GAMMA

was formed by **RONNIE MONTROSE**, retaining **ALCIVAR + FITZGERALD** plus **DAVEY PATTISON** – vocals / **SKIP GALLETTE** – drums

Elektra Elektra
Dec 79. (lp)(c) **GAMMA I**
– Thunder and lightning / I'm alive / Razor king / No tears / Solar heat / Ready for action / Wish I was / Fight to the finish.
Jan 80. (7") **I'M ALIVE. / SOLAR HEAT** - 60
Jun 80. (7") **THUNDER AND LIGHTNING. / RAZOR KING**

—— **GLENN LETSCH** – bass repl. FITZGERALD / **DENNY CARMASSI** – drums (ex-MONTROSE, ex-SAMMY HAGAR) repl. GALLETTE
Sep 80. (lp)(c) **GAMMA 2** 65
– Mean streak / Four horsemen / Dirty city / Voyager / Something in the air / Cat on a leash / Skin and bone / Mayday.
Oct 80. (7") **SOMETHING IN THE AIR. / MAYDAY**
Jan 81. (7") **VOYAGER. / ?** -
Mar 81. (7") **DIRTY CITY. / READY FOR ACTION**

—— **MITCHELL FROOM** – keyboards, synthe. repl. ALCIVAR
Feb 82. (7") **RIGHT THE FIRST TIME. / NO WAY OUT** - 77
Mar 82. (lp)(c) **GAMMA 3** 72
– What's gone is gone / Right the first time / Moving violation / Mobile devotion / Stranger / Condition yellow / Modern girl / No way out / Third degree.
Apr 82. (7") **RIGHT THE FIRST TIME. / CONDITION YELLOW** -
May 82. (7") **STRANGERS. /** -

—— Break-up again, PATTISON later joined ROBIN TROWER Band in 1987.

RONNIE MONTROSE

went solo again with session people.

not issued Passport
1986. (lp)(c) **TERRITORY** -
– Catscan / I'm gonna be strong / Love you to / Odd man out / I spy / Territory / Synesthesia / Pentagon / Women of Ireland.

—— now with **JOHNNY EDWARDS** – vocals / **GLEN LETSCH** – bass / **JAMES KOTTAK** – drums

not issued Enigma
May 87. (lp)(c) **MEAN** -
– Don't damage the rock / Game of love / Pass it on / Hard headed woman / M for machine / Ready, willing and able / Man of the hour / Flesh and blood / Stand.

—— **JOHNNY BEE BEDANJEK** – vocals repl. EDWARDS who joined FOREIGNER / added **PAT FEEHAN** – synthesizer
Apr 88. (lp)(c) **THE SPEED OF SOUND** -
– March / Black box / Hyper-thrust / Monolith / Zero G / Telstar / Sindwinder / Windshear / VTOL / Outer marker inbound.

Road-runner Road-runner
Apr 90. (cd)(c)(lp) **THE DIVA STATION**
– Sorcerer / The diva station / Weirding way / New kid in town / Choke canyon / Little demons / Stay with me baby / Quid pro quo / High and dry / Solitaire.

MOODY BLUES

Formed: Birmingham, England ... May'64 by DENNY LAINE (who had just dissolved his DIPLOMATS band), PINDER, THOMAS, WARWICK and EDGE. They signed with manager Tony Secunda, who soon secured them a deal with 'Decca' records. Their debut 45 'LOSE YOUR MONEY', bombed, but by early '65, they were at the top spot with 'GO NOW'. They tried desperately to emulate hit, and although they scored with a few minor ones, they disbanded in Oct'66. They quickly re-united a month later, after finding JUSTIN HAYWARD and JOHN LODGE to replace DENNY LAINE and recent member ROD CLARKE. Late in the summer of '67, they switched to 'Deram', and hit immediately with concept lp 'DAYS OF FUTURE PASSED'. A piece from it 'NIGHTS IN WHITE SATIN', became a massive seller and an all-time classic in the process. After a rare concert at Queen Elizabeth Hall, London, they issued follow-up concept 'IN SEARCH OF THE LOST CHORD'. Another massive seller, it was pursued by their first 1969 UK No.1 album 'ON THE THRESHOLD OF A DREAM'. Later in '69, they founded own label 'Threshold', and soon became one of the world's top groups of the early 70's. • **Style:** Moved from mid-60's HOLLIES-style pop outfit, to neo-classical rock group, with own identifiable Mellotron organ sound fused with orchestral backing. Influenced a new generation of near copyists (aka BARCLAY JAMES HARVEST and early KING CRIMSON, etc). • **Songwriters:** LAINE wrote most of material, until LODGE or HAYWARD took over late '66. Also covered; GO NOW (Bessie Banks) / I DON'T WANT TO GO ON WITHOUT YOU (Drifters) / IT AIN'T NECESSARILY SO (Gershwin) / TIME IS ON MY SIDE (Rolling Stones) / BYE BYE BIRD (Sonny Boy Williamson) / etc. • **Trivia:** 10cc produced 1975 BLUE JAYS (HAYWARD & LODGE)'s album.

Recommended: VOICES IN THE SKY – THE BEST OF... (*8)

DENNY LAINE (b.BRIAN HINES, 29 Oct'44) – vocals, guitar (ex-DIPLOMATS) / **MIKE PINDER** (b.12 Dec'41) – keyboards, vocals (ex-CREWCATS) / **RAY THOMAS** (b.29 Dec'42, Stourport, England) – flute, vocals, harmonica / **CLINT WARWICK** (b.CLINTON ECCLES, 25 Jun'40) – bass, vocals / **GRAHAM EDGE** (b.30 Mar'42) – drums (ex-GERRY LEVENE AND THE AVENGERS)

Decca London
Aug 64. (7") **LOSE YOUR MONEY (BUT DON'T LOSE YOUR MIND). / STEAL YOUR HEART AWAY** -
Nov 64. (7") **GO NOW. / IT'S EASY CHILD** 1 -
Feb 65. (7") **I DON'T WANT TO GO ON WITHOUT YOU. / TIME IS ON MY SIDE** 33
Feb 65. (7") **GO NOW. / LOSE YOUR MONEY (BUT DON'T LOSE YOUR MIND)** - 10
May 65. (7") **FROM THE BOTTOM OF MY HEART (I LOVE YOU). / AND MY BABY'S GONE** 22 93
Jul 65. (lp) **THE MAGNIFICENT MOODIES** (US-title 'GO NOW – THE MOODY BLUES')
– I'll go crazy / Something you got / Go now / Can't nobody love you / I don't mind / I've got a dream / Let me go / Stop! / Thank you baby / It ain't necessarily so / True story / Bye bye bird. *(re-iss.cd Jan93 on 'Polydor') (re-issued again Mar93 on 'Repertoire' +=)*– Steal your heart away / Lose your money (but don't lose your mind) / It's easy child / I don't want to go on without you (come back) / Time is on my side / From the bottom of my heart / And my baby's gone.
Oct 65. (7") **EVERYDAY. / YOU DON'T (ALL THE TIME)** 44
Mar 66. (7") **STOP! / BYE BYE BIRD** - 98

—— (Jul66) **ROD CLARKE** – bass repl. WARWICK
Oct 66. (7") **BOULEVARD DE LA MADELAINE. / THIS IS MY HOUSE (BUT NOBODY CALLS)**

—— (Nov66) **JUSTIN HAYWARD** (b.14 Oct'46, Swindon, England) – vocals, guitar (ex-solo artist) repl. DENNY who went solo (and later to WINGS) / **JOHN LODGE** (b.20 Jul'45) – bass, vocals (ex-EL RIOT & THE REBELS) repl. CLARKE
Jan 67. (7") **LIFE'S NOT LIFE. / HE CAN WIN**
(above withdrawn after a day)
May 67. (7") **FLY ME HIGH. / REALLY HAVEN'T GOT THE TIME**
Aug 67. (7") **LOVE AND BEAUTY. / LEAVE THIS MAN ALONE**

Deram Deram
Nov 67. (7") **NIGHTS IN WHITE SATIN. / CITIES** 19
(re-iss.Sep72 reached UK no.9 / US no.2, re-Mar76, re-Oct79 no.14 all on 'Deram')(re-Oct83,Jun88 'Old Gold')
Nov 67. (lp) **DAYS OF FUTURE PASSED** 27 3 Apr 68
– The day begins / Dawn:- Dawn is a feeling / The morning:- Another morning / Lunch break:- Peak hour / The afternoon:- Forever afternoon (Tuesday) / Time to get away / Evening:- The sunset / Twilight time / The night:- Nights in white satin. *(re-iss.Sep72 hit No.3 US) (cd-iss.Nov84 on 'Decca')*
Jul 68. (7") **TUESDAY AFTERNOON (FOREVER AFTERNOON). / ANOTHER MORNING** - 24
Jul 68. (7") **VOICES IN THE SKY. / DR. LIVINGSTONE, I PRESSUME** 23
Jul 68. (lp) **IN SEARCH OF THE LOST CHORD** 5 23 Sep 68
– Departure / Ride my see-saw / Dr. Livingstone, I pressume / House of four doors (part 1) / Legend of a mind / House of four doors (part 2) / Voices in the sky / The best way to travel / The actor / The word / Om. *(re-iss.Nov84) (cd-iss.1986 on 'London')*
Oct 68. (7") **RIDE MY SEE-SAW. / VOICES IN THE SKY** - 61
Nov 68. (7") **RIDE MY SEE-SAW. / A SIMPLE GAME** 42 -
Apr 69. (7") **NEVER COMES THE DAY. / SO DEEP WITHIN YOU** 91
Apr 69. (lp) **ON THE THRESHOLD OF A DREAM** 1 20 May 69
– In the beginning / Lovely to see you / Dear diary / Send me no wine / To share our love / So deep within you / Never comes the day / Lazy day / Are you sitting comfortably / The dream / Have you heard (part 1) / The voyage / Have you heard (part 2). *(cd-iss.1986 on 'London')*

Threshold Threshold

Oct 69. (7") **WATCHING AND WAITING. / OUT AND IN** [ ] [-]

Nov 69. (lp)(c) **TO OUR CHILDREN'S CHILDREN'S CHILDREN** [2] [14] Jan70
– Higher and higher / Eyes of a child (part 1) / Floating / Eyes of a child (part 2) / I never thought I'd live to be a hundred / Beyond / Out and in / Gypsy / Eternity road / Candle of life / Sun is still shining / I never thought I'd live to be a million / Watching and waiting. *(cd-iss.Aug86 on 'London')*

Apr 70. (7") **QUESTION. / CANDLE OF LIFE** [2] [21]
(re-iss.Oct83 on 'Old Gold')

Aug 70. (lp)(c) **A QUESTION OF BALANCE** [1] [3] Sep 70
– Question / How is it (we are here) / And the tide rushes in / Don't you feel small / Tortoise and the hare / It's up to you / Minstrel's song / Dawning is the day / Melancholy man / The balance. *(cd-iss.Aug86 on 'London')*

Jul 71. (lp)(c) **EVERY GOOD BOY DESERVES FAVOUR** [1] [2] Aug 71
– Procession / The story in your eyes / Our guessing game / Emily's song / After you came / Riches more than these / Nice to be here / You can never go home / My song. *(cd-iss.Aug86 on 'London')*

Aug 71. (7") **THE STORY IN YOUR EYES. / MELANCHOLY MAN** [-] [23]

Apr 72. (7") **ISN'T LIFE STRANGE. / AFTER YOU CAME** [13] [29]

Nov 72. (lp)(c) **SEVENTH SOJOURN** [5] [1]
– Lost in a lost world / New horizons / For my lady / Isn't life strange / You and me / The land of make-believe / When you're a free man / I'm just a singer (in a rock'n'roll band). *(cd-iss.Sep86 on 'London')*

Jan 73. (7") **I'M JUST A SINGER (IN A ROCK'N'ROLL BAND). / FOR MY LADY** [36] [12]

— Split early '73 but only for a 5 year trial period, releasing own solos released (2) compilations while they split

Nov 74. (d-lp)(d-c) **THIS IS THE MOODY BLUES** [14] [11]
– Question / The actor / The word / Eyes of a child / Dear diary / Legend of a mind / In the beginning / Lovely to see you / Never comes the day / Isn't life strange / The dream / Have you heard / Voyage / Ride my see-saw / Tuesday afternoon / And the tide rushes in / New horizons / Simple game / Watching and waiting / I'm just a singer (in a rock'n'roll band) / For my lady / Story in your eyes / Melancholy man / Nights in white satin. *(d-cd.iss.Aug89)*

Decca London

Apr 77. (d-lp)(d-c) **CAUGHT LIVE + 5** (live '69 +1 studio side) [ ] [26] Jun 77
– Gypsy / The sunset / Dr. Livingstone, I pressume / Never comes the day / Peak hour / Tuesday afternoon / Are you sitting comfortably / Have you heard (part 1) / The voyage / Have you heard (part 2) / Nights in white satin / Legend of a mind / Ride my see-saw / Gimme a little somethin' / Please think about it / Long summer day / King and Queen / What am I doing here.

— Re-formed mid 1978. **(HAYWARD, LODGE, EDGE, PINDER** and **THOMAS)**

Decca London

Jun 78. (lp)(c) **OCTAVE** [6] [13]
– Steppin' in a slide zone / Under moonshine / Had to fall in love / I'll be level with you / Driftwood / Top rank suite / I'm your man / Survival / One step into the light / The day we meet again. *(cd-iss.Oct86) (re-iss.cd Jan93)*

Jul 78. (7") **STEPPIN' IN A SLIDE ZONE. / I'LL BE LEVEL WITH YOU** [ ] [39]

Oct 78. (7") **DRIFTWOOD. / I'M YOUR MAN** [ ] [59]

— **PATRICK MORAZ** – keyboards (ex-YES, solo artist, ex-REFUGEE) repl. PINDER

Threshold Threshold

May 81. (lp)(c) **LONG DISTANCE VOYAGER** [7] [1] Jun 81
– The voice / Talking out of turn / Gemini dream / In my world / 22,000 days / Nervous / Painted smile / Reflection smile / Veteran cosmic rocker. *(cd-iss.Oct86)*

Jun 81. (7") **GEMINI DREAM. / PAINTED SMILE** [ ] [12]

Jul 81. (7") **THE VOICE. / 22,000 DAYS** [ ] [15]

Nov 81. (7")(7"pic-d) **TALKING OUT OF TURN. / VETERAN COSMIC ROCKER** [ ] [65]

Aug 83. (7")(12") **BLUE WORLD. / GOING NOWHERE** [35] [-]

Sep 83. (lp)(c)(cd) **THE PRESENT** [15] [26]
– Blue world / Meet me halfway / Sitting at the wheel / Going nowhere / Hole in the world / Under my feet / It's cold outside of your heart / Running water / I am / Sorry. *(cd re-iss. Apr91 on 'London')*

Sep 83. (7") **SITTING AT THE WHEEL. / GOING NOWHERE** [-] [27]

Oct 83. (7") **SITTING AT THE WHEEL. / SORRY** [ ] [-]
(12"+=) – Gemini dream.

Nov 83. (7") **BLUE WORLD. / SORRY** [-] [62]

Feb 84. (7") **UNDER MY FEET. / RUNNING WATER** [-] [ ]

Polydor Polydor

Mar 86. (7")(12") **YOUR WILDEST DREAM. / TALKIN' TALKIN'** [ ] [9] Apr 86

May 86. (lp)(c)(cd) **OTHER SIDE OF LIFE** [24] [9]
– Your wildest dreams / Talkin' talkin' / Rock'n'roll over you / I just don't care / Running out of love / The other side of life / The spirit / Slings and arrows / It may be a fire.

Aug 86. (7") **THE OTHER SIDE OF LIFE. / NIGHTS IN WHITE SATIN (live)** [ ] [58]
(12"+=) – The spirit. *(US; b-side)*

May 88. (7") **I KNOW YOU'RE OUT THERE SOMEWHERE. / MIRACLE** [52] [30]
(12"+=) – ('A'extended).
(cd-s+=) – Rock'n'roll over you (live).

Jun 88. (lp)(c)(cd) **SUR LA MER** [21] [38]
– I know you're out there somewhere / Want to be with you / River of endless love / No more lies / Here comes the weekend / Vintage wine / Breaking point / Miracle / Love is on the run / Deep.

Dec 88. (7") **NO MORE LIES. / RIVERS OF ENDLESS LOVE** [ ] [ ]
(12"+=) – The other side of life.

Jun 91. (7")(c-s) **SAY IT WITH LOVE. / LEAN ON ME (TONIGHT)** [ ] [ ]
(12"+=)(cd-s+=) – Highway.

Aug 91. (cd)(c)(lp) **KEYS OF THE KINGDOM** [54] [94]
– Say it with love / Bless the wings (that bring you back) / Is this Heaven? / Say what you mean (pt.1 & 2) / Lean on me (tonight) / Hope and pray / Shadows on the wall / Celtic sonant / Magic / Never blame the rainbows for the rain. *(re-iss.cd,c,lp Jan93)*

Mar 93. (cd)(c) **LIVE AT RED ROCKS (live)** [ ] [ ]
– Overture / Late lament / Tuesday afternoon (forever afternoon) / For my lady / Lean on me (tonight) / Lovely to see you / I know you're out there somewhere / The voice / Your wildest dreams / Isn't life strange / The other side of life / I'm just a singer (in a rock and roll band) / Nights in white satin / Question / Ride my see-saw.

– other compilations, etc. –

May 65. Decca; (7"ep) **THE MOODY BLUES** [ ] [-]
– Go now / Lose your money (but don't lose your mind) / Steal your heart away / I don't want to go on without you.

Nov 84. Threshold; (7") **THE VOICE. / GEMINI DREAM** [ ] [ ]
(12"+=) – Nights in white satin.

Nov 84. Threshold; (lp)(c)(cd) **VOICES IN THE SKY – THE BEST OF THE MOODY BLUES** [ ] [ ] Mar 85
– Ride my see-saw / Talking out of turn / Driftwood / Never comes the day / I'm just a singer (in a rock and roll band) / Gemini dream / The voice / After you came / Question / Veteran cosmic rocker / Isn't life strange / Nights in white satin. *(cd re-iss. Apr91)*

Oct 79. K-Tel; (lp)(c) **OUT OF THIS WORLD** [15] [-]

Sep 83. A.K.A.; (lp)(c) **GO NOW** [ ] [-]

Sep 85. Old Gold; (7") **GO NOW. / I DON'T WANT TO GO ON WITHOUT YOU** [ ] [-]

Sep 85. Castle; (d-lp)(c) **THE MOODY BLUES COLLECTION** [ ] [-]
(cd-iss.1986)

Sep 87. London; (cd) **PRELUDE** [ ] [-]

Nov 89. Polydor; (lp)(c)(cd) **GREATEST HITS** [71] [ ]

Sep 93. Threshold; (cd)(c) **GO NOW** [ ] [-]

Sep 94. Polydor; (5xcd-box) **THE TRAVELLER** [ ] [ ]

— below: solo work, etc. they released during 5 year trial split.

JUSTIN HAYWARD & JOHN LODGE

Threshold Threshold

Apr 75. (7") **I DREAMED LAST NIGHT. / REMEMBER ME (MY FRIEND)** [ ] [ ]

Apr 75. (lp)(c) **BLUE JAYS** [4] [16] Mar 75
– This morning / Remember me (my friend) / My brother / You / Nights, winters, years / Saved by the music / I dreamed last night / Who are you now / Maybe / When you wake up. *(re-iss.Nov84) (cd-iss.1988 on 'London')*

Sep 75. (7") **BLUE GUITAR. / WHEN YOU WAKE UP** [8] [94]
(re-iss.1989 on 'Old Gold')

JUSTIN HAYWARD

Deram Deram

Jan 77. (7") **LAY IT ON ME. / SONGWRITER (part 2)** [-] [ ]

Jan 77. (7") **ONE LOVELY ROOM. / SONGWRITER (part 2)** [ ] [-]

Feb 77. (lp)(c) **SONGWRITER** [28] [37]
– Tightrope / Songwriter (pt.1 – vocal & pt.2 – instrumental) / Country girl / One lonely room / Lay it on me / Stage door / Raised on love / Doin' time / Nostradamus. *(cd-iss.Dec87)* (cd+=) – Music / Learning the game.

Apr 77. (7") **COUNTRY GIRL. / DOIN' TIME** [ ] [-]

Apr 77. (7") **COUNTRY GIRL. / SONGWRITER (part 2)** [-] [ ]

Jul 77. (7") **STAGE DOOR. / LAY IT ON ME** [ ] [ ]

— Appeared on JEFF WAYNE'S 'WAR OF THE WORLDS' Various Artists Jun78 album Below 2 'A'singles credited to "JUSTIN HAYWARD".

C.B.S. Columbia

Jun 78. (7") **FOREVER AUTUMN. / THE FIGHTING MACHINE** [5] [ ]
(re-iss. Oct84 & Jan87 on 'Old Gold')

Aug 78. (7") **EVE OF THE WAR. / THE RED WEED** [36] [ ]

Decca Deram

Apr 79. (7") **MARIE. / HEART OF STEEL** [ ] [ ]

May 80. (7") **NIGHT FLIGHT. / SUITCASE** [ ] [ ]

Jul 80. (lp)(c) **NIGHT FLIGHT** [41] [ ]
– Night flight / Maybe it's just love / Crazy lovers / Penumbra moon / Nearer to you / Face in the crowd / Suitcase / It's not on / Bedtime stories. *(cd-iss.Jan89)*

Towerbell not issued

Aug 85. (7")(12") **SILVERBIRD. / TAKE YOUR CHANCES** [ ] [ ]

Sep 85. (lp)(c)(cd) **MOVING MOUNTAINS** [78] [ ]
– One again / Take your chances / Moving mountains / Silverbird / Is it just a game / Lost and found / Goodbye / Who knows / The best is yet to come.

Nov 85. (7") **THE BEST IS YET TO COME. / MARIE** [ ] [ ]

B.B.C. not issued

Jul 87. (7") **STAR COPS (IT WON'T BE LONG). / OUTER SPACE** [ ] [ ]

— next with guests **MIKE BATT** and **The LONDON PHILHARMONIC ORCHESTRA**

Trax not issued

Oct 89. (lp)(c)(cd) **CLASSIC BLUE** [47] [-]
– The racks of my tears / MacArthur Park / Blackbird / Vincent / God only knows / Bright eyes / A whiter shade of pale / Scarborough fair / Railway hotel / Man of the world / Forever autumn / As long as the Moon can shine / Stairway to Heaven.

JOHN LODGE

Decca London

Jan 77. (7") **SAY YOU LOVE ME. / NATURAL AVENUE** [ ] [ ]

Feb 77. (lp)(c) **NATURAL AVENUE** [38] [ ]
– (Introduction to Children of rock'n'roll) / Natural avenue / Summer breeze / Carry me / Who could change / Broken dreams, hard road / Piece of my heart / Rainbow / Say you love me / Children of rock'n'roll. *(cd-iss.May87 on 'London')*

Mar 77. (7") **CHILDREN OF ROCK'N'ROLL. / PIECE OF MY HEART** [ ] [-]

Jul 77. (7") **SUMMER BREEZE. / RAINBOW** [ ] [-]

Oct 80. (7") **STREET CAFE. / THREW IT ALL AWAY** [ ] [-]

GRAEME EDGE BAND

with **ADRIAN GURVITZ** – guitar, vocals, keyboards and **PAUL GURVITZ** – bass, vocals / **MICK GALLAGHER** – keys / plus sessioners

Threshold London

Jul 74. (7") **WE LIKE TO DO IT. / SHOTGUN** [ ] [ ]

Sep 75. (lp)(c) **KICK OFF YOUR MUDDY BOOTS**
– Bareback rider / In dreams / Lost in space / Have you ever wondered / My life's not wasted / The tunnel / Gew Janna women / Shotgun / Something we'd like to say. *(cd-iss.Aug89 on 'London')*

Nov 75. (7") **THE TUNNEL. / BAREBACK RIDER**

Decca London

Apr 77. (7") **EVERYBODY NEEDS SOMEBODY. / BE MY EYES** -

Apr 77. (lp)(c) **PARADISE BALLROOM**
– Paradise ballroom / Human / Everybody needs somebody / All is fair / Down down down In the night of the light / Caroline. *(cd-iss.Jan89 on 'London')*

RAY THOMAS

Threshold London

Jun 75. (7") **HIGH ABOVE MY HEAD. / LOVE IS THE KEY**

Jul 75. (lp)(c) **FROM MIGHTY OAKS** 23
– From mighty oaks / Hey mama life / Play it again / Rock-abye baby blues / High above my head / Love's the key / You make me feel alright / Adam and I / I wish we could fly. *(cd-iss.Aug89 on 'London')*

Jun 76. (7") **ONE NIGHT STAND. / CAROUSEL**

Jun 76. (lp)(c) **HOPES, WISHES AND DREAMS**
– In your song / Friends / We need love / Within your eyes / One stand stand / Keep on searching / Didn't I / The last dream / Migration / Carousel. *(cd-iss.Jan89 on 'London')*

MICHAEL PINDER

Threshold London

Apr 76. (lp)(c) **THE PROMISE**
– Free as a dove / You'll make it through / I only want to love you / Someone to believe in / Carry on / Air / Message / The seed / The promise. *(cd-iss.Aug89 on 'London')*

May 76. (7") **CARRY ON. / I ONLY WANT TO LOVE YOU**

Keith MOON (see under ⇒ WHO)

Michael MOORCOCK (see under ⇒ HAWKWIND)

Gary MOORE

Born: 4 Apr'52, Belfast, N.Ireland. in the mid-60's, he formed school group GRANNY'S INTENTIONS, which included NOEL BRIDGEMAN on drums, before he went to SKID ROW in 1969. A year later, they recorded 'HONEST INJUN' for 'Deram', but this was without GARY and NOEL. GARY then did on stage guest work for DR.STRANGELY STRANGE and appeared on their 'Heavy Pettin'' lp in 1970. He left SKID ROW in 1971, after they released 'SKID' lp for 'C.B.S.'. In 1972, GARY formed own band GRINDING STONE, who released lp for 'CBS' in '73. In 1974, he joined THIN LIZZY, but left to join COLOSSEUM II in Spring '75. He returned to THIN LIZZY early '77 but left again only to return once more on a full-time basis Aug'78. This time, MOORE stayed long enough to be part of their UK Top 3 album 'BLACK ROSE (A ROCK LEGEND)'. Around the same time, Spring 1979, after releasing solo album 'BACK ON THE STREETS' early '79 for 'MCA', he hit UK Top 10 with single 'PARISIENNE WALKWAYS'. This featured THIN LIZZY frontman PHIL LYNOTT on vocals, and enjoyed the usual '93 charting remix. In 1980, GARY formed G-FORCE, but gave this up after joining The GREG LAKE BAND in 1981. In 1982, he signed another solo deal with 'Virgin', and breached the UK Top 30 with album 'CORRIDORS OF POWER'. Continued to go from strength to strength for the next decade. • **Style:** Initially influenced by JEFF BECK, GARY's guitar work shifted through blues, jazz-rock with COLOSSEUM II, heavy rock with G-FORCE, and returning to basic blues in the early 90's. • **Songwriters:** MOORE penned most, and covered; DON'T LET ME BE MISUNDERSTOOD (hit; Animals) / SHAPES OF THINGS (Yardbirds) / FRIDAY ON MY MIND (Easybeats) / DON'T YOU TO ME (Hudson Whittaker) / THE BLUES IS ALRIGHT (Milton Campbell) / KEY TO LOVE (John Mayall) / JUMPIN' AT SHADOWS (Duster Bennett) / etc. • **Trivia:** GARY sessioned also on 1975's 'Peter & The Wolf', and ANDREW LLOYD WEBBER's 1978 lp 'Variations'. In 1980, he was heard on ROD ARGENT's 'Moving Home' & COZY POWELL's 'Over The Top'. The CHIEFTAINS guested on his 'WILD FRONTIER' album.

Recommended: WILD FRONTIER (*6) / BALLADS AND BLUES 1982-1994 (*6)

GARY MOORE BAND

GARY MOORE – guitar, vocals (ex-SKID ROW) with **JAN SCHELHAAS** – keyboards (ex-NATIONAL HEAD BAND) / **JOHN CURTIS** – bass / **PEARCE KELLY** – drums / plus session man **PHILIP DONNELLY** – guitar

C.B.S. Peters

1973. (lp) **GRINDING STONE**
– Grinding stone / Time to heal / Sail across the mountain / The energy dance / Spirit / Boogie my way back home. *(re-iss.Nov85) (re-iss.+cd.Oct90 & Dec92)*

—— In 1974 GARY joined THIN LIZZY ⇒ for 3 mths. May75 he joined COLOSSEUM II before returning to THIN LIZZY p/t for 5 mths early'77 and f/t Aug'78.

GARY MOORE

also started a new solo career at this time with friends **DON AIREY** – keyboards (of COLOSSEUM) / **JOHN MOLE** – bass / **SIMON PHILLIPS** – drums / plus THIN LIZZY'S – **PHIL LYNOTT** and **BRIAN DOWNEY**.

M.C.A. Jet

Dec 78. (7") **BACK ON THE STREETS. / TRACK NINE**

Jan 79. (lp) **BACK ON THE STREETS** 70
– Back on the streets / Don't believe a word / Fanatical fascists / Flight of the snow moose / Hurricane / Song for Donna / What would you rather bee or wasp / Parisian walkways. *(re-iss.Aug81.)*

Apr 79. (7") **PARISIAN WALKWAYS. / FANATICAL FASCISTS** 8

—— (above 'A' featured **PHIL LYNOTT** – vocals – (of THIN LIZZY)

Oct 79. (7") **SPANISH GUITAR. / SPANISH GUITAR (instrumental)**

G-FORCE

GARY MOORE – vocals / **TONY NEWTON** – vocals / **WILLIE DEE** – keyboards, bass, vocals / **MARK NAUSEEF** – drums, percussion (ex-THIN LIZZY, ex-ELF, ex-IAN GILLAN BAND)

Jet Jet

Jun 80. (7") **HOT GOSSIP. / BECAUSE OF YOUR LOVE**

Jun 80. (lp)(pic-lp) **G-FORCE**
– You / White knuckles – Rockin' & rollin' / She's got you / I look at you / Because of your love / You kissed me sweetly / Hot gossip / The woman's in love / Dancin'. *(re-iss.Mar87) (re-iss.Feb91 on 'Castle')*

Aug 80. (7") **YOU. / TRUST YOUR LOVIN'**

Nov 80. (7") **WHITE KNUCKLES – ROCKIN' & ROLLIN'. / I LOOK AT YOU**

—— In '81 and '83 he was part of the GREG LAKE BAND. Although he did continue solo career

GARY MOORE

with **CHARLIE HUHN** – vocals (ex-JACK LANCASTER) / **TOMMY EYRE** – keyboards (ex-GREG LAKE BAND) / **NEIL MURRAY** – bass (ex-WHITESNAKE) / **IAN PAICE** – drums (ex-WHITESNAKE, ex-DEEP PURPLE, ex-PAICE, ex-ASHTON & LORD)

Virgin Mirage

Sep 82. (7")(7"pic-d) **ALWAYS GONNA LOVE YOU. / COLD HEARTED**

Oct 82. (lp)(c) **CORRIDORS OF POWER** 30 Apr 83
– Don't take me for a loser / Always gonna love you / Wishing well / Gonna break my heart again / Falling in love with you / End of the world / Rockin' every night / Cold hearted / I can't wait until tomorrow. *(free live 7"ep)* – PARISIAN WALKWAYS / ROCKIN' EVERY NIGHT / BACK ON THE STREETS

—— **JOHN SLOMAN** – vocals, keyboards repl. HUHN / **DON AIREY** – keyboards (see above) (ex-OZZY OSBOURNE) repl. EYRE

Feb 83. (7")(7"pic-d) **FALLING IN LOVE WITH YOU. / ('A'instrumental)** -
(12"+=) – Wishing well.

—— GARY MOORE recruited new personnel after SLOMAN departed / **NEIL CARTER** – keyboards, guitar (ex-UFO, ex-WILD HORSES) repl. AIREY / **BOBBY CHOUINARD** – drums 1/2 repl. PAICE (he appeared on most of next 2 lp's) / on tour Mar 84 **CRAIG GRUBER** – bass (ex-BILLY SQUIER) 1/2 replaced MURRAY (he appeared on lp) (note that all: MURRAY, AIREY and PAICE rejoined past bands WHITESNAKE, OZZY OSBOURNE and DEEP PURPLE respectively.)

Ten-Virgin Mirage

Jan 84. (7")(7"sha-pic-d) **HOLD ON TO LOVE. / DEVIL IN HER HEART** 65 -
(12"+=) – Law of the jungle.

Feb 84. (lp)(c) **VICTIMS OF THE FUTURE** 12 May 84
– Victims of the future / Teenage idol / Shapes of things / Empty rooms / Murder in the skies / All I want / Hold on to love / Law of the jungle. *(cd-iss.Jun88)*

Mar 84. (7")(7"sha-pic-d) **SHAPES OF THINGS. / BLINDER** -
(12"+=) – (an interview with Alan Freeman).

Aug 84. (7") **EMPTY ROOMS. / NUCLEAR ATTACK (live)** 51 -
(12"+=) – ('A'extended version).
(d-12"+=) – Rockin' every night (live) / Empty rooms (live).

Aug 84. (7") **EMPTY ROOMS. / MURDER IN THE SKIES** -

Oct 84. (d-lp)(d-c)(d-cd) **WE WANT MOORE (live)** 32 Dec 84
– Murder in the skies / Shapes of things / Victims of the future / Cold hearted / End of the world / Back on the streets / So far away / Empty rooms / Don't take me for a loser / Rockin' and rollin'.

—— **GLENN HUGHES** – bass (ex-DEEP PURPLE) repl. BOB DAISLEY who repl. GRUBER / **PAUL THOMPSON** (ex-ROXY MUSIC) and **TED McKENNA** (ex-SAHB) took over drums

May 85. (7")(7"sha-pic-d) **OUT IN THE FIELDS. ("GARY MOORE & PHIL LYNOTT") / MILITARY MAN** 5 -
(12"+=) – Still in love with you.
(d7"+=) – Stop messin' around (live).

Jul 85. (7") **EMPTY ROOMS. / OUT OF MY SYSTEM** 23 -
(12"+=) – Parisienne walkways (live) / Empty rooms (summer '85).
(d7"+=) – Parisienne walkways (live) / Murder in the skies (live).

Sep 85. (lp)(c)(pic-lp) **RUN FOR COVER** 12 Feb 86
– Run for cover / Reach for the sky / Military man / Empty rooms / Out in the fields / Nothing to lose / Once in a lifetime / All messed up / Listen to your heartbeat. *(cd-iss.Feb86, re-iss.1989, c+cd+=)* – Out of my system.

—— **GARY** now used members of **The CHIEFTAINS.** Retained **CARTER + DAISLEY.**

Dec 86. (7")(7"sha-pic-d) **OVER THE HILLS AND FAR AWAY. / CRYING IN THE SHADOWS** 20 -
(d7"+=) – All messed up (live) / Out in the fields (live).
(12"+=) – All messed up (live) / ('A'version).

Feb 87. (7") **WILD FRONTIER. / RUN FOR COVER (live)** 35 -
(12"+=) – ('A'live) / ('A'extended).
(d7"+=) – Murder in the skies (live) / Wild frontier (live).
(cd-s+=) – Over the hills and far away / Empty rooms / Out in the fields / Shapes of things.

Mar 87. (lp)(c)(cd) **WILD FRONTIER** 8 May 87
– Over the hills and far away / Wild frontier / Take a little time / The loner / Friday on my mind / Strangers in the darkness / Thunder rising / Johnny boy. *(cd+=)* – Crying in the shadows / Over the hills and far away (12"version) / Wild frontier (12"version) *(re-iss.Sep87. WILD FRONTIER (SPECIAL EDITION) (incl.extra 12"ep) (re-iss.cd Jan89 & Apr90 on 'Virgin')*

Apr 87. (7")(7"pic-d) **FRIDAY ON MY MIND. / REACH FOR THE SKY (live)** 26 -
(12"+=) – ('A'version).
(cd-s+=) – Parisian walkways (live).

Aug 87. (7") **THE LONER. / JOHNNY BOY** 53 -
(12"+=) – ('A'live).
(c-s+=) – ('A'extended version).

Nov 87. (7") **TAKE A LITTLE TIME. / OUT IN THE FIELDS** 75 -
(d7"+=) – All messed up (live) / Thunder rising (live).

— brought back **COZY POWELL** – drums

Virgin Virgin

Jan 89. (7")(7"pic-d) **AFTER THE WAR. / THIS THING CALLED LOVE** 37
(12"+=) – Over the hills and far away.
(cd-s+=) – Emerald / Thunder rising.

Jan 89. (lp)(c)(cd) **AFTER THE WAR** 23 Mar 89
– After the war / Speak for yourself / Livin' on dreams / Led clones / Running from the storm / This thing called love / Ready for love / Blood of emeralds. *(c+=)(cd+=)* – Dunlace (pt.1 & 2) / The messiah will come.

Mar 89. (7") **READY FOR LOVE. / WILD FRONTIER** 56 -
(12"+=)(cd-s+=) – The loner (live).

Apr 89. (7") **SPEAK FOR YOURSELF. / LED CLONES** -

— **CHRIS SLADE** – drums (ex-MANFRED MANN'S EARTH BAND, ex-FIRM) repl. COZY POWELL

Oct 89. (7") **LIVIN' ON DREAMS. / THE MESSIAH WILL COME AGAIN**

— His band were now **DON AIREY** – keyboards / **BOB DAISLEY + ANDY PYLE** – bass / **GRAHAM WALKER + BRIAN DOWNEY** – drums / **FRANK MEAD** – tenor sax / **NICK PAYN** – sax

Mar 90. (7")(c-s) **OH PRETTY WOMAN. / KING OF BLUES** 48
(12"+=)(cd-s+=) – The stumble.

Mar 90. (cd)(c)(lp) **STILL GOT THE BLUES** 13 83 Jun 90
– Moving on / Oh pretty woman / Walking by myself / Still got the blues (for you) / Texas street / All your love / Too tired / King of the blues / Midnight blues / As the years go passing by / That kind of woman / Stop messin' around.

May 90. (7")(c-s) **STILL GOT THE BLUES (FOR YOU). / LET ME WITH THE BLUES** 31 97 Jan 91
(12"+=) – ('A'extended) / The sky is crying.
(cd-s++=) – Further on up the road / Mean cruel woman.

Aug 90. (7") **WALKING BY MYSELF. / STILL GOT THE BLUES (FOR YOU) (live)** 48
(12"+=) – ('A'live).
(cd-s++=) – Still got the blues (live).

Dec 90. (7") **TOO TIRED ("GARY MOORE featuring ALBERT COLLINS"). / TEXAS STRUT** 71
(12"+=) – ('A'live).
(cd-s) – ('A'side) / All your love (live) / The stumble.

— He featured on TRAVELLING WILBURYS single 'She's My Baby'.

— **WILL LEE + JOHNNY B.GAYDON** – bass repl. PYLE / **ANTON FIG** – drums repl. DOWNEY / **TOMMY EYRE** – keyboards repl. AIREY / added on horns **MARTIN DROVER, NICK PENTELOW, ANDREW LOVE + WAYNE JACKSON RICHARD MORGAN** – oboe / backing vocals – **CAROLE KENYON + LINDA TAYLOR**

Feb 92. (7") **COLD DAY IN HELL. ("GARY MOORE & THE MIDNIGHT BLUES BAND") / ALL TIME LOW** 24
(cd-s+=) – Stormy Monday (live) / Woke up this morning.

Mar 92. (cd)(c)(lp) **AFTER HOURS** 4
– Cold day in Hell / Don't lie to me (I get evil) / Story of the blues / Since I met you baby / Separate ways / Only fool in town / Key to love / Jumpin' at shadows / The blues is alright / The hurt inside / Nothing's the same.

May 92. (7")(c-s) **STORY OF THE BLUES. / MOVIN' ON DOWN THE ROAD** 40
(cd-s+=) – King of the blues / Midnight blues (live).
(cd-s+=) – ('A'dry mix).

Jul 92. (7")(c-s) **SINCE I MET YOU BABY. ("GARY MOORE & B.B.KING") / THE HURT INSIDE** 59
(cd-s+=) – ('A'mix) / Moving on (live) / Texas strut (live).
(cd-s+=) – Don't start me talking / Once in a blue mood (instrumental)

Oct 92. (7")(c-s) **SEPARATE WAYS. / ONLY FOOL IN TOWN** 59
(12"+=)(cd-s+=) – Farther on up the road / Caledonia.
(cd-s+=) You don't love me / Stumble.

Apr 93. (7")(c-s) **PARISIENNE WALKWAYS (live '93). / STILL GOT THE BLUES** 32
(cd-s+=) – Stop messin' around / You don't love me.
(cd-s) – ('A'side) / Since I met you baby (live with B.B.KING) / Key to love.

Pointblank Virgin

May 93. (cd)(c)(d-lp) **BLUES ALIVE** 8
– Cold day in Hell / Walking by myself / Story of the blues / Oh pretty woman / Separate ways / Too tired / Still got the blues / Since I met you baby / The sky is crying / Further on up the road / King of the blues / Parisienne walkways / Jumpin' at shadows.

— In Jun 94, MOORE teamed up with JACK BRUCE + GINGER BAKER (ex-CREAM, and both solo artists) to form BBM. They had UK Top10 album 'AROUND THE NEXT DREAM' for 'Virgin' records.

Virgin Virgin

Nov 94. (cd)(c)(lp) **BALLADS AND BLUES 1982-1994** (compilation) 33

below a tribute to PETER GREEN (ex-Fleetwood Mac) guitarist

May 95. (cd)(c)(lp) **BLUES FOR GREENY** 14
– If you be my baby / Long grey mare / Merry go round / I loved another woman / Need your love so bad / The same way / The super-natural / Driftin' / Showbiz blues / Love that burns / Looking for somebody.

Jun 95. (7"ep)(12"ep)(cd-ep) **NEED YOUR LOVE SO BAD / THE SAME WAY (acoustic). / THE WORLD KEEPS ON TURNIN' (acoustic) / STOP MESSIN' AROUND (acoustic)** 48

– compilations, etc. –

Jun 84. Jet; (lp)(c) **DIRTY FINGERS**
(re-iss.1987 on 'Castle')

Jun 84. Jet; (7") **DON'T LET ME BE MISUNDERSTOOD. / SHE'S GOT YOU (live)**

1984. Jet; (lp) **LIVE AT THE MARQUEE (live)**
(re-Jun87 on 'Raw Power')

Oct 85. Raw Power; (lp)(c)(cd) **WHITE KNUCKLES** -

Sep 86. Raw Power; (d-lp)(d-c) **ANTHOLOGY** -

Jun 86. 10-Virgin; (lp)(c)(cd) **ROCKIN' EVERY NIGHT (live Japan)** 99
(re-iss.cd Jun88)

Nov 87. M.C.A.; (lp)(c) **PARISIENNE WALKWAYS**
(cd-iss.May90)

Mar 88. Castle; (d-cd) **G-FORCE / LIVE AT THE MARQUEE**

Oct 90. Castle; (cd)(c)(lp) **THE COLLECTION** -
– Nuclear attack / White knuckles – Rockin' & rollin' / Grinding stone / Spirit / Run to your mama / Don't let me be misunderstood / Bad news / I look at you / She's got you / Back on the streets (live) / Hiroshima / Parisienne walkways (live) / Dancin' / Really gonna rock tonight / Dirty fingers.

Mar 91. Castle; (cd)(c)(lp) **LIVE AT THE MARQUEE (live)** -

Jun 90. Nightriding; (cd) **GOLDEN DECADE OF GARY MOORE** -

— next when as SKID ROW

Sep 90. Essential; (cd)(c)(lp) **GARY MOORE, BRUSH SHIELDS, NOEL BRIDGEMAN** -

Sep 94. Spectrum; (cd)(c) **WALKWAYS** -

Alanis MORISSETTE

Born: 1975, Ottawa, Canada, to a French-Canadian father and Hungarian mother, who were both teachers. She began writing songs at age ten and became a regular on cable show 'You Can't Do That On Television'. Her first single was released at the same time, and by 16 she had made two disco/pop albums. She then headed for LA, where she hawked around her demo which was refused by nearly every major. In 1994, along came MADONNA, who duly signed her to 'Maverick'. The resulting album 'JAGGED LITTLE PILL' in 1995, was heralded by critics and public alike and soon went No.1 Stateside. It won 4 Grammys and a Brit award early '96. • **Style:** Evocative and emotional singer, with a confrontational approach to all life's subjects; especially love. • **Songwriters:** Writes all music with GLEN BALLARD, who also plays guitar and keyboards. • **Trivia:** Guests on her debut included FLEA (Red Hot Chilis) and DAVE NAVARRO (ex-Jane's Addiction)

Recommended: JAGGED LITTLE PILL (*9)

ALANIS MORISSETTE – vocals/ with **BENMONT TENCH** organ (ex-TOM PETTY) / **LANCE MORRISON** – bass / **MATT LAUG** – drums

Maverick Maverick

Jun 95. (cd)(c)(lp) **JAGGED LITTLE PILL** 12 1
– All I really want / You oughta know / Perfect / Hand in my pocket / Right through you / Forgiven / You learn / Head over feet / Mary Jane / Ironic / Not the doctor / Wake up.

Jul 95. (c-s) **YOU OUGHTA KNOW / ('A'-Jimmy The Saint version)** 22
(cd-s+=) – Perfect (acoustic) / Wake up.

Oct95. (c-s) **HAND IN MY POCKET / HEAD OVER FEET (live)** 26
(cd-s+=) – Not the doctor (live).
(cd-s) – ('A'side) / Right through (live) / Foreign (live).

Van MORRISON

Born: GEORGE IVAN, 31 Aug'45, Belfast, N.Ireland. In the early 60's, he formed The MONARCHS, who evolved into THEM in 1963. With MORRISON at the helm, they had a number of chart hits, namely 'HERE COMES THE NIGHT' & 'GLORIA', before he moved to New York early '67, to sign contract with Bert Berns of 'Bang' records. His debut 45 'BROWN-EYED GIRL', reached the US Top 10, but his partnership with BERNS came to an end when BERNS died of a heart attack late '67. After a debut lp 'BLOWIN' YOUR MIND', MORRISON moved to Cambridge, Massachusetts and was snapped up by 'Warner Bros.', where he recorded in 2 days 'ASTRAL WEEKS' with producer Lewis Merenstein. Although its sales were only moderate, it became critics' seminal lp of the decade. His next album 'MOONDANCE' was another gem, but this got deserved commercial success, and hit both US & UK Top 40's. He continued to be major album orientated star of the 70's, 80's & 90's. His 1971 album 'TUPELO HONEY', was written for his wife Janet Planet, whom he divorced in '73. • **Style:** Magical and melancholy jazz-influenced songer/songwriter, whose lyrics explore a deep spiritual mood, mixed with joy and romanticism. • **Songwriters:** Self-penned except covers; CALEDONIA (Fleecie Moore) / HELP ME (Sonny Boy Williamson) / BRING IT HOME TO ME (Sam Cooke) / SANTA FE (co-written w / Jackie DeShannon) / LONELY AVENUE (Doc Pomus) / GOOD MORNING LITTLE SCHOOLGIRL (Soony Boy Williamson) / THE

LONESOME ROAD (N.Shikret – G.Austin) / MOODY'S MOOD FOR LOVE (James Moody) / I'LL TAKE CARE OF YOU (Brook Benton) / BEFORE THE WORLD WAS MADE (W.B.Yeats / music; Kenny Craddock) / YOU DON'T KNOW ME (hit; Ray Charles) / I'LL NEVER BE FREE (Benjamin-Weiss) / THAT OLD BLACK MAGIC (hit; Sammy Davis Jnr). • **Trivia:** Early in the 70's, still having a love for the blues, he jammed with JOHN LEE HOOKER on 2 songs. They were to re-unite on stage late '89, singing 'Boom Boom' & 'It Serves You Right To Suffer'.

Recommended: ASTRAL WEEKS (*10) / MOONDANCE (*9) / TUPELO HONEY (*8) / VEEDON FLEECE (*7) / INARTICULATE SPEECH OF THE HEART (*7) / AVALON SUNSET (*8) / THE BEST OF VAN MORRISON (*9) / ENLIGHTENMENT (*7)

VAN MORRISON – vocals, guitar, saxophone (ex-THEM) with loads of session persons.

London / Bang

Jun 67. (7") **BROWN EYED GIRL. / GOODBYE BABY (BABY GOODBYE)** [ ] [10]
(re-iss Mar71 on 'President' & Apr74 on 'London' records)

Sep 67. (7") **RO RO ROSEY. / CHICK-A-BOO** [-] [ ]

Nov 67. (7") **SPANISH ROSE / MIDNIGHT ROSE** [-] [ ]

Feb 68. (lp) **BLOWIN' YOUR MIND** [ ] [ ] Sep 67
– Brown eyed girl / He ain't give you none / T.B. sheets / Spanish rose / Goodbye baby (baby goodbye) / Ro Ro Rosey / Who drove the red sports car? / Midnight special. *(cd-iss.Jul95 on 'Epic')*

— now with **LARRY FALLON** – conductor, arranger / **JAY BERLINER** – guitar / **RICHARD DAVIS** – bass / **CONNIE KAY** – drums / **JOHN PAYNE** – flute, sporano sax / **WARREN SMITH JR** – percussion, vibraphone

Warners / Warners

Sep 69. (lp)(c) **ASTRAL WEEKS** [ ] [ ] Nov 68
– In the beginning: Astral weeks / Beside you / Sweet thing / Cypress avenue / Afterwards: Young lovers do / Madame George / Ballerina / Slim slow rider. *(re-iss.Aug 71) (cd-iss.May87, re-iss.1989)*

— now with **JOHN PLATANIA** – guitar / **JEFF LABES** – keys / **JACK SHROER** – sax / **GARY MALLABER** – drums / **JOHN KLINGBERG** – bass.

Mar 70. (lp)(c) **MOONDANCE** [32] [29]
– And it stoned me / Moondance / Crazy love / Into the mystic / Caravan / Come running / These dreams of you / Brand new day / Everyone / Glad tidings. *(re-iss Aug 71) (cd-iss Jan86)*

May 70. (7") **COME RUNNING. / CRAZY LOVE** [ ] [39] Apr 70

Dec 70. (lp)(c) **HIS BAND AND THE STREET CHOIR** [ ] [32] Nov 70
– Domino / Crazy face / I've been working / Call me up in Dreamland / I'll be your lover, too / Blue money / Virgo clowns / Gypsy queen / Sweet Janine / If I ever needed someone / Street choir. *(re-iss.Aug 71) (re-iss.cd Feb93)*

Dec 70. (7") **DOMINO. / SWEET JANINE** [ ] [9] Oct 70
(re-iss Jul 71)

Feb 71. (7") **BLUE MONEY. / SWEET THING** [-] [23]

Apr 71. (7") **CALL ME UP IN DREAMLAND. / STREET CHOIR** [-] [95]

— now with **MALLABER, SHROER + BILL CHURCH** – bass / **RONNIE MONTROSE** – guitar / **RICK SCHLOSSER** – drums + **CONNIE KAY** – drums.

Sep 71. (7") **WILD NIGHT. / WHEN THAT EVENING SUN GOES DOWN** [-] [28]

Nov 71. (lp)(c) **TUPELO HONEY** [ ] [27] Oct 71
– Wild night / (Straight to your heart) Like a cannonball / Old old Woodstock / Starting a new life / You're my woman / Tupelo honey / I wonna roo you / When that evening sun goes down / Moonshine whiskey. *(re-iss.+cd. Aug89 on 'Polydor') (re-iss.cd+c Feb94 on 'Polydor')*

Dec 71. (7") **TUPELO HONEY. / STARTING A NEW LIFE** [-] [47]

Mar 72. (7") **(STRAIGHT TO YOUR HEART) LIKE A CANNON-BALL. / OLD OLD WOODSTOCK** [-] [ ]

— **LEROY VINNEGAR** – bass repl. CHURCH (who later joined MONTROSE) / **ROY ELLIOT** – guitar + **MARK NAFTALIN** – piano repl. SCHOSSLER + MALLABER

Jul 72. (7") **JACKIE WILSON SAID (I'M IN HEAVEN WHEN YOU SMILE). / YOU'VE GOT THE POWER** [ ] [61]

Aug 72. (lp)(c) **SAINT DOMINIC'S PREVIEW** [ ] [15]
– Jackie Wilson said (I'm in Heaven when you smile) / Gypsy / I will be there / Listen to the lion / Saint Dominic's preview / Redwood tree / Almost Independance day. *(re-iss.1974) (re-iss.+cd.Aug89 on 'Polydor' cd-iss.Apr95)*

Oct 72. (7") **REDWOOD TREE. / SAINT DOMINIC'S PREVIEW** [-] [98]

— RONNIE now formed MONTROSE went through various session personnel: **DAVID HAYES** – bass and most of new band.

Jul 73. (7") **WARM LOVE. / I WILL BE THERE** [ ] [ ] Jun 73

Jul 73. (lp)(c) **HARD NOSE THE HIGHWAY** [22] [27]
– Snow in San Anselmo / Warm love / Hard nose the highway / Wild children / The great deception / Green / Autumn song / Purple heather. *(re-iss.+cd.Aug89 on 'Polydor', cd-iss.Apr95)*

Sep 73. (7") **GREEN. / WILD CHILDREN** [-] [ ]

Feb 74. (7") **AIN'T NOTHING YOU CAN DO. / WILD CHILDREN** [-] [ ]

Feb 74. (d-lp)(d-c) **IT'S TOO LATE TO STOP NOW (live)** [ ] [53]
– Ain't nothing you can do / Warm love / Into the mystic / These dreams of you / I believe to my soul / I've been working / Help me / Wild children / Domino / I just wanna make love to you / Bring it on home to me / Saint Dominic's preview / Take your hand out of my pocket / Listen to the lion / Here comes the night / Gloria / Caravan / Cypress Avenue. *(re-iss.+d-cd.Aug89 on 'Polydor', cd-iss.Apr95)*

May 74. (7") **CALDONIA (WHAT MAKES YOUR BIG HEAD HARD?). / WHAT'S UP, CRAZY PUP** [ ] [ ]

Oct 74. (lp)(c) **VEEDON FLEECE** [41] [53]
– Streets of Arklow / Country fair / Cul de sac / Linden Arden stole the highlights / Fair play / Bulbs / You don't pull no punches but you don't push the river / Comfort you / Come here my love / Who was that masked man. *(re-iss.+cd.Aug89 on 'Polydor', cd-iss.Apr95)*

Jul 74. (7") **BULBS. / CUL DE SAC** [-] [ ]

Nov 74. (7") **BULBS. / WHO WAS THAT MASKED MAN** [ ] [-]

Mar 77. (lp)(c) **A PERIOD OF TRANSITION** [23] [43]
– You gotta make it through the world / It fills you up / The eternal Kansas City / Joyous sound / Flamingoes fly / Heavy connection / Cold wind in August. *(re-iss.+cd.Aug89 on 'Polydor')*

Apr 77. (7") **THE ETERNAL KANSAS CITY. / JOYOUS SOUND** [ ] [-]

Jul 77. (7") **JOYOUS SOUND. / MECHANICAL BLISS** [-] [ ]

Oct 77. (7") **COLD WIND IN AUGUST. / MOONDANCE** [-] [ ]

— **PETER VAN HOOKE** – drums / **HERBIE ARMSTRONG** – guitar etc

Oct 78. (lp)(c) **WAVELENGTH** [27] [28]
– Kingdom hall / Checkin' it out / Natalia / Venice U.S.A. / Lifetimes / Wavelength / Santa Fe / Beautiful obsession / Hungry for your love / Take it where you find it. *(re-iss.+cd.Aug89 on 'Polydor') (re-iss.cd+c Feb94 on 'Polydor')*

Oct 78. (7") **WAVELENGTH. / CHECKIN' IT OUT** [ ] [42]

Feb 79. (7") **NATALIA. / LIFETIMES** [ ] [ ]

Apr 79. (7") **CHECKIN' IT OUT. /** [-] [ ]

— now with **HOOKE, ARMSTRONG, HAYES / + MARK JORDAN** – keyboards / **MARK ISHAM** – trumpet / **PEE WEE ELLIS** – saxophone

Vertigo / Warners

Aug 79. (lp)(c) **INTO THE MUSIC** [21] [43]
– Bright side of the road / Full force gale / Stepping out queen / Troubadours / Rolling hills / You make me feel so free / Angeliou / And the healing has begun / It's all in the game / You know what they're writing about. *(re-iss.+cd.May83 on 'Mercury') (re-iss.+cd.Aug89 on 'Polydor') (re-iss.cd+c Feb94 on 'Polydor')*

Sep 79. (7") **BRIGHT SIDE OF THE ROAD. / ROLLING HILLS** [63] [ ]

Dec 79. (7") **FULL FORCE GALE. / YOU MAKE ME FEEL SO FREE** [-] [ ]

— **JOHN ALLAIR** – keyboards + **MICK COX** – guitar repl. JORDAN + MARCUS

Mercury / Warners

Sep 80. (lp)(c) **COMMON ONE** [53] [73]
– Haunts of ancient peace / Summertime in England / Satisfied / Wild honey / Spirit / When heart is open. *(re-iss.May83, cd-iss.1986) (re-iss.+cd.Aug89 on 'Polydor'; cd-iss.Apr95)*

— added **TOM DONLINGER** – drums

Feb 82. (lp)(c) **BEAUTIFUL VISION** [31] [44]
– Celtic Ray / Northern muse (solid sound) / Dweller on the threshold / Beautiful vision / She gives me religion / Cleaning windows / Vanlose stairway / Aryan mist / Scandinavia / Across the bridge where angels dwell / Scandinavia. *(cd-iss.1983) (re-iss.Mar85) (re-iss.+cd.Aug89 on 'Polydor') (re-iss.cd+c Feb94 on 'Polydor')*

Mar 82. (7") **CLEANING WINDOWS. / SCANDINAVIA** [-] [ ]

Mar 82. (7") **CLEANING WINDOWS. / IT'S ALL IN THE GAME** [ ] [-]

Jun 82. (7") **SCANDINAVIA. / DWELLER ON THE THRESHOLD** [ ] [ ]

— **CHRIS MICHIE** – guitar repl. COX

Feb 83. (7") **CRY FOR HOME. / SUMMERTIME IN ENGLAND (live)** [ ] [ ]
(12"+=) – All Saint's day.

Mar 83. (lp)(c)(cd) **INARTICULATE SPEECH OF THE HEART** [14] [ ]
– Higher than the world / Connswater / River of time / Celtic swing / Rave on, John

Donne / Inarticulate speech of the heart No.1 / Irish heartbeat / The street only knew your name / Cry for home / Inarticulate speech of the heart No.2 / September night. *(re-iss.May86) (re-iss.+cd.Aug89 on 'Polydor') (re-iss.cd+c Feb94 on 'Polydor')*

May 83. (7") **CELTIC SWING. / MR. THOMAS** [ ] [ ]
(12"+=) – Rave on, John Donne.

Feb 84. (lp)(c)(cd) **LIVE AT THE GRAND OPERA HOUSE, BELFAST (live)** [47] [ ]
– (intro) / Into the music / Inarticulate seech of the heart / Dweller on the threshold / It's all in the game – You know what they're writing about / She gives me religion / Haunts of ancient peace / Full force gale / Beautiful vision / Vanlose stairway / Rave on, John Donne – Rave on (part 2) / Northern muse (solid ground) / Cleaning windows. *(re-iss.+cd.Aug89 on 'Polydor')*

Mar 84. (7") **DWELLER ON THE THRESHOLD (live). / NORTHERN MUSE (SOLID GROUND)** [ ] [ ]

Nov 84. (7") **A SENSE OF WONDER. / HAUNTS OF ANCIENT PEACE (live)** [ ] [ ]

Feb 85. (lp)(c)(cd) **A SENSE OF WONDER** [25] [61]
– Tore down a La Rimbaud / Ancient of days / Evening meditation / The master's eyes / What would I do / A sense of wonder / Boffyflow and Spike / If you only knew / Let the slave / A new kind of man. *(re-iss.+cd.May90 on 'Polydor', cd-iss.Apr95)*

Jul 86. (lp)(c)(cd) **NO GURU, NO METHOD, NO TEACHER** [27] [70]
– Got to go back / Oh the warm feeling / Foreign window / Town called Paradise / In the garden / Tir na nog / Here comes the night / Thanks for the information / One Irish rover / Ivory tower. *(re-iss.Sep91) (re-iss.cd/c Feb94 on 'Polydor')*

Aug 86. (7") **GOT TO GO BACK. / IN THE GARDEN** [ ] [ ]

—— note: HOOKE + ISHAM left early '84 / **ELLIS + DONLINGER** in '85 / now new band

Sep 87. (lp)(c)(cd) **POETIC CHAMPIONS COMPOSE** [26] [90]
– Spanish steps / The mystery / Queen of the slipstream / I forgot that love existed / Sometimes I feel like a motherless child / Celtic excavation / Someone like you / Alan Watts blues / Give me my rapture / Did ye get healed? / Allow me.

Sep 87. (7") **DID YE GET HEALED?. / ALAN WATTS BLUES** [ ] [ ]

Apr 88. (7") **QUEEN OF THE SLIPSTREAM. / SPANISH STEPS** [ ] [ ]

Jun 88. (lp)(c)(cd) **IRISH HEARTBEAT ("VAN MORRISON & THE CHIEFTAINS")** [18] [ ]
– Star of the County Down / Irish heartbeat / Ta mo chleamhnas deanta / Raglan road / She moved through the fair / I'll tell me ma / Carrickfergus / Celtic Ray / My lagan love / Marie's wedding.

Jun 88. (7") **I'LL TELL ME MA. / TA MO CHLEAMHNAS DEANTA** [ ] [ ]
(12"+=)(cd-s+=) – Carrickfergus.

Polydor Mercury

May 89. (lp)(c)(cd) **AVALON SUNSET** [13] [91]
– Whenever God shines his light / Contacting my angel / I'd love to write another love song / Have I told you lately (that I love you) / Coney Island / I'm tired Joey boy / When will I ever learn to live in God / Orangefield / Daring night / These are the days.

Jun 89. (7") **HAVE I TOLD YOU LATELY (THAT I LOVE YOU). / CONTACTING MY ANGEL** [74] [ ]
(12"+=) – Listen to the lion.
(cd-s+=) – Irish heartbeat.

Sep 89. (7")(12") **ORANGEFIELD. / THESE ARE THE DAYS** [ ] [ ]
(cd-s+=) – And the healing has begun.

Nov 89. (7")(c-s) **WHENEVER GOD SHINES HIS LIGHT. (by "VAN MORRISON & CLIFF RICHARD") / I'D LOVE TO WRITE ANOTHER LOVE SONG** [20] [ ]
(12"+=) – Cry for home.
(cd-s++=) – ('A'-lp version).

Feb 90. (7") **CONEY ISLAND. / HAVE I TOLD YOU LATELY (THAT I LOVE YOU)** [ ] [ ]
(12"+=) – A sense of wonder.
(c-s++=)(cd-s++=) – Spirit.

Sep 90. (7")(c-s) **REAL REAL GONE. / START ALL OVER AGAIN** [ ] [ ]
(12"+=)(cd-s+=) – Cleaning windows.

Oct 90. (cd)(c)(lp) **ENLIGHTENMENT** [5] [62]
– Real real gone / Enlightenment / So quiet in here / Avalon of the heart / See me through / Youth of 1,000 summers / In the days before rock'n'roll / Start all over again / She's a baby / Memories.

Nov 90. (7")(c-s) **IN THE DAYS BEFORE ROCK'N'ROLL. / I'D LOVE TO WRITE ANOTHER LOVE SONG** [ ] [ ]
(12"+=)(cd-s+=) – Coney Island.

Jan 91. (7") **ENLIGHTENMENT. / AVALON OF THE HEART** [ ] [ ]
(12"+=)(cd-s+=) – Jackie Wilson said.

(VAN is credited w / TOM JONES on his Mar91 single 'CARRYING A TORCH')

May 91. (7")(c-s) **I CAN'T STOP LOVING YOU. ("VAN MORRISON & CHIEFTAINS") / ALL SAINTS DAY** [ ] [ ]
(12"+=)(cd-s+=) – Carrying a torch. (w / "TOM JONES")

Aug 91. (7")(c-s) **WHY MUST I ALWAYS EXPLAIN?. / SO COMPLICATED** [ ] [ ]
(12"+=)(cd-s+=) – Enlightenment.

Sep 91. (d-cd)(d-c)(d-lp) **HYMNS OF THE SILENCE** [5] [99]
– Professional jealousy / I'm not feeling it anymore / Ordinary life / Some peace of mind / So complicated / I can't stop loving you / Why must I always explain? / Village idiot / See me through part II (just a closer walk with thee) / Take me back / By his Grace / All Saints day / Hymns to the silence / On Hyndford Street / Be thou my vision / Carrying a torch / Green mansions / Pagan streams / Quality Street / It must be you / I need your kind of loving.

May 93. (7")(c-s) **GLORIA. ("VAN MORRISON & JOHN LEE HOOKER") / IT MUST BE YOU (live)** [31] [ ]
(cd-s+=) – The healing has begun (live) / See me through (live).
(cd-s) – ('A'side) / Whenever God shines his light (live) / It fills you up (live) / The star of County Down (live).

Jun 93. (cd)(c)(lp) **TOO LONG IN EXILE** [4] [29]
– Too long in exile / Big time operators / Lonely avenue / Ball & chain / In the forest / Till we get the healing done / Gloria / Good morning little schoolgirl / Wasted years / The lonesome road / Moody's mood for love / Close enough for jazz / Before the world was made / I'll take care of you – Instrumental – Tell me what you want.

Apr 94. (d-cd)(d-c) **A NIGHT IN SAN FRANCISCO (live)** [8] [ ]
– Did ya get healed? / It's all in the game / Make it real one more time / I've been working / I forgot that love existed / Vanlose stairway / Trans-Euro train / Fool for you / You make me feel so real / Beautiful vision / See me through / Soldier of fortune / Thankyoufalettinmebemiseldagain / Ain't that lovin' you baby / Stormy Monday / Have you ever loved a woman / No rollin' blues / Help me / Good morning little schoolgirl / Tupelo honey / Moondance / My funny valentine / Jumpin' with Symphony Sid / It fills you up / I'll take care of you / It's a man's man's man's world / Lonely avenue / 4 o'clock in the morning / So quiet in here / That's where it's at / In the garden / You send me / Allegheny / Have I told you lately that I love you / Shakin' all over / Gloria.

Jun 95. (cd-s) **DAYS LIKE THIS / YO** [65] [ ]
(7"+=)(c-s+=)(cd-s+=) – I don't want to go on without you / That old black magic.

Jun 95. (cd)(c)(lp) **DAYS LIKE THIS** [5] [33]
– Perfect fit / Russian roulette / Rain check / You don't know me / No religion / Underlying depression / Songwriter / Days like this / I'll never be free / Melancholia / Ancient highway / In the afternoon.

Sep 95. (c-s) **PERFECT FIT / RAINCHECK** [ ] [ ]
(cd-s+=) – Cleaning windows.

Nov 95. (cd-s) **NO RELIGION / HAVE I TOLD YOU LATELY** [54] [ ]
(cd-s+=) – Whenever God shines his light / Gloria.
(cd-s) – ('A'side) / Days like this / Raincheck.

– compilations, others, etc. –

May 71. President/ US= Bang; (lp) **THE BEST OF VAN MORRISON** [ ] [ ] 1970
(nearly a re-iss of debut '67 lp)

Mar 74. London/ US= Bang; (lp) **T.B. SHEETS** [ ] [ ] Jan 74
(nearly a re-iss of debut '67 lp) *(re-iss. Sep 88 on 'Bellaphon')(re-iss.+cd.May91 on 'C.B.S.')*

Sep 77. Bang; (lp) **THIS IS WHERE I CAME IN** [ ] [ ]
(nearly a re-iss of debut '67 lp)

Oct 75. Warners; (d-lp) **TWO ORIGINALS OF VAN MORRISON** [ ] [ ]
(VAN MORRISON, HIS BAND AND STREET CHOIR / TUPELO HONEY)

Oct 77. Warners; (7") **MOONDANCE. / ?** [-] [92]

Oct 82. Warners; (d-c) **MOONDANCE / . . . HIS BAND AND STREET CHOIR** [ ] [-]

Mar 90. Polydor/ US= Mercury; (cd)(c)(lp) **THE BEST OF VAN MORRISON** [4] [41] May 90
– Bright side of the road / Gloria (THEM) / Moondance / Baby please don't go (THEM) / Have I told you lately / Brown eyed girl / Sweet thing / Warm love / Wonderful remark / Jackie Wilson said (I'm in Heaven when you smile) / Full force gale / And it stoned me / Here comes the night (THEM) / Domino / Did ye get healed / Wild night / Cleaning windows / Whenever God shines his light (w / CLIFF RICHARD). *(c+cd.iss.has extra tracks)*

Jul 90. Polydor; (7") **GLORIA. / RAVE ON** [ ] [ ]

Feb 93. Polydor; (cd)(c) **THE BEST OF VAN MORRISON VOLUME 2** [31] [ ]
– Real real gone / When will I ever learn to live in God / Sometimes I feel like a motherless child / In the garden / A sense of wonder / I'll tell me ma / Coney Island / Enlightenment / Rave on john Donne – Rave on part two live / Don't look back / It's all over now, baby blue / One Irish Rover / The mystery / Hymns to the silence / Evening meditation.

Jan 92. Moles; (c) **CUCHULAINN** (spoken word) [ ] [-]

Mar 92. Sony; (d-cd)(c) **BANG MASTERS** [ ] [-]

Jan 93. Movieplay Gold; (cd) **THE LOST TAPES VOLUME 1** [ ] [-]

Jan 93. Movieplay Gold; (cd) **THE LOST TAPES VOLUME 1** [ ] [-]

May 94. Charly; (cd) **PAYIN' DUES** [ ] [-]

Oct 95. Verve; (cd)(c)(lp) **HOW LONG HAS THIS BEEN GOING ON ("VAN MORRISON with GEORGIE FAME & FRIENDS") (live 3 May'95 at Ronnie Scott's)** [ ] [ ]
– I will be there / The new symphony Sid / Early in the morning / Who can I turn to? / Sack o'woe / Moondance / Centerpiece / How long has this been going on? / Your mind is on vacation / All saint's day / Blues in the night / Don't worry about a thing / That's life / Heathrow shuffle.

MORRISSEY

Born: STEPHEN PATRICK MORRISSEY, 22 May'59, Manchester, England. Former SMITHS frontman, until his fall-out with their guitarist JOHNNY MARR in August 1987. The SMITHS had already progressed from top indie 'Rough Trade' to 'EMI', but as there was now no band, MORRISSEY's releases were switched to EMI's re-activated 'HMV'. His debut single 'SUEDEHEAD', was his first ever entry into UK Top 5, early in '88. It was hastily pursued by Top 3 album 'VIVA HATE', which brought in new band and producer STEPHEN STREET. From then on, MORRISSEY was a regular feature in the charts, and surprised many when 1991 album 'KILL UNCLE', nearly hit the US Top 50. • **Style:** Intellectual, overtly confident chanter, who was best described as 'The Oscar Wilde of Rock'. • **Songwriters:** Writes all lyrics, with music by STEPHEN STREET until 1991, when MARK NEVIN augmented. Producers now being CLIVE LANGER and ALAN WINSTANLEY. Covered; THAT'S ENTERTAINMENT (Jam) / SKIN STORM (Bradford). • **Trivia:** In the late 80's, he made a cameo appearance in Channel 4's 'Brookside' off-shoot 'South'. MICK RONSON (ex-BOWIE) produced 1992 album.

Recommended: VIVA HATE (*9) / KILL UNCLE (*8) / YOUR ARSENAL (*8) / VAUXHALL AND I (*9).

MORRISSEY – vocals (ex-SMITHS) with **STEPHEN STREET** – guitar, bass, producer, co-writer / **ANDREW PARESI** – drums / **VINI REILLY** – guitar, keyboards (of DURUTTI COLUMN)

H.M.V. Sire

Feb 88. (7") **SUEDEHEAD. / I KNOW VERY WELL HOW I GOT MY NAME** [5] [ ]
(12"+=) – Hairdresser on fire.
(c-s++=)(cd-s++=) – Oh well, I'll never learn.

Mar 88. (lp)(c)(cd) **VIVA HATE** [2] [48]

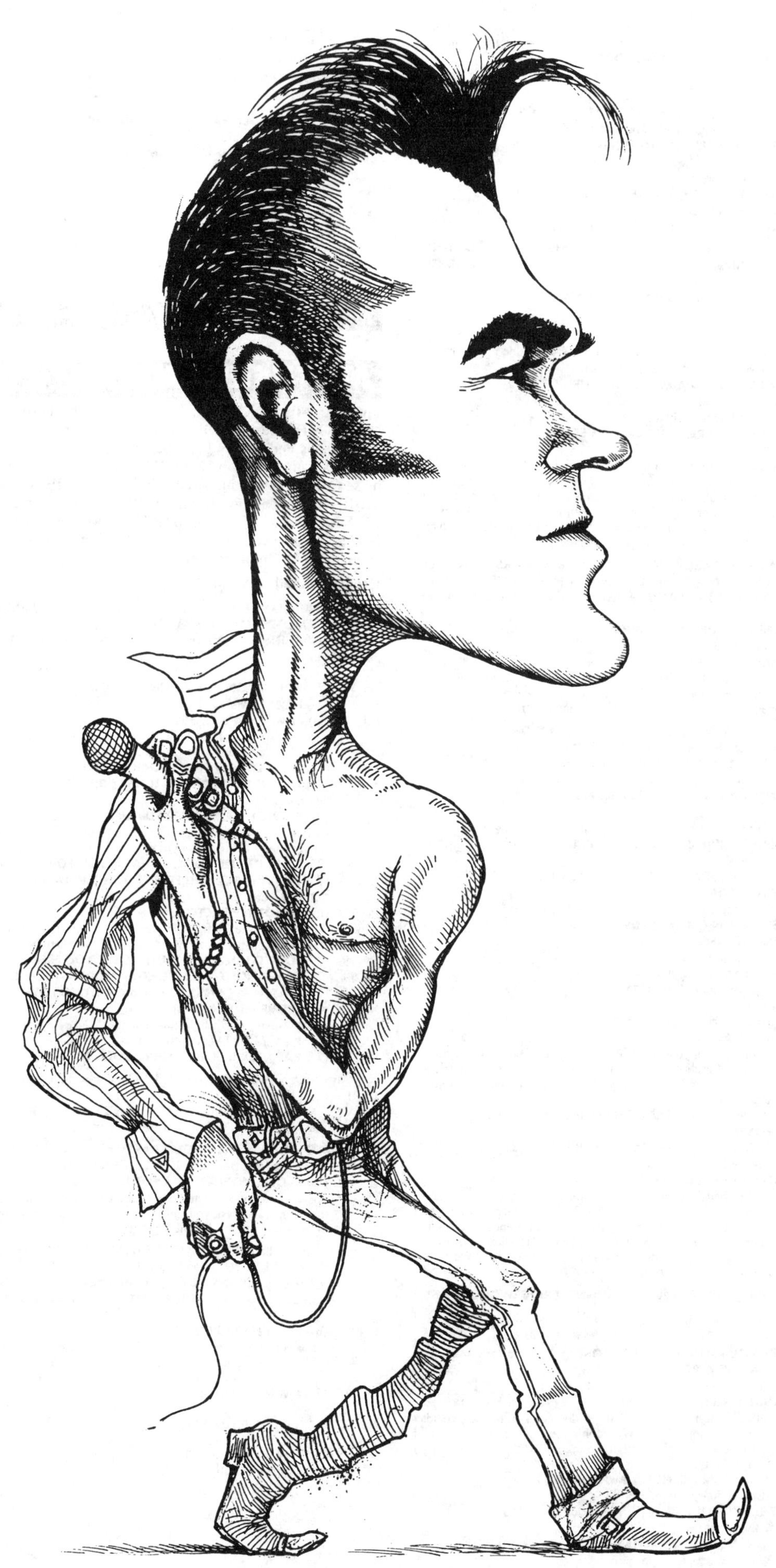

– Alsatian cousin / Little man, what now? / Everyday is like Sunday / Bengali in platforms / Angel, angel, down we go together / Late night, Maudlin Street / Suedehead / Break up the family / The ordinary boys / I don't mind if you forget me / Dial-a-cliche / Margaret on the guillotine. *(re-iss.cd+c Mar94 on 'Parlophone')*

Jun 88. (7") **EVERYDAY IS LIKE SUNDAY. / DISAPPOINTED** [9] [ ]
(12"+=) – Sister I'm a poet.
(c-s++=)(cd-s++=) – Will never marry.

— **MORRISSEY** only retained **STREET.** He brought in **NEIL TAYLOR** – guitar and re-united with (ex-SMITHS):- **CRAIG GANNON, ANDY ROURKE + MIKE JOYCE**

Feb 89. (7") **THE LAST OF THE FAMOUS INTERNATIONAL PLAYBOYS. / LUCKY LIPS** [6] [ ]
(12"+=)(cd-s+=) – Michael's bones.

Apr 89. (7") **INTERESTING DRUG. / SUCH A LITTLE THING MAKES SUCH A BIG DIFFERENCE** [9] [ ]
(12"+=)(c-s+=)(cd-s+=) – Sweet and tender hooligan (live).

— He brought in complete new line-up:- **KEVIN ARMSTRONG** – guitar / **MATTHEW SELIGMAN** – bass / **STEVE HOPKINS** – drums and returning **ANDREW PARESI** – keys

Nov 89. (7")(c-s) **OUIJA BOARD, OUIJA BOARD. / YES, I AM BLIND** [18] [ ]
(12"+=)(cd-s+=) – East west.

— **ANDY ROURKE** returned to repl. SELIGMAN + HOPKINS / added guest **MARY MARGARET O'HARA** – vocals (up & coming solo artist)

Apr 90. (7")(c-s) **NOVEMBER SPAWNED A MONSTER. / HE KNOWS I'D LOVE TO SEE HIM** [12] [ ]
(12"+=)(cd-s+=) – The girl least likely to.

Oct 90. (7")(c-s) **PICCADILLY PALAVARE. / GET OFF THE STAGE** [18] [ ]
(12"+=)(cd-s+=) – At amber.

Oct 90. (cd)(c)(lp) **BONA DRAG** (compilation of recent material) [9] [59]
– Piccadilly palavre / Interesting drug / November spawned a monster / Will never marry / Such a little thing makes such a big difference / The last of the famous international playboys / Ouija board, ouija board / Hairdresser on fire / Everyday is like Sunday / He knows I'd love to see him / Yes, I am blind / Lucky lisp / Suedehead / Disappointed. *(re-iss.cd/c Mar94 on 'Parlophone')*

— He now retained **ANDREW PARESI.** Newcomers were **BEDDERS** – bass (ex-MADNESS) / **MARK E.NEVIN** – guitars, co-composer (ex-FAIRGROUND ATTRACTION) plus **STEVE HEART + SEAMUS BEAGHAN** – keyboards / **NAWAZISH ALI KHAN** – violin

Feb 91. (7")(c-s) **OUR FRANK. / JOURNALISTS WHO LIE** [26] [ ]
(12"+=)(cd-s+=) – Tony the pony.

Feb 91. (cd)(c)(lp) **KILL UNCLE** [8] [52] Mar 91
– Our Frank / Asian rut / Sing your life / Mute witness / King Leer / Found found found / Driving your girlfriend home / The harsh truth of the camera eye / (I'm) The end of the family line / There's a place in Hell for me and my friends.

— His tour band Spring '91; **ALAIN WHYTE** – guitar / **GARY DAY** – bass / **BOZ BOORER** – guitar (ex-POLECATS) / **SPENCER COBRIN** – drums

Apr 91. (7")(c-s) **SING YOUR LIFE. / THAT'S ENTERTAINMENT** [33] [ ]
(12"+=)(cd-s+=) – The loop.

Jul 91. (7")(c-s) **PREGNANT FOR THE LAST TIME. / SKIN STORM** [25] [ ]
(12"+=)(cd-s+=) – Cosmic dancer (live) / Disappointed (live).

Oct 91. (7")(c-s) **MY LOVE LIFE. / I'VE CHANGED MY PLEA TO GUILTY** [29] [ ]
(12"+=)(cd-s+=) – There's a place in Hell for me and my friends.

late 91. (cd-ep) **MORRISEY AT KROQ (live)** [-] [ ]
– There's a place in Hell for my friends / My love life / Sing your life.

Apr 92. (7")(c-s) **WE HATE IT WHEN OUR FRIENDS BECOME SUCCESSFUL. / SUEDEHEAD** [17] [ ]
(12"+=) – Pregnant for the last time.
(cd-s+=) – I've changed my plea to guilty.

Jul 92. (7")(c-s) **YOU'RE THE ONE FOR ME, FATTY. / PASHERNATE LOVE** [19] [ ]
(12"+=)(cd-s+=) – There speaks a true friend.

Jul 92. (cd)(c)(lp) **YOUR ARSENAL** [4] [21]
– You're gonna need someone on your side / Glamorous glue / We'll let you know / The National Front disco / Certain people I know / We hate it when our friends become successful / You're the one for me, Fatty / Seasick, yet still docked / I know it's gonna happen someday / Tomorrow.

Aug 92. (12"ep)(cd-ep) **TOMORROW / LET THE RIGHT ONE SLIP IN / PAHERNATE LOVER** [-] [ ]

Nov 92. (7")(c-s) **CERTAIN PEOPLE I KNOW. / JACK THE RIPPER** [35] [ ]
(12"+=)(cd-s+=) – You've had her.

May 93. (cd)(c)(lp) **BEETHOVEN WAS DEAF (live)** [13] [ ]
– You're the one for me, Fatty / Certain people I know / National Front disco / November spawned a monster / Seasick, yet still docked / The loop / Sister I'm a poet / Jack the ripper / Such a little thing makes such a big difference / I know it's gonna happen someday / We'll let you know / Suedehead / He knows I'd love to see him / You're gonna need someone on your side / Glamorous glue / We hate it when our friends become successful. *(re-iss.cd+c Sep94)*

— **BOZ BOORER + ALAIN WHYTE** – guitars / **JONNY BRIDGEWOOD** – bass / **WOODIE TAYLOR** – drums

Parlophone | Sire

Mar 94. (7")(c-s) **THE MORE YOU IGNORE ME, THE CLOSER I GET. / USED TO BE A SWEET BOY** [8] [46]
(12"+=)(cd-s+=) – I'd love to.

Mar 94. (cd)(c)(lp) **VAUXHALL AND I** [1] [18]
– Now my heart is full / Spring-heeled Jim / Billy Budd / Hold on to your friends / The more you ignore me, the closer I get / Why don't you find out for yourself / I am hated for loving / Lifeguard sleeping, girl drowning / Used to be a sweet boy / The lazy sunbathers / Speedway.

Jun 94. (7")(c-s) **HOLD ON TO YOUR FRIENDS. / MOONRIVER** [47] [ ]
(12")(cd-s) – (extended versions).

Aug 94. (7")(c-s) **INTERLUDE. (w/ SIOUXSIE) / ('A'extended)** [25] [ ]
(12"+=)(cd-s+=) – ('A'mix).

Jan 95. (7")(c-s) **BOXERS. / HAVE-A-GO MERCHANT** [23] [ ]
(12"+=)(cd-s+=) – Whatever happens, I love you.

Feb 95. (cd)(c)(lp) **WORLD OF MORRISSEY** (part compilation) [15] [ ]
– Whatever happens, I love you / Billy Budd / Jack the ripper (live) / Have-a-go merchant / The loop / Sister I'm a poet (live) / You're the one for me, Fatty (live) / Boxers / Moon river (extended) / My love life / Certain people I know / The last of the famous international playboys / We'll let you know / Spring-heeled Jim.

— **SPENCER JAMES COBRIN** – drums repl.WOODIE

RCA Victor | RCA Victor

Aug 95. (7")(c-s) **DAGENHAM DAVE. / NOBODY LOVES US** [26] [ ]
(cd-s+=) – You must please remember.

Aug 95. (cd)(c)(lp) **SOUTHPAW GRAMMAR** [4] [66]
– The teachers are afraid of the pupils / Reader meet author / The boy racer / The operation / Dagenham Dave / Do your best and don't worry / Best friend on the payroll / Southpaw.

Nov 95. (7")(c-s) **THE BOY RACER. / LONDON (live)** [36] [ ]
(cd-s+=) – Billy Budd (live).
(cd-s) – Spring heeled Jim (live) / Why don't you find out for yourself (live).

Dec 95. (7")(c-s) **SUNNY. / BLACK-EYED SUSAN** [42] [ ]
(cd-s+=) – A swallow on my neck.

MOTHER LOVE BONE (see under ⇒ PEARL JAM)

MOTHER'S FINEST

Formed: Atlanta, Georgia, USA . . . 1974 by husband annd wife GLENN MURDOCH and JOYCE KENNEDY. Gained European success in the Netherlands and 4 Top 200 albums in the States. • **Style:** A blend of R&B /funk rock, that fused between VAN HALEN or BUDGIE, although fronted by sensual and attacking strikeforce of BABY JEAN KENNEDY and GLEN MURDOCK. • **Songwriters:** MURDOCH and some group except MICKEY'S MONKEY (Miracles) / STRAWBERRY FIELDS FOREVER (Beatles) / **Note:** Not to be confused with other band of the same name, who released an eponymous US lp in 1972 on 'RCA'.

Recommended: LIVE MUTHA (*6)

BABY JEAN (b.JOYCE KENNEDY) – vocals, percussion / **GLENN MURDOCK** – vocals, percussion / **MOSES MO** (b.GARY MOORE) – guitar, vocals / **MIKE KECK** – keyboards / **WIZZARD** (b.JERRY SEAY) – bass, vocals / **B.B. QUEEN** (b.BARRY BORDEN) – drums, percussion

Epic | Epic

Sep 76. (7") **FIRE. / DONCHA WANNA LOVE ME** [ ] [93] Aug76
Jan 77. (7") **RAIN. / MY BABY** [ ] [ ]
Feb 77. (lp)(c) **MOTHER'S FINEST** [ ] [ ] Sep76
– Fire / Give you all the love / Niggizz can't sing rock and roll / My baby / Fly with me / Doncha wanna love me / Rain.
Sep 77. (7") **BABY LOVE. / HARD ROCK LOVERS** [-] [58]
Nov 77. (7") **THANK YOU FOR THE LOVE. / DIS GO DIS WAY DIS GO DAT WAY** [-] [ ]
Apr 78. (lp)(c) **ANOTHER MOTHER FURTHER** [ ] [ ] Sep77
– Mickey's monkey / Baby love / Thank you for the love / Piece of the rock / Truth'll set you free / Burning love / Dis go dis way, dis go that way / Hard rock lovers.
Jul 78. (7") **PIECE OF THE ROCK. / THANK YOU FOR THE LOVE** [-] [ ] Apr 78
Nov 78. (7") **TRUTH'LL SET YOU FREE. / DON'T WANNA COME BACK** [-] [ ]
Jan 79. (lp)(c) **MOTHER FACTOR** [ ] [ ] Sep78
– Can't fight the feeling / Tell me / Watch my stylin' / Love changes / Don't wanna come back / Give it up / Mr.Goodbar / I can't believe / More and more.
Feb 79. (7") **LOVE CHANGES. / TRUTH'LL SET YOU FREE** [-] [ ]
Jun 79. (7") **CAN'T FIGHT THE FEELING. / MORE AND MORE** [-] [ ]
Sep 79. (7") **WATCH MY STYLIN'. / SOMEBODY TO LOVE** [-] [ ]
Nov 79. (lp)(c) **LIVE MUTHA (live)** [ ] [ ]
– Baby love / Can't fight this feeling / Mickey's monkey / Love changes / Watch my stylin' / Don't wanna come back / Fire / Give you all the love.
Dec 79. (7") **BABY LOVE (live). / HARD ROCK LOVERS (live)** [-] [ ]

— In 1980, MIKE departed. (MURDOCK now added guitar)

Jul 81. (lp)(c) **IRON AGE** [ ] [ ] May81
– Movin' on / All the way / Earthling / Luv drug / Evolution / Gone with th' rain / Illusion / Rock'n'roll nite / Time / U turn me on.

— **GREG WILLIS** – guitar / **DOUG BARE** – keyboards / **HAROLD SEAY** – drums **+ MATT GREELY** – percussion repl. B.B. QUEEN who joined MOLLY HATCHET.

Aug 83. (lp)(c) **ONE MOTHER TO ANOTHER** [ ] [ ]
– Everybody needs somebody / Secret service / Victory / What kind of fool / Take me to the middle (of your luv) / Love me too / Big shot Romeo / In my baby's arms / What you do to me / Some kind of madness.

— Disbanded in 1984, and MOSES (GARY MOORE) teamed up with B.B.QUEEN to form ILLUSION. JOYCE was heard on GEORGE DUKE's eponymous album. In 1989, they (**KENNEDY** – vocals, **MURDOCK** – vocals **+ WIZZARD** – bass, vocals) re-formed, recruiting **JOHN HAYES** – guitar / **DION DEREK** – drums

Capitol | Capitol

Oct 89. (lp)(c)(cd) **LOOKS COULD KILL** [ ] [ ]
– For your love / I'm 'n danger / Legs and lipstick / Dream come true / Stilloveach other / I'll never be the same / Brave and strong / Your wish is my command / Cherish your lover / Heartbreaker. (c+cd+=) – Call me mister / Too serious.
Oct 89. (7") **I'M 'N DANGER. /** [-] [ ]

R.C.A. | R.C.A.

Nov 90. (cd)(c)(lp) **SUBLUXATION (live)** [ ] [ ]
– Chain / Truth'll set you free / Call me mister / Mandela song / Mickey's monkey / Give you all the love / Think about me / Cheap spot / Piece of the rock / Strawberry fields forever / Baby love / Somebody to love.

MOTHERS (OF INVENTION)
(see under ⇒ ZAPPA, Frank)

MOTLEY CRUE

Formed: Los Angeles, California, USA . . . early 1981 by NIKKI SIXX, etc (see below). In 1982, they issued lp 'TOO FAST FOR LOVE', on own US label 'Leathur'. This was re-issued the following year as their debut for 'Elektra'. Later in 1983, their 2nd album 'SHOUT AT THE DEVIL', which was produced by Tom Werman. After a nationwide tour supporting KISS, it hit the US Top 20. For the rest of the 80's, the band became one of top attractions and had a US No.1 album 'DR.FEELGOOD' in 1989. However on the 8 Dec'84, VINCE NEIL was involved in a serious accident while driving his car. A passenger NICK 'RAZZLE' DINGLEY was killed in the crash, and 2 others were injured. VINCE was ordered to pay $2• 5 million compensation and was sentenced to 20 days in jail, after being convicted of vehicle manslaughter. Early in 1988, MATTHEW TRIPPE sued the CRUE for royalties, alleging he masqueraded and wrote songs as NIKKI SIXX, while he recovered from a 1983 car crash. This was later proved to be false, although there is still much speculation on how SIXX's face was bloated on some mug pics. • **Style:** Theatrical and aggressive heavy-metal outfit, influenced by KISS or The TUBES. • **Songwriters:** All written by SIXX (in Dec'87 he was clinically dead for 2 minutes, after taking heroin). Covered; SMOKIN' IN THE BOYS ROOM (Brownsville Station) / HELTER SKELTER (Beatles) / JAILHOUSE ROCK (Leiber-Stoller). • **Trivia:** Late 1985, TOMMY LEE married actress Heather Lockear. On Dec'87, MICK married one-time PRINCE girlfriend VANITY (star of 'Purple Rain')?. In May'90, NIKKI was hitched to former Playboy centre-fold Brandi Brandt.

Recommended DR. FEELGOOD (*7) / SHOUT AT THE DEVIL (*7) / DECADE OF DECADENCE (*8)

VINCE NEIL (b. VINCENT NEIL WHARTON, 8 Feb'61) – vocals (ex-ROCK CANDY) / **NIKKI SIXX** (b. FRANK FARRANO, 11 Dec'58, Seattle, DC) – bass (ex-LONDON) / **MICK MARS** (b. ROB DEAL, 4 Apr'55, Terre Haute, Indiana) – guitar / **TOMMY LEE** (b. 3 Oct'62, Athens, Greece) – drums (ex-SUITE 19)

not issued | Leathur

1981. (lp) **TOO FAST FOR LOVE** [-] [ ]
– Live wire / Public enemy No.1 / Take me to the top / Merry-go-round / Piece of your action / Starry eyes / Come on and dance / Too fast for love / On with the show. *(UK iss.Oct82 as 'MOTLEY CRUE' on 'Elektra') (US re-iss.Nov83 on 'Elektra') (cd-iss.Feb93 on 'Elektra')*
1982. (7") **TOAST OF THE TOWN. / STICK TO YOUR GUNS** [-] [ ]
(above a US gig freebie)

Elektra | Elektra

Sep 83. (lp)(c) **SHOUT AT THE DEVIL** [ ] [17]
– In the beginning / Shout at the Devil / Looks that kill / Bastard / Knock 'em dead, kid / Danger / Too young to fall in love / Helter skelter / Red hot / Ten seconds 'til love / God bless the children of the beast. *(cd-iss.Jan86)*
Jul 84. (7") **LOOKS THAT KILL. / PIECE OF THE ACTION** [ ] [54] Jan 84
(12"+=) – Live wire.
Oct 84. (7")(12") **TOO YOUNG TO FALL IN LOVE (remix). / TAKE ME TO THE TOP** [ ] [90] Jun 84
Jul 85. (lp)(c) **THEATRE OF PAIN** [36] [6]
– City boy blues / Smokin' in the boys' room / Louder than Hell / Keep your eye on the money / Home sweet home / Tonight (we need a lover) / Use it or lose it / Save our souls / Raise your hands to rock / Fight for your rights. *(cd-iss.Jul86)*
Aug 85. (7")(12") **SMOKIN' IN THE BOYS ROOM. / USE IT OR LOSE IT** [71] [16] Jul 85
(US-12") – ('A'side) / Helter skelter / Piece of your action / Live wire.
Oct 85. (7") **HOME SWEET HOME. / RED HOT** [-] [89]
Jan 86. (7")(7"pic-d) **SMOKIN' IN THE BOYS ROOM. / HOME SWEET HOME** [51] [-]
(12"+=) – Shout at the Devil.
Jun 87. (lp)(c)(cd) **GIRLS, GIRLS, GIRLS** [14] [2]
– Wild side / Girls, girls, girls / Dancing on glass / Bad bad boogie / Nona / Five years dead / All in the name of . . . / Sumthin' for nuthin' / You're all I need / Jailhouse rock (live).
Jul 87. (7") **GIRLS, GIRLS, GIRLS. / SUMTHIN' FOR NUTHIN'** [26] [12] May 87
(12"+=)(12"pic-d+=) – Smokin' in the boys room.
Nov 87. (7") **WILD SIDE. / FIVE YEARS DEAD** [-] [ ]
Jan 88. (7") **YOU'RE ALL I NEED. / ALL IN THE NAME OF ROCK** [-] [83]
Jan 88. (7") **YOU'RE ALL I NEED. / WILD SIDE** [23] [-]
(12"+=)(12"pic-d+=) – Home sweet home / Looks that kill.
Jul 88. (m-lp)(c)(cd) **HOME SWEET HOME** (RAW TRACKS) [-] [ ]
– Live wire / Piece of your action / Too young to fall in love / Knock 'em dead, kid / Home sweet home.
Sep 89. (lp)(c)(cd) **DR. FEELGOOD** [4] [1]
– Same ol' situation (S.O.S.) / Slice of your pie / Rattlesnake shake / Kickstart my heart / Without you / Don't go away mad (just go away) / She goes down / Sticky sweet / Time for a change / T.N.T. (Terror 'n' Tinseltown) / Dr. Feelgood.
Oct 89. (7")(c-s)(7"pic-d) **DR. FEELGOOD. / STICKY SWEET** [50] [6] Sep 89
(12")(3"cd-s) – ('A'extended) / All in the name of rock.
Dec 89. (7")(c-s) **KICKSTART MY HEART. / SHE GOES DOWN** [-] [27]
Feb 90. (7") **WITHOUT YOU. / SLICE OF YOUR LIFE** [-] [8]
Apr 90. (7")(c-s)(7"pic-d) **WITHOUT YOU. / LIVE WIRE** [39] [-]
(12"+=)(cd-s+=) – Girls, girls, girls / All in the name of rock.
May 90. (c-s)(cd-s) **DON'T GO AWAY MAD (JUST GO AWAY). / ?** [-] [19]
Aug 90. (c-s)(cd-s) **SAME OL' SITUATION (S.O.S.). / ?** [-] [78]
Aug 91. (7")(c-s) **PRIMAL SCREAM. / DANCING ON GLASS** [32] [63]
(12"+=)(cd-s+=) – Red hot (live) / Dr.Feelgood (live).
Oct 91. (cd)(c)(lp) **DECADE OF DECADENCE** (compilation) [20] [2]
– Live wire / Piece of your action / Shout at the Devil / Looks that kill / Home sweet home / Smokin' in the boys room / Girls, girls, girls / Wild side / Dr. Feelgood / Kickstart my heart / Teaser / Rock'n'roll junkie / Primal scream / Angela / Anarchy in the UK.
Dec 91. (7") **HOME SWEET HOME ('91 remix). / YOU'RE ALL I NEED** [37] [37] Nov 91
(12"+=)(cd-s+=)(12"pic-d+=) – Without you / ('A'original mix).

—— Had already split temporarily Apr'91 to do own projects. The group parted company with VINCE NEIL, who went solo early 1992.

—— **JOHN CORABI** – vocals (ex-SCREAM) repl. VINCE

Mar 94. (7"yellow) **HOOLIGAN'S HOLIDAY. / HYPNOTISED (demo)** [36] [ ]
(12"+=)(cd-s+=) – ('A'mixes).
Mar 94. (cd)(c)(d-lp) **MOTLEY CRUE** [17] [7]
– Power to the music / Uncle Jack / Hooligan's holiday / Misunderstood / Loveshine / Poison apples / Hammered / 'Til death us do part / Welcome to the numb / Smoke the sky / Droppin' like flies / Driftaway.

MOTORHEAD

Formed: London, England . . . Jun'75 by LEMMY who had just been sacked from HAWKWIND for spending 5 days in a Canadian jail, following his arrest for a drug offence. After toying with the idea of name BASTARD, he opted for MOTORHEAD, named after a recent song he wrote for HAWKWIND. He recruited LARRY WALLIS – guitar, vocals (of PINK FAIRIES) and LUCAS FOX – drums, but by early 1976, they had been deposed by 'FAST' EDDIE CLARKE and PHIL 'ANIMAL' TAYLOR. The initial line-up, had recorded album 'ON PAROLE' for 'United Art', but label shelved it until exploiting their success in 1979. More bad luck ensued, when late '76, new 'Stiff' records, also withdrew their debut 45 'WHITE LINE FEVER' & 'LEAVIN' HERE', and they too gave it light in 1979. In Apr'77, they found solace in Ted Carroll's 'Chiswick', who 2 months later released eponymous single and lp. The latter made the UK Top 50, and prompted major 'Bronze' records to give them contract the next year. After a minor hit with cover 'LOUIE LOUIE', they went Top 40 in 1979 with 'OVERKILL' 45 and album. They grew with every subsequent release, peaking in 1981 with the live No.1 'NO SLEEP TIL HAMMERSMITH'. • **Style:** Hard-drinking, leather-clad, speed-metal rock outfit, whose loudness was their forte. • **Songwriters:** LEMMY or group penned except covers; LOUIE LOUIE (Kingsmen) / TRAIN KEPT A-ROLLIN' (Yardbirds) / PLEASE DON'T TOUCH (Johnny Kidd) / (I'M YOUR) HOOCHIE COOCHIE MAN (Willie Dixon) / CAT SCRATCH FEVER (Ted Nugent). • **Trivia:** In 1987, LEMMY appeared in the Comic Strip movie 'Eat The Rich'.

Recommended: NO SLEEP TIL HAMMERSMITH (*8) / NO REMORSE (*8).

LEMMY (b.IAN KILMISTER, 24 Dec'45, Stoke-On-Trent, England) – vocals, bass (ex-HAWKWIND, ex-OPAL BUTTERFLY, ex-SAM GOPAL'S DREAM, ROCKIN' VICKERS) / **PHIL 'ANIMAL' TAYLOR** (b.21 Sep'54, Chesterfield, England) – drums / **FAST EDDIE CLARKE** – guitar, vocals (ex-BLUE GOOSE, ex-CURTIS KNIGHT & ZEUS) (below withdrawn)

Stiff | not issued

Dec 76. (7") **WHITE LINE FEVER. / LEAVING HERE** [-] [-]
(withdrawn but iss.Dec78 in 'Stiff' box set Nos.1-10)

Chiswick | not issued

Jun 77. (7") **MOTORHEAD. / CITY KIDS** [ ] [-]
(re-iss.1979 diff.colrd 7") (re-iss.Feb82 in diff.colrd pic-d)
Aug 77. (lp)(c) **MOTORHEAD** [43] [-]
– Motorhead / Vibrator / Lost Johnny / Iron Horse – Born to lose / White line fever / Keepers on the road / The Watcher / Born to lose / Train kept a-rollin'. *(re-white-lp 1978) (re-iss.Sep81 on red / clear, cd-iss.1987 on 'Big Beat')* (re-iss.Feb91 on 'Big Beat')

Bronze | not issued

Sep 78. (7") **LOUIE LOUIE. / TEAR YA DOWN** [68] [-]
(re-iss.Dec82)
Feb 79. (7") **OVERKILL. / TOO LATE, TOO LATE** [39] [-]
(re-iss.Dec82)
Mar 79. (lp)(c)(green-lp) **OVERKILL** [24] [-]
– Overkill / Stay clean / Pay your price / I'll be your sister / Capricorn / No class / Damage case / Tear ya down / Metropolis / Limb for limb. *(cd-iss.Jul87 on 'Legacy') (re-iss.+cd.May90 on 'Fame') (re-iss.+cd.Feb91 on 'Castle')*
Jun 79. (7") **NO CLASS. / LIKE A NIGHTMARE** [61] [-]
(re-iss.Dec82)
Oct 79. (lp)(c)(blue-lp) **BOMBER** [12] [-]
– Dead men tell no tales / Lawman / Sweet revenge / Sharpshooter / Poison / Stone dead forever / All the aces / Step down / Talking head / Bomber. *(cd-iss.Jul87 on 'Legacy') (re-iss.+cd.Apr91 on 'Castle')*
Nov 79. (7")(7"pic-d) **BOMBER. / OVER THE TOP** [34] [-]
Apr 80. (7"ep)(12"ep) **THE GOLDEN YEARS (live)** [8] [-]
– Dead men don't tell tales / Too late, too late / Leaving here / Stone dead forever. *(re-iss.Dec82)*

Bronze | Mercury

Oct 80. (7")(12") **ACE OF SPADES. / DIRTY LOVE** [15] [ ]
(re-iss.Dec82)
Oct 80. (lp)(c)(gold-lp) **ACE OF SPADES** [4] [ ]
– Ace of spades / Bite the bullet / The chase is better than the catch / Dance / Fast and loose / Fire fire / The hammer / Jailbait / Live to win / Love me like a reptile / (We are) The road crew / Shoot you in the back. *(re-iss.Mar85) (cd-iss.Aug87 on 'Legacy')*
Feb 81. (7"ep) **ST.VALENTINE'S DAY MASSACRE (as "HEADGIRL")** [5] [ ]
– Please don't touch (by MOTORHEAD & GIRLSCHOOL) / Bomber (by GIRLSCHOOL) / Emergency (by MOTORHEAD).

Jun 81. (lp)(c)(gold-lp) **NO SLEEP TIL HAMMERSMITH (live)** [1] [ ]
– Ace of spades / Stay clean / Metropolis / The hammer / Iron horse / No class / Overkill / (We are) The road crew / Capricorn / Bomber / Motorhead. *(cd-iss.Aug87 on 'Legacy') (re-iss.+cd.Feb90 on 'Castle')*

Jul 81. (7")(7"pic-d) **MOTORHEAD (live). / OVER THE TOP (live)** [6] [ ]

—— below, one-off (MOTORHEAD and The NOLANS)

Nov 81. (7") **DON'T DO THAT ("YOUNG AND MOODY BAND"). / HOW CAN I HELP YOU TONIGHT** [ ] [ ]

Mar 82. (7")(7"red)(7"blue) **IRON FIST. / REMEMBER ME I'M WRONG** [29] [ ]

Apr 82. (lp)(c) **IRON FIST** [6] [ ]
– Iron fist / Heart of stone / I'm the doctor / Go to Hell / Loser / Sex and outrage / America / Shut it down / Speed freak / (Don't let 'em) Grind ya down / (Don't need) Religion / Bang to rights. *(re-iss.Mar87 +cd.on 'Castle')*

Sep 82. (7"m) **STAND BY YOUR MAN. (by "LEMMY & WENDY" O'WILLIAMS) / NO CLASS (By "PLASMATICS") / MASTERPLAN (by "MOTORHEAD")** [ ] [-]

—— **BRIAN ROBERTSON** (b. 2 Feb'56, Clarkston, Scotland) – guitar, vocals (ex-THIN LIZZY, ex-WILD HORSES) repl. CLARKE who formed FASTWAY

May 83. (7") **I GOT MINE. / TURN YOU AROUND AGAIN** [46] [ ]
(12"+=) – Tales of glory.

May 83. (lp)(c) **ANOTHER PERFECT DAY** [20] [-]
– Back at the funny farm / Shine / Dancing on your grave / Rock it / One track mind / Another perfect day / Marching off to war / I got mine / Tales of glory / Die you bastard. *(re-iss.+cd.Feb91 on 'Castle')*

Jul 83. (7") **SHINE. / (I'M YOUR) HOOCHIE COOCHIE MAN (live)** [59] [-]
(12"+=) – (Don't need) Religion.

—— LEMMY with **PHIL CAMPBELL** (b. 7 May'61, Pontypridd, Wales) – guitar / **WURZEL** (b.MICHAEL BURSTON, 27 Oct'49, Cheltenham, England) – guitar both replace ROBERTSON who joined FRANKIE MILLER BAND / **PETE GILL** (b.9 Jun'51, Sheffield, England) – drums (ex-SAXON) repl. TAYLOR

Aug 84. (7")(7"sha-pic-d) **KILLED BY DEATH. / UNDER THE KNIFE** [51] [-]
(12"+=) – ('B'version).

Sep 84. (d-lp)(d-c) **NO REMORSE** (compilation) [14] [ ]
– Ace of spades / Motorhead / Jailbait / Stay clean / Killed by death / Bomber / Iron fist / Shine / Dancing on your grave / Metropolis / Snaggletooth / Overkill / Please don't touch / Stone dead forever / Like a nightmare / Emergency / Steal your face / Louie Louie / No class / Iron horse / (We are) The road crew / Leaving here / Locomotive. *(cd-iss.Dec86 on 'Castle') (cd contains 4 new tracks)*

—— (couldn't record for a couple of years)

G.W.R. — GWR-Profile

Jun 86. (7") **DEAF FOREVER. / ON THE ROAD** [67] [ ]
(12"+=) – Steal your face.

Jul 86. (lp)(c)(cd) **ORGASMATRON** [21] [ ] Nov 86
– Deaf forever / Nothing up my sleeve / Claw / Mean machine / Ain't my crime / Built for speed / Riding with the driver / Doctor Rock / Orgasmatron. *(pic-lp.Aug89)*

—— **PHILTHY ANIMAL** – drums returned to repl. GILL

Aug 87. (lp)(c)(cd) **ROCK'N'ROLL** [43] [ ] Oct 87
– Rock'n'roll / Eat the rich / Blackheart / Stone deaf in the U.S.A. / The wolf / Traitor / Dogs / All for you / Boogeyman.

Nov 87. (7") **EAT THE RICH. / CRADLE TO GRAVE** [ ] [ ]
(12"+=) – Power.

Oct 88. (lp)(c)(cd) **NO SLEEP AT ALL (live)** [79] [ ]
– Doctor Rock / Stay clean / Traitor / Metropolis / Dogs / Ace of spades / Eat the rich / Built for speed / Deaf forever / Just cos you got the power / Killed by death / Overkill.

Epic — W.T.G.

Jan 91. (7")(c-s)(7"sha-pic-d) **THE ONE TO SING THE BLUES. / DEAD MAN'S HAND** [45] [ ]
(12"+=)(cd-s+=) – Eagle rock / Shut you down.

Jan 91. (cd)(c)(lp)(pic-lp)(pic-cd) **1916** [24] [ ]
– The one to sing the blues / I'm so bad (baby I don't care) / No voices in the sky / Going to Brazil / Nightmare / The dreamtime / Love me forever / Angel city / Make my day / Ramones / Shut you down / 1916.

Aug 92. (cd)(c)(lp) **MARCH OR DIE** [60] [ ]
– Stand / Cat scratch fever / Bad religion / Jack the ripper / I ain't no nice guy / Hellraiser / Asylum choir / Too good to be true / You better run / Name in vain / March or die.

Nov 92. (7"ep)(c-ep)(cd-ep) **'92 TOUR (live)** [63] [ ]
– Hellraiser / You better run / Going to Brazil / Ramones.

Above 1st track co-written w / OZZY OSBOURNE.

not issued — ZYX

Nov 93. (cd)(c) **BASTARDS** [-] [ ]

Arista — Arista

Nov 94. (7")(12")(c-s)(cd-s) by MOTORHEAD with ICE-T & WHITFIELD CRANE) **BORN TO RAISE HELL. / ('A'mixes)** [49] [ ]

Plastic H. — Plastic H.

Apr 95. (cd)(c)(lp) **SACRIFICE** [ ] [-]

– compilations, others, etc. –

Oct 79. United Artists; (lp)(c) **ON PAROLE** [65] [ ]
(was to be have been released Dec75) *(re-iss.May82 on 'Fame', cd-iss.1986)*

Nov 80. Big Beat; (7"ep)(12"blue-ep)(12"pink)(12"orange) **BEER DRINKERS EP** [43] [ ]
– Beer drinkers and Hell raisers / On parole / Instro / I'm your witchdoctor.

Mar 83. Big Beat; (lp)(c) **WHAT'S WORDS WORTH (live at the Roundhouse 18/2/78)** [71] [-]
(re-iss.Jan90)

Aug 82. Bronze; (d-c) **OVERKILL. / BOMBER** [ ] [ ]

Nov 84. Astan; (lp)(c) **RECORDED LIVE (live)** [ ] [ ]

Apr 86. Raw Power; (lp)(c) **ANTHOLOGY** [ ] [ ]
(cd-iss.Dec86)

Apr 86. Dojo; (lp)(c) **BORN TO LOSE** [ ] [ ]

Apr 88. That's Original; (cd) **OVERKILL / ANOTHER PERFECT DAY** [ ] [ ]

1988. Castle; (3"cd-ep) **MOTORHEAD / ACE OF SPADES / BOMBER / OVERKILL** [ ] [-]

Apr 90. Castle; (cd)(d-lp) **WELCOME TO THE BEAR TRAP** [ ] [-]

Apr 90. Castle; (cd)(d-lp) **BOMBER / ACE OF SPADES** [ ] [-]

Nov 93. Castle; (cd)(c)(lp) **ALL THE ACES** [ ] [-]

Nov 89. Receiver; (lp)(cd) **BLITZKREIG ON BIRMINGHAM LIVE '77 (live)** [ ] [-]

Jan 90. Receiver; (cd)(c)(lp) **DIRTY LOVE** [ ] [-]

Jul 90. Receiver; (cd)(c)(lp) **LOCK UP YOUR DAUGHTERS (live 1977)** [ ] [-]

Feb 92. Receiver; (cd)(c)(lp) **LIVE JAILBAIT (live)** [ ] [-]

Jun 93. Receiver; (4xcd-box) **MOTORHEAD BOX SET** [ ] [-]

Jul 90. Action Replay; (cd)(c) **THE BEST OF MOTORHEAD** [ ] [-]
(re-iss.Jul93)

Jul 93. Action Replay; (cd)(c) **BEST OF THE REST** [ ] [-]

Nov 90. Musidisc; (cd)(c)(lp) **THE BIRTHDAY PARTY (live '85)** [ ] [-]
(cd has 3 extra tracks)

Nov 90. Knight; (cd)(c)(lp) **FROM THE VAULTS** [ ] [-]

Jul 91. Essential; (3xcd-box) **MELTDOWN** [ ] [-]

Sep 92. Roadrunner; (cd)(c)(lp) **THE BEST OF MOTORHEAD** [ ] [-]

Mar 94. Roadrunner; (cd) **LIVE AT BRIXTON ACADEMY (live)** [ ] [-]

Apr 93. Tring; (cd)(c) **LIVE (live)** [ ] [-]

Aug 93. W.G.A.F.; (12")(c-s)(cd-s) **ACE OF SPADES (THE C.C.N.remix). /** [23] [-]

Jul 94. Success; (cd)(c) **GRIND YA DOWN** [ ] [-]

Aug 94. Spectrum; (cd)(c) **ACES HIGH** [ ] [-]

Sep 94. Cleopatra; (cd) **IRON FIST AND THE HORDES FROM HELL** [ ] [-]

May 95. Spectrum; (cd) **ULTIMATE METAL** [ ] [-]

Jul 95. Emporio; (cd)(c) **THE BEST OF MOTORHEAD** [ ] [-]

Jul 95. Griffin; (box-cd) **FISTFUL OF ACES – THE BEST OF MOTORHEAD** [ ] [-]

MOTT THE HOOPLE

Formed: Herefordshire, England . . . Jun'69 by WATTS, GRIFFIN, ALLEN and RALPHS, who were part of The SHAKEDOWN SOUND, with singer STAN TIPPINS. In '69, with new manager and producer Guy Stevens placing ad in music paper, they found new singer IAN HUNTER, who had guested on 45 by CHARLIE WOLFE. They named themselves MOTT THE HOOPLE (after a recent novel by Willard Manus), and soon signed to Chris Blackwell's 'Island'. Their eponymous debut, gained minor chart placing, as did their 2 follow-ups in the early 70's. In 1972, after a brief split, they transferred to 'CBS', where they immediately made impact with Top 3 single 'ALL THE YOUNG DUDES'. This was written by for them by DAVID BOWIE after he encouraged them to re-form. For the next 2 years, they enjoyed fruitful period that ended late '74, with the exit of IAN HUNTER and recent member MICK RONSON. Without them, the group MOTT carried on, but with little success. • **Style:** BOB DYLAN influenced rock'n'rollers, fronted by FREDDIE MERCURY's good friend IAN HUNTER. • **Songwriters:** HUNTER or others wrote most except; YOU REALLY GOT ME (Kinks) / LAUGH AT ME (Sonny Bono) / ? (Sir Douglas Quintet) / KEEP A KNOCKIN' (Little Richard) / WHOLE LOTTA SHAKIN' GOIN' ON (Jerry Lee Lewis) / etc.

Recommended: THE BALLAD OF MOTT THE HOOPLE – A RETROSPECTIVE (*8)

IAN HUNTER (b. 3 Jun'46, Shrewsbury, England) – vocals, guitar, piano / **MICK RALPHS** (b.31 May'44, Hereford, Wales) – guitar, vocals / **VERDEN ALLEN** (b.26 May'44, Hereford) – organ / **OVEREND WATTS** (b.13 May'49, Birmingham, England) – bass, vocals / **DALE 'BUFFIN' GRIFFIN** (b.24 Oct'48, Hereford) – drums, vocals

Island — Atlantic

Oct 69. (7") **ROCK AND ROLL QUEEN. / ROAD TO BIRMINGHAM** [ ] [ ]

Nov 69. (lp) **MOTT THE HOOPLE** [66] [ ]
– You really got me / At the crossroads / Laugh at me / Backsliding fearlessly / Rock and roll queen / Rabbit foot and Toby time / Half Moon Bay / Wrath and wroll. *(re-iss.+c.1974)*

Jan 70. (7") **ROCK AND ROLL QUEEN. / BACKSLIDING FEARLESSLY** [-] [ ]

Sep 70. (lp) **MAD SHADOWS** [48] [ ]
– Thunderbuck ram / No wheels to ride / You are one of us / Walkin' with a mountain / I can feel / Threads of iron / When my mind's gone. *(re-iss.+c.1974)*

Feb 71. (lp) **WILD LIFE** [44] [ ]
– Whisky woman / Angel of 8th avenue / Wrong side of the river / Waterloo / Lay down / It must be love / Original mixed-up lad / Home is where I want to be / Keep a knockin'. *(re-iss.+c.1974)*

Sep 71. (lp) **BRAIN CAPERS** [ ] [ ]
– Death maybe your Santa Claus / Darkness darkness / Your own backyard / Journey / Sweet Angeline / Wheel of the quivering meat conception / Second love / Moon upstairs. *(re-iss.+c.1974)*

Oct 71. (7") **MIDNIGHT LADY. / THE DEBT** [ ] [ ]

Dec 71. (7") **DOWNTOWN. / HOME IS WHERE I WANT TO BE** [ ] [ ]

C.B.S. — Columbia

Jul 72. (7") **ALL THE YOUNG DUDES. / ONE OF THE BOYS** [3] [37]

Sep 72. (lp)(c) **ALL THE YOUNG DUDES** [21] [89] Nov 72
– Sweet Jane / Momma's little jewel / All the young dudes / Sucker / Jerkin' crocus / One of the boys / Soft ground / Ready for love – After lights / Sea diver. *(re-iss.1974)*

Jan 73. (7") **ONE OF THE BOYS. / SUCKER** [-] [96]

Mar 73. (7") **SWEET JANE. / JERKIN' CROCUS** [-] [ ]

—— **MICK BOLTON** – keyboards filled in for departing VERDEN who went solo

May 73. (7") **HONALOOCHIE BOOGIE. / ROSE** [12] [ ]

Jul 73. (lp)(c) **MOTT** [7] [35] Aug 73
– All the way from Memphis / Whizz kid / Hymn for the dudes / Honaloochie

boogie / Violence / Drivin' sister / Ballad of Mott The Hoople (March 26, 1972 – Zurich) / I'm a Cadillac – El Camino Dolo Roso / I wish I was your mother. *(cd-iss.Mar95 on 'Rewind')*

Aug 73. (7") **ALL THE WAY FROM MEMPHIS. / BALLAD OF MOTT THE HOOPLE (MARCH 26, 1972 – ZURICH)** [10] [-]
Sep 73. (7") **ALL THE WAY FROM MEMPHIS. / I WISH I WAS YOUR MOTHER** [-] [ ]

— **ARIEL BENDER** (b.LUTHER GROSVENOR) – guitar (ex-SPOOKY TOOTH) replaced RALPHS who joined BAD COMPANY / **MORGAN FISHER** – keyboards (ex-LOVE AFFAIR) repl. BOLTON (above 2 with HUNTER, WATTS and GRIFFIN.)

Nov 73. (7") **ROLL AWAY THE STONE. / WHERE DO YOU ALL COME FROM** [8] [-]
Mar 74. (7") **THE GOLDEN AGE OF ROCK'N'ROLL. / REST IN PEACE** [16] [96] Feb 74
Mar 74. (lp)(c) **THE HOOPLE** [11] [28] Apr 74
– The golden age of rock'n'roll / Marionette / Alice / Crash Street kids / Born late '58 / Trudi's song / Pearl 'n' Roy (England) / Through the looking glass / Roll away the stone.
Apr 74. (7") **ROLL AWAY THE STONE. / THROUGH THE LOOKING GLASS** [-] [ ]
Jun 74. (7") **FOXY FOXY. / TRUDI'S SONG** [33] [-]

— **BLUE WEAVER**" – organ on tour (ex-AMEN CORNER)

Nov 74. (lp)(c) **LIVE** (live; Broadway-Nov73 / Hammersmith-May74) [32] [23]
– All the way from Memphis / Sucker / Rest in peace / All the young dudes / Walkin' with a mountain / Sweet Angeline / Rose / Medley; (a) Jerkin' crokus – (b) One of the boys – (c) Rock and roll queen – (d) Get back – (e) Whole lotta shakin' goin' on – (f) Violence.

— **MICK RONSON** – guitar, vocals (Solo artist, ex-DAVID BOWIE; SPIDERS FROM MARS) repl. ARIEL who formed WIDOWMAKER

Oct 74. (7") **SATURDAY GIGS. / MEDLEY; JERKIN' CROCUS – SUCKER (live)** [41] [-]
Dec 74. (7") **ALL THE YOUNG DUDES (live). / ROSE** [-] [ ]

— Split Dec74. HUNTER and RONSON formed duo and went solo.

MOTT

(OVEREND, DALE and **MORGAN**) were joined by **NIGEL BENJAMIN** – vocals (ex-ROYCE) / **RAY MAJORS** – guitar (ex-HACKENSHACK)

C.B.S. | Columbia

Aug 75. (7") **MONTE CARLO. / SHOUT IT ALL OUT** [ ] [ ]
Sep 75. (lp)(c) **DRIVE ON** [45] [ ]
– By tonight / Monte Carlo / She does it / I'll tell you something / Stiff upper lip / Love now / Apologies / The great white wall / Here we are / It takes one to know one / I can show you how it is.
Oct 75. (7") **BY TONIGHT. / I CAN SHOW YOU HOW IT IS** [ ] [ ]
Feb 76. (7") **IT TAKES ONE TO KNOW ONE. / I'LL TELL YOU SOMETHING** [ ] [ ]
Jun 76. (lp)(c) **SHOUTING AND POINTING** [ ] [ ]
– Shouting and pointing / Collision course / Storm / Career (no such thing as rock'n'roll) / Hold on, you're crazy / See you again / Too short arms (I don't care) / Broadside outcasts / Good times.

– compilations, etc. –

Oct 72. Island/ US= Atlantic; (lp)(c) **ROCK'N'ROLL QUEEN** [ ] [ ] Jul 74
1980. Island; (lp)(c) **TWO MILES FROM HEAVEN** [ ] [-]
Jun 90. Island; (cd) **WALKING WITH A MOUNTAIN (BEST OF 1969-1972)** [ ] [ ]
– Rock'n'roll queen / At the crossroads / Thunderbuck ram / Whiskey woman / Waterflow / The Moon upstairs / Second love / The road to Birmingham / Black scorpio (mama's little jewel) / You really got me / Walking with a mountain / No wheels to ride / Keep a knockin' / Midnight lady / Death may be your Santa Claus / Darkness darkness / Growing man blues / Black hills.
Mar 76. CBS/ US= Columbia; (lp)(c) **GREATEST HITS** [ ] [ ]
– All the way from Memphis / Honaloochie boogie / Hymn for the dudes / Born late '58 / All the young dudes / Roll away the stone / Ballad of Mott The Hoople / Golden age of rock'n'roll / Foxy lady / Saturday gigs. *(re-iss.Jun81) (cd-iss.1989)*
Jul 84. CBS; (7") **ALL THE YOUNG DUDES. / HONALOOCHIE BOOGIE** [ ] [ ]
Jun 92. Columbia; (7")(c-s) **ALL THE YOUNG DUDES. / ONCE BITTEN TWICE SHY (IAN HUNTER)** [ ] [ ]
(cd-s+=) – Roll Away The Stone
Mar 81. Hallmark; (lp)(c) **ALL THE WAY FROM MEMPHIS** [ ] [ ]
Apr 83. Old Gold; (7") **ALL THE YOUNG DUDES. / ROLL AWAY THE STONE** [ ] [-]
1988. Castle; (d-lp)(c)(cd) **THE COLLECTION** [ ] [-]
Jun 93. See For Miles; (cd) **MOTT THE HOOPLE FEATURING STEVE HYAMS** [ ] [-]
Nov 93. Legacy; (d-cd) **THE BALLAD OF MOTT THE HOOPLE – A RETROSPECTIVE** [ ] [-]

— In Feb80, MOTT THE HOOPLE tracks were included on album SHADES OF IAN HUNTER – THE BALLAD OF IAN HUNTER & MOTT THE HOOPLE

BRITISH LIONS

MOTT + **JOHN FIDDLER** – vocals (ex-MEDICINE HEAD) repl. NIGEL who joined ENGLISH ASSASSINS

Vertigo | not issued

Feb 78. (7") **ONE MORE CHANCE TO RUN. / BOOSTER** [ ] [-]
Feb 78. (lp)(c) **BRITISH LIONS** [ ] [-]
– Big drift away / Booster / Break this fool / Eat the rich / Fork talking man / International heroes / My life in your hands / One more chance to run / Wild in the street.
Apr 78. (7") **INTERNATIONAL HEROES. / EAT THE RICH** [ ] [-]

Cherry Red | not issued

May 80. (lp) **TROUBLE WITH WOMEN** [ ] [-]
– Trouble with women / Any port in a storm / Lady don't fall backwards / High noon / Lay down your love / Waves of love / Electric chair / Won't you give him up.

— When they split MORGAN FISHER went solo. GRIFFIN and WATTS went into production incl. HANOI ROCKS.

MORGAN FISHER

solo.

Cherry Red | not issued

Sep 79. (7"ep) **GENEVE / ROLL AWAY THE STONE '78. / SLEEPER / LYDIA'S THEME** [ ] [-]

Bob MOULD (see under ⇒ HUSKER DU)

MOUNTAIN

Formed: Bronx, New York, USA ... 1969 by producer FELIX PAPPALARDI and guitarist LESLIE WEST. PAPPALARDI (father Itaian) had produced the likes of LOVIN' SPOONFUL, JOAN BAEZ, YOUNGBLOODS, etc, before working with CREAM. He met the bulky WEST, while trying to produce his VAGRANTS in 1968. When they split, PAPPALARDI produced 1969 solo effort 'LESLIE WEST – MOUNTAIN'. After this collaboration, they decided to form MOUNTAIN with other 2, in time for Aug'69 Woodstock Festival. Their first lp 'MOUNTAIN CLIMBING', did just that, and stormed into the US Top 20 by mid 1970. Lifted from it 'MISSISSIPPI QUEEN' made No.21 there, and group looked set to take off where CREAM left off. However after more album success, they too fell from peak and split. • **Style:** CREAM influenced outfit, with heavy-rock and dynamic guitar-work their forte. • **Songwriters:** WEST-PAPPALARDI penned except; THIS WHEEL'S ON FIRE (Bob Dylan) / ROLL OVER BEETHOVEN (Chuck Berry) / WHOLE LOTTA SHAKIN' GOIN' ON (Jerry Lee Lewis). LESLIE WEST solo covered; RED HOUSE (Jimi Hendrix) / SPOONFUL (Cream) / THE STEALER (Free) / I PUT A SPELL ON YOU (Screaming Jay Hawkins) / HALL OF THE MOUNTAIN KING (Grieg) / DREAM LOVER (Bobby Darin) / THEME FROM EXODUS (Gold) / SEA OF FIRE (Cintron). • **Trivia:** On their live double album 'TWIN PEAKS', they used 1 album and a bit for track 'NANTUCKET SLEIGHRIDE'.

Recommended: THE BEST OF MOUNTAIN (FEATURING LESLIE WEST & FELIX PAPPALARDI) (*8).

LESLIE WEST

(b.LESLIE WEINSTEIN, 22 Oct'45, Queens, New York) – vocals, lead guitar (ex-VAGRANTS) / with **FELIX PAPPALARDI** (b.1939) – bass, keys / **NORMAN LANDSBERG** – keyboards / **NORMAN D.SMART** (b.Boston) – drums

Bell | Windfall

Sep 69. (lp) **MOUNTAIN** [ ] [72]
– Blood of the sun / Long red / Better watch out / Blind man / Baby I'm down / Dreams of milk & honey / Storyteller man / This wheel's on fire / Look to the wind / Southbound train / Because you are my friend.
Oct 69. (7") **DREAMS OF MILK AND HONEY. / THIS WHEEL'S ON FIRE** [ ] [ ]
Jan 70. (7") **BLOOD OF THE SUN. / LONG RED** [-] [ ]

MOUNTAIN

named after last album. **STEVE KNIGHT** – keyboards (ex-DEVIL'S ANVIL) repl. LANDSBERG (This line-up appeared at 'Woodstock' festival)

— **CORKY LAING** (b.28 Jan'48, Montreal, Canada) – drums repl. SMART

Mar 70. (lp) **MOUNTAIN CLIMBING!** [ ] [17]
– Mississippi queen / Theme for an imaginary western / Never in my life / Silver paper / For Yasgur's farm / To my friend / The laird / Sittin' on a rainbow / Boys in the band. *(re-iss.+cd.Aug91 on 'B.G.O.') (re-iss.cd Mar95 on 'Rewind')*
May 70. (7") **MISSISSIPPI QUEEN. / THE LAIRD** [ ] [21] Mar 70
Jun 70. (7") **FOR YASGUR'S FARM. / TO MY FRIEND** [ ] [-]
Oct 70. (7") **SITTIN' ON A RAINBOW. / TO MY FRIEND** [ ] [-]

Island | Windfall

May 71. (lp)(c) **NANTUCKET SLEIGHRIDE** [43] [16] Jan 71
– Don't look around / Taunta (Sammy's tune) / Nantucket sleighride / You can't get away / Tired angels / The animal trainer and the toad / My lady / Travelin' in the dark / The great train robbery. *(re-iss.1974) (re-iss.+cd.Jun89 on 'B.G.O.')*
Mar 71. (7") **THE ANIMAL TRAINER AND THE TOAD. / TIRED ANGELS** [-] [76]
Jul 71. (7") **TRAVELIN' IN THE DARK. / SILVER PAPER** [-] [ ]
Jan 72. (lp)(c) **FLOWERS OF EVIL** [ ] [35] Dec 71
– Flowers of evil / King's chorale / One last cold kiss / Crossroader / Pride and passion / (Dream sequence: Guitar solo) / Roll over Beethoven / Dreams of milk and honey – Variations – Swan theme / Mississippi queen. *(re-iss.1974) (re-iss.+cd.Dec91 on 'B.G.O.')*
Feb 72. (7") **ROLL OVER BEETHOVEN. / CROSSROADER** [ ] [ ]
Jun 72. (lp)(c) **MOUNTAIN LIVE – THE ROAD GOES EVER ON (live)** [21] [63] May 71
– Long red / Waiting to take you away / Crossroader / Nantucket sleighride. *(re-iss.1974) (re-iss.+cd.Dec91 on 'B.G.O.')*

Jul 72. (7") **WAITING TO TAKE YOU AWAY. / NANTUCKET SLEIGHRIDE (live excerpt)** -
Feb 73. (lp)(c) **THE BEST OF MOUNTAIN (FEATURING LESLIE WEST & FELIX PAPPALARDI)** (compilation) 72
– Never in my life / Taunta (Sammy's tune) / Nantucket sleighride / Roll over Beethoven / For Yasgur's farm / The animal trainer and the toad / Mississippi queen / King's chorale / Boys in the band / Don't look around / Theme for an imaginary western / Crossroader. *(re-iss.+cd.Apr89 on 'B.G.O.') (cd re-iss.Dec92 on 'Columbia')*

— Disbanded mid 1972.

WEST, BRUCE & LAING

were formed by ex-MOUNTAIN men and **JACK BRUCE** – vocals, bass (ex-CREAM, etc)

C.B.S. Columbia

Nov 72. (lp)(c) **WHY DON'CHA** 26 Oct 72
– Why don'cha / Out in the fields / The doctor / Turn me over / Third degree / Shake ma thing (Rollin' Jack) / While you sleep / Pleasure / Love is worth the blues / Pollution woman *(re-iss.Aug85 on 'R.S.O.') (cd-iss.Apr93 on 'Sony Europe')*
Dec 72. (7") **SHAKE MA THING (ROLLIN' JACK). / THE DOCTOR** -
Mar 73. (7") **WHY DON'CHA. / MISSISSIPPI QUEEN** -

R.S.O. Windfall

1973. (7") **DIRTY SHOES. / BACKFIRE**
Jul 73. (lp)(c) **WHATEVER TURNS YOU ON**
– Backfire / Token / Shifting sand / November song / Rock and roll machine / Scotch krotch / Slow blues / Dirty shoes / Like a plate.
– (re-iss.Aug76) (cd-iss.Apr93 on 'Sony Europe')
May 74. (lp)(c) **LIVE AND KICKIN' (live)**
– Play with fire / The doctor / Politician / Powerhouse sod. *(cd-iss.Apr93 on 'Sony Europe')*

MOUNTAIN

had already re-formed late in 1973 with **WEST + PAPPALARDI** bringing in **ALLEN SCHWARZBERG** – drums / **ROBERT MANN** – keyboards

C.B.S. Columbia

Feb 74. (d-lp)(c) **TWIN PEAKS (live Japan '73)** -
– Never in my life / Theme for an imaginary western / Blood of the sun / Crossroader / Mississippi queen / Silver paper / Roll over Beethoven / Nantucket sleighride (part 1 & 2).
– (iss.UK Nov77)

— **DAVID PERRY** – rhythm guitar repl. ALLEN + ROBERT (FELIX now + keyboards)
Nov 74. (lp)(c) **AVALANCHE**
– Whole lotta shakin' goin' on / Sister justice / Alisan / Swamp boy / Satisfaction / Thumbsucker / You better believe it / I love to see you fly / Back where I belong / Last of the sunshine days. *(re-iss.+cd.1987 on 'Castle')*

— Split again late in '74. FELIX PAPPALARDI signed to 'A&M' and released 2 albums **FELIX PAPPALARDI AND CREATION** (1976) and **DON'T WORRY MUM?** (1979). He retired to Japan, and later (17 Apr'83) was dead, shot by his wife GAIL COLLINS.

LESLIE WEST

went solo with band **CORKY LAING** – drums / **DON KRETMMAR** – bass / **FRANK VICARI** – horns / **etc.**

R.C.A. Phantom

Mar 75. (lp)(c) **THE GREAT FATSBY**
– Don't burn me / House of the rising sun / High roller / I'm gonna love you thru the night / E.S.P. / Honky tonk woman / If I still had you / Doctor Love / If I were a carpenter / Little bit of love.
Mar 76. (lp)(c) **THE LESLIE WEST BAND**
– Money (watcha gonna do) / Dear Prudence / Get it up / Singapore sling / By the river / The twister / Setting sun / See of heartache / We'll find a way / We gotta get out of this place.

— LESLIE WEST retired for a while, until . . .

MOUNTAIN

re-formed in 1981. (**WEST, PAPPALARDI, LAING** and 2 others). In 1984, after death of PAPPALARDI. added **MARK CLARKE** – bass, keyboards (ex-URIAH HEEP, ex-RAINBOW, etc)

Scotti Brothers Scotti Brothers

Apr 85. (lp)(c) **GO FOR YOUR LIFE**
– Hard times / Spark / She loves her rock (and she loves it hard) / Bardot damage / Shimmy on the footlights / I love young girls / Makin' it in your car / Babe in the woods / Little bit of insanity.

Legacy Columbia

Jun 95. (d-cd) **OVER THE TOP**

LESLIE WEST

brought in **JACK BRUCE** – vocals, bass / **JOE FRANCO** – drums (ex-TWISTED SISTER)

not issued Passport

Apr 88. (lp)(c)(cd) **THEME**
– Talk dirty / Motherlode / Theme for an imaginary western / I'm crying / Red house / Love is forever / I ate it / Spoonful / Love me tender.

— In Apr '89, he appeared on Various Artists live cd,c,d-lp,video 'NIGHT OF THE GUITAR' on his next label.

I.R.S. I.R.S.

Oct 89. (lp)(c)(cd) **ALLIGATOR**
– Sea of fire / Waiting for the F change / Whiskey / Alligator / I put a spell on you / All of me / The stealer / Medley: Hall of the mountain king – Theme from Exodus / Dream lover.

MOVE

Formed: Birmingham, England ... early 1966 by ROY WOOD, CARL WAYNE, TREVOR BURTON, ACE KEFFORD and BEV BEVAN. By the summer, they had found manager Tony Secunda, who helped them sign to 'Deram'. Early the next year, their debut 45 'NIGHT OF FEAR' (based on the 1812 Overture), had crashed into UK Top 3. After another Top 5 hit, their 3rd single 'FLOWERS IN THE RAIN' (the first record to be played on newly launched BBC Radio 1), was another to make the Top 3 in Oct'67 on new 'Regal Zono.' label. Their 4th successive Top 5 hit arrived early '68 with 'FIRE BRIGADE', and was quickly followed by Top 20 self-titled album. After a surprise flop, they scored first No.1 early '69 with 'BLACKBERRY WAY'. They never emulated this, and WOOD became increasingly involved with his new 1970 project The ELECTRIC LIGHT ORCHESTRA. He soon left JEFF LYNNE to take over leadership, after he ended The MOVE on a high-note mid 1972 with Top 10 hit 'CALIFORNIA MAN'. Sticking with 'Harvest' records, he formed WIZZARD after a live June '72 debut at Wembley's Rock'n'roll festival. They hit Top 10 with first 45 'BALL PARK INCIDENT' late '72, and followed this with two No.1's 'SEE MY BABY JIVE' & 'ANGEL FINGERS'. Around the same time (mid-'73), WOOD entered the albums' Top 20 with totally solo 'BOULDERS'. He continued to pursue both activities and scored many times in the Top 20, until a new contract was signed in 1975 with 'Jet'. • **Style:** The talented multi-instrumentalist WOOD shifted from The MOVE's bubblegum psychedelia to teenybop 50's pastiche rock'n'roll with WIZZARD. They were part of the glam-rock scene, due to ROY's attire of tartan trousers and multi-coloured robe, topped with war-paint face and multi-coloured hair-do. • **Songwriters:** WOOD wrote mostly everything, except B-sides for WIZZARD, which were credited to the band members. He covered; LOVELY RITA + POLYTHENE PAM (Beatles). • **Trivia:** ROY also produced and wrote for DARTS, etc

Recommended: THE ROY WOOD STORY (*6)

MOVE

ROY WOOD (b.ULYSSES ADRIAN WOOD, 8 Nov'46) – guitar, vocals (ex-MIKE SHERIDAN & NIGHTRIDERS, ex-GERRY LEVENE & THE AVENGERS) / **TREVOR BURTON** (b. 9 Mar'44) – guitar, vox (ex-DANNY KING & THE MAYFAIR SET) / **CARL WAYNE** (b.18 Aug'44) – vocals (ex-CARL WAYNE & THE VIKINGS) / **ACE KEFFORD** (b.CHRIS, 10 Dec'46) – bass, vox (ex-CARL WAYNE & THE VIKINGS) / **BEV BEVAN** (b.24 Nov'44) – drums (ex-CARL WAYNE & THE VIKINGS, ex-DENNY LAINE & THE DIPLOMATS)

Deram Deram

Dec 66. (7") **NIGHT OF FEAR. / DISTURBANCE** 2
Apr 67. (7") **I CAN HEAR THE GRASS GROW. / WAVE THE FLAG, STOP THE TRAIN** 5

Regal Zono. A&M

Sep 67. (7") **FLOWERS IN THE RAIN. / (HERE WE GO ROUND) THE LEMON TREE** 2 -
Feb 68. (7") **FIRE BRIGADE. / WALK UPON THE WATER** 3
Mar 68. (lp) **THE MOVE** 15
– Yellow rainbow / Kilroy was here / (Here we go round) The lemon tree / Weekend / Walk upon the water / Flowers in the rain / Useless information / Zing went the strings of my heart / The girl outside / Fire brigade / Mist on a Monday morning / Cherry blossom clinic. *(cd-iss.Nov92 on 'Repertoire' += 8 bonus tracks)*

— quartet, (**BURTON** – bass, vocals) when KEFFORD formed ACE KEFFORD STAND
Jul 68. (7") **WILD TIGER WOMAN. / OMNIBUS** -
Sep 68. (7"ep) **SOMETHING ELSE FROM THE MOVE** -
– Stephanie knows who / So you want to be a rock 'n' roll star / Something else / It'll be me / Sunshine help me.
Sep 68. (7") **SOMETHING. / YELLOW RAINBOW** -

— added **RICHARD TANDY** – hapsicord, keyboards (of The UGLYS)
Jan 69. (7") **BLACKBERRY WAY. / SOMETHING** 1

— **RICK PRICE** (b.10 Jun'44) – bass (ex-SIGHT'N'SOUND) repl. BURTON + TANDY whom became part of The UGLYS
Aug 69. (7") **CURLY. / THIS TIME TOMORROW** 12
Feb 70. (lp)(c) **SHAZAM**
– Hello Susie / Beautiful daughter / Cherry blossom clinic revisted / Fields of people / Don't make my baby blue / The last thing on my mind. *(re-iss.1982 on 'Cube') (cd-iss.Mar93 on 'Repertoire' +=)–* Stephanie knows who / So you want to be a rock'n'roll star / Something else / It'll be me / Sunshine help me.

— now trio of **WOOD, PRICE** and **BEVAN.** (WAYNE became cabaret singer)
Mar 70. (7") **BRONTOSAURUS. / LIGHTNING NEVER STRIKES TWICE** 7

— added **JEFF LYNNE** (b.30 Dec'47) – vocals, guitar, keys (ex-IDLE RACE)

Fly Capitol

Sep 70. (7") **WHEN ALICE COMES BACK TO THE FARM. / WHAT?**
Oct 70. (lp)(c) **LOOKING ON**
– Looking on / Turkish tram conductor blues / What? / When Alice comes back to the farm / Open up said the world at the door / Brontosaurus / Feel too good. *(cd-iss.Mar93 on 'Repertoire' +=)–* Blackberry way / Something / Curly / This time tomorrow / Lightning never strikes twice.

Harvest Capitol

May 71. (7") **ELLA JAMES. / NO TIME** (withdrawn) - -
Jun 71. (7") **TONIGHT. / DON'T MESS ME UP** 11
Jul 71. (lp)(c) **MESSAGE FROM THE COUNTRY**
– Message from the country / Ella James / No time / Don't mess me up / Until your moma's gone / It wasn't my idea to dance / The minister / Ben Crawley Steel

Company / The words of Aaron / My Marge. *(cd-iss.Jul94 on 'B.G.O.')*

Oct 71. (7") **CHINATOWN. / DOWN ON THE BAY** 23

—— (Aug71) Now a trio when RICK PRICE left to go solo. The other three (WOOD, LYNNE and BEVAN) continued with The MOVE although they formed ELECTRIC LIGHT ORCHESTRA. The MOVE made one more new single below

May 72. (7"m) **CALIFORNIA MAN. / DO YA. / ELLA JAMES** 7

– compilations, etc. –

Mar 71. Fly; (lp)(c) **THE BEST OF THE MOVE** -

Apr 72. Fly; (7"ep) **FIRE BRIGADE. / I CAN HEAR THE GRASS GROW. / FLOWERS IN THE RAIN / NIGHT OF FEAR** -

Feb 73. United Artists; (7") **TONIGHT. / MY MARGE** -

Feb 73. United Artists; (lp) **SPLIT ENDS** -

May 74. A&M; (lp) **THE BEST OF THE MOVE** -

Jun 74. A&M; (7") **WILD TIGER WOMAN. / ZING WENT THE STRINGS OF MY HEART** -

Jul 74. M.F.P.; (lp)(c) **ROY WOOD AND THE MOVE** -

Sep 74. Harvest/ US= United Artists; (7") **DO YA. / NO TIME** 93 Oct 72

Oct 74. Harvest; (lp)(c) **CALIFORNIA MAN** -

Mar 78. Cube; (d-lp) **SHAZAM / THE MOVE** -

May 78. Hallmark; (lp)(c) **THE GREATEST HITS VOL.1** -

Oct 81. Hallmark; (d-lp)(d-c) **THE PLATINUM COLLECTION** -

Aug 82. Dakota; (7") **BLACKBERRY WAY. / I CAN HEAR THE GRASS GROW** -

Aug 82. Dakota; (7") **NIGHT OF FEAR. / FIRE BRIGADE** -

Aug 82. Dakota; (7") **FLOWERS IN THE RAIN. / BRONTOSAURUS** -

Nov 84. Sierra; (d-lp)(d-c) **OFF THE RECORD WITH THE MOVE** -

Apr 86. Castle; (d-lp)(c)(cd) **THE COLLECTION** -

Sep 86. Archive 4; (12"ep) **ARCHIVE 4** -
– I can hear the grass grow / Flowers in the rain / Fire brigade / Blackberry way.

Jul 82. Old Gold; (7") **NIGHT OF FEAR. / I CAN HEAR THE GRASS GROW** -

Mar 90. Old Gold; (7") **FLOWERS IN THE RAIN. / FIRE BRIGADE** -

Jul 88. Knight; (lp)(c) **NIGHTRIDING** -

Mar 91. Music Club; (cd)(c) **THE BEST OF THE MOVE** -

Nov 92. Dojo; (cd) **THE EARLY YEARS** -

May 94. BR Music; (cd)(c) **THE DEFINITIVE ALBUM (ROY WOOD)** -

Oct 94. Disky; (cd) **THE MOVE** -

ROY WOOD

in two bands (MOVE and ELO) had also gone solo. Roy played mostly every instrument himself.

Harvest | United Art

Feb 72. (7") **WHEN GRANDMA PLAYS THE BANJO. / WAKE UP**

—— ROY WOOD solo (although he continued with his new band WIZZARD, see below)

Jun 73. (lp)(c) **BOULDERS** 15
– Songs of praise / Wake up / Rock down low / Nancy sing me a song / Dear Elaine / a) All the way over the hill, b) Irish loafer (and his hen) / Miss Clarke and the computer / When gran'ma plays the banjo / Rock medley: a) Rockin' shoes, b) She's too good for me, c) Locomotive. *(re-iss.Oct77) (cd-iss.Mar94 on 'B.G.O.')*

Sep 73. (7") **DEAR ELAINE. / SONGS OF PRAISE** 18

Nov 73. (7") **FOREVER. / MUSIC TO COMMIT SUICIDE BY** 8

Jun 74. (7") **GOING DOWN THE ROAD. / THE PREMIUM BOND THEME** 13

Jet | United A..

May 75. (7") **OH WHAT A SHAME. / BENGAL JIM** 13

Nov 75. (7") **LOOKING THRU' THE EYES OF A FOOL. / STRIDER**

Dec 75. (lp)(c) **MUSTARD**
– Mustard / Any old time will do / The rain came down on everything / You sure got it now / Why does such a pretty girl sing those sad songs / The song / Look thru' the eyes of a fool / Interlude / Get on down home / Rock'n'roll winter. *(re-iss. as 'THE WIZZARD – ROY WOOD')*

Mar 76. (7") **INDIANA RAINBOW. (as "ROY WOOD'S WIZZARD") / THE THING IS THIS (THIS IS THE THING)** -

May 76. (7") **ANY OLD TIME WILL DO. / THE RAIN CAME DOWN ON EVERYTHING** -

May 76. (7") **ANY OLD TIME WILL DO. / WHY DOES SUCH A PRETTY GIRL SING THOSE SAD SONGS** -

—— In Oct77, ROY WOOD made a duo single with ANNIE HASLAM of RENAISSANCE 'I NEVER BELIEVED IN LOVE. / INSIDE MY LIFE'. (from HASLAM's lp 'ANNIE IN WONDERLAND')

WIZZARD

(were formed August 1972 by **ROY WOOD** with **RICK PRICE**, plus others)(ex-MONGREL musicians) **CHARLIE GRIMA** – drums and **KEITH SMART** – drums also **HUGH McDOWELL** – cello and **BILL HUNT** – keyboards (both ex-ELO) and **NICK PENTELOW** – saxophone and **MICK BURNEY** – saxophone (ex-DALTONS)

Harvest | United Art

Nov 72. (7") **BALL PARK INCIDENT. / THE CARLSBERG SPECIAL** 6

Apr 73. (7") **SEE MY BABY JIVE. / BEND OVER BEETHOVEN** 1

Apr 73. (lp)(c) **WIZZARD BREW** 29
– You can dance the rock & roll / Meet me at the jailhouse / Jolly cup of tea / Buffalo station – Get down to Memphis / Gotta crush / Wear a fast gun.

Aug 73. (7") **ANGEL FINGERS. / YOU GOT THE JUMP ON ME** 1

—— (Sep73) trimmed slightly when McDOWELL returned to ELECTRIC LIGHT ORCH. (Nov73) **BOB BRADY** – keyboards (ex-APPLEJACKS) repl. HUNT

Nov 73. (7") **I WISH IT COULD BE CHRISTMAS EVERY DAY. / ROB ROY'S NIGHTMARE** 4

Warners | United Art

Apr 74. (7") **ROCK AND ROLL WINTER. / DREAM OF UNWIN** 6

Aug 74. (7") **THIS IS THE STORY OF MY LOVE (BABY). / NIXTURE** 34

Aug 74. (lp)(c) **INTRODUCING EDDY AND THE FALCONS** 19
– (intro) / Eddy's rock / Brand new '88' / You got me runnin' / I dun lotsa cryin' over you / This is the story of my love / Everyday I wonder / Crazy jeans / Come back Karen / We're gonna rock & roll tonight.

Oct 74. (7") **YOU'VE GOT ME RUNNIN'. / IT'S JUST MY IMAGINATION**

Dec 74. (7") **ARE YOU READY TO ROCK. / MARATHON MAN** 8

—— (Feb75) **WOOD** was just left with **PRICE** and **BURNEY,** and sessioners. (BRADY joined FAIRPORT CONVENTION) (SMART joined ROCKIN' BERRIES)

Jet | not issued

Oct 75. (7") **RATTLESNAKE ROLL. / CAN'T HELP MY FEELINGS**

ROY WOOD'S WIZZO BAND

(**ROY** only retained stalwart **RICK PRICE** now on pedal steel) also **GRAHAM GALLERY** – bass / **DAVE DONOVAN** – drums / **PAUL ROBBINS** – keyboards / **BILLY PAUL** – alto sax / **BOB WILSON** – trombone

Jet | Warners

Aug 77. (7") **THE STROLL. / JUBILEE**

Sep 77. (lp)(c) **SUPERACTIVE WIZZO**
– Life is wonderful / Waitin' at the door / Another wrong night / Sneakin' / Giant footsteps (jubilees) / Earthrise.

ROY WOOD

continued solo work

Warners | Warners

Feb 78. (7") **DANCING AT RAINBOW'S END. / WAITING AT THE DOOR** -

Nov 78. (7") **KEEP YOUR HANDS ON THE WHEEL. / JUBILEE**

Automatic | Warners

May 79. (7")(7"pic-d) **(WE'RE) ON THE ROAD AGAIN. / SAXMANIACS**

Aug 79. (lp)(c) **ON THE ROAD AGAIN**
– (We're) On the road again / Wings over the sea / Keep your hands on the wheel / Colourful lady / Road rocket / Backtown sinner / Jimmy lad / Dancin' at the rainbow's end / Another night / Way beyond the rain.

ROY WOOD'S HELICOPTERS

with **MIKE DEACON** (ex-DARTS) / + members of RENAISSANCE & MAGNUM

Cheapskate | not iss.

1980. (7") **GIVIN' YOUR HEART AWAY. / ROCK CITY** -

E.M.I. | not issued

Mar 81. (7") **GREEN GLASS WINDOWS. / DRIVING SONG** -

—— (released album in Jun81 'THE MANCUNIAN WAY' with 'Roy Perry'? on Deroy)

Jun 81. (7") **DOWN TO ZERO. / OLYMPIC FLYER** -

Jan 82. (7") **IT'S NOT EASY. / MOONRISER** -

Cheapskate | not issued

Dec 82. (7") **SING OUT THE OLD . . . BRING IN THE NEW. / WATCH THIS SPACE** -

Legacy | not issued

May 85. (7")(12") **UNDERFIRE. / ?** -

Nov 85. (7")(12") **SING OUT THE OLD . . . BRING IN THE NEW. / WATCH THIS SPACE** -

Oct 86. (7") **RAINING IN THE CITY. / ('A'instrumental)** -

Feb 87. (lp)(c) **STARTING UP** -
– Red cars are after me / Raining in the city / Under fire / Turn your body to the light / Hot cars / Starting up / Keep it steady / On top of the world / Ships in the night. *(cd-iss.1995 on 'Castle Classics')*

—— WOOD had earlier (late '86) featured on DOCTOR & THE MEDICS Top 50 version of ABBA's 'Waterloo'.

Woody | not issued

Dec 95. (c-s)(cd-s) **I WISH IT WOULD BE CHRISTMAS EVERYDAY. ("The ROY WOOD BIG BAND") /** -

– (ROY WOOD) compilations, etc. –

Apr 76. Harvest; (d-lp)(d-c) **THE ROY WOOD STORY** (solo unless stated) -
– Ball park incident (WIZZARD) / Until you moma's gone / Dear Elaine / Ella James (MOVE) / First movement (ELECTRIC LIGHT ORCHESTRA) / California man (MOVE) / Whisper in the night / Chinatown (MOVE) / You can dance your rock'n'roll / Forever / Angel fingers (WIZZARD) / Look at me now (ELECTRIC LIGHT ORCHESTRA) / Tonight (MOVE) / See me baby jive (WIZZARD). *(re-iss.+cdJul89 as 'YOU CAN DANCE THE ROCK'N'ROLL (THE ROY WOOD YEARS 1971-73', +=) Wake up / It wasn't my idea to dance / Nancy, sing me a song / Songs of praise.*

Apr 85. M.F.P.; (lp)(c) **THE BEST OF ROY WOOD (1970-1974)** -

Jul 82. Speed; (lp) **THE SINGLES** (all his bands' work) 37 -
– See my baby jive / Are you ready to rock / Oh what a shame / Fire brigade / Forever / I can hear the grass grow / O.T.T. / Blackberry way / Angel fingers / We're on the road again / Flowers in the rain / Green grass windows / Keep your hands on the wheel / Rock & roll winter / This is the story of my love (baby). *(re-iss.cd+c Sep93 on 'Connoisseur')*

Nov 82. Speed; (7") **O.T.T. / MYSTERY SONG** -

Feb 90. Action Replay; (cd)(c) **THE BEST AND THE REST OF ROY WOOD & WIZZARD** -
(re-iss.May91) (re-iss.Jul95 on 'Emporio')

– other WIZZARD compilations –

Oct 74. Harvest; (lp)(c) **SEE MY BABY JIVE** -

Oct 92. Old Gold; (cd-ep) **SEE MY BABY JIVE / ANGEL FINGERS / BALL PARK INCIDENT** *(re-iss.Nov95)* -

MOVING SIDEWALKS (see under ⇒ ZZ TOP)

Alison MOYET

Born: GENEVIEVE ALISON MOYET, 18 Jun'61, Basildon, Essex, England. Nicknamed ALF by her French father, she joined Southend R&B groups The VICARS and The SCREAMING ABDABS. Early in 1982, she was invited by ex-DEPECHE MODE mainman VINCE CLARKE, to become singer in duo YAZOO. For the next 18 months, they produced a number of Top 20 hits, from 2 top selling albums, before their split. She signed solo contract with 'CBS-Columbia', around the same time as marrying long-time hairdresser boyfriend Malcolm Lee, and setting up home in Hertfordshire. In the summer of '84, her first 45 'LOVE RESURRECTION', broke the UK Top 10, as did her next 'ALL CRIED OUT'. These were highlights on her late 1984 No.1 debut album 'ALF'. She continued to be a top artist for the rest of the 80's, while also bringing up new family. However in 1989, she divorced her husband after they had lived separately for last two years. • **Style:** Bluesy jazz pop singer, with an enormous soulful vocal-range and figure. • **Songwriters:** TONY SWAIN and STEVE JOLLEY wrote, produced and played on her debut album. She also covered; INVISIBLE (Lamont-Dozier) / THAT OLE DEVIL CALLED LOVE (Billy Holiday) / LOVE LETTERS (Ketty Lester) / ROCK AND ROLL (Led Zeppelin). • **Trivia:** Female comedy duo FRENCH & SAUNDERS featured on the video of 'LOVE LETTERS'.

Recommended: ALF (*7)

ALISON MOYET – vocals with session people

C.B.S. Columbia

Jun 84. (7") **LOVE RESURRECTION. / BABY I DO** 10 82 Jul 85
(12") – ('A'love injected mix).
Sep 84. (7")(12") **ALL CRIED OUT. / STEAL ME BLIND** 8
(12") – ('A'remixed).
Nov 84. (lp)(c)(cd) **ALF** 1 45 Mar 85
– Love resurrection / Honey for the bees / For you only / Invisible / Steal me blind / All cried out / Money mile / Twisting the knife / Where hides sleep.
Nov 84. (7")(12") **INVISIBLE. / HITCH HIKE** 21 31 Feb85
(12") – ('A'transparent mix).
Mar 85. (7") **THAT OLE DEVIL CALLED LOVE. / DON'T BURN DOWN THE BRIDGE** 2
(12"+=) – ('A' jazz version).
(d7"+=) – ('A' live version) / Twisting the knife (live).
Aug 85. (7") **MONEY MILE. / FOR YOU ONLY** -
Nov 86. (7") **IS THIS LOVE?. / BLOW WIND BLOW** 3
(12"+=) – ('A'-L.A. mix).
(12") – ('A'side) / For you only (Europa mix).
Mar 87. (7") **WEAK IN THE PRESENCE OF BEAUTY. / TO WORK ON YOU** 6
(12"+=) – ('A'extended remix).
(12"+=) – Take my imagination to bed.
(d7"+=) – Is this love / Blow wind blow.
Apr 87. (lp)(c)(cd) **RAINDANCING** 2 94 Jun 87
– Weak in the presence of beauty / Ordinary girl / You got me wrong / Without you / Sleep like breathing / Is this love? / Blow wind blow / Glorious love / When I say no (no giveaway) / Stay. *(re-iss.Mar90)*
May 87. (7") **ORDINARY GIRL. / PALM OF YOUR HAND (CLOAK AND DAGGER)** 43
(12"+=) – ('A'remix).
(12"+=) – ('A'special dance mix).
Sep 87. (7") **SLEEP LIKE BREATHING. / LOVE RESURRECTION (live)**
(12"+=) – Ne me quitte pas (live).
Nov 87. (7") **LOVE LETTERS. / THIS HOUSE** 4
(12"+=) – ('A'extended).
(cd-s++=) – Ne me quitte pas (live).

Columbia Columbia

Mar 91. (7")(c-s) **IT WON'T BE LONG. / MY RIGHT A.R.M.** 50
(12"+=)(cd-s+=) – Take of me.
Apr 91. (cd)(c)(lp) **HOODOO** 11
– Footsteps / It won't be long / This house / Rise / Wishing you were here / (Meeting with my) Main man / Hoodoo / Back where I belong / My right A.R.M. / Never too late / Find me.
May 91. (7")(c-s) **WISHING YOU WERE HERE. / BACK WHERE I BELONG** 72
(12"+=)(cd-s+=)(pic-cd-s+=) – ('B'-soft mix) / ('B'-polite mix).
Oct 91. (7")(c-s) **THIS HOUSE. / COME BACK HOME** 40
(cd-s+=) – Love letters / That ole Devil called love.
Oct 93. (7")(c-s)(cd-s) **FALLING. / ODE TO A BOY** 44
Feb 94. (c-s) **WHISPERING YOUR NAME / F.O.S.** 18
(12") – ('A'extended mixes) / ('A'-Vince Clarke mix).
(cd-s) – ('A'side) / Rise / Wishing you were here / Rock and roll (all live).
(12")(cd-s) – ('A'side) / Hoodoo / Back where I belong.
Mar 94. (cd)(c)(lp) **ESSEX** 24
– Falling / Whispering your name / Getting into something / Dorothy / So am I / And I know / Ode to boy / Satellite / Another living day / Boys own / Take of me / Ode to boy II / Whispering your name (single mix).
May 94. (c-s) **GETTING INTO SOMETHING. / ('A'mix)** 51
(12"+=)/ /(cd-s++=) – Never too late. / / Ne me quitte pas.
Oct 94. (c-s) **ODE TO BOY. / LIFE IN A HOLE** 59
(cd-s) – (2-'A'mixes) / Sunderland Glynn.
(12") – (5-'A'mixes).
May 95. (cd)(c) **SINGLES** (compilation) 1
– The first time ever I saw your face / Only you (YAZOO) / Nobody's diary (YAZOO) / Situation (YAZOO) / Love resurrection / All cried out / Invisible / That ole Devil called love / Is this love? / Weak in the presence of beauty / Ordinary girl / Love letters / It won't be long / Wishing you were here / This house / Falling / Whispering your name / Getting into somthing / Ode to boy II / Solid wood.
Aug 95. (c-s) **SOLID WOOD / BLUE** 44
(cd-s+=) – Ode to boy / There are worse things I could do.
(cd-s+=) – Whispering your name / The first time ever I saw your face.

– compilations, others, etc. –

1988. C.B.S.; (cd) **ALF / RAINDANCING** -

MR.BIG

Formed: San Francisco then Los Angeles, California, USA ... Sep'88 by ERIC MARTIN and BILLY SHEEHAN, who named themselves after a FREE track. Made progress in the late 80's to score US No.1 hit in '92 'TO BE WITH YOU'. • **Style:** Hard-rock & ballad outfit, similar to EXTREME. • **Songwriters:** Group or MARTIN who collaborated with either TONY FANUCCHI or ANDRE PESSIS. • **Trivia:** The ERIC MARTIN BAND released one 'CBS' 1983 lp 'SUCKER FOR A PRETTY FACE', before gong solo for 'Capitol', and issuing mid-80's albums 'ERIC MARTIN' & 'I'M ONLY FOOLING MYSELF'.

Recommended: LEAN INTO IT (*6).

ERIC MARTIN – vocals (ex-solo artist) / **PAUL GILBERT** – guitar (ex-RACER X) / **PAT DORPEY** – drums / **BILLY SHEEHAN** – bass (ex-TALAS, ex-DAVID LEE ROTH)

Atlantic Atlantic

Jul 89. (lp)(c)(cd) **MR.BIG** 60 46
– Addicted to that rush / Wind me up / Merciless / Had enough / Blame it on my youth / Take a walk / Big love / How can you do what you do / Anything for you / Rock and roll over. *(cd+=)*– 30 days in a hole.
Aug 89. (7") **ADDICTED TO THAT RUSH. / BLAME IT ON MY YOUTH** -
Jan 90. (7") **WIND ME UP. / MERCILESS** -
Mar 91. (7")(c-s) **THE DRILL SONG (DADDY, BROTHER, LOVER, LITTLE BOY). / ROAD TO RUIN**
(12"+=)(cd-s+=) – Addicted to that rush (live) / Strike like lightning.
Apr 91. (cd)(c)(lp) **LEAN INTO IT** 52 15
– Daddy, brother, lover, little boy (the electric drill song) / Alive and kickin' / Green-tinted sixties mind / CDFF lucky this time / Voodoo kiss / Never say never / Just take my heart / My kinda woman / A little too loose / Road to ruin / To be with you. *(Feb92 re-entered UK chart hit 28) (re-iss.cd/c Feb95)*
May 91. (7") **GREEN TINTED SIXTIES MIND. / SHADOWS**
(12"+=)(12"pic-d+=) – Take a walk (live).
(cd-s++=) – Drilled and confused. *(re-iss.Aug92)*
Dec 91. (7") **TO BE WITH YOU. / GREEN TINTED SIXTIES MIND** - 1
Feb 92. (7")(c-s) **TO BE WITH YOU. / THE DRILL SONG (DADDY, BROTHER, LOVER, LITTLE BOY) (live)** 3 -
(cd-s+=) – Shy boy (live) / Woman from Tokyo (live).
(12"+=) – Lean into it (live) / A little too loose (live) / Alive and kickin' (live).
May 92. (7"c-s) **JUST TAKE MY HEART. / GREEN TINTED SIXTIES MIND** 26 16 Apr 92
(cd-s+=) – To be with you (live) / Lucky this time (live).
(cd-s+=) – Shadow / Strike like lightning.
Jul 92. (7")(c-s) **GREEN TINTED SIXTIES MIND. / LOVE MAKES YOU STRONG** 72
(12")(pic-cd-s) – ('A'side) / Just take my heart (acoustic) / Big love / Dirty days in the hole.
Sep 93. (cd)(c)(lp) **BUMP AHEAD** 61
– Colorado bulldog / The price you gotta pay / Promise her the Moon / What's it gonna be / Wild world / Mr.Gone / The whole world is gonna know / Nothing but love / Temperamental / Ain't seen love like that / Mr.Big.
Oct 93. (7")(c-s) **WILD WORLD. / TEMPERAMENTAL** 59 27
(12"+=) – Long way down.
(cd-s) – ('A'side) / Rock and roll over / Let yourself go / Voodoo kiss (live).
Feb 94. (c-s)(cd-s) **AIN'T SEEN LOVE LIKE THAT. /** - 83

MR.BUNGLE (see under ⇒ FAITH NO MORE)

M.S.G. (see under ⇒ SCHENKER GROUP, Michael)

MUDHONEY

Formed: Seattle, USA ... 1988 by ex-GREEN RIVER members MARK ARM and STEVE TURNER. They were soon joined by MATT LUKIN (ex-MELVINS) and DAN PETERS (ex-BUNDLES OF PISS). Signed to Bruce Pavitt's 'Sub Pop' label and issued UK debut 'TOUCH ME, I'M SICK' (later covered by SONIC YOUTH). Debut album 'SUPERFUZZ BIGMUFF' (named after TURNER's favourite effects pedals), failed to impress many, although success found them in 1991 with 'EVERY GOOD BOY DESERVES FUDGE'. The following year, they moved to 'Warners' and enjoyed another album UK chart entry with 'PIECE OF CAKE'. • **Style:** Garageland fuzz/thrash outfit, hot on the heels of The STOOGES, SONIC YOUTH or The HEARTBREAKERS. • **Songwriters:** ARM-TURNER? except; HATE THE POLICE (Dicks) / EVOLUTION (Spacemen 3) / OVER THE TOP (Motorhead) / PUMP IT UP (Elvis Costello). MARK ARM solo:- MASTERS OF WAR (Bob Dylan).

Recommended: EVERY GOOD BOY DESERVES FUDGE (*7).

MARK ARM – vocals, guitar / **STEVE TURNER** – guitar (both ex-GREEN RIVER) / **MATT LUKIN** – bass (ex-MELVINS) / **DAN PETERS** – drums

Glitterhouse / Sub Pop

Aug 88. (7")(7"brown) **TOUCH ME I'M SICK. / SWEET YOUNG THING AIN'T SWEET NO MORE**

Oct 88. (12"ep) **SUPERFUZZ BIGMUFF**
– No one has / If I think / In 'n' out of grace / Need / Chain that door / Mudride. *(re-iss.+cd-ep.Apr89)*

Jan 89. (7")(7"clear) **('A'side by 'Sonic Youth'). / TOUCH ME I'M SICK**

Jun 89. (7")(7"white)(12") **YOU GOT IT (KEEP IT OUTTA MY FACE). / BURN IT CLEAN / NEED (demo)**
(re-iss.May93)

Oct 89. (7")(7"purple)(12") **THIS GIFT. / BABY HELP ME FORGET / REVOLUTION**
(re-iss.May93)

Oct 89 (m-lp)(c)(cd) **MUDHONEY**
– This gift / Flat out f***ed / Get into yours / You got it / Magnolia caboose babyshit / Come to mind / Here comes sickness / Running loaded / The further I go / By her own hand / When tomorrow hits / Dead love.

Jun 90. (7")(7"pink) **YOU'RE GONE. / THORN / YOU MAKE ME DIE** [60]
(re-iss.Jun93)

Sub Pop / Sub Pop

Jul 91. (7")(12"grey) **LET IT SLIDE. / OUNCE OF DECEPTION / CHECKOUT TIME** [60]
(cd-s+=) – Paperback life / The money will roll right in.

Aug 91. (cd)(c)(lp) **EVERY GOOD BOY DESERVES FUDGE** [34]
– Generation genocide / Let it slide / Good enough / Something so clear / Thorn / Into the drink / Broken hands / Who you drivin' now / Move out / Shoot the Moon / Fuzzgun '91 / Poking around / Don't fade IV / Check out time.

— MARK + STEVE took up time in MONKEYWRENCH, and DAN joined SCREAMING TREES, after below album.

Warners / Reprise

Oct 92. (7")(c-s) **SUCK YOU DRY. / DECEPTION PASS** [65]
(12"+=)(cd-s+=) – Underride / Over the top.

Oct 92. (cd)(c)(lp) **PIECE OF CAKE** [39]
– No end in sight / Make it now / Suck you dry / Blinding Sun / Thirteenth floor opening / Youth body expression explosion / I'm spun / Take me there / Living wreck / Let me let you down / Ritzville / Acetone.

Oct 93. (cd)(c)(m-lp) **FIVE DOLLAR BOB'S MOCK COOTER STEW**
– In the blood / No song III / Between you and me kid / Six two one / Make it now again / Deception pass / Underide.

— In Apr'94, they released with JIMMIE DALE GILMOUR a 7"yellow and cd-s 'TONIGHT' for 'Sub Pop'.

Reprise / Reprise

Mar 95. (cd)(c)(lp) **MY BROTHER THE COW** [70]
– Judgement, rage, retribution and thyme / Generation spokesmodel / What moves the heart? / Today, is a good day / Into yer schtik / In my finest suit / F.D.K. (Fearless Doctor KIllers) / Orange ball-pen hammer / Crankcase blues / Execution style / Dissolve / 1995.

Apr 95. (7") **INTO YOUR SCHTIK. / YOU GIVE ME THE CREEPS**

— above single on 'Super Electro'

May 95. (7"colrd)(c-s) **GENERATION SPOKESMODEL. / NOT GOING DOWN THAT ROAD AGAIN**
(cd-s+=) – What moves the heart live) / Judgement, rage, retribution and thyme (live).

Amphetami. / Amphetami.

Aug 95. (7") **GOAT CHEESE. /**

– compilations, etc. –

Nov 89. Tupelo; (12"ep)(cd-ep) **BOILED BEEF AND ROTTING TEETH**

THE FREEWHEELIN' MARK ARM

Sub Pop / Sub Pop

Feb 91. (7")(7"red)(7"green) **MASTERS OF WAR. / MY LIFE WITH RICKETS** [ ] [ ] Dec 90

MONKEYWRENCH

— **MARK ARM / STEVE TURNER / TOM PRICE / TIM KERR / MARTIN BLAND**

Sub Pop / Sub Pop

1992. (7") **BOTTLE UP AND GO /**

MUNGO JERRY

Formed: London, England ... 1969 out of GOOD EARTH and The MUNGOES, by RAY DORSET, etc (see below). Just signed to 'Dawn' and after a superb performance at the Hollywood festival in Newcastle May'70, their appropriately titled debut 45 'IN THE SUMMERTIME', hit No.1. It soon managed a Top 3 placing in the States (their only hit), and was quickly followed by an eponymous Top 20 debut lp. Early in '71, their next 45 (another EP) 'BABY JUMP', gave them another top spot, but they couldn't match GERRY & THE PACEMAKERS record of 3 novice consecutive hits, when 3rd single 'LADY ROSE', hit No.5. This was probably due to its 'B'side, 'HAVE A WHIFF ON ME', being banned by the BBC. They sustained an up and down run of hits, until the mid-70's, when 'Polydor' took over. • **Style:** Jug-band skiffle pop-rock outfit, fronted by the frizzy Afro-haired RAY DORSET, known to the uninitiated as MUNGO JERRY. Also part of the glam-rock scene of the early 70's, alongside SWEET, GARY GLITTER and T.REX. • **Songwriters:** DORSET wrote most, and did a few covers. • **Trivia:** In 1980, disco singer KELLY MARIE had a UK No.1 smash with RAY DORSET penned & produced 'FEELS LIKE I'M IN LOVE'.

Recommended: ALL THE HITS PLUS MORE (*5)

RAY DORSET (b.21 Mar'46, Ashford, Kent, England) – vocals, guitar, washboard / **COLIN EARL** (b. 6 May'42, Hampton Court, England) – piano, vocals / **PAUL KING** (b. 9 Jan'48, Dagenham, England) – guitar, banjo / **MIKE COLE** – drums

Dawn / Janus

May 70. (7"m) **IN THE SUMMERTIME. / MIGHTY MAN / DUST PNEUMONIA BLUES** [1] [3]

Jul 70. (lp)(c) **MUNGO JERRY** [13] [64] Aug 70
– Baby let's play house / Johnny B. Badde / San Francisco Bay blues / Sad eyed Joe / Maggie / Peace in the country / See me my friend / Mother Boogie / Tramp / Daddie's brew. *(re-iss.+c.Mar86 on 'P.R.T.', cd-iss.Apr89)*

Nov 70. (7") **JOHNNY B. BADDE. / SEE ME MY FRIEND** [-]

Jan 71. (7"m) **BABY JUMP / THE MAN BEHIND THE PIANO. / MAGGIE / MIDNIGHT SPECIAL / MIGHTY MA** [1]

— **JOHN GODFREY** – bass, vocals, keyboards repl. COLE

Dawn / Bell

Apr 71. (lp)(c) **ELECTRONICALLY TESTED** [14]
– She rowed / I just wanna make love to you / In the summertime / Somebody stole my wife / Baby jump / Follow me down / Memoirs of a stockbroker / You better leave that whisky alone / Coming back to you.

May 71. (7"m) **LADY ROSE / HAVE A WHIFF ON ME. / MILK COW BLUES / LITTLE LOUIS** [5]

— (after above was withdrawn, 'SHE ROWED' repl. 'Have A Whiff . . . ')

Dawn / Pye

Sep 71. (7"m) **YOU DON'T HAVE TO BE IN THE ARMY TO FIGHT IN THE WAR / O'REILLY WE SHALL BE FREE. / THE SUN IS SHINING** [13]

1971. (lp)(c) **YOU DON'T HAVE TO BE IN THE ARMY**
– You don't have to be in the army to fight in the war / Ella Speed / Pigeon stew / Take me back / Give me love / Hey Rosalyn / Northcote Arms / There's a man going round taking names / Simple things / Keep your hands off her / On a Sunday / That old dust storm. *(US-title 'MEMOIRS OF A STOCKBROKER')*

— **JOHN POPE** – keyboards repl. COLIN who formed KING-EARL BOOGIE BAND / **TIM REEVES** – drums repl. PAUL who also joined above

Apr 72. (7"m) **OPEN UP / GOING BACK HOME. / I DON'T WANNA GO BACK TO SCHOOL / NO GIRL REACTION** [21] [-]
(in the US, only first 2 songs from EPs were released A+B)

1972. (7"m) **MY GIRL AND ME / 46 AND ON. / IT'S A GOODIE BOOGIE WOOGIE / SUMMER'S GONE** [ ] [-]

1972. (lp)(c) **BOOT POWER**
– Open up / She's gone / Lookin' for my girl / See you again / The demon / My girl and me / Sweet Mary Jane / Lady Rose / Dusty road / Brand new car / 46 an' on.

Jun 73. (7") **ALRIGHT ALRIGHT ALRIGHT. / LITTLE MISS HIPSHAKE** [3]

1973. (lp)(c) **GREATEST HITS** (compilation) [ ] [-]

Pye / Bell

Oct 73. (7") **WILD LOVE. / GLAD I'M A ROCKER** [32]

Mar 74. (7") **LONGLEGGED WOMAN DRESSED IN BLACK. / GONNA BOP TILL I DROP** [13]

Sep 74. (lp)(c) **LONG LEGGED WOMAN** [ ] [-]
– Long legged woman dressed in black / Glad I'm a rocker / Gonna bop 'til I drop / Wild love / O'Reilly / The sun is shining / Summer's gone / Don't stop / Going back home / No girl reaction / Little Miss hipshake / Milk cow blues / I don't wanna go back to school / Alright alright alright.

Nov 74. (7"m) **ALL DRESSED UP / SHAKE TILL I BREAK. / TOO FAST TO LIVE / BURNIN' UP** [ ] [-]

Polydor / not issued

Jul 75. (7") **CAN'T GET OVER LOVING YOU. / LET'S GO** [ ] [-]

Nov 75. (7") **HELLO NADINE. / BOTTLE OF BEER** [ ] [-]

Feb 76. (lp)(c) **IMPALA SAGA** [ ] [-]
– Hello Nadine / Never mind I've still got my rock'n'roll / Ain't too bad / Too fast / It's a secret / Impala saga / Bottle of beer / Get down on your baby / Hit me / Quiet man / Never mind I've got my rock'n'roll (reprise).

Jul 76. (7") **DON'T LET GO. / GIVE ME BOP** [ ] [-]

RAY DORSET & MUNGO JERRY

with **COLIN EARL** returning alongside **CHRIS WARNES** – bass / **PETE SULLIVAN** – drums

Apr 77. (7") **HEAVY FOOT STOMP. / THAT'S MY BABY** [ ] [-]

May 77. (lp)(c) **LOVIN' IN THE ALLEYS, FIGHTIN' IN THE STREETS** [ ] [-]
– All that a woman should be / I could never start lovin' you / Lovin' in the alleys, fightin' in the streets / The grease / Dragster queen / Heavy foot stomp / Gone to Malaya / Can't keep it down / Lovin' in the morning / Just can't say goodbye.

Jul 77. (7"m) **ALL THAT A WOMAN SHOULD BE. / DRAGSTER QUEEN / GET DOWN ON YOUR BABY** [ ] [-]

Nov 77. (7") **WE'RE O.K. / LET'S MAKE IT** [ ] [-]

Jul 79. (7") **DANCIN' IN THE STREET. / ROCKIN' ON THE ROAD** [ ] [-]

Dec 79. (lp)(c) **RAY DORSET & MUNGO JERRY** [ ] [-]

Satellite / not issued

Dec 79. (7") **FORGOTTEN LAND. (as "RAY DORSET" solo) / NEW WAY OF LIFE** [ ] [-]

Feb 80. (7") **WHAT'S HER NAME. / WHY D'YOU LIE TO ME** [ ] [-]

Stage Coach / not issued

1981. (7") **KNOCKIN' ON HEAVEN'S DOOR. / HAZEL EYES** [ ] [-]

Jun 83. (7") **THERE GOES MY HEART AGAIN. ("MUNGO JERRY & The TARTS") / THINKING OF YOU** [ ] [-]

MUNGO JERRY & HORIZON

Orbit / not issued

Jun 84. (7") **SUNSHINE REGGAE. / NIGHTLIFE** [ ] [-]

MUNGO JERRY & The BROTHERS GRIMM

Illegal | not issued

Aug 87. (7")(12") **IN THE SUMMERTIME. / GET A JOB** -

—— disbanded.

- more compilations, etc. -

May 75. Dawn; (7") **IN THE SUMMERTIME. / SHE ROWED** -
Nov 74. Pye; (lp)(c) **THE GOLDEN HOUR PRESENTS MUNGO JERRY'S GREATEST HITS** -
Nov 77. Pye; (d-lp)(c) **MUNGO JERRY FILE** -
Sep 77. Pye; (12"ep) **IN THE SUMMERTIME / MIGHTY MAN. / LADY ROSE / BABY JUMP** -
Apr 79. Pye; (7") **IN THE SUMMERTIME. / BABY JUMP** -
(re-iss.May80)
Aug 80. Scratch; (7"ep) **SUMMERTIME HOLIDAY / HOORAY IT'S PARTY TIME. / NIGHT ON THE TOWN / REALLY HAD A GOOD TIME** -
Jul 89. Old Gold; (7") **IN THE SUMMERTIME. / LONGLEGGED WOMAN DRESSED IN BLACK** -
Jul 82. Old Gold; (7") **BABY JUMP. / ALRIGHT ALRIGHT ALRIGHT** -
May 89. Old Gold; (cd-ep) **IN THE SUMMERTIME / BABY JUMP / LONGLEGGED WOMAN DRESSED IN BLACK** -
Nov 82. P.R.T.; (c) **100 MINUTES OF MUNGO JERRY** -
Oct 87. P.R.T.; (lp)(c)(cd) **TOO FAST TO LIVE AND TOO YOUNG TO DIE** -
Oct 85. Flashback; (lp)(c) **IN THE SUMMERTIME** -
Nov 84. Astan; (lp)(c) **GREATEST HITS** -
Nov 84. Astan; (c) **SIX-A-SIDE** -
Apr 85. Autograph; (c) **SOUL PARTY** -
May 90. Prestige; (cd)(c)(lp) **ALL THE HITS PLUS MORE** -
Nov 90. B.B.C.; (7") **IN THE SUMMERTIME (Dance Rave Medley 1990)** -
(cd-s+=) – Lady Rose / Alright, Alright, Alright / Hello Nadine / In The Summertime.
Aug 91. Topline; (7")(c-s) **IN THE SUMMERTIME /**
Dec 91. Dojo; (cd) **THE EARLY YEARS** -
1992. Dojo; (cd) **GREATEST HITS** -
– Maggie / Sad eyed Joe / Peace in the country / In the summertime / Midnight special (live) / Might man (live) / Baby jump / The man behind the piano / Somebody stole my wife / Have a whiff on me / Lady Rose / You don't have to be in the army to fight in the war / Open up / Going back home / Alright alright alright / Wild love / Long legged woman dressed in black.
Jul 94. Success; (cd)(c) **GREATEST HITS VOLUME 1** -
Jul 94. Success; (cd)(c) **GREATEST HITS VOLUME 2** -
Jan 95. Spectrum; (cd) **SUMMERTIME** -
Nov 95. BGO; (cd) **MUNGO JERRY / ELECTRONICALLY TESTED** -

RAY DORSET

with **MIKE McNAUGHT** – piano / **DAVE MARKEE** – bass / **MIKE TRAVIS** – drums

Dawn | not issued

1971. (7") **COLD BLUE EXCURSION. / I NEED IT** -
1972. (lp)(c) **COLD BLUE EXCURSION** -
– Got to be free / Cold blue excursion / With me / Have pity on me / Time is now / Livin' ain't easy / Help your friends / I need it / Because I want you / Nightime / Maybe that's the way / Always on my mind. *(cd-iss.Jul95 on 'BGO')*

RAY DORSET & The FABULOUS LATICS

Pier | not issued

Mar 87. (7") **COME ON YOU LATICS. / WE'RE GONNA BLAZE AWAY** -

Peter MURPHY (see under ⇒ BAUHAUS)

Pauline MURRAY & INVISIBLE GIRLS (see under ⇒ PENETRATION)

MY BLOODY VALENTINE

Formed: Dublin, Ireland ... 1984 by KEVIN SHIELDS and COLM CUSACK. Late that year, they went to Germany and recorded mini-lp 'THIS IS YOUR BLOODY VALENTINE', for small 'Tycoon' records. It was issued the next year, but only 50 copies seemed to emerge, which are now very rare. They moved to London and soon issued 'GEEK!' EP for 'Fever'. After more 45's for 'Kaleidoscope' then 'Lazy' (home of The PRIMITIVES), they were transferred to 'Creation' in 1988 by SLAUGHTER JOE FOSTER (ex-TV PERSONALITIES). They finally made the breakthrough in 1990, when the 'GLIDER' EP, nearly went Top 40 UK. • **Style:** Twangly fuzzy IGGYPOP-like beginnings, progressed into dreamy psychedelia and uncompromising rock, with a new complete concept and landscape of sound. • **Songwriters:** SHIELDS writes most of material, with words after 1987 by BILINDA. • **Trivia:** A track 'SUGAR' was given away free with 'The Catalogue' magazine of Feb '89.

Recommended: LOVELESS (*8) / ISN'T ANYTHING (*8) / ECSTASY AND WINE (*7).

KEVIN SHIELDS – guitar, vocals, occasional bass / **DAVE CONWAY** – vocals / **COLM CUSACK** (b. O'COISDIG) – drums / **TINA** – keyboards

Tycoon | not issued

1985. (m-lp) **THIS IS YOUR BLOODY VALENTINE** - - GERM
– Forever and again / Homelovin' guy / Don't cramp my style / Tiger in my tank / The love gang / Inferno / The last supper.

—— **DEBBIE GOOGE** – bass repl. TINA

Fever | not issued

Apr 86. (12"ep) **GEEK!** -
– No place to go / Moonlight / Love machine / The sandman never sleeps.
Jun 86. (7") **NO PLACE TO GO. / MOONLIGHT** -

Kaleidoscope | not issued

Oct 86. (12"ep) **THE NEW RECORD BY MY BLOODY VALENTINE** -
– Lovelee sweet darlene / By the danger in your eyes / We're so beautiful / On another rainy Sunday.

Lazy | not issued

Feb 87. (7") **SUNNY SUNDAE SMILE. / PAINT A RAINBOW** -
(12"+=) – Kiss the eclipse / Sylvie's head.

—— **BILINDA BUTCHER** – vocals, guitar repl. CONWAY

Nov 87. (m-lp) **ECSTASY** -
– (Please) Lose yourself in me / The things I miss / I don't need you / Clair / (You're) Safe in your sleep / She loves you no less / Strawberry wine / Lovelee sweet darlene.
Nov 87. (12") **STRAWBERRY WINE. / NEVER SAY GOODBYE / CAN I TOUCH YOU** -

Creation | not issued

Jul 88. (7") **YOU MADE ME REALISE. / SLOW** -
(12"+=) – Thorn / Cigarette in your bed / Drive it all over me. *(above 12" tracks re-iss.Mar90 as cd-ep)*
Oct 88. (7") **FEED ME WITH YOUR KISSES. / EMPTINESS INSIDE** -
(12"+=) – I believe / I need no trust. *(re-iss.Mar90 as cd-ep)*
Nov 88. (lp)(c)(cd) **ISN'T ANYTHING** -
– Soft as snow (but warm inside) / Lose my breath / Cupid come / (When you wake) You're still in a dream / No more sorry / All I need / Feed me with your kiss / Sue is fine / Several girls galore / You never should / Nothing much to lose / I can see it (but I can't feel it). *(free 7"w.a.)* – INSTRUMENTAL. / INSTRUMENTAL
Apr 90. (7"ep)(12"ep)(cd-ep) **GLIDER** 41 -
– Soon / Glider / Don't ask why / Off your face.
Feb 91. (7"ep)(12"ep)(cd-ep) **TREMOLO** 29
– To here knows when / Swallow / Honey power / Moon song.
Apr 91. (cd)(c)(lp) **LOVELESS** 24
– Only shallow / Loomer / Touched / To here knows when / When you sleep / I only said / Come in alone / Sometimes / Blown a wish / What you want / Soon.

Signed to 'Island' records in Oct'92.

- compilations, others, etc. -

Feb 89. Lazy; (lp)(c)(cd) **ECSTASY AND WINE** -
– Strawberry wine / Never say goodbye / Can I touch you / She loves you no less / The things I miss / I don't need you / Safe in your sleep / Clair / You've got nothing / Lose yourself in me.

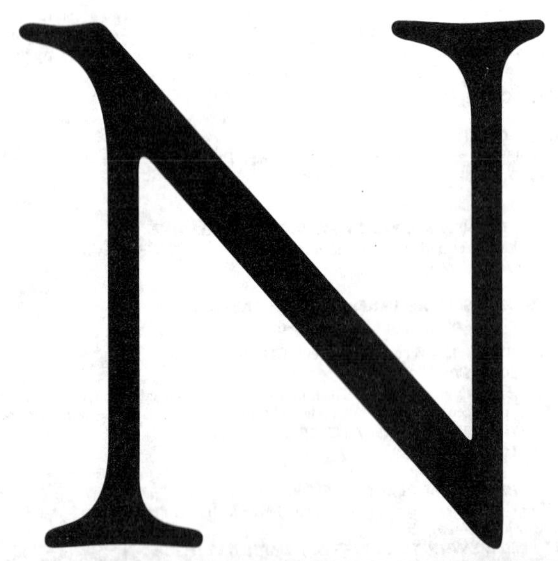

NAILBOMB (see under ⇒ SEPULTURA)

NAPALM DEATH

Formed: Ipswich, England . . . 1982 by DORRIAN and STEER. Finally made it onto vinyl (after a few John Peel sessions), on their own 'Earache' label. In 1987, they unveiled 'SCUM', a 27-track lp of song spurts. Were making headway into UK brains, when they split with surviving originals, and brought in some easier going Americans. • **Style:** Innovators of hardcore grindcrushing rock. A hybrid of death speed-metal and greasy haired punk. Their short abrupt ditties, were carcassed with inaudible vox, which virtually brain-washed their lemmingmania audience. In the 90's with changed line-up, they opted for a more longer-tuned heavy-metal song. • **Songwriters:** All written by DORRIAN (lyrics) and STEER (music!!), until their departure. • **Trivia:** Recorded the shortest track ever (1 second), for a free 7", given away with an 'Earache' sampler 'Grindcrusher'. SHANE EMBURY exchanged death threats with another teeth-grinding outfit SORE THROAT (mainly band member RICH MILITIA).

Recommended: DEATH BY MANIPULATION (*7)

LEE DORRIAN – vocals (also runs own label 'Rise Above') / **BILL STEER** – guitar (also of CARCASS) / **SHANE EMBURY** – bass (also drummer of UNSEEN TERROR) / **MICK HARRIS** – drums (also vocals of EXTREME NOISE TERROR) repl. FRANK HEALEY (other early drummer JUS of HEAD OF DAVID)

Earache | not issued

Jul 87. (lp) **SCUM** [ ] [-]
– Multinational corporations / Instinct of survival / The kill / Scum / Caught in a dream / Polluted minds / Sacrificied / Stage of power / Control / Born on your knees / Human garbage / You suffer / Life? / Prison without walls / Negative approach / Success? / Deceiver / C.S. / Parasites / Pseudo youth / Divine death / As the machine rolls on / Common enemy / Moral crusade / Stigmatized / M.A.D. / Dragnet. *(c-iss.May89) (re-iss.cd Sep94)*

Nov 88. (lp)(c)(cd) **FROM ENSLAVEMENT TO OBLITERATION** [ ] [-]
– Evolved as one / It's a man's world / Lueid fairytale / Private death / Impressions / Unchallenged hate / Uncertainty blurs the vision / Cock rock alienation / Retreat to nowhere / Think for a minute / Display to me . . . / From enslavement to obliteration / Blind to the truth / Social sterility / Emotional suffocation / Practise what you preach / Inconceivable / Worlds apart / Obstinate direction / Mentally murdered / Sometimes / Make way. *(pic-lp iss.Jul90) (re-iss.cd Sep94)*

Aug 89. (7") **MENTALLY MURDERED. / CAUSE AND EFFECT** [ ] [-]
(12"ep) **MENTALLY MURDERED EP** (+=) – Rise above / Missing link – Mentally murdered / Walls of confinement / Cause and effect – No manual effort.

— (Aug89) **MARK 'Barney' GREENWAY** – vocals (ex-BENEDICTION) repl. LEE (LEE was to join CATHEDRAL, another 'Earache' band) **MITCH HARRIS** (b.Las Vegas, USA) + **JESSE PINTADO** (b.Mexico) – guitars repl. BILL who went full-time with CARCASS)

Aug 90. (7") **SUFFER THE CHILDREN. / SIEGE OF POWER** [ ] [-]
(12"+=) – Harmony corruption.

Sep 90. (cd)(c)(lp) **HARMONY CORRUPTION** [67] [-]
– Vision conquest / If the truth be known / Inner incineration / Malicious intent / Unfit Earth / Circle of hypocrisy / Suffer the children / The chains that bind us / Mind snare / Extremity retained. (some w/free 12") *(re-iss.cd Sep94)*

May 91. (7") **MASS APPEAL MADNESS. / PRIDE ASSASSIN** [ ] [-]
(12"+=) – Unchallenged hate / Social sterility.

— MICK HARRIS was arrested for jewel shop robbery & he left to join SCORN. He was soon replaced by **DANNY HERARRA** – drums

May 92. (cd)(c)(lp) **UTOPIA BANISHED** [58] [-]
– Discordance / I abstain / Dementia access / Christening of the blind / The world keeps turning / Idiosyncratic / Arayanisus / Cause and effect / Judicial slime / Distorting the medium / Got time to kill / Upward and Uninterested / Exile / Awake (to a life of misery) / Contemptious. (free 4 track 7"ep). *(re-iss.cd Sep94)*

Jun 92. (12"ep)(cd-ep) **THE WORLD KEEPS TURNING. / A MEANS TO AN END / INSANITY EXCURSION** [ ] [-]

Jul 93. (7")(cd-s) **NAZI PUNKS FUCK OFF. / ARYANISMS / ('A' version) / CONTEMPTUOUS (xtreem mix)** [ ] [-]
(above a cover of a DEAD KENNEDYS single)

May 94. (cd)(c)(lp) **FEAR, EMPTINESS, DESPAIR** [ ] [-]
– Twist the knife (slowly) / Hung / Remain nameless / Plague rages / More than meets the eye / Primed time / State of mind / Armageddon X7 / Retching on the dirt / Fasting on deception / Throwaway.

Nov 95. (m-cd)(m-c)(10"m-lp) **GREED KILLING** [ ] [-]
– Greed killing / My own worst enemy / Self betrayal / Finer truths, white lies / Antibody / All links severed / Plague rages (live).

– compilations, others, etc. –

May 88. Strange Fruit; (12"ep) **THE PEEL SESSIONS** (13.9.87) [ ] [-]
– The kill / Prison without walls / Dead part one / Deceiver / Lucid fairytale / In extremis / Blind to the trash / Negative approach / Common enemy / Obstinate direction / Life? / You suffer (Part 2). *(re-iss.as d12"/c-ep/cd-ep.May89, cont. += Mar88 sessions)*

Feb 92. Earache; (cd)(lp) **DEATH BY MANIPULATION** [ ] [-]
(free cd-ep) *(re-iss.Oct92) (re-iss.cd Sep94)*

Graham NASH (see under ⇒ CROSBY, STILLS, NASH & YOUNG)

NAZARETH

Formed: Dunfermline, Scotland . . . 1969 by McCAFFERTY, AGNEW and SWEET. For a number of years they had toured Scotland as The SHADETTES, until the addition of CHARLTON in '69. In 1971, they turned pro and moved to London, where they gained deal with 'Pegasus'. After 2 albums in the early 70's, they careered into the UK Top 10 in 1973 with single 'BROKEN DOWN ANGEL'. For the next 2 years, they enjoyed fruitful period, helped by the services of producer ROGER GLOVER (ex-DEEP PURPLE). • **Style:** No frills, hard-rock outfit, fronted by mean-looking screecher McCAFFERTY. • **Songwriters:** Group penned, except SHAPES OF THINGS (Yardbirds) / DOWN HOME GIRL (Leiber-Stoller) / I WANT TO DO EVERYTHING FOR YOU (Joe Tex) / THIS FLIGHT TONIGHT (Joni Mitchell) / TEENAGE NERVOUS BREAKDOWN (Little Feat) / THE BALLAD OF HOLLIS BROWN (Bob Dylan) / MY WHITE BICYCLE (Tomorrow) / YOU'RE THE VIOLIN (Golden Earring) / WILD HONEY (Beach Boys) / SO YOU WANT TO BE A ROCK'N'ROLL STAR (Byrds) / I DON'T WANT TO GO ON WITHOUT YOU (Berns/Wexler) / LOVE HURTS (Boudleaux Bryant) / etc. DAN McCAFFERTY solo covered OUT OF TIME (Rolling Stones) / WHATCHA GONNA DO ABOUT IT (Small Faces) / etc. • **Trivia:** Also internationally known, especially in Canada and mosts parts of Europe.

Recommended: THE SINGLES COLLECTION (*8)

DAN McCAFFERTY – vocals / **MANNY CHARLTON** – guitar, vocals / **PETE AGNEW** (b.14 Sep'48) – bass / **DARRYL SWEET** – drums, percussion

Pegasus | Warners

Nov 71. (lp) **NAZARETH** [ ] [ ] Feb 73
– Witchdoctor woman / Dear John / Empty arms, empty heart / If I had a dream / Red light lady / Fat man / Country girl / Morning dew / King is dead. *(re-iss.Apr 74 on 'Mooncrest') (re-iss.Nov 75 on 'Mountain')*

Jan 72. (7") **DEAR JOHN. / FRIENDS** [ ] [-]

Jul 72. (7") **MORNING DEW. / SPINNING TOP** [ ] [-]

Jul 72. (7") **MORNING DEW. / DEAR JOHN** [-] [ ]

Jul 72. (lp) **EXERCISES** [ ] [ ] Nov 72
– Fool about you / Love now you're gone / Madelaine / Sad song / 1692 (Glencoe massacre) / I will not be led / Cat's eye, apple pie / In my time / Woke up this morning / Called her name. *(re-iss. Apr 74 on 'Mooncrest') (re-iss. Nov 75+ Apr 80 on 'Mountain') (re-iss.May85 on 'Sahara') (cd-iss.Feb91 on 'Castle')*

Sep 72. (7") **IF YOU SEE MY BABY. / HARD LIVING** [ ] [-]

Mooncrest | A & M

Apr 73. (7") **BROKEN DOWN ANGEL. / WITCHDOCTOR WOMAN** [9] [-]

May 73. (lp)(c) **RAZAMANAZ** [11] [ ]
– Razamanaz / Alcatraz / Vigilante man / Woke up this morning / Night woman / Bad, bad boy / Sold my soul / Too bad, too sad / Broken down angel. *(re-iss. Nov75 + Apr80 on 'Mountain') (re-iss.Oct82 on 'NEMS') (re-iss.+cd.Dec89 on 'Castle')*

Jul 73. (7"m) **BAD, BAD BOY. / HARD LIVING / SPINNING TOP** [10] [-]

Sep 73. (7") **BROKEN DOWN ANGEL. / HARD LIVING** [-] [ ]

Oct 73. (7") **THIS FLIGHT TONIGHT. / CALLED HER NAME** [11] [-]

Nov 73. (lp)(c) **LOUD 'N' PROUD** [10] [ ]
– Go down fighting / Not faking it / Turn on your receiver / Teenage nervous breakdown / Freewheeler / This flight tonight / Child in the sun / The ballad of Hollis Brown. *(re-iss. Nov75 & Apr80 on 'Mountain') (re-iss.May85 on 'Sahara') (re-iss.+cd.Dec89 on 'Castle')*

Nov 73. (7") **BAD BAD BOY. / RAZAMANAZ** [-] [ ]

Feb 74. (7") **THIS FLIGHT TONIGHT. / GO DOWN FIGHTING** [-] [ ]

Mar 74. (7") **SHANGHAI'D IN SHANGHAI. / LOVE, NOW YOU'RE GONE** [41] [ ]

May 74. (lp)(c) **RAMPANT** [13] [ ]
– Silver dollar forger (parts 1 & 2) / Glad when you're gone / Loved and lost / Shanghai'd in Shanghai / Jet lag / Light my way / Sunshine / a) Shapes of things – b) Space safari. *(re-iss. Nov75+Apr80 on 'Mountain')*

Jul 74. (7") **SUNSHINE. / THIS FLIGHT TONIGHT** [-] [ ]

Nov 74. (7") **LOVE HURTS. / DOWN** [ ] [8] Nov 75

Mar 75. (7") **HAIR OF THE DOG. / TOO BAD, TOO SAD** [ ] [-]

Apr 75. (lp)(c) **HAIR OF THE DOG** [ ] [17]
– Hair of the dog / Miss Misery / Guilty * / Changin' times / Beggars day / Rose in the heather / Whiskey drinkin' woman / Please don't Judas me. *(In the US, track* repl.*

by 'Love hurts') *(re-iss.Nov75 + Apr80 on 'Mountain') (re-iss.Oct82 on 'NEMS') (re-iss.May85 on 'Sahara')*

May 75. (7") **HAIR OF THE DOG. / LOVE HURTS** | - | |
May 75. (7") **MY WHITE BICYCLE. / MISS MISERY** | 14 | |

Mountain A & M

Oct 75. (7") **HOLY ROLLER. / RAILROAD BOY** | 36 | - |
Nov 75. (lp)(c) **GREATEST HITS** (compilation) | 54 | |
– Razamanaz / Holy roller / Shanghai'd in Shanghai / Love hurts / Turn on your receiver / Bad bad boy / This flight tonight / Broken down angel / Hair of the dog / Sunshine / My white bicycle / Woke up this morning *(re-iss.Apr80) (re-iss.Oct82 on 'NEMS') (re-iss.+cd. Apr89 on 'Castle')*

Feb 76. (7") **CARRY OUT FEELINGS. / LIFT THE LID** | | |
Mar 76. (lp)(c) **CLOSE ENOUGH FOR ROCK'N'ROLL** | | 24 |
– Telegram (part 1:- On your way / part 2:- So you want to be a rock'n'roll star / part 3:- Sound check / part 4:- Here we are again) / Vicki / Homesick again / Vancouver shakedown / Born under the wrong sign / Loretta / Carry out feelings / Lift the lid / You're the violin. *(re-iss.Apr80) (re-iss.May85 on 'Sierra') (cd-iss.Feb91 on 'Castle')*

Jun 76. (7") **YOU'RE THE VIOLIN. / LORETTA** | | - |
Sep 76. (7") **LIFT THE LID. / LORETTA** | - | |
Nov 76. (7") **I DON'T WANT TO GO ON WITHOUT YOU. / GOOD LOVE** | | - |
Nov 76. (lp)(c) **PLAY 'N' THE GAME** | | 75 |
– Somebody to roll / Down home girl / Flying / Waiting for the man / Born to love / I want to (do everything for you) / I don't want to go on without you / Wild honey / L.A. girls. *(cd-iss.Feb91 on 'Castle')*

Dec 76. (7") **I WANT TO (DO EVERYTHING FOR YOU). / BLACK CATS** | - | |
Jan 77. (7") **SOMEBODY TO ROLL. / VANCOUVER SHAKEDOWN** | | |
Feb 77. (7") **I DON'T WANT TO GO ON WITHOUT YOU. / I WANT TO DO (EVERYTHING FOR YOU)** | - | |
Apr 77. (7") **SOMEBODY TO ROLL. / THIS FLIGHT TONIGHT** | - | |
Jun 77. (lp)(c) **HOT TRACKS** (compilation) | - | |
Sep 77. (7"ep) **HOT TRACKS** (compilation) | 15 | |
– Love hurts / This flight tonight / Broken down angel / Hair of the dog. *(re-iss.1983 on pic-ep 'NEMS')*

Nov 77. (lp)(c) **EXPECT NO MERCY** | | 82 |
– Expect no mercy / Gone dead train / Shot me down / Revenge is sweet / Gimme what's mine / Kentucky fried blues / New York broken toy / Busted / A place in your heart / All the king's horses. *(re-iss.May85 on 'Sierra')(cd-iss.Sep93 on 'Elite') (re-iss+cd. Jun 90 on 'Castle')*

Jan 78. (7"m) **GONE DEAD TRAIN. / GREENS / DESOLATION ROAD** | 49 | - |
Apr 78. (7") **A PLACE IN YOUR HEART. / KENTUCKY FRIED BLUES** | 70 | |
Apr 78. (7") **SHOT ME DOWN. / KENTUCKY FRIED BLUES** | - | |
Jul 78. (7") **GONE DEAD TRAIN. / KENTUCKY FRIED BLUES** | - | |

— added **ZAL CLEMINSON** – guitar, synth. (ex-SENSATIONAL ALEX HARVEY BAND)

Jan 79. (7") **MAY THE SUN SHINE. / EXPECT NO MERCY** | 22 | |
Jan 79. (lp)(c) **NO MEAN CITY** | 34 | 88 |
– Just to get into it / May the sun shine / Simple solution / Star / Claim to fame / Whatever you want babe / May the Sun shine / What's in it for me / No mean city. *(re-iss.May85 on 'Sahara') (re-iss. +cd May 91 on 'Castle')*

Apr 79. (7")(7"purple) **WHATEVER YOU WANT BABE. / TELEGRAM (PARTS 1, 2 & 3)** | | |
Jul 79. (7") **STAR. / EXPECT NO MERCY** | - | |
Jul 79. (7") **STAR. / BORN TO LOVE** | 54 | - |
Jan 80. (7") **HOLIDAY. / SHIP OF DREAMS** | | 87 |
Jan 80. (lp)(c) **MALICE IN WONDERLAND** | | 41 |
– Holiday / Showdown at the border / Talkin' to one of the boys / Heart's grown cold / Fast cars / Big boy / Talkin' 'bout love / Fallen angel / Ship of dreams / Turning a new leaf. *(cd-iss.Feb91 on 'Castle')*

Apr 80. (7") **SHIP OF DREAMS. / HEARTS GROWN COLD** | - | |

NEMS A & M

Dec 80. (d7") **NAZARETH LIVE (live)** | | - |
– Hearts grown cold / Talkin' to one of the boys / Razamanaz / Hair of the dog.

— added **JOHN LOCKE** – keyboards (ex-SPIRIT)

Feb 81. (lp)(c) **THE FOOL CIRCLE** | 60 | 70 |
– Dressed to kill / Another year / Moonlight eyes / Pop the Silo / Let me be your leader / We are the people / Every young man's dream / Little part of you / Cocaine (live) / Victoria. *(re-iss. +cd Feb91 on 'Castle')*

Mar 81. (7") **DRESSED TO KILL. / POP THE SILO** | | |

— **BILLY RANKIN** – guitar (ex-SPIRIT) repl. ZAL who joined TANDOORI CASSETTE

Sep 81. (d-lp)(c) **SNAZ (live)** | 78 | 83 |
– Telegram (part 1:- On your way – part 2:- So you want to be a rock'n'roll star – part 3:- Sound check) / Razamanaz / I want to (do everything for you) / This flight tonight / Beggars day / Every young man's dream / Heart's grown cold / Java blues / Cocaine / Big boy / So you want to be a rock'n'roll star / Holiday / Dressed to kill / Hair of the dog / Expect no mercy / Shape of things / Let me be your leader / Love hurts / Tush / Juicy Lucy / Morning dew. *(re-iss+cd. Jan 87 on 'Castle')*

Sep 81. (7") **MORNING DEW (live). / JUICY LUCY (live)** | | |
Dec 81. (7") **HAIR OF THE DOG (live). / HOLIDAY (live)** | - | |
Jun 82. (lp)(c) **2 x 5** | | |
– Love will lead to madness / Boys in the band / You love another / Gatecrash / Games / Back to the trenches / Dream on / Lonely in the night / Preservation / Take the rap / Mexico. *(cd-iss.Feb91 on 'Castle')*

Jul 82. (7") **LOVE LEADS TO MADNESS. / TAKE THE RAP** | | |
Aug 82. (7") **DREAM ON. / TAKE THE RAP** | - | |
Jan 83. (7") **GAMES. / YOU LOVE ANOTHER** | | - |
Jun 83. (7") **DREAM ON. / JUICY LUCY** | | - |

Vertigo Capitol

Jun 83. (lp)(c) **SOUND ELIXIR** | | |
– All nite radio / Milk and honey / Whippin' boy / Rain on the window / Backroom boys / Why don't you read the book / I ran / Rags to riches / Local still / Where are you now. *(re-iss.Jul85 on 'Sahara') (cd-iss.Feb91 on 'Castle')*

Sep 84. (lp)(c) **THE CATCH** | | |
– Party down / Ruby Tuesday / Last exit Brooklyn / Moondance / Love of freedom / This month's Messiah / You don't believe in us / Sweetheart tree / Road to nowhere.

Sep 84. (7") **RUBY TUESDAY. / SWEETHEART TREE** | | |
(12"+=) – This month's Messiah / Do you think about it.

1986. (lp)(c) **CINEMA** | - | - | Europe
– Cinema / Juliet / Just another heartache / Other side of you / Hit the fan / One from the heart / Salty salty / White boy / A veterans song / Telegram / This flight tonight.

1989. (cd)(c)(lp) **SNAKES AND LADDERS** | - | - | Europe
– We are animals / Lady luck / Hang on to a dream / Piece of my heart / Trouble / The key / Back to school / Girls / Donna – Get off that crack / See you, see you / Helpless.

— **BILLY RANKIN** – guitar now totally repl. CHARLTON

Mausoleum not issued

Nov 91. (cd)(c)(lp) **NO JIVE** | | - |
– Hire and fire / Do you wanna play house / Right between the eyes / Every time it rains / Keeping our love alive / Thinkin' man's nightmare / Cover your heart / Lap of luxury / The Rowan tree / Tell me that you love me / Cry wolf. *(cd+=)* – This flight tonight.

Jan 92 (7")**EVERY TIME IT RAINS / THIS FLIGHT TONIGHT 1991** | | - |
(12"+=)(cd-s+=) – Lap of Luxury.

Mar 92. (cd-ep) **TELL ME THAT YOU LOVE ME / RIGHT BETWEEN THE EYES / ROWAN TREE / TELL ME THAT YOU LOVE ME (extended)** | | - |

– more compilations, others, etc. –

Jun 85. Sahara; (d-lp) **20 GREATEST HITS** | | - |
Jan 89. Castle; (cd-ep)**THIS FLIGHT TONIGHT / BROKEN DOWN / ANGEL / LOVE HURTS / BAD BAD BOY** | | - |
Jan 91. Castle; (cd)(c)(d-lp) **THE SINGLES COLLECTION** | | - |
– Broken down angel / Bad, bad boy / This flight tonight / Shanghai'd in Shanghai / Love hurts / Hair of the dog / My white bicycle / Holy roller / Carry out feelings / You're the violin / Somebody to roll / I don't want to go on without you / Gone dead train / A place in your heart / May the Sun shine / Star / Dressed to kill / Morning dew / Games / Love will lead to madness.

Dec 88. Raw Power; (lp)(c)(cd) **ANTHOLOGY** | | - |
Jun 88. That's Original; (d-lp)(c)(cd) **RAMPANT / HAIR OF THE DOG** | | - |
Oct 88. Old Gold; (7") **LOVE HURTS. / BAD BAD BOY** | | - |
Oct 88. Old Gold; (7") **THIS FLIGHT TONIGHT. / BROKEN DOWN ANGEL** | | - |
(above 4 tracks were also featured on a 'Special Edition' cd-ep)

Oct 91. Essential; (3xcd-box) **ANTHOLOGY** | | - |
Nov 91. Windsor; (cd) **BBC RADIO 1 LIVE IN CONCERT** | | - |
Dec 91. Dojo; (cd) **THE EARLY YEARS** | | - |
Jun 93. Optima; (cd)(c) **ALIVE AND KICKING** | | - |
Apr 93. Elite; (cd) **FROM THE VAULTS** | | - |

DAN McCAFFERTY

with some members of NAZARETH and SAHB.

Mountain A & M

Aug 75. (7") **OUT OF TIME. / CINNAMON GIRL** | 41 | |
Oct 75. (lp)(c) **DAN McCAFFERTY** | | |
– The honky tonk down stairs / Cinnamon girl / The great pretender / Boots of Spanish leather / Watcha gonna do about it / Out of time / You can't lie to a liar / Troubles / You got me hummin' / Stay with me baby. *(cd-iss.Jul94 on 'Sequel')*

Oct 75. (7") **WHAT'CHA GONNA DO ABOUT IT. / NIGHTINGALE** | | |
Mar 78. (7") **STAY WITH ME, BABY. / OUT OF TIME / WHAT('CHA GONNA DO ABOUT IT** | | - |
Aug 78. (7") **THE HONKY TONK DOWNSTAIRS. / TROUBLE** | | - |
Aug 79. (7") **BOOTS OF SPANISH LEATHER. / WHAT('CHA GONNA DO ABOUT IT** | | - |

— with German musicians + **PETE AGNEW** – bass

Mercury not issued

1987 (lp)(cd) **INTO THE RING** | - | - | Germ'y
– Into the ring / Backstage pass / Starry eyes / My sunny island / For a car / Caledonia / Headin' for South America / The departure (instrumental) / Southern Cross / Where the ocean ends we'll find a new born land / Sally Mary / Island in the Sun / Albatross / The last ones will be the first after all / Reprise.

1987. (7") **STARRY EYES. / SUNNY ISLAND** | - | - | Germ.
(12"+=)(cd-s+=) Where the ocean ends, we'll find a new born land.

NAZZ (see under ⇒ RUNDGREN, Todd)

Youssou N'DOUR

Born: Senegal. After quitting IBRA HASSE'S NIGHTCLUB STARBAND in 1977, he formed The SUPER ETOILE DE DAKAR band, who recorded homeland SANTANA /HENDRIX inspired albums from early 80's noteably 'YAROU', 'DJAMIL', 'DABY' and 1984's 'IMMIGRES', which was finally released in Britain 1988 after he accompanied PETER GABRIEL on his 1987 'SO' world tour. In fact it was PETER who influenced his record company 'Virgin' to sign him and they combined talents on GABRIEL-N'DOUR's minor hit single 'SHAKIN' THE TREE'. Signed to film-maker SPIKE LEE's '40 Acres And A Mule' label in 1990. Commercial success eluded N'DOUR until 1994, when now on 'Columbia' records, he shared vocal duties with NENEH CHERRY on massive hit single '7 SECONDS'. • **Style:** World music superstar waiting to be appreciated by the masses. • **Songwriters:** Self-penned except SHAKIN' THE TREE (w / P.Gabriel). • **Trivia:** DAVID SANCIOUS

& DAVID SANBORN were noted session men on 1989's 'THE LION'.

Recommended: HEY YOU! (THE BEST OF YOUSSOU N'DOUR) (*7)

YOUSSOU N'DOUR – vocals with **PAPE OHMAR NGOMN + JIMMY MBAYE** – guitar / **ASSANE THAIM** – percussion / **BABACAR FAYE** – percussion + others on session

Rough Trade / not issued

Mar 86. (12") **THE RUBBERBAND MAN. / NELSON MANDELA** [ ] [-]

Earthworks / Celluloid

Apr 86. (lp) **NELSON MANDELA** [ ] [ ]
– N'Dobine / Donkassi gi / Wareff / Magninde / The rubberband man / Moule moule / Samayaye / Nelson Mandela.

Aug 88. (lp)(c)(cd) **IMMIGRES** [ ] [ ]
– Immigres – Britim rew / Pitche mi / Taaw / Badou.

Virgin / 40 Acres . . .

May 89. (7") **SHAKIN' THE TREE. (with PETER GABRIEL) / OLD TUCSON** [61] [ ]
(12"+=)(cd-s+=) – Sweeping the leaves. *(re-iss.Dec90 hit 57)*

May 89. (lp)(c)(cd) **THE LION** [ ] [ ]
– The lion-Gaiende / Shakin' the tree / Kocc barma / The truth / Old Tucson / Macoy / My daughter (Sama Doom) / Bes.

Feb 90. (7") **THE LION. / MACOY** [ ] [ ]
(12"+=) – Gaiende (African mix).

Sep 90. (cd)(c)(lp) **SET** [ ] [ ]
– Set / Alboury / Sabar / Toxiques / Sinebar / Medina / Hyoko / Xale rewmi / Fenene / Fakastela / Hey you! / One day / Ay chono la.

Columbia / Columbia

May 92. (cd)(c)(lp) **EYES OPEN** [ ] [ ]
– New Africa / Live television / No Moe / Country boy / Hope / Africa remembers / Coupi's choice / Yo le le (Fulani groove) / Survive / Am am / Marie-Madelaine la Sainte-Louisieene / Useless weapons / The same / Things unspoken.

Jun 94. (c-s) **7 SECONDS. (with NENEH CHERRY) / MAME BAMBA** [2] [98]
(12"+=)/ /(cd-s++) – (2 'A' mixes). / / (1 more 'A'mix).

Jun 94. (cd)(c) **THE GUIDE WOMMAT** [ ] [ ]
– Leaving (Dem) / Old man (Gorgui) / Without smile (Same) / Mame bamba / 7 seconds / How you are (No mele) / Generations (Diamono) / Tourista / Undecided (Japoula) / Love one another (Beagante) / Life (Adouna) / My people (Samay nit) / Silence (Tongo) / Chimes of freedom.

Jan 95. (12")(c-s) **UNDECIDED. / ('A'mix)** [53] [ ]
(cd-s+=) – (2-'A'mixes).

– compilations, etc –

Jan 90. Jacot; (14xc-box) **SENGALESE ALBUMS VOLS.1-14** (all early material) [ ] [-]
– (Vols. 1-4 ? / Vol.5 =YAROU / Vol.6 =DJAMIL / Vol.7 =DABY / Vol.8 IMMIGRES / Vol.9-10 ? / Vol.11 =BEKOOR / Vol.12 =JAMM / Vol.13 =KOCC BARMA / Vol.14 =GAINDE)

Oct 93. Music Club; (cd)(c) **HEY YOU! (THE BEST OF YOUSSOU N'DOUR)** [ ] [-]
– The lion-Gaiende / Hey you! / Fenene / Sinebêr / Fakastalu / Set / Bes / Miyoko / Shakin' the tree / Immigres-Britim rew / Madina / Sabar / Banako / Toxiques / Macoy.

Nov 94. Virgin; (cd) **THE BEST OF YOUSSOU N'DOUR** [ ] [ ]

NECTARINE No.9 (see under ⇒ FIRE ENGINES)

NED'S ATOMIC DUSTBIN

Formed: Stourbridge, W.Midlands, England . . . Nov'87 by JOHN PENNEY, RAT, MATT CHESLIN, ALEX GRIFFIN and DAN WARTON. Surfaced on own 'Furtive' label in 1990, which after a few minor hits, was taken over by 'Sony'. Their debut album 'GOD FODDER', became their first to hit UK Top 5. • **Style:** Alternative pop-rock outfit, similar to WONDER STUFF or JESUS JONES. • **Songwriters:** Group compositions. • **Trivia:** Took their name from a character on BBC TV's 'Goon Show'.

Recommended: GOD FODDER (*8) / ARE YOU NORMAL (*7)

JOHN PENNEY (b.17 Sep'68) – vocals / **RAT** (b.GARETH PRING, 8 Nov'70) – guitar / **ALEX GRIFFIN** (b.29 Aug'71) – bass / **MAT CHESLIN** (b.28 Nov'70) – bass / **DAN WARTON** (b.28 Jul'72) – drums

Furtive / not issued

Mar 90. (12"ep) **THE INGREDIENTS** [ ] [-]
– Aim / Plug me in / Grey cell green / Terminally groovy.

Chapter 22 / not issued

Jul 90. (7"ep)(12"ep)(cd-ep) **KILL YOUR TELEVISION** [53] [-]
– Kill your television / That's nice / Sentence / Kill your remix.

Oct 90. (7")(c-s) **UNTIL YOU FIND OUT. / FLEXIBLE HEAD** [51] [-]
(12"+=)(cd-s+=) – Bite.

Furtive – Sony / Columbia

Feb 91. (7")(c-s) **HAPPY. / TWENTY-THREE HOUR TOOTHACHE** [16] [ ]
(12"+=)(cd-s+=) – Aim (at the Civic live) / 45 second blunder.

Apr 91. (cd)(c)(lp) **GOD FODDER** [4] [91]
– Kill your television / Less than useful / Selfish / Grey cell green / Cut up throwing things / Capital letters / Happy / Your complex / Nothing like until you find out / You / What gives my son. *(re-iss.cd May95)*

Sep 91. (7") **TRUST. / FACELESS** [21] [ ]
(12"+=)(cd-s+=) – Titch.
(US-cd-ep++=) – Grey cell green / Until you find out (live).

Feb 92. (c-s) **GREY CELL GREEN. / TRUST** [-] [ ]

Apr 92. (cd-ep) **KILL YOUR TELEVISION. / TERMINALLY GROOVIE / SENTENCE / KILL YOUR REMIX** [-] [ ]

Furtive / Chaos

Oct 92. (7") **NOT SLEEPING AROUND. / CUT UP** [19] [ ]
(12"+=)(cd-s+=) – Scrawl.
(US c-s+=) – N. S. A. (NAD VS. NOX).

Oct 92. (cd)(c)(lp) **ARE YOU NORMAL?** [13] [ ]
– Suave and suffocated / Walking through syrup / Legoland / Swallowing air / Who goes first / Tantrum / Not sleeping around / You don't want to do that / Leg end in his own boots / Two and two made five / Fracture / Spring / Intact.

Nov 92. (7") **INTACT. / PROSTRATE** [36] [ ]
(10"+=) – NAD & NDX =Intact.
(12"+=)(cd-s+=) – Swiss legoland (live).

Mar 95. (c-s) **ALL I ASK OF MYSELF IS THAT I HOLD TOGETHER / CAPSIZE** [33] [ ]
(12"+=) – ('A'-Just together mix) / ('A'-No answer mix).
(cd-s++=) – ('A'-In control mix).
(cd-s+=) – Take me to the cleaners / Premonition (need to know mix).

Jul 95. (7") **STUCK. / A TEMPTED FATE** [64] [-]
(cd-s+=) – . . .To be right (acoustic) / ('A'acoustic).
(12") – ('A'side) / Premonition (as I thought mix) / Premonition (dirty caller mix).

Jul 95. (cd)(c)(lp) **BRAINBLOODVOLUME** [ ] [ ]
– All I ask of myself is that I hold together / Floote / Premonition / Talk me down / Borehole / Your only joke / Stuck / . . .To be right / I want it over / Traffic / Song eleven could take forever.

— Disbanded October 1995.

– compilations, etc. –

Jan 91. R.T.D.Euro; (lp) **BITE** (imported) [72] [-]

Bill NELSON

Born: 18 Dec'48, Wakefield, Yorkshire, England. In the late 60's, after a job as government officer, he joined local groups GLOBAL VILLAGE TRUCKING COMPANY and GENTLE REVOLUTION. He then released an obscure and limited solo lp on own label. The album in 1971 'NORTHERN DREAM', found its way to Radio 1 DJ John Peel, who gave it night-time airplay. That year, NELSON formed BE-BOP DELUXE (see below), and after one single, signed to 'Harvest'. Their first album 'AXE VICTIM' in 1974, was followed by a tour supporting COCKNEY REBEL. In Aug'74, NELSON split band up, but quickly re-formed group with unhappy ex-REBELS. After a well-received album 'FUTURAMA', they followed it early next year, with a UK Top 30 hit single 'SHIPS IN THE NIGHT', from parent hit album 'SUNBURST FINISH'. They experienced a couple of years in the top flight, until NELSON decided to form other project RED NOISE. After a promising 1979 album, NELSON went solo, and hit Top 10 immediately with adventurous double-lp 'QUIT DREAMING AND GET ON THE BEAM'. For the rest of the 80's, NELSON packed in loads of albums, mostly released on his own obscure 'Cocteau' label. • **Style:** Gifted multi-instrumentalist and guitarist, who shifted from contemporary rock with BE-BOP DELUXE, to more experimental instrumental work. • **Songwriters:** All penned by NELSON. • **Trivia:** His younger brother IAN (of RED NOISE), also had minor hit with FIAT LUX.

Recommended: RAIDING THE DIVINE ARCHIVES (*8; BE BOP DELUXE) / SOUND ON SOUND (*7; RED NOISE) / QUIT DREAMING AND GET . . . (*9) CHIMERA (*7)

BILL NELSON

– vocals, lead guitar

1971 (lp) **NORTHERN DREAM** [ ] [-]
– Photograph (a beginning) / Everyone's hero / House of sand / End of the seasons / Rejoice / Love's a way / Northern dreamer (1957) / Bloo blooz / Sad fellings / See it through / Smiles / Chymepeace (an ending). *(re-iss.Feb81, Mar82 & Aug86 on 'Butt')*

BE-BOP DELUXE

was formed by **BILL NELSON** plus **IAN PARKIN** – rhythm guitar / **ROBERT BRYAN** – bass / **NICHOLAS CHATTERTON-DEW** – drums / **RICHARD BROWN** – keyboards

Smile / not issued

1973. (7") **TEENAGE ARCHANGEL. / JETS AT DAWN** [ ] [-]

— became trio, when BROWN departed.

Harvest / Harvest

May 74. (7") **JET SILVER & THE DOLLS OF VENUS. / THIRD FLOOR HEAVEN** [ ] [-]

Jun 74. (lp)(c) **AXE VICTIM** [ ] [ ]
– Axe victim / Love is swift arrows / Jet Silver & the dolls of Venus / Third floor Heaven / Night creatures / Rocket cathedrals / Adventures in a Yorkshire landscape / Jets at dawn / No trains to Heaven / Darkness (l'immoralise). *(cd-iss.Feb91 with 3 extra)*

— Aug74, **NELSON** recruited entire new line-up **MILTON REAME-JAMES** – keyboards (ex-COCKNEY REBEL) repl. IAN / **PAUL AVRON JEFFRYS** – bass (ex-COCKNEY REBEL) repl. ROBERT / **SIMON FOX** – drums (ex-HACKENSHACK) repl. NICHOLAS

— (late 1974) **BILL** and **SIMON** were joined by **CHARLIE TUMAHAI** (b. New Zealand) – bass who repl. MILTON & PAUL

Feb 75. (7") **BETWEEN THE WORLDS. / LIGHTS** (withdrawn) [-] [-]

May 75. (lp)(c) **FUTURAMA** [ ] [ ]
– Stage whispers / Love with the madman / Maid in Heaven / Sister seagull / Sound track / Music in Dreamland / Jean Cocteau / Between the worlds / Swan song. *(cd-iss.Feb91)*

Jun 75. (7") **MAID IN HEAVEN. / LIGHTS** [ ] [-]

Jul 75. (7") **MAID IN HEAVEN. / SISTER SEAGULL** [-] [ ]

— added **ANDREW CLARKE** – keyboards

Jan 76. (7") **SHIPS IN THE NIGHT. / CRYING TO THE SKY** [23] [ ]

Jan 76. (lp)(c) **SUNBURST FINISH** [17] [96]
– Fair exchange / Heavenly homes / Ships in the night / Crying to the sky / Sleep that burns / Beauty secrets / Life in the air age / Like an old blues / Crystal gazing / Blazing apostles. *(re-iss.Mar82 on 'Fame') (re-iss.Jun86 on 'Revolver') (cd-iss.Feb91 with 3 extra tracks)*

Aug 76. (7") **THE KISS OF LIGHT. / SHINE** [ ] [ ]

— (above 'B'side as "FUNKY PHASER UNEARTHLY MERCHANDISE")

Sep 76. (lp)(c) **MODERN MUSIC** [12] [88]
– Orphans of Babylon / Twilight capers / Kiss of light / The bird charmer's destiny / The gold at the end of my rainbow / Bring back the spark / Modern music / Dancing in the moonlight / Honeymoon on Mars / Lost in the neon world / Dance of the Uncle Sam humanoids / Modern music / Forbidden lovers / Down on Terminal street / Make the music magic. *(cd-iss.Feb91 with 3 extra)*

Jul 77. (white-lp)(c) **LIVE IN THE AIR AGE (live)** [10] [65]
– Life in the air age / Ships in the night / Piece of mine / Fair exchange / Mill street junction / Adventures in a Yorkshire landscape / Blazing apostles. (free-7"ep) **SHINE. / SISTER SEAGULL / MAID IN HEAVEN** *(cd-iss.Feb91 with the 3 extra free tracks)*

Sep 77. (7") **JAPAN. / FUTURIST MANIFESTO** [ ] [ ]

Feb 78. (7") **PANIC IN THE WORLD. / BLUE AS A JEWEL** [ ] [ ]

Feb 78. (lp)(c) **DRASTIC PLASTIC** [22] [95]
– Electrical language / New precision / New mysteries / Surreal estate / Love in flames / Panic in the world / Dangerous stranger / Superenigmatix (lethal appliances for the home) / Islands of the dead / Visions of endless hopes / Possession / Islands of the dead. *(cd-iss.Feb91 with 3 extra)*

May 78. (7") **ELECTRICAL LANGUAGE. / SURREAL ESTATE** [ ] [ ]

— Disbanded Spring 1978. TUMAHAI joined The DUKES, SIMON joined JACK GREEN. CLARKE joined NICO's band.

– (BE-BOP DELUXE) compilations, others –

Oct 76. Harvest; (7"ep) **HOT VALVES** [36] [ ]
– Maid in Heaven / Blazing apostles / Jet Silver and the dolls of Venus / Bring back the spark.

1978. Harvest; (d-lp)(c) **THE BEST OF AND THE REST OF BE-BOP DELUXE** [ ] [ ]
(cd-iss.May90)

May 81. Harvest; (lp)(c) **THE SINGLES A & B** [ ] [-]

Sep 83. Harvest; (d-lp) **AXE VICTIM / FUTURAMA** [ ] [-]

Mar 87. Harvest; (lp)(c) **RAIDING THE DIVINE ARCHIVES** [ ] [-]
– Jet silver and the dolls of Venus / Adventures in a Yorkshire landscape / Maid in Heaven / Ships in the night / Life in the air age / Kiss of light / Sister seagull / Modern music / Japan / Panic in the world / Bring back the spark / Forbidden lovers / Electrical language. *(re-iss.+cd.Apr90 on 'EMI'+=)* – Fair exchange / Sleep that burns / Between the worlds / Music in Dreamland.

Feb 83. Cocteau; (12"ep) **ELECTRICAL LANGUAGE** [ ] [-]
– Electrical language / Panic in the world / Maid in Heaven. *(re-1985)*

Aug 83. Cocteau; (7") **PANIC IN THE WORLD. / MAID IN HEAVEN** [ ] [-]

May 84. EMI Gold; (7") **SHIPS IN THE NIGHT. / MAID IN HEAVEN** [ ] [-]

Aug 86. Dojo; (lp) **BOP TO THE NOISE** [ ] [-]

Sep 94. Windsong; (cd) **RADIOLAND – BBC RADIO 1 LIVE IN CONCERT (live)** [ ] [-]

BILL NELSON'S RED NOISE

BILL NELSON with **ANDREW CLARKE** – keyboards / **RICK FORD** – drums / **IAN NELSON** (brother) – saxophone / **STEVE PEER** – drums

Harvest Harvest

Feb 79. (7")(7"red) **FURNITURE MUSIC. / WONDERTOYS THAT LAST FOREVER / ACQUITTED BY MIRRORS** [59] [ ]

Feb 79. (lp)(c) **SOUND ON SOUND** [33] [ ]
– Don't touch me, I'm electric / For young moderns / Stop – go – stop / Furniture music / Radar in my heart / Stay young / Out of touch / A better home in the phantom zone / Substitute flesh / The atom age / Art – empire – industry / Revolt into style. *(re-iss.Nov85 on 'Cocteau')*

Apr 79. (7")(7"blue) **REVOLT INTO STYLE. / OUT OF TOUCH** [69] [ ]
(12") – ('A'side) / Stay young / Furniture music. *(re-iss.Aug83 on 'Cocteau')*

BILL NELSON

solo, with **TOM KELLICHAN** – drums / with sessioners

Cocteau not issued

Jun 80. (7"ep) **DO YOU DREAM IN COLOUR? / IDEAL HOMES. / INSTANTLY YOURS / ATOM MAN LOVES RADIUM GIRL** [52] [ ]

Crepescule not issued

Mar 81. (7") **ROOMS WITH BRITTLE VIEWS. / DADA GUITARS** [ ] [-]

Mercury Mercury

Mar 81. (7") **BANAL. / MR. MAGNETISN HIMSELF** [ ] [ ]
(12"+=) – Turn to fiction.

May 81. (lp)(c) **QUIT DREAMIMG AND GET ON THE BEAM** [7] [ ]
– Banal / Living in my limousine / Vertical games / Disposable / False alarms / Decline and fall / Life runs out like sand / A kind of loving / Do you dream in colour? / U.H.F. / Youth of nation on fire / Quit dreaming and get on the beam. *(cd-iss Jul86 on 'Cocteau')* (cd+=) – White sound. (free-lp.w.a.) **SOUNDING THE RITUAL ECHO** – Annuciation / The ritual echo / Sleep / Near east / Emak bakia / My intricate image / Endless orchids / The heat in the room / Another willingly opened window / Vanishing parades / Glass fish (for the final aquarium) / Cubical domes / Ashes of roses / The shadow garden (opium). *(iss.on own.Jun85 on 'Cocteau')(cd-iss.on own.Sep89)*

Jun 81. (7") **YOUTH OF NATION ON FIRE. / BE MY DYNAMO** [73] [ ]
(d7"+=) – Rooms with brittle views / All my wives were iron.

Sep 81. (7") **LIVING IN MY LIMOUSINE. / BIRDS OF TIME** [ ] [ ]
(12"+=) – Love in the abstract.

Apr 82. (7") **EROS ARRIVING. / HAUNTING IN MY HEAD** [ ] [-]
(d7"+=) – Flesh / He and sleep were brothers.

Jun 82. (d-lp)(c) **THE LOVE THAT WHIRLS** [28] [ ]
– Empire of the senses / Hope for the heartbeat / Waiting for the voices / Private view / Eros arriving / Bride of Christ in Autumn / When your dream of perfect beauty comes true / Flaming desire / Portrait of Jan with flowers / Crystal escalator in the palace of God department store / Echo in her eyes / October man. *(re-iss.+cd.Jul86 on 'Cocteau', cd+=)* – Flesh / He and sleep were brothers.

Jul 82. (7")(12") **FLAMING DESIRE. / THE PASSION** [ ] [-]

May 83. (lp)(c) **CHIMERA** [30] [ ]
– The real adventure / Acceleration / Every day feels like another new drug / Tender is the night / Glow world / Another day, another ray of hope. *(cd-iss.Sep87 on 'Cocteau', re-iss.Apr89)*

Cocteau Portrait

Aug 83. (7"m) **TOUCH AND GLOW. / DANCING IN THE WILD / LOVE WITHOUT FEAR** [ ] [-]

Dec 83. (m-lp) **SAVAGE GESTURES FOR CHARMS SAKE** [ ] [ ]
– The man in the exine suit / Watching my dream boat go down in flames / The meat room / Another happy thought (carved forever in your cortex) / Portrait of Jan with Moon and stars. *(re-iss.Feb85)*

Aug 84. (7") **ACCELERATION. / HARD FACTS FROM THE FICTION DEPARTMENT** [ ] [-]
(12"+=)(12"pic-d+=) – ('A'short version) / ('A'long version).

Oct 84. (lp) **VISTAMIX** [-] [ ]
– The real adventure / Flaming desire / Acceleration / Empire of the senses / Everyday feels like another new drug / Do you dream in color? / A kind of loving / Tender is the night / Glow world / Another day, another ray of hope.

Portrait Portrait

Mar 86. (7")(12") **WILDEST DREAMS. / SELF IMPERSONATION** [ ] [ ]

Apr 86. (lp)(c) **GETTING THE HOLY GHOST ACROSS** [91] [ ]
– Suvasini / Contemplation / Theology / Wildest dreams / Lost in your mystery / Rise like a fountain / Age of reason / Hidden flame / Because of you / Living for the spangled moment / Word for word / Illusions of you / Heart and soul / Finks and stooges of the spirit. *(cd-iss.1988 on 'C.B.S.')*

Cocteau Enigma

Jun 86. (lp) **CHAMBER OF DREAMS** [ ] [-]
– The blazing memory of innuendo / Into the luminous future / Dip in the swimming pool / Reactor / Tomorrowland (the threshold of 1947) / Listening to lizards / Endless torsion / My sublime perversion / Eros in Autumn / Sleeplessness / The latest skyline / Train of thought / Packs and fountains clouds and trees / Golden bough / Forever Orpheus / In arcadia / Sentimental / Autumn fires / Wild blue yonder. *(cd-iss.Aug89)*

Oct 86. (lp)(c) **SUMMER OF GOD'S PIANO** [ ] [-]
– Antennae two / N.B.C.97293 / The sleep of Hollywood / The celestial bridegroom / Under the red arch / Orient pearl / Sacrament / Falling blossoms / The difficulty of being / Zanoni / The Chinese nightingale / Soon September (another enchantment) / Rural shires / Perfido incanto / The lost years / The charm of transit / Night thoughts (twilight radio) / Wysteria / Swing / Snowfall / Real of dusk / Over ocean. *(cd-iss.Aug89)*

Jan 87. (lp)(c)(cd) **MAP OF DREAMS** [ ] [-]
– Legions of the endless night / Spinning creatures / At the gates of the singing garden / Heavenly message No.1, 2 & 3 / Fellini's picnic / Dark angel / Infernal regions / Dance of the fragrant woman / The alchemy of ecstasy / Aphrodite adorned / The wheel of fortune and the hand of fate / Forked tongues, mixed blessings / Another tricky mission for the celestial pilot / Water of life (transfiguration).

May 87. (12") **SECRET CEREMONY (theme from 'BROND'). / WIPING A TEAR FROM THE ALLSEEING EYES** [ ] [-]

— (above by "SCALA" (BILL NELSON & DARYL RUNSWICK)

Nov 87. (d-lp)(c)(cd) **CHANCE ENCOUNTERS IN THE GARDEN OF LIGHT** [ ] [-]
– My dark demon / The dove consumed (the serpent slumbers) / Calling Heaven, calling Heaven overs / Path of return / Theurgia / Staircase to no place / Evocation of a radiant childhood / The kingdom of consequence / Divine raptures of a radiant childhood / Bright star (moonlight over the ocean blue) / A bird of the air shall earn the voice / Clothed in light amongst the stars / Hastening the chariot of my hearts desire / Transcendant conversation / West deep / The spirit cannot fail / Pilots of kite / Phantom gardens / The angel of hearth and home / Villefranche interior / Night tides / First memory / Azure extention / Radiant spires / Evening peal / Thremodia / Short drink for a certain fountain / Body of light / At the centre / Self-initiation / The word that became flesh / The hermetic garden / Revolving globes / The four square citadel / Orient of Memphis / Little daughters of light / Angel at the western window.

Sep 88. (lp)(c)(cd) **OPTIMISM (by "BILL NELSON ORCHESTRA ARCANA")** [ ] [ ]
– Exactly the way you want it / Why be lonely / Everyday is a better day / The receiver and the fountain pen / Welcome home Mr. Kane / This is true / Greeting a new day / The breath in my father's saxophone / Our lady of apparations / The whole city between us / Deva dance / Always looking forward to tomorrow / Profiles, hearts, stars / Alchemia.

Dec 88. (7") **LIFE IN YOUR HANDS. / DO YOU DREAM IN COLOUR** [ ] [-]
(12"+=) – Get out of that hole / Drean demon.

Aug 89. (lp)(cd) **PAVILLIONS OF THE HEART AND SOUL** [ ] [-]
– Gift of the August tide / Loving tongues / Blue nude / In the realms of bells / Your nebulous smile / The glance of a glittering stranger / Another kiss for your slender neck / The warmth of women's eyes / Seduction (ritual with roses) / Dreamed entrances / Four pieces for imaginary strings:- Herself with her shadow – The exquisite corpse – Ardent hands – Her laughing torso / Migrating angels / Les amoureaux / Meshes of the afternoon / Mountains of the heart / Willow silk / Tender encounters (states of grace) / Melancholia / The eternal female.

Aug 89. (lp)(cd) **CATALOGUE OF OBSESSIONS** [ ] [-]
– Sex party six / Tune in Tokyo / Promise of perfume / View from a balcony / Test of affection / Birds in two hemispheres / Wider windows for the walls / The boy pilots of Bangkok / Talk technique / Glass breakfast / Edge of tears / Erotikon.

Imaginary not issued

Apr 91. (cd)(c) **LUMINOUS** [ ] [-]

1992. (cd) **BLUE MOONS AND LAUGHING GUITARS** [ ] [ ]

Resurgence not issued

Feb 95. (cd) **CRIMSWORTH (FLOWERS STONES FOUNTAINS AND FLAMES)** [ ] [-]
– (part 1) / (part 2).

Nov 95. (cd) **CULTUREMIX WITH BILL NELSON** [ ] [-]

All Saints not issued

Mar 95. (cd) **PRACTICALLY WIRED** [ ] [-]
– Roses and rocketships / Spinning planet / Thousand fountain island / Piano 45 / Pink buddha blues / Kid with cowboy tie / Royal ghosts / Her presence in flowers / Big noise in Twangtown / Tiny little thing / Wild blue cycle / Every moment infinite / Friends from Heaven / Eternal for Eniko.

– (BILL NELSON) compilations, specials, others –

Nov 81. Cocteau; (d-lp)(c) **DAS KABINET (OF DR.CAGLIARI)** [ ] [-]
– The asylum / Waltz / The fairground / Doctor Cagliari / Cesare the somnabulist / Murder / The funeral / The somnabulist and the children / The children / Cagliari disciplines Cesare / Cagliari opens the cabinet / Jane discovers Cesare / The attempted murder of Jane / The dream dance of Jane and the somnabulist / Escape over the rooftops / The unmasking / The shot / The cabinet closes.

1982. Cocteau; (lp)(c) **LA BELLE ET LA BETE (THE BEAUTY AND THE BEAST)** [ ] [-]
– Overture / The family / Sisters and Sedan chairs / In the forest of storms / The castle / The gates / The corridor / The great hall / Dreams (the merchant sleeps) / The rose and the beast / Magnificent (the white horse) / Beauty enters the castle / The door / The mirror / Candelabra and the gargoyles / Beauty and the beast / Transition No.1, 2 – The gift / The garden / Transitions No.3, 4 – The tragedy / Transitions No.5 – The enchanted glove / Tears as diamonds (the gift reverses) / The beast in solitude / Return of the magnificent / Transition No.6-The journey / The pavillion of Diana / Transformation No.1 & 2 / The final . . . *(above 2 albums re-iss.Jun85)*

Nov 82. Cocteau; (5x7"box) **PERMANENT FLAME** [ ] [-]

Jan 85. Cocteau; (4xlp-box) **TRIAL BY INTAMACY** [ ] [-]
– (DAS KABINET / BEAUTY & . . . / CHAMBER OF . . . / SUMMER OF . . .)

Feb 85. Cocteau; (d-lp)(cd) **THE TWO-FOLD ASPECT OF EVERYTHING** [-] [ ]

Jul 85. Cocteau; (7"pic-d) **ACCELERATION. / ('A'instrumental)** [ ] [-]

Sep 87. Cocteau; (d-cd) **CHIMERA / SAVAGE GESTURES FOR CHARMS SAKE** [ ] [-]

Sep 89. Cocteau; (d-lp)(c)(cd) **DUPLEX: THE BEST OF BILL NELSON** [ ] [-]
– Flaming desire / Acceleration (remix) / hope for the heartbeat (remix) / Here and now / Life in your hands / Glow world / The blazing memory of the innuendo / The angel at the western window / The man in the Rexine suit / Right then left / Half asleep in the hall of mirrors / Opening / Metaphysical jerks / Loving tongues / Radiant spires / Do you dream in clour / Living in my limousine (remix) / October man / Private view / Contemplation / Another day, another ray of hope / Another tricky mission / Portrait of Jan with flowers / Wiping a tear from the all-seeing eye / Secret ceremony (theme from 'Brond') / Broadcast news (from 'Right To Reply') / Loosening up with lady luck / The garden / Burning the groove of Satyre / Set me a seal upon thine heart.

Dec 89. Cocteau; (4xlp)(4xc)(4xcd) **DEMONSTRATIONS OF AFFECTION** (new) [ ] [-]

Aug 92. Magpie; (3xcd-box) **QUIT DREAMING AND GET ON THE BEAM / CHIMERA – SAVAGE GESTURES / THE LOVE THAT WHIRLS** [ ] [-]

Dec 95. Resurgence; (4xcd-box) **BOXED SET** [ ] [-]

NEU!

Formed: Dusseldorf, Germany . . .Autumn 1971 by breakaway KRAFTWERK member KLAUS DINGER and THOMAS HOMANN. The latter was soon deposed by MICHAEL ROTHER, who with borrowed finances, appeared on eponymous debut in 1972. Live gigs were augmented by EBERHARD KRAKNENN, who had also guested for KRAFTWERK. After only three acclaimed underground albums, they split in the mid-70's, when ROTHER went solo. • **Style:** Trance-rock similar to early KRAFTWERK, AMON DUUL II or HAWKWIND (their DAVE BROCK was a great fan). • **Songwriters:** ROTHER-DINGER. • **Trivia:** Produced by CONNY PLANK except 2nd lp.

Recommended: NEU! (*8) / NEU II (*8) / NEU '75 (*9) / BLACK FOREST GATEAU (*9)

MICHAEL ROTHER – guitar, bass, keyboards, synths, percussion / **KLAUS DINGER** – guitar, vocals, drums, keyboards (ex-KRAFTWERK)

United Art Billingsg.

1972. (lp) **NEU!** [ ] [ ]
– Hallo Gallo / Sonderangebot / Weissensee / Jahresuebersicht / Im glueck / Negativland / Lieber honig. *(re-iss.May80 as 'HALLO GALLO' on 'Brain')*

Jan 73. (7") **SUPER. / NEUSCHNEE** [ ] [-]

1973. (lp) **NEU II** [ ] [-]
– Fur immer / Spitzenqualitat / Gedenkminute / Lila engel / Neuschnee / Super 16 / Neuschnee / Cassetto / Super 78 / Hallo exentrico / Super.

added **HANS LAMPE + THOMAS HOMANN – drums (ex-KRAFTWERK)**

Jun 75. (7") **ISI. / AFTER EIGHT** [ ] [-]

1975. (lp) **NEU '75** [ ] [-]
– Isi / Seeland / Leb' wohl / Hero / E-Musik / After eight.

— Split after above.

compilations, others

Nov 82. (lp) **BLACK FOREST GATEAU** [ ] [-]
– Hallo Gallo / Isi / E-Musik / Negativland / Seeland / Leb' wohl / After eight.

MICHAEL ROTHER

with **JAKI LIEBEZEIT** – drums (ex-CAN) (debut was w/drawn by UK 'Radar')

Sky not issued

1977. (lp) **FLAMMENDE HERZEN** [-] [-] Germ'y
– Flammende herzen / Zyklodrom / Karussell / Feuerland. *(cd-iss.??? on 'Polydor')*

1978. (lp) **STERNTALER** [-] [-] Germ'y
– Sonnenrad / Blauer Regen / Stromlinien / Sterntaler / Fontana di luna / Orches trion.

1979. (lp) **KATZENMUSIK** [-] [-] Germ'y
– Katzenmusik (1-12). *(cd-iss.??? on 'Polydor')*

Polydor not issued

1982. (lp) **FERNWARME** [-] [-] Germ'y
– Silberstrei F / Elfenbein / Erikoenig / Fortuna / Klangkoerper / Hohe luft / Fernwarme.

— now without JAKI who was solo artist before slight return to CAN

1984. (lp) **LUST** [-] [-] Germ'y
– Palmengarten / Primadonna / Dynamotron / Lust / Cascadia / Pulsar. *(cd-iss.1988)*

Aug 85. (lp) **SUSSHERZ UND TIEFENSCHARFE** [-] [-] Germ'y
– Sussherz / Tiefenscharfe / Glitzerglanz / Rapido / Daisy / Blaus licht. *(cd-iss.??? on 'Steamhammer-SPV')*

1987. (lp)(cd) **TRAUMREISEN** [-] [-] Germ'y
– Sudseewellen / Reiselust / Schwarze augen / Lucky stars / Lichtermeer / Gloria / Happy end.

— Seems to have retired from recording.

NEVILLE BROTHERS

Formed: New Orleans, USA . . . mid-60's as The NEVILLE SOUNDS, by ART and younger brother AARON. They had previously had solo careers from 1955, some in the early 60's, under the guidance of ALLEN TOUSSAINT. Early in 1967, AARON hit US No.2 with soul gem 'TELL IT LIKE IT IS', but couldn't sustain any major follow-up. In 1968, ART formed The METERS, with NEVILLE SOUNDS backers; GEORGE PORTER, ZIGGY MODELISTE and LEO NOCENTELLI. They had first hit in 1969 with 'SOPHISTICATED CISSY'. After several more hits, and some fine albums (CYRIL joined in 1975 for 'FIRE ON THE BAYOU'), the brothers (ART, AARON, CYRIL & CHARLES) re-united for one album as The WILD TCHOUPITOULAS, before becoming the better known NEVILLE BROTHERS. In 1978, their eponymous first album was issued by 'Capitol', which gained attention of singer/comedienne BETTE MIDLER, who encouraged her stable 'A&M' to sign them early in the 80's. By the end of the decade, they are the toast of the critics, after the release of 'YELLOW MOON' album'. Meanwhile AARON was continuing a fruitful solo career, which also encompassed a Top 3 duet with LINDA RONSTADT: 'Don't Know Much'. This was to win a Grammy for AARON, as he and the brothers also picked up best singer and group awards respectively for 1990 Rolling Stone magazine. A year later, AARON and LINDA won another duo award for 'All My ife'. • **Style:** The METERS were similiar in rhythm to BOOKER T. & THE MG's, due to instrumental numbers. • **Songwriters:** Each contributed, collaborating with other writers including more brothers IVAN and GAYNEILLE. Also HAWK WOLINSKI was added in 1992 alongside DARYL JOHNSON. Other recent collective contributors PHIL ROY, BOB THEILE and BILLY VALENTINE. Covered; BIRD ON A WIRE (Leonard Cohen) / WITH GOD ON OUR SIDE + THE BALLAD OF HOLLIS BROWN (Bob Dylan) / FLY LIKE AN EAGLE (Steve Miller Band) / IN THE STILL OF THE NIGHT (Cole Porter) / IT FEELS LIKE RAIN (John Hiatt) / LOUISIANA 1927 (RANDY NEWMAN) / DON'T GO PLEASE STAY (Bacharach-Milliard) / WITH YOU IN MIND + THAT'S THE WAY SHE LOVES (Allen Toussant) / CLOSE YOUR EYES (. . .Willis) / AVE MARIA (Mozart) / LOVE THE ONE YOU'RE WITH (Stephen Stills) / YOU CAN'T ALWAYS GET WHAT YOU WANT (Rolling Stones) / LET MY PEOPLE GO + AMAZING GRACE (trad) / ONE LOVE – PEOPLE GET READY (Bob Marley). Aaron also covered: YOU NEVER CAN TELL (Chuck Berry) / SONG OF BERNADETTE + AIN'T NO CURE FOR LOVE (Leonard Cohen) / BETCHA BY GOLLY WOW (Stylistics). • **Trivia:** AARON's son IVAN NEVILLE, had a US Top 30 hit in 1988 with 'NOT JUST ANOTHER GIRL'. DAVE STEWART of EURYTHMICS produced the brothers' 1990 album 'BROTHER'S KEEPER'. The METERS sessioned for DR.JOHN (In The Right Place + Desitively Bonaroo) and ROBERT PALMER (Sneaking Sally Through The Alley).

Recommended: TREACHEROUS: A HISTORY OF THE NEVILLE BROTHERS 1955-1985 (*9) / YELLOW MOON (*8) / BROTHER'S KEEPER (*7) / THE ORIGINAL FUNKMASTERS (METERS; *7).

The HAWKETTS

(7-piece New Orleans band with **ART NEVILLE** (b.17 Dec'37) – vocals / **GEORGE DAVIS** – ? / etc.

1955. (7") **MARDI GRAS MAMBO. / ?** [-] [ ]
(re-iss.annually by 'Chess' US)

— ART still performed with them, and released solo singles for 'Speciality' in 1957; ZING ZING + CHA DOOKY-DOO. Both re-issued 1976 as double 'A'side. A year later, ART joined the US Navy and was replaced by brother **AARON** (b.1941) – vocals. He also issued duo 45 with ALLEN TOUSSAINT

Minit Minit

Jun 60. (7") **OVER YOU. / EVERY DAY** [-] [ ]

Dec 60. (7") **GET OUT OF MY LIFE. / SHOW ME THE WAY** [-] [ ]

Mar 61. (7") **DON'T CRY. / REALITY** [-] [ ]

Feb 62. (7") **HOW MANY TIMES. / I'M WAITIN' AT THE STATION** [-] [ ]

Aug 62. (7") **SWEET LITTLE MAMA. / HUMDINGER** [-] [ ]

Jan 63. (7") **WRONG NUMBER. / HOW COULD I HELP BUT LOVE YOU** [-] [ ]

— Early 1962, ART re-joined The HAWKETTS, and released solo single 'ALL THESE THINGS'. To end the year, they became The NEVILLE SOUNDS, whom were an 8-piece band with ART, AARON & CYRIL, plus MODELISTE & PORTER.

AARON NEVILLE

Stateside | Par-Lo

Dec 66. (7") **TELL IT LIKE IT IS. / WHY WORRY** [ ] [2]
(re-iss.Sep69 on 'B&C') (re-iss.Aug74 on 'Cooltempo') (re-iss.1976 on 'Island')

Mar 67. (7") **SHE TOOK YOU FOR A RIDE. / ?** [ ] [ ]

Liberty | Mint

1967. (lp) **LIKE IT 'TIS** [ ] [ ]
– Over you / Get out of my life / I found another love / Don't cry / Sweet little mama / I'm waitin' at the station / How many times / Let's live / Everyday / Reality / Wrong number (I'm sorry, goodbye) / How dould I help but love you. *(cd-iss.ul91 on 'Music Club')*

not issued | Bell

Nov 68. (7") **WHERE IS MY BABY. / YOU CAN GIVE, BUT YOU CAn"T TAKE** [–] [ ]

Jun 69. (7") **YOU DON'T LOVE ME ANYMORE. / SPEAK TO ME** [–] [ ]

— The NEVILLE SOUNDS break-up with AARON + CYRIL forming SOUL MACHINE.

The METERS

were founded by ex-NEVILLE SOUNDS people **ART NEVILLE** – keys / **ZIGGY MODELISTE** – drums / **GEORGE PORTER** – bass / **LEO NOCENTELLI** – guitar

Stateside | Josie

Feb 69. (7") **SOPHISTICATED CISSY. / SEHORNS FARM** [ ] [34]

May 69. (7") **CISSY STRUT. / HERE COMES THE METER MAN** [ ] [23] Apr 69

May 69. (lp) **THE METERS** (instrumental) [ ] [ ]

Jul 69. (7") **EASE BACK. / ?** [–] [61]

Direction | Josie

Oct 69. (7") **LOOK KA-PY-PY. / DRY SPELL** [–] [56]

Dec 69. (7") **LOOK KA-PY-PY. / THIS IS MY LAST AFFAIR** [ ] [–]

Jan 70. (lp) **LOOK KA-PY-PY** [ ] [ ]
– (you'll find most of early tracks of UK Charly 80's compilations)

Apr 70. (7") **CHICKEN STRUT. / HEY! LAST MINUTE** [ ] [50]

May 70. (lp) **STRUTTIN'** [ ] [ ]
– Tippi toes / Sophisticated Cissy / Rigor mortis / Little old money maker / Look ka-py-py / Cissy strut / Ease back / Chicken strut / A message from The Meters / Ride your pony / Dry spell / Handclapping song / Liver splash / Same old thing / Sehorns farm / Yeah you're right / 9 till 5 / Pungee. *(re-iss.+cd.Feb87 on 'Charly')*

Jun 70. (7") **HANDCLAPPING SONG. / JOOG** [–] [89]

Sep 70. (7") **A MESSAGE FROM THE METERS. / ZONY MASH** [–] [ ]

Feb 71. (7") **GROOVY LADY. / STRETCH YOUR RUBBER BAND** [–] [ ]

Apr 71. (7") **I NEED MORE TIME. / DOUBLE OOP** [–] [ ]

Jul 71. (7") **SASSY LADY. / GOOD OLD FUNKY MUSIC** [–] [ ]

Reprise | Reprise

1972. (lp) **CABBAGE ALLEY** [ ] [ ]
– You've got to change (You've got to reform) / Stay away / Birds / Flower song / Soul island / Do the dirt / Smiling / Lonesome and unwanted people / Gettin' funkier all the time / Cabbage alley.

1972. (7") **DO THE DIRT. / SMILING** [–] [ ]

1972. (7") **CABBAGE ALLEY. / THE FLOWER SONG** [–] [ ]

1973. (7") **CHUG CHUG CHUG-A-LUG. / (part 2)** [–] [ ]

The METERS did session work for DR.JOHN and ROBERT PALMER.

Jun 74. (7") **AFRICA. / HEY ROCK-A-WAY** [–] [ ]

Aug 74. (7") **PEOPLE SAY. / LOVING YOU IS ON MY MIND** [–] [ ]

Sep 74. (7") **PEOPLE SAY. / AFRICA** [ ] [–]

Oct 74. (lp)(c) **REJUVENATION** [ ] [ ]
– People say / Love is for me / Just kissed me baby / What'cha say / Jungle man / Hey rocky a-way / It ain't no use Loving you is on my mind / Africa.

— added **CYRIL NEVILLE** – percussion, vocals (ex-SOUL MACHINE)

Aug 75. (lp)(c) **FIRE ON THE BAYOU** [ ] [ ]
– Out in the country / Fire in the bayou / Love slip upon ya / Talkin' about New Orleans / They all asked for you / Can you do without / Liar / You're a friend of mine / Middle of the road / Running fast / Mardi Gras mambo.

Nov 75. (7") **FIRE ON THE BAYOU. / THEY ALL ASKED FOR YOU**

— added **AARON + CHARLES NEVILLE** – vocals

Sep 76. (7") **DISCO IS THE THING TODAY. / MISTER MOON** [–] [ ]

Sep 76. (lp)(c) **TRICK BAG** [ ] [ ]
– Disco is the thing today / Find your self / All these things / I want to be loved by you / Suite for 20 G / The world is a little bit under the weather / Trick bag / Mister Moon / Chug-a-lug / Hang 'em high / Honky tonk women.

Nov 76. (7") **TRICK BAG. / FIND YOURSELF** [–] [ ]

WILD TCHOUPITOULAS

aka The METERS

Island | Island

Feb 77. (7") **MEET DE BOYS ON THE BATTLEFRONT. / BIG CHIEF GOT A GOLDEN CROWN** [–] [ ]

Apr 77. (lp)(c) **THE WILD TCHOUPITOULAS** [ ] [ ]
– Brother John / Meet de boys on de battlefront / Here dey come / Hey pocky-a-way / Indian red / Big chief got a golden crown / Hey mama, hey hey. *(re-iss.+cd.Apr88 + Feb90)*

May 77. (7") **BROTHER JOHN. / HERE DEY COME** [–] [ ]

METERS

Warners | Warners

Jun 77. (lp)(c) **NEW DIRECTIONS** [ ] [ ]
– No more okey doke / I'm gone / Be my lady / My name up in lights / Funkify your life / Stop that train / we got the kind of love / Give it all you can.

Oct 77. (7") **BE MY LADY. / NO MORE OKEY DOKE** [ ] [78] Sep 77

AARON NEVILLE

not issued | Polydor

Nov 77. (7") **GREATEST LOVE. / PERFORMANCE** [–] [ ]

The NEVILLE BROTHERS

(with all brothers except CHARLES)

Capitol | Capitol

Oct 78. (7") **SPEED OF LIGHT. / IF IT TAKES ALL NIGHT** [–] [ ]

Mar 79. (lp)(c) **THE NEVILLE BROTHERS** [ ] [ ] Mar 78
– Dancing Jones / Washable ink / All nights all right / Audience for my pain / Break away / If it takes all night / Viclux carre rouge / Arianne / Speed of light.

— 4 brothers again (**AARON, ART, CYRIL + CHARLES**)

A & M | A & M

Sep 81. (lp)(c) **FIYO ON THE BAYOU** [ ] [ ] Aug 81
– Hey pocky way / Sweet honey dripper / Fire on the bayou / The ten commandments of love / Sitting in limbo / Brother John / Iko Iko / Mona Lisa / Run Joe. *(re-iss.Jul86 on 'Demon') (re-iss.cd+c Mar93)*

Sep 81. (7") **WHY ME?. / BROHER JOHN – IKO IKO** [–] [ ]

Nov 81. (7") **SWEET HONEY DRIPPER. / BROTHER JOHN – IKO IKO** [–] [ ]

Jan 82. (7") **FIRE ON THE BAYOU. / MONA LISA** [–] [ ]

Demon | Black Top

Jun 84. (lp)(c) **NEVILLE-IZATION (live '82 New Orleans)** [ ] [ ]
– Fever / Woman's gotta have it / Mojo Hannah / Tell it like it is / Why you wanna hurt my heart? / Fear, hate, envy, jealousy / Caravan / Big chief / Africa. *(cd-iss.Nov86)*

Late in 1988, AARON teamed up with WAS (NOT WAS) and BONNIE RAITT on 'A&M' single 'BABY MINE'.

A & M | A & M

Mar 89. (lp)(c)(cd) **YELLOW MOON** [ ] [66]
– My blood / Yellow Moon / Fire and brimstone / A change is gonna come / Sister Rosa / With God on our side / Wake up / Voodoo / The ballad of Hollis Brown / Will the circle be unbroken / Healing chant / Wild Injuns. *(re-iss.cd May95)*

Apr 89. (7")(12") **A CHANGE IS GONNA COME. / SISTER ROSA** [ ] [ ]

May 89. (7") **YELLOW MOON. / HEALING CHANCE** [–] [ ]
(re-iss.Nov89)

Jun 89. (7") **YELLOW MOON. / WITH GOD ON OUR SIDE** [ ] [–]
(12"+=)(cd-s+=) – Healing chant.

Jul 89. (7") **VOODOO. / SISTER ROSA** [–] [ ]

Oct 89. (7") **SISTER ROSA. / ('A'-long version)** [–] [ ]

Nov 89. (7") **WITH GOD ON OUR SIDE. / VOODOO** [47] [ ]
(12"+=)(cd-s+=) – Healing chant

Jan 90. (7") **A CHANGE IS GONNA COME. / WAKE UP (live)** [ ] [ ]
(12"+=)(cd-s+=) – Sister Rosa (live).

— Late 1989 & early 1990, AARON duetted on 2 hit singles; 'DON'T KNOW MUCH' & 'ALL MY LIFE', with LINDA RONSTADT. Below 'A'side from film of same name.

— with band **WILLIE GREEN** – drums / **TONY HALL** – bass / **ERIC STRUTHERS** – guitar

Jun 90. (7") **BIRD ON A WIRE. / BLACK DIAMOND PEARL** [72] [ ]
(12"+=)(cd-s+=) – ('A' version)

Aug 90. (cd)(c)(lp) **BROTHER'S KEEPER** [35] [60]
– Brother blood / Brother Jake / Steer me right / Fearless / Sons and daughters / Fallin' rain / Jah love / River of life / Witness / My brother's keeper / Sons and daughters (reprise) / Mystery train / Bird on a wire.

Aug 90. (7") **RIVER OF LIFE. / TELL IT LIKE IT IS (live)** [ ] [ ]
(12"+=)(cd-s+=) – Sister Rosa

Oct 90. (7") **FEARLESS. / SHAKE YOUR TAMBOURINE** (live) [ ] [ ]
(12"+=)(cd-s+=) – A change is gonna come (live).

AARON NEVILLE

A & M | A & M

Jun 91. (7")(c-s) **EVERYBODY PLAYS THE FOOL. / ANGELA BOUND** [ ] [8]
(12"+=)(cd-s+=) – ('A' lovin' eyes mix) / Hard times come around no more.

Jul 91. (cd)(c)(lp) **WARM YOUR HEART** [ ] [44]
– Louisiana 1927 / Everybody plays the fool / It feels like rain / Somewhere, somebody / Don't go, please stay / With you in mind / That's the way she looks / Angela bound / Close your eyes / La vie dansette / Warm your heart / I bid you goodnight / Ave Maria.

Aug 91. (7")(c-s) **SOMEWHERE SOMEBODY. / BROTHER JAKE** [ ] [ ]
(12"+=)(cd-s+=) – Yellow moon.

Jan 92. (7") **LOUISIANA 1927. / HOUSE ON A HILL** [ ] [ ]
(12"+=)(cd-s+=) – A change is gonna come (live).

NEVILLE BROTHERS

A & M | A & M

Sep 92. (cd)(c) **FAMILY GROOVE** [ ] [ ]
– Fly like an eagle / One more day / I can see it in your eyes / Day to day thing / Line of fire / Take me to heart / Maori chant / It takes more / Family groove / True love / On the other side of Paradise / Let my people go / Saxafunk / Good song.

Oct 92. (7")(c-s) **FLY LIKE AN EAGLE. / ('A'instrumental)** [ ] [ ]
(+cd-s+=) – ('A' 3 dub mixes) / ('A' other mix).
(12"++=) (1 extra dub mix)

Apr 94. (cd)(c) **LIVE ON PLANET EARTH** [ ] [ ]
– Shake your tambourine / Voodoo / Dealer / Junk man / Brother Jake / Sister Rosa / Yellow Moon / Her African eyes / Sands of time / Congo Square / Love the one you're with / You can't always get what you want / Let my people go / Get up stand up / Amazing Grace / One love – People get ready. *(re-iss.cd May95)*

— In Jun 94, he duetted with TRICIA YEARWOOD on 'MCA' single 'I FALL TO

PIECES'.

AARON NEVILLE

A & M A & M

May 93. (c-s) **DON'T TAKE AWAY MY HEAVEN. /** -
Aug 93. (cd)(c) **THE GRAND TOUR** 37
– Don't take away my Heaven / I owe you one / Don't fall apart on me tonight / My brother, my brother / Betcha by golly wow / Song of Bernadette / You never can tell / The bells / These foolish things / The roadie song / Ain't no way / The grand tour / The Lord's prayer / Ronnie-O.
Sep 93. (c-s) **THE GRAND TOUR. /** -
Nov 93. (cd) **AARON NEVILLE'S SOULFUL CHRISTMAS** (festive) 53
Apr 95. (cd)(c) **TATTOOED HEART** 64
–
Jun 95. (c-s)(cd-s) **CAN'T STOP MY HEART FROM LOVING YOU (THE RAIN SONG) /** - 99

– (METERS) compilations, others, etc. –

Jan 76. Reprise; (lp) **THE BEST OF THE METERS**
May 79. Pye; (lp) **GOOD OLD FUNKY MUSIC** -
(re-iss.Oct90 on 'Special Delivery') (cd-iss.Jan95 on 'Rounder')
Jul 80. Charly; (7"ep) **LOOK KA-PY-PY. / TIPPI TOES / CISSY STRUT** -
1980. Charly; (lp) **SECOND LINE STRUT** -
Apr 86. Charly; (lp) **HERE COMES THE METERMEN** -
Mar 91. Charly; (cd) **FUNKY MIRACLE** -
May 92. Special Delivery; (cd) **JAM** -
Nov 92. Instant; (cd) **ORIGINAL FUNKMASTERS** -
– Sophisticated Cissy / Funky miracle / Look-ka py py / Till 5 / Ease back / Ride your pony / Stormy / Dry spell / Cissy strut / Tippi-toes / Chicken strut / I need more time / Live wire / Handclapping song / Message from the Metermen.
Dec 92. Sequel; (cd) **UPTOWN RULERS!! (LIVE ON THE QUEEN MARY) (live)** -

– (NEVILLE BROTHERS) comps, others. –

Feb 86. Rhino; (d-lp)(c) **TREACHEROUS!** (all work from over 30 years) Apr 87
Jul 91. Rhino; (cd) **TREACHEROUS TOO!** (more of the same)
1987. E.M.I./ US= Capitol; (lp) **UPTOWN**
(cd-iss.Jul88) (re-iss.+cd.May91 on 'Fame')
Jun 88. Demon; (lp) **LIVE AT TIPITINA'S VOL.II (live)** -
(re-iss.1990 on 'Essential')
Apr 90. Charly; (cd-box)(c-box) **LEGACY (A HISTORY OF THE NEVILLES)** -
Aug 94. Charly; (cd) **FUNDAMENTALLY FUNKY (METERS)** -
Nov 94. Charly; (cd) **CRESCENT CITY** -
May 94. Traditional Line; (cd) **LIVE AT TIPITINA'S (live)** -
May 94. Castle; (cd) **LIVE (live)** -
Nov 95. One Way; (cd) **THE NEVILLE BROTHERS** -
Apr 86. Demon; (lp) **ORCHID IN THE STORM (AARON NEVILLE)** -
(cd-iss.May95 on 'Rhino')
Sep 86. Stateside; (lp)(c) **HUMDINGER (AARON NEVILLE)** -
Feb 87. Charly; (c)(cd) **MAKE ME STRONG (AARON NEVILLE)** -
Aug 89. Charly; (lp)(c)(cd) **SHOW ME THE WAY (AARON NEVILLE)** -
Nov 93. Charly; (cd) **HERCULES (AARON NEVILLE)** -
Nov 86. Ace; (lp) **MARDI GRAS ROCK'N'ROLL (ART NEVILLE)** -
(cd-iss.1991)
Jan 93. Ace; (cd) **HIS SPECIALITY RECORDINGS: 1956-1958 (ART NEVILLE)** -
Sep 88. Charly; (lp) **ROCK'N'ROLL HOOTENANNY (ART NEVILLE)** -

NEW CHURCH (see under ⇒ KORNER, Alexis)

NEW FAST AUTOMATIC DAFFODILS

Formed: Manchester, England ... 1988 out of punk group PARIAH. Unleashed indie 45 'LIONS' which was heralded as best debut for years. By late 1990 a fresh move to a new label gave them a brief entry into UK album chart with 'PIGEONHOLE'. • **Style:** Reminiscent of the alternative funk rock early 80's (i.e. PIGBAG, ACR, FIRE ENGINES or 23 SKIDOO). • **Songwriters:** Group penned except; I'M SET FREE (Velvet Underground). • **Trivia:** Around mid'91, 20,000 copies of 'Getting Better' were stolen by Basque separatists of Spain. The NEW FADS '94 album was produced by JEREMY ALLOM (Massive Attack).

Recommended: PIGEONHOLE (*7) / BODY EXIT MIND (*8)

ANDY SPEARPOINT – vocals / **DOLAN HEWISON** (b.Newcastle) – guitar / **JUSTIN CRAWFORD** – bass / **PERRY SAUNDERS** – drums / **ICARUS WILSON-KNIGHT** – percussion

Playtime not issued

Jun 89. (12"ep) **LIONS / FATE DON'T FAIL ME NOW. / YOUR DREAMS, MY NIGHTMARES** -
Oct 89. (12"ep) **MUSIC IS SHIT** -
– Beam me up / Men without qualities / Music is shit (parts 1, 2 & 3) / Lions. *(re-iss.+cd-ep Apr92)*
Mar 90. (12"ep)(cd-ep) **BIG. / ('A'instrumental) / Baka / ('A'-Baka mix)** -

P.I.A.S. Elektra

Sep 90. (7") **FISHES EYES. / FISHES EYES (UNDERWATER)** -
('A'ext-12"+=)(cd-s+=) – White.
Nov 90. (cd)(c)(lp) **PIGEONHOLE** 49 1991
– Get better / Fishes eyes / Working for him / Part 4 / Big / You were lying when you said you loved me / Amplifier / Reprise / Partial.
(free-7") – I'M SET FREE. / PENGUINS *(re-iss.cd Sep93)*
Apr 91. (7") **GET BETTER. / PIGEONHOLE** -
('A'ext-12"+=) – I found myself in another room.
(cd-s++=) – ('A'extended).
Nov 91. (7") **ALL OVER MY FACE. / WHY THE HARD MEN FAIL**
(12")(cd-s) – ('A'-split decision mix) / ('A'-off the road mix) / ('B'side).
Aug 92. (7") **IT'S NOT WHAT YOU KNOW. / BEAUTIFUL**
(12"+=)(cd-s+=) – Head on / Beatlemania.
Sep 92. (7") **STOCKHOLM (radio mix). / CANNES**
(12"+=)(cd-s+=) – ('A'extended).
(10") – ('A'demo) / Hexagon spray / It's not what you know (demo).
Oct 92. (cd)(c)(lp) **BODY EXIT MIND** 57 -
– Bong / It's not what you know / Stockholm / I take you to sleep / Bruises / Kyphos / Beatlemania / What kind of Hell is this? / American money / Missing parts of famous people / Patchwork lies / Music.
(cd+=) – How much longer shall we tolerate mass culture? / Teenage combo / Exit body, exit mind.

NEW FADS

P.I.A.S. Elektra

Sep 94. (12"m) **LIFE IS AN ACCIDENT. / EVERY ONCE IN A WHILE (Fuzzy Logic remix) / MAD POP**
(cd-s) – (1st & 3rd tracks) / PSV (VPL remix).
(cd-s) – (1st 2 tracks) / Aches and pains.
Oct 94. (cd)(c)(lp) **LOVE IT ALL**
– These foolish things / Life is an accident / Left right / Every once in a while / Why waste your love / What I feel / Saxophone / Monday it is / P.S.V. / Kill my instincts / Souvenir.
Nov 94. (10") **THESE FOOLISH THINGS. / EVERY ONCE IN A WHILE**
(cd-s+=) – Bassdrum (H.Nicholson mix) / Lions (live).
Jan 95. (cd)(c)(lp) **LOVE IT ALL**
– These foolish things / Life is an accident / Left right / Every once in a while / Why waste your love / Monday it is / What I feel / Saxophone / P.S.V. / Kil my instincts / Souvenir.

– compilations, others, etc. –

Jul 91. Strange Fruit; (cd)(c)(lp) **THE PEEL SESSIONS** (late '89) -
– Purple haze / Man without qualities II / Jaggerbog / Big II (instrumental) / Get better / Part 4 / Man without qualities I.

Colin NEWMAN (see under ⇒ WIRE)

Randy NEWMAN

Born: RANDOLPH NEWMAN, 28 Nov'43, New Orleans, Louisiana, USA. At the age of 10, he moved with his Jewish family to Los Angeles. His uncle, Alfred Newman, had written over 200 scores for 20th Cent Fox films, including 'Wuthering Heights' & 'Airport'. In 1961, RANDY issued one-off 45 'GOLDEN GRIDIRON BOY' for 'Dot', which was produced by singer PAT BOONE. After its flop, he became staff-writer for 'Liberty' records. He wrote hits for VIC DANA, GENE McDANIELS, CILLA BLACK!, GENE PITNEY, etc in the mid-60's. In 1967, ALAN PRICE started borrowing his songs, and had UK hit with 'SIMON SMITH AND HIS AMAZING DANCING BEAR'. That year, RANDY became staff arranger/producer for 'Warners', working with VAN DYKE PARKS, BEAU BRUMMELS and HARPER'S BIZARRE. In 1968, he finally issued eponymous debut for Warners subsidiary 'Reprise'. In Mar'70, another solo artist NILSSON, released a whole album of his songs as 'NILSSON SINGS NEWMAN'. A month later, NEWMAN issued 2nd album '12 SONGS', which included 'MAMA TOLD ME NOT TO COME', which went on to become a US No.1 for THREE DOG NIGHT. On 5 Oct'74, he played The Atlanta Symphony Hall with their 87-piece orchestra, conducted by another uncle; Emil Newman. His first major chart album (Top 40), 'GOOD OLD BOYS' soon followed, but this was surpassed in 1977, when RANDY hit US Top 3 with single 'SHORT PEOPLE', from Top 10 album 'LITTLE CRIMINALS'. Although his commercial appeal declined over the next decade and he concentrated on more film soundtracks, he still had numerous songs covered. • **Style:** Classy singer-songwriter, capable of writing songs for anybody from cabaret to hard-rock. • **Songwriters:** As said except; TIME OF THE SEASON (Zombies). • **Trivia:** His 1988 comeback album 'LAND OF DREAMS' was co-produced with JEFF LYNNE and MARK KNOPFLER.

Recommended: LONELY AT THE TOP – THE BEST OF RANDY NEWMAN (*8)

RANDY NEWMAN – vocals, piano

not issued Dot

1962. (7") **GOLDEN GRIDIRON BOY. / COUNTRY BOY** -

— RANDY became semi-successful songwriter for other established acts. He eventually embarked an a long awaited solo career, after a US instrumental 1966 lp 'THE RANDY NEWMAN ORCHESTRA PLAYS MUSIC FROM THE HIT TELEVISION SERIES 'PEYTON PLACE' for 'Epic'. In 1968, he used over 30-piece orchestra.

Reprise Reprise

Jun 68. (lp) **RANDY NEWMAN**

– Love story / Bet no one ever hurt this bad / Living without you / So long dad / I think he's hiding / Linda / Laughing boy / Cowboy / The beehive state / I think it's going to rain today / Davy the fat boy. *(cd-iss.May95 on 'Warners')*

1968. (7") **BEEHIVE STATE. / I THINK IT'S GOING TO RAIN TODAY** [-] [ ]

Jul 68. (7") **LOVE STORY. / I THINK IT'S GOING TO RAIN TODAY** [ ] [ ]

— his guests included **RY COODER** – slide guitar / **RON ELLIOTT** – guitar / **GENE PARSONS** – drums / **CLARENCE WHITE** – guitar / **AL McKIBBON** – bass / etc.

Apr 70. (lp)(c) **12 SONGS** [ ] [ ]
– Have you seen my baby / Let's burn the cornfield / Mama told me not to come / Suzanne / Lover's prayer / Lucinda / Underneath the Harlem moon / Yellow man / Old Kentucky home / Rosemary / If you need oil / Uncle Bob's midnight oil. *(re-iss.1971 & 1974)*

May 70. (7") **HAVE YOU SEEN MY BABY. / HOLD ON** [-] [ ]

(below from the soundtrack of the film 'Performance')

Nov 70. (7") **GONE DEAD TRAIN. / HARRY FLOWERS** [ ] [ ]

— **RANDY** – just vocals and piano only.

Nov 71. (lp)(c) **RANDY NEWMAN LIVE (live)** [ ] [ ] Sep 71
– Mama told me not to come / Tickle me / I'll be home / So long dad / Living without you / Last night I had a dream / I think it's going to rain today / Lover's prayer / Maybe I'm doing it wrong / Yellow man / Old Kentucky home / Davy the fat boy / Lonely at the top. *(cd-iss.May95 on 'Warners')*

Mar 72. (7") **LONELY AT THE TOP (live). / MY OLD KENTUCKY HOME (live)** [ ] [ ]

— Reverted to solo / orchestra plus past and new session people. From then after he continued to employ famous musicians and singers.

Jul 72. (lp)(c) **SAIL AWAY** [ ] [ ] Jun 72
– Political science / Burn on / Memo to my son / Dayton, Ohio – 1903 / You can leave your hat on / God's song (that's why I love mankind) / Sail away / Lonely at the top / He gives us all his love / Last night I had a dream / Simon Smith and his amazing dancing bear / Old man.

Jul 72. (7") **SAIL AWAY. / POLITICAL SCIENCE** [ ] [ ]

Sep 72. (7") **MEMO TO MY SON. / YOU CAN LEAVE YOUR HAT ON** [-] [ ]

Sep 74. (7") **NAKED MAN. / GUILTY** [-] [ ]

Oct 74. (lp)(c) **GOOD OLD BOYS** [ ] [36]
– Rednecks / Birmingham / Marie / Mr. President (have pity on the working man) / Guilty / Louisiana 1927 / Every man a king / Kingfish / Naked man / Wedding in Cherokee County / Back on my feet again / Rollin'.

Nov 75. (7") **LOUISIANA 1927. / MARIE** [-] [ ]

Warners Warners

Sep 77. (lp)(c) **LITTLE CRIMINALS** [ ] [9]
– Short people / You can't fool the fat man / Little criminals / Texas girl at the funeral of her father / Jolly coppers on parade / In Germany before the war / Sigmund Freud's impersonation of Albert Einstein in America / Baltimore / I'll be home / Rider in the rain / Kathleen / Old man on the farm.

Oct 77. (7") **SHORT PEOPLE. / OLD MAN ON THE FARM** [ ] [2]

Jun 78. (7") **RIDER IN THE RAIN. / LITTLE CRIMINALS** [ ] [ ]

Aug 78. (7") **BALTIMORE. / YOU CAN'T FOOL THE FATMAN** [-] [ ]

Oct 78. (7") **RIDER IN THE RAIN. / SIGMUND FREUD'S IMPERSONATION OF ALBERT EINSTEIN IN AMERICA** [-] [ ]

Aug 79. (7") **THE STORY OF A ROCK AND ROLL BAND. / PRETTY BOY** [ ] [ ]

Sep 79. (lp)(c) **BORN AGAIN** [ ] [41] Aug 79
– It's money that I love / The story of a rock and roll band / Mr. Sheep / Pretty boy / They just got married / Ghosts / Spies / The girls in my life (part 1) / Half a man / William Brown / Pants. *(cd-iss.Feb93)*

Nov 79. (7") **IT'S MONEY THAT I LOVE. / GHOSTS** [ ] [ ] Sep 79

Nov 79. (7") **THE STORY OF A ROCK AND ROLL BAND. / HALF A MAN** [-] [ ]

Feb 80. (7") **SPIES. / POLITICAL SCIENCE** [-] [ ]

Feb 82. (lp)(c) **RAGTIME (Original Soundtrack on 'Elektra')** [ ] [ ]
– Main title / Newsreel / I could love a million girls / Train ride / Tateh's picture book / Lower East Side / Delmonico polka / Coalhouse and Sarah / Waltz for Evelyn / One more hour / Sarah's responsibility / Change your way / Clef club No.1 / Atlantic City / Clef club No.2 / arah's funeral / Denouncement: Morgan Library takeover – Rhinelander Waldo / Coalhouse's prayer / Ragtime. *(re-iss.Jan89 on 'Screen')*

Jan 83. (lp)(c) **TROUBLE IN PARADISE** [ ] [64]
– I love L.A. / Christmas in Capetown / The blues / Same girl / The Mikey's / My life is good / Miami / Real emotional girl / Take me back / There's a party at my house / I'm different / Song for the dead. *(re-iss.Mar89 on 'Edsel')(cd-iss.Nov93)*

Jan 83. (7") **THE BLUES (with "PAUL SIMON"). / SOME GIRL** [ ] [51]
(12") – ('A'side) / Simon Smith and the amazing dancing bear / Short people / Mama told me not to come.

Apr 83. (7") **I LOVE L.A. / SONG FOR THE DEAD** [ ] [ ]

Oct 84. (lp)(c) **THE NATURAL (Film Soundtrack)** [ ] [ ]
– The natural / Prologue 1915-1923 / The whammer strike out / The old farm 1939 / The Majors: the mind is a strange thing / Knock the cover off the ball / Memo / Wrigley field / Iris and Roy / Winning / A father makes a difference / Penthouse party / The end title / The final game – take me to the ballroom.

Sep 88. (lp)(c)(cd) **LAND OF DREAMS** [ ] [80]
– Dixie flyer / New Orleans wins the war / Four eyes / Falling in love / Something special / Bad news from home / Roll with the punches / Masterman and Baby J. / Follow the flag / It's money that matters / I want you to hurt like I do.

Oct 88. (7") **IT'S MONEY THAT MATTERS. / ROLL WITH THE PUNCHES** [ ] [60]
(12"+=)(cd-s+=) – Short people.

Feb 89. (7") **FALLING IN LOVE. / BAD NEWS FROM HOME** [ ] [ ]
(12"+=)(cd-s+=) – Miami.

(above 'A'side from film of the same name)

Sep 89. (7") **I'D LOVE TO SEE YOU SMILE. / END TITLE (I LOVE TO SEE YOU SMILE)** [-] [ ]

Jun 90. (cd)(c)(lp) **PARENTHOOD (Soundtrack)** [ ] [ ] Sep 89
– Introduction – I love to see you smile / Kevin's graduation / Helen and Julie / Kevin's party (cowboy Gil) / Gary's in trouble / Father and son / Drag race / Todd and Julie / Kevin comes through / Karen and Gil (montage) / End title (I love to see you smile).

Mar 91. (cd)(c)(lp) **AWAKENINGS (Soundtrack)** [ ] [ ]
– Leonard / Dr.Sayer / Lucy / Catch / Rilke's panther / L dopa / Awakenings / Outside / Escape attempt / Ward five / Dexter's tune / The reality of miracles / End title.

May 94. (cd) **THE PAPER – ORIGINAL SOUNDTRACK** [ ] [ ]

— with guest singers BONNIE RAITT / DON HENLEY / RY COODER / JAMES TAYLOR / LINDA RONSTADT / ELTON JOHN

A&M A&M

Sep 95. (cd)(c) **RANDY NEWMAN'S FAUST** [ ] [ ]
– Glory train / Can't help a good man down / How great our Lord / Best little girl / Northern boy / Bless the children of the world / Gainesville / Relax, enjoy yourself / Life has been good to me / Little island / The man / My hero / I gota be your hero / Feels like home / Bleeding all over the place / Sandman's coming / Happy ending.

– compilations, etc. –

May 84. Warners; (lp)(c) **LONELY AT THE TOP – THE BEST OF RANDY NEWMAN** [ ] [ ]
– Love story / Living without you / I think it's going to rain today / Mama told me not to come / Sail away / Simon Smith and his amazing dancing bear / Political science / God's song (that's why I love mankind) / Rednecks / Birmingham / Louisiana 1927 / Marie / Baltimore / Jolly coppers on parade / Rider in the rain / Short people / I love L.A. / Lonely at the top. *(re-iss.+c/cd.Jul87+=)* – My life is good / In Germany before the war / Christmas in Capetown / My old Kentucky home. *(re-iss.cd/c Nov93)*

Jun 87. Atlantic; (lp)(c) **THREE AMIGOS (Soundtrack)** [ ] [ ]
– (including several NEWMAN songs)

NEW MODEL ARMY

Formed: Bradford, England ... 1980 by SLADE THE LEVELLER (aka JUSTIN SULLIVAN). After their own 45 'BITTERSWEET' on 'Quiet', they moved to bigger indie 'Abstract' in 1983, for a single and a mini-lp 'VENGEANCE'. Early in '85, they were given contract by 'EMI', who gave them free reign of output. Their first 45 for the label 'NO REST' / 'HEROIN', saw them banned by the IBA for the latter's subject matter. The Americans also initially banned them from arriving there, reputedly citing their lack of artistic quality. In 1985, their first full album 'NO REST FOR THE WICKED', went into the UK Top 30, thus rendering all banning efforts pointless. • **Style:** A blend of raw punk, protest and politics. • **Songwriters:** All written by SULLIVAN / HEATON. • **Trivia:** Their name was taken from Oliver Cromwell's forces in the 11th century English civil war. SULLIVAN and HEATON played back-up to the former's girlfriend poet JOOLZ on many stage shows.

Recommended: HISTORY THE SINGLES (*7) / VENGEANCE (*8)

SLADE THE LEVELLER (b. JUSTIN SULLIVAN, 1956) – vocals, guitar / **STUART MORROW** – bass / **ROBB HEATON** (b.1962) -drums

Quiet not issued

May 83. (7") **BITTERSWEET. / BETCHA / TENSION** [ ] [-]
(w/free flexi-7") – FASHION / CAUSE.

Abstract not issued

Nov 83. (7") **GREAT EXPECTATIONS. / WAITING** [ ] [-]
(re-iss.Feb90 on colour vinyl)

Apr 84. (m-lp) **VENGEANCE** [73] [-]
– Christian militia / Notice me / Smalltown England / A liberal education / Vengeance / Sex (the black angel) / Running / Spirit of the Falklands. *(c-iss.Nov85) (cd-iss.Jun87 +=)* – Great expectations / Waiting / The price / 1984 / No man's land. *(blue-lp iss.Nov87 w / 6xbox-set of 'Abstract' label records: 'SIX DISQUES BLEU')*

Oct 84. (7") **THE PRICE. / 1984** [ ] [-]
(12"+=) – No man's land / Notice me / Great expectations.

E.M.I. Capitol

Apr 85. (7")(c-s) **NO REST. / HEROIN** [28] [-]
(d12"+=) – Vengeance / The price / No greater love (all 3 live).

May 85. (lp)(c) **NO REST FOR THE WICKED** [22] [-]
– Frightened / Ambition / Grandmother's footsteps / Better than them / My country / No greater love / No rest / Young, gifted & skint / Drag it down / Shot 18 / The attack. *(re-iss.May88 on 'Fame', cd-iss.Jul89)*

Jun 85. (d7")(7"ep)(12"ep) **BETTER THAN THEM. / NO SENSE/ / ADRENELIN. / TRUST** [49] [-]

— **JASON 'MOOSE' HARRIS** repl. MORROW

Nov 85. (7") **BRAVE NEW WORLD. / R.I.P.** [57] [-]
(12"+=) – Brave new world 2.
(d12"+=) – Young, gifted & skint (live) / Sex (the black angel) (live)

Sep 86. (lp)(c) **THE GHOST OF CAIN** [45] [-]
– The hunt / Lights go out / 51st state / All of this / Poison street / Western dream / Love songs / Heroes / Ballad / Master race. *(re-iss.+cd.Jul89)*

Oct 86. (7")(12") **51st STATE. / TEN COMMANDMENTS** [71] [-]
(d12"+=) – A liberal education / No rest / No man's land (all 3 live).

Feb 87. (7")(7"red) **POISON STREET. / COURAGE** [64] [-]
(12"+=) – ('A'extended version).
(d12"+=) – All of this (live) / My country (live).

Jun 87. (7"ep)(12"ep) **WHITE COATS / THE CHARGE. / CHINESE WHISPERS / MY COUNTRY** [50] [-]

Dec 88. (m-lp) **SEVEN SONGS** [-] [ ]
– My country (live) / Waiting / 51st state / The hunt (live) / White coats / The charge / Chinese whispers.

Jan 89. (7") **STUPID QUESTIONS. / NOTHING TOUCHES** [31] [ ]
(12") – ('A'extended) / Betcha (live).
(cd-s++=) – 51st state.

Feb 89. (lp)(c)(cd) **THUNDER AND CONSOLATION** [20] [ ]
– I love the world / Stupid questions / 225 / Inheritence / Green and grey / Ballad of Bodmin Pill / Family / Family life / Vagabonds / Archway towers. *(re-iss.Aug91 on*

'Fame', *cd+=)*– The charge / Chinese whispers / Nothing changes / White coats.

Feb 89. (7")(7"pic-d) **VAGABONDS. / DEAD EYE** [37] [ ]
(12"+=) – ('A'extended) / White coats (live).
(cd-s++=) – Lights go out (extended).

Jun 89. (7")(c-s)(7"pic-d) **GREEN AND GREY. / THE CHARGE (live)** [37] [ ]
(12") – ('A'side) / Family life (live) / 125 mph (live).
(cd-s+=) – Green and grey (live).

—— **NELSON** – bass (ex-HIDING PLACE) repl. JASON

Aug 90. (7") **GET ME OUT. / PRISON** [34] [ ]
(10"+=) – ('A'extended) / Waiting (live).
(12"+=) – ('A'extended) / White coats (live).
(cd-s+=) – White coats (live) / Waiting (live).

Sep 90. (cd)(c)(lp) **IMPURITY** [23] [ ]
– Get me out / Space / Innocense / Purity / Whirlwind / Lust for power / Bury the hatchet / 11 years / Lurkstop / Before I get old / Vanity. (cd+=) – Marrakesh.

Oct 90. (7") **PURITY (IS A LIE). / CURSE** [61] [-]
(12"+=)(cd-s+=) – ('A'extended) / Vengeance (live).

May 91. (7")(c-s) **SPACE (live). / FAMILY LIFE** [39] [ ]
(12") – ('A'side) / No rest (live) / Stupid questions (live).
(cd-s) – ('A'side) / 225 (live) / Ambition (live).
(10") – ('A'side) / Bury the hatchet (live) / Stupid questions (live).

Jun 91. (cd)(c)(lp) **RAW MELODY MEN (live)** [43] [ ]
– Whirlwind / The charge / Space / Purity / White coats / Vagabonds / Get me out / Lib. fol / Better than them / Innocense / Love songs / Innhstaap / Archway towers / Smalltown England / Green & grey / The world. *(re-iss.cd+c Jun93 on 'Fame')*

Apr 92. (cd)(c)(lp) **HISTORY THE SINGLES 1985-91** (compilation) [ ] [ ]
– No rest / Better than them / Brave new world / 51st state / Poison street / White coats / Stupid questions / Vagabonds / Green and grey / Get me out / Purity / Space (live). *(incl.free 12")*– Far Better Thing / Higher Wall / Adrenalin (version) Luurstaap (acoustic). *(cd+c+=) – (2 extra tracks *)*

—— Jun'92, JUSTIN was nearly killed when he was electrocuted on stage.

Epic Epic

Jan 93. (7") **HERE COMES THE WAR. / MODERN TIMES** [25] [ ]
(12"+=)(cd-s+=) – Ghost of your father.

Mar 93. (cd)(c)(lp) **THE LOVE OF HOPELESS CAUSES** [22] [ ]
– Here comes the war / Fate / Living in the rose / White light / Believe it / Understand U / My people / These words / Afternoon song / Bad old world.

Jul 93. (12"ep)(cd-ep) **THE BALLADS EP** [51] [ ]
– Living in a rose / Drummy B / Marry the sea / Sleepwalking.

– compilations, others, etc. –

Apr 88. Abstract; (m-lp)(cd) **RADIO SESSIONS (1983-1984 rare)** [ ] [-]
Dec 93. Windsong; (cd) **BBC RADIO 1 LIVE IN CONCERT (live)** [ ] [-]
Sep 94. E.M.I.; (cd) **B SIDES AND ABANDONED TRACKS** [ ] [-]
Oct 94. Abstract; (12"ep)(cd-ep) **VENGEANCE 1994. / ('A'-Zion Train mix) / ('A'-The Headman mix) / ('A'-Pressure Of Speech mix)** [ ] [-]
Jun 95. Abstract; (d-cd) **VENGEANCE / RADIO SESSIONS** [ ] [-]

NEW ORDER

Formed: Manchester, England . . . Jun'80, after the death of JOY DIVISION frontman IAN CURTIS on 18 May'80. The remaining JOY DIVISION members ALBRECHT (now SUMNER), HOOK & MORRIS stayed with 'Factory' records, and played some gigs until Mar'81, when they issued debut 45 'CEREMONY'. This broke the Top 40, as did the Martin Hannett produced follow-up 'PROCESSION' / 'EVERYTHING'S GONE GREEN', which introduced 4th member GILLIAN GILBERT. Their first lp 'MOVEMENT', scraped into the UK Top 30 late in '81. By 1989, they had hit the UK No.1 for the first time with Stephen Hague co-produced album 'TECHNIQUE'. In between these in 1983, they had Top 10 for the first time with classic 12"only 45 'BLUE MONDAY', which also went down well on the US dancefloors. • **Style:** Sombre but infectious alternative rock outfit, who ventured into the techno-rock field after 1982. Their 1983 singles 'BLUE MONDAY' and 'CONFUSION', were produced by US dance producer ARTHUR BAKER, who also co-wrote the latter. He also collaborated on the 1984 follow-up 'THIEVES LIKE US'. • **Songwriters:** All group compositions except; TURN THE HEATER ON (Keith Hudson). • **Trivia:** In 1987, they contributed some tracks to the movie 'SALVATION'.

Recommended: POWER, CORRUPTION AND LIES (*9) / TECHNIQUE (*9) / MOVEMENT (*8) / SUBSTANCE 1980-1987 (*10) / LOW-LIFE (*8) / BROTHERHOOD (*8) / ELECTRONIC (*8; ELECTRONIC) / THE BEST OF NEW ORDER (*9).

BERNARD SUMNER (b.BERNARD DICKEN, 4 Jan'56) – vocals, guitar / **PETER HOOK** (b.13 Feb'56) – bass / **STEPHEN MORRIS** (b.28 Oct'57) – drums

Factory Streetwise

Mar 81. (7") **CEREMONY. / IN A LONELY PLACE** [34] [-]
(12"+=) – ('B'extended). *(12"w/re-recorded 'A'version re-issJul81)*

—— added **GILLIAN GILBERT** (b.27 Jan'61) – keyboards, synth., guitar

Sep 81. (7") **PROCESSION. / EVERYTHING'S GONE GREEN** [38] [-]
Nov 81. (lp) **MOVEMENT** [30] [-]
– Dreams never end / Truth / Senses / Chosen time / I.C.B. / The him / Doubts even here / Denial. *(re-iss.+c+cd.Nov86)(re-iss.cd+c Jul93 on 'Centredate')*

May 82. (7") **TEMPTATION. / HURT** [29] [-]
(12"+=) – ('A'&'B'extended).

Mar 83. (12") **BLUE MONDAY. / THE BEACH** [9] [ ]
(re-iss.Dec83)

May 83. (lp) **POWER, CORRUPTION AND LIES** [4] [ ]
– Your silent face / Ultraviolence / Ecstasy / Leave me alone / Age of consent / We all stand / The village / 5-8-6. *(c-iss.Nov84 +=)*
-Blue Monday / The beach. *(cd-iss.Nov86) (re-iss.cd+c Jul93 on 'Centredate')*

Jul 83. (12"ep) **CONFUSION. / CONFUSED BEATS / CONFUSION (instrumental & Rough mixes)** [12] [ ]

May 84. (12") **THIEVES LIKE US. / LONESOME TONIGHT** [18] [ ]

Factory Qwest

May 85. (7") **THE PERFECT KISS. / THE KISS OF DEATH** [46] [ ]
(12"+=) – Perfect pit (US mix). (US; b-side)

May 85. (lp)(c)(cd) **LOW-LIFE** [7] [94]
– Sooner than you think / Sub-culture / Face up / Love vigilantes / Elegia / The perfect kiss / This time of the night / Sunrise. *(c+=) – (3 extra tracks =last single). (re-iss.cd+c Jul93 on 'Centredate')*

Nov 85. (7")(12") **SUB-CULTURE. / DUB-CULTURE** [63] [-]
Mar 86. (7") **SHELLSHOCK (edit). / THIEVES LIKE US (instrumental)** [28] [-]
(12") – ('A'extended) / Shellshock (dub).

Sep 86. (7")(12") **STATE OF THE NATION. / SHAME OF THE NATION** [30] [-]

Oct 86. (lp)(c)(cd) **BROTHERHOOD** [9] [ ]
– Paradise / Weirdo / As it was when it was / Broken promise / Way of life / Bizarre love triangle / All day long / Angel dust / Every little counts. *(cd+=)* – State of the nation. *(re-iss.cd+c Jul93 on 'Centredate')*

Nov 86. (7")(12") **BIZARRE LOVE TRIANGLE. / BIZARRE DUB TRIANGLE** [56] [-]

Mar 87. (7") **BIZARRE LOVE TRIANGLE. / EVERY LITTLE COUNTS** [-] [ ]
Jul 87. (7")(12") **TRUE FAITH. / 1963** [4] [32]
(12"+=) – True dub.

Aug 87. (d-lp)(d-c)(d-cd) **SUBSTANCE (1980-1987)** (compilation) [3] [36]
– Ceremony / Everthing's gone green / Temptation / Blue Monday / Confusion / Thieves like us / Perfect kiss / Subculture / Shellshock / State of the nation / Bizarre love triangle / True faith.
(d-c+=)– Procession / Mesh / Hurt / In a lonely place / The beach / Confused / Murder / Lonesome tonight / Kiss of death / Shame of the nation / 1963. *(cd++=)*– Cries and whispers / Dub culture / Shellcock / Bizarre dub triangle. *(re-iss.cd+c Jul93 on 'Centredate', hit UK No.32)*

Dec 87. (7") **TOUCHED BY THE HAND OF GOD. / TOUCHED BY THE HAND OF DUB** [20] [-]
(12") – ('A'&'B'extended).
(cd-s) – ('A'extended) / Confusion (dub '87) / Temptation (original).

Mar 88. (7") **TOUCHED BY THE HAND OF GOD. / BLUE MONDAY 1988** [-] [ ]

Nov 88. (7") **FINE TIME. / DON'T DO IT** [11] [ ]
(12"+=) – Fine line.
(cd-s+=) – ('A'silk mix) / ('A'messed around mix).

Jan 89. (lp)(c)(cd)(dat) **TECHNIQUE** [1] [32]
– Fine time / All the way / Love less / Round & round / Guilty partner / Run / Mr. Disco / Vanishing point / Dream attack. *(re-iss.cd+c Jul93 on 'Centredate')*

Mar 89. (7") **ROUND & ROUND. / BEST AND MARSH** [21] [64]
(12") – ('A'&'B'extended).
(12"+=)(3"cd-s) – ('A'club mix) / ('A'Detroit mix) / ('B'extended).
(cd-s+=) – Vanishing point (instrumental 'Making Out' mix) / ('A'-12"mix).

Sep 89. (12"ep) **RUN 2 / RUN 2 (extended). / MTO / MTO (minus mix)** [49] [-]

May 90. (7")(12")(c-s) **WORLD IN MOTION. (as "ENGLAND / NEW ORDER") / THE B SIDE** [1] [-]
(cd-s+=) – ('A' no alla violenzia / ('A'subbuteo mix).
(12") – ('A'subbuteo mix) / ('A'subbuteo dub). / ('A' no alla violenzia mix) / ('A' Carabinieri mix).

—— Around the late 80's/early 90's, all members splintered to do own projects

Centredate-London Qwest

Apr 93. (7")(c-s) **REGRET ('A' mix)** [4] [28]
(cd-s+=) – ('A' Fire Isalnd mix) / ('A'-Junior's dub mix).
(12") – ('A'-Fire Island mix) / ('A'-Junior's dub mix) / (2-'A' Sabres mixes)

May 93. (cd)(c)(lp) **REPUBLIC** [1] [11]
– Regret / World / Ruined in a day / Spooky / Everyone everywhere / Young offender / Liar / Chemical / Times change / Special / Avalanche.

Jun 93. (7")(c-s) **RUINED IN A DAY. / VICIOUS CIRCLE (mix)** [22] [ ]
(cd-s+=)/ /(cd-s) – ('A'mixes)./ / ('A'mixes).
(12") – ('A'side) / World (the price of dub mix).

Aug 93. (c-s) **WORLD (THE PRICE OF LOVE). / ('A'mixes)** [13] [92]
(12"+=)(cd-s+=) ('A' perfecto + sexy club mixes)
(cd-s) – ('A' Brothers in rhythm mix) / ('A' dubstramental mix) / ('A' World in action mix) / ('A' pharmacy dub)

Dec 93. (12")(c-s)(cd-s) **SPOOKY. / (3 'A' mixes-magimix-minimix-moulimix)** [22] [ ]
(cd-s) – ('A' out of order mix) / ('A' stadium mix) / ('A'-in Heaven mix) / ('A'-Boo-dub mix) / ('A' stadium instrumental).

Nov 94. (7")(c-s) **TRUE FAITH '94. / ('A'-Perfecto mix)** [9] [ ]
(12"+=) – ('A'-sexy disco dub mix) / ('A'-TWA Gim Up North mix).
(cd-s++=) – ('A'radio mix).

Nov 94. (cd)(c)(d-lp) **? (THE BEST OF)** (compilation) [4] [78]
– True faith '94 / Bizarre love triangle '94 / 1963 / Regret / Fine time / The perfect kiss / Shellshock / Thieves like us / Vanishing point / Run (2) / Round and round '94 / World (price of love) / Ruined in a day / Touched by the hand of God / Blue Monday '88 / World in motion.

Jan 95. (c-s)(cd-s) **NINETEEN63 (Arthur Baker remix)./ ('A'-'94 album version)/ ('A'-Lionrock full throttle mix)/ ('A'-Joe T Venelli remix)** [21] [ ]
(12") – ('A'-Lionrock & Joe T mixes / True faith (Eschreamer mix)/ ('A'-Eschreamer dub).
(cd-s) – ('A'-Arthur Baker remix) / Let's go/ Spooky (Nightstripper mix)/ True faith '87 (Shep Pettibone mix).

Jul 95. (c-s) **BLUE MONDAY - 95 / ('A'-original)** [17] [ ]
(12"+=)(cd-s+=) – ('A'-Hardfloor mix) / ('A'-Jam & Spoon mix).

Jul 95. (c-s)(cd-s) **BIZARRE LOVE TRIANGLE (new mix)** [-] [98]
Aug 95. (cd)(c) **THE REST OF NEW ORDER** (remixes, etc) [ ] [ ]

– other compilations, etc. –

Dec 81. Factory Benelux; (12"m) **EVERYTHING'S GONE GREEN (extended). / MESH / CRIES AND WHISPERS** [-] [-] Belg'm

(cd-ep iss.Jul90)
Nov 82. Factory Benelux; (m-lp) **NEW ORDER 1981-82** [-] [-] Belg'm
Jun 84. Factory Benelux; (12") **MURDER. / THIEVES LIKE US (instrumental)** [-] [-] Belg'm
Sep 86. Strange Fruit; (12"ep) **THE PEEL SESSIONS** (1.6.82) [54] [-]
– Turn the heater on / We all stand / 586 / Too late.
(c-ep Jul87) (cd-ep Aug88)
Oct 87. Strange Fruit; (12"ep) **THE PEEL SESSIONS** (29.1.81) [ ] [-]
– Truth / Senses / I.C.B. / Dreams never end. *(cd-ep.May88)*
Mar 88. Factory/ US= Qwest; (7")(12") **BLUE MONDAY 1988. / THE BEACH** [3] [68]
(cd-s+=) – ('A'original).
Sep 90. Strange Fruit; (cd)(c)(m-lp) **THE PEEL SESSIONS** (above tracks) [ ] [-]
Feb 92. Windsong; (cd)(c)(lp) **BBC RADIO 1 LIVE IN CONCERT (live Jun'87)** [33] [-]
– Touched by the hand of God / Temptation / True faith / Your silent face / Every second counts / Bizarre love triangle / Perfect kiss / Age of consent / Sister Ray.

— In Mar'89, issued two 5"cd-videos of TRUE FAITH + BLUE MONDAY '88.

ELECTRONIC

BERNARD SUMNER – vocals, guitar / **JOHNNY MARR** – guitar (ex-SMITHS) + both programmers. also with **NEIL TENANT** – vocals (of PET SHOP BOYS)

Factory Warners
Dec 89. (7")(c-s) **GETTING AWAY WITH IT. / LUCKY BAG** [12] [38]
(12"+=)(cd-s+=)/ /(12"ltd.+=) – ('A'extended)./ / ('A'extra mixes).

— added further guests **CHRIS LOWE, DONALD JOHNSON, DAVID PALMER, DENISE JOHNSON, HELEN POWELL + ANDREW ROBINSON** (on same track)

Apr 91. (7")(c-s) **GET THE MESSAGE. / FREE WILL** [8] [ ]
(cd-s+=)/ /(12"+=) – ('A' DNA groove mix)./ / ('A' 2 other mixes).
May 91. (cd)(c)(lp) **ELECTRONIC** [2] [ ]
– Idiot country / Reality / Tighten up / The patience of a saint / Gangster / Soviet / Get the message / Try all you want / Some distant memory / Feel every beat
Sep 91. (7")(c-s) **FEEL EVERY BEAT. / LEAN TO THE INSIDE** [39] [ ]
(12"+=) – ('A'dub version).
(cd-s+=) – Second to none / ('A' DNA mix)

Next with NEIL TENANT again.

Parlophone Warners
Jun 92. (7") **DISAPPOINTED. / IDIOT COUNTRY TWO** [6] [ ]
(12"+=)(cd-s+=) – ('A'-808 State mix) /('B'ultimatum mix).

REVENGE

PETER HOOK – bass with **DAVE HICKS** – words, vocals / **C.JONES**

Factory Warners
Nov 89. (7") **REASONS. / JESUS I LOVE YOU** [ ] [ ]
(12"+=) – Love you 2.
(cd-s+=) – ('B'version) / Bleach boy.
May 90. (7")(c-s) **PINEAPPLE FACE. / 14K** [ ] [ ]
(12"+=) – ('A'-Revenge version).
(cd-s+=) – ('A'-Last Lunge version).
Jun 90. (cd)(c)(lp) **ONE TRUE PASSION** [ ] [ ]
– Pineapple face / Big bang / Lose the chrome / Slave / Bleachman / Surf Nazi / Fag hag / It's quiet.
Sep 90. (7") **(I'M NOT YOUR) SLAVE. / AMSTERDAM** [ ] [ ]
(12"+=)(cd-s+=) – ('A' II version) / Slave.

— DAVE HICKS departed Apr'91, replaced by **POTTSY**

Dec 91. (12"ep)(cd-ep) **GUN WORLD PORN** [ ] [-]
– Deadbeat (remix) / Cloud nine / State of shock / Little pig.

The OTHER TWO

STEPHEN + GILLIAN

Parlophone Warners
Oct 91. (7")(c-s) **TASTY FISH (Pascal mix). / ('A'mix)** [ ] [-]
(12"+=)(cd-s+=) – ('A'-almond slice mix).

London London
Oct 93. (7")(c-s) **SELFISH. / SELFISH (that pop mix)** [46] [ ]
(12") (all 4 versions)
(cd-s+=) – ('A'-East Village vocal mix) / ('A'-Waterfront mix).
Nov 93. (cd)(c)(lp) **THE OTHER TWO AND YOU** [ ] [ ]
– Tasty fish / The greatest thing / Selfish / Movin' on / Ninth configuration / Feel this love / Spirit level / Night voice / Innocence.
(cd+=) Love it.

NEW POWER GENERATION (see under ⇒ PRINCE)

NEW RIDERS OF THE PURPLE SAGE

Formed: San Francisco, California, USA ... 1970, by NELSON and DAWSON, who incorporated the services of JERRY GARCIA (GRATEFUL DEAD), for their self-titled album in 1971 for 'Columbia'. They had been support band to GD, as a project for GARCIA, PHIL LESH and MICKEY HART, but the latter 2 were soon deposed by SPENCER DRYDEN and DAVE TORBERT. Their 2nd album 'POWERGLIDE', also reached the US Top 40, but with now no GRATEFUL DEAD connection, others failed to score. • **Style:** Country-rock outfit, incorporating hillbilly and rock'n'roll. • **Songwriters:** DAWSON penned most on their debut, but all group shared duties on follow up. Covered; HELLO MARY LOU (Ricky Nelson) / WILLIE AND THE HAND JIVE (Johnny Otis) / LONESOME L.A.COWBOY (Peter Rowan) / KICK IN THE HEAD (Robert Hunter) / etc. • **Trivia:** ROBERT HUNTER of GD, also initially wrote lyrics.

Recommended: THE BEST OF NEW RIDERS OF THE PURPLE SAGE (*7)

JOHN 'Marmaduke' DAWSON – acoustic guitar, vocals (ex-NEW DELHI RIVER BAND) / **DAVID NELSON** – vocals, guitars, mandolin / **DAVE TORBERT** – bass, acoustic guitar, vocals (ex-NEW DELHI RIVER BAND) / with **SPENCER DRYDEN** – drums, percussion (ex-JEFFERSON AIRPLANE) repl. MICKEY HART (of GRATEFUL DEAD) except 2 tracks / **JERRY GARCIA** – guitars, banjo (of GRATEFUL DEAD) / **COMMANDER CODY** – piano (2)

C.B.S. Columbia
Oct 71. (lp)(c) **THE NEW RIDERS OF THE PURPLE SAGE** [ ] [39] Sep 71
– I don't know you / Whatcha gonna do / Portland woman / Henry / Dirty business / Glendale train / Garden of Eden / All I ever wanted / Last lonely eagle / Louisiana lady. *(re-iss.Feb88 on 'Edsel')*
Oct 71. (7") **LOUISIANA LADY. / LAST LONELY LADY** [-] [ ]
Jan 72. (7") **I DON'T KNOW YOU. / GARDEN OF EDEN** [-] [ ]

— Basic 4-piece (DAWSON, NELSON, TORBERT and **DRYDEN** – now full-time) / added **BUDDY CAGE** – pedal steel guitar

Jun 72. (lp)(c) **POWERGLIDE** [ ] [33] May 72
– Dim lights, thick smoke (and loud, loud music) / Rainbow / California day / Sweet lovin' one / Lochinvar / I don't need no doctor / Contract / Runnin' back to you / Hello Mary Lou / Duncan and Brody / Willie and the hand jive.
Jun 72. (7") **I DON'T NEED NO DOCTOR. / RUNNIN' BACK TO YOU** [-] [81]
Dec 72. (7") **I DON'T NEED NO DOCTOR. / CALIFORNIA DAY** [ ] [-]
Dec 72. (7") **DIM LIGHTS, THICK SMOKE (AND LOUD, LOUD MUSIC). / RAINBOW** [-] [ ]
Dec 72. (lp)(c) **GYPSY COWBOY** [ ] [85]
– Gypsy cowboy / Whiskey / Groupie / Sutter's mill / Death and destruction / Linda / On my way back home / Superman / She's no angel / Long black veil / Sailin'.
Feb 73. (7") **GROUPIE. / SHE'S NO ANGEL** [-] [ ]
Oct 73. (lp)(c) **THE ADVENTURES OF PANAMA RED** [ ] [55]
– Panamas red / It's alright with me / Lonesome L.A. cowboy / Important exportin' man / One too many stories / Kick in the head / You should have seen me running / L.A. lady / Thank the day / Cement, clay and glass. *(re-iss.Feb89 on 'B.G.O.', cd-iss.Aug92)*
Feb 74. (7") **PANAMA RED. / CEMENT, CLAY AND GLASS** [-] [ ]
Jun 74. (lp)(c) **HOME, HOME ON THE ROAD (live)** [ ] [68] Apr 74
– Hi, hello, how are you / She's no angel / Groupie / Sunday Susie / Kick in the head / Truck drivin' man / Hello Mary Lou / Sutter's mill.

— **SKIP BATTIN** – bass (ex-BYRDS, ex-Solo artist) repl. TORBERT to KINGFISH

Nov 74. (7") **YOU ANGEL YOU. / PARSON BROWN** [-] [ ]
Jan 75. (lp)(c) **BRUJO** [ ] [68] Oct 74
– Old man Noll / Ashes of love / You angel you / Instant armadillo blues / Workingman's woman / On the Amazon / Big wheels / Singing cowboy / Crooked judge / Parson Brown / Neon rose.
Dec 75. (lp)(c) **OH, WHAT A MIGHTY TIME** [ ] [ ] Nov 75
– Mighty time / I heard you been layin' my old lady / Strangers on a train / Up against the wall Redneck / Take a letter to Maria / Little old lady / On top of old Smokey / Over and over / La bamba / Going round the Horn / Farewell Angelina.

M.C.A. M.C.A.
May 76. (7") **FIFTEEN DAYS UNDER THE HOOD. / DON'T PUT HER DOWN** [-] [ ]
Jul 76. (lp)(c) **NEW RIDERS** [ ] [ ] Jun 76
– Fifteen days under the hood / Annie May / You never can tell / Hard to handle / Dead flowers / Don't put her down / The honky tonkin' (I guess I done me some) / She's looking better after every beer / Can't get over you / The swimming song.
Aug 76. (7") **DEAD FLOWERS. / SHE'S LOOKING BETTER AFTER EVERY BEER** [ ] [ ]

STEVE LOVE – bass (ex-RICK NELSON's STONE CANYON BAND) repl. BATTIN who joined FLYING BURRITO BROTHERS.

Feb 77. (7") **JUST ANOTHER NIGHT IN RENO. / HOME GROWN** [-] [ ]
Apr 77. (lp)(c) **WHO ARE THOSE GUYS** [ ] [ ]
– I can heal you / High rollers / Peggy Sue / Just another night in Reno / It never hurts to be nice to somebody / Love has strange ways / Hold on it's coming / By and by / When I need you / Home grown / Red hot woman and ice cold beer.
May 77. (7") **LOVE HAS STRANGE WAYS. / RED HOT WOMAN AND ICE COOL BEER** [ ] [ ]
Feb 78. (lp)(c) **MARIN COUNTY LINE** [ ] [ ]
– Jasper / Twenty good men / Echoes / Take a red / Knights and queens / A good woman likes to drink with the boys / Turkeys in a straw / Green eyes a flashing / Little Miss Bad / Echoes / Till I met you / Oh what a night / Llywelyn.

— **ALLEN KEMP** – guitar, vocals / **PATRICK SHANAHAN** – drums / **MICHAEL WHITE** – bass repl. DRYDEN + LOVE

not issued A & M
Feb 81. (lp)(c) **FEELIN' ALRIGHT** [-] [ ]
– Night for making love / No other love / The way she dances / Tell me / Fly right / Crazy little girl / Full Moon at midnite / Pakalolo man / Daydreamin' girl / Saralyn.
Apr 81. (7") **NIGHT FOR MAKING LOVE. / FLY RIGHT** [-] [ ]
Jul 81. (7") **FULL MOON AT MIDNIGHT. / NO OTHER LOVE** [-] [ ]

not issued M.U.
1982?. (lp) **KEEP ON KEEPIN' ON** [-] [ ]
– Keep on keepin' on / Now I call it love / It's o.k. to cry / Bounty hunter / Barbaric splendor / Senorita / Night of the living lonely / Rancher's daughter / Big Ed / Friend of the Devil.

— Disbanded after last independent album.

– compilations, others, etc. –

Dec 76. CBS/ US= Columbia; (lp)(c) **THE BEST OF NEW RIDERS OF THE PURPLE SAGE** [ ] [ ]
1988. Relix; (lp)(cd) **VINTAGE** [-] [ ]

NEW YORK DOLLS

Formed: New York, USA ... Dec'71 by THUNDERS, JOHANSEN, MURCIA, KANE & RIVETS. In Mar'72, RIVETS left to form The BRATS, and was replaced by SYLVAIN. On 6 Nov'72, MURCIA died after drowning in his own bath (not to contrary belief from a drug overdose). He was soon superseded by NOLAN, as they signed to 'Mercury', Mar'73. Their TODD RUNDGREN produced eponymous debut album came out in the summer of '73, but sold moderately enough for a GEORGE MORTON produced 2nd, 'TOO MUCH TOO SOON' in 1974. Early the following year, they brought in Londoner MALCOLM McLAREN as manager, but it was clear their short trail was at an end. • **Style:** Comparisons drew on the ROLLING STONES, as JOHANSEN was a dead-ringer in voice and looks for MICK JAGGER. THUNDERS too, was similar to the other 'Glimmer Twin' KEITH RICHARDS. Their trashy transvestite attire, also was derived from The STONES (circa '66 'Have You Seen Your Mother . . . '). Their other sources of inspiration came from MC5, The PRETTY THINGS, PINK FAIRIES and The SHANGRI-LAS'S! Their double-axed guitar sound, although limited and punk-rock like, was effective nonetheless. • **Songwriters:** JOHANSEN with THUNDERS or SYLVAIN. Covered PILLS (Bo Diddley) / DON'T START ME TALKIN' (Sonny Boy Williamson) / SHOWDOWN (Archie Bell) / SOMETHIN' ELSE (Eddie Cochran) / etc. • **Trivia:** 2 songs 'PERSONALITY CRISIS' & 'WHO ARE THE MYSTERY GIRLS', appeared on the 1977 Various Artists compilation 'NEW WAVE'. • **Johansen's filmography:** Married To The Mob + Scrooged.

Recommended: NEW YORK DOLLS (*8) / TOO MUCH TOO SOON (*7)

DAVID JOHANSEN (b. 9 Jan'50, Staten Island, New York) – vocals / **JOHNNY THUNDERS** (b.JOHN GENZALE, 15 Jul'54) – guitar, vocals / **SYLVAIN SYLVAIN** (b.SIL MIZRAHI) – guitar, vocals repl. RICK RIVETS / **ARTHUR KANE** (b. 3 Feb'51) – bass JERRY NOLAN (b. 7 May'51) – drums repl. BILLY MURCIA who died.

Mercury / Mercury

Jul 73. (7") **TRASH. / PERSONALITY CRISIS** -

Aug 73. (lp)(c) **NEW YORK DOLLS** Jul 73
– Personality crisis / Looking for a kiss / Vietnamese baby / Lonely planet boy / Frankenstein / Trash / Bad girl / Subway train / Pills / Private world / Jet boy. *(US re-iss.1984)*

Nov 73. (7") **JET BOY JET GIRL. / VIETNAMESE BABY** -

Jul 74. (lp)(c) **TOO MUCH TOO SOON** May 74
– Babylon / Stranded in the jungle / Who are the mystery girls? / (There's gonna be a) Showdown / It's too late / Puss 'n' boots / Chatterbox / Bad detective / Don't start me talkin' / Human being. *(US re-iss.1984)*

Jul 74. (7") **STRANDED IN THE JUNGLE. / WHO ARE THE MYSTERY GIRLS?**

not issued / Fan Club

1974. (7"ep) **LOOKING FOR A KISS (live). / WHO ARE THE MYSTERY GIRLS? (live) / SOMETHIN' ELSE (live)** -

— **PETER JORDAN** – bass (the roadie filled in on stage when KANE was drunk)

— Disbanded mid 1975, after **BOBBY BLAIN** – keyboards repl. CHRIS ROBINSON who had repl. THUNDERS (he formed The HEARTBREAKERS with NOLAN). **TOMMY MACHINE** (was last drummer). The NEW YORK DOLLS reformed again with JOHANSEN and SYLVIAN but only toured until late '76. SYLVIAN later formed The CRIMINALS.

– compilations, others, etc. –

Jun 77. Mercury; (7"m) **JET BOY, JET GIRL. / BABYLON / WHO ARE THE MYSTERY GIRLS?** -

Jul 77. Mercury; (d-lp) **NEW YORK DOLLS / TOO MUCH TOO SOON** -
(re-iss.Apr89)

1985. Mercury; (lp) **NIGHT OF THE LIVING DOLLS** -

1983. R.O.I.R.; (c) **LIPSTICK KILLERS – MERCER ST.SESSIONS** -
(lp/cd. iss.May90 on 'Danceteria') (cd-iss.Feb95 on 'ROIR Europe')

Sep 82. Kamera; (12"ep) **PERSONALITY CRISIS / LOOKING FOR A KISS. / SUBWAY TRAIN / BAD GIRL** -
(re-iss.Feb86) (cd-ep re-iss.Jul90 on 'See For Miles')

1985. Antler; (7")(12"pic-d)(12"red) **PERSONALITY CRISIS. / SUBWAY TRAIN** -

1985. Antler; (7")(12"pic-d)(12"blue) **LOOKING FOR A KISS. / BAD GIRL** -

1986. Receiver; (lp) **AFTER THE STORM** -

Sep 84. Fan Club; (red-m-lp) **RED PATENT LEATHER (rec. 75)** - - France
– Girls / Downtown / Private love / Personality crisis / Pills / Something else / Daddy rollin' stone / Dizzy Miss Lizzy. *(cd-iss.Oct88) (cd-iss.Feb93 on 'Receiver')*

Oct 84. Fan Club; (7"white) **PILLS (live). / DOWN, DOWN, DOWN TOWN (live)** - -

Oct 94. Mercury; (cd) **ROCK'N'ROLL**

DAVID JOHANSEN

–.vocals, keyboards with his group **STATEN ISLAND BOYS: THOMAS TRASK** – guitar / **JOHHNY RAO** – guitar / **BUZZ VERNO** – bass (ex-CHERRY VANILLA) / **FRANKI LA ROCKA** – drums (ex-CHERRY VANILLA)

Blue Sky / Blue Sky

Jul 78. (lp)(c) **DAVID JOHANSEN** May 78
– Funky but chic / Girls / Pain in my heart / Not that much / Donna / Cool metro / I'm a lover / Lonely tenement / Frenchette.

Sep 78. (7") **FUNKY BUT CHIC. / THE ROPE (THE LET GO SONG)**

Sep 79. (lp)(c) **IN STYLE**
– Melody / She / Big city / She knew she was falling in love / Swaheto woman / Justine / In style / You touched me too / Wreckless crazy / Flamingo road.

Sep 79. (7") **MELODY. / RECKLESS CRAZY** -

Mar 80. (7")(12") **SWAHETO WOMAN. / SHE KNEW SHE WAS FALLING IN LOVE** 1979

— with new band **BLONDIE CHAPLIN** – guitar, vocals / **ERNIE BROOKS** – bass / **TOM MANDEL** – organ / **BOBBY BLAIN** – piano / **TONY MACHINE** – drums

Aug 81. (lp)(c) **HERE COMES THE NIGHT**
– She loves strangers / Bohemian love pad / You fool me / My obsession / Marquesa de Sade / Here comes the night / Suspicion / Party tonight / Havin' so much fun / Rollin' job / Heart of gold. *(cd-iss.Oct94 on 'Rewind')*

Sep 81. (7") **HERE COMES THE NIGHT. / SHE LOVES STRANGERS** -

Jun 82. (7") **BOHEMIAN LOVE PAD. / MEDLEY: WE GOTA GET OUT OF THIS PLACE – DON'T BRING ME DOWN (live)** -

1982. (lp) **LIVE IT UP** -
(cd-iss.Jan 94 on 'Legacy')

— now with **JOE DELIA** – keyboards / **DAVID NELSON** – guitar / **BRETT CARTWRIGHT** – bass / **DENNIS McDERMOTT** – drums

10-Virgin / Passport

Feb 85. (lp)(c) **SWEET REVENGE**

Mar 85. (7")(12") **HEARD THE NEWS. / KING OF BABYLON**

BUSTER POINDEXTER & HIS BANSHEES OF BLUE

(aka DAVID JOHANSEN)

R.C.A. / R.C.A.

Jun 88. (7")(12") **HOT HOT HOT. / CANNIBAL** 45 Nov 87

Jul 88. (lp)(c)(cd) **BUSTER POINDEXTER** 90 Jan 88
– Smack dab in the middle / Bad boy / Hot hot hot / Are you lonely for me baby / Screwy music / Good morning judge / Oh me oh my (I'm a fool for you baby) / Whadaya want? / House of the rising sun / Cannibal / Heart of gold.

Jul 88. (7") **OH ME, OH MY (I'M A FOOL FOR YOU BABY). / CANNIBAL** -

Sep 88. (7") **HEART OF GOLD. / HIT THE ROAD JACK** -

1989. (7") **ALL NIGHT PARTY. / ('A'-hot mix)** -

1989. (7") **UNDER THE SEA. / DEBOURGE YOURSELF** -

Oct 94. Sequel-Rhino; (cd) **BUSTER'S HAPPY HOUR**

NICE

Formed: London, England . . . Oct'67 by ex-GARY FARR & THE T-BONES members KEITH EMERSON and LEE JACKSON, who had just previously with DAVID O'LIST and BRIAN DAVISON, been back-up to British black soul singer P.P.ARNOLD. Being part of Andrew Loog Oldham's 'Immediate' label, they moved to different musical direction, and issued first 45 'THOUGHTS OF EMERLIST DAVJACK'. This flopped, as did its same titled debut lp containing their show-stopper 'RONDO', early in '68. In the summer, they surprised nearly everyone, when their re-indition of Leonard Bernstein's 'AMERICA' (from 'West Side Story'), nearly hit UK Top 20. It was banned in the States, however, when their promotional poster featured recently deceased Martin Luther King, Bobby and John F.Kennedy. At a concert at The Royal Albert Hall, they burned an American flag, which riled Bernstein enough to prevent the 45 being issued in the US. Although their next lp failed, their subsequent ones all went Top 5. • **Style:** Pioneers of classical-rock, they at times dislocated classic music, arranging new interpretations, around the keyboard-stabbing showman KEITH EMERSON. He also went on to become the greatest ivory-tinkler after forming EMERSON, LAKE & PALMER. • **Songwriters:** Group compositions, using first letters of forenames (aka 'EMERLIST DAVJACK' until O'LIST left in 1968). Covered AMERICA (Sondheim / Bernstein) / INTERMEZZO FROM KARELIA SUITE (Sibelius) / HANG ON TO A DREAM (Tim Hardin) / SHE BELONGS TO ME + MY BACK PAGES + COUNTRY PIE (Bob Dylan) / and other classical re-inditions.

Recommended: THE NICE COLLECTION (*8)

KEITH EMERSON (b. 2 Nov'44) – keyboards / **DAVID O'LIST** – guitar, vocals / **BRIAN DAVISON** (b.25 May'42, Leicester, England) – drums / **LEE JACKSON** (b. 8 Jan'43, Newcastle, England) – vocals, bass

Immediate / Immediate

Nov 67. (7") **THE THOUGHTS OF EMERLIST DAVJACK. / AZRIAL (ANGEL OF DEATH)**

Dec 67. (lp) **THE THOUGHTS OF EMERLIST DAVJACK**
– Flower king of flies / The thoughts of Emerlist Davjack / Bonnie K. / Rondo / War and peace / Tantalising Maggie / Dawn / The cry of Eugene / Angel of death / America: 1A (adapted from 'West Side Story') – 1B second amendment / The diamond hard apples of the Moon. *(re-iss.Jul 68) (re-iss.1978 on 'Charly') (cd-iss.1988 on 'Line') (cd-iss.1990's on 'Repertoire')*

Jun 68. (7") **AMERICA. / THE DIAMOND HARD APPLES OF THE MOON** 21
(re-iss.Dec82)

— now a trio, when O'LIST departed, later joining ROXY MUSIC

Dec 68. (lp) **ARS LONGA VITA BREVIS**
– Daddy, where did I come from? / Little Arabella / Happy Freuds / Intermezzo from Karelia / Don Edito el Gruva / Ars longa vita brevis – Prelude: 1st movement – Wakening ; 2nd movement – Realisation ; 3rd movement – Acceptance – Brandenburger ; 4th movement – Denial / Coda – Extention to the big note. *(cd-iss.1990's on 'Castle')*

Dec 68. (7") **BRANDENBURGER. / HAPPY FREUDS** -

Jul 69. (7") **SHE BELONGS TO ME. / ('A'version)** -

Aug 69. (lp) **THE NICE** 3
– Azrael revisited / Hang on to a dream / Diary of an empty day / For example / Rondo 69 / She belongs to me. *(cd-iss.1990's on 'Repertoire')*

Charisma / Mercury

Jun 70. (lp)(c) **FIVE BRIDGES SUITE** 2

– The five bridges suite:- Fantasia, 1st bridge – 2nd bridge – Choral, 3rd bridge – High level fugue, 4th bridge – Finale, 5th bridge / Intermezzo Karelia suite:- Pathetique, 'Symphony No.6. 3rd movement' / Country pie – Bach: Brandenburg concerto No.6 / One of those people. *(cd-iss.Feb91 on 'Virgin')*

Jul 70. (7") **COUNTRY PIE. / ONE OF THOSE PEOPLE** | | |

— Disbanded mid 1970. KEITH formed EMERSON, LAKE AND PALMER. LEE and BRIAN later surfaced as REFUGEE and made one eponymous album in 1974 for 'Charisma', which featured future YES man, PATRICK MORAZ.

– compilations, others, etc. –

Apr 71. Charisma/ US= Mercury; (lp)(c) **ELEGY (live)** | 5 | |
– Hang on to a dream / My back pages / 3rd movement – Pathetique / America (from 'West Side Story'). *(cd-iss.Feb91 on 'Virgin') (cd-iss.Jun93 on 'Virgin' +=)* – Diamonds blue apples of the Moon / Dawn / Tantalising Maggie / The cry of Eugene / Daddy, where did I come from? / Aziral.

1972. Charisma/ US= Mercury; (lp)(c) **AUTUMN 67 SPRING 68** | | |

Mar 83. Charisma; (d-c) **FIVE BRIDGES SUITE / AUTUMN 67 AND SPRING 68** | | - |

Mar 76. Immediate; (lp) **AMOENI REDIVI** | | - |

Jan 78. Immediate; (lp) **THE NICE GREATEST HITS** | | - |

Dec 93. Immediate; (cd) **THE BEST OF THE NICE – AMERICA** | | - |

Nov 85. Castle; (d-lp)(d-c)(cd) **THE NICE COLLECTION** | | - |
– America 1A (adapted from 'West Side Story') – 1B Second amendment / Happy Freuds / The cry of Eugene / The thoughts of Emerlist Davjack / Rondo / Daddy, where did I come from? / Little Arabella / Intermezzo from Karelia / Hang on to a dream / The diamond hard apples of the Moon / Angel of death / Ars longa vita brevis – Prelude:- 1st movement – Wakening, 2nd movement – Realisation, 3rd movement – Acceptance, Brandenburger, 4th movement – Denial / Coda – Extention to the big note. *(re-iss.cd Apr94)*

Aug 87. Seal; (lp)(c) **THE 20th ANNIVERSARY OF THE NICE** | | - |
(cd-iss.Apr88 on 'Bite Back')

Feb 72. Mercury; (d-lp) **KEITH EMERSON WITH THE NICE** (4th + 5th albums) | - | |
(cd-iss. 1988)

Mar 94. Laserlight; (cd)(c) **AMERICA** | | - |

Nov 95. Charly; (3xcd-box) **THE IMMEDIATE YEARS** | | - |

Stevie NICKS

Born: STEPHANIE NICKS, 26 May '48, Phoenix, Arizona, USA. Raised in California, she was part of early 70's Bay Area duo BUCKINGHAM-NICKS, who issued one self-titled album in 1973. Early in 1975, guitarist LINDSEY BUCKINGHAM was asked by the troubled and strife UK/US outfit FLETWOOD MAC to replace BOB WELCH. He said yes on the assurance that they also took on STEVIE. They did and the results were the most fruitful of MAC's long history. The album 'FLEETWOOD MAC' soon climbed to US No.1 and was followed in 1977 by an even greater seller 'RUMOURS', which like it's predessor stayed in the charts for nearly three years. During the next decade and a bit, she appeared on 'TUSK' (1979) / 'LIVE' (1980) / 'MIRAGE' (1982) / 'TANGO IN THE NIGHT' (1987) + her last before she departed; 'BEHIND THE MASK'. During the period, she also carved out own solo career, beginning with 1981's US No.1 album 'BELLA DONNA'. It's success was due to hit single augmented by TOM PETTY & THE HEART-BREAKERS; 'STOP DRAGGIN' MY HEART AROUND'. For the rest of the 80's and early 90's, she continued to have hit after hit. • **Style:** Angelic looking and dreamy sounding AOR songstress. • **Songwriters:** Writes herself except; covers MAYBE LOVE (Nowells-Stewart) / JUST LIKE A WOMAN (Bob Dylan) / DOCKLANDS (Trevor Horn- Betsy Cook).

Recommended: BELLA DONNA (*6) / TIMESPACE – THE BEST OF (*7)

W.E.A. | Modern

Jul 81. (7") **STOP DRAGGIN' MY HEART AROUND. ("STEVIE NICKS with TOM PETTY & THE HEARTBREAKERS") / KIND OF WOMAN** | 50 | 3 |

Jul 81. (lp)(c) **BELLA DONNA** | 11 | 1 |
– The highwayman / Stop draggin' my heart around / Bella Donna / Edge of 17 / Kind of woman / Leather and lace / Outside the rain / After the glitter fades / Think about it / How still my love. *(cd-iss.Jan84) (re-iss.+cd.Aug89 & Mar91 on 'EMI')*

Sep 81. (7") **LEATHER AND LACE (w/DON HENLEY). / BELLA DONNA** | - | 6 |

Oct 81. (7") **LEATHER AND LACE. / OUTSIDE THE RAIN** | | - |

— (above featured DON HENLEY duet)

Feb 82. (7") **EDGE OF 17. / ('A' live)** | - | 11 |

May 82. (7") **EDGE OF 17. / OUTSIDE THE RAIN** | | - |

Jun 82. (7") **AFTER THE GLITTER FADES. / THINK ABOUT IT** | - | 32 |

Jun 83. (7") **STAND BACK. / GARBO** | | 5 |
(12"+=) – Wild heart.

Jun 83. (lp)(c)(cd) **THE WILD HEART** | 28 | 5 |
– If anyone falls / Gate and garden / Enchanted / Sable on blond / Nightbird / Stand back / I will run to you / The wild heart / Nothing ever changes / Beauty and the beast. *(cd-iss.Jan84) (re-iss.+cd.Oct89 on 'EMI')*

Aug 83. (7") **IF ANYONE FALLS. / WILD HEART** | - | 14 |

Sep 83. (7") **IF ANYONE FALLS. / GATE & GARDEN** | | - |

Jan 84. (7") **NIGHTBIRD. / NOTHING EVER CHANGES** | | - |

Jan 84. (7") **NIGHTBIRD. / GATE AND GARDEN** | - | 33 |

— (above featured SANDY STEWART duet)

Parlophone | Modern

Dec 85. (lp)(c)(cd) **ROCK A LITTLE** | 30 | 12 |
– Sister honey / I can't wait / Rock a little / Imperial hotel / I sing for the things / Some become strangers / The nightmare / Has anyone ever written anything for you / If I were you / No spoken word / Talk to me.

Dec 85. (7")(12") **I CAN'T WAIT. / ROCK A LITTLE** | 54 | - |

Feb 86. (7") **I CAN'T WAIT. / THE NIGHTMARE** | - | 16 |

Mar 86. (7") **TALK TO ME . / ONE MORE BIG TIME ROCK'N'ROLL STAR** | 68 | 4 | Nov 85
(12"+=) – Imperial hotel.

Aug 86. (7") **HAS ANYONE EVER WRITTEN ANYTHING FOR YOU. / IMPERIAL HOTEL** | - | 60 |

Aug 86. (7") **HAS ANYONE EVER WRITTEN ANYTHING FOR YOU. / I CAN'T WAIT** | | - |
(12"+=) – No spoken word.

E.M.I. | Modern

Apr 89. (7")(c-s) **ROOMS ON FIRE. / ALICE** | 16 | 16 |
(12"+=)(cd-s+=) – Has anyone ever written anything for you.

Jun 89. (7") **TWO KINDS OF LOVE (w/BRUCE HORNSBY). / REAL TEARS** | - | |

Jun 89. (lp)(c)(cd) **THE OTHER SIDE OF THE MIRROR** | 3 | 10 |
– Rooms on fire / Long way to go / Two kinds of love / Oh my love / Ghosts / Whole lotta trouble / Fire burning / Cry wolf / Alice / Juliet / Doing the best I can (escape from Berlin) / I still miss someone. *(re-iss.cd+c Mar94)*

Jul 89. (7") **LONG WAY TO GO. / REAL TEARS** | 60 | |
(12"+=) – ('A' remix).
(c-s+=)(cd-s+=) – No spoken word.

Oct 89. (7") **WHOLE LOTTA TROUBLE. / GHOSTS** | - | |

Nov 89. (7") **WHOLE LOTTA TROUBLE. / EDGE OF 17** | 62 | |
(12"+=) – Beauty and the beast (live).
(c-s+=)(cd-s+=) – Rooms on fire.

Aug 91. (7")(c-s) **SOMETIMES IT'S A BITCH. / DESERT ANGEL** | 40 | 56 |
(12"+=)(cd-s+=) – Battle of the dragons.

Aug 91. (cd)(c)(lp) **TIMESPACE – THE BEST OF STEVIE NICKS** (compilation) | 15 | 30 |
– Sometimes it's a bitch / Stop draggin' my heart / Whole lotta trouble / Talk to me / Stand back / Beauty and the beast / If anyone falls / Rooms on fire / Love's a hard game to play / Edge of seventeen / Leather and lace / I can't wait / Has anyone ever written anything for you. *(cd+=)* Desert angel.

Nov 91. (7")(c-s) **I CAN'T WAIT (remix). / EDGE OF 17 (live)** | 47 | |
(cd-s+=) – ('A'version) / Sleeping angel.
(12") – ('A'side) / ('A'dub version) / Sleeping angel.

— with **MICHAEL CAMPBELL** (co-writer) **+ BERNIE LEADON + ANDY FAIRWEATHER LOW + WADDY WACHTEL** – guitars / **PETER MICHAEL** – percussion / **PAT DONALDSON** – bass / **BENMONT TENCH** – hammond organ / **ROY BITTAN** – piano / **KENNY ARONOFF** – drums

May 94. (cd)(c) **STREET ANGELS** | 16 | 45 |
– Blue denim / Gretta / Street angel / Docklands / Listen to the rain / Destiny / Unconditional love / Love is like a river / Rose garden / Maybe love will change your mind / Just like a woman / Kick it / Jane.

Jun 94. (7")(c-s) **MAYBE LOVE WILL CHANGE YOUR MIND. / ('A'mix)** | 42 | 57 |
(cd-s+=) – Inspiration / Has anyone ever written anything for you.
(cd-s) – ('A'side) / Thousand days / I can't wait / Stand back.

NICO

Born: CHRISTA PAFFGEN, 1938, Cologne, W.Germany. Her father died in a concentration camp, and she travelled as a girl with her mother through Europe. Having a liking for opera, she learned to play classical piano and harmonium. In 1959, while vacationing in Italy, she was introduced by new friends to film director Federico Fellini. After a bit-part in 'La Dolce Vita', she became top model and appeared in Vogue magazine. In the early 60's, while working in films, she became girlfriend of French actor Alain Delon. She later give birth to his son, to add to her daughter of actor/dancer Eric Emerson. In 1963, she fell in love with up and coming folk-star BOB DYLAN, who wrote 'I'LL KEEP IT WITH MINE' for her. In 1965, at his suggestion, she moved to London and also signed for Andrew Loog Oldham's new label 'Immediate'. One single 'I'M NOT SAYING' (written by GORDON LIGHTFOOT) was issued, but this flopped, even after an appearance on 'Ready Steady Go'. She then moved to New York, where she met pop-artist ANDY WARHOL, who asked her to feature in avant-garde film 'Chelsea Girl'. He also asked her to join LOU REED, JOHN CALE, MO TUCKER, etc. in his managerial group The VEL-VET UNDERGROUND. Together they made one glorious late 1966 lp 'THE VELVET UNDERGROUND AND NICO', but she decided again to try solo work in 1967. After a liason with BRIAN JONES of The ROLLING STONES, she became girlfriend of teenager and new pensmith JACKSON BROWNE, who wrote songs for her debut 1968 lp 'CHELSEA GIRL' (notebly 'THESE DAYS'). Regarded as an artistic triumph, she didn't agree with producer Tom Wilson's string arrangements. She now moved to Los Angeles, and started writing own material for follow-up 'Elektra' album 'THE MARBLE INDEX'. She travelled constantly between America and Europe, and starred in another underground film 'La Cicatrice Interieupe' for Philippe Garrel. In 1971, she was on vinyl again, this time 'DESERTSHORE' was produced by CALE, and guested her son on 1 song 'Le Petit Chevalier'. She fled New York to France, after she was involved in a bottle fight with a girl Black Panther member. On 1st Jun'74, she appeared at The Rainbow, London, alongside JOHN CALE, ENO and KEVIN AYERS. A track 'THE END', was recorded for an album, and 'Island' records promptly signed her, for same titled album, with ENO and PHIL MANZANERA at the helm. That year, she also contributed vocals to KEVIN AYERS' album 'Confessions Of Dr. Dream', but she retired from music to live between Berlin, Los Angeles and Spain. In 1981, she made a comeback album, appropriately titled 'DRAMA OF EXILE', but after poor audience response on a SIOUXSIE & THE BANSHEES support slot, she again went AWOL. She stayed in Manchester, England around this time with her live-in-boyfriend / poet JOHN COOPER CLARKE. After another dismissed vinyl return in 1985, she retired only to re-appear at a 1987 ANDY WARHOL tribute. Tragically on 18 Jul'88, on a holiday in Ibiza with CLARKE, she fell off her bike, and died of a brain haemorrhage. • **Style:** Described as 'The Edith Piaf of the Blank Generation'. An avant-garde moody songstress, who was anti-pop music in every sense. • **Songwriters:** As said, and other covers; THE END (Doors) / DEUTSCHLAND UBER ALLES (German national anthem) / HEROES (David Bowie) / etc. Plus there are obviously a number of VELVET UNDERGROUND re-inditions littered about. • **Trivia:** In 1974, she joined LOU REED and JOHN CALE for a French filmed VELVET UNDERGROUND reunion.

Recommended: CHELSEA GIRL (*7) / THE MARBLE INDEX (*8) / THE BLUE ANGEL (*8).

NICO – vocals (plus session people)

Immediate / not issued

Aug 65. (7") **I'M NOT SAYING. / THE LAST MILE** [ ] [-]
(re-iss.May82) (above 'B'side featured JIMMY PAGE as guitarist/writer)

— In 1966, she teamed up with The VELVET UNDERGROUND on their eponymous lp. Breaking from them the following year, she returned to solo work, augmented by JOHN CALE + LOU REED. Her beau JACKSON BROWNE also became her main songwriter.

not issued / Verve

Feb 68. (lp) **CHELSEA GIRL** [ ] [ ]
– The fairest of the seasons / These days / Little sister / Winter song / It was a pleasure then / Chelsea girls / I'll keep it with mine / Somewhere there's a father / Wrap your troubles in dreams / Eulogy to Lenny Bruce. *(UK-iss.Sep71 on 'M.G.M.') (re-iss.1974 on 'Polydor', cd-iss.May88 & Apr94)*

— Retained JOHN CALE as producer, etc.

Elektra / Elektra

Jul 69. (lp) **THE MARBLE INDEX** [ ] [ ]
– Prelude / Lawns of dawns / No one is there / Ari's song / Facing the wind / Julius Caesar (memento Hodie) / Frozen warnings / Evening of light. *(cd-iss.Apr91 +=)* – Roses in the snow / Nibelungen.

Reprise / Reprise

Jan 71. (lp) **DESERTSHORE** [ ] [ ]
– Janitor of lunacy / Falconer / My only child / Le petit chevalier / Abschied / Afraid / Mutterlein / All that is my own. *(re-iss.1974)*

— She retained **CALE** and brought in **ENO** – synthesizer / **PHIL MANZANERA** – guitar / **STERLING MORRISON** – guitar

Island / Island

Oct 74. (lp)(c) **THE END** [ ] [ ]
– It has not taken long / Secret side / You forgot to answer / Innocent and vain / Valley of the kings / We've got the gold / The end / Das lied der Deutschen. *(cd-iss.Apr94)*

— now with **ANDY CLARKE** – keyboards / **MUHAMMED HADI** – guitar / **DAVEY PAYNE** – sax / **STEVE CORDONA** – drums / **PHILIPPE QUILICHINI** – bass.

Aura / not issued

Jul 81. (lp) **DRAMA OF EXILE** [ ] [-]
– Genghis Khan / Purple lips / One more chance / Henry Hudson / I'm waiting for the man / Sixty forty / The sphinx / Orly flight / Heroes. *(re-iss.1982) (cd-iss.Jul92 on 'Great Expectations')*

Flicknife / not issued

Sep 81. (7") **VEGAS. / SAETA** [ ] [-]

Half / not issued

Jul 82. (7") **PROCESSION. / ALL TOMORROW'S PARTIES** [ ] [-]
(12"+=) – Secret side (live) / Femme fatale (live).

NICO / The FACTION

with **JAMES YOUNG** – keyboards / **GRAHAM DIDS** – percussion

Beggar's B. / not issued

Jun 85. (7")(12") **MY FUNNY VALENTINE. / MY HEART IS EMPTY** [ ] [-]

Jun 85. (lp)(c) **CAMERA OBSCURA** [ ] [ ]
– Camera obscura / Tananore / Win a few / My funny valentine / Das lied von einsamen Madchens / Fearfully in danger / My heart is empty / Into the arena / Konig. *(re-iss.+cd.Jan89 on 'Lowdown-Beggar's')*

— added **ERIC RANDOM** – percussion, etc / **TOBY TOMAN** – drums

Dojo / not issued

Apr 86. (d-lp)(c)(cd) **BEHIND THE IRON CURTAIN (live 1985)** [ ] [-]
– All saints night from a Polish motorway / One more chance / Frozen warnings / The song of the lonely girl / Win a few / Konig / Purple lips / All tomorrow's parties / Fearfully in danger / The end / My funny valentine / 60-40 / Tananoori / Janitor of lunacy / My heart is empty / Femme fatale.

— NICO died 18 Jul'88 (see info above).

– compilations, others, etc. –

1983. R.O.I.R.; (c) **DO OR DIE** [-] [ ]
(re-iss.cd+c May93)

Jun 83. Aura; (7") **HEROES. / ONE MORE CHANCE** [ ] [-]

Sep 85. Aura; (lp)(c)(cd) **THE BLUE ANGEL** (best of) [ ] [ ]
– Femme fatale / All tomorrow's parties / I'll keep it with mine / Chelsea girls / Janitor of lunacy / Heroes / One more chance / Sixty forty / Waiting for the man / The end.

Oct 85. Aura; (7") **I'M WAITING FOR THE MAN. / PURPLE LIPS (live)** [ ] [-]

1987. Dojo; (lp) **LIVE IN TOKYO, JAPAN (live)** [ ] [-]
(cd-iss.1988 & Jun95)

Feb 87. Archive 4; (12"ep) **LIVE (live)** [ ] [-]

Mar 87. V.U.; (pic-lp) **LIVE IN DENMARK (live)** [ ] [-]

May 88. One Over Two; (c) **ON PERSONNE EN EUROPE** [ ] [-]

Nov 88. Strange Fruit; (12"ep)(cd-ep) **THE PEEL SESSIONS** (2/2/71) [ ] [-]
– Secret side / No one is there / Janitor of lunacy / Frozen warnings.

Jun 89. Performance; (lp)(cd) **LIVE HEROES (live)** [ ] [-]

Nov 90. Restless; (cd)(c)(lp) **HANGING GARDENS** [ ] [-]

Jul 92. Great Expectations; (cd) **CHELSEA LIVE (live)** [ ] [-]
(re-iss.Jun94 on 'Cleopatra')

Sep 94. Anagram; (cd) **HEROINE** [ ] [-]

NIGHTMARES IN WAX (see under ⇒ DEAD OR ALIVE)

NIGHT RANGER

Formed: San Francisco, California, USA ... 1981 by BLADES, GILLIS and FITZGERALD. They signed to 'Boardwalk' in the States in 1982, after supporting the likes of Doobie Brothers. • **Style:** Pomp-rock heavies. • **Songwriters:** Mainly BLADE Compositions. • **Trivia:** RUBICON had a US Top 30 hit 'I'M GONNA TAKE CARE OF EVERYTHING' in 1978. Keith Olson produced their album 'MAN IN MOTION'.

Recommended: GREATEST HITS (*5)

JACK BLADES (b.24 Apr'54) – vocals, bass (ex-RUBICON) / **BRAD GILLIS** – guitar (ex-RUBICON, ex-OZZY OSBOURNE) / **JEFF WATSON** (b. 4 Nov'56) – guitar / **ALAN 'FITZ'GERALD** (b.16 Jun'54) – keyboards (ex-SAMMY HAGAR, ex-MONTROSE) / **KELLY KEAGY** (b.15 Sep'52) – drums, vocals

Boardwalk / Boardwalk

Feb 83. (7") **DON'T TELL ME THAT YOU LOVE ME. / NIGHT RANGER** [ ] [40] Jan 83

Feb 83. (lp)(c) **DAWN PATROL** [ ] [38] Dec 82
– Don't tell me that you love me / Sing me away / At night she sleeps / Call my name / Eddie's comin' out tonight / Can't find me a thrill / Young girl in love / Play rough / Penny / Night ranger. *(US cd-iss.Jun88)*

Apr 83. (7") **SING ME AWAY. / PLAY ROUGH** [-] [54]

Jul 83. (7") **CALL MY NAME. / YOUNG GIRL IN LOVE** [-] [ ]

M.C.A. / Camel-MCA

Nov 83. (7") **YOU CAN STILL ROCK IN AMERICA. / LET HIM RUN** [-] [51]

Apr 84. (7") **SISTER CHRISTIAN. / CHIPPIN' AWAY** [ ] [5] Mar 84

Jul 84. (lp)(c) **MIDNIGHT MADNESS** [ ] [15] Nov 83
– Sister Christian / Rumours in the air / Touch of madness / Passion play / When you close your eyes / Chippin' away / Let him run / (You can still) Rock in America / Why does love have to change. *(US cd-iss.Jun88)*

Jul 84. (7") **WHEN YOU CLOSE YOUR EYES. / WHY DOES LOVE HAVE TO CHANGE** [ ] [14]

May 85. (7")(12") **SENTIMENTAL STREET. / NIGHT MACHINE** [ ] [8]

Jun 85. (lp)(c) **7 WISHES** [ ] [10]
– Seven wishes / Faces / Four in the morning (I can't take any more) / I need a woman / Sentimental street / This boy needs to rock / I will follow you / Interstate love affair / Night machine / Goodbye. *(US cd-iss.Jun88)*

Sep 85. (7") **FOUR IN THE MORNING (I CAN'T TAKE ANY MORE). / THE BOY NEEDS TO ROCK** [ ] [19]

Nov 85. (7") **GOODBYE. / SEVEN WISHES** [-] [17]

Apr 87. (7") **COLOUR OF YOUR SMILE. / GIRLS WILL LIKE IT** [ ] [ ]
(12"+=) – When you close your eyes / Don't tell me that you love me.

Apr 87. (lp)(c)(cd) **BIG LIFE** [ ] [28]
– Big life / Color of your smile / Love is standing near / Rain comes crashing down / The secret of my success / Carry on / Bedtter let it go / I know tonight / Hearts away.

Jun 87. (7") **THE SECRET OF MY SUCCESS. / CARRY ON** [ ] [64] Mar 87
(12"+=) – Sister Christian (live).

Jul 87. (7") **HEARTS AWAY. / BETTER LET IT GO** [-] [90]

— **JESS BRADMAN** – keyboards repl. FITZGERALD

Sep 88. (7") **I DID IT FOR LOVE. / WOMAN IN LOVE** [-] [75]

Oct 88. (lp)(c)(cd) **MAN IN MOTION** [ ] [81]
– Man in motion / Reason to be / Don't start thinking (I'm alone tonight) / Woman in love / Love shot me down / Restless kind / Halfway to the sun / Here she comes again / Right on you / Kiss me where it hurts / Woman in love.

Nov 88. (7") **KISS ME WHERE IT HURTS. / DON'T START THINKING (I'M ALONE TONIGHT)** [-] [ ]

— Disbanded Apr'89, BLADES joined DAMN YANKEES with TED NUGENT. BRADMAN joined the band of JIMMY BAIN.

BRAD, JEFF & KELLY re-formed NIGHT RANGER in Mar'91.

– compilations, others, etc. –

Jul 89. M.C.A.; (lp)(c)(cd) **GREATEST HITS** [ ] [ ]
– You can still rock in America / Goodbye / Sister Christian / The secret of my success / Rumours in the air / Sing me away / When you close your eyes / Sentimental street / Restless kind / Eddie's comin' out tonight.

Nov 90. M.C.A.; (cd)(c)(lp) **LIVE IN JAPAN (live '88)** [ ] [ ]
– Touch of madness / When you close your eyes / Man in motion / Don't start thinking (I'm alone tonight) / Let him run / Goodbye / Reason to be / Four in the morning (I can't take any more) / Sister Christian / Don't tell me you love me / Halfway to the sun / (You can still) Rock in America.

JEFF WATSON

(solo) with **BRAD GILLIS / SAMMY HAGAR / BOB DAISLEY / CARMINE APPICE / STEVE SMITH + ALLAN HOLDSWORTH**

Road-runner / Road-runner

Apr 92. (cd)(c)(lp) **LONE RANGER** [ ] [ ]
– Late one night / Cement shoes / Forest of feelings / Night lifer / Picnic island / Morse minor / Osaka rot / Echo chalet / Talking hands / Pipedream / Song for Rebecca.

NILSSON

Born: HARRY NELSON, 15 Jun'41, Brooklyn, New York, USA. Raised in California, he became a computer worker at The First National Bank in Van Nuys. Around the mid-60's, he started songwriting part-time. His first song recorded 'CUDDLY TOY', which appeared on The MONKEES 1967 lp 'Pisces, Aquarius, Capricorn & Jones Ltd'. He signed to 'RCA' that year, and released debut 45 'YOU CAN'T DO THAT'. In 1969, his version of 'EVERYBODY'S TALKIN'', was chosen for the soundtrack of movie 'Midnight Cowboy', and this became his first US Top 10 hit. Early in 1972, with help from producer Richard Perry, he recorded his finest 3 minutes 'WITHOUT YOU'. It soared to the top on both sides of the Atlantic, and was soon regarded as a classic of the era. For the rest of the 70's, his commerciality waned, and by the early 80's, he was all but forgotten. • **Style:** Classy musical pop star/balladeer, who never quite fulfilled early promise, after his magnus-opus 'WITHOUT YOU'. • **Songwriters:** Wrote own material, alongside covering loads of others; YOU CAN'T DO THAT + SHE'S LEAVING HOME + MOTHER NATURE'S SON (Beatles) / RIVER DEEP, MOUNTAIN HIGH (Phil Spector) / EVERYBODY'S TALKIN' (Fred Neil) / SIMON SMITH AND HIS AMAZING DANCING BEAR (Randy Newman) + all album 'NILSSON SINGS NEWMAN'. / WITHOUT YOU (Badfinger). His album A LITTLE TOUCH OF SCHMILSSON was a set of old standards, and PUSSY CATS (produced by his pal JOHN LENNON) was rock'n'roll covers album. NILSSON's songs that have been hits for others:- ONE (Three Dog Night) / THE STORY OF ROCK AND ROLL (Turtles) / THE PUPPY SONG (David Cassidy) / etc. • **Trivia:** Early in 1969, he wrote first film score 'Skidoo', and even had bit part as a security guard. Two years later, he wrote, narrated and sang songs for the children's fantasy film 'The Point'. In 1974, he provided the score and starred alongside RINGO STARR for the film 'Son Of Dracula'.

Recommended: ALL THE BEST (*7)

NILSSON – vocals, piano with session people and orchestra

not issued | Tower

1964. (7") **I'M GONNA LOSE MY MIND. / 16 TONS** [-] [ ]
1965. (7") **YOU CAN'T AKE YOUR LOVE AWAY FROM ME. / BORN IN GRENADA** [-] [ ]
1966. (7") **GROWING UP. / SHE'S YOURS** [-] [ ]

R.C.A. | R.C.A.

Jun 67. (7") **WITHOUT HER. / FRECKLES** [-] [ ]
Sep 67. (7") **YOU CAN'T DO THAT. / TEN LITTLE INDIANS** [ ] [ ]
Dec 67. (7") **RIVER DEEP, MOUNTAIN HIGH. / SHE BANGS HYMNS OUT OF TUNE** [-] [ ]
Mar 68. (lp) **PANDEMONIUM SHADOW SHOW** [ ] [ ]
– Ten little Indians / 1941 / Cuddly toy / She sang hymns out of tune / You can't do that / Sleep late, my lady friend / She's leaving home / There will never be / Without her / Freckles / It's been so long / River deep, mountain high.
Mar 68. (7") **ONE. / SISTER MARIE** [ ] [ ]
Aug 68. (lp) **AERIAL BALLET** [ ] [ ]
– Good old desk / Don't leave me / Mr. Richland's favorite song / Little cowboy / Together / Everybody's talkin' / I said goodbye to me / Mr. Tinker / One / The wailing of the willow / Bath. *(re-iss.1974)*
Aug 68. (7") **EVERYBODY'S TALKIN'** (withdrawn). / ONE [-] [ ]
—— (Below 'A'side was now used in the film 'Midnight Cowboy')
Aug 69. (7") **EVERYBODY'S TALKIN'. / DON'T LEAVE ME** [ ] [6]
Sep 69. (lp) **HARRY** [ ] [ ] Aug 69
– The puppy song / Nobody cares about the railroads anymore / Open your window / Mother nature's son / Fairfax rag / City life / Mournin' glory story / Marchin' down Broadway / I guess the Lord must be in New York City / Rainmaker / Mr. Bojangles / Simon Smith & his amazing dancing bear. *(re-iss.1974)*
Sep 69. (7") **RAINMAKER. / I WILL TAKE YOU THERE** [-] [ ]
Oct 69. (7") **MAYBE. / THE PUPPY SONG** [ ] [ ]
Oct 69. (7") **I GUESS THE LORD MUST BE IN NEW YORK CITY. / GOOD OLD DESK** [ ] [34] Nov 69
Feb 70. (7") **I'LL BE HOME. / WAITING** [ ] [ ]
Mar 70. (lp) **NILSSON SINGS NEWMAN** [ ] [ ]
– Vine Street / Love story (you and me) / Yellow man / Caroline / Cowboy / The beehive state / I'll be home / Living without you / Dayton Ohio, 1903 / So long, dad. *(re-iss.Sep77, cd-iss.Feb89)*
May 70. (7") **DOWN TO THE JALLY. / BUY MY ALBUM** [ ] [ ]
Apr 71. (lp)(c) **THE POINT!** (animated TV film soundtrack) [46] [25] Mar 71
– Everything's got 'em / The town (narration) / Me and my arrow / The game (narration) / Poli high / The trial and banishment (narration) / Think about your troubles / Thursday (why I did not go to work today) / Blanket for a sail / Down to the valley / The pointed man (narration) / P.O.V. waltz / The clearing in the woods (narration) / Are you sleeping? / Oblio's return (narration). *(re-iss.+cd.Aug91 & Sep93 on 'Demon')*
Mar 71. (7") **ME AND MY ARROW. / ARE YOU SLEEPING?** [-] [34]
Jan 72. (7") **WITHOUT YOU. / GOTTA GET UP** [1] [1] Dec 71
(re-iss.Feb79 on 'RCA Gold')
Jan 72. (lp)(c) **NILSSON SCHMILSSON** [4] [3] Nov 71
– Gotta get up / Driving along / Early in the morning / Moonbeam / Down / Without you / Coconut / Let the good times roll / Jump into the fire / I'll never leave you. *(also in quad-lp) (re-iss.Apr80 & Nov84, cd-iss.Oct87) (re-iss.Sep86 on 'Fame')*
Mar 72. (7") **JUMP INTO THE FIRE. / MOONBEAM** [-] [27]
May 72. (7") **COCONUT. / MOONBEAM** [42] [-]
Jun 72. (7") **COCONUT. / DOWN** [-] [8]
Jul 72. (lp)(c) **SON OF SCHMILSSON** [41] [12]
– Take 54 / Remember (Christmas) / Joy / Turn on your radio / You're breakin' my heart / Spaceman / The lottery song / At my front door / Ambush / I'd rather be dead / The most beautiful girl in the world.
Oct 72. (7") **SPACEMAN. / YOU'RE BREAKIN' MY HEART** [ ] [23] Sep 72
Dec 72. (7") **REMEMBER (CHRISTMAS). / THE LOTTERY SONG** [ ] [53]
Jul 73. (lp)(c) **A LITTLE TOUCH OF SCHMILSSON IN THE NIGHT** [20] [46]
– Lazy Moon / For me and my gal / It had to be you / Always / Makin' whoopee / You made me love you (I didn't want to do it) / Lullaby in ragtime / I wonder who's kissing her now / What'll I do / Nevertheless (I'm in love with you) / This is all I ask / As time goes by. *(cd-iss.Aug91)*
Jul 73. (7") **AS TIME GOES BY. / MAKIN' WHOOPEE!** [ ] [86]
Apr 74. (7") **DAYBREAK. / DAWN** [ ] [39]
May 74. (lp)(c) **SON OF DRACULA (Soundtrack)** [ ] [ ]
– It is he who will be King / Daybreak / At my front door / Count Down meets Merlin and Amber / Moonbeam / Perhaps this is all a dream / Remember (Christmas) / Intro: Without you / The Count's vulnerability / Down / Frankenstein, Merlin and the operation / Jump into the fire / The abdication of Count Down / The end (moonbeam).
—— (above was iss.UK on 'Rapple' & part compilation)
Sep 74. (7") **MANY RIVERS TO CROSS. / DON'T FORGET ME** [ ] [ ]
Sep 74. (lp)(c) **PUSSY CATS** [ ] [60]
– Many rivers to cross / Subterranean homesick blues / Don't forget me / All my life / Old forgotten soldier / Save the last dance for me / Mucho Mungo – Mt. Elga / Loop de loop / Black sails / Rock around the clock. *(cd-iss.Jan92 on 'Demon')*
Nov 74. (7") **MUCHO MUNGO – MT. ELGA. / SUBTERRANEAN HOMESICK BLUES** [-] [ ]
Jan 75. (7") **SAVE THE LAST DANCE FOR ME. / ALL MY LIFE** [ ] [-]
Feb 76. (7") **DON'T FORGET ME. / LOOP DE LOOP** [-] [ ]
Mar 75. (lp)(c) **DUIT EN MON DEI** [ ] [ ]
– It's a jungle out there / Down by the sea / Kojak Columbo / Easier for me / Turn out the light / Salmon falls / Puget sound / What's your sign / Home / Good for God. *(also in quad-lp)*
Jun 75. (7") **KOJAK COLOMBO. / TURN OUT THE LIGHT** [ ] [ ]
Sep 75. (lp)(c)(quad-lp) **SANDMAN** [ ] [ ]
– I'll take a tango / Something true / Pretty soon there'll be nothing left for everybody / The ivy covered walls / Here's why I did not go to work today / How to write a song / The flying saucer song / Will she miss me / Jesus Christ you're tall.
Jan 76. (7") **SOMETHING TRUE. / PRETTY SOON THERE'LL BE NOTHING** [ ] [ ]
May 76. (7") **SAIL AWAY. / MOONSHINE BANDIT** [ ] [ ]
Jul 76. (lp)(c) **NILSSON . . . THAT'S THE WAY IT IS** [ ] [ ]
– That is all / Just one look – Baby I'm yours / Moonshine bandit / I need you / A thousand miles away / Sail away / She sits down on me / Daylight has caught me / Zombie jambouree (back to back) / That is all (reprise).
Jan 77. (7") **WHO DONE IT. / PERFECT DAY** [-] [ ]
Mar 77. (7") **MOONSHINE BANDIT. / SHE SITS DOWN ON ME** [ ] [-]
Jun 77. (7") **ALL I THINK ABOUT IS YOU. / I NEVER THOUGHT I'D GET THIS LONELY** [-] [ ]
Jun 77. (7") **ALL I THINK ABOUT IS YOU. / OLD BONES** [43] [-]
Jul 77. (lp)(c) **KNNILLSSONN** [ ] [ ]
– All I think about is you / I never thought I'd get this lonely / Who done it / Lean on me / Goin' down / Old bones / Sweet surrender / Blanket for a sail / Laughin' man / Perfect day.
Nov 77. (7") **AIN'T IT KINDA WONDERFUL. / I'M BRINGING A RED RED ROSE** [-] [ ]
Nov 77. (7") **LEAN ON ME. / WILL SHE MISS ME** [ ] [ ]

HARRY NILSSON

Mercury | Mercury

Sep 80. (7") **I DON'T NEED YOU. / IT'S SO EASY** [ ] [ ]
Sep 80. (lp)(c) **FLASH HARRY** [ ] [ ]
– Harry / Cheek to cheek / Best move / Old dirt road / I don't need you / Rain / I've got it / It's so easy / How long can disco go on / Bright side of life.
Nov 80. (7") **RAIN. / BRIGHT SIDE OF LIFE** [ ] [ ]

Polydor | Polydor

Aug 84. (7") **LONLINESS. / SILVER HORSE** [ ] [ ]
—— Virtually retired from music business. Died of a heart attack on the 15 Jan'94, aged 52.

– compilations, others, etc. –

Jun 71. RCA; (lp)(c) **AERIAL PANDEMONIUM BALLET** [ ] [ ]
Sep 76. RCA; (7"m) **WITHOUT YOU. / EVERYBODY'S TALKIN' / KOJAK, COLOMBO** [22] [ ]
Jan 77. RCA; (7") **ME AND MY ARROW. / SPACEMAN** [-] [ ]
Jan 77. RCA; (7") **ME AND MY ARROW. / THURSDAY** [ ] [-]
Jun 78. RCA; (lp)(c) **GREATEST HITS** [ ] [ ]
(re-iss.1982, cd-iss.1984)
Jul 81. RCA; (7") **WITHOUT YOU. / EVERYBODY'S TALKIN'** [ ] [ ]
(re-iss.Oct86 on 'Old Gold')
Sep 81. RCA; (lp)(c) **NILSSON'S GREATEST MUSIC** [ ] [ ]
Apr 88. RCA; (cd) **NILSSON** ('RCA Diamond' series) [ ] [ ]
Sep 93. RCA; (cd)(c) **ALL THE BEST** [ ] [-]
– Without you / Everybody's talkin' / Mother nature's son / It's been so long / Good old desk / Without her / Mournin' glory story / Mr. Richland's favourite song / Mr.Bojangles / She's leaving home / Lulaby in ragtime / Makin' whoopee! / Cuddly toy / River deep, mountain high / Little cowboy / As time goes by.
Feb 94. RCA; (7")(c-s) **WITHOUT YOU. / EVERYBODY'S TALKIN'** [47] [ ]
(cd-s+=) – Over the rainbow.
1969. Tower; (7") **GOOD TIME. / GROWING UP** [-] [ ]
Oct 77. D.J.M.; (lp)(c) **EARLY TIMES** [ ] [-]
Oct 79. K-Tel; (lp)(c) **HARRY AND . . .** [ ] [-]
Feb 82. Orchid; (c) **ALL FOR YOUR LOVE** [ ] [-]
Dec 88. BMG; (lp) **A TOUCH MORE SCHMILSSON IN THE NIGHT** (out-takes) [ ] [ ]
Oct 90. BMG; (cd)(c)(lp) **WITHOUT HER – WITHOUT YOU** [ ] [ ]
Oct 92. Old Gold; (cd-ep) **WITHOUT YOU / EVERYBODY'S TALKIN' / COCONUT** [ ] [-]
Oct 94. Woodford; (cd) **SIMPLY THE BEST** [ ] [ ]
Oct 95. Retro-RPM; (cd) **NILSSON '62 – THE DEBUT SESSIONS** [ ] [-]

NINE INCH NAILS

Formed: San Francisco, California, USA . . . 1989 by REZNOR. Toured on the 'Lolla palooza' tour with JANE'S ADDICTION around the same time as they unleashed their debut album 'PRETTY HATE MACHINE'. • **Style:** Violent hard-core alternative metal influenced by KILLING JOKE and obsessed with Charles Manson. They smashed up gear and soaked electrical equipment on stage!!! • **Songwriters:** 'The Terminator' REZNOR penned except PHYSICAL YOU'RE SO (Adam Ant). • **Trivia:** REZNOR appeared in the 1987 film 'LIGHT OF DAY'. ALAN MOULDER is the mixing engineer.

Recommended: PRETTY HATE MACHINE (*7) / BROKEN (*7) / THE DOWNWARD SPIRAL (*8)

TRENT REZNOR – vocals, guitar / **JAMES WOOLEY** – keyboards / **RICHARD** – guitar / **CHRIS VRENNA** – drums

TVT-Island | Nothing-Interscope

Nov 90. (12"ep)(cd-ep) **DOWN IN IT (skin). / TERRIBLE LIE (mix) / DOWN IN IT (shred)** [ ] [ ]
(12"ep)(cd-ep) – (1st 2 tracks) / Down in it (demo)

Sep 91. (7")(10") **HEAD LIKE A HOLE. / ('A'copper mix)** [45] [ ]
(cd-s+=) – ('A'opal mix).

Sep 91. (cd)(c)(lp) **PRETTY HATE MACHINE** [67] [75] Nov 90
– Head like a hole / Terrible lie / Down in it / Sanctified / Something I can never have / Kinda I want to / Sin / That's what I get / The only time / Ringfinger.

Nov 91. (7") **SIN. / GET DOWN MAKE LOVE** [35] [ ]
(10"+=)(cd-s+=) – Sin (dub).

Sep 92. (cd)(c)(lp) **BROKEN** [18] [7]
– Pinion / Wish / Last / Help me I am in Hell / Happiness is slavery / Gave up.
(free 7"+cd+=) – Physical (you're so) / Suck.

Nov 92. (cd)(c)(m-lp) **FIXED** (remixes) [ ] [ ]
– Gave up / Wish / Happiness is slavery / Throw this away / Fist fuck / Screaming slave.

— Below controversially recorded at the house of the Charles Manson murders (some produced by /with FLOOD). Guests on 1 track each were **ADRIAN BELEW + DANNY LOHNER** – guitar / **CHRIS VRENNA + STEPHEN PERKINS + ANDY KUBISZEWSKI +** – drums (live:- **VRENNA, LOHNER, WOOLLEY + ROBIN FINCK**)

Mar 94. (cd)(c)(d-lp) **THE DOWNWARD SPIRAL** [9] [2]
– Mr.Self destruct / Piggy / Heresy / March of the pigs / Closer / Ruiner / The becoming / I do not want this / Big man with a gun / A warm place / Eraser / Reptile / The downward spiral / Hurt.

Mar 94. (etched-7") **MARCH OF THE PIGS. / A VIOLENT FLUID** [45] [59]
(9"+=) – All the pigs, all lined up / Underneath the skin.
(cd-s) – ('A'side) / Underneath the skin / Reptillian.
(cd-s+=) – All the pigs, all lined up / Big man with a gun.

Jun 94. (12")(cd-s) **CLOSER / CLOSER TO GOD / MARCH OF THE FUCKHEADS / HERESY (BLIND) / MEMORABILIA** [25] [41] Sep94
(cd-s) – ('A'side) – (deviation) – (further away) / ('A'original) / ('A'precursor) / ('A'internal).

May 95. (cd)(c) **FURTHER DOWN THE SPIRAL** (remixes) [ ] [23]
– Piggy (nothing can stop me) / The art of destruction (part one) / Self destruction (part three) / Heresy (version) / The downward spiral (the bottom) / Hurt / At the heart of it all / Ruiner (version) / Eraser (denial: realization) / Self destruction: final.

NIRVANA (UK)

Formed: Based in London, England . . . 1967 by former Trinity College, Dublin student PATRICK CAMPBELL-LYONS. After a brief spell in R&B group SECOND THOUGHTS who became JULY, he studied film-making at St.Martin's school. He found partnership with ALEX SPYROPOULOS and RAY SINGER, and became NIRVANA. They interested MUFF WINWOOD (Steve's brother), and signed to 'Island' records in '67. Two singles were issued that year, and one of them 'PENTECOST HOTEL', went to No.1 in parts of Scandanavia, where they attracted a major following. Their debut album, the concept sci-fi pantomine 'THE STORY OF SIMON SIMOPATH', was released early '68, but did little apart from gain airplay on John Peel's Perfumed Garden radio 1 show. In April that year, they had first and only UK Top 40 hit with 'RAINBOW CHASER', but by 1969 they were dropped by Chris Blackwell at 'Island'. That year they had trimmed to a duo, when RAY departed, and after their 1970 'Pye' album 'TO MARKOS III', ALEX thought it better to exit. This left PATRICK to control activities, as his future flitted between NIRVANA and solo releases. • **Style:** Pastel and dreamy psychedelic outfit, run by the talented CAMPBELL-LYONS and SPYROPOULOS. • **Songwriters:** CAMPBELL-LYONS – lyrics, duo penned. • **Trivia:** CAMPBELL-LYONS was also a noted early 70's producer of CLEAR BLUE SKY, JADE WARRIOR and SUNBURST.

Note:- Nothing whatsoever to do with grunge-metal US stars NIRVANA, whom PATRICK thought of sueing for the right of group name.

Recommended: TRAVELLING ON A CLOUD (*7)

PATRICK CAMPBELL-LYONS (b.Waterford, Ireland) – vocals, keyboards, multi / **ALEX SPYROPOULOS** (b.Greece) – keyboards, choral arrangements, multi / **RAY SINGER** – guitar / with **BRIAN HENDERSON** – bass / **MICHAEL COE** – viola, F.horn / **SYLVIA SCHUSTER** – cello / and on session **PETER KESTER** – drums

Island | Bell

Jul 67. (7") **TINY GODDESS. / I BELIEVE IN MAGIC** [ ] [-]

Sep 67. (7") **PENTECOST HOTEL. / FEELIN' SHATTERED** [ ] [-]

Feb 68. (lp) **THE STORY OF SIMON SIMOPATH** [ ] [ ]
– Wings of love / Lonely boy / We can help you / You are just the one / Satellite jockey / In the courtyard of the stars / Pentecost hotel / I never had a love like this before / Take this hand / 1999.

Mar 68. (7") **RAINBOW CHASER. / FLASHBULB** [34] [ ]

May 68. (7") **PENTECOST HOTEL. / WE CAN HELP YOU** [-] [ ]

Sep 68. (lp) **ALL OF US** [ ] [ ]
– Rainbow chaser / Tiny goddess / The touchables (all of us) / Melanie blue / Trapeze / The show must go on / Girl in the park / Miami masquerade / Frankie the great / You can try it / Everybody loves the clown / St. John's Wood affair.

Sep 68. (7") **GIRL IN THE PARK. / C SIDE IN OCHO RIOS** [ ] [-]

Oct 68. (7") **GIRL IN THE PARK. / YOU ARE JUST THE ONE** [-] [ ]

Nov 68. (7") **THE TOUCHABLES (ALL OF US). / TRAPEZE** [ ] [ ] Dec 69

Jan 69. (7") **WINGS OF LOVE. / REQUIEM TO JOHN COLTRANE** [ ] [-]

— Now down to basic duo of PATRICK and ALEX. (RAY went into producing)

1969. (7") **OH! WHAT A PERFORMANCE. / DARLING DARLENE** [ ] [-]

— added on session **BILLY BREMNER** – guitar / **LESLIE DUNCAN** – b.vocals

Pye | Metromedia

1970. (lp) **NIRVANA – TO MARKOS III** [ ] [ ]
– The world is cold without you / Black flower / etc.

Feb 70. (7") **THE WORLD IS COLD WITHOUT YOU. / CHRISTOPHER LUCIFER** [ ] [-]

— NIRVANA were now just PATRICK CAMPBELL-LYONS and session people, incl. JADE WARRIOR + MEL COLLINS (ALEX went on to do TV work, and produce AQUILA) .

Vertigo | not issued

1970. (lp) **LOCAL ANAESTHETIC** [ ] [-]
– Modus operandi (method of work) / Home:- Salutation – Construction – Destruction – Re-construction – Fanfare. *(cd-iss.Jul93 on 'Repertoire')*

1970. (7") **THE SADDEST DAY OF MY LIFE. / (I WANNA GO) HOME** [ ] [-]

Phillips | not issued

1971. (7") **PENTECOST HOTEL. / LAZY DAY DRIFT** [ ] [-]

1972. (7") **RAINBOW CHASER. / AD LIB** [ ] [-]

1972. (lp) **SONGS OF LOVE AND PRAISE** [ ] [-]
– Rainbow chaser / Please believe me / Lord up above / She's lost it / Nova sketch / Pentecost hotel / I need your love tonight / Will there be me / Stadium. *(cd-iss.Sep95 on 'Background')*

1972. (7") **STADIUM. / PLEASE BELIEVE ME** [ ] [-]

PATRICK CAMPBELL-LYONS

went solo with session players and a choir.

Sovereign | not issued

1973. (lp) **ME AND MY FRIEND** [ ] [-]
– Out of nowhere / Friends / Mother England / Everybody should fly a kite / Tomorrow I'll make you smile / Me and my friend / Jesus Christ Junior / I think I want him too / 1974 / Watch out Cassius Clay.

Jan 73. (7") **EVERYBODY SHOULD FLY A KITE. / I THINK I WANT HIM TOO** [ ] [-]

1973. (7") **OUT ON THE ROAD. / ME AND MY FRIEND** [ ] [-]

NIRVANA

were re-formed in name only by sole member PATRICK.

Bradleys | not issued

Feb 76. (7") **TWO OF A KIND. / BEFORE MIDNIGHT** [ ] [-]

PATRICK CAMPBELL-LYONS

again went solo, augmented by ARTHUR BROWN + ALIKI ASHMAN.

Electric | not issued

Mar 77. (7") **THE GURU SONG. / WHISLING FIDDLER** [ ] [-]

NIRVANA

PATRICK tried yet again.

United A. | not issued

Oct 78. (7") **LOVE IS. / PASCALE** [ ] [-]

Apr 79. (7") **RESTLESS WIND. / THANK YOU AND GOODNIGHT** [ ] [-]

PATRICK CAMPBELL-LYONS

again went solo.

Public | Shanachie

1981. (lp) **THE ELECTRIC PLOUGH (concept)** [ ] [-]
(US-title 'THE HERO I MIGHT HAVE BEEN')

Nov 81. (7") **NAKED ROBOTS. / WATCHING BREAKFAST TV** [ ] [-]

NIRVANA

(aaargh!).

Zilch | not issued

Sep 81. (7") **THE PICTURE OF DORIAN GRAY. / NO IT ISN'T** [ ] [-]

Feb 82. (7") **BLACK AND WHITE OR COLOUR. / TALL TREES AND MANSIONS** [ ] [-]

— PATRICK retired from recording, although he tried to keep NIRVANA name alive, especially after formation of the US grunge band.

– compilations, etc. –

Aug 76. Island; (7") **RAINBOW CHASER. / TINY GODDESS** [ ] [-]

Sep 92. Island; (cd) **TRAVELLING ON A CLOUD** [ ] [-]

Apr 87. Bam Caruso; (7") **BLACK FLOWER. / SAVE MY SOUL** [ ] [-]

May 87. Bam Caruso; (lp) **BLACK FLOWER** [ ] [-]
(cd-iss.1994 on 'Edsel')

Feb 95. Edsel; (cd) **SECRET THEATRE** [ ] [-]

Geffen

NIRVANA (US)

Formed: Aberdeen, Washington, USA . . . 1987 by KURT & CHRIS. Released debut 45 'LOVE BUZZ' on US indie label 'Sub Pop' in 1988, before finally issuing first lp 'BLEACH' in 1989. After a quiet following year, they returned in 1991 with a classic! 'NEVERMIND'. It soon raced up the US and UK charts, helped by the lifted track 'SMELLS LIKE TEEN SPIRIT', smashing the hit parade. • **Style:** A blend of punk Pixies, power GUNS'N'ROSES and even melodie of R.E.M.. Their "New-wave" grunge metal shifted music finally into the 90's. • **Songwriters:** COBAIN wrote late 80's work. In the 90's, the group were credited with COBAIN lyrics. Covers; LOVE BUZZ (Shocking Blue) / HERE SHE COMES NOW (Velvet Underground) / DO YOU LOVE ME? (Kiss) / TURNAROUND (Devo) / MOLLY'S LIPS + SON OF A GUN + JESUS WANTS ME FOR A SUNBEAM (Vaselines) / D7 (Wipers) / THE MAN WHO SOLD THE WORLD (David Bowie) / WHERE DID YOU SLEEP LAST NIGHT (Leadbelly). FOO FIGHTERS covered OZONE (Kiss). • **Trivia:** KURT married COURTNEY LOVE (of Hole) in Feb'92, who gave a him child in Aug'92.

Recommended: NEVERMIND (*10) / IN UTERO (*9) / BLEACH (*7) / UNPLUGGED IN NEW YORK (*9) / FOO FIGHTERS (*8; FOO FIGHTERS)

KURT COBAIN (b.20 Feb'67) – vocals, guitar / **CHRIS NOVOSELIC** (b.16 May'65) – bass / **CHAD CHANNING** – drums

Tupelo / Sub Pop

Oct 88. (7") **LOVE BUZZ. / BIG CHEESE** [-] [ ]

— Early '89, added **JASON EVERMAN** – guitar Also guest drummer on 2 tracks **DALE CROVER**

Aug 89. (lp)(cd)(white-lp)(green-lp) **BLEACH** [ ] [ ] Jun 89
– Blew / Floyd the barber / About a girl / School / Paper cuts / Negative creep / Scoff / Swap meet / Mr.Moustache / Sifting / Big cheese. (cd+=) – Love buzz / Downer. *(US re-iss.Dec 91 hit 89) (re-iss.+cd+c.Feb92 on 'D.G.C.', hit UK No.33)* (c+=) – Big cheese. *(re-iss.cd/c Oct95 on 'Geffen')*

Dec 89. (12"ep)(cd-ep) **BLEW / LOVE BUZZ. / BEEN A SON / STAIN** [ ] [-]

— **DAN PETERS** – drums (of MUDHONEY) repl. CHANNING (Apr90)

Jan 91. (7")(7"green) **SLIVER. / DIVE** [ ] [ ] Sep 90
(12"+=) – About a girl (live). *(US-iss.7"blue)*
(cd-s++=) – Spank thru (live).

Feb91. (7")(7"green) **MOLLY'S LIPS. / FLUID** [-] [ ]

not issued / Communion

Mar 91. (7"colrd) **HERE SHE COMES NOW. /('B'by "Melvins")** [-] [ ]

— (Apr91 trio) **DAVID GROHL** (b.14 Jan'69) – drums, vocals (ex-SCREAM) repl. PETERS and EVERMAN, who joined MIND FUNK.

D.G.C. / D.G.C.

Sep 91. (cd)(c)(lp) **NEVERMIND** [7] [1]
– Smells like teen spirit / In bloom / Come as you are / Breed / Lithium / Polly / Territorial pissings / Drain you / Lounge act / Stay away / On a plain / Something in the way. *(cd+=)*– Endless nameless.

Oct 91. (7") **SMELLS LIKE TEEN SPIRIT. / EVEN IN HIS YOUTH** [-] [6]

Nov 91. (7")(c-s) **SMELLS LIKE TEEN SPIRIT. / DRAIN YOU** [7] [-]
(12"+=)/ /(12"pic-d+=) – Even in his youth./ / Aneurysm.
(cd-s+=) – Even in his youth / Aneurysm.

(above only issued in US on c-s/cd-s)

Mar 92. (7") **COME AS YOU ARE. / DRAIN YOU (live)** [-] [32]

Mar 92. (7")(c-s) **COME AS YOU ARE. / ENDLESS NAMELESS** [9] [-]
(12"+=)/ /(cd-s++=) – Drain you (live)./ / School (live).

Jul 92. (7")(c-s) **LITHIUM. / BEEN A SON (live)** [11] [ ]
(12"pic-d+=)/ /(cd-s++=) – Curmudgeons./ / D7.

Nov 92. (7")(c-s) **IN BLOOM. / POLLY** [28] [ ]
(cd-s+=)(12"pic-d+=) – Sliver (live)

Dec 92. (cd)(c)(lp) **INCESTICIDE** (rare material) [14] [39]
– Dive / Sliver / Stain / Been a son / Turnaround / Molly's lips / Son of a gun / (New wave) Polly / Beeswax / Downer / Mexican seafood / Hairspray queen / Aero zeppelin / Big long now / Aneurysm.

— In Feb'93, NIRVANA's 'OH, THE GUILT' appeared on double'A'side with JESUS LIZARD's 'Puss'. Issued on 'Touch & Go' 7"blue +cd-s, it made UK No.12, and crashed out of the Top 60 the following week!.

— GOODBYE MR MACKENZIE's BIG JOHN played guitar live for them in mid'93. In Aug'93, KURT KOBAIN and WILLIAM S.BURROUGHS narrated 'The Priest, They Call Him By' on 10"lp,cd 'T.K.'.

Aug 93. (7")(c-s) **HEART-SHAPED BOX. / MARIGOLD** [5] [ ]
(12"+=)(cd-s+=) – Milk it.

Sep 93. (cd)(c)(lp)(clear-lp) **IN UTERO** [1] [1]
– Serve the servants / Scentless apprentice / Heart-shaped box / Rape me / Frances Farmer will have her revenge on Seattle / Dumb / Very ape / Milk it / Penny royal tea / Radio friendly unit shifter / Tourette's / All apologies / Gallons of rubbing alcohol flow through the strip.

Dec 93. (7")(c-s) **ALL APOLOGIES. / RAPE ME** [32] [ ]
(12"+=)(cd-s+=) – MV.

— On the 4th March '94, KURT overdosed while on holiday in Italy and went into a coma. A month later, on the 8th April he committed suicide, by shooting himself through the mouth. He was only 27, and this was certainly the biggest rock star death since JOHN LENNON. For more details see HOLE and the COURTNEY LOVE story.

— below album featured **LORI GOLDSTON** – cello + **MEAT PUPPETS' Curt & Cris Kirkwood** on 3rd, 4th & 5th last songs.

Nov 94. (cd)(c)(white-lp) **UNPLUGGED IN NEW YORK** (live acoustic) [1] [1]
– About a girl / Come as you are / Jesus doesn't want me for a sunbeam / Dumb / The man who sold the world / Pennyroyal tea / Polly / On a plain / Something in the way / Plateau / Oh me / Lake of fire / All apologies / Where did you sleep last night.

— GROHL (now vox, guitar) formed The FOO FIGHTERS, taking their name from the mysterious lights that were reported by fighter pilots during World War 2. He recruited ex-GERMS guitarist PAT SMEAR. Meanwhile NOVOSELIC formed the trio SWEET 75.

compilations, etc

Nov 95. Geffen; (6xcd-s) **6 CD SINGLE BOXED SET** [ ] [-]

FOO FIGHTERS

DAVE GROHL – vocals, guitar / **PAT SMEAR** – guitar (ex-GERMS) / **NATE MANDEL** – bass / **WILLIAM GOLDSMITH** – drums (both of SUNNY DAY REAL ESTATE) – signed to 'Capitol' through below . . .

Rosswell / Rosswell

Jun 95. (7") **THIS IS A CALL. / WINNEBAGO** [5] [ ]
(12"+=)(cd-s+=) – Podunk.

Jun 95. (cd)(c)(lp) **FOO FIGHTERS** [3] [23]
– This is a call / I'll stick around / Big me / Alone and easy target / Good grief / Floaty / Weenie beenie / Oh, George / For all the cows / X-static / Watershed / Exhausted.

Sep 95. (7"red)(c-s) **I'LL STICK AROUND. / HOW I MISS YOU** [18] [ ]
(12"+=)(cd-s+=) – Ozone.

Nov 95. (7"blue)(c-s) **FOR ALL THE COWS. / WATTERSHED (live)** [28] [ ]
(cd-s+=) – ('A'live at Reading).

NORTHSIDE

Formed: Manchester, England . . . mid '88, by DERMO, etc (see below). Like so many other Mancunian outfits, found local contract at Tony Wilson's 'Factory' records early in 1990, and soon released debut single 'SHALL WE TAKE A TRIP', which scraped into UK Top 50. • **Style:** Psychedelic rock/rave band typical of the new drug-influenced scene. • **Songwriters:** Group compositions, although they did SOLISBURY HILL (Peter Gabriel) on stage.

Recommended: CHICKEN RHYTHMS (*7)

WARREN 'Dermo' DERMODY – vocals / **TIMMY WALSH** – guitar repl. ? / **CLIFF OGIER** – bass / **PAUL 'Walt' WALSH** – drums

Factory / Qwest

May 90. (7")(12") **SHALL WE TAKE A TRIP. / MOODY PLACES** [50] [ ]

Oct 90. (7")(12")(c-s) **MY RISING STAR. / ('A'instrumental)** [32] [ ]
(cd-s+=) – Shall we take a trip / Moody places.

May 91. (7")(12")(c-s) **TAKE 5. / WHO'S TO BLAME (instrumental)** [40] [ ]
(cd-s+=) – ('A'other version).

Jun 91. (cd)(c)(lp) **CHICKEN RHYTHMS** [19] [ ]
– Take 5 / Weight of air / Funky Munky / A change is on it's way / Yeah man / Tour de world / Wishful thinking / Shall we take a trip / Who's to blame / Practice makes perfect.

— Disbanded later in the year.

NOTTING HILLBILLIES (see under ⇒ DIRE STRAITS)

NOVA MOB (see under ⇒ HUSKER DU)

Ted NUGENT

Born: 13 Dec'49, Detroit, Michigan, USA. In 1966, he formed garage-rock Chicago band The AMBOY DUKES, who quickly signed to 'Mainstream' US, releasing debut 'BABY PLEASE DON'T GO' in 1967. Their eponymous lp, early '68 broke into the Top 200, and by the Summer, the 45 'JOURNEY TO THE CENTER OF THE MIND', was in the US Top 20. Although they toured constantly in the US for the next couple of years, the band only managed minor chart placings. In 1971, they transgressed to TED NUGENT & THE AMBOY DUKES, who were snapped up by FRANK ZAPPA's 'Discreeet' label and unleashed 2 albums in the mid-70's, before dissolving. In 1975, NUGENT subscribed to a solo deal with 'Epic', and hit US Top 30 with eponymous Tom Werman produced debut early '76. His next album in 1977, 'FREE FOR ALL' (which featured MEAT LOAF) ventured further, and was first to earn him a Top 40 placing in UK. • **Style:** Controversial heavy-metal axeman, whose love of hunting animals and blood sports was well-publicised. A vehement non-drug taker, he sacked anyone in the band who dabbled with them. Early in 1978, he enscribed his name with a bowie knife on the arm of a fan! • **Songwriters:** NUGENT penned, except BABY PLEASE DON'T GO (hit; Them). The DAMN YANKEES credited TED, TOM & JACK. • **Trivia:** In 1973 while working on new record deal, he featured alongside other stars MIKE PINERA (Iron Butterfly), WAYNE KRAMER (MC5) and FRANK MARINO (Mahogany Rush), on 'battle of the guitarists' stage shows.

Note: There was another UK group called The AMBOY DUKES, and they released several singles on 'Polydor', around the mid 60's to '68.

Recommended: GREAT GONZOS (*8)

AMBOY DUKES

(UK = "AMERICAN AMBOY DUKES"). **TED NUGENT** – guitar, vox / plus **JOHN DRAKE** – vocals / **STEVE FARMER** – guitar / **BILL WHITE** – bass / **RICK LOBER** – keys / **DAVID PALMER** – drums

Fontana / Mainstream

1967. (7") **BABY PLEASE DON'T GO. / PSALMS OF AFTERMATH** [-] [ ]
1967. (7") **LET'S GO GET STONED. / IT'S NOT TRUE** [ ] [-]
1968. (lp) **THE AMBOY DUKES** [ ] [ ] Jan 68
– Baby please don't go / I feel free / Young love / Psalms of aftermath / Colors / Let's go get stoned / Down on Philips escalator / The lovely lady / Night time / It's not true / Gimme love. *(cd-iss.Dec92 on 'Repertoire' +=)*– J.B. special.

— **RUSTY DAY** – vocals repl. DRAKE and FARMER / **ANDY SOLOMAN** – keyboards repl. LOBER **GREG ARAMA** – bass repl. WHITE

London / Mainstream

Jul 68. (7") **JOURNEY TO THE CENTER OF THE MIND. / MISSISSIPPI MURDERER** [ ] [16]
Aug 68. (lp) **JOURNEY TO THE CENTER OF THE MIND** [ ] [74]
– Mississippi murderer / Surrender to your kings / Flight of the Byrd / Scottish tea / Dr. Slingshot / Journey to the center of the mind / Ivory castles / Why is a carrot more orange than an orange? / Missionary Mary / Death is life / Saint Philips friend / I'll prove I'm right / (Conclusion). *(cd-iss.Dec92 on 'Repertoire' +=)*– You talk sunshine, I breathe fire.
Oct 68. (7") **SCOTTISH TEA. / YOU TALK SUNSHINE, I BREATHE FIRE** [-] [ ]
1969. (lp) **MIGRATION** [ ] [ ]
– Migration / Prodigal man / For his namesake / I'm not a juvenile delinquent / Good natured Emma / Inside the outside / Shades of green and grey / Curb your elephant / Loaded for bear. *(cd-iss.Dec92 on 'Repertoire' +=)*– Sobbin' in my mug of bear.
1969. (7") **PRODIGAL SON. / GOOD NATURED EMMA** [-] [ ]
1969. (7") **MIGRATION. / FLIGHT OF THE BIRDS** [-] [ ]

Polydor / Polydor

Mar 70. (lp) **MARRIAGE ON THE ROCKS – ROCK BOTTOM** [ ] [ ]
– Marriage:- (a) Part 1 – Man / (b) Part 2 – Woman / (c) Part 3 – Music / Breast-fed 'gator (bait) / Get yer guns / Non-conformist wilderbeast man / Today's lesson / Children of the woods / Brain games of the yesteryear / The inexhaustable quest for the cosmic garbage (part 1 & 2) / (excerpt from Bartok).

— **NUGENT** brought in new members **BOB GRANGE** – bass / **KJ KNIGHT** – drums retaining also **ANDY SOLOMAN** (RUSTY DAY joined CACTUS)

TED NUGENT & THE AMBOY DUKES

Mar 71. (lp) **SURVIVAL OF THE FITTEST** (live) [ ] [ ]
– Survival of the fittest / Rattle my snake / Mr. Jones' hanging party / Papa's will / Slidin' on / Prodigal man.

— Disbanded in the early 70's, but in 1973 re-surfaced as

TED NUGENT'S AMBOY DUKES

with others **BOB GRANGE** – bass / **ANDY JEZOWSKI** – vocals / **GABRIEL MAGNO** – keyboards / **VIC MASTRIANNI** – drums

Discreet / Discreet

Jun 74. (lp)(c) **CALL OF THE WILD** [ ] [ ]
– Call of the wild / Sweet revenge / Pony express / Ain't it the truth / Renegade / Rot gut / Below the belt / Cannon balls. *(re-iss.+cd.Oct89 on 'Edsel')*
Jun 74. (7") **SWEET REVENGE. / AIN'T IT THE TRUTH** [ ] [ ]

— **Rev.ATROCIOUS THEODOLIUS** – guitar, vocals repl. MAGNO
1975. (lp)(c) **TOOTH FANG & CLAW** [ ] [ ]
– No holds barred / Sacha / The great white buffalo / Maybelline / Free flight / Hibernation / Living in the woods / Lady luck.

— TED finally gave up AMBOY DUKES in 1975.

TED NUGENT

(solo) with **ROB GRANGE** – bass / **DEREK ST.HOLMES** – vocals, guitar (ex-SCOTT) / **CLIFF DAVIS** – drums / plus guests.

Epic / Epic

Nov 75. (7") **MOTORCITY MADNESS. / WHERE HAVE YOU BEEN ALL MY LIFE** [-] [ ]
Mar 76. (lp)(c) **TED NUGENT** [56] [28] Nov 75
– Stranglehold / Stormtroopin' / Hey baby / Just what the doctor ordered / Snakeskin cowboy / Motor city madhouse / Where have you been all my life / You make me feel right at home / Queen of the forest. *(re-iss.Mar81)*
Mar 76. (7") **HEY BABY. / STORMTROOPIN'** [ ] [72]
(above poss.rel.UK Feb77)
Oct 76. (lp)(c) **FREE-FOR-ALL** [33] [24] Sep 76
– Dog eat dog / Free-for-all / Together / Hammerdown / Writing on the wall / Light my way / Street rats / I love you so I told you a lie / Turn it up. *(re-iss.Jan84)*
Nov 76. (7") **DOG EAT DOG. / LIGHT MY WAY** [-] [91]
Nov 76. (7") **DOG EAT DOG. / I LOVE YOU SO I TOLD YOU A LIE** [ ] [-]
Jan 77. (7") **FREE-FOR-ALL. / STREET RAGS** [ ] [-]
Jun 77. (lp)(c) **CAT SCRATCH FEVER** [28] [17]
– Cat scratch fever / Wang dang sweet poontang / Death by misadventure / Live it up / Home bound / Workin' hard, playin' hard / Sweet Sally / A thousand nights / Fist fightin' son of a gun / Out of control. *(cd-iss.Jun89)*
Jun 77. (7") **CAT SCRATCH FEVER. / WANG DANG SWEET POONTANG** [-] [ ]
Jul 77. (7") **CAT SCRATCH FEVER. / A THOUSAND NIGHTS** [ ] [-]
Feb 78. (7") **HOME BOUND. / DEATH BY MISADVENTURE** [ ] [70]
Feb 78. (d-lp)(c) **DOUBLE LIVE GONZO! (live)** [47] [13]
– Just what the doctor ordered / Wang dang sweet poontang / Cat scratch fever / Stormtroopin' / Hibernation / Motor city madhouse / Stranglehold / Gonzo / Baby please don't go / Yank me, crank me / Great white buffalo.
Mar 78. (7") **YANK ME, CRANK ME (live). / CAT SCRATCH FEVER (live)** [-] [58]

— **CHARLIE HUHN** – vocals, vocals repl. ST.HOLMES (to ST.PARADISE, etc) **DAVID HULL** – bass repl. BOB GRANGE (also to ST.PARADISE)
Nov 78. (lp)(c) **WEEKEND WARRIORS** [ ] [24]
– Tight spots / Weekend warriors / Need you bad / Smokescreen / Cruisin' / Name your poison / Venom soup / Good friends and a bottle of wine / I got the feelin' / One woman.
Dec 78. (7") **NEED YOU BAD. / I GOT THE FEELIN'** [-] [84]

— **WALTER MONAHAN** – bass repl. HULL
Jun 79. (lp)(c)(US-pic-lp) **STATE OF SHOCK** [ ] [18] May 79
– Alone / Bite down hard / I want to tell you / It doesn't matter / Paralyzed / Saddle sore / Satisfied / Snake charmer / State of shock / Take it or leave it.
Jun 79. (7") **I WANT TO TELL YOU. / BITE DOWN HARD** [-] [ ]
Jul 79. (7") **I WANT TO TELL YOU. / PARALYSED** [ ] [-]
May 80. (7")(12") **FLESH AND BLOOD. / MOTOR CITY MADHOUSE** [ ] [-]
Jun 80. (lp)(c) **SCREAM DREAM** [37] [13] May 80
– Wango tango / Scream dream / Hard as nails / I gotta move / Violent love / Flesh and blood / Spit it out / Come and get it / Terminus Eldorada / Don't cry.
Jul 80. (7") **WANGO TANGO. / SCREAM DREAM** [-] [86]
Feb 81. (7") **LAND OF A THOUSAND DANCES. / THE TNT OVERTURE** [-] [ ]
Apr 81. (lp)(c) **(INTENSITIES) IN 10 CITIES** [75] [51]
– Put up or shut up / Spontaneous combustion / My love is like a tire iron / Jailbait / I am a predator / Heads will roll / The flying lip lock / Land of a thousand dances / The TNT overture / I take no prisoners.
Dec 81. (lp)(c) **GREAT GONZOS! THE BEST OF TED NUGENT** (compilation) [ ] [ ]
– Cat scratch fever / Just what the doctor ordered / Free-for-all / Dog eat dog / Motor city madness / Paralysed / Stranglehold / Baby please don't go / Wango tango / Wang dang sweet poontang.

— **DEREK ST.HOLMES** – vocals returned from WHITFORD / ST.HOLMES to repl. HUHN / **DAVE KISWINEY** – bass repl. MONAGHAN / **CARMINE APPICE** – drums (ex-VANILLA FUDGE, ex-CACTUS, etc.) repl. DAVIS

Atlantic / Atlantic

Aug 82. (lp)(c) **NUGENT** [ ] [51] Jul 82
– No, no, no / Bound and gagged / Habitual offender / Fightin' words / Good and ready / Ebony / Don't push me / Can't stop me now / We're gonna rock tonight / Tailgunner.
Sep 82. (7") **BOUND AND GAGGED. / HABITUAL OFFENDER** [-] [ ]
Nov 82. (7") **NO, NO, NO. / HABITUAL OFFENDER** [-] [ ]

— **NUGENT** recruited entire new band again! **BRIAN HOWE** – vocals / **ALAN ST.JOHN** – keyboards / **DOUG LABAHN** – bass / **BOBBY CHOUINARD** – drums
Feb 84. (lp)(c) **PENETRATOR** [ ] [56]
– Tied up in love / (Where do you) Draw the line / Knockin' at your door / Don't you want my love / Go down fighting / Thunder thighs / No man's land / Blame it on the night / Lean mean R&R machine / Take me home.
Feb 84. (7") **TIED UP IN LOVE. / LEAN MEAN R&R MACHINE** [ ] [-]
Apr 84 (7") **(WHERE DO YOU) DRAW THE LINE. / LEAN MEAN R&R MACHINE** [ ] [-]

— Took time out to appear in 'Miami Vice' US TV programme. He also played on charity single 'Stars' by aggregation 'HEAR'N AID' circa Spring 1986.

— **DAVE AMATO** – guitar, vocals repl. HOWE who joined BAD COMPANY / **RICKY PHILIPS** – bass (ex-BABYS) repl. LABAHN
Nov 86. (lp)(c)(cd) **LITTLE MISS DANGEROUS** [ ] [76] Mar 86
– High heels in motion / Strangers / Little Miss Dangerous / Savage dancer / Crazy ladies / When your body talks / My little red book / Take me away / Angry young man / Painkiller.
Apr 86. (7") **HIGH HEELS IN MOTION. / ANGRY YOUNG MAN** [-] [ ]
Jul 86. (7") **LITTLE MISS DANGEROUS. / ANGRY YOUNG MAN** [-] [ ]

— **NUGENT** re-recruited **DEREK ST.HOLMES** – vocals, guitar / **DAVE KISWINEY** – bass / plus new drummer – **PAT MARCHINO**
Feb 88. (lp)(c)(cd) **IF YOU CAN'T LICK 'EM . . . LICK 'EM** [ ] [ ]
– Can't live with 'em / She drives me crazy / If you can't lick 'em . . . lick 'em / Skintight / Funlover / Spread your wings / The harder they come (the harder I get) / Separate the men from the boys, please / Bite the hand / That's the story of love.

DAMN YANKEES

TED NUGENT – guitar / **TOMMY SHAW** – vocals (ex-STYX) / **JACK BLADES** – bass (ex-NIGHT RANGER) / **MICHAEL CARTELLONE** – drums, non-s/writer

Warners / Warners

Apr 90. (cd)(c)(lp) **DAMN YANKEES** [26] [13] Mar 90
– Coming of age / Bad reputation / Runaway / High enough / Damn Yankees / Come again / Mystified / Rock city / Tell me how you want it / Piledriver.
Apr 90. (c-s)(cd-s) **COMING OF AGE. / TELL ME HOW YOU WANT IT** [-] [60]
Jan 91. (7") **HIGH ENOUGH. / PILEDRIVER** [ ] [3] Oct 90
(12"+=)(cd-s+=) – Bonestripper.
Apr 91. (c-s) **COME AGAIN. / ('A' radio version)** [-] [50]
Aug 92. (cd)(c)(lp) **DON'T TREAD** [ ] [22]
– Don't tread on me / Fifteen minutes of fame / Where you goin' now / Dirty dog / Mister please / Silence is broken / Firefly / Someone to believe / This side of Hell / Double coyote / Uprising. *(re-iss.cd Feb95)*
Jan 93. (7")(c-s) **WHERE YOU GOIN' NOW. / THIS SIDE OF HELL** [ ] [20] Sep 92
(12"+=)(cd-s+=) – ('A'version).
Apr 93. (c-s)(cd-s) **SILENCE IS BROKEN. /** [-] [62]
(12"+=)(cd-s+=) – High enough (live) / ('A'live version).

Ted NUGENT

— returned w/ **ST.HOLMES / LUTZ**

Atlantic / Atlantic

Dec 95. (cd)(c) **SPIRIT OF THE WILD** [ ] [86] May95
– Thighraceous / Wrong side of town / I shoot back / Tooth, fang and claw / Lovejacker / Fred bear / Primitive man / Hot or cold / Kiss my ass / Heart and soul / Spirit of the wild / Just do it like this.

– more compilations, others, etc. –

Feb 83. Epic; (d-c) **TED NUGENT / FREE FOR ALL** [ ] [-]
Sep 86. Raw Power; (d-lp)(d-c) **ANTHOLOGY** [ ] [-]
(re-iss.cd+c.Feb91 on 'Castle')
May 91. Thunderbolt; (cd)(c) **ON THE EDGE** [ ] [-]
Jun 93. Sony; (cd) **THE VERY BEST OF TED NUGENT** [ ] [ ]
May 94. Epic-Legacy; (d-cd)(d-c) **OUT OF CONTROL** [ ] [ ]
1975. Mainstream; (lp) **DR.SLINGSHOT (AMBOY DUKES)** [-] [ ]
Apr 75. Polydor; (d-lp) **JOURNEYS & MIGRATIONS (AMBOY DUKES)** [ ] [ ]
Jun 77. Polydor; (d-lp) **MARRIAGE ON THE ROCKS – ROCK BOTTOM / SURVIVAL OF THE FITTEST (AMBOY DUKES)** [ ] [ ]
1977. Warners; (d-lp) **TWO ORIGINALS OF . . . (AMBOY DUKES)** [ ] [ ]
– (CALL OF THE WILD & TOOTH, FANG & CLAW) albums

Gary NUMAN

Born: GARY WEBB, 8 Mar'58, Hammersmith, London, England. In 1977, he formed punk outfit MEAN STREET, who appeared on Various Artists live compilation 'Live At The Vortex'. To end the year, he set up TUBEWAY ARMY, which was basically his solo project, accompanied on live work by PAUL GARDINER and uncle GERALD LIDYARD. Their debut vinyl outing 'THAT'S TOO BAD', was issued by indie punk label 'Beggar's B.' early '78. Their eponymous debut lp, virtually went unnoticed, but things dramatically changed in Jun'79, when they/he had first No.1 with 'ARE FRIENDS ELECTRIC', spurred on by a stunning appearance on UK's 'Top Of The Pops'. Its parent album 'REPLICAS', also shot to the top in the same month. In August, he decided to release next '45 'CARS' as GARY NUMAN. This quickly shot to the top, as did yet another 1979 album 'THE PLEASURE PRINCIPLE'. The following year, he had a few Top 10 hits, and another No.1 lp 'TELEKON'. He continued throughout the 80's as mainly Top 50 artist. In 1984 he formed his own label 'Numa', to issue own product, plus brother JOHN's outfit HOHOKAM. • **Style:** NUMAN played futuristic-synth based rock-pop, and was a confessed plagiarist of BOWIE. NUMAN found his own clone-type fans, as BOWIE had ventured into other areas of rock and pop. • **Songwriters:** Wrote own material, with inspiration from psi-fi writers (i.e. WILLIAM S.BURROUGHS). Covered 1999 + U GOT THE LOOK (Prince). • **Trivia:** NUMAN appeared on ROBERT PALMER's 'Clues' album in 1980, and was part of initial off-shoot outfit DRAMATIS. In the early 80's, he took up flying planes, and bought own aircrafts (mainly warplanes).

Recommended: THE GARY NUMAN COLLECTION (*7) / THE PLEASURE PRINCIPLE (*6) / REPLICAS (*7; TUBEWAY ARMY)

TUBEWAY ARMY

GARY NUMAN – vocals, guitar, synthesizer, keyboards (ex-MEAN STREET) / **PAUL 'Scarlett' GARDINER** – bass / **GERALD 'Rael' LIDYARD** – drums

Beggars Banquet / not issued

Feb 78. (7") **THAT'S TOO BAD. / OH! DIDN'T I SAY** [ ] [-]

— **BARRY BENN** – drums repl. BOB SIMMONDS who had repl. LIDYARD / added **SEAN BURKE** – guitar

Jul 78. (7") **BOMBERS. / O.D. RECEIVER. / BLUE EYES** [ ] [-]
Aug 78. (lp)(c)(blue-lp) **TUBEWAY ARMY** [ ] [-]
– Listen to the sirens / My shadow in vain / The life machine / Friends / Something's in the house / Every day I die / Steal and you / My love is a liquid / Are you real / The dream police / Jo the waiter / Zero bass. *(re-iss.Aug79 reached No.14) (re-iss.May83 on 'Fame') (re-iss.Jul88)*

— **JESS LIDYARD** – drums returned to replace BARRY and SEAN

Mar 79. (7") **DOWN IN THE PARK. / DO YOU NEED THE SERVICE?** [ ] [-]
(12"+=) – I nearly married a human 2.

Beggars Banquet / Warners

May 79. (7")(7"pic-d)(US-7")(US-c-s) **ARE 'FRIENDS' ELECTRIC. / WE ARE SO FRAGILE?** [1] [ ]
Jun 79. (lp)(c) **REPLICAS** [1] [ ]
– Me I disconnect from you / Are 'friends' electric / The machman / Praying to the aliens / Down in the park / You are in my vision / Replicas / It must have been years / When the machines rock / I nearly married a human. *(re-iss.+cd.Sep88) (re-iss.cd/c Apr95 on 'Music Club')*

GARY NUMAN

solo retaining **PAUL GARDINER** – bass / **CEDRIC SHARPLEY** – drums / **CHRIS PAYNE** – synth, viola / **BILLY CURRIE** – keyboards.

Beggars Banquet / Atco

Aug 79. (7") **CARS. / ASYLUM** [1] [-]
Sep 79. (lp)(c) **THE PLEASURE PRINCIPLE** [1] [16] Jan 80
– Airplane / Metal / Complex / Films / M.E. / Tracks / Observer / Conversation / Cars / Engineers. *(re-iss.Sep88)*
Nov 79. (7") **COMPLEX. / BOMBERS (live)** [6] [ ]
(12"+=) – Me I disconnect from you (live).
Feb 80. (7") **CARS. / METAL** [-] [9]

— **DENNIS HAINES** – keyboards repl. CURRIE who returned to ULTRAVOX and VISAGE; added **RUSSELL BELL** – guitar (on tour) .

May 80. (7") **WE ARE GLASS. / TROIS GYMNPEDIES (1st MOVEMENT)** [5] [ ]
Aug 80. (7") **I DIE: YOU DIE. / DOWN IN THE PARK (piano version)** [6] [-]
Sep 80. (lp)(c) **TELEKON** [1] [64]
– This wreckage / The aircrash bureau / Telekon / Remind me to smile / Sleep by windows / I'm an agent / I dream of wires / Remember I was a vapour / Please push no more / The joy circuit. *(free-7"w.a.)* – REMEMBER I WAS A VAPOUR. / ON BROADWAY *(re-iss.Jul88)*
Sep 80. (7") **I DIE: YOU DIE. / SLEEP BY WINDOWS** [-] [ ]
Dec 80. (7") **REMIND ME TO SMILE. /** [-] [ ]
Dec 80. (7") **THIS WRECKAGE. / PHOTOGRAPH** [20] [ ]
Apr 81. (d-lp)(d-c) **LIVING ORNAMENTS 1979-1980 (live)** [2] [ ]
Apr 81. (lp)(c) **LIVING ORNAMENTS 1979** [47] [ ]
– Airplane / Cars / We are so fragile? / Films / Something's in the house / My shadow in vain / Conversation / The dream police / Metal. *(re-iss.1988)(both available as single lp)*
Apr 81. (lp)(c) **LIVING ORNAMENTS 1980** [39] [ ]
– This wreckage / I die: you die / M.E. / Everyday I die / Down in the park / Remind me to smile / The joy circuit / Tracks / Are 'friends' electric / We are glass. *(re-iss.1988)*

— GARY now recruited famous stars to replace BELL, SHARPLEY, HAINES and PAYNE. They became DRAMATIS. Jul'81 he guested on PAUL GARDINER single STORMTROOPER IN DRAG, which hit UK No.49. Next with The stars were **MICK KARN** – bass (of JAPAN) / **ROGER TAYLOR** – drums (of QUEEN) and **NASH THE SLASH** – violin (solo artist from Canada).

Aug 81. (7") **SHE'S GOT CLAWS. / I SING RAIN** [6] [ ]
(12"+=) – Exhibition.
Sep 81. (lp)(c) **DANCE** [3] [ ]
– Slowcar to China / Night talk / A subway called you / Cry the clock said / She's got claws / Crash / Boys like me / Stories / My brother's time / You are you are / Moral. *(re-iss.Jan89)*
Nov 81. (7") **LOVE NEEDS NO DISGUISE. (as "GARY NUMAN & DRAMATIS") / TAKE ME HOME** [33] [ ]
(12"+=) – Face to face.

— GARY NUMAN now used session people.

Feb 82. (7") **MUSIC FOR CHAMELEONS. / NOISE NOISE** [19] [ ]
(12") – ('A'extended) / Bridge? what bridge.
Jun 82. (7") **WE TAKE MYSTERY (TO BED). / THE IMAGE IS** [9] [ ]
(12") – ('A'extended) / ('A'early version).
Aug 82. (7") **WHITE BOYS AND HEROES. / WAR GAMES** [20] [ ]
(12") – ('A'extended) / Glitter and ash.
Sep 82. (lp)(c) **I, ASSASSIN** [8] [ ]
– White boys and heroes / War songs / A dream of Siam / Music for chameleons / This is my house / I, assassin / The 1930's rust / We take mystery (to bed). *(re-iss.Jan89)*
Aug 83. (7")(7"sha-pic-d) **WARRIORS. / MY CAR SLIDE (1)** [20] [ ]
(12") – ('A'extended) / My car slides (2).
Sep 83. (lp)(c) **WARRIORS** [12] [ ]
– Warriors / I am render / The iceman comes / This prison moon / My centurion / Sister surprise / The tick tock man / Love is like clock law / The rhythm of the evening. *(re-iss.Jan89)*
Oct 83. (7") **SISTER SUPRISE. / POETRY AND POWER** [32] [ ]
(12") – ('A'extended) / Letters.

Numa / Numa

Oct 84. (7")(7"sha-pic-d) **BERSERKER. / EMPTY BED, EMPTY HEART** [32] [ ]
(12"+=) – ('A'extended version).
Nov 84. (lp)(c) **BERSERKER** [45] [ ]
– Berserker / This is new love / The secret / My dying machine / Cold warning / Pump it up / The God film / A child with the ghost / The hunter. *(c+=) – (6 extra tracks). (cd-iss.Dec95)*
Dec 84. (7") **MY DYING MACHINE. / HERE I AM** [66] [ ]
(12") – ('A'extended) / She cries.

— next single on 'Polydor' by (SHARPE of SHAKATAK)

Feb 85. (7")(7"pic-d) **CHANGE YOUR MIND.(as "SHARPE & NUMAN") / REMIX, REMAKE, REMODEL** [17] [ ]
(12")(12"pic-d) – ('A'extended) / ('B'side) / Fools in a world of fire.
Apr 85. (d-lp)(c) **WHITE NOISE (live)** [29] [ ]
– (intro) / Berserker / Metal / Me, I disconnect from you / Remind me to smile / Sister surprise / Music for chameleons / The iceman comes / Cold warning / Down in the park / This prison moon / I die; you die / My dying machine / Cars / We take mystery (to bed) / We are glass / This is new love / My shadow in vain / Are 'friends' electric.
May 85. (7")(12")(12"blue)(12"white) **THE LIVE EP (live)** [27] [ ]
– Are 'friends' electric / Cars / We are glass / Beserker.
Jul 85. (7")(7"pic-d) **YOUR FASCINATION. / WE NEED IT** [46] [ ]
(12")(12"pic-d) – ('A'extended) / Anthem.
Sep 85. (7") **CALL OUT THE DOGS. / THIS SHIP COMES APART** [49] [ ]
(12") – ('A'extended) / No shelter.
Sep 85. (lp)(c)(cd)(pic-lp) **THE FURY** [24] [ ]
– Call out the dogs / This disease / Your fascination / Miracles / The pleasure skin / Creatures / ricks / God only knows / Creatures / I still remember. (c+)– (all tracks extended).
Nov 85. (7")(7"red)(7"white) **MIRACLES. / THE FEAR** [49] [ ]
(12")(12"red)(12"white+=) – ('A'&'B'extended).
Apr 86. (7")(7"pic-d) **THIS IS LOVE. / SURVIVAL** [28] [ ]
(12")(12"pic-d) – ('A'extended). (all w/free 7"flexi)
(d12"+=) – Call out the dogs (extended) / No shelter / This ship comes apart.
Jun 86. (7")(7"pic-d) **I CAN'T STOP. / FACES** [27] [ ]
(12") – ('A'extended). *(all w/free 7"flexi).*
(12"pic-d)/ /(10") – ('A' picture mix)./ / ('A'club mix).
Sep 86. (7")(7"pic-d) **NEW THING FROM LONDON TOWN. (as "SHARPE & NUMAN") / TIME TO DIE** [52] [ ]
(12")(12"pic-d) – ('A'&'B'extended).
Oct 86. (lp)(c)(cd) **STRANGE CHARM** [59] [ ]
Nov 86. (7")(7"pic-d) **I STILL REMEMBER (new version). / PUPPETS** [74] [ ]
(12")(12"pic-d) – ('A'&'B'extended).

— Early in 1987, he teamed up with RADIO HEART (see below)
Aug 87. (7")(7"pic-d) **CARS (E-REG MODEL). / ARE FRIENDS ELECTRIC?** [16] [ ]
(12")(c-s) – ('A'extended) / We are glass / I die: you die (US mix).
(12"+=) – ('A'extended) / ('A'motorway mix).
Sep 87. (d-lp)(c)(d-cd) **EXHIBITION** – (compilation) [43] [ ]
– Me, I disconnect from you / That's too bad / My love is a liquid / Music for chameleons / We are glass / Bombers / Sister Surprise / Are 'friends' electric / I dream of wires / Complex / Noise noise / Warriors / Everyday I die / Cars / We take mystery to bed / I'm an agent / My centurion / Metal / You are in my vision / I die: you die / She's got claws / This wreckage / My shadow in vain / Down in the park / The iceman comes. *(d-cd += 11 tracks)*

SHARPE AND NUMAN

Polydor Warners
Jan 88. (7")(7"pic-d)(7"white)(7"blue)(7"clear) **NO MORE LIES. / VOICES** [34] [ ]
(12"+=)(12"pic-d+=) – ('A'extended).
(cd-s++=) – Change your mind.

GARY NUMAN

Illegal I.R.S.
Sep 88. (7") **NEW ANGER. / I DON'T BELIEVE** [46] [ ]
(12"+=)/ /(cd-s+=) – Children./ / Creatures / I can't stop.
Oct 88. (lp)(c)(cd) **METAL RHYTHM** [48] [ ]
– Respect / Don't call my name / New anger / America / Hunger / Voix / Young heart / Cold metal rhythm / This is emotion. *(pic-lp iss.Mar89)*
Nov 88. (7")(7"pic-d) **AMERICA. / RESPECT (live)** [49] [ ]
(12"+=) – New anger (live).
(cd-s++=) – Call out the dogs (live).

SHARPE & NUMAN

again with **ROGER ODELL** – drums / **TESSA MILES + LINDA TAYLOR** – backing vocals
Polydor M.C.A.
May 89. (7")(7"pic-d) **I'M ON AUTOMATIC. / LOVE LIKE A GHOST** [44] [ ]
(12") – ('A'extended) Voices / ('89 mix).
(7") – ('A'side) / No more lies (new version).
(cd-s+=) – (all 4 above).
Jun 89. (lp)(c)(cd) **AUTOMATIC** [59] [ ]
– Change your mind / Turn off the world / No more lies / Breathe in emotion / Some new game / I'm on automatic / Rip it up / Welcome to love / Voices / Nightlife. *(cd+=)*– (2 extended mixes).

GARY NUMAN

solo with **RUSSELL BELL** – guitar / **CHRIS PAYNE** – keyboards, violin / **ADE ORANGE** – keyboards / **CEDRIC SHARPLY** – drums / **JOHN WEBB** – saxophone / **ANDY COUGHLAN** – bass / **VAL CHALMERS + EMMA CHALMER** – backing vocals
I.R.S. I.R.S.
Oct 89. (lp)(c)(cd) **THE SKIN MECHANIC (live Sep88)** [55] [ ]
– Survival / Respect / Call out the dogs / Cars / Hunger / Down in the park / New anger / Creatures / Are 'friends' electric / Young heart / We are glass / I die: you die.
Mar 91. (7")(c-s)(7"red) **HEART. / SHAME** [ ] [ ]
(12") – ('A'side) / Icehouse.
(cd-s) – ('A'side) / Tread careful.
(12") – ('A'side) / Are 'friends' electric.
Apr 91. (cd)(c)(lp) **OUTLAND** [39] [ ]
– Confession / My world storm / Interval 1 / From Russia infected / Interval 2 / They whisper you / Dark Sunday / Heart / Devotion / Outland / Interval 3 / 1999 / Dream killer.
Sep 91. (7")(c-s) **EMOTION. / IN A GLASSHOUSE** [43] [ ]
(12"+=) – Hanoi.
(cd-s++=) – ('A'diff.mix).
Mar 92. (7")(c-s) **THE SKIN GAME. / DARK MOUNTAIN** [68] [ ]
(12"+=)(cd-s+=) – U got the look / ('A'digi mix).
Jul 92. (7") **MACHINE AND SOUL. / ('A'promo mix)** [72] [-]
(cd-s+=) – 1999 / The hauntings.
(cd-s) ('A' side) / Soul protection (live) / Confession (live) / From Russia infected (live).
(12"+=) – Your fascination (live) / Outland (live) / Respect (live).
(cd-s+=) – Cry baby / Wonder eye.
Jul 92. (cd)(c)(lp) **MACHINE AND SOUL** [42] [ ]
– Machine and soul / Generator / The skin game / Poison / I wonder / Emotion / Cry / U got the look / Love isolation. *(ext.cd re-iss.Sep93 on 'Numa')*
— Apr 94; He guested for GENERATOR on their version of 'ARE FRIENDS' ELECTRIC'.
— NUMAN & DADAGANG; Apr 94 12"/cd-s LIKE A REFUGEE (I WON'T CRY) on 'Record Label', re-iss.Aug 94 as GARY NUMAN & FRIENDS.
Numa Numa
Aug 94. (d-cd)(d-c)(t-lp) **DREAM CORROSION** [ ] [-]
Oct 94. (12")(cd-s) **A QUESTION OF FAITH** [ ] [-]
Mar 95. (cd)(c)(lp) **SACRIFICE** [ ] [-]
Mar 95. (12")(cd-s) **ABSOLUTION. / MAGIC (trick mix) / MAGIC (extended)** [ ] [-]
Jun 95. (12"ep)(cd-ep) **DARK LIGHT LIVE E.P. (live)** [ ] [-]
– Bleed / Everyday I die / The dream police / Listen to the sirens.
Jul 95. (d-cd)(c) **DARK LIGHT (live)** [ ] [ ]
– Pray / A question of faith / I dream of wires / Noise noise / Listen to the sirens / Everyday I die / Desire / Friens / Scar / Magic / Praying to the aliens / Replicas I / Mean street / Stormtrooper in drag / Dead liner / Bleed / The dream police / I die, you die / The hunter / Remind me to smile / Are friends "electric"? / Do you need the service? / Love and napalm / Jo the waiter / I'm an agent.
Nov 95. (cd)(c) **HUMAN** (with MICHAEL R. SMITH) [ ] [-]

– compilations, etc. (TUBEWAY ARMY *)

Aug 79. Beggar's Banquet; (d7") * **THAT'S TOO BAD. / OH! I DIDN'T SAY/ / BOMBERS. / O.D. RECEIVER / BLUE EYES** [ ] [-]
Apr 83. Beggar's Banquet; (12"ep) * **TUBEWAY ARMY '78 VOL.1** [ ] [-]
– (same tracks as above +) Do you need the service? *(re-iss.1985 on 12"yellow)*
Sep 84. Beggar's Banquet; (lp)(c)(pic-lp) * **THE PLAN (by "TUBEWAY ARMY /GARY NUMAN)** [29] [-]
(re-iss.1989)
1985. Beggar's Banquet; (12"red-ep) **TUBEWAY ARMY '78-'79 VOL.2** [ ] [-]
– Fade out / 1930 / The crazies / Only a downstate / We have a technical.
1985. Beggar's Banquet; (12"blue-ep) **TUBEWAY ARMY '78-'79 VOL.3** [ ] [-]
– The Monday troup / Crime of assikon / The life machine / A game called Echo / Random / Oceans.
Dec 87. Beggar's Banquet; (cd) * **REPLICAS / * THE PLAN** [ ] [-]
(re-iss.d-cd Dec93)
Dec 87. Beggar's Banquet; (cd) * **TUBEWAY ARMY / DANCE** [ ] [-]
(re-iss.d-cd Dec93)
Dec 87. Beggar's Banquet; (cd) **THE PLEASURE PRINCIPLE / WARRIORS** [ ] [-]
(re-iss.d-cd Dec93)
Dec 87. Beggar's Banquet; (cd) **TELEKON / I, ASSASSIN** [ ] [ ]
(re-iss.d-cd Dec93)
(above series of cd's, omitted some tracks on each)
1990. Beggar's Banquet; (pic-cd-ep) **THE SELECTION** [ ] [-]
– Cars('E' reg.model) / Down in the park / I die: you die / Are 'friends' electric? / We are glass / Music for chameleons.
Aug 93. Beggar's Banquet; (7")(c-s) **CARS. / ('A'mix)** [53] [ ]
(12"sha-pic-d+=)(cd-s+=) – CARS ('93 SPRINT) / CARS (TOP GEAR)
Sep 93. Beggar's Banquet; (d-cd)(c) **THE BEST OF GARY NUMAN 1978-1983** [70] [-]
Apr 81. Old Gold; (7") * **ARE 'FRIENDS' ELECTRIC. / DOWN IN THE PARK** [ ] [-]
1990. Old Gold; (7") * **ARE FRIENDS ELECTRIC?. / I DID YOU** [ ] [-]
1990. Old Gold; (7") **CARS. / WE ARE GLASS** [ ] [-]
Nov 82. TV-Virgin; (lp)(c) **NEW MAN NUMAN – THE BEST OF GARY NUMAN** [45] [-]
Aug 87. Strane Fruit; (12"ep)(c-ep) * **THE PEEL SESSIONS** [ ] [-]
– Me I disconnect from you / Down in the park / I nearly married a human.
Dec 89. Strange Fruit; (m-lp)(cd) **DOUBLE PEEL SESSIONS** [ ] [-]
Oct 89. Castle; (d-lp)(cd) **THE GARY NUMAN COLLECTION** [ ] [-]
Dec 92. Connoisseur; (cd)(c) **DOCUMENT SERIES** [ ] [-]
— GARY has also contributed to other DRAMATIS recordings.
Jul 94. Receiver; (cd) **HERE I AM** [ ] [-]

RADIO HEART

with **DAVID + HUGH NICHOLSON**
G.F.M. not issued
Mar 87. (7")(7"sha-pic-d) **RADIO HEART. / ('A'instrumental)** [35] [ ]
(12"+=)(12"pic-d+=) – Mistasax version 2.
May 87. (7")(7"sha-pic-d) **LONDON TIMES. / RUMOUR** [48] [ ]
(12"+=) – ('A'extended).
Oct 87. (7") **ALL ACROSS THE NATION** [ ] [-]
(12"+=)/ /(cd-s+=) – ('A'extended)./ / ('A'instrumental).
Nov 87. (lp)(c)(cd) **RADIO HEART** [ ] [-]
– All across the nation / London times / Radio heart / Blue nights / Starlight jingles / Strange thing / I'm alone / Mad about the girl / Victim.

NUTTY BOYS (see under ⇒ MADNESS)

N.W.A.

Formed: NIGGAS WITH ATTITUDE, Los Angeles, California, USA ... 1988 by (see below). Gathered local COMPTON momentum and angst when they unleashed debut anti-everything album 'STRAIGHT OUTTA COMPTON'. Mainman ICE CUBE departed for slightly more laid-back solo approach in 1990, but group went straight to No.1 slot with follow-up 'EFIL4ZAGGIN'. • **Style:** Rebelious and violent rapping gangstas, who spray a barrage of expletives to show their anger against racist peers. • **Songwriters:** Group penned plus samples. DR.DRE (a half-bro to WARREN G) sampled on 'NUTHIN' BUT A G THANG'; I Want'a Do Somethin' Freakey To You (Leon Haywood). Also on 'LET ME RIDE'; Mothership Connection (Parliament). His 1993 album also featured rapper SNOOP DOGGY DOGG. • **Trivia:** Album 'EFIL4ZAGGIN' is actually NIGGAZ4LIFE spelt backwards (as seen on sleeve).

Recommended: STRAIGHT OUTTA COMPTON (*9) / EFIL4ZAGGIN (*7) / THE CHRONIC (DR. DRE *7)

ICE CUBE (b. OSHEA JACKSON) – vocals (ex-C.I.A.) / **DR DRE** (b. ANDRE YOUNG) – vocals (also of WORLD CLASS WRECKIN' CREW) / **EAZY-E** (b. ERIC WRIGHT, 7 Sep'73) – vocals / **MC REN** (b. LORENZO PATTERSON) – vocals / **DJ YELLA** (b. ANTOINE CARRABY) – turntables
4th & Broad. Ruthless
Aug 89. (7") **EXPRESS YOURSELF. / STRAIGHT OUTTA COMPTON** [50] [ ]
(ext-12"+=)(cd-s+=) – ('A'bonus beats) / A bitch is a bitch. *(re-iss.May90, hit Uk 26)*
Aug 89. (lp)(c)(cd) **STRAIGHT OUTTA COMPTON** [41] [37]
– Straight outta Compton / Fu** the police / Gangsta gangsta / If it ain't ruff / Parental discretion iz advised / 8 ball (remix) / Something like that / Express yourself / Compton's in the house (remix) / I ain't tha 1 / Dopeman (remix) / Quiet on the set /

Something to dance to.
Aug 90. (7") **GANGSTA, GANGSTA / IF IT AIN'T RUFF** 70
(12"+=)(cd-s+=) – Dopeman (remix).
— now without ICE CUBE who was now solo.
Oct 90. (7") **100 MILES AND RUNNIN'. / REAL NIGGAZ** 38 27 Aug90
(12")(cd-s) – ('A'side) / Just don't bite it / Sa prize (pt.2) / Kamurshoi.
Apr 91. (12")(cd-s) **F*** THE POLICE. / ('A'mixes)**
— (above written for RODNEY KING, who was the black motorist beat up by police. The court case instigated the race riots all around America.
Jun 91. (cd)(c)(lp) **EFIL4ZAGGIN** 25 1
– Prelude / Real niggaz don't die / Real niggaz 4 life / Protest / Appetite for destruction / Don't drink that wine / Alwayz into somethin' / Message to B.A. / Real niggaz / To kill a hooker / One less bitch / Findum, f***um and flee / Automobile / She swallowed it / I'd rather f*** you / Approach to danger / 1-900-2 Compton / The dayz of wayback.
Nov 91. (7") **ALWAYZ INTO SOMETHIN'. / EXPRESS YOURSELF** 60
(12"+=)(cd-s+=) – Something 2 dance 2.
— Disbanded and all went solo.

EAZY-E

4th & Broad. Ruthless
Sep 89. (lp)(c)(cd) **EAZY-DUZ-IT** 41 Dec88
– (Prelude) Still talkin' / Nobody move / 2 Hard muthas (featuring MC REN) / Boyz-n-the-hood (remix) / Eazy-duz-it / We want Eazy / Eazy-er said than dunn / Radio / No more ?'s / Imma break it down / Eazy – Chapter 8, verse 10. *(re-iss.Jun91)*
Jan 93. (cd)(c) **5150 HOME FOR THA SICK** 70
–
Oct 93. (cd)(c) **IT'S ON (DR.DRE 187 UM) KILLA** 5
–
Jan 94. (c-s)(cd-s) **REAL MUTHAPHUCKIN' G'S. /** - 42
— Early in 1995, EAZY-E featured on BONE THUGS N HARMONY's hit single 'Foe Tha Love Of'.
— EAZY-E died of AIDS on the 26th March 1995 after only being diagnosed HIV a month earlier.
Epic Epic
Dec 95. (c-s) **JUST TAH LET U KNOW / THE MUTHAPHU**IN' REAL** 30 51
(12"+=)(cd-s+=) – ('A'-Ruthless "G" mix) / ('A'-Ba-da-ba-do acappella mix).
Dec 95. (cd)(c) **ETERNAL E** - 84

MC REN

4th & Broad. Ruthless
Jul 92. (cd)(c) **KIZZ MY BLACK AZZ** 12
– Check it out y'all / Behind the scenes / Hound dogz / Kiss my black azz / Right up my alley / Final frontier.
Nov 93. (cd)(c) **SHOCK OF THE HOUR** 22
–
Nov 93. (c-s)(cd-s) **SAME OL' SHIT. / ?** - 90
— Above sampled; LET'S GET IT ON (Marvin Gaye) / I GOT A GOOD THING (James Brown) / LAD DI DA DI (Doug E.Fresh).

DR. DRE

Interscope Death Row
Feb 93. (cd)(c) **THE CHRONIC** 3
– The chronic / Fuck wit Dre day (and everybody's celebrating) / Let me ride / The day the niggaz took over / Nuthin' but a "G" thang / Dreeez nuuuts / Bitches ain't shit / Lil' ghetto boy / A nigga witta gun / Rat-tat-tat-tat / The $20 sack pyramid / Lyrical gangbang / High powered / The doctor's office / Stranded on death row / The roach (the chronic outro).
Mar 93. (7") **NUTHIN' BUT A "G" THANG. / ('A'mix)** 2 Jan93
(club-12"+=) – ('A'-freestyle mix).
May 93. (7")(c-s) **DRE DAY. / ('A'-flavour mix)** 8
(cd-s+=) – ('A'extended club) / ('A'-UK Flavour mix) / ('A'instrumental) / ('A'again).
(12") – (A+B) / (above 2) / Puffin' on blunts and drinkin' tanqueray.
Aug 93. (c-s)(cd-s)(12") **LET ME RIDE / ('A'mixes)** 34
Jan 94. (12"ep) **NUTHIN' BUT A G THANG (club) / ('A'red-eye mix) / ('A'mix) / LET ME RIDE (remix)** 31
(12") – (1st & 4th tracks) / Let me ride (extended club mix).
(cd-s) – (1st & 4th tracks) + their club mixes.
Aug 94. (7") **DRE DAY. / ('A'-UK radio mix)** 59
(12"+=) – puffin' on blunts and drinkin' tanqueray.
(cd-s+=) – ('A'-radio remix) / ('A'instrumental) / ('A'-2 other mixes).
— In Sep'94, DR.DRE was convicted of battery (assault) and imprisoned for 8 months, although it seems likely he'll be out a lot sooner.
Interscope Triple X
Oct 94. (cd)(c) **CONCRETE ROOTS** 43
— DR.DRE & ICE CUBE; below from the film 'Murder Was The Case'.
Mar 95. (c-s) **NATURAL BORN KILLAZ / THA DOGG POUND: What Would U Do?** 45 ?
(12"+=)(cd-s+=) – (2 'A'versions).
Virgin Priority
May 95. (c-s) **KEEP THEIR HEADS RINGIN'. / TAKE A HIT (mix)** 25 10 Mar 95
(12"+=)(cd-s+=) – (other mixes).
above 'A' from the film 'Friday'.

Michael NYMAN

Born: Signed to ENO's 'Obscure' records in 1978. Was a regular on each Peter Greenaway film soundtracks, including 'THE DRAUGHTMAN'S CONTRACT', 'A ZED AND TWO NOUGHTS', 'DROWNING BY NUMBERS', 'THE COOK, THE THIEF . . . ' and 'PROSPERO'S BOOKS'. Finally found commercial success in 1993, after tackling the more accessible worldwide score for the Jane Campion film 'THE PIANO'. • **Style:** Minimalist similiar to STOCKHAUSEN or JOHN CAGE. • **Songwriters:** Self-penned bar some w / GEESE. • **Trivia:** Wrote a track for The FLYING LIZARDS on 1981 album 'The Fourth Wall'.

Recommended: THE PIANO (*6) / THE COMPLETE PETER GREENAWAY COLLECTION (*7)

MICHAEL NYMAN – keyboards, piano, synthesizers

Obscure not issued
Apr 78. (lp) **DECAY MUSIC** -
– One hundred / Bell set No.1. *(re-iss.Jan87 on 'Editions-EG')*
Crepescule not issued
Jan 81. (7") **MOZART. /** -
Piano not issued
Feb 82. (7") **IN RE DON GIOVANNI. / LAST BUT ONE** -
Sheet not issued
Mar 82. (lp) **MICHAEL NYMAN** -
Charisma D.R.G.
Dec 82. (lp) **THE DRAUGHTMAN'S CONTRACT (soundtrack)** 1988
– Chasing sheep is best left to shepherds / The disposition of the linen / A watery death / The garden is becoming a robe room / Queen of the night / An eye for official theory / Bravery in the face of grief. *(cd-iss.Apr89) (cd re-iss.Feb90 on 'Silva Screen')*
Editions-EG E.G.
Jul 85. (lp)(c) **THE KISS AND OTHER MOVEMENTS** -
– The kiss / Noselist song / Tango between the lines / Images were introduced / Water dances (making a splash):- Stroking – Gliding – Synchronising. *(cd-iss.Jan87)*
T.E.R. not issued
Dec 85. (lp)(c) **A ZED AND TWO NOUGHTS (soundtrack by The ZOO ORCHESTRA)** -
– Anglefish decay / Car crash / Time lapse / Prawn watching / Biscosis Populi / Swan rot / Delft waltz / Up for crabs / Verneer's wife / Venus De Milo / Lady in the red hat / L'escargot. *(cd-iss.Jan90 on 'Venture')*
Dec 86. (lp)(c)(cd) **AND DO THEY DO (MICHAEL NYMAN BAND) / ZOO CAPRICES (w / ALEXANDER BALANESCU)** -
– AND DO THEY DO: Song I / Song II / Song III / Song IV / ZOO CAPRICES: The lady in the red hat / Swan rot / Up for crabs / Car crash / Bisocosis popull / Venus de Milo / Anglefish decay / Vermeer's wife watches prawns / Timeplace.
C.B.S. not issued
Jul 88. (c)(cd) **THE MAN WHO MISTOOK HIS WIFE FOR A HAT (soundtrack with EMILE BELCOURT & SARAH LEONARD)** -
Venture Virgin
Aug 88. (lp)(c)(cd) **DROWNING BY NUMBERS (soundtrack)** -
– Trysting fields / Sheep and tides / Great death game / Drowning by number 3 / Wheelbarrow walk / Dead man's catch / Drowning by number 2 / Bees in trees / Fish beach / Wedding tango / Crematorium conspiracy / Knowing the ropes / End game.
Oct 89. (c)(cd) **THE COOK, THE THIEF, HIS WIFE AND HER LOVER (soundtrack)**
– Memorial / Miserere paraphrase (w / ALEXANDER BALANESCU) / Book depository / Coupling / Miserere (by LONDON VOICES).
— next by MICHAEL NYMAN BAND, with **SARAH LEONARD, MARIE ANGEL, UTE LEMPER** and **DEBORAH CONWAY**. It was also a one-off for 'Decca'.
Sep 91. (cd)(c) **PROSPERO'S BOOKS (soundtrack)**
– Full fathom five / Prospero's curse / While you here do snoring lie / Prospero's magic / Miranda / Twelve years since / Come into these yellow sands / History of Sycorax / Come and go / Cornfield / While the bee sucks / Caliban's pit / Reconciliation / The masque.
Venture Virgin
Jun 93. (cd)(c) **THE PIANO (soundtrack)** 31 41
– To the edge of the Earth / Big mystery secret / A wild and distant shore / The heart asks pleasure first – The promise / Here to there / A bed of ferns / The fling / The scent of love / Deep into the forest / The mood that passes through you / Lost and found / The embrace / Little impulse / The sacrifice / I clipped your wing / The wounded / All imperfect things / Dreams of a journey.
Mar 94. (7")(c-s) **THE HEART ASKS PLEASURE FIRST – THE PROMISE. / BIG MYSTERY SECRET** 60
(cd-s+=) – Trysting fields / The garden is becoming a robe room.
(cd-s) – ('A'side) / All perfect things / Delft waltz / Coupling.
Oct 94. (cd)(c) **LIVE (live)**
– In re Don Giovanni / Bird list / Queen of the night / Water dances / The upside down violin / The piano (concert suite).
SilvaScreen SilvaScreen
Apr 95. (cd) **THE COLD ROOM (soundtrack with The WEMBLEY STUDIO CHAMBER CHOIR)**
– The cold room (main theme) / The nightmare begins / The closet / Sorcerer / Sounds of the night / Her man awaits / Ghosts of the past / The damned / Thoughtful / Spectral movements / Macabre piano / A cold spot / Red drum / Chase / The nightmare ends / The cold room (main theme).

– compilations, etc. –

Dec 89. Venture; (4xcd-box) **THE COMPLETE PETER GREENAWAY COLLECTION** -
– THE DRAUGHTMAN'S CONTRACT / A ZED AND TWO NOUGHTS / DROWNING BY NUMBERS / THE COOK, THE THIEF, HIS WIFE AND HER LOVER
— Also released THE ESSENTIAL MICHAEL NYMAN BAND on cd+c / OUT ON THE RUN (TV original soundtrack).

Laura NYRO

Born: LAURA NIGRO, 18 Oct'47, Bronx, New York, USA, of Italian/Jewish parentage. Started writing songs at 8 and later attended Manhattan's High School of Music and Art, where she underwent a bad LSD trip. In 1966 she signed to folk-rock label 'Verve', and soon released debut album 'MORE THAN A NEW DISCOVERY'. At the 1967 Monterey Festival, she made a disastrous attempt to do a soul-revue show, which was unfairly booed off by large hippie audience. This was to later affect her permanently, when she again suffered stage fright. In 1968, she went under the management of David Geffen, who guided her into a new contract with 'Columbia', where she was produced by Charlie Callello. In 1970, she finally broke through with US Top 40 album 'NEW YORK TENDABERRY'. • **Trivia:** Her songs were being successfully recorded by major stars FIFTH DIMENSION (Stoned Soul Picnic; 1968-Top 3 US) + (Sweet Blindness; 1968-Top 20 US) + (Wedding Bell Blues; 1969-No.1 US) / BLOOD, SWEAT & TEARS (And When I Die; 1969 – No.2 US) / THREE DOG NIGHT (Eli's Coming; 1969-Top 10 US) / BARBRA STREISAND (Stoney End; 1970-Top 10). **Style & Songwriters:** Cult singer/songwriter, who mixed her lyrically excellent fusion of white soul and gospel with R&B. Covered Motown 60s classics on collaboration album 'GONNA TAKE A MIRACLE' alongside LaBELLE.

Recommended: CLASSICS (*6)

LAURA NYRO – vocals, piano

Date	Release	UK	US
		Verve	Verve
1966.	(lp) **MORE THAN A NEW DISCOVERY**		
	– Wedding bells blues / Goodbye Joe / Billy's blues / And when I die / Stoney end / Lazy Susan / Hands off the man / Buy and sell / He's a runner / Blowin' away / I never meant to hurt you / California shoeshine boys. *(UK-iss.+c.Feb73 as 'THE FIRST SONGS' on 'CBS' hit No.97)*		
Oct 66.	(7") **WEDDING BELL BLUES. / STONEY END**		
May 67.	(7") **GOODBYE JOE. / BILLY'S BLUES**	-	
Dec 67.	(7") **AND WHEN I DIE. / FLIM FLAM MAN**	-	
		C.B.S.	Columbia
Jul 68.	(7") **ELI'S COMIN'. / SWEET BLINDNESS**		
Aug 68.	(lp) **ELI AND THE THIRTEENTH CONFESSION**		
	– Luckie / Lu / Sweet blindness / Poverty train / Lonely women / Eli's comin' / Timer / Stoned good picnic / Emmie / Woman's blues / Once it was alright now (farmer Joe) / December's boudoir / The confession. *(re-iss.+c.1974)*		
Oct 68.	(7") **SAVE THE COUNTRY. / TIMER**	-	
Feb 69.	(7") **ONCE IT WAS ALRIGHT NOW (FARMER JOE). / WOMAN'S BLUES**		Jan69
Jan 70.	(7") **TIME AND LOVE. / THE MAN WHO SENDS ME HOME**		
Jan 70.	(lp) **NEW YORK TENDABERRY**		32 Oct 69
	– You don't love me when I cry / Captain for dark mornings / Tom cat good by / Mercy on Broadway / Save the country / Gibson Street / Time and love / The man who sends me home / Sweet lovin' baby / Captain Saint Lucifer / New york tendaberry. *(re-iss.+c.1974)*		
Mar 70.	(7") **SAVE THE COUNTRY. / NEW YORK TENDABERRY**	-	

— with session people.

Date	Release	UK	US
Oct 70.	(7") **UP ON THE ROOF. / CAPTAIN SAINT LUCIFER**		92
Dec 70.	(lp) **CHRISTMAS AND THE BEADS OF SWEAT**		
	– Brown earth / When I was a freeport and you were the main drag / Blackpatch / Been on a train / Upon the roof / Upstairs by a Chinese lamp / Map to the treasure / Beads of sweat / Christmas in my soul. *(re-iss.+c.1974)*		
Feb 71.	(7") **WHEN I WAS A FREEPORT AND YOU WERE THE MAIN DRAG. / BEEN ON A TRAIN**		
Feb 72.	(lp)(c) **GONNA TAKE A MIRACLE**		46 Dec 71
	– I met him on a Sunday / The bells / Monkey time – Dancing in the street / Desiree / You've really got a hold on me / Spanish harlem / Jimmy Mack / Wind / Nowhere to run / It's gonna take a miracle. *(re-iss.Feb89 on 'B.G.O.', cd-iss.Nov91)*		
Feb 72.	(7") **IT'S GONNA TAKE A MIRACLE. / DESIREE**		

— (above as "LAURA NYRO AND LaBELLE") She retired for 4 years after getting married.

Date	Release	UK	US
Mar 76.	(lp)(c) **SMILE**		60
	– Sexy mama / Children of the junks / Money / I am the blues / Stormy love / The cat-song / Midnite blue / Smile.		
Aug 77.	(lp)(c) **SEASONS OF LIGHT . . . LAURA NYRO IN CONCERT (live)**		Jun 77
	– The confession / And when I die / Upstairs by a Chinese lamp / Sweet blindness / Captain Saint Lucifer / Money / The cat-song / When I was a freeport and you were the main drag / Timer / Emmie.		
Aug 78.	(lp)(c) **NESTED**		
	– Mr. Blue (the song of communications) / Rhythm and blues / My innocence / Crazy love / The nest / American dreamer / Spring blown / Sweet sky / Light pops principle / Child in a universe.		
Mar 84.	(lp)(c) **MOTHER'S SPIRITUAL**		
	– To a child / The right to vote / A wilderness / Melody in the sky / Late for love / A free thinker / Man in the Moon / Talk on a green tree / Trees of the ages / The brighter song / Roadnotes / Sophia / Mother's spiritual / Refrain.		

— She virtually retired from the music business around the mid-80's.

Date	Release	UK	US
		Cypress	Cypress
Oct 89.	(lp)(cd) **LIVE AT THE BOTTOM LINE (live)**		
	– Medley:- The confession – Hi heel sneakers / Roll of the ocean / Companion / Wild world / Medley:- My innocence – Sophia / To a child / And when I die / Park song / Broken rainbow / Women of the one world / Emmie / Wedding bell blues / The Japanese restaurant song / Stoned soul picnic / Medley:- La la means I love you – Trees of the ages – Up on the roof.		
		not issued	Columbia
Nov 90.	(7") **LET IT BE ME. (w/ SHAWN COLVIN) / CHRISTMAS SONG; CHESTNUTS ROASTING ON AN OPEN FIRE / (other track by SHAWN)**	-	
		Sony	Sony
Jan 94.	(cd) **WALK THE DOG AND LIGHT THE LIGHT**		
	– Oh yeah, oh yeah (the heebie jeebies) / A woman of the world / The descent of Luna Rose / Art of love / Like a flame (the animal rights song) / Louise's church / Broken rainbow / Walk the dog and light the light (song of the road) / To a child / I'm so proud / Dedicated to the one I love.		

– compilations, others, etc. –

Date	Release	UK	US
1969.	Columbia; (7") **STONEY END. / FLIM FLAM MAN**	-	
1969.	Columbia; (7") **GOODBYE JOE. / I NEVER MEANT TO HURT YOU**	-	
Feb 73.	CBS; (7") **WEDDING BELL BLUES. / HANDS OFF THE MAN (FLIM FLAM MAN)**		
Dec 80.	CBS/ US= Columbia; (lp)(c) **IMPRESSIONS**		
Jul 91.	Elite; (cd)(c) **CLASSICS** *(re-iss.Sep93)*		-

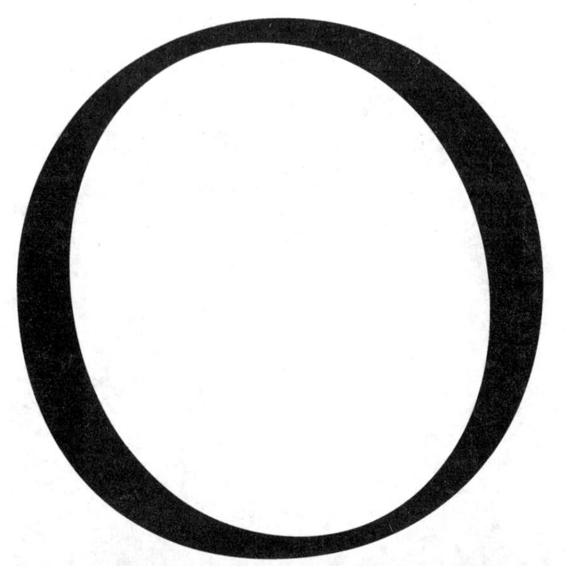

Phil OAKEY & Giorgio MORODER (see under ⇒ HUMAN LEAGUE)

OASIS

Formed: Manchester, England . . . summer 1992, by LIAM, BONEHEAD, PAUL & TONY. Initially called RAIN, they were soon joined by LIAM's older brother NOEL who was a roadie for The INSPIRAL CARPETS. After a year of rehearsals and occasional local gigs, they were signed by Creation's ALAN McGEE, who caught them playing at a Glasgow gig mid 1993. With plenty hype behind them, they secured a near UK Top 30 debut single with 'SUPERSONIC'. They went from strength to strength with each release and topped the album charts with 'DEFINITELY MAYBE' (most critics' choice for album of the year award). Certainly 1994 had belonged to this self-proclaimed 'best band in the world' and they even tried to knock popstarts EAST 17 off the Christmas No.1 slot with 'WHATEVER'. • **Style:** The BEATLES, The SEX PISTOLS and The SMITHS all rolled into one delicious and most exciting rock group since the aforementioned! • **Songwriters:** NOEL, except I AM THE WALRUS (Beatles) / FEELIN' LONELY by Noel (Small Faces). • **Trivia:** NOEL wrote 'SLIDE AWAY' on a Les Gibson guitar, which he bought from friend JOHNNY MARR (ex-Smiths) and which was once the property of PETE TOWNSHEND (The Who). LIAM has now an on-off relationship with PATSY KENSIT (singer/actress and estranged wife of Simple Minds voxman JIM KERR). It is common knowledge, JUSTINE FRISCHMANN of ELASTICA (girlfriend of rival DAMON ALBARN) has knocked back his blatant advances.

Recommended: DEFINITELY MAYBE (*10) / (WHAT'S THE STORY) MORNING GLORY? (*10)

LIAM GALLAGHER (b.21 Sep'72) – vocals / **NOEL GALLAGHER** (b.29 May'67) – guitar / **PAUL 'BONEHEAD' ARTHURS** (b.23 Jun'65) – guitar / **PAUL McGUIGAN** (b.19 May'71) – guitar / **TONY McCARROLL** – drums

Creation Creation

Apr 94. (7") **SUPERSONIC. / TAKE ME AWAY** [31] [ ]
(12"+=) – I will believe (live).
(cd-s++=) – Columbia (demo).

Jun 94. (7")(c-s) **SHAKER MAKER. / D'YER WANNA BE A SPACEMAN?** [11] [ ]
(12"+=) – Alive (demo).
(cd-s+==) – Bring it on down (live).

Aug 94. (7")(c-s) **LIVE FOREVER. / UP IN THE SKY (acoustic)** [10] [ ]
(12"+=) – Cloudburst.
(cd-s++=) – Supersonic (live).

Aug 94. (cd)(c)(lp) **DEFINITELY MAYBE** [1] [58] Jan95
– Rock'n'roll star / Shaker maker / Live forever / Up in the sky / Columbia / Supersonic / Bring it down / Cigarettes and alcohol / Digsy's dinner / Slide away / Married with children.(lp+=) – Sad song.

Oct 94. (7")(c-s) **CIGARETTES AND ALCOHOL. / I AM THE WALRUS (live)** [7] [ ]
(12"+=) – Fade away.
(cd-s++=) – Listen up.

Dec 94. (7")(c-s) **WHATEVER. / (IT'S GOOD) TO BE FREE** [3] [ ]
(12"+=) – Slide away.
(cd-s++=) – Half the world away.

— After a punch-up McCARROLL left and was replaced by drummer **ALAN WHITE (b.26 May'72, London)** (ex-IDHA) and brother of STEVE WHITE (long-time sticksman with PAUL WELLER)

Apr 95. (c-s) **SOME MIGHT SAY / TALK TONIGHT** [1] [ ]
(12"+=) – Acquiesce.
(cd-s++=) – Headshrinker.

— Their first 5 singles re-entered UK Top 60 in Jun'95. The next single lost the battle with rivals BLUR to the No.1 spot. It was a year of running verbal battles between them, although LIAM's arrogance and NOEL's songwriting abilities on next album, finally won over the public.

Aug 95. (c-s) **ROLL WITH IT / IT'S BETTER, PEOPLE** [2] [ ]
(12"+=) – Rockin' chair.
(cd-s+=) – Live forever (live).

Oct 95. (cd)(c)(lp) **(WHAT'S THE STORY) MORNING GLORY?** [1] [72]
– Hello / Roll with it / Wonderwall / Don't look back in anger / Hey now! / Some might say / Cast no shadow / She's electric / Morning glory / Champagne supernova. (lp+=) Bonehead's bank holiday.

Oct 95. (c-s) **WONDERWALL / ROUND ARE WAY** [2] [ ]
(12"+=) – The swamp song.
(cd-s+=) – The masterplan.

OBLIVION EXPRESS (see under ⇒ AUGER, Brian)

Ric OCASEK (see under ⇒ CARS)

Phil OCHS

Born: 19 Dec'40, El Paso, Texas, USA. Raised by Scottish/Polish parents in Perrysburg, Ohio. Having spent time following his family tradition in the military, he studied journalism at local university. He became more aware of economics and socialism, after meeting room-mate JIM GLOVER. The two became country-folk duo The SUNDOWNERS, but split in 1963 when PHIL moved to Greenwich Village, New York. His solo debut came on 15th Mar'63, when supporting JOHN HAMMOND. After writing future hit 'THERE BUT FOR FORTUNE' for JOAN BAEZ, he appeared at many Newport folk festivals. In 1964, he was signed to 'Elektra' by owner Jac HOLZMAN. His debut lp 'ALL THE NEWS THAT'S FIT TO SING', despite an American TV ban, made the US Top 100, and was an early example of his past journalistic attitude. In 1965, he issued debut 45 'I AIN'T MARCHING ANYMORE', but its anti-Vietnam stance, only irritated the media and his folk contemporary DYLAN. In 1966, his label dropped him, but after rejecting 'Columbia', he opted to sign for 'A&M'. His songs were now being covered by artists such as CRISPIAN ST.PETERS, FOUR SEASONS and PETER AND GORDON. He made 4 albums with the label, the last being in 1970 'PHIL OCH'S GREATEST HITS'. This despite its title, was not a compilation, but a joke that was to backfire on him. To promote it, he dressed as ELVIS in a gold ELVIS-suit and was promptly booed off stage. He basically retired after this, and wrote for 'Time Out' magazine in 1973. His self-belief had all but left him, and he committed suicide 8 Apr'76 (see below). • **Style:** Political/protest folk singer, whose anthems were always unfairly in the shadow of BOB DYLAN. • **Songwriters:** Writes own material. • **Trivia:** Featured in mid-80's on a Channel 4 documentary 'Chords Of Fame'.

Recommended: CHORDS OF FAME (*7)

PHIL OCHS – vocals, acoustic guitar / with **DANNY KALE** – acoustic guitar

Elektra Elektra

Mar 65. (lp) **ALL THE NEWS THAT'S FIT TO SING** [ ] [ ] Nov 64
– One more parade / The thresher / Talking Vietnam / Lou Marsh / Power and the glory / Celia / The bells / Automation song / Ballad of William Worthy / Knock on the door / Talking Cuban crisis / Bound for glory / Too many martyrs / What's that I hear. *(re-iss.Oct87 on 'Edsel') (re-iss.+c. May89 on 'Carthage') (cd-iss.May94 on 'Hannibal' +=)*– Bullets of Mexico.

Aug 65. (lp) **I AIN'T MARCHING ANYMORE** [ ] [ ] May 65
– I ain't marching anymore / In the heat of the summer / Draft dodger rag / That's what I want to hear / That was the president / Iron lady / The highway man / Links on the chain / Hills of West Virginia / The men behind the guns / Talking Birmingham jam / Ballad of the carpenter / Days of decision / Here's to the state of Mississippi. *(re-iss.+c.May89 on 'Carthage') (cd-iss.May94 on 'Hannibal')*

Dec 65. (7") **I AIN'T MARCHING ANYMORE. / THAT WAS THE PRESIDENT** [ ] [ ]

May 66. (lp) **PHIL OCHS IN CONCERT (live)** [ ] [ ] Feb66
– I'm going to say it now / Bracero / Ringing of revolution / Is there anybody here? / Canons of Christianity / There but for fortune / Cops of the world / Santo Domingo / Changes / Love me, I'm a Liberal / When I'm gone.

A & M A & M

Nov 67. (7") **CROSS MY HEART. / FLOWER LADY** [-] [ ]

Jan 68. (lp) **PLEASURES OF THE HARBOR** [ ] [ ] Oct 67
– Cross my heart / Flower lady / Outside of a small circle of friends / I've had her / Miranda / The party / Pleasures of the harbor / The crucifixion.

Jan 68. (7") **OUTSIDE A SMALL CIRCLE OF FRIENDS. / MIRANDA** [ ] [ ]

Jul 69. (7") **THE WAR IS OVER. / THE HARDER THEY FALL** [-] [ ]

Oct 68. (lp) **TAPE FROM CALIFORNIA** [ ] [ ] Jul 68
– Tape from California / White boots marching in a yellow land / Half a century high / Joe Hill / The war is over / The harder they fall / When in Rome / Floods of Florence.

May 69. (lp) **REHEARSALS FOR RETIREMENT** [ ] [ ]
– Pretty smart on my part / The doll house / I kill therefore I am / William Butler Yeats visits Lincoln Park and escapes unscathed / My life / The scorpion, departs but never returns / The world began in Eden and ended in Los Angeles / Doesn't Lenny live here anymore / Another age / Rehearsals for retirement.

Mar 70. (lp) **PHIL OCHS GREATEST HITS** (not compilation) [ ] [ ]
– One way ticket home / Jim Dean of Indiana / My kingdom for a car / Boy in Ohio / Gas station women / Chords of fame / Ten cents a coup / Bach, Beethoven, Mozart and me / Basket in the pool / No more songs. *(re-iss.Jun86 on 'Edsel', cd-iss.Jul90)*

Mar 70. (7") **ONE WAY TICKET HOME. / MY KINGDOM FOR A CAR** [-] [ ]

PHIL semi-retired after recording Apr70 live album 'GUNFIGHT AT CARNEGIE HALL'. It was only issued in Canada 1975.

Sep 72. (7") **KANSAS CITY BOMBER. / GAS STATION WOMEN** [-] [ ]

Feb 74. (7") **HERE'S TO THE STATE OF RICHARD NIXON. / POWER & THE GLORY** [-] [ ]

DUBLIN
12 m
MANCHESTER

1974. (7") **BWATUE. / NIKO MCHUMBA NGOMBE** [-] [-] Kenya

1975. (lp) **GUNFIGHT AT CARNEGIE HALL (live)** [-] [ ]
– Mona Lisa / I ain't marchin' anymore / Oakie from Meskogee / Chords of fame / Buddy Holly medley:- Not fade away – I'm gonna love you too – Think it over – Oh boy – Everyday – It's so easy – Not fade away / Pleasures of the harbor / Tape from California / Elvis medley:- My baby left me – I'm ready – Heartbreak hotel – All shook up – Are you lonesome tonight – My baby left me (encore) / A fool such as I.

— While visiting friend/singer/protester Victor Jaro in Chile, he was robbed and suffered throat damage which prevented him from singing. After bouts of heavy drinking and schizophrenia, he hanged himself on 9 Apr'76.

– compilations, others, etc. –

1976. Folkways; (lp) **SINGS FOR BROADSIDES** [-] [ ]

1976. Folkways; (lp) **BROADSIDE MAGAZINE INTERVIEWS** [-] [ ]

1980. Folkways; (lp) **THE BROADSIDE TAPES** [-] [ ]

Jan 77. A&M; (d-lp) **CHORDS OF FAME** [ ] [ ] 1974
– I ain't marchin' anymore / No more parades / Draft dodger rag / Here's to the state of Richard Nixon / The bells / Bound of glory / Too many martyrs / There but for fortune / I'm going to say it now / Santo Domingo / Changes / Is there anybody here? / Love me, I'm a Liberal / When I'm gone / Outside of a small circle of friends / Pleasures of the harbor / Tape from California / Chords of fame / Crucifixion / War is over / Jim Dean of Indiana / The power and the glory / Flower lady / No more songs.

Mar 88. Edsel/ US= Rhino; (lp) **A TOAST TO THOSE WHO ARE GONE** (lost tapes) [ ] [-] 1986
– Do what I have to do / Ballad of Billie Sol / Coloured town / A.M.A. song / William Moore / Paul Crump / Going down to Mississippi / I'll be there / Ballad of Oxford / No Christmas in Kentucky / A toast to those who are gone / I'm tired / City boy / Song of my returning. *(cd-iss.195 on 'Diablo')*

May 89. Elektra; (d-lp)(c)(cd) **THERE BUT FOR FORTUNE** (some live 1965-66) [ ] [ ]

Mar 91. Rhino; (cd) **THERE AND NOW: LIVE IN VANCOUVER 1968 (live)** [ ] [ ]

Sinead O'CONNOR

Born: 12 Dec'66, Glenageary, Ireland. Raised in Dublin, her parents divorced when she was 8, and she was later put to a Dominican nun-run center for girls with behavioural problems. In 1985, after attending Dublin's College of Music, she joined local band TON TON MACOUTE, where she met boyfriend and future manager FACHTNA O'CEALLAIGH. In 1986, he arranged for her to guest on U2's The EDGE's soundtrack album 'Captive'. She was soon spotted by Nigel Grainge and Chris Hill of 'Ensign' records, who contracted her that year. In April the following year, she guested for stablemates WORLD PARTY (aka KARL WALLINGER) on album 'Private Revolution'. Two months later, she and new boyfriend / drummer John Reynolds, had a son, Jake. At the end of '87, she issued debut solo 45 'TROY', but this failed to sparkle commercially. Early the next year, she scored first Top 20 hit with 'MANDINKA', which re-actified sales of earlier released album 'THE LION AND THE COBRA'. Early in 1990, she unleashed the excellent PRINCE-penned 'NOTHING COMPARES 2 U', which hit Top spot on both sides of the Atlantic. It was quickly pursued by her second album 'I DO NOT WANT WHAT I HAVEN'T GOT', which also made No.1 in both UK & US. Throughout the rest of early 90's, she was surrounded by controversy for her outspoken views on abortion, religion, AIDS, etc, etc, etc (see further below). • **Style:** Shaven-headed, angel-faced nightingale, whose well intentioned public out-bursts have overshadowed her classy contributions to rock and pop. In 1992, she and her orchestra gave her a more BARBRA STREISAND feel, taking her further back to classic renditions of past standards. **The covers:** YOU DO SOMETHING TO ME + MY HEART BELONGS TO DADDY (Cole Porter) / SOMEONE TO WATCH OVER ME (Ira Gershwin) /DAMN YOUR EYES (Etta James) / SECRET LOVE (Doris Day) / ALL APOLOGIES (Nirvana). Her 1992 album was filled with covers originally sung by; WHY DONT YOU DO RIGHT? (Julie London; J.McCoy) / BEWITCHED, BOTHERED AND BEWILDERED (Ella Fitzgerald; L.Hart & R.Rodgers) / SECRET LOVE + BLACK COFFEE (Sarah Vaughan; F.Webster & S.Burke) / SUCCESS HAS MADE A FAILURE OF OUR HOME (Loretta Lynn; J.Mullins) / DON'T CRY FOR ME ARGENTINA (Elaine Page; Tim Rice & Andrew Lloyd Webber) / I WANT TO BE LOVED BY YOU (Marilyn Monroe; H.Stothart, H.Ruby & B.Kalmar) / GLOOMY SUNDAY (Billie Holiday; L.Javor, R.Seress & Lewis) / LOVE LETTERS (Alison Moyet; E.Heyman & V.Young) / HOW INSENSITIVE (Astrud Gilberto; V.de Morales, A.C.Jobim & Gimbel) / SCARLET RIBBONS (her mum & dad; J.Segal & E.Danzig). She co-writes w/COULTER or REYNOLDS and sample merchant TIM SIMENON for return 1994 album. Other covers; YOU MAKE ME FEEL SO REAL (Van Morrison) • **Miscellaneous:** She married John Reynolds in Mar'89, but soon split from him 18 months later. Early in 1991, she moved in to a house with long-time friend Ciara O'Flanagan.

Recommended: I DO NOT WANT WHAT I HAVEN'T GOT (*9) / THE LION AND THE COBRA (*7).

SINEAD O'CONNOR – vocals (ex-TON TON MACOUTE) / with **ENYA** + **MARCO PIRRONI**

Ensign Chrysalis

Oct 87. (7")(12") **TROY. / STILL LISTENING** [ ] [ ]

Nov 87. (lp)(c)(cd) **THE LION AND THE COBRA** [27] [36]
– Jackie / Mandinka / Jerusalem / Just like U said it would B / Never get old / Troy / I want your (hands on me) / Drink before the war / Just call me Joe. *(re-iss.Jan90 hit No.37)*

Dec 87. (7") **MANDINKA. / DRINK BEFORE THE WAR** [17] [ ]
(12"+=)/ /(12"+=) – ('A'dub mix)./ / ('A'remix).
(cd-s+=) – ('A'instrumental dub) / Still listening.

Apr 88. (7") **I WANT YOUR (HANDS ON ME). / JUST CALL ME JOE** [ ] [ ]

— ('B'side as "SINEAD O'CONNOR with MC LYTE")
(12"+=)(cd-s+=) – ('A'dance) / ('A'street).
(12"+=) – ('A'-2 different mixes).

Oct 88. (7") **JUMP IN THE RIVER. / NEVER GET OLD (live)** [ ] [ ]
(12"+=)(cd-s+=) – ('A'duet with KAREN FINLAY).

— Early 1989, she appeared on THE THE's album 'Mind Bomb', singing on 'Kingdom Of Rain'.

Ensign Ensign

Jan 90. (7") **NOTHING COMPARES 2 U. / JUMP IN THE RIVER** [1] [1] Ma4 90
(12"+=)(cd-s+=) – ('B'instrumental).

Mar 90. (cd)(c)(lp) **I DO NOT WANT WHAT I HAVEN'T GOT** [1] [1]
– Feel so different / I an stretched on your grave / Three babies / The Emperor's new clothes / Black boys in mopeds / Nothing compares 2 U / Jump in the river / You cause as much sorrow / The last day of our acquaintance / I do not want what I haven't got. *(re-iss.cd Mar94)*

Jul 90. (7") **THE EMPEROR'S NEW CLOTHES. / WHAT DO YOU WANT** [31] [60] Jun 90
(c-s+=) – I am stretched on your grave.
(12")(cd-s) – ('A'side remixed) / I am stretched on your grave (mix) / ('A'dub mix).

Oct 90. (7") **THREE BABIES. / DAMN YOUR EYES** [42] [ ]
(12"+=)(c-s+=)(cd-s+=) – Troy (live) / The value of ignorance.

May 91. (7") **MY SPECIAL CHILD. / NOTHING COMPARES 2 U (live)** [42] [ ]
(12"+=)(cd-s+=) – ('A'instrumental) / The Emperor's new clothes (live).
(12"+=)(c-s+=)(cd-s+=) – Standing on your grave.

Dec 91. (7")(cd-s) **SILENT NIGHT. / IRISH WAYS & IRISH LAWS (live)** [60] [ ]

— Early in 1991, she was the first ever person to refuse her Grammy for alternative 1990 album. She protested about anti-legalizing Irish abortion on TV and press. After earlier ripping a photo of Pope John Paul II on US Saturday Night Live, she was booed off-stage (Oct92) at a Bob Dylan tribute concert at Madison Square Garden. Due to crowd noise which drowned out backing band, she eventually sang unaccompanied a Bob Marley! song 'War'. She announced that month she was to retire, although thankfully she retracted press statements by late '92.

— now with **CHRIS PARKER** – drums / **DAVID FINCK** – bass / **RICHARD TEE** – piano / **IRA SIEGAL** – guitar / **DAVE LEBOLT** – synthesizer / plus a host of saxists, flautists, violinists, trumpeters & backing singers.

Sep 92. (cd-s) **SUCCESS HAS MADE A FAILURE OF OUR HOME / YOU DO SOMETHING TO ME / I WANT TO BE LOVED BY YOU** [18] [ ]
(cd-s) – (1st track) / Someone to watch over me / My heart belongs to daddy.

Sep 92. (cd)(c)(lp) **AM I NOT YOUR GIRL?** [6] [27]
– Why don't you do right? / Bewitched, bothered and bewildered / Secret love / Black coffee / Success has made a failure of our lives / Don't cry for me Argentina / I want to be loved by you / Gloomy Sunday / Love letters / How insensitive / Scarlet ribbons / Don't cry for me Argentina (inst.).

In Oct'92, she collaborated on MARXMAN single 'Ship Ahoy'.

Dec 92. (7")(c-s) **DON'T CRY FOR ME ARGENTINA. / AVE MARIA** [53] [ ]
(cd-s+=) – Scarlet ribbons.
(cd-s) – ('A'side) / Love letters / Scarlet ribbons.

In Jun'93, she was credited on WILLIE NELSON single 'Don't Give Up'.

Feb 94. (7")(c-s) **YOU MADE ME THE THIEF OF YOUR HEART. / THE FATHER AND HIS WIFE THE SPIRIT** [42] [ ]
(12"+=)(cd-s+=) – ('A'mixes).

(above single from film 'In The Name Of The Father'; on 'Island' records)

— now with **JOHN REYNOLDS** – drums / **PHIL COULTER** – piano / **DAVE CLAYTON** – keyboards / **MARCO PIRRONI + VAN GILLIANO** – guitar / **TIM SIMENON** etc.

Sep 94. (cd)(c)(lp) **UNIVERSAL MOTHER** [19] [37]
– Fire on Babylon / John I love you / My darling child / Am I human? / Red football / All apologies / A perfect Indian / Scorn not his simplicity / All babies / In this heart / Tiny grief song / Famine / Thank you for hearing me.

Nov 94. (12")(c-s)(cd-s) **THANK YOU FOR HEARING ME. / FIRE ON BABYLON (remix)** [13] [ ]
(cd-s) – ('A'side) / I believe in you / Streets of London / House of the rising Sun.

— In Apr'95, she duetted with SHANE MacGOWAN on his 'HAUNTED' hit.

Aug 95. (c-s)(cd-s) **FAMINE (extended) / FAMINE / ALL APOLOGIES** [51] [ ]
(12") – ('A'extended) / Fire On Babylon (M Beat remix).

OFFSPRING

Formed: Orange County, California, USA . . . 1991 by DEXTER HOLLAND, etc. After one lp and a 45 as THE OFFSPRING, they quickly signed to other DIY label 'Epitaph' run by BRAD GUREWITZ (ex-BAD RELIGION's guitarist), where they unleashed follow-up album 'IGNITION'. However it wasn't until 1994 and their follow-up 'SMASH', that their breakthrough came to light. It went onto sell over a million copies in the States and was awaiting deserved recognition in the UK. • **Style:** Underground punk skatecore rock, hard on the heels of GREEN DAY, but more like BLACK FLAG. • **Songwriters:** HOLLAND most.

Recommended: SMASH (*8)

DEXTER HOLLAND – vocals, guitar / **NOODLES** (KEVIN WASSERMAN) – guitar / **GREG KRIESEL** – bass / **RON WELTY** – drums

not issued Nitro

1989. (lp) **THE OFFSPRING** [-] [ ]

– Jennifer lost the war / Elders / Out on patrol / Crossroads / Demons / Beheaded / Tehran / A thousand days / Black ball / I'll be waiting / Kill the president. *(re-iss.cd/c Nov95 on 'Nitro')*

not issued — Plastic Head

1991. (7") **BAGHDAD. /** – [ ]

Epitaph — Epitaph

Oct 92. (cd)(c)(lp) **IGNITION** – [ ]

Sep 94. (cd)(c)(lp) **SMASH** 21 4 Apr94

– Time to relax / Nitro (youth energy) / Bad habit / Gotta get away / Genocide / Something to believe in / Come out and play / Self esteem / It'll be a long time / Killboy powerhead / What happened to you / So alone / Not the one / Smash.

Sep 94. (c-s)(12")(cd-s) **COME OUT AND PLAY. / SESSION / ('A'acoustic)** [ ] [ ]

Feb 95. (7")(c-s)(12")(cd-s) **SELF ESTEEM. / JENNIFER LOST THE WAR / BURN IT UP** 37 [ ]

OutOfStep — Epitaph

Aug 95. (7")(c-s)(cd-s) **GOTTA GET AWAY. / SMASH** 43 [ ]

Mike OLDFIELD

Born: 15 May'53, Reading, Berkshire, England. Started playing guitar at age 7, and by 1968, had formed SALLYANGIE with sister SALLY. They signed to folk-orientated label 'Transatlantic', who issued lp 'CHILDREN OF THE SUN'. After releasing a single 'TWO SHIPS'. / 'COLOURS OF THE WORLD' in Sep69, they broke partnership to concentrate on other projects. After a spell in short-lived BAREFOOT, MIKE became bassist in Mar70 for KEVIN AYERS' band The WHOLE WORLD. He appeared on 2 of his albums 'SHOOTING AT THE MOON' & 'WHATEVERSHE-BRINGSWESING' between 1971 & 1972, before they dissolved. Around this time, MIKE started work on his own solo project, which gained financial support in 1972 from Richard Branson's newly formed 'Virgin' label. The same year, MIKE also contributed session work for EDGAR BROUGHTON BAND and DAVID BEDFORD. The project 'TUBULAR BELLS', finally saw light of day in May73, and soon stirred critical acclaim from music press. A near 50-minute concept piece, played and overdubbed many times by now multi-instrumentalist MIKE, it went into UK Top 3 a year later. Helped by an unusual Top 10 single cut in the US that was used for the horror movie 'The Exorcist', it hit Top 3. In Sep'74, his follow-up 'HERGEST RIDGE', was complete, and this went straight to UK No.1. Critically lambasted by some critics as "Son of Tubular Bells", it only managed to hit No.87 in the States. OLDFIELD continued to surface with some work during the next couple of decades, but never quite regained earlier impact of the then and still now classic 'TUBULAR BELLS'. In 1992 (19 years after), 'WEA' records returned MIKE to UK No.1, with the almost identical but still appealling 'TUBULAR BELLS II'. • **Style:** Multi-talented introverted genius, with an over-the-top approach to his music, due to his move into more commercially based rock in the 80's. However his contribution to the 70's, in both classical and rock-pop fields, were only matched by PINK FLOYD in that era. 1975-1978, saw him even branch into African and folk-type origins on albums 'OMMADAWN' & 'INCANTATIONS'. Although he embarrassed his rock following by releasing mainly Christmassy hit 45's around same time. • **Songwriters:** Writes own material except; SAILOR'S HORNPIPE (trad.) / IN DULCE JUBILO (R.L. Pearsall) / WILLIAM TELL OVERTURE (Korsokov) / BLUE PETER (BBC copyright) / ARRIVAL (Abba) / WONDERFUL LAND (Shadows) / ETUDE (Franscisco Tarrega). In 1982, he was augmented in writing by group. • **Trivia:** In the mid-70's, MIKE also had time to session on albums by Virgin artists; DAVID BEDFORD (Star's End) / ROBERT WYATT (Rock Bottom) / TOM NEWMAN (Fine Old Tom). MIKE's sister SALLY also went on to have a UK Top 20 hit late '78 with 'MIRRORS'.

Recommended: TUBULAR BELLS (*10) / HERGEST RIDGE (*7) / OMMADAWN (*8) / INCANTATIONS (*8).

MIKE OLDFIELD – guitar, bass, everything (ex-KEVIN AYERS, ex-SALLYANGIE) with **TOM NEWMAN** – guitar / **JON FIELD** – flute / **STAN BROUGHTON** – drums / **LINDSAY COOPER** – wind. plus **VIVIAN STANSHALL** – narration (ex-BONZO DOG BAND)

Virgin — Virgin

May 73. (lp)(c) **TUBULAR BELLS** 1 3 Nov 73

– Tubular bells (side 1) / Tubular bells (side 2). *(Finally hit UK No.1 in Oct74) (quad-lp iss.Jul74) (pic-lp Dec78) (cd-iss.Jun83 hit No.28)*

Feb 74. (7") **TUBULAR BELLS (edit). / TUBULAR BELLS (excerpt)** – 7

Jun 74. (7") **MIKE OLDFIELD'S SINGLE (THEME FROM TUBULAR BELLS). / FROGGY WENT A-COURTIN'** 31 –

— now with **TERRY OLDFIELD** – wind / etc.

Sep 74. (lp)(c) **HERGEST RIDGE** 1 87

– Hergest ridge (side 1) / Hergest ridge (side 2). *(re-iss.+cd.Apr86)*

Jan 75. (lp)(c) **THE ORCHESTRAL TUBULAR BELLS (WITH THE ROYAL PHILHARMONIC ORCHESTRA)** 17 [ ]

– The orchestral Tubular Bells part 1 / The orchestral Tubular Bells part 2. (Rec.live Sep'74, conducted by DAVID BEDFORD, with MIKE OLDFIELD – guitar) *(cd-iss.Jul87) (re-iss.+cd.Sep89)*

Feb 75. (7") **DON ALFONSO. / IN DULCE JUBILO** [ ] –

— back-up were **JUBULA** (African musicians) / **PIERRE MOERLEN** (of GONG) / backing vocals by sister **SALLY OLDFIELD + CLODAGH SIMMONDS**

Nov 75. (lp)(c) **OMMADAWN** 4 [ ]

– Ommadawn (side 1) / Ommadawn (side 2). *(quad-lp Feb86) (cd-iss.1986)*

Nov 75. (7") **IN DULCE JUBILO. / ON HORSEBACK** 4 –

Nov 75. (7") **OMMADAWN (excerpt). / ON HORSEBACK** – [ ]

Oct 76. (7") **PORTSMOUTH. / SPEAK (THO' YOU ONLY SAY FAREWELL)** 3 –

Nov 76. (7") **PORTSMOUTH. / ALGIERS** – [ ]

Feb 77. (7") **WILLIAM TELL OVERTURE. / ALGIERS** [ ] –

Dec 77. (7") **THE CUCKOO SONG. / PIPE TUNE** [ ] –

— added from last album. (see most musicians from following live album)

Nov 78. (d-lp)(d-c) **INCANTATIONS** 14 [ ]

– Incantations (part 1) / Incantations (part 2) / Incantations (part 3) / Incantations (part 4). *(cd-iss.Feb87, omits 4 mins.of side 3)*

Apr 79. (7") **GUILTY. / INCANTATIONS (excerpt)** 22 –

(12"blue) – ('A'side) / Guilty (live).

— MIKE with **PIERRE MOERLEN** – drums, percussion / **RINGO McDONOUGH** – bodhran / **MIKE FRYE, BENOIT MOERLEN, DAVID BEDFORD** (also string arrangements) / **NICO RAMSDEN** – guitar / **PHIL BEER** – guitar, vocals / **PEKKA POHJOLA** – bass / **RAY GAY, RALPH IZEN, SIMO SALMINEN, COLIN MOORE** – trumpets / **SEBASTIAN BELL, CHRIS NICHOLLS** – flutes / **PETE LEMER, TIM CROSS** – keyboards / **MADDY PRIOR** – vocals / **JONATHAN KAHAN, DICK STUDT, BEN CRUFT, JANE PRYCE, LIZ EDWARDS, NICOLA HURTON** – violins / **VANESSA PARK, DAVID BUCKNALL, JESSICA FORD, NIGEL WARREN-GREEN** – cellos / **NICK WORTERS, JOE KIRBY** – bass / **DON McVAY, PAULINE MACK, DANNY DAGGERS, MELINDA DAGGERS, LIZ BUTLER, ROSS COHEN** – vocals, plus 11 piece choir.

Aug 79. (d-lp)(d-c) **EXPOSED (live)** 16 –

– Incantations (parts 1 and 2) / Incantations (parts 3 and 4) / Tubular bells (part 1) / Tubular bells (part 2) / Guilty. *(also on quad) (d-cd-iss.Jul86)*

— Trimmed backing group down.

Nov 79. (7") **BLUE PETER. / WOODHENGE** 19 –

Dec 79. (lp)(c) **PLATINUM** 24 –

– Platinum:- Airborne – Platinum – Charleston North star – Platimun finale / Woodhenge / Sally / Punkadiddle / I got rhythm. *(cd-iss.1989)*

— next featured **PHIL COLLINS** – drums

Sep 80. (7") **ARRIVAL. / POLKA** [ ] –

Oct 80. (lp)(c) **QE2** 27 –

– Taurus I / Sheba / Conflict / Arrival / Wonderful land / Mirage / QE2 / Celt / Molly. *(cd-iss.1989)*

Nov 80. (7") **WONDERFUL LAND. / SHEBA** [ ] –

Dec 80. (d-lp)(d-c) **AIRBORN** – [ ]

– (see PLATINUM tracks, except 'Guilty' repl. – / / Tubular bells live part 1 / Incantations (segue of 20+ mins. studio and live recordings)

— MIKE brought in **MAGGIE REILLY** – vocals (ex-CADO BELLE) / **TIM CROSS** – keys / **MORRIS PERT** – percussion, drums (ex-BRAND X) / **RICK FENN** – bass, guitar / **PIERRE MOERLEN** – drums, percussion returned to repl. MIKE FRYE / added **TIM RENWICK** – bass, guitar

Mar 82. (7")(7"pic-d) **FIVE MILES OUT. / LIVE PUNKADIDDLE** 43 [ ]

Mar 82. (lp)(c) **FIVE MILES OUT** 7 [ ]

– Taurus II / Family man / Orabidoo / Mount Teidi / Five miles out. *(cd-iss.1983) (re-iss.Apr90) (re-iss.cd+c Oct94 on 'Virgin-VIP')*

Jun 82. (7")(7"pic-d) **FAMILY MAN. / MOUNT TEIDI** 45 [ ]

Sep 82. (7")(7"pic-d) **MISTAKE. / (THE PEAK) WALDBERG** [ ] [ ]

— MIKE retained REILLY + MOERLEN. New members were **SIMON PHILLIPS** – drums / **PHIL SPALDING** – bass / **GRAEME PLEETH** – keyboards / **SIMON HOUSE** – violin

May 83. (7")(7"pic-d) **MOONLIGHT SHADOW. / RITE OF MAN** 4 [ ]

(12"+=) – ('A'extended).

May 83. (lp)(c)(cd) **CRISES** 6 [ ]

– Crises / Moonlight shadow / In high places / Foreign affair / Taurus III / Shadow on the wall *. (* vocals by **ROGER CHAPMAN, ex-FAMILY**) *(re-iss.cd+c May94 on 'Virgin-VIP')*

Sep 83. (7") **SHADOW ON THE WALL. / TAURUS III** [ ] [ ]

(12") – ('A'extended).

Jan 84. (7") **CRIME OF PASSION. / JUNGLE GARDENIA** 61 [ ]

(12") – ('A'extended).

— He retained **REILLY, PHILLIPS + SPALDING** – adding guitar / plus **BARRY PALMER** – vocals / **MICKEY SIMMONDS** – keyboards / **HAROLD ZUSCHRADER** – synth.

Jun 84. (7") **TO FRANCE. / IN THE POOL** 48 [ ]

(12"+=) – Bones.

Jul 84. (lp)(c)(cd) **DISCOVERY** 15 [ ]

– To France / Poison arrows / Crystal gazing / Tricks of the light / Discovery / Talk about your life / Saved by a bell / The lake.

Sep 84. (7") **TRICKS OF THE LIGHT. / APEMAN** [ ] [ ]

(12"+=) – ('A'instrumental).

Nov 84. (7") **ETUDE. / EVACUATION** [ ] [ ]

(12") – ('A' & 'B'extended).

Dec 84. (lp)(c)(cd) **THE KILLING FIELDS (Film Soundtrack)** 97 [ ]

– Pran's theme / Requiem for a city / Evacuation / Pran's theme 2 / Capture / Execution / Bad news / Pran's departure / Worksite / The year zero / Blood sucking / The year zero 2 / Pran's escape – The killing fields / The trek / The boy's burial – Pran sees the red cross / Good news / Etude. *(re-iss.Jun88)*

— **ANITA HEGERLAND + ALED JONES** – vocals repl. REILLY

Nov 85. (7") **PICTURES IN THE DARK. / LEGEND** 50 [ ]

('A'ext-12") – The trap.

Apr 86. (7")(7"sha-pic-d) **SHINE. / THE PATH** [ ] [ ]

('A'ext-12") – (as above)

May 87. (7") **IN HIGH PLACES. / POISON ARROWS** [ ] –

(12"+=) – Jungle Gardenia.

— vocalists – **JON ANDERSON / KEVIN AYERS / BONNIE TYLER**

Sep 87. (7") **ISLANDS. / THE WIND CHIMES (part one)** [ ] [ ]

(c-s+=)(cd-s+=)(12"+=) – When the night's on fire.

(12"='A'extended).

Oct 87. (lp)(c)(cd) **ISLANDS** 29 [ ]

– The wind chimes (parts 1 & 2) / Islands / Flying start / North point / Magic touch / The time has come. *(cd+=)*– When the night's on fire.

Nov 87. (7") **THE TIME HAS COME. / (Final extract from) THE WIND CHIMES** [ ] –

(12"+=) – ('A'original mix).

Nov 87. (7") **MAGIC TOUCH. / THE WIND CHIMES (part 1)** -
Feb 88. (7")(12") **FLYING START. / THE WIND CHIMES (part 2)**
Jul 89. (7") **EARTHMOVING. / BRIDGE TO PARADISE**
(12"+=)(cd-s+=) – ('A'disco mix).
Jul 89. (lp)(c)(cd) **EARTHMOVING** 30
– Holy / Hostage / Far country / Innocent / Runaway son / See the light / Earthmoving / Blue night / Nothing but – Bridge to Paradise.
Oct 89. (7") **INNOCENT. / EARTHMOVING (club mix)**
(12"+=)(cd-s+=) – ('A'version).
Jun 90. (cd)(c)(lp) **AMAROK** 49
– Amarok (part 1) / Amarok (part 2).

MICHAEL OLDFIELD

with **SIMON PHILLIPS** – drums / **DAVE LEVY** – bass / **MICKEY SIMMONDS** – keyboards / **ANDY LONGHURST** – keyboards / **COURTNEY PINE** – sax
Jan 91. (7")(12")(cd-s) **HEAVEN'S OPEN. / EXCERPT FROM AMAROK** -
Mar 91. (cd)(c)(lp) **HEAVEN'S OPEN**
– Make make / No dream / Mr.Shame / Gimme back / Heaven's open / Music from the balcony.

MIKE OLDFIELD

solo again playing most instruments, except some guests & a bagpipe band.
W.E.A. W.E.A.
Sep 92. (cd)(c)(lp) **TUBULAR BELLS II** 1
– Sentinel / Dark star / Clear light / Blue saloon / Sunjammer / Red dawn / The bell / Weightless / The great pain / Sunset door / Tattoo / Altered state / Maya gold / Moonshine.
Sep 92. (7")(c-s)(cd-s) **SENTINEL (SINGLE RESTRUCTION). / EARLY STAGES** 10
Dec 92. (7")(c-s) **TATTOO. / SILENT NIGHT / SENTINEL (live)** 33
(cd-ep+=) – Live At Edinburgh Castle:- Moonshine / Reprise / Maya gold.
Apr 93. (7")(c-s) **THE BELL. / SENTINEL** 50
(cd-s+=) – ('A' 3 mixes).
(cd-s) – (5 'A'mixes).
Nov 94. (cd)(c)(lp) **THE SONGS OF DISTANT EARTH** 24
– In the beginning / Let there be light / Supernova / Magellan / First landing / Oceania / Only time will tell / Prayer for the Earth / Lament for Atlantis / The chamber / Hibernaculum / Tubular world / The shining ones / Crystal clear / The sunken forest / Ascension / A new beginning. *(re-iss.cd/c Oct95)*
Dec 94. (cd-s) **HIBERNACULUM. / MOONSHINE (mixes)** 47
(c-s)(cd-s) – ('A'side) / The spectral Song of the boat men.
Aug 95. (cd-s) **LET THERE BE LIGHT (Indian Lake mix) / LET THERE BE LIGHT (BT's entropic dub)** 51
(12") – ('A'-BT's pure luminescence remix) / ('A'-Hardfloor mix) / ('A'club mix).
(cd-s) – (above club mix) repl.by – ('A'-Ultraviolet mix).

– compilations, etc. –

Nov 76. Virgin; (4xlp-box) **BOXED** 22 -
– (TUBULAR BELLS / HERGEST RIDGE / OMMADAWN / + COLLABORATIONS (singles, etc.) *(re-iss.+4xc+4xcd. 1985) (cd-box re-iss.1990)*
Dec 78. Virgin; (7"ep)(12"ep) **TAKE 4** 72 -
– Portsmouth / In dulce jubilo / Wrekorder wrondo / Sailor's hornpipe.
Oct 85. Virgin; (d-lp)(c)(cd) **THE COMPLETE MIKE OLDFIELD** 36 -
– Arrival / In dulce jubilo / Portsmouth / Jungle gardenia / Guilty / Blue Peter / Waldberg (the peak) / Etude / Wonderful land / Moonlight shadow / Family man / Mistake / Five miles out / Crime of passion / To France / Shadow on the wall / Excerpt from Tubular Bells / Sheba / Mirage / Platinum / Mount Tiede / Excerpt from Ommadawn / Excerpt from Hergest Ridge / Excerpt from Incantations / Excerpt from Killing Fields.
Jun 88. Virgin; (3"cd-ep) **MOONLIGHT SHADOW (extended) / RITE OF MAN / TO FRANCE / JUNGLE GARDENIA** -
Jun 88. Virgin; (cd-video) **THE WIND CHIMES (Soundtrack 1986)** -
Dec 90. Virgin; (7")(c-s) **ETUDE. / GAKKAEN** -
(12"+=)(cd-s+=) – ('A'extended) (with "ONO GAGUKU KAI").
—— (The above 'A'side was now used on TV ad for 'Nurofen'.)
Sep 93. Virgin; (cd)(c)(d-lp) **ELEMENTS: THE BEST OF MIKE OLDFIELD** 5
– Tubular bells – opening hteme / Family man / Moonlight shadow / Heaven's open / Five miles out / To France / Foreign affair / In dulce jubilo / Shadow on the wall / Islands / Etude / Sentinel / Ommadawn – excerpt / Incantations part four – excerpt / Amarok – excerpt / Portsmouth.
Sep 93. Virgin; (4xcd-box) **ELEMENTS – MIKE OLDFIELD 1973-1991**
– (all TUBULAR BELLS & other album excerpts, plus singles to 1991)
Oct 93. Virgin; (7")(c-s) **MOONLIGHT SHADOW. / MOONLIGHT SHADOW (extended version)** 52
(cd-s+=) – In The Pool (Instrumental) / Bones (Instrumental)
Nov 93. Virgin; (c-ep)(cd-ep) **THE MIKE OLDFIELD CHRISTMAS EP**
– In dulce jubilo / Portsmouth

OMD (see under ⇒ ORCHESTRAL MANOEUVRES IN THE DARK)

ONLY ONES

Formed: South London, England . . . 1976 by singer/guitarist PERRETT out of recently defunct ENGLAND'S GLORY, who also comprised HARRY KAKOULLI – bass & JON NEWEY – drums. They were managed by Harry's sister ZENA, who also provided some backing vocals alongside 4th member; MICHAEL KEMP – keyboards. When HARRY, quit to join SQUEEZE in 1974, PERRETT found new veteran musicians JOHN PERRY, MIKE KELLIE and ALAN MAIR, who became The ONLY ONES. Their vinyl debut 'LOVERS OF TODAY', came out in Summer '77 on Zena & Peter's own 'Vengeance', and sold enough to attract major 'CBS'. In April '78, their exhilarating 'ANOTHER GIRL, ANOTHER PLANET', was issued, and remains to this day in the "One That Got Away" bracket. Their eponymous self-produced debut soon followed, and this scraped into UK Top 60, paving the way for 2 more chart albums, before their ill-timed demise. • **Style:** New wave/punk balladeers, fronted by the charismatic PERRETT, whose laid back dragging lyrical style, was reminiscent of LOU REED. • **Songwriters:** PERRETT compositions except; FOOLS (Johnny Duncan) / MY WAY OF GIVING (Small Faces) / SILENT NIGHT (trad.carol). • **Trivia:** PERRETT is known to have made recordings with SQUEEZE man GLENN TILBROOK in the mid-70's.

Recommended: THE ONLY ONES (*8) / THE IMMORTAL STORY (*8).

PETER PERRETT – vocals, guitar (ex-ENGLAND'S GLORY) / **JOHN PERRY** – lead guitar, keyboards (ex-RATBITES FGROM HELL) / **MIKE KELLIE** (b.24 Mar'47, Birmingham, England) – drums (ex-SPOOKY TOOTH, ex-FRAMPTON'S CAMEL) / **ALAN MAIR** – bass (ex-BEATSTALKERS)
Vengeance not issued
Jun 77. (7")(12") **LOVERS OF TODAY. / PETER AND THE PETS** -
C.B.S. Epic
Apr 78. (7") **ANOTHER GIRL, ANOTHER PLANET. / SPECIAL VIEW**
May 78. (lp)(c) **THE ONLY ONES** 56
– The whole of the law / Another girl, another planet / Breaking down / City of fun / The beast / Creature of doom / It's the truth / Language problem / No peace for the wicked / Immortal story. *(re-iss.1984) (re-iss.cd Sep94 on 'Rewind')*
Aug 78. (12") **ANOTHER GIRL, ANOTHER PLANET. / AS MY WIFE SAYS** -
Feb 79. (7") **YOU'VE GOT TO PAY. / THIS AIN'T ALL (IT'S MADE OUT TO BE)**
Mar 79. (lp)(c) **EVEN SERPENTS SHINE** 42
– From here to eternity / Flaming touch / You've got to pay / No solution / In betweens / Out there in the night / Curtains for you / Programme / Someone who cares / Miles from nowhere / Instrumental. *(re-iss.1985)*
Apr 79. (12"blue) **OUT THERE IN THE NIGHT. / LOVERS OF TODAY / PETER AND THE PETS** -
Jun 79. (lp)(c) **SPECIAL VIEW** (compilation 77-79) -
– Another girl, another planet / Lovers of today / Peter and the pets / The beast / City of fun / The whole of the law / Out there in the night / Someome who cares / You've got to pay / Flaming torch / Curtains for you / From here to eternity.
Nov 79. (7") **TROUBLE IN THE WORLD. / YOUR CHOSEN LIFE** -
Apr 80. (lp)(c) **BABY'S GOT A GUN** 37
– The happy pilgrim / Why don't you kill yourself / Me and my shadow / Deadly nightshade / Strange mouth / The big sleep / Oh Lucinda (love becomes a habit) / Reunion / Trouble in the world / Castle built on sand / Fools / My way out of here. *(re-iss.1985)*
(on below 45; PAULINE MURRAY, ex-PENETRATION)
May 80. (7") **FOOLS. (by "The ONLY ONES featuring PETER & PAULINE") / CASTLE BUILT ON SAND** -
—— Disbanded March '81, PERRY formed DECLINE AND FALL but soon disappeared. In Autumn 91, PERRETT augmented the HEARTTHROBS live in Canada.

– compilations, others, etc. –

Jan 83. Vengeance; (7") **BABY'S GOT A GUN. / SILENT NIGHT ('B' by PETER PERRETT)** -
(re-iss.Aug85)
(next lp featured on session **GLENN TILBROOK + GORDON EDWARDS** to repl. KELLIE + MAIR.
Jun 84. Closer; (m-lp) **REMAINS** (out-takes from last album) - - France
(cd-iss.Dec88)
Oct 86. Dojo; (lp) **ALONE IN THE NIGHT** -
Aug 89. Mau Mau; (lp)(c)(cd) **THE ONLY ONES LIVE (live)** -
Dec 89. Strange Fruit; (lp)(c)(cd) **DOUBLE PEEL SESSIONS** -
(re-iss.Jul94)
Jan 92. Columbia; (7") **ANOTHER GIRL, ANOTHER PLANET. / ('B' by 'Psychedelic Furs')** 57 -
(12"+=)(12"red+=)(cd-s+=) – Lovers of today.
May 92. (cd)(c)(d-lp) **THE IMMORTAL STORY** -
– Lovers of today / Peter and the pets / The whole of the law / Another girl, another planet / Special view (aka Telescopic love) / The beast / It's the truth / No peace for the wicked / The immortal story / From here to eternity / In betweens / No solution / Curtains for you / Someone who cares / Miles from nowhere / Instrumental / Your chosen life / Baby's got a gun / Why don't you kill yourself / Oh Lucinda (love becomes a habit) / Big sleep.
Dec 93. Jungle; (cd) **THE BIG SLEEP** -
Dec 95. Windsong; (cd) **IN CONCERT** -

ENGLAND'S GLORY

(The band featuring PERRETT)
May 87. 5 Hours Back; (lp) **ENGLAND'S GLORY – THE LEGENDARY LOST RECORDINGS** -

The ONE

PETER PERRETT – vocals, guitar
Dwarf not issued
Nov 94. (12"ep)(cd-ep) **CULTURED PALATE** -
– Baby don't talk / etc.

ORANGE JUICE (see under ⇒ COLLINS, Edwyn)

ORB

Formed: South London, England … 1989 by remix supremo and ex-KILLING JOKE roadie Dr.ALEX PATERSON. He took the name from a Woody Allen psi-fi film 'Sleepers' and found ex-BRILLIANT guitarist JIM CAUTY. They broke through in the early 90's when 'BLUE ROOM' hit UK Top 10. Their label 'Wau! Mr. Modo' had by now been taken over by 'Big Life'. • **Style:** Ambient electronic rave project, whose lengthy ep's & lp's, have graced the new dancefloors of the 90's, although influenced by TANGERINE DREAM or ENO. • **Songwriters:** Most by WESTON and PATERSON. • **Trivia:** The ORB have remixed many including 'Mute' label stars; DEPECHE MODE / ERASURE & WIRE. In 1992, caused upset in the Asian community when using their religious chant.

Recommended: UF ORB (*9) / ADVENTURES BEYOND THE ULTRAWORLD (*9)

ALEX PATERSON – synth, keyboards / with **JIM CAUTY**

Wau! Mr.Modo | not issued

May 89. (ltd.12"ep) **KISS (as "ROCKMAN ROCK & LX DEE")** [ ] [–]
– Kiss your love / Suck my kiss mix / The roof is on fire / Ambiorix mix.

Oct 89. (12") **A HUGE EVER GROWING PULSATING BRAIN THAT RULES FROM THE CENTRE OF THE ULTRAWORLD: LOVIN' YOU (Orbital mix). / ('A'bucket and spade mix) / WHY IS 6 SCARED OF 7?** [ ] [–]
(re-iss.+cd-ep Jun90 on next new label, remixed Jul90)

In Nov90, they collaborated on STEVE HILLAGE's SYSTEM 7 release 'Sunburst'.

Big Life | Mercury

Nov 90. (7") **LITTLE FLUFFY CLOUDS. / ('A'ambient mix Mk.1)** [ ] [ ]
(dance mix-12"+=)(cd-s+=) – Into the fourth dimension (Essenes beyond..)

— CAUTY was replaced by **STEVE HILLAGE** – guitar (ex-Solo artist, ex-GONG) / **MIQUETTE GIRAUDY** (ex-GONG) + **ANDY FALCONER**

Apr 91. (d-cd)(d-c)(d-lp) **ADVENTURES BEYOND THE ULTRAWORLD** [29] [ ] Nov 91
– Little fluffy clouds / Earth (Gaia) / Supernova at the end of the universe / Back side of the Moon / Spanish castles in space / Perpetual dawn / Into the fourth dimension / Outlands / Star 6 & 7 8 9 / A huge ever growing pulsating brain that rules from the centre of the Ultraworld.

Jun 91. (7")(c-s) **PERPETUAL DAWN (SOLAR YOUTH). / STAR 6&789 (phase II)** [61] [ ]
(ext-12"+=)(cd-s+=) – ('A'ultrabass 1 mix).
(12"ep 'ORB IN DUB' Andy Weatherall ultrabass mixes += Towers Of Dub')

— In Nov91, SYSTEM 7 issued another release on '10-Virgin'; 'Miracle'.

Dec 91 (cd)(c)(lp) **THE AUBREY MIXES: THE ULTRAWORLD EXCURSIONS (deleted after 1 day)** [44] [ ]
– Little fluffy clouds / (Pal Joey mix) / Black side of the moon (Steve Hillage remix) / Spanish castles in Spain (Youth remix) / Outlands (Ready made remix) / A huge overgrowing pulsating brain (Jim Caldy & Dr. Alex Patterson remix).

— **PATERSON** now with **THRASH** – guitars? plus guests **YOUTH, STUART McMILLAN, GUY PRATT, JAH WOBBLE, STEVE HILLAGE, MIQUETTE GIRAUDY, THOMAS FEHLMANN, GREG HUNTER, ORDE MEIKLE, TOM GREEN, MARNEY PAX.**

Jun 92. (12"ep)(c-ep)(cd-ep) **THE BLUE ROOM** [8] [ ]
– The blue room (nearly 40 mins.)
(cd-ep+=) – The blue room (2 shorter 4 minute versions) / Towers of dub (mad professor mix).

Jul 92. (d-cd)(d-c)(t-lp) **UF ORB** [1] [ ]
– O.O.B.E. / U.F. Orb / Blue room / Towers of dub / Close encounters / Majestic / Sticky end.
– (free live lp at some shops 'Soundtrack To The Film: ADVENTURES BEYOND THE ULTRAWORLD: PATTERNS & TEXTURES')

Oct 92. (12"-box)(c-box)(d-cd-box) **ASSASSIN (the oasis of rhythms mix). / U.F.ORB (Bandalu mix)** [12] [ ]
(d-cd+=) – ('A'another live version mix).

Nov 93. (12"ep)(c-ep)(cd-ep) **LITTLE FLUFFY CLOUDS. / ('A'mixes)** [10] [ ]

Island | Island

Nov 93. (d-cd)(d-c)(d-lp) **LIVE 93 (live)** [23] [ ]
– Plateau / The valley / Oobe / Little fluffy clouds / Star 6, 7, 8 & 9 / Towers of dub / Spanish castles in space / The blue room / Perpetual dawn / Assassin / Outlands / Huge ever pulsating brain …

Jan 94. (12")(c-s)(cd-s) **PERPETUAL DAWN. / TOWERS OF DUB (ambient mix)** [18] [ ]
(12") – ('A'-Andy Weatherall mixes) / Towers of dub (ambient mix).

Jun 94. (cd)(c)(lp) **POMMEFRITZ** [6] [ ]
– Pommefritz / More gills less fishcakes / We're paste to be grill you / Banger'n'chips / Allers ist schoen / His immortal logness.

— now w /out KRIS WESTON, who was repl. (after 1995 recording by) **ANDREW HUGHES**

Mar 95. (cd)(c)(d-lp) **ORBUS TERRARUM** [20] [ ]
– Valley / Plateau / Oxbow lakes / Montagne d'or (der gute berg) / White river junction / Occidental / Slug dub.

May 95. (cd-s) **OXBOW LAKES / ('A'-Everglades mix)** [38] [ ]
(12") – ('A'-Everglades mix) / ('A'-Sabres No.1 mix).
(cd-s) – (3 tracks above).
(12") – ('A'-Carl Craig psychic pals family wealth plan mix). / ('A'-Evensong string arrangement mix).
(cd-s) – (all 5 mixes above).

FFWD

aka **ROBERT FRIPP / THOMAS FEHLYN / KRIS WESTON / DR.ALEX PATTERSON**

Intermodo | Intermodo

Aug 94. (cd)(c)(d-lp) **FFWD** [48] [ ]
– Hidden / Lucky saddle / Drone / Hempire / Collosus / What time is clock / Can of bliss / Elauses / Meteor storm / Buckwheat and grits / Klangtest / Suess wie eine nuss.

– compilations, others, etc. –

Nov 91. Strange Fruit; (cd)(c)(lp) **THE PEEL SESSIONS** [ ] [–]

Feb 92. Strange Fruit; (cd-ep) **THE PEEL SESSIONS** [ ] [–]
– A huge ever growing brain that rules from the centre of the ultraworld.

APOLLO XI

DR. ALEX PATTERSON + guest **BEN WATKINS** (of SUNSONIC)

Wau! Mr. Modo | not issued

Feb 91. (12")(cd-s) **PEACE (IN THE MIDDLE EAST) /** [ ] [–]

Roy ORBISON

Born: 23 Apr'36, Vernon, Texas, USA. After stints with local hillbilly groups The WINK WESTERNERS and The TEEN KINGS, he cut solo single for 'Jewel' label in 1955. A successful audition for Sam Phillips' 'Sun' records, broke him into the US Top 60 in 1956 with 'OOBY DOOBY'. It was written by 2 college friends WADE MOORE and DICK PENNER. His further 50's singles for 'Sun' and 'R.C.A.' all failed, and after moving to Nashville with his wife, he concentrated on songwriting. 'CLAUDETTE' (written for his wife), was gifted to The EVERLY BROTHERS who scraped into the US Top 30. In 1959, his solo career was re-activated when 'Monument' took reins. The following year, 'ONLY THE LONELY' was first of many million sellers in the early to mid-sixties. His most famous being; RUNNING SCARED / CRYING / DREAM BABY / IN DREAMS / BLUE BAYOU / IT'S OVER + OH PRETTY WOMAN. In Nov'64, at the height of his success, he divorced Claudette due to her infidelity. Reconciled, they remarried in Aug'65, but 10 months later she was killed, when her motorcycle hit a truck. Later that year, he began short-lived acting career, but the film 'The Fastest Guitar Alive' did poorly at box-office. His solo career was still flourishing, especially in the UK, when another tragedy befell him. On the 14 Sep'68, while he was on tour, his home caught fire, killing his 2 oldest sons Roy Jr. and Tony. In 1970, he semi-retired to Bielefeld, Germany, with his remaining son and new German born wife Barbara Wellhonen. She soon gave him another son; Roy Kelton. His recording career went through a minor comeback (i.e. a cameo in the film 1980 'Roadie', with Emmylou Harris duetting 'You've Lost That Lovin' Feelin') before he sued Wesley Rose (head of 'Monument') for $50m in backdated royalties. In 1987, he signed to 'Virgin' records and re-started inroads into world popularity. In 1988, he joined TRAVELING WILBURYS, alongside other superstars BOB DYLAN, GEORGE HARRISON, JEFF LYNNE and TOM PETTY. Their 'VOLUME 1', reached a US Top 3 & UK Top 20 album later in the year. Tragically ROY O was to die of a heart attack on the 6th Dec'88. He had just completed a tremendous comeback album 'MYSTERY GIRL', which posthumously peaked in the UK+US Top 5 (would've anyway). Lifted from it 'YOU GOT IT', gave him his first entry into the US Top 10 for nearly 25 years. • **Style:** Moved from 50's rockabilly, to 60's ballad themes, with lyrical brilliance sang with operatic/falsetto vox, which nearly always ending in tearful crescendo. His (trademark) dark glasses were initially worn in 1963, when he left his regular specs on a plane. Dogged by domestic bad luck, he moved into country music in the late 60's. • **Songwriters:** A brilliant poet of our time, ROY wrote most of the songs himself, at times collaborating in the 60's with JOE MELSON (1960-1963 + 1967) and BILL DEES (1964-66). His final material in the late 80's, was co-written w / JEFF LYNNE & TOM PETTY. Covered CANDY MAN (Fred Neil) / MEAN WOMAN BLUES (Elvis Presley) / LET THE GOOD TIMES ROLL (Shirley & Lee) / THE COMEDIANS (Elvis Costello) / SHE'S A MYSTERY TO ME (U2) / I DROVE ALL NIGHT (Cyndi Lauper) / AFTER THE LOVE HAS GONE (Earth, Wind & Fire). His song DISTANT DRUMS was posthumously a UK No.1 hit for JIM REEVES. Others, BLUE BAYOU and CRYING, were huge hits for LINDA RONSTADT and DON McLEAN respectively. • **Trivia:** His concert 'A BLACK AND WHITE NIGHT' in Sep'87, featured guest appearances by k.d. LANG (on 'CRYING' duet which in 1992 became UK Top 10 hit), BRUCE SPRINGSTEEN, TOM WAITS, BONNIE RAITT, JACKSON BROWNE, ELVIS COSTELLO, JENNIFER WARNES, J.D.SOUTHER among others …

Recommended: THE LEGENDARY ROY ORBISON (*9) / MYSTERY GIRL (*7)

ROY ORBISON – vocals with early **BOB MOORE** – bass / **BILLY PAT ELLIS** – drums

not issued | Jewel

Jan 56. (7") **TRYING TO GET TO YOU. / OOBY DOOBY** [–] [ ]

Sun | Sun

May 56. (7") **OOBY DOOBY. / GO GO GO** [–] [59]

Sep 56. (7") **ROCKHOUSE. / YOU'RE MY BABY** [–] [ ]
(UK-iss.1964 on 'Ember')

Mar 57. (7") **CHICKEN HEARTED. / DEVIL DOLL** [–] [ ]

1957. (7") **OOBY DOOBY. / DEVIL DOLL** [ ] [–]
(UK-iss.Nov71)

Dec 57. (7") **CHICKEN HEARTED. / I LIKE LOVE** [–] [ ]

not issued | RCA Victor

Sep 58. (7") **SWEET AND INNOCENT. / SEEMS TO ME** [-] [ ]
Dec 58. (7") **ALMOST 18. / JOLIE** [-] [ ]
— (first 3 singles also on 78 rpm)

London Monument

1959. (7") **PAPER BOY. / WITH THE BUG** [-] [ ]
Dec 59. (7") **UPTOWN. / PRETTY ONE** [ ] [72]
Jun 60. (7") **ONLY THE LONELY. / HERE COMES THAT SONG AGAIN** [1] [2] May 60
Oct 60. (7") **BLUE ANGEL. / TODAY'S TEARDROPS** [11] [9] Sep 60
1961. (lp) **LONELY AND BLUE** [ ] [ ] Dec 60
– Only the lonely / Bye bye love / Cry / Blue avanue / I can't stop loving you / Come back to me (my love) / Blue angel / Raindrops / (I'd be) A legend in my time / I'm hurtin' / Twenty-tow days / I'll say it's my fault. *(UK re-iss.May63, hit No.15)*
Mar 61. (7") **I'M HURTIN'. / I CAN'T STOP LOVING YOU** [ ] [27] Dec 60
May 61. (7") **RUNNING SCARED. / LOVE HURTS** [9] [1] Apr61
(re-iss.1975 on 'Monument')
Sep 61. (7") **CRYING. / CANDY MAN** [25] [2]
[25] Aug 61
(re-iss.1975 on 'Monument')
Feb 62. (7") **DREAM BABY. / THE ACTRESS** [2] [4]
May 62. (lp) **CRYING** [ ] [21] Apr 62
– Crying / The great pretender / Love hurts / She wears my ring / Wedding day / Summersong / Dance / Lana / Loneliness / Let's make a memory / Nite life / Running scared. *(UK re-iss.Jun63, hit No.17)*
Jun 62. (7") **THE CROWD. / MAMA** [40] [26]
Oct 62. (lp) **ROY ORBISON'S GREATEST HITS** (compilation) [ ] [14] Aug62
– The crowd / Love star / Crying / Evergreen / Running scared / Mama / Candy man / Only the lonely / Dream baby / Blue angel / Uptown / I'm hurtin'. *(UK re-iss.Sep67, hit No.40)*
Oct 62. (7") **WORKIN' FOR THE MAN. / LEAH** [50] [33]
[25]
(re-iss.1975 on 'Monument')
Feb 63. (7") **IN DREAMS. / SHAHDOROBA** [6] [7]
May 63. (7") **FALLING. / DISTANT DRUMS** [9] [22]
Sep 63. (7") **BLUE BAYOU. / MEAN WOMAN BLUES** [3] [29]
[5]
(re-iss.1975 on 'Monument')
Nov 63. (lp) **IN DREAMS** [6] [35] Aug 63
– In dreams / Lonely wine / Shahdaroba / No one will ever know / Sunset / House without windows / Dream / Blue bayou / (They call you) Gigolette / All I have to do is dream / Beautiful dreamer / My prayer.
Dec 63. (7") **PRETTY PAPER. / BEAUTIFUL DREAMER** [-] [15]
(UK-iss.1975 on 'Monument')
Feb 64. (7") **BORNE ON THE WIND. / WHAT'D I SAY** [15] [-]
Apr 64. (7") **IT'S OVER. / INDIAN WEDDING** [1] [9]
Aug 64. (7") **OH PRETTY WOMAN. / YO TE AMO MARIA** [1] [1]
— (above featured/credited The CANDYMEN)
Sep 64. (lp) **MORE OF ROY ORBISON'S GREATEST HITS** [ ] [19]
– (compilation)
Nov 64. (7") **PRETTY PAPER. / SUMMER SONG** [6] [-]
Nov 64. (lp) **OH PRETTY WOMAN** (compilation) [4] [-]
– Oh pretty woman / It's over / Falling / Indian wedding / Borne on the wind / Distant drums / The crowd / Yo te amo / Maria / Candy man / Mama.
Feb 65. (7") **GOODNIGHT. / ONLY WITH YOU** [14] [21]
Jul 65. (7") **(SAY) YOU'RE MY GIRL. / SLEEPY HOLLOW** [23] [39]

London M.G.M.

Aug 65. (7") **RIDE AWAY. / WONDERIN'** [34] [25]
Sep 65. (lp) **THERE IS ONLY ONE ROY ORBISON** [10] [55]
– Ride away / You fool you / Two of a kind / This is your song / I'm in a blue, blue mood / If you can't say something nice / Claudette / Afraid to sleep / Sugar and honey / Summer love / Big as I can dream / Wondering.
Oct 65. (7") **CRAWLIN' BACK. / IF YOU CAN'T SAY SOMETHING NICE** [19] [46]
Jan 66. (7") **BREAKIN' UP IS BREAKIN' MY HEART. / WAIT** [22] [31]
Feb 66. (lp) **THE ORBISON WAY** [11] [ ]
– Crawling back / It ain't no big thing / Time changed everything / This is my land / The loner / Maybe / Breakin' up is breakin' my heart / Go away / A new star / Never / It wasn't very long ago / Why hurt the one who loves you.
Mar 66. (7") **TWINKLE TOES. / WHERE IS TOMORROW** [29] [39]
Jun 66. (7") **LANA. / OUR SUMMER SONG** [15] [-]
— (above 45 an older 'Monument' recording)
Jul 66. (7") **TOO SOON TO KNOW. / YOU'LL NEVER BE SIXTEEN AGAIN** [-] [68]
Aug 66. (7") **TOO SOON TO KNOW. / SWEET DREAMS** [3] [-]
Sep 66. (lp) **THE CLASSIC ROY ORBISON** [12] [ ]
– You'll never be sixteen again / Pantomine / Twinkle toes / Losing you / City life / Wait / Growing up / Where is tomorrow / I'll never get over you / Going back to Gloria / Never love again / Just another name for rock'n'roll. *(re-iss.+c+cd.Apr89 on 'Ocean' UK / 'Rhino' US)*
Nov 66. (7") **THERE WON'T BE MANY COMING HOME. / GOING BACK TO GLORIA** [18] [-]
Dec 66. (7") **COMMUNICATION BREAKDOWN. / GOING BACK TO GLORIA** [-] [60]
Feb 67. (7") **SO GOOD. / MEMORIES** [32] [ ]
1967. (lp) **SINGS DON GIBSON** [ ] [ ]
– A legend in my time / I'm hurtin' / The same street / Far far away / Big hearted me / Sweet dreams / Oh, such a stranger / Blue blue day / What about me / Give myself a party / Too soon to know / Lonesome number one.
Aug 67. (7") **CRY SOFTLY, LONELY ONE. / PISTOLERO** [ ] [52]
Sep 67. (lp) **CRY SOFTLY, LONELY ONE** [ ] [ ]
– She / Communication breakdown / Cry softly, lonely one / Girl like me / It takes one to know one / That's a no-no / Just let me make believe / Here comes the rain baby / Memories / Time to cry / Only alive / Just one time.
Oct 67. (7") **SHE. / HERE COMES THAT SONG AGAIN** [ ] [ ]
Jan 68. (7") **BORN TO BE LOVED BY YOU. / SHY AWAY** [ ] [ ]
Jan 68. (lp) **FASTEST GUITAR ALIVE (1966 Soundtrack)** [ ] [-]
– Whirlwind / Medicine man / River / The fastest guitar alive / Rollin' on / Pistolero / Good time party / Heading south / Best friend / There won't be many coming home.
Jul 68. (7") **WALK ON. / FLOWERS** [39] [ ]
Sep 68. (7") **HEARTACHE. / SUGARMAN** [44] [ ]
1969. (lp) **GREAT SONGS** [-] [ ]
Apr 69. (7") **MY FRIEND. / SOUTHBOUND JERICO PATHWAY** [35] [ ]
May 69. (lp) **MANY MOODS** [-] [ ]
– Truly, truly, true / Unchained melody / I recommend her / More / Heartache / Amy / Good morning, dear / What now my love / Walk on / Yesterday's child / Try to remember.
Aug 69. (7") **PENNY ARCADE. / TENNESSEE OWNS MY SOUL** [27] [ ]
1969. (lp) **HANK WILLIAMS – THE ROY ORBISON WAY** [-] [ ]
– Kaw-liga / Jambalaya (on the bayou) / (Last night) I heard you crying in your sleep / You win again / Your cheatin' heart / Cold, cold heart / A mansion on the hill / I can't help it (if I'm still in love with you) / There'll be no teardrops tonight / I'm so lonesome I could cry.
Nov 69. (7") **BREAK MY MIND. / HOW DO YOU START OVER** [ ] [-]
Nov 69. (lp) **THE BIG 'O'** [ ] [ ]
– Break my mind / Help me Rhonda / Money / Only you / Down the line / When I stop dreaming / Living touch / Land of 1000 dances / Scarlet ribbons / She won't head her love out / Casting spell / Penny arcade. *(UK iss.Oct75 & 1982 on 'Charly') (re-iss.+cd.May89 on 'Pickwick')(cd-iss.Feb93)*
— (above credited The ART MOVEMENT)
1970. (7") **SHE CHEATS ON ME. / HOW DO YOU START OVER** [-] [ ]
Apr 70. (7") **SO YOUNG. / IF I HAD A WOMAN LIKE YOU** [ ] [ ]
Aug 71. (7") **(LOVE ME LIKE YOU DID IT) LAST NIGHT. / CLOSE AGAIN** [ ] [ ]
Feb 72. (7") **GOD LOVE YOU. / CHANGES** [ ] [ ]
1972. (7") **REMEMBER THE GOOD. / HARLEM WOMAN (or) IF ONLY FOR A WHILE** [-] [ ]
Sep 72. (7") **MEMPHIS TENNESSEE. / I CAN READ BETWEEN THE LINES** [ ] [ ]
1973. (lp)(c) **MEMPHIS** [ ] [ ]
– Memphis, Tennessee / Why a woman cries / Run baby run (back into my arms) / Take care of your woman / I'm the man on Susie's mind / I can't stop loving you / Run the engines up high / It ain't no big thing / I fought the law / The three bells / Danny boy.
1973. (7") **BLUE RAIN (COMING DOWN). / SOONER OR LATER** [-] [ ]
1973. (7") **I WANNA LIVE. / YOU LAY EASY ON MY MIND** [-] [ ]
1974. (lp)(c) **MILESTONES** [-] [ ]

Mercury Mercury

Sep 74. (7") **SWEET MAMA BLUE. / HEARTACHE** [ ] [ ]
Apr 75. (7") **HUNG UP ON YOU. / SPANISH NIGHTS** [ ] [ ]
1975. (7") **IT'S LONELY. / STILL** [-] [ ]
1976. (lp)(c) **I'M STILL IN LOVE WITH YOU** [-] [ ]
– Pledging my love / Rainbow love / Heartache / Still / Circle / All I need is time / Spanish nights / It's lonely / Crying time / Hung up on you / Sweet mama blue. *(cd-iss.Aug89)*

Monument Monument

May 76. (7") **BELINDA. / NO CHAIN AT ALL** [ ] [ ]
Nov 76. (7") **(I'M A) SOUTHERN MAN. / BORN TO LOVE ME** [ ] [ ]
Feb 77. (lp)(c) **REGENERATION** [ ] [ ]
– (I'm a) Southern man / N chain at all / Old love song / Can't wait / Born to love me / Blues in my mind / Something they can't take away / Under suspicion / I don't really want you / Belinda.
Apr 77. (7") **DRIFTING AWAY. / UNDER SUSPICION** [ ] [ ]
— In 1978, he underwent major heart surgery, but steadily recovered.

Asylum Asylum

May 79. (7") **EASY WAY OUT. / TEARS** [ ] [ ]
Jul 79. (lp)(c) **LAMINAR FLOW** [ ] [ ]
– Easy way out / Love is a cold wind / Lay it down / I care / We're into something good / Movin' / Poor baby / Warm spot hot / Tears / Friday night / Hound dog man. *(cd-iss.Feb93)*
Sep 79. (7") **LAY IT DOWN. / POOR BABY** [-] [ ]
Nov 79. (7") **LAY IT DOWN. / WARM SPOT HOT** [ ] [-]
— (below duet with **EMMYLOU HARRIS** from the film 'Roadie')

Warners Warners

Jun 80. (7") **THAT LOVING YOU FEELING AGAIN. / (b-by Craig Hindley)** [ ] [55]
Apr 81. (7") **UNTIL THE NIGHT IS OVER. / LONG WAY BACK TO LOVE** [ ] [ ]

ZTT-Island Island

Aug 85. (7") **WILD HEARTS (TIME). / WILD HEARTS (VOICELESS)** [ ] [ ]
(d7"+=) – Ooby dooby (revive) / Crying (live).
(12"+=) – Ooby dooby / Wild hearts (and time again).

Virgin Virgin

Jun 87. (7") **IN DREAMS. / LEAH** [ ] [ ]
Jul 87. (d-lp)(c)(cd) **IN DREAMS: THE GREATEST HITS** [86] [95] Jan 89
– (new versions of old songs) Only the lonely / Leah / In dreams / Uptown / It's over / Crying / Dream baby / Blue angel / Working for the man / Candy man / Running scared / Falling / I'm hurtin' / Claudette / Oh pretty woman / Mean woman blues / Ooby dooby / Lana / Blue bayou.
— In the fall of 1988, he teamed up with DYLAN, PETTY, HARRISON and LYNNE to form The TRAVELING WILBURYS. Tragedy struck on the 7th Dec'88, when he died of a heart attack. He had coincidentally just released comeback solo album.
Dec 88. (7") **YOU GOT IT. / THE ONLY ONE** [3] [9]
(12"+=)(3"cd-s+=) – Crying (with k.d.LANG).
Jan 89. (lp)(c)(cd) **MYSTERY GIRL** [2] [5]
– You got it / In the real world / (All I can do is) Dream you / A love so beautiful / California blue / She's a mystery to me / The comedians / The only one / Windsurfer / Careless heart.
Feb 89. (7") **SHE'S A MYSTERY TO ME. / CRYING** [27] [ ]
(12"+=)(cd-s+=) – Dream baby (live).
Jul 89. (7") **CALIFORNIA BLUE. / BLUE BAYOU (live with k.d.LANG)** [ ] [ ]
(12"+=)/ /(3"cd-s++=) – Leah (live)./ / In dreams (live).

Nov 89. (lp)(c)(cd) **ROY ORBISON AND FRIENDS – A BLACK AND WHITE NIGHT (live Sep'87)** [51] [ ]
– Oh pretty woman / Only the lonely / In dreams / Dream baby (how long must I dream) / Leah / Move on down the line / Crying / Mean woman blues / Running scared / Blue bayou / Candy man / Uptown / Ooby dooby / The comedians / (All I can do is) Dream is you / It's over. *(re-iss.c+cd.Aug91)*
Nov 89. (7") **OH PRETTY WOMAN ('87 version). / CLAUDETTE** [ ] [ ]
(12"+=)(cd-s+=) – ('A'-lp version).

– other compilations, etc. –

Sep 57. London; (7"ep) **HILLBILLY ROCK** [ ] [-]
Dec 60. London; (7"ep) **ONLY THE LONELY** [ ] [ ]
1961. Sun; (lp) **ROY ORBISON AT THE ROCKHOUSE** [-] [ ]
(re-iss.Feb81 on 'Charly')
Mar 63. London; (7"ep) **ROY ORBISON** [ ] [-]
Jun 63. London; (7"ep) **IN DREAMS** [ ] [-]
Aug 64. London; (7"ep) **IT'S OVER** [ ] [-]
Dec 64. London; (7"ep) **OH PRETTY WOMAN** [ ] [-]
Feb 65. London; (7"ep) **ROY ORBISON'S STAGE SHOW HITS** [ ] [-]
Jun 65. London; (7"ep) **LOVE HURTS** [ ] [-]
– Love hurts / All I have to do is dream / I can't stop loving you / The crowd.
1970. London/ US= Sun; (lp) **THE ORIGINAL SOUNDS OF . . .** [ ] [ ]
1972. London/ US= Sun; (lp) **ROY ORBISON SINGS** [ ] [ ]
Jul 76. London; (d-lp)(c) **FOCUS ON ROY ORBISON** [ ] [-]
Jan 90. Sun; (lp)(c)(cd) **ROY ORBISON** [ ] [-]
Jul 64. Ember; (lp) **THE EXCITING SOUNDS OF ROY ORBISON** [17] [-]
Jul 64. Ember; (7") **YOU'RE MY BABY. / ROCK HOUSE** [ ] [-]
Sep 64. Ember; (7") **THIS KIND OF LOVE. / I NEVER KNEW** [ ] [-]
1964. Ember; (7"ep) **SWEET AND EASY TO LOVE** [ ] [-]
1964. Ember; (7"ep) **TRYIN' TO GET TO YOU** [ ] [-]
Mar 65. Ember; (7") **SWEET AND EASY TO LOVE. / YOU'RE GONNA CRY** [ ] [-]
1965. Ember; (7"ep) **DEVIL DOLL** [ ] [-]
1964. Allegro; (lp) **ROY ORBISON SINGS** [ ] [-]
Oct 64. Monument; (lp) **EARLY ORBISON** [ ] [ ]
Oct 65. Monument; (7") **LET THE GOOD TIMES ROLL. / DISTANT DRUMS** [ ] [81]
Dec 65. Monument; (lp) **ORBISONGS** [ ] [ ]
(UK-iss.Jul67, hit No.40) (cd-iss.Dec95)
Sep 66. Monument; (lp) **THE VERY BEST OF ROY ORBISON** [ ] [94]
1967. Monument; (lp) **ROY ORBISON'S GREATEST HITS** [ ] [-]
(re-iss.1972)
1969. Monument; (lp) **MORE OF ROY ORBISON'S GREATEST HITS** [ ] [ ]
1972. Monument; (7") **DREAM BABY. / BLUE ANGEL** [ ] [ ]
Jan 73. Monument; (d-lp)(d-c) **ALL-TIME GREATEST HITS** [39] [ ]
(cd-iss.Jan89) (re-iss.+cd.Dec88 on 'Skyline')
1975. Monument; (lp)(c) **THE MONUMENTAL ROY ORBISON** [ ] [-]
1975. Monument; (7") **I'M HURTIN'. / DREAM BABY (HOW LONG MUST I DREAM)** [ ] [-]
Jul 75. Monument; (7") **IT'S OVER. / OH PRETTY WOMAN** [ ] [-]
(re-iss.Jan78)
1975. Monument; (7") **THE CROWD. / IN DREAMS** [ ] [ ]
1975. Monument; (7") **ONLY THE LONELY. / UPTOWN** [ ] [ ]
Nov 75. Monument; (lp)(c) **THE MONUMENTAL ROY ORBISON VOL.2** [ ] [-]
Mar 76. Monument; (7") **ONLY THE LONELY. / IT'S OVER** [ ] [ ]
Jan 78. Monument; (7") **ONLY THE LONELY. / DREAM BABY** [ ] [ ]
Jul 81. Monument-CBS; (lp)(c) **GOLDEN DAYS** [63] [ ]
(cd-iss.Jun92)
May 89. Monument; (lp)(c)(cd) **BEST LOVED STANDARDS** [ ] [ ]
(re-iss.+cd.Dec92)
May 89. Monument; (lp)(c)(cd) **RARE ORBISON** [ ] [ ]
May 89. Monument; (lp)(c)(cd) **OUR LOVE SONG** [ ] [ ]
Nov 93. Monument; (cd) **LONELY AND BLUE / CRYING** [ ] [ ]
Nov 93. Monument; (cd) **IN DREAMS / ORBISONGS** [ ] [ ]
Jul 67. MGM; (7") **CRAWLIN' BACK. / RIDE AWAY** [-] [ ]
Jul 67. MGM; (7") **BREAKIN' UP IS BREAKIN' MY HEART. / TOO SOON TO KNOW** [-] [ ]
Jul 67. MGM; (7") **TWINKLE TOES. / WHERE IS TOMORROW** [-] [ ]
Jul 67. MGM; (7") **SWEET DREAMS. / GOING BACK TO GLORIA** [-] [ ]
Jul 67. MGM; (7") **YOU'LL NEVER BE SIXTEEN AGAIN. / THERE WON'T BE MANY COMING HOME** [-] [ ]
1974. Hallmark; (lp) **THE EXCITING ROY ORBISON** [ ] [-]
Nov 75. Arcade; (lp)(c) **THE BEST OF ROY ORBISON** [1] [-]
Dec 76. Charly; (7"ep) **ROY ORBISON: OOBY DOOBY** [ ] [-]
Sep 78. Charly; (7") **OOBY DOOBY. / CURTIS LEE** [ ] [-]
1980. Charly; (lp) **ROY ORBISON AT THE ROCK HOUSE** [ ] [-]
Sep 84. Charly; (d-lp) **THE SUN YEARS 1956-1958: THE DEFINITIVE COLLECTION** [ ] [-]
(cd-iss.Apr89 on 'Bear Family')
Oct 86. Charly; (cd) **GO GO GO** [ ] [-]
Aug 83. Decca; (lp)(c) **THE BIG O COUNTRY** [ ] [-]
Sep 86. Castle; (d-lp)(c) **THE ROY ORBISON COLLECTION** [ ] [-]
(cd-iss.Jul91 on 'Pickwick')
Jan 88. Point; (lp) **DANCIN' WITH ROY ORBISON** [ ] [-]
Jan 88. Point; (lp) **DREAMIN' WITH ROY ORBISON** [ ] [-]
Sep 82. Bear Family; (7"ep) **ALMOST EIGHTEEN / JOLIE / SWEET AND INNOCENT / THE BUG / PAPER BOY / SEEMS TO ME** [-] [-] Germ
Jul 87. Bear Family; (cd) **THE RCA SESSIONS: ROY ORBISON & SONNY JAMES** [-] [-]
May 88. Zu-Jazz; (7") **PROBLEM CHILD. / ?** [ ] [-]
May 88. Zu-Jazz; (lp) **PROBLEM CHILD** [ ] [-]
Oct 88. Telstar; (lp)(c)(cd) **THE LEGENDARY ROY ORBISON** [1] [-]
– It's over / Only the lonely / Goodnight / Lana / The crowd / All I have to do is dream / Dream baby / Mean woman blues / Oh pretty woman / Love hurts / My prayer / Falling / Blue angel / In dreams / Blue bayou / The great pretender / Pretty paper.
Jan 89. Rhino; (d-lp)(c)(cd) **FOR THE LONELY; ROY ORBISON ANTHOLOGY, 1956-1965** [-] [ ]
Oct 90. Rhino; (cd)(c)(lp) **BALLADS – 22 CLASSIC LOVE SONGS** [38] [-]
Feb 89. Venus; (c) **THE MAGIC OF ROY ORBISON** [ ] [-]
May 89. Pickwick; (c,cd) **THE LEGEND** [ ] [-]
May 90. Pickwick; (cd)(c)(lp) **THE HITS 1** [ ] [-]
May 90. Pickwick; (cd)(c)(lp) **THE HITS 2** [ ] [-]
Jul 91. Pickwick; (cd) **ROY ORBISON VOL.2** [ ] [-]
Feb 89. Old Gold; (7") **ONLY THE LONELY. / BLUE ANGEL** [ ] [-]
Feb 89. Old Gold; (7") **RUNNING SCARED. / CRYING** [ ] [-]
Feb 89. Old Gold; (7") **OH PRETTY WOMAN. / MEAN WOMAN BLUES** [ ] [-]
Feb 89. Old Gold; (7") **IN DREAMS. / FALLING** [ ] [-]
Feb 89. Old Gold; (7") **DREAM BABY. / PRETTY PAPER** [ ] [-]
Feb 89. Old Gold; (7") **IT'S OVER. / BLUE BAYOU** [ ] [-]
Feb 89. Old Gold; (7") **THE CROWD. / LANA** [ ] [-]
May 89. Polydor; (d-lp)(cd) **THE SINGLES COLLECTION 1965-1973** [ ] [-]
Sep 89. Instant; (lp)(c)(cd) **THE EARLY YEARS** [ ] [-]
Dec 89. Raven; (lp) **COMMUNICATION BREAKDOWN** [ ] [-]
(cd-iss.Feb91)
Jul 90. Knight; (cd-box)(c-box)(lp-box) **GOLDEN DECADE BOXED SET (1960-1970)** [ ] [-]
Jun 92. MCA; (7")(c-s) **I DROVE ALL NIGHT. / FOREVER FRIENDS (with SHEENA EASTON)** [7] [ ]
(cd-s+=) – Trickster:- Line of fire.
Aug 92. Virgin America; (7")(c-s) **CRYING. ("ROY ORBISON & k.d.LANG") / FALLING** [13] [ ]
(cd-s+=) – Oh pretty woman / She's a mystery to me.
(cd-s+=) – Only the lonely / It's over.
Oct 92. Virgin America; (7")(c-s) **HEARTBREAK RADIO. / CRYING (with k.d.LANG)** [36] [ ]
(cd-s) ('A" side) / In dreams / You got it / Dream baby.
(cd-s) ('A' side) / Blue angel / Claudette / Lana.
Nov 92. Virgin; (cd)(c)(lp) **KING OF HEARTS** (1988 recordings) [23] [ ]
– You're the one / Heartbreak radio / We'll take the night / Crying (with k.d.LANG) / After the love has gone / Love in time / I drove all night / Wild hearts run out of time / Coming home / Careless heart (original demo).
Nov 93. Virgin; (7")(c-s) **I DROVE ALL NIGHT. / CRYING** [47] [ ]
(cd-s+=) – Oh pretty woman / After the love has gone.
Jun 93. Sequel; (3xcd) **THE GOLDEN YEARS 1960-1969** [ ] [-]
Apr 93. Ariola; (cd)(c) **ROY ORBISON / RAY PETERSON** [ ] [-]
May 94. Laserlight; (cd)(c) **ROY ORBISON** [ ] [-]
Aug 94. Legends In Music; (cd) **ROY ORBISON** [ ] [-]
Oct 94. Pickwick; (3xcd-box) **THE HITS** [ ] [-]
Oct 94. Monument; (cd) **THE BEST** [ ] [-]
Mar 95. Collection; (cd) **THE COLLECTION** [ ] [-]
Sep 95. Spectrum; (cd) **CLASS OF '55 – MEMPHIS ROCK'N'ROLL HOMECOMING (with JOHNNY CASH/ JERRY LEE LEWIS/ CARL PERKINS)** [ ] [-]
Nov 95. The Collection; (3xcd-box) **ROY ORBISON** [ ] [-]

ORBITAL

Formed: Seven Oaks, London, England . . . late 80's by brothers PHIL and PAUL HARTNOLL. Issued own label release, which gained attention of London's 'Ffrr' records, who duly signed them, unleashing revised debut 'CHIME'. They were soon starring on Top Of The Pops early 1991, when 'SATAN' (complete with BUTTHOLE SURFERS sample) nearly hit UK 30. • **Style:** Techno-electro sample duo, with KRAFTWERK-like keys backing pulsating infectious dance themes. • **Songwriters:** The duo, except noted samples; O EUCHARI (performed by Emily Van Evera). • **Trivia:** Vox on tracks 'SAD BUT TRUE' & 'ARE WE HERE?' by ALISON GOLDFRAPP.

Recommended: UNTITLED (ORBITAL 1) (*7) / UNTITLED (ORBITAL II) (*7) / SNIVILIZATION (*8)

PHIL HARTNOLL – keyboards / **PAUL HARTNOLL** – keyboards

Oh-Zone / not issued
Dec 89. (12"ep) **CHIME. / DEEPER (full version)** [ ] [-]
Ffrr-London / Ffrr-London
Mar 90. (7")(ext.12") **CHIME. / DEEPER** [ ] [-]
(cd-ep+=) – ('A'version).
(12"ep) – ('A'-JZM remix) / ('A'-Bacardi mix)
Jul 90. (12"ep) **OMEN. / 2 DEEP / OPEN MIND** [ ] [-]
(cd-ep) – (1st & 3rd track) / ('A'edit)
(12"ep) – Omen: The chariot / The tower / Wheel of fortune / The fool.
Jan 91. (7") **SATAN. / BELFAST** [31] [-]
(12"ep+=)(cd-ep+=) – L.C.1.
(12"ep) – ('A'-rhyme & reason mix) / L.C.2 (outer limits mix) / Chime.
Aug 91. (12") **MIDNIGHT. / CHOICE** [ ] [-]
(12"ep) – Midnight (Sasha mix) / Choice (Orbital & Eye & I mix).
(cd-ep+=) – Analogue test Feb'90.
Sep 91. (cd)(c)(lp) **UNTITLED (ORBITAL 1)** [71] [ ]
– The moebius / Speed freak / Oolaa / Desert storm / Fahrenheit 303 / Steel cube idolatry / High rise / Chime (live) / Midnight (live) / Belfast / Macrohead. (cd w /out last track, repl. by – I Think It's Disgusting
(c+=) – Untitled.
Feb 92. (12"ep) MUTATIONS (I): OOLAA (Joey Beltram remix) / OOLAA (Meat Beat Manifesto mix) / CHIME (Joey Beltram). / SPEED FREAK (Moby mix) [24] [-]

(12"ep) MUTATIONS (II): Chime (Ray Keith mix) / Chime (Crime remix) / Steel cube idolatory / Farenheit 303.
(cd-ep) Oolaa (Joey Beltram mix) / Chime (Ray Keith mix) / Speed freak / Fahrenheit 303.

Internal | Ffrr-London

Sep 92. (12"ep) **RADICCIO EP: THE NAKED AND THE DEAD. / SUNDAY** [37] [ ]
(cd-ep+=) – Halycon.
Apr 93. (12"ep) LUSH 3-1. / LUSH 3-2 / LUSH 3-3 (underworld) [ ] [-]
(12"ep) **LUSH 3-4 (Psychick Warriors Ov Gaia) / LUSH 3-5 (CJ Bollard).**
(cd-ep) **(all 5 tracks).**
Jun 93. (cd)(c)(lp) **UNTITLED (ORBITAL II)** [28] [-]
– Time becomes / Planet of the shapes / Lush 3-1 / Lush 3-2 / Impact (the Earth is burning) / Remind / Walk now . . . / Monday / Halycon + on + on / Input out.
Mar 94. (m-cd)(m-lp) **PEEL SESSION EP** [ ] [-]
– Lush (Euro-tunnel disaster '94) / Walk about / Semi detached / Attached.
(cd-ep) DIVERSIONS EP – Impact USA / Lush 3 (Euro-Tunnel disaster '94) / Walk-about / Lush 3-5 (CJ Bolland) / Lush 3-4 (Warrior drift) / Lush 3-4 (Underworld).
Aug 94. (cd)(c) **SNIVILIZATION** [4] [ ]
– Forever / I wish I had duck feet / Sad but true / Crash and carry / Science friction / Philosophy by numbers / Kein trink wasser / Quality seconds / Are we here? / Attached.
Sep 94. (12")(c-s)(cd-s) **ARE WE HERE? EP** [33] [ ]
– Are we here: Who are they? / Do they here? / They did it (mix) / What was that? / Criminal Justice Bill? / Industry standard?.

— In May'95, they covered THERAPY?'s 'Belfast' on special cd-s which hit UK No.53. THERAPY? gave us interpretation of 'INNOCENT X'.

Aug 95. (d7"ep)(d12"ep)(cd-ep) **UNTITLED EP** [ ] [-]
– Times fly (slow) / Sad but new / Times fly (fast) / The tranquilizer.
(above was not eligible for UK chart position due to it's length)

ORCHESTRAL MANOEUVRES IN THE DARK

Formed: West Kirby, Liverpool, England . . . Autumn 1978, initially as The ID, by McCLUSKEY and HUMPHREYS. After one-off indie single 'ELECTRICITY' for 'Factory', they signed to 'Virgin' subsidiary label 'Dindisc'. Early in 1980, they hit UK Top 75 with 'RED FRAME – WHITE LIGHT', which paved the way for eponymous parent album, which made Top 30. In the summer of 1980, they hit the Top 20 with 'MESSAGES' & 'ENOLA GAY' (the name of the plane which dropped the Hiroshima bomb). They remained in the chart limelight for the next decade plus. • **Style:** Electronic pop-rockers, influenced by KRAFTWERK, although they drifted into more mainstream sound, away from experimental period of the early 80's. • **Songwriters:** All material written by McCLUSKEY & HUMPHREYS, until latter's exit in '89. Covered; I'M WAITING FOR THE MAN (Velvet Underground) / NEON LIGHTS (Kraftwerk). • **Trivia:** An ID track 'JULIA'S SONG', appeared on an 'Open Eye' indie compilation lp 'Street To Street' in 1978.

Recommended: THE BEST OF O.M.D. (*8)

ANDREW McCLUSKEY (b.24 Jun'59, Wirral, England) – vocals, bass (ex-DALEK I) / **PAUL HUMPHRIES** (b.27 Feb'60, London, England) – keys, synths. (ex-The ID) with backing from computer 'Winston'.

Factory | not issued

May 79. (7") **ELECTRICITY. / ALMOST** [ ] [-]
(re-iss.Sep79 on 'Dindisc')

Dindisc | not issued

Feb 80. (7")(12") **RED FRAME – WHITE LIGHT. / I BETRAY MY FRIENDS** [67] [-]

— guests **DAVID FAIRBURN** – guitar / **MALCOLM HOLMES** – drums / **MARTIN COOPER** – sax

Feb 80. (lp)(c) **ORCHESTRAL MANOEUVRES IN THE DARK** [27] [-]
– Bunker soldiers / Almost / Mystereality / Electricity / The Messerschmit twins / Messages / Julia's song / Red frame – white light / Dancing / Pretending to see the future. *(re-iss.Aug84 on 'Virgin') (cd-iss.Jul87)*
May 80. (7") **MESSAGES. / TAKING SIDES AGAIN** [13] [-]
(10") – ('A'extended) / Waiting for the man.

— added **DAVID HUGHES** – keyboards (ex-DALEK I LOVE YOU, ex-SECRETS) and now f/t member **MALCOLM HOLMES** – drums (ex-CLIVE LANGER & THE BOXES, ex-ID)

Sep 80. (7")(12") **ENOLA GAY. / ANNEX** [8] [-]
Oct 80. (lp)(c) **ORGANISATION** [6] [-]
– Enola Gay / 2nd thought / VCL XI / Motion and heart / Statues / The misunderstanding / The more I see you / Promise / Stanlow. *(free 7"ep)*– INTRODUCING RADIOS / PROGRESS. / DISTANCE FADES BETWEEN US / WHEN I WAS SIX *(re-iss.Aug88 on 'Virgin') (cd-iss.Jul87)*

— **MALCOLM COOPER** – saxophone, keyboards (ex-DALEK I LOVE YOU) repl. HUGHES

Dindisc | Epic

Aug 81. (7")(10") **SOUVENIR. / MOTION AND HEART (Amazon version) / SACRED HEART** [3] [-]
Oct 81. (7")(12") **JOAN OF ARC. / THE ROMANCE OF THE TELESCOPE (unfinished version)** [5] [ ]
Nov 81. (lp)(c) **ARCHITECTURE & MORALITY** [3] [ ]
– New stone age / She's leaving / Souvenir / Sealand / Joan Of Arc / Joan Of Arc (Maid of Orleans) / Architecture and morality / Georgia / The beginning and the end. *(cd-iss.1988 on 'Virgin') (re-iss.Apr90)*
Jan 82. (7")(12") **MAID OF ORLEANS (THE WALTZ JOAN OF ARC). / NAVIGATION** [4] [ ]
(12"+=) – Of all the things we've made. *(3"cd-s iss.Jun88)*
Jan 82. (7") **SOUVENIR. / NEW STONE AGE** [-] [ ]

Virgin | Epic-Virgin

Feb 83. (7")(12")(7"pic-d) **GENETIC ENGINEERING. / 4-NEU** [20] [-]
Mar 83. (lp)(c) **DAZZLE SHIPS** [5] [ ]
– Radio Prague / Genetic engineering / ABC auto-industry / Telegraph / This is Helena / International / Dazzle ships / The romance of the telescope / Silent running / Radio waves / Time zones / Of all the things we've made. *(re-iss.1987, cd-iss.1985)*
Apr 83. (7")(7"pic-d) **TELEGRAPH. / 66 AND FADING** [42] [-]
(12") – ('A'extended).
May 83. (7") **TELEGRAPH. / THIS IS HELENA** [-] [ ]

Virgin | A & M

Apr 84. (7")(7"pic-d) **LOCOMOTION. / HER BODY IN MY SOUL** [5] [ ] Nov 84
(12") – ('A'extended) / The avenue. *(3"cd-s iss.Jun88)*
May 84. (lp)(c) **JUNK CULTURE** [9] [ ] Nov 84
– Junk culture / Tesla girls / Locomotion / Apollo / Never turn away / Apollo / Love and violence / Hard day / All wrapped up / White trash / alking loud and clear. *(cd-iss.1986 & Mar90)*
Jun 84. (7")(7"pic-d) **TALKING LOUD AND CLEAR. / JULIA'S SONG** [11] [-]
(12") – ('A'&'B'extended).
Aug 84. (7")(c-s) **TESLA GIRLS. / TELEGRAPH (live)** [21] [-]
(12"+=) – Garden city.
Oct 84. (7")(7"pic-d) **NEVER TURN AWAY. / WRAP-UP** [70] [-]
(12") – ('A'extended) / Waiting for the man (live).
May 85. (7") **SO IN LOVE. / CONCRETE HANDS** [27] [26] Aug85
(12")(12"pic-d) – ('A'&'B'extended) / Maria Gallante.
(d12"++=) – White trash (live).
Jun 85. (lp)(c) **CRUSH** [13] [38] Jul 85
– So in love / Secret / Bloc bloc bloc / Women III / Crush / 88 seconds in Greensboro / The native daughters of the west / La femme accident / Hold you / The lights are going out. *(cd-iss.Jan86 & Mar90)*
Jul 85. (7") **SECRET. / DRIFT** [34] [-]
(12"+=) – ('A'extended).
(d12"+=) – Red frame – white light / I betray my friends.
Oct 85. (7")(7"sha-pic-d) **LA FEMME ACCIDENT. / FIREGUN** [42] [ ]
(12"+=) – ('A'extended).
(d12"++=) – Locomotion (live) / Enola Gay (live).
Nov 85. (7") **SECRET. / FIREGUN** [-] [63]
Mar 86. (7") **IF YOU LEAVE. / LA FEMME ACCIDENT** [-] [ ]
Apr 86. (7") **IF YOU LEAVE. / 88 SECONDS IN GREENSBORO** [48] [-]
(12") – ('A'extended) / Locomotion (live).

— added The **WEIR BROTHERS** (NEIL & GRAHAM) (had guested on earlier songs)

Aug 86. (7")(7"pic-d) **(FOREVER) LIVE AND DIE. / THIS TOWN** [11] [19]
(12"+=) – ('A'extended).
Sep 86. (lp)(c)(cd) **THE PACIFIC AGE** [15] [47]
– Stay (the black rose and the universal wheel) / (Forever) Live and die / The Pacific age / The dead girls / Shame / Southern / Flame of hope / Goddess of love / We love you / Watch us fall. *(re-iss.Mar90)*
Nov 86. (7") **WE LOVE YOU. / WE LOVE YOU (dub)** [54] [ ]
(12"+=) – ('A'extended).
(d7"+=) – If you leave / 88 seconds on Greensboro.
(free c-s w7"+=) – Souvenir / Electricity / Enola Gay / Joan of Arc.
Apr 87. (7") **SHAME (re-recorded). / GODDESS OF LOVE** [52] [ ]
(12"+=) – ('B're-recorded version).
(cd-s+=) – (Forever) Live and die / Messages.
Jan 88. (7") **DREAMING. / SATELLITE** [50] [16] Feb 88
(12")(12"pic-d) – ('A'extended) / Gravity never failed.
(cd-s+=)(3"cd-s++=) – Dreaming. *(re-distJun88, hit 60)*
(10") – ('A'side) / ('A'William Orbit mix) / Messages / Secret.
Feb 88. (lp)(c)(cd)(pic-cd) **IN THE DARK – THE BEST OF O.M.D.** (compilation) [2] [46]
– Electricity / Messages / Enola Gay / Souvenir / Joan of Arc / Maid of Orleans (Joan Of Arc waltz) / Talking loud and clear / Tesla girls / Locomotion / So in love / Secret / If you leave / (Forever) Live and die / Dreaming. *(cd+=)*– Telegraph / We love you (12"version) / La femme accident (12"version) / Genetic engineering.

OMD

ANDY McCLUSKEY now sole survivor after others left 1989. HUMPHREYS formed The LISTENING POOL in the early 90's. / added **STUART BOYLE** – guitar plus additional 8 vocalists.

Mar 91. (7")(c-s) **SAILING ON THE SEVEN SEAS. / BURNING** [3] [ ]
(12") – ('A'extended) / Floating on the seven seas.
(cd-s) – ('A'extended) / Dancing on the seven seas / Big town.
(cd-s) – ('A'side) / Floating on the seven seas / Dancing on the seaven seas (Larrabee mix) / Sugartax.
May 91. (cd)(c)(lp) **SUGAR TAX** [3] [ ]
– Sailing on the seven seas / Pandora's box / Then you turn away / Speed of light / Was it something I said / Big town / Call my name / Apollo XI / Walking on air / Walk tall / Neon lights / All that glitters.
Jun 91. (7")(c-s) **PANDORA'S BOX. / ALL SHE WANTS IS EVERYTHING** [7] [ ]
(cd-s+=) – ('A'constant pressure mix) / ('A'diesel fingers mix).
(12")/ /(cd-s) – (2 'A'mixes)./ / (3 'A'mixes).
Sep 91. (7")(c-s) **THEN YOU TURN AWAY. / SUGAR TAX** [50] [ ]
(cd-s+=) – Area / ('A'inforce repeat mix).
(cd-s) – ('A'side) / ('A'repeat mix) / Sailing on the seven seas / Vox humana.
Nov 91. (7")(c-s) **CALL MY NAME. / WALK TALL** [50] [ ]
(12") – ('A'side) / Brides of Frankenstein.
(cd-s++=) – ('A'side) / ('A'version) / Brides . . . (dub).
May 93. (7")(c-s) **STAND ABOVE ME. / CAN I BELIEVE YOU** [21] [ ]
(cd-s+=) – ('A' transcendental mix) / ('A' hynofunk mix).
(12") – ('A'side) / ('A'transcendental mix) / ('A'-10 minute version)
Jun 93. (cd)(c)(lp) **LIBERATOR** [14] [ ]
– Stand above me / Everyday / King of stone / Dollar girl / Dream of me (based on Love's theme) / Sunday morning / Agnus Dei / Love and hate you / Heaven is / Best years of our lives / Christine / Only tears.

Jul 93. (7")(c-s) **DREAM OF ME (BASED ON LOVE'S THEME). / ('A' mix)** [24] [ ]
(cd-s+=) – Strange sensations / The place you fear the most.
(cd-s) ('A' side) / Enola Gay / Dreaming / Call my name
Sep 93. (7")(c-s) **EVERYDAY. / ELECTRICITY (live)** [59] [ ]
(cd-s+=) – Walk tall (live) / Locomotion (live).

– other compilations, etc. –

May 84. Epic; (lp) **ORCHESTRAL MANOEUVRES IN THE DARK** [-] [ ]
– (compilation of first 2 albums)
Feb 89. Old Gold; (7") **ENOLA GAY. / ELECTRICITY** [ ] [-]
Mar 89. Old Gold; (12") **SOUVENIR (extended). / TALKING LOUD AND CLEAR (ext.)** [ ] [-]
Feb 89. Virgin/ US= A&M; (12") **BRIDES OF FRANKENSTEIN (OMD megaremixes: LOCOMOTION / SO IN LOVE / SECRET / IF YOU LEAVE / WE LOVE YOU)** [-] [ ]
Nov 90. Virgin; (3xpic-cd-box) **CD BOXED SET** [ ] [-]
– (first 3 albums)
Sep 94. Virgin; (cd)(c) **THE BEST OF OMD** [69] [ ]

ORGANISATION (see under ⇒ KRAFTWERK)

Benjamin ORR (see under ⇒ CARS)

Ozzy OSBOURNE

Born: JOHN MICHAEL OSBOURNE, 3 Dec'48, Aston, Birmingham, England. After 11 years as frontman for BLACK SABBATH, he formed own BLIZZARD OF OZZ in 1980. They signed to Don Arden's 'Jet', and released self-titled album, which hit UK Top 10 & US No.21. Their next album 'DIARY OF A MADMAN' in 1981, credited to OZZY solo, also went into cross-Atlantic Top 20. For the rest of the 80's, OZZY became renowned for his upsetting stage shows, where he used to bite the heads off doves, bats, etc. • **Miscellaneous:** He divorced wife Thelma in 1981, and married Don Arden's daughter Sharon on 4 Jul'82, who became his manager. Ozzy was always a hard drinker and drug user, although she forced him to attend the Betty Ford Clinic in 1984. He was taken to court a few times around the mid-80's, for people committing suicide while listening to his music, mainly citing the track 'SUICIDE SOLUTION'. • **Style:** Aleister Crowley influenced heavy-metal, lyrically evil, but taken seriously?. OZZY's screach was well-matched for this near SABBATH-like sound. • **Songwriters:** OZZY lyrics, RHOADS music, until his tour bus / plane-crash death on 19 Mar'82. In 1982, the group recorded a live album 'TALK OF THE DEVIL', full of BLACK SABBATH covers. OZZY later collaborated with BOB DAISLEY. • **Trivia:** In 1987, he played a bible-punching preacher in the film 'Trick Or Treat'.

Recommended: NO MORE TEARS (*7) / DIARY OF A MADMAN (*7) / OZZY OSBOURNE'S BLIZZARD OF OZZ (*6) / THE ULTIMATE SIN (*6).

OZZY OSBOURNE'S BLIZZARD OF OZZ

OZZY OSBOURNE – vocals (ex-BLACK SABBATH) / **RANDY RHOADS** – guitar (ex-QUIET RIOT) / **LEE KERSLAKE** – drums (ex-URIAH HEEP) / **BOB DAISLEY** – bass (ex-RAINBOW, ex-CHICKEN SHACK) / **DON AVERY** – keyboards

Jet Jet-CBS

Sep 80. (7") **CRAZY TRAIN. / YOU LOOKING AT ME LOOKING AT YOU** [49] [-]
Sep 80. (lp)(c) **OZZY OSBOURNE'S BLIZZARD OF OZZ** [7] [21] Mar81
– I don't know / Crazy train / Goodbye to romance / Dee / Suicide solution / Mr. Crowley / No bone movies / Revelation (Mother Earth) / Steal away (the night). *(re-iss.Nov87 on 'Epic', cd-iss.on 'Jet' & Nov95 on 'Epic')*
Nov 80. (7") **MR.CROWLEY. / YOU SAID IT ALL** [46] [-]
(12"+=) – Suicide solution.
Feb 81. (7") **CRAZY TRAIN. / STEAL AWAY (THE NIGHT)** [-] [ ]

OZZY OSBOURNE

(same line-up, except AVERY)
Oct 81. (lp)(c) **DIARY OF A MADMAN** [14] [16]
– Over the mountain / Flying high again / You can't kill rock and roll / Believer / Little dolls / Tonight / S.A.T.O. / Diary of a madman. *(cd-iss.May87) (re-iss.+cd.Apr91 & Nov95 on 'Epic')*
Nov 81. (7") **OVER THE MOUNTAIN. / I DON'T KNOW** [ ] [-]

— (Nov81) **RUDY SARZO** – bass (ex-QUIET RIOT) repl. DAISLEY (to URIAH HEEP) **TOMMY ALDRIDGE** – drums (ex-BLACK OAK ARKANSAS, etc) repl. KERSLAKE

— (Apr'82) **BRAD GILLIS** – guitar (of NIGHT RANGER) repl. RANDY RHOADS who was killed in a light aeroplane crash on 19th Mar'82.

Nov 82. (d-lp)(d-c) **TALK OF THE DEVIL** (live at Ritz Club, NY) [21] [14]
– Symptom of the universe / Snowblind / Black sabbath / Fairies wear boots / War pigs / The wizard / N.I.B. / Sweet leaf / Never say die / Sabbath bloody sabbath / Iron man / Children of the grave / Paranoid. *(cd-iss.Jan89 omits dialogue) (re-iss.complete cd+c.Jul91 on 'Castle') (re-iss.cd Nov95 on 'Epic')*
Dec 82. (7")(7"pic-d) **SYMPTOM OF THE UNIVERSE (live). / N.I.B. (live)** [ ] [-]
(12"+=) – Iron man – Children of the grave (live).
Feb 83. (7") **NEVER SAY DIE (live). / PARANOID (live)** [-] [ ]

— (Dec82) **JAKE E.LEE** (b.JAKEY LOU WILLIAMS, San Diego, California, USA) – guitar (ex-RATT) repl. GILLIS who returned to NIGHT RANGER / **DON COSTA** – bass repl. PETE WAY (ex-UFO) who had deputised for the departing RUDY SARZO who had returned to QUIET RIOT. (He later joined WHITESNAKE)

— **OZZY, JAKE E + TOMMY** re-recruit **BOB DAISLEY** to repl. COSTA

Epic CBS Assoc.

Nov 83. (7") **BARK AT THE MOON. / SPIDERS** [-] [ ]
Nov 83. (7") **BARK AT THE MOON. / ONE UP ON THE B-SIDE** [21] [ ]
(12"+=)(12"silver+=)(12"pic-d+=) – Slow down.
Dec 83. (lp)(c) **BARK AT THE MOON** [24] [19]
– Rock'n'roll rebel / Bark at the Moon / You're no different / Now you see it (now you don't) / Forever / So tired / Waiting for darkness / Spiders. *(re-iss.Apr86, cd-iss.Oct88 & Nov95)*
Mar 84. (7") **SO TIRED. / FOREVER (live)** [ ] [ ]
(12"+=)(d7"+=) – Waiting for darkness / Paranoid (live).

— ALDRIDGE was briefly replaced (Mar-May84) on tour by CARMINE APPICE.

May 84. (7") **SO TIRED. / BARK AT THE MOON (live)** [20] [ ]
(12"+=)(12"gold+=) – Waiting for darkness (live) / Suicide solution (live) / Paranoid (live).

— **PHIL SOUSSAN** – bass repl. DAISLEY / **RANDY CASTILLO** – drums (ex-LITA FORD BAND) repl. ALDRIDGE

Jan 86. (7")(12") **SHOT IN THE DARK. / ROCK'N'ROLL REBEL** [20] [-]
Feb 86. (lp)(c) **THE ULTIMATE SIN** [8] [6]
– Lightning strikes / Killer of giants / Thank God for the bomb / Never / Shot in the dark / The ultimate sin / Secret loser / Never know why / Fool like you. *(cd-iss Jul86 & Feb89 & Nov95) (pic-lp Aug86)*
Mar 86. (7") **SHOT IN THE DARK. / YOU SAID IT ALL** [-] [69]
Jul 86. (7")(12") **THE ULTIMATE SIN. / LIGHTNING STRIKES** [72] [ ]

— (Aug88) **ZAKK WILDE** (b.ZACH ADAMS, 14 Jan'66) – guitar repl. JAKE who formed BADLANDS. / **DAISLEY** returned to repl. SOUSSAN (to BILLY IDOL) / added **JOHN SINCLAIR** – keyboards

Oct 88. (lp)(c)(cd) **NO REST FOR THE WICKED** [23] [13]
– Miracle man / Devil's daughter / Crazy babies / Breaking all the rules / Bloodbath in Paradise / Fire in the sky / Tattooed dancer / The demon alcohol. *(cd+=)– Hero. (re-iss.cd+c Jun94 & Nov95)*
Oct 88. (7")(7"pic-d) **MIRACLE MAN. / CRAZY BABIES** [ ] [-]
(12"+=)(cd-s+=) – The liar.
Dec 88. (7") **MIRACLE MAN. / MAN YOU SAID IT ALL** [-] [ ]
Feb 89. (7") **CRAZY BABIES. / THE DEMON ALCOHOL** [-] [ ]

— Earlier in the year OZZY had accompanied LITA FORD on 45 'CLOSE MY EYES FOREVER'. In Apr'89, it was to reach UK/US Top50.

— **TERRY 'GEEZER' BUTLER** – bass was used for tour work late 1988.

Feb 90. (cd)(c)(lp) **JUST SAY OZZY (live)** [69] [58]
– Miracle man / Bloodbath in Paradise / Shot in the dark / Tattooed dancer / Sweet leaf / War pigs. *(re-iss.cd Nov95)*

— In the late 80's, OZZY retired to his Buckinghamshire mansion with his manager/wife Sharon Arden and 3 kids. He had also kicked his alcohol addiction.

Returned 1991 after being cleared of causing death of fan. See last studio line-up. Augmented also by **MICHAEL INEZ** – bass, inspiration repl. BUTLER

Sep 91. (7") **NO MORE TEARS. / S.I.N.** [32] [71]
(12"+=)(c-s+=)(cd-s+=)(12"pic-d+=) – Party with the animals.
Oct 91. (cd)(c)(lp) **NO MORE TEARS** [17] [7]
– Mr.Tinkertrain / I don't want to change the world / Mama, I'm coming home / Desire / S.I.N. / Hellraiser / Time after time / Zombie stomp / A.V.H. / Road to nowhere. *(re-iss.cd Nov95)*
Nov 91. (7") **MAMA, I'M COMING HOME. / DON'T BLAME ME** [46] [28] Feb 92
(12"+=) – I don't know / Crazy train.
(cd-s+=) – (Steve Wright interview)
(12"+=) – Time after time / Goodbye to romance.
(US-cd-ep+=) Party with the animals.
Jun 93. (d-cd) **LIVE & LOUD (live)** [ ] [22]
– Intro / Paranoid / I don't want to change the world / Desire / Mr.Crowley / I don't know / Road to nowhere / Flying high again / Guitar solo / Suicide solution / Goodbye to romance / Shot in the dark / No more tears / Miracle man / Drum solo / War pigs / Bark at the Moon / Mama, I'm coming home / Crazy train / Black sabbath / Changes. *(re-iss.Nov95)*
Jun 93. (12")(cd-s) **CHANGES (live). / CHANGES / NO MORE TEARS / DESIRE** [ ] [ ]
Oct 95. (cd)(c)(lp) **OZZMOSIS** [22] [4]
– Perry Mason / I just want you / Ghost behind my eyes / Thunder underground / See you on the other side / Tomorrow / Denial / My little man / Mr. Jekyll doesn't hide / Old L.A. tonight.
Nov 95. (7"pic-d) **PERRY MASON. / LIVING WITH THE ENEMY** [23] [ ]
(cd-s+=) – The whole world's falling down.
(cd-s) – ('A'side) / No more tears / I don't want to change the world / Flying high again.

– compilations, others, etc. –

May 87. Epic/ US= CBS; (d-lp)(c)(cd) **TRIBUTE (live)** [13] [6]
– I don't know / Crazy train / Revelation (Mother Earth) / Believer / Mr.Crowley / Flying high again / No bone movies / Steal away (the night) / Suicide solution / Iron man – Children of the grave / Goodbye to romance / Paranoid / Dee. *(cd-omits studio track 'Dee') (re-iss.cd+c Apr93 & Nov95 on 'Epic')*

(Album + 45 were recorded 1981 with the deceased RANDY RHOADS)

Jun 87. Epic/ US= CBS; (7")(12") **CRAZY TRAIN (live). / CRAZY TRAIN** [ ] [ ]
Jul 88. Epic; (12"ep)(cd-ep) **THE ULTIMATE SIN / BARK AT THE MOON. / MR.CROWLEY / DIARY OF A MADMAN** [ ] [-]
Mar 93. Epic; (cd) **BARK AT THE MOON / BLIZZARD OF OZ** [-] [ ]
Aug 90. Priority; (cd)(c)(lp) **TEN COMMANDMENTS** (rare) [-] [ ]

Lee OSKAR (see under ⇒ WAR)

OTHER TWO (see under ⇒ NEW ORDER)

John OTWAY (& Wild Willy BARRETT)

Born: 2 Oct'52, Aylesbury, Buckinghamshire, England. In 1972, after earlier supporting The GROUNDHOGS, he hired a proper musician WILD WILLY BARRETT, a school friend of his older bullying brother. WILLY augmented on JOHN's self-financed (borrowed) bluegrass 45 MISTY MOUNTAIN', cut in a shed. A copy was sent to DJ JOHN PEEL, who played it's B-side on Radio One. Another managed to be heard by PETE TOWNSHEND (of The Who) who offered to produce it properly. The limitation of OTWAY on his 3-chords while TOWNSHEND bashed away skillfully at his Gibson, left OTWAY a little embarrassed but in awe. It did bear fruit though as TOWNSHEND's label at the time 'Track' signed OTWAY and his first real recording 'MURDER MAN' was issued (even in the States!) late 1973. After it's flop, 'Track' became uninterested and OTWAY returned to a day-time job. In 1975 still desperate to hit big-time, he self-financed another TOWNSHEND produced track 'LOUISA ON A HORSE'. He wrote to all (nearly 200) record companies at the time but failed to receive much of a reply, although 'Track' re-issued 'LOUISA' in 1976. He re-united with BARRETT, who had invented an unusual fix-on-distortion pedal to help on their song 'RACING CARS'. In 1977, PUNK ROCK was taking over and through this and their eccentric appearance, several regular gigs started to come their way. They then went to Chalk Farm to record other tracks for an lp, but after it's completion 'Track' showed no interest. Undaunted, OTWAY encouraged his parents to re-mortgage their house, to pay for it's release. In the Spring of '77 it hit the shops on pun intended 'Extracted' records. It sold over 2,000 copies within a month and they were rewarded when 'Polydor' signed them for a 5-figure sum, re-releasing the eponymous gem late in the summer. To end the year, they released their best 3 minutes on two sides 'REALLY FREE' & 'BEWARE OF THE FLOWERS'. Promoted on BBC2's 'Old Grey Whistle Test' with daft-as-ever OTWAY knocking out BARRETT's lead leaving him near silent, it made the UK Top 30. Not for the first or last time, OTWAY & BARRETT disagreed and a solo ballad 45 'GENEVE' appeared early '78. 'Polydor' soon offered him a renewed 6-figure sum to stay with them, while BARRETT's advance was only a fraction of this. After both being dismal solo failures in 1979, they decided to re-unite for 'WAY & BAR', which contained 2 more gems 'BIRTHDAY BOY' & 'DK 50-80', the latter having returned them to Top 50 status. Later in 1980 they signed to 'Stiff', but only a few 45's were issued. The song 'HEADBUTTS' (wriiten by BARRETT whose inspiration came from a headbutting pub-goer) caused the label to reject it, although it could be found cheekily on own 'Stiff Indie'. The 1980's saw OTWAY & BARRETT head-off on solo projects, although they did clash again sporadically. In 1990, 'Omnibus' pressed OTWAY's hilarious autobiography 'Cor Baby, That's Really Me', which is obviously more comprehensive. Recently OTWAY & BARRETT re-formed partnership and OTWAY has surpassed his 2,000th gig!. • **Style:** DIY hairy-hippie with punk attitude and whose somersault guitar playing must be seen. OTWAY's early use of hillbilly country sound used to for me, conjure up images of a madcap RAY DAVIES (Kinks) fused with NEIL INNES (Bonzos). His/their "novelty" songs should have given him more chart appeal. • **Songwriters:** OTWAY or OTWAY-BARRETT except covers; RIDERS IN THE SKY (Jones)/ THE ALAMO (Bowers)/ CHERYL'S GOING HOME (Bob Lind)/ GREEN GREEN GRASS OF HOME (Tom Jones)/ THE NEW JERUSALEM (William Blake)/ IN DREAMS (Roy Orbison)/ YOU AIN'T SEEN NOTHIN' YET (Bachman-Turner Overdrive)/ TWO LITTLE BOYS (Rolf Harris)/ I WILL SURVIVE (Gloria Gaynor). In the mid-90's, he co-wrote with HOLGARTH. • **Trivia:** Apart from appearing in an episode of 'Supergran' (children's TV serial), OTWAY has been seen in several TV ads for companies; Toshiba/ Bradford & Bingley/ Boots/ Danepak Bacon (2)/ McDonald's/ Irn Bru/ Wickes DIY.

Recommended: COR BABY, THAT'S REALLY ME (*7)

JOHN OTWAY – vocals, guitar

County / not issued

Sep 72. (7") **MISTY MOUNTAIN. / GYPSY** [ ] [-]

Track / M.C.A.

Oct 73. (7") **MURDER MAN. / IF I DID** [ ] [ ]

(above by "JOHN OTWAY & WILD WILLY BARRETT")

Viking / not issued

Feb 76. (7") **LOUISA ON A HORSE. / BEWARE OF THE FLOWERS** [ ] [-]

JOHN OTWAY AND WILD WILLY BARRETT

OTWAY – vocals, guitar / **WILD WILLY BARRETT** – guitar, violin / **NIGEL PEGRUM** – drums / and session people

Track / not issued

Nov 76. (7") **LOUISA ON A HORSE. / MISTY MOUNTAIN** [ ] [-]

Extracted / not issued

May 77. (lp) **JOHN OTWAY & WILD WILLY BARRETT** [ ] [-]
– Misty mountain / Murder man / If I did / Racing cars (jet spotter of the track) / Louisa on a horse / Gypsy / Really free / Bluey green / Cheryl's going home / Trying times / Geneve. *(re-iss.Aug77 on 'Polydor')*

Polydor / not issued

Aug 77. (7") **RACING CARS (JET SPOTTER OF THE TRACK). / RUNNING FROM THE LAW** [ ] [-]

Nov 77. (7") **REALLY FREE. / BEWARE OF THE FLOWERS ('CAUSE I'M SURE THEY'RE GOING TO GET YOU, YEH)** [27] [-]

In Nov'77 also gave out 250 copies of 'OTWAY & BARRETT LIVE AT THE ROUND-HOUSE 14/8/77')

Mar 78. (7") **GENEVE. ("JOHN OTWAY") / IT'S A LONG TIME SINCE I HEARD HOMESTEAD ON THE FARM** [ ] [-]

May 78. (lp) **DEEP & MEANINGLESS** [44] [-]
– Place Farm Way / To Anne / Beware of the flowers ('cause I'm sure they're going to get you, yeh) / The Alamo / Oh my body is making me / Josephine / Schnot / Riders in the sky- Running from the law- Riders in the sky / I wouldn't wish it on you / Can't complain. (free 7" w/some lp) RACING CARS (JET SPOTTER OF THE TRACK). / DOWN THE ROAD *(cd-iss.1993 on 'The Music Corporation' with 1977 & 1978 lp tracks)*

JOHN OTWAY

now w/ **OLLIE HALSALL** – guitar / **MORGAN FISHER** – keyboards / **PAUL MARTINEZ** – bass / **CHARLIE MORGAN** – drums

Polydor / not issued

Sep 78. (7") **BABY'S IN THE CLUB. / JULIE JULIE JULIE** [ ] [-]

Mar 79. (7") **FRIGHTENED AND SCARED./ ARE YOU ON MY SIDE** [ ] [-]

Apr 79. (lp) **WHERE DID I GO RIGHT?** [ ] [-]
– Makes good music / It's a pain / Blue eyes of the belle / Best dream / What a woman / Frightened and scared / Waiting / Hurting her more / The highwayman.

— In Aug'79, JOHN OTWAY featured on WILD WILLY BARRETT's debut solo lp 'CALL OF THE WILD' (Polydor). Lifted from it in Mar79 was the single 'LET'S PLAY SCHOOLS'. / 'I DID IT OTWAY' (Polydor). In Nov77, BARRETT on 'Logo' issued 'RETURN OF KONG'. / 'NICE TO KNOW YOU'RE MY FRIEND'. In 1981 he surfaced on 'Black Eye' records issuing a number of singles and an lp 'KRAZY KONG ALBUM'. In 1983, he signed to 'Carrere' (3 singles), before moving to 'Strike Back'. In 1986 with STEPHEN TWO NAMES, he issued for 'Galvanised' lp 'ORGANIC BONDAGE'.

OTWAY & BARRETT

Polydor / not issued

Apr 80. (7") **BIRTHDAY BOY. / WHAT A WOMAN** [ ] [-]

Jun 80. (7") **DK 50-80. / IT'S A LONG LONG TIME SINCE I HEARD HOMESTEAD ON THE FARM (Otway)/ HOMESTEAD ON THE FARM (Barrett)** [45] [-]

Aug 80. (lp) **WAY & BAR** [ ] [-]
– Birthday boy / DK 50-80 / Cry cry / 21 days / Medieval dance / Body talk / Baby's in the club / The man who shot Liberty Valance / When love's in bloom / Day after day / Come back darling.

JOHN OTWAY

Stiff / Stiff

Oct 80. (7") **GREEN GREEN GRASS OF HOME. / WEDNES-DAY CLUB** [ ] [-]

Dec 80. (7"ep) **LIBERTY VALANCE. / BIRTHDAY BOY/ RACING CARS (JET SPOTTER OF THE TRACK)** [-] [ ]

Jan 81. (lp) **DEEP THOUGHT** [-] [ ]

Apr 81. (7") **THE TURNING POINT. / TOO MUCH AIR NOT ENOUGH OXYGEN** [ ] [-]

May 81. (12"ep) **I DID IT OTWAY EP** [-] [ ]
– Running from the law / Turning point / Headbutts / Green green grass of home / Highway man / I did it Otway. *(Canada Stiff)*

Stiff Indie / not issued

Dec 81. (7") **HEADBUTTS. / HEADBUTTS (live)** [76] [-]

next featured The EUROPEANS as backing band

Empire / not issued

Jul 82. (lp) **JOHN OTWAY (ALL BALLS AND NO WILLY)** [ ] [-]
– Nothing's gone / Mass communication / In dreams / Too much air, not enough oxygen / Montreal / Middle of winter / Turn off your dream / Telex/ etc. ???

Aug 82. (12"ep) **12 STITCH EP** [ ] [-]
– Headbutts (live at Capitol Radio) / Best dream jingle / Auld Lang Sammy / Headbutts jingle / Headbutts (original) / Raving cars jingle.

— (above 2 singles by "JOHN OTWAY & WILD WILLY BARRETT")

Oct 82. (7") **IN DREAMS. ("JOHN OTWAY SWEAT") / YOU AIN'T SEEN NOTHIN' YET** [ ] [-]

May 83. (7"green) **MASS COMMUNICATION. / BABY IT'S THE REAL THING** [ ] [-]

StrikeBack / not issued

Nov 84. (7") **MIDDLE OF WINTER. / IT MAKES ME SEE RED** [ ] [-]

Feb 86. (lp)(c)(cd) **GLEATEST HITS - YAWTO SINGS** (compilation) [ ] [-]

(above lp by "JOHN OTWAY & WILD WILLY BARRETT")

W.E.A. / not issued

Nov 86. (7") **THE NEW JERUSALEM. / THE TYGER** [ ] [-]

(above was originally a private pressing sent a month earlier to 'Warners' alongside their logo accompanied with a 3-figure cheque and a letter stating he had signed them and not the reverse!. They didn't sue and signed him!.

Mar 87. (7")(12") **WHOOPS APOCALYPSE. / LOSING** [ ] [-]

JOHN OTWAY & WILD WILLY BARRETT

VM / not issued

Sep 87. (7") **THE LAST OF THE MOHICANS. / FASHION** [ ] [-]

Sep 87. (ltd.lp) **THE WIMP AND THE WILD** [ ] [-]

JOHNNY JAPES & HIS JESTICLES

aka JOHN OTWAY & ANDY PARTRIDGE (XTC)

Viz Comics / not issued

Dec 87. (7") **BAGS OF FUN WITH BUSTER. / SCROTAL SCRATCH MIX** [ ] [-]

JOHN OTWAY with ATTILA THE STOCKBROKER

StrikeBack / not issued

Oct 91. (7") **CHERYL. / BOYS IN THE HOOD (trainspotter rap) (by MC Trainspotter & The Platform 2 Live Crew)** [ ] [-]
Oct 91. (lp) **CHERYL A ROCK OPERA** [ ] [-]

JOHN OTWAY

John Otway / not issued

Sep 92. (cd-ep) **TWO LITTLE BOYS / I WILL SURVIVE / JOSEPHINE (w/ Wild Willy Barrett) / THE HIGHWAYMAN** [ ] [-]
Oct 92. (cd) **UNDER THE COVERS AND OVER THE TOP** [ ] [-]

Amazing Feet / not issued

Jan 94. (cd)(c) **JOHN OTWAY AND THE BIG BAND LIVE (live)** [ ] [-]
– In dreams / Misty mountain / Really free / Bluey green / Racing cars (jet spoter of the track) / Beware of the flowers / Josephine / Louisa on a horse / It's the real thing / Two little boys / Best dream / Frightened and scared / Cheryl's going home / The house of the rising sun / Geneve.
Apr 95. (cd) **PREMATURE ADULATION** [ ] [-]
– Judgement day / oetry and jazz / Duet / We know what she's doing (she's in love) / The saddest sound since the blues / Entertainment (not) / Photograph / Please don't read my poetry / Nothing at all / God's camera / Willy (in the air) / Typewriter.

Strikeback / not issued

Oct 95. (cd-ep) **DELILAH (THE OTWAY SINGS JONES EP)** [ ] [-]
– Delilah / It's not unusual / Green green grass of home (live).

compilations, others

Aug 81. Polydor; (lp)(c) **GONE WITH THE BIN (THE BEST OF OTWAY & BARRETT)** [ ] [-]
– Beware of the flowers ('cause I'm sure they're going to get you, yeh) / Racing cars (jet spotter of the track) / Oh my body is making me / Running from the law / Riders in the sky / Cheryl's going home / Birthday boy / Geneve / Really free / DK 50-80 / Louisa on a horse / Body talk / The man who shot Liberty Valance / Baby's in the club / I did it Otway.
May 90. StrikeBack; (cd) **COR BABY, THAT'S REALLY ME!** [ ] [-]

OZRIC TENTACLES

Formed: London, England . . . after meeting at Stonehenge in 1982. Brothers ED and ROLY WYNNE with the others, decamped to Trowbridge, Somerset in the early 90's, having issued second album (a double) 'ERPLAND' on managers' JOHN BENNETT own 'Dovetail' label. • **Style:** Psychedelic /progressive festival crusty band, who had similiar inclinations to STEVE HILLAGE, CAMEL or HAWKWIND. • **Songwriters:** Group / or ED and JOIE. • **Trivia:** JOIE bet their record company that aliens!!! would land on Earth by the year 2000.

Recommended: STRANGEITUDE (*7) / JURASSIC SHIFT (*6) / ARBORESCENCE (*6)

ED WYNNE – guitar, synthesizers / **ROLY WYNNE** – bass / **JOIE 'OZROONICULATOR' HINTON** – synthesizers / **NICK 'TIG' VAN GELDER** – drums / **GAVIN GRIFFITHS** – guitar / added in 1983; **TOM BROOKES** – synthesizers / **PAUL HANKIN** – percussion

— In 1984, GRIFFITHS left to form ULLINATORS, and a year later BROOKES also left. HINTON sidelined with group ULLINATORS and OROONIES. Released cassette-only albums which I think were untitled.

— **MERV PEPLER** – drums, percussion repl. VAN GELDER

Demi-Monde / not issued

Feb 89. (lp) **PUNGENT EFFULGENT** [ ] [-]
– Dissolution (the clouds disperse) / 0-1 / Phalam dawn / The domes of G'bal / Shaping the pelm / Ayurvedic / Kick muck / Agog in the ether / Wreltch. *(re-iss.+cd/c Mar91 on 'Dovetail')*

Dovetail / not issued

Nov 90. (cd)(d-lp) **ERPLAND** [ ] [-]
– Eternal wheel / Toltec spring / Tidal convergence / Sunscape / Mysticum Arabicola / Crackerblocks / The throbbe / Erpland / Valley of a thousand thoughts / Snakepit / Iscence / A gift of wings.
Jul 91. (12")(cd-s) **SPLOOSH!. / LIVE THROBBE** [ ] [-]
Aug 91. (cd)(c)(lp) **STRANGEITUDE** [70] [-]
– White rhino tea / Sploosh / Saucers / Strangeitude / Bizzare bazaar / Space between your ears. (cd+=) – Live Throbbe.

— **STEVE EVERETT** – synthesizers repl. BROOKES

— added **MARCUS CARCUS** – percussion / **JOHN EGAN** – flute

Jan 92. (d-cd) **AFTERWISH** (compilation 1984-1991) [ ] [ ]
– Guzzard / Chinatype / The sacred turf / Og-ha-be / Thyroid / Omnidibectional Bhadba / Afterwish / Velmwend / Travelling the great circle / Secret names / Soda water / Fetch me the pongmaster / Zall! / Abul Hagag / It's a hup ho world / The dusty pouch / Thrashing breath texture / Floating seeds / Invisible carpet / The code for Chickendon / Kola b'pep / Mae Hong song / Symetricum / Jabular / Sliding and gliding.
Apr 92. (cd)(c)(d-lp) **LIVE UNDERSLUNKY (live)** [ ] [-]
– Dot thots / Og-ha-be / Erpland / White rhino tea / Bizzare bazaar / Sunscrape / Erpsongs / Snake pit / Kick muck / 0-1 / Ayurvedic.

— **ZIA** – bass repl. ROLY (late'92)

— (5-piece **ED, JOIE, JON, MERV + ZIA**)

Apr 93. (cd)(c)(lp) **JURASSIC SHIFT** [11] [-]
– Sun hair / Stretchy / Feng Shui / Jurassic shift / Pteranodon / Train oasis / Vita voom.
Jul 94. (cd)(c)(d-lp) **ARBORESCENCE** [18] [ ]
– Astro Cortez / Yog-bar-og / Arborescence / Al-salooq / Dance of the Loomi / Myriapod / There's a planet here / Shima Koto.

— JOIE + MERV were now EAT STATIC full-time. They had splintered as said outfit since summer '92.

Oct 95. (cd) **BECOME THE OTHER** [ ] [-]
– Og-ha-be / Shards of ice / Sniffing dog / Music to gargle at / Ethereal cereal / Atmosphear / Ulluvar gate / Tentacles of Erpmiad / Trees of eternity / Mescalito / Odhanshan / Become the other / Gnuthlia / Sorry style / The Aun shuffle.

– compilations, etc. –

Nov 93. Dovetail; (6xcd-box) **VITAMIN ENHANCED** [ ] [-]
Feb 94. Dovetail; (cd) **ERPSONGS** [ ] [-]
Feb 94. Dovetail; (cd) **TANTRIC OBSTACLES** [ ] [-]
Feb 94. Dovetail; (cd) **LIVE ETHEREAL CEREAL** [ ] [-]
Feb 94. Dovetail; (cd) **THERE IS NOTHING** [ ] [-]
Feb 94. Dovetail; (cd) **SLIDING GLIDING WORDS** [ ] [-]
Feb 94. Dovetail; (cd) **THE BITS BETWEEN THE BITS** [ ] [-]
(all 6 above re-iss.Mar94)

EAT STATIC

JOIE + MERV + STEVE

Alien / not issued

1992. (c) **PREPARE YOUR SPIRIT** [ ] [-]
– Hallucinate / Fudge / Wormlips / Instinct / Eat-Static / Destroy / Raga / Almost human / Om machine / Cyper-funk / The watcher / Higher-state / Woman is life / Medicine wheel / Fourt dimension.
Nov 92. (12"ep)(cd-ep) **ALMOST HUMAN / FOURTH DIMENSION. / PUPAE (THE LOCUST SONG) / MOTHER PLANET** [ ] [-]

Ultimate-Planet Dog / not issued

May 93. (cd)(c)(lp) **ABDUCTION** [62] [-]
– Prana / Gulf breeze / Kalika / Splitting world / Kinetic flow / Forgotten rites / Abduction / Intruder / Xenomorph / Inner peace.
Nov 93. (12"ep)(cd-ep) **LOST IN TIME. / GULF BREEZE / THE BRAIN** [ ] [-]
Mar 94. (12"ep)(cd-ep) **GULF BREEZE (remix). / ('A'-Ashoshashoz mix) / ('A'cat mix)** [ ] [-]
Jun 94. (cd)(c)(lp) **IMPLANT** [13] [ ]
– Implant.
Jul 94. (1 track; 12"ep/cd-ep) **SURVIVORS** [ ] [-]
Mar 95. (12"ep)(d12"ep)(c-ep)(cd-ep) **EPSYLON EP** [ ] [-]
– Epsylon / Dionsyiac / Peeou / Undulattice.

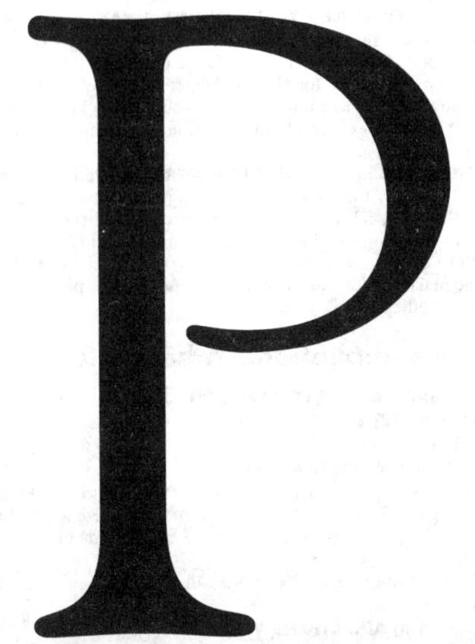

Jimmy PAGE (see under ⇒ LED ZEPPELIN)

PAICE, ASHTON & LORD (see under ⇒ DEEP PURPLE)

PALE SAINTS

Formed: Leeds, England ... 1987 by MASTERS, COOPER and NAYSMITH. Their first ever gig in London, was seen by '4 a.d.' records, who signed them promptly in '89. Their debut album 'THE COMFORT OF MADNESS', earned them a top indie seller, which also breached the Top 40. Their follow-up mini-lp to end the year 'HALF LIFE REMEMBERED' was certainly their finest to date. • **Style:** Textured and layered alternative rock group, fused between The CHAMELEONS and The BOO RADLEYS. • **Songwriters:** Group penned except; KINKY LOVE (Nancy Sinatra) / REFLECTIONS FROM A WATERY WORLD (Slapp Happy) /FELL FROM THE SUN (opal). • **Trivia:** They issued a Japanese-only album in 1991 'MRS.DOLPHIN'. MERIEL guested on BOO RADLEY'S 1993 album.

Recommended: THE COMFORT OF MADNESS (*8) / IN RIBBONS (*9).

IAN MASTERS (b.4 Jan'64, Potters Bar, Hertfordshire, England) – vocals, bass / **GRAEME NAYSMITH** (b. 9 Feb'67, Edinburgh, Scotland) – guitar / **CHRIS COOPER** (b.17 Nov'66, Portsmouth, England) – drums

		4 a.d.	Relativity
Sep 89.	(12"ep)(cd-ep) **BARGING INTO THE PRESENCE OF GOD**		-
	– Sight of you / She rides the waves / Mother might.		
——	added **ASHLEY HORNER** – guitar		
Feb 90.	(cd)(c)(lp) **THE COMFORT OF MADNESS**	40	
	– True coming dream / Little hammer / You tear the world in two / The sea of sound / Way the world is / A deep sleep for Steven / Fell from the Sun / Time thief / Insubstantial / Language of flowers / Sight of you.		
——	**MERIEL BARHAM** (b.15 Oct'64, Germany) – guitar, vocals repl. HORNER who concentrated on own group EDSEL AUCTIONEER, whom he spent the last 2 years with		
Oct 90.	(12"ep)(cd-ep) **HALF-LIFE**		-
	– Half-life remembered / Baby maker / Two sick sisters / A revelation.		
Jun 91.	(7") **KINKY LOVE. / HAIR SHOES**	72	-
	(12"+cd-ep+=) **FLASH BALLOON**(EP) – Hunted / Porpoise.		
Mar 92.	(cd)(c)(lp) **IN RIBBONS**	61	
	– Throwing back the apple / Ordeal / Thread of light / Shell / There is no day / Hunted / Hair shoes / Babymaker / Liquid / Neverending night / Featherframe / A thousand stars bust open. (free 12"w.a. as "The TINWISTLE BRASS BAND") **A THOUSAND STARS BUST OPEN. / A REVELATION**		
May 92.	(12"ep)(cd-ep) **THROWING BACK THE APPLE**		-
	– Throwing back the apple / Blue flower / Half-life remembered / Reflections from a watery world.		
Aug 94.	(12")(cd-s) **FINE FRIEND. / SPECIAL PRESENT / MARIMBA / SURPRISE**		
Sep 94.	(cd)(c)(lp) **SLOW BUILDINGS**		
	– King Fade / Angel (will you be my) / One blue hill / Henry / Under your nose / Little gesture / Song of Solomon / Fine friend / Gesture of a fear / Always I / Suggestion.		

Robert PALMER

Born: ALAN ROBERT PALMER, 19 Jan'49, Batley, Yorkshire, England. From the age of 3, lived with family in Malta, due to father being in the services. In 1969 after being in semi-pro group MANDRAKE PADDLE STEAMER, he moved to London. He joined ALAN BOWN SET, replacing solo bound JESS RODEN. Late that year, he featured on 'Deram' 45 'GYPSY GIRL'. The following year, he joined jazz-rockers DADA, who also had on their eponymous 'Atco' album debut, singer ELKIE BROOKS. In 1971, they evolved into VINEGAR JOE, but after 3 poor selling albums for 'Island' (VINEGAR JOE / ROCK'N'ROLL GYPSIES + SIX-STAR GENERAL), they split-up Mar'74. After nearly replacing LOWELL GEORGE in LITTLE FEAT, PALMER was retained by 'Island'. His first album release 'SNEAKING SALLY . . . ', failed in the UK, but sales in the US, nearly made it crack the Top 100. The next year, he flitted to New York with his wife. After his follow-up album 'PRESSURE DROP', and support slot on LITTLE FEAT tour, he again relocated, this time to Nassau, Bahamas. After making inroads into Transatlantic charts in the mid-70's, he broke through in the US with 1978 singles 'EVERY KINDA PEOPLE' & 'BAD CASE OF LOVING YOU (DOCTOR, DOCTOR)'. He gained deserved commercial leap in the early 80's, with album 'CLUES'. In 1985, he teamed up with DURAN DURAN members to become The POWER STATION. They scored with a few hits including 'SOME LIKE IT HOT'. In 1987, now as an accomplished worldwide artist, he emigrated to Lugano, Switzerland, although he and his wife also stayed in Milan, Italy. • **Style:** BRYAN FERRY like in image/smart attire. His use of stunning female filled videos also drew attention to American AOR reggae beat/disco leanings. • **Songwriters:** PALMER penned, except SNEAKING SALLY THROUGH THE ALLEY + FROM A WHISPER TO A SCREAM (Allen Toussaint) / PRESSURE DROP (Lee Perry) / EVERY KINDA PEOPLE (Andy Fraser) / YOU REALLY GOT ME (Kinks) / JEALOUS + THE SILVER GUN (Alan Powell) / YOU ARE IN MY SYSTEM (System) / CAN WE STILL BE FRIENDS (Todd Rundgren) / SOME GUYS HAVE ALL THE LUCK (Persuaders) / BAD CASE OF LOVING YOU (Moon Martin) / I DIDN'T MEAN TO TURN YOU ON (hit; Cherrelle) / EARLY IN THE MORNING (Gap Band) / I'LL BE YOUR BABY TONIGHT (Bob Dylan) / MERCY MERCY ME (THE ECOLOGY) – I WANT YOU (Marvin Gaye) / WITCHCRAFT (hit; Frank Sinatra) / GIRL U WANT (Devo) / RESPECT YOURSELF (Staple Singers) / etc. • **Trivia:** GARY NUMAN featured on his 1980 'CLUES' album. PALMER produced The COMSAT ANGELS, DESMOND DEKKER and PETER BAUMANN.

Recommended: ADDICTIONS VOL.1 (*7) / ADDICTIONS 2 (*5).

ROBERT PALMER – vocals with various session people

		Island	Island
Sep 74.	(lp)(c) **SNEAKIN' SALLY THROUGH THE ALLEY**		May 75
	– Sailing shoes / Hey Julia / Sneakin' Sally through the alley / Through it all there's you / Get outside / Blackmail / How much fun / From a whisper to a scream / Through it all there's you. *(re-iss.Jan87, cd-iss.Aug89)*		
Nov 74.	(7") **SNEAKIN' SALLY THROUGH THE ALLEY. / EPIDEMIC**	-	
Oct 75.	(7") **WHICH OF US IS THE FOOL. / GET OUTSIDE**		
Feb 76.	(7") **GIMME AN INCH. / PRESSURE DROP**		
Mar 76.	(lp)(c) **PRESSURE DROP**		Nov 75
	– Give me an inch / Work to make it work / Back in my arms / Riverboat / Pressure drop / Here with you tonight / Trouble / Fine time / Which of us is the fool. *(re-iss.Jan87, cd-iss.Apr87 + Aug89)*		
Oct 76.	(7") **MAN SMART, WOMAN SMARTER. / FROM A WHISPER TO A SCREAM**		-
Oct 76.	(lp)(c) **SOME PEOPLE CAN DO WHAT THEY LIKE**	46	68
	– One lost look / Keep in touch / Man smart, woman smarter / Spanish moon / Have mercy / Gotta get a grip on you (part II) / What can you bring me / Hard head / Off the bone / Some people can do what they like.		
Oct 76.	(7") **MAN SMART, WOMAN SMARTER. / KEEP IN TOUCH**	-	63
Mar 77.	(7") **SOME PEOPLE CAN DO WHAT THEY LIKE. / ONE LOST LOOK**	-	
Jan 78.	(lp)(c) **DOUBLE FUN**		45 Mar 78
	– Every kinda people / Best of both worlds / Come over / Where can it go / Night people / Love can run faster / You overwhelm me / You really got me / You're gonna get what's coming. *(re-iss.Jan87, cd-iss.Nov87 + Aug89)*		
Mar 78.	(7") **EVERY KINDA PEOPLE. / HOW MUCH FUN**	-	16
Mar 78.	(7") **EVERY KINDA PEOPLE. / KEEP IN TOUCH**	53	-
May 78.	(7") **COME OVER. / YOU OVERWHELM ME**	-	
Jun 78.	(7") **BEST OF BOTH WORLDS. / ('A'dub version)**		
	(12"+=) – Pressure drop.		
May 79.	(7") **BAD CASE OF LOVIN' YOU (DOCTOR, DOCTOR). / LOVE CAN RUN FASTER**	61	14 Jul 79
Jun 79.	(lp)(c) **SECRETS**	54	19 Jul 79
	– Bad case of loving you (doctor, doctor) / Too good to be true / Can we still be friends / In walks love again / Mean old world / Love stop / Jealous / Under suspicion / Woman you're wonderful / What's it take / Remember to remember. *(re-iss.Jan87, cd-iss.1988 + Aug89)*		
Jul 78.	(7") **YOU'RE GONNA GET WHAT'S COMING. / WHERE CAN IT GO**	-	
Aug 79.	(7") **JEALOUS. / WOMAN YOU'RE WONDERFUL**		-
Sep 79.	(7") **JEALOUS. / IN WALKS LOVE AGAIN**	-	
Nov 79.	(7") **CAN WE STILL BE FRIENDS. / BACK IN MY ARMS**	-	
Dec 79.	(7") **CAN WE STILL BE FRIENDS. / REMEMBER TO REMEMBER**	-	52
Aug 80.	(7") **JOHNNY AND MARY. / STYLE KILLS**	-	
Aug 80.	(7") **JOHNNY AND MARY. / WHAT'S IT TAKE**	44	-
	(12"+=) – Remember to remember.		
Aug 80.	(lp)(c) **CLUES**	31	59 Oct 80
	– Looking for clues / Sulky girl / Johnny and Mary / What do you care / I dream of wires / Woke up laughing / Not a second time / Found you now. *(re-iss.+cd.Jan87, cd-iss.Jan89)*		
Oct 80.	(7") **LOOKING FOR CLUES. / WOKE UP LAUGHING**	-	
Nov 80.	(7") **LOOKING FOR CLUES. / IN WALKS LOVE AGAIN**	33	-
	(12") – ('A'side) / Good care of you / Style kills.		
Jun 81.	(7") **NOT A SECOND TIME. / WOKE UP LAUGHING**		
Jan 82.	(7")(7"pic-d) **SOME GUYS HAVE ALL THE LUCK. / TOO GOOD TO BE TRUE**	16	

(12")(12"pic-d) – ('A'side) / Style kills / Si Chatouillieux / What do you care.

Mar 82. (lp)(c) **MAYBE IT'S LIVE (live)** [32] [ ] May 82
– Sneakin' Sally through the alley / What's it take / Best of both worlds / Every kinda people / Bad case of loving you (doctor, doctor) / Some guys have all the luck / Style kills / Si Chatouillieaux / Maybe it's you / What do you care. *(cd+c.-iss.Apr91) (re-iss.cd+cMay93 on 'Spectrum')*

Nov 82. (7")(7"pic-d) **PRIDE. / PRIDE (instrumental)** [ ] [ ]
(12") – ('A'side) / Parade of the obliterators.

Mar 83. (7")(12") **YOU ARE IN MY SYSTEM. / DEADLINE** [53] [78] Jun 83

Apr 83. (lp)(c) **PRIDE** [37] [ ]
– Pride / Deadline / Want you more / Dance for me / You are in my system / It's not difficult / Say you will / You can have it (take my heart) / What you waiting for / The silver gun. *(re-iss.+cdJan87, cd-issJun89)*

Jun 83. (7")(12")(7"pic-d) **YOU CAN HAVE IT (TAKE MY HEART). / THE SILVER GUN** [66] [ ]

— From early '85, PALMER became lead singer of DURAN DURAN off-shoot band The POWER STATION. Their eponymous lp, hit both UK + US Top 20's, and spawned a few hits 'SOME LIKE IT HOT', 'GET IT ON' & 'COMMUNICATION'. (see DURAN DURAN ⇒).

Oct 85. (7") **DISCIPLINE OF LOVE. / DANCE FOR ME** [ ] [82]
(12"+=) – Woke up laughing.

Nov 85. (lp)(c)(cd) **RIPTIDE** [5] [8]
– Riptide / Hyperactive / Addicted to love / Trick bag / Get it through your heart / I didn't mean to turn you on / Flesh wound / Discipline of love / Riptide (reprise). *(cd-iss.1988) (re-iss.+cd.Apr91)*

Dec 85. (7") **RIPTIDE. / BACK IN MY ARMS** [ ] [ ]
(12") – ('A'side) / No not much (live) / Trick bag (live)
(d7"++=) – (12"tracks) / Johnny and Mary.

Feb 86. (7") **ADDICTED TO LOVE. / LET'S FALL IN LOVE TONIGHT** [-] [1]

Apr 86. (7")(12") **ADDICTED TO LOVE. / REMEMBER TO REMEMBER** [5] [-]
(7"sha-pic-d) – ('A'side) / More.

May 86. (7") **HYPERACTIVE. / WOKE UP LAUGHING** [-] [33]

Jun 86. (7")(12") **I DIDN'T MEAN TO TURN YOU ON. / GET IT THROUGH YOUR HEART** [9] [2] Aug 86
(d7"+=) – You are in my system / Johnny and Mary.

Oct 86. (7")(12") **DISCIPLINE OF LOVE. / DANCE FOR ME** [68] [-]
(12"+=) – Riptide (medley).
(d7"+=) – Remember to remember / Addicted to love.

Mar 88. (7") **SWEET LIES. / WANT YOU MORE** [ ] [94]
(12"+=) – Riptide.
(cd-s++=) – ('A'extended).

E.M.I. Manhattan

Jun 88. (7")(7"pic-d) **SIMPLY IRRESISTABLE. / NOVA** [44] [2]
(12"+=)(cd-s+=) – ('A'extended version) / ('A'instrumental).

Jun 88. (lp)(c)(cd) **HEAVY NOVA** [17] [13]
– Simply irresistable / More than ever / Change his ways / Disturbing behaviour / Early in the morning / It could happen to you / She makes my day / It could happen to you / Tell me I'm not dreaming / Between us / Casting a spell. *(re-iss.cd+c Mar94)*

Oct 88. (7") **SHE MAKES MY DAY. / DISTURBING BEHAVIOUR** [6] [ ]
(12"+=)(cd-s+=) – Simply irresistable (extended).

Oct 88. (7") **EARLY IN THE MORNING. / ?** [-] [19]

May 89. (7")(7"pic-d) **CHANGE HIS WAYS. / MORE THAN EVER** [28] [ ]
(12") – (2 diff.mixes).
(cd-s++=) – She makes my day.

Jun 89. (7") **TELL ME I'M NOT DREAMING. / ?** [-] [60]

Aug 89. (7")(c-s) **IT COULD HAPPEN TO YOU. / CHANGE HIS WAYS** [71] [ ]
(12"+=) – Early in the morning (get up mix).
(cd-s++=) – Casting a spell.

E.M.I. E.M.I.

Oct 90. (7")(c-s) **I'LL BE YOUR BABY TONIGHT. ("ROBERT PALMER & UB40") / DEEP END** [6] [ ]
(12"+=)(cd-s+=) – ('A'version).

Nov 90. (cd)(c)(d-lp) **DON'T EXPLAIN** [9] [88]
– Your mother should have told you / Light-years / You can't get enough of a good thing / Dreams to remember / You're amazing / Mess around / Happiness / History / I'll be your baby tonight / Housework / Mercy mercy me – I want you / Don't explain / Aeroplane / People will say we're in love / Not a word / Top 40 / You're so desirable / You're my thrill. *(re-iss.cd+c Sep94)*

Nov 90. (c-s) **YOU'RE AMAZING. / ?** [-] [28]

Dec 90. (7")(c-s) **MERCY MERCY ME (THE ECOLOGY) – I WANT YOU. / OH YEAH** [9] [16] Feb 91
(12"+=)(cd-s+=) – (2 'A'&'B'versions).

Apr 91. (7")(c-s) **HAPPINESS. / ALL SHOOK UP** [ ] [ ]
(12"+=)(cd-s+=) – ('A'extended).

Jun 91. (7")(c-s) **DREAMS TO REMEMBER. / MESS AROUND** [68] [ ]
(12"+=) – Happiness.
(cd-s+=) – Mercy mercy me / I want you.

Oct 92. (7")(c-s) **WITCHCRAFT. / CHANCE** [50] [ ]
(cd-s) – ('A'side) / She makes my day / Mercy mercy me – I want you.

Oct 92. (cd)(c)(d-lp) **RIDIN' HIGH** [32] [ ]
– Love me or leave me / (Love is) The tender trap / You're my thrill / Want you more / Baby it's cold outside / Aeroplane / Witchcraft / What a little moonlight can do / Don't explain / Chance / Goody goody / Do nothin' till you hear from me / Honeysuckle rose / No not much / Ridin' high / Hard head.
(above featured many 40's + 50's covers)

Jul 94. (7")(c-s) **GIRL U WANT. / NO FUSS** [57] [ ]
(cd-s+=) – ('A'mixes).

Aug 94. (7")(c-s) **KNOW BY NOW. / MERCY MERCY ME** – I WANT YOU [25] [ ]
(cd-s+=) – Simply irrestible.
(cd-s) – ('A'side) / ('A'mixes) / In the stars / She makes my day.

Sep 94. (cd)(c)(lp) **HONEY** [25] [ ]
– Honey A / Honey B / You're mine / Know by now / Nobody but you / Love takes time / Honeymoon / You blow me away / Close to the edge / Closer to the edge / Girl u want / Wham bam boogie / Big trouble / Dreams come true.

Dec 94. (7")(c-s) **YOU BLOW ME AWAY. / SIMPLY IRRESISTABLE** [38] [ ]
(cd-s) – ('A'side) / No control / ('A'mix) / Know by now.
(cd-s) – ('A'side) / ('A'mixes) / Change his ways.

Sep 95. (c-s) **RESPECT YOURSELF / YOU BLOW ME AWAY** [45] [ ]
(cd-s+=) – Girl u want / Race to the end of the set medley:- Bad case of loving you (doctor, doctor) – Simply irrisistible – Some guys have all the luck – I didn't mean to turn you on – Looking for clues – Addicted to love – You are in my system – Know by now – Some like it hot – I want you – Every kinda people.
(cd-s) – ('A'side) / Get it on (45 mix) / Some like it hot (7"mix) / Respect yourself (FX mix).

Oct 95. (cd)(c) **THE VERY BEST OF ROBERT PALMER** (compilation) [4] [ ]
– Addicted to love / Bad case of loving you (doctor, doctor) / Simply irresistable / Get it on (POWER STATION) / Some guys have all the luck / I didn't mean to turn you on / Looking for clues / You are in my system / Some like it hot (POWER STATION) / Respect yourself / I'll be your baby tonight (w/ UB40) / Johnny & Mary / She makes my day / Know by now / Every kinda people / Mercy mercy me – I want you (medley).

– compilations, others, etc. –

Nov 89. Island; (7") **BAD CASE OF LOVING YOU (DOCTOR, DOCTOR). / SWEET LIES** [ ] [ ]
(12"+=)(cd-s+=) – What's it take.

Nov 89. Island; (lp)(c)(cd) **ADDICTIONS VOL.1** [7] [79]
– Bad case of loving you (doctor, doctor) / Pride / Addicted to love / Sweet lies / Woke up laughing / Looking for clues / Some guys have all the luck / Some like it hot (POWER STATION) / What's it take? / Every kinda people / Johnny & Mary / Simply irristible / Style kills.

Feb 92. Island; (7")(12")(c-s)(cd-s) **EVERY KINDA PEOPLE. / ('A'radio mix)** [43] [ ]

Mar 92. Island; (cd)(c)(lp) **ADDICTIONS VOL.2** [12] [ ]
– Remember to remember / Sneakin' Sally through the alley / Maybe it's you / You are in my system / I didn't mean to turn you on / Can we still be friends / Man smart, woman smarter / Too good to be true / Every kinda people / She makes my day / Best of both worlds / Give me an inch / You're gonna get what's coming / I dream of wires / The silver gun.

Jun 92. Island; (7")(c-s)(cd-s) **YOU ARE IN MY SYSTEM. / YOU'RE GONNA GET WHAT'S COMING / TOO GOOD TO BE TRUE** [ ] [ ]

Jul 87. See For Miles; (lp)(c) **THE EARLY YEARS** [ ] [-]
– (above featured before solo work with The ALAN BOWN SET)

Nov 95. Island; (d-cd) **ADDICTIONS VOL.1 & 2** [ ] [ ]

PANTERA

Formed: Texas, USA . . .1981 by TERRY GLAZE, DARRELL ABBOTT, (brother) VINCE ABBOTT and REX ROCKER. After 4 albums on own homegrown 'Metal Magic' (and recommendation from ROB HALFORD of JUDAS PRIEST), they switched to 'Atco' for the 90's. • **Style:** Power groove heavy-metal similiar to KISS, which progressed into anthemic grindcore NAPALM DEATH sound by the 90's. • **Songwriters:** Group, except PLANET CARAVAN (Black Sabbath) / THE BADGE (Poison Idea). • **Trivia:** Means PANTHER in Spanish. In the late 80's, DARRELL turned down the chance to join MEGADETH.

Recommended: A VULGAR DISPLAY OF POWER (*6)

TERRY GLAZE – vocals, guitar / **DARRELL ABBOTT** – guitar / **REX ROCKER** – bass / **VINCE ABBOTT** – drums

not issued Metal Magic

1983. (lp) **METAL MAGIC** [-] [ ]
– Ride my rocket / I'll be alright / Tell me if you want it / Latest lover / Biggest part of me / Metal magic / Widowmaker / Nothin' on (but the radio) / Sad lover / Rock out!.

— GLAZE became TERRENCE LEE, DARRELL prefixed the word DIMEBAG and VINCE was now VINNIE PAUL.

1984. (lp) **PROJECTS IN THE JUNGLE** [-] [ ]
– All over tonite / Out for blood / Blue lite turnin' red / Like fire / In over my head / Projects in the jungle / Heavy metal rules! / Heartbeat away / Killers / Takin' my life.

1985. (lp) **I AM THE NIGHT** [-] [ ]
– Hot and heavy / I am the night / Onward we rock! / D.S.G.S.T.S.T.S.M. / Daughters of the queen / Down below / Come-on eyes / Right on the edge / Valhalla / Forever tonight.

— **PHILIP ANSELMO** – vocals repl. TERRY

May 88. (lp) **POWER METAL** [-] [ ]
– Rock the world / Power metal / We'll meet again / Over and out / Proud to be loud / Down below / Death trap / Hard ride / Burnnn! / P.S.T. 88.

Atco Atco

Jul 90. (cd)(c)(lp) **COWBOYS FROM HELL** [ ] [ ]
– Cowboys from Hell / Primal concrete sledge / Psycho holiday / Heresy / Cemetery gates / Domination / Shattered / Clash with reality / Medicine man / Message in blood / The sleep / The art of shredding.

Feb 92. (cd)(c)(lp) **A VULGAR DISPLAY OF POWER** [64] [44]
– Mouth for war / A new level / Walk / F**king hostile / This love / Rise / No good (attack the radical) / Live in a hole / Regular people (conceit) / By demons be driven / Hollow.

Oct 92. (7")(c-s) **MOUTH FOR WAR. / RISE** [73] [ ]
(cd-s+=) – Cowboys from Hell / Heresy.
(12") – ('A'side) / ('A'-superloud mix) / Domination / Primal concrete sledge.

Feb 93. (12"m) **WALK. / COWBOYS FROM HELL / PSYCHO HOLIDAY (live)** [34] [ ]
(cd-ep) – ('A'side) / Fucking hostile / By demons be driven.
(cd-ep) – ('A'side) / No good (attack the radical)/ A new level / Walk (extended).
(cd-ep) – ('A'side) / ('A'remixes by Jim 'Foetus' Thirlwell).

East West Atco

Mar 94. (12")(cd-s) **I'M BROKEN. / SLAUGHTERED** [19] [ ]
(cd-s+=) – Domination (live) / Primal concrete sledge.

(cd-s) – ('A'side) / Cowboys from Hell (live) / Psycho holiday (live).
(12") – ('A'side) / Walk (cervical edit) / Fuckin' hostile.

Mar 94. (cd)(c)(lp) **FAR BEYOND DRIVEN** [3] [1]
– Strength beyond strength / Becoming / 5 minutes alone / I'm broken / Good friends and a bottle of pills / Hard lines, sunken cheeks / Slaughtered / 25 years / Shedding skin / Use my third arm / Throes of rejection / Planet Caravan.

May 94. (7"white) **5 MINUTES ALONE. / THE BADGE** [ ] [ ]

Oct 94. (12") **PLANET CARAVAN. / COWBOYS FROM HELL / HERESAY** [26] [ ]
(cd-s) – ('A'side) / The badge / New level / Becoming.
(cd-s) – ('A'side) / Domination / Hollow.

PARADISE LOST

Formed: Halifax, England . . .1988. Took their name from poet Milton. Debutted early in 1990 with 'IN DUB' single. Finally found fortune in 1995, when their 5th album 'DRACONIAN TIMES' briefly hit the UK Top 20. • **Style:** Initially a death-metal band in mould of OBITUARY or NAPALM DEATH. Evolved with slower songs, into a fusion of METALLICA and SISTERS OF MERCY. • **Songwriters:** McINTOSH-HOLMES except DEATH WALKS BEHIND YOU (Atomic Rooster) / WALK AWAY (Sisters Of Mercy). • **Trivia:** Produced by SIMON EFFEMEY.

Recommended: GOTHIC (*7) / DRACONIAN TIMES (*8)

NICK HOLMES – vocals / **GREGOR McINTOSH** – lead guitar / **AARON AEDY** – guitars / **STEHEN EDMONDSON** – bass / **MATT ARCHER** – drums, percussion

Peaceville Rough Trade

Apr 90. (12") **IN DUB** [ ] [-]
– Rotting misery (doom dub) / Breeding fear (demolition dub).

Apr 90. (cd)(c)(lp) **LOST PARADISE** [ ] [-]
– Intro / Deadly inner sense / Paradise lost / Our saviour / Rotting misery / Frozen illusion / Breeding fear / Lost Paradise. (cd+=) – Internal torment II. *(re-iss.cd Apr95)*

Apr 91. (cd)(c)(lp) **GOTHIC** [ ] [ ]
– Gothic / Dead emotion / Shattered / Rapture / Eternal / Falling forever / Angel tears / Silent / The painless / Desolate.

1992. (cd-ep) **GOTHIC EP** [ ] [-]
– Gothic / IN DUB (tracks) / The painless (mix).

M.F.N. M.F.N.

Jun 92. (cd)(c)(lp) **SHADES OF GOD** [ ] [ ]
– Mortals watch the day / Crying for eternity / Embraced / Daylight torn / Pity the sadness / No forgiveness / Your hand in mine / As I die / The word made flesh.

Oct 92. (12"ep)(cd-ep) **AS I DIE / RAPE OF VIRTUE. / DEATH WALKS BEHIND YOU / ETERNAL (live)** [ ] [ ]

Sep 93. (cd)(c)(d-lp) **ICON** [ ] [ ]
– Embers fire / Remembrance / Forging sympathy / Joys of the emptiness / Dying freedom / Widow / Colossal rains / Weeping words / Poison / True belief / Shallow seasons / Christendom / Deus miseratur.

Feb 94. (12"ep)(cd-ep) **SEALS THE SENSE** [ ] [ ]
– Embers fire / Sweetness / True belief / Your hand in mine.

—— now without ARCHER

May 95. (12"ep)(c-ep)(cd-ep) **LAST TIME. / WALK AWAY / LAID TO WASTE / MASTER OF MISRULE** [60] [ ]

Jun 95. (cd)(c)(lp)(pic-lp) **DRACONIAN TIMES** [16] [ ]
– Enchantment / Hallowed land / The last time / Forever failure / Once solemn / Shadowkings / Elusive cure / Yearn for change / Shades of God / Hands of reason / I see your face / Jaded.

Oct 95. (12"ep)(c-ep)(cd-ep) **FOREVER FAILURE. / ANOTHER DESIRE / FEAR** [66] [ ]

PARAMOUNTS (see under ⇒ PROCOL HARUM)

Graham PARKER

Born: 18 Nov'50, East London, England. After spending time in Guernsey in The Channel Islands, he returned to London in 1975. With the help of future 'Stiff' manager Dave Robinson, he sent solo tape to 'Phonogram', with credited augmentation from back-up The RUMOUR. In 1976, he/they signed to subsidiary label 'Vertigo' and released Nick Lowe produced album 'HOWLIN' WIND'. They cracked the UK singles Top 30 with 1977 EP 'THE PINK PARKER', which spawned cover 'HOLD BACK THE NIGHT'. His appeal fizzed out around the mid-80's, after US Top 40 hit 'WAKE UP (NEXT TO YOU)'. • **Style:** Emerged out of the pub-rock / new wave scene, likened to SPRINGSTEEN or COSTELLO. • **Songwriters:** PARKER penned, except covers HOLD BACK THE NIGHT (Trammps) / CUPID + A CHANGE IS GONNA COME (Sam Cooke) / SUBSTITUTE (Who) / etc. • **Trivia:** In 1980, PARKER had book 'The Great Trouser Mystery' published.

Recommended: THE BEST OF GRAHAM PARKER (*6)

GRAHAM PARKER & THE RUMOUR

GRAHAM PARKER – vocals, guitar / **MARTIN BELMONT** – guitar (ex-DUCKS DELUXE) / **BRINSLEY SCHWARZ** – guitar (ex-BRINSLEY SCHWARZ) / **BOB ANDREWS** – keys, sax, guitar (ex-BRINSLEY SCHWARZ) / **ANDREW BODNAR** – bass / **STEVE GOULDING** – drums (both ex-BONTEMPS ROULEE)

Vertigo Mercury

Mar 76. (7") **SILLY THING. / I'M GONNA USE IT NOW** [ ] [-]

Apr 76. (lp)(c) **HOWLIN' WIND** [ ] [ ]
– White honey / Nothin's gonna pull us apart / Silly thing / Gypsy blood / Between you and me / Back to schooldays / Soul shoes / Lady doctor / You've got to be kidding / Howlin' wind / Not if it pleases me / Hey Lord, don't ask me questions. *(free live 7"+=)* – KANSAS CITY. / SILLY THING *(re-iss.Apr89 on 'B.G.O.') (cd-iss.May90 on 'Polydor')*

Jul 76. (7") **SOUL SHOES. / WILD HONEY** [ ] [-]

Oct 76. (7") **HOTEL CHAMBERMAID. / DON'T ASK ME QUESTIONS** [ ] [ ]

Oct 76. (lp)(c) **HEAT TREATMENT** [52] [ ]
– Heat treatment / That's what they all say / Turned up too late / Black honey / Hotel chambermaid / Pourin' it all out / Back door love / Something you're goin' thru / Help me shake it / Fool's gold. *(re-iss.May89 on 'B.G.O.')*

Jan 77. (7") **POURIN' IT ALL OUT. / HELP ME SHAKE IT** [ ] [ ]

Mar 77. (7"pink-ep) **THE PINK PARKER** [24] [58]
– Hold back the night / (Let me get) Sweet on you / White honey / Soul shoes.

Oct 77. (lp)(c) **STICK TO ME** [19] [ ]
– Stick to me / I'm gonna tear your playhouse down / Problem child / Soul on ice / Clear head / The New York shuffle / Watch the Moon come down / Thunder and rain / The heat in Harlem / The raid.

Nov 77. (7") **THE NEW YORK SHUFFLE. / BLEEP** [ ] [ ]

Apr 78. (7") **HEY LORD, DON'T ASK ME QUESTIONS (live). / FOOL'S GOLD** [32] [ ]

May 78. (d-lp)(c) **THE PARKERILLA (live)** [14] [ ]
– Lady doctor / Fool's gold / I'm gonna tear your playhouse down / Hey Lord, don't ask me questions / Silly thing / The heat in Harlem / Gypsy blood / Back to schooldays / Heat treatment / Watch the Moon come down / The New York shuffle / Soul shoes / Hey Lord, don't ask me questions (studio 45 rpm).

GRAHAM PARKER

solo but still augmented by The RUMOUR

Vertigo Arista

Feb 79. (7")(12") **PROTECTION. / I WANT YOU BACK (live)** [ ] [-]

Mar 79. (lp)(c) **SQUEEZING OUT SPARKS** [18] [40]
– Discovering Japan / Local girls / Nobody hurts you / You can't be too strong / Passion is no ordinary word / Saturday nite is dead / Love gets you twisted / Protection / Waiting for the UFO's / Don't get excited.

May 79. (7") **DISCOVERING JAPAN. / LOCAL GIRLS** [ ] [-]

GRAHAM PARKER & THE RUMOUR

Stiff Arista

Apr 80. (7") **STUPEFACTION. / WOMEN IN CHARGE** [ ] [-]

Apr 80. (lp)(c) **THE UP ESCALATOR** [11] [40]
– Up / No holding back / Devil's sidewalk / Stupefaction / Love without greed / Jolie Jolie / Endless night / Paralyzed / Manoeuvres / Empty lives / Beating of another heart. *(c+=)* – Women in charge. *(re-iss.Jun90 on 'Demon')*

Jun 80. (7") **LOVE WITHOUT GREED. / MERCURY POISONING** [ ] [ ]

GRAHAM PARKER

solo, without The RUMOUR. PARKER now used **NICKY HOPKINS** – piano / **GEORGE SMALL** – keyboards / **HUGH McCRACKEN** – guitars, harmonica / **DAVID BROWN** – guitars / **DOUG STEGMEYER** – bass / **MICHAEL BRAUN** – drums / **KURT McKETTRICK** – sax, flute / **JIM CLOUSE** – sax / **PAUL PRESTINO** – banjo / **JACK DOUGLAS** – percussion / +backing vocalists

R.C.A. Arista

Feb 82. (7") **TEMPORARY BEAUTY. / NO MORE EXCUSES** [50] [ ]

Mar 82. (lp)(c) **ANOTHER GREY AREA** [40] [51]
– Temporary beauty / Another grey area / No more excuses / Dark side of the bright lights / Can't waste a minute / Big fat zero / You hit the spot / It's all worth nothing alone / Crying for attention / Thankless task / Fear not. *(re-iss.+cd.Jul91 on 'Great Expectations')*

Jul 82. (7") **NO MORE EXCUSES. / YOU HIT THE SPOT** [ ] [ ]
(12"+=) – Another grey area.

—— now with **SMALL** + **KEVIN JENKINS** – bass / **GILSON LAVIS** – drums (ex-SQUEEZE)

Jul 83. (7")(12") **LIFE GETS BETTER. / ANNIVERSARY** [ ] [-]

Sep 83. (lp)(c) **THE REAL MACAW** [ ] [59]
– You can't take love for granted / Glass jaw / Just like a man / assive resistance / Sounds like chains / Life gets better / A miracle a minute / Beyond a joke / Last couple on the dance floor / Anniversary / (Too late) The smart bomb. *(re-iss.+cd.Jul91 on 'Great Expectations')*

Sep 83. (7") **LIFE GETS BETTER. / BEYOND A JOKE** [-] [94]

Oct 83. (7") **YOU CAN'T TAKE LOVE FOR GRANTED. / GLASS JAW** [ ] [ ]

GRAHAM PARKER & THE SHOT

with **SMALL, JENKINS** + **SCHWARTZ** plus **MICHAEL BRAUN** – drums repl. LAVIS

Elektra Elektra

Apr 85. (7")(12") **BREAK THEM DOWN. / EVERYONE'S HAND IS ON THE SWITCH** [ ] [-]
(d7"+=) – Bricks and mortar / Too much to think.

Apr 85. (lp)(c)(cd) **STEADY NERVES** [ ] [57]
– Break them down / Mighty rivers / Lunatic fringe / Wake up (next to you) / When you do that to me / The weekend's too short / Take everything / Black Lincoln Continental / Canned laughter / Everyone's hand is on the switch / Locked into green. *(cd+=)*– Too much time to think.

Jun 85. (7") **WAKE UP (NEXT TO YOU). / CANNED LAUGHTER** [ ] [39] Apr 85
(12"+=) – Locked into green.

GRAHAM PARKER

solo, with backers **BRINSLEY** / **ANDREW BODNAR** – bass / **JAMES HALLAWELL** – keyboards / **TERRY WILLIAMS** – drums (on all but 3).

Demon R.C.A.

Jul 88. (7") **I'M JUST YOUR MAN. / I DON'T KNOW** [ ] [ ]

Jul 88. (lp)(c)(cd) **THE MONA LISA'S SISTER** | | 77 May 88
– Don't let it break you down / Under the mask of happiness / Back in time / I'm just your man / OK Hieronymous / Get started, start a fire / The girl isn't ready / Blue highways / Success / I don't know / Cupid.

Nov 88. (7") **CUPID. / BLUE HIGHWAYS**

Apr 89. (lp)(c)(cd) **LIVE! ALONE IN AMERICA (live)**
– White honey / Watch the moon come down / Black honey / Protection / Soul corruption / Gypsy blood / Back to schooldays / Durban poison / The 3 Martini lunch / Back in time / Hotel chambermaid / Don't let it break you down / You can't be too strong / A change is gonna come.

—— retained **SCHWARZ, BODNAR, HALLIWELL. PETE THOMAS** – drums repl. TERRY Also incl.**STEVE NIEVE** – synth. / **BEIZEL SICKS** – percussion / **SONIA JONES MORGAN + CARMEN DAYE** – backing vox / **MOLLY DUNCAN** – tenor sax / **J. NEIL SIDWELL** – trombone / **MARTIN DROVER** – trumpet

Oct 89. (lp)(c)(cd) **HUMAN SOUL** | | Feb 90
– Little Miss understanding / My love's strong / Dancing for money / Call me your doctor / Big man on paper / Soultime / Everything goes / Sugar gives you energy / Daddy's a postman / Green monkeys / I was wrong / You got the world (rightwhere you want it) / Slash and burn.

Demon B.M.G.

Feb 91. (cd)(c)(d-lp) **STRUCK BY LIGHTNING**
– She wants so many things / They murdered the clown / Strong winds / The kid with the butterfly net / And it shook me / That's where she ends up / A brand new book / Weeping statues / Wrapping paper / Ten girls ago / I'm into something good / Over the border (to America) / The Sun is gonna shine again / Guardian angels / Children and dogs / When I was king / Museum piece / Museum of stupidity.

Jul 92. (cd)(c)(lp) **BURNING QUESTIONS**
– Release me / Too many knots to untangle / Just like Joe Meek's blues / Love is a burning question / Platinum blonde / Long stem rose / Short memories / Here it comes again / Mr.Tender / Just like Herm & Hesse / Yesterdays cloud / Oasis / Worthy of your love / Substitute.

Aug 92. (cd-ep) **BURNING QUESTIONS / RELEASE ME / PLATINUM BLONDE / SHORT MEMORIES** | | -

Aug 93. (cd) **LIVE! ALONE IN JAPAN (live)**
– That's what they all say / Platinum blonde / Mercury poisoning / Sweet 16 / No woman no cry / Lunatic fringe / Long stem rose / Discovering Japan / Hey Lord, don't ask me questions / Watch the Moon come down (revisited) / Just like Herman Hesse / Too many knots to untabgle / Chopsticks / Short memories.

Dec 94. (cd-ep) **GRAHAM PARKER'S CHRISTMAS CRACKER** | | -
– Christmas is for mugs / New Year's revolution / Soul Christmas.

Grapevine Asylum?

Apr 95. (cd)(c)(lp) **12 HAUNTED EPISODES**
– Partner for life / Pollinate / Force of nature / Disney's America / Haunted episodes / Next phase / Honest work / Cruel stage / See yourself / Loverman / Fly / First day of Spring.

– compilations, others, etc. –

May 80. Vertigo/ US= Mercury; (lp)(c) **THE BEST OF GRAHAM PARKER & THE RUMOUR**
– Soul shoes / Heat reatment / Howling wind / Hold back the night / Back to schooldays / You can't be too strong / Kansas City / Stick to me / The New York shuffle / Local girls / White honey / Hotel chambermaid / Between you and me / Hey Lord, don't ask me questions.

May 84. Philips; (lp)(c) **IT DON'T MEAN A THING IF IT AIN'T GOT THAT SWING** | | -

1991. Demon; (4xcd-box) **GRAHAM PARKER** | | -
– (MONA LISA'S SISTER / HUMAN SOUL / LIVE ALONE IN AMERICA / THE UP ESCALATOR)

Sep 93. Polygram; (cd)(c) **THE BEST OF GRAHAM PARKER**
– Silly thing / I'm gonna use it now / Between you and me / Back to schooldays / White honey / You can't hurry love / Pourin' it all out / That's what they all say / Hotel chambermaid / Fool's gold / Watch the Moon come down / I'm gonna tear your playhouse down / Thunder and rain / Hold back the night / New York shuffle / Soul shoes / Hey Lord, don't ask me questions / I want you back / Discovering Japan / Local girls / You can't be too strong / Mercury poisoning.

Jun 94. Windsong; (cd) **LIVE ON THE TEST (live)** | | -

—— In the US, 1976 a ltd 1,000 bootleg lp 'LIVE AT MARBLE ARCH' was issued. The **RUMOUR** also branched out with own releases includung several 45s and albums MAX (Jul 77, Vertigo) / FROGS, SPROUTS, CLOGS & KRAUTS (Apr 79, Stiff) / PURITY OF PRESENCE (Jul 80, Stiff).

Van Dyke PARKS

Born: 3 Jan'41, Mississippi, USA. As a young teenager he moved to Hollywood, California, where he studied classical piano, while becoming child- actor in the film 'The Swan' alongside Grace Kelly. In the mid-60's, he was signed by 'MGM', initially to score soundtracks for Walt Disney!. He issued a 1966 solo debut 45 'NUMBER NINE', and penned a well recorded song 'HIGH COIN'. He went into production for US hitmakers The MOJO MEN and HARPER'S BIZARRE. In 1967, he worked with The BEACH BOYS on their 'Smile' lp, but this remained unreleased for the next half decade. In 1968, while working on albums by RANDY NEWMAN, RY COODER, PHIL OCHS and ARLO GUTHRIE, he released debut solo lp 'SONG CYCLE' for 'Warners'. It took 4 years for his follow-up 'DISCOVER AMERICA', and his output was never prolific for the next 2 decades. • **Style:** Art-rock talent, who delved into Caribbean sound from 1972-75. • **Songwriters:** Wrote own material, and re-arranged Beethoven's Ninth Symphony on his debut 45. • **Trivia:** In 1979, he contributed to the Robert Altman film 'Popeye'.

Recommended: IDIOSYNCRATIC PATH: THE BEST OF . . . (*7).

VAN DYKE PARKS – vocals, piano with session people

M.G.M. M.G.M.

Mar 66. (7") **NUMBER NINE. / DO WHAT YOU WANTA**

1967. (7") **COME TO THE SUNSHINE. / FARTHER ALONG** | - |

Warners Warners

1968. (lp) **THE SONG CYCLE**
– Vine street / Palm desert / Widow's talk / The all golden / Van Dyke Parks / Public domain / Donovan's colours / The attic / Laurel Canyon Blvd. / By the people / Pot porri. *(re-iss.Nov86 on 'Edsel', cd-iss. Jul88)(re-iss.cd+lp Sep93 on 'Demon')*

—— PARKS became session pianist and producer for many including RY COODER, LITTLE FEAT, ARLO GUTHRIE, TIM BUCKLEY, JUDY COLLINS, PHIL OCHS, etc.

1970. (7") **ON THE ROLLING SEA WHEN JESUS SPEAKS TO ME. / EAGLE & ME** | - |

1972. (7") **ODE TO TOBAGO. / OCCAPELLA** | - |

1972. (lp)(c) **DISCOVER AMERICA**
– Jack Palance / Introduction / Bing Crosby / Steelband music / The four Mills brothers / Be careful / John Jones / FDR in Trinidad / Sweet Trinidad / Occapella / Sailin' shoes / Riverboat / Ode to Tobago / Your own comes first / G-man Hoover / Stars & stripes forever. *(re-iss.Nov86 on 'Edsel', cd-iss.1988)*

1972. (7") **RIVERBOAT. / JOHN JONES** | - |

Dec 75. (lp)(c) **THE CLANG OF THE YANKEE REAPER**
– Clang of the yankee reaper / City on the hill / Pass that stage / Another dream / You're a real sweetheart / Love is the answer / Iron man / Tribute to space / Soul train / Cannon in D. *(re-iss.Nov86 on 'Edsel', cd-iss.Aug88)*

1984. (lp)(c) **JUMP**
– Jump / Opportunity for two / Come along / I ain't goin' home / Many a mile to go / Taps / An invitation to say / Mona / After the ball / Look away / Homing grove.

Aug 89. (lp)(c)(cd) **TOKYO ROSE**
– America / Tokyo Rose / Yankee go home / Cowboy / Manzanar / Calypso / White chrysanthnum / Trade war / Out of love / One home run.

Nov 95. (cd)(c) **ORANGE CRATE ART (with BRIAN WILSON)**
– Orange crate art / Sail away / My hobo heart / Wings of a dove / Palm tree and Moon / Summer in Monterey / San Francisco / Hold back time / My Jeanine / Movies is magic / This town goes down at sunset / Lullaby.

– compilation –

Mar 94. Demon; (cd) **IDIOSYNCRATIC PATH: THE BEST OF VAN DYKE PARKS**
– Donovan's colours / John Jones / Pass that stage / Ode to Tobago / The attic / Clang of the yankee reaper / The four Mills brothers / You're a real sweetheart / Sailin' shoes / Vine Street / Palm desert / Tribute to Spree / Iron man / Sweet Trinidad / Be careful / Bing Crosby / Steelband music / Your own comes first / Stars and stripes forever. *(re-iss.Nov95 on 'Diablo')*

PARLIAMENT (see under ⇒ CLINTON, George)

Alan PARSONS PROJECT

Formed: London, England . . . 1975 by the man who engineered 'Abbey Road' – BEATLES and 'Dark Side Of The Moon' – PINK FLOYD. While working at Abbey Road studios with groups STEVE HARLEY AND COCKNEY REBEL and PILOT, he formed partnership / group with ERIC WOOLFSON. Their first project intended as a one-off 'TALES OF MYSTERY AND IMAGINATION', was released on 'Charisma' in 1976, and surprised critics, when it hit the US Top 40. In 1977, they signed a new contract with 'Arista' and issued follow-up 'I ROBOT', based on science fiction writers' Isaac Asimov's book. The group/project became major success, especially in the States, where they were to hit Top 3 with 1982 title track single 'EYE IN THE SKY'. • **Style:** Concept pop-rock outfit, which hosted an array of guest vocal talent. • **Songwriters:** PARSONS – music / WOOLFSON – words. • **Trivia:** EYE IN THE SKY was inspired by the Philip K.Dick novel which was about technology.

Recommended: TALES OF MYSTERY AND IMAGINATION (*7) / THE BEST OF THE ALAN PARSONS PROJECT (*6).

ALAN PARSONS – guitar, keyboards, vocals, producer, engineer with **ERIC WOOLFSON** – keyboards, vocals / **IAN BAIRNSON** – guitars (ex-PILOT) / **DAVID PATON** – bass, vocals, guitar / **STUART TOSH** – drums

Charisma 20th Cent.

Jun 76. (lp)(c) **TALES OF MYSTERY AND IMAGINATION** | 56 | 38 May 76
– A dream within a dream / The raven / The tell-tale heart / The cask of Amontillado / (The system of) Doctor Tarr and Professor Feather / The fall of the House of Usher: Prelude – Arrival – Intermezzo – Pavane / Fall / To one in Paradise.

Jul 76. (7") **(THE SYSTEM OF) DOCTOR TARR AND PROFESSOR FEATHER. / A DREAM WITHIN A DREAM** | | 37

Sep 76. (7") **THE RAVEN. / PRELUDE TO THE FALL OF THE HOUSE OF USHER** | - | 80

Oct 76. (7") **TO ONE IN PARADISE. / THE CASK OF AMONTILLADO** | | -

—— added **DUNCAN MACKAY** – keyboards

Arista Arista

Jun 77. (lp)(c) **I ROBOT** | 30 | 9
– I robot / I wouldn't want to be like you / Some other time / Breakdown / Don't let it show / The voice / Nucleus / Day after day / Total eclipse / Genesis Ch.1 V.32.

Aug 77. (7") **I WOULDN'T WANT TO BE LIKE YOU. / NUCLEUS** | | 36

—— (above 'A' feat. **LENNY ZAKATEK** – vox) / (below **DAVID TOWNSHEND** – vox)

Dec 77. (7") **DON'T LET IT SHOW. / I ROBOT** | - | 92

Feb 78. (7") **I ROBOT. / SOME OTHER TIME** | | -

Feb 78. (7") **BREAKDOWN. / DAY AFTER DAY** | - |

—— added **STUART ELLIOTT** – drums (ex-10cc) repl. TOSH

May 78. (lp)(c) **PYRAMID** | 49 | 26
– Voyager / What goes up / The eagle will rise again / One more river / Can't take

it with you / In the lap of the gods / Pyramania / Hyper-gamma-spaces / Shadow of a lonely man. *(re-iss.+cd.Apr88)*

Jun 78. (7") **PYRAMANIA. / IN THE LAP OF THE GODS** □ [-]
Sep 78. (7") **WHAT GOES UP. / IN THE LAP OF THE GODS** [-] [87]
Aug 79. (lp)(c) **EVE** [74] [13]
– Lucifer / You lie down with dogs / I'd rather be a man / You won't be there / Winding me up / Damned if I do / Don't hold back / Secret garden / If I could change your mind. *(re-iss.Jul83 on 'Fame') (re-iss.+cd.May88)*
Aug 79. (7") **LUCIFER. / I'D RATHER BE A MAN** □ [-]
(12") – ('A'side) / Damned if I do / Secret garden.
(below feat. **ZAKATEK – vocals** (also on Jan81, Dec83 singles)
Nov 79. (7") **DAMNED IF I DO. / IF I COULD CHANGE YOUR MIND** □ [27] Sep 79
Jan 80. (7") **SECRET GARDEN. / YOU WON'T BE THERE** [-] □
Mar 80. (7") **LUCIFER. / YOU LIE DOWN WITH DOGS** [-] □
—— now w/out MACKAY
Nov 80. (lp)(c) **THE TURN OF A FRIENDLY CARD** [38] [13]
– May be a price to pay / ames people play / Time / I don't wanna go home / The gold bug / The turn of a friendly card: (part 1 – Snake eyes – The ace of swords; part 2 – Nothing left to lose). *(re-iss.+cd.May88)*
Nov 80. (7") **THE TURN OF A FRIENDLY CARD. / MAY BE A PRICE TO PAY** □ □
Jan 81. (7") **GAMES PEOPLE PLAY. / ACE OF SWORDS** □ [16] Nov 80
Aug 81. (7") **TIME. / THE GOLD BUG** □ [15] Apr 81
Oct 81. (7") **SNAKE EYES. / I DON'T WANNA GO HOME** [-] [67]
—— (above feat. **CHRIS RAINBOW** – vocals) (also on May85 single)
May 82. (lp)(c) **EYE IN THE SKY** [28] [7]
– Sirius / Eye in the sky / Children of the Moon / Gemini / Silence and I / You're gonna get your finger burned / Psychobabble / Mammagamma / Step by step / Old and wise. *(re-iss.+cd.May87)*
May 82. (7") **EYE IN THE SKY. / GEMINI** □ [3]
—— (below feat. **COLIN BLUNSTONE** – vocals (ex-ZOMBIES) (below **ELMER GANTRY**)
Nov 82. (7") **PSYCHOBABBLE. / CHILDREN OF THE MOON** [-] [57]
Dec 82. (7") **OLD AND WISE. / CHILDREN OF THE MOON** [74] [-]
Feb 83. (7") **OLD AND WISE. / YOU'RE GONNA GET YOUR FINGERS BURNED** [-] □
Oct 83. (lp)(c) **THE BEST OF THE ALAN PARSONS PROJECT** (compilation) [99] [53]
– I wouldn't want to be like you / Eye in the sky / Games people play / Time / Pyramania / You don't believe / Lucifer / Psychobabble / Damned if I do / Don't let it show / Can't take it with you / Old and wise. *(cd-iss.Feb87 & 1988)*
Feb 84. (7") **YOU DON'T BELIEVE. / LUCIFER** [-] [54]
Feb 84. (lp)(c)(cd) **AMMONIA AVENUE** [24] [15]
– Prime time / Let me go home / One good reason / Since the last goodbye / Don't answer me / Dancing on a high wire / You don't believe / Pipeline / Ammonia Avenue.
Feb 84. (7")(7"sha-pic-d) **DON'T ANSWER ME. / YOU DON'T BELIEVE** [58] [-]
(12"+=) – Games people play / Old and wise.
Feb 84. (7")(12") **DON'T ANSWER ME. / PRIME TIME** [-] [15]
Jun 84. (7") **PRIME TIME. / THE GOLD BUG** □ [34] May 84
(12"+=) – Pipeline (instrumental) / Sirius (instrumental).
(below feat. **DAVID PATON** – vocals)
Jan 85. (7") **LET'S TALK ABOUT ME. / HAWKEYE** □ [56]
(12+=) – Pipeline.
Feb 85. (lp)(c)(cd) **VULTURE CULTURE** [40] [46]
– Let's talk about me / Separate lives / Days are numbered (the traveller) / Sooner or later / Vulture culture / Hawkeye / Somebody out there / The same old sun. *(re-iss.May88)*
Apr 85. (7") **DAYS ARE NUMBERED (THE TRAVELLER). / SOMEBODY OUT THERE** □ [71]
—— next feat. vocalists **JOHN MILES, CHRIS RAINBOW, GARY BROOKER**
Jan 86. (lp)(c)(cd) **STEREOTOMY** □ [43]
– Stereotomy / Beaujolais / Urbania / Limelight / In the real world / Where's the walrus? / Light of the world / Chinese whispers / Stereotomy two.
Mar 86. (7")(12") **STEREOTOMY. / URBANIA (instrumental)** □ [82] Feb 86
—— added **LAURIE COTTLE** – bass / **RICHARD COTTLE** – saxophone, synthesizers / **GEOFF BARRADALE** – vocals (with usual vocalists) repl. BROOKER
Jan 87. (7") **STANDING ON HIGHER GROUND. / INSIDE LOOKING OUT** [-] □
Jan 87. (lp)(c)(cd) **GAUDI** [66] [57]
– La Sagrada familia / Too late / Closer to Heaven / Standing on higher ground / Money talks / Inside looking out / Paseo de gracia (instrumental). *(re-iss.Feb90)*
Jan 88. (lp)(c)(cd) **LIMELIGHT: THE BEST OF THE ALAN PARSONS PROJECT VOL.2** (compilation) □ □
– Limelight / Same old sun / Ammonia avenue / Mammagamma / Since the last goodbye / I robot / Prime time / Hawkeye / Return of the friendly card / Silence and I. *(re-iss.cd Oct95)*
Oct 93. (cd)(c)(lp) **TRY ANYTHING ONCE** □ □
– The three of me / Turn it up / Wine from the water / Breakaway / Jigue / Mr.Time / Siren song / Back against the wall / Re-jigue / Oh life (there must be more). *(cd+c+=)* I'm talking to you / Dreamscape.

– other compilations, etc. –

Nov 87. Mercury; (cd) **TALES OF MYSTERY AND IMAGINATION** □ □
– (remixed debut with new synth/guitar touches + narration by ORSON WELLS)
Nov 88. RCA/ US= Arista; (lp)(c)(cd) **THE INSTRUMENTAL WORKS** □ □
– Pipeline / Where's the walrus? / I robot / Mammagamma / Hawkeye / Voyager / Paseo de Gracia / Urbania / The gold bug / Genesis Ch.1 V.32.
Dec 90. Arista; (cd-box)(c-box) **ALAN PARSONS BOX SET** □ □

Gram PARSONS

Born: CECIL INGRAM CONNOR, 5 Nov'46, Winterhaven, Florida, USA. Raised in Georgia, but moved to New Orleans when his ranch hand father BULL DOG CONNOR committed suicide. His mother died of alcoholism on the day he graduated from high school. In Between 1963-65, he formed The SHILOS, having previously sang in duo with KENT LAVOIE (aka hitmaker LOBO). In 1966 while at Harvard University, Boston, he formed second band The INTERNATIONAL SUBMARINE BAND, with others JOHN NUESE – guitar / IAN DUNLOP – bass / MICKEY GAUVIN – drums. With new personnel changes (JON CORNEAL – drums repl. GAUVIN / CHRIS ETHRIDGE – bass repl. DUNLOP / and addition of guitarist BOB BUCHANAN), they made one album 'SAFE AT HOME' for the Lee Hazlewood label in Apr'68. By this time, GRAM had already been drafted into becoming integral part of The BYRDS. This line-up made one critically well-received country album 'SWEETHEART OF THE RODEO', before he left with others SNEAKY PETE & CHRIS HILLMAN, to form The FLYING BURRITO BROTHERS. Their 1969 debut 'THE GILDED PALACE OF SIN', also gathered rave reviews, but only managed to scrape into US Top 200. GRAM stayed for another album 'BURRITO DELUXE', before falling into heavy drug habit by Spring 1970. He left the group at this time, but re-emerged early 1973 with debut solo album for 'Warners'; 'G.P.'. It contained dual vocals with EMMYLOU HARRIS, and was another excellent piece of work. Tragically, he was to die on 19 Sep'73, in a desert outside Los Angeles. Mysteriously at an alleged earlier request, his friend and road manager PHIL KAUFMAN, had cremated his body at The Joshua Tree National Monument. Cause of death therefore, could not be established. With an album nearly completed, EMMYLOU decided to issue it as 'GREVIOUS ANGEL' early '74. • **Style:** Pioneer of the country-rock sound, that heralded a new generation of bands EAGLES, POCO, etc. • **Songwriters:** Self-penned. • **Trivia:** In 1974, The EAGLES / BERNIE LEADON paid homage on song 'MY MAN'. Further vinyl tributes were paid to him by EMMYLOU HARRIS (Boulder To Birmingham) + CRAZY EYES (Poco).

Recommended: G.P. (*8) / GREVIOUS ANGEL (*8)

GRAM PARSONS – vocals, guitar / with **EMMYLOU HARRIS** – vocals / **JAMES BURTON** – guitar / **GLEN D.HARDIN** – piano / **RIK GRECH** – bass / etc.

Reprise Reprise

Jan 73. (7") **SHE. / THAT'S ALL IT TOOK** [-] □
Mar 73. (lp)(c) **G.P.** □ □
– Still feeling blue / We'll sweep out the ashes in the morning / A song for you / Streets of Baltimore / She / That's all it took / The new soft shoe / Kiss the children / Cry one more time / How much I've lied / Big mouth blues.
Mar 73. (7") **THE NEW SOFT SHOE. / SHE** □ [-]
Apr 73. (7") **CRY ONE MORE TIME. / STREETS OF BALTIMORE** [-] □
Jan 74. (lp)(c) **GREVIOUS ANGEL** □ □
– Return of the grevious angel / Hearts on fire / I can't dance / Brass buttons / $1000 wedding / Medley:- (a) Cash on the barrel head – (b) Hickory wind / Love hurts / Las Vegas / In my hour of darkness.
Jan 74. (7") **LOVE HURTS. / IN MY HOUR OF DARKNESS** [-] □
—— GRAM died 19 Sep'73, after recording 90% of above album.

– compilations, others, etc. –

May 76. A&M; (lp)(c) **SLEEPLESS NIGHTS ("GRAM PARSONS WITH THE FLYING BURRITO BROTHERS")** □ □
Mar 79. Shiloh; (lp) **LUXURY LINER** [-] □
May 79. Shiloh; (lp) **GRAM PARSONS – THE EARLY YEARS 1963-65** [-] □
(UK-iss.May84 on 'Sundown')
Feb 83. Sundown/ US= Sierra; (7"ep) **THE BIG FINISH (with EMMYLOU HARRIS & The FALLEN ANGELS)** [-] □
1983. Sierra; (7") **LOVE HURTS. / THE NEW SOFT SHOE (live)** [-] □
Nov 83. Sundown; (lp) **LIVE '73 (live with The FALLEN ANGELS / EMMYLOU HARRIS)** *(re-iss.+cd.1989)* □ □ Apr 82
May 84. Sundown; (lp)(c) **MELODIES** □ [-]
Dec 81. Warners; (7") **THE RETURN OF THE GREVIOUS ANGEL (alt.take). / HEARTS ON FIRE** [-] □
Jun 82. Warners; (lp)(c) **GRAM PARSONS** □ □
1989. Warners; (cd) **G.P. / GREVIOUS ANGEL** □ □
(re-iss.Nov93)
Aug 92. Raven; (lp) **WARM EVENINGS, PALE MORNINGS, BOTTLED BLUES** □ [-]
Jun 94. Sierra; (cd) **LIVE 1973 (live w / The FALLEN ANGELS)** □ □

INTERNATIONAL SUBMARINE BAND

not issued Ascot

1967. (7") **THE RUSSIANS ARE COMING. / TRUCK DRIVING MAN** [-] □

not issued Columbia

1967. (7") **SUM UP BROKE. / ONE DAY WEEK** [-] □

not issued L.H.I.

1967. (7") **LUXURY LINER. / BLUE EYES** [-] □
Apr 68. (lp) **SAFE AT HOME** [-] □
– Blue eyes / I must be somebody else you've known / A satisfied mind / Polson Prison blues / That's all right / Miller's cave / I still someone / Luxury liner / Strong boy / Do you know how it feels to be lonesome. *(US re-iss.1979 by "GRAM PARSONS" on 'Shiloh') (re-iss.1985 on 'Rhino' US / 'Statik' UK) (cd-iss.Jun94 on 'Shiloh')*
1968. (7") **MILLER'S CAVE. / SOMEBODY ELSE YOU'VE KNOWN** [-] □

Andy PARTRIDGE (see under ⇒ XTC)

PASSENGERS (see under ⇒ U2)

PASTELS

Formed: Glasgow, Scotland . . . 1982 by STEPHEN McROBBIE, who changed surname to PASTEL. After a few indie outings, they settle for Alan McGee's 'Creation' records late 1983. In 1986 'Glass' took over, and they finally succumbed to 33 rpm with 1987 lp 'UP FOR A BIT WITH . . . '. • **Style:** Alternative rock outfit influenced by The VELVET UNDERGROUND. • **Songwriters:** All written by STEPHEN and group except SPEEDING MOTORCYCLE (Daniel Johnson) / BOARDWALKIN' (. . .Larson) • **Trivia:** STEPHEN formed own indie label '53rd & 3rd', who signed new Scots acts BMX BANDITS + SOUP DRAGONS.

Recommended: SUCK ON THE PASTELS (*8).

STEPHEN PASTEL (b.STEPHEN McROBBIE) – vocals / **BRIAN SUPERSTAR** (b.BRIAN TAYLOR) – guitar / **MARTIN** – bass / **BERNICE** – drums

Whaam / not issued

Oct 82. (7") **HEAVENS ABOVE. / TEA TIME TALES** [ ] [-]

Creation / not issued

Apr 83. (7"flexi) **I WONDER WHY** (1 sided) [ ] [-]

Rough Trade / not issued

Oct 83. (7") **I WONDER WHY. / SUPPOSED TO UNDERSTAND** [ ] [-]

Creation / not issued

Mar 84. (7") **SOMETHING GOING ON. / STAY WITH ME TILL MORNING** [ ] [-]

Oct 84. (12") **MILLION TEARS. / SUPRISE ME / BABY HONEY** [ ] [-]

Nov 85. (12") **I'M ALRIGHT WITH YOU. / WHAT'S IT WORTH / COULDN'T CARE LESS** [ ] [-]

Glass / not issued

Jul 86. (7") **TRUCK TRAIN TRACTOR. / BREAKING LINES** [ ] [-]
(12"+=) – ('A'version 2). *(re-iss.Aug88)*

— (in '87) added **AGGI** – keyboards (ex-BUBA & THE SHOP ASSISTANTS) and **NORMAN BLAKE** – guitar (of The BOY HAIRDRESSERS)

Feb 87. (lp) **UP FOR A BIT WITH THE PASTELS** [ ] [-]
– Ride / Up for a bit / Crawl babies / Address book / I'm alright with you / Hitchin' a ride / Get round town / Baby honey / Automatically yours / If I could tell you. *(cd-iss.Oct88) (re-iss.Sep91 on 'Paperhouse')*

Feb 87. (7") **CRAWL BABIES. / EMPTY HOUSE** [ ] [-]
(12"+=) – The day I got certified.

Oct 87. (7") **COMING THROUGH. / SIT ON IT MOTHER** [ ] [-]
(12"+=) – Lonely planet boy / Not unloved.

— guest **EUGENE KELLY** (of VASELINES) who later formed CAPTAIN AMERICA then EUGENIUS.

Chapter 22 / Homestead

Apr 89. (12") **BABY YOU'RE JUST YOU. / HOLY MOLY. / UGLY TOWN** [ ] [-]

Jun 89. (lp)(c)(cd) **SITTIN' PRETTY** [ ] [ ]
– Nothing to be done / Anne Boleyn / Sit on it mother / Holy moly / Ugly town / Zooom / Baby you're just you / Ditch the fool / Sittin' pretty / Swerve. *(lp re-iss.Feb95 on 'Homestead')*

— now a trio **STEPHEN, AGGI + KATRINA MITCHELL** also with **FRANCES McDONALD** – drums (ex-BOY HAIRDRESSERS)

Paperhouse / not issued

Sep 91. (7") **SPEEDING MOTORCYCLE. / SPEEDWAY STAR** [ ] [-]
(12"+=)(cd-s+=) – 4th band.

Nov 91. (7") **THRU YOUR HEART. / FIREBELL RINGING** [ ] [-]
(12"+=)(cd-s+=) – My heart's my badge / Sign across me / Thru' your heart (home recording).

— In Feb + Jun 92, they teamed up with JAD FAIR (ex-HALF JAPANESE) on his singles; THIS COULD BE THE NIGHT + HE CHOSE HIS COLOURS WELL from his 1991 album 'JAD FAIR AND THE PASTELS'.

Nov 92. (cd)(c)(lp) **TRUCKLOAD OF TROUBLE** [ ] [-]
– Thank you for being you / Thru' your heart / Kitted out / Comin' through / Over my shoulder / Truck train tractor / Crawl babies / Nothing to be done / Different drum / Not unloved / Baby honey / Speeding motorcycle / Speedway star / What you said / Dark side of your world / Sometimes I think of you / Sign across me.

May 93. (7") **THANK YOU FOR BEING YOU. / KITTED OUT** [ ] [-]
(cd-s+=) Sometimes I think about you.

— now w/ guests: **GERARD LOVE** (Teenage Fanclub) / **DEAN WAREHAM** (Galaxie 500).

May 94. (7"ep)(cd-ep) **OLYMPIC WORLD OF PASTELISM** [-] [ ]
– Hot wheels / Three strip dynamite / Feedback Olympics.

— **STEPHEN/ AGGI/ KATRINA MITCHELL**

Domino / Domino

Oct 94. (12"ep)(cd-ep) **YOGA / BOARDWALKIN'. / WINTER OLYMPIC GLORY / YOGA** [ ] [-]

Feb 95. (cd)(c)(lp) **MOBILE SAFARI** [ ] [ ]
– Exploration team / Mandarin / Yoga / Mobile deli / Exotic arcade / Classic line-up / Flightpaths to each other / Basement scam / Strategic gear / Token collecting / Coolport / Worlds of possibility. (lp w/free 7") **SAFARI COMPANION** – 1 / 2 / 3 / 4.

Apr 95. (12"ep)(cd-ep) **WORLDS OF POSSIBILITY / PHOTO-GRAM. / EVER FAR / LOVE IT'S GETTING BETTER** [ ] [ ]

– compilations, etc. –

Mar 85. Villa 21; (7") **HEAVENS ABOVE. / I WONDER WHY** [ ] [-]

Dec 87. Glass; (d12") **TRUCK TRAIN TRACTOR. / BREAKING LINES / TRUCK TRAIN TRACTOR 2/ / CRAWL BABIES. / EMPTY HOUSE / THE DAY I GOT CERTIFIED** [ ] [-]

Jun 88. Creation; (lp)(cd) **SUCK ON THE PASTELS** [ ] [-]
– Baby honey / I wonder why / Something going on / Million tears / Surprise me / She always cries on Sunday / Baby honey / I'm alright with you / Couldn't care less / What's it worth. *(cd-iss.Mar94 on 'Rockville')*

— (above was to be have been released Mar85 as 'SHE ALWAYS CRIES ON SUNDAY')

PAVEMENT

Formed: Stockton, North California, USA . . . 1989 by GARY YOUNG and STEVEN MALKMUS. Only part-time they released a number of US 7" singles, before record companies fell at their feet in 1992. Two years later they had first outing into UK Top 20 with album 'CROOKED RAIN CROOKED RAIN'. • **Style:** Quirky, chaotic avant-garde rock, similiar to early FALL, PIXIES, The VELVET UNDERGROUND or KING CRIMSON!. • **Songwriters:** MALKMUS. • **Trivia:** MALMUS produced early 90's album 'Eyes Wide Smile' for FAITH OVER REASON. BOB and STEVEN played on SILVER JEW's (David Berman) album 'Starlite Walter'.

Recommended: SLANTED AND ENCHANTED (*7) / WESTING (BY MUSKET & SEXTANT) (*8) / CROOKED RAIN CROOKED RAIN (*7) / WOWEE ZOWEE (*8)

STEVEN MALKMUS – vocals, guitar

not issued / Treble Kicker

1989. (7"ep) **SLAY TRACKS 1933-1969** [-] [ ]
– You're killing me / Box elder / Maybe maybe / She believes / Price yeah!.

— added **GARY YOUNG** (b.1953, Stockton) – drums

not issued / Drag City

1990. (7"ep) **DEMOLITION PLOT J-7** [-] [ ]
– Forklift / Spizzle trunk / Recorder grot / Internal K-dart / Perfect depth / Recorder grot (rally).

— (Aug90) added **BOB NASTANOVICH** – drums

1991. (10"m-lp) **PERFECT SOUND FOREVER** [-] [ ]
– Heckler spray / From now on /Angel carver blues – Mellow jazz docent / Drive by fader / Debris slide / Home / Krell vid-user.

— (mid '91) added **MARK IBOLD** (b. New York) – bass

Jan 92. (7"ep) **SUMMER BABE (Winter version) / MERCY: THE LAUNDROMAT. / BAPTISS BLACKTICK / MY FIRST MINE / MY RADIO** [-] [ ]

— added **SCOTT KANNBERG** – guitar, vocals (ex-SPIRAL STAIRS)

Big Cat / Matador

Mar 92. (cd)(c) **SLANTED AND ENCHANTED** [72] [ ]
– Summer babe (winter version) / Trigger cut – Wounded – Kite at: 17 / No life singed her / In a mouth of a desert / Conduit for sale / Chesleys little wrists / Loretta's scars / Here / Two states / Perfume-V / Fame throwa / Jackals, false grails – The lonesome era / Our singer / Zurich is stained.

Jul 92. (7"ep)(12"ep)(cd-ep) **TRIGGER CUT. / SUE ME JACK / SO STARK (YOU'RE A SKYSCRAPER)** [ ] [ ]

Nov 92. (12"ep)(cd-ep) **WATERY, DOMESTIC EP** [58] [ ]
– Brick wall / Sick profile / Annual report / Fear the Panzers.
(12"pic-d) – Texas never whispers / Frontwards / Feed 'em to the (Linden) lions / Shoot the singer (1 sick verse).

Mar 93. (cd)(c)(lp) **WESTING (BY MUSKET & SEXTANT)** (all first 4 US ep material) [30] [ ]

STEVE WEST – drums repl. GARY YOUNG – solo (single; 'PLANET MAN' 94)

Jan 94. (7") **CUT YOUR HAIR. / CAMERA** [52] [ ]
(12"+=)(cd-s+=) – Stare.

Feb 94. (cd)(c)(lp) **CROOKED RAIN CROOKED RAIN** [15] [ ]
– Silence kit / Elevate me later / Stop breathin / Cut your hair / Newark wilder / Unfair / Gold sound Z / 5-4 = unity / Range life / Heaven is a truck / Hit the plane down / Fillmore jive.

Jul 94. (7") **GOLD SOUNDZ. / KNEELING BUS** [ ] [ ]
(12"+=)(cd-s+=) – Strings of Nashville / The exit theory.

line-up= **S.M. JENKINS/ MARK IBOLD/ ROBERT NASTANOVICH/ STEVE WEST/ SPIRAL STAIRS/ FATAH RUARK**

Jan 95. (7") **RANGE LIFE. / COOLIN' BY SOUND** [ ] [ ]
(12"+=)(cd-s+=) – Raft.

Mar 95. (7")(12") **RATTLED BY THE RUSH. / FALSE SKORPION / EASILY FOOLED** [ ] [ ]
(cd-s+=) – Brink of the clouds.

Apr 95. (cd)(c)(3-sided-d-lp) **WOWEE ZOWEE!** [18] [ ]
– We dance / Rattled by the rush / Black out / Brinx job / Grounded / Serpentine pad / Motion suggests / Father to a sister of thought / Extradition / Best friends arm / Grave architecture / At & t / Flux = rad / Fight this generation / Kennel district / Pueblo / Half a canyon / Western homes.

Jun 95. (7"ep)(12"ep)(cd-ep) **FATHER TO A SISTER OF THOUGHT. / KRIS KRAFT / MUSSLE ROCK (IS A HORSE IN TRANSITION)** [ ] [ ]

PAVLOV'S DOG

Formed: St.Louis, Missouri, USA . . . 1973 by SURKAMP, HAMILTON, RAYBURN, SCORFINA, SAFRON and CARVER. Now based in New York, they signed to 'ABC' records in 1974, and surfaced in '75 as 'PAMPERED MENIAL', and although not a commercial triumph, it became a college cult favourite throughout the the next few years. Their follow-up 'AT THE SOUND OF THE BELL', disappointed new faithful, and the band disintegrated soon after. • **Style:** Hard rock outfit, spearheaded by the astonishing vox of SURKAMP, described as a vocal gymnast with tonsils similar to a choirboy on speed. • **Songwriters:** Group compositions / SURKAMP-SCORFINA. • **Trivia:** Production and management was by Murray Krugman and Sandy Pearlman.

Recommended: PAMPERED MENIAL (*9).

DAVID SURKAMP – vocals, acoustic guitar / **DAVID HAMILTON** – keyboards / **STEVE SCORFINA** – guitar (ex-REO SPEEDWAGON) / **DOUG RAYBURN** – organ, bass / **SIEGRIED CARVER** – violin / **MIKE SAFRON** – drums (ex-CHUCK BERRY)

C.B.S. A.B.C.

Oct 75. (lp)(c) **PAMPERED MENIAL** [ ] [ ] Mar 75
– Julia / Late November / Song dance / Fast gun / Natchez trace / Theme from Subway Sue / Episode / Preludin / Of once and future kings. *(cd-iss.Mar95 on 'Rewind')*

Oct 75. (7") **JULIA. / EPISODE** [ ] [ ]

— **TOM NICKESON** – guitar, vocals repl. CARVER / on session **BILL BRUFORD** – drums (ex-KING CRIMSON, ex-YES) repl. SAFRON / added guests **ANDY MACKAY** – saxophone (of ROXY MUSIC) / **GAVIN WRIGHT** – violin / **RICHARD STOCKTON** – bass / **ELLIOTT RANDALL** – guitar, bass / **LES NICOL** – guitar

Apr 76. (lp)(c) **AT THE SOUND OF THE BELL** [ ] [ ]
– She came shining / Standing here with you (Megan's song) / Mersey / Valkerie / Try to hang on / Gold nuggets / She breaks like a morning sky / Early morning on / Did you see him cry.

— **SURKAMP, RAYBURN, SCORFINA + RANDALL** brought in **JEFF BAXTER** – guitar / **KIRK SARKESIAN** – drums

not issued Hounds

Nov 77. (lp) **THE ST.LOUIS 'HOUNDS'** [-] [ ]
– Only you / Painted ladies / Falling in love / Today / Trafalgar / I love you still / Jenny / It's all for you / Suicide / While you were out.

— They disbanded early 1977, but briefly reformed in 1983.

DAVID SURKAMP

1980. Butt; (7") **LOUIE LOUIE. / SUMMERTIME** [ ] [-]

— SURKAMP formed HI-FI with British folk-star **IAN MATTHEWS** – guitar and released 12"ep DEMONSTRATION RECORD lp MUSIC FOR MALLARDS (1983).

PEARL JAM

Formed: Seattle, USA ... 1991 by ex-GREEN RIVER members AMENT and GOSSARD. Their debut album 'TEN', soon smashed its way into the US Top 10. • **Style:** Moved through grunge-metal with GREEN RIVER to more late 60's type DOORS, STOOGES or MC5, which gave credibility in the alternative and heavy circuit. Competed from 1992 with NIRVANA and SOUNDGARDEN. • **Songwriters:** VEDDER wrote lyrics / GOSSARD and AMENT the songs. GREEN RIVER covered QUEEN BITCH (David Bowie). • **Trivia:** Their album 'TEN' was named after the number of basketball player Mookie Blaylock, whre they also took group title.

Recommended: TEN (*9) / VS (*8) / VITALOGY (*7) / MOTHER LOVE BONE (*8).

GREEN RIVER

MARK ARM – vocals / **STEVE TURNER** – guitar / **STONE GOSSARD** – guitar / **JEFF AMENT** – bass / **ALEX VINCENT** – drums

not issued Homestead

Sep 85. (12"ep) **COME ON DOWN** [-] [ ]
– New god / Swallow my pride / Ride of your life / Corner of my eye / Tunnel of love. *(cd-iss.May94)*

— **BRUCE FAIRWEATHER** – guitar repl. TURNER who later joined MUDHONEY

not issued I.P.C.

Nov 86. (7"green) **TOGETHER WE'LL NEVER. / AIN'T NOTHIN' TO DO** [-] [ ]

Glitterhouse Sup Pop

Jun 87. (12"ep) **DRY AS A BONE** [-] [ ]
– Unwind / Baby takes / This town / PCC / Ozzie. *(UK-iss.Mar91 on 'Tupelo') (cd-iss.May94)*

Feb 88. (12"ep) **REHAB DOLL** [ ] [ ] May 88
(c-ep+=) – Queen bitch. *(US re-iss.c+cd-lp Jul88 as 'DRY AS A BONE'/'REHAB DOLL')*

— MARK ARM formed MUDHONEY ⇒ .

MOTHER LOVE BONE

formed by **AMENT, GOSSARD + FAIRWEATHER** plus **ANDREW WOOD** (b.1966) – vocals (ex-MALFUNKSHUN) / **GREG GILMORE** – drums

Polydor Stardog

1989. (m-lp) **SHINE** [-] [ ]
– Thru fade away / Midshaker meltdown / Halfass monkey boy / Medley:- Chloe dancer / Lady Godiva blues.

Jul 90. (cd)(c)(lp) **APPLE** [ ] [ ] Mar 90
– This is Shangri-la / Stardog champion / Holy roller / Bone China / Come bite the apple / Stargazer / Heartshine / Captain hi-top / Man of golden words / Mr.Danny boy / Capricorn sister / Crown of thorns. *(above 2 re-iss.as 'STAR DOG CHAMPION' cd Sep92 on 'Polydor', hit US No.77)*

— ANDREW WOOD died 19 Mar'90 after heroin overdose. AMENT and GOSSARD paid tribute to him by teaming with SOUNDGARDEN ⇒ members in off-shoot TEMPLE OF THE DOG. After this project was completed,

PEARL JAM

AMENT + GOSSARD with **EDDIE VEDDER** – vocals / **MIKE McCREADY** – lead guitar / **DAVE ABBRUZZESE** – drums repl. DAVE KRUZON

Epic Epic

Feb 92. (cd)(c)(lp)(pic-lp) **TEN** [18] [2] Dec 91
– Once / Even flow / Alive / Why go / Black / Jeremy / Oceans / Porch / Garden / Deep / Release. *(re-dist.Dec92, will still be in US Top 10)* (re-cd+=) – Alive (live) / Wash / Dirty Frank.

Feb 92. (7")(c-s)(7"white) **ALIVE. / WASH** [16] [ ]
(12"+=)(pic-cd-s+=) – Once.

Apr 92. (7")(c-s) **EVEN FLOW (remix). / OCEANS** [27] [ ]
(12"white+=)(cd-pic-s+=) – Dirty Frank.

Sep 92. (7"white)(c-s) **JEREMY. / ALIVE (live)** [15] [ ]
(12"pic-d+=) – Footsteps (live).
(pic-cd-s+=) – Yellow Ledbetter.

Oct 93. (cd)(c)(lp) **VS** [2] [1]
– Go / Animal / Daughter / Glorified G / Dissident / W.M.A. / Blood / Rear view mirror / Rats / Elderly woman behind the counter in a small town / Leash / Indifference.

Oct 93. (12"ep)(cd-ep) **GO. / ALONE / ELDERLY WOMAN BEHIND THE COUNTER IN A SMALL TOWN (acoustic)** [ ] [ ]
(free c-s+=) – Animal (live).

Dec 93. (7"red)(c-s) **DAUGHTER. / BLOOD (live)** [18] [ ]
(12"+=)(cd-s+=) – Yellow leadbetter (live).

May 94. (7")(c-s) **DISSIDENT. / REARVIEWMIRROR (live)** [14] [ ]
(cd-s+=) – Release / Even flow (versions).
(cd-s) – ('A'side) / Deep / Even flow / Why go (versions).

— ABBRUZZESE departed and was repl. after below album by **JACK IRONS** (ex-RED HOT CHILI PEPPERS)

Nov 94. (7")(c-s) **SPIN THE BLACK CIRCLE. / TREMOR CHRIST** [10] [18]

Nov 94. (cd)(c)(d-lp) **VITALOGY** [6] [1]
– Last exit / Spin the black circle / Not for you / Tremor Christ / Nothingman / Whipping / Pry, to / Corduroy / Bugs / Satan's bed / Better man / Aye davanita / Immortality / Stupid mop.

— McCREADY now also moonlighted for MAD SEASON (see under ALICE IN CHAINS) due to lead singer being LAYNE STALEY. Meanwhile, STONE GOSSARD set up own record label 'Loosegroove' and signed MALFUNKSHUN, DEVILHEAD, WEAPON OF CHOICE, BRAD and PROSE AND CONCEPTS.

Feb 95. (7"colrd)(c-s)(cd-s) **NOT FOR YOU. / OUT OF MY MIND (live)** [34] [ ]

Jul 95. (c-s)(cd-s) **JEREMY / YELLOW LEDBETTER** [-] [79]

Dec 95. (7")(cd-s) **MERKINBALL** [25] [7]
– I got I.D. / Long road. (both rec. w/ NEIL YOUNG)

PEDAL POINT (see under ⇒ FOCUS)

PENETRATION

Formed: Newcastle / Middlesborough, England ... 1977 by PAULINE MURRAY, who was brought up in Ferrybridge, before going to Darlington College. Signed to Richard Branson's 'Virgin' label, and built up healthy audience, which stirred debut 1978 album 'MOVING TARGETS', into UK Top 30. • **Style:** Socially aware punk/new wave outfit, that were heavier than most. • **Songwriters:** MURRAY lyrics / group music except NOSTALGIA (Buzzcocks). PAULINE solo: – CLOSE WATER (John Cale). • **Trivia:** In 1979, Pauline guested for THE ONLY ONES on last album 'Baby's Got A Gun' and dueted with their PETER PERRETT on song 'Fools'

Recommended: DON'T DICTATE – THE BEST OF PENETRATION (*8) / PAULINE MURRAY & THE INVISIBLE GIRLS (*7).

PAULINE MURRAY (b. 8 Mar'58, Durham, England) – vocals / **GARY CHAPLIN** – guitar / **ROBERT BLAMIRE** – bass / **GARY SMALLMAN** – drums

Virgin not issued

Nov 77. (7") **DON'T DICTATE. / MONEY TALKS** [ ] [-]

— **NEALE FLOYD** – guitar repl. CHAPLIN. / added **FRED PURSER** – keyboards

May 78. (7") **FIRING SQUAD. / NEVER ARE** [ ] [-]

Sep 78. (7") **LIFE'S A GAMBLE. / V.I.P.** [ ] [-]

Oct 78. (lp)(c)(luminous-lp) **MOVING TARGETS** [22] [-]
– Future daze / Life's a gamble / Lovers of outrage / Vision / Silent community / Stone heroes / Movement / Too many friends / Reunion / Nostalgia / Free money. *(re-iss.Mar84, cd-iss.1989) (cd-iss.Mar94)*

Apr 79. (7") **DANGER SIGNS. / STONE HEROES** [ ] [-]
(12"+=) – Vision. (live).

Aug 79. (7") **COME INTO THE OPEN. / LIFELINE** [ ] [-]

Sep 79. (lp)(c) **COMING UP FOR AIR** [36] [-]
– Shout about the noise / She is the slave / Last saving grace / Killed in the rush / Challenge / Come into the open / What's going on / The party's over / On reflection / Lifeline / New recruit. *(re-iss.1988)*

— (split late 1979) **CHAPLIN** later formed SOUL ON ICE. PURSER later to TYGERS OF PANG TANG.

– compilations, etc. –

Oct 79. Cliffdayn; (lp) **RACE AGAINST TIME** (official bootleg) [ ] [-]

May 83. Virgin; (12"ep) **DON'T DICTATE / FREE MONEY. / LIFE'S A GAMBLE / DANGER SIGNS** [ ] [-]

— Next album other side by The RUTS

Jan 92. Windsong; (cd)(lp) **BBC RADIO 1 LIVE IN CONCERT (live)** [ ] [-]

Nov 93. Burning Airlines; (cd) **PENETRATION** [ ] [-]
– (live / demos / Peel sessions / solo PAULINE MURRAY)

Mar 95. Virgin; (cd) **DON'T DICTATE ...THE BEST OF PENETRATION** [ ] [-]

– Come into the open / Lifeline / Firing squad / Never / Life's a gamble / V.I.P. / Danger signs / Stone heroes / Don't dictate / Free money / Shout above the noise / She is the slave / Party's over / Future daze.

PAULINE MURRAY & THE INVISIBLE GIRLS

with **ROBERT BLAMIRE** – bass / **STEVE HOPKINS** – keyboards / **JOHN MAHER** – drums (ex-BUZZCOCKS) / **MARTIN HANNETT** – keyboards.

Illusive / not issued

Jul 80. (7")(10") **DREAM SEQUENCE 1. / DREAM SEQUENCE 2** [ ] [-]
Sep 80. (lp)(c) **PAULINE MURRAY & THE INVISIBLE GIRLS** [25] [-]
– Screaming in the darkness / Dream sequence 1 / European eyes / Shoot you down / Sympathy / Time slipping / Drummer boy / Thunder tunes / When will we learn / Mr. X / Judgement day.
Oct 80. (7") **MR. X. / TWO SHOTS** [ ] [-]
Apr 81. (7") **SEARCHING FOR HEAVEN. / ANIMAL CRAZY** [ ] [-]
(10"+=) – The Visitor.

— (split 1981)

PAULINE MURRAY & THE STORM

with **ROBERT BLAMIRE** – bass / **PAUL HARVEY** – guitar / **TIM JOHNSON** – drums.

Polestar / not issued

Oct 84. (7") **HOLOCAUST. / DON'T GIVE UP** [ ] [-]
(12"+=) – ('A'version). *(above 'B'side by* **"PAULINE MURRAY & THE SAINT"**)
Oct 86. (7") **NEW AGE. / BODY MUSIC** [ ] [-]
(12"+=) Archangel.

PAULINE MURRAY & THE SAINT

Mar 87. (12"ep) **HONG KONG EP** [ ] [-]
– Close watch / All I want / Body music / Holocaust.

PAULINE MURRAY

Cat & Mouse / not issued

Apr 89. (12"m) **THIS THING CALLED LOVE. / MR.MONEY / PRESSURE ZONE** [ ] [-]
Jul 89. (lp) **STORM CLOUDS** [ ] [-]
– This thing called love / Holocaust / Soul power / No one like you / Another world / Don't give up / Pressure zone / Close watch / Everybody's talkin' / New age / Time.
(all 1989 'Cat & Mouse' material was re-iss.mid 1991 on 'Polestar')

PENGUIN CAFE ORCHESTRA

Formed: By Londoner SIMON JEFFES in 1976 as a studio ensemble. SIMON produced early tracks by The 101'ERS, who included JOE STRUMMER. He then went onto create string arrangement for SID VICIOUS on his 1978 version of 'My Way'. In the early 80's, he became musical director for BOW WOW WOW; another SEX PISTOLS / MALCOLM McLAREN connection. • **Style:** Chamber classical music, with a touch of new-age and whatever. • **Songwriters:** JEFFES. • **Trivia:** Now used for many TV ads, documentaries & other TV intros etc.

Recommended: SIGNS OF LIFE (*8) / WHEN IN ROME (*7) / UNION CAFE (*6)

SIMON JEFFES – bass, synthesizers, guitar, multi / **STEVE NYE** – piano / **HELEN LIEBMANN** – cello / **GAVYN WRIGHT** – violin, viola / **NEIL RENNIE** – ukelele / **EMILY YOUNG** – vocals

E.G. / not issued

1976. (lp) **MUSIC FROM THE PENGUIN CAFE ORCHESTRA** [ ] [-]
– Penguin Cafe single / Zopf:- From the colonies – In a Sydney motel – Surface tension – Milk / Coronation – Giles Farnaby's dream – Pigtail / The sound of someone you love who's going away and it doesn't matter / Hugebaby / Chartered flight. *(re-iss.Mar78) (cd-iss.Jun87 & Apr92)*

— added **GEOFFREY RICHARDSON** – viola, guitar, bass, multi / **PETER VEITCH** – accordion, violin / **GILES LEAMAN** – oboe / **JULIO SEGOVIA** – cymbals (EMILY not in line-up)

Jul 81. (lp) **PENGUIN CAFE ORCHESTRA** [ ] [-]
– Air a danser / Yodel 1 / Telephone and rubber band / Cutting branches for a temporary shelter / Pythagora's trousers / Numbers 1-4 / Yodel 2 / Salty bean fumble / Paul's dance / The ecstasy of dancing fleas / Walk don't run / Flux / Simon's dream / Harmonic necklace / Steady state. *(re-iss.+c Jul83) (cd-iss.Jul87 & Apr92 +c)*

— added **KUMA HARADA** – bass

Jul 83. (lp)(c) **THE PENGUIN CAFE ORCHESTRA MINI-LP** [ ] [-]
– The Penguin Cafe single / Air a danser / The toy / Number 1-4 (live) / Salty bean fumble / Piano music.
Sep 84. (lp)(c) **BROADCASTING FROM HOME** [ ] [ ]
– Music for a found harmonium / Prelude & yodel / More milk / Sheep dip / White mischief / In the back of a taxi / Music by numbers / Another one from the colonies / Air / Heartwind / Isle of view (music for helicopter pilots) / Now nothing. *(cd-iss.Jan87 & Apr92)*
Apr 85. (7") **MUSIC FOR A FOUND HARMONIUM. / AIR A DANSER** [ ] [-]

— Above 'A'side came to be used for 'The Independent' newspaper.

Mar 87. (7") **MUSIC FOR A FOUND HARMONIUM. / IN THE BACK OF A TAXI** [ ] [ ]
– (12"+=) – Bean fields / Penguin Cafe single.

— **ELIZABETH PERRY** – violin / **BOB LOVEDAY** – violin, kalimba / **DANNY CUMMINGS** – percussion repl. GILES, PETER + KUMA

Mar 87. (lp)(c)(cd) **SIGNS OF LIFE** [49] [ ]
– Bean fields / Southern jukebox music / Horns of the bull / Oscar tango / The snake and the Lotus (the pond) / Sketch / Rosasolis / Dirt / Perpetuum mobile / Swing the cat / Wildlife.
May 87. (7") **DIRT. / AIR A DANSER** [ ] [ ]
(12"+=) – Air.

— **IAN MAIDMAN** – percussion, bass / **JULIO SEGOVIA** – percussion / **PAUL STREET** – guitar? repl.DANNY, ELIZABETH + GAVYN

Sep 88. (lp)(c)(cd) **WHEN IN ROME (live at The Festival Hall)** [ ] [ ]
– Air a danser / Yodel 1 / From the colonies / Southern jukebox music / Number 1-4 / Bean fields / Paul's dance / Oscar tango / Music for a found harmonium / Isle of view (music for helicopters pilots) / Prelude & yodel / Giles Farnaby's dream. (c/cd+=) – Air / Dirt / Cutting branches for a temporary shelter / Telephone and rubber band.

— group now; **SIMON JEFFES** – instruments / **GEOFFREY RICHARDSON** – viola, cello / **HELEN LIEBMANN** – cello / **PETER McGOWAN** – violin / **ANNIE WHITEHEAD** – trombone / **GAVYN WRIGHT** – violin / +others

Zopf / Zopf

Oct 93. (cd)(c) **UNION CAFE** [ ] [ ]
– Scherzo and trio / Lifeboat (lovers rock) / Nothing really blue / Cage dead / Vega / Yodel / Organum / Another one from Porlock / Thorn tree wind / Silver star of Bologna / Discover America / Pythagoras on the line / Kora Kora / Lie back and think of England / Red shorts / Passing through.
Jul 95. (d-cd)(d-c)(d-lp) **CONCERT PROGRAM (live)** [ ] [ ]

– compilations, etc. –

Apr 82. E.G.; (d-c) **MUSIC FROM THE PENGUIN CAFE ORCHESTRA / PENGUIN CAFE ORCHESTRA** [ ] [-]

PENTANGLE

Formed: based London, England . . . late 1967 by mid-60's solo artists BERT JANSCH and JOHN RENBOURN, who were joined by JACQUI McSHEE, plus session men DANNY THOMPSON and TERRY COX. They released their eponymous debut in the summer of '68, and this surprised most when it knocked on the door of the UK Top 20. After an adventurous double set to end the year, they were hitting the Top 5 late in 1969 with 3rd and best album 'BASKET OF LIGHT'. • **Style:** Contemporary folk outfit, featuring the clean and tidy guitar pickin' of the legendary BERT JANSCH. He and RENBOURN crafted together an experimentation of folk baroque, blues and jazz, which fused beautiful with the clear soprano vox of JACQUI. BERT's pre-PENTANGLE solo work, was influenced by BIG BILL BROONZY and DAVY GRAHAM. In 1967, his 'NICOLA' album unsuccessfully experimented with orchestra. • **Songwriters:** JANSCH, RENBOURN and McSHEE, who also arranged traditional tunes. Amongst several covers, JANSCH did a fine version of HEARTBREAK HOTEL (hit; Elvis Presley). • **Trivia:** Shel Talmy produced most of their albums. The 45 'LIGHT FLIGHT' was used for BBC-TV series 'Take 3 Girls'.

Recommended: BASKET OF LIGHT (*8) / THE ESSENTIAL PENTANGLE VOL.1 & 2 (*6) / JACK ORION (BERT JANSCH *8) / BERT JANSCH (BERT JANSCH *8) / THE GARDENER: THE ESSENTIAL BERT JANSCH 1965-1971 (*7) / THE ESSENTIAL JOHN RENBOURN (A BEST OF) (*5).

BERT JANSCH (b. 3 Nov'43, Glasgow, Scotland) – acoustic guitar, vocals / **JOHN RENBOURN** – guitars, sitar, vocals (ex-Solo artist) / **JACQUI McSHEE** – vocals / **DANNY THOMPSON** – bass (ex-ALEXIS KORNER'S BLUES INC.) / **TERRY COX** – drums, percussion, glockenspiel (ex-ALEXIS KORNER'S BLUES INC.)

Transatla. / Reprise

May 68. (7") **TRAVELIN' SONG. / MIRAGE** [ ] [-]
Jun 68. (lp) **THE PENTANGLE** [21] [ ]
– Let no man steal your thyme / Bells / Hear my call / Pentangling / Mirage / Way behind the Sun / Burton Town / Waltz. *(re-iss.1974)*
Dec 68. (7") **LET NO MAN STEAL YOUR THYME. / WAY BEHIND THE SUN** [-] [ ]
Dec 68. (d-lp) **SWEET CHILD (half live / half studio)** [ ] [ ]
– Market song / No more my Lord / Turn your money green / Haitian fight song / A woman like you / Goodbye pork pie hat / Three dances / Brentzal gay / La rotta / The Earl of Salisbury / Watch the stars / So early in the Spring / No exit / The time has come / Burton town / Sweet child / I loved a lass / Three part thing / Sovay / In time / In your mind / I've got a feeling / The trees they do grow high / Moon dog / Hole in my coal. *(cd-iss.1988, omits 3)*
May 69. (7") **ONCE I HAD A SWEETHEART. / I SAW AN ANGEL** [46] [ ]
Oct 69. (lp) **BASKET OF LIGHT** [5] [ ]
– Light flight / Once I had a sweetheart / Springtime promises / Lyke Wyke dirge / Train song / Hunting song / Sally go round the roses / The cuckoo / House carpenter. *(re-iss.1974 +c.Oct81, cd-iss.Jul87) (re-iss.Feb89 on 'Demon')*
Feb 70. (7") **LIGHT FLIGHT. / COLD MOUNTAIN** [43] [-]
Nov 70. (lp) **CRUEL SISTER** [51] [ ]
– Cruel sister / A maid that's deep in love / When I was in my prime / Lord Franklin / Jack Orion. *(re-iss.Mar77) (cd-iss.1988)*
Oct 71. (lp) **REFLECTION** [ ] [ ]
– Wedding dress / Omie wise / Will the circle be unbroken / When I get home / Rain and snow / Helping hand / So clear / Reflection. *(re-iss.1974) (cd-iss.1988)*

Reprise / Reprise

Sep 72. (lp)(c) **SOLOMON'S SEAL** [ ] [ ]
– Sally free and easy / The cherry tree carol / The snows / High Germany / People on the highway / Willy O'Winsbury / No love is sorrow / Jump baby jump / Lady old Carlisle.

— Disbanded Mar'73. THOMPSON and COX returned to session work. THOMPSON also went solo and joined JOHN MARTYN's group, to mention just one. JANSCH and RENBOURN continued to work on solo albums, with the latter being augmented by McSHEE.

- compilations, etc. -

Jul 72. Transatlantic; (lp) **HISTORY BOOK**
Aug 73. Transatlantic; (lp) **PENTANGLING**
(re-iss.Aug 77 on 'Hallmark') (re-iss.May81)
1973. Transatlantic; (7"m) **LIGHT FLIGHT. / MARKET SONG / THE TIME HAS COME** *(re-issJul78)*
1975. Transatlantic; (d-lp) **THE PENTANGLE COLLECTION** - -
(Europe only, re-iss.Apr88 +c+cd.Apr88 on 'Castle')
Jul 78. Transatlantic; (lp) **ANTHOLOGY** -
Jul 87. Transatlantic; (cd) **THE ESSENTIAL PENTANGLE VOL.1** -
– Once I had a sweetheart / Hear my call / Hole in the coal / Omie Wise / Waltz / The trees they do grow / Sweet child / A woman like you / Reflection / Will the circle be unbroken / Watch the stars / Helping hand / Goodbye pork pie hat / When I was in my prime.
Sep 87. Tranatlantic; (cd) **THE ESSENTIAL PENTANGLE VOL.2** -
– Pentangling / Bruton Town / Shake shake mama / Let no man steal your thyme / Soho / The cruel sister / Bells / Wedding dress / I've got a feeling / Three part thing / Rain and snow / Way behind the Sun / When I get home / The time has come.
Mar 82. Cambra; (d-lp)(c) **AT THEIR BEST** -
(c-iss.1985 on 'Autograph')
Jul 90. Shanachie; (cd) **A MIND THAT'S DEEP DEEP IN LOVE** -
Aug 92. Shanachie; (cd) **EARLY CLASSICS** -
Apr 94. Castle; (cd)(c) **THE COLLECTION** -
Jan 95. Ariola Express; (cd)(c) **IN YOUR MIND** -
Sep 95. Band Of Joy; (cd) **LIVE AT THE BBC** -

BERT JANSCH

Transatla. Vanguard

1965. (lp) **BERT JANSCH** -
– Strolling down the highway / Smokey river / Oh how your love is strong / I have no time / Finches / Rambling's going to be the death of me / Veronica / Needle of death / Do you hear me now? / Alice's wonderland / Running from home / Courting blues / Casbah / Dreams of love / Angie. *(re-iss.1980 + Jan88) (re-iss.Jun88 on 'Demon')*
Dec 65. (lp) **IT DON'T BOTHER ME** -
– Oh my babe / Ring-a-ding bird / Tinker's blues / Anti apartheid / The wheel / A man I'd rather be / My lover / It don't bother me / Harvest your thoughts of love / Lucky thirteen / As the day grows longer now / So long (been on the road so long) / Want my daddy now / 900 miles. *(re-issJul76 as 'EARLY BERT' on 'Xtra') (cd-iss.1994 +=)*– The times has come / Soho / In this game / Dissatisfied blues.
1966. (lp) **JACK ORION** -
– The waggoner's lad / The first time ever I saw your face / Jack Orion / The gardener / Nottamun Town / Henry Martin / Black water side / Pretty Polly. *(re-issJul76 as 'EARLY BERT VOL. 2' on 'Xtra')*
1966. (lp) **BERT AND JOHN ("BERT JANSCH & JOHN RENBOURN")** -
– Eastwind / Piano time / Goodbye pork pie hat / Soho / Tie tocative / Orlando / Red favourite / No exit / Along the way / The time has come / Stepping stones / After the dance. *(re-iss.1974)*
1966. (7"ep) **NEEDLE OF DEATH** -
– Running from home / Tinker's blues / Needle of death / The wheel.

Transatla. Reprise

Jun 67. (7") **LIFE DEPENDS ON LOVE. / A LITTLE SWEET SUNSHINE** -
Jul 67. (lp) **NICOLA** -
– Go your way my love / Woe is love, my dear / Nicola / Come back baby / A little sweet sunshine / Love is teasing / Rabbit run / Life depends on love / Weeping willow blues / Box of love / Wish my baby was here / If the world isn't there / Come sing me a happy song to prove we can all get along the lumpy, bumpy road. *(re-issJul76 as 'EARLY BERT VOL. 3' on 'Xtra')*
Dec 68. (lp) **BIRTHDAY BLUES**
– Come and sing me a happy song / To prove / The bright new year / Tree song / Poison / Miss Heather / Rosemary Sewell / I've got a woman / A woman like you / I'm lonely / Promised land / Birthday blues / Wishing well blues.
Jun 71. (lp) **ROSEMARY LANE**
– Tell me what is true love / Rosemary Lane / M'lady Nancy / A dream, a dream, a dream / Alman / Wayward child / Nobody's bar / Reynardine / Silly women / Peregrinations / Sylvie / Sarabanda / Bird song. *(cd-iss.Sep94 on 'Traditional Line') (re-iss.Jan77 as 'EARLY BERT VOL. 4' on 'Xtra')(cd-iss.1990)*

Reprise Reprise

Feb 73. (lp) **MOONSHINE**
– Yarrow / Brought with the rain / January man / Night time blues / Moonshine / First time ever I saw your face / Rambleaway / Twa corbies / Oh my father. *(cd-iss.Sep95 on 'Fledg'ling')*
Mar 73. (7") **OH MY FATHER /THE FIRST TIME EVER I SAW YOUR FACE**

Charisma Charisma

Sep 74. (lp) **L.A. TURNAROUND**
– Fresh as a sweet Sunday morning / Chambertin / One for Jo / Travelling man / Open up the Watergate (let the sunshine in) / Stone monkey / Of love and lullaby / Needle of death / Lady nothing / There comes a time / Cluck old hen / The blacksmith.
Oct 74. (7") **IN THE BLEAK MIDWINTER. / ONE FOR JO**
Oct 75. (lp) **SANTA BARBARA HONEYMOON**
– Love a new / Mary and Joseph / Be my friend / Baby blue / Dance lady dance / You are my sunshine / Lost and gone / Blues run the game / Built another band / When the teardrops fell / Dynamite / Buckrabbit.
Nov 75. (7") **DANCE LADY DANCE. / BUILD ANOTHER BAND**
May 77. (lp) **A RARE CONUNDRUM**
– Daybreak / One to a hundred / Pretty Saro / Doctor, doctor / 3 a.m. / The Curragh of Kildare / Instrumentally Irish / St.Flacre / If you see my love / Looking for a home / Poor mouth / Cat and mouse / Three chord trick / Lost love.

— In 1978 he appeared on CONUNDRUM & RICHARD HARVEY single 'Black Birds of Brittany'.

Feb 79. (lp) **AVOCET**
– Avocet / Bittern / Kingfisher / Kittiwake / Lapwing / Osprey.

Sonet KIcking Mule

Apr 80. (7") **TIME AND TIME. / UNA LINEA DI DOLCEZZA** -
Jul 80. (lp) **13 DOWN** (as "BERT JANSCH CONUNDRUM")
– Una linea di dolcezza / Let me sing / Down river / Nightfall / If I had a lover / Time and time / In my mind / Sovay / Where did my life go / Single Nose / Ask your daddy / Sweet mother Earth / Bridge.

Logo Kicking Mule

Feb 82. (lp) **HEARTBREAK**
– Is it real? / Up to the stars / Give me the time / If I were a carpenter / Wild mountain thyme / Heartbreak hotel / Sit down beside me / No rhyme nor reason / Blackwater side / And not a word was said. *(re-iss.May89 on 'Hannibal', cd-iss.Jul93)*
Feb 82. (7") **HEARTBREAK HOTEL. / UP TO THE STARS**

Mausoleum not issued

Sep 85. (lp) **FROM THE OUTSIDE**
– Sweet rose in the garden / Black bird in the morning / Read all about it / Change the song / Shout / From the outside / If you're thinking 'bout me / Silver raindrops / Why me? / Get out of my life / Time is an old friend. *(cd-iss. Aug93 on 'Hypertension')(+=)* River running / High emotion / From the inside.

Black Crow not issued

Mar 88. (lp)(c)(cd) **LEATHER LAUNDERETTE ("BERT JANSCH & ROD CLEMENTS")** -
– Strolling down the highway / Sweet Rose / Brafferton / Ain't no more cane / Why me? / Sundown station / Knight's move / Brownsville / Bogie's bonny belle / Leather launderette / Been on the road so long.

— his backers now **PETER KIRTLEY** – guitar, b.vocals, percussion / **DANNY THOMPSON** – double bass, percussion, chimes / **STEVE BAKER** – blues harp / **STEFAN WULFF** – percussion / **FRANK WULFF** – percussion, alto-flute, etc.

Temple Hypertens.

Nov 90. (cd)(c)(lp) **SKETCHES** Germ'y
– Ring-a-ding bird / One for Jo / Poison / The old routine / Needle of death / Oh my father / Running, running from home / Afterwards / Can't hide love / Moonshine / A woman like you / A windy day. *(cd+=)*– As the day grows longer now.

Run River not issued

Nov 90. (cd)(c)(lp) **THE ORNAMENT TREE** -

Cooking V. not issued

Sep 95. (cd) **WHEN THE CIRCUS COMES TO TOWN** -
– Walk quietly by / Open road / Back home / No-one around / Step back / When the circus comes to town / Summer heat / Just a dream / The lady doctor from Ashington / Stealing the night away / Honey don't you understand / Born with the blues / Morning brings peace of mind / Living in the shadows.

- (BERT JANSCH) compilations, etc. -

1966. Transatlantic; (lp) **LUCKY THIRTEEN** -
1969. Vanguard; (lp) **STEPPING STONES** -
Nov 69. Transatlantic; (lp) **THE BERT JANSCH SAMPLER** -
Dec 72. Transatlantic; (lp) **BOX OF LOVE - THE BERT JANSCH SAMPLER VOL. 2** -
– Oh how your love is strong / In this game / The gardener / Soho / I am lonely / Renegrinations / Casbah / Dissatisfied blues / As the day grows longer now / Box of love / Birthday blues / Nobody's bar.
Mar 78. Transatlantic; (lp) **ANTHOLOGY** -
Jul 87. Transatlantic; (cd) **THE ESSENTIAL COLLECTION VOL.1** -
Sep 87. Transatlantic; (cd) **THE ESSENTIAL COLLECTION VOL.2** -
Jul 93. Transatlantic; (cd) **BERT JANSCH / JACK ORION** -
Dec 93. Transatlantic; (cd) **NICOLA / BIRTHDAY BLUES** -
1980. Kicking Mule; (lp) **THE BEST OF BERT JANSCH** -
Jul 92. Demon; (cd) **THE GARDENER: THE ESSENTIAL BERT JANSCH 1965-1971** -
– The gardener / Alice's wonderland / Running from home / Tinker's blues / It don't bother me / The waggoner's lad / The first ever I saw your face / Go your way my love / My lover / Woe is love my dear / Black waterside / Rabbit run / A woman like you (studio) / Market song / A woman like you (live) / Wishing well / Rosemary Lane / Peregrinations / Poison / Miss Heather Rosemary Sewell / Reynardine / Bird song / When I get home / I am lonely.
Jul 93. Virgin; (cd) **THREE CHORD TRICK** (74-79 material) -
Sep 93. Windsong; (cd) **BBC RADIO 1 LIVE IN CONCERT (live 1980-82 with CONUNDRUM)** -

JOHN RENBOURN

Transatlan Reprise

1965. (lp) **JOHN RENBOURN** -
– Judy / Beth's blues / Song / Down on the barge / John Henry / Plainsong / Louisianna blues / Blue bones / Train time / Candy man / The wildest pig in captivity / National seven / Motherless children / Winter is gone / Noah and rabbit. *(re-iss.1974)*
1966. (lp) **ANOTHER MONDAY** -
– Another Monday / Lady Nothing's tongue puffe / I know my babe / Waltz / Lost lover blues / One for William / Buffalo / Sugar babe / Debbie Anna / Can't keep from crying / Day at the seaside / Nobody's fault but mine. *(re-issJun88 on 'Demon')*
Jun 68. (lp) **SIR JOHN ALOT OF MERRIE ENGLANDE'S MUSICK THYNGE AND YE GREENE KNIGHT**
– The Earl of Salisbury / The trees they do grow high / Lady goes to church / Morgana / Transfusion / Forty-eight / My dear boy / White fishes / Sweet potato / seven up. *(re-iss.1974)*
Oct 70. (lp) **THE LADY & THE UNICORN**
– Trotto saltarello / Lamenta di Tristan / La rotta / Veri Floria / Triple ballade / Brentzel gay / Brentzel de bourgoyne / Alman / Melancholy galliard / Sarabande / The lady & the unicorn / My Johnny was a shoemaker / Western wynde / Scarborough fair. *(re-iss.1974)*
Jan 72. (lp) **FARO ANNIE**
– White house blues / Buffalo skinners / Kokomo blues / Little Sadie / Shake shake mama / Willy o' Winsbury / The cuckoo / Come on in my kitchen / Country blues / Faro Annie / Back on the road again. *(re-iss.1974)*
1974. (lp) **HEADS AND TAILS ("JOHN RENBOURN & STEFAN GROSSMAN")** -
Nov 76. (lp) **THE HERMIT** (rec. 1973) -
– John's tune / Little Alice / Old McBladgitt / Faro's rag / Caroline's tune / Three

pieces by O'Carolan; a) The lamentation of Owen Rae O'Neil, b) Lord Inchiquin, c) Mrs.Power (O'Carolan's concerts) / Princess and the puddings / Pavanna (Anna-Pavanna) a) A toye (Thomas Robinson). b) Lord Willoughby's welcome home.

1977. (lp) **A MAID IN BEDLAM**
– Black waterside / Nacht tanz – shaeffertane / A maid in bedlam / Gypsy dance / Jews dance / John Barleycorn / Reynardine / My Johnny was a shoemaker / Death and the lady / The battle of Augrham / Talk about suffering.

Transatlan Kicking Mu

1978. (lp) **JOHN RENBOURN AND STEFAN GROSSMAN – LIVE IN CONCERT (live)**
– Looper's corner / The shoes of the fisherman's wife / Are some jive ass slippers / Twelve sticks / Cocaine blues / Tightrope / Sheebeg an Sheemore – Drunken wagoner (medley) / Cincinnati flow rag – New York City rag – Hot dogs (medley) / Judy – Angie (medley) / Lament for Owen Roe O'Neill – Mist covered mountains of home (medley) / Great dreams from Heaven / Sweet potato / Goodbye pork pir hat / Midnight on the water / Spirit levels / Mississippi blues No.2. *(re-iss.Aug85 on 'Spindrift')*

Apr 79. (lp) **THE BLACK BALLOON**
– The Moon Shines Bright / English Dance / Medley / Bourre 1 / Bourre 2 / Medley / Mist Covered Mountains Of Home / The Orphan / The Tarboulton / The Pelican / The Black Balloon. *(re-iss.Jul87 on 'Zu Zazz')*

JOHN RENBOURN GROUP

with some trad.song & contributions from group **JACQUI McSHEE** – vocals (ex-PENTANGLE) / **TONY ROBERTS** – wind, vocals, percussion, glockenspiel / **JOHN MOLINEUX** – mandolin, volin, dulcimer, vocals / **KESHAV SATHE** – tabla, perc. / **GLEN TOMMY** – snare drum

Feb 80. (lp) **THE ENCHANTED GARDEN**
– (a) Pavane 'Belle, qui tiens ma vie', (b) Tourdion / The truth about above / Le tambourin / The plans of waterloo / The maid on the shore / Douce Dame Jolie / A bold young farmer / Sidi Brahim.

Sonet Kicking Mu

1980. (lp) **UNDER THE VOLCANO**
– Idaho potato / Medley: Shheberg and Sheemor – Drunken wagoner / Under the volcano / Resurrection of blind Joe Death – For the roses – Mantagu's pact – The rights of man / Medley: Bonaparte's retreat – Billy in the Lowgrounds / Swedish jig / Water gypsy / All things parallel must converge / The Blarney pilgrim / Missisippi blues No.3.

Spindrift FlyingFish

1986. (lp) **NINE MAIDENS**
– New nothynge / The fish in the well / Pavan d'Aragon / Variations on my Lady Carey's dompe / Circle dance / The nine maidens: Clarsach – The nine maidens – The fiddler.

FlyingFish FlyingFish

1995. (cd) **WHEEL OF FORTUNE** ("JOHN RENBOURNE & ROBIN WILLIAMSON")
– South wind – Blarney pilgrim / The Curragh of Kildare – Millner's daughter / Bunyan's hymn – I saw three ships – English dance / The lights of sweet St. Anne's / The snows / Finn and the old man's house / Matt highland / Little Niles / The rocks of Bawn / Lindsay / Port Partrick / Wheel of fortune.

– (JOHN RENBOURN) compilations, etc. –

Note below on 'Transatlantic' until otherwise mentioned.

Jun 71. (lp) **THE JOHN RENBOURN SAMPLER** [ ] [-]
May 73. (lp) **SO CLEAR (THE JOHN RENBOURN SAMPLER VOL.II)** [ ] [-]
1987. (cd) **THE SOHO YEARS – THE ESSENTIAL COLLECTION VOL.1** [ ] [-]
May 85. Cambra; (d-lp)(d-c) **JOHN RENBOURN & BERT JANSCH** [ ] [-]
Jul 92. Demon; (cd) **THE ESSENTIAL JOHN RENBOURN (A BEST OF)** [ ] [-]
– Wildest pig in captivity / Beth's blues / Winter is gone / Train tune / I know my babe / Nobody's fault but mine / Debbie Anne / White House blues / Can't keep from crying sometime / After the dance / Piano tune / The cuckoo / Country blues / Faro's rag / The hermit / Lord Franklin / My sweet potato / Kokomo blues / Goodbye pork pie hat / Will the circle be unbroken? / Sally go round the roses / So clear.
Apr 95. Castle; (cd) **THE COLLECTION** [ ] [-]

PENTANGLE

re-formed in the early 80's. **MIKE PIGGOTT** – guitar repl. JOHN

Spindrift Varrick

Jul 85. (lp) **OPEN THE DOOR** [ ] [ ] 1988
– Open the door / Dragonfly / Mother Earth / Child of the winter / The dolphin / Lost love / Sad lady / Taste of love / Yarrow / Street song. *(cd-iss. 1990 on 'Plane')*
1985. (7") **DRAGON FLY. / THE DOLPHIN**

—— **NIGEL PORTMAN SMITH** – bass, keyboards, accordian, vocals repl. DANNY

Feb 86. (7") **PLAY THE GAME. / SATURDAY MOVIE** [ ] [-]
1986. (cd)(c)(d-lp) **IN THE ROUND** [ ] [ ] 1988
– Play the game / Open sea / She moved through the fair / Set me free / When the night is over come to me baby / Sunday morning blues / Chase that devil away / The Saturday movie / Suilagrar / Circle the Moon / Let me be. *(re-iss.d-lp,c,cd.Apr90 on 'Episode')*
1986. (7") **SET ME FREE. / COME TO ME BABY** [ ] [-]

—— **ROD CLEMENTS** – guitar, mandolin / **GERRY CONWAY** – drums, percussion repl. PIGGOTT + COX

Plane Green Linnet

Aug 89. (lp) **SO EARLY IN THE SPRING** [ ] [ ] 1990
– New nothynge / The fish in the well / Pavan d'Aragon / Variations on my Lady Carey's dompe / Circle dance / The nine maidens: Clarsach – The nine maidens – The fiddler.

—— again re-formed:- **BERT JANSCH** – vocals, banjo, acoustic guitar / **JACQUI McSHEE** – vocals / **PETER KIRTLEY** – vocals, guitars / **GERRY CONWAY** – drums, percussion, conga / **NIGEL PORTMAN SMITH** – bass, banjo, keyboards

Permanent not issued

May 93. (cd)(c) **ONE MORE ROAD**
– Travelling solo / Oxford City / Endless sky / The lily of the west / One more road / High Germany / Hey, hey soldier / Willy of Winsbury / Somali / Manuel / Are you going to Scarborough fair.

—— (also some obvious trad. covers)

Hypertens. not issued

Jun 95. (cd) **THINK OF TOMORROW (live 1994?)** [ ] [-]
– O'er the lonely mountain / Baby now it's over / Share a dream / he storyteller / Meat on the bone / Ever yes ever no / Straight ahead / The toss of golden hair / The lark in the clear air / The bonny boy / Colour my paintbook.

PERE UBU

Formed: Akron & Cleveland, Ohio, USA . . . Sep'75 by DAVID THOMAS (aka CROCUS BEHEMOTH; his alter-ego). They formed own 'Hearthan' label, and released 4 rare and brilliant 45's, before debuting on 12" in 1977 with classic lp 'THE MODERN DANCE'. The next year, they signed to major 'Chrysalis' label, and brought out another creative 'DUB HOUSING' album. Became mainly a cult band for the next decade or so, remarkably never gaining any chart success, even after a 1988 comeback album 'THE TENEMENT YEARS'. • **Style:** Underground avant-garde synth. orientated rock'n'roll outfit, capturing a collective array of influences from CAPTAIN BEEFHEART, CAN or ROXY MUSIC. The large-framed eccentric DAVID THOMAS, never quite appealed commercially, although music press and night time Radio 1 DJ John Peel, gave them acolade and deserved airplay. • **Songwriters:** All group compositions, except MIRROR MAN (Captain Beefheart) / DOWN BY THE RIVER (Neil Young) / LIKE A ROLLING STONE (Bob Dylan). THOMAS collaborated with others on solo work. • **Trivia:** The name PERE UBU, was taken from the French writer Alfred Jarry's book.

Recommended: TERMINAL TOWER: AN ARCHIVAL COLLECTION (*9) / THE MODERN DANCE (*9) / DUB HOUSING (*7) / NEW PICNIC TIME (*7) / CLOUDLAND (*6). DAVID THOMAS & THE PEDESTRIANS:- THE SOUND OF THE SAND . . . (*5).

DAVID THOMAS – vocals / **PETER LAUGHNER** – guitar / **TIM WRIGHT** – bass, guitar / **TOM HERMAN** – guitar, bass / **R.SCOTT KRAUSE** – drums / **ALLEN RAVENSTINE** – synthesizer

not issued Hearthan

Dec 75. (7"ltd) **30 SECONDS OVER TOKYO. / HEART OF DARKNESS** [-] [ ]

—— **DAVE TAYLOR** – synthesizer repl. RAVENSTINE

Mar 76. (7"ltd) **FINAL SOLUTION. / CLOUD 149** [-] [ ]

—— **ALLEN RAVELSTINE** – synthesizer returned to repl. TAYLOR / **ALAN GREENBLATT** – guitar repl. LAUGHNER who formed FRICTION (he died Jun77).

—— **TONY MAIMONE** – bass, piano repl. WRIGHT who joined DNA. (GREENBLATT left too) (were now a quintet with **THOMAS, HERMAN, KRAUSE MAIMONE** and **RAVELSTINE**).

Nov 76. (7"ltd) **STREET WAVES. / MY DARK AGES** [-] [ ]
Aug 77. (7"ltd) **UNTITLED (aka THE MODERN DANCE). / HEAVEN** [-] [ ]

not issued Blank

Jan 78. (lp) **THE MODERN DANCE** [-] [ ]
– Non-alignment pact / The modern dance / Laughing / Street waves / Chinese radiation / Life stinks / Real world / Over my head / Sentimental journey / Humor me. *(UK-iss.+re-US-iss.Apr78 on 'Mercury') (UK re-iss.Jan81 on 'Rough Trade') (re-iss.+cd+c.Feb88 on 'Fontana' ltd)*

Chrysalis Chrysalis

Nov 78. (lp)(c) **DUB HOUSING**
– Navy / On the surface / Dub housing / Cagliari's mirror / Thriller / I will wait / Drinking wine Spodyody / Ubu dance party / Blow daddy-o / Codex. *(cd-iss.Mar89 on 'Rough Trade')*

Sep 79. (lp)(c) **NEW PICNIC TIME**
– One less worry / Make hay / Goodbye / The voice of the sand / Jehovah's kingdom comes / Have shoes will walk / 49 guitars and 1 girl / A small dark cloud / Small was fast / All the dogs are barking. *(cd-iss.Mar89 on 'Rough Trade')*

Oct 79. (7") **THE FABULOUS SEQUEL (HAVE SHOES WILL WALK). / HUMOR ME (live). / THE BOOK IS ON THE TABLE**

—— **MAYO THOMPSON** – guitar (ex-RED CRAYOLA) repl. HERMAN who went solo

Rough Trade not issued

Sep 80. (lp) **THE ART OF WALKING**
– Go / Rhapsody in pink / Arabia * / Miles * / Misery goats / Loop / Rounder / Birdies / Lost in art / Horses / Crush this horn. *(re-iss.1981 * tracks became 'Arabian nights' & 'Tribute to Miles') (cd-iss.Apr89 tracks as re-issue)*

Feb81. (7") **NOT HAPPY. / LONESOME COWBOY DAVE**

—— added **ANTON FIER** – drums, percussion (ex-FEELIES) / guest **EDDIE THORNTON** – trumpet

Jun 82. (lp) **SONG OF THE BAILING MAN**
– The long walk home / Use of a dog / Petrified / Stormy weather / West Side story / Thoughts that go by steam / Big Ed's used farms / A day such as this / The vulgar boatman bird / My hat / Horns are a dilemma. *(cd-iss.Apr89)*

—— Split mid'82. MAYO returned to RED CRAYOLA (which also incl. most UBU's) **KRAUSE** and **MAIMONE** formed HOME AND GARDEN, (see below for more).

DAVID THOMAS

had already gone solo.

Rough Tr. Recomm.

1981. (12") **VOCAL PERFORMANCES. /** [ ] [-]

DAVID THOMAS & THE PEDESTRIANS

included **THOMPSON, KRAUSE, FIER & RAVENSTINE** plus **CHRIS CUTLER** – drums / **JOHN GREAVES** – bass (both ex-HENRY COW) / **PHILIP MOXHAM** – multi (ex-YOUNG MARBLE GIANTS) / **RICHARD THOMPSON** – guitar

Jan 82. (lp) **THE SOUND OF THE SAND AND OTHER SONGS OF THE PEDESTRIANS**
– The birds are good ideas / Yiki Tiki / The crickets in the flats / Sound of the sand / The new atom mine / Big dreams / Happy to see you / Crush this horn – part 2 / Confuse did / Sloop John B. / Man's best friend.

Oct 82. (7") **PETRIFIED. / ?** –

—— next 1 credited to back. group HIS LEGS:- **CHRIS CUTLER & LINDSAY COOPER** – bassoon (ex-MIKE OLDFIELD) Issued on 'Recommended' US.

Feb 83. (lp) **WINTER COMES HOME (live Munich, 1982)**
– A day such as this / Winter comes home / West side story / Sunset / Stormy weather / Poetic license / Rhapsody in pink / Dinosaurs like me / Petrified / Bones in action / Contrasted views of the archaeopterix

—— added **RICHARD THOMPSON** etc. (CUTLER, COOPER)

Dec 83. (lp) **VARIATIONS ON A THEME** –
– A day at the Botanical Gardens / Pedestrians walk / Bird town / The egg and I / Who is it / Song of hoe / Hurry back / The ram / Semaphore.

—— **TONY MAIMONE** – bass repl. GREAVES who joined The FLYING LIZARDS

May 85. (lp) **MORE PLACES FOREVER**
– Through the magnifying glass / Enthusiastic / Big breezy day / About true friends / Whale head king / Song of the bailing man / The farmer's wife / New broom.

DAVID THOMAS & THE WOODEN BIRDS

(**DAVID** retained **MAIMONE** and **CUTLER**) brought in **RAVENSTINE** again. (**DAVID HILD** – accordion of LOS LOBOS guested)

Apr 86. (lp) **MONSTER WALKS THE WINTER LAKE**
– My theory of similtanious similtude – Red tin bus / What happened to me / Monster walks the winter lake / Bicycle / Coffee train / My town / Monster Magge king of the seas / Monster thinks about the good days / What happened to us.

—— **JIM JONES** – guitar was added

Mar 87. (lp) **BLAME THE MESSENGER**
– The long rain / My town / King Knut / A fact about trains / When love is uneven / Storm breaks / Having time / Velikovsky / The two-step.

PERE UBU

(**THOMAS, RAVENSTINE, MAIMONE, CUTLER, JONES** and **KRAUSE**)

Fontana Fontana

Mar 88. (lp)(c)(cd) **THE TENEMENT YEARS**
– Something's gotta give / George had a hat / Talk to me / Busman's honeymoon / Say goodbye / Universal vibration / Miss you / Dream the Moon / Rhythm kind / The hollow Earth / We have the technology.

Jul 88. (7") **WE HAVE THE TECHNOLOGY. / THE B-SIDE**
(12"+=)(cd-s-ltd.+=) – The postman drove a caddy / ('A'diff.mix).

—— **ERIC DREW FELDMAN** – drums (ex-CAPTAIN BEEFHEART) repl. RAVENSTINE + CUTLER

Mar 89. (7") **WAITING FOR MARY (WHAT ARE WE DOING HERE?). / WINE DARK SPARKS**
(12"+=)(cd-s+=) – Flat.

May 89. (lp)(c)(cd) **CLOUDLAND**
– Breath / Bus called happiness / Race the sun / Waiting for Mary / Cry / Flat * / Ice cream truck / Lost nation road / Monday night / Pushin' / The wire * / The waltz. *(cd+= *)*

Jun 89. (7") **LOVE LOVE LOVE. / FEDORA SATELLITE**
(cd-s+=) – Say goodbye.
(12") – ('A'side) / (2 diff.'A'mixes).

Oct 89. (7") **BREATH. / BANG THE DRUM**
(12"+=) – Over my head (live) / Universal initiation (live).
(cd-s+=) – Humor me (live).

Mar 91. (7")(c-s) **I HEAR THEY SMOKE THE BARBEQUE. / INVISIBLE MAN**
(12"+=)(cd-s+=) – Around the fire.

May 91. (cd)(c)(lp) **WORLD'S IN COLLISION**
– Oh Catherine / I hear they smoke the barbeque / Turpentine / Goodnight Irene / Mirror man / Cry cry / World's in collision / Life of Riley / Over the Moon / Don't look back / Playback / Nobody knows / Winter in the Netherlands.

May 91. (7") **OH CATHERINE. / LIKE A ROLLING STONE**
(12"+=)(cd-s+=) – Down by the river.

Jan 93. (cd)(c)(lp) **THE STORY OF MY LIFE**
– Wasted / Come home / Louisiana train wreck / Fedora satellite II / Heartbreak garage / Postcard / Kathleen / Honey Moon / Sleep walk / The story of my life / Last will and testament.

—— **THOMAS / KRAUSS / JONES / TEMPLE / YELLIN**

Cooking V. ???

Aug 95. (cd) **RAY GUN SUITCASE**
– Folly of youth / Electricity / Beach Boys / Turquoise fins / Vacuum in my head / Memphis / Three things / Horse / Don't worry / Ray gun suitcase / Surfer girl / Red sky / Montana / My friend is a stooge for the media priests / Down by the river II.

Nov 95. (cd-ep) **FOLLY OF YOUTH / BALL 'N' CHAIN (jam) / DOWN BY THE RIVER II (demo) / MEMPHIS (demo)**

– (PERE UBU) compilations, others, etc. –

Apr 78. Radar; (12"ep) **DATAPANIK IN THE YEAR ZERO (remixes)**
– Heart of darkness / 30 seconds over Tokyo / Cloud 149 / Untitled / Heaven.

Jun 80. Rough Trade; (7") **FINAL SOLUTION. / MY DARK AGES**

May 81. Rough Trade; (lp) **390° OF SIMULATED STEREO – UBU LIVE: VOLUME 1 (live 76-79)**
– Can't believe it / Over my head / Sentimental journey / 30 seconds over Tokyo / Humor me / Rea world / My dark ages / Street waves / Laughing / Non-alignment pact / Heart of darkness / The modern dance. *(cd-iss.Apr89)*

Nov 85. Rough Trade; (lp) **TERMINAL TOWER: AN ARCHIVAL COLLECTION**
– (early 'Hearthan' sides + rare)

Mar 89. Rough Trade; (cd) **ONE MAN DRIVES WHILE THE OTHER MAN SCREAMS – LIVE VOL.2: PERE UBU ON TOUR**

Nov 95. Cooking Vinyl; (4x7"box) **(the 4 'Hearthan' 45's)** –

Nov 95. Movieplay Gold; (d-cd) **MODERN DANCE / TERMINAL TOWER** –

Carl PERKINS

Born: CARL LEE PERKINGS, 9 Apr'32, Ridgely, Tennessee, USA. In 1950, he and brothers JAY & CLAYTON formed honky tonk band The PERKINS BROTHERS. They continued to back him on newly launched solo career in 1954. After moving to Jackson, Memphis with his wife and inspiration Valda Crider, he signed to Sam Phillips' 'Sun' records. Early 1956, his third single 'BLUE SUEDE SHOES', nearly hit the No.1 spot and became future classic. The brothers had a lucky escape in March that year, when their car collided with another vehicle, and put them in hospital for a few weeks. Around the same time, ELVIS covered the hit song, which also got him a place in the Top 30. After a few more Hot 100 entries and a shift to 'Columbia', CARL's career slid into decline. He pursued relentlessly releasing more records and constantly touring. His songs, became many standards for other singers and groups such as The BEATLES. • **Style:** Blues orientated country rocker that inspired many, but didn't reap the rich rewards he rightly deserved. In the mid-60's, he became a pure country singer and a devout Christian with great friend JOHNNY CASH. • **Songwriters:** Wrote most of his own material and covered RUBY (DON'T TAKE YOUR LOVE TO TOWN) (Kenny Rogers) / etc. • **Trivia:** (see further discography)

Recommended: THE LEGENDARY CARL PERKINS (*5)

CARL PERKINS – vox, electric guitar / with brothers **JAY** – acoustic guitar / **CLAYTON** – bass / **W.S.HOLLAND** – drums

not issued Flip

Jan 55. (7") **MOVIE MAGG. / TURN AROUND** –

London Sun

Jul 55. (7") **GONE, GONE, GONE. / LET THE JUKEBOX KEEP ON PLAYING** –

Apr 56. (7") **BLUE SUEDE SHOES. / HONEY DON'T** 10 2 Feb 56

Apr 56. (7") **SURE TO FAIL. / TENNESSEE** –

Jun 56. (7") **BOPPIN' THE BLUES. / ALL MAMA'S CHILDREN** – 70

Nov 56. (7") **DIXIE FRIED. / I'M SORRY, I'M NOT SORRY** –

Apr 57. (7") **YOUR TRUE LOVE. / MATCHBOX** 67 Feb 57

May 57. (7") **THAT'S ALL RIGHT. / FOREVER YOURS** –

Dec 57. (7") **GLAD ALL OVER. / FOREVER YOURS** – –

Dec 57. (7") **GLAD ALL OVER. / LEND ME YOUR COMB** –

Apr 58. (7") **THAT'S ALL RIGHT. / LEND ME YOUR COMB** – –

1958. (lp) **CARL PERKINS** (US-title 'CARL PERKINS' DANCE ALBUM – TEENBEAT') –
– Blue suede shoes / Movie Magg / Sure to fall / Gone gone gone / Honey don't / Only you / All mama's children / Tennessee / Wrong yo-yo / Everybody's trying to be my baby / Matchbox / Your true love / Boppin' the blues. *(UK-iss.Nov59 on 'London') (UK-iss.'THE DANCE ALBUM' Jul81 on 'Charly', cd-iss.Apr87 on 'Topline')*

Philips Columbia

Apr 58. (7") **PINK PEDAL PUSHERS. / JIVE AFTER JIVE** – 91

Aug 58. (7") **LEVI JACKET. / POP, LET ME HAVE THE CAR** –

—— In Oct'58, brother JAY died of cancer, after a car accident 2 years prev.

Feb 59. (7") **Y-O-U. / THIS LIFE I LEAD** –

May 59. (7") **POINTED TOE SHOES. / HIGHWAY OF LOVE** – 93

Jan 60. (7") **ONE TICKET TO LONELINESS. / I DON'T SEE ME IN YOUR ARMS ANYMORE** Oct 59

1960. (7") **L-O-V-E-V-I-L-L-E. / TOO MUCH FOR A MAN TO UNDERSTAND** –

1960. (7") **HONEY, 'CAUSE I LOVE YOU. / JUST FOR YOU** –

Sep 61. (7") **ANYWAY THE WIND BLOWS. / THE UNHAPPY GIRLS** – Jul 61

1961. (7") **HOLLYWOOD CITY. / THE FOOL I USED TO BE** –

1962. (7") **HAMBONE. / TWISTER SISTER** –

1962. (7") **FORGET ME NEXT TIME AROUND. / I JUST CAN'T GET BACK FROM THERE** –

—— Next 45, featured The NASHVILE TEENS.

Brunswick Decca

1963. (7") **HELP ME FIND MY BABY. / FOR A LITTLE WHILE** –

1963. (7") **AFTER SUNDOWN. / I WOULDN'T HAVE YOU**

Apr 64. (7") **HELP ME FIND MY BABY. / I WOULDN'T HAVE YOU** –

Jun 64. (7") **BIG BAD BLUES. / LONELY HEART**

Nov 64. (7") **THE MONKEY SHINE. / LET MY BABY BE**

1964. (7") **MAMA OF MY SONG. / ONE OF THESE DAYS** –

—— CARL became live guitarist for friend and country singer JOHNNY CASH, as well as continuing solo, signing for . . .

Realm not issued

1966. (lp) **WHOLE LOTTA CARL PERKINS** –
– Whole lotta shakin' goin' on / Tutti frutti / Shake, rattle and roll / Sittin' on top of the world / Ready Teddy / Long tall Sally / That's all right / Where the Rio Rosa flows / Good rockin' tonight / I got a woman / Hey, good lookin' / Jenny, Jenny.

Stateside Dollie

Mar 67. (7") **A COUNTRY BOY'S DREAM. / IF I COULD COME BACK**

1967. (7") **SHINE, SHINE, SHINE. / ALMOST LOVE** –

1967. (7") **WITHOUT YOU. / YOU CAN TAKE THE BOY OUT OF THE COUNTRY** –

Spark / Dollie

·1968. (7") **MY OLD HOMETOWN. / BACK TO TENNESSEE** [-] [ ]

London / Dollie

May 68. (7") **LAKE COUNTY COTTON COUNTRY. / IT'S YOU** [ ] [ ]

Sep 68. (lp) **COUNTRY BOY'S DREAMS** [ ] [ ]
– Country boys's dreams / If I could come back / Sweet misery / Stateside / Detroit City / Unmitigated gall / Shine, shine, shine / Dream on little dreamer / You can take the boy out of the door / The star of the show / Home (that's where the heart is) / Poor boy blues. *(cd-iss.May92 with extra tracks)*

C.B.S. / Columbia

Feb 69. (7") **RESTLESS. / 1143** [ ] [ ] 1968
1969. (7") **FOR YOUR LOVE. / FOUR LETTER WORD** [-] [ ]
1969. (7") **SOUL BEAT. / C.C.RIDER (YOU'RE SO BAD)** [-] [ ]
1969. (lp) **ON TOP** [-] [ ]
– Superfool / I'm gonna set my foot down / A lion in the jungle / Baby, what you want me to do / Soul beat / Riverboat Annie / Champaign, Illinois / Power of my soul / Brown-eyed handsome man / C.C.rider *(UK-iss.1972 as 'BROWN-EYED HANDSOME MAN')*

— Next with country rock revival band **N.B.R.Q.; STEVE FERGUSON** – guitar / **JODY ST.NICHOLAS** – bass / **TOM STANLEY** – drums / **DON ADAMS** – trombone / **FRANK GADLER**

Mar 70. (lp) **BOPPIN' THE BLUES** [ ] [ ]
– Blue suede shoes / I'm sorry, I'm not sorry / Let the juke box keep on playing / All mama's children / Honey don't / Dixie fried / Boppin' the blues / Your true love / That's alright / Matchbox / Lend me your comb / Gone, gone, gone. *(re-iss.Nov84 on 'Topline')*

May 70. (7") **ALL MAMA'S CHILDREN. / STEP ASIDE** [ ] [ ]
1970. (7") **STATE OF CONFUSION. / MY SON MY SUN** [-] [ ]
1970. (7") **JUST AS LONG. / WHAT EVERY BOY OUGHT TO KNOW** [-] [ ]
1971. (7") **ME WITHOUT YOU. / RED HEADED WOMAN** [-] [ ]
1971. (7") **COTTON TOP. / ABOUT ALL I CAN GIVE YOU IS LOVE** [-] [ ]
1971. (7") **HIGH ON LOVE. / TAKE ME BACK TO MEMPHIS** [-] [ ]
1971. (7") **SOMEDAY. / THE TRIP** [-] [ ]

Mercury / Mercury

1974. (7") **HELP ME DREAM. / YOU TORE MY HEAVEN ALL TO HELL** [-] [ ]

Mar 74. (lp)(c) **MY KIND OF COUNTRY** [ ] [ ]
– (Let's get) Dixiefried / You tore my Heaven to hell / Love sweet love / One more loser going home / Just as long / Goin' to Memphis / Never look back / Honky tonk song / Lord, I sinned again last night / Help me dream / Ruby, don't take your love to town.

1974. (7") **(LET'S GET) DIXIE FRIED. / ONE MORE LOSER GOIN' HOME** [-] [ ]
1974. (7") **RUBY (DON'T TAKE YOUR LOVE TO TOWN). / SING MY SONG** [-] [ ]

— In Dec'74, his brother CLAYTON, takes his own life.

1975. (7") **YOU'LL ALWAYS BE A LADY TO ME. / LOW CLASS** [-] [ ]
Oct 77. (7") **THE EP EXPRESS. / BIG BAD BLUES** [-] [ ]

— (above was a tribute to the recently departed ELVIS PRESLEY)

— toured with sons **GREG** – bass / **STAN** – drums, plus **LEE McALPIN** – piano / **DAVID SEA** – saxophone

not issued / Suede

1976. (lp) **CARL PERKINS SHOW (live)** [-] [ ]

not issued / Musichill

1970's. (7") **BORN TO BOOGIE. / TAKE ME BACK** [-] [ ]

Jet / Jet

Mar 78. (7"m) **BLUE SUEDE SHOES. / THAT'S ALL RIGHT / ROCK ON AROUND THE WORLD** [ ] [ ]

Mar 78. (lp)(c) **OL' BLUE SUEDES IS BACK** [38] [ ]
– Rock around the clock / That's alright mama / Kaw-liga / Tutti frutti / I'm in love again / Blue suede shoes / Be-bop-a-lula / Maybellene / Whole lotta shakin' goin' on / Hang up my rock'n'roll shoes / Shake, rattle and roll / Rock around the world.

Aug 78. (7") **MUSTANG WINE. / THE WHOLE WORLD MISSES YOU** [ ] [-]

Nov 80. (7"ep) **TWENTY-FIVE** [ ] [-]
– Lovesick blues / Turn around / Miss misunderstood / Blue suede shoes.

— Next album 'THE SURVIVORS' in May '82 was shared with **JOHNNY CASH** and **JERRY LEE LEWIS** and issued on 'CBS'.

— The previous year, CARL guested on album 'Tug Of War' w / PAUL McCARTNEY. In 1985, he appeared in the John Landis film 'Into The Night'. Later that year, a British TV special 'BLUE SUEDE SHOES' is recorded with many rock celebrities incl. GEORGE HARRISON, RINGO STARR, ERIC CLAPTON, DAVE EDMUNDS, etc.

M.C.A. / M.C.A.

Mar 86. (lp)(c) **CARL PERKINS** [ ] [ ]
– Matchbox / If I had a' known / Green green grass of home / Texas woman / Signs / Blue sued shoes / Honey don't / I'm walking / Matchbox / Susie Q / Memphis / Maybellene / Slippin' and slidin' / Be-bop-a-lula / Roll over Beethoven / Hound dog / Whole lotta shakin' goin' on / Lucille / Jailhouse rock / All shook up / That's alright mama / Bird dog / Rock Island line.

Universal / Universal

Jun 89. (lp)(c)(cd) **BORN TO ROCK** (with the JORDANAIRES) [ ] [ ]
– Born to rock / Charlene / The rain / Might wash your love away / Hambone / A lifetime last night / Cotton top / Baby, please answer the phone / Till I couldn't stand no more / Don't let go / Love makes dreams come true.

– (UK) compilations, others, etc. –

May 68. London; (7") **BLUE SUEDE SHOES. / MATCHBOX** [ ] [-]
(re-iss.Jul76 & Feb78 on 'Charly')
May 68. CBS/ US= Columbia; (lp) **KING OF ROCK** [ ] [ ]
Aug 69. CBS/ US= Columbia; (lp) **CARL PERKINS' GREATEST HITS** [ ] [ ]
(re-iss.Jul77 on 'CBS-Embassy')
May 77. Embassy; (lp) **LONG TALL SALLY** [ ] [-]
Oct 70. Sun; (lp) **ORIGINAL GOLDEN HITS** [ ] [-]
Oct 70. Sun; (7") **BLUE SUEDE SHOES. / ONLY YOU** [ ] [-]
Feb 71. Sun; (lp) **BLUE SUEDE SHOES** [ ] [-]
Jan 82. Sun; (3xlp-box) **THE SUN YEARS** [ ] [-]
(cd-box iss.Feb90)
Aug 88. Sun; (lp) **BLUE SUEDE SHOES** [ ] [-]
Aug 88. Sun; (lp) **PUT YOUR CAT CLOTHES ON** [ ] [-]
Dec 76. Charly; (7"ep) **BOPPIN' THE BLUES** [ ] [-]
– Boppin' the blues / Dixie fried / Sure to fall / Movie Magg.
Feb 78. Charly; (lp) **THE ROCKIN' GUITARMAN** [ ] [-]
(re-iss.1982) (re-iss.Sep83 on 'Magnum F.')(cd-iss.Feb93)
Mar 78. Charly; (lp) **THE ORIGINAL CARL PERKINS** [ ] [-]
Jul 78. Charly; (7"ep) **PUT YOU CAT CLOTHES ON** [ ] [-]
– Put your cat clothes on / Right string but the wrong yo-yo / Tennessee / Honey don't.
1978. Charly; (7") **BLUE SUEDE SHOES. / MATCHBOX** [ ] [-]
Sep 78. Charly; (lp) **SUN SOUNDS SPECIAL** [ ] [-]
Jan 82. Charly; (10"lp) **HEP CATS SESSION ("& SONNY BURGESS")** [ ] [-]
Mar 86. Charly; (cd) **DIXIE FRIED** [ ] [-]
Feb 89. Charly; (cd-ep) **BLUE SUEDE SHOES / BOPPIN' THE BLUES / HONEY DON'T / EVERYBODY'S TRYING TO BE MY BABY** [ ] [-]
Jan 90. Charly; (cd-box) **THE CARL PERKINS CD BOX SET** [ ] [-]
Apr 77. MCA; (7"m) **THE MONKEY SHINE. / AFTER SUNDOWN / BIG BAD BLUES** [ ] [-]
Aug 83. Cambra; (d-lp) **CARL PERKINS** [ ] [-]
Nov 83. Bulldog; (lp)(c) **20 GOLDEN PIECES OF CARL PERKINS** [ ] [-]
Apr 84. Allegience; (lp)(c) **THE HEART AND SOUL OF CARL PERKINS** [ ] [-]
Sep 84. Boplicity; (lp) **INTRODUCING CARL PERKINS** [ ] [-]
Nov 84. Astan; (lp) **DISCIPLE IN BLUE SUEDE SHOES** [ ] [-]
Nov 84. Astan; (lp) **SWEETER THAN CANDY** [ ] [-]
Nov 84. Warwick; (lp)(c) **THE CARL PERKINS' ROCK'N'ROLL PARTY** [ ] [-]
Sep 85. Cultue; (lp) **TURN AROUND** [ ] [-]
Nov 85. Network; (d-lp)(d-c) **ROCKIN' THE HOUSE DOWN** [ ] [-]
Feb 86. Magnum Force; (lp) **GOIN' BACK TO MEMPHIS** [ ] [-]
1986. Magnum Force; (7"ep) **ROCK AND ROLL & COUNTRY SOUL** [ ] [-]
– Didn't the 50's rock / Country soul / I don't like what I'm seeing in you.
Oct 86. Magnum Force; (d-lp) **THE MAN & THE LEGEND** [ ] [-]
(cd-iss.May95)
Jan 93. Magnum Force; (cd) **FRIENDS, FAMILY & LEGENDS** [ ] [-]
Oct 87. Demand; (lp) **MR.COUNTRY ROCK** [ ] [-]
1987. Old Gold; (7") **BLUE SUEDE SHOES. / THAT'S ALL RIGHT** [ ] [-]
May 88. Rhino; (cd-ep) **LIL' BIT OF GOLD** [ ] [-]
– Blue suede shoes / Honey don't / Everybody's trying to be my baby / Matchbox.
1988. Country Store; (lp)(c)(cd) **CARL PERKINS** [ ] [-]
1988. Joker; (lp)(c) **EVERY ROAD** [-] [-]
1988. Joker; (lp) **GOIN' BACK TO MEMPHIS VOL.2** [-] [-]
1988. Ditto; (d-c) **CARL PERKINS** [-] [-]
Apr 89. Rounder; (lp) **HONKY TONK GAL** [-] [-]
Jun 89. Ocean; (lp)(c)(cd) **THE CLASSIC CARL PERKINS** [ ] [-]
Feb 90. Instant; (cd)(c)(lp) **TENNESSEE BOP** [ ] [-]
Nov 86. Bear Family; (cd) **UP THROUGH THE YEARS 1954-1957** [ ] [-]
Apr 90. Bear Family; (5xlp-box) **THE CLASSIC CARL PERKINS** [ ] [-]
May 90. Pickwick; (cd)(c) **THE LEGENDARY CARL PERKINS** [ ] [-]
– Born to boogie / I can feel it / Don't get off gettin' it on / Take me back / Redneck / The hurt put on by you / Sweeter than candy / Boppin' the blues / We did it in '54 / Mama / Standing in the need of love / What am I living for / '21 / Country soul / Georgia courtroom / I didn't want to fall in love again. *(re-iss.Jun91)*
Apr 93. Sony; (cd) **RESTLESS** [ ] [-]
Nov 93. Fat Boy; (cd) **ROCK'N'ROLL GREATS** [ ] [-]
May 94. Charly; (cd) **TWO ON ONE** (w / JERRY LEE LEWIS) [ ] [-]
Jul 94. Success; (cd)(c) **THIS OLD HOUSE** [ ] [-]
Nov 94. Music Club; (cd)(c) **THE SUN SESSIONS** [ ] [-]
Feb 95. Marble Arch; (cd) **THE BEST OF CARL PERKINS** [ ] [-]
Apr 95. Muskateer; (cd)(c) **HOUND DOG** [ ] [-]
May 95. Pickwick; (cd)(c) **KING OF ROCKABILLY** [ ] [-]
Jul 95. Charly; (cd) **THE ROCKBILLY KING** [ ] [-]
Jul 95. Charly; (cd) **BOPPIN' BLUE SUEDE SHOES** [ ] [-]
Jul 95. Summit; (cd) **LUE SUEDE SHOES** [ ] [-]

Mark PERRY (see under ⇒ ALTERNATIVE TV)

Steve PERRY (see under ⇒ JOURNEY)

Mike PETERS (see under ⇒ ALARM)

PET SHOP BOYS

Formed: London, England . . . Aug'81 by assistant editor of Smash Hits NEIL TENNANT and CHRIS LOWE (ex-DUST). After 2 years making demos, they met disco producer Bobby 'O' Orlando, and worked on debut 1984 'Epic' single 'WEST END GIRLS'. After it flopped in Britain (it was a French & Belguin hit), they signed with manager Tom Watkins, who attained a deal with 'Parlophone' early in 1985. Their first 45 for the label 'OPPORTUNITIES' failed to make impact, but early the next year a Stephen Hague produced remake of 'WEST END GIRLS', finally gave them major breakthrough, hitting No.1 in many countries including UK + US. They soon became top stars of the 80's, hitting UK top spot again another 3 times with 'IT'S A SIN', 'ALWAYS

ON MY MIND' & 'HEART'. • **Style:** Intelligent and classy electro-pop disco rock duo, with perfectionist production and social comment lyrics their forte. • **Songwriters:** All written by duo, except ALWAYS ON MY MIND (Elvis Presley) / WHERE THE STREETS HAVE NO NAME (U2) / CAN'T TAKE MY EYES OFF YOU (Frankie Valli). • **Trivia:** Early in 1988, they produced EIGHTH WONDER's (w / Patsy Kensit) first Top 10 hit 'I'm Not Scared'. The following year, they were behind the controls for the rejuvenated careers of DUSTY SPRINGFIELD (Nothing Has Been Proved) and LISA MINNELLI (Losing My Mind).

Recommended: DISCOGRAPHY – THE COMPLETE SINGLES COLLECTION (*9) / VERY (*7)

NEIL TENNANT (b.10 Jul'54, Gosforth, Northumberland, England) – vocals / **CHRIS LOWE** (b. 4 Oct'59, Blackpool, England) – keyboards, synthesizers

Epic Bobcat 12"

Apr 84. (7")(12") **WEST END GIRLS. / PET SHOP BOYS** [ ] [-]

Parlophone EMI Amer..

Jun 85. (7") **OPPORTUNITIES (LET'S MAKE LOTS OF MONEY). / IN THE NIGHT** [ ] [ ]
(12") – ('A'dance mix). / ('B'extended).
(12") – ('A' Latin version). / ('B'dub for money remix).

Nov 85. (7")(7"pic-d) **WEST END GIRLS. / A MAN COULD GET ARRESTED** [1] [1] Feb 86
(10") – ('A'remixed). / ('B'extended).
(12"+=) – ('A'dance mix).
(12") – ('A' Shep Pettibone mix). / (A'dub mix) / ('B'extended).

Mar 86. (7") **LOVE COMES QUICKLY. / THAT'S MY IMPRESSION** [19] [62] Aug 86
(10")(12") – ('A'dance mix). / ('B'disco mix).

Mar 86. (lp)(c)(cd) **PLEASE** [3] [7]
– Two divide by zero / West End girls / Opportunities (let's make lots of money) / Love comes quickly / Suburbia / Tonight is forever / Violence / I want a lover / Later tonight / Why don't we live together / Opportunities (reprise).

May 86. (7") **OPPORTUNITIES (LET'S MAKE LOTS OF MONEY) (remix). / WAS THAT WHAT IT WAS** [11] [10]
(12") – ('A'&'B' Shep Pettibone mastermixes) / Opportunities (original dance mix) / Opportunities (reprise Shep Pettibone mix).

Sep 86. (7") **SUBURBIA. / PANINARO** [8] [70] Nov 86
('A'full horror mix – 12") – Jack the lad.
(c-s++=) – Love comes quickly (Shep Pettibone remix).
(c-s) – ('A'-J.Mendelsohn remixed) (was 'A'side + others)
(d7") – (same as above 4) (+=) – Suburbia pt.2.

Nov 86. (lp)(c)(cd) **DISCO** (The 12"mixes) [15] [95]
– In the night / Suburbia / Opportunities / Paninaro / Love comes quickly / West end girls.

Jun 87. (7") **IT'S A SIN. / YOU KNOW WHERE YOU WENT WRONG** [1] [9] Aug 87
(12"+=)(c-s+=)(cd-s+=) – ('A'disco mix).
(12") – ('A'-Ian Levene remix). / ('B'-rough mix).

Aug 87. (7") **WHAT HAVE I DONE TO DESERVE THIS? (by "PET SHOP BOYS & DUSTY SPRINGFIELD"). / A NEW LIFE** [2] [2] Dec 87
('A'ext-12"+=)(c-s+=)(cd-s+=) – ('A'disco mix).

Sep 87. (lp)(c)(cd) **ACTUALLY** [2] [25]
– One more chance / What have I done to deserve this? / Shopping / Rent / Hit music / It couldn't happen here / It's a sin / I want to wake up / Heart / King's Cross. *(re-iss.May88 w/free US 12" or cd-s)*

Oct 87. (7") **RENT. / I WANT A DOG** [8] [ ]
(12"+=)(c-s+=)(cd-s) – ('A'extended). / ('B'side) / ('A'dub version).

Nov 87. (7") **ALWAYS ON MY MIND. / DO I HAVE TO?** [1] [4] Mar 88
(12"+=)(c-s+=)(cd-s+=) – ('A'extended dance mix).
(12") – ('A' Phil Harding remix). / ('A'dub) / ('B'side).

Mar 88. (7") **HEART. / I GET EXCITED (YOU GET EXCITED TOO)** [1] [ ]
(12")(c-s)(cd-s) – ('A'disco mix). / ('B'side) / ('A'dance mix).
(12") – ('A' J.Mendelsohn mix). / ('A'dub mix) / ('B'side).

Jun 88. (7")(12"(c-s)(cd-s) **ACTUALLY. / ALWAYS ON MY MIND** [ ] [ ]

Sep 88. (7") **DOMINO DANCING. / DON JUAN** [7] [18]
(12")(c-s)(cd-s) – ('A'&'B'disco mixes) / ('A'alternative mixes).
(12") – ('A'remix). / ('A'&'B'demos).

Oct 88. (lp)(c)(cd) **INTROSPECTIVE** (12"mixes) [2] [34]
– Left to my own devices / I want a dog / Domino dancing / I'm not scared / Always on my mind – In my house / It's alright. *(re-iss.as 3x12" Mar89) (re-iss.cd+c Mar94)*

Nov 88. (7") **LEFT TO MY OWN DEVICES. / THE SOUND OF THE ATOM SPLITTING** [4] [84] Jan 89
(12"+=)(c-s+=)(cd-s+=) – ('A'disco mixes).

Jun 89. (7")(c-s)(ext.-12")(ext-cd-s) **IT'S ALRIGHT. / ONE OF THE CROWD / YOUR FUNNY UNCLE** [5] [ ]
(10") – ('A'alternative mix). / ('A'extended dance mix).
(12") – ('A' Tyree mix). / ('A' Sterling Void mix).

— NEIL and CHRIS had guested late '89-91 for BERNARD SUMNER & JOHNNY MARR on their ELECTRONIC project. (see ⇒ NEW ORDER)

— On tour augmented by **COURTNEY PINE / PETE GLEADALAS / DANNY CUMMINGS**

— next featured **JOHNNY MARR** – guitar

Sep 90. (7")(c-s) **SO HARD. / IT MUST BE OBVIOUS** [4] [62]
(12"+=) – ('A'dub mix).
(cd-s++=) – ('A'dance mix).

Oct 90. (cd)(c)(lp) **BEHAVIOUR** [2] [45]
– Being boring / This must be the place I waited years to leave / To face the truth / How can you expect to be taken seriously? / Only the wind / My October symphony / So hard / Nervously / The end of the world / Jealousy.

Nov 90. (7")(c-s) **BEING BORING. / WE ALL FEEL BETTER IN THE DARK** [20] [ ]
(12"+=)(cd-s+=) – ('A'&'B'extended mixes).

Feb 91. (c-s) **HOW CAN YOU EXPECT TO BE TAKEN SERIOUSLY. /** [-] [93]

Mar 91. (7")(c-s) **WHERE THE STREETS HAVE NO NAME – CAN'T TAKE MY EYES OFF YOU. / HOW CAN YOU EXPECT TO BE TAKEN SERIOUSLY (remix)** [4] [72]
(ext-'A'12"+=)(cd-s+=) – But she's not your girlfriend.
(cd-s+=) – ('B'classical).

May 91. (7")(c-s) **JEALOUSY. / LOSING MY MIND** [12] [ ]
(12"+=)(cd-s+=) – ('A'&'B'extended).
(cd-s+=) – This must be the place / Waited for the years to leave (extended) / So hard (eclipsed mix).

May 91. (c-s) **WHERE THE STREETS HAVE NO NAME – I CAN'T TAKE MY EYES OFF YOU** [-] [ ]

Oct 91. (7") **DJ CULTURE. / MUSIC FOR BOYS** [13] [ ]
(12"+=)(c-s+=)(cd-s+=) – ('A' II version).

Nov 91. (cd)(c)(lp) **DISCOGRAPHY – THE COMPLETE SINGLES COLLECTION** (compilation) [3] [ ]
– West End girls / Love comes quickly / Opportunities (let's make lots of money) / Suburbia / It's a sin / What have I done to deserve this? / Rent / Always on my mind / Heart / Domino dancing / Left to my own devices / It's alright / So hard / Being boring / Where the streets have no name (I can't take my eyes off you)/ Jealousy / DJ culture / Was it worth it?.

Dec 91. (7")(c-s) **WAS IT WORTH IT? / MISERABLISM** [24] [ ]
(12"+=)(cd-s+=) – ('A'remixes).

Jun 93. (7")(c-s) **CAN YOU FORGIVE HER? / HEY, HEADMASTER** [7] [ ]
(12"+=)(cd-s+=) – ('A'rollo remix) / ('A'rollo dub).
(cd-s) – ('A'remix) / I want to wake up (Johnny Marr remix) / What keeps mankind alive? / ('A' MK dub).

Sep 93. (7")(c-s) **GO WEST. / SHAMELESS** [2] [ ]
(12"+=)(cd-s+=) – ('A'mixes).

Oct 93. (cd)(c)(lp) **VERY** [1] [20]
– Can you forgive her? / I wouldn't normally do this kind of thing / Liberation / A different point of view / Dreaming of the Queen / Yesterday, when I was mad / The theatre / One and one make five / To speak is a sin / Young offender / One in a million / Go west. *(free-cd)* **RELENTLESS** – My head is spinning / Forever is love / KDX 125 / We came from outer space / The man who has everything / One thing leads to another.

Dec 93. (7")(c-s) **I WOULDN'T NORMALLY DO THIS KIND OF THING. / TOO MANY PEOPLE** [13] [ ]
(cd-s+=) – Violence (Hacienda mix) / West End girls (Sasha mix).
(cd-s) – ('A'side) / ('A'mixes).

Re-issued all 14 singles from 1987-1992 on cd-ep's Nov93.

Apr 94. (7")(c-s) **LIBERATION. / DECADENCE** [14] [ ]
(cd-s+=) – ('A'-E Smoove mix).
(cd-s)(d12") – ('A'-Murk mix) / ('B'unplugged mix) / Young offender (jam & spoon mix).

— Below a second Comic Relief charity single, featuring vox from the TV series of that name; JENNIFER 'Edina' SAUNDERS and JOANNA 'Patsy' LUMLEY.

May 94. (7")(c-s) **ABSOLUTELY FABULOUS (by ABSOLUTELY FABULOUS). / ('A'mix)** [6] [-]
(cd-s+=) – ('A'mixes).

Sep 94. (c-s) **YESTERDAY, WHEN I WAS MAD. / EUROBOY** [13] [ ]
(cd-s) – ('A'side) / If love were all / Can you forgive her? (swing version) / ('A'-Jam & Spoon mix).
(cd-s) – ('A'-Coconut 1 remix) / ('A'-Junior Vasquez dub & RAF zone mix) / Some speculation.
(12") – ('A'-Jam & Spoon mix) / ('A'-Junior Vasquez dub & RAF zone mix).

Sep 94. (cd)(c)(lp) **DISCO 2** (remixes) [6] [75]

Jul 95. (c-s) **PANINARO '95 / IN THE NIGHT** [15] [ ]
(cd-s+=) – Girls and boys (live in Rio).
(12") – ('A'-Tracy's mix) / ('A'-Sharon's Sexy Boyz dub) / ('A'-Tin Tin Out mix) / ('A'extended).
(12") – ('A'-Angel Morales deep dance mix) / ('A'-Girls Boys in dub mix) / ('A'-Hot'n'spicy dub mix).

Aug 95. (d-cd)(d-c)(t-lp) **ALTERNATIVE** (B-sides) [2] [ ]
– In the night / A man could get arrested / That's my impression / Was that what it was? / Paninaro / Jack the lad / You know where you went wrong / A new life / I want a dog / Do I have to? / I get excited (you get excited too) / Don Juan / The sound of the atom splitting / One of the crowd / Your funny uncle. // It must be obvious / We all feel better in the dark / Bet she's not your girlfriend / Losing my mind / Music for boys / Miserablism / Hey, headmaster / What keeps mankind alive? / Shameless / Too many people / Violence (Hacienda version) / Decadence / If love were all / Euroboy / Some speculation.

Tom PETTY

Born: 20 Oct'53, Gainesville, Florida, USA. In 1968, he formed school band The SUNDOWNERS, who later became The EPICS. In 1971, they evolved into MUDCRUTCH who also had in their ranks MIKE CAMPBELL – guitar, TOMMY LEADON (brother of EAGLES man BERNIE) – lead guitar & RANDALL MARSH – drums. They made demo tape, which was heard by Denny Cordell's 'Shelter' records, who signed band in 1975. They released a single 'DEPOT STREET', and recorded an album which did not see the light of day due to their demise. PETTY was retained by Shelter in 1976, and he instigated The HEARTBREAKERS, with CAMPBELL and TENCH, plus RON BLAIR, STAN LYNCH and JEFF JOURARD. The latter soon left to form The MOTELS with brother Marty. Late '76 the album 'TOM PETTY & THE HEARTBREAKERS' was released, but it initially flopped until it is resurrected by well-received tour of US in summer of '77. They had already hit UK Top 40, with 2 classic singles 'ANYTHING THAT'S ROCK'N'ROLL' & 'AMERICAN GIRL'. In May78, their first US Top 40 hit 'BREAKDOWN', was used on the movie 'FM'. Two months later their second album 'YOU'RE GONNA GET IT', hit both US & UK Top 40. A year on, PETTY filed for bankruptcy owing more than half a million dollars, due to Shelter being sold to 'ABC' and then 'MCA', who sued him for breach of contract. Luckily they came to an agreement, when MCA decided to put band on their Danny Bramson run 'Backstreet' label. Their first output late 1979 'DAMN THE TORPEDOES', sold only moderately in the UK, but smashed into the US Top 3, due to lifted Top 10 cut 'DON'T DO ME LIKE THAT'. • **Style:** Influenced by the early BYRDS, but soon became embodiment of US mainstream rock. • **Songwriters:** PETTY wrote material, except; SO YOU WANT TO BE A ROCK'N'ROLL STAR (Byrds) / NEEDLES AND PINS (Searchers) /FEEL A WHOLE LOT BETTER (Byrds) / SOMETHING IN THE AIR (Thunderclap Newman). • **Trivia:** In 1983, PETTY produced DEL SHANNON's 'Drop Down And Get Me', with backing from The HEARTBREAKERS. In 1985, PETTY co-produced album 'SOUTHERN ACCENTS' with Jimmy Iovine and Eurythmics guitarist Dave Stewart.

Recommended: GREATEST HITS (*9) / DAMN THE TORPEDOES (*8) / FULL MOON FEVER (*7) / TOM PETTY & THE HEARTBREAKERS (*6)

TOM PETTY AND THE HEARTBREAKERS

TOM PETTY – vocals, guitar (ex-MUDCRUTCH) / **MIKE CAMPBELL** (b. 1 Feb'54, Panama City, Florida) – guitar (ex-MUDCRUTCH) / **BELMONT TENCH** (b. 7 Sep'54, Gainesville) – keyboards (ex-MUDCRUTCH) / **RON BLAIR** (b.16 Sep'52, Macon, Georgia, USA) – bass / **STAN LYNCH** (b.21 May'55, Gainsville) – drums

		Island	Shelter
Jan 77.	(7") **BREAKDOWN. / THE WILD ONE, FOREVER**	-	
Feb 77.	(7") **AMERICAN GIRL. / THE WILD ONE, FOREVER**		-
May 77.	(lp)(c) **TOM PETTY AND THE HEARTBREAKERS** – Rockin' around (with you) / Breakdown / Hometown blues / The wild one, forever / Anything that's rock'n'roll / Strangered in the night / Fooled again (I don't like it) / Mystery man / Luna / American girl. *(cd-iss.Jul87 on 'MCA')*	24	55
May 77.	(7") **AMERICAN GIRL. / FOOLED AGAIN (I DON'T LIKE IT)**	-	
Jun 77.	(7")(12") **ANYTHING THAT'S ROCK'N'ROLL. / FOOLED AGAIN (I DON'T LIKE IT)**	36	
Jul 77.	(7")(12") **AMERICAN GIRL. / LUNA**	40	-
Oct 77.	(7") **BREAKDOWN. / FOOL AGAIN (I DON'T LIKE IT)**	-	40
May 78.	(lp)(c) **YOU'RE GONNA GET IT** – When the time comes / You're gonna get it / Hurt / Magnolia / Too much ain't enough / I need to know / Listen to her heart / No second thoughts / Restless / Baby's a rock'n'roller. *(cd-iss.Jun88 on 'MCA')*	34	23
Jun 78.	(7")(12")**I NEED TO KNOW. / NO SECOND THOUGHTS**		41
Sep 78.	(7")(12")**LISTEN TO HER HEART. / I DON'T KNOW WHAT TO SAY TO YOU**		59
		M.C.A.	Backstreet
Nov 79.	(lp)(c) **DAMN THE TORPEDOES** – Refugee / Here comes my girl / Even the losers / Century city / Don't do me like that / Shadows of a doubt (a complex kind) / What are you doin' in my life? / Louisiana rain / You tell me. *(re-iss,+cd.Oct87, cd-iss.Jul88 + 89)*	57	2
Nov 79.	(7") **HERE COMES MY GIRL. / DON'T BRING ME DOWN** (12"+=) – Casa Dega.		59 Apr 80
Feb 80.	(7")(7"pic-d) **REFUGEE. / IT'S RAINING AGAIN**		15 Jan 80
Jul 80.	(7") **DON'T DO ME LIKE THAT. / CENTURY CITY** (d7"+=) – Somethin' else / Stories we can tell.		10 Nov 79

— **DONALD DUNN** – bass replaced RON BLAIR

Apr 81.	(7") **THE WAITING. / NIGHTWATCHMAN**		19
May 81.	(lp)(c) **HARD PROMISES** – The waiting / A woman in love (it's not me) / Nightwatchman / Something big / King's road / Letting you go / A thing about you / Insider / The criminal kind / You can still change your mind. *(re-iss.+cd.May86, re-cd.1988)*	32	5
Jul 81.	(7") **A WOMAN IN LOVE (IT'S NOT ME). / GATOR ON THE LAWN**		79

— PETTY and his band then were credited with backing STEVIE NICKS of FLEETWOOD MAC on a single 'Stop Draggin' My Heart Around' Aug81 hit US No.3.

Jul 82.	(7") **REFUGEE. / THE INSIDER ("with STEVIE NICKS")**		

— **HOWARD EPSTEIN** – bass repl. DUNN

Nov 82.	(7") **YOU GOT LUCKY. / BETWEEN TWO WORLDS**		20
Nov 82.	(lp)(c) **LONG AFTER DARK** – A one story town / You got lucky / Deliver me / Change of heart / Finding out / We stand a chance / Straight into darkness / The same old you / Between two worlds / A wasted life. *(re-iss.May86, cd-iss.Oct87)*	45	9
Dec 82.	(7") **STRAIGHT INTO DARKNESS. / HEARTBREAKERS BEACH PARTY**		
Apr 83.	(7") **CHANGE OF HEART. / HEARTBREAKERS BEACH PARTY**		21 Feb 83
Apr 85.	(7")(12") **DON'T COME AROUND HERE NO MORE. / TRAILER**	50	13 Mar 85
Apr 85.	(lp)(c) **SOUTHERN ACCENTS** – Rebels / It ain't nothin' to me / Don't come around here no more / Southern accents / Make it better (forget about me) / Spike / Dogs on the run / Mary's new car / The best of everything. *(cd-iss.1986)*	23	7
Jun 85.	(7") **MAKE IT BETTER (FORGET ABOUT ME). / CRACKING UP** (12") – ('A'side) / ('A'instrumental).		54
Aug 85.	(7") **REBELS. / SOUTHERN ACCENTS (live)**	-	74
Jan 86.	(d-lp)(d-c) **PACK UP THE PLANTATION (live)** – So you want to be a rock'n'roll star / Needles and pins / The waiting / Breakdown / American girl / It ain't nothin' to me / Insider / Rockin' around (with you) / Refugee / I need to know * / Southern accents / Rebels / Don't bring me down / You got lucky * / Shout / The stories we can tell. *(cd-iss.Oct87, omits *)*		22 Dec 85
Jan 86.	(7") **NEEDLES AND PINS (live). / SPIKE (live)**	-	37
Feb 86.	(7") **SO WANT TO BE A ROCK'N'ROLL STAR (live). / AMERICAN GIRL (live)** (12"+=) – Spike (live).		-
Aug 86.	(7")(12") **BAND OF THE HAND. ("with BOB DYLAN") / THEME FROM 'JOE'S DEATH'**		
Apr 87.	(7") **JAMMIN' ME. / LET ME UP (I'VE HAD ENOUGH)** (12"+=) – Make that connection.		18
Apr 87.	(lp)(c)(cd) **LET ME UP (I'VE HAD ENOUGH)** – Jammin' me / Runaway trains / The damage you've done / It'll all work out / My life – Your world / Think about me / All mixed up / A self made man / Ain't love strange / How many more days / Let me up (I've had enough).	59	20
Sep 87.	(7") **ALL MIXED UP. / LET ME UP (I'VE HAD ENOUGH)** (12"+=) – Little bit of soul.		
Nov 87.	(7") **THINK ABOUT ME. / MY LIFE – YOUR WORLD** (12"+=) – The damage you've done.		

In 1988, before he went solo, TOM PETTY teamed up with BOB DYLAN, GEORGE HARRISON, JEFF LYNNE and ROY ORBISON in The TRAVELLING WILBURYS (see ⇒)

TOM PETTY

solo with **JEFF LYNNE** – guitar, bass keyboards, vocals, co-writer / **MIKE CAMPBELL** – guitar, bass mandolin, keyboards, co-writer / **PHIL JONES** – drums, percussion / +guests **GEORGE HARRISON, ROY ORBISON, BENMONT TENCH, JIM KELTNER, HOWIE EPSTIEN, KELSEY CAMPBELL.**

		M.C.A.	M.C.A.
Apr 89.	(7") **I WON'T BACK DOWN. / THE APARTMENT SONG** (12"+=)(cd-s+=) – Don't treat me like a stranger.	28	12
Jun 89.	(lp)(c)(cd) **FULL MOON FEVER** – Free fallin' / I won't back down / Love is a long road / A face in the crowd / Runnin' down a dream / Feel a whole lot better / Yer so bad / Depending on you / The apartment song / Alright for now / A mind with a heart of it's own / Zombie zoo.	8	3 May 89
Aug 89.	(7")(c-s) **RUNNIN' DOWN A DREAM. / ALRIGHT FOR NOW** (12"+=)(cd-s+=) – Down the line.	55	23 Jul 89
Nov 89.	(7") **FREE FALLIN'. / DOWN THE LINE**	-	7
Nov 89.	(7") **FREE FALLIN'. / LOVE IS A LONG ROAD** (12"+=)(cd-s+=) – ('A'live version).	64	-
Feb 90.	(c-s) **A FACE IN THE CROWD. / A MIND WITH A HEART OF ITS OWN**	-	46

TOM PETTY AND THE HEARTBREAKERS

(originals reformed)

		M.C.A.	M.C.A.
Jun 91.	(7")(c-s) **LEARNING TO FLY. / TOO GOOD TO BE TRUE** (12"+=)(cd-s+=) – Baby's a rock'n'roller / I need to know.	46	28
Jul 91.	(cd)(c)(lp) **INTO THE GREAT WIDE OPEN** – Learning to fly / Into the great wide open / Two gunslingers / The dark of the Sun / All or nothin' / All the wrong reasons / Too good to be true / Out in the cold / You and I will meet again / Makin' some noise / Built to last.	3	13
Aug 91.	(7")(c-s) **INTO THE GREAT WIDE OPEN. / MAKIN' SOME NOISE** (cd-s+=) – Strangered in the night / Listen to her heart.		92 Nov 91
Jan 92.	(7")(c-s) **KING'S HIGHWAY. / I WON'T BACK DOWN** (cd-s+=) – Into the great wide open / Learning to fly.		
Mar 92.	(7")(c-s) **TOO GOOD TO BE TRUE. / THE DARK SIDE OF THE SUN** (cd-s+=) – Hurt / Don't come around here no more. (cd-s+=) – Psychotic reaction / I'm tired / Lonely.	34	
Oct 93.	(7")(c-s) **SOMETHING IN THE AIR. / THE WAITING** (cd-s+=) – American girl.	53	
Nov 93.	(cd)(c)(lp) **GREATEST HITS** (compilation) – American girl / Breakdown / Anything that's rock'n'roll / Listen to her heart / I need to know / Refugee / Don't do me like that / Even the losers / Here comes my girl / The waiting / You got lucky / Don't come around here no more / I won't back down / Runnin' down a dream / Free fallin' / Learning to fly / Into the great wide open / Jane's last dance / Something in the air.	10	8
Feb 94.	(c-s) **MARY JANE'S LAST DANCE. / KING'S HIGHWAY (live)** (cd-s+=) – Make that connection (live) / Take out some insurance (live). (cd-s) – ('A'side) / Casa dega / Gator on the lawn / Down the line.	52	14
		Warners	Warners
Oct 94.	(c-s) **YOU DON'T KNOW HOW IT FEELS. / HOUSE IN THE WOODS** (cd-s+=) – Girl on L.S.D.		13
Nov 94.	(cd)(c)(lp) **WILDFLOWERS** – Wildflowers / You don't know how it feels / Time to move on / You wreck me / It's good to be king / Only a broken heart / Honey bee / Don't fade on me Hard on me / Cabin down below / To find a friend / A higher place / House in the woods / Crawling back to you / Wake up time.	36	8
Feb 95.	(c-s) **YOU WRECK ME / CABIN DOWN BELOW (acoustic)** (cd-s+=) – Only a broken heart.		
May 95.	(c-s)(cds) **IT'S GOOD TO BE KING /**	-	68

– compilations, others, etc. –

Sep 84.	MCA; (d-c) **DAMN THE TORPEDOES. / HARD PROMISES**		-
Apr 86.	MCA; (12"ep) **REFUGEE / DON'T DO ME LIKE THAT. / HERE COMES MY GIRL / THE WAITING**		
Nov 95.	MCA; (cd) **PLAYBACK**		

Liz PHAIR

Born: 1967, Chicago based, USA. After graduating in Art History, she signed to semi-indie 'Matador' early in 1992, where she has so far made 2 albums, the second of which has hit US Top 30. • **Style:** Folk grunge fusing wry life-in-America / hard-hitting sexual lyrics with beautiful country harmonies similiar to MAZZY STAR or THROWING MUSES. • **Songwriters:** Herself except; TURNING JAPANESE (Vapors). • **Trivia:** She became to the first woman since JONI MITCHELL in 1974, to win the prestigious 'Village Voice' annual award for her 1993 debut album.

Recommended: EXILE IN GUYVILLE (*8) / WHIP-SMART (*7)

LIZ PHAIR – vocals, guitar / **BRAD WOOD** – drums, percussion / **CASEY RICE** – guitar / **LEROY BACH** – bass

		Minty Fresh	Matador	
Aug 93.	(7")(cd-s) **CARNIVORE. /**			
		Matador	**Matador**	
Aug 93.	(cd)(c)(lp) **EXILE IN GUYVILLE**			Jun 93

– 6'1" / Help me Mary / Glory / Dance of the seven veils / Never said / Soao star Joe / Explain it to me / Carnivore / Mesmerizing / Fuck and run / Girls, girls, girls / Divorce song / Shatter / Flatter / Flower / Johnny Sunshine / Gunshy / Stratford-On-Guy / Strange loop.

Aug 94.	(7") **SUPERNOVA. / COMBO PLATTER (GIRLYSOUND)**		78	

(cd-s+=) – ('A'clean version).
(7")(c-s) – ('A'side) / X-ray man (remix). *(re-iss.Oct94 on 'Atlantic')*

Sep 94.	(cd)(c)(lp) **WHIP-SMART**		27	

– Chopsticks / Supernova / Support system / X-ray man / Shane / Nashville / Go west / Cince de Mayo / Dogs of L.A. / Whip-smart / Jealousy / Crater lake / Alice Springs / May queen.

Aug 95.	(d7"ep)(cd-ep) **JUVENILIA**		-	

– Jealousy / Turning Japanese / Animal girl / California / South Dakota / Batmobile / Dead shark / Easy.

PHANTOM, ROCKER & SLICK (see under ⇒ STRAY CATS)

John PHILLIPS (see under ⇒ MAMAS & THE PAPAS)

Wilson PICKETT

Born: 18 Mar'41, Prattville, Alabama, USA. As a teenager, he moved to Detroit where he sang in various gospel choirs. In 1961, he joined The FALCONS, who were already famous for their US Top20 hit 'You're So Fine'. In Spring '62, with PICKETT on lead vox, they scraped into the US Top75 with 'I FOUND A LOVE'. Through their producer Robert Bateman, he gained solo deal with LLOYD PRICE's label 'Double L' early '63. After 3 mildly successful US hits, he signed for 'Atlantic' worldwide. In the summer of '65, his classic 'IN THE MIDNIGHT HOUR' hit UK/US Top 30, ascending 'The Wicked Pickett' quickly to top new breed soul singer. • **Style:** Crossover R&B/soul man, shifting danceable sound somewhere between OTIS REDDING and a black TOM JONES. • **Songwriters:** PICKETT penned himself and with collaboraters, including STEVE CROPPER on IN THE MIDNIGHT HOUR. In 1967, he sessioned In Memphis alongside BOBBY WOMACK. His 1970 work was recorded in Philadelphia with producers Kenny Gamble and Leon Huff. Covered many including singles: LAND OF A 1000 DANCES (c. Chris Kenner) / MUSTANG SALLY (Mack Rice) / EVERYBODY NEEDS SOMEBODY TO LOVE (Solomon Burke) / FUNKY BROADWAY (Dyke & The Blazers) / STAG-O-LEE (Lloyd Price) / HEY JUDE* (Beatles) / BORN TO BE WILD* (Steppenwolf) / SUGAR SUGAR (Archies) / HEY JOE (Jimi Hendrix) / YOU KEEP ME HANGIN' ON (Supremes) / FIRE AND WATER (Free) / MAMA TOLD ME NOT TO COME (Randy Newman) / etc. • **Trivia:** Guitarist DUANE ALLMAN guested on *. Bouts of heavy drinking and volatile off-stage temperament, climaxed with him being arrested on 21 Nov'74 for threatening behaviour with a gun.

Recommended: HEART AND SOUL OF WILSON PICKETT (*6)

FALCONS

WILSON PICKETT – vocals / **MACK RICE** – vocals / **EDDIE FLOYD** – vocals / **+2**

		London	Lupine	
Jun 62.	(7") **I FOUND A LOVE. / SWIM**		75	Apr 62
1962.	(7") **ANNA. / YOU'RE ON MY MIND**	-		
		not issued	**Correctone**	
1962.	(7") **MY HEART BELONGS TO YOU. / LET ME BE YOUR BOY**	-		

(re-iss. US+UK Oct 65 on 'MGM/VERVE')

WILSON PICKETT

		not issued	Cub	
1963.	(7") **MY HEART BELONGS TO YOU. / LET ME BE YOUR BOY**	-		
		Liberty	**Double L**	
May 63.	(7") **IF YOU NEED ME. / BABY CALL ON ME**	-	64	
Aug 63.	(7") **IT'S TOO LATE. / I'M GONNA LOVE YOU**	-	49	Jul 63
Oct 63.	(7") **I'M DOWN TO MY LAST HEARTBREAK. / I CAN'T STOP**	-	95	
		Atlantic	**Atlantic**	
1964.	(7") **I'M GONNA CRY. / FOR BETTER OR WORSE**	-		
1964.	(7") **COME HOME BABY. / TAKE A LITTLE LOVE**	-		
Sep 65.	(7") **IN THE MIDNIGHT HOUR. / I'M NOT TIRED**	12	21	Jul 65
Nov 65.	(7") **DON'T FIGHT IT. / IT'S ALL OVER**	29	53	
Dec 65.	(lp) **IN THE MIDNIGHT HOUR**			Oct 65

– In the midnight hour / Teardrops will fall / Take a little love / For better or worse / I found a love / That;s a man's way / I'm gonna cry / Don't fight it / Take this love I've got / Come home baby / I'm not tired / Let's kiss and make up. *(cd-iss Aug93 on 'Rhino')*

Feb 66.	(7") **634-5789 (SOULSVILLE, U.S.A.). / THAT'S A MAN'S WAY**	36	13	Jan 66
Jun 66.	(7") **NINETY-NINE AND A HALF (WON'T DO). / DANGER ZONE**		53	May 66
Aug 66.	(7") **LAND OF A 1000 DANCES. / YOU'RE SO FINE**	22	6	Jul 66
Sep 66.	(lp) **THE EXCITING WILSON PICKETT**		21	Aug 66

– Land of 100 dances / Something you got / 634-5789 / Barefootin' / Mercy, mercy / You're so fine / In the midnight hour / 99 and a half (won't do) / Danger zone / I'm drifting / It's all over / She's so good to me *(re-iss.Jun88)(cd-iss.Aug93 on 'Rhino')*

Nov 66.	(7") **MUSTANG SALLY. / THREE TIME LOSER**	28	23	
Feb 67.	(7") **EVERYBODY NEEDS SOMEBODY TO LOVE. / NOTHING YOU CAN DO**		29	
Feb 67.	(lp) **THE WICKED PICKETT**		42	Jan 67

– Mustang Sally / New Orleans / Sunny / Everybody needs somebody to love / Ooh poo pah doo / She ain't gonna do right / Knock on wood / Time is on my side / Up tight good woman / You left the water running / Three time loser / Nothing you can Do

Mar 67.	(7") **I FOUND A LOVE (pt.1). / (pt.2)**	-	32	
May 67.	(7") **NEW ORLEANS. / SOUL DANCE NUMBER THREE**		-	
May 67.	(7") **SOUL DANCE NUMBER THREE. / YOU CAN'T STAND ALONE**	-	55	
			70	
Aug 67.	(lp) **THE SOUND OF WILSON PICKETT**		54	

– Soul dance number three / Funky Broadway / I need a lot of loving every day / I found a love (part 1) / I found a love (part 2) / You can't stand alone / Mojo mamma / I found the one / Something within me / I'm sorry about that / Love is a beautiful thing

Sep 67.	(7") **FUNKY BROADWAY. / I'M SORRY ABOUT THAT**	43	8	Aug 67
Oct 67.	(lp) **THE BEST OF WILSON PICKETT**		35	

– (compilation) *(re-iss.Apr82, cd-iss.Jul87)(cd-iss.Aug93)*

Oct 67.	(7") **STAGGER-LEE. / I'M IN LOVE**		22	
			45	
Feb 68.	(7") **JEALOUS LOVE. / I'VE COME A LONG WAY**	-	50	
Feb 68.	(lp) **I'M IN LOVE**		70	

– Jealous love / Stagger lee / That kind of love / I'm in love / Hello sunshine / Don't cry no more / We've got to have love / Bring it on home to me / She's looking good / I've come a long way

Mar 68.	(7") **THAT KIND OF LOVE. / I'VE COME A LONG WAY**			
May 68.	(7") **SHE'S LOOKIN' GOOD. / WE'VE GOT TO HAVE LOVE**		15	Apr 68
Aug 68.	(7") **I'M A MIDNIGHT MOVER. / DEBORAH**	38	24	Jun 68
Sep 68.	(lp) **THE MIDNIGHT MOVER**		91	Jul 68

– I'm a midnight mover / It's a groove / Remember, I been good to you / I'm gonna cry / Deborah / I found a true love / Down by the sea / Trust me / Let's get an understanding / For better or worse

Nov 68.	(7") **I FOUND A TRUE LOVE. / FOR BETTER OR WORSE**		42	Sep 68
Nov 68.	(7") **A MAN AND A HALF. / PEOPLE MAKE THE WORLD (WHAT IT IS)**	-	42	
Dec 68.	(7") **HEY JUDE. / NIGHT OWL**	16	-	
Jan 69.	(7") **HEY JUDE. / SEARCH YOUR HEART**	-	23	
Feb 69.	(lp) **HEY JUDE**		97	

– Save me / Hey Jude / Back in your arms / Toe hold / Night owl / My own style of loving / A man and a half / Sit down and talk this over / Search your heart / Born to be wild / People make the world (what it is).

Mar 69.	(7") **MINI SKIRT MINNIE. / BACK IN YOUR ARMS**		50	
Apr 69.	(lp) **RIGHT ON**			

– Groovy little woman / Funky way / Sugar sugar / Sweet inspiration / This old town / You keep me hangin' on / Lord pity us all / It's still good / Woman likes to hear that / She said yes / Hey Joe / Steal away.

May 69.	(7") **BORN TO BE WILD. / TOE HOLD**	-	64	
Jul 69.	(7") **HEY JOE. / NIGHT OWL**	-	59	
Jan 70.	(7") **YOU KEEP ME HANGIN' ON. / NOW YOU SEE ME, NOW YOU DON'T**	-	92	Nov 69
May 70.	(7") **SUGAR SUGAR. / COLE, COOKE AND REDDING**		25	
			91	
Jul 70.	(7") **HEY JOE. / BORN TO BE WILD**		-	
Aug 70.	(7") **SHE SAID YES. / IT'S STILL GOOD**	-	68	
Oct 70.	(lp) **WILSON PICKETT IN PHILADELPHIA**		64	

– Run Joey run / Help the needy / Come right here / Bumble bee (sting me) / Don't let the green grass fool you / Get me back on time, engine number 9 (part 1) / Get me back on time, engine number 9 (part 2) / Days go by / International playboy / Ain't no doubt about it

Oct 70.	(7") **ENGINE No.9. / INTERNATIONAL PLAYBOY**		14	
Feb 71.	(lp)(c) **ENGINE NO.9**			Sep 70

– Run Joey run / Help the needy / Come right here / Bumble bee (sting me) / Don't let the green grass fool you / Get me back on time, engine No.9 (part 1 & 2) / The days go by / International playboy / Ain't no doubt about it.

Mar 71.	(7") **DON'T LET THE GRASS FOOL YOU. / AIN'T NO DOUBT ABOUT IT**	-		
Apr 71.	(7") **FIRE AND WATER. / DON'T LET THE GREEN GRASS FOOL YOU**		-	
Jun 71.	(lp) **THE BEST OF WILSON PICKETT, VOL.II** (compilation)		73	May 71

– Don't let the green grass fool you / Sugar sugar / Get me back on time, engine No.9 / I'm a midnight mover / A man and a half / Born to be wild / She's lookin' good / I'm in love / Hey Joe / Cole, Cooke & Redding / Hey Jude / You keep me hangin' on / I found a true love.

Oct 71.	(7") **CALL MY NAME, I'LL BE THERE. / WOMAN LET ME BE DOWN HOME**		52	Aug 71
Dec 71.	(7") **FIRE AND WATER. / PLEDGING MY LOVE**	-	24	
Jan 72.	(lp) **DON'T KNOCK MY LOVE**			Dec 71

– Fire and water / (Your love has brought me) A mighty long way / Covering the same old ground / Don't knock my love (part 1) / Don't knock my love (part 2) / Call my name, I'll be there / Hot love / Not enough love to satisfy / You can't judge a book by its cover / Pledging my love / Mama told me not to come / Woman let me be down home

Feb 72. (7") **DON'T KNOCK MY LOVE. / (part 2)** [ ] [13] Apr 71
Apr 72. (7") **DON'T LET THE GREEN GRASS FOOL YOU. / COVERING THE SAME OLD GROUND** [ ] [17] Jan 71
Jun 72. (7") **FUNK FACTORY. / ONE STEP AWAY** [ ] [58] May72
Oct 72. (7") **MAMA TOLD ME NOT TO COME. / COVERING THE SAME OLD GROUND** [-] [99]
1973. (7") **INTERNATIONAL PLAYBOY. / COME RIGHT HERE** [ ] [-]

R.C.A. R.C.A.

Mar 73. (7") **MR.MAGIC MAN. / I SHO' LOVE YOU** [ ] [98]
Mar 73. (lp)(c) **MIZ LENA'S BOY (US title 'MR. MAGIC MAN')** [ ] [ ]
– Take a closer look at the woman you're with / Memphis, Tennessee / Soft spoul boogie woogie / Help me make it through the night / Never my love / You lay'd it on me / Is your love life better / Two women and a wife / Why don't you make up your mind / Take the pollution out your throat.
Nov 73. (7") **TAKE A CLOSER LOOK AT THE WOMAN YOU'RE WITH. / TWO WOMEN AND A WIFE** [ ] [90] Sep 73
Feb 74. (7") **SOFT SOUL BOOGIE WOOGIE. / TAKE THE POLLUTION OUT OF YOUR THROAT** [ ] [ ]
May 74. (lp)(c) **TONIGHT I'M MY BIGGEST AUDIENCE** [ ] [ ]
– Mr.Magic man / Only I can sing this love / Love is beautiful / I sure love you / Baby man / Sin was the blame / What it is / If you need me / I can't slip my true love away / I keep walking straight ahead.
Aug 74. (7") **TAKE YOUR PLEASURE WHERE YOU FIND IT. / WHAT GOOD IS A LIE** [ ] [ ]
Sep 74. (lp)(c) **PICKETT IN THE POCKET** [-] [ ]
Nov 74. (7") **I WAS TOO NICE. / ISN'T THAT SO** [-] [ ]
Dec 74. (d-lp) **LIVE IN JAPAN (live)** [ ] [-]
– T.S.O.P. (The Sound Of Philadelphia) / Proud Mary / People make the world / Sugar sugar / Don't let the green grass fool you / I'm in love / In the midnight hour / Fire and water / I found a love / Never my love / Glory hallelujah / Mustang Sally / Land of a 1000 dances / Soft soul boogie / Mr.Magic man / Don't knock my love / Goodnight my love.
Jul 75. (lp)(c) **JOIN ME AND LET'S BE FREE** [ ] [ ]
– Join me and let's be free / Let's make love right / I've got a good friend / Smokin' in the United Nations / Gone / Good things / Higher consciousness / Bailin' hay on a rainy day / Mighty mouth.

D.J.M. Wicked

Nov 76. (7") **HOW WILL I EVER KNOW. / THE BEST PART OF A MAN** [-] [ ]
Nov 76. (lp)(c) **PEACE BREAKER** [ ] [ ]
Feb 77. (7") **LOVE WILL KEEP US TOGETHER. / IT'S GONNA BE GOOD** [-] [ ]

Atlantic Big Tree

Aug 78. (7") **WHO TURNED YOU ON. / DANCE YOU DOWN** [ ] [ ]
Aug 78. (lp)(c) **A FUNKY SITUATION** [-] [ ]
– Dance with me / She's so tight / The night we called a day / Dance you down / Hold on to your hiney / Groovin' / Lay me like you hate me / Funky situation / Time to let the sunshine on me / Who turned you on.
Dec 78. (7") **GROOVIN'. / TIME TO LET THE SUNSHINE ON ME** [-] [ ]

United Art EMI America

Sep 79. (7")(12") **GROOVE CITY. / YOU ARE THE LOVE OF MY LIFE** [ ] [ ]
(re-iss.Nov79 on 'EMI America')
Nov 79. (7") **I WANT YOU. / LOVE OF MY LIFE** [-] [ ]
Nov 79. (lp)(c) **I WANT YOU** [ ] [ ]
– I want you / Love of my life / Shameless / Live with me / Groove city / Superstar / Granny.
Jan 80. (7") **LIVE WITH ME. / GRANNY** [-] [ ]

Liberty EMI America

Apr 80. (7") **SHAMELESS. / SUPERSTAR** [ ] [-]

EMI America EMI America

Feb 81. (7") **DON'T UNDERESTIMATE THE POWER OF LOVE. / AIN'T GONNA GIVE YOU NO MORE** [ ] [ ]
(12"+=) – I want you.
Mar 81. (lp)(c) **THE RIGHT TRACK** [ ] [ ]
– Back on the right track / If you can't beat 'em join 'em / Help me be without / I ain't gonna give you no more / Maybe this time / Don't underestimate the power of love / It's you.
May 81. (7") **BACK ON THE RIGHT TRACK. / IT'S YOU** [-] [ ]

not issued Erva

mid80s. (7") **LOVE DAGGER. / TIME TO LET THE SUNSHINE ON ME** [-] [ ]

not issued Precision

mid80s. (7") **MUSTANG SALLY (THE BOSS IS BACK). / ('A'instrumental)** [-] [ ]

Motown Motown

Oct 87. (7") **IN THE MIDNIGHT HOUR (remix). / ('A'original)** [62] [ ]
(12"+=) – ('A'dub version).
Oct 87. (lp)(c)(cd) **AMERICAN SOUL MAN** [ ] [ ]
– A thing called love / When your heart speaks / Love never let me down / A man of value / (I wanna) Make love to you / In the midnight hour / Don't turn away / Just let her know / Can't stop now.

New York Montage

Feb 88. (7")(12") **SECONDS. ("WILSON PICKETT & JACKIE MOORE") / SECONDS (instrumental)** [ ] [ ]
— in Oct'93, WILSON was given a 1-year jail sentence, after being found guilty of drunk driving and killing a pensioner.

– more compilations, etc. –

Jun 67. London; (7") **BILLY THE KID. / I DON'T WANT NO PART TIME LOVE** [ ] [-]
1967. Wand; (lp) **GREAT HITS** [-] [ ]
(cd-iss.May93)
Feb 68. Atlantic; (7") **IN THE MIDNIGHT HOUR. / DANGER ZONE** [ ] [ ]
(re-iss.1972)
1972. Atlantic; (7"m) **EVERYBODY NEEDS SOMEBODY TO LOVE. / DON'T FIGHT IT / FIRE AND WATER** [ ] [-]
Feb 73. Atlantic; (lp)(c) **WILSON PICKETT'S GREATEST HITS** [-] [ ]
1974. Atlantic; (7"m) **IN THE MIDNIGHT HOUR. / LAND OF 1000 DANCES / FUNKY BROADWAY** [ ] [-]
(re-iss.Nov76)
Jul 78. Atlantic; (lp) **STAR COLLECTION** [ ] [-]
Apr 80. Atlantic; (7"ep) **LAND OF A 1000 DANCES / IN THE MIDNIGHT HOUR. / (2 tracks by 'Sam & Dave')** [ ] [-]
Nov 73. President; (7") **I CAN'T STOP. / DOWN TO MY LAST HEARTBREAK** [ ] [-]
1974. Joy; (lp) **IF YOU NEED ME** [-] [ ]
Jan 85. Old Gold; (7") **IN THE MIDNIGHT HOUR. / 634-5789** [ ] [-]
Apr 91. Knight; (cd)(c) **THE HEART AND SOUL OF WILSON PICKETT** [ ] [-]
Jul 92. Rhino-Atlantic; (d-cd) **A MAN AND A HALF** [ ] [-]
(d-cd.iss.Aug93 on 'Rhino')
Jul 92. Castle; (cd) **THE COLLECTION** [ ] [-]
– Hey Jude / You keep me hangin' on / Born to be wild / Sunny / Sugar sugar / Time is on my side / In the midnight hour / Knock on wood / Barefootin' / Fire and water / Stagger Lee / Hey Joe / Mama told me not to come / Land of a 1,000 dances.
Mar 94. Spectrum; (cd)(c) **AMERICAN SOUL MAN** [ ] [-]

Jeffrey Lee PIERCE (see under ⇒ GUN CLUB)

PIERRE ETOILE (see under ⇒ GALAXIE 500)

PIGBAG

Formed: Bristol / Cheltenham, Gloustershire / Avon, England ... 1980 by JAMES JOHNSTONE and ex-POP GROUP member SIMON UNDERWOOD. Managed by Linda Neville, they formed own label 'Y', through 'Rough Trade', and issued classic debut 'PAPA'S GOT A BRAND NEW PIGBAG' (based on a JAMES BROWN song). Although it flopped first time around in Mar'81, it shot to No.3 a year later. At the same time, their debut album 'DR.HECKLE & MR.JIVE', broke through into the UK Top 20, but things drew to an end, 12 months later. • **Style:** Instrumental dance-floor combo, who used salsa, jerky jazz and Afro rhythms to boost energetic experimentation. Vocalist ANGELA JAEGER, gave them a new dimension to sound, although many fans bailed out. • **Songwriters:** All group compositions.

Recommended: DR.HECKLE & MR.JIVE (*8).

JAMES JOHNSTONE – guitar, alto sax, steel drums / **OLLIE MOORE** – tenor sax, clarinet, sanza / **CHRIS LEIGH** – trumpet, percussion / **CHIP CARPENTER** – drums, percussion, tumbas / **SIMON UNDERWOOD** – bass, cello, violin (ex-POP GROUP) / **ROGER FREEMAN** – percussion, trombone, keyboards, piano

Y not issued

May 81. (7") **PAPA'S GOT A BRAND NEW PIG BAG. / BACKSIDE** [ ] [-]
(12"+=) – Another orangutango. *(re-iss.Mar82 hit No.3)*
Oct 81. (7")(12") **SUNNY DAY. / ELEPHANTS WISH TO BECOME NIMBLE** [53] [-]
Jan 82. (7") **GETTING UP. / GIGGLING MUD** [61] [-]
(12"+=) – Go cat.
Mar 82. (lp)(c) **DR HECKLE AND MR JIVE** [18] [-]
– Getting up / Bigbag / Dozo Don / Brian the snail / Wiggling / Brazil nuts / Orangutango / As it will be.
— **BRIAN** – drums / + **OSCAR** – trombone repl. ROGER who joined DISCONNECTION.
Jul 82. (7")(12") **THE BIG BEAN. / SCUMDA** [40] [-]
— **ANGELA JAEGAR** (OLIVER) – vox (ex-RIP, RIG & PANIC, ex-DROWNING CRAZE)
Feb 83. (7")(12") **HIT THE 'O' DECK. / SIX O ONE** [ ] [-]
Feb 83. (lp)(c) **LEND AN EAR** [ ] [-]
– Weak at the knees / Hit the 'O' deck / Ubud / One way ticket to Cubesville / Jump the line / Can't see for looking / No such thing as / Listen listen (litle man).
Jun 83. (m-lp)(c) **PIGBAG LIVE (live)** [ ] [-]
– Shack of scraps / Smiling faces / Sunny day / Papa's got a brand new pigbag / Jump the line / Global terrain / End of Ubud / Can't see for looking.
— Had already disbanded early '83, SIMON joined RIP, RIG & PANIC.

– compilations, others, etc. –

Nov 87. Kaz; (cd) **THE BEST OF PIGBAG** [ ] [-]
– Papa's got a brand new Pigbag (extended) / Weak at the knees / Hit the 'O' deck / Getting up / Brazil nuts / Jump the line / Another orangutango (extended) / Sunny day (extended) / Big bean (extended) / Can't see for looking / Six of one / Big bag. *(re-iss cd+=)* / Listen listen little man / Papa's got a brand new Pigbag.

PiL (see under ⇒ PUBLIC IMAGE LTD.)

Michael PINDER (see under ⇒ MOODY BLUES)

PINK FAIRIES

Formed: London, England ... 1966 as The SOCIAL DEVIANTS, by RUSSELL HUNTER, MICK FARREN – vocals, SID BISHOP – guitar,

CORD REES – bass & two others. In 1967, they shortened to The DEVIANTS, and self-financed an album 'PTOOF', which sold reasonably well on mail order. With DUNCAN SANDERSON replacing CORD, and the recruitment of new manager Canadian Jamie Mandelkau, they issued second lp 'DISPOSABLE' in 1968 on 'Stable' records. Early in 1969, PAUL RUDOLPH replaced BISHOP, and their third lp 'DEVIANTS' was issued by 'Transatlantic'. When FARREN left to go solo in Oct'69, the new line-up (HUNTER, SANDERSON & RUDOLPH) augmented SHAGRAT member TWINK on his debut 'Polydor' album 'THINK PINK'. TWINK had already initiated the idea of The PINK FAIRIES in Colchester, so he just teamed up with said trio with that name. TWINK had also drummed at various stages with The IN-CROWD, who evolved with TOMORROW, and The PRETTY THINGS. Early 1971, The PINK FAIRIES unleashed their first official 'Polydor' single 'THE SNAKE', which preceeded joyous album 'NEVER NEVER LAND'. Their 1972 follow-up 'WHAT A BUNCH OF SWEETIES' without TWINK (who had briefly formed The STARS, with another acid casualty SYD BARRETT) scraped into the UK 50. With numerous personnel changes, they decided to disband Mar'74, although many re-incarnations were ahead of them, but only to tour. • **Style:** Hippie drug-orientated rock'n'roll band. • **Songwriters:** Group compositions?, except; WALK DON'T RUN (Ventures) / etc. • **Trivia:** They toured constantly with friends HAWKWIND, with constant scirmishes with the law.

Recommended: FLASHBACK: PINK FAIRIES (*7).

DEVIANTS

DUNCAN SANDERSON – bass / **SID BISHOP** – guitar, sitar / **MICK FARREN** – vocals, piano / **CORD REES** – bass, guitar / **RUSS HUNTER** – drums

Under-ground | not issued

1967. (lp) **PTOOF!**
– Opening / I'm coming home / Child of the sky / Charlie / Nothing man / Garbage / Bun / Deviation street. *(re-iss.May69 on 'Decca') (re-iss.Dec83 on 'Psycho') (cd-iss.Sep95 on 'Alive')*

— **PAUL RUDOLPH** – guitar repl. CORD

Stable | not issued

Oct 68. (lp) **DISPOSABLE**
– Somewhere to go / Sparrows and wires / Jamie's song / You've got to hold on / Fire in the city / Let's loot the supermarket / Papa – oo-Mao-Mao / Slum lord / Blind Joe McTurk's last session / Normality jam / Guaranteed too dead / Sidney B. Goode / Last man

Nov 68. 7") **YOU'VE GOT TO HOLD ON. / LET'S LOOT THE SUPERMARKET**

— now a trio of SANDERSON, RUDOLPH + HUNTER when BISHOP left, FARREN went solo and released lp in 1970 'MONA (THE CARNIVEROUS CIRCUS).'

Transatla. | not iss.

Jan 70. (lp) **DEVIANTS**
– Billy the monster / Broken biscuits / First line / The people suite / Rambling 'B'ask transit blues / Death of dream machine / Play time / Black George does it weith his mouth / Junior narco raiders / People of the city / Metamorphosis exploration. *(re-iss. 1987 on 'Logo') (re-iss. Oct 88 on 'Demon')*

TWINK

TWINK (b. JOHN ADLER) – drums, vocals (ex-SHAGRAT) (solo, with DEVIANTS)

Polydor | not issued

Jul 70. (lp) **THINK PINK**
– Coming of the other side / Ten thousand words in a cardboard box / Dawn of magic / Tiptoe on the highest hill / Fluid / Mexican grass war / Rock an' roll the joint / Suicide / Three little piggies / Sparrow is a sign.

PINK FAIRIES

PAUL RUDOLPH – guitar, vocals / **DUNCAN SANDERSON** – bass, vocals / **RUSSELL HUNTER** – drums now with **TWINK**

Polydor | Polydor

Jan 71. (7") **THE SNAKE. / DO IT**

May 71. (lp)(c)(red-lp) **NEVER NEVER LAND**
– Do it / Heavenly man / Say you love me / War girl / Never never land / Track one side two / Thor / Teenage rebel / Uncle Harry's last freak-out / The dream is just beginning. *(re-iss.1974)*

— Trimmed to a trio when TWINK joined STARS, before flitting to Morocco. His spot filled by guest **TREVOR BURTON** – guitar (ex-MOVE)

Jul 72. (lp)(c) **WHAT A BUNCH OF SWEETIES** [48]
– Right on, fight on / Portobello shuffle / Marilyn / The pigs of Uranus / Walk, don't run / Middle run / I went up, I went down / X-ray / I saw her standing there. *(re-iss.1974)*

— **MICK WAYNE** – guitar, vox (ex-JUNIOR'S EYES) repl. RUDOLPH (to UNCLE DOG)

Nov 72. (7") **WELL, WELL, WELL. / HOLD ON**

— **LARRY WALLIS** – guitar, vocals (ex-UFO, ex-SHAGRAT, ex-BLODWYN PIG) repl. MICK. (trio now consisted of LARRY, DUNCAN + RUSSELL)

Jun 73. (lp)(c) **KINGS OF OBLIVION**
– City kids / I wish I was a girl / When's the fun begin / Chromium plating / Raceway / Chambermaid / Street urchin.

— Break-up Mar74, although **DUNCAN, RUSSELL, PAUL, TWINK & LARRY** re-formed for one-off reunion gig at The Roundhouse 13th Jul'75. Autumn 1975, they officially re-united w / **DUNCAN, RUSSELL & LARRY.** When they added (mid'76) **MARTIN STONE** – guitar (ex-CHILI WILLI, ex-MIGHTY BABY, ex-ACTION, etc.) they returned to studio.

Stiff | not issued

Sep 76. (7") **BETWEEN THE LINES. / SPOILING FOR A FIGHT**

— Break again, LARRY went solo in 1977.

TWINK

solo with ex-PINK FAIRIES (**PAUL RUDOLPH**; who had been recently seen in HAWKWIND, etc. / **DUNCAN + RUSSELL).**

Chiswick | not issued

Feb 78. (12"ep) **DO IT '77. / THE PSYCHEDELIC PUNKAROO / ENTER THE DIAMONDS**

— Disbanded once again when TWINK moved to Belguim. DUNCAN joined LIGHTNING RAIDERS.

MICK FARREN

with **TWINK** – drums, percussion, vocals / **SHAGRAT THE VAGRANT** – vocals, percussion / **STEVE HAMMOND** – guitar / **JOHNNY GUSTAFSON** – bass / **PETE ROBINSON** – keyboards

Transatla. | not iss.

1970. (lp) **MONA (THE CARNIVEROUS CIRCUS)**
– Mona (a fragrant) / Carniverous circus part 1: The whole thing starts – But Charlie it's still moving – Observe the ravens – Society 4 the horsemen – Summertime blues / Carniverous circus part 2: Don't talk to Mary – You can't move me – In my window box – An epitaph can point the way – Mona (the whole trip). *(re-iss.Mar 84 on 'Psycho'0*

Stiff | not issued

Nov 77. (7"ep) **SCREWED UP ("MICK FARREN & DEVIANTS")**
– Outragious contagious / Let's loot the supermarket / Screwed up / Shock horror

— now with **WILKO JOHNSON** – guitar / **ALAN POWER** – drums / **ANDY COLQUHOUN** – bass / **WILL STALL** – brass / **CHRISSIE JANE + SONJA KRISTINA** – b. vox.

Logo | not issued

1978. (lp) **VAMPIRES STOLE MY LUNCH MONEY**
– Trouble coming every day / Half price drinks / I don't want to go this way / I want a drink / Son of a millionaire / Zombie (live) / Bela Lugosi / People call you crazy / Fast Eddie / Let me in damn you / Self destruction / Drunk in the morning.

1978. (7") **HALF PRICE DRINKS. / I DON'T WANT TO GO THIS WAY**

May 79. (7") **BROKEN STATUE. / IT'S ALL IN THE PICTURE**

DEVIANTS

— reformed with **MICK FARREN** – vocals / **LARRY WALLIS + WAYNE KRAMER** – guitar / **DUNCAN SANDERSON** – bass / **GEORGE BUTLER** – drums

May 84. (lp) **HUMAN GARBAGE** (live at Dingwalls 1984)
– Outragious contagious / Broken statue / Rambli' Rose / Hey thanks / Screwed up / I wanna drink / Takin' LSD / Police car / Trouble coming every day.

PINK FAIRIES

re-formed 1987 with **TWINK, LARRY, RUSSELL, ANDY + SANDY** (aka DUNCAN).

Demon | not issued

Oct 87. (lp)(cd) **KILL 'EM AND EAT 'EM**
– Broken statue / Fear of love / Undercover of confusion / Waiting for the ice-cream to melt / Taking LSD / White girls on amphetamine / Seeing double / Fool about you / Bad attitude / I might be lying.

— Once again, bit the dust, and TWINK joined MAGIC MUSCLE who made live lp in 1989 'ONE HUNDRED MILES BELOW'. TWINK released another solo lp 'MR.RAINBOW', and then 'MAGIC EYE' both in 1990 for 'Woronzow' label.

– compilations, others, etc. –

Jul 75. Flashback-Polydor; (lp) **PINK FAIRIES**
– The snake / City kids / Wargirl / Portobello shuffle / Heavenly man / Do it / pigs of Uranus / Well well well / Chromium plating / I went up, I went down / Say you love me / Street urchin.

Jun 82. Big Beat; (m-lp) **AT THE ROUNDHOUSE (live Jul'75)**
– City kids / Waiting for the man / Lucille / Uncle Harry's last freakout / Going down.

Oct 84. Big Beat; (m-lp) **PREVIOUSLY UNRELEASED**
– As long as the price is right / Waiting for the lightning to strike / Can't find a lady / No second chance / Talk of the Devil / I think it's coming back again. *(both above iss. 1-cd Aug91)*

TWINK

Twink | not issued

Mar 86. (7") **APOCALIPSTIC. / HE'S CRYING**

Jul 86. (12"ep) **SPACE LOVER (Rock'n'roll mix 1 & 2). / ('A'percussion mix) / ('A'psychedelic mix) / ('A'instrumental)**

Jun 87. (7") **DRIVING MY CAR. / WAR GIRL**

PINK FLOYD

Formed: London, England . . . 1965 by WATERS, WRIGHT and MASON, initially as The SCREAMING ABDABS, with 3 others CLIVE METCALFE – bass, KEITH NOBLE and JULIETTE GALE on vocals. They were dismissed, after finding SYD BARRETT and becoming PINK FLOYD (the name taken from bluesman PINK ANDERSON and the FLOYD district council). In Mar'66, they became regulars at London's Marquee club, where their Sunday afternoon gigs were described as "spontaneous underground". Having played the UFO club late in 1966, they were surprisingly signed to EMI's 'Columbia' early 1967, helped by new management team of Peter Jenner and Andrew King. FLOYD's debut outing 'ARNOLD LAYNE' (about a transvestite washing-line thief), was not banned by the BBC and managed a UK Top 20 spot. Their follow-up 'SEE EMILY PLAY', hit UK No.6, and preceeded their debut Top 10 classic lp 'THE PIPER AT THE GATES OF DAWN'. Their 3rd 45 'APPLES AND ORANGES' (another not featured on debut lp) flopped late in 1967 and BARRETT started to suffer bad LSD (drug) trips. Early in 1968, DAVE GILMOUR an old school friend of SYD's, was added for live gigs to augment the spaced out BARRETT. In April '68, BARRETT was asked to leave group, and he retreated to a life of reclusiveness in Cambridge home. After another flop 45 'IT WOULD BE SO NICE', they unleashed their second lp 'A SAUCERFUL OF SECRETS', which again hit the UK Top 10. On 29 June, they played first free concert at London's Hyde Park, alongside JETHRO TULL and ROY HARPER. They finished the year, with another flop single 'POINT ME TO THE SKY', which was their last one in the UK for 11 years. They now concentrated on albums, with disappointing Barbet Schroeder soundtrack 'MORE' being last Top tenner for 'Columbia'. They now moved to EMI's new 'Harvest' label, and issued part live/part solo 'UMMA GUMMA' double album to end 1969. A year later, they achieved first No.1 album, with 'ATOM HEART MOTHER', which contained the excellent title track on one side, with trumpeter RON GEESIN given co-credit. He was to collaborate with ROGER WATERS the same year, on a soundtrack for the Roy Battersby documentary film 'THE BODY'. On the 15th May'71, they played at a Crystal Palace Garden Party, and introduced a new piece of music 'RETURN TO THE SUN OF NOTHING', which in 6 months time, became 'ECHOES', and took up one side of their UK Top 3 album 'MEDDLE'. In 1972, they were used on another Schroeder film 'LA VALLEE', which recorded in France became Top 10 album 'OBSCURED BY CLOUDS', and although disappointing many die hard FLOYD fans, hit the Top 50 in the States. The same year, the group premiered own Italian-made music film 'LIVE AT POMPEII', at Edinburgh Theater. In March 1973, after its spectacular January showing at the Planetarium, the master-piece 'DARK SIDE OF THE MOON' was unveiled. A concept piece taking a year of meticulous crafting, which dealt with lunacy, depression and death. It hit No.1 in the US, and No.2 in the UK, also amassing over 10 million sales, while staying in the chart for nearly 300 weeks. It became regarded by many as the greatest album of all time, and gave new meaning to stereo headphones. They returned to London's Earl's Court for a spectacular laser show, which featured albums' all-girl backing singers The BLACKBERRIES. In 1974, they did benefit gig raising £10,000 for their recently disabled friend ROBERT WYATT. In the same year, NICK MASON also produced his 'Rock Bottom' album. In the summer of '75, their stupendous Knebworth Festival concert, previewed another best selling album 'WISH YOU WERE HERE', which went straight to No.1 on both sides of the Atlantic. Late in 1976, they lost their 40 foot inflatable pig on their Top 3 to be 'ANIMALS' album sleeve shot. The Civil Aviation Authority was alerted to warn pilots of the danger, but it was never found. In 1978, DAVID GILMOUR and RICHARD WRIGHT released own solo project albums, and MASON also produced The DAMNED (late '77) and STEVE HILLAGE ('Green' lp). FLOYD returned late 1979, with a new ROGER WATERS written concept double lp 'THE WALL', which lifted a Christmas No.1 single 'ANOTHER BRICK IN THE WALL (PART II)'. The next couple of years were spent making it into a film, which was directed by Alan Parker and issued in 1982, with BOB GELDOF playing the main character Pink. WRIGHT had already quarrelled with WATERS and left in 1980. In Spring 1983, they/WATERS issued follow-up album 'THE FINAL CUT' which hit UK No.1 but was found too depressing, and called by critics as a poor "son of The Wall". The year ended with WATERS departing to go solo, leaving GILMOUR and MASON to fight him in court for the use of the PINK FLOYD name. In 1984, GILMOUR released another solo album 'ABOUT FACE', which was followed a year later by a NICK MASON / RICK FENN album 'PROFILES'. In 1987, after WRIGHT returned to boost live shows (which helped them win court battle with WATERS), PINK FLOYD returned with Transatlantic Top 3 album 'A MOMENTARY LAPSE OF REASON'. A live double album followed a year later, but this was first album not to hit UK + US Top 10. • **Style:** Psychedelic rock outfit, who progressed into more experimental and percussive sound after the departure of SYD. • **Songwriters:** BARRETT wrote nearly all of compositions, until he left after writing 'JUGBAND BLUES' for A SAUCERFUL OF SECRETS album. WATERS and sometimes WRIGHT, took over writing credits. By the late 70's, WATERS had virtually taken full control, until he left. • **Trivia:** MASON also made a 30 minute autobiographical film 'Life Could Be A Dream' with his other outlet, racing driving, the main feature. In 1995, GILMOUR featured on JOHN 'RABBIT' BUNDRICK's ambient album 'Dream Jungle'.

Recommended: THE DARK SIDE OF THE MOON (*10) / MEDDLE (*9) / THE PIPER AT THE GATES OF DAWN (*9) / WISH YOU WERE HERE (*10) / THE WALL (*8) / ATOM HEART MOTHER (*8) / ANIMALS (*8) / A SAUCERFUL OF SECRETS (*8) / UMMA GUMMA (*8) / THE DELICATE SOUND OF THUNDER (*7) / THE DIVISION BELL (*7).

SYD BARRETT (b.ROGER KEITH BARRETT, 6 Jan'46) – vocals, guitar / **RICHARD WRIGHT** (b.28 Jul'45, London) – keyboards / **ROGER WATERS** (b.GEORGE WATERS, 9 Sep'44) – bass, vocals, percussion / **NICK MASON** (b.27 Jan'45, Birmingham, England) – drums, percussion

Columbia Tower

Mar 67. (7") **ARNOLD LAYNE. / CANDY AND THE CURRENT BUN** [20] [ ]
Jun 67. (7") **SEE EMILY PLAY. / THE SCARECROW** [6] [ ]
Aug 67. (lp) **THE PIPER AT THE GATES OF DAWN** [6] [-]
– Astronomy domine / Lucifer Sam / Matilda mother / Flaming / Pow R. Toc H. / Take up thy stethoscope and walk / Interstellar overdrive / The gnome / Chapter 24 / Scarecrow / Bike. *(re-iss.May83 on 'Fame') (cd-iss.Feb87 on 'EMI') (re-iss.cd+c Oct94 on 'EMI')*
Nov 67. (lp) **PINK FLOYD** (nearly as above) [-] [ ]
Nov 67. (7") **APPLES AND ORANGES. / PAINTBOX** [ ] [-]
Jan 68. (7") **FLAMING. / THE GNOME** [-] [ ]

—— added **DAVID GILMOUR** – guitar who soon repl. BARRETT who later went solo.

Apr 68. (7") **IT WOULD BE SO NICE. / JULIA DREAM** [ ] [ ]
Jun 68. (lp) **A SAUCERFUL OF SECRETS** [9] [ ]
– Let there be more light / Remember a day / Set the controls for the heart of the sun / Corporal Clegg / A saucerful of secrets / See saw / Jugband blues. *(re-iss.May83 on 'Fame') (cd-iss.Feb87 on 'EMI') (re-iss.cd+c Jul94 on 'EMI')*
Jul 68. (7") **LET THERE BE MORE LIGHT. / REMEMBER A DAY** [-] [ ]
Dec 68. (7") **POINT ME TO THE SKY. / CAREFUL WITH THAT AXE, EUGENE** [ ] [-]
Jul 69. (lp)(c) **MORE (Film Soundtrack)** [9] [ ]
– Cirrus minor / The Nile song / Crying song / Up the khyber / Green is the colour / Cymbaline / Party sequence / Main theme / Ibiza bar / More blues / Quicksilver / A Spanish piece / Dramatic theme. *(cd-iss.Apr87)*

Harvest Harvest

Nov 69. (d-lp)(d-c) **UMMA GUMMA** (live */ others solo) [5] [74]
– Astronomy domine * / Careful with that axe, Eugene * / Set the control for the heart of the sun * / A saucerful of secrets * / RICHARD WRIGHT:- Sysyphus (parts 1-4) / ROGER WATERS:- Grantchester Meadows / Several species of small furry animals gathered together in a cave and grooving with a pict / DAVID GILMOUR: – The narrow way (parts 1-3) / NICK MASON:- The Grand Vizier's garden party – part 1; Entrance – part 2; Entertainment / part 3; Exit. *(re-iss.Dec79 on 'EMI', d-cd-iss.Mar87) (re-iss.d-cd,d-c Oct94 on 'EMI')*
Oct 70. (lp)(c) **ATOM HEART MOTHER** [1] [55]
– Atom heart mother; (a) Father's shout – (b) Breast milky – (c) Mother fore – (d) Funky dung – (e) Mind your throats please – (f) Remergence / If / Summer '68 / Fat old Sun / Alan's psychedlic breakfast / Rise and shine / Sunny side up / Morning glory. *(quad-lp 1973) (cd-iss.Mar87) (re-iss.cd+c Oct94 on 'EMI')*

—— (above featured **RON GEESIN** – horns, co-writer)

Nov 71. (lp)(c) **MEDDLE** [3] [70]
– One of these days / A pillow of winds / Fearless (interpolating 'You'll never walk alone') / San Tropez / Seamus / Echoes. *(re-iss.Nov83 on 'Fame') (cd-iss.Aug84) (cd-iss. Apr89 on 'Mobile Fidelity') (re-iss.cd+c Aug94 on 'EMI')*
Dec 71. (7") **ONE OF THESE DAYS. / FEARLESS** [-] [ ]
Jun 72. (lp)(c) **OBSCURED BY CLOUDS** [6] [46]
– Obscured by clouds / When you're in / Burning bridges / The gold it's in the . . . / Wots . . . uh the deal / Mudmen / Childhood's end / Free four / Stay / Absolute curtains. *(cd-iss.Apr87 on 'EMI')*
Jul 72. (7") **FREE FOUR. / STAY** [-] [ ]
Mar 73. (lp)(c) **THE DARK SIDE OF THE MOON** [2] [1]
– Speak to me / Breathe / On the run / Time / The great gig in the sky / Money / Us and them / Any colour you like / Brain damage / Eclipse. *(cd-iss.Aug84) (re-iss.cdMar93, hit UK No.4) (re-iss.cd+c. Jul94 on 'EMI') (also on quad-lp + US pic-lp)*
May 73. (7") **MONEY. / ANY COLOUR YOU LIKE** [-] [13]

Harvest Columbia

Sep 75. (lp)(c)(quad-lp) **WISH YOU WERE HERE** [1] [1]
– Shine on you crazy diamond (parts 1-5) / Welcome to the machine / Have a cigar / Wish you were here / Shine on you crazy diamond (parts 6-9). *(cd-iss.Aug84) (re-iss.cd+c Jul94 on 'EMI')*
Oct 75. (7") **HAVE A CIGAR. / SHINE ON YOU CRAZY DIAMOND (excerpt)** [-] [ ]
Jan 77. (lp)(c) **ANIMALS** [2] [3] Feb 77
– Pigs on the wing (part 1) / Dogs / Pigs (three different ones) / Sheep / Pigs on the wing (part 2). *(cd-iss.Jul86) (re-iss.cd+c Jul94 on 'EMI')*
Nov 79. (7") **ANOTHER BRICK IN THE WALL (PART 2). / ONE OF MY TURNS** [1] [1] Jan 80
Dec 79. (d-lp)(c) **THE WALL** [3] [1]
– In the flesh / The thin ice / The happiest days of our lives / Another brick in the wall (part 2) / Mother / Goodbye blue sky / Empty spaces / Young lust / One of my turns / Don't leave me now / Another brick in the wall (part 3) / Goodbye cruel world / Hey you / Is there anybody out there? / Nobody home / Vera / Comfortably numb / The show must go on / Run like hell / Waiting for the worms / Stop / The trial / Outside the wall. *(cd-iss.Sep84) (re-iss.UK & US Jul90) (re-iss.cd+c Oct94 on 'EMI')*
Apr 80. (7") **RUN LIKE HELL. / DON'T LEAVE ME NOW** [-] [53]
Jun 80. (7") **COMFORTABLY NUMB. / HEY YOU** [-] [ ]
Jul 82. (d-lp) **SOUNDTRACK FROM THE FILM 'THE WALL'** [ ] [ ]
– (tracks from above + new singles)
Aug 82. (7") **WHEN THE TIGERS BROKE FREE. / BRING THE BOYS BACK HOME** [39] [ ]

—— Now just main trio **WATERS, GILMOUR, MASON.**(WRIGHT left to form ZEE) guests on lp were **ANDY BROWN** – organ, **RAY COOPER** – perc., **MICHAEL KAMEN** – piano, **RALPH RAVENSCROFT** – saxophone.

Mar 83. (lp)(c) **THE FINAL CUT** [1] [6]
– The post war dream / Your possible pasts / One of the few / The hero's return / The gunners dream / Paranoid eyes / Get your filthy hands off my desert / The Fletcher memorial home / Southampton dock / The final cut / Not now John / Two suns in the sunset. *(cd-iss.Jul86) (re-iss.cd+c Oct94 on 'EMI')*
May 83. (7") **NOT NOW JOHN. / THE HERO'S RETURN (pt.1)** [30] [ ]
(12"+=) – The hero's return (part 2).

—— **MASON** and **GILMOUR** recruited new members below to replace WATERS who went solo. **TIM RENWICK** – guitar (ex-SUTHERLAND BROTHERS & QUIVER, ex-TV SMITH) / **GUY PRATT** – bass (ex-KILLING JOKE, ex-ICEHOUSE) / **SCOTT PAGE** – saxophone.**RICK WRIGHT** – keyboards also returned p/t.

E.M.I. Columbia

Sep 87. (lp)(c)(cd) **A MOMENTARY LAPSE OF REASON** [3] [3]
– Signs of life / Learning to fly / The dogs of war / One slip / On the turning away / Yet another movie / Round and around / A new machine (part 1) / Terminal frost /

A new machine (part 2) / Sorrow.

Sep 87. (cd-ep) **LEARNING TO FLY (edit) / ONE SLIP (edit) / TERMINAL FROST (lp version) / TERMINAL FROST (DYOL version)** [ ] [70]

Dec 87. (7") **ON THE TURNING AWAY. / RUN LIKE HELL (live)** [55] [ ]
(12"+=)(cd-s+=) – ('A'live).

Jun 88. (7") **ONE SLIP. / TERMINAL FROST** [50] [ ]
(12"+=)(cd-s+=) – Dogs of war (live).

Nov 88. (d-lp)(d-c)(d-cd) **THE DELICATE SOUND OF THUNDER (live)** [11] [11]
– Shine on you crazy diamond / Learning to fly / Yet another movie / Round and around / Sorrow / The dogs of war / On the turning away / One of these days / Time / Wish you were here / Us and them * / Money / Another brick in the wall (part 2) / Comfortably numb / Run like hell. *(d-cd+= *)*

— with **GILMOUR, MASON + WRIGHT** plus **GUY PRATT / TIM RENWICK / BOB EZRIN** – keyboards, percussion / **DICK PARRY** – tenor sax / **GARY WALLIS** – percussion / **JON CARIN** – programming + add.keyboards / + backing vocalists

Apr 94. (cd)(c)(lp) **THE DIVISION BELL** [1] [1]
– Cluster one / What do you want from me / Poles apart / Marooned / A great day for freedom / Wearing the inside out / Take it back / Coming back to life / Keep talking / Lost for words / High hopes.

May 94. (7"colrd)(c-s) **TAKE IT BACK. / ('A'mix)** [23] [73]
(cd-s+=) – Astronomy Domine (live).

Oct 94. (7")(c-s) **HIGH HOPES. / KEEP TALKING** [26] [ ]
(12"+=)(cd-s+=) – One of these days.

Jun 95. (d-cd)(d-c)(q-lp)(video) **PULSE (live)** [1] [1]
– Shine on you crazy diamond / Astronomy domine / What do you want from me / Learning to fly / Keep talking / Coming back to life / Hey you / A great day for freedom / Sorrow / High hopes / Another brick in the wall (part 2) / One of these days *[not on cd]* / Speak to me / Breathe / On the run / Time / The great gig in the sky / Money / Us and them / Any colour you like / Brain damage / Eclipse / Wish you were here / Comfortably numb / Run like hell.

– compilations, etc. –

May 71. Starline/ US= Harvest; (lp) **RELICS** – (early 45's and rare) [32] [ ]
(re-iss.Oct78 on 'MFP')

Jan 74. Harvest; (d-lp)(c) **A NICE PAIR** (re-issue of first 2 lps) [21] [36] Dec 73

Nov 81. Harvest/ US= Columbia; (lp)(c) **A COLLECTION OF GREAT DANCE SONGS** (remixes) [37] [31]
– One of these days / Money / Another brick in the wall (part 2) / Wish you were here / Shine on you crazy diamond / Sheep.
(re-iss.85 on 'Fame') (cd-iss.Nov88)

Nov 81. Harvest; (7") **MONEY. / LET THERE BE MORE LIGHT** [ ] [-]

1979. Harvest; (11xlp-box) **THE FIRST XI (67-77)** (boxed lp's) [ ] [ ]

Jun 83. Capitol; (lp)(c) **WORKS (68-73)** [-] [68]

Nov 92. EMI/ US= Columbia; (7xcd)(7xc)(7xlp) **SHINE ON** [ ] [ ]
– (A SAUCERFUL OF SECRETS – MOMENTARY LAPSE . . . + rare singles)

Nov 93. See For Miles; (cd) **TONITE LET'S ALL MAKE LOVE IN LONDON . . . PLUS** [ ] [-]

Nov 95. See For Miles; (cd) **LONDON '66-'67** [ ] [-]

DAVID GILMOUR

solo with **MICK WEAVER** – keyboards / **RICK WILLIS** – bass / **JOHN WILLIE WILSON** – drums

Harvest Columbia

Jun 78. (lp)(c) **DAVID GILMOUR** [17] [29]
– Mihalis / There's no way out of it / Cry from the street / So far away / Short and sweet / Raise my rent / No way / Deafinitely / I can't breathe anymore. *(re-iss.1983 on 'Fame')*

Jun 78. (7") **THERE'S NO WAY OUT OF IT. / DEAFINATELY** [ ] [ ]

— Now with various sessioners incl.STEVE WINWOOD, JEFF PORCARO & JON LORD

Feb 84. (7")(12") **BLUE LIGHT. / CRUISE** [ ] [62]

Mar 84. (lp)(c)(cd) **ABOUT FACE** [21] [32]
– Until we sleep / Murder / Love on the air / Blue light / Out of the blue / All lovers are deranged / You know I'm right / Cruise / Let's get metaphysical / Near the end. *(re-iss.Mar87 on 'Fame')*

May 84. (7")(7"pic-d) **LOVE ON THE AIR. / LET'S GET METAPHYSICAL** [ ] [ ]

RICHARD WRIGHT

solo with **SNOWY WHITE** – guitar / **MEL COLLINS** – saxophone / **LARRY STEELE** – bass / **REG ISADORE** – drums

Harvest Columbia

Sep 78. (lp)(c) **WET DREAM** [ ] [ ]
– Medterranean c / Against the odds / Cat cruise / Summer elegy / Waves / Holiday / Mad Yannis dance / Drop in from the top / Pink's song / Funky deux.

— In 1984, he formed ZEE duo, and still appeared with FLOYD later in the 80's..

ZEE

RICHARD WRIGHT / DAVE HARRIS – guitar, vocals, keyboards, synth (ex-FASHION)

Harvest Columbia

Apr 84. (7")(12") **CONFUSION. / EYES OF A GYPSY** [ ] [ ]

Apr 84. (lp) **IDENTITY** [ ] [ ]
– Confusion / Voices / Private person / Strange rhythm / Cuts like a diamond / By touching / How do you do it / Seems we are dreaming.

NICK MASON

solo with **CARLA BLEY** and **ROBERT WYATT**

Harvest Columbia

May 81. (lp)(c) **FICTITIOUS SPORTS** [ ] [ ]
– Can't get my motor to start / I was wrong / Siam / Hot river / Boo to you too / Do ya / Wervin' / I'm a mineralist.

NICK MASON with RICK FENN

Harvest Columbia

Aug 85. (lp)(c) **PROFILES** [ ] [ ]
– Malta / Lie for a lie / Rhoda / Profiles (part 1 & 2) / Israel / And the address / Mumbo jumbo / Zip code / Black ice / At the end of the day / Profiles (part 3).

Sep 85. (7") **LIE FOR A LIE. / AND THE ADDRESS** [ ] [ ]
(12"+=) – Mumbo jumbo.

PIRATES (see under ⇒ KIDD, Johnny)

PIXIES

Formed: Boston, Massachusetts, USA . . . 1986 by L.A.born BLACK FRANCIS. Alongside fellow Bostonians THROWING MUSES, they were a surprise signing for Ivo's UK indie label '4 a.d.'. Their first vinyl outing 'COME ON PILGRIM', came out late '87, receiving plaudets from NME and Radio 1 DJ John Peel. By 1989, they had first UK Top 10 album 'DOOLITTLE'. • **Style:** Alternative hard-rock band, moving from underground PERE UBU/HUSKER DU type sound to more accessible IGGY POP influenced punk. • **Songwriters:** BLACK FRANCIS penned except; WINTERLONG + I'VE BEEN WAITING FOR YOU (Neil Young) / EVIL HEARTED YOU (Yardbirds) / HEAD ON (Jesus & Mary Chain) / CECELIA ANN (Surftones) / BORN IN CHICAGO (Paul Butterfield's Blues Band). • **Trivia:** STEVE ALBINI (Big Black) produced 1988 album, with GIL NORTON producing further material. In the 90's, KIM moved to Ohio and JOEY to Los Angeles.

Recommended: SURFER ROSA (*8) / DOOLITTLE (*9) / BOSSANOVA (*8) / TROMPE LE MONDE (*9) / FRANK BLACK (*8).

BLACK FRANCIS (b.CHARLES MICHAEL KITRIDGE THOMPSON IV) – vocals, guitar / **JERRY SANTIAGO** – lead guitar / **KIM DEAL** (Mrs.JOHN MURPHY) – bass, vocals / **DAVE LOVERING** – drums

4.a.d. Elektra

Oct 87. (m-lp)(c) **COME ON PILGRIM** [ ] [-]
– Caribou / Vamos / Islade encounter / Ed is dead / The holiday song / Nimrod's son / I've been tried / Levitate me.

Mar 88. (lp)(c)(cd) **SURFER ROSA** [ ] [-]
– Bone machine / Break my body / Something against you / Broken face / Gigantic / River Euphrates / Where is my mind? / Cactus / Tony's theme / Oh my golly! / Vamos / I'm amazed / Brick is red. *(cd+=)* – COME ON PILGRIM (m-lp)

Aug 88. (12"ep)(cd-ep) **GIGANTIC. / RIVER EUPHRATES. / VAMOS. / IN HEAVEN (LADY IN THE RADIATOR SONG)** [ ] [-]

Mar 89. (7") **MONKEY GONE TO HEAVEN. / MANTA RAY** [60] [ ]
(12"+=)(cd-s+=) – Weird at my school / Dancing the manta ray.

Apr 89. (lp)(c)(cd) **DOOLITLE** [8] [98]
– Debaser / Tame / Wave of mutilation / I bleed / There goes my gun / Here comes your man / Dead / Monkey gone to Heaven / La la love / Mr. Grieves / Crakity Jones / 13 baby / Silver / Hey / Gouge away.

Jun 89. (7") **HERE COMES YOUR MAN. / INTO THE WHITE** [54] [ ]
(12"+=)(cd-s+=) – Wave of mutilation / Bailey's walk.

— KIM DEAL was also part of amalgamation The BREEDERS (see: THROWING MUSES ⇒)

Jul 90. (7")(c-s) **VELOURIA. / I'VE BEEN WAITING FOR YOU** [28] [ ]
(12"+=)(cd-s+=) – Make believe / The thing.

Aug 90. (cd)(c)(lp) **BOSSANOVA** [3] [70]
– Cecilia Ann / Rock music / Velouria / Allison / Is she weird / Ana / All over the world / Dig for fire / Down to the wall / The happening / Blown away / Hang fire / Stormy weather / Havalina.

Oct 90. (7")(c-s) **DIG FOR FIRE. / VELVETY (instrumental)** [62] [ ]
(12"+=)(cd-s+=) – Santo / Winterlong.

May 91. (7") **PLANET OF SOUND. / BUILD HIGH** [27] [ ]
(12"+=)(c-s+=)(cd-s+=) – Evil hearted you / Theme from Narc.

Sep 91. (cd)(c)(lp) **TROMPE LE MONDE** [7] [92]
– Trompe de Monde / Planet of sound / Alec Eiffel / The sad punk / Head on / U-mass / Palace of the brine / Letter to Memphis / Bird dream Of the Olympus mons / Space (I believe in) / Subbacultha / Distance equals rate times time / Lovely day / Motorway to Roswell / The Navajo know.

— Disbanded late in '92, with BLACK FRANCIS going solo as FRANK BLACK.

FRANK BLACK

With **ERIC DREW FELDMAN** – bass, keyboards, synthetics (ex-CAPTAIN BEEFHEART) / **NICK VINCENT** – drums, percussion / + extra guitars **SANTIAGO, MORRIS TEPPER + DAVID SARDY.**

4 a.d. Elektra

Mar 93. (cd)(c)(lp) **FRANK BLACK** [9] [ ]
– Los Angeles / I heard Ramona sing / Hang on to your ego / Fu Manchu / Places named after numbers / Czar / Old black dawning / Ten percenter / Brackish boy / Two spaces / Tossed (instrumental version) / Parry the wind high, low / Adda Lee / Every time I go around here / Don't ya rile 'em.

Apr 93. (7")(c-s) **HANG ON TO YOUR EGO. / THE BALLAD OF JOHNNY HORTON** [ ] [ ]
(12"+=)(cd-s+=) – Surf epic.

— same trio augmented by **SANTIAGO, TEPPER + LYLE WORKMAN** – guitars

May 94. (7") **HEADACHE. / ('A'mix)** [53] [ ]
(10")(cd-s) – ('A'side) / Men in black / At the end of the world / Oddball.
(cd-s) – ('A'side) / Hate me / This is where I belong / Amnesia.

May 94. (cd)(c)(d-lp) **TEENAGER OF THE YEAR** [21] [ ]
– Whatever happened to Pong? / Thalassocracy / (I want to live on an) Abstract plain / Calistan / The vanishing spies / Speedy Marie / Headache / Sir Rockaby / Freedom rock / Two reelers / Fiddle riddle / Ole Mulholland / Fazer eyes / I could stay here forever / The hostess with the mostess / Superabound / Big red / Space is gonna do me good / White noise maker / Pure denizen of the citizens band / Bad, wicked world / Pie in the sky.

— FRANK BLACK had earlier in the year teamed up with ex-SEX PISTOL; GLEN MATLOCK to form tribute band FRANK BLACK & THE STAX PISTOLS.

PLAINSONG (see under ⇒ MATTHEWS, Ian)

Robert PLANT (see under ⇒ LED ZEPPELIN)

PLASTIC ONO BAND (see under ⇒ LENNON, John)

P.M. (see under ⇒ EMERSON, LAKE & PALMER)

P.M.DAWN

Formed: New Jersey, USA ... 1988 by Christian brothers ATTRELL (PRINCE BE) and JARRETT CORDES (MINUTEMIX), sons of BUCK, a KOOL AND THE GANG member. They scored massive international hit in 1991 with 'SET ADRIFT ON MEMORY BLISS'. • **Style:** Soft-soul daisy-age rappers/samplers in the mould of DE LA SOUL. The weighty PRINCE BE and slim MINUTEMIX, were also inspired by GEORGE MICHAEL and PRINCE. • **Songwriters:** ATTRELL is main pensmith, with JARRETT contributing. Covers: NORWEGIAN WOOD (THIS BIRD HAS FLOWN) (Beatles) / sampled HUSH (Deep Purple) on 1995 return single. • **Trivia:** In 1991, they lost their attire, when British Airways mislaid their gear.

Recommended: OF THE HEART, OF THE SOUL AND OF THE CROSS (*7).

PRINCE BE (ATTRELL CORDES) – vocals / **MINUTEMIX** (JARRETT CORDES) – DJ

not iss. / Wizard

1989. (7") **ODE TO A FORGETFUL MIND. / ?** [-] [ ]

Gee Street / Gee Street

May 91. (7")(c-s) **A WATCHER'S POINT OF VIEW (DON'T 'CHA THINK). / TWISTED MELLOW** [36] [ ]
(12"+=)(cd-s+=) – ('A'radio mix) / ('A'acapella mix).

Aug 91. (7")(c-s) **SET ADRIFT ON MEMORY BLISS. / FOR THE LOVE OF PEACE** [3] [1]
(12"+=)(cd-s+=) – ('A'extended).

Sep 91. (cd)(c)(lp) **OF THE HEART, OF THE SOUL AND OF THE CROSS** [8] [48]
– Intro / Reality used to be a friend of mine / Paper doll / To serenade a rainbow / Comatose / A watcher's point of view (don't 'cha think) / Even after I die / In the presence of mirrors / Set adrift on memory bliss / Shake / If I wuz u / On a clear day / The beautiful. *(cd+=)(c+=)–* Ode to a forgetful mind (the more than words mix) / Twisted mellow / For the love of peace / Reality (US mix).

Oct 91. (7")(c-s) **PAPER DOLL. / ODE TO A FORGETFUL MIND (THE MORE THAN WORDS MIX)** [49] [28]
(12"+=)(cd-s+=) – ('A'radio mix) / ('A'instrumental) / ('A'club).

Feb 92. (7")(c-s) **REALITY USED TO BE A FRIEND OF MINE (mix). / COMATOSE** [29] [ ]
(cd-s+=) – Set adrift on memory bliss.
(12"+=) – A watcher's point of view (melody mix).

— Below from the film 'Boomerang'.

Nov 92. (7")(c-s) **I'D DIE WITHOUT YOU. / ON A CLEAR DAY** [30] [3] Aug 92
(cd-s+=) – ('A'club mix).

Mar 93. (7")(c-s) **LOOKING THROUGH PATIENT EYES. / PLASTIC** [11] [6]
(12"+=)(cd-s+=) – ('A'&'B'mixes).

Mar 93. (cd)(c)(lp) **P.M.DAWN THE BLISS ALBUM ... ? (VIBRATIONS OF LOVE AND ANGER AND THE TOLERANCE OF LIFE AND EXISTENCE)** [9] [30]
– Intro / When the midnight sighs / So on and so on / Plastic / The ways of the wind / To love me more / About nothing (for the love of destiny) / Norwegian wood (this bird has flown) / Beyond infinite affections / Looking through patient eyes / Filthy rich (I don't wanna be) / More than likely / The nocturnal is in the house / When it's raining cats and dogs / I'd die without you.

Jun 93. (7")(c-s) **MORE THAN LIKELY. ("P.M.DAWN featuring BOY GEORGE"). / WHEN IT'S RAINING CATS AND DOGS** [40] [ ]
(cd-s+=) – ('A'mixes).
(cd-s) – ('A'strings mix) / You, me and the electric vibe / Fly me to the Moon / Frostbite.

Jul 93. (c-s)(cd-s) **THE WAYS OF THE WIND. /** [-] [ ]

Nov 93. (7")(c-s) **NORWEGIAN WOOD (THIS BIRD HAS FLOWN). / TAKE CARE OF MY HEART** [ ] [ ]
(cd-s+=) – Looking through patient eyes / When midnight sighs.

Sep 95. (c-s)(cd-s) **DOWNTOWN VENUS / SHE DREAMS PERSISTANT MAYBES** [58] [48]
(cd-s+=)(12"+=) – ('A'-Kiss my wife remix) / ('A'-I want to be with you mix).

Oct 95. (cd)(c)(d-lp) **JESUS WEPT** [ ] [ ]
–

Dec 95. (c-s)(cd-s) **SOMETIMES I MISS YOU SO MUCH (DEDICATED TO THE CHRIST CONSCIOUSNESS) /** [-] [97]

— Late in '95, DJ JARRETT was charged with aggrevated sexual assault on his 14 year-old cousin.

POCO

Formed: Los Angeles, California, USA ... Aug'68 as POGO, by ex-BUFFALO SPRINGFIELD members FURAY and MESSINA, plus ex-BOENZEE CRYQUE partners YOUNG and GRANTHAM. MEISNER from band The POOR, also joined but departed to join RICK NELSON's STONE CANYON BAND and later The EAGLES. Early in '69, POGO signed to 'Epic', but due to a comic strip of the same name threatening legal action, they changed to POCO. Their debut album 'PICKIN' UP THE PIECES' managed a US Top 75 placing, and by 1970 they invited again TIM SCHMIT to make up the 5-piece. Their self-titled FURAY produced second album hit No.58, but live reputation was rewarded when the following year's 'DELIVERIN'' live album made the US Top 30. Continued to be fruitful throughout the 70's, and even returned in the late 80's, with a Top 20 single 'CALL IT LOVE'. • **Style:** Country-rock outfit, flying the same airways as The EAGLES. • **Songwriters:** Group penned together and individually, with FURAY and COTTON contributing the most. Covered BRASS BUTTONS (Gram Parsons) / etc? • **Trivia:** STEELY DAN's DONALD FAGEN provided them with synthesized sound on their 'INDIAN SUMMER' album.

Recommended: POCO: THE FORGOTTEN TRAIL 1969-1974 (*6) / ROSE OF CIMARRON (*6) / PICKIN' UP THE PIECES (*7).

RICHIE FURAY (b. 9 May'44, Yellow Springs, Ohio) – guitar, vocals / **JIM MESSINA** (b. 5 Dec'47, Maywood, California) – guitar, vocals / **RUSTY YOUNG** (b.23 Feb'46, Long Beach, California) – pedal steel guitar / **GEORGE GRANTHAM** (b.20 Nov'47, Cordell, Oklahoma) – drums, vocals / **RANDY MEISNER** (b. 8 Mar'46, Scottsbluff, Nebraska) – bass, vocals (RANDY left before debut recording)

Epic / Epic

JUn 69. (7") **PICKIN' UP THE PIECES. / FIRST LOVE** [-] [ ]

Jun 69. (lp) **PICKIN' UP THE PIECES** [-] [63]
– Foreward – What a day / Nobody's fool / Calico lady / First love / Make me smile – Short changed / Pickin' up the pieces / Grand junction / Oh yeah / Just in case it happens / Tomorrow / Consequently so long. *(UK-iss.1974) (re-iss.Mar86 on 'Edsel')*

Nov 69. (7") **MY KIND OF LOVE. / HARD LUCK** [-] [ ]

— added **TIM SCHMIT** (b.30 Oct'47) – bass, vocals (ex-NEW BREED)

Jul 70. (lp)(c) **POCO** [ ] [58] Jun 90
– Hurry up / You better think twice / Honky tonk downstairs / Keep on believin' / Anyway bye bye / Don't let it pass by / Nobody's fool / El Tonto de Nadie Regrasa.

Aug 70. (7") **YOU BETTER THINK TWICE. / ANYWAY BYE BYE** [ ] [72]

Feb 71. (lp)(c) **DELIVERIN' (live)** [ ] [26]
– I guess you made it / C'mon / Hear that music / Kind woman / Hard luck – Child's claim to fame / Pickin' up the pieces / You'd better think twice / A man like me / Just in case it happens, yes indeed / Grand junction / Consequently so long. *(re-iss.1974 quad)*

Apr 71. (7") **C'MON. / I GUESS YOU MADE IT** [ ] [69] Mar 71

— **PAUL COTTON** (b.26 Feb'43) – guitar, vocals (ex-ILLINOIS SPEED PRESS) repl. MESSINA. (He joined LOGGINS & MESSINA)

Nov 71. (7") **JUST FOR ME AND YOU. / OL' FORGIVER** [ ] [ ]

Dec 71. (lp)(c) **FROM THE INSIDE** [ ] [52] Sep 71
– Bad weather / Ol' forgiver / Railroad days / From the inside / Hoe down / Just for me and you / What am I gonna do / You are the one / Do you feel it too / What if I should say I love you. *(re-iss.1974)*

Nov 72. (7") **I CAN SEE EVERYTHING. / GO AND SAY GOODBYE** [-] [ ]

Jan 73. (7") **A GOOD FEELIN' TO KNOW. / EARLY TIMES** [ ] [-]

Jan 73. (lp)(c) **A GOOD FEELIN' TO KNOW** [ ] [69] Nov 72
– And settling down / Ride the country / I can see everything / Go and say goodbye / Keeper of the fire / Early times / A good feelin' to know / Restrain / Sweet lovin'.

Mar 73. (7") **AND SETTLING DOWN. / I CAN SEE EVERYTHING** [ ] [-]

Nov 73. (lp)(c)(quad-lp) **CRAZY EYES** [ ] [38] Sep 73
– Blue water / Fool's gold / Here we go again / Brass buttons / A right along / Crazy eyes / Magnolia / Let's dance tonight.

Nov 73. (7") **FOOL'S GOLD. / HERE WE GO AGAIN** [-] [ ]

Feb 74. (7") **BLUE WATER. / MAGNOLIA** [-] [ ]

— Trimmed to a quartet when RICHIE formed SOUTHER-HILLMAN-FURAY.

Jun 74. (lp)(c) **SEVEN** [ ] [68] May 74
– Skatin' / Drivin' wheel / You've got your reasons / Just call my name / Faith in the families / Krikkit's song (passing through) / Rocky mountain breakdown / Angel.

Jun 74. (7") **ROCKY MOUNTAIN BREAKDOWN. / FAITH IN THE FAMILIES** [-] [ ]

Nov 74. (7") **BITTER BLUE. / HIGH AND DRY** [-] [ ]

Dec 74. (lp)(c) **CANTAMOS** [ ] [76] Nov 74
– Sagebush serenade / Susannah / High and dry / Western Waterloo / One horse blue / Bitter blue / Another time around / Whatever happened to your smile / All the ways.

A.B.C. / A.B.C.

Jul 75. (lp)(c) **HEAD OVER HEELS** [ ] [43]
– Keep on tryin' / Lovin' arms / Let me turn back to you / Makin' love / Down in the quarter / Sittin' on a fence / Georgia, bind my ties / Us / Flyin' solo / Dallas / I'll be back again.

Sep 75. (7") **KEEP ON TRYIN'. / GEORGIA, BIND MY TIES** [ ] [50]

Feb 76. (7") **MAKIN' LOVE. / FLYIN' SOLO** [ ] [ ]

— added **AL GARTH** – fiddle, saxophone(to **YOUNG, GRANTHAM, SCHMIT & COTTON)**

May 76. (lp)(c) **ROSE OF CIMARRON** [ ] [89]
– Rose of cimarron / Stealaway / Just like me / Company's comin' / Slow poke / Too many nights too long / P.N.S. (when you come around) / Starin' at the sky / All alone together / Tulsa turnaround. *(re-iss.Feb82 on 'MCA')*

Jul 76. (7") **ROSE OF CIMARRON. / TULSA TURNAROUND** [-] [94]

Oct 76. (7") **STARIN' AT THE SKY. / P.N.S. (WHEN YOU COME AROUND)** [ ] [-]

— Returned to a quartet when AL GARTH departed.

Apr 77. (7") **INDIAN SUMMER. / ME AND YOU** - [ ]
Apr 77. (lp)(c) **INDIAN SUMMER** [ ] 57
– Indian summer / Twenty years / Me and you / Downfall / Win or lose / Living in the band / Stay (night until noon) / Find out in time / The dance medley:- When the dance is over – Never gonna stop – When the dance is over (reprise).
Apr 77. (7") **INDIAN SUMMER. / ME AND YOU** - 50
May 77. (7") **INDIAN SUMMER. / FIND OUT IN TIME** [ ] -

—— **CHARLIE HARRISON** – bass, vocals (ex-AL STEWART) repl. TIM to EAGLES / **STEVE CHAPMAN** – drums, vocals (ex-AL STEWART) repl. GEORGE to The SECRETS / added **KIM BULLARD** – keyboards (ex-CROSBY, STILLS & NASH) (US tour)

Jan 79. (lp)(c) **LEGEND** [ ] 14 Nov 78
– Boomerang / Spellbound / Barbados / Little darlin' / Love comes love goes / Heart of the night / Crazy love / The last goodbye / Legend. *(re-iss.Jun88 on 'MCA')*
Jan 79. (7") **CRAZY LOVE. / BARBADOS** [ ] 17
Jun 79. (7") **HEART OF THE NIGHT. / THE LAST GOODBYE** [ ] 20 May 79
Sep 79. (7") **LEGEND. / INDIAN SUMMER** - [ ]

M.C.A. M.C.A.

Jul 80. (7") **UNDER THE GUN. / REPUTATION** [ ] 48
Aug 80. (lp)(c) **UNDER THE GUN** [ ] 46 Jul 80
– Under the gun / While we're still young / The everlasting kind / Down to the wire / Footsteps of a fool / Reputation / Midnight rain / A fool's Paradise / Friends in the distance / Made of stone.
Oct 80. (7") **MIDNIGHT RAIN. / FOOL'S PARADISE** - 74
Jan 81. (7") **FRIENDS IN THE DISTANCE. / EVERLASTING KIND** - [ ]
Jul 81. (7") **WIDOWMAKER. / DOWN ON THE RIVER AGAIN** - [ ]
Jul 81. (lp)(c) **BLUE AND GRAY** - 76
– Glorybound / Blue and gray / Streets of Paradise / The writing on the wall / Down the river again / Please wait for me / Widowmaker / Here comes that girl again / Sometime / The land of glory.
Mar 82. (lp)(c) **COWBOYS AND ENGLISHMEN** - [ ] Feb 82
– Sea of heartbreak / No relief in sight / There goes my heart / Ashes / Feudin' / Cajun Moon / Ribbon of darkness / If you could read my mind / While you're on your way / The price of love.
Mar 82. (7") **SEA OF HEARTBREAK. / FEUDIN'** - [ ]

Atlantic Atlantic

Oct 82. (7") **GHOST TOWN. / HIGH SIERRA** - [ ]
Oct 82. (lp)(c) **GHOST TOWN** [ ] [ ]
– Ghost town / How will you feel tonight / Shoot for the Moon / The midnight rodeo / Cry no more / Break of hearts / Love's so cruel / Special care / When hearts collide / High Sierra.
Feb 83. (7") **SHOOT FOR THE MOON. / MIDNIGHT RODEO** - 50
JUn 83. (7") **BREAK OF HEARTS. /** - [ ]

—— **FURAY** returned reforming early line-up with **GRANTHAM, COTTON, SCHMIT + YOUNG.**

Jun 84. (lp)(c) **INAMORATA** - [ ] May 84
– Days gone by / This old flame / Daylight / Odd man out / How many moons / When you love someone / Brenda X / Standing in the fire / Save a corner of your heart / The storm.
Apr 84. (7") **DAYS GONE BY. / DAYLIGHT** - 80
Jun 84. (7") **THE STORM. / SAVE A CORNER OF YOUR HEART** - [ ]
Aug 84. (7") **SAVE A CORNER OF YOUR HEART. /** - [ ]

—— They split 1984 but reformed 5 years later. **FURAY, MESSINA, GRANTHAM, MEISNER + RUSTY YOUNG.**

R.C.A. R.C.A.

Oct 89. (7") **CALL IT LOVE. / LOVIN' YOU EVERY MINUTE** [ ] 18 Aug 89
(12"+=) – Who else?.
Nov 89. (lp)(c)(cd) **LEGACY** [ ] 40 Sep 89
– When it all began / Call it love / The nature of love / What do people know / Nothin' to hide / Look within * / Rough edges / Who else? / Lovin' you every minute / If it wasn't for you / Follow your dreams. *(cd+= *)*
Nov 89. (7") **NOTHIN' TO HIDE. / IF IT WASN'T FOR YOU** - 39

– compilations, others, etc. –

Aug 75. Epic; (d-lp)(d-c) **THE VERY BEST OF POCO** [ ] 90 Jul 75
(US-cd. iss. 1989 omits 2 tracks)
Mar 76. Epic; (lp)(c) **POCO LIVE (live Nov 74)** [ ] [ ]
– Blue water / Fools gold / Rocky mountain breakdown / Bad weather / Ride the country / Angel / High and dry / Restrain / A good feelin' to know.
1979. Epic; (lp) **POCO: THE SONGS OF PAUL COTTON** (his POCO compositions) - [ ]
Nov 77. ABC; (12"ep) **ROSE OF CIMARRON. / INDIAN SUMMER. / KEEP ON TRYIN'. / STARIN' AT THE SKY** [ ] [ ]
Mar 80. CBS/ US= Columbia; (lp)(c) **POCO: THE SONGS OF RICHIE FURAY**(his POCO compositions) [ ] [ ]
May 80. MCA; (7") **ROSE OF CIMARRON. / LEGEND** [ ] [ ]
Jan 90. CBS-Legacy; (cd) **POCO: THE FORGOTTEN TRAIL (1969-74)** [ ] [ ]

RICHIE FURAY

Elektra Asylum

Aug 76. (lp)(c) **I'VE GOT A REASON** [ ] [ ]
– Look at the sun / We'll see / Starlight / Gettin' through / I've got a reason / Mighty maker / You're the one I love / Still rolling stones / Over and over again. *(re-iss.May82 on 'Myrrh')*
Jul 78. (7") **THIS MAGIC MOMENT. / BITTERSWEET LOVE** - [ ]
Jul 78. (lp)(c) **DANCE A LITTLE LIGHT** [ ] [ ]
– It's your love / Your friends / Ooh dreamer / Yesterday's gone / Someone who cares / Dance a little light / This magic moment / Bittersweet love / You better believe it / Stand your guard.
Nov 78. (7") **DANCE A LITTLE LIGHT. / OOH DREAMER** - [ ]
Oct 79. (7") **I STILL HAVE DREAMS. / HEADIN' SOUTH** - 39
Jan 80. (7") **LONELY TOO LONG. / HEADIN' SOUTH** - [ ]
Feb 80. (lp) **I STILL HAVE DREAMS** - [ ]
May 80. (7") **COME ON. / OOOH CHILD** - [ ]

Myrrh Myrrh

May 82. (lp)(c) **SEASONS OF CHANGE** [ ] [ ]
– Hallelujah / Endless flight / Yellow moon rising / Seasons of change / My Lord and my God / Rise up / Promise of love / Home to my lord / For the prize / Through it all.

POET & THE ROOTS (see under ⇒ JOHNSON, Linton Kwesi)

POGUES

Formed: North London, England ... late 1983 by Tipperary raised MacGOWAN, STACEY and FINER. Originally calling themselves POGUE MAHONE (Gaelic for 'kiss my arse'), they added drinking buddies RANKEN and FEARNLEY, plus female singer / bassist CAIT O'RIORDAN. In Spring 1984, they formed own self-named label, and issued 'DARK STREETS OF LONDON', which received an official BBC radio ban, after they found out what their name meant. A month later they secured a deal with 'Stiff', and became The POGUES. Their debut album 'RED ROSES FOR ME' produced by Stan Brennan, broke into the UK Top 100, as they acquired growing support from live audiences around the country. In Apr'85, they released 45 'A PAIR OF BROWN EYES' which was produced by ELVIS COSTELLO, who stayed on for their Top 20 album 'RUM, SODOMY & THE LASH'. On the 16th May'86, COSTELLO married CAIT, and she left them in Nov'86 after writing Top 50 hit 'HAUNTED' for the Alex Cox film 'SID & NANCY'. Around the same time, the group played 'The McMahon Gang' in Cox's movie 'Straight To Hell'. They met ex-CLASH singer JOE STRUMMER on the set, and he even temporarily deputised for the absent MacGOWAN on early 1988 US tour. This period also saw them peak at No.3 in the album charts with 'IF I SHOULD FALL FROM GRACE WITH GOD', which parented the No.2 Christmas 1987 hit 'FAIRY TALE OF NEW YORK', which featured solo artist KIRSTY MacCOLL on dual vox with SHANE. • **Style:** Pioneers of a new wave of Celtic punk-folk. A cross between The DUBLINERS (who they jointly hit the Top 10 with in 1987's version of 'THE IRISH ROVER') and The CLASH. MacGOWAN was/is a renowned heavy drinker, with a spacious set of front teeth and an uncompromising on/off stage appeal. • **Songwriters:** Group compositions, except; THE BAND PLAYED WALTZING MATILDA (Eric Bogle) / DIRTY OLD TOWN (Ewan MacColl) / WILD ROVER + MADRA RUM (trad.) / THE IRISH ROVER (Dubliners) / MAGGIE MAY (Rod Stewart) / HONKY TONK WOMAN (Rolling Stones) / WHISKEY IN THE JAR (Thin Lizzy) / MISS OTIS REGRETS (Cole Porter) / GOT A LOT O' LIVIN' TO DO (Elvis Presley) / HOW COME (Ronnie Lane) / WHEN THE SHIP COMES IN (Bob Dylan). FINER became main writer in the mid-90's with others contributed some material. • **Trivia:** FEARNLEY married actress Danielle Von Zerneck on 7th Oct'89. In the early '90s, they supplied the soundtarack for TV play 'A MAN YOU DON'T MEET EVERY DAY'. The song 'Fiesta' is used on Vauxhall-Tigra TV ad, after rights were sold from 1988 album.

Recommended: RED ROSES FOR ME (*8) / RUM, SODOMY & THE LASH (*9) / IF I SHOULD FALL FROM GRACE WITH GOD (*8) / PEACE AND LOVE (*6) / HELL'S DITCH (*6) / WAITING FOR HERB (*5) / POGUE MAHONE (*5) / THE BEST OF THE POGUES (*9) / THE BEST OF THE REST OF THE POGUES (*7)

SHANE MacGOWAN (b.25 Dec'57, Kent, England) – vocals, guitar (ex-NIPS) / **JAMES FEARNLEY** (b.10 Oct'54, Manchester, England) – accordion (ex-NIPS) / **SPIDER STACEY** (b.PETER, 14 Dec'58, Eastbourne, UK) – tin whistle (ex-NIPS) / **JEM FINER** (b.JEREMY, 29 Jul'55, Dublin, Ireland) – banjo / **CAIT O'RIORDAN** – bass, vocals / **ANDREW RANKEN** (b.13 Nov'53, London) – drums

Pogue Mahone not issued

May 84. (7") **DARK STREETS OF LONDON.(as "POGUE MAHONE") / THE BAND PLAYED WALTZING MATILDA** [ ] -
(soon re-iss.Jun84 on 'Stiff' by **"The POGUES"** *their new adopted name)*

Stiff not issued

Sep 84. (lp)(c) **RED ROSES FOR ME** 89 -
– Transmetropolitan / The battle of Brisbane / The auld triangle / Waxie's dargle / Boys from the county Hell / Sea shanty / Dark streets of London / Streams of whiskey / Poor daddy / Dingle regatta / Greenland whale fisheries / Down in the ground where the dead men go / Kitty. *(cd-iss.May87) (re-iss.Jan89 on 'WEA')*
Oct 84. (7") **BOYS FROM THE COUNTY HELL. / REPEAL OF THE LICENSING LAWS** [ ] -
Mar 85. (7")(7"pic-d) **A PAIR OF BROWN EYES. / WHISKEY YOU'RE THE DEVIL** 72 -
(12"+=) – Muirshin Durkin.

—— added p/t **PHIL CHEVRON** (b.RYAN, 17 Jun'57, Dublin) – guitar, producer (ex-RADIATORS FROM SPACE)

Jun 85. (7")(7"pic-d)(7"green) **SALLY MacLENNANE. / WILD ROVER** 51 -
(12"+=) – The leaving of Liverpool.
Aug 85. (lp)(c)(cd) **RUM, SODOMY & THE LASH** 13 -
– The sick bed of Cuchulainn / The old main drag / Wild cats of Kilkenny / I'm a man you don't meet every day / A pair of brown eyes / Sally MacLennane / Dirty old town / Jesse James / Navigator / Billy's bones / The gentleman soldier / And the band played waltzing Matilda. *(cd+=)* – A pistol for Paddy Garcia. *(re-iss.Jan89 on 'WEA')*
Aug 85. (7")(7"pic-d) **DIRTY OLD TOWN. / A PISTOL FOR PADDY GARCIA** 62 -
(12"+=) – The parting glass.
Feb 86. (7"ep)(12"ep)(c-ep)(7"pic-ep) **POGUETRY IN MOTION** 29 -
– A rainy night in Soho / The body of an American / London girl / Planxty Noel Hill.

M.C.A. M.C.A.

Aug 86. (7") **HAUNTED. / JUNK THEME** [42] [ ]
(12"+=) – Hot-dogs with everything.

— (above single from the motion picture 'Sid & Nancy')

— **DARRYL HUNT** (b. 4 May'50, Bournemouth, England) – bass (ex-PRIDE O' THE CROSS) replaced CAIT

Stiff not issued

Mar 87. (7") **THE IRISH ROVER. (as "POGUES & The DUBLINERS") / THE RARE OLD MOUNTAIN DEW** [8] [ ]
(12"+=) – The Dubliners fancy.

— added **TERRY WOODS** (now 8-piece)

Pogue Mahone-EMI Island

Nov 87. (7") **FAIRYTALE OF NEW YORK. ("POGUES featuring KIRSTY MacCOLL) / BATTLE MARCH MEDLEY** [2] [ ]
(12"+=)(c-s+=)(cd-s+=) – Shanne Bradley.

Jan 88. (lp)(c)(cd) **IF I SHOULD FALL FROM GRACE WITH GOD** [ ] [88]
– If I should fall from grace with God / Turkish song of the damned / Bottle of smoke / Fairytale of New York (featuring KIRSTY MacCOLL) / Metropolis / Thousands are sailing / Fiesta / Medley:- The recruiting sergeant – The rocky road to Dublin – Galway races / Streets of Sorrow – Birmingham Six / Lullaby of London / Sit down by the fire / The broad majestic Shannon / Worms. *(cd+=)* – South Australia / The battle march medley. *(re-iss.Jan89 on 'WEA')*

Feb 88. (7") **IF I SHOULD FALL FROM GRACE WITH GOD. / SALLY MacLENNANE (live)** [58] [ ]
(7"ep)(12"red-ep)(cd-ep+=) – A pair of brown eyes / Dirty old town (both live).

Jul 88. (7") **FIESTA. / SKETCHES OF SPAIN** [24] [ ]
(12"+=)(cd-s+=) – South Australia.

Dec 88. (7") **YEAH YEAH YEAH YEAH YEAH. / LIMERICK'S RAKE** [43] [ ]
(12"+=)(cd-s+=) – Honky tonk women.

WEA WEA

Jun 89. (7")(c-s) **MISTY MORNING ALBERT BRIDGE. / COTTONFIELDS** [41] [ ]
(12"+=)/ /(cd-s+=) – Young Ned of the hill./ / Train of love.

Jul 89. (lp)(c)(cd) **PEACE AND LOVE** [5] [ ]
– White City / Young Ned of the hill / Misty morning, Albert Bridge / Cotton fields / Blue heaven / Down all the days / U.S.A. / Lorelei / Gartloney rats / Boat train / Tombstone / Night train to Lorca / London you're a lady / Gridlock.

Aug 89. (7")(c-s) **WHITE CITY. / EVERYMAN IS A KING** [ ] [ ]
(12")(cd-s) – ('A'side) / Maggie May / Star of the County Down.

May 90. (7")(c-s) **JACK'S HEROES. ("POGUES & THE DUBLINERS") / WHISKEY IN THE JAR** [63] [ ]
(12"+=)(cd-s+=) – ('B'extended). *('A'side used by Eire in World Cup)*

Aug 90. (7") **SUMMER IN SIAM. / BASTARD LANDLORD** [64] [ ]
(12"+=)(cd-s+=) – Hell's ditch (instrumental) / The Irish rover.

Sep 90. (cd)(c)(lp) **HELL'S DITCH** [12] [ ]
– The sunnyside of the street / Sayonara / The ghost of a smile / Hell's ditch / Lorca's novena / Summer in Siam / Rain street / Rainbow man / The wake of the Medusa / House of the gods / Five green onions and Jean / Maidria Rua / Six to go.

Apr 91. (cd-s) **SAYONARA / CURSE OF LOVE / INFINITY** [-] [ ]

Sep 91. (7") **A RAINY NIGHT IN SOHO (remix). / SQUID OUT OF WATER** [67] [ ]
(12"+=)/ /(cd-ep+=) – Infinity./ / POGUETRY IN MOTION (ep).

Sep 91. (cd)(c)(lp) **THE BEST OF THE POGUES** (compilation) [11] [ ]
– Fairytale of New York / Sally MacLennane / Dirty old town / The Irish rover / A pair of brown eyes / Streams of whiskey / A rainy night in Soho / Fiesta / Rain street / Misty morning, Albert Bridge / White City / Thousand are sailing / The broad majestic Shannon / The body of an American.

Dec 91. (7") **FAIRYTALE OF NEW YORK. / FIESTA** [36] [ ]
(12"+=)(cd-s+=) – A pair of brown eyes / Sick bed of Cuchulainn / Maggie May.

— p/t JOE STRUMMER is deposed by member SPIDER who takes over vox.

May 92. (7")(c-s) **HONKY TONK WOMAN. / CURSE OF LOVE** [56] [ ]
(12"+=)/ /(cd-s+=) – Infinity./ / The parting glass.

Jun 92. (cd)(c)(lp) **THE BEST OF THE REST OF THE POGUES** [ ] [ ]
(compilation out-takes)
– If I should fall from grace with God / The sick bed of Cuchulainn / The old main drag / Boys from the County Hell / Young Ned of the hill / Dark streets of London / The auld triangle / Repeal of the licensing laws / Yeah yeah yeah yeah yeah / London girl / Honky tonk women / Summer in Siam / Turkish song of the damned / Lullaby of London / The sunnyside of the street / Hell's ditch.

— (Sep91) **SHANE McGOWAN** left when his health deteriorated. **JOE STRUMMER** (ex-CLASH) deputised for him on tour.

— added 8th member & producer **MICHAEL BROOK** – infinite guitar

W.E.A. W.E.A.

Aug 93. (7")(c-s) **TUESDAY MORNING. / FIRST DAY OF FOREVER** [18] [ ]
(cd-s+=) – Turkish song of the damned (live).
(cd-s) – ('A'side) / London calling / I fought the law (both live with JOE STRUMMER).

Sep 93. (cd)(c)(lp) **WAITING FOR HERB** [20] [ ]
– Tuesday morning / Smell of petroleum / Haunting / Once upon a time / Sitting on top of the world / Drunken boat / Big city / Girl from the Wadi Hammamat / Modern world / Pachinko / My baby's gone / Small hours.

Jan 94. (7")(c-s) **ONCE UPON A TIME. / TRAIN KEPT ROLL-ING ON** [66] [ ]
(12"+=)(cd-s+=) – Tuesday morning / Paris St.Germain.

— FEARNEY and WOODS departed, apparently due to the brief Christmas comeback of SHANE McGOWAN.

— **SPIDER / JEM / DARRYL + RANKEN** added **JAMIE CLARKE** – banjo / **JAMES McNALLY** – accordion, uilleann pipes / **DAVID COULTER** – mandolin, tambourine

Sep 95. (7"colrd)(c-s) **HOW COME. / EYES OF AN ANGEL** [ ] [ ]
(cd-s+=) – Tuesday morning (live) / Big city (live).

Oct 95. (cd)(c)(lp) **POGUE MAHONE** [ ] [ ]
– How come / Living in a world without her / When the ship comes in / Anniversary / Amadie / Love you 'till the end / Bright lights / Oretown / Pont Mirabeau / Tosspint / Four o'clock in the morning / Where that love's been gone / The Sun and the Moon.

– other special POGUES releases, etc. –

Nov 90. Chrysalis; (7")(c-s) **MISS OTIS REGRETS. (by "KIRSTY MacCOLL") / JUST ONE OF THOSE THINGS (by "The POGUES")** [ ] [ ]
(12"+=)(cd-s+=) (song by "Aztec Camera", all 3 songs on 'Chrysalis' Cole Porter tribute album 'Red, White & Blue').

Buster POINDEXTER (see under ⇒ NEW YORK DOLLS)

POISON

Formed: Harrisburg, Pennsylvania, USA . . . Mar'84 by former SPECTRES members MICHAELS and ROCKETT. In 1985, they moved to Los Angeles, where they signed to 'Enigma' records which was licensed to 'Capitol'. Their first album 'LOOK WHAT THE CAT DRAGGED IN', was first of many albums to hit the Top 3. Early in 1989, they had massive selling US No.1 with single 'EVERY ROSE HAS ITS THORN'. • **Style:** Glamourous heavy/soft metal outfit, similar to GUNS'N' ROSES, but with the bleached hair look, except DALL. • **Songwriters:** MICHAELS – DEVILLE penned, except YOUR MAMA DON'T DANCE (Loggins & Messina). • **Trivia:** Late in 1990, BRETT co-wrote and produced girlfriend SUSIE HATTON's debut lp.

Recommended: LOOK WHAT THE CAT DRAGGED IN (*6) / OPEN UP AND SAY . . . AAH! (*6).

BRET MICHAELS (b.15 Mar'?, Pittsburgh, Pennsylvania) – vocals / **C.C.DEVILLE** – lead guitar (ex-SCREAMING MIMI) repl. SLASH to GUNS'N'ROSES / **BOBBY DALL** (b. 2 Nov'?, Florida) – bass / **RIKKI ROCKETT** (b. 8 Aug'61, Mechanicsburg, Pennsylvania) – drums

M.F.N. Capitol

Oct 86. (lp)(c)(pic-lp) **LOOK WHAT THE CAT DRAGGED IN** [ ] [3] Jul 86
– Cry tough / I want action / I won't forget you / Play dirty / Look what the cat dragged in / Talk dirty to me / Want some, need some / Blame it on you / £1 bad boy / Let me go to the show. *(re-iss.lp/c/pic-lp/cd.Apr89) (re-iss.cd+c Jul94)*

May 87. (7") **TALK DIRTY TO ME. / WANT SOME, NEED SOME** [67] [9] Mar 87
(12"+=)(12"pic-d+=) – (interview).

Jun 87. (7") **I WANT ACTION. / PLAY DIRTY** [-] [50]

Aug 87. (7") **CRY TOUGH. / LOOK WHAT THE CAT DRAGGED IN** [ ] [ ]
(12"+=)(12"pic-d+=) – ('A'-US mix). *(re-iss.Apr89)*

Capitol Enigma

Sep 87. (7") **I WON'T FORGET YOU. / BLAME IT ON YOU** [-] [13]

Apr 88. (7") **NOTHIN' BUT A GOOD TIME. / LOOK BUT YOU CAN'T TOUCH** [35] [6]
(12"+=) – Livin' for a minute.

May 88. (lp)(c)(cd)(pic-lp)(pic-cd) **OPEN UP AND SAY . . .AAH!** [23] [2]
– Love on the rocks / Nothin' but a good time / Back to the rocking horse / Good love / Tearin' down the walls / Look but you can't touch / Fallen angel / Every rose has its thorn / Your mama can't dance / Bad to be good. *(re-iss.cd+c Mar94)*

Oct 88. (7") **FALLEN ANGEL. / BAD TO BE GOOD** [59] [12] Jul 88
(12"+=)(12"pic-d+=) – (interview).

Oct 88. (7") **EVERY ROSE HAS ITS THORN. / LIVING FOR THE MINUTE** [-] [1]

Jan 89. (7")(7"sha-pic-d) **EVERY ROSE HAS ITS THORN. / BACK TO THE ROCKING HORSE** [13] [-]
(12"+=)(cd-s+=) – Gotta face the hangman.

Apr 89. (7")(7"green) **YOUR MAMA DON'T DANCE. / TEARIN' DOWN THE WALLS** [13] [10] Feb 89
(12"+=)(cd-s+=)(12"green+=) – Love on the rocks.

Jul 89. (7")(c-s) **NOTHIN' BUT A GOOD TIME. / LIVIN' FOR THE MINUTE** [48] [-]
(12"+=)(cd-s+=)(12"pic-d+=) – Look what the cat dragged in (live).

Jun 90. (7")(c-s) **UNSKINNY BOP. / SWAMP JUICE (SOUL-O)** [15] [3]
(12"+=)(cd-s+=)(12"pic-d+=) – Valley of lost souls / Poor boy blues.

Jul 90. (cd)(c)(lp) **FLESH & BLOOD** [3] [2]
– Strange days of Uncle Jack / Valley of lost souls / Unskinny bop / (Flesh and blood) Sacrifice / Swamp juice (soul-o) / Let it play / Life goes on / Come Hell or high water / Ride the wind / Don't give up an inch / Something to believe in / Ball and chain / Life loves a tragedy / Poor boy blues. *(re-iss.cd Sep94)*

Oct 90. (7")(c-s) **SOMETHING TO BELIEVE IN. / BALLS AND CHAIN** [ ] [4]
(12"+=) – Look what the cat dragged in / Your mama don't dance / Every rose has its thorn.
(10"yellow+=)(cd-s+=) – (Bret Michaels interview).

Jan 91. (c-s)(12") **RIDE THE WIND. / ?** [-] [38]

Apr 91. (c-s)(12") **LIFE GOES ON. / ?** [-] [35]

Nov 91. (7")(7"clear) **SO TELL ME WHY. / GUITAR SOLO** [25] [ ]
(12"+=)(cd-s+=) – Unskinny bop (live) / Ride the wind (live).
(12"+=)(cd-s+=) – Only time will tell / No more Lookin' back (poison jazz)

Nov 91. (cd)(c)(d-lp) **SWALLOW THIS LIVE** (live / +studio tracks *) [52] [51]
– Intro / Look what the dragged in / Look but you can't touch / Good love / I want action / Something to believe in / Poor boy blues / Unskinny bop / Every rose has its thorn / Fallen angel / Your mama don't dance / Nothin' but a good time / Talk dirty to me / So tell me why* / Souls on fire* / Only time will tell* / No more lookin' back (poison jazz).

— (Nov91) DeVILLE left, and was replaced by **RICKIE KOTZEN** (Jun92)

Feb 93. (7")(c-s) **STAND. / STAND (CHR edit)** [25] [50] Jan 93
(cd-s) – ('A'side) / Native tongue / Scream / Whip comes down / ('A'lp version).

Feb 93. (cd)(c)(lp) **NATIVE TONGUE** [20] [16]
– Native tongue / THe scream / Stand / Stay alive / Until you suffer some (Fire and ice) / Body talk / Bring it home / 7 days over you / Richie's acoustic thang / Ain't that the truth / Theatre of the soul / Strike up the band / Ride child ride / Blind faith / Bastard son of a thousand blues.

Apr 93. (7"pic-d)(c-s) **UNTIL YOU SUFFER SOME (FIRE AND ICE). / STAND (acoustic)** [32] [ ]

(cd-s+=) – Bastard son of a thousand blues / ('A'mix).
(12"colrd+=) – Strike up the band / ('A'mix).

POLICE

Formed: London, England based . . . early 1977 by COPELAND, STING and PADOVANI. In May'77, they released debut 45 'FALL OUT' for Miles Copeland's (Stewart's brother) indie label 'Illegal'. Immediately after this, they were invited by GONG member MIKE HOWLETT to join veteran guitarist ANDY SUMMERS in live band STRONTIUM 90. When PADOVANI left in August, SUMMERS decided to join. They first sessioned on German artist EBERHARD SCHOENER's 'Video Flashback' album. Early 1978, while recording debut album, they were seen with new dyed blonde look for a Wrigley's Spearmint Gum TV ad. After a support slot on a SPIRIT tour, they signed to 'A&M'. Their first 'A&M' 45, 'ROXANNE' was well-received but fails to hit chart. Their follow-up 'CAN'T STAND LOSING YOU' broke into the 50, and helped debut album 'OUTLANDOS D'AMOUR', sell well. With a re-release of 'ROXANNE' in Apr'79 which hit UK No.12, it eventually climbed into the Top 10. In the US, the single also peaked at 32, and a revived 'CAN'T STAND LOSING YOU', hit the Top 3 in Britain. By Autumn of '79, they were at No.1 with both single 'MESSAGE IN A BOTTLE' and album 'REGGATTA DE BLANC' (aka WHITE REGGAE). For the next half a decade they became worldwide superstars, until their unofficial split around mid-80's. • **Style:** New wave / reggae rock band with a social comment and an aspiration for experimentation. (see also; STING ⇒). • **Songwriters:** Mainly STING compositions, with some by or with either COPELAND or SUMMERS. STING also wrote lyrics. • **Trivia:** NIGEL GRAY produced or co-produced 70's albums. HUGH PADGHAM co-produced 'GHOST IN THE MACHINE'.

Recommended: EVERY BREATH YOU TAKE – THE SINGLES (*9) / OUTLANDOS D'AMOUR (*8) / REGGATTA DE BLANC (*7) / ZENYATTA MONDATTA (*7) / GHOST IN THE MACHINE (*7) / SYNCHRONICITY (*9)

STING (b.GORDON SUMNER, 2 Oct'51, Wallsend, England) – vocals, bass (ex-LAST EXIT) / **HENRY PADOVANI** (b. Corsica) – guitar, vocals / **STEWART COPELAND** (b.19 Jul'52, Egypt) – drums, vocals (ex-CURVED AIR)

Illegal / not issued

May 77. (7") **FALL OUT. / NOTHING ACHIEVING** [ ] [-]
(re-iss.Dec79 reached UK No.47)

—— **ANDY SUMMERS** (b.ANDREW SOMERS, 31 Dec'42, Lanc., England) – guitar (ex-KEVIN AYERS, ex-KEVIN COYNE, ex-ERIC BURDON, ex-SOFT MACHINE) soon repl. HENRY (after brief spell as 4-piece) left to form his FLYING PADOVANI BROTHERS

A & M / A & M

Apr 78. (7")(12") **ROXANNE. / PEANUTS** [ ] [-]
(re-iss.Apr79 reached UK No.12)

Aug 78. (7")(7"sha-pic-d)(7"in most colours) **CAN'T STAND LOSING YOU. / DEAD END JOB** [42] [-]
(re-iss.Jun79 hit UK No.2)

Oct 78. (lp)(c)(blue-lp) **OUTLANDOS D'AMOUR** [ ] [23] Feb 79
– Next to you / So lonely / Roxanne / Hole in my life / Peanuts / Can't stand losing you / Truth hits everybody / Born in the 50's / Be my girl – Sally / Masoko tanga. *(resurrected Apr79 made No.6) (cd-iss.1983 + Aug91)*

Oct 78. (7") **SO LONELY. / NO TIME THIS TIME** [ ] [ ]
(re-iss.Feb80 made No.6)

Jan 79. (7") **ROXANNE. / DEAD END JOB** [-] [32]

Apr 79. (7") **CAN'T STAND LOSING YOU. / NO TIME THIS TIME** [-] [ ]

Sep 79. (7")(7"green)(7"sha-pic-d) **MESSAGE IN A BOTTLE. / LANDLORD** [1] [74] Nov 79

Oct 79. (lp)(c)(2x10") **REGGATTA DE BLANC** [1] [25]
– Message in a bottle / Reggata de blanc / It's alright for you / Bring on the night / Deathwish / Walking on the Moon / On any other day / The bed's too big without you / Contact / Does everybody stare / No time this time. *(cd-iss.1983)*

Nov 79. (7")(12") **WALKING ON THE MOON. / VISIONS OF THE NIGHT** [1] [-]

Jan 80. (7") **BRING ON THE NIGHT. / VISIONS OF THE NIGHT** [-] [ ]

Sep 80. (7")(7"sha-pic-d) **DON'T STAND SO CLOSE TO ME. / FRIENDS** [1] [-]

Oct 80. (lp)(c) **ZENYATTA MONDATTA** [1] [5]
– Don't stand so close to me / Driven to tears / When the world is running down, you make the best of what's still around / Canary in a coalmine / Voices in my head / Bombs away / De do do do, de da da da / Behind my camel / Man in a suitcase / Shadows in the rain / The other way of stopping. *(re-iss.+cd.Sep86)*

Oct 80. (7") **DE DO DO DO, DE DA DA DA. / FRIENDS** [-] [10]

Dec 80. (7")(7"pic-d) **DE DO DO DO, DE DA DA DA. / A SERMON** [5] [-]

Feb 81. (7") **DON'T STAND SO CLOSE TO ME. / A SERMON** [-] [10]

Sep 81. (7") **INVISIBLE SUN. / SHAMELLE** [2] [ ]

Sep 81. (7") **EVERY LITTLE THING SHE DOES IS MAGIC. / SHAMBELLE** [-] [3]

Oct 81. (lp)(c) **GHOSTS IN THE MACHINE** [1] [2]
– Spirits in the material world / Every little thing she does is magic / Invisible sun / Hungry for love / emolition man / Too much information / Rehumanize yourself / One world (not there) / Omega man / Darkness / Omega man / Secret journey / Darkness. *(cd-iss.1983)*

Oct 81. (7")(7"pic-d) **EVERY LITTLE THING SHE DOES IS MAGIC. / FLEXIBLE STRATEGIES** [1] [-]

Dec 81. (7") **SPIRITS IN THE MATERIAL WORLD. / LOW LIFE** [12] [-]

Jan 82. (7") **SPIRITS IN THE MATERIAL WORLD. / FLEXIBLE STRATEGIES** [-] [11]

Apr 82. (7") **SECRET JOURNEY. / DARKNESS** [-] [46]

May 83. (7")(7"pic-d) **EVERY BREATH YOU TAKE. / MURDER BY NUMBERS** [1] [1]
(d-7"+=) – Truth hits everybody / Man in a suitcase.

Jun 83. (lp)(c)(cd) **SYNCHRONICITY** [1] [1]
– Synchronicity / alking in your footsteps / O my God / Mother / Miss Gradenko / Synchronicity II / Every breath you take / King of pain / Wrapped around your finger / Tea in the sahara. *(c+cd+=)* – Murder by numbers. *(re-iss.cd+c Mar93)*

Jul 83. (7")(7"pic-d-x3) **WRAPPED AROUND YOUR FINGER. / SOMEONE TO TALK TO** [7] [-]
(12"+=) – Message in a bottle / I burn for Mary.

Aug 83. (7") **KING OF PAIN. / SOMEONE TO TALK TO** [-] [3]

Oct 83. (7")(12") **SYNCHRONICITY II. / ONCE UPON A DAYDREAM** [17] [16] Nov 83

Jan 84. (7")(12") **KING OF PAIN. / TEA IN THE SAHARA** [17] [-]

Jan 84. (7") **WRAPPED AROUND YOUR FINGER. / TEA IN THE SAHARA** [-] [8]

—— Split up although not officially, until 1986. All members went solo.

– compilations, etc. –

Jun 80. A&M; (6x7"box) **SIX PACK** [17] [ ]
– (first 5 – A&M singles re-issued in blue vinyl, plus added 45 below) **THE BED'S TOO BIG WITHOUT YOU. / TRUTH HITS EVERYBODY**

Sep 86. A&M; (7")(12") **DON'T STAND SO CLOSE TO ME '86. / (live version)** [24] [46]

Nov 86. A&M; (lp)(c)(cd) **EVERY BREATH YOU TAKE – THE SINGLES** [1] [7]
– Roxanne / Can't stand losing you / Message in a bottle / Walking on the Moon / Don't stand so close to me '86 / De do do do, de da da da / Every little thing she does is magic / Invisible Sun / Spirits in the material world / Every breath you take / King of pain / Wrapped around your finger. *(c/cd+=)* – So lonely. *(re-iss.UK Mar92 hit No.31)*

Nov 86. A&M; (7")(12") **ROXANNE '86. / SYNCHRONICITY II** [ ] [7]

Jan 87. A&M; (7") **WALKING ON THE MOON. / MESSAGE IN A BOTTLE** [-] [ ]

Apr 88. A&M; (3"cd-ep) **COMPACT HITS** [ ] [ ]
– Roxanne / Can't stand losing you / Canary in a coalmine / Bed's too big without you.

Jun 89. A&M; (d-c) **REGATTA DE BLANC / SYNCHRONICITY** [ ] [-]

Oct 92. A&M; (cd)(c)(lp) **THE POLICE: GREATEST HITS (like above)** [10] [ ]

Oct 93 A&M; (cd)(c) **MESSAGE IN A BOX: THE COMPLETE RECORDINGS** [-] [79]

May 95. A&M; (7"sha-pic-d)(12") **CAN'T STAND LOSING YOU (live). / VOICES IN MY HEAD (mix)** [27] [ ]
(cd-s+=) – Roxanne live).
(d12") – Voices in my head (8 remixes).

May 95. A&M; (d-cd)(d-c)(d-lp) **THE POLICE LIVE! (live)** [25] [86]
– Next to you / So lonely / Truth hits everybody / Walking on the Moon / Hole in my life / Fall out / Bring on the night / Message in a bottle / The bed's too big without you / Peanuts / Roxanne / Can't stand losing you / Landlord / Born in the 50's / Be my girl – Sally / Synchronicity I / Synchronicity II / Walking in your footsteps / Message in a bottle / O my God / De do do do, de da da da / Wrapped around your finger / Tea in the Sahara / Spirits in the material world / King of pain / Don't stand so close to me / Every breathe you take / Roxanne / Can't stand losing you / So lonely.

KLARK KENT

Pseudonym used by **STEWART COPELAND**.

Kryptone / not issued

May 78. (7"green) **DON'T CARE. / THRILLS / OFFICE GIRLS** [ ] [ ]
(re-iss.Jul78 on green vinyl 'A&M', hit No.48)

Nov 78. (7"green) **TOO KOOL TO KALYPSO. / THEME FROM KINETIC RITUAL** [ ] [ ]

A & M / A & M

May 80. (7"green) **AWAY FROM HOME. / OFFICE TALK** [ ] [ ]

Jul 80. (10"green-lp) **KLARK KENT** (compilation) [ ] [ ]

Aug 80. (7"green) **RICH IN A DITCH. / GRANDELINQUENT** [ ] [ ]

STEWART COPELAND

A & M / A & M

Jan 84. (7") **DON'T BOX ME IN. (by "STEWART COPELAND & STAN RIDGWAY") / DRAMA AT HOME** [ ] [ ]

Jan 84. (lp)(c) **RUMBLE FISH (Soundtrack)** [ ] [ ]
– Don't box me in / Tulsa tango / Our mother is alive / Party at someone's else place / Biff gets stomped by Rusty James / Brothers on wheels / Weat Tulsa story / Tulsa rags / Father on the stairs / Hostile bridge to Benny's / Your mother is not crazy / Personal midget – Clain's ballroom / Motorboy's fate.

—— Soundtrack also feat. vocals of ex-WALL OF VOODOO man STAN RIDGWAY.

Apr 85. (7") **KOTEJA. (by "STEWART COPELAND & RAY LEMA") / GONG ROCK** [ ] [ ]

—— Next featured numerous African musicians.

May 85. (lp)(c) **THE RHYTHMATIST** [ ] [ ]
– Koteja (oh Bolilla) / Brazzaville / Liberte / Coco / Kemba / amburu sunset / Gong rock / Franco / Serengeti / Long walk / African dream. *(cd-iss.1988)*

I.R.S. / I.R.S.

Aug 86. (7"w/ ADAM ANT) **OUT OF BOUNDS. / ('A' solo)** [-] [ ]

Aug 86. (7")(12") **LOVE LESSONS. (by "STEWART COPELAND & DEREK HOLT") / AMY (SILENT MOVIES)** [ ] [-]

—— DEREK HOLT from CLIMAX BLUES BAND.

M.C.A. / M.C.A.

Nov 87. (7") **THE EQUALIZER (from US TV series). / ('A'instrumental)** [ ] [ ]
(12"+=) – Love lessons.

Dec 87. (lp)(c)(cd) **THE EQUALIZER (AND OTHER CLIFFHANGERS)** [ ] [ ]

– Lurking solo / Music box / Screaming Lord Cole and the Commanches / The Equalizer busy equalizing / Green fingers (ten thumbs) / Archie David in overtime / Tancred ballet / Dark ships / Flowership quintet / Rag pole dance.

— COPELAND went on to writes scores for films 'Talk Radio', 'Wall Street', 'First Power', etc. The first were combined on cd for US release on 'Varese Sarabande'. He has since went on to form ANIMAL LOGIC with bassist STANLEY CLARKE ⇒ and vocalist DEBORAH HOLLAND. They made one eponymous album in 1989. He also in 1988 composed an opera 'Holy Blood And Crescent Moon', for The CLEVELAND OPERATIC SOCIETY.

ANDY SUMMERS / ROBERT FRIPP

FRIPP – guitar, synths (of KING CRIMSON)

A & M A & M

Oct 82. (lp)(c) **I ADVANCE MASKED**
– I advance masked / Under bridges of silence / China, yellow leader / In the cloud forest / New marimba / Girl on a swing / Hardy country / Truth of skies / Painting and dance / Still point / Lakeland, Aquarelle / Steven on seven / Stultified. *(cd-iss.1986 on 'E.G.')*

Oct 82. (7") **I ADVANCE MASKED. / HARDY COUNTRY**

Sep 84. (lp)(c) **BEWITCHED**
– Parade / What kind of man reads Playboy? / Begin the day / Train / Bewitched / Maquillage / Guide / Forgotten steps / Image and likeness. *(cd-iss.1988)*

Sep 84. (7") **PARADE. / TRAIN**
(12"+=) – Hardy country.

Dec 84. (7") **2010. / TO HELL AND BACK** -

ANDY SUMMERS

now solo, augmented by **DAVID HENTSCEL** – keyboards, drum programmes / **NAN VERNON** – vocals and **MICHAEL G.FISHER.**

M.C.A. M.C.A.

Jul 87. (lp)(c)(cd) **XYZ**
– Love is the strangest way / How many days / Almost there / Eyes of a stranger / The change / Scary voices / Nowhere / XYZ / The only road / Hold me.

Jul 87. (7")(12") **LOVE IS THE STRANGEST WAY. / XYZ**

— now with **PAUL McCANDLESS / DOUG LUNN / KURT WORTMAN / JIMMY HASLIP**

not issued Private . . .

Apr 89. (lp)(c)(cd) **THE GOLDEN WIRE** -
– A piece of time / The golden wire / Earthly pleasures / Imagine you / Vigango / Blues for snake / The island of silk / Journey through blue regions / Piya tose / Rain forest in Manhattan / A thousand stones.

Oct 89. (lp)(c)(cd) **MYSTERIOUS BARRICADE** -
– Red balloon / Mysterious barricades / When that day comes / Train song / Luna / Satyric dancer / Shiny sea / Emperor's last straw / Rain / Tomorrow / In praise of shadows / The lost marbles / How can I forget.

— **ANDY SUMMERS w / JOHN ETHERIDGE** iss UK-cd 'INVISIBLE THREADS' on 'Inak' Jan 94.

Jean-Luc PONTY

Born: 29 Sep'42, Arranches, Normandy, France. Classically trained at an early age, by his violin-professor father and piano-teacher mother. Recorded with JOHN COLTRANE in the early 60's and in 1966 released 'VIOLIN SUMMIT' with STEFAN GRAPPELLI, STUFF SMITH and SVEN ASMUSSON. His first American appearance was at the 1967 Monterey Jazz Festival. In 1969, he struck up a friendship with FRANK ZAPPA and his MOTHERS OF INVENTION. The following year, he turned up on ZAPPA's 'Hot Rats', with the great man producing PONTY's 'KING KONG'. In 1971, he returned to Europe and gigged extensively, while issuing a few instrumental albums and sessioning on ELTON JOHN's 'Honky Chateau'. Early in 1973, he emigrated to the States and joined The MOTHERS OF INVENTION, but later in the year he left to join JOHN McLAUGHLIN's MAHAVISHNU ORCHESTRA. In the Spring of 1975, he left and signed a solo deal with 'Atlantic', for whom he had first of many US Top 200 album appearances; 'UPON THE WINGS OF MUSIC'. Hit his commercial and critical peak during the late 70's and early 80's. • **Style:** Avant-garde electric violin virtuoso. • **Songwriters:** Writes most of material.

Recommended: IMAGINARY VOYAGE (*6) / ENIGMATIC OCEAN (*6) / COSMIC MESSENGER (*7) / A TASTE FOR PASSION (*6)

JEAN-LUC PONTY – violin; with **WOLFGANG DAUNER** – piano / **NIELS HENNING OERSTED PEDERSON** – bass / **DANIEL HUMAIR** – drums

M.P.S. not issued

1967. (lp) **SUNDAY WALK** - - Germ'y
– Sunday walk / Carole's garden / Cat coach / You've changed / Suite for Claudia.

— **GEORGE GRUNTZ** – piano / **CARMELL JONES** – trumpet / **LEO WRIGHT** – sax, flute – repl.DAUNER + PEDERSON

Liberty Pacific J.

1968. (lp) **MORE THAN MEETS THE EAR** -
– With a little help from my friends / 3+2=1 / California / Gimme little sign / Pata pata / Pebble beach walk / Pacific drove / Fort Old Canon.

— **GEORGE DUKE** – piano / **WILBERT LONGMIRE – guitar / BOB WEST** – bass / **PAUL HUMPHREY** – drums / **BUD SHANK + RICHARD APLANALP – saxes / TONY ORTEGA** – flute / others repl.all

1969. (lp) **ELECTRIC CONNECTION**
– Summit soul / Hypomode del Sol / Scarborough fair – Canticle / The name of the game / The loner / Waltz for Clara / Forget / Eighty-one.

— **PONTY + DUKE** recruited **JOHN HEARD** – bass / **DICK BERK** – drums

1969. <lp> **EXPERIENCE** -
– Foosh / Pamukkale / Contact / Cantaloupe Island / Starlight, starbright. *(UK-iss.1971 as 'WITH THE GEORGE DUKE TRIO' on 'Sunset') (US re-iss.1980 on 'Pausa')*

— now with most of FRANK ZAPPA's band incl. the man himself

1970. (lp)
– King Kong / Idiot bastard son / Twenty small cigars /How would you like to have a head like that / Music for electric violin and low budget orchestra / America drinks and goes home. *(re-iss.lp/c on 'E.M.I.')*

not issued Far East

1970. (lp) **ASTRORAMA** -

— now with **PHILIP CATHERINE** – guitar / **JOACHIM KUEHN** – piano / **PETER WARREN** – bass / **OLIVER JOHNSON** – drums

not issued M.P.S.

1972. (lp) **OPEN STRINGS** -
– Flipping (parts 1-3) / Open strings / Sad ballad.

— **JENNY CLARKE** – bass / **NANA VASCONCELOS** – percussion repl.CATHERINE + WARREN

not issued Inner City

1972. (lp) **LIVE FROM MONTREUX (live)** -
– Sonata erotica: Preludio – Pizzicato con fuoco e con echo – Appassionato – Con sensualita – Accelerando e rallentendo. *(UK-iss.Sep79 as 'SONATA EROTICA' on 'Atmosphere') (re-iss.May85 on 'Affinity')*

— next credited other violinist STEPHANE GRAPPELLI

not issued America

1973. (lp) **PONTY & GRAPPELLI** - - Germ'y
– Bowing-bowing / Golden green / Memorial jam for Stuff Smith / Violin summit No.2 / Valerie.

— next featured **GIORGIO GASLINI** – piano

not issued Associati

1974. (lp) **MEETS GIORGIO GASLINI** -
– Fabbiciccato occupata / The woman I love.

— now with **PATRICE RUSHEN** – keyboards, synthesizers / **RAY PARKER Jr. + DAN SAWYER** – guitar / **RALPHE ARMSTRONG** – bass / **NDUGU LEON CHANCLER** – drums, percussion

Atlantic Atlantic

Aug 75. (lp) **UPON THE WINGS OF MUSIC** Jul75
– Upon the wings of music / Question with no answer / Now I know / Polyfolk dance / Waving memories / Echoes of the future / Bowing-bowing / Fight for life.

— **DARRYL STUERMER** – guitar / **TOM FOWLER** – bass / **NORMAN FEARRINGTON** – drums – repl. everyone except RUSHEN

Apr 76. (lp) **AURORA**
– Is once enough? / Renaissance / Aurora / Passenger of the dark / Lost forest / Between you and me / Waking dream.

— **ALLAN ZAVOD** – keyboards / **MARK CRANEY** – drums – repl.RUSHEN (went solo) + NORMAN

Nov 76. (lp) **IMAGINARY VOYAGE** 67
– New country / The gardens of Babylon / Wandering on the Milky Way / Once upon a dream / Tarantula / Imaginary voyage (part I, II, III & IV).

Apr 77. (7") **NEW COUNTRY. / RENAISSANCE**

— **ALLAN HOLDSWORTH** – guitar / **RALPHE ARMSTRONG** – bass / **STEVE SMITH** – drums – repl.FOWLER + CRANEY

Sep 77. (lp) **ENIGMATIC OCEAN** 35
– Overture: The Trans-Love express / Mirage / Enigmatic ocean (parts I, II, III & IV) / Nostalgic lady / The struggle of the turtle to the sea (parts I, II & III).

— **PETER MAUNU + JOAQUIN LIEVANO** – guitar / **CASEY SCHEUERELL** – drums, percussion – repl.STUERMER, HOLDSWORTH + SMITH

Feb 79. (lp) **COSMIC MESSENGER** 36 Aug78
– Cosmic messenger / The art of happiness / Don't let the world pass you by / I only feel good with you / Puppet's dance / Fake Paradise / Ethereal mood / Egocentric molecules.

— **JAMIE GLASER** – guitar – repl.MAUNU

May 79. (lp) **JEAN-LUC PONTY: LIVE (live)** 68
– Aurora (part I & II) / Imaginary voyage (parts I, II, III & IV) ? Mirage / No strings attached / Egocentric molecules.

Oct 79. (lp) **A TASTE FOR PASSION** 54
– Stay with me / Sunset drive / Dreamy eyes / Beach girl / A taste for passion / Life cycles / Reminiscene / Give us a chance / Obsession / Farewell.

Jan 80. (7") **BEACH GIRL. / SUNSET DRIVE**

now with returning **STUERMER + CRANEY + LIEVANO / CHRIS RHYNE** – keyboards / **RANDY JACKSON** – bass

Nov 80. (lp) **CIVILIZED EVIL** 73 Oct80
– Demagomania / In case we survive / Forms of life / Peace crusaders / Happy robots / Shape up your mind / Good guys, bad guys / Once a blue planet.

Dec 80. (7") **DEMAGOMANIA. / HAPPY ROBOTS**

— now with **RHYNE + GLASER / RANDY JACKSON** – bass / **RAYFORD GRIFFIN** – drums, percussion, vocals / **PAULINHO DA COSTA** – percussion

Feb 82. (lp) **MYSTICAL ADVENTURES** 44
– Mystical adventures (suite): (parts I, II, III, IV & V) / Rhythms of hope / As / Final truth (parts I & II) / Jig.

— **GEORGE DUKE** – synthesizer / **ALLAN HOLDSWORTH** – guitar – repl.DA COSTA + GLASER

Polydor Atlantic

Apr 84. (lp)(cd) **INDIVIDUAL CHOICE** 85 Aug83
– Computer incantations for world peace / Far from the beaten paths / In spiritual love / Eulogy to Oscar Romero / Nostalgia / Individual choice / In spite of all.

— guests on next; GEORGE BENSON + CHICK COREA

Nov 84. (lp)(c)(cd) **OPEN MIND**
– Open mind / Solitude / Watching birds / Modern times blues / Orbital encounters / Intuition.

— with **SCOTT HENDERSON** – guitar / **NARON BROWNE** – bass / **RAYFORD GRIFFIN** – drums

Atlantic Atlantic

Jan 86. (lp)(c)(cd) **FABLES** Oct85
– Infinite pursuit / Elephants in love / Radioactive legacy / Cats tales / Perpetual rondo / In the kingdom of peace / Plastic idols.

— **PAT THOMI** – guitar – repl.HENDERSON

C.B.S. Columbia

Nov 87. (lp)(c)(cd) **THE GIFT OF TIME**
– Prologue / New resolutions / Faith in you / No more doubts / Between sea and sky / Metamorphosis / Introspective perceptions / The gift of time.

— with **RUSHEN / BROWNE / GLASER / WALLY MINKO** – keyboards / **CLARA PONTY + KURT WORTMAN** – percussion

1989. (cd) **STORYTELLING**
–

compilations, others, etc

Jul 86. Timeless Treasures; (c) **JAZZ FIRST (w/ CLEO LAINE)** -
Aug 88. MPS Jazz; (c)(cd) **JEAN-LUC PONTY & STEPHANE GRAPPELLI** -

Iggy POP

Born: JAMES JEWEL OSTERBURG, 21 Apr'47, Muskegan, Ann Arbor, Michegan, USA. Son of an English father and American mother, he joined The IGUANAS as a drummer in 1964. They issued a cover of Bo Diddley's 'MONA', which was limited to a 1,000 copies sold at gigs. In 1965, he became IGGY POP and joined The PRIME MOVERS, with bassist RON ASHETON, but they folded and IGGY moved to Chicago. In 1967, he returned to Michegan and formed The (PSYCHEDELIC) STOOGES, with RON and his drummer brother SCOTT. They were soon joined by DAVE ALEXANDER, and IGGY made celluloid debut on avant-garde film 'Francois De Moniere' with girlfriend NICO. In 1968, the band gigged more constantly, and on 1 occasion, IGGY was charged with indecent exposure. In 1969, A&R man Danny Fields while looking to sign MC5, signed The STOOGES to 'Elektra', with a $25,000 advance. Their eponymous debut, produced by JOHN CALE (another VELVET UNDERGROUND connection), nearly broke into the US Top 100. It proved later to be ahead of its time, with gems such as; NO FUN (later rec.'77 by punks SEX PISTOLS) / 1969 (later rec.'83 by goths SISTERS OF MERCY). After another semi-clasic lp in 1970, they disbanded due to dissentions in line-up and drug related circumstances. He moved to Florida, where he became a greenkeeper while taking up golf. In 1972, he met DAVID BOWIE and his manager TONY DeFRIES, who persuaded IGGY & THE STOOGES to sign to a MainMan management deal, leading to 'CBS' contract. After one album 'RAW POWER', they folded again citing drugs as cause. In 1975, IGGY checked in to a psychiatric institute weaning himself off heroin. His only true friend BOWIE, who regularly visited him in hospital, invited him to appear on his 'LOW' lp. He signed to 'RCA' (home of BOWIE) in 1977, and issued BOWIE produced debut solo album 'THE IDIOT', which due to recent 'New wave' explosion, broke into the UK Top 30 and US Top 75. It contained first BOWIE-POP collaboration 'CHINA GIRL', which was later a smash hit for BOWIE. His 2nd solo release 'LUST FOR LIFE' (also produced by BOWIE in '77), was another gem and deservedly again reached UK Top 30. In 1979, IGGY moved to 'Arista' records, and shifted through various famous personnel (see discography), but found commercial appeal leaving him behind. Until, that is, in 1987, when his revival of a 1957 Johnny O'Keefe hit 'REAL WILD CHILD', cracked the UK Top 10. • **Style:** Proclaimed 'The Godfather of Punk', he pioneered in the 60's what was to burgeon in the 70's. Psychotic gravel-voxed contortionist, whose early stage shows saw him slash his chest with a razor. He finally recovered in the mid-80's from drug addiction. • **Songwriters:** IGGY and STOOGES. In 1977 he collaborated with BOWIE, and 1986 with ex-SEX PISTOLS guitarist; STEVE JONES. Others covered; SOMETHING WILD (John Hiatt) / LIVIN' ON THE EDGE OF THE NIGHT (Rifkin / Rackin) / LOUIE LOUIE (Kingsmen). • **Trivia:** In 1987, he made a cameo appearance in the pool film 'The Colour Of Money'. In 1990, his film & TV work included 'Cry Baby', 'Shannon's Deal', Tales From The Crypt' & 'Miami Vice'. In 1991, he starred in the opera! 'The Manson Family'.

Recommended: THE STOOGES (*8) / FUN HOUSE (*9) / RAW POWER (*7) / THE IDIOT (*9) / LUST FOR LIFE (*9) / BLAH-BLAH-BLAH (*7) / INSTINCT (*8) / BRICK BY BRICK (*7).

STOOGES

IGGY POP – vocals / **RON ASHETON** – guitar / **DAVE ALEXANDER** – bass / **SCOTT ASHETON** – drums

Elektra Elektra

Sep 69. (lp) **THE STOOGES** Aug 69
– 1969 / I wanna be your dog / We will fall / No fun / Real cool time / Ann / Not right / Little doll. *(re-iss.Mar77) (US cd-iss.1988)(cd-iss.Nov93)*

Oct 69. (7") **I WANNA BE YOUR DOG. / 1969** -

— added guests **STEVE MACKAY** – saxophone / **BILL CHEATHAM** – 2nd guitar

Dec 70. (lp) **FUN HOUSE**
– Down on the street / Loose / T.V. eye / Dirt / I feel alright (1970) / Fun house / L.A. blues. *(re-iss.Mar77) (US cd-iss.1988)(cd-iss.Nov93)*

Dec 70. (7") **I FEEL ALRIGHT (1970). / DOWN ON THE STREET** -

— Break-up in 1972. Soon **IGGY** re-formed with **SCOTT** and **RON** (now bass) .

IGGY AND THE STOOGES

JAMES WILLIAMSON – guitar repl. DAVE

C.B.S. Columbia

May 73. (lp)(c) **RAW POWER**
– Search and destroy / Gimme danger / Hard to beat * / Penetration / Raw power / I need somebody / Shake appeal / Death trip. *(re-iss.May77 on 'CBS-Embassy', hit UK No.44*, *track repl. by – Your pretty face is going to Hell. *(re-iss.Nov81) (US cd-iss.1988 on 'Columbia') (UK cd-iss.May89 on 'Essential') (cd-iss.all tracks) (re-iss.cd+c May94 on 'Columbia').*

Jun 73. (7") **SEARCH AND DESTROY. / PENETRATION** -

— added **SCOTT THURSTON** – keyboards (on last 1974 tour, before disbanding) The ASHETONS formed The NEW ORDER (US version), with RON moving on to DESTROY ALL MONSTERS who had three 45's for UK label 'Cherry Red' in the late 70's.

- compilations, other, etc. -

(* = as "IGGY & THE STOOGES")

1976. Visa; (white-d-lp) * **METALLIC KO** -
(re-iss.+cd.May88 on 'Skydog') (cd-iss.Sep94 on 'Skydog')

1977. Bomp; (7"ep) * **I'M SICK OF YOU. / TIGHT PANTS / SCENE OF THE CRIME** -

1977. Bomp; (7"ep) * **JESUS LOVES THE STOOGES ("IGGY POP & JAMES WILLIAMSON")** -
– Jesus loves the Stooges / Consolation prizes / Johanna *(re-iss. 10"ep. Nov 94)*

1977. Skydog France; (7") **I GOT NOTHIN'. / GIMME DANGER** - -
(12"+=) – Heavy liquid.

1977. Siamese; (7") **I GOT A RIGHT. / GIMME SOME SKIN** -
(UK-iss.Dec95 on 'Bomp')

Feb 78. Radar/ US= Bomp; (lp) **KILL CITY (as "IGGY POP with James Williamson")**
– Sell your love / Kill city / I got nothin' / Beyond the law / Johanna / Night theme / Night theme reprise / Master charge / No sense of crime / Lucky monkeys / Consolation prizes. *(re-iss.! on 'Elektra') (cd-iss.Feb89 on 'Line') (cd-iss.Jan93) (re-iss.10"lp Feb95 on 'Bomp')*

Apr 78. Radar/ US= Bomp; (7") **KILL CITY. / I GOT NOTHIN'**
Aug 80. Elektra; (lp)(c) **NO FUN** (1969-70 best of THE STOOGES)
1983. Invasion; (lp) **I GOT A RIGHT** -
Dec 87. Fan Club; (lp) **RUBBER LEGS** -
Feb 95. Bomp; (10"lp) **ROUGH POWER** -

— Also in France 1988 on 'Revenge' records, a number of releases were issued. **GIMME DANGER** (12") / **OPEN UP AND BLEED** (cd) / **DEATH TRAP** (pic-lp) / **LIVE AT THE WHISKEY A-GO-GO**(lp) / **THE STOOGES**(12"ep) / **SHE CREATURES OF HOLLYWOOD HILLS**

IGGY POP

had already went solo, augmented by **DAVID BOWIE** – producer, keyboards / **RICKY GARDINER** – guitar / **TONY SALES** – bass / **HUNT SALES** – drums (latter 2; ex-TODD RUNDGREN) / guest **CARLOS ALOMAR** – guitar

R.C.A. R.C.A.

Feb 77. (7") **SISTER MIDNIGHT. / BABY** -
Mar 77. (lp)(c) **THE IDIOT** 30 72
– Sister midnight / Nightclubbing / Fun time / Baby / China girls / Dum dum boys / Tiny girls / Mass production. *(re-iss.+cd.Apr90 on 'Virgin')*

May 77. (7") **CHINA GIRL. / BABY**

— **STACEY HEYDON** – guitar / **SCOTT THURSTON** – keys repl. BOWIE + ALOMAR

Sep 77. (lp)(c) **LUST FOR LIFE** 28
– Lust for life / Sixteen / Some weird sin / The passenger / Tonight / Success / Turn blue / Neighbourhood threat / Fall in love with me. *(re-iss.1984) (re-iss.+cd.Apr90 on 'Virgin')*

Oct 77. (7") **SUCCESS. / THE PASSENGER**

— **IGGY** retained **THURSTON**, and recruited **SCOTT ASHETON** – drums / **FRED 'SONIC' SMITH** – guitar (ex-MC5) / **GARY RAMUSSEN** – bass (The SALES bros.later to BOWIE's TIN MACHINE)

Apr 78. (7") **I GOT A RIGHT (live). / SIXTEEN (live)**
May 78. (lp)(c) **TV EYE (live 1977)**
– T.V. eye / Funtime / Sixteen / I got a right / Lust for life / Dirt / Nightclubbing / I wanna be your dog. *(cd-iss.Jul94 on 'Virgin')*

— **IGGY / THURSTON** now with **JAMES WILLIAMSON** – guitar, producer / **JACKIE CLARKE** – bass (ex-IKE & TINA TURNER) / **KLAUS KREUGER** – drums (ex-TANGERINE DREAM) / **JOHN HORDEN** – saxophone

Arista Arista

Apr 79. (lp)(c) **NEW VALUES** 60
– Tell me a story / New values / Girls / I'm bored / Don't look down / The endless sea / Five foot one / How do ya fix a broken part / Angel / Curiosity / African man / Billy is a runaway. *(re-iss.Mar87)*

May 79. (7") **I'M BORED. / AFRICAN MAN**
Jul 79. (7")(7"pic-d) **FIVE FOOT ONE. / PRETTY FLAMINGO**

— **IGGY / KREUGER** recruited **IVAN KRAL** – guitar (ex-PATTI SMITH) / **PAT MORAN** – guitar / **GLEN MATLOCK** – bass (ex-SEX PISTOLS, ex-RICH KIDS) / **BARRY ANDREWS** – keyboards (ex-XTC, ex-LEAGUE OF GENTLEMEN) (THURSTON formed The MOTELS)

Jan 80. (lp)(c) **SOLDIER** 62
– Knockin' 'em down (in the city) / I'm a conservative / I snub you / Get up and get out / Ambition / Take care of me / I need more / Loco mosquito / Mr.Dynamite / Play it safe / Dog food. *(US re-iss.Oct87) (UK re-iss.+cd.Apr91)*

Jan 80. (7") **LOCO MOSQUITO. / TAKE CARE OF ME**

— **IGGY / KRAL** now with **ROB DuPREY** – guitar / **MICHAEL PAGE** – bass / **DOUGLAS BROWNE** – drums (BARRY ANDREWS formed SHRIEKBACK)

May 81. (7") **BANG BANG. / SEA OF LOVE**
Jun 81. (lp)(c) **PARTY**
– Pleasure / Rock and roll party / Eggs on plate / Sincerity / Houston is hot tonight / Pumpin' for Jill / Happy man / Bang bang / Sea of love / Time won't let me. *(re-*

'LUST FOR LIFE'

iss.Jan87) (cd-iss.Sep89 on 'RCA')

— **IGGY / DuPREY** found new people **CHRIS STEIN** – guitar, producer (ex-BLONDIE) / **CLEM BURKE** – drums (ex-BLONDIE)

Animal-Chrysalis / Animal

Aug 82. (7") **RUN LIKE A VILLAIN. / PLATONIC** [ ] [ ]
Sep 82. (lp)(c) **ZOMBIE BIRDHOUSE** [ ] [ ]
– Run like a villain / The villagers / Angry hills / Life of work / The ballad of Cookie McBride / Ordinary bummer / Eat to be eaten / Bulldozer / Platonic / The horse song / Watching the news / Street crazies.

— In 1984, he sang the title song on Alex Cox's movie 'REPO MAN'. For the same director, he appeared in the 1985 film 'SID & NANCY' about SID VICIOUS.

— **IGGY** now with **ERDAL KIZILCAY** – drums, bass, synthesizers / **KEVIN ARMSTRONG** – guitar / **BOWIE + STEVE JONES** (guest writers)

A& M / A & M

Sep 86. (7") **CRY FOR LOVE. / WINNERS & LOSERS** [ ] [ ]
Oct 86. (lp)(c)(cd) **BLAH-BLAH-BLAH** [43] [75]
– Real wild child (wild one) / Baby, it can't fail / Shades / Fire girl / Isolation / Cry for love / Blah-blah-blah / Hideaway / Winners and losers. (cd+=) Little Miss Emperor. *(re-cd-iss.1989)*
Nov 86. (7")(12") **REAL WILD CHILD (WILD ONE). / LITTLE MISS EMPEROR** [10] [ ]
Feb 87. (7") **SHADES. / BABY IT CAN'T FAIL** [ ] [ ]
(12"+=) – Cry for love.
Apr 87. (7")(12") **FIRE GIRL. / BLAH-BLAH-BLAH (live)** [ ] [ ]
Jun 87. (7") **ISOLATION. / HIDEAWAY** [ ] [ ]
(12"+=) – Fire girl (remix).

— IGGY now with **STEVE JONES** – guitar / **PAUL GARRISTO** – drums (ex-PSYCHEDELIC FURS) / **SEAMUS BEAGHEN** – keyboards / **LEIGH FOXX** – bass

Jul 88. (lp)(c)(cd) **INSTINCT** [61] [ ]
– Cold metal / High on you / Strong girl / Tom tom / Easy rider / Power & freedom / Lowdown / Tuff baby / Squarehead.
Aug 88. (7") **COLD METAL. / INSTINCT** [ ] [ ]
(12"+=)(12"pic-d+=) – Tuff baby.
Nov 88. (7") **HIGH ON YOU. / SQUAREHEAD** [ ] [ ]
(12"+=) – Tuff baby (remix).

— **ALVIN GIBBS** – guitar (ex-UK SUBS) repl. STEVE JONES (continued solo) / **ANDY McCOY** – bass (ex-HANOI ROCKS) repl. FOXX (to DEBORAH HARRY)

Nov 88. (lp)(c)(cd) **LIVE AT THE CHANNEL (live 17.9.88)** [-] [ ]

— now with **SLASH** – guitar / **DUFF McKAGAN** – bass (both of GUNS'N'ROSES) / **KENNY ARONOFF** – drums

Virgin America / Virgin America

Jan 90. (7")(c-s) **LIVIN' ON THE EDGE OF THE NIGHT. / THE PASSENGER** [51] [ ]
(12"+=)(cd-s+=)(12"pic-d+=) – Nightclubbing / China girl.
Jun 90. (7")(c-s) **HOME. / LUST FOR LIFE** [ ] [ ]
(12"+=)(cd-s+=) – Pussy power / Funtime.
Jul 90. (cd)(c)(lp) **BRICK BY BRICK** [50] [90]
– Home / Main street eyes / I won't crap out / Candy / Butt town / The undefeated / Moonlight lady / Something wild / Neon forest / Stormy night / Pussy power / My baby wants to rock & roll / Brick by brick / Livin' on the edge of the night.

— (below 'A'side feat. **KATE PIERSON – vox (of B-52's)**)

Dec 90. (7")(c-s) **CANDY. / PUSSY POWER (acoustic demo)** [67] [28] Nov 90
(12")(cd-s) – ('A'side) / The undefeated / Butt town (acoustic demo).
(10"+=)(cd-s+=) – My baby wants to rock'n'roll (acoustic demos).

— Oct 90, IGGY dueted with DEBORAH HARRY on UK Top 50 single 'DID YOU EVAH')

— with **LARRY MULLINS** (U2) – drums, percussion / **HAL CRAGIN** – bass / **ERIC SCHERMERHORN** – guitar plus guests **MALCOLM BURN** – guitars, etc

Aug 93. (7"ep)(12"ep)(c-ep)(cd-ep) **THE WILD AMERICA EP** [63] [ ]
– Wild America / Credit card / Come back tomorrow / My angel.
Sep 93. (cd)(c)(d-lp) **AMERICAN CAESAR** [43] [ ]
– Character / Wild America / Mixin' the colors / Jealousy / Hate / It's our love / Plastic & concrete / F***in' alone / Highway song / Beside you / Sickness / Boogie boy / Perforation / Problems / Social life / Louie Louie / Caesar / Girls of N.Y
May 94. (10"ep) **BESIDE YOU / EVIL CALIFORNIA. / POEM (live) / FUCKIN' ALONE** [47] [ ]
(cd-s) – ('A'side) / Les amants / Louie Louie (live) / ('A'acoustic).

– his compilations, etc. –

May 82. RCA; (7") **THE PASSENGER. / NIGHTCLUBBING** [ ] [-]
Sep 84. RCA; (lp)(c) **CHOICE CUTS** [ ] [-]
Apr 88. A&M; (cd-ep) **COMPACT HITS** [ ] [-]
– Real wild child (the wild one) / Isolation / Cry for love / Shades.
Jun 93. Revenge; (cd) **LIVE NYC RITZ '86 (live)** [ ] [-]
Aug 93. Revenge; (cd)(c) **SUCK ON THIS!** [ ] [-]
Aug 95. Skydog; (cd) **WE ARE NOT TALKING ABOUT COMMERCIAL SHIT** [ ] [-]
Aug 95. Skydog; (cd) **WAKE UP SUCKERS** [ ] [-]

POP GROUP

Formed: Bristol, England . . . 1978 by MARK STEWART, etc (see below). In 1979, they debuted on Jake Riviera's 'Radar' records with the seminal classic 'SHE IS BEYOND GOOD AND EVIL', but the break through was not to be, even with reggae producer DENNIS BOVELL at the controls of album 'Y'. • **Style:** A fusion of jazzy rock and Afro-new wave, fronted by STEWART's weird vox. Described as a rhythmic jam session, waiting to explode. • **Songwriters:** STEWART lyricist / group compositions. • **Trivia:** Legal wrangles culminated after owing £100,000 to 'Rough Trade', and thus their untimely demise. Sadly, early member SEAN OLIVER, co-writer of 'Wishing Well' for TERENCE TRENT D'ARBY, was to die on 30 Mar'90 of heart failure.

Recommended: Y (*7) / FOR HOW MUCH LONGER (*8).

MARK STEWART – vocals / **JOHN WADDINGTON** – guitar / **DAVID WRIGHT** – saxophone / **SEAN OLIVER** – bass / **BRUCE SMITH** – drums, percussion

Radar / not issued

Mar 79. (7")(12") **SHE IS BEYOND GOOD AND EVIL. / 3:38** [ ] [-]

— **SIMON UNDERWOOD** – bass repl. OLIVER who joined ESSENTIAL LOGIC / **GARETH SAGER** – guitar, saxophone repl. WRIGHT who joined ESSENTIAL LOGIC

Apr 79. (lp)(c) **Y** [ ] [-]
– Thief of fire / Snowgirl / Blood money / Savage sea / We are time / Words disobey me / Don't call me Pain / The boys from Brazil / Don't sell your dreams.

— **DAN KATSIS** – bass (also of GLAXO BABOES) repl. SIMON who joined PIGBAG / added **TRISTAN HONSINGER** – cello.

Rough Trade / not issued

Oct 79. (7") **WE ARE ALL PROSTITUTES. / OUR CHILDREN SHALL RISE UP AGAINST** [ ] [ ]

— **PAUL STUART** – drums repl. SMITH who joined SLITS.

Mar 80. (lp) **FOR HOW MUCH LONGER DO WE TOLERATE MASS MURDER** [ ] [-]
– Forces of oppression / Feed the hungry / One out of many / Blind faith / How much longer . . . / Justice / There are no spectators / Communicate / Rob a bank.
Mar 80. (7") **(In The Beginning – by SLITS). / WHERE THERE'S A WILL THERE'S A WAY** [ ] [-]
Dec 80. (lp) **WE ARE TIME (live)** [ ] [-]
– Kiss the book / Amnesty report / Springer / Sense of purpose / We are time / Trap / Thief of fire / Genius or lunatic / Colour blind / Spanish inqusition. *(re-iss.Aug84)*

— (split 1980) MARK and GARETH joined RIP, RIG & PANIC, with other ex-members.

— **MAXIMUM JOY** were formed by WADDINGTON and CATSIS with JOHN RAINFORTH – vocals, clarinet TONY WRAFTER – saxophone (ex-GLAXO BABIES) **CHARLIE LLEWELLYN** – drums (ex-GLAXO BABIES). They released a number of singles, plus an album 'STATION WX JY' in 1982.

POP WILL EAT ITSELF

Formed: Stourbridge, Midlands, England . . . early 1985 initially as WILD AND WONDERING, by CLINT, ADAM and GRAHAM, out of the ashes of EDEN. After a ROLLING STONES inspired EP '2000 LIGHT ALES FROM HOME', they became POP WILL EAT ITSELF, early '86. The PWEI debut 'POPPIES SAY GRRRR . . . EP', was originally sold at a Dudley gig, but when given more DIY copies were in the shops, it became NME single of the week, and playlisted on night time Radio 1. In the summer of '86, they signed to Craig Jennings' indie 'Chapter 22' label, and after a few more releases, he became their manager. After becoming resident in the indie charts for the next years, they finally shifted to major 'RCA', with their first hit 'CAN U DIG IT', breaking into the 40 early 1989. • **Style:** Grebo pop-rock gurus, who were a hybrid of heavy punk (aka KILLING JOKE) and psychedelia, fused with samples and over-the-top sexist lyrics (aka 'BEAVER PATROL'). • **Songwriters:** Group compositions except; LOVE MISSILE F1-11 (Sigue Sigue Sputnik) / LIKE AN ANGEL (Mighty Lemon Drops) / ORGONE ACCUMULATOR (Hawkwind) / EVERYTHING THAT RISES (Eno) / ROCK-A-HULA BABY (Elvis Presley). • **Trivia:** MILES and MALCOLM of The WONDER STUFF co-wrote and guested on W&W 1986 debut.

Recommended: BOX FRENZY (*8) / NOW FOR A FEAST (*7) / THIS IS THE DAY (*7).

WILD & WONDERING

CLINT MARSELL – vocals, guitar / **ADAM MOLE** – guitar, keyboards / **GRAHAM CRABB** – drums / **RICHARD MARCH** – bass

Iguana / not issued

Feb 86. (12"ep) **2000 LIGHT ALES FROM HOME** [ ] [-]
– Dust me down / Stand by me / Real cool time / Interlong / Apple tree (pt.1 & 2).

POP WILL EAT ITSELF

Desperate / not issued

May 86. (12"ep) **POPPIES SAY GRRRR . . . EP** [ ] [-]
– (see below Aug86 for the 5 tracks).
Jun 86. (7") **THERE'S A PSYCOPATH IN MY SOUP. / CANDIOSES** [ ] [-]

Chapter 22 / not issued

Aug 86. (7") **I'M SNIFFING WITH YOU-HOO. / SICK LITTLE GIRL** [ ] [-]
(12"+=) – Mesmerised / There's a psychopath in my soup / Candioses.
Oct 86. (7"ep)(12"ep) **POPPIECOCK** [ ] [-]
– Oh Grebo I think I love you / Black country chainsaw massacre manogamy / Titanic clown / B-b-breakdown. (12"ep incl. – May86 ep).
Jan 87. (7") **SWEET SWEET PIE. / THE DEVIL INSIDE** [ ] [-]
(12"+=) – Runaround.
May 87. (7") **LOVE MISSILE F1-11 (remix). / ORGONE ACCUMULATOR** [ ] [-]
THE COVERS EP (12"+=) – Like an angel / Everything that rises.
(12"+=) – ('A'designer Grebo mix). repl. 'Like an angel'.
Sep 87. (7")(7"pink)(7"clear) **BEAVER PATROL. / BUBBLES** [ ] [-]
(12"+=) – Oh Grebo I think I love you (new version).
(12"+=) – Ugly.

Oct 87. (lp)(c)(cd) **BOX FRENZY** [ ] [-]
– Grebo guru / Beaver patrol / Let's get ugly / U.B.L.U.D. / Inside you / Evelyn / There is no love between us anymore / She's surreal / Intergalactic love mission / Love missile F1-11 / Hit the hi-tech groove / Razorblade kisses.

Jan 88. (7")(7"pic-d) **THERE IS NO LOVE BETWEEN US ANY-MORE. / PICNIC IN THE SKY** [66] [-]
(12"+=) – On the razor's edge / Kiss that girl.

Jul 88. (7") **DEF CON ONE. / INSIDE YOU** [63] [-]
(12"+=) – She's surreal / ('A'remix).
(12"+=)(cd-s+=) – Hi-tech groove (live) / She's surreal (live).

Dec 88. (lp)(c)(cd) **NOW FOR A FEAST** (compilation) [ ] [-]
– Black country chainstore massacre / Monogamy / Oh Grebo I think I love you / Titanic clown / B-B-B Breakdown / Sweet sweet pie / Like an angel / I'm sniffin' with you hoo / Sick little girl / Mesmerized / There's a psychopath in my soup / Candyiosis / The devil inside / Orgone accumulator.

R.C.A. R.C.A.

Jan 89. (7")(7"orange)(7"green) **CAN U DIG IT. / POISON TO THE MIND** [38] [ ]
(cd-s+=) – Radio PWEI (acapella) / ('A'-12"version).
(12"++=) – The fuses have been lit.

Apr 89. (7")(7"pic-d) **WISE UP! SUCKER. / ORGYONE STIMU-LATOR** [41] [ ]
(12"+=)(c-s+=)(cd-s+=) – ('A'remix) / Can u dig it (riffs mix).
(10") – ('A'side) / ('A'-2 other versions).

May 89. (lp)(c)(cd) **THIS IS THE DAY, THIS IS THE HOUR, THIS IS THIS** [24] [ ]
– PWEI is a four letter word / Preaching to the peverted / Wise up! sucker / Sixteen different flavours of Hell / Inject me / Can u dig it? / The fuses have been lit / Poison to the mind / Def con one / Radio PWEI / Shortwave transmission on up to the minuteman / Satellite ecstatica / Now now James, we're busy / Wake up! time to die . . . *(cd+=)*– Wise up sucker (mix). *re-iss.cd Nov93)*

Aug 89. (7"ep)(12"ep)(c-ep)(cd-ep)(7"sha-pic-d-ep) **VERY METAL NOISE POLLUTION EP** [45] [ ]
– Pweization / 92 degrees f / Def con one (remix) / Preaching to the converted.

May 90. (7")(c-s) **TOUCHED BY THE HAND OF CICCIOLINA. / THE INCREDI-BULL MIX** [28] [ ]
(12"+=) – ('A'extra time mix).
(cd-s) – ('A'extra time mix). / ('A' Diva mix) / ('A' Renegade Sound..)
(12") – ('A' Diva futura mix). / ('A' Renegade Soundwave mix).

Oct 90. (7")(c-s) **DANCE OF THE MAD BASTARDS. / PREACHING TO THE PERVERTED** [32] [ ]
PWEI VS. THE MORAL MAJORITY
(12"ep+=)(cd-ep+=) – ('A'other mix).

Oct 90. (cd)(c)(lp) **THE POP WILL EAT ITSELF CURE FOR SANITY** [33] [ ]
– Incredible PWEI vs. The Moral Majority / Dance of the mad bastards / 88 seconds... and still counting / X, Y and Zee / City Zen radio 1990-2000 FM / Dr.Nightmares medication time / Touched by the hand of Cicciolina / 1000 x no! / Psycho sexual / Axe of men / Another man's rhubarb / Medicine man speaks with forked tongue / Nightmare at 20,000 feet / Very metal noise pollution / 92 degrees F (the 3rd degree) / Lived in splendour, died in chaos / The beat that refused to die. *(re-iss.+pic-lp.May91)(re-iss.cd Nov93)*

Jan 91. (7")(c-s) **X, Y AND ZEE. / AXE OF MEN** [15] [ ]
(12"box+=) – Psychosexual.
(12"+=)(cd-s+=) – ('A'intergalactic mix) / ('A'sensory amp mix).

May 91. (7")(c-s) **92 f. / INCREDIBLE PWEI VS. DIRTY HARRY** [23] [ ]
(10"+=)(12"+=)(cd-s+=) – Another man's rhubarb.

May 92. (7")(c-s) **ARMADROME. / EAT ME DRINK ME LOVE ME KILL ME** [17] [ ]
(12"+=) – Dread alert in the karmadrome / Eat me drink me dub me kill me.
(cd-s) – ('A'side) / PWEI-zation (original metal noise pollution).
(12"pic-d+=) – PWEI-zation (original . . .) / Eat me drink me dub . . .

Aug 92. (7")(c-s) **BULLETPROOF. / ('A'-On-U-Sound mix)** [24] [ ]
(cd-s+=)(12"pic-d+=) – Good from far, far from good.
(12") – ('A'-mile high mix) / ('A'-no half measures mix).

Sep 92. (cd)(c)(lp) **THE LOOKS OF THE LIFESTYLE** [15] [ ]
– England's finest / Eat me, drink me, love me, kill me / Mother / Get the girl, kill the baddies! / I've always been a coward baby / Spoken drug song / Karmadrome / Urban futuristic (son of South Central) / Pretty pretty / I was a teenage grandad / Harry Dean Stanton / Bulletproof. *(re-iss.re-iss.cd Nov93)*

— added 5th member **FUZZ** – drums

Jan 93. (7")(c-s) **GET THE GIRL! KILL THE BADDIES!. / ('A' Adrian Sherwood mix)** [9] [ ]
(12"+=)(cd-s+=) – ('A' black country & western mix) or ('A'boilerhouse mix)
(cd-s) – ('A'side) / Urban futuristic (live) / Can u dig it? (live) / Wise up! sucker! (live).

Feb 93. (cd)(c)(lp) **WEIRDS, BARS AND GRILLS (live)** [44] [ ]
– England's finest / Eat me drink me love me kill me / Get the girl, kill the baddies!! / Wise up! sucker / 88 seconds and counting / Karmadrome / Token drug song mother / Preaching to the perverted / Axe of men / Nightmare at 20,000 feet / Always been a coward / Can U dig it / Bullet proof / Urban futuristic / There is no love between us anymore / Def con one. (cd/c+=) – Harry Dean Stanton teenage grandad.

Oct 93. (cd)(c)(lp) **16 DIFFERENT FLAVOURS OF HELL** (compilation) [73] [ ]
– Def con one / Wise up! sucker / Can U dig it / Touched by the hand of Cicciolina (extra time mix) / Dance of the mad / X Y and Zee (sunshine mix) / 92 degrees (boilerhouse The Birth mix) / Karmadrome / Bullet proof / Get the girl kill the baddies / Another man's rhubarb / Rockahula baby / Wise up sucker / Cicciolina (Renegade Soundwave mix). (cd=) Preaching to the perverted (remix) / Eat me drink me love me kill me / PWElzatin.

Infectious ???

Oct 93. (12"ep)(c-ep)(cd-ep) **R.S.V.P. / FAMILUS HORRIBILUS** [27] [ ]
(cd-ep+=) – ('B' remixes) / ('B' live)
(12"ep+=)(cd-ep+=) – ('A'side) / ('B'-higher later space mix agency vocal).

Feb 94. (7")(c-s)(7"pic-d) **ICH BIN EIN AUSLANDER. ("POP WILL EAT ITSELF & FUN-DA-MENTAL") / CP1£2** [28] [-]
(12"+=)(cd-s+=) – ('A'-Fun-Da-Mental instrumental) / ('A'-Fun-Da-Mental extra).
(12"+=) – ('A'-drone ranger mix) / Intense.

Aug 94. (7"colrd) **EVERYTHING'S COOL?. / LET IT FLOW** [23] [ ]
(7"colrd) – ('A'side) / WILD WEST
(cd-s) – ('A'side) / ('A'-Youth remix) / R.S.V.P. (Fluke mix).
(cd-s) – ('A'side) / Ich bin ein Auslander (live) / Familus horribilus (live) / R.S.V.P. (live).

Sep 94. (cd)(c)(lp) **DOS DEDOS MIS AMIGOS** [11] [ ]
– Ich bin ein Auslander / Kick to kill / Familus horribilus / Underbelly / Fatman / Home / Cape connection / Menofearthereaper / Everything's cool / R.S.V.P. / Babylon.

Mar 95. (d-cd)(d-c)(d-lp) **TWO FINGERS MY FRIENDS!** (remixes) [25] [ ]
– Ich bin ein Auslander (Fun-Da-Mental) / Kick to kill (Jim Foetus seersucker mix) / Familus horribilus (mega web 2) / Underbelly (Renegade Soundwave blackout mix) / Fatman (Hoodlum Priest Fatboy mix) / Home (Orb sweet sin and salvation mix) / Cape Connection (Transglobal Underground Cossack in UFO encounter mix) / Menofearthereaper (concrete no fee, no fear mix) / Everything's cool (safe as milk mix) / R.S.V.P. (made in Japan, live at the Budokan double live Gonzo F mix) / Babylon (Loop Guru Babylon a dub fire mix) // Ich bin ein Auslander (Die Krupps mix) / Familus horribilus (Hia Nyg vocal mix) / Cape Connection (golden claw versus clock and dagger mix) / Intense / C.P.I. £2 / Cape Connection (TGV aliens, bodacious aliens mix) / Everything's cool (Dragonfly mix) / RSVP (Fluke lunch mix) / Cape Connection (Secret Knowledge transfered up mix) / Underbelly (The Drum Club bugsong mix).

PORNO FOR PYROS (see under ⇒ JANE'S ADDICTION)

PORTISHEAD

Formed: Bristol, England . . . 1993 by duo GEOFF BARLOW and BETH GIBBONS. Signed to 'Chrysalis – Go! Discs' off-shoot 'Go Beat' and created quite a stir in 1994, with the release of their critically acclaimed debut album 'DUMMY'. This is currently breaking new chart ground and the UK Top 10. • **Style:** Melancholy cool jazz soul, chameleoned somewhere between a pastel SADE / SINEAD / BILLE HOLIDAY, fellow scratch Bristolites MASSIVE ATTACK and 60's spy-film soundtracks. In fact they also released a film 'TO KILL A DEAD MAN'. • **Songwriters:** BARROW-GIBBONS, but most with UTLEY. Sample; MORE MISSION IMPOSSIBLE (Lalo Schifrin) / SPIN IT JIG (Smokey Brooks) / ELEGANT PEOPLE (Weather Report) / MAGIC MOUNTAIN (War) / I'LL NEVER FALL IN LOVE AGAIN (Johnnie Ray; at slow speed!) / ISAAC MOODS (Isaac Hayes). • **Trivia:** Have remixed for the likes of DEPECHE MODE (In Your Room) / RIDE (I Don't Know Where It Comes From) / GRAVEDIGGAZ (Nowhere To Run).

Recommended: DUMMY (*10)

BETH GIBBONS – vocals / **GEOFF BARLOW** (b.1971) – programming, synthesizer with **ADRIAN UTLEY** – guitar, bass / **CLIVE DEAMER** – drums / **DAVE McDONALD** – nose flute / **RICHARD NEWELL** – drum programme / **NEIL SOLMAN** – synthesizers, organ / **ANDY HAGUE** – trumpet

Go Beat Go! Discs

Jun 94. (c-s)(cd-s) **NUMB / NUMBED IN MOSCOW** [ ] [ ]
(12"+=)(cd-s+=) – Revenge of the numbed / Numb: Earth under / Extra numb.
(cd-s++=) – A tribute to Monk and Cantella.

Aug 94. (c-s)(cd-s) **SOUR TIMES / SOUR SOUR TIMES** [57] [ ]
(12"+=)(cd-s+=) – Lot more / Sheared times.
(cd-s++=) – Airbus reconstruction.
(cd-s) – ('A'side) / It's a fire / Pedestal / Theme from 'To Kill A Dead Man'.
(re-iss.Apr95, hit UK No.13/ issued US hit 53)

Aug 94. (cd)(c) **DUMMY** [2] [79] Jan 95
– Mysterons / Sour times / Strangers / It could be sweet / Wandering star / Numb / Roads / Pedestal / Biscuit / Glory box.

Oct 94. (c-s)(cd-s) **GLORY BOX / ('A'version)** [13] [ ]
(12"+=)(cd-s+=) – ('A'versions).

POWER STATION (see under ⇒ DURAN DURAN)

PREFAB SPROUT

Formed: Consett, Durham, England . . . 1982 by Newcastle University student PADDY McALOON, with his brother MARTIN, plus WENDY SMITH and MICK SALMON. Their debut release 'LIONS IN MY OWN GARDEN' was rejected by many majors but its 1,000 copies shift quickly enough on own 'Candle' records, for local man Keith Armstrong to sign them to new 'Kitchenware' label. After a good showing in the indie charts with follow-up 'THE DEVIL HAS ALL THE BEST TUNES', the label moved with 'CBS', who released first Top 75 entry 'DON'T SING' early '84. Their first album 'SWOON', gained a Top 30 placing, and was followed the next year by another, 'STEVE McQUEEN'. Later that year (1985) at its third attempt, the single 'WHEN LOVE BREAKS DOWN', cracked the UK Top 30. A hiatus followed, but their return in 1988 heralded a UK Top 5 album 'FROM LANGLEY PARK TO MEMPHIS', which parented Top 10 single 'THE KING OF ROCK'N'ROLL'. • **Style:** Intelligent and romantic pop-rock outfit, initially likened to AZTEC CAMERA, but progressing to bedroom college circuit. • **Songwriters:** PADDY McALOON wrote all material. 'CARS AND GIRLS' was a swipe at BRUCE SPRINGSTEEN's alleged narrow song repertoire. PADDY has also attributed on songs, singing stars 'FARON YOUNG' (a gem) and 'DONNA SUMMER'. • **Trivia:** THOMAS DOLBY produced most of their work from 1985 onwards, bar a period in 1988 when he was ill.

Recommended: STEVE McQUEEN (*9) / FROM LANGLEY PARK TO MEMPHIS (*8) / JORDAN: THE COMEBACK (*8) / SWOON (*6) / A LIFE OF SURPRISES –

THE BEST OF PREFAB SPROUT (*9).

PADDY McALOON (b.PATRICK, 7 Jun'57) – vocals, guitar / **WENDY SMITH** (b.31 May'63) – some guitar, vocals / **MARTIN McALOON** (b. 4 Jan'62) – bass / **MICK SALMON** – drums

Candle — not issued

Aug 82. (7") **LIONS IN MY OWN GARDEN (EXIT SOMEONE). / RADIO LOVE** [ ] [-]
(re-iss.May83. on 'Kitchenware-Rough Trade')

Kitchenware — Epic

Oct 83. (7") **THE DEVIL HAS ALL THE BEST TUNES. / WALK ON** [ ] [-]
(re-iss.Jun86)
Dec 83. (12"+=) – Lions in my own garden / Radio love.
Jan 84. (7") **DON'T SING. / GREEN ISAAC II** [64] [-]
(12"+=) – He'll have to go.

—— **GRAHAM LANT** – drums repl. SALMON

Feb 84. (lp)(c) **SWOON** [22] [ ]
– Don't sing / Cue fanfare / Green Isaac I / Here on the eerie / Cruel / Couldn't bear to be special / I never play basketball now / Ghost town blues / Elegance / Technique / Green Isaac II. *(re-iss.+cd.Mar88) (re-iss.cd+c Mar93)*
Mar 84. (7") **COULDN'T BEAR TO BE SPECIAL. / SPINNING BELINDA** [ ] [ ]
(12"+=) – Donna Summer.

—— **NEIL CONTI** – drums repl. GRAHAM

Oct 84. (7") **WHEN LOVE BREAKS DOWN. / DIANA** [ ] [-]
(d7"+=) – Yearning loins / Donna Summer.
(12"++=) – Cruel.
Mar 85. (7") **WHEN LOVE BREAKS DOWN (remix). / THE YEARNING LOINS** [ ] [ ]
(d7"+=) – The Devil has all the best tunes / Walk on.
(d7"+=) – Lions in my own garden (exit someone). / Radio love.
Jun 85. (7") **FARON YOUNG. / SILHOUETTES** [74] [ ]
(d7"+=) – When love breaks down / The yearning loins.
(12") – ('A'truckin' mix). / ('B'full version).
Jun 85. (lp)(c)(cd) **STEVE McQUEEN** [21] [ ]
– Faron Young / Bonny / Appetite / When love breaks down / Goodbye Lucille (Johnny Johnny) / Hallelujah / Moving the river / Horsin' around / Desire as / Blueberry pies / When the angels. *(US-title 'TWO WHEELS GOOD')* (+=) – The yearning loins / He'll have to go / Faron (truckin' mix).
Aug 85. (7") **APPETITE. / HEAVEN CAN WAIT** [ ] [ ]
(d12"+=) – Oh, the Swiss / Faron Young (truckin' mix) / Silhouettes.
Oct 85. (7") **WHEN LOVE BREAKS DOWN. / THE YEARNING LOINS** [25] [ ]
(12"+=) – Spinning Belinda / He'll have to go / Donna Summer.
(extra 12"+=) – Real life lies.
Feb 86. (7")(7"sha-pic-d) **JOHNNY JOHNNY. / WIGS** [64] [ ]
(12"+=) – The guest who stayed forever.
Feb 88. (7")(7"pic-d) **CARS AND GIRLS. / VENDETTA** [44] [ ]
(10"+=) – Real life (just around the corner).
(12"++=)(pic-cd-s++=) – Faron Young (truckin' mix).
Mar 88. (lp)(c)(cd) **FROM LANGLEY PARK TO MEMPHIS** [5] [ ]
– The king of rock'n'roll / Cars and girls / I remember that / Enchanted / Nightingales / Hey Manhattan! / Knock on wood / The golden calf / Nancy (let your hair down for me) / The Venus of the soup kitchen.
Apr 88. (7") **THE KING OF ROCK'N'ROLL. / THE MOVING RIVER** [7] [ ]
(12"+=) – Dandy of the blue river / Tin can pot.
(cd-s+=) – Dandy of the blue river / He'll have to go.
Jul 88. (7") **HEY MANHATTAN!. / TORNADO** [72] [ ]
(12"+=) – ('A'-JFK version) / Donna Summer.

—— Below 'A'side featured **STEVIE WONDER on harmonica**

Nov 88. (7") **NIGHTINGALES. / LIONS IN MY OWN GARDEN** [ ] [ ]
(d7"ep+=) – The devil has all the best tunes.
(12"+=)(cd-s+=) – Life of suprise / Bearpark.
(12") – ('A'side) / The king of rock'n'roll (live).
Feb 89. (7")(7"pic-d) **THE GOLDEN CALF. / THE VENUS OF THE SOUP KITCHEN** [ ] [ ]
(12"+=)(cd-s+=) – ('A'long version) / Bonny (live).
Jun 89. (lp)(c)(cd) **THE PROTEST SONGS** (was scheduled for 1985 release) [18] [ ]
– The world awake / Life of suprise / Horse chimes / Wicked things / Dublin / Tiffany's / Diana / Talkin' Scarlet / 'Till the cows come home / Pearly gates. *(re-iss.May91 & Mar93 on 'Columbia')*
Aug 90. (7")(c-s) **LOOKING FOR ATLANTIS. / MICHAEL** [51] [ ]
(12"+=) – King of rock'n'roll / Cars and girls.
(cd-s++=) – When love breaks down.
Aug 90. (cd)(c)(lp) **JORDAN: THE COMEBACK** [7] [ ]
– Looking for Atlantis / Wild horses / Machine gun Ibiza / We let the stars go / Carnival 2000 / Jordan: the comeback / Jesse James symphony / Jesse James bolero / Moon dog / All the world loves lovers / All boys believe anything / The ice maiden / Paris Smith / The wedding march / One of the broken / Michael / Mercy / Scarlet nights / Doo wop in Harlem. *(re-iss.cd+c May94)*
Oct 90. (7")(c-s) **LET THE STARS GO. / CRUEL** [50] [ ]
(12"+=) – Don't sing / Couldn't bear to be special.
(cd-s+=) – Faron Young / Hey Manhattan (JFK version).
Dec 90. (7")(12")(cd-ep) **JORDAN: THE EP** [35] [ ]
– Carnival 2000 / One of the broken / The ice maiden / Jordan: The comeback.

Kitchenware-Columbia — Columbia

Jun 92. (7")(c-s) **THE SOUND OF CRYING. / ONE OF THE BROKEN** [23] [ ]
(cd-s+=) – Nightingales / Faron Young.
(cd-s) – ('A'full version) / The golden calf / Looking for Atlantis.
Jul 92. (cd)(c)(lp) **A LIFE OF SURPRISES – THE BEST OF PREFAB SPROUT** (compilation) [3] [ ]
– The king of rock'n'roll / When love breaks down / The sound of crying / Faron Young / Carnival 2000 / Goodbye Lucille 1 (Johnny Johnny) / I remember that / Cruel / Cars and girls / We let the stars go / Life of surprises / Appetite / If you don't love me / Wild horses / Hey Manhattan! / All the world loves lovers.
Jul 92. (7")(c-s) **IF YOU DON'T LOVE ME. / ('A'mix)** [33] [ ]
(cd-s) – ('A'side) / ('A'string driven thing mix) / Nero the zero / Real life (just around the corner).
(cd-s) – ('A'side) / ('A'no strings attached mix) / Lions in my own garden (exit someone) / Hey Manhattan (JFK mix).
Sep 92. (7")(c-s) **ALL THE WORLD LOVES LOVERS. / MACHINE GUN IBIZA** [61] [ ]
(cd-s) – ('A'side) / Knock on wood / Desire as / Moondog.
(cd-s+=) – Till the cows come home / Enchanted.
Jan 93. (7")(c-s) **LIFE OF SURPRISES. / THE KING OF ROCK 'N' ROLL** [24] [ ]
(cd-s+=) – If you don't love me
(12") – ('A'side) / If you don't love me (2 mixes)
Mar 93. (cd-s) **I REMEMBER THAT. / THE WORLD AWAKE** [ ] [ ]

– more compilations, etc. –

1988. CBS; (cd) **SWOON / STEVE McQUEEN** [ ] [-]
Feb 95. Columbia; (d-cd) **STEVE McQUEEN / FROM LANGLEY PARK TO MEMPHIS** [ ] [-]

PADDY McALOON

solo, with **LOUISE** and **DEIRDRE RUTKOWSKI** (of SUNSET GUN)
Jan 84. (7") **HORSIN' AROUND.** / (withdrawn) [ ] [ ]

Elvis PRESLEY

Born: ELVIS AARON PRESLEY, 8 Jan'35, Tupelo, Mississippi, USA. One of twin sons (the other Jesse was stillborn), he was raised in Memphis, Tennessee. Between the summer of '53 & '54, he spent time in Sam Phillips' 'Sun' studios, cutting demos. He finally produced first fruits, after the arrival of back-up session players SCOTTY MOORE and BILL BLACK. His first single 'THAT'S ALL RIGHT MAMA' gained local airplay before its release, and he soon signed to 'Sun'. He attempted a few country styles at this time, but after his young audiences saw his pelvic action on stage, he opted for R&B. Note:- Sam Phillips at first thought ELVIS was a black blues singer. It was Sam who chose to still feature ELVIS's country recordings on the flip sides. Colonel Tom Parker became his manager in 1955, and soon attained a large 5 figure deal with 'RCA', who also bought out his contract with 'Sun' records. The attention ELVIS's riotous stage shows had received prompted many bids from others. His major debut 'HEARTBREAK HOTEL', sparked off new phenomenom at the start of 1956, and soon exploded into a massive selling No.1. He appeared on many TV shows at this time and went on to star in his first feature film 'Love Me Tender' (named after his song, see also further film discography). The constant demand for ELVIS's records saw many similtaneous releases which choked the charts. He had a further 9 US No.1's in the States, before being controversially drafted into the army on 24 Mar'58. While serving his country for a two-year period, his mother Gladys died 14 Aug'58. In this period, several singles were issued, which were recorded just before the draft. After being promoted to Sergeant, his army time expired on 5 Mar'60. He returned to the Nashville studios and began new ballad-style mixed with uptempo beat, that was vaguely reminiscent of his pre-Army days. His films too, (around 3 a year in the 60's), contained a sort of manufactured pop, guided no doubt by the vast sums of money it stimulated. However, in spells between 1960 & 1965, he did create some truly wonderful pop records, including IT'S NOW OR NEVER / ARE YOU LONESOME TONIGHT? / WOODEN HEART / RETURN TO SENDER / DEVIL IN DISGUISE / VIVA LAS VEGAS / CRYING IN THE CHAPEL / to name several. In 1965, he also released first of a series of gospel albums 'HIS HAND IN MINE'. On the 1 May'67, he married long-time girlfriend Priscilla Beaulieu. After having a child, Lisa Marie, in 1968, they seperated 1972 and divorced 1973 (Priscilla Presley later became actress on 'Dallas' soap). In the late 1960's, he revived a somewhat commercialy declining singles career, when 'IN THE GHETTO' then 'SUSPICIOUS MINDS' hit the Top 3. His work in the 70's showed him moving into cabaret style as his live appearances were mainly in Las Vegas & Hawaii. He was still a top performer, as loyal fans old and new flocked to see his larger frame with white glitzy suit, churn out another exhaustive show. He was certainly not a shadow of the rock'n'roll hero he once was. His special diet he was on, combatted between prescribed drugs, junk food binges and alcohol. Tragically on the 16th August 1977, he was found dead in his Graceland home by girlfriend Ginger Alden. The coroner's unsurprising report was heart failure. His funeral had over 75,000 fans attending outside the gates of his home. THE KING OF ROCK was dead. I must write also that, following the death of ELVIS, many tabloids have reported sightings of a living Elvis. Speculation has been catapulted into untold heights of human degradation, The KING should be laid to rest in peace, and let only what he would've wanted, his music, to live on. • **Style:** (see also above plus . . .) • **Songwriters:** Covered (singles only):- THAT'S ALL RIGHT MAMA + MY BABY LEFT ME (Arthur 'Big Boy' Crudup) / BLUE MOON OF KENTUCKY (Bill Monroe) / BABY LET'S PLAY HOUSE (Arthur Gunter) / BLUE SUEDE SHOES (Carl Perkins) / TUTTI FRUTTI + RIP IT UP (Little Richard) / HOUND DOG (Freddie Bell . . . & Big Mama Thornton) / ALL SHOOK UP (Otis Blackwell) / ONE BROKEN HEART FOR SALE (Blackwell-Scott) / ONE NIGHT (Smiley Lewis) / A FOOL SUCH AS I (Hank Snow) / MY WISH CAME TRUE (Ivory Joe White) / IT'S NOW OR NEVER + SURRENDER + ASK ME (Italian trad.) / ARE YOU LONESOME TONIGHT? (Vaughn Deleath) / I FEEL SO BAD (Chuck Willis) / WITCHCRAFT (Spiders) / WHAT'D I SAY (Ray Charles) / BOSSA NOVA BABY (Lieber-Stoller) / SUCH A NIGHT (Johnnie Ray) / FRANKIE & JOHNNY (?) / LOVE LETTERS (Dick Haymes) / BIG BOSS MAN (Jimmy Reed) / U.S. MALE (Jerry Reed) / YOU'LL NEVER WALK ALONE (hit. Gerry & The Pacemakers) / IN THE GHETTO (Mac Davis) / SUSPICIOUS MINDS (Mark James) / THE WONDER OF YOU (Ray Peterson) / KENTUCKY RAIN (Eddie Rabbit) / YOU DON'T HAVE TO SAY YOU LOVE ME (Dusty Springfield) / THERE GOES MY EVERYTHING (Engelbert Humperdink) / I REALLY WANT TO KNOW (Les Paul & Mary Ford) / RAGS TO RICHES (Tony Bennett) / I JUST CAN'T HELP BELIEVIN' (B.J.Thomas) / UNTIL IT'S TIME FOR YOU TO GO (Buffy Sainte-Marie) / AN AMERICAN TRILOGY (Mickey Newbury) / BURNING LOVE (Arthur Alexander) / STEAMROLLER BLUES (James Taylor) / POLK SALAD ANNIE (Tony Joe White) / I'VE GOT A THING ABOUT YOU BABY (Billy Lee Riley) / PROMISED LAND (Chuck Berry) / MY BOY (hit. Richard Harris) / HURT (Timi Yuro) / GREEN, GREEN GRASS OF HOME (Tom Jones) / MY WAY (Paul Anka) / TOMORROW'S A LONG TIME (Bob Dylan) / etc. • **Miscellaneous:** He bought his Whitehaven, Memphis mansion GRACELAND in 1957.

— **Filmography:** LOVE ME TENDER (1956) / LOVING YOU (1957) / JAILHOUSE ROCK (1957) / KING CREOLE (1958) / G.I.BLUES (1960) / WILD IN THE COUNTRY (1961) / FLAMING STAR (1961) / BLUE HAWAII (1961) / FOLLOW THAT DREAM (1962) / KID GALAHAD (1962) / GIRLS! GIRLS! GIRLS! (1962) / IT HAPPENED AT THE WORLD'S FAIR (1963) / FUN IN ACAPULCO (1963) / KISSIN' COUSINS (1964) / VIVA LAS VEGAS (1964) / ROUSTABOUT (1964) / GIRL HAPPY (1965) / TICKLE ME (1965) / HAREM HOLIDAY (1965, 'HARUM SCARUM'-US title) / FRANKIE AND JOHNNY (1966) / PARADISE, HAWAIIAN STYLE (1966) / CALIFORNIA HOLIDAY (1966, 'SPINOUT'-US title) / DOUBLE TROUBLE (1967) / CLAMBAKE (1968) / STAY AWAY JOE (1968) / SPEEDWAY (1968) / LIVE A LITTLE, LOVE A LITTLE (1968) / CHARRO (1969) / THE TROUBLE WITH GIRLS (1969) / CHANGE OF HABIT (1970) / (This was his last feature film, but many concerts were recorded)

Recommended: A DATE WITH ELVIS (*7) / PRESLEY – THE ALL TIME GREATEST HITS (*9)

with **SCOTTY MOORE** – guitar / **BILL BLACK** – bass / + session drums
(iss.+ 78 rpm until Oct60)

not issued | Sun

Aug 54. (7") **THAT'S ALL RIGHT MAMA. / BLUE MOON OF KENTUCKY** [-] [ ]
Oct 54. (7") **GOOD ROCKIN' TONIGHT. / I DON'T CARE IF THE SUN DON'T SHINE** [-] [ ]
Jan 55. (7") **MILK COW BLUES BOOGIE. / YOU'RE A HEART-BREAKER** [-] [ ]
May 55. (7") **I'M LEFT, YOU'RE RIGHT, SHE'S GONE. / BABY LET'S PLAY HOUSE** [-] [ ]
Aug 55. (7") **MYSTERY TRAIN. / I FORGOT TO REMEMBER TO FORGET** [-] [ ]
(above all re-iss.Nov55 on 'RCA' US) (UK rel.Feb59 & Mar64 on 'RCA')

— added **D.J. FONTANA** – drums (on tour and then on session)

— now adding on session **FLOYD CRAMER** – piano / **CHET ATKINS** – guitar / **HANK GARLAND** – guitar / **'BOOTS' RANDOLPH** – saxophone.
His vocals were also backed and at times credited with **The JORDANAIRES; GORDON STOKER, HOYT HAWKINS, NEAL MATTHEWS** and **HUGH JARRETT.**

H.M.V. | R.C.A.

Mar 56. (7") **HEARTBREAK HOTEL. / I WAS THE ONE** [2] [1]
[19] Jan 56
Mar 56. (lp) **ELVIS PRESLEY** [NO] [1]
– Blue suede shoes* / I'm counting on you* / Money honey* / I got a sweetie (I got a woman)* / One sided love affair* / I'm gonna sit right down and cry over you* / Tryin' to get to you* / I love you because / Just because / Blue moon / I'll never let you go / Tutti frutti. (tracks * =on next album too) *(UK release Oct56, lp,c,cd-iss.Mar85 & Oct88 on 'RCA')*
May 56. (7") **BLUE SUEDE SHOES. / TUTTI FRUTTI** [9] [-]
Jul 56. (7") **I WANT YOU, I NEED YOU, I LOVE YOU. / MY BABY LEFT ME** [14] [1]
[31] May 56
Sep 56. (7") **HOUND DOG. / DON'T BE CRUEL** [2] [1] Jul 56
(re-iss.Jun78 on 'R.C.A.', hit UK No.24)
Sep 56. (7") **LOVE ME TENDER. / ANYWAY YOU WANT ME (THAT'S HOW I WILL BE)** [11] [1]
[20] Oct 56
Oct 56. (lp) **ROCK'N'ROLL NO.1** [NO] [-]
– (see last lp)+ / Mystery train / Lawdy Miss Clawdy / I'm left, you're right, she's gone / Shake rattle and roll. (US-title 'ELVIS') *(re-iss.Mar59 hit No.4) (re-iss.May72 as 'ROCK'N'ROLL', hit No.34) (re-iss.+c.Sep81 on 'RCA')*
Nov 56. (7") **BLUE MOON. / I DON'T CARE IF THE SUN DON'T SHINE** [9] [-]
[23]
Feb 57. (7") **MYSTERY TRAIN. / LOVE ME** [25] [ ]
Mar 57. (7") **RIP IT UP. / BABY LET'S PLAY HOUSE** [27] [ ]
Apr 57. (lp) **ROCK'N'ROLL NO.2** [NO] [-]
– Rip it up / When my blue moon turns to gold again / Love me / Long tall Sally / First in line / Old Shep / So glad you're mine / How's the world treating you / Any place is Paradise / Paralysed / Ready Teddy / How do think I feel.
Apr 57. (lp) **ELVIS** (finally iss.) [NO] [1] Nov 56
– (see other earlier lp's for tracks) *(cd-iss.Dec84 on 'RCA')*
May 57. (7") **TOO MUCH. / PLAYING FOR KEEPS** [6] [1]
[21] Jan 57
Jun 57. (7") **ALL SHOOK UP. / THAT'S WHEN YOUR HEART-ACHES BEGIN** [1] [1]
[58] Mar 57

(all 'H.M.V.' singles were re-iss.UK Oct57.)

— ELVIS was now backed by a variety of session men. SCOTTY and BILL left. In Jun'58, **BOB MOORE** – bass / **HANK GARLAND** – guitar repl. them

R.C.A. | R.C.A.

Jul 57. (7") **(LET ME BE YOUR) TEDDY BEAR. / LOVING YOU** [3] [1]
[20] Jun 57
Aug 57. (10"lp) **LOVING YOU (film)** [NO] [1] Jul 57
– Mean woman blues / (Let me be your) Teddy bear / Loving you / Got a lot o' livin' to do / Lonesome cowboy / I need you so / Have I told you lately that I love you / True love / Party / Blueberry hill / Hot dog / Don't leave me now. *(US rel. + re-iss.12" Sep77 +=4 extra) (re-iss.+c.Aug81)(cd-iss.Oct87)*
Oct 57. (7") **PARTY. / GOT A LOT OF LIVIN' TO DO** [2] [ ]
17 [ ]
Nov 57. (7") **SANTA BRING MY BABY BACK TO ME. / SANTA CLAUS IS COMING TO TOWN** [7] [ ]
Nov 57. (lp) **ELVIS' CHRISTMAS ALBUM** [NO] [1]
– Santa Claus is coming to town / White Christmas / Precious Lord it is no secret (what God can do) / Blue Christmas / Santa bring my baby back to me / I'll be home for Christmas / Here comes Santa Claus (right down Santa Claus lane) / O little town of Bethlehem / Silent night / Take my hand / I believe / (There'll be) Peace in the valley (for me). *(re-iss.Nov58, Nov71, hit No.7) (re-iss. Nov80, Nov85) (re-iss.Nov70 & Oct79 on 'RCA-Camden') (re-iss.Nov75 on 'Pickwick' diff) (cd-iss.Dec57 on 'RCA')*
Jan 58. (7") **JAILHOUSE ROCK. / TREAT ME NICE** [1] [1]
[18] Oct 57
(re-iss.May77, hit UK chart Aug77 – No.44) (re-iss.Jan83, hit No.27, also on 7"pic-d diff B-side THE ELVIS MEDLEY)
Feb 58. (7") **DON'T. / I BEG OF YOU** [2] [1]
[8] Jan 58

— ELVIS was served US army draft notice in Dec'57. He finally – after much fan/film producer protest – joined army on 24 Mar'58. He has had enough time to record many songs and appeared on celluloid once again (aka KING CREOLE film).

Apr 58. (7") **WEAR MY RING ROUND YOUR NECK. / DON'T CHA THINK IT'S TIME** [3] [2]
[15] Jun 58
Jul 58. (7") **HARD HEADED WOMAN. / DON'T ASK ME WHY** [2] [1]
[25] Jun 58
Sep 58. (7") **KING CREOLE. / DIXIELAND ROCK** [2]
Oct 58. (lp) **KING CREOLE (film soundtrack)** [4] [2] Sep 58
– King Creole / As long as I have you / Crawfish / Lover doll / Hard headed woman / Don't ask me why / Trouble / New Orleans / Dixieland rock / Steadfast, loyal and true / Young dreams. *(re-iss.1963, Feb69) (re-iss.Aug81, Apr84 +c) (cd-iss.Oct87*
Jan 59. (7") **ONE NIGHT. / I GOT STUNG** [1] [4]
[8] Oct 58
(re-iss.May77 UK)
Apr 59. (7") **(NOW AND THEN THERE'S) A FOOL SUCH AS I. / I NEED YOUR LOVE TONIGHT** [1] [2]
[4] Mar 59
(re-iss.May77 UK)
Jul 59. (7") **A BIG HUNK O' LOVE. / MY WISH CAME TRUE** [4] [1]
[12] Jun 59
(all singles from Jul57 were re-iss. Mar60)
He was now demobbed from the army 5 Mar'60. His session men now are **FLOYD CRAMER** – piano / **SCOTTY MOORE** – guitar
Mar 60. (7") **STUCK ON YOU. / FAME AND FORTUNE** [3] [1]
[17]
Jun 60. (lp) **ELVIS IS BACK** [1] [2] May 60
– Make me no it / The girl of my best friend / Dirty dirty / I will be home again / The thrill of your love / Feeling / Soldier boy / Such a night / It feels so right / Like a baby / Fever / Reconsider baby / The girl next door. *(re-iss.Sep81 + Jun84 +c) (cd-iss.Jul89)*
Jul 60. (7") **A MESS OF BLUES. / THE GIRL OF MY BEST FRIEND** [2] [-]
Jul 60. (7") **IT'S NOW OR NEVER. / A MESS OF BLUES** [-] [1]
[32]
Oct 60. (7") **IT'S NOW OR NEVER. / MAKE ME KNOW IT** [1] [-]
(re-iss.May77, hit UK chart Aug77 – No.39)
Dec 60. (lp) **G.I. BLUES (Film soundtrack)** [1] [1] Oct 60
– Tonight is so right for love / What's she really like / Big boots / Frankfurt special / Wooden heart / Shoppin' around / Pocketful of rainbows / G.I. blues / Doin' the best I can / Didja ever / Blue suede shoes. *(re-iss.Sep77, hit UK No.14, re-iss.Aug81 & Jan84) (cd-iss.1987 & 1990)*
Jan 61. (7") **ARE YOU LONESOME TONIGHT?. / I GOTTA KNOW** [1] [1]
[20] Nov 60
(re-iss.May77, hit UK chart Aug77 – No.46)
Mar 61. (7") **WOODEN HEART. / TONIGHT IS SO RIGHT FOR LOVE** [1] [-]
(re-iss.May77, hit UK chart Aug77 – No.49)
May 61. (lp) **HIS HAND IN MINE** [3] [13] Jan 61
– His hand in mine / I'm gonna walk dem golden stairs / Milky white way / My father's house / Known only to him / Mansions over the hilltop / I believe in the sky / If we never meet again / Working on the building / Jesus knows what I need / Joshua fit the battle / Swing low sweet chariot. *(re-iss.Aug81 & Apr84 +c) (cd-iss.Oct88)*
May 61. (7") **SURRENDER (TORNA A SURRIENTO). / LONELY MAN** [4] [1]
[32] Feb 61
(re-iss.May77 UK)
Aug 61. (7") **WILD IN THE COUNTRY. / I FEEL SO BAD** [1] [26]
[5] May 61
Oct 61. (7") **(MARIE'S THE NAME) HIS LATEST FLAME. / LITTLE SISTER** [4] [26]
[5] Aug 61
(re-iss.May77 UK)
Oct 61. (lp) **SOMETHING FOR EVERYBODY** [2] [1] Jul 61
– There's always me / Give me the right / Gently / It's a sin / Sentimental me / Starting today / I'm coming home / I slipped I stumbled I fell / Put the blame on me / I want you with me / Judy / In your arms. *(re-iss.Sep81 & Aug84 +c)(cd-iss.Dec90)*
Dec 61. (lp) **BLUE HAWAII (Soundtrack)** [1] [1] Oct 61

– Blue hawaii / Almost always true / Moonlight swim / No more / Can't help falling in love / Rock a hula baby / Island of love / Hawaiin sunset / Hawaiin wedding song / Alohaoe / Beach boy blues / Slicin' sands / Ku ui Po / Ito eats. *(re-iss.Sep81, hit UK No.26. re-iss. Aug84 +c) (cd-iss.Oct87)*

Jan 62. (7") **ROCK-A-HULA-BABY. / CAN'T HELP FALLING IN LOVE** 1 23
2 Dec 61
(re-iss.May77 UK)

May 62. (7") **GOOD LUCK CHARM. / ANYTHING THAT'S PART OF YOU** 1 1
31 Mar 62
(re-iss.May77 UK)

Jun 62. (lp) **POT LUCK** 1 4
– Kiss me quick / Just for old times sake / Fountain of love / Gonna get back home somehow / Such an easy question / Night rider / Suspicion / Stepping out of line / I fell I've known you forever / That's someone you never forget / Something blue / I'm yours. *(re-iss.Apr81 & Jul84 +c) (cd-iss.Apr88)*

Aug 62. (7") **SHE'S NOT YOU. / JUST TELL HER JIM SAID HELLO** 1 5
55 Jul 62
(re-iss.May77 UK)

Nov 62. (7") **RETURN TO SENDER. / WHERE DO YOU COME FROM** 1 2
99 Oct 62
(re-iss.May77, hit UK chart Aug77 – No.42)

Jan 63. (lp) **GIRLS! GIRLS! GIRLS! (Film soundtrack)** 2 3 Dec 62
– Girls girls girls / I don't wanna be tired / Because of love / Return to sender / Where do you come from / I don't want to / We'll be together / A boy like me a girl like you / Song of the shrimp / The walls have ears / Earth boy / Thanks to the rolling sea / We're coming in loaded. *(re-iss.Oct77, Aug81 & Jun84) (re-iss.Sep86 on 'Camden')*

Feb 63. (7") **ONE BROKEN HEART FOR SALE. / THEY REMIND TO MUCH OF YOU** 12 11
53

May 63. (lp) **IT HAPPENED AT THE WORLD'S FAIR (Film Soundtrack)** 4 4 Apr 63
– Beyond the bend / Relax / Take me to the fair / Happy ending / They remind to much of you / One broken heart for sale / I'm falling in love tonight / Cotton candy land / A world of our own / How would you like to be. *(?)*

Jun 63. (7") **(YOU'RE THE) DEVIL IN DISGUISE. / PLEASE DON'T DRAG THAT STRING AROUND** 1 3
(re-iss.May77)

Oct 63. (7") **BOSSA NOVA. / WITCHCRAFT** 13 8
32

Dec 63. (7") **KISS ME QUICK. / SOMETHING BLUE** 14 34 May 64

Dec 63. (lp) **FUN IN ACAPULCO (Film Soundtrack)** 9 3 Mar 64
– Fun in Acapuco / The bullfighter was a lady / Marguerritta / There's no room to rhumba in a sports car / Dinero y amor / Mexico / I think I'm gonna like it here / Bossa nova baby / Vino / El Toro / You can't say no to acapulco / Guadalajara / Love me tonight / Slowly but surely. *(re-iss.Oct77, Aug81 + Nov84)*

Mar 64. (7") **VIVA LAS VEGAS. / WHAT'D I SAY** 17 29
21 May 64

Jun 64. (7") **KISSIN' COUSINS. / IT HURTS ME** 10 12
29 Feb 64

Jun 64. (lp) **KISSIN' COUSINS (Film Soundtrack)** 5 6 Apr 64
– Kissin' cousins / Smokey mountain boy / Anyone could fall in love with you / Catchin' on fast / Tender feeling / Once is enough / (It's a) Long lonely highway / Barefoot ballet / Echoes of love / Kissin' cousins (reprise). *(re-iss.Oct77, Aug81 + Nov84) (re-iss.Sep86 on 'Camden')*

Aug 64. (7") **SUCH A NIGHT. / NEVER ENDING** 13 16 Jul 64

Oct 64. (7") **AIN'T THAT LOVIN' YOU BABY. / ASK ME** 15 16
12

Nov 64. (7") **BLUE CHRISTMAS. / WHITE CHRISTMAS** 11

Jan 65. (lp) **ROUSTABOUT (Film Soundtrack)** 12 1 Nov 64
– Roustabout / Little Egypt / Poison Ivy league / Hard knocks / It's a wonderful world / Big love big heartache / There's a brand new day on the horizon / Wheels of my heels / Carny town / One track heart / It's carnival time. *(re-iss.Oct77, Aug81 + Nov84 +c.)*

Mar 65. (7") **DO THE CLAM. / YOU'LL BE GONE** 19 21 Feb 64

Apr 65. (lp) **GIRL HAPPY (Film Soundtrack)** 8 8
– Girl happy / Spring fever / Fort Lauderdale / You'll be gone / Chamber of commerce / Startin' tonight / Puppet on a string / Do not disturb / Cross my heart and hope to die / Wolf call / The meanest girl in town / I've got to find my baby / Do the clam. *(re-iss.Aug80, Nov84 +c.)*

May 65. (7") **CRYING IN THE CHAPEL. / I BELIEVE IN THE MAN IN THE SKY** 1 3
(re-iss.May77, hit UK chart Aug77 – No.43)

Jun 65. (7") **(SUCH AN) EASY QUESTION. / IT FEELS SO RIGHT** - 11
55

Sep 65. (7") **I'M YOURS. / (IT'S A) LONG LONELY HIGHWAY** - 11

Sep 65. (lp) **FLAMING STAR AND SUMMER KISSES** 11
– (compilation of 'FLAMING STAR' Film soundtrack EP + 'LOVING YOU' lp) *(re-iss.Jun69 as 'FLAMING STAR' hit UK No.2) (re-iss.Apr79 on 'Camden' +c.)*

Nov 65. (7") **PUPPET ON A STRING. / ?** - 14

Nov 65. (7") **TELL ME WHY. / PUPPET ON A STRING** 15 -

Nov 65. (lp) **ELVIS FOR EVERYONE!** 8 10 Sep 65
– You're cheatin' heart / Summer kisses / Winter tears / For the millionth and the last time / Finders keepers losers weepers / In my way / Tomorrow night / Forget me never / Met her tonight / Memphis Tennessee / Sound advice / Santa Lucia / When it rains it really pours. *(re-iss.Feb81 & Apr84 +c.) (cd-iss.Apr95)*

Jan 66. (7") **TELL ME WHY. / BLUE RIVER** - 33
95

Jan 66. (lp) **HAREM HOLIDAY (Film Soundtrack)** 11 8 Nov 65
– Harem holiday / My desert serenade / Go west young man / Hey little girl / Mirage / Shake that tambourine / Golden coins / So close yet so far (from Paradise) / Animal instinct / Wisdom of ages. (US title 'HARUM SCARUM') *(re-iss.Aug80 + Apr84)*

Feb 66. (7") **BLUE RIVER. / DO NOT DISTURB** 22

Mar 66. (7") **FRANKIE AND JOHNNY. / PLEASE DON'T STOP LOVING ME** 21 25

Apr 66. (lp) **FRANKIE AND JOHNNY (Film Soundtrack)** 11 20
– Frankie and Johnny / Come along / What every woman lives for / Petunia the gardeners daughter / Beginners luck / Chesay / Down by the riverside / When the saints go marching in / Please don't stop loving me / Look out / Everybody come aboard / Shout it out / Hard luck. *(re-iss.Aug80 + Apr84)*

Jun 66. (7") **LOVE LETTERS. / COME WHAT MAY** 6 19

Jul 66. (lp) **PARADISE, HAWAIIAN STYLE (Film Soundtrack)** 7 15
– Paradise Hawaiian style / Queenie Wamine's papaya / Scratch my back (then I'll scratch yours) / House of sand / Datin' / Drums of the islands / Stop where you are / A dogs life / Sand castles / This is my heaven. *(re-iss.Aug80 & Apr84)*

Oct 66. (7") **ALL THAT I AM. / SPINOUT** 17 40 Bside

Nov 66. (lp) **CALIFORNIA HOLIDAY (Film Soundtrack)** 17 18
– Stop look and listen / Adam and evil / All that Iam / Am I ready / Never say yes / Beach shack / Spinout / Smorgasbord / Tomorrow is a long time / Down in the alley / I'll be back / I'll remember you. (US title 'SPINOUT') *(re-iss. Aug80 + Nov84)*

Nov 66. (7") **IF EVERYDAY WAS LIKE CHRISTMAS. / HOW WOULD YOU LIKE TO BE** 13

Feb 67. (7") **INDESCRIBABLY BLUE. / FOOLS FALL IN LOVE** 21 33

Apr 67. (lp) **HOW GREAT THOU ART** 11 18
– How great thou art / In the garden / Without him / By and by / Somebody bigger than you and I / Stand by me / Farther along / Where could I go to but the Lord / Crying in the chapel / If the Lord wasn't by my side / So high / Run on / Where no one stands alone. *(re-iss.Sep82 + Jul84) (cd-iss.Apr88)*

May 67. (7") **YOU GOTTA STOP. / LOVE MACHINE** 38

Aug 67. (7") **LONG LEGGED GIRL (WITH THE SHORT DRESS ON). / THAT'S SOMEONE YOU NEVER FORGET** 49 63
92

Aug 67. (lp) **DOUBLE TROUBLE (Film Soundtrack)** 34
– Double trouble / Baby if you'll give me all your love / City by night / Could I fall in love / Old McDonald / I love only one girl / Long legged girl (with the short dress on) / It won't be long / There is so much world to see / Blue river / Never ending / What now what next where to. *(re-iss.Aug80)*

Sep 67. (7") **THERE'S ALWAYS ME. / JUDY** 56
78

Nov 67. (7") **BIG BOSS MAN. / YOU DON'T ME** 38 Oct 67

Feb 68. (7") **GUITAR MAN. / HI-HEEL SNEAKERS** 19 43

Apr 68. (lp) **CLAMBAKE (Film Soundtrack)** 19 40 Feb 68
– Clambake / Who needs money / A house that has everything / Confidence / Hey hey hey / You don't know me / Guitar man / The girl I never loved / How can you lose what you never had / Big boss man / Singing trees / Just call me lonesome. *(re-iss.Aug80)*

May 68. (7") **U.S. MALE. / STAY AWAY** 15 28
67 Mar 68

Jul 68. (7") **YOUR TIME HASN'T COME YET BABY. / LET YOURSELF GO** 22 72
71 Jun68

Aug 68. (lp) **SPEEDWAY (Film Soundtrack)** 82
– Speedway / There ain't nothing like a song / Your time hasn't come yet baby / Who are you (who am I) / He's your uncle not your dad / Let yourself go / Your groovy self / Western union / Five sleepy heads / Mine / Goin' home / Suppose.

Oct 68. (7") **YOU'LL NEVER WALK ALONE. / WE CALL ON HIM** 44 90 Apr 68

Dec 68. (7") **A LITTLE LESS CONVERSATION. / ALMOST IN LOVE** 69
95 Sep68

Feb 69. (7") **IF I CAN DREAM. / MEMORIES** 11 12 Nov 68
(above iss.separately in the US, 'B' side hit No.35)

Jun 69. (7") **IN THE GHETTO. / ANY DAY NOW** 2 3 May69

Aug 69. (lp) **FROM ELVIS IN MEMPHIS** 1 13 Jun 69
– Wearin that loved-in look / Only the strong survive / I'll hold you in my heart / Long black limousine / It keeps right on a-turnin' / I'm moving on / Power of my love / Gentle on my mind / After loving you / True love travels on a gravel road / Any day now / In the ghetto. *(cd-iss.Mar91) (re-iss.cd+c Mar94)*

Aug 69. (7") **CLEAN UP YOUR OWN BACK YARD. / THE FAIR'S MOVING ON** 21 35 Jul 69

Nov 69. (7") **SUSPICIOUS MINDS. / YOU'LL THINK OF ME** 2 1 Sep 69

Feb 70. (7") **DON'T CRY DADDY. / RUBBERNECKIN'** 8 6 Nov 69

— His live band mid '69 for album **JAMES BURTON** – lead guitar / **JOHN WILKINSON** – guitar / **CHARLIE HODGE** – guitar / **JERRY SCHEFF** – bass / **LARRY MUHOBERAC** – keyboards / **RONNIE TUTT** – drums back up groups were The IMPERIALS and also The SWEET INSPIRATIONS.

Mar 70. (d-lp)(d-c) **FROM MEMPHIS TO VEGAS – FROM VEGAS TO MEMPHIS** 3 12 Nov 69
– FROM MEMPHIS TO VEGAS (live at the International, Vegas) – Blue suede shoes / Johnny B.Goode / All shook up / Hound dog / Are you lonesome tonight / I can't stop loving you / Me babe / Medley; Mystery train – Tiger man / Words / In the ghetto / Suspicious minds / Can't help falling in love. FROM VEGAS TO MEMPHIS (studio sessions) – Elvis back in Memphis / Inherit the wind / This is the story / Stranger in my hometown / A little bit of green / The fair's moving on / And the grass don't pay no mind / From a jack to a king / You'll think of me / Without love (there's nothing). *(re-iss.Jun84) (cd-iss.Dec91, first lp only)*

— **GLEN D. HARDIN** – drums (ex-CRICKETS) repl. TOTT

May 70. (7") **KENTUCKY RAIN. / MY LITTLE FRIEND** 21 16 Feb 70

Jul 70. (7") **THE WONDER OF YOU (live). / MAMA LIKE ROSES** 1 9 May 70
(re-iss.May77, hit UK No.48)

Jul 70. (lp)(c) **ON STAGE – FEBUARY 1970 (live)** 2 13 Jun 70
– See see rider blues / Release me (and let me live again) / Sweet Caroline / Runaway / The wonder of you / Polka salad Annie / Yesterday / Proud Mary / Walk a mile in my shoes / Let it be me (je't appartiens). *(re-iss.1974)(re-iss.+cd.Mar91)*

Nov 70. (7") **I'VE LOST YOU. / THE STEP IS LOVE** 9 32 Aug 70

Jan 71. (7") **YOU DON'T HAVE TO SAY YOU LOVE ME. / PATCH IT UP** 9 11 Oct 70

Jan 71. (lp)(c) **THAT'S THE WAY IT IS (live Las Vegas)** 12 21 Dec 70
– I just can't help believin' / Twenty days and twenty nights / How the web was woven / Patch it up / Mary in the morning / You don't have to say you love me / You've lost that lovin' feeling / I've lost you / Just pretend / Stranger in the crowd / The next step is love / Bridge over troubled water. *(re-iss.1984)(re-iss.cd+c Jul93)*

Mar 71. (7") **THERE GOES MY EVERYTHING. / I REALLY DON'T WANT TO KNOW** 6 21 Dec 70

Mar 71. (lp)(c) **ELVIS COUNTRY (I'M 10,000 YEARS OLD)** 6 12 Jan 71
– Snowbird / Tomorrow never comes / Little cabin on the hill / Whole lotta shakin'

goin' on / Funny how time slips away / I really don't want to know / There goes my everything / It's your baby / You rock it / Fool / Faded love / I washed my hands in muddy water / Make the world go away / I was born about 10,000 years ago *(re-iss.Aug84)(re-iss.cd+c Jul93)*

May 71. (7") **RAGS TO RICHES. / WHERE DID THEY GO, LORD** 9 33 Mar 71

May 71. (7") **LIFE. / ONLY BELIEVE** - 53

Jul 71. (lp)(c) **LOVE LETTERS FROM ELVIS** 7 33 Jun 71

– Love letters / When I'm over you / I'll never know / Got my mojo working / Heart of Rome / It ain't no big thing (but it's growing) / Only believe / This is our dance / Cindy Cindy / Life. *(re-iss.Nov84) (cd-iss.Jun88)*

Sep 71. (7") **I'M LEAVIN'. / HEART OF ROME** 23 36 Aug 71

Oct 71. (7") **IT'S ONLY LOVE. / THE SOUND OF YOUR CRY** - 51

Nov 71. (7") **I JUST CAN'T HELP BELIEVIN'. / HOW THE WEB WAS WOVEN** 6

Mar 72. (7") **UNTIL IT'S TIME FOR YOU TO GO. / WE CAN MAKE THE MORNING** 5 40 Feb 72

May 72. (lp)(c) **ELVIS NOW** 12

– Help me make it through the night / Miracle of the rosary / Hey Jude / Put your hand in the hand / Until it's time for you to go / We can make the morning / Early mornin' rain / Sylvia / Fools rush in (where angels feare to tread) / I was born about ten thousand years ago. *(re-iss.1974)(re-iss.cd+c Jul93)*

Jun 72. (7") **AN AMERICAN TRILOGY. / THE FIRST TIME EVER I SAW YOUR FACE** 8 66 Apr 72

Jul 72. (lp)(c) **ELVIS IS RECORDED AT MADISON SQUARE GARDEN (live)** 3 11

– Introduction; / Theme from 2001 – a space odyssey / That's all right / Proud Mary / Never been to Spain / You don't have to say you love me / You've lost that lovin' feelin' / Polk salad Annie / Love me / All shook up / Heartbreak hotel / Medley; / (Let me your) Teddy bear – Don't be cruel – Love me tender – The impossible dream / Hound dog / Suspicious minds / For the good times / An American trilogy / Funny how time slips away / I can't stop loving you / Can't help falling in love. *(re-iss.1974)*

Aug 72. (lp)(c) **HE TOUCHED ME (gospel)** 38 79

– He touched me / I've got confidence / Amazing Grace / Seeing is believing / He is my everything / Bosom of Abraham / An evening prayer / Lead me, guide me / There is no god but God / Thing called love / I, John / Reach out to Jesus.

Sep 72. (7") **BURNING LOVE. / IT'S A MATTER OF TIME** 7 2 Aug 72

Dec 72. (7") **ALWAYS ON MY MIND. / SEPERATE WAYS** 9 20 b-side

Feb 73. (d-lp)(d-c) **ALOHA FROM HAWAII VIA SATELLITE** (TV special rec. 14 Jan73) 11 1

– Theme from 2001 (a space odyssey) / See see rider / Burning love / Something / You gave me a mountain / Steamroller blues / My way / Love me Johnny B.Goode / It's over / I can't stop loving you / Blue suede shoes / I'm so lonesome I could cry / Hound dog / What now my love / Fever / Welcome to my world / Suspicious minds / I'll remember you / Medley; Long tall Sally- Whole lotta shakin goin' on – An American trilogy – A big hunk o' love – I can't help falling in love. *(re-iss.Aug84) (cd-iss.Sep86 & Oct95)*

May 73. (7") **POLK SALAD ANNIE. / SEE SEE RIDER** 23

Jul 73. (7") **FOOL. / STEAMROLLER BLUES** 16 17

Sep 73. (lp)(c) **ELVIS** 16 52

– Fool / Where do I go from here / Love me, love the life I lead / I'm still here / It's impossible / (That's what you get) For lovin' me / Padre / I'll take you home again Kathleen / I will be true / Don't think twice, it's alright. *(re-iss.cd+c Mar94)*

Nov 73. (7") **RAISED ON ROCK. / FOR OL' TIMES SAKE** 36

Nov 73. (lp)(c) **RAISED ON ROCK**

– Raised on rock / Are you sincere / Find out what's happening / I miss you / Girl of mine / For 'ol times sake / If you don't come back / Just a little bit / Sweet Angeline / Three corn patches. *(re-iss.cd+c Mar94)*

Mar 74. (7") **TAKE GOOD CARE OF HER. / I'VE GOT A THING ABOUT YOU BABY** 33 39 Mar 74

May 74. (lp)(c) **GOOD TIMES** 42 90

– Take good care of her / Loving arms / I got a feeling in my body / If that isn't love / She wears my ring / I've got a thing about you baby / My boy / Spanish eyes / Talk about the good times / Good time Charlie got the blues. *(re-iss.cd+c Mar94)*

Jun 74. (7") **IF YOU TALK IN YOUR SLEEP. / HELP ME** 40 17

Aug 74. (lp)(c) **ELVIS RECORDED LIVE ON STAGE (live in Memphis)** 44 33

– See see rider / I got a woman / Love me / Trying to get to you / Medley; Long tall Sally – Whole lotta shakin' goin on / Mama don't dance / Flip flop and fly / Jailhouse rock / Hound dog / Why me Lord / How great thou art / Blueberry hill / Can't stop loving you / Help me / An American trilogy / Let there be me / My baby left me / Lawdy Miss Clawdy / Can't help falling in love / Closing vamp.

Oct 74. (7") **MY BOY. / LOVING ARMS** 5 20 Feb 75

Dec 74. (7") **PROMISED LAND. / IT'S MIDNIGHT** 9

Feb 75. (lp)(c) **PROMISED LAND** 21 47

– Promised land / There's a honky tonk angel (who will take me back in) / Help me / Mr.Songman / Love song of the year / It's midnight / Your love's been a long time comin' / If you talk in your sleep / Thinking about you / You ask me to. *(cd-iss.Dec91)*

May 75. (7") **T-R-O-U-B-L-E. / MR.SONGMAN** 31 35

Jun 75. (lp)(c) **TODAY** 48 57

– T.R.O.U.B.L.E. / And I love you so / Susan when she tried / Woman without love / Shake a hand / Pieces of my life / Fairy tale / I can help / Bringin' it back / Green green grass of home.

Oct 75. (7") **BRINGING IT BACK. / PIECES OF MY LIFE** - 65

Nov 75. (7") **GREEN, GREEN GRASS OF HOME. / THINKING ABOUT YOU** 29 -

Apr 76. (7") **HURT. / FOR THE HEART** 37 28

Jun 76. (lp)(c) **FROM ELVIS PRESLEY BOULEVARD, MEMPHIS, TENNESSEE** 29 41

– Hurt / Never again / Blue eyes crying in the rain / Danny boy / The last farewell / For the heart / Bitter they are, harder they fall / Solitaire / Love coming down / I'll never fall in love again. *(re-iss.Jan85)(re-iss.cd+c Jul93)*

Feb 77. (7") **MOODY BLUE. / SHE THINKS I STILL CARE** 6 31

Jul 77. (7") **WAY DOWN. / PLEDGING MY LOVE** 1 18

—— On the 16th August 1977, ELVIS died of heart failure. Below are songs he recorded just prior to death.

Aug 77. (lp)(c) **MOODY BLUE** (4 live) 3 3

– Unchained melody / If you love me (let me know) / Little darlin' / He'll have to go / Let me be there / Way down / Pledging my love / Moody blue / She thinks I still care. *(re-iss.Sep81 + Jan85) (cd-iss.Oct88)*

– postumous compilations, others, etc. –

Note; All below releases were issued on 'RCA' until otherwise stated

Aug 77. (lp)(c) **WELCOME TO MY WORLD** 7

– Welcome to my world / Help me make it through the night / Release me (and let me love again) / I really don't know what to know / For the good times / Make the world go away / Gentle on my mind / I'm so lonesome I could cry / Your cheatin' heart / I can't stop loving you. *(re-iss.Sep81)*

Oct 77. (lp)(c) **A LEGENDARY PERFORMER VOL.2**

Oct 77. (lp)(c) **LOVING YOU** 24

Nov 77. (d-lp)(d-c) **ELVIS IN CONCERT (live)** 13 5

– (Elvis' fans comment, and opening riff to 2001) / See see rider / That's alright / Are you lonesome tonight? / You gave me a mountain / Jailhouse rock / How great thou art / I really don't want to know / (Elvis introduces his father) / Hurt. *(re-iss.Oct85)(re-iss.cd+c Jul93)*

Nov 77. (7") **MY WAY (live). / AMERICA, THE BEAUTIFUL (live)** 9 22

Apr 78. (lp)(c) **HE WALKS BESIDE ME (gospel)** 37

– He is my everything / Miracle of the rosary / Where did they go Lord / Somebody bigger than you and I / An evening prayer / The impossible dream / If I can dream / Padre / Known only to him / Who am I / How great thou art.

May 78. (lp)(c) **THE '56 SESSIONS VOL.1** 47 -

1978. (lp)(c) **THE '56 SESSIONS VOL.2** -

(above 2 re-iss.Sep81)

Nov 78. (lp)(c) **ELVIS – A CANADIAN TRIBUTE** -

Nov 78. (7") **OLD SHEP. / PARALYZED**

Jan 79. (lp)(c) **A LEGENDARY PERFORMER VOL.3** 43

Apr 79. (lp)(c) **OUR MEMORIES OF ELVIS** 72

Sep 79. (lp)(c) **MEMORIES OF ELVIS VOL.2**

Oct 79. (d-lp) **ELVIS PRESLEY**

Nov 79. (lp)(c) **ELVIS SINGS THE WONDERFUL WORLD OF CHRISTMAS**

Dec 79. (7")(12") **IT WON'T SEEM LIKE CHRISTMAS (WITHOUT YOU). / MERRY CHRISTMAS BABY** 13

Mar 80. (lp)(c) **PICTURES OF ELVIS**

Jun 80. (lp)(c) **ELVIS PRESLEY SINGS LEIBER AND STOLLER** 32

(re-iss.Apr84)

Aug 80. (8xlp,8xc) **ELVIS AARON PRESLEY** 21 27

– (AN EARLY LIVE PERFORMANCE / AN EARLY BENEFIT PERFORMANCE / COLLECTOR'S GOLD FROM THE MOVIE YEARS / THE TV SPECIALS / THE LAS VEGAS YEARS / LOST SINGLES / ELVIS AT THE PIANO – THE CONCERT YEARS (PART 1) / THE CONCERT YEARS (concluded).

Aug 80. (7")(12") **IT'S ONLY LOVE. / BEYOND THE REEF** 3 -

Nov 80. (7") **SANTA CLAUS IS BACK IN TOWN. / I BELIEVE** 41

Feb 81. (7") **GUITAR MAN (remix). / FADED LOVE** 43 28

Mar 81. (lp)(c) **GUITAR MAN** 33 49

– Guitar man / After loving you / Too much monkey business / Just call me lonesome / Lovin' arms / You asked me to / Clean up your own backyard / She thinks I still care / Faded love / I'm movin' on.

Apr 81. (7") **LOVIN' ARMS. / YOU ASKED ME TO** 47

May 81. (d-lp)(d-c) **THIS IS ELVIS (Soundtrack)** 47

(re-iss.Apr81 + May84)

Sep 81. (lp)(c) **ELVIS'S GOLDEN RECORDS VOL.1**

Sep 81. (lp)(c) **ELVIS'S GOLDEN RECORDS VOL.2**

Sep 81. (lp)(c) **ELVIS'S GOLDEN RECORDS VOL.3**

Sep 81. (lp)(c) **ELVIS'S GOLDEN RECORDS VOL.4**

Sep 81. (lp)(c) **ELVIS'S GOLDEN RECORDS VOL.5**

(all 5 volumes re-iss. again separately Nov84)

Oct 81. (lp)(c) **20 GREATEST HITS VOL.1**

Mar 82. (lp)(c) **20 GREATEST HITS VOL.2**

(above 2 re-dist.Apr84)

Feb 82. (lp)(c) **THE SOUND OF YOUR CRY** 31 -

Feb 82. (7") **ARE YOU LONESOME TONIGHT? (live version). / FROM A JACK TO A KING (live)** 25

Mar 82. (lp)(c) **ELVIS PRESLEY EP PACK** 97

Jun 82. (7")(7"pic-d) **THE SOUND OF YOUR CRY. / I'LL NEVER KNOW** 59

Aug 82. (d-lp)(d-c) **ROMANTIC ELVIS 20 LOVE SONGS – ROCKIN' ELVIS 60's** 62 -

(re-iss.2 diff.lp's.May84)

1982. (7"ep) **G.I. BLUES – THE ALTERNATIVE TAKES** -

– Shoppin' around / Big boots / Frankfurt special / Tonight's all right for love.

Oct 82. (11x7"ep-box) **THE EP COLLECTION VOL.3**

– THE REAL ELVIS / ELVIS PRESLEY / LOVE ME TENDER / HEARTBREAK HOTEL / JAILHOUSE ROCK / LOVING YOU / KING CREOLE VOL.1 / SUCH A NIGHT / FOLLOW THAT DREAM / KID GALAHAD)

Nov 82. (7")(7"pic-d) **THE ELVIS MEDLEY: Jailhouse Rock-Teddy Bear-Hound Dog-Don't Be Cruel-Burning Love-Suspicious Minds. / JAILHOUSE ROCK** - 71

Dec 82. (lp)(c) **THE ELVIS MEDLEY** -

Dec 82. (lp)(c) **IT WON'T SEEM LIKE CHRISTMAS WITHOUT YOU** 80

(re-dist.Nov84)

Feb 83. (pic-lp) **PICTURES OF ELVIS II** -

Apr 83. (pic-lp)(c) **JAILHOUSE ROCK / LOVE IN LAS VEGAS** 40

– (compilation of music from the 2 films)

Apr 83. (7") **(YOU'RE SO SQUARE) BABY, I DON'T CARE. / TRUE LOVE** 61

(12"pic-d) – ('A'side) / One-side love affair / Tutti frutti.

May 83. (c-ep) **CASSETTE EP** -

– I just can't help believin' / Always on my mind / Seperate ways / I've lost you.

Jul 83. (c-ep) **FLIP HITS** -

– It's now or never / The girl of my best friend / Are you lonesome tonight? / Surrender.

Aug 83. (lp)(c) **I WAS THE ONE** 83

Nov 83. (7") **I CAN HELP. / THE LADY LOVES ME (w/ ANN-MARGARET)** 30

(10"pic-d+=) – If every day was like Christmas.

Nov 83. (lp)(c) **A LEGENDARY PERFORMER VOL.4** 91
Mar 84. (lp)(c) **I CAN HELP** 71
Apr 84. (lp)(c) **ELVIS – THE FIRST LIVE RECORDINGS** 69
May 84. (7"m) **GREEN, GREEN GRASS OF HOME. / RELEASE ME (AND LET ME LOVE AGAIN) (live) / SOLITAIRE (live)**
Jun 84. (c) **MAGIC MOMENTS** -
Aug 84. (d-lp)(c) **THE COMPLETE SONGS** -
Aug 84. (lp)(c) **ELVIS IN GERMANY (live)**
Aug 84. (d-lp)(d-c)(cd) **32 FILM HITS** -
Oct 84. (7") **THE LAST FAREWELL. / IT'S EASY FOR YOU** 48
(12"+=) – Shake, rattle and roll / Flip, flop and fly / That's all right (mama) / My heart cries for you.
Nov 84. (6xlp-box) **ELVIS – A GOLDEN CELEBRATION**
Jan 85. (7") **THE ELVIS MEDLEY. / BLUE SUEDE SHOES** 51
Jan 85. (lp)(c) **GOLDEN RECORDS VOL.5**
(cd-iss.1986)
Jan 85. (lp)(c) **20 GREATEST HITS VOLUME 2** 98
Feb 85. (lp)(c)(cd) **A VALENTINE GIFT FOR YOU** -
Mar 85. (lp)(c) **RARE ELVIS VOL.1**
Mar 85. (lp)(c) **RARE ELVIS VOL.2**
Mar 85. (lp)(c) **RARE ELVIS VOL.3**
Mar 85. (lp)(c)(cd) **THE ROCKER**
May 85. (lp)(c)(cd) **RECONSIDER BABY** 92
Jul 85. (d-lp,d-c,cd) **32 FILM HITS VOL.2**
Jul 85. (7") **ALWAYS ON MY MIND. / TOMORROW NIGHT** 59
(12"+=) – Ain't that loving you baby / Dark moon.
Jul 85. (lp)(c)(cd) **ALWAYS ON MY MIND**
Feb 86. (cd) **ELVIS: THE COLLECTION VOL.1** -
Feb 86. (cd) **ELVIS: THE COLLECTION VOL.2** -
Feb 86. (cd) **ELVIS: THE COLLECTION VOL.3** -
Feb 86. (cd) **ELVIS: THE COLLECTION VOL.4** -
(was originally issued w / same track in 1983 on 3xcd)
Jul 86. (cd) **RARE ELVIS** -
Jul 86. (lp)(c) **FOREVER** -
Dec 86. (lp)(c)(cd) **ESSENTIAL ELVIS**
Mar 87. (7") **BOSSA NOVA BABY (remix). / AIN'T THAT LOVIN' YOU BABY** 47
(12"+=) – I'm coming home / Rock-a-hula baby.
(12") – ('A'side) / ('A'stretch mix) / I'm coming home.
Aug 87. (d-lp)(d-c)(d-cd) **PRESLEY – THE ALL TIME GREATEST HITS** 4 -
– Heartbreak Hotel / Blue suede shoes / Hound dog / Love me tender / Too much / All shook up / Teddy bear / Paralysed / Party / Jailhouse rock / Don't / wear my ring around your neck / Hard headed woman / King Creole / One night / A fool such as I / Big hunk o' love / Stuck on you / Girl of my best friend / It's now or never / Are you lonesome tonight? / Wooden heart / Surrender / His latest flame / Can't help falling in love / Good luck charm / She's not you / Return to sender / Devil in disguise / Crying in the chapel / Love letters / If I can dream / In the ghetto / Suspicious minds / Don't cry daddy / The wonder of you / I just can't help believing / American trilogy / Burning love / Always on my mind / My boy / Suspicion / Moody blue / Way down / It's only love.
Aug 87. (d-lp)(d-c)(d-cd) **THE TOP 10 HITS** (as above) -
Aug 87. (cd) **THE COMPLETE SUN SESSIONS** -
Aug 87. (7") **LOVE ME TENDER. / TEDDY BEAR** 56
(12"+=) – If I can dream / Bossa nova baby (extended).
Aug 87. (cd) **THE MEMPHIS RECORD** -
Dec 87. (cd) **I WISH YOU A MERRY CHRISTMAS**
Jan 88. (7")(12")(cd-s) **STUCK ON YOU. / ANYWAY YOU WANT ME** 58 -
Aug 88. (cd) **THE ALTERNATIVE ALOHA**
Jan 89. (7") **MEAN WOMAN BLUES. / I BEG OF YOU**
(12"+=)(cd-s+=) – (A'dub version) / Party.
Jan 89. (lp)(c)(cd) **ESSENTIAL ELVIS VOLUME 2: STEREO '57** 60
Feb 89. (cd-ep) **HEARTBREAK HOTEL / I WAS THE ONE / DON'T BE CRUEL / HOUND DOG**
Jul 90. (cd)(c)(lp) **ESSENTIAL ELVIS – VOLUME 3: HITS LIKE NEVER BEFORE** 71
Aug 90. (cd)(c)(lp) **THE GREAT PERFORMANCES** 62
Nov 90. (cd) **FOR THE ASKING**
Jul 91. (7") **ARE YOU LONESOME TONIGHT? (live'69). / RUNAWAY (live)** 68
(12"+=)(cd-s+=) – / Baby, What You Want Me To Do (Live) / Reconsider Baby (Live)
Aug 91. (3xcd)(3xc) **COLLECTOR'S GOLD** 57
Jul 92. (cd-box)(c-box)(lp-box) **THE COMPLETE 50's MASTERS**
1992. (cd)(c)(d-lp) **FROM THE HEART – HIS GREATEST LOVE SONGS** 4
Aug 92. (7")(c-s) **DON'T BE CRUEL. / ALL SHOOK UP** 42
(cd-s+=) – Jailhouse rock / I need your love tonight.
Mar 93. (cd) **KID GALAHAD / GIRLS! GIRLS! GIRLS!**
Mar 93. (cd) **IT HAPPENED AT THE WORLD'S FAIR / FUN IN ACAPULCO**
Mar 93. (cd) **VIVA LAS VEGAS / ROUSTABOUT**
Mar 93. (cd) **HARUM SCARUM / GIRL HAPPY**
Nov 93. (cd)(c) **THE DEFINITIVE R'N'R ALBUM**
Nov 93. (cd)(c) **THE DEFINITIVE GOSPEL ALBUM**
Nov 93. (cd)(c) **THE DEFINITIVE COUNTRY ALBUM**
Nov 93. (cd)(c) **THE DEFINITIVE FILM ALBUM**
Nov 93. (cd)(c) **THE DEFINITIVE LOVE ALBUM**
Nov 93. (cd)(c) **ELVIS' CHRISTMAS ALBUM**
Nov 93. (cd)(c) **ELVIS SINGS THE WONDERFUL WORLD OF CHRISTMAS**
Sep 77. RCA Starcall; (lp)(c) **PICTURES OF ELVIS** 52 -
(re-iss.Apr80 on 'RCA Int.')
Apr 79. RCA Camden; (lp)(c) **PLEASE DON'T STOP LOVING ME** -
Jan 80. RCA Camden; (lp)(c) **DOUBLE DYNAMITE VOL.1** -
Jan 80. RCA Camden; (lp)(c) **DOUBLE DYNAMITE VOL.2** -
(also iss. as d-lp/d-c on Jan80)

Jan 80. RCA Camden; (lp)(c) **THE KING . . . ELVIS** -
Jan 81. RCA Camden; (lp)(c) **ELVIS PRESLEY** -
Jan 81. RCA Camden; (d-lp)(d-c) **THE WONDERFUL WORLD OF ELVIS** -
Jan 81. RCA Camden; (lp)(c) **RETURN TO SENDER** -
Sep 81. RCA Camden; (lp)(c) **IT'S NOW OR NEVER** -
Sep 81. RCA Camden; (lp)(c) **HEARTBREAK HOTEL** -
Mar 82. RCA Camden; (lp)(c) **ARE YOU LONESOME TONIGHT?** -
Mar 82. RCA Camden; (lp)(c) **SUSPICIOUS MINDS** -
Apr 83. RCA Camden; (lp)(c) **CAN'T HELP FALLING IN LOVE AND OTHER GREAT MOVIE HITS** -
Aug 83. RCA Camden; (lp)(c) **LOVE SONGS** -
Nov 83. RCA Camden; (lp)(c) **THE LEGEND** -
Sep 84. RCA Camden; (lp)(c) **THE FIRST TEN YEARS** -
(cd-iss.1984 in silver or gold box on 'RCA')
Apr 86. RCA Camden; (lp)(c) **THE ROCK HITS** -
Jul 81. RCA Golden Grooves; (7") **I JUST CAN'T HELP BELIEVIN'. / BRIDGE OVER TROUBLED WATER (live)** -
Jul 81. RCA Golden Grooves; (7") **AN AMERICAN TRILOGY. / SUSPICIOUS MINDS (live)** -
Jul 81. RCA Golden Grooves; (7") **THE GIRL OF MY BEST FRIEND. / SUSPICION** -
Aug 81. RCA Golden Grooves; (7") **THAT'S ALL RIGHT (MAMA). / HARBOUR LIGHTS** -
Oct 81. RCA Golden Grooves; (7") **GOOD ROCKIN' TONIGHT. / MYSTERY TRAIN** -
Nov 81. RCA Golden Grooves; (7") **IF EVERY DAY WAS LIKE CHRISTMAS. / BLUE CHRISTMAS** -
May 82. RCA Golden Grooves; (7") **WAY DOWN. / MOODY BLUE** -
Apr 88. RCA Diamond; (cd) **DIAMOND SERIES – ELVIS PRESLEY** -
Oct 77. Charly; (lp) **THE SUN YEARS** 31 -
Aug 83. Charly; (lp) **THE FIRST YEAR**
(originally iss.ltd.Nov79 on 'Golden First') (re-iss.Jan85 on 'RCA')
Jan 88. Charly; (cd) **THE COMPLETE MILLION DOLLAR SESSIONS** -
—— (above featured songs with JERRY LEE LEWIS, JOHNNY CASH, etc)
Mar 79. Ace; (lp) **THE ELVIS TAPES** (press conference 1957) -
(cd-iss.Dec91)
Nov 84. Topline; (lp)(c) **IN THE BEGINNING** -
(cd-iss.Apr87)
Jun 85. Topline; (lp)(c) **ELVIS, SCOTTY & BILL** -
(actually iss.earlier 1979 on 'Virgin')((cd-iss.Feb93 on 'Charly')
Mar 82. Audio Fidelity; (d-lp) **PERSONALLY ELVIS** -
Mar 84. Audio Fidelity; (pic-lp) **AN HISTORICAL DOCUMENTARY** -
Jul 82. Everest; (lp)(c) **ELVIS IN HOLLYWOOD** -
Dec 83. Everest; (d-lp)(d-c) **BLUE RHYTHMS** -
(both these re-iss.Dec84 on 'Premier')
Jun 78. Pickwick; (d-lp)(d-c) **ELVIS PRESLEY COLLECTION VOL.2** -
Apr 79. Pickwick; (d-lp)(d-c) **ELVIS PRESLEY COLLECTION VOL.3** -
Oct 79. Hammer; (lp) **THE KING SPEAKS** (dialogue) -
(re-iss.Mar81)
Nov 79. K-Tel; (d-lp)(d-c) **LOVE SONGS** 4 -
Nov 80. K-Tel; (lp)(c) **INSPIRATION** (gospel) 6 -
Nov 81. K-Tel; (lp)(c) **THE ULTIMATE PERFORMANCE** 45 -
Jun 82. K-Tel; (lp)(c) **ROCK'N'ROLL REBEL (20 ROCK'N'ROLL ORIGINALS)** -
Mar 81. Buttons; (lp) **ELVIS ANSWERS BACK** -
Jan 85. V.F.M.; (c) **1935-1977** -
Mar 85. Cambra; (d-lp)(d-c) **IMAGES** -
Oct 85. Telstar; (lp)(c)(cd) **BALLADS** 23 -
All below on 'Old Gold' until otherwise mentioned.
Oct 86. (7") **IN THE GHETTO. / SUSPICIOUS MINDS** -
Oct 86. (7") **PARTY. / A LOT O' LIVIN' TO DO** -
Oct 86. (7") **BLUE MOON. / I DON'T CARE IF THE SUN DON'T SHINE** -
Oct 86. (7") **HIS LATEST FLAME. / GIRL OF MY BEST FRIEND** -
Oct 86. (7") **AN AMERICAN TRILOGY. / UNTIL IT'S TIME FOR YOU TO GO (live)** -
Apr 87. (7") **HOUND DOG. / DON'T BE CRUEL** -
Apr 87. (7") **ARE YOU LONESOME TONIGHT?. / WOODEN HEART** -
Apr 87. (7") **HEARTBREAK HOTEL. / ALL SHOOK UP** -
Apr 87. (7") **WILD IN THE COUNTRY. / I FEEL SO BAD** -
Jan 88. (7") **JAILHOUSE ROCK. / TREAT ME NICE** -
Jan 88. (7") **IT'S NOW OR NEVER. / SURRENDER** -
Jan 88. (7") **ALWAYS ON MY MIND. / BURNING LOVE** -
Jan 88. (7") **LOVING YOU. / PARALYSED** -
Jan 88. (7") **KING CREOLE. / HARD HEADED WOMAN** -
Jan 88. (7") **DON'T. / WEAR MY RING AROUND YOUR NECK** -
Jan 88. (7") **CAN'T HELP FALLING IN LOVE. / ROCK-A-HULA BABY** -
Jan 88. (7") **MY BOY. / MY WAY (live)** -
Jan 88. (7") **WAY DOWN. / MOODY BLUE** -
Jan 88. (7") **THE WONDER OF YOU. / IF I CAN DREAM** -
Nov 90. Reader's Digest; (5xcd-box) **THE LEGEND LIVES ON** -
Mar 94. RCA; (cd) **KNOWN ONLY TO HIM: ELVIS GOSPEL 1957-1971** -
Mar 94. RCA; (cd) **THE MEMPHIS RECORD**
Jun 94. RCA; (cd)(c) **FRANKIE & JOHNNY / PARADISE, HAWAIIAN STYLE**
Jun 94. RCA; (cd)(c) **SPINOUT / DOUBLE TROUBLE**
Jun 94. RCA; (cd)(c) **KISSIN' COUSINS / CLAMBAKE / STAY AWAY, JOE**
Sep 94. RCA; (cd)(c)(d-lp) **THE ESSENTIAL COLLECTION** 6
Sep 94. RCA; (cd)(c) **AMAZING GRACE**
Nov 94. RCA; (cd) **IF EVERY DAY WAS LIKE CHRISTMAS**
Jun 94. Javelin; (cd) **THE ONE AND ONLY** -

Jan 95. Thunderbolt; (cd) **FROM CALYPSO TO CALLAPSO** [ ] [-]
Jan 95. Simon & Schuster; (d-c) **ELVIS: AN AUDIO SCRAPBOOK** [ ] [-]

– (pre – death) compilations, others, etc. –

Mar 56. RCA; (7"ep) **ELVIS PRESLEY** [-] [20]
– Blue suede shoes No.20 /
May 56. RCA; (7"ep) **HEARTBREAK HOTEL** [-] [ ]
Sep 56. RCA; (7"ep) **ELVIS PRESLEY (SHAKE, RATTLE AND ROLL)** [-] [ ]
Sep 56. RCA; (7"ep) **THE REAL ELVIS** [-] [ ]
– Don't be cruel / Hound dog / My baby left me / I want you, I need you, I love you. *(re-iss.Apr61 on 'RCA-Gold')*
Oct 56. RCA; (7"ep) **ANYWAY YOU WANT ME** [-] [ ]
Nov 56. RCA; (7"ep) **ELVIS, VOLUME 1** [-] [ ]
– Love me No. 2 / When my blue moon turns to gold again No.19 / (2 tracks).
Dec 56. RCA; (7"ep) **LOVE ME TENDER** [ ] [ ]
– Love me tender / Let me / Poor boy No.24 / We're gonna move. *(UK re-iss.Mar60)*
Sep 57. RCA; (7"ep) **GOOD ROCKING TONIGHT** [ ] [-]
– Good rocking tonight / Blue Moon of Kentucky / Milkcow blues boogie / Just because.
Dec 56. RCA; (7"ep) **ELVIS, VOLUME 2** [-] [ ]
Jun 57. RCA; (7"ep) **PEACE IN THE VALLEY** [ ] [3] Apr 57
– (There'll be) Peace in the valley (for me) No.25 / It is no secret / I believe / Take my hand precious Lord. *(UK re-iss.Mar60 + Oct82) (US re-iss.Apr61 on 'RCA Gold')*
Jun 57. RCA; (7"ep) **LOVING YOU** [-] [ ]
– Loving you / Let's have a party / Teddy bear / Gotta lotta lovin' to do. *(re-iss.Oct77)*
Jun 57. RCA; (7"ep) **LOVING YOU, VOLUME 2** [-] [18] lp-chart
Aug 57. RCA; (7"ep) **JUST FOR YOU** [-] [18] lp-chart
Oct 57. RCA; (7"ep) **ELVIS PRESLEY** [ ] [-]
– I need you so / Have I told you lately that I love you / Blueberry Hill / Don't leave me now. *(re-iss.Mar60)*
Jan 58. RCA; (7"ep) **JAILHOUSE ROCK** [18] [ ] Nov 57
– Jailhouse rock / Young and beautiful / Don't leave me now / Baby I don't care / I want to be free. *(re-iss.Mar60 + Feb82)*
Sep 58. RCA; (7"ep) **KING CREOLE VOLUME 1** [ ] [ ]
– King Creole / New Orleans / As long as I have you / Lover doll. *(re-iss.Mar60 + Feb82) (US re-iss.Apr61 on 'RCA Gold')*
Sep 58. RCA; (7"ep) **KING CREOLE VOLUME 2** [ ] [ ]
– Trouble / Young dreams / Crawfish / Dixieland rock. *(re-iss.Mar60 + Feb82) (US re-iss.Apr61 on 'RCA Gold')*
Oct 58. RCA; (lp) **ELVIS' GOLDEN RECORDS** [ ] [3] Apr 58
(re-iss.Jul84 as 'GOLDEN RECORDS VOL.1') (cd-iss.1988)
Nov 58. RCA; (7"ep) **ELVIS SINGS CHRISTMAS SONGS** [ ] [ ] Nov57
– Santa bring my baby back to me / Blue Christmas / Santa Claus is back in town / I'll be home for Christmas.
Nov 58. RCA; (7"ep) **ELVIS SAILS** (dialogue) [ ] [ ] Mar59
Dec 58. RCA; (7"ep) **CHRISTMAS WITH ELVIS** [-] [ ]
Feb 59. RCA; (7"ep) **ELVIS IN TENDER MOOD** [ ] [-]
– Young and beautiful / True love / Lover doll / Love me tender. *(re-iss.Mar60)*
Mar 59. RCA; (lp) **FOR LP FANS ONLY** [-] [19]
(cd-iss.Nov89)
Jul 59. RCA; (lp) **A DATE WITH ELVIS (early Sun recordings)** [4] [32] Sep 59
– Blue Moon of Kentucky / Young and beautiful / Baby I don't care / Milk cow blues boogie / Baby let's play house / Good rockin' tonight / Is it so strange / I forgot to remember to forget.
(re-iss.Aug80 + Apr84) (cd-iss.Nov89)
Dec 59. RCA; (7"ep) **A TOUCH OF GOLD, VOLUME 1** [ ] [-]
– Hard headed woman / Good rockin' tonight / Don't / Teddy bear. *(re-iss.Mar60 + Oct82)*
Feb 60. RCA; (7"ep) **STRICTLY ELVIS** [26] [ ] Jan 57
– Old Shep / Any place is Paradise / Paralysed / Is it so strange.
Jun 60. RCA; (lp) **50,000,000 ELVIS FANS CAN'T BE WRONG – ELVIS' GOLDEN RECORDS VOLUME 2** [4] [31]
(re-iss.Nov83, 'ELVIS GOLDEN VOL.2', cd-iss.Nov84)
(these early collections vary in track listings UK/US).
1960. RCA; (7"ep) **A TOUCH OF GOLD, VOLUME 2** [ ] [-]
– Wear my ring around your neck / Treat me nice / One night / That's all right mama.
Nov 60. RCA; (7"ep) **SUCH A NIGHT** [ ] [-]
– Such a night / It feels so right / Like a baby / Make me know it.
Apr 61. RCA; (7"ep) **ELVIS BY REQUEST** [-] [ ]
– Flaming star No.14 / (3 tracks).
Jun 62. RCA; (7"ep) **FOLLOW THAT DREAM** [34] [ ]
– Follow that dream No.15 / Angel / What a wonderful world / I'm not the marrying kind.
Jan 63. RCA; (7"ep) **KID GALAHAD** [16] [ ] Sep 62
– King of the whole wide world No.30 / This is living / Riding the rainbow / Home is where the heart is / I got lucky / Whistling tune.
Apr 64. RCA; (lp) **ELVIS' GOLDEN RECORDS, VOLUME 3** [6] [3] Sep 63
(re-iss.Nov84) (cd-iss.Dec90)
Apr 64. RCA; (7"ep) **LOVE IN LAS VEGAS** [ ] [92]
– If you think I don't need you / I need somebody to lean on / C'mon everybody / Today tomorrow and forever.
May 64. RCA; (7"ep) **ELVIS FOR YOU VOLUME 1** [ ] [ ]
– Rip it up / Love me / When my blue moon turns to gold / Paralysed.
May 64. RCA; (7"ep) **ELVIS FOR YOU VOLUME 2** [ ] [ ]
– Long tall Sally / First in line / How do you think I feel / How's the world treating you.
Jul 65. RCA; (7"ep) **TICKLE ME VOLUME 1** [ ] [70]
– I feel that I've known you forever / Night rider / Slowly but surely / Dirty dirty feeling / Put the blame on me.
Jul 65. RCA; (7"ep) **TICKLE ME VOLUME 2** [ ] [ ]
– I'm yours / Long lonely highway / It feels so right / Such an easy question.
Sep 65. RCA; (lp) **ELVIS FOR EVERYONE!** [8] [10]
(UK – ELVIS FOR EVERYBODY) (UK re-iss.+c.May72, hit No.48)
Jun 67. RCA; (7") **EASY COME EASY GO** [ ] [-]
– Easy come easy go / Yoga is as Yoga does / Sing you children / I'll take love.

Note: All below also on 'RCA' unless mentioned.
Apr 68. (lp) **ELVIS' GOLD RECORDS, VOLUME 4** [ ] [33]
(re-iss.Apr84) (cd-iss.Dec90)
Apr 69. (lp) **ELVIS – N.B.C. TV SPECIAL** [2] [8] Jan 69
(re-iss.UK Aug78 hit No.50) (re-iss.Aug81 & Nov84) (cd-iss.Mar91)
Feb 70. (lp) **PORTRAIT IN MUSIC** [36] [ ]
Nov 70. (4xlp) **WORLD WIDE 50 GOLD AWARD HITS** [49] [45]
(c-iss.May72 – 2 Volumes 25 hits in each)
May 71. (c) **WORLD WIDE 25 GOLD AWARD HITS Vol.3** [ ] [ ]
Jul 71. (7"m) **HEARTBREAK HOTEL. / HOUND DOG / DON'T BE CRUEL** [10] [-]
Jul 71. (lp)(c) **C'MON EVERYBODY** [5] [ ]
—— (above & below album were budget, below on 'RCA Camden').
Jul 71. (lp)(c) **YOU'LL NEVER WALK ALONE** (gospel) [20] [ ] Apr 71
Sep 71. (lp)(c) **ALMOST IN LOVE** [38] [ ]
Nov 71. (7"m) **JAILHOUSE ROCK. / ARE YOU LONESOME TONIGHT?. / (LET ME BE YOUR) TEDDY BEAR / STEADFAST, LOYAL AND TRUE** [42] [-]
Nov 71. (lp)(c) **ELVIS SINGS THE WONDERFUL WORLD OF CHRISTMAS** [7] [ ]
(cd-iss.Nov89)
Dec 71. (lp)(c) **I GOT LUCKY** [26] [ ]
(re-iss.Nov75 on 'RCA Camden')
Feb 74. (lp)(c) **A LEGENDARY PERFORMER VOL.1** [20] [ ]
Dec 74. (lp)(c) **HITS OF THE 70'S** [ ] [ ]
(re-iss.Sep77, hit No.30)
Mar 75. (lp)(c) **HAVING FUN WITH ELVIS ON STAGE (live)** [ ] [ ]
Mar 75. (c) **WORLD WIDE 25 GOLD AWARD HITS Vol.4** [ ] [ ]
Sep 75. (7"m) **BLUE MOON / YOU'RE A HEARTBREAKER. / I'M LEFT, YOU'RE RIGHT, SHE'S GONE** [ ] [-]
Sep 76. (7") **THE GIRL OF MY BEST FRIEND. / A MESS OF BLUES** [9] [-]
Nov 76. (7") **SUSPICION. / (IT'S A) LONG LONELY HIGHWAY** [9] [-]
Feb 77. (lp)(c) **ELVIS IN DEMAND** [12] [ ]
(re-iss.Sep81)
May 77. (7") **ALL SHOOK UP. / HEARTBREAK HOTEL** [41] [ ]
Jul 72. RCA Camden; (lp)(c) **ELVIS SINGS HITS FROM HIS MOVIES, VOL.1** [ ] [ ]
Nov 72. RCA Camden; (lp)(c) **BURNING LOVE AND HITS FROM HIS MOVIES, VOL.2** [ ] [22]
1973. RCA Camden; (lp)(c) **SEPARATE WAYS** [ ] [46]
Jun 75. RCA Camden; (lp)(c) **U.S. MALE** [ ] [ ]
1975. RCA Camden; (lp)(c) **EASY COME EASY GO** [ ] [ ]
Aug 75. RCA Starcall; (lp)(c) **THE ELVIS PRESLEY SUN COLLECTION** [16] [ ]
(re-iss.Mar79) (re-iss.Oct83, cd-iss.Aug88 on 'RCA')
Jun 78. RCA Starcall; (d-lp)(d-c) **THE ELVIS PRESLEY COLLECTION VOL.2** [ ] [-]
Jun 75. Arcade; (d-lp)(d-c) **40 GREATEST HITS** [1] [-]
(re-iss.Nov78 on 'RCA', hit No.40)
Jul 76. Pickwick; (d-lp)(d-c) **ELVIS PRESLEY COLLECTION** [ ] [-]
– (50,000,000 FANS lp / +) *(cd-iss.!)*
Apr 95. RCA; (cd) **FLAMING STAR / WILD IN THE COUNTRY / FOLLOW THAT DREAM** [ ] [ ]
Apr 95. RCA; (cd) **EASY COME EASY GO / SPEEDWAY** [ ] [ ]
Apr 95. RCA; (cd) **LIVE A LITTLE, LOVE A LITTLE / CHARRO / THE TROUBLE . . .** [ ] [ ]
May 95. Pickwick; (cd)(c) **THE LEGEND BEGINS – LIVE 1954-56 (with interviews)** [ ] [-]
Jul 95. RCA; (d-cd) **THE ESSENTIAL 60'S MASTERS VOLUME 2** [ ] [-]
Oct 95. RCA; (cd) **THE COLLECTION 1** [ ] [ ]
Oct 95. RCA; (cd-ep) **TWELTH OF NEVER / BURNING LOVE / WALK A MILE IN MY SHOES** [21] [ ]

Reg PRESLEY (see under ⇒ TROGGS)

Billy PRESTON

Born: 9 Sep'46, Houston, Texas, USA. As a young boy he and his family moved to L.A., where he became child prodigy. Aged 10-12 he conducted his church choir, played organ behind gospel legend MAHALIA JACKSON and landed a part in the film 'St.Louis Blues'. In the early 60's, he toured with LITTLE RICHARD and SAM COOKE, eventually releasing debut 45 for COOKE's label 'SAR'. In the mid-60's, he had resident spot on TV show 'Shindig', which enabled 'Capitol' records to promote 1966 album 'THE WILDEST ORGAN IN TOWN'. Through RAY CHARLES, he was introduced to The BEATLES, who invited him to guest on their 'GET BACK' 45. He was in turn, credited on the 1969 No.1, and was given a contract by The BEATLES' label 'Apple'. Their first collaboration 'THAT'S THE WAY GOD PLANNED IT', saw the title track nearly hit the UK Top 10 that year. In 1971, he moved to 'A&M', where he soon scored at US No.2 with instrumental 'OUTA-SPACE'. The following couple of years, saw him hit again with No.1's 'WILL IT GO ROUND IN CIRCLES?' & 'NOTHING FROM NOTHING'. In the late 70's, 'Motown' teamed him up with STEVIE WONDER's ex-wife SYREETA (WRIGHT), to score smash hit duet 'WITH YOU I'M BORN AGAIN'. (see further on) • **Style:** Influenced initially by RAY CHARLES, he played instrumental R&B gospel. In the 70's, his remarkable ability organ techniques were intertwined with uptempo soul. These were smoothed down to love ballads with the arrival of SYREETA. • **Songwriters:** Wrote own material, except selective covers IN THE MIDNIGHT HOUR (Wilson Pickett) / MY SWEET LORD (George Harrison) / DAY TRIPPER + BLACKBIRD

(Beatles) / SIGNED, SEALED, DELIVERED (Stevie Wonder) / KEEP ON TRUCKIN' (Eddie Kendricks) / etc. • **Trivia:** He also played on albums by SLY & THE FAMILY STONE and toured with The ROLLING STONES in the mid-70's.

Recommended: THE COLLECTION (*6).

BILLY PRESTON – vocals, keyboards

not issued — Sar

1964. (7") **SIXTEEN YEAR OLD SOUL. / ?** — -

Joy — Vee-Jay

1964. (lp) **GOSPEL IN MY SOUL**
(UK-iss.1977 on 'Peacock')

Jun 65. (lp) **MOST EXCITING ORGAN EVER**
– If I had a hammer / Low down / Slippin' and slidin' / Drown in my own tears / I am coming through / The octopus / Don't let the sun catch you crying / Soul meetin' / Let me know / Billy's bag / The masquerade is over / Steady gettin' it.

May 66. (7") **BILLY'S BAG. / DON'T LET THE SUN CATCH YOU CRYING**

JUl 66. (7") **DROWN IN MY OWN TEARS. / LOG CABIN** — -

Sep 66. (7") **SUNNY. / LET THE MUSIC PLAY** — -

Capitol — Vee-Jay

Jul 66. (7") **IN THE MIDNIGHT HOUR. / ADVICE**

Sue — Vee-Jay

Jul 66. (lp) **WILDEST ORGAN IN TOWN**
– In the midnight hour / Uptight / A hard day's night / Ain't got no time to play / Love makes me do foolish things / Duck / Advice / Satisfaction / I got you / It's got to happen / Free funk / The in crowd. *(re-iss.1976)*

Sep 68. (7") **HEY BROTHER. / (prt 2)** –

Soul City — Soul City

1969. (7") **GREAZEE. / (part 2)** — -

1969. (lp) **GREAZEE SOUL** — -

President — President

1969. (lp) **THE APPLE OF THEIR EYES**
– You've lost that lovin' feeling / Eight days a week / Downtown / Ferry 'cross the Mersey / My girl / Go now / Goldfinger / Shotgun / Stop! in the name of love / King of the road / The birds and the bees / Can't you hear my heartbeat. *(re-iss.1974)*

Apple — Apple

Jun 69. (7") **THAT'S THE WAY GOD PLANNED IT. / WHAT ABOUT YOU?** — 11 — 62
(re-iss. US Jul72, hit No.65)

Aug 69. (lp) **THAT'S THE WAY GOD PLANNED IT**
– Do what you want / I want to thank you / Everything's all right / She belongs to me / It doesn't matter / Morning star / Hey brother / What about you? / Let us get together right now / This is it / Keep it to yourself / That's the way God planned it. *(cd-iss.Oct91)* (+=) – Through all times / As I get older / That's the way God planned it (alternate version).

Oct 69. (7") **EVERYTHING'S ALRIGHT. / I WANT TO THANK YOU** — -

Jan 70. (7") **ALL THAT I'VE GOT. / AS I GET OLDER** — -

Sep 70. (lp) **ENCOURAGING WORDS**
– Right now / Little girl / Use what you got / My sweet Lord / Let the music play / The same thing again / I've got a feeling / Sing one for the lord / When you are mine / I don't want you to pretend / Encouraging words / All things (must) pass / You've been acting strange / As long as i got my baby / All that I've got (I'm gonna give it to you) *(re-iss.cd+c Mar93)*

Jan 71. (7") **MY SWEET LORD. / LITTLE GIRL** — - — 90

Jan 71. (7") **MY SWEET LORD. / LONG AS I GOT MY BABY** — -

A & M — A & M

Dec 71. (lp)(c) **I WROTE A SIMPLE SONG** — 32
– Should've known better / I wrote a simple song / John Henry / Without a song / The bus / Outa-Space / The looner tune / You done got older / Swing down chariot / God is great. *(re-iss.1974)*

Apr 72. (7") **OUTA-SPACE. / I WROTE A SIMPLE SONG** — - — 2

77

Jul 72. (7") **SHOULD'VE KNOWN BETTER. / THE BUS** — -

Sep 72. (7") **OUTA-SPACE. / THE BUS** — 44 — -

Sep 72. (7") **SLAUGHTER. / GOD LOVES YOU** — - — 50

May 73. (7") **WILL IT GO ROUND IN CIRCLES?. / BLACKBIRD** — 1 Mar 73

Jun 73. (lp)(c) **MUSIC IS MY LIFE** — 32 Dec 72
– We're gonna make it / One time or another / Blackbird / I wonder why / Goin' around in circles / Ain't that nothin' / God loves you / Make the Devil mad / Heart full of sorrow / Music is my life.

Oct 73. (7") **SPACE RACE. / WE'RE GONNA MAKE IT** — 4

Nov 73. (lp)(c) **EVERYBODY LIKES SOME KIND OF MUSIC** — 52
– Everybody likes some of music / You're so unique / How long has the train been gone / My soul is a witness / Sunday morning / You've got me for company / Listen to the wind / Everybody likes some kind of music (reprise) / Space race / Do you love me / I'm so tired / It's alright ma / Minuet for me.

Jan 74. (7") **HOW LONG HAS THIS TRAIN BEEN GONE. / YOU'RE SO UNIQUE** — 48 b-side

May 74. (7") **MY SOUL IS A WITNESS. / CREATURE FEATURE** — -

Jul 74. (7") **NOTHING FROM NOTHING. / MY SOUL IS A WITNESS** — 1

Aug 74. (lp)(c) **LIVE EUROPEAN TOUR (live)**
– Day tripper / The bus / Let it be / Let's go get started / Billy's bag / Will it go round in circles? / Outa space / Higher (vamp) / Get back.

Oct 74. (lp)(c) **THE KIDS & ME** — 17 Sep 74
– Tell me you need my loving / Nothing from nothing / Struttin' / Sister Sugar / You are so beautiful / Sad sad song / St.Elmo / Sometimes I love you / John The Baptist / Little black boys and girls / Creature feature.

Dec 74. (7") **STRUTTIN'. / YOU ARE SO BEAUTIFUL** — 22

Jul 75. (lp)(c) **IT'S MY PLEASURE** — 43
– Fancy lady / Found the love / That's life / Do it while you can / It's my pleasure / Song of joy / I can't stand it / All of my life.

Oct 75. (7") **FANCY LADY. / SONG OF JOY** — 71

Nov 76. (lp)(c) **BILLY PRESTON**
– Do what you want / Girl / Bells / I've got the spirit / When you are mine / Bad case of ego / Take time to figure it out / Let the music play / Simplify your life / Let's make love / Ecstasy.

Nov 76. (7") **GIRL. / ECSTASY** — -

Jun 77. (7") **WHEN YOU ARE MINE. / WIDE STRIDE** — -

Jan 78. (lp)(c) **WHOLE NEW THING**
– Whole new thing / Disco dancing / Complicated sayings / Attitudes / I'm really gonna miss you / Wide stride / You got me buzzin' / Sweet Marie / Happy / Touch me love / You don't have to go.

Mar 78. (7") **WIDE STRIDE. / WHOLE NEW THING** — -

May 78. (7") **ATTITUDES. / I REALLY MISS YOU** — -

Feb 79. (7") **GET BACK. / SPACE RACE** — 86 Oct 78

not issued — Myrrh

1979. (lp)(c) **BEHOLD** — -
– I'm giving up my life to Christ / Heavenly / Born again / All to Jesus I surrender / He will see you through / He brought me out / Motherless child / Yes my God is real / Behold / For you my Lord. *(re-iss.May82)*

BILLY PRESTON & SYREETA

Motown — Motown

May 79. (lp)(c) **FASTBREAK**
– More than just a friend / He didn't say / Go for it / With you I'm born again / Instrumentals – Welcome to Cadwalder / With you I'm born again / Books and basketball / Half time / The big game. *(re-iss.Oct81)*

Jul 79. (7") **GO FOR IT. / WITH YOU I'M BORN AGAIN**
(12"+=) – ('A'instrumental).

Dec 79. (7") **WITH YOU I'M BORN AGAIN. / SOCK IT ROCK IT** — 2 — 4
(re-iss.Mar83)

Mar 80. (lp)(c) **LATE AT NIGHT** — 49
– Give it up / Hot / Late at night / All I wanted was you / You / I come to rest in you / It will come in time / Lovely lady / With you I'm born again. *(re-iss.Oct81)*

Feb 80. (7") **IT WILL COME IN TIME. / ALL I WANTED WAS YOU**
(re-iss.Oct81)

Jun 80. (7") **ONE MORE TIME FOR LOVE. / DANCE FOR ME CHILDREN** — 52
(re-iss.Oct81)

Nov 80. (7") **PLEASE STAY. / SIGNED, SEALED, DELIVERED (I'M YOURS)**
(re-iss.Oct81)

Oct 81. (lp)(c) **BILLY PRESTON & SYREETA** — Aug 81
– Someone special / Searchin' / Just for love / It's so easy / A long and lasting love / One more try / Hey you / A new way to say I love you / What we did for love.

Feb 82. (7") **NEW WAY TO SAY I LOVE YOU. / HEY YOU**
(12"+=) – ('A'version).

BILLY PRESTON

Motown — Motown

Apr 81. (lp)(c) **THE WAY I AM**
– Hope / Good life boogie / Keep on truckin' / A change is gonna come / Let your feeling on me / I won't mistreat your love / Baby I'm yours / Until then / The way I am. *(re-iss.Oct81)*

Apr 81. (7") **A CHANGE IS GONNA COME. / YOU**

Oct 81. (7") **HOPE. / GIVE IT UP / HOT**

Oct 82. (7") **I'M NEVER GONNA SAY GOODBYE. / I LOVE YOU SO** — 88 Sep 82

Nov 82. (lp)(c) **PRESSIN' ON**
– Pressin' on / I'd like to go back home again / Loving you is easy (cause you're beautiful) / Turn it out / I'm never gonna say goodbye / Thanks but no thanks / Don't try to fight it / I love you so / I come on.

E.R.C. — E.R.C.

Jun 84. (7")(12") **AND DANCE. / KICK IN**

Blow Up — not issued

1984. (lp) **ON THE AIR** — - — - Germ
– And dance / Kick-it / Come to me little darlin' / Beatle tribute / If you let me love you / You can't hide from love / Oh Jamaica / Here, there and everywhere.

Outerspace — Outerspace

May 91. (12") **HEROES. / HEROES (Short Club Mix)**

—— In Aug'91, BILLY is arrested for attacking an 11 year-old under the influence of cocaine while also watching porn movies.

– compilations, others, etc. –

1975. Springboard; (lp) **THE GENIUS OF BILLY PRESTON** — - — -

Oct 76. D.J.M.; (lp)(c) **BILLY'S BAG** — -
(re-iss.+cd.Feb87 on 'Topline')

Apr 77. GNP Crescendo; (lp) **SOUL'D OUT** — - — -

Apr 80. Old Gold; (7") **BILLY'S BAG. / ?** — - — -

1980. Myrrh; (lp) **UNIVERSAL LOVE** — -

1982. A&M; (lp)(c) **THE BEST OF BILLY PRESTON**
(cd-iss.1988)

Jan 85. Pickwick; (d-c) **BILLY PRESTON** — -

Mar 89. Castle; (d-lp)(c)(cd) **THE COLLECTION** — -
– The bus / How long has the train been gone / It's alright ma (I'm only bleeding) / Blackbird / Let's make love / Will it go round in circles / Outa space / Let it be / I can't stand it (live) / You are so beautiful / Should've known better / You got me buzzin' / Billy's bag / Listen to the wind (live) / I'm so tired / Struttin' / Space race / It's my pleasure / Nothing from nothing / Disco dancin' / Get back.

PRETENDERS

Formed: London, England ... Mar'78 by American CHRISSIE HYNDE, with Hereford based musicians; HONEYMAN-SCOTT, FARNDON and MACKLEDUFF. HYNDE's past had included spending the early 70's at Kent State University, before moving to London in 1973 to become an NME journalist. In 1974, she relocated to Paris to join The FRENCHIES, where she met CHRIS SPEDDING. He invited her to sing backing vocals on his 1977 released lp 'HURT'. Prior to this, she had returned to homeland Ohio in 1975 to join R&B group JACK RABBIT. A year later, she came back to London to form The BERK BROTHERS (DAVE & FRED), before they replaced her with JOHNNY MOPED. In Aug'77, she cut a demo tape for Dave Hill's new 'Real' records, who asked her to form a band; The PRETENDERS. Early in '79, their first 45 'STOP YOUR SOBBING', produced by NICK LOWE and written by Kinks' RAY DAVIES (her future beau, common-law husband, they were refused a marriage certificate by registrar annoyed by their arguing), and father of her child Natalie). They began the 80's, hitting the UK top spot with 'BRASS IN POCKET' and a No.1 eponymous album, which was first of many top sellers throughout the decade. Tragedy struck the band twice between 1982 and 1983, when HONEYMAN-SCOTT then the already departed FARNDON, both overdosed on heroin. • **Style:** New wave / power pop, smoothed down by the sultry goddess of rock'n'roll CHRISSIE HYNDE. • **Songwriters:** Group compositions, except as said plus; MAY THIS BE LOVE (Jimi Hendrix) / IF THERE WAS A MAN (co-w/ John Barry) / NOT A SECOND TIME (Beatles) / CREEP (Radiohead). • **Trivia:** After her relationship ended with DAVIES in 1984, she quickly married JIM KERR (Simple Minds) on the 5th May'85. They split in the 80's, after she gave birth to another child. She caused controversy in June '89, when she attended a Greenpeace Rainbow Warriors press conference, and told of how she (a staunch vegetarian) once firebombed McDonalds burger shop. The day after, one of their shops in Milton Keynes was firebombed and CHRISSIE was asked / told to sign a retracting statement, or be taken to court.

Recommended: THE SINGLES (*8) / PRETENDERS (*8) / PRETENDERS II (*7)

CHRISSIE HYNDE (b. 7 Sep'51, Akron, Ohio, USA) – vocals, guitar / **JAMES HONEYMAN-SCOTT** (b. 4 Nov'57) – guitar, keyboards (ex-CHEEKS) / **PETE FARNDON** (b.1953, Hereford, Wales) – bass / **GERRY MACKLEDUFF** – drums

Real / Sire

Jan 79. (7") **STOP YOUR SOBBING. / THE WAIT** — 34 / -

— **MARTIN CHAMBERS** (b. 4 Sep'51) – drums repl. GERRY

Jun 79. (7") **KID. / TATTOOED LOVE BOYS** — 33 / [ ] Jul 80

Nov 79. (7") **BRASS IN POCKET. / SWINGING LONDON** — 1 / -
(12"+=) – Nervous but shy. *(c-ep iss.Apr81) ?*

Jan 80. (lp)(c) **PRETENDERS** — 1 / 9
– Precious / The phone call / Up the neck / Tattooed love boys / Space invader / The wait / Stop your sobbing / Kid / Private life / Brass in pocket / Lovers of today / Mystery achievement. *(cd-iss.1983)*

Feb 80. (7") **BRASS IN POCKET. / SPACE INVADER** — - / 14

Apr 80. (7") **TALK OF THE TOWN. / CUBAN SLIDE AND SLIDE** — 8 / [ ]

May 80. (7") **STOP YOUR SOBBING. / PHONE CALL** — - / 65

Feb 81. (7") **MESSAGE OF LOVE. / PORCELAIN** — 11 / 27 Apr 81
(7"ep+=) – Talk of the town / Cuban slide and slide.

Aug 81. (lp)(c) **PRETENDERS II** — 7 / 10
– The adultress / Bad boys get spanked / Message of love / I go to sleep / Birds of Paradise / Talk of the town / Pack it up / Waste not, want not / Day after day / Jealous dogs / Waste not want not / English rose / Louie Louie. *(cd-iss.Nov86)*

Aug 81. (7") **LOUIE LOUIE. / IN THE STICKS** — - / [ ]

Aug 81. (7") **DAY AFTER DAY. / IN THE STICKS** — 45 / [ ]
(12"+=) – The adultress.
(7"ep+=)(c-ep+=) – Stop your sobbing / Kid.

Nov 81. (7") **I GO TO SLEEP. / THE ENGLISH ROSE** — 7 / [ ]
(12"+=) – Waste not, want not. *(US; b-side)*

— (Sep82) **BILLY BREMNER** – guitar (ex-NICK LOWE, ex-DAVE EDMUNDS' ROCKPILE) repl. HONEYMAN-SCOTT who died of drug overdose 16 Jun'82 / **TONY BUTLER** – bass (of BIG COUNTRY) repl. FARNDON (died o.d. 14 Apr'83)

Sep 82. (7") **BACK ON THE CHAIN GANG. / (part 2)** — 17 / 5 Dec 82
(12"+=) – My city was gone. *(US; b-side)*

— (Feb83) **HYNDE** and **CHAMBERS** brought in new members **ROBBIE McINTOSH** (25 Oct'57) – guitar (ex-MANFRED MANN'S EARTH BAND, ex-NIGHT) repl. BREMNER who rejoined NICK LOWE etc. / **MALCOLM FOSTER** (b.13 Jan'56) – bass repl. BUTLER who rejoined BIG COUNTRY.

Nov 83. (7") **2000 MILES. / THE LAW IS THE LAW** — 15 / -
('A'fast or slow versioned 12"+=) – Money (live).

Nov 83. (7") **MIDDLE OF THE ROAD. / 2,000 MILES** — - / 19

Jan 84. (lp)(c)(cd) **LEARNING TO CRAWL** — 11 / 5
– Middle of the road / Back on the chain gang / Time the avenger / Watching the clothes / Show me / Thumbelina / My city was gone / Thin line between love and hate / I hurt you / 2000 miles.

Feb 84. (7")(12") **MIDDLE OF THE ROAD. / WATCHING THE CLOTHES** — [ ] / -

— added **PAUL CARRACK** – keyboards (ex-ACE, ex-ROXY MUSIC, ex-solo artist)

Mar 84. (7") **SHOW ME. / FAST OR SLOW (THE LAW IS THE LAW)** — - / 28

Apr 84. (7") **THIN LINE BETWEEN LOVE AND HATE. / TIME THE AVENGER** — 49 / 83 Jun 84
(12"+=) – Bad boys get spanked.

— Sep 85, CHRISSIE HYNDE guests on UB40's 'I Got You Babe' which hits No.1. Three years later the same team hit no.6 with 'Breakfast In Bed'. **PRETENDERS** re-group with **HYNDE, McINTOSH** and **TIM STEVENS** – bass / **BLAIR CUNNINGHAM** – drums (ex-HAIRCUT 100) repl. CHAMBERS (on some) and **BERNIE WORRELL** – keyboards

W.E.A. / Warners

Sep 86. (7") **DON'T GET ME WRONG. / DANCE** — 10 / 10
(12"+=) – ('A'extended).

Oct 86. (lp)(c)(cd) **GET CLOSE** — 6 / 25
– My baby / When I change my life / Light of the Moon / Dance * / Tradition of love / Don't get me wrong / I remember you / How much did you get for your soul / Chill factor / Hymn to her / Room full of mirrors. *(c+cd+= *)*

Nov 86. (7") **HYMN TO HER. / ROOM FULL OF MIRRORS** — 8 / [ ]
(12"+=) – Stop your sobbing (demo).

Feb 87. (7") **MY BABY. / ROOM FULL OF MIRRORS** — - / 64

Mar 87. (7") **MY BABY. / TRADITION OF LOVE (remix)** — [ ] / -
(12"+=) – Thumbelina.
(7"ep+=) – Private life / Middle of the road.

Apr 87. (7") **HYMN TO HER. / TRADITION OF LOVE** — - / [ ]

Aug 87. (7") **IF THERE WAS A MAN. (as "PRETENDERS 007") / WHERE HAS EVERYBODY GONE** — 49 / [ ]
(12"+=) – Into Vienna. (US; b-side)

Oct 87. (lp)(c)(cd) **THE SINGLES** (compilation) — 6 / 69
– Stop your sobbing / Kid / Brass in pocket / Talk of the town / I go to sleep / Day after day / Message of love / Back on the chain gang / Middle of the road / 2000 miles / Show me / Thin line between love and hate / Don't get me wrong / Hymn to her / My baby / I got you babe (w / UB40) / What you gonna do about it.

Oct 87. (7") **KID (remix). / STOP YOUR SOBBING (original)** — [ ] / [ ]
(12"+=)(cd-s+=) – ('B' 1978 demo) / What you gonna do about it ('87 remix)

Jun'88, she guested again with UB40 on hit single 'BREAKFAST IN BED'.

— added guest **JOHNNY MARR** – guitar (ex-SMITHS) repl. McINTOSH

Apr 89. (7")(12")(3"cd-s) **WINDOWS OF THE WORLD. / 1969** — [ ] / [ ]

— (above from the film '1969', a one-off on label 'Polydor')

— now virtually **CHRISSIE** solo, augmented by **BLAIR CUNNINGHAM** – drums / **BILLY BREMNER + DOMINIC MILLER** – guitar / **JOHN McKENZIE** – bass / plus others

May 90. (7")(c-s) **NEVER DO THAT. / NOT A SECOND TIME** — [ ] / [ ]
(12"+=) – The wait.
(cd-s++=) – Spirit of life.

May 90. (cd)(c)(lp) **PACKED!** — 19 / 48
– Never do that / Let's make a pact / Millionaires / May this be love / No guarentee / When will I see you / Sense of purpose / Downtown (Akron) / How do I miss you / Hold a candle to this / Criminal. *(re-iss.cd Nov94)*

Oct 90. (7") **SENSE OF PURPOSE. / SPIRIT OF LIFE** — [ ] / [ ]
(12"+=) – Brass in pocket.
(cd-s++=) – Not a second time.

— Oct 91, CHRISSIE's vox was credited on single 'SPIRITUAL HIGH', by MOOD SWINGS. It finally hit UK no. 47 early '93.

— She wrote most with B.STEINBERG + T.KELLY. Covered; FOREVER YOUNG (Bob Dylan).

— **CHRISSIE** + main band **MARTIN CHAMBERS** – drums / **ADAM SEYMOUR** – guitar / **ANDY HOBSON** – bass

Apr 94. (7")(c-s) **I'LL STAND BY YOU. / REBEL ROCK ME** — 10 / 16 Aug94
(cd-s+=) – Bold as love.
(cd-s) – ('A'side) / Message of love / Brass in pocket / Don't get me wrong.

May 94. (cd)(c) **LAST OF THE INDEPENDENTS** — 8 / 41
– Hollywood perfume / Night in my veins / Money talk / 977 / Revolution / All my dreams / I'll stand by you / I'm a mother / Tequila / Every mother's son / Rebel rock me / Love colours / Forever young.

Jun 94. (7")(c-s) **NIGHT IN MY VEINS. / BAD BOYS GET SPANKED** — 25 / 72
(cd-s+=) – My city was gone / Tattooed love boys.

Oct 94. (7")(c-s) **977. / I'LL STAND BY YOU (live)** — 66 / [ ]
(cd-s+=) – Hollywood perfume (live) / Kid (live).
(cd-s) – ('A'side) / Back on the chain gang (live) / Night in my veins (live) / Precious (live).

Sep 95. (c-s) **KID (acoustic) / THE ISLE OF VIEW (acoustic)** — 73 / [ ]
(cd-s+=) – Creep (acoustic).

Oct 95. (cd)(c) **THE ISLE OF VIEW (live acoustic)** — 23 / 100
– Sense of purpose / Chill factor / Private life / Back on the chain gang / Kid / I hurt you / Criminal / Brass in pocket / 2000 miles / Hymn to her / Lovers of today / The phone call / I go to sleep / Revolution. (cd+=) – The Isle of View.

Nov 95. (c-s) **2000 MILES (acoustic) / TEQUILA** — [ ] / [ ]
(cd-s+=) – Happy Christmas / Night in my veins.

– compilations –

Jul 94. Warners; (cd)(c) **DON'T GET ME WRONG** — [ ] / -
(re-iss.Sep95)

PRETTY THINGS

Formed: Dartford, Kent, England . . . 1963 by DICK TAYLOR and PHIL MAY. DICK had once been a member of LITTLE BOY BLUE & THE BLUE BOYS, which was an embryonic version of The ROLLING STONES. Taking their name from a BO DIDDLEY song, they soon signed to 'Fontana', employing management team of Bryan Morrison and James Duncan, the latter of whom, wrote 1964 debut Top 50 hit 'ROSALYN'. Their follow-up 'DON'T BRING ME DOWN', dented the UK Top 10, and preceeded their eponymous Top 10 debut album early '65. Unlike The STONES, the hits dried up in 1967, and they moved to 'Columbia' records, who released first rock opera album 'S.F.SORROW' which flopped late in '68. They struggled on relentlessly, moving on to 'Harvest' in 1970 and LED ZEPPELIN's 'Swan Song' in '74. • **Style:** Rougher looking than even The STONES, their pure roots R&B sound, relied on black American blues artists of the 50's, for much inspiration and music. In 1968, they broke away from R&B to try underground psychedelic scene. • **Songwriters:** Most by PHIL MAY, except covers; PRETTY THING + ROADRUNNER + MONA (Bo Diddley) / CRY TO ME (Bert Berns) / A HOUSE IN THE COUNTRY (Ray Davies; Kinks) / REELIN' AND ROCKIN' (Chuck Berry) / I'M A KING BEE (Muddy Waters) / SHAKIN' ALL OVER (Johnny Kidd & The Pirates) / etc. • **Trivia:** Made cameo appearances in the films 'What's Good For The Goose' (1969 w / Norman Wisdom) and 'The Monster Squad' (1980 w / Vincent Price). They were given tribute by BOWIE in 1973, when he covered their first 2 hits on his 'PIN-UPS' album.

Recommended: THE PRETTY THINGS (*7) / S.F.SORROW (*7) / PARACHUTE (*6) / THE THINGS (*7).

PHIL MAY (b. 9 Nov'44, Kent, England) – vocals / **DICK TAYLOR** (28 Jan'43) – lead guitar (ex-LITTLE BOY BLUE & THE BLUE BOYS) / **BRIAN PENDLETON** (b.13 Apr'44, Wolverhampton, England) – rhythm guitar / **JOHN STAX** (b.JOHN FULLEGAR, 6 Apr'44) – bass / **VIV PRINCE** (b. 9 Aug'44, Loughborough, Leicestershire, England) – drums(PETE KITLEY then VIV ANDREWS sessioned on 1st-2 45's)

Fontana / Fontana

Jun 64. (7") **ROSALYN. / BIG BOSS MAN** 41 Oct 64
Oct 64. (7") **DON'T BRING ME DOWN. / WE'LL BE TOGETHER** 10 Jan 65
Feb 65. (7") **HONEY I NEED. / I CAN NEVER SAY** 13
Mar 65. (lp) **THE PRETTY THINGS** 6
– Roadrunner / Judgement day / 13 Chester street / Honey I need / Big city / Unkown blues / Mama, keep your big mouth shut / Oh baby doll / She's fine she's mine / Don't you lie to me / The Moon is rising / Pretty thing. *(re-iss.1967 on 'Wing') (cd-iss. Jul 90)*
Jul 65. (7") **CRY TO ME. / JUDGEMENT DAY** 28
Dec 65. (7") **MIDNIGHT TO SIX MAN. / CAN'T STAND THE PAIN** 46
Dec 65. (lp) **GET THE PICTURE**
– Get the picture / You don't believe me / We'll play house / Can't stand the pain / Rainin' in my heart / Buzz the jerk / London town / You'll never do it to me baby / Cry to me / I had a dream / Gonna find me a substitute / I want your love. *(re-iss.Mar84, cd-iss.Jul90)*

— **SKIP ALAN** (b.ALAN SKIPPER, 11 Jun'44) – drums repl. PRINCE on some

Fontana / Blue Thumb

Apr 66. (7") **COME SEE ME. / L.S.D.** 43
Jul 66. (7") **A HOUSE IN THE COUNTRY. / ME NEEDING YOU** 50
Dec 66. (7") **PROGRESS. / BUZZ IN THE JERK**
Apr 67. (7") **CHILDREN. / MY TIME**
May 67. (lp) **EMOTIONS** -
– Death of a socialite / Children / The Sun / There will never be another day / House of ten / Out in the night / One long glance / Growing in my mind / Photographer / Bright lights of the city / Tripping / My time / A house in the country / Me needing you / Progress. *(re-iss.Apr91)*

— **PHIL** and **DICK** were left to recruit new members **JOHN POVEY** (b.20 Aug'44) – keyboards, vocals (ex-FENMEN) repl. PENDLETON / **WALLY ALLEN** – bass, vocals (ex-FENMEN) repl. SKIP / **MITCH MITCHELL** – (session) drums repl. SKIP

Columbia / Rare Earth

Nov 67. (7") **DEFLECTING GREY. / MR. EVASION** -

— **BOBBIE GRAHAM** – drums (also on session) repl. MITCHELL

Feb 68. (7") **TALKIN ABOUT THE GOOD TIMES. / WALKING THROUGH MY DREAMS** -

— **JOHN 'TWINK' ADLER** – percussion, vocals (ex-TOMORROW, etc) repl. GRAHAM

Nov 68. (7") **PRIVATE SORROW. / BALLROOM BURNING**
Dec 68. (lp) **S.F. SORROW** Feb 70
– S.F. sorrow / Bracelets of fingers / She says good morning / Private sorrow / Balloon burning / Death / Baron Saturday / I see you / The journey / Well of destiny / Trust / Old man going / Lonliest person. *(cd-iss. Apr 91)*

— **SKIP ALAN** – drums, vocals (returned from SUNSHINE) repl. TWINK who joined PINK FAIRIES (new one joining MAY, POVEY and ALLEN plus below) **VICTOR UNITT** – guitar, vocals (ex-EDGAR BROUGHTON) repl. TAYLOR (⇒ producer)

Harvest / Rare Earth

Apr 70. (7") **THE GOOD MR.SQUARE. / BLUE SERGE BLUES**
Jun 70. (lp)(c) **PARACHUTE** 43
– Parachute / Scene 1: The good Mr. Square, she was tall, she was high / Rare Earth / In the square, the letter, rain / Miss Fay regrets / Cries from the midnight circus / Grass / Sickle clowns / She's a lover / What's the use. *(re-iss.+cd.Sep88 on 'Edsel')*

— **PETER TOLSON** (b.10 Sep'51, Bishops Stortford, England) – guitar, vocals (ex-EIRE APPARANT) repl. UNITT (who returned to EDGAR BROUGHTON BAND)

Oct 70. (7") **OCTOBER 26. / COLD STONE**
May 71. (7"m) **STONE HEARTED MAMA. / SUMMERTIME / CIRCUS MIND**

— **STUART BROOKS** – bass, vocals repl. WALLY who went into producing

Warners / Warners

Dec 72. (lp)(c) **FREEWAY MADNESS**
– Love is good / Havana bound / Peter / Rip off train / Over the Moon / Religion's dead / Country road / All night sailor / Onion soup / Another bowl?.
Jan 73. (7") **OVER THE MOON. / HAVANA BOUND**

— added **GORDON EDWARDS** (b.26 Dec'46, Southport, England) – keyboards (to **MAY, ALAN, POVEY, TOLSON and BROOKS)**

Swan Song / Swan Song

Oct 74. (lp)(c) **SILK TORPEDO**
– Dream / Joey / Maybe you tried / Atlanta / L.A.N.T.A. / Is it only love / Come home / Bridge of God / Singapore silk torpedo / Belfast cowboy / Bruise in the sky.
Jan 75. (7") **JOEY. / IS IT ONLY LOVE**
Jun 75. (7") **I'M KEEPING. / ATLANTA**

— **JACK GREEN** (b.12 Mar'51, Glasgow, Scotland) – bass, vocals (also as EDWARDS, ex-SUNSHINE) repl. BROOKS

Sep 75. (7") **JOEY. / COME HOME MOMMA**
Feb 76. (7") **SAD EYE . / REMEMBER THAT BOY** -
Apr 76. (7") **REMEMBER THAT DAY. / IT ISN'T ROCK 'N' ROLL** -
May 76. (lp)(c) **SAVAGE EYE** Feb 76
– Under the volcano / My song / Sad eye / Remember that boy / It isn't rock'n' roll / I'm keeping / It's been so long / Drowned man / Theme for Michelle.
May 76. (7") **TONIGHT. / IT ISN'T ROCK'N'ROLL** -

— Last original PHIL MAY went solo augmented by the FALLEN ANGELS (see below). POVEY also departed leaving only 4 (SKIP, PETER, JACK and GORDON) calling themselves METROPOLIS between mid '76-late'77. JACK also joined T.REX and GORDON went to The KINKS.

PHIL MAY & THE FALLEN ANGELS

with **MICKEY FINN** – guitar (ex-T.REX) / **BILL LOVELADY** – guitar / **BRIAN JOHNSTON** – keyboards (ex-STREETWALKERS) / **WALL ALLEN** – bass / **CHICO GREENWOOD** – drums / etc.

Philips / not issued

1978. (lp) **PHIL MAY & THE FALLEN ANGELS** - - Holl.
– Fallen angels / California / 13 floor suicide / Dance again / Shine on baby / My good friend / Cold wind / I keep on / Dogs of war / Girl like you. *(UK-iss.1982, re-iss.Feb85)*

PRETTY THINGS

re-formed ex-members in 1980. (**PHIL MAY, DICK TAYLOR, JOHN POVEY, PETER TOLSON, WALLY ALLEN** and **SKIP SLAN)**

Warners. / Warners

Aug 80. (lp)(c) **CROSS TALK**
– I'm calling / Edge of the night / Sea of blue / Office love / Lost that girl / Bitter end / Falling again / It's so hard / She don't / No future.
Aug 80. (7") **I'M CALLING. / SEA OF BLUE**

— Disbanded 1981. Reformed briefly as

ZAC ZOLAR AND ELECTRIC BANANA

Butt / not issued

1984. (7") **TAKE ME HOME. / JAMES MARSHALL** -

— (above appeared on 'Minder' TV series) *(re-iss.Aug86 on 'Shanghai')*

PRETTY THINGS

reformed by **MAY + TAYLOR** in 1984. Now with **JOE SHAW** – guitar / **DAVE WINTOUR** – bass / **KEVIN FLANAGAN** – saxophone / **JOHN CLARKE** – drums

Big Beat / not issued

Aug 84. (lp) **LIVE AT THE HEARTBREAK HOTEL (live)** -
– Big boss man / Midnight to six man / I'm a king bee / Honey I need / Shakin' all over / Rosalyn / Roadrunner / Mama keep your big mouth shut / Raining in my heart / Reelin' and rockin' / Don't bring me down / Mona.

— **ROLF TER VELD** – bass + **BERTRAM ENGEL** – drums (ex-UDO LINDENBERG, ex-PANIKORCHESTER) repl.WINTOUR, FLANAGAN + CLARKE

In-Akustik / not issued

Jun 88. (cd) **OUT OF THE ISLAND** -
– Cry to me / Baby doll / She's fine, she's mine / Get the picture / Havana bound / Can't stop / Loneliest person / L.S.D. / Private sorrow / The Moon is rising / Big city / Cause and effect / Well known blues / You don't believe me / Judement day. *(re-iss.May95)*

— **MAY + TAYLOR** again reformed them in 1989, with new **GLEN MATLOCK** – bass, vocals (ex-SEX PISTOLS, ex-RICH KIDS) / **FRANK HOLLAND** – guitar, keyboards / **BOBBY WEBB** – keyboards, vocals / **MARK ST.JOHN** – drums, bass, vocals

Trax / not issued

Sep 89. (7") **EVE OF DESTRUCTION. / GOIN' DOWNHILL** -

— (on tour) **STEVE BROWNING** – bass repl. MATLOCK

— Re-formed again in 1991, with **PHIL MAY / DICK TAYLOR** (ex-MEKONS) / **JIMMY McCARTY** (ex-YARDBIRDS) / **RICHARD HITE** (ex-CANNED HEAT)

PRETTY THINGS & THE YARDBIRD BLUES BAND

Superbluesgroup / collab with ex-YARDBIRDS and plenty covers

Demon / not issued

Oct 91. (cd) **CHICAGO BLUES TAPE 1991** -
– Can't judge the book / Down in the bottom / Hush hush / Can't hold out / Spoonful / She fooled me / Time is on my side / Scratch my back / Long tall Shorty / Diddley daddy / Ain't got you / Caress my baby / Here's my picture / Chain of fools / Don't start crying now.
Feb 94. (cd) **WINE, WOMEN & WHISKEY** -
– Wine, women and whiskey / Sure look good to me / No questions / The amble / It's all over now / Bad boy / Spoonful (bare bones remix) / French champagne / My back scratcher / Can't hold out (big city remix) / Diddley daddy (street corner remix) / I'm cryin' / Gettin' all wet.

PRETTY THINGS 'N MATES (WITH MATTHEW FISHER)

featuring a plethora of famous cover versions

Kingdom / not issued

May 94. (cd) **A WHITER SHADE OF DIRTY WATER** -
– He's waitin' / Strychnine / Pushing too hard / Kicks / Candy / Louie, Louie / 96 tears / Let's talk about girls / Sometimes good guys don't wear black / I'm a man / Red river rock / Midnight to 6 man '93.

PRETTY THINGS

not issued / Medicine

1994. (7") **HAVANA BOUND. / RELIGION'S DEAD** -

— re-formed again 1995, **MAY, TAYLOR, POVEY, ALEN, ALAN + HOLLAND**

Fragile / not issued

Oct 95. (d-cd) **UNREPENTANT – BLOODY BUT UNBOWED** -
–

– compilations, others, etc. –

Dec 64. Fontana; (7"ep) **PRETTY THINGS** -
Aug 65. Fontana; (7"ep) **RAINING IN MY HEART** -
Jan 66. Fontana; (7"ep) **ON FILM** -
Jun 69. Fontana; (7") **ROSALYN. / DON'T BRING ME DOWN** -
1968. Phonogram; (lp) **GREATEST HITS** -

(cd-iss.1991 on 'Carnaby')

Jun 75. Harvest/ US= Rare Earth; (d-lp) **REAL PRETTY:- S.F. SORROW / PARACHUTE** 1976

Jul 77. Harvest; (lp) **SINGLES A's & B's** -

May 86. Harvest; (lp)(c) **CRIES FROM THE MIDNIGHT CIRCUS** (1968-1971) -

1976. Sire; (d-lp) **THE VINTAGE YEARS** -

1979. Butt; (lp) **ELECTRIC BANANA – THE SEVENTIES** -
(recordings 1973-78 / + from 'De Wolfe' label of late 60's)

Film music lp's:- 1967; ELECTRIC BANANA/ 1968; MORE ELECTRIC BANANA/ 1969; EVEN MORE ELECTRIC BANANA/ 1973; HOT LICKS/ 1978; THE RETURN OF THE ELECTRIC BANANA.

Mar 82. See For Miles; (lp)(c) **THE PRETTY THINGS 1967-1971** -
(cd-iss.Oct89)

Jul 82. Old Gold; (7") **DON'T BRING ME DOWN. / HONEY I NEED** -

Jun 84. Edsel; (lp) **LET ME HEAR THE CHOIR SING** -

Feb 86. Bam Caruso; (lp) **CLOSED RESTAURANT BLUES** -

Apr 92. Band Of Joy; (cd) **ON AIR** -

Mar 94. Spectrum; (cd)(c) **MIDNIGHT TO 6** -

PRIMAL SCREAM

Formed: Glasgow, Scotland . . . mid'84 by JESUS & MARY CHAIN drummer BOBBY GILLESPIE. Signed to up and coming indie label 'Creation' early '85, and made 2 singles there, which led to GILLESPIE leaving J&MC. After spending 1987 on WEA subsidiary label 'Elevation', they returned to 'Creation'. They finally hit the UK Top 20 singles chart with 'LOADED', in the early 90's. • **Style:** Influenced by 60's flower-power scene, which evolved into indie disco by the early 90's. • **Songwriters:** GILLESPIE, YOUNG and BEATTIE, until the latter's replacement by INNES. Covered CARRY ME HOME (Dennis Wilson) / UNDERSTANDING (Small Faces). • **Trivia:** In 1991, they re-located to Tennessee, USA, recording highly acclaimed album 'SCREAMADELICA' in the process.

Recommended: SCREAMADELICA (*10) / PRIMAL SCREAM (*8) / GIVE OUT BUT DON'T GIVE UP (*7).

BOBBY GILLESPIE (b.22 Jun'64) – vocals (ex-WAKE) (also drummer of JESUS & MARY CHAIN) / **JIM BEATTIE** – guitar / **ROBERT YOUNG** – bass / **TOM McGURK** – drums / **MARTIN ST.JOHN** – tambourine

Creation / not issued

May 85. (7") **ALL FALL DOWN. / IT HAPPENS** -

— added **PAUL HARTE** – rhythm guitar (GILLESPIE left JESUS & MARY)

Apr 86. (7") **CRYSTAL CRESCENT. / VELOCITY GIRL** -
(12"+=) – Spirea X.

— **STUART MAY** – rhythm guitar (ex-SUBMARINES) repl. HARTE (Dec86) / **ANDREW INNES** – rhythm guitar (of REVOLVING PAINT DREAM) repl. MAY / Guest drummers **PHIL KING** (studio) + **DAVE MORGAN** (tour) repl. McGURK

Elevation / not issued

Jun 87. (7") **GENTLE TUESDAY. / BLACK STAR CARNIVAL** -
(12"+=) – I'm gonna make you mine.

Sep 87. (7") **IMPERIAL. / STAR FRUIT SURF RIDER** -
(12"+=) – So sad about us / Imperial (demo).

Oct 87. (lp)(c) **SONIC FLOWER GROOVE** 62
– Gentle Tuesday / Treasure trip / May the sun shine bright for you / Sonic sister love / Silent spring / Imperial / Love you / Leaves / Aftermath / We go down slowly. *(re-iss.Jul91)*

— (Jun87) **GAVIN SKINNER** – drums repl. ST.JOHN

— (Feb88) Now a trio **GILLESPIE, YOUNG + INNES** augmented by **JIM NAVAJO** – guitar. (BEATTIE formed SPIREA X, and SKINNER also left)

— (Feb89) added **HENRY OLSEN** – bass (ex-NICO) / **PHILIP 'TOBY' TOMANOV** – drums (ex-NICO, ex-DURUTTI COLUMN, ex-BLUE ORCHIDS)

Creation / Sire

Jul 89. (7") **IVY, IVY, IVY. / YOU'RE JUST TOO DARK TO CARE**
(12"+=)(cd-s+=) – I got you split wide open over me.

Sep 89. (lp)(c)(cd) **PRIMAL SCREAM**
– Ivy, Ivy, Ivy / You're just dead skin to me / She power / You're just too dark to care / I'm losing more than I'll ever have / Gimme gimme teenage head / Lone star girl / Kill the king / Sweet pretty thing / Jesus can't save me. *(free 7"ltd.)* – SPLIT WIDE OPEN (demo). / LONE STAR GIRL (demo)

— Trimmed to a trio again (**GILLESPIE, YOUNG + INNES**)

Feb 90. (7") **LOADED. / I'M LOSING MORE THAN I'LL EVER HAVE** 16
(12")(cd-s) – ('A'-Terry Farley extended remix) / Rambling Rose (live).

Jul 90. (7") **COME TOGETHER (Terry Farley remix). / COME TOGETHER (Andrew Weatherall mix)** 26
(12"+=)(cd-s+=) – ('A'extended).

Jun 91. (7")(12") **HIGHER THAN THE SUN. / ('A' American mix)** 40
(cd-s+=) – Higher than the Orb.

— guest spot on above 'A' by **JAH WOBBLE** – bass

Aug 91. (7")(12") **DON'T FIGHT IT, FEEL IT. / ('A'scat mix)** 41
(cd-s+=) – ('A'extended version).

('A'vocals **DENISE JOHNSON**)

Sep 91. (cd)(c)(d-lp) **SCREAMADELICA** 8
– Movin' on up / Slip inside this house / Don't fight it, feel it / Higher than the Sun / Inner flight / Come together / Loaded / Damaged / I'm comin' down / Higher than the Sun (a dub symphony in two parts) / Shine like stars.

Jan 92. (7"ep)(c-ep) **DIXIE NARCO** 11
– Movin' on up / Carry me home / Screamadelica.
(12"ep+=)(cd-ep+=) – Stone my soul.

— In Jan'94, MARTIN DUFFY was stabbed in Memphis, although he recovered.

— Line-up:- **GILLESPIE, YOUNG, INNES, DUFFY + DAVID HOOD + DENISE JOHNSON** + guest **GEORGE CLINTON** – vocals

Mar 94. (7")(c-s) **ROCKS. / FUNKY JAM** 7
(12")(cd-s) – ('A'side) / Funky jam (hot ass mix) / Funky jam (club).

Apr 94. (cd)(c)(lp) **GIVE OUT BUT DON'T GIVE UP** 2
– Jailbird / Rocks / (I'm gonna) Cry myself blind / Funky jam / Big jet plane / Free / Call on me / Struttin' / Sad and blue / Give out but don't give up / I'll be there for you.

Jun 94. (7")(c-s) **JAILBIRD. / ('A'-Dust Brothers mix)** 29
(12"+=) – ('A'-Toxic Trio stay free mix) / ('A'-Weatherall dub chapter 3 mix).
(cd-s++=) – ('A'-Sweeney 2 mix).

Nov 94. (7")(c-s) **(I'M GONNA) CRY MYSELF BLIND (George Drakoulias mix). / ROCKS (live)** 51
(cd-s+=) – I'm losing more than I'll ever have (live) / Struttin' (back in our minds) (Brendan Lynch remix).
(10") – ('A'side) / Struttin' (back in our minds) (Brendan Lynch remix) / Give out but don't give up (Portishead remix) / Rockers dub (Kris Needs mix).

PRIMITIVES

Formed: Coventry, England . . . Sep'85 by TWEEDIE, DULLAHAN and COURT, who had been part of EUROPEAN SUN with male singer KEIRON. Now as The PRIMITIVES, they found blonde female TRACY, and through manager Wayne Morris, signed to new indie label 'Lazy'. After 4 well-received singles playlisted on the John Peel Radio 1 show, their label got taken over by 'RCA'. Early in 1988, they had first and biggest hit 'CRASH', which broke them into UK Top 5. • **Style:** Power pop psychedelic outfit, lying somewhere between BLONDIE (although TRACY turned ginger in 1989), a melodic JESUS & MARY CHAIN or The BUZZCOCKS. • **Songwriters:** Penned by COURT, except I'LL BE YOUR MIRROR (Velvet Underground) / I WANNA BE YOUR DOG (Stooges; Iggy Pop) / AS TEARS GO BY (Rolling Stones) / (YOU'RE SO SQUARE) BABY I DON'T CARE (Elvis Presley). • **Trivia:** So far TRACY has still to reveal her surname, which is slightly irritating for a discographer.

Recommended: LOVELY (*7) / LAZY 86-88 (*8).

TRACY TRACY (b.18 Aug'67, Australia) – vocals repl. KIERON / **PAUL COURT** (b.27 Jul'65) – guitar, vocals / **STEVE DULLAHAN** (b.18 Dec'66) – bass / **PETE TWEEDIE** – drums

Lazy / not issued

May 86. (12"ep) **THRU THE FLOWERS / ACROSS MY SHOULDER. / SHE DON'T NEED YOU** -

Oct 86. (7") **REALLY STUPID. / WE FOUND A WAY TO THE SUN** -
(12"+=) – Where the wind blows.

Feb 87. (7") **STOP KILLING ME. / BUZZ BUZZ BUZZ** -
(12"+=) – Laughing up my sleeve.

Aug 87. (7") **THRU THE FLOWERS (new version). / EVERYTHING SHINING BRIGHT** -
(12"+=) – Across my shoulder (original).
(7"ltd.+=) – ('A'original).

— **TIG WILLIAMS** – drums repl. TWEEDIE who joined HATE

Lazy-RCA / R.C.A.

Feb 88. (7") **CRASH. / I'LL STICK WITH YOU** 5 Apr88
(7"ep+=)/ /(10"ep+=) – ('A'extended) / ('A'mix)./ / Crash (live).
(12"+=) – Crash (demo) / Things get in your way.

Mar 88. (lp)(c)(cd) **LOVELY** 6
– Crash / Spacehead / Carry me home / Shadow / Thru the flowers / Dreamwalk baby / I'll stick with you / Nothing left / Stop killing me / Out of reach / Ocean blue / Run, baby, run / Anything to change / Buzz buzz buzz.

Apr 88. (7") **OUT OF REACH (remix). / REALLY STUPID (live)** 25 -
(7"ep+=) – Crash (live) / Dreamwalk baby (live).
(12"+=) – Crash (live) / ('A'lp version).
(cd-s+=) – Ocean blue (lp version) / I wanna be your dog (live).

Aug 88. (7")(7"red)(7"green)(7"yellow)(7"blue) **WAY BEHIND ME. / ALL THE WAY DOWN** 36 -
(12"+=)(c-s+=) – ('A'acoustic version) / ('B'beat version).

Sep 88. (7") **WAY BEHIND ME. / THRU THE FLOWERS (lp version)** -

— Trimmed to a trio when DULLAHAN also departed to join HATE

Jul 89. (7")(c-s) **SICK OF IT. / NOOSE** 24
(12"+=)(cd-s+=) – I'll be your mirror.
(12"blue++=) – As tears go by.

— added **ANDY HOBSON** – bass (ex-JUNK)

Sep 89. (7")(c-s) **SECRETS. / I ALMOST TOUCHED YOU** 49
(7"ep+=)/ /(12"ep+=) – Dizzy heights./ / Secrets (demo).
(7"ep)(12"red-ep)(3"cd-ep) – (all 4 above).

— **PAUL SAMPSON** – bass repl. HOBSON (on lp)

Oct 89. (lp)(c)(cd) **PURE** 33
– Outside / Summer rain / Sick of it / Shine / Dizzy heights / All the way down / Secrets / Keep me in mind / Lonely streets / Can't bring me down / Way behind me / Never tell / Noose / I'll be your mirror. *(cd+=)*– All the way down (beat version) / I almost touched you.

Jul 91. (7")(c-s) **YOU ARE THE WAY. / IN MY DREAM** 58 -
(12"+=)(cd-s+=) – Sunpulse / Stop killing me.

Oct 91. (7") **EARTH THING. / EMPHASISE** -
('THE SPELLS EP' 12"ep+=)(cd-ep+=) – Under my spell / Haunted.
('THE SPELLS EP' 12"+=) – All the way down / Way behind me (2 live).

Mar 92. (7")(c-s) **LEAD ME ASTRAY. / OUTSIDE (live) / YOU ARE THE WAY (live)**
(12") – ('A'side) / Slip away (live) / Earth thing (live) / Outside.
(12") – ('A'side) / See thru the dark (live) / Stop killing me (live).
(cd-s) – ('A'side) / Sick of it (live) / Give this world to me (live).

Apr 92. (cd)(c)(lp) **GALORE**
– You are the way / Lead me astray / Earth thing / Give this world to you / Slip

away / Cold enough to kill / Hello Jesus / Empathise / See thru the dark / Kiss mine / Smile / The little black egg.

— Disbanded around Spring 1992.

– compilations, others, etc. –

Aug 89. Lazy; (lp)(c)(cd) **LAZY 86-88** (early materiel) [73] [-]

PRIMUS

Formed: Bay Area, San Francisco, USA . . . mid-80's by LEE CLAYPOOL and TODD HUTH initially as PRIMATE until the late 80's. During the early 90's, they were regular guests of MTV, while signing big time to 'Interscope'. • **Style:** Psychedelic and experimental polka /thrash-funk, trio similiar to a very bassy RED HOT CHILI PEPPERS, but with weird humour staccato-snorkle vox of CLAYPOOL whose sound could fuse elements of TALKING HEADS, VERY THINGS or STUMP. • **Songwriters:** CLAYPOOL except; MAKING PLANS FOR NIGEL (XTC). • **Trivia:** TOM WAITS guests on their 1991 album.

Recommended: SAILING THE SEAS OF CHEESE (*8) / PORK SODA (*9)

LEE CLAYPOOL – vocals, bass / LARRY LALONDE – guitar repl. TODD HUTH who joined BLIND ILLUSION / **JAY LANE** – drums, repl. drum machine

not issued Prawnsong

1989. (lp) **SUCK ON THIS (live)** [ ] [ ]
– John the fisherman / Groundhog's day / The heckler / Pressman / Jelikit / Tommy the cat / Pudding time / Harold of the rocks / Frizzle fry. *(UK-iss.cd+c Mar92 on 'Interscope-Atlantic')*

— **TIM 'HERB' ALEXANDER** – drums repl. JAY who joined SAUSAGE

Virgin Caroline

Jul 90. (cd)(c)(lp) **FRIZZLE FRY** [ ] [ ]
– To defy the laws of tradition / Ground hog's day / Too many puppies / Mr.Know-it-all / Frizzle fry / John the fisherman / You can't kill Michael Malloy / The toys go winding down / Pudding time / Sathington Willoby / Spaghetti western / Harold of the rocks / To defy.

Atlantic Interscope

May 91. (cd)(c)(lp) **SAILING THE SEAS OF CHEESE** [ ] [ ]
– Seas of cheese / Here come the bastards / Sgt. Baker / American life / Jerry was a race car driver / Eleven / Is it luck? / Grandad's lil ditty / Tommy the cat / Sathington waltz / Those damned blue collar tweekers / Fish on / Los bastardos. *(re-iss.Feb95)*

Jun 92. (7"ep)(cd-ep) **CHEESY EP 1 (US title 'MISCELLANEOUS DEBRIS')** [ ] [ ]
– Making plans for Nigel / Tommy the cat / Tippy toes / Have a cigar.
(cd-s'CHEESY 2') – (1st 2 tracks) / Sinister exaggerator / Intruder.

Interscope Interscope

May 93. (cd)(c)(lp) **PORK SODA** [56] [7]
– Pork chop's little ditty / My name is mud / Welcome to this world / Bob / D.M.V. / The ol' Diamondback sturgeon (Fisherman's chronicles, part 3) / Nature boy / Wounded Knee / Pork soda / The pressman / Mr.Krinkle / The air is getting slippery / Hamburger train / Pork chop's little ditty / Hail Santa.

Jun 95. (cd)(c) **TALES FROM THE PUNCHBOWL** [ ] [8]
– Professor Nutbutter's house of treats / Mrs. Blaileen / Wynona's big brown beaver / Southbound pachydern / Space farm / Year of the parrot / Hellbound 17 1/2 (theme from) / Glass sandwich / Del Davis tree farm / De Anza jig / On the tweak again / Over the electric grapevine / Captain Shiner.

PRINCE

Born: PRINCE ROGERS NELSON, 7 Jun'58, Minneapolis, Minnesota, USA. Named so after his father's jazz band The PRINCE ROGER TRIO, who featured his mother Mattie on vocals. When his parents divorced, he was taken to a JAMES BROWN concert in 1968 (an experience to influence his future solo work), by his stepfather. In 1970, he absconded from home to sleep rough while also finding father. He taught him guitar, and was eventually adopted by the ANDERSON family, whose son ANDRE (later ANDRE CYMONE) became friend. At this time, PRINCE learnt numerous other instruments and found he had writing ability. In 1972, he was invited to play in cousin CHARLES SMITH's junior high school band GRAND CENTRAL. The following year, they became CHAMPAGNE, with PRINCE becoming leader after SMITH was replaced by MORRIS DAY. In 1976, he sessioned guitar for Sound 80 studios' PEPE WILLIE. At this time he made a demo for producer Chris Moon, who also taught him studio skills. In 1977, PRINCE landed a solo deal with 'Warners', which gave him control of production, etc. The following year, his debut 'FOR YOU' was finally released and started the steady road to superstardom. In the late 70's, he had first US Top 30 album with 'PRINCE', which contained a near Top 10 single 'I WANNA BE YOUR LOVER' and a future No.1 for CHAKA KHAN; 'I FEEL FOR YOU'. By the mid-80's, PRINCE had become one of the world's top stars, especially after near biographical film 'PURPLE RAIN' and its soundtrack, smashed into No.1 spot. At this time, he also formed own record company 'Paisley P.', to issue not just his records, but also for friends The FAMILY, SHEILA E., GEORGE CLINTON, etc. In 1988, he mysteriously recalled his 'BLACK ALBUM' from its German pressing plant, and shelved album although many copies were bootlegged. • **Style:** Moved from R&B disco-funk multi-instrumentalist to experimental pop-rock artist, whose erotic sexy stage routines were likened to JAMES BROWN or MICHAEL JACKSON. • **Songwriters:** Prolific pensmith writing, unusually for the 80's, an album a year. He also wrote songs under pseudonyms CAMILLE, JAMIE STARR, CHRISTOPHER, etc., and has written hits especially for SHEENA EASTON (Sugar Walls) and BANGLES (Manic Monday). Note: WENDY AND LISA wrote 'MOUNTAINS' before departing for own duo. • **Trivia:** In 1988, his sister TYKA NELSON signed for 'Chrysalis', and issued poor selling album. • **Filmography:** PURPLE RAIN (1984) / UNDER THE CHERRY MOON (1986) / GRAFFITI BRIDGE (1990). He also wrote score for BATMAN (1989).

Recommended: SIGN 'O' THE TIMES (*9) / PARADE (*8) / LOVESEXY (*8) / 1999 (*8) / PURPLE RAIN (*8) / DIAMONDS AND PEARLS (*8) / THE HITS 1 (*9) / THE HITS 2 (*9) / SYMBOL (*8) / MUSIC FROM GRAFITTI BRIDGE (*8).

PRINCE – vocals, multi-instrumentalist, synthesizers, producer, everything

Warners Warners

Oct 78. (lp)(c) **FOR YOU** [-] [ ]
– For you / In love / Soft and wet / Crazy you / Just as long as we're together / Baby / My love is forever / So blue / I'm yours. *(UK-iss.Sep86, cd-iss. Oct87)*

Nov 78. (7") **SOFT AND WET. / SO BLUE** [-] [92]

Jan 79. (7") **JUST AS LONG AS WE'RE TOGETHER. / IN LOVE** [-] [ ]

— **PRINCE** – vocals, guitar live back-ups **DEZ DICKERSON** – guitar / **GAYLE CHAPMAN** – keyboards / **ANDRE CYMONE** – bass / **MATT FINK** – keyboards / **BOBBY Z** – drums

Nov 79. (7") **I WANNA BE YOUR LOVER. / MY LOVE IS FOREVER** [-] [11]

Dec 79. (7")(12") **I WANNA BE YOUR LOVER. / JUST AS LONG AS WE'RE TOGETHER** [41] [-] Nov 79

Jan 80. (lp)(c) **PRINCE** [ ] [22] Oct 79
– I wanna be your lover / Why you wanna treat me so bad? / Sexy dancer / When we're dancing close and slow / With you / Bambi / Still waiting / I feel for you / It's gonna be lonely.

Feb 80. (7") **WHY YOU WANNA TREAT ME SO BAD?. / BAD** [-] [ ]

— (Feb80) live **LISA COLEMAN** – keyboards repl. GAYLE

Apr 80. (7")(12") **SEXY DANCER. / BAMBI** [ ] [ ]

May 80. (7") **STILL WAITING. / BAMBI** [-] [ ]

Sep 80. (7") **UPTOWN. / CRAZY YOU** [-] [ ]

Oct 80. (lp)(c) **DIRTY MIND** [ ] [45]
– Dirty mind / When you were mine / Do it all night / Gotta broken heart again / Uptown / Head / Sister / Party up. *((re-iss.1989) (cd-iss.Dec85)*

Nov 80. (7") **DIRTY MIND. / WHEN WE'RE DANCING CLOSE AND SLOW** [-] [ ]

Mar 81. (7")(12") **DO IT ALL NIGHT. / HEAD** [ ] [ ]

Jun 81. (7") **GOTTA STOP (MESSIN' ABOUT). / UPTOWN (live)** [ ] [ ]
(12"+=) – Head (live).
(12") – ('A'side) / I wanna be your lover (live).

— (mid'81) live **BROWN MARK** – bass repl. ANDRE who ventured solo

Oct 81. (7")(12") **CONTROVERSY. / WHEN YOU WERE MINE** [ ] [70]

Nov 81. (lp)(c) **CONTROVERSY** [ ] [21]
– Controversy / Sexuality / Do me, baby / Private joy / Ronnie talk to Russia / Let's work / Annie Christian / Jack u off. *(cd-iss.1984)*

Apr 82. (7")(12") **LET'S WORK. / RONNIE TALK TO RUSSIA** [ ] [ ]

Jun 82. (7") **DO ME, BABY. / PRIVATE JOY** [-] [ ]

PRINCE & THE REVOLUTION

live **WENDY MELVOIN** – guitar repl. DEE

Jan 83. (7") **1999. / HOW COME U DON'T CALL ME ANYMORE** [25] [44] Oct 82
(free c-s w/7") – 1999 / Controversy. / Dirty mind / Sexuality.
(12"+=) – D.M.S.R. *(US re-dist.Jun83 hit No.12)*

Feb 83. (lp)(c) **1999** [ ] [26]
– 1999 / Little red Corvette / Delirious / Let's pretend we're married / D.M.S.R. * / Delirious / Automatic / Something in the water / Free / Lady cab driver / All the critics love u in New York / International lover. *(re-iss.Nov83 as d-lp/d-c, hit UK No.30 in Sep84 +cd.omits *)*

Feb 83. (7") **LITTLE RED CORVETTE. / ALL THE CRITICS LOVE U IN NEW YORK** [-] [6]

Apr 83. (7") **LET'S PRETEND WE'RE MARRIED. / IRRESISTIBLE BITCH** [-] [52]

Apr 83. (7") **LITTLE RED CORVETTE. / LADY CAB DRIVER** [54] [-]
(12") – ('A'extended) / Automatic lover / International lover.

Sep 83. (7") **DELIRIUS. / HORNY TOAD** [-] [8]

Sep 83. (7")(12") **LET'S PRETEND WE'RE MARRIED. / ALL THE CRITICS LOVE U IN NEW YORK** [ ] [-]

Nov 83. (7") **LITTLE RED CORVETTE. / HORNY TOAD** [66] [ ]
('A'extended-12"+=) – D.M.S.R.

Jun 84. (7")(12") **WHEN DOVES CRY. / 17 DAYS** [4] [1] May84
(d12"+=)(c-s+=) – 1999 / D.M.S.R.

Jul 84. (lp)(c)(cd)(purple-lp) **PURPLE RAIN** (Music From The Motion Picture) [7] [1]
– Let's go crazy / Take me with u / The beautiful ones / Computer blue / Darling Nikki / When doves cry / I would die 4 U / Baby I'm a star / Purple rain. (US-iss.as d-lp, w / += tracks by The TIME + APOLLONIA 6) *(re-iss.Jan92 hit UK No.59) (re-iss.cd/c Feb95)*

Jul 84. (7") **LET'S GO CRAZY. / EROTIC CITY** [-] [1]

Sep 84. (7")(7"sha-pic-d) **PURPLE RAIN. / GOD** [8] [2]
(12") – ('A'side) / ('A'vocal + instrumental).

Nov 84. (7") **I WOULD DIE 4 U. / ANOTHER LONELY CHRISTMAS** [58] [8]
(12"+=)/ /(12") – Free./ / ('A'&'B' US remixes).

Jan 85. (7")(12") **1999. / LITTLE RED CORVETTE** [2] [-]
(free c-s w/7"+=) – 1999 / Uptown / Controversy / D.M.S.R. / Sexy dancer.

Feb 85. (7") **LET'S GO CRAZY. / TAKE ME WITH U** [7] [-]
('A'extended-12"+=) – Erotic city.

Feb 85. (7") **TAKE ME WITH U. / BABY I'M A STAR** [-] [25]

— added live **SHEILA E.** (b.ESCOVEDO) – percussion, vocals / **ERIC LEEDS** – saxophone

Paisley P. Paisley P.

Apr 85. (lp)(c)(cd) **AROUND THE WORLD IN A DAY** [5] [1]

SLAVE

– Around the world in a day / Paisley Park / Condition of the heart / Raspberry beret / Tambourine / America / Pop life / The ladder / Temptation.

May 85. (7")(7"sha-pic-d) **PAISLEY PARK. / SHE'S ALWAYS IN MY HAIR** 18 2
(12"+=)/ /(12"++=) – ('A'extended)./ / ('B'extended).

May 85. (7") **RASPBERRY BERET. / SHE'S ALWAYS IN MY HAIR** - 2

Jul 85. (7") **RASPBERRY BERET. / HELLO** 25 -

Jul 85. (7") **POP LIFE. / HELLO** - 7
(12") – ('A'&'B'extended remixes).

Oct 85. (7") **AMERICA. / GIRL** - 46

Oct 85. (7")('A'ext-12") **POP LIFE. / GIRL** 60 -

Feb 86. (7")(7"pic-d)('A'ext-12") **KISS. / LOVE OR MONEY** 6 1

Apr 86. (lp)(c)(cd)(pic-lp) **PARADE (Music from the film 'Under The Cherry Moon')** 4 3
– Christopher Tracey's parade / New position / I wonder u / Under the cherry moon / Girls and boys / Life can be so nice / Venus de Milo / Mountains / Do u lie / Kiss / Anotherloverholdenyohead / Sometimes it snows in April.

May 86. (7") **MOUNTAINS. / ALEXA DE PARIS** 45 23
(10"white)(12") – ('A'&'B'extended).

Aug 86. (7")(7"sha-pic-d) **GIRLS AND BOYS (edit). / UNDER THE CHERRY MOON** 11
(12"+=) – Erotic city.
(d7"+=) – She's always in my hair / 17 days.

Oct 86. (7") **ANOTHERLOVERHOLDENYOHEAD. / GIRLS AND BOYS** - 63

Oct 86. (7") **ANOTHERLOVERHOLDENYOHEAD. / I WANNA BE YOUR LOVER** 36 -
('A'ext-12")(12"pic-d) – (same tracks).
(d7"+=) – Mountains / Alexa de Paris.

PRINCE

solo, without WENDY & LISA who formed own duo. He retained live **FINK, LEEDS & SHEILA E.** adding **MICO WEAVER** – guitar / **BONI BOYER** – keyboards / **LEVI STEACER JR.** – bass / **CAT GLOVER** – dancer, vocals

Mar 87. (7") **SIGN 'O' THE TIMES. / LA LA LA LA HE HE HE HE** 10 3
(12")(12"pic-d) – ('A'&'B'extended).

Mar 87. (d-lp)(c)(cd) **SIGN 'O' THE TIMES** 4 6
– Sign 'o' the times / Play in the sunshine / Housequake / Ballad of Dorothy Parker / It / Starfish and coffee / Slow love / Hot thing / Forever in my life / U got the look / If I was your girlfriend / Strange relationship / I could never take the place of your man / The cross / It's gonna be a beautiful night / Adore.

Jun 87. (7")(c-s)(7"peach)(ext-12")(ext.12"pic-d) **IF I WAS YOUR GIRLFRIEND. / SHOCKADELICA** 20 May 87

— (next 'A'side featured backing vocals by ex-Scots solo artist SHEENA EASTON now living in California with all her well-invested millions!)

Aug 87. (7")(c-s) **U GOT THE LOOK. / HOUSEQUAKE** 11 2 Jul 87
('B'ext-12"+=)(12"pic-d+=) – ('A'long version).

Nov 87. (7")(c-s) **I COULD NEVER TAKE THE PLACE OF YOUR MAN. / HOT THING** 29 10
(12"+=)(12"pic-d+=) – ('B'extended).

Feb 88. (7") **HOT THING. /** - 63

Apr 88. (7")(c-s) **ALPHABET ST. / THIS IS NOT MUSIC, THIS IS A TRIP** 9 8
(12")(cd-s) – ('A'&'B'extended).

May 88. (lp)(c)(cd) **LOVESEXY** 1 11
– I no / Alphabet St. / Glam slam / Anna Stesia / Dance on / Lovesexy / When 2 r in love / I wish U Heaven / Positivity. *(re-iss.cd/c Feb95)*

Jul 88. (7")(12") **GLAM SLAM. / ESCAPE** 29
(cd-s+=) – Escape (free yo mind from this rat race).

Oct 88. (7") **I WISH U HEAVEN. / SCARLET PUSSY (by 'Camille')** 24
(12"+=)(cd-s+=) – ('A' pts.2 & 3).

Jun 89. (7")(c-s)('A'ext-12")(c-s)(cd-s)(3"cd-s)(12"pic-d) **BATDANCE. / 200 BALLOONS** 2 1
(12"+=) – ('A'batmix) / ('B'side) / ('A' Vicki Vale mix).

Jun 89. (lp)(c)(cd)(pic-lp) **BATMAN** 1 1
– The future / Electric chair / The arms of Orion / Partyman / Vicki waiting / Trust / Lemon crush / Scandalous / Batdance. *(re-iss.cd/c Feb95)*

Aug 89. (7")(c-s)('A'remix-12")('A'ext-12") **PARTYMAN. / FEEL U UP** 14 18
(12"pic-d)(cd-s) – ('A'video mix). / ('B'long stroke mix)

Oct 89. (7")(c-s) **THE ARMS OF ORION. ("PRINCE & SHEENA EASTON") / I LUV U IN ME** 27 36
(12"+=)(cd-s+=)(12"pic-d+=) – ('A'extended).

— live **PATRICE RUSHDEN** – keyboards (solo artist) repl. BOYER + GLOVER / **MICHAEL BLAND** – drums repl. SHEILA E. / **CANDY DULFER** – saxophone repl. LEEDS

Jul 90. (7")(c-s) **THIEVES IN THE TEMPLE. / (Part 2)** 7 6
(12")(cd-s)(12"pic-d) – ('A'side) / ('A'remix) / ('A'dub version).

Aug 90. (cd)(c)(d-lp) **MUSIC FROM GRAFFITI BRIDGE (soundtrack)** 1 6
– Can't stop this feeling I got / New power generation / The question of U / Elephants and flowers / Joy in repetition / Tick, tock, bang / Thieves in the temple. *(also other tracks by 'The TIMES' etc.)*

Oct 90. (7")(c-s) **NEW POWER GENERATION. / (Part 2)** 26 64
(12"+=)(cd-s+=)(12"pic-d+=) – Melody cool (extended remix).

PRINCE & THE NEW POWER GENERATION

with **LEVI SEACER JR.** – guitar, vox / **TOMMY BARBARELLA** – keys, synths / **SONNY T.** – bass, vox / **ROSIE GAINES** – co-vocals, organ, synths / **MICHAEL B.** – drums / **TONY M.** – rap/vox / **KIRKY JOHNSON** – perc., vox / **DAMON DICKSON** – perc., vox.

Aug 91. (7")(c-s) **GETT OFF (remix). / HORNY PONY** 4 21
(12"+=)/ /(cd-s+=) – ('A'thrust mix)./ / ('A'purple pump mix).
(above: as a m-lp, its US import hit UK chart! at No.33)

Sep 91. (7")(c-s) **CREAM. / HORNY PONY** 15 1
(12"+=)(cd-s+=) – Gangster glam.

Sep 91. (cd)(c)(d-lp) **DIAMONDS AND PEARLS** 2 3
– Thunder / Daddy pop / Diamonds and pearls / Cream / Strollin' / Willing and able / Gett off / Walk don't walk / Jughead / Money don't matter 2 night / Push / Insatiable / Live 4 love. *(re-iss.cd/c Feb95)*

Nov 91. (7") **DIAMONDS AND PEARLS. / LAST DANCE** 25 4
(cd-s+=) – 2 the wire (Grammy instrumental) / Do you dance (remix).

Dec 91. (c-s) **INSATIABLE. / I LOVE YOU IN ME** - 77

Mar 92. (7")(c-s)(cd-s) **MONEY DON'T MATTER 2 NIGHT. / CALL THE LAW** 19 23
(12"+=) – Push.

Jun 92. (7")(c-s) **THUNDER. / VIOLET THE ORGAN DRIVER** 28
(12"+=)(cd-s+=)(12"pic-d+=) – Gett off (thrust dub).

— **MAYTE** – vocals repl. ROSIE

Jul 92. (7")(c-s) **SEXY M.F. / STROLLIN'** 4 66
(12"+=)(cd-s+=) – Daddy Pop.

Sep 92. (7")(c-s) **MY NAME IS PRINCE. / 2 WHOM IT MAY CONCERN** 7 36
(12"+=)/ /(cd-s++=) – Sexy mutha./ / ('A'extra mix).

Nov 92. (12")(cd-s) **MY NAME IS PRINCE (remixes). / (other mixes)** 51

Oct 92. (cd)(c)(d-lp) **(SYMBOL)** 1 5
– My name is Prince / Sexy MF / Love 2 the 9's / The morning papers / The Max / Segue / Blue light / I wanna melt with U / Sweet baby / The continental / Dawn U / Arrogance / The flow / 7 / And God created woman / 3 chains o' gold / Segue / The sacrifice of Victor.

Nov 92. (7")(c-s) **7. / 7 (mix)** 27 7
(cd-s+=) – ('A'other mixes).

Mar 93. (7")(c-s) **THE MORNING PAPERS. / LIVE FOR LOVE** 52 44
(cd-s+=) – Love 2 the 9's.

Sep 93. (cd)(c)(d-lp) **THE HITS 1** (compilation) 5 46
– When doves cry / Pop life / Soft and wet / I feel for you / Why you wanna treat me so bad? / When you were mine / Uptown / Let's go crazy / 1999 / I could never take the place of your man / Nothing compares 2 U / Adore / Pink cashmere / Alphabet St. / Sign 'o' the times / Thieves in the temple / Diamonds and pearls / 7.

Sep 93. (cd)(c)(d-lp) **THE HITS 2** (compilation) 5 54
– Controversy / Dirty mind / I wanna be your lover / Head / Do me, baby / Delirious / Little red Corvette / I would die 4 U / Raspberry beret / If I was your girlfriend / Kiss / Peach / U got the look / Sexy M.F. / Gett off / Cream / Pope / Purple rain.

Sep 93. (3xcd)(3xc) **THE HITS / THE B-SIDES** 4 19
– (all of above plus corresponding 'B'sides)
+ Hello / 200 ballooons / Escape / Gotta stop (messin' about) / Horny toad / Feel u up / Girl / I love u in me / Erotic city / Shockadelica / Irresistable bitch / Scarlet pussy / La, la, la, he, he, hee / She's always in my hair / 17 days / How come u don't call me anymore / Another lonely Christmas / God / Tears in your eyes / Power fantastic.

Sep 93. (c-s) **PINK CASHMERE. / ?** - 50

Oct 93. (7")(c-s) **PEACH. / WISH U HEAVEN** 14 -
(cd-s+=) – Girls & boys / My name is Prince.
(cd-s) – ('A'side) / Money don't matter 2 nite / Partyman / Mountains.

Dec 93. (7"pic-d)(c-s) **CONTROVERSY. / THE FUTURE** 5 -
(cd-s) – ('A'side) / The future (remix) / Glam slam / D.M.S.R.
(cd-s) – ('A'side) / Paisley Park / Anotherloverholenyohead / New power generation.

Mar 94. (7")(c-s) **THE MOST BEAUTIFUL GIRL IN THE WORLD. / BEAUTIFUL** 1 3
(12"+=)(cd-s+=) – ('A'mixes).

May 94. (cd)(c)(m-lp) **THE BEAUTIFUL EXPERIENCE** 18 92
– (7 versions of last single)

— Musicians: **PRINCE / MICHAEL B. / SONNY T. / TOMMY BARBARELLA / MR.HAYES / MAYLE**

Aug 94. (cd)(c)(lp) **COME** 1 15
– Come / Space / Pheromone / Loose! / Papa / Race / Dark / Solo / Letitgo / Orgasm.

Aug 94. (7"pic-d+c-s) **LETITGO. / SOLO** 30 31
(cd-s+=) – Alexa de Paris / Pope.

Mar 95. (cd-ep) **PURPLE MEDLEY / PURPLE MEDLEY (extended)/ PURPLE MEDLEY (Kirk J's B-side remix)** 33 84

NEW POWER GENERATION

Due to contractual problems with Warners (only allowed 1 album a year), PRINCE (aka SLAVE/ VICTOR/ THE ARTIST FORMERLY KNOWN AS . . ./ TORA TORA) took to wearing a mask on stage, etc (or was it him?)

N.P.G. N.P.G.

Mar 95. (7"ep)(c-ep)(12"ep)(cd-ep) **GET WILD / BEAUTIFUL GIRL (sax version) / HALLUCINATION RAIN**

Apr 95. (cd)(c)(lp) **EXODUS** 11
– N.P.G. operator intro / Get wild / Segue / DJ gets jumped / New power soul / DJ seduces Sonny / Segue / Count the days / The good life / Cherry, Cherry / Segue / Return of the bump squad / Mashed potato girl intro / Segue / Big fun / New power day / Segue / Hallucination rain / N.P.G. bum rush the ship / The exodus has begun / Outro.

Aug 95. (c-s) **THE GOOD LIFE /** 29
(cd-s)(12") –

Oct 95. (c-s) **COUNT THE DAYS /**
(cd-s) –

PRINCE (symbol)

or T.A.F.K.A.P. (The Artist Formerly Known As PRINCE)

Warner-NPG Warner-NPG

Sep 95. (c-s) **EYE HATE U /** 20 12
(cd-s) –

Sep 95. (cd)(c)(lp) **THE GOLD EXPERIENCE** 4 6
– P control / npq operator / Endorphinmachine / Shhh / We march / npq operator / The most beautiful girl in the world / Dolphin / npq operator / Now / npq operator / 319 / npq operator / Shy / Billy Jack bitch / Eye hate u / npq operator / Gold.

Nov 95. (c-s) **GOLD / ROCK AND ROLL IS ALIVE! (AND IT LIVES IN MINNEAPOLIS)** 10 58 (cd-s+=) – Eye hate U (extended remix).

– compilations, others, etc. –

Oct 88. WEA; (cd-s) **WHEN DOVES CRY / PURPLE RAIN** [ ] [ ]
Oct 88. WEA; (cd-s) **LET'S GO CRAZY (extended) / TAKE ME WITH U** [ ] [ ]
Oct 88. WEA; (cd-s) **LITTLE RED CORVETTE (dance mix) / 1999 (extended)** [ ] [ ]
Oct 88. WEA; (cd-s) **KISS / GIRLS AND BOYS / UNDER THE CHERRY MOON** [ ] [ ]
Nov 94. Warners; (cd)(c) **THE BLACK ALBUM** (finally released!) [36] [47]
– Le grind / Cindy C. / Dead on it / When 2 R in love / Bob George / Superfunkycalifragisexy / 2 nigs united for West Compton / Rockhard in a funky place.

Maddy PRIOR (see under ⇒ STEELEYE SPAN)

PROCLAIMERS

Formed: Auchtermuchty, Scotland ... 1986 by twin brothers CRAIG and CHARLIE REID, who had progressed from local bands The HIPPIE HASSLERS and REASONS FOR EMOTIONS. After a bemusing but stunning appearance on Channel 4's 'The Tube', and through fan/manager Kenny McDonald, they were given deal by 'Chrysalis' records, who employed GERRY RAFFERTY to produce debut work. Their second 45 in 1987 'LETTER FROM AMERICA' peaked at UK No.3, and paved the way for a fruitful next couple of years. • **Style:** Acoustic and heavily-accented balladeers, whose bespectacled looks, put heart back into C&W based rock-pop. • **Songwriters:** All written by REID brothers, except TWENTY FLIGHT ROCK (Eddie Cochran) / KING OF THE ROAD (Roger Miller) / THESE ARMS OF MINE (Otis Redding) / etc. • **Trivia:** The twins were proudly both activist members of the SNP (Scottish National Party).

Recommended: THIS IS THE STORY (*7).

CRAIG REID – vocals, tambourine, bongos, maracas / **CHARLIE REID** – acoustic guitar, 12-string bass, vocals plus sessioners

Chrysalis Chrysalis

Apr 87. (lp)(c) **THIS IS THE STORY** [43] [ ]
– Throw the 'R' away / Over and done with / Misty blue / The part that really matters / (I'm gonna) Burn your Playhouse down / Letter from America (acoustic) / Sky takes the soul / It broke my heart / The first attack / Make my heart fly / Beautiful truth / The joyful Kilmarnock blues / Letter from America (band version) *re-iss.cd+c Mar93)*
May 87. (7") **THROW THE 'R' AWAY. / A TRAIN WENT PAST THE WINDOW** [ ] [ ]
(12"+=) – Long gone lonesome / I can't be myself tomorrow (both live).
Oct 87. (7") **LETTER FROM AMERICA (band version). / LETTER FROM AMERICA (acoustic version)** [3] [ ]
(10"+=)(12"+=) – I'm lucky / Just because / Twenty flight rock.
Feb 88. (7") **MAKE MY HEART FLY. / WISH I COULD SAY** [63] [ ]
(12"+=) – (I'm gonna) Burn your playhouse down (live) / Throw the 'R' away.
(cd-s+=) – Letter from America (band version).

— (1988) with **JERRY DONAHUE** – guitar / **PETE WINGFIELD** – keyboards, producer / **PHIL CRANHAM** – bass / **PAUL ROBINSON** – drums / etc.

Aug 88. (7") **I'M GONNA BE (500 MILES). / BETTER DAYS** [11] [ ]
(12"+=) – Teardrops.
(cd-s++=) – I can't be myself.
Sep 88. (lp)(c)(cd) **SUNSHINE ON LEITH** [6] [ ]
– I'm gonna be (500 miles) / Cap in hand / Then I met you / My old friend the blues / Sean / Sunshine on Leith / Come on nature / I'm on my way / What do you do / It's Saturday night / Teardrops / Oh Jean. *(re-iss.cd+c Jul93, hit US No.31; above single had already made No.3 in June 93.) (re-iss.cd Mar94)*
Oct 88. (7") **SUNSHINE ON LEITH. / LEAVING HOME** [41] [ ]
(12"+=)(cd-s+=) – The first attack / Letter from America (live).
Feb 89. (7") **I'M ON MY WAY. / OVER AND DONE WITH** [43] [ ]
(12"+=)(cd-s+=) – Throw the 'R' away / Cap in hand.
Nov 90. (7")(c-s) **KING OF THE ROAD. / LONG BLACK VEIL** [9] [ ]
(7"ep)(12"ep+=)(cd-ep+=) – Lulu selling tea / Not ever.
Feb 94. (7")(c-s) **LET'S GET MARRIED. / I'M GONNA BE (500 MILES)** [21] [ ]
(cd-s+=) – Gentle on my mind / Waiting for a train.
(cd-s) – ('A'side) / Invitation to the blues / Letter from America / ('A'acoustic).
Mar 94. (cd)(c)(lp) **HIT THE HIGHWAY** [8] [ ]
– Let's get married / The more I believe / What makes you cry / Follow the money / These arms of mine / Shout shout / The light / Hit the highway / A long long long time ago / I want to be a Christian / Your childhood / Don't turn out like your mother.
Apr 94. (7")(c-s) **WHAT MAKES YOU CRY. / GUESS WHO WON'T BEG** [38] [ ]
(cd-s+=) – Shout shout (acoustic) / Follow the monkey (acoustic).
(cd-s) – ('A'side) / Bobby / King of the road / ('A'acoustic).
Oct 94. (7")(c-s) **THESE ARMS OF MINE. / SUNSHINE ON LEITH** [51] [ ]
(cd-s+=) – Joyful KIlmarnock blues / What makes you cry.
(cd-s) – ('A'side) / I'm on my way / Let's get married / I'm gonna be (500 miles).

PROCOL HARUM

Formed: Southend, Essex, England ... 1959 as The PARAMOUNTS, by five schoolboys; BOB SCOTT – vocals / GARY BROOKER – keyboards / ROBIN TROWER – guitar / CHRIS COPPING – bass / MICK BROWNLEE – drums. They played a number of local gigs, and GARY soon took over vocal chores, when SCOTT didn't turn up. In 1962, they left school and acquired manager Peter Martin. The following year with a few personnel changes, they signed to EMI's 'Parlophone' label, and soon hit the UK Top 40 with Coasters R&B cover 'POISON IVY'. Their follow-up of Thurston Harris's 'LITTLE BITTY PRETTY ONE', failed to emulate debut, and after a few more covers, they folded late summer '66. Note other covers:- I FEEL GOOD ALL OVER (Drifters) / I'M THE ONE WHO LOVES YOU (Major Lance) / BAD BLOOD (Coasters) / BLUE RIBBONS (Jackie DeShannon) / CUTTIN' IN (Johnny Guitar Watson) / YOU'VE NEVER HAD IT SO GOOD (P.F.Sloan). In 1967, BROOKER and lyricist KEITH REID, advertised in the Melody Maker for musicians, and soon settled with FISHER, ROYER, KNIGHTS and HARRISON. They became PROCOL HARUM (taking name from Latin "procul" meaning "far from these things"), and with help from producer Denny Cordell, unleashed mesmeric debut 45 'A WHITER SHADE OF PALE' for 'Deram'. It soon sold over half a million copies in the UK and stayed at No.1 for 6 weeks. With pressures to tour, ROYER and HARRISON departed from group, and were deposed by former PARAMOUNTS; TROWER and WILSON. Later in 1967, they moved with producer CORDELL, to 'Regal Zono.', and had another smash hit 'HOMBURG'. In 1969, the band line-up was same as The PARAMOUNTS of 1963, having brought back COPPING to replace management bound FISHER and KNIGHTS. In the 70's PROCOL HARUM continued to have album success, more so in the States and Canada. • **Style:** Gothic pop-rock outfit, who were never quite unpigeonholed from classical rock tag, although bluesy sounding BROOKER tried hard to disperse this. Mystical surreal lyrics were provided by non-playing member KEITH REID, until 1975. • **Songwriters:** BROOKER wrote music, except; A WHITER SHADE OF PALE (adapted from J.S.Bach's 'Suite No.3 in D Major (Air On The G String) / I KEEP FORGETTING (Leiber & Stoller; producers of 1975 lp) / EIGHT DAYS A WEEK (Beatles). • **Trivia:** CHRIS THOMAS produced their 3 albums in the early 70's.

Recommended: THE COLLECTION (*8) / BROKEN BARRICADES (*7).

PARAMOUNTS

GARY BROOKER (b.29 May'45) – vocals, keyboards / **ROBIN TROWER** (b. 9 Mar'45) – guitar / **DIZ DERRICK** – bass repl. CHRIS COPPING who went to Leicester University (Sep63) / **B.J. WILSON** (b.18 Mar'47) – drums repl. MICK BROWNLEE (Jan63).

Parlophone not issued

Dec 63. (7") **POISON IVY. / I FEEL GOOD ALL OVER** [35] [-]
Feb 64. (7") **LITTLE BIT PRETTY ONE. / A CERTAIN GIRL** [ ] [-]
Mar 64. (7"ep) **THE PARAMOUNTS** (see above 4 tracks) [ ] [-]
Jun 64. (7") **I'M THE ONE WHO LOVES YOU. / IT WON'T BE LONG** [ ] [-]
Nov 64. (7") **BAD BLOOD. / DO I** [ ] [-]
Mar 65. (7") **BLUE RIBBONS. / CUTTIN' IN** [ ] [-]
Oct 65. (7") **YOU'VE NEVER HAD IT SO GOOD. / DON'T YA LIKE MA LOVE** [ ] [-]

PROCOL HARUM

BROOKER with also **MATTHEW FISHER** (b. 7 Mar'46) – organ (ex-SCREAMING LORD SUTCH) / **RAY ROYER** (b. 8 Oct'45) – guitar / **DAVE KNIGHTS** (b.28 Jun'45) – bass / **BOBBY HARRISON** (b.28 Jun'43) – drums / **KEITH REID** (b.10 Oct'46) – lyrics

Deram Deram

May 67. (7") **A WHITER SHADE OF PALE. / LIME STREET BLUES** [1] [5]
(re-iss. US Jan 73 on 'A&M')

— **ROBIN TROWER** – guitar (ex-PARAMOUNTS) repl. ROYER who formed FREEDOM / **B.J. WILSON** – drums (ex-PARAMOUNTS) repl. HARRISON who also formed FREEDOM

Regal Zono. A & M

Sep 67. (7") **HOMBURG. / GOOD CAPTAIN CLACK** [6] [34]
(re-iss.Oct75 on 'Cube')
Dec 67. (lp) **PROCOL HARUM** (US-version w/the 2 single tracks) [ ] [47] Sep 67
– A whiter shade of pale / Conquistador / She wandered through the garden fence / Something following me / Mabel / Cerdes (outside the gate of) / Homburg / Christmas camel / Kaleidoscope / Salad days / Good Captain Clack / Repent Walpurgis. *(re-iss.+c.May85 as 'A WHITER SHADE OF PALE' on 'Sierra')*
Apr 68. (7") **QUITE RIGHTLY SO. / IN THE WEE SMALL HOURS OF SIXPENCE** [50] [ ]
Dec 68. (lp) **SHINE ON BRIGHTLY** [ ] [24] Oct 68
– Quite rightly so / Shine on brightly / Skip softly (my moonbeams) / Wish me well / Rambling on / Magdalene (my regal zonophone) / In held twas I:- a) Glimpses of Nirvana – (b) Twas tea-time at the circus – (c) In the Autumn of my madness – (d) Look to your soul – (e) Grand finale. *re-iss.+c+cd Sep 85 on 'Sierra')*
May 69. (lp) **A SALTY DOG** [27] [32]
– A salty dog / The milk of human kindness / Too much between us / The Devil came from Arkansas / Boredom / Juicy John Pink / Wreck of the Hesperus / All this and more / Crucifiction Lane / Pilgrim's progress. *(re-iss. 1971 on 'MFP')(re-iss.+c+cd May85 on 'Sierra') (cd-iss.1986 on 'Mobile Fidelity')*
Jun 69. (7") **A SALTY DOG. / LONG GONE CREEK** [44] [-]
Jul 69. (7") **THE DEVIL CAME FROM KANSAS. / BOREDOM** [-] [ ]

— **CHRIS COPPING** – organ, bass (ex-PARAMOUNTS) repl. FISHER + KNIGHTS

Jun 70. (7") **WHISKEY TRAIN. / ABOUT TO DIE** [-] [ ]
Jun 70. (lp)(c) **HOME** [49] [34]
– Whiskey train / Dead man's dream / Still there'll be more / Nothing that I didn't know / About to die / Barnyard story / Piggy pig pig / Whaling stories / Your own choice. *(re-iss.+cd.Apr89 on 'Castle')*

Chrysalis A & M

Jun 71. (lp)(c) **BROKEN BARRICADES** [42] [32] May 71
– Simple sister / Broken barricades / Memorial drive / Luskus Delph / Power failure /

Song for a dreamer / Playmate of the mouth / Poor Mohammed. *(re-iss.1974)*

Jun 71. (7") **BROKEN BARRICADES. / POWER FAILURE** [-] [ ]

Oct 71. (7") **SIMPLE SISTER. / SONG FOR A DREAMER** [-] [ ]

— **DAVE BALL** (b.30 Mar'50) – guitar repl. ROBIN TROWER (later solo) / added **ALAN CARTWRIGHT** (b.10 Oct'45) – bass (to **BROOKER, COPPING, WILSON, REID + BALL)**

Apr 72. (lp)(c) **PROCOL HARUM IN CONCERT WITH THE EDMUNTON SYMPHONY ORCHESTRA (live)** [48] [5]
– Conquistador / Whaling stories / A salty dog / All this and more / In held 'twas I; a) Glimpses of Nirvana – (b) 'Twas teatime at the circus – (c) In the Autumn of my madness – (d) I know if I'd been wiser – (e) Grand finales. *(re-iss.1974) (re-iss.c+cd Aug 86)*

May 72. (7") **CONQUISTADOR (live). / A SALTY DOG (live)** [-] [16]

Jul 72. (7") **CONQUISTADOR (live). / LUSKUS DELPH** [22] [-]

Chrysalis Chrysalis

Mar 73. (lp)(c) **GRAND HOTEL** [ ] [21]
– Grand hotel / Toujours l'amour / A rum tale / T.V. Ceaser / Souvenir of London / Bringing home the bacon / Robert's box / For licorice John / Fires (which burnt brightly) / Robert's box.

Apr 73. (7") **ROBERT'S BOX. / A RUM TALE** [ ] [-]

Apr 73. (7") **BRINGING HOME THE BACON. / TOUJOURS L'AMOUR** [-] [ ]

Aug 73. (7") **GRAND HOTEL. / FIRE'S (WHICH BURNT BRIGHTLY)** [-] [ ]

Aug 73. (7") **SOUVENIR OF LONDON. / TOUJOURS L'AMOUR** [ ] [-]

— **MICK GRABHAM** – guitar (ex-PLASTIC PENNY, ex-COCHISE) repl. BALL to BEDLAM

Apr 74. (lp)(c) **EXOTIC BIRDS AND FRUIT** [ ] [86]
– Nothing but the truth / Beyond the pale / As strong as Samson / The idol / The thin edge of the wedge / Monsieur R. Monde / Fresh fruit / Butterfly boys / New lamps for old.

Apr 74. (7") **NOTHING BUT THE TRUTH. / DRUNK AGAIN** [ ] [ ]

Jul 75. (7") **PANDORA'S BOX. / THE PIPER'S TUNE** [16] [ ]

Aug 75. (lp)(c) **PROCOL'S NINTH** [41] [52]
– Pandora's box / Fools gold / Taking the time / The unquiet zone / The final thrust / I keep forgetting / Without a doubt / The piper's tune / Typewriter torment / Eight days a week.

Oct 75. (7") **THE FINAL THRUST. / TAKING THE TIME** [ ] [-]

Jan 76. (7") **AS STRONG AS SAMSON. / THE UNQUIET ZONE** [ ] [-]

— **PETE SOLLEY** – keyboards (ex-ARTHUR BROWN, ex-SNAFU, ex-CHRIS FARLOWE) repl. CARTWRIGHT (COPPING now bass only)

Feb 77. (7") **WIZARD MAN. / BACKGAMMON** [ ] [-]

Mar 77. (lp)(c) **SOMETHING MAGIC** [ ] [ ]
– Something magic / Skating on thin ice / Wizard man / The mark of the claw / Strangers in space / The worm and the tree.

Mar 77. (7") **WIZARD MAN. / SOMETHING MAGIC** [-] [ ]

— Disbanded mid-77. WILSON joined JOE COCKER. GRABHAM to MICKEY JUPP. GARY BROOKER joined ERIC CLAPTON band and went solo. PROCOL HARUM reformed Oct'91, TIM RENWICK instead of TROWER.

– compilations, others, etc. –

1971. Fly; (lp) **THE BEST OF PROCOL HARUM** [ ] [-]
(US-iss.Oct 73 on 'A&M')

Apr 72. Magnifly; (7"m) **A WHITER SHADE OF PALE. / HOMBURG / A SALTY DOG** [13] [-]

Apr 72. Cube; (d-lp)(d-c) **PROCOL HARUM – A WHITER SHADE OF PALE / A SALTY DOG** [26] [-]
(re-iss.Jan75, Mar78, Oct81)

Mar 78. Cube; (7") **A WHITER SHADE OF PALE. / CONQUISTADOR** [ ] [ ]
(re-iss.12"white-Mar79) (re-iss.7"-Aug82 on 'Dakota')

Mar 78. Cube; (d-lp)(d-c) **SHINE ON BRIGHTLY / HOME** [ ] [-]

Oct 81. Cube; (d-lp)(c) **THE PLATINUM COLLECTION** [ ] [-]

Jun 83. Cube; (7") **A WHITER SHADE OF PALE. / HOMBURG** [ ] [-]
(12"+=) – Conquistador.

Mar 76. Decca; (lp) **ROCK ROOTS** [ ] [-]

May 78. Hallmark; (lp)(c) **PROCOL HARUM'S GREATEST HITS** [ ] [-]

Aug 78. Chrysalis; (7") **CONQUISTADOR. / A SALTY DOG** [ ] [-]

Aug 78. E.M.I.; (7"ep) **THE PARAMOUNTS** [ ] [-]
– Poison Ivy / I feel glad all over / Blue ribbons / Cuttin' in.

1981. E.M.I.; (cd)(c)(lp) **PORTFOLIO** [ ] [-]

Apr 82. Ace; (lp) **PROCOL HARUM** (67-69) [ ] [-]

Aug 82. Dakota; (7") **HOMBURG. / A SALTY DOG** [ ] [-]

Oct 82. Dakota; (lp)(c) **PROCOL HARUM** (67-70) [ ] [-]

Oct 84. Sierra; (d-lp)(c) **OFF THE RECORD WITH PROCOL HARUM** [ ] [-]

Apr 86. Castle; (d-lp)(d-c)(cd) **THE COLLECTION** [ ] [-]
– A whiter shade of pale / Homburg / Too much between us / A salty dog / The Devil came back from Kansas / Whaling stories / Good Captain Clack / All this and more / Quite rightly so / Shine on brightly / Grand hotel / Bringing home the bacon / Toujours l'armour / Broken barricades / Power failure / Conquistador (live) / Nothing but the truth / Butterfly boys / Pandora's box / Simple sister.

Mar 88. Castle; (d-lp)(c)(cd) **SHINE ON BRIGHTLY. / A SALTY DOG** [ ] [-]

Mar 88. Castle; (cd-ep) **A WHITER SHADE OF PALE / HOMBURG / CONQUISTADOR / A SALTY DOG** [ ] [-]

Feb 92. Castle; (cd-box) **PROCOL HARUM** [ ] [-]

Feb 87. Old Gold; (7") **CONQUISTADOR. / PANDORA'S BOX** [ ] [-]

Jun 88. Old Gold; (7") **A WHITER SHADE OF PALE. / HOMBURG** [ ] [-]

Jul 88. Knight; (lp)(c)(cd) **NIGHTRIDING** [ ] [-]

Dec 88. Fun; (lp)(c)(cd) **20 GREATEST HITS** [ ] [-]

Apr 83. Edsel; (lp) **WHITER SHADES OF R'N'B (PARAMOUNTS)** [ ] [-]
(cd-iss. Aug 87 + Sep 91)

Jun 88. A&M; (cd) **CLASSICS** [ ] [-]

Jun 92. Dojo; (cd) **THE EARLY YEARS** [ ] [-]

Oct 94. Disky; (cd) **PROCOL HARUM** [ ] [-]

Jul 95. Essential; (cd-ep) **A WHITER SHADE OF PALE / A SALTY DOG / REPENT WALPURGIS** [ ] [-]

Sep 95. Essential; (cd)(c) **THE BEST OF PROCOL HARUM** [ ] [-]

GARY BROOKER

Chrysalis Chrysalis

Apr 79. (7") **SAVANNAH. / S.S. BLUES** [ ] [ ]

May 79. (lp)(c) **NO MORE FEAR OF FLYING** [ ] [ ]
– Savannah / Pilot / (No more) Fear of flying / Get up and dance / Give me something to remember / Say it ain't so Joe / Old Manhattan melodies / Angelina / Let me in / Switchboard Susan.

Aug 79. (7")(7"pic-d) **SAY IT AIN'T SO JOE. / ANGELINA** [ ] [ ]

Apr 80. (7") **LEAVE THE CANDLE. / CHASING THE CHOP** [ ] [ ]

Mercury Mercury

May 81. (7") **HOMELOVIN'. / CHASING THE CHOP** [ ] [ ]

Feb 82. (lp)(c) **LEAD ME TO THE WATER** [ ] [ ]
– Mineral man / Another way / Hang on Rose / Home loving / The cycle (let it flow) / Lead me to the water / The angler / Low flying birds / Sympathy for the hard of hearing.

Mar 82. (7") **THE CYCLE (LET IT FLOW). / BADLANDS** [ ] [ ]

Nov 84. (7") **THE LONG GOODBYE. / TRICK OF THE LIGHT** [ ] [ ]

Apr 85. (7") **TWO FOOLS IN LOVE. / SUMMER NIGHTS** [ ] [ ]

Sep 85. (lp)(c) **ECHOES IN THE NIGHT** [ ] [ ]
– Count me out / Two fools in love / Echoes in the night / Ghost train / Mr. Blue day / Saw the fire / The long goodbye / Hear what you're saying / Missing person / Trick of the night.

GARY was still a member of ERIC CLAPTON's band.

PROCOL HARUM

re-formed in 1991. **BROOKER** – vocals, piano / **KEITH REID** – words / **ROBIN TROWER** – lead guitar / **MATTHEW FISHER** – hammond organ / with guests **DAVE BRONZE** – bass / **MARK BRZEZICKI** – drums / **JERRY STEVENSON** – mandolin, guitar.

B.M.G. B.M.G.

Feb 92. (cd)(c)(lp) **THE PRODIGAL STRANGER** [ ] [ ]
– The truth won't fade away / Holding on / Man with a mission / (You can't) Turn back the page / One more time / A dream in ev'ry home / The hand that rocks the cradle / The king of hearts / All our dreams are sold / Perpetual motion / Learn to fly / The pursuit of happiness.

PRODIGY

Formed: London, England . . . early 90's by LIAM HOWLETT. Signed to 'X.L.' and scored UK Top 3 hit, with 2nd single 'CHARLY' (LIAM's cats name). Deservedly topped the UK charts in 1994 with album 'MUSIC FOR THE JILTED GENERATION'. • **Style:** Hardcore techno punk rock /dance outfit, conjuring images of KRAFTWERK at 100 mph, although with a harder danceable edge (very danceable!). • **Songwriters:** HOWLETT except samples of BABY D ('Casanova') on 'BREAK & ENTER', and KELLY CHARLES on 'YOU'RE NO GOOD FOR ME'. 'FULL THROTTLE' is also reminiscent of JOAN ARMATRADING's 'Me Myself I'. • **Trivia:** POP WILL EAT ITSELF co-wrote and featured on the track 'THEIR LAW'. 'CHARLY' sampled from TV ad, which featured a cartoon cat telling children not to talk to strangers!!!

Recommended: EXPERIENCE (*7) / MUSIC FOR THE JILTED GENERATION (*9)

LIAM HOWLETT – keyboards / **MC MAXIM REALITY** – rapper-vox / **LEEROY THORNHILL + KEITH FLINT** – dancers

X.L. Elektra

Mar 91. (12"ep) **WHAT EVIL LURKS / WE GONNA ROCK. / ANDROID / EVERYBODY IN THE PLACE** [ ] [-]

Aug 91. (7")(c-s) **CHARLY. / CHARLY (original mix)** [3] [-]
(12"+=)(cd-s+=) – Pandemonium / Your love.

Dec 91. (7")(c-s) **EVERYBODY IN THE PLACE. / G-FORCE (ENERGY FLOW)** [2] [-]
(12"+=) – Crazy man / Rip up the sound system.
(cd-s++=) – ('A'remix).

Feb 92. (c-ep+cd-ep) **CHARLY (Beltram says mix) / CHARLY (alley cat mix) / EVERYBODY IN THE PLACE (dance hall version) / EVERYBODY IN THE PLACE (fairground mix) / YOUR LOVE (the original excursion) / G-FORCE (Part 1)** [-] [ ]

Sep 92. (7")(c-s) **FIRE. / JERICHO (original mix)** [11] [-]
(12"+=)(cd-s+=) – Fire (sunrise version) / Jericho (genaside II remix).

Oct 92. (c-ep)(cd-ep) **FIRE (edit) / JERICHO (original version) / FIRE (sunrise version) / JERICHO (genaside II remix) / PANDEMONIUM** [-] [ ]

Oct 92. (cd)(c)(lp) **EXPERIENCE** [12] [ ]
– Jericho / Music reach (1,2,3,4) / Wind it up / Your love (remix) / Hyperspeed (G-Force part 2) / Charly (trip into drum and bass version) / Out of space / Everybody in the place (155 and rising) / Weather experience / Fire (sunrise version) / Ruff in the jungle bizness / Death of the Prodigy dancers (live).

Nov 92. (7")(c-s) **OUT OF SPACE (remix). / RUFF IN THE JUNGLE BIZNESS (uplifting vibes remix)** [5] [-]
(12"+=)(cd-s+=) – ('A'techno underworld remix) / Music reach (1,2,3,4) (live).

Dec 92. (c-ep)(cd-ep) **OUT OF SPACE (edit) / OUT OF SPACE (techno underworld remix) / UT OF SPACE (millenium mix) / OUT OF SPACE (celestial bodies mix) / RUFF IN THE JUNGLE BIZNESS (uplifting vibes remix) / JERICHO (live)** [-] [ ]

Apr 93. (7")(c-s) **WIND IT UP (REWOUND). / WE ARE THE RUFFEST** [7] [ ]
(12"+=) – Weather experience (remix).
(cd-s++=) – ('A'edit).

May 93. (c-ep)(cd-ep) **WIND IT UP (the rewound edit) / WIND IT UP (tightly wound) / WIND IT UP (forward wind) / WIND IT UP (unwind) / WE ARE THE RUFFEST / WEATHER EXPERIENCE (top buzz remix) / WIND IT UP (bonus beats)** [-] [ ]

Oct 93. (12"ep)(c-ep)(cd-ep) **ONE LOVE / RHYTHM OF LIFE (original mix) / FULL THROTTLE (original mix) / ONE LOVE (Johny L remix)** [8] [ ]

May 94. (12")(c-s) **NO GOOD (START THE DANCE) / NO GOOD (bad for you mix) / NO GOOD (CJ Bolland's museum mix)** [4] [ ]
(cd-s+=) – No Good (original mix).

— below album with **PHIL BENT** – flute / **LANCE RIDDLER** – guitar

X.L. / Mute

Jul 94. (cd)(c)(d-lp) **MUSIC FOR THE JILTED GENERATION** [1] [-] Mar95
– Intro / Break & enter / Their law (featuring POP WILL EAT ITSELF) / Full throttle / Voodoo people / Speedway (theme from 'Fastlane') / The heat (the energy) / Poison / No good (start the dance) / One love (edit) – The narcotic suite / 3 kilos / Skylined / Claustrophobic sting.

Sep 94. (12"ep)(cd-ep) **VOODOO PEOPLE (original mix) / VOODOO PEOPLE (Dust Brothers mix) / VOODOO PEOPLE** (12"= Haiti Island mix / cd= edit) / GOA (THE HEAT, THE ENERGY PART 2) [13] [ ]

Mar 95. (c-s) **POISON ('95) / ('A'-Rat Poison mix) / SCIENIDE** [15] [ ]
(12"+=)(cd-s+=) – ('A'-Environmental science dub mix).

PROFESSIONALS (see under ⇒ SEX PISTOLS)

PROPAGANDA

Formed: Dusseldorf, Germany ... 1983 by DORPER, who recruited MERTENS, plus girls BRUCKEN and FREYTAG. Signed to Paul Morley & Trevor Horn's 'ZTT' label, and with promotion from Channel 4's 'The Tube', their debut single 'DR.MABUSE', cracked the UK Top 30 in 1984. • **Style:** Rhythmic and heavily synthesized outfit, initially influenced by KRAFTWERK and The HUMAN LEAGUE. • **Songwriters:** DORPER composed except covers; DISCIPLINE (Throbbing Gristle) / SORRY FOR LAUGHING (Josef K) / FEMME FATALE (Velvet Underground). • **Trivia:** The track DREAM WITHIN A DREAM contained a poem by Edgar Allan Poe.

Recommended: A SECRET WISH (*7).

RALF DORPER

Operation Twilight / not issued

Nov 82. (12"ep) **RALF DORPER'S ERASERHEAD** [ ] [-]
– Dizziplin / Assault / Lorelia.

PROPAGANDA

were formed by **DORPER** (b.11 Jan'60) – instruments / **MICHAEL MERTENS** (b.23 Oct'63) – keyboards, synth. (ex-DUSSELDORF SYMPHONY) / **SUSANNE FREYTAG** – synthesizers, vocals / **CLAUDIA BRUCKEN** (b.12 Dec'63) – vocals (ex-TOPPOLINOS) / with **ANDREAS THEIN** – tapes

ZTT-Island / Island

Mar 84. (7") **DR.MABUSE. / DR.MABUSE DER SPIELER (instrumental)** [27] [ ]
(12") – Das testaments des Mabuse / Femme fatale (the woman with the orchid) / The 9th life (of Dr.Mabuse).
(12") – The 13th life of Dr.Mabuse / Das testaments des Mabuse.
(c-s) – ('A'side) / Das testaments . . . / The last word.

— Now a quartet when ANDREAS bailed out.

Apr 85. (7")(7"sha-pic-d) **DUEL. / JEWEL** [21] [ ]
(d7"+=) – Lied / The lesson.
(12") – Duel (bittersweet). / Jewel (cut rough).
(some copies of above version incl.free 12") – Dr.Mabuse
(12")(c-s) – Do well (mixes of single) / Wonder.

Jul 85. (lp)(c)(cd) **A SECRET WISH** [16] [ ]
– Dream within a dream / The murder of love / Duel / P-machinery / Sorry for laughing / Dr. Mabuse (first life) / The chase / The last word / Strength to dream. *(cd+=) – Frozen faces. (re-iss.cd/c May94)*

Aug 85. (7")(7"clear) **P-MACHINERY. / FROZEN FACES** [50] [ ]
(12")(12"clear) – ('A' Polish). / ('A'passive) / ('B'side).
(12")(c-s) – P-Machinery (beta). / Extracts from complete machinery. *(re-iss.Dec85 with different versions)*

Nov 85. (m-lp)(c) **WISHFUL THINKING** (remixes) [82] [ ]
– Abused / Machined / Laughed / Loving / Jewelled / Loved / Abuse / Thought. *(re-iss.cd+c May94)*

— Split late 1986, when CLAUDIA married ZTT boss Paul Morley. She made one-off single with GLENN GREGORY (of HEAVEN 17) before forming ACT with soloist THOMAS LEER. **PROPAGANDA** re-formed in 1989 with **DORPER** bringing in **BETSY MILLER** – vocals / **DEREK FORBES** – bass (ex-SIMPLE MINDS)

Virgin / Virgin

Apr 90. (7")(c-s) **HEAVEN GIVE ME WORDS. / COUNT ZERO** [36] [ ]
(12")(cd-s) – (2 different versions)

May 90. (cd)(c)(lp) **1 2 3 4** [46] [ ]
– Vicious circle / Heaven give me words / Your wildlife / Only one word / How much love / Vicious (reprise) / Ministry of fear / Wound in my heart / La carne, la morte e il diavolo.

Aug 90. (7")(c-s) **ONLY ONE WORD. / LA CARTE, LA MORTE E IL DIAVOLO** [71] [ ]

(12"+=)(cd-s+=) – ('A'extended).

Seven / not issued

Jul 95. (12")(cd-s) **P-MACHINERY. / ('A'mixes)** [ ] [-]

PSYCHEDELIC FURS

Formed: London, England ... 1977 by RICHARD and TIM BUTLER, etc (see below). After a Radio 1 John Peel session, they signed to 'Epic-CBS' in 1978. In 1980, they dented the UK Top 20 album charts with self-titled debut, which featured the classic 45 'SISTER EUROPE'. They soon moved to New York and continued to have run of UK Top 30 album successes, until the late 80's when another comeback album 'BOOK OF DAYS', failed miserably. • **Style:** Post-punk alternative rock band, fronted by BOWIE / IGGY POP clone RICHARD BUTLER. • **Songwriters:** RICHARD BUTLER + FURS, except MACK THE KNIFE (Bobby Darin). • **Trivia:** TODD RUNDGREN produced their 1982 'FOREVER NOW' album.

Recommended: THE PSYCHEDELIC FURS (*8) / TALK TALK TALK (*7) / FOREVER NOW (*7) / ALL OF THIS AND NOTHING (*7).

RICHARD BUTLER – vocals / **JOHN ASHTON** – lead guitar / **ROGER MORRIS** – guitar / **TIM BUTLER** – bass / **DUNCAN KILBURN** – saxophone, keyboards / **VINCE ELY** – drums (ex-UNWANTED)

Epic / not issued

Oct 79. (7") **WE LOVE YOU. / PULSE** [ ] [ ]

C.B.S. / Columbia

Feb 80. (7") **SISTER EUROPE. / ****** [ ] [ ]

Mar 80. (lp)(c) **THE PSYCHEDELIC FURS** [18] [ ]
– India / Sister Europe / Imitation of Christ / Fall / Pulse / We love you / Wedding song / Blacks / Radio / Flowers. *(re-iss.Mar83) (cd-iss.Apr89)*

Oct 80. (7") **MR.JONES. / SUSAN'S STRANGE** [ ] [ ]

Apr 81. (7") **DUMB WAITERS. / DASH** [59] [ ]

May 81. (lp)(c) **TALK TALK TALK** [30] [89]
– Dumb waiters / Pretty in pink / I wanna sleep with you / No tears / Mr. Jones / Into you like a train / It goes on / So run down / All of this and nothing / She is mine. *(re-iss.Nov84, cd-iss.Apr89)*

Jun 81. (7")(7"pic-d) **PRETTY IN PINK. / MACK THE KNIFE** [43] [ ]
(12"+=) – Soap commercial.

— **PHIL CALVERT** – drums (ex-BIRTHDAY PARTY) repl. ELY (to ROBYN HITCHCOCK)

Jul 82. (7") **LOVE MY WAY. / AEROPLANE (dance mix)** [42] [-]

Sep 82. (lp)(c) **FOREVER NOW** [20] [61]
– Love my way / President Gas / Sleep comes down / Forever now / Danger / You and I / Run and run / Merry-go-round / Goodbye / No easy street. *(c+=) – Shadow. (re-iss.Apr86)*

Oct 82. (7") **DANGER. / (I DON'T WANT TO BE YOUR) SHADOW** [ ] [ ]
(12"+=) – Goodbye (mix).

Jan 83. (7") **LOVE MY WAY. / SHADOW** [-] [44]

May 83. (7") **PRESIDENT GAS. / RUN AND RUN** [-] [ ]

— **KEITH FORSEY** – drums repl. CALVERT who joined CRIME & THE CITY SOLUTION / **MARS WILLIAMS** – saxophone (ex-WAITRESSES) repl. KILBURN + MORRIS

Mar 84. (7")(12") **HEAVEN. / HEARTBEAT (remix)** [29] [-]

May 84. (lp)(c) **MIRROR MOVES** [15] [43]
– The ghost in you / Here come cowboys / Heaven / Heartbeat / My time / Like a stranger / Alice's house / Only a game / Highwire days. *(re-iss.+cd.Jan87) (re-iss.cd+c Jun94 on 'Columbia')*

May 84. (7")(7"pic-d) **THE GHOST IN YOU. / CALYPSO DUB** [68] [59]
(12"+=) – President Gas (live).

Jul 84. (7") **HERE COME COWBOYS. / ANOTHER EDGE** [-] [ ]

Sep 84. (7") **HEAVEN. / ALICE'S HOUSE** [-] [ ]

Oct 84. (7")(12") **HEARTBEAT (Mendelssohn mix). / MY TIME** [ ] [ ]
(d7"+=) – Here comes cowboys / Heaven.

— **PAUL GARISTO** – drums repl. DORSEY. (below 45 on 'A&M' US)

Aug 86. (7")(7"pic-d) **PRETTY IN PINK (film version). / LOVE MY WAY** [18] [-]
(12"+=)/ /(d7"+=) – ('A'version)./ / Heaven / Heartbeat.

Oct 86. (7") **HEARTBREAK BEAT. / NEW DREAM** [ ] [26] Mar 87
(12"+=) – ('A'version).
(free c-s w/7"+=) – Sister Europe / Into you like a train / President Gas.

Jan 87. (7") **ANGELS DON'T CRY. / NO RELEASE** [ ] [ ]
(12"+=) – ('A'version).
(free c-s w/7"+=) – We love you / Pretty in pink / Love my way.

Feb 87. (lp)(c)(cd) **MIDNIGHT TO MIDNIGHT** [12] [29]
– Heartbreak beat / Shock / Shadow in my heart / Angels don't cry / Midnight to midnight / One more word / Torture / All of the law / No release * / Petty in pink. *(cd+= *) (re-iss.Feb89)*

Apr 87. (7") **SHOCK. / PRESIDENT GAS (live)** [-] [ ]

Jun 87. (7") **ANGEL'S DON'T CRY. / MACK THE KNIFE** [-] [ ]

— **VINCE ELY** – drums returned to repl. GARISTO (to CURE) + WILLIAMS

Jul 88. (7") **ALL THAT MONEY WANTS. / BIRDLAND** [75] [ ]
(12"+=) – No easy street (live).
(d7"++=)/ /(cd-s++=) – Heaven (live)./ / No tears (live).

Aug 88. (lp)(c)(cd) **ALL OF THIS AND NOTHING** (compilation) [67] [ ]
– President Gas / All that money wants / Imitation of Christ / Sister Europe / Love my way / Highwire days / Dumb waiters / Pretty in pink / Ghost in you / Heaven / Heartbreak beat / All of this and nothing. *(cd+=) – No easy street / She is mine. (re-iss.cd,c.Apr91)*

Nov 88. (7") **HEAVEN. / INDIA** [-] [ ]

Nov 89. (lp)(c)(cd) **BOOK OF DAYS** [74] [ ]
– Entertain me / Book of days / Should God forget / Torch / Parade / Mother-son / House / Wedding / I don't mine.

Jan 90. (7")(7"pic-d) **HOUSE. / WATCHTOWER** [ ] [ ]

(12"+=) – ('A'versions).
(10"+=)(cd-s+=) – Badman / Torch (electric).

— **BUTLER, ASHTON + BUTLER** recruited **DON YALLITCH** – drums repl. ELY

East West | Epic

Jun 91. (7")(c-s) **UNTIL SHE COMES. / MAKE IT MINE**
(12"+=)(cd-s+=) – Sometimes (US; b-side) / ('A'remix).

Jul 91. (cd)(c)(lp) **WORLD OUTSIDE** | 68 |
– Valentine / In my head / Until she comes / Don't be a girl / Sometimes / Tearing down / There's a world / Get a room / Better days / All about you. *(re-iss.cd Feb95)*

Sep 91. (7")(c-s) **DON'T BE A GIRL. / GET A ROOM (acoustic)**
(12"+=)(cd-s+=) – (2 'A'versions).

– other compilations, etc. –

Nov 82. CBS; (c-ep) **GREATEST ORIGINAL HITS** | – |
– Sister Europe / Pretty in pink / Dumb waiters / Love my way. *(re-iss.Mar83.as 7"ep.)*

Sep 86. CBS; (c-ep) **THE 12" TAPE** | – |
– Pretty in pink / Love my way / Heaven / Heartbeat / Ghost in you.

Jan 92. CBS; (7") **PRETTY IN PINK. / ('B'by 'Only Ones')** | – |
(cd-s+=) – (other track by Only Ones).

May 95. Columbia; (cd) **B SIDES AND LOST GROOVES** | – |

LOVE SPIT LOVE

RICHARD BUTLER – vocals / **RICHARD FORTUS** – guitar / TIM BUTLER – bass / drums?

Imago-RCA | Imago-RCA

Oct 94. (cd)(c)(lp) **LOVE SPIT LOVE**
– Seventeen / Superman / Half a life / Jigsaw / Change in the weather / Wake up / Am I wrong / Green / Please / Codeine / St. Mary's gate / More.

Oct 94. (c-s)(cd-s) **AM I WRONG. /** | – | 83 |

PUBLIC ENEMY

Formed: New York, USA . . . 1984 by CHUCK D and co-producer & future co-manager WILLIAM SHOCKLEE, who mixed some tapes for co-(as said) BILL STEPNEY. In 1986, 'Def Jam' owner Rick Rubin, signed CHUCK D and others (see below). Their debut self-titled single, hit the shops early in '87. By the end of the year, their 3rd single 'REBEL WITHOUT A PAUSE', cracked the UK Top 40. In 1990, they at last crossed over from R&B charts to mainstream US Top 10 with album 'FEAR OF A BLACK PLANET'. • **Style:** Pro-black urban rappers/samplers, who remonstrated white authoritarism with violent anthemic lyrics, on and off record. • **Songwriters:** CHUCK D, with managers SHOCKLEE and STEPNEY, taking mostly samples from JAMES BROWN. • **Miscellaneous:** PROFESSOR GRIFF (whose father was killed by the Ku Klux Klan when he was a boy), was sacked from the band in mid-89, after allegedly making an anti-Semetic statement to Washington Times.

Recommended: YO! BUM RUSH THE SHOW (*9) / IT TAKES A NATION OF MILLIONS TO HOLD US BACK (*10) / FEAR OF A BLACK PLANET (*10) / APOCALYPSE 91 . . .THE ENEMY STRIKES BACK (*8)

CHUCK D (b.CARLTON RIDENHOUR, 1960) – vocals / **FLAVOR FLAV** (b.WILLIAM DRAYTON) – multi-instrumentalist, classically trained pianist / **TERMINATOR X** (b.NORMAN RODGERS) – DJ / **PROFESSOR GRIFF** (b.RICHARD GRIFFIN) – vocals / plus part-time **JAMES ALLEN + JAMES NORMAN**
(Please note they never released a 7" in US)

Def Jam | Def Jam

Mar 87. (7") **PUBLIC ENEMY No.1. / TIMEBOMB**
(12"+=) – Son of public enemy No.1 ('A'instrumental version).

Apr 87. (lp)(c)(cd) **YO! BUM RUSH THE SHOW**
– You're gonna get yours / Sophisticated bitch / Miuzi weighs a ton / Timebomb / Too much posse / Rightstarter (message to a black man) / Public enemy No.1 / M.P.E. / Yo! bum rush the show / Raise the roof / Megablast / Terminator X speaks with his hands. *(re-iss.cd+c Sep93 & Jul95)*

Jun 87. (7") **YOU'RE GONNA GET YOURS. / MUIZI WEIGHS A TON**
(12"+=) – ('A'dub) / ('A' terminator X mix) / Rebel without a pause.

Nov 87. (7") **REBEL WITHOUT A PAUSE (vocal). / ('A'instrumental)** | 37 | – |
(12"+=)(cd-s+=) – Terminator X speaks with his hands / Sophisticated bitch.

Dec 87. (12") **ARE YOU MY WOMAN? (by "The BLACK FLAMES") / BRING THE NOISE** | – |
(12"+=) – ('A'noise version) / ('A'a cappella mix).

Jan 88. (7") **BRING THE NOISE. / SOPHISTICATED BITCH** | 32 | – |
(12"+=) – ('A'noise version) / ('A'accapella version).

Jun 88. (7") **DON'T BELIEVE THE HYPE. / PROPHETS OF RAGE** | 18 |
(12"+=) – Rhythm & the rebel (accapella) / ('B'power version).
(cd-s+=) – Bring the noise / ('B'power version).

Jul 88. (lp)(c)(cd) **IT TAKES A NATION OF MILLIONS TO HOLD US BACK** | 8 | 42 |
– Countdown to armageddon / Bring the noise / Don't believe the hype / Cold lampin' with Flavor / Terminator X to the edge of panic / Mind terrorist / Louder than a bomb / Caught, can we get a witness? / Show 'em whatcha got / She watch Channel Zero?! / Night of the living baseheads / Black steel in the hour of chaos / Security of the first world / Rebel without a pause / Prophets of rage / Party for your right to fight. *(re-iss.cd Jul95)*

Oct 88. (7") **NIGHT OF THE LIVING BASEHEADS. / TERMINATOR X TO THE EDGE OF PANIC (or) ('A' instrumental version)** | 63 |
(12"+=)/ /(cd-s+=) – (all 3) / / ('A'anti-high blood . . . mix).
(US-12"+=) – Cold lampin' with Flavor.

1989. (12") **BLACK STEEL IN THE HOUR OF CHAOS (radio version) / ('A' instrumental). / TOO MUCH POSSE / CAUGHT, CAN I GET A WITNESS (dub mix) / B-SIDE WINS AGAIN** | – |

Jun 89. (7")(c-s) **FIGHT THE POWER. / ('A'version)** | 29 |
('A'ext-12"+=)(cd-s+=) – ('A'Flavor meets Spike Lee mix).

— (above was issued in the States on a one-off 'Motown' deal).

Jan 90. (7")(c-s) **WELCOME TO THE TERRORDOME. / ('A'terromental version)** | 18 |
(12"+=) – Black steel in the hour of chaos.
(cd-s+=) – Terrorbeat.

— Trimmed when PROFESSOR GRIFF left permanently to go solo. He soon released debut 'PAWNS IN THE GAME' with his LAST ASIATIC DISCIPLES. A year later he followed this with second album 'KAD'S II WIZ *7* DOME'.

Apr 90. (7")(c-s) **911 IS A JOKE. / REVOLUTIONARY GENERATION** | 41 |
(12"+=)(cd-s+=) – ('A'&'B'instrumentals).
(12") – ('A'side) / Son of Public Enemy / Bring the noise / Rebel without a pause.

Apr 90. (cd)(c)(lp) **FEAR OF A BLACK PLANET** | 4 | 10 |
– Contract on the world love jam / Brothers gonna work it out / 911 is a joke / Incident at 66.6 FM / Welcome to the terrordome / Meet the G that killed me / Pollywanacraka / Anti-nigger machine / Burn Hollywood burn / Power to the people / Who stole the soul / Fear of a black planet / Revolutionary generation / Can't do nuttin' for ya man / Reggae Jax / Leave this off your fuckin' charts / B side wins again / War at 33 1/3 / Final count of the collision between us and the damned. *(re-iss.cd Jul95)*

Jun 90. (7")(c-s) **BROTHERS GONNA WORK IT OUT (remix). / WAR AT 33 1/3** | 46 |
(12"+=) – Bring the noise (no noise instrumental) / ('B'instrumental).
(cd-s+=) – Anti-nigger machine / Don't believe the hype.

Oct 90. (7")(c-s) **CAN'T DO NUTTIN' FOR YA MAN. / ('A'version)** | 53 |
(12"+=)(cd-s+=) – ('A'full rub mix).
(12") – ('A'version) / Get the f . . . out of Dodge (uncensured) / Powersave / Burn Hollywood burn.

— added **SISTER SOULJAH** – vocals

— (May91) FLAVOR FLAV served 30 days in jail for an earlier incident in which he hit the mother of his 3 children Karen Ross.

— Jun91, teamed up with ANTHRAX on a hit single version of 'BRING THE NOISE'.

Sep 91. (7")(c-s) **CAN'T TRUSS IT (new bootleg mix). / ('A'radio mix)** | 22 | 50 |
(cd-s+=) – Move (censored radio mix).
(12"++=) – ('A'instrumental).

Oct 91. (cd)(c)(d-lp) **APOCALYPSE 91 . . .THE ENEMY STRIKES BACK** | 8 | 4 |
– Lost at birth / Rebirth / Night train / Can't truss it / I don't wanna be called yo niga / How to kill a radio consultant / By the time I get to Arizona / Move! / 1 million bottlebags / More news at 11 / Shut 'em down / A letter to the New York post / Get the f . . . outta Dodge / Bring the noise (w/ ANTHRAX). *(re-iss.cd Jul95)*

Jan 92. (7")(c-s) **SHUT 'EM DOWN (remix). / BY THE TIME I GET TO ARIZONA** | 21 |
(12"+=)(cd-s+=)(12"pic-d+=) – ('A'rock mixx instrumental) / ('A'bald beat acapella) / ('B'side dubbed).

Mar 92. (7")(c-s) **NIGHT TRAIN (mixx). / MORE NEWS AT 11 (mixx)** | 55 |
(12"+=)(cd-s+=)(12"pic-d+=) – ('A'funk mixx) / ('A'instrumental mixx).

Sep 92. (cd)(c)(d-lp) **GREATEST MISSES DON'T MISS IT** | 14 | 13 |
– Tie goes to the runner / Hitt da road Jack / Get off my back / Air hoodlum got ta do what I gotta do / Hazy shade of criminal megablast (remix) / Louder than a bomb (telephone groove) / How to kill a radio consultant (DJ check chillout..) / Who stole the soul (mixx) / Party for your right to fight (metromix) / You're gonna get yours (version). (cd+=) – Shut 'em down (live in the UK). *(re-iss.cd Jul95)*

— PROFESSOR GRIFF, TERMINATOR X, and newcomer SISTER SOULJAH all had own releases for various labels from 1990 onwards.

FLAVOR FLAV was charged late '93, for drunkenly attempting to shoot his neighbour, after he allegedly thought his wife was committing adultery.

Aug 94. (12"ep)(c-ep)(cd-ep) **GIVE IT UP. / ('A'-main version) / ('A'-bedlam instrumental)** | 18 | 33 | Jul94
(cd-s+=) – Live and undrugged (part 2) / Harry Allen interactive highway / Bedlam instrumental.

Aug 94. (cd)(c) **MUSE SICK-N-HOUR MESS AGE** | 12 | 14 |
– Whole lotta love / Theatrical / Give it up / What side you on? / Body count / Stop in the name / What kind of power we got? / So watcha gone do now? / White Heaven – black Hell / Race against time / Used to call it dope / Aintnuthin' buttersong / Live & undrugged parts I & II / I ain't madd at all / Death of carjacka / I stand accused / Gold complexx / Hitler day / Harry Allen superhighway.

Nov 94. (12"ep)(cd-ep) **I STAND ACCUSED / WHAT KIND OF POWER WE GOT**
(cd-s+=) – I stand accused (Sleek'sschool of self-defence mix) / Mao Tse Tung.

— On 26th May'95, FLAVOR was jailed for drug possession. He was sent to a rehab centre and given three years probation. While in Italy in July, he broke his leg in a motorcycle accident.

Jul 95. (c-s) **SO WHATCHA GONNA DO NOW? / BLACK STEEL IN THE HOUR OF CHAOS** | 50 |
(12"+=)(cd-s+=) – ('A'-Drive by s**t mix) / ('A'-Drive by inst.).

– compilations, etc. –

Mar 93. Def Jam; (cd)(c) **THE 12" MIXES**

PUBLIC IMAGE LTD.

Formed: London, England . . . Jul'78 by ex-SEX PISTOLS singer JOHNNY ROTTEN who reverted to his real name JOHN LYDON. He recruited local friends KEITH LEVENE, JAH WOBBLE and Canadian JIM WALKER, and re-signed to 'Virgin'. Their near self-titled debut 45, which was wrapped in a mock-newspaper cover, reached the UK Top 10 late 1978, and preceeded an eponymous Top 30 album. A year later, they issued 'METAL BOX 1',

which was packaged as three 12" 45's inside a metal box. It reached No.18, and when re-issued in normal format 2 months later, even managed a Top 50 placing. LYDON and various line-ups continued to score in the charts, but things slowed down in 1983, when he moved to New York. That year, he had also starred alongside Harvey Keitel in the film 'Out Of Order' (US title 'Cop Killer'). • **Style:** LYDON quickly abandoned initial punk rock sound, for more Eastern influenced experimental alternative rock. His cynical yet poignant attitude, had been both a commercial asset and a put off for many, but no one can deny his phenomanal contribution to rock, both in the PISTOLS and PIL. • **Songwriters:** LYDON and PIL compositions. • **Trivia:** On 13 Feb'80, LYDON's home was raided by police, who found virtually nothing. 8 months later in Ireland, he was arrested for assault. He was sentenced to 3 months imprisonment, but was acquited on appeal.

Recommended: PUBLIC IMAGE (*9) / METAL BOX 1 (*10) / GREATEST HITS – SO FAR (*9).

JOHN LYDON (b.31 Jan'56, Finsbury Park, London) – vocals (ex-SEX PISTOLS) / **KEITH LEVENE** – guitar (ex-CLASH) / **JAH WOBBLE** (b.JOHN WORDLE) – bass / **JIM WALKER** – drums (ex-FURIES) (most singles just credit "PIL")

Virgin Island

Oct 78. (7") **PUBLIC IMAGE. / THE COWBOY SONG** 9 —
Dec 78. (lp)(c) **PUBLIC IMAGE** 22 —
– Theme / Religion I / Religion II / Annalisa / Public image / Low life / Attack / Fodderstompf. *(re-iss.Apr86) (cd-iss.Oct86)*

— **DAVE CROWE** – drums repl. WALKER who joined The PACK (with KIRK BRANDON) added **JEANNETTE LEE** – keyboards, synthesizer

Jun 79. (7") **DEATH DISCO. / NO BIRDS DO SING** 20 —
(12") – ('A'extended) / Megamix (Fodderstompf remixed).
Sep 79. (7")('A'ext-12") **MEMORIES. / ANOTHER** 60 —
Nov 79. (3x12"lp-box) **METAL BOX 1** 18 —
– Albatross / Memories / Swan lake/ / Poptones / Careering / No birds / Graveyard / / The suit / Bad baby / Socialist – Chant – Radio 4. *(cd-iss.Jun90) (re-iss.Jan80 as d-lp/c- 'SECOND EDITION', hit No.46) (cd-iss.Jun87)*

— **RICHARD DUDANSKI** – drums (ex-101'ERS, ex-BASEMENT 5) repl. CROWE (above had joined during Apr-Sep'79) (below French titles of above songs)

Nov 80. (lp)(c) **PARIS AU PRINTEMPS (live 'PARIS IN THE SPRING')** 61 —
– Theme / Psalmodie (Chant) / Precipitamment (Careering) / Sale bebe (Bad baby) / La vie ignoble (Low life) / Attaque (Attack) / Timbres de pop (Poptones). *(re-iss.Mar84)*

— (Jul80) Trimmed to a quartet when JAH WOBBLE went solo. / **MARTIN ATKINS** (b. 3 Aug'59, Coventry, England) (aka BRIAN BRAIN) – drums repl. DUDANSKI who joined RAINCOATS. (ATKINS was sacked Jul80, most of drums by LYDON and LEVENE) . ('B'side recorded 1978)

Virgin Warner

Mar 81. (7") **FLOWERS OF ROMANCE. / HOME IS WHERE THE HEART IS** 24 —
(12"+=) – ('A'instrumental).
Apr 81. (lp)(c) **FLOWERS OF ROMANCE** 11 —
– Four enclosed walls / Track 8 / Phenagen / Flowers of romance / Under the house / Hymie's him / Banging the door / Go back / Francis massacre. *(re-iss. Mar84, cd-iss.Apr90) (cd-iss.Mar94)*

— **KEN LOCKIE** – keyboards (ex-COWBOYS INTERNATIONAL, ex-Solo) repl. LEE / added (May82) **MARTIN ATKINS** – drums / **PETE JONES** – bass

Aug 83. (7") **THIS IS NOT A LOVE SONG. / PUBLIC IMAGE** 5 —
(12"+=) – Blue water / ('A'remix). *(cd-ep iss.Jun88)*

— LYDON + ATKINS were joined by US session people from New Jersey; **JOSEPH GUIDA** – guitar / **TOM ZVONCHECK** – keyboards / **LOUIE BERNARDI** – bass

Sep 83. (2xm-lp)(c) **LIVE IN TOKYO (live)** 28 —
– Annalisa / Religion / Low life / Solitaire / Flowers of romance / This is not a love song / Death disco / Bad life / Banging the door / Under the house. *(cd-iss.1986)*
May 84. (7")('A'ext-12") **BAD LIFE. / QUESTION MARK** 71 —
Jul 84. (lp)(c) **THIS IS WHAT YOU WANT . . . THIS IS WHAT YOU GET** 56 —
– Bad life / This is not a love song / Solitaire / Tie me to the length of that / The pardon / Where are you? / 1981 / The order of death. *(re-iss.1986, cd-iss.Apr90)* (US-iss.Aug84 as 'COMMERCIAL ZONE' by "KEITH LEVENE & PIL").

— Disbanded mid'84, but reformed by LYDON late '85 with on session **STEVE VAI** – guitar (ex-ALCATRAZZ) / **RYUICHI SAKAMOTO** – keys (ex-YELLOW MAGIC ORCHESTRA) / **GINGER BAKER** (ex-CREAM, etc) / **TONY WILLIAMS** (ex-MILES DAVIES, etc) / **RAVI SHANKER** – violin

Virgin Elektra

Jan 86. (7")(12") **SINGLE ('RISE'). / ('A'instrumental)** 11 —
Feb 86. (lp)(c)(cd) **ALBUM (CASSETTE / COMPACT DISC)** 14 —
– FFF / Rise / Fishing / Round / Bags / Home / Ease. *(re-iss.1989)*
Apr 86. (7") **HOME. / ROUND** 75 —
(12"+=) – ('A'-lp version).
(d7"+=) – Rise / ('A'instrumental).

— (Feb86) **LYDON** recruited **LU EDMUNDS** – guitar, keys (ex-DAMNED, ex-MEKONS) / **JOHN McGEOGH** – guitar (of ARMOURY SHOW, ex-SIOUXSIE & THE BANSHEES) / **ALAN DIAS** – bass / **BRUCE SMITH** – drums (ex-RIP, RIG & PANIC, ex-SLITS, ex-POP GROUP)

Virgin Virgin

Aug 87. (7") **SEATTLE. / SELFISH RUBBISH** 47 —
(12"+=)(c-s+=) – The suit.
Sep 87. (lp)(c)(cd) **HAPPY?** 40 —
– Seattle / Rules and regulations / The body / Save me / Hard times / Open and revolving / Angry / Fat chance hotel.
Oct 87. (7") **THE BODY. / RELIGION (new version)** — —
(12"+=) – Angry.
(12") – ('A'extended remix). / ('A'-US remix) / Angry.

— trimmed to a quartet when EDMUNDS dispersed.

Apr 89. (7") **DISAPPOINTED. / SAME OLD STORY** 38 —
('A'ext-12"+=)(12"pic-d+=)(3"cd-s+=) – ('A'version).
Jun 89. (lp)(c)(cd) **9** 36 —
– Happy / Disappointed / Warrior / U.S.L.S. 1 / Sand castles in the snow / Worry / Brave new world / Like that / Same old story / Armada.
Jul 89. (7") **WARRIOR (edit). / U.S.L.S. 1** — —
('A'extended-12"+=) – ('A'instrumental).
(3"cd-s+=) – ('A'extended).
(12") – ('A'-Dave Dorrell remix). / ('A'instrumental)
Oct 90. (7")(c-s) **DON'T ASK ME. / RULES AND REGULATIONS** 22 —
(12") – ('A'extended) / Warrior (remix).
(cd-s+=) – Warrior (original).
Oct 90. (cd)(c)(lp) **GREATEST HITS – SO FAR** (compilation) 20 —
– Public image / Death disco / Memories / Careering / Flowers of romance / This is not a love song / Rise / Home / The body / Rules and regulations / Disappointed / Warrior / Don't ask me / Seattle.

— **MIKE JOYCE** – drums (ex-SMITHS, ex-BUZZCOCKS) repl. BRUCE

P.I.L.

Feb 92. (7")**CRUEL. / LOVE HOPE** 49 —
(cd-s+=)/ /(10"+=) – Rise (live) / Home (live)./ / Happy (live).
Feb 92. (cd)(c)(lp) **THAT WHAT IS NOT** 46 —
– Acid drops / Lucks up / Cruel / God / Covered / Love hope / Unfairground / Think tank / Emperor / Good things.

— In Nov'93, LYDON was credited on acclaimed dance hit & UK No.19 'Open Up' by LEFTFIELD / LYDON on 'Hard Hands' records.

— Stop press:- Early '96, JOHN LYDON (ROTTEN) re-grouped with The SEX PISTOLS for summer tours in Britain, Europe and America.

PULP

Formed: Sheffield, England . . . 1981 originally as ARABACUS PULP by JARVIS COCKER. In the mid-80's after release of 'IT' debut mini-lp, JARVIS was confined to a wheel-chair for a year, after falling from a window. They were releasing material for 'Fire' around this time and finally released first full album 'FREAKS' in 1987. Most of the band moved to London in the late 80's and it wasn't long before the enigmatic JARVIS and crew were on the roster of 'Island' and in chartland. • **Style:** A fusion between LEONARD COHEN and The FALL in their early days to mid-80's; MONOCHROME SET, ULTRAVOX! (John Foxx era). Later with fashion (aka Bri-Nylon, glitter-boots, early 70's), COCKER was to become a star on the same scale as BRETT ANDERSON (Suede) and LAWRENCE (ex-Felt; now Denim). • **Songwriters:** COCKER + SIMON HINKLER collaborated on debut. COCKER, SENIOR, C.DOYLE, MANSELL penned, until 90's when COCKER was main contributor. • **Trivia:** COCKER and MACKAY directed videos for TINDERSTICKS and The AMPHEX TWINS.

— **Note:** Not to be confused with other band fronted by ANDY BEAN + PAUL BURNELL, who released in 1979; LOW FLYING AIRCRAFT single.

Recommended: HIS 'N' HERS (*9) / DIFFERENT CLASS (*9) / MASTERS OF THE UNIVERSE (*7)

JARVIS COCKER (b. Sep'62) – vocals, guitar, piano / **SIMON HINKLER** – keyboards, vocals repl. PETER DALTON / **PETER BOAM** – bass repl. JAMIE PINCHBECK who had repl. DAVID LOCKWOOD / **DAVID HINKLER** – keyboards, trombone / **GARY WILSON** – drums (of ARTERY) repl. WAYNE FURNISS who had repl. JIMMY SELLERS who had repl. MARK SWIFT
plus guests **SASKIA COCKER + GILL TAYLOR** – b.vox / **TIMM ALLCARD** – keyboards.

Red Rhino not issued

Apr 83. (m-lp) **IT** — -
– My lighthouse / Wishful thinking / Joking aside / Boats and trains / Blue girls / Love love / In many ways. *(cd-iss.Mar94 on 'Cherry Red')* (cd+=) – Looking for life / Everybody's problem / There was. *(re-iss.cd Dec94 on 'Fire')* (cd+=) – Looking for life.
May 83. (7") **MY LIGHTHOUSE (remix). / LOOKING FOR LIFE** — -
Sep 83. (7") **EVERYBODY'S PROBLEM. / THERE WAS** — -

— **RUSSELL SENIOR** – guitar, violin, vocals repl. DAVID
CANDIDA DOYLE – keyboards, vocals repl. SIMON who joined ARTERY then the MISSION)

— **MAGNUS DOYLE** – drums repl. GARY, SASKIA, GILL + TIMM

— **PETER MANSELL** – bass repl. BOAM

Fire not issued

Nov 85. (12"ep) **LITTLE GIRL AND OTHER PIECES** — -
– Little girl (with blue eyes) / Simultaneous / Blue glow / The will to power. *(re-iss.Oct91)*
Jun 86. (12"ep) **DOGS ARE EVERYWHERE / THE MARK OF THE DEVIL. / 97 LOVERS / ABORIGINE / GOODNIGHT** — -
(re-iss.Oct91)
Jan 87. (7")(ext-12") **THEY SUFFOCATE AT NIGHT. / TUNNEL** — -
Mar 87. (7")(12") **MASTER OF THE UNIVERSE (sanitised version). / MANON / SILENCE** — -
(re-iss.Oct91)
May 87. (lp) **FREAKS** — -
– Fairground / I want you / Being followed home / Master of the universe / Life must be so wonderful / There's no emotion / Anorexic beauty / The never ending story / Don't you know / They suffocate at night. *(cd-iss.Apr93)*

— **STEPHEN MACKAY** – bass repl. STEPHEN HAVENLAND who had repl. PETER

— **NICHOLAS BANKS** – drums, percussion repl. MAGNUS

Sep 90. (12"ep) **MY LEGENDARY GIRLFRIEND. / IS THIS HOUSE? / THIS HOUSE IS CONDEMNED** — -

(re-iss.Oct91)

Aug 91. (12"ep)(cd-ep) **COUNTDOWN. / DEATH GOES TO THE DISCO / COUNTDOWN (edit)** [ ] [-]
(re-iss.Oct91)

Oct 91. (cd)(c)(lp) **SEPARATIONS** [ ] [-]
– Love is blind / Don't you want me anymore / She's dead / Separations / Down by the river / Countdown / My legendary girlfriend / Death II / This house is condemned. *(re-iss.Jun92)*

Gift | not issued

May 92. (12"ep)(cd-ep) **O.U. (GONE GONE) / SPACE / O.U. (GONE GONE) (radio edit)** [ ] [-]

Oct 92. (12"ep)(cd-ep) **BABIES. / STYLOROC (NIGHTS OF SUBURBIA) / SHEFFIELD** – SEX CITY [ ] [-]

Feb 93. (12"ep)(cd-ep) **RAZZAMATAZZ. / MEDLEY (abridged)** [ ] [-]

Island | Island

Oct93. (cd)(c)(lp) **INTRO** – THE GIFT RECORDINGS [ ] [-]
– Space / Ou (gone gone) / Babies / Styloroc (nights of suburbia) / Razzamatazz / Sheffield-Sex city / Medley of stacks: Inside Susan (a story in 3 songs) Stacks – Inside Susan – 59 Lyndhurst Grove.

Nov 93. (7") **LIPGLOSS. / YOU'RE A NIGHTMARE** [50] [ ]
(12"+=)(cd-s+=) – Deep fried in Kelvin.

Mar 94. (7")(c-s) **DO YOU REMEMBER THE FIRST TIME?. / STREET LITES** [33] [ ]
(12"+=)(cd-s+=) – Babysitter.

Apr 94. (cd)(c)(lp) **HIS'N'HERS** [9] [ ]
– Joyriders / Lipgloss / Acrylic afternoons / Have you seen her lately? / She's a lady / Happy endings / Do you remember the first time? / Pink glove / Someone like the Moon / David's last summer.(cd,c+=) – Babies (remix).

May 94. (7"ep)(12"ep)(cd-ep) **THE SISTERS EP** [19] [ ]
– Babies / Your sister's clothes / Seconds / His'n'hers.

May 95. (c-s)(cd-s) **COMMON PEOPLE / UNDERWEAR** [2] [ ]
(cd-s) – ('A'side) / Razzmatazz (acoustic) / Dogs are everywhere (acoustic) / Joy-riders (acoustic).

—— Below second side (double A) caused controversy with tabloids and parents, due to it's mis-use of drugs in JARVIS's lyrics. JARVIS was to become the hero to most and villain to the few early in 1996 at a certain awards ceremony (skinny J.C. vs. St.MICHAEL & the bouncers; who won – you decide).

Sep 95. (c-s) **MIS-SHAPES / SORTED FOR E'S AND WIZZ** [2] [ ]
(cd-s+=) P.T.A. (Parent Teacher Association) / Common people (live at Glastonbury).
(cd-s+=) – Common people (Motiv8 mix).

Oct 95. (cd)(c)(lp) **DIFFERENT CLASS** [1] [ ]
– Mis-shapes / Pencil skirt / Common people / I spy / Disco 2000 / Live bed show / Something changed / Sorted out for E's and wizz / F.E.E.L.I.N.G.S.C.A.L.L.E.D.L.O.V.E. / Underwear / Monday morning / Bar Italia.

Nov 95. (c-s) **DISCO 2000 / ('A'mix)** [7] [ ]
(cd-s+=) – Ansaphone / Live bed show (extended).
(cd-s+=) – ('A'-Motiv8 discoid mixes).

– compilations, etc. –

Jun 94. Fire; (cd)(c)(lp) **MASTERS OF THE UNIVERSE** (1985-86 singles) [ ] [-]
– Little girl (with blue eyes) / Simultaneous / Blue glow / The will to power / Dogs are everywhere / The mark of the Devil / 97 lovers / Aborigine / Goodnight / They suffocate at night / Tunnel / Master of the universe (sanitised version) / Manon.

Jimmy PURSEY (see under ⇒ SHAM 69)

PYRAMID (see under ⇒ MATTHEWS, IAN)

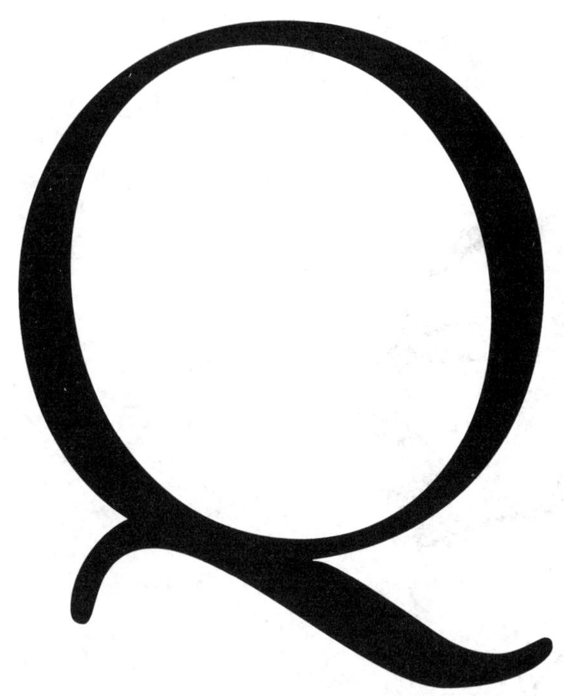

Q-TIPS (see under ⇒ YOUNG, Paul)

QUARTERFLASH

Formed: Portland, Oregon, USA . . . 1980 by husband/wife team MARV and RINDY ROSS, the former having quit teaching in 1977. Originally called SEAFOOD MAMA, until they signed to the David 'Geffen' label in 1981. Their debut 45 'HARDEN MY HEART', found its way to US No.3 by that Christmas, and was followed by an eponymous Top 10 debut album the next year. • **Style:** Mainstream AOR ballad outfit. • **Songwriters:** The ROSS's penned most, except some by CHARLES. • **Trivia:** 1985 album produced by STEVE LEVINE.

Recommended: QUARTERFLASH (*5)

CINDY ROSS – vocals, saxophone / **MARV ROSS** – guitar / **JACK CHARLES** – guitar, vocals / **RICK DiGIALLONARDO** – keyboards / **RICK GOOCH** – bass / **BRIAN WILLIS** – drums

		Geffen	Geffen
Feb 82.	(7") **HARDEN MY HEART. / DON'T BE LONELY**	49	3 Oct 81
Apr 82.	(lp)(c) **QUARTERFLASH**		8 Oct 81
	– Harden my heart / Find another fool / Critical times / Valerie / Try to make it true / Right kind of love / Cruisin' with the deuce / Love should be so kind / Williams Avenue. *(re-iss.Sep86) (cd-iss.1983)*		
Apr 82.	(7") **FIND ANOTHER FOOL. / CRUISIN' WITH THE DEUCE**		16 Feb 82
Aug 82.	(7") **RIGHT KIND OF LOVE. / YOU'RE HOLDING ME BACK**		56 May 82
Aug 82.	(7") **NIGHT SHIFT. / LOVE COULD BE SO KIND**	-	60
	(above 'A' from 'Warners' film of same name)		
Oct 82.	(7") **TRY TO MAKE IT TRUE. / CRITICAL TIMES**	-	
Jun 83.	(7") **TAKE ME TO HEART. / NOWHERE LEFT TO HIDE**		14
Sep 83.	(lp)(c) **TAKE ANOTHER PICTURE**		34 Jul 83
	– Take me to heart / Take another picture / Shane / Eye to eye / It don't move me / Shakin' the jinx / Made it shine / One more round to go / Nowhere left to hide / It all becomes clear. *(re-iss.Sep86)*		
Sep 83.	(7") **TAKE ANOTHER PICTURE. / ONE MORE ROUND TO GO**	-	58

—— trimmed to a quartet, when JACK and RICK bailed out.

Aug 85.	(7") **GRACE UNDER FIRE. / TALK TO ME**	-	
Sep 85.	(lp)(c) **BACK INTO BLUE**		
	– Walking on ice / Caught in the rain / Back into blue / Talk to me / I want to believe it's you / Love without a net / Come to me / Grace under fire / Just for you / Welcome to the city.		
Oct 85.	(7") **WALKING ON ICE. / GRACE UNDER FIRE**		
Oct 85.	(7") **TALK TO ME. / WALKING ON ICE**	-	83

—— Disbanded in 1986. Re-formed in the 90's.

		Epic	Epic
Nov 90.	(7")(c-s) **IS IT ANY WONDER. / ONE LESS LIE**		
	(12"+=)(cd-s+=) – Girl in the wind.		
Feb 92.	(cd)(c)(lp) **GIRL IN THE WIND**		

QUEEN

Formed: London, England . . . early 1971 by MAY, TAYLOR, MERCURY and DEACON. MAY had left school in 1963, with 10 O-levels and joined teenage group The OTHERS, who issued one single 'OH YEAH' for 'Fontana' in 1965. He & TAYLOR formed as SMILE in 1969 and released 45 'EARTH. / STEP ON ME' for 'Mercury US'. After spending most of 1972 in the studio, QUEEN signed to 'EMI' after sending demo tape through engineer John Anthony. In April 1973, they played The Marquee in London, but prior to any QUEEN release, FREDDIE MERCURY (as LARRY LUREX) issued a one-off 45 in Jun'73 for 'EMI'; I CAN HEAR MUSIC. / GOIN' BACK, (the former an old BEACH BOYS number). A month later, QUEEN unleashed similtaneously their eponymous Roy Thomas-Baker produced debut album, and single 'KEEP YOURSELF ALIVE'. In Nov'73, they supported friends to be MOTT THE HOOPLE, and early next year dented the UK Top 10 with 'SEVEN SEAS OF RHYE'. This was quickly followed by 'QUEEN II', which managed a Top 5 placing, thus rendering 'Elektra' records, to give them chance in the States. Became top group by Christmas 1975, when the near 6-minute epic 'BOHEMIAN RHAPSODY', made UK No.1 for record breaking 9 weeks. It was obviously helped by a masterful video, made for just £5,000, and a pioneer of the video-promo age. QUEEN went on to have over 35 Top 50 UK hits over the next 15 years. Tragically FREDDIE MERCURY was to die of AIDS on 23 Nov'91, after just announcing he had the dreaded disease the day before. • **Style:** Initially a LED ZEPPELIN influenced hard-rock act. The flamboyant FREDDIE MERCURY used large range of vox styles (falsetto or aggressive) for tremendous live sets, although it was largely known that he was a shy bi-sexual in real life. MAY also quiet off-stage, used new coin-pick and own custom made guitars to produce own unique sound. • **Songwriters:** Group or individual compositions. MAY covered: SINCE YOU'VE BEEN GONE (Rainbow; c.Russ Ballard). Note: In QUEEN, MAY wrote most of songs, except some by either MERCURY or group. MERCURY covered: THE GREAT PRETENDER (Platters). The CROSS covered FOXY LADY (Jimi Hendrix) and MAY did ROLLIN' OVER (Small Faces). • **Trivia:** In 1987, MAY began relationship with 'Eastenders' actress Anita Dobson. He also produced a few of her solo singles, and sessioned for LIVING IN A BOX.

Recommended: QUEEN (*7) / QUEEN II (*6) / SHEER HEART ATTACK (*7) / QUEEN'S GREATEST HITS (*9) / GREATEST HITS II (*8).

FREDDIE MERCURY (b.FREDERICK BULSARA, 5 Sep'46, Zanzibar, Africa. In 1959, he moved with family to Feltham, Middlesex, England) – vocals, piano / **BRIAN MAY** (b.19 Jul'47, Twickenham, Middlesex) – guitar, vocals, keyboards / **ROGER MEDDOWS-TAYLOR** (b.26 Jul'49, King's Lynn, England) – drums, vocals / **JOHN DEACON** (b.19 Aug'51, Leicester, England) – bass, vocals

		E.M.I.	Elektra
Jul 73.	(7") **KEEP YOURSELF ALIVE. / SON AND DAUGHTER**		
Jul 73.	(lp)(c) **QUEEN** (hit chart Mar74-)	24	83 Oct 73
	– Keep yourself alive / Doing all right / Great King Rat / My fairy king / Liar / The night comes down / Modern times rock'n'roll / Son and daughter / Jesus / Seven seas of rhye. *(US-only last track) (re-iss.Aug82 on 'Fame') (cd-iss.May88 on 'Fame') (US cd-iss.Jun91 on 'Hollywood', +=)*– Mad the swine, keep yourself alive (long lost retake) / Liar (1991 remix) *(re-iss.cd+c Apr94 on 'Parlophone')*		
Nov 73.	(7") **LIAR. / DOING ALL RIGHT**	-	
Feb 74.	(7") **SEVEN SEAS OF RHYE. / SEE WHAT A FOOL I'VE BEEN**	10	
	(re-iss.Nov88 as 3" cd-s, += Funny how love is)		
Mar 74.	(lp)(c) **QUEEN II**	5	49 May 74
	– Procession / Father to son / White queen (as it began) / Some day one day / The loser in the end / Ogre battle / The fairy feller's master-stroke / Nevermore / The march of the black queen / Funny how love is / Seven seas of rhye. *(re-iss.Apr84 on 'Fame', cd-iss.Nov86 + May88) (US cd-iss.Oct91 on 'Hollywood', +=)*– See what a fool I've been / Ogre battle – 1991 remix / Seven seas of rhye – 1991 remix. *(re-iss.cd+c Apr94 on 'Parlophone')*		
Oct 74.	(7") **KILLER QUEEN. / FLICK OF THE WRIST**	2	12 Feb 75
	(re-iss.Nov88 as 3" cd-s, += Brighton rock)		
Nov 74.	(lp)(c)(red-lp) **SHEER HEART ATTACK**	2	12 Dec 74
	– Brighton rock / Killer Queen / Tenement funster / Flick of the wrist / Lily of the valley / Now I'm here / In the lap of the gods / Stone cold crazy / Dear friends / Misfire / Bring back that Leroy Brown / She makes me (stormtrooper in stilettos) / In the lap of the gods (revisited). *(re-iss.1985, cd-iss.Jun88) (US cd-iss.Nov88 on 'Hollywood', +=)*– Stone cold sober – 1991 remix) *(re-iss.cd+c Aug93)*		
Jan 75.	(7") **NOW I'M HERE. / LILY OF THE VALLEY**	11	-
Apr 75.	(7") **LILY OF THE VALLEY. / KEEP YOURSELF ALIVE**	-	
Nov 75.	(7") **BOHEMIAN RHAPSODY. / I'M IN LOVE WITH MY CAR**	1	9 Dec 75
	(re-iss.Nov88 as 3" cd-s, += You're my best friend)		
Dec 75.	(lp)(c) **A NIGHT AT THE OPERA**	1	4
	– Death on two legs (dedicated to . . .) / Lazing on a Sunday afternoon / I'm in love with my car / You're my best friend / '39 / Sweet lady / Seaside rendezvous / The prophet's song / Love of my life / Good company / Bohemian rhapsody / God save the Queen. *(re-iss.1985, cd-iss.Jun88) (US cd-iss.Aug91 on 'Hollywood', +=)*– I'm in love with my car – 1991 remix / You're my best friend – 1991 remix. *(re-iss.cd+c Aug93)*		
Jun 76.	(7") **YOU'RE MY BEST FRIEND. / '39**	7	16 May 76
Nov 76.	(7") **SOMEBODY TO LOVE. / WHITE MAN**	2	13
	(re-iss.Nov88 as 3" cd-s, += Tie your mother down)		
Dec 76.	(lp)(c) **A DAY AT THE RACES**	1	5 Jan 77
	– Tie your mother down / You take my breath away / Long away / The millionaire waltz / You and I / Somebody to love / White man / Good old fashioned lover boy / Drowse / Teo Torriate (let us cling together). *(re-iss.1984, cd-iss.Jun88) (US cd-iss.Mar91 on 'Hollywood', +=)*– Tie your mother down – remix / Somebody to love – remix.		
Mar 77.	(7") **TIE YOUR MOTHER DOWN. / YOU AND I**	31	-
Mar 77.	(7") **TIE YOUR MOTHER DOWN. / DROWSE**	-	49
May 77.	(7"ep) **QUEEN'S FIRST EP**	17	-
	– Good old fashioned lover boy / Death on two legs / White Queen (as it began) / Tenement funster. *(re-iss.Nov88 as 3" cd-ep)*		
Jun 77.	(7") **LONG AWAY. / YOU AND I**	-	
Oct 77.	(7") **WE ARE THE CHAMPIONS. / WE WILL ROCK YOU**	2	4

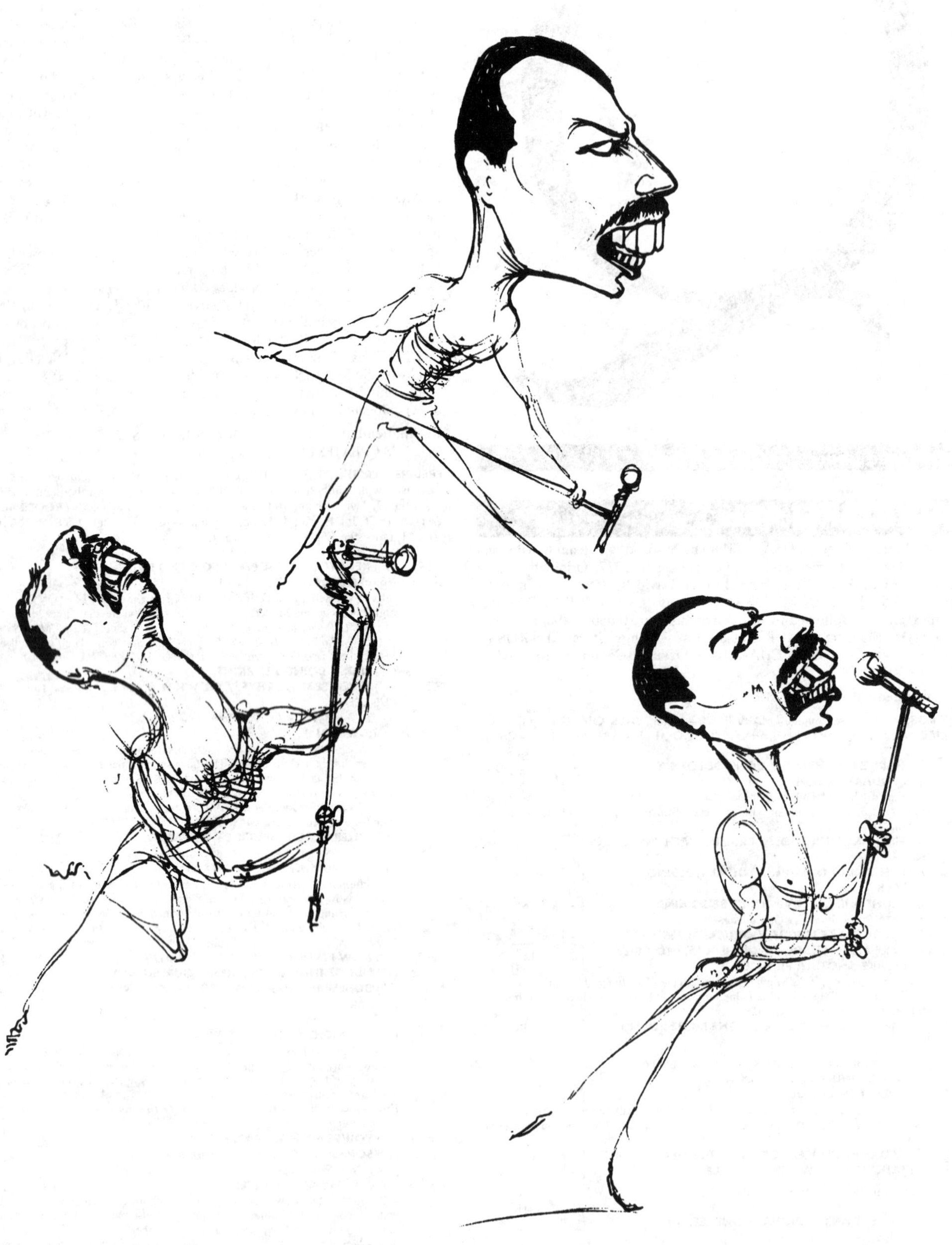

(re-iss.Nov88 as 3" cd-s, += Fat bottomed girls)

Nov 77. (lp)(c) **NEWS OF THE WORLD** [4] [3]
– We will rock you / We are the champions / Sheer heart attack / All dead, all dead / Spread your wings / Fight from the inside / Get down make love / Sleeping on the sidewalk / Who needs you / It's late / My melancholy blues. *(re-iss.1985, cd-iss.Jun88) (US cd-iss.Mar91 on 'Hollywood', +=)–* We will rock you – 1991 remix.

Feb 78. (7") **SPREAD YOUR WINGS. / SHEER HEART ATTACK** [34] [-]
Apr 78. (7") **IT'S LATE. / SHEER HEART ATTACK** [-] [74]
Oct 78. (7") **BICYCLE RACE. / FAT BOTTOMED GIRLS** [11] [24] Nov 78
Nov 78. (lp)(c) **JAZZ** [2] [6]
– Mustapha / Fat bottomed girls / Jealousy / Bicycle race / If you can't beat them / Let me entertain you / Dead on time / In only seven days / Dreamer's ball / Fun it / Leaving home ain't easy / Don't stop me now / More of that jazz. *(re-iss. 1985, cd-iss.Jun88) (US cd-iss.Jun91 on 'Hollywood', +=)–* Fat bottomed girls – 1991 remix / Bicycle race – 1991 remix. *(re-iss.cd+c Feb94 on 'Parlophone')*

Feb 79. (7") **DON'T STOP ME NOW. / IN ONLY SEVEN DAYS** [9] [-]
Feb 79. (7") **DON'T STOP ME NOW. / MORE OF THAT JAZZ** [-] [86]
Apr 79. (7") **JEALOUSY. / FUN IT** [-] [ ]
Jun 79. (d-lp)(c) **LIVE KILLERS (live)** [3] [16]
– We will rock you / Let me entertain you / Death on two legs (dedicated to . . .) / Killer Queen / Bicycle race / I'm in love with my car / Get down, make love / You're my best friend / Now I'm here / Dreamer's ball / '39 / Keep yourself alive / Don't stop me now / Spread your wings / Brighton rock / Bohemian rhapsody / Tie your mother down / Sheer heart attack / We will rock you / We are the champions / God save the Queen. *(re-iss.1985, cd-iss.Jun88) (US cd-iss.Nov88 on 'Hollywood') (re-iss.cd+c Apr94 on 'Parlophone')*

Jul 79. (7") **LOVE OF MY LIFE (live). / NOW I'M HERE (live)** [63] [-]
Aug 79. (7") **WE WILL ROCK YOU (live). / LET ME ENTERTAIN YOU (live)** [-] [ ]
Oct 79. (7") **CRAZY LITTLE THING CALLED LOVE. / WE WILL ROCK YOU (live)** [2] [-]
Dec 79. (7") **CRAZY LTTLE THING CALLED LOVE. / SPREAD YOUR WINGS** [-] [1]
Feb 80. (7") **SAVE ME. / LET ME ENTERTAIN YOU (live)** [11] [-]
Jun 80. (7") **PLAY THE GAME. / HUMAN BODY** [14] [42]
Jul 80. (lp)(c) **THE GAME** [1] [1]
– Play the game / Dragon attack / Another one bites the dust / Need your loving tonight / Crazy little thing called love / Rock it (prime jive) / Don't try suicide / Sail away sweet sister / Coming soon / Save me. *(re-iss.1985, cd-iss.Jun88) (US cd-iss.Jun91 on 'Hollywood', +=)–* Dragon attack – 1991 remix. *(re-iss.cd+c Feb94 on 'Parlophone')*

Aug 80. (7") **ANOTHER ONE BITES THE DUST. / DRAGON ATTACK** [7] [-]
Aug 80. (7") **ANOTHER ONE BITES THE DUST. / DON'T TRY SUICIDE** [-] [1]
(re-iss.Nov88 as 3" cd-s, += Las Palabras de amor)
Oct 80. (7") **NEED YOUR LOVING TONIGHT. / ROCK IT (PRIME JIVE)** [-] [44]
Nov 80. (7") **FLASH. / FOOTBALL FIGHT** [10] [42] Jan 81
Dec 80. (lp)(c) **FLASH GORDON (Soundtrack)** [10] [23]
– Flash's theme / In the space capsule (the love theme) / Ming's theme (in the court of Ming the merciless) / The ring (hypnotic seduction of Dale) / Football fight / In the death cell (love theme reprise) / Execution of Flash / The kiss (Aura resurrects Flash) / Arboria (planet of the tree men) / Escape from the swamp / Flash to the rescue / Vultan's theme (attack of the hawk men) / Battle theme / The wedding march / The marriage of Dale and Ming (and Flash approaching) / Flash's theme reprise (victory celebrations) / The hero. *(re-iss. 1985, cd-iss.Jun88) (US cd-iss.Aug91 on 'Hollywood', +=)–* Flash – 1991 remix. *(re-iss.cd+c Apr94 on 'Parlophone')*

Nov 81. (lp)(c) **QUEEN'S GREATEST HITS** (compilation) [1] [14]
– Bohemian rhapsody / Another one bites the dust / Killer queen / Fat bottomed girls / Bicycle race / You're my best friend / Don't stop me now / Save me / Crazy little thing called love / Now I'm here / Good old-fashioned lover boy / Play the game / Flash / Seven seas of Rhye / We will rock you / We are the champions / Somebody to love. *(re-iss.Aug84) (re-iss.Dec91 on 'Parlophone', hit UK 7) (re-iss.cd+c Jun94 on 'Parlophone')*

Nov 81. (7") **UNDER PRESSURE. ("QUEEN and DAVID BOWIE") / SOUL BROTHER** [1] [29]
(re-iss.Nov88 as 3" cd-s, += Body language)
Apr 82. (7") **BODY LANGUAGE. / LIFE IS REAL (SONG FOR LENNON)** [25] [11]
May 82. (lp)(c) **HOT SPACE** [4] [22]
– Staying power / Dancer / Back chat / Body language / Action this day / Put out the fire / Life is real (song for Lennon) / Calling all girls / Las Palabras de amor / Cool cat / Under pressure. *(cd-iss.Jun88) (re-is.+cd.Aug89 on 'Fame') (US cd-iss.Mar91 on 'Hollywood', += Body language – 1991 remix) (re-iss.cd+c Feb94 on 'Parlophone')*

Jun 82. (7") **LAS PALABRAS DE AMOR. / COOL CAT** [17] [-]
Jul 82. (7") **CALLING ALL GIRLS. / PUT OUT THE FIRE** [-] [60]
Aug 82. (7")(12") **BACKCHAT. / STAYING POWER** [40] [ ]

E.M.I. Capitol

Jan 84. (7") **RADIO GA-GA (edit). / I GO CRAZY** [2] [16]
('A'ext-12") – ('A'dub version). *(re-iss.Nov88 as 3"cd-s += Hammer to fall +7"tracks)*
Mar 84. (lp)(c)(cd) **THE WORKS** [2] [23]
– Radio Ga-ga / Tear it up / It's a hard life / Man on the prowl / Machines (or back to humans) / I want to break free / Keep passing the open windows / Hammer to fall / Is his he world we created?. *(re-US cd-iss.Dec91 on 'Hollywood', +=)–* Radio Ga Ga (12"mix) / I want to break free (12"mix) / I go crazy) (re-iss.cd+c Feb94 on 'Parlophone')

Apr 84. (7")(12") **I WANT TO BREAK FREE (remix). / MACHINES (OR BACK TO HUMANS)** [3] [45]
(re-iss.Nov88 as 3" cd-s, += It's a hard life)
Jul 84. (7")(12"pic-d) **IT'S A HARD LIFE. / IS THIS THE WORLD WE CREATED?** [6] [72]
(12"+=) – ('A'extended remix).
Sep 84. (7") **HAMMER TO FALL (edit). / TEAR IT UP** [13] [ ]
(12") – ('A'headbangers mix).
Dec 84. (7") **THANK GOD IT'S CHRISTMAS. / MAN ON THE PROWL / KEEP PASSING OPEN WINDOWS** [21] [-]
(12") – ('B'side extended).

note:- In the mid 80's and earlier, each individual had also launched solo ⇒

Nov 85. (7")('A'ext-12") **ONE VISION. / BLURRED VISION** [7] [61]
Feb 86. (7") **PRINCESS OF THE UNIVERSE. / A DOZEN RED ROSES FOR MY DARLING** [-] [ ]
Mar 86. (7") **A KIND OF MAGIC. / A DOZEN RED ROSES FOR MY DARLING** [3] [42] Jun 86
('A'ext-12")(12"pic-d) – (as above) *(re-iss.Nov88 as 3" cd-s, += One vision)*
May 86. (lp)(c)(cd) **A KIND OF MAGIC** [1] [46]
– One vision / A kind of magic / One year of love / Pain is so close to pleasure / Friends will be friends / Who wants to live forever / Gimme the prize / Don't lose your head / Princes of the universe. *(cd+=)–* A kind of 'A kind of magic – Friends will be friends – Who wants to live forever). *(re-US cd-iss. Jun91 on 'Hollywood', +=)–* Forever, One vision.

Jun 86. (7")(7"pic-d) **FRIENDS WILL BE FRIENDS. / SEVEN SEAS OF RHYE** [14] [-]
(12"+=) – ('A'extended mix).
Jul 86. (7") **DON'T LOSE YOUR HEAD. / PAIN IS SO CLOSE TO PLEASURE** [-] [ ]
Sep 86. (7") **WHO WANTS TO LIVE FOREVER (edit). / KILLER QUEEN** [24] [-]
(12"+=) – ('A'lp version) / Forever.
Dec 86. (d-lp)(c)(cd) **LIVE MAGIC (live)** [3] [ ]
– One vision / Tie your mother down / I want to break free / Hammer to fall / Seven seas of rhye / We are the champions / Another one bites the dust / Is this the world we created? / Bohemian rhasody / Radio Ga Ga / Friends will be friends / We will rock you / Under pressure / A kind of music / God save the Queen. *(re-iss.Dec91 on 'Parlophone', hit UK No.51)*

— During this lull in QUEEN activity, FREDDIE MERCURY had released some solo singles and collaborated with MONTSERRAT CABALLE. TAYLOR had formed The CROSS ⇒

Apr 89. (7")(c-s) **I WANT IT ALL. / HANG ON IN THERE** [3] [50]
(12"+=)(cd-s+=) – ('A'album version).
May 89. (lp)(c)(cd) **THE MIRACLE** [1] [24]
– Party / Khashoggi's ship / The miracle / I want it all / The invisible man / Breakthru / Rain must fall / Scandal / Was it all worth it / My baby does me. *(cd+=)–* Hang on in there / Chinese torture / The invisible man (ext). *(re-US cd-iss.Oct91 on 'Hollywood', ++= Scandal – 12"mix)*

Jun 89. (7")(c-s)(7"sha-pic-d) **BREAKTHRU. / STEALIN'** [7] [ ]
(12"+=)(cd-s+=) – ('A'extended).
Aug 89. (7")(c-s)(7"clear) **INVISIBLE MAN. / HIJACK MY HEART** [12] [ ]
(12"+=)(cd-s+=)(12"clear+=) – ('A'extended).
Oct 89. (7")(c-s) **SCANDAL. / MY LIFE HAS BEEN SAVED** [25] [ ]
(12"+=)(cd-s+=) – ('A'extended).
Dec 89. (7")(c-s) **THE MIRACLE. / STONE COLD CRAZY (live)** [21] [ ]
(12"+=)(cd-s+=) – My melancholy blues (live '77).

Parlophone Hollywood

Jan 91. (7")(c-s) **INNUENDO. / BIJOU** [1] [ ]
(12"+=)(cd-s+=)(12"pic-d+=) – Under pressure (extended).
Feb 91. (cd)(c)(lp) **INNUENDO** [1] [30]
– Innuendo / I'm going slightly mad / Headlong / I can't live without you / Don't try so hard / Ride the wild wind / All God's people / These are the days of our lives / Delilah / Hit man / Bijou / The show must go on. *(re-hit.34 Dec91)*

Mar 91. (7")(c-s)(7"sha-pic-d) **I'M GOING SLIGHTLY MAD. / HIT MAN** [22] [ ]
(12"+=)(cd-s+=) – Lost opportunity.
May 91. (7")(c-s) **HEADLONG. / ALL GOD'S PEOPLE** [14] [ ]
(12"+=)(cd-s+=)(12"pic-d+=) – Mad the swine.
Sep 91. (7")(c-s) **THE SHOW MUST GO ON. / KEEP YOURSELF ALIVE** [16] [ ]
(12"+=) – (Queen talks – interview). (cd-s++=) – Body language.
(cd-s) – ('A'side) / Now I'm here / Fat bottomed girls / Los Parabras de amor.
Oct 91. (cd)(c)(d-lp) **GREATEST HITS II** (compilation) (US title 'CLASSIC QUEEN') [1] [4]
– A kind of magic / Under pressure / Radio Ga Ga / I want it all / I want to break free / Innuendo / It's a hard life / Breakthru / Who wants to live forever / Headlong / The miracle / I'm going slightly mad / The invisible man / Hammer to fall / Friends will be friends / The show must go on / One vision. *(hit UK No.29 in May93)*

— On the 23 Nov'91, FREDDIE lost his 2 year silent battle against AIDS. The previous day, it was announced in the news. The rumours had now ended.

Dec 91. (7")(12")(c-s)(cd-s) **BOHEMIAN RHAPSODY. / THESE ARE THE DAYS OF OUR LIVES** [1] [2]
Jun 92. (c-s)(cd-s) **WE WILL ROCK YOU. / WE ARE THE CHAMPIONS** [-] [52]
Sep 92. (cd)(c) **GREATEST HITS** [-] [11]
Apr 93. (7"ep)(c-ep)(cd-ep) **FIVE LIVE EP ("GEORGE MICHAEL / QUEEN")** [1] [46] album
– Somebody to love / Medley: Killer / Papa was a rollin' stone / These are the days of our lives (with LISA STANSFIELD) / Calling you.
(cd-s) – ('A'side) / Medley: Killer / Papa was a rollin' stone (with PM DAWN).
(12"+=) – Medley: Killer / Papa was a rollin' stone – instrumental.

— (In the US, the EP's main track 'SOMEBODY TO LOVE', hit No.30)

— In Feb95, FREDDIE and BRIAN featured on EDDIE HOWELL's re-issued 1977 single 'THE MAN FROM MANHATTAN'.

Oct 95. (c-s) **HEAVEN FOR EVERYONE / IT'S A BEAUTIFUL DAY** [2] [ ]
(cd-s+=) – ('A'-lp version).
(cd-s) – ('A'sie) / Keep yourself alive / Seven seas of rhye / Killer queen.
Nov 95. (cd)(c)(lp) **MADE IN HEAVEN** [1] [58]
– It's a beautiful day / Made in Heaven / Let me live / Mother love / My life has been saved / I was born to love you / Heaven for everyone / Too much love will kill you / You don't fool me / A winter's tale / It's a beautiful day (reprise) / Yeh / Track 13.
Dec 95. (7")(c-s) **A WINTER'S TALE. / THANK GOD IT'S CHRISTMAS** [6] [ ]
(cd-s+=) – Rock in Rio blues.
(cd-s) – ('A'side) / Now I'm here / You're my best friend / Somebody to love.

- more compilations, etc. -

Dec 85. EMI/ US= Capitol; (14xlp-box) **THE COMPLETE WORKS** [ ] [ ]
Nov 88. EMI; (3"cd-s) **CRAZY LITTLE THING CALLED LOVE / SPREAD YOUR WINGS / FLASH** [ ] [-]
Dec 89. Band Of Joy; (lp)(c)(cd) **QUEEN AT THE BEEB (live)** [67] [-]
Jun 92. Parlophone/ US= Hollywood; (cd) **QUEEN: LIVE AT WEMBLEY (live)** [2] [53]
– (above was originally issued UK on video)
Oct 94. Parlophone; (d-cd)(d-c) **GREATEST HITS 1 & 2** [37] [ ]
Dec 95. EMI; (cd-box) **ULTIMATE QUEEN** [ ] [ ]

FREDDIE MERCURY

C.B.S. Columbia
Sep 84. (7")(7"pic-d)('A'ext-12") **LOVE KILLS. / ROT WANG'S PARTY** [10] [69]
(above from film 'Metropolis' & co-written w / Georgio Moroder)
Apr 85. (7")('A'ext-12") **I WAS BORN TO LOVE YOU. / STOP ALL THE FIGHTING** [11] [ ]
(d7"+=) – Love kills (extended) / Stop all the fighting (extended).
May 85. (lp)(c)(cd) **MR. BAD GUY** [6] [ ]
– Let's turn it on * / Made in Heaven / I was born to love you * / Foolin' around / Mr. Bad guy / Man made Paradise / There must be more to life than this / Living on my own * / Your kind of lover / My love is dangerous / Love me like there's no tomorrow. *(c+cd+=)*– (* extended tracks).
Jul 85. (7")(7"sha-pic-d) **MADE IN HEAVEN (remix). / SHE BLOWS HOT AND COLD** [57] [-]
('A'&'B'extended-12") – (also 'A'side version).
Sep 85. (7") **LIVING ON MY OWN. / MY LOVE IS DANGEROUS** [50] [-]
(12") – ('A'&'B'extended).
Oct 85. (7") **LIVING ON MY OWN. / SHE BLOWS HOT AND COLD** [-] [ ]
Nov 85. (7") **LOVE ME LIKE THERE IS NO TOMORROW. / LET'S TURN IT ON** [ ] [-]
(12") – ('A'&'B'extended).
(below from Dave Clark musical 'Time')

E.M.I. not issued
May 86. (7")(ext-12") **TIME. / TIME (instrumental)** [ ] [ ]

Parlophone Capitol
Feb 87. (7")(7"sha-pic-d) **THE GREAT PRETENDER. / EXERCISES IN FREE LOVE** [4] [ ]
(12"+=) – ('A'extended).

FREDDIE MERCURY with MONTSERRAT CABALLE

(female Spanish opera star)

Polydor Polydor?
Oct 87. (7") **BARCELONA. / EXERCISES IN FREE LOVE** (her version) [8] [ ]
(12"+=)(c-s+=)(cd-s+=)(12"pic-d+=) – ('A'extended version).
Oct 88. (lp)(c)(cd) **BARCELONA** [25] [ ]
– Barcelona / La Japonaise / The fallen priest / Ensueno / The golden boy / Guide me home / How can I go on / Overture piccante. *(re-iss.Aug92, hit UK No.15)*
Oct 88. (7") **THE GOLDEN BOY. / THE FALLEN PRIEST** [ ] [ ]
(12"+=)(cd-s+=) – ('A'instrumental).
Jan 89. (7")(7"pic-d) **HOW CAN I GO ON. / OVERTUREPICCANTE** [ ] [ ]
(12"+=)(cd-s+=) – Guide me home.

- (FREDDIE MERCURY) compilations, others, etc. -

Jul 92. Polydor; (7")(c-s)(cd-s) **BARCELONA. / EXCERCISES IN FREE LOVE** [2] [ ]
(12"+=) – ('A'extended).
Oct 92. Polydor; (7")(c-s) **HOW CAN I GO ON. / THE GOLDEN BOY** [ ] [ ]
(cd-s+=) – The fallen priest.
(12"+=)(cd-s+=) – Guide me home / Overture paccante.
Nov 92. Parlophone/ US= Maverick; (cd)(c)(lp) **THE FREDDIE MERCURY ALBUM** [4] [ ]
– The great pretender / Foolin' around / Time / Your kind of love / Exercises in free love / In my defence / Mr.Bad guy / Let's turn it on / Living on my own / Love kills / Barcelona (w / MONSERRAT CABALLE). *(re-iss.Jul93, hit UK No.13)*
Dec 92. Parlophone; (7")(c-s) **IN MY DEFENCE. / LOVE KILLS (original)** [8] [ ]
(cd-s+=) – Mr.Bad guy / Living on my own (mix).
Jan 93. Parlophone; (7")(c-s) **THE GREAT PRETENDER. / STOP ALL THE FIGHTING** [29] [ ]
(cd-s+=) – Exercises in free love / ('A'malouf mix).
Jul 93. (7")(12")(c-s)(cd-s) **LIVING ON MY OWN. / ('A'mixes)** [1] [ ]

BRIAN MAY & FRIENDS

with **EDDIE VAN HALEN** – guitar / **PHIL CHEN** – bass / **FRED MANDEL** – keyboards / **ALAN GRATZER** – drums etc.

E.M.I. Capitol
Oct 83. (7") **STARFLEET. / SON OF STARFLEET** [65] [-]
Oct 83. (7") **STARFLEET. / STARFLEET (extended)** [-] [-]
Oct 83. (m-lp)(c) **STARFLEET PROJECT** [35] [ ]
– Starfleet / Let me out / Bluesbreaker.

BRIAN MAY

E.M.I. Capitol
Sep 89. (7") **WHO WANTS TO LIVE FOREVER.** (by **"IAN MEESON & BELINDA GHILETT"**) **/** ('A'instrumental) [ ] [-]
(12"+=)(cd-s+=) – ('A'version by LOUISA MAY – original demo).

Parlophone Capitol
Nov 91. (7")(c-s) **DRIVEN BY YOU. / JUST ONE LIFE (DEDICATED TO THE MEMORY OF PHILIP SAYER)** [6] [ ]
(cd-s+=) – ('B'guitar version) / ('A' Ford ad 1:30 version).
Sep 92. (7") **TOO MUCH LOVE WILL KILL YOU. / I'M SCARED** [5] [ ]
(cd-s+=) – ('A'guitar version) / Driven by you (feat. COZY POWELL + NEIL MURRAY).
Oct 92. (cd)(c)(lp) **BACK TO THE LIGHT** [6] [ ]
– The dark / Back to the light / Love token / Resurrection / Too much love will kill you / Driven by you / Nothin' but blue / I'm scared / Last horizon / Let your heart rule your head / Just one life / Rollin' over.

—— In Oct'92, BRIAN featured on HANK MARVIN's (Shadows) version of QUEEN's song 'WE ARE THE CHAMPIONS'.

Nov 92. (7") **BACK TO THE LIGHT. / NOTHING BUT BLUE (guitar version)** [19] [ ]
(cd-s+=) – Blues breaker. (cd-s+=) – Star fleet / Let me out.
Jun 93. (c-s) **RESURRECTION. ("BRIAN MAY with COZY POWELL") / LOVE TOKEN** [23] [ ]
(cd-s+=)(12"pic-d+=) – Too much love will kill you (live).
(cd-s) – ('A'side) / Drive by you (two) / Back to the light (live) / Tie your mother down (live).
Dec 93. (7")(c-s) **LAST HORIZON. / LET YOUR HEART RULE YOUR HEAD** [51] [ ]
(cd-s) – ('A'side) / ('A'live) / We will rock you (live) / ('A'lp mix).

The BRIAN MAY BAND

MAY – vox, guitar with **COZY POWELL** – drums / **NEIL MURRAY** – bass / **SPIKE EDNEY** – keyboards / **JAMIE MOSES** – guitar, vocals / **CATHY PORTER + SHELLEY PRESTON** – vox

Feb 94. (cd)(c)(d-lp) **LIVE AT THE BRIXTON ACADEMY (live London, 15th June 1993)** [20] [ ]
– Back to the light / Driven by you / Tie your mother down / Love token / Headlong / Love of my life / 39 – Let your heart rule your head / Too much love will kill you / Since you've been gone / Now I'm here / Guitar extravagance / Resurrection / Last horizon / We will rock you / Hammer to fall.

- his compilations, etc -

Dec 95. Javelin; (cd) **THEMES AND DREAMS** [ ] [-]
Dec 95. Koch; (cd-s) **BLACK WHITE HOUSE** [ ] [-]

ROGER TAYLOR

E.M.I. Elektra
Aug 77. (7") **I WANNA TESTIFY. / TURN ON THE T.V.** [ ] [-]
Apr 81. (7") **FUTURE MANAGEMENT. / LAUGH OR CRY** [49] [-]
Apr 81. (lp)(c) **FUN IN SPACE** [18] [ ]
– No violins / Laugh or cry / Future management / Let's get crazy / My country I & II / Good times are now / Magic is loose / Interlude in Constantinople / Airheads / Fun in space.
Apr 81. (7") **LET'S GET CRAZY. / LAUGH OR CRY** [-] [ ]
Jun 81. (7") **MY COUNTRY (edit). / FUN IN SPACE** [ ] [-]

E.M.I. Capitol
Jun 84. (7")(12") **MAN ON FIRE. / KILLING TIME** [66] [-]
Jul 84. (lp)(c) **STRANGE FRONTIER** [30] [-]
– Strange frontier / Beautiful dreams / Man on fire / Racing in the street / Masters of war / Killing time / Abandon fire / Young love / It's an illusion / I cry for you (love, hope & confusion).
Aug 84. (7") **STRANGE FRONTIER. / I CRY FOR YOU (remix)** [ ] [-]
('A'&'B'extended-12"+=) – Two sharp pencils.

The CROSS

ROGER with **PETER NOONE** – bass / **CLAYTON MOSS** – guitar / **SPIKE EDNEY** – keyboards / **JOSH MacRAE** – drums

Virgin Virgin
Sep 87. (7") **COWBOYS AND INDIANS. / LOVE LIES BLEEDING** [74] [ ]
(12"+=)(c-s+=) – ('A'extended).
Jan 88. (7") **SHOVE IT. / ROUGH JUSTICE** [ ] [ ]
(12"+=) – ('A'metropolis mix).
(cd-s++=) – Cowboys and Indians.
Jan 88. (lp)(c)(cd) **THE CROSS** [58] [ ]
– Shove it / Heaven for everyone / Love on a tightrope (like an animal) / Cowboys and Indians / Stand up for love / Love lies bleeding (she was a wicked, wily waitress) / Contact. (cd+=) – Rough justice – 2nd shelf mix.
Mar 88. (7") **HEAVEN FOR EVERYONE. / LOVE ON A TIGHTROPE (LIKE AN ANIMAL)** [ ] [ ]
(12"+=) – Contact.
Jul 88. (7") **MANIPULATOR. / STAND UP FOR LOVE** [ ] [ ]
(12"+=) – ('A'extended).
Apr 90. (7") **POWER TO LOVE. / PASSION FOR TRASH** [ ] [ ]
(12"+=)(cd-s+=) – ('A'extended).
May 90. (cd)(c)(lp) **MAD, BAD AND DANGEROUS TO KNOW** [ ] [ ]
– On top of the world ma / Liar / Closer to you / Breakdown / Penetration guru / Power to love / Sister blue / Better things / Old men (lay down) / Final destination. (cd+=) – Foxy lady.

ROGER TAYLOR

with **JASON FALLOON** – guitars / **PHIL SPALDING** – bass / **MIKE CROSSLEY** – piano, keyboards / **CATHERINE PORTER** – backing vocals / **JOSHUA J. MacRAE** – programming

Parlophone Capitol
Apr 94. (7")(c-s) **NAZIS 1994. / ('A'radio mix)** [22] [ ]
(12"red+=) – ('A'extended) / ('A'big science mix).
(cd-s++=) – ('A'kick mix) / ('A'-Schindler's extended mix).
Sep 94. (cd)(c) **HAPPINESS?** [22] [ ]
– Nazis 1994 / Happiness / Revelations / Touch the sky / Foreign sand / Freedom

train / You had to be there / The key / Everybody hurts sometime / Loneliness . . . / Dear Mr.Murdoch / Old friends.

— Below featured a Japanese classically trained drummer, pianist & co-composer **YOSHIKI** plus **JIM CREGAN** – guitars / **PHIL CHEN** – bass / **DICK MARX** – strings arr.

Sep 94. (7"colrd)(c-s) **FOREIGN SAND. ("ROGER TAYLOR & YOSHIKI") / ('A'mix)** 26 —
(12"pic-d+=)(cd-s+=) – You had to be there / Final destination.

Nov 94. (7") **HAPPINESS. / RIDE THE WILD WIND (live)** 32 —
(12") – ('A'side) / Dear Mr.Murdoch / Everybody hurts sometime (live) / Old friends (live).
(cd-s) – ('A'side) / Loneliness / Dear Mr.Murdoch / I want to break free (live).

The IMMORTALS

— **JOHN DEACON** played bass on their (May86 'M.C.A.'(7")(12") **NO TURNING BACK. / ('A'mix)**from the film 'Biggles'.

QUEENSRYCHE

Formed: Bellevue, Seattle, Washington, USA . . . 1980 initially as THE MOB by high school friends (see line-up). After releasing debut EP on Diana Harris' '206' label in '83, they signed to 'EMI America', and re-issued it. Made commercial headway for the rest of the 80's, and finally cracked the US & UK market in the early 90's, with Top 20 album 'EMPIRE'. • **Style:** Heavy techno rockers whose 1988 concept album 'OPERATION: MINDCRIME', was inspired by the psi-fi writer George Orwell. It also featured Michael Kamen who arranged string and choir. • **Trivia:** Peter Collins produced this album JAMES GUTHRIE their debut + NEIL KERNON the follow-up. PAMELA MOORE was guest singer on 'SUITE SISTER MARY'. • **Songwriters:** DeGARMO or TATE / WILSON except; SCARBOROUGH FAIR – CANTICLE (Simon & Garfunkel) / GONNA GET CLOSE TO YOU (Lisa Diabello).

Recommended: OPERATION: MINDCRIME (*8) / EMPIRE (*7).

GEOFF TATE (b.14 Jan'59) – vocals / **CHRIS DeGARMO** (b.14 Jun'63) – guitar / **MICHAEL WILTON** (b.23 Feb'62) – guitar / **EDDIE JACKSON** (b.29 Jan'61) – bass / **SCOTT ROCKENFIELD** (b.15 Jun'50) – drums

EMI America / EMI America

Sep 83. (12"ep) **QUEENSRYCHE** — —
– Queen of the Reich / Nightrider / Blinded / The lady wore black.

Sep 84. (7") **TAKE HOLD OF THE FLAME. / NIGHTRIDER** — —

Sep 84. (lp)(c) **THE WARNING** — 61
– The warning / En force / Deliverance / No sanctuary / N.M. 156 / Take hold of the flame / Before the storm / Child of fire / Roads to madness. *(cd-iss.Mar87) (cd+c.re-iss.Aug91) (re-iss.cd Oct94)*

Jul 86. (lp)(c)(cd) **RAGE FOR ORDER** 66 47
– Walk in the shadows / I dream in infrared / The whisper / Gonna get close to you / The killing words / Surgical strike / Neue regel / Chemical youth (we are rebellion) / London / Screaming in digital / I will remember. *(cd+c.re-iss.Aug91) (re-iss.cd Oct94)*

Aug 86. (7") **GONNA GET CLOSE TO YOU. / PROPHECY** — —
(d7"+=) – Queen of the Reich / Deliverance.

Manhattan / Manhattan

May 88. (lp)(c)(cd) **OPERATION: MINDCRIME** 58 50
– I remember now / Anarchy-X / Revolution calling / Operation: Mindcrime / Speak / Spreading the disease / The mission / The needle lies / Suite Sister Mary / Electric requiem / Breaking the silence / I don't believe in love / Waiting for 22 / My empty room / Eyes of a stranger. *(re-iss.cd Oct94)*

Oct 88. (10"ep) **OVERSEEING THE OPERATION. / EXCERPTS FROM OPERATION MINDCRIME: SUITE SISTER MARY – I Remember Now / Revolution Calling / Operation: Mindcrime / Breaking The Silence / Eyes Of A Stranger.** — —

Apr 89. (7") **EYES OF A STRANGER. / QUEEN OF THE REICH** 59 —
(12"+=) – Walk in the shadows / Take hold of the flame.
(cd-s+=) – Prophecy / Take hold of the flame.

E.M.I. USA / Manhattan

Sep 90. (7")(7"sha-pic-d) **EMPIRE. / SCARBOROUGH FAIR – CANTICLE** 61 —
(12"+=)(cd-s+=) – Prophecy.

Sep 90. (cd)(c)(d-lp) **EMPIRE** 13 7
– Best I can do / The thin line / Jet city woman / Della Brown / Another rainy night (without you) / Empire / Resistance / Silent lucidity / Hand on heart / One and only / Anybody listening? *(re-iss.cd Oct94)*

Apr 91. (7")(c-s) **SILENT LUCIDITY. / THE MISSION (live)** 34 9 Mar 91
(12"+=) – Eyes of a stranger.
(cd-s++=) – Della Brown.

Jun 91. (7")(c-s) **BEST I CAN DO. / I DREAM IN INFRARED (acoustic)** 36 —
(10"+=) – Prophecy.
(12"++=)(cd-s++=) – ('A'radio edit).

Aug 91. (7")(7"sha-pic-d) **JET CITY WOMAN. / EMPIRE (live)** 39 —
(12"+=) – Walk in the shadows (live).
(cd-s) ('A' side) / Queen of The Reich. / Walk in the shadows (live)

Nov 91. (cd)(c) **OPERATION: LIVECRIME (live)** - 38

Aug 92. (7")(c-s) **SILENT LUCIDITY. / I DON'T BELIEVE IN LOVE** (live) 18 —
(12") – Last time in Paris / Take hold of the fame.
(cd-s) ('A' side) / Eyes of a stranger (live) / Operation: Mindcrime.
(cd-s) ('A' side) / Suite Sister Mary (live) / Last time in Paris.

Oct 94. (cd)(c)(lp) **PROMISED LAND** 13 3
– 9:28 a.m. / I am I / Damaged / Out of mind / Bridge / Promised land / Disconnected / Lady Jane / My global mind / One more time / Someone else?.

Jan 95. (12"gold) **I AM I. / REAL WORLD / SOMEONE ELSE?** 40 —
(cd-s+=) – Dirty li'l secret.

Mar 95. (7"pic-d)(c-s) **BRIDGE. / THE KILLING WORDS (live)** 40 —
(cd-s+=) – The lady wore black (live) / Damaged (live).
(cd-s) – ('A'side) / Silent lucidity (live) / My empty room (live) / Real world (live).

? & THE MYSTERIANS

Formed: Saginaw, Michegan, USA . . . 1964, after abandoning the name XYZ, and their Texan upbringing. Early 1966, their manager LILY GONZALES dispatched 750 copies of their first single '96 TEARS'. This sparked off interest from major US record company 'Cameo', who re-issued it later in the year, when it topped the US charts. Another hit followed, but this was their last glory call. • **Style:** Organ orientated garage outfit. • **Songwriters:** RUDY MARTINEZ penned except; SHOUT (Isley Brothers). • **Trivia:** In 1967, The SEMI-COLONS featured The MYSTERIANS on 2 instrumental tracks. ALICE COOPER later covered I NEED SOMEBODY, and STRANGLERS were one of several who resurrected 96 TEARS.

Recommended: 96 TEARS (*6)

? (aka RUDY MARTINEZ, 1945, Mexico) – vocals / **FRANK RODRIGUEZ JNR.** (b. 9 Mar'51, Crystal City, Texas) – Farfisa organ / **FRANK LUGO** (b.FRANCISCO HERNANDEZ LUGO, 15 Mar'47, Weslaco, Texas) – bass / **LARRY BORJAS** – guitar / **ROBERT MARTINEZ** – drums

Cameo / Cameo

Sep 66. (7") **96 TEARS. / MIDNIGHT HOUR** 37 1 Jan66
(originally issued as The MYSTERIANS – US Jan66 on 'Pa-Go-Go')

— **BOBBY BALDERRAMA** (b.27 Feb'50, O'Donnell, Texas) – guitar repl. ROBERT / **EDDIE SERRATO** (b. 5 Dec'45, Encial, Texas) – drums repl. LARRY

— Both of the outgoing members were drafted into the army.

Nov 66. (lp) **96 TEARS** - 66
– I need somebody / Stormy Monday / You're telling me lies / Ten o'clock / Set aside / Upside / Don't tease me / Don't break this heart of mine / Why me / Midnight hour / 96 tears.

Dec 66. (7") **I NEED SOMEBODY. / 8 TEEN** — 22

Feb 67. (7") **CAN'T GET ENOUGH OF YOU, BABY. / SMOKES** - —

Apr 67. (7") **GIRL (YOU CAPTIVATE ME). / GOT TO** - —

Jun 67. (lp) **ACTION** - —
– Girl (you captivate me) / Can't get enough of you baby / Got to / I'll be back / Shout / Hangin' on a string / Smokes / It's not easy / Don't hold it against me / Just like a rose / Do you feel it.

Jul 67. (7") **DO SOMETHING TO ME. / LOVE ME BABY** - —

— Their label 'Cameo Parkway' folded early in '68.

not issued / Chicory

Feb 68. (7") **TALK IS CHEAP. / SHE GOES TO CHURCH ON SUNDAY** - —

not issued / Capitol

May 68. (7") **MAKE YOU MINE. / I LOVE YOU BABY** - —

not issued / Tangerine

Dec 68. (7") **AIN'T IT NO SHAME. / TURN AROUND, BABY** - —

not issued / Super K

Jan 69. (7") **SHA LA LA. / HANG IN** - —

— Disbanded in 1969, although they re-united in 1975.

not issued / Luv

1975. (7") **FUNKY LADY. / HOT'N'GROOVIN'** - —

— Disbanded once again, although they did concerts early 1980.

– compilations, etc. –

Jul 76. London; (7") **96 TEARS. / 8 TEEN** — -

1983. Abkco; (7") **96 TEARS. / CAN'T GET ENOUGH OF YOU, BABY** - —

1983. Abkco; (7") **I NEED SOMEBODY. / GIRL (YOU CAPTIVATE ME)** - —

1985. R.O.I.R.; (c) **THE DALLAS REUNION TAPES – 96 TEARS FOREVER** - —
(cd-iss.Feb90, lp-iss.Sep90)

QUICKSILVER MESSENGER SERVICE

Formed: San Francisco, California, U.S.A . . . late 1964 by JIM MURRAY, JOHN CIPOLLINA, DAVID FREIBERG and CASEY SONOBAN. Also present at early rehearsals were SKIP SPENCE and DINO VALENTI, who was jailed for possession of drugs. In June '65, CIPOLLINA, MURRAY and FREIBERG were joined by GREG ELMORE and GARY DUNCAN. Two years later, they received a great reception at Monterey International Pop Festival, but MURRAY soon left as group signed to 'Capitol'. They had just previously recorded 2 tracks 'Codine' & 'Babe, I'm Gonna Leave You', for the Dec '67 Various Artists soundtrack album 'REVOLUTION' on 'United Art'. In the summer of '68, they finally released eponymous debut which with anticipation reached the US Top 75. Their follow-up in 1969 'HAPPY TRAILS', featuring a 25 minute improvised version of 'WHO DO YOU LOVE', crashed into the US Top 30. For the next couple of years with VALANTI back out of prison, they enjoyed huge fortunes on the other side of the water. • **Style:** Excellent live outfit, who transgressed through drug-orientated psychedelic rock to more basic rock'n'roll. • **Songwriters:** CIPOLINA + FREIBERG, until VALENTI's virtual take-over in 1970 as alter-ego JESSE ORIS FARROW, although others still individually contributed. Covered WHO DO YOU LOVE + MONA (Bo Diddley) / etc. • **Trivia:** Debut lp produced by NICK GRAVENITES and HARVEY BROOKS of ELECTRIC FLAG.

Recommended: THE ULTIMATE JOURNEY (*7)

JOHN CIPOLLINA (b.24 Aug'43, Berkeley, USA) – guitar, vocals (ex-DEACONS) / **GARY DUNCAN** (b.GRUBB, 4 Sep'46) – guitar, vocals repl. SKIP SPENCE / **DAVID FREIBERG** (b.24 Aug'38, Boston, USA) – bass, vocals / **GREG ELMORE** (b. 4 Sep'46) – drums repl. CASEY SONOBAN

Capitol / Capitol

May 68. (lp) **QUICKSILVER MESSENGER SERVICE** [ ] [63]
– Pride of man / Light your windows / Dino's song / Gold and silver / It's been too long / The fool. *(re-iss.+cd.Aug86) (re-iss.cd Jul92 on 'Edsel')*

Jun 68. (7") **PRIDE OF MAN. / DINO'S SONG** [-] [ ]

Nov 68. (7") **BEARS. / STAND BY ME** [-] [ ]

Mar 69. (lp) **HAPPY TRAILS** [ ] [27]
– Who do you love suite:- Who do you love (pt.1) – Who do you love – Where do you love – How do you love – Which do you love – Who do you love (pt.2) / Mona / Maiden of the Cancer Moon / Calvary / Happy trails. *(re-iss.Jun81 on 'Greenlight') (cd-iss.Dec92 on 'B.G.O.')*

Jul 69. (7") **WHO DO YOU LOVE (edit). / WHICH DO YOU LOVE** [-] [91]

— **NICKY HOPKINS** – keyboards (ex-STEVE MILLER BAND) repl. DUNCAN

Nov 69. (7") **HOLY MOLY. / WORDS CAN'T SAY** [-] [ ]

Jan 70. (lp) **SHADY GROVE** [ ] [25]
– Shady Grove / Flute song / Three or feet from home / Too far / Holy Moly / Joseph's coat / Flashing lonesome / Words can't say / Edward, the mad shirt grinder. *(re-iss.Feb87 on 'Edsel', cd-iss.1990's)*

Feb 70. (7") **SHADY GROVE. / THREE OR FOUR FEET FROM HOME** [-] [ ]

— added now officially ex-part time member **DINO VALENTI** (b. 7 Nov'43, New York City) – guitar, vocals / **GARY DUNCAN** – guitar, vocals returned to 6-piece w / **JOHN, NICKY, DAVID + GREG**

Aug 70. (lp) **JUST FOR LOVE** [ ] [27]
– Wolf run (part 1) / Just for love (part 1) / Cobra / The hat / Freeway flyer / Gone again / Fresh air / Just for love (part 2) / Wolf run (part 2). *(cd-iss.Dec92 on 'B.G.O.')*

Sep 70. (7") **FRESH AIR. / FREEWAY FLYER** [-] [49]

— **MARK NATALFIN** – keyboards (ex-PAUL BUTTERFIELD) repl. (on 3 tracks) HOPKINS. Also on below lp: **JOSE RICO REYES** – percussion / **MARTINE FIERRO** – wind / **RON TAORMINA** – saxes / **FRANK MORIN** – sax / **PAT O'HARA** – trombone / **KEN BALZELL** – trumpet

Feb 71. (lp)(c) **WHAT ABOUT ME** [ ] [26] Jan 71
– What about me / Local color / Baby baby / Won't kill me / Long haired lady / Subway / Spindrifter / Good old rock and roll / All in my mind / Call on me. *(cdiss.1991 on 'BGO')*

Mar 71. (7") **WHAT ABOUT ME. / GOOD OLD ROCK AND ROLL** [-] [100]

— Now a quintet when CIPOLLINA left to form COPPERHEAD / **MARK RYAN** – bass (ex-COUNTRY JOE & THE FISH) repl. DAVID to JEFFERSON STARSHIP

Nov 71. (lp)(c) **QUICKSILVER** [ ] [ ]
– Hope / I found love / Song for Frisco / Play my guitar / Rebel / Fire Brothers / Out of my mind / Don't cry my lady love / The truth. *(cd-iss.Jan94 on 'B.G.O.')*

Nov 71. (7") **HOPE. / I FOUND LOVE** [-] [ ]

— **CHUCK STEAKS** – organ repl. NATAFLIN

May 72. (lp)(c) **COMIN' THRU** [ ] [ ]
– Doin' time in the U.S.A. / Chicken / Changes / California state correctional facility blues / Forty days / Mojo / Don't lose it. *(cd-iss.1993 on 'BGO')*

May 72. (7") **DOIN' TIME IN THE U.S.A. / CHANGES** [-] [ ]

— Mid'72, contributed 2 tracks for live lp 'The Last Days Of Fillmore'.

— (May73) **JOHN NICHOLAS** – bass (ex-IT'S A BEAUTIFUL DAY) repl. RYAN / added **HAROLD ACEVES** – 2nd drummer (6-piece DINO, GARY, GREG + CHUCKS)

— (Feb74) **BOB HOGAN** – keyboards (ex-MILES DAVIS) repl. STEAKS / **SKIP OLSEN** – bass repl. BOB FLURIE who had repl. JOHN NICHOLAS

— (Mar75) **DINO, GARY, GREG, SKIP** plus the returning **JOHN CIP . . . + DAVID** on tour / added **MICHAEL LEWIS** – piano

Oct 75. (lp)(c) **SOLID SILVER** [ ] [89]
– Gypsy lights / Heebie jeebies / Cowboy on the run / I heard you singing / Worryin' shoes / The letter / They don't know / Flames / Witches' moon / Bittersweet Moon. *(cd-iss.Sep93 on 'Edsel')*

Nov 75. (7") **GYPSY LIGHTS. / WITCHES MOON** [-] [ ]

— Had already broke-up, after brief re-union. CIPOLLINA joined MAN. He was to die 30 May'89 of emphysema lung disease. FREIBERG returned to STARSHIP. In 1987, **GARY DUNCAN** resurrected **QUICKSILVER MESSENGER SERVICE** for an album 'PEACE BY PIECE'. Unfortunately on the 29th May 1989, CIPOLLINA died from emphysema. All group members, included others from The GRATEFUL DEAD, JEFFERSON AIRPLANE and (HUEY LEWIS &) THE NEWS, played benefit in San Francisco.

– compilations, others, etc. –

Oct 73. Capitol; (lp)(c) **ANTHOLOGY** [ ] [ ] May 73
(cd-iss.Jun95 on 'BGO')

Sep 83. Psycho; (d-lp) **MAIDEN OF THE CANCER MOON** (live Fillmore, Jun'68) [ ] [-]

Apr 86. See For Miles; (lp) **THE ULTIMATE JOURNEY** [ ] [-]
– Who do you love / Pride of man / Codine / Dino's song / Gold and silver / Joseph's coat / Shady grove / Fresh air / Too far / Stand by me / What about me / Mona. *(re-iss.cd Aug93)*

Oct 89. B.G.O.; (lp)(c) **WHAT GOES ON** [ ] [-]

Aug 91. Rhino; (d-cd) **SONS OF MERCURY (1968-1975)** [ ] [ ]

QUIET RIOT

Formed: Los Angeles, California, USA . . . 1975 by DuBROW, etc (see below). Went to Japan in 1977, and recorded two enthusiastically accepted albums I & II before disbanding in the early 80's. After a near 3-year hiatus, they returned in 1983 on new 'Pasha' label, and unleashed a Top 5 single 'CUM ON FEEL THE NOIZE', lifted from US No.1 album 'METAL HEALTH'. • **Style:** Heavy metal glam-pop/rock. • **Songwriters:** DuBROW penned except; CUM ON FEEL THE NOIZE + MAMA WEER ALL CRAZEE NOW (Slade)

Recommended: WILD, YOUNG AND CRAZEE (*5)

KEVIN DuBROW (b.29 Oct'56) – vocals / **RANDY RHOADS** – guitar / **KELLY GARNI** – bass / **DREW FORSYTH** – drums

Columbia JAPAN / not iss

1978. (lp) **QUIET RIOT** [-] [-]
– It's not so funny / Mama's little angels / Tin soldier / Ravers / Back to the coast / Glad all over / Get your kicks / Look in any window / Just how you want it / Riot reunion / Fit to be tied / Demolition derby.

1979. (lp) **QUIET RIOT II** [-] [-]
– Slick black Cadillac / You drive me crazy / Afterglow (of your love) / Eye for an eye / Trouble / Killer girls / Face to face / Inside you / We've got the magic.

— **RUDY SARZO** (b.Havana, Cuba) – bass repl. GARNI. Disbanded in 1979 when RHOADS joined OZZY OSBOURNE. He was killed in a plane crash in Mar'82. **KEVIN** formed own self-named outfit **DuBROW**, with **SARZO** + drummer **FRANKIE BANALI.**

QUIET RIOT

reformed with **DUBROW, SARZO, BANALI + CARLOS CAVAZO** (b. 8 Jul'59) – guitar

Epic / Pasha

May 83. (lp)(c)(pic-lp) **METAL HEALTH** [ ] [1] Apr 83
– Metal health (bang your head) / Cum on feel the noize / Don't wanna let you go / Slick black Cadillac / Love's a bitch / Breathless / Run for cover / Battle axe / Let's get crazy / Thunderbird. *(re-iss.Jan87, cd-iss.1988) (cd-iss.Jul93 on 'Sony Europe')*

Jul 83. (7") **BANG YOUR HEAD. / ('A'live version)** [-] [ ]

Jul 83. (7") **CUM ON FEEL THE NOIZE. / RUN FOR COVER** [ ] [5] Sep 83

Nov 83. (7") **METAL HEALTH. / CUM ON FEEL THE NOIZE** [45] [31] Jan 84
(12"+=)(d7"+=) – Love's a bitch / Let's get crazy.

Mar 84. (7") **BAD BOY. / METAL HEALTH (BANG YOUR HEAD)** [ ] [ ]
(12"+=) – Slick black Cadillac.

Jul 84. (lp)(c) **CONDITION CRITICAL** [71] [15]
– Sign of the times / Mama weer all crazee now / Party all night / Stomp your hands, clap your feet / Winners take all / Condition critical / Scream and shout / Red alert / Bad boy / (We were) Born to rock. *(cd-iss.1988) (re-iss.cd+c Oct94)*

Aug 84. (7") **MAMA WEER ALL CRAZEE NOW. / BAD BOY** [ ] [51] Jul 84
(12"+=) – Love's a bitch.

Oct 84. (7") **WINNERS TAKE ALL. / RED ALERT** [ ] [ ]

— (1985) **CHUCK WRIGHT** – bass (ex-GUIFFRA) repl. SARZO to WHITESNAKE

Aug 86. (lp)(c)(cd) **QR III** [ ] [31] Jul 86
– Main attraction / The wild and the young / Twilight hotel / Down and dirty / Rise or fall / Put up or shut up / Still of the night / Bass case / The pump / Slave to love / Helping hands.

Sep 86. (7")(12") **WILD AND THE YOUNG. / RISE OR FALL** [ ] [ ]

— **PAUL SHORTINO** (b.14 May'58) – vocals (ex-ROUGH CUTT) repl. DuBROW to LITTLE WOMEN / **SEAN McNABB** – bass repl. WRIGHT

Oct 88. (7") **STAY WITH ME TONIGHT. / CALLING THE SHOTS** [-] [ ]

Nov 88. (lp)(c)(cd) **POWER AND GROOVE** (US – 'QUIET RIOT') [ ] [ ]
– Stay with me tonight / Callin' the shots / Run to you / I'm king of the hill / The joker / Lunar obsession / Don't wanna be your fool / Coppin' a feel / In a rush / Empty promises.

— Disbanded finally when SHORTINO joined MITCH PERRY. BANALI went on to WASP and later FASTER PUSSYCAT. In 1991, CAVAZO re-united with DuBROW in HEAT. They are joined by KENNY HILARY – bass + PAT ASHBY – drums

– compilations, others, etc. –

May 87. Raw Power; (lp)(c) **WILD, YOUNG AND CRAZEE** [ ] [-]
– Metal health / Cum on feel the noize / Love's a bitch / Mama weer all crazee now / Winner takes all / Condition critical / Bad boy / Main attraction / Wild and the young / Put up or shut up / Slave to love / Let's get crazy.

Feb 94. Rhino-Atlantic; (cd) **THE RANDY RHOADS YEARS** [ ] [ ]

QUIET SUN (see under ⇒ ROXY MUSIC)

QUIREBOYS

Formed: Newcastle, England . . . 1987 initially as The QUEERBOYS by MOGG (younger cousin of UFO's PHIL MOGG). In 1988 they decided to become The QUIREBOYS, after riotous homophobic gigs. Signed to indie 'Survival' label, they issued 2 singles that year, before moving up to 'Parlophone'. They dented the UK Top 40 in 1989 with single '7 O'CLOCK', which was pursued the following year by 3 more and a UK No.2 album 'A LITTLE BIT OF WHAT YOU FANCY'. • **Style:** Retro heavy rock band, influenced by NAZARETH & The FACES (SPIKE resembles ROD STEWART in sound and vision). Their acoustic ballads were very reminiscent of pop band SMOKIE! • **Songwriters:** GRAY-BAILEY penned except HEARTBREAKER (Rolling Stones) / HOLD ON, I'M COMING (Hayes-Porter) / BROTHER LOUIE (Hot Chocolate). • **Trivia:** JIM CREGAN produced debut album. Were named LONDON QUIREBOYS for U. S. releases.

Recommended: A LITTLE BIT OF WHAT YOU FANCY (*6)

SPIKE GRAY – vocals, acoustic guitar, mouth harp / **GUY BAILEY** – guitars, vocals / **NIGEL MOGG** – bass, vocals / **GINGER** – guitar / **CHRIS JOHNSTONE** – keyboards / **NICK 'COZY' CONNEL** – drums

Survival / not issued

May 88. (7") **MAYFAIR. / MISLED** [ ] [-]
(12"+=) – Man on the loose.

Oct 88. (7")(7"pic-d) **THERE SHE GOES AGAIN. / HOW DO YA FEEL** [ ] [-]

— guest **IAN WALLACE** – drums repl. CONNEL / **GUY GRIFFIN** – guitar repl. GINGER

Parlophone / Capitol

Sep 89. (7")(c-s)(7"pic-d) **7 O'CLOCK. / PRETTY GIRLS** [36] [ ]
(12"+=)(cd-s+=) – How do ya feel.

— **RUDY RICHMOND** – drums, percussion repl. WALLACE

Jan 90. (7")(c-s) **HEY YOU. / SEX PARTY** [14] [ ]
(12"+=)(cd-s+=) – Hoochie coochie man.

Feb 90. (cd)(c)(lp) **A BIT OF WHAT YOU FANCY** [2] [ ]
– 7 o'clock / Man on the loose / Whippin' boy / Sex party / Sweet Mary Ann / I don't love you anymore / Hey you / Misled / Long time comin' / Roses and rings / There she goes again / Take me home. *(re-iss.cd+c Mar94)*

Mar 90. (7")(c-s)(7"sha-pic-d) **I DON'T LOVE YOU ANYMORE. / MAYFAIR (original)** [24] [ ]
(12"+=)(cd-s+=) – Hey you (live).

Aug 90. (7")(c-s)(7"sha-pic-d) **THERE SHE GOES AGAIN. / MISLED** [37] [ ]
(12"+=) – Heartbreaker (live).
(cd-s++=) – I don't love you anymore (live).

Dec 90. (cd)(c)(lp) **LIVE AROUND THE WORLD (live)** [ ] [ ]
– Hey you / Sex party / Whippin' boy / Sweet Mary Ann / I don't love you anymore / Heartbreaker / Hold on I'm coming / There she goes again.

Oct 92. (7")(c-s) **TRAMPS AND THIEVES. / AIN'T LOVE BLIND** [41] [ ]
(12"+=) – Wild, wild, wild / Can't park here.
(cd-s+=) – Wild, wild, wild / Pleasure and pain / Best jobs.
(cd-s+=) – Can't park here / Hold on, I'm comin' / Heartbreaker.

Feb 93. (7")(c-s) **BROTHER LOUIE. / CAN'T GET THROUGH** [31] [ ]
(12"+=) – I don't love you anymore (live).
(cd-s++=) – 7 o'clock (live).
(cd-s) – ('A'side) / Tramps and thieves (live) / Hey you (live) / Sweet Mary Ann (live).

Mar 93. (cd)(c)(lp) **BITTER SWEET & TWISTED** [31] [ ]
– Tramps and thieves / White trash blues / Can't park here / King of New York / Don't bite the hand / Last time / Debbie / Brother Louie / Ode to you (baby just walk) / Hates to please / My Saint Jude / Takes no revenge / Wild, wild, wild / Ain't love blind. *(re-iss.cd+c Dec94 on 'Fame')*

– compilations –

Oct 94. Essential; (cd)(c) **(UNDONE) FROM TOOTING TO BARKING** (early demos) [ ] [-]

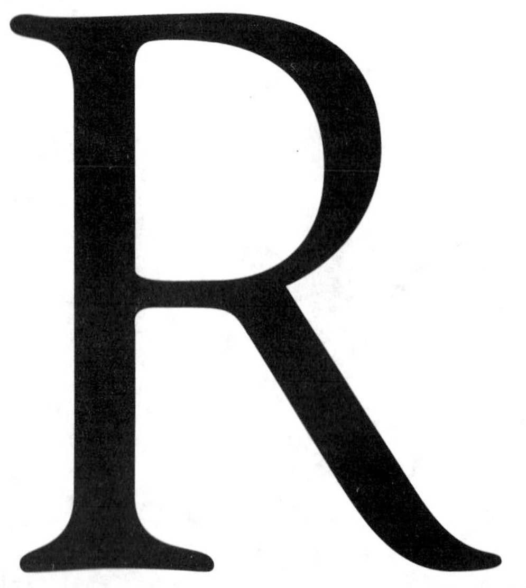

RADIOHEAD

Formed: Oxford, England . . . 1988 by YORKE, etc. Quickly found contract on 'Parlophone / Capitol', and ventured to the US in 1992, where their debut album 'PABLO HONEY', was selling like hotcakes, due to playlisting on MTV. By the end of the year, they were the toast of Britain as well, after their 'CREEP' single hit the Top 10. • **Style:** Grunge guitar punk-rock lying somewhere between NIRVANA or The ONLY ONES, although YORKE's image is certainly his own. • **Songwriters:** YORKE lyrics / group music. • **Trivia:** NME readers voted them in Top 10 bands of '92!, after hearing only singles.

Recommended: PABLO HONEY (*8) / THE BENDS (*9)

THOM YORKE – vocals, guitar / **ED O'BRIEN** – guitar, vocals / **JON GREENWOOD** – guitar / **COLIN GREENWOOD** – bass / **PHIL SELWAY** – drums

Date	Release	Parlophone	Capitol
May 92.	(12"ep)(c-ep)(cd-ep) **PROVE YOURSELF / STUPID CAR. / YOU / THINKING ABOUT YOU**		
Sep 92.	(12"ep)(c-ep)(cd-ep) **CREEP / LURCEE. / INSIDE MY HEAD / MILLION DOLLAR QUESTION**		
Feb 93.	(12"ep)(c-ep)(cd-ep) **ANYONE CAN PLAY GUITAR. / COKE BABIES / FAITHLESS, THE WONDER BOY**	32	
Feb 93.	(cd)(c)(lp) **PABLO HONEY** – You / Creep / How do you? / Stop whispering / Thinking about you / Anyone can play guitar / Ripcord / Vegetable / Prove yourself / I can't / Lurgee / Blow out.	25	32 Jun 93
May 93.	(12"ep)(c-ep)(cd-ep) **POP IS DEAD / BANANA CO. (live). / CREEP (live) / RIPCORD (live)**	42	
Sep 93.	(7"clear-ep)(c-ep)(cd-ep) **CREEP / YES I AM. / BLOW OUT (remix) / INSIDE MY HEAD (live)** (12"ep) – ('A'side) / Vegetable (live) / Killer cars (live) / You (live).	7	34 Jun 93
Oct 94.	(12"ep)(c-ep) **MY IRON LUNG E.P.** – Lewis (mistreated) / The trickster / Punchdrunk lovesick singalong. (cd-s) – (2nd + 3rd tracks) / Lozenger of love. (cd-s) – (1st track) / Permanent daylight / You never wash up after yourself.	24	
Mar 95.	(c-s) **HIGH & DRY. / PLANET TELEX** (cd-s+=) – Maquiladora / Planet Telex (hexidecimal mix). (cd-s+=) – Killer cars / (Planet Telex (L.F.O. JD mix). (12") – Planet Telex (hexidecimal mix) / Planet Telex (L.F.O. JD mix) / Planet Telex (hexidecimal dub) / High & dry.	17	
Mar 95.	(cd)(c)(lp) **THE BENDS** – Planet telex / The bends / High & dry / Fake plastic trees / Bones / Nice dream / Just / My iron lung / Bulletproof . . .I wish I was / Black star / Sulk / Street spirit.	6	
May 95.	(c-s)(cd-s) **FAKE PLASTIC TREES / INDIA RUBBER / HOW CAN YOU BE SURE?** (cd-s) – ('A'side) / ('A'acoustic) / Bullet proof..I wish I was (acoustic) / Street spirit (fade out) (acoustic).	20	
Aug 95.	(c-s)(cd-s) **JUST / PLANET TELEX (Karma Sunra mix) / KILLER CARS (mogadon mix)** (cd-s) – ('A'side) / Bones (live) / Planet Telex (live) / Anyone can play guitar (live).	19	

RADIO HEART (see under ⇒ NUMAN, Gary)

RADIO STARS (see under ⇒ JOHN'S CHILDREN)

Gerry RAFFERTY

Born: 16 Apr'47, Paisley, Scotland. In 1968, he joined The HUMBLEBUMS, alongside future comedian BILLY CONNOLLY and TAM HARVEY. They gave signature to folk label 'Transatlantic', who released 2 lp's 'HUMBLEBUMS' (1969) & 'OPEN UP THE DOOR' (1970), before parting ways. In 1971, RAFFERTY released debut solo album 'CAN I HAVE MY MONEY BACK', before he moved to London and formed STEALER'S WHEEL with RAB NOAKES and JOE EGAN. They signed to 'A&M', but band went through some major personnel changes, before the release of their eponymous album late '72 (see below). The next year, they made Top 10 on both sides of the Atlantic with 'STUCK IN THE MIDDLE WITH YOU'. After two more albums, RAFFERTY went solo for 'United Art', releasing US No.1 album 'CITY TO CITY' early 1978. Taken from it, the classy 'BAKER STREET', hit Top 3 on both sides of the Atlantic. He soon became an established artist for the next 5 years, taking a hiatus around 1983. • **Style:** Singer-songwriter who progressed from CROSBY, STILLS & NASH like STEALER'S WHEEL, to becoming easy-listening smooth pop-rock star. • **Songwriters:** STEALER'S WHEEL was virtually a writing partnership for RAFFERTY and EGAN. GET OUT OF MY LIFE WOMAN (Allen Toussaint). • **Trivia:** The first album by STEALER'S WHEEL was produced by LEIBER & STOLLER.

Recommended: RIGHT DOWN THE LINE – THE BEST OF . . . (*7)

GERRY RAFFERTY – vocals, guitar with session people including future STEALER'S WHEEL members.

Date	Release	Transatla.	Blue Thumb
1971.	(lp) **CAN I HAVE MY MONEY BACK** – New street blues / Didn't I / Mr. Universe / Mary Skeffington / Long way round / Can I have my money back / Sign on the dotted line / Make you break you / To each and everyone / One drink down / Don't count me out / Half a chance / Where I belong. *(re-iss.+c.Sep81) (re-iss.cd+c Apr93 on 'Ariola Express')*		
1972.	(7") **CAN I HAVE MY MONEY BACK. / SO SAD THINKING**		-
1972.	(7") **CAN I HAVE MY MONEY BACK. / SIGN ON THE DOTTED LINE**	-	

STEALER'S WHEEL

GERRY with **JOE EGAN** – vocals, keyboards / **PAUL PILNICK** – guitar (ex-BIG THREE) repl. RAB NOAKES who went solo / **TONY WILLIAMS** – bass repl. IAN CAMPBELL / **ROD COOMBES** – drums repl. ROGER BROWN

Date	Release	A & M	A & M
Nov 72.	(7") **LATE AGAIN. / I GET BY**		
Dec 72.	(lp)(c) **STEALER'S WHEEL** – Late again / Stuck in the middle with you / Another meaning / I get by / Outside looking in / Johnny's song / Next to me / Josie / Gets so lonely / You put something better inside of me.		50
Feb 73.	(7") **YOU PUT SOMETHING BETTER INSIDE OF ME. / NEXT TO ME**		-
May 73.	(7") **STUCK IN THE MIDDLE WITH YOU. / JOSE**	8	6

—— Group had disbanded when RAFFERTY had been replaced by **LUTHER GROSVENOR** (ex-SPOOKY TOOTH) for 2 months. **DELISLE HARPER** – bass repl. others

—— By mid'73, they were a basic duo (**RAFFERTY & EGAN**) augmented by **BERNIE HOLLAND** – guitar / **CHRIS MERCER** – saxophone / **ANDREW STEELE** – drums / **CHRIS NEILL** – harmonica and loads more sessioners.

Date	Release	A & M	A & M
Aug 73.	(7") **EVERYTHING'L TURN OUT FINE. / JOHNNY'S SONG**	33	-
Aug 73.	(7") **(EVERYONE'S AGREED THAT) EVERYTHING'L TURN OUT FINE. / NEXT TO ME**	-	49
Nov 73.	(lp)(c) **FERGUSLIE PARK** – Good businessman / Star / Wheelin' / Waltz (you know it makes sense!) / What more could you want / Over my head / Blind faith / Nothing's gonna change my mind / Steamboat row / Back on my feet again / Who cares / (Everyone's agreed that) Everything'l turn out fine.		
Dec 73.	(7") **STAR. / WHAT MORE COULD I WANT**	25	29
Apr 74.	(7") **WHEELIN'. / YOU PUT SOMETHING BETTER INSIDE OF ME**	-	
Feb 75.	(7") **RIGHT OR WRONG. / THIS MORNING**		
Feb 75.	(lp)(c) **RIGHT OR WRONG** – Benediction / Found my way to you / This morning / Let yourself go / Home from home / Go as you please / Wishbone / Don't get me wrong / Monday morning / Right or wrong.		
May 75.	(7") **FOUND MY WAY TO YOU. / WISHBONE**		-
May 75.	(7") **FOUND MY WAY TO YOU. / THIS MORNING**	-	

—— Broke again later in the year. JOE EGAN went solo, as did GERRY.

– compilations, others, etc. –

Date	Release		
Sep 78.	A&M; (lp)(c) **THE BEST OF STEALER'S WHEEL** *(re-iss.1981 on 'M.F.P.')*		
Sep 78.	A&M; (7") **(EVERYONE AGREED THAT) EVERYTHING'L TURN OUT FINE. / WHO CARES**	-	
Mar 82.	Old Gold; (7") **STUCK IN THE MIDDLE WITH YOU. / STAR**		-

GERRY RAFFERTY

with many session people.

Date	Release	United Art	United Art
Oct 77.	(7") **CITY TO CITY. / MATTIE'S RAG**		
Jan 78.	(lp)(c) **CITY TO CITY** – he ark / Baker Street / Right down the line / City to city / Stealin' time / Mattie's rag / Whatever's written in your heart / Home and dry / Island / Waiting for the day. *(re-iss.Mar85 on 'Fame', cd-iss.Jul89)*	6	1
Feb 78.	(7") **BAKER STREET. / BIG CHANGE IN THE WEATHER**	3	2 Apr 78

—— above featured **RAPHAEL RAVENSCROFT** – saxophone

Date	Release	United Art	United Art
May 78.	(7") **WHATEVER'S WRITTEN IN YOUR HEART. / WAITING FOR THE DAY**		-
Aug 78.	(7") **RIGHT DOWN THE LINE. / WAITING FOR THE DAY**	-	12

Sep 78. (7") **RIGHT DOWN THE LINE. / ISLAND** [ ] [-]
Nov 78. (7") **HOME AND DRY. / MATTIE'S RAG** [-] [28]
May 79. (7") **NIGHT OWL. / WHY DON'T YOU TALK TO ME** [5] [-]
May 79. (lp)(c) **NIGHT OWL** [9] [29]
– Days gone down (still got the light in your eyes) / Night owl / The way that you do it / Why don't you talk to me / Get it right next time / Take the money and run / Family tree / Already gone / The tourist / It's gonna be a long night. *(re-iss.1985 on 'Liberty') (re-iss.Jul86 on 'Fame', cd-iss.Jul89)*
May 79. (7") **DAYS GONE DOWN (STILL GOT THE LIGHT IN YOUR EYES). / WHY DON'T YOU TALK TO ME** [-] [17]
Aug 79. (7") **GET IT RIGHT NEXT TIME. / IT'S GONNA BE A LONG NIGHT** [30] [21]
Mar 80. (7") **BRING IT ALL HOME. / IN TRANSIT** [54] [ ]
Mar 80. (lp)(c) **SNAKES AND LADDERS** [15] [61]
– The Royal Mile / I was a boy scout / Welcome to Hollywood / Wastin' away / Look at the Moon / Bring it all home / The garden of England / Johnny's song / Didn't I / Syncopatin' Sandy / Cafe le Cabotin / Don't close the door. *(cd-iss.Mar89 on 'Liberty')*
Oct 80. (7") **THE ROYAL MILE. / WASTIN' AWAY** [67] [54] Jul 80

Liberty Liberty

Aug 82. (7") **SLEEPWALKING. / WHEN I REST** [ ] [ ]
Sep 82. (lp)(c) **SLEEPWALKING** [39] [ ]
– Standing at the gates / Good intentions / A change of heart / On the way / Sleepwalking / Cat and mouse / The right moment / As wise as a serpent. *(re-iss.Sep84 on 'Fame') (re-iss.Aug86, cd-iss.Mar89)*
Nov 82. (7") **A CHANGE OF HEART. / GOOD INTENTIONS** [ ] [ ]
Nov 82. (7") **STANDING AT THE GATES. / GOOD INTENTIONS** [-] [ ]

—— Took some time off, although he did appear on MARK KNOPFLER's 'Local Hero' 1983 soundtrack and in 1987 produced 'Letter From America' by The PROCLAIMERS.

London London

Apr 88. (7") **SHIPYARD TOWN. / HEARTS DESIRE** [ ] [ ]
(12"+=)(cd-s+=) – ('A'lp version).
May 88. (lp)(c)(cd) **NORTH AND SOUTH** [43] [ ]
– North and south / Moonlight and gold / Tired of talking / Hearts run dry / A dangerous age / Shipyard town / Winter's come / Nothing ever happens down here / On a night like this / Unselfish love. *(re-iss.+cd.Apr91)*

—— with **PAVEL ROSAK** – keyboards, drums, bass, percussion, programming / **HUGH BURNS** – electric guitars, co-producer / **MEL COLLINS** – sax / **B.J. COLE** – pedal steel / **ARRAN AHMUN** – percussion / **MO FOSTER** – bass / **BRYN HAWORTH** – bottleneck guitar / etc. Note: Brother **JIM RAFFERTY** also provided backing vocals & co-songwriting.

A & M A & M

Nov 92. (7")(c-s)(cd-s) **I COULD BE WRONG. / BAKER STREET / LIFE GOES ON** [ ] [ ]
Feb 93. (cd)(c) **ON A WING & A PRAYER** [73] [ ]
– Time's caught up on you / I see red / It's easy to talk / I could be wrong / Don't speak of my heart / Get out of my life woman / Don't give up on me / Hang on / Love and affection / Does he know what he's taken on / The light of love / Life goes on.

Polydor Polydor

Jun 95. (cd) **OVER MY HEAD** [ ] [-]
– Bajan moon / The waters of forgetfulness / Down and out / Over my head / The girl's got no confidence / Wrong thinking / Lonesome polecat / Right or wrong / Late again / Clear day / Out the blue / A new beginning / Her father didn't like me anyway.

– (his) compilations, others, etc. –

Apr 74. Transatlantic; (lp) **GERRY RAFFERTY REVISITED** [ ] [-]
Jul 87. Transatlantic; (cd) **THE COLLECTION** [ ] [-]
Apr 78. Logo; (7") **MARY SKEFFINGTON. / SHOESHINE BOY** [ ] [-]
Sep 78. Logo; (lp) **GERRY RAFFERTY** [ ] [-]
Apr 84. Cambra; (lp)(c) **THE FIRST CHAPTER** [ ] [-]
Jun 88. Demon; (lp) **BLOOD AND GLORY** [ ] [-]
Nov 89. E.M.I.; (lp)(c)(cd) **RIGHT DOWN THE LINE – THE BEST OF GERRY RAFFERTY** [ ] [-]
– Baker Street / Whatever's written in your heart / Bring it all home / Right down the line / Get it right next time / Night owl / A dangerous age / Family tree / Shipyard town / The right moment / Look at the Moon.
(cd+=) – The way that you do it / Tired of talking / The garden of England / Sleepwalking / As wise as a serpent.
Feb 90. E.M.I.; (7") **BAKER STREET (remix). / NIGHT OWL (remix)** [53] [ ]
(12"+=)/ /(cd-s++=) – ('A'extended)./ / Bring it all home (remix).
Apr 95. Castle; (cd) **THE TRANSATLANTIC YEARS** [ ] [-]
Oct 95. Polygram TV; (cd)(c) **ONE MORE DREAM – THE VERY BEST OF ...** [17] [-]

RAGE AGAINST THE MACHINE

Formed: Los Angeles, California, USA . . . 1992 by ZACK and TOM. In 1992 they signed to 'Epic', and due to early '93 appearance on 'The Word', soared into UK charts with riotous classic 'KILLING IN THE NAME'. With their eponymous debut album, making inroads into US charts, they made dramatic entrance in Philadelphia. In front of a 14,000 audience, they walked onto a stage naked with PMRC (Parents Music Resource Committee) written across their chests. This was to protest against the birthplace of American censorship. • **Style:** Multi-racial non-conformist heavy-rock rappers, against the hypocritical money power-whores of their homeland. • **Songwriters:** ROCHA lyrics / group music. • **Trivia:** TOM's father was part of the Mau Maus (Kenyan guerrillas) who fought to end British colonialism there. His uncle JOMO KENYATTA was imprisoned during this period, but went on to become the first Kenyan president. ZACK's father was a Spanish muralist and political activist in L.A.

Recommended: RAGE AGAINST THE MACHINE (*8).

ZACK DE LA ROCHA (b.1971) – vocals / **TOM MORELLO** (b.1965) – guitar / **TIMMY C.** – bass / **BRAD WILK** – drums

Epic Epic

Feb 93. (7")(12"white)(cd-s) **KILLING IN THE NAME. / CLEAR THE LANE / DARKNESS OF GREED** [25] [ ]
Feb 93. (cd)(c)(lp) **RAGE AGAINST THE MACHINE** [17] [45]
– Bombtrack / Killing in the name / Take the power back / Bullet in your head / Know your enemy / Wake up / Fistful of steel / Township rebellion / Freedom.
Apr 93. (7")(12")(cd-s) **BULLET IN THE HEAD. / BULLET IN THE HEAD (remix)** [16] [ ]
– Bullet in the head / Settle for nothing.
Sep 93. (7") **BOMBTRACK. / BOMBTRACK** [37] [ ]
(12"+=)(cd-s+=) – ('A'version).

RAINBOW (see under ⇒ DEEP PURPLE)

RAINCOATS

Formed: Ladbroke Grove, London, England . . . late 1977 by ANA DA SILVA and GINA BIRCH, who were joined by NICK TURNER and ROSS CRIGHTON. In 1978, they left and were replaced by PALMOLIVE and VICKY ASPINALL. Fifth members at the time were KATE KORUS (ex-SLITS), JEREMIE FRANK – guitar, and later in the year; SHIRLEY O'LOUGHLIN. They signed to 'Rough Trade' in 1979, and after a John Peel session, eleased debut 'FAIRYTALE IN A SUPERMARKET'. • **Style:** Quirky punk outfit, not too dissimilar to The SLITS. • **Songwriters:** BIRCH and ASPINALL, except LOLA (Kinks) / RUNNING AWAY (Sly & The Family Stone)/ STILL WAITING (Prince). • **Trivia:** GINA was also part of RED CRAYOLA, and VICKY played violin for NEW AGE STEPPERS.

Recommended: THE RAINCOATS (*7) / ODYSHAPE (*8) / MOVING (*8)

ANA DA SILVA – vocals, guitar / **VICKY ASPINALL** – guitar, violin / **GINA BIRCH** – bass / **PALMOLIVE** (b.Spain) – drums (ex-SLITS)

Rough Trade Rough Trade

Apr 79. (7"m) **FAIRYTALE IN A SUPERMARKET. / IN LOVE / ADVENTURES CLOSE TO HOME** [ ] [-]
Nov 79. (lp) **THE RAINCOATS** [ ] [-]
– Fairytale in a supermarket / No side to fall in / Adventures close to home / Off duty trip / Black and white / Lola / The void / Life on the line / You're a million / In love / No looking. *(re-iss.+cd Jan94)*

—— **INGRID WEISS** – drums repl. PALMOLIVE who returned to Spain.

—— guests on next album **ROBERT WYATT** and **CHARLES HAYWARD** (of THIS HEAT)

Jun 81. (lp) **ODYSHAPE** [ ] [ ]
– The Raincoats / Shouting out loud / Family treat / Only loved at night / Dancing in my head / And then it's o.k. / Baby song / Red shoes / Go away. *(re-iss.+cd Jan94)*

—— **RICHARD DUDANSKI** – drums repl. INGRID

Jul 82. (7") **RUNNING AWAY. / NO-ONE'S LITTLE GIRL** [ ] [-]

—— basic trio **BIRCH, DA SILVA, ASPINALL + DUDANSKI** plus guests **PADDY O'CONNELL** – saxophone / **DEREK GODDARD** – percussion

Nov 83. (7") **ANIMAL RHAPSODY. / NO-ONE'S LITTLE GIRL** [ ] [-]
(12"+=) – ('A'version) / Honey mad woman.
Feb 84. (lp) **MOVING** [ ] [-]
– Ooh ooh la la la / Dreaming in the past / Mouth of a story / Hoey mad woman / Rainstorm / The dance of the hopping mad / Balloon / I saw a hill / Overheard / The body / Avidoso / Animal rhapsody. *(cd-iss.Feb94)*

—— Disbanded after above album.

– compilations, etc. –

1983. R.O.I.R.; (c) **THE KITCHEN TAPES (live)** [-] [ ]
(cd-iss.Feb 95 on 'ROIR Europe')

DOROTHY

were a duo formed by **GINA + VICKY**

Blue Guitar not issued

Jul 88. (7")(12") **STILL WAITING. / FROG PRINCE** [ ] [-]
Jan 89. (7")(12")(cd-s) **LOVING FEELING. / SEXUAL OBSESSION** [ ] [-]

Cooltempo not issued

Jul 89. (7")(12") **REFLECTIONS. / ('A'version)** [ ] [-]

They split after above dance flop.

RAINCOATS

—— re-formed w / **BIRCH, DE SILVA,** etc.

BlastFirst BlastFirst

Jun 94. (12"ep)(cd-ep) **EXTENDED PLAY** [ ] [ ]
– Don't be mean / We smile / No-one's little girl / Shouting out loud.

RAIN PARADE

Formed: Los Angeles, California, USA . . . 1982 by ROBACK brothers. After a few releases on US indie labels (the latter being 'EXPLOSIONS IN

THE GLASS PARADE' for 'Zippo'), they signed to major 'Island' records. They made 2 albums there (the first being a dissapointing live set), before disbanding much too soon. • **Style:** West Coast 60's influenced outfit, fusing psychedelia with tints of early PINK FLOYD. • **Songwriters:** All written by the ROBACKS and group, except AIN'T THAT NOTHIN' (Television).

Recommended: EMERGENCY THIRD POWER RAIL TRIP (*8)

DAVE ROBACK – vocals, guitar, percussion / **MATT PUICHI** – guitar, vocals, sitar / **WILL GLENN** – keyboards / **STEVEN ROBACK** – bass, vocals / **EDDIE KALWA** – drums

not issued Llama

1982. (7") **WHAT'S SHE DONE TO YOUR MIND?. / ?** [-] [ ]

not issued Enigma

1983. (lp) **EMERGENCY THIRD RAIL POWER TRIP** [-] [ ]
– Talking in my sleep / This can't be today / I look around / 1 hr. half ago / Carolyn's song / What she's done to your mind / Look at Merri / Saturday's asylum / Kaleidoscope / Look both ways. *(UK-iss.Aug84 on 'Zippo', cd-iss.1988)*

— trimmed to a quartet when DAVE left to form RAINY DAY (later OPAL). He is now part of MAZZY STAR

Zippo Zippo

1984. (m-lp) **EXPLOSIONS IN THE GLASS PALACE** [ ] [ ]
– You are my friend / Prisoners / Blue / Broken horse / No easy way down. *(re-iss.1988)*

Feb 85. (7") **YOU ARE MY FRIEND. / THIS CAN'T BE TODAY** [ ] [ ] 1984

— **MARK MARCUM** – drums repl. KALWA / added **JOHN THOMAN** – guitar, vocals

Island Island

Jun 85. (lp)(c) **BEYOND THE SUNSET** (live in Tokyo 1984) [78] [ ]
– Night shade / Prisoners / This can't be today / Blue / Eyes closed / Ain't that nothin' / Don't feel bad / 1 hr. half ago / Blue / No easy way down / Cheap wine.

Oct 85. (lp)(c) **CRASHING DREAM** [ ] [ ]
– Depending on you / My secret country / Don't feel bad / Mystic green / Sad eyes kill / Shoot down the railroad man / Fertile crescent / Invisible people / Gone west / Only business.

— Disbanded when PUICHI formed GONE FISHIN'.

– compilations, others, etc. –

Feb 92. Mau Mau; (cd) **EMERGENCY THIRD RAIL POWER / EXPLOSIONS IN THE GLASS PALACE** [ ] [-]

RAIN TREE CROW (see under ⇒ JAPAN)

Bonnie RAITT

Born: 8 Nov'49, Burbank, California, USA. Daughter of Broadway musical star of ('Oklahoma', 'Carousel' & 'Kiss Me Kate') JOHN RAITT, who was a Quaker. In 1967 she relocated to Radcliffe College in Massachusetts, until 1969 when she moved to Cambridge in Boston with boyfriend/manager Dick Waterman. By the early 70's, she was enjoying underground status mostly at The Gaslite in New York. The following year, she was snapped up by to 'Warners' who released eponymous debut. After a follow-up in 1972, she moved back to Los Angeles and released John Hall (of band Orleans) produced album 'TAKIN' MY TIME', which was her first to crack the US Top 100. • **Style:** White country blues singer who mixed contemporary ballads with basic Dixieland R&B. Her constant touring in the early 70's, finally paid off late by the next decade, when 'NICK OF TIME' album reached US No.1. • **Songwriters:** Wrote some herslf, but covered many including WALKING BLUES (Robert Johnson) / UNDER THE FALLING SKY (Jackson Browne) / LOVE HAS NO PRIDE + CRY LIKE A RAINSTORM (Eric Kaz) / GUILTY (Randy Newman) / WHAT IS SUCCESS (Allen Toussaint) / WOMEN BE WISE (Wallace-Beach) / LOVE ME LIKE A MAN (. . . Smither) / ANGELS FROM MONTGOMERY (John Prine) / MY FIRST NIGHT ALONE WITH YOU (. . . Vassey) / SUGAR MAMA (McClinton-Clark) / LOUISE (Paul Siebel) / NO WAY TO TREAT A LADY (Bryan Adams) / RUNAWAY (Del Shannon) / THE GLOW (. . . Hildebrand) / BUILT TO MAKE ME LEAVE HOME (. . . Randle) / WITH YA, WON'T CHAS (. . . Schell) / YOUR GOOD THING (Hayes-Porter) / YOUR GONNA GET WHAT'S COMING (Robert Palmer) / TRUE LOVE IS HARD TO FIND (Toots & The Maytals) / GOIN' WILD FOR YOU BABY (Snow-Batteau) / BURNING DOWN THE HOUSE (Talking Heads) / etc. In 1989 most were written by JOHN HIATT and others including SOMETHING TO TALK ABOUT (S.Eikhardt) / I CAN'T MAKE YOU LOVE ME (Reid / Shamblin). • **Trivia:** Her album NICK OF TIME won a Grammy in 1990 for Best Female Performance. On 28 Apr'91, she married actor Michael O'Keefe.

Recommended: THE BONNIE RAITT COLLECTION (*7)

BONNIE RAITT – vocals, guitar, steel guitar / **FREEBO** – bass / **A.C.REID** – tenor sax / etc.

Warners Warners

Nov 71. (lp)(c) **BONNIE RAITT** [ ] [ ]
– Bluebird revisited / I'm a mighty tight woman / Thank you / Finest lovin' man / Any day woman / Big road / Walking blues / Danger heartbreak dead ahead / Since I fell for you / I ain't blue / Woman be wise. *(re-iss.Jun76)*

Dec 71. (7") **BLUEBEARD. / WOMAN BE WISE** [-] [ ]

Nov 72. (lp)(c) **GIVE IT UP** [ ] [ ] Oct 72
– Give it up or let me go / Nothing seems to matter / I know / If you gotta make a fool of somebody / Love me like a man / Stayed too long at the fair / Under the falling sky / You got to know how / You told me baby / Love has no pride. *(re-iss.Jun76)*

Dec 72. (7") **STAYED TOO LONG AT THE FAIR. / UNDER THE FALLING SKY** [ ] [ ]

— now on session **LOWELL GEORGE / BILL PAYNE / JIM KELTNER + TAJ MAHAL**

Oct 73. (7") **YOU'VE BEEN IN LOVE TOO LONG. / EVERYBODY'S CRYIN' MERCY** [-] [ ]

Nov 73. (lp)(c) **TAKIN' MY TIME** [ ] [87] Oct 73
– You've been in love too long / I gave my love a candle / Let me in / Everybody's cryin' mercy / Cry like a rainstorm / Wah she go do / I feel the same / I thought I was a child / Write me a few of your lines – Kokomo blues / Guilty. *(re-iss.Jun76) (cd-iss.Feb93)*

Oct 74. (7") **I GOT PLENTY. / YOU GOTTA BE READY FOR LOVE (IF YOU WANNA BE MINE)** [-] [ ]

Nov 74. (lp)(c) **STREETLIGHTS** [ ] [80] Oct 74
– That song about the Midway / Rainy day man / Angel from Montgomery / I got plenty / Streetlights / What is success / Ain't nobody home / Everything that touches you / Got you on my mind / You gotta be ready for love (if you wanna be mine). *(cd-iss.1989)*

Nov 75. (7") **MY FIRST NIGHT ALONE WITH YOU. / GOOD ENOUGH** [-] [ ]

Dec 75. (lp)(c) **HOME PLATE** [ ] [43] Oct 75
– What do you want the boy to do / Good enough / Run like a thief / Fool yourself / My first night alone with you / Walk out the front door / Sugar mama / Pleasin' each other / I'm blowin' away / Your sweet and shiny eyes.

May 76. (7") **WALK OUT THE FRONT DOOR. / RUN LIKE A THIEF** [-] [ ]

Jun 76. (7") **I'M BLOWIN' AWAY. / RUN LIKE A THIEF** [ ] [ ]

— In 1976, she duetted w/**GEOFF MULDAUR** on single 'WHEN YOU TOUCH ME THIS WAY' / SINCE I'VE BEEN WITH YOU BABE'.

— Her touring band were **WILL McFARLANE** – guitar / **JEFF LABES** – keyboards / **DENNIS WHITTED** – drums / **FREEBO** – bass (as always) + guests **MICHAEL McDONALD + J.D.SOUTHER** on guest backing vocals

Apr 77. (lp)(c) **SWEET FORGIVENESS** [ ] [25]
– Sweet forgiveness / Gamblin' man / Two lives / Runaway / About to make me leave home / Three time loser / My opening farewell / Takin' my time / Home / Louise. *(cd-iss.Feb93)*

May 77. (7") **RUNAWAY. / LOUISE** [-] [57]

May 77. (7") **RUNAWAY. / HOME** [ ] [-]

Aug 77. (7") **THREE TIME LOSER. / TWO LIVES** [-] [ ]

Aug 77. (7") **THREE TIME LOSER. / LOUISE** [ ] [-]

Nov 77. (7") **GAMBLIN' MAN. / ABOUT TO MAKE ME LEAVE HOME** [-] [ ]

Oct 79. (lp)(c) **THE GLOW** [ ] [30]
– I thank you / Your good thing (is about to end) / Sleep's dark and silent gate / The glow / Bye bye baby / The boy can't help it / (I could have been your) Best old friend / You're gonna get what's coming / (Goin') Wild for you baby. *(cd-iss.Feb93)*

Nov 79. (7") **YOU'RE GONNA GET WHAT'S COMING. / THE GLOW** [-] [73]

Mar 80. (7") **(I COULD HAVE BEEN YOUR) BEST OLD FRIEND. / (GOIN') WILD FOR YOU BABY** [-] [ ]

— In mid-80's, she released 'Asylum' 45; 'DON'T IT MAKE YOU WANNA DANCE'. At the same time she and J.D. SOUTHER issued 'ONCE IN A LIFE-TIME' / 'YOU'RE ONLY LONELY'.

— next feat. **The BUMP BAND** incl. **IAN McLAGAN** – keyboards (ex-SMALL FACES) / **JOHNNY LEE SCHELL** – guitar / **RAY O'HARA** – bass / **RICKY FATAAR** – drums

Feb 82. (7") **CAN'T GET ENOUGH. / KEEP THIS HEART IN MIND** [-] [ ]

Feb 82. (lp)(c) **GREEN LIGHT** [ ] [38]
– Keep this heart in mind / River of tears / Can't get enough / Me and the boys / I can't help myself / Willya wontcha / Let's keep it between us / Baby come back / Talk to me / Green light.

Apr 82. (7") **ME AND THE BOYS. / RIVER OF TEARS** [-] [ ]

Apr 82. (7") **ME AND THE BOYS. / KEEP THIS HEART IN MIND** [ ] [-]

— She semi-retired in 1982 to go through a period of drug rehabilitation and attend a form of alcoholics anonymous.

Sep 86. (lp)(c)(cd) **NINE LIVES** [ ] [ ] Aug 86
– No way to treat a lady / Runnin' back to me / Who but a fool / Crime of passion / All day, all night / Stand up to the night / Excited / Freezin' (for a little human love) / True love is hard to find / Angel.

Sep 86. (7") **NO WAY TO TREAT A LADY. / STAND UP TO THE NIGHT** [-] [ ]

Feb 87. (7") **CRIMES OF PASSION. / STAND UP TO THE NIGHT** [-] [ ]

— In Oct '88, she teamed up with DON WAS of WAS (NOT WAS) on 'A&M' single 'BABY MINE'. Their vocalists **SWEAT PEA ATKINSON + SIR HARRY BOWENS** plus guests **DAVID CROSBY & GRAHAM NASH, FATAAR & SCHELL, KIM WILSON**, etc.

Capitol Capitol

Apr 89. (lp)(c)(cd) **NICK OF TIME** [51] [1]
– Nick of time / A thing called love / Love letter / Cry on my shoulder / Real man / Nobody's girl / Have a heart / Too soon to tell / I will not be denied / I ain't gonna let you break my heart again / The road's my middle name. *(re-iss.Apr90)*

May 89. (7")(c-s) **NICK OF TIME. / THE ROAD'S MY MIDDLE NAME** [ ] [92] May 90
(12"+=)(cd-s+=) – I ain't gonna let you break my heart again. *(re-iss.Mar90)*

Mar 90. (7") **HAVE A HEART. / ?** [-] [49]

May 90. (7") **A THING CALLED LOVE. / NOBODY'S GIRL** [ ] [ ]
(12"+=)(cd-s+=) – The road's my middle name.

— next also feat. **HIATT**, plus **BRUCE HORNSBY + RICHARD THOMPSON**

Jul 91. (cd)(c)(lp) **LUCK OF THE DRAW** [38] [2]
– Something to talk about / Good man, good woman / I can't make you love me / Tangled and dark / Come to me / No business / One part of my lover / Not the only one / Papa come quick (Jody and Chico) / Slow ride / Luck of the draw / All at once.

Jul 91. (7")(c-s) **SOMETHING TO TALK ABOUT. / ONE PART OF MY LOVER** [ ] [5]
(12"+=) – I ain't gonna let you break my heart again.
(cd-s++=) – Nick of time. *(re-iss.Feb92)*

Aug 91. (7")(c-s) **NOT THE ONLY ONE. / COME TO ME** [ ] [34] Mar 92
(12"+=)(cd-s+=) – Papa come quick (Jody and Chico).

Dec 91. (7")(c-s) **I CAN'T MAKE YOU LOVE ME. / COME TO ME** [50] [18] Nov 91
(cd-s+=) – Tangled and dark.

Jun 92. (7") **GOOD MAN, GOOD WOMAN. / NICK OF TIME** [ ] [ ]
(cd-s+=) – Thing called love / One part be my lover.
Apr 94. (c-s) **LOVE SNEAKIN' UP ON YOU / NICK OF TIME / HELL TO PAY** [69] [19] Mar94
(cd-s+=) – Baby mine.
Apr 94. (cd)(c)(lp) **LONGING IN THEIR HEARTS** [26] [1] Mar94
– Love sneakin' up on you / Longing in their hearts / You / Cool, clear water / Circle dance / I sho do / Dimming of the day / Feeling of falling / Steal your heart away / Storm warning / Hell to pay / Shadow of doubt.
Jun 94. (c-s) **YOU. / I CAN'T MAKE YOU LOVE ME** [31] [92]
(cd-s+=) – I ain't gonna let you break my heart again / All at once.
(cd-s) – ('A'side) / This thing called love / Longing in their hearts / Good man, good woman.
May 95. (c-s) **YOU GOT IT / FEELING OF FALLING** [ ] [33] Feb 95
(cd-s+=) – Circle dance.
— (above single issued on 'Arista')
Nov 95. (c-s) **ROCK STEADY ("BONNIE RAITT & BRYAN ADAMS" live) / COME TO ME (live) / FEELING OF FALLING (live)** [50] [73]
(cd-s+=) – Thing called love (live with BRUCE HORNSBY).
Nov 95. (cd)(c) **ROAD TESTED (live)** [69] [44]
– Thing called love / Something to talk about / Never make your move too soon / Shake a little / Matters of the heart / Love me like a man / The Kokomo medley: Write me a few of your lines – Kokomo blues / My opening farewell / Dimming of the day / Longing in their hearts / Love sneakin' up on you / Burning down the house / I can't make you love me / I believe I'm in love / Rock steady / Angel from Montgomery.

– compilations, others, etc. –

Aug 90. Warners; (cd)(c)(lp) **THE BONNIE RAITT COLLECTION** [ ] [61] Jul 90
– Finest lovin' man / Give it up or let me go / Women be wise (live with SIPPIE WALLACE) / Under the falling sky / Love me like a man / Love has no pride / I feel the same / Guilty / Angel from Montgomery / What is success / My first night alone without you / Sugar mama / Louise / About to make me leave home / Runaway / The glow / (Goin') Wild for you baby / Willya wontcha / True love is hard to find / No way to treat a lady.

RAMONES

Formed: Forest Hills, New York, USA . . . Aug'74 as a trio by JOHNNY, JOEY and DEE DEE, who all took the working surname RAMONE. Began residency at The CBGB's with TOMMY being added to let JOEY sing. In June 1975, they failed an audition for RICK DERRINGER's 'Blue Sky' label in front of 20,000 fans at a JOHNNY WINTER concert. Later that year, their new manager Danny Fields, obtained a deal with up and coming new wave label 'Sire' run by Seymour Stein. They soon recorded Craig Leon produced eponymous debut lp. In mid-76, its release caused minor stir and nearly made the US Top 100. With the new wave scene now burgeoning in the UK, they arrived to play a tour supporting FLAMIN' GROOVIES. The following year 1977, saw their second album 'LEAVE HOME', break into the UK Top 50, with it being closely chased by a hit single 'SHEENA IS A PUNK ROCKER'. They continued to compete in the charts until in 1980, when they lost credibility and past fans, by breaking the UK Top 10 with a PHIL SPECTOR produced 'BABY I LOVE YOU'. • **Style:** Innovators of 70's punk rock, famous for their high-speed 2 minute buzz-saw classics about girls, solvent-abuse and sunny weather. Their usual cartoon punk image, 1-2-3-4 intro and 'Gabba Gabba Hey', was shelved in the 80's, for a more sedated 3-4 minute song (a RAMONES epic!). • **Songwriters:** DEE DEE and group, except; DO YOU WANNA DANCE (Bobby Freeman) / SURFIN' BIRD (Trashmen) / BABY I LOVE YOU (Ronettes; Phil Spector) / NEEDLES AND PINS (Searchers) / STREET FIGHTIN' MAN (Rolling Stones) / TAKE IT AS IT COMES (Doors) / etc. In '77, DEE DEE co-wrote 'CHINESE ROCKS' for The HEARTBREAKERS. • **Trivia:** The RAMONES featured in the films 'Blank Generation' (1976) & 'Rock'n'roll High School' (Roger Corman 1979).

Recommended: RAMONES (*9) / LEAVE HOME (*8) / ROCKET TO RUSSIA (*8) / RAMONES MANIA (*9).

JOEY RAMONE (b.JEFFREY HYMAN, 19 May'52) – vocals (was drummer) / **JOHNNY RAMONE** (b.JOHN CUMMINGS, 8 Oct'48, Long Island) – guitar, vocals / **DEE DEE RAMONE** (b.DOUGLAS COLVIN, 18 Sep'52, Fort Lee, VA) – bass, vocals / **TOMMY RAMONE** (b.TOMMY ERDELYI, 29 Jan'49, Budapest, Hungary) – drums

Sire Sire
Jul 76. (lp) **RAMONES** [ ] [ ] May 76
– Blitzkreig bop / Beat on the brat / Judy is a punk / I wanna be your boyfriend / Chain saw / Now I wanna sniff some glue / I don't wanna go down to the basement / Loudmouth / Havana affair / Listen to my heart / 53rd & 3rd / Let's dance / I don't wanna walk around with you / Today your love, tomorrow the world. *(re-iss.Sep78) (US re-iss.Sep87)*
Jul 76. (7") **BLITZKREIG BOP. / HAVANA AFFAIR** [ ] [ ] May 76
Oct 76. (7"m) **I WANNA BE YOUR BOYFRIEND. / CALIFORNIA SUN (live) / I DON'T WANNA WALK AROUND WITH YOU (live)** [-] [ ]
Feb 77. (7"m) **I REMEMBER YOU. / CALIFORNIA SUN (live) / I DON'T WANNA WALK AROUND WITH YOU (live)** [ ] [ ]
Mar 77. (lp)(c) **LEAVE HOME** [45] [ ] Feb 77
– Glad to see you go / Gimme gimme shock treatment / I remember you / Oh oh I love her so / Babysitter * / Suzy is a headbanger / Pinhead / Now I wanna be a good boy / Swallow my pride / What's your game / California sun / Commando / You're gonna kill that girl / You should never have opened that door / California sun. *(re-iss.Jun77 'Carbona Not Glue' replaced *; other re-iss's same) (re-iss.Sep78) (re-iss.Nov87 on 'Mau Mau')*
May 77. (7"m)(12"m) **SHEENA IS A PUNK ROCKER. / COMMANDO / I DON'T CARE** [22] [81]
Jul 77. (7"m) **SWALLOW MY PRIDE. / PINHEAD / LET'S DANCE (live)** [36] [ ] Mar 77
Nov 77. (7"m)(12"m) **ROCKAWAY BEACH. / TEENAGE LOBOTOMY / BEAT ON THE BRAT** [ ] [-]
Nov 77. (7") **ROCKAWAY BEACH. / LOCKET LOVE** [-] [66]
Dec 77. (lp)(c) **ROCKET TO RUSSIA** [60] [49] Nov 77
– Cretin hop / Rockaway beach / Here today, gone tomorrow / Locket love / I don't care / Sheena is a punk rocker / We're a happy family / Teenage lobotomy / Do you wanna dance? / I wanna be well / I can't give you anything / Ramona / Surfin' bird / Why is it always this way. *(re-iss.Sep78)*
Feb 78. (7") **DO YOU WANNA DANCE?. / BABYSITTER** [-] [86]
Mar 78. (7"m) **DO YOU WANNA DANCE?. / IT'S A LONG WAY BACK TO GERMANY / CRETIN HOP** [ ] [-]
— **MARKY RAMONE** (b.MARC BELL) – drums (ex-RICHARD HELL & THE VOIDOIDS, ex-DUST) repl. TOMMY who continued producing others.
Sep 78. (7")(7"yellow)(12"yellow)(12"red) **DON'T COME CLOSE. / I DON'T WANT YOU** [38] [ ]
Oct 78. (lp)(c)(yellow-lp) **ROAD TO RUIN** [32] [ ]
– I just want to have something to do / I wanted everything / Don't come close / I don't want you / Needles and pins / I'm against it / I wanna be sedated / Go mental / Questioningly / She's the one / Bad brain / It's a long way back.
Nov 78. (7") **NEEDLES AND PINS. / I WANTED EVERYTHING** [-] [ ]
Jan 79. (7") **SHE'S THE ONE. / I WANNA BE SEDATED** [ ] [ ]
May 79. (d-lp)(c) **IT'S ALIVE (live)** [27] [ ]
– Rockaway beach / Teenage lobotomy / Blitzkreig bop / I wanna be well / Glad to see you go / Gimme gimme shock treatment / You're gonna kill that girl / I don't care / Sheena is a punk rocker / Havana affair / Commando / Here today, gone tomorrow / Surfin' bird / Cretin hop / Listen to my heart / California sun / I don't wanna walk around with you / Pinhead / Do you wanna dance? / Chain saw / Today your love, tomorrow the world / Now I wanna be a good boy / Judy is a punk / Suzy is a headbanger / Let's dance / Oh oh I love her so / Now I wanna sniff some glue / We're a happy family. *(album features TOMMY on drums) (cd-iss.Nov93 on 'Warners')*
Sep 79. (7") **ROCK'N'ROLL HIGH SCHOOL. / I WANT YOU AROUND** [-] [ ]
Sep 79. (7") **ROCK'N'ROLL HIGH SCHOOL. / SHEENA IS A PUNK ROCKER (live) / ROCKAWAY BEACH (live)** [67] [-]
Jan 80. (lp)(c) **END OF THE CENTURY** [14] [44]
– Do you remember rock'n'roll radio? / I'm affected / Danny says / Chinese rock / The return of Jackie and Judy / Let's go / Baby I love you / I can't make it on time / This ain't Havana / Rock'n'roll high school / All the way / High risk insurance. *(US re-iss.May88) (re-iss.cd Mar94)*
Jan 80. (7") **BABY I LOVE YOU. / HIGH RISK INSURANCE** [8] [ ]
Apr 80. (7") **DO YOU REMEMBER ROCK'N'ROLL RADIO?. / LET'S GO** [-] [ ]
Apr 80. (7") **DO YOU REMEMBER ROCK'N'ROLL RADIO?. / I WANT YOU AROUND** [54] [-]
Jul 81. (7") **WE WANT THE AIRWAVES. / ALL'S QUIET ON THE EASTERN FRONT** [ ] [ ]
Jul 81. (lp)(c) **PLEASANT DREAMS** [ ] [58]
– We want the airwaves / All's quiet on the Eastern front / The KKK took my baby away / Don't go / You sound like you're sick / It's not my place / She's a sensation / 7-11 / You didn't mean anything to me / Come on now / This business is killing me / Sitting in my room. *(US re-iss.May88) (re-iss.cd Mar94)*
Oct 81. (7") **SHE'S A SENSATION. / ALL'S QUIET ON THE EASTERN FRONT** [ ] [ ]
May 83. (lp)(c) **SUBTERRANEAN JUNGLE** [ ] [83]
– Little bit o' soul / I need your love / Outsider / What'd ya do / Highest trails above / Somebody like me / Psycho therapy / Time has come today / My-my kind of girl / In the park / Time bomb / Everytime I eat vegetables It makes me think of you. *(re-iss.cd Mar94)*
Jun 83. (7") **TIME HAS COME TODAY. / PSYCHO THERAPY** [ ] [ ]
(12"+=) – Baby I love you / Don't come close.
— **RICKY RAMONE** (b.RICHARD BEAU) – drums (ex-VELVETEENS) repl. MARC

Beggar's B. Sire
Nov 84. (7") **HOWLING AT THE MOON (SHA LA LA). / WART HOG** [-] [ ]
Jan 85. (lp)(c) **TOO TOUGH TO DIE** [63] [ ] Oct 84
– Mama's boy / I'm not afraid of life / Too young to die / Durango 95 / Wart hog / Danger zone / Chasing the night / Howling at the Moon (sha-la-la) / Daytime dilemma (dangers of love) / Planet Earth 1988 / Human kind / Endless vacation / No go.
Jan 85. (7") **HOWLING AT THE MOON (SHA-LA-LA). / SMASH YOU** [ ] [-]
(12"+=) – Street fighting man.
Mar 85. (d7")(12"pic-d) **CHASING THE NIGHT. / HOWLING AT THE MOON (SHA-LA-LA)/ / SMASH YOU. / STREET FIGHTING MAN** [ ] [ ]
Jun 85. (7") **BONZO GOES TO BITBURG. / DAYTIME DILEMMA (DANGERS OF LOVE)** [ ] [-]
(12"+=) – Go home Annie.
Apr 86. (7") **SOMETHING TO BELIEVE IN. / SOMEBODY PUT SOMETHING IN MY DRINK** [69] [ ]
(12"+=) – Can't say anything nice.
May 86. (lp)(c)(cd) **ANIMAL BOY** [38] [ ]
– Somebody put something in my drink / Animal boy / Love kills / Apeman hop / She belongs to me / Crummy stuff / My brain is hanging upside down (Bonzo goes to Bitburg) / She belongs to me / Mental hell / Eat that rat / Freak of nature / Hair of the dog / Something to believe in.
Jul 86. (7") **CRUMMY STUFF. / SHE BELONGS TO ME** [ ] [ ]
(12"+=)(12"red+=) – I don't want to live this life.
— **MARC RAMONE** – drums returned to repl. CLEM BURKE (ex-BLONDIE) who had repl. RICKY (above now with originals JOEY, DEE DEE and JOHNNY.)
Sep 87. (7") **A REAL COOL TIME. / INDIAN GIVER** [ ] [ ]
(12"+=) – Life goes on.
Sep 87. (lp)(c)(cd) **HALFWAY TO SANITY** [78] [ ]
– I wanna live / Bop 'til you drop / Garden of serenity / Weasel face / Go lil' Camaro go / I know better now / Death of me / I lost my mind / A real cool time / I'm not Jesus / Bye bye baby / Worm man. *(cd+=)*– Indian giver / Life goes on.

Nov 87. (7")(12") **I WANNA LIVE. / MERRY CHRISTMAS (I DON'T WANT TO FIGHT TONIGHT)**

Jun 88. (d-lp)(c)(cd) **RAMONES MANIA** (compilation)
– I wanna be sedated / Teenage lobotomy / Do you remember rock'n'roll radio? / Gimme gimme shock treatment / Beat on the brat / Sheena is a punk rocker / I wanna live / Pinhead / Blitzkreig bop / Cretin hop / Rockaway beach / Commando / I wanna be your boyfriend / Mama's boy / Bop 'til you drop / We're a happy family / Bonzo goes to Bitburg / The outsider / Psycho therapy / Wart hog / Animal boy / Needles and pins / Howlin' at the Moon / Somebody put something in my drink / We want the airwaves / Chinese rocks / I just want to have something to do / The KKK took my baby away / Indian giver / Rock'n'roll high school.

Chrysalis Sire

Aug 89. (lp)(c)(cd) **BRAIN DRAIN** 75 Jun 89
– I believe in miracles / Zero zero UFO / Don't bust my chops / Punishment fits the crime / All screwed up / Palisades Park / Pet sematary / Learn to listen / Can't get you outta my mind / Ignorance is bliss / Come back, baby / Merry Christmas (I don't want to fight tonight). *(re-iss.cd+c Mar93)*

Sep 89. (7") **PET SEMATARY. / ALL SCREWED UP** -
(12"+=) – Zero zero UFO.

Sep 89. (7") **PET SEMATARY. / SHEENA IS A PUNK ROCKER** -

— **C.J.RAMONE** – bass repl. DEE DEE who became rap artist DEE DEE KING

Oct 91. (cd)(c)(d-lp) **LIVE LOCO (live)**
– The good, the bad and the ugly / Django 95 / Teenage lobotomy / Psycho therapy / Blitzkreig bop / Rock'n'roll radio / I believe in miracles / Gimme gimme shock treatment / Rock'n'roll high school / I wanna be sedated / The KKK took my baby away / I wanna live / Bonzo goes to Bitzburg / Too tough to die / Sheena is a punk rocker / Rockaway beach / Pet semetary / Don't bust my shape / Palisades park / Mama's boy / Animal boy / Wart hog / Surfin' bird / Cretin hop / I don't wanna walk around with you / Today your love, tomorrow the world / Pinhead / Somebody put something in my drink / Beat on the brat / Judy is a punk / Chinese rocks / Love kills / Ignorance is bliss.

Chrysalis Radio-active

Sep 92. (cd)(c)(lp) **MONDO BIZARRO**
– Censorshit / The job that ate my brain / Poison heart / Anxiety / Strength to endure / It's gonna be alright / Take it as it comes / Main man / Tomorrow she goes away / I won't let it happen again / Cabbies on crack / Heidi is a heartache / Touring.

Oct 92. (7")(c-s)(7"yellow) **POISON HEART. / CENSORSHIT (live)** 69
(12"+=) – Chinese rocks (live) / Sheena is a punk rocker (live).
(cd-s+=) – Rock and roll radio (live).

Dec 93. (cd)(c)(lp) **ACID EATERS**
– Journey to the center of the mind / Substitute / Out of time / The shape of things to come / Somebody to love / When I was young / 7 and 7 is / My back pages / Can't seem to make you mine / Have you ever seen the rain / I can't control myself / Surf city.

— Album of covers; SUBSTITUTE (Who) / I CAN'T CONTROL MYSELF (Troggs) / SURF CITY (Jan & Dean) / OUT OF TIME (Rolling Stones) / THE SHAPE OF THINGS TO COME (Headboys) / etc.

Jun 95. (cd)(c)(lp) **IL ADIOS AMIGOS!** 62
– I don't want to grow up / I'm makin' monsters for my friends / It's not for me to know / The crusher / Life's a gas / Take the pain away / I love you / Cretin family / Have a nice day / Scattergun / Got a lot to say / She talks to rainbows / Born to die in Berlin.

DEE DEE RAMONE

writes with **REY**

World Dom. World Dom.

Jun 94. (cd)(lp) **I HATE FREAKS LIKE YOU**
– I'm making monsters for my friends / Don't look in my window / Chinese bitch / It's not for me to know / Runaway / All's quiet on the Eastern Front / I hate it / Life is like a little smart Alleck / I hate creeps like you / Trust me / Curse on me / I'm seeing strawberry's again / Lass mich in Fuhe / I'm making monsters for my friends.

– (RAMONES) compilations, others, etc. –

Aug 80. RSO; (7") **I WANNA BE SEDATED. / THE RETURN OF JACKIE AND JUDY**

— (above from Various Artists Film Soundtrack 'Rock'n'roll High School' also incl.Medley: Blitzkreig / Lobotomy / California / Pinhead / She's the one)

Nov 80. Sire; (7"ep) **MELTDOWN WITH THE RAMONES**
– I just wanna have something to do / Questioningly / I wanna be your boyfriend / Here today, gone tomorrow.

Sep 90. (cd)(c)(d-lp) **ALL THE STUFF (AND MORE)**
(demos 1976-1977, etc.)

Mar 93. Selfless; (lp) **THE SCREECHING WEASEL**

— JOEY also on "HOLLY & JOEY" 7" – 1982 'I Got You Babe' on 'Virgin'.
In Aug88, JOHNNY teamed up with DEBBIE HARRY for 7" – 'Go Lil Camara Go'.

Lee RANALDO (see under ⇒ SONIC YOUTH)

RAPEMAN (see under ⇒ BIG BLACK)

RASCALS

Formed: New York, USA ... 1964 by ex-JOEY DEE & THE STARLIGHTERS members FELIX CAVALIERE, EDDIE BRIGATI and GENE CORNISH. They recruited past friend of FELIX's and jazz sessioner DINO DANELLI. After meeting promoter/manager Sid Bernstein, they received contract with 'Atlantic' records and due to age, became The YOUNG RASCALS. On 15 August 1965, they supported The BEATLES at their final live concert at The Shea Stadium. To end the year, they issued a near US Top 50 entry 'I AIN'T GONNA EAT MY HEART OUT ANYMORE'. Their follow-up in 1966 'GOOD LOVIN', smashed into the No.1 spot, and was the first of a string of hits, during the 60's, the latter half as The RASCALS. • **Style:** White soul/R&B outfit, who mellowed with romance and flower-power peacefulness by 1967. • **Songwriters:** CAVALIERE-BRIGATI penned except; I AIN'T GONNA EAT MY HEART OUT ANYMORE (Pam Sawyer & Lori Burton) / GOOD LOVIN' (Rudy Clark & Artie Resnick) / etc. • **Trivia:** Early in 1968 while on tour in Florida, their trailer broke down and they received anti-rock music backlash from local rednecks. After their escape, they always toured with at least 1 black supporting act as a way of protest.

Recommended: IN RETROSPECTIVE (*5)

FELIX CAVALIERE (b.29 Nov'44, Pelham, New York) – vocals, keyboards / **EDDIE BRIGATI** (b.22 Oct'46, Garfield, New Jersey) – vocals, percussion / **GENE CORNISH** (b.14 May'45, Rochester, New York) – guitar / **DINO DANELLI** (b.23 Jul'45, New York) – drums

YOUNG RASCALS

Atlantic Atlantic

Dec 65. (7") **I AIN'T GONNA EAT OUT MY HEART ANYMORE. / SLOW DOWN** 52

Mar 66. (7") **GOOD LOVIN'. / MUSTANG SALLY** 1

Jun 66. (7") **YOU BETTER RUN. / LOVE IS A BEAUTIFUL THING** 20

Jun 66. (lp) **THE YOUNG RASCALS** 15 May 66
– Slow down / Baby let's wait / Just a little / I believe / Do you feel it / Good lovin' / Like a rolling stone / Mustang Sally / I ain't gonna eat out my heart anymore / In the midnight hour.

Sep 66. (7") **COME ON UP. / WHAT IS THE REASON** 43

Dec 66. (7") **TOO MANY FISH IN THE SEA. / NO LOVE TO GIVE** -

Feb 67. (7") **I'VE BEEN LONELY TOO LONG. / IF YOU KNEW** 16 Jan 67

Feb 67. (lp) **COLLECTIONS** 14 Jan 67
– What is the reason / Since I fell for you / Lonely too long / No love to give / Mickey's monkey – Love lights / Come on up / Too many fish in the sea / More / 1956 / Love is a beautiful thing / Land of 1000 dances.

Apr 67. (7") **GROOVIN'. / SUENO** 8 1

Jul 67. (7") **A GIRL LIKE YOU. / IT'S LOVE** 37 10

Aug 67. (lp) **GROOVIN'** 4
– A girl like you / Find somebody / I'm so happy now / Sueno / How can I be sure / Groovin' / If you knew / I don't love you anymore / You better run / A lace in the Sun / It's love.

Sep 67. (7") **HOW CAN I BE SURE. / I'M SO HAPPY NOW** - 4

Sep 67. (7") **HOW CAN I BE SURE. / I DON'T LOVE YOU ANYMORE** -

Dec 67. (7") **IT'S WONDERFUL. / OF COURSE** 20

The RASCALS

Apr 68. (7") **A BEAUTIFUL MORNING. / RAINY DAY** 3

Apr 68. (lp) **ONCE UPON A DREAM** 9 Mar 68
– Intro / Easy rollin' / Rainy day / Please love me / It's wonderful / I'm gonna love you / My Hawaii / My world / Silly girl / Singin' the blues too long / Sattva / Finale: Once upon a dream.

Jul 68. (7") **PEOPLE GOT TO BE FREE. / MY WORLD** 1

Aug 68. (lp) **TIME PEACE – THE RASCALS' GREATEST HITS** (compilation) 1 Jul 68
– How can I be sure / Groovin' / I've been lonely too long / In the midnight hour / I ain't gonna eat my heart out anymore / Good lovin' / You better run / Come on up / Mustang Sally / Love is a beautiful thing / A girl like you / It's wonderful / Easy rollin' / Beautiful morning. *(cd-iss.Aug93 & May95 on 'Rhino')*

Nov 68. (7") **A RAY OF HOPE. / ANY DANCE'LL DO** - 24

Feb 69. (7") **HEAVEN. / BABY I'M BLUE** - 39

Apr 69. (d-lp) **FREEDOM SUITE** 17 Mar 69
– America the beautiful / Me and my friends / Any dance'll do / Look around / A ray of hope / Island of love / Of course / Love was so easy to give / People got to be free / Baby I'm blue / Heaven / Adrian's birthday / Boom / Cute.

May 69. (7") **SEE. / AWAY, AWAY** 27

Sep 69. (7") **CARRY ME BACK. / REAL THING** 26

Dec 69. (lp) **SEE** 45
– See / I'd like to you home / Remember me / I'm blue / Stop and think / Temptations 'bout to get me / Nubia / Carry me back / Away away / Real thing / Death's reply / Hold on.

Jan 70. (7") **HOLD ON. / I BELIEVE** 51

Aug 70. (7") **GLORY GLORY. / YOU DON'T KNOW** 58 Jul 70
(above featured backing by SWEET INSPIRATIONS gospel choir)

Jan 71. (lp) **SEARCH AND NEARNESS**
– Right on / I believe / Thank you baby / You don't know / Mama / Almost home / The letter / Ready for love / Fortunes / Glory glory.

Jan 71. (7") **RIGHT ON. / ALMOST HOME** -

— **ROBERT POPWELL** – bass repl. EDDIE / **BUZZY FEITEN** – guitar repl. GENE / added **ANN SUTTON** – vocals

C.B.S. Columbia

Jun 71. (7") **LOVE ME. / HAPPY SONG** - 95

Jun 71. (lp) **PEACEFUL WORLD**
– Sky trane / In and out of love / Bit of Heaven / Love me / Peaceful world / Mother Nature land / Icy water / Happy song / Love letter / Little dove / Visit to Mother Nature land / Getting nearer.

Dec 71. (7") **LUCKY DAY. / LOVE LETTER**

Apr 72. (lp) **THE ISLAND OF REAL**
– Lucky day / Saga of New York / Be on the real side / Jungle walk / Brother Tree / Island of real / Hummin' song / Echoes / Buttercup / Time will tell / Lament.

Apr 72. (7") **BROTHER TREE. / SAGA OF NEW YORK** -

Jun 72. (7") **HUMMIN' SONG. / ECHOES** -

Aug 72. (7") **JUNGLE WALK. / SAGA OF NEW YORK** -

— Disbanded May'72. DANELLI re-united with CORNISH to form BULLDOG. In 1978, also as a 5-piece they became FOTOMAKER. When they split DANELLI joined LITTLE STEVEN & THE DISCIPLES OF SOUL. POPWELL joined The CRUSADERS in 1976.

– compilations, others, etc. –

Mar 67. Atlantic; (7") **I AIN'T GONNA EAT OUT MY HEART. / GOOD LOVIN'** | | – |
Jul 71. Atlantic; (7") **GROOVIN'. / YOU BETTER RUN** | | – |
Jul 92. Raven-Topic; (cd) **IN RETROSPECTIVE** | | – |
– I ain't gonna eat out my heart anymore / Slow down / Good lovin' / Mustang Sally / You better run / Come on up / Love is a beautiful thing / What is the reason? / I've been lonely too long / Baby let's wait / Groovin' / A girl like you / How can I be sure? / It's wonderful / Beautiful morning / It's love / Easy rollin' / Rainy day / Silly girl / People got to be free / A ray of hope / Heaven / See / Carry me back / Glory glory.
Aug 93. Rhino; (d-cd) **ANTHOLOGY**

FELIX CAVALIERE

went solo after going into production (aka LAURA NYRO)
next with **TODD RUNDGREN** – producer

Bearsville Bearsville

1974. (lp) **FELIX CAVALIERE**
– A high price to pay / I am a gambler / I've got a solution / Everlasting love / Summer in El Barrio / Long times gone / Future train / Mountain man / Funky Friday / It's been a long time / I'm free.
1974. (7") **A HIGH PRICE TO PAY. / MOUNTAIN MAN** | – | |
1974. (7") **EVERLASTING LOVE. / FUTURE TRAIN** | – | |
1975. (7") **NEVER FELT LOVE BEFORE. / LOVE CAME** | – | |
Sep 75. (lp) **DESTINY**
– Destiny / Flip flop / Never felt love before / I can remember / Light of my life / Can't stop loving you / Try to believe / You came and set me free / Love came / Hit and run.
Sep 75. (7") **FLIP FLOP. / CAN'T STOP LOVIN' YOU** | | – |

— FELIX continues to produce others until;

Epic Epic

Jan 80. (7") **CASTLES IN THE AIR. / OUTSIDE YOUR WINDOW** | – | |
Mar 80. (7") **ONLY A LONELY HEART SEES. / YOU TURNED ME AROUND** | | 36 |
Jul 80. (lp)(c) **CASTLES IN THE AIR** | | | Apr 80
– Good to have you back / Only a lonely heart sees / All or nothing / Castles in the air / People got to be free / Dancin' the night away / Love is the first day of Spring / Outside your window / Don't hold back your love / You turned me around.
Sep 80. (7") **GOOD TO HAVE YOU BACK. / DANCIN' THE NIGHT AWAY** | – | |

– (CAVALIERE) compilations, etc. –

Jul 88. See For Miles; (lp)(c)(cd) **A RASCAL ALONE** | | – |
(lp re-iss 1992)

— In 1988, The Original RASCALS reformed without BRIGATI for US tours. The following year, DANELLI and CORNISH sued CAVALIERE, and prevented him touring as The YOUNG RASCALS. They also continued to tour as The NEW RASCALS.

RATT

Formed: Los Angeles, California, USA . . . 1982 by PEARCY, etc (see below) out of original name MICKEY RATT. After eponymous debut for indie 'Time Coast' in '83, they signed major deal with 'Atlantic'. 1984 saw album 'OUT OF THE CELLAR' bite into the US Top 10, helped by a hit 45 'ROUND AND ROUND'. • **Style:** Heavy-metal pop-rock outfit, filling a gap for AEROSMITH and CHEAP TRICK fans, who were obviously trapped by their use of sexist videos. • **Songwriters:** Group compositions, except WALKING THE DOG (Rufus Thomas). In 1990, hard-rock writer DESMOND CHILDS helped them hold the pen.

Recommended: RATT & ROLL (*5)

STEPHEN PEARCY (b. 3 Jul'59) – vocals / **JAKE E.LEE** – guitar / **WARREN DeMARTINI** (b.10 Apr'63) – guitar / **JUAN CROUCHER** (b.22 Aug'59) – bass (ex-DOKKEN) / **BOBBY BLOTZER** (b.22 Oct'58) – drums

M.F.N. Time Coast

Jun 83. (lp)(c) **RATT**
– You think you're tough / Sweet cheater / U got it / Tell the world / Back for more / Walkin' the dog. *(re-iss.Sep86 on 'Time Coast')*

— **ROBBIN CROSBY** – guitar repl. LEE (to ROUGH CUTT then OZZY OSBOURNE)

Atlantic Atlantic

Apr 84. (lp)(c) **OUT OF THE CELLAR** | | 7 | Mar 84
– Wanted man / You're in trouble / Round and round / In your direction / She wants money / Lack of communication / Back for more / The morning after / I'm insane / Scene of the crime. *(cd-iss.1988)*
Jun 84. (7") **ROUND AND ROUND. / THE MORNING AFTER** | – | 12 |
Aug 84. (7") **WANTED MAN. / SHE WANTS MONEY** | – | 87 |
Sep 84. (7") **ROUND AND ROUND. / YOU THINK YOU'RE TOUGH** | | – |
(12"+=) – Sweet cheater.
Oct 84. (7") **SCENE OF THE CRIME. / LACK OF COMMUNICATION** | – | |
Jun 85. (7")(12") **LAY IT DOWN. / GOT ME ON THE LINE** | | 40 |
Jul 85. (lp)(c)(cd) **INVASION OF YOUR PRIVACY** | 50 | 7 | Jun 85
– You're in love / Never use love / Lay it down / Give it all / Closer to my heart / Between the eyes / What you give is what you get / Got me on the line / You should know by now / Dangerous but worth the risk.
Jan 86. (7") **YOU'RE IN LOVE. / BETWEEN THE EYES** | | 89 | Oct 85
Oct 86. (7") **DANCE. / TAKE A CHANCE** | | 59 | Feb 87
Oct 86. (lp)(c)(cd) **DANCING UNDERCOVER** | 51 | 26 |
– Dance / One good lover / Drive me crazy / Slip of the lip / Body talk / Looking for love / 7th Avenue / It doesn't matter / Take a chance / Enough is enough.
Oct 88. (lp)(c)(cd) **REACH FOR THE SKY** | 82 | 17 |
– City to city / I want a woman / No surprise / Way cool Jr. / Don't bite the hand that feeds / I want to love you tonight / Chain reaction / No surprise / Bottom line / What's it gonna be / What I'm after.
Jan 89. (c-s)(cd-s) **WAY COOL JR. / CHAIN REACTION** | – | 75 |
Apr 89. (7") **WHAT I'M AFTER. / I WANT A WOMAN** | – | |
Aug 90. (cd)(c)(lp) **DETONATOR** | 55 | 23 |
– Intro to shame / Shame shame shame / Lovin' you is a dirty job / Scratch that itch / One step away / Hard time / Heads I win, tails you lose / All or nothing / Can't wait on love / Givin' yourself away / Top secret.
Oct 90. (7")(c-s) **LOVIN' YOU IS A DIRTY JOB. / WHAT'S IT GONNA BE**
(12"+=)(cd-s+=) – ('A'version).

— Now a quartet, when ROBBIN left. In 1992 PEARCY quit also.

Sep 91. (cd)(c)(lp) **RATT & ROLL** (compilation) | | 57 |
– Tell the world / Round and round / Wanted man / Back for more / Lack of communication / Lay it down / You're in love / Slip of the lip / Body talk / Way cool Jr. / Lovin' you's a dirty job / Shame shame shame / Givin' yourself away / Nobody rides for free. *(cd+c+=)* You think you're tough / Dance (part 1) / I want a woman / One step away / Heads I win, tails you lose.

Chris REA

Born: 4 Mar'51, Middlesborough, England . . . out of Irish/Italian parentage. He learned guitar in the early 70's and by 1973 had joined local band MAGDALENE, taking the place of DAVID COVERDALE, who had just joined DEEP PURPLE. In 1974, he signed one-off with 'Magnet', who released flop 45 'SO MUCH LOVE' (see below). In 1977, he guested on HANK MARVIN's 'Guitar Syndicate' album and soon re-signed to 'Magnet'. In 1978, he issued another 45 'FOOL (IF YOU THINK IT'S OVER)', which initially failed in the UK, but hit No.12 in America. In the Autumn it was re-promoted in the UK and scraped into the Top 30. In between all this, Gus Dungeon produced debut album 'WHATEVER HAPPENED TO BENNY SANTINI?' (referring to the name his label wanted to have him adopt). He continued to plod on with minor degrees of album successes, apart from Germany, where he had superstar status. He finally cracked the big time again in the mid-80's, when 'STAINSBY GIRLS' became a UK Top 30 hit, and preceeded his first of many Top 20 albums 'SHAMROCK DIARIES'. Around the same time, he was invited to join BILL WYMAN, in his project 'WILLIE & THE POOR BOYS'. • **Style:** Gruff vocalled down-to-earth singer-songwriter, in the mould of MARK KNOPFLER (Dire Straits), and also an accomplished guitarist with AOR appeal. • **Songwriters:** As said. • **Trivia:** He guested on CATHERINE HOWE's 1978 album 'Truth Of The Matter'. In 1982, ELKIE BROOKS scored a UK Top 20 hit, with her interpretation of 'FOOL'.

Recommended: NEW LIGHT THROUGH OLD WINDOWS (*7)

CHRIS REA – vocals, guitar with various session people.

Magnet United Art

May 74. (7") **SO MUCH LOVE. / BORN TO LOSE** | | – |

— Returned to MAGDELENE who changed their name to The BEAUTIFUL LOSERS in 1975. They won 'Melody Maker's Best Newcomers award', but in 1977, they disbanded. REA returned to solo work, re-signing longer term contract for 'Magnet'.

Apr 78. (7") **FOOL (IF YOU THINK IT'S OVER). / MIDNIGHT LOVE** | | 12 | Jul 78
(re-iss.UK Sep78, hit No.30)
Jun 78. (lp)(c) **WHATEVER HAPPENED TO BENNY SANTINI?** | | 49 |
– Whatever happened to Benny Santini? / he closer you get / Because of you / Dancing with Charlie / Bows and bangles / Fool (if you think it's over) / Three angels / Just one of these days / Standing in your doorway / Fires of Spring. *(re-iss.+cd.Feb88 on 'WEA') (re-iss.cd+c Mar93 on 'Pickwick') (re-iss.cd/c Sep95 on 'Warners')*
Jun 78. (7")(7"red) **WHATEVER HAPPENED TO BENNY SANTINI?. / THREE ANGELS** | | 71 | Nov 78
Feb 79. (lp)(c)(blue-lp) **DELTICS** | 54 | |
– Twisted wheel / The things lovers should do / Dance (don't think) / Raincoat and a rose / Cenotaph – Letter from Amsterdam / Deltics / Diamonds / She gave it away / Don't want your best friend / Diamonds / No qualifications / Seabird. *(re-iss.+cd. Feb88 on 'WEA')*
Mar 79. (7") **DIAMONDS. / CLEVELAND CALLING** | 44 | 44 |
Jun 79. (7") **RAINCOAT AND A ROSE. / NO QUALIFICATIONS**

Magnet Columbia

Feb 80. (7") **TENNIS. / IF YOU REALLY LOVE ME**
Feb 80. (lp)(c) **TENNIS** | 60 | |
– Tennis / Since I don't see you anymore / Dancing girls / No work today / Everytime I see you smile / For ever and ever / Good news / Friends across the water / Only with you / Stick it / Tennis.
May 80. (7") **DANCING GIRLS. / FRIENDS ACROSS THE WATER**
Jan 82. (7") **LOVING YOU. / LET ME BE THE ONE** | 65 | 88 | Mar 88
Mar 82. (lp)(c) **CHRIS REA** | 52 | |
– Loving you / If you choose to go / Guitar Street / Do you still dream / Every beat of my heart / Goodbye little Colombus / One sweet tender touch / Do it for love / Just want to be with you / Runaway / When you know your love has died. *(re-iss.+cd.Feb88 on 'WEA')*
May 82. (7") **EVERY BEAT OF MY HEART. / DON'T LOOK BACK**
Jul 82. (7") **LET IT LOOSE. / SIERRA SIERRA**
(12"+=) – Urban Samurai.
(free-7"ep+=) – Fool (if you think it's over) / The closer you get / Diamonds / Guitar Street.
Apr 83. (7") **I CAN HEAR YOUR HEARTBEAT. / FROM LOVE TO LOVE** | 60 | |

Jun 83. (lp)(c) **WATER SIGN** [64] [ ]
– Nothing's happening by the sea / Deep water / Candles / Love's strange ways / Texas / Let it loose / I can hear your heartbeat / Midnight blue / Hey you / Out of the darkness. *(re-iss.+cd.Feb88 on 'WEA')*

Jul 83. (7") **LOVE'S STRANGE WAYS. / SMILE** [ ] [ ]

Feb 84. (7")(12") **I DON'T KNOW WHAT IT IS BUT I LOVE IT. / MYSTERY MAN** [65] [ ]

Apr 84. (lp)(c) **WIRED TO THE MOON** [35] [ ]
– Bombollini / Touche d'amour / Shine, shine, shine / Wired to the Moon / easons / I don't know what it is but I love you / Ace of hearts / Holding out / Winning. *(re-iss.+cd.Feb88 on 'WEA') (re-iss.+cd.Jul91 on 'East West')*

May 84. (7") **BOMBOLLINI. / TRUE LOVE** [ ] [ ]
(12"+=) – Excerpts from Bombollini.

Jun 84. (7") **TOUCHE D'AMOUR. / ('A'instrumental)** [ ] [ ]
(12"+=) – ('A'extended remix).
(12") – ('A'side) / Let it loose – I can hear your heartbeat – I don't know what it is but I love it (medley).

Sep 84. (7") **ACE OF HEARTS. / I CAN HEAR YOUR HEARTBEAT** [ ] [ ]
(12"+c-s+=) – From love to love / True love / Smile.

Mar 85. (7") **STAINSBY GIRLS. / AND WHEN SHE SMILES** [27] [ ]
(12"+=)(c-s+=) – Sunrise / Dancing shoes / September blue.
(d7"+=) – Bittersweet / Auf Immer und Ewig.

May 85. (lp)(c)(cd) **SHAMROCK DIARIES** [15] [ ]
– Steel river / Stainsby girls / Chisel Hill / Josephine / One golden rule / All summer long / Stone / Shamrock diaries / Love turns to lies / Hired gun. *(re-iss.+cd.Feb88 on 'WEA') (re-iss.+cd.Jul91 on 'East West')*

Jun 85. (7") **JOSEPHINE (remix). / DANCING SHOES** [67] [ ]
(12"+=) – Every time it rains.

Nov 85. (7") **ACE OF HEARTS (remix). / I CAN HEAR YOUR HEARTBEAT (live)** [ ] [ ]
(12"+=) – From love to love / True love / Smile.

Mar 86. (7") **IT'S ALL GONE. / BLESS THEM ALL** [69] [ ]
(12"+=)(c-s+=) – Crack that mould / Look out for me / Let's dance.

Apr 86. (lp)(c)(cd) **ON THE BEACH** [11] [ ]
– On the beach / Little blonde plaits / Giverny / Lucky day / Just passing through / It's all gone / Hello friend / Two roads / Light of hope / Auf immer und ewig. *(c+cd+=)–* Bless them all / Freeway / Crack that mould. *(re-iss.+cd.Feb88 on 'WEA') (re-iss.+cd.Jun91 on 'East West')*

Jun 86. (7") **ON THE BEACH. / IF ANYBODY ASKS YOU** [57] [ ]
(12"+=) – ('A'extended remix).
(d7"+=) – One golden rule (live) / Midnight blue (live).

Dec 86. (7") **DRIVING HOME FOR CHRISTMAS. / HELLO FRIEND** [ ] [ ]
(d7"+=) – It's all gone (live) / Steel river (live).

Magnet Motown

May 87. (7")(c-s) **LET'S DANCE. / I DON'T CARE ANYMORE** [12] [81]
(12"+=)/ /(cd-s+=) – ('A'extended)./ / Josephine (French version).

Aug 87. (7") **LOVING YOU AGAIN. / DONAHUE'S BROKEN WHEEL** [47] [ ]
(12"+=) – ('A'extended).

Sep 87. (lp)(c)(cd) **DANCING WITH STRANGERS** [2] [ ]
– Joys of Christmas / I can't dance to that / Windy Town / Gonna buy a hat / Curse of the traveller / Let's dance / Que sera / Josie's tune / Loving you again / That girl of mine / September blue. *(cd+=)–* I don't care anymore / Donaue's broken wheel / Danielle's breakfast. *(re-iss.+cd.Jul91 on 'East West')*

Nov 87. (7") **JOYS OF CHRISTMAS. / DRIVING HOME FOR CHRISTMAS** [67] [ ]
(12"+=)/ /(cd-s+=) – Hello friend (remix)./ / Yes I do.

Jan 88. (7") **QUE SERA. / SE SEQUI (instrumental)** [73] [ ]
(12"+=)/ /(cd-s+=) – ('A'extended)./ / One sweet tender touch.

W.E.A. Motown

Jul 88. (7") **ON THE BEACH (SUMMER '88). / I'M TAKING THE DAY OUT** [12] [ ]
(12"+=)(cd-s+=) – It's all gone (live).

Oct 88. (7") **I CAN HEAR YOUR HEARTBEAT. / LOVING YOU AGAIN (live)** [74] [ ]
(12"+=)(cd-s+=) – Giverny.

W.E.A. Geffen

Oct 88. (lp)(c)(cd) **NEW LIGHT THROUGH OLD WINDOWS – THE BEST OF CHRIS REA** (compilation) [5] [92]
– Let's dance / Working on it / Ace of hearts / Josephine / Candles / On the beach / Fool (if you think it's over) / I can hear your heartbeat / Shamrock diaries / Stainsby girls / Windy town / Driving home for Christmas / Steel river.

Dec 88. (d7")(12"ep)(3"cd-ep) **DRIVING HOME FOR CHRISTMAS. / FOOTSTEPS IN THE SNOW/ / JOYS OF CHRISTMAS. / SMILE** [53] [ ]

Jan 89. (7") **WORKING ON IT. / ONE GOLDEN RULE** [53] [73] Mar 89
(12"+=)/ /(cd-s+=) – ('A'extended)./ / Stainsby girls.

Sep 89. (7") **THE ROAD TO HELL. / HE SHOULD KNOW BETTER** [10] [ ]
(12") – ('A'side) / The road to Hell (pt.2) / Josephine (French re-recorded).
(cd-s) – (all 4 tracks).

Oct 89. (lp)(c)(cd) **THE ROAD TO HELL** [1] [ ]
– The road to Hell (part 1 & 2) / You must be evil / Texas / Looking for a rainbow / Your warm and tender love / Daytona / That's what they all say / I just wanna be with you / Tell me there's a Heaven. *(re-iss.cd/c Feb95)*

Nov 89. (7") **THAT'S WHAT THEY ALL SAY. / 1975** [ ] [ ]
(12"+=) – ('A'extended rainbow mix).
(cd-s++=) – Driving home for Christmas.

Feb 90. (7")(c-s) **TELL ME THERE'S A HEAVEN. / AND WHEN SHE SMILES** [24] [ ]
(12"+=) – Curse of the traveller.
(cd-s++=) – Little blonde plaits.

Apr 90. (7")(c-s) **TEXAS. / LET'S DANCE** [69] [ ]
(12"+=) – ('A'side) / ('B'live) / The road to Hell (part 1 & 2)
(cd-s+=) – Working on it.

East West East West

Feb 91. (7")(c-s) **AUBERGE. / HUDSON'S DREAMS** [16] [ ]
(cd-s) – ('A'side) / Let's dance / On the beach / The road to Hell (pt.2).

Feb 91. (cd)(c)(lp) **AUBERGE** [1] [ ]
– Auberge / Gone fishing / You're not a number / Heaven / Set me free / Red shoes / Sing a song of love to me / Every second counts / Looking for the summer / And you my love / The mention of your name.

Apr 91. (7")(c-s) **HEAVEN. / THEME FROM THE PANTILE JOURNALS** [57] [ ]
(12"+=) – Teach me to dance.
(cd-s) – ('A'side) / Stainsby girls / Josephine / Tell me there's a Heaven.

Jun 91. (7")(c-s) **LOOKING FOR SUMMER. / SIX UP** [49] [ ]
(12"+=)(cd-s+=) – Urban Samurai / Theme from the Pantile / Teach me to dance.

Nov 91. (7")(c-s) **WINTER SONG. / FOOTPRINTS IN THE SNOW / TELL ME THERE'S A HEAVEN** [27] [ ]
(cd-s+=) – True to you.

Oct 92. (7")(c-s) **NOTHING TO FEAR. / STRANGE DANCE** [16] [ ]
(cd-s+=) – Daytona (live).
(cd-s) – ('A'side) / Road to Hell (live) / Working on it (live).

Nov 92. (cd)(c)(lp) **GOD'S GREAT BANANA SKIN** [4] [ ]
– Nothing to fear / Miles is a cigarette / God's great banana skin / Nineties blues / Too much pride / Boom boom / I ain't the fool / There she goes / I'm ready / Black dog / Soft top hard shoulder.

Nov 92. (7")(c-s) **GOD'S GREAT BANANA SKIN. / I SAW YOU COMING** [31] [ ]
(cd-s+=) – Just passing through (live).
(cd-s+=) She's gonna change everything / You must be evil.

—— his band: **ROBERT AHWAI** – guitar / **MAX MIDDLETON** – piano, keyboards / **SYLVIN MARC** – bass / **MARTIN DITCHAM** – drums, percussion

Jan 93. (7")(c-s) **SOFT TOP HARD SHOULDER. / MELANCHOLY** [53] [ ]
(cd-s+=) – The van stomp – Glasgow horizon.
(cd-s) – ('A'side) / One fine day / One seet & tended touch / Sierra Sierra.

Jul 93. (7")(c-s) **TOO MUCH PRIDE (new version). / MUNICH 1993 IMPROVISED INTRO (live)** [ ] [ ]
(cd-s+=) – On the beach (live).
(cd-s) – ('A'side) / Gone fishing (live) / Nothing to fear (live) / Soft top, hard shoulder (live).

Oct 93. (7")(c-s)(cd-s) **JULIA. / I THOUGHT I WAS GOING TO LOSE YOU / JORDAN 191** [18] [ ]

Nov 93. (cd)(c)(lp) **ESPRESSO LOGIC** [8] [ ]
– Espresso logic / Red / Soup of the day / Johnny needs a fast guitar / Between the Devil and the deep blue sea / Julia /Summer love / New way / Stop / She closed her eyes.

Dec 93. (7")(c-s) **ESPRESSO LOGIC. / WE DON'T HAVE A PROBLEM** [ ] [ ]
(cd-s+=) – That's the way it goes.

Oct 94. (cd)(c) **THE BEST OF CHRIS REA** (compilation) [3] [ ]
– Road to Hell / Josephine / Let's dance / Fool if you think it's over / Auberge / Julia / Stainsby girls / If you were me (with ELTON JOHN) / On the beach / Looking for the summer / I can hear your heartbeat / Go your own way / God's great banana skin / Wintersong / Gone fishing / Tell me there's a Heaven.

Nov 94. (c-s) **YOU CAN GO YOUR OWN WAY. / ESPRESSO LOGIC (mixes)** [28] [ ]
(12")(cd-s) – ('A'side) / Ruby blue / Three little green candles.

Dec 94. (7")(c-s) **TELL ME THERE'S A HEAVEN. / AND WHEN SHE SMILES** [70] [-]
(cd-s+=) – Curse of the traveller / Little blonde plaits.

Eddi READER

Born: 28 Aug'59, Glasgow, Scotland. In 1987 the one-time backing singer for GANG OF FOUR, WATERBOYS, etc formed FAIRGROUND ATTRACTION with Englishman MARC B. NEVIN. After literally busking around city centres, they progressed to gigs and soon signed to 'RCA' records. Their early 1988 debut single 'PERFECT', made it's way to No.1 in the UK, and was a preview for Top 3 album 'THE FIRST OF A MILLION KISSES'. A few years later they were no more and EDDI soon forged out some solo successes; mainly with eponymous 1994 album. • **Style:** Dreamy angel-voiced singer, whose range included folk based pop, tinged with smooth jazzy sound. • **Songwriters:** NEVIN penned all FAIRGROUND ATTRACTION, except YOU SEND ME (Sam Cooke) / MYSTERY TRAIN (Elvis Presley) / DO YOU WANT TO KNOW A SECRET (Beatles) / WALKING AFTER MIDNIGHT (Patsy Cline) / AY FOND KISS (trad. Robert Burns) / TRYING TIMES (Donny Hathaway) / SUNDAY MORNING (Velvet Underground) / JACK O'HAZLEDEAN (trad.Walter Scott) / OLE BUTTERMILK SKY (Hoagy Carmichael). EDDI READER solo:- MY OLD FRIEND THE BLUES (Steve Earle) / WHAT YOU DO (S.W. Kahn) / SPIRIT (Waterboys). • **Trivia:** In 1990, their PERFECT, was used for a supermarket TV ad.

Recommended: THE FIRST OF A MILLION KISSES (FAIRGROUND ATTRACTION *5) / EDDI READER (*6).

FAIRGROUND ATTRACTION

EDDI READER – vocals / **MARC B. NEVIN** – guitars / **SIMON EDWARDS** – guitaron (Mexican accoustic bass) / **ROY DODDS** – drums

R.C.A. R.C.A.

Mar 88. (7") **PERFECT. / MYTHOLOGY** [1] [80] Nov 88
(12"+=)(cd-s+=) – Falling backwards / Mystery train.
(re-iss.+c-s. Feb93, B-side 'CAPTURED')

May 88. (lp)(c)(cd) **THE FIRST OF A MILLION KISSES** [2] [ ]
– A smile and a whisper / Perfect / Moon on the rain / Find my love / Fairground attraction / The wind knows my name / Clare / Comedy waltz / The moon is mine / Station street / Whispers / Allelujah. (cd+=) – Falling backwards / Mythology. *(re-iss.cdMay93)*

Jul 88. (7")(12") **FIND MY LOVE. / WATCHING THE PARTY** [7] [ ]
(cd-s+=) – You send me / Ay fond kiss.

Nov 88. (7") **A SMILE AND A WHISPER. / WINTER ROSE** [75] [ ]
(12"+=)(cd-s+=) – A walk after midnight / Trying times.
Jan 89. (7") **CLARE. / GAMES OF LOVE** [49] [ ]
(12"+=)(cd-s+=) – Do you want to know a secret / Jack O'Hazeldean.

— Disbanded early 1990. EDDI went into acting career, noteably Scots TV 'C&W' drama Your Cheatin' Heart. NEVIN joined MORRISSEY in '91 and formed SWEETMOUTH.

May 90. (7")(c-s) **WALKING AFTER MIDNIGHT. / COMEDY WALTZ (live)** [ ] [ ]
(12"+=)(cd-s+=) – Clare (live).
Jun 90. (cd)(c)(lp) **AY FOND KISS** (rare + demos, etc) [55] [ ]
(re-iss.cd Apr94)

compilations, etc –

Sep 94. R.C.A.; (cd) **THE COLLECTION** [ ] [ ]
Apr 95. R.C.A.; (cd) **AY FOND KISS / FIRST OF A MILLION KISSES** [ ] [-]

EDDI READER with The PATRON SAINTS OF IMPERFECTION

with **ROY DODDS** – drums, percussion / **PHIL STERIOPULOS** – 5-string double bass / **NEIL MacCOLL** – guitar / **DOMINIC MILLER** – guitar / and guest **JOOLS HOLLAND** – piano

B.M.G.-RCA | R.C.A.

Nov 91. (7"ep)(12"ep)(c-ep) **ALL OR NOTHING** [ ] [ ]
– All or nothing / Sunday morning / Ole buttermilk sky / Broken vows.
(cd-ep) – (first + last track+) – The blacksmith / The girl with the weight of the world in her hands.
Feb 92. (7")(c-s) **WHAT YOU DO WITH WHAT YOU'VE GOT. / I WISH YOU WERE MY BOYFRIEND** [ ] [ ]
(cd-s+=) – Broken vows / Ole buttermilk sky (take 2).
Mar 92. (cd)(c)(lp) **MIRMAMA** [34] [ ]
– What you do with what you've got / Honeychild / All or nothing / Hello in there / Dolphins / The blacksmith / That's fair / Cinderellas downfall / Pay no mind / The swimming song / My old friend the blues. *(re-iss.cd.May93)*
Apr 92. (7")(c-s) **HONEYCHILD. / SPIRIT (live)** [ ] [ ]
(cd-s+=) – All or nothing (live).

Haven | not issued

Mar 93. (cd-ep) **WONDERFUL LIE / LAST NIGHT I DREAMT SOMEBODY LOVED ME / WHO'S YOUR JAILER NOW** [ ] [-]

— Below written by BOO HEWERDINE (ex-BIBLE)

Blanco Y Negro | Sire

May 94. (7")(c-s) **PATIENCE OF ANGELS. / RED FACE BIG SKY** [33] [ ]
(cd-s+=) – Shirt & comb.
Jun 94. (cd)(c) **EDDI READER** [4] [ ]
– The right place / Patience of angels / Dear John / Scarecrow / East of us / Joke / The exception / Red face big sky / Howling in Ojai / When I watch you sleeping / Wonderful lie / Siren.
Aug 94. (7")(c-s) **JOKE (I'M LAUGHING). / 3 CROSSES** [42] [ ]
(cd-s+) – Go and sit upon the grass.
(cd-s) – ('A'side) / Saturday night / Wonder boy.
Oct 94. (7")(c-s) **DEAR JOHN. / BATTERSEA MOONWALK** [48] [ ]
(cd-s+=) – When I watch you sleeping / What you do with what you've got / That's fair.
Sep 95. (c-s) **NOBODY LIVES WITHOUT LOVE / WONDERFUL LIE** [ ] [ ]
(cd-s+=) – Red face, big sky.

Mac REBENNACK (see under ⇒ DR. JOHN)

Otis REDDING

Born: 9 Sep'41, Dawson, Georgia, USA. He left school in Macon and soon gigged with local R&B outfit JOHNNY JENKINS & THE PINETOPPERS. His/their first release in 1960 was SHOUT BAMALAMA on 'Confederate' label. The following year after OTIS married Zelda, they issued GETTIN' HIP on 'Alshire'. At this time he was only given vocal stints, due to his driving them to concerts. Early in 1962, another single LOVE TWIST was given light by 'Gerald' records. In Oct'62, with groups' recording sessions for 'Atlantic' now over, 2 solo songs were listened to by new 'Stax' subsidiary label 'Volt'. The 45 'B'side; THESE ARMS OF MINE became minor US hit mid 1963. By mutual agreement and special contract, 'Atlantic (aka Atco)' decided to let 'Volt' continue releasing 45's, etc. After a few minor hits, he broke through in summer '65 with near Top20 hit I'VE BEEN LOVING YOU TOO LONG. Chalked up several more cross-Atlantic hits, before tragically he and most of his back-up group The BAR-KEYS, were killed in a charter plane crash on 10 Dec'67. His postumously-released next single became regarded as his greatest. '(SITTIN' ON) THE DOCK OF THE BAY' became a million selling US No.1 also hitting Top3 in the UK. • **Style:** Progressed from being a LITTLE RICHARD copyist (in the early 60's), to being a classic soul balladeer. • **Songwriters:** Penned own material, except singles DOCK OF THE BAY (c. Steve Cropper) / MY GIRL (Temptations) / PAIN IN MY HEART (Irma Thomas) / SATISFACTION (Rolling Stones) / DAY TRIPPER (Beatles) / SHAKE! (Sam Cooke) / KNOCK ON WOOD (Eddie Floyd) / PAPA'S GOT A BRAND NEW BAG (James Brown) / A LOVER'S QUESTION (Clyde McPhatter) / AMEN (Impressions) / etc. • **Trivia:** Late in 1973, his son DEXTER issued single GOD BLESS. In the early 80's, he was joined by other son OTIS and their cousin MARK LOCKET who transpired as The REDDINGS. All on vocals and instruments, they released 2 albums THE AWAKENING and CLASS on the 'Believe' label.

Recommended: THE COLLECTION (*9)

OTIS REDDING – vocals solo with sessioners

London | Volt

Oct 62. (7") **THESE ARMS OF MINE. / HEY HEY BABY** [-] [85]
Jul 63. (7") **THAT'S WHAT MY HEART NEEDS. / MARY'S LITTLE LAMB** [-] [ ]
Nov 63. (7") **PAIN IN MY HEART. / SOMETHING IS WORRYING ME** [ ] [61]

— His backing included BOOKER T. & THE MG'S plus JOHNNY JENKINS.

Mar 64. (7") **COME TO ME. / DON'T LEAVE ME THIS WAY** [ ] [69]
Apr 64. (lp) **PAIN IN MY HEART** [-] [ ]
– Pain in my heart / The dog / Stand by me / Hey hey baby / You send me / I need your lovin' / Louie Louie / These arms of mine / Something is worrying me / Security / That's what my heart needs / Lucille. *(UK-iss.Apr67 on 'Atlantic', hit No.28) (cd-iss.Aug93)*
May 64. (7") **SECURITY. / WONDERFUL WORLD** [ ] [-]
Jun 64. (7") **SECURITY. / I WANT TO THANK YOU** [-] [97]
Oct 64. (7") **CHAINED AND BOUND. / YOUR ONE AND ONLY MAN** [-] [70]

Atlantic | Volt

Apr 65. (7") **MR.PITIFUL. / THAT'S HOW STRONG MY LOVE IS** [ ] [41] [74] Feb 65
May 65. (7") **I'VE BEEN LOVING YOU TOO LONG (TO STOP NOW). / I'M DEPENDING ON YOU** [-] [21]
Aug 65. (7") **I'VE BEEN LOVING YOU TOO LONG. / RESPECT** [ ] [-]
Sep 65. (lp) **THE GREAT OTIS REDDING SINGS SOUL BALLADS** [ ] [ ] Mar 65
– That's how strong my love is / Chained and bound / A woman, a lover, a friend / Your one and only man / Nothing can change this love / It's too late / For your precious love / I want to thank you / Come to me / Home in your heart / Keep your arms around me / Mr. Pitiful. *(hit UK chart No.30, Apr66) (re-iss.Jun88 on 'Atco', cd-iss.Jul91) (cd-iss.May93)*
Sep 65. (7") **RESPECT. / OLE MAN TROUBLE** [-] [35]
Nov 65. (7") **MY GIRL. / DOWN IN THE VALLEY** [11] [-]
Nov 65. (7") **JUST ONE MORE DAY. / I CAN'T TURN YOU LOOSE** [-] [85]
Feb 66. (lp) **OTIS BLUE (OTIS REDDING SINGS SOUL)** [6] [75] Oct 65
– My girl / (I can't get no) Satisfaction / Respect / Shake! / I've been loving you too long / You don't miss your water / Rock me baby / Wonderful world / Down in the valley / Change gonna come / Ole man trouble. *(UK re-iss.Jan67, hit No.7) (re-iss.1974 + Dec83 +c) (cd-iss.Jun91 on 'Atco')*
Mar 66. (7") **(I CAN'T GET NO) SATISFACTION. / ANY OLE WAY** [33] [31]
Jul 66. (7") **MY LOVER'S PRAYER. / DON'T MESS WITH CUPID** [37] [61] Jun 66
Jul 66. (lp) **THE SOUL ALBUM** [22] [54] Apr 66
– Just one more day / It's growing / Cigarettes and coffee / Chain gang / Nobody knows you (when you're down and out) / Good to me / Scratch my back / Treat her right / Everybody makes a mistake / Any ole way / 634-5789. *(cd-iss.Jul91 on 'Atco') (cd-iss.Jun93)*
Aug 66. (7") **I CAN'T TURN YOU LOOSE. / JUST ONE MORE DAY** [29] [-]
Nov 66. (7") **FA FA FA FA FA (SAD SONG). / GOOD TO ME** [23] [29] Sep 66
Jan 67. (lp) **OTIS REDDING'S DICTIONARY OF SOUL** [23] [73] Nov 66
– Fa-fa-fa-fa-fa (sad song) / I'm sick y'all / Tennessee waltz / Sweet Lorene / Try a little tenderness / Day tripper / My lover's prayer / She put the hurt on me / Ton of joy / You're still my baby / Hawg for you / Love have mercy. *(re-iss.Jun88, cd-iss.Jul91 on 'Atco') (cd-iss.Jun93)* (US-title 'COMPLETE AND UNBELIEVABLE . . . THE OTIS REDDING DICTIONARY OF SOUL')
Jan 67. (7") **TRY A LITTLE TENDERNESS. / I'M SICK Y'ALL** [46] [25] Dec 66
Mar 67. (7") **RESPECT. / THESE ARMS OF MINE** [ ] [-]
(re-iss.Feb72)

Stax | Volt

Mar 67. (7") **DAY TRIPPER. / SHAKE!** [43] [-]
Apr 67. (7") **LET ME COME ON HOME. / I LOVE YOU MORE THAN WORDS CAN SAY** [48] [78] B-side
May 67. (7") **TRAMP. ("OTIS & CARLA THOMAS"). / TELL IT LIKE IT IS** [-] [26]
Jun 67. (7") **SHAKE (live). / 634-5789 (live)** [28] [-]
Jun 67. (7") **SHAKE. / YOU DON'T MISS YOUR WATER** [-] [ ]

— Some releases on 'Stax' now with CARLA THOMAS, daughter of singer RUFUS.

Jun 67. (lp) **KING AND QUEEN ("OTIS REDDING & CARLA THOMAS")** [18] [36] Apr 67
– Knock on wood / Let me be good to you / Tramp / Tell it like it is / When something is wrong with my baby / Lovey dovey / New Year's resolution / It takes two / Are you lonely for me baby / Bring it on home to me / Ooh Carla, Ooh Otis.
– (re-iss.Jun88, cd-iss.Jul91 on 'Atco')
Jul 67. (7") **TRAMP. ("OTIS REDDING & CARLA THOMAS") / OOH CARLA OOH OTIS** [18] [ ]
Aug 67. (7") **GLORY OF LOVE. / I'M COMING HOME** [ ] [60] Jul 67
Sep 67. (lp) **LIVE IN EUROPE (live)** [-] [32] Aug 67
– Respect / Can't turn you loose / I've been loving you too long / My girl / Shame / Satisfaction / Fa-fa-fa-fa-fa (sad song) / These arms of mine / Day tripper / Try a little tenderness. *(UK-iss.Mar68, hit No.2) (re-iss.Aug69 on 'Atco') (cd-iss.Aug93) (cd-iss.Feb95 & Sep95 on 'Warners')*
Oct 67. (7") **KNOCK ON WOOD. ("OTIS REDDING & CARLA THOMAS") / LET ME BE GOOD TO YOU** [35] [30] Aug 67
Nov 67. (7") **SATISFACTION. / I'VE BEEN LOVING YOU TOO LONG** [ ] [-]

— On 10th Dec'67, OTIS was killed in a plane crash (see biography)

– immediate postumous releases, etc. –

Dec 67. Volt; (lp)(c) **THE HISTORY OF OTIS REDDING** [2] [9]
(re-iss.1974 on 'Atlantic')
Below released on 'Volt'/ 'Stax' unless mentioned.
Feb 68. (7") **(SITTIN' ON) THE DOCK OF THE BAY. / MY SWEET LORENE** [3] [1] Jan 68

Mar 68. (7") **LOVEY DOVEY. ("OTIS REDDING & CARLA THOMAS") / NEW YEAR'S RESOLUTION** [ ] [68] Feb 68

May 68. (lp) **DOCK OF THE BAY** (late 1967 sessions) [1] [4] Mar 68
– The dock of the bay / Home in your heart / I want to thank you / Your one and only man / Nothing can change this love / It's too late / For your precious love / Keep your arms around me / Come to me / A woman, a lover, a friend / Chained and bound / That's how strong my love is. *(re-iss.Jul69 on 'Atco') (re-iss.Nov71)*

May 68. (7") **THE HAPPY SONG (DUM DUM). / OPEN THE DOOR** [24] [25] Apr 68

Below released on 'Atlantic' UK/ 'Atco' US unless mentioned.

Feb 68. (7") **MY GIRL. / MR.PITIFUL** [36] [ ]
(re-iss.1972, 1980 & Mar84)

Jul 68. (7") **HARD TO HANDLE. / AMEN** [15] [36] B-side

Aug 68. (lp) **THE IMMORTAL OTIS REDDING** [19] [58] Jul 68
(re-iss.Jan72 on 'Atco') (cd-iss.Aug93)

Sep 68. (7") **I'VE GOT DREAMS TO REMEMBER. / NOBODY'S FAULT BUT MINE** [ ] [41]

Oct 68. (7") **I'VE GOT DREAMS TO REMEMBER. / CHAMPAGNE AND WINE** [ ] [-]

Nov 68. (lp) **OTIS REDDING IN PERSON AT THE WHISKEY A GO-GO (live 1966)** [ ] [82]
– I can't turn you loose / Pain in my heart / Just one more day / Mr.Pitiful / (I can't get no) Satisfaction / I'm depending on you / Any ole way / These arms of mine / Papa's got a brand new bag / Respect. *(cd-iss.Dec94 & Sep95 on 'Warners')*

Dec 68. (7") **MERRY CHRISTMAS BABY. / WHITE CHRISTMAS** [ ] [ ]

Dec 68. (7") **PAPA'S GOT A BRAND NEW BAG (live). / DIRECT ME** [ ] [21] Nov 68

Below released on 'Atco' unless mentioned.

Mar 69. (7") **A LOVER'S QUESTION. / YOU MADE A MAN OUT OF ME** [ ] [48] Feb 69

Apr 69. (7") **WHEN SOMETHING IS WRONG WITH MY BABY (w/CARLA THOMAS) / OOH CARLA, OOH OTIS** [-] [ ]

May 69. (7") **LOVE MAN. / CAN'T TURN YOU LOOSE** [-] [72]

Jun 69. (7") **LOVE MAN. / THAT'S HOW STRONG MY LOVE IS** [43] [-]

Jun 69. (lp) **LOVE MAN** [ ] [46]
(re-iss.Nov71 on 'Atlantic') (cd-iss.Jul92 on 'Rhino')

Aug 69. (7") **FREE ME. / (YOUR LOVE HAS LIFTED ME) HIGHER AND HIGHER** [ ] [ ]

Feb 70. (7") **LOOK AT THE GIRL. / THAT'S A GOOD IDEA** [ ] [ ]

1970. (7") **DEMONSTRATION. / JOHNNY'S HEARTBREAK** [-] [ ]

1970. (7") **GIVE AWAY NONE OF MY LOVE. / SNATCH A LITTLE PIECE** [-] [ ]

– other compilations, etc. –

Feb 68. Marble Arch; (lp) **HERE COMES SOME SOUL FROM OTIS REDDING AND LITTLE JOE CURTIS (W / LITTLE JOE CURTIS)** [ ] [-]

Jun 68. Pye Int.; (7") **SHE'S ALRIGHT. / GAMA LAMA** [ ] [-]

— Above and below single rec.1959

Sep 69. Evolution; (7") **SHE'S ALRIGHT. / TUFF ENUFF** [ ] [-]

— In Sep70, shared live lp with JIMI HENDRIX (rec.Jun67) 'MONTEREY INTERNATIONAL POP FESTIVAL' on 'Reprise', hit US No.16.

Below releases on 'Atlantic' UK/ 'Atco' US unless mentioned.

Jul 70. (7") **WONDERFUL WORLD. / SECURITY** [ ] [-]

Jul 70. (7") **I LOVE YOU. / I NEED YOU** [ ] [-]

Jan 71. (lp) **TELL THE TRUTH** (rec.1967) [ ] [ ] Aug70
– Demonstration / Tell the truth / Out of sight / Give away none of my love / Wholesale love / I got the will / Johnny's heartbreak / Snatch a little piece / Slippin' and slidin' / The match game / A little time / Swingin' on a string. *(cd-iss.Jul92 on 'Rhino')*

Mar 71. (7") **I'VE BEEN LOVIN' YOU TOO LONG. / TRY A LITTLE TENDERNESS** [ ] [-]

Aug 71. (7"m) **(SITTIN' ON) THE DOCK OF THE BAY. / RESPECT / MR.PITIFUL** [ ] [-]
(re-iss.Jan72, 1974, Jul84)

Aug 71. (7") **MY GIRL. / GOOD TO ME** [-] [ ]

Nov 71. (7") **WHITE CHRISTMAS. / MERRY CHRISTMAS BABY** [ ] [ ]

Jan 73. (7"m) **(SITTIN' ON) THE DOCK OF THE BAY. / SATISFACTION / I CANT TURN YOU LOOSE** [ ] [-]

Feb 73. (7") **TRAMP. ("OTIS REDDING & CARLA THOMAS"). / KNOCK ON WOOD** [ ] [-]

Jul 73. (d-lp)(c) **THE BEST OF OTIS REDDING** [ ] [76] Sep 72
(cd-iss.Mar87)

Aug 73. (7") **MY GIRL. / HARD TO HANDLE** [ ] [-]

Jun 79. (lp)(c) **PURE OTIS** [ ] [ ]

Apr 80. (12") **I CAN'T TURN YOU LOOSE. / (SITTIN' ON) THE DOCK OF THE BAY** [ ] [-]

May 81. (lp)(c) **OTIS REDDING VOL.1** [ ] [ ]

Apr 82. (lp)(c) **RECORDED LIVE (live)** [ ] [ ]

Oct 84. (7") **(SITTIN' ON) THE DOCK OF THE BAY. / YOU DON'T MISS YOUR WATER** [ ] [ ]

May 87. (7") **TRY A LITTLE TENDERNESS. / I'VE BEEN LOVING YOU TOO LONG** [ ] [-]
(12"+=) – Hard to handle.

Jul 87. (lp)(c)(cd) **DOCK OF THE BAY – THE DEFINITIVE COLLECTION** [ ] [ ]
(re-iss.cd+c.Aug93,hit UK No.50)

Dec 88. (lp)(c) **THE OTIS REDDING STORY** [ ] [ ]

Nov 93. Rhino; (4xcd-box) **THE DEFINITIVE OTIS REDDING** [ ] [ ]

May 94. Rhino; (7")(c-s) **(SITTIN' ON THE) DOCK OF THE BAY. / ?** [ ]
(cd-s+=) –

Aug 74. WEA; (lp) **STAR COLLECTION** [ ] [-]

Jul 84. WEA; (lp)(c) **THE BEST OF OTIS REDDING** [ ] [ ]

Apr 84. Charly; (lp)(c) **COME TO ME** [ ] [-]

Jan 85. Old Gold; (7") **(SITTIN' ON) THE DOCK OF THE BAY. / MY GIRL** [ ] [-]

Apr 91. Knight; (cd)(c) **HEART AND SOUL OF OTIS REDDING** [ ] [-]

— (below from film 'The Commitments')

Aug 91. MCA; (7")(c-s) **TRY A LITTLE TENDERNESS. / I'VE BEEN LOVING YOU TOO LONG** [ ] [ ]
(12"+=)(cd-s+=) – ?'

Sep 91. Traditional Line; (cd) **SOUL EXPLOSION** [ ] [-]

Sep 91. Traditional Line; (cd) **LIVE IN CONCERT 1965 (live)** [ ] [-]

Oct 91. Stax; (cd) **1000 VOLTS OF STAX** [ ] [ ]

Dec 91. Stax; (cd) **IT'S NOT JUST SENTIMENTAL** [ ] [ ]

May 93. Stax; (cd)(lp) **GOOD TO ME – RECORDED LIVE AT THE WHISKEY A-GO-GO** [ ] [ ]

Nov 92. East West; (7")(12")(c-s)(cd-s) **(SITTIN' ON) THE DOCK OF THE BAY. / SWEET LORRAINE** [ ] [ ]

Jul 92. Castle; (cd)(c) **THE COLLECTION** [ ] [-]
– My girl / Stand by me / Higher and higher / The happy song / I love you more than words can say / Amen / Fa-fa-fa-fa-fa (sad song) / I've been losing you too long / The glory of love / I've got dreams to remember / Love man / Free me / Papa's got a brand new bag / (Sittin' on) The dock of the bay.

Apr 94. That's Soul; (cd) **I'VE BEEN LOVIN' YOU TOO LONG** [ ] [-]

Feb 95. Atlantic; (cd)(c) **THE DOCK OF THE BAY** [54] [ ]

RED HOT CHILI PEPPERS

Formed: Los Angeles, California, USA . . . 1983 after 4 years as ANTHEM. The CHILIS (see below line-up), signed to 'EMI' stark naked, as part of a now famous publicity stunt. They were later to feature naked (all but one sock each strategically placed; you guessed where), on a photo shoot (on Beatles' ABBEY ROAD). Their eponymous debut in 1984 and FREAKIE STYLIE follow-up, saw light of day only in America, but by 1988, the band had begun to venture over the Atlantic, soon issuing 'UPLIFT MOFO PARTY PLAN'. By the early 90's, although depleted somewhat by the death of HILLEL SLOVAK, the group had become red hot property. • **Miscellaneous:** In Apr'90, KIEDIS was given a 60-day jail sentence for sexual battery and indecent exposure to a female student. • **Style:** A hybrid of jazzy funksters PARLIAMENT/FUNFADELIC and 70's punk, fused together with inspiration from JIMI HENDRIX, due to the fact FLEA often played his bass upside down, hanging feet up by a rope!!!. • **Songwriters:** Group compositions except; SUBTERANEAN HOMESICK BLUES (Bob Dylan) / HOLLYWOOD (AFRICA) (Meters) / FIRE + CASTLES MADE OF SAND (Jimi Hendrix) / HIGHER GROUND (Stevie Wonder) / IF YOU WANT ME TO STAY / Sly & Family Stone) / MOMMY WHERE'S DADDY (Frank Zappa) / THEY'RE RED HOT (Robert Johnson) / SEARCH AND DESTROY (Iggy Pop). **Producers:** ANDY GILL (Gang Of Four) produced debut, GEORGE CLINTON of PARLIAMENT produced the 1985 follow-up. In 1991, RICK RUBINS of Def Jam label, held the reins.

Recommended: WHAT HITS? (*8) / BLOOD SUGAR SEX MAGICK (*8) / ONE HOT MINUTE (*7) / MOTHER'S MILK (*7)

ANTHONY KIEDIS (ANTWAN THE SWAN) (b. Michegan) – vocals / **HILLEL SLOVAK** (b. Israel) – guitar / **MICHAEL 'Flea' BALZARY** (b. Melbourne, Australia) – bass / **JACK IRONS** (b. California) – drums

EMI America / EMI America

1984. (lp)(c) **THE RED HOT CHILI PEPPERS** [-] [ ]
– True me don't kill coyotes / Baby appeal / Buckle down / Get up and jump / Why don't you love me / Green heaven / Mommy where's daddy? / Out in L.A. / Police helicopter / You always sing / Grand pappy du plenty. *(UK-iss.+cd.Aug90) (re-iss.cd+c Jun93 on 'Fame')*

(Due to contractual reasons, SLOVAK and IRONS couldn't play on debut. They were deputised by session men **JACK SHERMAN** – guitar (ex-CAPTAIN BEEFHEART) / & **CLIFF MARTINEZ** – drums (ex-WEIRDOS, ex-TEENAGE JESUS & THE JERKS)

— **HILLEL SLOVAK** returned from (**WHAT IS THIS?**) to repl. SHERMAN guests included **MACEO PARKER + FRED WESLEY** (of FUNKADELIC / PARLIAMENT)

1985. (lp)(c) **FREAKY STYLIE** [-] [ ]
– Jungle man / Hollywood (Africa) / American ghost dance / If you want me to stay / Never mind / Freaky stylie / Blackeyed blonde / The brothers cup / Battle ship / Lovin' and touchin' / Catholic school girls rule / Sex rap / Thirty dirty birds / Yertle the turtle. *(UK-iss.+cd.Aug90) (re-iss.cd+c Dec94 on 'Fame')*

Aug 85. (7") **HOLLYWOOD (AFRICA). / NEVER MIND** [ ] [ ]
('A'remixed-12"+=) – ('A'dub version).

— **JACK IRONS** returned from **WHAT IS THIS?** to repl. MARTINEZ

Jan 88. (7") **FIGHT LIKE A BRAVE. / FIRE** [ ] [ ]
(12"+=)(12"pic-d+=) – ('A' mofo mix) / ('A'knucklehead mix).

Mar 88. (lp)(c)(cd) **UPLIFT MOFO PARTY PLAN** [ ] [ ] Nov 87
– Fight like a brave / Funky crime / Me and my friends / Backwoods / Skinny sweaty man / Behind the sun / Subterranean homesick blues / Special secret song inside / No chump love sucker / Walkin' on down the road / Love trilogy / Organic anti-beat box band.

— **ANTWAN & FLEA** (now adding trumpet) brought in new lads **JOHN FRUSCIANTE** – guitar repl. HILLEL who died (of heroin OD) 20 Jun'88. **CHAD SMITH** – drums repl. IRONS who later formed ELEVEN

EMI Manhattan / Manhattan

Aug 89. (7")(7"pic-d) **KNOCK ME DOWN. / PUNK ROCK CLASSIC / PRETTY LITTLE DITTY** [ ] [ ]
(12") – (first 2 – 7"tracks) / Special secret song inside / Magic Johnson
(cd-s) – (first 2 – 7"tracks) / Jungle man / Magic Johnson.

Aug 89. (lp)(c)(cd) **MOTHER'S MILK** [ ] [52]
– Good time boys / Higher ground / Subway to Venus / Magic Johnson / Nobody weird like me / Knock me down / Taste the pain / Stone cold bush / Fire / Pretty little ditty / Punk rock classic / Sexy Mexican maid / Johnny kick a hole in the sky.

Dec 89. (7") **HIGHER GROUND. / MILLIONAIRES AGAINST HUNGER** 55
(12") – ('A' Munchkin mix) / ('A'dub mix) / Politician.
(12") – ('A' Munchkin mix)(++=) – Mommy where's daddy.
('A' Munchkin mix – cd-s+=) – Mommy where's daddy / Politician (mini rap).
Jun 90. (7")(c-s) **TASTE THE PAIN. / SHOW ME YOUR SOUL** 29
(12"+=)(9"square-pic-d+=) – Castles made of sand (live).
(cd-s++=) – Never mind.
(remixed-12"+=) – If you want me to stay / Never mind.
Aug 90. (7")(c-s) **HIGHER GROUND. / FIGHT LIKE A BRAVE** 54
(12"+=)(cd-s+=) – ('A'mix) / Out in L.A.
(cd-s+=) – Behind the Sun.

Warners Warners

Sep 91. (cd)(c)(d-lp) **BLOOD SUGAR SEX MAGIK** 25 3
– The power of equality / If you have to ask / Breaking the girl / Funky monks / Suck my kiss / I could have lied / Mellowship slinky in B major / The righteous & the wicked / Give it away / Blood sugar sex magik / Under the bridge / Naked in the rain / Apache Rose peacock / The greeting song / My lovely man / Sir psycho sexy / They're red hot. *(re-iss.Mar92)*
Dec 91. (c-s) **GIVE IT AWAY. / ?** - 73
(US re-iss.Jul92, hit No.73)
Mar 92. (7") **UNDER THE BRIDGE. / GIVE IT AWAY** 26 2
(12")(cd-s) – ('A'side) / Search and destroy / Soul to squeeze / Skiamikanico.

— (the last track also featured on 'Wayne's World' film/single)

— **ZANDER SCHLOSS** (THELONIUS MONSTER) – guiter, repl. FRUSCANTE
Jun 92. (c-s) **IF YOU HAVE TO ASK. / ?** -
Aug 92. (7") **BREAKING THE GIRL. / FELA'S COOK** 41
(12"+=)(cd-s+=) – Suck my kiss (live) / I could have lied (live).

— (Aug92) **ERIC MARSHALL** – guitar (ex-MARSHALL LAW) repl. SCHLOSS
Aug 93. (c-s)(cd-s) **SOUL TO SQUEEZE. / ?** - 22
Jan 94. (7")(c-s) **GIVE IT AWAY. / IF YOU HAVE TO ASK (remix)** 9 -
(cd-s+=) – Nobody weird like me (live).
(cd-s) – ('A'side) / Soul to squeeze.
Apr 94. (7"blue)(c-s) **UNDER THE BRIDGE. / SUCK MY KISS (live)** 13 -
(cd-s+=) – Sikamikanico / Search and destroy.
(cd-s) – ('A'side) / I could have lied / Sela's cock / Give it away.

— **DAVE NAVARRO** – guitar (ex-JANE'S ADDICTION) repl.MARSHALL
Aug 95. (c-s) **WARPED / PEA** 31
(cd-s+=) – Melancholy maniacs.
Sep 95. (cd)(c)(lp) **ONE HOT MINUTE** 2 4
– Warped / Aeroplane / Deep kick / My friends / Coffee shop / Pea / One big mob / Walkabout / Tearjerker / One hot minute / Falling into grace / Shallow be thy name / Transcending.
Oct 95. (c-s) **MY FRIENDS / LET'S MAKE EVIL** 29
(12"+=)(cd-s+=) – Coffee / Stretch.

– compilations, others, etc. –

May 88. EMI Manhattan; (7"ep) **THE ABBEY ROAD EP** -
– Backwoods / Hollywood (Africa) / True men don't kill coyotes.
(12"ep+=) – Catholic school girls rule.
Oct 92. EMI Manhattan; (cd)(c)(d-lp) **WHAT HITS?** 23 22
– Higher ground / Fight like a brave / Behind the Sun / Me & my friends / Backwoods / True men don't kill coyotes / Fire / Get up and jump / Knock me down / Under the bridge / Show me your soul / If you want me to stay / Hollywood / Jungle man / The brothers cup / Taste the pain / Catholic school girls rule / Johnny kick a hole in the sky.
Oct 94. Warners; (d-cd) **PLASMA SHAFT** (rare mixes/live)
Nov 94. EMI; (cd)(c)(lp) **OUT IN L.A.** (rare remixes, demos & live) 61 82
Nov 95. EMI; (3xcd-box) **THE RED HOT CHILI PEPPERS / FREAKY STYLIE / UPLIFT MOFO PARTY PLAN**

RED HOUSE PAINTERS

Formed: San Francisco, USA . . .1989 by MARK KOZELEK, who had earlier sang in GOD FORBID. In 1989, he moved from Ohio to Atlanta and met ANTHONY KOUTSOS who helped him form RED HOUSE PAINTERS. They relocated again. This time to San Francisco, where they met GORDON MACK and JERRY VESSEL. Their demos found their way to the doors of UK's '4 a.d.', via the ears of MARK EITZEL (American Music Club). The early 1990 demos soon becam their debut album; 'DOWN COLOURFUL HILL'. • **Style:** Moody alternative pastel-rock outfit, fronted by drug & drink-free near solo KOZELEK. • **Songwriters:** All by KOSELER except 'Dragonflies' by ROBYN RIEL-NAIL. Covers; I AM A ROCK (Paul Simon) / STAR SPANGLED BANNER (US National Anthem) / SHOCK ME (Kiss) / LONG DISTANCE RUNAROUND (Yes). • **Trivia:** Their UK first gig (very rare) was at The Borderline in London in the Autumn of '92.

Recommended: RED HOUSE PAINTERS (*9; Jun93 double album)

MARK KOZELEK – vocals / **GORDON MACK** – guitar / **JERRY VESSEL** – bass / **ANTHONY KOUTSOS** – drums

4 a.d. 4 a.d.

Sep 92. (cd)(c)(lp) **DOWN COLOURFUL HILL**
– 24 / Medicine bottle / Down colourful hill / Japanese to English / Lord kill the pain / Michael.
Jun 93. (cd)(c)(d-lp) **RED HOUSE PAINTERS** 63
– Grace cathedral park / Down through / Katy song / Mistress / Things mean a lot / Funhouse / Take me out / Rollercoaster / New Jersey / Dragonflies / Mistress (piano version) / Mother / Strawberry hill / Brown eyes.
Oct 93. (m-cd)(m-c)(m-lp) **RED HOUSE PAINTERS** 68
– Evil / Bubble / I am a rock / Helicopter / New Jersey / Uncle Joe / Blindfold / Star spangled banner.
Feb 94. (12"ep)(cd-ep) **SHOCK ME / SHOCK ME (mix). / SUNDAYS AND HOLIDAYS / THREE-LEGGED CAT**
Mar 95. (cd)(c)(2x10"lp) **OCEAN BEACH**
– Cabezon / Summer dress / San Geronimo / Shadows / Over my head / Red carpet / Brockwell Park / Moments / Drop. *(lp+=)*– Long distance runaround.

RED NOISE (see under ⇒ NELSON, Bill)

Dan REED NETWORK

Formed: Portland, Oregon, USA . . . 1982 by DAN REED, etc (see below). They signed worldwide deal with 'Mercury' in 1987, and after 3 flop 45's, released eponymous album late '88. They cracked the UK market in the early 90's, with a few hit singles and a Top 20 album 'THE HEAT'. • **Style:** Guitar-based funk-metal band, in the mould of MOTHER'S FINEST, FAITH NO MORE and LIVING COLOUR. REED's long black locks were swapped for the shaven-head look in Apr'90. • **Songwriters:** REED penned except; YOU CAN LEAVE YOUR HAT ON (Randy Newman) / MONEY (Pink Floyd). • **Trivia:** First & third albums were produced by Bruce Fairburn, the second by Nile Rodgers (ex-Chic).

Recommended: DAN REED NETWORK (*6) / THE HEAT (*6).

DAN REED (b. South Dakota) – vocals / **BRIAN JAMES** (b. New York) – guitar / **BLAKE SAKAMOTO** (b. Japan) – keyboards / **DAN PRED** (b.Jewish parents) – drums / **MELVIN BRANNON** (black American) – bass repl. ?

Mercury Mercury

1987. (7"ep) **BREATHLESS** -
Apr 88. (7") **RITUAL. / ?** 38 Mar 88
(12"+=) – ?
Oct 88. (7") **GET TO YOU. / ?**
(12"+=)(cd-s+=) – Tatiana.
Nov 88. (lp)(c)(cd) **DAN REED NETWORK** 95 Mar 88
– The world has a heart too / Get to you / Ritual / Forgot to make her mine / Tamin' the wild nights / I'm so sorry / Resurrect / Baby don't fade / Human / Halfway around the world / Rock you all night long. *(cd+=)*– Tatiana.
Sep 89. (7") **TIGER IN A DRESS. / AFFECTION**
(12"+=)/ /(c-s+=)(cd-s+=) – Seven sisters road./ / Get to you.
Oct 89. (lp)(c)(cd) **SLAM** 66
– Make it easy / Slam / Tiger in a dress / Rainbow child / Doin' the love thing / Stronger than steel / Cruise together / Under my skin / Lover / I'm lonely, please stay / Come back baby / All my lovin' / Seven Sisters road.
Jan 90. (7")(c-s) **COME BACK BABY. / BURNIN' LOVE** 51
(12"+=)(12"pic-d) – ('A'side) / Come alive / Make it easy.
(cd-s) – (all 4 tracks)
Mar 90. (7")(c-s) **RAINBOW CHILD. / YOU CAN LEAVE YOUR HEART ON** 60
(12"+=)(12"yellow+=) – Ritual.
(cd-s++=) – Tamin' the wild nights.
Jun 90. (7")(c-s) **STARDATE 1990. / RAINBOW CHILD (live)** 39
(12"+=)(cd-s+=)(12"pic-d+=) – Without you / Come to me.
(12"+=)(12"pic-d+=) – Ritual / Under my skin.
Aug 90. (7")(c-s) **LOVER. / MONEY** 45
(12"+=)(cd-s+=)(12"yellow+=) – Ritual (mix).
(12"blue+=) – Forgot to make her mine / Tiger in a dress.
Jul 91. (7")(c-s) **MIX IT UP. / THE HEAT** 49
(10"orange+=)/ /(12"+cd-s+=) – Slavery./ / The lonely sun.
Jul 91. (cd)(c)(lp) **THE HEAT** 15
– Baby now I / Blame it on the Moon / Mix it up / The heat / Let it go / Love don't work that way / Money / Chill out / Life is sex / The salt of joy / Take my hand / Thje lovely Sun / Thy will be done / Wake up / Long weay to go. *(re-iss.cd+c Mar93)*
Sep 91. (7")(c-s) **BABY NOW I. / THY WILL BE DONE** 65
(10"pic-d+=)(12"black+=)(12"white+=) – Living with a stranger.
(cd-s++=) – Stronger than steel.

— Disbanded around 1992.

– compilations, etc. –

Jul 93. Mercury; (cd)(c)(lp) **MIXING IT UP (THE BEST OF)**
(re-iss.cd/c Apr95)

Lou REED

Born: LOUIS FIRBANK, 2 Mar'42, Freeport, Long Island, New York, USA. In 1958, he formed the JADES who released 2 singles written by him 'LEAVE HER FOR ME / SO BLUE' plus 'LEAVE HER FOR ME / BELINDA' for 'Time' and 'Dot' respectively. Late in '64 he joined the 'Pickwick' stable of writers and achieved local minor hit when The PRIMITIVES issued his 'The Ostrich / Sneaky Pete' 45. Later in the year, he became part leader of seminal supergroup The VELVET UNDERGROUND. He departed in Sep'70, and went solo after signing to 'RCA'. His eponymous debut in 1972 with Richard Robinson on production, scraped into The US Top 200 but gained nothing in renewed respect. The following year, helped by RCA stablemates/fans DAVID BOWIE and MICK RONSON, he unleashed 'TRANSFORMER', which gave him first major taste of triumph, when it reached Top 30 on both sides of the Atlantic. It was boosted by a superb single lifted from it 'WALK ON THE WILD SIDE', which also broke into each Top 20. His next album 'BERLIN', although unfairly panned by US critics, still managed a Top 10 placing in Britain. On reflection, its subject matter like suicide and child neglect, didn't help win any new friends. • **Style:** Cult experimental rock artist, whose socially aware narratively sung lyrics and extreme looks made him punk superstar of the 70's and 80's. In 1975, he shot himself in the foot, when releasing in the US, an experimental double album 'METAL MACHINE MUSIC', which consisted of ENO type unaccessible pieces of noise interrupted with feedback, screams, hums, etc. • **Songwriters:** REED compositions except, SEPTEMBER SONG (Kurt Weill) / SOUL MAN (Sam & Dave). In 1979 & 1980, he co-wrote with MICHAEL FORFARA plus other group members. The single 'CITY LIGHTS' was co-written with NILS LOFGREN. • **Trivia:** Surprisingly in 1973, WALK ON THE WILD SIDE was not banned from airplay. It contained lyrics 'giving head', which had been overlooked by unstreet-wise cred. radio producers. LOU has been married twice. The first to cocktail waitress Betty on 9 Jan'73, the second to Sylvia Morales on 14 Feb'80. He played guitar and composed 4 tracks on NICO'S 'Chelsea Girl' lp in 1967. Nine years later he produced NELSON SLATER'S 'Wild Angel' album, also contributing guitar, piano and vocals. In 1979 & 1981 he co-composed with NILS LOFGREN and KISS on their 'NILS' and 'THE ELDER' albums respectively. In the late 80's, he guested for RUBEN BLADES and his old friend MAUREEEN TUCKER. He was also backing vocalist on SIMPLE MINDS' 'This is Your Land' / DION'S 'King of The New York Streets' and TOM TOM CLUB'S version of 'Femme Fatale'.

Recommended: TRANSFORMER (*10) / BERLIN (*8) / RETRO (*8) / NEW YORK (*9) / MAGIC AND LOSS (*8) / SONGS FOR DRELLA (*7).

LOU REED – vocals, guitar (ex-VELVET UNDERGROUND) / with **STEVE HOWE** – guitar / **RICK WAKEMAN** – keyboards (both of YES) / **CLEM CATTINI** – drums (ex-TORNADOES)

R.C.A. R.C.A.

Jun 72. (7") **GOING DOWN. / I CAN'T STAND IT** [-] [ ]
Jul 72. (lp)(c) **LOU REED** [ ] [ ] May 72
– I can't stand it / Going down / Walk and talk it / Lisa says / Berlin / I love you / Wild child / Love makes you feel / Ride into the Sun / Ocean.
Aug 72. (7") **WALK AND TALK IT. / WILD CHILD** [ ] [ ]

—— now with **MICK RONSON** – guitar / **HERBIE FLOWERS + KLAUS VOORMANN** – bass / **JOHN HALSEY + RITCHIE DHARMA + BARRY DE SOUZA** – drums / **RONNIE ROSS** – saxophone / **DAVID BOWIE** – backing vocals, producer

Nov 72. (lp)(c) **TRANSFORMER** [13] [29]
– Vicious / Andy's chest / Perfect day / Hangin' round / Walk on the wild side / Make up / Satellite of love / Wagon wheel / New York telephone conversation / I'm so free / Goodnight ladies. *(re-iss.Feb81, Jun82 hit 91, 1984, cd-iss.1985 + Oct87)*
Nov 72. (7") **WALK ON THE WILD SIDE. / PERFECT DAY** [10] [16]
(re-iss.May79.on'RCA Gold')
Feb 73. (7") **SATELLITE OF LOVE. / WALK AND TALK IT** [-] [ ]
Mar 73. (7") **SATELLITE OF LOVE. / VICIOUS** [ ] [-]
Apr 73. (7") **VICIOUS. / GOODNIGHT LADIES** [-] [ ]

—— all new band **DICK WAGNER + STEVE HUNTER** – guitar (both ex-ALICE COOPER) / **STEVE WINWOOD** – keyboards / **JACK BRUCE** – bass / **AYNSLEY DUNBAR** – drums / etc.

Oct 73. (7") **HOW DO YOU THINK IT FEELS. /LADY DAY** [-] [ ]
Oct 73. (lp)(c) **BERLIN** [7] [98]
– Berlin / Lady day / Men of good fortune / Caroline says I / How do think it feels / Oh Jim / Caroline says II / The kids / The bed / Sad song. *(re-iss. Oct81, re-iss.+cdJun86)*
Feb 74. (7") **CAROLINE SAYS I. / CAROLINE SAYS II** [ ] [-]

—— **PRAKASH JOHN** – bass (ex-ALICE COOPER) repl. TONY LEVIN / **JOSEF CHIROWSKY** – keyboards / **WHITNEY GLEN** – drums (ex-ALICE COOPER)

Mar 74. (lp)(c) **ROCK'N'ROLL ANIMAL (live)** [26] [45] Feb 74
– (intro) – Sweet Jane / Heroin / White light – white heat / Lady day / Rock and roll. *(re-iss.May81 + 1984, re-iss.+cdJun86)*
Apr 74. (7") **SWEET JANE (live). / LADY DAY (live)** [ ] [ ]

—— **MICHAEL FORFARA** – keyboards repl. JOSEF

Aug 74. (7") **SALLY CAN'T DANCE. / VICIOUS** [-] [ ]
Sep 74. (lp)(c) **SALLY CAN'T DANCE** [ ] [10]
– Ride Sally ride / Animal language / Baby face / N.Y. stars / Kill your sons / Billy / Sally can't dance / Ennui. *(re-iss.Feb81 + 1984, cd-iss.Mar87 + Feb89)*
Oct 74. (7") **SALLY CAN'T DANCE. / ENNUI** [ ] [ ]
Mar 75. (lp)(c) **LOU REED LIVE (live)** [ ] [62]
– Walk on the wild side / I'm waiting for the man / Vicious / Oh Jim / Satellite of love / Sad song. *(re-iss.Feb81 + 1984, cd-iss.Mar87 + Feb90)*

—— LOU now used synthesizer only.

Jul 75. (d-lp) **METAL MACHINE MUSIC – (THE AMINE B RING)** [-] [ ]
– Metal machine music A1 / A2 / A3 / A4. *(quad-lp also iss.) (re-iss.+cd.Mar91 on 'Great Expectations')*

—— Band now featured **MICHAEL SUCHORSKY** – percussion / **BOB KULICK** – guitar / **BRUCE YAW** – bass

Jan 76. (lp)(c) **CONEY ISLAND BABY** [52] [41]
– Crazy feeling / Charley's girl / She's my best friend / Kicks / A gift / Oooh baby / Nobody's business / Coney Island baby. *(re-iss.Mar81 + 1984, cd-iss. Dec86)*
Mar 76. (7") **CHARLEY'S GIRL. / NOWHERE AT ALL** [ ] [ ]
May 76. (7") **CRAZY FEELING. / NOWHERE AT ALL** [-] [ ]

Arista Arista

Nov 76. (lp)(c) **ROCK AND ROLL HEART** [ ] [64]
– I believe in love / Banging on my drum / Follow the leader / You wear it so well / Ladies pay / Rock and roll heart / Temporary thing.
Nov 76. (7") **I BELIEVE IN LOVE. / SENSELESSLY CRUEL** [-] [ ]
Apr 77. (7") **ROCK AND ROLL HEART. / SENSELESSLY CRUEL** [ ] [-]

—— **STUART HEINRICH** – guitar, vocals repl. KULICK / **MARTY FOGEL** – saxophone repl. YAW

Apr 78. (lp)(c) **STREET HASSLE** [ ] [89]
– Gimme some good times / Dirt / Street hassle / I wanna be black / Real good time together / Shooting star / Leave me alone / Wait.
Apr 78. (12") **STREET HASSLE. / (same track)** [-] [ ]
Jul 78. (12"ep) **STREET HASSLE. / Waiting For The Man + Venus In Furs (by "The VELVET UNDERGROUND")** [ ] [-]

—— **ELLARD BOLES** – bass, guitar repl. HEINRICH. (Below released 'RCA' UK)

Mar 79. (d-lp)(c) **LIVE – TAKE NO PRISONERS (live)** [ ] [ ] Nov 78
– Sweet Jane / I wanna be black / Satellite of love / Pale blue eyes / Berlin / I'm waiting for the man / Coney Island baby / Street hassle / Walk on the wild side / Leave me alone. *(US-iss.red or blue-lp)*

—— **REED** now with **FORFARA, BOLES, SUCHORSKY, FOGEL** and **DON CHERRY** – trumpet

Oct 79. (lp)(c) **THE BELLS** [ ] [ ] May 79
– Stupid man / Disco mystic / I want to boogie with you / With you / Looking for love / City lights / All through the night / Families / The bells.
Jun 79. (7") **CITY LIGHTS. / I WANT TO BOOGIE WITH YOU** [-] [ ]
Oct 79. (7") **CITY LIGHTS. / SENSELESSLY CRUEL** [ ] [-]

—— **CHUCK HAMMER** – synthesizer, guitar repl. FOGEL & CHERRY

May 80. (lp)(c) **GROWING UP IN PUBLIC** [ ] [ ] Apr 80
– How do you speak to an angel / My old man / Keep away / Growing up in public / Standing on ceremony / So alone / Love is here to stay / The power of positive drinking / Smiles / Think it over / Teach the gifted children.
Jun 80. (7") **THE POWER OF POSITIVE DRINKING. / GROWING UP IN PUBLIC** [-] [ ]

—— **ROBERT QUINE** – guitar repl. HAMMER

R.C.A. R.C.A.

Mar 82. (lp)(c) **THE BLUE MASK** [ ] [ ] Feb 82
– My house / Women / Underneath the bottle / The gun / The blue mask / The gun / The heroine / Waves of fear / The day John Kennedy died / Heavenly arms.
Mar 83. (lp)(c) **LEGENDARY HEARTS** [ ] [ ] Dec 82
– Legendary hearts / Don't talk to me about work / Make up mind / Martial law / The last shot / Turn out the light / ow wow / Betrayed / Bottoming out / Home of the brave / Rooftop garden. *(re-iss.Oct86, re-iss.+cd.Apr91)*
Jan 84. (d-lp)(c) **LIVE IN ITALY (live)** [ ] [-]
– Sweet Jane / I'm waiting for the man / Martial law / atellite of love / Kill your sons / Betrayed / Sally can't dance / Waves of fear / Average guy / White light – white heat / Some kinda love / Sister Ray / Walk on the wild side / Heroin / Rock and roll.

—— Line-up now **FERNANDO SAUNDERS** – bass, rhythm guitar / **FRED MAHER** – drums / **PETER WOOD** – piano, synthesizer, accordion / **L. SHANKER** – electric violin

Apr 84. (12") **MY RED JOY STICK. / ('A' remix)** [-] [ ]
May 84. (lp)(c) **NEW SENSATIONS** [92] [56]
– I love you, Suzanne / Endlessly jealous / My red joystick / Turn to me / New sensations / Doin' the things that we want to / What becomes a legend most / Fly into the Sun / High in the city / My friend George / Down at the arcade. *(cd-iss.Jul86)*
May 84. (7") **I LOVE YOU, SUZANNE. / VICIOUS** [ ] [-]
(12"+=) – Walk on the wild side.
Apr 86. (12") **THE ORIGINAL WRAPPER. / (2 'A' versions)** [-] [ ]
Apr 86. (lp)(c)(cd) **MISTRIAL** [69] [47]
– Mistrial / No money down / Outside / Don't hurt a woman / Video violence / Spit it out / The original wrapper / Mama's got a lover / I remember you / Tell it to your heart. *(re-iss.+cd.Oct88)*
Jun 86. (7") **NO MONEY DOWN. / DON'T HURT A WOMAN** [ ] [-]
(12"+=) – ('A'dub version).

—— Next from the film 'Soul Man'.

A & M A & M

Jan 87. (7") **SOUL MAN. (by "LOU REED and SAM MOORE") / Sweet Sarah (by 'Tom Scott')** [30] [ ]
(US-12"+=) – My love is chemical.

—— new band **MIKE RATHKE** – guitar / **ROB WASSERMAN** – bass / **FRED MAHER** – drums / **MAUREEN TUCKER** – drums on 2 (ex-VELVET UNDERGROUND)

Sire Sire

Jan 89. (lp)(c)(cd) **NEW YORK** [14] [40]
– Romeo had Juliette / Halloween parade / Dirty Blvd. / Endless cycle / There is no time / The last great American whale / Beginning of a great adventure / Busload of faith / Sick of you / Hold on / Good evening Mr.Waldheim / Xmas in February / Strawman / Dime store mystery. *(re-iss.cd/c Feb95)*
Feb 89. (7") **ROMEO HAD JULIETTE. / BUSLOAD OF FAITH (live)** [-] [ ]
Feb 89. (7") **DIRTY BLVD. / THE LAST GREAT AMERICAN WHALE** [ ] [-]
(12"+=) – The room.
Apr 90. (cd)(c)(lp) **SONGS FOR DRELLA ("LOU REED – JOHN CALE")** [22] [ ]
– Smalltown / Open house / Style it takes / Work / Trouble with classicists / Starlight / Faces and names / Images / Slip away (a warning) / It wasn't me / I believe / Nobody but you / A dream / Forever changed / Hello it's me. *(re-iss.Feb91)*

—— (above re-united the two VELVET UNDERGROUND members, tributing the recently deceased ANDY WARHOL)

—— **MICHAEL BLAIR** – percussion, drums, vocas repl. MAHER

Jan 92. (cd)(c)(lp) **MAGIC AND LOSS** [6] [80]
– Dorita – the spirit / What's good – the thesis / Power and glory – the situation / Magician – internally / Sword of Damocles – eternally / Goodby mass – in a chapel bodily termination / Cremation – ashes to ashes / Dreamin' – escape / No chance – regret / Warrior king – revenge / Harry's circumcision – reverie gone astray / Gassed and stoked – loss / Power and glory part II – magic transformation / Magic and loss – the summation.
Mar 92. (7")(c-s) **WHAT'S GOOD. / THE ROOM** [ ] [ ]
(12"+=)(cd-s+=) – Mary's circumcision / A dream.

– compilations, others, etc. –

Below releases issued on 'RCA' unless mentioned.

Apr 77. (lp)(c) **WALK ON THE WILD SIDE – THE BEST OF LOU REED** *(cd-iss.Mar87)* [ ] [ ]
Jan 79. (lp)(c) **VICIOUS** [ ] [ ]
Aug 81. (lp) **ROCK GALAXY** [ ] [ ]
Aug 81. (7") **WALK ON THE WILD SIDE. / VICIOUS** [ ] [-]
(re-iss.Oct86 + Mar89 on 'Old Gold')

Sep 82. (lp)(c) **I CAN'T STAND IT**
May 86. (c) **MAGIC MOMENTS**
Feb 89. (3"cd-ep) **WALK ON THE WILD SIDE / PERFECT DAY / SATELLITE OF LOVE / VICIOUS**
Sep 89. (lp)(c)(cd) **RETRO** 29
– Walk on the wild side / Satellite of love / I love you Suzanne / Wild child / How do you think it feels / Lady day / Coney Island baby / Sweet Jane (live) / Vicious / Sally can't dance / Berlin / Caroline says II / Kill your sons / White light – white heat (live). (cd+=) – I'm waiting for the man (VELVET UNDERGROUND) / Heroin (VELVET UNDERGROUND).
Dec 80. Arista; (d-lp)(c) **ROCK AND ROLL DIARY 1967-1980**
above featured 8 tracks by VU.
Sep 86. Fame; (lp)(c) **NEW YORK SUPERSTAR** -
Oct 85. A&M; (7") **SEPTEMBER SONG. / Oh Heavenly Action (by 'Mark Bingham with Johnny Adams & Aaron Neville')**
Mar 92. BMG; (3xcd)(3xc) **BETWEEN THOUGHT AND EXPRESSION**
Aug 92. Arista; (cd) **THE BELLS / GROWING UP IN PUBLIC**

REEF

Formed: London-based from Bath, England . . .1994. Hit the ears of the nation in 1995, when a Sony Minidisc TV commercial featured their song 'NAKED'. This became their second! Top 30 hit, although they shunned STILTSKIN-like now-made-it-through-TV-ad comparisons. • **Style:** Funky country blues fusing American-like sound of BLACK CROWES or LENNY KRAVITZ with LED ZEPPELIN. • **Songwriters:** Group? / STRINGER.

Recommended: REPLENISH (*6)

GARY STRINGER – vocals / **KENWYN HOUSE** – guitar / **JACK BESSANT** – bass / **DOMINIC GREENSMITH** – drums

S2 – Sony Sony

Apr 95. (c-s) **GOOD FEELING / WAKE** 24
(cd-s+=) – End.
(12"pic-d+=) – Water over stone.
May 95. (7"colrd)(c-s) **NAKED. / CHOOSE TO LIVE** 11
(cd-s+=) – Fade.
Jun 95. (cd)(c)(lp) **REPLENISH** 9
– Feed me / Naked / Good feeling / Repulsive / Mellow / Together / Replenish / Choose to live / Comfort / Loose / End / Reprise.
Jul 95. (7"colrd)(c-s) **WEIRD. / ACOUSTIC ONE** 19
(cd-s) – ('A'side) / Sunrise shakers / Together / End (live).

REEGS (see under ⇒ CHAMELEONS)

Martha REEVES (see under ⇒ MARTHA & THE VANDELLAS)

Terry REID

Born: 13 Nov'49, Cambridge, England. Left school at 15 and moved to London, where he played guitar for PETER JAY's JAYWALKERS. With the aid of said soulful outfit, he made first recording for 'Columbia' early in 1967; 'THE HAND DON'T FIT THE GLOVE'. TERRY had previously supported The ROLLING STONES in 1966. He then joined the stable of producer /manager MICKIE MOST, who groomed /guided him in a wrong direction, with the results being an ill-conceived debut lp 'BANG BANG . . .' which only gained a US-release. He then toured the States supporting CREAM and did a well-received stint at The Miami Pop Festival. Earlier that year, he turned down the chance to join LED ZEPPELIN, although he did suggest to JIMMY PAGE another vocalist ROBERT PLANT!. A second album simply called 'TERRY REID', regained due respectability when issued Autumn '69. Due to a fall-out over direction with MICKIE MOST, he moved to California while his contract expired. In 1973, he returned with a third album 'RIVER', which gained rave reviews again while suffering another commercial flop. Each release from then on, took three years and a change of labels to see light of day. He retired in 1980, but was back along 11 years later with 'THE DRIVER' album. • **Style:** At first groomed as the new LONG JOHN BALDRY, he quickly gruffed his vocal chords back to life by 1969. Regarded by many as a great white-soul balladeer although similiar to PAUL RODGERS, ROD STEWART or even his idol OTIS REDDING. • **Songwriters:** Self-penned except covers; SOMETHING'S GOTTEN HOLD OF MY HEART (Gene Pitney) / SUMMERTIME BLUES (Eddie Cochran) / HIGHWAY 61 REVISITED (Bob Dylan) / WALK AWAY RENEE (Four Tops) / ALL I HAVE TO DO IS DREAM (Everly Brothers) / GIMME SOME LOVIN' (Spencer Davis Group) / WHOLE OF THE MOON (Waterboys) / etc. • **Trivia:** Produced by MICKIE MOST between 1968-69. In 1973, TOM DOWD and EDDIE OFFORD took over, but were replaced by GRAHAM NASH in 1976. A couple of years later TERRY co-produced with CHRIS KIMSEY. His early 90's return saw TREVOR HORN (ex-BUGGLES, ex-YES) take the controls.

Recommended: TERRY REID (*7) / RIVER (*8).

TERRY REID – vocals, guitar, bass with **The JAYWALKERS** who included **PETER JAY**

Columbia Epic

Apr 67. (7") **THE HAND DON'T FIT THE GLOVE. / THIS TIME** -

— with **PETE SOLLEY** – keyboards / **KEITH WEBB** – drums

May 68. (7") **BETTER BY FAR. / FIRES ALIVE** -
Oct 68. (lp) **BANG BANG, YOU'RE TERRY REID** -
– Bang, bang / Tinker tailor / Erica / Without expression / Sweater / Something's gotten hold of my heart / Season of the witch / Writing on the wall / Summertime blues / When you get home / Loving time. *(cd-iss.Dec92 on 'B.G.O.')*

— **ERIC LEESE** – keyboards repl. SOLLEY

Jul 69. (7") **MAYFLY. / SUPERLUNGS MY SUPERGIRL** -
Sep 69. (lp) **TERRY REID**
– Superlungs my supergirl / Silver white light / July / Marking time / Stay with me baby / Highway 61 revisited / Mayfly / Speak now or forever hold your peace / Rich kid blues. *(re-iss.Jun85 as 'THE HAND DON'T FIT THE GLOVE!' on 'See For Miles'; += first 2 singles) (cd-iss.Dec92 on 'B.G.O.')*

— Moved to California and couldn't record for 3 years due to his producer and manager MICKIE MOST holding his contract.

M.F.P. not issued

Sep 71. (lp) **THE MOST OF MICKIE MOST** (compilation) -

— now with **DAVID LINDLEY** – steel & slide guitars (ex-KALEIDOSCOPE) / **LEE MILES** – bass / **CONRAD ISODORE** – drums / **WILLIE BOBO** – percussion

Atlantic Atlantic

Mar 73. (lp)(c) **RIVER**
– Dean / Avenue / Things to try / Live life / River / Dream / Milestones.

— **JOEL BERNSTEIN** – guitar / **BEN KEITH** – steel guitar / **SOKO RICHARDSON** – drums repl. ISODORE + BOBO

A.B.C. A.B.C.

May 76. (lp)(c) **SEED OF MEMORY**
– Faith to arise / Seed of memory / Brave awakening / To be treated rite / Ooh baby (make me feel so young) / The way you walk / The frame / Fooling you. *(cd-iss.May95 on 'Demon')*
Aug 76. (7") **OOH BABY (MAKE ME FEEL SO YOUNG). / BRAVE AWAKENING** May76

— now with The CLOSE QUARTERS: **DOUG RODRIGUES** – guitar / **STERLING SMITH + JAMES E.JOHNSON** – organ / **JOHN SIOMOS** – drums, percussion

Capitol Capitol

Feb 79. (lp)(c) **ROGUE WAVES**
– Ain't no shadow / Baby, I love you / Stop and think it over / Rogue waves / Walk away Renee / Believe in magic / Then I kissed her / Bowangi / All I have to do is dream. *(cd-iss.Jun92 on 'B.G.O.')*
Mar 79. (7") **AIN'T NO SHADOW. / BOWANGI**

Semi-retired for the 80's, to get married and help bring up his 2 children.

— with guests **JOE WALSH, TIM SCHMIDT, STEWART COPELAND, HOWARD JONES, ENYA**

W.E.A. not issued

Apr 91. (7") **WHOLE OF THE MOON. / LAUGH AT LIFE** -
(cd-s+=) – Gimme some lovin'.
May 91. (7")(c-s) **FIFTH OF JULY. / CINDY** -
(cd-s) – ('A'side) / River / July (1969).
Jun 91. (cd) **THE DRIVER** -
– Fifth of July / There's nothing wrong / Right to the end / The whole of the Moon / Hand of dimes / The driver (part 1) / If you let her / Turn around / Gimme some lovin' / Laugh at life / The driver (part 2).

R.E.M.

Formed: Athens, Georgia, USA . . . Spring 1980 by STIPE and BUCK, who met MILLS and BERRY at a party. In 1981, through manager Jefferson Holt, they released debut Mitch Easter produced 45 'RADIO FREE EUROPE', which made its way the ears of 'IRS' label boss Miles Copeland, who signed them in 1982. He retained Easter for their mini-lp 'CHRONIC TOWN', which gained heavy praise by critics. In 1983 their full album debut 'MURMUR' (co-produced by Easter & Don Dixon), became college favourite and soon broke into the US Top 40. They progressed steadily, bettering each album throughout the 80's. They superseded all before them in the 90's, when albums 'OUT OF TIME' & 'AUTOMATIC FOR THE PEOPLE' both made trans-Atlantic No.1's. For me and millions of others, the greatest band to come out of America. • **Style:** Moved from underground 60's influenced rock, similar to CREEDENCE CLEARWATER REVIVAL or The BYRDS, to a more country/folk tinted rock, mixed with new psychedelia, sifted from remains of the new wave. Unusually they have not toured since the 'GREEN' tour of early '89, and they intended being a studio outfit until 1994 at least. • **Songwriters:** Group compositions except 'B'side covers; THERE SHE GOES AGAIN + PALE BLUE EYES + FEMME FATALE (Velvet Underground) / TOYS IN THE ATTIC (Aerosmith) / KING OF THE ROAD (Roger Miller) / CRAZY (Pylon) / AFTER HOURS (Lou Reed) / LOVE IS ALL AROUND (Troggs) / FIRST WE TAKE MANHATTAN (Leonard Cohen) / LAST DATE (Floyd Cramer) / TIGHTEN UP (Booker T. & The MG's) / SEE NO EVIL (Television) / ACADEMY EIGHT SONG (Mission of Burma) / SUMMERTIME (Gershwin) / BABY BABY (Vibrators) / WHERE"S CAPAIN KICK? (Spizz) / PARADE OF WOODEN SOLDIERS (Tchaikovsky) / MOON RIVER (Henry Mancini) / THE ARMS OF YOU (Robyn Hitchcock) / THE LION SLEEPS TONIGHT (Tokens) / DARK GLOBE (Syd Barrett). • **Trivia:** R.E.M. stands for Rapid Eye Movement. The great STIPE, has been acquaintance of 10,000 MANIACS' singer NATALIE MERCHANT. Their other albums were produced by Joe Boyd (1985) / Don Gehman (1986) / Scott Litt & group (1987-1990's).

Recommended: AUTOMATIC FOR THE PEOPLE (*10) / OUT OF TIME (*10) / GREEN (*9) / DOCUMENT (*8) / LIFE'S RICH PAGEANT (*8) / FABLES OF THE

RECONSTRUCTION (*9) / RECKONING (*9) / MURMUR (*9) / DEAD LETTER OFFICE (*7) / THE BEST OF R.E.M. (*9) / MONSTER (*8).

MICHAEL STIPE (b. 4 Jan'60) – vocals / **PETER BUCK** (b. 6 Dec'56) – guitar / **MIKE MILLS** (b.17 Dec'58) – bass / **BILL BERRY** (b.31 Jul'58) – drums

not issued Hib-tone

Jul 81. (7") **RADIO FREE EUROPE. / SITTING BULL** [-] [ ]

I.R.S. I.R.S.

Aug 82. (m-lp) **CHRONIC TOWN** [-] [ ]
– Wolves, lower / 1,000,000 / Gardening at night / Stumble / Carnival of sorts (box cars).

Aug 83. (7") **RADIO FREE EUROPE. / THERE SHE GOES AGAIN** [ ] [78] Jul 83

Aug 83. (lp)(c) **MURMUR** [ ] [36] May 83
– Radio free Europe / Pilgrimage / Laughing / Talk about the passion / Moral kiosk / Perfect circle / Catapult / Sitting bull / 9-9 / Shaking through / We walk / West of the fields. *(re-iss.1986, cd-iss.1988 & Mar91)*

Nov 83. (7") **TALK ABOUT THE PASSION. / SHAKING THROUGH** [ ] [ ]
(12"+=) – Carnival of sorts (box cars) / 1,000,000.

Mar 84. (7") **SO. CENTRAL RAIN. / KING OF THE ROAD** [ ] [85] Jun 84
(12"+=) – Voice of Harold / Pale blue eyes.

Apr 84. (lp)(c) **RECKONING** [91] [27]
– Harborcoat / 7 Chinese Bros. / So. central rain (I'm sorry) / Pretty persuasion / Time after time (Annelise) / Second guessing / Letter never sent / Camera / (Don't go back to) Rockville / Little America. *(cd-iss.1988 & 1992 +=)*– Wind out (with Friends) / Pretty persuasion (live in studio) / White tornado (live in studio) / Tighten up / Moon river. *(re-iss.cd+c Oct94 on 'A&M')*

Jun 84. (7") **(DON'T GO BACK TO) ROCKVILLE. / WOLVES, LOWER** [ ] [ ]
(12"+=) – Gardening at night (live) / 9-9.

Jun 84. (7") **(DON'T GO BACK TO) ROCKVILLE. / CATAPULT (live)** [-] [ ]

Jul 85. (7") **CAN'T GET THERE FORM HERE. / BANDWAGON** [-] [ ]
(extended 12"+=) Burning Hell.

Jul 85. (lp)(c) **FABLES OF THE RECONSTRUCTION – RECONSTRUCTION OF THE FABLES** [35] [28] Jun 85
– Feeling gravitys pull / Maps and legends / Driver 8 / Life and how to live it / Old Man Kensey / Can't get there from here / Green grow the rushes / Kokoutek / Auctioneer (another engine) / Good advices / Wendell Gee. *(cd-iss. Apr87 + Jan90 +=)*– Crazy / Burning Hell / Bandwagon / Driver 8 (live) / Maps of legends (live).

Oct 85. (7") **DRIVER 8. / CRAZY** [-] [ ]

Oct 85. (7") **WENDELL GEE. / CRAZY** [ ] [ ]
(12"+=)/ /(d7"+=) – Driver 8./ / Ages of you / Burning down.

Aug 86. (7") **FALL ON ME. / ROTARY TEN** [ ] [94]
(12"+=) – Toys in the attic.

Aug 86. (lp)(c)(cd) **LIFE'S RICH PAGEANT** [43] [21]
– Begin the begin / These days / Fall on me / Cuyahoga / Hyena / Underneath the bunker / The flowers of Guatemala / I believe / What if we give it away? / Just a touch / Swan swan H / Superman. *(re-iss.cd.1992)*

Mar 87. (7") **SUPERMAN. / WHITE TORNADO** [ ] [ ]
(12"+=) – Femme fatale.

Aug 87. (7") **IT'S THE END OF THE WORLD AS WE KNOW IT (AND I FEEL FINE). / (THIS ONE GOES OUT TO) THE ONE I LOVE (live)** [ ] [69] Jan 88

Oct 87. (lp)(c)(cd) **DOCUMENT** [28] [10] Sep 87
– Finest worksong / Welcome to the occupation / Exhuming McCarthy / Disturbance at Heron House / Strange / It's the end of the world as we know it (and I feel fine) / The one I love / Fireplace / Lightnin' Hopkins / King of birds / Oddfellows local 151. *(re-iss.cd.1992)*

Nov 87. (7")(12") **THE ONE I LOVE. / LAST DATE (live)** [51] [9]
(cd-s+=) – Disturbance at the Heron House (live).

Jan 88. (7") **FINEST WORKSONG. / TIME AFTER TIME (live)** [50] [ ]
(12"+=) – ('A'club mix).
(12"+=) – Red rain / S.central rain (live).
(cd-s+=) – It's the end of the world and we know it (and I feel fine).

Mar 88. (12") **FINEST WORKSONG (lengthy club mix). / ('A'mix) / TIME AFTER TIME, ETC** [-] [ ]

Warners Warners

Nov 88. (lp)(c)(cd) **GREEN** [27] [12]
– Pop song 89 / Get up / You are the everything / Stand / World leader pretend / The wrong child / Orange crush / Turn you inside – out / Hairshirt / I remember California / Untitled song.

Jan 89. (7") **STAND. / MEMPHIS TRAIN BLUES** [51] [6]
(12"+=)(cd-s+=) – Eleventh untitled song.

Mar 89. (7") **ORANGE CRUSH. / GHOST RIDERS** [28] [ ]
(12"+=)(7"box+=)(3"cd-s+=) – Dark globe.

Jul 89. (7") **STAND. / POP SONG '89 (acoustic)** [48] [86] B-side
(12"+=)(cd-s+=) – Skin tight (live).
(all above 7"singles were re-iss. in 4xbox Dec89)

Sep 89. (7") **GET UP. / FUNTIME** [-] [ ]

—— R.E.M. toured early '91 as BINGO HAND JOB.

Feb 91. (7")(c-s) **LOSING MY RELIGION. / ROTARY ELEVEN** [19] [4]
(12"+=) – After hours (live).
(cd-s) – ('A'side) / Stand (live) / Turn you inside out (live) / World leader pretend (live).

Mar 91. (cd)(c)(lp) **OUT OF TIME** [1] [1]
– Radio song / Losing my religion / Low / Near wild Heaven / Endgame / Shiny happy people / Belong / Half a world away / Texarkana / Country feedback / Me in honey. *(re-entered UK chart Dec92, peaked 50)*
(the album feat. PETER HOLSAPPLE – guitar (ex-DB'S) / KRS-1 – rapper) MICHAEL STIPE released album with KRS-1 'CIVILIZATION VS.TECHNOLOGY' Oct91.

May 91. (7") **SHINY HAPPY PEOPLE. / FORTY SECOND SONG** [6] [10] Jul 91
(12"+=)(cd-s+=) – Losing my religion (live acoustic version).
(cd-s) – ('A'side) / I remember California / Get up / Pop song '89 (live).
(above 'A'side feat. KATE PIERSON of The B-52'S)

Aug 91. (7") **NEAR WILD HEAVEN. / POP SONG '89** [27] [ ]
(12"+=) – Half a world away (acoustic live).
(cd-s) – ('A'side) / Tom's diner (live) / Low (live) / Endgame (live).

Nov 91. (7") **RADIO SONG. / LOVE IS ALL AROUND** [28] [ ]
(12"+=) – Shiny hapy people (remix).
(cd-s+=) – You are the everything / Orange crush / Belong (all live).

Oct 92. (7")(c-s) **DRIVE. / IT'S A FREE WORLD BABY** [11] [28]
(cd-s+=) – World leader pretend / First we take Manhattan / Winged manual thorn.

Oct 92. (cd)(c)(lp) **AUTOMATIC FOR THE PEOPLE** [1] [2]
– Drive / Try not to breathe / The sidewinder sleeps tonight / Everybody hurts / New Orleans instrumental No.1 / Sweetness follows / Monty got a raw deal / Ignoreland / Star me kitten / Man on the Moon / Nightswimming / Find the river. *(re-hit UK No.1 Apr93)*

Nov 92. (7")(c-s) **MAN ON THE MOON. / TURN YOU INSIDE OUT** [18] [30] Feb 93
(cd-s+=) – Fruity organ / New Orleans instrumental No.1.
(cd-s+=) – The arms of you.

Feb 93. (7")(c-s) **THE SIDEWINDER SLEEPS TONIGHT. / GET UP** [17] [ ]
(cd-s) – ('A'side) / The lion sleeps tonight (live) / Fretless.
(cd-s) – ('A'side) / Star me kitten (demo) / Organ song.

Apr 93. (7")(c-s) **EVERYBODY HURTS. / POP SONG '89** [7] [-]
(cd-s) – ('A'side) / Dark globe / Chance (dub).
(cd-s) – ('A'side) / Mandolin strum / New Orleans instrumental No.1.

Jul 93. (7")(c-s) **NIGHTSWIMMING. / LOSING MY RELIGION (live)** [27] [ ]
(cd-s+=)(one-sided-12"pic-d) – ('A'side) / World leader pretend / Low / Belong (all 3 live).

Aug 93. (12"orange) **EVERYBODY HURTS. / MANDOLIN STRUM / BELONG / ORANGE CRUSH (live)** [-] [29]
(12"white)(12"blue)(cd-ep+=) – ('A'side) / Star me kitten (demo) / Losing my religion (live) / Organ song

Dec 93. (7")(c-s) **FIND THE RIVER. / EVERYBODY HURTS (live)** [54] [ ]
(cd-s+=)/ /(cd-s+=) – World leader pretend (live)./ / Orange crush.

Sep 94. (7")(c-s) **WHAT'S THE FREQUENCY, KENNETH?. / ('A'instrumental)** [9] [21]
(cd-s) – ('A'side) / Monty got a raw deal (live) / Everybody hurts (live) / Man on the Moon (live).

Oct 94. (cd)(c)(lp) **MONSTER** [1] [1]
– What's the frequency, Kenneth? / Crush with eyeliner / King of comedy / I don't sleep I dream / Star 69 / Strange currencies / Tongue / Bang and blame / I took your name / Let me in / Circus envy / You.

Nov 94. (c-s) **BANG AND FLAME. / ('A'instrumental)** [15] [19]
(cd-s) – ('A'side) / Losing my religion (live) / Country feedback (live) / Begin the begin (live).

Jan 95. (7")(c-s) **CRUSH WITH EYELINER. / ('A'instrumental)** [23] [ ]
(cd-s) – ('A'side) / Calendar bag / Fall on me (live) / Me in honey (live) / Finest worksong (live).

—— On 1st March, 1995, BILL BERRY suffered a brain haemorrhage, after collapsing during a concert in Switzerland. Thankfully, he steadily recovered during the following few months.

Apr 95. (7")(c-s) **STRANGE CURRENCIES. / ('A'instrumental)** [9] [47]
(cd-s) – ('A'side) / Drive (live) / Funtime (live) / Radio free Europe (live).

Jul 95. (c-s) **TONGUE / ('A'instrumental)** [13] [ ]
(cd-s) – ('A'side) / Bang and flame (live) / What's the frequency, Kenneth? (live) / I don't sleep, I dream (live).

– compilations, others, etc. –

May 87. IRS; (lp)(c)(cd) **DEAD LETTER OFFICE** ('B' sides, rarities, etc.) [60] [52]
– Crazy / There she goes again / Burning down / Voice of Harold / Burning Hell / White tornado / Toys in the attic / Windout / Ages of you / Pale blue eyes / Rotary ten / Bandwagon / Femme fatale / Walters theme / King of the road. *(re-iss.cd+c Oct94 on 'A&M')* (cd+=) – CHRONIC TOWN (tracks).

Oct 88. IRS; (lp)(c)(cd) **EPONYMOUS** [69] [ ]

Oct 88. IRS; (7") **THE ONE I LOVE. / FALL ON ME** [ ] [-]
(12"+=)(cd-s+=) – So. central rain (I'm sorry).

Sep 91. IRS-MCA; (cd)(c)(lp) **THE BEST OF R.E.M.** [7] [ ]
– Carnival of sorts / Radio free Europe / Perfect circle / Talk about the passion / So. central rain / (Don't go back to) Rockville / Pretty persuasion / Green grow the rushes / Can't get there from here / Driver 8 / Fall on me / I believe / Cuyahoga / The one I love / Finest worksong / It's the end of the world as we know it (and I feel fine).

Sep 91. IRS-MCA; (cd-s) **THE ONE I LOVE. / MAPS AND LEGENDS** [16] [ ]
(cd-ep+=) – Driver 8 / Disturbance at the Heron House.

Dec 91. IRS-MCA; (7")(c-s) **IT'S THE END OF THE WORLD (AS WE KNOW IT). / RADIO FREE EUROPE** [39] [ ]
(cd-s+=) – Time after time / Red rain / So.central rain (all live).

May 90. A&M; (c) **MURMUR / RECKONING** [ ] [ ]

—— When MICHAEL STIPE went off guesting for others incl.GOLDEN PALOMINOS; others splintered off into . . .

HINDU LOVE GODS

not issued I.R.S.

Sep 85. (7") **NARRATOR. / GONNA HAVE A GOOD TIME TONIGHT** [-] [ ]

with **WARREN ZEVON** – vocals They guested on his late '89 album; SENTIMENTAL HYGIENE.

Reprise Giant

Nov 90. (7") **RASPBERRY BERET. / WANG DANG DOODLE** [ ] [ ]
(12"+=)(cd-s+=) – Mannish boy.

Nov 90. (cd)(c)(lp) **HINDU LOVE GODS** [ ] [ ]
– Walkin' blues / Travelin' riverside blues / Raspberry beret / Crosscut saw / Junco pardner / Mannish boy / Wang dang doodle / Battleship chains / I'm a one woman man / Vigilante man.
(all above HINDU songs were covers)

RENAISSANCE

Formed: Surrey, England . . . 1969 by KEITH RELF and JIM McCARTY, both ex-YARDBIRDS. After debut 45 for 'Polydor', they signed to 'Island', but fell apart after dismal reviews of misguided debut. By '72, the group had completely changed personnel, with ANNIE HASLAM, taking the lead. After better press reception for 'PROLOGUE' album, especially in the States, they based themselves there and signed to 'Capitol'. • **Style:** Their debut album was a directionless mismatch of folk, classical, R&B and jazz. After their big break-up, they opted for quasi-classical sound, until 1978, when the folky 'NORTHERN LIGHTS' broke through. • **Songwriters:** Originally RELF, until break-up early 70's. By 1973, DUNFORD wrote music / BETTY THATCHER – lyrics. • **Trivia:** The original line-up, went on to release self-titled 'Island' album in 1977 as ILLUSION.

Recommended: DA CAPO – THE STORY OF RENAISSANCE (*8)

KEITH RELF – vocals, mouth harp (ex-YARDBIRDS, ex-Solo, ex-TOGETHER, ex-REIGN) **JANE RELF** – vocals / **JOHN HAWKEN** – keyboards (ex-NASHVILLE TEENS) / **LOUIS CENNAMO** – bass (ex-CHIGAGO BLUES) / **JIM McCARTY** – drums (ex-YARDBIRDS, ex-TOGETHER)

Polydor / not issued

1969. (7") **MARY JANE (GET OFF THE DEVIL'S MERRY-GO-ROUND). / DAYTIME LOVERS** [ ] [-]

Island / Elektra

Dec 69. (lp) **RENAISSANCE** [60] [ ]
– Kings and queens / Innocence / Island / Wanderer / Bullet. *(cd-iss.Jan95 on 'Repertoire')*

Jan 70. (7") **ISLAND. / THE SEA** [ ] [-]

— They split many times, with McCARTHY joining SHOOT and KEITH RELF becoming producer and joining MEDICINE HEAD. Finally evolved again with no originals remaining. These original members re-formed as ILLUSION in 1970 for unreleased (until later) lp for 'Island'. In 1976, ILLUSION were once more and they released 2 more lp's. RENAISSANCE were now in 1972; **ANNIE HASLAM** – vocals / **JOHN TOUT** – keyboards / **ROB HENDRY** – guitar / **JON CAMP** – bass, vocals / **TERRENCE SULLIVAN** – percussion

Sovereign / Capitol

Oct 72. (lp) **PROLOGUE** [ ] [ ]
– Prologue / Kiev / Sounds of the sea / Spare some love / Bound for infinity / Rajah Khan. *(cd-iss.Jun95 on 'Repertoire')*

Nov 72. (7") **PROLOGUE. / SPARE SOME LOVE** [-] [ ]

— **MICHAEL DUNFORD** – acoustic guitar, vocals repl. HENDRY

Oct 73. (7") **CARPET OF THE SUN. / BOUND FOR INFINITY** [-] [ ]

Oct 73. (lp) **ASHES ARE BURNING** [ ] [ ]
– Can you understand / Let it grow / On the frontier / Carpet of the Sun / At the harbour / Ashes are burning. *(cd-iss.Jun95 on 'Repertoire')*

B.T.M. / Sire

Nov 74. (7") **I THINK OF YOU. / MOTHER RUSSIA** [-] [ ]

Mar 75. (lp)(c) **TURN OF THE CARDS** [ ] [94] Jul 74
– Running hard / I think of you / Things I don't understand / Black flame / Cold is being / Mother Russia. *(cd-iss.Sep94 on 'Repertoire')*

Sep 75. (lp)(c) **SCHEHERAZADE & OTHER STORIES** [ ] [48] Aug 75
– Trip to the fair / The vultures fly high / Ocean gypsy / Song of Scheherazade: – Fanfare – The betrayal – The sultan – Love theme – The young prince and princess – Festival preparations – Fugue for the sultans – The festival – Finale. *(cd-iss.Sep94 on 'Repertoire')*

Sep 76. (d-lp)(c) **RENAISSANCE LIVE AT THE CARNEGIE HALL (live 1975)** [ ] [55] Jun 76
– Prologue / Ocean gypsy / Can you understand / Carpet of the Sun / Running hard / Mother Russia / Song of Scheherazade: Fanfare – The betrayal – The sultan – Love theme – The young prince and princess – Festival preparations – Fugue for the sultan – The festival – Finale / Ashes are burning. *(d-cd-iss.Sep94 on 'Repertoire') (re-iss.d-cd Sep95 on 'HTD')*

Oct 76. (7") **CARPET OF THE SUN. / (part 2)** [-] [ ]

Warners / Sire

Aug 77. (lp)(c) **NOVELLA** [ ] [46] Feb 77
– Can you hear me / The sisters / Midas man / The captive heart / Touching once (is so hard to keep).

Aug 77. (7") **THE CAPTIVE HEART. / MIDAS MAN** [-] [ ]

Sep 77. (7") **THE CAPTIVE HEART. / BACK HOME ONCE AGAIN** [ ] [-]

Mar 78. (lp)(c) **A SONG FOR ALL SEASONS** (Aug78:-) [35] [58]
– Opening out / Day of the dreamer / Closer than yesterday / Kindness (at the end) / Back home once again / She is love / Northern lights / A song for all seasons.

May 78. (7") **NORTHERN LIGHTS. / OPENING OUT** [10] [ ]

Apr 79. (7") **WINTER TREE. / ISLAND OF AVALON** [ ] [ ]

May 79. (lp)(c) **AZURE D'OR** [73] [ ]
– Jekyll and Hyde / The winter tree / Only angels have wings / Golden key / Forever changing / Secret mission / Kalynda / The discovery / Friends / The flood at Lyons. *(re-iss.+cd.Jan88 on 'Thunderb.')*

Jun 79. (7") **JEKYLL AND HYDE. / FOREVER CHANGING** [-] [ ]

— **PETER GOSLING** – keyboards repl. TOUT **PETER BARRON** – percussion repl. SULLIVAN

Illegal / I.R.S.

Sep 81. (7") **FAIRIES (LIVING AT THE BOTTOM OF MY GARDEN). / REMEMBER** [ ] [-]

Sep 81. (lp)(c) **CAMERA CAMERA** [ ] [ ]
– Camera camera / Faeries (living at the bottom of my garden) / Remember / Tyrant-Tula / Okichi-San / Jigsaw / Running away from you / Ukraine ways. *(cd-iss.Nov95 on 'HTD')*

Jan 82. (7") **BONJOUR SWANSONG. / UKRAINE WAYS** [ ] [-]

Jan 82. (7") **BONJOUR SWANSONG. / REMEMBER** [-] [ ]

Apr 83. (lp)(c) **TIME LINE** [ ] [ ]
– Flight / Missing persons / Chagrin boulevard / Richard IX / The entertainer / Electric avenue / Majik / Distant horizons / Orient express / Auto-tech. *(cd-iss.Nov95 on 'HTD')*

Apr 83. (7") **RICHARD IX. / (part 2)** [-] [ ]

— Disbanded in 1983.

ANNIE HASLAM

with **ROY WOOD** – instruments, vocals (ex-MOVE, ex-WIZZARD) / **JON CAMP** – bass / **DAVE DONOVAN** – drums / **LOUIS CLARK** – synthesizers.

Warners / Sire

Oct 77. (7") **I NEVER BELIEVED IN LOVE. ("ANNIE HASLAM & ROY WOOD") / INSIDE MY LIFE** [ ] [ ]

Jan 78. (7") **GOING HOME. / INSIDE MY LIFE** [ ] [ ]

Apr 78. (lp)(c) **ANNIE IN WONDERLAND** [ ] [ ]
– Introlise / If I were made of music / I never believed in love / If I loved you / Humicoco / Rockalise / Nature boy / Inside my life / Going home.

— In Aug95, ANNIE released cd 'BLESSING IN DISGUISE' for 'Thunderbolt'.

RENAISSANCE

MICHAEL DUNFORD re-formed with new female lead singer **STEPHANIE ADLINGTON** – vocals/ + **STUART BRADBURY** – guitars/ **ANDY SPILLAR** – keyboards, programming/ **PHIL MALFORD** – bass/ **DAVE DOWLY** – drums

H.T.D. / not issued

Jan 95. (cd) **THE OTHER WOMAN** [ ] [-]
– Deja vu / Love lies, love dies / Don't talk / The other woman / Lock in on love / Northern lights / So blase / Quicksilver / May you be blessed / Somewhere west of here.

compilations, etc

Jun 95. Repertoire; (d-cd) **DA CAPO – THE STORY OF RENAISSANCE** [ ] [-]
– Kings and queens / Island / Love goes on / Love is all / Prologue / Bound for infinity / Carpet of the sun / Ashes are burning / Black flame / Running hard / Mother Russia / Africa / Trip to the fair / Ocean gypsy / The young prince and the princess / Midas man / Captive heart / Northern lights / Song for all seasons / Forever changing / Flood at Lyons / Bonjour swansong / Ukraine ways / The entertainer / Writers wronged.

John RENBOURN (see under ⇒ PENTANGLE)

REO SPEEDWAGON

Formed: Champaign, Illinois, USA . . . 1968 by DOUGHTY and GRATZER, who soon brought in RICHRATH, LUTTRELL and PHILBIN. With help from manager Irving Azoff, they signed to 'Epic' records in 1971, and released eponymous debut. They built up national following, but only managed minor US chart placing until the late 70's, when their 9th album 'NINE LIVES', hit the Top 40. Eighteen months later they had dual US No.1's with single 'KEEP ON LOVING YOU' & lp 'HI INFIDELITY'. Continued to be major stars throughout the 80's. • **Style:** Faceless soft-rock ballad group (harder on stage), similar to JOURNEY, STYX, BOB SEGER or KANSAS. • **Songwriters:** RICHRATH until 1976 when CRONIN returned to co-write most. • **Trivia:** Took their name from a 1911 fire truck.

Recommended: A SECOND DECADE OF ROCK'N'ROLL 1981-1991 (*6) / A DECADE OF ROCK'N'ROLL 1970 TO 1980 (*6).

GARY RICHRATH (b.18 Oct'49, Peoria, Illinois) – lead guitar / **NEAL DOUGHTY** (b.29 Jul'46, Evanston, Illinois) – keyboards, organ / **ALAN GRATZER** (b. 9 Nov'48, Syracuse, New York) – drums / **TERRY LUTTRELL** – vocals / **GREGG PHILBIN** – bass

Epic / Epic

Jan 72. (7") **PRISON WOMAN. / SOPHISTICATED LADY** [-] [ ]

Mar 72. (lp) **REO SPEEDWAGON** [ ] [ ] Dec 71
– Gypsy woman's passion / 157 Riverside Avenue / Anti-establishment man / Lay me down / Sophisticated lady / Five men were killed today / Prison women / Dead at last. *(re-iss.+c.Nov81) (re-iss.cd+c Jun93 on 'Sony Collectors')*

Apr 72. (7") **GYPSY WOMAN'S PASSION. / LAY ME DOWN** [-] [ ]

Jun 72. (7") **157 RIVERSIDE AVENUE. / FIVE MEN WERE KILLED TODAY** [ ] [ ]

— **KEVIN CRONIN** (b. 6 Oct'51, Evanston) – vocals, guitar repl. LUTTRELL

Apr 73. (lp) **R.E.O.T.W.O.** [ ] [ ] Dec 72
– Let me ride / How the story goes / Little Queenie / Being kind / Music man / Like you do / Flash tan queen / Golden country.

Apr 73. (7") **GOLDEN COUNTRY. / LITTLE QUEENIE** [-] [ ]

— **MIKE MURPHY** – vocals repl. CRONIN who became unrecorded solo artist.

Feb 74. (7") **RIDIN' THE NIGHT STORM. / WHISKEY NIGHT** [-] [ ]

Jun 74. (lp) **RIDIN' THE STORM OUT** [ ] [ ] Jan 74
– Ridin' the storm out / Whiskey night / Oh woman / Find my fortune / Open up / Movin' / Son of a poor man / Start a new life / It's everywhere / Without expression.

Jun 74. (7") **OPEN UP. / START A NEW LIFE** [-] [ ]

Apr 75. (lp) **LOST IN A DREAM** [ ] [98] Nov 74
– Give me a ride / Throw the chains away / Sky blues / You can fly / Lost in a dream / Down by the dam / Do your best / Wild as the western wind / They're on the road / I'm feeling good.

Apr 75. (7") **THROW THE CHAINS AWAY. / SKY BLUES** [-] [ ]

— **KEVIN CRONIN** returned to repl. MURPHY

Aug 75. (7") **OUT OF CONTROL. / RUNNING BLIND** [-] [ ]

Nov 75. (lp) **THIS TIME WE MEAN IT** [ ] [74] Jul 75
– Reelin' / Headed for a fall / River of life / Out of control / You better realise / Gambler / Candalera / Lies / Dance / Dream weaver.

Nov 75. (7") **HEADED FOR A FALL. / REELIN'** [-] [ ]

Jun 76. (7") **KEEP PUSHIN' / TONIGHT** [-] [ ]

Jul 76. (lp) **R.E.O.** [ ] [ ] Jun 76
– Keep pushin' / Any kind of love / Summer love / Our time is gonna come / Breakaway / Flying turkey trot / Tonight / Lightning.

Nov 76. (7") **FLYING TURKEY TROT. / KEEP PUSHIN'** –
May 77. (7") **RIDIN' THE STORM OUT (live). / BEING KIND (live)** – 94
Aug 77. (d-lp) **REO SPEEDWAGON LIVE / YOU GET WHAT YOU PLAY FOR (live)** 72 Mar 77
– Like you do / Lay me down / Any kind of love / Being kind (can hurt someone sometimes) / Keep pushin' / (Only) A summer love / Son of a poor man / (I believe) Our time is gonna come / Flying turkey trot / Gary's guitar solo / 157 Riverside Avenue / Ridin' the storm out / Music man / Little Queenie / Golden country. *(re-iss.Aug87)*
Aug 77. (7") **FLYING TURKEY TROT (live). / KEEP PUSHIN' (live)** –

—— **BRUCE HALL** (b. 3 May'53) – bass repl. PHILBIN

Jul 78. (lp)(c) **YOU CAN TUNE A PIANO, BUT YOU CAN'T TUNA FISH** 29 Apr 78
– Roll with the changes / Time for me to fly / Runnin' blind / Blazin' your own trail again / Sing to me / Lucky for you / Do you know where your woman is tonight / The unidentified flying tuna trot / Say you love me or say goodnight. *(re-iss.Sep82)*
Jun 78. (7") **ROLL WITH THE CHANGES. / THE UNIDENTIFIED FLYING TUNA TROT** 58 May 78
Jul 78. (7") **TIME FOR ME TO FLY. / RUNNIN' BLIND** – 56
Jul 79. (7") **EASY MONEY. / I NEED YOU TONIGHT** –
Aug 79. (lp)(c) **NINE LIVES** 33
– Heavy on your love / Drop it (an old disguise) / Only the strong survive / Easy money / Rock'n 'roll music / Take me / I need you tonight / Meet me on the mountain / Back on the road again.
Oct 79. (7") **ONLY THE STRONG SURVIVE / DROP IT (AN OLD DISGUISE)** –
Aug 80. (7") **ONLY THE STRONG SURVIVE. / MEET ME ON THE MOUNTAIN** –
Nov 80. (7") **KEEP ON LOVING YOU. / TIME FOR ME TO FLY** – 1
Feb 81. (7") **KEEP ON LOVING YOU. / FOLLOW MY HEART** 7 –
Apr 81. (lp)(c) **HI INFIDELITY** 6 1 Dec 80
– Don't let him go / Keep on loving you / Follow my heart / In your letter / Take it on the run / Tough guys / Out of season / Shakin' it loose / Someone tonight / I wish you were there. *(re-iss.Nov84)*
Jun 81. (7") **TAKE IT ON THE RUN. / SOMEONE TONIGHT** 19 5 Mar 81
Jun 81. (7") **DON'T LET HIM GO. / I WISH YOU WERE THERE** – 24
Sep 81. (7") **IN YOUR LETTER. / SHAKIN' IT LOOSE** 20 Aug 81
Jul 82. (7") **KEEP THE FIRE BURNIN'. / I'LL FOLLOW YOU** 7 Jun 82
Jul 82. (lp)(c) **GOOD TROUBLE** 29 7
– Keep the fire burnin' / Sweet time / Girl with the heart of gold / Every now and then / I'll follow you / The key / Back in my heart again / Let's bebop / Stillness of the night / Good trouble. *(re-iss.1986)*
Sep 82. (7") **SWEET TIME. / STILLNESS OF THE NIGHT** 26 Aug 82
Oct 82. (7") **THE KEY. / LET'S BEBOP**
Nov 84. (7") **I DO WANNA KNOW. / ROCK AND ROLL STAR** 29 Oct 82
Nov 84. (lp)(c)(cd) **WHEELS ARE TURNIN'** 7
– I do wanna know / One lonely night / Thru the window / Rock and roll star / Live every moment / Can't fight this feeling / Gotta feel more / Break his spell / Wheels are turnin'.
Jan 85. (7") **CAN'T FIGHT THIS FEELING. / BREAK HIS SPELL** – 1
Feb 85. (7") **CAN'T FIGHT THIS FEELING. / ROCK AND ROLL STAR** 16 –
(12"+=) – Keep on loving you.
May 85. (7") **ONE LONELY NIGHT. / WHEELS ARE TURNIN'** 19 Mar 85
(12"+=) – Take it on the run.
Jul 85. (7") **LIVE EVERY MOMENT. / GOTTA FEEL MORE** 34
Nov 85. (7") **WHEREVER YOU'RE GOING. / SHAKIN' IT LOOSE**
Mar 87. (7") **THAT AIN'T LOVE. / ACCIDENTS CAN HAPPEN** 16 Jan 87
Apr 87. (lp)(c)(cd) **LIFE AS WE KNOW IT** 28 Feb 87
– New way to love / That ain't love / In my dreams / One too many girlfriends / Variety tonight / Screams and whispers / Can't get you out of my heart / Over the edge / Accidents can happen / Tired of getting nowhere.
May 87. (7") **VARIETY TONIGHT. / TIRED OF GETTING NOWHERE** – 60
Oct 87. (7") **IN MY DREAMS. / OVER THE EDGE** 19 Jul 87

—— **GRAHAM LEAR** – drums (ex-SANTANA) repl. GRATZER

Sep 88. (7") **HERE WITH ME. / WHEREVER YOU'RE GOIN' (IT'S ALRIGHT)** 20 Jun 88
(12"+=)(cd-s+=) – Keep on loving you / Take it on the run.
Nov 88. (7") **I DON'T WANT TO LOSE YOU. / ON THE ROAD AGAIN** –

—— (Apr89) **MILES JOSEPH** – guitar (ex-PLAYER) repl. RICHRATH

—— (1990) **CRONIN, DOUGHTY & HALL** brought in new members **DAVE AMATO** – lead guitar, vocals (ex-TED NUGENT) repl. MILES JOSEPH / **BRYAN HITT** – drums (ex-WANG CHUNG) repl. LEAR / added **JESSE HARMS** – keyboards, vocals (ex-JOHN HIATT, ex-RY COODER)

Aug 90. (7") **LIVE IT UP. / ALL HEAVEN BROKE LOOSE** –
Sep 90. (cd)(c)(lp) **THE EARTH, A SMALL MAN, HIS DOG AND A CHICKEN** Aug 90
– Love is a rock / The heart survives / Live it up / All Heaven broke loose / Love in the future / Half way / Love to hate / You won't see me / Can't lie to my heart / L.I.A.R. / Go for broke.
Oct 90. (7") **LOVE IS A ROCK. / GO FOR BROKE** 65
(12"+=)(cd-s+=) – ?
Jan 91. (7") **L.I.A.R. / HALF WAY** –

– compilations, others, etc. –

Below releases on 'Epic' unless mentioned.
May 80. (7") **TIME FOR ME TO FLY. / LIGHTNING** – 77
Jul 80. (d-lp)(d-c) **A DECADE OF ROCK'N'ROLL 1970 TO 1980** 55 Apr 80
– Sophisticated lady / Music man / Golden country / Son of a poor man / Lost in a dream / Reelin' / Keep pushin' / Our time is gonna come / Breakaway / Lightning / Like you do / Flying turkey trot / 157 Riverside Avenue / Ridin' the storm out / Roll with the changes / Time for me to fly / Say you love me or say goodnight / Only the strong survive / Back on the road again. *(re-iss.Jul82)*
Nov 85. (lp)(c) **BEST FOOT FORWARD – THE BEST OF REO SPEEDWAGON** –
(re-iss.+cd Jan92)
Jun 88. (lp)(c)(cd) **THE HITS** 56
Aug 88. (3"cd-s) **KEEP ON LOVIN' YOU. / TIME FOR ME TO FLY** –
Oct 91. (cd)(c)(lp) **A SECOND DECADE OF ROCK'N'ROLL 1981-1991**
– Don't let him go / Tough guys / Take it on the run / Shakin' it loose / Keep the fire burnin' / Roll with the changes / I do wanna know / Can't fight this feeling / Live every moment / That ain't love / One too many girlfriends / Variety tonight / Back on the road again / Keep on loving you '89 / Love is a rock / All Heavens broke loose / L.I.A.R. / Live it up.
Oct 94. (cd) **THE BEST**
Aug 84. Scoop; (7"ep)(c-ep) **6 TRACK HITS** –
– Only the strong survive / Meet me on the mountain / Shakin' it loose / In your letter / I need you tonight / Roll with the changes.
Feb 86. Old Gold; (7"ep) **KEEP ON LOVIN' YOU. / (2 other tracks by 'Journey' & 'Meat Loaf')** –

REPLACEMENTS

Formed: Minneapolis, Minnesota, USA . . . 1980 originally as The IMPEDIMENTS by the STINSON brothers plus WESTERBERG and MARS. After 3 well-received albums for US label 'Twin Tone', they moved to US based indie label 'Zippo', who found an outley in 'Demon' for 1984 lp 'LET IT BE'. In 1985, they transferred to major 'Sire' records, and made headway with album 'TIM'. • **Style:** Raw HUSKER DU type R&B/punk rock, whose courseness mellowed somewhat by the mid 80's, when stage eccentric BOB departed (he often played guitar in the nude or in a dress). • **Songwriters:** Penned by WESTERBERG, except; I WILL DARE (Kiss) / ROUTE 66 (Nelson Riddle Orchestra) / 20TH CENTURY BOY (T-Rex) / HEY GOOD LOOKING (Bo Diddley) / CRUELLA DE VILLE (from '1001 Dalmations'). • **Trivia:** Were quoted after a saying 'Better hours, 9 to 5; 9 at night to 5 in the morning, that is'. Their '87 single 'ALEX CHILTON', was dedicated to legendary BOX TOPS leader.

Recommended: BOINK!! (*8) / LET IT BE (*8) / TIM (*7).

PAUL WESTERBERG (b.31 Dec'60) – vocals, rhythm guitar / **BOB STINSON** (b.17 Dec'59) – lead guitar / **TOMMY STINSON** (b. 6 Oct'66, San Diego, California) – bass / **CHRIS MARS** (b.26 Apr'61) – drums

not issued Twin Tone
1981. (lp) **SORRY MA, FORGOT TO TAKE OUT THE TRASH** –
– Takin' a ride / Careless / Customer / Hanging downtown / Kick your door down / Otto / I bought a headache / Rattlesnake / I hate music / Johnny's gonna die / Shiftless when idle / More cigarettes / Don't ask why / Something to do / I'm in trouble / Love you till Friday / Shut up / Raised in the city. *(UK-iss.Mar88 on 'What Goes On') (cd-iss.Apr93 on 'Roadrunner') (cd-iss.Mar95)*
1981. (7") **I'M IN TROUBLE. / IF ONLY YOU WERE LONELY** –
1982. (lp) **STINK** –
– Kids don't follow / Fuck school / Stuck in the middle / God damn job / White and lazy / Dope smokin' moron / Go / Gimme noise. *(UK-iss.Mar88 on 'What Goes On') (cd-iss.Apr93 on 'Roadrunner') (cd-iss.Mar95)*
1983. (lp) **HOOTENANNY** –
– Hootenanny / Run it / Color me impressed / Will power / Take me down to the hospital / Mr. Whirly / Within your reach / Buck hill / Lovelines / You lose / Hayday / Treatment bound. *(UK-iss.Mar88 on 'What Goes On') (cd-iss.Mar95)*
1984. (12") **I WILL DARE. / 20TH CENTURY BOY / HEY GOOD LOOKING (live)** –

Zippo Twin Tone
Oct 84. (lp) **LET IT BE**
– I will dare / We're comin' out / Tommy gets his tonsels out / Black diamond / Androgynous / Unsatisfied / Seen your video / Gary's got a boner / Sixteen blue / Answering machine. *(cd-iss.Apr93 on 'Roadrunner') (cd-iss.Mar95)*

Sire Sire
Nov 85. (lp)(c) **TIM**
– Hold my life / I'll buy / Kiss me on the bus / Dose of thunder / Waitress in the sky / Swingin' party / Bastards of young / Lay it down clown / Left of the dial / Litle mascara / Here comes a regular. *(cd-iss Jul93)*
Mar 86. (7") **SWINGIN' PARTY. / LEFT OF THE DIAL**
May 86. (7") **KISS ME ON THE BUS. / LITTLE MASCARA**

—— **SLIM DUNLAP** – keyboards repl. BOB (he was to die 18th February 1995 of a drug overdose)

Apr 87. (lp)(c)(cd) **PLEASED TO MEET ME**
– I.O.U. / Alex Chilton / I don't know / Nightclub jitters / The ledge / Never mind / Valentine / Shooting dirty pool / Red red wine / Skyway / Can't hardly wait. *(re-iss.cd Jul93)*
Jun 87. (7") **ALEX CHILTON. / ELECTION DAY**
(12"+=) – Nightclub jitters / Route 66.
Jul 87. (7") **CAN'T HARDLY WAIT. / COOL WATER** –

—— **BOB STINSON** – guitar returned to repl. SLIM who went solo.

Jan 89. (lp)(c)(cd) **DON'T TELL A SOUL** 57
– Talent show / Back to back / We'll inherit the Earth / Achin' to be / They're blind / Anywhere's better than here / Asking me lies / I won't / Rock'n'roll ghost / Darlin' one. *(re-iss.cd Jul93)*
Apr 89. (7") **I'LL BE YOU. / DATE TO CHURCH (with TOM WAITS)** – 51

—— (Below w/guests **STEVE BERLIN / MICHAEL BLAIR / BELMONT TENCH / JOHN CALE /** etc.

Sep 90. (cd)(c)(lp) **ALL SHOOK DOWN** 69
– Merry go round / One wink at a time / Nobody / Bent out of shape / Sadly beautiful / Someone takes the wheel / When it began / All shook down / Attitude / Happy town / Torture / My little problem / The lost. *(re-iss.cd Jul93 & Feb95)*

—— (Mar91) **STEVE FOLEY** – drums repl. MARS who went solo.

—— Disbanded 1992, TOMMY formed BASH & POP, who released album 'FRIDAY

NIGHT IS KILLING ME'.

– compilations, others, etc. –

Apr 86. Glass; (m-lp)(c) **BOINK!!** [ ] [-]
– Color me impressed / White and lazy / Within your reach / If only you were lonely / Kids don't follow / Nowhere is my home / Take me down to the hospital / Go.

PAUL WESTERBERG

Sire | Warners

Jun 93. (cd)(c) **14 SONGS** [ ] [44]
– Knockin' on mine / First glimmer / World class fad / Runaway wind / Dice behind your shades / Even here we are / Silver naked ladies / A few minutes of silence / Someone I once knew / Black eyed Susan / things / Something is me / Mannequin shop / Down love.
Jul 93. (7")(c-s) **WORLD CLASS FAD. / SEEING HER** [ ] [ ]
(12")(cd-s) – ('A'side) / Men without ties / Down love.
Oct 93. (7")(c-s) **WORLD CLASS FAD. / CAN'T HARDLY WAIT (live)** [ ] [ ]
(cd-s+=) – Left of the dial / Another girl another planet (both live).
(cd-s) – ('A'side) / Waiting for somebody / Dyslexic heart / Answering machine (live).

RESIDENTS

Formed: Shrieveport, Louisiana, USA . . .1966 by mysterious line-up. They soon moved to San Mateo, California and in early 70's made a few homemade recordings under no name. They sent these to Hal Haverstadt of 'Warners' who sent them back to address marked 'for the attention of The Residents'. Issued the 2 tapes around the early 70's; 'RUSTY COAT HANGER FOR THE DOCTOR' & 'THE BALLAD OF STUFFED TRIGGER'. In 1972, they shifted base to San Francisco and founded 'Ralph' records. Their real debut lp 'MEET THE RESIDENTS' was issued in 1974. In 1980 the 'COMMERCIAL ALBUM' contained 40 tracks exactly 1 minute long. Continued through the 80's with even more obscurity than their earlier 70's work. Wore hilarious head covers including eyeballs, etc. • **Style:** Initially compared to FRANK ZAPPA's MOTHER OF INVENTION, although their 60's pastiche sound was rare and weird in the extreme. • **Songwriters:** Group penned except tribute /covers lp's of ELVIS PRESLEY, HANK WILLIAMS, GEORGE GERSHWIN and JAMES BROWN material. • **Trivia:** SNAKEFINGER (r.n. PHILIP LITHMAN) ex-CHILI WILLI & THE RED HOT PEPPERS, joined part-time in 1971.

Recommended: THE COMMERCIAL ALBUM (*7)

not issued | Ralph

Dec 72. (d-7"ltd.) **SANTA DOG** [-] [ ]
– Aircraft damage (cred. ARR + OMEGA)
Feb 74. (lp-ltd.) **MEET THE RESIDENTS** [-] [ ]
– Boots . . . Numb erone . . . Guylum Bardot . . . Breath and length . . . Consuelo's departure . . . Smelly tongues . . . Rest aria . . . Skratz . . . Spotted pinto bean . . . Infant tango . . . Seasoned greetings . . . N-er-gee (crisis blues). *(re-iss.+re-mixed Aug77, lost 7 minutes) (re-iss.+cd Dec88 on 'Torso')*
In Oct'75 they issued 500 copies US of lp 'BLORP ESETTE' for 'Lafms'.
Feb 76. (lp-ltd.) **THE THIRD REICH AND ROLL** [-] [ ]
– Hitler was a vegetarian / Hey Jude / Swastikas on parade / The twist / Land of 1000 dances / Hanky panky. *(re-iss. in 1978)*
Sep 76. (7"ltd.) **SATISFACTION. / LOSER = WEED** [-] [ ]
(re-iss.yellow-7" Aug78)
Jan 77. (7"ep-ltd.) **BABYFINGERS** [-] [-]
Feb 77. (lp-ltd.) **FINGERPRINCE** [ ] [-]
– You yesyesyes / Home age conversation / Godsong / March de la winni / Bos sy / Boo who / Tourniquet of roses / You yesyesyes again / Six things to a cycle. *(re-iss.twice 1978) (cd-iss.Dec87 on 'Torso')*
Aug 77. (7") **(THE BEATLES PLAY THE RESIDENTS AND THE RESIDENTS PLAY THE BEATLES)** [-] [ ]
Feb 78. (7"ep) **DUCK STAB / BUSTER AND GLEN** [-] [ ]
– Constantinople / Sinister exaggerator / The Booker tease / Blue rosebuds / Laughing song / Bach is dead / Elvis and his boss / Lizard lady / Semolina / Birthday boy / Weight-lifting Lulu / Krafty cheese / Hello skinny / The electrocutioner. *(cd-iss.Jul87 on 'Torso')*
Oct 78. (lp) **NOT AVAILABLE** [-] [ ]
– Edweena / The making of a soul / Ships a going down / Never known questions epilogue.
Mar 79. (lp-ltd.) **PLEASE DO NOT STEAL IT** (DJ compilation) [-] [ ]
– Yesyesyesyes / Santa dog '78 / Gloria / Rest aria / Semolina / The spot / Never known questions / Constantinople / Laughing song / The mocking of a soul / Skratz / Good lovin' / Blue rosebuds / Six things to a cycle / The electrocutioner. *(iss.as Aug79 on 'Virgin' with SNAKEFINGER)*
Aug 79. (lp) **SUBTERRANEAN MODERN** [-] [-]
Sep 79. (lp) **ESKIMO** [ ] [ ]
– The walrus hunt / Birth / Arctic hysteria / The angry Angakok / A spirit steals a child / The festival of death. *(cd-iss.Jul87 on 'Torso')*

Pre | Ralph

Oct 80. (lp) **COMMERCIAL ALBUM** [ ] [ ]
– Easter woman / Perfect love / Picnic boy / End of home / Amber / Japanes watercolour / Red rider / My second wife / Suburban bathers / Floyd / Dimples and toes / The nameless souls / Die in terror / Love leaks out / Act of being polite / Medicine man / Tragic bells / Loss of innocence / The simple song / Ups and downs / Possessions / Give it someone else / Phantom / Less not more / My work is so behind / Birds in the trees / Handful of desire / Moisture / Love is . . . / Troubled man / La la loneliness / Nice old man / The talk of creatures / Fingertips / In between dreams / Margaret Freeman / The coming of the crow / When we were young.
Oct 80. (7"ep) **AMBER / RED RIDER / PICNIC BOY. / WHEN WE WERE YOUNG / PHANTOM / MOISTURE** [ ] [ ]
1981. (lp) **MARK OF THE MOLE** [-] [ ]
– Hole-worker at the mercies of nature / Voices of the air / The ultimate disaster / Won't you keep us working / First warning / Back to normality / The sky falls / Why are we crying / The tunnels are filling / It never stops / Migration / March to the sea / The observer / Hole-worker's new hymn / Hole-worker's vs Man and machine / Another land / Rumors / Arrival / Deployment / Saturation / The new machine / Idea / Construction / Failure / Reconstruction / Success / Final confrontation / Success / Final confrontation / Driving the moles away / Don't tread on me / The short war / Resolution.

Ralph | Recommended

May 82. (lp) **THE TUNES OF TWO CITIES** [ ] [ ] Mar82
– Serenade for Missy / Mousetrap / Smack your lips clap your teeth / A maze of jigsaws / God of darkness / Smokebams / Mourning the undead / Song of the wild / Happy home / The secret seed / The evil disposer.
Jul 83. (12"ep) **INTERMISSION – LIGHTS OUT. / SHORTY'S LAMENT / MOLES ARE COMING / WOULD WE BE ALIVE / NEW HYMN** [-] [ ]
1983. (lp) **RESIDUE OF THE RESIDENTS** [-] [ ]
– The sleeper / Whoopy snorp / Kamakazi lady / Boy in love / Shut up! shut up! / Anvil forest / Diskomo / Jailhouse rock / Up & down / Walter Westinghouse / Saint Nix / Open up.

New Ralph | New Ralph

Jan 84. (lp) **TIME IN LIMBO** (w / RENALDO & THE LOAF) [ ] [ ]

Korova | Recommended

Jul 84. (7") **IT'S A MAN'S MAN'S MAN'S WORLD. / I'LL GO CRAZY** [ ] [ ]
Aug 84. (lp)(c) **GEORGE & JAMES** (some live) [ ] [ ]
– Rhapsody in blue / I got rhythm / Summertime / Live at the Apollo: I'll go crazy / Try me / Think / I don't mind / Lost someone / Please please please / Night train.
Oct 84. (lp)(c) **RALPH BEFORE '84 – VOLUME 1** (compilation) [ ] [-]
– It's a man's man's man's world / Diskomo / Hello skinny / (I left my heart in) San Francisco / Happy home / Smack your lips / Yesyesyesyes / Jailhouse rock / Monkey and Bunny / Festival of death.
Dec 84. (lp) **WHATEVER HAPPENED TO VILENESS FATS** [-] [ ]
– Whatever happened to Vileness Fats / Atomic shopping carts / Adventures of a troubled heart / Search for the short man / The importance of evergreen / Broccoli and saxophone / Disguised as meat / Thoughts busily betraying / Lord, it's lonely / The knife fight.
Jan 85. (lp) **BEFORE RALPH VOLUME 2** (compilation) [ ] [ ]
– Eva's warning / Halloween / Evolution / What use / Mahogany wood / Same ole me / Tritone / Melvyn's repose / Yeti: what are you / Nelda danced at day break / Norrgarden nyvia.
1985. (lp) **THE BIG BUBBLE – PART 4 OF THE MOLE TRILOGY** [-] [ ]
– Sorry / Hop a little / Go where ya wanna go / Gotta gotta get / Cry for the fire / Die stay-go / Vinegar / Fire fly / The big bubble / Fear for the future / Kula bocca says so. *(cd-iss.1990's)*

DoubleVision | Rykodisc

1985. (cd) **HEAVEN** [-] [ ]
– The importance of evergreen / It's a man's man's man's world / H.E.L.L. no! / Japenese watercolours / I got rhythm / Ups and downs / Serenade for Missy / Eastern woman / Amber / The census taker / Happy home / Crashing / Redrider / Floyd / The moles are coming / Resolution / Mahogany wood / Simple song / Kula bocca says no / Love leaks out / New hymn / Whater happened to Vileness Fats / Twinkle / Festival of death (excerpt).
1985. (cd) **HELL!** [-] [ ]
– The ultimate disaster (excerpt) / Lights out / Where is she? / The coming of the crow / Lizard lady / Die interior / Shut up! shut up! / Shorty's lament / Hello skinny / Kamikaze lady / Secret seed / Sonny / Smelly tongues / Monkey and Bunny / Farmers / Satisfaction / Sinister exaggerator / Loss of innocence / The sleeper / Final confrontation (excerpt).
Sep 85. (lp) **PAL TV** [ ] [-]

Torso | Torso

Oct 86. (d-lp) **13TH ANNIVERSARY SHOW (live in Japan & Holland)** [ ] [ ]
– Jailhouse rock / Where is she? / Picnic in the jungle / I got rhythm / Passing in the bottle / Monkey and Bunny / This is a man's man's man's world / Walter Westinghouse / Easter woman guitar solo / Diskomo / Hello skinny / Constantinople / Hop a little / Cry for the fire / Kamikaze.
Nov 86. (lp) **THE AMERICAN COMPOSERS SERIES VOL.2 – STARS AND HANK FOREVER** [ ] [ ]
– Hey good lookin' / Six more miles / Kaw-liga / Ramblin' man / Jambalaya / John Philip Sousa: Souaside: Nobles of the mystic shrine – The stars and stripes forever – El capitan – The liberty bell – Semper fidelis – Washington post.
Dec 86. (7")(12")(cd-s) **KAW-LIGA. / ?** [ ] [ ]
(12" re-iss.Mar89)
Jun 87. (7")(12") **HIT THE ROAD. / ?** [ ] [ ]
Aug 88. (d-lp)(cd)(dat) **GOD IN THREE PERSONS** [ ] [ ]
– Hard and tenderly / Devotion / The thing about them / Their early yearsx / Loss of a loved one / The touch / The service / Confused / Fine fat flies / Time / Silver sharp / Kiss of flesh / Pain and pleasure.
1989. (lp)(cd) **THE MOLE SHOW LIVE (live)** [-] [ ]
– Voices of the air / The secret seed / Narration / The ultimate disaster / God of darkness / Migration / Smack your lips clap your feet / Another land / The new machine / Call of the wild / Final confrontation / Satisfaction / Happy home.
1989. (lp)(cd) **THE KING AND EYE** [-] [ ]
– Blue suede shoes / Don't be cruel / Heartbreak hotel / All shook up / Return to sender / Teddy bear / Devil in disguise / Stuck on you / Big hunk o' love / A fool such as I / Little sister / His latest flame / Burning love / Viva Las Vegas / Love me tender / Hound dog.
May 90. (7"ep)(12"ep)(cd-ep) **DON'T BE CRUEL. / DISKOMO / DISCO WILL NEVER DIE** [ ] [ ]
1991. (cd)(lp) **FREAKSHOW** [ ] [ ]

Euro Ralph | Ralph

Nov 92. (cd)(c)(lp) **PRESENT OUR FINEST FLOWERS** [ ] [ ]

RETURN TO FOREVER (see under ⇒ COREA, Chick)

Martin REV (see under ⇒ SUICIDE)

REVENGE (see under ⇒ NEW ORDER)

Paul REVERE & THE RAIDERS

Formed: Caldwell, Idaho, USA ... 1960 originally as The DOWNBEATS by PAUL REVERE (real name) and MARK LINDSAY. Signed to local label 'Gardena', and hit US Top40 with 'LIKE, LONG HAIR'. In 1963, they moved to Portland, Oregon, where they gained deal with 'Columbia'. After unsuccessful attempt to out-do The KINGSMEN with their version of LOUIE LOUIE, they finally broke through late in '65 with JUST LIKE ME. Throughout the 60's, a string of US hits secured them their little piece of history. • **Trivia:** Of course, the name PAUL REVERE had already made impact for America nearly 200 years before. Their stage attire, during mid-60's, depicted dress-sense of that 18th century period. • **Style:** After initial early semi-instrumental period in the early 60's, their sound lay between MONKEES, KINKS or ROLLING STONES. • **Songwriters:** REVERE-LINDSAY or other members, except LOUIE LOUIE (c.Richard Berry) / KICKS + HUNGRY (B.Mann-C.Weil) / STEPPING STONE (Boyce-Hart) / INDIAN RESERVATION (hit.Don Fardon). MARK LINDSAY covered ARIZONA (Family Dogg) / AND THE GRASS WON'T PAY YOU NO MIND (Neil Diamond) / BEEN TOO LONG ON THE ROAD (Bread).

Recommended: KICKS (*6)

PAUL REVERE (b. 7 Jan'42, Boise, Idaho) – organ / **MARK LINDSAY** (b. 9 Mar'42, Cambridge, Idaho) – saxophone, vocals

not issued | Sande

1960. (7") **LOUIE LOUIE. / NIGHT TRAIN** [-] [ ]

Top Rank | Gardena

1960. (7") **BEATNIK STICKS. / ORBIT (THE SPY)** [-] [ ]
1961. (7") **PAUL REVERE'S RIDE. / UNFINISHED FIFTH** [-] [ ]
Apr 61. (7") **LIKE, LONG HAIR. / SHARON** [-] [38] Mar 61
1961. (lp) **LIKE, LONG HAIR** [-] [ ]
1961. (7") **LIKE CHARLESTON. / MIDNITE RIDE** [-] [ ]
1962. (7") **ALL NIGHT LONG. / GROOVEY** [-] [ ]
1962. (7")LIKE BLUEGRASS. / LEATHERNECK [-] [ ]
1962. (7") **SHAKE IT UP. / (part 2)** [-] [ ]
1962. (7") **TALL COOL ONE. / ROADRUNNER** [-] [ ]

— REVERE was drafted into the army, but quickly recorded a number of singles before departure. He re-grouped with MARK LINDSAY in 1963, adding **MIKE 'Smitty' SMITH** – drums / **PHILIP 'Fang' VOLK** – bass / **DRAKE 'Kid' LEVIN** – guitar

not issued | Jerdon

1963. (7") **SO FINE. / BLUES STAY AWAY** [-] [ ]

— MARK LINDSAY now took on all vocals.

C.B.S. | Columbia

Jun 63. (7") **LOUIE LOUIE. / NIGHT TRAIN** [-] [ ]
1964. (7") **LOUIE, GO HOME. / HAVE LOVE, WILL TRAVEL** [-] [ ]
1964. (7") **OVER YOU. / SWIM** [-] [ ]

— In 1964, MARK vacationed from group but returned in 1965.

Apr 65. (7") **OOH POO PAH DOO. / SOMETIMES** [-] [ ]
Jun 65. (lp) **HERE THEY COME!** [-] [71]
– You can't sit down / Money / Louie Louie / Do you love me / Big boy Pete / Oo poo pah doo / Sometimes / Gone / Time is on my side / A kiss to remember.
Oct 65. (7") **STEPPIN' OUT. / BLUE FOX** [ ] [46] Sep 65
Dec 65. (7") **JUST LIKE ME. / B.F.D.R.F. BLUES** [ ] [11]
Apr 66. (lp) **PAUL REVERE & THE RAIDERS** [ ] [5] Feb 66
– Steppin' out / Doggone / Out of sight / Baby, please don't go / I know / Night train / Just like me / Catch the wind / Satisfaction / I'm crying / New Orleans / Action. *(US-title 'JUST LIKE US!')*
Apr 66. (7") **KICKS. / SHAKE IT UP** [ ] [4] Mar 66
Jul 66. (7") **HUNGRY. / THERE SHE GOES** [-] [6] Jun 66
Sep 66. (lp) **MIDNIGHT RIDE** [ ] [9] Jun 66
– Kicks / There's always tomorrow / Little girl in the 4th row / Ballad of a useless man / I'm not your stepping stone / There she goes / All I really need is you / Get it on / Louie, go home / Take a look at yourself / Melody for an unknown girl. *(cd-iss.!)*

— **FREDDY WELLER** (b. 9 Sep'47, Georgia) – lead guitar repl. LEVIN who was drafted solo / **CHARLIE COE** (b.19 Nov'44) – bass repl. VOLK and who formed BROTHERHOOD with DRAKE LEVIN.

— **JIM VALLEY** – drums repl. SMITH.

Nov 66. (7") **THE GREAT AIRPLANE STRIKE. / IN MY COMMUNITY** [ ] [20] Sep 66
Jan 67. (7") **GOOD THING. / UNDECIDED MAN** [ ] [4] Dec 66
Mar 67. (lp) **GOOD THING** [ ] [9] Dec 66
– Good thing / All about her / Louise / In my community / Why why why / Oh to be a man / Hungry / Undecided man / 1001 Arabian nights / Our candidate / Great airplane strike. *(US-title 'THE SPIRIT OF '67')*
Mar 67. (7") **UPS AND DOWNS. / LESLIE** [ ] [22] Feb 67
May 67. (lp) **GREATEST HITS** (compilation) [-] [15]
– Ups and downs / Steppin' out / Just like me / Louie Louie / Louie go home / Kicks / Hungry / The great airplane strike / Good thing / Legend of Paul Revere / Melody for an unknown girl. *(re-iss.+c+cd.Oct89 on 'Black Tulip')*
Jun 67. (7") **HIM OR ME - WHAT'S IT GONNA BE?. / THE LEGEND OF PAUL REVERE** [ ] [5] Apr 67
Sep 67. (7") **I HAD A DREAM. / UPON YOUR LEAVING** [ ] [17] Aug 67
Nov 67. (lp) **REVOLUTION!** [ ] [25] Sep 67
– Him or me, what's it gonna be / I had a dream / Reno / Upon your leaving / Mo'reen / I hear a voice / Wanting you / Gone movin' on / Tighter / Make it with me / Ain't nobody who can do it like Leslie can.
Nov 67. (7") **PEACE OF MIND. / DO UNTO OTHERS** [-] [42]
Jan 68. (7") **MO'REEN. / OH! TO BE A MAN** [ ] [ ]

— LINDSAY became their producer as well as combining a solo career.

Feb 68. (7") **TOO MUCH TALK. / HAPPENING '68** [-] [19]
Mar 68. (lp) **GOIN' TO MEMPHIS** [ ] [61]
– Boogaloo down Broadway / Every man needs a woman / My way / One night stand / Love you so / Soul man / I don't want nobody (to lead me on) / I'm a loser too / No sad songs / Cry on my shoulder / Peace of mind / Goin' to Memphis.
Jul 68. (7") **DON'T TAKE IT SO HARD. / OBSERVATIONS FROM FLIGHT 285** [ ] [27] Jun 68
Sep 68. (7") **CINDERELLA SUNSHINE. / THEME FROM "IT'S HAPPENING"** [-] [58]
Oct 68. (7") **CINDERELLA SUNSHINE. / MR.SUN, MR.MOON** [ ] [-]
Oct 68. (lp) **SOMETHING HAPPENING** [-] [-]
– Happening intro / Too much talk / Don't take it so hard / Good times / Happens every day / Communications / Burn like a candle / Free / Get out of my mind / Happening '68 / Love makes the world go 'round / Observation from Flight 285.
Nov 68. (7") **MR. SUN, MR. MOON. / WITHOUT YOU** [-] [18]

— **JOE CORRERO** (b.19 Nov'46) – drums + **KEITH ALLISON** – bass repl. VALLEY + COE

Apr 69. (lp) **HARD'N'HEAVY (WITH MARSHMALLOW)** [ ] [51]
– Mr.Sun, Mr.Moon / Money can't buy me / Time after time / Time on my shoulder / Without you / Trishalana / Out on that road / Hard and heavy / 5 string soul banjo / Where you goin' girl / Cinderella sunshine / Call on me.
Jun 69. (7") **LET ME. / I DON'T KNOW** [ ] [20] May 69

— In Aug69, MARK LINDSAY issued debut 45 'FIRST HYMN FROM GRAND TERRACE' / OLD MAN AT THE FAIR, hit US No.1

Sep 69. (lp) **ALIAS PINK FUZZ** [-] [ ] Aug 69
– Let me thank you / Frankfort side street / Louisiana redbone / Here comes the pain / The original handy man / I need you / Down in Amsterdam / I don't know / Freeborn man.
Oct 69. (7") **WE GOTTA ALL GET TOGETHER. / FRANKFORT SIDE STREET** [ ] [50] Sep 69

The RAIDERS

(same line-up and label)

Jan 70. (7") **JUST 17. / SORCERESS WITH BLUE EYES** [-] [82]
May 70. (lp) **COLLAGE** [ ] [ ] Apr 70
– Just 17 / We gotta all get together / Save the country / The boys in the band / Wednesday child / Sorceress with blue eyes / Dr.Fine / Tighter / Think twice / Interlude / Gone movin' on.
May 70. (7") **GONE MOVIN' ON. / INTERLUDE** [ ] [ ]
Nov 70. (lp) **GREATEST HITS VOL.2** (compilation) [-] [ ]

— **WELLER** was now main singer (LINDSAY stayed on as producer and continued solo career). Group only continued as a studio set-up with retirement from live

May 71. (7") **INDIAN RESERVATION (THE LAMENT OF THE CHEROKEE RESERVATION INDIAN). / TERRY'S TUNE** [ ] [1] Apr 71
Jul 71. (lp)(c) **INDIAN RESERVATION** [ ] [19] Jun 71
– Indian reservation / Birds of a feather / Just remember you're my sunshine / Prince of peace / Eve of destruction / Come in, you'll get pneumonia / Shape of things to come / Take me home / Heaven help us all / The turkey.
Sep 71. (7") **BIRDS OF A FEATHER. / THE TURKEY** [ ] [23]
Jan 72. (7") **COUNTRY WINE. / IT'S SO HARD GETTIN' UP TODAY** [ ] [51]
Feb 72. (lp) **COUNTRY WINE** [ ] [ ]
– Country wine / Powder blue Mercedes queen / Hungry for some lovin' / Baby make up your mind / Take a stand / Where are your children / Ballad of the unloved / American family / Golden girls sometimes / Farewell to a golden girl.
May 72. (7") **POWDER BLUE MERCEDES QUEEN. / GOLDEN GIRLS SOMETIMES** [ ] [54]
Jun 72. (d-lp) **ALL-TIME GREATEST HITS** (compilation) [-] [ ]
– Louie Louie / Steppin' out / Just like me / Kicks / Hungry / The great airplane strike / Good thing / Ups and downs / Him or me, what's it gonna be / Legend of Paul Revere / I had a dream / Too much talk / Do unto others / Peace of mind / Don't take it so hard / Cinderella sunshine / Mr.Sun, Mr.Moon / Let me / We gotta all get together / Just 17.
Oct 72. (7") **SONG SELLER. / A SIMPLE SONG** [-] [96]
Jan 73. (7") **LOVE MUSIC. / GOODBYE £9** [-] [97]
1973. (7") **ALL OVER YOU. / SEABOARD LINE BOOGIE** [-] [ ]
1975. (7") **GONNA HAVE A GOOD TIME. / YOUR LOVE (IS THE ONLY LOVE)** [-] [ ]

not iss. | 20th Cent

Jun 76. (7") **THE BRITISH ARE COMING. / SURRENDER AT APPOMATOX** [-] [ ]

PAUL REVERE & THE RAIDERS

Jayboy | Drive

Aug 76. (7") **AIN'T NOTHING WRONG. / YOU'RE REALLY SAYING SOMETHING** [ ] [ ]

— Finally disbanded in 1977. Re-formed in 1983 to issue new album? 'PAUL REVERE RIDES AGAIN'.

– more compilations, etc. –

Below releases issued on 'CBS' UK/ 'Columbia' US unless mentioned.

Dec 67. (lp) **CHRISTMAS PAST AND PRESENT** [-] [ ]
1975. (7") **LOUIE LOUIE. / LOUIE, GO HOME** [ ] [-]
1975. (7") **KICKS. / JUST LIKE ME** [ ] [-]
1975. (7") **THE GREAT AIRPLANE STRIKE. / HUNGRY** [ ] [-]
1975. (7") **UPS AND DOWNS. / GOOD THING** [ ] [-]
1975. (7") **STEPPIN' OUT. / HIM OR ME, WHAT'S IT GONNA BE** [ ] [-]
1975. (7") **DON'T TAKE IT SO HARD. / CINDERELLA SUNSHINE** [ ] [-]
1975. (7") **LET ME. / WE GOTTA ALL GET TOGETHER** [ ] [-]

1975. (7") **INDIAN RESERVATION (THE LAMENT OF THE CHEROKEE RESERVATION INDIAN). / BIRDS OF A FEATHER** [ ] [-]
1966. Gardena; (lp) **IN THE BEGINNING** [-] [ ]
1972. Harmony; (lp) **MOVIN ON** [-] [ ]
Jan 84. Edsel; (lp) **KICKS!** [ ] [-]
Jun 86. Timeless; (c) **PAUL REVERE & THE RAIDERS** [ ] [-]

MARK LINDSAY

(solo 1970-onwards)

C.B.S. Columbia

Jan 70. (7") **ARIZONA. / MAN FROM HOUSTON** [ ] [10] Dec 69
Mar 70. (lp) **ARIZONA** [ ] [36]
– First hymn from Grand Terrace / Leaving on a jet plane / Something / The name of my sorrow / Miss America / Man from Houston / Love's been good to me / Sunday mornin' comin' down / Small town woman / I'll never fall in love again / Arizona.
Apr 70. (7") **MISS AMERICA. / SMALL TIME WOMAN** [ ] [44]
Jul 70. (7") **SILVER BIRD. / SO HARD TO LEAVE YOU** [ ] [25] Jun 70
Sep 70. (7") **SILVER BIRD** [ ]
– Silver bird / We've only just begun / So hard to leave you / Bookends / And the grass won't pay you no mind / The long and winding road / Yesterday / Funny how little men care / Come Saturday morning / Feel.
Sep 70. (7") **AND THE GRASS WON'T PAY YOU NO MIND. / FUNNY HOW LITTLE MEN CARE** [-] [44]
Dec 70. (7") **PROBLEM CHILD. / BOOKENDS** [-] [ ]
Mar 71. (7") **COUNTER CLOCKWISE. / ALL I REALLY SEE IS YOU** [-] [ ]
Jun 71. (7") **BEEN TOO LONG ON THE ROAD. / ALL I REALLY SEE IS YOU** [ ] [ ]
Oct 71. (lp) **YOU'VE GOT A FRIEND** [-] [ ]
– You've got a friend / Been too long on the road / Help me make it through the night / Pretty pretty / Need a little time / It's too late / Never can say goodbye / If you could read my mind / The old man and the fair / All I really see is you.
Oct 71. (7") **ARE YOU OLD ENOUGH. / DON'T YOU KNOW** [ ] [ ]
Jan 72. (7") **PRETTY PRETTY. / SOMETHING BIG** [-] [ ]
1972. (7") **CALIFORNIA. / SOMEONE'S BEEN HIDING** [-] [ ]
1974. (7") **MAMACITA. / SONG FOR A FRIEND** [-] [ ]
1974. (7") **PHOTOGRAPH. / SONG FOR A FRIEND** [-] [ ]
Oct 74. (7") **ARIZONA. / MISS AMERICA** *(re-issued)* [ ] [-]

not issued Greedy

1974. (7") **SING YOUR OWN SONG. / (theme)** [-] [ ]

not issued Warners

1975. (7") **SONG ME HIGH, SING ME LOW. / FLIPS-EYED** [-] [ ]
1975. (7") **LITTLE LADIES OF THE NIGHT. / FLIPS-EYED** [-] [ ]

REVILLOS (see under ⇒ REZILLOS)

REVOLTING COCKS (see under ⇒ MINISTRY)

REZILLOS

Formed: Edinburgh, Scotland . . . Mar'76 by EUGENE REYNOLDS and JO CALLIS, plus other ex-art school colleagues. Early 1977, they signed one-off deal with Lawrie Love's 'Sensible' records, who released debut 45 'CAN'T STAND MY BABY'. Immediately after this, they were snapped up by US label 'Sire', who gave them 1978 Top 20 hit 'TOP OF THE POPS', which also featured on same named TV music show. • **Style:** Colourful new wave ouftit, influenced by DR.FEELGOOD, ROXY MUSIC and 60's beat groups, although fronted by quickfire dual vox of FAY and EUGENE. • **Songwriters:** EUGENE and JO penned most, except; I WANNA BE YOUR MAN (Beatles) / I LIKE IT (Gerry & The Pacemakers) / GLAD ALL OVER (Dave Clark Five) / TWIST AND SHOUT (Isley Brothers) / BALLROOM BLITZ (Sweet) / TELL HIM (Exciters) / LAND OF A 1,000 DANCES (Cannibal & The Headhunters) / ON THE BEACH (Cliff Richard) / THUNDERBIRDS ARE GO (Barry Gray). • **Trivia:** Toured North America in the Summer of 1982, but with only moderate cult success.

Recommended: CAN'T STAND THE REZILLOS (*7)

FAY FIFE (b. SHEILAGH HYNDE) – vocals / **EUGENE REYNOLDS** (b.ALAN FORBES) – vocals / **LUKE WARM** (b. JO CALLIS) – guitar, vocals (both ex-KNUTSFORD DOMINATORS) / **MARK 'HI-FI' HARRIS** – guitar / **Dr. D.K.SMYTHE** – bass / **ANGEL PATERSON** – drums / **GAYLE WARNING** – backing vocals

Sensible not issued

Aug 77. (7") **CAN'T STAND MY BABY. / I WANNA BE YOUR MAN** [ ] [-]
(re-iss.Aug79, hit 71)

— **WILLIAM MYSTERIOUS** (b.DONALDSON) – bass finally repl. SMYTHE, HARRIS & WARNING

Sire Sire

Nov 77. (7") **(MY BABY DOES) GOOD SCULPTURES. / FLYING SAUCER ATTACK** [ ] [-]
May 78. (7") **COLD WARS. / WILLIAM MYSTERIOUS OVERTURE** [ ] [-]
(withdrawn)
Jul 78. (7") **TOP OF THE POPS. / 20,000 REZILLOS UNDER THE SEA** [17] [ ]
(c-s) – ('A'side) / Destination Venus.
Jul 78. (lp)(c) **CAN'T STAND THE REZILLOS** [16] [ ]
– Flying saucer attack / No / Someone's gonna get their heads kicked in tonight / Top Of The Pops / 2000 AD / It gets me / Can't stand my baby / Glad all over / My baby does good sculptures / I like it / Gettin' me down / Cold wars / Bad guy reaction.

— **SIMON TEMPLAR** (b.BLOOMFIELD) – bass, vocals repl. WILLIAM

Nov 78. (7") **DESTINATION VENUS. / MYSTERY ACTION** [43] [ ]

— Disbanded late '78. JO, SIMON & ANGEL formed SHAKE who at varying times joined BOOTS FOR DANCING. The REZILLOS gave us a few more exploitation releases

Apr 79. (7"m) **COLD WARS. / FLYING SAUCER ATTACK (live) / TWIST AND SHOUT (live)** [ ] [-]
Apr 79. (lp)(c) **MISSION ACCOMPLISHED . . . BUT THE BEAT GOES ON (live)** [30] [-]
– Top of the pops / Mystery action / Somebody's gonna get their head kicked in tonight / Thunderbirds are go / Cold wars / Teenbeat / Land of 10,000 dances / I need you / Gettin' me down / Culture shock / Ballroom blitz / Destination Venus / (my baby does) Good sculptures.

The REVILLOS

(a slight change) brought together again **FAY & EUGENE** (also now on bass) / **HI-FI HARRIS** – guitar / **ROCKY RHYTHM** (b. NICKY FORBES) – drums (ex-PORK DUKES) / **JANE WHITE, JANE BROWN, TRICIA BRYCE** – backing vocals

Dindisc not issued

Sep 79. (7") **WHERE'S THE BOY FOR ME?. / THE FIEND** [ ] [-]

— (Aug79) added **KID KRUPA** – guitar (on tour) / **FELIX** – bass / **CHERIE & BABS REVETTE** – backing vocals repl. last backing trio

Jan 80. (7") **MOTORBIKE BEAT. / NO SUCH LUCK** [45] [-]

— **WILLIAM MYSTERIOUS** – bass returned to repl. FELIX (to HEY ELASTICA)

Apr 80. (7") **SCUBA SCUBA. / BOY BOP** [ ] [-]
Sep 80. (lp)(c) **REV UP** [ ] [-]
– Secret of the shadow / Rev up / Rock-a-boom / Voodoo / Bobby come back to me / Scuba scuba / Boy bop / Yeah yeah / Hungry for love / Jukebox sound / On the beach / Cool jerk / Hippy hippy sheik / Motorbike beat.
Sep 80. (7") **HUNGRY FOR LOVE. / VOODOO 2** [ ] [-]

— **KID KRUPA** (b. JON McLOUGHLIN) – guitar now totally repl. HARRIS / **DRAX** – b.vox repl. BABS / **VINCE SANTINI** – bass repl. MYSTERIOUS

Superville not issued

Sep 81. (7") **(SHE'S FALLEN IN LOVE WITH A) MONSTER MAN. / MIND BENDING CUTIE DOLL** [ ] [-]
Jan 82. (lp)(c) **ATTACK** (withdrawn) [ ] [-]
Feb 82. (7"m) **BONGO BRAIN. / HIP CITY / YOU WERE MEANT FOR ME** [ ] [-]

— **MAX ATOM** – guitar repl. KRUPA / **TERRI REVETTE** – b.vox repl. DRAX

Aura not issued

Nov 82. (7") **TELL HIM. / GRAVEYARD GROOVE** [ ] [-]

— **FABIAN WONDERFUL** – guitar repl. ATOM

E.M.I. not issued

Oct 83. (7") **BITTEN BY A LOVE BUG. / TRIGGER HAPPY JACK** [ ] [-]
(12"+=) – Cat call.
Mar 84. (7") **MIDNIGHT. / Z-X-7** [ ] [-]
(12"+=) – ('A'extended).

— **BUDDY MOON** – bass repl. SANTINI.

— Disbanded early 1985, FAY went into acting and later featured in 'Taggart' and 'The Bill'.

– other (REZILLOS) compilations, etc. –

Apr 81. Sire; (7") **TOP OF THE POPS. / DESTINATION VENUS** [ ] [-]

REVILLOS

— re-formed with main originals (see above)

Dec 94. Vinyl Japan; (12"ep)(cd-ep) **YEAH YEAH / CRUSH. / SCUBA SCUBA / SCUBA SCUBA (Japanese version)** [ ] [-]
May 95. (cd)(lp) **LIVE AND ON FIRE IN JAPAN (live)** [ ] [-]
– Secret of the shadow / Bongo brain / Rockaboom / She's fallen in love with a monster man / Where's the boy for me? / Rev up! / Bitten by a lovebug / Mad from birth to death / Bobby come back to me / The fiend / Scuba scuba / My baby does good sculptures / Do the mutilation / Somebody's gonna get their head kicked in tonight / Yeah yeah.

RHYTHM DEVILS (see under ⇒ GRATEFUL DEAD)

Keith RICHARDS (see under ⇒ ROLLING STONES)

Jonathan RICHMAN

Born: 16 May'51, Boston, Massachusetts, USA. After a period in the late 60's being a contributor for local music papers 'Vibrations' & 'Fusion', he formed first real MODERN LOVERS in 1971. With the help of producer KIM FOWLEY, they recorded successful demo for 'Warners' in 1972. The following year, the label shelved their JOHN CALE produced lp and soon dropped group. They split late in '74, but re-formed again 6 months later to record debut 7" 'ROADRUNNER' for 'United Art'. They then moved to West Coast label 'Beserkley', who bought the Warners tapes, and released the songs as an eponymous album in 1976. RICHMAN then recruited his new MODERN LOVERS, who finaly re-issued 'ROADRUNNER', which zoomed up to a near UK Top 10 placing in 1977. They followed this, with an unusual instrumental 'EGYPTIAN REGGAE', which dented the Top 5. • **Style:** New wave eccentric, who was likened to a minimalist LOU REED, but with a sense of tongue-in-cheek humour. • **Songwriters:** RICHMAN compositions.

• **Trivia:** JOHN CALE (ex-Velvet Underground), went on to record his brilliant 'PABLO PICASSO'.

Recommended: 23 GREAT RECORDINGS (*8)

The MODERN LOVERS

were formed by **RICHMAN** – vocals, guitar / with **JERRY HARRISON** – keyboards, vocals / **ERNIE BROOKS** – bass, vocals / **DAVID ROBINSON** – drums (left Nov73 to DMZ, after recording debut)

United Art United Art

Jun 75. (7") **ROADRUNNER (once). / IT WILL STAND**

Beserkley Beserkley

Jul 76. (lp) **THE MODERN LOVERS** (1972 demos) 1975
– Roadrunner / Astral plane / Old world / Pablo Picasso / I'm straight / She cracked / Hospital / Someone I care about / Girlfriend / Modern world. *(re-iss.Nov87) (cd-iss.Nov89 on 'Rhino') (cd-iss.Dec92 on 'Rev-ola', 3 extra tracks)*

— HARRISON (also to TALKING HEADS) and BROOKS joined ELLIOTT MURPHY.

JONATHAN RICHMAN & THE MODERN LOVERS

with also **LEROY RADCLIFFE** – guitar, vox / **GREG KERANEN** – bass, vox / **DAVID ROBINSON** – drums

Oct 76. (lp) **JONATHAN RICHMAN & THE MODERN LOVERS** [-]
– Rockin' shopping center / Back in the U.S.A. / Important in your life / New England / Lonely financial zone / Hi dear / Abominable snowman in the market / Hey there little insect / Here comes the Martian Martians / Springtime / Amazing Grace. *(UK-iss.Oct77) (re-iss.Nov86, cd-iss.Mar89)*

Feb 77. (7") **NEW ENGLAND. / HERE COME THE MARTIAN MARTIANS** [-]

Jun 77. (7") **ROADRUNNER (once). / ROADRUNNER (twice)** [11] [-]
(re-iss.Jul82 on 'Old Gold')

Aug 77. (lp)(c) **ROCK'N'ROLL WITH THE MODERN LOVERS** [50]
– The sweeping wind (kwa ti feng) / Ice cream man / Rockin' rockin' leprechauns / Summer morning / Afternoon / Fly into the mystery / South American folk song / Roller coaster by the sea / Dodge veg-o-matic / Egyptian reggae / Coomyah / The wheels on the bus / Angels watching over you. *(re-iss.Nov87) (cd-iss.Mar93 on 'Rev-ola')*

Sep 77. (7") **EGYPTIAN REGGAE. / ROLLER COASTER BY THE SEA** [5]

The MODERN LOVERS

D.SHARPE – drums repl. ROBINSON / **ASA BREMNER** – bass repl. KERANEN

Jan 78. (7") **MORNING OF OUR LIVES (live). / ROADRUNNER (thrice)** [28]

Apr 78. (7") **NEW ENGLAND. / ASTRAL PLANE**

Jul 78. (7") **ABDUL & CLEOPATRA. ("JONATHAN RICHMAN & THE MODERN LOVERS") / OH CAROL**

Dec 78. (lp)(c) **THE MODERN LOVERS LIVE (live)**
– I'm a little airplane / Hey there little insect / Egyptian reggae / Ice cream man / I'm a little dinosaur / My little kookenhaken / South American folk song / New England / Morning of our lives. *(re-iss.Nov86)*

JONATHAN RICHMAN

is credited solo, but still uses same backers.

Dec 78. (7") **BUZZ BUZZ BUZZ. / HOSPITAL**

Feb 79. (lp)(c) **BACK IN YOUR LIFE**
– Abdul and Cleopatra / (She's gonna) Respect me / Lover please / Affection / Buz buzz buzz / Back in your life / Party in the woods tonight / My love is a flower (just beginning to bloom) / I'm nature's mosquito / Emaline / Lydia / I hear you calling me. *(US re-iss.Nov86)*

Mar 79. (7") **LYDIA. / IMPORTANT IN YOUR LIFE**

Jan 80. (lp)(c) **JONATHAN RICHMAN SONGBOOK – THE BEST OF . . .** – (compilation)

— JONATHAN retired in the late 70's, until 1982. Joining him were **KEN FORFIA** – keyboards / **BETH HARRINGTON** – guitar / **GREG KERANEN** – bass, vocals / **MICHAEL GUARDABASCIO** – drums, vocals / **ELLIE MARSHALL** – backing vocals

Rough Trade Sire

Aug 84. (lp)(c) **JONATHAN SINGS**
– That summer feeling / This kind of music / The neighbors / Somebody to hold me / These conga drums / Stop this car / Not yet three / Give Paris one more chance / You're the one for me / When I'm walking.

Jun 85. (7") **THAT SUMMER FEELING. / THIS KIND OF MUSIC**
(12"+=) – The tag game.

JONATHAN RICHMAN & THE MODERN LOVERS

re-formed with **JONATHAN, ELLIE, MICHAEL** and newcomer **ANDY PALEY** – toy piano

Jun 85. (lp)(c) **ROCKIN' AND ROMANCE**
– The beach / My jeans / Bermuda / The U.F.O. man / Down in Bermuda / V. Van Gogh / Walter Johnson / I'm just beginning to live / The fenway / Chewing gum wrapper / The Baltimores / Up in the sky sometime / Now is better than before.

Aug 85. (7") **I'M JUST BEGINNING TO LIVE. / CIRCLE 1**
(12"+=) – Shirlin & Fahrad.

Feb 86. (lp)(c) **IT'S TIME FOR JONATHAN RICHMAN & THE MODERN LOVERS**
– It's you / Let's take a trip / This love of mine / Neon sign / Double chocolate malted / Just about seventeen / Corner store / The desert / Yo Jo Jo / When I dance / Shirlin & Fahrad / Ancient and long ago.

— **JONATHAN** recruited complete new line-up **BRENDAN TOTTEN** – guitar / **JOHNNY AVILA** – drums

Demon Rounder

Feb 88. (lp)(cd) **MODERN LOVERS '88**
– Dancin' late at night / When Harpo played his harp / Gail loves me / New kind of neighborhood / African lady / I love hot nights / California desert party / Everything's gotta be right / Circle 1 / I have come out to play / The theme from 'Moulin Rouge'!.

JONATHAN RICHMAN

Special D. Rounder

Aug 89. (lp)(c)(cd) **JONATHAN RICHMAN**
– Malagueno de Jojo / Action packed / Everyday clothes / Fender Stratocaster / Blue Moon / Closer / I eat with Gusto / Damn!! you bet / Miracles will start to happen / Sleepwalk / Que reste t'll de nos amours / A mistake today for me / Cerca.

— now with **TOM BRUMLEY** – guitar

Aug 90. (cd)(c)(lp) **JONATHAN GOES COUNTRY**
– Since she started to ride / Reno / You're the one for me / Your good girl's gonna go bad / I must be king / You're crazy for takin' the blues / Rodeo wind / Corner store / The neighbours / Men walks among us / I can't stay mad at you / Satisfied mind.

Cheree Cheree

Nov 91. (cd)(lp) **HAVING A PARTY (live US tour)**
– The girl stands up to me now / Cappuccino bar / my career as a homewrecker / She doesn't laugh at my jokes / When she kisses me / They're not tryin' on the dance floor / At night / When I say wife / 1963 / Monologue about bermuda / Our swingin' pad / Just for fun

Rounder Rounder

May 94. (cd) **¡JONATHAN, TE VAS A EMOCIONAR!**
– Pantomima de el amor Brujo / Harpo en su Harpa / No te oye / No mas por fun / Papel de chicle / Los vecinos / Compadrito corazon / Melodia tradicional Ecuadoriana / Shirin y Farad / Reno / Cerca / El U.F.O. man / Ahora es Mejor / Sabor A.Mi / Una Fuerza alla.

May 95. (cd)(c) **YOU MUST ASK THE HEART**
– To hide a little thought / The heart of Saturday night / Vampire girl / Just because I'm Irish / That's how I feel / Let her go into darkness / The rose / You must ask the heart / Nothing can change this love / Amorcito corazon / City vs. country / Walter Johnson / Nishi.

– other compilations, etc. –

Oct 81. Bomp; (lp) **THE ORIGINAL MODERN LOVERS** [-]
(UK-iss.Jun87 on 'Link')

Jul 82. Old Gold; (7") **EGYPTIAN REGGAE. / MORNING OF OUR LIVES (live)** [-]

1988. Rounder; (cd) **JONATHAN RICHMAN & BARRENCE WHITFIELD** [-]

Sep 90. Castle; (cd) **23 GREAT RECORDINGS** [-]
– Roadrunner / Dignified & old / Pablo Picasso / I'm straight / Astral plane / Girl friend / Government centre / New teller / It will stand / Morning of our lives / Abominable snowman in the market / Important in your life / My little kookenhaken / Dodge veg-o-matic / Lonely financial zone / Roller coaster by the sea / New England / Egyptian reggae / Ice cream man / Buzz buzz buzz / Abdul & Cleopatra / Roadrunner (twice).

Apr 94. Castle; (cd) **THE COLLECTION** [-]

Apr 95. Rounder; (cd) **PRECISE MODERN LOVERS ORDER** [-]

Jun 95. Nectar; (cd) **A PLEA FOR TENDERNESS** [-]

RIDE

Formed: Oxford, England . . . 1989 by Oxford University students (see below). Immediately signed to 'Creation' records, and stirred up enough support through tour to generate eponymous 1990 debut EP into the UK Top 75. It was quickly followed by 2 more Top 40 EP's, and a near UK Top 10 album 'NOWHERE'. • **Style:** Solemn and dreamy psychedelic rock band, taking influences from The BYRDS, STOOGES and The JESUS & MARY CHAIN. • **Songwriters:** Lyrics MARK or ANDY / group compositions except EIGHT MILES HIGH (Byrds) / THE MODEL (Kraftwerk) / HOW DOES IT FEEL TO FEEL (Creation) / THAT MAN (Small Faces). • **Trivia:** In 1991, they headlined the Slough Music Festival in front of over 8,000 fans.

Recommended: NOWHERE (*8) / GOING BLANK AGAIN (*8).

MARK GARDENER – vocals, guitar / **ANDY BELL** – guitar, vocals / **STEPHAN QUERALT** – bass / **LAURENCE COLBERT** – drums

Creation Creation

Jan 90. (12"ep)(cd-ep) **RIDE** [71] [-]
– Chelsea girl / Drive blind / Close my eyes / All I can see. *(re-iss.Oct90)*

Apr 90. (12"ep)(cd-ep) **PLAY** [32]
– Like a daydream / Silver / Furthest sense / Perfect time.

Oct 90. (7"ep) **FALL** [34]
– Dreams burn down / Taste / Here and now / Nowhere.

Jul 90. (cd)(c) **SMILE** (above tracks) [-]

Oct 90. (cd)(c)(lp) **NOWHERE** [11]
– Seagull / Kaleidoscope / Polar bear / Dreams burn down / In a different place / Decay / Paralysed / Vapour trail.
(cd+=) Taste / Here and now / Nowhere

Mar 91. (12"ep)(c-ep)(cd-ep) **TODAY FOREVER** [14]
– Unfamiliar / Sennen / Beneath / Today.

Feb 92. (12"ep)(c-ep)(cd-ep) **LEAVE THEM ALL BEHIND. / CHROME WAVES / GRASSHOPPER** [9]

Mar 92. (cd)(c)(2x12"lp) **GOING BLANK AGAIN** [5]
– Leave them all behind / Twisterella / Not fazed / Chrome waves / Mouse trap / Time of her life / Cool your boots / Making Jusy smile / Time machine / OX4.

Apr 92. (12"ep)(c-ep)(cd-ep) **TWISTERELLA / GOING BLANK AGAIN. / HOWARD HUGHES / STAMPEDE** [36]

Apr 94. (12"ep)(12"clear-ep)(cd-ep) **BIRDMAN / ROLLING THUNDER £2. / LET'S GET LOST / DON'T LET IT DIE** [38]

Jun 94. (7")(c-s) **HOW DOES IT FEEL TO FEEL?. / CHELSEA GIRL** [58]
(12")(cd-s) – ('A'side) / Walkabout / At the end of the universe.

Jun 94. (pic-cd)(c)(d-lp) **CARNIVAL OF LIGHT** [5] [ ]
– Moonlight medicine / 1000 miles / From time to time / Natural grace / Only now / Birdman / Crown of creation / How does it feel to feel? / Endless road / Magical spring / Rolling thunder / I don't know where it comes from.

Sep 94. (c-s) **I DON'T KNOW WHERE IT COMES FROM. / TWISTERELLA** [46] [ ]
(12")(cd-s) – ('A'side) / Drive blind / From time to time / How does it feel to feel (live w / The CREATION).
(cd-s) – ('A'-Apollo 11 mix) / Moonlight medicine (ride on the wire mix by Portishead) / A journey to the end of the universe (version).

— They disbanded late 1995, although final album will be issued 1996.

RIFF RAFF (see under ⇒ BRAGG ,Billy)

RIGOR MORTIS (see under ⇒ WHO)

Penny RIMBAUD (see under ⇒ CRASS)

Brian RITCHIE (see under ⇒ VIOLENT FEMMES)

ROACHFORD

Born: England . . .1987 by ANDY ROACHFORD. Quickly signed to 'CBS-Columbia', who released eponymous debut in 1988, which hit UK Top 20 lists. They finally made the UK + US singles Top 20, when a re-issue of 'CUDDLY TOY' became a hit early 1989. • **Style:** Soulful rock. • **Songwriters:** ANDY except; CHILDREN OF THE REVOLUTION (T.Rex) / MANIC DEPRESSION (Jimi Hendrix). • **Trivia:** Co-produced with synth-electronics man FAYNEY.

Recommended: ROACHFORD (*6)

ANDY ROACHFORD – vocals, keyboards, percussion / **HAWI GONDWE** – guitar / **DERRICK TAYLOR** – bass / **CHRIS TAYLOR** – drums, percussion

C.B.S. Epic

Feb 88. (7") **FAMILY MAN. / GIVE IT UP** [ ] [ ]
(12"+=)(cd-s+=) – ('A'extended).
(7"ep+=) – Since / Why.

May 88. (7") **CUDDLY TOY. / LION'S DEN** [61] [ ]
(12"+=)/ /(cd-s+=) – ('A'live). / / ('A'mix).

May 88. (lp)(c)(cd) **ROACHFORD** [18] [ ]
– Give it up / Family man / Cuddly toy / Find me another love / No way / Kathleen / Beautiful morning / Lying again / Since / Nobody but you. *(re-dist.Feb89, hit UK No.11)*

Oct 88. (7") **FIND ME ANOTHER LOVE. / LYING AGAIN** [ ] [ ]
(12"+=) – Just can't go / Real gone kid.
(cd-s+=) – ('A'mix).
(7"ep+=) – Born again / It's not funny anymore.

Jan 89. (7") **CUDDLY TOY. / LYING AGAIN** [-] [25]

Jan 89. (7") **CUDDLY TOY. / LION'S DEN** [4] [-]
(12"+=)(cd-s+=) – Nobody but you (live) / Family man (live).
(7"ep+=) – Nobody but you (live) / Lovers leap.

Mar 89. (7") **FAMILY MAN. / NEVER** [25] [-]
(d7"+=) – Gun crazy / Way.
(12"+=) – ('A'mix) / Cuddly toy.
(cd-s+=) – ('A'mix).

Jun 89. (7") **KATHLEEN. / JUST CAN'T GO** [43] [ ]
(7"+=)(c-s+=) – Lying again (live) / Beautiful morning (live).
(12"+=)(cd-s+=) – Kathy's house / ('A'extended).

Columbia Columbia

Apr 91. (7")(c-s) **GET READY. / DO MY THANG** [22] [ ]
(cd-s+=)/ /(12"++=) – ('A'extended). / / Believe.
(7"ep+=) – Family man / Shadow girl.

May 91. (cd)(c)(lp) **GET READY!** [20] [ ]
– Get ready! / Survival / Funky Chile / Stone city / Wannabee loved bayou / Innocent eyes / Hands of fate / Takin' it easy / Higher / Vision of the future / Get ready (reprise). *(re-iss.cd May95)*

Jun 91. (7")(c-s) **STONE CITY. / REAL WORLD** [ ] [ ]
(12"+=)(cd-s+=) – ('A'extended).

Nov 91. (7")(c-s) **INNOCENT EYES. / KATHLEEN** [ ] [ ]
(cd-s+=) – Cuddly toy (live) / Give it up (live).

Mar 94. (7")(c-s) **ONLY TO BE WITH YOU. / FUNKY AFFAIR** [21] [ ]
(cd-s+=) – ('A'extended).
(cd-s) – ('A'side) / Kathleen / Nobody but you / Innocent eyes.

Apr 94. (cd)(c)(lp) **PERMANENT SHADE OF BLUE** [25] [ ]
– Only to be with you / Johnny / Emergency / Lay your love on me / Ride the storm / This generation / I know you don't love me / Gus's blues (intro) / Do we wanna live together / Cry for me / Guess I must be crazy / Higher love.

Jun 94. (7")(c-s) **LAY YOUR LOVE ON ME. / INNOCENT EYES (live)** [36] [ ]
(cd-s+=) – I know you don't love me (live) / Ride the storm (live).
(cd-s) – ('A'side) / Needs / Tied down man / Can't take away the music.

Aug 94. (c-s) **THIS GENERATION. / CUDDLY TOY** [38] [ ]
(cd-s+=) – Children of the revolution / Manic depression.
(cd-s) – ('A'side) / Shotgun / Stone City (Keith LeBlanc mix) / Funky chile.

Nov 94. (c-s) **CRY FOR ME. / RIDE THE STORM (live)** [46] [ ]
(cd-s+=) – I know you don't love me (live) / Innocent eyes (live).
(cd-s) – ('A'side) / Nobody but you (live) / Johnny (live) / Lay your love on me (live).

Mar 95. (c-s) **I FEEL YOU DON'T LOVE ME / THIS GENERATION** [42] [ ]
(cd-s+=) – Cry / ('A'mix).

Robbie ROBERTSON

Born: JAMIE ROBERTSON, 4 July 1944, Toronto, Canada. Was an integral part of the BAND ⇒ in the late 60s and 70s before going into acting work. He starred and wrote the score for 'CARNY' in 1980. He produced NEIL DIAMOND's album 'Beautiful Noise' in 1976. His first solo outing finally arrived in 1987 when 'Geffen' released his eponymous debut. Lifted from it was the deep 'SOMEWHERE DOWN THE CRAZY RIVER'. • **Songwriters:** Self-penned. • **Trivia:** Other film parts; 'The Coal Miner's Daughter' (1980) + 'The Right Stuff' (1983).

Recommended: ROBBIE ROBERTSON (*7)

ROBBIE ROBERTSON – vocals, guitar, keyboards / with **BILL DILLON** – guitar / **TONY LEVIN** – bass / **MANU KATCHE** – drums, percussion / **DANIAL LANOIS** – percussion, guitar, bass, co-producer / **PETER GABRIEL** – vocals / **U2 / GARTH HUDSON + RICK DANKO**, etc

Geffen Geffen

Oct 87. (7") **SHOWDOWN AT THE BIG SKY. / HELL'S HALF ACRE** [-] [ ]

Oct 87. (lp)(c)(cd) **ROBBIE ROBERTSON** [47] [38]
– Fallen angel / Showdown at the big sky / Broken arow / Sweet fire of love / American roulette / Somewhere down the crazy river / Hell's half acre / Sonny get caught in the moonlight / Testimony. *(re-iss.Jan91) (re-iss.cd Oct95)*

Oct 87. (7") **FALLEN ANGEL. / HELL'S HALF ACRE** [ ] [ ]
(12"+=) – Tailgate. *(re-iss.Sep88)*

Jun 88. (7") **SOMEWHERE DOWN THE CRAZY RIVER. / BROKEN ARROW** [15] [ ]
(12"+=) – Tailgate.

Sep 91. (cd)(c)(lp) **STORYVILLE** [30] [69]
– Night parade / Hold back the dawn / Go back to your woods / Soap box preacher / Day of reckoning (burnin' for you) / What about now / Shake this town / Break in the rules / Resurrection / Sign of the rainbow. *(re-iss.cd Oct95)*

— now with **The RED ROAD ENSEMBLE**

Capitol Capitol

Oct 94. (cd)(c) **THE NATIVE AMERICANS** [ ] [ ]
– Coyote dance / Mahk tchi (heart of the people) / Ghost dance / The vanishing breed / It's a good day to die / Golden feather / Akua Tutu / Words of fire, deeds of blood / Cherokee morning song / Skinwalker / Ancestor song / Twisted hair.

Smokey ROBINSON

Born: WILLIAM ROBINSON, 19 Feb'40, Detroit, Michigan, USA. In 1954 he formed the MATADORS who 3 years later became The MIRACLES (⇒ see). At the end of a 6-month tour in Jul'72, SMOKEY decided to leave the MIRACLES for a solo career. In 1973, he received lukewarm response after the appearance of his debut 'SMOKEY'. For most of the 70's, his career did little more than mediocre sales, but this ceased when 1979's 'CRUISIN'' 45, hit the US Top 5. He was back again at his best 2 years later when 'BEING WITH YOU' gave him a UK No.1 & US No.2. He continued to be a major star and well-liked personality during the 80's. • **Style:** Classy soul poet with voice of silk. He had forsaken the MIRACLES uptempo trademark for a more sophisticated love ballad. • **Songwriters:** Has written all or most of his own material since the 50's. Was a main writer for the 'Tamla Motown' label. • **Trivia:** SMOKEY married MIRACLES singer CLAUDETTE ROGERS on 7 Nov'59.

Recommended: BLAME IT ON LOVE . . . (*7)

SMOKEY ROBINSON – vocals (with session people)

Tamla Motown Tamla

Jul 73. (7") **SWEET HARMONY. / WANT TO KNOW MY MIND** [-] [48]

Oct 73. (lp)(c) **SMOKEY** [ ] [70] Jul 73
– Holly / Medley: Never my love – Never can say goodbye / A silent partner in a three-way love affair / Just my soul responding / Sweet harmony / Will you love me tomorrow / Wanna know my mind / The family song / Baby come close. *(re-iss.Aug81)*

Jan 74. (7") **JUST MY SOUL RESPONDING. / SWEET HARMONY** [35] [-]

May 74. (7") **BABY COME CLOSE. / A SILENT PARTNER IN A THREE-WAY LOVE AFFAIR** [ ] [27]

Jun 74. (lp)(c) **PURE SMOKEY** [ ] [99] Apr 74
– It's her turn to live / The love between me and the kids / Asleep on my love / I am I am / Just passing through / Virgin man / She's only a baby herself / Fulfill your need / A tattoo. *(re-iss.Feb82)*

May 74. (7") **IT'S HER TURN TO LIVE. / JUST MY SOUL RESPONDING** [-] [82]

Sep 74. (7") **VIRGIN MAN. / FULFILL YOUR NEED** [-] [56]

Dec 74. (7") **I AM I AM. / THE FAMILY SONG** [-] [56]

May 75. (7") **BABY THAT'S BACKATCHA. / JUST PASSING THROUGH** [ ] [26] Apr 75

Jun 75. (lp,c **A QUIET STORM** [ ] [36] Apr 75
– A quiet storm / The agony and the ecstasy / Baby that's backatcha / Wedding song / Happy-love theme (from the film 'Lady Sings The Blues') / Love letters / Coincidentely. *(re-iss.Feb82)*

Sep 75. (7") **THE AGONY AND THE ECSTASY. / WEDDING SONG** [-] [36]

Jan 76. (7") **A QUIET STORM. / ASLEEP ON MY LOVE** [ ] [61]

Apr 76. (lp)(c) **SMOKEY'S FAMILY ROBINSON** [ ] [57]
– When you came / Get out of town / Do like I do / Open / So in love / Like nobody can / Castles made of sand.

May 76. (7") **OPEN. / COINCIDENTALLY** [-] [81]

Motown Tamla

Mar 77. (7") **THERE WILL COME A DAY (I'M GONNA TO HAPPEN TO YOU). / OLD-FASHIONED MAN** [ ] [-]

Apr 77. (lp)(c) **DEEP IN MY SOUL** [ ] [47] Feb 77
– Vitamin U / There will come a day (I'm gonna happen to you) / It's been a long time (since I been in love) / Let's do the dance of life together / If you want my love / You cannot laugh alone / In my corner / The humming song (lost for words).

Jun 77. (7") **VITAMIN U. / HOLLY** [ ] [ ]

Sep 77. (7") **THEME FROM BIG TIME. / (part 2)** [ ] [ ]

Sep 77. (lp)(c) **BIG TIME (Film Soundtrack)** [ ] [ ]
– Theme from Big Time / J.J.'s theme / Hip trip / He is the light of the world / So nice to be with you / Shona's theme (with dialogue) / If we're gonna act like lovers / The agony and the ecstasy / Theme from Big Time (reprise).

Feb 78. (lp)(c) **SMOKEY'S WORLD** [ ] [ ]
– (compilation)

Apr 78. (7") **MADAM X. / THE AGONY AND ECSTASY** [ ] [-]

May 78. (lp)(c) **LOVE BREEZE** [ ] [75] Apr 78
– Why you wanna see my bad side / Love so fine / Feeling you feeling me / Madam X / Shoe soul / Trying it again / Daylight and darkness / I'm loving you softly.

Jul 78. (7") **DAYLIGHT AND DARKNESS. / WHY YOU WANNA SEE MY BAD SIDE** [ ] [75] Jun 78

Nov 78. (7") **SHOE SOUL. / I'M LOVING YOU SOFTLY** [ ] [ ]

Jan 79. (d-lp) **SMOKIN' (live)** [-] [ ]

— Early '79, SMOKEY featured with STEVIE WONDER, DIANA ROSS and MARVIN GAYE on minor hit single POPS WE LOVE YOU.

Jul 79. (7") **GET READY. / EVER HAD A DREAM** [ ] [ ]

Aug 79. (lp)(c) **WHERE THERE'S SMOKE** [ ] [17] Jun 79
– Smoke / It's a good night / I love the nearness of you / The hurt on you / Ever had a dream / Fire get ready / Share it / Cruisin'. *(re-iss.Oct81)*

Sep 79. (7") **CRUISIN'. / EVER HAD A DREAM** [-] [4]

Sep 79. (7") **CRUISIN'. / THE HUMMING SONG (LOST FOR WORDS)** [ ] [-]
(re-iss.Aug81)

Apr 80. (7") **LET ME BE THE CLOCK. / TRAVELLIN' THROUGH** [ ] [31] Mar 80

Apr 80. (lp)(c) **WARM THOUGHTS** [ ] [14] Mar 80
– Let me be the clock / Heaven on pride / Into each rain some life must fall / Wine, women and song / Melody man / What's in your life for me / I want to be your love / Travellin' through. *(re-iss.Oct81)*

Jun 80. (7") **HEAVY ON PRIDE. / I LOVE THE NEARNESS OF LOVE** [ ] [ ]

Feb 81. (7") **BEING WITH YOU. / WHAT'S IN YOUR LIFE FOR ME** [1] [2]

Apr 81. (lp)(c) **BEING WITH YOU** [17] [10] Mar 81
– Being with you / Food for thought / If you wanna make love (come round here) / Who's sad / Can't fight love / You are forever / As you do / I hear the children singing. *(re-iss.Oct81 & Apr85) (cd-iss.Sep93)*

Oct 81. (7") **YOU ARE FOREVER. / I HEAR THE CHILDREN SINGING** [ ] [ ] Jun 81

Feb 82. (7") **TELL ME TOMORROW. / (part 2)** [51] [33] Jan 82
(12"+=) – Being with you / Aqui con tigo.

Feb 82. (lp)(c) **YES IT'S YOU LADY** [ ] [33]
– Tell me tomorrow / Yes it's you lady / Old fashioned love / Are you still here / The only game in town / International baby / Merry go ride / I'll try something new / Destiny.

May 82. (7")(12") **AN OLD FASHIONED LOVE. / DESTINY** [ ] [60] Apr 82

Feb 83. (7") **I'VE MADE LOVE TO YOU A THOUSAND TIMES. / INTO EACH RAIN SOME LIFE MUST FALL** [ ] [ ]
(12"+=) – (Greatest hits medley).

Mar 83. (lp)(c) **TOUCH THE SKY** [ ] [50] Jan 83
– Touch the sky / Gimme what you want / Even tho' / Gone again / All my life's a lie / Sad time / Dynamite / I've made love to you a thousand times.

May 83. (7") **TOUCH THE SKY. / ALL MY LIFE'S A LIE** [ ] [ ]

Aug 83. (7") **BLAME IT ON LOVE. ("SMOKEY ROBINSON & BARBARA MITCHELL") / EVEN THO'** [ ] [48] Jun 83

Sep 83. (lp)(c) **BLAME IT ON LOVE & ALL THE GREAT HITS** [ ] [ ]
– (compilation)

— In Dec 83. SMOKEY was credited on RICK JAMES' US Top 50 hit 'EBONY EYES'.

Jun 84. (7")(12") **AND I DON'T LOVE YOU. / DYNAMITE** [ ] [ ]

Jul 84. (lp)(c) **ESSAR** [ ] [ ] Jun 84
– And I don't love you / Train of thought / I can't find / Why are you running from my love / Gone forever / Close encounters of the first kind / Little girl, little girl / Girl I'm standing there / Driving thru life in the fast lane.

— Early 1985, he guested on the WE ARE THE WORLD charity No.1 single.

Jan 86. (7")(12") **HOLD ON TO YOUR LOVE. / TRAIN OF THOUGHT** [ ] [ ]

Mar 86. (lp)(c)(cd) **SMOKE SIGNALS** [ ] [ ] Feb 86
– Some people (will do anything for love) / Sleepless nights / Because of you (it's the best it's ever been) / Be kind to the growing mind / Te quiero como si no hubicra un manama / Hold on to your love / Photograph in my mind / No time to stop believing / Wishful thinking / Hanging on by a thread.

May 86. (7")(12") **SLEEPLESS NIGHTS. / CLOSE ENCOUNTERS OF THE FIRST KIND** [ ] [ ]

Mar 87. (7") **JUST TO SEE HER. / I'M GONNA LOVE YOU LIKE THERE'S NO TOMORROW** [52] [8]
(12"+=) – You really got a hold on me / That's what love is made of / Ooh baby baby. (3 extra by SMOKEY ROBINSON & THE MIRACLES)

May 87. (lp)(c)(cd) **ONE HEARTBEAT** [ ] [26] Mar 87
– Just to see her / One heartbeat / It's time to stop shoppin' around / Why do happy memories hurt so bad / You don't know what it's like / What's too much / Love brought us here tonight / Love don't give no reason / Keep me.

Jun 87. (7") **ONE HEART BEAT. / LOVE WILL SET YOU FREE** [-] [ ]

Jul 87. (7")(12") **ONE HEARTBEAT. / JUST TO SEE HER** [ ] [-]

Nov 87. (7") **WHAT'S TOO MUCH. / I'VE MADE LOVE TO YOU A THOUSAND TIMES** [-] [79]

— Early in '88, SMOKEY dueted on DOLLY PARTON single I KNOW YOU BY HEART.

Mar 88. (7") **LOVE DON'T GIVE NO REASON. / ('A'instrumental)** [ ] [ ]
(12"+=) – ('A'dance mix) / ('A'dub mix).
(cd-s+=) – Going to a go-go / You've really got a hold on me.

S.B.K. / S.B.K.

Feb 90. (cd)(c)(lp) **LOVE SMOKEY** [ ] [ ]

Jan 92. (7") **DOUBLE GOOD EVERYTHING. / GUESS WHAT I GOT FOR YOU** [ ] [91] Nov 91
(12"+=)(c-s+=)(cd-s+=) – Skid row.

Feb 92. (cd)(c)(lp) **DOUBLE GOOD EVERYTHING** [ ] [ ]
– Why / Double good everything / Be who you are / I love your face / Can't get enough / Rack me back / When a woman cries / You take me away / Skid row.

– more compilations, etc. –

Below releases issued on 'Tamla Motown' unless mentioned.

Jul 82. (lp)(c) **HOT SMOKEY** [ ] [ ]

Aug 82. (7")(12") **CRUISIN'. / THE ONLY GAME IN TOWN** [ ] [-]

Sep 82. (d-lp)(d-c) **ANTHOLOGY (w/ MIRACLES)** [ ] [ ]
(d-cd-iss.Jan87)

Jun 83. K-Tel; (lp)(c) **THE SMOKEY ROBINSON STORY** [ ] [-]

Nov 88. Telstar; (lp)(c)(cd) **LOVE SONGS** (side by MARVIN GAYE) [69] [-]

Nov 92. K-Tel; (cd)(c) **THE GREATEST HITS** [65] [ ]

Jun 94. Motown; (4xcd-box) **35th ANNIVERSARY COLLECTION** [ ] [ ]

Tom ROBINSON

Born: 1 Jun'50, Cambridge, England. After being part of the group DAVANQ in the early 70's, he formed acoustic folk-rock outfit CAFE SOCIETY in 1973. They released one self-titled album for Ray Davies' (KINKS) label 'Konk', before disbanding soon after. The following year, he formed The TOM ROBINSON BAND, with fellow reform school pupil DANNY KUSTOW. In 1977 and after many personnel changes, they signed to 'EMI'. Their debut single '2-4-6-8 MOTORWAY' gave them immediate impact, and rose to No.5 in the UK charts. For the next year or so, the band toured constantly, but after their TODD RUNDGREN produced 2nd album, which hit the Top 20, they disbanded. This led to TOM having a nervous breakdown, although he recovered in 1980 to form a new group SECTOR 27, and start new label 'Panic'. He moved to Hamburg, Germany in early 1982, and was soon back in the Top 10 with thought-provoking solo 45 'WAR BABY'. • **Style:** College new-wave anthem rock, with TOM an articulate forefront for the Gay radical activist movements. In the 80's, his music mellowed somewhat, and he confessed to actually being bi-sexual, not homosexual. • **Songwriters:** Most written by ROBINSON, except covers; RIKKI DON'T LOSE THAT NUMBER (Steely Dan) / etc? • **Trivia:** In 1978, he helped arrange a 'Rock Against Fascism' rally in East London, which was a protest against the anti-Nazi league.

Recommended: BACK IN THE OLD COUNTRY (*7)

TOM ROBINSON BAND

– vocals, bass (ex-CAFE SOCIETY, ex-DAVANQ) / **DANNY KUSTOW** – guitar (ex-DAVANQ) / **MARK AMBLER** – keyboards repl. ANTON MAUVE, BRET SINCLAIR & MARK GRIFFITHS / **DOLPHIN TAYLOR** – drums, vocals repl. NICK TREVISICK (ex-CAFE SOCIETY)

E.M.I. / Harvest

Oct 77. (7") **2-4-6-8 MOTORWAY. / I SHALL BE RELEASED** [5] [ ]

Feb 78. (7"ep) **RISING FREE (live)** [18] [ ]
– Don't take no for an answer / Right on sister / Sing if you're glad to be gay / Martin.

May 78. (7") **UP AGAINST THE WALL. / I'M ALRIGHT JACK** [33] [-]

May 78. (lp)(c) **POWER IN THE DARKNESS** [4] [ ]
– Up against the wall / Grey Cortina / Too good to be true / Ain't gonna take it / Long hot summer / Winter of 79 / Man you never saw / Better decide which side you're on / You gotta survive / Power in the darkness / 2-4-6-8 Motorway. *(re-iss.Aug83) (re-iss.cd+c Oct94 on 'Cooking Vinyl')*

Aug 78. (7") **TOO GOOD TO BE TRUE. / POWER IN THE DARKNESS** [ ] [-]

Sep 78. (7") **RIGHT ON SISTERS. / GLAD TO BE GAY** [-] [ ]

— (mid'78) **IAN PARKER** – keyboards repl. NICK PLYTAS (ex-ROOGALATOR) who had repl. AMBLER (Apr'78).

— (Dec78) **PRESTON HEYMAN** – drums (ex-BRAND X) repl. DOLPHIN who joined STIFF LITTLE FINGERS.

Mar 79. (7") **BULLY FOR YOU. / OUR PEOPLE** [68] [ ]

Mar 79. (lp)(c) **TRB TWO** [18] [ ]
– All right all night / Why should I mind / Black angel / Let my people be / Blue murder / Bully for you / Crossing over the road / Sorry Mr. Harris / Law and order / Days of rage / Hold out. *(re-iss.Aug83) (re-iss.cd+c Oct94 on 'Cooking Vinyl')*

May 79. (7") **ALRIGHT ALL NIGHT. / BLACK ANGEL** (withdrawn) [ ] [-]

— **CHARLIE MORGAN** – drums repl. the returning TREVISICK who had repl. HEYMAN. The latter joined KATE BUSH. **GEOFF SHARKEY** – guitar repl. KUSTOW / added **GRAHAM COLLIER** – double bass / **GEOFF DALY** – saxophone

Aug 79. (7") **NEVER GONNA FALL IN LOVE (AGAIN). / GETTING TIGHTER** [ ] [-]

— Disbanded late summer '79. **TOM ROBINSON** now vocals, guitar went solo with back-up from SECTOR 27. **STEVE BLANCHARD** – guitar / **DEREK QUINTON** – drums / **JO BURT** – bass. They recorded one withdrawn lp 'SECTOR 27' on 'Regal Zono.'

SECTOR 27

were now given full billing.

Panic / not issued

Jul 80. (7")(12") **NOT READY. / CAN'T KEEP AWAY** [ ] [-]

Oct 80. (7") **INVITATION, WHAT HAVE WE GOT TO LOSE?. / DUNGANNON** [ ] [-]

Fontana Int.Record

Nov 80. (lp)(c) **SECTOR 27** [ ] [ ]
– Invitation / Not ready / Mary Lynne / Looking at you / 523 / Total recall / Where can we go tonight / Take it or leave it / Bitterly disappointed / One fine day.

Panic not issued

Jan 81. (7") **TOTAL RECALL. / STORNOWAY** [ ] [-]
May 81. (7") **MARTIN'S GONE. / CHRISTOPHER CALLING** [ ] [-]

TOM ROBINSON

went solo again. (SECTOR 27 as a trio branched out on own). **TOM** added **STEVE LAURIE** – drums / **RICHARD MAZDA** – guitar, producer / etc

Jun 82. (lp)(c) **NORTH BY NORTHWEST** [ ] [ ]
– Now Martin's gone / Atmospherics / Can't keep away (part 2) / Looking for a bonfire / Merrily up on high / Those days / In the cold / The night tide / Dungannon / Love comes. *(cd-iss.1986 on 'Castle')*
Jul 82. (7") **NOW MARTIN'S GONE. / ATMOSPHERICS** [ ] [-]
(re-iss.Feb83 as 5-track-12"ep. 'ATMOSPHERICS')

Panic Geffen

Jun 83. (7") **WAR BABY. / HELL YES** [6] [ ] Sep 84
(12"+=) – Martin's gone (original).
Nov 83. (7") **LISTEN TO THE RADIO: ATMOSPHERICS. / DON'T DO ME ANY FAVOURS** [39] [ ]
(12"+=) – Out to lunch.

Castaway-RCA R.C.A.

Jun 84. (7") **BACK IN THE OLD COUNTRY. / BEGGIN'** [ ] [ ]
(12"+=) – ('A'live version).
Sep 84. (7")(12") **RIKKI DON'T LOSE THAT NUMBER. / CABIN BOY (live)** [58] [-]
Sep 84. (lp)(c) **HOPE AND GLORY** [21] [ ]
– War baby / Atmospherics: Listen to the radio / Cabin boy / Blond and blue / Hope and glory / Murder at the end of the day / Prison / Rikki don't lose that number / Old friend / Looking for a bonfire.
May 85. (7")(12") **PRISON. / MORE LIVES THAN ONE** [ ] [-]

— TOM brought back **BLANCHARD + BURT** plus **RED** – drums

Jul 86. (7") **(IT AIN'T NOTHIN' LIKE) THE REAL THING. / THE WEDDING** [ ] [ ]
(12"+=) ('A'extended).
Sep 86. (lp)(c)(cd) **STILL LOVING YOU** [ ] [ ]
– Feel so good – Hurt so bad / (It nothin' like) The real thing / Still loving you / Take me home again / You tattooed me / Drive all night / Living in a love town / Spain / This little romance / The wedding.
Sep 86. (7")(12") **STILL LOVING YOU. / THE SATURDAY DISCO** [ ] [ ]

— (next featured duet with KIKI DEE)

Jan 87. (7") **FEEL SO GOOD. / NORTHERN RAIN** [ ] [-]
(12"+=) – You tattooed me / Change.
Jun 87. (7") **SPAIN. / DRIVE ALL NIGHT** [ ] [-]
(12"+=) – (It ain't nothin' like) The real thing.

Musidisc not issued

Oct 90. (cd)(c)(lp) **WE NEVER HAD IT SO GOOD ("TOM ROBINSON & JAKKO M. JAKSYSK")** [ ] [-]
– We never had it so good / Drinking through the desert / Blood brother / What have I ever done to you / The baby rages on / Tomboy / Kiss and roll over / Hard cases / Can't stop: Peter's theme / My own sweet way.
Nov 90. (7") **BLOOD BROTHER. / ('A'version)** [ ] [-]
(12"+=) – What have I ever done to you / Rigging.

Cooking V. not issued

Sep 92. (cd)(c)(lp) **LIVING IN A BOOM TIME** [ ] [-]
– Folk song (intro) / Living in a boom time / More lives than one / Yuppie scum / My own sweet way / Castle island / Digging it up / The Brits / War baby / Back in the old country. *(re-iss.cd+c Mar94)*
Jan 93. (c-ep)(cd-ep) **WAR BABY. / BLOOD BROTHER / WE DIDN'T KNOW WHAT WAS GOING ON / WAR BABY** [ ] [-]

— now w / **ROBIN MILLAR** – rhythm guitar / **CHRIS REA** – slide guitar / **MARK AMBLER** – keyboards / **WINSTON BLISSETT** – bass / **MARTIN DITCHAM** – drums / **MARK RAMSDEN** – saxophone / **T.V.SMITH + ANDY MITCHELL** – backing vocals

May 94. (cd)(c)(lp) **LOVE OVER RAGE** [ ] [ ]
– Roaring / Hard / Loved / Days / Driving / Green / DDR / Fifty / Silence / Chance.
Jun 94. (cd-ep) **HARD / GREEN / LIVING IN A BOOM TIME / PORTOBELLO TERRACE** [ ] [ ]
Jul 94. (cd-ep) **LOVED / FIFTY / YUPPY SCUM / GLAD TO BE GAY '94** [ ] [ ]
Sep 94. (cd-ep) **DAYS (THAT CHANGED THE WORLD) / ROARING / THE BRITS COME ROLLING BACK** [ ] [ ]

– compilations, others, etc. –

Dec 81. EMI; (lp)(c) **TOM ROBINSON BAND** [ ] [-]
(re-iss.May82 on 'Fame')
Sep 87. EMI; (7")(12") **2-4-6-8 MOTORWAY. / SING IF YOU'RE GLAD TO BE GAY** [ ] [-]
Sep 87. EMI; (lp)(c)(cd) **COLLECTION 77-87** [ ] [-]
Nov 82. Panic; (lp) **CABARET '79 (live)** [ ] [-]
Oct 83. Old Gold; (7") **2-4-6-8 MOTORWAY. / DON'T TAKE NO FOR AN ANSWER** [ ] [-]
Apr 87. Dojo; (lp)(c) **MIDNIGHT AT THE FRINGE (live with The CREW)** [ ] [-]
Mar 89. Line; (lp)(cd) **GLAD TO BE GAY CABARET** [ ] [-]
Jun 89. Line; (cd) **LAST TANGO** [ ] [-]
Oct 89. Connoisseur; (d-lp)(c)(cd) **BACK IN THE OLD COUNTRY** [ ] [-]
– Listen to the radio: Atmospherics / Too good to be true / Up against the wall / Northern rain / I shall be released / 2-4-6-8 motorway / Drive all night / Don't take no for an answer / Where can we go tonight / Back in the old country / Alright all night / War baby / Power in the darkness / Crossing over the road / Rikki don't lose that number / Looking for a bonfire / Hard cases / Still loving you / Not ready / Bully for you / Long hot summer. (d-lp/c+=) – Mary Lynne / Bitterly disappointed.
Jun 93. Optima; (cd) **TOM ROBINSON** [ ] [-]
Jul 94. Music De-Luxe; (cd) **MOTORWAY** [ ] [-]
Aug 95. Line; (d-cd) **GLAD TO BE GAY / LAST TANGO** [ ] [-]

ROCKPILE (see under ⇒ EDMUNDS, Dave)

Nile RODGERS (see under ⇒ CHIC)

Paul RODGERS

Born: 17 Dec '49, Middlesborough, England. After fronting massive selling hard rockers FREE (1968-1973) + BAD COMPANY (1974-1982), he ventured solo. In 1983, he issued his debut album 'CUT LOOSE' for 'Atlantic'. Early in 1985, he teamed up with ex-LED ZEPPELIN members to form supergroup 'The FIRM'. Early in the 90s RODGERS teamed up with KENNY JONES to form the LAW. They released one-off eponymous album in 1991, before they went their separate ways. He returned to solo work in 1993, giving tribute to blues legend Muddy Waters.

Recommended: MUDDY WATERS BLUES (*6)

Atlantic Atlantic

Nov 83. (lp)(c) **CUT LOOSE** [ ] [ ]
– Fragile / Cut loose / Live in peace / Sweet sensation / Rising sun / Boogie mama / Morning after the night before / Northwinds / Superstar woman / Talking guitar blues.
Nov 83. (7") **CUT LOOSE / TALKING GUITAR BLUES** [ ] [ ]
Jan 84. (7") **MORNING AFTER THE NIGHT BEFORE. / NORTHWINDS** [-] [ ]

— Early in 1985, he joined The Firm (see under ⇒ LED ZEPPELIN). In the 90's he returned to the studio.

The LAW

RODGERS wrote some material w/ **BRYAN ADAMS / DAVID GILMORE / CHRIS REA.** Covered: MISS YOU IN A HEARTBEAT (Def Leppard).
RODGERS – vocals / **KENNY JONES** – drums (ex-WHO, ex-SMALL FACES).

Atlantic Atco

Mar 91. (7") **LAYING DOWN THE LAW / TOUGH LOVE** [ ] [ ]
(12"+=)(cd-s+=) That's when you fall.
Apr 91. (cd)(c)(lp) **THE LAW** [61] [ ]
– For a little ride / Miss you in a heartbeat / Stone cold / Come save me (Julianne) / Laying down the law / Nature of the beast / Stone / Anything for you / Best of my love / Missing you bad girl.

Paul RODGERS

(solo) with **JASON BONHAM** – drums / **PINO PALLADINO** – bass / **IAN HATTON** – rhythm guitar / plus **JIMMIE WOOD** – harmonica / **RONNIE FOSTER** – organ / **MARK T.WILLIAMS** – bass drum and guest lead guitarists on each of the 15 tracks; **BUDDY GUY / TREVOR RABIN / BRIAN SETZER / JEFF BECK / JEFF BECK / STEVE MILLER / TREVOR RABIN / DAVID GILMOUR / SLASH / GARY MOORE / BRIAN MAY / JEFF BECK / NEAL SCHON / RICHIE SAMBORA / NEAL SCHON**

Victory Victory

Jun 93. (cd)(c) **MUDDY WATERS BLUES: A TRIBUTE TO MUDDY WATERS** [9] [91]
– Muddy Water blues (acoustic version) / Louisiana blues / I can't be satisfied / Rollin' stone / Good morning little school girl (part 1) / I'm your hoochie coochie man / She's alright / Standing around crying / The hunter / She moves me / I'm ready / I just want to make love to you / Born under a bad sign / Good morning little school girl (part 2) / Muddy Water blues (electric version). (free-cd 'THE HISTORY'; re-recordings of FREE and BAD COMPANY hits) – All right now / Wishing well / Fire & water / Bad company / Feel like making love / Can't get enough.

Album 'MUDDY WATER BLUES' songs stemming from MUDDY WATERS, RODGERS, SONNY BOY WILLIAMSON, WILLIE DIXON or BOOKER T.JONES.

Feb 94. (cd-ep) **MUDDY WATER BLUES / PURPLE HAZE / STONE FREE / LITTLE WING** [45] [ ]
(cd-ep) ('A'side) / The hunter / Stone free / Nature of the beast.

— More covers; PURPLE HAZE + STONE FREE + LITTLE WING (Jimi Hendrix).

ROLLING STONES

Formed: London, England ... mid-1962 by JONES, JAGGER and RICHARDS. In May'63 they were signed by A&R man Dick Rowe for 'Decca', who had just rejected The BEATLES. (Decca slightly re-christened Keith as KEITH RICHARD, although he regained real name by the late 70's). Their debut single 'COME ON' nearly hit UK Top 20, although by the next year, they had first of many No.1's with 'IT'S ALL OVER NOW'. In 1965, they scored their first US No.1 with gem '(I CAN'T GET NO) SATISFACTION'. After The BEATLES disbanded in 1969, The STONES took over the mantle in the 70's as the hottest property in rock and popular music. **Style & Trivia:** R&B rebels from the early 60's, who progressed through controversial lyrically hard-edged rock, that never wained throughout 3 decades. Constantly in the press headlines for drug-taking/busts. Tragically JONES was to die 3 Jul'69, when drowning after a drink and drugs binge, He had left The STONES a month previously. JAGGER also an early drug taker, was more in the papers for his love-life. His 60's relationship with singer MARIANNE FAITHFULL

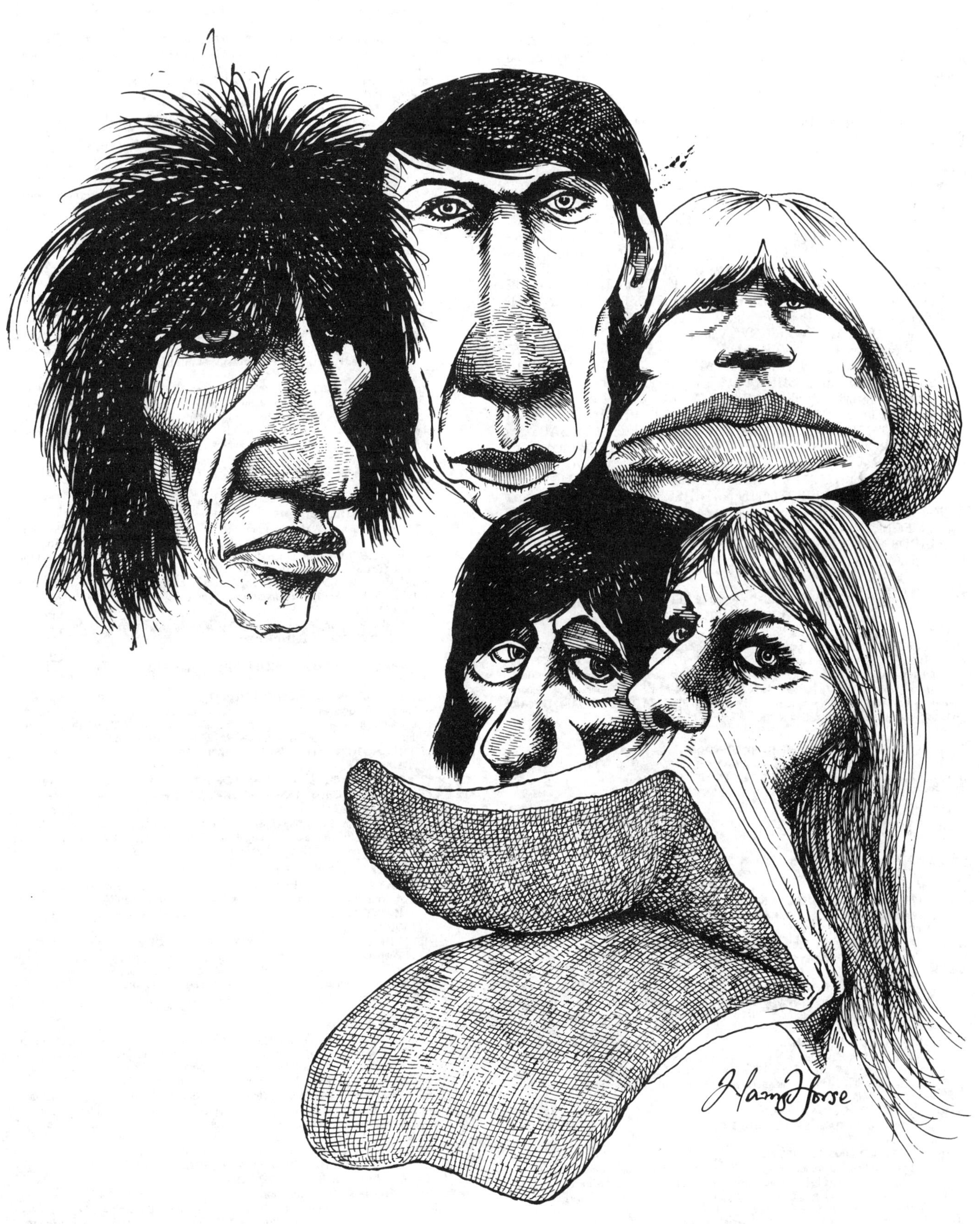

ended in 1970. He met and married Nicaraguan model Bianca Rosa Perez-Mora on 12 May'71. They split in 1978, probably over Marsha Hunt's allegations that MICK was the father of her child. He later married ex-Bryan Ferry girlfriend Jerry Hall on 21 Nov'90 after a long relationship. JAGGER's film work included:- NED KELLY (1969) / PERFORMANCE (1970) / FITZCARALDO (1981). The other glimmer-twin RICHARDS, relationship with actress Anita Pallenberg ended and he later married Patti Hansen on 18 Dec'83. WYMAN's marriage since 1959 ended abruptly in the mid-80's. In 1988, his 2-year relationship with a 16 year-old Mandy Smith was revealed in The News Of The World Sunday tabloid. They married relatively quietly on 2 Jun'89, but controversially divorced in 1992, with now-famous Mandy sueing for a half million. • **Songwriters:** JAGGER-RICHARDS mostly except covers; NOT FADE AWAY (Buddy Holly) / ROUTE 66 (Nelson Riddle Orchestra) / I JUST WANT TO MAKE LOVE TO YOU (Willie Dixon) / HONEST I DO (Jimmy Reed) / I NEED YOU BABY (Bo Diddley) / POISON IVY (Coasters) / NOW I'VE GOT A WITNESS . . . (Gene Pitney) / LITTLE BY LITTLE (Pitney / Spector) / COME ON + CAROL + YOU CAN'T CATCH ME + TALKIN' 'BOUT YOU + LITTLE QUEENIE + AROUND AND AROUND + BYE BYE JOHNNY (Chuck Berry) / CAN I GET A WITNESS (Holland-Dozier-Holland) / MONEY (Barrett Strong) / I WANNA BE YOUR MAN (Beatles) / LITTLE BY LITTLE (w/Spector) / YOU CAN MAKE IT IF YOU TRY (Gene Allison; hit) / WALKING THE DOG (Rufus Thomas) / SUSIE Q (Dale Hawkins) / UNDER THE BOARDWALK (Drifters) / I CAN'T BE SATISFIED + MANNISH BOY (Muddy Waters) / DOWN HOME GIRL (Jerry Butler) / IT'S ALL OVER NOW (Valentinos) / PAIN IN MY HEART + MY GIRL (Otis Redding) / EVERYBODY NEEDS SOMEBODY TO LOVE (Solomon Burke) / DOWN THE ROAD APIECE (?. Raye) / TIME IS ON MY SIDE (Irma Thomas) / SHE SAID YEAH (Jackson/Christy) / I DON'T KNOW WHY (Stevie Wonder) / MERCY, MERCY (Don Covay) / GOOD TIMES (Sam Cooke) / CRY TO ME (Betty Harris; hit) / HITCH HIKE (Marvin Gaye) / THAT'S HOW STRONG MY LOVE IS (?. Jamison) / OH BABY . . . (?. Ozen) / PRODIGAL SON (Robert Wilkins) / YOU BETTER MOVE ON (Arthur Alexander) / LOVE IN VAIN (Robert Johnson; trad.) / AIN'T TOO PROUD TO BEG + JUST MY IMAGINATION (Temptations) / I'M A KING BEE + SHAKE YOUR HIPS (Slim Harpo) / CHERRY OH BABY (? reggae) / GOING TO A GO-GO (Smokey Robinson / Miracles) / HARLEM SHUFFLE (Bob & Earl) / TWENTY FLIGHT ROCK (Eddie Cochran) / etc. KEITH RICHARDS solo wrote with JORDAN. RONNIE WOOD covered TESTIFY (Parliaments) / AM I GROOVIN' YOU (Bert Berns) / SEVEN DAYS (Bob Dylan) / SHOW ME (J. Williams).

Recommended: EXILE ON MAIN ST. (*9) / ROLLED GOLD (*10) / MADE IN THE SHADE (*8) / BEGGAR'S BANQUET (*8) / STICKY FINGERS (*7).

MICK JAGGER (b.26 Jul'43, Dartford, Kent, England) – vocals, harmonica / **KEITH RICHARDS** (b.18 Dec'43, Dartford) – rhythm guitar / **BRIAN JONES** (b.28 Feb'43, Cheltenham, England) – lead guitar / **CHARLIE WATTS** (b. 2 Jun'41, Islington, London) – drums (ex-BLUES INC.) / **BILL WYMAN** (b.WILLIAM PERKS, 24 Oct'36, Lewisham, London) – bass repl. DICK TAYLOR who later joined PRETTY THINGS / **IAN STEWART** – piano (was 6th member, pushed to the background by manager)

Decca London

Jun 63. (7") **COME ON. / I WANT TO BE LOVED** 21 -

Nov 63. (7") **I WANNA BE YOUR MAN. / STONED** 12 [ ] Jan 64

Feb 64. (7") **NOT FADE AWAY. / LITTLE BY LITTLE** 3 -

Mar 64. (7") **NOT FADE AWAY. / I WANNA BE YOUR MAN** - 48

Apr 64. (lp) **THE ROLLING STONES** 1 11 Jun 64
– (Get your kicks on) Route 66 / I just want to make love to you / Honest I do / I need you baby (Mona) / Now I've got a witness (like uncle Phil and uncle Gene) / Little by little / I'm a king bee / Carol / Tell me (you're coming back) / Can I get a witness / You can make it if you try / Walking the dog. *(US title 'ENGLAND'S NEWEST HITMAKERS – THE ROLLING STONES')(+=)* – Not fade away. / =Mona *(in the US) re-iss.+c+cd.Jul84 & Jun95 on 'London')*

Jun 64. (7") **IT'S ALL OVER NOW. / GOOD TIMES, BAD TIMES** 1 26 Aug 64

Jul 64. (7") **TELL ME (YOU'RE COMING BACK). / I JUST WANT TO MAKE LOVE TO YOU** - 24

Oct 64. (7") **TIME IS ON MY SIDE. / CONGRATULATIONS** - 6

Nov 64. (7") **LITTLE RED ROOSTER. / OFF THE HOOK** 1 -

Nov 64. (lp) **12 x 5** - 3
– Around and around / Confessin' the blues / Empty heart / Time is on my side / Good times bad times / It's all over now / 2120 South Michigan Avenue / Under the boardwalk / Congratulations / Grown up wrong / If you need me / Susie Q. *(UK-iss.+c+cd-Aug84 & Jun95 on 'London', as US cd-iss.!)*

Jan 65. (lp) **THE ROLLING STONES No.2** 1 -
– Everybody needs somebody to love / Down home girl / You can't catch me / Time is on my side / What a shame / Grown up wrong / Down the road apiece / Under the boardwalk / I can't be satisfied / Pain in my heart / Off the hook / Susie Q. *(re-iss.c+cd.1986)*

Jan 65. (7") **HEART OF STONE. / WHAT A SHAME** - 19

Feb 65. (7") **THE LAST TIME. / PLAY WITH FIRE** 1 9
96 Mar65

Mar 65. (lp) **THE ROLLING STONES NOW!** - 5
– Everybody needs somebody to love / Down home girl / You can't catch me / Heart of stone / I need you baby (Mona) / Down the road apiece / Off the hook / Pain in my heart / Oh baby (we got a good thing goin') / Little red rooster / Surprise surprise. *(UK-iss.+c+cd Aug88 + Jun95 on 'London')*

May 65. (7") **(I CAN'T GET NO) SATISFACTION. / THE SPIDER AND THE FLY** 1 -

Jun 65. (7") **(I CAN'T GET NO) SATISFACTION. / THE UNDER ASSISTANT WEST COAST MAN** - 1

Sep 65. (lp) **OUT OF OUR HEADS** 2 1 Aug 65
– She said yeah* / Mercy, mercy / Hitch hike / That's how strong my love is / Good times / Gotta get away* / Talkin' 'bout you* / Cry to me / Oh baby (we got a good thing going)* / Heart of stone / The under assistant west coast man / I'm free. (in the US; tracks above* were repl. by) – I'm alright (live) / (I can't get no) Satisfaction / Play with fire / The spider and the fly / One more try. *(re-iss.+c+cd.Jul84 & Jun95 on 'London')*

Sep 65. (7") **GET OFF OF MY CLOUD. / I'M FREE** - 1

Oct 65. (7") **GET OFF OF MY CLOUD. / THE SINGER NOT THE SONG** 1 -

Nov 65. (lp) **DECEMBER'S CHILDREN (AND EVERYBODY'S)** - 4
– She said yeah / Talkin' 'bout you / You better move on / Look what you've done / The singer not the song / Route 66 (live) / Get off of my cloud / I'm free / As tears go by / Gotta get away / Blue turns to grey / I'm movin' on (live). *(UK-iss.+c+cd.Aug88 & Jun95 on 'London')*

Dec 65. (7") **AS TEARS GO BY. / GOTTA GET AWAY** - 6

Feb 66. (7") **19th NERVOUS BREAKDOWN. / AS TEARS GO BY** 1 -

Feb 66. (7") **19th NERVOUS BREAKDOWN. / SAD DAY** - 2

Apr 66. (lp) **AFTERMATH** 1 2 Jul 66
– Mother's little helper / Stupid girl / Lady Jane / Under my thumb / Doncha bother me / Goin' home / Flight 505 / High and dry / Out of time / It's not easy / I am waiting / Take it or leave it / Think / What to do. (US version incl.) – Paint it black. *(re-iss.+c+cd.May85 & Jun95 on 'London')*

May 66. (7") **PAINT IT BLACK. / STUPID GIRL** - 1

May 66. (7") **PAINT IT BLACK. / LONG LONG WHILE** 1 -

Jul 66. (7") **MOTHER'S LITTLE HELPER. / LADY JANE** - 8
24

Sep 66. (7") **HAVE YOU SEEN YOUR MOTHER BABY, STANDING IN THE SHADOW?. / WHO'S DRIVING YOUR PLANE?** 5 9

Nov 66. (lp) **BIG HITS (HIGH TIDE AND GREEN GRASS)** 4 3 Apr 66
(compilation) – Have you seen your mother baby, standing in the shadows? / Paint it black / It's all over now / The last time / Heart of stone / Not fade away / Come on / (I can't get no) Satisfaction / Get off my cloud / As tears go by / 19th nervous breakdown / Lady Jane / Time is on my side / Little red rooster. *(re-iss.+c+cd Jun95 on 'London')*

Dec 66. (lp) **GOT LIVE IF YOU WANT IT (live, Royal Albert Hall)** - 6
– Under my thumb / Get off of my cloud / Lady Jane / Not fade away / I've been loving you too long (to stop now) (studio) / Fortune teller (studio) / The last time / 19th nervous breakdown / Time is on my side / I'm alright / Have you seen your mother baby, standing in the shadow? / (I can't get no) Satisfaction. *(UK-iss.+c+cd.Aug88 & Jun95 on 'London', also in US on 'London')*

Jan 67. (7") **LET'S SPEND THE NIGHT TOGETHER. / RUBY TUESDAY** 3 55
1

Jan 67. (lp) **BETWEEN THE BUTTONS** 3 2 Feb 67
– Yesterday's papers / My obsession / Back street girl* / Connection / She smiled sweetly / Cool, calm and collected / All sold out / Please go home* / Who's been sleeping here? / Complicated / Miss Amanda Jones / Something happened to me yesterday. *(US version*; = tracks repl. by)*
– Let's spend the night together / Ruby Tuesday. *(cd-iss.Jan83) (re-iss.+c+cd.Apr85 + Jun95 on 'London') (re-iss.lp/cd. Dec91 on 'UFO' with free booklet)*

Jul 67. (lp) **FLOWERS** - 3
– (compilation of singles and out-takes) *(UK cd-iss.Aug88 & Jun95 on 'London')*

Aug 67. (7") **WE LOVE YOU. / DANDELION** 8 50
14

Nov 67. (7") **SHE'S A RAINBOW. / 2,000 LIGHT YEARS FROM HOME** - 25

Dec 67. (lp) **THEIR SATANIC MAJESTIES REQUEST** 3 2
– Sing this all together / Citadel / In another land / 2,000 man / Sing this all together (see what happens) / She's a rainbow / The lantern / Gomper / 2,000 light years from home / On with the show. *(re-iss.+c+cd.Feb86 + Jul90 + Jun95 on 'London')*

Dec 67. (7") **IN ANOTHER LAND. ("BILL WYMAN") / THE LANTERN** - 87

May 68. (7") **JUMPIN' JACK FLASH. / CHILD OF THE MOON** 1 3

Aug 68. (7") **STREET FIGHTING MAN. / NO EXPECTATIONS** - 48

Dec 68. (lp) **BEGGAR'S BANQUET** 3 5
– Sympathy for the Devil / No expectations / Dear doctor / Parachute woman / Jigsaw puzzle / Street fighting man / Prodigal son / Stray cat blues / Factory girl / Salt of the Earth. *(re-iss.+c+cd.Jul84 & JUn95 on 'London', +US-cd)*

—— (Jun69) **MICK TAYLOR** (b.17 Jan'48, Hertfordshire, England) – lead guitar (ex-JOHN MAYALL's BLUESBREAKERS) repl. BRIAN JONES who tragically after a bout of drink/drugs was found dead by his girlfriend on 3 Jul'69.

Jul 69. (7") **HONKY TONK WOMEN. / YOU CAN'T ALWAYS GET WHAT YOU WANT** 1 1

Sep 69. (lp)(c) **THROUGH THE PAST DARKLY (BIG HITS VOL.2)** 2 2
– Look what you've done / It's all over now / Confessin' the blues / One more try / As tears go by / The spider and the fly / My girl / Paint it black / If you need me / The last time / Blue turns to grey / Around and around. – (compilation of hits 1967-1969) *(re-iss.cd/c/lp Jun95 on 'London')*

(all UK singles so far were re-iss.Mar82).

Dec 69. (lp)(c) **LET IT BLEED** 1 3
– Gimme shelter / Love in vain / Country honk / Live with me / Let it bleed / Midnight rambler / You got the silver / Monkey man / You can't always get what you want. *(re-iss.+c+cd.Feb86 & Jun95 UK+US on 'London')*

(Mid-1970, MICK JAGGER finally appears as 'Ned Kelly' in the film of same.)

Sep 70. (lp)(c) **GET YER YA YA'S OUT** (live, New York, Nov'69) 1 6 Oct 69
– Jumpin' Jack Flash / Carol / Stray cat blues / Love in vain / Midnight rambler / Sympathy for the Devil / Live with me / Little Queenie / Honky tonk women. *(cd-iss.mid-80's & Jun95 on 'London')*

In 1970, MICK JAGGER starred in his second feature film 'Performance'.

Nov 70. (7") **MEMO FROM TURNER. (by "MICK JAGGER" from the film) / ('B'side by 'Jack Nitzsche')** 32 [ ]

Apr 71. (lp)(c) **STONE AGE** (compilation) 4 -
– Look what you've done / It's all over now / Confessin' the blues / One more try / As tears go by / The spider and the fly / My girl / Paint it black / If you need me / The last time / Blue turns to grey / Around and around.

Rolling St. Rolling St.

Apr 71. (7"m) **BROWN SUGAR. / BITCH / LET IT ROCK** 2 1

Apr 71. (lp)(c) **STICKY FINGERS** 1 1
– Brown sugar / Sway / Wild horses / Can't you hear me knocking? / You gotta move / Bitch / I got the blues / Sister Morphine / Dead flowers / Moonlight mile.

(re-iss.Mar80 + Sep87) (re-iss.+cd.Nov89 on 'CBS' UK/US) (re-iss.cd Jun94 + c Aug94 on 'Virgin')

Jun 71. (7") **WILD HORSES. / SWAY** [-] [28]

Apr 72. (7") **TUMBLING DICE. / SWEET BLACK ANGEL** [5] [7]

Jun 72. (d-lp)(c) **EXILE ON MAIN ST.** [1] [1]
– Rocks off / Rip this joint / Shake your hips / Casino boogie / Tumbling dice / Sweet Virginia / Torn and frayed / Sweet black angel / Loving cup / Happy / Turd on the run / Ventilator blues / I just want to see his face / Let it loose / All down the line / Stop breaking down / Shine a light / Soul survivor. *(re-iss.Mar80 + Sep87) (re-iss.+cd.Nov89 on 'CBS' UK/US) (re-iss.cd+c Aug94 on 'Virgin')*

Jun 72. (7") **HAPPY. / ALL DOWN THE LINE** [-] [22]

Aug 73. (7") **ANGIE. / SILVER TRAIN** [5] [1]

Sep 73. (lp)(c) **GOAT'S HEAD SOUP** [1] [1]
– Dancing with Mr.D / 100 years ago / Coming down again / Doo doo doo doo doo (heartbreaker) / Angie / Silver train / Hide your love / Winter / Can you hear the music / Star star. *(re-iss.Mar80 + Jan88) (re-iss.+cd.Nov89 on 'CBS' UK/US) (re-iss.cd+c Aug94 on 'Virgin')*

Jan 74. (7") **DOO DOO DOO DOO DOO (HEARTBREAKER). / DANCING WITH MR.D** [-] [15]

Jul 74. (7") **IT'S ONLY ROCK'N'ROLL. / THROUGH THE LONELY NIGHTS** [10] [16]

Oct 74. (lp)(c) **IT'S ONLY ROCK'N'ROLL** [2] [1]
– If you can't rock me / Ain't too proud to beg / It's only rock'n'roll / Till the next goodbye / Time waits for no one / Luxury / Dance little sister / If you really want to be my friend / Short and curlies / Fingerprint file. *(re-iss.Mar80 + Jan88) (re-iss.+cd.Nov89 on 'CBS' UK/US) (re-iss.cd+c Aug94 on 'Virgin')*

Oct 74. (7") **AIN'T TOO PROUD TO BEG. / DANCE LITTLE SISTER** [-] [17]

Jun 75. (lp)(c) **MADE IN THE SHADE** [14] [6]
– Brown sugar / Tumbling dice / Happy / Dance little sister / Wild horses / Angie / Bitch / It's only rock'n'roll (but I like it) / Doo doo doo doo doo (heartbreaker) / Rip this joint. *(re-iss.Mar80 + Mar88) (re-iss.+cd.Nov89 on 'CBS' UK/US)*

— (Apr-Dec75) **RON WOOD** – lead guitar (ex-FACES, ex-CREATION, etc) repl. MICK TAYLOR who left Dec74 and later joined JACK BRUCE BAND

Apr 76. (7") **FOOL TO CRY. / CRAZY MAMA** [6] [-]

Apr 76. (7") **FOOL TO CRY. / HOT STUFF** [-] [10] [49]

May 76. (lp)(c) **BLACK AND BLUE** [2] [1]
– Hot stuff / The hand of fate / Cherry oh baby / Memory motel / Hey Negrita / Melody / Fool to cry / Crazy mama. *(re-iss.Mar80 + Jan88) (re-iss.+cd.Nov89 on 'CBS' UK/US) (re-iss.cd+c Aug94 on 'Virgin')*

Sep 77. (d-lp)(d-c) **LOVE YOU LIVE (live)** [3] [5]
– Fanfare for the common man / Honky tonk woman / If you can't rock me / Get off of my cloud / Happy / Hot stuff / Star star / Tumbling dice / Fingerprint file / You gotta me / You can't always get what you want / Mannish boy / Crackin' up / Little red rooster / Around and around / It's only rock'n'roll / Brown sugar / Jumpin' Jack Flash / Sympathy for the Devil. *(re-iss.Mar80 + Sep87) (re-iss. +d-cd.Nov89 on 'CBS' UK/US)*

May 78. (7"pink)(12"pink) **MISS YOU. / FARAWAY EYES** [3] [1]

Jun 78. (lp)(c) **SOME GIRLS** [2] [1]
– Miss you / When the whip comes down / Just my imagination / Some girls / Lies / Far away etes / Respectable / Before they make me run / Beast of burden / Shattered. *(re-iss.Sep87) (re-iss.+cd.Nov89 on 'CBS' UK/US) (re-iss.cd+c Aug94 on 'Virgin')*

Sep 78. (7") **BEAST OF BURDEN. / WHEN THE WHIP COMES DOWN** [-] [8]

Sep 78. (7") **RESPECTABLE. / WHEN THE WHIP COMES DOWN** [23] [-]

Dec 78. (7") **SHATTERED. / EVERYTHING IS TURNING TO GOLD** [-] [31]

Jun 80. (7") **EMOTIONAL RESCUE. / DOWN IN THE HOLE** [9] [3]

Jul 80. (lp)(c) **EMOTIONAL RESCUE** [1] [1]
– Dance (pt.1) / Summer romance / Send it to me / Let me go / Indian girl / Where the boys go / Down in the hole / Emotional rescue / She's so cold / All about you. *(re-iss.+cd.Nov89 on 'CBS' UK/US) (re-iss.cd+c Aug94 on 'Virgin')*

Sep 80. (7") **SHE'S SO COLD. / SEND IT TO ME** [33] [26]

Mar 81. (lp)(c) **SUCKING IN THE 70'S** (comp. + new) [ ] [15]
– Shattered / Everything is turning to gold / Hot stuff / Time waits for no one / Fool to cry / Mannish boy / When the whip comes down (live) / I was a dancer (part 2) / Crazy mama / Beast of burden. *(re-iss.+cd.Nov89 on 'CBS' UK/US)*

Aug 81. (7") **START ME UP. / NO USE IN CRYING** [7] [2]

Sep 81. (lp)(c) **TATTOO YOU** [2] [1]
– Start me up / Hang fire / Slave / Little T & A / Black limousine / Neighbours / Worried about you / Tops / Heaven / No use in crying / Waiting on a friend. *(re-iss.+cd.Nov89 on 'CBS' UK/US) (re-iss.cd+c Aug94 on 'Virgin')*

Nov 81. (7") **WAITING ON A FRIEND. / LITTLE T & A** [50] [13]

Mar 82. (7") **HANG FIRE. / NEIGHBORS** [-] [20]

Jun 82. (7") **GOING TO A GO-GO (live). / BEAST OF BURDEN (live)** [26] [25]

Jun 82. (lp)(c)(pic-lp) **STILL LIFE (AMERICAN CONCERTS 1981)** [4] [5]
– Under my thumb / Let's spend the night together / Shattered / Twenty flight rock / Going to a go-go / Let me go / Time is on my side / Just my imagination / Start me up / (I can't get no) Satisfaction / Take the A train / Star-spangled banner. *(re-iss.+cd.Nov89 on 'CBS' UK/US)*

Sep 82. (7") **TIME IS ON MY SIDE (live). / TWENTY FLIGHT ROCK (live)** [ ] [ ]
(12"+=) – Under my thumb (live).

Nov 83. (7") **UNDERCOVER OF THE NIGHT. / ALL THE WAY DOWN** [11] [9]
(12"+=) – Feel on baby (instrumental dub).

Nov 83. (lp)(c)(cd) **UNDERCOVER** [3] [4]
– Undercover of the night / She was hot / Tie you up / Wanna hold you / Feel on baby / Too much blood / Pretty beat up / Too tough / All the way down / It must be hell. *(re-iss.Apr86) (re-iss.all.Nov89 on 'CBS' UK/US) (re-iss.cd+c Aug94 on 'Virgin')*

Jan 84. (7") **SHE WAS HOT. / I THINK I'M GOING MAD** [42] [44]
(12"pic-d+=) – ('A'extended).

Jul 84. (lp)(c)(cd) **REWIND 1971-1984 (THE BEST OF THE ROLLING STONES)** (compilation) [23] [86]
– Brown sugar / Undercover of the night / Start me up / Tumbling dice / It's only rock'n'roll (but I like it) / She's so cold / Hang fire / Miss you / Beast of burden / Fool to cry / Waiting on a friend / Angie / Emotional rescue. (cd+= 2 extra) *(re-iss. all Nov89 on 'CBS' UK/US)*

— In 1984, JAGGER guested dual vocals w / MICHAEL JACKSON on The JACKSONS' 'State Of Shock'. He also recorded debut solo album 'She's The Boss', which was released 1985. Later mid'85, he appeared at LIVE AID with DAVID BOWIE duetting on (Martha & The Vandellas) song 'DANCING IN THE STREET'. When issued as a charity single, it made UK No.1 / US No.7 (see BOWIE ⇒).

— 12th Dec'85, IAN STEWART their long-serving 6th member died of a heart attack.

C.B.S. Columbia

Mar 86. (7") **HARLEM SHUFFLE. / HAD IT WITH YOU** [13] [5]
(12"+=)/ /(12"+=) – ('A'-London mix)./ / ('A'-New York mix).

Mar 86. (lp)(c)(cd) **DIRTY WORK** [4] [4]
– One hit (to the body) / Fight / Harlem shuffle / Hold back / Too rude / Winning ugly / Back to zero / Dirty work / Had it with you / Sleep tonight. *(re-iss.all.Nov89 on 'CBS' UK/US) (re-iss.cd+c Aug94 on 'Virgin')*

May 86. (7") **ONE HIT (TO THE BODY). / FIGHT** [ ] [28]
(12") – ('A'London mix) / ('B'side)

— During this lull in group activity, JAGGER and RICHARDS ventured solo amidst rumours of disbandment. In 1989, they re-surfaced.

Aug 89. (7") **MIXED EMOTIONS. / FANCY MAN'S BLUES** [36] [5]
(12"+=)(c-s+=) – ('A'remixed version).
(cd-s+=) – Tumbling dice / Miss you.
(cd-s+=) – Shattered / Waiting on a friend.

Sep 89. (lp)(c)(cd) **STEEL WHEELS** [2] [3]
– Sad sad sad / Mixed emotions / Terrifying / Hold on to your hat / Hearts for sale / Blinded by love / Rock and a hard place / Can't be seen / Almost hear you sigh / Continental drift / Break the spell / Slipping away. *(cd re-iss.Dec92) (re-iss.cd+c Aug94 on 'Virgin')*

Nov 89. (7") **ROCK AND A HARD PLACE. / COOK COOK BLUES** [63] [23]
(12")(c-s) – ('A'dance mix) / ('A'dub mix) / ('B'side).
('A'mixed-cd-s+=) – Emotional rescue / Some girls.
(12") – ('A'side) / ('A'Michael Brauer mix) / ('A'dub).

Jun 90. (7") **ALMOST HEAR YOU SIGH. / BREAK THE SPELL** [-] [50]

Jun 90. (7") **ALMOST HEAR YOU SIGH. / WISH I'D NEVER MET YOU** [31] [-]
(c-s+=) – Mixed emotions.
(cd-s+=) – Miss you / Waiting on a friend.
(12")(cd-s) – ('A'side) / Beast of burden / Angie / Fool to cry.

Aug 90. (7")(c-s) **TERRIFYING (remix). / ROCK AND A HARD PLACE (remix)** [ ] [ ]
(cd-s+=) – ('A'-12"remix) / Harlem shuffle.
('A'diff.remix/'B'dance mixed 12"+=) – Harlem shuffle (London mix).
(cd-s) – ('A'side) / Start me up / Shattered / If you can't rock me.

Mar 91. (7")(c-s) **HIGH WIRE. / 2,000 LIGHT YEARS FROM HOME (live)** [29] [57]
(12"+=)(cd-s+=) – Sympathy for the Devil / I just want to make love to you (both live).
(cd-s+=) – Light my fire / Factory girl (both live).

Apr 91. (cd)(c)(lp) **FLASHPOINT (live)** [6] [16]
– Start me up / Sad sad girl / Miss you / Ruby Tuesday / Tou can't always get what you want / Factory girl / Little red rooster / Paint it black / Sympathy for the Devil / Brown sugar / Jumpin' Jack Flash / (I can't get no) Satisfaction / Sexdrive (studio) / High wire (studio). (cd+=) – Rock and a hard place / Can't be seen. *(cd re-iss.Dec92)*

May 91. (7")(c-s) **RUBY TUESDAY (live). / PLAY WITH FIRE (live)** [59] [ ]
(12"+=)(cd-s+=) – You can't always get what you want / Rock and a hard place (both live).
(cd-s+=) – Harlem shuffle / Winning ugly VI (mix).

— In Nov'91, The STONES signed to 'Virgin', and BILL WYMAN soon quit.

Virgin Virgin

Nov 93. (cd)(c)(d-lp) **JUMP BACK: THE BEST OF THE ROLLING STONES 1971-1993** (compilation) [16] [ ]
– Start me up / Brown sugar / Harlem shuffle / It's only rock'n'roll (but I like it) / Mixed emotions / Angie / Tumbling dice / Fool to cry / Rock and a hard place / Miss you / Hot stuff / Emotional rescue / Respectable / Beast of burden / Waiting on a friend / Wild horses / Bitch / Undercover of the night. *(re-iss.Oct94 & Jun95)*

— WYMAN replaced by sessioners **DARRYL JONES** – bass / **CHUCK LEAVELL** – piano

Virgin Virgin

Jul 94. (7")(c-s) **LOVE IS STRONG. / ('A'mix)** [14] [93]
(cd-s+=) – The storm / So strong.

Jul 94. (cd)(c)(d-lp) **VOODOO LOUNGE** [1] [2]
– Love is strong / You got me rocking / Sparks will fly / The worst / New faces / Moon is up / Out of tears / I go wild / Brand new car / Sweethearts together / Suck on the jugular / Blinded by rainbows / Baby break it down / Thru and thru. *(re-iss.Jun95)*

Oct 94. (7")(c-s) **YOU GOT ME ROCKING. / JUMP ON TOP OF ME** [23] [ ]
(12"+=)(cd-s+=) – (2 'A'mixes).

Dec 94. (7")(c-s) **OUT OF TEARS. / I'M GONNA DRIVE** [38] [60] Oct94
(cd-s+=)/ /(cd-s+=) – ('A'mix). / / Sparks will fly.

Jul 95. (7")(c-s) **I GO WILD. / ('A'-Scott Litt remix)** [29] [ ]
(cd-s+=) – ('A'version) / ('A'-Luis Resto straight vocal mix).

Nov 95. (c-s) **LIKE A ROLLING STONE / BLACK LIMOUSINE / ALL DOWN THE LINE** [12] [ ]
(cd-s+=) – ('A'edit).

Nov 95. (cd)(c)(d-lp) **STRIPPED (live)** [9] [9]
– Street fighting man / Like a rolling stone / Not fade away / Shine a light / The spider and the fly / I'm free / Wild horses / Let it bleed / Dead flowers / Slipping away / Angie / Love in vain / Sweet Virginia / Little baby.

– other compilations, etc. –

Below releases issued on 'Decca' UK/ 'Abkco' US unless mentioned.

Jan 64. (7"ep) **THE ROLLING STONES** [ ] [-]
– Bye bye Johnny / Money / You better move on / Poison Ivy. *(re-iss.Mar82) (12"ep-iss.Dec83)*

Aug 64. (7"ep) **5 X 5** [ ] [-]
– If you need me / Empty heart / 2120 South Michegan Avenue / Confessin' the blues / Around and around. *(re-iss.Mar82) (12"ep-iss.Dec83)*

Jun 65. (7"ep) **GOT LIVE IF YOU WANT IT (live)** [ ] [-]
– We want the Stones / Everybody needs somebody to love / Pain in my heart / Route

66 / I'm moving on / I'm alright. *(re-iss.Mar82) (12"ep-iss.Dec83)*
Jul 71. (7") **STREET FIGHTING MAN. / SURPRISE SURPRISE** [21] [-]
Aug 71. (lp)(c) **GIMME SHELTER** [19] [-]
Jan 72. (d-lp)(c) **HOT ROCKS 1964-1971** [-] [4]
(UK cd-iss.1983 on 'Decca', re-iss.all Jul90) (US cd-iss.1989 on 'Abko') (hit UK 66 Oct93) (re-iss.cd/c/d-lp Jun95 on 'London')
Feb 72. (lp)(c) **MILESTONES** [14] [-]
Jun 72. (7") **EVERYBODY NEEDS SOMEBODY TO LOVE. / SURPRISE SURPRISE** [ ] [-]
Nov 72. (lp)(c) **ROCK'N'ROLLING STONES** [41] [-]
Dec 72. (lp)(c) **MORE HOT ROCKS (BIG HITS & FAZED COOKIES)** [-] [9]
(UK re+cd-iss.Aug88 + Nov90 + Jun95 on 'London')
Apr 73. (7") **YOU CAN'T ALWAYS GET WHAT YOU WANT. / SAD DAY** [ ] [42]
Oct 73. (lp)(c) **NO STONE UNTURNED** [ ] [-]
May 75. (7") **I DON'T KNOW WHY. / TRY A LITTLE HARDER** [ ] [42]
Jun 75. (lp)(c) **METAMORPHISIS** (early demos) [45] [8]
Sep 75. (7") **OUT OF TIME. / JIVING SISTER FANNY** [45] [81]
Nov 75. (d-lp)(d-c) **ROLLED GOLD – (THE VERY BEST OF THE ROLLING STONES)** [7] [-]
– Come on / I wanna be your man / Not fade away / Carol / It's all over now / Little red rooster / Time is on my side / The last time / (I can't get no) Satisfaction / Get off my cloud / 19th nervous breakdown / As tears go by / Under my thumb / Lady Jane / Out of time / Paint it black / Have you seen your mother baby, standing in the shadows? / Let's spend the night together / Ruby Tuesday / Yesterday's papers / We love you / She's a rainbow / Jumpin' Jack Flash / Honky tonk women / Sympathy for the Devil / Street fighting man / Midnight rambler / Gimme shelter.
Apr 76. (7") **HONKY TONK WOMAN. / SYMPATHY FOR THE DEVIL** [ ] [-]
(re-iss.Mar82)
Oct 77. (lp)(c) **GET STONED** [13] [-]
Aug 80. (12x7"box) **BOXED SET SINGLES 1963-1969** [ ] [ ]
COME ON. / I WANNA BE YOUR MAN // **IT'S ALL OVER NOW. / I WANT TO BE LOVED // (I CAN'T GET NO) SATISFACTION. / LITTLE BY LITTLE // NOT FADE AWAY. / LITTLE RED ROOSTER // THE LAST TIME. / PAINT IT BLACK // GET OFF OF MY CLOUD. / PLAY WITH FIRE // JUMPIN' JACK FLASH. / AS TEARS GO BY // 19th NERVOUS BREAKDOWN. / HAVE YOU SEEN YOUR MOTHER BABY, STANDING IN THE SHADOWS? // LET'S SPEND THE NIGHT TOGETHER. / YOU CAN'T ALWAYS GET WHAT YOU WANT // HONKY TONK WOMAN. / RUBY TUESDAY STREET FIGHTING MAN. / OUT OF TIME // SYMPATHY FOR THE DEVIL. / GIMME SHELTER**
Oct 80. (lp)(c) **SOLID ROCK** [ ] [-]
Nov 81. (lp)(c) **SLOW ROCKERS** [ ] [-]
Jan 86. (d-cd-box) **HOT ROCKS 1 & 2** [ ] [-] 1985
Sep 89. (d-lp)(d-c)(d-cd) **SINGLES COLLECTION: THE LONDON YEARS** [-] [91]
(on 'Abkco' US) (re-iss.Jun95)
Jun 90. (7") **PAINT IT BLACK / HONKY TONK WOMAN** [61] [-]
Jan 74. Atlantic; (7") **BROWN SUGAR. / HAPPY / ROCKS OFF** [ ] [-]
May 79. Rolling Stones; (lp)(c) **TIME WAITS FOR NO ONE** [ ] [-]
Jul 82. Decca Holland; (lp)(c) **IN CONCERT (live)** [94] [-]
Jul 84. Rolling Stones; (7")(7"pic-d) **BROWN SUGAR. / BITCH** [58] [-]
Oct 82. K-Tel; (d-lp)(d-c) **THE STORY OF THE STONES** [24] [-]
Jul 90. Columbia; (cd) **COLLECTOR'S EDITION** [ ] [ ]
Mar 92. Circus; (cd)(c)(lp)(video) **LIVE AT THE HOLLYWOOD PALLADIUM DECEMBER 15, 1988 (live)** [ ] [ ]

– solo releases –

MICK JAGGER

(see also other Nov70 ⇒)

C.B.S. Columbia
Feb 85. (7") **JUST ANOTHER NIGHT. / TURN THE GIRL LOOSE** [32] [12]
('A'extended-12"+=) – ('A'dub version).
Mar 85. (lp)(c)(cd) **SHE'S THE BOSS** [6] [13]
– Lonely at the top / Half a loaf / Hard woman / Lucky in love / Secrets / Just another night / She's the boss / Running out of luck / Turn the girl loose. *(re-iss.cd Aug95 on 'WEA')*
Apr 85. (7")(12") **LUCKY IN LOVE. / RUNNING OUT OF LUCK** [ ] [38]
Jul 86. (7") **RUTHLESS PEOPLE. / I'M RINGING** [-] [51]
—— (above from the film 'Ruthless People', issued on 'Epic' records)
Aug 87. (7") **LET'S WORK. / CATCH US IF YOU CAN** [31] [39]
(12"+=) – ('A'dance mix).
Sep 87. (lp)(c)(cd) **PRIMITIVE COOL** [26] [41]
– Throwaway / Peace for the wicked / Say you will / Primitive cool / Kow Tow / Shoot off your mouth / Party doll / War baby. *(re-iss.cd Aug95 on 'WEA')*
Nov 87. (7")(7"pic-d) **THROWAWAY. / PEACE FOR THE WICKED** [ ] [67]
('A'remixed-12"+=)(cd-s+=) – ('A'vocal dub mix).
Feb 88. (7") **SAY YOU WILL. / SHOOT OFF YOUR MOUTH** [-] [ ]
Atlantic Epic
Jan 93. (7")(c-s) **SWEET THING. / WANDERING SPIRIT** [24] [84]
(12"+=)(cd-s+=) – ('A'dub mix).
Feb 93. (cd)(c)(lp) **WANDERING SPIRIT** [12] [11]
– Wired all night / Sweet thing / Out of focus / Don't tear me up / Put me in the trash / Use me / Evening gown / Mother of a man / think / Wandering spirit / Hang on to me tonight / I've been lonely for so long / Angel in my heart / Handsome Molly. *(re-iss.cd Aug95 on 'WEA')*
Apr 93. (7")(c-s) **DON'T TEAR ME UP. / EVERYBODY KNOWS ABOUT MY GOOD THING** [ ] [ ]
(12"+=)(cd-s+=) – Sweet thing (funky guitar edit).
Jul 93. (7")(12")(c-s)(cd-s) **OUT OF FOCUS. / HIPGRASS** [ ] [ ]

KEITH RICHARDS

(covers 'A'side= Chuck Berry / 'B'= Jimmy Cliff)

Rolling St. Rolling St.
Nov 78. (7") **RUN RUDOLPH RUN. / THE HARDER THEY COME** [ ] [ ]
C.B.S. Virgin
Oct 88. (lp)(c)(cd) **TALK IS CHEAP** [37] [24]
– Talk is cheap / Take it so hard / Struggle / I could have stood you up / Make no mistake / You don't move me / It means a lot / Whip it up / How I wish / Rock awhile / Locked away. (re-iss.Sep90 on 'Virgin')
Oct 88. (7") **TAKE IT SO HARD. / I COULD HAVE STOOD YOU UP** [ ] [ ]
(12"+=)(cd-s+=) – It means a lot.
Apr 89. (7") **MAKE NO MISTAKE. / IT MEANS A LOT** [ ] [ ]
(12"+=)(cd-s+=) – ('A'extended).
Virgin Virgin
Nov 91. (cd)(c)(lp) **KEITH RICHARDS AND THE X-PENSIVE WINOS LIVE AT THE HOLLYWOOD, PALLADIUM, DECEMBER 15, 1988 (live)** [ ] [ ]
– Take it so hard / How I wish / I could have stood you up / Too rude / Make no mistake / Time is on my side / Big enough / Whip it up / Locked away / Struggle / Happy / Connection / Rockawhile.
Oct 92. (cd)(c)(lp) **MAIN OFFENDER** [45] [99]
– 999 / Wicked as it seems / Eileen / Words of wonder / Yap yap / Bodytalks / Hate it when you leave / Runnin' too deep / Will but you don't / Demon.
RICHARDS writes with JORDAN and some with WACHTEL.

BILL WYMAN

solo (see also 1967 R.S. releases)

Rolling St. Rolling St.
May 74. (lp)(c) **MONKEY GRIP** [39] [99]
– I wanna get me a gun / Crazy woman / Pussy / Mighty fine time / Monkey grip glue / What a blow / White lightnin' / I'll pull you thro' / It's a wonder.
– *(US iss.quad !)*
Jun 74. (7") **MONKEY GRIP GLUE. / WHAT A BLOW** [ ] [ ]
Nov 74. (7") **WHITE LIGHTNIN'. / PUSSY** [ ] [ ]
Feb 76. (lp)(c) **STONE ALONE** [ ] [ ]
– A quarter to three / Gimme just one chance / Soul satisfying / Apache woman / Every sixty seconds / Get it on / Feet / Peanut butter time / Wime and wimmen / If you wanna be happy / What's the point / No more foolin'.
Apr 76. (7") **A QUARTER TO THREE. / SOUL SATISFYING** [ ] [ ]
Sep 76. (7") **APACHE WOMAN. / SOUL SATISFYING** [ ] [ ]
A & M A & M
Jul 81. (7") **(SI SI) JE SUIS UN ROCK STAR. / RIO DE JANEIRO** [14] [ ]
Oct 81. (7") **COME BACK SUZANNE. / SEVENTEEN** [ ] [ ]
Mar 82. (7") **A NEW FASHION. / GIRLS** [37] [ ]
Apr 82. (lp)(c)(pic-lp) **BILL WYMAN** [55] [ ]
– Ride on baby / A new fashion / Nuclear reactions / Jump up / Come back Suzanne / (Si si) Je suis en rock star / Visions / Seventeen / Rio de Janeiro / Girls.
May 82. (7") **VISIONS. / NUCLEAR REACTION** [ ] [ ]
—— (next from film 'GREEN ICE' for which he provided the soundtrack)
Polydor Polydor
Jun 82. (7") **GREEN ICE THEME. / COULD HOPPERS** [ ] [ ]
—— BILL also recorded live jamming lp's with BUDDY GUY and JUNIOR WELLS. Alongside CHARLIE WATTS & FRIENDS, they released an album 'WILLIE & THE POOR BOYS' (May86). From it was taken single THESE ARMS OF MINE. / POOR BOY BOOGIE.
CHARLIE WATTS formed **ROCKET 88**, who released one eponymous lp Jan '81 on 'Atlantic'.

CHARLIE WATTS & FRIENDS

released lp (Dec86) on CBS **LIVE AT THE FULHAM TOWN HALL**.
In 1991, his quintet issued 10"lp,c,cd **FROM ONE CHARLIE** (which was on 'UFO Jazz').

RON WOOD

solo (74-75; while still with The FACES)

Warners Warners
Sep 74. (lp)(c) **I'VE GOT MY OWN ALBUM TO DO** [ ] [ ]
– I can feel the fire / Far east man / Mystifies me / Take a look at the guy / Act together / Am I grooving you / Shirley / Cancel everything / Sure the one you need / If you gotta make a fool of somebody / Crutch music. *(re-iss.Oct85 as 'CANCEL EVERYTHING' on 'Thunderbolt', cd-iss.Jun87, pic-lp iss.1989) (cd-iss.Sep94)*
Nov 74. (7") **I CAN FEEL THE FIRE. / BREATHE ON ME** [ ] [ ]
Jul 75. (lp)(c) **NOW LOOK** [ ] [ ]
– I got lost when I found you / Big bayou / Breathe on me / If you don't want my love for you / I can say she's alright / Caribbean boogie / Now look / Sweet baby of mine / I can't stand the rain / It's unholy / I got a feeling. *(re-iss. +cd.Nov87 on 'Thunderbolt', pic-lp iss.1989) (cd-iss.Sep94)*
Oct 75. (7") **IF YOU DON'T WANT MY LOVE. / I GOT A FEELING** [ ] [ ]
Jan 76. (7") **BIG BAYOU. / SWEET BABY MINE** [ ] [ ]
Atlantic Atlantic
Sep 76. (lp)(c) **MAHONEY'S LAST STAND ("RONNIE WOOD & RONNIE LANE")** [ ] [ ]
– Tonight's number / From the late to the early / Chicken wired / I'll fly away / Title one / Just for a momoent / Mons the blues / Car radio / Hay tumble / Wooly's thing / Rooster funeral. *(re-iss.+cd.Dec88 on 'Thunderbolt', pic-lp May89)*
C.B.S. Columbia
May 79. (lp)(c) **GIMME SOME NECK** [ ] [45]
– Worry no more / Breaking my heart / Delia / Buried alive / Come to realise / Infekshun / Seven days / We all get old / F.U.C. her / Lost and lonely / Don't worry.
Aug 79. (7") **SEVEN DAYS. / COME TO REALISE** [ ] [ ]
Nov 81. (lp)(c) **1, 2, 3, 4** [ ] [ ]
– Fountain of love / 1, 2, 3, 4 / Outlaws / Down to the ground / Wind howlin' through / She never told me / Red eyes / Priceless / She was out there. *(re-iss.d-lp+d-cd.May90*

on 'Castle', incl+= GIMME SOME NECK) (cd-iss.Apr93 on 'Sony Europe')

— Nov 90, had both his legs broken in a car accident.

RONNIE WOOD

w/ **BERNARD FOWLER** – vocals, co-producer / **JOHNNY LEE SCHELL** – guitars / **WAYNE P. SHEEKY** – drums / **SHAWN SOLOMON** – bass / **IAN McLAGEN** – keyboards / plus **CHUCK LEAVELL** – additional keyboards

Continuum Continuum

Aug 92. (cd-s) **SHOW ME. / BREATHE ON ME**

Mar 93. (cd-s) **SOMEBODY ELSE MIGHT (slidin' on this mix). / AIN'T ROCK & ROLL**

Sep 93. (12")(cd-s) **STAY WITH ME. / JOSEPHINE / SOMEBODY ELSE MIGHT (remix)**

Nov 93. (cd)(c) **SLIDE ON LIVE – PLUGGED IN AND STANDING (live)**
– Testify / Josephine / Pretty beat up / Am I groovin' you? / Flying / Breathe on me / Silicon grown / Seven days / Show me & show me (groove) / Ican feel the fire / Around the plinth / Gasoline alley / Traditional / Stay with me.

Henry ROLLINS

Born: HENRY GARFIELD, 13 Feb '61, Washington DC, USA. (see BLACK FLAG) After several albums released during the late 80's, he (ROLLINS BAND) broke through into UK charts 1992 with 'THE END OF THE SILENCE!' • **Style:** Aggressive but intelligent hard man of rock, playing hard core punk, curbed by anti-establishment talk/comedy gigs. • **Songwriters:** Writes own work except; EX-LION TAMER (Wire) / DO IT (Pink Fairies) / LET THERE BE ROCK (Ac-Dc) / FRANKLIN'S TOWER (Grateful Dead). • **Trivia:** A few lp's are spoken word/poetry and offensively straight to the point.

Recommended: END OF SILENCE (*7)

HENRY ROLLINS – vocals (ex-BLACK FLAG, ex-SOA) / with **CHRIS HASKETT** (b. Leeds, England) – guitar (ex-SURFIN' DAVE) / **BERNIE WANDEL** – bass / **MICK GREEN** – drums

Fundamental Fundamental

Jul 87. (lp)(cd) **HOT ANIMAL MACHINE**
– Black and white / Followed around / Lost and found / There's a man outside / Crazy lover / A man and a woman / Hot animal machine I / Ghost rider / Move right in / Hot animal machine 2 / No one. *(re-iss.cd Mar94 on 'Intercord')*

Sep 87. (m-lp) **DRIVE BY SHOOTING (as "HENRIETTA ROLLINS & THE WIFE-BEATING CHILD HATERS")**
– Drive by shooting (watch out for that pig) / Ex-lion tamer / Hey Henriezza / Can you speak this? / I have come to kill you / Men are pigs.

HENRY ROLLINS BAND

retained **HASKETT** and recruited **ANDREW WEISS** – bass / **SIMEON CAIN** – drums

Sep 88. (lp)(cd) **LIFE TIME**
– Burned beyond recognition / What am I doing here / 1000 times blind / Lonely / Wreck-age / Gun in mouth blues / You look at you / If you're alive / Turned out. *(cd+=)*– What am I doing here? / Burned beyond recognition / Move right in / Hot animal machine 2. *(re-iss.cd Mar94 on 'Intercord')*

World Service World Service

Mar 89. (lp) **OVER**
– (cd-iss.+= Joyriding with Frank (30 minutes live))

Nov 89. (lp)(cd) **HARD VOLUME**
– Hard / What have I got / I feel like this / Planet Joe / Love song / Turned inside out / Down and away / Joyriding with Frank. *(re-iss.cd Mar94 on 'Intercord')*

ROLLINS BAND

Touch & Go Touch & Go

Nov 90. (cd)(lp) **TURNED ON (live '89)**
– Lonely / Do it / What have I got / Tearing / Out there / You didn't need / Hard // Followed around / Mask / Down & away / Turned inside out / The Dietmar song / Black & white / What do you do / Crazy lover.

HENRY ROLLINS & THE HARD-ONS

(Australian back-up)

Vinyl Sol. Touch & Go

Jul 91. (12")(cd-s) **LET THERE BE ROCK. / CARRY ME DOWN**

ROLLINS BAND

retained same band.

Imago-RCA Imago-RCA

Feb 92. (12") **LOW SELF OPINION. / LIE, LIE, LIE**

Feb 92. (cd)(c)(lp) **THE END OF SILENCE**
– The end of silence / Grip / Tearing / You didn't need / Almost real / Obscene / What do you do? / Blues jam / Another life / Just like you.

Aug 92. (7") **TEARING. / EARACHE IN MY EYE (live)** 54
(12"+=)(cd-s+=) – (There'll be no) Next time / Ghost rider.

Jan 93. (2xcd-box,2xc-box) **BOXED LIFE**

— In early '94, he acted in the film 'The Chase', and was about to be seen in 'Johnny Mnemonic'.

— **MELVIN GIBBS** – bass repl. HASKINS who left in 1993.

Apr 94. (cd)(c)(clear-lp) **WEIGHT** 22 33
– Disconnect / Fool / Icon / Civilized / Divine object of hatred / Liar / Step back / Wrong man / Volume 4 / Tired / Alien blueprint / Shine.

Aug 94. (7")(c-s) **LIAR. / DISCONNECT** 27
(cd-s+=) – Right here too much / Nightsweat.

– others, imports, etc. –

Eksakt not issued

Oct 87. Eksakt Dutch; (lp) **HENRY ROLLINS LIVE / GORE LIVE** - -

Dec 87. Texas Hotel; (lp) **BIG UGLY MOUTH (spoken word live Feb'87)** -
(UK-cd-iss.Mar93)

Apr 89. Texas Hotel; (lp-box) **SWEAT BOX** -
(UK-cd-iss.Mar93)

1989. Texas Hotel; (lp)(cd) **DO IT** -
– Do it / Move light in / Next time / Joe is everything, everything is Joe / Black and white / Lost and found / Followed around / Wreck age / Lonely / Hot animal machine £1 / You look at you / Gun in mouth blues / Turned out / Thousand times blind / No one. *(re-iss.cd Mar94 on 'Intercord')*

1992. 1/4 Stick/ US= Touch & Go; (lp-box) **DEEP THROAT**

Mar 93. 1/4 Stick/ US= Touch & Go; (cd) **LIVE AT McCABES**

Mar 93. 1/4 Stick/ US= Touch & Go; (cd) **HUMAN BUTT**

Nov 94. Imago; (cd)(c) **HENRY: PORTRAIT OF A SINGER SINGER** (spoken word)

Nov 94. Imago; (cd)(c) **GET IN THE VAN** (life on the road with BLACK FLAG)

RONETTES

Formed: 1961, New York, USA . . . by sisters VERONICA and ESTELLE BENNETT with cousin NEDRA TALLEY. In 1961, they broke through after appearing in dance film 'Twist Around The Clock' as The DOLLY SISTERS. Their dance routines were seen by Murray K, who invited them to become regulars in his stage shows. The next two years saw little success, until they met PHIL SPECTOR who guided them to superstardom. The 1963 songs 'BE MY BABY' & 'BABY I LOVE YOU' became massive hits and future classics. By the mid-60's, their fame was over, and RONNIE married PHIL, although this only lasted 'til '74. **Style & Songwriters:** Classic all-girl singing group created by PHIL SPECTOR's 'Wall Of Sound' production technique. He also co-wrote many of their songs. TRY SOME, BUY SOME was written by GEORGE HARRISON. • **Trivia:** Supported The ROLLING STONES early 1964 on their UK tour.

Recommended: THE BEST OF THE RONETTES (*6)

VERONICA 'Ronnie' BENNETT (b.10 Aug'43) – lead vocals / **ESTELLE BENNETT** (b.22 Jul'44) + **NEDRA TALLEY** (b.27 Jan'46) – vocals

RONNIE & THE RELATIVES

not issued Colpix

Jul 61. (7") **I WANT A BOY. / SWEET 16** -

The RONETTES

not issued May

Jan 62. (7") **I'M GONNA QUIT WHILE I'M AHEAD. / I'M ON THE WAGON** -

Feb 62. (7") **MY GUIDING ANGEL. / I'M GONNA QUIT WHILE I'M AHEAD** -

Apr 62. (7") **SILHOUETTES. / YOU BET I WOULD** -

Aug 62. (7") **GOOD GIRLS. / MEMORIES** -

not issued Dimension

1962. (7") **RECIPE FOR LOVE. / HE DID IT** -

London Philles

Oct 63. (7") **BE MY BABY. / TEDESCO AND PITMAN** 4 2 Aug 63

Jan 64. (7") **BABY I LOVE YOU. / MISS JOAN AND MR.SAM** 11 24 Dec 63

In Apr'64, RONNIE BENNETT issued single 'SO YOUNG' on 'Phil Spector' label.

Jul 64. (7") **(THE BEST PART OF) BREAKIN' UP. / BIG RED** 43 39 Mar 64

Jul 64. (7") **DO I LOVE YOU?. / BEBE & SUSAN** - 34

Sep 64. (7") **DO I LOVE YOU?. / WHEN I SAW YOU** 35 -

Nov 64. (7") **(WALKING) IN THE RAIN. / HOW DOES IT FEEL?** 23 Oct 64

Feb 65. (7") **BORN TO BE TOGETHER. / BLUES FOR BABY** 52 Jan 65

May 65. (lp) **(PRESENTING) THE FABULOUS RONETTES (FEATURING VERONICA)** 96 Nov 64
– Walking in the rain / Do I love you / So young / Breakin' up / I wonder / What'd I say / Be my baby / Baby I love you / How does it feel / When I saw you / Chapel of love.

May 65. (7") **IS THIS WHAT I GET FOR LOVING YOU?. / OH, I LOVE YOU** - 75

Jul 65. (7") **IS THIS WHAT I GET FOR LOVING YOU?. / YOU BABY** -

— (Aug65) cousin **ELAINE BENNETT** – lead vocals repl. VERONICA who married PHIL SPECTOR

Oct 66. (7") **I CAN HEAR MUSIC. / WHEN I SAW YOU** - 100

— They split later in '66. ESTELLE and NEDRA quit music scene. Meanwhile RONNIE SPECTOR (aka VERONICA BENNETT) went solo as . . .

The RONETTES featuring The Voice of VERONICA

A & M A & M

Mar 69. (7") **YOU CAME, YOU SAW, YOU CONQUERED. / OH I LOVE YOU** -

Apr 69. (7") **YOU CAME, YOU SAW, YOU CONQUERED. / I CAN HEAR MUSIC** □ -

RONNIE SPECTOR

Apple Apple

Apr 71. (7") **TRY SOME, BUY SOME. / TANDOORI CHICKEN** □ □

— Her proposed album produced by PHIL and co-penned with GEORGE HARRISON is shelved. In '73,

RONNIE & THE RONETTES

re-form. **RONNIE** recruiting **DENISE EDWARDS + CHIP FIELDS** – vocals

Buddah Buddah

Nov 73. (7") **LOVER, LOVER. / GO OUT AND GET IT** □ □
May 74. (7") **I WISH I NEVER SAW THE SUNSHINE. / I WONDER WHAT HE'S DONE** □ □

RONNIE SPECTOR

(although it was actually The RONETTES). She was divorced from PHIL in 1973.

Warner-Spector Warner-Spector

1975. (7") **PARADISE. / WHEN I SAY YOU** □ □

— Late '76, RONNIE joined BRUCE SPRINGSTEEN & THE E-STREET SHUFFLE on tour.

RONNIE & THE RONETTES

Epic Epic

Apr 77. (7") **SAY GOODBYE TO HOLLYWOOD. / BABY PLEASE DON'T GO** □ □

RONNIE SPECTOR

not issued Tom Cat

1977. (7") **YOU'D BE GOOD FOR ME. / SOMETHING TELLS ME** - □

not issued Alston

1978. (7") **IT'S A HEARTACHE. / I WANNA COME OVER** □ □

Red Shadow Polish

Jan 81. (7") **DARLIN'. / TONIGHT** - □
Jan 81. (7") **DARLIN'. / SETTIN' THE WOODS ON FIRE** □ -
Jan 81. (lp) **SIREN** □ □
– Here today, gone tomorrow / Darlin' / Any way that you want me / Tonight / Boys will be boys / Hell of a nerve / Settin' the woods on fire / Let your feelings show / Dynamite / Happy birthday rock'n'roll.
Mar 81. (7") **HERE TODAY GONE TOMORROW. / HELL OF A NERVE** □ -

C.B.S. Columbia

Jun 87. (7")(12") **WHO CAN SLEEP. / WHEN WE DANCED** □ □
Jul 87. (lp)(c) **UNFINISHED BUSINESS** □ □
– Who can sleep / Love on a rooftop / Dangerous / Burning love / Unfinished business / (If I could) Walk away / Heart song / True to you / When we danced / Good love is hard to find.
1988. (7") **LOVE ON A ROOFTOP. / GOOD LOVE IS HARD TO FIND** - □

— In 1990, RONNIE disclosed untold events in her book 'Be My Baby'.

– (RONETTES) compilations, etc. –

Jun 65. Colpix; (lp) **THE RONETTES** - □
Jan 69. London; (7") **BE MY BABY. / BABY I LOVE YOU** □ -
1974. Phil Spector; (7"m) **FROSTY THE SNOWMAN. / (2 by CRYSTALS + ?)** □ -
(re-iss.Dec82)

Below releases issued on 'London' unless mentioned.

Jul 75. (7") **BE MY BABY. / OH, I LOVE YOU** □ -
Sep 75. (lp) **THE RONETTES SING THEIR GREATEST HITS** □ -
Oct 75. (7") **I'M A WOMAN IN LOVE. / WHEN I SAW YOU** - -
Mar 76. (7") **I CAN HEAR MUSIC. / HOW DOES IT FEEL** □ -
Jul 76. (7") **(WALKING) IN THE RAIN. / I WONDER** □ -
Nov 81. Polydor; (7") **DO I LOVE YOU. / (THE BEST PART OF) BREAKIN' UP** □ -

— Also featured on VOL.II of a multi-'Phil Spector' boxed set WALL OF SOUND.

Aug 87. Murray Hill; (lp) **THE COLPIX YEARS 1961-63** □ -
Aug 92. Sequel; (cd) **THE COLPIX AND BUDDAH YEARS** □ -
Oct 92. EMI; (cd)(c)(lp) **THE BEST OF THE RONETTES** □ □
– Be my baby / Why don't they let us fall in love / I wonder / Baby, I love you / (The best part of) Breakin' up / So young / When I saw you / Do I love you? / You baby / How does it feel? / WAlking in the rain / Born to be together / Is this what I get for loving you? / Paradise / Here I sit / I wish I never saw the sunshine / Everything under the Sun / You came, you saw, you conquered.

Mick RONSON

Born: 1947, Hull, England. Formed first band The RATS in 1964, but they were to disperse late the following year. Guitarist RONSON then went into sessions, noteably for 'Fully Qualified Survivor' MICHAEL CHAPMAN in 1969, before being first associated with BOWIE under group name HYPE. Alongside drummer WOODY WOODMANSEY on BOWIE's 'Man Who Sold The World', they soon became known as The SPIDERS FROM MARS, named after BOWIE's 1972 album 'Ziggy Stardust & The Spiders From Mars'. RONSON left for a solo career in 1974, after featuring on late 1973 album 'Bowie Pin-Ups'. Retained by MainMan productions & 'RCA' records, he issued solo debut 'SLAUGHTER ON 10th AVENUE'. In between his 1975 follow-up 'PLAY DON'T WORRY', he had a short spell with MOTT THE HOOPLE, who were shortly to disband. Their frontman IAN HUNTER, who MICK had also toured alongside, formed a partnership with him as HUNTER-RONSON BAND. For the next decade and a half, RONSON was his guitarist, with a dual album 'YUI ORTA' finally being issued in 1990. Years previous to this, MICK had played for BOB DYLAN on his ROLLING THUNDER REVUE of '75-76, where he met ROGER McGUINN of The BYRDS. MICK produced his 'Cardiff Rose' album soon after. He also went on to work in the late 70's for JOHN COUGAR (Chestnut Street Incident), RICH KIDS (Ghosts Of Princes In Towers) & DAVID JOHANSEN (In Style). After a relatively quiet 80's, he was back with IAN HUNTER, and went into a busy 1992 producing MORRISSEY (Your Arsenal), and guesting alongside old mates BOWIE and HUNTER at FREDDIE MERCURY's Wembley Tribute that April. Sadly it was known at the time, that MICK was suffering from cancer. He was to die on 29th April 1993, just after completing most of his long-awaited 3rd album, scheduled for 1994 release. • **Style:** Superb quality guitarist, at his height when with The SPIDERS. His solo work was worthy of note, although his songwriting and singing was questionable. • **Songwriters:** Self-penned except; LOVE ME TENDER (Elvis Presley) / THE GIRL CAN'T HELP IT (Little Richard) / WHITE LIGHT WHITE HEAT (Velvet Underground) / GROWING UP AND I'M FINE + MOONAGE DAYDREAM (live encore) (Bowie). The RATS covered; PARCHMAN FARM (Mose Allison) / EVERY DAY I HAVE THE BLUES (Arthur Alexander) / SPOONFUL (Willie Dixon) / I'VE GOTTA SEE MY BABY EVERYDAY (Chris Andrews). • **Trivia:** His sister MARGARET RONSON provided backing vocals for debut album. MICK's 80's production work was for The PAYOLAS and LOS ILLEGALS.

Recommended: SLAUGHTER ON 10th AVENUE (*6) / PLAY DON'T WORRY (*5)

RATS

MICK RONSON – guitar / + unknown

Oriole not issued

Nov 64. (7") **PARCHMAN FARM. / EVERY DAY I HAVE THE BLUES** □ -

— **WOODY WOODMANSEY** – drums repl. ? / (entire new members with RONSON)

Columbia not issued

Mar 65. (7") **SPOONFUL. / I'VE GOT MY EYES ON YOU BABY** □ -
Jun 65. (7") **I GOTTA SEE MY BABY EVERYDAY. / HEADIN' BACK (TO NEW ORLEANS)** □ -

— Disbanded. (see biography for BOWIE details, etc.)

RONNO

MICK RONSON – guitar / **BENNY MARSHALL** / etc.

Vertigo Vertigo

Jul 71. (7") **4th HOUR OF MY SLEEP. / POWERS OF DARKNESS** □ □

— He then played on BOWIE albums 'ZIGGY STARDUST', 'ALADDIN SANE' & 'PIN-UPS'.

MICK RONSON

solo with **AYNSLEY DUNBAR** – drums / **TREVOR BOLDER** – bass / **MIKE GARSON** – piano

R.C.A. R.C.A.

Jan 74. (7") **LOVE ME TENDER. / ONLY AFTER DARK** □ □
Mar 74. (lp)(c) **SLAUGHTER ON 10th AVENUE** 9 □
– Love me tender / Growing up and I'm fine / Only after dark / Music is lethal / I'm the one / Medley: Pleasure man – Hey ma get papa / Slaughter on 10th Avenue.
Apr 74. (7") **SLAUGHTER ON 10th AVENUE. / LEAVE MY HEART ALONE** □ □

— From Sep-Dec'74, RONSON joined MOTT THE HOOPLE, and featured on only one single 'SATURDAY GIGS'. He continued on already recorded 2nd solo album.

Feb 75. (7") **BILLY PORTER. / HAZY DAYS** □ □
Feb 75. (lp)(c) **PLAY DON'T WORRY** 29 □
– Billy Porter / Angel No.9 / This is for you / White light – white heat / Play don't worry / Hazy days / The girl can't help it / Empty bed (lo me ne andrail) / Woman.

— MICK lost contract, and went off to play for BOB DYLAN, IAN HUNTER, and produce many (see biography). In 1990 he was on record again with IAN HUNTER on album 'YUI ORTA'. (see under ⇒)

Epic Epic

Apr 94. (12"pic-d)(cd-s) **DON'T LOOK DOWN. / SLAUGHTER ON 10th AVENUE / BILLY PORTER / LOVE ME TENDER** 55 □

Above with JOE ELLIOTT of DEF LEPPARD on vocals.

May 94. (cd)(c)(lp) **FROM HEAVEN TO HULL** □ □
– Don't look down / Like a rolling stone / When the world falls down / Trouble with me / Life's a river / You and me / Colour me / Takes a long line / Midnight love / All the young dudes.

– compilations, etc. –

May 82. RCA Gold; (7") **BILLY PORTER. / SLAUGHTER ON 10th AVENUE** □ -
Sep 94. Trident; (d-cd) **ONLY AFTER DARK** □ □

Linda RONSTADT

Born: 15 Jul'46, Tucson, Arizona, USA. Raised by Mexican/German parents. In the mid-60's, she formed folk trio The STONE PONEYS, with guitarists BOB KIMMEL and KENNY EDWARDS. After appearing regularly at the Troubadour club in Los Angeles, they were signed to 'Capitol' by Herb Cohen. In 1968, they enjoyed Top 20 US hit with 'DIFFERENT DRUM', but they soon split in 1969, with LINDA staying on at Capitol as a solo artist. After 2 flop albums at the turn of the decade, they broke through with US Top 30 single 'LONG LONG TIME'. Early in 1975, she topped the American charts with 45 'YOU'RE NO GOOD', and album 'HEART LIKE A WHEEL'. • **Style:** Scrumptious country-rock/pop artist. • **Songwriters:** Owes much to other artists' material; DIFFERENT DRUM (Mike Nesmith) / I'LL BE YOU BABY TONIGHT (Bob Dylan) / SILVER THREADS AND GOLDEN NEEDLES (Springfields) / DESPERADO (Eagles) / YOU'RE NO GOOD (Betty Everett) / WHEN WILL I BE LOVED (Everly Brothers) / IT DOESN'T MATTER ANYMORE + THAT'LL BE THE DAY + IT'S SO EASY (Buddy Holly) / THE TRACKS OF MY TEARS (Miracles) / HEATWAVE (Martha & The Vandellas) / CRAZY (Patsy Cline) / SOMEONE TO LAY DOWN BESIDE ME (Karla Bonoff) / TUMBLING DICE (Rolling Stones) / BLUE BAYOU (Roy Orbison) / BACK IN THE USA (Chuck Berry) / LOVE ME TENDER (Elvis Presley) / OOH BABY BABY (Smokey Robinson) / JUST ONE LOOK (Doris Troy) / ALISON + GIRLS TALK (Elvis Costello) / HURT SO BAD (Little Anthony & The Imperials) / I KNEW YOU WHEN (Billy Joe Royal) / EASY FOR YOU TO SAY + SHATTERED (Jimmy Webb) / DON'T KNOW MUCH (Bill Medley) / WHEN SOMETHING IS WRONG WITH MY BABY (Sam & Dave) / FEELS LIKE HOME (Randy Newman) / AFTER THE GOLDRUSH (Neil Young) / THE WAITING (Tom Petty) / etc. She made standards albums WHAT'S NEW + LUSH LIFE + FOR SENTIMENTAL REASONS, plus a Spanish-sung Mexican trad.songs CANCIONES DE MI PADRE (MY FATHER'S SONGS). • **Trivia:** In 1980, she made her acting debut on stage production of 'The Pirates Of Penzance'. In 1983, she starred in the film version.

Recommended: GREATEST HITS (*6) / GREATEST HITS VOL.2 (*5).

The STONE PONEYS

featured **LINDA** – vocals / plus **BOB KIMMEL** – guitar / **+ KENNY EDWARDS** with sessioners / **BILLY MUNDI** – drums

not issued Sidewalk

1966. (7") **SO FINE. / EVERYBODY HAS THEIR OWN IDEAS** [-] [ ]

Capitol Capitol

Mar 67. (lp) **THE STONE PONEYS** [-] [ ]
– Sweet summer blue and gold / If I were you / Just a little bit of rain / Bicycle song (soon now) / Orion / Wild about my lovin' / Back home / Meredith (on my mind) / Train and the river / All the beautiful things / 2:10 train.

Mar 67. (7") **ALL THE BEAUTIFUL THINGS. / SWEET SUMMER BLUE AND GOLD** [-] [ ]

Jun 67. (7") **EVERGREEN. / ONE FOR ALL** [-] [ ]

—— She was now credited/billed with The STONE PONEYS.

Dec 67. (7") **DIFFERENT DRUM. / I'VE GOT TO KNOW** [ ] [13] Nov 67

Dec 67. (lp) **EVERGREEN VOLUME 2** [-] [100] Jun 67
– December dream / Song about the rain / Autumn afternoon / I've got to know / Evergreen (parts 1 & 2) / Different drum / Driftin' / One for one / Back on the street again / Toys in time / New hard times.

Feb 68. (7") **UP TO MY NECK IN MUDDY WATER. / CARNIVAL BEAR** [-] [93]

Apr 68. (lp) **LINDA RONSTADT, STONE PONEYS & FRIENDS: VOL 3** [-] [ ]
– Golden song / Merry-go-round / Love is a child / By the fruits of their labors / Hobo (morning glory) / Star and a stone / Let's stick together / Up to my neck in muddy water / Aren't you the one / Wings / Some of Shelly's blues / Stoney end.

May 68. (7") **SOME OF SHELLY'S BLUES / HOBO (MORNING GLORY)** [-] [ ]

—— When EDWARDS left, group fold.

LINDA RONSTADT

went solo, after she made a US Christmas 45 with the TURTLES.

Capitol Capitol

Apr 69. (lp) **HAND SOWN – HOME GROWN** [ ] [ ]
– Baby you've been on my mind / Silver threads and golden needles / Bet no one ever hurt this bad / A number and a name / The only mamma that'll walk the line / Break my mind / I'll be your baby tonight / It's about time / We need a lot more of Jesus (and a lot less of rock and roll) / The dolphins. *(US re-iss.1975)*

Apr 69. (7") **THE DOLPHINS. / THE WRONG WAY AROUND** [ ] [ ]

Oct 69. (7") **BABY YOU'VE BEEN ON MY MIND. / I'LL BE YOUR BABY TONIGHT** [ ] [ ]

Sep 70. (lp) **SILK PURSE** [ ] [ ]
– Lovesick blues / Are my thoughts with you? / Will you love me tomorrow? / Nobody's / Louise / Long long time / Mental revenge / I'm leaving it all up to you / He darkens the Sun / Life is like a mountain railway.

Sep 70. (7") **LONG LONG TIME. / NOBODY'S** [ ] [25] Aug70

Dec 70. (7") **WILL YOU LOVE ME TOMORROW?. / LOVESICK BLUES** [-] [ ]

Jan 71. (7") **(SHE'S A) VERY LOVELY WOMAN. / THE LONG WAY AROUND** [ ] [70]

—— She recruited tour/studio band of future EAGLES / **BERNIE LEADON** – guitar / **GLEN FREY** – guitar / **RANDY MEISNER** – bass / **DON HENLEY** – drums

Feb 72. (lp)(c) **LINDA RONSTADT** [ ] [ ]
– Rock me on the water / Crazy arms / I won't be hangin' around / I still miss someone / In my reply / I fall to pieces / Ramblin' round / Birds / Rescue me. *(re-iss.May82 on 'Fame')*

Apr 72. (7") **ROCK ME ON THE WATER. / CRAZY ARMS** [ ] [85] Feb 72

Apr 72. (7") **I FALL TO PIECES. / CAN IT BE TRUE?** [-] [ ]

(She now used numerous sessioners)

Asylum Asylum

Nov 73. (lp)(c) **DON'T CRY NOW** [ ] [45]
– I can almost see it / Love has no pride / Silver threads and golden needles / Desperado / Don't cry now / Sail away / Colorado / The fast one / Everybody loves a winner / I believe in you. *(re-iss.Jun76)*

Dec 73. (7") **LOVE HAS NO PRIDE. / I CAN ALMOST SEE IT** [-] [51]

Apr 74. (7") **SILVER THREADS AND GOLDEN NEEDLES. / DON'T CRY FOR NOW** [-] [67]

—— With PETE ASHER for the second time producing, she had to make contractual album for 'Capitol'. Augmented by **ANDREW GOLD** – guitar, keyboards, etc.

Dec 74. (7") **YOU'RE NO GOOD. / WHEN WILL I BE LOVED** [-] [1]

Jan 75. (lp)(c) **HEART LIKE A WHEEL** [ ] [1] Nov 74
– You're no good / It doesn't matter anymore / Faithless love / The dark end of the street / Heart like a wheel / When will I be loved / Willin' / I can't help it (if I'm still in love with you) / Keep me blowing away / You can close your eyes. *(re-iss.Dec86)*

Jan 75. (7") **YOU'RE NO GOOD. / I CAN'T HELP IT** [ ] [-]

Apr 75. (7") **WHEN WILL I BE LOVED. / IT DOESN'T MATTER ANYMORE** [ ] [2]

[47]

Asylum Asylum

Oct 75. (7") **HEAT WAVE. / LOVE IS A ROSE** [ ] [5]

[63]

Nov 75. (7") **SILVER BLUE. / LOVE IS A ROSE** [-] [ ]

Jan 76. (lp)(c) **PRISONER IN DISGUISE** [ ] [4] Sep 75
– Love is a rose / Hey mister, that's me up on the jukebox / Roll um easy / The tracks of my tears / Prisoner in disguise / Herat wave / Many rivers to cross / The sweetest gift / You tell me that I'm falling down / I will always love you / Silver blue.

Jan 76. (7") **THE TRACKS OF MY TEARS. / THE SWEETEST GIFT** [-] [25]

Mar 76. (7") **THE TRACKS OF MY TEARS. / PRISONER IN DISGUISE** [42] [-]

Aug 76. (lp)(c) **HASTEN DOWN THE WIND** [32] [3]
– Lose again / The tattler / If he's ever near / That'll be the day / Lo siento mi vida / Hasten down the wind / Rivers of Babylon / Give one heart / Try me again / Crazy / Down so low / Someone to lay down beside me. *(cd-iss.Sep89)*

Sep 76. (7") **THAT'LL BE THE DAY. / TRY ME AGAIN** [ ] [11] Aug 76

Oct 76. (7") **LOSE AGAIN. / LO SIENTO MI VIDA** [ ] [76] May77

Dec 76. (lp)(c) **GREATEST HITS** (compilation) [37] [6]
– You're no good / Silver threads and golden needles / Desperado / Love is a rose / That'll be the day / Long long time / Different drum / When will I be loved? / Love has no pride / Heat wave / It doesn't matter anymore / Tracks of my tears. *(cd-iss.1984)*

Feb 77. (7") **SOMEONE TO LAY DOWN BESIDE ME. / CRAZY** [ ] [42] Dec 76

Sep 77. (7") **BLUE BAYOU. / OLD PAINT** [-] [3]

Sep 77. (7") **POOR POOR PITIFUL ME. / OLD PAINT** [ ] [-]

Nov 77. (lp)(c) **SIMPLE DREAMS** [15] [1] Sep 77
– It's so easy / Carmelita / Simple man, simple dream / Sorrow lives here / I will never marry / Blue bayou / Poor poor pitiful me / Maybe I'm right / Tumbling dice / Old paint. *(cd-iss.Jan87)*

Nov 77. (7") **IT'S SO EASY. / SORROW LIVES HERE** [ ] [5] Oct 77

Jan 78. (7") **BLUE BAYOU. / MAYBE I'M RIGHT** [35] [-]

Feb 78. (7") **POOR POOR PITIFUL ME. / SIMPLE MAN, SIMPLE DREAM** [-] [31]

Mar 78. (7") **TUMBLING DICE. / CARMELITA** [ ] [-]

May 78. (7") **TUMBLING DICE. / I WILL NEVER MARRY** [-] [32]

Sep 78. (7") **BACK IN THE U.S.A. / WHITE RHYTHM & BLUES** [ ] [16] Aug 78

Oct 78. (lp)(c) **LIVING IN THE U.S.A.** [39] [1] Sep 78
– Back in the U.S.A. / When I grow too old to dream / Just one look / Alison / White rhythm & blues / All that you dream / Ooh baby baby / Mohammed's radio / Blowing away / Love me tender.

Oct 78. (7") **OOH BABY BABY. / BLOWIN' AWAY** [-] [7]

Nov 78. (7") **OOH BABY BABY. / BLACK ROSES** [ ] [-]

Feb 79. (7") **JUST ONE LOOK. / LOVE ME TENDER** [-] [44]

Apr 79. (7")(7"pic-d) **ALISON. / ALL THAT YOU DREAM** [66] [-]

Apr 79. (7") **ALISON. / MOHAMMED'S RADIO** [-] [ ]

Feb 80. (7") **HOW DO I MAKE YOU. / RAMBLER GAMBLER** [ ] [10] Jan 80

Feb 80. (lp)(c) **MAD LOVE** [65] [3]
– Mad love / Party girl / How do I make you / I can't let go / Hurt so bad / Look out for my love / Cost of love / Justine / Girls talk / Talking in the dark.

—— (above has backing from The CRETONES)

Jun 80. (7") **HURT SO BAD. / JUSTINE** [ ] [8] Apr 80

Jul 80. (7") **I CAN'T LET GO. / LOOK OUT FOR MY LOVE** [-] [31]

Nov 80. (lp)(c) **GREATEST HITS, VOLUME 2** (compilation) [ ] [26]
– It's so easy / I can't let go / Hurt so bad / Blue bayou / How do I make you / Back in the U.S.A. / Ooh baby baby / Poor poor pitiful me / Tumbling dice / Just one look / Someone to lay down beside me. *(cd-iss.1983)*

—— (next featured **J.D. SOUTHER** – vocals)

Elektra Elektra

Oct 82. (7") **GET CLOSER. / SOMETIMES YOU JUST CAN'T WIN** [ ] [29]

Oct 82. (lp)(c) **GET CLOSER** [ ] [31]
– Get closer / The Moon is a harsh mistreess / I knew you when / Easy for you to say / People gonna talk / Talk to me of Mendocino / I think it's gonna work out fine / Mr. Radio / Lies / Tell him / Sometimes you just can't win / My blue tears. *(cd-iss.Jan84)*

Jan 83. (7")(12") **I KNEW YOU WHEN. / TALK TO ME OF MENDOCINO** [ ] [37]

Mar 83. (7")(12") **TELL HIM. / MR. RADIO** [ ] [ ]

Apr 83. (7") **EASY FOR YOU TO SAY. / MR. RADIO** [-] [54]

—— next 2 albums credit The NELSON RIDDLE ORCHESTRA.

Nov 83. (lp)(c)(cd) **WHAT'S NEW** [31] [3]
– What's new / I've got a crush on you / Guess I'll hang my tears out to dry / Crazy

he calls me / Someone to watch over me / I don't stand a ghost of a chance with you / What'll I do / Lover man (oh where can you be) / Good-bye. *(re-iss.Nov 86)*
Mar 84. (7") **WHAT'S NEW. / CRAZY HE CALLS ME** 53 Nov 83
Dec 84. (lp)(c) **LUSH LIFE** 100 13 Nov 84
– When I fall in love / Skylark / It never entered my mind / Mean to me / When your lover has gone / I'm a fool to want you / You took advantage of me / Sophisticated lady / Can't we be friends / My old flame / Falling in love again / Lush life. *(cd-iss.Jun87)*
Jan 85. (7") **FALLING IN LOVE AGAIN. / SOPHISTICATED LADY**
— next credited NELSON RIDDLE & HIS ORCHESTRA (NELSON died mid-80's)
Sep 86. (lp)(c)(cd) **FOR SENTIMENTAL REASONS**
– When you wish upon a star / Bewitched, bothered & bewildered / You go to my head / But not for me / My funny valentine / I get along without you very well / Am I blue / I love you for sentimental reasons / Straighten up and fly right / Little girl blue / 'Round midnight.
Jun 87. (7") **SOMEWHERE OUT THERE. ("LINDA RONSTADT & JAMES INGRAM") / ('A'instrumental)** 8 2 Dec 86
(12"+=) – ('A'version).
— (above 45 on 'MCA' and lifted from the cartoon film 'An American Tail')
Mar'87, she teamed up with DOLLY PARTON & EMMYLOU HARRIS (⇒) on album TRIO. It hits No.6 in the States, and a number of 45's are lifted from it by Warners.
Nov 87. (lp)(c)(cd) **CANCIONES DE MI PADRE (MY FATHER'S SONG)** 42
– Por un amor / Los Laureles / Hay unos ojos / La cigarra / Tu solo tu / Y andale / Rogaciano el huapanguero / La charreada / Dos arbolitos / Corrido de cananea / La barca de guaymas / La calandria / El sol que tu eres. *(re-iss.cd Nov93)*
Elektra Elektra
Oct 89. (lp)(c)(cd) **CRY LIKE A RAINSTORM – HOWL LIKE THE WIND** 43 7
– Still within the sound of my voice / Cry like a rainstorm / All my life / I need you / Don't know much / Adios / Trouble again / I keep it hid / So right, so wrong / Shattered / When something is wrong with my baby / Goodbye my friend.
Nov 89. (7")(c-s) **DON'T KNOW MUCH ("LINDA RONSTADT featuring AARON NEVILLE"). / HURT SO BAD** 2 2 Sep 89
(12"+=)(cd-s+=) – I can't let go.
Jan 90. (7") **ALL MY LIFE. / SHATTERED** 11
(12"+=)(cd-s+=) – Love has no pride.
May 90. (7") **WHEN SOMETHING IS WRONG WITH MY BABY. /** - 78
— Oct 91, she again duetted with AARON NEVILLE on his 'A&M' 45 'CLOSE YOUR EYES'
Nov 91. (cd)(c)(lp) **MAS CANCIONES** 88
– Tata dios / El Toro Relajo / Mi ranchito / La Mariquita / Gritenme Piedras del Campo / Siempre hace Frio / El Curcifijo de Piedra / Palomita de ojos negros / Pena de los amores / El Camino / El Gustito / El Sueno.
Nov 93. (7")(c-s) **WINTER LIGHT. / DON'T KNOW MUCH**
(cd-s+=) – Blue bayou / Alison.
Dec 93. (cd)(c) **WINTER LIGHT** 92
– Heartbeats accelerating / Do what you gotta do / Anyone who had a heart / Don't talk (put your head on my shoulder) / Oh no, not my baby / It's too soon to know / I just don't know what to do with myself / A river for him / Adonde voy / You cant treat the wrong man right / Winter light.
Feb 94. (7")(c-s) **HEARTBEATS ACCELERATING. / THE SECRET GARDEN**
(cd-s) – ('A'side) / Don't know much / Desperado / A river for him.
Mar 95. (cd)(c) **FEELS LIKE HOME** 75
– The waiting / Walk on / High Sierra / After the gold rush / The blue train / Feels like home / Teardrops will fall / Morning blues / Women 'cross the river / Lover's return.
Mar 95. (c-s) **THE WAITING / DESPERADO**
(cd-s+=) – Poor poor pitiful me / Cry like a rainstorm.

– more compilations, etc. (STONE PONEYS =*) –

1972. Pickwick; (lp)(c) **STONEY END *** -
Jun 75. Capitol; (lp) **THE STONE PONEYS FEATURING LINDA RONSTADT ***
Apr 77. Capitol; (lp)(c) **DIFFERENT DRUM *** 92 Feb 74
Jul 77. Capitol; (7") **DIFFERENT DRUM. * / IT DOESN'T MATTER ANYMORE**
Jul 77. Capitol; (d-lp) **A RETROSPECTIVE** May 77
Sep 76. Asylum; (7") **DESPERADO. / SILVER THREADS AND GOLDEN NEEDLES**
Nov 86. Asylum; (c-box)(cd-box) **ROUND MIDNIGHT**
– (WHAT'S NEW /LUSH LIFE /FOR SENTIMENTAL REASONS)

ROOSTERS (see under ⇒ IMPRESSIONS)

Tim ROSE

Born: September 1940, Washington DC, U.S.A. Was a member of folk trio The BIG THREE, which included CASS ELLIOTT, future MAMAS & THE PAPAS. He signed to 'Columbia' in 1966, and soon unleashed eponymous debut album. It contained the classic one-that-got-away 'MORNING DEW', and a version of traditional 'HEY JOE'. Never quite gained the attention he deserved, even after moving to London in the mid-70's and forming duo with TIM HARDIN. • **Style:** Cult folk-rock artist with powerful gravel larynx**. • **Songwriters:** Self-penned and several recorded covers.

Recommended: I'VE GOT TO GET A MESSAGE TO YOU (*7) / TIM ROSE (*6)

TIM ROSE – vocals, guitar with session people **HUGH McCRACKEN** + **JAY BERLINER** – guitar / **FELIX PAPPALARDI** – bass, producer (CREAM producer) / **BERNARD PURDIE** – drums
C.B.S. Columbia
Mar 67. (7") **MORNING DEW. / YOU'RE SLIPPING AWAY FROM ME**
Nov 67. (7") **COME AWAY MELINDA. / LONG THE MAN** -
Feb 68. (7") **I GOT A LONELINESS. / LONG TIME MAN**
Feb 68. (lp) **TIM ROSE**
– I got a loneliness / I'm gonna be strong / I gotta do things my way / Fare thee well / Eat, drink and be merry / Hey Joe / Morning dew / Where was I / You're slipping away from me / Long time man / Come away, Melinda. *(re-iss.+cd Apr88 as 'MORNING DEW' on 'Edsel')*
May 68. (7") **I GUESS IT'S OVER. / HELLO SUNSHINE**
Jul 68. (7") **LONG-HAIRED BOY. / LOOKING AT MY BABY**
— now totally solo.
Apr 69. (7") **ANGELA. / WHATCHA GONNA DO** -
Jun 69. (7") **ROANOKE. / BABY YOU TURN ME ON**
Jul 69. (lp) **THROUGH ROSE COLOURED GLASSES**
– The days back when / Roanoke / Hello sunshine / When I was a young man / Whatcha gonna do / Let there be love / Baby you turn me on / Apple truck swamper / Angela / You'd laugh / You ain't my girl no more.
Capitol Capitol
Nov 70. (lp)(c) **LOVE – A KIND OF HATE STORY**
– I've gotta get a message to you / Dimlight / Where do you go to my lovely / You can't stop yourself / Sad song / Georgia by morning / Ode to an old ball / Sympathy / I know these two people / Jamie Sue.
Jan 71. (7") **I'VE GOTTA GET A MESSAGE TO YOU. / JAMIE SUE** -
— added **GARY WRIGHT** – keyboards, producer / **MICK JONES** – guitar / **ARCHIE LEGGETT** – bass / **BRYSON GRAHAM** – drums
1972. (7") **IT TAKES A LITTLE LONGER. / HIDE YOUR LOVE AWAY** -
1973. (7") **GOIN' DOWN TO HOLLYWOOD** -
Dawn Playboy
1974. (lp)(c) **TIM ROSE** 1972
– It takes a little longer / You can't keep me / Hide your love away / Boogie woogie / If I were a carpenter / Cryin' shame / Darling you were all that I had / Cotton growin' man / Goin' down in Hollywood.
now with a plethara of musicians.
Atlantic Atlantic
1975. (lp)(c) **THE MUSICIAN**
– 7:30 song / Small town talk / The musician / Loving arms / Old man / It's not my life that's been changin' / The day I spent with you / Second avenue / Now you're a lady / Where is the good life. *(cd-iss.Nov95 on 'Edsel')*
— Retired from music business until below.
President not issued
Nov 91. (cd)(c) **THE GAMBLER** -
– I just wanna make love to you / He was born to be a lady / Dancing on ma belle / It'll be alright on the night / Runaway / Moving targets / The gambler / Blow me back Santa Ana / So much to lose / Is there something 'bout the way I hold my gun / Bowery Avenue / Laurie.

– compilations, etc. –

Dec 87. See For Miles; (lp) **I'VE GOT TO GET A MESSAGE TO YOU** -

ROSSINGTON-COLLINS BAND (see under ⇒ LYNYRD SKYNYRD)

David Lee ROTH

Born: 10 Oct'55, Bloomington, Indiana, USA. After suffering from hyperactivity from an early age, he attended a child clinic at age 8. His family moved to Pasadena, where he joined group MAMMOTH in 1973, who were to become VAN HALEN in 1975. Following 10 years of phenomenal success, he departed for a solo career in 1985. He immediately struck gold for 'Warners', when his debut 45 'CALIFORNIA GIRLS', complete with raunchy video, made the US Top 3. • **Style:** Hard but commercial rock artist, relying on his stage antics and extrovert persona. • **Songwriters:** ROTH written (most with STEVE VAI '86-88), except JUST A GIGOLO (Ted Lewis) / I AIN'T GOT NOBODY (Marian Harris) / CALIFORNIA GIRLS (Beach Boys) / THAT'S LIFE (hit; Frank Sinatra) / TOBACCO ROAD (Nashville Teens). • **Trivia:** In August 1988, ROTH appeared at Britain's premier Castle Donnington festival.

Recommended: SKYSCRAPER (*5)

DAVID LEE ROTH – vocals (ex-VAN HALEN) with **DEAN PARKS** + **EDDIE MARTINEZ** + **SID McGINNIS** – guitar / **EDGAR WINTER** – keyboards, sax, synthesizers, vocals / **JAMES NEWTON HOWARD** – synthesizers / **WILLIE WEEKS** – bass / **JOHN ROBINSOB** – drums / **SAMMY FIGUEROA** – percussion / **BRIAN MANN** – synthesizers
Warners Warners
Feb 85. (7") **CALIFORNIA GIRLS. / ('A'version)** 68 3 Jan 85
— (above feat. CARL WILSON of The BEACH BOYS on backing vocals)
Feb 85. (m-lp)(c) **CRAZY FROM THE HEAT** 91 15
– Easy street / Just a gigolo – I ain't got nobody / Coconut Grove / California girls.
Apr 85. (7") **JUST A GIGOLO – I AIN'T GOT NOBODY. / ?** 12 Mar 85
— **STEVE VAI** – guitar (ex-FRANK ZAPPA) / **BILLY SHEEHAN** – bass (ex-TALAS) / **BRETT TUGGLE** – keyboards / **GREGG BISSONETTE** (b. 9 Jun'59) – drums
Jul 86. (7")(7"sha-pic-d) **YANKEE ROSE. / SHYBOY** 16
(12"+=) – Easy street.
Jul 86. (lp)(c)(cd) **EAT 'EM AND SMILE** 28 4
– Yankee Rose / Shyboy / I'm easy / Ladies' nite in Buffalo? / Goin' crazy / Tobacco Road / Elephant gun / Big trouble / Bump and grind / That's life.
Sep 86. (7") **GOIN' CRAZY. / OOCO DEO CALOR** - 66
Nov 86. (7") **THAT'S LIFE. / BUMP AND GRIND** - 85
— **MATT BISSONETTE** – bass repl. SHEEHAN who joined OZZY OSBOURNE
Jan 88. (lp)(c)(cd) **SKYSCRAPER** 11 6
– Hot dog and a shake / Stand up / Hina / Perfect timing / Two fools a minute /

Knucklebones / Just like Paradise / Bottom line / Skyscraper / Damn good. *(cd+=)–* California girls / Just a gigolo – I ain't got nobody.

Feb 88. (7") **JUST LIKE PARADISE. / THE BOTTOM LINE** 27 6 Jan 88
(12"+=)(12"pic-d+=) – Yankee Rose.

Apr 88. (7") **STAND UP. / KNUCKLEBONES** – 64

Jul 88. (7") **DAMN GOOD. / SKYSCRAPER** –

Jul 88. (7")(12") **DAMN GOOD. / STAND UP** 72 –

Nov 88. (7") **CALIFORNIA GIRLS. / JUST A GIGOLO** –
(12"+=) – I ain't got nobody. (cd-s++=) – Yankee Rose.

— (Apr89-Jan90) **ROCKY RICHETTE** – guitar (ex-STEPPENWOLF, ex-BLACK ROSE) repl. STEVE VAI who went solo and joined WHITESNAKE

— (Oct90) **TODD JENSEN** – bass (ex-HARLOW) repl. MATT / **DEZZI REXX + JOE HOLMES** – guitar repl. JASON BECKER + ROCKY RICHETTE

W.E.A. Warners

Dec 90. (7")(c-s) **A LITTLE AIN'T ENOUGH. / BABY'S ON FIRE** 32
(12"+=)(cd-s+=) – Tell the truth.

Jan 91. (cd)(c)(lp) **A LITTLE AIN'T ENOUGH** 4 18
– A little ain't enough / Shoot it / Lady Luck / Hammerhead shark / Tell the truth / Baby's on fire / 40 below / Sensible shoes / Last call / The dogtown shuffle / It's showtime! / Drop in the bucket.

Mar 91. (7")(c-s)(7"pic-d) **SENSIBLE SHOES. / A LIL AIN'T ENOUGH**
(12")(cd-s) – ('A'side) / California girls / Just a gigolo / I ain't got nobody.

Feb 94. (7")(c-s) **SHE'S MY MACHINE. / MISSISSIPPI POWER** 64
(cd-s+=) – Land's edge / Yo breathin' it.

Mar 94. (cd)(c)(lp) **YOUR FILTHY LITTLE MOUTH** 28 78
– She's my machine / Everybody's got the monkey / Big train / Experience / A little luck / Cheatin' heart cafe / Hey, you never know / No big 'ting / Yo breathin' it / Your filthy little mouth / Land's edge / Night life / Sunburn / You're breathin' it (urban NYC mix).

May 94. (7")(c-s) **NIGHT LIFE. / JUMP (live)** 72
(cd-s+=) – She's my machine (live).
(cd-s) – ('A'side) / Panama (live) / Big train (live) / Experience (live).

Michael ROTHER (see under ⇒ NEU!)

Kevin ROWLAND (see under ⇒ DEXY'S MIDNIGHT RUNNERS)

ROXY MUSIC

Formed: Newcastle, England . . . 1970 by art school graduate and teacher BRYAN FERRY with GRAHAM SIMPSON. Early in 1971, they invited ANDY MACKAY and electronic wizard BRIAN ENO, to join. They finally settled with debut album line – up a year later, when they added PHIL MANZANERA. Already signed to 'Island', they issued PETE SINFIELD (King Crimson lyricist) produced debut, which with airplay on John Peel's Radio 1 show, hit UK Top 10. In August '72, they broke into the singles chart with 'VIRGINIA PLAIN', regarded then and now, as an all-time classic. Their follow-up album 'FOR YOUR PLEASURE', made the Top 5, with their second 1973, giving them their first No.1. In the same year, ENO argued with FERRY, and departed for a solo career. FERRY too, also controlled a largely successful solo career side by side with ROXY. When they finally split in 1983, FERRY continued to hit the UK Top 30 with many releases. • **Style:** Moved through futurist experimental, but melodic rock to a more sophisticated rock-pop, highlighting the crooning of the smooth and image conscious FERRY. The inspiration for many 'New wave-futurist' bands of the 80's. • **Songwriters:** FERRY / MANZANERA with contributions from MACKAY and ENO until latter left. Covered IN THE MIDNIGHT HOUR (Wilson Pickett) / EIGHT MILES HIGH (Byrds) / JEALOUS GUY (John Lennon) / LIKE A HURRICANE (Neil Young). FERRY's solo covers:- A HARD RAIN'S A-GONNA FALL (Bob Dylan) / SYMPATHY FOR THE DEVIL (Rolling Stones) / DON'T EVER CHANGE (Crickets) / THESE FOOLISH THINGS (Cole Porter?) / PIECE OF MY HEART (hit; Janis Joplin) / I LOVE HOW YOU LOVE ME (Paris Sisters) / DON'T WORRY BABY (Beach Boys) / TRACKS OF MY TEARS (Miracles) / IT'S MY PARTY (Leslie Gore) / BABY I DON'T CARE (Leiber-Stoller) / WALK A MILE IN MY SHOES (Joe South) / THE IN-CROWD (Dobie Gray) / WHAT A WONDERFUL WORLD (Sam Cooke) / YOU ARE MY SUNSHINE (Ray Charles) / SMOKE GETS IN YOUR EYES (Platters) / HELP ME MAKE IT THROUGH THE NIGHT (Kris Kristofferson) / FINGERPOPPIN' (Hank Ballard) / FUNNY HOW TIME SLIPS AWAY (Jimmy Ellidge) / LET'S STICK TOGETHER (Wilbert Harrison) / THE PRICE OF LOVE (Everly Brothers) / IT'S ONLY LOVE (Barry White) / SHAME SHAME SHAME (Shirley & Company) / HEART ON MY SLEEVE (Gallagher & Lyle) / SHE'S LEAVING HOME + YOU WON'T SEE ME (Beatles) / WHEN SHE WALKS IN THE ROOM (Searchers) / TAKE ME TO THE RIVER (Al Green) / YOU DON'T KNOW (Sam & Dave) / PARTY DOLL (Buddy Knox) / FEEL THE NEED (Detroit Emeralds). Note:- JOHNNY MARR (ex-Smiths) co-wrote THE RIGHT STUFF with him. FERRY returned in 1993 with a covers album #096TAXI'. • **Trivia:** FERRY married model Lucy Helmore on 26 Jun'82, after a 70's relationship with Jerry Hall had finished. He was said to have turned down the Keith Forsey penned song 'DON'T YOU FORGET ABOUT ME', which was a No.1 for SIMPLE MINDS.

Recommended: ROXY MUSIC (*8) / FOR YOUR PLEASURE (*9) / STRANDED (*7) / COUNTRY LIFE (*6) / STREETLIFE (*8).

BRYAN FERRY (b.26 Sep'45, County Durham, England) – vocals, piano / **ANDY MACKAY** (b.23 Jul'46, London, England) – saxophone, oboe, wind inst. / (BRIAN) **ENO** (b.15 May'48, Woodbridge, Suffolk, England) – synthesizers-keys / **GRAHAM SIMPSON** – bass, vocals / **PHIL MANZANERA** (b.31 Jan'51, London) – guitar (ex-QUIET SUN) repl. DAVID O'LIST (ex-NICE) wo had repl. original ROGER BUNN (Jul'71). / **PAUL THOMPSON** (b.13 May'51, Jarrow, Northumberland, England) – drums repl. original DEXTER LLOYD (Jul71).

Island Reprise

Jun 72. (lp)(c) **ROXY MUSIC** 10
– Bitters end / The bob / Chance meeting / If there is something / Ladytron / Re-make/re-model / 2HB / Would you believe? / Sea brrezes. *(re-iss. Feb77 on 'Polydor') (re-iss.+cdJan87 on 'EG' +=)* – Virginia Plain. *(re-iss.cd+c.Sep91 on 'EG')*

— (May72) **RIK KENTON** – bass repl. SIMPSON

Aug 72. (7") **VIRGINIA PLAIN. / THE NUMBERER** 4

— (Jan73) **JOHN PORTER** – bass repl. KENTON who went solo.

Island Warners

Mar 73. (7") **PJAMARAMA. / THE PRIDE AND THE PAIN** 10

Mar 73. (lp)(c) **FOR YOUR PLEASURE** 4
– Do the strand / Beauty queen / Strictly confidential / Editions of you / In every dream home a heartache / The bogus man / Grey lagoons / For your pleasure. *(re-iss.Feb77 on 'Polydor') (re-iss.+cd.Jan87 cd+c.Sep91 on 'EG')*

Jul 73. (7") **DO THE STRAND. / EDITIONS OF YOU** –

— (Jul73) **EDDIE JOBSON** (b.28 Apr'55, Billingham, Teeside, England) – keyboards, violin (ex-CURVED AIR) repl. ENO who went solo.

ROXY MUSIC

session bassmen **JOHN GUSTAFSON** (studio) / **SAL MAIDA** (tour)repl. PORTER (other 5= **FERRY, MANZANERA, MACKAY, JOBSON & THOMPSON)**

Island Atco

Nov 73. (7") **STREET LIFE. / HULA KULA** 9 –

Nov 73. (lp)(c) **STRANDED** 1
– Street life / Just like you / Amazona / Psalm / Serenade / A song for Europe / Mother of pearl / Sunset. *(re-iss.Feb77 on 'Polydor') (re-iss.+cd.Jan87, cd+c.Sep91 on 'EG')*

— brought in **JOHN WETTON** – tour bass (ex-FAMILY, ex-KING CRIMSON, etc.) repl. MAIDA

Oct 74. (7") **ALL I WANT IS YOU. / YOUR APPLICATIONS FAILED** 12 –

Nov 74. (lp)(c) **COUNTRY LIFE** 3 37 Jan 75
– The thrill of it all / Three and nine / All I want is you / Out of the blue / If it takes all night / Bitter-sweet / Triptych / Casanova / A really good time / Prairie rose. *(re-iss.Feb77 on 'Polydor') (re-iss.+cd.Jan87, cd+c.Sep91 on 'EG')*

Nov 74. (7") **THE THRILL OF IT ALL. / YOUR APPLICATIONS FAILED** –

Sep 75. (7") **LOVE IS THE DRUG. / SULTANESQUE** 2 –

Oct 75. (lp)(c) **SIREN** 4 50
– Love is the drug / End of the line / Sentimental fool / Whirlwind / She sells / Could it hapen to me / Both ends burning / Nightingale / Just another high. *(re-iss.Feb77 on 'Polydor') (re-iss.+cd.Jan87, cd+c.Sep91 on 'EG')*

Dec 75. (7") **BOTH ENDS BURNING. / FOR YOUR PLEASURE** 25

Dec 75. (7") **LOVE IS THE DRUG. / BOTH ENDS BURNING** – 30

— **RICK WILLS** – tour bass repl. WETTON who stayed on with FERRY (see below)

— Disbanded officially mid'76, leaving behind one more album

Jul 76. (lp)(c) **VIVA! ROXY MUSIC (live 1973-1975)** 6 81
– Out of the blue / Pjamarama / The bogus man / Chance meeting / Both ends burning / If there is something / In every dream home a heartache / Do the strand. *(re-iss.Feb77 on 'Polydor') (re-iss.+cd.Jan87, cd+c.Sep91 on 'EG')*

— After split ANDY MACKAY continued solo work, as did PHIL MANZANERA. EDDIE JOBSON joined FRANK ZAPPA.

BRYAN FERRY

also had simultaneous solo career. (same labels). He used various session people, including many members of ROXY MUSIC.

Sep 73. (7") **A HARD RAIN'S GONNA FALL. / 2HB** 4

Oct 73. (lp)(c) **THESE FOOLISH THINGS** 5
– A hard rain's a-gonna fall / River of salt / Don't ever change / Piece of my heart / Baby I don't care / It's my party / Don't worry baby / Sympathy for the Devil / Tracks of my tears / You won't see me / I love how you love me / Loving you is sweeter than ever / These foolish things. *(re-iss.+cd.Aug84 on 'Polydor') (re-iss.+cd.Jan87, cd+c.Sep91 on 'EG')*

May 74. (7") **THE IN-CROWD. / CHANCE MEETING** 13 –

Jul 74. (lp)(c) **ANOTHER TIME, ANOTHER PLACE** 4
– The in-crowd / Smoke gets in your eyes / Walk a mile in my shoes / Funny how time slips away / You are my sunshine / (What a) Wonderful world / It ain't me babe / Fingerpoppin' / Help me make it through the night. *(re-iss.+cd.Aug84 on 'Polydor') (re-iss.+cd.Jan87, cd+c.Sep91 on 'EG')*

Aug 74. (7") **SMOKE GETS IN YOUR EYES. / ANOTHER TIME, ANOTHER PLACE** 17 –

Jun 75. (7") **YOU GO TO MY HEAD. / RE-MAKE RE-MODEL** –

— Solo again, with ex-ROXY MUSIC men **PAUL THOMPSON + JOHN WETTON**. Added **CHRIS SPEDDING** – guitar (ex-SHARKS)

Island Atlantic

Jun 76. (7") **LET'S STICK TOGETHER. / SEA BREEZES** 4

Aug 76. (7"ep) **EXTENDED PLAY** 7 –
– The price of love / Shame shame shame / Heart on my sleeve / It's only love.

Sep 76. (lp)(c) **LET'S STICK TOGETHER** 19
– Let's stick together / Casanova / Sea breeze / Shame shame shame / 2HB / The price of love / Chance meeting / It's only love / You go to my head / Re-make/re-model / Heart on my sleeve. *(re-iss.+cd.Aug84 on 'Polydor') (re-iss.+cd.Jan87, cd+c.Sep91 on 'EG')*

Oct 76. (7") **HEART ON MY SLEEVE. / RE-MAKE/RE-MODEL** –

— added **PHIL MANZANERA** – guitar / **ANN ODELL** – keyboards / **MEL COLLINS** – sax/ plus many backing singers.

Polydor Atlantic

Jan 77. (7") **THIS IS TOMORROW. / AS THE WORLD TURNS** [9] [ ]

Feb 77. (lp)(c) **IN YOUR MIND** [5] [ ]
– This is tomorrow / All night operator / One kiss / Love me madly again / Tokyo Joe / Party doll / Rock of ages / In your mind. *(re-iss.+cd Jan87, cd+c Sep91 on 'EG')*

Apr 77. (7") **TOKYO JOE. / SHE'S LEAVING HOME** [15] [-]

Jun 77. (7") **TOKYO JOE. / AS THE WORLD TURNS** [-] [ ]

— FERRY continued to use many different musicians, too many to mention.

Apr 78. (7") **WHAT GOES ON. / CASANOVA** [67] [ ]

Apr 78. (lp)(c) **THE BRIDE STRIPPED BARE** [13] [ ]
– Sign of the times / Can't let go / Hold on (I'm coming) / The same old blues / When she walks in the room / Take me to the river / What goes on / Carrickfergus / That's how strong my love is / This island Earth. *(re-iss Jan87, cd+c Sep91 on 'EG')*

Jul 78. (7") **SIGN OF THE TIMES. / FOUR LETTER LOVE** [37] [-]

Nov 78. (7") **SIGN OF THE TIMES. / CAN'T LET GO** [-] [ ]

Nov 78. (7") **CARRICKFERGUS. / WHEN SHE WALKS IN THE ROOM** [ ] [ ]

ROXY MUSIC

re-formed with **FERRY, MANZANERA, MACKAY, THOMPSON,** plus **PAUL CARRACK** – studio keyboards (ex-ACE) / **DAVID SKINNER** – tour keyboards / **GARY TIBBS** – bass (ex-VIBRATORS)

Polydor Atco

Feb 79. (7") **TRASH. / TRASH 2** [40] [-]

Mar 79. (lp)(c)(pic-lp) **MANIFESTO** [7] [23]
– Manifesto / Trash / Angel eyes / Still falls the rain / Stronger through the years / Ain't that so / My little girl / ance away / Cry cry cry / Spin me round. *(re-iss.+cd Jan87, cd+c Sep91 on 'EG'+=)* – Angel eyes (12"disco version).

Apr 79. (7") **DANCE AWAY. / CRY CRY CRY** [2] [-]

Apr 79. (7") **DANCE AWAY. / TRASH 2** [-] [44]

Aug 79. (7")(disco-12") **ANGEL EYES. / MY LITTLE GIRL** [4] [ ]

May 80. (7") **OVER YOU. / MANIFESTO** [5] [ ]

May 80. (lp)(c) **FLESH + BLOOD** [1] [35]
– In the midnight hour / Oh yeah (on the radio) / Same old scene / Flesh and blood / My only love / Over you / Eight miles high / Rain rain rain / No strange delight / Running wild. *(re-iss.+cd Jan87, cd+c Sep91 on 'EG')*

May 80. (7") **OVER YOU. / MY ONLY LOVE** [-] [80]

Jul 80. (7") **OH YEAH (ON THE RADIO). / SOUTH DOWNS** [5] [ ]

Nov 80. (7") **SAME OLD SCENE. / LOVER** [12] [-]

Dec 80. (7") **IN THE MIDNIGHT HOUR. /** [-] [ ]

— Earlier 1980, CARRACK joined SQUEEZE, and TIBBS joined ADAM & THE ANTS. Session men used at the time **NEIL HUBBARD** – guitar / **ALAN SPENNER** – bass / **ANDY NEWMARK** – drums repl. THOMPSON

Feb 81. (7") **JEALOUS GUY. / TO TURN YOU ON** [1] [ ]

Apr 82. (7") **MORE THAN THIS. / INDIA** [6] [-]

May 82. (lp)(c) **AVALON** [1] [53]
– More than this / The space between / India / While my heart is still beating / Main thing / Take a chance with me / Avalon / To turn you on / True to life / Tara. *(re-iss.+cd Jan87 on 'EG')*

Jun 82. (7") **AVALON. / ALWAYS UNKNOWING** [13] [ ]

Sep 82. (7")(12") **TAKE A CHANCE WITH ME. / THE MAIN THING** [26] [-]

Sep 82. (7") **TAKE A CHANCE ON ME. / INDIA** [-] [ ]

Nov 82. (7") **MORE THAN THIS. / ALWAYS UNKNOWING** [-] [ ]

— added **GUY FLETCHER + JIMMY MAELEN** – keys / **MICHELLE COBBS + TAWATHA AGEE**

Mar 83. (m-lp)(c) **THE HIGH ROAD (live)** [26] [67]
– Can't let go / My only love / Like a hurricane / Jealous guy.

— Had already disbanded again late 1982. MANZANERA and MACKAY became The EXPLORERS, and FERRY went solo again (see further on).

BRYAN FERRY

solo again.

E.G. Warners

May 85. (7") **SLAVE TO LOVE. / VALENTINE (instrumental)** [10] [ ]
(12"+=) – ('A'instrumental).

Jun 85. (lp)(c)(cd) **BOYS AND GIRLS** [1] [63]
– Sensation / Slave to love / Don't stop the dance / A wasteland / Windswept / The chosen one / Valentine / Stone woman / Boys and girls. *(re-iss.cd+c Sep91)*

Aug 85. (7") **DON'T STOP THE DANCE. / NOCTURNE** [21] [ ]
(12"+=) – Windswept (instrumental).

Nov 85. (7")(7"pic-d) **WINDSWEPT. / CRAZY LOVE** [46] [ ]
(12"+=) – Feel the need / Broken wings.

Mar 86. (7") **IS YOUR LOVE STRONG ENOUGH. / WINDSWEPT (instrumental)** [22] [ ]
(12"+=) – ('A'mix).

Jul 86. (7") **HELP ME. / BROKEN WINGS** [-] [ ]

EG-Virgin Reprise

Sep 87. (7")(12") **THE RIGHT STUFF. / ('A'instrumental)** [37] [ ]
(c-s+=)(cd-s+=) – ('A'extended) / ('A'dub version).

Nov 87. (lp)(c)(cd) **BETE NOIRE** [9] [63]
– Limbo / Kiss and tell / New town / Day for night / Zamba / The right stuff / Seven deadly sins / The name of the game / Bete noire. *(cd-re-iss.Dec88)*

Feb 88. (7") **KISS AND TELL. / ZAMBA** [41] [31]
(12"+=)(cd-s+=) – ('A'&'B'remixes).

Jun 88. (7") **LIMBO (Latin mix). / BETE NOIRE (instrumental)** [ ] [ ]
(12"+=)(cd-s+=) – ('A'mix).

Feb 93. (7")(c-s) **I PUT A SPELL ON YOU. / THESE FOOLISH THINGS** [18] [ ]
(cd-s+=) – Ladytron (live) / While my heart is still beating (live).

Mar 93. (cd)(c)(lp) **TAXI** [2] [79]
– I put a spell on you / Will you love me tomorrow / Answer me / Just one look / Rescue me / All tomorrow's parties / Girl of my best friend / Amazing Grace / Taxi / Because you're mine.

May 93. (7")(c-s) **WILL YOU LOVE ME TOMMOROW. / A HARD RAIN'S AGONNA FALL** [23] [ ]
(cd-s+=) – A wasteland (live) / Windswept (live).
(cd-s) – ('A'side) / Crazy love / Feel the need / When she walks in the room.

Aug 93. (c-s) **GIRL OF MY BEST FRIEND /** [57] [ ]
(cd-s) – Nocturne / Are you lonesome tonight? / Valentine.
(cd-s) – Let's stick together / Boys and girls (live) / The bogus man (live).

— now with a plethora of musicians **BRIAN ENO, PHIL MANZANERA, ANDY MACKAY, STEVE FERRONE, NEIL HUBBARD, NATHAN EAST, NILE RODGERS, ROBIN TROWER, GUY FLETCHER, PINO PALLADINO, CARLEEN ANDERSON, LUKE CRESSWELL, RHETT DAVIES, YANNICK ETIENNE, LUIS JARDIM, NEIL JASON, JHELISA, PAUL JOHNSON, CHESTER KAMEN, NAN KIDWELL, MIKE PAICE, MACEO PARKER, GUY PRATT, RICHARD T. NORRIS, STEVE SCALES, DAVID WILLIAMS, JEFF THALL + FONZI THORNTON**

Sep 94. (cd)(c) **MAMOUNA** [11] [94]
– Don't want to know / N.Y.C. / Your painted smile / Mamouna / The only face / The 39 steps / Which way to turn / Wildcat days / Gemini Moon / Chain reaction.

Oct 94. (7")(c-s) **YOUR PAINTED SMILE. / DON'T STOP THE DANCE** [ ] [ ]
(cd-s+=) – In every dream home a heartache (live) / Bete noire (live).

Feb 95. (7")(c-s) **MAMOUNA. / THE 39 STEPS (Brian Eno mix)** [57] [ ]
(cd-s+=) – Jealous guy (live) / Slave to love (live).

– (FERRY) compilations, others, etc. –

Jun 88. EG; (3"cd-ep) **LET'S STICK TOGETHER / SHAME SHAME SHAME / CHANCE MEETING / SEA BREEZES** [ ] [-]

Oct 88. EG; (7") **LET'S STICK TOGETHER ('88 remix). / TRASH** [12] [ ]
(12"+=) – Shame shame shame / Angel eyes.
(cd-s+=) – Casanova / Sign of the times.

Nov 88. EG/ US= Reprise; (lp)(c)(cd)(pic-lp) **THE ULTIMATE COLLECTION ("BRYAN FERRY & ROXY MUSIC")** [6] [ ]
– Let's stick together ('88 remix) / The in-crowd / Angel eyes (ROXY MUSIC) / He'll have to go / Tokyo Joe / All I want is you (ROXY MUSIC) / Jealous guy (ROXY MUSIC) / The price of love / Don't stop the dance / Love is the drug (ROXY MUSIC) / This is tomorrow / Slave to love / Help me / Avalon (ROXY MUSIC) / Dance away (ROXY MUSIC).

Feb 89. EG; (7") **THE PRICE OF LOVE (R&B mix). / LOVER** [49] [ ]
(12"+=) – Don't stop the dance (remix) / Nocturne.
(cd-s+=) – Don't stop the dance (remix) / Slave to love (remix).

Apr 89. EG; (7") **HE'LL HAVE TO GO. / CARRICKFERGUS** [63] [ ]
(12") – ('A'side) / Windswept / Is your love strong enough.
(cd-s+=) – Take me to the river / Broken wings.

Dec 89. EG; (3xlp-box)(3xc-box)(3xcd-box) **THESE FOOLISH THINGS / LET'S STICK TOGETHER / BOYS AND GIRLS** [ ] [-]
(free w / Island Various Artists compilations)

Oct 95. Virgin; (cd)(c)(d-lp) **MORE THAN THIS – THE BEST OF BRYAN FERRY & ROXY MUSIC** [15] [ ]

– (ROXY MUSIC) compilations, etc. –

Oct 77. Polydor/ US= Atco; (7") **VIRGINIA PLAIN. / PJAMARAMA** [11] [ ]

Nov 77. Polydor/ US= Atco; (lp)(c) **GREATEST HITS** [20] [ ]
– Virginia Plain / Do the strand / All I want is you / Out of the blue / Pjamarama / Editions of you / Love is the drug / Mother of pearl / Song for Europe / Thrill of it all / Street life. *(re-iss.+cd Jan87 on 'EG')*

Jan 78. Polydor; (7")(12") **DO THE STRAND. / EDITIONS OF YOU** [ ] [-]

Dec 81. EG; (7xlp-box) **BOXED SET** (all albums exc.'Viva') [ ] [-]

Nov 83. EG; (lp)(c)(cd) **THE ATLANTIC YEARS 1973-1980** [23] [ ]

Apr 86. EG/ US= Reprise; (d-lp)(c)(cd) **STREETLIFE (as "BRYAN FERRY & ROXY MUSIC")** [1] [100] Aug 89
– Virginia plain / A hard rain's a-gonna fall (BRYAN FERRY) / Pjamarama / Do the strand / These foolish things (BRYAN FERRY) / Street life / Let's stick together (BRYAN FERRY) / Smoke gets in your eyes (BRYAN FERRY) / Love is the drug / Sign of the times (BRYAN FERRY) / Dance away / Angel eyes / Oh yeah / Over you / Same old scene / The midnight hour / More than this / Avalon / Slave to love (BRYAN FERRY) / Jealous guy.

Jun 88. EG; (3"cd-ep) **JEALOUS GUY / LOVER / SOUTHDOWN** [ ] [ ]

Dec 89. EG; (3xlp)(3xc)(3xcd) **THE EARLY YEARS** [ ] [ ]
– (ROXY MUSIC / FOR YOUR PLEASURE / STRANDED albums)

Dec 89. EG; (3xlp)(3xc)(3xcd) **THE LATER YEARS** [ ] [ ]
– (MANIFESTO / FLESH AND BLOOD / AVALON albums)

Oct 90. EG; (cd)(c)(d-lp) **HEART STILL BEATIN' (live in France '82)** [ ] [ ]

Oct 90. EG; (7") **LOVE IS THE DRUG (live). / EDITIONS OF YOU (live)** [ ] [-]
(12"+=)(cd-s+=) – Do the strand (live).

Oct 94. EG; (3xcd-box) **THE COMPACT COLLECTION** [ ] [ ]

Nov 95. Virgin; (4xcd-box) **THE THRILL OF IT ALL – ROXY MUSIC 1972-1982** [ ] [ ]

ANDY MACKAY

Island not issued

Jun 74. (lp)(c) **IN SEARCH OF EDDIE RIFF** [ ] [-]
– The end of the world / Walking the whippet / What becomes of the broken-hearted / An die musik / The hour before dawn / Past, present and future * / Ride of the Valkyries / Summer Sun * / A four-legged friend *. *(re-iss Feb77 on 'Polydor'* tracks* repl. by) – Wild weekend / Pyramid of night / Time regained / The long and winding road.

Aug 74. (7") **WILD WEEKEND. / WALKING THE WHIPPET** [ ] [-]

— In 1976-77, MACKAY wrote music for hit UK No.1 TV series 'ROCK FOLLIES'.

Bronze not issued

Oct 78. (lp)(c) **RESOLVING CONTRADICTIONS** [ ] [-]
– Iron blossom / Trumpets on the mountains / Off to work / Unreal city / The Loyang tractor factory / Rivers / Battersea Rise / Skill and sweat / The Ortolan bunting (a

sparrow's fall) / The inexorable sequence / A song of friendship (the Renmin hotel) / Medley: Alloy blossom – Trumpets in the Sabu – Green and gold. *(re-iss.+cd.Nov90 on 'Expression')*

Oct 78. (7") **A SONG FOR FRIENDSHIP. / SKILL AND SWEAT** [ ] [-]

PHIL MANZANERA

Island Atco

May 75. (lp)(c) **DIAMOND HEAD** [40] [ ]
– Frontera / Diamond head / Big day / The flex / Same time next week / Miss Shapiro / East of echo / Lagrima / Alma. *(re-iss.Mar77 on 'Polydor') (re-iss. 1980 on 'EG', cd-iss.1988)*

QUIET SUN

formed earlier by **MANZANERA, DAVE JARRETT** – keyboards / **BILL McCORMICK** – bass / **CHARLES HAYWARD** – drums

Help-Island Antilees

Aug 75. (lp)(c) **MAINSTREAM** [ ] [ ]
– Sol Caliente / Trumpets with motherhood / Trot / Rongwrong / Bargain classics / R.F.D. / Mummy was an asteroid, daddy was a small non-stick kitchen utensil. *(re-iss.Oct77 on 'Polydor') (re-iss.+cd.Jan87 on 'EG')*

801

featured **MANZANERA, McCORMICK, ENO** plus **LLOYD WATSON** – guitar / **FRANCIS MONKMAN** – piano, clarinet (ex-CURVED AIR) / **SIMON PHILLIPS** – drums

Island Polydor

Oct 76. (lp)(c) **801 LIVE (live)** [ ] [ ]
– Lagima / T.N.K. (Tomorrow Never Knows) / East of asteroid / Rongwrong / Sombre reptiles / Baby's on fire / Diamond head / Miss Shapiro / You really got me / Third uncle. *(re-iss.Feb77 on 'Polydor') (re-iss.+cd.Jan87 on 'EG')*

— retained **McCORMICK**, and brought in **PAUL THOMPSON** – drums (ROXY MUSIC) **SIMON AINLEY** – guitar, vocals / **DAVID SKINNER** – keyboards, vocals / etc.

Polydor Polydor

Sep 77. (7") **FLIGHT 19. / CAR RHUMBA** [ ] [-]
Oct 77. (lp)(c) **LISTEN NOW!** [ ] [ ]
– Listen now / Flight 19 / Island / Law and order / ? Que ? / City of light / Initial speed / Postcard love / That falling feeling. *(re-iss.+cd.Jan87 on 'EG')*
Nov 77. (7") **FLIGHT 19. / INITIAL SPEED** [-] [ ]

PHIL MANZANERA

went solo again, using past QUIET SUN + 801 members.

Nov 78. (lp)(c) **K-SCOPE** [ ] [ ]
– K-scope / Remote control / Cuban crisis / Hot spot / Numbers / Slow motion T.V. / Gone flying / N-shift / Walking through Heaven's door / You are here.
Nov 78. (7") **REMOTE CONTROL. / K-SCOPE** [ ] [-]

E.G. not issued

Mar 82. (lp)(c) **PRIMITIVE GUITARS** [ ] [-]
– Criollo / Caracas / La nueva ola / Bogota / Ritmo de Los Angeles / Europe 70-1 / Impossible guitar / Europe 80-1. *(re-iss.Jan87 on 'Editions-EG')*
Apr 87. (lp)(c)(cd) **GUITARISSMO** (compilation) [ ] [-]
(cd-iss.3 extra tracks)

Expression not issued

May 90. (7") **A MILLION REASONS WHY. / SOUTHERN CROSS** [ ] [-]
(12"+=) – Blood brother.
Jun 90. (cd)(c)(lp) **SOUTHERN CROSS** [ ] [-]
– A million reasons why / Tambor / The great leveller / Astrud / Southern cross / Guantanemera / Rich and poor / Verde / Dr.Fidel / Venceremos.
May 95. Virgin; (cd) **THE MANZANERA COLLECTION** (compilation) [ ] [-]

The EXPLORERS

PHIL MANZANERA / ANDY MACKAY plus **JAMES WRAITH** – vocals (ex-FLYING TIGERS)

Virgin Virgin?

Jun 84. (7")(12") **LORELEI. / YOU GO UP IN SMOKE** [ ] [ ]
Oct 84. (7")(12") **FALLING FOR NIGHTLIFE. / CRACK THE WHIP** [ ] [ ]
Apr 85. (7") **TWO WORLDS APART. / IT ALWAYS RAINS IN PARADISE** [ ] [ ]
(12"+=) – Voodoo isle.
May 85. (lp)(c)(cd) **THE EXPLORERS** [ ] [ ]
– Ship of fools / Lorelei / Breath of life / Venus de Milo / Soul fantasy / Prussian blue / Two worlds apart / Robert Louis Stevenson / You go up in smoke.
Jun 85. (7")(12") **VENUS DE MILO. / ANOTHER LOST SOUL ON THE RUN** [ ] [ ]

PHIL MANZANERA & ANDY MACKAY

retained **WRAITH**

Expression not issued

Nov 90. (cd)(c)(lp) **MANZANERA & MACKAY** [ ] [-]
– Black gang chime / Free yourself / Built for speed / Many are the ways / I can be tender / Dreams of the East / Sacrosanct / Every kind of stone / Man with extraordinary ways / Safe in the arms of love / Forgotten man.

RTZ (see under ⇒ BOSTON)

RUBICON (see under ⇒ FIELDS OF THE NEPHILIM)

RUBY (see under ⇒ SILVERFISH)

RUFUS

Formed: Chicago, USA . . . 1972 as ASK RUFUS and stemming from successful 60's pop band The AMERICAN BREED. This outfit had 3 US hits in 1967-68 'STEP OUT OF YOUR MIND' (No.24), 'BEND ME, SHAPE ME' (No.5) & 'GREEN LIGHT' (No.39). Now called ASK RUFUS, they met CHAKA in 1971 (who had just married at 17). She replaced PAULINE McWILLIAMS as lead vocalist. They shortened group name and signed to 'ABC', where their debut lp broke into the US Top 200. In 1974, they surpassed expectations, when their version of 'TELL ME SOMETHING GOOD' raced into the US Top 3. Their albums 'RAGS TO RUFUS' & 'RUFUSIZED' went platinum, before they fronted CHAKA KHAN as their credited leader. In 1978, CHAKA even launched a solo career, hitting Top 20 with dance classic 'I'M EVERY WOMAN'. She left, then returned to combine both activities in the early 80's. In 1984, CHAKA had her first chart-topper with 'I FEEL FOR YOU'. • **Style:** Bi-racial outfit, whose soul sound encompassed jazzy funk and disco rock. Group or BELLFIELD compositions except; TELL ME SOMETHING GOOD (Stevie Wonder) / LOVE THE ONE YOU'RE WITH – SIT YOURSELF DOWN (Stephen Stills) / STOP ON BY (Bobby Womack) / etc. CHAKA KHAN covered many including I'M EVERY WOMAN (c.Ashford & Simpson) / TWISTED (Annie Ross) / WE CAN WORK IT OUT (Beatles) / STRONGER THAN BEFORE (Bacharach / Bayer-Sager) / GOT TO BE THERE (Michael Jackson) / I FEEL FOR YOU (c.Prince) / IT'S MY PARTY (Womack And Womack) / SIGNED, SEALED, DELIVERED (Stevie Wonder) / LOVE OF A LIFETIME (Green of Scritti Politti) / etc. • **Trivia:** In 1986, she duetted on DAVID BOWIE's single 'Underground' (see further on).

Recommended: LIVE – STOMPIN' AT THE SAVOY (*6)

CHAKA KHAN (b.YVETTE MARIE STEVENS, 23 Mar'53, Great Lakes, Illinois) – vox KEVIN MURPHY – keyboards (ex-AMERICAN BREED) / **RON STOCKERT** – vocals, keyboards / **AL CINER** (b.14 May'47) – guitar, vocals (ex-AMERICAN BREED) / **DENNIS BELFIELD** – bass / **ANDRE FISCHER** – drums (ex-AMERICAN BREED)

A.B.C. A.B.C.

Aug 73. (7") **SLIP 'N' SLIDE. / I FINALLY FOUND YOU** [-] [ ]
Aug 73. (lp)(c) **RUFUS** [-] [ ]
– Slip 'n' slide / Keep it coming / There's no tellin' / Maybe your baby / I finally found you / Feel good / Satisfied / Haulin' coal / Whoever's thrilling you / Medley: Love the one you're with – Sit yourself down. *(UK-iss.Feb75)*
Dec 73. (7") **WHOEVER'S THRILLING YOU. / I FINALLY FOUND YOU** [-] [ ]
Mar 74. (7") **KEEP IT COMING. / FEEL GOOD** [-] [ ]
Sep 74. (7") **TELL ME SOMETHING GOOD. / SMOKIN' ROOM** [ ] [3] Jun 74
Oct 74. (lp)(c) **RAGS TO RUFUS** [ ] [4] Jul 74
– You got the love / I got the right street (but the wrong direction) / Walkin' in the Sun / Rags to Rufus / Swing down chariot / Sideways / Ain't nothin' but a maybe / Tell me something good / Look through my eyes / In love we grow / Smokin' room.
Oct 74. (7") **YOU GOT THE LOVE. / RAGS TO RUFUS** [-] [11]

— **TONY MAIDEN** – guitar, vocals (ex-BILLY PRESTON) repl. CINER / **NATE MORGAN** – piano repl. STOCKERT / **BOBBY WATSON** – bass (ex-BILLY PRESTON) repl. BELFIELD.

Feb 75. (7") **STOP ON BY. / RUFUSIZED** [ ] [ ]
Feb 75. (7") **ONCE YOU GET STARTED. / RUFUSIZED** [-] [10]
Mar 75. (lp)(c) **RUFUSIZED** [48] [7] Jan 75
– Once you get started / Somebody's watching / Pack'd my bags / Your smile / Rufusized / I'm a woman (I'm a backbone) / Right is right / Half Moon / Please pardon me (you remind me of a friend) / Stop on by. *(also on quad-lp 1977)*
May 75. (7") **ONCE YOU GET STARTED. / RIGHT IS RIGHT** [ ] [-]
Jul 75. (7") **PLEASE PARDON ME (YOU REMIND ME OF A FRIEND). / SOMEBODY'S WATCHING YOU** [ ] [48] May 75

RUFUS FEATURING CHAKA KHAN

Jan 76. (7") **SWEET THING. / CIRCLES** [ ] [5]
Mar 76. (lp)(c) **RUFUS FEATURING CHAKA KHAN** [ ] [7] Nov75
– Fool's Paradise / Have a good time / Oh I like your loving / Everybody has an aura / Circles / Sweet thing / Dance with me / Little boy blue / On time / Jive talkin'.
Apr 76. (7") **DANCE WIT ME. / EVERYBODY'S GOT AN AURA** [ ] [39]
Aug 76. (7") **JIVE TALKIN'. / ON TIME** [ ] [ ]
Jan 77. (7") **AT MIDNIGHT (MY LOVE WILL LIFT YOU UP). / BETTER DAYS** [ ] [30]
Jan 77. (lp)(c) **ASK RUFUS** [ ] [12]
– At midnight / Close the door / Slow screw against the wall / A flat fry / Earth song / Everlasting love / Hollywood / Majic in your eyes / Better days / Egyptian song.
May 77. (7") **HOLLYWOOD. / EARTHSONG** [ ] [38]
Jul 77. (7") **CLOSE THE DOOR. / EVERLASTING LOVE** [-] [ ]

— **DAVID 'The Hawk' WOLINSKI** – synth. (ex-SHADOWS OF KNIGHT) repl. MORGAN / **JOHN ROBINSON** – drums repl. FISCHER

Feb 78. (7") **CHANGE YOUR WAYS. / MY SHIP WILL SAIL** [-] [ ]
Feb 78. (lp)(c)(US-pic-lp) **STREET PLAYER** [ ] [14]
– Destiny / Stranger to love / Stay / Best of your heart / Finale / Take time / Blue love / Turn / Street player / Change your ways.
Mar 78. (7") **BLUE LOVE. / TAKE TIME** [ ] [ ]
Apr 78. (7") **STAY. / ?** [-] [38]

— CHAKA provided the vocals for QUINCY JONES's hit 45 'STUFF LIKE THAT'. Late 1978, she left RUFUS already signed to 'Warners' as a solo artist. Her debut single I'M EVERY WOMAN hit Top30 UK/**US** (see further on . . .)

RUFUS

continued with WOLINSKI and MAIDEN taking over vocals

Feb 79. (7") **KEEP IT TOGETHER (DECLARATION OF LOVE). / RED HOT POKER** [-] [ ]

Apr 79. (lp)(c)(US-pic-lp) **NUMBERS** 81 Feb 79
– Ain't nobody like you / You're to blame / Keep it together (declaration of love) / Dancin' mood / Red hot poker / Don't you sit alone / Bet my dreams / Pleasure dome / Are we / Life in the city.
Apr 79. (7") **AIN'T NOBODY LIKE YOU. / (part 2)** -
Apr 79. (7") **AIN'T NOBODY LIKE YOU. / YOU'RE TO BLAME** -

— CHAKA returned to the fold, combining also a continuous solo career.

RUFUS & CHAKA KHAN

M.C.A. M.C.A.

Oct 79. (7")(12") **DO YOU LOVE WHAT YOU FEEL. / DANCIN' MOOD** 30
(re-iss.Jun84)
Dec 79. (lp)(c) **MASTERJAM** 14 Nov 79
– Do you love what you feel / Any love / Heaven bound / Walk the rockway / Live in me / Body heat / I'm dancing for your love / What am I missing / Masterjam.
Mar 80. (7")(12") **ANY LOVE. / WHAT AM I MISSING**

RUFUS

without CHAKA
Mar 81. (7")(12") **TONIGHT WE LOVE. / PARTY TILL YOU'RE BROKE**
Apr 81. (lp)(c) **PARTY TILL YOU'RE BROKE** 73 Mar 81
– Tonight we love / Hold on to a friend / Love is taking over / Secret love / Party till you're broke / Can I show you / You're made for me / What is it / We got the way / Afterwards.

— **RUFUS** and the record co. again invited CHAKA do honour contract.
Nov 81. (7") **SHARING THE LOVE. / WE GOT THE WAY** -
Dec 81. (lp)(c) **CAMOUFLAGE** 98 Oct 81
– Better together / Jigsaw / Secret friend / Music man (the D.J. song) / True love / Sharing the love / Quandary / Lilah / Losers in love / Highlight.

Warners Warners

Mar 83. (7") **TAKE IT TO THE TOP. / DISTANT LOVER**
(12"+=) – You turn me around.
Mar 83. (lp)(c) **SEAL IN RED**
– Take it to the top / The time is right / When I get over you / You turn me all around / You, the night and the music / Blinded by the boogie / I'm saving this love song / You're really out of line / Distant lovers / No regrets.
May 83. (7") **BLINDED BY THE BOOGIE. / YOU'RE REALLY OUT OF LINE** -

RUFUS & CHAKA KHAN

Sep 83. (d-lp)(d-c) **LIVE – STOMPIN' AT THE SAVOY** (live Feb'72 / 1 studio side) 64 50
– You got the love / Once you get started / Dance wit me / Sweet thing / Tell me something good / Stop on by / Pack'd my bags / I'm a woman (I'm a backbone) / At midnight (my love will lift you up) / Ain't that peculiar / Stay / What'cha gonna do for me / Do you love what you feel / Ain't nobody / One million kisses / Try a little understanding / Don't go to strangers.
Nov 83. (7") **AIN'T NOBODY. / STOP ON BY (live)** 22 Sep 83
(12"+=) – Don't go to strangers (live).
Mar 84. (7")(12"- as above) 8 -
(c-s++=) – One million kisses / Stay.
Jun 84. (7") **ONE MILLION KISSES. / ANY OLD SUNDAY**
(12"+=) – Do you love what you feel.

— RUFUS were finally defunct, with CHAKA KHAN continuing to go solo.

CHAKA KHAN

(includes all from 1978 onwards)

Warners Warners

Nov 78. (7") **I'M EVERY WOMAN. / WOMAN IN A MAN'S WORLD** 11 21
Jan 79. (lp)(c) **CHAKA** 12 Nov 78
– I'm every woman / Love has fallen on me / Roll me through the rushes / Sleep on it / Life is a dance / We got the love / Some love / Woman in a man's world / Message in the middle of the bottom / I was made to love him.
Mar 79. (7") **LIFE IS A DANCE. / SOME LOVE** Feb79
May 80. (12") **CLOUDS. / WHAT YOU DID**
May 80. (lp)(c) **NAUGHTY** 43
– Clouds / Get ready get set / Move me no mountain / Nothing's gonna take me away / Do naughty / Too much love / All night's alright / What you did / Papillion / Our love's in anger.
Apr 81. (7")(12") **HEED THE WARNING. / NIGHT MOODS**
Apr 81. (lp)(c) **WHAT'CHA GONNA DO FOR ME** 17
– We can work it out / What'cha gonna do for me / I know you, I live you / Any ole Sunday / We got each other / Night in Tunisia / Night moods / Heed the warning / Father he said / Fate / I know you, I live you (reprise).
May 81. (7") **WHAT'CHA GONNA DO FOR ME. /** - 53

— 1982, she contributed vocals to LENNY WHITE's jazz album ECHOES OF AN ERA.
Nov 82. (7") **GOT TO BE THERE. / PASS IT ON, A SURE THING**
Jan 83. (lp)(c) **CHAKA KHAN** 52 Dec 82
– Tearin' it up / Slow dancin' / Best in the west / Got to be there / Be bop medley: a) Hot house, b) East of Suez, c) Epistoophy, d) Yard bird suite, e) Con alma, f) Giant steps / Twisted / So not to worry / Pass it on, a sure thing.
Feb 83. (7") **BEST IN THE WEST. / BE BOP MEDLEY**
(12"+=) – I know I love you.
Oct 84. (7")(12") **I FEEL FOR YOU. / CHINA TOWN** 1 3

— Above 45 featured **STEVIE WONDER** – harmonica / **MELLE MEL** – rapper
Oct 84. (lp)(c)(cd) **I FEEL FOR YOU** 15 14
– This is my night / Stronger than before / My love is alive / Eye to eye / Laflamme / I feel for you / Hold her / Through the fire / Caught in the act / Chinatown.
Jan 85. (7") **THIS IS MY NIGHT. / CAUGHT IN THE ACT** 14 60
(12"+=) – Got to be there.
Apr 85. (7")(12") **EYE TO EYE. / LAFLAMME** 16 -
Aug 85. (7") **THROUGH THE FIRE. / LAFLAMME** 60 Apr85
(12"+=) – I'm every woman.
Sep 85. (7")(12") **KRUSH GROOVE (CAN'T STOP THE STREET). / ?**
Nov 85. (7") **OWN THE NIGHT. / ?** - 57
Jun 86. (7")(12") **LOVE OF A LIFETIME. / COLTRANE DREAMS** 52 53
Jul 86. (lp)(c)(cd) **DESTINY** 77 67
– Love of a lifetime / Earth to Mickey / Watching the world / Other side of the world / My destiny / I can't be loved / It's you / So close / Tight fit / Who's it gonna be / Coltrane dreams.
Nov 86. (7")(12") **WATCHING THE WORLD. / I CAN'T BE LOVED**
Nov 88. (7")(12") **IT'S MY PARTY. / WHERE ARE YOU TONIGHT** 71
Nov 88. (lp)(c)(cd) **CK**
– Signed, sealed, delivered (I'm yours) / Soul talkin' / It's my party / Eternity / Sticky wicket / The end of a love affair / Baby me / Make it last / Where are you tonight / I'll be around.
Apr 89. (7")(c-s) **I'M EVERY WOMAN ('89 remix). / BABY ME** 8 -
(12"+=)(cd-s+=) – ('A'extended)
May 89. (lp)(c)(cd) **LIFE IS A DANCE (The Remix Project)** 14
– (Best of remixed)
Sep 89. (7")(c-s) **I FEEL FOR YOU (remix). / I KNOW I LOVE YOU** 45
(12"+=)/ /(cd-s) – ('A'-L.A.mix)./ / (3 'A'mixes).
Mar 92. (7")(c-s) **LOVE YOU ALL MY LIFETIME. / KEEP GIVIN' ME LOVIN'** 49 68
(12")(cd-s) – (5 'A'mixes incl. garage / love suite 1 & 2 / diva mix).
Apr 92. (cd)(c)(lp) **THE WOMAN I AM** 92
– Everything changes / Give me all / Telephone / Keep givin' me your lovin' / Facts of lovbe / Love you all my lifetime / I want / You can make the story right / Be my eyes / This time / The woman I am / Don't look at me that way.
May 92. (7")(12")(c-s)(cd-s) **DON'T LOOK AT ME THAT WAY. / I'M EVERY WOMAN (remix)**
(re-is.Jul93 hit UK 73)
Jul 92. (7")(c-s) **GIVE ME ALL. / THE WOMAN I AM**
(12"+=)(cd-s+=) – ('A'extended) / ('A'club).
Jan 93. (c-s)(cd-s) **FEELS LIKE HEAVEN. (PETER CETERA with CHAKA KHAN) /** - 71

RUNAWAYS

Formed: Los Angeles, California, USA . . . mid-1974 by record producer KIM FOWLEY, who wanted to run a female RAMONES, after finding JOAN JETT and SANDY WEST. After a rooftop session on a Los Angeles apartment block in early 1976, he secured a record deal with 'Mercury'. Their eponymous debut lp that year, just cracked the US Top 200, but after 2 more minor flops they went separate ways. • **Style:** All-girl new wave punks, with brazen attitude supplanted over some fine heavy tunes. • **Songwriters:** Group co-wrote debut with FOWLEY. The JOAN JETT & THE RUNAWAYS album, was entirely made up of covers; MAMA WENT ALL CRAZEE NOW (Slade). • **Trivia:** They made New York debut at CBGB's in Sep'76, supporting TELEVISION and TALKING HEADS! The RUNAWAYS featured on Various Artists lp 'NEW WAVW' (tracks; 'Cherry Bomb' + 'Hollywood')

Recommended: THE RUNAWAYS (*7)

CHERRIE CURRIE – vocals who repl. MICKI STEELE (was part-time vox, bass) / **LITA FORD** – lead guitar, vocals / **JOAN JETT** – rhythm guitar, vocals / **JACKIE FOX** – bass / **SANDY WEST** – drums

Mercury Mercury

Sep 76. (7") **CHERRY BOMB. / BLACKMAIL**
Nov 76. (lp)(c) **THE RUNAWAYS** - Jun 76
– Cherry bomb / You drive me wild / Is it day or night? / Thunder / Rock and roll / Lovers / American nights / Blackmail / Secrets / Dead end justice. *(re-iss.Sep82)*
Feb 77. (lp)(c) **QUEENS OF NOISE** Jan 77
– Queens of noise / Take it or leave it / Midnight music / Born to be bad / Neon angels on the road to ruin / Midnight music / I love playin' with fire / California Paradise / Hollywood heartbeat / Johnny Guitar.
Feb 77. (7") **HEARTBEAT. / NEON ANGELS ON THE ROAD TO RUIN** -
Feb 77. (7") **QUEENS OF NOISE. / BORN TO BE BAD** -
Oct 77. (lp) **LIVE IN JAPAN (live)** - - Japan
– Queens of noise / California Paradise / All right you guys / Wild thing / Gettin' hot / Rock and roll / You drive me wild / Neon angels on the road to ruin / I wanna be where the boys are / Cherry bomb / American nights.

— (Jul77) **VICKI BLUE** – bass repl. FOX who suffers from nervous exhaustion. **JETT** took over lead vocals, when CURRIE left to go solo.
Oct 77. (7") **SCHOOL DAYS. / WASTED**
Dec 77. (lp)(c) **WAITIN' FOR THE NIGHT**
– Little sister / Wasted / Gotta get out tonight / Wait for me / Fantasies / School days / Trash can murder / Don't go away / Waitin' for the night / You're too possessive.

— **LAURIE McALLISTAR** – bass repl. VICKI BLUE when she attempted suicide. Split late 1978. LITA FORD went solo after recording of final album below.

Cherry Red not issued

Jul 79. (lp)(c)(colrd-lp) **AND NOW . . . THE RUNAWAYS** -
– Saturday night special / Eight days a week / Mama weer all crazee now / I'm a million / Right now / Take over / My buddy and me / Little lost girls / Black leather. *(US re-iss. pic-lp, 1981 as 'LITTLE LOST GIRLS' on 'Rhino') (cd-iss.Jul93 on 'Anagram')*
Aug 79. (7") **RIGHT NOW. / BLACK LEATHER** -

— Disband again in 1979. JOAN JETT went solo backed by her BLACKHEARTS.

– compilations, others, etc. –

Feb 80. Cherry Red; (lp) **FLAMING SCHOOLGIRLS** (live/studio) [ ] [-]
Sep 82. Mercury; (lp) **THE BEST OF THE RUNAWAYS** [ ] [ ]
1981. Rhino; (lp) **MAMA WEER ALL CRAZEE NOW** [-] [ ]
Apr 82. Cherry Red; (lp)(pic-lp) **I LOVE PLAYING WITH FIRE ("JOAN JETT & THE RUNAWAYS")** [ ] [-]
Jun 94. Marilyn; (10"lp) **BORN TO BE BAD** [ ] [-]

Todd RUNDGREN

Born: 22 Jun'48, Upper Derby, Philadelphia, USA. In 1967, he and another ex-WOODY'S TRUCK STOP member CARSTEN VAN OSTEN formed The NAZZ, taking group name from a YARDBIRDS B-side. In 1968 after supporting The DOORS a year earlier, they signed to 'Screen Gems/Columbia'. Their eponymous debut album sold moderately, and RUNDGREN left band mid-69, after 2 more were completed. In 1970, he became an in-house producer for Albert Grossman's 'Bearsville', his first job being for The AMERICAN DREAM. Later in the year, he formed own band 'RUNT' (his nickname), and released RUNT, which fathered his first Top 20 hit 'WE GOTTA GET YOU A WOMAN'. After one more album, he decided to use his own name for further releases. In 1972, after taking over the production duties from GEORGE HARRISON on BADFINGER's 'Straight Up' lp, he unleashed a truly wonderful solo work 'SOMETHING/ANYTHING'. The double album reached US No.29, with a cut from it 'I SAW THE LIGHT' making the Top 20 US & a year later Top 40 in UK. He continued solo and production work, and even formed another outfit 'UTOPIA', to develop a more mystical lyrical side to his genius. • **Style:** Multi-talented rock star, progressing from NAZZ's metal psychedelia into solo experimentation that went from extreme avant-garde to pop/soul pastiche. • **Songwriters:** Phenomenal pensmith, although he did fit in a number of near perfect covers; DO YA (Move) / GOOD VIBRATIONS (Beach Boys) / LOVE OF THE COMMON MAN (from West Side Story?) / MOST LIKELY TO GO YOUR WAY (Bob Dylan) / TIN SOLDIER (Small Faces) / STRAWBERRY FIELDS FOREVER + RAIN (Beatles) / IF SIX WAS NINE (Jimi Hendrix) / HAPPENINGS TEN YEARS TIME AGO (Yardbirds) / etc? • **Trivia:** In 1983, TODD co-wrote the Top 20 hit 'KISSING WITH CONFIDENCE' for WILL POWERS (see under Carly SIMON). TODD's others major productions have included GRAND FUNK (1973) / HALL & OATES (1974) / MEAT LOAF (Bat Out Of Hell) / TOM ROBINSON (1978) / TUBES (1979) / PSYCHEDELIC FURS (1982) / etc. Note:- TODD has just released in 1992 a compilation album of his production work.

Recommended: SOMETHING / ANYTHING (*9) / INITIATION (*8) / THE COLLECTION (UTOPIA; *7) / THE EVER POPULAR TORTURED ARTIST (*7) / ANTHOLOGY (*8) / RA (*7)

NAZZ

TODD RUNDGREN – lead guitar, vocals, composer / **ROBERT 'Stewkey' ANTONI** (b.17 Nov'47, Rhode Island, USA) – vocals, piano / **CARSTEN VAN OSTEN** (b.24 Sep'46, New Jersey, USA) – bass, vocals / **THOM MOONEY** (b. 5 Jan'48, Pennsylvania, USA) – drums

Screen Gems / Screen Gem

Sep 68. (7") **OPEN MY EYES. / HELLO IT'S ME** [ ] [71]
Oct 68. (lp) **NAZZ** [-] [ ]
– Back of your mind / Open my eyes / When I get my plane / If that's the way you feel / Hello it's me / Wildwood blues / She's going down / The lemming song / etc. *(US re-iss.Oct83 on 'Rhino')*
Apr 69. (7") **HELLO IT'S ME. / CROWDED** [ ] [66]
May 69. (lp)(red-lp) **NAZZ NAZZ** [-] [80]
– Forget all about it / Not wrong long / Rain rider / Gonna cry today / Meridian Leeward / Under the ice / Hang on Paul / Kiddie boy / Featherbedding lover / Letters don't count / A beautiful song. *(US re-iss.Oct83 on 'Rhino')*
May 69. (7") **UNDER THE ICE. / NOT WRONG LONG** [ ] [ ]
1970. (7") **SOME PEOPLE (or) KIDS. / MAGIC ME** [-] [ ]
Dec 70. (lp,green-lp) **NAZZ III** [-] [ ]
– You are my window / Old time lovemaking / Loosen up / Kicks / Take the hand / How can you call that beautiful / Only one winner / etc. *(US re-iss.Nov83 on 'Rhino')*

— Had already disbanded early 1970, after completion of III'rd album.

RUNT

was formed by **RUNDGREN** now on – lead vocals, guitar / **TONY SALES** – bass / **HUNT SALES** – drums

not issued / Ampex

Nov 70. (7") **WE GOTTA GET YOU A WOMAN. / BABY LET'S SWING** [-] [20]
Dec 70. (lp) **RUNT** [-] [ ]
– Broke down and busted / Believe in me / We gotta get you a woman / Who's that man / Once burned / Devil's bite / I'm in the cliche / There are no words / Baby let's swing / The last thing you said / Don't tie my hands / Birthday carol. *(UK-iss.Apr72 on 'Bearsville') (US re-iss.Oct87 on 'Rhino') (re-iss.cd May93 on 'Rhino-Bearsville')*

— **N.D.SMART** – drums repl. HUNT who later joined IGGY POP then TIN MACHINE

May 71. (7") **BE NICE TO ME. / BROKE DOWN AND BUSTED** [-] [71]
May 71. (lp) **THE BALLAD OF TODD RUNDGREN** [-] [ ]
– Long flowing robe / The ballad / Bleeding / Wailing wall / The range war / Chain letter / A long time, a long way to go / Boat on the Charles / Be nice to me / Hope I'm around / Parole / Remember me. *(UK-iss.Apr72 on 'Bearsville') (US re-iss.Oct87 on 'Rhino') (re-iss.cd May93 on 'Rhino-Bearsville')*
Aug 71. (7") **A LONG TIME, A LONG WAY TO GO. / PAROLE** [-] [92]

TODD RUNDGREN

now completely solo except for one side of the d-lp which was frequented by session people.

Bearsville / Bearsville

Mar 72. (d-lp) **SOMETHING / ANYTHING?** [ ] [29]
– I saw the light / It wouldn't have made any difference / Wolfman Jack / Cold morning light / It takes two to tango (this is for the girls) / Sweeter memories / (intro) Breathless / The night the carousel burned down / Saving grace / Marlene / Song of the Viking / I went to the mirror / Black Maria / One more day (one word) / Couldn't I just tell you / Torch song / Little red lights / Dust in the wind / Piss Aaron / Hello it's me / Some folks is even whiter than me / You left me sore / Slut. *(US re-iss.Nov87 on 'Rhino') (d-cd-iss. Jul89 on 'Essential') (re-iss.cd Jun93 on 'Rhino-Bearsville')*
Mar 72. (7") **I SAW THE LIGHT. / BLACK MARIA** [-] [16]
Mar 72. (7") **I SAW THE LIGHT. / MARLENE** [ ] [-]
Jul 72. (7") **COULDN'T I JUST TELL YOU. / WOLFMAN JACK** [-] [93]
May 73. (7"m) **I SAW THE LIGHT. / BLACK MARIA / LONG FLOWING ROBE** *(re-iss.Nov76)* [36] [-]
Jun 73. (lp) **A WIZARD, A TRUE STAR** [ ] [86]
– International feel / Never never land / Tic tic tic it wear off / You need your head / Rock and roll pussy / Dogfight giggle / You don't have to camp around / Flamingo / Zen archer / Just another onionhead – Da da Dali / When the shit hits the fan – Sunset Blvd. / Le feel internacionale / Sometimes I don't know what to feel / Does anybody love you? / I'm so proud – Ooh ooh baby – La la means I love you – Cool jerk / Is it my name? / Just one victory. *(re-iss.Nov80 on 'Island') (re-iss.+cd.1987 on 'Castle') (re-iss.cd May93 on 'Rhino-Bearsville')*
Jul 73. (7") **SOMETIMES I DON'T KNOW WHAT TO FEEL. / DOES ANYONE LOVE YOU?** [-] [ ]
Oct 73. (7") **WE GOTTA GET YOU A WOMAN. / COULDN'T I JUST TELL YOU** [ ] [-]
Dec 73. (7") **HELLO IT'S ME. / COLD MORNING LIGHT** [ ] [5] Sep 73.

— He now used many musicians that were to appear as first UTOPIA incarnation

Mar 74. (d-lp) **TODD** [ ] [54]
– How about a little fanfare? / I hink you know / The spark of life / An elpee's worth of toons / A dream goes on forever / Lord Chancelor's nightmare song / Drunken blue rooster / The last ride / Everybody's going to Heaven / King Kong reggae / Number one lowest common denominator / Useless begging / Sidewalk cafe / Izzat love / Heavy metal kids / In and out of Chakras we go / Don't you ever learn / Sons of 1984. *(re-iss.+cd.Dec89 on 'Castle') (re-iss.cd May93 on 'Rhino-Bearsville')*
May 74. (7") **A DREAM GOES ON FOREVER. / HEAVY METAL KIDS** [ ] [69]

— **TODD** formed UTOPIA with **MOODY KLINGMAN** – keyboards / **RALPH SHUCKETT** – bass / **JOHN SIEGLER** – bass, cello / **M.FROG LABAT** – synthesizers

Nov 74. (lp)(c) **TODD RUNDGREN'S UTOPIA ("TODD RUNDGREN'S UTOPIA")** [ ] [34]
– Utopia (theme) / Freak parade / Freedom fighter / The ikon. *(re-iss.cd May93 on 'Rhino-Bearsville')*
Jun 75. (lp)(c) **INITIATION ("TODD RUNDGREN")** [ ] [86]
– Real man / Born to synthesize / The death of rock and roll / Eastern intrigue / Initiation / Fair warning / A treatise on cosmic fire (intro- Prana): (a) The fire of mind or solar fire – (b) The fire of spirit or electric fire – (c) The internal fire or fire by friction / (outro- Prana). *(re-iss.cd May93 on 'Rhino-Bearsville')*
Sep 75. (7") **REAL MAN. / PRANA ("TODD RUNDGREN")** [ ] [83]

— trimmed slightly when LABAT departed.

Oct 75. (lp)(c) **ANOTHER LIVE (live "TODD RUNDGREN'S UTOPIA")** [ ] [66]
– Another life / The wheel / The seven rays / (intro) – Mister Triscuts / West Side Story theme / Something's coming / Just one victory / Heavy metal kids / Do ya / Just one victory. *(re-iss.cd Aug93 on 'Rhino-Bearsville')*
Apr 76. (lp)(c) **FAITHFULL ("TODD RUNDGREN")** [ ] [54]
– Happenings ten years time ago / Good vibrations / Rain / Most likely you go your way and I'll go mine / If six was nine / Strawberry fields forever / Black and white / Love of the common man / When I pray / Cliche / The verb "to love" / Boogies (hamburger hell). *(re-iss.cd Jun93 on 'Rhino-Bearsville')*
Jun 76. (7") **GOOD VIBRATIONS. / LOVE OF THE COMMON MAN** [-] [-]
Jun 76. (7") **GOOD VIBRATIONS. / WHEN I PRAY** [-] [34]
Nov 76. (7") **LOVE OF THE COMMON MAN. / BLACK AND WHITE** [-] [ ]

UTOPIA

with **TODD** now completely changed line-up into **ROGER POWELL** – keyboards (from late '75) / **JOHN 'Willie' WILCOX** – drums / **KASIM SULTON** – bass

Jan 77. (lp)(c) **RA** [27] [79]
– (overture) / Communion with the sun / Magig dragon theatre / Jealousy / Eternal love / Sunburst finish / Hiroshima / Singing and the glass guitar. *(re-iss.cd May93 on 'Rhino-Bearsville')*
Feb 77. (7") **COMMUNION WITH THE SUN. / SUNBURST FINISH** [ ] [ ]

— TODD played/produced 'BAT OUT OF HELL' album for MEAT LOAF, which included some UTOPIANS and was massive seller from 1978 onwards.

Sep 77. (lp)(c) **OOPS! WRONG PLANET** [59] [73]
– Trapped / Windows / Love in action / Crazy lady blue / Back on the street / Marriage of Heaven and Hell / The martyr / Abandon city / Gangrene / My angel / Rape of the young / Love is the answer. *(re-iss.cd Jun93 on 'Rhino-Bearsville')*
Oct 77. (7") **LOVE IS THE ANSWER. / THE MARRIAGE OF HEAVEN AND HELL** [ ] [ ]

TODD RUNDGREN

Apr 78. (lp)(c) **HERMIT OF MINK HOLLOW** [42] [36]
– All the children sing / Can we still be friends / Hurting for you / Too far gone / Onomatopoeia / Determination / Bread / Bag lady / You cried wolf / Lucky guy / Out of control / Fade away. *(re-iss.Nov80 on 'Island') (re-iss.cd May93 on 'Rhino-Bearsville')*

May 78. (7") **CAN WE STILL BE FRIENDS. / DETERMINATION** [ ] [29]
(some US copies had 'OUT OF CONTROL' on B-side)
Jul 78. (7") **YOU CRIED WOLF. / ONOMATOPOEIA** [-] [ ]
Nov 78. (7") **ALL THE CHILDREN SING. / BAG LADY** [ ] [ ]
Dec 78. (d-lp)(c) **BACK TO THE BARS (live)** [ ] [75]
– Real man / Love of the common man / The verb "to love" / Love in action / A dream goes on forever / Sometimes I just don't know what to think / The range war / Black and white / The last ride / Cliche / Don't you ever learn / Never never land / Black Maria / Zen archer / Medley: I'm so proud – Ooh ooh baby – La la means I love you / I saw the light / It wouldn't have made any difference / Eastern intrigue / Initiation / Couldn't I just tell you / Hello it's me. *(re-iss.cd Jun93 on 'Rhino-Bearsville')*
Feb 79. (7") **IT WOULDN'T HAVE MADE ANY DIFFERENCE. / DON'T YOU EVER LEARN** [-] [ ]

UTOPIA

Island Bearsville

Jan 80. (lp)(c) **ADVENTURES IN UTOPIA** [57] [32]
– The road to Utopia / You make me crazy / Second nature / Set me free / Caravan / Last of the new wave riders / Shot in the dark / The very last time / Love alone / Rock love. *(re-iss.cd May93 on 'Rhino-Bearsville')*
Mar 80. (7") **SET ME FREE. / THE UMBRELLA MAN** [ ] [27]
May 80. (7") **THE VERY LAST TIME. / LOVE ALONE** [-] [76]
Oct 80. (lp)(c) **DEFACE THE MUSIC** [ ] [65]
– I just want to touch you / Crystal ball / Where does the world go to hide / Silly boy / Alone / That's not right / Take it home / Hoi poloi / Life goes on / Feel too good / Always late / All smiles / Everybody else is wrong. *(re-iss.cd May93 on 'Rhino-Bearsville')*
Oct 80. (7") **SECOND NATURE. / YOU MAKE ME CRAZY** [-] [ ]
Nov 80. (7"ep) **I JUST WANT TO TOUCH YOU. / SILLY BOY / LIFE GOES ON / ALL SMILES** [ ] [-]
Dec 80. (7") **I JUST WANT TO TOUCH YOU. / ALWAYS LATE** [-] [ ]

TODD RUNDGREN

Feb 81. (7") **TIME HEALS. / TINY DEMONS** [-] [ ]
Feb 81. (lp)(c) **HEALING** [ ] [48]
– Healer / Pulse / Flesh / Golden goose / Compassion / Shine / Healing (part 1, 2 & 3). *(free-7"ltd.w.a.)–* TIME HEALS. / TINY DEMONS *(lp,c / re-iss.Dec81 on 'Avatar') (re-iss.cd May93 on 'Rhino-Bearsville')*
Jan 82. (7") **COMPASSION. / HEALING** [-] [ ]

UTOPIA

Avatar Bearsville

Mar 82. (lp)(c) **SWING TO THE RIGHT** [ ] [ ]
– Swing to the right / Lysistrata / The up / Junk rock (million monkeys) / Shinola / For the love of money / Last dollar on Earth / Fahrenheit 451 / Only human / One world.
Apr 82. (7") **ONE WORLD. / SPECIAL INTEREST** [-] [ ]
May 82. (7") **ONE WORLD. / JUNK ROCK (MILLION MONKEYS)** [ ] [-]
Jun 82. (7") **LYSISTRATA / JUNK ROCK (MILLION MONKEYS)** [-] [ ]
Nov 82. (7"ep) **TIME HEALS / TINY DEMONS / I SAW THE LIGHT / WHY CAN'T WE BE FRIENDS** [ ] [-]

Epic Network

Nov 82. (7") **FEET DON'T FAIL ME NOW. / FORGOTTEN BUT NOT GONE** [ ] [82]
Nov 82. (lp)(c) **UTOPIA** [ ] [84]
– Libertine / Bad little actress / Feet don't fail me now / Neck on up / Say yeah / Call it what you will / I'm looking at you but I'm talking to myself / Hammer in the heart / Burn three times / There goes my inspiration. *(w/ free UK+US m-lp)–* Princess of the universe / Infrared and ultraviolet / Forgotten but not gone / Private Heaven / Chapter and verse. *(re-iss.cd Aug93 on 'Rhino-Bearsville')*
Jan 83. (7") **HAMMER IN MY HEART. / I'M LOOKING AT YOU BUT I'M TALKING TO MYSELF** [-] [ ]

TODD RUNDGREN

Lamborghini Bearsville

Mar 83. (7") **BANG THE DRUM ALL DAY. / CHANT** [-] [63]
Aug 83. (lp)(c) **THE EVER POPULAR TORTURED ARTIST EFFECT** [ ] [66] Feb 83
– Hideaway / Influenza / Don't hurt yourself / There goes my baybay / Tin soldier / Emperor of the highway / Bang the drum all day / Drive / Chant. *(re-iss.cd Jun93 on 'Rhino-Bearsville')*
Aug 83. (7") **BANG THE DRUM ALL DAY. / DRIVE** [ ] [-]
Sep 83. (7") **HIDEAWAY. / EMPEROR OF THE HIGHWAY** [-] [ ]

UTOPIA

W.E.A. Passport

Apr 84. (lp)(c) **OBLIVION** [ ] [74]
– Itch in my brain / Love with a thinker / Bring me my longbow / If I didn't try / Too much water / Maybe I could change / Crybaby / Welcome to my revolution / Winston Smith takes it on the jaw / I will wait.
May 84. (7") **CRYBABY. / WINSTON SMITH TAKES IT ON THE JAW** [ ] [ ]
Jul 84. (7") **LOVE WITH A THINKER. / WELCOME TO MY REVOLUTION** [ ] [-]

Food for Tht. Passport

Jun 85. (lp)(c) **P.O.V.** [ ] [ ] May 85
– Play this game / Style / Stand for something / Secret society / Zen machine / Mated / Wildlife / Mimi gets mad / Mystified / More light.
Jun 85. (7") **MATED. / MAN OF ACTION** [ ] [-]
Jun 85. (7") **MATED. / STAND FOR SOMETHING** [-] [ ]
— (Oct85) TODD is credited on duet with BONNIE TYLER on single 'LOVING YOU IS A DIRTY JOB'.

TODD RUNDGREN

W.E.A. Warners

Oct 85. (7") **SOMETHING TO FALL BACK ON. / LOCKJAW** [ ] [ ]
(UK-12"+=) – ('A'dance mix).
Nov 85. (lp)(c) **A CAPPELLA** [ ] [ ]
– Blue Orpheus / Johnee Jingo / Pretending to care / Hodja / Lost horizon / Something to fall back on / Miracle in the bazaar / Lockjaw / Honest work / Mighty love.
— Early in 1986, UTOPIA split and ROGER POWELL went solo. TODD returned to solo work in 1988 augmented by **ROSS VALORY** – bass (ex-JOURNEY) / **PRAIRIE PRINCE** – drums (ex-TUBES) (same label)
May 89. (lp)(c)(cd) **NEARLY HUMAN** [ ] [ ]
– The want of a nail / The waiting game / Parallel lines / Can't stop running / Unloved children / Fidelity / Feel it / Hawking / I love my life. *(cd+=)–* Two little Hitlers.
May 89. (7") **PARALLEL LINES. / I LOVE MY LIFE** [-] [ ]
Feb 91. (cd)(c)(lp) **SECOND WIND** [ ] [ ]
– Change myself / Love science / Who's sorry now / The smell of money / If I have to be alone / Love in disguise / Kindness / Public servant / Goya's eyes / Second wind.
Jun 93. (cd)(c) **REDUX '92: LIVE IN JAPAN (Utopia live)** [ ] [ ]
Sep 94. (d-cd) **NO WORLD ORDER – LITE** [ ] [ ]
– Worldwide epiphany / No world order / Worldwide epiphany / Day job / Property / Fascist Christ / Love thing / Time stood still / Proactivity / No world order / World epiphany / Time stood still / Love thing / Time stood still / World made flesh / Fever broke. (d-cd+=) – (10 different versions of above).

– compilations, others, etc. (UTOPIA =*) –

Feb 75. Bearsville; (7") **WOLFMAN JACK. / BREATHLESS** [ ] [ ]
Nov 87. Passport; (lp)(c)(cd) **TRIVIA** * [-] [ ]
Feb 88. Raw Power/ US= Rhino; (d-lp)(c)(cd) **ANTHOLOGY** [ ] [ ] 1989
– Can we still be friends / All the children sing / Too far gone / Sweet memories / It wouldn't have made any difference / Hello it's me / I saw the light / Just one victory / Love of the common man / The verb 'to love' / Sometimes I don't know what to feel / Couldn't I just tell you / Tiny demons / Initiation / Real man / A long time a long way to go / Long flowing robe / Compassion / We gotta get you a woman / A dream goes on forever / The last ride / Don't you ever learn / Bang the drum all day / Zen archer. *(cd-omits some+US diff. track listings) (re-iss.d-cd Aug93 on 'Rhino-Bearsville') (re-iss.cd Aug93 on 'Rhino-Bearsville')*
Mar 88. That's Original; (d-lp)(d-c)(d-cd) **RUNT / HERMIT OF MINK HOLLOW** [ ] [-]
Mar 88. That's Original; (d-lp)(d-c)(d-cd) **OOPS! SORRY WRONG PLANET * / ADVENTURES IN UTOPIA *** [ ] [-]
Jun 88. Castle; (d-lp)(d-c)(d-cd) **THE UTOPIA COLLECTION *** [ ] [-]
– Where does the world go to hide / Freedom fighters / All smiles / Lysistrata / Always late / Love in action / Rock love / Set me free / The seven rays / Traped / Swing to the right / One world / Heavy metal kids / The very last time / Crazy lady blue / Feel too good / Love alone / Love is the answer.
Sep 88. WEA; (3"cd-ep) **BANG THE DRUM ALL DAY / I SAW THE LIGHT / CAN WE STILL BE FRIENDS / ALL THE CHILDREN SING** [ ] [-]
Oct 88. Old Gold; (7") **I SAW THE LIGHT. / (other artist)** [ ] [-]
1989. Rhino; (lp) **THE BEST OF NAZZ** [-] [ ]
May 95. Rhino; (cd) **ANTHOLOGY *** [ ] [ ]
Apr 92. Rhino; (cd) **AN ELPEE'S WORTH OF PRODUCTIONS** [ ] [-]
(various)

RUN DMC

Formed: Hollis, New York, USA . . . 1982 by SIMMONS, McDANIELS and MIZEL. In '83, SIMMONS' brother RUSSELL obtained deal with 'Profile' records, for whom they released acclaimed eponymous debut lp, which earned raps first gold disc. In 1985, they starred in first rap film 'Krush Groove', which was based on life story of RUSSELL, who had just become co-chairman of Rick Rubin's 'Def Jam' label. In 1986, their third album 'RAISING HELL' broke through to make US Top 3, and they soon became rappin' buddies with tour partners The BEASTIE BOYS. • **Style:** Fused a mixture of rap, sampling and heavy rock. • **Songwriters:** Group compositions, except WALK THIS WAY (Aerosmith) / MARY MARY (Mike Nesmith). • **Trivia:** In Mar'88, they lost legal battle with 'Profile', who had contracted them to 10 albums. This delayed and probably cancelled their much touted expensive movie 'TOUGHER THAN LEATHER'.

Recommended: RUN DMC'S GREATEST HITS TOGETHER FOREVER (*8) / RAISING HELL (*8)

JOSEPH 'Run' SIMMONS (b.'64) – vocals / **MC DARRYL 'D' McDANIELS** (b.'64) – vocals / **JASON MIZEL** (JAM-MASTER JAY) (b.'65) – DJ

4th & Broad. Profile

Jun 84. (lp) **RUN – D.M.C.** [-] [53]
– Hard times / Rock box / Jam-master Jay / Hollis Crew (krush-groove 2) / Sucker M.C.'s (krush-groove 1) / It's like that / Wake up / 30 days / Jay's game. *(UK-iss.+c.May85 on '4th & Broadway', re-iss.+cd.Apr91*
Jun 84. (7") **ROCK BOX. / ('A'vocal dub)** [ ] [ ]
(12"+=) – ('A'dub version).
Sep 84. (7") **30 DAYS. / ('A' instrumental)** [-] [ ]
Jan 85. (7") **HOLLIS CREW. / ('A' instrumental)** [-] [ ]
Feb 85. (lp)(c)(pic-lp) **KING OF ROCK** [ ] [52]
– Rock the house / King of rock / You talk too much / Jam-master jammin' / Roots, rap, reggae / Can you rock it like this / You're blind / It's not funny / Daryll and Joe (krush-groove 3). *(cd-iss.May88) (re-iss.+cd.Apr91)*
Mar 85. (7") **KING OF ROCK. / ROCK BOX (vocal)** [ ] [ ]
(12"+=) – ('A'instrumental).
Mar 86. (7") **YOU TALK TOO MUCH. / DARRYL AND JOE (KRUSH-GROOVE 3)** [ ] [ ]

(12"+=) – ('A'instrumental) / Sucker M.C.'s (krush-groove 1).
Apr 86. (7") **JAM-MASTER JAMMIN'. / (part 2)** [-] [ ]
May 86. (7") **CAN YOU ROCK IT LIKE THIS. / TOGETHER FOREVER** [-] [ ]

London Profile

Jun 86. (7") **MY ADIDAS. / PETER PIPER** [62] [ ]
(12"+=) – ('A'instrumental).
Jul 86. (lp)(c)(cd) **RAISING HELL** [41] [3] Jun 86
– Peter Piper / It's tricky / My Adidas / Walk this way / Is it live / Perfection / Hit it run / Raising Hell / You be illin' / Dumb girl / Son of Byford / Proud to be black.
Aug 86. (7") **WALK THIS WAY. ("RUN DMC featuring AEROSMITH"). / KING OF ROCK** [-] [4]
Aug 86. (7") **WALK THIS WAY. ("RUN DMC featuring AEROSMITH") / ('A' instrumental)** [8] [-]
(12"+=)(12"pic-d+=) – My Adidas.
Sep 86. (7") **KING OF ROCK. / JAM MASTER JAY** [ ] [-]
(12"+=) Rock box / Jay's game / You talk too much.
Feb 87. (7") **YOU BE ILLIN'. / HIT IT RUN** [42] [29] Oct 86
(12"+=) – ('A'instrumental).
May 87. (7") **IT'S TRICKY. / PROUD TO BE BLACK** [16] [57] Feb 87
(12"+=) – ('A'club tempo) / ('A'scratchapella) / ('A'reprise).
Sep 87. (7") **PETER PIPER. / MY ADIDAS** [ ] [-]
(12"+=) – Walk this way / King of rock.
Nov 87. (7") **XMAS IN HOLLIS. / PETER PIPER** [56] [-]
(12"+=) – My Adidas / Walk this way / King of rock.
Apr 88. (7") **RUN'S HOUSE. / BEATS TO THE RHYME** [37] [ ]
(12"+=)(cd-s+=) – ('A'&'B'instrumental).
Jun 88. (lp)(c)(cd) **TOUGHER THAN LEATHER** [13] [9]
– Run's house / Mary, Mary / They call us Run DMC / Beats to the rhyme / Radio station / Papa crazy / Tougher than leather / I'm not going out like that / How d'ya do it Dee? / Miss Elaine / Soul to rock and roll / Ragtime.
Aug 88. (7") **MARY, MARY. / RAISING HELL** [ ] [75] Jul 88
(12"+=) – ('A'instrumental).

M.C.A. M.C.A.

Aug 89. (7")(c-s) **GHOSTBUSTERS THEME II. / ('A'instrumental)** [65] [ ]
(12"+=)(cd-s+=) – Pause.

Profile Profile

Nov 90. (7")(c-s) **WHAT'S IT ALL ABOUT. / THE AVE** [48] [ ]
(12"+=) – ('A'&'B'instrumentals).
(cd-s+=) – ('A'instrumental) / ('A'version).
Dec 90. (cd)(c)(lp) **BACK FROM HELL** [-] [81]
– Back from hell / Bob your head / Livin' in the city / Sucker DJs / What's it all about / Word is born / Pause / Not just another groove / P upon a tree / Party time / Naughty / Kick the frama lama lama / Groove to the sound / Don't stop.
Mar 91. (7")(c-s) **FACES. / BACK FROM HELL (remix)** [ ] [ ]
(12"+=) – ('A'radio mix) / ('A'instrumental).
(cd-s) – (2 'A'versions see above) / (2 'B'versions).
(12") – (4 'A'mixes – 3 above).
Nov 91. (cd)(c)(lp) **RUN DMC GREATEST HITS TOGETHER FOREVER 1983-1991** (compilation) [ ] [ ]
– Sucker M.C.'s (krush groove 1) / Walk this way / Together forever (krush groove 4) (live at Hollis Park '84) / King of rock / Run's house / It's tricky / Pause / You be illin' / My Adidas / Here we go (live at The Funhouse) / Rock box / What's it all about / Hard times / Beats to the rhyme / Jam-master Jay / Peter Piper / It's like that / Christmas in Hollis.

—— Earlier 1991, JOSEPH SIMMONS was charged with raping a 22-year female fan.

Mar 93. (12")(cd-s) **DOWN WITH THE KING. / ('A'mixes)** [69] [21]
(re-iss. Nov '93 UK)
May 93. (cd)(c)(lp) **DOWN WITH THE KING** [44] [7]
– Down with the king / C'mon everybody / Can I get it to yo / Hit 'em hard / To the maker / In the head / Ooh, what ya gonna do / Big Willie / Three little Indians / In the house / Kick it (can I get a witness) / Get open / What's next / Wreck shop / For ten years.
Jul 93. (12")(cd-s) **OOH, WHATCHA GONNA DO. / ('A'mixes)** [ ] [ ]
Apr 94. (12")(cd-s) **WHAT'S NEXT. / CAN I GET IT, YO / PIED PIPER** [ ] [ ]

compilations, etc

Nov 95. Profile; (10x12"box) **12" SINGLES BOX SET** [ ] [-]

RUNRIG

Formed: North Uist, Outer Hebrides, Scotland . . . 1973 as The RUN-RIG DANCE BAND, by brothers RORY and CALUM McDONALD plus BLAIR DOUGLAS. After many comings and goings throughout the next 6 years, RUNRIG issued debut album 'THE HIGHLAND CONNECTION' for own self-financed label 'Ridge'. After building up home support on the live front, and releasing 3 more albums during a 9 year period, they finally secured nationwide outlet when signing to 'Chrysalis'. Their first taste of success came in the late 80's, when album 'SEARCHLIGHT', nearly made the British Top 10. • **Style:** Traditional Celtic-rock outfit, who retained Gaelic roots and language throughout career. Described as a cross between BIG COUNTRY, The CHIEFTAINS or HORSLIPS. • **Songwriters:** McDONALD brothers / JONES write instrumental songs. Also play traditional songs. • **Trivia:** Due to religious beliefs, they never play live on a Sunday.

Recommended: ONCE IN A LIFETIME (*7).

DONNIE MUNRO (b. 2 Aug'53, Uig, Isle Of Skye, Scotland) – vocals / **RORY McDONALD** (b.RODERICK, 27 Jul'49, Dornoch, Scotland) – bass, vocals, acoustic guitar, accordion / **BLAIR DOUGLAS** – harmonica, organ (re-joined Jun78) / **CALUM McDONALD** (b.MALCOLM MORRISON McDONALD, 12 Nov'53, Lochmaddy, North Uist, Scotland) – drums, percussion

Neptune not issued

Apr 78. (c) **PLAY GAELIC** [ ] [-]
– Duisg mo run / Sguaban arbhair / Tillidh mi / Criogal cridhe / Nach neonach neiad a tha E / Sunndach / Air an traigh / De ni mi – pulp / An ros / Ceolan danasa / Chi'n geamhradh / Cum 'ur n'aire. *(lp-iss.Sep84) (re-iss.+c+cd.Jul95 as 'RUNRIG PLAY GAELIC – THE FIRST LEGENDARY RECORDINGS' on 'Lismor')*

—— added **MALCOLM ELWYN JONES** (b.12 Jul'59, Inverness, Scotland) – guitar, bagpipes, mandolin to repl. BLAIR (who still guested later)

Ridge not issued

Oct 79. (lp)(c) **THE HIGHLAND CONNECTION** [ ] [-]
– Gamhna gealla / Mairi / What time? / Fichead bliadhna / Na luing air scoladh / Loch Lomond / Na h-vain a's t-earrach / Foghar nan Eilean / The twenty-five pounder / Going home / Morning tide / Cearcal a chuain. *(re-iss.Sep84 + Feb86) (cd-iss.Aug89)*

—— added on tour '81, **RICHARD CHERNS** (b.England) – keyboards

Dec 82. (7") **LOCH LOMOND. / TUIREADH IAIN RUAIDH** [72] [-]
Aug 84. (7") **DANCE CALLED AMERICA. / NA H-UAIN A'S T-ERRACH** [ ] [-]
(12"+=) – Ribhinn o.

—— added guests **BLAIR DOUGLAS / JOHN MARTIN** – cello / **RONNIE GERRARD** – fiddle

Sep 84. (lp)(c) **RECOVERY** [ ] [-]
– An toll dubh / Rubh nan cudaigean / 'Ic lain 'ic Sheimas / Recovery / Instrumental / 'S tu mo Leannan – Nightfall in Marsco / Breakin' the chains / Fuaim a bhlair / Tir an airna / The old boys / Dust. *(re-iss.Feb86, c-iss.May88, cd-iss.Aug89)*
Nov 84. (7")(12") **SKYE. / HEY MANOU** [ ] [-]

—— The 1984 singles were issued on 'Simple')

—— **PETER WISHART** (b. 9 Mar'52, Dunfermline, Scotland) – keyboards, vocals (ex-BIG COUNTRY) repl. CHERNS / added **IAIN BAYNE** (b.22 Jan'60, St.Andrews, Scotland) – drums, percussion

Feb 86. (lp)(c) **HEARTLAND** [ ] [-]
– O cho mealdt / This darkest winter / Life line / Air a' chuain / Dance called America / The everlasting gun / Skye / Choc na feille / The wire / An atalreaachd Ard / The ferry / Tuireadh Iain ruaidh. *(cd-iss.1989)*
1986. (7") **THE WORK SONG. / THIS TIME OF YEAR** [ ] [-]
Nov 87. (7") **ALBA. / WORKER FOR THE WIND** [ ] [-]
Dec 87. (lp)(c)(cd) **THE CUTTER AND THE CLAN** [ ] [-]
– Alba / The cutter / Hearts of olden glory / Pride of the summer / Worker for the wind / Rocket to the Moon / The only rose / Protect and survive / Our Earth was once green / An ubhal as airde. *(re-iss.Jul88 on 'Chrysalis') (re-iss.cd Mar94) (re-iss.cd May95, hit No.45)*

Chrysalis Chrysalis?

Aug 88. (7") **PROTECT AND SURVIVE. / HEARTS OF OLDEN GLORY** [ ] [-]
(12"+=)(cd-s+=) – ('A'live).
Nov 88. (lp)(c)(cd) **ONCE IN A LIFETIME (live)** [61] [ ]
– Dance called America / Protect and survive / Chi mi'n geamhradh / Rocket to the Moon / Going home / Choc na feille / Nightfall on Marsco / 'S tu mo Leannan / Skye / Loch Lomond / Hearts of olden glory.
Aug 89. (7")(c-s)(7"pic-d) **NEWS FROM HEAVEN. / SMALLTOWN** [ ] [ ]
(12"+=) – Chi min fir.
(12"pic-d+=)(cd-s+=) – The times they are a-changin'.
Sep 89. (lp)(c)(cd) **SEARCHLIGHT** [11] [ ]
– News from Heaven / Every river / City of lights / Eirinn / Tir a'mhurain / World appeal / Tear down these walls / Only the brave / Siol ghoraidh / That final mile / Smalltown / Precious years.
Nov 89. (7")(c-s) **EVERY RIVER. / THIS TIME OF YEAR** [ ] [ ]
(12"+=)(cd-s+=) – Once our Earth was green.
Sep 90. (10"ep)(12"ep)(cd-ep) **CAPTURE THE HEART** [49] [ ]
– Stepping down the glory road / Satellite flood / Harvest Moon / The apple came down.
Jun 91. (cd)(c)(lp) **THE BIG WHEEL** [4] [ ]
– Headlights / Healer in your heart / Abhainn an t-sluaigh – The crowded river / Always the winner / This beautiful pain / An cuibhle mor – The big wheel / Edge of the world / Hearthammer / I'll keep coming home / Flower of the West.
Aug 91. (7")(c-s) **HEARTHAMMER. / BEAT THE DRUM** [25] [ ]
(12")(cd-s) – ('A'side) / Loch Lomond (live) / Solus na madainn (live).
(7"ep+=) – Pride of the summer (live).
Nov 91. (7")(c-s) **FLOWER OF THE WEST (live). / CHI M'N GEAMHRADH** [43] [ ]
(12"+=)(cd-s+=) – Ravenscraig / Harvest Moon (live).
Feb 93. (7")(7"blue)(c-s) **WONDERFUL. / APRIL COME SHE WILL** [29] [ ]
(cd-s) – ('A'side) / Straidean na roinn Eorpa (Streets of Europe) / On the edge.
Mar 93. (cd)(c)(lp) **AMAZING THINGS** [2] [ ]
– Amazing things / Wonderful / The greatest flame / Move a mountain / Pog aon oidhche earraich (A kiss one evening Spring) / Dream fields / Song of the Earth / Forever eyes of blue / Sraidean na roinn-earpa (Streets of Europe) / Canada / Ard (High) / On the edge.
Apr 93. (7")(c-s) **THE GREATEST FLAME. / SUILVAN** [36] [ ]
(cd-s+=) – Saints of the soil / An t-lasgair (the fisherman).
(cd-s) – ('A'side) / The fisherman / Morning tide (re-recorded) / Chi m'in tir (I see the land).
Nov 94. (cd)(c)(lp) **TRANSMITTING LIVE (live)** [41] [ ]
– Urlar / Ard / Edge of the world / The greatest flame / Harvest Moon / The wire / Precious years / Every river / Flower of the west / Only the brave / Alba / Pog aon oidche earraich (one kiss one Spring evening).
Dec 94. (12"ep)(c-ep)(cd-ep) **THIS TIME OF YEAR / WONDERFUL (live). / DREAM FIELDS (live) / I'LL KEEP COMING HOME (live) / THIS TIME OF YEAR (re-recorded)** [38] [-]
Apr 95. (7")(c-s)(cd-s) **AN UBHAL AS AIRDE (THE HIGHEST APPLE). / ABHAINN AN T-SLUIGH / THE GREATEST FLAME** [18] [ ]
(cd-s+=) – Flower of the west.
Oct 95. (7")(c-s) **THINGS THAT ARE. / AN UBHAL AS AIRDE (THE HIGHEST APPLE)** [40] [ ]
(cd-s+=) – Amazing things (remix) / That other landscape.
Nov 95. (cd)(c)(lp) **MARA** [24] [ ]

– Day in a boat / Nothing but the sun / The mighty Atlantic / Things that are / Road and the river / Meadhan Oidhche air an Acairseid / The wedding / The dancing floor / Thairis air a ghleann / Lighthouse.

RUSH

Formed: Toronto, Canada . . . 1969 by LIFESON, LEE and RUTSEY. They toured local clubs, and by 1973 were supporting The NEW YORK DOLLS in their hometown. They released own financed eponymous Terry Brown produced debut album early '74, which was soon picked up by DJ Donna Halper, who sent a copy to 'Mercury' records. They signed the band for a 6-figure sum, and also re-released debut, which nearly made US Top 100. By 1976, they had built up large following, which enabled live double album 'ALL THE WORLD'S A STAGE' to creep into the 40. They grew from strenth to strength during next decade and a half, to stronger commercial triumphs in the UK. • **Style:** Spectacular sci-fi influenced heavy rock trio, who mixed ambitious concept pieces, with unique but complex lyrical content. They went into more sophisticated progressive rock during the 80's. • **Songwriters:** Group compositions / PEART lyrics from 1974 onwards. Covered NOT FADE AWAY (Buddy Holly). • **Trivia:** The concept album 2112, was based on the work by novelist and philosopher Ayn Rand. Early in 1982, GEDDY guests for BOB & DOUG McKENZIE (aka Rick Moranis & Dave Thomas) on their US Top 20 single 'Take Off'.

Recommended: ALL THE WORLD'S A STAGE (*9) / 2112 (*8) / CHRONICLES (*7).

GEDDY LEE (b.29 Jul'53, Willowdale, Toronto, Canada) – vocals, bass, keyboards / **ALEX LIFESON** (b.27 Aug'53, Fernie, British Columbia, Canada) – lead guitar / **JOHN RUTSEY** – drums

not issued / Moon

1973. (7") **NOT FADE AWAY. / YOU CAN'T FIGHT IT** [-] [ ]

Mercury / Mercury

Feb 75. (lp)(c) **RUSH** [ ] [ ] Jul 74
– Finding my way / Need some love / Take a friend / Here again / What you're doing / In the mood / Before and after / Working man. *(re-iss.Jun83, cd-iss.Apr87)*

— (Autumn '74) **NEIL PEART** (b.12 Sep'52, Hamilton, Ontario, Canada) – drums, vocals, lyrics repl. RUTSEY

Apr 75. (lp)(c) **FLY BY NIGHT** [ ] [ ] Feb 75
– Anthem / Best I can / Beneath, between and behind / By-Tor and the snowdog:- At the tobes of Hades – Across the styx – Of the battle – Epilogue / Fly by night / Making memories / Rivendell / In the end. *(re-iss.Jun83, cd-iss.Apr87)*

May 75. (7") **FLY BY NIGHT. / ANTHEM** (re-iss.Dec 77) [-] [ ]

Nov 75. (7") **BASTILLE DAY. / LAKESIDE PARK** [-] [ ]

Mar 76. (lp)(c) **CARESS OF STEEL** [ ] [ ] Oct 75
– Bastille day / The fountain of Lamneth: In the valley – Didacts and narpets – No one at the bridge – Panacea – Bacchus plateau – The fountain / I think I'm going bald / Lakeside Park / Necromancer:- Into the darkness – Under the shadow – Return of the prince. *(re-iss.Jun83, cd-iss.Apr87)*

Jun 76. (lp)(c) **2112** [61] [ ] Apr 76
– A passage to Bangkok / The twilight zone / Lessons / Tears / Something for nothing / 2112: (a) Overture – (b) The Temples of Syrinx – (c) Discovery – (d) Presentation – (e) Oracle – (f) The dream – (g) Soliliquy – (h) Grand finale. *(re-iss.Jan85, cd-iss.Apr87)*

Jun 76. (7") **LESSONS. / THE TWILIGHT ZONE** [-] [ ]

Mar 77. (d-lp)(d-c) **ALL THE WORLD'S A STAGE (live)** [ ] [40] Sep 76
– Anthem / Bastille day / By-Tor and the snowdog: At the tobes of Hades – Across the styx – Of the battle – Epilogue / Fly by night / In the mood / Lakeside park / Something for nothing / 2112: (a) Overture – (b) The Temples of Syrinx – (c) Discovery – (d) Presentation – (e) Oracle – (f) The dream – (g) Soliliquy – (h) Grand finale / What you're doing / Working man / Finding my way. *(re-iss.Sep84, cd-iss.Apr87)*

Dec 76. (7") **FLY BY NIGHT (live). / IN THE MOOD (live)** [-] [88]

Feb 77. (7") **THE TEMPLES OF SYRINX. / MAKING MEMORIES** [-] [ ]

Sep 77. (lp)(c) **A FAREWELL TO KINGS** [22] [33]
– A farewell to kings / Xanadu / Closer to the heart / Cinderella man / Madrigal / Cygnus X-1. *(cd-iss.Apr87)*

Nov 77. (7") **CLOSER TO THE HEART. / MADRIGAL** [-] [76]

Jan 78. (7"ep) **CLOSER TO THE HEART. / BASTILLE DAY / THE TEMPLES OF SYRINX** [36] [-]
(12"ep+=) – Anthem.

Nov 78. (lp)(c)(pic-lp) **HEMISPHERES** [14] [47]
– Cygnus X-1 Book 2; Hemispheres: Prelude – Apollo, bringer of wisdom – Dionysus, bringer of love – Armageddon, the battle of heart and mind – Cygnus, bringer of balance / Circumstances / The trees / La villa Strangiato. *(re-iss.Mar88, cd-iss.Apr87)*

Jan 79. (7") **CIRCUMSTANCES. / THE TREES** [-] [ ]

Jan 80. (lp)(c) **PERMANENT WAVES** [3] [4]
– The spirit of radio / Freewill / Jacob's ladder / Entre nous / Different strings / Natural science. *(cd-iss.Apr87)*

Feb 80. (7") **THE SPIRIT OF RADIO. / CIRCUMSTANCES** [-] [51]

Feb 80. (7") **THE SPIRIT OF RADIO. / THE TREES** [13] [-]
(12"+=) – Working man.

Apr 80. (7") **DIFFERENT STRINGS. / ENTRE NOUS** [-] [ ]

Feb 81. (7") **LIMELIGHT. / XYZ** [-] [55]

Feb 81. (lp)(c) **MOVING PICTURES** [3] [3]
– Tom Sawyer / Red Barchetta / XYZ / Limelight / The camera eye / Witch hunt (part III of fear) / Vital signs. *(cd-iss.1983)*

Mar 81. (7") **VITAL SIGNS. / IN THE MOOD** [41] [ ]
(12"+=) – A passage to Bangkok / Circumstances.

May 81. (7") **TOM SAWYER. / WITCH HUNT** [-] [ ]

Oct 81. (7") **FREEWILL (live). / CLOSER TO THE HEART (live)** [-] [ ]

Oct 81. (d-lp)(d-c) **EXIT . . . STAGE LEFT (live)** [6] [10]
– The spirit of radio / Red Barchetta / YYZ / A passage to Bangkok / Closer to the heart / Beneath, between and behind / Jacob's ladder / Broon's bane / The trees / Xanadu / Freewill / Tom Sawyer / La villa Strangiato. *(cd-iss.Apr87)*

Oct 81. (7") **TOM SAWYER (live). / A PASSAGE TO BANGKOK (live)** [25] [-]
(12"+=) – Red Barchetta (live).

Dec 81. (7") **CLOSER TO THE HEART (live). / THE TREES (live)** [ ] [69]

Aug 82. (7") **NEW WORLD MAN. / VITAL SIGNS (live)** [42] [21]
(12"+=) – Freewill (live).

Sep 82. (lp)(c) **SIGNALS** [3] [10]
– Subdivisions / The analog kid / Chemistry / Digital man / The weapon / New world man / Losing it / Countdown. *(cd-iss.1983)*

Oct 82. (7") **SUBDIVISIONS. / COUNTDOWN** [-] [ ]

Oct 82. (7")(7"pic-d) **SUBDIVISIONS. / RED BARCHETTA (live)** [53] [-]
(12"+=) – Jacob's ladder (live).

Apr 83. (7")(7"sha-pic-d) **COUNTDOWN. / NEW WORLD MAN** [36] [ ]
(12"+=) – The spirit of radio (live) / (interview excerpts).

Apr 84. (lp)(c)(cd) **GRACE UNDER PRESSURE** [5] [10]
– Distant early warning / After image / Red sector A / The enemy within / The body electric / Kid gloves / Red lenses / Between the wheels.

May 84. (7") **THE BODY ELECTRIC. / THE ANALOG KID** [56] [ ]
(12"+=)(10"red+=) – Distant early warning.

Oct 85. (7") **THE BIG MONEY. / TERRITORIES** [ ] [45]
(12"+=) – Red sector A.
(d7"+=) – Closer to the heart / The spirit of radio.
(7") – ('A'side). / Middletown dreams.

Nov 85. (lp)(c)(cd)(pic-lp) **POWER WINDOWS** [9] [10] Oct 85
– The big money / Grand designs / Manhattan project / Marathon / Territories / Middletown dreams / Emotion detector / Mystic rhythms.

Oct 87. (7") **TIME STAND STILL. / FORCE TEN** [41] [ ]
(12"pic-d+=) – The enemy within (live).
(12"++=) – Witch hunt (live).

Nov 87. (lp)(c)(cd) **HOLD YOUR FIRE** [10] [13] Sep 87
– Force ten / Time stand still / Open secrets / Second nature / Prime mover / Lock and key / Mission / Turn the page / Tai Shan / High water.

Mar 88. (7") **PRIME MOVER. / TAI SHAN** [ ] [ ]
(12"+=) – Open secrets.
(12"++=)(cd-s++=) – New world man (live).
(7"white) – ('A'side). / DISTANT EARLY WARNING (live)

Jan 89. (d-lp)(c)(cd) **A SHOW OF HANDS (live)** [12] [21]
– (intro) / The big money / Subdivisions / Marathon / Turn the page / Manhattan project / Mission / Distant early warning / Mystic rhythms / Witch hunt (part III of fear) / The rhythm method / Force ten / Time stand still / Red sector A / Closer to the heart.

Atlantic / Atlantic

Nov 89. (lp)(c)(cd) **PRESTO** [27] [16]
– Show don't tell / Chain lightning / The pass / War paint / Scars / Presto / Superconductor / Anagram (for Mongo) / Red tide / Hands over fist / Available light.

Jan 90. (7") **SHOW DON'T TELL. / ?** [-] [ ]

Sep 91. (cd)(c)(lp) **ROLL THE BONES** [10] [3]
– Dreamline / Bravado / Roll the bones / Face up / Where's my thing? (part IV 'Gangster Of Boats' trilogy) / The big wheel / Heresy / Ghost of a chance / Neurotica / You bet your life.

Feb 92. (7")(7"sha-pic-d) **ROLL THE BONES. / SHOW DON'T TELL** [49] [ ]
(cd-s+=) – (interviews) / Anagram.

Apr 92. (7")(c-s) **GHOST OF A CHANCE. / DREAMLINE** [ ] [ ]
(12"+=)(cd-s+=) – Chain lightning / Red tide.

Oct 93. (cd)(c)(lp) **COUNTERPARTS** [14] [2]
– Animate / Stick it out / Cut to the chase / Nobody's hero / Between Sun and Moon / Alien shore / The speed of love / Double agent / Leave that thing alone / Cold fire / Everyday glory.

– compilations, others, etc. –

May 78. Mercury; (t-lp)(d-c) **ARCHIVES** (first 3 lp's) [ ] [ ] Apr 78

1981. Mercury; (lp)(c)(pic-lp) **RUSH THROUGH TIME** [-] [ ]

Feb 88. Old Gold; (7") **THE SPIRIT OF RADIO. / CLOSER TO THE HEART** [ ] [-]

Sep 90. Vertigo/ US= Mercury; (d-cd)(d-c)(t-lp) **CHRONICLES** [42] [51]
– Finding my way / Working man / Fly by night / Anthem / Bastille day / Lakeside park / 2112: a) Overture, b) The temples of Syrinx / What you're doing (live) / A farewell to kings / Closer to the heart / The trees / La villa Strangiato / Freewill / The spirit of radio/ / Tom Sawyer / Red barchetta / Limelight / A passage to Bangkok (live) / Subdivisions / New world man / Distant early warning / Red sector A / The big money / Manhattan project / Force ten / Time stand still / Mystic rhythms (live) / Show don't tell.

Leon RUSSELL

Born: HANK WILSON, 2 Apr'41, Lawton, Oklahoma, USA. Having learned to play the piano at an early age, he soon learnt other instruments, and by the late 50's still in his teens, progressed to nightclubs augmenting RONNIE HAWKINS and JERRY LEE LEWIS. By the early 60's, he had moved to California, and was session man under the name of RUSSELL BRIDGES. Soon became a regular member of PHIL SPECTOR's "wall of sound". His sessions included HERB ALPERT's 'Taste Of Honey' & The BYRDS 'Mr.Tambourine Man'. In the mid-60's, he arranged a hit for GARY LEWIS & THE PLAYBOYS; 'This Diamond Ring', and also signed for 'A&M' records. His work for others continued including sessions for GENE CLARK (ex-Byrds) and arranging a hit single 'Feelin' Groovy' for HARPER'S BIZARRE. In 1968 he formed ASYLUM CHOIR with MARC BENNO, and recorded 2 albums. Around the same time, he worked and produced for DELANEY & BONNIE (BRAMLETT), on their 'Accept No Substitute' album. After this, he and JOE COCKER's manager DENNY CORDELL formed own label 'Shelter', and released LEON's solo debut in 1970. Prior to this, LEON had been organizer of JOE COCKER's live tour 'Mad Dogs And Englishmen', which had helped hoist debut into minor chart placing. His next album 'LEON RUSSELL & THE SHELTER PEOPLE', made both US + UK Top 30, with LEON also joining GEORGE HARRISON's 'Concert For Bangla Desh' at Madison Square Garden in August '71. The following year, he was at No.2 with album 'CARNEY', and was writing and producing 2 songs with BOB DYLAN; 'Watching The River Flow' & 'When I Paint My Masterpiece'. • **Style:** Talented singer-songwriter, who shifted from a workaholic session man and rock-pop star to a more melodic country-bluegrass artist, by the late 70's. **Covers:** BEWARE OF DARKNESS (George Harrison) / THE BATTLE OF NEW ORLEANS (Jimmy Driftwood) / MASTERS OF WAR + IT'S A HARD RAIN GONNA FALL + THE MIGHTY QUINN + IT'S ALL OVER NOW, BABY BLUE (Bob Dylan) / ROLL IN MY SWEET ARMS BABY (Lester Flatt) / IF I WERE A CARPENTER (Tim Hardin) / JAMBALAYA + I'M SO LONESOME I COULD CRY (Hank Williams) / and other covers from 'HANK WILSON'S BACK'.JUMPING JACK FLASH (Rolling Stones) / YOUNG BLOOD + IDOL WITH THE GOLDEN HEAD (Leiber-Stoller) / SWEEPING THROUGH THE CITY (. . . Casal) / I SERVE A LIVING SAVOIR (. . . Watson) / SOME DAY (. . . Henderson) / TOO MUCH MONKEY BUSINESS (Chuck Berry) / JEZEBEL (. . . Shanklin) / etc. • **Trivia:** In 1977, his song 'THIS MASQUERADE', won a Grammy award for GEORGE BENSON. In the late 60's JOE COCKER successfully cvered 'Delta Lady'.

Recommended: THE COLLECTION (*6)

LEON RUSSELL – vocals, piano, trumpet, guitar, etc.

		not issued	A & M
1964.	(7") **MISTY. / CINDY**	-	
		Dot	Dot
Nov 65.	(7") **EVERYBODY'S TALKIN' 'BOUT THE YOUNG. / IT'S ALRIGHT WITH ME**		

ASYLUM CHOIR

with **MARC BENNO** (b.1 Jul'47, Dallas, Texas) – guitar

		Mercury	Smash
1968.	(lp) **LOOKING INSIDE**		

– Welcome to Hollywood / Soul food / Icicle star tree / Death of the flowers / Indian style / Episode containing three songs: N.Y. – Land of dog / Mr. Henry the clown / Thieves in the choir / Black sheep boogaloo. *(cd-iss.Apr91 as 'ASYLUM CHOIR' by "LEON RUSSELL & MARC BENNO" on 'Sequel' += 'ASYLUM CHOIR II tracks)–* Sweet home Chicago / Down on the base / Hello little friend / Salty Candy / Tryin' to stay 'live / Intro to Rita / Straight brother / Learn how to boogie / Ballad for a soldier / When you wish upon a fag / Lady in waiting.

— A second lp 'ASYLUM CHOIR II' was shelved in 1969 and they folded. This was re-issued by own label 'Shelter' Nov 71 & hit US No.70, when both were having own solo careers. Early in 1970, RUSSELL augmented both DELANEY & BONNIE plus JOE COCKER.

LEON RUSSELL

		A & M	Shelter
May 70.	(7") **ROLL AWAY THE STONE. / HUMMINGBIRD**	-	
Jun 70.	(lp)(c) **LEON RUSSELL**		60 Dec 69

– A song for you / Dixie lullaby / I put a spell on you / Shoot out on the plantation / Hummingbird / Delta lady / Prince of peace / Old masters / Give peace a chance / Hurt somebody / Pisces apple lady / Roll away the stone. *(re-iss.Apr76)*

May 71.	(7") **THE BALLAD OF MAD DOGS AND ENGLISHMEN. / LET IT BE**	-	
		A&M	Shelter
May 71.	(lp)(c) **LEON RUSSELL AND THE SHELTER PEOPLE**	29	17

– Stranger in a strange land / Of thee I sing / Hard rain's a-gonna fall / Crystal closet queen / Home sweet Oklahoma / Alcatraz / The ballad of mad dogs and Englishmen / It takes a lot to laugh, it takes a train to cry / She smokes like a river / Sweet Emily / Beware of darkness. *(re-iss.Apr76 on 'Island') (cd-iss. 1991 on 'Sequel' +=)–* It's all over now, baby blue / Love minus zero – No limit / She belongs to me.

May 71.	(7") **HOME SWEET OKLAHOMA. / IT TAKES A LOT TO LAUGH, IT TAKES A TRAIN TO CRY**	-	
Apr 72.	(7") **ME AND BABY JANE. / HARD RAIN'S A-GONNA FALL**	-	
Jun 72.	(7") **A SONG FOR YOU. / HARD RAIN'S A-GONNA FALL**	-	
Aug 72.	(lp)(c) **CARNEY**		2 Jul 72

– Tight rope / Out in the woods / Me and baby Jane / Manhattan island serenade / Cajun love song / Roller derby / Carney / Acid Annapolis / If the shoe fits / My cricket / This masquerade / Magic mirror.

Aug 72.	(7") **TIGHTROPE. / THIS MASQUERADE**	-	11
Sep 72.	(7") **TIGHT ROPE. / DELTA LADY**		-
Sep 72.	(7") **SLIPPING INTO CHRISTMAS. / CHRISTMAS IN CHICAGO**		
Aug 73.	(t-lp) **LEON LIVE (live Long Beach Arena)**	-	9 Jul 73

– Medley:- I'll take you there – Idol with the golden head – The mighty Quinn – I serve a living savior – The mighty Quinn / Shoot out on the plantation / Dixie lullaby / Queen of the roller derby / Roll away the stone / It's been a long time baby / Great day / Alcatraz / Crystal closet queen / Prince of peace / Sweet Emily / Stranger in a strange land / Out in the woods / Some day / Sweeping through the city / Medley:- Jumping Jack Flash – Young blood / Medley:- Of thee I sing – Yes I am – Delta lady / It's all over now, baby blue. *(UK-iss.d-cd.Jan92 on 'Sequel')*

Aug 73.	(7") **QUEEN OF THE ROLLER DERBY (live). / ROLL AWAY THE STONE**	-	89
Sep 73.	(lp)(c) **HANK WILSON'S BACK**		28

– Roll in my sweet baby's arms (part 1 & 2) / She thinks I still care / I'm so lonesome I could cry / I'll sail my ship alone / Jambalaya / A six pack to go / Battle of New Orleans / Uncle Pen / Am I that easy to forget / Truck drivin' man / The window up above / Lost highway / Goodnight Irene.

(above album & below 2 singles were credited to real name **"HANK WILSON"**)

Sep 73.	(7") **ROLL IN MY SWEET BABY'S ARMS. / I'M SO LONESOME I COULD CRY**		78
Nov 73.	(7") **UNCLE PEN. / SIX PACK TO GO**	-	
Apr 74.	(7") **IF I WERE A CARPENTER. / WILD HORSES**		73
Jul 74.	(lp)(c) **STOP ALL THAT JAZZ**		34

– If I were a carpenter / Smashed / Leaving Whipporwhill / Spanish Harlem / Streaker's ball / Working girl / Time for love / The ballad of Hollis Brown / Mona Lisa please / Stop all that jazz. *(re-iss.Apr76 on 'Island') (cd-iss.Apr91 on 'Sequel')*

Jul 74.	(7") **TIME FOR LOVE. / LEAVING WHIPPORWHILL**	-	
Jun 75.	(lp)(c) **WILL O' THE WISP**		30

– Will o' the wisp / Little hideaway / Make you feel good / Can't get over losing you / My father's shoes / Stay away from sad songs / Back to the island / Down on deep river / Bluebird / Laying right here in Heaven / Lady blue. *(re-iss.Apr76 on 'Island') (cd-iss.Apr91 on 'Sequel')*

Aug 75.	(7") **LADY BLUE. / LAYING RIGHT HERE IN HEAVEN**		14
Dec 75.	(7") **BACK TO THE ISLAND. / BLUEBIRD**	-	53

LEON & MARY RUSSELL

Mary was his wife. **MARY McCREARY** – vocalist with LITTLE SISTER (ex-SLY & THE FAMILY STONE).

		Paradise	Paradise
Jun 76.	(lp)(c) **THE WEDDING ALBUM**		34 Apr 76

– Rainbow in your eyes / Like a dream come true / Love's supposed to be that way / Fantasy / Satisfy you / You are on my mind / Lavender blue / Quiet nights / Windsong / Daylight.

Jun 76.	(7") **RAINBOW IN YOUR EYES. / LOVE'S SUPPOSED TO BE THAT WAY**	-	52
Sep 76.	(7") **SATISFY YOU. / WINDSONG**	-	
Jun 77.	(lp)(c) **MAKE LOVE TO THE MUSIC**		

– Easy love / Joyful noise / Now now boogie / Say you will / Make love to the music / Love crazy / Love is in your eyes / Hold on to this feeling / Island in the Sun.

Jun 77.	(7") **SAY YOU WILL. / LOVE CRAZY**	-	
Oct 77.	(7") **EASY LOVE. / HOLD ON TO THIS FEELING**	-	

LEON RUSSELL

solo again on same label.

Aug 78.	(lp)(c) **AMERICANA**		

– Let's get started / Elvis and Marilyn / From Maine to Mexico / When a man loves a woman / It's only me / Midnight lover / Housewife / Ladies of the night / Shadow and me / Jesus on my side.

Oct 78.	(7") **ELVIS AND MARILYN. / ANITA BRYANT**		
Jan 79.	(7") **FROM MAINE TO MEXICO. / MIDNIGHT LOVER**	-	

— Mid'79, he partners WILLIE NELSON for d-lp 'WILLIE AND LEON', see further.

1979.	(lp)(c) **LIFE & LOVE**		

– One more love song / You girl / Struck by lightning / Strange love / Life and love / On the first day / High horse / Sweet mystery / On the borderline.

LEON RUSSELL & THE NEW GRASS REVIVAL

		Warners	Paradise
Jan 81.	(7") **OVER THE RAINBOW. / I'VE JUST SEEN A FACE**	-	
Mar 81.	(lp)(c) **THE LIVE ALBUM (live)**		

– Over the rainbow / I've just seen a face / One more love song / I believe to my soul / Pilgrim land / Georgia blues / Prince of peace / Rollin' in my sweet baby's arms / Stranger in a strange land / I want to be at the meeting / Wild horses / Jambalaya / Caribbean / Jumpin' Jack Flash.

HANK WILSON

		not issued	Paradise
1984.	(lp) **HANK WILSON VOL.II**	-	

— Retired from solo music biz, until 1992, when he co-wrote songs with BRUCE HORNSBY.

		Virgin Am.	Virgin Am.
May 92.	(cd)(c)(lp) **ANYTHING CAN HAPPEN**		

– Anything can happen / Black halos / No man's land / Too much monkey business / Angel ways / Life of the party / Stranded on Easy Street / Jezebel / Love slave / Faces of the children.

– compilations, others, etc. –

Jan 72.	Shelter; (7") by 'ASYLUM CHOIR') **STRAIGHT BROTHER. / TRYIN' TO STAY ALIVE**	-	
1973.	Olympic; (lp) **LOOKING BACK**	-	
Nov 76.	Island/ US= Shelter; (lp)(c) **THE BEST OF LEON**		40 Oct 76
Jan 77.	Island; (7") **TIGHT ROPE. / THIS MASQUERADE**		
Jan 92.	Castle; (cd)(c) **THE COLLECTION**		-

– A song for you / Lady blue / Tight rope / Blue bird / This masquerade / Roll away the stone / Beware of darkness / Crystal closet queen / Delta lady / Back to the island / Stranger in a strange land / Hummingbird / Queen of the roller derby / Of thee I sing / Streaker's ball / Roll in my sweet baby's arms / Magic mirror / If I were a carpenter / Out in the woods / The battle of New Orleans.

WILLIE NELSON & LEON RUSSELL

		C.B.S.	Columbia
Jul 79.	(d-lp)(c) **WILLIE AND LEON – ONE FOR THE ROAD (live)**		25

– Detour / I saw the light / Heartbreak hotel / Let the rest of the world go by / Trouble in mind / Don't fence me in / Wild side of life / Ridin' down the canyon / Sioux City Sue / You are my sunshine / Danny boy / Always / Summertime / Because of you / Am I blue / Tenderly / Far away places / That lucky old Sun / Stormy weather / One for my baby.

Jul 79.	(7") **HEARTBREAK HOTEL. / SIOUX CITY SUE**	-	

Mike RUTHERFORD (see under ⇒ GENESIS)

RUTS

Formed: London, England . . . 1978 by MALCOLM OWEN, etc (see below). After a few John Peel sessions and a one-off 45 for reggae label 'People Unite' in 1979, they sign to 'Virgin' records. Their first major 45 'BABYLON'S BURNING', hits the UK Top 10, and is followed by 2 more gems, but tragedy befalls them in July 1980 when MALCOLM died of a drug overdose. • **Style:** Anthemic, raw punk-rock group who dabbled with a splash of reggae and politics, similar to The CLASH. • **Songwriters:** Group compositions. • **Trivia:**

Recommended: SOMETHING THAT I SAID – THE BEST OF . . . (*8) / THE CRACK (*7)

MALCOLM OWEN – vocals / **PAUL FOX** – guitar, vocals / **SEGS** (b.JOHN JENNINGS) – bass / **DAVE RUFFY** – drums

		People Unite	not issued
Jan 79.	(7") **IN A RUT. / H-EYES**		-
		Virgin	not issued
May 79.	(7")(12") **BABYLON'S BURNING. / SOCIETY**	7	-
Aug 79.	(7") **SOMETHING THAT I SAID. / BLACK MAN'S PINCH**	29	-
Oct 79.	(lp)(c) **THE CRACK**	16	-

– Babylon's burning / Dope for guns / S.U.S. / Something that I said / You're just a . . . / It was cold / Savage circle / Jah war / Criminal mind / Backbiter / Out of order / Human punk. *(re-iss.+cd.Aug88 +=)*– Give youth a chance / I ain't so satisfied / The crack. *(cd-iss.Mar94)*

Nov 79.	(7") **JAH WARS. / I AIN'T SOPHISTICATED**		-
Apr 80.	(7") **STARING AT THE RUDE BOYS. / LOVE IN VAIN**	22	-

—— In Jul'80, MALCOLM OWEN died of a drug overdose. Postumous releases below

Aug 80.	(7") **WEST ONE (SHINE ON ME). / THE CRACK**	43	-
Oct 80.	(lp)(c) **GRIN AND BEAR IT** (new, live & rare)	28	-

– In a rut / Love in vain / S.U.S. / Babylon's burning / Society / West one (shine on me) / Staring at the rude boys / Demolition dancing / Secret soldier / H eyes. *(re-iss.Mar84)*

RUTS D.C.

remaining trio (with **PAUL** – lead vocals / added **GARY BARNACLE** – saxophone, keyboards

Feb 81.	(7") **DIFFERENT VIEW. / FORMULA BOYS**		-
May 81.	(lp)(c) **ANIMAL NOW**		-

– Mirror smashed / Dangerous minds / Slow down / Despondency / Different view / No time to kill / Fools / Walk or run / Parasites.

		Bohemian	not issued
Jul 82.	(7") **WHATEVER WE DO. / PUSH YOURSELF (MAKE IT WORK)**		-
Jul 82.	(lp) **RHYTHM COLLISION**		-

– Whatever we do / Militant / Push yourself (make it work) / Rhythm collision / Accusation / Pleasures of the dance / Weak heart (dub) / Love and fire. *(a dub version credited w/ MAD PROFESSOR is iss.on c.Aug87 on 'R.O.I.R.', re-iss.Mar91)*

Mar 83.	(7") **WEAK HEART. / MILITANT**		-

(12"+=) – Accusation.

May 83.	(7"m) **STEPPING BONDAGE. / LOBOTOMY / RICH BITCH**		-

—— Folded mid'83. BARNACLE joined VISAGE, etc. and RUFFY joined AZTEC CAMERA.

– more (RUTS) compilations, etc. –

Apr 83.	Virgin; (12"ep) **BABYLON'S BURNING / SOMETHING THAT I SAID. / STARING AT THE RUDE BOYS / WEST ONE (SHINE ON ME)**		-
1987.	Virgin; (cd) **YOU'VE GOTTA GET OUT OF IT**		-
Dec 86.	Strange Fruit; (12"ep)(c-ep) **THE PEEL SESSIONS** (21.5.79)		-

– S.U.S. / Society / You're just a . . . / It was cold / Something that I said.

May 87.	Strange Fruit; (12"ep)(c-ep) **THE PEEL SESSIONS** (27.11.78)		-
May 90.	Strange Fruit; (cd)(c)(lp) **THE COMPLETE PEEL SESSIONS**		-
Mar 87.	Dojo; (lp) **LIVE! (live)**		-
Dec 87.	Link; (lp) **LIVE AND LOUD (live)** *(cd-iss.Aug92)*		-
Nov 88.	Old Gold; (7") **BABYLON'S BURNING. / STARING AT THE RUDE BOYS**		-

—— (next shared with PENETRATION).

Jan 92.	Windsong; (cd)(lp) **BBC RADIO 1 LIVE IN CONCERT (live)**		-
Mar 94.	Receiver; (cd) **DEMOLITION DANCING**		-
Mar 95.	Virgin; (cd) **SOMETHING THAT I SAID . . .THE BEST OF THE RUTS**		-

– In a rut / Babylon's burning / Dope for guns / Sus / Something that I said / You're just a . . . / It was cold / Savage circle / Jah war / Criminal mind / Backbiter / Out of order / Human punk / Staring at the rude boys / Love in vain / West one (shine on me).

Mar 95.	Step 1; (cd) **LIVE AND LOUD (live) (w/ ADVERTS)**		-

Mitch RYDER

Born: WILLIAM LEVISE JR., 26 Feb'45, Hamtramack, Michegan, USA. In 1963, after leaving local group The PEPS, he formed BILLY LEE & THE RIVIERAS, who recorded 2 singles for local labels, before in 1965 becoming MITCH RYDER & THE DETROIT WHEELS. On the recommendation of DJ Dave Prince, they were signed by producer Bob Crewe to his 'New Voice' label. Their second 45 'JENNY TAKES A RIDE!' (a medley of oldies 'C. C. Rider' & 'Jenny Jenny'), scraped into the US Top 10, and was the first of a string of hits up to 1968. • **Style:** Blue-eyed soul outfit, fronted by R&B screecher RYDER, who was inspired by Motown and JAMES BROWN. • **Songwriters:** Mainly revivals of 50's rock'n'roll medleys; LITTLE LATIN LUPE LU (Righteous Brothers) /JENNY JENNY (Little Richard) / DEVIL WITH THE BLUE DRESS ON (Shorty Long) / C. C. RIDER (Chuck Willis) / THREE LITTLE FISHES (hit; Kay Lyser) / WHAT NOW MY LOVE (Gilbert Becaud) / YOU ARE MY SUNSHINE (Jimmie Davis) / WHEN YOU WERE MINE (Prince) / etc, etc. • **Trivia:** Took the name MITCH RYDER, from a phone directory. His 1983 album for 'Riva' was produced by JOHN COUGAR MELLENCAMP.

Recommended: REV UP – THE BEST OF MITCH RYDER (*6) / NEVER KICK A SLEEPING DOG (*6).

BILLY LEE & THE RIVIERAS

MITCH RYDER – vocals / with **JIM McCARTY** – guitar / **JOE KUBERT** – guitar / **EARL ELLIOTT** – bass / **JOHN BADANJEK** – drums

		not issued	Carrie
1962.	(7") **FOOL FOR YOU. / THAT'S THE WAY IT'S GONNA BE**	-	

BILLY LEE & THE RIVIERAS

		not issued	Hyland
1964.	(7") **WON'T YOU DANCE WITH ME. / YOU KNOW**	-	

MITCH RYDER & THE DETROIT WHEELS

		Stateside	New Voice	
Jun 65.	(7") **I NEED HELP. / I HOPE**	-		
Jan 66.	(7") **JENNY TAKES A RIDE!. / BABY JANE**	33	10	Dec 65
Apr 66.	(7") **LITTLE LATIN LUPE LU. / I HOPE**	48	17	Mar 66
May 66.	(lp) **TAKE A RIDE**		78	Feb 66

– Jenny take a ride / Come see about me / I'll go crazy / Please, please, please / Shake a tail feather / Let your lovelight shine / I hope / Just a little bit / Sticks and stones / Bring it on home to me / Baby Jane (Mo-Mo Jane) / I got you.

Jun 66.	(7") **BREAKOUT. / I NEED HELP**		62	May 66
Jul 66.	(7") **TAKIN' ALL I CAN GET. / YOU GET YOUR KICKS**	-	100	
Oct 66.	(7") **DEVIL WITH A BLUE DRESS ON – GOOD GOLLY MISS MOLLY (medley). / I HAD IT MADE**		4	
Dec 66.	(lp) **BREAKOUT . . . !!!**		23	Aug 66

– Little Latin Lupe Lu / Breakout / In the midnight hour / Walking the dog / I had it made / So papa do / I like it like that / You got your kicks / Shakin' with Linda / Stubborn kind of fellow / Any day now / I need help.

—— **JIM McCALLISTER** – bass repl. ELLIOTT who was drafted

Feb 67.	(7") **SOCK IT TO ME – BABY!. / I NEVER HAD IT BETTER**		6
Apr 67.	(7") **TOO MANY FISH IN THE SEA – THREE LITTLE FISHES (medley) . / ONE GRAIN OF SAND**		24
Apr 67.	(lp) **SOCK IT TO ME!**		34

– Sock it to me baby! / I can't hide it / Takin' all I can get / Slow fizz / Walk on by / Devil with the blue dress on / Good golly Miss Molly / I never had it better / Shakedown / A face in the crowd / I'd rather go to jail / Wild child. *(cd-iss. US-1993 on 'Sundazed' w/extra 3 tracks)*

MITCH RYDER

went solo, groomed for the Las Vegas cabaret circuit.

Jun 67.	(7") **JOY. / I'D RATHER GO TO JAIL**		41
		Stateside	Dynovoice
Sep 67.	(7") **WHAT NOW MY LOVE. / BLESSING IN DISGUISE**		30
Nov 67.	(lp) **WHAT NOW MY LOVE**		

– Let it be me / I make a fool of myself / Born to lose / If you go away / What now my love / Whole lotta shakin' goin' on / Sally go round the roses / Brown-eyed handsome man / I need lovin' you / That's it . . .I quit..

Jan 68.	(7") **(YOU'VE GOT) PERSONALITY – CHANTILLY LACE (medley). / I MAKE A FOOL OF MYSELF**		87
1968.	(7") **I NEED YOUR LOVIN'. / THE LIGHTS OF NIGHT**	-	
1968.	(7") **RING YOUR BELL. / BABY I NEED YOUR LOVIN' – THEME FOR MITCH**	-	

—— now backed by BOOKER T & THE MG'S

		not issued	Dot
1969.	(lp) **THE DETROIT – MEMPHIS EXPERIMENT**	-	

– Liberty / Eenie meenie minie moe / Boredom / Push aroun' / Sugar bee / I get hot / I believe / Direct me / Long, long time / Raise your hand / Wear and tear on my heart / Meat.

1969.	(7") **SUGAR BEE. / I BELIEVE (THERE MUST BE SOMEONE) (WE THREE)**	-	
1969.	(7") **DIRECT ME. / LONG, LONG TIME**	-	

DETROIT

RYDER with **JOHN BADANJEK** – drums / **BRETT TUGGLE** – guitar / **JIM McCARTY + STEVE HUNTER** – guitar / **HARRY PHILIPS** – keyboards / **W.R.COOKE** – bass / **DIRTY ED** – percussion

		not issued	Paramount
Nov 71.	(7") **I CAN'T SEE NOBODY. / ?**	-	
Dec 71.	(lp) **DETROIT**	-	

– Long neck goose / Is it you (or is it me) / It ain't easy / Rock'n'roll / Let it rock / Drink / Box of old roses / I found a love. *(cd-iss.1988, w/extra track += Gimme shelter)*

1972.	(7") **IT AIN'T EASY. / LONG NECK GOOSE**	-	
1972.	(7") **ROCK 'N' ROLL. / BOX OF OLD ROSES**	-	
1972.	(7") **GIMME SHELTER. / OO LA LA LA DEE DA DOO**	-	

— In 1972, he retired from music business due to throat infection. BADANJEK + McCARTY later formed the ROCKETS.

MITCH RYDER

returned w/new backing band **RICHARD SCHEIN & WAYNE GABRIEL** – guitars / **BILLY CSERNITS** – keyboards / **MARK GOUGEON** – bass / **WILSON OWENS** – drums

Line Germany / Seeds & Stems

1978. (lp) **HOW I SPENT MY VACATION** [-] [ ]
– Tough kid / Dance ourselves to death / Passions wheel / Cherry poppin' / Freezin' in Hell / Nice'n'easy / The Jon / Falling forming / Poster.

— **JOE GUTC** – guitar repl. WAYNE

1980. (lp) **NAKED BUT NOT DEAD** [-] [ ]
– Ain't nobody white / Corporate song / War / Future looks brite / I got mine / Spitting lizard / True love / I don't wanna hear it / Hometown. *(cd-iss. 1992 w/1979 lp)*

1980. (7"ep) **WE'RE GONNA WIN** [-] [ ]

1981. (lp) **GOT CHANGE FOR A MILLION** [-] [-]
– My heart belongs to me / Back at work / That's charm / Red scar eyes / Bang bang / Betty's too tight / Ich bin aus America / Bare your soul / We're gonna win.

1979. (12"ep) **ROCK'N'ROLL LIVE (live)** [-] [-]
– Rock & roll / Soul kitchen.

1982. (d-lp) **LIVE TALKIES (live)** [-] [-]
– It's all over now / Corporate song (it's not for me) / Bang bang / Subterranean homesick blues / Er ist nicht mein praesi dent / Take me to the river / Tough kid / Red scar eyes / Liberty / Ain't nobody white / Nice and easy / Long tall Sally / I'm gonna be a wheel someday.
– (free 7"m) – Wicked Messenger / True Love *(cd-iss.1987)*

— **AL WOTTON** – drums repl. OWENS.

Safari / Line

Sep 82. (lp) **SMART ASS** [ ] [ ] Germ
– Hot house / You better stop / Try and must / Code dancing / Tape's rolling / One room world / Hands high / It keeps you alive / Berlin.

— now w/**LARRY CRANE + MIKE WANCHIC** – guitars / **KENNY ARONOFF** – drums / **MARK GOUGEON** – bass / **HARRY PHILLIPS** – organ

Towerbell / Riva

Oct 83. (lp)(c) **NEVER KICK A SLEEPING DOG** [ ] [ ] Jul 83
– B.I.G.T.I.M.E / When you were mine / A thrill is a thrill (w/ MARIANNE FAITHFULL) / Come again / Cry to me / The thrill of it all / Stand / Rue de Thahir / Code dancing. *(cd-iss. 1987 on 'Line')*

Nov 83. (7") **WHEN YOU WERE MINE. / COME AGAIN** [ ] [87] Jul 83

1984. (7") **THE THRILL OF IT ALL. / ?** [-] [ ]

— **OWENS** returned to replace WOTTON

— **ROBERT GILLESPIE** – guitar repl. SCHEIN

Line / Line

1986. (lp)(c)(cd) **IN THE CHINA SHOP** [ ] [ ]
– Where is the next one coming from? / Like a worm / Rock 'n' roll skin / All the way / Looks are deceiving / I'm not sad tonite / End of the line / Uncle Sam & the Russian bear / Young blood.

— **JOHN BADANJEK** – drums repl. OWENS

1988. (cd) **RED BLOOD & WHITE MINK (live)** [ ] [ ]
– Little Latin Lupe Lu / Rock & roll / Heart of stone / Gimme shelter / War / Freezin' in hell / Bang bang / Red scar eyes / Where's the next one coming from? / I feel good / Bridge of sympathy / Big time / Ain't nobody white / Berlin.

— with **JOE GUTC + RAY GOODMAN** – guitar / **DENNIS "MOON" WEZALIS** – keyboards / **BARRY GEORGE** – bass / **DANNY McALEER** – drums

1992. (cd) **LA GASH** [ ] [ ]
– It must be in her genes / Argyle / Do you feel alright? / Child of rage / Bye-bye love / Dr. Margaret Smith / It's your birthday / Arms without love / Correct me if I'm wrong / One thing / Almost bigamy / The terrorist. (some w/extra tracks; Long neck goose / Devil with the blue dress on – Good golly Miss Molly.

Sep 94. (cd) **RITE OF PASSAGE** [ ] [ ]
– See her again / Sex you up / Actually 101 / It wasn't me / We are helpless / Into the blue / Mercy / Too sentimental / Let it shine / Hermasn's garden / I'm starting all over again / By the feel.

– compilations, others, etc. –

Below released on 'New Voice' unless stated.

Nov 67. (7") **YOU ARE MY SUNSHINE. / WILD CHILD** [-] [88] Oct 67

Nov 67. (lp) **ALL MITCH RYDER HITS!** (solo + band) [-] [37]
– Devil with the blue dress on & Good golly Miss Molly / Jenny take a ride / Joy / Breakout / In the midnight hour / Sock it to me – baby! / Little Latin Lupe Lu / Takin' all I can get / Too many fish in the sea & Three little fishes / I'd rather go to jail / Shake a tail feather.

1968. (7") **COME SEE ABOUT ME. / A FACE IN THE CROWD** [-] [ ]

1968. (7") **RUBY BABY & PEACHES ON A CHERRY TREE. / YOU GET YOUR KICKS** [-] [ ]

1968. (lp) **SINGS THE HITS** [-] [ ]

1971. Avco; (7") **JENNY TAKES A RIDE!. / I NEVER HAD IT BETTER** [ ] [ ]

Mar 75. Disco D; (7") **YOU GET YOUR KICKS. / BREAKOUT** [ ] [-]

1967. Bell; (lp) **ALL TIME HEAVY HITS** [ ] [-]

1972. Virgo; (lp) **GREATEST HITS** [ ] [-]

Oct 80. Classic Cuts; (7") **JENNY TAKE A RIDE. / (other artist?)** [ ] [-]

Apr 83. PRT; (10"lp)(c) **WHEELS OF STEEL** [ ] [-]

Jan 90. Roulette; (cd)(c)(lp) **REV UP – THE BEST OF MITCH RYDER & THE DETROIT WHEELS** [ ] [-]
– Jenny take a ride / Little Latin lupe lu / Shakin' with Linda / I like it like that / I had it made / Breakout / Shake a tail feather / Devil with a blue dress on / Good golly Miss Molly / Sock it to me baby / Too many fish in the sea / Three little fishes / I'd rather go to jail / Ooh papa doo / I hope / I never had it better. (cd+=) – Takin' all I can get / You get your kicks / Sticks and stones / Baby Jane (Mo-Mo Jane) / Joy / Just a little bit.

1990. Line; (cd) **THE BEAUTIFUL TOULANG SUNSET** [-] [ ]

Nov 92. Document; (cd) **DOCUMENT SERIES PRESENTS MITCH RYDER & THE DETROIT WHEELS** [ ] [-]

SABRES OF PARADISE

Formed: London, England ... 1993 by mixer to the masses ANDY WEATHERALL, plus ALEX KNIGHT and NINA WALSH. That year they / he completed a debut album, which was another of the new music that broke new ground and the Top 30. • **Style:** Ambient dance mixer. • **Songwriters:** WEATHERALL with samples. • **Trivia:** WEATHERALL's numerous remixes have included ONE DOVE / BJORK / LEFTFIELD-LYDON / JAMES / ESPIRITU / BOMB THE BASS & K-CLASS.

Recommended: SABRESONIC (*7)

ANDY WEATHERALL – keyboards, synthesizers / **JAGZ KOONER** – keyboards, synthesizers / **GARY BURNS** – keyboards, synthesizers

		S.O.P.	not issued
Sep 93.	(12") **SMOKEBELCH II. / (2 'A'mixes)** (cd-s+=)/ /(12") – ('A'mix). / / ('A'-4 mixes).	55	
Oct 93.	(cd)(c)(lp) **SABRESONIC** – Still fighting / Smokebelch I / Clock factory / Ano electric endante / R.S.D. / Inter-Lergen-Tan-Ko / Ano electro allegro.	29	
Mar 94.	(12"ep)(cd-ep) **THE THEME / ('A'mix). / EDGE / RETURN OF CARTER** (10") – (2 mixes of 'A').	56	
		Warp	Warp
Sep 94.	(10"ep)(12"ep)(c-ep)(cd-ep) **WILMOT / WILMOT MEETS LORD SCRUFFAGE / SIEGE REFRAIN / WILMOT (edit)**	36	
Nov 94.	(cd)(c)(d-lp) **HAUNTED DANCEHALL** – Bubble and slide / Bubble and slide II / Duke of Earlsfield / Flight path estate / Planet D / Wilmot / Tow truck / Theme / Theme 4 / Return to Planet D / Ballad of Nicky McGuire / Jacob Street 7 a.m. / Chapel Street Market 9 a.m. / Haunted dancehall.	58	
May 95.	(12"ltd.) **TOW TRUCK (Depth Charge remix). / TOW TRUCK (Chemical Brothers remix)**		-
May 95.	(10"ltd.) **DUKE OF EARLSFIELD (LFO remix). / BUBBLE & SLIDE (Nightmares On Wax remix)**		-
May 95.	(7"ltd.) **HAUNTED DANCEHALL (In The Nursery mix)**		-
May 95.	(m-cd) **VERSUS** – (all 3 similtaneous releases + extra Depth Charge mix).		-

SADE

Born: HELEN FOLASADE ADU, 16 Jan'59, Ibadan, Nigeria. Raised by her mother in Clacton, Essex, England, in '84 she moved to Camden Town, London. The previous year, after spells with ARRIVA and funk outfit PRIDE, she launched solo career, having signed to 'Epic' records for a large advance. Helped by an appearance on Channel 4's 'The Tube', her first 45 'YOUR LOVE IS KING', broke her into the UK Top 10. Her debut album 'DIAMOND LIFE', made UK No.2, and steadily found an audience in the States, where it hit Top 5. • **Style:** A fashion model from the early 80's, she turned her head to sophisticated, romantic pop/soul music, ideal for the new compact disc era. • **Songwriters:** SADE writes own lyrics, with her music a collaboration with MATTHEWMAN and HALE. • **Trivia:** She appeared in the 1986 film musical 'Absolute Beginners'.

Recommended: DIAMOND LIFE (*8) / PROMISE (*7) / STRONGER (*7).

SADE ADU – vocals / with **STUART MATTHEWMAN** (b.1961) – guitar, sax / **PAUL DENHAM** (b.1958) – bass / **ANDREW HALE** (b.1963) – keyboards / **PAUL COOK** – drums

		Epic	Portrait
Jan 84.	(7") **YOUR LOVE IS KING. / LOVE AFFAIR WITH LIFE** (12"+=) – Smooth operator / Snake bite.	6	54 Jun 85
May 84.	(7") **WHEN AM I GONNA MAKE A LIVING. / SHOULD I LOVE YOU** (12"+=) – Why can't we live together.	36	-
Jul 84.	(lp)(c)(cd) **DIAMOND LIFE** – Smooth operator / Your love is king / Hang on to your love / Frankie's first affair / When am I going to make a living / Cherry pie / Sally / I will be your friend / Why can't we live together.	2	5 Jan 85
Sep 84.	(7") **SMOOTH OPERATOR. / SPIRIT** (12"+=) – Red eyes.	19	-
Sep 84.	(7") **HANG ON TO YOUR LOVE. / CHERRY PIE**	-	
Jan 85.	(7") **SMOOTH OPERATOR. / SALLY**	-	5
Oct 85.	(7")(12") **THE SWEETEST TABOO. / YOU'RE NOT THE MAN**	31	5 Nov 85
Nov 85.	(lp)(c)(cd) **PROMISE** – Is it a crime / The sweetest taboo / War of the hearts / Jezebel / Mr. Wrong / Never as good as the first time / Fear / Tar baby / Maureen. *(c+=)* – Punch drunk / You're not the man. *(re-iss.Mar90)*	1	1
Dec 85.	(7")(12") **IS IT A CRIME. / PUNCH DRUNK**	49	-
May 86.	(7")(12") **NEVER AS GOOD AS THE FIRST TIME. / KEEP HANGIN' ON**		20
Jul 86.	(7") **IS IT A CRIME. / ('A' long version)**	-	
		Epic	Epic
Mar 88.	(7") **LOVE IS STRONGER THAN PRIDE. / SUPER BIEN TOTAL** (12"+=)(cd-s+=) – ('B'extended).	44	-
May 88.	(lp)(c)(cd) **STRONGER THAN PRIDE** – Love is stronger than pride / Paradise / Nothing can come between us / Haunt me / Turn my back on you / Keep looking / Clean heart / Give it up / I never thought I'd see the day / Siempre hay esperanza.	3	7
May 88.	(7") **PARADISE (remix). / ('A'instrumental)** (12"+=) – ('A'extended). (cd-s+=) – Hang on to your love (US remix) / Keep hanging on (live).	29	-
May 88.	(7") **PARADISE. / SUPER BIEN TOTAL**	-	16
Aug 88.	(7") **NOTHING CAN COME BETWEEN US. / MAKE SOME ROOM** (12"+=)(cd-s+=) – You're not the man.		
Nov 88.	(7") **TURN MY BACK ON YOU. / KEEP LOOKING** (12"+=)(cd-s+=) – ('A'extended) / ('A'mix).		
Jan 89.	(7") **LOVE IS STRONGER THAN PRIDE. / MAKE SOME ROOM**	-	
Oct 92.	(7")(c-s) **NO ORDINARY LOVE. / PARADISE (Remix)** (cd-s+=) – ('A' version). (12"+=) – ('B'-drums and Sade mix). (returned to UK chart in 1993 and hit No.4)	26	28
Nov 92.	(cd)(c)(lp) **LOVE DELUXE** – No ordinary love / Feel no pain / I couldn't love you more / Like a tattoo / Kiss of life / Cherish the day / Pearls / Bullet proof soul / Mermaid.	10	3
Nov 92.	(7")(c-s) **FEEL NO PAIN. / LOVE IS STRANGER THAN PRIDE (Mad Professor remix)** (cd-s+=) ('A' version)	56	
May 93.	(7")(c-s) **KISS OF LIFE. / ROOM 55** (12"+=)(cd-s+=) – Kiss Of Life	44	78 Mar 93
Jul 93.	(c-s) **CHERISH THE DAY. / CHERISH THE DAY (Ronin Remix)** (12"+=)(cd-s+=) – Cherish The Day (Pal Joey Remix)	53	
Nov 94.	(cd)(c)(lp) **THE BEST OF SADE** (compilation) – Your love is king / Hang on to your love / Smooth operator / Jezebel / The sweetest taboo / Is it a crime / Never as good as the first time / Love is stronger than pride / Paradise / Nothing can come between us / No ordinary love / Like a tattoo / Kiss of life / Please send me someone to love / Cherish the day / Pearls.	6	9

– compilations, etc. –

1992.	Old Gold; (7") **YOUR LOVE IS KING. / SMOOTH OPERATOR**		-
Feb 95.	Epic; (d-cd) **PROMISE / STRONGER THAN PRIDE**		-

Buffy SAINTE-MARIE

Born: 20 Feb'41, Piapot Reservation, Saskatchewan, Canada. From Cree Indian descent she moved to New York in the 60's where she signed to 'Vanguard'. She was to have biggest hit in 1971, when 'SOLDIER BLUE' cracked the UK Top 10. • **Style:** Shifted from folk rock in the mid 60's, to Nashville style country in the late 60's. Her distinctive vocal sound and pasts roots secured her a few hits in the early 70's. • **Songwriters:** She wrote nearly all her material which was used by many, including COD'INE (Quicksilver Messenger Service) / UNTIL IT'S TIME FOR YOU TO GO (Elvis Presley) / UNIVERSAL SOLDIER (Donovan) / etc. She herself covered THE CIRCLE GAME + SONG TO A SEAGULL (Joni Mitchell) / YOU'RE GONNA NEED SOMEBODY ON YOUR BOND (Robert Johnson) / and some traditional material, etc. • **Trivia:** She guested on lp's by NEVILLE BROTHERS and NEW RIDERS OF THE PURPLE SAGE. In 1982, BUFFY co-wrote w / JACK NITZSCHE 'UP WHERE WE BELONG' which hit US No.1 for 'JOE COCKER & JENNIFER WARNES'.

Recommended: THE BEST OF BUFFY SAINTE-MARIE VOL.1 (*7) / COINCIDENCE AND LIKELY STORIES (*8)

BUFFY SAINTE-MARIE – vocals, guitar with **PATRICK SKY** (b.Oct'40 near Atlanta, Georgia, USA) – guitar (also a solo artist for same label) / **ART DAVIS** – bass

		Fontana	Vanguard
1964.	(lp) **IT'S MY WAY!** – Now that the buffalo's gone / The old man's lament / Ananias / Mayoo sto hoon / Cod'ine / Cripple creek / Universal soldier / Babe in arms / He lived alone in town / You're gonna need somebody on your bond / The incest song / Eyes of amber / It's my way. *(re-iss.Apr74 on 'Vanguard') (cd-iss.Feb93 on 'Vanguard')*		

— **RUSS SAVAKUS** – bass + **DADDY BONES** – guitar repl. DAVIS
Jun 65. (7") **UNTIL IT'S TIME FOR YOU TO GO. / THE FLOWER AND THE APPLE TREE**
1965. (lp) **MANY A MILE**
– Must I go bound / Los Pescadores / Groundhog / On the banks of red roses / Fixin' to die / Until it's time for you to go / The Piney Wood Hills / Welcome welcome emigrante / Brokedown girl / Johnny be fair / Maple sugar boy / Lazarus / Come all ye fair and tender girls / Many a mile. *(re-iss.May74 on 'Vanguard')*
Sep 65. (7") **UNIVERSAL SOLDIER. / CRIPPLE CREEK**
— **BRUCE LANGHORNE + ERIC WEISSBERG** – guitar repl. BONES
May 66. (7") **TIMELESS LOVE. / LADY MARGARET**
May 66. (lp) **LITTLE WHEEL SPIN AND SPIN** — 97
– Little wheel spin and spin / Waly, Waly / Rolling log blues / My country 'tis of thy people you're dying / Men of the fields / Timeless love / Sir Patrick Spens / Poor man's daughter / Lady Margaret / Sometimes when I get to thinkin' / Winter boy. *(re-iss.Feb74 on 'Vanguard')(cd-iss.Feb93 on 'Vanguard')*
Jan 67. (7") **JUSQU'AU JOUR OU TU PARTIRAS. / UNTIL IT'S TIME FOR YOU TO GO** — -
— **AL ROGERS** – drums / **MONTE DUNN** – mandolin / **BOB SIGGINS** – banjo repl. SKY + WEISSBERG. From the 1968 onwards, her albums featured heap many session people.
Jul 67. (lp) **FIRE & FLEET & CANDLELIGHT** — -
– The seeds of brotherhood / Summer boy / The circle game / Lyke wake dirge / Song to a seagull / Doggett's gap / The wedding song / 97 men in this here town would give a half a grand in silver just to follow me down / Lord Randall / The carousel / T'es pas un autre / Little boy dark eyes / Reynardine – a vampire legend / Hey, little boy. *(UK-iss.Jan72 on 'Vanguard')*
Jul 67. (7") **THE CIRCLE GAME. / UNTIL IT'S TIME FOR YOU TO GO** — -
Jun 68. (7") **THE PINEY WOOD HILLS. / SOULFUL SHADE OF BLUE** — -
Jul 68. (lp) **I'M GONNA BE A COUNTRY GIRL AGAIN** — -
– I'm gonna be a country girl again / He's a pretty good man if you ask me / Uncle Joe / A soulful shade of blue / From the bottom of my heart / Sometimes when I get to thinkin' / The Pine Wood Hills / How that the buffalo's gone / They outta quit kickin' my dawg around / Tall trees in Georgia / The love of a good man / Take my hand for awhile / Gonna feel much better when you're gone. *(UK-iss.Apr72 on 'Vanguard')*
Nov 68. (7") **BETTER TO FIND OUT FOR YOURSELF. / SOMETIMES WHEN I GET TO THINKIN'** — -
1969. (7") **I'M GONNA BE A COUNTRY GIRL AGAIN. / FROM THE BOTTOM OF MY HEART** — -
Dec 69. (lp) **ILLUMINATIONS** — -
– God is alive, magic is a foot / Mary / Better to find out for yourself / The vampire / Adam / The dream tree / Suffer the little children / The angel / With you honey / Guess who I saw in Paris / He's a keeper of the fire / Poppies. *(UK-iss.Dec71 on 'Vanguard')(cd-iss.Feb93 on 'Vanguard')*
Dec 69. (7") **HE'S A KEEPER OF THE FIRE. / BETTER TO FIND OUT FOR YOURSELF** — -
Aug 70. (7") **BETTER TO FIND OUT FOR YOURSELF. / THE CIRCLE GAME** — -
Feb 71. (7") **SOLDIER BLUE. / UNTIL IT'S TIME FOR YOU TO GO** — -
— (below 45 from the film 1970 'Soldier Blue')

R.C.A. R.C.A.

Jun 71. (7") **SOLDIER BLUE. / MORATORIUM** — 7

Vanguard Vanguard

May 71. (7") **SHE USED TO BE A BALLERINA. / MORATORIUM** — -
Sep 71. (lp)(c) **SHE USED TO WANNA BE A BALLERINA** — Apr 71
– Rollin' mill man / Smack water Jack / Sweet September morning / She used to be a ballerina / Bells / Helpless / Moratorium – Bring our brothers home / The surfer / Song of the French partisans / Soldier blue / Now you've been gone a long time. *(cd-iss.Oct95)*
Sep 71. (7") **HELPLESS. / NOW YOU'VE BEEN GONE A LONG TIME** — -
Sep 71. (7") **SHE USED TO WANNA BE A BALLERINA. / UNTIL IT'S TIME FOR YOU TO GO**
Jan 72. (7") **I'M GONNA BE A COUNTRY GIRL AGAIN. / THE PINEY WOOD HILLS** — 34 — 98 Nov 71
Jun 72. (7") **MISTER CAN'T YOU SEE. / MOONSHOT** — 38 Mar 72
Jul 72. (lp)(c) **MOONSHOT** — May 72
– Not the lovin' kind / You know how to turn on those lights / I wanna hold your hand forever / He's an Indian cowboy in the rodeo / Lay it down / Moonshot / Native North American child / My baby left me / Sweet memories / Jeremiah / Mister can't you see. *(cd-iss.Feb93)*
Aug 72. (7") **HE'S AN INDIAN COWBOY IN THE RODEO. / NOT THE LOVIN' KIND** — - — 98
Feb 73. (7") **JEREMIAH. / I WANNA HOLD YOUR HAND FOREVER** — -
Nov 73. (lp)(c) **QUIET PLACES**
– Why you been gone so long / No one told me / For free / She'll be comin' 'round the mountain when she comes / Clair Vol's young son / Just that kind of man / Quiet places / Have you seen my baby / There's no gone in the world like Caleb / Civilization / Eventually / The jewels of Hanalei. *(cd-iss.Jan94)*

M.C.A. M.C.A.

Feb 74. (7") **CAN'T BELIEVE THE FEELING. / WHEN YOU'RE GONE** — -
Mar 74. (7") **CAN'T BELIEVE THE FEELING. / WAVES** — -
Mar 74. (lp)(c) **BUFFY**
– Can't believe the feeling when you're gone / I've really fallen for you / Sweet little Vera / Star boy / Sweet, fast hooker blues / Generation / Hey, baby howdja do me this way / I can't take it no more / Waves / That's the way you fall in love.
May 74. (7") **WAVES. / SWEET LITTLE VERA** — -
Sep 74. (7") **GENERATION. / SWEET, FAST HOOKER BLUES** — -
Mar 75. (7") **LOVE'S GOT TO BREATHE AND FLOWER. / NOBODY WILL EVER KNOW IT'S REAL BUT YOU**
Mar 75. (lp)(c) **CHANGING WOMAN**
– Eagle man – Changing woman / Can't you see the way I love you / Love's got to breathe and fly / You take me away / 'Til I see you again / Mongrel pup / The beauty way / Nobody will ever know it's real but you / All around the world / A man.

A.B.C. A.B.C.

Feb 76. (lp)(c) **SWEET AMERICA**
– Sweet America / Wynken, Blynken and Nod / Where poets go / Free the lady / America my home / Look at the facts / I don't need no city life / Sweet January / Q'appelle Valley, Saskatchewan / Honey can you hang around / I been down / Starwalker / Ain't no time for the worryin' blues.
Mar 76. (7") **STARWALKER. / FREE THE LADY** — -
Apr 76. (7") **SWEET AMERICA. / STAR WALKER**
Jul 76. (7") **LOOK AT THE FACTS. / WHERE POETS GO**
— She retired from the studio, but in the late 70's was invited to appear on US children's show 'Sesame Street'. She stayed on the show for over 5 years, helping to initiate their attitude to racism in America. She returned to the studio in 1991 with new band **ROGER JACOBS** – bass, drums, percussion / **CHRIS BIRETT** – samples / **RICK MARVIN** – keyboards / etc.

Ensign Chrysalis

Jan 92. (7")(c-s) **THE BIG ONES GET AWAY. / I'M GOING HOME** — 39
(12"pic-d+=)(cd-s+=) – Contrahosophy.
Mar 92. (cd)(c)(lp) **COINCIDENCE AND LIKELY STORIES** — 39
– The big ones get away / Fallen angels / Bad end / Emma Lee / Starwalker / The priests of the golden bull / Disinformation / Getting started / I'm going home / Bury my heart at Wounded Knee / Goodnight.
Jun 92. (7")(c-s) **FALLEN ANGELS. / SOLDIER BLUE**
(cd-s+=) – ('A'mixes).

– compilations, others, etc. –

Note; on 'Vanguard' until otherwise mentioned.
May 73. (d-lp)(c) **THE BEST OF BUFFY SAINTE-MARIE**
– Soulful shade of blue / Soldier blue / Universal soldier / Better to find out for yourself / Cod'ine / He's a keeper of the fire / Take my hand for a while / Ground hog / The circle game / My country 'tis of thy people you're dying / Many a mile. *(re-iss.+cd.Mar89 on 'Start') (US re-iss.Nov84)*
1974. (d-lp)(c) **THE BEST OF BUFFY SAINT-MARIE VOL.II**
1974. (7") **SOLDIER BLUE. / ('A' version)** — -
Oct 74. (lp)(c) **NATIVE NORTH AMERICAN: AN ODYSSEY**
Jul 75. (7") **I'M GONNA BE A COUNTRY GIRL AGAIN. / NOW THAT THE BUFFALO'S GONE**
Mar 76. (7") **TAKE MY HAND FOR A WHILE. / TALL TREES IN GEORGIA**
Oct 76. Golden Hour; (lp)(c) **A GOLDEN HOUR OF BUFFY SAINTE-MARIE** — -
Nov 81. PRT; (d-lp)(c) **SPOTLIGHT ON BUFFY SAINTE-MARIE** — -
Jan 83. Flashback; (7") **SOLDIER BLUE. / I'M GONNA BE A COUNTRY GIRL AGAIN** — -
(re-iss.Jan90 on 'Old Gold')

SAINT ETIENNE

Formed: North London, England . . . early 90's by BOB STANLEY and PETER WIGGS. Named themselves after French football team St Etienne, after once toying with idea REARDON (the snooker player). They signed to up-and-coming indie label 'Heavenly', where they quickly secured chart status. • **Style:** Psychedelic dance and dub outfit, fronted by the dreamy vox of SARAH CRACKNELL. • **Songwriters:** STANLEY-WIGGS except a few with CRACKNELL plus outside covers ONLY LOVE CAN BREAK YOUR HEART (Neil Young) / WHO DO YOU THINK YOU ARE (Scott-Dyer) / MY CHRISTMAS PRAYER (Billy Fury) / WESTERN WIND (trad.) / STRANGER IN PARADISE (hit; Tony Bennett) / IS IT TRUE (Marc Bolan) / HOW I LEARNED TO LOVE THE BOMB (TV Personalities). • **Trivia:** Sang a version of RIGHT SAID FRED's 'I'M TOO SEXY' on a 1992 'Heavenly' compilation ep.

Recommended: FOXBASE ALPHA (*8) / SO TOUGH (*7) / TIGER BAY (*6).

BOB STANLEY (b.Peterborough) – keyboards / **PETE WIGGS** – keyboards, synthesizers / **DONNA SAVAGE** – vocals

Heavenly ???

Jul 90. (7") **ONLY LOVE CAN BREAK YOUR HEART. / ('A'version)**
(12") – ('A'-Andy Weatherall mix) / The Official Saint Etiene world cup theme.
Sep 90. (7") **KISS AND MAKE UP. / SKY'S DEAD**
(cd-s+=) – ('A'extended).
(12") – (2-'A'mixes by Pete Helber incl. dub version).
— **SARAH CRACKNELL** – vocals repl. DONNA
May 91. (7") **NOTHING CAN STOP US. / SPEEDWELL** — 54
(12"+=)/ /(cd-s+=) – (2 'B'mixes) / 3-D tiger./ / ('A'instrumental).
Aug 91. (7") **ONLY LOVE CAN BREAK YOUR HEART. / FILTHY** — 39 — 97 Feb 92
(12"+=)(cd-s+=) – ('A'extended).
(cd-s) – ('A'side) / (2 half mixes by Andy Weatherall).
Oct 91. (cd)(c)(lp) **FOXBASE ALPHA** — 34
– This is Radio Etienne / Only love can break your heart / Wilson / Carnt sleep / Girl VII / Spring / She's the one / Stoned to say the least / Nothing can stop us / Etienne gonna die / London belongs to me / Like the swallow / Dilworth's theme.
May 92. (7")(c-s) **JOIN OUR CLUB. / PEOPLE GET REAL** — 21
(12"+=)(cd-s+=) – ('A'chemically friendly mix) / Scene '93.
Sep 92. (12"ep)(cd-ep) **AVENUE (club) / ('A'-Butlins mix) / ('A'marital mix) / ('A'-Venusian mix)** — 40
(12")(cd-s) – ('A'side) / Some place else / Paper / Johnny in the Echo cafe.
— added **IAN CATT** – guitar, programmer
Feb 93. (7")(c-s) **YOU'RE IN A BAD WAY. / CALIFORNIA SNOW STORY** — 12

(12"+=)(cd-s+=) – Archway people / Duke Duvet.
Mar 93. (cd)(c)(lp) **SO TOUGH** 7
– Mario's cafe / Railway jam / Date with Spelman / Calico / Avenue / You're in a bad way / Memo to Pricey / Hobart paving / Leafhound / Clock milk / Conchita Martinez / No rainbows for me / Here come clown feet / Junk the morgue / Chicken soup. *(re-iss.Jun93 with free ltd.cd 'YOU NEED A MESS OF HELP TO STAND ALONE' compilation)* – Who do you think you are / Archway people / California snow storm / Kiss and make up / Duke duvet / Filthy / Join our club / Paper / Some place else / Speedwell.
May 93. (7")(c-s) **HOBART PAVING. / WHO DO YOU THINK YOU ARE** 23
(cd-s+=) – Hobart Paving / Who Do You Think You Are
Dec 93. (7")(c-s) **I WAS BORN ON CHRISTMAS DAY. / MY CHRISTMAS PRAYER** 37
(12"+=)(cd-s+=) – Snowplough / Peterloo.
(above 'A' featured dual vocals with TIM BURGESS of The CHARLATANS)
Dec 93. (cd)(c)(lp) **YOU NEED A MESS OF HELP TO STAND ALONE**
– (see last album)
Feb 94. (7")(c-s) **PALE MOVIE. / HIGHGATE ROAD INCIDENT** 28
(12")(cd-s) – ('A'side) / ('A'-Stetorian dub) / ('A'-Secret Knowledge mix) / ('A'-Lemonentry mix).
Feb 94. (cd)(c)(lp) **TIGER BAY** 8
– Urban clearway / Former lover / Hug my soul / Like a motorway / On the shore / Marble lions / Pale movie / Cool kids of death / Western wind / Tankerville / Western wind / Boy scouts of America.
May 94. (7")(c-s) **LIKE A MOTORWAY. / YOU KNOW I'LL MISS YOU WHEN YOU'RE GONE / SUSHI RIDER** 47
(12")(cd-s) – ('A'side) / ('A'-Dust Brothers mix) / ('A'-David Holmes mix) / ('A'-Autechre mix).
Sep 94. (12"ep)(c-ep) **HUG MY SOUL / I BUY AMERICAN RECORDS / HATE YOUR DRUG** 32
(cd-ep+=) – No, no, no.
(remixed-cd-ep) – ('A'side) / ('A'-Sure Is Pure) / ('A'-Motiv8) / ('A'-Juan 'Kinky' Hernandez) / ('A'-Secret Knowledge).
Oct 95. (c-s) **HE'S ON THE PHONE / ('A'-Motiv8 mix)** 11
(cd-s) – ('A'-Motiv8 mix) / Cool kids of death (Underworld mix) / How I learned to love the bomb.
(cd-s) – ('A'side) / Groveley Road / Is it true / The process.
Nov 95. (cd)(c)(d-lp) **TOO YOUNG TO DIE – THE SINGLES** (compilation) 17
– Only love can break your heart / Kiss and make up / Nothing can stop us / Join our club / People get real / Avenue / You're in a bad way / Who do you think you are / Hobart paving / I was born on Christmas day / Pale movie / Like a motorway / Hug my soul / He's on the phone. (cd+=) – (9 remixes).

SAINTS

Formed: Sydney & Melbourne, Australia ... 1976 by KUEPPER and BAILEY. Their debut 45 '(I'M) STRANDED', issued by 'Fatal' in Australia, was noticed by UK 'Harvest' records, who immediately signed them in '77. Their third single 'THIS PERFECT DAY', was their first, but only Top 40 hit. They split the following year, and attention drifted a little to KUEPPER's new outfit The LAUGHING CLOWNS. The SAINTS re-formed in the early 80's and signed to French label 'New Rose'. • **Style:** Punk/R&B rock band, who brought in brassy experimental sound in 1978. • **Songwriters:** Penned by BAILEY and KUEPPER, until the latter's departure. Covered RIVER DEEP MOUNTAIN HIGH (Phil Spector) / LIPSTICK ON YOUR COLLAR (Connie Francis).

Recommended: SONGS OF SALVATION (*8)

CHRIS BAILEY – vocals / **ED KUEPPER** – guitar / **KYM BRADSHAW** – bass / **IVOR HAY** – drums

Power Exchange / Fatal AUST
Dec 76. (7") **(I'M) STRANDED. / NO TIME** – Sep 76
(US iss. Jun '77 on 'Sire')

Harvest / Sire
May 77. (7") **EROTIC NEUROTIC. / ONE WAY STREET** –
May 77. (lp)(c) **(I'M) STRANDED**
– (I'm) Stranded / One way street / Wild about you / Messin' with the kid / Erotic neurotic / No time / Kissin' cousins / Story of love / Demolition girl / Nights in Venice.
Jul 77. (7") **THIS PERFECT DAY. / LIES** 34
(12") – ('A'side) / Do the robot.
— **ALGY WARD** – bass repl. BRADSHAW who joined The LURKERS
Sep 77. (7"ep) **ONE TWO THREE FOUR** –
– Lipstick on your collar / One way street / Demolition girl / River deep mountain high.
Feb 78. (7") **KNOW YOUR PRODUCT. / RUN DOWN**
Mar 78. (lp)(c) **ETERNALLY YOURS**
– Know your product / Lost and found / Memories are made of this / Private affair / A minor aversion / No, your product / This perfect day / Run down / Ostralia / New center of the universe / Untitled / Misunderstood. *(re-iss.Nov87 on 'Fan Club')*
Aug 78. (7") **SECURITY. / ALL TIMES THROUGH PARADISE**
Sep 78. (lp)(c) **PREHISTORIC SOUNDS**
– Swing for the crime / All times through Paradise / Everyday's a holiday, every night's a party / Brisbane / Church of indifference / Crazy Googenheimer blues / Everything's fine / The prisoner / Security / This time / This heart of mine / The chameleon / Save me. *(re-iss.Nov87 on 'Fan Club')*
— Disbanded late 1978. KUEPPER formed The LAUGHING CLOWNS and WARD joined The DAMNED. In 1980, **CHRIS BAILEY** re-formed The SAINTS recruiting **CHRIS BARRINGTON** – guitar / **JANINE HALL** – bass / **MARK BIRMINGHAM** – drums / guest **IVOR HAY** – keyboards

New Rose / not issued
Oct 80. (7") **IN THE MIRROR. / ALWAYS** –
Jan 81. (lp) **THE MONKEY PUZZLE** –
– Miss wonderful / Always / Paradise / Let's pretend / Someday / Monkeys (let's go) / Mystery dream / Simple love / The ballad / Dizzy Miss Lizzy. *(free live 7"m w.a.)* – **(I'M) STRANDED. / SECURITY / THIS PERFECT DAY** *(cd-iss.! += Below 12"ep)*
Jul 82. (12"ep) **PARALYTIC TONIGHT DUBLIN TOMORROW** –
Feb 83. (7") **FOLLOW THE LEADER. / ANIMAL** –

CHRIS BAILEY

New Rose / not issued
1983. (lp) **CASABLANCA** –
1984. (lp) **WHAT WE DID ON OUR HOLIDAYS** –
– In the midnight hour / Ghost ships / Cherokee dance / I'm drinking / Bring it on home to me / Careless love / I heard it through the grapevine / Amsterdam / All night long / Wak on / Another Saturday night / Home again / It's only time / Insurance on me / Junko partner / Look at me / Always the same / Why does it make me feel / Country boy. *(cd-iss.Aug90)*

SAINTS

were back again. **TRACY PEW** – bass (ex-BIRTHDAY PARTY) repl. JANINE HALL

New Rose / not issued
Dec 84. (7") **IMAGINATION. / PRISONER (live)** –
Dec 84. (lp) **A LITTLE MADNESS TO BE FREE** –
– (cd-iss.!, += extra live tracks)
Mar 85. (7") **GHOST SHIP. / WRAPPED UP & BLUE** –
May 85. (lp) **LIVE IN A MUD HUT (live)** –
– Ghost ship / Imagination / Follow the leader / Know your product / etc.
— TRACY PEW died Nov86 of cancer.
— **BAILEY + HAY** with **RICHARD BURGMANN** – bass + **ARTURO LaRIZZA** – drums

Polydor / not issued
Oct 86. (7") **THE TEMPLE OF THE LORD. / CELTIC BALLAD** –
(12"+=) – How to avoid disaster.
Oct 86. (lp)(c) **ALL FOOL'S DAY** –
– Just like fire would / First time / Hymn to Saint Jude / See you in Paradise / Love or imagination / Celtic ballad / Empty page / Big hits (on the underground) / How to avoid disaster / Blues on my mind / Temple of the Lord / All fools day.
Mar 87. (7") **JUST LIKE FIRE WOULD. / EAST IS EAST** –
(12"+=) – Casablanca.
— Split but BAILEY re-formed 1989 with **ARTURO, IAIN SHEDDON, BARRINGTON FRANCIS + JOE CHIOFALO**

Mushroom / not issued
Oct 89. (7")(12") **PRODIGAL SON. / ?** –
Jan 90. (cd)(c)(lp) **PRODIGAL SON** –
– Grain of sand / Fire and brimstone / Friend of the people / Before Hollywood / Sold out / Ghost ships / Massacre / Tomorrow / Stay / Shipwreck / The music goes round my head.
Jan 90. (7") **GRAIN OF SAND. / MAD RACE** –
(12"+=) – Minus a ride.
1992. (cd) **PERMANENT REVOLUTION** –
– Grain of sand (zydeco version) / One night with you / Wild and wicked world / Pick up the pieces / Running away / Revolution in my life / Friday the 13th / Love or imagination / Cartoon life / Idiot blues.
1992. (12"etched) **GRAIN OF SAND. / CARTOON** –
— band now disbanded.

CHRIS BAILEY

East West / East West
Mar 91. (cd)(lp) **DEMONS**
– Demons / Marquis of Queensberry / Return to zero / Bridges / Edgar Allan Poe / Running away from home / Fade away / Marie Antoinette / Rusting in the moonlight / That's the way it goes / Up all night.

Mushroom / not issued
Mar 94. (cd) **54 DAYS AT SEA** –

– compilations, others, etc. –

Aug 77. Power Exchange; (7") **(I'M) STRANDED. / ('B' by 'Chuck Stanley')** –
Nov 86. Razor; (lp) **THE BEST OF THE SAINTS (77-78)** –
1980s. New Rose; (cd) **OUT IN THE JUNGLE** –
Dec 89. Raven; (lp) **SCARCE SAINTS** –
Feb 91. Raven; (cd) **SONGS OF SALVATION 1976-1988** –
Jan 90. Fan Club; (cd)(c)(lp) **THE NEW ROSE YEARS (GREATEST HITS)** –
(cd+= 5 extra tracks)
Jul 95. Hot; (cd)(lp) **THE MOST PRIMITIVE BAND IN THE WORLD (live from The Twilight Zone, Brisbane 1974)** –
– Wild about you / Do the robot / One way street / Knock on wood / Erotic neurotic / River deep mountain high / Lies / Stranded / Messin' with the kid / Misunderstood.

SALAD

Formed: London, England . . .1992 by ex-MTV presenter and fashion model MARIJNE with her fellow ex-film student and boyfriend PAUL KENNEDY. After a few 45's in 1993, they signed to Island's new indie offshoot label 'Island Red' and soon made inroads into charts with classy singles 'ON A LEASH', 'YOUR MA', 'DRINK THE ELIXIR' and The Shangri-la's influenced 'MOTORBIKE TO HEAVEN'. All were included on their long-awaited

UK Top 20 album 'DRINK ME' in 1995. • **Style:** Raw-edged alternative pop/rock, lying somewhere between ALL ABOUT EVE, The PRIMITIVES or BLONDIE. • **Songwriters:** KENNEDY, WAKEMAN or VAN DER VLUGT, except IT'S FOR YOU (Lennon-McCartney; hit Cilla Black).

Recommended: DRINK ME (*9)

MARIJNE VAN DER VLUGT – vocals, keyboards / **PAUL KENNEDY** – guitar, vocals / **PETE BROWN** – bass / **ROB WAKEMAN** – drums, samples

Waldorf not issued

Jun 93. (12"ep) **KENT EP** [ ] [-]
– Kent / The king of love / Heaven can wait / Mistress.

Oct 93. (12")(cd-s) **DIMINISHED CLOTHES. / CLEAR MY NAME / COME BACK TOMORROW** [ ] [-]

Island Red not issued

Apr 94. (7") **ON A LEASH. / WHAT DO YOU SAY ABOUT THAT?** [ ] [ ]
(12"+=)(cd-s+=) – Planet in the ocean / Problematique.

Jul 94. (7") **YOUR MA. / PLANK** [ ] [ ]
(12"+=)(cd-s+=) – Open.

Feb 95. (7")(c-s) **DRINK THE ELIXIR. / KISS MY LOVE** [66] [ ]
(12"+=)(cd-s+=) – Julius / Diminished clothes (live).

Apr 95. (7")(c-s) **MOTORBIKE TO HEAVEN. / DIARY HELL** [42] [ ]
(cd-s+=) – I am December.

May 95. (cd)(c)(lp) **DRINK ME** [16] [ ]
– Motorbike to Heaven / Drink the elixir / Granite statue / Machine of menace / Overhear me / Shepherds' isle / Muscleman / Your ma / Warmth of the hearth / Gertrude Campbell / Nothing happens / No.1's cooking / A man with a box / Insomnia.

Aug 95. (7")(c-s) **GRANITE STATUE. / IT'S FOR YOU** [50] [ ]
(cd-s+=) – Ici les amigos.
(cd-s) – ('A'side) / Rip goes love and lust / Roadsex.

Richie SAMBORA (see under ⇒ BON JOVI)

Joe SAMPLE (see under ⇒ CRUSADERS)

SAMSON

Formed: London, England ... 1978 by PAUL SAMPSON. After a brief spell with 'Lightning' then 'Lazer' records in the late 70's, they signed to 'RCA' subsidiary label 'Gem' in 1980. Their second album 'HEAD ON', made the UK Top 40 lists, but commercial appeal meandered in 1981, when BRUCE DICKINSON jumped ship to IRON MAIDEN. • **Style:** Co-founders of NWOBHM (New Wave Of Britsh Heavy Metal), with publicity stunts by the masked drummer THUNDERSTICKS, who was replaced in March 1982 by himself! (BARRY GRAHAM). In 1981, NICKY MOORE lent new gritty vox to some melodic bluesy hard-rock numbers. • **Songwriters:** SAMPSON and McCOY penned from the mid-80's. • **Trivia:** MEL GAYNOR of SIMPLE MINDS, was once a brief member in 1981!. The 80's SAMSON are not to be confused with progressive band of the early 70's, who issued an album 'Are You Samson?'.

Recommended: PILLARS OF ROCK (*6)

BRUCE BRUCE (b. DICKINSON) – vocals / **PAUL SAMPSON** – guitar, vocals / **THUNDERSTICKS** (b. BARRY GRAHAM) – drums repl. BURR who joined IRON MAIDEN / **CHRIS AYLMER** – bass

Lightning not issued

Oct 78. (7") **TELEPHONE. / LEAVING YOU** [ ] [-]

Lazer not issued

Jun 79. (lp) **SURVIVORS** [ ] [-]
– It's not as easy as it seems / I wish I was the saddle of a schoolgirl's bike / Big brother / Tomorrow or yesterday / Koz / Six foot under / Inside out / Wrong side of time. *(cd-iss.Jul93 on 'Repertoire')*

Jun 79. (7") **MR. ROCK'N'ROLL. / DRIVIN' MUSIC** [ ] [-]

E.M.I. not issued

May 80. (7") **VICE VERSA. / HAMMERHEAD** [ ] [-]

Gem-R.C.A. not issued

Jun 80. (lp)(c) **HEAD ON** [34] [ ]
– Hard times / Take it like a man / Vice versa / Man watcher / Too close to rock / Thunderburst / Hammerhead / Hunted / Take me to your leader / Walking out on you. *(cd-iss.Jul93 on 'Repertoire')*

Aug 80. (7") **HARD TIMES. / ANGEL WITH A GUN** [ ] [-]

R.C.A. not issued

May 81. (7")(7"pic-d) **RIDING WITH THE ANGELS. / LITTLE BIG MAN** [55] [-]

May 81. (lp)(c) **SHOCK TACTICS** [ ] [ ]
– Riding with the angels / Earth mother / Nice girl / Blood lust / Go to Hell / Bright lights / Once bitten / Gimme crime / Communion. *(cd-iss.Jul93 on 'Repertoire')*

— **NICKY MOORE** – vocals (ex-TIGER) repl. BRUCE who joined IRON MAIDEN / **PETE JUPP** – drums repl. MEL GAYNOR (future SIMPLE MINDS) who repl. THUNDERSTICKS

Polydor not issued

Jul 82. (7")(7"pic-d) **LOSING MY GRIP. / PYRAMID TO THE STARS** [63] [-]
(12"+=) – ('A'extended).

Oct 82. (7") **LIFE ON THE RUN. / DRIVING WITH ZZ!** [ ] [ ]
(d7"+=) – Walkin' out on you / Bright lights.

Nov 82. (lp)(c) **BEFORE THE STORM** [ ] [-]
– Danger zone / Stealing away / Red skies / I'll be round / Test of time / Life on the run / Turn out the light / Losing my grip / Young idea.

Feb 83. (7")(7"pic-d) **RED SKIES. / LIVING LOVING LYING** [65] [-]
(12"+=) – Running out of time.

Feb 84. (7")(7"pic-d) **ARE YOU READY. / FRONT PAGE NEWS** [ ] [-]
(12"+=) – La grange.

Mar 84. (lp)(c) **DON'T GET MAD – GET EVEN** [ ] [-]
– Are you ready / ove hungry / Burning up / The fight goes on / Don't get mad – get even / Into the valley / Bite on the bulet / Doctor Ice / Front page news / Leaving love (behind).

Apr 84. (7") **THE FIGHT GOES ON. / RIDING WITH THE ANGELS** [ ] [-]
(12"+=)(12"pic-d+=) – Vice versa.

— Disbanded 1985, after **DAVE COLWELL** – rhythm guitar / **MERV GOLDWORTHY** – bass repl. AYLMER.

Metal Masters not issued

Mar 85. (lp) **THANK YOU AND GOOD NIGHT (live)** [ ] [-]
– Bite on the bullet / Into the valley / Losing my grip / Vice versa / Love hungry / Tomorrow or yesterday / Mr. Rock and roll / Don't get mad, get even / Test of time / Are you ready?. *(re-iss.Oct86 on 'Razor') (cd-iss.Feb95 on 'Thunderbolt')*

— NICKY MOORE joined ULI ROTH.

PAUL SAMSON'S EMPIRE

with **NICKY MOORE** – vocals / **JO JULIAN** – guitar / **JOHN McCOY** – bass / **EDGAR PATRICK** – drums

Raw Power not issued

May 86. (lp)(c) **JOINT FORCES** [ ] [-]
– Burning emotion / No turning back / Russians / Tales of the fury / Reach out to love / Chosen few / Tramp / The power of love / Tell me. *(cd-iss.Jul93 on 'Repertoire') (cd-iss.Sep94 on 'Thunderbolt')*

— To tour PAUL brought in **DAVE COLWELL** – guitar, keyboards (ex-SAMSON) / **MARK BRABBS** – drums (ex-TANK, ex-DUMPY'S RUSTY NUTS) / **SAM BLUE** – vocals / **KEVIN RIDDLES** – bass, synth. (ex-ANGELWITCH, ex-TITAN)

SAMSON

re-formed with **PAUL** bringing in **MICK WHITE** – vocals / **TOBY SADLER** – keyboards / **DAVE BOYCE** – bass / **CHARLIE MACK GOLIE** – drums

Razor not issued

Jul 88. (m-lp) **AND THERE IT IS** [ ] [-]
– Tomorrow / Don't turn away / I must be crazy / Good to see you / The silver screen.

— (Jan89) **PETER SCANLON** – vocals repl. WHITE

Communique not issued

Aug 90. (cd)(c)(lp) **REFUGEE** [ ] [-]
– Good to see you / Can't live without your love / Turn on the lights / Love this time / Room 109 / State of emergency / Look to the future / Someone to turn to / Too late / Samurai sunset / The silver screen.

Aug 93. (cd) **SAMSON** [ ] [-]

– compilations, others, etc. –

Apr 84. Thunderbolt; (12"ep) **MR. ROCK'N'ROLL / PRIMROSE SHUFFLE. / TELEPHONE / LEAVIN' YOU** [ ] [-]

Sep 84. Thunderbolt; (lp) **LAST RITES** [ ] [-]

Mar 86. Capitol; (7") **VICE VERSA. / LOSING MY GRIP** [ ] [-]

Mar 86. Capitol; (lp)(c) **HEAD TACTICS ("SAMSON featuring BRUCE DICKINSON")** [ ] [-]

1990. Castle; (cd)(c)(lp) **THE BEST OF SAMSON – HAMMERHEAD** [ ] [-]

Dec 90. Raw Fruit; (cd)(lp) **LIVE AT READING 1981** [ ] [-]
(re-iss.cd Jul93 on 'Repertoire')

Jan 91. Connoisseur; (cd)(lp) **PILLARS OF ROCK** [ ] [-]
– Danger zone / Stealing away / Red skies / Losing my grip / Running out of time / Driving with ZZ! / Young idea / Test of time / Leaving love (behind) / The fight goes on / Don't get mad get even / Doctor Ice / Front page news / Bite on the bullet / Into the valley / Tomorrow or yesterday / Mr.Rock and roll / Love hungry.

Ed SANDERS (see under ⇒ FUGS)

SANTANA

Formed: San Francisco, California, USA ... Oct'66 as The SANTANA BLUES BAND by CARLOS SANTANA. In 1968 as SANTANA, they played concert at The Fillmore West. Later in the year, CARLOS guested on album 'THE LIVE ADVENTURES OF AL KOOPER and MIKE BLOOMFIELD', which brought him to the attention of 'Columbia' records. Their long-awaited eponymous debut lp late in '69, cracked the US Top 5 due to an August appearance at the now famous 'Woodstock' festival. Became massive group in the 70's, after 2 consecutive No.1 albums 'ABRAXAS' and 'SANTANA III'. • **Style:** Blues based Latin-American orientated rock, jazzily fused with percussive instrumentals mixed with CARLOS's clear guitar technique. • **Songwriters:** CARLOS penned with group except covers:- JIN-GO-LA-BA (Michael Babatunde Olatunji) / BLACK MAGIC WOMAN (Fleetwood Mac) / OYO COMO VA (c.Tito Puente) / GYPSY WOMAN (Curtis Mayfield) / PEACE ON EARTH (Alice Coltrane) / STORMY (Classics IV) / SHE'S NOT THERE (Zombies) / WELL ALL RIGHT (Buddy Holly) / ONE CHAIN (Four Tops) / WINNING (Russ Ballard) / THIRD STONE FROM THE SUN (Jimi Hendrix) / WHO'S THAT LADY (Isley Brothers) / FULL MOON (Paola Rustichelli) / RIGHT ON (Marvin Gaye) / I'VE BEEN TO THE MOUNTAIN TOP (... King) / etc. • **Trivia:** In 1973, CARLOS married Urmila, a Sri Chimnoy devotee. He also became highly religious and changed his name to DEVADIP, which means 'The Light Of The Lamp Supreme'. In the mid-

70's, Bill Graham took over management of SANTANA. For all the lovers of anything, SANTANA, his brother JORGE (in Latin-rock band MALO) had success in Apr '72 with eponymous lp, which hit no. 14 US. A single lifted from it 'SALI VECITO' made no. 18. They went on to release 3 more 'Warner Bros.' albums; DOS (1972) / EVOLUTION (1973) + ASCENSION (1974).

Recommended: SANTANA (*7) / ABRAXAS (*8) / SANTANA III (*6) / CARAVANSERAI (*8) / VIVA! SANTANA (*8)

CARLOS SANTANA (b.20 Jul'47, Autlan de Navarro, Mexico. Raised in Tijuana then San Francisco, USA) – lead guitar / **GREGG ROLIE** – keyboards, vocals / **DAVID BROWN** – bass repl. GUS RODRIGUES (in 1967) / **MIKE SHRIEVE** – drums repl. BOB LIVINGSTONE (in '67). He had repl. ROD HARPER / **JOSE 'CHEPITO' AREAS** – perc. + **MIKE CARABELLO** – congas repl. TOM FRAZER – guitar

C.B.S. Columbia

Oct 69. (7") **PERSUASION. / SAVOR** Sep 69

Oct 69. (7") **JIN-GO-LA-BA. / PERSUASION** – 56

Nov 69. (lp)(c) **SANTANA** (UK re-dist.Mar70) 26 4 Sep 69
– Waiting / Evil ways / Shades of time / Savor / Jingo / Persuasion / Treat / You just don't care / Soul sacrifice. *(re-iss.Mar81, cd-iss.May87 & May92)*

Jan 70. (7") **EVIL WAYS. / WAITING** – 9

Apr 70. (7") **EVIL WAYS. / JINGO**

Nov 70. (lp)(c) **ABRAXAS** 7 1 Sep 70
– Singing winds, crying beasts / Black magic woman – Gypsy queen / Oyo como va / Incident at Neshabur / Se a cabo / Mother's daughter / Samba pa ti / Hope you're feeling better / El Nicoya. *(re-iss.Mar81) (re-iss.+cd.Mar86)*

Dec 70. (7") **BLACK MAGIC WOMAN. / HOPE YOU'RE FEELING BETTER** 4 Nov 70

Mar 71. (7") **OYE COMO VA. / SAMBA PA TI** 13 Feb 71

— added **NEIL SCHON** – guitar / **COKE ESCOVEDO** – percussion

Oct 71. (lp)(c) **SANTANA III** 6 1
– Batuka / No one to depend on / Taboo / Toussaint l'overture / Everybody's everything / Guajira / Everything's coming our way / Jungle strut / Para los rumberos. *(re-iss.Mar82, cd-iss.Mar87) (re-iss.cd+c Jun94 on 'Columbia')*

Nov 71. (7") **EVERYBODY'S EVERYTHING. / GUAJIRA** 12 Oct 71

Mar 72. (7") **NO ONE TO DEPEND ON. / TABOO** 36 Feb72

Jul 72. (lp)(c) **CARLOS SANTANA & BUDDY MILES LIVE (live) ("CARLOS SANTANA & BUDDY MILES")** 29 8
– Marbles / Lava / Evil ways / Faith interlude / Them changes / Free form funkafide filth. *(re-iss.Sep84)*

Oct 72. (7") **EVIL WAYS (live). / THEM CHANGES (live)** 84 Sep 72

(above was also credited to "CARLOS SANTANA & BUDDY MILES")

— **ARMANDO PERAZA** – percussion repl. CARABELLO and ESCOVEDO / **TOM RUTLEY** – bass repl. BROWN

Nov 72. (lp)(c) **CARAVANSERAI** 6 8
– Eternal caravan of reincarnation / Waves within / Look up (to see what's coming down) / Just in time to see the sun / Song of the wind / All the love of the universe / Future primitive / Stone flower / La fuente del ritmo / Every step of the way. *(re-iss.Nov81, cd-iss.1988)*

Jan 73. (7") **LOOK UP (TO SEE WHAT'S COMING DOWN). / ALL THE LOVE OF THE UNIVERSE** –

Jul 73. (lp)(c) **LOVE DEVOTION SURRENDER ("CARLOS DEVADIP SANTANA AND MAHAVISHNU JOHN McLAUGHLIN")** 7 14
– A love supreme / Naima / The lie divine / Let us go into the house of the Lord / Meditation. *(re-iss.cd+c Jun94 on 'Columbia')*

(Above album feat. below newcomers (**RAUCH + LEWIS**) + **PERAZA, JAN HAMMER** – keyboards / **BILLY COBHAM** – drums / **LARRY YOUNG** – keyboards)

— **CARLOS** retained **AREAS, PERAZA + SHRIEVE** and brought in newcomers **TOM COSTER** – keyboards, vocals repl. ROLIE who formed JOURNEY / **RICHARD KERMODE** – keyboards repl. SCHON who also formed JOURNEY / **DOUG RAUCH** – bass repl. RUTLEY / added **LEON THOMAS** – vocals / **JAMES MINGO LEWIS** – congas

Nov 73. (lp)(c) **WELCOME** 8 25
– Going home / Love, devotion and surrender / Samba de sausalito / When I look into your eyes / Yours is the light / Mother Africa / Light of life / Flame-sky / Welcome. *(re-iss.1984)*

Nov 73. (7") **WHEN I LOOK INTO YOUR EYES. / SAMBA DE SAUSALITO**

Sep 74. (lp)(c) **ILLUMINATIONS ("CARLOS SANTANA & ALICE COLTRANE")** 40 79
– Guru Sri Chimnoy aphorism / Angel of air – Angel of water / Bliss: The eternal now / Angel of sunlight / Illuminations. (**ALICE** – keyboards, etc.)

— **GREG WALKER** – vocals + sessioners repl. KERMODE, LEWIS and THOMAS

Nov 74. (lp)(c) **BORBOLETTA** 18 20
– Spring manifestations / Canto de los flores / Life is anew / Give and take / One with the Sun / Aspirations / Practice what you preach / Mirage / Here and now / Flor de canela / Promise of a fisherman / Borboletta. *(re-iss.Nov83)(re-iss.cd Nov93 on 'Sony Collectors')*

Nov 74. (7") **PRACTICE WHAT YOU PREACH. / CANTO DE LOS FLORES**

Jan 75. (7") **MIRAGE. / FLOR DE CANELA**

Mar 75. (7") **GIVE AND TAKE. / LIFE IS ANEW** –

(Below triple album was issued initially in Japan 1973)

Dec 75. (t-lp) **LOTUS (live)**
– Meditation / Going home / A-1 funk / Every step of the way / Black magic woman – Gypsy queen / Oye como va / Yours is the light / Batuka / Xibaba (she-ba-ba) / Savor / Stone flower / (introduction) / Castillos de arena (pt.1) / Waiting / Se a cabo / Samba pa ti / Toussaint l'overture / Incident at Neshabur. *(re-iss.d-c+d-cd.Dec90)*

— **LEON NDUGU CHANCLER** – drums repl. SHRIEVE and AREAS / **IVORY STONE** – bass repl. RAUCH

Mar 76. (7") **EUROPA. / TAKE ME WITH YOU**

Apr 76. (lp)(c) **AMIGOS** 21 10
– Dance sister dance (baila mi Hermana) / Take me with you / Let me / Gitano / Tell me are you tired / Europa (Earth's cry, Heaven's smile) / Let it shine. *(re-iss.Jun84, cd-iss.Mar87 & Jun92)*

May 76. (7") **LET IT SHINE. / TELL ME ARE YOU TIRED** 77

Aug 76. (7") **DANCE SISTER DANCE (BAILA MI HERMANA). / LET ME**

— **JOSE AREAS** returned to repl. PERAZA / **PABLO TELEZ** – bass repl. STONE

Dec 76. (lp)(c) **FESTIVAL** 27 27
– Carnaval / Let the children play / Jugando / Carnival / Give me love / Verao Vermelho / Let the music set you free / Revelations / Reach up / The river / Try a little harder / Maria Caracoles.

Jan 77. (7") **REVELATIONS. / REACH UP** –

Jan 77. (7") **REVELATIONS. / GIVE ME LOVE** –

Mar 77. (7") **LET THE CHILDREN PLAY. / CARNAVAL**

— Trimmed slightly when CHANCLER vacated

Sep 77. (7") **SHE'S NOT THERE. / ZULU** 11 27

Oct 77. (d-lp)(c) **MOONFLOWER (live + studio)** 7 10
– Dawn – Go within / Carnaval / Let the children play / Jugando / I'll be waiting / Zulu / Bahia / Black magic woman – Gypsy queen / Dance sister dance (baila mi Hermana) / Europa (Earth's cry, Heaven's smile) / She's not there / Flor de Luna (Moonflower) / Soul sacrifice / Heads, hands & feet / El Morocco / Transcendance / Savor / Toussaint l'overture. *(re-iss.Apr85, cd-iss.Apr89)*

Jan 78. (7") **BLACK MAGIC WOMAN (live). / TRANSCENDANCE** –

Jan 78. (7") **BLACK MAGIC WOMAN (live). / I'LL BE WAITING (live)** –

Aug 78. (7") **I'LL BE WAITING. ("CARLOS SANTANA") / FLOR DE LUNA (MOONFLOWER)**

— **CARLOS** retained only **WALKER + COSTER** and introduced **ARMANDO PERAZA** returned to repl. AREAS / **DAVID MARGEN** – bass repl. TELLEZ / added **GRAHAM LEER** – drums / **CHRIS RHYME** – keyboards / **RAUL REKOW** – percussion / **CHRIS SOLBERG** – guitar, keyboards, vocals

Oct 78. (7") **WELL ALL RIGHT. / JERICHO** – 69

Oct 78. (7") **WELL ALL RIGHT. / WHAM!** 53 –
(12"+=) – Life is a lady – Holiday.

Nov 78. (lp)(c) **INNER SECRETS** 17 27
– Dealer / Spanish rose / Well all right / One chain (don't make no prison) / Stormy / Open invitation / Wham! / The facts of love / Life is a lady – Holiday / Move on. *(cd-iss.Jun92)*

Jan 79. (7") **ONE CHAIN (DON'T MAKE NO PRISON). / MOVE ON** –

Jan 79. (7") **STORMY. / MOVE ON** – 32

Mar 79. (lp)(c) **ONENESS: SILVER DREAMS, GOLDEN REALITY ("CARLOS SANTANA")** 55 87
– The chosen hour / Arise awake / Light versus darkness / Jim Jeannie / Transformation day / Victory / Silver dreams golden smiles / Cry of the wilderness / Guru's song / Oneness / Life is just a passing parade / Golden dawn / Free as the morning sun / Song for Devadip.

Apr 79. (7") **ONE CHAIN (DON'T MAKE NO PRISON). / LIFE IS A HOLIDAY** – 59

— **ALEX LIGERTWOOD** – vocals (ex-BRIAN AUGER) repl. WALKER / **ALAN PASQUE** – keyboards, vocals repl. COSTER + RHYME

Oct 79. (7") **YOU KNOW THAT I LOVE YOU. / AQUA MARINE** – 35

Oct 79. (lp)(c) **MARATHON** 28 25
– Marathon / Lightning in the sky / Aqua marine / You know that I love you / All I ever wanted / Stand up – Runnin' / Summer lady / Love / Stay / Hard times. *(cd-iss.May87)*

Feb 80. (7") **ALL I EVER WANTED. / LOVE** 57 –

Feb 80. (7") **ALL I EVER WANTED. / LIGHTNING IN THE SKY** –

Jun 80. (7") **AQUA MARINE. / STAND UP - RUNNIN'**

Sep 80. (d-lp)(d-c) **THE SWING OF DELIGHT ("CARLOS SANTANA")** 65 65
– Swapan tari / Love theme from 'Sparticus' / Phuler Matan / Song for my brother / Jharna kala / Gardenia / La Llave / Golden hours / Shere Khan, the tiger. *(this featured The MILES DAVIS QUINTET of the 60's)*

— added **ORESTES VILATO** – percussion / **RICHARD BAKER** – keyboards

Apr 81. (7") **WINNING. / BRIGHTEST STAR** 17

Apr 81. (lp)(c) **ZEBOP!** 33 9
– Changes / E papa re / Primera invasion / Searchin' / Over and over / Winning / Tales of Kilimanjaro / The sensitive kind / American gypsy / I love you much too much / Brightest star / Hannibal. *(cd-iss.Dec85)*

Jun 81. (7") **CHANGES. / AMERICAN GYPSY**

Sep 81. (7") **THE SENSITIVE KIND. / AMERICAN GYPSY** 56 Aug 81

Jan 82. (7") **SEARCHIN'. / TALES OF KILIMANJARO** –

— **CARLOS** retained only **LEAR, MARGEN, BAKER + VILATO**

Aug 82. (lp)(c) **SHANGO** 35 22
– The Nile / Hold on / Night hunting time / Nowhere to run / Nueva York / Oxun / Body surfing / What does it take / Let me inside / Warrior / Shango. *(cd-iss.1988)*

Aug 82. (7") **HOLD ON. / OXUN** – 15

Nov 82. (7") **NOWHERE TO RUN. / NUEVA YORK** – 66

CARLOS SANTANA

solo again, featuring **WILLIE NELSON, BOOKER T.JONES & The FABULOUS THUNDERBIRDS.**

Apr 83. (7") **WATCH YOUR STEP. / TALES OF KILIMANJARO** –

Apr 83. (7") **WATCH YOUR STEP. / LIGHTNIN'** –

Apr 83. (lp)(c) **HAVANA MOON** 84 31
– Watch your step / Lightnin' / Who do you love / Mudbone / One with you / Ecuador / Tales of Kilimanjaro / Havana Moon / Daughter of the night / They all went to Mexico / Vereda tropical. *(cd-iss.May87) (cd re-iss.Jun88 on 'Collector's Choice')*

May 83. (7") **THEY ALL WENT TO MEXICO. / MUDBONE** –

Jun 83. (7") **HAVANA MOON. / LIGHTNIN'** –

SANTANA

CARLOS only retained **VILATO** plus sessioners

Mar 85. (7") **SAY IT AGAIN. / TOUCHDOWN RAIDERS** 46 Feb 85

(12"+=) – She's not there / ('A'instrumental).
Mar 85. (lp)(c) **BEYOND APPEARANCES** [58] [50]
– Breaking out / Written in sand / How long / Brotherhood / Spirit / Say it again / Who loves you / I'm the one who loves you / Touchdown raiders / Right now. *(re-iss.+cd.Mar86)*
May 85. (7") **HOW LONG. / RIGHT NOW** [ ] [-]
(12"+=) – She's not there.
May 85. (7") **I'M THE ONE WHO LOVES YOU. / RIGHT NOW** [-] [ ]
—— **CARLOS** re-united **GREGG ROLIE, MIKE SHRIEVE, JOSE AREAS** +sessioners
Feb 87. (lp)(c)(cd) **FREEDOM** [ ] [95]
– Vera Cruz / She can't let go / Once it's gotcha / Love is you / Songs of freedom / Deeper, dig deeper / Praise / Mandela / Before we go / Victim of circumstance.
Feb 87. (7") **PRAISE. / LOVE IS YOU** [-] [ ]
May 87. (7")(12") **VERA CRUZ. / MANDELA** [ ] [ ]
—— SANTANA touring band **ROLIE, CHESTER THOMPSON** – keyboards / **TOM COSTER** – synthesizers / **ALFONSO JOHNSON** – bass / **GRAHAM LEER** – drums / **BUDDY MILES** – vocals / **ARMANDO PERAZA, PAUL REKOW + ORESTES VILATO** – percussion
Nov 87. (lp)(c)(cd) **BLUES FOR SALVADOR ("CARLOS SANTANA")** [ ] [ ]
– Bailando / Aquatic park / Bella / I'm gone / 'Trane / Deeper, dig deeper / Mingus / Now that you know / Hannibal / Blues for Salvador.
(above featured mainly session people)
—— **CARLOS** retained **THOMPSON + PERAZA,** plus recruited **BENNY RIETVELD** – bass / **ALEX LIGERTWOOD** – vocals, guitar / **WALFREDO REYES** – drums, timbales, perc with host of guests (over 15).
Jun 90. (cd)(c)(lp) **SPIRITS DANCING IN THE FLESH** [68] [85]
– Let there be light – Spirits dancing in the flesh / Gypsy woman / It's a jungle out there / Soweto (African libre) / Choose / Peace on Earth . . . Mother Earth . . . Third stone from the Sun / Full Moon / Who's that lady / Jin-go-la-ba / Goodness and mercy.
Jun 90. (7") **GYPSY WOMAN. / GOODNESS AND MERCY** [ ] [ ]
(12"+=)(cd-s+=) – Black magic woman / Oye como va / She's not there (live)
—— Next with samples from MILES DAVIS and JOHN COLTRANE.

Polydor Polydor
Apr 92. (cd)(c)(d-lp) **MILAGRO** [ ] [ ]
– Medley:- Introduction by BILL GRAHAM – Milagro / Medley:- I've been to the mountain top – Somewhere in Heaven / Medley:- Saja – Right on / Your touch / Life is for living / Red prophet / Aqua que va ceer / Make somebody happy / Free all the people (South Africa) / Medley:- Gypsy – Grajoonca / We don't have to wait / Adios.
Nov 93. (cd)(c) **SACRED FIRE** (live in S. America) [ ] [ ]
– Angels all around us / Vive le Vada (life is for living) / Esperando / No one to depend on / Black magic woman – Gypsy queen / Oye como va / Samba pa ti / Guajira / Make somebody happy / Toussaint l'overture / Soul sacrifice / Don't try this at home / Europa / Jingo-la-ba.
—— now with brother **JORGE** – guitar (ex-MALO)

Island Island
Sep 94. (cd)(c) **BROTHERS ("SANTANA BROTHERS")** [ ] [ ]
– Transmutation industrial / Thoughts / Luz amor y vida / En aranjouz con tu amour / Contigo / Blues Latino / La olaza / Brujo / The trip / Reflections / Morning in Marin.

– (SANTANA) compilations, others, etc. –

Below released on 'CBS/ Columbia' until mentioned otherwise.
Mar 73. (7") **OYE COMO VA. / BLACK MAGIC WOMAN** [ ] [ ]
(re-iss.Feb76)
Aug 74. (lp)(c) **SANTANA'S GREATEST HITS** [14] [17] Jul 74
(re-iss.Feb88, cd-iss.Jun87)
Sep 74. (7") **SAMBA PA TI. / INCIDENT AT NESHABUR** [27] [ ]
(re-iss.Feb79)
Oct 80. (t-lp) **BOX SET** (first 3 albums) [ ] [ ]
Jul 84. (7") **SHE'S NOT THERE. / SAMBA PA TI** [ ] [-]
(re-iss.Jan88 on 'Old Gold')
Oct 88. (t-lp)(d-c)(d-cd) **VIVA! SANTANA** (best + live) [ ] [ ]
– Everybody's everything / Black magic woman – Gypsy queen / Guajira / Jungle strut / Jingo / Ballin' / Bambara / Angel Negro / Incident at Neshabur / Just let the music speak / Super boogie – Hong Kong blues / Song of the wind / Abi cama / Vitalo / Paris finale / Brotherhood / Open invitation / Aqua marine / Dance, sisters, dance / Europa / Peraza 1 / She's not there / Bambele / Evil ways / Daughter of the night / Peraza II / Black magic woman – Gypsy woman (live) / Oyo como va / Persuasion / Soul sacrifice.
May 89. (3"cd-ep) **BLACK MAGIC WOMAN / SAMBA PA TI / OYE COMO VA / JIN-GO-LA-BA** [ ] [-]
Jun 92. (cd)(c)(lp) **THE BEST OF SANTANA** [ ] [ ]
Mar 93. Columbia; (cd) **SANTANA / ABRAXAS** [ ] [ ]
Feb 86. Old Gold; (12"ep) **SAMBA PA TI / JIN-GO-LA-BA. / SHE'S NOT THERE / EVIL WAYS** [ ] [-]
Oct 86. K-Tel; (lp)(c)(cd) **VIVA! SANTANA – THE VERY BEST OF SANTANA** [50] [-]
May 88. Arcade; (d-cd) **THE VERY BEST OF SANTANA – VOLUME 1 & 2** [ ] [-]
Jun 89. Thunderbolt; (lp)(cd) **PERSUASION** [ ] [-]
Jan 90. Thunderbolt; (cd)(lp) **LATIN TROPICAL** [ ] [-]
Jun 88. That's Orginal; (d-lp)(c)(d-cd) **WELCOME / CARLOS SANTANA & BUDDY MILES LIVE** [ ] [-]
Nov 93. Sony Collectors; (cd)(c) **SAMBA PA TI** [ ] [-]
(re-iss.cd Dec95 on 'Columbia')
Sep 93. Sony Collectors; (cd)(c) **SALSA, SAMBA & SANTANA** [ ] [-]
May 93. F.N.A.C.; (cd) **NINETEEN SIXTY EIGHT** [ ] [-]
Feb 94. Thunderbolt; (cd) **EVOLUTION** [ ] [-]
Mar 94. Charly; (cd) **SOUL SACRIFICE** [ ] [-]
Oct 94. Charly; (cd) **LATIN ROCK FUSIONS** [ ] [-]
Apr 94. Pulsar; (3xcd) **THE SUPER COLLECTION** [ ] [-]
Jul 94. Success; (cd)(c) **AS YEARS GO BY** [ ] [-]
Jul 94. Success; (cd)(c) **SANTANA JAM** [ ] [-]
Jul 94. Success; (cd)(c) **EVERY DAY I HAVE THE BLUES** [ ] [-]
Jul 94. Success; (cd)(c) **WITH A LITTLE HELP FROM MY FRIENDS** [ ] [-]
Oct 94. Columbia; (cd) **THE BEST** [ ] [-]
Feb 95. B.A.M.; (cd) **PEARLS OF THE PAST** [ ] [-]
Apr 95. Muskateer; (cd)(c) **THE EARLY YEARS** [ ] [-]
Nov 95. The Collection; (3xcd-box) **THE COLLECTION** [ ] [-]
—— Note: Most albums up to 1974, were also issued ! on quad-lp.

Joe SATRIANI

Born: Bay Area, San Francisco, USA. Raised in Carle Place, Long Island. After a time overseas, he formed The SQUARES in 1984. Played sessions on GREG KIHN's mid-80's album, before going solo in 1986 and releasing eponymous EP. • **Style:** New-age techno guitar-solo orientated rock. • **Songwriters:** Writes all his own work. • **Trivia:** Famous for having taught young guitarists STEVE VAI and Metallica's KIRK HAMMETT. He also guested on ALICE COOPER's 'Hey Stoopid' & SPINAL TAP's 'Break Like The Wind'.

Recommended: SURFING WITH THE ALIEN (*7) / FLYING IN A BLUE DREAM (*7)

JOE SATRIANI – guitar, bass, keyboards, percussion, etc. / with band **JEFF CAMPITELLI** – drums, percussion, DX / **JOHN CUNIBERTI** – percussion, vocals / **BONGO BOB SMITH** – electronics, drums / **JEFF KREEGER** – synth.

F.F.Thought Relativity
1986. (12"ep) **JOE SATRIANI** [-] [ ]
Feb 87. (lp) **NOT OF THIS EARTH** [ ] [ ] Nov 86
– Not of this Earth / The snake / Rubina / Memories / Brother John / The enigmatic / Driving at night / Hordes of locusts / New day / The headless horseman. *(c+cd-iss.Sep88)(re-iss.cd+c May93 on 'Relativity')*
—— He was now joined by **STU HAMM** – bass / **JONATHAN MOVER** – drums
Nov 87. (lp)(c)(cd) **SURFING WITH THE ALIEN** [ ] [29]
– Surfing with the alien / Ice 9 / Crushing day / Always with you, always with me / Satch boogie / Hill of the skull / Circles / Lords of Karma / Midnight / Echo. *(re-iss.cd+c May93 on 'Relativity')*
Jun 88. (7") **ALWAYS WITH YOU, ALWAYS WITH ME. / SURFING WITH THE ALIEN** [ ] [ ]
Dec 88. (m-lp) **DREAMING £11** [ ] [42]
– The crush of love / Ice 9 / Memories (live) / Hordes of locusts (live). *(re-iss.cd-ep/c-ep May93 on 'Relativity')*
—— SATRIANI now supplied vocals for 6 tracks & returned to original line-up.
Nov 89. (lp)(c)(cd) **FLYING IN A BLUE DREAM** [ ] [23]
– Flying in a blue dream / The mystical potato head groove thing / Can't slow down / Headless / Strange / I believe / One big rush / Big bad Moon / The feeling / The phone call / Day at the beach (new rays from an ancient Sun) / Back to Shalla-bal / Ride / The forgotten (part one & two) / The bells of Lal (part one & two) / Into the light. *(re-iss.cd+c May93 on 'Relativity')*
Mar 90. (7") **BIG BAD MOON. / DAY AT THE BEACH (NEW RAYS FROM AN ANCIENT SUN)** [ ] [ ] 1989
(12"+=)(cd-s+=) – ('A'extended).
Mar 91. (7") **I BELIEVE. / FLYING IN A BLUE DREAM** [ ] [ ]
(12"+=)(cd-s+=) – ('A'remix).
—— Now with **ANDY JOHNS** on production, etc.
Aug 92. (cd)(c)(lp) **THE EXTREMIST** [13] [22]
– Friends / The extremist / War / Cryin' / Rubina's blue sky happiness / Summer song / Tears in the rain / Why / Motorcycle driver / New blues.

Epic Epic
Feb 93. (12"ep)(cd-ep) **THE SATCH EP** [53] [ ]
– The Extremist / Cryin' / Banana Mango / Crazy
Nov 93. (2xcd)(2xc)(3xlp) **TIME MACHINE** [32] [95]
– Time machine / The mighty turtle head / All alone (a.k.a. left alone) / Banana mango 11 / Thinking of you / Crazy / Speed of light / Baroque / Dweller of the threshold / Banana mango / Dreaming £11 / I am become death / Saying goodbye / Woodstock jam / Satch boogie / Summer song / Flying in a blue dream / Cryin' / The crush of love / Tears in the rain / Always with me, always with you / Big bad Moon / Surfing with the alien / Rubina / Circles / Drum solo / Lords of Karma / Echo.
Oct 95. (cd)(c) **JOE SATRIANI** [21] [51]
– Cool £9 / If / Down down down / Luminous flesh giants / SMF / Look my way / Home / Moroccan sunset / Killer bee bop / Slow down blues / (You're) My world / Sittin' 'round.

– compilations, etc. –

Oct 94. Relativity; (3xcd-box) **NOT OF THIS EARTH / SURFING WITH THE ALIEN / FLYING IN A BLUE DREAM** [ ] [ ]

SAVOY BROWN

Formed: London, England . . . 1966 as SAVOY BROWN BLUES BAND by teenager at the time KIM SIMMONDS. After brief spell on MIKE VERNON's 'Purdah' label, they signed to 'Decca' in 1967. Due to increasing sales in the US, they emigrated there in 1973. • **Style:** Boogie-blues similar to CHICKEN SHACK, etc. • **Songwriters:** Most written by SIMMONDS and group, except covers WHOLE LOTTA SHAKIN' GOIN' ON (Jerry Lee Lewis) / LITTLE QUEENIE (Chuck Berry) / I AIN'T SUPERSTITIOUS (Willie Dixon) / PURPLE HAZE (Jimi Hendrix) / ENDLESS SLEEP (Joey Reynolds) / JUST FOR KICKS (Russ Ballard) / ON THE PROWL + SHOT IN THE HEAD (Vanda-Young) / I HATE TO SEE YOU GO (Little Walter Jacobs) / HOWLING FOR MY DARLING (Dixon-Burnette) / SHE'S THE ONE (Brown-Ballard) / etc. • **Trivia:** During their best period in early 1971, they headlined over ROD STEWART & THE FACES on a US tour.

Recommended: THE BEST OF SAVOY BROWN (*6)

SAVOY BROWN BLUES BAND

BRUCE PORTIUS – vocals / **KIM SIMMONDS** – guitar / **MARTIN STONE** – guitar / **BOB HALL** – piano / **RAY CHAPPELL** – bass / **LEO MANNINGS** – drums / **BILL BRUFORD** was also member 67-68

Purdah / not issued

1966. (7") **I TRIED. / CAN'T QUIT YOU BABY** [ ] [-]

Decca / Parrot

1967. (lp) **SHAKE DOWN** [ ] [-]
– Ain't superstitious / Let me love you baby / Black night / High rise / Rock me baby / I smell trouble / Oh pretty woman / Little girl / The doormouse rides the rails / It's all my fault / Shake 'em down. *(cd-iss.Jan89 on 'London')*

1967. (7") **SHAKE 'EM DOWN. / (part 2)** [-] [ ]

— **DAVE PEVERETT** – guitar, vocals repl. STONE who joined MIGHTY BABY / **CHRIS YOULDEN** – vocals repl. PORTIUS / **RIVERS JOBE** – bass repl. CHAPPELL / **ROGER EARL** – drums repl. MANNINGS who joined SUNFLOWER BLUES BAND

Nov 67. (7") **TASTE AND TRY, BEFORE YOU BUY. / SOMEDAY PEOPLE** [ ] [-]

Sep 68. (lp) **GETTING TO THE POINT** [ ] [ ]
– Flood in Houston / Stay with me baby / Honey bee / Give me a penny / The incredible gnome meets Jaxman / Downchild / Getting to the point / Big city lights / You need love. *(cd-iss.Jun90 on 'Deram')*

SAVOY BROWN

TONE STEVENS – bass repl. JOBE

Jun 68. (7") **WALKING BY MYSELF. / VICKSBURG BLUES** [ ] [-]

Dec 68. (7") **TRAIN TO NOWHERE. / TOLLING BELLS** [ ] [-]

Dec 68. (7") **SHE'S GOT A RING IN HIS NOSE AND A RING ON HER HAND. / GRITS AIN'T GROCERIES** [-] [ ]

Apr 69. (lp) **BLUE MATTER** [ ] [ ]
– Train to nowhere / Tolling bells / She's got a ring in his nose and a ring on her hand / Vicksburg blues / Don't turn me on your door / Maybe wrong / Louisiana blues / It hurts me too. *(cd-iss.May90 on 'Deram')*

Aug 69. (7") **MAKE UP MY MIND. / TRAIN TO NOWHERE** [-] [ ]

Sep 69. (lp) **A STEP FURTHER** [ ] [71]
– Make up my mind / Waiting in the bamboo groove / Life's one act play / I'm tired / Where I am / Whole lotta shakin' goin' on / Savoy Brown boogie (incl. Feels so good) / Purple haze / Little Queenie / Hernando's hideaway. *(re-iss.+cd.Aug91 on 'Deram')*

Nov 69. (7") **I'M TIRED. / STAY WITH ME BABY** [ ] [74]

— Trimmed to a quintet when BOB HALL left to form The SUNFLOWER BLUES BAND.

May 70. (7") **A HARD WAY TO GO. / WAITING IN THE BAMBOO GROOVE** [ ] [-]

May 70. (lp) **RAW SIENNA** [ ] [ ] Apr 70
– A hard way to go / That same feelin' / Master hare / I'm crying / Needle and spoon / A little more wine / Is that so / Stay while the night is young / When I was a young boy.

Jun 70. (7") **A HARD WAY TO GO. / THE INCREDIBLE GNOME MEETS JAXMAN** [-] [ ]

— Now trim to a quartet, when CHRIS YOULDEN left later going solo.

Oct 70. (lp)(c) **LOOKING IN** [ ] [39]
– Poor girl / Money can't save your soul / Sunday night / Looking in / Take it easy / Sittin' an' thinkin' / Leavin' again / Romanoff. *(re-iss.+cd.Aug91 on 'Deram')*

Nov 70. (7") **POOR GIRL. / MASTER HARE** [ ] [ ]

Feb 71. (7") **SITTIN' AN' THINKIN'. /** [-] [ ]

— (Jan71) **KIM SIMMONDS** now the sole original survivor, recruited new men **PAUL RAYMOND** – keyboards (ex-CHICKEN SHACK) repl. PEVERETT who formed FOGHAT / **ANDY SYLVESTER** – bass (ex-CHICKEN SHACK) repl. STEVENS who formed FOGHAT / **DAVE BIDWELL** – drums (ex-CHICKEN SHACK) repl. ROGER EARL who formed FOGHAT / added **DAVE WALKER** – vocals

Sep 71. (lp)(c) **STREET CORNER TALKING** [ ] [75]
– Tell mama / Let it rock / I can't get next to you / Time does tell / Street corner talking / All I can do / Wang dang doodle.

Oct 71. (7") **LET IT ROCK. / TELL MAMA** [ ] [-]

Oct 71. (7") **TELL MAMA. / ROCK AND ROLL ON THE RADIO** [-] [83]

Mar 72. (lp)(c) **HELLBOUND TRAIN** [ ] [34]
– Doin' fine / Lost and lonely child / I'll make everything alright / Troubled by these days and times / If I could see and end / I'll make you happy / Hellbound train. *(re-iss.+cd.Aug91 on 'Deram')*

May 72. (7") **LOST AND LONELY CHILD. / IF I COULD SEE AN END** [-] [ ]

— (a member early '71) **ANDY PYLE** – bass (ex-JUICY LUCY, ex-BLODWYN PIG) repl. SYLVESTER who went into session work.

Nov 72. (lp) **LION'S SHARE** [ ] [ ]
– Shot in the head / Second try / The saddest feeling / I can't find you / Howling for my darling / So tired / Damn demon / Love me please / I hate to see you go.

Jan 73. (7") **SO TIRED. / THE SADDEST FEELING** [ ] [-]

— (Sep72) **JACKIE LYNTON** – vocals repl. WALKER who joined FLEETWOOD MAC / **RON BERG** – drums (ex-JUICY LUCY) repl. BIDWELL (he died 70's, heroin O.D.)

Jun 73. (lp)(c) **JACK THE TOAD** [ ] [84]
– Coming down your way / Ride on babe / Hold your fire / If you want to / Endless sleep / Casting my spell / Just 'cos you got the blues don't mean you gotta sing / Some people / Jack the toad.

Aug 73. (7") **COMING DOWN YOUR WAY. / I CAN'T FIND YOU** [ ] [ ]

— (Jan74) **SIMMONDS** recruited entire new line-up. **STAN WEBB** – guitar, vocals (ex-CHICKEN SHACK) repl. LYNTON / **MILLER ANDERSON** – guitar, vocals repl. RAYMOND who joined UFO / **JIMMY LEVERTON** – bass repl. PYLE who rejoined BLODWYN PIG **ERIC DILLON** – drums repl. BERG who joined NETWORK.

Decca / London

Apr 74. (lp)(c) **BOOGIE BROTHERS** [ ] [ ]
– Highway blues / Me and the preacher / My love's lying down / You don't love me / Always the same / Everybody loves a drinking man / Rock'n'roll star / Boogie brothers / Threegy blues.

— After brief break-up, **KIM** re-formed new line-up late 1974. **IAN ELLIS** – bass (ex-CLOUDS) repl. LEVERTON (WEBB rejoined CHICKEN SHACK) / **TOM FARNELL** – drums (ex-FAIRPORT CONVENTION) repl. DILLON (ANDERSON to T.REX)

Nov 75. (lp) **WIRE FIRE** [-] [ ]
– Put your hands together / Stranger blues / Here comes the music / Ooh what a feeling / Hero to zero / Deep water / Can't get on / Born into pain.

1976. (lp) **SKIN'N'BONE** [-] [ ]
– Get on up and do it / Part time lady / This day is gonna be our last / She's the one / Skin'n'bone / Walkin' and talkin' (live).

1978. (lp) **SAVAGE RETURN** [-] [ ]
– The first night / Don't do it baby, do it / Spirit high / Play it right / Walk before you run / My own man / I'm alright now / Rock'n'roll man / Double lover.

— (1980) **KIM** again recruited entire new formation **BARRY PAUL** – guitar / **JOHN SINCLAIR** – keyboards / **JOHN HUMPHREY** – bass / **KEITH BOYCE** – drums / **RALPH MOMAN** – vocals / + female backing vocalists

Town House / Town House

Jul 81. (lp)(c) **ROCK'N'ROLL WARRIORS** [ ] [ ]
– Cold hearted woman / Georgie / Bad dreams / Don't tell me I told you / This could be the night / Run to me / Shot down by love / Bad girls / Got lover if you want it / Nobody's perfect.

Oct 85. (7") **RUN TO ME. /** [-] [68]

Town House / Accord

1981. (lp)(c) **GREATEST HITS – LIVE IN CONCERT (live)** [ ] [ ]
– Street corner talkin' / I'm tired / Hellbound train / Train to nowhere / I can't get next to you / All I can do is cry / Needle and spoon / Tell mama / Run to me / Wang dang doodle / Louisiana blues / The boogie.

— Disband again 1982. Five years later KIM was back in the studio with **DAVE WALKER / JIMMY DAGNESI** – bass / **AL MACOMBER** – drums (latter 2 joined '89)

Sonet / G.N.P.

Jan 88. (lp)(c)(cd) **MAKE ME SWEAT** [ ] [ ]
– Limousine boogie (hey hey mama) / Just for kicks / Good time lover / Goin' down / Hard way to go / Don't tell me it's over / Runnin' with a bad crowd / Tell mama / Shot in the head / Breaking up / On the prowl.

Apr 89. (lp)(c)(cd) **KINGS OF BOOGIE** [-] [ ]
– Kings of boogie / Deep in my heart / A man alone / No win love / Mean business / Bad state of mind / Heartbreaks make you strong / Since you've been gone / Caught in the saddle / All burned out / Until the sky fades away.

– compilations, others, etc. –

1977. Decca/ US= London; (lp) **THE BEST OF SAVOY BROWN** [-] [ ]
– Train to nowhere / Mr.Downchild / Stay with me baby / Shake 'em on down / Leaving again / Needle & spoon / Hellbound train / Coming down your way / Made up my mind / Let it rock / Highway blues. *(UK-iss.May82 on 'Decca') (re-iss.+c.Oct 87 on 'C5', cd-iss.May 90)(cd-iss.Apr 93 on 'C5')*

1978. Decca; (lp) **BLUES ROOTS** [ ] [-]

May 85. See For Miles; (lp) **HIGHWAY BLUES** [ ] [-]

Oct 85. Platinum; (lp)(c) **A HARD WAY TO GO** [-] [-] Germ'y

Jun 93. Relix; (cd) **LIVE IN CENTRAL PARK (live)** [ ] [ ]

Jun 93. Relix; (cd) **SLOW TRAIN** [ ] [ ]

Jun 95. Coast To Coast; (cd) **BRING IT HOME** [ ] [-]

SAW DOCTORS

Formed: Tuam, Galway, Ireland . . . late 70's by MORAN, CARTON, etc. Dropped their daytime jobs to support The WATERBOYS on UK tour. The following year, they released debut 45 'I USETA LOVE HER', which climbed to the top of the Irish charts. It stayed there for many a week, and became biggest seller ever a year later. After two more singles scored, their first album, poignantly titled 'IF THIS IS ROCK'N'ROLL I WANT MY OLD JOB BACK', made them stars. • **Style:** An unusual bunch, described as raggle-taggle showband with rock-pop attributions, or even folk-punk with pathos similiar to POGUES or the early BEATLES. • **Songwriters:** Most by MORAN-CARTON except THE WEST'S AWAKE (trad). • **Trivia:** The 1991 track 'SING A POWERFUL SONG', was used on film '????' about the L.A. riots. Loved by MIKE SCOTT (Waterboys), who produced their debut 'N 17', before PHIL TENNANT took over.

Recommended: IF THIS IS ROCK'N'ROLL, I WANT MY OLD JOB BACK (*5)

JOHN 'TURPS' BURKE – mandolin, organ, guitars, vocals / **DAVY CARTON** – vocals, guitars / **LEO MORAN** – guitars, vocals, organ, etc / **TONY LAMBERT** – accordion, organ / **PEARSE 'BLACKIN' DOHERTY** – bass, vocals, piano, flute / guest **JOHN 'TANK' DONNELLY** – drums, percussion

Solid / WEA

1989. (7") **n17. / ?** [-] [ ] IRE

Oct 90. (7"m) **I USETA LOVE HER. / CAPTAIN JOE FIDDLE'S / I USED TO LOVER HER BLAZE X** [ ] [-]

May 91. (cd)(c)(lp) **IF THIS IS ROCK'N'ROLL, I WANT MY OLD JOB BACK** [69] [ ]
– I useta lover / Only one girl / Why do I always want you / It won't be tonight / Irish poet / Sing a powerful song / Freedom fighters / That's what she said last night / Red Cortina / Presentation boarder / Don't let me down / £25 / What a day / n17 / I hope you meet again. *(re-iss.Dec93)(re-iss.cd+c Dec94 on 'Shamtown')*

Jul 91. (7")(c-s) **N17. / N17 LIVE (including PADDY'S POEM)** [ ] [ ]
(cd-s+=) – At least pretend.

Nov 91. (7")(c-s) **THAT'S WHAT SHE SAID LAST NIGHT. / HAY WRAP: HAY WRAP – THE WEST'S AWAKE** – HAY WRAP [ ] [ ]
(cd-s+=) – The trip to Tipp.

W.E.A. / Warners

Oct 92. (cd)(c)(lp) **ALL THE WAY FROM TUAM** [33] [ ]

– Green and red of Mayo / You got me on the run / Pied piper / My heart is livin' in the sixties still / Hay wrap / Wake up sleeping / Midnight express / Broke my heart / Exhilarating sadness / All the way from Tuam / Music I love / Yvonne / Never mind the strangers. *(re-iss.Dec93)(re-iss.cd+c Dec94 on 'Shamtown')*

Feb 93. (7")(c-s) **WAKE UP SLEEPING. / JOE WALL BROKE MY HEART**
(cd-s+=) – Thank God it's a Tuesday / I hope you melt again.
(cd-s) – ('A'side) / Why do I always want you / What a day / N17 (all live).

— **ANTO THISTLETHWAITE** – saxophone, etc (ex-WATERBOYS, ex-solo artist 1993 album; AESOP WROTE . . .) repl. BURKE

May 94. (7")(c-s) **TO WIN JUST ONCE. / ?**
(cd-s+=) –

— Above the unofficial Irish World Cup theme.

— now without THISTLETWAITE who was now solo

Shamtown | Warners

Oct 94. (c-ep)(cd-ep) **SMALL BIT OF LOVE / MICHAEL D. ROCKING IN THE DAIL / I'D LOVE TO KISS THE BANGLES / WHERE'S THE PARTY (live)** — 24

SAXON

Formed: Barnsley, Yorkshire, England . . . 1977 by BIFF BYFORD and crew (see below), after initially calling themselves SON OF A BITCH. In 1978, they signed to French based label 'Carrere', where they finally hit big in 1980 with 2nd album 'WHEELS OF STEEL'. • **Style:** Under the banner of NWOBHM (New Wave Of British Heavy Metal), this leather-clad brigade, mixed their own blend of hard rock, fused with lyrical sword and sorcery. • **Songwriters:** Group compositions, except; S.O.S. (TOO BAD) (Saxon) / RIDE LIKE THE WIND (Christopher Cross). • **Trivia:** In 1981, they appeared at Castle Donnington's 'Monster Of Rock' festival.

Recommended: BACK ON THE STREETS (*7).

BIFF BYFORD (b.PETER BYFORD, 5 Jan'51) – vocals / **PAUL QUINN** – lead guitar / **GRAHAM OLIVER** – lead guitar / **STEVE DAWSON** – bass / **PETE GILL** – drums (ex-GLITTER BAND)

Carrere | Carrere

Mar 79. (7") **STALLIONS OF THE HIGHWAY. / BIG TEASER**
May 79. (lp)(c) **SAXON**
– Rainbow theme / Frozen rainbow / Big teaser / Judgement day / Stallions of the highway / Backs to the wall / Still fit to boogie / Militia guard.
Jun 79. (7") **BIG TEASER. / STALLIONS OF THE HIGHWAY**
Nov 79. (7") **BACKS TO THE WALL. / MILITIA GUARD**
(re-iss.Jun80 on 'Atlantic', hit Uk 64)
Mar 80. (7") **WHEELS OF STEEL. / STAND UP AND BE COUNTED** — 20
Mar 80. (lp)(c) **WHEELS OF STEEL** — 5
– Motorcycle man / Stand up and be counted / 747 (strangers in the night) / Wheels of steel / Freeway mad / See the light shining / Street fighting gang / Suzi hold on / Machine gun. *(re-iss.Mar85)(re-iss.cd+c Jun93 on 'Optima')*
Jun 80. (7") **747 (STRANGERS IN THE NIGHT). / SEE THE LIGHT SHINING** — 13
Sep 80. (7") **SUZI HOLD ON. / JUDGEMENT DAY (live)**
Nov 80. (lp)(c) **STRONG ARM OF THE LAW** — 11
– Heavy metal thunder / To Hell and back again / Strong arm of the law / Taking your chances / 20,000 ft. / Hungry years / Sixth form girls / Dallas 1 p.m. *(re-iss.Dec84) (re-iss.May87 on 'Fame')*
Nov 80. (7")(12") **STRONG ARM OF THE LAW. / TAKING YOUR CHANCES** — 63
Apr 81. (7")(12")(7"pic-d) **AND THE BANDS PLAYED ON. / HUNGRY YEARS / HEAVY METAL THUNDER** — 12
Jul 81. (7") **NEVER SURRENDER. / 20,000 FT.** — 18
(d7"+=) – Bap-shoo-ap! (live) / Street fighting gang.
Sep 81. (lp)(c)(blue-lp) **DENIM AND LEATHER** — 9
– Princess of the night / Never surrender / Out of control / Rough and ready / Play it loud / And the bands played on / Midnight rider / Fire in the sky / Denim and leather. *(re-iss.+cd.May87 on 'Fame')*
Oct 81. (7") **PRINCESS OF THE NIGHT. / FIRE IN THE SKY** — 57

— **NIGEL GLOCKER** – drums (ex-TOYAH, etc.) repl. GILL who joined MOTORHEAD

May 82. (lp)(c)(pic-lp) **THE EAGLE HAS LANDED (live)**
– Motorcycle man / 747 (strangers in the night) / Princess of the night / Strong arm of the law / Heavy metal thunder / See the light shining / 20,000 ft. / Wheels of steel / Never surrender / Fire in the sky / Machine gun. *(re-iss.May86 on 'E.M.I.', cd-iss.Jul89)*
Mar 83. (lp)(c)(pic-lp) **POWER AND THE GLORY** — 15
– Power and the glory / Redline / Warrior / Nightmare / This town rocks / Watching the sky / Midas touch / The eagle has landed. *(re-iss.1986 on 'E.M.I.', cd-iss.Jul89)*
Apr 83. (7")(7"pic-d) **POWER AND THE GLORY. / SEE THE LIGHT SHINING** — 32 | -
(12"+=) – Denim and leather.
Jul 83. (7")(7"pic-d) **NIGHTMARE. / MIDAS TOUCH** — 50 | -
(12"+=) – 747 (strangers in the night).
Jan 84. (7")(12") **SAILING TO AMERICA. / A LITTLE BIT OF WHAT YOU FANCY** — | -
Feb 84. (lp)(c)(pic-lp) **CRUSADER** — 18
– (prelude) / Crusader / A little bit of what you fancy / Sailing to America / Set me free / Just let me rock / Bad boys (like to rock'n'roll) / Do it all for you / Rock city / Run for your lives. *(re-iss. Mar85, cd-iss.1986)*
Mar 84. (7")(12") **DO IT ALL FOR YOU. / JUST LET ME ROCK** — | -

Parlophone | Capitol

Aug 85. (7")(7"sha-pic-d) **BACK ON THE STREETS. / LIVE FAST DIE YOUNG** — 75
(12"+=) ('A'extended version).
Sep 85. (lp)(c)(pic-lp) **INNOCENCE IS NO EXCUSE** — 36
– Rockin' again / Call of the wild / Back on the streets / The Devil rides out / Rock'n'roll gypsy / Broken heroes / Gonna shout / Everybody up / Raise some hell / Give it everything you've got.
Oct 85. (7") **ROCKIN' AGAIN. / KRAKATOA**
(12"+=) – Gonna shout (live).
Mar 86. (7")(7"pic-d) **ROCK'N'ROLL GYPSY. / KRAKATOA** — 71
(12"+=) – Medley: Heavy metal thunder – Stand up and be counted – Taking your chances – Warrior.

— **PAUL JOHNSON** – bass repl. DAWSON. (GLOCKER briefly joined G.T.R.)

E.M.I. | Capitol

Aug 86. (7") **WAITING FOR THE NIGHT. / CHASE THE FADE** — 66
(12"+=) – ('A'extended).
Aug 86. (lp)(c)(cd) **ROCK THE NATIONS** — 34
– Rock the nations / Battle cry / Waiting for the night / We came here to rock / You ain't no angel / Running hot / Party 'til you puke / Empty promises / Northern lady.
Oct 86. (7")(12")(7"pic-d)(12"pic-d) **ROCK THE NATIONS. / 747 / AND THE BANDS PLAYED ON**
Jan 87. (7") **NORTHERN LADY. / EVERYBODY UP (live)**
(12"+=) – Dallas 1 p.m.

— **NIGEL DURHAM** – drums repl. GLOCKER

Feb 88. (7")(7"pic-d) **RIDE LIKE THE WIND. / RED ALERT** — 52
(12"+=) – Back on the streets (live).
(cd-s+=) – Rock the nations (live).
Mar 88. (lp)(c)(cd) **DESTINY** — 49
– Ride like the wind / Where the lightning strikes / I can't wait anymore / Calm before the storm / S.O.S. (too bad) / Song for Emma / For whom the bells toll / We are strong / Jericho siren / Red alert.
Apr 88. (7") **I CAN'T WAIT ANYMORE. / BROKEN HEROES (live)** — 71
(12"+=) – Gonna shout.

— **TIM NIBBS CARTER** – bass repl. JOHNSON.

M.F.N. | Road-runner

Nov 89. (lp)(c)(cd) **ROCK'N'ROLL GYPSIES** (live '88 Hungary)
– Power and the glory / And the bands played on / Rock the nations / Dallas 1 p.m. / Broken heroes / Rock'n'roll gypsies / Northern lady / I can't wait anymore / This town rocks. *(cd+=)*– The eagle has landed / Just let me rock.

Virgin Int. | Enigma

Jan 91. (cd)(c)(lp) **SOLID BALL OF ROCK**
– Solid ball of rock / Alter of the gods / Requiem (we will remember) / Lights in the sky / I just can't get enough / Baptism of fire / Ain't gonna take it / I'm on fire / Overture in b minor refugee / Bavarian beaver / Crash dive.
Mar 91. (7") **REQUIEM (WE WILL REMEMBER). / ALTAR OF THE GODS**
(12"+=)(cd-s+=) – Reeperbahn stomp.

Warhammer | not issued

Apr 93. (12")(cd-s) **IRON WHEELS. / WHATEVER FREE** — | -

– compilations, others, etc. –

Jun 80. Atlantic; (7") **BIG TEASER. / RAINBOW THEME / FROZEN RAINBOW** — 66 | -
Apr 81. Atlantic; (7") **WHEELS OF STEEL. / 747 (STRANGERS IN THE NIGHT)** — | -
Jul 83. Carrere; (c-ep) **FLIPHITS** — | -
– 747 (strangers in the night) / And the bands played on / Never surrender / Princess of the night.
Dec 84. Carrere; (lp)(c) **GREATEST HITS – STRONG ARM METAL**
(re-iss.Jan86 on 'Parlophone', cd-iss.1988)
Oct 88. Castle; (d-lp)(c)(cd) **ANTHOLOGY** — | -
Jan 90. Connoisseur; (cd)(c)(d-lp) **BACK ON THE STREETS** — | -
– Power & the glory / Backs to the wall / Watching the sky / Never surrender / Princess of the night / Motorcycle man / 747 (Strangers in the night) / Wheels of steel / Nightmare / Back on the streets / Rock'n'roll gypsy / Broken heroes / Devil rides out / Party 'til you puke / Rock the nations / Waiting for the night / I can't wait anymore / We are the strong. (d-lp+=) – Midnight rider / Ride like the wind.
Mar 91. EMI; (cd)(c)(lp) **THE BEST OF SAXON** — | -
Oct 92. Old Gold; (cd-ep) **AND THE BAND PLAYED ON / 747 (AND THE BAND PLAYED ON) / NEVER SURRENDER** — | -
Aug 95. Smashing; (cd) **THE BEST OF SAXON** — | -

Sky SAXON (see under ⇒ SEEDS)

Boz SCAGGS

Born: WILLIAM ROYCE SCAGGS, Ohio, USA. In the late 50's, having learnt guitar from Texas schoolpal STEVE MILLER, he joined The MARKSMEN. The pair soon enrolled at Wisconsin University, where they joined The ARDELLS, who soon became FABULOUS NIGHT TRAIN. In 1963, he returned to Texas where he formed The WIGS. The following year, he moved to the UK, but soon was living in Sweden, where he released lp 'BOZ' for 'Polydor' in 1966. In Sep'67, he joined The STEVE MILLER BAND and played on 2 albums, CHILDREN OF THE FUTURE + SAILOR, before going on to solo work again. After one unsuccessful eponymous attempt on 'Atlantic', he signed contract on 'CBS/Columbia' in 1970. He steadily built up audiences in the US, and by 1976 was sitting at No.2 with album 'SILK DEGREES'. • **Style:** Innovative white soul-rock balladeer, who won a Grammy in 1977 for his 'LOWDOWN' single. • **Songwriters:** Wrote own material. In 1988 his comeback album 'OTHER ROADS' featured a couple of songs co-written with JIM CARROLL. • **Trivia:** RITA COOLIDGE reached both US + UK Top 10's, with her version of 'WE'RE ALL ALONE'.

Recommended: BOZ SCAGGS HITS (*6).

BOZ SCAGGS – vocals, guitar, with session people.

Polydor / not issued

1966. (lp) **BOZ** – / – Sweden

—— Joined STEVE MILLER BAND for 2 albums (see above). Solo again with Muscle Shoals session people, plus **DUANE ALLMAN** – slide guitar.

Atlantic / Atlantic

Aug 69. (lp) **BOZ SCAGGS**
– I'm easy / I'll be long gone / Another day (another letter) / Now you're gone / Finding her / Look what I got / Waiting for a train / Loan me a dime / Sweet release. *(re-iss.Jul74)*

—— with **JOACHIM JIMMY YOUNG** – keyboards / **GEORGE RAINS** – drums / **DAVID BROWN** – bass / + many others

C.B.S. / Columbia

Apr 71. (7") **WE WERE ALWAYS SWEETHEARTS. / PAINTED BELLS** 61
Apr 71. (lp) **MOMENTS**
– We were always sweethearts / Downright woman / Painted bells / Alone, alone / Near you / I will forever sing (the blues) / Moments / Hollywood blues / We been away / Can I make it last (or will it just be over).
Jun 71. (7") **NEAR YOU. / DOWNRIGHT WOMAN** – 96
Dec 71. (lp) **BOZ SCAGGS AND BAND**
– Monkey time / Runnin' blue / Up to you / Love anyway / Flames of love / Here to stay / Nothing will take your place / Why why / You're so good. *(re-iss.Oct80)*
Jan 72. (7") **HERE TO STAY. / RUNNIN' BLUE** –
Feb 72. (7") **UP TO YOU. / RUNNIN' BLUE**
Sep 72. (lp) **MY TIME**
– Dinah Flo / Slowly in the west / Full lock power-slide / Old time lovin' / Might have to cry / Hello my lover / Freedom for the stallion / He's a fool for you / We're gonna roll / My time.
Sep 72. (7") **DINAH FLO. / HE'S A FOOL FOR YOU** 86

—— Toured with guests STEVE MILLER and GEORGE RAINS. Late 1972, his new band were **LES DUDEK** – guitar / **JIMMY YOUNG** – keyboards / **TOM RUTLEY** – bass / **RICK SCHLOSSER** – drums / **JACK SCHROEDER** – sax

Apr 74. (7") **YOU MAKE IT SO HARD (TO SAY NO). / THERE IS SOMEONE ELSE**
Apr 74. (lp)(c) **SLOW DANCER** 81 Mar 74
– You make it so hard (to say no) / Slow dancer / Angel lady (come just in time) / There is someone else / Hercules / Pain of love / Let it happen / Sail on white Moon / I got your number / Take it for granted. *(re-iss.Mar82) (re-iss.cd Apr94 on 'Sony Collectors)*
Jul 74. (7") **I GOT YOUR NUMBER. / SLOW DANCER**
Jul 74. (7") **PAIN OF LOVE. / SLOW DANCER** –

—— next with also future members of TOTO (aka PORCARO's & STEVE LUKATHER)

Apr 76. (7") **GEORGIA. / JUMP STREET**
May 76. (7") **IT'S OVER. / HARBOUR LIGHTS** 38 Apr 76
Jul 76. (7") **LOWDOWN. / HARBOR LIGHTS** – 3
Aug 76. (lp)(c) **SILK DEGREES** 20 2 Mar 76
– What can I say / Georgia / Jump Street / What do you want the girl to do? / Harbor lights / Lowdown / It's over / Love me tomorrow / Lido shuffle / We're all alone. *(re-iss.Mar81 & 1984, cd-iss. 1986) (re-iss.cd Mar94 on 'Sony Collectors') (re-iss.Feb95 on 'Columbia')*
Oct 76. (7") **LOWDOWN. / JUMP STREET** 28 –
Jan 77. (7") **WHAT CAN I SAY!. / HARBOUR LIGHTS** 10 42 Nov 76
Apr 77. (7") **LIDO SHUFFLE. / WE'RE ALL ALONE** 13 11 Feb 77
Nov 77. (7") **HARD TIMES. / WE'RE WAITING** 58 Sep 77
Nov 77. (lp)(c) **DOWN TWO, THEN LEFT** 55 11
– Still falling for you / Hard times / A clue / Whatcha gonna tell your man? / We're waiting / Hollywood / Then she walked away / Gimme the goods / 1993 / Tomorrow never came / Tomorrow never came (reprise).
Nov 77. (7") **HOLLYWOOD. / WE'RE WAITING** 33 –
Dec 77. (7") **HOLLYWOOD. / A CLUE** – 49
Feb 78. (7") **1993. / A CLUE** –
Sep 78. (7") **IT'S OVER. / LOVE ME TOMORROW** –
Apr 80. (7") **BREAKDOWN DEAD AHEAD. / ISN'T IT TIME** 15 Mar 80
May 80. (lp)(c) **MIDDLE MAN** 52 8 Apr 80
– JoJo / Breakdown dead ahead / Simone / You can have me anytime / Middle man / Do like you do in New York / Angel you / Isn't it time / You got some imagination.
Jul 80. (7") **JOJO. / DO LIKE YOU DO IN NEW YORK** 17 Jun80
Jul 80. (7") **SIMONE. / DO LIKE YOU DO IN NEW YORK** –
Aug 80. (7") **LOOK WHAT YOU'VE DONE TO ME. / SIMONE** – 14
Sep 80. (7") **LOOK WHAT YOU'VE DONE TO ME. / YOU GOT SOME IMAGINATION** –
Dec 80. (lp)(c) **BOZ SCAGGS HITS** (compilation) 24 Nov 80
– Lowdown / You make it so hard (to say no) / Miss Sun / Lido shuffle / We're all alone / Breakdown dead ahead / Look what you've done to me / What can I say / Dinah Flo / You can have me anytime.

—— (below featured b.vox by LISA DAL BELLO)

Jan 81. (7") **MISS SUN. / DINAH FLO** 14 Nov 80
Mar 81. (7") **YOU CAN HAVE ME ANYTIME. / GEORGIA** –

—— He retired from music scene to run Southern style restaurant in San Francisco. He returned to the studio in 1987 for 'CBS-Columbia'.

May 88. (7") **HEART OF MINE. / YOU'LL NEVER KNOW** 35 Apr 88
(12"+=) – We're all alone / Slow dancer.
(cd-s++=) – Soul to soul / What can I say.
Jul 88. (lp)(c)(cd) **OTHER ROADS** 47 Jun 88
– What's number one? / Claudia / Heart of mine / Right out of my head / I don't hear you / Mental shakedown / Crimes of passion / Funny / Cool running / The night of Van Gogh.
Jul 88. (7") **COOL RUNNING. / YOU'LL NEVER KNOW** –
Sep 88. (7") **WHAT'S NUMBER ONE?. / CLAUDIA** –

—— In 1990, SCAGGS produced debut album for local SMOKING SECTION group.

Virgin / Virgin

Jun 94. (cd)(c) **SOME CHANGE** 91
– You got my letter / Some change / I'll be the one / Call me / Fly like a bird / Sierra / Lost it / Time / Illusion / Follow that man.

– more compilations, etc. –

Feb 83. CBS; (d-c) **SLOW DANCER / SILK DEGREES** –
Feb 89. Old Gold; (7") **WHAT CAN I SAY. / LIDO SHUFFLE** –

Michael SCHENKER GROUP

Born: 10 Jan'55, Savstedt, W.Germany. In 1971 he formed The SCORPIONS with brother RUDOLPH, but left in mid-73 to be part of English group UFO. He stayed there for 4 albums (PHENOMENON / FORCE IT / NO HEAVY PETTIN' / LIGHTS OUT), before returning in 1978 to Germany to re-join SCORPIONS. He guested on their 1979 album 'LOVEDRIVE', and featured in new live set-up, before moving on to form own outfit MICHAEL SCHENKER GROUP in 1980. He signed to 'Chrysalis' that year and surprisingly triumphed with UK Top 10 album. Continued to stir audiences, until he took break in the mid-80's. In 1988, MSG were based in L.A. • **Style:** Heavy rockers, in the mould of RAINBOW (70's style), with variations of axe-grinding by SCHENKER. • **Songwriters:** SCHENKER compositions. plus revived past SCORPIONS tracks. • **Trivia:** SCHENKER was also part of 1991 semi-supergroup CONTRABAND (see below). They covered Mott The Hoople's:- ALL THE WAY FROM MEMPHIS.

Recommended: PORTFOLIO (*6)

MICHAEL SCHENKER – lead guitar (ex-SCORPIONS, ex-UFO) / **GARY BARDEN** – vocals / **DON AIREY** – keyboards (ex-COLOSSEUM II) / **MO FOSTER** – bass / **SIMON PHILLIPS** – drums

Chrysalis / Chrysalis

Aug 80. (lp)(c) **MICHAEL SCHENKER GROUP** 8 100
– Armed and ready / Cry for the nations / Victim of illusion / Bijou pleasurette / Feels like a good thing / Into the arena / Looking out from nowhere / Tales of mystery / Lost horizons. *(re-iss.Jun84 on 'Fame')*
Aug 80. (7")(7"colrd) **ARMED AND READY. / BIJOU PLEASURETTE** 53
Oct 80. (7")(7"clear) **CRY FOR THE NATIONS. / INTO THE ARENA (live)** 56
(12"+=) – Armed and ready (live).

—— **PAUL RAYMOND** – keyboards (ex-UFO, etc.) repl. AIREY / **CHRIS GLEN** – bass (ex-SENSATIONAL ALEX HARVEY BAND) repl. FOSTER / **COZY POWELL** – drums (ex-RAINBOW, ex-Solo artist) repl. PHILLIPS

Aug 81. (7")(7"clear) **READY TO ROCK. / ATTACK OF THE MAD AXEMAN**
Sep 81. (lp)(c) **MSG** 14 81
– Are you ready to rock / Attack of the mad axeman / On and on / Let sleeping dogs lie / But I want more / Never trust a stranger / Looking for love / Secondary motion. *(cd-iss.May86)*
Feb 82. (d-lp)(d-c) **ONE NIGHT AT BUDOKAN (live)** 5
– Armed and ready / Cry for the nations / Attack of the mad axeman / But I want more / Victim of illusion / Into the arena / On and on / Never trust a stranger / Let sleeping dogs lie / Courvoisier concert / Lost horizon / Doctor doctor / Are you ready to rock.

—— **GRAHAM BONNET** – vocals (ex-RAINBOW, ex-Solo) repl. BARDEN + RAYMOND / **TED McKENNA** – drums (ex-SENSATIONAL ALEX HARVEY BAND, ex-RORY GALLAGHER) repl. COZY WHO joined WHITESNAKE

Sep 82. (7")(7"clear)(7"pic-d) **DANCER. / GIRL FROM UPTOWN** 52
(12"+=) – ('A'extended).
Oct 82. (lp)(c)(pic-lp) **ASSAULT ATTACK** 19
– Assault attack / Rock you to the ground / Dancer / Samurai / Desert song / Broken promises / Searching for a reason / Ulcer.

—— **GARY BARDEN** – vocals returned to repl. BONNET who went solo / added **DEREK ST.HOLMES** – keyboards (ex-TED NUGENT) (on tour **ANDY NYE** – keyboards)

Sep 83. (lp)(c)(pic-lp) **BUILT TO DESTROY** 23
– Rock my nights away / I'm gonna make you mine / The dogs of war / Systems failing / Captain Nemo / Still love that little devil / Red sky / Time waits (for no one) / Walk the stage. *(re-iss.1986)*
Jun 84. (lp)(c) **ROCK WILL NEVER DIE (live)** 24
– Captain Nemo / Rock my nights away / Are you ready to rock / Attack of the mad axeman / Into the arena / Rock will never die / Desert song / I'm gonna make you mine / Doctor, doctor.

—— When CHRIS GLEN departed, most of others also folded.

McAULEY-SCHENKER GROUP

added **ROBIN McAULEY** (b.20 Jan'53, County Meath, Eire) – vox (ex-FAR CORPORATION) / **MITCH PERRY** – guitar / **ROCKY NEWTON** – bass / **BOBO SCHOPF** – drums

E.M.I. / Capitol

Oct 87. (7") **GIMME YOUR LOVE. / ROCK TILL YOU'RE CRAZY**
(12"+=)(12"pic-d+=) – ('A'extended).
Oct 87. (lp)(c)(cd) **PERFECT TIMING** 65 95
– Gimme your love / Here today, gone tomorrow / Don't stop me now / No time for losers / Follow the night / Get out / Love is not a game / Time / I don't wanna lose / Rock 'til you're crazy.
Jan 88. (7")(12") **LOVE IS NOT A GAME. / GET OUT**
Apr 88. (7") **FOLLOW THE NIGHT. / DON'T STOP ME NOW** –

—— **McAULEY & SCHENKER** now with **BOBO SCHOPF** – drums / **STEVE MANN** (b.9 Aug'56) – rhythm guitar / **ROCKY NEWMAN** (b.11 Sep'57) – bass (ex-LIONHEART)

Oct 89. (lp)(c)(cd) **SAVE YOURSELF** 92
– Save yourself / Bad boys / Anytime / Get down to bizness / I am your radio / Shadow of the night / What we need / There has to be another way / This is my heart / Destiny. *(cd+=)*– Take me back.
Apr 90. (7")(c-s) **ANYTIME. / WHAT WE NEED**
(12"+=)(12"pic-d+=)(cd-s+=) – ('A'-lp version).

—— **SCHENKER** with **ROBIN McAULEY** – vocals / **JEFF PILSON** – bass (ex-DOKKEN) / **JAMES KOTTAK** – drums (ex-KINGDOM COME)

E.M.I. Impact

Feb 92. (12"ep)(cd-ep) **NEVER ENDING NIGHTMARE**
Feb 92. (cd)(c)(lp) **M.S.G. ("SCHENKER / McAULEY")**
– Eve / Paradise / When I'm gone / This broken heart / We believe in love / Crazy / Invincible / What happens to me / Lonely nights / This night is gonna last forever / Never ending nightmare.

– compilations, others, etc. –

Jun 87. Chrysalis; (d-lp)(c)(cd) **PORTFOLIO** -
– Doctor doctor (UFO) / Rock bottom (UFO) / Rock will never die / Armed and ready / Ready to rock / Assault attack / Ulcer / Attack of the mad axeman / I'm a loser / Reasons to love / Too hot to handle / Only you can rock me (UFO) / Lights out (UFO) / Arbory hill / Love drive (SCORPIONS) / Searching for a reason / Rock my nights away / Captain Nemo.
Jul 91. Castle; (cd)(lp) **THE COLLECTION** -
Nov 93. Windsong; (cd) **BBC RADIO 1 LIVE IN CONCERT (live)** -
Jun 94. Music Club; (cd)(c) **ARMED AND READY – THE BEST OF** -
Aug 95. Griffin; (d-cd) **ANTHOLOGY** -

CONTRABAND

MICHAEL SCHENKER – guitar / **RICHARD BLACK** – vocals (of-SHARK ISLAND) / **TRACII GUNS** – guitar (of-L.A.GUNS) / **SHARE PEDERSON** – bass (of-VIXEN) / **BOBBY BLOTZER** – drums (of-RATT)

E.M.I. Impact-EMI

Mar 91. (cd)(c)(lp) **CONTRABAND**
– All the way from Memphis / Kiss by kiss / Ultimate outrage / Bad for each other / Loud guitars, fast cars and wild, wild living / Good rockin' tonight / Stand / Tonight you're mine / Hang on to yourself.
Jul 91. (7")(c-s) **ALL THE WAY FROM MEMPHIS. / LOUD GUITARS, FAST CARS AND WILD, WILD LIVING** 65
(12"+=)(cd-s+=) – ('A'versions-3)
(12"+=) – ('A'-balls to the wall version).

Irwin SCHMIDT (see under ⇒ CAN)

Fred SCHNEIDER (see under ⇒ B-52's)

Neal SCHON & Joe HAMMER (see under ⇒ JOURNEY)

SCORPIONS

Formed: Hanover, W.Germany . . . 1971 by SCHENKER brothers and others (see below). Signed worldwide to 'RCA' in 1974, but didn't make big time until '79 when 'Harvest' took over. • **Style:** Initially a jazzy-hard rock outfit, that shifted into more basic heavy-rock, characterised by homeland accent. • **Songwriters:** SCHENKER / SCHENKER / MEINE wrote most. RAREBELL was co-credited when MICHAEL SCHENKER broke loose. Now mainly group compositions. • **Trivia:** Another heavy band to have colossal success in Japan.

Recommended: LOVEDRIVE (*8) / ANIMAL MAGNETISM (*6) / BLACKOUT (*7) / LOVE AT FIRST STING (*7) / THE BEST OF THE SCORPIONS (*7)

KLAUS MEINE (b.25 May'52) – vocals / **MICHAEL SCHENKER** – lead guitar / **RUDOLPH SCHENKER** (b.31 Aug'52) – guitar (ex-COPERNICUS) / **LOTHAR HEINBERG** – bass / **WOLFGANG ZIONY** – drums

Brain not issued

1973. (lp) **LONESOME CROW** - - Germ'y
– It all depends / Action / Lonesome crow / I'm goin' mad / Leave me / In search of the peace of mind / Inheritance. *(UK-iss.1979 on 'Logo-RCA') (pic-lp Nov82) (re-iss.Jul85 on 'Heavy Metal', cd-iss.1987) (re-iss.Oct86 on 'Razor', cd-iss. 1988) (re-iss.May80 as 'ACTION' on 'Logo-RCA') (re-iss.Nov77 as 'GOLD ROCK' on 'Brain') (re-iss.Aug74 as 'I'M GOIN' MAD & OTHERS' on 'Billingsgate')*

—— (Jun73) **ULRICH ROTH** – lead guitar repl. MICHAEL who joined UFO / **JURGEN ROSENTHAL** – drums repl. WOLFGANG / **FRANCIS BUCHHOLZ** (b.19 Feb'50) – bass repl. LOTHAR

R.C.A. R.C.A.

Nov 74. (lp)(c) **FLY TO THE RAINBOW**
– Speedy's coming / They need a million / Drifting Sun / Fly, people, fly / This is my song / Fly away / Fly to the rainbow. *(re-iss.Oct85, cd-iss.Apr88)*

—— (1975) **RUDY LENNERS** – drums repl. JURGENS

Mar 76. (lp)(c) **IN TRANCE**
– Dark lady / In trance / Life's like a river / Top of the bill / Living and dying / Robot man / Evening wind / Sun in my hand / Longing for fire / Night lights. *(re-iss.Jun83, cd-iss.Feb90)*
Nov 76. (7") **IN TRANCE. / NIGHT LIGHTS** -
Feb 77. (lp)(c) **VIRGIN KILLERS**
– Pictured life / Catch your train / In your park / Backstage queen / Virgin killer / Hell cat / Crying days / Polar nights / Yellow raven. *(cd-iss.Apr88)*

—— **HERMAN RAREBELL** (b.18 Nov'53) – drums (ex-STEPPENWOLF) repl. RUDY

Apr 78. (lp)(c) **TAKEN BY FORCE**
– Steamrock fever / We'll burn the sky / I've got to be free / The riot of your time / The sails of Charon / Your light / He's a woman, she's a man / Born to touch your feelings. *(re-iss.Sep81) (re-iss.+cd.Oct88)*
Feb 79. (d-lp)(d-c) **THE TOKYO TAPES (live)**
– All night long / Pictured life / Backstage queen / Polar nights / In trance / We'll burn the sky / Surrender love / In search of the peace of mind / Fly to the rainbow. *(re-iss.1984, d-cd-iss.Nov88)*

—— (Dec78) **MATHIAS JABS** (b.25 Oct'56) – lead guitar repl. ULRICH who formed ELECTRIC SUN. **MICHAEL SCHENKER** also guested on 3 tracks on next album, joining **KLAUS, RUDOLF, HERMAN, FRANCIS & MATHIAS**

Harvest Mercury

Mar 79. (7") **LOVING YOU SUNDAY MORNING. / COAST TO COAST** -
Apr 79. (lp)(c) **LOVEDRIVE** 36 55
– Loving you Sunday morning / Another piece of meat / Always somewhere / Coast to coast / Can't get enough / Is there anybody there? / Lovedrive / Holiday. *(re-iss.Nov83 on 'Fame', cd-iss.Nov88)*
May 79. (7") **IS THERE ANYBODY THERE?. / ANOTHER PIECE OF MEAT** 39
Aug 79. (7")(12") **LOVEDRIVE. / COAST TO COAST** 69
Apr 80. (lp)(c) **ANIMAL MAGNETISM** 23 52
– Make it real / Don't make no promises (your body can't keep) / Hold me tight / 20th century man / Lady starlight / Fallin' in love / Only a man / The zoo / Animal magnetism. *(re-iss.+cd.May89 on 'Fame')*
Apr 80. (7") **LADY STARLIGHT. /** -
May 80. (7") **MAKE IT REAL. / DON'T MAKE NO PROMISES (YOUR BODY CAN'T KEEP)** 72
Aug 80. (7") **THE ZOO. / HOLIDAY** 75

—— In 1981, MICHAEL SCHENKER briefly returned to repl. JABS while MEINE had throat surgery. Everything resumed as 1980 line-up re-appeared in 1982.

Mar 82. (lp)(c) **BLACKOUT** 11 10
– Blackout / Can't live without you / You give me all I need / Now! / No one like you / Dynamite / Arizona / China white / When the smoke is going down. *(re-iss.May85 on 'Fame') (re-iss.+cd.Nov88)*
Mar 82. (7")(7"pic-d) **NO ONE LIKE YOU. / NOW!** 64 65 Jun 82
Jul 82. (7") **CAN'T LIVE WITHOUT YOU. / ALWAYS SOMEWHERE** 63
Feb 84. (7") **ROCK YOU LIKE A HURRICANE. / COMING HOME** 25
Mar 84. (lp)(c) **LOVE AT FIRST STING** 17 6
– Bad boys running wild / Rock you like a hurricane / I'm leaving you / Coming home / The same thrill / Big city nights / As soon as the good times roll / Crossfire / Still loving you. *(re-iss.Nov87) (re-iss.+cd.Aug89 on 'Fame')*
Aug 84. (7")(12")(12"pic-d) **BIG CITY NIGHTS. / BAD BOYS RUNNING WILD**
Mar 85. (7") **STILL LOVING YOU. / HOLIDAY** 64 Jun 84
(12"+=)(12"pic-d+=) – Big city nights.
Jun 85. (d-lp)(d-c) **WORLD WIDE LIVE (live)** 18 14
– Countdown / Coming home / Blackout / Bad boys running wild / Loving you Sunday morning / Make it real / Big city nights / Coast to coast / Holiday / Still loving you / Rock you like a hurricane / Can't live without you / Another piece of meat / Dynamite / The zoo / No one like you / Can't get enough (part 1: Six string sting – part 2: Can't get enough). *(d-cd.Feb86)*
Jun 85. (7") **NO ONE LIKE YOU (live). / THE ZOO (live)**
Apr 88. (lp)(c)(cd)(pic-lp) **SAVAGE AMUSEMENT** 18 5
– Don't stop at the top / Rhythm of love / Passion rules the game / Media overkill / Walking on the edge / We let it rock . . . you let it roll / Every minute every day / Love on the run / Believe in love.
May 88. (7")(7"pic-d) **RHYTHM OF LOVE. / WE LET IT ROCK . . . YOU LET IT ROLL** 59 75
(12"+=) – Love on the run (mix).
Aug 88. (7")(7"pic-d) **BELIEVE IN LOVE. / LOVE ON THE RUN**
(12"+=)(12"pic-d+=) – ('A' lp version).
Feb 89. (7")(7"pic-d) **PASSION RULES THE GAME. / EVERY MINUTE EVERY DAY** 74
(12"+=)(12"pic-d+=) – Is there anybody there?
(cd-s++=) – ('A' other mix).

Vertigo Mercury

Nov 90. (cd)(c)(lp) **CRAZY WORLD** 21
– Tease me please me / Don't believe her / Wind of change / To be with you in Heaven / Kicks after six / Send me an angel / Crazy world / Money and fame / Lust or love / Hit between the eyes / Restless nights. *(re-iss.Oct91, hit UK No.27)*
Dec 90. (7") **DON'T BELIEVE HER. / KICKS AFTER SIX**
(12"+=)(cd-s+=) – Big city nights / Holiday (live).
May 91. (7")(c-s)(7"red) **WIND OF CHANGE. / RESTLESS NIGHTS** 53 4
(12"+=) – Hit between the eyes / Blackout (live).
(cd-s+=) – To be with you in Heaven / Blackout (live). *(re-iss.Sep91, hit UK No.2 / US No.21)*
Nov 91. (7") **SEND ME AN ANGEL. / WIND OF CHANGE (Russian)** 27 44
(12"+=)(cd-s+=) – (2 live tracks).

—— (May92) FRANCIS BUCHOLZ departed.

Sep 93. (cd)(c)(lp) **FACE THE HEAT** 51 24
– Alien nation / No pain, no gain / Someone to touch / Under the same sun / Unholy alliance / Woman / Hate to be nice / Taxman woman / Ship of fools / Nightmare Avenue / Lonely nights / Destin / Daddy's girl
Nov 93. (c-s) **UNDER THE SAME SUN. / SHIP OF FOOLS**
(12"+=) – Alien nation / Rubberfucker.
(cd-s+=) – Partners in crime.
Apr 95. (cd) **LIVE BITES (live)**
– Tease me, please me / Is there anybody there? / Rhythm of love / In trance / No pain, no gain / When the smoke is going down / Ave Maria no morro / Living for tomorrow / Concerto in V / Alien nation / Hit between the eyes / Crazy world / Wind of change / Heroes / Don't cry / White dove.

– compilations, others, etc. –

Nov 79. RCA; (lp)(c) **THE BEST OF THE SCORPIONS**
– Steamrock fever / Pictured life / Robot man / Backstage queen / Speedy's coming / Hell-cat / He's a woman, she's a man / In trance / Dark lady / The sails of Charon / Virgin killer. *(re-iss.Sep81) (re-iss.+cd.Feb89)*
Apr 80. RCA; (12") **ALL NIGHT LONG. / ?** -
Jul 84. RCA; (lp)(c) **THE BEST OF THE SCORPIONS, VOL.2**
(re-iss.+cd Feb 90)
Feb 90. RCA; (cd) **HOT AND HEAVY**
Mar 90. RCA; (cd) **TAKE OFF**
Sep 93. RCA; (cd) **HOT AND HARD**
Nov 89. Harvest/ US= Mercury; (lp)(c)(cd) **BEST OF ROCKERS'N'BALLADS** 43

Mar 90. Connoisseur; (cd) **HURRICANE ROCK**
Apr 92. EMI; (cd)(c)(lp) **STILL LOVING YOU**

Andy SCOTT (see under ⇒ SWEET)

Mike SCOTT (see under ⇒ WATERBOYS)

Gil SCOTT-HERON

Born: 1 Apr'49, Chicago, Illinois, USA. Raised in Jackson, Tennessee, but later moved to New York, where he studied at Lincoln University. He met fellow poet BRIAN JACKSON, and had two novels 'The Vulture' & 'The Nigger Factory' published in the late 60's. The next decade started with him signing to Bob Thiele's 'Flying Dutchman' label, where he issued debut album of poetry 'SMALL TALK AT 125th AND LENNOX'. In 1975, he signed to 'Arista', where he cracked US Top 30 with lp 'THE FIRST MINUTE OF A NEW DAY'. • **Style:** Black political poet/rapper, who branched out into disco and jazz-funk in the mid to late 70's. • **Songwriters:** Collaborated with BRIAN JACKSON until 1978. Wrote own words and music from then on. Covered; INNER CITY BLUES (Marvin Gaye). • **Trivia:** In the early '60s his father played professional football with Glasgow Celtic, known as the Black Arrow. LaBELLE covered his song 'THE REVOLUTION WILL NOT BE TELEVISED' in 1974.

Recommended: THE BEST OF GIL SCOTT-HERON (*8) / THE REVOLUTION WILL NOT BE TELEVISED (*9) / REFLECTIONS (*7)

GIL SCOTT-HERON – vocals, piano, guitar

Philips F.Dutchman

1972. (lp) **SMALL TALK AT 125th AND LENNOX** [-]
– (rap poems)
1972. (lp) **FREE WILL** [-]

—— added **BRIAN JACKSON** – keyboards / **DANNY BOWENS** – bass / **BOB ADAMS** – drums

Apr 73. (lp) **PIECES OF A MAN**
– Lady Day and John Coltrane / When you are who you are / The revolution will not be televised / Home is where the hatred is / I think I'll call it morning / Save the children / The needle's eye / Pieces of a man / A sign of the ages / Or down you fall / The prisoner.
Apr 73. (7") **WHEN YOU ARE WHO YOU ARE. / LADY DAY AND JOHN COLTRANE**

not issued Stata East

1974. (lp) **WINTER IN AMERICA** [-]

—— next featured The MIDNIGHT BAND.

—— **JOSEF BLOCKER + REGGIE BRISBANE** – drums repl. ADAMS

Arista Arista

Jul 75. (lp)(c) **THE FIRST MINUTE OF A NEW DAY (by "GIL SCOTT-HERON & BRIAN JACKSON")** [30] Jun 75
– Offering / The liberation song (red, black and green) / Must be something / Ain't no such thing as Superman / Pardon our analysis (we beg your pardon AMerica) / Winter in America / Guerilla / Western sunrise / Alluswe.
Jul 75. (7") **AIN'T NO SUCH THING AS SUPERMAN. / WE BEG YOUR PARDON AMERICA** [-]
Oct 75. (7") **(WHAT'S THE WORD) JOHANNESBURG. / FELL TOGETHER**
Jan 76. (lp)(c) **FROM SOUTH AFRICA TO SOUTH CAROLINA** Oct 75
– Johannesburg / A toast to the people / The summer of '42 / Beinnings (first minute of a new day) / South Carolina (Barnwell) / Essex / Fell together / A lovely day.
Nov 76. (lp)(c) **IT'S YOUR WORLD** (live)
– Seventeenth street / Tomorrow's trane (gospel trane) / Must be something / It's your world / New York City / The bottle / Possum Slim / Home is where the hatred is / Bicentennial blues / Sharing.

—— **JOSEF BLOCKER + REGGIE BRISBANE** – drums repl. ADAMS

Dec 77. (lp)(c) **BRIDGES** Oct 77
– Hello Sunday! hello road! / Song of the wind / Racetrack in France / Vildgolia (deaf, dumb and blind) / Under the hammer / We almost lost Detroit / Tuskeegee No.626 / Delta man (where I'm coming from) / 95 South (all of the places we've been).
Dec 77. (7") **HELLO SUNDAY, HELLO ROAD. / THE BOTTLE (live)**
Dec 77. (7") **HELLO SUNDAY, HELLO ROAD. / SONG OF THE WIND** [-]
Mar 78. (7") **UNDER THE HAMMER. / RACETRACK IN FRANCE** [-]

—— **GREG PHILLINGANES** – keyboards repl. BOWENS

Jul 78. (7") **ANGEL DUST. / THIRD WORLD REVOLUTION** [-]
Sep 78. (lp)(c) **SECRETS**
– Angel dust / Madison Avenue / Cane / Third world revolution / Better days ahead / Three miles down / Angola, Louisiana / Show bizness / A prayer for everybody / To be free.
Oct 78. (7") **SHOW BIZNESS. / BETTER DAYS AHEAD** [-]

—— retained only **JACKSON** + recruited **ED GRADY** – guitar / **KENNY POWELL** – drums / **GLEN TURNER** – keyboards / **CARL CORNWALL + VERNON JAMES** – tenor sax, flute / **KENNY SHEFFIELD** – trumpet

Feb 80. (lp)(c) **1980** [-]
– Shut 'um down / Alien / Willing / Corners / 1980 / Push comes to shove / Shah mot / Late last night. *(UK-iss.Jul85)*
Mar 80. (7")('A'ext-12") **SHUT 'EM DOWN. / BALTIMORE**
May 80. (7") **WILLIN'. /** [-]
Dec 80. (lp)(c) **REAL EYES**
– The train from Washington / Not needed / Waiting for the axe to fall / Combinations / A legend in his own mind / You could be my brother / The Klan / Your daddy loves you.
Dec 80. (7") **LEGEND IN HIS OWN MIND. /** [-]
Oct 81. (7") **STORM MUSIC. /** [-]
Dec 81. (lp)(c) **REFLECTIONS**
– Storm music / Grandma's hands / Is that jazz? / Morning thoughts / Inner city blues (poem – The siege of New Orleans) / Gun / B-movie.
Feb 82. (7") **STORM MUSIC. / B-MOVIE**
(12"+=) – Gun.
Sep 82. (7") **FAST LANE. / BLUE COLLAR** [-]
Sep 82. (lp)(c) **MOVING TARGET**
– Fast lane / Washington D.C. / No exit / Blue collar / Ready or not / Explanations / Black history – The word.
May 83. (7") **(WHAT'S THE WORD) JOHANNESBURG. / WAITING FOR THE AXE TO FALL**
(12"+=) – B-Movie (intro, poem, song).
Aug 84. (7") **RE-RON. / B-MOVIE**
(12") – Re-Ron (the missing brain mix). / B-Movie (intro, poem, song).
Sep 84. (lp)(c) **THE BEST OF GIL SCOTT-HERON** (compilation)
– The revolution will not be televised / The bottle / Winter in America / Ain't no such thing as Superman / Re-Ron / Shut 'em down / Angel dust / B-movie.
Nov 85. (7")(10") **WINTER IN AMERICA. / JOHANNESBURG**

—— now with **ROBBIE GORDON** – bass, percussion / **RON HOLLOWAY** – saxophone

Essential Rykodisc

Mar 90. (7") **SPACE SHUTTLE (vocal). / ('A'original mix)**
(12"+=) – ('A'deep club mix) / Pieces of gold – medley.
(12"+=) – ('A'deep club dub) / War is very ugly.
(cd-s+=) – The bottle / Pieces of gold – medley.
Mar 90. (cd)(c)(d-lp) **THE TALES OF GIL SCOTT-HERON AND HIS AMNESIA EXPRESS (live)**
– Washington DC / Save the children / Angel dust / Gun / Blue collar / Amen (hold on to your dream) / Three miles down / The bottle.

Mother Mother

Jul 94. (cd)(c) **SPIRITS**
– Message to the messengers / Spirits / Give her a call / Laly's song / Spirits past / The other side (parts 1-3) / Work for peace / Don't give up.
Oct 94. (12")(cd-s) **DON'T GIVE UP. / MESSAGE TO THE MESSENGERS / THE BOTTLE (live)**

– others, etc. –

Jul 75. RCA; (lp) **THE REVOLUTION WILL NOT BE TELEVISED** [-]
(cd-iss.May89 on 'Bluebird', += extra track)
Jul 80. Inferno; (7")(12") **THE BOTTLE (drunken mix). / THE BOTTLE (sober mix)**
(re-iss.Jan 81 on 'Champagne')

—— (above as "GIL SCOTT-HERON & BRIAN JACKSON")

1981. Audio Fidelity; (lp) **THE BOTTLE** (1973) [-]
Mar 88. Old Gold; (12"m) **THE BOTTLE. / JOHANNESBURG / WINTER IN AMERICA** [-]
Apr 94. Castle; (cd)(c) **MINISTRY OF INFORMATION (live)** [-]
– Winter in America / Alien / The bottle / Is that jazz / Washington DC / Gun / B-movie.

SCRATCH ACID (see under ⇒ JESUS LIZARD)

SCREAMING TREES

Formed: Ellensburg, Washington, USA . . . 1985 by MARK LANEGAN and brothers GARY and VAN CONNER. Had spells with now famous US indies, before being transferred to 'Epic' in the early 90's. • **Style:** Grunge metal rock. • **Songwriters:** CONNER / LANEGAN / CONNER. • **Trivia:** Produced by CHRIS CORNELL (Soundgarden) on 'UNCLE ANAESTHESIA' album of '92.
Note: Not to be confused with English band on 'Native' records.

Recommended: ANTHOLOGY – THE S.S.T. YEARS 1985-1989 (*7)

MARK LANEGAN – vocals / **GARY LEE CONNER** – guitar, vocals / **VAN CONNER** – bass, vocals / **MARK PICKEREL** – drums, percussion

S.S.T. S.S.T.

1985. (lp) **OTHER WORLDS** [-]
– *(cd+c UK-iss.1992)*
Sep 87. (lp)(c)(cd) **EVEN IF AND ESPECIALLY WHEN**
– Transfiguration / Straight out to any place / World painted / Don't look down / Girl behind the mask / Flying / Cold rain / Other days and different planets / The pathway / You know where it's at / Back together / In the forest.
Sep 88. (lp)(c)(cd) **INVISIBLE LANTERN**
– Ivy / Walk through to the other side / Line & circles / Shadow song / Grey diamond desert / Smokerings / The second I awake / Invisible lantern / Even if / Direction of the Sun / Night comes creeping / She knows.
Mar 89. (m-lp)(c)(cd) **BUZZ FACTORY**
– Where the twain shall meet / Windows / Black Sun morning / Too far away / Subtle poison / Yard trip / Flower web / Wish bringer / Revelation revolution / The looking glass cracked / End of the universe.

Glitterhouse Sub Pop

Dec 89. (d7"w /1-white) **CHANGE HAS COME. / DAYS / / FLASHES. / TIME SPEAKS HER GOLDEN TONGUE**
(c-ep/cd-ep iss.Dec90) (+=) – I've seen you before.

Epic Epic

1991. (12"ep) **UNCLE ANAESTHESIA / WHO LIES IN DARKNESS. / OCEAN OF CONFUSION / SOMETHING ABOUT TODAY (numb inversion version)** [-]
Jun 91. (cd)(lp) **UNCLE ANAESTHESIA** Mar91
– Beyond this horizon / Bed of roses / Uncle anaesthesia / Story of her fate / Caught between / Lay your head down / Before we arise / Something about today / Alice

said / Time for light / Disappearing / Ocean of confusion / Closer.

— **BARRETT MARTIN** – drums repl. PICKEREL

Oct 92. (cd)(c)(lp) **SWEET OBLIVION**
– Shadow of the season / Nearly lost you / Dollar bill / More or less / Butterfly / For celebrations past / The secret kind / Winter song / Troubled times / No one knows / Julie Paradise.

Feb 93. (12"ep)(pic-cd-ep) **NEARLY LOST YOU. / E.S.K. / SONG OF A BAKER / WINTER SONG (acoustic)** 50

Apr 93. (7"pic-d-ep)(12"colrd-ep)(cd-ep) **DOLLAR BILL. / (THERE'LL BE) PEACE IN THE VALLEY FOR ME (acoustic) / TOMORROW'S DREAM** 52

– compilations, others, etc. –

Nov 91. S.S.T.; (cd)(d-lp) **ANTHOLOGY . . . THE S.S.T. YEARS 1985-1989**

May 93. Sub Pop; (cd)(m-lp) **CHANGE HAS COME**

MARK LANEGAN

Sub Pop | Sub Pop

May 90. (cd)(c)(lp)(red-lp) **THE WINDING SHEET**
(c+cd+=) – I love you little girl. *(re-iss.Apr94)*

Sep 90. (7") **DOWN IN THE DARK. /**

— next w / **J.MASCIS + MARK JOHNSON** (Dinosaur Jr.) / **TAD DOYLE** (Tad) / **DAN PETERS** (Mudhoney) / **KURT FEDORA** (Gobblehoof)

Jan 93. (cd)(lp) **WHISKEY FOR THE HOLY GHOST**
– The river rise / Borracho / House a home / Kingdoms of rain / Carnival / Riding the nightingale / El Sol / Dead on you / Shooting gallery / Sunrise / Pendulum / Jesus touch / Beggar's blues. *(re-iss.Mar94)*

May 94. (cd-ep) **HOUSE A HOME / SHOOTING GALLERY / UGLY SUNDAY / SUNRISE**

SCRITTI POLITTI

Formed: London, England ... late 1977 by Leeds art school student GREEN GARTSIDE. Their first release 'SKANK BLOG BOLOGNA' on own 'St.Pancras' label, did little, except ensure a John Peel Session, which got own release on 'Rough Trade' in 1979. In 1982, he/they finally released debut album 'SONGS TO REMEMBER', which described it perfectly as it hit No.12 in the UK. The following year, he switched to major 'Virgin' label, and triumphed again with 1984-85 singles 'WOOD BEEZ', 'ABSOLUTE' & 'THE WORD GIRL'. They even surprised many, by conquering the States, with hit single 'PERFECT WAY', which was later covered by the legendary trumpeter MILES DAVIS. He also guested on their return 1988 single 'OH PATTI'. GREEN had already moved in 1983 to New York, where he found American session musicians MAHER and GAMSON. • **Style:** Dreamy art skank / shambolic dreadlock outfit (i.e. a mixture of new wave + white reggae). SCRITTI POLITTI were basically a solo studio outing for the fresh-faced GREEN. • **Songwriters:** GREEN penned all material, except SHE'S A WOMAN (Beatles) / TAKE ME IN YOUR ARMS AND LOVE ME (hit; Gladys Knight). • **Trivia:** SCRITTI POLITTI is nearly Italian for political writing. MADNESS had a 1986 hit with 'THE SWEETEST GIRL'. That year also saw GREEN and GAMSON write the title track for AL JARREAU's album 'L Is For Lover'.

Recommended: SONGS TO REMEMBER (*8) / CUPID & PSYCHE (*8).

GREEN (b.GREEN STROHMEYER-GARTSIDE, 22 Jun'56, Cardiff, Wales) – vox, guitar / **TOM MORLEY** – linn drum / **MATTHEW 'K'** – programme organiser / **NIAL JINKS** – bass

St.Pancras | not issued

Nov 78. (7") **SKANC BLOG BOLOGNA. / IS AND OUGHT OF THE WESTERN WORLD** -

Rough Trade | not issued

Sep 79. (12"ep) **FOUR 'A' SIDES** -
– Doubt beat / Confidences / Bibbly O'tek / P.A.'s.

Nov 79. (7"ep) **WORK IN PROGRESS (John Peel Sessions)** -
– Hegamony / Scritlocks door / Opec-Immac / Messthetics.

— added **MIKE MacEVOY** – synthesizers, vocoder / **MGOTSE** – d.bass / guest **ROBERT WYATT** – piano

Aug 81. (7")(12") **THE SWEETEST GIRL. / LIONS AFTER SLUMBER** 64 -

— **JOE CANG** – bass repl. NIAL / **STEVE SIDWELL** – trumpet / **JAMIE TALBOT** – saxophone repl. MGOTSE

Apr 82. (7")(12") **FAITHLESS. / FAITHLESS PART II (instrumental)** 56 -

Jul 82. (7")(7"pic-d) **ASYLUMS IN JERUSALEM. / JAQUES DERRIDA** 43 -
(12"+=) – ('A'extended).

Aug 82. (lp)(c) **SONGS TO REMEMBER** 12 -
– Asylums in Jerusalem / A slow soul / Jacques Derrida / Lions after slumber / Faithless / Sex / Rock-a-boy blue / Gettin' havin' & holdin' / The sweetest girl. *(cd-iss.May87)*

— **GREEN** recruited US musicians **MARCUS MILLER** – bass (ex-MILES DAVIS) / **STEVE FERRONE** – drums (ex-BRIAN AUGER) / **PAUL JACKSON Jnr.** – guitar (MORLEY went solo)

Virgin | Warners

Mar 84. (7")(7"pic-d) **WOOD BEEZ (PLAY LIKE ARETHA FRANKLIN). / ('A'dub version)** 10 91 Jan 86
(12"+=) – ('A'extended).

— **GREEN** with **ROBBIE BUCHANAN + DAVID FRANK** – keys / **FRED MAHER** – drums

Jun 84. (7")(7"pic-d) **ABSOLUTE. / ('A'version)** 17
(12"+=) – ('A'extended).

— **GREEN** now with **DAVID GAMSON** – keyboards / **ALLAN MURPHY** – guitar

Nov 84. (7")(7"pic-d) **HYPNOTISE. / ('A'version)** 68
(12"+=) – ('A'extended version).

— **NICK MOROCH** – guitar was added to above guests for album below.

May 85. (7")(7"sha-pic-d) **THE WORD GIRL. / FLESH AND BLOOD** 6
(12"+=) – ('A'&'B'versions).

Jun 85. (lp)(c)(cd) **CUPID AND PSYCHE '85** 5 50
– The word girl / Small talk / Absolute / A liitle knowledge / Don't work that way / Perfect way / Lover to fall / Wood beez (pray like Aretha Franklin) / Hypnotize. *(cd+=)* – (other versions).

Aug 85. (7") **PERFECT WAY. / ('A'version)** 48 11
(12"+=) – ('A'extended).

— **GREEN** with numerous session people, + next single guest MILES DAVIS

Apr 88. (7") **OH PATTI (DON'T FEEL SORRY FOR LOVERBOY). / ('A'instrumental)** 13
(12"+=)(12"pic-d+=) – ('A'extended).
(cd-s+=) – Best thing ever.
(c-s++=) – ('A'drumless mix).

Jun 88. (lp)(c)(cd) **PROVISION** 8
– Boom! there she was / Overnite / First boy in this town / All that we are / Best thing ever / Oh Patti (don't feel sorry for loverboy) / Bam salute / Sugar and spice / Philosophy now. *(cd+=)* – Oh Patti (extended) / Boom! . . . (dub). *(re-iss.c+cd.Aug91)*

Jul 88. (7") **FIRST BOY IN TOWN (LOVESICK). / WORLD COME BACK TO LIFE** 63
(12"+=)/ /(cd-s+=) – ('A'instrumental)./ / ('A'extended).

Oct 88. (7") **BOOM! THERE SHE WAS. / PHILOSOPHY NOW** 55 53 Jun 88
(12"+=)(3"cd-s+=) – ('A'mix) / ('A'dub version).

Mar 91. (7") **SHE'S A WOMAN. ("SCRITTI POLITTI & SHABBA RANKS") / LITTLE WAY (diff.)** 20
(12"+=) – ('A'-Apollo 440 remix).
(cd-s+=) – Wood beez (pray like Aretha Franklin).
(12") – ('A'-William Orbit remix) / ('A'-Tutology business mix).

Jul 91. (7")(c-s) **TAKE ME IN YOUR ARMS. ("SCRITTI POLITTI & SWEETIE IRIE") / ('A' instrumental) / ('A' mix)** 47
(12"+=)(cd-s+=) – She's a woman.

— Does look as if GREEN has abandoned SCRITTI, but still writes for and with others.

– compilations, others, etc. –

1988. Virgin; (3"cd-ep) **WOOD BEEZ (PRAY LIKE ARETHA FRANKLIN) / ('A'dub) / SMALL TALK** -

1988. Virgin; (3"cd-ep) **THE WORD GIRL / FLESH AND BLOOD / ('A'turntable . . .)** -

Apr 90. Virgin; (3"cd-ep) **ABSOLUTE. / (3 other tracks by other artists)** -

SEAL

Born: SEALHENRY SAMUEL, Paddington, London, England of Nigerian-Brazilian parentage. Went solo in 1990, after previously providing guest vocals for ADAMSKI's UK No.1 'KILLER'. Signed to Island's 'ZTT', his debut outing 'CRAZY', broke into the UK Top 20 by Christmas 1990. His next Top 20 follow-up 'THE FUTURE LOVE', preceded an eponymous No.1 album in 1991. • **Style:** Soul rock giant (6 and a half foot) with acoustic & synthesized side, drawing similarities to MARVIN GAYE. • **Songwriters:** Writes all material, including the lyrics for 'KILLER'. Covered HEY JOE + THE WIND CRIES MARY (Jimi Hendrix).

Recommended: SEAL (*6).

SEAL – vocals, acoustic guitar (ex-ADAMSKI) with many session people

Z.T.T. | Sire

Nov 90. (7")(c-s) **CRAZY. / SPARKLE** 2 7 May 91
(12"+=)(cd-s+=) – ('A'extended).

Apr 91. (7"ep)(c-ep) **THE FUTURE LOVE. / A MINOR GROOVE / VIOLET** 12
(12"+=)(cd-s+=) – ('A'extended Future Love Paradise mix).

May 91. (cd)(c)(lp) **SEAL** 1 24
– The beginning / Deep water / Crazy / Killer / Whirlpool / Future love Paradise / Wild / Show me / Violet.

Jul 91. (7")(c-s) **THE BEGINNING. / DEEP WATER (acoustic)** 24
(cd-s+=) – ('A'giro mix) / ('A'remix).
(12") – ('A'remix) / ('A'giro mix) / ('A'dub mix).

Nov 91. (7")(c-s) **KILLER . . . ON THE LOOSE. / HEY JOE / COME SEE WHAT LOVE HAS DONE** 8 100 Mar 92
(12"+=)(cd-s+=) – ('A'remixes).

Feb 92. (7")(c-s)(7"sha-pic-d) **VIOLET. / WILD** 39
(cd-s+=) – Show me / Whirlpool.

— with a plethora of musicians, the principals being; **GUS ISIDORE, WENDY MELVOIN, LISA COLEMAN & JAMIE MUHOBERAC** (the first 3 co-writers). Guests incl. **JEFF BECK, JONI MITCHELL, LUIS JARDIM, ANNE DUDLEY, ANDY NEWMARK, WILLIAM ORBIT, PINO PALLADINO, GAVIN WRIGHT, BETSY COOK** + producer **TREVOR HORN**

May 94. (c-s) **PRAYER FOR THE DYING. / DREAMING IN METAPHORS** 14 21
(cd-s+=) – Crazy (acoustic).

May 94. (cd)(c)(lp) **SEAL** 1 16
– Bring it on / Prayer for the dying / Dreaming in metaphors / Don't cry / Fast changes / Kiss from a rose / People asking why / Newborn friend / If I could / I'm alive / Bring it on (reprise).

Jul 94. (7")(c-s) **KISS FROM A ROSE. / I'M ALIVE** 20
(cd-s) – ('A'mixes) / The wind cries Mary / Blues in E.

Oct 94. (12")(c-s) **NEWBORN FRIEND. / ('A'mix)** 45
(12"+=)/ /(cd-s++=) – ('A'mix). / / ('A'mix).

Jul 95. (c-s)(cd-s)(12") **A KISS FROM A ROSE. / I'M ALIVE (SON OF BONTEMPI) / I'M ALIVE (Sasha & B.T.remix)** 5 1 Jun95
(cd-s) – ('A'side) / The wind cries Mary / Blues in E.

Nov 95. (c-s) **DON'T CRY / PRAYER FOR THE DYING / DON'T CRY (YOU'RE NOT ALONE)** 51
(cd-s+=) – ('B'extended).

SEARCHERS

Formed: Kirkdale, Liverpool, England . . . 1961 by PENDER and McNALLY. Named themselves after a famous John Wayne film. Like The BEATLES, they played The Cavern, and recorded at The Star-Club in Germany and backed a local singer Johnny Sandon. They were soon signed for 'Pye' by Tony Hatch in 1963. Their first 45 'SWEETS FOR MY SWEET', hit UK No.1 and was first of string of hits during the next 3 years. • **Style:** Harmonious pop band, similar to The BEATLES and jangly folk affitionados The BYRDS. They later moved into the cabaret circuit in the 70s & 80's. • **Songwriters:** Mostly re-activated cover versions; SWEETS FOR MY SWEET (Drifters) / NEEDLES AND PINS + WHEN YOU WALK IN THE ROOM (Jackie DeShannon) / DON'T THROW YOUR LOVE AWAY (Shirelles) / SOME DAY WE'RE GONNA LOVE AGAIN (Barbara Lewis) / WHAT HAVE THE DONE TO THE RAIN? (Malvina Reynolds) / LOVE POTION 9 (Clovers) / BUMBLE BEE (LaVern Baker) / TAKE ME FOR WHAT I'M WORTH (P.F.Sloan) / TAKE IT OR LEAVE IT (Rolling Stones) / and loads of lp tracks. • **Trivia:** In 1981, they play a Royal Variety Show alongside Cliff Richard, Lonnie Donegan and Adam & The Ants.

Recommended: THE ULTIMATE COLLECTION (*6).

MIKE PENDER (b.PRENDERGAST, 3 Mar'42) – vocals, lead guitar / **JOHN McNALLY** (b.30 Aug'41) – vocals, rhythm guitar / **TONY JACKSON** (b.16 Jul'40) – vocals, bass / **CHRIS CURTIS** (b.CHRIS CRUMMY, 26 Aug'41, Oldham) – vocals, drums repl. NORMAN McGARRY who joined RORY STORME & THE HURRICANES replacing RINGO STARR.

Pye Mercury

Jun 63. (7") **SWEETS FOR MY SWEET. / IT'S ALL BEEN A DREAM** 1 Mar 64

Aug 63. (lp) **MEET THE SEARCHERS** 2 -
– Sweets for my sweet / Alright / Love potion No.9 / Farmer John / Stand by me / Money / Da doo ron ron / Ain't gonna love ya / Since you broke my heart / Tricky Dickey / Where have all the flowers gone / Twist and shout. *(re-iss.1966 on 'Golden Guinea') (re-iss.+cd.Feb87 on 'PRT') (re-cd-iss.Dec89 on 'Castle')*

Pye Liberty

Oct 63. (7") **SUGAR AND SPICE. / SAINTS AND SEARCHERS** 2 Dec 63
(re-iss. US Apr 64 hit No. 44)

Nov 63. (lp) **SUGAR AND SPICE** 5 -
– Sugar and spice / Don't cha know? / Some other guy / One of these days / Listen to me / Unhappy girls / (Ain't that) Just like me / Oh my lover / Saints and searchers / Cherry stones / All my sorrows / Hungry for love. *(re-iss.1967 on 'Marble A.') (re-iss.+cd.Feb87 on 'PRT') (re-cd-iss.Dec89 on 'Castle')*

Pye Kapp

Jan 64. (7") **NEEDLES AND PINS. / SATURDAY NIGHT OUT** 1 13 Feb 64

Mar 64. (lp) **MEET THE SEARCHERS – NEEDLES AND PINS** - 22
– (tracks from last 2 albums plus title track)

Mar 64. (7") **AIN'T THAT JUST LIKE ME. / AIN'T GONNA KISS YA** - 61

Apr 64. (7") **DON'T THROW YOUR LOVE AWAY. / I PRETEND I'M WITH YOU** 1 16 May 64

May 64. (lp) **IT'S THE SEARCHERS** 4 -
– Sea of heartbreak / Glad all over / It's in her kiss / Livin' lovin' wreck / Where have you been / Shimmy shimmy / Needles and pins / This empty place / Gonna send you back to Georgia / I count the tears / High heel sneakers / Can't help forgiving you / Sho' know a lot about love / Don't throw your love away. *(re-iss.1968 on 'Marble A.') (re-iss.+cd.Feb87 on 'PRT')*

Jul 64. (7") **SOMEDAY WE'RE GONNA LOVE AGAIN. / NO ONE ELSE COULD LOVE YOU** 11 34 Aug 64

— **FRANK ALLEN** (b.FRANCIS McNIECE, 14 Jul'43, Hayes, Middlesex, England) – vocals, bass (ex-CLIFF BENNETT & THE REBEL ROUSERS) repl. JACKSON (solo)

Sep 64. (7") **WHEN YOU WALK IN THE ROOM. / I'LL BE MISSING YOU** 3 35 Oct 64

Oct 64. (lp) **THIS IS US** - 97

Nov 64. (7") **WHAT HAVE THEY DONE TO THE RAIN?. / THIS FEELING INSIDE** 13 29 Jan 65

Dec 64. (7") **LOVE POTION NO.9. / HI HEEL SNEAKERS** - 3

Feb 65. (7") **GOODBYE MY LOVE. / TILL I MET YOU** 4 52 Mar 65

— (US-title of above 'GOODBYE MY LOVER GOODBYE')

Mar 65. (lp) **SOUNDS LIKE THE SEARCHERS** 8
– Everybody come and clap your hands / If I could fine someone / Magic potion / I don't want to go on without you / Bumble bee / Something you got baby / Let the good times roll / A tear fell / Till you say you'll be mine / You wanna make her happy / Everything you do / Goodnight baby. *(re-iss.+cd.Feb87 on 'PRT')*

— (US-title 'THE NEW SEARCHERS', diff.tracks)

Mar 65. (7") **BUMBLE BEE. / A TEAR FELL** - 21

Jul 65. (7") **HE'S GOT NO LOVE. / SO FAR AWAY** 12 79

Oct 65. (7") **WHEN I GET HOME. / I'M NEVER COMING HOME** 35 -

Oct 65. (7") **DON'T YOU KNOW WHY. / YOU CAN'T LIE TO A LIAR** -

Nov 65. (7") **TAKE ME FOR WHAT I'M WORTH. / TOO MANY MILES** 20 76 Jan 66

Nov 65. (lp) **TAKE ME FOR WHAT I'M WORTH**
– I'm ready / I'll be doggone / Does she really care for me / It's time / Too many miles / You can't lie to a liar / Don't you know why / I'm your loving man / Each time / Be my baby / Four strong winds / Take me for what I'm worth. *(re-iss.+cd.Feb87 on 'PRT')*

— (US title 'THE SEARCHERS No.4')

— **JOHN BLUNT** – drums repl. CURTIS

Apr 66. (7") **TAKE IT OR LEAVE IT. / DON'T HIDE IT AWAY** 31 -

Oct 66. (7") **HAVE YOU EVER LOVED SOMEBODY?. / IT'S JUST THE WAY LOVE WILL COME AND GO** 48 94

Jan 67. (7") **POPCORN DOUBLE FEATURE. / LOVERS**

Apr 67. (7") **WESTERN UNION. / I'LL CRY TOMORROW**

1967. (7") **SECOND HAND DEALER. / CRAZY DREAMS**

Liberty Liberty

Nov 68. (7") **UMBRELLA MAN. / OVER THE WEEKEND**

Jul 69. (7") **KINKY CATHY ABERNATHY. / SUZANNA**

— (Late 1969) **BILLY ADAMSON** – drums, vocals repl. BLUNT

R.C.A. R.C.A.

Aug 71. (7") **DESDEMONA. / THE WORLD IS WAITING FOR TOMORROW** 94

Oct 71. (7") **LOVE IS EVERYWHERE. / AND A BUTTON** -

1972. (lp) **SECOND TAKE**
– Sugar and spice / Don't throw your love away / Farmer John / Come on back to me / When you walk in the room / Needles and pins / Desdemona / Goodbye my love / Love potion No.9 / Sweets for my sweet / Take me for what I'm worth / What have they done to the rain.

Apr 72. (7") **SING SINGER SING. / COME ON BACK TO ME** -

Aug 72. (7"m) **NEEDLES AND PINS. / WHEN YOU WALK IN THE ROOM / COME ON BACK TO ME** -

Oct 72. (7") **VALHELLA. / MADMAN** -

Feb 73. (7") **SOLITAIRE. / SPICKS AND SPECKS** -

— Resigned themselves to oldies circuit in the US.

Sire Sire

Oct 79. (7") **HEARTS IN HER EYES. / DON'T HANG ON** -

Feb 80. (7") **IT'S TOO LATE. / THIS KIND OF LOVE AFFAIR** -

Feb 80. (7") **IT'S TOO LATE. / DON'T HANG ON** -

Mar 80. (lp)(c) **THE SEARCHERS**
– Hearts in her eyes / Switchboard Susan / Felling fine / Back to the war / This kind of love affair / Lost in your eyes / It's too late / Love's melody / No dancing / Love's gonna be strong / Don't hang on. *(US tracks differed)*

Jul 80. (7") **LOVE'S MELODY. / CHANGING** -

Mar 81. (7") **ANOTHER NIGHT. / BACK TO THE WAR** -

May 81. (lp)(c) **PLAY FOR TODAY** (US title 'LOVE'S MELODY')
– Another night / September girls / Murder in my heart / She made a fool of you / Silver / Sick and tired / Radio romance / Infatuation / Almost Saturday night / Everything but a heartbeat / Little bit of Heaven / New day.

May 81. (7") **LOVE'S MELODY. / LITTLE BIT OF HEAVEN** -

— Around mid-80's, group dispersed into 2 sections (aka MIKE PENDER'S SEARCHERS and other SEARCHERS). The others took MIKE to court in 1988.

Arista Coconut

Apr 90. (cd)(c)(lp) **HUNGRY HEART**
– Forever in love (near to Heaven) / Love lies bleeding / Lonely weekend / Somebody told me / Every little tear / Sweets for my sweet (new 1988 version) / No other love / This boy's in love / Fooled myself once again / Baby, I do / Push, push / Needles and pins.

– compilations, others, etc. –

Sep 63. Philips; (7") **SWEET NOTHINGS (live in Hamburg). / WHAT'D I SAY** 48 -

Jun 64. Mercury; (lp) **HEAR! HEAR! (live in Hamburg)** -

1963. Pye; (7"ep) **SWEETS FOR MY SWEETS** -

Oct 63. Pye; (7"ep) **AIN'T GONNA KISS YA** 12 -

1964. Pye; (7"ep) **HUNGRY FOR LOVE** -

Apr 64. Mercury; (7") **(AIN'T THAT) JUST LIKE ME. / I CAN TELL** -

1964. Pye; (7"ep) **THE SEARCHERS PLAY THE SYSTEM** -

1964. Pye; (7"ep) **WHEN YOU WALK IN THE ROOM** -
(re-iss.Jul80 on 'Flashback-Pye')

1965. Pye; (7"ep) **HITMAKERS VOL.1** -

1965. Pye; (7"ep) **BUMBLE BEE** -

1965. Pye; (7"ep) **THE SEARCHERS '65** -

Nov 65. Pye; (7"ep) **TAKE ME FOR WHAT I'M WORTH** -

1966. Pye; (7"ep) **FOUR BY FOUR** -

1966. Pye; (7"ep) **HITMAKERS VOL.3** -

1970. Pye; (lp)(c) **THE GOLDEN HOUR OF THE SEARCHERS** -
(re-iss.+c.Jan74)

1973. Pye; (lp)(c) **THE GOLDEN HOUR OF THE SEARCHERS VOL.2** -

May 76. Pye; (7") **NEEDLES AND PINS. / SUGAR AND SPICE** -

1976. Mercury; (lp) **HISTORY OF BRITISH POP** -

1976. Mercury; (lp) **HISTORY OF BRITISH POP VOL.2** -

Nov 77. Pye; (d-lp) **THE SEARCHERS FILE** -

Jul 78. Pye; (7") **WHEN YOU WALK IN THE ROOM. / DON'T THROW YOUR LOVE AWAY**

May 80. Pye; (lp) **WHEN YOU WALK IN THE ROOM** -

Apr 79. Pye; (7") **NEEDLES AND PINS. / SWEETS FOR MY SWEET** -

— (above on 'Flashback-Pye')

Jan 77. Big Deal; (12"ep) **WHEN YOU WALK IN THE ROOM / NEEDLES AND PINS. / DON'T THROW YOUR LOVE AWAY / GOODBYE MY LOVE** -

1966. Marble Arch; (lp) **SEARCHERS' SMASH HITS** -

1967. Marble Arch; (lp) **SEARCHERS' SMASH HITS VOL.2** -

1971. Hallmark; (lp)(c) **NEEDLES AND PINS** -

Jan 80. PRT; (d-lp)(d-c) **SPOTLIGHT ON THE SEARCHERS** -

Jun 82. PRT; (c) **100 MINUTES OF THE SEARCHERS** -

Nov 82. PRT; (7") **I DON'T WANT TO BE THE ONE. / HOLLYWOOD** [ ] [-]
Jul 83. PRT; (lp)(c) **LOVE LIES BLEEDING** [ ] [-]
Dec 85. PRT; (lp)(c) **SWEETS FOR MY SWEET** [ ] [-]
Apr 87. PRT; (7")(12") **WHEN YOU WALK IN THE ROOM. / BE MY BABY** [ ] [-]
Apr 87. PRT; (lp)(c)(cd) **SILVER SEARCHERS** [ ] [-]
Sep 87. PRT; (lp)(c)(cd) **THE HITS COLLECTION** [ ] [-]
Oct 87. PRT; (lp)(c)(cd) **THE SEARCHERS PLAY THE SYSTEM** [ ] [-]
Jul 82. Old Gold; (7") **NEEDLES AND PINS. / DON'T THROW YOUR LOVE AWAY** [ ] [-]
Jul 84. Old Gold; (7") **SWEETS FOR MY SWEET. / WHEN YOU WALK IN THE ROOM** [ ] [-]
Apr 86. Showcase/ US= Rhino; (lp)(c) **GREATEST HITS** [ ] [ ]
1988. Castle; (d-lp)(c)(cd) **THE COMPLETE COLLECTION** [ ] [-]
– Sweets for my sweet / Listen to me / When you walk in the room / Goodbye my love / i don't want to go on without you / What have they done to the rain / Don't throw your love away / Ain't gonna kiss ya / Since you broke my heart / Goodnight baby / Hungry for love / When I get home / Needles and pins / (Ain't that) Just like me / Take it or leave it / Bumble bee / Someday we're gonna love again / Farmer John / Sugar and spice / Have you ever loved somebody / Take me for what I'm worth / Western Union / He's got no love / Love potion No.9.
May 90. Castle; (lp)(c)(cd) **THE ULTIMATE COLLECTION** [ ] [-]
May 90. Knight; (cd)(c) **THE GOLDEN HOUR OF THE SEARCHERS** [ ] [-]
Feb 92. Sequel; (3xcd-box) **30th ANNIVERSARY COLLECTION** [ ] [-]
Jul 89. See For Miles; (lp)(c)(cd) **THE EP COLLECTION** [ ] [-]
Nov 92. See For Miles; (cd) **THE EP COLLECTION VOL.2** [ ] [-]
Jul 94. Success; (cd)(c) **DON'T THROW YOUR LOVE AWAY** [ ] [-]
Sep 94. Spectrum; (cd)(c) **SWEETS FOR MY SWEET** [ ] [-]
Feb 95. B.A.M.; (cd) **PEARLS OF THE PAST** [ ] [-]

SEASTONES (see under ⇒ GRATEFUL DEAD)

SEBADOH

Formed: Boston, USA . . . 1989 by LOU BARLOW, former DINOSAUR JR. employee. After 2 albums in 1992 they finaly dented charts (UK) for 1993's 'BUBBLE AND SCRAPE'. • **Style:** NIRVANA + STOOGES-like eccentric alternative grunge rocker. • **Songwriters:** BARLOW and GAFFNEY (until latter repl. by FAY), some by LOWENSTEIN after 1992. Covered REJECT (Negros) / EVERYBODY'S BEEN BURNED (Byrds) / PINK MOON (Nick Drake) / NAIMA (John Coltrane?). FOLK IMPLOSION covered SCHOOL (Nirvana) / WON'T BACK DOWN (Tom Petty).

Recommended: BAKESALE (*8)

LOU BARLOW – vocals, guitar (ex-DINOSAUR JR) / **ERIC GAFFNEY** – drums

Homestead Homestead

Dec 89. (lp)(c) **THE FREED MAN** [ ] [ ]
1990. (lp) **WEED FORESTIN'** [ ] [ ]
(UK cd-iss of above 2 albums 'FREED WEED' in Nov92)

—— added **JASON LOEWENSTEIN** – bass, guitar

Jul 91. (7") **GIMME INDIE ROCK** [-] [ ]
1991. (cd)(lp) **SEBADOH III** *(UK-iss.Jul94)* [-] [ ]

not issued Siltbreeze

1991. (7") **OVEN IS MY FRIEND. / ?** [-] [ ]

—— In 1991, Sonic Life fanzine issued 'SPLIT WITH BIG STICK' for 'Blast First'.

not issued Vertical

1992. (7") **ASSHOLE** [-] [ ]

20 /20 Sub Pop

Aug 92. (cd)(m-lp) **ROCKIN' THE FOREST** [ ] [ ]
– Gimme indie rock / Ride the darker wave / It's so hard to fall in love / Cry sis / Really insane II / Vampire / Junk bands / Mind-held.

—— Sep 92; split an EP release w/AZALIA SNAIL on 'Dark Beloved Cloud'.

Oct 92. (cd)(m-lp) **SEBADOH VS HELMET** [ ] [ ]
– Notsur dnuora selcric / Brand new love / Mean distance / . . . Burned / New worship / Good things, proud man / P.Moon / Cecilia chime in Melee / Soulmate.
(2 albums above issued in US together as 'SMASH YOUR HEAD ON THE PUNK ROCK')

Domino Sub Pop

Mar 93. (7") **SOUL AND FIRE. / FANTASTIC DISASTER (amateur mix)** [ ] [ ]
(12"+=)(cd-s+=) – Emma get wild / Reject.
Apr 93. (cd)(lp) **BUBBLE AND SCRAPE** [63] [ ]
– Soul and fire / Two years two days / Telecosmic alchemy / Fantastic disaster / Happily divided / Sister / Cliche / Sacred attention / Elixir is Zog / Emma get wild / Sixteen / Homemade / Forced love / No way out / Bouquet for a siren / Think (let tomorrow be) / Flood.
Dec 93. (7") **REBOUND. / CAREFUL** [ ] [ ]
– (12"ep/cd-ep 'FOUR SONGS EP'+=) – Mar backlash / Not a friend / Foreground / Naima / 40203 / Mystery man / Drumstick jumble / Lime kiln.

—— **BOB FAY** – drums repl. GAFFNEY who went solo (although still on below album)

Jul 94. (7")(cd-s) **SKULL. / PUNCHING MYSELF IN THE FACE REPEATEDLY, PUBLICLY / SING SOMETHING – PLATE O'HATRED** [ ] [ ]
Aug 94. (cd)(c)(lp) **BAKESALE** [40] [ ]
– License to confuse / Careful / Magnet's coil / Not a friend / Not too amused / Dreams / Skull / Got it / S. soup / Give up / Rebound / Mystery man / Temptation tide / Drama mine / Together or alone. *(ltd. w / free 7")*
Jun 95. (7")(cd-s) **NOT TOO AMUSED. / HANK WILLIAMS** [ ] [ ]

LOU BARLOW

not issued Sub Pop

1993. (7") **I AM NOT MOCKING YOU. /** [-] [ ]

LOU BARLOW AND HIS SENTRIDOH

not issued Smells Like R.

1992. (7") **LOSERCORE. / REALLY INSANE** [-] [ ]

not issued Little Bro.

1993. (7"ep) **THE MYSTERIOUS SENTRIDOH** [-] [ ]

LoFi

1994. (7"ep) **LOU BARLOW'S ACOUSTIC SENTRIDOH** [-] [ ] France

City Slang Sub Pop

Jun 94. (cd)(d-lp) **A COLLECTION OF PREVIOUSLY RELEASED SONGS** (compilation) [ ] [ ]

FOLK IMPLOSION

LOU BARLOW + JOHN DAVIS

Chocolate Drunken F.

1993. (c) **FOLK IMPLOSION** [-] [ ]
(5 tracks were featured in Sep94 on cd+10"m-lp 'TAKE A LOOK INSIDE THE FOLK IMPLOSION' om 'Tupelo-Communion' UK / 'Shrimper' US)

imported Drunken F.

Aug 94. (7"ep) **WALK THRU THIS WORLD WITH THE FOLK IMPLOSION** [-] [ ]
– My head really hurts / End of the first side / Won't back down / School.

Communion Communion

Sep 94. (cd)(lp) **TAKE A LOOK INSIDE** [ ] [ ]

not issued London

Dec 95. (cd-s) **NATURAL ONE /** [-] [42]

—— above from the film 'Kids'.

SEEDS

Formed: Los Angeles, California, USA . . . 1965 by solo artist SKY SAXON. They signed to 'GNP Crescendo' in 1965, and cracked the charts early in 1967, when a re-issue of '(YOU'RE) PUSHIN' TOO HARD', hit US Top 40. They then found it hard to maintain any more substantial success, and they were soon pushed back into underground scene. • **Style:** Weird psychedelic blues-rock outfit, who mixed sexual lyric content with usual drug connotations. • **Songwriters:** SKY SAXON penned.

Recommended: EVIL HOODOO (*7)

LITTLE RICHIE MARSH

(aka SKY SAXON)

not issued Ava

1961. (7") **GOODBYE. / CRYING INSIDE MY HEART** [-] [ ]

not issued Shepherd

1962. (7") **THEY SAY. / DARLING I SWEAR IT'S TRUE** [-] [ ]

SKY SAXON

not issued Conquest

1962. (7") **THEY SAY. / GO AHEAD AND CRY** [-] [ ]

—— For the rest of 1962, SKY SAXON formed his ELECTRA FIRES. The following 2 years he founded SKY SAXON & The SOUL ROCKERS. At the beginning of 1965,

The SEEDS

were formed by **SKY SAXON** – vocals, bass, saxophone / plus **JAN SAVAGE** – guitar / **DARYLL HOOPER** – keyboards / **RICK ANDRIDGE** – drums

Vocalion GNP Cresc.

Jun 65. (7") **CAN'T SEEM TO MAKE YOU MINE. / DAISY MAE** [-] [ ]
1965. (7") **(YOU'RE) PUSHIN' TOO HARD. / OUT OF THE QUESTION** [-] [ ]
1966. (7") **THE OTHER PLACE. / TRY TO UNDERSTAND** [-] [ ]
Apr 66. (lp) **THE SEEDS** [-] [ ]
– Can't seem to make you mine / No escape / Lose your mind / Evil hoodoo / Girl I want you / Pushin' too hard / Try to understand / Nobody spoil my fun / It''s a hard life / You can't be trusted / Excuse excuse / Fallin' in love. *(UK-iss.1977 on 'Sonet') (re-iss.+cd 1988 US) (UK-iss. Feb 84 on 'Line', cd-iss. Sep 89)*
Oct 66. (7") **PUSHIN' TOO HARD. / TRY TO UNDERSTAND** [ ] [36]

—— added **HARVEY SHARPE** – bass

Oct 66. (lp) **A WEB OF SOUND** [ ] [ ]
– Mr.Farmer / Pictures and designs / Tripmaker / I tell myself / A fasded picture / Rollin' machine / Just let go / Up in her room. *(US re-iss.Oct75) (re-iss. +cd 1988 US)*
Feb 67. (7") **MR.FARMER. / NO ESCAPE (or) UP IN HER ROOM** [-] [86]
Apr 67. (7") **CAN'T SEEM TO MAKE YOU MINE. / I TELL MYSELF** [ ] [41]
Jun 67. (7") **A THOUSAND SHADOWS. / MARCH OF THE FLOWER CHILDREN** [-] [72]
Aug67. (lp) **FUTURE** [ ] [87]
– Introduction / March of the flower children / Travel with your mind / Out of the question / Painted doll / Flower lady & her assistant / Now a man / A thousand shadows / Two fingers pointing at you / Where is the entrance way to play / Six dreams / Falin'. *(re-iss.+cd 1988 US)*

1967. (7") **THE WIND BLOWS YOUR HAIR. / SIX DREAMS** -

SKY SAXON BLUES BAND

(same line-up & label, except HARVEY)

1967. (lp) **A FULL SPOON OF SEEDY BLUES** -
– Pretty girl / Moth and the flame / I'll help you / Cry wolf / Plain spoken / The gardener / One more time blues / Creepin' about / Buzzin' around. *(US re-iss.Sep76) (UK-iss.May87 on 'Music Box') (re-iss. +cd 1988 US)*

The SEEDS

again, but basically **SKY SAXON** + session people.

1968. (lp) **RAW AND ALIVE (MERLIN'S MUSIC BOX) (live)** -
– Introduction by Humble Harv / Mr.Farmer / No escape / Satisfy you / Night time girl / Up in her room / Gypsy plays his drums / Can't seem to make you mine / Mumble and bumble / Forest outside your door / 900 million people daily all making love / Pushin' too hard. *(re-iss.+cd 1988 US)*

1968. (7") **SATISFY YOU (live). / 900 MILLION PEOPLE DAILY MAKING LOVE (live)** -

not issued M.G.M.

1971. (7") **BAD PART OF TOWN. / WISH ME UP** -
1971. (7") **LOVE IN A SUMMER BASKET. / DID HE DIE** -

not issued Production

1972. (7") **SHUCKIN' AND JIVIN'. / YOU TOOK ME BY SURPRISE** -

— SKY SAXON folded SEEDS and formed various bands SKY SUNLIGHT / SUNLIGHT / SKY SUNLIGHT SAXON.

SKY SAXON

New Rose not issued

Nov 84. (lp) **MASTERS OF PSYCHEDELIA** -
Aug 86. (lp) **A GROOVY THING** -
Dec 88. (lp,cd) **IN SEARCH OF BRIGHTER COLOURS (by "SKY SUNLIGHT SAXON & FIRE WALL")** -
– I hear the mountains crash / Lightning lightning / Put something sweet between your lips / Barbie doll look / The big screen / Baby baby / Come on pretty girl / Kick kick / Paisley rocker / Come a here right now.

SKY SUNLIGHT SAXON

& THE STARRY SEEDS BAND:- ELLIOTT INGBAR / MARS BONFIRE / RON BUSHY / RAINBOW STARDUST

Psycho not issued

Feb 85. (m-lp) **STARRY RIDE** (various aggregations) -
– Starry ride / I'm in love with life / Drums, stars & guitars / 24 hour rocker.

Line not issued

Jun 87. (lp) **TAKES ON GLORY** (as 'SKYLIGHT / SKY SAXON') -
– As much as I love you / Born to be wild / In Paradise / Swim / Aphrodite / Sodom & Gomorrah / 30 seconds over Hollywood / Love dog / Wish me up / Statue of stone / Picnic in the grass / Pushin' too far too hard / Skid row children.

— **SKY + MARS** now with **TOM AZEVEDO** – guitar / **GARY STERN** – bass, guitar / **PAUL SCHOFIELD** – drums

not issued Pinpoint

1989. (lp) **JUST IMAGINE** -
– Black & red / Focus point / Wild roses / Just imagine / Black beans / Some people / Million miles / World tribute / Thriller riff / Mr.Farmer.

– (SEEDS) compilations, etc. –

Sep 76. GNP Crescendo; (lp) **THE SEEDS IN CONCERT (live)** -
1977. GNP Crescendo; (lp) **FALLIN' OFF THE EDGE** -
(re-iss.May87 on 'Music Box')
Aug 78. Sonet; (lp) **LEGENDARY MASTER RECORDINGS** -
Apr 88. Bam Caruso; (lp)(cd)(colrd-lp) **EVIL HOODOO** -
– March of the flower children / The wind blows your hair / Tripmaker / Try to understand / Evil hoodoo / Chocolate river / Pushing too hard / Falling off the edge / Mr.Farmer / Up in her room / Can't seem to make you mine / Pictures and designs / Flower lady and her assistant / Rollin' machine / Out of the question / Satisfy you.
Apr 88. Bam Caruso; (7") **PUSHIN' TOO HARD. / GREENER DAY** -
Nov 91. Drop Out; (cd) **A FADED PICTURE** -
– (FIRE ESCAPE – Psychotic Reaction / SEEDS – RAW AND ALIVE – LIVE AT MERLIN'S MUSIC BOX
Jul 95. GNP Crescendo; (cd) **TRAVEL WITH YOUR MIND**

Bob SEGER

Born: 6 May'45, Ann Arbor, Michigan, USA; but raised in Detroit. In 1964 he joined (DOUG BROWN &) The OMENS contributing keyboards. He and the lead singer BROWN wrote their material, even managing a spoof of BARRY SADLER's 'The Ballad Of The Green Berets' under the "The BEACH BUMS" pseudonym early '66. The OMENS now became BOB SEGER & THE LAST HEARD, releasing a couple of 45's on local 'Hideout' label. Early in '68, Eddie Punch Andrews became manager and band were now billed as BOB SEGER SYSTEM gaining contract for 'Capitol'. In 1969, he had first US top 20 hit with 'RAMBLIN' GAMBLIN' MAN'. Commercially things dried up until 1976 + 1977 when with The SILVER BULLET BAND, he began to hit top 10 mainly in the US. Continued to have many hit albums and singles there, even in the 90's, when he returned after 4 year hiatus. • **Style:** 60's college rock band mould, until early 70's when he unsuccessfully tried out singer/troubadour image w / BRAND NEW MORNING lp. By the mid 70's, he had drifted into SPRINGSTEEN mould, although many could differentiate his gritty vocals. • **Songwriters:** SEGER wrote most except, RIVER DEEP MOUNTAIN HIGH + NUTBUSH CITY LIMITS (Ike & Tina Turner) / BO DIDDLEY (Bo Diddley) / IF I WERE A CARPENTER (Tim Hardin) / LOVE THE ONE YOU'RE WITH (Stephen Stills) / FORTUNATE SON (Creedence Clearwater Revival) / BLIND LOVE + 16 SHELLS FROM A 30.6 (Tom Waits) / SHE CAN'T DO ANYTHING WRONG (C. Davis-Richmond) / C'EST LA VIE (Chuck Berry) / etc. • **Trivia:** SEGER's songs have been covered by many including ROSALIE (Thin Lizzy) / GET OUT OF DENVER (Eddie & The Hot Rods) / WE'VE GOT TONITE (Kenny Rogers & Sheena Easton).

Recommended: GREATEST HITS (*8)

BOB SEGER & The LAST HEARD

BOB SEGER – vocas, guitar with **DAN HONAKER** – bass, guitar, vocals / **PEP PERRINE** – drums, vocals / **DOUG BROWN** – keyboards

not issued Hideout

May 66. (7") **EAST SIDE STORY. / EAST SIDE SOUND** -

— (Above & below 45's, were soon distributed by 'Cameo')

Jul 66. (7") **PERSECUTION SMITH. / CHAIN SMOKIN'** -

not issued Cameo

Dec 66. (7") **SOCK IT TO ME, SANTA. / FLORIDA TIME** -
1967. (7") **VAGRANT WINTER. / VERY FEW** -
1967. (7") **HEAVY MUSIC (part 1). / HEAVY MUSIC (part 2)** -

BOB SEGER SYSTEM

repl BROWN who departed.

— **BOB SCHULTZ** – keyboards, saxophone / **TONY NEME** – guitar, keyboards

Capitol Capitol

Jan 68. (7") **2 + 2 = WHAT?. / DEATH ROW** -
Dec 68. (7") **RAMBLIN' GAMBLIN' MAN. / TALES OF LUCY BLUE** 17
Jan 69. (lp) **RAMBLIN' GAMBLIN' MAN** - 62
– Ramblin' gamblin' man / Tales of Lucy Blue / Ivory / Gone / Down home / Train man / White wall / Black eyed girl / 2 + 2 = what? / Doctor Fine / The lost song (love needs to be loved). *(UK-iss.Nov77) (re-iss.Jun81 on 'Greenlight')*
May 69. (7") **IVORY. / LOST SONG (LOVE NEEDS TO BE LOVED)** - 97
Mar 70. (7") **LENNIE JOHNSON. / NOAH (or) OUT LOUD** -
Apr 70. (lp) **NOAH** -
Jun 70. (7") **INNERVENUS EYES. / LONELY MAN** -

BOB SEGER

now solo, after disbanding The SYSTEM. / added **DON WATSON** – keyboards to repl SCHULTZ + NEME

Oct 70. (7") **LUCIFER. / BIG RIVER** 84 Mar 70
Oct 70. (lp) **MONGREL** -
– Song to Rufus / Evil Edna / Highway child / Big river / Mongrel / Lucifer / Teachin' blues / Leavin' on my dream / Mongrel too / River deep mountain high. *(UK-iss.Nov77) (re-iss.Jun81 on 'Greenlight') (re-iss.Jul83 on 'Fame')*

— now with **DAVE TEEGARDEN** – drums / **SKIP VANWINKLE KNAPE** – keyboards, bass / **MICHAEL BRUCE** – guitar

Nov 71. (lp) **BRAND NEW MORNING** -
Nov 71. (7") **LOOKIN' BACK. / HIGHWAY CHILD** 96

Reprise Palladium

Jul 72. (7") **IF I WERE A CARPENTER. / JESSE JAMES** - 76
Aug 72. (lp)(c) **SMOKIN' O.P.'s** Jul 72
– Bo Diddley / Love the one you're with / If I were a carpenter / Hummingbird / Let it rock / Turn on your love light / Jesse James / Someday / Heavy music. *(re-iss.Apr80)*
Nov 72. (7") **TURN ON YOUR LOVE LIGHT. / BO DIDDLEY** -

— SEGER's back-up back included **DICK SIMS** – keyboards / **TOM CARTMELL** – sax / **JAMIE OLDAKER** – drums / **SERGIO PASTORA** – percussion / **MARCY LEVY** – backing vocals

Mar 73. (lp)(c) **BACK IN '72**
– Midnight rider / So I wrote you a song / Stealer / Rosalie / Turn the page / Back in '72 / Neon sky / I've been working / I've got time.
Apr 73. (7") **ROSALIE. / NEON SKY** -
Nov 73. (7") **ROSALIE. / BACK IN '72** -

— His band all left to join ERIC CLAPTON. Newcomers **KENNY BUTTREY** – drums / **RANDY MEYERS** – drums / **RICK MANSKA** – keyboards / **TOMMY COGBILL** – bass / + guitars.

Jun 74. (7") **NEED YA. / SEEN A LOT OF FLOORS** -
Jul 74. (lp)(c) **SEVEN / CONTRASTS**
– Get out of Denver / Long song comin' / Need ya / School teacher / Cross of gold / U.M.C. (Upper Middle Class) / Seen a lot of floors / 20 years from now / All your love. *(re-iss.Apr80) (re-iss.Jun81 on 'Greenlight')*
Aug 74. (7") **GET OUT OF DENVER. / LONG SONG COMIN'** 80
Nov 74. (7") **U. M. C. (UPPER MIDDLE CLASS). . THIS OLD HOUSE** -

— New line-up were **DREW ABBOTT** – guitar / **ROBIN ROBBINS** – keyboards / **CHRIS CAMPBELL** – bass / **ALTO REED** – saxophone / **CHARLIE ALLEN MARTIN** – drums

Capitol Capitol

May 75. (7") **BEAUTIFUL LOSER. / FINE MEMORY** -
Aug 75. (lp)(c) **BEAUTIFUL LOSER** Apr 75
– Beautiful loser / Black night / Katmandu / Jody girl / Travellin' man / Momma / Nutbush city limits / Sailing nights / Fine memory. *(re-iss.Apr80)*
Aug 75. (7") **KATMANDU. / BLACK NIGHT** 43
Nov 75. (7") **NUTBUSH CITY LIMITS. / TRAVELIN' MAN** -

BOB SEGER & THE SILVER BULLET BAND

Aug 76. (d-lp)(d-c) **LIVE BULLET (live Detroit)** [ ] [34] Apr 76
– Nutbush city limits / Travellin' man / Beautiful loser / Jody girl / Lookin' back / Get out of Denver / Let it rock / I've been workin' / Turn the page / U.M.C. (Upper Middle Class) / Bo Diddley / Ramblin' gamblin' man / Heavy music / Katmandu. *(cd-iss.Feb95)*

Jun 76. (7") **NUTBUSH CITY LIMITS (live). / LOOKIN' BACK** [-] [69] May 76

Aug 76. (7") **TRAVELLIN' MAN (live). / BEAUTIFUL LOSER (live)** [ ] [ ]

— Next 2 albums also credited The MUSCLE SHOALS RHYTHM SECTION on one side apiece. They were **DAVID HOOD** – bass / **ROGER HAWKINS** – drums / **BARRY BECKETT + JIMMY JOHNSON** – horns / **DOUG RILEY** – keyboards / **PETE CARR** – guitar / + **GLENN FREY**

Nov 76. (7") **MAINSTREET. / COME TO POPPA** [ ] [-]

Mar 77. (lp)(c) **NIGHT MOVES** [ ] [8] Nov 76
– Rock and roll never forgets / Night moves / The fire down below / Sunburst / Sunspot baby / Mainstreet / Come to poppa / Ship of fools / Mary Lou. *(re-iss. May82 on 'Fame') (cd-iss.Feb95)*

Mar 77. (7") **NIGHT MOVES. / SHIP OF FOOLS** [ ] [4] Dec76

Apr 77. (7") **MAINSTREET. / JODY GIRL** [-] [24]

Jul 77. (7") **ROCK AND ROLL NEVER FORGETS. / THE FIRE DOWN BELOW** [-] [41]

Sep 77. (7") **ROCK AND ROLL NEVER FORGETS. / SHIP OF FOOLS** [ ] [-]

— **DAVE TEEGARDEN** – drums (ex-STK) repl. CHARLIE (was paralysed from car crash)

May 78. (lp)(c)(silver-lp) **STRANGER IN TOWN** [31] [4]
– Hollywood nights / Still the same / Old time rock & roll / Till it shines / Feel like a number / Ain't got no money / We've got tonite / Brave strangers / The famous final scene. *(cd-iss.Feb95)*

May 78. (7") **STILL THE SAME. / FEEL LIKE A NUMBER** [ ] [4]

Jul 78. (7") **HOLLYWOOD NIGHTS. / BRAVE STRANGERS** [-] [ ]

Aug 78. (7")(7"silver) **HOLLYWOOD NIGHTS. / OLD TIME ROCK & ROLL** [42] [-]

Jan 79. (7") **WE'VE GOT TONITE. / AIN'T GOT NO MONEY** [41] [13] Oct 78

Mar 79. (7") **TILL IT SHINES. / BEAUTIFUL LOSER** [ ] [-]
(12"+=) – Get out of Denver.

Apr 79. (7") **OLD TIME ROCK & ROLL. / SUNSPOT BABY** [-] [28]

Mar 80. (7") **FIRE LAKE. / LONG TWIN SILVER LINE** [ ] [6] Feb 80

Mar 80. (lp)(c) **AGAINST THE WIND** [26] [1]
– The horizontal bop / You'll accomp'ny me / Her strut / No man's land / Long twin silver line / Against the wind / Good for me / Betty Lou's getting out tonight / Fire Lake / Shinin' brightly. *(cd-iss. 1986 & Feb95)*

May 80. (7") **AGAINST THE WIND. / NO MAN'S LAND** [ ] [5] Apr 80

Aug 80. (7") **YOU'LL ACCOMP'NY ME. / BETTY LOU'S GETTING OUT TONIGHT** [ ] [14] Jul 80

Oct 80. (7"m) **AGAINST THE WIND. / GET OUT OF DENVER / NUTBUSH CITY LIMITS** [ ] [-]

Nov 80. (7") **THE HORIZONTAL BOP. / HER STRUT** [-] [42]

Sep 81. (d-lp)(d-c) **NINE TONIGHT (live)** [24] [3]
– Nine tonight / Tryin' to live my life without you / You'll accomp'ny me / Hollywood nights / Old time rock & roll / Mainstreet / Against the wind / The fire down below / Her strut / Feel like a number / Fire Lake / Betty Lou's gettin' out tonight / We've got tonight / Night moves / Rock and roll never forgets / Let it rock. *(cd-iss.Feb95)*

Sep 81. (7") **TRYIN' TO LIVE MY LIFE WITHOUT YOU (live). / BRAVE STRANGERS (live)** [-] [5]

Oct 81. (7")(12") **HOLLYWOOD NIGHTS (live). / BRAVE STRANGERS (live)** [49] [-]

Dec 81. (7") **WE'VE GOT TONIGHT (live). / FEEL LIKE A NUMBER (live)** [60] [-]
(12"+=)(12"red+=) – Brave strangers (live).

Dec 81. (7") **FEEL LIKE A NUMBER (live). / HOLLYWOOD NIGHTS (live)** [-] [48]

— **SEGER** retained **CHRIS CAMPBELL + ALTO REED,** and recruited **ROY BITTAN** – keyboards (of BRUCE SPRINGSTEEN's E-STREET BAND) / **RUSS KUNKEL** – drums / **WADDY WACHTEL** – guitar / **CRAIG FROST** – keyboards (ex-GRAND FUNK RAILROAD)

Dec 82. (7") **SHAME ON THE MOON. / HOUSE BEHIND A HOUSE** [ ] [2]

Dec 82. (lp)(c) **THE DISTANCE** [45] [5]
– Even now / Makin' Thunderbirds / Boomtown blues / Shame on the Moon / Love's the last to know / Roll me away / House behind a house / Comin' home / Little victories. *(cd-iss.1983)*

Mar 83. (7") **EVEN NOW. / LITTLE VICTORIES** [73] [12]
(d7"+=) – We've got tonight / Brave strangers.

Jun 83. (7") **ROLL ME AWAY. / BOOMTOWN BLUES** [ ] [27] May 83

(below 'A'side was used on the film 'Teachers')

Jan 85. (7") **UNDERSTANDING. / EAST L.A.** [ ] [11] Nov 84
(12"+=) – We've got tonite.

— **DON BREWER** – drums (ex-GRAND FUNK RAILROAD) repl. KUNKEL

Mar 86. (7") **AMERICAN STORM. / FORTUNATE SON (live)** [ ] [13]
(12"+=) – Hollywood nights (live).
(d7"++=) – Hollywood nights.

Apr 86. (lp)(c)(cd) **LIKE A ROCK** [35] [3]
– American storm / Like a rock / Miami / The ring / Tightrope / The aftermath / Sometimes / It's you / Somewhere tonight. *(cd+=)*– Living inside my heart / Like a rock (edit) / Fortunate son (live).

Jul 86. (7") **LIKE A ROCK. / LIVING INSIDE MY HEART** [ ] [12] May 86
(12"+=) – Katmandu.

Aug 86. (7") **IT'S YOU. / THE AFTERMATH** [-] [52]

Nov 86. (7") **MIAMI. / SOMEWHERE TONIGHT** [-] [70]

— (below solo 45 from the 'Beverley Hills Cop II' film on 'M.C.A.')

Aug 87. (7")(12") **SHAKEDOWN. / THE AFTERMATH** [ ] [1] May87

Sep 91. (cd)(c)(lp) **THE FIRE INSIDE** [54] [7]
– Take a chance / The real love / Sightseeing / Real at the time / Always in my heart / The fire inside / Which way / New coat of paint / The mountain / The long way home / Blind love / She can't do anything wrong.

Sep 91. (7") **THE REAL LOVE. / WHICH WAY** [ ] [24] Aug 91
(12"+=) – The mountain.
(cd-s++=) – Hollywood nights.

Mar 92. (7")(c-s)(cd-s) **THE FIRE INSIDE. / THE REAL LOVE** [ ] [ ]

Jan 95. (7") **WE'VE GOT TONIGHT. / HOLLYWOOD NIGHTS** [22] [ ]
(c-s+=)(cd-s+=) – C'est la vie.
(cd-s) – ('A'side) / Night moves (live) / Nutbush city limits (live).

Feb 95. (cd)(c)(lp) **GREATEST HITS** (compilation) [6] [8] Nov94
– Roll me away / Night moves / Turn the page / You'll accomp'ny me / Hollywood nights / Still the same / Old time rock & roll / We've got tonight / Against the wind / Main street / The fire inside / Like a rock / C'est la vie / In your time.

Apr 95. (c-s) **NIGHT MOVES / EVEN NOW / WE'VE GOT TONIGHT (live)** [50] [ ]
(cd-s+=) – American storm.
(cd-s) – ('A'side) / Katmandu (live) / The fire down below / The famous final scene.

Jul 95. (c-s)(cd-s) **HOLLYWOOD NIGHTS / ROCK AND ROLL NEVER FORGETS / HOLLYWOOD NIGHTS (live)** [52] [ ]
(cd-s) – ('A'side) / Come to poppa / Fire lake.

Nov 95. (cd)(c) **IT'S A MYSTERY** [ ] [27]
– Rite of passage / Lock and load / By the river / Manhattan / I wonder / It's a mystery / Revisionism street / Golden boy / I can't save you, Angelene / 16 shells from a 30.6 / West of the Moon / Hands in the air.

– compilations, others, etc. –

Jun 77. Reprise; (7"ep) **EXTENDED PLAY** [ ] [-]
– Get out of Denver / Back in '72 / Midnight rider / Rosalie.

Below releases on 'Capitol' unless mentioned.

Nov 77. (7"m) **TURN THE PAGE. / GET OUT OF DENVER (live) / HEAVY MUSIC (live)** [ ] [-]

Sep 83. (7") **OLD TIME ROCK & ROLL. / TILL IT SHINES** [-] [48]

Mar 84. (7") **OLD TIME ROCK & ROLL. / ROLL ME AWAY** [ ] [-]
(12"+=) – Makin' Thunderbirds.

SELECTER

Formed: Birmingham, England . . . mid-79 by NOEL DAVIS with help from JOHN BRADBURY of The SPECIAL AKA who wanted a B-side instrumental filler for the 'Gangsters' 45. After it made the UK Top 10, they branched out on own, having been retained on '2-Tone' label by JERRY DAMMERS, who had set up co-deal with 'Chrysalis'. Their first real debut 'ON MY RADIO', also hit the Top 10, and they enjoyed a degree of fame in the next 18 months. • **Style:** Ska-pop revivalists, with female lead singer, PAULINE BLACK, the difference between them and The SPECIALS, MADNESS and The BEAT. • **Songwriters:** All written by DAVIS and group, except JAMES BOND (John Barry) / TRAIN TO SKAVILLE (Ethiopians) / etc. PAULINE BLACK also covered singles by Johnny Nash & Betty Wright. • **Trivia:** PAULINE went on to host children's TV quiz show 'Hold Tight'.

Recommended: TOO MUCH PRESSURE (*7).

JOHN BRADBURY – drums (of The SPECIAL AKA) / **DESMOND BROWN** – keyboards / **NOEL DAVIS** – guitar / **KEVIN HARRISON** – guitar / **STEVE** – bass

2-Tone / not issued

Jul 79. (7") **Gangsters (by The Special AKA). / THE SELECTER** [6] [-]

— **DESMOND + KEVIN** recruited entire new band. (BRADBURY re-to SPECIALS) new **PAULINE BLACK** – vocals / **CHARLEY ANDERSON** – bass / **COMPTON AMANOUR** – guitar / **CHARLEY 'H' BEMBRIDGE** – drums / **ARTHUR 'GAPS' HENDRICKSON** – vocals

2-Tone/Chrysalis / Chrysalis

Oct 79. (7") **ON MY RADIO. / TOO MUCH PRESSURE** [8] [ ]

Jan 80. (7") **THREE MINUTE HERO. / JAMES BOND** [16] [ ]

Feb 80. (lp)(c) **TOO MUCH PRESSURE** [5] [ ]
– Three minute hero / Every day / They make me mad / Missing words / Danger / Street feeling / My Collie (not a dog) / On my radio / Too much pressure / Murder / Out on the streets / Carry go bring home / Black and blue / James Bond.

Mar 80. (7") **MISSING WORDS. / CARRY GO BRING HOME** [23] [ ]

— **ADAM WILLIAMS** – bass repl. ANDERSON / **JAMES MACKIE** – keyboards, sax repl. BROWN

Chrysalis / Chrysalis

Aug 80. (7") **THE WHISPER. / TRAIN TO SKAVILLE** [36] [ ]

— **NORMAN WATT-ROY** – bass (ex-IAN DURY / BLOCKHEADS) repl. WILLIAMS

Feb 81. (7")(12") **CELEBRATE THE BULLET. / LAST TANGO** [ ] [ ]

Feb 81. (lp)(c) **CELEBRATE THE BULLET** [41] [ ]
– Celebrate the bullet / Tell me what's wrong / (Who likes) Facing situations / Bristol and Miami / Their dream goes on / Cool blue lady / Red reflections / Bombscare / Washed up and left for dead / Selling out your future / Deep water.

— Disbanded mid 1981, but re-formed 11 years later.

Jan 94. (cd-ep) **THE MADNESS EP** [ ] [-]
– Madness / Madness (mix) / The Selecter / On my radio.

Demon / not issued

Jul 94. (cd) **THE HAPPY ALBUM** [ ] [-]
– Reselecterisation / Whip them down / Sweet and dandy / Neurotica / California screaming / I want justice / Trout / Copasetic / Mother knows best / Ladders. *(re-iss.cd Aug95)*

Triple X / not issued

Aug 95. (cd-s) **MADNESS. (with PRINCE BUSTER) /** [ ] [-]

— **BLACK + WELSH** covered RAINY DAY WOMAN (Bob Dylan) / SUGAR TOWN (Lee Hazlewood).

Dojo / not issued

Aug 95. (cd-ep) **HAIRSPRAY EP** [ ] [-]

– Hairspray / Die happy / On my radio (live) / Missing words (live).

Aug 95. (cd) **PUCKER!** -
– My perfect world / Hearsay / Die happy / Sugar town / Hairspray / Chocolate whip / Not so tall / Then she did / Rainy day women / Vicky's magic garden.

– compilations, others, etc. –

Feb 87. Old Gold; (7") **ON MY RADIO. / THREE MINUTE HERO** -
(12"+=) – Missing words / The whisper.

1992. Receiver; (cd)(c)(lp) **OUT IN THE STREETS** -
(re-iss.Oct93) (re-iss.cd Aug95 on 'Triple X')

— In Dec'92, shared an album with The SPECIALS 'BBC RADIO 1 LIVE IN CONCERT'.

— The following year, they scraped into the UK Top 30 with 'ON MY RADIO' from '2-Tone' ep alongside SPECIALS, MADNESS & The BEAT.

Nov 94. Dojo; (cd) **RARE** -
Mar 95. Dojo; (cd) **RARE VOLUME TWO** -
Jun 95. Dojo; (cd) **RARE VOLUME 3 – VERSIONS** -

PAULINE BLACK

Chrysalis not issued

Oct 82. (7")(12") **SHOO-RAH SHOO-RAH. / CALL OF THE WILD** -
Oct 83. (7")(12") **THREW IT AWAY. / I CAN SEE CLEARLY NOW** -

SENATE (see under ⇒ SPEAR OF DESTINY)

SENSATIONAL ALEX HARVEY BAND (see under ⇒ HARVEY, Alex)

SENSELESS THINGS

Formed: Twickenham, London, England ... late '86 by KEDS and NICHOLLS. A year later, they finally got to vinyl, after a session on the John Peel show. This flexi-7" was given free with a fanzine, and led to real debut for 'Red' records late 1988. Further indie 45's appeared, but things really took off in 1992, when on the major 'Epic' label, they smashed into UK Top 20 with 'EASY TO SMILE'. • **Style:** Thrashy amphetamine-rifled rock, lying somewhere between NIRVANA and The JAM!. • **Songwriters:** KEDS penned most, except; SHOPLIFTING (Slits) / BREAK IT AWAY (Perfect Daze) / APACHE (Shadows) / ANSWERING MACHINE (Replacements). • **Trivia:** BEN HARDING was once a clerk for the BBC.

Recommended: THE FIRST OF TOO MANY (*7)

MARK KEDS – vocals, guitar / **BEN HARDING** – lead guitar / **MORGAN NICHOLLS** – bass, guitar / **CASS BROWNE** – drums

Yo Jo Jo not issued

Feb 88. (7"flexi) **I'M MOVING / LOW TIME / (ALL YOU'VE GOT TO DO IS) STAY TOGETHER** -

— (above was given free with 'Shy Like You' fanzine)

Red not issued

Nov 88. (12"ep) **UP AND COMING** -
– Where the secret lies / I want to go back / I don't want to talk about it / You don't want me / When you let me down. *(re-iss.+cd-ep.Feb91)* (+=) – Girlfriend / Standing in the rain.

Way Cool not issued

Mar 89. (7") **GIRLFRIEND. / STANDING IN THE RAIN** -
Oct 89. (7") **TOO MUCH KISSING. / TREVOR** -
Dec 89. (lp)(c)(cd) **POSTCARD C.V.** -
– Trevor / Come together / Sneaking kisses / Laura Lamona / Shoplifting / Drunk & soppy / Back to nowhere / Teenage / Someone in you / Too much kissing / Girlfriend / Standing in the rain. (cd+)(c+=) – UP AND COMING EP.

Decoy not issued

May 90. (7") **IS IT TOO LATE?. / LEO** -
(12"+=)(cd-s+=) – Andi in a karmann / Ponyboy.

May 90. (cd)(m-lp) **IS IT TOO LATE?** - -
– Is it too late? / Leo / Andi is a karmann / Ponyboy / Celebrity / Tricia don't belong. *(only for European export)*

Jul 90. (12"ep)(cd-ep) **CAN'T DO ANYTHING. / CAN'T EXPLAIN / TANGLED LINES** -
(re-issued 2 above in '92)

Epic Epic

Jun 91. (7")(c-s) **EVERYBODY'S GONE. / MYSTERY TRAIN** 73 -
(12"+=)(cd-s+=) – I'm on black and white.

Sep 91. (7") **GOT IT AT THE DELMAR. / FISHING AT TESCOS** 50 -
(12"+=)(c-s+=)(cd-s+=) – Beat to Blondie / Can't remember.

Oct 91. (cd)(c)(lp) **THE FIRST OF TOO MANY** 66
– Everybody's gone / Best friend / Ex teenager / It's cool to hang out with your ex / 19 blues / Should I feel it / Lip radio / In love again / Got it at the Delmar / American dad / Radio Spiteful / Chicken / Wrong number / Different tongues / Fishing at Tescos. *(re-iss.purple-lp Feb92)*

Dec 91. (7"pink)(c-s) **EASY TO SMILE. / HAZEL** 18
(12"+=)(cd-s+=) – Mollylove.

Mar 92. (7"orange)(c-s) **HOLD IT DOWN. / CRUCIAL JUVENILIA** 19
(12"+=)(pic-cd-s+=) – Splitting hairs.

Nov 92. (7")(c-s) **HOMOPHONIC ASSHOLE. / BODY BAG** 52
(12"+=) – Just flirting.
(cd-s++=) – ('A' radio edit).

Feb 93. (7") **PRIMARY INSTINCT. / RUNAWAYS** 41
(12"colrd+=)(cd-s+=) – Too much like I know you.

Mar 93. (cd)(c)(lp) **EMPIRE OF THE SENSELESS** 37
– Homophobic asshole / Keepsake / Tempting Kate / Hold it down / Counting friends / Just one reason / Cruel Moon / Primary instinct / Rise (song for Dean & Gene) / Ice skating at the Milky Way / Say what you will / Runaways. *(re-iss.Jun93 which incl. 'POSTCARD CV')*

Jun 93. (7")(c-s) **TOO MUCH KISSING (remix). / KEEPSAKE / SAY WHAT YOU WILL (demo)** 69
(cd-s) – (1st 2 tracks) / Cruel dub / ('A'original).

Oct 94. (7") **CHRISTINE KEELER. / HIGH ENOUGH** 56
(12") – ('A'side) / Jerk / The revivalist / Can't go back.
(cd-s) – ('A'side) / Jerk / The revivalist / Driving on the right.

Jan 95. (7"colrd) **SOMETHING TO MISS. / 16.18.21** 61
(12"+=)(cd-s+=) – Never haunted / Answering machine.

Feb 95. (cd)(c)(lp) **TAKING CARE OF BUSINESS**
– Christine Keeler / Something to miss / Page 3 valentine / Any which way / Marlene / Role models / Watching the pictures go / Scapegoats / 16.18.21 / Touch me on the heath / Wanted / Too late / Dead sun / The way to the drugstore.

— now without KEDS who joined WILDHEARTS for 2 months before going AWOL

– compilations, etc. –

Feb 94. Strange Fruit; (cd) **THE PEEL SESSIONS** -

SENSER

Formed: Wimbledon, London, England ... late 1990 initially as a trio by NICK MICHAELSON, KERSTIN HAIGH and JAMES BARRETT. Added 4 others including dual singer; male HEITHAM AL-SAYED. Debut single 'EJECT' in 1993, was quickly followed by UK Top 50 single 'THE KEY'. • **Style:** Thrash-metal hip-hop rap, described as Britain's answer to RAGE AGAINST THE MACHINE. • **Songwriters:** Group except; SHE WATCH CHANNEL ZERO (Public Enemy). 'PEACE' was co-written w / TIM MORTON. • **Trivia:** Produced by HAGGIS.

Recommended: STACKED UP (*8)

HEITHAM AL-SAYED (b.1970, Riyadh, Saudi Arabia) – vocals, piano, bongos / **KERSTIN HAIGH** (b.1969, Balham, London) – vocals, flute / **NICK MICHAELSON** (b.1969, London) – guitar / **JAMES BARRETT** (b. 1970, London) – guitar / **ANDY CLINTON** (b. 1969, Buckinghamshire) – DJ / **HAGGIS** (b. 1966, Edinburgh, Scotland) – soundman, engineer / **JOHN MORGAN** (b.London, 1970) – drums

Ultimate Ultimate?

Jun 93. (12")(cd-s) **EJECT / DON'T LOSE YOUR SOUL. / (other mixes)**

Sep 93. (7") **THE KEY. / NO COMPLY** 47
(12"+=)(cd-s+=) – ('A'-radio mix) / ('A'-liquid lunch mix).

Mar 94. (7") **SWITCH. / CHANNEL ZERO**
(12"+=)(cd-s+=) – ('A'-Depth Charge mix) / Age of panic (Eat Static mix).

Apr 94. (cd)(c)(d-lp) **STACKED UP** 4
– States of mind / The key / Switch / Age of panic / What's going on / One touch one bounch / Stubborn / Door game / Peanut game / Peace / Eject / No comply / Worth.

Jul 94. (c-s) **AGE OF PANIC. / LOOKING DOWN THE BARREL OF A GUN (live)** 52
(12"+=)(cd-s+=) – ('A'-sick man mix).

SENTRIDOH (see under ⇒ SEBADOH)

SEPULTURA

Formed: Sao Paolo, Brazil ... 1983 by brothers MAX and IGOR CAVELERA, who took the name SEPULTURA from the MOTORHEAD song 'Dancing On Your Grave'. (Sepultura =Grave; in Spanish). After a few releases on homeland label, they signed in 1986 to 'Roadrunner'. Fortunes changed in 1989, when GLORIA BUJNOWSKI took over management and then married MAX! Their 4th album for the label 'ARISE', surprised many by denting UK Top 40 in 1991. • **Style:** Heavy-metal thrash outfit, influenced by SLAYER and ANTHRAX. **Songwriters:** Group penned, except ORGASMATRON (Motorhead) / DRUG ME (Dead Kennedys) / SYMPTOM OF THE UNIVERSE (Black Sabbath) / THE HUNT (New Model Army) / CLENCHED FIST (Ratos De Porao). • **Trivia:** Drummer IGOR was 14 years old when he played on their 1984 debut release 'BESTIAL DEVASTATION'.

Recommended: ARISE (*7).

MAX CAVELERA – vocals, guitar / **JAIRO T** – guitar/ **PAOLO JR.** – bass / **IGOR CAVELERA** – drums

Cogumelo Brazil not issued

Nov 84. (m-lp) **BESTIAL DEVASTATION (shared with OVERDOSE)** - -
– Bestial devastation / Antichrist / Necromancer / Warriors of death.

Nov 85. (lp) **MORBID VISIONS** - -
– Morbid visions / Mayhem / Troops of doom / War / Crucifixion / Show me the wrath / Funeral rites / Empire of the damned / The curse. *(UK-iss.Apr89 on 'Shark') (UK iss.cd Nov 91 on 'Roadrunner' w/'BESTIAL DEVASTATION') (re-iss.cd/c/lp Apr94 & Aug95)*

— **ANDREAS KISSER** – lead guitar repl.JAIRO T

Roadracer New Renaissance

Feb 87. (lp) **SCHIZOPHRENIA**
– Intro / From the past comes the storms / To the wall / Escape from the void / Inquisition symphony / Screams behind the shadows / Septic schizo / The abyss / R.I.P. (Rest In Peace). *(cd+c+=)* Troops of doom. *(re-iss.+cd.May88 on 'Shark')*

(re-iss.cd/c/lp Apr94 & Aug95)

		Road-runner	Road-runner
Apr 89.	(lp)(c)(cd) **BENEATH THE REMAINS**	[ ]	[ ]

– Beneath the remains / Mass hypnosis / Inner self / Lobotomy / Sarcastic existence / Slaves of pain / Primitive future / Hungry / Stronger than hate. *(re-iss.cd/c/lp Apr94 & Aug95)*

Mar 91. (cd)(c)(lp) **ARISE** — 40 — [ ]
– Arise / Dead embryonic cells / Desperate cry / Murder / Subtraction / Altered states / Under siege (regnum Irae) / Meaningless movements / Infected voice. (pic-lp+=) – Orgasmatron. *(re-iss.cd/c/lp Apr94 & Aug95)*

Mar 91. (12"ep)(c-ep)(cd-ep) **UNDER SIEGE (REGNUM IRAE). / ORGASMATRON / TROOPS OF DOOM (re-recorded)** — [ ] — [ ]

Feb 92. (12"ep)(cd-ep) **ARISE. / TROOPS OF DOOM (live) / INNER SELF (live)** — [ ] — [ ]

(Road-runner / Epic)

Sep 93. (7"pic-d)(c-s)(12")(cd-s) **TERRITORY. / POLICIA / BIOTECH IS GODZILLA** — 66 — [ ]

Oct 93. (cd)(c)(lp)(ltd-cd) **CHAOS A.D.** — 11 — 32
– Refuse-Resist / Territory / Slave new world / Amen / Kaiowas / Propaganda / Biotech is Godzilla / Nomad / We who are not as others / Manifest / The Hunt / Clenched fist *(re-iss.cd-tin Mar94 w/2 extra)*– Policia / Inhuman nature. *(re-iss.Aug95)*

Early in '94, MAX was arrested and fined for stamping on the Brazilian flag. He is said to have done it accidentally.

Feb 94. (7")(c-s)(12"purple)(cd-s) **REFUSE – RESIST. / INHUMAN NATURE / PROPAGANDA** — 51 — [ ]

May 94. (10"colrd-ep)(c-ep)(cd-ep)(12"ep) **SLAVE NEW WORLD. / CRUCIFICADOS PELO SYSTEMA / DRUG ME / ORGASMATRON (live)** — 46 — [ ]
(cd-s) – ('A'side) / Desperate cry.

– compilations, others, etc. –

Nov 89. Shark; (cd) **MORBID VISIONS / CEASE TO EXIST** — [ ] — -
May 90. Shark; (cd) **SCHIZOPHRENIA / MORBID VISIONS** — [ ] — -
Sep 91. Roadrunner; (cd) **BEASTIAL DEVASTATION / MORBID VISIONS** — [ ] — [ ]

NAILBOMB

MAX CAVALERA + ALEX NEWPORT (of FUDGE TUNNEL)

(Road-runner / Roadracer)

Mar 94. (cd)(c)(lp) **POINT BLANK** — 62 — [ ]
– Wasting away / Vai toma no cu / 24 hour bullshit / Guerillas / Blind and lost / Sum of your achievements / Cockroaches / For f***'s sake / World of shit / Exploitation / Religious cancer / Shit panata / Sick life. *(re-iss.Aug95)*

Oct 95. (cd)(c)(lp) **PROUD TO COMMIT COMMERCIAL SUICIDE** — [ ] — [ ]

Will SERGEANT (see under ⇒ ECHO & THE BUNNYMEN)

Brian SETZER (see under ⇒ STRAY CATS)

SEX PISTOLS

Formed: London, England ... Summer 1975 out of THE SWANKERS by COOK, JONES and MATLOCK, whom through their manager MALCOLM McLAREN, found the green-haired JOHN LYDON. He was re-named JOHNNY ROTTEN by JONES, who informed his farting rear-end 'You're rotten, you are'. After a few local gigs, they supported The 101'ers (JOE STRUMMER's band) in April '76. The rest of the year was spent causing havoc and controversy, which led to a £40,000 contract with 'EMI'. Their debut 45 'ANARCHY IN THE UK', having already shocked many on the 'So It Goes' pop TV show, was released Nov'76. It climbed into the Top 40, but after riotous appearances on the 'Today' show, in which they swore at interviewer Bill Grundy, they had single withdrawn from shops. They were also dropped by 'EMI', with label still honouring contract. In Feb'77, they fired MATLOCK, for being too nice, and brought in another violent and abusive character; SID VICIOUS. The next month they signed to 'A&M' for another six-figure sum, but due to protests from other A&M artists, they were dropped once again. Their follow-up single 'GOD SAVE THE QUEEN' had 25,000 copies pressed but it didn't hit the shops, until Richard Branson's 'Virgin' records took the reigns for a meagre £15,000 advance in May'77. It outsold its competing rivals for a No.1 spot, but due to its ban from airplay and major chainstores, it only unjustly reached No.2. Two more classics, 'PRETTY VACANT' & 'HOLIDAYS IN THE SUN', hit the Top 10, before debut album 'NEVER MIND THE BOLLOCKS, HERE'S THE SEX PISTOLS' controversially hit No.1, despite nearly contravening the 1889 indecent advertising act for the use of the word bollocks!. 1978 yet again started with more outrage, with US tours, COOK and JONES flying to Rio in Brazil to see train robber RONNIE BIGGS and JOHN LYDON leaving to form PUBLIC IMAGE LTD (see further below for more). • **Style:** The first punk-rock outfit to break into chart scene, due to their raw heavy R&B garage sound and anarchic attitude of frontman ROTTEN. Their influences ranged from The STOOGES to The NEW YORK DOLLS. • **Songwriters:** Group compositions, until COOK & JONES took over in 1978. They also covered; NO FUN (Stooges) / MY WAY (Paul Anka) / ROCK AROUND THE CLOCK (Bill Haley) / SOMETHIN' ELSE + C'MON EVERYBODY (Eddie Cochran) / JOHNNY B.GOODE (Chuck Berry) / STEPPING STONE (Boyce-Hart) / etc. • **Trivia:** In 1979, they took McLAREN to court for unpaid royalties. In 1986, the official receiver, through McLAREN paid a 7 figure out-of-court settlement to LYDON, JONES, COOK and SID's mother.

Recommended: NEVER MIND THE BOLLOCKS, HERE'S THE SEX PISTOLS (*10) / THE GREAT ROCK'N'ROLL SWINDLE (*8).

JOHNNY ROTTEN (b.JOHN LYDON, 31 Jan'56) – vocals / **STEVE JONES** (b. 3 Sep'55) – guitar / **GLEN MATLOCK** (b.27 Aug'56) – bass / **PAUL COOK** (b.20 Jul'56) – drums

(E.M.I. / not issued)

Nov 76. (7") **ANARCHY IN THE UK. / I WANNA BE ME** — 38 — -

— (Feb77) **SID VICIOUS** (b.JOHN RITCHIE, 10 May'57) – bass, vocals (ex-SIOUXSIE & THE BANSHEES) repl. MATLOCK who soon formed RICH KIDS (Mar77: They signed to 'A&M', but were soon paid off yet again. Some copies of next 45 filtered through and soon w/pic-cover became collector's items).

(Virgin / Warners)

May 77. (7") **GOD SAVE THE QUEEN. / DID YOU NO WRONG** — 2 — -

— (above was banned by the BBC, and outsold the official No.1 at the time; Rod Stewart's 'I Don't Want To Talk About It'.)

Jul 77. (7") **PRETTY VACANT. / NO FUN** — 6 — -
Oct 77. (7") **HOLIDAYS IN THE SUN. / SATELLITE** — 8 — -
Nov 77. (7") **PRETTY VACANT. / SUBMISSION** — - — [ ]
Nov 77. (lp)(c) **NEVER MIND THE BOLLOCKS, HERE'S THE SEX PISTOLS** — 1 — 106
– Holidays in the sun / Bodies / No feelings / Liar / God save the Queen / Problems / Seventeen / Anarchy in the UK / Submission / Pretty vacant / New York / E.M.I. *(7" free w/some copies of above)*- **SUBMISSION** (one-sided). *(pic-lp 1979) (re-iss.+cd.Oct86)(re-iss.cd+c May93)*

— ROTTEN left, reverted to JOHN LYDON and created new band PUBLIC IMAGE LTD. His place was temporarily taken by **RONNIE BIGGS** (the Great Train Robber escapee now exiled in Brazil) 'A'-side vocals / **SID VICIOUS** – 'B'side vocals

Jun 78. (7") **NO ONE IS INNOCENT. / MY WAY** — 7 — [ ]
(some-12"+=) – (interview).

— On 11 Oct'78, SID was charged with the murder of girlfriend NANCY SPUNGEN. MALCOLM McLAREN/'Virgin' bailed him out, but he died 2 Feb'79 of drug overdose. The 1979/80 singles were all taken from THE GREAT ROCK'N'ROLL SWINDLE film.

Feb 79. (7") **SOMETHING ELSE. / FRIGGIN' IN THE RIGGIN'** — 3 — [ ]
Mar 79. (d-lp)(d-c) **THE GREAT ROCK'N'ROLL SWINDLE (Film Soundtrack)** — 7 — [ ]
– God save the Queen symphony / Rock around the clock / Johnny B. Goode / Roadrunner / Black Arabs / Watcha gonna do about it (* on some) / Who killed Bambi? / Silly thing / Substitute / No lip / (I'm not your) Stepping stone / Lonely boy / Somethin' else / Anarchie pour le UK / Einmal war Belsen vortrefflich / No one is innocent / My way / C'mon everybody / E.M.I. / The great rock'n'roll swindle / You need hands / Friggin' in the riggin'. *(re-iss.1-lp May80) (d-cd iss.Jul86, re-iss.+d-cd.1989)(re-iss.cd+cMay93)*

Apr 79. (7") **SILLY THING. / WHO KILLED BAMBI?** — 6 — [ ]

— (above 'A'vocals – **STEVE JONES**, 'B'vocals – **EDDIE TENPOLE TUDOR**) (below 'A'vocals – **SID VICIOUS**)

Jun 79. (7") **C'MON EVERYBODY. / GOD SAVE THE QUEEN SYMPHONY / WATCHA GONNA DO ABOUT IT** — 3 — [ ]
Aug 79. (lp)(c) **SOME PRODUCT: CARRI ON SEX PISTOLS** — 6 — -
– The very name (the Sex Pistols) / From beyond the grave / Big tits across America / The complex world of Johnny Rotten / Sex Pistols will play / Is the Queen a moron / The fuckin' rotter.

Oct 79. (7") **THE GREAT ROCK'N'ROLL SWINDLE. / ROCK AROUND THE CLOCK** — 21 — [ ]
Dec 79. (lp)(c) **SID SINGS ("SID VICIOUS")** — 30 — -
– Born to lose / I wanna be your dog / Take a chance on me / (I'm not your) Stepping stone / My way / Belsen was a gas / Somethin' else / Chatterbox / Search and destroy / Chinese rocks / My way.

Feb 80. (lp)(c) **FLOGGIN' A DEAD HORSE** — 23 — [ ]
– (singles compilation) *(re-iss.+cd.Apr86)*

Jun 80. (7") **(I'M NOT YOUR) STEPPING STONE. / PISTOLS PROPAGANDA** — 21 — -

— COOK and JONES were now The PROFESSIONALS (see further below)

– more compilations, exploitation releases –

Note; on 'Virgin' until mentioned otherwise.

Dec 80. (6x7"box) **PISTOLS PACK** — [ ] — -
– GOD SAVE THE QUEEN. / PRETTY VACANT / / HOLIDAYS IN THE SUN. / MY WAY / / SOMETHING ELSE. / SILLY THING / / C'MON EVERYBODY. / THE GREAT ROCK'N'ROLL SWINDLE / / STEPPING STONE. / ANARCHY IN THE UK / / BLACK LEATHER. / HERE WE GO AGAIN

(below 45 credited EDDIE TENPOLE TUDOR)

Sep 81. (7") **WHO KILLED BAMBI?. / ROCK AROUND THE CLOCK** — [ ] — -
1983. (7") **ANARCHY IN THE UK. / NO FUN** — [ ] — -
(12"+=) – E.M.I. *(cd-ep-iss.Jun88)*
1988. (7") **GOD SAVE THE QUEEN. / DID YOU NO WRONG** — [ ] — -
(cd-s+=) – Don't give me no lip child.
Sep 92. (7")(c-s) **ANARCHY IN THE UK. / I WANNA BE ME** — 33 — [ ]
(cd-s+=) – ('A'demo).
Oct 92. (d-cd)(c)(d-lp) **KISS THIS** — 10 — [ ]
– Anarchy in the UK / God save the Queen / Pretty vacant / Holidays in ther Sun / I wanna be me / Did you no wrong / No fun / Satellite / Don't give me no lip child / (I'm not your) Stepping stone / Bodies / No feelings / Liar / Problems / Seventeen / Submission / New York / E.M.I. / My way / Silly thing / Live in Trondheim 21st July 1977:- Anarchy in the UK / I wanna be me / Seventeen / New York / E.M.I. / No fun / No feelings / Problems / God save the Queen.
Nov 92. (7") **PRETTY VACANT. / NO FEELINGS (demo)** — 56 — [ ]
(cd-s+=) – E.M.I. (demo) / Satellite (demo).
(cd-s) – ('A'side) / Seventeen (demo) / Submission (demo) / Watcha gonna do

about it.
(12"+=) – Satellite (demo) / Seventeen (demo).

Jan 80. Flyover; (lp) **THE BEST OF . . . AND WE DON'T CARE** [ ] [-]
Jan 85. Cherry Red; (7") **LAND OF HOPE AND GLORY. ("EX-PISTOLS") / FLOWERS OF ROMANSK** [69] [-]
Jan 85. Chaos; (m-lp) **THE MINI-ALBUM** [ ] [-]
(re-iss.pic-lp Jan86) (re-iss.as 2-12"pic-dJan89 on 'Antler')
Mar 87. Chaos; (7")(7"yellow)(7"pink) **SUBMISSION. / NO FEELINGS** [ ] [-]
(12")(12"various colours) – ('A'side) / Anarchy in the UK.
Jul 85. Receiver; (lp) **ORIGINAL PISTOLS LIVE (live)** [ ] [-]
(re-iss.+pic-lp Jun86 on 'Demon', re-iss.+cd.Jan89) (re-iss.Dec86 on 'Dojo') (re-iss.May86 on 'Fame', cd-iss.Jul89)
Nov 85. Receiver; (lp) **WHERE WERE YOU IN '77** [ ] [-]
Dec 89. Receiver; (lp)(c)(cd) **NO FUTURE UK?** [ ] [-]
Jan 91. Receiver; (cd)(d-lp) **PRETTY VACANT** [ ] [-]
Aug 85. Konnexion; (lp) **LIVE WORLDWIDE (live)** [ ] [-]
Aug 85. Link; (lp) **LIVE AND LOUD (live)** [ ] [-]
(re-iss.Jun89)
Nov 85. Bondage; (lp)(pic-lp) **BEST OF SEX PISTOLS LIVE (live)** [ ] [-]
Nov 85. Hippy; (lp) **NEVER TRUST A HIPPY** [ ] [-]
Nov 85. '77 Records; (lp) **POWER OF THE PISTOLS** [ ] [-]
Feb 86. McDonald-Lydon; (lp) **THE LAST CONCERT ON EARTH (live)** [ ] [-]
Apr 86. McDonald-Lydon; (12") **ANARCHY IN THE UK (live). / FLOGGING A DEAD HORSE** [ ] [-]
Aug 86. McDonald-Lydon; (lp) **10th ANNIVERSARY ALBUM** [ ] [-]
Jan 87. McDonald-Lydon; (6xlp-box) **THE FILTH AND THE FURY** [ ] [-]
– FILTH & THE FURY / LAST SHOW ON EARTH / 10th ANNIVERSARY ALBUM / ITALIAN DOMOS / NO FUTURE USA / THE REAL SID & NANCY
Aug 86. Archive 4; (12"ep) **ANARCHY IN THE UK / I'M A LAZY SOD. / PRETTY VACANT / SUBSTITUTE** [ ] [-]
May 88. Restless; (lp)(cd) **BETTER LIVE THAN DEAD (live)** [-] [ ]
Jun 88. MBC; (lp)(cd) **IT SEEMED TO BE THE END UNTIL THE NEXT BEGINNING** [ ] [-]
Oct 88. Specific; (cd) **ANARCHY WORLDWIDE** [ ] [-]
Oct 88. Specific; (cd-ep) **CASH FOR CHAOS** [ ] [-]
Feb 90. Action Replay; (cd)(c) **THE BEST OF AND THE REST OF THE SEX PISTOLS** [ ] [-]
Jul 95. Dojo; (cd) **WANTED – THE GOODMAN TAPES** [ ] [-]

PROFESSIONALS

STEVE JONES – vocals, guitar / **PAUL COOK** – drums / **ANDY ALLEN** – guitar, vocals / **RAY McVEIGH** – guitar, vocals / **PAUL MYERS** – bass (ex-SUBWAY SECT)

Virgin — not issued

Jul 80. (7") **JUST ANOTHER DREAM. / ACTION MAN** [ ] [-]
Aug 80. (lp)(c) **THE PROFESSIONALS** [ ] [-]
– All the way / Are you? / Kick down the doors / Crescendo / Little boys in blue / Does anybody care / Kamikaze / 1-2-3 / Rockin' Mick.
Sep 80. (7"m) **1-2-3. / BABY I DON'T CARE / WHITE LIGHT, WHITE HEAT** [43] [-]
May 81. (7") **JOIN THE PROFESSIONALS. / HAS ANYBODY GOT AN ALIBI** [ ] [-]
Oct 81. (7") **THE MAGNIFICENT. / JUST ANOTHER DREAM** [ ] [-]
Nov 81. (lp)(c) **I DIDN'T SEE IT COMING** [ ] [-]
– The magnificent / Payola / Northern slide / Friday night square / Kick down the doors / Little boys / All the way / Crescendo / Madhouse / Too far to fall.

— PROFESSIONALS split early in '82 and COOK joined CHIEFS OF RELIEF. STEVE JONES joined IGGY POP and went solo in 1987 releasing 'MERCY'.

— — Stop press; the original SEX PISTOLS have re-formed at the back end of '95. Messrs LYDON, JONES, COOK + MATLOCK will tour summer '96.

SHADOWS

Formed: London, England . . . 1958 as the FIVE CHESTERNUTS by HANK MARVIN, BRUCE WELCH and PETE CHESTER (son of comedian Charlie Chester). They signed to EMI's 'Columbia' label and issued one flop single which was aired for BBC TV's '6.5 Special'. In Sep'58, they were spotted by CLIFF RICHARD's manager John Foster, who needed a replacement for guitarist KEN PAVEY. Called The DRIFTERS at this time, HANK MARVIN agreed to join, but only if WELCH joined as well. The next month, the pair teamed up with IAN SAMWELL (now on bass) & TERRY SMART to augment CLIFF on tour. In Nov'58, CLIFF brought in new replacement for IAN SAMWELL (who stays on as manager, etc.); JET HARRIS, and they appeared on 'LIVIN' LOVIN' DOLL'. To end this hectic year, TONY MEEHAN replaced SMART and they soon had own debut 'FEELIN' FINE' released. After another flop and an injunction served on them by the American group of the same name, they became The SHADOWS. Following their first vocal miss, they hit No.1 in July 1960 with an instrumental classic 'APACHE'. They went on to be the biggest UK group of the early 60's. The decided to disband late in 1968, after heated arguments and decreasing record sales. They re-formed again in various guises, but were not really in public eye again until April 1975, when they were the dreaded entry in The Eurovision Song Contest. Their vocal song 'LET ME BE THE ONE' came second, but had consolation in the fact, that it gave them their first Top 20 hit in just under 10 years. Early in 1979, their version of Evita's 'DON'T CRY FOR ME ARGENTINA' hit No.5, and paved the way for a middle-aged comeback in the 80's, although mainly with albums. • **Style:** Initially a mainly instrumental guitar-based beat combo, led by bespectacled HANK MARVIN (the boyhood hero of many). In the mid-60's they added more vocal songs to their repertoire, and lost their musical identity in the process, thus leading to eventual failure. In 1979, the clear sound of HANK and The SHADOWS were back once more, producing fine although not specky tackular re-inditions of classic standards (see below). • **Songwriters:** First songs written by/with PETE CHESTER or IAN SAMWELL. The group, mainly MARVIN and WELCH pen some, but mainly use other worldly sources; JERRY LORDAN wrote APACHE / WONDERFUL LAND / etc. His wife PETRINA penned A PLACE IN THE SUN. Their producer NORRIE PARAMOUR wrote THE FRIGHTENED CITY + THE SAVAGE. MAN OF MYSTERY + KON-TIKI (Michael Carr). They also covered ('A'singles only, their were loads more); DANCE ON (Avons) / DON'T MAKE MY BABY BLUE (hit; Frankie Laine) / THE WARLORD (Jerome Moross) / MAROC 7 + LET ME BE THE ONE (Paul Ferris; a friend) / SLAUGHTER ON 10th AVENUE (Richard Rodgers) / DON'T CRY FOR ME ARGENTINA (Tim Rice-Andrew Lloyd Webber) / DEER HUNTER (John Williams) / RODRIGO'S GUITAR CONCERTO (Manuel; Geoff Love) / RIDERS IN THE SKY (Stan Jones; hit, Ramrods) / EQUINOXE V (Jean-Michel Jarre) / MOZART FORTE (Mozart; hit, Waldo De La Rios) / TELSTAR (Tornados) / TREAT ME NICE (Elvis Presley) / MISSING (Vangelis) / GOIN' HOME (Mark Knopfler) / MOONLIGHT SHADOW (Mike Oldfield) / DANCING IN THE DARK (Bruce Springsteen) / EASTENDERS-HOWARD'S WAY + PULASKI (TV themes) / SNOWMAN (hit; Aled Jones) / etc, etc, etc. • **Trivia:** WELCH married in 1959, but left her 8 years later for singer OLIVIA NEWTON JOHN. They did not marry and broke up in 1972, which led to an attempted suicide by WELCH. He married again in '79 to close friend Lynne. The group appeared in CLIFF's films; THE YOUNG ONES / SUMMER HOLIDAY (title track penned by MARVIN & BENNETT) / WONDERFUL LIFE / ALADDIN . . . + CINDERELLA (wrote and performed the pantomimes).

Recommended: 20 GOLDEN GREATS (*8)

FIVE CHESTERNUTS

HANK MARVIN (b.BRIAN RANKIN, 28 Nov'41, Newcastle, England) – lead guitar / **BRUCE WELCH** (b.CRIPPS, 2 Nov'41, Bognor Regis, England) – rhythm guitar / **GERALD HURST** – vocals / **PETER CHESTER** – drums / **NEIL JOHNSON** – bass

Columbia — not issued

Aug 58. (7") **TEENAGE LOVE. / JEAN DOROTHY** [ ] [-]

DRIFTERS

Oct'58. They were also backing CLIFF RICHARD. **IAN SAMWELL** – bass + **TERRY SMART** – drums repl. all bar **MARVIN + WELCH**(Oct-Dec58) / **JET HARRIS** (b.TERRENCE, 6 Jul'39, London) – bass (ex-VIPERS) repl. IAN SAMWELL who became their manager in 1959) / **TONY MEEHAN** (b.DANIEL, 2 Mar'43, London) – drums (ex-VIPERS) repl. TERRY SMART who joined the merchant navy.

Columbia — not issued

Feb 59. (7") **FEELIN' FINE. / DON'T BE A FOOL WITH LOVE** [ ] [-]
Jul 59. (7") **JET BLACK. / DRIFTIN'** [ ] [ ]

— Above single released in the US as "The FOUR JETS" (see below)

SHADOWS

Name was taken to avoid confrontation with American soul/R&B group.
They remained CLIFF RICHARD's backers.

Columbia — Atlantic

Dec 59. (7") **SATURDAY DANCE. / LONESOME FELLA** [ ] [-]

— (above 'A'side featured vocals by BRUCE)

Jul 60. (7") **APACHE. / QUARTERMASTER'S STORES** [1] [-]
Oct 60. (7") **MAN OF MYSTERY. / THE STRANGER** [5] [ ]
Jan 61. (7") **F.B.I. / MIDNIGHT** [6] [-]
May 61. (7") **FRIGHTENED CITY. / BACK HOME** [3] [-]
Jun 61. (7") **FRIGHTENED CITY. / F.B.I.** [-] [ ]
Aug 61. (7") **KON TIKI. / 36-24-36** [1] [ ]
Sep 61. (lp) **THE SHADOWS** [1] [-]
– Shadoogie / Nivram / Blue star / Theme from a filletted plaice / Sleepwalk / See you in my dreams / Stand up and say that / All my sorrows / That's my desire / Find me a golden street / Big boy / Gonzales / My resistance is low / Baby my heart. *(re-iss.+c.May83 on 'Fame')*

— **BRIAN BENNETT** (b. 9 Feb'40, London) – drums repl. MEEHAN (see below)

Nov 61. (7") **THE SAVAGE. / PEACE PIPE** [10] [-]
Feb 62. (7") **WONDERFUL LAND. / STARS FELL ON STOCKTON** [1] [ ]

— **BRIAN 'Licorice' LOCKING** – bass repl. JET HARRIS to own duo with MEEHAN

Jul 62. (7") **GUITAR TANGO. / WHAT A LOVELY TUNE** [4] [ ]
Oct 62. (lp) **OUT OF THE SHADOWS** [1] [-]
– The rumble / The bandit / Perfidia / Cosy / Some are lonely / Little B / Spring is nearly here / Bo Diddley / Kinda cool / 1861 / South of the border / Are they all like you / Tales of a raggy tramline. *(re-iss.+c.Aug86 on 'Awareness')*
(above album still featured JET on some tracks)
Dec 62. (7") **DANCE ON. / ALL DAY** [1] [-]
Dec 62. (7") **DANCE ON. / RUMBLE** [-] [-]
Mar 63. (7") **FOOT TAPPER. / THE BREEZE AND I** [1] [-]
May 63. (7") **ATLANTIS. / I WANT YOU TO BUY ME** [2] [-]
Jun 63. (lp) **GREATEST HITS** (compilation) [2] [-]
– Apache / Man of mystery / F.B.I. / Midnight / Frightened city / Kon-tiki / 36-24-36 / The savage / Peace pipe / Wonderful land / Stars fell on Stockton / Guitar tango / The boys / Dance on / The stranger.
(re-iss.Aug71 / re-iss.May74, hit No.48) (cd-iss.May89 on 'E.M.I.')
Sep 63. (7") **SHINDIG. / IT'S BEEN A BLUE DAY** [6] [-]

— **JOHN ROSTILL** (b.16 Jun'42, Birmingham, England) – bass (ex-INTERNS) repl. LOCKING. They shared duties on below album.

Nov 63. (7") **GERONIMO. / SHAZAM** 11 -
Feb 64. (7") **THEME FOR YOUNG LOVERS. / THIS HAMMER** 12 -
May 64. (7") **THE RISE & FALL OF FLINGEL BUNT. / IT'S A MAN'S WORLD** 5 -
May 64. (lp) **DANCE WITH THE SHADOWS** 2 -
– Chattanooga choo choo / Blue shadows / Fandango / Tonight / That's the way it goes / Don't it make you feel good / Big 'B' / Dakota / In the mood / The lonely bull / French dressing / The high and the mighty / Zambesi / Temptation.
Jun 64. (7") **THE RISE AND FALL OF FLINGEL BUNT. / THEME FOR YOUNG LOVERS** -
Aug 64. (7") **RHYTHM AND GREENS. / THE MIRACLE** 22
Nov 64. (7") **GENIE WITH THE LIGHT BROWN LAMP. / PRINCESS** 17 -

— Next 45 with vocals, as was alternate singles until MAROC 7 instrumental.

— **HANK + BRIAN** also added keyboards to repertoire.

Feb 65. (7") **MARY ANNE. / CHU-CHI** 17 -
May 65. (7") **STINGRAY. / ALICE IN SUNDERLAND** 19 -
Jul 65. (lp) **SOUND OF THE SHADOWS** 4 -
– A little bitty tear / Five hundred miles / Let it be me / Brazil / Lost city / Blue sky, blue sea, blue me / Bossa roo / Cotton pickin' / Santa Ana / The windjammer / Deep purple / Dean's theme / Breakthru / National provincial samba.
Jul 65. (7") **DON'T MAKE MY BABY BLUE. / MY GRANDFATHER** 10 -
Nov 65. (7") **WARLORD. / WISH I COULD SHIMMY** 18 -
Dec 65. (lp) **MORE HITS!** (compilation) -
– Foot tapper / Atlantis / Shindig / Theme for young lovers / Geronimo / Shazam / The rise and fall of Flingel Bunt / Genie with the light brown lamp / Mary-Anne / Stingray / Rhythms and greens / Don't make my baby blue / Lute number / Drum number. *(re-iss.Aug85) (cd-iss.May89 on 'E.M.I.')*
Mar 66. (7") **I MET A GIRL. / LATE LAST NIGHT** 22 -
May 66. (lp) **SHADOW MUSIC** 5 -
– Razzamatazz / I only want to be with you / Babes in the wood / Only one way to love / Stay around / In the past / Bento-San / Fly me to the Moon / 4th street / A sigh (un sospero) / Don't stop now / March to Drina / The magic doll / Now that you're gone / Maid Marion's theme.
Jun 66. (7") **A PLACE IN THE SUN. / WILL YOU BE THERE** 24 -
Oct 66. (7") **THE DREAMS I DREAM. / SCOTCH ON THE SOCKS** 42 -
Mar 67. (7") **MAROC 7. / BOMBAY DUCK** 24 -
Jul 67. (lp) **JIGSAW** 8 -
– Prelude in E major / Jigsaw / Waiting for Rosie / With a hym hym on my knee / Chelsea boot / Winchester cathedral / Green eyes / Stardust / Marie Elena / Tennessee waltz / Trains and boats and planes / Cathy's clown / Semi-detached Mr.James / Friday on my mind. *(re-iss.+cd+c.Apr90 on 'B.G.O.')*
Sep 67. (7") **TOMORROW'S CANCELLED. / SOMEWHERE** -
Dec 67. (lp) **FROM HANK, BRUCE, BRIAN AND JOHN** -
– Snap, crackle and how's your dad / Evening glow / A thing of beauty / Naughty Nippon nights / The wild roses / The letter / San Francisco / The day I met Marie / Holy cow / I'm a believer. *(re-iss.+cd+c.Apr90 on 'B.G.O.')*
Jan 68. (7") **LONDON'S NOT TOO FAR. (as "HANK MARVIN & THE SHADOWS") / RUNNING OUT OF THE WORLD** -
Mar 68. (7") **DEAR OLD MRS.BELL. / TRYING TO FORGET THE ONE YOU LOVE** -

— The SHADOWS split late '68, after release in October of shared lp 'ESTABLISHED 1958' with CLIFF RICHARD.

BRIAN BENNETT

— had already issued solo tracks with sextet group.

Columbia / not issued

Oct 67. (lp) **CHANGE OF DIRECTION** -
– Memphis / Sunshine Superman / Sunny afternoon / 98.6 / Canvas / Slippery Jim De Grize / Whisper not / Tricycle / On Broadway / Little old lady / Can Alma / Change of direction.
Oct 67. (7") **SLIPPERY JIM DE GRIZE. / CANVAS** -

Studio One / not issued

Sep 69. (lp) **THE ILLUSTRATED LONDON NOISE** -
– Love and occasional rain / I heard it through the grapevine / Chameleon / Witchita lineman / Just lookin' in / General Mojo's well-laid plan / In the heat of the night / Soul mission / Take me in your arms and love me / Rocky Racoon / Air / Ticket to ride. *(re-iss.both as d-lp.Nov87 on 'See For Miles')*

HANK MARVIN

solo, augmented by **BENNETT,** etc.

Columbia / not issued

Mar 69. (7") **GOODNIGHT DICK. / WAHINE** -
1969. (7") **SUNDAY FOR SEVEN DAYS. / SASHA** -
1969. (7") **BREAK ANOTHER DAWN. / MORNING STAR** -

— In Sep'69, HANK's duet with CLIFF 'Throw Down A Line' hits No.7. March the next year, another duet 'Joy Of Living' hits No.25.

Nov 69. (lp) **HANK MARVIN** 14 -
– Aquarius / Born free / This guy's in love with you / The big country / Tokyo guitar / Chameleon / Georgia on my mind / The windmills of your mind / Somewhere my love (Lara's theme) / Love and occasional rain / Sasha / High Sierra.

SHADOWS

re-formed in mid'69. **ALAN HAWKSHAW** – guitar, keyboards repl. WELCH (see further below)

Parlophone / not issued

Oct 69. (7") **SLAUGHTER ON 10th AVENUE. / MIDNIGHT COWBOY (by "HANK MARVIN")** -

— Now augmented by bassmen; **HERBIE FLOWERS, DAVE RICHMOND + BRIAN HODGES**

Oct 70. (lp)(c) **SHADES OF ROCK** -
– Proud Mary / My babe / Lucille / Johnny B.Goode / Paperback writer / (I can't get no) Satisfaction / Bony Moronie / Get back / Something / River deep, mountain high / Memphis / What'd I say.

— They disbanded again in 1970. ROSTILL re-joined TOM JONES band, he was later electrocuted on 26 Nov'73, when playing guitar in his home.

MARVIN, WELCH & FARRAR

formed singing trio (**FARRAR** – b.Australia), augmented by **HAWKSHAW, RICHMOND / CLEM CATTINI** – drums / **PETER VINCE** – organ

Regal Zono. / not issued

Jan 71. (7") **FAITHFUL. / MR.SUN** -
Feb 71. (lp)(c) **MARVIN, WELCH & FARRAR** 30 -
– You're burning bridges / A thousand conversations / Brownie Kentucky / My home town / Silvery rain / Throw down a line / Baby I'm calling you / Faithful / Mistress Fate & Father Time / Take her away / Wish you were here / Mr. Sun / Strike a light. *(cd-iss.Aug91 on 'See For Miles', with extra tracks)*

— The trio now augmented by **BENNETT, HAWKSHAW + RICHMOND**

May 71. (7") **LADY OF THE MORNING. / TINY ROBIN** -
Nov 71. (lp)(c) **SECOND OPINION** -
– Black eyes / Tiny Robin / Ronnie / Far away falling / Lady of the morning / Let's say goodbye / Lonesome mole / The time to come / Thank Heaven's I've got you / Come back to natre / All day, all night blues. *(cd-iss.Aug91 on 'See For Miles', with extra tracks)*
Apr 72. (7") **MARMADUKE. / STRIKE A LIGHT** -

— Early in 1972, when WELCH's girlfriend (OLIVIA NEWTON-JOHN) broke off engagement, he attempted suicide. The remaining 5 members became part of

MARVIN & FARRAR

E.M.I. / not issued

Aug 73. (7") **MUSIC MAKES MY DAY. / SKIN DEEP** -
Aug 73. (lp)(c) **HANK MARVIN AND JOHN FARRAR** -
– So hard to live with / Music makes my day / Skin deep / If I rewrote yesterdays / Galadrie / Love oh love / Help me into your wagon / Small and lonely night / You never can tell / Nobody cares / Lord how it's hurting. *(cd-iss.Aug91 on 'See For Miles' with extra tracks)*

SHADOWS

reformed (**MARVIN, WELCH, FARRAR + BENNETT**)

E.M.I. / not issued

Nov 73. (7") **TURN AROUND AND TOUCH ME. / JUNGLE JAM** -

— added **ALAN TARNEY** – bass

Dec 73. (lp)(c) **ROCKIN' WITH CURLY LEADS** 45 -
– Pinball wizard – See me, feel me / Years away / Deep roots / Humbucker / Jungle jam / Gracie / Good vibrations / Rockin' with curly leads / Turn around and touch me / Wide mouthed frog / Gutbucket / Jumpin' Jack input.
Apr 74. (7") **PLEASE MR.PLEASE ("BRUCE WELCH" solo). / SONG OF YESTERDAY** -

— same 5-piece, but **WELCH** now vocals, **TARNEY** – piano. Below was second in The Eurovision Song Contest.

Mar 75. (7") **LET ME BE THE ONE. / STAND UP LIKE A MAN** 12 -
Apr 75. (lp)(c) **SPECS APPEAL** 30 -
– God only knows / Cool clear air / Rose, Rose / This house runs on sunshine / Colarado songbird / No no Nina / Don't throw it all away / Honourable puff-puff / Spider juice / Let me be the one / Like strangers / Stand up like a man.
Jun 75. (7") **RUN BILLY RUN. / HONOURABLE PUFF-PUFF** -
Oct 75. (7") **SMALL AND LONELY NIGHT. ("MARVIN & FARRAR") / GALADRIEL (SPIRIT OF STARLIGHT)** -
Nov 75. (lp)(c) **LIVE AT THE PARIS OLYMPIA (live April'75)** -
– The rise and fall of Flingel Bunt / Man of mystery / Lady of the morning / Nivram / Tiny Robin / Sleepwalk / Guitar tango / Honourable puff-puff / Apache / Shadoogie / Marmaduke / Somewhere / Little 'B' / Medley (Lucille – Rip it up – Blue suede shoes). *(re-iss.Apr81 on 'M.F.P.', w/free other live at Sankei Hall) (cd-iss.Feb92)*
Jun 76. (7") **IT'LL BE ME BABE. / LIKE STRANGERS** -

— In Jan'77, the TV advertised compilation '20 GOLDEN GREATS' hit No.1

— **FRANCIS MONKMAN** – keyboards repl. FARRAR who went to solo & Australia. / **ALAN JONES** – bass repl. TARNEY

Jul 77. (7") **ANOTHER NIGHT. / CRICKET BAT BOOGIE** -
Aug 77. (lp)(c) **TASTY** -
– Cricket bat boogie / Return to the Alamo / Another night / Goodbye yellow brick road / Honky tonk woman / Montezuma's revenge / Walk don't run / Superstar / Bermuda triangle / The most beautiful girl in the world / Creole nights.
Aug 78. (7") **LOVE DE LUXE. / SWEET SATURDAY NIGHT** -

— **CLIFF HALL** – keyboards (ex-CLIFF RICHARD Band) repl. MONKMAN to SKY They were now virtually a trio of **MARVIN, WELCH & BENNETT**

Nov 78. (7") **DON'T CRY FOR ME ARGENTINA. / MONTEZUMA'S REVENGE** 5 -

— In Feb79, their album with CLIFF 'THANK YOU VERY MUCH' hit No.5.

Apr 79. (7") **THEME FROM 'THE DEER HUNTER'. / BERMUDA TRIANGLE** 9 -
Sep 79. (lp)(c) **STRING OF HITS** 1 -
– Riders in the sky / Parisienne walkways / Heart of glass / Classical gas / You're the one that I want / Theme from 'The Deer Hunter' / Bridge over troubled water / Don't cry for me Argentina / Song for Duke / Bright eyes / Rodrigo's guitar de Aranjuez / Baker street. *(re-iss.Sep85 on 'M.F.P.', cd-iss.Sep88) (cd-iss.Oct87)*
Oct 79. (7") **RODRIGO'S GUITAR CONCERTO. / SONG FOR DUKE** -
Jan 80. (7") **RIDERS IN THE SKY. / RUSK** 12 -
Jul 80. (7") **HEART OF GLASS. / RETURN OF THE ALAMO** -

Polydor / not issued

Aug 80. (7") **EQUINOXE V. / FENDER BENDER** 50 -
Sep 80. (lp)(c) **CHANGE OF ADDRESS** 17 -

– Mozart forte / Midnight creeping / Change of address / Just the way you are / Indigo-Outdigo / Arty's party / Albatross / Hello Mr.W.A.M. / Temptation / If you leave me now / Equinoxe V. *(re-iss.Aug83)*
Nov 80. (7") **MOZART FORTE. / MIDNIGHT CREEPING** [ ] [-]
Apr 81. (7") **THE THIRD MAN. / THE FOURTH MAN** [44] [-]
Sep 81. (7") **TELSTAR. / SUMMER LOVE '59** [ ] [-]
Sep 81. (lp)(c) **HITS RIGHT UP YOUR STREET** [15] [-]
– Telstar / Chi Mai (theme from 'The Life & Times Of David Lloyd George') / We don't talk anymore / Imagine; Woman / Hats off to Wally / One day I'll fly away / Summer love '59 / Misty / This ole house / The winner takes all / Sailing / Nut rocker / Thing-me-jig / More than I can say / Cowboy cafe / The third man.
Nov 81. (7") **IMAGINE; WOMAN. / HATS OFF TO WALY** [ ] [-]
May 82. (7") **TREAT ME NICE. / SPOT THE BALL** [ ] [-]
Jul 82. (7") **THE THEME FROM 'MISSING'. / THE SHADY LADY** [ ] [-]
Sep 82. (2xlp)(d-c) **LIFE IN THE JUNGLE** [24] [-]
– Life in the jungle / High noon / The theme from 'Missing' / Treat me nice / Cat'n'mouse / Chariots of fire / No dancing / Riders of the range / The old romantics / You rescue me / Lili Marlene / Raunchy. *(re-iss.as lp Jan85) (cd-iss.May89)* **LIVE AT ABBEY ROAD (live)** – The third man / Thing-me-jig / Runaway / All I have to do is dream / It doesn't matter anymore / Johnny B.Goode / Over in a flash / Summer love '59 / Oh! boy / Crying in the rain / Arty's party. *(cd-iss.May89)*
Aug 83. (7") **DIAMONDS. / ELEVEN IS** [ ] [-]
Oct 83. (lp)(c) **XXV** [34] [-]
– Africa / Goin' home (theme from 'Local Hero') / Up where we belong / You don't have to say you love me / The modern way / Diamonds / Time is tight / Memory / Liverpool days / Queen of hearts / A whiter shade of pale. *(cd-iss.1988)*
Oct 83. (7") **GOIN' HOME. / CAT'N'MOUSE** [ ] [-]
Aug 84. (7") **ON A NIGHT LIKE THIS. / THING-ME-JIG** [ ] [-]
Nov 84. (lp)(c)(cd) **GUARDIAN ANGEL** [98] [-]
– How do I love thee / Hammerhead / The Saturday western / On a night like this / Look back on love / Johnny Staccato / I will return / (I'm gonna be your) Guardian angel / Can't play your game / Turning point / Our Albert.
May 86. (7") **MOONLIGHT SHADOW. / JOHNNY STACCATO** [ ] [-]
May 86. (lp)(c)(cd) **MOONLIGHT SHADOWS** [6] [-]
– Moonlight shadow / Walk of life / I just called to say I love you / Hello / Every breath you take / Nights in white satin / The power of love / Three times a lady / Against all odds / Hey Jude / Dancing in the dark / Imagine / I know him so well / Memory / Sailing / A whiter shade of pale. *(re-iss.cd/c Apr95)*
Aug 86. (7") **DANCING IN THE DARK. / TURNING POINT** [ ] [-]
(12"+=) – ('A'version).
Nov 86. (7") **EASTENDERS; HOWARD'S WAY. / NO DANCING!** [ ] [-]
Oct 87. (7") **PULASKI. / CHANGE OF ADDRESS** [ ] [-]
Oct 87. (lp)(c)(cd) **SIMPLY SHADOWS** [11] [-]
– I knew you were waiting (for me) / We don't need another hero / Theme from 'The Snowman' / Careless whisper / Don't give up / I guess that's why they call it the blues / A heart will break tonight / The lady in red / Pulaski / Take my breath away / Eastenders / I want to know what love is / Skye boat song / Jealous guy / Chain reaction / Howard's way.
Nov 87. (7") **THEME FROM THE SNOWMAN. / OUTDIGO** [ ] [-]
Apr 89. (7") **MOUNTAINS OF THE MOON. / STACK-IT** [ ] [-]
(cd-s+=) – Turning point.
May 89. (lp)(c)(cd) **STEPPIN' TO THE SHADOWS** [11] [-]
– You win again / I wanna dance with somebody (who loves me) / He ain't heavy, he's my brother / Candle in the wind / Farewell my lovely / Mountains of the Moon / Nothing's gonna change my love for you / Heaven is a place on Earth / When the going gets tough / Alone / All I ask of you / Stack-it / Shoba / You keep me hangin' on / Some people / One moment in time. *(re-iss.cd+c May93 on 'Spectrum')*
Oct 90. (cd)(c)(lp) **REFLECTION** [6] [-]
– Eye of the tiger / Crockett's theme / Right here waiting / Every little thing she does is magic / Sealed with a kiss / Uptown girl / Strawberry fields forever / Riders in the sky '90 / Flashdance / Something's gotten hold of my heart / Love changes everything / Nothing's gonna stop us now / Bilitis / You'll never walk alone / Always on my mind / Megamix.
Oct 91. (cd)(c)(lp) **THEMES AND DREAMS** [21] [-]
– Crockett's theme / Up where we belong / Take my breath away / Theme from The Deerhunter / Walking in the air / If you leave me now / One day I'll fly away / Africa / Every breath you take / Memory / Nights in white satin / Candle in the wind / You win again / Sailing / Just the way you are / Moonlight shadow.

– more compilations, etc. –

Oct 62. Columbia; (7"ep) **THE BOYS** [ ] [-]
– The boys / The girls / Sweet dreams / (1 CLIFF RICHARD track).
Aug 83. Columbia; (d-lp)(c) **SOUND OF THE SHADOWS / DANCE WITH THE SHADOWS** [ ] [-]
(re-iss.Sep86 on 'M.F.P.') (cd-iss.Mar91 on 'E.M.I.')
Nov 69. Regal Starline; (lp)(c) **SOMETHIN' ELSE** [ ] [-]
Oct 72. MFP; (lp)(c) **MUSTANG** [ ] [-]
Jan 78. MFP; (lp)(c) **THE SHADOWS AT THE MOVIES** [ ] [-]
Feb 80. MFP; (lp)(c) **ROCK ON WITH THE SHADOWS** [ ] [-]
Sep 89. MFP; (lp)(c)(cd) **THE SHADOWS IN THE 60's** [ ] [-]
May 89. CMP; (cd) **LISTEN TO THE SHADOWS** [ ] [-]
Nov 72. Parlophone; (7"m) **APACHE. / WONDERFUL LAND / F.B.I.** [ ] [-]
(re-iss.Feb77 on 'E.M.I.')
Jan 75. Ember; (lp)(c) **THE SHADOWS** [ ] [-]
Nov 76. Nut-EMI; (lp)(c) **RARITIES** [ ] [-]
(cd-iss.Mar93)
Jan 77. EMI; (lp)(c) **20 GOLDEN GREATS** [1] [-]
– Apache / Frightened city / Guitar tango / Kon-tiki / Genie with the light brown lamp / The warlord / A place in the Sun / Atlantis / Wonderful land / F.B.I. / The savage / Geronimo / Shindig / Stingray / Theme for young lovers / The rise and fall of Flingel Bunt / Maroc 7 / Dance on / Man of mystery / Foot tapper. *(cd-iss. Aug 87)*
Feb 79. EMI; (lp)(c) **THANK YOU VERY MUCH (with "CLIFF RICHARD")** [5] [-]
Jul 80. EMI; (lp)(c) **ANOTHER STRING OF HOT HITS** [ ] [-]
(re-iss.Nov83 on 'M.F.P.', cd-iss.Oct87)
May 84. EMI; (lp)(c) **THE SHADOWS' VOCALS** [ ] [-]
Feb 90. EMI; (d-cd)(d-c)(d-lp) **THE ORIGINAL CHART HITS 1960-1980** [ ] [-]
(d-cd+=) – (11 tracks).
Mar 91. EMI; (cd) **THE SHADOWS / OUT OF THE SHADOWS** [ ] [-]
Feb 92. EMI; (cd) **SHADOW MUSIC / SHADES OF ROCK** [ ] [-]
Nov 93. EMI; (d-cd)(d-c) **THE DEFINITIVE GUITAR ALBUM** [ ] [-]
Sep 83. Tellydisc; (d-lp) **SHADOWS SILVER ALBUM** [ ] [-]
Sep 84. Polydor; (cd) **COMPACT SHADOWS** [ ] [-]
Dec 89. Polydor; (lp)(c)(cd) **AT THEIR VERY BEST** [ ] [-]
Sep 90. Polydor; (7"ep)(12"ep)(cd-ep) **SHADOWFAX** [ ] [-]
– Apache – Wonderful land – Rise and fall of Flingel Bunt – Kon Tiki – F.B.I. – Man of mystery – Apache.
Jan 85. VFM; (c) **HITS OF THE SHADOWS VOLUME 1** [ ] [-]
May 86. Hour Of Pleasure; (c) **AN HOUR OF THE SHADOWS** [ ] [-]
1987. Exclusive; (pic-lp) **DRIFTIN'** [ ] [-]
Jun 87. Pathe Marconi; (d-lp)(c) **DOUBLE ALBUM** [ ] [-]
Jan 89. See For Miles; (cd) **THE EP COLLECTION** [ ] [-]
Nov 89. See For Miles; (cd) **STEP FROM THE SHADOWS ("MARVIN, WELCH & FARRAR")** [ ] [-]
(re-iss.cd/lp Apr93)
Oct 93. See For Miles; (cd)(c) **THE EP COLLECTION VOLUME 3** [ ] [-]
Dec 89. Pickwick; (lp)(c)(cd) **THE COLLECTION** [ ] [-]
Jul 92. Magpie; (3xcd-box) **THE EP COLLECTIONS** [ ] [-]
– (1 EP is by CLIFF RICHARD & THE SHADOWS)
May 93. Polygram TV; (cd)(c) **SHADOWS IN THE NIGHT - 16 CLASSIC TRACKS** [22] [-]
Oct 93. Polygram TV; (cd)(c) **DREAMTIME** [ ] [-]
Apr 94. Polygram TV; (cd)(c) **AT THEIR VERY BEST** [ ] [-]
Oct 94. Polygram TV; (cd)(c) **THE BEST OF HANK MARVIN & THE SHADOWS** [19] [-]
May 94. BR Music; (cd)(c) **THE SHADOWS AND FRIENDS** [ ] [-]
May 95. EMI; (3xcd) **THE FIRST 20 YEARS AT THE TOP - 75 ORIGINALS 1959-1979** [ ] [-]
Aug 95. Ichiban; (cd) **THE DARK SIDE OF THE SHADOWS** [ ] [-]

HANK MARVIN

E.M.I. not issued
Nov 77. (lp)(c) **THE HANK MARVIN GUITAR SYNDICATE** [ ] [-]
– New Earth / Bird of beauty / Have you never been mellow / You are everything / Thunder thumbs and lightnin' licks / I've got you under my skin / Silvery rain / St.Louis blues / Ebb tide / Flamingo / Syndicated. *(re-iss.+cd Jan90 + Apr 93 on 'See For Miles')*
Feb 78. (7") **FLAMINGO. / SYNDICATED** [ ] [-]
Polydor not issued
Feb 82. (7") **DON'T TALK. / LIFELINE** [48] [-]
Feb 82. (lp)(c) **WORDS AND MUSIC BY HANK MARVIN** [ ] [-]
– Don't talk / Slow down / Bad cop / Tahlia take your time / China town / Captain Zlogg / The trouble with me is you / Oh Suzie / Night nurse / Go Jimmy / Then I found love / Life line.
Feb 83. (7") **THE TROUBLE WITH ME IS YOU. / CAPTAIN ZLOGG** [ ] [-]
Apr 83. (7") **THE HAWK AND THE DOVE. / JANINE** [ ] [-]
May 83. (lp)(c) **ALL ALONE WITH FRIENDS** [ ] [-]
– Just another heartbreak / The hawk and the dove / The invisible man / Lelia (Danny's got a song) / Where do you go when you dream / Don't answer / Stardom / Rainy day goodbye / 99 days / All alone with friends. *(re-iss.cd+c.Aug91 on 'Pickwick')*
Jun 83. (7") **THE INVISIBLE MAN. / ALL ALONE WITH FRIENDS** [ ] [-]
— Below single features **BRIAN MAY** (Queen) on guitar.
Oct 92. (7")(c-s) **WE ARE THE CHAMPIONS. / MOONTAN** [66] [-]
(cd-s+=) – Into the light.
Dec 92. (cd)(c)(lp) **INTO THE LIGHT** [18] [-]
– We are the champions (featuring BRIAN MAY) / Pipeline (featuring DUANE EDDY) / Sylvia / Jessica / Another day in Paradise/ Everybody wants to rule the world / Don't know much / Road train / Sumiko / Into the light / (Everything I do) I do it for you / Rikki don't lose that number / Scirocco / Moontalk / Tailspin / Steel wheel.
Oct 93. (7")(c-s)(cd-s) **WONDERFUL LAND. (HANK MARVIN featuring MARK KNOPFLER") / NIVRAM** [ ] [ ]
Nov 93. (cd)(c) **HEARTBEAT** [17] [-]
– Heartbeat / Oxygene (part IV) / Mrs.Robinson / Space oddity / Achy breaky heart / I will always love you / The crying game / Cable beach / Wonderful land / Hot rox / Rocket man / Take five / Wichita lineman / Live and let die / Crying / Limited slip.
— More obvious covers, plus appearances by BRIAN BENNETT/ MARK GRIFFITHS/ WARREN BENNETT/ ALAN HAWKSHAW/ MARK KNOPFLER/ BEN MARVIN/ CLIFF RICHARD/ TAHLIA MARVIN
PolygramTV not issued
Nov 95. (cd)(c) **HANK PLAYS CLIFF** [39] [-]
–

BRIAN BENNETT

Fontana not issued
Aug 74. (7") **CHASE SIDE SHOOT-UP. / PEGASUS** [ ] [-]
E.M.I. not issued
Dec 74. (7") **MELISSA. / LITTLE MISS BRISTOL** [ ] [-]
D.J.M. not issued
Sep 76. (7") **THUNDERBOLT. / CLEARING SKIES** [ ] [-]
Mar 77. (7") **SATURDAY NIGHT SPECIAL. / FAREWELL TO A FRIEND** [ ] [-]
Apr 77. (lp)(c) **ROCK DREAMS** [ ] [-]
– Rock dreams – introduction / Rock and roll dreamer / Banja boogie / Rave on / Milwaukee massacre / C'mon everybody / Thunderb. / Saturday night special / Girls back home / Wallop / Farewell to a friend / Drum odyssey / Rock dreams-finale.
Jun 77. (7") **GIRLS BACK HOME. / JONY JUMP** [ ] [-]
Mar 78. (7") **PENDULUM FORCE. / OCEAN GLIDE** [ ] [-]
May 78. (lp)(c) **VOYAGE** [ ] [-]
– Voyage / Solstice / Chain reaction / Pendulum force / Airquake / Ocean glide.

Jan 79. (7") **TOP OF THE WORLD. / SOUL ICE** [ ] [-]

— In Oct'89, BENNETT has his TV Soundtrack for 'RUTH RENDELL MYSTERIES' issued on 'Pickwick'.

SHADOWS OF KNIGHT

Formed: Chicago, Illinois, USA . . . 1965 by JIM SOHNS, etc (see below). That year they signed to Bill Traut & George Badowski's 'Dunwich' label. Their debut single, the Van Morrison penned 'GLORIA', gave them US Top 10 triumph, but after one more hit, success eluded them. • **Style:** Pioneers of garage punk – rock which was inspired by BO DIDDLEY-like R&B rhythms, soon tempered in 1968 by pop industry sound, copyright of The KASENETZ-KATZ production. • **Songwriters:** Group compositions except; GLORIA (Them) / OH YEAH + GOT MY MOJO WORKING (Muddy Waters) / HOOCHIE COOCHIE MAN + I JUST WANNA MAKE LOVE TO YOU + SPOONFUL (Willie Dixon) / BOOM BOOM (John Lee Hooker) / I'M NOT TALKIN' (Yardbirds) / BAD LITTLE WOMEN (Wheels) / TOMORROW'S GONNA BE ANOTHER DAY (Boyce-Hart) / • **Trivia:** Their final sessions were at Paragon studios in May 1970, although they did re-form for live gigs in the 70's.

Recommended: GEE-EL-O-ARE-I-AY (*8)

JIM SOHNS – vocals / **WARREN ROGERS** – lead guitar / **JERRY McGEORGE** – rhythm guitar / **NORM GOTSCH** – bass / **TOM SCHIFFOUR** – drums

Atlantic Dunwich

Mar 66. (7") **GLORIA. / DARK SIDE** [ ] [10] Jan 66
(US re-iss.1971 on 'Atlantic')

— **JOE KELLEY** – lead guitar repl. GOTSCH (WARREN now on bass)

Jun 66. (7") **OH YEAH. / LIGHT BULB BLUES** [ ] [39]

Jun 66. (lp) **GLORIA** [-] [46] May 66
– Gloria / Light bulb blues / I got my mojo working / Dark side / Let it rock / Oh yeah / It always happens that way / You can't judge a book (by looking at the cover) / I just want to make love to you / Bad little woman / Gospel zone / Hey Joe / I'll make you sorry / Peepin' and hidin' / Tomorrow's going to be another day / Spoonful. *(UK-iss.Mar79 on 'Radar')*

Sep 66. (7") **BAD LITTLE WOMAN. / GOSPEL ZONE** [ ] [91]

— **DAVE 'The Hawk' WOLINSKI** – keyboards repl. ROGERS who was drafted.

Dec 66. (7") **I'M GONNA MAKE YOU MINE. / I'LL MAKE YOU SORRY** [-] [90]

1967. (lp) **BACK DOOR MEN** [-] [ ]
– Bad little women / Gospel zone / The behemoth / Three for love / Hey Joe / I'll make you sorry / Peepin' and hidin' / Tomorrow's going to be another day / New York bullseye / High blood pressure / Spoonful.

1967. (7") **THE BEHEMOTH. / WILLIE JEAN** [-] [ ]

— (Jul67) **JIM SOHNS** now sole survivor, with hired session musicians. (McGEORGE joined H.P. LOVECRAFT)

Sep 67. (7") **SOMEONE LIKE ME. / THREE FOR LOVE** [ ] [ ]

— (1968) **SOHNS** brought in **JOHN FISHER / DAN BAUGHMAN / WOODY WOODRUFF / KENNY TURKIN**

Buddah Team

Dec 68. (7") **SHAKE. / FROM WAY OUT TO WAY UNDER** [ ] [46] Oct 68

not issued Super K

1969. (7") **TAURUS. / MY FIRE DEPARTMENT NEEDS A FIREMAN** [-] [ ]

1969. (7") **RUN RUN BILLY PORTER. / MY FIRE DEPARTMENT NEEDS A FIREMAN** [-] [ ]

1969. (lp) **THE SHADOWS OF KNIGHT** [-] [ ]
– Follow / Alone / Times & places / I am what I am / Uncle Wiggley's airship / I wanna make you all mine / Shake revisited '69 / I'll set you free / Under acoustic control / Bluebird / Back door man.

not issued Atco

1969. (7") **GLORIA '69. / SPANIARD AT MY DOOR** [-] [ ]

Jun 70. (7") **I AM THE HUNTER. / WARWICK COURT AFFAIR** [-] [ ]

— Disbanded 1970, although SOHNS re-united them for one-off tour in 1974.

– compilations, others, etc. –

Apr 85. Edsel; (lp) **GEE-EL-O-ARE-I-AY** [ ] [-]
– Gloria / Light bulb blues / I got my mojo working / Dark side / Let it rock / Oh yeah / It always happens that way / You can't judge a book by the cover / I just wanna make love to you / Bad little woman / Gospel zone / Hey Joe / I'll make you sorry / Peepin' and hidin' / Tomorrow's gonna be another day / Spoonful.

Nov 92. Sundazed; (cd) **RAW'N ALIVE AT THE CELLAR, CHICAGO 1966 (live)** [ ] [-]

SHAKESPEAR'S SISTER

Formed: London, England . . . 1988 by ex-BANANARAMA singer SIOBHAN FAHEY, who teamed up with former session guitarist & American singer MARCELLA DETROIT (aka MARCY LEVY). They signed to 'London' subsidiary label 'FFRR' in '88 after initial gigs in Leningrad, but flopped with debut 45 'BREAK MY HEART'. The following year, they made amends by hitting UK Top 10 with 'YOU'RE HISTORY'. • **Style:** Weird but diverse pop duo, who transferred from pop world, into a more visual outfit in the late 80's. • **Songwriters:** STEWART/DETROIT collaborated with FERRARA/FELDMAN/SEYMOUR, except COULD YOU BE LOVED (Bob Marley) / AIN'T NOTHING LIKE THE REAL THING (Ashford & Simpson) / I WANT TO TAKE YOU HIGHER (Sly & The Family Stone) / OUT OF MY MIND (Lance Aston). • **Trivia:** SIOBHAN married The EURYTHMICS mainman DAVE STEWART on 1 Aug'87.

Recommended: HORMONALLY YOURS (*6).

MARCY LEVY

original stage name

R.S.O. R.S.O.

Oct 80. (7"w/ROBIN GIBB) **HELP ME. / ('A' instrumental)** [ ] [ ]

Epic Epic

1982. (lp)(c) **MARCELLA** [-] [ ]
– Close to her / First invasion / All my love / Waiting on you / Life is on the vine / I can't stand it / Got to know you / I can't wait that long / T oyou / Love side

Aug 82. (7") **CLOSE TO HER. / WAITING ON YOU** [ ] [ ]

SHAKESPEAR'S SISTER

SIOBHAN STEWART (b.SIOBHAN FAHEY, 10 Sep'58, Dublin, Ireland) – vox, etc. / **MARCELLA DETROIT** (b.21 Jun'59, Detroit) – guitar (ex-ERIC CLAPTON Band) with 3rd member **RICHARD FELDMAN** – keyboards

ffrr-London London

Nov 88. (7")(12") **BREAK MY HEART (YOU REALLY). / ('A'version)** [ ] [-]
(cd-s+=) – ('A'acid mix).

Jul 89. (7")(c-s)(7"pic-d) **YOU'RE HISTORY. / DIRTY MIND** [7] [ ]
(12"+=)(cd-s+=) – Heroine / You're history (parts 2-4).

Aug 89. (lp)(c)(cd) **SACRED HEART** [9] [ ]
– Heroine / Run silent, run deep / Dirty mind / Sacred heart / Heaven is in your arms / Twist the knife * / You're history / Break my heart / Red rocket / Electric Moon / Primitive love / Could you be loved / You made me come to this *. *(cd+= *)*

Sep 89. (7")(c-s) **RUN SILENT. / MR.WRONG** [54] [ ]
(12"+=)/ /(cd-s+=) – ('A'dub version)./ / ('A'deep mix).

Feb 90. (7") **DIRTY MIND. / ('A'-1990 version)** [71] [ ]
(12"+=)(c-s+=)(cd-s+=) – Electric Moon.

— now with **MICK COZZI** – guitar (on 1) / **JONATHON PERKINS** – keyboards / **IAN MAIDMAN** – bass, keys / **STEVE FERRARA** – drums, keys / **ED SHEAMUR** – keyboards /

Sep 91. (7")(c-s) **GOODBYE CRUEL WORLD. / BLACK SKY (mix)** [59] [ ]
(12"+=) – ('A'dub versions) / ('B'black widow mix).
(cd-s+=) – You're history.

Jan 92. (7") **STAY. / THE TROUBLE WITH ANDRE** [1] [4] Jun 92
(c-s+=)(cd-s+=) – Remixes: Run silent / Dirty mind / ('A'-lp sample).

Feb 92. (cd)(c)(lp) **HORMONALLY YOURS** [3] [56]
– Goodbye cruel world / I don't care / My 16th apology / Are we in love yet / Emotional thing / Stay / Black sky / The trouble with Andre / Moonchild / Catwoman / Let me entertain you / Hello (turn your radio on).

Mar 92. (7")(c-s) **I DON'T CARE. / REMEMBER MY NAME** [7] [55] Nov 92
(pic-cd-s+=) – You're history / Catwoman.

Jul 92. (7")(c-s) **GOODBYE CRUEL WORLD. / MOONCHILD** [32] [ ]
(cd-s+=) – Are we in love yet?

Oct 92. (7")(c-s) **HELLO (TURN YOUR RADIO ON). / STAY (remix)** [14] [ ]
(cd-s+=) – Black sky (dubextravaganza) / Goodbye cruel world (bio remix)

Feb 93. (7"ep)(c-ep)(cd-ep) **MY 16th APOLOGY. / CAT WOMEN / HOT LOVE / DIRTY MIND** [61] [ ]
(cd-s+=) ('A' alternative piano mix) / ('A' version).

— Split early in '93, after which the admittedly volatile SIOBHAN admitted herself into a psychiatric unit. She is currently putting together a new version of SS with Scottish musicians.

MARCELLA DETROIT

with **PHIL SPALDING** – bass, vocals / **CHRIS SABO** – drums / **CHRIS THOMAS** – flute, keyboards / **JOOLS HOLLAND** – piano / **PHIL MANZANERA** – guitars / **MATTHEW VAUGHN** – programming / etc.

London London

Feb 94. (7")(c-s) **I BELIEVE. / I WANT TO TAKE YOU HIGHER** [11] [ ]
(cd-s+=)/ /(12"+=) – Shadow. / / (2-'A'mixes).

Mar 94. (cd)(c)(lp) **JEWEL** [15] [ ]
– Jewel / I believe / Perfect world / Art of melancholy / James Brown / Detroit / Ain't nothing like the real thing / I'm no angel / I want to take you higher / You don't tell me everything / Cool people / Out of my mind / Prima Donna.

Apr 94. (7")(c-s); & ELTON JOHN) **AIN'T NOTHIN' LIKE THE REAL THING. / BREAK THE CHAIN** [24] [ ]
(cd-s+=) – I feel free.

Jun 94. (7")(c-s) **I'M NO ANGEL. / YOU OWN THE MOON** [33] [ ]
(cd-s+=) – Cool people.
(cd-s) – ('A'side) / Lay down Sally / Crucify me / Monday morning.

Mar 95. (7")(c-s) **PERFECT WORLD. / ('A'-95 version)** [ ] [ ]
(cd-s+=) – ('A'-Youth vocal session) / ('A'-Youth dub session).
(cd-s) – ('A'acoustic) / I believe (acoustic) / I'm no angel (acoustic) / You don't tell me everything (acoustic).

SHAMEN

Formed: Aberdeen, Scotland . . . 1984 as ALONE AGAIN OR (named after a LOVE track from '67) by COLIN ANGUS and McKENZIE brothers DEREK and KEITH. After 2 singles (1 for 'Polydor'; DREAM COME TRUE), they became The SHAMEN, and released mainly singles on own label 'Mouska' in 1986-87. In the late 80's, they signed to Derek Schulman's indie 'O. L. Indian' label, and soon secured UK chart placings by the early 90's. • **Style:**

Shifted from psychedelic experimental rock in the mid-80's, to drug invoking rave-disco outfit during the 90's. Their No.1 single 'EBENEEZER GOODE', referred to the drug Ecstasy in the lyrics 'E's are good'. • **Songwriters:** All written by COLIN and DEREK, until latter's departure and replacement by the late WILL SINNOTT. ANGUS & WEST took over in '91. Covered; GRIM REAPER OF LOVE (Turtles) / FIRE ENGINE (13th Floor Elevators) / LONG GONE (Syd Barrett) / SWEET YOUNG THING (Monkees) / PURPLE HAZE (Jimi Hendrix). • **Trivia:** In Apr'88, they were dropped from a McEwans lager TV ad, because of their then anti-commercial approach.

Recommended: IN GORBACHEV WE TRUST (*7) / BOSS DRUM (*8) / EN-TACT (*9).

ALONE AGAIN OR

COLIN ANGUS (b.24 Aug'61) – keyboards / **DEREK McKENZIE** (b.27 Feb'64) – vocals, guitar / **KEITH McKENZIE** (b.30 Aug'61) – drums

All One | not issued

Dec 84. (7") **DRUM THE BEAT (IN MY SOUL). / SMARTER (edit)** [ ] [-]

Polydor | not issued

Mar 85. (7") **DREAM COME TRUE. / SMARTER THAN THE AVERAGE BEAR** [ ] [-]
(12") – ('A'&'B'-diff.versions) / Drum the beat (shall we dance?).

SHAMEN

added **ALISON MORRISON** – bass, keyboards

One Big Guitar | not issued

Apr 86. (12"ep) **THEY MAY BE RIGHT . . . BUT THEY'RE CERTAINLY WRONG** [ ] [-]
– Happy days / Velvet box / I don't like the way the world is turning.

—— **PETER STEPHENSON** (b. 1 Mar,62, Ayrshire) – keyboards repl. ALISON

Mouska | not issued

Nov 86. (7"m) **YOUNG TILL YESTERDAY. / WORLD THEATRE / GOLDEN HAIR** [ ] [-]
(12"m) – (first 2 tracks) / Strange days dream / It's all around.

May 87. (7") **SOMETHING ABOUT YOU. / DO WHAT YOU WILL** [ ] [-]
(12"+=) – Grim reaper of love.

Jun 87. (lp)(c) **DROP** [ ] [-]
– Through with you / Something about you / Four letter girl / The other side / Passing away / Young till yesterday / Happy days / Where do you go / Through my window / I don't like the way the world is turning / World theatre / Velvet box. *(c+=)* – Do what you will. *(cd-iss.Nov88, +=)* – Strange days dream. *(re-iss.Jan92 on 'Mau Mau')*

Sep 87. (7") **CHRISTOPHER MAYHEW SAYS. / SHITTING ON BRITAIN** [ ] [-]
(12"+=) – Fire engine / Christopher Mayhew says a lot.

—— **WILL SINNOTT** (b.23 Dec'60, Glasgow, Scotland) – bass repl. DEREK (COLIN now vocals, guitar)

Feb 88. (7") **KNATURE OF A GIRL. / HAPPY DAYS** [ ] [-]
(12"+=)(cd-s+=) – What's going down / Subknature of a girl.

Ediesta | not issued

Jun 88. (7") **JESUS LOVES AMERIKA. / DARKNESS IN ZION** [ ] [-]
(12"+=) – Do what you will.
(cd-s++=) – Sub knature dub.

—— now a duo of **COLIN + WILL**

Desire | not issued

Nov 88. (12") **TRANSCENDENTAL.(as "The SHAMEN Vs. BAM BAM") / ('A'lounge mix)** [ ] [-]

Demon | not issued

Jan 89. (lp)(c)(cd) **IN GORBACHEV WE TRUST** [ ] [-]
– Synergy / Sweet young thing / Raspberry infundibulum / War prayer / Adam Strange / Jesus loves Amerika / Transcendental / Misinformation / Raptyouare / In Gorbachev we trust / (Fundamental). *(c+=)* – Resistance (once again). *(cd+=)* – Yellow cellaphane day / Mayhew speaks out.

added **SANDRA** – percussion

Moshka | not issued

Apr 89. (7") **YOU, ME & EVERYTHING. / RERAPTYOUARE** [ ] [-]
(12"+=)(cd-s+=) – Ed's bonus beats.

May 89. (10"m-lp)(c)(cd) **PHORWARD** [ ] [-]
– You, me & everything (else) / Splash 2 / Negation state / Reraptyouare / SDD 89 / Phorward. *(free 7")* – (The S&N Sessions) *(c+cd+=)* – (2 extra mixes of last single).

—— **JOHN DELAFONS** – percussion repl. SANDRA

One Little Indian | Epic

Nov 89. (12"ep)(cd-ep) **OMEGA AMICO / OMEGA A. / OMEGA PRE-MIX / PH 1** [ ] [-]

Mar 90. (7")(c-s) **PRO-GEN. / ('A'dub version)** [55] [-]
(12"+=) – Lightspan (Ben Chapman mix).
(c-s++=)(cd-s++=) – ('A'-Paul Oakenfield mix).

Sep 90. (7")(c-s) **MAKE IT MINE (PROGRESS). / ('A'evil Ed mix)** [42] [ ]
(12"+=)(cd-s+=) – Something wonderful / ('A'-Lenny D mix).
(12"+=) – Progen (Land of Oz mix) / ('A'other version).

Oct 90. (cd)(c)(2x12"lp) **EN-TACT** [31] [ ]
– Human N.R.G. / Progen (land of Oz) / Possible worlds / Omega amigo / Evil is even / Hypereal / Lightspan / Make it mine V 2.5 / Oxygen restriction / Here are my people (orbital delays expected). *(cd+=) – (extra tracks + mixes) (re-iss.Jul91, hit No.45)*

Mar 91. (7")(c-s) **HYPERREAL (William Orbit mix). / ('A'-lp version)** [29] [ ]
(12"+=)(cd-s+=) – ('A'dub or 'Meatbeat Manifesto' versions) / In the bag.
(12") – ('A' Meatbeat Manifesto mixes). / ('A'dub mix).

—— (above featured **PLAVKA** (b. Poland) – vocals

On the 23 May'91, WILL drowned while on holiday in Ibiza. He was just 30.

Jul 91. (7")(c-s) **MOVE ANY MOUNTAIN – PROGEN '91. / ('A'well hung parliament mix)** [4] [38] Nov 91
(12"+=)//(cd-s+=) – (2 other mixes, diff.on each version).

Sep 91. (cd)(c)(lp) **PROGENCY** [23] [ ]
– Progency (8 versions).

—— New line-up **COLIN** plus **MR.C** – vocals, rhythm / **+ JHELSA ANDERSON** – backing vox (ex-SOUL FAMILY SENSATION) / **BOB BREEKS** – live keyboards / **GAVIN KNIGHT** – live drums / **RICHARD SHARPE** – occasional analogue

Jun 92. (7")(12") **L.S.I. (LOVE SEX INTELLIGENCE). / POSSIBLE WORLDS** [6] [ ]
(c-s+=)(cd-s+=) – Make it mine (Moby mix).

Aug 92. (7")(c-s) **EBENEEZER GOODE. / ('A'dub)** [1] [ ]
(12"+=)(cd-s+=) – ('A'mix) / L.S.I. (mix).

Oct 92. (cd)(c)(lp) **BOSS DRUM** [3] [ ]
– Boss drum / L.S.I.: Love Sex Intelligence / Space time / Librae solidi denari / Ebeneezer Goode (Beatmasters mix) / Comin' on / Phorever people / Fatman / Scientas / Re: evolution.

Oct 92. (7") **BOSS DRUM. / OMEGA AMIGO** [4] [ ]
(cd-s+=) – (3 'A'mixes).
(12"-2 diff.) – (5 'A'mixes either J.Robertson or Beatmasters).
(c-s++=) – ('A'-Steve Osbourne mixes & Youth).

Dec 92. (7"ep)(c-ep)(cd-ep) **PHOREVER PEOPLE. / ('A'dub + 'A'hypereal orbit mix)** [5] [ ]

—— now with vocalist **VICTORIA WILSON-JAMES**

Aug 95. (7")(c-s) **DESTINATION ESCHATON (Beatmasters mix). / ('A'-Deep melodic mix)** [15] [ ]
(cd-s) – ('A'-Shamen acid: Escacid) / (2 'A'-Hardfloor mixes). / (cd-s) – (2 'A'-Basement Boys mixes) / (3 'A'-Beatmasters mixes).

Oct 95. (c-s) **TRANSAMAZONIA (Beatmasters mix) / ('A'-Visnadi mix) / ('A'-Watershed instrumental) / ('A'-LTJ Bukin mix)** [28] [ ]
(12"+=) – ('A'-Deep dish mix).
(cd-s) – (6 'A'mixes including; Alex Party Aguirre / Zion Train).
(cd-s+=) – ('A'-Nuv Idol mix).

Oct 95. (d-cd)(d-c)(d-lp) **AXIS MUTATIS** [27] [ ]
– Destination Eschaton / Transamazonia / Conquistador / Mauna Kea to Andromeda / Neptune / Prince of Popacatapertl / Heal the separation / Persephone's quest / Moment / Axis mundi / Eschaton omega (deep melodic techno). (d-lp w/other d-lp) – **ARBOR BONA / ARBOR MALA** – Asynptotic Escaton / Sefirotic axis (a)(b)(c) Formation (d) Action / Extraterrestrial / Deneter / Beneath the underworld / Xochipilis return / Rio Negro / Above the underworld / A moment in dub / Pizarro in Paradiso / West of the underworld / Anticipation Escaton (be ready for the storm) / Out in the styx.

– compilations, others, etc. –

Aug 88. Materiali Italy; (lp)(c)(cd) **STRANGE DAY DREAMS** [-] [-]
(re-iss.+cd.Oct91)(re-iss.all formats Jan93)

Dec 89. Communion; (m-lp)(cd) **WHAT'S GOING DOWN** [-] [ ]

Nov 93. Band Of Joy; (cd)(c)(lp) **ON AIR (live session)** [61] [-]

SHAM 69

Formed: London, England . . . 1976 by JIMMY PURSEY, etc (see below). After one 45 for indie 'Step Forward' in 1977, they signed to 'Polydor'. Their third 45 'ANGELS WITH DIRTY FACES', broke them into the UK 20 in 1978, and was followed by a string of hits up to the early 80's. • **Style:** Anthem political punk-rock outfit, who suffered anti-commercial "sell-out" press backlash. This was not helped by anti-social overtones, and riotous skinhead fans, which was main cause for PURSEY to hang up mits. • **Songwriters:** Penned by PURSEY-PARSONS except; YOU'RE A BETTER MAN THAN I (Yardbirds) / WITH A LITTLE HELP FROM MY FRIENDS (Beatles). The WANDERERS covered THE TIMES THEY ARE A-CHANGIN' (Bob Dylan). • **Trivia:** PURSEY appeared on Various Artists lp 'The Whip' in '83.

Recommended: THE FIRST, THE BEST AND THE LAST (*7)

JIMMY PURSEY (b. Hersham, Surrey, England) – vocals / **DAVE PARSONS** – guitar repl. NEIL HARRIS who had repl. JOHNNY GOODFORNOTHING / **ALBIE SLIDER** (b. ALBERT MASKAIL) – bass, vocals / **MARK CAIN** – drums repl. BILLY BOSTIK

Step Forward | not issued

Oct 77. (7"m)(12"m) **I DON'T WANNA. / RED LONDON / ULSTER** [ ] [-]

—— **DAVE TREGANNA** – bass, vocals repl. ALBIE

Polydor | Sire

Jan 78. (7") **BORSTAL BREAKOUT. / HEY LITTLE RICH BOY** [ ] [-]

Feb 78. (lp)(c) **TELL US THE TRUTH** (some live) [25] [ ]
– We gotta fight / Rip off / Ulster / George Davis is innocent / They don't understand / Borstal breakout / Family life / Hey little rich boy / I'm a man, I'm a boy / What about the lonely / Tell us the truth / It's never too late / Whose generation. *(re-iss.Mar89 on 'Receiver')*

Apr 78. (7") **ANGELS WITH DIRTY FACES. / COCKNEY KIDS ARE INNOCENT** [19] [ ]

Jul 78. (7") **IF THE KIDS ARE UNITED. / SUNDAY MORNING NIGHTMARE** [9] [ ]

Oct 78. (7") **HURRY UP HARRY. / NO ENTRY** [10] [ ]

Nov 78. (lp)(c) **THAT'S LIFE** [27] [ ]
– Leave me alone / Who gives a damn / Everybody's right, everybody's wrong / That's life / Win or lose / Hurry up Harry / Evil way (live) / Reggae pick up (part 1) / Sunday morning nightmare / Reggae pick up (part 2) / Angels with dirty faces / Is this me or is this you. *(re-iss.Jul88 on 'Skunx')*

Mar 79. (7"m) **QUESTIONS AND ANSWERS. / I GOTTA SURVIVE (live) / WITH A LITTLE HELP FROM MY FRIENDS** [18] [ ]

Jul 79. (7"m)(12"m) **HERSHAM BOYS. / I DON'T WANNA (live) / TELL US THE TRUTH (live)** [6] [ ]

Sep 79. (lp)(c) **THE ADVENTURES OF THE HERSHAM BOYS** 8
– Money / Fly dark angel / Joey's on the street / Cold blue in the night / You're a better man than I / Hersham boys / Lost on Highway 46 / Voices / Questions and answers / What have we got. *(free 12")* – IF THE KIDS ARE UNITED. / BORSTAL BREAKOUT

Oct 79. (7") **YOU'RE A BETTER MAN THAN I. / GIVE A DOG A BONE** 49 -

— Disbanded for 2 months Jul'79. **MARK GOLDSTEIN** – drums repl. CAIN

Mar 80. (7") **TELL THE CHILDREN. / JACK** 45 -

May 80. (lp)(c) **THE GAME** -
– The game / Human zoo / Lord of the flies / Give a dog a bone / In and out / Tell the children / Spray it on the wall / Dead or alive / Simon / Deja vu / Poor cow / Run wild run free / Unite and win. *(re-iss.Mar89 on 'Receiver')*

Jun 80. (7") **UNITE AND WIN. / I'M A MAN** -

Nov 80. (lp)(c) **THE FIRST, THE BEST AND THE LAST** (compilation) -
– Borstal breakout / Hey little rich boy / Angels with dirty faces / Cockney kids are innocent / If the kids are united / Sunday morning nightmare / Hurry up Harry / Questions and answers / Give the dog a bone / Hersham boys / Tell the children / Unite & win. *(free 7"ep live) (re-iss.cd+c Apr94).*

— Had already splintered, with PURSEY going solo (see further below).

WANDERERS

(**TREGANNA, PARSONS + GOLDSTEIN**) added **STIV BATORS** – vocals (ex-DEAD BOYS)

Polydor / not issued

Mar 81. (7") **READY TO SNAP. / BEYOND THE LAW** -

May 81. (lp)(c) **THE ONLY LOVERS LEFT ALIVE** -
– Fanfare for 1984 / No dreams / Dr.Baker / Take them and break them / Little bit frightening / It's all the same / The times they are a-changin' / Ready to snap / Can't take you anymore / Sold your soul for fame / Circles of time / There'll be no end fanfare.

Jun 81. (7") **THE TIMES THEY ARE A-CHANGIN'. / (IT'S A) LITTLE BIT FRIGHTENING** -

— Split Aug'81, TREGANNA followed BATORS into LORDS OF THE NEW CHURCH. PARSONS formed FRAMED later in 1982.

JIMMY PURSEY

Polydor / not issued

Sep 80. (7") **LUCKY MAN. / BLACK AND WHITE ROCK REGGAE** -

Oct 80. (lp)(c) **IMAGINATION CAMOUFLAGE** -
– Moon morning funday / Have a nice day / Lucky man / You never can tell / Situation's vacant / Playground soldier / White trash / Fifty-fifty / Freak show / Your mother should have told you / Just another memory.

Epic / not issued

Jun 81. (7") **ANIMALS HAVE MORE FUN. / SUS** -

Nov 81. (7") **NAUGHTY BOYS LIKE NAUGHTY GIRLS. / WHO'S MAKING YOU HAPPY** -

Feb 82. (lp)(c) **ALIEN ORPHAN** -
– Alien orphan / The first deadly kiss / I'm a human being / One invite only / Why (he shouldn't be here) / Who's making you happy / Spies / Jungle west one / Oh isn't it a weird weird world / One night in Paris / Technical / Naughty boys like naughty girls.

Feb 82. (7") **ALIEN ORPHAN. / CONVERSATIONS** -

Code Black / not issued

Jan 83. (lp) **REVENGE IS NOT THE PASSWORD** -

Feb 83. (7") **MAN WORRIES MAN. / ?** -

An Eskimo / not issued

May 84. (7")(12") **IF ONLY BEFORE. (as "JAMES T.PURSEY") / ABOVE AND BEYOND** -

Videocat / not issued

Sep 86. (7")(12") **ZAP POW. / ('A'bass camp mix)** -

SHAM 69

re-formed in '87. (**PURSEY, PARSONS,** +2)

Legacy / not issued

Jul 87. (7") **RIP AND TEAR. / THE GREAT AMERICAN SLOW-DOWN** -
(12"+=) – ('A'extended).

Feb 88. (7") **OUTSIDE THE WAREHOUSE. / ('A'version)** -
(12"+=) – How the west was won.

Jun 88. (lp)(c) **VOLUNTEER** -
– Outside the warehouse / Wicked tease / Wallpaper / Mr.Know it all / As black as sheep / How the west was won / That was the day / Rip and tear / Bastard club / Volunteer. *(cd-iss.Dec89)*

Nov 92. (12") **M25. / ?** -

Nov 92. (cd)(lp) **INFORMATION LIBRE** -
– Break on through / Uptown / Planet trash / Information libretaire / Caroline's suitcase / Feel it / King Kong drinks Coca-Cola / Saturdays and Strangeways / Breeding dinosaurs / Wild and wonderful.

C.M.P. / not issued

Mar 93. (7") **UPTOWN. / BORSTAL BREAKOUT** -
(12"+=) – Flowers / Wild and wonderful.

Nov 93. (cd) **KINGS & QUEENS** -
– Action time vision / I don't wanna / Ulster boy / They don't understand / Tell us the truth / Borstal breakout / Family life / The kids are united / Hurry up Harry / Hey little rich boy / Bosnia / Reggae giro. *(re-iss.Jul95 on 'Dojo')*

Red Cat / not issued

Jul 95. (cd)(c) **SOAPY WATER & MR. MARMALADE** -

– compilations, others, etc. –

Oct 82. Polydor; (12"ep) **ANGELS WITH DIRTY FACES / BORSTAL BREAKOUT. / HURRY UP HARRY / IF THE KIDS ARE UNITED** -

Nov 86. Receiver; (lp)(c) **ANGELS WITH DIRTY FACES – THE BEST OF SHAM 69** -

May 89. Receiver; (lp)(cd) **THE BEST OF THE REST OF SHAM 69** -

Aug 90. Receiver; (cd)(lp) **LIVE AT THE ROXY (live tapes '77)** -

Feb 87. Link; (lp) **LIVE AND LOUD (live)** -
(re-iss.Dec87)

Apr 88. Link; (lp) **LIVE AND LOUD VOL.2** -

Oct 89. Castle; (lp)(c)(cd) **COMPLETE LIVE (live)** -

Apr 90. Action Replay; (cd)(c) **SHAM 69 LIVE (live)** -

Oct 93. Windsong; (cd) **BBC RADIO 1 LIVE IN CONCERT (Live)** -

Mar 94. Spectrum; (cd) **LIVE IN JAPAN (live)** -

Mar 95. Step-1; (cd) **LIVE AND LOUD (one side 999)** -

Sep 95. Emporio; (cd)(c) **SHAM 69 LIVE** -

Dec 95. Essential; (cd) **THE BEST OF SHAM 69** -

SHANGRI-LA'S

Formed: Andrew Jackson High, Queens, New York, USA . . .1963 by two sets of sisters BETTY & MARY WEISS, plus twins MARY-ANN & MARGIE GANSER. Discovered in 1963 by producer GEORGE 'Shadow' MORTON, who changed their group name from The BON BONS to The SHANGRI-LAS. Their first two singles in 1964 'REMEMBER (WALKING IN THE SAND)' & 'LEADER OF THE PACK' were both smash hits worldwide and have since become classics of that era. The latter 'death disc' featured motor bike revs over the tearful chorus. Sadly a sharp decline in record sales the following few years, made them give up. • **Style & Songwriters:** Melodramatic girl-group pop with a hint of pastiche rock'n'roll thrown in by background puppet master SHADOW MORTON.

Recommended: MYRMIDONS OF MELODRAMA (*7)

BON BONS

MARY WEISS – lead vocals / **BETTY WEISS** – vocals / **MARY-ANN GANSER** – vocals / **MARGE GANSER** – vocals

SHANGRI-LAS

Red Bird / Red Bird

Sep 64. (7") **REMEMBER (WALKING IN THE SAND). / IT'S EASIER TO CRY** 14 5 Aug64

Dec 64. (7") **LEADER OF THE PACK. / WHAT IS LOVE?** 11 1 Oct64

Jan 65. (7") **GIVE HIM A GREAT BIG KISS. / TWIST AND SHOUT** 18 Dec64

Jan 65. (7") **MAYBE. / SHOUT** 91 Dec64

1965. (lp) **THE SHANGRI-LAS – LEADER OF THE PACK** Mar65
– Give him a great big kiss / Leader of the pack / Bull dog / It's easier to cry / What is love? / Remember (walking in the sand) / Twist and shout / Maybe / So much in love / Shout / Good night, my love / Pleasant dreams / You can't sit down. *(re-iss.1983 on 'Charly')*

1965. (7") **OUT IN THE STREETS. / THE BOY** 53 Mar65

1965. (7") **GIVE US YOUR BLESSINGS. / HEAVEN ONLY KNOWS** 29 May65

1965. (7") **RIGHT NOW AND NOT LATER. / TRAIN FROM KANSAS CITY** 99 Sep65

1965. (lp) **SHANGRI-LAS '65** -
– Right now and not later / Never again / Give us your blessings / Sophisticated boom boom / I'm blue / Heaven only knows / The train from Kansas City / Out in the streets / What's a girl supposed to do / The dum dum ditty / You cheated, you lied / The boy. *(UK-iss.Mar84 on 'Charly')*

1966. (7") **I CAN NEVER GO HOME ANYMORE. / BULLDOG** 6 Nov65

1966. (7") **LONG LIVE OUR LOVE. / SOPHISTICATED BOOM BOOM** 33 Jan66

— now without MARGE

May 66. (7") **HE CRIED. / DRESSED IN BLACK** 65 Apr66

1966. (7") **PAST, PRESENT AND FUTURE. / PARADISE** 59 Jun66

Mercury / Mercury

1966. (lp) **GOLDEN HITS** (compilation)
– Leader of the pack / The train from Kansas City / Heaven only knows / Remember (walking in the sand) / I can never go home anymore / What is love? / Past, present and future / Out in the streets / Give him a great big kiss / Long live our love / Give us your blessings / Sophisticated boom boom. *(re-iss.1973 lp/c on 'Philips')*

1967. (7") **THE SWEET SOUND OF SUMMER. / I'LL NEVER LEARN**

1967. (7") **TAKE YOUR TIME. / FOOTSTEPS ON THE ROOF**

— Split in 1967. In 1971 MARY ANN died of encephalitis. MARGE died of a drug overdose.

compilations, etc.

1965. Red Bird; (7"ep) **THE SHANGRI-LAS** -

1971. Philips; (7") **PAST, PRESENT AND FUTURE. / THE TRAIN FROM KANSAS CITY** -

Oct72. Kama Sutra; (7") **LEADER OF THE PACK. / REMEMBER (WALKING IN THE SAND)** 3 -
(re-iss.Jul82 & Jun88 on 'Old Gold')

1973. Buddah; (7"m) **GIVE HIM A GREAT BIG KISS. / NEW YORK IS A LONELY TOWN / THE BOY FROM NEW YORK CITY** -

May 76. Charly; (7") **LEADER OF THE PACK. / GIVE HIM A GREAT BIG KISS** 7 -

May 76. Contempo; (7") **LEADER OF THE PACK. / REMEMBER (WALKING IN THE SAND)** 7 -

1976. Charly; (7"ep) **REMEMBER (WALKING IN THE SAND) / LEADER OF THE PACK. / GIVE HIM A GREAT BIG KISS / PAST, PRESENT AND FUTURE** -

(cd-ep iss.Feb89)

Aug 76. Philips; (7"m) **PAST, PRESENT AND FUTURE. / GIVE HIM A GREAT BIG KISS / REMEMBER (WALKING IN THE SAND)** [ ] [-]
Sep 78. Charly; (7") **LEADER OF THE PACK. / THE BOY FROM NEW YORK CITY** [ ] [-]
1978. Charly; (lp) **TEEN ANGUISH VOL.2** [ ] [-]
Nov 84. Topline / Astan US (lp)(c) **LEADER OF THE PACK** [ ] [-]
May 87. Topline; (cd) **GREATEST HITS** [ ] [-]
Aug 87. The Collection; (cd) **SHANGRI-LAS** [ ] [-]
Jun 88. Spectrum; (cd) **GREATEST HITS** [ ] [-]
Feb 89. Old Gold; (cd-s) **LEADER OF THE PACK / REMEMBER (WALKING IN THE SAND) / CHAPEL OF LOVE** [ ] [-]
Mar 89. Crusader; (cd) **LEADER OF THE PACK** [ ] [-]
Feb 90. Instant; (cd)(c)(lp) **REMEMBER** [ ] [-]
– Leader of the pack / Give him a great big kiss / Maybe / Out in the streets / Give us your blessings / Right now and not later / Remember (walking in the sand) / I can never go home anymore / Long live our love / Past, present and future / The train from Kansas City / Shout / Twist and shout / I'm blue / You cheated, you lied / So much in love.
1995. RPM; (cd) **MYRMIDONS OF MELODRAMA** [ ] [-]

Del SHANNON

Born: CHARLES WEEDON WESTOVER, 30 Dec'34, Coopersville, Michegan, USA. In 1960 he met keyboard player MAX CROOK and they became CHARLIE JOHNSON & HIS BIG LITTLE SHOW BAND. They gained attention of DJ Ollie McLaughlin, who introduced them to Harry Balk and Irving Micahnik, owners of 'Big Top' records. They signed him as DEL SHANNON, retaining CROOK as his co-writer sidekick. His 1961 DEL's debut 'RUNAWAY' quickly soared high to be a chart-topper on both sides of the Atlantic. This classic formula was repeated when 'HATS OFF TO LARRY' also peaked into both Top 10's. A string of hits followed until 1964, when most American artists were swamped by the British invasion (BEATLES, etc). The year previous, he had severed ties with management to form own 'Berlee' label. When he moved to New York in '64, he signed to 'Amy'. In the late 60's, he became noted producer for The SHIRELLES and BRIAN HYLAND. In 1974 & 1982, he was produced by DAVE EDMUNDS then TOM PETTY, with the latter heralding him a return into the US Top 40, with single 'Sea Of Love'. In 1989, he signed to UK label 'Silvertone', but after recording another JEFF LYNNE produced album, he committed suicide on 8th Feb'90 by shooting himself. He had always suffered from depression and alcoholism, and in the 80's had seemed to have overcome the latter. It was rumoured he was to be the replacement for ROY ORBISON in The TRAVELING WILBURYS. • **Style:** The 60's introduced DEL's falsetto vox, intertwined with understated CROOK, whose invention/trademark was an electronic organ 'The Musitron'. After his fame was over in the 60's, DEL turned to folk and country pop. • **Songwriters:** DEL and MAX wrote initial batch of songs. DEL wrote the rest except covers; THE SWISS MAID (Roger Miller) / FROM ME TO YOU (Beatles) / HANDY MAN (Jimmy Jones) / DO YOU WANT TO DANCE? (Bobby Freeman) / MEMPHIS (Chuck Berry) / TWIST AND SHOUT (Isley Brothers) / CRYING + RUNNING SCARED + PRETTY WOMAN (Roy Orbison) / NEEDLES AND PINS + WHEN YOU WALK IN THE ROOM (Searchers) / RAG DOLL (Four Seasons) / A WORLD WITHOUT LOVE (hit; Peter & Gordon) / THE BIG HURT (Toni Fisher) / MOVE IT ON OVER (Hank Williams) / UNDER MY THUMB (Rolling Stones) / KICKS (Paul Revere) / RED RUBBER BALL (Cyrkle) / PIED PIPER (Crispian St.Peters) / SUMMER IN THE CITY (Lovin' Spoonful) / SUNNY (Bobby Hebb) / TELL HER NO (Zombies). Billy Nichols wrote 3 tracks for him on the withdrawn 'AND THE MUSIC PLAYS ON' lp. • **Trivia:** PETER AND GORDON had a 1965 hit with his 'I GO TO PIECES'.

Recommended: LOOKING BACK: HIS BIGGEST HITS (*6)

DEL SHANNON – vocals (with session people, incl. MAX CROOK – keyboards)

London / Big Top

Mar 61. (7") **RUNAWAY. / JODY** [1] [1]
Sep 61. (7") **HATS OFF TO LARRY. / DON'T GILD THE LILY, LILY** [6] [5] Jun 61
Nov 61. (7") **SO LONG BABY. / THE ANSWER TO EVERYTHING** [10] [28] Sep 61
Nov 61. (lp) **RUNAWAY WITH . . .** [ ] [ ]
– Misery / Daydreams / His latest flame / The prom / The search / Runaway / I wake up crying / Wide wide world / I'll always love you / Lies / He doesn't care / Jody. *(cd+c-iss.Sep93 on 'Remember')*
Nov 61. (7") **HEY! LITTLE GIRL. / I DON'T CARE ANYMORE** [-] [38]
Mar 62. (7") **HEY! LITTLE BABY. / YOU NEVER TALKED ABOUT ME** [2] [-]
Mar 62. (7") **GINNY IN THE MIRROR. / I WON'T BE THERE** [-] [ ]
Aug 62. (7") **CRY MYSELF TO SLEEP. / I'M GONNA MOVE ON** [29] [99] Jun 62
Sep 62. (7") **THE SWISS MAID. / YOU NEVER TALKED ABOUT ME** [-] [64]
Oct 62. (7") **THE SWISS MAID. / GINNY IN THE MIRROR** [2] [-]
Jan 63. (7") **LITTLE TOWN FLIRT. / THE WAMBOO** [4] [12] Dec 62
Apr 63. (7") **TWO KINDS OF TEARDROPS. / KELLY** [5] [50]
May 63. (lp) **HATS OFF TO LARRY** (compilation) [ ] [-]
– The Swiss maid / Cry myself to sleep / Ginny in the mirror / You never talked about me / Don't gild the lily, Lily / I won't be there / Hats off to Larry / The answer to everything / Hey little girl / I'm gonna move on / I don't care anymore / So long baby.
Jun 63. (7") **FROM ME TO YOU. / TWO SILHOUETTES** [-] [77]
Aug 63. (7") **TWO SILHOUETTES. / MY WILD ONE** [23] [-]
Oct 63. (lp) **LITTLE TOWN FLIRT** [15] [12] Jun 63
– Two kinds of teardrops / Dream baby / Happiness / Two silhouettes / She thinks I still care / My wild one / Runaround Sue / From me to you / Kelly / Hey baby / Go away little girl / Little town flirt.

London / Berlee

Oct 63. (7") **SUE'S GONNA BE MINE. / SINCE SHE'S GONE** [21] [71]
Mar 64. (7") **THAT'S THE WAY LOVE IS. / TIME OF THE DAY** [ ] [ ]

Stateside / Amy

Mar 64. (7") **MARY JANE. / STAINS ON MY LETTER** [35] [ ]
Jul 64. (7") **HANDY MAN. / GIVE HER LOTS OF LOVIN'** [36] [22]
Oct 64. (7") **DO YOU WANT TO DANCE?. / THIS IS ALL I HAVE TO GIVE** [ ] [43] Sep 64
Jan 65. (lp) **HANDY MAN** [ ] [ ] Nov 64
– Memphis / That's the way love is / Ruby baby / I'll be lonely tomorrow / I can't fool around anymore / Handy man / Crying / Mary Jane / World without love / I ran all the way home / Give her lots of lovin' / Twist and shout.
Jan 65. (7") **KEEP SEARCHIN' (WE'LL FOLLOW THE SUN). / BROKEN PROMISES** [3] [9] Nov 64
Mar 65. (7") **STRANGER IN TOWN. / OVER YOU** [40] [30] Feb 65
May 65. (lp) **DEL SHANNON SINGS HANK WILLIAMS**
– Your cheatin' heart / Kaw-liga / I can't help it / Honky tonk blues / (See I hear) That lonesome whistle / You win again / Ramblin' man / Hey good looking / Long gone lonesome blues / Weary blues / I'm so lonesome, I could cry / Cold cold heart.
Jun 65. (7") **BREAK UP. / WHY DON'T YOU TELL HIM** [ ] [95] May 65
Sep 65. (7") **MOVE IT ON OVER. / SHE STILL REMEMBERS TONY** [ ] [ ]
Sep 65. (lp) **1,661 SECONDS WITH DEL SHANNON** [ ] [ ]
– Stranger in town / She cried / Needles and pins / Broken promises / Why don't you tell him / Do you wanna dance / I go to pieces / I'm gonna be strong / Rag doll / Over you / Running scared / Keep searchin'.
Mar 66. (7") **I CAN'T BELIEVE MY EARS. / I WISH IT WASN'T ME TONIGHT** [ ] [ ]

Liberty / Liberty

Apr 66. (7") **THE BIG HURT. / I GOT IT BAD** [ ] [94]
Jun 66. (7") **FOR A LITTLE WHILE. / HEY LITTLE STAR** [ ] [ ]
Sep 66. (7") **SHOW ME. / NEVER THOUGHT I COULD** [-] [ ]
Nov 66. (7") **UNDER MY THUMB. / SHE WAS MINE** [-] [ ]
Nov 66. (lp) **THIS IS MY BAG** [ ] [ ]
– Lightnin' strikes / The cheater / Kicks / Action / It's too late / Never thought I could / The big hurt / Everybody loves a clown / Hey! little star / When you walk in the room / For a little while / Oh pretty woman.
Jan 67. (7") **SHE. / WHAT MAKES YOU RUN** [ ] [ ]
Feb 67. (lp) **TOTAL COMMITMENT** [ ] [ ]
– Under my thumb / Red rubber ball / She was mine / Where were you when I needed you / The joker went wild / The Pied Piper / Sunny / Show me / Time won't let me / What makes you run / I can't be true / Summer in the city.
Jun 67. (7") **MIND OVER MATTER. / LED ALONG** [ ] [-]
Jun 67. (7") **LED ALONG. / I CAN'T BE TRUE** [-] [ ]
Oct 67. (7") **RUNAWAY (live '67). / HE CHEATED** [-] [ ]
Oct 67. (7") **RUNAWAY '67. / SHOW ME** [ ] [-]

—— Early in '68, 'Liberty' shelved album AND THE MUSIC PLAYS ON. It featured famous session men JIMMY PAGE, JOHN PAUL JONES and NICKY HOPKINS.

Mar 68. (7") **THINKIN' IT OVER. / RUNNING ON BACK** [ ] [ ]
May 68. (7") **GEMINI. / MAGICAL MUSICAL BOX** [ ] [ ]
Jul 68. (lp) **THE FURTHER ADVENTURES OF CHARLES WESTOVER** [ ] [ ]
– Thinkin' it over / Be my friend / Silver birch / I think I love you / River cool / Colour flashing hair / Gemini / Runnin' on back / Conquer / Been so long / Magical music box / New Orleans (Mardi Gras).
Feb 69. (7") **RAINDROPS. / YOU DON'T LOVE ME** [-] [ ]

Stateside / Dunhill

Sep 69. (7") **COMIN' BACK TO ME. / SWEET MARY LOU** [ ] [ ]
Mar 70. (7") **SISTER ISABELLE. / COLORADO RAIN** [ ] [ ]

United Art / United Art

Oct 72. (7") **WHAT'S A MATTER, BABY. / EARLY IN THE MORNING** [ ] [-]
May 73. (7") **KELLY. / COOPERSVILLE YODEL** [ ] [-]
Jun 73. (lp)(c) **LIVE IN ENGLAND (live)** [ ] [ ]
– Hats off to Larry / Handy man / The Swiss maid / Hey! little girl / Little town flirt / Kelly / Crying / Two kinds of teardrops / Coopersville yodel / The answer to everything / Keep searchin' (We'll follow the Sun) / What's a matter, baby / So long baby / Runaway. *(re-iss.May82 on 'Fame')*
Oct 74. (7") **AND THE MUSIC PLAYS ON. / IN MY ARMS AGAIN** [ ] [-]

not issued / Island

1975. (7") **TELL HER NO. / RESTLESS** [-] [ ]
1975. (7") **CRY BABY CRY. / IN MY ARMS AGAIN** [-] [ ]

—— Between 1975-76, he issued Australian 45; OH HOW HAPPY. / THE GHOST Retired for the rest of the 70's, but returned in the early 80's after bout of alcoholism. First batch of releases co-produced with TOM PETTY.

Demon / Network

Dec 81. (7") **SEX OF LOVE. / MIDNIGHT TRAIN** [-] [33]
Apr 82. (7") **TO LOVE SOMEONE. / LIAR** [-] [ ]
May 83. (lp) **DROP DOWN AND GET ME** [ ] [ ] Dec 81
Sea of love / Life without you / Out of time / Sucker for your love / To love someone / Drop down and get me / Maybe tomorrow / Liar / Never stop tryin' / Midnight train. (UK-version +=) Cheap love.
May 83. (7") **CHEAP LOVE. / DISTANT GHOST** [ ] [-]
Nov 83. (7") **SEA OF LOVE. / HELP ME** [ ] [-]

not issued / Warners

1985. (7") **IN MY ARMS AGAIN. / YOU CAN'T FORGIVE ME** [-] [ ]
1985. (7") **STRANGER ON THE RUN. / WHAT YOU GONNA DO WITH THAT BEAUTIFUL MODY OF YOURS** [-] [ ]

After another Australian-only single WALK AWAY in 1987, he signed to 'Silvertone' in the UK 1989. Tragically, after more fits of depression, he committed suicide on 8th Feb'90.

Silvertone / Silvertone

Mar 91. (7") **WALK AWAY. / NOBODY'S BUSINESS** [ ] [-]
(cd-s+=) – Let's dance.
Apr 91. (cd)(c)(lp) **ROCK ON** [ ] [ ]
– Walk away / Who left who / Are you lovin' me too / Callin' out my name / I go to pieces / Lost in a memory / I got you / What kind of fool do you think I am? / When I had you / Let's dance. *(re-iss.cd/c Apr95)*

Jun 91. (7") **ARE YOU LOVIN' ME TOO. / ONE WOMAN MAN** [ ] [-]
(cd-s+=) – Who left who.

– more compilations, etc. –

Jan 62. London/ US= Big Top; (7"ep) **DEL SHANNON** [ ] [ ]
Feb 63. London/ US= Big Top; (7"ep) **DEL SHANNON No.2** [ ] [ ]
Oct 63. London/ US= Big Top; (7"ep) **DEL'S OWN FAVOURITES** [ ] [ ]
Nov 63. London/ US= Big Top; (7"ep) **FROM DEL TO YOU** [ ] [ ]
Jul 80. London; (lp) **THE DEL SHANNON HIT PARADE** [ ] [-]
May 65. Stateside/ US= Amy; (7"ep) **DEL SHANNON HITS** [ ] [ ]
Mar 67. Liberty; (7"ep) **THE NEW DEL SHANNON** [ ] [ ]
Aug 91. Liberty; (cd) **THE LIBERTY YEARS** [ ] [ ]
Apr 71. Sunset; (lp) **TENTH ANNIVERSARY ALBUM** [ ] [ ]
Mar 78. Sunset; (lp)(c) **AND THE MUSIC PLAYS ON** (unissued lp from 1968) [ ] [ ]
– It's the feeling / Mind over matter / Silently / Cut and come again / My love has gone / Led along / Life is but nothing / And the music plays on / Easy to say, easy to do / Friendly with you / Raindrops / He cheated / Leaving you behind / Runaway '67.
Jun 73. Contour; (lp) **THE BEST OF DEL SHANNON** [ ] [-]
Nov 74. Cooltempo; (7") **THE SWISS MAID. / HEY! LITTLE GIRL** [ ] [-]
Jan 75. Cooltempo; (7") **RUNAWAY. / KEEP SEARCHIN' (WE'LL FOLLOW THE SUN)** [ ] [-]
Mar 75. Cooltempo; (7") **KELLY. / THE ANSWER TO EVERYTHING** [ ] [-]
Jul 75. Cooltempo; (d-lp) **THE VERY BEST OF DEL SHANNON** [ ] [-]
Aug 76. DJM; (7"ep) **RUNAWAY** [ ] [-]
Jun 79. Creole; (7") **RUNAWAY (new version). / HATS OFF TO LARRY (new version)** [ ] [-]
Jun 80. J.B.; (7") **RUNAWAY. / KEEP SEARCHIN' (WE'LL FOLLOW THE SUN)** [ ] [-]
(re-iss.Jan81 on 'London')
Jun 80. J.B.; (7") **HATS OFF TO LARRY. / LITTLE TOWN FLIRT** [ ] [-]
Oct 82. Dakota; (lp) **DEL SHANNON** [ ] [-]
1983. Audio Fidelity; (lp) **20 GREATEST HITS** [ ] [-]
Note; Below releases on 'Old Gold' until mentioned otherwise.
Apr 83. (7") **RUNAWAY. / JODY** [ ] [-]
Apr 83. (7") **HATS OFF TO LARRY. / HEY! LITTLE GIRL** [ ] [-]
Apr 83. (7") **THE SWISS MAID. / SO LONG BABY** [ ] [-]
Apr 83. (7") **LITTLE TOWN FLIRT. / TWO KINDS OF TEARDROPS** [ ] [-]
Apr 83. (7") **KEEP SEARCHIN' (WE'LL FOLLOW THE SUN). / KELLY** [ ] [-]
Feb 89. (cd-s) **RUNAWAY / HATS OFF TO LARRY / KEEP SEARCHIN' (WE'LL FOLLOW THE SUN)** [ ] [-]
Mar 84. Edsel; (lp)(c) **RUNAWAY HITS** [ ] [-]
(cd-iss.1986) (below cd-iss.1990)
Apr 86. Edsel; (lp) **I GO TO PIECES** [ ] [-]
Apr 86. MFP; (lp) **ROCK'N'ROLL GREATS** [ ] [-]
Jul 91. Connoisseur; (cd) **LOOKING BACK: HIS BIGGEST HITS** [ ] [-]
– Runaway / Hats off to Larry / Don't gild the lily / So long baby / The answer to everything / Hey little girl / I don't care anymore / You never talked about me / I won't be there / Ginny in the mirror / cry myself to sleep / Swiss maid / little town flirt / Two kinds of teardrops / Kelly / Two silhouettes / From me to you / Sue's gonna be mine / That's the way love is / Mary Jane / Handy man / World without love / Do you wanna dance / Keep searchin' / Broken promises / I go to pieces / Stranger in town / Break up / Why don't you tell him / Move it on over.
Nov 93. Charly; (cd) **GREATEST HITS** [ ] [-]
Jul 94. Success; (cd)(c) **RUNAWAY** [ ] [-]
Feb 95. B.A.M.; (cd) **PEARLS OF THE PAST** [ ] [-]
Apr 95. Muskateer; (cd)(c) **20 GREATEST HITS** [ ] [-]
Jun 95. BGO; (cd) **LIVE IN ENGLAND / . . .AND THE MUSIC PLAYS ON** [ ] [-]

Feargal SHARKEY (see under ⇒ UNDERTONES)

SHARPE & NUMAN (see under ⇒ NUMAN, Gary)

Tommy SHAW (see under ⇒ STYX)

SHED SEVEN

Formed: York, England . . . late 1991 by (see below). Signed to 'Polydor' late in '93 and with press adulation (NME, etc) they secured a near Top 75 hit with double-A side 'MARK' / 'CASINO GIRL'. In the summer of '94, they were on TOTP with high charting 'DOLPHIN'. • **Style:** Young indie-pop outfit like SUEDE, CHARLATANS, glam/mod. Singer WITTER has remarkable vox fusion lying somewhere between BRETT ANDERSON & ADAM ANT! • **Songwriters:** WITTER lyrics / group compositions. • **Trivia:** Said to have taken their group name, after it was revealed by ALAN the drummer that he lost his virginity in a shed aged only 7!. (eh!)

Recommended: CHANGE GIVER (*7)

RICK WITTER – vocals / **PAUL BANKS** – guitar / **TOM GLADWIN** – bass / **ALAN LEACH** – drums

Polydor Polydor
Mar 94. (7"green)(c-s) **MARK. / CASINO GIRL** [77] [ ]
(12"+=)(cd-s+=) – Mobile 10.
Jun 94. (7")(c-s) **DOLPHIN. / IMMOBILITIES** [28] [ ]
(12"+=)(cd-s+=) – ('A'remix).
Aug 94. (7")(c-s) **SPEAKEASY. / AROUND YOUR HOUSE** [24] [ ]
(12"+=)(cd-s+=) – Your guess is as good as mine / Dolphin.
Sep 94. (cd)(c)(lp) **CHANGE GIVER** [16] [ ]
– Dirty soul / Speakeasy / Long time dead / Head and hands / Casino girl / Missing out / Dolphin / Stars in your eyes / Mark / Ocean pie / On an island with you.
Nov 94. (7")(c-s) **OCEAN PIE. / NEVER AGAIN** [33] [ ]
(12"+=)(cd-s+=) – Sleepeasy / Sensitive.
Apr 95. (7"green)(c-s) **WHERE HAVE YOU BEEN TONIGHT?. / SWING MY WAVE** [23] [ ]
(cd-s+=) – This is my house.

Pete SHELLEY (see under ⇒ BUZZCOCKS)

Michelle SHOCKED

Born: KAREN MICHELLE JOHNSON, 1962, Gilmer, East Texas, USA. Spent years travelling around army bases in 1977, until she went to New York in 1978 to live with father. In 1986, after spending time busking around Europe, she recorded on one take 'THE TEXAS CAMPFIRE TAPES', with help from Englishman PETE LAWRENCE, and her Dylan-like song introductions. It was released in the UK by indie label 'Cooking V.', which led to a deal with 'London'. Her next album 'SHORT SHARP SHOCKED', complete with controversial lp sleeve, depicting police brutality, cracked the UK Top 40 in 1988. Six months later she ordered her American record label 'Polygram' to destroy all copies going to South Africa. • **Style:** Folk-rock protester, influenced by blueglass and dustbowl WOODY GUTHRIE. Her near MELANIE vocal style, progressed into jazz-swing era for her 1989 album 'CAPTAIN SWING'. • **Songwriters:** Writes all material and borrows some trad., except ZIP-A-DEE-DOO-DAH (Wrubel-Gilbert) / GOODNIGHT IRENE (?). • **Trivia:** Her 1988 album was produced by PETE ANDERSON. The HOTHOUSE FLOWERS guested on a track 'Over The Waterfall' off 1992 album.

Recommended: TEXAS CAMPFIRE TAPES (*8) / SHORT SHARP SHOCKED (*7).

MICHELLE SHOCKED – vocals, acoustic guitar

Cooking V. Mercury
Nov 86. (lp)(c) **THE TEXAS CAMPFIRE TAPES** [ ] [ ]
– 5 a.m. in Amsterdam / The secret admirer / The incomplete image / Who cares? / Down on St. Thomas St. / Fogtown / Steppin' out / The hepcat / Necktie / (Don't you mess around with) My little sister / The ballad of Patch eye & Meg / The secret to a long life (is knowing when it's time to go). *(cd-iss.Apr88 +=)*– The chain smoker / Stranded in a limousine / Goodnight Irene. *(re-iss.cd+c Nov93)*
Jun 87. (7") **DISORIENTATED. / IF LOVE WAS A TRAIN** [ ] [-]
(12"+=) – Chain smoker / Stranded in a limousine / Goodnight Irene.

—— now added numerous session people.

London Mercury
Aug 88. (lp)(c)(cd) **SHORT SHARP SHOCKED** [33] [73]
– When I grow up / Hello Hopeville / Memories of East Texas / (Making the run to) Gladewater / Graffiti limbo / If love was a train / Anchorage / The L&N don't stop here anymore / V.F.D. / Black widow.
Sep 88. (7") **ANCHORAGE. / FOGTOWN** [60] [66] Nov 88
(10"+=) – Remodelling the Pentagon / Penny Evans (live).
(12"+=)(cd-s+=) – Strawberry jam (live) / Penny Evans (live).
Dec 88. (7") **IF LOVE WAS A TRAIN. / MEMORIES OF EAST TEXAS** [63] [ ]
(12"+=) – Graffiti limbo (live).
(cd-s+=) – V.F.D. / Jambouree queen.
Feb 89. (7") **WHEN I GROW UP. / 5 A.M. IN AMSTERDAM (live)** [67] [ ]
(12"+=)/ /(cd-s+=) – Goodnight Irene./ / Camper crusade.
Nov 89. (lp)(c)(cd) **CAPTAIN SWING** [31] [95]
– God is a real estate developer / On the greener side / Silent ways / Sleep keeps me awake / The cement lament / (You don't mess around with) My little sister / Looks like Mona Lisa / Too little too late / Street corner ambassador / Must be luff.
Nov 89. (7")(c-s) **ON THE GREENER SIDE. / RUSSIAN ROULETTE** [ ] [ ]
(12"+=)(cd-s+=) – The Titanic / Old paint.
Mar 92. (7")(c-s) **COME A LONG WAY. / OVER THE WATERFALL** [ ] [ ]
(cd-s+=) – Contest coming / Jump Jim Crow-Zip-a-dee-doo-dah.
(cd-s+=) – Worth the weight / Shaking hands (soldier's toy).
Apr 92. (cd)(c)(lp) **ARKANSAS TRAVELER** [46] [ ]
– 33 r.p.m. soul / Come a long way / Secret to a long life / Contest coming (Cripple Creek) / Over the waterfall / Shaking hands (Soldier's joy) / Medley:-Jump Jim crow – Zip-a-dee-doo-dah / Hold me back / Strawberry jam / Prodigal daughter (Cotton-eyed Joe) / Blackberry blossom / Weaving way / Arkansas traveler / Woody's rag.
May 92. (7") **33 R.P.M. SOUL. / BLACKBERRY BLOSSOM (live)** [ ] [ ]
(cd-s+=) – Over the waterfall (live) / ('A'live).

SIGUE SIGUE SPUTNIK

Formed: London, England . . . 1985 by extrovert fashion conscious punk TONY JAMES + CHRIS KAVANAGH. They were soon hyped by music press for outrageous image and sound, which enabled them to sign reputed £4 million deal with 'EMI'. Early in 1986, their label's high exposure, paid off when debut 'LOVE MISSILE FX-1', broke them into the UK Top 3. After another Top 20 hit, they issued weird first album 'FLAUNT IT', which came complete with real commercials between tracks!. Their stay at top level was short-lived, as public and press all but abandoned them by the late 80's. • **Style:** As said, plus a mixture/barrage of technical glam-punk/pop sounds, which relied very heavily on unusual haircuts and clothes. A case of image over talent. • **Songwriters:** TONY JAMES wrote & produced songs. • **Trivia:** TONY JAMES previously produced for goth band SEX GANG CHILDREN.

Recommended: FLAUNT IT (*5)

TONY JAMES – space guitar, bass, producer (ex-GENERATION X) / **MARTIN DEGVILLE** – vocals / **NEIL X** (WHITMORE) – guitar / **RAY MAYHEW** –

drums / **CHRIS KAVANAGH** (b. 4 Jun'64) – drums / **JANE FARRIMOND** – sound mixer

Parlophone Manhattan

Feb 86. (7") **LOVE MISSILE F1-11. / HACK ATTACK** [3] [ ]
(12"+=) – ('A'extended dance).
(12") – ('A'side) / ('A'mixes).

May 86. (7")(12") **21st CENTURY BOY. / BUY E.M.I.** [20] [-]

Jul 86. (lp)(c)(cd) **FLAUNT IT** [11] [96]
– Love missile F1-11 / Atari baby / Sex bomb boogie / Rockit Miss U.S.A. / 21st century boy / Massive retaliation / Teenage thunder / She's my man.

Aug 86. (7") **MASSIVE RETALIATION. / TEENAGE THUNDER** [-] [ ]

Dec 86. (video-single) **SEX BOMB BOOGIE. / LOVE MISSILE F1-11 (US mix)** [ ] [-]

Nov 88. (7") **SUCCESS. / FRANKENSTEIN CHA CHA CHA** [31] [ ]
(12"+=)(12"pic-d+=) – Last temptation of Sputnik.
(cd-s++=) – Bodaera city

E.M.I. EMI America

Mar 89. (7")(7"pic-d) **DANCERAMA. / BARBARANDROID** [50] [ ]
(12")(cd-s)(12"pic-d) – ('A'club mix) / ('A'extended) / ('A'lp mix).

Apr 89. (lp)(c)(cd) **DRESS FOR EXCESS** [53] [ ]
– Albinoni vs. star wars (part 1 & 2) / Boom boom satellite / Hey Jayne Mansfield superstar! / Super crook blues / Success / Dancerama / Orgasm / M.A.D. (Mutual Assured Destruction) / Is this the future?.

May 89. (7") **ALBINONI VS. STAR WARS. / ('A' part 2)** [75] [ ]
(12"+=)(cd-s+=) – ('A'extended).

Jul 89. (7") **RIO ROCKS. / ALIENS** [ ] [ ]
(12")(cd-s) – ('A'side) / ('A'samba mix ext.) / ('A'acid mix).

—— Disbanded when TONY JAMES joined The SISTERS OF MERCY. KAVANAGH later went to BIG AUDIO DYNAMITE II.

– compilations, others, etc. –

Jun 90. Jungle; (cd)(c)(lp) **THE FIRST GENERATION** (demos, rarities, etc.) [ ] [-]

MARTIN DEGVILLE

solo, augmented by **MICK ROSSI** – guitar (ex-SLAUGHTER & THE DOGS)

Receiver not issued

Feb 91. (cd)(lp) **WORLD WORLD FAIR** [ ] [-]
– Nuclear sex machine / Judge Dread on a B.S.A. / Only the lonely / Saturn 5 / Sexy robot / Transformer transex / Freak show city / Wild is the wind / Space rider / Planet Mars.

SILVERCHAIR

Formed: Australia . . .early 90's by schoolmates DANIEL, CHRIS and BEN. Made a huge impact in homeland with 1995 debut album 'FROGSTOMP', before repeating the formula ten-fold in the States. • **Style:** Teenage heavy-rock influenced by ROLLINS BAND, HELMET and BLACK SABBATH. • **Songwriters:** JOHNS-GILLIES.

Recommended: FROGSTOMP (*7)

DANIEL JOHNS – vocals, guitar / **CHRIS JOANNOU** – bass / **BEN GILLIES** – drums

Columbia Columbia

Jul 95. (12"ep) **PURE MASSACRE. / ACID RAIN / BLIND** [71] [ ]
(cd-ep+=) – Stoned.

Sep 95. (7")(c-s) **TOMORROW. / BLIND (live)** [59] [ ]
(cd-s) – ('A'side) / Leave me out / Undecided.

Sep 95. (cd)(c)(lp) **FROGSTOMP** [49] [9] Aug95
– Israel's son / Tomorrow / Faultline / Pure massacre / Shade / Blind / Leave me out / Suicidal dream / Madman / Undecided / Cicada / Findaway.

SILVERFISH

Formed: London, England . . . 1988 by FUZZ DUPREY, who soon found WATSON and MOWFORTH. They spotted female LESLEY RANKINE, bopping around at a hard-core gig, and quickly recruited her. After a few Peel Sessions and releases on indie 'Wiiija', they signed to 'Creation' in 1991. Their second album 'ORGAN FAN' achieved minor chart placing in Top 75, before they toured the States. • **Style:** Punk noise you can dance to, fronted by what was described by press as the female 'fat Axl Rose' (a title they used for debut lp). Manic LESLEY howled her way high-pitched vox effectively, through a chainsaw barrage of blues-ish guitar-rock. • **Songwriters:** Most by RANKINE-DUPREY or group, except ROCK ON (David Essex). • **Trivia:** Their song 'DOLLY PARTON' contained thigh-slapping lyrics 'Jolene, Jolene, oh f . . . off'. JIM THIRLWELL (Foetus) produced and played brass on 1992 album. It was his idea to bring in guest trumpeter JOE COLARUSSO (ex-Vegas years ELVIS P).

Recommended: ORGAN FAN (*7)

ANDREW 'FUZZ' DUPREY (b.14 Jun'63, Kent, England) – guitar / **LESLEY RANKINE** (b.11 Apr'65, Edinburgh, Scotland) – vocals / **CHRIS POWFORTH** (b.30 May'64, Middlesex, England) – bass / **STUART WATSON** (b.10 Nov'62, Northamptonshire, England) – drums

Wiiija not issued

Jul 89. (12"ep) **SILVERFISH EP** [ ] [-]
– Weird shit / Don't fuck / Dolly Parton / On the motorway. *(re-iss.Feb93 as 'DOLLY PARTON EP')*

Feb 90. (7"ep)(12"ep) **TOTAL FUCKING ASSHOLE. / DIE / DRILLER** [ ] [-]

Jan 91. (cd)(c)(lp) **FAT AXL** [ ] [-]
– Pink and lively / Fat painted carcass / Harry Butcher / Shit out of luck / White lines / Two marines / Spoon / Baby baby baby / Ich bin eih- / Schifttek trauser. *(re-iss.Feb93 on 'Southern')*

Creation Creation ?

Aug 91. (12"ep)(cd-ep) **F***IN' DRIVIN' OR WHAT . . . E.P.** [ ] [-]
– Big bad baby pig squeal / Puppy truck / Texas tea.

—— In Nov 91, LESLEY SILVERFISH was credited on 'Clawfist' collaboration with The ROCKINGBIRDS:- 'Your Good Girl's Gonna Go Bad'.

Mar 92. (12"ep)(cd-ep) **SILVERFISH WITH SCRAMBLED EGGS** [ ] [ ]
– Crazy / Jimmy / Vitriola / Jenny.

Jun 92. (cd)(c)(lp) **ORGAN FAN** [65] [ ]
– This bug / Mary Brown / Suckin' gas / Petal / Fuckin' strange way to get attention / Big bad baby pig squeal / Elvis leg / Dechainee / Scrub me mama with that boogie beat / Rock on / Joos.

Mar 93. (7") **DAMN FINE WOMAN. / SUCKING GAS** [ ] [ ]
(12")(cd-s) – ('A'side) / Scrub me mama / Petal / F.S.W.T.G.A.

– compilations, others, etc –

Aug 90. Touch & Go; (cd)(c)(lp) **COCKEYE** [ ] [ ]

RUBY

LESLEY RANKINE – vocals (now living New Orleans) with co-writer **MARK WALK** (named after both grandmothers' name)

Creation Creation

Sep 95. (c-s) **PARAFFIN / THE WHOLE IS EQUAL TO THE SUM OF IT'S PARTS** [ ] [ ]
(cd-s) – ('A'-Red Snapper remix) / ('A'-Wagon Christ remix) / ('A'-Dead Elvis remix) / ('A'-Mark Walk remix).
(cd-s) – ('A'-Harpie mix) / ('A'-album version) / ('A'-Wagon Christ vocal) / ('A'-Richard Fearless dub).

Oct 95. (cd)(c) **SALT PETER** [ ] [ ]
– Flippin' the bird / Salt water fish / Heidi / Tiny meat / Paraffin / Hoops / Pine / Swallow baby / The whole is equal to the sum of the parts / Bud / Carondelet.

Patrick SIMMONDS (see under ⇒ DOOBIE BROTHERS)

Gene SIMMONS (see under ⇒ KISS)

Carly SIMON

Born: 25 Jun'45, New York City, USA. In 1963 she formed folk duo The SIMON SISTERS with older sister LUCY. They recorded a few 45's on 'Kapp' label, before parting ways in 1966. She went solo in the early 70's after signing to 'Elektra'. Her eponymous debut album in 1971, was the first of many US Top 30 successes. 18 months later, she was at the top of the US singles chart with gem 'YOU'RE SO VAIN'. • **Style:** Sophisticated pop/rock star who mixed classy love songs with uptempo AOR tunes. • **Songwriters:** Initially worked with film critic JACOB BRACKMAN on debut album. She also covered MOCKINGBIRD (Charlie & Inez Foxx) / IT KEEPS YOU RUNNING (Doobie Brothers) / NOBODY DOES IT BETTER (Marvin Hamlisch & Carole Bayer Sager) / DEVOTED TO YOU (Everly Brothers) / WHY (Chic) / etc. She recorded 2 standards/covers albums TORCH and MY ROMANCE. CARLY also collaborated on several numbers. • **Trivia:** She married singer JAMES TAYLOR on 3rd Nov'72, whom she wrote some songs with during the 70's. They separated in 1982 and divorced the year after.

Recommended: THE BEST OF CARLY SIMON (*7).

SIMON SISTERS

CARLY & LUCY – dual vocals

London Kapp

Apr 64. (7") **WINKIN', BLINKIN' AND NOD. / SO GLAD I'M HERE** [ ] [73]

Aug 65. (7") **CUDDLEBUG. / NO ONE TO TALK MY TROUBLES TO** [ ] [ ]

—— Split in 1966, when LUCY went off to get married. The following year, CARLY moved to France but returned to sign for Albert Grossman management. After dispute with him, she met producer JAC HOLZMAN who signed her to 'Elektra' in 1969.

CARLY SIMON

CARLY – vocals, piano, guitar was augmented by session musicians.

Elektra Elektra

Apr 71. (lp)(c) **CARLY SIMON** [ ] [30]
– That's the way I've always heard it should be / Alone / One more time / The best thing / Just a sinner / Dan, my fling / Another door / Reunions / Rolling down the hills / The love's still growing. *(quad-lp iss.Apr77)*

May 71. (7") **THAT'S THE WAY I'VE ALWAYS HEARD IT SHOULD BE. / ALONE** [ ] [10] Apr 71

Dec 71. (lp)(c) **ANTICIPATION** [ ] [30] Nov 71
– Anticipation / Legend in your own time / Our first day together / The girl you think you see / Summer's coming around again / Share the end / The garden / Three days / Julie through the glass / I've got to have you. *(cd-iss.Oct89)*

Dec 71. (7") **ANTICIPATION. / THE GARDEN** [ ] [13]

Mar 72. (7") **LEGEND IN YOUR OWN TIME. / JULIE THROUGH THE GLASS** [ ] [50]

Sep 72. (7") **SHARE THE END. / THE GIRL YOU THINK YOU SEE** [-] [ ]

Nov 72. (7") **YOU'RE SO VAIN. / HIS FRIENDS ARE MORE THAN FOND OF ROBIN** [3] [1]

— (above 'A' featured uncredited MICK JAGGER on backing vocals)

Jan 73. (lp)(c) **NO SECRETS** [3] [1] Dec 72
– The right thing to do / The Carter family / You're so vain / His friends are more than fond of Robin / We have no secrets / Embrace me you child / Waited so long / It was so easy / Night owl / When you close your eyes. *(quad-lp Apr77)*

Mar 73. (7") **THE RIGHT THING TO DO. / WE HAVE NO SECRETS** [-] [17]

Mar 73. (7") **THE RIGHT THING TO DO. / THE WAY I'VE ALWAYS HEARD IT SHOULD BE** [17] [-]
(re-iss.1976)

Jan 74. (7") **HAVEN'T GOT TIME FOR THE PAIN. / MIND ON MY MAN** [ ] [14] May 74

Mar 74. (lp)(c) **HOTCAKES** [19] [3] Jan 74
– Just not true / Hotcakes / Misfit / Forever my love / Mockingbird / Grown up / Haven't got time for the pain / Safe and sound / Mind on my man / Think I'm gonna have a baby / Older sister. *(quad-lp iss.Apr77)*

Mar 74. (7") **MOCKINGBIRD. ("CARLY SIMON & JAMES TAYLOR") / GROWN UP** [34] [5] Jan 74

May 74. (7") **MIND ON THE MAN. / HAVEN'T GOT TIME FOR THE PAIN** [-] [ ]

May 75. (lp)(c) **PLAYING POSSUM** [ ] [10]
– After the storm / Love out on the street / Look me in the eyes / More and more / Slave / Attitude dancing / Waterfall / Sons of summer / Are you ticklish / Playing possum. *(quad-lp iss.Apr77)*

Jun 75. (7") **ATTITUDE DANCING. / ARE YOU TICKLISH** [ ] [21] May 75

Jun 75. (7") **LOOK ME IN THE EYES. / SLAVE** [-] [ ]

Aug 75. (7") **WATERFALL. / AFTER THE STORM** [ ] [78] Jul 75

Oct 75. (7") **MORE AND MORE. / LOVE OUT IN THE STREET** [-] [94]

Dec 75. (lp)(c) **THE BEST OF CARLY SIMON** (compilation) [ ] [17]
– That's the way I've always heard it / Should be / The right thing to do / Mockingbird / Legend in our own time / Haven't you got time for the pain / You're so vain / No secrets / Night owl / Anticipation / Attitude dancing. *(cd-iss. 1983) (re-iss.+cd.May91) (quad-lp iss.Apr77)*

Jun 76. (7") **IT KEEPS YOU RUNNIN'. / LOOK ME IN THE EYES** [-] [46]

Jun 76. (7") **IT KEEPS YOU RUNNIN'. / BE WITH ME** [ ] [-]

Jun 76. (lp)(c) **ANOTHER PASSENGER** [ ] [29]
– Half a chance / It keeps you runnin' / Fairweather father / Cowtown / He likes to roll / In times when my head / One love stand / Riverboat gambler / Darkness 'til dawn / Dishonesty modesty / Libby / Be with me.

Aug 76. (7") **HALF A CHANCE. / LIBBY** [ ] [ ]

Jul 77. (7") **NOBODY DOES IT BETTER. / AFTER THE STORM** [7] [2]
(re-iss.Mar82)

(above single from the James Bond film 'The Spy Who Loved Me')

Apr 78. (7") **YOU BELONG TO ME. / IN A SMALL MOMENT** [ ] [6]

Apr 78. (lp)(c) **BOYS IN THE TREES** [ ] [10]
– You belong to me / Boys in the trees / Back down to Earth / Devoted to you / De bat (fly in me face) / Haunting / Tranquillo (melt my heart) / You're the one / In a small moment / One man woman / For old times sake.

Aug 78. (7") **TRANQUILLO (MELT MY HEART). / FOR OLD TIMES SAKE** [ ] [-]

Nov 78. (7") **DEVOTED TO YOU. ("CARLY SIMON & JAMES TAYLOR") / BOYS IN THE TREES** [ ] [36] Aug 78

Feb 79. (7") **TRANQUILO (MELT MY HEART). / BACK DOWN TO EARTH** [-] [ ]

Jun 79. (lp)(c) **SPY** [ ] [45]
– Vengeance / We're so close / Just like you do / Coming to get you / Never been gone / Pure sin / Love you by heart / Spy / Memorial day.

Jun 79. (7") **VENGEANCE. / I LOVE YOU BY HEART** [ ] [48]

Aug 79. (7") **SPY. / PURE SIN** [ ] [ ]

Warners Warners

Jun 80. (7") **COME UPSTAIRS. / JAMES** [ ] [ ]

Jul 80. (lp)(c) **COME UPSTAIRS** [ ] [36]
– Come upstairs / Stardust / Them / Jesse / James / In pain / The three of us in the dark / Take me as I am / The desert.

Nov 80. (7") **JESSE. / STARDUST** [ ] [11] Jul 80

Sep 81. (lp)(c) **TORCH** [ ] [50]
– Blue of blue / I'll be around / I got it bad and that ain't good / I get along without you very well / Body and soul / Hurt / Spring is here / Pretty strange / What shall we do with the child / Not a day goes by.

Jan 82. (7") **HURT. / FROM THE HEART** [ ] [ ]

Jul 82. (7") **WHY. / WHY (instrumental)** [10] [74]
(12"+=) – ('A'extended). *(re-iss.Jun89, hit UK 56)*

(above single from the film 'Soup For One' on 'Mirage' records). In Aug'83, she provided the singing part on UK No.17 hit single 'Kissing With Confidence' by WILL POWERS.

Sep 83. (lp)(c) **HELLO BIG MAN** [ ] [69]
– You know what to do / Menemsha / Damn you get to me / Is this love / Orpheus / It happens everyday / Such a goody boy / Hello big man / You don't feel the same / Floundering. *(cd-iss.Jul86)*

Sep 83. (7") **YOU KNOW WHAT TO DO. / ORPHEUS** [ ] [83]

Feb 84. (7") **HELLO BIG MAN. / DAMN YOU GET TO ME** [-] [ ]

not issued Planet

1984. (7") **SOMEONE WAITS FOR YOU. / ('A'version)** [-] [ ]

Epic Epic

Jun 85. (7")(12") **TIRED OF BEING BLONDE. / BLACK HONEY-MOON** [ ] [70]

Aug 85. (lp)(c)(cd) **SPOILED GIRL** [ ] [88] Jul 85
– My new boyfriend / Come back home / Tonight and forever / Spoiled girl / Tired of being blonde / The wives are in Connecticut / Anyone but me / Interview / Make me feel something / Can't give it up. *(c+cd+=)* – Black honeymoon. *(cd re-iss.Jun91)*

Aug 85. (7")(12") **MY NEW BOYFRIEND. / THE WIVES ARE IN CONNECTICUT** [ ] [ ]

next 45 was from film 'Heartburn'.

Arista Arista

Jan 87. (7") **COMING AROUND AGAIN. / ITSY BITSY SPIDER** [12] [18] Oct 86
(12"+=) – If it wasn't love.

Apr 87. (7") **GIVE ME ALL NIGHT. / TWO HOT GIRLS (ON A HOT SUMMER'S NIGHT)** [ ] [61]
(12"+=) – Hold what you've got.

Jun 87. (lp)(c)(cd) **COMING AROUND AGAIN** [25] [25] Apr 87
– Coming around again / Give me all night / As time goes by / Do the walls come down / It should have been me / The stuff that dreams are made of / Two hot girls (on a hot summer's night) / You have to hurt / All I want is you / Hold what you've got / Itst bitsy spider.

Aug 87. (7") **THE STUFF THAT DREAMS ARE MADE OF. / AS TIME GOES BY** [ ] [ ]
(12"+=) – Sleight of hand.

Oct 87. (7") **ALL I WANT IS YOU. / TWO HOT GIRLS (ON A HOT SUMMER NIGHT)** [-] [ ]

Nov 87. (7") **ALL I WANT IS YOU. / YOU HAVE TO HURT** [ ] [54]

Sep 88. (lp)(c)(cd) **GREATEST HITS LIVE (live)** [49] [87]
– You're so vain / Nobody does it better / Coming around again / It happen every day / Anticipation / Right thing to do / Do the walls come down / You belong to me / Two hot girls (on a hot summer night) / All I want is you / Never been gone. *(re-iss.cd Oct95)*

Sep 88. (7")(US-c-s) **YOU'RE SO VAIN (live). / DO THE WALLS COME DOWN (live)** [ ] [ ]
(12"+=)(cd-s+=) – Coming around again (live) / Itsy bitsy spider (live).

Nov 88. (7") **NOBODY DOES IT BETTER (live). / ALL I WANT IS YOU (live)** [ ] [ ]
(12"+=)(cd-s+=) – Never been gone (live).

Below 45 was from the movie 'Working Girl'.

Feb 89. (7") **LET THE RIVER RUN. / THE TURN OF THE TIDE** [-] [49]

Mar 89. (7")(c-s) **LET THE RIVER RUN. / CARLOTTA'S HEART** [ ] [-]
(12"+=)(cd-s+=) – Medley: Coming around again – Itsy bitsy spider.

Mar 90. (cd)(c)(lp) **MY ROMANCE** [ ] [46]
– My romance / By myself / I see your face / When your lover is gone / In the wee small hours / My funny valentine / Something wonderful / Little girl blue / He was good to me / What has she got / Bewitched / Danny boy / Time after time.

Oct 90. (cd)(c)(lp) **HAVE YOU SEEN ME LATELY?** [ ] [60]
– Better not tell her / Didn't I? / Have you seen me lately? / Life is eternal / Waiting at the gate / Happy birthday / Holding me tonight / It's not like him / Don't wrap it up / Fisherman's song / We just got here.

Oct 90. (7") **BETTER NOT TELL HER. / HAPPY BIRTHDAY** [-] [ ]

Jan 91. (7") **LIFE IS ETERNAL. / WE JUST GOT HERE** [-] [ ]

Nov 94. (cd)(c) **LETTERS NEVER SENT** [ ] [ ]
– (intro) / Letters never sent / LOst in your love / Like a river / Time works on all the wild young men / Touched by the Sun / Davy / Halfway 'round the world / What about a holiday / The reason / Private / Catch it like a fever / Born to break my heart / I'd rather it was you.

Dec 95. (cd)(c) **CLOUDS IN MY COFFEE** (compilation) [ ] [ ]

– more compilations, etc. –

On 'Elektra' unless otherwise mentioned.

Sep 76. (7") **YOU'RE SO VAIN. / ANTICIPATION** [ ] [ ]
(re-iss.Sep85 on 'Old Gold')

Sep 76. (7") **MOCKINGBIRD. ("CARLY SIMON & JAMES TAYLOR") / LEGEND IN** [ ] [-]

Oct 82. (d-c) **ANTICIPATION / NO SECRETS** [ ] [-]

Apr 91. (7")(c-s) **YOU'RE SO VAIN. / DO THE WALLS COME DOWN** [41] [ ]
(12"+=) – Coming around again / Itsy bitsy spider.
(cd-s) – ('A'side) / The girl you think you see / Anticipation.

Apr 81. Hallmark; (lp)(c) **YOU'RE SO VAIN** [ ] [-]

Dec 82. Mirage; (7") **COME UPSTAIRS. / JESSE** [ ] [-]
(12"+=) – ('A'version).

SIMON AND GARFUNKEL

Formed: New York, USA ... 1957 as TOM & JERRY by ART GARFUNKEL (b. ARTHUR GARFUNKEL, 5 Nov'41, Queens, New York) & PAUL SIMON (b.13 Oct'41, Newark, New Jersey). After a number of singles from 1958-1962, and PAUL's excursion into solo pseudonym territory, they finally teamed up together in 1964 as SIMON & GARFUNKEL. They signed to 'Columbia' that year, and issued debut lp 'WEDNESDAY MORNING 3 A.M.'. After it flopped, PAUL ventured to the UK, where he wrote 'HOMEWARD BOUND' on the Platform of Widnes railway station. It was included on his 1965 solo album ' . . . SONGBOOK'. In Oct'65, producer Tom Wilson decided to re-record 1964 track 'THE SOUNDS OF SILENCE' with electric backing, without informing the duo. Their protests were put aside, when the re-vamped track topped the US chart for 2 weeks early in '66. Pop trio The BACHELORS scored a Top 3 hit with it in Britain. S&G chose to issue 'HOMEWARD BOUND' as a duo, and this gave them worldwide smash. After a string of other hits, they were invited to supply music for the 1968 film 'THE GRADUATE' (which starred Dustin Hoffman & Anne Bancroft). In 1970, before their demise, they went into rock/pop history when 'BRIDGE OVER TROUBLED WATER' made UK + US No.1, staying in UK charts for over 300 weeks, and receiving a US grammy. The rest of the 70's saw ART going into acting and sparse solo work, while PAUL was the more successful having solo 70's Top 5 albums 'PAUL SIMON', 'THERE GOES . . . ' & 'STILL CRAZY AFTER ALL THESE YEARS'. In 1980, he signed a new deal with 'Warners'. His first venture was to write a soundtrack & script for his self-directed/acted movie 'ONE TRICK PONY'. After a disappointing follow-up in 1983, PAUL was back in the limelight in 1986 with a superb 'GRACELANDS' album, which featured South African dancers, musicians & singers. The following year, after being removed from anti-apartheid blacklists, it won a Grammy. • **Style:** Overly influenced by The EVERLY BROTHERS, although in the mid-60's, they caught on to burgeoning folk pop scene. Their clean-cut acoustic ballads were beautifully harmonised by both parties. In 1986, PAUL was inspired by African rhythms, etc on his album

'GRACELANDS'. • **Songwriters:** PAUL SIMON penned most. They covered THE TIMES THEY ARE A-CHANGIN' (Bob Dylan) / BYE BYE LOVE (Everly Brothers). PAUL SIMON covered GO TELL IT TO THE MOUNTAIN (trad). GARFUNKEL covered loads including ALL I KNOW (Jimmy Webb) / SECOND AVENUE (Tim Moore) / BREAKAWAY (Gallagher & Lyle) / I ONLY HAVE EYES FOR YOU (Flamingos) / WONDERFUL WORLD (Sam Cooke) / BRIGHT EYES (Mike Batt) / SINCE I DON'T HAVE YOU (Skyliners) / SO MUCH IN LOVE (Tymes) / MISS YOU NIGHTS (Cliff Richard) / WHEN A MAN LOVES A WOMAN (Percy Sledge) / RAG DOLL (Four Seasons) / etc. **ART's filmography:** CATCH 22 (1970 w/Alan Arkin) / CARNAL KNOWLEDGE (1971 w/Ann-Margret, Candice Bergen & Jack Nicholson) / BAD TIMING (1979 w/Teresa Russell) / ILLUSIONS (1980) / GOOD TO GO (1986) / MOTHER GOOSE ROCK'N'RHYME (1989 TV Disney musical with PAUL). Note PAUL cameod in the 1977 Woody Allen film 'Annie Hall'. • **Trivia:** PAUL's video for the 1986 single 'YOU CAN CALL ME AL' featured comic actor Chevy Chase. PAUL married long-time fiance and actress Carrie Fisher, on 16th May '83.

Recommended: THE DEFINITIVE SIMON & GARFUNKEL (*9). PAUL SIMON:- NEGOTIATIONS AND LOVE SONGS 1971-1986 (*8). ART GARFUNKEL:- THE ART GARFUNKEL ALBUM (*5).

TOM AND JERRY

(TOM = ART GARFUNKEL / JERRY = PAUL SIMON)

not issued | Big

Dec 57. (7") **HEY SCHOOLGIRL. / DANCIN' WILD** [-] [49]
(US re-iss.on 'King')
1958. (7") **OUR SONG. / TWO TEENAGERS** [-] [ ]
1959. (7") **THAT'S MY STORY. / DON'T SAY GOODBYE** [-] [ ]
(US re-iss.on 'Hunt')
1959. (7") **BABY TALK. / TWO TEENAGERS** [-] [ ]
(US re-iss.on 'Bell')

not issued | ABC Para..

1960. (7") **SURRENDER. / FIGHTING MAD** [-] [ ]
1960. (7") **THAT'S MY STORY. / TIJUANA BLUES** [-] [ ]

TRUE TAYLOR

(aka PAUL SIMON)

not issued | Big

1958. (7") **TRUE OR FALSE. / TEENAGE FOOL** [-] [ ]

JERRY LANDIS

not issued | M.G.M.

1959. (7") **ANNA BELLE. / LONELINESS** [-] [ ]

not issued | Warwick

1960. (7") **JUST A BOY. / SHY** [-] [ ]
1960. (7") **ID LIKE TO BE THE LIPSTICK ON YOUR COLLAR. / JUST A BOY** [-] [ ]

not issued | Amy

Dec 62. (7") **THE LONE TEEN RANGER. / LISA** [-] [97]

TICO & THE TRIUMPHS, PASSIONS

not issued | Amy

1961. (7") **PLAY ME A SAD SONG. / IT MEANS A LOT TO THEM** [-] [ ]

not iss. | Con-Am

1961. (7") **I'M LONELY. / I WISH I WEREN'T IN LOVE** [-] [ ]

not iss. | Amy

Dec 61. (7") **MOTORCYCLE. / I DON'T BELIEVE THEM** [-] [99]
1962. (7") **EXPRESS TRAIN. / WILDFLOWER** [-] [ ]
1962. (7") **CRY, LITTLE BOY, CRY. / GET UP & DO THE WONDER** [-] [ ]
1962. (7") **CARDS OF LOVE. / NOISE** [-] [ ]

JERRY LANDIS (UK), PAUL KANE (US)

(different credits across the ocean)

Oriole | Tribute

May 64. (7") **HE WAS MY BROTHER. / CARLOS DOMINGUEZ** [ ] [ ]

—— ART also recorded 3 unknown US singles as ARTIE GARR.
In-between their re-united SIMON & GARFUNKEL debut & follow-up albums,

PAUL SIMON

released solo below.

C.B.S. | Columbia

May 65. (lp) **THE PAUL SIMON SONGBOOK** [ ] [ ]
– I am a rock / Leaves that are green / A church is burning / April come she will / The sound of silence / Patterns / A most peculiar man / He was my brother / Kathy's song / The side of a hill / A simple desultory Philippic / Flowers never bend with the rainfall. *(cd-iss.Jan88)*
Jul 65. (7") **I AM A ROCK. / LEAVES THAT ARE GREEN** [ ] [ ]

SIMON AND GARFUNKEL

both vocals, acoustic guitar

C.B.S. | Columbia

Oct 64. (lp) **WEDNESDAY MORNING 3 A.M.** [-] [ ]
– You can tell the world / Last night I had the strangest dream / Bleecker Street / Sparrow / Benedictus / The sound of silence / He was my brother / Peggy-O / Go tell it to the mountain / The sun is burning / The times they are a-changin' / Wednesday morning 3 a.m. *(US re-dist.Jan66, hit No.30) (UK-iss.Nov68, hit No.24) (re-iss.+c+cd.Nov85)*
Jul 65. (7"ep) **SIMON AND GARFUNKEL** [ ] [ ]
– Bleecker Street / Sparrow / Wednesday morning 3 a.m. / The sound of silence.
Dec 65. (7") **THE SOUND OF SILENCE. / WE'VE GOT A GROOVY THING GOIN'** [ ] [1] Nov 65
Mar 66. (lp) **SOUND OF SILENCE** [13] [21] Feb 66
– The sound of silence / Leaves that are green / Blessed / Kathy's song / Somewhere they can't find me / Anji / Homeward bound / Richard Cory / A most peculiar man / April come she will / We've got a groovy thing goin' / I am a rock. *(re-iss.Mar81 hit UK 68, cd-iss.Dec85)*
Mar 66. (7") **HOMEWARD BOUND. / LEAVES THAT ARE GREEN** [9] [5] Feb 66
Jun 66. (7") **I AM A ROCK. / FLOWERS NEVER BEND WITH THE RAINFALL** [17] [3] May 66
(7"ep+=) – The sound of silence / Blessed.
Sep 66. (7") **THE DANGLING CONVERSATION. / THE BIG BRIGHT GREEN PLEASURE MACHINE** [ ] [25] Aug 66
Oct 66. (lp) **PARSLEY, SAGE, ROSEMARY & THYME** [ ] [4]
– Dangling conversation / Scarborough fair – Canticle / Patterns / For Emily, whenever I may find her / The big bright green pleasure machine / A poem on the underground all / Cloudy / A simple desultory Philippic (or how I was Robert McNamara'd into submission) / The 59th Street Bridge song (feelin' groovy) / Flowers never bend with the rainfall / 7 o'clock news – Silent night / Parsley, sage, Rosemary and thyme. *(UK re-dist.Aug68, hit No.13) (re-iss.Mar81) (re-iss.+c+cd.Jul87 + Apr89)*
Nov 66. (7") **A HAZY SHADE OF WINTER. / FOR EMILY, WHENEVER I MAY FIND HER** [ ] [13]
Mar 67. (7") **AT THE ZOO. / THE 59th STREET BRIDGE SONG (FEELIN' GROOVY)** [ ] [16]
Jun 67. (7"ep) **FEELIN' GROOVY** [ ] [-]
– The 59th Street bridge song (feelin' groovy) / The big bright green pleasure machine / A hazy shade of winter / Homeward bound.
Aug 67. (7") **FAKIN' IT. / YOU DON'T KNOW WHERE YOUR INTEREST LIES** [ ] [23] Jul 67
Mar 68. (7") **SCARBOROUGH FAIR; CANTICLE. / APRIL COME SHE WILL** [ ] [11] Feb 68
Jul 68. (7") **MRS. ROBINSON. / OLD FRIENDS; BOOKENDS** [4] [1] Apr 68
Jul 68. (lp) **BOOKENDS** [1] [1] May 68
– Bookends theme / Save the life of my child / America / Overs / (voices of old people) – Old friends / Bookends / Fakin' it / Punky's dilemma / Mrs. Robinson / A hazy shade of winter / At the zoo. *(re-iss.+c.Nov82) (cd-iss. Dec 85)*
Oct 68. (lp) **THE GRADUATE (Film Soundtrack; with tracks by DAVE GRUISIN *)** [3] [1] Mar 68
– The sound of silence / The singleman party foxtrot * / On the strip * / Sunporch cha-cha-cha * / Mrs.Robinson / A great effect * / Scarborough fair – Canticle / April come she will / Whew * / The folks * / The big bright green pleasure machine. *(re-iss.Feb84 + 1987, cd-iss.Dec85 + Apr89) (cd-iss.Apr91 on 'Sequel') (re-iss.cd+c Feb94 on 'Columbia')*
Dec 68. (7"ep) **MRS. ROBINSON** [9] [-]
– Mrs.Robinson / April come she will / Scarborough fair – Canticle / The sound of silence.
Apr 69. (7") **THE BOXER. / BABY DRIVER** [6] [7]
Feb 70. (7") **BRIDGE OVER TROUBLED WATER. / KEEP THE CUSTOMER SATISFIED** [1] [1]
(re-entered UK chart Aug70, at No.45) (re-iss.Feb78 + Jul84)
Feb 70. (lp)(c) **BRIDGE OVER TROUBLED WATER** [1] [1]
– Bridge over troubled water / El Condor Pasa / Cecilia / Keep the customer satisfied / So long, Frank Lloyd Wright / The boxer / Baby driver / The only living boy in New York / Why don't you write me / Bye bye love / Song for the asking. *(re-iss.on quad 1974) (cd-iss.Dec82) (re-iss.cd+c Sep93 & Feb95 & Dec95 on 'Columbia')*
Apr 70. (7") **CECILIA. / THE ONLY LIVING BOY IN NEW YORK** [ ] [4]
Sep 70. (7") **EL CONDOR PASA. / WHY DON'T YOU WRITE ME** [-] [18]

—— Both went solo, after ART wanted to concentrate on acting career.

– compilations, exploitation releases, etc. –

1967. Allegro; (lp) **SIMON AND GARFUNKEL** [ ] [-]
Note; Released on 'CBS/ Columbia' unless otherwise mentioned.
Sep 70. (7") **THE SOUND OF SILENCE. / THE 59th STREET BRIDGE SONG** [ ] [-]
Jul 72. (lp)(c) **SIMON AND GARFUNKEL'S GREATEST HITS** [2] [5] Jun 72
– Mrs.Robinson / For Emily, wherever I may find her / The boxer / Feelin' groovy / The sound of silence / I am a rock / Scarborough fair (Canticle) / Homeward bound / Bridge over troubled water / America / Kathy's song / If I could / Bookends / Cecilia.
Sep 72. (7") **AMERICA. / FOR EMILY, WHENEVER I MAY FIND HER** [25] [97]
[53]
Apr 73. (7") **MRS. ROBINSON. / SCARBOROUGH FAIR; CANTICLE** [ ] [ ]
Mar 76. (7") **HOMEWARD BOUND. / THE SOUND OF SILENCE** [ ] [-]
Nov 81. (lp)(c) **THE SIMON AND GARFUNKEL COLLECTION** [4] [-]
– I am a rock / Homeward bound / America / 59th Street Bridge song / Wednesday morning 3 a.m. / El condor pasa / At the Zoo / Scarborough fair (Canticle) / The boxer / The sound of silence / Mrs.Robinson / Keep the customer satisfied / Song for the asking / Hazy shade of winter / Cecilia / Old friends / Bookends / Bridge over troubled water. *(cd-iss.Apr85 + 1988)*
Dec 81. (7") **HOMEWARD BOUND. / THE 59TH STREET BRIDGE SONG** [ ] [-]

—— SIMON AND GARFUNKEL re-united for one-off concert 20 Dec'81.

Geffen | Warners

Mar 82. (d-lp)(d-c) **THE CONCERT IN CENTRAL PARK (live)** [6] [6]
– Mrs. Robinson / Homeward bound / America / Scarborough fair / Me and Julio down by the schoolyard / Wake up little Susie / April come she will / Slip slidin' away / Still crazy after all these years / American tune / 50 ways to leave your lover / Late in the evening / Bridge over troubled water / A heart in New York / The

59th Street bridge song (feelin' groovy) / The sound of silence / Kodachrome / Old friends: bookends / Maybellene / The boxer. *(re-iss.+cd.May88)*

Mar 82. (7") **WAKE UP LITTLE SUSIE (live). / THE BOXER (live)** [ ] [-]

Mar 82. (7") **WAKE UP LITTLE SUSIE (live). / ME AND JULIO DOWN BY THE SCHOOLYARD (live)** [-] [27]

Jun 82. (7") **MRS. ROBINSON (live). / BRIDGE OVER TROUBLED WATER (live)** [ ] [ ]

– more compilations, etc. –

1988. CBS; (cd) **BRIDGE OVER TROUBLED WATER / PARSLEY, SAGE, ROSEMARY & SAGE** [ ] [ ]

May 88. Arcade; (cd) **COLLECTION** [ ] [-]

Nov 91. Sony-Columbia; (7")(c-s)(cd-s) **A HAZY SHADE OF WINTER. / SILENT NIGHT – SEVEN O'CLOCK NEWS (Medley)** [30] [ ]

Nov 91. Sony-Columbia; (cd)(c) **THE DEFINITIVE SIMON & GARFUNKEL** [8] [ ]
– Wednesday morning 3 a.m. / The sound of silence / Homeward bound / Cathy's song / I am a rock / For Emily wherever I may find her / Scarborough fair (canticle) / The 59th Street bridge song (feelin' groovy) / Seven o'clock news – Silent night / A hazy shade of winter / El Condor pasa (If I could) / Mrs.Robinson / America / At the zoo / Old friends / Bookends theme / Cecilia / The boxer / Bridge over troubled water / Song for the asking.

Feb 92. Sony-Columbia; (7") **THE BOXER. / CECILIA** [75] [ ]
(cd-ep+=)(cd-ep+=) –

Aug 92. Sony; (2xcd) **PARSLEY, SAGE, ROSEMARY & SAGE / BOOKENDS** [ ] [ ]

PAUL SIMON

(solo with session people)

C.B.S. | Columbia

Feb 72. (7") **MOTHER AND CHILD REUNION. / PARANOIA BLUES** [5] [4]

Feb 72. (lp)(c) **PAUL SIMON** [1] [4]
– Mother and child reunion / Duncan / Everything put together falls apart / Run that body down / Armistice day / Me and Julio down by the schoolyard / Peace like a river / Papa hobo / Hobo's blues / Paranoia blues / Congratulations. *(re-iss. 1974 on quad) (re-iss.+cd.Dec87 on 'WEA')*

Apr 72. (7") **ME AND JULIO DOWN BY THE SCHOOLYARD. / CONGRATULATIONS** [15] [22]

Jul 72. (7") **DUNCAN. / RUN THAT BODY DOWN** [-] [52]

May 73. (lp)(c) **THERE GOES RHYMIN' SIMON** [4] [2]
– Kodachrome / Tenderness / Take me to the Mardi Gras / Something so right / One man's ceiling is another man's floor / American tune / Was a sunny day / Learn how to fall / St. Judy's comet / Loves me like a rock. *(re-iss.1974 on quad) (re-iss.+cd.Dec87 on 'WEA')*

May 73. (7") **KODACHROME. / TENDERNESS** [-] [2]

May 73. (7") **TAKE ME TO THE MARDI GRAS. / KODACHROME** [7] [-]

Sep 73. (7") **LOVES ME LIKE A ROCK. / LEARN HOW TO FALL** [39] [2] Aug 73

Feb 74. (7") **AMERICAN TUNE. / ONE MAN'S CEILING IS ANOTHER MAN'S FLOOR** [ ] [35] Nov 73

— Below in concert with URUBOMBA and The JESE DIXON SINGERS.

Mar 74. (lp)(c) **PAUL SIMON IN CONCERT / LIVE RHYMIN' (live)** [ ] [33]
– Jesus is the answer / The boxer / Duncan / El Condor pasa (if I could) / Me and Julio down by the schoolyard / American tune / Homeward bound / America / Mother and child reunion / Loves me like a rock / Bridge over troubled water / The sound of silence. *(re-iss.+cd.Dec87 on 'WEA')*

May 74. (7") **THE SOUND OF SILENCE (live). / MOTHER AND CHILD REUNION (live)** [ ] [ ]

Nov 74. (7") **SOMETHING SO RIGHT. / TENDERNESS** [ ] [ ]

Aug 75. (7") **GONE AT LAST (w/ PHOEBE SNOW). / TAKE ME TO THE MARDI GRAS** [-] [23]

Oct 75. (7") **GONE AT LAST. ("PAUL SIMON & PHOEBE SNOW with The JESSE DIXON SINGERS") / TENDERNESS** [ ] [-]

Oct 75. (lp)(c) **STILL CRAZY AFTER ALL THESE YEARS** [6] [1]
– Still crazy after all these years / My little town / I do it all for love / 50 ways to leave your lover / Night game / Gone at last / Some folks lives roll easy / Have a good time / You're kind / Silent eyes. *(re-iss.1976 on quad)(cd-iss.Dec85, re-iss.+cd.Dec87 on 'WEA')*

Oct 75. (7") **MY LITTLE TOWN ("SIMON & GARFUNKEL"). / RAG DOLL ("ART GARFUNKEL")** [-] [9]

Nov 75. (7"m) **MY LITTLE TOWN. ("SIMON AND GARFUNKEL") / RAG DOLL ("ART GARFUNKEL") / YOU'RE KIND** [ ] [-]

Dec 75. (7") **50 WAYS TO LEAVE YOUR LOVER. / SOME FOLKS LIVES ROLL EASY** [23] [1]

Apr 76. (7") **STILL CRAZY AFTER ALL THESE YEARS. / I DO IT FOR YOUR LOVE** [-] [40]

Apr 76. (7") **STILL CRAZY AFTER ALL THESE YEARS. / SILENT EYES** [ ] [-]

Nov 77. (7") **SLIP SLIDIN' AWAY. / SOMETHING SO RIGHT** [36] [5] Oct 77

Nov 77. (lp)(c) **GREATEST HITS, ETC.** (part compilation) [6] [18]
– Something so right / 50 ways to leave your lover / Kodachrome / Me and Julio down by the schoolyard / American tune / Gone at last / Still crazy after all these years / My little town / Mother and child reunion / Loves me like a rock / Stranded in a limousine / Slip slidin' away / Take me to the Mardi Gras. *(re-iss.+cd.Jan87, hit 73 UK)*

— See ART GARFUNKEL discography further on for other single

May 78. (7") **STRANDED IN A LIMOSINE. / HAVE A GOOD TIME** [ ] [ ]

Warners | Warners

Aug 80. (lp)(c) **ONE-TRICK PONY** [17] [12]
– Late in the evening / That's why God made the movies / One-trick pony / How the heart approaches what it yearns / Oh, Marion / Ace in the hole / Nobody / God bless the absentee / Jonah / Long, long day. *(cd-iss.1987)*

Aug 80. (7") **LATE IN THE EVENING. / HOW THE HEART APPROACHES WHAT IT YEARNS** [58] [6]

Nov 80. (7") **ONE TRICK PONY. / LONG, LONG DAY** [ ] [40] Oct 80

Jan 81. (7") **OH, MARION. / GOD BLESS THE ABSENTEE** [ ] [ ]

— See ART GARFUNKEL discography again for duet A HEART IN NEW YORK single

Early '83, PAUL collaborated with RANDY NEWMAN on US No.51 single THE BLUES

Nov 83. (lp)(c)(cd) **HEARTS AND BONES** [34] [35]
– Allergies / Hearts and bones / When numbers get serious / Think too much (part 1) / Song about the Moon / Think too much (part 2) / Train in the distance / Renee and Georgette Margritte with the dog after the war / Cars are cars / The late great Johnny Ace.

Nov 83. (7") **ALLERGIES. / THINK TOO MUCH** [ ] [44]

Feb 84. (7") **SONG ABOUT THE MOON. / THINK TOO MUCH** [-] [ ]

Aug 86. (7")(12") **YOU CAN CALL ME AL. / GUMBOOTS** [4] [44]
(re-iss.Mar87 US, hit No.23)

Sep 86. (lp)(c)(cd) **GRACELAND** [1] [3]
– The boy in the bubble / Graceland / I know what I know / Gumboots / Diamonds on the sole of her shoes / You can call me Al / Under African skies / Homeless / Crazy love Vol.2 / That was your mother / All around the world of the myth of fingerprints.

Nov 86. (7") **THE BOY IN THE BUBBLE. / ('A'remix)** [33] [-]
(12"+=) – Hearts and bones.

Dec 86. (7") **GRACELAND. / HEARTS AND BONES** [-] [81]
(re-iss.US 1988)

Feb 87. (7") **THE BOY IN THE BUBBLE. / CRAZY LOVE VOL. 2** [-] [86]

Feb 87. (7")(12") **DIAMONDS ON THE SOLES OF HER SHOES. / ALL AROUND THE WORLD OF THE MYTH OF FINGER-PRINTS** [ ] [ ] Apr 87

Apr 87. (7") **GRACELAND. / CRAZY LOVE VOL.2** [ ] [-]
(12"+=) – The late great Johny Ace.

Aug 87. (7") **UNDER AFRICAN SKIES. / I KNOW WHAT I KNOW** [ ] [ ]
(12"+=) – Homeless. (above w/LINDA RONSTADT)

Oct 90. (7") **THE OBVIOUS CHILD. / THE RHYTHM OF THE SAINTS** [15] [92]
(12"+=)/ /(cd-s++=) – You can call me Al./ / The boy in the bubble.

Oct 90. (cd)(c)(lp) **THE RHYTHM OF THE SAINTS** [1] [4]
– The obvious child / Can't run but / The coast / Proof / Further to fly / She moves on / Born at the right time / The cool cool river / Spirit voices / The rhythm of the saints.

Feb 91. (7")(c-s) **PROOF. / THE OBVIOUS CHILD** [ ] [ ]
(12")(cd-s) – ('A'side) / The cool cool river / American tune.

Apr 91. (7") **BORN AT THE RIGHT TIME. / FURTHER TO FLY** [ ] [ ]
(12"+=) – You can call me Al.
(cd-s++=) – Me and Julio down by the schoolyard / 50 ways to leave your lover.

Nov 91. (cd)(c)(d-lp) **THE CONCERT IN THE PARK – AUGUST 15th 1991 (live)** [60] [ ]
–

– (PAUL SIMON) compilations, others, etc. –

Nov 88. CBS/ US= Columbia; (d-lp)(c)(cd) **NEGOTIATIONS AND LOVE SONGS** [17] [ ]
– Mother and child reunion / Me and Julio down by the schoolyard / Something so right / St.Judy's comet / Loves me like a rock / Have a good time / 50 ways to leave your lover / Still crazy after all these years / Late in the evening / Slip slidin' away / Hearts and bones / Train in the distance / Rene and Georgette Magritte with their dog after the war / Diamonds on the soles on her shoes / You can call me Al / Kodachrome. (d-lp+=) – Graceland.

Nov 88. CBS; (7") **MOTHER AND CHILD REUNION. / TRAIN IN THE DISTANCE** [ ] [ ]
(12"+=)(cd-s+=) – The boy in the bubble.

Feb 89. Venus; (c) **THE MAGIC OF PAUL SIMON** [ ] [-]

May 93. Royal; (cd)(c) **PAUL SIMON & FRIENDS** [ ] [-]

Sep 93. Warners; (3xcd) **1964-1993** [ ] [ ]

Sep 93. Warners; (cd)(c) **ANTHOLOGY** [ ] [ ]

ART GARFUNKEL

(solo with session people)

C.B.S. | Columbia

Sep 73. (7") **ALL I KNOW. / MARY WAS AN ONLY CHILD** [ ] [9]

Oct 73. (lp)(c) **ANGEL CLARE** [14] [5] Sep 73
– Travelling boy / Down in the willow garden / I shall sing / Old man / Feuilles oh! – Do spacemen pass dead souls on their way to the Moon? / All I know / Woyaya / Mary was an only child / Barbara Allen / Another lullaby. *(also on quad-lp) (cd-iss.1988) (re-iss.Jul89 on 'Pickwick')*

Feb 74. (7") **I SHALL SING. / FEUILLES OH! – DO SPACEMEN PASS DEAD SOULS ON THEIR WAY TO THE MOON?** [ ] [38] Dec 73

Sep 74. (7") **SECOND AVENUE. / WOYAYA** [ ] [34]
(re-iss. UK Nov76)

— (above 1973/74 releases as "GARFUNKEL")

Sep 75. (7") **I ONLY HAVE EYES FOR YOU. / LOOKING FOR THE RIGHT ONE** [1] [18] Aug 75

Oct 75. (lp)(c) **BREAKAWAY** [7] [7]
– I believe (when I fall in love it will be forever) / Rag doll / Breakaway / Disney girls / Waters of March / My little town / I only have eyes for you / Looking for the right one / 99 miles from L.A. / The same old tears on a new background. *(re-iss.Nov85, cd-iss.Ar86) (re-iss.+cd.Sep89 on 'Pickwick')(re-iss.cdSep93 on 'Sony Collectors')*

— See PAUL SIMON section, for their hit duet MY LITTLE TOWN.

Dec 75. (7") **BREAKAWAY. / DISNEY GIRLS** [-] [ ]

Jan 76. (7") **BREAKAWAY. / THE SAME OLD TEARS ON A NEW BACKGROUND** [ ] [-]

May 76. (7") **I BELIEVE (WHEN I FALL IN LOVE IT WILL BE FOREVER). / WATERS OF MARCH** [ ] [ ]

Nov 77. (7") **CRYING IN MY SLEEP. / MR.SHUCK'N'JIVE** [ ] [ ]

Jan 78. (7") **(WHAT A) WONDERFUL WORLD. ("ART GARFUNKEL, PAUL SIMON & JAMES TAYLOR") / WOODEN PLANES** [ ] [17]

Feb 78. (lp)(c) **WATERMARK** [25] [19]

– Crying in my sleep / Marionette / Shine it on me / Watermark / Saturday suit / All my love's laughter / (What a) Wonderful world / Mr. Shuck 'n' jive / Paper chase / She moved through the fair / Someone else (1958) / Wooden planes. *(re-iss.Jan87) (cd-iss.Apr94 on 'Sony')*

Apr 78. (7") **MARIONETTE. / ALL MY LOVE'S LAUGHTER** [ ] [-]
Feb 79. (7") **BRIGHT EYES. / KEHAAR'S THEME** [1] [-]
(above from animated film 'Watership Down') *(re-iss.Jul84)*
Mar 79. (7") **AND I KNOW. / IN A LITTLE WHILE (I'LL BE ON MY WAY)** [-] [ ]
Apr 79. (lp)(c) **FATE FOR BREAKFAST** [2] [67]
– In a little while (I'll be on my way) / Since I don't have you / And I know / Sail on a rainbow / Miss you nights / Bright eyes / Finally a reason / Beyond the tears / Oh how happy / When someone doesn't want you / Take me away.
May 79. (7") **SINCE I DON'T HAVE YOU. / WHEN SOMEONE DOESN'T WANT YOU** [-] [53]
Jun 79. (7") **SINCE I DON'T HAVE YOU. / AND I KNOW** [38] [-]
Aug 79. (7") **BRIGHT EYES. / SAIL ON A RAINBOW** [-] [ ]
Aug 81. (7") **A HEART IN NEW YORK. ("ART GARFUNKEL & PAUL SIMON") / IS THIS LOVE** [ ] [66]
Sep 81. (lp)(c) **SCISSORS CUT** [51] [ ]
– Scissors cut / A heart in New York / Up in the world / Hang on in / So easy to begin / Can't turn my heart away / The French waltz / The romance / In cars / That's all I've got to say.
Oct 81. (7") **SCISSORS CUT. / SO EASY TO BEGIN** [ ] [-]

— Late 1981, he had re-united with PAUL SIMON for live one-off album.

Oct 84. (7") **SOMETIME WHEN I'M DREAMING. / SCISSORS CUT** [ ] [-]
Nov 84. (lp)(c)(cd) **THE ART GARFUNKEL ALBUM** (compilation) [12] [-]
– Bright eyes / Break away / A heart in New York / I shall sing / 99 miles from L.A. / All I know / I only have eyes for you / Watermark / Sometimes when I'm dreaming / Travelin' boy / The same old tears on a new background / (What a) Wonderful world / I believe (when I fall in love it will be forever) / Scissors cut.
Nov 86. (7"w/AMY GRANT) **CAROL OF THE BIRDS. / THE DECREE** [-] [ ]
Dec 86. (lp)(c) **THE ANIMALS CHRISTMAS** [ ] [ ]
– The annunciation / The creatures of the field / Just a simple little tune / The decree / Incredible phat / The friendly beasts / The song of the camel / Words from an old Spanish carol / Carol of the birds / The frog / Herod / Wild geese.
Jan 88. (7") **SO MUCH IN LOVE. / KING OF TONGA** [-] [ ]
Feb 88. (7") **SO MUCH IN LOVE. / SLOW BREAKUP** [ ] [-]
(12"+=)(cd-s+=) – (What a) Wonderful world / I only have eyes for you.
Mar 88. (7") **THIS IS THE MOMENT. / SLOW BREAKUP** [-] [ ]
Mar 88. (lp)(c)(cd) **LEFTY** [ ] [ ]
– This is the moment / I have a love / So much in love / Slow breakup / Love is the only chain / When a man loves a woman / I wonder why / King of Tonga / If love takes you away / The promise.
May 88. (7") **WHEN A MAN LOVES A WOMAN. / KING OF TONGA** [ ] [-]
May 88. (7") **WHEN A MAN LOVES A WOMAN. / I HAVE A LOVE** [-] [ ]

Columbia Columbia
Nov 93. (cd)(c)(lp) **UP UNTIL NOW** [ ] [ ]
– Crying in the rain (w/ JAMES TAYLOR) / All I know / Just over the Brooklyn Bridge / The sound of silence / The breakup / Skywriter / The decree / It's all in the game / One less holiday / Since I don't have you / Two sleepy people / Why worry / All my love's daughter.

– (ART GARFUNKEL) compilation, etc. –

Oct 79. CBS; (3xlp-box) **ART GARFUNKEL** [ ] [ ]
(first 3 albums)
1984. Columbia; (7") **BRIGHT EYES. / THE ROMANCE** [-] [ ]

SIMPLE MINDS

Formed: Gorbals, Glasgow, Scotland, early 1978 after 4 members (KERR, BURCHILL, BARNWELL and McGEE) had left punk band JOHNNY & THE SELF-ABUSERS. In 1978, after taking group name from a line in a BOWIE song, SIMPLE MINDS gigged constantly at Glasgow's Mars Bar. They sent demo to record store owner BRUCE FINDLEY, who duly signed them to his independent Edinburgh label 'Zoom'. They were soon licensed to major 'Arista', after release of debut album, 'LIFE IN A DAY', scraped into the UK Top 30. In 1981, they transferred to 'Virgin' records and gained first Top 50 hit with 'LOVE SONG'. It was lifted from joint lp 'SONS AND FASCINATION' / 'SISTER FEELINGS CALL', which was produced by STEVE HILLAGE. In the mid-80's, they competed with U2 for stadium rock supremacy, while their albums 'SPARKLE IN THE RAIN' & 'ONCE UPON A TIME', hit No.1 in the UK. Between these, they also smashed the American charts with No.1 'DON'T YOU FORGET ABOUT ME'. (It's now cheapified on a UK TV ad for milk!). • **Style:** Initially a mix of experimental pop + rock, which progressed in the 80's to electro disco rock and sophisto-pop. • **Songwriters:** All group compositions or KERR-BURCHILL. Covered BIKO (Peter Gabriel) / SIGN O' THE TIMES (Prince) / DON'T YOU FORGET ABOUT ME (Keith Forsey-Steve Chiff). • **Trivia:** On the 5th May'84, JIM KERR married CHRISIE HYNDE of The PRETENDERS and settled in Queensferry. They divorced in the late 80's, and KERR soon married another singer and actress PATSY KENSIT. Needless to say, The MINDS have played both LIVE AID and MANDELA DAY concerts in 1985 and 1988 respectively.

Recommended: GLITTERING PRIZE 81-91 (*9) / CELEBRATION (*7) / EMPIRES AND DANCE (*8) / SONS AND FASCINATION (*8) / NEW GOLD DREAM (*8) / ONCE UPON A TIME (*7) / SPARKLE IN THE RAIN (*8) / LIFE IN A DAY (*7).

JOHNNY & THE SELF ABUSERS

JIM KERR (b. 9 Jul'59) – vocals / **CHARLIE BURCHILL** (b.27 Nov'59) – guitar / **DUNCAN BARNWELL** – guitar / **BRIAN McGEE** – drums / + 3 future CUBAN HEELS members.

Chiswick not issued
Nov 77. (7") **SAINTS AND SINNERS. / DEAD VANDALS** [ ] [-]

SIMPLE MINDS

(KERR, BURCHILL, McGEE) recruited **MICK McNEILL** (b.20 Jul'58) – keyboards / **DEREK FORBES** (b.22 Jun'56) – bass

Zoom not issued
Apr 79. (7") **LIFE IN A DAY. / SPECIAL VIEW** [62] [-]
Apr 79. (lp)(c) **LIFE IN A DAY** [30] [-]
– Someone / Life in a day / Sad affair / All for you / Pleasantly disurbed / No cure / Chelsea girl / Wasteland / Destiny / Murder story. *(re-iss.Oct82 + 1985 on 'Virgin', cd-iss.Jul86)*
Jun 79. (7") **CHELSEA GIRL. / GARDEN OF HATE** [ ] [-]

Arista Arista
Nov 79. (lp)(c) **REAL TO REAL CACOPHONY** [ ] [ ]
– Real to real / Naked eye / Citizen (dance of youth) / Carnival (shelter in a suitcase) / Factory / Cacophony / Veldt / Premonition / Changeling / Film theme / Calling your name / Scar. *(re-iss.Oct82 + 1985 on 'Virgin', cd-iss.May88)*
Jan 80. (7") **CHANGELING. / PREMONITION (live)** [ ] [-]
Sep 80. (lp)(c) **EMPIRES AND DANCE** [41] [ ]
– I travel / Today I died again / Celebrate / This fear of gods / Capital city / Constantinople line / Twist-run-repulsion / Thirty frames a seconds / Kant-kino / Room. *(re-iss.Oct82 on 'Virgin', cd-iss.May88)*
Oct 80. (7") **I TRAVEL. / NEW WARM SKIN** [ ] [ ]
(free 7"blue flexi) – KALEIDOSCOPE. / FILM DUB THEME
(12") – ('A'side) / Film dub theme.
Feb 81. (7") **CELEBRATE. / CHANGELING (live)** [ ] [ ]
(12"+=) – I travel (live).

Virgin A&M
May 81. (7")(12") **THE AMERICAN. / LEAGUE OF NATIONS** [59] [-]

— **KENNY HYSLOP** – drums (ex-SKIDS, ex-ZONES, ex-SLIK) repl. McGEE, who in 1994 became a songwriter for LES McKEOWN (ex-BAY CITY ROLLERS)

Aug 81. (7")(12") **LOVE SONG. / THE EARTH THAT YOU WALK UPON (instr.)** [47] [-]
Sep 81. (2xlp)(d-c) **SONS AND FASCINATION / SISTER FEELINGS CALL** [11] [ ]
– SONS AND FASCINATION – In trance as mission / Sweat in bullet / 70 cities as love brings the fall / Boys from Brazil / Love song / This Earth that you walk upon / Sons and fascination / Seeing out the angels. SISTER FEELINGS CALL – Theme for great cities * / The American / 20th Century promised land / Wonderful in young life / League of nations / Careful in career / Sound in 70 cities. *(iss.separately Oct81) (cd-iss.Apr86 + Apr90, omits*)*
Oct 81. (7") **SWEAT IN BULLET. / 20th CENTURY PROMISED LAND** [52] [-]
(d7"+=) – League of nations (live) / Premonition (live).
(12"+=) – League of nations (live) / In trance as mission (live).
Apr 82. (7") **PROMISED YOU A MIRACLE. / THEME FOR GREAT CITIES** [13] [-]
(12"+=) – Seeking out the angel (instrumental mix).

— **MIKE OGLETREE** – drums repl. HYSLOP who formed SET THE TONE

Aug 82. (7")(12") **GLITTERING PRIZE. / GLITTERING THEME** [16] [ ]

— **MEL GAYNOR** – drums (ex-sessions) repl. MIKE who joined FICTION FACTORY

Sep 82. (lp)(c) **NEW GOLD DREAM (81-82-83-84)** [3] [69] Jan 83
– Someone somewhere in summertime / Colours fly and the Catherine wheel / Promised you a miracle / Big sleep / Somebody up there likes you / New gold dream (81-82-83-84) / Glittering prize / Hunter and the hunted / King is white and in the crowd. *(cd-iss.Jul83) (iss.US on gold-lp)*
Nov 82. (7")(7"pic-d) **SOMEONE SOMEWHERE IN SUMMERTIME. / KING IS WHITE AND IN THE CROWD** [36] [ ]
(12"+=) – Soundtrack for every Heaven.
Nov 82. (7") **PROMISED YOU A MIRACLE. / THE AMERICAN** [-] [ ]
Nov 83. (7")(12") **WATERFRONT. / HUNTER AND THE HUNTED (live)** [13] [ ]
Jan 84. (7")(7"pic-d) **SPEED YOUR LOVE TO ME. / BASS LINE** [20] [ ]
(12"+=) – ('A'extended).
Feb 84. (lp)(c)(cd)(white-lp) **SPARKLE IN THE RAIN** [1] [64]
– Up on the catwalk / Book of brilliant things / Speed your love to me / Waterfront / East at Easter / White hot day / Street hassle / "C" Moon cry like a baby / The kick inside of me / Shake off the ghosts. *(re cd-iss.1986 + Mar91)*
Mar 84. (7")(7"pic-d) **UP ON THE CATWALK. / A BRASS BAND IN AFRICA** [27] [ ]
(12"+=) – ('B'other version).
Apr 85. (7")(7"sha-pic-d) **DON'T YOU (FORGET ABOUT ME). / A BRASS BAND IN AFRICA** [7] [1] Feb 85
(12"+=) – ('B'other version). *(cd-s iss.Jun88)*

— **KERR, BURCHILL, McNEILL + GAYNOR** brought in new member **JOHN GIBLING** – bass (ex-PETER GABRIEL sessions) to repl. FORBES

Oct 85. (7") **ALIVE AND KICKING. / ('A'instrumental)** [7] [3]
(12"+=) – Up on the catwalk (live). (US; b-side)
Oct 85. (lp)(c)(cd)(pic-lp) **ONCE UPON A TIME** [1] [10]
– Once upon a time / All the things she said / Ghost dancing / Alive and kicking / Oh jungleland / I wish you were here / Sanctify yourself / Come a long way.
Jan 86. (7") **SANCTIFY YOURSELF. / ('A'instrumental)** [10] [14]
(d7"+=) – Love song (live) / Street hassle (live).
(12") – ('A'mix). / ('A'dub instrumental)
Apr 86. (7") **ALL THE THINGS SHE SAID. / DON'T YOU (FORGET ABOUT ME)** [9] [28]
(12"+=) – Promised you a miracle (US mix).
Nov 86. (7") **GHOSTDANCING. / JUNGLELAND (instrumental)** [13] [ ]
(ext-12"+=)(cd-s+=) – ('A'instrumental) / ('B'mix).
May 87. (d-lp)(d-c)(d-cd) **LIVE IN THE CITY OF LIGHT (live)** [1] [96]
– Ghostdancing / Big sleep / Waterfront / Promised you a miracle / Someone some-

where in summertime / Oh jungleland / Alive and kicking / Don't you forget about me / Once upon a time / Book of brilliant things / East at Easter / Sanctify yourself / Love song / Sun City – Dance to the music / New gold dream (81-82-83-84).

Jun 87. (7")(10") **PROMISED YOU A MIRACLE (live). / BOOK OF BRILLIANT THINGS (live)** [19] [ ]
(12"+=)(c-s+=) – Glittering prize (live) / Celebrate (live).

— **KERR, BURCHILL + McNEILL** were basic trio, w/other 2 still sessioning.

Feb 89. (7") **BELFAST CHILD. / MANDELA DAY** [1] [ ]
(12"ep+=)(12"box-ep+=)(c-ep+=)(cd-ep+=) – BALLAD OF THE STREETS – Biko.

Apr 89. (7") **THIS IS YOUR LAND. / SATURDAY GIRL** [13] [ ]
(12"+=)(c-s+=)(3"cd-s+=) – Year of the dragon.

May 89. (lp)(c)(cd) **STREET FIGHTING YEARS** [1] [70]
– Soul crying out / Wall of love / This is your land / Take a step back / Kick it in / Let it all come down / Biko / Mandela day / Belfast child / Street fighting years. *(re-iss.box-lp+cd.Dec89, +=Interview)*

Jul 89. (7")(c-s) **KICK IT IN. / WATERFRONT ('89 mix)** [15] [ ]
(12"+=)/ /(12"+=)(cd-s+=) – ('A'mix)./ / Big sleep (live).

Dec 89. (7"ep)(12"ep)(c-ep)(cd-ep) **THE AMSTERDAM EP** [18] [ ]
– Let it all come down / Sign o' the times / Jerusalem.
(12"ep+=)(cd-ep+=) – Sign o' the times (mix).

— **KERR, BURCHILL + GAYNOR** brought in sessioners **MALCOLM FOSTER** – bass / **PETER JOHN VITESSE** – keyboards / **STEPHEN LIPSON** – bass, keyboards / **ANDY DUNCAN** – percussion / **GAVIN WRIGHT** – string leader / **LISA GERMANO** – violin

Mar 91. (7") **LET THERE BE LOVE. / GOODNIGHT** [6] [ ]
(12"+=) – Alive and kicking (live).
(cd-s++=) – East at Easter (live).

Apr 91. (cd)(c)(lp) **REAL LIFE** [2] [74]
– Real life / See the lights / Let there be love / Woman / Stand by love / African skies / Let the children speak / Ghostrider / Banging on the door / Travelling man / Rivers of ice / When two worlds collide.

May 91. (7")(c-s) **SEE THE LIGHTS. / THEME FOR GREAT CITIES ('91 edit)** [20] [40]
(12"+=)(cd-s+=) – Soul crying out (live).

Aug 91. (7")(c-s) **STAND BY LOVE. / KING IS WHITE AND IN THE CROWD (live)** [13] [ ]
(12"+=)(cd-s+=) – Let there be love (live).

Oct 91. (7")(c-s) **REAL LIFE. / SEE THE LIGHTS** [34] [ ]
('A'extended-12"+=) – Belfast child (extended).
(cd-s++=) – Ghostrider.

— **KERR + BURCHILL** with guests **MARK BROWNE, MALCOLM FOSTER, MARCUS MILLER + LANCE MORRISON – bass/ MARK SCHULMAN, TAL BERGMAN + VINNIE CALAIUTA – drums**

Jan 95. (7")(c-s) **SHE'S A RIVER. / E55 / ('A'mix)** [9] [52]
(cd-s+=) – Celtic strings.

Jan 95. (cd)(c)(lp) **GOOD NEWS FROM THE NEXT WORLD** [2] [87]
– She's a river / Night music / Hypnotised / Great leap forward / 7 deadly sins / And the band played on / My life / Criminal world / This time.

Mar 95. (7")(c-s) **HYPNOTISED. / £4** [18] [ ]
(cd-s+=) – ('A'-Tim Simenon extended remixes) / ('A'-Malfunction mix).
(cd-s) – ('A'side) / Up on the catwalk (live) / And the band played on (live) / She's a river (live).

– compilations, others, etc. –

Jan 82. Arista; (7") **I TRAVEL. / THIRTY FRAMES A SECOND (live)** [ ] [-]
(12"+=) – ('A'live).

Feb 82. Arista; (lp)(c) **CELEBRATION** [45] [ ]
(re-iss.Oct82 on 'Virgin', re-iss.+cd.Apr89)

Apr 83. Virgin; (12") **I TRAVEL (mix). / FILM THEME** [ ] [-]

Aug 90. Virgin; (5xcd-box-ep) **THEMES – VOLUME ONE** [ ] [ ]
– (Apr79 – LIFE IN A DAY – Apr82 – PROMISED YOU A MIRACLE singles)

Sep 90. Virgin; (5xcd-box-ep) **THEMES – VOLUME TWO** [ ] [ ]
– (Aug82 – GLITTERING PRIZE – Apr85 – DON'T YOU (FORGET ABOUT ME) singles)

Oct 90. Virgin; (5xcd-box-ep) **THEMES – VOLUME THREE** [ ] [ ]
– (Oct85 – ALIVE AND KICKING – Jun87 – PROMISED YOU A MIRACLE (live) singles)

Nov 90. Virgin; (5xcd-box-ep) **THEMES – VOLUME FOUR** [ ] [ ]
– (Feb89 – BELFAST CHILD, Dec 89 – THE AMSTERDAM EP)

Oct 92. Virgin; (7")(c-s) **LOVE SONG. / ALIVE AND KICKING** [6] [ ]
('A'&'B'ext-cd-s+=) – ('B'instrumental).

Oct 92. Virgin; (cd)(c)(lp) **GLITTERING PRIZE – SIMPLE MINDS 81-92** [1] [ ]
– Waterfront / Don't you (forget about me) / Alive and kicking / Sanctify yourself / Love song / Someone somewhere in summertime / See the lights / Belfast child / The American / All the things she said / Promised you a miracle / Ghostdancing / Speed your love to me / Glittering prize / Let there be love / Mandela Day.

SIMPLY RED

Formed: Manchester, England . . . 1984 by MICK HUCKNALL, who had been frontman for power-punk group The FRANTIC ELEVATORS. They had made 4 singles for local indie labels, the last of which 'HOLDING BACK THE YEARS', later became a massive SIMPLY RED hit. Signed worldwide deal with 'Elektra' in 1985, but after Top 20 hit with 'MONEY'S TOO TIGHT', found it difficult to emerge until 1986 when the smoochy 'HOLDING BACK THE YEARS' hit US No.1. The following year, their 2nd album 'MEN AND WOMEN', crashed into the UK Top 3, and they were soon one of the top bands of the 90's. • **Style:** Romantic ballad soul-pop & dance outfit. Ginger-haired frontman HUCKNALL, could smoothly woo anyone to moondance, with tight highly strung vox. • **Songwriters:** HUCKNALL compositions, some with LAMONT DOZIER. Covered:- MONEY'S TOO TIGHT (Valentine Brothers) / LET ME HAVE IT ALL (Sly Stone) / EV'RY TIME WE SAY GOODBYE (Cole Porter) / LOVE FIRE (Bunny Wailer) / IF YOU DON'T KNOW ME BY NOW (Harold Melvin) / IT'S ONLY LOVE (Barry White; c. J & V Cameron). • **Trivia:** STEWART LEVINE produced all albums, except MEN AND WOMEN which was worked on by ALEX SADKIN.

Recommended: STARS (*9) / A NEW FLAME (*9) / MEN AND WOMEN (*8) / PICTURE BOOK (*7).

MICK HUCKNALL (b. 8 Jun'61) – vocals (ex-FRANTIC ELEVATORS) / **DAVID FRYMAN** – guitar (originals EDDIE SHERWOOD, OJO & MOG repl. by below) / **TONY BOWERS** – bass (ex-DURUTTI COLUMN, ex-MOTHMEN) / **CHRIS JOYCE** – drums (ex-DURUTTI COLUMN, ex-MOTHMEN, ex-PINK MILITARY) / **FRITZ McINTYRE** – guitar / **TIM KELLETT** – brass (ex-DURUTTI COLUMN)

Elektra Elektra

Jun 85. (7")(7"pic-d) **MONEY$ TOO TIGHT (TO MENTION). / OPEN UP THE RED BOX** [13] [ ]
(12"+=) – No direction.
(12") – ('A'remix). / ('B'side)

Aug 85. (7") **COME TO MY AID. / VALENTINE** [66] [ ]
('A'extended-12"+=) – Granma's hand.

— **SYLVAN RICHARDSON** – guitar repl. FRYMAN (although he did appear on lp)

Oct 85. (lp)(c)(cd) **PICTURE BOOK** [34] [16] Apr 86
– Come to my aid / Sad old Red / Look at you now / Heaven / Jericho / Money's too tight (to mention) / Holding back the years / Open up the red box / No direction / Picture book. *(pic-lp iss.May86) (album hit UK No.2 in May87) (re-entered UK Top50 Feb92 peaked at 39 May92)*

Nov 85. (7")(7"pic-d) **HOLDING BACK THE YEARS. / I WON'T FEEL BAD** [51] [1] Mar 86
(12"+=) – Drowning in my own tears.

Feb 86. (7")(7"red) **JERICHO. / JERICHO (THE MUSICAL)** [53] [ ]
(12"+=) – Money's too tight (to mention) (live) / Heaven (live).

May 86. (7") **HOLDING BACK THE YEARS. / DROWNING IN MY OWN TEARS** [2] [-]
(12"+=) – Picture Book.

Jul 86. (7") **MONEY'S TOO TIGHT (TO MENTION). / PICTURE BOOK (dub)** [-] [28]

Jul 86. (7") **OPEN UP THE RED BOX (remix). / LOOK AT YOU NOW** [61] [ ]
(12"+=) – Heaven (the musical).
(w/free 7"pic-d) – Money's too tight to mention / Open the red box.
(d7"+=) – Holding back the years / I won't feel bad.

— **AZIZ IBRAHIM** – guitar repl. SYLVAN / added **IAN KIRKHAM** – saxophone / **JANETTE SEWELL** – b.vocals

Feb 87. (7")(7"pic-d) **THE RIGHT THING. / THERE'S A LIGHT** [11] [27]
(12"+=)(12"pic-d+=) – Ev'rytime we say goodbye.
(d7"+=) – Holding back the years / Drowning in my own tears.

Mar 87. (lp)(c)(cd) **MEN AND WOMEN** [2] [31]
– The right thing / Infielity / Suffer / I won't feel bad / Ev'ry time we say goodbye / Let me have it all / Love fire / Move on out / Shine / Maybe someday. *(re-iss.cd/c Feb95)*

May 87. (7") **INFIDELITY. / LADY GODIVA'S ROOM** [31] [ ]
('A'stretch mix-12"+=)(12"pic-d+=) – Love fire (massive red mix).

Jul 87. (7") **MAYBE SOMEDAY. / LET ME HAVE IT ALL (remix)** [ ] [ ]
(12"+=) – Broken man. *(US; b-side)*

Nov 87. (7") **EV'RY TIME WE SAY GOODBYE. / LOVE FOR SALE (live)** [11] [-]
(12"+=)/ /(10"+=)(cd-s+=) – ('A'live)./ / Sad old Red / Broken man.

Mar 88. (7") **I WON'T FEEL BAD. / LADY GODIVA'S ROOM** [68] [ ]
(12"+=)/ /(cd-s+=) – ('A' Arthur Baker remix)./ / The right thing.

Jul 88. (7") **LET ME HAVE IT ALL. / SUFFER** [-] [ ]

— **HEITOR T.P.** – guitar repl. IBRAHIM and SEWELL

Jan 89. (7") **IT'S ONLY LOVE. / TURN IT UP** [13] [57]
('A'valentine-3"cd-s+=)(10"+=)(12"+=) – I'm gonna lose you.
(cd-s++=) – The right thing.

Feb 89. (lp)(c)(cd) **A NEW FLAME** [1] [22]
– It's only love / A new flame / You've got it / To be with you / More / Turn it up / Love lays its tune / She'll have to go / If you don't know me by now / Enough. *(re-entered UK chart 49 on Feb92 / 44 on May92)*

Apr 89. (7") **IF YOU DON'T KNOW ME BY NOW. / MOVE ON OUT (live)** [2] [1]
(12"+=) – Shine (live).
(cd-s++=) – Sugar daddy.
(10"+=) – Great divide.

Jul 89. (7")(c-s) **A NEW FLAME. / MORE** [17] [ ]
(12"+=)(cd-s+=) – I asked her for water (live) / Resume (live).
(10"+=) – I asked her for water (live) / Funk on out (live).

Oct 89. (7")(c-s) **YOU'VE GOT IT. / HOLDING BACK THE YEARS (acoustic)** [46] [-]
(12"+=)(cd-s+=)/ /(10"+=) – I wish./ / I know you got soul.

Oct 89. (7") **YOU'VE GOT IT. / SHE'LL HAVE TO GO** [-] [ ]

— **HUCKNALL, McINTYRE, KELLETT, HEITOR + KIRKHAM** recruit newcomers **GOTA** – drums, percussion, programs repl. JOYCE / **SHAUN WARD** – bass repl. BOWERS. added guest **JESS BAILEY** – key programmer

East West East West

Sep 91. (7")(c-s) **SOMETHING GOT ME STARTED. / A NEW FLAME** [11] [27]
(12"+=)/ /(cd-s+=) – ('A'instrumental)./ / Come on in my kitcken.

Oct 91. (cd)(c)(lp) **STARS** [1] [76]
– Something got me started / Stars / Thrill me / Your mirror / She's got it bad / For your babies / Model / How could it fall / Freedom / Wonderland.

Nov 91. (7")(c-s) **STARS. / ('A' PM DAWN remix)** [8] [44] Jan 92
(12"+=)(cd-s+=) – Rambling on my mind / Something got me started (remix).

Feb 92. (7")(c-s) **FOR YOUR BABIES. / ('A'french version)** [9] [ ]
(cd-s+=) – Me and the Devil blues / Freedom (how long mix).
(12") – ('A'side) / Freedom (perfecto mix).

Apr 92. (7")(c-s) **THRILL ME. / ('A'-Nellie Hooper mix)** [33] [ ]

(cd-s+=) – ('A'live) / When you've got a good friend.
(12") – (3 'A'mixes:- connoisseurs-club – dub).

Jul 92. (7")(c-s) **YOUR MIRROR. / MORE (live) / SOMETHING'S GOT ME STARTED (live)** [17] [ ]
(cd-s) – ('A'side) / Same old Red (live) / She's got it bad (live).

Nov 92. (7"ep)(12"ep)(c-ep)(cd-ep) **MONTREAUX EP** [11] [ ]
– Love for sale / Grandma's house / Drowning in my own tears / Lady Godiva's room.

—— **DEE JOHNSON** – backing vocals repl.TIM

Sep 95. (c-s) **FAIRGROUND / ('A'extended)** [1] [ ]
(cd-s+=) – Stars (live) / The right thing (live).
(cd-s+=) – ('A'-In the Garden mix) / ('A'-Too precious mix) / ('A'-Rollo and Sister Bliss remix).

Oct 95. (cd)(c)(lp) **LIFE** [1] [75]
– You make me believe / So many people / Lives and loves / Fairground / Never never love / So beautiful / Hillside avenue / Remembering the first time / Out on the range / We're in this together.

Dec 95. (c-s)(cd-s) **REMEMBERING THE FIRST TIME / ENOUGH (live) / A NEW FLAME (live)** [22] [ ]
(cd-s) – ('A'-radio disco mix) / ('A'-Hucknall – Herrington remix) / ('A'-Self Preservation Society remix) / ('A'-Satoshi Tomiie remix) / ('A'-Too Precious remix).

FRANTIC ELEVATORS

releases **MICK HUCKNALL** – vocals, guitar / **NEIL MOSS** – guitar, piano / **BRIAN TURNER** – piano, bass / **KEVIN WILLIAMS** – drums

T.J.M. / not issued

Jun 79. (7"m) **VOICES IN THE DARK. / PASSION / EVERY DAY I DIE** [ ] [-]

Eric's / not issued

Nov 80. (7") **YOU KNOW WHAT YOU TOLD ME. / PRODUCTION PREVENTION** [ ] [-]

Crackin' Up / not issued

Apr 81. (7") **SEARCHING FOR THE ONLY ONE. / HUNCHBACK OF NOTREDAME** [ ] [-]

No Waiting / not issued

Oct 82. (7") **HOLDING BACK THE YEARS. / PISTOLS IN MY BRAIN** [ ] [-]

—— MICK took time off to form SIMPLY RED in '84 (see above).

– compilation –

Jan 87. TJM; (m-lp) **THE EARLY YEARS** (soon w/drawn) [ ] [-]

Richard SINCLAIR'S CARAVAN OF DREAMS (see under ⇒ CARAVAN)

SIOUXSIE & THE BANSHEES

Formed: London, England . . . Sep'76 by punkette SIOUXSIE SIOUX and STEVE SEVERIN. Throughout 1977, they toured constantly and signed to 'Track' records, who folded early 1978. Undeterred, they flitted to cousin label 'Polydor', who finally released debut 45 'HONG KONG GARDEN' in August '78. It raced up into the UK Top 10, and was soon followed by classic debut album 'THE SCREAM'. During the late 70's and throughout the 80's, the BANSHEES notched up a run of 20 consecutive Top 50 UK hits, not including 3 off-shoot CREATURES hits between 1981 and 83. • **Style:** Alternative punk-rock, that moved quickly into haunting cult rock that oozed sensuality and the imagery of SIOUXSIE. • **Songwriters:** All written by SIOUXSIE / SEVERIN except; HELTER SKELTER + DEAR PRUDENCE (Beatles) / 20th CENTURY BOY (T.Rex) / THE LORD'S PRAYER (trad.prayer re-arranged) / IL EST NE LE DIVIN ENFANT (French festive song) / ALL TOMORROW'S PARTIES (Velvet Underground). THROUGH THE LOOKING GLASS was a covers album containing THIS WHEEL'S ON FIRE (Bob Dylan) / THE PASSENGER (Iggy Pop) / YOU'RE LOST LITTLE GIRL (Doors) / GUN (John Cale) / THIS TOWN AIN'T BIG ENOUGH FOR THE BOTH OF US (Sparks) / SEA BREEZES (Roxy Music) / STRANGE FRUIT (Billie Holiday) / WALL OF MIRRORS (Kraftwerk) / LITTLE JOHNNY JEWEL (Television) / TRUST IN ME ('Jungle Book' animated film). CREATURES re-done RIGHT NOW (Mel Torme). • **Trivia:** SEVERIN produced ALTERED IMAGES debut 45 'Dead Pop Stars'. SIOUXSIE married BUDGIE May'91 after long relationship.

Recommended: THE SCREAM (*10) / JOIN HANDS (*8) / KALEIDOSCOPE (*7) / HYAENA (*8) / JU JU (*7) / ONCE UPON A TIME – THE SINGLES (*9) / TWICE UPON A TIME (*7) / A KISS IN THE DREAMHOUSE (*7).

SIOUXSIE SIOUX (b.SUSAN DALLION, 27 May'57) – vocals / **STEVEN SEVERIN** (b.STEVEN BAILEY, 1955) – bass / **JOHN McKAY** – guitar repl. PT FENTON who had repl. MARCO PIRRONI (who joined MODELS and later ADAM & THE ANTS) / **KENNY MORRIS** – drums repl. SID VICIOUS who later became bassman for SEX PISTOLS

Polydor / Polydor

Aug 78. (7") **HONG KONG GARDEN. / VOICES** [7] [-]

Oct 78. (7") **HONG KONG GARDEN. / OVERGROUND** [-] [ ]

Nov 78. (lp)(c) **THE SCREAM** [12] [ ]
– Pure / Jigsaw feeling / Overground / Carcass / Helter skelter / Mirage / Metal postcard / Nicotine stain / Suburban relapse / Switch. *(cd-iss.Mar89 & Mar95 on 'Wonderland')*

Mar 79. (7") **THE STAIRCASE (MYSTERY). / 20th CENTURY BOY** [24] [-]

Jun 79. (7") **PLAYGROUND TWIST. / PULLED TO BITS** [28] [-]

Sep 79. (lp)(c) **JOIN HANDS** [13] [-]
– Poppy day / Regal zone / Placebo effect / Icon / Premature burial / Playground twist / Mother / Oh mein papa / The Lord's prayer. *(cd-iss.Mar89 & Mar95 on 'Wonderland')*

Sep 79. (7") **MITTAGEISEN (METAL POSTCARD). / LOVE IN A VOID** [47] [-]

—— **BUDGIE** (b.PETER CLARK, 21 Aug'57, St.Helens, N.England) – drums (ex-SLITS, ex-PLANETS, ex-BIG IN JAPAN, etc.) repl. MORRIS who decamped / **JOHN McGEOGH** (b. 1955, Greenock, Scotland) – guitar (of MAGAZINE) finally repl. ROBERT SMITH (of The CURE) + JOHN CARRUTHERS who repl. disappearing McKAY

Mar 80. (7") **HAPPY HOUSE. / DROP DEAD** [17] [ ]

May 80. (7") **CHRISTINE. / EVE WHITE EVE BLACK** [24] [ ]

Aug 80. (lp)(c) **KALEIDOSCOPE** [5] [ ]
– Happy house / Tenant / Trophy / Hybrid / Lunar camel / Christine / Desert kisses / Red light / Paradise place / Skin. *(cd-iss.Mar89 & Mar95 on 'Wonderland')*

Nov 80. (7")('A'dance-12") **ISRAEL. / RED OVER WHITE** [41] [ ]

May 81. (7") **SPELLBOUND. / FOLLOW THE SUN** [22] [ ]
(12"+=) – Slap dash snap.

Jun 81. (lp)(c) **JU JU** [7] [ ]
– Spellbound / Into the light / Arabian knights / Halloween / Monitor / Night shift / Sin in my heart / Head cut / Voodoo dolly. *(cd-iss.Mar89 & Mar95 on 'Wonderland')*

Jul 81. (7") **ARABIAN KNIGHTS. / SUPERNATURAL THING** [32] [ ]
(12"+=) – Congo conga.

—— In Sep81, SIOUXSIE & BUDGIE as The CREATURES hit Top 30 w / WILD THINGS EP.

Dec 81. (lp)(c) **ONCE UPON A TIME – THE SINGLES** [21] [ ]
– Hong Kong garden / Mirage / The staircase (mystery) / Playground twist / Happy house / Christine / Israel / Spellbound / Arabian knights / Fireworks. *(cd-iss.Mar89 & Mar95 on 'Wonderland')*

May 82. (7") **FIREWORKS. / COAL MIND** [22] [ ]
(12"+=) – We fall.

Sep 82. (7") **SLOWDIVE. / CANNIBAL ROSES** [41] [ ]
(12"+=) – Obsession II.

Nov 82. (lp)(c) **A KISS IN THE DREAMHOUSE** [11] [ ]
– Cascade / Green fingers / Obsession / She's a carnival / Circle / Melt! / Painted bird / Cocoon / Slowdive. *(cd-iss.Apr89 & Mar95 on 'Wonderland')*

Nov 82. (7") **MELT!. / IL EST NE LE DIVIN ENFANT** [49] [ ]
(12"+=) – A sleeping rain.

—— **ROBERT SMITH** – guitar (of The CURE) returned part-time to repl. McGEOGH who later joined The ARMOURY SHOW.

—— In 1983, SMITH and SEVERIN had also splintered into The GLOVE, with SIOUXSIE and BUDGIE re-uniting as The CREATURES (see further on).

Wonderland-Polydor / Geffen

Sep 83. (7") **DEAR PRUDENCE. / TATTOO** [3] [ ]
(12"+=) – There's a planet in my kitchen.

Nov 83. (d-lp)(c) **NOCTURNE (live)** [29] [-]
– Intro – The rite of Spring / Israel / Dear Prudence / Paradise place / Melt! / Cascade / ulled to bits / Night shift / Sin in my heart / Slowdive / Painted bird / Happy house / Switch / Spellbound / Helter skelter / Eve white eve black / Voodoo dolly. *(cd-iss.Apr89 & Mar95)*

Mar 84. (7") **SWIMMING HORSES. / LET GO** [28] [-]
(12"+=) – The humming wires.

May 84. (7") **DAZZLE. / I PROMISE** [33] [-]
(12"+=) – Throw them to the lions / ('A'mix).

Jun 84. (lp)(c)(cd) **HYAENA** [15] [ ]
– Dazzle / We hunger / Take me back / Belladonna / Swimming horses / Bring me the head of the preacher man / Running town / Pointing bone / Blow the house down. *(re-iss.cd Mar95)*

—— **JOHN CARRUTHERS** – guitar (ex-CLOCKDVA, ex-JEFFREY LEE PIERCE) returned to repl. SMITH who had CURE commitments.

Oct 84. (12"ep) **THE THORN (live)** [47] [-]
– Voices / Placebo effect / Red over white / Overground.

Oct 85. (7") **CITIES IN DUST. / AN EXECUTION** [21] [ ]
(12"+=) – Quarter drawing of the dog.

Feb 86. (7") **CANDYMAN. / LULLABY** [34] [-]
(12"+=) – Umbrella.

Apr 86. (lp)(c)(cd) **TINDERBOX** [13] [88]
– Candyman / The sweetest chill / This unrest / Cities in dust / Cannons / Partys fall / 92° / Lands End. *(cd+=)* – An execution / Quarter drawing of the dog / Lullaby / Umbrella / Candyman (extended). *(re-iss.cd Mar95)*

Jan 87. (7") **THIS WHEEL'S ON FIRE. / SHOOTING SUN** [14] [ ]
(12"+=) – Sleepwalking (on the high wire).

Feb 87. (lp)(c)(cd) **THROUGH THE LOOKING GLASS** [15] [ ]
– Hall of mirrors / Trust in me / This wheel's on fire / Strange fruit / This town ain't big enough for the both of us / You're lost little girl / The passenger / Gun / Sea breezes / Little Johnny Jewel. *(re-iss.cd Mar95)*

Mar 87. (7") **THE PASSENGER. / SHE'S CUCKOO** [41] [ ]
(12"+=) – Something blue.

—— **JON KLEIN** – guitar (ex-SPECIMEN) repl. CARRUTHERS / added **MARTIN McCARRICK** – cello, keysboards (ex-MARC ALMOND, ex-The GLOVE) (to SIOUXSIE, SEVERIN, BUDGIE + KLEIN)

Jul 87. (7")(c-s)(7"pic-d) **SONG FROM THE EDGE OF THE WORLD. / THE WHOLE PRICE OF BLOOD** [59] [-]
(12"+=) – Mechanical eyes.

Jul 88. (7") **PEEK-A-BOO. / FALSE FACE** [16] [53]
(c-s+=)(cd-s+=)(vid-cd+=) – Catwalk / ('A'big suspender mix).
(12"+=) – ('A'-2 other mixes).

Sep 88. (lp)(c)(cd) **PEEPSHOW** [20] [68]
– Peek-a-boo / Killing jar / Scarecrow / Carousel / Burn-up / Ornaments of gold / Turn to stone / Rawhead and bloodybones / The last beat of my heart / Rhapsody. *(re-iss.cd Mar95)*

Sep 88. (7")(7"pic-d) **KILLING JAR. / SOMETHING WICKED (THIS WAY COMES)** [41] [ ]
(12"+=)(cd-s+=) – Are you still dying, darling.

Nov 88. (7") **THE LAST BEAT OF MY HEART. / EL DIABLO LOS MUERTOS** [44] [ ]
(12"+=) – Sunless.
(cd-s++=) – ('B'mix).

—— In Autumn'89, The CREATURES issued singles and 'BOOMERANG' album.

May 91. (7")(c-s) **KISS THEM FOR ME. / RETURN** [32] [23]
('A'version-12"+=)(12"pic-d+=) – Staring back.
(cd-s++=) – ('A'side).

Jun 91. (cd)(c)(lp) **SUPERSTITION** [25] [65]
– Kiss them for me / Fear (of the unknown) / Cry / Drifter / Little sister / Shadowtime / Silly thing / Got to get up / Silver waterfalls / Softly / The ghost in you. *(re-iss.cd Mar95)*

Jul 91. (7")(c-s) **SHADOWTIME. / SPIRAL TWIST** [57] [ ]
(12"+=)(cd-s+=) – Sea of light. / ('A'-eclipse mix).

—— Below single from the film 'Batman Returns'.

Jul 92. (7")(c-s) **FACE TO FACE. / I COULD BE AGAIN** [21] [ ]
(cd-s+=) – ('A'-catatonic mix) / Hothead.
(12") – ('A'side) / ('A'-catatonic mix) / Hothead.

Oct 92. (cd)(c)(lp) **TWICE UPON A TIME – THE THING** [26] [ ]
– Fireworks / Slowdive / Melt / Dear Prudence / Swimming horses / Dazzle / Overground (from The Thorn) / Cities in dust / Candyman / This wheel's on fire / The passenger / Peek-a-boo / The killing jar / The last beat of my heart / Kiss them for me / Shadowtime / Fear (of the unknown) / Face to face. *(re-iss.cd Mar95)*

—— In Aug 94, SIOUXSIE partnered MORRISSEY on his single 'INTERLUDE'.

Dec 94. (c-s) **O BABY. / OURSELVES** [34] [ ]
(cd-s+=) – ('A'-Manhattan mix).
(cd-s) – ('A'side) / Swimming horses (live) / All tomorrow's parties (live).

Jan 95. (cd)(c)(lp) **THE RAPTURE** [33] [ ]
– O baby / Tearing apart / Stargazer / Fall from grace / Not forgotten / Sick child / The lonely one / Falling down / Forever / The rapture / The double life / Love out me.

Feb 95. (7")(c-s) **STARGAZER. / HANG ME HIGH** [64] [ ]
(cd-s+=) – Black Sun.
(cd-s) – ('A'-Mambo sun) / ('A'-Planet queen mix) / ('A'-Mark Saunders mix).

– compilations, others, etc. –

Feb 87. Strange Fruit; (12"ep) **THE PEEL SESSIONS (29.11.77)** [ ] [-]
– Love in a void / Mirage / Suburban relapse / Metal postcard. *(c-ep iss. Jun87, cd-ep iss.Mar88)*

Feb 89. Strange Fruit; (12"ep)(cd-ep) **THE PEEL SESSIONS (Feb78)** [ ] [-]
– Hong Kong garden / Carcass / Helter skelter / Overground.

Apr 93. ZYX; (cd) **THE BEST OF THE CREATURES (CREATURES)** [ ] [-]

CREATURES

(SIOUXSIE & BUDGIE)

Polydor / not issued

Sep 81. (d7"ep) **WILD THINGS** [24] [-]
– Mad-eyed screamer / So unreal / But not them / Wild thing / Thumb.

Wonderland-Polydor / Geffen

May 83. (7") **MISS THE GIRL. / HOT SPRING IN THE SNOW** [21] [-]

May 83. (lp)(c) **FEAST** [17] [ ]
– Morning dawning / Inoa 'ole / Ice house / Dancing on glass / Gecko / Sky train / Festival of colours / Miss the girl / A strutting rooster / Flesh.

Jul 83. (7") **RIGHT NOW. / WEATHERCADE** [14] [-]
(12"+=) – Festival of colours.

Oct 89. (7") **STANDING THERE. / DIVIDED** [53] [-]
(10"+=)(12"+=)(cd-s+=) – Solar choir.

Nov 89. (lp)(c)(cd) **BOOMERANG** [ ] [ ]
– Standing there / Manchild / You! / Pity / Killing time / Willow / Pluto drive / Solar choir * / Speeding * / Fury eyes / Fruitman / Untiedundone * / Simoom * / Strolling wolf / Venus sands / Morriha. (*= extra tracks on cd)

Feb 90. (7")(c-s)(cd-s) **FURY EYES. / ABSTINENCE** [ ] [-]
(12") – ('A'side) / ('A'-2 dub + fever mixes).

The GLOVE

(SEVERIN & ROBERT SMITH) also incl. **MARTIN McCARRICK** – cello / **ANNE STEPHENSON + GINNY HEWES** – strings / **ANDY ANDERSON** – drums / (JEANETTE) **LANDRAY** – dual vocals w/**SMITH**

Wonderland-Polydor / Geffen

Aug 83. (7") **LIKE AN ANIMAL. / MOUTH TO MOUTH** [52] [-]
(12"+=) – Animal (club mix).

Aug 83. (lp)(c) **BLUE SUNSHINE** [35] [ ]
– Like an animal / Looking glass girl / Sex-eye-make-up / Mr. Alphabet says / A blues in drag / Punish me with kisses / This green city / Orgy / Perfect murder / Relax. *(re-iss.+cd.Sep90 +=)–* Mouth to mouth / The tightrope / Like an animal (club mix).

Nov 83. (7") **PUNISH ME WITH KISSES. / THE TIGHTROPE** [ ] [-]

SIREN (see under ⇒ COYNE, Kevin)

SISTERS OF MERCY

Formed: Leeds, England . . . 1980 by ELDRITCH and MARX. Formed own indie 'Merciful' records in 1980, to release debut 'DAMAGE DONE'. After a tour supporting The BIRTHDAY PARTY and The PSYCHEDELIC FURS, they appeared on Leeds Futurama festival in the early 80's. In 1984, their label, received distribution from 'WEA' and they finally made UK Top 50 with 'BODY AND SOUL'. • **Style:** Atmospheric goth-punk outfit fronted by the deep, black-attired ELDRITCH. When PATRICIA MORRISON was added in 1986, it added glam to already heavy alternative disco-goth. • **Songwriters:** All ELDRITCH written, except period between 1983-85 when HUSSEY was writing partner. Covered:- EMMA (Hot Chocolate) / 1969 (Stooges) / GIMME SHELTER (Rolling Stones) / KNOCKIN' ON HEAVEN'S DOOR (Bob Dylan). In 1990, ELDRITCH co-wrote 'VISION THING' album with JIM STEINMAN. • **Trivia:** In 1982, they argued with stablemates The MARCH VIOLETS, who immediately left for new pastures 'Rebirth'.

Recommended: SOME GIRLS WANDER BY MISTAKE (*9) / FIRST AND LAST AND ALWAYS (*8) / FLOODLAND (*8) / VISION THING (*7). The SISTERHOOD:- GIFT (*7).

ANDREW ELDRITCH (b.ANDREW TAYLOR, 15 May'59, East Anglia, England) – vocals / **GARRY MARX** – guitar / + drum machine DOKTOR AVALANCHE

Merciful / not issued

1980. (7"m) **DAMAGE DONE. / WATCH / HOME OF THE HITMAN** [ ] [-]

—— added **BEN GUNN** – guitar / **CRAIG ADAMS** – bass (ex-EXPELAIRES)

C.N.T. / not issued

Feb 82. (7") **BODY ELECTRIC. / ADRENOCHROME** [ ] [-]

Merciful / not issued

Nov 82. (7") **ALICE. / FLOORSHOW** [ ] [-]

Mar 83. (7") **ANACONDA. / PHANTOM** [ ] [-]

Apr 83. (12"ep) **ALICE. / FLOORSHOW / 1969 / PHANTOM** [ ] [-]

May 83. (12"ep) **THE REPTILE HOUSE** [ ] [-]
– Kiss the carpet / Lights / Valentine / Burn / Fix. *(re-iss.Apr94)*

—— **WAYNE HUSSEY** – guitar (ex-DEAD OR ALIVE, ex-HAMBI & THE DANCE) repl. BEN

Oct 83. (7") **TEMPLE OF LOVE. / HEARTLAND** [ ] [-]
(12"+=) – Gimme shelter.

Merciful-WEA / Warners

Jun 84. (7") **BODY AND SOUL. (as "The SISTERS") / TRAIN** [46] [-]
(12"+=) – After hours / Body electric.

Oct 84. (7") **WALK AWAY. / POISON DOOR** [45] [-]
(above w/free 7"flexi) – Long Train.
(12"+=) – On the wire.

Feb 85. (7") **NO TIME TO CRY. / BLOOD MONEY** [63] [-]
(12"+=) – Bury me deep.

Mar 85. (lp)(c) **FIRST AND LAST AND ALWAYS** [14] [ ]
– Black planet / Walk away / No time to cry / A rock and a hard place / Marian / First and last and always / Possession / Nine while nine / Amphetamine logic / Some kind of stranger. *(cd-iss.Jul88) (re-iss.re-mastered.Jul92 on 'East West')*

—— Disbanded mid'85 . . . GARRY MARX helped form GHOST DANCE. HUSSEY and ADAMS formed The MISSION after squabbles with ANDREW over use of group name.

—— **ELDRITCH** with ever faithful drum machine adopted

The SISTERHOOD

recruited **PATRICIA MORRISON** (b.14 Jan'62) – bass, vocals (ex-FUR BIBLE, ex-GUN CLUB) **JAMES RAY** – guitar / **ALAN VEGA** – synthesizers (ex-SUICIDE) / **LUCAS FOX** – drums. (ELDRITCH moved to Berlin, Germany.)

Merciful / not issued

Feb 86. (7") **GIVING GROUND (remix). / GIVING GROUND (album version)** [ ] [-]

Jul 86. (lp)(c) **GIFT** [90] [-]
– Jihad / Colours / Giving ground / Finland red, Egypt white / Rain from Heaven. *(cd-iss.Sep89 & Jul94)*

The SISTERS OF MERCY

were again as **ELDRITCH** and **MORRISON** obtained rights to name. (drum machine)

Merciful-WEA / Elektra

Sep 87. (7") **THIS CORROSION. / TORCH** [7] [ ]
(c-s+=)/ /(12"+=)(cd-s+=) – ('A'version)./ / Colours.

Nov 87. (lp)(c)(cd) **FLOODLAND** [9] [ ]
– Dominion / Mother Russia / Flood I / Lucretia my reflection / 1959 / This corrosion / Flood II / Driven like the snow / Neverlan. *(c+=)–* Torch. *(cd-s++=)–* Colours.

Feb 88. (7") **DOMINION. / SANDSTORM / UNTITLED** [13] [-]
(d12"+=)/ /(c-s+=)(cd-s+=) – Emma./ / Ozy-Mandias.

May 88. (7") **LUCRETIA MY REFLECTION. / LONG TRAIN** [20] [ ]
(12"+=)(cd-s+=) – ('A'extended).

—— (Feb90) **ELDRITCH** w/drum machine, recruited complete new line-up / **TONY JAMES** – bass, vocals (ex-SIGUE SIGUE SPUTNIK, ex-GENERATION X) / **ABDREAS BRUHN** – guitar / **TIM BRICHENO** – guitar (ex-ALL ABOUT EVE) / guests were **MAGGIE REILLY** – b.vocals (ex-MIKE OLDFIELD) / **JOHN PERRY** – guitar (ex-ONLY ONES)

Oct 90. (7")(c-s) **MORE. / YOU COULD BE THE ONE** [21] [ ]
(12"+=)(cd-s+=) – ('A'extended).

Oct 90. (cd)(c)(lp) **VISION THING** [11] [ ]
– Vision thing / Ribons / Destination Boulevard / Something fast / When you don't see me / Doctor Jeep / More / I was wrong.

Dec 90. (7") **DOCTOR JEEP. / KNOCKIN' ON HEAVEN'S DOOR (live)** [37] [ ]
(12"+=)(cd-s+=) – ('A'extended).
('A'ext-12") – Burn (live) / Amphetamine logic (live).

—— (Oct91) **TONY JAMES** split from ELDRITCH amicably.

—— Next featured vocals by **OFRA HAZA**

East West / East West

Apr 92. (7") **TEMPLE OF LOVE (1992). / I WAS WRONG (American fade)** *(re-iss.Apr94)* [3] [ ]

('A'ext-12"+=) – Vision thing (Canadian club mix).
(cd-s+=) – When you don't see me (German release).

Apr 92. (cd)(c)(d-lp) **SOME GIRLS WANDER BY MISTAKE** (1980-1983 material) | 5 |
– Alice / Floorshow / Phantom / 1969 / Kiss the carpet / Lights / Valentine / Fix / Burn / Kiss the carpet (reprise) / Temple of love / Heartland / Gimme shelter / Damage done / Watch / Home of the hitmen / Body electric / Adrenochrome / Anaconda.

— now just **ANDREW ELDRITCH** on own with guests

Aug 93. (7")(c-s) **UNDER THE GUN. / ALICE (1993)** | 19 |
(12"+=)(cd-s+=) – ('A'-Jutland mix).

Aug 93. (cd)(c)(d-lp) **GREATEST HITS VOLUME 1 – A SLIGHT CASE OF OVERBOMBING** (compilation) | 14 |
– Under the gun / Temple of love (1992) / Vision thing / Detonation boulevard / Doctor Jeep / More / Lucretia my reflection / Dominion – Mother / This corrosion / No time to cry / Walk away / Body and soul.

SKID ROW

Formed: New Jersey, USA . . . late '86 by Canadian born BACH. Signed worldwide to 'Atlantic' in 1988, and soon released eponymous debut hit album. • **Style:** Hard-rock outfit influenced by KISS, DOKKEN, MOTLEY CRUE or even SEX PISTOLS. • **Songwriters:** BOLAN w/SNAKE + BACH or BOLAN w / AFFUSO + HILL. Covered C'MON AND LOVE ME (Kiss) / HOLIDAYS IN THE SUN (Sex Pistols) / WHAT YOU'RE DOING (Rush). • **Trivia:** Run by the same management team as BON JOVI.

Recommended: SKID ROW (*6) / SLAVE TO THE GRIND (*7).

SEBASTIAN BACH (b. BIERK, 3 Apr'68, Toronto) – vocals / **DAVE 'Snake' SABO** – guitar / **SCOTTI HILL** – guitar / **RACHEL BOLAN** – bass / **ROB AFFUSO** – drums

Atlantic | Atlantic

Nov 89. (7")(7"sha-pic-d) **YOUTH GONE WILD. / SWEET LITTLE SISTER** | 42 | 99 Jun 89
(12"+=) – Makin' a mess (live).

Dec 89. (lp)(c)(cd) **SKID ROW** | 30 | 6 Feb 89
– Big guns / Sweet little sister / Can't stand the heartache / Piece of me / 18 and life / Rattlesnake shake / Youth gone wild / Here I am / Makin' a mess / I remember you / Midnight – Tornado. *(re-iss.cd/c Feb95 on 'Warners')*

Jan 90. (7"one-sided)(7"sha-pic-d) **18 AND LIFE. / MIDNIGHT TORNADO** | 12 | 4 Jul 89
(12"+=)(c-s+=)(cd-s+=) – Here I am (live).

Mar 90. (7")(c-s) **I REMEMBER YOU. / MAKIN' A MESS** | 36 | 6 Nov 89
(12"+=)(cd-s+=)/ /(10"+=) – Big guns./ / ('A'live).

East West | Atlantic

Jun 91. (7")(7"sha-pic-d) **MONKEY BUSINESS. / SLAVE TO THE GRIND** | 19 |
(12"+=)(cd-s+=) – Riot act.

Jun 91. (cd)(c)(lp) **SLAVE TO THE GRIND** | 5 | 1
– Monkey business / Slave to the grind / The threat / Quicksand Jesus / Psycho love / Get the fuck out / Lovin' on a chain gang / Creepshow / In a darkened room / Riot act / Mud kicker / Wasted time.

Sep 91. (7")(c-s) **SLAVE TO THE GRIND. / C'MON AND LOVE ME** | 43 |
(12") – ('A'side) / Creepshow / Beggar's day.
(cd-s++=) – (above 'B'side).

Nov 91. (7") **WASTED TIME. / HOLIDAYS IN THE SUN** | 20 | 88
(12"+=) – What you're doing / Get the fuck out (live).
(cd-s+=) – Psycho love / Get the fuck out (live).
(12"pic-d) – ('A'side) / Psycho love.

Aug 92. (7")(c-s) **YOUTH GONE WILD. / DELIVERIN' THE GOODS** | 22 |
(12"+=)(cd-s+=) – Get the funk out / Psycho therapy.

Sep 92. (m-cd)(m-c) **B-SIDES OURSELVES** (as said) | - | 58

Mar 95. (cd)(c)(lp) **SUBHUMAN RACE** | 8 | 35
– My enemy / Firesign / Bonehead / Beat yourself blind / Eileen / Remains to be seen / Subhuman race / Frozen / Into another / Face against my soul / Medicine jar / Breakin' down / Ironwill.

Nov 95. (7"colrd) **BREAKIN' DOWN. / RIOT ACT (live)** | 48 |
(cd-s) – ('A'side) / Firesign (demo) / Slave to the grind (live) / Monkey business (live).
(cd-s) – ('A'side) / Frozen (demo) / Beat yourself blind (live) / Psychotherapy (live).

SKIDS

Formed: Dunfermline, Scotland . . . Spring 1977 by JOBSON and ADAMSON. After one-off 45 on indie label 'No-Bad', they signed to major 'Virgin' mid-'78. Success developed relatively quickly, when their 4th single 'INTO THE VALLEY' scraped into UK Top 10, followed by their debut album hitting Top 20. Hits continued until departure of ADAMSON, and JOBSON's diversion into poetry in '81. They had also flitted to London around this time. • **Style:** Initially a clever visual (i.e. JOBSON's kick-dance and ultra-combed hairdo) punk/new wave outfit, who eased into semi-stardom. Bit the dust when they opted for more trad/folk sound in 1981. • **Songwriters:** JOBSON lyrics / group compositions, except ALL THE YOUNG DUDES (hit; Mott The Hoople) / BAND PLAYED WALTZING MATILDA (Australian trad.). • **Trivia:** In 1981, JOBSON published book of poetry 'A MAN FOR ALL SEASONS'.

Recommended: SCARED TO DANCE (*8) / SWEET SUBURBIA – THE BEST OF THE SKIDS (*8)

RICHARD JOBSON (b. 6 Apr'60) – vocals, guitar / **STUART ADAMSON** (b.WILLIAM STUART ADAMSON, 11 Apr'58, Manchester, England) – lead guitar, vocals / **BILL SIMPSON** – bass / **TOM KELLICHAN** – drums

No-Bad | not issued

Mar 78. (7"m) **CHARLES. / REASONS / TEST-TUBE BABIES** | | -

Virgin | Virgin?

Sep 78. (7")(7"white) **SWEET SUBURBIA. / OPEN SOUND** | 70 | -

Oct 78. (7"red-ep)(12"red-ep) **WIDE OPEN** | 48 | -
– The saints are coming / Of one skin / Confusion / Night and day.

Feb 79. (7")(7"white) **INTO THE VALLEY. / T.V. STARS** | 10 |

Feb 79. (lp)(c) **SCARED TO DANCE** | 19 |
– Into the valley / Scared to dance / Of one skin / Dossier (of fallibility) / Melancholy soldiers / Hope and glory / The saints are coming / Six times / Calling the tune / Integral plot / Charles / Scale. *(re-iss.Apr84, cd-iss.Jun90)*

May 79. (7") **MASQUERADE. / OUT OF TOWN** | 14 |
(d7"+=) – Another emotion / Aftermath dub.

— **RUSTY EGAN** – drums (ex-RICH KIDS) repl. KELLICHAN

Sep 79. (7") **CHARADE. / GREY PARADE** | 31 |

Oct 79. (lp)(c) **DAYS IN EUROPA** | 32 |
– Animation * / Charade / Dulce et decorum (pro patria mor) / Pros and cons / Home of the saved / Working for the Yankee dollar / The olympian / Thanatos / Masquerade / A day in Europa / Peaceful times. *(re-dist.Mar80 += *) (re-iss.Mar84)*

Nov 79. (7") **WORKING FOR THE YANKEE DOLLAR. / VANGUARD'S CRUSADE** | 20 |
(d7"+=) – All the young dudes / Hymns from a haunted ballroom.

— **RUSSELL WEBB** – bass, vocals (ex-ZONES, ex-SLIK) repl. SIMPSON / **MIKE BAILLIE** – drums (ex-INSECT BITES) repl. EGAN who joined VISAGE

Feb 80. (7") **ANIMATION. / PROS AND CONS** | 56 |

Jul 80. (7") **CIRCUS GAMES. / ONE DECREE** | 32 |

Sep 80. (lp)(c) **THE ABSOLUTE GAME** | 9 |
– Circus games / Out of town / Goodbye civilian / The children saw the shame / A woman in winter / Hurry on boys / Happy to be with you / The Devil's decade / One decree / Arena. *(free-lp w.a.)* **STRENGTH THROUGH JOY** *(re-iss.Mar84)*

Oct 80. (7")(7"pic-d) **GOODBYE CIVILIAN. / MONKEY McGUIRE MEETS SPECKY POTTER BEHIND THE LOCHORE INSTITUTE** | 52 |

Nov 80. (7") **A WOMAN IN WINTER. / WORKING FOR THE YANKEE DOLLAR (live)** | 49 |

— **KENNY HYSLOP** (b.14 Feb'51, Helensburgh, Scotland) – drums (ex-ZONES, ex-SLIK) repl. BAILLIE who joined EPSILON.

Aug 81. (7") **FIELDS. / BRAVE MAN** | | -

— **JOBSON + WEBB** recruited **PAUL WISHART** – saxophone, flute to repl. ADAMSON who formed BIG COUNTRY and HYSLOP who joined SIMPLE MINDS. Session people on album incl. **J.J. JOHNSON** – drums / **The ASSOCIATES / VIRGINIA ASTLEY / MIKE OLDFIELD** – guitar / **KEN LOCKIE / TIM CROSS** – piano / **ALAN DARBY** – guitar

Oct 81. (7") **IONA. / BLOOD AND SPOIL** | | -

Nov 81. (lp)(c) **JOY** | | -
– Blood and soil / A challenge, the wanderer / Men of mercy / A memory / Iona / In fear of fire / Brothers / And the band played Waltzing Matilda / The men of the fall / The sound of retreat (instrumental) / Fields. *(re-iss.1988)*

— Folded early '82, with JOBSON already concentrating on poetry & solo work.

– compilations, others, etc. –

May 82. Virgin; (lp)(c) **FANFARE** | | -

May 83. Virgin; (12"ep) **INTO THE VALLEY / MASQUERADE. / SCARED TO DANCE / WORKING FOR THE YANKEE DOLLAR** | | -

1987. Virgin; (cd) **DUNFERMLINE** *(re-iss.Jul93)* | | -

Feb 92. Windsong; (cd) **BBC RADIO 1 LIVE IN CONCERT (live)** | | -

Jan 95. Virgin; (cd) **SWEET SUBURBIA – THE BEST OF THE SKIDS** | | -
– Into the valley / Charles / The saints are coming / Scared to dance / Sweet suburbia / Of one skin / Night and day / Animation / Working for the Yankee dollar / Charade / Masquerade / Circus games / Out of town / Goodbye civilin / A woman in winter / Hurry on boys / Iona / Fields.

RICHARD JOBSON

solo with **JOHN McGEOGH** – guitar / **VIRGINIA ASTLEY** – piano, flute / **JOSEPHINE** – wind, piano

Cocteau | not issued

Oct 81. (lp) **THE BALLAD OF ETIQUETTE** (some poetry) | | -
– India song / Don't ever tell anybody anything / Pavillion pole / Etiquette / Joy / Thomas / Anonymous / The night of crystal / Orphee / Stormy weather. *(re-iss.Jul85)*

Crepescule | not issued

Feb 83. (lp) **10:30 ON A SUMMER NIGHT** | | -

— with **VINI RELLY** – guitar (of DURUTTI COLUMN) / **WIM MERTENS** (of SOFT VERDICT) / **BLAINE L. REININGER** (of TUXEDO MOON) / **PAUL HAIG** – synthesizers (ex-JOSEF K) / **STEVEN BROWN** – sax

Jul 84. (lp) **AN AFTERNOON IN COMPANY (as "THOMAS THE IMPOSTER")** | | -
– Autumn / The return to England / Auden / The Pyrenees / Verbier / The Rhur Valley / Hollow men / Savannah / Jericho 1 / Meditation / Oran / Aragon / Jericho 2 / Dignity / Mount Fuji / The end of the era.

Feb 86. (d-lp) **THE OTHER MAN** | | -

Jan 87. (lp) **16 YEARS OF ALCOHOL** | | -

ARMOURY SHOW

was formed by **RICHARD JOBSON** – vocals + RUSSELL WEBB – bass / plus **JOHN McGEOGH** – guitar (ex-SIOUXSIE & THE BANSHEES, ex-MAGAZINE) / **JOHN DOYLE** – drums (ex-MAGAZINE) / **EVAN CHARLES** – keyboards (ex-COWBOYS INTERNATIONAL)

Parlophone | Capitol

Aug 84. (7") **CASTLES IN SPAIN. / INNOCENTS ABROAD** | 69 | -
(12"+=) – Is it a wonder.

Jan 85. (7") **WE CAN BE BRAVE AGAIN. / A FEELING** 66 -
(12"+=) – Catherine.
Jul 85. (7") **GLORY OF LOVE. / HIGHER THAN THE WORLD (instrumental)** -
(12"+=) – ('A'part 2) / ('A'instrumental).
Sep 85. (lp)(c) **WAITING FOR THE FLOODS** 57
– Castles in Spain / Kyria / A feeling / Jungle of cities / We can be brave again / Higher than the world / Glory of love / Waiting for the floods / Sense of freedom / Sleep city sleep / Avalanche.
Oct 85. (7") **CASTLES IN SPAIN. / A GATHERING**
(12"+=) – Ring those bells.
Jan 87. (7")(12") **LOVE IN ANGER. / TENDER IS THE NIGHT** 63
Apr 87. (7") **NEW YORK CITY. / WHIRLWIND**
(12"+=) – ('A'versions).

— Crumbled around mid'87, with . . .

RICHARD JOBSON

again trying solo career augmented by co-writer RUSSELL WEBB.

Parlophone not issued

Aug 88. (7")(12") **BADMAN. / THE HEAT IS ON** -
(cd-s+=) – Big fat city.
Nov 88. (lp)(c)(cd) **BADMAN** -
– Badman / This thing caled love / Monkey's cry / The heat is on / Uptown – downtown / A boat called Pride / Angel / Fire.

— JOBSON, who was now a successful male model and also took up TV work mainly interviews. Most now know of his winning battle against alcohol and epilepsy. In the late 80's, his marriage to TV presenter MARIELLA FROSTRUP folded although they remained very good friends. He is currently presenting late night TV show 'Holywood Report'.

SKIN

Formed: London, England . . . 1991 briefly as TASTE, by MYKE GRAY (ex-JAGGED EDGE) and Welsh heavies KOUGAR. Early 1994, they scored first of 5 hits that year with 'SKIN UP' EP. • **Style:** Metal-pop /rock similiar to WHITESNAKE with hard blues. • **Songwriters:** GRAY, some w/others, except HANGIN' ON THE TELEPHONE (Blondie) / PUMP IT UP (Elvis Costello). • **Trivia:** Produced by KEITH OLSEN.

Recommended: SKIN (*5)

NEVILLE MacDONALD – vocals (ex-KOOGA) / **MYKE GRAY** (b.12 May'68) – guitar (ex-JAGGED EDGE) / **ANDY ROBBINS** – bass, vocals / **DICKIE FLISZAR** – drums, vocals (ex-BRUCE DICKINSON)

Parlophone Capitol

Dec 93. (12"ep)(cd-ep) **SKIN UP EP** 67
– Look but don't touch / Shine your light / Monkey.
Mar 94. (12"ep)(c-ep)(cd-ep) **HOUSE OF LOVE / GOOD TIME LOVIN'. / THIS PLANET'S ON FIRE / TAKE IT EASY** 45
Apr 94. (c-s) **MONEY. / ALL I WANT / FUNKTIFIED** 18
(cd-s) – (1st 2 tracks) / Unbelievable / Down down down.
(12"pic-d) – (1st & 3rd tracks) / Express yourself.
(cd-s) – (1st & 3rd tracks) / Express yourself / Unbelievable.
May 94. (cd)(c)(lp) **SKIN** 9
– Money / Shine your light / House of love / Colourblind / Which are the tears / Look but don't touch / Nightsong / Tower of strength / Revolution / Raised on radio / Wings of an angel. *(re-iss.Oct94)*
Jul 94. (c-s) **TOWER OF STRENGTH. / LOOK BUT DON'T TOUCH (live) / UNBELIEVABLE (live)** 19
(12"+=)(cd-s+=) – ('A'live).
(cd-s) – ('A'side) / Money (live) / Shine your light (live) / Colourblind (live).
Oct 94. (c-s) **LOOK BUT DON'T TOUCH. / HANGIN' ON THE TELEPHONE** 33
(cd-s+=) – Should I stay or should I go / Dog eat dog.
(12"pic-d)(cd-s) – ('A'side) / Should I stay or should I go / Pump it up / Money.
May 95. (12"ep) **TAKE ME DOWN TO THE RIVER. / SPEED KING (live) / NEED YOUR LOVE SO BAD (live) / HOUSE OF LOVE (live)** 26
(cd-s) – ('A'side) / Rock and roll (live) / Ain't talkin' 'bout love (live) / Rock candy (live).
(cd-s) – ('A'side) / Radar love (live) / Come together (live) / My generation (live).

SKUNK ANANSIE

Formed: London, England . . .1994 by aggressive shaven-headed black lesbian SKIN and guitarist ACE. Quickly made an impact on British audiences with three Top 50 singles and a Top 10 album in 1995. • **Style:** As said with anti-rascist overtones fused with blasting indie-metallic and punk rock. • **Songwriters:** SKIN – ARRAN.

Recommended: PARANOID & SUNBURNT (*7)

SKIN (DYER) – vocals / **ACE** (L.ARRAN) – guitar / **CASS** – bass / **ROBBIE** – drums

One Little Indian ???

Mar 95. (c-s)(10"white) **SELLING JESUS. / THROUGH RAGE / YOU WANT IT ALL** 46
(cd-s+=) – Skunk song.
Jun 95. (10"lime)(c-s) **I CAN DREAM. / AESTHETIC ANARCHIST / BLACK SKIN SEXUALITY** 41
(cd-s+=) – Little baby Swastikkka.

— **LOUIE** – drums repl.ROBBIE

Aug 95. (c-s) **CHARITY / I CAN DREAM (version)** 40
(cd-s+=) – Punk by numbers.
(cd-s+=) – Kept my mouth shut.
(10"colrd) – ('A'side) / Used / Killer's war.
Sep 95. (cd)(c)(lp) **PARANOID & SUNBURNT** 8
– Selling Jesus / Intellectualise my blackness / I can dream / Little baby swastikkka / All in the name of pity / Charity / It takes blood and guts / Weak / And here I stand (nigger rage) / 100 ways to be a good girl / Rise up.

SLADE

Formed: Wolverhampton, England . . . 1964 as The VENDORS by DAVE HILL and DON POWELL. The next year they became The IN-BETWEENS and recorded a demo EP for French label 'Barclay'. Their official debut 'YOU BETTER RUN' (with newcomers HOLDER and LEA), flopped late in '66, and they retired from studio until 1969 when they became AMBROSE SLADE. By now living in London, they were spotted by ex-ANIMALS bass player CHAS CHANDLER, who became their manager and producer, after arranging deal with 'Fontana' records. Their first product 'BEGINNINGS' sold badly, and they shortened name to SLADE. After a few more flops, they finally cracked the UK Top 20 in 1971 with 'GET DOWN AND GET WITH IT'. Their follow-up 'COZ I LUV YOU' hit the top for 4 weeks, and was the start of lucrative 5 years in which they scored another 5 No.1's, 3 of them 'CUM ON FEEL THE NOIZE', 'SKWEEZE ME PLEEZE ME' & 'MERRY XMAS EVERYBODY', peaking there on first week of release. • **Style:** From 1969, they were first to wear skinhead clothing (Dr.Marten's boots / braces / etc). Their anthemic pop-metal from 1971 which included some ballads, changed with HOLDER's gritty vox into harder rock – pop for the 80's. • **Songwriters:** HOLDER-LEA or LEA-POWELL penned except IN-BETWEENS:- TAKE A HEART (Sorrows) / CAN YOUR MONKEY DO THE DOG (Rufus Thomas) / YOU BETTER RUN (Rascals). AMBROSE SLADE:- BORN TO BE WILD (Steppenwolf) / AIN'T GOT NO HEAT (Frank Zappa) / IF THIS WORLD WERE MINE (Marvin Gaye) / FLY ME HIGH (Justin Hayward) / MARTHA MY DEAR (Beatles) / JOURNEY TO THE CENTER OF MY MIND (Ted Nugent). SLADE:- THE SHAPE OF THINGS TO COME (Max Frost & The Troopers; Mann-weill) / ANGELINA (Neil Innes) / COULD I (Griffin-Royer) / JUST A LITTLE BIT (?) / GET DOWN AND GET WITH IT (Bobby Marchin) / DARLING BE HOME SOON (Lovin' Spoonful) / LET THE GOOD TIMES ROLL (Shirley & Lee) / MY BABY LEFT ME – THAT'S ALL RIGHT (Elvis Presley) / PISTOL PACKIN' MAMA (Gene Vincent) / SOMETHIN' ELSE (Eddie Cochran) / OKEY COKEY (seasonal; trad) / HI HO SILVER LINING (Jeff Beck) / STILL THE SAME (Bob Seger) / YOU'LL NEVER WALK ALONE (Rogers-Hammerstein) / AULD LANG SYNE (trad.) / SANTA CLAUS IS COMING TO TOWN (festive) / LET'S DANCE (Chris Montez) / etc. • **Miscellaneous:** On 4 Jul'73, POWELL was seriously injured in a car crash, in which his girlfriend Angela Morris was killed, and he suffered amnesia. After SLADE split again in '88, he became an antique dealer.

Recommended: WALL OF HITS (*7).

The IN-BETWEENS

JOHNNY HOWELLS – vocals / **MICKEY MARSTON** – guitar / **DAVE HILL** (b. 4 Apr'52, Fleet Castle, Devon, England) – guitar / **DAVE JONES** – bass / **DON POWELL** (10 Sep'50, Bilston, Staffordshire) – drums

Barclay not issued

1965. (7"ep) **TAKE A HEART / LITTLE NIGHTINGALE. / (2 tracks by 'The Hills')** - France
1965. (7"ep) **TAKE A HEART. / CAN YOUR MONKEY DO THE DOG / OOP OOP I DO** - -

— **NODDY HOLDER** (b.NEVILLE, 15 Jun'50, Walsall, England) – vox, guitar repl. HOWELLS / **JIM LEA** (b.14 Jun'52, Wolverhampton) – bass, piano repl. MARSTON + JONES

Columbia not issued

Nov 66. (7") **YOU BETTER RUN. / EVIL WITCHMAN** -

AMBROSE SLADE

(**HOLDER, HILL, LEA + POWELL**)

Fontana not issued

Apr 69. (lp) **BEGINNINGS** -
– Genesis / Everybody's next one / Knocking nails into my house / Roach daddy / Ain't got no heat / Pity the mother / Mad dog Cole / Fly me high / If this world were mine / Martha my dear / Born to be wild / Journey to the centre of my mind. *(cd+c-iss.Jun91)*
May 69. (7") **GENESIS. / ROACH DADDY** -

SLADE

(same line-up & label) (issued in the States on 'Cotillion' and 'Polydor' until 1972)
Oct 69. (7") **WILD WINDS ARE BLOWING. / ONE WAY HOTEL** -
Mar 70. (7") **SHAPE OF THINGS TO COME. / C'MON C'MON** -

Polydor Cotillion

Sep 70. (7") **KNOW WHO YOU ARE. / DAPPLE ROSE** -
Nov 70. (lp) **PLAY IT LOUD** -
– Raven / See us here / Daple rose / Could I / One way hotel / The shape of things to come / Know who you are / I remember / Pouk Hill / Angelina / Dirty joker / Sweet box. *(cd-iss.Jun91)*

May 71. (7"m) **GET DOWN AND GET WITH IT. / DO YOU WANT ME / THE GOSPEL ACCORDING TO RASPUTIN** [16] [ ]
Oct 71. (7") **COZ I LUV YOU. / LIFE IS NATURAL** [1] [–]
Jan 72. (7") **COZ I LOVE YOU. / GOTA KEEP A-ROCKIN' (live)** [–] [ ]
Jan 72. (7") **LOOK WOT YOU DUN. / CANDIDATE** [4] [ ]
Mar 72. (lp)(c) **SLADE ALIVE! (live)** [2] [ ]
– Hear me calling / In like a shot from my gun / Darling be home soon / Know who you are / Gotta keep on rockin' / Get down and get with it / Born to be wild. *(re-iss. Feb 83 + Nov84) (cd-iss.Jun91)*

Polydor Polydor

May 72. (7") **TAKE ME BAK 'OME. / WONDERIN'** [1] [97] Sep 72
Aug 72. (7") **MAMA WEER ALL CRAZEE NOW. / MAN WHO SPEAKS EVIL** [1] [76] Nov 72
Nov 72. (7") **GUDBUY T'JANE. / I WON'T LET IT 'APPEN AGAIN** [2] [68] Mar 73
Dec 72. (lp)(c) **SLAYED?** [1] [69]
– How d'you ride / The whole world's goin' craze / Look at last nite / I won't let it 'appen again / Move over / Gudbuy t'Jane / Gudbuy gudbuy / Mama weer all crazee now / I don't mind / Let the good times roll. *(cd-iss.Nov91)*
Feb 73. (7") **CUM ON FEEL THE NOIZE. / I'M MEE, I'M NOW AN' THAT'S ORL** [1] [98] May 73
Jun 73. (7") **SKWEEZE ME PLEEZE ME. / KILL 'EM AT THE HOT CLUB TONITE** [1] [–]
Jul 73. (7") **LET THE GOOD TIMES ROLL. / FEEL SO FINE – I DON' MINE** [–] [ ]

Polydor Reprise

Sep 73. (7") **SKWEEZE ME PLEEZE ME. / MY TOWN** [–] [ ]
Sep 73. (7") **MY FRIEND STAN. / MY TOWN** [2] [ ]
Sep 73. (lp)(c) **SLADEST** (compilation) [1] [ ]
– Wild things are blowing / Shape of things to come / Know who you are / Pounk Hill / One way hotel / Get down and get with it / Coz I luv you / Look wot you dun / Tak me bak ome / Mama weer all crazee now / Gudbuy t'Jane / Look at last nite / Cum on feel the noize / Skweeze me pleeze me. *(cd-iss.Mar93)*

Polydor Warners

Dec 73. (7") **MERRY XMAS EVERYBODY. / DON'T BLAME ME** [1] [ ]
(re-iss.Dec80, Dec81 (No.32), Dec82 (No.67), Dec83 (No.20), Dec84 (No.47).
Feb 74. (lp)(c) **OLD NEW BORROWED AND BLUE** (US title **'STOMP YOUR HANDS, CLAP YOUR FEET'**) [1] [ ]
– Just want a little bit / When the lights are out / My town / Find yourself a rainbow / Miles out to sea / We're really gonna raise the roof / Do we still do it / How can it be / Don't blame me / My friend Stan / Everyday / Good time gals. *(cd-iss.Nov91)*
Mar 74. (7") **EVERYDAY. / GOOD TIME GALS** [3] [ ]
Jun 74. (7") **THE BANGIN' MAN. / SHE DID IT TO ME** [3] [ ]
Oct 74. (7") **FAR FAR AWAY. / OK YESTERDAY WAS YESTERDAY** [2] [–]
Nov 74. (lp)(c) **SLADE IN FLAME (Film Soundtrack)** [6] [93]
– Standin' on the corner / Them kinda monkeys can't swing / How does it feel / Far far away / O.K. yesterday was yesterday / This girl / Heaven knows / Summer song / So far so good / Lay it down. *(re-iss.Jun82, cd-iss.Nov91)*
Feb 75. (7") **HOW DOES IT FEEL. / SO FAR SO GOOD** [15] [–]
Apr 75. (7") **HOW DOES IT FEEL. / O.K. YESTERDAY WAS YESTERDAY** [–] [ ]
May 75. (7") **THANKS FOR THE MEMORY (WHAM BAM THANK YOU MAM). / RAINING IN MY CHAMPAGNE** [7] [–]
Nov 75. (7") **IN FOR A PENNY. / CAN YOU JUST IMAGINE** [11] [–]
Jan 76. (7") **LET'S CALL IT QUITS. / WHEN THE CHIPS ARE DOWN** [11] [–]
Mar 76. (lp)(c) **NOBODY'S FOOLS** [14] [ ]
– Nobody's fools / Do the dirty / Let's call it quits / Pack up your troubles / In for a penny / Get on up / L.A. jinx / Did your mama ever tell ya / Scratch my back / I'm a talker / All the world is a stage. *(cd-iss.Jul92)*
Apr 76. (7") **NOBODY'S FOOL. / L.A. JINX** [ ] [–]
Apr 76. (7") **NOBODY'S FOOL. / WHEN THE CHIPS ARE DOWN** [–] [ ]

Barn-Polydor not issued

Feb 77. (7") **GYPSY ROADHOG. / FOREST FULL OF NEEDLES** [48] [–]
Mar 77. (lp)(c) **WHATEVER HAPPENED TO SLADE** [ ] [–]
– Be / Lightning never strikes twice / Gypsy roadhog / Dogs of vengeance / When fantasy calls / One eyed Jacks with moustaches / Big apple blues / Dead men tell no tales / She's got the lot / It ain't love but it ain't bad / The soul, the fall and the motion. *(cd-iss.Jul92)*
Apr 77. (7") **BURNING IN THE HEAT OF LOVE. / READY STEADY KIDS** [ ] [–]
Oct 77. (7") **MY BABY LEFT ME – THAT'S ALL RIGHT (Medley). / O.H.M.S.** [32] [–]
Mar 78. (7") **GIVE US A GOAL. / DADDIO** [ ] [–]
Oct 78. (7") **ROCK'N'ROLL BOLERO. / MY BABY'S GOT IT** [ ] [–]
Nov 78. (lp)(c) **SLADE ALIVE VOL.2** [ ] [–]
– Get on up / Take me bak 'ome / Medley: My baby left me – That's all right / Be / Mama weer all crazee now / Burning in the heat of love / Everyday / Gudbuy t'Jane / One-eyed Jacks with moustaches / C'mon feel the noize. *(cd-iss.Mar93)*

Barn not issued

Mar 79. (7"yellow) **GINNY GINNY. / DIZZY MAMA** [ ] [–]
Oct 79. (7") **SIGN OF THE TIMES. / NOT TONIGHT JOSEPHINE** [ ] [–]
Oct 79. (lp)(c) **RETURN TO BASE** [ ] [–]
– Wheels ain't coming down / Hold on to your hats / Chakeeta / Don't waste your time / Sign of the times / I'm a rocker / Nuts, bolts and screws / My baby's got it / I'm mad / Lemme love into ya / Ginny, Ginny.
Dec 79. (7") **OKEY COKEY. / MY BABY'S GOT IT** [ ] [–]
(re-iss.Jan80 on 'R.S.O.')

Cheapskate not issued

Sep 80. (7"ep) **SLADE ALIVE AT READING '80 (live)** [44] [–]
– When I'm dancing I ain't fightin' / Born to be wild / Somethin' else / Pistol packin' mama / Keep a rollin'.
Nov 80. (7") **MERRY XMAS EVERYBODY. / OKEY COKEY / GET DOWN AND GET WITH IT** [70] [–]
Jan 81. (7") **WE'LL BRING THE HOUSE DOWN. / HOLD ON TO YOUR HATS** [10] [–]
Mar 81. (lp)(c) **WE'LL BRING THE HOUSE DOWN** [25] [–]
– Night starvation / Wheels ain't coming down / I'm a rocker / Nuts, bolts and screws / We'll bring the house down / Dizzy mama / Hold on to your hats / Lemme love into ya / My baby's got it / When I'm dancing I ain''t fightin'.
Mar 81. (7") **WHEELS AIN'T COMING DOWN. / NOT TONIGHT JOSEPHINE** [60] [–]
May 81. (7") **KNUCKLE SANDWICH NANCY. / I'M MAD** [ ] [–]

R.C.A. CBS-Assoc.

Sep 81. (7") **LOCK UP YOUR DAUGHTERS. / SIGN OF THE TIMES** [29] [–]
Nov 81. (lp)(c) **TILL DEAF US DO PART** [ ] [–]
– Rock and roll preacher (hallelujah I'm on fire) / Ruby red / Lock up your daughters / Till deaf us do part / That was no lady that was my wife / She brings out the devil in me / A night to remember / M'hat m'coat / It's your body not your mind / Let the rock and roll out of control / Knuckle sandwich Nancy / Till deaf resurrected.
Mar 82. (d7") **RUBY RED. / FUNK PUNK AND JUNK/ / ROCK AND ROLL PREACHER. / TAKE ME BAK 'OME** [51] [–]
Nov 82. (7") **(AND NOW – THE WALTZ) C'EST LA VIE. / MERRY XMAS EVERYBODY (ALIVE & KICKIN')** [50] [–]
Dec 82. (lp)(c) **ON STAGE (live)** [ ] [–]
– Rock and roll preacher / When I'm dancing I ain't fightin' / Take me bak 'ome / Everyday / Lock up your daughters / We'll bring the house down / A night to remember / Mama weer all crazee now / Gudbuy t'Jane / You'll never walk alone. *(cd-iss. Jul93 on 'Castle')*
Nov 83. (7") **MY OH MY. / KEEP YOUR HANDS OFF MY POWER SUPPLY** [2] [–]
Dec 83. (lp)(c) **THE AMAZING KAMIKAZE SYNDROME** [49] [–]
– Slam the hammer down / In the doghouse / Run runaway / High and dry / My oh my / Cocky rock boys / Ready to explode / (And now – The waltz) C'est la vie / Cheap 'n' nasty love / Razzle dazzle man.
Jan 84. (7") **RUN RUNAWAY. / TWO TRACK STEREO ONE TRACK MIND** [7] [–]
Apr 84. (lp)(c) **KEEP YOUR HANDS OFF MY POWER SUPPLY** [–] [33]
Apr 84. (7") **RUN RUNAWAY. / DON'T TAME A HURRICANE** [–] [20]
Jul 84. (7") **OH MY MY. / HIGH AND DRY** [–] [37]
Nov 84. (7")(12") **ALL JOIN HANDS. / HERE'S TO . . .** [15] [ ]
(other 12"+=) – My oh my / Merry xmas everybody (live).
Jan 85. (7") **7 YEAR (B)ITCH. / LEAVE THEM GIRLS ALONE** [60] [–]
Mar 85. (lp)(c) **ROGUES GALERY** [ ] [ ]
– Hey ho wish you well / Little Sheila / Harmony / Myzsterious Mizster Jones / Walking on water, running on alcohol / 7 year (b)itch / I'll be there / I win, you lose / Time to rock / All join hands.
Mar 85. (7")(7"pic-d) **MYZSTERIOUS MIZSTER JONES. / MAMA NATURE IS A ROCKER** [50] [ ]
(12"+=) – My oh my (demo version).
Apr 85. (7") **LITTLE SHEILA. /** [–] [86]
Nov 85. (7") **DO YOU BELIEVE IN MIRACLES. / MY OH MY (version)** [54] [–]
(12"+=) – Time to rock.
(12"++=) – Santa Claus is coming to town / Auld lang syne.
Feb 87. (7")(12") **STILL THE SAME. / GOTTA GO HOME** [73] [–]
(d7"+=) – Roaring silence / Don't talk to me about love.
Apr 87. (7") **THAT'S WHAT FRIENDS ARE FOR. / WILD WILD PARTY** [ ] [–]
(12"+=) – Hi ho silver lining / Lock up your daughters (live).
Apr 87. (lp)(c) **YOU BOYZ MAKE BIG NOIZE** [ ] [–]
– Love is like a rock / That's what friends are for / Still the same / Fools go crazy / She's heavy / We won't give in / Won't you rock with me / Ooh la la in L.A. / Me and the boys / Sing shout (knock yourself out) / The roaring silence / It's hard having fun nowadays / You boyz make big noize / Boyz (instrumental).

Cheapskate-RCA not issued

Jun 87. (7") **YOU BOYZ MAKE BIG NOIZE. / ('A'instrumental)** [ ] [–]
(12"+=) – ('A'-USA mix).
Nov 87. (7") **WE WON'T GIVE IN. / LA LA IN L.A.** [ ] [–]
Nov 88. (7") **LET'S DANCE. / STANDING ON THE CORNER** [ ] [–]
(cd-s+=) – Far far away / How does it feel.
Oct 91. (7") **RADIO WALL OF SOUND. / LAY YOUR LOVE ON THE LINE** [21] [ ]
(12"+=)(cd-s+=) – Cum on feel the noize.
Nov 91. (cd)(c)(lp) **WALL OF HITS** (compilation & new hits) [34] [ ]
– Get down and get with it / Coz I luv you / Look wot you dun / Take me bak 'ome / Gudbuy t'Jane / Cum on feel the noize / Skweeze me pleeze me / My friend Stan / Everyday / Bangin' man / Far far away / Let's call it quits / My oh my / Run run away / Radio wall of sound / Universe / Merry Xmas everybody. (cd/c+=) How does it feel / Thanks for the memory (wham bam thank you mam).
Nov 91. (7")(c-s) **UNIVERSE. / MERRY CHRISTMAS EVERYBODY** [ ] [ ]
(12"+=)(cd-s+=) – Gypsy roadhog.

– other compilations, etc. –

Jun 80. Six Of The Best; (12"ep) **SIX OF THE BEST** [ ] [–]
– Night starvation / When I'm dancing I ain't fightin' / I'm a rocker / Don't waste your time / Wheels ain't coming down / Nine to five.
Nov 80. Polydor; (lp)(c) **SLADE SMASHES** [21] [–]
Apr 81. Polydor; (d-lp)(d-c) **THE STORY OF SLADE** [ ] [–]
(cd-iss.VOL.1 & VOL.2 Nov90 on 'Bear Tracks')
Dec 81. Polydor; (12"ep) **CUM ON FEEL THE NOIZE / COZ I LUV YOU. / TAKE ME BAK 'OME / GUDBUY T'JANE** [ ] [–]
Dec 83. Polydor; (7"m) **CUM ON FEEL THE NOIZE. / TAKE ME BAK 'OME / GUDBUY T'JANE** [ ] [–]
(12"ep+=) – Coz I luv you.
May 84. Polydor; (lp)(c) **SLADE'S GREATS** [ ] [–]
Nov 85. Polydor; (7")(12") **MERRY CHRISTMAS EVERYBODY (remix). / DON'T BLAME ME** [48] [–]
(re-iss.Dec86, hit No.71)
Dec 82. Speed; (7")(7"pic-d) **THE HOKEY COKEY. / GET DOWN AND GET WITH IT** [ ] [–]
Nov 85. Telstar; (lp)(c)(cd) **CRACKERS – THE SLADE CHRISTMAS PARTY ALBUM** [34] [–]

Mar 89. RCA; (3"cd-ep) **MY OH MY / KEEP YOUR HANDS OFF MY POWER SUPPLY / RUNAWAY / ONE TRACK STEREO, ONE TRACK MIND** [ ] [-]

Apr 91. RCA; (cd)(c)(lp) **COLLECTION 81-87** [ ] [-]

1988. Classic Cuts; (cd-ep) **HOW DOES IT FEEL / FAR FAR AWAY / (2 tracks by Wizzard)** [ ] [-]

Dec 90. Receiver; (7") **MERRY CHRISTMAS EVERYBODY. / DON'T BLAME ME** [ ] [-]
(12"+=)/ /(cd-s+=) – ('A'original version)./ / Far far away.

Apr 93. Castle; (cd)(c) **THE SLADE COLLECTION 81-87** [ ] [-]

DUMMIES

(aka **JIMMY & FRANKIE LEA**)

Cheapskate / not issued

Dec 79. (7") **WHEN THE LIGHTS ARE OUT. / SHE'S THE ONLY WOMAN** [ ] [-]
(re-iss.Jan80 on 'Pye')

Aug 80. (7") **DIDN'T YOU USE TO BE YOU. / MILES OUT TO SEA** [ ] [-]

Feb 81. (7") **MAYBE TONITE. / WHEN I'M DANCIN' I AIN'T FIGHTIN'** [ ] [-]

BLESSINGS IN DISGUISE

(**NODDY + DAVE**)

Mooncrest / not issued

Nov 89. (7") **CRYING IN THE RAIN. / WILD NIGHTS** [ ] [-]

SLASH'S SNAKEPIT (see under ⇒ GUNS 'N' ROSES)

SLAUGHTER

Formed: USA ... Sep'88 by MARK SLAUGHTER and DANA STRUM (both ex-VINNIE VINCENT'S INVASION). That year they stuck with past 'Chrysalis' label. Scored massive selling US Top 20 debut album in 1990 with 'STICK IT TO YA'. • **Style:** Heavy-metal, similar to KISS or BON JOVI, featuring the high-pitched vox of MARK. • **Songwriters:** MARK and DANA.

Recommended: STICK IT TO YA (*5).

MARK SLAUGHTER – vocals / **TIM KELLY** – guitar / **DANA STRUM** – bass / **BLAS ELIAS** – drums

Chrysalis / Chrysalis

Apr 90. (cd)(c)(lp) **STICK IT TO YA** [ ] [18] Feb 90
– Eye to eye / Burnin' bridges / Up all night / Spend my life / Thinking of June / She wants more / Fly to the angels / Mad about you / That's not enough / You are the one / Give me your heart / Desperately / Loaded gun. *(cd+=)*– Fly to the angels (acoustic) / Wingin' it.

May 90. (7") **UP ALL NIGHT. / EYE TO EYE** [62] [27] Apr 90
(12"+=)(cd-s+=) – Stick it to ya (medley); Mad about you – Burning bridges – Fly to the angels.

Aug 90. (7")(c-s)(7"pic-d) **FLY TO THE ANGELS. / UP ALL NIGHT (live)** [55] [19]
(12"+=)(12"pic-d+=) – Loaded gun.
(cd-s++=) – ('A'acoustic version). *(re-iss.Jan91, hit UK No.55)*

Nov 90. (m-cd)(m-c)(m-lp) **STICK IT LIVE (live)** [-] [ ]
– Burnin' bridges / Eye to eye / Fly to the angels / Up all night / Loaded gun.

Dec 90. (c-s)(cd-s) **SPEND MY LIFE. / ?** [-] [39]

Mar 92. (cd)(c)(lp) **WILD LIFE** [64] [8]
– Reach for the sky / Out for love / The wild life / Days gone by / Dance for me baby / Times they change / Move to the music / Real love / Shake this place / Streets of broken hearts / Hold on / Do ya know. (cd+=) – Old man / Days gone by (acoustic version).

Aug 92. (c-s)(cd-s) **REAL LOVE. / ?** [-] [69]

S.P.V. / ???

Jun 95. (cd) **FEAR NO EVIL** [ ] [ ]

SLAYER

Formed: Los Angeles, California, USA ... late 1981 by ARAYA, HANNEMAN and former jazz drummer LOMBARDO. Following releases on indie labels, they agreed terms with 'Def American' in 1986. With Rick Rubin (co-owner of rap label 'Def Jam') producing 'REIGN IN BLOOD', they hit UK Top 50 and rose substantially in the States. The controversy over the track 'Angel Of Death', made 'Geffen' (UK distributers) pull out of agreement. 'London' records bailed them out in 1987, with new contract. It payed off, when their 1990 album 'SEASONS IN THE ABYSS' hit UK Top20 / US Top40. • **Style:** Heavy thrash-metal played with spitfire repitition and flavoured with grim occult lyrics. • **Songwriters:** ARAYA words / HANNEMAN music, also covering DISSIDENT AGGRESSOR (Judas Priest) / IN-A-GADDA-DA-VIDA (Iron Butterfly). • **Trivia:** Maiden track recording was on 'Metal Blade''s Various Artists gathering 'METAL MASSACRE II'.

Recommended: SOUTH OF HEAVEN (*7)

TOM ARAYA – vocals, bass / **JEFF HANNEMAN** – lead guitar / **KERRY KING** (b. 3 Jun'64) – lead guitar / **DAVE LOMBARDO** (b.16 Feb'54) – drums

M.F.N. / Metal Blade

Jun 84. (lp) **SHOW NO MERCY** [ ] [ ]
– Evil has no boundaries / The antichrist / Die by the sword / Fight till death / Metalstorm – Face the slayer / Black magic / Tormentor / The final command / Crionics / Show no mercy. *(US re-iss.pic-lp Dec88)*

Roadrunner / Metal Blade

Oct 84. (12"ep) **HAUNTING THE CHAPEL. / CHEMICAL WARFARE / CAPTOR OF SIN** [ ] [ ]
(re-iss.c-ep/cd-ep.Oct89)

Roadrunner / Enigma

1984. (lp) **LIVE UNDEAD (live)** [ ] [ ]
– Black magic / Die by the sword / Captor of sin / The antichrist / Evil has no boundaries / Show no mercy / Aggressive perfector / Chemical warfare. *(re-iss.pic-lp/cd/lp Dec88) (US re-iss.Oct87)*

May 85. (lp) **HELL AWAITS** [ ] [ ]
– Hell awaits / Kill again / At dawn they sleep / Praise of death / Necrophiliac / Crypts of eternity / Hardening of the arteries. *(re-iss.c+d.Feb89)*

London / Def Jam

Apr 87. (lp)(c)(cd)(pic-lp) **REIGN IN BLOOD** [47] [94] Nov 86
– Angel of death / Piece by piece / Necrophobic / Jesus saves / Altar of sacrifice / Criminally insane / Reborn / Epidemic / Post mortem / Raining blood.

May 87. (7") **CRIMINALLY INSANE. / AGGRESSIVE PERFECTER** [64] [ ]
(12"+=) – Post mortem.

Jun 88. (lp)(c)(cd) **SOUTH OF HEAVEN** [25] [57]
– South of Heaven / Silent scream / Live undead / Behind the crooked cross / Mandatory suicide / Ghosts of war / Cleanse the soul / Read between the lies / Dissident aggressor / Spill the blood.

Sep 88. (12")(7") **SOUTH OF HEAVEN. / ?** [ ] [ ]

Def Amer.. / Def Amer..

Oct 90. (cd)(c)(lp) **SEASONS IN THE ABYSS** [18] [40]
– War ensemble / Blood red / Spirit in black / Expendable youth / Dead skin mask / Hallowed point / Skeletons of society / Temptation / Born of fire / Seasons in the abyss.

Def Amer. / Def Amer.

Oct 91. (cd)(c)(d-lp) **DECADE OF AGGRESSION (live)** [29] [ ]
– Hell awaits / The anti-Christ / War ensemble / South of Heaven / Raining blood / Altar of sacrifice / Jesus saves / Dead skin mask / Seasons in the abyss / Mandatory suicide / Angel of death / Hallowed paint / Blood red / Die by the sword / Black magic / Captor of sin / Born of fire / Post mortem / Spirit in black / Expendable youth / Chemical warfare.

Oct 91. (7")(7"pic-d) **SEASONS IN THE ABYSS (live). / AGGRESSIVE PERFECTOR (live)** [51] [ ]
(12"+=) – Chemical warfare.
(cd-s+=)(12"pic-d+=) – ('A'-experimental).

—— (May92) **PAUL BOSTOPH** – drums repl.LOMBARDO

Oct 94. (cd)(c)(lp) **DIVINE INTERVENTION** [15] [8]
– Killing fields / Sex, murder, art / Fictional reality / Ditto head / Divine intervention / Circle of beliefs / SS III / Serenity in murder / Two-thirteen / Mind control.

Sep 95. (7"ep) **SERENITY IN MURDER / RAINING BLOOD. / DITTOHEAD / SOUTH OF HEAVEN** [ ] [ ]
(cd-s) – ('A'side) / At dawn they sleep / Dead skin mask / Divine intervention.
(cd-s) – ('A'side) / Angel of death / Mandatory suicide / War ensemble.

Percy SLEDGE

Born: 1941, Leighton, Alabama, USA. Went solo in 1966, after a spell in the ESQUIRES COMBO. His debut 45 'WHEN A MAN LOVES A WOMAN', hit the top spot in the US, and became a classic standard for most up and coming singers. Never quite capitalised on this arrangement, but succeeded to have more hits in the US. • **Style:** Soul ballad vocalist. • **Songwriters:** Writes own songs, except LOVE ME TENDER (Elvis Presley) / etc. • **Trivia:** A little mysterious, sorry!. Recently MICHAEL BOLTON has re-recorded his debut to return it again into the charts.

Recommended: THE ULTIMATE COLLECTION (*6)

PERCY SLEDGE – vocals with session people.

Atlantic / Atlantic

May 66. (7") **WHEN A MAN LOVES A WOMAN. / LOVE ME LIKE YOU MEAN IT** [4] [1] Apr 66
(re-iss.1974) (12"iss.Apr80)

Jul 66. (7") **WARM AND TENDER LOVE. / SUGAR PUDDIN'** [34] [17]

Jul 66. (lp) **WHEN A MAN LOVES A WOMAN** [ ] [37] May 66
– When a man loves a woman / You're pouring water on a drowning man / Love makes the world go round / Love me like you meant it / My adorable one / Put a little lovin' on me / Love me all the way / When she touches me / Thief in the night / You fooled me / Success.
(re-iss. 1970)

Nov 66. (7") **HEART OF A CHILD. / MY ADORABLE ONE** [ ] [ ] Sep 66

Nov 66. (7") **IT TEARS ME UP. /HEART OF A CHILD** [ ] [20]

Jan 67. (7") **IT TEARS ME UP. / OH HOW HAPPY** [ ] [20] Oct 66

Feb 67. (lp) **WARM AND TENDER SOUL** [ ] [ ] Nov 66
– Make it good and make it last / When a man loves a woman / Walkin' in the Sun / Warm and tender love / The God love / Out of left field / Behind closed doors / Just out of reach / I believe in you / I believe in you / Take time to know her. *(re-iss.+c.Aug86 on 'Blue Moon')*

Feb 67. (7") **BABY HELP ME. / YOU'VE LOST THAT SOMETHING WONDERFUL** [-] [87]

Apr 67. (7") **OUT OF LEFT FIELD. / IT CAN'T BE STOPPED** [ ] [59]

Jun 67. (7") **LOVE ME TENDER. / WHAT AM I LIVING FOR** [-] [40] [91]

Aug 67. (7") **JUST OUT OF REACH (OF MY TWO EMPTY ARMS). / HARD TO BELIEVE** [-] [66]

Oct 67. (7") **PLEDGING MY LOVE. / YOU DON'T MISS YOUR WATER** [ ] [ ]

Nov 67. (lp) **THE PERCY SLEDGE WAY** [ ] [ ] Aug 67

– Dark end of the street / You send me / I had a talk with my woman / What am I living for / I've been loving you too long / Drown in my own tears / My special prayer / Just out of reach / Pledging my love / You don't miss your water . . .

Nov 67. (7") **COVER ME. / BEHIND EVERY GREAT MAN THERE IS A WOMAN** [-] [42]

Apr 68. (7") **TAKE TIME TO KNOW HER. / IT'S ALL WRONG BUT IT'S ALRIGHT** [ ] [11] Mar 68

May 68. (lp) **TAKE TIME TO KNOW HER** [-] [ ]
– Take time to know her / Feed the flame / Out of left field / Cover me / Come softly to me / Sudden stop / Spooky / Baby help me / It's all wrong but it's alright / High cost of leaving / Between these arms / I love everything about you.

Jul 68. (7") **SUDDEN STOP. / BETWEEN THESE ARMS** [-] [63]

Sep 68. (7") **YOU'RE ALL AROUND ME. / SELF PRESERVATION** [-] [ ]

Nov 68. (7") **COME SOFTLY TO ME. / YOU'RE ALL AROUND ME** [ ] [ ]

Jan 69. (7") **MY SPECIAL PRAYER. / BLESS YOUR SWEET LITTLE SOUL** [-] [93]

May 69. (7") **ANY DAY NOW. / THE ANGELS LISTENED IN** [ ] [86] Apr 69

Aug 69. (7") **KIND WOMAN. / WOMAN OF THE NIGHT** [ ] [ ]

Nov 69. (7") **TRUE LOVE TRAVELS ON A GRAVEL ROAD. / FAITHFUL AND TRUE** [ ] [ ]

Nov 69. (lp) **THE BEST OF PERCY SLEDGE** (compilation) [ ] [ ] Feb 69
– When a man loves a woman / Out of left field / Take time to know her / Warm and tender / Just out of reach (of my two empty arms) / Dark end of the street / Cover me / Sudden stop / Baby help me / It tears me up / My special prayer / You're all around me. *(re-iss.1972 & 1980)*

Feb 70. (7") **TOO MANY RIVERS TO CROSS. / PUSHING MY PRIDE AGAIN** [-] [ ]

1970. (7") **HELP ME MAKE IT THROUGH THE NIGHT. / THIEF IN THE NIGHT** [-] [ ]

1970. (7") **THAT'S THE WAY I WANT TO LIVE MY LIFE. / STOP THE WORLD TONIGHT** [-] [ ]

1970. (lp) **IN SOUTH AFRICA (live)** [-] [ ] S.Africa
– My special prayer / Cover me / Heart of a child / Take time to know her / Warm and tender love / I gotta get a message to you / Silent night / Come softly to me / What am I living for / When a man loves a woman.

Mar 72. (7") **RAINBOW ROAD. / STANDING ON THE MOUNTAIN** [ ] [ ]

Jun 72. (7"m) **BABY HELP ME. / WARM AND TENDER LOVE / TAKE TIME TO KNOW HER** [ ] [-]

Aug 73. (7") **SUNSHINE. / UNCHANGING LOVE** [ ] [ ]

Capricorn Capricorn

Oct 74. (7") **I'LL BE YOUR EVERYTHING. / BLUE WATER** [-] [62]

Nov 74. (7") **I'LL BE YOUR EVERYTHING. / WALKIN' IN THE SUN** [ ] [-]

Nov 74. (lp)(c) **I'LL BE YOUR EVERYTHING** [-] [ ]
– Walkin' in the sun / Behind closed doors / Make it good and make it last / The good love I believe in you / I'll be your everything / If this is the last time / Hard to be friends / Blue water / Love among people.

Feb 75. (7") **BEHIND CLOSED DOORS. / IF THIS IS THE LAST TIME** [-] [ ]

1975. (7") **WHEN A BOY BECOMES A MAN. / WHEN SHE TOUCHES ME** [-] [ ]

— Retired from music business after being dogged by ill health.

not issued Monument

1983. (7") **SHE'S TOO PRETTY TO CRY. / ?** [-] [ ]

1983. (lp) **PERCY** [-] [ ]
– Bring your lovin' to me / You had to be there / All night rain / She's too pretty to cry / I still miss someone / The faithful kind / Home type thing / Personality / I'd put angels around you / Hard lovin' woman.

Pointblank not issued

Nov 94. (cd)(c) **BLUE NIGHT** [ ] [ ]
– You got away with love / Love come knockin' / Why did you stop / I wish it would rain / Blue night / These ain't teardrops / Your love will save the world / First you cry / Going home tomorrow / The grand blvd. / I've got dreams to remember.

– compilations, others, etc. –

Note; Below releases on 'Atlantic' unless otherwise mentioned.

Apr 80. (7"ep) **WHEN A MAN LOVES A WOMAN** [ ] [-]
– When a man loves a woman / You're pouring water on a drowning man / Love makes the world go round / Love me like you mean it / My adorable one / Put a little lovin' on me / Love me all this way / When she touches me / Thief in the night / You fooled me / Success.

Jan 87. (7") **WHEN A MAN LOVES A WOMAN. / WARM AND TENDER LOVE** [2] [ ]
(12"+=)(cd-s+=) – ?

Feb 87. (lp)(c)(cd) **WHEN A MAN LOVES A WOMAN (THE ULTIMATE COLLECTION)** [36] [ ]
– When a man loves a woman / It tears me up / Take time to know her / My special prayer / Baby help me / It's all wrong but it's right / You're all around me / Dark end of the street / Warm and tender love / Love me tender / Out of left field / Come softly to me / What am I living for? / You're pouring water on a drowning man / Just out of reach / Cover me / Sudden stop / You really got a hold on me / That's how strong my love is / Put a little lovin' in me.

May 87. (7")(12") **COVER ME. / IT TEARS ME APART** [ ] [ ]

Jun 81. Hallmark; (lp)(c) **WHEN A MAN LOVES A WOMAN** [ ] [-]
(re-iss.Oct89 on 'Pickwick')

Mar 84. Charly; (lp)(c) **ANY DAY NOW** [ ] [-]

Aug 87. Charly; (lp) **IF LOVING YOU IS WRONG** [ ] [-]
(cd-iss.Feb93)

Aug 84. Goldmasters; (c) **GREATEST HITS** [ ] [-]

Jan 85. Old Gold; (7") **WHEN A MAN LOVES A WOMAN. / WARM AND TENDER LOVE** [ ] [-]
(re-iss.Mar90)

Jul 86. Timeless; (cd) **HIS TOP HITS** [ ] [-]

Feb 88. Sonet; (7") **JUST CAN'T STOP. / ?** [ ] [-]

May 88. Streetlife; (lp)(c) **GREATEST HITS** [ ] [-]

Dec 88. Spectrum; (cd) **GREATEST HITS** [ ] [-]
(re-iss.cd+c May93 on 'Prestige')

Dec 88. Magnum Force; (cd) **WHEN A MAN LOVES A WOMAN** [ ] [-]

Jul 89. Demon; (lp)(cd) **WANTED AGAIN** [ ] [-]

May 92. Rhino; (cd) **IT TEARS ME UP: THE BEST OF PERCY SLEDGE** [ ] [ ]

Jul 94. Success; (cd)(c) **WHEN A MAN LOVES A WOMAN** [ ] [-]

Aug 94. Legends In Music; (cd) **PERCY SLEDGE** [ ] [-]

Apr 95. Muskateer; (cd)(c) **20 GREATEST HITS** [ ] [-]

Jun 95. Collection; (cd) **THE COLLECTION** [ ] [-]

Jul 95. Summit; (cd) **A LITTLE TENDERNESS** [ ] [-]

— Also shared an album SOUL SENSATION in Dec 87 with ARETHA FRANKLIN.

SLEEPER

Formed: Ilford, Essex, England ... 1993 by LOUISE and her boyfriend JOHN STEWART, who soon found ANDY McCLURE and DIID. Were indie successes of 1994 and were about to breakthrough into the pop charts early '95. • **Style:** On the same Wave as ELASTICA but with fuzzy WIRE guitars. • **Songwriters:** Most by WENER or some w/ STEWART. • **Trivia:** LOUISE had earlier attended Manchester Uni to study English and politics.

Recommended: SMART (*9)

LOUISE WENER – vocals, guitar / **JOHN STEWART** – lead guitar / **DIID OSMAN** – bass / **ANDY MacCLURE** – drums, percussion

Indolent not issued

Nov 93. (7"ep)(12"ep)(cd-ep) **ALICE IN VAIN. / HA HA YOU'RE DEAD / BIG NURSE** [ ] [-]

Feb 94. (7"ep)(cd-ep) **SWALLOW. / TWISTED / ONE GIRL DREAMING** [ ] [-]

May 94. (7"ep)(cd-ep) **DELICIOUS. / LADY LOVE YOUR COUNTRYSIDE / BEDSIDE MANNERS** [75] [-]
(12"ep+=) – Tatty.

Oct 94. (7"mail-order) **BUCKET AND SPADE (live)** [-] [-]
– Bedhead / Alice in vain / Swallow.

Jan 95. (7")(c-s) **INBETWEENER. / LITTLE ANNIE** [16] [ ]
(cd-s+=) – Disco Duncan.
(12"++=) – Bank.

Feb 95. (cd)(c)(lp) **SMART** [5] [ ]
– Inbetweener / Swallow / Delicious / Hunch / Amuse / Bedhead / Lady love your countryside / Vegas / Poor flying man / Alice in vain / Twisted / Pyrotechnician.

Mar 95. (7"blue)(c-s) **VEGAS. / HYMN TO HER** [33] [ ]
(12"pic-d)(cd-s+=) – It's wrong to breed / Close.

Sep 95. (7")(c-s) **WHAT DO I KNOW?. / PAINT ME / ROOM AT THE TOP** [14] [ ]
(cd-s) – ('A'side) / Vegas (live) / Amuse (live) / Disco Duncan (live).

Grace SLICK (see under ⇒ JEFFERSON AIRPLANE)

SLIM HARPO

Born: JAMES MOORE, 11 January 1924, Baton Rouge, Louisiana. From the early 50's, he was known as HARMONICA SLIM, as he worked in juke joints, etc. His first recording was in 1953, when Nashville blues label 'Excello' (subsidiary of 'Nashboro'), cut ARTHUR GUNTER's 'BABY LET'S PLAY HOUSE'. Another now semi-famous recording was 'LIL' DARLIN'', which stemmed from GLADIOLAS. He worked from mid-50's to late 50's, with brother-in-law singer /guitarist LIGHTNIN' SLIM (born OTIS HICKS, 13 March 1913, St.Louis; died 27 July 1974, Detroit), who had a R&B hit 'ROOSTER BLUES'. HARPO had two years previously, cracked that market with excellent 'I'M A KING BEE'. In the 60's, he went onto score with 'RAININ' IN MY HEART' & 'BABY SCRATCH MY BACK'. He died at his birthplace 31 Jan'70. **Blues style:** Swamp blues giant, who was self-taught in guitar and harmonica. • **Songwriters:** Wrote most himself, until he co-penned in the late 50's & 60's with wife LOVELL. Covered; FOLSOM PRISON BLUES (Johnny Cash), and others already mentioned. • **Miscellaneous:** LONESOME SUNDOWN (aka CORNELIUS GREEN, was another to highlight HARPO's songs during the 50's & 60's. • **Legacy:** I'M A KING BEE (for DAVID BOWIE ? early) / I GOT LOVE IF YOU WANT IT + SHAKE YOUR HIPS (Rolling Stones).

Recommended: THE BEST OF SLIM HARPO (* 7)

SLIM HARPO – vocals, harmonica

not issued Excello

1957. (7") **I'M A KING BEE. / I'VE GOT LOVE IF YOU WANT IT** [-] [ ]
(UK-iss.Nov66 on 'Stateside')

1959. (7") **WONDERIN' AND WORRYIN'. / STRANGE LOVE** [-] [ ]

1959. (7") **YOU'LL BE SORRY ONE DAY. / ONE MORE DAY** [-] [ ]

1960. (7") **BUZZ ME BABE. / LATE LAST NIGHT** [-] [ ]

1960. (7") **BLUES HANGOVER. / WHAT A DREAM** [-] [ ]

Pye Int. Excello

Aug 61. (7") **RAININ' IN MY HEART. / DON'T START CRYIN' NOW** [ ] [ ]
(re-iss.Sep63)

1962. (lp) **SINGS RAININ' IN MY HEART** [-] [ ]
– Rainin' in my heart / Blues hangover / I got love if you want it / Bobby sox baby / I'm a King Bee / Snoopin' around / Buzz me baby / What a dream / Don't start cryin' now / My home is a prison / Moody baby / Dream girl. *(re-iss.Dec87) (UK cd-iss.Mar94 on 'El Dianblo')*

1963. (7") **I LOVE THE LIFE I'M LIVING. / BUZZIN'** [-] [ ]

1964. (7") **I NEED MONEY. / LITTLE QUEEN BEE** [-] [ ]

1964. (7") **WE'RE TWO OF A KIND. / STILL RAININ' IN MY HEART** [-] [ ]

1965. (7") **STILL HERE WONDERIN'. / WHAT'S GOING ON BABY** [-] [ ]

1965. (7") **HARPO'S BLUES. / PLEASE DON'T TURN ME DOWN** [-] [ ]

Stateside Excello

Feb 66. (7") **BABY SCRATCH MY BACK. / I'M GONNA MISS YOU (LIKE THE DEVIL)** [ ] [ ]
Apr 66. (7") **GOIN' AWAY BLUES. / JUST A LONELY STRANGER** [-] [ ]
Jul 66. (7") **SHAKE YOUR HIPS. / MIDNIGHT BLUES** [ ] [ ]
Sep 66. (lp) **SLIM HARPO** [-] [ ]
– Baby scratch my back / Wonderin' blues / I love the life I'm living / Rainin' in my heart / Little queen bee / We're two of a kind / Harpo's blues / I'm gonna miss you (like the Devil) / Shake your hips / Midnight blues.
Jan 67. (7") **I'M YOUR BREADMAKER BABY. / LOVING YOU (THE WAY I DO)** [ ] [ ]
Mar 67. (7") **TIP ON IN. / (part 2)** [-] [ ]
Oct 67. (7") **I'VE GOT TO BE WITH YOU TONIGHT. / I'M GONNA KEEP WHAT I'VE GOT** [-] [ ]
Jul 68. (7") **MAILBOX BLUES. / TE-NI-LEE-NI-NU** [-] [ ]
Jan 69. (7") **MOHAIR SAM> / I JUST CAN'T LEAVE YOU** [-] [ ]

President Excello

1968. (lp) **TIP ON IN WITH SLIM HARPO** [ ] [ ]
– Tip on in / Te-ni-nee-ni-nu / Mailbox blues / I've been a good thing for you / Hey little Lee / I'm gonna keep what I got / I've got to be with you tonight / I'm so sorry / My baby / She's got it / It just can't leave you. *(re-iss.Dec87 on 'Excello' US)*

— next 1969 recording w / **GUITAR GABLE + JAMES JOHNSON + RUDOLF RICHARD** – guitar / **GEESE AUGUST + FATS PERRODIN** – bass / **JERRY WEST + SAMMY K.BROWN** – drums

— HARPO was to die 31 Jan'70.

Blue Horizon Excello

Jun 70. (7") **JUST FOR YOU. / THAT'S WHY I LOVE YOU** [-] [ ]
Jul 70. (7") **FOLSOM PRISON BLUES. / MUTUAL FRIEND** [ ] [ ]
Sep 70. (7") **I'VE GOT MY FINGER ON THE TRIGGER. / THE PRICE IS TOO HIGH** [-] [ ]
Dec 70. (7") **RAININ' IN MY HEART. / JODY MAN** [-] [ ]
1971. (lp) **TRIGGER FINGER** [ ] [ ]
– Wonderin' and worryin' / Strange love / You'll be sorry one day / One more day / Late last night / Buzzin' / Sittin' here wondering / What's goin' on baby / Please don't turn me down / Tip on in (part 2) / I just can't leave you / That's why I love you / Just for you / I've got my finger on your trigger / The price is too high / Rainin' in my heart.

- compilations, etc. -

1983. Excello; (lp) **THE ORIGINAL KING BEE – THE BEST OF** [-] [ ]
– Baby scratch my back / Got love if you want it / I'm a King Bee / Shake your hips / Te-ni-nee-ni-nu / I've been a good thing (for you) / Rainin' in my heart / The music's hot / Mohair Sam / Tip on in / Moody blues / The hippy song / Don't start crying now / Rock me, baby.
Oct 86. Flyright; (lp) **SHAKE YOUR HIPS** [ ] [-]
– Wonderin' blues / Baby scratch my back / I'm gonna miss you / Rainin' in my heart / We're two of a kind / I need money / Shake your hips / Midnight blues / Harpo's blues / Buzzin' / My little Queen Bee / I love the life I'm livin'.
Dec 88. Flyright; (lp) **GOT LOVE IF YOU WANT IT** [ ] [ ]
May 89. Flyright; (cd) **I'M A KING BEE** [ ] [ ]
(re-iss.Oct93 on 'Ace')
1989. Flyright; (lp) **BLUES HANGOVER (The JAY MILLER SESSIONS)** [ ] [-]
Jul 88. Sonet; (lp) **HE KNEW THE BLUES** [ ] [-]
Jul 92. Ace; (cd) **THE BEST OF SLIM HARPO** [ ] [-]
Mar 95. Ace; (cd) **SHAKE YOUR HIPS** [ ] [-]

SLITS

Formed: London, England . . . early 1977 as foremost all-girl punk rock outfit (until BUDGIE joined that is). Supported The CLASH on Spring 1977 tour, but amazingly never secured a record deal until 1979 when 'Island' knocked on door. The 'Real' label (home of HEARTBREAKERS and PRETENDERS) were turned down the preceeding year. The two and a half year wait was over, when their vinyl debut (oddly not a 45! but the album CUT), controversially revealing on its sleeve the trio naked but coated with mud. This DENNIS BOVELL produced seminal classic album, scraped into the 30 and was astonishingly their commercial peak. The untitled follow-up jam/bootleg disaster saw to that. Anti-conventional attitudes were once more thrown away, when 'CBS' re-kindled aspirations for brief 'RETURN OF THE GIANT SLITS' lp. • **Style:** Anti-pro feminists who fused punk ideals/sounds with unorthodox tribal rhythm. • **Songwriters:** Group compositions, except I HEARD IT THROUGH THE GRAPEVINE (Marvin Gaye) / MAN NEXT DOOR (John Holt). • **Trivia:** Early 1978, they were sighted in the punk film 'JUBILEE'.

Recommended: CUT (*9) / RETURN OF THE GIANT (*7)

ARI UP (b.ARIANNA FOSTER) – vocals / **VIVIEN ALBERTINE** – guitar (ex-FLOWERS OF ROMANCE) repl. KATE KORUS to KLEENEX (Feb77) / **TESSA POLLITT** – bass repl. SUZI GUTSY who formed The FLICKS. / **PALM OLIVE** – drums (ex-FLOWERS OF ROMANCE) was repl. (Oct78) by **BUDGIE** (b.PETER CLARK) – percussion, drums (ex-BIG IN JAPAN, ex-SECRETS,etc)

Island Antilles

Sep 79. (lp)(c) **CUT** [30] [ ]
– Instant hit / So tough / Spend spend spend / Shoplifting / FM / Newtown / Ping pong affair / Love and romance / Typical girls / Adventures close to home. *(cd-iss.Apr90)*
Sep 79. (7") **TYPICAL GIRLS. / I HEARD IT THROUGH THE GRAPEVINE** [60] [ ]
(12"+=) – Typical girls – brink style / Liebe and romance.

— **BRUCE SMITH** – drums (of POP GROUP) repl. BUDGIE to SIOUXSIE & BANSHEES jazz-trumpeter **DON CHERRY** guested

Y-Rough not issued

Mar 80. (7") **IN THE BEGINNING THERE WAS RHYTHM. / ('B'by Pop Group)** [ ] [-]
May 80. (lp) **UNTITLED (Y3)** (bootleg demo jam) [ ] [-]
– A boring life / Slime / Or what it is / No.1 enemy / Once upon a time in a living room / Bongos on the lawn / Face place / Let's do the split / Mosquitos / Vaseline / No more rock and roll for you.
Jun 80. (7") **MAN NEXT DOOR. / MAN NEXT DOOR (dub)** [ ] [-]

— added guest **STEVE BERESFORD** – keyboards, guitar (of FLYING LIZARDS)

Human not issued

Jun 81. (7")(12") **ANIMAL SPACE. / ANIMAL SPACIER** [ ] [-]

C.B.S. Epic

Oct 81. (7") **EARTHBEAT. / BEGIN AGAIN RHYTHM** [ ] [-]
(12"+=) – Earthdub.
Oct 81. (12"m) **ANIMAL SPACE. / ANIMAL SPACE (dub) / IN THE BEGINNING** [-] [ ]
Oct 81. (lp)(c) **RETURN OF THE GIANT SLITS** [ ] [ ]
– Earthbeat / Or what it is? / Face place / Walkabout / Difficult fun / Animal space – Spacier / Improperly dressed / Life on Earth. *(free-7"w.a.)* – (INTERVIEW). / FACE DUB
Dec 81. (7") **EARTHBEAT. / OR WHAT IT IS?** [-] [ ]

— Parted ways early 1982. BRUCE joined RIP, RIG & PANIC. All except TESSA were part of colossus band NEW AGE STEPPERS.

- compilations, others, etc. -

Feb 87. Strange Fruit; (12"ep) **THE PEEL SESSIONS** (19.9.77) [ ] [-]
– Love and romance / Vindictive / Newtown / Shoplifting.
Dec 88. Strange Fruit; (m-lp)(c)(cd) **DOUBLE PEEL SESSIONS** [ ] [-]

SLOWDIVE

Formed: Thames Valley, Reading, England . . . 1989 by RACHEL GOSWELL, etc (see below). They broke through in 1991, when EP 'HOLDING OUR BREATH' nearly hit UK Top 50. • **Style:** Dreamy guitar-based shoegazing outfit, complete with splendid atmospheric harmonies. • **Songwriters:** HALSTEAD penned, except GOLDEN HAIR (Syd Barrett).

Recommended: JUST FOR A DAY (*7)

RACHEL GOSWELL (b.16 May'71, Hampshire, England) – vocals, guitar / **NEIL HALSTEAD** (b. 7 Oct'70, Luton, England) – vocals, guitar / **BROOK CHRISTIAN SAVILL** (b. 6 Dec'70, Bury, England) – guitar / **NICK CHAPLIN** (b.23 Dec'70, Slough, England) – bass / **SIMON SCOTT** (b. 3 Mar'71, Cambridge, England) – drums (ex-CHARLOTTES) repl. NEIL CARTER (ex-COLOUR MARY), who had repl. original ADRIAN SELL

Creation Creation

Nov 90. (12"ep)(cd-ep) **SLOWDIVE:- AVALYN I. / SLOWDIVE:- AVALYN II** [ ] [-]
Feb 91. (12"ep)(cd-ep) **MORNINGRISE. / SHE CALLS / LOSING TODAY** [ ] [-]
Jun 91. (7") **CATCH THE BREEZE. / SHINE** [52] [ ]
(12"ep+=)(cd-ep+=) **HOLDING OUR BREATH – Albatross / Golden hair.**
Aug 91. (cd)(c)(lp) **JUST FOR A DAY** [32] [ ]
– Spanish air / Cedlia's dream / Catch the breeze / Ballad of Sister Sue / Erik's song / Waves / Brighter / The sadman / Primal.
1992. (cd)(lp) **BLUE DAY** [ ] [ ]
– Slowdive:- Avalyn I / Morningrise / She calls / Losing today / Shine / Albatross.

— now without CHAPLIN

May 93. (12"ep)(cd-ep) **OUTSIDE YOUR ROOM** [69] [ ]
– Alison / So tired / Souvlaki space station / Moussaka chaos.
Jun 93. (cd)(c)(lp) **SOUVLAKI** [51] [ ]
– Alison / Machine gun / 40 days / Sing / Here she comes / Souvlaki space station / When the Sun hits / Altogether / Melon yellow / Dagger.
Nov 93. (12"ep)(cd-ep) **5 EP** [ ] [ ]
– Bandulu (in mind mix) / (open mind mix) / (in mind mix) / Reload (remix – the 147 take).
Feb 95. (cd)(c)(lp) **PYGMALION** [ ] [ ]
– Rutty / Crazy for you / Miranda / Trellisaze / Cello / Jay's heaven / Visions of L.A. / Blue skied and clear / All of us.

MOJAVE 3

— **RACHEL + NEIL** plus drummer **IAN McCUTCHESON + POPPY + SIMON**

4 a.d. 4 a.d.

Oct 95. (cd)(c) **ASK ME TOMORROW** [ ] [ ]
– Love songs on the radio / Sarah / Tomorrow's taken / Candle song 3 / You're beautiful / Where is the love / After all / Pictures / Mercy.

SLY & ROBBIE

Formed: Kingston, Jamaica . . . 1978 when collaborating on DUNBAR's solo lp 'SIMPLY SLY MAN'. Their partnership, finally bore fruit in 1985 when 'Island' give the ex-BLACK UHURU members acclaimed album 'LANGUAGE BARRIER'. The 1987 follow-up 'RHYTHM KILLERS' on '4th & Bro.', secured them a deserved place in the UK Top 40. • **Style:** Reggae fundamentalists, who progressed into funk and soul during the mid to late 80's. • **Songwriters:** Most written by DUNBAR or duo, except TICKET TO

RIDE (Beatles) / INNER CITY BLUES (Marvin Gaye / YES WE CAN CAN (Allen Toussaint). • **Trivia:** Both were seasoned session men for black acts; PETER TOSH, BUNNY WAILER, BURNING SPEAR, etc. They continued to produce many other acts; IAN DURY and YOKO ONO.

Recommended: RHYTHM KILLERS (*6).

SLY DUNBAR

(solo) (b.NOEL CHARLES DUNBAR, 10 May'52) – drums / with **ROBBIE SHAKESPEARE** (b.27 Sep'53) – bass (ex-BIG YOUTH)

Virgin / not issued

Apr 78. (7") **COCAINE, COCAINE. / A WHO SAY** [ ] [-]

Frontline / not issued

Jun 78. (lp) **SIMPLE SLY MAN** [ ] [-]
– Cocaine, cocaine / Top rank / Mr.Bassie / Dope addict (Sun is shining) / A who say / Nigger whitie / Dance and shake your tambourine.

Apr 79. (7") **RASTA FIESTA. / DIRTY HARRY** [ ] [-]

May 79. (lp) **SLY, WICKED AND SLICK** [ ] [-]
– Rasta fiesta / Sesame street / Lover's top / Senegal market / Mr.Music / Queen of the minstrels / Dirty Harry / Oriental taxis. *(re-iss.Jun88, cd-iss.Jul91 with extra tracks) (cd-iss.Mar94)*

— Both SLY & ROBBIE went into writing and producing partnership, and back acts including GREGORY ISAACS, GRACE JONES and BLACK UHURU. A compilation of this work by other artists, but credited to

SLY & ROBBIE

was issued on Island.

Jun 81. (lp) **THE 60's, 70's & 80's = SLY & ROBBIE** [ ] [-]

— both were on The COMPASS POINT ALL-STARS

Island / not iss.

Mar 81. (12") **PEANUT BUTTER. / ('B'by Junior Tucker)** [ ] [-]

BITS AND PIECES

Island / not issued

Dec 81. (7") **DON'T STOP THE MUSIC. / (part 2)** [ ] [-]

SLY DUNBAR

solo once more with more session people.

(same label)

May 82. (12") **HOT YOU'RE HOT. / ('A'diff.mix)** [ ] [-]

Aug 82. (lp)(c) **SLY-GO-VILLE** [ ] [-]
– Slippin' into darkness / Gonna love you / Inner city blues / The battle of Jerico / If you want it / River Niger / Hot you're hot / Unmetred taxi.

SLY & ROBBIE

duo, originally imports some collaborations with TAXI GANG

Taxi / not issued

Oct 83. (12") **AYATOLLAH. / ('A'version)** [ ] [-]

Oct 83. (12") **INSIDE OUTSIDE. / ('A'version)** [ ] [-]

Oct 83. (12") **RIVER NIGER. / ('A'version)** [ ] [-]

Dec 83. (12") **('A'by Jimmy Riley). / SEARCH AND DESTROY** [ ] [-]

Dec 83. (12") **('A'by Struggle). / TAXI CONNECTION** [ ] [-]

Dec 83. (12") **('A'by Carlton Livingstone). / AYATOLLAH** [ ] [-]

Dec 83. (12") **('A'by Ken Boothe). / RAIN FROM THE SKIES / YOU HAVE CAUGHT ME** [ ] [-]

Dec 83. (12") **('A'by Sugar Minott). / CONQUER ME / SWING EAST** [ ] [-]

Dec 83. (12"ep) **TRIPLET / INTERPOLAXING: DON'T GO / WATERBED** [ ] [-]

Apr 84. (12") **('A' by STRUGGLE WITH ROBBIE SHAKESPEARE). / ('B'by DEAN FRAZIER) / BILLIE JEAN** [ ] [-]

Apr 84. (12") **(track by SUGAR MINOTT) / RUB A DUB / RED HOT (version)** [ ] [-]

C.S.A. / not issued

Feb 84. (d-lp) **A DUB EXTRAVAGANZA** [ ] [-]
– (BLACK UHURU IN DUB / JOHNNY OSBOURNE IN DUB) *(c-iss.Dec86)*

SLY & ROBBIE + The TAXI GANG

S & R / not issued

Mar 85. (12") **LAND OF RIDIM** [ ] [-]

SLY & ROBBIE

had previously joined BLACK UHURU in 1983 before again forming duo with session people.

Island / Island

Jul 85. (7")(12") **GOT TO GET THIS TO THAT. / ('A'dub version)** [ ] [ ]

Jul 85. (lp)(c) **LANGUAGE BARRIER** [ ] [ ]
– Make 'em move / No name on the bullet / Miles (black satin) / Bass & trouble / Language barrier / Get to this, get to that. *(cd-iss.Dec85, re-iss.Apr87)*

Oct 85. (7") **MAKE 'EM MOVE. / MOVE A LITTLE MORE** [ ] [ ]
(12") – ('A'side) / ('A'riot zone parts 1 & 2) / Bass & trouble.

Mar 86. (12") **('A'by Ruddy Thomas). / TWILIGHT ZONE / PETER GUNN** [ ] [ ]

— In 1987 duo featured **HERBIE HANCOCK** – synthesizers / **BOOTSY COLLINS** – vox / **BERNIE WORRELL** – keyboards / etc.

4th & Bro. / Isalnd

Mar 87. (7") **BOOPS (HERE TO GO). / DON'T STOP THE MUSIC** [12] [-]
(12"+=)/ /(cd-s+=) – ('A'instrumental)./ / Ticket to ride.

Apr 87. (7") **BOOPS (HERE I GO). / LANGUAGE BARRIER** [-] [ ]

Apr 87. (lp)(c)(cd) **RHYTHM KILLERS** [35] [ ]
– Fire / Boops (here to go) / Let's rock / Yes, we can (can) / Rhythm killer / Bank job.

Jul 87. (7") **FIRE. / TICKET TO RIDE** [ ] [ ]
(12"+=) – Miles.

Aug 87. (7") **YES WE CAN (CAN). / NO NAME ON THE BULLET** [-] [ ]

Sep 88. (lp)(c)(cd) **THE SUMMIT** [ ] [-]
– All aboard / Spy vs. spy / Super cool / First light / My fure / Free at last / Rice and peas / Here and beyond.

(above album released on UK 'R. A. S.')

4th & Broad. / 4th & Broad.

Oct 89. (7") **DANCEHALL. / JAM FIERCE HOUSE** [ ] [ ]
(12"+=)(cd-s+=) – No bass to yo face.

Mar 90. (cd)(c)(lp) **SILENT ASSASSINS** [ ] [ ]
– Rebel / Adventures of a bullet / Woman for the job / Man on a mission / Steppin' / Under arrest / No one can top this boy / Dance hall / Party together / Living a lie / Come again / Letters to the President / Ride this riddim / It's me.

— They both joined BILL LASWELL in his group MATERIAL. Summer'94; they contributed to RED DRAGON hit 'Compliments On Your Kiss'.

– other (SLY & ROBBIE) releases –

Jun 85. Island; (lp)(c) **REGGAE GREATS** [ ] [-]

Jun 85. Island; (lp) **A DUB EXTRAVAGANZA SLY & ROBBIE** [ ] [-]
(both above issued together on cd+c Sep91)

Oct 88. RDL; (lp) **SENSI DUB (with The REVOLUTIONARIES)** [ ] [-]

Jul 88. Mango-Island; (lp) **THE TAXI GANG PRESENTS . . . ("The TAXI GANG")** [ ] [-]

Jul 90. Mango-Island; (cd)(c)(lp) **DJ RIOT** [ ] [-]

— The rest by The TAXI GANG.

Aug 85. Taxi; (7")(12") **DOWN ON THE CORNER. / COMPUTER MALFUNCTION** [ ] [-]

Jul 86. Taxi; (lp) **ELECTRO REGGAE VOL.1** [ ] [-]

Jul 86. Taxi; (lp) **THE STING** [ ] [-]

Apr 89. Taxi; (12") **DANCING DIRTY. / MASS BRASS** [ ] [-]

Apr 93. R.A.S.; (cd) **REMEMBER PRECIOUS TIMES** [ ] [-]

Jul 93. Original; (lp) **SENSI DUB 4** [ ] [-]

Jul 93. Original; (cd) **SENSI DUB 4 & 5 (with JAH SHAKA)** [ ] [-]

Sep 93. Rhino; (cd) **THE BEST OF LOVERS ROCK VOLUME 1** [ ] [-]

Aug 94. Rhino; (cd) **MONEY DUB** [ ] [-]

Jan 94. Sonic; (cd) **OVERDRIVE IN OVERDUB** [ ] [-]

Jun 95. Island Red; (cd)(c)(lp) **HAIL UP THE TAXI** (SLY & ROBBIE PRESENT THE TAXI GANG) [ ] [ ]

Jul 95. M.S.; (cd) **BASS RIFF & DRUM DROPS** [ ] [-]

Oct 95. Original; (cd) **SENSI DUB 1 & 2 (SLY & THE REVOLUTIONARIES / JAH POWER BAND)** [ ] [-]

ROBBIE

Rob's / not issued

Jan 95. (12") **GET BACK 2 U. /** [ ] [-]

SLY & THE FAMILY STONE

Formed: San Francisco, California, USA . . . 1966 initially as The STONERS by SLY STONE with brother FREDDIE, sister ROSEMARY and cousin LARRY GRAHAM. They soon became SLY & THE FAMILY STONE after gigging in local bars / clubs in Oakland. In 1967, they signed to 'Epic', and issued debut album 'A WHOLE NEW THING'. The following year, they broke through commercially with US Top 10 single 'DANCE TO THE MUSIC'. In 1969, they were given massive accolade, for their performance on the now famous 'Woodstock' festival. • **Style:** Pioneers of the psychedelic soul movement in 1967, which re-influenced older groups TEMPTATIONS and The ISLEY BROTHERS. One of the first inter-racial, inter-gender and inta-drugs outfits to emerge from the rock-soul world. • **Songwriters:** All by SLY and group except; I CAN'T TURN YOU LOOSE (Otis Redding)/ YOU REALLY GOT ME (Kinks). • **Trivia:** On 5 Jun'74, SLY married Kathy Silva on stage at Madison Square Garden. Two months earlier, she had given him first child Bubb Ali (all 3 pictured on album cover of SMALL TALK). She divorced SLY in '75, and he filed for bankruptcy early '76.

Recommended: STAND (*9) / THERE'S A RIOT GOIN' ON (*9) / TAKIN' YOU HIGHER – THE BEST OF (*8)

SLY STONE (b.SYLVESTER STEWART, 15 Mar'44, Dallas, Texas) – vox, guitar, keyboards (ex-SLY & THE MOJO MEN) / **FREDDIE STONE** (b.FREDDIE STEWART, 5 Jun'46, Dallas) – guitar / **CYNTHIA ROBINSON** (b.12 Jan'46) – trumpet / **ROSEMARY STONE** (b.ROSEMARY STEWART, 21 Mar'45) – vocals, piano / **LARRY GRAHAM** (b.14 Aug'46, Beaumont, Texas) – bass / **JERRY MARTINI** – saxophone / **GREG ERRICO** – drums

not iss. / Loadstone

1966. (7") **I AIN'T GOT NOBODY. / I CAN'T TURN YOU LOOSE** [-] [ ]

Columbia / Epic

1967. (lp) **A WHOLE NEW THING** [-] [ ]
– Underdog / If this room could talk / Run run run / Turn me loose / Let me hear it from you / Advice / I cannot make it / Trip to your heart / I hate to love her / Bad risk / That kind of person / Day.

1967. (7") **HIGHER. / UNDERDOG** [-] [ ]

Mar 68. (7") **DANCE TO THE MUSIC. / LET ME HEAR IT FROM YOU** [ ] [8] Jan 68

Direction / Epic

Jun 68. (7") **DANCE TO THE MUSIC. / LET ME HEAR IT FROM YOU** [7] [-]

Sep 68. (lp) **DANCE TO THE MUSIC** [ ] [ ] Apr 68

– Dance to the music / Higher / I ain't got nobody (for real) / Dance to the medley: Music is alive – Dance in – Music lover / Ride the rhythm / Color me true / Are you ready / Don't burn baby / I'll never fall in love again. *(re-iss.Oct73 on 'CBS-Embassy')*

Sep 68. (7") **M'LADY. / LIFE** [32] [93]
[93] Jun 68

Jan 69. (lp) **M'LADY** (US-title 'LIFE') [ ] [ ] Nov68
– Dynamite! / Chicken / Plastic Jim / Fun / Into my own thing / Harmony / Life / Love city / I'm an animal / M'lady / Jane is a groupie.

Mar 69. (7") **EVERYDAY PEOPLE. / SING A SIMPLE SONG** [36] [1]
[89] Nov 68
(re-iss.1975 on 'Epic')

Jul 69. (lp) **STAND!** [ ] [13] Apr 69
– Stand! / Don't call me nigger, Whitey / I want to take you higher / Somebody's watching you / Sing a simple song / Everyday people / Sex machine / You can make it if you try. *(re-iss.cd Feb95)*

Aug 69. (7") **HOT FUN IN THE SUMMERTIME. / FUN** [ ] [2]

Oct 69. (7") **STAND!. / I WANT TO TAKE YOU HIGHER** [ ] [22]
[60] Apr 69
(re-iss.1975 on 'Epic')

Feb 70. (7") **THANK YOU (FALLETTINME BE MICE ELF AGIN). / EVERYBODY IS A STAR** [ ] [1] Dec 69

C.B.S. Epic

May 70. (7") **I WANT TO TAKE YOU HIGHER. / YOU CAN MAKE IT IF YOU TRY** [ ] [ ]

Jan 71. (lp)(c) **GREATEST HITS** (compilation) [ ] [2] Oct 70
– I want to take you higher / Everybody is a star / Stand / Life / Fun / You can make it if you try / Dance to the music / Everyday people / Hot fun in the summertime / M'lady / Sing a simple song / Thank you (falletinme be mice elf agin). *(re-iss.Mar81, cd-iss.Jun90) (quad-lp 1975)*

Epic Epic

Nov 71. (7") **FAMILY AFFAIR. / LUV 'N' HAIGHT** [15] [1] Oct 71

Jan 72. (lp)(c) **THERE'S A RIOT GOIN' ON** [31] [1] Nov 71
– Luv 'n' haight / Just like a baby / Poet / Family affair / Africa talks to you 'The Asphalt Jungle' / Brave & strong / (You caught me) Smilin' / Time / Spaced cowboy / Runnin' away / Thank you for talkin' to me Africa. (free ltd.12"w.a) *(re-iss.Feb86 on 'Edsel', cd-iss.Jan91) (re-iss.cd+c May94)*

Mar 72. (7") **RUNNIN' AWAY. / BRAVE & STRONG** [17] [23] Jan 72

Apr 72. (7") **(YOU CAUGHT ME) SMILIN'. / LUV 'N' HAIGHT** [-] [42]

— (Jan73) **RUSTEE ALLEN** – bass repl. LARRY (formed GRAHAM CENTRAL STATION) **ANDY NEWMARK** – drums repl. ERRICO. / added **PAT RICCO** – saxophone

Jun 73. (lp)(c) **FRESH** [ ] [7]
– In time / If you want me to stay / Let me have it all / Frisky / Thankful 'n' thoughtful / The skin I'm in / I don't know (satisfaction) / Keep on dancin' / Que sera sera / If it were left up to me / Babies makin' babies. *(re-iss.+cd.May87 on 'Edsel')*

Aug 73. (7") **IF YOU WANT ME TO STAY. / THANKFUL 'N' THOUGHTFUL** [ ] [12] Jun 73

Oct 73. (7") **FRISKY. / IF IT WERE LEFT UP TO ME** [-] [79]

Nov 73. (7") **QUE SERA SERA. / IF IT WERE LEFT UP TO ME** [ ] [-]

— **BILL LORDAN** – drums repl. NEWMARK who became session man

Jul 74. (lp)(c) **SMALL TALK** [ ] [15]
– Small talk / Say you will / Mother beautiful / Time for livin' / Can't strain my brain / Loose booty / Holdin' on / Wishful thinking / Better thee than me / Livin' while I'm livin' / This is love.

Jul 74. (7") **TIME FOR LIVIN'. / SMALL TALK** [ ] [32]

Jan 75. (7") **LOOSE BOOTY. / CAN'T STRAIN MY BRAIN** [ ] [84] Oct 84

— Discontinued for a while, as

SLY STONE

went solo (same label).

Oct 75. (lp)(c) **HIGH ON YOU** [ ] [45]
– I get high on you / Crossword puzzle / That's lovin' you / Who do you love / Green-eyed monster girl / Organize / Le lo li / My world / So good to me / Greed.

Oct 75. (7") **I GET HIGH ON YOU. / THAT'S LOVIN' YOU** [ ] [52] Sep 75

Dec 75. (7") **LE LO LI. / WHO DO YOU LOVE** [-] [ ]

Mar 76. (7") **CROSSWORD PUZZLE. / GREED** [-] [ ]

SLY & THE FAMILY STONE

reformed (same label)

Dec 76. (lp)(c) **HEARD YA MISSED ME, WELL I'M BACK** [ ] [ ]
– Heard ya missed me, well I'm back / What was I thinkin' / In my head / Sexy situation / Blessing in disguise / Everything in you / Mother is a hippie / Let's be together / The thing / Family again.

Feb 77. (7") **FAMILY AGAIN. / NOTHING LESS THAN HAPPINESS** [-] [ ]

Warners Warners

Sep 79. (7") **REMEMBER WHO YOU ARE. / SHEER ENERGY** [ ] [ ]

Oct 79. (lp)(c) **BACK ON THE RIGHT TRACK** [ ] [ ]
– Remember who you are / Back on the right track / If it's not addin' up . . . / The same thing (makes you laugh, makes you cry) / Shine it on / It takes all kinds / Who's to say / Sheer energy.

Dec 79. (7") **THE SAME THING (MAKES YOU LAUGH, MAKES YOU CRY). / WHO'S TO SAY** [-] [ ]

— In 1981, SLY guested on album 'THE ELECTRIC SPANKING OF WAR BABIES' by George Clinton's FUNKADELIC.

Mar 83. (lp)(c) **AIN'T BUT THE ONE WAY** [-] [ ]
– L.O.V.I.N.U. / One way / Ha ha, hee hee / Hobo Ken / Who in the funk do you think we are / You really got me / Sylvester / We can do it / High, y'all.

— In 1984, SLY joined BOBBY WOMACK on tour. He later guested on JESSE JOHNSON's 'A&M' US No.53 hit single 'Crazay' (Oct86).

SLY STONE

A & M A & M

Oct 86. (7") **EEK-A-BO-STATIK. / BLACK GIRLS (RAE DAWN CHONG)** [-] [ ]

Dec 86. (7"w/ MARTHA DAVIS) **STONE LOVE AND AFFECTION. / BLACK GIRLS** [-] [ ]

– (SLY & FAMILY . . .) compilations, others, etc. –

Mar 73. Epic; (7") **FAMILY AFFAIR. / DANCE TO THE MUSIC** [ ] [ ]

Feb 75. Epic; (7"ep) **DANCE TO THE MUSIC / COLOUR ME TRUE. / STAND! / RIDE THE RHYTHM** [ ] [ ]

May 75. Epic; (d-lp) **HIGH ENERGY** [ ] [ ]
– (A WHOLE NEW THING / LIFE)

1975. Epic; (7") **DANCE TO THE MUSIC. / LIFE** [ ] [ ]

1975. Epic; (7") **HOT FUN IN THE SUMMERTIME. / M'LADY** [ ] [ ]

1975. Epic; (7") **HOT FUN IN THE SUMMERTIME. / FUN** [-] [ ]

1975. Epic; (7") **FAMILY AFFAIR. / RUNNIN' AWAY** [ ] [ ]

1975. Epic; (7") **IF YOU WANT ME TO STAY. / FRISKY** [ ] [ ]

Jan 77. Epic; (7") **DANCE TO THE MUSIC. / I WANT TO TAKE YOU HIGHER** [ ] [-]

Mar 79. Epic; (7") **DANCE TO THE MUSIC. / STAND!** [ ] [-]

Nov 79. Epic; (7") **DANCE TO THE MUSIC. / SING A SIMPLE SONG** [ ] [-]

Aug 80. Epic; (7") **DANCE TO THE MUSIC. / EVERYDAY PEOPLE** [ ] [ ]
(re-iss.Jul82 on 'Old Gold')

Mar 82. Epic; (d-lp)(d-c) **ANTHOLOGY** [ ] [ ]
(re-iss.Sep87)

Apr 85. Epic; (lp)(c)(cd) **DANCE TO THE MUSIC** [ ] [ ]

Sep 87. Epic; (7") **DANCE TO THE MUSIC. / FAMILY AFFAIR** [ ] [ ]
(12"+=) – Everyday people / Runnin' away.

Oct 94. Epic; (cd) **THE BEST** [ ] [ ]

1979. Sculpture; (lp) **RECORDED IN SAN FRANCISCO 1964-67** [ ] [-]

Jan 80. CBS; (lp) **TEN YEARS TOO SOON ("SLY STONE")** [ ] [-]

Dec 91. CBS; (cd) **IN THE STILL OF THE NIGHT** [ ] [-]

Nov 91. Castle; (cd) **THE COLLECTION** [ ] [-]

1992 Sony; (cd)(c) **TAKIN' YOU HIGHER – THE BEST OF SLY & THE FAMILY STONE** [ ] [ ]
– Dance to the music / I want to take you higher / Family affair / Thank you (falletinme be mice elf agin) / I get high on you / Stand / M'lady / Skin I'm in / Everyday people / Sing a simple song / Hot fun in the summertime / Don't call me nigger, Whitey / Brave & strong / Life / Everybody is a star / If you want me to stay / (You caught me) Smilin' / Que sera sera / Running away / Family affair (remix).

Feb 94. Javelin; (cd)(c) **SPOTLIGHT ON SLY & THE FAMILY STONE** [ ] [-]

Mar 94. Charly; (cd) **REMEMBER WHO YOU ARE** [ ] [-]

Sep 94. Ace; (cd) **PRECIOUS STONE: IN THE STUDIO WITH SLY STONE** [ ] [-]

Dec 94. Prestige; (cd)(c) **EVERY DOG HAS IT'S DAY** [ ] [-]

Feb 95. B.A.M.; (cd) **PEARLS OF THE PAST ("SLY STONE & THE MOJO MEN")** [ ] [-]

— Thunderbolt records issued 2 albums of SLY STONE productions in Apr87 + Oct87 respectively, named 'DANCE TO THE MUSIC' & 'FAMILY AFFAIR'.

— **SLY STONE's** early US recordings under various pseudonyms (label in brackets)

STEWART BROTHERS

doo-wop outfit with brother FREDDIE and sister ROSE?

1959. (7") **THE RAT. / RA RA ROO** (Ensign)

1960. (7") **SLEEP ON THE PORCH. / YUM YUM YUM** (Keen)

LUKE STEWART

1961. (7") **A LONG TIME ALONE. / I'M JUST A FOOL** (Luke)

SYLVESTER STEWART

1961. (7") **A LONG TIME ALONE. / HELP ME WITH MY BROKEN HEART** (G&P)

The VISCANES

another doo-wop outfit.

1961. (7") **STOP WHAT YOU ARE DOING. / I GUESS I'LL BE** (Trop-po)

1961. (7") **YELLOW MOON. / UNCLE SAM NEEDS YOU** (V.P.M.)

SLY STEWART

1962. (7") **YELLOW MOON. / HEAVENLY ANGEL** (V.P.M.)

1963. (7") **I JUST LEARNED HOW TO SWIM. / SCAT SWIM** (Autumn)

SLY

1964. (7") **BUTTERMILK. / (part 2)** (Autumn)

1965. (7") **TEMPTATION WALK. / (part 2)** (Autumn)

— SLY at this time was producing Autumn acts The BEAU BRUMMELS, BOBBY FREEMAN and The MOJO MEN. He also became well-known local DJ for K-DIA.

SMALL FACES

Formed: East London, England . . . mid '65 by LANE, JONES and WINSTON who quickly found lead singer and ex-child actor STEVE MARRIOTT. They soon signed to 'Decca' records, and released Top 20 hit 'WHATCHA GONNA DO ABOUT IT?'. The following year, they deposed The BEATLES' Eleanor

Rigby at the top of charts with 'ALL OR NOTHING'. In 1968, they were No.1 in the album charts with concept 'OGDEN'S NUT GONE FLAKE', which was sleeved in a circle cover. Early in 1969, MARRIOTT departed from them, but they renewed band as The FACES with ex-JEFF BECK singer ROD STEWART. They quickly established themselves as UK/US top act after hitting big with 45 'STAY WITH ME'. The SMALL FACES re-united with MARRIOTT in 1977, but after 2 mediocre albums they finally folded. • **Style:** R&B mod outfit who branched out into pop psychedelia in 1967. The FACES were a high energy rock band, popular with live audiences, due to ROD STEWART's husky vox. • **Songwriters:** MARRIOTT and LANE except; WHATCHA GONNA DO ABOUT IT (Ian Samwell-Smith; their early producer) / SHA-LA-LA-LA-LEE (c.Kenny Lynch & Mort Schuman) / EVERY LITTLE BIT HURTS (Brenda Holloway) / TAKE THIS HURT OFF ME (Don Covay) / YOU'VE REALLY GOT A HOLD ON ME (Miracles) / etc. The FACES covered MAYBE I'M AMAZED (Paul McCartney) / I WISH IT WOULD RAIN (Temptations) / WICKED MESSENGER (Bob Dylan) / etc. • **Trivia:** The FACES had come together initially as supergroup QUIET MELON, which included ART WOOD, LONG JOHN BALDRY and JIMMY HOROWITZ.

Recommended: OGDEN'S NUT GONE FLAKE (*8) / THE ULTIMATE COLLECTION (*7) / The FACES:- SNAKES AND LADDERS – THE BEST OF THE FACES (*7)

STEVE MARRIOTT (b.30 Jan'47, Bow, London) – vocals, guitar (ex-solo artist) / **JIMMY WINSTON** (b.JAMES LANGWITH, 20 Apr'45, Stratford, London) – organ / **RONNIE LANE** (b. 1 Apr'45, Plaistow, London) – bass, vocals / **KENNEY JONES** (b.16 Sep'48, Stepney, London) – drums

Decca / Press

Aug 65. (7") **WHATCHA GONNA DO ABOUT IT?. / WHAT'S A MATTER, BABY** [14] [ ] Jan66

— **IAN McLAGAN** (b.12 May'45) – keyboards repl. WINSTON who went solo

Nov 65. (7") **I'VE GOT MINE. / IT'S TOO LATE** [ ] [-]
Jan 66. (7") **SHA-LA-LA-LA-LEE. / GROW YOUR OWN** [3] [ ] Apr66
May 66. (7") **HEY GIRL. / ALMOST GROWN** [10] [ ] Jul66
May 66. (lp) **SMALL FACES** [3] [-]
– Shake / Come on children / You better believe it / It's too late / One night stand / Whatcha gonna do about it? / Sorry she's mine / E to D / You need loving / Don't stop what you're doing / Own up / Sha-la-la-la-lee. *(cd-iss.Jul88 on 'London' +=)* – What's a matter baby / I've got mine / Grow your own / Almost grown.

Decca / RCA Victor

Aug 66. (7") **ALL OR NOTHING. / UNDERSTANDING** [1] [ ] Sep66
Nov 66. (7") **MY MIND'S EYE. / I CAN'T DANCE WITH YOU** [4] [ ] Dec66
Feb 67. (7") **I CAN'T MAKE IT. / JUST PASSING** [26] [-]
Apr 67. (7") **PATTERNS. / E TO D** [ ] [-]
May 67. (lp) **FROM THE BEGINNING** (out-takes, demos, etc) [17] [-]
– Runaway / My mind's eye / Yesterday, today and tomorrow / That man / My way of giving / Hey girl / Tell me have you ever seen me? / Come back and take this hurt off me / All or nothing / Baby don't do it / Plum Nellie / Sha-la-la-la-lee / You really got a hold on me / Whatcha gonna do about it?. *(re-iss.Aug84) (cd-iss.Jan89 on 'London')*

Immediate / Immediate

Jun 67. (7") **HERE COMES THE NICE. / TALK TO YOU** [12] [ ]
Jun 67. (lp) **SMALL FACES** [12] [-]
– Green circles / Become like you / Get yourself together / All our yesterdays / Talk to you / Show me the way / Up the wooden hills to Bedfordshire / Eddie's dreaming / (Tell me) Have you ever seen me / Something I want to tell you / Feeling lonely / Happy boys happy / Things are going to get better / My way of giving. *(cd-iss.May91 as 'GREEN CIRCLES (FIRST IMMEDIATE ALBUM)' on 'Sequel' +=)* Green circles (take 2) / Donkey rides, a penny, a glass / Have you ever seen me (take 2).
Aug 67. (7") **ITCHYCOO PARK. / I'M ONLY DREAMING** [3] [16] Nov 67
Nov 67. (7") **TIN SOLDIER. / I FEEL MUCH BETTER** [9] [73] Mar 68
Feb 68. (lp) **THERE ARE BUT FOUR SMALL FACES** [-] [ ]
– Here comes the nice / All or nothing / Lazy Sunday / Sha-la-la-la-lee / Collibosher / The Autumn stone / Whatcha gonna do about it? / My mind's eye / Itchyco Park / Hey girl / The universal / Runaway / Call it something nice / I can't make it / Afterglow (of your love) / Tin soldier.
Apr 68. (7") **LAZY SUNDAY. / ROLLIN' OVER** [2] [ ]
Jun 68. (lp) **OGDENS NUT GONE FLAKE** [1] [ ]
– Ogden's nut gone flake / Afterglow (of your love) / Long agos and worlds apart / Rene / Son of a baker / Lazy Sunday / Happiness Stan / Rollin' over / The hungry intruder / The journey / Mad John / Happy days / Toy town. *(US re-iss. Mar 73 on 'Abkco') (re-iss.Mar80 on 'Virgin') (re-iss.+cd.Sep86) (re-iss.+cd.Oct86 on 'Castle', cd+=)*– Tin soldier (live).
Jul 68. (7") **THE UNIVERSAL. / DONKEY RIDES, A PENNY, A GLASS** [16] [ ]
Nov 68. (7") **THE JOURNEY. / MAD JOHN** [-] [ ]
Mar 69. (7") **AFTERGLOW (OF YOUR LOVE). / WHAM BAM, THANK YOU MAM** [36] [ ]
Mar 69. (d-lp) **THE AUTUMN STONE** (rarities, live, etc) [ ] [ ]
– Here comes the nice / The Autumn stone / Collibosher / All or nothing / Red balloon / Lazy Sunday / Rollin' over / If I were a carpenter / Every litle bit hurts / My mind's eye / Tin soldier / Just assing / Call it something nice / I can't make it / Afterglow (of your love) / Sha-la-la-la-lee / The universal / Itchycoo Park / Hey girl / Wide eyed girl / On the wall / Whatcha gonn do about it / Wham bam thank you mam. *(re-iss.Jul84) (re-iss.lp/c/cd May86 on 'Castle')*

— Disbanded Mar'69. STEVE MARRIOTT formed HUMBLE PIE. The remaining formed . . .

The FACES

alongside **ROD STEWART** – vocals (also Solo artist, ex-JEFF BECK) / **RON WOOD** – guitar (ex-JEFF BECK GROUP, ex-CREATION)
(note: in the US, debut lp still credited to The SMALL FACES)

Warners / Warners

Feb 70. (7") **FLYING. / THREE BUTTON HAND ME DOWN** [ ] [-]
Mar 70. (lp)(c) **FIRST STEP** [45] [ ]
– Wicked messenger / Devotion / Shake, shudder, shiver / Stone / Around the plynth / Flying / Pineapple and the monkey / Nobody knows / Looking out the window / Three button hand me down. *(re-iss.Jul87 & Sep91 on 'Edsel') (cd-iss.Sep93)*
Mar 71. (7") **HAD ME A REAL GOOD TIME. / REAR WHEEL SKID** [ ] [-]
Mar 71. (lp)(c) **LONG PLAYER** [31] [29]
– Bad 'n' ruin / Tell everyone / Sweet lady Mary / Richmond / Maybe I'm amazed / Had a real good time / On the beach / I feel so good / Jerusalem. *(cd-iss.Sep93)*
Apr 71. (7") **MAYBE I'M AMAZED. / OH LORD I'M BROWNED OFF** [-] [ ]
Nov 71. (7") **STAY WITH ME. / DEBRIS** [6] [-]
Nov 71. (lp)(c) **A NOD'S AS GOD AS A WINK (TO A BLIND HORSE)** [2] [6]
– Miss Judy's farm / You're so rude / Love lives here / Last orders please / Stay with me / Debris / Memphis / Too bad / That's all I need. *(cd-iss.Sep93)*
Nov 71. (7") **STAY WITH ME. / YOU'RE SO RUDE** [-] [ ]
Feb 73. (7") **CINDY INCIDENTALLY. / SKEWIFF** [2] [48]
Apr 73. (lp)(c) **OOH LA LA** [1] [21]
– Silicone grown / Cindy incidentally / Flags and banners / My fault / Borstal boys / Fly in the ointment / If I'm on the late side / Glad and sorry / Just another monkey / Ooh la la. *(cd-iss.Sep93)*
May 73. (7") **OOH LA LA. / BORSTAL BOYS** [-] [ ]

— **TETSU YAMAUCHI** – bass (ex-FREE) repl. RONNIE LANE who went solo.

Nov 73. (7") **POOL HALL RICHARD. / I WISH IT WOULD RAIN** [8] [ ]

ROD STEWART & THE FACES

due to ROD's solo successes.

Jan 74. (lp)(c) **COAST TO COAST – OVERTURE FOR BEGINNERS (live)** [3] [63]
– It's all over now / Cut across Shorty / Too bad / Every picture tells a story / Angel / Stay with me / I wish it would rain / I'd rather go blind / Borstal boys / Amazing Grace / Jealous guy. *(cd-iss.Nov87)*

— (above featured ROD's song from solo career and was on 'Mercury')

Nov 74. (7") **YOU CAN MAKE ME DANCE SING OR ANYTHING. / AS LONG AS YOU TELL HIM** [12] [ ]

— Late '75, crumbled again, as ROD STEWART enjoyed overwhelming solo stardom. RON WOOD went off to join The ROLLING STONES.

– (FACES) compilations, others, etc. –

Oct 75. Warners; (d-lp) **TWO ORIGINALS OF THE FACES** [ ] [-]
– (FIRST STEP / LONG PLAYER)
Apr 77. Riva; (lp)(c) **SNAKES AND LADDERS – THE BEST OF THE FACES** [24] [ ]
– Pool hall Richard / Cindy incidentally / Ooh la la / Sweet Lady Mary / Flying / Pineapple and the monkey / You can make me dance, sing or anything / Had me a real good time / Stay with me / Miss Judy's farm / Silicone grown / That's all you need.
May 77. Riva; (7"ep) **THE FACES** [41] [ ]
– Cindy incidentally / Stay with me / Memphis / You can make me dance, sing or anything.
Sep 80. Pickwick; (lp)(c) **THE FACES FEATURING ROD STEWART** [ ] [-]
Nov 92. Mercury; (cd)(c) **THE BEST OF ROD STEWART & THE FACES** [58] [-]
May 93. Spectrum; (cd)(c) **AMAZING GRACE (ROD STEWART & THE FACES)** [ ] [-]

SMALL FACES

were re-formed by **JONES, McLAGAN** + reinstated **MARRIOTT** incomer **RICKY WILLS** – bass (ex-Peter FRAMPTON'S CAMEL, ex-ROXY MUSIC, etc)

Atlantic / Atlantic

Jul 77. (7") **LOOKIN' FOR A LOVE. / KO'D (BY LUV)** [ ] [ ]
Aug 77. (lp)(c) **PLAYMATES** [ ] [ ]
– High and happy / Never too late / Tonight / Say larvee / Find it / Lookin' for a love / Playmates / Drive in romance / This song's just for you / Smilin' in tune. *(cd-iss.Jun92 on 'Repertoire')*

— added on tour **JIMMY McCULLOCH** – guitar (of WINGS)

Jun 78. (7") **FILTHY RICH. / OVER TOO SOON** [ ] [ ]
Sep 78. (lp)(c) **78 IN THE SHADE** [ ] [ ]
– Over too soon / Too many crossroads / Let me down gently / Thinkin' about love / Stand by me (stand by you) / Brown man do / Soldier / Reel sour / You ain''t seen nothin' yet / Filthy rich. *(cd-iss.Nov93 on 'Repertoire')*
Nov 78. (7") **STAND BY ME (STAND BY YOU). / HUNGRY AND LOOKING** [ ] [ ]

— Disbanded again mid'78. KENNY JONES joined The WHO. MARRIOTT re-formed HUMBLE PIE. He was to tragically die in his Essex home after it went on fire 20 Apr'91.

– compilations, others, etc. –

1972. Pride; (7") **RUNAWAY./ SHAKE** [-] [ ]
Jul 72. Pride; (lp) **EARLY YEARS** [-] [ ]
1972. Pride; (lp) **THE HISTORY OF THE SMALL FACES** [-] [ ]
Jun 77. Decca; (lp) **ROCK ROOTS: THE SMALL FACES** [ ] [ ]
('A'&'B'sides)
Sep 77. Decca; (7"m) **SHA-LA-LA-LA-LEE. / WHAT'CHA GONNA DO ABOUT IT / ALL OR NOTHING** [ ] [-]
(re-iss.Mar82)
Sep 79. Decca; (7"ep) **THE LONDON BOYS EP** [ ] [-]
– (shared EP w / DAVID BOWIE / DOBIE GRAY / +1)
Mar 81. Decca; (lp) **SHA-LA-LA-LA-LEE** [ ] [-]
Sep 81. Decca; (7") **SHA-LA-LA-LA-LEE. / ALL OR NOTHING** [ ] [-]
(re-iss.Oct83 on 'Old Gold')

Nov 75. Immediate; (7") **ITCHYCOO PARK. / MY MIND'S EYE** [9] [ ]
1975. Immediate; (7") **LAZY SUNDAY./ THE AUTUMN STONE** [ ] [ ]
(re-iss.Sep81)
Mar 76. Immediate; (7") **LAZY SUNDAY. / (TELL ME) HAVE YOU EVER SEEN ME** [36] [ ]
Jan 78. Immediate; (lp)(c) **GREATEST HITS** [-] [ ]
May 75. Sire; (d-lp) **VINTAGE YEARS – THE IMMEDIATE STORY VOL.2** [-] [ ]
1978. Charly; (lp) **LIVE UK 1969 (live)** [ ] [-]
May 80. New World; (lp) **THE SMALL FACES** (shared w / AMEN CORNER) [ ] [-]
Jul 80. Virgin; (lp)(c) **BIG HITS** [ ] [-]
Jul 80. Virgin; (7"m) **TIN SOLDIERS./ TIN SOLDIERS (live) / RENE (live)** [ ] [-]
Oct 80. Virgin; (lp) **FOR YOUR DELIGHT THE DARLINGS OF WAPPING WHARF LAUNDERETTE** [ ] [-]

Below released on 'Old Gold' unless otherwise stated.
Oct 83. (7") **ALL OR NOTHING. / MY MIND'S EYE** [ ] [-]
Jan 85. (7") **LAZY SUNDAY. / TIN SOLDIER** [ ] [-]
Jan 85. (7") **ITCHYCOO PARK. / HERE COMES THE NICE** [ ] [-]
Feb 89. (cd-ep) **ITCHYCOO PARK / LAZY SUNDAY / TIN SOLDIER** [ ] [-]
Nov 84. Astan; (lp) **GOLDEN HITS** [ ] [-]
Nov 85. Castle; (d-lp,c,cd) **SMALL FACES COLLECTION** [ ] [-]
May 88. Castle; (3"cd-ep); (Special Edition) **ITCHYCOO PARK / LAZY SUNDAY / ALL OR NOTHING (live)/ AUTUMN STONE** [ ] [-]
Apr 89. Castle; (lp)(c)(cd) **GREATEST HITS** [ ] [-]
May 90. Castle; (cd)(c)(lp) **THE ULTIMATE COLLECTION** [ ] [-]
Jun 86. Archive 4; (12"ep) **CLASSIC CUTS** [ ] [-]
– Itchycoo park / Lazy Sunday / Here comes the nice / Sha la la la lee.
Sep 86. Showcase; (lp)(c) **QUITE NATURALLY** [ ] [-]
(cd-iss.Dec87)
Jul 88. Knight; (c) **NIGHTRIDING** [ ] [-]
Jun 90. See For Miles; (cd)(c)(lp) **THE SINGLES A's & B's** [ ] [-]
May 93. Spectrum; (cd)(c) **IT'S ALL OR NOTHING** [ ] [-]
Sep 93. Laserlight; (cd)(c) **ITCHYCOO PARK** [ ] [-]
Mar 94. Laserlight; (cd)(c) **HERE COMES THE NICE** [ ] [-]
Apr 94. Disky; (cd-ep) **ITCHYCOO PARK / TIN SOLDIER / LAZY SUNDAY** [ ] [-]
Jul 95. Summit; (cd) **THE BEST OF THE SMALL FACES** [ ] [-]
Jul 95. Repertoire; (cd) **BOXED** [ ] [-]
Nov 95. Charly; (4xcd-box) **THE IMMEDIATE YEARS** [ ] [-]

S*M*A*S*H

Formed: Welwyn Garden City, Hertfordshire, England ... early 90's as SMASH AT THE BLUES. In 1993, after controversial singles released on own label were lambasted by Tory councils, they signed to 'Hi-Rise', where their debut mini-album 'S*M*A*S*H SPRING 1994' hit UK Top 30. • **Style:** New wave of the new wave, anti-government punks inspired by The SEX PISTOLS, ANGELIC UPSTARTS and being on the dole. • **Songwriters:** ED and group. • **Trivia:** Played London's 100 Club late in 1993 alongside other NWOTNW hopefuls THESE ANIMAL MEN.

Recommended: SELF ABUSED (*6)

ED BORRIE – vocals, guitar / **SALVADOR ALESSI** – bass / **ROB HAIGH** – drums (ex-NIGHTMARE, ex-ASTRONAUTS)

Les Disques / not issued

Jul 93. (7") **REAL SURREAL. / DRUGS AGAIN / REVISITED NO.3** [ ] [-]
Dec 93. (c-ep) **WHEELERS, DEALERS & CHRISTINE KEELERS** [ ] [-]
– Self-abused / Kill somebody / Altruism / Bang bang bang / (5 other tracks by THESE ANIMAL MEN)
Feb 94. (7")(7"pink)(7"red-one-sided) **LADY LOVE YOUR C***. / SHAME** [ ] [-]

Hi-Rise / not issued

Mar 94. (m-cd)(m-c)(m-lp) **S*M*A*S*H SPRING 1994** [28] [-]
– Real surreal / Drugs again / Revisited No.3 / Lady love your c*** / Shame.
Jul 94. (12"ep)(c-ep)(cd-ep) **(I WANT TO) KILL SOMEBODY (Topper mix). / ('A'-Keith LeBlanc mix) / ('A'Gunshot headhunter mix) / ('A'-Bragg reshuffle mix)** [26] [ ]
Sep 94. (cd)(c)(lp) **SELF ABUSED** [59] [ ]
– Revisited No.5 / Barrabas / Oh ovary / Altruism / Reflections of you (remember me) / Self abused / Scream silent / Another love / Another shark in the deep end of my swimming pool / Real surreal / Dear Lou / Bang bang bang (granta 25) / Time / A.L.L.Y.C.
Nov 94. (7") **BARRABAS (PILOTED). / TURN ON THE WATER** [ ] [ ]
—— (above single on 'Sub Pop')
Feb 95. (m-cd)(m-c)(m-lp) **ANOTHER LOVE** [ ] [-]
– Another love (Bobbit mix) / Petal buzz / You've got a friend who's a friend of mine / Reflections of you (live) / Time (live) / Self abused (live) / Another love (uncut).

SMASHING PUMPKINS

Formed: Chicago, Illinois, USA ... 1986 by BILLY CORGAN (son of a jazz guitarist), JAMES IHA, female D'ARCY WRETZKY and JIMMY CHAMBERLAIN. After one 45 for local label, they moved on to 'Sub Pop' in 1990. Three years later now signed to Virgin subsidiary 'Hut', they made Top 10 on both sides of the Atlantic with classic ground-breaking album 'SIAMESE DREAM'. • **Style:** Influenced by an acoustic LED ZEPPELIN fused with slices of 70's PINK FLOYD. CORGAN's croaky but effective vox was at its best on his pastel NIRVANA-like grunge classics (i.e. 'TODAY', 'DISARM', 'BULLET WITH BUTTERFLY WINGS', '1979' & 'TONIGHT, TONIGHT. • **Songwriters:** CORGAN, except several with IHA. Covered; A GIRL NAMED SANDOZ (Eric Burdon & The Animals) / LANDSLIDE (Fleetwood Mac) / DANCING IN THE MOONLIGHT (Thin Lizzy) / NEVER LET ME DOWN (Depeche Mode). • **Trivia:** Initially co-produced by BUTCH VIG (he of NIRVANA fame) and CORGAN. Album named after actress LILIAN GISH.

Recommended: GISH (*7) / SIAMESE DREAM (*9) / MELLON COLLIE AND THE INFINITE SADNESS (*10)

BILLY CORGAN (b.17 Mar'67) – vocals, guitar / **JAMES IHA** – guitar / **D'ARCY** – bass, vocals / **JIMMY CHAMBERLIN** – drums

not issued / Potential

1989. (7") **I AM ONE. / NOT WORTH ASKING** [-] [ ]

Glitterhouse / Sub Pop

Dec 90. (7")(7"pink) **TRISTESSA. / HONEY SPIDER** [ ] [ ]
(12"+=) La Dolly Vita *(re-iss.12"-cd-s May93)*

Hut-Virgin / Caroline

Aug 91. (12") **SIVA. / WINDOW PAINE** [ ] [ ]
Feb 92. (12"ep)(cd-ep) **LULL** [ ] [ ]
– Rhinoceros / Blue / Slunk / Bye June (demo).
Feb 92. (cd)(c)(lp) **GISH** [ ] [ ] Sep 91
– I am one / Siva / Rhinoceros / Bury me / Crush / Suffer / Snail / Tristessa / Window paine / Daydream. *(re-iss.May94)*
Aug 92. (12"ep)(cd-ep) **I AM ONE. / PLUME / STARLA** [73] [ ]
(10") – ('A'side) / Terrapin / Bullet train to Osaka.
Jun 92. (12"ep)(c-ep)(cd-ep) **THE PEEL SESSIONS** [ ] [-]
– Siva / Smiley / A girl named Sandoz.

Hut-Virgin / Virgin

Jun 93. (7"clear) **CHERUB ROCK. / PURR SNICKETY** [31] [ ]
(12"+=)(cd-s+=) Pissant/ French movie theme.
Jul 93. (cd)(c)(lp) **SIAMESE DREAM** [4] [10]
– Cherub rock / Quiet / Today / Hummer / Rocket / Disarm / Soma / Geek U.S.A. / Mayonaise / Spaceboy / Silverfuck / Sweet sweet / Luna.
Sep 93. (7")(c-s) **TODAY. / HELLO KITTY KAT** [44] [ ]
(12"+=)(cd-s+=) – Obscured
Feb 94. (7"purple) **DISARM. / SIAMESE DREAM** [11] [ ]
(12")(cd-s) – ('A'side) / Soothe (demo) / Blew away.
(12") – ('A'side) / Dancing in the moonlight / Landslide.
Oct 94. (cd)(c)(lp) **PISCES ISCARIOT** (compilation of B-sides) [ ] [4]
Dec 94. (7") **ROCKET. / NEVER LET ME DOWN** [ ] [ ]
– (4x7"box-set) **SIAMESE SINGLES** – (last 3 singles 1993-94 + above)
Oct 95. (c-s)(cd-s) **BULLET WITH BUTTERFLY WINGS / ...SAID SADLY** [20] [25]
Oct 95. (d-cd)(d-c) **MELLON COLLIE AND THE INFINITE SADNESS** [4] [1]
– DAWN TO DUSK:- Mellon Collie and the infinite sadness / Tonight, tonight / Jellybelly / Zero / Here is no why / Bullet with butterfly wings / To forgive / An ode to no one / Love / Cupid de Locke / Galapogos / Muzzle / Porcelina of the vast oceans / Take me down. // TWILIGHT TO STARLIGHT:- Where boys fear to tread / Bodies / Thirty-three / In the arms of sleep / 1979 / Tales of a scorched Earth / Thru the eyes of Ruby / Stumbleine / X.Y.U. / We only come out at night / Beautiful / Lily (my one and only) / By starlight / Farewell and goodnight.

Kendra SMITH (see under ⇒ DREAM SYNDICATE)

Patti SMITH

Born: 30 Dec'46, Chicago, Illinois, USA. She started to write for New York magazine 'Rock' in 1969, having earlier being shipped around by her family between Paris and London. In the early 70's, she began writing poetry full-time and met LENNY KAYE, who became her accompaniment at readings/gigs. In 1971, she scribed for 'Creem' mag, and soon developed professional musical partnership with playwright Sam Shepherd. By Christmas '72, she had 2 books of poetry 'Witt' & '7th Heaven', in the stores, and TODD RUNDGREN gave her credit on his 'A WIZARD A TRUE STAR' album, for nicknaming him 'Runt'. In 1974, she issued debut single 'HEY JOE' / 'PISS FACTORY' on a local label 'MER', which gained airplay when picked up by 'Sire' records. Early in 1975, she landed a contract with 'Arista', and by end of that year 'HORSES' was in the US Top 50. In 1978, she co-wrote 'BECAUSE THE NIGHT' with BRUCE SPRINGSTEEN, and this gave her a Top 10 hit, helping establish her return to the album charts. • **Style:** New wave/rock'n'roll poetess, influenced by JIM MORRISON and LOU REED. Her self-indulgence was forgotten in the late 70's, after 2 fine comeback albums. • **Songwriters:** Lyrics PATTI, some music KAYE. Covered HEY JOE (Jimi Hendrix) / LAND OF 1000 DANCES (Cannibal & The Headhunters) / MY GENERATION (The Who) / GLORIA (Them) / SO YOU WANNA BE A ROCK'N'ROLL STAR (Byrds) / 5-4-3-2-1 (Manfred Man) / DOWNTOWN TRAIN (Tom Waits). • **Trivia:** In 1974, she co-wrote with ex-boyfriend ALLEN LANIER, his groups' (BLUE OYSTER CULT) 'Career Of Evil'. Her albums were produced by JOHN CALE (1st) / JACK DOUGLAS (2nd) / JIMMY IOVINE (3rd) / TODD RUNDGREN (4th) / FRED SMITH and JIMMY IOVINE (1988). • **Miscellaneous:** Her career nearly ended abruptly in Jan'77, when she fell off stage at a concert in Tampa Bay, breaking a vertebrae in her neck.

Recommended: HORSES (*9) / EASTER (*7) / WAVE (*7)

PATTI SMITH – vocals, poetry / with **LENNY KAYE** – guitar / **RICHARD SOHL** – piano

not issued / M.E.R.

Aug 74. (7") **HEY JOE. / PISS FACTORY** [-] [ ]
(UK-iss.Mar78 on 'Sire')

— added **IVAN KRAAL** – bass, guitar, piano / **JAY DAUGHERTY** – drums

Arista / Arista

Dec 75. (lp,c,silver+grey-lp) **HORSES** [ ] [47]
– Gloria / Redondo Beach / Birdland / Free monkey / Kimberley / Break it up / Land / Elegie. *(re-iss.+cd.Aug88)*

Apr 76. (7") **GLORIA. / MY GENERATION** [ ] [ ]
(re-iss.12"-Sep77)

Oct 76. (lp)(c) **RADIO ETHIOPIA** [ ] [ ]
– Ask the angels / Ain't it strange / Poppies / Pissing in the river / Pumping (my heart) / Distant fingers / Radio Ethiopia / Abyssinia. *(re-iss.+cd.Aug88)*

— Her tour featured **LEIGH FOXX** – bass repl. SOHL. Others augmenting at the time **ANDY PALEY** (ex-ELLIOT MURPHY) + **BRUCE BRODY** – keyboards (ex-JOHN CALE)

PATTI SMITH GROUP

with **KAYE / KRAAL / DAUGHERTY / BRODY + SOHL**

Mar 78. (7") **BECAUSE THE NIGHT. / GOD SPEED** [5] [13]

Mar 78. (lp)(c) **EASTER** [16] [20]
– Till victory / Space monkey / Because the night / Ghost dance / Babelogue / Rock'n'roll nigger / Privilege (set me free) / We three / 25th floor / High on rebellion / Easter. *(re-iss.Jan83 on 'Fame') (cd-iss.Aug88)*

Jun 78. (7") **PRIVILEGE (SET ME FREE). / ASK THE ANGELS** [72] [ ]
(12"+=) – 25th floor (live) / Babelogue (live).

— **FRED 'Sonic' SMITH** – drums (ex-MC5) repl. DAUGHERTY to TOM VERLAINE

May 79. (7") **FREDERICK. / FIRE OF UNKNOWN ORIGIN** [63] [-]

May 79. (lp)(c) **WAVE** [41] [18]
– Frederick / Dancing barefoot / Citizen ship / Hymn / Revenge / So you want to be a rock'n'roll star / Seven ways of going / Broken flag / Wave. *(re-iss.+cd.Aug88)*

Jun 79. (7") **FREDERICK. / FREDERICK (live)** [-] [90]

Jul 79. (7") **DANCING BAREFOOT. / FIVE, FOUR, THREE, TWO, ONE (live)** [ ] [-]

Aug 79. (7"m) **SO YOU WANT TO BE A ROCK 'N' ROLL STAR. / 5-4-3-2-1 / FIRE OF UNKNOWN ORIGIN** [-] [ ]

Sep 79. (7") **SO YOU WANT TO BE A ROCK'N'ROLL STAR. / FREDERICK (live)** [ ] [-]

— PATTI retired Mar'80 with her new husband FRED SMITH to bring up children. BRUCE BRODY was another to join ex-TELEVISION singer TOM VERLAINE's band.

PATTI SMITH

re-appeared in 1988 with still **SOHL, DAUGHERTY & SONIC**

Fierce / Fierce

Feb 88. (7"m) **BRIAN JONES. / STOCKINGED FEET / JESUS CHRIST . . .** [ ] [ ]

Arista / Arista

Jul 88. (7") **PEOPLE HAVE THE POWER. / WILD LEAVES** [ ] [ ]
(12"+=)/ /(cd-s+=) – Where duty calls./ / ('A'-album version).

Jul 88. (lp)(c)(cd) **DREAM OF LIFE** [70] [65]
– People have the power / Going under / Up there, down there / Paths that cross / Dream of life / Where duty calls / (I was) Looking for you / The Jackson song. *(re-iss.cd.Apr92)*

— RICHARD SOHL was to die from a cardiac arrest on 3 Jun'90. PATTI returned to reciting and recording her poetry in 1995.

– compilations, others, etc. –

Apr 83. Arista; (7") **BECAUSE THE NIGHT. / GLORIA** [ ] [-]
(12") – ('A'side) / Redondo beach / Dancing barefoot / Free money.

Jul 84. Old Gold; (7") **BECAUSE THE NIGHT. / GLORIA** [ ] [-]

Sep 91. RCA; (3xcd-box) **BOX SET** [ ] [ ]
– (RADIO ETHIOPIA / HORSES / WAVE albums)

t.v. SMITH (see under ⇒ ADVERTS)

SMITHEREENS

Formed: New Jersey, USA . . . 1980 by JIM BABJAK and DENNIS DIKEN, who had played in bands together since the early 70's. They recruited other 2 (see below), and backed singer OTIS BLACKWELL on a couple of recordings. In 1983, they signed to 'Enigma', and eventually had breakthrough late 80's with 'SMITHEREENS II' album. • **Style:** Described as being between The BEATLES, The BYRDS and AC/DC!. • **Songwriters:** DiNIZIO penned, except THE SEEKER (Who). • **Trivia:** SUZANNE VEGA guested on 1986 album. Amongst soundtracks they appear on was 1991 film 'Class Of Nuke 'Em High'. **Note:** Not to be confused with a Dutch band of same name, circa mid-80's.

Recommended: ESPECIALLY FOR YOU (*7).

PAT DiNIZIO – vocals, guitar / **JIM BABJAK** – guitar / **MIKE MESAROS** – bass / **DENNIS DIKEN** – drums

not issued / D-Tone

1980. (7"ep) **GIRLS ABOUT TOWN / GIRL DON'T TELL ME. / GOT ME A GIRL / GIRLS ARE LIKE THAT** [-] [ ]

not iss. / Little Ricky

1983. (m-lp) **BEAUTY & SADNESS** [-] [ ]
– Beauty & sadness / Some other guy / Tracey's world / Much too much / Beauty and sadness (instrumental). *(UK-iss.+cd.Jul89 on 'Virgin')*

Enigma / Enigma

Dec 86. (lp,cd) **ESPECIALLY FOR YOU** [ ] [51] Aug 86
– *(pic-lp Nov87)*

Jan 87. (7"+7"red) **IN A LONELY ROOM. ("SMITHEREENS with SUZANNE VEGA") / BEAUTY AND SADNESS** [ ] [-]
(12"+=) – Blood and roses / Mr. Eliminator.

Jan 87. (7") **IN A LONELY ROOM ("SMITHEREENS with SUZANNE VEGA"). / BLOOD AND ROSES (live)** [-] [ ]

Mar 87. (7") **BEHIND THE WALL OF SLEEP. / BLOOD AND ROSES** [ ] [ ] Sep 86
(12"+=) – ?

Enigma-MCA / Enigma

Jul 87. (12"m) **STRANGERS WHEN WE MEET. / THE SEEKER / HANG TEN HIGH** [ ] [ ]

1987. (lp) **SMITHEREENS LIVE (live)** [-] [ ]
– Blood and roses / Behind the wall of sleep / Beauty and sadness / Alone at midnight / Strangers when we meet / The seeker.

Feb 88. (7") **ONLY A MEMORY. / THE SEEKER** [-] [92]

Mar 88. (7") **ONLY A MEMORY. / LUST FOR LIFE** [ ] [92]
(12"+=) – Something new.

Apr 88. (lp)(c)(cd) **GREEN THOUGHTS** [ ] [60]
– Only a memory / House we used to live in / Something new / The world we knew / Especially for you / Drown in my own tears / Deep black / Elaine / Spellbound / If the Sun doesn't shine / Green thoughts.

Jun 88. (7") **THE HOUSE WE USED TO LIVE IN. / ONLY A MEMORY** [-] [ ]

Oct 88. (7") **THE HOUSE WE USED TO LIVE IN. / RULER OF MY HEART** [ ] [ ]
(12"+=) – Blood and roses (live).
(cd-s++=) – ('A'live version).

Dec 88. (7") **DROWN IN MY OWN TEARS. / THE HOUSE WE USED TO LIVE IN** [-] [ ]

Enigma-EMI / Enigma

Nov 89. (lp)(c)(cd) **11** [ ] [41]
– Girl like you / Blues before and after / Blue period / Baby be good / Room without a view / Yesterday girl / Cut flowers / Willian Wilson / Maria Elana / Kiss your tears away.

Feb 90. (7") **A GIRL LIKE YOU. / CUT FLOWERS** [ ] [38] Dec 89
(12"+=)(cd-s+=) – Someone in love. (US; b-side)

May 90. (7") **BLUE PERIOD. / MARIA ELENA** [ ] [-]
(12"+=)(cd-s+=) – Room without a view.

May 90. (c-s) **BLUES BEFORE AND AFTER. / MARIA ELENA (acoustic)** [-] [94]

Capitol / Capitol

Sep 91. (cd)(c)(lp) **BLOW UP** [ ] [ ]
– Top of the pops / Too much passion / Tell me when did things go so wrong / Evening dress / Get a hold of my heart / Indigo blues / Now and then / Girl in room 12 / Anywhere you are / Over and over again / It's alright / If you want to see to shine.

Feb 92. (7")(c-s) **TOO MUCH PASSION. / ?** [ ] [37]
(12"+=)(cd-s+=) – ?

not issued / R.C.A.

May 94. (cd)(c) **A DATE WITH THE SMITHEREENS** [-] [ ]

SMITHS

Formed: Manchester, England . . . Nov'82 by MORRISSEY and MARR. MORRISSEY had recently had book 'James Dean Isn't Dead' published by Babylon, and had been UK president of The NEW YORK DOLLS fan club. Following rave reviews on debut UK tour, they signed one-off deal with 'Rough Trade' in March 1983, after turning down local 'Factory' records. Their first single 'HAND IN GLOVE', topped the indie charts, after being played on the nightly John Peel Radio 1 show. They turned down offers from major companies, to re-sign a long-term contract with 'Rough Trade'. To end 1983, they had first of many Top 30 hits with classic 'THIS CHARMING MAN'. Early in 1984, their eponymous debut album (John Porter taking over from Troy Tate on production) nearly hit No.1, and they were soon to become household names. • **Style:** Non-comformist alternative rock band, that featured superb guitarist MARR, and the extroverted Oscar Wilde of the pop/rock world MORRISSEY. • **Songwriters:** Lyrics – MORRISSEY / music – MARR, except HIS LATEST FLAME (Elvis Presley). • **Trivia:** HOW SOON IS NOW? was sampled in 1990 by duo SOHO on their hit 45 'Hippychick'.

Recommended: THE SMITHS (*10) / MEAT IS MURDER (*10) / THE QUEEN IS DEAD (*10) / HATFUL OF HOLLOW (*9) / THE WORLD WON'T LISTEN (*9) / STRANGEWAYS HERE WE COME (*9). / BEST . . . I (*10) / BEST II (*9)

MORRISSEY (b.STEPHEN PATRICK MORRISSEY, 22 May'59) – vocals (ex-NOSEBLEEDS) / **JOHNNY MARR** (b.JOHN MAHER, 31 Oct'63) – guitar, harmonica, mandolins, piano / **ANDY ROURKE** – bass / **MIKE JOYCE** (b. 1 Jun'63) – drums

Rough Trade / Sire

May 83. (7") **HAND IN GLOVE. / HANDSOME DEVIL** [ ] [-]

Nov 83. (7") **THIS CHARMING MAN. / JEANE** [25] [ ]
(12") – ('A'side) / Accept yourself / Wonderful woman.

Jan 84. (7") **WHAT DIFFERENCE DOES IT MAKE?. / BACK TO THE OLD HOUSE** [12] [ ]
(12"+=) – These things take time.

Feb 84. (lp)(c) **THE SMITHS** [2] [ ]
– Reel around the fountain / You've got everything now / Miserable lie / Pretty girls make graves / The hand that rocks the cradle / Still ill / Hand in glove / What difference does it make? / I don't owe you anything / Suffer little children. *(cd-*

iss.May87) (re-cd-iss.1989) (re-iss.cd/c/ltd-10"lp Nov93 on 'WEA')

May 84. (7") **HEAVEN KNOWS I'M MISERABLE NOW. / SUFFER LITTLE CHILDREN** 10
(12"+=) – Girl afraid.

Aug 84. (7") **WILLIAM, IT WAS REALLY NOTHING. / PLEASE PLEASE PLEASE LET ME GET WHAT I WANT** 17
(12"+=) – How soon is now?.

Nov 84. (lp)(c) **HATFUL OF HOLLOW** (with BBC sessions *) 7
– William, it was really nothing / What difference does it make? * / These things take time * / This charming man * / How soon is now? / Handsome devil * / Hand in glove / Still ill * / Heaven knows I'm miserable now / This night has opened my eyes * / You've got everything now * / Accept yourself * / Girl afraid / Back to the old house * / Reel around the fountain * / Please please please let me get what I want. *(cd-iss.May87) (re-iss.cd/c/ltd-d10"lp Nov93 on 'WEA')*

Jan 85. (7") **HOW SOON IS NOW?. / WELL I WONDER** 24 -
(12"+=) – Oscillate wildly.

Feb 85. (7") **HOW SOON IS NOW?. / THE HEADMASTER RITUAL** -

Feb 85. (lp)(c) **MEAT IS MURDER** 1
– The headmaster ritual / Barbarism begins at home / Rusholme ruffians / I want the one I can't have / What she said / Nowhere fast / That joke isn't funny anymore / Nowhere fast / Well I wonder / Meat is murder. *(cd-iss.May87) (re-iss.cd/c/ltd-d10"lp Nov93 on 'WEA')*

Mar 85. (7") **SHAKESPEARE'S SISTER. / WHAT SHE SAID** 26
(12"+=) – Stretch out and wait.

Jul 85. (7") **THAT JOKE ISN'T FUNNY ANYMORE. / MEAT IS MURDER (live)** 49
(12"+=) – Nowhere fast / Shakespeare's siste / Stretch out and wait (all live).

Sep 85. (7") **THE BOY WITH THE THORN IN HIS SIDE. / ASLEEP** 23
(12"+=) – Rubber ring.

— added **CRAIG GANNON** – guitar, bass (ex-AZTEC CAMERA, ex-BLUEBELLS)

May 86. (7") **BIGMOUTH STRIKES AGAIN. / MONEY CHANGES EVERYTHING** 26
(12"+=) – Unloveable.

Jun 86. (lp)(c) **THE QUEEN IS DEAD** 2 70
– Frankly Mr. Shankly / I know it's over / Never had no one ever / Cemetery gates / Big mouth strikes again / Vicar in a tutu / There is a light that never goes out / Some girls are bigger than others / The queen is dead / The boy with the thorn in his side. *(cd-iss.May87) (re-iss.cd/c/ltd-d10"lp Nov93 on 'WEA')*

Jul 86. (7") **PANIC. / VICAR IN A TUTU** 11
(12"+=) – The draize train.

Oct 86. (7") **ASK. / CEMETRY GATES** 14
(12"+=)(c-s+=) – Golden lights. *(re-iss.Feb95 on 'Warners', hit No.62)*

— Reverted to a quartet, when GANNON left to join The CRADLE.

Feb 87. (7") **SHOPLIFTERS OF THE WORLD UNITE. / HALF A PERSON** 12
(12"+=) – London.

— ('A'side on some 'YOU JUST HAVEN'T EARNED IT YET BABY')

Feb 87. (lp)(c)(cd) **THE WORLD WON'T LISTEN** (part compilation) 7
– Panic / Ask / London / Big mouth strikes again / Shakespeare's sister / There is a light that never goes out / Shoplifters of the world unite / The boy with the thorn in his side / Asleep / Unloveable / Half a person / Stretch out and wait / That joke isn't funny anymore / Oscillate wildly / You just haven't earned it yet baby / Rubber ring. (c+=) – Money changes everything. *(re-iss.cd/c/ltd-d10"lp Nov93 on 'WEA')*

Apr 87. (7") **SHEILA TAKE A BOW. / IS IT REALLY SO STRANGE?** 10
(12"+=) – Sweet and tender hooligan.

Aug 87. (7") **GIRLFRIEND IN A COMA. / WORK IS A FOUR-LETTER WORD** 13
(12"+=)(c-s+=) – I keep mine hidden.

Sep 87. (lp)(c)(cd) **STRANGEWAYS HERE WE COME** 2 55
– A rush and a push and the land is ours / I started something I couldn't finish / Death of a disco dancer / Girlfriend in a coma / Stop me if you think you've heard this one before / Last night I dreamt that somebody loved me / Unhappy birthday / Paint a vulgar picture / Death at one's elbow / I won't share you. *(re-iss.cd/c/ltd-d10"lp Nov93 on 'WEA')*

Oct 87. (7") **STOP ME IF YOU THINK YOU'VE HEARD THIS ONE BEFORE. / I KEEP MINE HIDDEN** -

Nov 87. (7") **I STARTED SOMETHING I COULDN'T FINISH. / PRETTY GIRLS MAKE GRAVES** 23
(12"+=) – Some girls are bigger than others (live).
(c-s++=) – What's the world (live).

Dec 87. (7") **LAST NIGHT I DREAMT THAT SOMEBODY LOVED ME. / NOWHERE FAST (BBC version)** 30
(12"+=) – Rusholme Russians (BBC version).
(cd-s++=) – William, it was really nothing (BBC version).

— In August '87, although signed to 'EMI', they had already broken-up. Cited for reasons, were MARR's increasing session work for PRETENDERS, BRYAN FERRY, etc. ROURKE and JOYCE splintered with ADULT NET before joining MORRISSEY when he went solo.

– other compilations, etc. –

Note; on 'Rough Trade' UK / 'Sire' US, unless otherwise mentioned.

Jun 87. (d-lp)(d-c) **LOUDER THAN BOMBS** 38 62 Apr 86
– Is it really so strange? / Sheila take a bow / Sweet and tender hooligan / Shoplifters of the world unite / Half a person / London / Panic / Girl afraid / Shakespeare's sister / William, it was really nothing / You just haven't earned it yet, baby / Golden lights / Ask / Heaven knows I'm miserable now / Unloveable / Asleep / Oscillate wildly / These things take time / Rubber ring / Back to the old house / Hand in glove / Stretch out and wait / This night has opened my eyes / Please, please, please, let me get what I want. *(re-iss.+cd.Nov88)*

Aug 88. (lp)(c)(cd)(dat) **RANK (live Oct'86)** 2 77
– The queen is dead / Panic / Vicar in a tutu / Ask / Rusholme ruffians / The boy with the thorn in his side / What she said / Is it really so strange? / Cemetry gates / London / I know it's over / The draize train / Still ill / Bigmouth strikes again / (Marie's the name) His latest flame – Take me back to dear old blighty. *(re-iss.cd/c/ltd-d10"lp Nov93 on 'WEA')*

Nov 88. (3"cd-ep) **THE HEADMASTER RITUAL / NOWHERE FAST (live) / MEAT IS MURDER (live) / STRETCH OUT AND WAIT (live)** -

Nov 88. (3"cd-ep) **BARBARISM BEGINS AT HOME / SHAKESPEARE'S SISTER / STRETCH OUT AND WAIT** -

— (Note:- 12"singles from Jan84 / May84 / Sep85 / Jul86 / Oct86 were issued on 3"cd-ep Nov88).

Oct 88. Strange Fruit; (12"ep)(cd-ep) **THE PEEL SESSIONS** (18.5.83) -
– What difference does it make? / Reel around the fountain / Miserable lie / Handsome devil.

Note; Below on 'WEA' UK/ 'Sire' US unless otherwise mentioned.

Jul 92. (7")(c-s) **THIS CHARMING MAN. / WONDERFUL WOMAN / ACCEPT YOURSELF** 8
(cd-s+=) – Jeane.

Aug 92. (cd)(c)(lp) **BEST . . . 1** 1
– This charming man / William, it was really nothing / What difference does it make / Stop me if you think you've heard it before / Girlfriend in a coma / Half a person / Rubber ring / How soon is now? / Hand in glove / Shoplifters of the world unite / Sheila take a bow / Some girls are bigger than others / Panic / Please please please let me get what I want.

Sep 92. (7")(c-s) **HOW SOON IS NOW. / HAND IN GLOVE** 16
(cd-s+=) – The queen is dead / Handsome devil / I started something I couldn't finish.
(cd-s+=) – I know it's over / Suffer little children / Back to the old house.

Oct 92. (7")(c-s) **THERE IS A LIGHT THAT NEVER GOES OUT. / HANDSOME DEVIL (live)** 25
(cd-s+=) – I don't owe you anything / Hand in glove / Jeane.
(cd-s+=) – Money changes everything (live) / Some girls are bigger than others (live) / Hand in glove (live).

Nov 92. (cd)(c)(lp) **BEST II** 29
– The boy with a thorn in his side / The headmaster ritual / Heaven knows I'm miserable now / Ask / Osciliate wildly / Nowhere fast / Still ill / That joke isn't funny anymore / Shakespeare's sister / Girl afraid / Reel around the fountain / Last night I dreamt somebody loved me / There is a light that never goes out.

Mar 95. (cd)(c) **"SINGLES"** 5
– Hand in glove / This charming man / What difference does it make? / Heaven knows I'm miserable now / William, it was really nothing / How soon is now? / Shakespeare's sister / That joke isn't funny anymore / The boy with the thorn in his side / Bigmouth strikes again / Panic / Ask / Shoplifters of the world unite / Sheila take a bow / Girlfriend in a coma / I started something I couldn't finish / Last night I dreamt that somebody loved me / There is a light that never goes out.

SNAPE (see under ⇒ KORNER, Alexis)

SNOOP DOGGY DOGG

Born: CALVIN BROADUS, 1971, Long Beach, California, USA. Unleashed in 1993, when his debut DR.DRE (ex-N.W.A.) produced album 'DOGGYSTYLE' created furore amongst the moral majority in America. Once again this was hype that any up and coming controversial star needs and the album shot straight to No.1 with record sales for a debut. However before the time of its release (August '93) and after guesting on DR.DRE's 'Nuthin' But A G Thang', convicted teenage drug-dealer SNOOP was arrested, when a local hood was killed after shots were allegedly fired by his bodyguard MALIK out of SNOOP's car. SNOOP was released after being bailed for $1million. Early in 1994, he hit London under a storm of protest, not least from tabloid press, including The Daily Star who headlined on the front page; 'KICK THIS EVIL BASTARD OUT!'. This only spurred the Brits to buy the album, especially after he was premiered on C4's 'The Word', complete with interview. • **Style:** Crude hard-core gangsta rapper, who portrays himself like a Doberman on heat. Music that broke the bounds of censorship and which was definitely not for the easily offended. • **Songwriters:** Himself and various samples. • **Trivia:** He was given his nickname by his mother!. Featured, as did DR.DRE and The DOGG POUND posse on film soundtrack 'Above The Rim'. Another mate of SNOOP's; WARREN G was also a massive hit in the summer of '94 with single 'REGULATE' from the album 'REGULATE ... G FUNK ERA'.

Recommended: DOGGYSTYLE (*7)

with The DOGG POUND & The DRAMATICS plus **WARREN G / KURUPT / NANCY FLETCHER / DAT NIGGA DAZ / D.O.C. RBX / THE LADY OF RAGE / LIL HERSHEY LOC (MALIK) / NATE DOGG**

		Death Row-East West	Death Row-Interscope
Dec 93.	(7")(c-s) **WHAT'S MY NAME. / ('A'club mix)** (12"+=)(cd-s+=) – ('A'explicit mix) / ('A'instrumental) / Who am I (what's my name?).	20	8 Nov93
Dec 93.	(cd)(c) **DOGGYSTYLE** – Bathtub / G funk intro / Gin and juice / Tha shiznit / Lodi dodi / Murder was the case / Seria killa / Who am I (what's my name)? / For all my niggaz & bitches / Aint no fun (if the homies cant have none) / Doggy Dogg world / GZ and hustlas / Pump pump.	38	1 Nov93
Feb 94.	(c-s) **GIN AND JUICE. / ('A'-laid back mix)** (12"+=)(cd-s+=) – (2-'A'mixes).	39	8
Aug 94.	(7")(c-s) **DOGGY DOGG WORLD. / ('A'-Perfecto mix)** (12"+=)(cd-s+=) – ('A'-Dr.Dre mix) / ('A'-Perfecto x-rated mix).	32	

— He is still to stand trial for murder 13 Jan'95. At the end of '94, he and 3 band members (RICHARD BROWN, DARRYL DANIEL + DELMAR ARNAUDE) were arrested and charged with possession of drugs. In Oct'95, SNOOP'S trial finally got underway, due to his attorney Johnnie Cochran being slightly busy with the O.J. Simpson case!.

SOFT BOYS

Formed: Cambridge, England ... 1976 by ROBYN HITCHCOCK, a one-time busker who had surfaced as The WORST FEARS, The BEETLES and MAUREEN & THE MEATPACKERS, etc. In 1977, one-time DENNIS AND THE EXPERTS members became The SOFT BOTS who issued debut release 'GIVE IT TO THE SOFT BOYS EP' on indie label 'Raw'. The following years saw them only actify cult interest. • **Style:** New wave rock, influenced by West Coast psychedelia, SYD BARRETT with tongue-in-cheek humour. • **Songwriters:** HITCHCOCK penned, some with REW.

Recommended: WADING THROUGH A VENTILATOR (*7) / ROBYN HITCHCOCK & THE EGYPTIANS :- INVISIBLE HITS (*7).

ROBYN HITCHCOCK (b. 3 Mar '52, East Grinstead, England) – vocals, guitar, bass / **ALAN DAVIS** – guitar / **ANDY METCALFE** – bass / **MORRIS WINDSOR** (aka OTIS FAGG) – drums

		Raw	not issued
Nov 77.	(7"ep) **GIVE IT TO THE SOFT BOYS** – Wading through a ventilator / The face of death / Hear my brane. *(re-iss.Oct79)*		-

— **KIMBERLEY REW** – guitar, harmonica, vocals repl. DAVIS

		Radar	not issued
May 78.	(7") **(I WANT TO BE AN) ANGLEPOISE LAMP. / FAT MAN'S SON**		-

— In Oct79, 'Raw' quickly withdrew release of 45 'WHERE ARE THE PRAWNS'.

		Aura	not issued
Feb 80.	(lp) **A CAN OF BEES** – Give it to the soft boys / The pigworker / Human music / Leppo and the jooves / The rat's prayer / Do the chisel / Sandra's having her brain out / The return of the sacred crab / Cold turkey / Skool dinner blues / Wading through a ventilator. *(re-iss.Jun84 on 'Two Crabs') (cd-iss.Feb95 on 'Rhino' +=)* – Leppo and the jooves / Sandra's having her brain out / Skool dinner blues / Fatman's son / (I want to be an) Anglepoise lamp / Ugly Nora.		-

— **MATTHEW SELIGMAN** – bass, keyboards (ex-SW9) repl. ANDY to FISH TURNED HUMAN

		Armageddon	Armageddon
Jun 80.	(7"ep) **NEAR THE SOFT BOYS** – Kingdom of love / Vegetable man / Strange. *(re-iss.Jul82)*		-
Jul 80.	(lp) **UNDERWATER MOONLIGHT** – I wanna destroy you / Kingdom of love / Positive vibrations / I got the job / Insanely jealous / Tonight / You'll have to go sideways / Old pervert / The queen of eyes / Underwater moonlight. *(cd-iss.Feb95 on 'Rhino' +=)* – Vegetable man / Strange / Only the stones remain / Where are the prawns / Dreams / Black snake diamond role / There's nobody like you / Song No.4.		-
Aug 80.	(7") **I WANNA DESTROY YOU. / (I'M AN) OLD PERVERT (DISCO)** *(re-iss.Jul81)*		-
Oct 81.	(7") **ONLY THE STONES REMAIN. / THE ASKING TREE**		
Mar 82.	(lp) **TWO HALVES FOR THE PRICE OF ONE** – Only the stones remain / Where are the prawns / The bells of Rhymney / There's nobody like you / Innocent box / Black snake diamond role / Underwater moonlight / Astronomy domine / Outlaw blues / Mystery train. (Half of above lp / half-live) (US-title; ONLY THE STONES REMAIN; rel; Oct 81)		

— Disbanded in 1982, SELIGMAN who THOMPSON TWINS

ROBYN HITCHCOCK

had already gone solo, using session people, including most ex-SOFT BOYS.

		Armageddon	not issued
Apr 81.	(7") **THE MAN WHO INVENTED HIMSELF. / DANCING ON GOD'S THUMB** (free 7"flexi w.a.) **IT'S A MYSTIC TRIP. / GROOVING ON AN INNER PLANE**		-
May 81.	(lp) **BLACK SNAKE DIAMOND ROLE** – The man who invented himself / Brenda's iron sledge / Do policemen sing? / The lizard / Meat / Acid bird / I watch the cars / Out of the picture / City of shame / Love. *(re-iss.May86 on 'Aftermath', cd-iss.1988) (cd-iss.Feb95 on 'Sequel' +=)* – Dancing on God's thumb / Happy the golden prince / I watch the cars / It was the night / Grooving on an inner plane.		-

— now w / **SARA LEE** – bass / **ANTHONY THISTLETWAITE** – sax / **ROD JOHNSON** – drums repl. SELIGMAN to THOMAS DOLBY (REW who formed KATRINA & THE WAVES

		Albion	not issued
Mar 82.	(7") **AMERICA. / IT WAS THE NIGHT / HOW DO YOU WORK THIS THING**		-
Mar 82.	(lp) **GROOVY DECAY** – Night ride to Trinidad / Fifty-two stations / Young people scream / The rain / America / The cars she used to drive / Grooving on an inner plane / St.Petersburg / When I was a kid / Midnight fish. *(re-iss.Dec85 on 'Midnight Music') (cd-iss.Nov89 on 'Line') (cd-iss.Feb95 as 'GRAVY DECO (THE COMPLETE GROOVY DECAY / DECOY SESSIONS)' on 'Sequel' + with extra mixes)*		-
May 83.	(12") **NIGHT RIDE TO TRINIDAD. / KINGDOM OF LOVE / MIDNIGHT FISH**		-

		Midnight	not issued
Nov 82.	(7") **EATEN BY HER OWN DINNER. / DR. STICKY / LISTENING TO THE HIGSONS**		-
Apr 83.	(7") **HE'S A REPTILE. (by "SOFT BOYS") / SONG No.4**		-

ROBYN HITCHCOCK

now w / **WINDSOR / METCALFE / + ROGER JACKSON** – keyboards

		Midnight	Slash
Aug 84.	(lp) **I OFTEN DREAM OF TRAINS** – Nocturne / Uncorrected personality traits / Sounds great when you're dead / Flavour of night / This could be the day / Trams of old London / Furry green atom bowl / Heart full of leaves / Autumn is your last chance / I often dream of trains. *(cd-iss.Oct86) (cd-iss.Feb95 on 'Sequel')* (cd+=) – Ye sleeping knights of Jesus / Sometimes I wish I was a pretty girl / Cathedral / Mellow together / Winter love / The bones in the ground / My favourite buildings / I used to say I love you.		-
Nov 84.	(12"m) **THE BELLS OF RHYMNEY / FALLING LEAVES. / WINTER LOVE / THE BONES IN THE GROUND**		-

ROBIN HITCHCOCK & THE EGYPTIANS

same as solo line-up and same label

Mar 85.	(lp) **FEGMANIA!** – Egyptian cream / Another bubble / I'm only you / My wife and my dead wife / Goodnight I say / The man with the lightbulb head / Insect mother / Strawberry mind / Glass / The fly / Heaven. *(cd-iss.1986 +=)* – The bells of rhymney / Dwarfbeat / Some body. *(re-iss.Mar95 on 'Rhino-Sequel' +=)* – Egyptian cream (demo) / Heaven (live) / Insect mother (demo) / Egyptian cream (live) / The pit of souls: I) The plateau – II) The descent – III) The spinal dance – IV) Flight of the iron lung.		
May 85.	(12"m) **HEAVEN. / DWARFBEAT / SOME BODY**		-

		Midnight	Relativity
Oct 85.	(lp)(c) **GOTTA LET THIS HEN OUT (live)** – Sometimes I wish I was a pretty girl / Kingdom of love / Acid bird / The cars she used to drive / My wife and my dead wife / Brenda's iron sledge / The fly * / Only the stones remain * / Egyptian cream * / Leppo & the Jooves / America / Heaven / Listening to The Higsons / Face of death. *(cd-iss.Oct86; c/cd+= *) (re-iss.cd Mar95 on 'Rhino-Sequel')*		-
Feb 86.	(12"ep) **BRENDA'S IRON SLEDGE (live). / ONLY THE STONES REMAIN (live) / PIT OF SOULS (parts 1-4)**		-
Mar 86.	(lp)(c)(pic-lp) **EXPLODING IN SILENCE** – *(cd-iss.Dec86)*		

		Glass Fish	Relativity
Sep 86.	(7") **IF YOU WERE A PRIEST. / THE CRAWLING** (12"+=) – Tell me about your drugs / The can opener.		-
Sep 86.	(lp)(cd) **ELEMENT OF LIGHT** – If you were a priest / Winchester / Somewhere apart / Ted, Woody and Junior / The president / Raymond Chandler evening / Bass / Airscape / Never stop bleeding / Lady Waters & the hooded one / The black crow knows / The crawling / The leopard / Tell me about your drugs. *(re-iss.cd Mar95 on 'Rhino-Sequel' +=)* – The can opener / Raymond Chandler evening (demo) / President (demo) / If you were a priest (demo) / Airscape (live) / The leopard (demo).		
Nov 86.	(lp)(cd) **INVISIBLE HITCHCOCK** (compilation) – All I wanna do is fall in love / Give me a spanner, Ralph / A skull, a suitcase, and a long red bottle of wine / It's a mystic trip / My favourite buildings / Falling leaves / Eaten by her own dinner / Pits of souls / Trash / Mr. Deadly / Star of hairs / Messages		

of dark / Vegetable friend / I got a message for you / Abandoned brain / Point it at gran / Let there be more darkness / Blues in A. *(re-iss.cd Mar95 on 'Rhino-Sequel' +=)* – Listening to the higsons / Dr. Sticky.

A & M A & M

Feb 88. (lp)(c)(cd) **GLOBE OF FROGS**
– Trapped flesh Mandela / Vibrating / Balloon man / Luminous rose / Sleeping with your devil mask on / Unsettled / Flesh number one / Chinese bones / A globe of frogs / Beatle Dennis / The shapes between us / Turn to animals.

Apr 88. (7") **GLOBE OF FROGS. / BALLOON MAN** -

— still with **METCALFE + WINDSOR** + guest **PETER BUCK** – guitar (of R.E.M.)

Jul 89. (7") **MADONNA OF THE WASPS. / RULING CLASS** -
(12"+=)(cd-s+=) – Veins of the queen (royal mix) / Freeze (shatter mix).

Dec 89. (lp)(c)(cd) **QUEEN ELVIS** -
– Madonna of the wasps / The Devils coachman / Wax doll / Knife / Swirling / One long pair of eyes / Veins of the Queen / Freeze / Autumn sea / Superman. *(cd+=)* – Veins of the Queen (royal mix) / Freeze (shatter mix).

ROBIN HITCHCOCK

Go! Discs Twin Tone

Nov 90. (cd)(c)(lp) **EYE** -
– Cynthia mask / Certainly clickot / Queen Elvis / Flesh cartoons / Chinese water python / Executioner / Linctus House / Sweet ghosts of light / College of ice / Transparent lover / Beautiful girl / Raining twilight coast / Clean Steve / Agony of pleasure / Glass hotel / Satellite / Aquarium / Queen Elvis II. *(UK-cd-iss.Mar95 on 'Rhino-Sequel' +=)* – Raining twilight coast (demo) / Agony of pleasure (demo) / Queen Elvis III (demo).

Oct 91. (cd)(c)(lp) **PERSPEX ISLAND**
– Oceanside / So you think you're in love / Birds in perspex / Ultra unbelievable love / Vegetations and dines / Lysander / Child of the universe / She doesn't exist / Ride / If you go away / Earthly Paradise.

Jan 92. (7") **SO YOU THINK YOU'RE IN LOVE. / WATCH YOUR INTELLIGENCE**
(12"+=)(cd-s+=) – Dark green energy (featuring STIPE + BUCK of R.E.M.).

1993. (cd) **RESPECT** -
–

1994. (cd) **YOU & OBLIVION** -
– You've got / Don't you / Birdshead / She reached for a light / Victorian squid / Captain Dry / Mr. Rock I / August hair / Take your knife out of my back / Surgery / The dust / Polly on the shore / Aether / Fiend before the shrine / Nothing / Into it / Stranded in the future / Keeping still / September clones / Ghost ship / You & me / If I could look. *(UK-iss.1995 on 'Rhino-Sequel')*

Volume LV not issued

Feb 95. (7") **I SOMETHING YOU. / ZIPPER IN MY SPINE / MAN WITH A WOMAN'S SHADOW** -

– (SOFT BOYS) compilations –

Nov 83. Midnight Music; (lp) **INVISIBLE HITS** -
– Wey-wey-hep-uh-hole * / Have a heart Betty (I'm not fireproof) * / The asking tree / Muriel's hoof / The rout of the clones / Let me put it next to you / When I was a kid * / Rock & roll toilet * / Love poisoning * / Empty girl / Blues in the dark / He's a reptile. *(cd-iss.Feb95 on 'Rhino" +=)* – (alt.takes of *)

Aug 85. De Laurean; (lp)(pic-lp) **WADING THROUGH A VENTILATOR** -

Oct 86. Midnight Music; (12"ep) **EATEN BY HER OWN DINNER / HAPPY THE GOLDEN PRINCE. / GROOVING ON AN INNER PLANE / MESSAGES OF DARK / THE ABANDONED BRAIN (all by "ROBYN HITCHCOCK")** -

Dec 87. Midnight Music; (lp) **LIVE AT PORTLAND ARMS** -

Sep 93. Rykodisc; (d-cd) **1976-81** -

Jul 94. Strange Roots; (cd) **THE KERSHAW SESSIONS** -

– (ROBYN HITCHCOCK) compilations, etc.

Mar 95. Rhino-Sequel; (cd) **RARE & UNRELEASED** -

SOFT CELL

Formed: Leeds, England . . . late 1979 by MARC ALMOND and DAVE BALL. With help from visual technician STEVEN GRIFFITHS, they embarked on studio and live work in 1980. After appearing on the now famous 'SOME BIZZARE ALBUM', with cut 'The Girl With The Patent Leather Face', they signed solo deal with said label. In 1981 their 2nd 45 for the label, 'TAINTED LOVE' made UK No.1 for 2 weeks. They continued to have string of hits up to their demise in 1984. MARC ALMOND, who had earlier splintered with his MARC & THE MAMBAS project, went solo and struggled to regain a top 20 placing, until early 1989, when GENE PITNEY provided old song and dual vox for the UK No.1 'SOMETHING'S GOTTEN HOLD OF MY HEART'. • **Style:** Northern electro-soul which fused sleazy sex with alternative disco rock-pop. ALMOND was always the brunt of slagging from the music press, for his extrovert homosexuality, which nearly made him retire for good during the mid-80's. • **Songwriters:** ALMOND lyrics / BALL music. SOFT CELL covered TAINTED LOVE (Gloria Jones; c.Ed Cobb) / WHERE DID OUR LOVE GO (Supremes) / HENDRIX MEDLEY (Jimi Hendrix). MARC & THE MAMBAS covered IF YOU GO AWAY + THE BULLS (Jacques Brel) / CAROLINE SAYS (Lou Reed) / TERRAPIN (Syd Barrett) / CATCH A FALLEN STAR (Perry Como). MARC ALMOND solo:- A WOMAN'S STORY (Cher) / A SALTY DOG (Procol Harum) / THE LITTLE WHITE CLOUD THAT CRIED (Johnnie Ray) / Album JACQUES (Jaques Brel). • **Trivia:** In 1983, DAVE BALL scored the music for Tennessee Williams' play 'Suddenly Last Summer'. In mid 1987, ALMOND guested and wrote on SALLY TIMMS' single 'This House Is A House Of Tears'.

Recommended: NON-STOP EROTIC CABARET (*9) / MEMORABILIA – THE SINGLES (*8) / MARC AND THE MAMBAS: – UNTITLED (*8) / MARC ALMOND:- THE SINGLES (1984-1987) (*7).

MARC ALMOND (b.PETER MARC ALMOND, 9 Jul'59, Southport) – vocals / **DAVE BALL** (b. 3 May'59, Blackpool, England) – keyboards, synthesizers, drum prog.

Big Frock not issued

1980. (7"ep) **MUTANT MOMENTS** -
– Potential / L.O.V.E. feelings / Metro MRX / Frustration.

Some Bizzare Sire

Mar 81. (7") **MEMORABILIA. / PERSUASION** -
(12"+=) – A man could get lost.

Jul 81. (7") **TAINTED LOVE. / WHERE DID OUR LOVE GO** 1 8 Jan 82
(12"+=) – ('A'version). *(UK re-iss.Jul82-hit 50, Jan85 – hit 43)*

Nov 81. (7") **BEDSITTER. / FACILITY GIRLS** 4
(12"+=) – ('A'extended version).

— guests **CINDY ECSTACY** – b.vox / **DAVE TOFANI** – sax / **JOHN GATHELL** – trumpet

Dec 81. (lp)(c) **NON-STOP EROTIC CABARET** 5 22
– Frustration / Tainted love / Seedy films / Youth / Sex dwarf / Entertain me / Chips on my shoulder / Bedsitter / Secret life / Say hello, wave goodbye. *(cd-iss.1988 & May90 & Mar92 with extra tracks)*

Jan 82. (7") **SAY HELLO, WAVE GOODBYE. / FUN CITY** 3
(12"+=) – ('A'instrumental).

May 82. (7")(12") **TORCH. / INSECURE ME** 2

— Duo carried on, without CINDY who later formed SIX SEE RED.

Jun 82. (m-lp)(c) **NON-STOP ECSTATIC DANCING** 6 57
– Memorabilia / Where did our love go / What! / A man could get lost / Chips on my shoulder * / Sex dwarf. *(US version repl.* w/)* – 'Insecure . . .me?') *(UK-cd-iss.Mar92)*

Aug 82. (7")(12") **WHAT!. / . . . SO** 3

Nov 82. (7") **WHERE THE HEART IS. / IT'S A MUG GAME** 21
(12"+=) – ('A'extended version).

Feb 83. (lp)(c) **THE ART OF FALLING APART** 5 84
– Forever the same / Where the heart is / Numbers / Heat / Kitchen sink drama / Baby doll / Loving you, hating me / The art of falling apart. *(12"ep w.a.+=)* **MARTIN. / HENDRIX MEDLEY: HEY JOE – PURPLE HAZE – VOODOO CHILE** *(re-iss.Nov87) (cd-iss.Mar92 with extra tracks)*

Feb 83. (7")(12") **NUMBERS. / BARRIERS** 25 -

Apr 83. (7") **HEAT. / IT'S A MUGS GAME** -

Sep 83. (7") **SOUL INSIDE. / YOU ONLY LIVE TWICE** 16
(12"+=) – Loving you, hating me / 007 theme.
(d7"+=) – Loving you, hating me / Her imagination.

Feb 84. (7") **DOWN IN THE SUBWAY. / DISEASE AND DESIRE** 24
(12"+=)(12"red+=)(12"gold+=) – Born to lose.

Mar 84. (lp)(c) **THIS LAST NIGHT . . . IN SODOM** 12
– Mr. Self destruct / Slave to this / Little rough rhinestone / Meet murder my angel / The best way to kill / L'Esqualita / Down in the subway / Surrender (to a stranger) / Soul inside / Where was your heart (when you needed it most). *(cd-iss.Aug84)*

— Waved goodbye, just prior to above album.

– compilations, others, etc. –

Dec 86. Some Bizzare/ US= Sire; (lp)(c)(cd) **SOFT CELL – THE SINGLES** 58

Mar 91. Mercury; (7") **SAY HELLO, WAVE GOODBYE '91. / MEMORABILIA (Grid remix)** 38
(12"+=)(cd-s+=) – ('A'-Mendelsohn extended remix).
(cd-s) – ('A'side) / Numbers / Torch (12"version).

May 91. Mercury; (7")(c-s) **TAINTED LOVE ('91 remix). / ('A'other remix)** 5
(12"+=)(cd-s+=) – Where did our love go.
(cd-s+=) – Where the heart is / Loving you, hating me.

May 91. Mercury; (cd)(c)(lp) **MEMORABILIA – THE SINGLES** 8
– Memorabilia '91 / Tainted love / Bedsitter / Torch / What was the matter with Rachmaninov? / Say hello wave goodbye '91 / Where the heart is / I feel love / Tears run rings / A lover spurned / Something's gotten hold of my heart. (cd+=) – (Soul inside / Say hello wave goodbye (12"mix) / Waifs and strays (Grid twilight mix).

Mar 94. Spectrum; (cd)(c) **DOWN IN THE SUBWAY** -

— In '82, ALMOND had already splintered with own band

MARC AND THE MAMBAS

with **ANNIE HOGAN** – piano / **TIM TAYLOR** – bass / **DAVE BALL** – multi instruments

Some Bizzare not issued

Mar 82. (12"m) **SLEAZE (TAKE IT, SHAKE IT). / FUN CITY / TAKING IT SHAKING IT** -

— guests on next 2 albums were **GENESIS P.ORRIDGE & MATT JOHNSON**

Sep 82. (lp)(c) **UNTITLED** 42 -
– Untitled / Empty eyes / Angels / Big Louise / Caroline says / Margaret / If you go away. *(free-12"ep.w.a+=)* – Terrapin / Twilights and lowlifes (street walking soundtrack) / Twilights and lowlifes.

Nov 82. (7") **BIG LOUISE. / EMPTY EYES** -
(12"+=) – The dirt behind the neon.

Jun 83. (7") **BLACK HEART. / YOUR AURA** 49 -
(12"+=) – Mamba.

Aug 83. (d-lp)(c) **TORMENT AND TOREROS** 28 -
– The animal in you / Narcissus / Gloomy Sunday / Vision / Your love is a lesson / The untouchable one / My little book of sorrows / In my room / First time / The bulls / Boss cat / Intro / Catch a fallen star / Beat out dat rhythm on a drum / A million manias / Torment / Black heart.

Nov 83. (12"m) **TORMENT / FIRST TIME. / YOU'LL NEVER SEE ME ON A SUNDAY / MAGAMILLIONMANIA-MULTIMANIAMIX** -

DAVE BALL

Some Bizzare / not issued

Nov 83. (lp)(c) **IN STRICT TEMPO** [ ] [-]
– Mirrors / Sincerity / Passion of a primitive / Strict tempo / Man in the man / Only time / Life of love / Rednecks / American stories.

— After SOFT CELL divided, BALL formed The OTHER PEOPLE in 1984, with wife GINI and ANDY ASTLE. They issued one single 'HAVE A NICE DAY' on 'Arcadia'. In 1986, he was credited on 'DECODER' album alongside GENESIS P. & THE THE. Early in 1988, his new trio ENGLISH BOY ON THE LOVE RANCH issued 7+12"; THE MAN IN YOUR LIFE on French label 'New Rose'. BALL joined The GRID in the late 80's, and had degree of success under this project and on its production hits.

MARC ALMOND

meantime had gone solo, augmented by **The WILLING SINNERS: ANNIE HOGAN** – piano / **BILLY McGEE** – bass / **RICHARD RILEY** – guitar / **STEPHEN HUMPHRIES** – drums / **MARTIN McCARRICK** – cello

Some Bizzare / Sire

May 84. (7")(10")(12") **THE BOY WHO CAME BACK. / JOEY DEMENTO** [52] [ ]
Sep 84. (7") **YOU HAVE. / SPLIT UP** [57] [ ]
(10"+=)(12"+=) – Black mountain blues.
Oct 84. (lp)(c)(cd) **VERMINE IN ERMINE** [36] [ ]
– Shining sinners / Hell was a city / You have / Crime sublime / Gutter hearts / Ugly head / The boy who came back / Solo adultos / Tenderness is a weakness. *(c+cd+=)* – Pink shack blues / Split lip / Joey Demento.
Nov 84. (7") **TENDERNESS IS A WEAKNESS. / LOVE FOR SALE** [ ] [ ]
(10"+=) – Blues the heel.

— In Apr 85, he teamed up with BRONSKI BEAT on Top 3 version of I FEEL LOVE. Two months later, he featured anonymously on 12" SKIN as BURMOE BROTHERS.

Aug 85. (7") **STORIES OF JOHNNY. / BLOND BOY** [23] [ ]
(12"+=) – Take my heart.
(d7"++=) – Stories of Johnny (WESTMINSTER CITY SCHOOL CHOIR)
Sep 85. (lp)(c)(cd) **STORIES OF JOHNNY** [22] [ ]
– Traumas, traumas, traumas / Stories of Johnny / The house is haunted (by the echoes of your last goodbye) / Love letter / The flesh is willing / Always / Contempt / I who never / My candle burns / Love and little white lies. *(c+cd+=)* – Take my heart / Blond boy / ('A'version with WESTMINSTER C.S.)
Oct 85. (7")(12") **LOVE LETTER. / ('A'version)** [68] [ ]
Jan 86. (7") **THE HOUSE IS HAUNTED (BY THE ECHO OF YOUR LAST GOODBYE). / BROKEN BARRICADES** [55] [ ]
(12"+=)(d7"+=) – Burning boats / ('A'version).
May 86. (7") **A WOMAN'S STORY. / FOR ONE MOMENT** [41] [ ]
(10"pic-d-ep+=)(12"ep+=)(c-ep+=) – SOME SONGS TO TAKE TO THE TOMB EP – The heel / A salty dog / The plague / The little white cloud that cried / Just good friends.
Oct 86. (7") **RUBY RED. / I'M SICK OF YOU TASTING OF SOMEONE ELSE** [47] [ ]
(12"+=) – Anarcoma / Broken-hearted and beautiful / Jackal jackal.
(12") – Ruby red (extended dance mix). / Ruby red (instrumental)
Jan 87. (7") **MELANCHOLY ROSE. / GYP THE BLOOD** [71] [ ]
(12"+=) – World full of people / Black lullaby.
(d7+=) – Surabaya Johnny / Pirate Jenny.
Mar 87. (lp)(c)(cd) **MOTHER FIST AND HER FIVE DAUGHTERS** [40] [ ]
– Mother Fist / There is a bed / Saint Judy / The room below / Angel in her kiss / The hustler / Melancholy rose / Mr. Sad / The sea says / Champ / Ruby red / The river.
Mar 87. (7") **MOTHER FIST. / TWO SAILORS ON THE BEACH** [ ] [ ]
(12"+=) – The hustler.
Nov 87. (lp)(c)(cd) **THE SINGLES 1984-1987** (compilation) [ ] [ ]
– The boy who came back / You have / Tenderness is a weakness / Stories of Johnny / Love letters / The house is haunted / A woman's story / Ruby red / Melancholy rose / Mother Fist.

— He was now backed by LA MAGIA. (aka HOGAN, HUMPHRIES + McGEE)

Parlophone / Capitol

Aug 88. (7") **TEARS RUN RINGS. / EVERYTHING I WANT TO BE** [26] [67]
(12"+=)(cd-s+=) – ('A'extended).
(12"+=) – ('A'&'B'-different mixes).
Sep 88. (lp)(c)(cd) **THE STARS WE ARE** [41] [ ]
– The stars we are / These my dreams are true / Bitter sweet / Only the moment / Your kisses burn / Tears run rings / Something's gotten hold of my heart / The sensualist / She took my soul in Instanbul. *(c+cd+=)* – The frost comes tomorrow / Kept boy.
Oct 88. (7")(7"clear) **BITTER SWEET. / KING OF THE FOOLS** [40] [ ]
(12"+=)(cd-s+=) – Tears run rings (mix).
Jan 89. (7") **SOMETHING'S GOTTEN HOLD OF MY HEART. ("MARC ALMOND & GENE PITNEY") / ('A'-solo version)** [1] [ ]
(12"+=)(cd-s+=) – The frost comes tomorrow.
Mar 89. (7")(7"clear) **ONLY THE MOMENT. / REAL EVIL** [47] [ ]
(12"+=) – ('A'extended).
(cd-s+=) – She took my soul in Instanbul.
Feb 90. (7") **A LOVER SPURNED. / EXOTICA ROSE** [29] [ ]
(12"+=)(cd-s+=)(10"square-pic-d+=) – ('A'version).
May 90. (7")(c-s) **THE DESPERATE HOURS. / THE GAMBLER** [45] [ ]
(12"+=)(12"clear-pic-d+=)(cd-s+=)(pic-cd-s+=) – ('A'extended mix).
Jun 90. (cd)(c)(lp) **ENCHANTED** [52] [ ]
– Madame de la luna / Waifs and strays / The desperate hours / Toreador in the rain / Widow weeds / A lover spurned / Death's diary / Sea still sings / Carnival of life / Orpheus in red velvet.
Oct 90. (7") **WAIFS AND STRAYS. / OLD JACK'S CHARM** [ ] [ ]
(12"+=)/ /(cd-s+=) – ('A'mix)./ / City of nights.

— Wrote w/**DAVE BALL + NORRIS** (The GRID)

W.E.A. / W.E.A.

Sep 91. (7")(c-s) **JACKY. / DEEP NIGHT** [17] [ ]
(12"+=)/ /(cd-s+=) – ('A' alpine dub)./ / A love outgrown.
(12") – ('A'side) / ('A' Youth remixes).
Oct 91. (cd)(c)(lp) **TENEMENT SYMPHONY** [48] [ ]
– Meet me in my dream / Beautiful brutal thing / I've never seen your face / Vaudeville and burlesque / Champagne / Tenement symphony (i) Prelude (ii) Jacky (iii) What is love? (iv) Trois Chansons de Bilitis – extract (v) The days of Pearly Spencer (vi) My hand over my heart. *(re-entered UK chart 39; Apr92) (re-iss.cd Feb95)*
Dec 91. (7") **MY HAND OVER MY HEART. / DEADLY SERENADE** [33] [ ]
(12"+=)(cd-s+=) – Money for love (2 versions).
Apr 92. (7")(c-s) **THE DAYS OF PEARLY SPENCER. / BRUISES** [4] [ ]
(12"+=)(cd-s+=) – Dancing in a golden cage / Extract from 'Trois Chansons'.

— with **DAVE CLAYTON** – keyboards, musical director / **MARTIN WATKINS** – piano / **ANDY HAMILTON** – saxophone / **MICHELE DREES** – drums, perc. / **CRIS BONACCI** – guitars / **SHIRLEY LEWIS, ANNA ROSS & AILEEN McLAUGHLIN** – b.vox / **TENEMENT SYMPHONY ORCH.**

Mar 93. (7")(c-s) **WHAT MAKES A MAN A MAN (live). / TORCH (live)** [60] [ ]
(cd-s+=) – Stars we are (live) / Tainted love (live).
(cd-s) – ('A'side) / Vision (live) / Only the moment (live).
Apr 93. (cd)(c)(lp) **12 YEARS OF TEARS – LIVE AT THE ROYAL ALBERT HALL (live)** [ ] [ ]
– Tears run rings / Champagne / Bedsitter / Mr.Sad / There is a bed / Youth / If you go away / Jacky / Desperate hours / Waifs and strays / Something's gotten hold of my heart / What makes a man a man / Tainted love / Say hello wave goodbye.
Sep 93. (cd)(c)(lp) **ABSINTHE** [ ] [ ]
– Undress me / Abel and Cain / Lost Paradise / Secret child / Rue Des Blancs Manteaux / The slave / Remorse of the dead / Incestuous love / A man / My little lovers / In your bed / Yesterday when I was young.

Mercury / Mercury

Apr 95. (c-s) **ADORNED AND EXPLORED / LOVELESS WORLD** [25] [ ]
(cd-s+=) – The user.
Jul 95. (c-s) **THE IDOL / ('A'-Tin Tin Out mix)** [44] [ ]
(cd-s+=) – ('A'-Idolized mix) / ('A'-Tenage dream mix).
(cd-s) – ('A'-part 1) / Law of the night / Adorned and explored / Bedsitter.
Nov 95. (c-ep)(cd-ep) **CHILD STAR EP** [41] [ ]
– Child star / The edge of heartbreak / Christmas in Vegas / My guardian angel.
(cd-ep) – ('A'side) / We need jealousy (live) / The idol (live) / Out there (live).

– more (MARC ALMOND) compilations, etc. –

Dec 89. Some Bizzare; (lp)(c)(cd) **JAQUES** (most rec.1986) [ ] [-]
– The Devil (okay) / If you need / The lockman / We must look / Alone / I'm coming / Litany for a return / If you go away / The town fell asleep / The bulls / (Never to be) Next / My death.

— (above a tribute to Belguin singer JAQUES BREL)

Sep 92. Virgin; (cd)(c)(d-lp) **A VIRGIN'S TALE VOL.1 (1985-1988)** [ ] [-]
Sep 92. Virgin; (cd)(c)(d-lp) **A VIRGIN'S TALE VOL.2 (1988-1991)** [ ] [ ]
(re-iss.both above Nov92 as d-cd)

SOFT MACHINE

Formed: Canterbury, England ... 1966 by ex-WILDE FLOWERS members WYATT and AYERS, who met up with Australian beatnik DAEVID ALLEN and former Oxford University student MIKE RATLEDGE. The others members of The WILDE FLOWERS (PYE HASTINGS & RICHARD COUGHLAN), went on to form CARAVAN. SOFT MACHINE phoned up novelist William Burroughs, to ask his permission on use of group name. Early 1967, they were signed to 'Polydor' by CHAS CHANDLER, who employed the services of JIMI HENDRIX on the B-side of debut single 'LOVE MAKES SWEET MUSIC'. The following two years saw them go to France, but return without ALLEN, who was refused re-entry. He stayed in Paris and formed GONG, while The SOFTS went to New York to support JIMI HENDRIX EXPERIENCE and signed a contract for 'Probe'. Their debut eponymous album late '68, was produced by CHANDLER and TOM WILSON, and only issued in the US. More personnel turmoil was created when AYERS quit to live and write in Ibiza. After another lp, they signed to 'CBS' in 1970, and they broke into the UK Top 20 with double album 'THIRD'. • **Style:** After initial pop 45, they spread themselves into avant-garde experimental jazz rock. • **Songwriters:** Either AYERS (on debut lp only), WYATT (first 4 albums), or RATLEDGE and group. • **Trivia:** A John Peel session was recorded on 21 Jun'69 with best 7 piece line-up. They were the first rock act to play the normally orchestrated 'Proms' at London's Albert Hall 1970. Non-originals RATLEDGE and JENKINS were ADIEMUS who had a UK Top 50 hit with 'ADIEMUS' single (theme from TV ad for Delta Airlines) which featured vocalist MIRIAM STOCKLEY.

Recommended: THIRD (*7) / THE PEEL SESSIONS (*7).

MIKE RATLEDGE – keyboards / **DAEVID ALLEN** – guitar / **KEVIN AYERS** – bass, vocals (ex-WILDE FLOWERS) / **ROBERT WYATT** (b.ROBERT ELLIDGE) – drums, vocals (ex-WILDE FLOWERS) / Note:- Other original guitarist LARRY NOLAN left before debut 45.

Polydor / not issued

Feb 67. (7") **LOVE MAKES SWEET MUSIC. / FEELIN' REELIN' SQUEELIN'** [ ] [-]

— trimmed to a trio, when DAEVID ALLEN went to France to form GONG. He was deputised on tour only by ANDY SUMMERS. First 2 albums guest **BRIAN HOPPER** – saxophone (ex-WILDE FLOWERS)

Probe Probe

Dec 68. (lp) **SOFT MACHINE** [-] [ ]
– Hope for happiness / Joy for a toy / Hope for happiness (reprise) / Why am I so short? / So boot it at all / A certain kind / Save yourself / Priscilla / Lullabye letter / We did it again / Plus belle qu'une poubelle / Why are we sleeping / Box 25-4 LID. *(UK-iss.+c.Mar87 on 'Big Beat'; see next for cd)*

— **HUGH HOPPER** – bass (ex-WILDE FLOWERS) repl. AYERS who went solo

Apr 69. (lp) **SOFT MACHINE VOL.2** [ ] [ ]
– Pataphysical introduction (part I) / A concise British alphabet (part I) / Hibou, Anemone and bear / A concise British alphabet (part II) / Hulloder / Dada was here / Thank you Pierrot Lunaire / Have you ever been green? / Pataphysical introduction (part II) / Out of tunes / As long as he lies perfectly still / Dedicated to you but you weren't listening / Fire engine passing with bells clanging / Pig / Orange skin food / A door opens and closes / 10.30 returns to the bedroom. *(re-iss.Oct74 as d-lp on 'A.B.C.' with debut lp) (d-cd with both iss.1995 on 'Big Beat')*

— added **ELTON DEAN** – saxophone (ex-BLUESOLOGY) / **LYN DOBSON** – flute, sax / **NICK EVANS** – trombone + **MARK CHARIG** – cornet (ex-BLUESOLOGY) both left before 3rd album. Added guests **JIMMY HASTINGS** – wind / **A. B. SPALL** – violin

C.B.S. Columbia

Jun 70. (d-lp)(d-c) **THIRD** [18]
– Facelift / Slightly all the time / Moon in June / Out-Bloody-Rageous. *(re-iss.Jun88 on 'Decal') (cd-iss.Mar93 on 'B.G.O.')*

— Now quartet, when LYN departed. Guests **HASTINGS + ALAN SKIDMORE** – sax

Feb 71. (lp)(c) **FOURTH** [32] [ ]
– Teeth / Kings and queens / Fletcher's blemish / Virtually (parts 1-4). *(cd-iss.Apr93 on 'Sony Europe') (re-iss.cd Oct95 on 'One Way')*

— **JOHN MARSHALL + PHIL HOWARD** – drums (shared) repl. WYATT who went solo. **ELTON DEAN** added electric piano + **ROY BABBINGTON** – double bass (guested 3)

Jun 72. (lp)(c) **SOFT MACHINE FIFTH** [ ] [ ]
– All white / Drop / Mc / As if / LBO / Pigling bland / Bone. *(re-iss.1979 on 'CBS-Embassy') (cd-iss.Apr93 on 'Sony Europe') (re-iss.Sep95 on 'One Way')*

— **KARL JENKINS** – piano, saxophone repl. DEAN who stayed with JUST US (above newcomer alongside **RATLEDGE, HOPPER + MARSHALL**)

Feb 73. (d-lp)(d-c) **SIX** (live, except for last 4) [ ] [ ]
– Fanfare / All white / Between / Riff / 37 and a half / Geseolveut / E.P.V. / Lefty / Stumble / 5 from 13 (for Phil Seaman with love and thanks) / Riff II / The soft weed factor / Stanley stamps gibbon album (for B.O.) / Chloe and the pirates / 1983. *(cd-iss.Apr93 on 'Sony Europe')*

— **ROY BABBINGTON** – bass (was guest) repl. HUGH HOPPER who went solo

Oct 73. (lp)(c) **SEVEN** [ ] [ ]
– Nettle bed / Carolyn / Day's eye / Bone fire / Tarabos / D.I.S. / Snodland / Penny hitch / Block / Down the road / The German lesson / The French lesson. *(cd-iss.Apr93 on 'Sony Europe')*

— added **ALAN HOLDSWORTH** – guitar

Harvest Harvest

Apr 75. (lp)(c) **BUNDLES** [ ] [ ]
– Hazard profile (parts 1-5) / Gone sailing / Bundles / Land of the bag snake / The man who waved at trains / Peff / Four gongs two drums / The floating world.

— With last original RATLEDGE going solo and HOLDWORTH joining GONG, the remainder (**BABBINGTON, JENKINS + MARSHALL**) were joined by **ALAN WAKEMAN** – saxophone + **JOHN ETHERIDGE** – guitar

Jun 76. (lp)(c) **SOFTS** [ ] [ ]
– Aubade / The tale of Taliesyn / Bab ban Caliban / Song of Aeolus / Out of season / Second bundle / Kayoo / The Camden tandem / Nexus / One over the eight / Etika.

— **RIC SAUNDERS** – violin + **STEVE COOKE** – bass repl. WAKEMAN + BABBINGTON

Mar 78. (lp)(c) **ALIVE AND WELL IN PARIS** [ ] [ ]
– White kite / Eos / Odds, bullets and blades (part 1 & 2) / Song of the sunbird / Puffin, huffin' / Number three / The nodder / Surrounder silence / Soft space.

Apr 78. (7") **SOFT SPACE. / (part 2)** [ ] [-]

— Folded 1979, but reformed for one-off studio outing below. Musicians:- **ETHRIDGE, MARSHALL, HOLDSWORTH** plus sessioners **DICK MORRISSEY** – saxophone / **ALAN PARKER** – guitar / **JOHN TAYLOR** – keyboards / **RAY WARLEIGH** – flute / **JACK BRUCE** – bass

E.M.I. E.M.I. ?

Mar 81. (lp)(c) **THE LAND OF COCKAYNE** [ ] [ ]
– Over 'n' above / Lotus groves / Isle of the blessed / Panoramania / Behind the crystal curtain / Palace of glass / Hot biscuit slim / (Black) Velvet mountain / Sly monkey / A lot of what you fancy.

— finally disbanded after above.

– compilations, others, etc. –

Jan 77. Charly; (lp) **AT THE BEGINNING** [ ] [-]
(re-iss.Feb81 + Mar83)

Mar 77. Harvest; (t-lp) **TRIPLE ECHO** [ ] [-]

Sep 87. Decal; (lp)(c) **JET PROPELLED PHOTOGRAPHS** [ ] [-]
– That's how much I need you now / Save yourself / I should've / Jet propelled photographs / When I don't want you / Memories / You don't remember / She's gone / I'd rather be with you. *(re-iss.Jul88) (cd-iss.Sep95 on 'Spalax')*

Aug 88. Reckless; (lp) **LIVE AT THE PROMS (live)** [ ] [-]

Sep 90. Strange Fruit; (cd)(d-lp) **THE PEEL SESSIONS** [ ] [-]

Dec 90. Castle; (cd)(c)(d-lp) **THE COLLECTION (75-78)** [ ] [-]

May 91. Elite; (cd)(c) **AS IF . . .** [ ] [-]
(cd-iss.Sep93)

Aug 92. See For Miles; (3xcd-box) **SOFTS / ALIVE & WELL / BUNDLES** [ ] [-]

Apr 93. Windsong; (cd) **BBC RADIO 1 LIVE IN CONCERT (live)** [ ] [-]

Jun 94. Windsong; (cd) **BBC RADIO 1 LIVE IN CONCERT (live)** [ ] [-]

Nov 94. Voiceprint; (cd) **RUBBER RIFF** [ ] [-]
– Crunch / Ravan / Joubles / A little fighting music / Hi power / Little Miss B / Splot / Rubber riff / Sam's short shuffle / Melina / City steps / Gentle turn – Porky – Travelogue.

Jan 95. Movieplay Gold; (cd) **LIVE AT THE PARADISO** [ ] [-]
(re-iss.Oct95 on 'Voiceprint')

Jun 95. C5; (cd) **THE BEST OF SOFT MACHINE: THE HARVEST YEARS** [ ] [-]

Nov 95. One Way; (d-cd) **LIVE IN FRANCE (live)** [ ] [-]

Jimmy SOMERVILLE (see under ⇒ COMMUNARDS)

SONIC BOOM (see under ⇒ SPACEMEN 3)

SONIC YOUTH

Formed: New York, USA . . . early 1981 by THURSTON, LEE and KIM. After numerous releases on various US indie labels (noteably Glenn Branca's 'Neutral' records), they signed to 'Blast First'. Finally secured a major deal with 'DGC' (David Geffen Company) in the early 90's, and smashed into the UK Top 40 with album 'GOO'. • **Style:** Underground experimental punk outfit, similar in ideals to VELVET UNDERGROUND, but fused with garage. • **Songwriters:** MOORE / RANALDO / GORDON compositions, except I WANNA BE YOUR DOG (Stooges) / TICKET TO RIDE (Beatles) / BEAT ON THE BRAT (Ramones) / TOUCH ME, I'M SICK (Mudhoney) / COMPUTER AGE (Neil Young). Their off-shoot CICCONE YOUTH covered INTO THE GROOVE (Madonna) / ADDICTED TO LOVE (Robert Palmer) / IS IT MY BODY (Alice Cooper) / PERSONALITY CRISIS (New York Dolls) / CA PLANE POUR MOI (Plastic Bertrand). • **Trivia:** Early in 1989, they were featured on hour-long special TV documentary for Melvyn Bragg's 'The South Bank Show'.

Recommended: BAD MOON RISING (*8) / EVOL (*8) / SISTER (*9) / DAYDREAM NATION (*9) / GOO (*9) / DIRTY (*8) / WASHING MACHINE (*8).

THURSTON MOORE – guitar / **KIM GORDON** – bass, vocals / **LEE RANALDO** – guitar, vocals repl. ANN DEMARIS / **RICHARD EDSON** – drums repl. DAVE KEAY

not issued Neutral

Mar 82. (m-lp) **SONIC YOUTH (live)** [-] [ ]
– The burning spear / I dreamt I dreamed / She's not alone / I don't want to push it / The good and the bad. *(US + UK re-iss.+cd.Oct87 on 'S.S.T.')*

— **JIM SCLAVUNOS** – drums repl. EDSON

Feb 83. (lp) **CONFUSION IS SEX** [-] [ ]
– Inhuman / The world looks red / Confusion is next / Making the nature scene / Lee is free / (She's in a) Bad mood / Protect me you / Freezer burn / I wanna be your dog / Shaking Hell. *(US + UK re-iss.+cd.Oct87 on 'S.S.T.')*

— **BOB BERT** – drums repl. SCLAVUNOS (still featured on 2 tracks)

not issued Zensor

Oct 83. (m-lp) **KILL YR. IDOLS** [-] [ ] Germ'y
– Protect me you / Shaking Hell / Kill yr. idols / Brother James / Early American.

not issued Ecstatic..

1984. (c) **SONIC DEATH (SONIC YOUTH LIVE)** [-] [ ]
– Sonic Death Side 1 / Sonic Death Side 2
(cd-iss.Jul88 on 'Blast First')

Blast First Iridescene

Mar 85. (12"ep) **DEATH VALLEY '69. ("SONIC YOUTH & LYDIA LUNCH") / I DREAMT I DREAMED / INHUMAN / BROTHER JAMES / SATAN IS BORING** [ ] [ ] Dec 84

Mar 85. (lp)(c) **BAD MOON RISING** [ ] [ ]
– Intro / Brave men rule / Society is a hole / I love her all the time / Ghost bitch / I'm insane / Justice is might / Death valley '69. *(cd-iss.Nov86 +=)* – Satan is boring / Flower / Halloween.

Jan 86. (7")(12"yellow) **HALLOWEEN. / FLOWER** [-] [ ]
(above single issued US on 'Homestead')

Jan 86. (7") **FLOWER. / REWOLF** [ ] [-]
(12") – ('A'side) / Satan is boring (live).

May 86. (12") **HALLOWEEN II. / ('A'version)** [ ] [-]

— **STEVE SHELLEY** – drums repl. BOB BERT who joined PUSSY GALORE

May 86. (lp)(c) **EVOL** [ ] [ ]
– Green light / Star power / Secret girl / Tom Violence / Death to our friends / Shadow of a doubt / Marilyn Moore / In the kingdom / Madonna, Sean and me. *(cd-iss.Nov86, (+=)* – Bubblegum.

Jul 86. (7")(12") **STAR POWER. / BUBBLEGUM** [ ] [ ]

Nov 86. (7")(12") **INTO THE GROOVE(Y). / TUFF TITTY RAP** [ ] [ ]

— (above single as **"CICCONE YOUTH"**, adding **MIKE WATT** – bass (of FIREHOSE))

Jun 87. (lp)(c)(cd) **SISTER** [ ] [ ]
– White cross / (I got a) Catholic block / Hot wire my heart / Tuff gnarl / Kotton crown / Schizophrenia / Beauty lies in the eye / Stereo sanctity / Pipeline – killtime / PCH. *(cd+=)* – Master-Dik (original).

Jan 88. (12"ep) **MASTER-DIK.-** [ ] [ ]
– Beat on the brat / Under the influence of The Jesus And Mary Chain: Ticket to ride.

Oct 88. (d-lp)(c)(cd) **DAYDREAM NATION** [99]
– Teenage riot / Silver rocket / The sprawl / 'Cross the breeze / Eric's trip / Total trash / Hey Joni / Providence / Candle? / Rain king / Kissability / Trilogy: The wonder – Hyperstation – Eliminator Jr.

— Late in '88, KIM teamed up with LYDIA LUNCH and SADIE MAE to form one-off project HARRY CREWS. Their live appearences were issued in Apr 90 as 'NAKED IN GARDEN HILLS' for 'Big Cat' UK + 'Widowspeak' US.

Jan 89. (lp)(c)(cd) **THE WHITEY ALBUM (as "CICCONE YOUTH")** [63] [ ]
– Needle-gun (silence) / G-force / Platoon II / Macbeth / Me & Jill / Hendrix Cosby / Burnin' up / Hi! everybody / Children of Satan / Third fig / Two cool rock chicks / Listening to Neu! / Addicted to love / Moby-Dik / March of the Ciccone robots / Making the nature scene / Tuff titty rap / Into the groovey.

Fierce Fierce

Feb 89. (12") **TOUCH ME, I'M SICK. / ('B'by 'Mudhoney')** [ ] [ ]

W.E.A. D.G.C.

Jun 90. (cd)(c)(lp) **GOO** [32] [96]
– Dirty boots / Tunic (song for Karen) / Mary-Christ / Kool thing / Mote / My friend Goo / Disappearer / Mildred Pierce / Cinderella's big score / Scooter + Jinx / Titanium expose. *(re-iss.Jun91 & Oct95 cd)*

Sep 90. (7")(c-s) **KOOL THING. / THAT'S ALL I KNOW (RIGHT NOW)** [ ] [ ]
(12"+=) – ('A'demo version).
(cd-s++=) – Dirty boots (rock & roll Heaven version).

—— In Autumn '90, THURSTON was part of 'Rough Trade' supergroup VELVET MONKEYS.

D.G.C. D.G.C.

Apr 91. (cd)(c)(m-lp) **DIRTY BOOTS** (all live, except the title track) [69] [ ]
– Dirty boots / The bedroom / Cinderella's big scene / Eric's trip / White kross .

—— Early in '92, THURSTON and STEVE also teamed up with RICHARD HELL's off-shoot group The DIM STARS.

Jun 92. (7") **100%. / CREME BRULEE** [28] [ ]
(12"+=)(10"orange+=) – Hendrix.
(cd-s++=) – Genetic.

Jul 92. (cd)(c)(d-lp) **DIRTY** [6] [83]
– 100% / Swimsuit issue / Theresa's sound-world / Drunken butterfly / Shoot / Wish fulfillment / Sugar Kane / Orange rolls, angel's spit / Youth against fascism / Nic fit / On the strip / Chapel Hill / JC / Purr / Creme brulee. *(d-lp+=)* – Stalker. *(re-iss.cd Oct95)*

Geffen Geffen

Oct 92. (7") **YOUTH AGAINST FASCISM. / PURR** [52] [ ]
(10"+=) – ('A'version).
(cd-s++=) – The destroyed room (radio version)

Apr 93. (7")(c-s) **SUGAR KANE. / THE END OF THE END OF THE UGLY** [26] [ ]
(10"blue+=)/ /(cd-s+=) – Is it my body./ / Personality crisis.

Apr 94. (c-s)(10"silver)(cd-s) **BULL IN THE HEATHER. / RAZORBLADE** [24] [ ]

May 94. (cd)(c)(blue-lp) **EXPERIMENTAL JET SET, TRASH AND NO STAR** [10] [34]
– Winner's blues / Bull in the heather / Starfield road / Skink / Self-obsessed and sexxee / Bone / Androgynous mind / Quest for the cup / Waist / Doctor's orders / Tokyo eye / In the mind of the bourgeois reader / Sweet shine.

—— In Sep 94; 'A&M' released CARPENTERS tribute album, which contained their single 'SUPERSTAR'. It was combined with also another cover from REDD KROSS, and reached UK No.45.

—— early '95, FREE KITTEN (aka KIM, JULIE CAFRITZ, MARK IBOLD + YOSHIMI) released album 'NICE ASS'.

Oct 95. (cd)(c)(d-lp) **WASHING MACHINE** [39] [58]
– Becuz / Junkie's promise / Saucer-like / Washing machine / Unwind / Little trouble girl / No queen blues / Panty lines / Becuz coda / Skip tracer / The diamond sea.

– compilations, others, etc. –

Feb 88. Fierce; (7")(d7"etched-one-sided) **STICK ME DONNA MAGICK MOMMA. / MAKING THE NATURE SCENE (live)** [ ] [ ]

Feb 92. Sonic Death; (cd) **GOO DEMOS LIVE AT THE CONTINENTAL CLUB (live)** [ ] [ ]

Mar 95. Blast First; (cd)(c) **CONFUSION IS SEX / KILL YR IDOLS** [ ] [-]

Mar 95. Warners; (cd) **MADE IN THE U.S.A.** [ ] [-]

Apr 95. Blast First; (cd) **SCREAMING FIELDS OF SONIC LOVE** [ ] [ ]

LEE RANALDO

Blast First Blast First

Jul 87. (m-lp)(c) **FROM HERE ⇒ ETERNITY** [ ] [ ]
– Time stands still / Destruction site / Ouroboron / Slodrown / New groove loop / Florida flower / Hard left / Fuzz-locusts / To Mary / Lathe speaks / The resolution / King's egg.

THURSTON MOORE

May 95. (cd)(c)(d-lp;colrd 3-sides) **PSYCHIC HEARTS** [ ] [ ]
– Queen bee and her pals / Ono soul / Psychic hearts / Pretty bad / Patti Smith math scratch / Blues from beyond the grave / See-through play-mate / Hang out / Feathers / Tranquilizor / Staring statues / Cindy (rotten tanx) / Cherry's blues / Female cop / Elegy for all dead rock stars.

SONNY & CHER (see under ⇒ CHER)

SOUL ASYLUM

Formed: Minneapolis, USA . . . 1983 by MURPHY and PIRNER. After releases on 'What Goes On', they signed to major 'A&M' in 1987. After 5 years on the label, they looked set to break through with album 'GRAVE DANCERS UNION'. • **Style:** Shifted from hard-core HUSKER DU metal to more easily accessible rock with vox similiar to TOM PETTY. • **Songwriters:** Mostly PIRNER except covers; BARSTOOL BLUES (Neil Young) / SEXUAL HEALING (Marvin Gaye) / ARE FRIENDS ELECTRIC (Tubeway Army). • **Trivia:** DAVE PIRNER is now the beau of actress WYNONA RYDER.

Recommended: HANG TIME (*6) / GRAVE DANCERS UNION (*7).

DAVE PIRNER – vocals, guitar / **DAN MURPHY** – guitar, vocals / **KURT MUELLER**– bass / **GRANT YOUNG** – drums, percussion

not issued Twin Tone

Aug 84. (m-lp) **SAY WHAT YOU WILL** [-] [ ]
– Long day / Voodoo doll / Money talks / Stranger / Sick of that song / Walking / Happy / Black and blue / Religiavision. *(US re-iss.May89, +=* Dragging me down / Do you know / Spacehead / Broken glass / Masquerade.) *(UK-iss.cd.Mar93 as 'SAY WHAT YOU WILL CLARENCE . . . KARL SOLD THE TRUCK' on 'Roadrunner') (cd-iss.Mar95)*

Rough Trade Roadrunner

Sep 86. (lp) **MADE TO BE BROKEN** [ ] [ ]
– Tied to the tracks / Ship of fools / Can't go back / Another world another day / Made to be broken / Never really been / Whoa / New feelings / Growing pain / Lone rider / Ain't that tough / Don't it (make your troubles seem small). *(cd-iss.Mar93 on 'Roadrunner'+=)*– Long way home) (cd-iss.Mar95)

Sep 86. (7") **TIED TO THE TRACKS. / ?** [-] [ ]

What Goes On Roadrunner

Mar 88. (lp) **WHILE YOU WERE OUT** [ ] [ ] 1987
– Freaks / Carry on / No man's land / Crashing down / The judge / Sun don't shine / Closer to the stars / Never too soon / Miracles mile / Lap of luxury / Passing sad daydream. *(cd-iss.Mar93 on 'Roadrunner') (cd-iss.Mar95)*

May 88. (m-lp) **CLAM DIP AND OTHER DELIGHTS** [ ] [ ] 1987
– Just plain evil / Chains / Secret no more / Artificial heart / P-9 / Take it to root. *(cd-iss.Mar93 on 'Roadrunner') (cd-iss.Mar95)*

—— split but re-formed adding guest **CADD** – sax, piano.

A & M A & M

Jun 88. (7")(12") **SOMETIME TO RETURN. / PUT THE BOOT IN** [ ] [ ]
(re-iss.Jun91, 12"+= Marionette)

Jun 88. (lp)(c)(cd) **HANG TIME** [ ] [ ]
– Down on up to me / Little too clean / Sometime to return / Cartoon / Beggars and choosers / Endless farewell / Standing in the doorway / Marionette / Ode / Jack of all trades / Twiddly dee / Heavy rotation. *(re-iss.cd+c.Sep93)*

Aug 88. (7") **CARTOON. / TWIDDLY DEE** [ ] [ ]
(12"+=) – Standing in the doorway.

Sep 90. (cd)(c)(lp) **SOUL ASYLUM & THE HORSE THEY RODE IN ON** [ ] [ ] 1988
– Spinnin' / Bitter pill / Veil of tears / Nice guys (don't get paid) / Something out of nothing / Gullible's travels / Brand new shine / Grounded / Don't be on your way / We / All the king's friends. *(re-iss.cd+c.Sep93)*

Jan 91. (7") **EASY STREET. / SPINNING** [ ] [ ]
(12"+=) – All the king's friends / Gullible's travels.

Columbia Columbia

Oct 92. (cd)(c)(lp) **GRAVE DANCERS UNION** [ ] [11]
– Somebody to shove / Black gold / Runaway train / Keep it up / Homesick / Get on out / New world / April fool / Without a trace / Growing into you / 99% / The Sun maid. *(re-dist.Jul93, hit UK No.52) (UK No.27 early '94)*

Mar 93. (10"ep)(cd-ep) **BLACK GOLD / BLACK GOLD (live). / THE BREAK / 99%** [ ] [ ]

Jun 93. (c-s) **RUNAWAY TRAIN. / BLACK GOLD (live)** [37] [5]
(12"+=) – By the way / Never really been (live).
(cd-s++=) – Everybody loves a winner. (- Black Gold).
(above single returned into UK chart Nov93 to hit No.7)

Aug 93. (12"ep)(cd-ep) **SOMEBODY TO SHOVE / SOMEBODY TO SHOVE (live). / RUNAWAY TRAIN (live) / BY THE WAY (demo)** [34] [ ]
(c-ep) – ('A'side) / Black gold (live) / Runaway train (live).

Jan 94. (7")(c-s) **BLACK GOLD. / SOMEBODY TO SHOVE** [26] [ ]
(cd-s+=) – Closer to the stairs / Square root.
(cd-s+=) – Runaway train (live).

Mar 94. (7")(c-s) **SOMEBODY TO SHOVE. / BY THE WAY** [32] [ ]
(cd-s+=) – Stranger (unplugged) / Without a trace (live).
(cd-s++=) – ('A'mix).

Jun 95. (cd)(c) **LET YOUR DIM LIGHT SHINE** [22] [6]
– Misery / Shut down / To my own devices / Hopes up / Promises broken / Bittersweetheart / String of pearls / Crawl / Caged rat / Eyes of a child / Just like anyone / Tell me when / Nothing to write home about / I did my best.

Jul 95. (7"white)(c-s) **MISERY. / STRING OF PEARLS** [30] [20] Jun95
(cd-s+=) – Hope (demo) / I did my best.

Nov 95. (c-s) **JUST LIKE ANYONE / DO ANYTHING YOU WANNA DO (live)** [52] [ ]
(cd-s+=) – Get on out (live).
(cd-s) – ('A'side) / You'll live forever (demo) / Fearless leader (demo).

SOUNDGARDEN

Formed: Seattle, Washington, USA . . . 1984 by CORNELL, THAYIL and YAMAMOTO. After recruiting CAMERON in '86 and enjoying periods on US labels 'Sub Pop' & 'SST', they signed to 'A&M' in 1989. Their classic second album for the label 'BADMOTORFINGER' in 1991, cracked open the US charts and soon made inroads into UK ears. • **Style:** Hardcore-metal punk influenced by LED ZEPPELIN, BLACK SABBATH and KILLING JOKE, but inspired by a new metal generation of NIRVANA and the likes. • **Songwriters:** Most by CORNELL and group permutations. Covered SWALLOW MY PRIDE (Ramones) / FOPP (Ohio Players) / INTO THE VOID tune only (Black Sabbath) / BIG BOTTOM (Spinal Tap) / EARACHE MY EYE (Cheech & Chong) / I CAN'T GIVE YOU ANYTHING (Ramones) / HOMOCIDAL SUICIDE (Budgie) / I DON'T CARE ABOUT YOU (Fear) / CAN YOU SEE ME (Jimi Hendrix) / COME TOGETHER (Beatles). • **Trivia:** LOUDER THAN LOVE was nominated for a Grammy in 1990.

Recommended: BADMOTORFINGER (*9) / ULTRAMEGA OK (*7) / LOUDER THAN LOVE (*8) / SUPERUNKNOWN (*9).

CHRIS CORNELL – vocals, guitar / **KIM THAYIL** – guitar / **HIRO YAMAMOTO** – bass / **MATT CAMERON** – drums

not issued Sub Pop

Jun 87. (7"blue) **HUNTED DOWN. / NOTHING TO SAY** [-] [ ]

Oct 87. (12"ep)(orange-12"ep) **SCREAMING LIFE** [-] [ ]

– Hunted down / Entering / Tears to forget / Nothing to say / Little Joe / Hand of God.

Aug 88. (12"ep) **FOPP** [-] [ ]
– Fopp / Fopp (dub) / Kingdom of come / Swallow my pride. *(above 2 re-iss.! on cd/c)*

S.S.T. S.S.T.

Nov 88. (m-lp)(c)(cd) **ULTRAMEGA OK** [ ] [ ]
– Flower / All your lies / 665 / Beyond the wheel / 667 / Mood for trouble / Circle of power / He didn't / Smokestack lightning / Nazi driver / Head injury / Incessant mace / One minute of silence. *(re-iss.cd/c/lp Oct95)*

May 89. (12")(c-s)(cd-s) **FLOWER. / HEAD INJURY / TOY BOX** [ ] [ ]

A & M A & M

Sep 89. (lp)(c)(cd) **LOUDER THAN LOVE** [ ] [ ]
– Ugly truth / Hands all over / Gun / Power trip / Get on the snake / Full on Kevin's mom / Loud love / I awake / No wrong no right / Uncovered / Big dumb sex / Full on (reprise).

Apr 90. (10"ep)(cd-ep) **HANDS ALL OVER** [ ] [ ]
– Hands all over / Heretic / Come together / Big dumb sex.

Jul 90. (7"ep)(12"ep) **THE LOUD LOVE E.P.** [ ] [ ]
– Loud love / Fresh deadly roses / Big dumb sex (dub) / Get on the snake.

—— **JASON EVERMAN** – bass (ex-NIRVANA) repl. HIRO

Sub Pop Sub Pop

Oct 90. (7")(7"purple/green) **ROOM A THOUSAND YEARS WIDE. / H.I.V. BABY** [-] [ ]

—— **BEN SHEPHERD** – bass repl. JASON

A & M A & M

Oct 91. (cd)(c)(lp) **BADMOTORFINGER** [39] [39]
– Rusty cage / Outshined / Slaves & bulldozers / Jesus Christ pose / Face pollution / Somewhere / Searching with my good eye closed / Room a thousand years wide / Mind riot / Drawing flies / Holy water / New damage. *(hit +re-iss.Mar92)*

Mar 92. (7") **JESUS CHRIST POSE. / STRAY CAT BLUES** [30] [ ]
(12"+=)(cd-s+=) – Into the void (sealth).

Jun 92. (7")(7"pic-d) **RUSTY CAGE. / TOUCH ME** [41] [ ]
(12"+=)(cd-s+=) – Show me.
(cd-s+=) – Big bottom / Earache my eye.

Nov 92. (7") **OUTSHINED. / I CAN'T GIVE YOU ANYTHING** [50] [ ]
(12"+=)(cd-s+=) – Homocidal suicide.
(cd-s+=) – I don't care about you / Can't you see me.

Feb 94. (7"pic-d)(c-s) **SPOONMAN. / FRESH TENDRILS** [20] [ ]
(12"clear+=)(cd-s+=) – Cold bitch / Exit Stonehenge.

Mar 94. (cd)(c)(d-lp) **SUPERUNKNOWN** [4] [1]
– Let me drown / My wave / Fell on black days / Mailman / Superunknown / Head down / Black hole Sun / Spoonman / Limo wreck / The day I tried to live / Kickstand / Fresh tendrils / 4th of July / Half / Like suicide / She likes surprises.

Apr 94. (7"pic-d)(c-s) **THE DAY I TRIED TO LIVE. / LIKE SUICIDE (acoustic)** [42] [ ]
(12"etched+=)(cd-s+=) – Kickstand (live).

Aug 94. (7"pic-d)(c-s) **BLACK HOLE SUN. / BEYOND THE WHEEL (live) / FELL ON BLACK DAYS (live)** [12] [ ]
(pic-cd-s+=) – Birth ritual (demo).
(cd-s) – ('A'side) / My wave (live) / Jesus Christ pose (live) / Spoonman (remix).

Jan 95. (7"pic-d)(c-s) **FELL ON BLACK DAYS. / KYLE PETTY, SON OF RICHARD / MOTORCYCLE LOOP** [24] [ ]
(cd-s) – ('A'side) / Kyle Petty, son of Richard / Fell on black days (video version).
(cd-s) – ('A'side) / Girl u want / Fell on black days (early demo).

– compilations, etc-

Oct 93. A&M; (cd) **LOUDER THAN LOUD / BADMOTORFINGER** [ ] [ ]

Oct 93. Sub Pop; (cd)(c) **SCREAMING LIFE / FOPP** [ ] [ ]

TEMPLE OF THE DOG

splinter-group feat. **CORNELL + CAMERON** plus **STONE GOSSARD / JEFF AMENT** (both ex-MOTHER LOVE BONE, future PEARL JAM)

A & M A & M

Apr 91. (cd)(c)(lp) **TEMPLE OF THE DOG** [ ] [ ]
– Say hello to Heaven / Reach down / Hunger strike / Pushing forward back / Call me a dog / Times of trouble / Wooden Jesus / Your saviour / 4-walled world / All night thing. *(above album, finally made US No.5 mid'92)*

Oct 92. (7"pic-d)(c-s) **HUNGER STRIKE. / ALL NIGHT THING** [51] [ ]
(12"+=)(cd-s+=) – Your saviour.

HATER

MATT + BEN plus ?

A & M A & M

Sep 93. (cd)(c)(lp) **HATER** [ ] [ ]
– Mona bone jakon / Who do I kill? / Tot finder / Lion and lamb / Roadside / Down undershoe / Circles / Putrid / Blistered / Sad McBain. *(re-iss.cd May95)*

not issued Sub Pop

Sep 93 (7"imp) **CIRCLES / GENOCIDE** [-] [ ]

SOUP DRAGONS

Formed: Bellshill, Lanarkshire, Scotland . . . 1985 by DICKSON and (see below). They signed to Martin Whitehead's indie label 'Subway' and released 2 singles before quickly moving to ex-WHAM managers Jaz Summers' label 'Raw TV'. In 1987 their 5th single 'CAN'T TAKE NO MORE', hit the UK Top 75, which led to 'Sire' records giving them disastrous deal in 1988. In 1989, they returned to 'Raw TV' unscathed, and were soon in the UK Top 5 with 'I'M FREE'. • **Style:** Moved from early BUZZCOCKS influences into burgeoning 'new rave' scene in the 90's, which was being led by STONE ROSES and The HAPPY MONDAYS. • **Songwriters:** DICKSON compositions, except PURPLE HAZE (Jimi Hendrix) / OUR LIPS ARE SEALED (Go-Go's) / I'M NOT YOUR STEPPING STONE (Monkees) / I'M FREE (Rolling Stones). • **Trivia:** They took group name from characters in children's TV programme 'The Clangers'.

Recommended: LOVEGOD (*7) / THIS IS OUR ART (*6).

SEAN DICKSON – vox, guitar / **JIM McCULLOCH** – guitar, vocals / **ROSS SINCLAIR** – drums / **SUSHILL K.DADE** – bass (ex-WAKE)

Subway not issued

Feb 86. (7"ep) **SUN IN THE SKY** (ltd.1,000 copies) [ ] [-]
– Quite content / Swirling round the garden with you / Fair's fair / Not for Humbert.

May 86. (7") **WHOLE WIDE WORLD. / I KNOW EVERYTHING** [ ] [-]
(12"+=) – Pleasantly surprised.

—— May 86, SEAN (bass) & JIM (guitar) were part-time auxiliaries of BMX BANDITS who were fronted by DUGLAS and released 'SAD'. / 'E102' on '53rd & 3rd' label. JIM played on their Jan87 follow-up 'WHAT A WONDERFUL WORLD'. / 'THE DAY BEFORE TOMORROW'.

Raw TV not issued

Sep 86. (7")(7"red)(7"blue) **HANG TEN!. / SLOW THINGS DOWN** [ ] [-]
(12"+=) – Just mind your step girl / Man about town with chairs.

Jan 87. (7") **HEAD GONE ASTRAY. / (IF YOU WERE THE ONLY) GIRL IN THE WORLD** [ ] [-]
(12"+=) – So sad I feel.

Jun 87. (7") **CAN'T TAKE NO MORE. / WHITEWASH** [65] [-]
(12"+=) – A-Ha experience.
(12"-'A'&'B'-live-ep+=) – Hang ten! / Purple haze.

Aug 87. (7") **SOFT AS YOUR FACE. / IT'S ALWAYS AUTUMN** [66] [-]
(12"+=) – Our lips are sealed / Soft as your face – arrangement.
(double-groove 12"+=) – Can't take no more / Whole wide world.

Mar 88. (7") **THE MAJESTIC HEAD. / 4-WAY BRAIN** [ ] [-]
(12"+=)/ /(12"pic-d+=) – Them./ / Corporation headlock.

Sire-WEA Sire

Apr 88. (lp)(c)(cd) **THIS IS OUR ART** [60] [ ]
– Kingdom chairs / Great empty space / The majestic head / Turning stone / Vacate my space / On overhead walkways / Passion protein / King of the castle / Another dream ticket / Soft as your face / Family ways. *(re-iss.cd Jul91)*

Jun 88. (7") **KINGDOM CHAIRS. / WHITE CRUISING** [ ] [ ]
(12") – ('A'side) / I'm not your stepping stone / All because of you.
(10"-'A'&'B'-live-ep+=) – Family way / King of the castle.

Raw TV Big Life

Jul 89. (7") **BACKWARDS DOG. / BURN OUT** [ ] [-]
(12"+=) – Supercherry / Kill kill kill me.

Oct 89. (7") **CROTCH DEEP TRASH. / YOU CAN FLY** [ ] [-]
('A'extended-12"+=) – Superangel / ('A'dub version).

—— **PAUL QUINN** – drums repl. ROSS. / added guest **ALEX McLAREN** – guitar

Mar 90. (7") **MOTHER UNIVERSE. / ('A'solar mix)** [ ] [-]
(12"+=) – ('A'love dub mix).
(cd-s++=) – 4-way brain.

May 90. (cd)(c)(lp) **LOVEGOD** [60] [88] Oct 90
– Mother Universe / Backwards dog / Softly / Drive the pain / Lovegod / Dream E-forever / Sweetmeat / Kiss the gun / Love you to death / Beauty freak / Lovedog (dub) / Crotch deep trash. *(cd+=)* – (2 extra mixes) *(re-dist.Aug90+=)* – I'm free. *(hit UK No.7.)*

Jul 90. (7")(c-s) **I'M FREE. (featuring JUNIOR REID) / LOVE GOD (dub)** [5] [79] Oct 90
('A'extended-12")/ /(cd-s+=) – (same as 7")./ / ('A'-12"version).
(12") – ('A'-Terry Farley mix). / Backwards dog (remix)

Oct 90. (7")(c-s) **MOTHER UNIVERSE. / BACKWARDS DOG** [26] [ ]
(12"+=)(cd-s+=) – ('A'dub remix) / ('A'-'89 remix).

Big Life Big Life

Aug 91. (7")(c-s) **ELECTRIC BLUES. / UNEARTHED** [ ] [ ]
(12"+=)(cd-s+=) – Solar rise / ('A'dub version).

Mar 92. (7")(c-s) **DIVINE THING. / DRIVING** [53] [35]
(12"+=)(cd-s+=) – ('A'revisited) / American sweetmeat.

Apr 92. (cd)(c)(lp) **HOTWIRED** [74] [97]
– Pleasure / Divine thing / Running wild / Getting down / Forever yesterday / No more / Understanding / Dream on (Solid gone) / Everlasting / Absolute heaven / Everything / Sweet layabout / Mindless.

Sep 92. (12"ep)(c-ep)(cd-ep) **PLEASURE / PLEASURE (revisited). / WHAT YOU WANT / DIVE-BOMBER** [ ] [69]
(cd-ep) – ('A'revisited) . . . repl. by 'Man'.
(cd-s+=) – ('A'revisited) / I'm free (original) / Mother universe / Electric blues.

SOUTHERN DEATH CULT (see under ⇒ CULT)

SPACE (see under ⇒ KLF)

SPACEMEN 3

Formed: Rugby, Warwickshire, England . . . 1983 by KEMBER and PIERCE. Through their manager Gerald Palmer, they signed to 'Glass' early in 1986. Just as they were about to breakthrough in the early 90's, they splintered into 2 projects SONIC BOOM and SPIRITUALIZED. • **Style:** Psychedelic noise outfit, intertwined with melancholy bursts of beauty and experimentation. • **Songwriters:** KEMBER or PIERCE material until the 90's when KEMBER penned all. Covered; CHE + ROCK'N'ROLL IS KILLING MY LIFE (Suicide) / COME TOGETHER + STARSHIP (MC5) / MARY-ANNE (. . .Campbell) / ROLLER COASTER (13th Floor Elevators). SPIRITUALIZED covered; ANYWAY THAT YOU WANT ME (Troggs) / BORN NEVER ASKED (Laurie Anderson). • **Trivia:** In the early 90's, SPIRITUAL-

IZED headlined at the ICA Rock Week sponsored by 'Irn Bru'.

Recommended: PLAYING WITH FIRE (*8) / LAZER GUIDED MELODIES (*9; SPIRITUALIZED) / PURE PHASE (*8; SPIRITUALIZED ELECTRIC MAINLINE)

SONIC BOOM (b.PETE KEMBER, 19 Nov'65) – vocals / **JASON PIERCE** (b.19 Nov'65) – guitar / **STEWART (ROSCO) ROSSWELL** – keyboards / **PETE (BASSMAN) BAINES** – bass

Glass | not issued

Jun 86. (lp) **SOUND OF CONFUSION** [ ] [-]
– Losing touch with my mind / Hey man / Roller coaster / Mary Anne / Little doll / 2:35 / O.D. catastrophe. *(re-iss.+cd.Sep89 on 'Fire')*

Dec 86. (12"m) **WALKIN' WITH JESUS (SOUND OF CONFUSION). / ROLLERCOASTER / FEEL SO GOOD** [ ] [-]

Jul 87. (12"ep) **TRANSPARENT RADIATION / ECSTASY SYMPHONY / TRANSPARENT RADIATION (FLASHBACK). / THINGS'LL NEVER BE THE SAME / STARSHIP** [ ] [-]

Aug 87. (lp)(c) **THE PERFECT PRESCRIPTION** [ ] [-]
– Take me to the other side / Walkin' with Jesus / Ode to street hassle / Ecstasy – Symphony / Feel so good / Things'll never be the same / Come down easy / Call the doctor / Soul 1 / That's just fine. *(re-iss.+cd.Dec89 on 'Fire')*

Mar 88. (7")(12") **TAKE ME TO THE OTHER SIDE. / SOUL 1 / THAT'S JUST FINE** [ ] [-]

— **WILLIE CARRUTHERS** – bass / **JON MATLOCK** – drums repl. ROSCO + BAINES who formed The DARKSIDE.

Fire | not issued

Nov 88. (7")(12") **REVOLUTION. / CHE** [ ] [-]
(cd-s+=) – May the circle be unbroken. *(re-iss.Oct91)*

Feb 89. (lp)(c)(cd) **PLAYING WITH FIRE** [ ] [-]
– Honey / Come down softly to my soul / How does it feel? / I believe it / Revolution / Let me down gently / So hot (wash away all my tears) / Suicide / Lord can you hear me. *(free-12"ep/cd-ep+=)* – Starship / Revolution / Suicide (live) / Repeater / Live intro theme (xtacy).

Jul 89. (7") **HYPNOTISED. / JUST TO SEE YOU SMILE HONEY (part 2)** [ ] [-]
(12"+=)(3"cd-s+=) – The world is dying. *(re-iss.Oct91)*
(free 7"flexi w.a) – EXTRACTS. / BARK PSYCHOSIS / FURY THINGS on 'Cheree' label.

Jan 91. (7") **BIG CITY. / DRIVE** [ ] [-]
(12"+=)(cd-s+=) – Big City (everybody I know can be found here).

Feb 91. (cd)(c)(lp) **RECURRING** [46] [-]
– Big city (everybody I know can be found here) / Just to see you smile (orchestral) / I love you / Set me free – I've got the key / Set me free (reprise) / Feel so bad (reprise) / Hypnotized / Sometimes / Feelin' just fine (head full of shit) / Billy Whizz – blue 1. (cd+=) When tomorrow hits / Why couldn't I see / Just to see you smile (instrumental) / Feel so sad (demo) / Drive.

May 91. (cd)(c)(lp) **PERFORMANCE** (live 1988 Holland) [ ] [-]
– Mary-Anne / Come together / Things'll never be the same / Take me to the other side / Roller coaster / Starship / Walkin' with Jesus.

— Had already folded Jun'90.

– compilations, etc. –

1991. Fierce; (cd)(d-lp) **DREAM WEAPON – ECSTASY IN SLOW MOTION** [ ] [-]
(re-iss.Nov95 on 'Space Age')

Nov 94. Bomp; (cd) **TAKING DRUGS TO MAKE MUSIC TO TAKE DRUGS TO** [ ] [-]

May 95. Sympathy For The . . . (cd)(lp) **FOR ALL FUCKED UP CHILDREN OF THE WORLD** [ ] [ ]

May 95. Bomp; (cd) **SPACEMEN ARE GO** [ ] [ ]

Nov 95. Space Age; (cd)(d-lp) **LIVE IN EUROPE 1989** [ ] [-]

SONIC BOOM

(PETE KEMBER solo with **WILLIE B. CARRUTHERS** and also **PHIL PARFITT + JO WIGGS** of PERFECT DISASTER)

Silvertone | not issued

Oct 89. (12") **ANGEL. / ANGEL (version) / HELP ME PLEASE** [ ] [-]

Feb 90. (cd)(c)(lp) **SPECTRUM** [65] [-]
– Pretty baby / If I should die / Lonely avenue / Help me please / Angel / Rock'n'roll is killing my life / You're the one. (free 10"w/lp) DRONE DREAM EP: OCTAVES. / TREMELOS.

Apr 91. (7" freebie gig) **(I LOVE YOU) TO THE MOON AND BACK. / CAPO WALTZ (live)** [-] [-]

SPECTRUM

KEMBER, CARRUTHERS, etc

Silvertone | Silvertone

Jun 92. (7")(12") **HOW YOU SATISFY ME. / DON'T GO (inst.2)** [ ] [-]
(12"clear+=)(cd-s+=) – My life spins around your every smile / Don't go (inst.1).

Jun 92. (cd)(c)(lp) **SOUL KISS (GLIDE DIVINE)** [ ] [-]
– How you satisfy me / Lord I don't even know my name / The drunk suite (overture) / Neon sigh / Waves wash over me / (I love you) To the moon and back / My love for you never died away but my soul gave out and wit / Sweet running water / Touch the stars / Quicksilver glide divine / The drunk suite / Phase me out (gently). *(re-iss.cd/c Apr95)*

Sep 92. (7") **TRUE LOVE WILL FIND YOU IN THE END. / MY LIFE SPINS AROUND YOUR EVERY SMILE** [70] [-]
(12")(cd-s) – ('A' side) / To the moon and back / Waves wash over me.

Aug 93. (7") **INDIAN SUMMER. / BABY DON'T YOU WORRY (California lullabye)** [ ] [ ]
(12"+=)(cd-s+=) – It's alright / True love will find you in the end.

Apr 94. (12")(cd-s) **SKY ABOVE** [ ] [-]
above single issued on 'Sub Assertive Sounds'.

Nov 94. (cd)(lp) **HIGHS LOWS AND HEAVENLY BLOWS** [ ] [ ]
– Undo the taboo / Feedback / Then I just drifted away / Take your time / Soothe me / All night long / Don't pass me by / I know they say / Take me away.

SPIRITUALIZED

were 5-piece **JASON, WILL & JON** plus girlfriend **KATE RADLEY** – organ, keyboards, vocals / **MARK REFOY** – guitar, dulcimer

Dedicated | not issued

Jun 90. (12") **ANYWAY THAT YOU WANT ME. / STEP INTO THE BREEZE** [75] [-]
(12"+=)(cd-s+=) – ('A'version)
(12")('A'side) / ('A'parts 2-3) / ('A'demo)

Jun 91. (7")(12")(cd-s) **FEEL SO SAD. / ('A'demos)** [ ] [-]

Aug 91. (7") **RUN. / I WANT YOU** [59] [-]
(12"+=)(cd-s+=) Luminescent (stay with me) / Effervescent.

Nov 91. (7") **WHY DON'T YOU SMILE NOW. / SWAY** [ ] [-]
(12"+=)(cd-s+=) – ('A'extended).

Apr 92. (cd)(c)(2x12"lp) **LAZER GUIDED MELODIES** [27] [ ]
– You know it's true / If I were with her now / I want you / Run / Smiles / Step into the breeze / Symphony space / Take your time / Shine a light / Angel sigh / Sway / 200 bars. (free-7" at 'Chain With No Name' shops) ANY WAY THAT YOU WANT ME / WHY DON'T YOU SMILE NOW.

Jul 92. (7"red) **MEDICATION. / SMILES (Peel session)** [55] [-]
(12"+=) – Feel so sad (Peel session) / Angel sigh.
(cd-s++=) – Space (instrumental).

Jun 93. (mail-order cd) **F***ED UP INSIDE** [-] [-]

Oct 93. (7" **GOOD TIMES / LAY BACK IN THE SUN** [49] [ ]
(12"ep+=)(cd-ep+=) – Electric Mainline 1 + 2

SPIRITUALIZED ELECTRIC MAINLINE

— **JASON + KATE RADLEY** – keyboards, vox/ **SEAN COOK** – synths/ plus **MARK REFOY** – guitar/ **JON MATTOCK** – percussion/ **LEON HUNT** – banjo/ **STEWART GORDON** – violin/ **THE BALANESCU QUARTET** – strings/ + others on wind instruments

Jan 95. (cd-ep) **LET IT FLOW / DON'T GO / STAY WITH ME / DON'T GO / STAY WITH ME (THE INDIVIDUAL)** [30] [ ]
(cd-ep) – ('A'side) / Take good care of it / Things will never be the same / Clear rush.
(cd-ep) – ('A'side) / Medication / Take your time / Smile.
(3xbox-cd-ep)(10"ep) – (all above).

Feb 95. (cd)(c)(d-lp) **PURE PHASE** [20] [ ]
– Medication / The slide song / Electric phase / All of my tears / These blues / Let it flow / Take good care of it / Born never asked / Electric mainline / Lay back in the sun / Good times / Pure phase / Spread your wings / Feel like goin' home.

Nov 95. (cd-ep) **LAY BACK IN THE SUN /** [ ] [ ]

— On Mar 92, HONEY TONGUES (aka MATTOCK + WIGGS) released lp 'NUDE NUDES' on 'Playtime'. *(re-iss.cd Oct93)*

SPANDAU BALLET

Formed: Islington, London, England . . . Nov'79 by brothers GARY and MARTIN KEMP, plus HADLEY, KEEBLE and NORMAN. With help from STEVE STRANGE and RUSTY EGAN, they found new manager Steve Dagger. He helped them form own label 'Reformation', which led to signature on the dotted line for 'Chrysalis' in 1980. Their first single 'TO CUT A LONG STORY SHORT', an innovator of the 'new romantic' scene, made the Top 5. They continued to grow bigger throughout the 80's, and peaked in 1983 with No.1 single 'TRUE'. They achieved a consecutive run of 20 UK Top 50 hits between 1980 + 1989. • **Style:** At first a highly hyped fashionable outfit, who branched out into funk-soul in 1981 and soul/pop ballads in '83. • **Songwriters:** All written by KEMP brothers. TONY HADLEY used writers SINFIELD-HILL, CLIMIE-FISHER or DIANE WARREN. HADLEY Covers: ROCK'N'ROLL SUICIDE (David Bowie) / THE BOYS OF SUMMER (Don Henley). • **Trivia:** In 1988, the KEMP brothers starred in the film 'The Krays' as the infamous twin gangsters.

Recommended: THE SINGLES COLLLECTION (*7).

TONY HADLEY (b. 2 Jun'59) – vocals, synthesizers / **GARY KEMP** (b.16 Oct'60) – keyboards, guitar / **STEVE NORMAN** (b.25 Mar'60) – saxophone, guitar / **MARTIN KEMP** (b.10 Oct'61) – bass / **JOHN KEEBLE** (b. 6 Jul'59) – drums

Chrysalis | Chrysalis

Nov 80. (7")(12") **TO CUT A LONG STORY SHORT. / ('A'instrumental)** [5] [ ]

Jan 81. (7")(12") **THE FREEZE. / ('A'instrumental)** [17] [ ]

Mar 81. (lp)(c) **JOURNEYS TO GLORY** [5] [ ]
– To cut a long story short / Reformation / Mandolin / Musclebound / Age of blows / The freeze / Confused / Toys. *(cd-iss.Dec82)*

Mar 81. (7")(12") **MUSCLEBOUND. / GLOW** [10] [ ]
(c-ep) **ACT 1** – ('A'side) / To cut a long story short / The freeze.

Jul 81. (7")(12") **CHANT No.1 (I DON'T NEED THIS PRESSURE ON). / FEEL THE CHANT** [3] [ ]
(above credited with BEGGAR & CO.)

Nov 81. (7")(12") **PAINT ME DOWN. / MAN WITH GUITAR (RE-PAINT)** [30] [ ]

Jan 82. (7")(12") **SHE LOVED LIKE DIAMOND. / ('A'version)** [49] [ ]

Mar 82. (lp)(c) **DIAMOND** [15] [ ]
– Chant No.1 (I don't need this pressure on) / Instinction / Paint me down / Coffee club / She loved like diamond / Pharoah / Innocence and science / Missionary.

Apr 82. (7")(7"pic-d) **INSTINCTION. / GENTLY** [10] [ ]
(12"+=) – Chant No.1 (remix).

Sep 82. (7")(12")(7"pic-d) **LIFELINE. / LIVE AND LET LIVE** [7] [ ]

Feb 83. (7")(12")(7"pic-d) **COMMUNICATION. / ('A'edited club mix)** [12] [-]

Mar 83. (lp)(c) **TRUE** [1] [19] May 83
– Pleasure / Communication / Code of love / Gold / Lifeline / Heaven is a secret /

Foundation / True. *(cd-iss.1986) (re-iss.cd Mar94)*
Apr 83. (7")(7"pic-d) **TRUE. / ('A'version)** [1] [-]
(12"+=) – Lifeline (acappella).
Aug 83. (7") **TRUE. / GENTLY** [-] [4]
Aug 83. (7")(7"pic-d) **GOLD. / ('A'instrumental)** [2] [-]
(12"+=) – Foundation.
Nov 83. (7") **GOLD. / ('A' live)** [-] [29]
Mar 84. (7") **COMMUNICATION. / ONLY WHEN YOU LEAVE** [-] [59]
May 84. (7")(7"pic-d) **ONLY WHEN YOU LEAVE. / PAINT ME DOWN** [3] [34] Jul 84
(12"+=) – ('A'live version).
Jun 84. (lp)(c) **PARADE** [2] [50] Aug 84
– Only when you leave / Highly strung / I'll fly for you / Nature of the beast / Revenge for love / Always in the back of my mind / With the pride / Round and round. *(cd-iss.Jun87)*
Aug 84. (7")(7"pic-d; 5-diff.) **I'LL FLY FOR YOU. / TO CUT A LONG STORY SHORT (live)** [9] [ ]
(12"+=) – ('A'live version).
Oct 84. (7")(7"silver) **HIGHLY STRUNG. / (part 2)** [15] [ ]
(12"+=) – ('A'extended).
Nov 84. (7") **ROUND AND ROUND. / TRUE (live)** [18] [ ]
(12"+=)(12"gold+=) – Gold (live).
Nov 85. (lp)(c)(cd) **THE SINGLES COLLECTION** (compilation) [3] [ ]
– Gold / Lifeline / Round and round / Only when you leave / Instinction / Highly strung / True / Communication / I'll fly for you / To cut a long story short / Chant No.1 (I don't need this pressure on) / She loved like diamond / Paint me down / The freeze / Musclebound. *(w/free 7") (c+= extra mixes)*

C.B.S. Epic
Jun 86. (7") **FIGHT FOR OURSELVES. / FIGHT . . . THE HEARTACHE** [15] [-]
(12"+=) – ('A'extended version).
Oct 86. (7")(7"pic-d) **THROUGH THE BARRICADES. / WITH THE PRIDE** [6] [-]
(12"+=) – ('A'extended).
Nov 86. (lp)(c)(cd) **THROUGH THE BARRICADES** [7] [ ]
– Barricades – introduction / Cross the line / Man in chains / How many lies / Virgin / Swept / Fight for ourselves / Swept / Snakes and lovers / Through the barricades. *(re-iss.cd+c Feb94 on 'Columbia')*
Jan 87. (7")(12") **HOW MANY LIES. / COMMUNICATION** [34] [-]
Mar 87. (7") **HOW MANY LIES. / SNAKES AND LOVERS** [-] [ ]
May 87. (7") **THROUGH THE BARRICADES. / SNAKES AND LOVERS** [-] [ ]
Aug 87. (7") **RAW. / ('A'version)** [47] [ ]
(12"+=)/ /(cd-s++=) – Raw (extended)./ / Raw (mix).
Aug 89. (7") **TO BE FREE WITH YOUR LOVE. / THROUGH THE BARRICADES (live)** [42] [ ]
(cd-s+=) – ('A'extended) / ('A'dance).
(12"++=) – ('A'dub version).
Sep 89. (lp)(c)(cd) **HEART LIKE A SKY** [31] [ ]
– Be free with your love / Crashed into love / Big feeling / A matter of time / Motivator / Raw / Empty spaces / Windy town / A handful of dust.
Nov 89. (7")(c-s) **EMPTY SACES. / FIGHT FOR OURSELVES (live)** [ ] [ ]
(12"+=)(cd-s+=) – Chant No.1 (I don't need this pressure on).
Feb 90. (7")(c-s) **CRASHED INTO LOVE. / HOW MANY LIES (live)** [ ] [ ]
(12"+=) – Through the barricades (live).
(12"+=)(cd-s+=) – With the pride / Gold (live) / True (live).

— Split when the KEMPS became 'The Krays' in the 1990 film. GARY went on to act in 'The Bodyguard' and married actress SADIE FROST, before embarking on a solo career in 1995.

– more compilations, etc. –

Feb 83. Chrysalis; (d-c) **JOURNEYS TO GLORY / DIAMOND** [ ] [-]
Dec 86. Chrysalis; (lp)(c)(cd) **THE 12" MIXES** [ ] [-]
(re-iss.Mar 94)
Aug 91. Chrysalis; (7")(c-s) **TRUE. / LIFELINE** [ ] [ ]
(12"+=)(cd-s+=) – Heaven is a secret / Pleasure.
Sep 91. Chrysalis; (cd)(c)(lp) **THE BEST OF SPANDAU BALLET** [44] [ ]
– (as THE SINGLES COLLECTION +) Fight for ourselves / Through the barricades / How many lies / Raw / Be free with your love.
Feb 87. Old Gold; (7") **TRUE. / GOLD** [ ] [-]
Feb 87. Old Gold; (7") **TO CUT A LONG STORY SHORT. / CHANT No.1 (I DON'T NEED THIS PRESSURE ON)** [ ] [-]
Nov 87. Telstar; (c)+book) **GREATEST HITS** [ ] [-]
Aug 95. Old Gold; (cd-s) **TRUE / GOLD** [ ] [-]

TONY HADLEY

E.M.I. E.M.I.
Feb 92. (7")(c-s) **LOST IN YOUR LOVE. / WHY CAN'T WE FALL IN LOVE** [42] [ ]
(12"+=)(cd-s+=) – Theme No.7.
Aug 92. (cd)(c)(lp) **THE STATE OF PLAY** [ ] [ ]
– Lost in your love / Just the thought of you / You keep coming back for more / For your blue eyes only / Fever / Riverside / Never get up on love / This time / Game of love / Freewheel / One good reason / Somebody up there.
Aug 92. (7")(c-s) **FOR YOUR BLUE EYES ONLY. / TONIGHT** [ ] [ ]
(cd-s+=) – Close-up.
Aug 93. (7")(c-s) **ABSOLUTION / ONE GOOD REASON** [ ] [ ]
(cd-s) – ('A'side) / Through the barricades (acoustic) / The boys of summer / Rock'n'roll suicide.
(12") – ('A'side) / ('A'mixes).

SPARKS

Formed: Los Angeles, California, USA ... 1968 as HALFNELSON by brothers RON and RUSSELL MAEL. After sending demo tape to TODD RUNDGREN, he as producer arranged for them to sign to Albert Grossman's 'Bearsville' label in 1970. Their eponymous debut sold poorly and they changed name to SPARKS. In 1973, they moved to London where they were given contract by 'Island', In 1974, they unleashed brilliant UK debut 45 'THIS TOWN AIN'T BIG ENOUGH FOR THE BOTH OF US', which quickly peaked at No.2. This was followed by a MUFF WINWOOD produced album and a string of UK-only hits, which ended late 1975 and their return to California. • **Style:** Weird, comic looking pop-rock brothers (RON the Hitler lookalike on keys and eyes, plus RUSS the near-falsetto singer) who succumbed to teenybop brigade. On their chart return in 1979, their music was smothered by effective Euro-disco beat which enlisted GIORGIO MORODER, who they had met since their stay in Germany from 1977. • **Songwriters:** RON MAEL wrote lyrics / music, and they also covered; I WANT TO HOLD YOUR HAND (Beatles) / FINGERTIPS (Stevie Wonder) / etc. • **Trivia:** In 1979, they produced NOEL'S album 'Is There More To Life Than Dancing'. They also worked for ADRIAN MUSSEY, BIJOU + TELEX. The 1980 single 'WHEN I'M WITH YOU', hit No.1 in France, but sold poorly in the UK & US.

Recommended: THE BEST OF SPARKS (*7).

RUSSELL MAEL (b.1953, Santa Monica, USA) – vocals, bass / **RON MAEL** (b.1948, Culver City, Los Angeles, California, USA) – keyboards / **EARLE MANKEY** – guitar / with **RALPH OSWALD** – bass / **JOHN HENDERSON** – drums

Bearsville Bearsville
Feb 72. (lp) **HALFNELSON (as "HALFNELSON")** [-] [ ]
– Wonder girl / Fa la fa lee / Roger / High C / Fletcher Honorama / Simple ballet / Slowboat / Biology 2 / Saccharin and the war / Big bands / Mr.Nice guys. *(UK cd-iss.Aug93 on 'Rhino')*

— **JIM MANKEY** – bass + **HARVEY FEINSTEIN** – drums repl. RALPH and JOHN
Nov 72. (7") **WONDER GIRL. / (NO MORE) MR.NICE GUYS** [ ] [ ]
Feb 73. (lp) **A WOOFER IN TWEETER'S CLOTHING** [ ] [ ]
– Girl from Germany / Beaver O'Lindy / Nothing is sacred / Here comes Bob / Moon over Kentucky / Do re mi / Argus desire / Underground / The louvre / Batteries not incuded / Whippings and apologies.

— The **MAELS** moved to London and recruited British musicians **ADRIAN FISHER** – guitar / **MARTIN GORDON** – bass, vocals / **DINKY DIAMOND** – drums / **PETER OXENDALE** – keyboards

Island Island
May 74. (7") **THIS TOWN AIN'T BIG ENOUGH FOR THE BOTH OF US. / BARBECUTIE** [2] [ ] Aug 74
May 74. (lp)(c) **KIMONO MY HOUSE** [4] [ ]
– This town ain't big enough for the both of us / Amateur hour / Falling in love with myself again / Here in Heaven / Thank God it's not Christmas / Hasta manana Monsieur / Talent is an asset / Complaints / In the family / Equator. *(cd-iss.Aug94)*
Jul 74. (7") **AMATEUR HOUR. / LOST AND FOUND** [7] [-]
Oct 74. (7") **TALENT IS AN ASSET. / LOST AND FOUND** [-] [ ]

— **TREVOR WHITE** – guitar repl. PETER / **IAN HAMPTON** – bass (ex-JOOK) repl. MARTIN who joined JET
Oct 74. (7") **NEVER TURN YOUR BACK ON MOTHER EARTH. / ALABAMY NIGHT** [13] [-]
Nov 74. (lp)(c) **PROPAGANDA** [9] [63] Feb 75
– Propaganda / At home, at work, at play / Reinforcements / B.C. / Thanks but no thanks / Don't leave me alone with her / Never turn your back on Mother Earth / Something for the girl with everything / Achoo / Who don't like kids / Bon voyage. *(cd-iss.Aug94)*
Jan 75. (7") **SOMETHING FOR THE GIRL WITH EVERYTHING. / MARRY ME** [17] [-]
Mar 75. (7") **SOMETHING FOR THE GIRL WITH EVERYTHING. / ACHOO** [-] [ ]
Jul 75. (7") **GET IN THE SWING. / PROFILE** [27] [ ]
Sep 75. (7") **LOOKS, LOOKS, LOOKS. / PINEAPPLE** [26] [ ]
Oct 75. (lp)(c) **INDISCREET** [18] [ ]
– Hospitality on parade / Happy hunting ground / Without using hands / Get in the swing / Under the table with her / How are you getting home / Pineapple / Tits / It ain't 1918 / The lady is lingering / In the future / Looks, looks, looks / Miss the start, miss the end. *(cd-iss.Aug94)*
Nov 75. (7") **LOOKS, LOOKS, LOOKS. / THE WEDDING OF JACQUELINE KENNEDY TO RUSSELL MAEL** [-] [ ]
Mar 76. (7") **I WANNA HOLD YOUR HAND. / ENGLAND** [ ] [-]
(withdrawn)

— The **MAELS** used session people incl. **SAL MAIDA** – bass (ex-ROXY MUSIC)
Oct 76. (7") **BIG BOY. / FILL 'ER UP** [ ] [-]
Oct 76. (lp)(c) **BIG BEAT** [ ] [ ]
– Big boy / I want to be like everybody else / Nothing to do / I bought the Mississippi River / Fill 'er up / Everybody's stupid / Throw her away / Confusion / Screwed up / White women / I like girls. *(cd-iss.Aug94)*
Dec 76. (7") **I LIKE GIRLS. / ENGLAND** [ ] [-]

C.B.S. Columbia
Sep 77. (7") **A BIG SURPRISE. / FOREVER YOUNG** [ ] [ ]
Oct 77. (lp)(c) **INTRODUCING SPARKS** [ ] [ ]
– A big surprise / Occupation / Ladies / I'm not / Forever young / Goofing off / Girls on the brain / Over the summer / Those mysteries.

— augmented by **GIORGIO MORODER** – electronics, producer

Virgin Elektra
Mar 79. (7")(12")(12"pic-d) **THE NUMBER ONE SONG IN HEAVEN. / ('A'-long version)** [14] [-]
Mar 79. (lp)(c) **NUMBER ONE IN HEAVEN** [73] [ ]
– Tryouts for the human race / Academy award performance / La dolce vita / Beat the clock / My other voice / The number one song in Heaven. *(re-iss.Aug82 on 'Fame-EMI')*
Jul 79. (7")(12")(12"blue) **BEAT THE CLOCK. / ('A'-long version)** [10] [-]
Oct 79. (7")(12")(12"pic-d) **TRYOUTS FOR THE HUMAN RACE. / ('A' long version)** [ ] [-]

Nov 79. (7") **TRYOUTS FOR THE HUMAN RACE. / NO. 1 SONG IN HEAVEN** [-] [ ]
Jan 80. (7") **WHEN I'M WITH YOU. / ('A'long version)** [ ] [-]
Feb 80. (lp)(c) **TERMINAL JIVE** [ ] [-]
– When I'm with you / Just because you love me / Rock and roll people in a disco world / When I'm with you (instrumental) / Young girls / Noisy boys / Stereo / The greatest show on Earth.
Apr 80. (7")('A'ext-12") **YOUNG GIRLS. / JUST BECAUSE YOU LOVE ME** [ ] [-]

—— added (ex-BATES MOTEL members) **BOB HAAG** – guitar / **LESLIE BOHEM** – bass / **DAVID KENDRICK** – drums

Why-Fi R.C.A.

Apr 81. (7")(12") **TIPS FOR TEENS. / DON'T SHOOT ME** [ ] [-]
May 81. (lp) **WHOMP THAT SUCKER** [ ] [ ]
– Tips for teens / Funny face / Where's my girl / Upstairs / I married a Martian / The willys / Don't shoot me / Suzie safety / That's not Nastassia / Wacky women.
Sep 81. (7") **FUNNY FACE. / THE WILLYS** [ ] [-]

—— The **MAELS + MORODER** added **JAMES GOODWIN** – synths.

Atlantic Atlantic

Jun 82. (7") **I PREDICT. / MOUSTACHE** [ ] [60] May 82
Jun 82. (lp)(c) **ANGST IN MY PANTS** [ ] [ ]
– Angst in my pants / I predict / Sextown U.S.A. / Sherlock Holmes / Nicotina / Mickey mouse / Moustache / Instant weight loss / Tarzan and Jane / The decline and fall of me / Eaten by the monster of love.
1982. (7") **EATEN BY THE MONSTER OF LOVE. / MICKEY MOUSE** [-] [ ]
Jun 83. (7") **COOL PLACES. / SPORTS** [ ] [49] Apr 83

—— Above credited with JANE WIEDLIN of the GO-GO's.

Jun 83. (lp)(c) **SPARKS IN OUTER SPACE** [ ] [88]
– Cool places / Popularity / Prayin' for a party / All you ever think about is sex / Please, baby please / Rockin' girls / I wish I looked a little better / Lucky me, lucky you / A fun bunch of guys from Outer Space / Dance godammit.
Nov 83 (7") **ALL YOU EVER THINK ABOUT IS SEX. / I WISH I LOOKED A LITTLE BETTER** [-] [ ]
(12") – ('A'club) / Dance goddamit (club version) / With all my might (extended club).
Jun 84. (lp)(c) **PULLING RABBITS OUT OF A HAT** [-] [ ]

—— MORODER moved on to produce PHIL OAKEY

Jun 84 (7") **PRETENDING TO BE DRUNK. / KISS ME QUICK** [-] [ ]

London Curb-MCA

Jun 85. (7")(12") **CHANGE. / THIS TOWN AIN'T BIG ENOUGH FOR THE BOTH OF US (acoustic)** [ ] [ ]

—— **JOHN THOMAS** – keyboards repl. GOODWIN

Consolidated M.C.A.

Nov 86. (7")(ext-12") **MUSIC THAT YOU CAN DANCE TO. / FINGERTIPS** [ ] [ ]
Nov 86. (lp)(c) **MUSIC THAT YOU CAN DANCE TO** [ ] [ ] Aug86
– Music that you can to / Rosebud / Fingertips / Armies of the night / The scene / Shopping mall of love / Modesty plays (new version) / Let's get funky. *(US version – Armies of the night (repl.)* Change.
Feb 87. (7") **ROSEBUD. / ('A'-cinematic version)** [ ] [ ]
(12") – ('A'extended) / ('A'-FM mix).

—— The MAELS retained **THOMAS + DAVID KENDRICK** ?, introducing **SPENCER SIRCOMBE** – guitar / **HANS CHRISTIAN REUMSCHUSSEL** – bass / **PAMELA STONEBROOK** – vocals

Carrere Fine Art

Jul 88. (7") **SO IMPORTANT. / BIG BRASS RING** [ ] [ ]
(12"+=) – ('A'extremely important mix).
(cd-s++=) – Madonna.

—— In Aug 88, SPARKS collaborated on 'SINGING IN THE SHOWER'. / 'SMOG' single by French husband and wife duo LES RITA MITSOUKO on 'Virgin' label.

Carrere Rhino

Jul 88. (lp)(c)(cd) **INTERIOR DESIGN** [ ] [ ] Aug 88
– So important / Just got back from Heaven / Lots of reasons / You got a hold of my heart / Love o rama / The toughest girl in town / Let's make love / Stop me if you've heard this before / A walk down memory lane / Madonna. *(cd+=)* – Madonna (French – German – Spanish; versions) / The big brass ring / So important. *(UK-iss.cd Aug92 on 'Magnum')*
Aug 89. (7")(12") **SO IMPORTANT. / JUST GOT BACK FROM HEAVEN** [ ] [-]

—— In 1991, the MAELS were working on own feature film 'Mai The Psychic Girl',

Fineflex Fineflex

Nov 93. (12") **NATIONAL CRIME AWARENESS WEEK. / (13 MINUTES OF HEAVEN) / ('A'-Perkins playtime mix)** [ ] [ ]
(cd-s) – ('A'side) / (3 other mixes).

Logic-BMG BMG

Oct 94. (12")(c-s)(cd-s) **WHEN DO I GET TO SING MY WAY. / ('A'-Grid mix) / ('A'-Rapino Brrothers mix)** [38] [ ]
(cd-s) – ('A'side) / ('A'-Vince Clarke mixes).
Nov 94. (cd)(c) **GRATUITOUS SAX & SENSELESS VIOLINS** [ ] [ ]
– Gratutous sex / When do I get to sing 'My Way' / (When I kiss you) I hear Charlie Parker playing / Frankly Scarlett I don't give a damn / I thought I told you to wait in the car / Hear no evil, see no evil, speak no evil / Now that I own the BBC / Tsui Hark (featuring TSUI HARK & BILL KONG) / The ghost of Liberace / Let's go surfing / Senseless violins.
Feb 95. (c-s) **WHEN I KISS YOU (I HEAR CHARLIE PARKER PLAYIN') / ('A'-Beatmasters mix)** [36] [ ]
(cd-s+=) – This town ain't big enough for the both of us.
(12"+=)(cd-s+=) – ('A'-Bernard Butler mix).
May 95. (c-s) **WHEN DO I GET TO SING 'MY WAY' / ('A'-Grid mix)** [32] [ ]
(12"+=) – National crime awareness week.
(cd-s++=) – (2 extra 'A'mixes).

– compilations, others, etc. –

Jul 74. Bearsville; (7") **GIRL FROM GERMANY. / BEAVER O'LINDY** [ ] [-]
Oct 74. Bearsville; (lp)(c) **SPARKS** (early 71-73) [ ] [-]
Mar 76. Bearsville; (d-lp) **TWO ORIGINALS OF SPARKS** [ ] [-]
– (the albums from 1972 + 1973)
Mar 77. Island; (lp)(c) **THE BEST OF SPARKS** [ ] [-]
– This town ain't big enough for the both of us / Hasta manana monsieur / Tearing the place apart / At home, at work, at play / Never turn your back on Mother Earth / Get in the swing / Amateur hour / Looks, looks, looks / Thanks but no thanks / Gone with the wind / Something for the girl with everything / Thank God it's not Christmas. *(re-iss.Sep79, cd-iss. Feb 90)*
Sep 79. Island; (7") **THIS TOWN AIN'T BIG ENOUGH FOR THE BOTH OF US. / LOOKS, LOOKS, LOOKS** [ ] [-]
May 80. Island; (7") **MAEL INTUITION** [ ] [-]
May 83. Virgin; (12"ep) **THE NUMBER ONE SONG IN HEAVEN / BEAT THE CLOCK. / WHEN I'M WITH YOU / YOUNG GIRLS** [ ] [-]
Nov 81. Underdog; (lp) **THE HISTORY OF THE SPARKS** [ ] [ ]
Jun 91. Rhino; (d-cd) **PROFILE: IT'S A MAEL MAEL MAEL MAEL WORLD** [ ] [ ]
(above was re-issue of BEST OF SPARKS)
May 93. Spectrum; (cd)(c) **IN THE SWING** [ ] [-]
Oct 93. Sony; (cd) **THE HEAVEN COLLECTION** [ ] [-]
Oct 93. Sony; (cd) **THE HELL COLLECTION** [ ] [-]
(above also issued both as d-cd)
Mar 94. Dojo; (cd) **SPARKS / A WOOFER IN TWEETER'S CLOTHING** [ ] [-]
Jul 94. Success; (cd)(c) **JUST GOT BACK FROM HEAVEN** [ ] [-]

SPARROW (see under ⇒ STEPPENWOLF)

SPEARHEAD (see under ⇒ DISPOSABLE HEROES OF HIPHOPRISY)

SPEAR OF DESTINY

Formed: Westminster, London, England . . . late 1982 by ex-THEATRE OF HATE mainmen KIRK BRANDON and STAN STAMMERS. KIRK had first ventured out in 1979 as leader of The PACK. The next year, he initiated the brilliant THEATRE OF HATE, who released smart double 'A'side debut 'ORIGINAL SIN' / 'LEGION' for his & Terry Razor's 'SS' label. In 1981, he formed own label 'Burning Rome', who finally came good early in 1982, when 'DO YOU BELIEVE IN THE WESTWORLD?', scraped the UK Top 40. This was quickly followed by a Top 20 album 'WESTWORLD', but BRANDON decided to forsake this project for the more accessible SPEAR OF DESTINY. Their 1983 debut 'GRAPES OF WRATH' album, sold moderately, although it contained an excellent near hit 45 'THE WHEEL'. In 1987, after completing two Top 30 albums in the mid-80's, they finally and deservedly broke the Top 20 singles chart with 'NEVER TAKE ME ALIVE'. After this, BRANDON experienced a set-back, when he underwent surgery for inflamation of the leg, a recurring illness. • **Style:** Alternative power rock, which leant on punk influence and the super high vocals chords of BRANDON. SOD were characterized by a well produced anthem sound backed by superb sax. • **Songwriters:** BRANDON penned material. • **Trivia:** MICK JONES of The CLASH, produced 1982's 'EASTWORLD'.

Recommended: S.O.D. – THE EPIC YEARS (*8) / OUTLAND (*7) THEATRE OF HATE:- WESTWORLD (*8) / REVOLUTION (*9)

The PACK

KIRK BRANDON (b. 3 Aug'56) – vocals, guitar / **SIMON WERNER** – guitar / **JONATHAN WERNER** – bass / **JIM WALKER** – drums (ex-PUBLIC IMAGE LTD.)

S.S. not issued

1979. (7") **BRAVE NEW SOLDIERS. / HEATHEN** [ ] [-]

Rough Trade not issued

Nov 79. (7") **KING OF KINGS. / NUMBER 12** [ ] [-]
(re-iss.1980 as 7"ep; all 4 tracks above on 'S.S.')

—— Early 1980, they had evolved into

THEATRE OF HATE

LUKE RANDALL – drums repl. WALKER

S.S. not issued

Nov 80. (7") **ORIGINAL SIN. / LEGION** [ ] [-]

—— **JAMIE STUART** – bass + **STEVE GUTHRIE** – guitar repl. both WERNERS

Mar 81. (lp) **HE WHO DARES WINS – LIVE AT THE WAREHOUSE, LEEDS (live)** [ ] [-]
– The original sin / Do you believe in the westworld / The klan / Conquistador / Poppies / Incinarator / Judgement hymn / 63 / Rebel without a brain / Legion.

Burning Rome not issued

Apr 81. (12") **REBEL WITHOUT A BRAIN. / MY OWN INVENTION** [ ] [-]
Jul 81. (12") **NERO. / INCINERATOR** [ ] [-]

—— **KIRK BRANDON** brought in entire new line-up **BILLY DUFFY** – guitar / **STAN STAMMERS** – bass (ex-STRAPS) repl. JAMIE who joined RITUAL then DEATH CULT / **NIGEL PRESTON** – drums / **JOHN BOY LENNARD** – saxophone

Jan 82. (7") **DO YOU BELIEVE IN THE WESTWORLD?. / PROPAGANDA** [40] [-]

(12"+=) – Original sin (version) / Ministry of broadcast.

Feb 82. (lp)(c) **WESTWORLD** [17] [ ]
– Do you believe in the westworld? / Judgement hymn / 63 / Love is a ghost / The wake / Conquistador / The new trail of tears / Freaks / Anniversary / The klan / Poppies. *(re-iss.+cd.May91 with free 7"ep)* **ORIGINAL SIN / LEGION./ / HEATHEN (The PACK) / BRAVE NEW SOLDIERS (The PACK)** (cd+=) – Incinerator / Rebel without a brain / Propaganda / Legion / Nero.

May 82. (7") **THE HOP. / CONQUISTADOR** [70] [-]

— reverted to a quartet, when DUFFY also joined The (DEATH) CULT.

Nov 82. (7") **EASTWORLD. / ASSEGAI** [ ] [-]
(12"+=) – Poppies.

— Had already disbanded Autumn '82. LENNARD moved to Canada to form DIODES. PRESTON joined The SEX GANG CHILDREN, and was later another to join The CULT.

SPEAR OF DESTINY

were almost immediately formed by **KIRK + STAN** with **CHRIS BELL** – drums (ex-KING TRIGGER, ex-THOMPSON TWINS) / **LASCELLES AMES** – saxophone (ex-MIGHTY DIAMONDS) ('Burning Rome' was taken over by 'Epic')

Epic / C.B.S.

Feb 83. (7") **FLYING SCOTSMAN. / THE MAN WHO TUNES THE DRUMS** [ ] [-]
(12"+=) – Africa.

Apr 83. (lp)(c) **GRAPES OF WRATH** [62] [-]
– The wheel / Flying Scotsman / Roof of the world / Aria / Solution / Murder of love / The preacher / Omen of the times / The man who tunes the drums / Grapes of wrath. *(re-iss.Apr86)*

May 83. (7")(7"pic-d) **THE WHEEL. / THE HOP** [59] [ ]
(d7"+=) – The preacher (live) / Grapes of wrath (live).
(12"+=) – Solution / Roof of the world / Love is a ghost (all live).

— **JOHN LENNARD** – saxophone returned to the fold repl. LASCELLES / **DOLPHIN TAYLOR** – drums (ex-STIFF LITTLE FINGERS, ex-TOM ROBINSON BAND) repl. BELL who joined The SPECIMEN then GENE LOVES JEZEBEL. / added **NEIL PYZER** – keyboards, saxophone (ex-HOWARD DEVOTO, ex-The CASE)

Jan 84. (7") **PRISONER OF LOVE. / ROSIE** [59] [ ]
(12"+=) – Grapes of wrath (1984).
(d7"+=) – Rainmaker (live) / Don't turn away (live).

— **BRANDON, STAMMERS, PYZER + TAYLOR** added **ALAN ST.CLAIRE** – guitar / **MICKEY DONNELLY** – saxophone (ex-The CASE) repl. LENNARD

Apr 84. (7") **LIBERATOR. / FORBIDDEN PLANET** [67] [ ]
(12"+=) – ('A'dub version) / ('A'extended).

Apr 84. (lp)(c) **ONE-EYED JACKS** [22] [ ]
– Rainmaker / Young men / Everything you ever wanted / Don't turn away / Liberator / Prisoner of love / Playground of the rich / Forbidden planet / Attica / These days are gone. *(re-iss.Feb88)*

May 85. (7") **ALL MY LOVE (ASK NOTHING). / LAST CARD** [61] [ ]
(12"+=) – Walk in the shadow.
(live-12"+=) – The wheel / Prisoner of love / Liberator.

Jul 85. (7") **COME BACK. / COLE YOUNGER** [55] [ ]
(12"+=) – Young men (the return of).

Aug 85. (lp)(c) **WORLD SERVICE** [11] [ ]
– Rocket ship / Up all night / Come back / World service / I can see / All my love (ask nothing) / Mickey / Somewhere in the east / Once in her lifetime / Harlan County.

— **BRANDON** recruited entire new band when STAMMERS + PYZER formed CRAZY PINK REVOLVERS. Newcomers:- **STEVIE BLANCHARD** – guitar (ex-TOM ROBINSON BAND) / **VOLKER JANSSON** – keyboards (ex-BERLIN) / **STEVE BARNACLE** – bass, keyboards / **PETE BARNACLE** – drums.

10-Virgin / Virgin

Jan 87. (7") **STRANGERS IN OUR TOWN. / SOMEWHERE OUT THERE** [49] [ ]
(12"+=) – Time of our lives / ('A'&'B'versions).
(d12"++=) – ('A'&'B'dub versions).

— **MIKE PROCTOR** – guitar repl. STEVIE B.

Mar 87. (7") **NEVER TAKE ME ALIVE. / LAND OF SHAME** [14] [ ]
('A'extended-12"+=) – Pumpkin man / Embassy song.
(3"cd-s+=) – Jack Straw / The man that never was.

— **MARCO PIRRONI** – guitar (ex-ADAM & THE ANTS, ex-MODELS) repl. PROCTOR

Apr 87. (lp)(c)(cd) **OUTLAND** [16] [ ]
– Outlands / Land of shame / The traveller / Was that you? / Strangers in our town / The whole world's waiting / Tonight / Miami vice / Never take me alive. *(c-ep+=)* – Time of our lives / Pumpkin man / Embassy song / Jack straw / The man that never was. *(re-iss.Oct87 w/free live lp, re-iss.Mar91)*

Jul 87. (7") **WAS THAT YOU?. / WAS THAT YOU? (live)** [55] [ ]
(12"+=)(12"pic-d+=) – Miami vice / Outlands.
(live-12"+=) – Land of shame / Jack Straw. (US-iss. 5 track cd-ep)

Sep 87. (7") **THE TRAVELLER. / LATE NIGHT PSYCHO** [44] [ ]
(12"+=) – Strangers in our town (live) / Mickey (live) –

— **ALAN ST.CLAIRE** – guitar returned to repl. PIRRONI / **CHRIS BOSTOCK** – bass (ex-JO BOXERS) repl. STEVE

Virgin / Virgin

Sep 88. (7") **SO IN LOVE WITH YOU. / MARCH OR DIE** [36] [ ]
(12"+=) – ('A'extended).
(cd-s+=)/ /(10"+=) – Junkman./ / Jungle.

Oct 88. (lp)(c)(cd) **THE PRICE YOU PAY** [37] [ ]
– So in love with you / Tinseltown / The price / I remember / Dreamtime / Radio radio / If the guns / View from a tree / Junkman. *(cd+=)* – Soldier soldier / Brave new world. *(re-iss.Mar91)*

Nov 88. (7") **RADIO RADIO. / LIFE GOES ON** [ ] [ ]
(10"+=)/ /(cd-s++=) – Made in London./ / ('A'extended).
(12"+=) – ('A'extended) / Spirits.

— In the 90's, **KIRK** brought back **STAN STAMMERS** – bass / + newcomers **MARK THWAITE** – guitar / **BOBBY RAE MAYHEM** – drums. Toured as TOH & SOD.

Burning Rome / not issued

Sep 92. (12")(cd-s) **BLACK COUNTRY GIRL. / BABYLON TALKING** [ ] [-]

Oct 92. (cd)(c)(lp) **SOD'S LAW** [ ] [-]
– Goldmine / Into the rising Sun / Black country girl / When the bull comes down / Slow me down / T.C.B. / In the city / Babylon talking / Crystalize / Killing ground. *(c+=)* – Rave on Albion. *(cd++=)* – Captain America.

KIRK BRANDON'S 10:51

Anagram / not issued

Mar 95. (c-s) **CHILDREN OF THE DAMNED / SATELLITE** [ ] [-]
(cd-s+=) – At her majesties request.

Apr 95. (cd) **STONE IN THE RAIN** [ ] [-]
– Stone in the rain / Communication ends / How long? / Satellite / Children of the damned / Europa / Psycho woman / Revolver / Propaganda / Heroes / Future world / Spirit tribe.

- compilations, others, etc. -

May 87. Epic; (lp)(c)(cd) **S.O.D. - THE EPIC YEARS** [53] [-]
– The wheel / Rainmaker / Prisoner of love / Playground of the rich / Young men / Up all night / Come back / All my love (ask nothing) / Mickey / Liberator.

Feb 86. Old Gold; (12"ep) **FLYING SCOTSMAN / THE WHEEL. / PRISONER OF LOVE / LIBERATOR** [ ] [-]

Jul 93. Mau Mau; (cd) **LIVE AT THE LYCEUM 22.12.85 (live)** [ ] [-]

Apr 94. Windsong; (cd) **THE BBC RADIO ONE LIVE IN CONCERT (live)** [ ] [-]

Mar 95. Virgin; (cd) **TIME OF OUR LIVES - THE BEST OF SPEAR OF DESTINY** [ ] [-]

- (THEATRE OF HATE) compilations, etc. -

Jun 81. Strange Music; (c) **LIVE AT THE LYCEUM (live)** [ ] [-]

Feb 82. S.S.; (lp) **HE WHO DARES WINS - LIVE IN BERLIN (live)** [ ] [-]

Aug 84. Burning Rome; (lp)(d-c) **REVOLUTION** (The Best Of . . .) [ ] [-]
– Legion / The original sin / Rebel without a brain / My own invention / Nero / Do you believe in the westworld? / Propaganda / The hop / Incinerator / Eastworld / Americanos. (d-c+=) – HE WHO DARES WINS *cd-iss.Feb93 on 'Line')*

Nov 85. Burning Rome; (12"ep) **THE HOP / CONQUISTADOR. / ORIGINAL SIN / WESTWORLD?** [ ] [-]

Mar 85. Bliss; (live-7"ep) **THE WAKE / LOVE IS A GHOST. / POPPIES / LEGION** [ ] [-]

Dec 85. Dojo; (lp) **ORIGINAL SIN LIVE (live)** [ ] [-]

Jul 93. Mau Mau; (cd) **THEATRE OF HATE** [ ] [-]

Jun 95. Anagram; (cd) **THE COMPLETE SINGLES COLLECTION** [ ] [-]

- (The PACK) compilations, etc. -

Apr 82. Cyclops; (7"ep) **LONG LIVE THE PAST (demos from Aug'78)** [ ] [-]
– Thalidomide / King of kings / St.Teresa / Abattoir.

1982. Donat; (c) **THE PACK LIVE 1979 (live)** [ ] [-]

The SENATE

(**KIRK BRANDON + RUSTY EGAN** ex-SKIDS, ex-VISAGE)

Jul 84. Burning Rome; (7") **THE ORIGINAL SIN. / DO YOU BELIEVE IN THE WESTWORLD?** [ ] [-]

Jul 84. W.A.R.; (7") **THE ORIGINAL SIN. / DO YOU BELIEVE IN THE WESTWORLD? (live)** [ ] [-]
(12"+=) – ('A'extended).

SPECIALS

Formed: Coventry, Midlands, England ... 1978 by DAMMERS, GOULDING and GENTLEMAN. After a brief spell with CLASH manager Bernie Rhodes, DAMMERS formed own label '2-Tone' in 1979 to release debut 45 'GANGSTERS'. It picked up airplay on The John Peel Radio 1 Show, with it eventually cracking the Top 10. It sparked off a ska-revival that year, that showcased other splendid acts The SELECTER, MADNESS and The BEAT. The 2-Tone label was picked up by 'Chrysalis', and after another Top 10 hit 'MESSAGE TO YOU RUDY', they unleashed fantastic ELVIS COSTELLO produced eponymous album. • **Style:** As said, ska revivalists with a mission of social protest. Loved by rude boys, punks/new wavees and mods alike. • **Songwriters:** DAMMERS wrote most of work. Covered GANGSTERS (Prince Buster; 'Al Capone' song) / GUNS OF NAVARONE (Skatelites) / CONCRETE JUNGLE (Bob Marley) / LONG SHOT KICK DE BUCKET (Pioneers) / LIQUIDATOR (Harry J. All Stars) / MONKEY MAN (Maytals) / MAGGIE'S FARM (Bob Dylan) / SKINHEAD MOONSTOMP (Symarip). • **Trivia:** In 1984, DAMMERS wrote 'NELSON MANDELA', a song that initiated the freedom of the jailed ANC South African leader. On 11 Jun'88, he organized MANDELA's 70th birthday benefit concert at Wembley Stadium, which featured artists EURYTHMICS, DIRE STRAITS, SIMPLE MINDS, STEVIE WONDER & TRACY CHAPMAN.

Recommended: THE SPECIALS (*8) / THE SPECIALS SINGLES (*9).

TERRY HALL (b.19 Mar'59) – vocals / **NEVILLE STAPLES** – vocals, percussion / **LYNVAL GOULDING** (b.24 Jul'51) – guitar, vocals / **JOHN BRADBURY** – drums / **JERRY DAMMERS** (b.GERALD DANKIN, 22 May'54, India) – keyboards / **RODDY RADIATION** (b.BYERS) – guitar / **HORACE GENTLEMAN** (b.PANTER) – bass

2-Tone / not issued

Jul 79. (7") **GANGSTERS. (as "The SPECIAL A.K.A.") / THE SELECTER (by "The SELECTER"),** the JOHN BRADBURY outfit) [6] [-]

— added (on some) guest **RICO RODRIQUEZ** – trombone

2-Tone-Chrysalis / Chrysalis

Oct 79. (7") **A MESSAGE TO YOU RUDY. / NITE CLUB** [10] [ ]
Oct 79. (lp)(c) **SPECIALS** [4] [84]
– A message to you Rudy / Do the dog / It's up to you / Nite club / Doesn't make it alright / Concrete jungle / Too hot / Monkey man / (Dawning of a) New era / Blank expression / Stupid marriage / Too much too young / Little bitch / You're wondering now. *(US-version w/)* – Gangsters. *(UK re-iss.Nov84 on 'Fame') (re-iss.cd Mar94)*
Jan 80. (7"ep) **TOO MUCH TOO YOUNG – GUNS OF NAVARONE (live). / LONG SHOT KICK DE BUCKET – LIQUIDATOR – SKINHHEAD MOONSTOMP (live)** [1] [ ]
May 80. (7") **RAT RACE. / RUDE BOYS OUTA JAIL** [5] [ ]
Sep 80. (7") **STEREOTYPES (part 1). / INTERNATIONAL JET SET** [6] [ ]
Sep 80. (lp)(c) **MORE SPECIALS** [5] [98]
– Enjoy yourself (it's later than you think) / Man at C & A / Hey little rich girl / Do nothing / Pearl's cafe / Sock it to 'em J.B. / Stereotypes / Stereotypes (part 2) / Holiday fortnight / I can't stand it / International jet set / Enjoy yourself (reprise). *(free-7"w.a.)* **BEGGIN' TRYING NOT TO LIE. / RUDE BOYS OUTA JAIL (diff.mix)**
Jan 81. (7") **DO NOTHING. / MAGGIE'S FARM** [4] [ ]
Jun 81. (7")(12") **GHOST TOWN. / WHY / FRIDAY NIGHT, SATURDAY MORNING** [1] [ ]

— Only two originals (DAMMERS & BRADBURY) remained, as GOULDING, STAPLES & HALL formed The FUN BOY THREE. RADIATION formed TEARJERKERS. RICO went solo. All repl. by **RHODA DAKAR** – vocals + **NICKY SUMMERS** – bass (ex-BODYSNATCHERS) / **JOHN SHIPLEY** – guitar / **DICK CUTHELL** – saxophone

RHODA with The SPECIAL A.K.A.

(same label)
Jan 82. (7") **THE BOILER. / THEME FROM THE BOILER** [35] [-]

The SPECIAL A.K.A.

HORACE PANTER – bass returned to repl. SUMMERS who joined The BELLE STARS / **STAN CAMPBELL** (b. 2 Jan'62) – vocals / **NICK PARKER** – violin repl. CUTHELL

(same label)
Dec 82. (7")(10") **WAR CRIMES (THE CRIME IS STILL THE SAME). / WAR CRIMES** [ ] [ ]

— **RODDY RADIATION** – guitar returned with newcomer **EGIDIO NEWTON** – vox

Aug 83. (7")(7"pic-d) **RACIST FRIEND. / BRIGHT LIGHTS** [60] [ ]

— **GARY McMANUS** – bass repl. PANTER who joined GENERAL PUBLIC guested on album **DICK CUTHELL** – cornet / **ANDY ADERINTO** – saxophone

Mar 84. (7")(12") **NELSON MANDELA. / BREAK DOWN THE DOOR** [9] [ ]
Jun 84. (lp)(c) **IN THE STUDIO** [34] [ ]
– Bright lights / Lonely crowd / House bound / War crimes / What I like most about you is your girlfriend / Night on the tiles / Nelso Mandela / War crimes / Rascist friend / Alcohol / Break down the door.
Aug 84. (7")(12") **WHAT I LIKE MOST ABOUT YOU IS YOUR GIRLFRIEND. / CAN'T GET A BREAK** [51] [ ]

— Folded late '84, STAN CAMPBELL went solo and BRADBURY formed The JB's ALL STARS. DAMMERS turned up on a charity single by STARVATION early 1985.

– compilations, others, etc. –

Dec 82. Chrysalis; (d-c) **SPECIALS / MORE SPECIALS** [ ] [-]
Jun 88. Chrysalis; (7")(12") **FREE NELSON MANDELA – 70th Birthday re-make). / ('A'original)** [ ] [-]
Aug 91. Chrysalis; (cd)(c)(lp) **THE SPECIALS SINGLES** [10] [ ]
– Gangsters / A message to you Rudy / Nite club / Too much too young – Guns of Navarone / Rat race / Rude boys outta jail / Stereotype / International jet set / Do nothing / Ghost town / Why? / Friday night, Saturday morning / Racist friend / Free Nelson Mandela / What I like most about you is your girlfriend.
Oct 91. Chrysalis; (7")(cd-s) **GHOST TOWN (REVISITED. / ('A'dub version)** [ ] [ ]
(12"+=) – Why / ('A'demo version).
Apr 92. Chrysalis; (cd)(c)(lp) **LIVE AT THE MOONLIGHT CLUB (live)** [ ] [-]
Feb 87. Strange Fruit; (12"ep) **THE PEEL SESSIONS** (23.5.79) [ ] [-]
– Gangsters / Too much too young / Concrete jungle / Monkey man.
Feb 87. Old Gold; (7") **TOO MUCH TOO YOUNG (live). / RAT RACE** [ ] [-]
Feb 87. Old Gold; (7") **GHOST TOWN. / RAT RACE** [ ] [-]
(re-iss.Mar90)
Apr 92. Receiver; (cd)(c)(lp) **TOO MUCH TOO YOUNG** [ ] [-]

— next shared with The SELECTER.

Dec 92. Windsong; (cd)(lp) **BBC RADIO 1 LIVE IN CONCERT (live)** [ ] [-]
Sep 93. 2-Tone; (12"ep)(c-ep)(cd-ep) **THE TWO-TONE EP ("Various Artists")** [30] [ ]
– Gangsters (SPECIAL AKA) / The Prince (MADNESS) / On my radio (SELECTER) / Tears of a clown (BEAT).

— In Oct'93, SPECIALS were credited on DESMOND DEKKER single 'Jamaica Sky'.

— re-form with **GOLDING, STAPLES + RADIATION** + featuring **SHEENA STAPLE + KENDELL**. Cover HYPOCRITE (Bob Marley).

Kuff-Virgin / not issued

Oct 95. (c-s) **HYPOCRITE (Stoker radio mix) / HYPOCRITE (Steely & Clevie radio mix)** [ ] [-]
(cd-s+=) – ('A'-Manual dub) / ('A'-Intelligent jungle mix) / ('A'-Steely & Clevie 12"mix) / ('A'-Early afternoon dubwise) / ('A'-Intelligent jungle instrumental).

SPECTRES (see under ⇒ STATUS QUO)

SPECTRUM (see under ⇒ SPACEMEN 3)

Alexander SPENCE (see under ⇒ MOBY GRAPE)

SPIDERS (see under ⇒ COOPER, Alice)

SPIN DOCTORS

Formed: New York, USA ... 1991 by students at the New York New School Of Jazz. They were soon hitting the Top 10 in America with classy 'TWO PRINCES' single. • **Style:** Funky-metal likened to The ALLMAN BROTHERS or STEVE MILLER BAND. • **Songwriters:** Group penned except WOODSTOCK (Joni Mitchell). • **Trivia:** Produced by themselves plus PETER DENENBERG and FRANKIE LA ROCKA.

Recommended: POCKETFULL OF KRYPTONYTE (*6).

CHRIS BARRON – vocals / **ERIC SCHENKMAN** – guitar / **MARK WHITE** – bass / **AARON COMESS** – drums

Epic / Epic

Sep 92. (7") **LITTLE MISS CAN'T BE WRONG. / TWO PRINCES** [-] [ ]
Feb 93. (7")(c-s) **LITTLE MISS CAN'T BE WRONG. / WHAT TIME IS IT?** [ ] [-]
(cd-s+=) – Big fat funky booty – At this hour (live)
(re-iss. Jul 93, hit UK No. 23)
Mar 93. (cd)(c) **POCKET FULL OF KRYPTONYTE** [2] [3] Aug 92
– Jimmy Olsen's blues / What time is it? / Little Miss can't be wrong / forty or fifty / Refrigerator car / More than she knows / Two princes / Off my line / How could you want him (when you know you could have me?) / Shinbone alley – Hard to exist.*(released a year earlier in US)*
May 93. (7")(c-s) **TWO PRINCES. / OFF MY LINE** [3] [7] Jan 93
(cd-s) – ('A'side) / Yo mamas a pasama (live) / Little miss can't be wrong (live).
Sep 93. (7")(c-s) **JIMMY OLSEN'S BLUES. / AT THIS HOUR** [40] [78]
(cd-s+=) – Rosetta stone.
Nov 93. (7")(c-s) **WHAT TIME IS IT?. / ('A'live)** [56] [ ]
(cd-s+=) – Two princess (live) / Forty or fifty (live).
Dec 93. (cd)(c) **HOMEBELLY GROOVE (live)** [ ] [ ]
– What time is it? – Off my line / Freeway of the plains – Lady Kerosene / Yo baby / Little Miss can't be wrong / Shinbone alley / Refrigerator car / Sweet widow / Stepped on a crack / Yo mamas a pajama / Rosetta Stone.
Jun 94. (7"pic-d)(c-s) **CLEOPATRA'S CAT. / URANIUM CENTURY** [29] [84]
(cd-s+=) – Stop breaking down (live).
Jun 94. (cd)(c)(lp) **TURN IT UPSIDE DOWN** [3] [28]
– Big fat funky booty / You let your heart go too fast / Cleopatra's cat / Hungry Hamed's / Biscuit head / Indifference / Bags of dirt / Mary Jane / More than meets the ear / Laraby's gang / At this hour / Someday all this will be road / Beasts in the woods.
Jul 94. (7")(c-s) **YOU LET YOUR HEART GO TOO FAST. / PIECE OF GLASS** [66] [42]
(cd-s+=) – I can't.
Oct 94. (c-s) **MARY JANE / WOODSTOCK** [55] [ ]
(cd-s+=) – Hungry Hamed's.

— **ANTHONY KRIZAN** – guitar repl. ERIC

SPIRIT

Formed: Los Angeles, California, USA . . . 1964 as The RED ROOSTERS by RANDY CALIFORNIA and his shaven-headed step-father ED CASSIDY. By late 1966, they became SPIRITS REBELLIOUS, but shortened to SPIRIT, with addition of other ex-RED ROOSTERS; JAY FERGUSON and MARK ANDES. Early in 1968, they signed to Lou Adler's 'Ode' records, which released eponymous debut soon after. The next year, they had first US Top 30 (and only) hit with drug-orientated 'I GOT A LINE ON YOU'. From 1970, they were haunted by numerous splits, and even a bogus SPIRIT!, which thought it could exist without RANDY + ED. • **Style:** Ecletic and progressive rock outfit, who diverted into psychedelia and the avant-garde. • **Songwriters:** CALIFORNIA and group, except YESTERDAY (Beatles) / HEY JOE (hit; Jimi Hendrix; c.William Roberts). CALIFORNIA covered solo:- MOTHER AND CHILD REUNION (Paul Simon) / RAIN + DAY TRIPPER (Beatles) / ALL ALONG THE WATCHTOWER (Bob Dylan) / WILD THING (Troggs). • **Trivia:** MARK ANDES played on BORIS PICKETT & THE CRYPT KICKER 5's hit single 'Monster Mash'. LED ZEPPELIN (Jimmy Page), must have listened to 1968 track 'TAURUS', before writing 'Stairway To Heaven'. Listen?

Recommended: TWELVE DREAMS OF DOCTOR SARDONICUS (*8) / THE BEST OF SPIRIT (*8) / POTATOLAND (*9)

RANDY CALIFORNIA (b.RANDY CRAIG WOLFE, 20 Feb'51, L.A., Calif) – guitar, vox / **JAY FERGUSON** (b.JOHN ARDEN FERGUSON, 10 May'47, Burnbank, Calif.) – vocals / **MARK ANDES** (b.19 Feb'48, Philadelphia) – bass (ex-YELLOW BALLOON, w /JAY) / **ED CASSIDY** (b. 4 May'31, Chicago) – drums (ex-NEW JAZZ TRIO) / **JOHN LOCKE** (b.25 Sep'53, L.A., Calif.) – keyboards (ex-NEW WORLD JAZZ CO.)

C.B.S. / Ode

Jun 68. (lp) **SPIRIT** [ ] [31] Jan 68
– Fresh garbage / Uncle Jack / Mechanical world / Taurus / Straight arrow / Topango windows / Gramophone man / Water woman / Great canyon fire in general / Elijah /

Girl in your eyes. *(re-iss.Apr79 as 'THE FIRST OF . . . ' on 'CBS-Embassy') (re-iss.+c+cd.Apr89 on 'Edsel')*

Jun 68. (7") **UNCLE JACK. / MECHANICAL WORLD**

Feb 69. (7") **I GOT A LINE ON YOU. / SHE SMILED** — 25 Dec 68

Apr 69. (lp) **THE FAMILY THAT PLAYS TOGETHER** — 22 Jan 69
– I got a line on you / Poor Richard / Aren't you glad / It shall be / The drunkard / It's all the same / Dream within a dream / Jewish / So little to say / Silky Sam. *(US re-iss.Jul72) (re-iss.+c+cd.Mar86 on 'Edsel'+=)* – She smiles / Darlin' if, repl. track) *(cd-iss.Sep94 on 'Rewind')*

Aug 69. (7") **DARK EYED WOMAN. / ICE** — -

Sep 69. (7") **DARK EYED WOMAN. / NEW DOPE AT TOWN**

Oct 69. (lp) **CLEAR SPIRIT** — 55 Jul 69
– Dark eyed woman / Apple orchard / So little time to fly / Groundhog / Cold wind / Policeman's ball / Ice / Give a life, take a life / I'm truckin' / Clear / Caught / New dope in town. *(re-iss.+cd.Mar88 on 'Edsel')*

Jan 70. (7") **1984. / SWEET STELLA BABY** — 69 Dec 69

Epic Epic

Sep 70. (7") **ANIMAL ZOO. / RED LIGHT, ROLL ON** — 97

Oct 70. (7") **MR. SKIN. / NATURE'S WAY** — - 92

Dec 70. (7") **NATURE'S WAY. / SOLDIER** — -

Feb 71. (lp) **TWELVE DREAMS OF DR. SARDONICUS** — 63 Dec 70
– Nothing to hide / Nature's way / Animal zoo / Love has found a way / Why can't I be free / Mr. Skin / Space child / When I touch you / Sweet worm / Life has just begun / Morning will come / Soldier. *(re-iss.+c.Mar81) (re-iss.+c+cd.Apr89 on 'Edsel') (re-iss.cd+c May94)*

Mar 71. (7") **SOLDIER. / MR.SKIN** — -

— (Dec70) **JOHN ARLISS** – bass repl. FERGUSON and ANDES who formed JO JO GUNNE (May71) **CASSIDY + LOCKE** recruited new men **AL STAEHELY** – bass (ex-PUMPKIN) / **J.CHRISTIAN** (b.CHRIS STAEHELY) – guitar repl. ARLISS + RANDY who went solo

May 72. (7") **CADILLAC COWBOYS. / DARKNESS**

Jun 72. (lp) **FEEDBACK** — 63 Mar 72
– Chelsea girl / Cadillac / Cowboys / Puesta del scam / Ripe and ready / Darkness / Earth shaker / Mellow morning / Trancas fog-out / The witch.

— (Aug72) Now a totally 'bogus' SPIRIT, fronted by The STAEHELY brothers. **STU PERRY** – drums repl. CASSIDY (see further below), and LOCKE who went solo. An album 'STA-HAY-LEE', included CASSIDY and LOCKE surfaced in US later? CHRIS was another to join JO JO GUNNE. Regarded as the 'real SPIRIT'

RANDY CALIFORNIA

(solo!) with **TIM McGOVERN** – drums, vocals / **CHARLIE BUNDY** – bass, b.vox / **HENRY MANCKATITZ** (aka MITCH MITCHELL) – drums / **CLIT McTORIUS**(aka NOEL REDDING) – bass / guests **CASS STRANGE** (aka ED CASSIDY) – bass / **FUZZY KNIGHT** (aka ARRY WEISBER) – keyboards

Sep 72. (7") **WALKIN' THE DOG. / LIVE FOR THE DAY** — -

Sep 72. (lp) **KAPTAIN KOPTER AND THE (FABULOUS) TWIRLY BIRDS**
– Downer / Devil / I don't want nobody / Day tripper / Mother and child reunion / Things yet to come / Rain / Rainbow. *(re-iss.+c.Jun80 on 'CBS') (re-iss. +c.Nov85 on 'Edsel'+=)* – Walkin' the dog / Live for the day. *(cd-iss.Aug93 on 'Edsel')*

— In 1973, CALIFORNIA attempted suicide by jumping off Chelsea Bridge.

SPIRIT

after a few other line-up's in 1974, settled with **CASSIDY, CALIFORNIA + MARK ANDES** who repl. FUZZY KNIGHT. **JOHN LOCKE** re-joined for short spell, until he went into sessions. Also ANDES (who joined FIREFALL) were repl. by **BARRY KEANE** – bass

Mercury Mercury

Jun 75. (d-lp)(d-c) **SPIRIT OF '76**
– America the beautiful / The times they are a-changin' / Victim of society / Lady of the lakes / Tampa man / Mounalo / What do I have / Sunrise / Walking the dog / Joker on the run / When? / Like a rolling stone / Once again / Feeling in time / Happy / Jack Bond (part 1) / Mr. Road / Thank you Lord / Urantia / Guide me / Veruska / Hey Joe / Jack Bond (part 2) / The star spangled banner. *(re-iss.May88 on 'Edsel') (cd-iss.Mar93)*

Aug 75. (7") **AMERICA THE BEAUTIFUL. / THE TIMES THEY ARE A-CHANGIN' / LADY OF THE LAKES** — -

— added **MATT ANDES** – guitar (ex-JO JO GUNNE)

Oct 75. (lp)(c) **SON OF SPIRIT** — -
– Holy man / Looking into darkness / Maybe you'll find / Don't go away / Family / Magic fairy princess / Circle / The other song / Yesterday / It's time now. *(UK-iss.+cd.May89 on 'Great Expectation')*

Oct 75. (7") **HOLY MAN. / LOOKING INTO DARKNESS** — -

Jul 76. (lp) **FARTHER ALONG**
– Farther along / Atomic boogie / World eat world dog / Stoney night / Pineapple / Colossus / Mega star / Phoebe / Don't look up your door / Once with you / Diamond spirit / Nature's way.

Sep 76. (7") **FARTHER ALONG. / ATOMIC BOOGIE** — -

— Now just a trio, when MARK re-joined FIREFALL and MATT & JOHN also left.

Apr 77. (lp)(c) **FUTURE GAMES (A MAGICAL KAHVANA DREAM)**
– CB talk / Stars are love / Kahouna dream / Brued my brain / Bionic unit / So happy now / All along the watchtower / Would you believe / Jack Bond speaks / Star Trek dreaming / Interlude XM / China doll / Hawaiian times / Gorn attack / Interlude 2001 / Detroit City / Freak out frog / The Romulan experiences / Monkey see, monkey do / Mt. Olympus / The journey of Nomad / Ending. *(re-iss.+cd.May89 on 'Great Expectations')*

May 77. (7") **ALL ALONG THE WATCHTOWER. / FARTHER ALONG**

— **LARRY KNIGHT** – bass returned to repl. KEENE

Illegal Potato

Dec 78. (7") **NATURE'S WAY (live). / STONE FREE (live)**

Jan 79. (lp) **SPIRIT LIVE** (live 11th Mar'78, Rainbow, London)
– Rock and roll planet / Nature's way / Animal zoo / 1984 / Looking down / It's all the same / I got a line on you / These are words / Hollywood dream.

— Disbanded yet again late 1978, RANDY formed own band with **STEVE LAURA** – bass / **JACK WILLOUGHBY** – drums.

SPIRIT

re-formed to re-record old unissued lost album below. **CALIFORNIA & CASSIDY** (alias KAPTAIN KOPTER & COMMANDER CASSIDY) enlisted **GEORGE VALUCK, JOHN LOCKE, MIKE BUNNELL + KARI NILE** – keys / **JEFF JARVIS, MIKE THORNBURGH + CHUCK SNYDER** – horns / **JOE GREEN** – strings

Beggar's B. Rhino

Apr 81. (lp)(c) **JOURNEY TO POTATOLAND** — 40
– We've got a lot to learn / Potatolandland theme / Open up your heart / Morning light / Potatoland prelude / Potatoland intro / Turn to the right / Donut house / Fish fry road / Information / My friend. *(re-iss.+cd+dat.1988 on 'Chord')*

Apr 81. (7") **WE'VE GOT A LOT TO LEARN. / FISH FRY ROAD**

Jun 81. (7") **TURN TO THE RIGHT. / POTATOLAND THEME**

— Band toured 1981:- **CALIFORNIA, CASSIDY, VALUCK + STEVE LAURA** (aka LIBERTY)

RANDY CALIFORNIA

solo including all present SPIRIT members and some past.

Apr 82. (lp)(c) **EURO AMERICAN**
– Easy love / Fearless leader / Five in the morning / Skull and crossbones / Breakout / Hand gun (toy guns) / This is the end / Mon ami / Rude reaction / Calling you / Wild thing. (free-7"w.a.) **SHATTERED DREAMS. / MAGIC WAND**

Apr 82. (7") **HAND GUNS (TOY GUNS). / THIS IS THE END**

Aug 82. (7") **ALL ALONG THE WATCHTOWER. / RADIO MAN**
(12"+=) – Breakout / Killer weed.

SPIRIT

originals re-formed re-recording material from that era.

Mercury Mercury

Jan 84. (7") **1984. / ELIJAH**
(12"+=) – I got a line on you.

Mar 84. (lp)(c)(cd) **THE THIRTEENTH DREAM** (remixes)
– Black satin nights / Mr. Skin / Mechanical world / Pick it up / All over the world / 1984 / Uncle Jack / Natures way / Fresh garbage / I got a line on you. *(c+=)* – Elijah.

Apr 84. (7")(6") **FRESH GARBAGE. / MR. SKIN**

RANDY CALIFORNIA

solo with live + studio **MIKE SHEPHERD** – bass / **NEIL MURRAY + ADRIAN LEE + NEAL DOUGHTY** – keyboards / **CURLY SMITH** – drums live: **SCOTT MONAHAN** – keys / **LES WARNER** – drums

Vertigo Mercury

May 85. (7") **RUN TO YOUR LOVER. / SECOND CHILD**
(12"+=) – Shane.

Jun 85. (lp)(c) **RESTLESS**
– Run to your lover / Restless nights / Second child / Jack Rabbit / Shane / One man's Heaven / Murphy's law / Camelot / Battle march of the overlords / Childhood's end.

Jun 85. (7") **JACK RABBIT. / SUPER CHILD**

Line not issued

1986. (lp) **SHATTERED DREAMS** — - — - Germ'y
– Hey Joe (live) / Shattered dreams / All along the watchtower / Don't bother me / Downer / Second child / Man at war / Killer weed / Hand guns (toy guns) / Radio man / Run to your lover.

— In Apr'89, RANDY appeared on Various Artists live d-lp,c,cd,video 'NIGHT OF THE GUITAR', which was on next label.

RANDY CALIFORNIA'S SPIRIT

gigged with various line-ups, until in 1989 settled with **RANDY, ED + SCOTT** plus **MIKE BUNNELL** – bass

I.R.S. I.R.S.

Jun 89. (7") **HARD LOVE. / THE PRISONER**
(12"+=) – Hey Joe.

Aug 89. (lp)(c)(cd) **RAPTURE IN THE CHAMBERS**
– Hard love / Love tonight / Thinking of / Rapture in the chambers / Mojo man / Contact / The prisoner / One track mind / Enchanted forest / Human sexuality / Shera, princess of power / End suite.

– compilations, others, etc. –

Apr 73. Epic; (7") **MR.SKIN. / NATURE'S WAY**

Aug 73. Epic; (d-lp) **SPIRIT. / CLEAR SPIRIT** — -

Oct 73. Epic; (lp)(c) **THE BEST OF SPIRIT** — Jul 73
(re-iss.Sep84, US re-iss.May89)

Dec 91. Columbia; (d-cd)(d-c) **TIME CIRCLE (1968-72)**

Jan 92. Castle; (cd)(c) **THE COLLECTION** — -

SPIRITUALIZED (see under ⇒ SPACEMEN 3)

SPLIT ENZ (see under ⇒ CROWDED HOUSE)

SPOOKY TOOTH

Formed: based London, England . . . out of LUTHER GROSVENOR's 1964 outfit The V.I.P.'s, who soon added MIKE HARRISON and GREG RIDLEY. In 1967, they evolved into ART and were joined by MIKE KELLIE. After one flop album, and the addition of American GARY WRIGHT, they became

SPOOKY TOOTH. Staying with 'Island' records, they recorded some fine albums, appreciated more on foreign soil. In 1976, after their demise, GARY WRIGHT became a near US No.1 success, with 'DREAM WEAVER'. • **Style:** Described somewhat unfairly as the poor man's TRAFFIC, who were also produced by American Jimmy Miller. Their hard-rock sound was bent a little to incorporate electronics wizard PIERRE HENRY on the 1970 album 'CEREMONY'. WRIGHT's solo stuff, was made for mainstream radio FM. • **Songwriters:** WRIGHT wrote most of material, except covers; I AM THE WALRUS (Beatles) / etc. • **Trivia:** Before his call-up to The SPOOKYS, GARY had stayed in Berlin.

Recommended: THE BEST OF SPOOKY TOOTH (*7).

The V.I.P.'s

LUTHER GROSVENOR (b.23 Dec'49) – guitar, vocals (ex-HELLIONS) / **FRANK KENYON** – rhythm guitar / **JIMMY HENSHAW** – guitar / **WALTER JOHNSTONE** – drums

R.C.A. | not issued

Nov 64. (7") **DON'T KEEP SHOUTING AT ME. / SHE'S NO GOOD** [ ] [-]

— **MIKE HARRISON** (b. 3 Sep'45, Carlisle) – vocals, piano (ex-RAMRODS) / **GREG RIDLEY** (b.23 Oct'41, Cumberland) – bass (ex-RAMRODS) both repl. JIMMY (single mis-credited as "The VIPPS")

C.B.S. | not issued

Jan 66. (7") **WINTERTIME. / ANYONE** [ ] [-]

Island | not issued

Oct 66. (7") **I WANNA BE FREE. / DON'T LET IT GO** [ ] [-]

Feb 67. (7") **STRAIGHT DOWN TO THE BOTTOM. / IN A DREAM** [ ] [-]

ART

(same label) **MIKE KELLIE** (b.24 Mar'47, Birmingham) – drums repl. WALTER

Aug 67. (7") **WHAT'S THAT SOUND. / ROME TAKE AWAY THREE** [ ] [-]

Dec 67. (lp) **SUPERNATURAL FAIRY TALES** [ ] [-]
– I think I'm going weird/ What's that sound (for what it's worth)/ African thing/ Room with a view/ Flying anchors/ Supernatural fairy tale/ Love is real/ Come on up/ Brothers, dads & mothers/ Talkin' to myself/ Alive not dead/ Rome take away three. *(cd-iss.Nov92 on Drop Out)*

— That year, the group also appeared on album 'Featuring The Human Host And The Heavy Metal Kids' by 'HAPHASH & THE COLOURED COAT'. They recorded 5 or 6 French-only 45's between 1966-68.

SPOOKY TOOTH

HARRISON now on keyboards / added **GARY WRIGHT** (b.26 Apr'45, Englewood, New Jersey, USA) – vocals, organ

Island | Mala

Jan 68. (7") **SUNSHINE HELP ME. / WEIRD** [ ] [ ]

Jun 68. (lp) **IT'S ALL ABOUT A ROUNDABOUT** [ ] [ ]
– Society's child / Love really changed me / Here I lived so well / Too much of nothing / Sunshine help me / It's all about a roundabout / / Tobacco road / It hurts so much / Forget it, I got it / Bubbles. *(re-iss.+c.1974) (US-issJun 71 as 'TOBACCO ROAD' for 'A&M')*

Jun 68. (7") **LOVE REALLY CHANGED ME. / LUGER'S GROVE** [ ] [ ]

Sep 68. (7") **THE WEIGHT. / DO RIGHT PEOPLE** [ ] [ ]

Island | A&M

Mar 69. (lp) **SPOOKY TWO** [ ] [44] Jul 69
– Waitin' for the wind / Feelin' bad / I've got enough heartaches / Evil woman / Lost in my dream / Better by you, better than me / Hangman hang my shell on a tree. *(re-is.+c.1974)*

Jun 69. (7") **SON OF YOUR FATHER. / I'VE GOT ENOUGH HEARTACHES** [ ] [-]

Jul 69. (7") **I'VE GOT ENOUGH HEARTACHES. / FEELIN' BAD** [-] [ ]

Nov 69. (7") **WAITIN' FOR THE WIND. / THAT WAS ONLY YESTERDAY** [-] [ ]

— trimmed to quartet (**GROSVENOR, WRIGHT, HARRISON & KELLIE**), after RIDLEY joined HUMBLE PIE. Below **PIERRE HENRY** was avant-garde electronic wizard.

Jan 70. (lp) **CEREMONY ("SPOOKY TOOTH with PIERRE HENRY")** [ ] [92] Mar 70
– Have mercy / Jubilation / Confession / Prayer / Offering / Hosana. *(re-iss.+c.1974)*

— GARY vacated to form WONDERWHEEL who made 2 albums on 'A&M';- EXTRACTION (1971) and FOOTPRINT (1972). He was replaced by **HENRY McCULLOCH** – guitar + **ALAN SPENNER** – bass, vocals (both ex-JOE COCKER's GREASE BAND)

Jul 70. (lp) **THE LAST PUFF** [ ] [84] Aug 70
– I am the walrus / The wrong time / Something to say / Nobody there at all / Down river / Son of your father / The last puff. *(re-iss.+c.1974)*

— **JOHN HAWKEN** – keyboards + **STEVE THOMPSON** – bass repl. last newboys to J.COCKER

— Disbanded Autumn 1970. KELLIE joined (PETER) FRAMPTON'S CAMEL. THOMPSON joined STONE THE CROWS and HAWKEN went to ILLUSION. GROSVENOR released solo lp 'UNDER OPEN SKIES' in Oct71, before joining STEALER'S WHEEL. In mid'73, he became ARIEL BENDER and joined MOTT THE HOOPLE. MIKE HARRISON went solo forming own band JUNKYARD ANGEL. They issued 2 albums for 'Island'; MIKE HARRISON (1971) and SMOKESTACK LIGHTNIN' (1972).

SPOOKY TOOTH

In 1973, **HARRISON + WRIGHT** reformed with **MICK JONES** – guitar / **BRYSON GRAHAM** – drums (both ex-WONDERWHEEL) / **IAN HERBERT** – bass (ex-JUNKYARD ANGELS).

Island | A&M

May 73. (lp)(c) **YOU BROKE MY HEART SO I BUSTED YOUR JAW** [ ] [84]
– Cotton growing man / Old as I was born / This time around / Holy water / Wildfire / Self seeking man / Times have changed / Moriah. *(re-iss.+c.1974)*

Aug 73. (7") **COTTON GROWING MAN. / TIMES HAVE CHANGED** [-] [ ]

— **MIKE KELLIE** returned to repl. BRYSON / **CHRIS STEWART** – bass repl. IAN

Island | Island

Oct 73. (7") **ALL SEWN UP. / AS LONG AS THE WORLD KEEPS ON TURNING** [ ] [-]

Nov 73. (lp)(c) **WITNESS** [ ] [99]
– Ocean of power / Wings on my heart / Things change / As long as the world keeps on turning / Don't ever stray away / All sewn up / Dream me a mountain / Sunlight of my mind / Pyramids. *(re-iss.+c.1974)*

Dec 73. (7") **ALL SEWN UP. / THINGS CHANGE** [-] [ ]

— **MIKE PATTO** – vocals (ex-TIMEBOX) / **KEITH ELLIS** – bass (ex-VAN DER GRAAF . . .) repl. HARRISON (who went solo) + **STEWART.** (May74) **WRIGHT, PATTO + JONES** enlisted **BRYSON GRAHAM** – drums returned to repl. KELLIE who joined ONLY ONES. **VAL MOORE** – bass repl. ELLIS to sessions.

Good Earth | Island

Aug 74. (7") **THE MIRROR. / HELL OR HIGH WATER** [-] [ ]

Aug 74. (7") **TWO TIME LOVE. / THE HOOFER** [ ] [-]

Sep 74. (lp) **THE MIRROR** [ ] [ ]
– Hell or high water / I'm alive / The mirror / The hoofer / Fantasy saisfier / Two time love / Kyle / Woman and gold / Higher circles. *(re-iss.May79 on 'Charly', cd-iss.Feb93)*

Feb 75. (7") **FANTASY SATISFIER. / THE HOOFER** [ ] [-]

— Inevitably bit the dust for final time 1975. JONES joined The LESLIE WEST BAND and later FOREIGNER. PATTO formed BOXER and BRYSON joined ALVIN LEE BAND.

– compilations, others, etc. –

Feb 75. Island; (7") **WHAT'S THAT SOUND. ("ART") / FLYING ANCHORS ("ART")** [ ] [-]

Mar 76. Island; (lp)(c) **THE BEST OF SPOOKY TOOTH** [ ] [-]
– Tobacco Road / Better by you, better than me / It's all about a roundabout / Waitin' for the wind / The last puff / Evil woman / That was only yesterday / I am the walrus / Self seeking man / All sewn up / Times have changed / As long as the world keeps turning / The weight.

Apr 76. A&M; (d-lp) **THAT WAS ONLY YESTERDAY** (includes stuff by GARY WRIGHT solo) [-] [ ]

GARY WRIGHT

Note; He released 4 singles for 'A&M' & 2 albums 'EXTRACTION' & 'FOOTPRINT' in the early 70's pre-SPOOKY

Warners | Warners

Jan 76. (lp)(c) **THE DREAM WEAVER** [ ] [7] Aug 75
– Love is alive / Let it out / Can't find the judge / Made to love you / Power of love / dream weaver / Blind feeling / Much higher / Feel for me. *(UK-iss.Nov76)*

Mar 76. (7") **DREAM WEAVER. / LET IT OUT** [ ] [2] Dec 75

Apr 76. (7") **LOVE IS ALIVE. /** [-] [2]

Sep 76. (7") **MADE TO LOVE YOU. / POWER OF LOVE** [-] [79]

Oct 76. (7") **LOVE IS ALIVE. / DREAM WEAVER** [ ] [-]

Jan 77. (lp)(c) **THE LIGHT OF SMILES** [ ] [23]
– Water sign / Time machine / I am the sky / Who am I / Silent fury / Phantom writer / The light of miles / I'm alright / Empty inside / Are you weepin' / Child of light.

Mar 77. (7") **ARE YOU WEEPIN'. / CHILD OF LIGHT** [ ] [ ]

May 77. (7") **PHANTOM WRITER. / CHILD OF LIGHT** [-] [43]

Jan 78. (lp)(c) **TOUCH AND GONE** [ ] [ ] Nov 77
– Touch and gone / Stay away / Lost in my emotions / Starry eyed / Sky eyes / Something very special / The love it takes / Night ride / Can't get above losing you.

Jan 78. (7") **TOUCH AND GONE. / LOST IN MY EMOTIONS** [-] [73]

Mar 79. (lp)(c) **HEADIN' HOME** [ ] [ ]
– I can feel you cryin' / I'm the one who'll be by your side / Keep love in your soul / Let me love you again / Love is why / Love's awake inside / Moonbeams / Stand / You don't own me.

Jun 81. (lp)(c) **THE RIGHT PLACE** [ ] [79]
– Heartbeat / Really wanna know you / Got the feelin' / Love is a rose / The right place / More than a heartache / Closer to you / Comin' apart / Positive feelings.

Jul 81. (7") **REALLY WANNA KNOW YOU. / MORE THAN A HEARTACHE** [ ] [16] Jun81

— GARY retired from music scene shortly after but retuned . . .

Cypress | Cypress

1988. (lp)(cd) **WHO AM I** [ ] [ ]
– Who am I / Voices / Love is on the line / Take a look / Blind alley / Sad eyes / Prey of your love / (I don't wanna) Hold back / It ain't right / Rose.

– his others, etc. –

Jul 92. Warners; (7")(c-s) **DREAM WEAVER. / ('Wayne's World' film theme)** [ ] [ ]
(12"+=)(cd-s+=) – (track by RED HOT CHILI PEPPERS).

Bruce SPRINGSTEEN

Born: 23 Sep'49, Freehold, New Jersey, USA. In 1969, he formed STEEL MILL, but they disbanded after 2 years, although 3 of them (VAN ZANDT, FEDERICKI + LOPEZ) soon became part of his 10-piece back-up band. In May'72, SPRINGSTEEN signed to 'Columbia' and set up recording debut album 'GREETINGS FROM ASBURY PARK, N.J.' with band. Released early '73, it originally sold poorly, as did his follow-up 'THE WILD, THE INNOCENT & THE E-STREET SHUFFLE'. After the latter's completion, he toured with backing band The E-STREET BAND, and gained enough renewed respect for his first two albums to both hit US Top 60 in mid-75. The much anticipated 3rd album 'BORN TO RUN', gave him breakthrough into superstardom, which stayed with him throughout the next 2 decades. • **Style:** Groomed by record co. as the next DYLAN, he moved into harder-edged rock'n'roll by the mid-70's and soon became known as 'The Boss'. After a very dissappointing 1982 folk/demo album 'NEBRASKA', he returned with the flag-waving multi-million selling 'BORN IN THE U.S.A.'. • **Songwriters:** All self-penned except; JERSEY GIRL (Tom Waits) / WAR (Edwin Starr) / SANTA CLAUS IS COMING TO TOWN (festive trad.) / VIVA LAS VEGAS (Elvis Presley) etc. • **Trivia:** SPRINGSTEEN produced 2 albums by GARY U.S.BONDS; DEDICATION (1981) / ON THE LINE (1982), which featured The BOSS's songs. He also provided songs for; SPIRIT IN THE NIGHT + BLINDED BY THE LIGHT for (Manfred Mann's Earth Band) / SANDY (Hollies) / FIRE (Robert Gordon) + (Pointer Sisters) / BECAUSE THE NIGHT (Patti Smith) / FOR YOU (Greg Kihn) / FROM SMALL THINGS (Dave Edmunds) / DANCING IN THE DARK (Big Daddy) / etc. On 13 May'85, BRUCE married model/actress Julianne Phillips, but she filed for divorce in August 1988, after seeing photographic newspaper evidence of a burgeoning relationship between BRUCE and backing singer PATTI SCIALFA. She had his child Evan James on 25 Jul'90.

Recommended: GREETINGS FROM ASBURY PARK, N.J. (*6) / THE WILD, THE INNOCENT & THE E-STREET SHUFFLE (*6) / BORN TO RUN (*9) / DARKNESS ON THE EDGE OF TOWN (*8) / THE RIVER (*7) / NEBRASKA (*7) / BORN IN THE U.S.A. (*8) / TUNNEL OF LOVE (*6) / HUMAN TOUCH (*5) / LUCKY TOWN (*5) / GHOST OF TOM JOAD (*6)

BRUCE SPRINGSTEEN – vocals, guitar / **DAVID SANCIOUS + DANNY FEDERICI** – keyboards / **GARRY TALLENT** – bass / **VINI LOPEZ** – drums / **CLARENCE CLEMENS** – saxophone / **STEVE VAN ZANDT** – lead guitar (left before recording of debut album)

C.B.S. | Columbia

Feb 73. (7") **BLINDED BY THE LIGHT. / ANGEL** [-] [ ]

Mar 73. (lp)(c) **GREETINGS FROM ASBURY PARK, N.J.** [ ] [ ] Jan73
– Blinded by the light / Growin' up / Mary Queen of Arkansas / Does this bus stop at 82nd Street / Lost in the flood / The angel / For you / / Spirit in the night / It's hard to be a saint in the city. *(hit No.60 in the US; Jul75) (UK re-iss.Nov82, re-iss.Jun85, hit No.41, cd-iss.1986)*

May 73. (7") **SPIRIT IN THE NIGHT. / FOR YOU** [-] [ ]

— For live appearances The BRUCE SPRINGSTEEN BAND now The E-STREET SHUFFLE. **ERNEST CARTER** – drums repl. LOPEZ

Feb 74. (lp)(c) **THE WILD, THE INNOCENT & THE E-STREET SHUFFLE** [ ] [ ] Nov 73
– The E-Street shuffle / 4th of July, Asbury Park (Sandy) / Kitty's back / Wild Billy's circus story / Incident on 57th Street / Rosalita (come out tonight) / New York City serenade. *(hit No.59 in the US; Jul75) (UK re-iss.Nov83, re-iss.Jun85, hit No.33, cd-iss.Apr89)*

— **ROY BITTAN** – piano / **MAX WEINBERG** – drums / and the returning **VAN ZANDT** repl. SANCIOUS and CARTER

Oct 75. (lp)(c) **BORN TO RUN** [17] [3] Sep 75
– Thunder road / Tenth Avenue freeze-out / Night / Backstreets / Born to run / She's the one / Meeting across the river / Jungleland. *(re-iss.Jan87 boxed w / free-7")* **BECAUSE THE NIGHT. / SSPIRIT IN THE NIGHT** *(cd-iss.1983 + 1988)(re-iss.cdJun93)*

Oct 75. (7") **BORN TO RUN. / MEETING ACROSS THE RIVER** [ ] [23] Sep 75

Feb 76. (7") **TENTH AVENUE FREEZE-OUT. / SHE'S THE ONE** [ ] [83] Jan 76

Jun 78. (7") **PROVE IT ALL NIGHT. / FACTORY** [ ] [33]

Jun 78. (lp)(c)(US-pic-d) **DARKNESS ON THE EDGE OF TOWN** [16] [5]
– Badlands / Adam raised a Cain / Something in the street / Candy's room / Racing in the street / Promised land / Factory / Streets of fire / Prove it all night / Darkness on the edge of town. *(re-iss.+cd Jul84)*

Jul 78. (7") **BADLANDS. / STREETS OF FIRE** [-] [42]

Jul 78. (7") **BADLANDS. / SOMETHING IN THE NIGHT** [ ] [-]

Oct 78. (7") **PROMISED LAND. / STREETS OF FIRE** [ ] [ ]

Oct 80. (d-lp)(d-c) **THE RIVER** [2] [1]
– The ties that bind / Sherry darling / Jackson cage / Two hearts / Independence day / Hungry heart / Out in the street / Crush on you / You can look (but you better not touch) / I wanna marry you / The river / Point blank / Cadillac ranch / I'm a rocker / Fade away / Stolen car / Ramrod / The price you pay / Drive all night / Wreck on the highway. *(d-cd-iss.1985) (re-iss.d-cd+d-c Oct94 on 'Columbia')*

Nov 80. (7") **HUNGRY HEART. / HELD UP WITHOUT A GUN** [44] [5]

Jan 81. (7") **FADE AWAY. / BE TRUE** [-] [20]

Feb 81. (7") **SHERRY DARLING. / BE TRUE** [ ] [ ]

May 81. (7") **THE RIVER. / INDEPENDENCE DAY** [35] [ ]
(12") – ('A'side) / Born to run / Rosalita.

Aug 81. (7") **CADILLAC RANCH. / WRECK ON THE HIGHWAY** [ ] [ ]

Sep 82. (lp)(c) **NEBRASKA** [3] [3]
– Nebraska / Atlantic City / Mansion on the hill / Johnny 99 / Highway patrolman / State trooper / Used cars / Open all night / My father's house / Reason to believe. *(re-iss.+cd.Feb89)*

Oct 82. (7") **ATLANTIC CITY. / MANSION ON THE HILL** [ ] [ ]

Nov 82. (7") **OPEN ALL NIGHT. / THE BIG PAYBACK** [ ] [ ]

— **NILS LOFGREN** – lead guitar (Solo artist) repl. VAN ZANDT to solo as LITTLE STEVEN / added **PATTI SCIALFA** – backing vox (ex-SOUTHSIDE JOHNNY)

May 84. (7")(12")(7"sha-pic-d) **DANCING IN THE DARK. / PINK CADILLAC** [28] [2]
(re-entered UK charts Jan85, hit No.4)

Jun 84. (lp)(c)(cd)(pic-lp) **BORN IN THE U.S.A.** [1] [1]
– Born in the U.S.A. / Cover me / Darlington County / Working on the highway / Downbound train / I'm on fire / No surrender / Bobby Jean / I'm goin' down / Glory days / Dancing in the dark / My hometown.

Sep 84. (7") **COVER ME. / JERSEY GIRL** [38] [7] Aug 84
(d7"+=) – Dancing in the dark / Pink Cadillac.
(12"+=) – Dancing in the dark (dub version).

Nov 84. (7") **BORN IN THE U.S.A. / SHUT OUT THE LIGHTS** [-] [9]

Jan 85. (7") **I'M ON FIRE. / JOHNNY BYE BYE** [-] [6]

Mar 85. (7")(7"sha-pic-d) **COVER ME. / JERSEY GIRL** [16] [-]
(12"+=) – Dancing in the dark (dub) / Shut out the light / Cover me (dub).

May 85. (7") **I'M ON FIRE. / BORN IN THE U.S.A. (mix)** [5] [-]
(12"+=) – Rosalita / Bye Bye Johnny.

Jul 85. (7")(12") **GLORY DAYS. / STAND ON IT** [17] [5] May 85

Aug 85. (7") **I'M GOIN' DOWN. / JANEY, DON'T YOU LOSE HEART** [-] [9]

Dec 85. (7")(12") **MY HOMETOWN. / SANTA CLAUS IS COMIN' TO TOWN** [9] [6]

Nov 86. (7") **WAR (live). / MERRY XMAS BABY** [18] [8]
(12"+=) – Incident on 57th Street.

Dec 86. (5xlp-box)(3xc-box)(3xcd-box) **LIVE 1977-1985 (live)** [4] [1] Nov 86
– Thunder road / Adam raised a Cain / Fire / Spirit in the night / 4th of July – Asbury Park (Sandy) / Paradise by the 'C' / Growin' up / It's hard to be a saint in the city / Backstreets / Rosalita (come out tonight) / Raise your hand / Hungry heart / Two hearts / Cadillac ranch / You can look (but you better not touch) / War / Candy's room / Badlands / Because the night / Independence day / Johnny 99 / Darkness on the edge of town / Racing in the street / Nebraska / This land is your land / Working on the highway / Reason to believe / Born in the U.S.A. / Seeds / The river / Born to run / Darlington County / Jersey girl / Bobby Jean / Cover me / My hometown / No surrender / I'm on fire / The promised land.

Jan 87. (7") **FIRE (live). / INCIDENT ON 57TH STREET** [-] [46]

Jan 87. (7")(12") **FIRE (live). / FOR YOU (live)** [54] [-]

May 87. (7") **BORN TO RUN (live). / JOHNNY 99 (live)** [16] [-]
(12"+=)/ /(d12"++=) – Seeds (live)./ / Because the night (live).
(cd-s+=) – Spirit in the night (live) / Seeds (live).

Sep 87. (7")(12") **BRILLIANT DISGUISE. / LUCKY MAN** [20] [5]

Oct 87. (lp)(c)(cd)(pic-lp)(pic-cd) **TUNNEL OF LOVE** [1] [1]
– Ain't got you / Tougher than the rest / All that Heaven will allow / Spare parts / Cautious man / Walk like a man / Tunnel of love / Two faces / Brilliant disguise / One step up / When you're alone / Valentine's day.

Dec 87. (7")(12")(7"sha-pic-d) **TUNNEL OF LOVE. / TWO FOR THE ROAD** [45] [9]
(cd-s+=) – Santa Claus is comin' to town.

Mar 88. (7") **ONE STEP UP. / ROULETTE** [ ] [13] Feb 88
(12"+=)(cd-s+=) – Lucky man.

Jun 88. (7") **TOUGHER THAN THE REST. / ROULETTE** [13] [ ]
(12"+=) – ('A'live) / Be true (live).
(cd-s+=) – Born to run (live).

Oct 88. (7")(12") **SPARE PARTS. / PINK CADILLAC** [32] [ ]
(cd-s+=) – ('A'live version) / Chimes of freedom.

— new band:- **SHANE FONTAYNE** – guitar / **ZACHERY ALFORD** – drums / **TOMMY SIMMS** – bass / **ROY BITTAN** – keyboards / **CRYSTAL TALIEFERO** – guitar, percussion, vocals / + backing vocalists.

Columbia | Columbia

Mar 92. (c-s) **HUMAN TOUCH. / BETTER DAYS** [-] [16]

Mar 92. (7")(c-s) **HUMAN TOUCH. / SOULS OF THE DEPARTED** [11] [-]
(12"+=)(cd-s+=)(pic-cd-d+=) – Long goodbye.

Mar 92. (cd)(c)(lp) **HUMAN TOUCH** [1] [2]
– Human touch / Soul driver / 57 channels (and nothin' on) / Cross my heart / Gloria's eyes / With every wish / Roll of the dice / Real world / All or nothin' at al / Man's job / I wish I were blind / Long goodbye / Real man / Pony boy.

Mar 92. (cd)(c)(lp) **LUCKY TOWN** [2] [3]
– Better days / Lucky town / Local hero / If I should fall apart / Leap of faith / Big Muddy / Living proof / Book of dreams / Souls of the departed / My beautiful reward.

May 92. (7")(c-s) **BETTER DAYS. / TOUGHER THAN THE REST** [34] [ ]
(12"+=)(cd-s+=) – Part man, part monkey.

Jun 92. (7") **57 CHANNELS (AND NOTHIN' ON). / PART MAN, PART MONKEY** [-] [68]

Jul 92. (7")(c-s) **57 CHANNELS (AND NOTHIN' ON). / STAND ON IT** [32] [-]
(cd-s+=) – Janey don't you lose heart.

Oct 92. (7")(c-s) **LEAP OF FAITH. / ('A'version)** [46] [ ]
(cd-s+=) – Shut out the light / The big payback.
(cd-s) – ('A'side) / 30 days out.

Apr 93. (7")(c-s) **LUCKY TOWN (live). / ('A' version)** [48] [ ]
(cd-s+=) – Human touch (live)

Apr 93. (cd)(c)(lp) **IN CONCERT – MTV PLUGGED (live)** [4] [ ]
– Red headed woman / Better days / Atlantic city / Darkness on the edge of town / Man's job / Human touch / Lucky town / I wish I were blind / Thunder Road / Light of day / If I should fall behind / Living proof / My beautiful reward.

Wife PATTI had child on 5th Jan'94.

Below from the film 'Philadelphia', which won an Oscar for Tom Hanks.

Mar 94. (7")(12")(c-s) **STREETS OF PHILADELPHIA. / IF I SHOULD FALL BEHIND** [2] [9] Feb94
(cd-s+=) – Growing up (live) / The big Muddy (live).

Feb 95. (cd)(c) **GREATEST HITS** (compilation) [1] [1]
– Born to run / Thunder road / Badlands / The river / Hungry heart / Atlantic city / Dancing in the dark / Born in the U.S.A. / My hometown / Glory days / Brilliant disguise / Human touch / Better days / Streets of Philadelphia / Secret garden / Murder incorporated / Blood brothers / This hard land.

Apr 95. (c-s) **SECRET GARDEN / THUNDER ROAD (plugged version)** [44] [63]
(cd-s+=) – Murder incorporated.
(cd-s) – ('A'side) / Because the night / Pink Cadillac / 4th Of July, Asbury Park (Sandy).

Oct 95. (7"pic-d)(c-s) **HUNGRY HEART. / STREETS OF PHILADELPHIA** [28] [ ]
(cd-s+=) – ('A'-Berlin '95 version) / Thunder Road.

Nov 95. (cd)(c) **THE GHOST OF TOM JOAD** [16] [11]
– The ghost of Tom Joad / Straight time / Highway 29 / Youngstown / Sinaola cowboys / The line / Balboa Park / Dry lightning / The new timer / Across the border /

Galveston Bay / The best was never good enough.

– compilations, others, etc. –

Nov 85. CBS; (lp-set) **BOXED SET 12" SINGLES** [ ] [ ]
1988. CBS; (d-cd) **NEBRASKA / BORN IN THE U.S.A.** [ ] [ ]
Mar 93. Columbia; (d-cd) **DARKNESS ON THE EDGE OF TOWN / NEBRASKA** [ ] [ ]
(re-iss.Feb95)
Jan 94. Dare Int.; (d-cd)(d-c)(d-lp) **PRODIGAL SON** [ ] [ ]

SQUEEZE

Formed: Deptford, South London, England ... Mar'74 by DIFFORD, TILBROOK and boogie pianist JOOLS HOLLAND. In 1976 they signed to 'BTM', but had debut 45 withdrawn. After releasing an indie EP, they transferred to major 'A&M' label late in '77. Early in 1978, they cracked the Top 20 with 'TAKE ME I'M YOURS', but this was surpassed the next year when they nearly hit No.1 twice with 'COOL FOR CATS' & 'UP THE JUNCTION'. • **Style:** Initially a pub rock / new wave outfit, who went into areas of pop, country, soul & AOR. • **Songwriters:** Mostly DIFFORD & TILBROOK compositions, and some by CARRACK who joined late 1980. Covered END OF THE CENTURY (Blur). • **Trivia:** JOOLS HOLLAND went on to become successful TV presenter, mainly for C4's 'The Tube' and BBC2's new 'Juke Box Jury'.

Recommended: ARGYBARGY (*7) / EAST SIDE STORY (*7) / GREATEST HITS (*8).

CHRIS DIFFORD (b. 4 Nov'54) – vocals, guitar / **GLENN TILBROOK** (b.31 Aug'57) – vocals, guitar / **JOOLS HOLLAND** (b.JULIAN, 24 Jan'58) – keyboards / **HARRY KAKOULI** – bass / **PAUL GUNN** – drums (below 45 withdrawn from release)

B.T.M. / not issued

Jan 77. (7") **TAKE ME I'M YOURS. / NO DISCO KID, NO** [-] [-]

— **GILSON LAVIS** (b.27 Jun'51) – drums (ex-MUSTARD) repl. GUNN

Deptford Fun City / not issued

Aug 77. (7"ep) **PACKET OF THREE** [ ] [-]
– Cat on a wall / Back track / Night ride. *(re-iss.12" Nov79)*

A & M / A & M

Feb 78. (7") **TAKE ME, I'M YOURS. / NIGHT NURSE** [19] [ ]
Mar 78. (lp)(c) **SQUEEZE** [ ] [ ]
– Sex master / Bang bang / Strong in reason / Wild sewerage tickles Brazil / Out of control / Take me, I'm yours / The call / Model / Remember what / First thing wrong / Hesitation (rool Britania) / Get smart. *(re-iss.Mar82)*
May 78. (7")(7"green) **BANG BANG. / ALL FED UP** [49] [-]

— **JOHN BENTLEY** (b.16 Apr'51) – bass repl. KAKOULI who went solo

Nov 78. (7") **GOODBYE GIRL. / SAINTS ALIVE** [63] [-]
Mar 79. (7")(12")(7"pink)(12"pink)(7"red) **COOL FOR CATS. / MODEL** [2] [ ]
Apr 79. (lp)(c) **COOL FOR CATS** [45] [ ]
– Slap and tickle / Revue / Touching me, touching you / It's not cricket / It's so dirty / The knack / Hop, skip and jump / Up the junction / Hard to find / Slightly drunk / Goodbye girl / Cool for cats. *(re-iss.Nov85, cd-iss.Mar91)*
May 79. (7")(7"lilac) **UP THE JUNCTION. / IT'S SO DIRTY** [2] [-]
Jun 79. (7") **SLIGHTLY DRUNK. / GOODBYE GIRL** [-] [ ]
Aug 79. (7")(7"red) **SLAP AND TICKLE. / ALL'S WELL** [24] [ ]
Nov 79. (7")(7"white) **CHRISTMAS DAY. / GOING CRAZY** [ ] [-]
Jan 80. (7")(7"clear) **ANOTHER NAIL IN MY HEART. / PRETTY THING** [17] [-]
Feb 80. (7") **IF I DIDN'T LOVE YOU. / PRETTY ONE** [-] [ ]
Feb 80. (lp)(c) **ARGYBARGY** [32] [71]
– Pulling mussels (from the shell) / Another nail in my heart / Seperate beds / Misadventure / I think I'm go go / Farfisa beat / Here comes that feeling / Vicky Verky / If I didn't love you / Wrong side of the Moon / There at the top.
Apr 80. (7")(7"red) **PULLING MUSSELS (FROM THE SHELL). / WHAT THE BUTLER SAW** [44] [-]
Jun 80. (7") **PULLING MUSSELS (FROM THE SHELL). / PRETTY ONE** [-] [ ]
Sep 80. (7") **ANOTHER NAIL IN MY HEART. / GOING CRAZY / WHAT THE BUTLER SAW** [-] [ ]
(re-iss. US Sep 82)

— **PAUL CARRACK** (b. Apr51, Sheffield) – keyboards (ex-ACE, ex-FRANKIE MILLER, ex-ROXY MUSIC) repl. JOOLS who formed his own MILLIONAIRES

Apr 81. (7") **IS THAT LOVE. / TRUST** [35] [ ]
May 81. (lp)(c) **EAST SIDE STORY** [19] [44]
– In quintessence / Someone else's heart / Tempted / Piccadilly / There's no tomorrow / A woman's world / Is that love / F-hole / Labelled with love / Someone else's bell / Mumbo jumbo / Vanity fair / Messed around. *(re-iss.Sep86, cd-iss.Jan87 & Mar91)*
Jul 81. (7") **TEMPTED. / YAP YAP YAP** [40] [-]
Jul 81. (7") **TEMPTED. / TRUST** [-] [49]
(free-5"w.a.) **ANOTHER NAIL IN MY HEART. / IF I DIDN'T LOVE YOU**
Sep 81. (7") **LABELLED WITH LOVE. / SQUABS ON FORTY FAB** [4] [ ]
Oct 81. (7") **MESSED AROUND. / YAP YAP YAP** [-] [ ]

— **DON SNOW** – keyboards (ex-VIBRATORS, ex-SINCEROS) repl. CARRACK (now solo)

Apr 82. (7")(7"pic-d) **BLACK COFFEE IN BED. / THE HUNT** [51] [ ] Jul 82
Apr 82. (12") **WHEN THE HANGOVER STRIKES. / I'VE RETURNED** [-] [ ]
May 82. (lp)(c) **SWEETS FROM A STRANGER** [37] [32]
– Out of touch / I can't hold on / Points of view / Stranger than the stranger on the shore / Onto the dance floor / When the hangover strikes / Black coffee in bed / I've returned / Tongue like a knife / His house her home / The very last dance / The elephant ride.
Jul 82. (7")(7"pic-d) **WHEN THE HANGOVER STRIKES. / THE ELEPHANT RIDE** [ ] [-]
Oct 82. (7") **ANNIE GET YOUR GUN. / SPANISH GUITAR** [43] [ ] Feb 83
Nov 82. (lp)(c) **THE SINGLES – 45 AND UNDER** (compilation) [3] [47]
– Take me I'm yours / Goodbye girl / Cool for cats / Up the junction / Slap and tickle / Another nail in my heart / Pulling mussels (from the shell) / Tempted / Is that love / Labelled with love / Black coffee in bed / Annie get your gun. *(cd-iss.Dec84, 1 diff. track)*

— Split at same time of compilation.

DIFFORD & TILBROOK

carried on as duo, augmented by **KEITH WILKINSON** – bass / other musicians

A & M / A & M

Jun 84. (7")(12") **LOVE'S CRASHING WAVES. / WITHIN THESE WALLS WITHOUT YOU** [57] [-]
Jun 84. (lp)(c) **DIFFORD & TILBROOK** [47] [55]
– Action speaks faster / Love's crashing waves / Picking up the pieces / On my mind tonight / Man for all seasons / Hope fell down / Wagon train / You can't hurt the girl / Tears for attention / The apple tree.
Jun 84. (7") **WITHIN THESE WALLS. / PICKING UP THE PIECES** [-] [ ]
Oct 84. (7")(12") **HOPE FELL DOWN. / ACTION SPEAKS FASTER** [ ] [-]

SQUEEZE

reformed '78 line-up. – **KEITH WILKINSON** – bass (not HARRY)

A & M / A & M

Jun 85. (7")(12") **LAST TIME FOREVER. / SUITE FROM FIVE STRANGERS** [45] [ ]
Aug 85. (lp)(c)(cd) **COSI FAN TUTTI FRUTTI** [31] [57]
– Big bang / By your side / King George Street / I learnt how to pray / Last time forever / No place like home / Heartbreakin' world / Hits of the year / Break my heart / I won't ever go drinking again.
Sep 85. (7") **HITS OF THE YEAR. / THE FORTNIGHT SAGA** [-] [ ]
Sep 85. (7") **NO PLACE LIKE HOME. / THE FORTNIGHT SAGA** [ ] [ ]
(12"+=) – Last time forever.
Nov 85. (7") **HEARTBREAKING WORLD. / BIG BANG** [ ] [ ]
(12"+=) – By your side (live) / Tempted (live) / Last time forever.
Apr 86. (7") **KING GEORGE STREET. / LOVE'S CRASHING WAVES (live)** [ ] [ ]
(12"+=) – Up the junction (live).

— added **ANDY METCALFE** – keyboards (ex-SOFT BOYS)

Aug 87. (7") **HOURGLASS. / WEDDING BELLS** [16] [15]
(12"+=) – Splitting into three.
Sep 87. (lp)(c)(cd) **BABYLON AND ON** [14] [36]
– Hourglass / Footprints / Tough love / The prisoner / 853-5937 / In today's room / Trust me to open my mouth / Striking matches / Cigarette of a single man / Who are you? / The waiting game / Some Americans.
Sep 87. (7") **TRUST ME TO OPEN MY MOUTH. / TAKE ME, I'M YOURS (live)** [72] [-]
(12"+=) – Black coffee in bed.
Nov 87. (7") **THE WAITING GAME. / LAST TIME FOREVER** [ ] [ ]
(12"+=) – The prisoner.
Dec 87. (7") **853-5937. / TAKE ME I'M YOURS (live)** [-] [32]
Jan 88. (7") **853-5937. / TOUGH LOVE** [ ] [-]
(12"+=) – ('A'bonus mix).
Apr 88. (7") **FOOTPRINTS. / BLACK COFFEE IN BED (live)** [-] [ ]
Jun 88. (7") **FOOTPRINTS. / STRIKING MATCHES – INSTANT BUFF** [ ] [-]
(12"+=) – In today's room.

— Reverted back to 5-piece when METCALFE departed.

Sep 89. (7") **IF IT'S LOVE. / FRANK'S HAG** [ ] [ ]
(12"+=)(cd-s+=) – Vanity fair.
Sep 89. (lp)(c)(cd) **FRANK** [58] [ ]
– Frank / If it's love / Peyton Place / Rose I said / Slaughtered, gutted and heartbroken / (This could be) The last time / She doesn't have to shave / Love circles / Melody hotel / Can of worms / Dr. Jazz / Is it too late.
Jan 90. (7") **LOVE CIRCLES. / RED LIGHT** [ ] [ ]
(12"+=)(cd-s+=) – Who's that.

— JOOLS left again to go solo and take up more TV work. In 1991 he was repl. by **MATT IRVING + STEVE NIEVE** – keyboards / **TONY BERG** – guitar, keyboards / **BRUCE HORNSBY** – accordion

Reprise / Reprise

Jul 91. (7")(c-s) **SUNDAY STREET. / MAIDSTONE** [ ] [ ]
(12"+=)(cd-s+=) – Mood swings.
Aug 91. (cd)(c)(lp) **PLAY** [41] [ ]
– Satisfied / Crying in my sleep / Letting go / The day I get home / The truck / House of love / Cupid's toy / Gone to the dogs / Walk a straight line / Sunday street / Wicked and cruel / There is a voice. *(re-iss.cd Feb95)*

— **DIFFORD + TILBROOK + WILKINSON** plus returning **PAUL CARRACK** – keyboards / **PETE THOMAS** – drums

A & M / A & M

Jul 93. (7")(c-s) **THIRD RAIL. / TAKE ME I'M YOURS (live)** [39] [ ]
(cd-s+=) – Cool for cats (live medley).
(cd-s) – ('A'side) / The truth (live) / Melody hotel (live) / Walk a straight line (live).
Sep 93. (7")(c-s) **SOME FANTASTIC PLACE. / JUMPING** [73] [ ]
(cd-s+=) – Dark saloons / Discipline.
(cd-s) – ('A'side) / Is that the time? / Don't be a stranger / Stark naked.
Sep 93. (cd)(c)(lp) **SOME FANTASTIC PLACE** [26] [ ]
– Everything in the world / Some fantastiv place / Third rail / Loving you tonight / It's over / Cold shoulder / Talk to him / Jolly comes home / Images of loving / True colours (the storm) / Pinocchio.
Oct 93. (7")(c-s) **LOVING YOU TONIGHT. / ('A'mix)** [ ] [ ]
(12"+=)(cd-s+=) – Tempted / Third rail.
Feb 94. (7")(c-s) **IT'S OVER. / IS THAT LOVE? (live)** [ ] [ ]
(cd-s+=) – Pulling mussels (from the shell) / Goodbye girl (live).
Aug 95. (c-s) **THIS SUMMER / GOODBYE GIRL (live)** [47] [ ]

(cd-s+=) – All the king's horses.
(cd-s) – ('A'side) / End of a century (live) / Periscope.

Nov 95. (c-ep)(cd-ep) **ELECTRIC TRAINS / CRACKER JACK / FIGHTING FOR PEACE / COLD SHOULDER (live)** [44] [ ]
(cd-ep) – ('A'side) / Some fantastic place / It's over / Hour glass.

Nov 95. (cd)(c) **RIDICULOUS** [50] [ ]
– Electric trains / Heaven knows / Grouch of the day / Walk away / This summer / Got to me / Long face / I want you / Daphne / Lost for words / Great escape / Temptation for love / Sound asleep / Fingertips.

– more compilations, etc. –

1981 A&M; (10"m-lp) **SIX SQUEEZE SONGS CRAMMED ONTO ONE TEN INCH RECORD** [-] [-]

Oct 83. Old Gold; (7") **TAKE ME, I'M YOURS. / UP THE JUNCTION** [ ] [-]

Sep 85. Old Gold; (7") **COOL FOR CATS. / LABELLED WITH LOVE** [ ] [-]

Mar 90. Deptford Fun City; (cd)(c)(d-lp) **ROUND AND A BOUT (live 1974-1989)** [50] [-]
– Footprints / Pulling mussels (from the shell) / Black coffee in bed / She doesn't have to shave / Is that love / Dr. Jazz / Up the junction / Slaughtered, gutted and heartbroken / Is it too late / Cool for cats / Take me, I'm yours / If it's love / Hourglass / Labelled with love / Annie get your gun / Boogie woogie country girl / Tempted. *(free 7"ep 'PACKET OF THREE').*

Apr 92. A&M; (7")(c-s) **COOL FOR CATS. / TRUST ME TO OPEN MY MOUTH** [62] [-]
(cd-s+=) – Squabs on forty fab (medley hits).

May 92. A&M; (cd)(c)(lp) **GREATEST HITS** [6] [ ]
– (as THE SINGLES 45 AND UNDER +) Take me, I'm yours / Goodbye girl / Cool for cats / Up the junction / Slap and tickle / Another nail in my heart / Pulling mussels (from the shell) / Tempted / Is that love / Labelled with love / Black coffee in bed / Annie get your gun / King George Street / Last time forever / No place like home / Hourglass / Trust me to open my mouth / Footprints / If it's love / Love circles.

Oct 93. A&M; (cd) **BABYLON AND ON / EAST SIDE STORY** [ ] [ ]

Billy SQUIER

Born: 12 May'50, Wellesley Hills, Massachusetts, USA. Moved to New York in the late 60's, but returned to Boston in the early 70's to join The SIDEWINDERS. Around the mid-70's, he formed PIPER, who made 2 albums for 'A&M' before disbanding. In 1979, SQUIER was offered a solo deal with 'Capitol', and not long after, he soared to No.5 in the charts with second album 'DON'T SAY NO'. • **Style:** Hard-rock power-pop artist, influenced by LED ZEPPELIN. • **Songwriters:** SQUIER wrote all material and collaborated with JIM STEINMAN (ex-MEAT LOAF) in 1984. • **Trivia:** The year previous, SQUIER wrote and performed in the film 'Fast Times At Ridgemont High'.

Recommended: DON'T SAY NO (*6).

PIPER

BILLY SQUIER – vocals, guitar (ex-SIDEWINDERS) / **ALAN LAINE NOLAN +TOMMY GUNN** – guitar / **DANNY McGARY** – bass / **RICHIE FONTANA** – drums

A & M A & M

Mar 77. (lp) **PIPER** [ ] [ ]
– Out of control / Whatcha gonna do / The road / Sail away / Who's your boyfriend (I gotta feelin') / Telephone relation / The last time / 42nd Street / Can't live with ya . . .can't live without ya.

May 77. (7") **THE ROAD. / WHO'S YOUR BOYFRIEND (I GOT A FEELIN')** [-] [ ]

Oct 77. (7") **CAN'T WAIT. / BLUES FOR THE COMMON PEOPLE** [-] [ ]

Nov 77. (lp) **CAN'T WAIT** [ ] [ ]
– Can't wait / Drop by and stay / See me through / Little Miss Intent / Now ain't the time / Bad boy / Comin' down off your love / Anyday / Blues for the common man

BILLY SQUIER

went solo with band **DAVID SANCIOUS** – keyboards / **BRUCE KULICK** – guitar / **BUCKY BALLARD** – bass / **BOBBY CHOUNARD** – drums

Capitol Capitol

May 80. (7") **THE BIG BEAT. / MUSIC'S ALRIGHT** [-] [ ]

Jul 80. (lp)(c) **THE TALE OF THE TAPE** [ ] [ ] Apr 80
– The big beat / Calley oh / Rich kid / Like I'm lovin' you / Who knows what a love can do / You should be high love / Who's your boyfriend / The music's all right / Young girls.

Aug 80. (7") **YOU SHOULD BE HIGH LOVE. / MUSIC'S ALL RIGHT** [ ] [ ]

— **SQUIER** retained only **CHOUNARD** and enlisted **GARY SHARAF** – guitar / **ALAN ST.JOHN** – keyboards / **MARK CLARK** – bass

May 81. (lp)(c) **DON'T SAY NO** [ ] [5]
– In the dark / The stroke / My kinda lover / Whadda you want from me / You know what I like / Too daze gone / I need you / Don't say no / Lonely is the night / Nobody knows. *(re-iss.+cd.Apr87)*

Jun 81. (7") **THE STROKE. / TOO DAZE GONE** [-] [17]

Aug 81. (7") **THE STROKE. / MY KINDA LOVER** [52] [-]

Aug 81. (7") **IN THE DARK. / WHADDA YOU WANT FROM ME** [-] [35]

Oct 81. (7") **IN THE DARK. / LONELY IS THE NIGHT** [-] [-]

Nov 81. (7") **MY KINDA LOVER. / CHRISTMAS IS THE TIME TO SAY I LOVE YOU** [-] [ ]

Feb 82. (7") **TOO DAZE GONE. / WHADDA YOU WANT FROM ME** [ ] [ ]

— **JEFF GOLUB** – guitar + **DOUG LABAHN** – bass repl. SHARAF and CLARK

Sep 82. (lp)(c) **EMOTIONS IN MOTION** [ ] [5] Aug 82
– Everybody wants you / Emotions in motion / Learn how to live / In your eyes / Keep me satisfied / It keeps you rockin' / One good woman / She's a runner / Catch 22 / Listen to her heart. *(re-iss.+cd.Apr87)*

Sep 82. (7") **EMOTIONS IN MOTION. / CATCH 22** [ ] [68]

Jan 83. (7") **EVERYBODY WANTS YOU. / KEEP ME SATISFIED** [ ] [32] Nov 82

Jan 83. (7") **SHE'S A RUNNERT. /** [-] [75]

— **SQUIER** with more session people employed collaborator **JIM STEINMAN**

Jun 84. (7") **ROCK ME TONITE. / CAN'T GET NEXT TO YOU** [ ] [15]
(d7"+=) – She's a runner / Listen to the heart.

Sep 84. (lp)(c) **SIGNS OF LIFE** [ ] [11] Aug 84
– All night long / Rock me tonite / Eye on you / Take a look behind you / Reach for the sky / Another 1984 / Can't get next to you / Fall for love / Hand me downs / Sweet release. *(cd-iss.Apr87)*

Oct 84. (7") **ALL NIGHT LONG. / CALLEY OH** [-] [75]

Dec 84. (7") **EYE ON YOU. / CALLEY OH** [-] [71]

— **T.M. STEVENS** – bass repl. DOUG

Sep 86. (7") **LOVE IS THE HERO. / LEARN HOW TO LIVE** [ ] [80]

Nov 86. (lp)(c)(cd) **ENOUGH IS ENOUGH** [ ] [61]
– Shot o' love / Love is the hero / Lady with a tenor sax / All we have to give / Come home / Break the silence / Lonely one / Powerhouse / Til it's over / Wink of an eye.

Nov 86. (7") **SHOT O' LOVE. / ONE GOD WOMAN** [-] [ ]

Jun 89. (lp)(c)(cd) **HEAR AND NOW** [ ] [64]
– Rock out – Punch someone / Don't say you love me / Don't let me go / Tied up / (I put a) Spell on you / G.O.D. / Mine tonite / The work song.

Jun 89. (7") **DON'T SAY YOU LOVE ME. / TOO MUCH** [-] [58]

Aug 89. (7") **DON'T LET ME GO. /** [-] [ ]

Apr 91. (cd)(c)(lp) **CREATURES OF HABIT** [-] [ ]
– Facts of life / Strange fire / Alone in your dreams (don't say goodbye) / (L.O.V.E.) Four letter world / Young at heart / Nerves on ice / She goes down / Lover / Hollywood / Hands of seduction / Conscience point.

Apr 93. (cd)(c) **TELL THE TRUTH** [ ] [ ]

Chris SQUIRE (see under ⇒ YES)

STANDELLS

Formed: Los Angeles, California, USA . . . 1962 by LARRY TAMBLYN, brother of actor RUSS. After the introduction of singer DICK DODD, they signed to 'Liberty' where they took off with 45 'PEPPERMINT BEATLES'. Early in 1966, they scored near US Top 10 hit with classic 'DIRTY WATER'. • **Style:** R&B first generation garage punks. • **Songwriters:** Producer ED COBB except LOUIE LOUIE (Kingsmen) / SO FINE (Johnny Otis) / I'LL GO CRAZY (James Brown) / MONEY (Barrett Strong) / BIG BOSS MAN (Willie Dixon) / BONY MORONIE (Larry Williams) / HEY JOE (hit; Jimi Hendrix) / MY LITTLE RED BOOK (Bacharach-David) / 19th NERVOUS BREAKDOWN + PAINT IT BLACK (Rolling Stones) / LAST TRAIN TO CLARKSVILLE (hit; Monkees) / WILD THING (Troggs) / SUNSHINE SUPERMAN (Donovan) / SUNNY AFTERNOON (Kinks) / ELEANOR RIGBY (Beatles) / BLACK IS BLACK (Los Bravos) / SUMMER IN THE CITY (Lovin' Spoonful) / WHEN I WAS A COWBOY (Leadbelly) / 99 AND A HALF WON'T DO (Wilson Pickett) / etc. • **Trivia:** CHER supplied backing vox on 45 'THE BOY NEXT DOOR' produced by SONNY BONO. Late in 1965, DEWEY MARTIN was a brief member before joining BUFFALO SPRINGFIELD.

Recommended: THE BEST OF THE STANDELLS (*6)

LARRY TAMBLYN – vocals, organ (ex-Solo artist) / **TONY VALENTINE** (b. Italy) – guitar / **GARY LANE** – bass / **GARY LEEDS** (b. New York) – drums

Linda not issued

1963. (7") **YOU'LL BE MONE SOMEDAY. ("LARRY TAMBLYN & THE STANDELLS") / THE GIRL IN MY HEART** [-] [ ]

— **DICK DODD** – vox, drums repl. LEEDS (to JOHNNY RIVERS then WALKERS BROTHERS)

Liberty Liberty

Jul 64. (7") **PEPPERMINT BEATLES. / THE SHAKE** [-] [ ]

Sep 64. (7") **HELP YOURSELF. / I'LL GO CRAZY** [-] [ ]

Nov 64. (7") **LINDA LOU. / SO FINE** [-] [ ]

1965. (lp) **THE STANDELLS IN PERSON AT P.J.'S (live)** [ ] [ ] 1964
– Help yourself / So fine / You can't do that / What have I got of my own / Money (that's what I want) / I'll go crazy / Bony Moronie / Ooh poo pah doo / Linda Lou / Louie Louie. *(US re-iss.1966 on 'Sunset', 3rd & 4th tracks repl. by 'Peppermint Beatles' & 'The Shake')*

not issued Vee Jay

1965. (7") **THE BOY NEXT DOOR. / B.J. QUETZAL** [-] [ ]

1965. (7") **DON'T SAY GOODBYE. / BIG BOSS MAN** [-] [ ]

not issued M.G.M.

1966. (7") **SOMEDAY YOU'LL CRY. / ZEBRA IN THE KITCHEN** [-] [ ]

Capitol Tower

Apr 66. (7") **DIRTY WATER. / RARI** [-] [11]

Jun 66. (lp) **DIRTY WATER** [-] [52]
– Dirty water / Little Sally tease / Black is black / Barracuda / Animal girl / St.James infirmary / Try it / Summer in the city / Why did you hurt me / Rari / Paint it black / Medication / Wht pick on me / Sunny afternoon / Mr. Nobody / Wild thing.

Aug 66. (7") **SOMETIMES GOOD GUYS DON'T WEAR WHITE. / WHY DID YOU HURT ME?** [-] [43]

Oct 66. (7") **WHY PICK ON ME?. / MR. NOBODY** [-] [54]

1966. (lp) **WHY PICK ON ME / SOMETIMES GOOD GUYS DON'T WEAR WHITE** [-] [ ]
– Sometimes good guys don't wear white / Paint it black / My little red book / Mi hai fatto innamorata / Have you ever spent the night in jail / Mainline / Black hearted woman / Mr.Nobody.

—— **DAVE BURKE** – bass repl. LANE

Nov 66. (lp) **THE HOT ONES** [-] [ ]
– Last train to Clarksville / Wild thing / Sunshine Superman / Sunny afternoon / Lil' Red Riding Hood / Eleanor Rigby / Black is black / Summer in the city / 19th nervous breakdown / Dirty water.

Nov 66. (7") **TRY IT. / POOR SHELL OF A MAN** [-] [ ]

—— **JOHN FLECK** – bass repl. BURKE

Jan 67. (7") **DON'T TELL ME WHAT TO DO. ("SLLEDNATS") / WHEN I WAS A COWBOY** [-] [ ]

Mar 67. (7") **RIOT ON SUNSET STRIP. / BLACK HEARTED WOMAN** [-] [ ]

Nov 67. (7") **CAN'T HELP BUT LOVE YOU. / 99 AND A HALF WON'T DO** [-] [78]

1967. (7") **ANIMAL GIRL. / SOUL DRIPPIN'** [-] [ ]

1967. (lp) **TRY IT** [-] [ ]
– Can't help but love you / 99 and a half won't do / Trip to Paradise / St.James Infirmary / Try it / Barracuda / Did you ever have that feeling / All fall down / Poor shell of a man / Riot on Sunset Strip.

—— Disbanded early '68, although in the early 70's VALENTINO and TAMBLYN re-formed. In the 80's, DODD was again added to 3 originals.

– compilations, etc. –

1966. Sunset; (7") **OOH POO PAH DOO. / HELP YOURSELF** [-] [ ]

1982. Rhino; (lp) **THE BEST OF THE STANDELLS** [-] [ ]
(re-iss.1986)

1984. Rhino; (lp) **RARITIES** [-] [ ]

Oct 92. Big Beat; (cd) **DIRTY WATER** [ ] [-]

Mar 93. Big Beat; (cd) **HOT ONES / TRY IT** [ ] [-]

Jun 93. Big Beat; (cd) **IS THIS THE WAY YOU GET YOUR HIGH** [ ] [-]

Sep 95. Sundazed; (7") **SITTING THERE STANDING. /** [ ] [-]

DICK DODD

went solo augmented by ED COBB

not issued / Attarack

1967. (7") **GUILTY. / REQUIEM: 820 LATHAM** [-] [ ]

not issued / Tower

Dec 67. (7") **LITTLE SISTER. / LONELY WEEKENDS** [-] [ ]

Feb 68. (7") **FANNY. / DON'T BE ASHAMED TO CALL MY NAME** [-] [ ]

Feb 68. (lp) **THE FIRST EVOLUTION OF DICK DODDS** [-] [ ]

Paul STANLEY (see under ⇒ KISS)

Vivian STANSHALL (see under ⇒ BONZO DOG BAND)

Ringo STARR

Born: RICHARD STARKEY, 7 Jul'40, Liverpool, England. The drummer of The BEATLES from Aug'62 to their final split in 1969. Early that year, he also appeared in the film 'Candy'. The next year he starred in 'The Magic Christian' film alongside Peter Sellers. This busy year also saw him release two solo albums; the George Martin produced covers lp 'SENTIMENTAL JOURNEY' and the Nashville recorded 'BEAUCOUPS OF BLUES'. He had his first major hit single in 1971, with 'IT DON'T COME EASY'. He also continued acting career throughout the 70's. **Filmography:** BLINDMAN (1971) / 200 MOTELS (1971 with Frank Zappa) / BORN TO BOOGIE (1972 T.Rex film he directed only) / THAT'LL BE THE DAY (1973) / LISZTOMANIA (1975) / SCOUSE THE MOUSE (1977) / PRINCESS DAISY (1983 TV mini-soap with Barbara) / THOMAS THE TANK ENGINE (1984-86; narrated children's TV) / GIVE MY REGARDS TO BROAD STREET (Paul McCartney's film 1984) / WATER (1985) / WILLIE AND THE POOR BOYS (1985 Bill Wyman video) / ALICE IN WONDERLAND (1985 TV). • **Style:** Pop rock legend whose patter and wit made up for his basic vocal talent. • **Songwriters:** As said above, wrote some himself and attempted covers YOU'RE SIXTEEN (Johnny Burnette) / ONLY YOU (Platters) / NO NO SONG (Hoyt Axton) / SNOOKEROO (elton John / Bernie Taupin) / IT'S ALL DOWN TO GOODNIGHT VIENNA (John Lennon) / HEY BABY (Bruce Channel). His 1978 album BAD BOY was another covers album. • **Miscellaneous:** In the early 80's, he met actress Barbara Bach, whom he married on 27 Apr'81. A year previous, they had survived a serious car crash.

Recommended: BLAST FROM THE PAST (*6).

RINGO STARR – vocals with session people

Apple / Apple

Mar 70. (lp)(c) **SENTIMENTAL JOURNEY** [7] [22]
– Sentimental journey / Night and day / Whispering grass / Bye bye blackbird / I'm a fool to care / Stardust / Blue, turning grey over you / Love is a many splendoured thing / Dream / You always hurt the one you love / Have I told you lately that I love you / Let the rest of the world go by. *(cd-iss.May 95 on 'EMI')*

Sep 70. (lp)(c) **BEAUCOUPS OF BLUES** [ ] [65]
– Beaucoups of blues / Love don't last long / Fastest growing heartache in the west / Without her / Woman of the night / I'd be talking all the time / $15 draw / Wine, women and loud happy songs / I wouldn't have you any other way / Loser's lounge / Waiting / Silent homecoming. *(cd-iss.May95 on 'EMI')*

Nov 70. (7") **BEAUCOUPS OF BLUES. / COOCHY-COOCHY** [-] [87]

Apr 71. (7") **IT DON'T COME EASY. / EARLY 1970** [4] [4]

Mar 72. (7") **BACK OFF BOOGALOO. / BLINDMAN** [2] [9]

Oct 73. (7") **PHOTOGRAPH. / DOWN AND OUT** [8] [1]

Nov 73. (lp)(c) **RINGO** [7] [2]
– You and me (babe) / I'm the greatest / Have you seen my baby / Photograph / Sunshine life for me / You're sixteen / Oh my my / Step lightly / Six o'clock * / Devil woman. *(US track *= extended) (re-iss.Nov80 on 'M.F.P.') (re-iss.+cd.Mar91 on 'EMI')*

Feb 74. (7") **YOU'RE SIXTEEN. / DEVIL WOMAN** [4] [8] Dec73

Mar 74. (7") **OH MY MY. / STEP LIGHTLY** [-] [5]

Nov 74. (7") **ONLY YOU. / CALL ME** [28] [6]

Nov 74. (lp)(c) **GOODNIGHT VIENNA** [30] [8]
– It's all down to goodnight Vienna / Occapella / Oo-wee / Husbands and wives / Snookeroo / All by myself / Call me / No no song / Only you / Easy for me / Goodnight Vienna (reprise).

Feb 75. (7") **SNOOKEROO. / OO-WEE** [ ] [-]

Feb 75. (7") **NO NO SONG. / SNOOKEROO** [-] [3]

Jun 75. (7") **IT'S ALL DOWN TO GOODNIGHT VIENNA. / OO-WEE** [-] [31]

Dec 75. (lp)(c) **BLAST FROM YOUR PAST** (compilation) [ ] [30]
– You're sixteen / No no song / It don't come easy / Photograph / Back off boogaloo / Only you / Beacoups of blues / Oh my my / Early 1970 / I'm the greatest. *(re-iss.Nov81 on 'M.F.P.') (cd-iss.1987 on 'E.M.I.')*

Jan 76. (7") **OH MY MY. / NO NO SONG** [ ] [-]

Polydor / Atlantic

Sep 76. (7") **A DOSE OF ROCK'N'ROLL. / CRYIN'** [ ] [26]

Sep 76. (lp)(c) **RINGO'S ROTOGRAVURE** [ ] [28]
– A dose of rock'n'roll / Hey baby / Pure gold / Cryin' / You don't know me at all / Cookin' / I'll still love you / This be called a song / La brisas / Lady Gaye.

Nov 76. (7") **HEY BABY. / LADY GAYE** [ ] [74]

Sep 77. (7") **DROWNING IN THE SEA OF LOVE. / GROWING** [-] [ ]

Sep 77. (7") **DROWNING IN THE SEA OF LOVE. / JUST A DREAM** [ ] [-]

Sep 77. (lp)(c) **RINGO THE 4th** [ ] [ ]
– Drowning in the sea of love / Tango all night / Wings / Gave it all up / Out on the streets / Can she do it like she dances / Sneaking Sally through the alley / It's no secret / Gypsies in flight / Simple love song.

Oct 77. (lp) **SCOUSE THE MOUSE** [ ] [ ]
– (8 children's songs)

Nov 77. (7") **WINGS. / JUST A DREAM** [-] [ ]

Apr 78. (lp)(c) **BAD BOY** [ ] [ ]
– Who needs a heart / Bad boy / Lipstick traces / Heart on my sleeve / Where did our love go / Hard times / Tonight / Monkey see monkey do / Old time relovin' / A man like me.

Jun 78. (7") **TONIGHT. / OLD TIME RELOVIN'** [ ] [ ]

not issued / Portrait

1980. (7") **OLD TIME RELOVIN'. / LIPSTICK TRACES (ON A CIGARETTE)** [-] [ ]

1980. (7") **HEART ON MY SLEEVE. / WHO NEEDS A HEART** [-] [ ]

—— Released US single 'OKEY COKEY' with NILSSON as "COLONEL DOUG BOGIE")

R.C.A. / Boardwalk

Nov 81. (7") **WRACK MY BRAIN. / DRUMMING IS MY MADNESS** [ ] [38]

Nov 81. (lp)(c) **STOP AND SMELL THE ROSES** [ ] [98]
– Private property / Wrack my brain / Drumming is my madness / Attention / Stop and take the time to smell the roses / Dead giveaway / You belong to me / Sure to fall (in love with you) / Nice way / Back off boogaloo.

Feb 82. (7") **STOP AND TAKE TIME TO SMELL THE ROSES. / PRIVATE PROPERTY** [-] [ ]

Bellaphon / not issued

Jun 83. (7") **IN MY CAR. / AS FAR AS WE CAN GO** [-] [-] GERM

Boardwalk / not issued

Jun 83. (lp) **OLD WAVE** [-] [-]
– In my car / Hopeless / Alibi / Be my baby / She's about a mover / Keep forgettin' / Picture show life / As far as we can go / Everybody's in a hurry but me / I'm going down.

—— Retired from solo work, guesting on ex-BEATLES' (PAUL McCARTNEY & GEORGE HARRISON solo). In '84, he narrated for children TV series 'Thomas The Tank Engine'. Returned to studio for 1990 album

RINGO STARR & HIS ALL-STAR BAND

DR.JOHN + BILLY PRESTON – keyboards / **NILS LOFGREN + JOE WALSH** – guitar / **RICK DANKO** – bass / **JIM KELTNER** – drums / **LEVON HELM** – perc. / **CLARENCE CLEMONS** – saxophone

R.C.A. / Arista

Nov 90. (cd)(c)(lp) **RINGO STARR AND HIS ALL-STARR BAND (live)** [ ] [ ]
– It don't come easy / The no-no song / Iko Iko / The weight / Shine silently / Honey don't / You're sixteen, you're beautifil, and you're mine / Quarter to three / Raining in my heart / Will it go round in circles / Life in the fast lane / Photograph.

May 92. (12") **WEIGHT OF THE WORLD. / AFTER ALL THESE YEARS** [74] [ ]

Rykodisc / Rykodisc

Oct 93. (cd)(c) **LIVE FROM MONTREUX (live)** [ ] [ ]
– Really serious introduction (QUINCY JONES & RINGO) / I'm the greatest (RINGO) / Don't go where the rain don't go (RINGO) / Desperado (JOE WALSH) / I can't tell you why (TIMOTHY B.SCHMIT) / Girls talk (DAVE EDMUNDS) / Weight of the world (RINGO) / Bang the drum all day (TODD RUNDGREN) / Walking nerve (NILS LOFGREN) / Black Maria (TODD RUNDGREN) / In the city (JOE WALSH) / American woman (BURTON CUMMINGS) / Boys (RINGO) / With a little help from my friends (RINGO).

– more compilations, etc. –

May 84. EMI Gold; (7") **IT DON'T COME EASY. / BACK OFF BOOGALOO** [ ] [-]

Feb 89. Rhino; (lp)(c)(cd) **STARRSTRUCK: RINGO'S BEST** [-] [ ]
(cd+=) – (4 tracks).

STARSHIP (see under ⇒ JEFFERSON AIRPLANE)

STATE OF PLAY (see under ⇒ CURVE)

STATUS QUO

Formed: London, England ... 1962 as The SPECTRES by schoolboys ALAN LANCASTER, ALAN KEY, MIKE ROSSI (aka FRANCIS) and JESS JAWORSKI. They soon added JOHN COUGHLAN to replace BARRY SMITH, and by the mid-60's were playing residency at Butlin's holiday camp, where ROY LYNES took over from JESS. In Jul'66 they signed to 'Piccadilly' records, but failed with a debut 45, a Leiber & Stoller cover 'I (WHO HAVE NOTHING)'. They released 2 more flops, before they changed name in Mar'67 to The TRAFFIC JAM. After one 45, it was thought best to become STATUS QUO, after another group called TRAFFIC were hitting Top 10. In Oct'67, MIKE reverted name to FRANCIS and STATUS QUO added a second guitarist RICK PARFITT. Now re-signed on 'Pye' records, they unleashed first single 'PICTURES OF MATCHSTICK MEN', which gave them breakthrough into the UK Top 10, with it also hitting US No.12 (their only Top 50 hit). The following year, they were again in the Top 10 with 'ICE IN THE SUN'. After 2 more Top 30 hits in the early 70's, they moved to 'Vertigo' records (1972), and became top selling group of the 70's, which continued into the 80's. • **Style:** Moved from a late 60's pastiche psychedelic outfit, into a blues & boogie hard rock band from the early 70's onwards. The English answer to CANNED HEAT, also attired themselves in jeans and T-shirt, which they retained up to the 90's. Their 3-chord wonder barrage of rock'n'roll, has had few variations throughout their career Suffered critical onslaught, deservedly given to them after their 90's 'ANNIVERSARY WALTZ' pop medleys which made them sound more like CHAS & DAVE. • **Songwriters:** LANCASTER or ROSSI or PARFITT. In the early 70's, ROSSI and tour manager BOB YOUNG took over duties. Covered; SPICKS AND SPECKS (Bee Gees) / GREEN TAMBOURINE (Lemon Pipers) / SHEILA (Tommy Roe) / ICE IN THE SUN + ELIZABETH DREAMS + PARADISE FLAT + others (Marty Wilde – Ronnie Scott) / JUNIOR'S WAILING (Steamhammer) / DOWN THE DUSTPIPE (Carl Grossman) / THE PRICE OF LOVE (Everly Brothers) / ROADHOUSE BLUES (Doors) / WILD SIDE OF LIFE (Tommy Quickly) / ROCKIN' ALL OVER THE WORLD (John Fogerty) / THE WANDERER (Dion) / IN THE ARMY NOW (Bolland-Bolland) / RESTLESS (Jennifer Warnes) / WHEN YOU WALK IN THE ROOM (Jackie DeShannon) / etc. • **Trivia:** In 1985, the group with LANCASTER still in tow, play The LIVE AID Wembley concert.

Recommended: QUOTATIONS VOL.1 (THE EARLY YEARS) (*6) / 12 GOLD BARS (*7).

SPECTRES

MIKE ROSSI (b.FRANCIS, 29 Apr'49, Forest Hill, London) – vocals, guitar / **ROY LYNES** (b.25 Oct'43, Surrey, Kent) – organ, vocals repl. JESS JAWORSKI / **ALAN LANCASTER** (b. 7 Feb'49, Peckham, London) – bass, vocals / **JOHN COGHLAN** (b.19 Sep'46, Dulwich, London) – drums repl. BARRY SMITH

		Piccadilly	not issued
Sep 66.	(7") **I (WHO HAVE NOTHING). / NEIGHBOUR, NEIGHBOUR**		–
Nov 66.	(7") **HURDY GURDY MAN. / LATICA**		–
——	(above was not later covered by DONOVAN)		
Feb 67.	(7") **(WE AIN'T GOT) NOTHIN' YET. / I WANT IT**		–

TRAFFIC JAM

		Piccadilly	not issued
Jun 67.	(7") **ALMOST THERE BUT NOT QUITE. / WAIT JUST A MINUTE**		–

The STATUS QUO

added **RICK PARFITT** (b.RICHARD HARRISON, 12 Oct'48, Woking, Surrey) – guitar, vocals / MIKE now **FRANCIS ROSSI**

		Pye	Cadet Con.
Nov 67.	(7") **PICTURES OF MATCHSTICK MEN. / GENTLEMAN JOE'S SIDEWALK CAFE**	7	12 May 68
Apr 68.	(7") **BLACK VEILS OF MELONCHOLY. / TO BE FREE**		Jul 69
Aug 68.	(lp) **PICTURESQUE MATCHSTICKABLE MESSAGES FROM THE STATUS QUO** (US-title 'MESSAGES FROM THE STATUS QUO')		

– Black veils of meloncholy / When my mind is not live / Ice in the Sun / Elizabeth dreams / Gentleman Joe's sidewalk cafe / Paradise flat / Technicolour dreams / Spicks and specks / Sheila / Sunny cellophane skies / Green tambourine / Pictures of matchstick men. *(re-iss.+c+cd.Oct87 on 'P.R.T.') (cd re-iss.Dec87 & Aug90 on 'Castle')*

Aug 68.	(7") **ICE IN THE SUN. / WHEN MY MIND IS NOT ALIVE**	8	70
Feb 69.	(7") **MAKE ME STAY A BIT LONGER. / AUNTIE NELLIE**		–
Mar 69.	(7") **TECHNICOLOR DREAMS. / SPICKS AND SPECKS**	–	
May 69.	(7") **ARE YOU GROWING TIRED OF MY LOVE. / SO ENDS ANOTHER LIFE**	46	–
Sep 69.	(lp)(c) **SPARE PARTS**		–

– Face without a soul / You're just what I'm looking for / Mr.Mind detector / Antique Angelique / So ends another life / Are you growing tired of my love / Little Miss Nothing / Poor old man / The clown / Velvet curtains / When I awake / Nothing at all. *(re-iss.+cd.Oct87 on 'P.R.T.') (re-cd-is.Aug90 on 'Castle')*

Oct 69.	(7") **THE PRICE OF LOVE. / LITTLE MISS NOTHING**		
		Pye	**Janus**
Mar 70.	(7") **DOWN THE DUSTPIPE. / FACE WITHOUT A SOUL**	12	
Sep 70.	(lp)(c) **MA KELLY'S GREASY SPOON**		

– Spinning wheel blues / Daughter / Everything / Shy fly / (April) Spring, Summer and Wednesdays / Junior's wailing / Lakky lady / Need your love / Lazy poker blues / Is it really me? – Gotta go home. *(re-iss.+cd.Oct87 on 'P.R.T.') (cd re-iss.Dec87 & Aug90 on 'Castle')*

STATUS QUO

now a quartet of **ROSSI, PARFITT, LANCASTER + COGHLAN** when LYNES departed.

Oct 70.	(7") **IN MY CHAIR. / GERDUNDULA** *(re-iss.Jun79)*	21	
		Pye	**Pye**
Jun 71.	(7") **TUNE TO THE MUSIC. / GOOD THINKING**		
Dec 71.	(lp)(c) **DOG OF TWO HEAD**		

– Umleitung / Nanana / Something going on in my head / Mean girl / Nanana / Gerdundula / Railroad / Someone's learning / Nanana. *(re-iss.+cd. Oct87 on 'P.R.T.') (cd re-iss.Aug90 on 'Castle')*

		Vertigo	A & M
Dec 72.	(7") **PAPER PLANE. / SOFTER RIDE**	8	–
Jan 73.	(lp)(c) **PILEDRIVER**	5	

– Don't waste my time / O baby / A year / Unspoken words / Big fat mama / Paper plane / All the reasons / Roadhouse blues. *(re-iss.May83, cd-iss.Feb91)*

May 73.	(7") **DON'T WASTE MY TIME. / ALL THE REASONS**	–	
Jul 73.	(7") **PAPER PLANE. / ALL THE REASONS**	–	
Sep 73.	(7") **CAROLINE. / JOANNE**	5	–
Sep 73.	(lp)(c) **HELLO!**	1	

– Roll over lay down / Claudie / A reason for living / Blue-eyed lady / Caroline / Softer ride / And it's better now / Forty-five hundred times. *(re-iss.May83, cd-iss.Feb91)*

Feb 74.	(7") **CAROLINE. / SOFTER RIDE**	–	
Apr 74.	(7") **BREAK THE RULES. / LONELY NIGHT**	8	–
May 74.	(lp)(c) **QUO**	2	

– Backwater / Just take me / Break the rules / Drifting away / Don't think it matters / Fine fine fine / Lonely man / Slow train. *(re-iss.Aug83, cd-iss.Feb91)*

		Vertigo	Capitol
Nov 74.	(7") **DOWN DOWN. / NIGHT RIDE**	1	
Feb 75.	(lp)(c) **ON THE LEVEL**	1	

– Little lady / Most of the time / I saw the light / Over and done / Night ride / Down down / Broken man / What to do / Where I am? / Bye bye Johnny. *(re-iss.Aug83, cd-iss.Feb91)*

May 75.	(7"ep) **EXTENDED PLAY (live)**	9	

– Roll over lay down / Gerdundula / Junior's wailing.

Feb 76.	(7") **RAIN. / YOU LOST YOUR LOVE**	7	
Mar 76.	(lp)(c) **BLUE FOR YOU** (US title 'STATUS QUO')	1	

– Is there a better way? / Mad about the boy / Ring of a change / Blue for you / Rain / Rolling home / That's a fact / Ease your mind / Mystery song. *(re-iss.Dec83, cd see-compilations)*

Jul 76.	(7") **MYSTERY SONG. / DRIFTING AWAY**	11	
Dec 76.	(7") **WILD SIDE OF LIFE. / ALL THROUGH THE NIGHT**	9	
Mar 77.	(d-lp)(d-c) **STATUS QUO LIVE! (live)**	3	

– Junior's wailing / Backwater / Just take me / Is there a better way? / In my chair / Little lady / Most of the time / Forty-five hundred times / Roll over lay down / Big fat mama / Caroline / Bye bye Johnny / Rain / Don't waste my time / Roadhouse blues. *(re-iss.Sep84)*

Oct 77.	(7") **ROCKIN' ALL OVER THE WORLD. / RING OF A CHANGE**	3	
Nov 77.	(lp)(c) **ROCKIN' ALL OVER THE WORLD**	5	

– Hard time / Can't give you more / Let's ride / Baby boy / You don't own me / Rockers rollin' / Rockin' all over the world / Who am I? / Too far gone / For you / Dirty water / Hold you back. *(re-iss.Aug85, cd-iss.Feb91)*

Aug 78.	(7") **AGAIN AND AGAIN. / TOO FAR GONE**	13	–
Oct 78.	(lp)(c) **IF YOU CAN'T STAND THE HEAT**	3	–

– Again and again / I'm giving up my worryin' / Gonna teach you to love me / Someone show me home / Long-legged Linda / Oh what a night / Accident prone / Stones / Let me fly / Like a good girl. *(cd-iss.see-compilations)*

Nov 78.	(7") **ACCIDENT PRONE. / LET ME FLY**	36	–
Sep 79.	(7") **WHATEVER YOU WANT. / HARD RIDE**	4	–
Oct 79.	(lp)(c) **WHATEVER YOU WANT**	3	–

– Whatever you want / Shady lady / Who asked you / Your smiling face / Living on an island / Come rock with me / Rockin' on / Runaway / High flyer / Breaking away. *(cd-iss.see-compilations)*

Nov 79.	(7") **LIVING ON AN ISLAND. / RUNAWAY**	16	–
Apr 80.	(lp)(c) **12 GOLD BARS** (compilation)	3	–

– Rockin' all over the world / Down down / Caroline / Paper plane / Break the rules / Again and again / Mystery song / Roll over lay down / Rain / The wild side of life / Whatever you want / Living on an island. *(cd-iss.Nov84)*

Oct 80.	(7") **WHAT YOU'RE PROPOSIN'. / A.B. BLUES**	2	–
Oct 80.	(lp)(c) **JUST SUPPOSIN'**	4	–

– What you're proposin' / Run to mummy / Don't drive my car / Lies / Over the edge / The wild ones / Name of the game / Coming and going / Rock'n'roll. *(cd-iss.see-compilations)*

Dec 80.	(7") **DON'T DRIVE MY CAR. / LIES**	11	–
Feb 81.	(7") **SOMETHING 'BOUT YOU BABY I LIKE. / ENOUGH IS ENOUGH**	7	–
Mar 81.	(lp)(c) **NEVER TOO LATE**	2	–

– Never too late / Something 'bout you baby I like / Take me away / Falling in falling out / Carol / Long ago / Mountain lady / Don't stop me now / Enough is enough / Riverside. *(cd-iss.Oct83, + see-compilations)*

Nov 81.	(7"m) **ROCK'N'ROLL. / HOLD YOU BACK / BACKWATER**	8	–

—— **PETE KIRCHNER** – drums (ex-ORIGINAL MIRRORS, ex-HONEYBUS, etc.) repl. COUGHLAN who formed PARTNERS IN CRIME

Mar 82.	(7") **DEAR JOHN. / I WANT THE WORLD TO KNOW**	10	–
Apr 82.	(lp)(c) **1+9+8+2**	1	–

– She don't fool me / Young pretender / Get out and walk / Jealousy / I love rock and roll / Resurrection / Dear John / Doesn't matter / I want the world to know / I should have known / Big man. *(cd-iss.Oct83, + see-compilations)*

Jun 82. (7") **SHE DON'T FOOL ME. / NEVER TOO LATE** [36] [-]

Oct 82. (7")(7"pic-d) **CAROLINE (live). / DIRTY WATER (live)** [13] [-]
(12"+=) – Down down (live).

Nov 82. (t-lp)(d-c) **FROM THE MAKERS OF . . .** (compilation & 2 lp-sides live) [4] [-]
– Pictures of matchstick men / Ice in the Sun / Down the dustpipe / In my chair / Junior's wailing / Mean girl / Gerdundula / Paper plane / Big fat mama / Roadhouse blues / Break the rules / Down down / Bye bye Johnny / Rain / Mystery song / Blue for you / Is there a better way / Again and again / Accident prone / The wild side of life / Living on an island / What you're proposing / Rock and roll / Something 'bout you baby I like / Dear John / Caroline / Roll over lay down / Backwater / Little lady / Don't drive my car / Whatever you want / Hold you back / Rockin' all over the world / Don't waste my time.

Sep 83. (7")(7"pic-d) **OL' RAG BLUES. / STAY THE NIGHT** [9] [-]
('A'extended-12"+=) – Whatever you want (live).

Oct 83. (lp)(c)(cd) **BACK TO BACK** [9] [-]
– A mess of the blues / Ol' rag blues / Can't be done / Too close to the ground / No contrast / Win or lose / Marguerita time / Your kind of love / Stay the night / Going down town tonight. *(cd re-iss. see-compilations)*

Oct 83. (7") **A MESS OF THE BLUES. / BIG MAN** [15] [-]
('A'extended-12"+=) – Young pretender.

Dec 83. (7")(7"pic-d) **MARGUERITA TIME. / RESURRECTION** [3] [-]
(d7"+=) – Caroline / Joanne.

May 84. (7") **GOING DOWN TOWN TONIGHT. / TOO CLOSE TO THE GROUND** [20] [-]

Oct 84. (7")(12")(7"pic-d)(12"clear) **THE WANDERER. / CAN'T BE DONE** [7] [-]

Nov 84. (d-lp)(c)(cd) **12 GOLD BARS VOL.2** (compilation) [12] [-]
– What you're proposing / Lies / Something 'bout you baby I like / Don't drive my car / Dear John / Rock and roll / Ol' rag blues / Mess of the blues / Marguerita time / Going down town tonight / The wanderer. (incl.VOL.1).

—— **ROSSI** + **PARFITT** enlisted **ANDY BOWN** – keyboards (ex-HERD) (He was p/t member since 1974) / **JEFF RICH** – drums (ex-CLIMAX BLUES BAND) repl. KIRCHNER / **RHINO EDWARDS** (r.n.JOHN) – bass (ex-CLIMAX BLUES BAND) repl. LANCASTER

May 86. (7")(7"sha-pic-d) **ROLLIN' HOME. / LONELY** [9] [-]
(12"+=) – Keep me guessing.

Jul 86. (7") **RED SKY. / DON'T GIVE IT UP** [19] [-]
(12"+=) – The Milton Keynes medley (live).
(d7"+=) – Marguerita time.

Aug 86. (lp)(c)(cd) **IN THE ARMY NOW** [7] [-]
– Rollin' home / Calling / In your eyes / Save me / In the army now / Dreamin' / End of the line / Invitation / Red sky / Speechless / Overdose.

Sep 86. (7")(7"pic-d) **IN THE ARMY NOW. / HEARTBURN** [2] [-]
('A'military mix-12"+=) – Late last night.
(d7"+=) – Whatever you want / Rockin' all over the world.

Nov 86. (7") **DREAMIN'. / LONG-LEGGED GIRLS** [15] [-]
('A'-wet mix-12"+=) – The Quo Christmas cake mix.

Mar 88. (7") **AIN'T COMPLAINING. / THAT'S ALRIGHT** [19] [-]
('A'extended-12"+=) – Lean machine.
(cd-s++=) – In the army now (remix).

May 88. (7") **WHO GETS THE LOVE?. / HALLOWEEN** [34] [-]
('A'extended-12"+=) – The reason for goodbye.
(cd-s++=) – The wanderer.

Jun 88. (lp)(c)(cd) **AIN'T COMPLAINING** [12] [-]
– Ain't complaining / Everytime I think of you / One for the money / Another shipwreck / Don't mind if I do / I know you're leaving / Cross that bridge / Cream of the crop / The loving game / Who gets the love? / Burning bridges / Magic.

—— (Below single was a re-working of 'ROCKIN' ALL . . . ' for Sport Aid)

Aug 88. (7") **RUNNING ALL OVER THE WORLD. / MAGIC** [17] [-]
(12"+=) – ('A'extended).
(cd-s++=) – Whatever you want.

Nov 88. (7") **BURNING BRIDGES (ON AND OFF AND ON AGAIN). / WHATEVER YOU WANT** [5] [-]
(12"+=)(cd-s+=) – ('A'extended) / Marguerita time.

Oct 89. (7")(c-s) **NOT AT ALL. / GONE THRU THE SLIPS** [50] [-]
(12"+=)(cd-s+=) – Every time I think of you.

Nov 89. (lp)(c)(cd) **PERFECT REMEDY** [49] [-]
– Little dreamer / Not at all / Heart on hold / Perfect remedy / Address book / The power of rock / The way I am / Tommy's in love / Man overboard / Going down for the first time / Throw her a line / 1,000 years.

Dec 89. (7")(c-s)(7"pic-d) **LITTLE DREAMER. / ROTTEN TO THE BONE** [ ] [-]
(12"+=)(cd-s+=) – Doing it all for you.

Oct 90. (7")(c-s)(7"silver) **THE ANNIVERSARY WALTZ – (PART 1). / THE POWER OF ROCK** [2] [-]
(12"+=)(cd-s+=) – Perfect remedy.

Oct 90. (cd)(c)(lp) **ROCKIN' ALL OVER THE YEARS** (compilation) [2] [-]
– Pictures of matchstick men / Ice in the Sun / Paper plane / Caroline / Break the rules / Down down / Roll over lay down / Rain / Wild side of life / Whatever you want / What you're proposing / Something 'bout you baby I like / Rock'n'roll / Dear John / Ol' rag blues / Marguerita time / The wanderer / Rollin' home / In the army now / Burning bridges / Anniversary waltz (part 1).

Dec 90. (7")(c-s) **THE ANNIVERSARY WALTZ – (PART 2). / DIRTY WATER (live)** [16] [-]
(12"+=)(cd-s+=) – Pictures of matchstick men / Rock'n'roll music / Lover please / That'll be the day / Singing the blues.

Aug 91. (7")(c-s) **CAN'T GIVE YOU MORE. / DEAD IN THE WATER** [37] [-]
(12"+=)(cd-s+=) – Mysteries from the ball.

Sep 91. (cd)(c)(lp) **ROCK 'TIL YOU DROP** [10] [-]
– Like a zombie / All we really wanna do (Polly) / Fakin' the blues / One man band / Rock 'til you drop / Can't give you more / Warning shot / Let's work together / Bring it on home / No problems / Good sign / Tommy / Nothing comes easy / Fame or money / Price of love / Forty-five hundred times. *(re-iss.Feb93)*

Jan 92. (7")(c-s) **ROCK 'TIL YOU DROP. / Awards Medley:- CAROLINE – DOWN DOWN – WHATEVER YOU WANT – ROCKIN' ALL OVER THE WORLD** [38] [-]
(12"+=)(cd-s+=) Forty-five hundred times.

Polydor Polydor

Oct 92. (7")(c-s)(cd-s) **ROADHOUSE BLUES MEDLEY (ANNIVERSARY WALTZ 25). / ('A'extended)** [21] [ ]
(cd-s+=) – Don't drive my car.

Nov 92. (cd)(c)(d-lp) **LIVE ALIVE QUO (live)** [37] [ ]
– Roadhouse medley:- Roadhouse blues – The wanderer – Marguerita time – Living on an island – Break the rules – Something 'bout you baby I like – The price of love – Roadhouse blues / Whatever you want / In the army now / Burning bridges / Rockin' all over the world / Caroline / Don't drive my car / Hold you back / Little lady. *(re-iss.cd Apr95)*

—— In May 94; their 'BURNING BRIDGES' tune, was used for Manchester United Football Squad's UK No.1 'Come On You Reds'.

Polydor M.C.A.

Jul 94. (7"colrd)(c-s) **I DIDN'T MEAN IT. / WHATEVER YOU WANT** [21] [ ]
(cd-s+=) – Down down / Rockin' all over the world.
(cd-s) – ('A'side) / Survival.
(cd-ep) – ('A'side) / ('A'-hooligan version) / Survival / She knew too much.

Aug 94. (cd)(c)(lp) **THIRSTY WORK** [13] [ ]
– Goin' nowhere / I didn't mean it / Confidence / Point of no return / Sail away / Like it or not / Soft in the head / Queenie / Lover of the human race / Sherri don't fail me now! / Rude awakening time / Back on my feet / Restless / Ciao ciao / Tango / Sorry.

Oct 94. (7"colrd)(c-s) **SHERRI DON'T FAIL ME NOW!. / BEAUTIFUL** [38] [ ]
(cd-s+=) – In the army now.
(cd-s) – ('A'side) / Tossin' and turnin' / Down to you.

Nov 94. (7")(c-s)(cd-s) **RESTLESS (re-orchestrated). / AND I DO** [39] [ ]

PolygramTV not issued

Oct 95. (7")(c-s) **WHEN YOU WALK IN THE ROOM. / TILTING AT THE MILL** [34] [ ]
(cd-s+=) – ('A'version).

– more compilations, etc. –

Dec 69. Marble Arch; (lp) **STATUS QUOTATIONS** [ ] [-]
May 78. Marble Arch; (lp)(c) **STATUS QUO** [ ] [-]
Mar 73. Pye; (7") **MEAN GIRL. / EVERYTHING** [20] [ ]
May 73. Pye; (lp)(c) **THE BEST OF STATUS QUO** [32] [ ]
– Down the dustpipe / Gerdundula / In my chair / Umleitung / Lakky lady / Daughter / Railroad / Tune to the music / April, Spring, Summer and Wednesdays / Mean girl / Spinning wheel blues. *(cd-iss.1986 on 'P.R.T.')*
Jul 73. Pye; (7") **GERDUNDULA. / LAKKY LADY** [ ] [-]
Sep 76. Pye; (lp)(c) **THE REST OF STATUS QUO** [ ] [-]
Jan 77. Pye; (lp)(c) **THE STATUS QUO FILE** [ ] [-]
(re-iss.Sep79 on 'P.R.T.')
Apr 77. Pye; (12"ep) **DOWN THE DUSTPIPE / MEAN GIRL. / IN MY CHAIR / GERDUNDULA** [ ] [-]
Oct 78. Pye; (7"yellow) **PICTURES OF MATCHSTICK MEN. / DOWN THE DUSTPIPE** [ ] [-]
(re-iss.7"black Apr83 on 'Old Gold')
May 79. Pye; (7") **PICTURES OF MATCHSTICK MEN. / ICE IN THE SUN** [ ] [-]
Jun 79. Pye; (lp)(c)(orange-lp) **JUST FOR THE RECORD** [ ] [-]
Jun 73. Golden Hour; (lp)(c) **A GOLDEN HOUR OF . . .** [ ] [-]
(c/cd-iss.Apr90 on 'Knight')
Oct 75. Golden Hour; (lp)(c) **DOWN THE DUSTPIPE** [20] [-]
Apr 78. Hallmark; (lp)(c) **PICTURES OF MATCHSTICK MEN** [ ] [-]
Aug 78. Pickwick; (d-lp)(d-c) **THE STATUS QUO COLLECTION** [ ] [-]
Sep 80. Pickwick; (d-lp)(d-c) **STATUS QUO** [ ] [-]
Jun 80. PRT; (d-lp)(d-c) **SPOTLIGHT ON . . .** [ ] [-]
Oct 81. PRT; (10"lp)(c) **FRESH QUOTA** (rare) [74] [-]
Jun 82. PRT; (c) **100 MINUTES OF . . .** [ ] [-]
Oct 82. PRT; (lp)(c) **SPOTLIGHT ON . . . VOL.II** [ ] [-]
Jul 83. PRT; (10"lp)(c) **WORKS** [ ] [-]
Oct 85. PRT; (lp)(c) **NA NA NA** [ ] [-]
Oct 87. PRT; (lp)(c)(cd) **QUOTATIONS VOL.1 – (THE EARLY YEARS)** [ ] [-]
Oct 87. PRT; (lp)(c)(cd) **QUOTATIONS VOL.2 – (ALTERNATIVES)** [ ] [-]
Sep 88. PRT; (lp)(c)(cd)(pic-lp) **FROM THE BEGINNING (1966-67)** [ ] [-]
Apr 83. Contour; (lp)(c) **TO BE OR NOT TO BE** [ ] [-]
(cd-iss.Apr91 on 'Pickwick')
1975. Starline; (lp) **ROCKIN' AROUND WITH** [ ] [-]
Jul 82. Old Gold; (7") **MEAN GIRL. / IN MY CHAIR** [ ] [-]
Sep 85. Old Gold; (7") **CAROLINE. / DOWN DOWN** [ ] [-]
Nov 85. Old Gold; (7") **ROCKIN' ALL OVER THE WORLD. / PAPER PLANE** [ ] [-]
(re-iss.Aug 89 + Sep 90)
Nov 85. Castle; (d-lp)(c) **THE COLLECTION** [ ] [-]
(cd-iss.1988)
Apr 89. Legacy; (c)(cd) **C90 COLLECTOR** [ ] [-]
Below 5 released on 'Vertigo'.
Jul 84. Dutch import; (lp) **LIVE AT THE N.E.C. (live)** [83] [-]
Feb 91. (cd) **WHATEVER YOU WANT / JUST SUPPOSIN'** [ ] [-]
Feb 91. (cd) **NEVER TOO LATE / BACK TO BACK** [ ] [-]
Feb 91. (cd) **QUO / BLUE FOR YOU** [ ] [-]
Feb 91. (cd) **IF YOU CAN'T STAND THE HEAT / 1+9+8+2** [ ] [-]
May 93. Spectrum; (cd)(c) **A FEW BARS MORE** [ ] [-]
Sep 94. Spectrum; (cd)(c) **IT'S ONLY ROCK'N'ROLL** [ ] [-]
Jul 94. Success; (cd)(c) **ICE IN THE SUN** [ ] [-]
Mar 95. Connoisseur; (cd) **THE OTHER SIDE OF STATUS QUO** [ ] [-]
May 95. Spectrum; (cd)(c) **PICTURES OF MATCHSTICK MEN** [ ] [-]
Jun 95. Savanna; (cd) **ICE IN THE SUN** [ ] [-]

FRANCIS ROSSI & BERNARD FROST

Vertigo not issued

Apr 85. (7")(ext-12") **MODERN ROMANCE (I WANT TO FALL IN LOVE AGAIN). / I WONDER WHY** 54 -

Oct 85. (7") **JEALOUSY. / WHERE ARE YOU NOW** -

('A'extended-12"+=) – That's all right.

STEALER'S WHEEL (see under ⇒ RAFFERTY, Gerry)

STEELEYE SPAN

Formed: St.Albans, England … 1969 by ASHLEY HUTCHINGS who teamed up with two duos MADDY PRIOR & TIM HART, plus GAY & TERRY WOODS. Under the direction of Sandy Robertson, they signed to 'RCA' and released 1970 album 'HARK! THE VILLAGE WAIT'. In 1972, they transferred to 'Chrysalis' records and had first singles success with surprise 1973 Christmas hit 'GAUDETE'. It sparked off further commercial fortunes during the mid-70's. • **Style:** Electric folk band who like the FAIRPORTS, crossed-over into pop charts. They retained traditional roots and instruments throughout, although they progressed into rock market. • **Songwriters:** All members through the years contributed their own songs; i.e. HUTCHINGS, PRIOR & HART, The WOODS, CARTHY, JOHNSON, etc. They also covered traditional Olde England folk tunes, reels and jigs, plus more regular classics RAVE ON (Buddy Holly) / GAUDETE (trad.Latin hymn) / TO KNOW HIM IS TO LOVE HIM (Teddy Bears) / TWINKLE TWINKLE LITTLE STAR (children's song) / etc. MADDY covered RAG DOLL (Four Seasons) / WHO'S SORRY NOW? (Connie Francis) / SWIMMING SONG (Loudon Wainwright III) / BOYS OF BEDLAM (Nick Jones-Dave Morgan) / WINTER WAKENETH (M.Kiszco). • **Trivia:** Their 1974 Top 20 album 'NOW WE ARE SIX' was produced by IAN ANDERSON (Jethro Tull), and featured DAVID BOWIE playing sax solo on track 'TO KNOW HIM IS TO LOVE HIM'. Their following album 'COMMONER'S CROWN', saw actor PETER SELLERS play ukelele on 'NEW YORK GIRLS'. 'ALL AROUND MY HAT' was produced by WOMBLES singer MIKE BATT.

Recommended: PLEASE TO SEE THE KING (*7) / BELOW THE SALT (*8) / PARCEL OF ROGUES (*6) / NOW WE ARE SIX (*7) / THE COLLECTION (*6).

MADDY PRIOR – vocals / **TIM HART** – guitar, vocals / **GAY WOODS** – vocals, concertina / **ASHLEY HUTCHINGS** – bass (ex-FAIRPORT CONVENTION) / **TERRY WOODS** – guitar, vocals with guest drummers **GERRY CONWAY + DAVE MATTACKS**

R.C.A. Chrysalis

Jun 70. (lp) **HARK! THE VILLAGE WAIT** 1976

– A calling – On song / The blacksmith / Fisherman's wife / Blackleg miner / Dark-eyed sailor / Copshawholme fair / All things are quite silent / The hills of Greenmore / My Johnny was a shoemaker / Lowlands of Holland / Twa corbies / One night as I lay on my bed. *(re-iss.Mar76 on 'Mooncrest', re-dist.1983) (re-iss.1988 on 'Shanachie')*

— **MARTIN CARTHY** (b.21 May'41, Hatfield, England) – electric guitar / **PETER KNIGHT** – fiddle repl. TERRY & GAY who formed own self-named duo.

B & C Chrysalis

Mar 71. (lp) **PLEASE TO SEE THE KING** 45 - 1976

– Blacksmith / Cold, haily, windy night / Bryan O'Lynn (jig) / The hag with the money / Prince Charlie Stuart / Boys of Bedlam / False knight on the road / The lark in the morning / Female drummer / The king / Lonely on the water. *(re-iss.Mar76 on 'Mooncrest', re-dist.1983) (re-iss.+cd.Mar91)*

1971. (7"m) **RAVE ON. / REELS / FEMALE DRUMMER** -

Pegasus Chrysalis

Jan 72. (lp) **TEN MAN MOP OR MR. RESERVOIR BUTLER RIDES AGAIN** - 1976

– Marrowbones / Captain Coulston / Reels: Dowd's favourite – 10 float – The morning dew / Wee weaver / Skewball / Gower wassail / Jigs: Paddy Clancy's jig – Willie Clancy's fancy / Four nights drunk / When I was on horseback. *(re-iss.Mar76 on 'Mooncrest', re-dist.1983) (re-iss.1988 on 'Shanachie') (re-iss.+cd.Aug91 on 'Total')*

— **BOB JOHNSON** – guitar, vocals repl. CARTHY who went solo / **RICK KEMP** – bass repl. HUTCHINGS who joined ALBION COUNTRY BAND

Chrysalis Chrysalis

Aug 72. (lp)(c) **BELOW THE SALT** 43

– Spotted cow / Rosebuds in June / Jigs / Sheepcrook and black dog / Royal forester / King Henry / John Barleycorn / Saucy sailor. *(re-iss.1974) (re-iss.Oct89 on 'Shanachie')*

Sep 72. (7") **JOHN BARLEYCORN. / JIGS** -

Nov 73. (7") **GAUDETTE. / ROYAL FORESTER** -

(re-iss. 1975)

Apr 73. (lp)(c) **PARCEL OF ROGUES** 26

– Alison Gross / One misty moisty morning / The bold poacher / The ups and downs / Robbery with violins / The wee wee man / Cam ye o'er fae France / The weaver and the factory maid / Rogues in a nation / Hares on a mountain. *(re-iss.1974) (re-iss.+cd.Nov88 on 'Shanachie')*

Nov 73. (7") **GAUDETE. / THE HOLLY & THE IVY** 14

— **PRIOR, HART, KNIGHT, JOHNSON + KEMP** added **NIGEL PEGRUM** – drums, percussion

Feb 74. (lp)(c) **NOW WE ARE SIX** 13

– Thomas the rhymer / Two magicians / Edwin / Twinkle twinkle little star / Seven hundred elves / The mooncoin jig / Drink down the Moon / Long a-growing / Now we are six / To know him is to love him. *(re-iss.Oct89 on 'Shanachie', cd-iss.Jun91)*

Feb 74. (7") **THOMAS THE RHYMER. / THE MOONCOIN JIG**

Jan 75. (lp)(c) **COMMONER'S CROWN** 21

– Little Sir Hugh / Bach goes to Limerick / Long Lankin / Dogs and ferrets / Galtee farmer / Demon lover / Elf call / Weary cutters / New York girls.

Mar 75. (7") **NEW YORK GIRLS. / TWO MAGICIANS**

Oct 75. (7") **ALL AROUND MY HAT. / BLACK JACK DAVY** 5

Oct 75. (lp)(c) **ALL AROUND MY HAT** 7

– Black Jack Davy / Hard times of old England / Cadgwith anthem / Sum waves (tunes) / The wife of Usher's Well / Gamble gold (Robin Hood) / All around my hat / Dance with me / Batchelor's hall. *(re-iss.Jul85 on 'M.F.P.') (re-iss.Oct89 on 'Shanachie') (re-iss.Mar94)*

Jan 76. (7") **HARD TIMES OF OLD ENGLAND. / CADGWITH ANTHEM**

Sep 76. (7") **LONDON. / SLIGO MAID**

Oct 76. (lp)(c) **ROCKET COTTAGE** 41

– London / The Bosnian hornpipes / Orfeo / Nathan's reel / The twelve witches / The brown girls / Fighting for strangers / Sligo maid / Sir James the rose / The drunkard.

Nov 76. (7") **FIGHTING FOR STRANGERS. / THE BOSNIAN HORNPIPES**

— **MARTIN CARTHY** – guitar, vocals returned to repl. JOHNSON / **JOHN KIRKPATRICK** – accordion repl. KNIGHT who formed duo with JOHNSON. They made one album 'KING OF ELFLAND'S DAUGHTER' in 1978 for 'Chrysalis'.

Nov 77. (7") **THE BOAR'S HEAD CAROL. / GAUDETE / SOME RIVAL** -

Nov 77. (lp)(c) **STORM FORCE TEN** -

– Awake, awake / Sweep, chimney sweep / The wife of the soldier / The victory / The black freighter / Some rival / Treadmill song / Seventeen come Sunday.

Nov 78. (lp)(c) **LIVE AT LAST**

– The Atholl highlanders / Walter Bulwer's polka / Saucy sailor / The black freighter / The maid and the palmer / Hunting the wren / Montrose / Bonnets so blue / The false knight on the road.

Nov 78. (7") **RAG DOLL. / HUNTING THE WREN** -

— Split May 78 until reformation 1980, **KNIGHT & JOHNSON** returned 1974 line-up

Nov 80. (7") **SAILS OF SILVER. / SENIOR SERVICE** -

Nov 80. (lp)(c) **SAILS OF SILVER** -

– Sails of silver / My love / Barnet fair / Senior service / Gone to America / Where are they now / Let her go now / Longbone / Marigold – Harvest home / Tell me why.

Feb 81. (7") **GONE TO AMERICA. / LET HER GO DOWN** -

— Disbanded 1981, MADDY PRIOR and TIM HART continued with solo work.

— **STEELEYE SPAN** returned sporadically in the 80's now without HART.

Flutterby not issued

Nov 85. (7") **SOMEWHERE IN LONDON. / LANERCROST** -

May 86. (lp)(cd) **BACK IN LINE** -

– Edward / Lanercrost / Lady Diamond / Isabel / A cannon by Telemann / Blackleg miner / Peace on the border / Scarecrow / Take my heart / White man. *(cd re-iss.Aug91 on 'Park' +=)*– Spotted cow / One misty moisty morning. (re-iss.c Jan94)

Supertrack not issued

Apr 89. (7") **PADSTOW. / REDS: THE FIRST HOUSE IN CONNAUGHT – SAILOR'S BONNET** -

Dover-Chrysalis not issued

Sep 89. (7") **FOLLOWING ME. / TWO BUTCHERS** -

Sep 89. (lp)(c)(cd) **TEMPTED AND TRIED** -

– Padstow / The fox / Two butchers / Following me / Seagull / The cruel mother / Jack Hall / Searching for lambs / Shaking of the sheets / Reels: The first house in Connaught – Sailor's bonnet – Betsy Bell and Mary Gray.

– compilations, others, etc. –

1972. Charisma; (lp) **INDIVIDUALLY AND COLLECTIVELY** -

Sep 76. Mooncrest; (7"ep) **RAVE ON. / (+3)** -

1977. Mooncrest; (d-lp) **TIMESPAN** -

(re-iss.Sep84)

May 77. Chrysalis; (d-lp)(c) **ORIGINAL MASTERS** -

Nov 82. Chrysalis; (7"ep) **ALL AROUND MY HAT / FIGHTING FOR STRANGERS. / GAUDETE / BOAR'S HEAD CAROL** -

Dec 82. Chrysalis; (d-c) **ALL AROUND MY HAT / ROCKET COTTAGE** -

Mar 84. Chrysalis; (lp)(c) **THE BEST OF STEELEYE SPAN** -

(cd-iss.1989)

Oct 88. Chrysalis; (lp)(c)(cd) **PORTFOLIO** -

Nov 79. Folktracks; (c) **FOLK ELECTRIC FOLK** -

May 80. Hallmark; (lp)(c) **STEELEYE SPAN** -

1980. P.E.L.; (7") **JIGS AND REELS (REELS MEDLEY). / ('A'version)** -

Sep 84. Cambra; (d-lp)(d-c) **STEELEYE SPAN** -

(re-iss.+cd.Apr90 on 'Action Replay')

Feb 87. Old Gold; (7") **ALL AROUND MY HAT. / GAUDETE** -

Apr 89. Connoisseur; (d-lp)(c)(cd) **EARLY YEARS** -

May 91. Action Replay; (cd) **THE BEST & THE REST OF …** -

Aug 91. Castle; (cd)(c) **THE COLLECTION** -

– Thomas the rhymer / Alison Gross / John Barleycorn / King Henry / One misty moisty morning / The mooncoin jig / Long Lankin / The fox / Shaking of the sheets / Rougues in a nation / Galtee farmer / All around my hat / Sailor's bonnet / Black Jack Davy / Gaudete / Seven hundred elves / Sligo maid / Following me / Robbery with violins / Seventeen come Sunday.

Nov 94. Park; (cd)(c) **THE COLLECTION: STEELEYE SPAN IN CONCERT (live)** -

Mar 95. Chrysalis; (cd) **SPANNING THE YEARS** -

TIM HART & MADDY PRIOR

1968. B&C; (lp) **FOLK SONGS OF YE OLDE ENGLAND VOL.1** -

(re-iss.+cd.Apr91 on 'Total')

1972. B&C; (lp) **SUMMER SOLTICE** -

(re-iss.Mar76 on 'Mooncrest') (re-iss.1988 on 'Shanachie')

1974. B&C; (lp) **FOLK SONGS OF YE OLDE ENGLAND VOL.2** -

(re-iss.Mar76 on 'Mooncrest')

MADDY PRIOR & JUNE TABOR

Chrysalis / not issued

Mar 76. (lp) **SILLY SISTERS**
– Doffin' mistress / Burning of Auchidoon / Lass of Loch Royal / The seven joys of Mary / My husband's got no courage in him / Singing the travels / Silver whistle / Geordie / The grey funnel line / The seven wonders / Four loom weaver / The game of cards / Dame Durdan. *(cd-iss.Jan94 on 'B.G.O.')*

— They combined again in the mid-90's as SILLY SISTERS on cd-album 'NO MORE TO THE DANCE' for 'Transatlantic'.

MADDY PRIOR

Chrysalis / Chrysalis

May 78. (7") **ROLLERCOASTER. / I TOLD YOU SO**
May 78. (lp)(c) **WOMAN IN THE WINGS**
– Woman in the wings / Cold flame / Mother and child / Gutter geese / Rollercoasters / Deep water / Long shadows / I told you so / Rosettes / Catseyes / Baggy pants. *(cd-iss.Mar94 on 'B.G.O.')*
Jul 78. (7") **RAG DOLL. / SAUCY SAILOR**
Sep 78. (7") **BAGGY PANTS. / WOMAN IN THE WINGS**
Nov 78. (lp)(c) **CHANGING WINDS**
– To have and to hold / Pity the poor night porter / Bloomers / Acappella Stella / Canals / The sovereign prince / Ali Baba / The mountain / In fighting / Another drink. *(re-iss.1986) (cd-iss.Dec93 on 'B.G.O.')*
Jan 79. (7") **JUST THE TWO OF US. / ACAPPELLA STELLA**

MADDY PRIOR BAND

MADDY with **RICK KEMP, RITCHIE CLOSE, MICK BYCHE & GARY WILSON**

E.M.I. / not issued

Aug 80. (7") **WAKE UP ENGLAND. / PARADISE**

Plant Life / not issued

May 82. (lp) **HOOKED ON WINNING**
– Hooked on winning / Anthem to failure / Long holiday / Nothing but the best / etc.
May 82. (7") **FACE TO FACE. / HALF LISTENING**

Spinthrift / not issued

Nov 83. (lp) **GOING FOR GLORY ("MADDY PRIOR & THE ANSWERS")**
– After the death / Saboteur / Morning girls / Half listening / Deep in the darkest night / Conversion / Oh no / God squad / Trivial hymn / Each heart / Hope lies now / Pater noster / Allelujah.

R.C.A. / not issued

Nov 83. (7") **DEEP IN THE DARKEST NIGHT. / WESTERN MOLLES**

Making W. / not issued

Sep 85. (7") **STOOKIE. / ('A'version)**

Skydisc / not issued

Dec 87. (lp)(c)(cd) **A TAPESTRY OF CAROLS**
– (Christmas songs by "MADDY PRIOR & THE CARNIVAL BAND")

— (another lp by this ensemble 'CAROLS AND CAPERS' was iss. Dec91 on 'Park' / re-iss.cd+c Dec94)

Sep 90. (cd)(c) **SING LUSTILY AND WITH GOOD COURAGE**

MADDY PRIOR & RICK KEMP

Park / not issued

Aug 91. (cd)(c)(lp) **HAPPY FAMILIES**
– Happy families / Good job / Rose / Mother and child / Here comes midnight / Bewcastle / Who's sorry now / Fire on the line / Goodbye / Alex / Low flying / Happy families (edit).
Aug 91. (7") **HAPPY FAMILIES. / WHO'S SORRY NOW?**

MADDY PRIOR

with **NICK HOLLAND** – piano, keyboards / **RICHARD LEE** – double bass / **MICK DYCHE** – acoustic guitar / **MARTIN LOVEDAY** – cello / **JOHN DOCHARY** – bass / guests **RICK KEMP / ANDY WATTS / LIAM GENOCKY**

Park / not issued

Oct 93. (cd)(c) **YEAR**
– Spring: Snowdrops – Birth / Summer: Swimming song / Autumn: Marigold – Harvest home / Winter: Red & green / Long shadows / Somewhere along the road / What had you for supper / Saucy sailor / The fabled hare: a) I sall goe until a hare, b) Scent of a dog, c) Winter wakeneth, d) The hare said, e) I shall run and run / Deep in the darkest night / Boys of bedlam / Twa corbies.
Dec 94. (cd) **MEMENTO – THE BEST OF MADDY PRIOR** (compilation)
Nov 95. (cd) **HANG UP SORROW AND CARE (w/ CARNIVAL BAND)**
Dec 95. (cd) **YEAR / HAPPY FAMILIES** (compilation)

TIM HART

Chrysalis / not issued

May 79. (lp)(c) **TIM HART**
– Keep on traveling / Tuesday afternoon / Hillman Avenger / Lovely lady / Nothing to hide / Come to my window / Time after time / Overseas / As I go on my way.
May 79. (7") **OVERSEAS. / HILLMAN AVENGER**

STEEL PULSE

Formed: Handsworth Wood, Birmingham, England ... 1976 by HINDS, GABBIDON and McQUEEN. After 2 singles flopped, they were snapped up by Chris Blackwell's 'Island' records. Their debut album 'HANDSWORTH REVOLUTION' received plenty airplay from early 1978, and finally breached the UK Top 10 later in the year. It contained two classic 45's 'KU KLUX KLAN' & 'PRODIGAL SON', which both hit the Top 50. • **Style:** Black political roots reggae, who fused melody and dance rhythms. • **Songwriters:** Most written by HINDS and co. • **Trivia:** Were regulars on the Rock Against Racism set of gigs and tours.

Recommended: HANDSWORTH REVOLUTION (*8).

DAVID HINDS – vocals, guitar / **BASIL GABBIDON** – lead guitar, vocals / **RONNIE 'Stepper' McQUEEN** – bass / **SELWYN BROWN** – keyboards / **STEVE NESBITT** – drums / **MICHAEL RILEY** – percussion, vocals / **ALPHONSO MARTIN** – percussion, vocals

Dip / not issued

1976. (7") **KIBUDO, MANSETTA AND ABUKI. / ?**

Anchor / not issued

Oct 77. (7") **NYAH LOVE. / LUV NYAH**

Island / Island

Jan 78. (lp)(c) **HANDSWORTH REVOLUTION** (hit Jul78) — 9
– Handsworth revolution / Bad man / Soldiers / Sound check / Prodigal son / Ku Klux Klan / Prediction / Makka splaff. *(cd-iss.1988 & Jan91 on 'Mango-Island')*
Feb 78. (7") **KU KLUX KLAN. / BUN DEM** — 41
Jun 78. (7") **PRODIGAL SON. / ('A'version)** — 35
Aug 78. (7")(12") **PREDICTION. / HANDSWORTH REVOLUTION (dub)**

— **GODFREY MADURA** – saxophone repl. RILEY

May 79. (7")(12") **SOUND SYSTEM. / CRAMPAS STYLE** — 71
Jun 79. (lp)(c) **TRIBUTE TO THE MARTYRS** — 42
– Unseen guest / Sound system / Uncle George / Blasphemy (selah) / Tribute to the martyrs / Biko's kindred lament / Babylon makes the rules / Jah Pickney. *(re-iss.1988 on 'Mango', cd-iss.Sep89 + Oct90)*
Mar 80. (7") **DON'T GIVE IN. / ('A'instrumental)**
May 80. (lp)(c) **CAUGHT YOU**
– Drug squad / Harassment / Reggae fever / Shining / Heart of stone / Rumours / Caught you dancing / Burning flame / Higher than high / Nyahbinghi voyage. *(cd-iss.1988 on 'Mango')*
May 80. (7")(12") **CAUGHT YOU DANCING. / HEART OF STONE**

— now without MADURA

Wiseman / Elektra

Apr 82. (7")(12") **THE RAVERS. / LEGGO BEAST (more dub Marcus say)**
Apr 82. (lp)(c) **TRUE DEMOCRACY**
– Chant a psalm / Ravers / Find it . . .quick! / A who responsible? / Worth his weight in gold / Leggo beast / Blues dance raid / Your house / Man no sober / Dub Marcus say.
Jan 83. (12"ep) **YOUR HOUSE / BLUES DANCE. / DOCTRINE RAID / WHO'S RESPONSIBLE**

— BASIL departed to form BASS DANCE.

Feb 84. (lp)(c) **EARTH CRISIS**
– Steppin' out / Tight rope / Throne of gold / Rollerskates / Earth crisis / Bodyguard / Grab education / Wild goose chase.
Mar 84. (12")(7") **STEPPIN' OUT. / BODY GUARD / RALLY GO ROUND**
Jul 84. (7") **ROLLERSKATES. /**

— **ALVIN EWAN** – bass repl. McQUEEN / added guest **CARLTON BRYAN** – guitar

Elektra / Elektra

Feb 86. (7") **LOVE WALK OUT. / KICK THAT HABIT (COLD TURKEY)**
(12"+=) – Save black music. *(US; b-side)*
Mar 86. (lp)(c) **BABYLON THE BANDIT**
– Save black music / Not King James version / School boy's crush (jail bait) / Sugar daddy / Kick that habit (cold turkey) / Blessed is the man / Love walks out / Don't be afraid / Babylon the bandit.

M.C.A. / M.C.A.

Oct 88. (7")('A'ext-12") **REACHING OUT. / ('A'dub version)**
Nov 88. (lp)(c)(cd) **STATE OF . . .EMERGENCY** — Jul 88
– State of emergency / Dead end circuit / Steal a kiss / Hijacking / P.U.S.H. / Love this reggae music / Said you was an angel / Reaching out / Melting pot / Disco drop out.
Apr 91. (cd)(c)(lp) **VICTIMS**
– Taxi driver / Can't get you (out of my system) / Soul of my soul / Grab a girlfriend / Feel the passion / Money / Victims / Gay warfare / To Tuta / Free the land / We can do it / Stay with the rhythm.
Apr 91. (12") **SOUL OF MY SOUL. / ('A' instrumental) / DUB OF MY DUB**
(c-s) – ("A" side) / Excerpts: Can't get you (out of my system) – We can do it – Grab a girlfriend.
Mar 93. (cd)(c)(lp) **RASTAFARI CENTENNIAL – (Live in Paris: Elysee Montmatre)**
– State of emergency / Blues dance raid / Taxi driver / Makka splaff – Drug squad – Handsworth revolution (makka medley) / Ku Klux Klan / Ravers / Soldiers / Steppin' out. (cd+=) – (4 extra tracks) Chant a psalm / Rally round / Taxi driver – Rebel on the pause / Taxi driver – Rebel on the pulse (dub).

– compilations, others, etc. –

May 85. Island; (lp)(c) **REGGAE GREATS**
– Sound system / Babylon makes the rules / Don't give in / Soldier / Prodigal son / Ku Klux Klan / Macka splaff / Drug squad / Reggae fever / Handsworth revolution. *(cd-iss.1988 + 1990 on 'Mango')*
Nov 90. Reggae Refreshers; (cd)(c) **PROTEST**

STEELY DAN

Formed: New York, USA . . . by DONALD FAGEN and WALTER BECKER initially as a writing partnership, after they left Bard's college in 1969. They recorded a soundtrack for the movie 'YOU GOTTA WALK IT LIKE YOU TALK IT', which starred Richard Pryor. In the early 70's, they joined JAY & THE AMERICANS, where they met producer GARY KATZ. When GARY was invited to be in-house producer for 'Dunhill-ABC', he secured a deal also for FAGEN and BECKER. In Jun'72, they added others (see below) and became STEELY DAN, taking name from the William Burroughs novel 'The Naked Lunch' describing a steam-powered dildo. Their debut album 'CAN'T BUY A THRILL' featuring the hit 45 'DO IT AGAIN', and this gave them their first of a string of Top 20 albums. • **Style:** Virtually a studio outlet, playing college loved laid back rock. They also added trad.jazz feel and clear production techniques that FM radio romantics loved. • **Songwriters:** BECKER-FAGEN except, EAST ST.LOUIS TOODLE-OO (Duke Ellington). • **Trivia:** In 1985, BECKER produced CHINA CRISIS' album 'Flaunt The Imperfection'. The duo teamed up yet again with KATZ when they sessioned on his 1987 production of ROSIE VELA's 1986 album 'ZAZU'. Scottish group DEACON BLUE, named themselves after a 1977 track of theirs 'DEACON BLUES'. **Recommended:** REELIN' IN THE YEARS – THE VERY BEST (*9).

DONALD FAGEN (b.10 Jan'48, Passaic, New Jersey, USA) – keyboards, vocals / **WALTER BECKER** (b.20 Feb'50, New York) – bass, vocals / **DAVID PALMER** – vocals (ex-MIDDLE CLASS) / **DENNY DIAS** – rhythm guitar / **JEFF BAXTER** – guitar (ex-HOLY MODAL ROUNDERS) / **JIM HODDER** – drums (ex-BEAD GAME)

Probe / A.B.C.

Sep 72. (7") **DALLAS. / SAIL THE WATERWAY**
Nov 72. (7") **DO IT AGAIN. / FIRE IN THE HOLE** — / 6
(re-iss.Sep75 on 'ABC', hit UK No.39)
Dec 72. (lp)(c) **CAN'T BUY A THRILL** — / 17 Nov 72
– Do it again / Dirty work / Kings / Midnite cruiser / Only a fool would say that / Reelin' in the years / Fire in the hole / Brooklyn (owes the charmer and me) / Change of the guard / Turn that heartbreak over again. *(re-iss.quad.Sep75 on 'ABC', hit UK No.38) (re-iss.1983 on 'MCA', cd-iss.Jul88)*
Mar 73. (7") **REELING IN THE YEARS. / ONLY A FOOL WOULD SAY THAT** — / 11

—— **BECKER & FAGEN** now on lead vocals, when PALMER left to BIG WHA-KOO.

Jul 73. (7") **SHOWBIZ KIDS. / RAZOR BOY** — / 61
Jul 73. (lp)(c) **COUNTDOWN TO ECSTACY** — / 35
– Bodhizattva / Razor boy / The Boston rag / Your gold teeth / Showbiz kids / My old school / Pearl of the quarter / King of the world. *(re-iss.Jul83 on 'Fame') (re-iss.Feb82 on 'MCA', cd-iss.Jun88)*
Oct 73. (7") **MY OLD SCHOOL. / PEARL OF THE QUARTER** — / 63
Mar 74. (lp)(c) **PRETZEL LOGIC** 37 / 8
– Rikki don't lose that number / Night by night / Any major dude / Barrytown / East St.Louis toodle-oo / Parker's bad / Thru with buzz / Pretzel logic / With a gun / Charlie Freak / Monkey in your soul. *(re-iss.quad.Oct74 on 'ABC') (re-iss.Feb84 on 'MCA', cd-iss.Aug88 + May90)*
May 74. (7") **RIKKI DON'T LOSE THAT NUMBER. / ANY MAJOR DUDE** — / 4
(re-iss.Oct78 on 'ABC', hit UK 58 Mar79)
Oct 74. (7") **PRETZEL LOGIC. / THRU WITH BUZZ** — / 57

—— **MICHAEL McDONALD** – keyboards, vocals repl. BAXTER to DOOBIE BROTHERS / **JEFF PORCARO** – drums repl. HODDER

A.B.C. / A.B.C.

Apr 75. (lp)(c) **KATY LIED** 13 / 13
– Black Friday / Bad sneakers / Rose darling / Daddy don't live in that New York City no more / Doctor Wu / Everyone's gone to the movies / Your gold teeth II / Chain lightning / Any world (that I'm welcome to) / Throw back the little ones. *(re-iss.Jun84 on 'MCA', cd-iss.Aug88)*
May 75. (7") **BLACK FRIDAY. / THROW BACK THE LITTLE ONES** — / 37
Sep 75. (7") **BAD SNEAKERS. / CHAIN LIGHTNING**

—— When McDONALD joined DOOBIE BROTHERS and PORCARO left later joining TOTO, **BECKER & FAGEN** employed session people incl. **DENNY DIAS** part-time

May 76. (lp)(c) **THE ROYAL SCAM** 11 / 15
– Kid Charemange / The caves of Altamira / Don't take me alive / Sign in stranger / The fez / Green earrings / Haitian divorce / Everything you did / The royal scam. *(re-iss.Sep82 on 'MCA', cd-iss.Jun88)*
May 76. (7") **KID CHARLEMANGE. / GREEN EARRINGS** — / 82
Sep 76. (7") **THE FEZ. / SIGN IN STRANGER** - / 59
Nov 76. (7") **HAITIAN DIVORCE. / SIGN IN STRANGER** 17 / -
Sep 77. (lp)(c) **AJA** 5 / 3
– Black cow / Aja / Deacon blues / Peg / Home at last / I got the news / Josie.. *(re-iss.1983 on 'MCA', cd-iss.1985 & 1991)*
Nov 77. (7") **PEG. / I GOT THE NEWS** — / 11
Apr 78. (7")(12") **DEACON BLUES. / HOME AT LAST** — / 19 Mar 78
Aug 78. (7") **JOSIE. / BLACK COW** — / 26

—— (Signed to new label earlier in the year)

M.C.A. / M.C.A.

Jul 78. (7") **FM (NO STATIC AT ALL). / FM (Reprise)** 49 / 22 Jun 78
Nov 80. (lp)(c) **GAUCHO** 27 / 9
– Babylon sisters / Hey nineteen / Glamour profession / Gaucho / Time out of mind / My rival / Third world man. *(re-iss.Sep86, cd-iss.Jan85)*
Nov 80. (7") **HEY NINETEEN. / BODHISATTVA (live)** — / 10
Mar 81. (7") **BABYLON SISTERS. / TIME OUT OF MIND** — / -
Mar 81. (7") **TIME OUT OF MIND. / BODHISATTVA** - / 22

Parted ways after 1980 album. FAGEN went solo and BECKER to production.

– compilations, others, etc. –

Jan 78. ABC; (12"ep) **+ FOUR** — / -
– Do it again / Haitian divorce / Dallas / Sail the waterway.
Nov 78. ABC; (d-lp)(c) **GREATEST HITS 1972-78** 41 / 30
(re-iss.Mar82 on 'MCA')
Apr 82. MCA; (d-c) **CAN'T BUY A THRILL / AJA** — / -
Jun 82. MCA; (lp)(c) **GOLD** 44 / —
(free-12"w.a) *(re-iss.+cd.Aug91)*
Jul 82. MCA; (7") **FM (NO STATIC AT ALL). / FM (REPRISE)**
(12"+=) – East St.Louis toodle-oo.
Oct 83. MCA; (d-c) **KATY LIED / THE ROYAL SCAM** — / -
Dec 83. MCA; (12"ep) **HAITIAN DIVORCE / DO IT AGAIN. / REELING IN THE YEARS / RIKKI DON'T LOSE THAT NUMBER** — / -
Sep 84. MCA; (d-c) **COUNTDOWN TO ECSTACY / PRETZEL LOGIC** — / -
Aug 85. MCA; (cd) **DECADE OF STEELY DAN – THE BEST OF STEELY DAN**
Oct 85. MCA; (lp)(c) **REELIN' IN THE YEARS – THE VERY BEST OF STEELY DAN** 43 / -
– Do it again / Reelin' in the years / My old school / Bodhisattva / Show biz kids / Rikki don't lose that number / Pretzel logic / Black Friday / Bad sneakers / Doctor Wu / Haitian divorce / Kid Charlemagne / The fez / Peg / Josie / Deacon blues / Hey nineteen / Babylon sisters. *(re-iss. cd/c. Dec 92)*
Nov 85. MCA; (7") **REELING IN THE YEARS. / RIKKI DON'T LOSE THAT NUMBER**
Oct 87. MCA; (7") **RIKKI DON'T LOSE THAT NUMBER. / DO IT AGAIN**
Nov 93. MCA; (cd)(c) **REMASTERED – THE BEST OF STEELY DAN** 49 / —
Dec 93. MCA; (cd) **CITIZEN STEELY DAN** — / —
Apr 83. Old Gold; (7") **DO IT AGAIN. / RIKKI DON'T LOSE THAT NUMBER** — / -
Oct 87. Telstar; (lp)(c)(cd) **DO IT AGAIN – THE VERY BEST OF STEELY DAN** 64 / -
Apr 86. Showcase; (c) **SUN MOUNTAIN** (early demos) — / -
May 86. Bellaphon; (lp)(c) **BERRYTOWN** (demos) - / —
May 87. Thunderbolt; (lp)(c)(cd) **OLD REGIME** (early material) — / -
(re-iss.cd+c Mar94 on 'Prestige')
Apr 88. Thunderbolt; (lp)(cd) **STONE PIANO** (early material) — / -
Jun 94. Thunderbolt; (d-cd) **CATALYST** — / -
Jun 88. Castle; (d-lp) **BECKER AND FAGEN – THE COLLECTION** — / -
(early pre-STEELY DAN material)
Mar 78. Spark/ US= Visa; (lp) **YOU GOTTA WALK IT (Film Soundtrack)** 1971
Mar 84. Aero; (lp) **THE EARLY YEARS – WALTER BECKER & DONALD FAGEN** - / —
Sep 93. Remember; (cd)(c) **FOUNDERS OF STEELY DAN ("WALTER BECKER & DONALD FAGEN")** — / -
Feb 94. Javelin; (cd)(c) **SPOTLIGHT ON STEELY DAN** — / -
Feb 95. B.A.M.; (cd) **PEARLS OF THE PAST ("BECKER & FAGEN")** — / -

DONALD FAGEN

Warners / Warners

Oct 82. (lp)(c) **THE NIGHTFLY** 44 / 11
– New frontier / Walk between the raindrops / Maxine / Green flower street / The goodbye look / The nightfly / I.G.Y. (what a wonderful world). *(cd-iss.Jul88)*
Oct 82. (7") **I.G.Y. (WHAT A WONDERFUL WORLD). / WALK BETWEEN THE RAINDROPS** — / 26
Jan 83. (7") **NEW FRONTIER. / MAXINE** — / 70
(12"+=) – The goodbye look.
Apr 83. (7") **RUBY BABY. / WALK BETWEEN THE RAINDROPS** — / -
(below 'A'single from the film 'Bright Lights, Big City')
Apr 88. (7") **CENTURY'S END. / SHANGHAI CONFIDENTIAL (instrumental)** — / 83 Mar 88
(12"+=)(3"cd-s+=) – The nightfly / The goodbye look.

—— with **WALTER BECKER** – bass, solo guitar, co-writer some / **GEORGE WADENIUS** – guitar / **PAUL GRIFFIN** – hamond organ / **LEROY CLOUDEN or CHRISTOPHER PARKER** – drums / **BASHIRI JOHNSON** – percussion / **RANDY BRECKER + others** – horns

Reprise / Reprise

May 93. (cd)(c) **KAMAKIRIAD** 3 / 10
– Trans-island skyway / Countermoon / Springtime / Snowbound / Tomorrow's girls / Florida room / On the dunes / Teahouse on the tracks.
Jun 93. (7")(c-s) **TOMORROW'S GIRL. / SHANGHAI CONFIDENTIAL** 46 / —
(cd-s+=) – Confide in me.
Aug 93. (7")(c-s) **TRANS-ISLAND SKYWAY. / BIG NOISE, NEW YORK**
(cd-s+=) – Home at last (live).
Nov 93. (7")(c-s) **SNOWBOUND. / TRANS-ISLAND SKYWAY**
(cd-s+=) – ('A'mix).

WALTER BECKER

Giant / Giant

Nov 94. (cd)(c) **ELEVEN TRACKS OF WHACK**
– Down in the bottom / Junkie girl / Surf and or die / Book of liars / Lucky Henry / Hard up case / Cringemaker / Girlfriend / My Waterloo / This moody bastard / Hat too flat.

STEELY DAN

duo re-formed for live appearances in the States.

Giant / Giant

Oct 95. (cd)(c) **ALIVE IN AMERICA (live 1994)** 62 / 40
– Babylon sister / Green earrings / Bodhisattva / Reelin' in the years / Josie / Book of liars / Peg / Third World man / Kid Charlemagne / Sign in stranger / Aja.

Jim STEINMAN

Born: 1956, New York, but raised in California, USA. In 1974, he formed own high school band CLITORIS THAT THOUGHT IT WAS A PUPPY and wrote off-Broadway musical 'More Than You Deserve'. This was followed by other plays 'Dream Engine' and 'Neverland', which set up a meeting with producer Joseph Papp. In 1975, he relocated himself to New York and toured alongside friend MEAT LOAF. Early in '77, he began partnership with MEAT LOAF, and with TODD RUNDGREN on production, wrote material for album 'BAT OUT OF HELL'. It became biggest seller in the next 6 years. In the early 80's, before he contributed to another MEAT LOAF album, STEINMAN put together first solo album 'BAD FOR GOOD', which hit UK Top 10. • **Style:** AOR'n'roll theatre, which missed the vocal power of MEAT LOAF, although similarities were rife. PANDORA'S BOX were a hard-rock opera outfit, filled with sexual concept overkills. • **Songwriters:** All STEINMAN penned. • **Trivia:** After splitting with MEAT LOAF in 1982, STEINMAN wrote and produced BONNIE TYLER's No.1 'Total Eclipse Of The Heart'. He went on to produce many acts including DEF LEPPARD, SISTERS OF MERCY. His song 'LEFT IN THE DARK' was later covered by BARBRA STREISAND.

Recommended: BAD FOR GOOD (*5).

JIM STEINMAN – keyboards, vocals (ex-MEAT LOAF) with **RORY DODD** – vox / **TODD RUNDGREN** – multi / **E-STREET BAND** (see; Bruce SPRINGSTEEN)

Epic Epic

May 81. (lp)(c)(pic-lp) **BAD FOR GOOD** [7] [63]
– Bad for good / Lost boys and golden girls / Love and death and an American guitar / Stark raving love / Out of the frying pan (and into the fire) / Surf's up / Dance in my pants / Left in the dark. *(re-iss.Aug86, cd, Jan 87)* (7"given away free with initial copies of debut album) – **THE STORM. / ROCK'N'ROLL DREAMS COME THROUGH**

Jun 81. (7") **ROCK'N'ROLL DREAMS COME THROUGH. / LOVE AND DEATH AND AN AMERICAN GUITAR** [52] [32] May 81
(12"blue+=) – The storm.

Aug 81. (7") **LOST BOYS AND GOLDEN GIRLS. / LEFT IN THE DARK** [ ] [ ]

Oct 81. (7") **DANCE IN MY PANTS. / LEFT IN THE DARK** [ ] [ ]

JIM STEINMAN'S FIRE INC.

M.C.A. M.C.A.

May 84. (7")(12") **TONIGHT IS WHAT IT MEANS TO BE YOUNG. / HOLD THAT SNAKE (RY COODER)** [67] [ ]

Sep 84. (7") **NOWHERE FAST. / THE SORCERER** [ ] [ ]

— Went back into production until the late 80's, when he formed

PANDORA'S BOX

with **ELAINE CASWELL** – vocals / **EDDIE MARTINEZ** – guitar / **STEVE BUSLOWER** – bass / **ROY BITTAN** – piano / **JEFF BITTAN** – piano / plus **backing singers ELLEN FOLEY, DELIRIA WILDE, GINA TAYLOR, HOLLY SHERWOOD + LAURA THEODORE.**

Vertigo Mercury

Oct 89. (7") **IT'S ALL COMING BACK TO ME NOW. / I'VE BEEN DREAMING UP A STORM RECENTLY** [51] [ ]
(c-s+=) – Pray lewd / Teenager in love.
(12"+=)(cd-s+=) – Pray lewd / Requiem metal.

Nov 89. (lp)(c)(cd) **ORIGINAL SIN** [ ] [ ]
– The invocation / Original sin (the natives are restless today) / 20th century fox / Safe sex (when it comes 2 loving U) / Good girls go to Heaven (bad girls go everywhere) / Requiem metal / I've been dreamin' up a storm recently / It's all coming back to me now / The opening of the box / The want ad / My little red book / It just won't quit / Pray lewd / The flute ain't what it used to be.

Mar 90. (7") **GOOD GIRLS GO TO HEAVEN (BAD GIRLS GO EVERYWHERE). / REQUIEM METAL** [ ] [ ]
(12"+=)(cd-s+=) – Pray lewd / Pandora's house; room to roam.

Jun 90. (7"m) **SAFE SEX. / I'VE BEEN DREAMIN' UP A STORM / REQUEIM METAL** [ ] [ ]
(12"+=)(cd-s+=) – Pray lewd.

Martin STEPHENSON & THE DAINTEES

Formed: Newcastle, England . . . 1983 as The DAINTEES, by former busker MARTIN STEPHENSON. They were soon snapped up by local label 'Kitchenware' boss Keith Armstrong, who soon licensed group to major 'London' records. In 1986, STEPHENSON also gave himself top billing, and in two years, it paid off with Top 40 album 'GLADSOME, HUMOUR AND BLUE'. • **Style:** Acoustic balladeer tinted with folk, country & blues, drawing on similarities to 70's artists LEONARD COHEN or AL STEWART. • **Songwriters:** MARTIN wrote material, except; HIGH COIN (Van Dyke Parks) / LET'S CALL THE WHOLE THING OFF (Ira & George Gershwin) / etc. • **Trivia:** LEFT US TO BURN was an indictment of Maggie Thatcher.

Recommended: BOAT TO BOLIVIA (*8). / THERE COMES A TIME

DAINTEES

MARTIN STEPHENSON (b.1965, Durham, England) – vocals, acoustic guitar / **JOHN STEEL** – piano, organ / **ANTHONY DUNN** – bass

Kitchen-ware not issued

Dec 83. (7") **ROLL ON SUMMERTIME. / INVOLVED WITH LOVE** [ ] [-]

Sep 84. (7") **TROUBLE TOWN. / BETTER PLAN** [ ] [-]
(12"+=) – Jealous mind. *(above re-iss.Jan87 with free ltd.c-s 'DAINTEES LIVE' hit No.58)* Running waters / Crocodile cryer / Boat to Bolivia / Tremelo man.

May 86. (7"ep) **INFERNO EP** [ ] [-]
– Running water / Look down, look down (live) / Synergy.

MARTIN STEPHENSON & THE DAINTEES

added guest **PAUL SMITH** – drums, percussion

May 86. (lp)(c) **BOAT TO BOLIVIA** [85] [ ]
– Crocodile cryer / Coleen / Little red bottle / Tribute to the late Reverand Gary Davis / Running water / Candle in the middle / Piece of the cake / Look down, look down / Slow lovin' / Caroline / Rain. *(re-iss.+cd.Mar87, c+=)* – Boat to Bolivia. *(cd+=)* – Slaughterman / Wholly humble heart.

Jun 86. (7") **CROCODILE CRYER. / LOUIS (acoustic version)** [ ] [ ]
(12") – ('A'full version) / ('B'live version).

Aug 86. (7") **SLOW LOVIN'. / TRIBUTE TO THE LATE REVEREND GARY DAVIS** [ ] [ ]
(12"+=) – Smile on the summertime / Look down, look down (live).

Oct 86. (7") **BOAT TO BOLIVIA. / SLAUGHTERMAN** [70] [ ]
(12"+=) – Wholly humble heart.
(d12"+=) – Crocodile cryer (full version) / Louis (live).

— **MICK WATSON** – keyboards, percussion, sax, string arr. repl. STEEL / added **GYPSY DAVE SMITH** – dobro guitar / **GARY DUNN** – lead + rhythm guitars Guests inc. **VIRGINIA ASTLEY** – flute / **ANNE STEPHENSON** – violin / **CAROLINE LAVELLE** – cello / **CAROLINE BARNES** – violin / **FAY EVANS** – viola / **D.BREWIS** – guitar, keyboards / **SHEILA & SHERYL PARKER** – backing vocals

Apr 88. (lp)(c)(cd) **GLADSOME, HUMOUR AND BLUE** [39] [ ]
– There comes a time / Slaughterman / The wait / I can see / The old church is still standing / Even the night / Wholly humble heart / Me and Matthew / Nancy / Goodbye John / I pray.

Jun 88. (7") **WHOLLY HUMBLE HEART. / GET GET GONE** [ ] [ ]
(12"+=) – Come back to me.
(12"+=) – I can see (live) / Slow lovin' (live).

Oct 88. (7") **THERE COMES A TIME. / RUNNING WATER** [ ] [ ]
(12"+=) – Little red bottle (live) / Coleen (live).
(12"+=) – Crocodile cryer (live) / Coleen (live).

— **MARTIN** retains **ANTHONY, GARY + MICK** (now bass), plus guests **ANDREA MACKIE** – vocals / **PETE ANDERSON** – producer, guitar, sitar / **JEFF DONOVAN** - **SKIP EDWARDS** – keyboards, organ / **LARRY KNIGHT** – guitar / **LENNY CASTRO** – perc. / **DUSTY WAKEMAN** – bass / **DON REED** – viola / **LEE THORNBERG** – trumpet / **LEN PRICE** – sax / **GREG SMITH** – baritone sax / **BEVERLEY DAHLHE SMITH** – flute / **STEVE GROVE** – tenor sax / **FREEBO** – tuba / **DONNIE GERRARD, SHAUN MURPHY, LAURA CREAMER** – backing vocals

Kitchenware-London London

Apr 90. (7")(c-s) **LEFT US TO BURN. / EYOT** [ ] [ ]
(12"+=)(cd-s+=) – Kathy (live).

May 90. (cd)(c)(lp) **SALUTATION ROAD** [35] [ ]
– Left us to burn / Endurance / In the heat of the night / Big north lights / Long hard road / Spoke in the weel / Heart of the city / Too much in love / We are storm / Migrants / Morning time / Salutation road.

Jun 90. (7")(c-s) **ENDURANCE. / MEN CAN BE FLUNG** [ ] [ ]
(12"+=)(cd-s+=) – Release the first.

— **PAUL SMITH** – drums returned adding also to The **DUNN's; BRENDAN HEALEY** – piano / **FRANKIE GIBBON** – organ, b.vocals / **PAULINE MURRAY, FRED PURSER** (both ex-PENETRATION) and **CATHAL COUGHAN** (of FATIMA MANSIONS) – backing vocals

Jun 92. (7")(c-s) **BIG SKY NEW LIGHT. / SONG ABOUT THE MEMBER / WAKE ME IN THE MORNING** [71] [ ]
(cd-s) – ('A'side) / You really had a heart / Peace of mind / Let's call the whole thing off.
(cd-s) – ('A'side) / Far away meadows / Should my friends be gone / Every night.

Jul 92. (cd)(c)(lp) **THE BOY'S HEART** [68] [ ]
– Big sky new light / The boy's heart / We can roll / Ballad of the English rose / Neon skies / Hollywood fields / Sentimental journey / Sunday halo / 8.30 Mowbray morning / (Least we're a) Map in the world / Him, her and the Moon / Cab attack.

Mar 93. (cd)(c) **THERE COMES A TIME – THE BEST OF MARTIN STEPHENSON & THE DAINTEES** (compilation) [ ] [ ]

Apr 93. (cd)(c) **HIGH BELLS RING THIN** (rec.1990) [ ] [ ]
– You really had a heart / Looking for some peace of mind / Song about the member / Should my friends be gone / Don't be afraid of the night / Far away meadows / Synergy / Wake me in the morning / I like in the east / Him, her and the Moon / Every night / Music and life / Let's call the whole thing off.

Demon-Fiend not issued

Feb 95. (cd)(c) **YOGI IN MY HOUSE** [ ] [ ]
– Solomon / In fire / Taker on the globe / Think only of the child / New wave / Spirit child / Bridge of nae hope / Fair company / Gone the gipsy Davey / Always us / Dance the last goodbye.

STEPPENWOLF

Formed: Toronto, Canada . . . 1967 as blues band SPARROW by JOHN KAY and (see below). After one-off 45 for 'Columbia', they soon relocated to Los Angeles after a brief stay in New York. They met producer Gabriel Mekler, who gave them STEPPENWOLF name (after a Herman Hesse novel). They quickly signed to 'Dunhill' and recorded eponymous 1968 debut. That year's summer saw them hit US No.2 with classic biker's anthem 'BORN TO BE WILD', thus resurrecting albums' appeal which finally hit Top 10. The track was used on the 1969 film 'Easy Rider' alongside another from the debut; 'THE PUSHER'. Became one of America's top attractions, until they faded away mid-70's. • **Style:** Politically aware hard rock act, anti-war, anti-drugs, pro-rock'n'roll. • **Songwriters:** KAY written, except; THE PUSHER + SNOW BLIND FRIEND (Hoyt Axton) / SOOKIE SOOKIE (Don Covay) / BORN

TO BE WILD (Dennis Edmonton; Jerry's brother) / I'M MOVIN' ON (Hank Snow) / HOOCHIE COOCHIE MAN (Muddy Waters). • **Trivia:** BORN TO BE WILD coined a new rock term in the their lyrics "heavy metal thunder". Early in 1969, they contributed some songs to another cult-ish film 'Candy'.

Recommended: GOLDEN GREATS (*8).

JOHN KAY (b.JOACHIM F.KRAULEDAT, 12 Apr'44, Tilsit, E.Germany) – vox, guitar / **MICHAEL MONARCH** (b. 5 Jul'50, Los Angeles, California, USA) – guitar / **GOLDY McJOHN** (b. 2 May'45) – organ / **RUSHTON MOREVE** (b.1948, Los Angeles) – bass / **JERRY EDMONTON** (b.24 Oct'46, Canada) – drums, vocals

The SPARROW

C.B.S. Columbia

1967. (7") **TOMORROW'S SHIP. / ISN'T IT STRANGE** [ ] [ ]
1967. (7") **GREEN BOTTLE LOVER. / DOWN GOES YOUR LOVE LIFE** [-] [ ]

JOHN KAY

1967. (7") **TWISTED. / SQUAREHEAD PEOPLE** [-] [ ]

STEPPENWOLF

JOHN RUSSELL MORGAN – bass repl. MOREVE. He was killed in car crash 1 Jul'81.

R.C.A. Dunhill

Nov 67. (7") **A GIRL I KNOW. / THE OSTRICH** [-] [ ]
Apr 68. (7") **SOOKIE SOOKIE. / TAKE WHAT YOU NEED** [ ] [ ] Jan 68

Stateside Dunhill

May 68. (lp) **STEPPENWOLF** [ ] [6] Jan 68
– Sookie Sookie / Everybody's next one / Berry rides again / Hoochie coochie man / Born to be wild / Your wall's too high / Desperation / The pusher / A girl I knew / Take what you need / The ostrich. *(hit UK No.59 Apr70) (re-iss.+cd.Jun87 on 'M.C.A.')*
Aug 68. (7") **BORN TO BE WILD. / EVERYBODY'S NEXT ONE** [-] [2] Jun 68
(above + below re-iss.in the UK May69 + Sep69, hit No.30 + 50)
Oct 68. (7") **MAGIC CARPET RIDE. / SOOKIE SOOKIE** [-] [3]
Jan 69. (lp) **STEPPENWOLF THE SECOND** [ ] [3] Nov 68
– Faster than the speed of life / Tighten up your wig / None of your doing / Spiritual fantasy / Don't step on the grass, Sam / 28 / Magic carpet ride / Disappointment / Number (unknown) / Lost and found by trial and error / Hodge, Podge strained through a Leslie / Resurrection / Reflections. *(re-iss.+cd.Jun87 on 'M.C.A.')*

— **LARRY BYROM** (b.27 Dec'48, USA) – guitar repl. MONARCH / **NICK ST.NICHOLAS** (b.28 Sep'43, Hamburg, W.Germany) – bass repl. RUSSELL

Feb 69. (7") **ROCK ME. / JUPITER CHILD** [ ] [10]
Jun 69. (lp) **AT YOUR BIRTHDAY PARTY** [ ] [7] Mar 69
– Don't cry / Chicken wolf / Lovely meter / Round and down / It's never too late / Sleeping dreaming / Jupiter child / She'll be better / Cat killer / Rock me / God fearing man / Mango juice / Happy birthday.
May 69. (7") **IT'S NEVER TOO LATE. / HAPPY BIRTHDAY** [-] [51]
Aug 69. (7") **MOVE OVER. / POWER PLAY** [-] [31]
Jan 70. (7") **MONSTER. / BERRY RIDES AGAIN** [-] [39]
Jan 70. (7") **MONSTER. / MOVE OVER** [ ] [-]
Jan 70. (lp)(c) **MONSTER** [43] [17] Nov 69
– Monster / Suicide / America / Draft resister / Power play / Move over / Fag / What would you do (if I did that to you) / From here to there eventually. *(cd-iss.Sep91 & Jul92 on 'B.G.O.')*
Mar 70. (7") **THE PUSHER (live). / YOUR WALL'S TOO HIGH (live)** [ ] [-]
Jun 70. (7") **HEY LAWDY MAMA (live). / TWISTED (live)** [ ] [35] Apr 70
Jun 70. (lp)(c) **STEPPENWOLF 'LIVE' (live)** [16] [7] Apr 70
– Sookie Sookie / Don't step on the grass, Sam / Tighten up your wig / Hey lawdy mama / Magic carpet ride / The pusher / Born to be wild / Monster / Draft resister / Power play / Corrina, Corrina / Twisted / From here to there eventually. *(re-iss.Oct74 on 'A.B.C.')*
Sep 70. (7") **SCREAMING NIGHT HOG. / SPIRITUAL FANTASY** [ ] [62] Aug 70

Probe Dunhill

Nov 70. (7") **WHO NEEDS YA. / EARSCHPLITTENLOUDENBOOMER** [ ] [54]
Nov 70. (lp)(c) **STEPPENWOLF 7** [ ] [19]
– Ball crusher / Forty days and forty nights / Fat Jack / Renegade / Foggy mental breakdown / Snow blind friend / Who needs ya / Earschplittenloudenboomer / Hippo stomp.
Mar 71. (7") **SNOW BLIND FRIEND. / HIPPO STOMP** [ ] [60]

— **KENT HENRY** – guitar repl. BYROM

— **GEORGE BIONDO** (b. 3 Sep'45, Brooklyn, New York) – bass repl. NICK

Jul 71. (7") **RIDE WITH ME. / FOR MADMEN ONLY** [ ] [52]
Oct 71. (7") **FOR LADIES ONLY. / SPARKLE EYES** [ ] [64]
Oct 71. (lp)(c) **FOR LADIES ONLY** [ ] [54]
– For ladies only / I'm asking / Snakes and chains / Tenderness / The night time's for you / Jadet strumpet / Sparkle eyes / Black pit / Ride with me / In hopes of a garden.

— Disbanded Feb'72, EDMUNTON and McJOHN formed MANBEAST.

JOHN KAY

went solo, augmented by **KENT HENRY + GEORGE BIONDO** plus **HUGH SULLIVAN** – keyboards / **PENTII WHITNEY GLEN** – drums / etc. (same label)

Apr 72. (lp)(c) **FORGOTTEN SONGS AND UNSUNG HEROES** [ ] [ ]
– Many a mile / Walk beside me / You win again / To be alive / Bold marauder / Two of a kind / Walking blues / Somebody / I'm moving on.
Apr 72. (7") **I'M MOVIN' ON. / WALK BESIDE ME** [-] [52]
Jul 72. (7") **YOU WIN AGAIN. / SOMEBODY** [-] [ ]
Jul 73. (7") **MOONSHINE. / NOBODY LIVES HERE ANYMORE** [-] [ ]
Jul 73. (lp)(c) **MY SPORTIN' LIFE** [ ] [ ]
– Moonshine / Nobody lives here anymore / Drift away / Heroes and devils / My sportin' life / Easy evil / Giles of the river / Dance to my song / Sing with the children.
Sep 73. (7") **EASY EVIL. / DANCE TO MY SONG** [ ] [ ]

STEPPENWOLF

re-formed (**KAY, McJOHN, EDMUNTON, BIONDO**) plus **BOBBY COCHRAN** – guitar repl. KENT (first and last with horn section)

C.B.S. Mums

Oct 74. (lp)(c) **SLOW FLUX** [ ] [47] Sep 74
– Gang war blues / Children of the night / Justice don't be slow / Get into the wind / Jeraboah / Straight shootin' woman / Smokey factory blues / Morning blue / A fool's factory / Fishin' in the dark.
Oct 74. (7") **STRAIGHT SHOOTIN' WOMAN. / JUSTICE DON'T BE SLOW** [ ] [29] Sep 74
Jan 75. (7") **GET INTO THE WIND. / MORNING BLUE** [-] [ ]
Apr 75. (7") **SMOKEY FACTORY BLUES. / A FOOL'S FANTASY** [ ] [ ]

— **ANDY CHAPIN** – keyboards repl. McJOHN who went solo

Aug 75. (7") **CAROLINE (ARE YOU READY). / ANGEL DRAWERS** [ ] [ ]
Sep 75. (lp)(c) **HOUR OF THE WOLF** [ ] [ ]
– Caroline (are you ready for the outlaw world) / Annie, Annie over / Two for the love of one / Just for tonight / Hard rock road / Someone told a lie / Another's lifetime / Mr. Penny pincher.

— **WAYNE COOK** – keyboards repl. ANDY

Epic Epic

May 77. (lp)(c) **SKULLDUGGERY** [ ] [ ]
– Skullduggery / Roadrunner / Rock and roll song / Train of thought / Life is a gamble / Pass it on / Sleep / Lip service.
Dec 77. (lp)(c) **REBORN TO BE WILD** [ ] [ ]
– Straight shootin' woman / Hard rock road / Another's lifetime / Mr.Penny pincher / Smokey factory blues / Caroline / Get into the wind / Gang war blues / Children of night / Skullduggery.

— Disbanded yet again.

JOHN KAY

with **LARRY BYROM** – slide guitar / **MAC McANALLY** – guitar / **CLAYTON IVEY** – keyboards / **BOB WRAY** – bass / **ROGER CLARK** – drums

Mercury Mercury

Jun 78. (lp)(c) **ALL IN GOOD TIME** [ ] [ ]
– Give me some news I can use / The best is barely good enough / That's when I think of you / Ain't nobody home / Ain't nothin' like it used to be / Business is business / Show me how you'd like it done / Down in New Orleans / Say you will / Hey, I'm alright.
Jun 78. (7") **GIVE ME SOME NEWS I CAN USE. / BUSINESS IS BUSINESS** [ ] [-]

— In the early 80's, KAY and group toured as

JOHN KAY & STEPPENWOLF

with **MICHAEL PALMER** – guitar / **BRETT TUGGLE** – keyboards / **CHAD PERRY** – bass / **STEVEN PALMER** – drums

not issued Allegiance

Dec 81. (lp) **LIVE IN LONDON (live)** [-] [ ]
– Sookie Sookie / Give me news I can use / You / Hot night in a cold town / Ain't nothin' like it used to be / Magic carpet ride / Five finger discount / Hey lawdy mama / Business is business / Born to be wild / The pusher.
Dec 81. (7") **HOT TOME IN A COLD TOWN. /** [-] [ ]

— **WELTON GITE** – bass repl. CHAD / added **MICHAEL WILK** – keyboards

not issued CBS-Sony

1983. (lp)(cd) **WOLFTRACKS** [-] [ ]
– All I want is all you got / None of the above / You / Every man for himself / Five finger discount / Hold your head up / Hot night in a cold town / Down to earth / For rock'n'roll / The balance.

— now with **ROCKET RITCHOTTE** – guitar, vocals + **MICHAEL WILK** – keyboards, bass / **RON HURST** – drums, vocals. Finally issued new material 1988.

Disky Qwil

May 88. (lp)(c)(cd) **ROCK'N'ROLL REBELS** [ ] [ ] Sep 87
– Give me life / Rock'n'roll rebels / Hold on / Man on a mission / Everybody knows you / Rock steady / Replace the face / Turn out the lights / Give me news I can use / Rage.

I.R.S. I.R.S.

Aug 90. (cd)(c)(lp) **RISE & SHINE** [ ] [ ]
– Let's do it all / Time out / Do or die / Rise & shine / The wall / The daily blues / Keep rockin' / Rock'n'roll war / Sign on the line / We like it, we love it (we want more of it).

– compilations, others, etc. –

Jul 69. Stateside/ US= Dunhill; (lp) **EARLY STEPPENWOLF** [ ] [29]
– Power play / Howlin' for my baby / Goin' upstairs / Corina Corina / Tighten up your wig / The pusher. *(live material from 1967 recorded as The SPARROW)*
Mar 71. Probe/ US= Dunhill; (lp)(c) **STEPPENWOLF GOLD** [ ] [24]
– Born to be wild / It's never too late / Rock me / Hey lawdy mama / Move over / Who needs ya / Magic carpet ride / The pusher / Sookie Sookie / Jupiter's child / Screaming night hog. *(re-iss.Oct74 on 'ABC') (re-iss.Aug80 on 'MCA') (re-iss.Jan83 on 'Fame')*
Jul 72. Probe/ US= Dunhill; (lp)(c) **REST IN PEACE** [ ] [62] Jun 72
Mar 73. Probe/ US= Dunhill; (lp)(c) **16 GREATEST HITS** [ ] [ ] Feb 73
(re-iss.Oct74 on 'ABC')
Jun 80. MCA; (7") **BORN TO BE WILD. / THE PUSHER** [ ] [ ]
(re-iss.Apr83 on 'Old Gold')
Jul 85. MCA; (lp)(c) **GOLDEN GREATS** [ ] [ ]
– Born to be wild / Magic carpet ride / Rock me / Move over / Hey lawdy mama / It's never too late / Who needs you? / Monster / Snow blind friend / The pusher / Sookie sookie / Jupiter's child / Screaming dog night / Ride with me / For ladies only / Tenderness.

Apr 93. Movieplay; (cd) **BORN TO BE WILD** -
Jan 94. Legacy; (cd) **TIGHTEN UP YOUR WIG – THE BEST OF JOHN KAY & SPARROW**

STEREOLAB

Formed: South London, England . . . early 1991 by ex-indie stalwards McCARTHY mainman TIM GANE and girlfriend LAETITIA SADIER. Formed own label 'Duophonic' and in 1993 signed in the States for 6 figure-sum to 'Elektra'. 1994 saw them unsurprisingly hit UK Top 20 with double album 'MARS AUDIAC QUINTET'. • **Style:** Indie electro-rock outfit influenced by minimalists VELVET UNDERGROUND, JOHN CAGE, NEU!, SPECEMEN 3 and The BEACH BOYS!. Lushishly fronted by NICO-like vox of LAETITIA (pronounced Le-ti-seaya). • **Songwriters:** GANE. • **Trivia:** Featured on Channel 4's TV show 'The Word' in 1993 promoting 'JENNY ONDIOLINE'.

Recommended: MARS AUDIAC QUINTET (*7) / TRANSIENT RANDOM . . . (*8) / MUSIC FOR THE AMORPHOUS BODY STUDY CENTER (*8)

TIM GANE (b. 1966) – guitar, vox organ, guitar (ex-McCARTHY) / **LAETITIA SADIER** (b.1968, Paris, France) – vocals, vox organ, guitar, tambourine, moog / **REBECCA MORRIS** – vocals / **JOE DILWORTH** – drums (of TH' FAITH HEALERS)

Duophonic not issued

May 91. (10"ep-mail order) **SUPER 45** -
– The light (that will cease to fail) / Au grand jour / Brittle / Au grand jour!. *(first 2 tracks re-iss.Jun92 7"pink on 'Big Money Incorporated')*

—— added **MARTIN KEAN** (b.New Zealand) – guitar (ex-CHILLS) / **RUSSELL YATES** – live guitar (of MOOSE). **MICK CONROY** (ex-MOOSE) was also a live member early '92.

Too Pure Slumberland

Sep 91. (10"ep) **SUPER ELECTRIC / HIGH EXPECTATION. / THE WAY WILL BE OPENING / CONTACT** -
Apr 92. (cd-ltd.) **SWITCHED ON** (compilation) -
– Super electric / Doubt / Au grand jour / The way will be opening / Brittle / Contract / Au grand jour / High expectation / The light that will cease to fail / Changer.

—— GINA departed after above. (when did she join?)

May 92. (cd)(c)(lp) **PENG!** -
– Super falling star / Orgiastic / Peng! 33 / K-stars / Perversion / You little shits / The seeming and the meaning / Mellotron / Enivrez-vous / Stomach worm / Surrealchemist.

—— added **MARY HANSEN** – vocals, tambourine, guitar / **ANDY RAMSAY** – percussion, vox organ, bazouki repl. DILWORTH

Sep 92. (10"ep)(10"clear-ep)(cd-ep) **LOW FI / (VAROOM!). / LAISSER-FAIRE / ELEKTRO (HE HELD THE WORLD IN HIS IRON GRIP)** - -

—— added **SEAN O'HAGAN** – vox organ, guitar (ex-MICRODISNEY, ex-HIGH LLAMAS)

Feb 93. (7")(7"pink) **JOHN CAGE BUBBLEGUM. / ELOGE D'EROS** -

—— added **DUNCAN BROWN** – bass, guitar, vocals

Mar 93. (cd)(c)(m-lp) **THE GROUP PLAYED SPACE AGE BACHELOR PAD MUSIC** -
– Avant-garde M.O.R. / Space age bachelor pad music (mellow) / The groop play chord X / Space age bachelor pad music / Ronco symphony / We're not adult orientated / UHF-MFP / We're not adult orientated (new wave).

Duophonic Elektra

Aug 93. (10"ep)(cd-ep) **JENNY ONDIOLINE / FRUCTION / GOLDEN BALL / FRENCH DISCO** 75
Sep 93. (cd)(c)(2xlp) **TRANSIENT RANDOM-NOISE BURSTS WITH ANNOUNCEMENTS** 62
– Tone burst / Our trinitone blast / Pack yr romantic mind / I'm going out of my way / Golden ball / Pause / Jenny Ondioline / Analogue rock / Crest / Lock-groove lullaby.
Nov 93. (7") **FRENCH DISKO (new version). / JENNY ONDIOLINE** -
Jul 94. (7"ltd) **PING PONG. / MOOGIE WONDERLAND** 45
(10"+=)(cd-s+=) – Pain et spectacles / Transcona (live).
Aug 94. (cd)(c)(d-lp) **MARS AUDIAC QUINTET** 16
– Three-dee melodie / Wow and flutter / Transona five / Des etoiles electroniques / Ping pong / Anamorphose / Three longers later / Nihilist assault group / International colouring contest / The stars of our destination / Transporte sans bouger / L'enfer des formes / Outer accelerator / New orthophony / Fiery yellow. (free clear-7" w /d-lp + cd-s on cd) – Klang-tang / Ulaan batter.
Oct 94. (7")(10")(cd-s) **WOW AND FLUTTER. / HEAVY DENIM** 70
Apr 95. (10"ep)(cd-ep) **AMORPHOUS BODY STUDY CENTRE** 59 -
– Pop quiz / The extension trip / How to explain your internal organs overnight / The brush descends the length / Melochord seventy five / Space moment.
Sep 95. (cd)(c)(colrd-d-lp) **REFRIED ECTOPLASM (SWITCHED ON – VOLUME 2)** (compilation on 'Duophonic Ultra High Frequency') 30 -

– more very limited mail order only singles, etc. –

Nov 91. Duophonic; (7"clear)(7"colrd) **STUNNING DEBUT ALBUM: Doubt / Changer** -
Jul 92. Duophonic; (7"colrd) **HARMONIUM. / FARFISA** -
Oct 93. Clawfist; (10"ep) **CRUMB DUCK (with NURSE WITH WOUND)** -
– Animal or vegetable / Exploding head movie.
Oct 93. Sub Pop; (7"clear) **LE BOOB OSCILLATOR. / TEMPTER** -
Nov 93. Teenbeat; (7") **MOUNTAIN. / ('B'by Unrest)** -

STEREO MC'S

Formed: Clapham, London, England . . . 1985 by NICK HALLAM and ROB BIRCH. They shared a flat with others, but were given £7,000 to vacate it by property developers. They used the money to set up own label 'Gee Street', which gained backing by '4th & Bro.' in the US. After a number of 45's & a debut album '33-45-78', they toured the States, supporting The HAPPY MONDAYS. They gained first taste of chart action there, when single 'ELEVATE MY MIND' broke the 40. In 1992, they scored 2 UK Top 20 hits with 'CONNECTED' & 'STEP IT UP', and were on their way to superstardom early '93. • **Style:** Cybernetic multi-racial hip hop, fronted by ginger-haired ROB B. Their sound was/is similar to tour mates HAPPY MONDAYS mixed with LL COOL J. • **Songwriters:** BIRCH-HALLAM, except SALSA HOUSE (Richie Rich) / BLACK IS BLACK (Jungle Brothers) / DANCE 4 ME (Queen Lafitah). • **Trivia:** CESARE left amicably after first release.

Recommended: CONNECTED (*8).

ROB B (b.ROB BIRCH) – rapper / **THE HEAD** (b.NICK HALLAM) – DJ / **OWEN IF** (b.ROSSITER) – drums / with **CATH COFFEY** – backing vocals

4th & Broad. 4th & Broad.

Mar 88. (7")(12") **MOVE IT. / FEEL SO GOOD**

—— above credited with **CESARE**, although he left soon after.

Oct 88. (7") **WHAT IS SOUL?. / ('A'-Rob B mix)**
(12"+=) – ('A'vocal mix) / ('A'instrumental) / ('A'accapella mix).
Jun 89. (7") **ON 33. / GEE STREET**
(10"+=)/ /(12"+=) – Non stop./ / ('A' DJ Mark the 45 King mix).
Jul 89. (lp)(c)(cd) **33-45-78**
– On 33 / Use it / Gee Street / Neighbourhood / Toe to toe / What is soul? / Use it (part 2) / Outta touch / Sunday 19th March / This ain't a love song / Ancient concept / On the mike / Back to the future.
Aug 89. (7") **LYRICAL MACHINE. / ON THE MIKE**
(12"+=) – Mechanical / Bring it on.
Sep 90. (7") **ELEVATE MY MIND. / SMOKIN' WITH THE MOTHERMAN (feat. Afrika)** 74 39 May 91
(12"+=)(cd-s+=) – ('A' dub version).
Sep 90. (cd)(c)(lp) **SUPERNATURAL**
– I'm a believer / Scene of the crime / Declaration / Elevate my mind / Watcha gonna do / Two horse town / Ain't got nobody / Goin' back to my roots / Lost in music / Life on the line / The other side / Set me loose / What's the word / Early one morning. (cd+c+=) Smokin' with the motherman / Relentless. *(re-iss.cd+c Apr94 on 'Island')*
Mar 91. (7")(c-s) **LOST IN MUSIC (Ultimatum Remix). / EARLY ONE MORNING** 46
(cd-s+=) – ('A' instrumental).
(12") – ('A'side) / ('A'-B.B.mix) / ('A'-B.B-instrumental).

—— now a 6-piece, added **VERONICA + ANDREA** – backing vox

Sep 92. (7")(c-s) **CONNECTED. / FEVER** 18 20 Mar 93
(cd-s+=) – ('A'-full version) / Disconnected.
Oct 92. (cd)(c)(lp) **CONNECTED** 2 92
– Connected / Ground level / Everything / Sketch / Fade away / All night long / Step it up / Playing with fire / Pressure / Chicken shake / Creation / The end.
Nov 92. (7")(c-s) **STEP IT UP.' / ('A'mix)** 12 58 Jun 93
(12"+=)(cd-s+=) – Lost in music (US mix).
Feb 93. (7")(c-s) **GROUND LEVEL. / EVERYTHING (EVERYTHING GROOVES pt.1)** 19
(12"+=)(cd-s+=) – (B'mixes pt.2).
May 93. (7")(c-s) **CREATION. / ('A'ultimation mix)** 19
(12"+=) – ('A'instrumental).
(cd-s+=) – All night long.

ST. ETIENNE (see under ⇒ SAINT ETIENNE)

Cat STEVENS

Born: STEVEN GEORGIOU, 21 Jul'47, Soho, London, England. Son of Greek restaurant owner and Swedish mother. While studying at Hammersmith college in 1966 he met Mike Hurst (ex-SPRINGFIELDS). He produced first single 'I LOVE MY DOG', after which CAT was signed by Tony Hall to new Decca subsidiary label 'Deram'. It reached the UK Top 30, but was surpassed the next year when follow-up 'MATTHEW AND SON' hit No.2. His songs were soon being covered by many, including P.P.ARNOLD (First Cut Is The Deepest) & TREMELOES (Here Comes My Baby). After a barren chart spell and recuperation from TB two years previous, he signed new deal with 'Island' in 1970 (A & M in America). He scored a comeback Top 10 hit with 'LADY D'ARBANVILLE', which lent on the production skills of ex-YARDBIRD Keith Relf. He stayed for the follow-up to 'MONA BONE JAKON', the 1970 classic album 'TEA FOR THE TILLERMAN'. CAT went on to become one of the biggest stars of the 70's until his retirement in 1979. He took up the Muslim faith and changed his name to Yusef Islam (see further on). • **Style:** Socially aware folk singer in the 60's, who progressed to classy rock-pop artist in the 70's, with hints of Eastern mysticism. • **Songwriters:** Self-penned except; MORNING HAS BROKEN (Eleanor Farjeon) / ANOTHER SATURDAY NIGHT (Sam Cooke). • **Trivia:** Other STEVENS' songs given new light were; WILD WORLD (Jimmy Cliff – 1970, Maxi Priest – 1988) / FIRST CUT IS THE DEEPEST (Rod Stewart) / PEACE TRAIN (10,000 Maniacs).

Recommended: THE VERY BEST OF CAT STEVENS (*9) / TEA FOR THE TILLERMAN (*8) / TEASER AND THE FIRECAT (*9).

CAT STEVENS – vocals, guitar, keyboards with orchestra

Deram / Deram

Sep 66. (7") **I LOVE MY DOG. / PORTOBELLO ROAD** [28] [ ]
Dec 66. (7") **MATTHEW AND SON. / GRANNY** [2] [ ]
(re-iss.Aug81 on 'Decca')
Mar 67. (lp) **MATTHEW AND SON** [7] [ ]
– Matthew and son / I love my dog / Here comes my baby / Bring another bottle baby / Portobello road / I've found a love / I see a road / Baby get your head screwed on / Granny / When I speak to the flowers / The tramp / Come on and dance / Hummingbird / Lady. *(cd-iss.Jul 88 on 'London')*
Mar 67. (7") **I'M GONNA GET ME A GUN. / SCHOOL IS OUT** [6] [ ]
Jul 67. (7") **A BAD NIGHT. / THE LAUGHING APPLE** [20] [ ]
Dec 67. (7") **KITTY. / BLACKNESS OF THE NIGHT** [47] [ ]
Dec 67. (lp) **NEW MASTERS** [ ] [ ]
– Kitty / I'm so sleepy / Northern wind / The laughing apple / Smash your heart / Moonstone / The first cut is the deepest / I'm gonna be king / Ceylon city / Blackness of the night / Come on baby / I love them all. *(re-iss.Nov84) (cd-iss.Apr89 +=)* – Image of Hell / Lovely city / Here comes my wife / The view from the top / It's a supa dupa life / Where are you / A bad night.
Feb 68. (7") **LOVELY CITY. / IMAGE OF HELL** [ ] [ ]

— Around early 1968, CAT slowly recovered from tuberculosis.

Oct 68. (7") **HERE COMES MY WIFE. / IT'S A SUPA DUPA LIFE** [ ] [-]
Jun 69. (7") **WHERE ARE YOU. / THE VIEW FROM THE TOP** [ ] [-]

— recruits band **ALUN DAVIES** – guitar / **JOHN RYAN** – bass / **HARVEY BURNS** – drums

Island / A & M

Jun 70. (7") **LADY D'ARBANVILLE. / TIME / FILL MY EYES** [8] [ ]
Jun 70. (lp)(c) **MONA BONE JAKON** [63] [ ]
– Lady D'Arbanville / Maybe you're right / Pop star / I think I see the light / Trouble / Mona bone Jakon / I wish, I wish / Katmandu / Time – Fill my eyes / Lilywhite. *(re-iss.1974 & Jan78)*
Nov 70. (lp)(c) **TEA FOR THE TILLERMAN** [20] [8] Feb 71
– Where do the children play / Hard headed woman / Wild world / Sad Lisa / Miles from nowhere / But I might die tonight / Longer boats / Into white / On the road to find out / Father and son / Tea for the tillerman. *(re-iss.1974 & Jan78, re-iss,+cd.Oct86) (re-iss.lp Jan94 + May94)*
Feb 71. (7") **WILD WORLD. / MILES FROM NOWHERE** [-] [11]

— **LARRY STEELE** – bass repl. RYAN

Jun 71. (7") **MOON SHADOW. / FATHER AND SON** [22] [30]
Sep 71. (7") **TUESDAY'S DEAD. / MILES FROM NOWHERE** [ ] [-]
Sep 71. (7") **PEACE TRAIN. / WHERE DO THE CHILDREN PLAY?** [-] [7]
Sep 71. (lp)(c) **TEASER AND THE FIRECAT** [3] [2]
– The wind / Ruby love / If I laugh / Changes IV / How can I tell you / Tuesday's dead / Morning has broken / Bitterblue / Moon shadow / Peace train. *(re-iss.1974 & Jan78, re-iss.+cd.Oct86)*

— (below 'A'side featured **RICK WAKEMAN** – piano)

Dec 71. (7") **MORNING HAS BROKEN. / I WANT TO LIVE IN A WIGWAM** [9] [6] Mar 72

In Apr72, STEVENS contributed tracks to film 'Harold And Maude'.

— added **JEAN ROUSELL** – piano / **CAT** – some synthesizers repl. WAKEMAN. **ALAN JAMES** – bass repl. LARRY

Sep 72. (lp)(c) **CATCH BULL AT FOUR** [2] [1]
– Sitting / Boy with a moon and star on his head / Angel sea / Silent sunlight / Can't keep it in / 18th Avenue / Freezing steel / O Caritas / Sweet Scarlet / Ruins. *(re-iss.1974 & Jan78, re-iss.+cd.Oct86)*
Nov 72. (7") **CAN'T KEEP IT IN. / CRAB DANCE** [13] [-]
(re-iss.Jul81)
Nov 72. (7") **SITTING. / CRAB DANCE** [-] [16]

— CAT now became tax exile in Brazil and donated his extras to charity.

— now w / **ROUSSEL, DAVIS, LYNCH + CONWAY** plus loads of sessioners

Jul 73. (7") **THE HURT. / SILENT SUNLIGHT** [ ] [31]
Jul 73. (lp)(c) **FOREIGNER** [3] [3]
– Foreigner suite / The hurt / How many times / Later / 100 I dream. *(re-iss.quad.1974)*

— **BRUCE LYNCH** – bass repl. PAUL

Mar 74. (7") **OH VERY YOUNG. / 100 I DREAMS** [ ] [10]
Mar 74. (lp)(c) **BUDDAH AND THE CHOCOLATE BOX** [3] [2]
– Music / Oh very young / Sun – C79 / Ghost town / Jesus / Ready / King of trees / Bad penny / Home in the sky.
Aug 74. (7") **ANOTHER SATURDAY NIGHT. / HOME IN THE SKY** [19] [6]
Sep 74. (lp)(c) **SATURDAY NIGHT (live)** [-] [ ]
– Wild world / Oh very young / Sitting / Where do the children play / Lady D'Arbanville / Another Saturday night / Hard-headed woman / Peace train / Father & son / King of trees / A bad penny / Bitter blue.
Dec 74. (7") **READY. / I THINK I SEE THE LIGHT** [-] [26]
Jul 75. (7") **TWO FINE PEOPLE. / BAD PENNY** [ ] [33]
Jul 75. (lp)(c) **GREATEST HITS** (compilation) [2] [6]
– Wild world / Oh very young / Can't keep it in / Hard headed woman / Moonshadow / Two fine people / Peace train / Ready / Father and son / Sitting / Morning has broken / Another Saturday night. *(cd-iss. Mar 93)*

— now w / **ROUSSEL, DAVIS, LYNCH + CONWAY** plus loads of sessioners

Dec 75. (lp)(c) **NUMBERS** [ ] [13]
– Whistlestar / Novim's nightmare / Majik of majiks / Dry wood / Banapple gas / Land o' free love and goodbye / Jzero / Home / Nomad's anthem.
Mar 76. (7") **BANAPPLE GAS. / GHOST TOWN** [ ] [41] Feb 76
Mar 76. (7") **LAND O' FREE LOVE AND GOODBYE. / (I NEVER WANTED) TO BE A STAR** [-] [ ]
Apr 77. (lp)(c) **IZITSO** [18] [7]
– (Remember the days of the) Old schoolyard / Life / Killin' time / Kypros / Bonfire / To be a star / Crazy / Sweet Jamaica / Was Dog a doughnut / Child for a day.
Jun 77. (7") **(REMEMBER THE DAYS OF THE) OLD SCHOOLYARD. / DOVES** [44] [-]
Jun 77. (7") **(REMEMBER THE DAYS OF THE) OLD SCHOOLYARD. / LAND O' FREE LOVE AND GOODBYE** [-] [ ]
Nov 77. (7") **WAS DOG A DOUGHNUT. / SWEET JAMAICA** [-] [70]
Jan 79. (7") **BAD BRAKES. / NASCIMENTO** [-] [83]
Jan 79. (lp)(c) **BACK TO EARTH** [ ] [33] Dec 78
– Just another night / Daytime / Bad brakes / Randy / The artist / Last love song / Nascimento / Father / New York times / Never.
Feb 79. (7") **LAST LOVE SONG. / NASCIMENTO** [ ] [-]
Apr 79. (7") **RANDY. / NASCIMENTO** [-] [ ]

— He retired from the music scene, due to newfound Muslim religion. He changed his name to YUSEF ISLAM and married Fouzia Ali in Sep'79. They lived in London where he taught his faith to local school. In the late 80's, he was back in the limelight, when he condoned the Muslim assassination sanction against writer Salman Rushdie.

– more compilations, etc. –

1970. Decca; (lp)(c) **THE WORLD OF CAT STEVENS** [ ] [-]
Aug 81. Decca; (lp)(c) **THE FIRST CUT IS THE DEEPEST** [ ] [-]
Mar 71. Deram; (d-lp) **MATTHEW AND SON / NEW MASTERS** [-] [ ]
(UK-iss.May75 as 'VIEW FROM THE TOP')
Jan 72. Deram; (lp) **VERY YOUNG AND EARLY SONGS** [-] [94]
Nov 73. Deram; (7") **I LOVE MY DOG. / MATTHEW AND SON** [ ] [-]
(re-iss.Oct83)
Aug 80. Deram; (7"ep) **MATTHEW AND SON / I LOVE MY DOG. / A BAD NIGHT / I'M GONNA GET ME A GUN** [ ] [-]
Nov 89. Deram; (cd) **FIRST CUTS** [ ] [-]
Apr 86. Castle; (d-lp)(c) **THE COLLECTION** [ ] [-]
Apr 86. Spot; (c) **CAT STEVENS** [ ] [-]
Nov 83. Island; (7") **MORNING HAS BROKEN. / MOON SHADOW** [ ] [-]
Jan 85. Island/ US= A&M; (lp)(c) **FOOTSTEPS IN THE DARK – GREATEST HITS VOL. 2** [ ] [ ] Dec 84
(US version +=) – (3 extra tracks).
Feb 90. Island; (cd)(c)(lp) **THE VERY BEST OF CAT STEVENS** [ ] [ ]
– Where do the children play / Wild world / Tuesday's dead / Lady D'Arbanville / The first cut is the deepest / Oh very young / Rubylove / Morning has broken / Moonshadow / Matthew and son / Father and son / Can't keep it in / Hard headed woman / (Remember the days of the) Old school yard / I love my dog / Another Saturday night / Sad Lisa / Peace train.*(re-iss Jul92)*
Apr 93. Pulsar; (cd) **WILD WORLD** [ ] [-]
Aug 93. Polygram TV; (cd)(c) **THE VERY BEST OF CAT STEVENS** (different) [47] [-]
Sep 93. Spectrum; (cd)(c) **EARLY TAPES** [ ] [-]

Al STEWART

Born: 5 Sep'45, Glasgow, Scotland. As a toddler, he moved to Bournemouth, England with his widowed mother, and learned guitar alongside ROBERT FRIPP. In the mid-60's, after briefly sharing a London flat with touring PAUL SIMON, he released one-off 45 'THE ELF' for 'Decca'. In 1967, he signed for 'C.B.S.' and issued debut album 'BED-SITTER IMAGES'. 9 years later, on his new label 'RCA', he broke through internationally with US Top 5 album 'YEAR OF THE CAT', which contained the classic title track. • **Style:** Initially a DYLAN influenced folk singer, who became self-analytic and lyrically controversial. Loved by college circuit, especially after Americanised YEAR OF THE CAT. • **Songwriters:** All self-penned. • **Trivia:** In 1962 AL played guitar in TONY BLACKBURN's band (who was later to become famous Radio 1 DJ). Future LED ZEPPELIN guitarist JIMMY PAGE sessioned on AL's second album. RICHARD BRANSON head of 'Virgin', rejected signing AL in 1976. Top producer ALAN PARSONS worked on the albums 'YEAR OF THE CAT' & 'TIME PASSAGES'.

Recommended: YEAR OF THE CAT (*7) / PAST, PRESENT AND FUTURE (*8) / LOVE CHRONICLES (*7).

AL STEWART – vocals, guitar with orchestra

Decca / not issued

Jul 66. (7") **THE ELF. / TURN INTO STONE** [ ] [-]

C.B.S. / Columbia

Sep 67. (7") **BEDSITTER IMAGES. / SWISS COTTAGE MANOEUVRES** [ ] [-]
Oct 67. (lp) **BEDSITTER IMAGES** [ ] [-]
– Bedsitter images / Swiss Cottage manoeuvres / Scandinavian girl * / Pretty golden hair * / Denise at 16 / Samuel, oh how you've changed! / Cleave to me * / A long way down from Stephanie / Ivich / Beleeka doodle day. *(re-iss.Jun70 as 'THE FIRST ALBUM (BED-SITTER IMAGES)'; tracks * repl. by)* – Lover man / Clifton in the rain.
Jan 69. (lp) **LOVE CHRONICLES** [ ] [ ]
– In Brooklyn / Old Compton Street blues / Ballad of Mary Foster / Life and life only / You should've listened to Al / Love chronicles. *(re-is.+c.May82 on 'R.C.A.')*
Mar 70. (7") **ELECTRIC LOS ANGELES SUNSET. / MY ENEMIES HAVE SWEET VOICES** [ ] [-]
Mar 70. (lp) **ZERO SHE FLIES** [40] [-]
– My enemies have sweet voices / A small fruit song / Gethsemane again / Burbling / Electric Los Angeles sunset / Manuscript / Black hill / Anna / Room of roots / Zero she flies. *(re-iss.+c.Oct85 on 'R.C.A.')*
Dec 71. (7") **THE NEWS FROM SPAIN. / ELVASTON PLACE** [ ] [-]
Feb 72. (7") **YOU DON'T EVEN KNOW ME. / I'M FALLING** [ ] [-]
Feb 72. (lp)(c) **ORANGE** [ ] [-]
– You don't even know me / Amsterdam / Songs out of clay / The news from Spain / I don't believe you / Once an orange, always an orange / I'm falling / Night of the 4th of May. *(re-iss.Nov81)*
Apr 72. (7") **AMSTERDAM. / SONGS OUT OF CLAY** [ ] [-]

C.B.S. / Janus

Sep 73. (7") **TERMINAL EYES. / LAST DAYS OF JUNE 1934** [ ] [-]
Oct 73. (lp)(c) **PAST, PRESENT & FUTURE** [ ] [ ] Jan 74

– Old admirals / Warren Harding / Soho (needless to say) / Last days of June 1934 / Post World War Two blues / Roads to Moscow / Terminal eyes / Nostradamus. *(re-iss.Jun81) (US cd-iss.1987 on 'Arista')*

Apr 74. (7") **NOSTRADAMUS. / TERMINAL EYES** [-] [ ]

— Around Spring'74, toured with backing band HOME.

Jun 74. (7") **SHALLOW WIND. / NOSTRADAMUS** [ ] [-]

— backed w / **GERRY CONWAY / SIMON NICOL / PAT DONALDSON & SIMON ROUSSEL**

Mar 75. (7") **CAROL. / SIRENS OF TITAN** [-] [ ]
Apr 75. (7") **CAROL. / NEXT TIME** [ ] [-]
Apr 75. (lp)(c) **MODERN TIMES** [ ] [30] Feb 75
– Carol / Sirens of Titan / What's going on / Not the one / Next time / Apple cider / Re-constitution / The dark and rolling sea / Modern times. *(re-iss.Mar81)*

R.C.A. Janus

Oct 76. (lp)(c) **YEAR OF THE CAT** [38] [5]
– Lord Grenville / On the border / Midas shadow / Sand in your shoes / If it doesn't come naturally, leave it / Flying sorcery / Broadway Hotel / One stage before / Year of the cat. *(re-iss.Sep81 & Dec87, cd-iss.Nov84)(re-iss.+cd.Apr91 on 'Fame')*

Jan 77. (7") **YEAR OF THE CAT. / BROADWAY HOTEL** [31] [8] Nov 76
Apr 77. (7") **ON THE BORDER. / FLYING SORCERY** [ ] [42]

R.C.A. Arista

Sep 78. (lp)(c) **TIME PASSAGES** [39] [10]
– Time passages / Valentina way / Life in dark water / A man for all seasons / Almost Lucy / Palace of Versailles / Timeless skies / Song on the radio / End of the day. *(re-iss.Sep81 & Aug84, cd-iss.Dec86) (cd re-iss.Oct91 on 'EMI')*

Sep 78. (7") **TIME PASSAGES. / ALMOST LUCY** [-] [7]
Feb 79. (7") **SONG ON THE RADIO. / A MAN FOR ALL SEASONS** [ ] [29] Jan 79
Aug 80. (7") **MONDO SINISTRO. / MERLIN'S TIME** [ ] [-]
Aug 80. (lp)(c) **24 CARROTS** [55] [37]
– Running man / Midnight rocks / Constantinople / Merlin's time / Mondo sinistro / Murmansk run – Ellis Island / Rocks in the ocean / Paint by numbers / Optical illusion. *(re-iss.Sep81)*

Aug 80. (7") **MIDNIGHT ROCKS. / CONSTANTINOPLE** [-] [24]
Nov 80. (7") **PAINT BY NUMBERS. / OPTICAL ILLUSION** [ ] [ ]
Jan 81. (7") **RUNNING MAN. / MERLIN'S TIME** [-] [ ]
Oct 81. (7") **INDIAN SUMMER. / PANDORA** [ ] [ ]
Nov 81. (d-lp)(d-c) **LIVE – INDIAN SUMMER (live)** [ ] [ ]
– Here in Angola / Pandora / Indian summer / Princess Olivia / Running man / Time passages / Merlin's time / If it doesn't come naturally, leave it / Roads to Moscow / Nostradamus (part 1) – World goes to Riyadah – Nostradamus (part 2) / Soho (needless to say) / On the border / Valentina way / Clarence frogman Henry / Year of the cat. *(re-iss.1984)*

R.C.A. Passport

May 84. (lp)(c) **RUSSIANS AND AMERICANS** [83] [ ]
– Strange girl / Russians and Americans / Cafe society / One, two, three / The candidate / 1-2-3 / Lori, don't go right now * / Rumours of war / The gypsy and the rose * / Accident on 3rd Street. *(US repl. * tracks)* – The one that got away / Night meeting. *(cd-iss.Jul93 on 'E.M.I.')*

Jun 84. (7") **LORI, DON'T GO RIGHT NOW. / ACCIDENT ON 3rd STREET** [ ] [-]
May 85. (lp)(c) **THE BEST OF AL STEWART** (compilation) [ ] [ ]
– Year of the cat / On the border / If it doesn't come naturally, leave it / Time passages / Almost lucky / Merlin's theme / Valentina way / Running man / Roads to Moscow / Here in Angola / Rumours of war. *(US cd 1988)*

Enigma Enigma

Sep 88. (lp)(c)(cd) **LAST DAYS OF THE CENTURY** [ ] [ ]
– Last days of the century / Real and unreal / King of Portugal / Red toupee / Where are they now / Bad reputation / Josephine Baker / License to steal / Fields of France / Antartica / Ghostly horses of the plain.

Oct 88. (7") **KING OF PORTUGAL. / JOSEPHINE BAKER** [ ] [ ]
(12"+=)/ /(3"cd-s+=) – Bad reputation./ / ('A'rock mix version).

E.M.I. E.M.I.

Feb 92. (cd)(c)(lp) **RHYMES IN ROOMS (live feat. PET)** [ ] [ ]
– Flying sorcery / Soho (needless to say) / Time passages / Josephine Baker / Nostradamus / On the border / Fields of France / Medley:- Clifton in the rain – A small fruit song / Broadway hotel / If it doesn't come naturally, leave it / Year of the cat. *(re-iss.cd Feb95 on 'Fame')*

Mar 92. (7") **RHYMES IN ROOMS (live). / YEAR OF THE CAT (live)** [ ] [ ]
(cd-s+=) – Songs on the radio.

Permanent Rykodisc?

Oct 93. (cd)(c) **FAMOUS LAST WORDS** [ ] [ ]
– Feel like / Angels of mercy / Don't forget me / Peter on the white sea / Genie on a table top / Trespasser / Trains / Necromancer / Charlotte Corday / Hippo song / Night rolls on.

E.M.I. Capitol?

Jun 95. (cd)(c) **BETWEEN THE WARS** [ ] [ ]
– Night train to Munich / The age of rhythm / Sampan / Lindy comes to town / Three mules / A league of notions / Between the wars / Betty Boop's birthday / Marion the Chatelaine / Joe the Georgian / Always the cause / Laughing into 1939 / The black Danube.

– more compilations, etc. –

Apr 78. RCA/ US= Arista; (lp)(c)(US-d-lp) **THE EARLY YEARS** (1967-1970) [ ] [ ]
(re-iss. Sep 86 on 'Fame')
1985. Arista; (7") **YEAR OF THE CAT / TIME PASSAGES** [-] [ ]
Nov 86. Old Gold; (7") **THE YEAR OF THE CAT. / ('B'by Climax Blues Band)** [ ] [-]
Jun 91. EMI; (cd) **CHRONICLES: THE BEST OF AL STEWART (1976-81)** [ ] [ ]
Oct 93. EMI; (cd) **TO WHOM IT MAY CONCERN** [ ] [ ]

Dave STEWART (see under ⇒ EURYTHMICS)

Eric STEWART (see under ⇒ 10cc)

Rod STEWART

Born: RODERICK DAVID STEWART, 10 Jan'45, Highgate, London. Out of Scottish parentage, where his roots still lie as a passionate Scotland supporter. In 1963, after a time as an apprentice for Brentford F.C. and busker in Spain, he joined West Midlands group The FIVE DIMENSIONS. He played harmonica on a Jimmy Powell 45, before lending same for a live LONG JOHN BALDRY & THE HOOCHIE COOCHIE MEN a year later. He soon became singer and signed to 'Decca' as a solo artist, releasing debut single 'GOOD MORNING LITTLE SCHOOLGIRL'. In 1965, he joined STEAMPACKET, who contained 2 other singers BALDRY and JULIE DRISCOLL. This set-up finally evolved into The BRIAN AUGER TRINITY, but without ROD, who was now part of THE JEFF BECK GROUP. ROD provided vocals on a B-side 'I'VE BEEN DRINKIN'' in 1968. In the mid-60's he was also part of live group SHOTGUN EXPRESS. In 1969, ROD left JEFF BECK to join SMALL FACES evolvement into The FACES, but continued a new solo career, which was re-activated by 'Phonogram' records. His debut album 'AN OLD RAINCOAT . . . ' which featured some FACES, failed to hit in Britain, but managed to sell moderately in the States. His second 1970 album 'GASOLINE ALLEY' surprisingly broke him into the US Top 30, but he really infiltrated worldwide, when double 'A'side 'MAGGIE MAY' / 'REASON TO BELIEVE' smashed into the top slot US + UK. Its parent album 'EVERY PICTURE TELLS A STORY' also made the top, and he was soon a major star on both sides of the Atlantic. His next 5 albums 'NEVER A DULL MOMENT', SING IT AGAIN ROD', 'SMILER', 'ATLANTIC CROSSING', + 'A NIGHT ON THE TOWN', all hit UK No.1, and he also delivered over 30 major hits over the next 2 decades. • **Style:** Charismatic singer-songwriter with large sandpapery vocal range. His glamorous looks (i.e. spiky top hair, large nose and extroverted self-confidence) made him surprise star of the 70's, which was often sent up by most comics. Moved from ballads to disco anthems with incredible ease. • **Songwriters:** ROD's cover versions:- STREET FIGHTING MAN (Rolling Stones) / SWEET SOUL MUSIC (Arthur Conley) / MAN OF CONSTANT SORROW (Bob Dylan) / HANDBAGS AND GLADRAGS (Mike D'Abo) / DIRTY OLD TOWN (Ewan MacColl) / I KNOW I'M LOSING YOU (Temptations) / IT'S ALL OVER NOW (Valentinos) / MY WAY OF GIVING (Small Faces) / CUT ACROSS SHORTY (hit; Eddie Cochran) / ANGEL (Jimi Hendrix) / AMAZING GRACE (trad. / hit; Judy Collins) / I'D RATHER GO BLIND (Etta James) / ONLY A HOBO + SWEETHEART LIKE YOU (Bob Dylan) / TWISTIN' THE NIGHT AWAY + BRING IT ON HOME TO ME + YOU SEND ME + HAVING A PARTY + SOOTHE ME (Sam Cooke) / OH NO NOT MY BABY + PRETTY FLAMINGO (Manfred Mann) / THE FIRST CUT IS THE DEEPEST (Cat Stevens) / COUNTRY COMFORTS + YOUR SONG (Elton John) / WHAT MADE MILWALKEE FAMOUS (hit; Jerry Lee Lewis) / SAILING (Sutherland Brothers) / THIS OLD HEART OF MINE (Isley Brothers) / GET BACK (Beatles) / YOU KEEP ME HANGIN' ON (Supremes) / I DON'T WANT TO TALK ABOUT IT (Crazy Horse member Danny Whitten) / SOME GUYS HAVE ALL THE LUCK (Robert Palmer) / HOW LONG (Ace) / SWEET LITTLE ROCK'N'ROLLER + LITTLE QUEENIE (Chuck Berry) / THE GREAT PRETENDER (Platters) / ALL RIGHT NOW (Free) / TRY A LITTLE TENDERNESS (Otis Redding) / THE MOTOWN SONG (L.J.McNally) / IT TAKES TWO (Marvin Gaye & Tammi Terrell) / DOWNTOWN TRAIN + TOM TRAUBERT'S BLUES + HANG ON ST.CHRISTOPHER (Tom Waits) / BROKEN ARROW (Robbie Robertson) / HAVE I TOLD YOU LATELY THAT I LOVE YOU (Van Morrison) / PEOPLE GET READY (Curtis Mayfield) / RUBY TUESDAY (Rolling Stones) / SHOTGUN WEDDING (Roy C.) / WINDY TOWN (Chris Rea) / DOWNTOWN LIGHTS (Blue Nile) / LEAVE VIRGINIA ALONE (Tom Petty) / SIMON CLIMIE began writing for him from 1988. YOU'RE THE STAR single written by Livesey, Lyle & Miller. **Trivia/Blondeography:** BRITT ECKLAND (marriage 5 Mar'75-1978) / ALANA HAMILTON (marriage 6 Apr'79-1984) / KELLY EMBERG (1985-1990) / RACHEL HUNTER (marriage 15 Dec'90-now).

Recommended: STORYTELLER – THE BEST OF ROD STEWART (*8)

ROD STEWART – vocals with session people

Decca Press

Oct 64. (7") **GOOD MORNING LITTLE SCHOOLGIRL. / I'M GONNA MOVE TO THE OUTSKIRTS OF TOWN** [ ] [ ]
(re-iss.Mar82)

In 1965, he joined STEAMPACKET, but they issued no 45's, and split Mar'66.

Columbia not issued

Nov 65. (7") **THE DAY WILL COME. / WHY DOES IT GO ON** [ ] [-]
Apr 66. (7") **SHAKE. / I JUST GOT SOME** [ ] [-]

— A month previous, he had joined SHOTGUN EXPRESS who released one 45, 'I COULD FEEL THE WHOLE WORLD TURN AROUND' Oct66 on 'Columbia'.

Immediate not issued

Nov 67. (7") **LITTLE MISS UNDERSTOOD. / SO MUCH TO SAY** [ ] [-]
(re-iss.Sep80 on 'Virgin') (re-iss.Feb83)

— In 1968, he joined JEFF BECK GROUP, appearing on 2 albums; 'TRUTH' & 'BECK-OLA'. Similtaneously joined The FACES and returned to solo work 1969.

Vertigo Mercury

Feb 70. (lp)(c) **AN OLD RAINCOAT WON'T EVER LET YOU DOWN** (US title 'THE ROD STEWART ALBUM') [ ] [ ]

– Street fighting man / Man of constant sorrow / Blind prayer / Handbags and gladrags / An old raincoat won't ever let you down / I wouldn't ever change a thing / Cindy's lament / Dirty old town. *(re-iss.Aug83 on 'Mercury', cd-iss.Nov87 & Sep95)*

Feb 70. (7") **AN OLD RAINCOAT WON'T LET YOU DOWN. / STREET FIGHTING MAN** -
May 70. (7") **HANDBAGS AND GLADRAGS. / MAN OF CONSTANT SORROW** -
(re-iss. US Feb '72; hit No. 42)
Sep 70. (7") **IT'S ALL OVER NOW. / JO'S LAMENT**
Sep 70. (lp)(c) **GASOLINE ALLEY** 62 27 Jun 70
– Gasoline alley / It's all over now / My way of giving / Country comfort / Cut across Shorty / Lady day / Jo's lament / I don't want to discuss it. *(re-iss.Aug83 on 'Mercury', cd-iss.Oct84 & Sep95)*
Nov 70. (7") **GASOLINE ALLEY. / ONLY A HOBO** -
Jan 71. (7") **CUT ACROSS SHORTY. / GASOLINE ALLEY** -
Mar 71. (7") **MY WAY OF GIVING. /** -
May 71. (7") **COUNTRY COMFORT. / GASOLINE ALLEY** -

Mercury Mercury
Jul 71. (7") **MAGGIE MAY. / REASON TO BELIEVE** 1 1 62

— (above was flipped over for BBC Radio One playlist. MAGGIE MAY was now bigger played hit) *(re-iss.Oct84)*

Jul 71. (lp)(c) **EVERY PICTURE TELLS A STORY** 1 1 Jun 71
– Every picture tells a story / Seems like a long time / That's all right / Tomorrow is such a long time / Amazing Grace / Henry / Maggie May / Mandolin wind / (I know) I'm losing you / Reason to believe. *(re-iss.May83, cd-iss.Nov87 & Sep95)*
Nov 71. (7") **(I KNOW) I'M LOSING YOU. / MANDOLIN WIND** - 24
Jul 72. (lp)(c) **NEVER A DULL MOMENT** 1 2
– True blue / Lost Paraguayos / Mama you been on my mind / Italian girls / Angel / Interludings / You wear it well / I'd rather go blind / Twisting the night away. *(re-iss.May83, cd-iss.Nov87 & Sep95)*
Aug 72. (7") **YOU WEAR IT WELL. / LOST PARAGUAYOS** 1 -
Aug 72. (7") **YOU WEAR IT WELL. / TRUE BLUE** - 13

— Sep72, a ROD STEWART early recording with PYTHON LEE JACKSON; 'In A Broken Dream' hits UK No.3 / US No.56.

Nov 72. (7") **ANGEL. / WHAT MADE MILWAUKEE FAMOUS (HAS MADE A LOSER OUT OF ME)** 4 -
Nov 72. (7") **ANGEL. / LOST PARAGUAYOS** - 40

— May73, older JEFF BECK & ROD STEWART recording 'I'VE BEEN DRINKIN' ' hit 27.

Aug 73. (7") **TWISTING THE NIGHT AWAY. / TRUE BLUE – LADY DAY** - 59
Aug 73. (lp)(c) **SING IT AGAIN ROD** (compilation of covers) 1 31 Jul 73
– Reason to believe / You wear it well / Mandolin wind / Country comforts / Maggie May / Handbags and gladrags / Street fighting man / Twisting the night away / Lost Paraguayos / (I know) I'm losing you / Pinball wizard / Gasoline alley. *(cd-iss.Oct84)*
Aug 73. (7") **OH! NO NOT MY BABY. / JODIE** 6 59 Oct 73
Sep 74. (7") **FAREWELL. / BRING IT ON HOME TO ME – YOU SEND ME (Medley)** 7 -
Oct 74. (lp)(c) **SMILER** 1 13
– Sweet little rock'n'roller / Lochinvar / Farewell / Sailor / Bring it on home to me – You send me (medley) / Let me be your car / A natural man / A natural man / Dixie toot / Hard road / I've grown accustomed to her face / Girl of the North Country / Mine for me. *(cd-iss.Nov87 & Sep95)*
Nov 74. (7") **MINE FOR ME. / FAREWELL** - 91
Jan 75. (7") **LET ME BE YOUR CAR. / SAILOR** -

Warners Warners
Aug 75. (7") **SAILING. / STONE COLD SOBER** 1 -
(re-activated Sep76, hit UK No.3, re-iss.Jan84) (re-iss.Jun77 on 'Riva') (re-iss.Mar87 for Channel Ferry disaster fund, hit No.41)
Aug 75. (lp)(c) **ATLANTIC CROSSING** 1 9
– Three time loser / Alright for an hour / All in the name of rock'n'roll / Drift away / Stone cold sober / I don't want to talk about it / It's not the spotlight / This old heart of mine / Still love you / Sailing. *(re-iss.Jan78 on 'Riva', hit UK 60) (cd-iss.Feb87 & 1989 on 'WEA') (blue-lp Jul77)*
Aug 75. (7") **SAILING. / ALL IN THE NAME OF ROCK'N'ROLL** - 58

Riva Warners
Nov 75. (7") **THIS OLD HEART OF MINE. / ALL IN THE NAME OF ROCK'N'ROLL** 4 83
May 76. (7") **TONIGHT'S THE NIGHT. / THE BALLTRAP** 5 -
Jun 76. (lp)(c) **A NIGHT ON THE TOWN** 1 2
– Tonight's the night / The first cut is the deepest / Fool for you / The killing of Georgie (part 1 & 2) / The balltrap / Pretty flamingo / Big bayou / The wild side of life / Trade winds. *(re-iss.Jun83 on 'Warner Bros', cd-iss.1989 on 'WEA')*
Aug 76. (7") **THE KILLING OF GEORGIE. / FOOL FOR YOU** 2 -
Sep 76. (7") **TONIGHT'S THE NIGHT. / FOOL FOR YOU** - 1
Nov 76. (7") **GET BACK. / TRADE WINDS** 11 -
Feb 77. (7") **THE FIRST CUT IS THE DEEPEST. / THE BALLTRAP** - 21
Apr 77. (7") **THE FIRST CUT IS THE DEEPEST. / I DON'T WANT TO TALK ABOUT IT** 1 -
Apr 77. (7") **THE KILLING OF GEORGIE. / ROSIE** - 30
Oct 77. (7") **YOU'RE IN MY HEART. / YOU GOT A NERVE** 3 4
Nov 77. (lp)(c) **FOOT LOOSE AND FANCY FREE** 3 2
– Hot legs / You're insane / You're in my heart / Born loose / You keep me hangin' on / (If loving you is wrong) I don't want to be right / You got a nerve / I was only joking. *(re-iss.Jun83 on 'Warner Bros.', cd-iss.Jun89)*
Jan 78. (7") **HOT LEGS. / I WAS ONLY JOKING** 5 -
Feb 78. (7") **HOT LEGS. / YOU'RE INSANE** - 28
Apr 78. (7") **I WAS ONLY JOKING. / BORN LOOSE** 22
May 78. (7") **OLE OLA (MUHLER BRASILEIRA). (as "ROD STEWART With The SCOTLAND WORLD CUP SQUAD") / I'D WALK A MILLION MILES FOR ONE OF YOUR GOALS** 4 -
Nov 78. (7") **D'YA THINK I'M SEXY?. / DIRTY WEEKEND** 1 -
Dec 78. (7")(12") **D'YA THINK I'M SEXY?. / SCARRED AND SCARED** - 1
Dec 78. (lp)(c)(US-pic-lp) **BLONDES HAVE MORE FUN** 3 1
– D'ya think I'm sexy / Dirty weekend / Ain't love a bitch / The best days of my life / Is that the thanks I get / Attractive female wanted / Blondes (have more fun) / Last summer / Standing in the shadows of love / Scarred and scared. *(re-iss.Jun83 on 'Warner Bros.')*
Jan 79. (7") **AIN'T LOVE A BITCH. / SCARRED AND SCARED** 11 -
Apr 79. (7") **AIN'T LOVE A BITCH. / LAST SUMMER** - 22
Apr 79. (7") **BLONDES (HAVE MORE FUN). / THE BEST DAYS OF MY LIFE** 63 -
Nov 79. (lp)(c) **GREATEST HITS VOLUME 1** (compilation) 1 22
– Hot legs / Maggie May / a ya think I'm sexy / You're in my heart / Sailing / I don't want to talk about it / Tonight's the night / The killing of Georgie (parts 1 & 2) / Maggie May / The first cut is the deepest / I was only joking. *(re-iss.Jun83, cd-iss.Jan84 on 'Warner Bros.')*
Dec 79. (7") **I DON'T WANT TO TALK ABOUT IT. / THE BEST DAYS OF MY LIFE** - 46
May 80. (7") **IF LOVING YOU IS WRONG (I DON'T WANT TO BE RIGHT). / LAST SUMMER** 23
Nov 80. (7")(12") **PASSION. / BETTER OFF DEAD** 17 5
Nov 80. (lp)(c) **FOOLISH BEHAVIOR** 4 12
– Better off dead / Foolish behaviour / My girl / She won't dance with me / Gi' me wings / So soon we change / Somebody special / Passion / Say it ain't true / Oh God, I wish I was home tonight. *(re-iss.Jun83 on 'Warner Bros.')*
Dec 80. (7") **MY GIRL. / SHE WON'T DANCE WITH ME** 32 -
Mar 81. (7")(c-s) **OH GOD, I WISH I WAS HOME TONIGHT. / SOMEBODY SPECIAL** -
Mar 81. (7") **SOMEBODY SPECIAL. / SHE WON'T DANCE WITH ME** - 71
Oct 81. (7") **YOUNG TURKS. / SONNY** - 5
Oct 81. (7") **TONIGHT I'M YOURS (DON'T HURT ME). / SONNY** 8 -
Nov 81. (lp)(c) **TONIGHT I'M YOURS** 8 11
– Tonight I'm yours (don't hurt me) / Only a boy / Just like a woman / How long / Never give up on a dream / Jealous / Tora, Tora, Tora (out with the boys) / Young Turks / Tear it up / Sonny. *(re-iss.Jun83)*
Dec 81. (7") **YOUNG TURKS. / TORA, TORA, TORA (OUT WITH THE BOYS)** 11 -
Jan 82. (7") **TONIGHT I'M YOURS (DON'T HURT ME). / TORA, TORA, TORA (OUT WITH THE BOYS)** - 20
Feb 82. (7") **HOW LONG. / JEALOUS** 41 49 Apr 82
Nov 82. (d-lp)(d-c) **ABSOLUTELY LIVE (live)** 35 46
– The stripper / Tonight I'm yours / Sweet little rock'n'roller / Hot legs / Tonight's the night / The great pretender / Passion / She won't dance with me / Little Queenie / You're in my heart / Rock my plimsoul / Young Turks / Guess I'll always love you / Gasoline alley / Maggie May / Tear it up / D'ya think I'm sexy / Sailing / I don't want to talk about it / Stay with me. *(re-iss.Mar84 on 'Warner Bros.', cd-iss.Mar87 on 'WEA')*
Nov 82. (7") **GUESS I'LL ALWAYS LOVE YOU (live). / ROCK MY PLIMSOUL (live)** -

Warner Warners
May 83. (7") **BABY JANE. / READY NOW** 1 14
(12"+=) – If loving you is wrong (live).
Jun 83. (lp)(c) **BODY WISHES** 5 30
– Dancin' alone / Baby Jane / Move me / Body wishes / Sweet surrender / What am I gonna do / Ghetto blaster / Ready now / Strangers again / Satisfied. *(cd-iss.Jul84)*
Aug 83. (7")(12") **WHAT AM I GONNA DO?. / DANCIN' ALONE** 3 35
Dec 83. (7") **SWEET SURRENDER. / GHETTO BLASTER** 23 -
(12"+=)(12"pic-d+=) – Oh God I wish I was home tonight.
May 84. (7") **INFATUATION. / SHE WON'T DANCE WITH ME** - 6
May 84. (7") **INFATUATION. / THREE TIME LOSER** 27 -
(12"+=) – Tonight's the night.
Jun 84. (lp)(c)(cd) **CAMOUFLAGE** 8 18
– Infatuation / All right now / Some guys have all the luck / Can we still be friends / Bad for you / Heart is on the line / Camouflage / Trouble. *(free 1-sided 7"pic-d w.a.)* – INFATUATION / (interview).
Jul 84. (7") **SOME GUYS HAVE ALL THE LUCK. / I WAS ONLY JOKING** 15 10
(12"+=) – The killing of Georgie.
Nov 84. (7") **TROUBLE. / TORA, TORA, TORA (OUT WITH THE BOYS)**
(12"+=) – This old heart of mine.
Dec 84. (7") **ALL RIGHT NOW. / DANCIN' ALONE** - 72

— In 1985, he was credited on 45 'PEOPLE GET READY' by JEFF BECK.

Jun 86. (7") **LOVE TOUCH. / HEART IS ON THE LINE** 27 6 May 86
(12"pic-d+=) – Hard lesson to learn.
Jun 86. (lp)(c)(cd) **EVERY BEAT OF MY HEART** (US-title 'ROD STEWART') 5 28
– Here to eternity / Another heartache / A night like this / Who's gonna take me home / Red hot in black / Love touch / In my own crazy way / Every beat of my heart / Ten days of rain / In my life. *(cd+=)* – Every beat of my heart (remix).
Jul 86. (7") **EVERY BEAT OF MY HEART. / TROUBLE** 2 83 Nov 86
(12"+=) – ('A'mix).
(12"pic-d+=) – Some guys have all the luck (live)
Sep 86. (7") **ANOTHER HEARTACHE. / YOU'RE IN MY HEART** 54 52
(12"+=) – ('A'extended).
Jul 87. (7") **TWISTING THE NIGHT AWAY. / LET'S GET SMALL** - 80
above was issued on 'Geffen' and on film 'Innerspace'.
May 88. (7")(US-c-s) **LOST IN YOU. / ALMOST ILLEGAL** 21 12
(12"+=)(12"pic-d+=) – ('A'extended).
(cd-s+=) – Baby Jane / Every beat of my heart.
May 88. (lp)(c)(cd) **OUT OF ORDER** 11 20
– Lost in you / The wild horse / Lethal dose of love / Forever young / My heart can't tell you no / Dynamite / Nobody loves you when you're down and out / Crazy about her / Try a little tenderness / When I was your man.
Jul 88. (7") **FOREVER YOUNG. / DAYS OF RAGE** 57 12
(12"+=)/ /(cd-s+=) – ('A'extended)./ / Every beat of my heart.
Jan 89. (7") **TRY A LITTLE TENDERNESS. / MY HEART CAN'T TELL YOU NO**
(12"+=)(cd-s+=) – Passion.

Apr 89. (7") **MY HEART CAN'T TELL YOU NO. / THE WILD HORSE** [49] [4] Nov 88
(12"+=)(cd-s+=)(12"pic-d+=) – Passion (live).
May 89. (7")(c-s) **CRAZY ABOUT HER. / DYNAMITE** [-] [11]
Nov 89. (7")(c-s)(7"pic-d) **THIS OLD HEART OF MINE. ("ROD STEWART with RONALD ISLEY") / TONIGHT I'M YOURS DON'T HURT ME)** [51] [-]
(12"+=)(cd-s+=)(12"pic-d+=) – Ain't love a bitch.
Nov 89. (d-lp)(d-c)(d-cd) **STORYTELLER – THE BEST OF ROD STEWART 1964-1990** (compilation) [3] [54]
— (was also issued UK on (7xlp)(4xc)(4xcd).
Jan 90. (7")(c-s) **DOWNTOWN TRAIN. / THE KILLING OF GEORGIE (pt.1 & 2)** [10] [3] Nov 89
(12")(cd-s) – ('A'side) / Hot legs.
(12"+=) – ('A'side) / Cindy incidentally / To love somebody.
Mar 90. (7") **THIS OLD HEART OF MINE (w/ RONALD ISLEY). / YOU'RE IN MY HEART** [-] [ ]
Mar 90. (cd)(c) **DOWNTOWN TRAIN – SELECTIONS FROM STORYTELLER** (compilation) [-] [20]
Nov 90. (7")(c-s) **IT TAKES TWO. ("ROD STEWART & TINA TURNER") / HOT LEGS (live)** [5] [ ]
(12"+=)(cd-s+=) – ('A'extended remix).
Mar 91. (7")(c-s) **RHYTHM OF MY HEART. / MOMENT OF GLORY** [3] [5] Feb 91
(12"+=)(cd-s+=) – I don't want to talk about it (re-recording).
Apr 91. (cd)(c)(lp) **VAGABOND HEART** [2] [10]
– Rhythm of my heart / Rebel heart / Broken arrow / It takes two / When a man's in love / You are everything / The Motown song / Go out dancing / No holding back / Have I told you lately that I love you / Moment of glory / Downtown train / If only.
Jun 91. (7")(c-s) **THE MOTOWN SONG. / SWEET SOUL MUSIC (live)** [10] [10]
(12"+=)(cd-s+=) – Try a little tenderness.
Aug 91. (7")(c-s) **BROKEN ARROW. / I WAS ONLY JOKING** [54] [20] Oct 91
(10"+=)(cd-s+=) – The killing of Georgie (parts 1 & 2).
Apr 92. (7")(c-s) **YOUR SONG. / BROKEN ARROW** [41] [48]
(12"+=)(cd-s+=) – Mandolin wind / The first cut is the deepest
Nov 92. (7")(c-s) **TOM TRAUBERT'S BLUES (WALTZING MATILDA). / NO HOLDING BACK** [6] [ ]
(cd-s+=) – Downtown train.
(cd-s) – ('A'side) / Sailing / I don't want to talk about it / Try a little tenderness.
Feb 93. (cd)(c)(lp) **ROD STEWART, LEAD VOCALIST** (part comp.) [3] [ ]
– I ain't superstitious / Handbags & gladrags / Cindy incidentally / Stay with me / True blue / Sweet Mary lady / Hot legs / Stand back / Ruby Tuesday / Shotgun wedding / First I look at the purse / Tom Traubert's blues.
Feb 93. (7")(c-s) **RUBY TUESDAY. / YOU'RE IN MY HEART** [11] [ ]
(cd-s+=) – Out of order / Passion.
(cd-s+=) – Crazy about her / Passion.
Apr 93. (7")(c-s) **SHOTGUN WEDDING. / EVERY BEAT OF MY HEART** [21] [ ]
(cd-s+=) – Sweet soul music (live).
(cd-s) – ('A'side) / Memphis / Maybe I'm amazed / Had me a real goodtime (all 3 by ROD STEWART & THE FACES).
— below with special guest **RONNIE WOOD** – guitar plus others **JEFF GOLUB** – guitar / **CARMINE ROJAS** – bass / **CHARLES KENTISS III** – piano, organ / **KEVIN SAVIGAR** – piano, organ & accordion / **JIM CREGAN** – guitar / **DON TESCHNER** – guitar, violin & mandolin / **PHIL PARLAPIANO** – accordion & mandolin / & backing singers
May 93. (cd)(c)(lp) **UNPLUGGED . . . AND SEATED** [2] [2]
– Hot legs / Tonight's the night / Handbags and gladrags / Cut across Shorty / Every picture tells a story / Maggie May / Reason to believe / People get ready / Have I told you lately / Tom Traubert's blues (waltzing Matilda) / The first cut is the deepest / Mandolin wind / Highgate shuffle / Stay with me / Having a party.
Jun 93. (7")(c-s) **HAVE I TOLD YOU LATELY THAT I LOVE YOU?. / LET THE DAY BEGIN** [5] [5] Apr 93
(cd-s+=) – Gasoline alley (live).
(cd-s) – ('A'side) / Love wars / One night.
Aug 93. (7")(c-s) **REASON TO BELIEVE (unplugged). / IT'S ALL OVER NOW (unplugged)** [51] [19]
(cd-s+=) – Love in the right hands.
(cd-s) – ('A'side) / Cindy incidentally / Stay with me (both w / FACES).
— In Dec '93, ROD & STING, teamed up with BRYAN ADAMS on his US Top 5 hit 'All For Love'.
Dec 93. (7")(c-s) **PEOPLE GET READY. / I WAS ONLY JOKING** [45] [ ]
(cd-s) – ('A'side) / Tonight's the night / If loving you is wrong (I don't want to be right).
(cd-s) – ('A'side) / Da ya think I'm sexy / Sweet little rock'n'roller (live) / Baby Jane.
— Late Nov '93, he BRYAN ADAMS and STING teamed up on a song from 'The Three Musketeers' film; 'ALL FOR LOVE', which hit UK No.2 (early '94) + US No.1.
Feb 94. (c-s)(cd-s) **HAVING A PARTY /** [-] [40]
May 95. (c-s) **YOU'RE THE STAR / SHOCK TO THE SYSTEM** [19] [ ]
(cd-s+=) – Have I told you lately.
May 95. (cd)(c)(lp) **A SPANNER IN THE WORKS** [4] [35]
– Windy town / Downtown lights / Leave Virginia alone / Sweetheart like you / This / Lady luck / You're the star / Muddy, Sam and Otis / Hang on St. Christopher / Delicious / Soothe me / Purple heather.
Jun 95. (c-s)(cd-s) **LEAVE VIRGINIA ALONE /** [-] [52]
Aug 95. (c-s) **LADY LUCK / HOT LEGS** [56] [ ]
(cd-s+=) – The groom still waiting at the altar / Young Turks.
(cd-s) – ('A'side) / The killing of Georgie / Sailing / The first cut is the deepest.

– more compilations, etc. –

Sep 72. Youngblood/ US= GNP Crescendo; (7") **IN A BROKEN DREAM. ("PYTHON LEE JACKSON") / THE BLUES** [3] [56]
(re-iss. Jul 80 +12"+=) – Cloud 9. *(re-iss.Aug87 as "PYTHON LEE JACKSON / ROD STEWART" on 'Bold Reprieve')*
— PYTHON LEE JACKSON was in fact an Australian 5-piece of the late 60s, headed by keyboard player **DAVID BENTLEY**, who employed ROD to sing on 3 tracks from their lp 'IN A BROKEN DREAM'.
1979. Lightning; (7") **IN A BROKEN DREAM. / IF THE WORLD STOPS STILL TONIGHT** [ ] [-]
Below releaes on 'Mercury' until otherwise mentioned.
Feb 76. (d-lp)(c) **THE VINTAGE YEARS 1969-70** [ ] [ ]
Feb 76. (7") **IT'S ALL OVER NOW. / HANDBAGS AND GLADRAGS** [ ] [-]
1976. (7") **EVERY PICTURE TELLS A STORY. / WHAT MADE MILWAUKEE FAMOUS (HAS MADE A LOSER OUT OF ME)** [-] [ ]
Jul 76. (lp)(c) **RECORDED HIGHLIGHTS AND ACTION REPLAYS** [ ] [ ]
Jun 77. (7"m) **MANDOLIN WIND. / GIRL FROM THE NORTH COUNTRY / SWEET LITTLE ROCK'N'ROLLER** [ ] [-]
Jun 77. (d-lp)(d-c) **THE BEST OF ROD STEWART** [18] [90]
(re-iss.1985)
Jul 77. (c) **THE MUSIC OF ROD STEWART (1970-71)** [ ] [-]
Aug 77. (d-lp)(d-c) **THE BEST OF ROD STEWART VOLUME 2** [ ] [ ]
Nov 79. (7") **MAGGIE MAY. / YOU WEAR IT WELL** [ ] [-]
(re-iss.Apr88 on 'Old Gold')
Sep 80. (lp)(c) **HOT RODS** [ ] [-]
May 81. (lp)(c) **BEST OF THE BEST** [ ] [-]
Nov 87. (cd) **THE ROD STEWART ALBUM** [ ] [-]
Jun 89. (lp)(c)(cd) **THE ROCK ALBUM** [ ] [-]
Jun 89. (cd) **THE BALLAD TIME** [ ] [-]
Feb 91. (cd)(c) **GASOLINE ALLEY / SMILER** [ ] [-]
Oct 92. (7")(c-s) **YOU WEAR IT WELL. / I WOULD RATHER GO BLIND** [ ] [ ]
(cd-s+=) – Angel.
Dec 78. St.Michael; (lp) **REASON TO BELIEVE** [ ] [-]
Sep 81. Contour; (lp)(c) **MAGGIE MAY** [ ] [-]
(cd-iss.Jul90 on 'Pickwick')
Oct 82. Contour; (lp)(c) **ROD STEWART** [ ] [-]
Sep 85. Contour; (lp)(c) **THE HITS OF ROD STEWART** [ ] [-]
Jan 87. Contour; (lp)(c) **JUKE BOX HEAVEN (14 ROCK'N'ROLL GREATS)** [ ] [-]
Jul 83. Cambra; (d-c) **ROD STEWART** [ ] [-]
Nov 83. Warners; (d-c) **ATLANTIC CROSSING / A NIGHT ON THE TOWN** [ ] [-]
Nov 84. Astan; (lp)(c) **CAN I GET A WITNESS** [ ] [-]
Jul 88. Knight; (lp)(c) **NIGHTRIDIN'** [ ] [-]
Feb 89. Venus; (c) **THE MAGIC OF ROD STEWART** [ ] [-]
Oct 89. K-Tel/ US- GNP; (lp)(c)(cd) **IN A BROKEN DREAM** [ ] [ ] 1988
Dec 92. M Classics; (cd)(c) **JUST A LITTLE MISUNDERSTOOD** [ ] [-]
Feb 93. Charly; (cd) **THE FIRST SUPER GROUP ("ROD STEWART & STEAMPACKET")** [ ] [-]
Jul 93. Ronco; (cd)(c) **THE FACE OF THE SIXTIES** [ ] [-]
Jul 94. Success; (cd)(c) **COME HOME BABY** [ ] [-]
Aug 95. Spectrum; (cd)(c) **MAGGIE MAY – THE CLASSIC YEARS** [ ] [-]

STIFF LITTLE FINGERS

Formed: Belfast, N.Ireland . . . 1977 by teenagers JAKE BURNS and co. They released a couple of singles on own 'Rigid Digit', before they moved to major indie label 'Rough Trade' in 1978. Their debut album 'INFLAMMABLE MATERIAL' hit the Top 20, due to more heavy airplay from Radio 1 DJ John Peel. In 1979, their fans cried "sell-out" when 'Chrysalis' records took them on board. They were soon chart regulars, although their loyal support soon dwindled. • **Style:** Protest punk rock (mainly about troubled homeland). In the early 80's, after SLF moved to London, England, BURNS's hoarse but effective vox had slightly succumbed to a more commercial attitude. • **Songwriters:** BURNS penned, some with OGILVIE. They also covered JOHNNY WAS (Bob Marley) / RUNNING BEAR (Johnny Preston) / WHITE CHRISTMAS (Bing Crosby) / LOVE OF THE COMMON PEOPLE (Nicky Thomas). • **Trivia:** JAKE once applied for a job of a Radio 1 producer.

Recommended: INFLAMMABLE MATERIAL (*9) / NOBODY'S HEROES (*8) / ALL THE BEST (*8).

JAKE BURNS – vocals, lead guitar / **HENRY CLUNEY** – guitar / **ALI McMORDIE** – bass / **BRIAN FALOON** – drums repl. GORDON BLAIR who later joined RUDI

Rigid Digit | not issued

Mar 78. (7") **SUSPECT DEVICE. / WASTED LIFE** [ ] [-]
(re-iss.Jun78) (re-iss.Mar79, Jan80 & Apr82 on 'Rigid Digit/Rough Trade')

Rough Trade | not issued

Oct 78. (7") **ALTERNATIVE ULSTER. / 78 R.P.M.** [ ] [-]
(above originally iss.Aug78 on 'Rigid Digit-Rough Trade')
Feb 79. (lp) **INFLAMMABLE MATERIAL** [14] [-]
– Suspect device / State of emergency / Here we are nowhere / asted life / No more of that / Barbed wire love / White noise / Breakout / Law and order / Rough trade / Johnny was / Alternative Ulster / Closed groove. *(re-iss.+c+cd.Mar89 on 'E.M.I.')*
— **JIM REILLY** – drums repl. FALOON
May 79. (7") **GOTTA GETAWAY. / BLOODY SUNDAY** [ ] [-]

Chrysalis | Chrysalis

Sep 79. (7") **STRAW DOGS. / YOU CAN'T SAY CRAP ON THE RADIO** [44] [ ]
Feb 80. (7") **AT THE EDGE. / SILLY ENCORES: RUNNING BEAR – WHITE CHRISTMAS** [15] [ ]
Mar 80. (lp)(c) **NOBODY'S HEROES** [8] [ ]
– Gotta getaway / Wait and see / Fly the flag / At the edge / Nobody's hero / Bloody dub / Doesn't make it alright / I don't like you / No change / Suspect device / Tin soldiers. *(re-iss.+c+cd.Mar89 on 'E.M.I.')*
May 80. (7") **TIN SOLDIERS. / NOBODY'S HERO** [36] [ ]
Jul 80. (7") **BACK TO FRONT. / MR.FIRE COAL-MAN** [49] [-]
Sep 80. (lp)(c) **HANX! (live)** [9] [-]

– Nobody's hero / Gotta getaway / Wait and see / Barbed wire love / Fly the flag / Alternative Ulster / Johnny was / At the edge / Wasted life / Tin soldiers / Suspect device. *(re-iss.+c+cd.Feb89 on 'Fame-EMI')*

Mar 81. (7"m) **JUST FADE AWAY. / GO FOR IT / DOESN'T MAKE IT ALRIGHT (live)** 47 -

Apr 81. (lp)(c) **GO FOR IT** 14 -
– Roots, radicals, rockers and reggae / Just fade away / Go for it / The only one / Hits and misses / Kicking up a racket / Safe as houses / Gate 49 / Silver lining / Piccadilly Circus. *(re-iss.+c+cd.Feb89 on 'Fame-EMI', cd+=)* – Back to front.

May 81. (7") **SILVER LINING. / SAFE AS HOUSES** 68 -

—— **BRIAN 'DOLPHIN' TAYLOR** – drums (ex-TOM ROBINSON BAND) repl. REILLY

Jan 82. (7"ep) **R.E.P. ONE POUND TEN PENCE OR LESS** 33 -
– Listen / Sad-eyed people / That's when your blood bumps / Two guitars clash.

Apr 82. (7") **TALK BACK. / GOOD FOR NOTHING** □ -

Aug 82. (7") **BITS OF KIDS. / STANDS TO REASON** 73 -

Sep 82. (lp)(c) **NOW THEN** 24 -
– Falling down / Won't be told / Love of the common people / The price of admission / Touch and go / Stands to reason / Bits of kids / Welcome to the whole week / Big city night / Talkback / Is that what you fought the war for. *(re-iss.cd Dec94 on 'Fame')*

Jan 83. (d-lp)(d-c) **ALL THE BEST** (compilation) 19 -
– Suspect device / Wasted life / Alternative Ulster / 78 rpm / Gotta getaway / Bloody Sunday / Straw dogs / You can't say crap on the radio / At the edge / Running bear / White Christmas / Nobody's hero / Tin soldiers / Back to front / Mr. Fire coal man / Just fade away / Go for it / Doesn't make it alright / Silver lining / Safe as houses / Sad eyed people / Two guitars clash / Listen / That's when your blood bumps / Good for nothing / Talkback / Stand to reason / Bits of kids / Touch and go / The price of admission. *(d-cd-iss.Jun88) (re-iss.d-cd+d-c.Sep91 on 'E.M.I.')*

Feb 83. (7") **THE PRICE OF ADMISSION. / TOUCH AND GO** □ -

—— Had already disbanded late 1982. McMORDIE joined FICTION GROOVE and DOLPHIN joined SPEAR OF DESTINY after stint with GO WEST.

JAKE BURNS & THE BIG WHEEL

were formed by **JAKE** plus **NICK MUIR** – keyboards / **SEAN MARTIN** – bass / **STEVE GRANTLEY** – drums

Survival / not issued

Jul 85. (7")(12") **ON FORTUNE STREET. / HERE COMES THAT SONG AGAIN** □ -

Mar 86. (7")(12") **SHE GREW UP. / RACE YOU TO THE GRAVE** □ -

Jive-CBS / not issued

Feb 87. (7")('A'ext-12") **BREATHLESS. / VALENTINE'S DAY** □ -

STIFF LITTLE FINGERS

re-formed in 1987 by **BURNS, TAYLOR, CLUNEY & McMORDIE**

Kaz / not issued

May 88. (lp)(c)(cd) **NO SLEEP TILL BELFAST (live)** □ -
– Alternative Ulster / Roots radicals rockers and reggae / Silver lining / Wait and see / Gotta getaway / Just fade away / Wasted life / The only one / Nobody's hero / At the edge / Listen / Barbed wire love / Fly the flag / Tin soldiers / No sleep till Belfast / Suspect device / Johnny was.

Skunx / not issued

Jun 88. (12"ep) **NO SLEEP TILL BELFAST (live)** □ -
– Suspect device / Alternative Ulster / Nobody's hero.

Virgin / Virgin

Mar 89. (12"ep)(3"cd-ep) **ST.PATRIX** (the covers live) □ -
– The wild rover / Johnny was / Love of the common people.

Apr 89. (d-lp)(d-c)(d-cd) **SEE YOU UP THERE! (live)** □ -
– (intro: Go for it) / Alternative Ulster / Silver lining / Love of the common people / Gotta getaway / Just fade away / Piccadilly Circus / Gate 49 / Wasted life / At the edge / Listen / Barbed wire love / Fly the flag / Tin soldiers / The wild rover / Suspect device / Johnny was.

—— (Mar91) **BRUCE FOXTON** – bass (ex-JAM, ex-Solo Artist) repl. McMORDIE

Essential / not issued

Oct 91. (cd)(c)(lp)(pic-lp) **FLAGS AND EMBLEMS** □ -
– (It's a) Long way to Paradise (from here) / Stand up and shout / Each dollar a bullet / The cosh / Beirut Moon / The game of life / Human shield / Johnny 7 / Dread burn / No surrender. *(re-iss.cd Jul95 on 'Dojo')*

Oct 91. (cd-ep) **BEIRUT MOON / STAND UP AND SHOUT / (interview)** □ -

Jan 94. (12"ep) **CAN'T BELIEVE IN YOU. / SILVER LINING (unplugged) / LISTEN (unplugged) / WASTED LIFE (unplugged)** □ -
(cd-ep) – ('A'side) / ('A'extended) / Alternative Ulster (featuring RICKY WARWICK of The ALMIGHTY) / Smithers-Jones (live with BRUCE FOXTON vocals).

Feb 94. (cd)(c) **GET A LIFE** □ -
– Get a life / Can't believe in you / The road to kingdom come / Walk away / No laughing matter / Harp / Forensic evidence / Baby blue ((what have they been telling you?) / I want you / The night that the wall came down / Cold / When the stars fall from the sky / What if I want more?.

Jun 94. (12")(cd-s) **HARP. / SHAKE IT OFF / NOW WHAT WE WERE (PRO PATRIA MORI)** □ □

– more compilations, etc. –

Sep 86. Strange Fruit; (12"ep) **THE PEEL SESSIONS** (12/9/78) □ -
– Johnny was / Law and order / Barbed wire love / Suspect device. *(c-ep iss. May87, cd-ep iss.Jul88)*

Nov 89. Strange Fruit; (lp)(c)(cd) **THE PEEL SESSIONS** □ -

Apr 88. Link; (d-lp)(green-d-lp) **LIVE AND LOUD (live)** □ -
(cd-iss.Sep89)

Oct 89. Link; (12"ep) **THE LAST TIME. / MR.FIRE-COAL MAN / TWO GUITARS CLASH** □ -

Apr 91. Link; (cd) **GREATEST HITS LIVE (live)** □ -

Oct 91. Link; (cd) **ALTERNATIVE CHARTBUSTERS** □ -

Oct 89. Limited; (green-lp)(cd) **LIVE IN SWEDEN (live)** □ -

Dec 92. Dojo; (cd) **FLY THE FLAGS – LIVE AT BRIXTON ACADEMY (27/9/91)** □ -

Aug 93. Windsong; (cd) **BBC RADIO 1 LIVE IN CONCERT (live)** □ -

Mar 95. Dojo; (cd) **PURE FINGERS LIVE – ST.PATRIX 1993** □ -

Stephen STILLS / MANASSAS
(see under ⇒ CROSBY, STILLS, NASH)

STILTSKIN

Formed: London, England ... 1989 by LAWLOR and FINNEGAN. The latter had played with Scots act HUE AND CRY, while LAWLOR had just returned from the States. They soon found ROSS McFARLANE, who had played with SLIDE, while 1993 saw them finding singer RAY WILSON. Came to light unusually when their track 'INSIDE' was aired on a Levi jeans TV commercial (the one where the quaker girls go to lake and see what appears to be a naked man in the water, only to find he is just breaking in his new jeans). The Television company were then inundated with enquiries on who was the group or person on its soundtrack, and where could they buy it. Unfortunately it hadn't been released, but was about to due to public demand. In April 1994, a version complete with words, crashed into the UK No.5 and soon was topping the charts. However by the end of the year, bad debut album reviews made them already yesterday's men. Maybe another quality song /advert will be on the cards for '95. • **Style:** Grunge rock, cloning NIRVANA. • **Songwriters:** LAWLOR. • **Trivia:** THE AMBROSIAN CHOIR sang choral on 'INSIDE'.

Recommended: THE MIND'S EYE (*4)

RAY WILSON – vocals / **PETER LAWLOR** – guitars, mandolin, vocals / **JAMES FINNIGAN** – bass, keyboards / **ROSS McFARLANE** – drums, percussion

Whitewater / Sony

Apr 94. (7")(c-s) **INSIDE. / AMERICA** 1 □
(12"+=)(cd-s+=) – ('A'extended).

Sep 94. (7")(c-s) **FOOTSTEPS. / SUNSHINE & BUTTERFLIES (live)** 34 □
(cd-s+=) – ('A'extended).

Oct 94. (cd)(c)(lp) **THE MIND'S EYE** 17 □
– Intro / Scared of ghosts / Horse / Rest in peace / Footsteps / Sunshine and butterflies / Inside / An illusion / America / When my ship comes in / Prayer before birth.

Mar 95. (7"ep)(c-ep)(cd-ep) **REST IN PEACE. / THE POLTROON / INSIDE (acoustic)** □ □

STING

Born: GORDON SUMNER, 2 Oct'51, Wallsend, nr.Newcastle, England. In the early 70's he gave up his job as a primary school teacher and joined a local group. He gained his nickname after wearing black and yellow hooped T-shirt. In 1974, he joined LAST EXIT, where he became lead singer on single 'WHISPERING VOICES'. Around this time, he enrolled with RADA and began on TV ad work. He was later to become successful actor later in the 70's. Early in 1977, he formed The POLICE, who became top selling outfit until their demise in 1983. STING had earlier branched out on a solo career while starring in the film 'BRIMSTONE AND TREACLE'. In 1985 he employed American musicians, to augment his new triumphant debut album 'DREAM OF THE BLUE TURTLES'. • **Style:** Popular rock tinged artist who fused his great voice into aspects of jazz and soul. • **Songwriters:** STING penned all work, except SPREAD A LITTLE HAPPINESS + SOMEONE TO WATCH OVER ME (George Gershwin) / TUTTI FRUTTI (Little Richard) / NEED YOUR LOVE SO BAD (Little Willie John) / MACK THE KNIFE (Bertold Brecht) / PURPLE HAZE (Jimi Hendrix) / SISTERS OF MERCY (Leonard Cohen) w/ CHIEFTAINS. • **Trivia:** He divorced actress Frances Tomelty in August of '82. In 1985, he dueted on singles MONEY FOR NOTHING (Dire Straits), which he co-wrote, plus LONG WAY TO GO (Phil Collins). That year he also guested on MILES DAVIS' album 'You're Under Arrest'. He was also another one of the stars on BAND AID and LIVE AID. **Filmography:** QUADROPHENIA (1979) / RADIO ON (1980) / ARTEMIS (1981 TV movie) / BRIMSTONE AND TREACLE (1982) / DUNE (1984) / THE BRIDE (1985) / PLENTY (1985) / STORMY MONDAY (1988) / JULIA JULIA (1987). In 1988 he also narrated Stravinsky's 'Soldier's Tale', which was soon issued on own 'Pangaea' label. He followed this by writing score for documentary about Quentin Crisp 'Crisp City'. He spent much of '89, campaigning for Brazilian rain forest projects before appearing in operatic play 'MacHeath'.

Recommended: NOTHING LIKE THE SUN (*8) / THE SOUL CAGES (*9) / FIELDS OF GOLD – THE BEST OF (*9).

STING – vocals, bass, etc. (with session people)

A & M / A & M

Aug 82. (7") **SPREAD A LITTLE HAPPINESS. / ONLY YOU** 16 □

Sep 82. (lp)(c) **BRIMSTONE AND TREACLE (Soundtrack)** □ □
– Spread a little happiness / Only you / Brimstone and treacle / You know I had the strangest dream / Brimstone 2 / (tracks by other artists).

—— Enlisted US musicians **KENNY KIRKLAND** – keyboards / **BRANFORD MARSALIS** – sax, percussion / **DARRYL JONES** – bass (ex-MILES DAVIS) / **OMAR HAKIM** – drums (WEATHER REPORT)

May 85. (7") **IF YOU LOVE SOMEBODY SET THEM FREE. / ANOTHER DAY** 26 3

(12"+=) – ('A'dance mix) / ('A'-Jellybean dance mix) / ('A'torch mix).

Jun 85. (lp)(c)(cd) **THE DREAM OF THE BLUE TURTLES** [3] [2]
– If you love somebody set them free / Love is the seventh wave / Russians / Children's crusade / Shadows in the rain / We work the black seam / Consider me gone / The dream of the blue turtles / Moon over Bourbon Street / Fortress around your heart. *(pic-lp Jan86)*

Aug 85. (7")(12") **LOVE IS THE SEVENTH WAVE. / CONSIDER ME GONE (live)** [41] [-]

Aug 85. (7") **FORTRESS AROUND YOUR HEART. / CONSIDER ME GONE** [-] [8]

Oct 85. (7")(12") **FORTRESS AROUND YOUR HEART. / SHADOWS IN THE RAIN** [49] [-]

Nov 85. (7") **LOVE IS THE SEVENTH WAVE. / DREAM OF THE BLUE TURTLES** [-] [17]

Dec 85. (7") **RUSSIANS. / GABRIEL'S MESSAGE** [12] [16]
(12"+=) – I burn for you (live).

Feb 86. (7") **MOON OVER BOURBON STREET. / MACK THE KNIFE** [44] [ ]
(12"+=) – Fortress around your heart.

Jul 86. (d-lp)(c)(cd) **BRING ON THE NIGHT (live)** [16] [-]
– Bring on the night – When the world is running down you make the best of what's still around / Consider me gone / Low life / We work the black seam / Driven to tears / The dream of the blue turtles – Demolition man / One world (not three) / Love is the seventh wave / Moon over Bourbon street / I burn for you / Another day / Children's crusade / Down so long / Tea in the Sahara.

— He retains **KIRKLAND + MARSALIS,** and recruited **MANU KATCHE** – drums / **MINO CINELU** – percussion, vocoder / **ANDY NEWMARK** – 2nd drummer / plus guests **ERIC CLAPTON, MARK KNOPFLER, ANDY SUMMERS + GIL EVANS**

Oct 87. (7") **WE'LL BE TOGETHER. / CONVERSATION WITH A DOG** [41] [7]
(12"+=)(3"cd-s+=) – ('A'extended mix) / ('A'instrumental).

Oct 87. (d-lp)(c)(cd) **NOTHING LIKE THE SUN** [1] [9]
– The Lazarus heart / Be still my beating heart / Englishman in New York / History will teach us nothing / They dance alone (gueca solo) / Fragile / We'll be together / Straight to my heart / Rock steady / Sister Moon / Little wing / The secret marriage.

Jan 88. (7") **BE STILL MY BEATING HEART. / GHOST IN THE STRAND** [-] [15]

Jan 88. (7")(12") **ENGLISHMAN IN NEW YORK. / GHOST IN THE STRAND (instrumental)** [51] [-]
(3"cd-s+=) – Bring on the night-When the world is running down (live)

Mar 88. (7") **ENGLISHMAN IN NEW YORK. / IF YOU'RE THERE** [-] [84]

Mar 88. (7") **FRAGILE. / FRAGIL (Portuguese mix)** [70] [-]
(12"+=)(cd-s+=) – Fragilidad (Spanish mix) / Mariposa libre.

Sep 88. (7") **THEY DANCE ALONE. / ELLAS DANZAN SOLAS (the Spanish version)** [ ] [ ]
(12"+=)(cd-s+=)/ /(10"+=) – We'll be together./ / Si Estamos juntos.

— He retained **MARSALIS, KIRKLAND, KATCHE.** New **DOMINIC MILLER** – guitar / **DAVID SANCIOUS** – keyboards / **KATHRYN TICKELL** – pipes / **PAOLA PAPAREUE** – oboe / **RAY COOPER, VINK, BILL SUMMERS, MUNYUNGO JACKSON, SKIP BURNEY, TONY VALCA** – percussion.

Dec 90. (7")(c-s) **ALL THIS TIME. / I MISS YOU KATE (instrumental)** [22] [5]
(12"+=)(cd-s+=)(pic-cd-s+=) – King of pain (live).

Jan 91. (cd)(c)(lp) **THE SOUL CAGES** [1] [2]
– Island of souls / All this time / Mad about you / Jeremiah blues (pt.1) / Why should I cry for you / Saint Agnes and the burning train / The wild wild sea / The soul cages / When the angels fall.

Feb 91. (7")(c-s) **MAD ABOUT YOU (remix). / TEMPTED (live)** [56] [ ]
(12"+=)(cd-s+=) – If you love somebody set them free (live).

Apr 91. (7")(c-s) **THE SOUL CAGES. / WALKING IN YOUR FOOTSTEPS (live)** [57] [ ]
(12"+=)(cd-s+=) – Don't stand so close to me / Oo la la Hugh (both live).
(12"+=) – The Lazarus heart / Too much inforation (live).

Aug 92. (7")(c-s)(cd-s) **IT'S PROBABLY ME. ("STING with ERIC CLAPTON") / ('A'long version)** [30] [ ]

— retained on album **MILLER, SANCIOUS & TICKELL** and brought in **VINNIE COLAIUTA** – drums / **LARRY ADLER + BRENDAN POWER** – chromatic harmonicas / **SIAN BELL** – cello / **DAVE HEATH** – flute / **PAUL FRANKLIN** – pedal steel / **JAMES BOYD** – viola / **KATHRYN GREELEY + SIMON FISCHER** – violins / **GUY BARKER + JOHN BARCLAY** – trumpets / **RICHARD EDWARDS + MARK NIGHTINGALE** – trombone / **DAVID ROXXE** – narration

Feb 93. (7")(c-s) **IF I EVER LOSE MY FAITH IN YOU. / ALL THIS TIME (live)** [14] [17]
(cd-s+=) – Mad about you (live) / Every breath you take (live).
(cd-s) – ('A'side) / Message in a bottle (live) / Tea in the Sahara (live) / Walking on the Moon (live).

Mar 93. (cd)(c)(lp) **TEN SUMMONER'S TALES** [2] [2]
– Prologue (If I ever lose my faith in you) / Love is stronger than justice (the magnificent seven) / Fields of gold / Heavy cloud no rain / She's too good for me / Seven days / Saint Augustine in Hell / It's probably me / Everybody laughed but you / Shape of my heart / Something the boy said / Epilogue (Nothing 'bout me).

Apr 93. (7")(c-s) **SEVEN DAYS. / JANUARY STARS** [25] [ ]
(cd-s+=) – Mad about you (live) / Ain't no sunshine (live).
(cd-s) – ('A'side) / Island of souls (live) / The wild wild sea (live) / The soul cages (live).

Jun 93. (7")(c-s) **FIELDS OF GOLD. / WE WORK THE BLACK SEAM** [16] [23]
(cd-s) – ('A'side) / King of pain / Fragile / Purple haze (all 3 live).
(cd-s) – ('A'side) / Message in a bottle (live) / Fortress around your heart (live) / Roxanne (live).

Aug 93. (7")(c-s) **SHAPE OF MY HEART. / WALKING ON THE MOON** [57] [ ]
(cd-s) – ('A'side) / The soul cages / The wild wild sea / All this time.

Nov 93. (7")(c-s) **DEMOLITION MAN. / ('A'mix)** [21] [ ]
(cd-s+=) – King of pain (live) / Shape of my heart (live).
(cd-s) – ('A'side) / It's probably me (live) / A day in the life of (live).

— Late 1993, he teamed up with BRYAN ADAMS & ROD STEWART to sing theme from 'The Three Musketeers'; ALL FOR LOVE, which hit UK No.2 & US No.1.

Feb 94. (7")(12")(c-s) **NOTHING 'BOUT ME. / IF I EVER LOSE MY FAITH IN YOU** [32] [57] Sep 93
(cd-s+=) – ('B'mixes) / Demolition man (soul power mix).

Oct 94. (12")(c-s) **WHEN WE DANCE. / FORTRESS AROUND YOUR HEART** [9] [38]
(cd-s) – ('A'side) / If you love somebody set them free (remix) / ('A'remix).

Nov 94. (cd)(c)(d-lp) **FIELDS OF GOLD – THE BEST OF STING 1984-1994** (compilation) [2] [7]
– When we dance / If you love somebody set them free / Fields of gold / All this time / Englishman in New York / Mad about you / It's probably me / They dance alone / If I ever lose my faith in you / Fragile / We'll be together / Nothing 'bout me / Love is the seventh wave / Russians / Seven days / Demolition man / This cowboy song.

— Around same time, Spanish crooner JULIO IGLESIAS covered his 'FRAGILE', which he accompanied with STING.

— (below single featured PATO BANTON)

Jan 95. (c-s) **THIS COWBOY SONG. / IF YOU LOVE SOMEBODY SET THE FREE (Brothers In Rhythm mix)** [15] [ ]
(cd-s+=) – Demolition man (Soul Power mix).
(12"++=) – If you love somebody set them free (extended).
(cd-s) – ('A'side) / ('A'extended) / When we dance (classic) / Take me to the sunshine.

– compilations, others, etc. –

Jul 88. A&M; (cd-ep) **COMPACT HITS** [ ] [-]
– Someone to watch over me / Englishman in New York / If you love somebody set them free / Spread a little happiness.

Feb 90. A&M; (d-c) **DREAM OF THE BLUE TURTLES / NOTHING LIKE THE SUN** [ ] [ ]

Aug 90. A&M; (7")(c-s) **ENGLISHMAN IN NEW YORK (Ben Liebrand mix). / IF YOU LOVE SOMEBODY SET THEM FREE** [15] [-]
(12"+=)(cd-s+=)(pic-cd-s+=) – ('A'original mix) / ('A' Jellybean dance mix).

Nov 91. A&M; (cd-box)(c-box)(lp-box) **ACOUSTIC LIVE IN NEWCASTLE – LIMITED EDITION BOXED SET** [ ] [ ]

Sly STONE (see under ⇒ SLY & THE FAMILY STONE)

STONE PONEYS (see under ⇒ RONSTADT, Linda)

STONE ROSES

Formed: Sale & Chorley, Gtr.Manchester, England ... 1984 by IAN BROWN, JOHN SQUIRE, etc, who took their name from a group called ENGLISH ROSE and The ROLLING STONES. After a MARTIN HANNETT produced 45, they signed a one-off deal with 'Black' records. In 1988, they were snapped up by ANDREW LAUDER's 'Jive' subsidiary label 'Silvertone'. They soon became darlings of the music press after indie success of single 'ELEPHANT STONE'. The following year, when their hit eponymous album was riding high in the UK charts, they exploded into the Top 10 with 'FOOL'S GOLD'. They were then chased by many record labels, but went to court many times in the 90's with Silvertone, who had tied them to a long-term contract. • **Style:** Pioneers of rave psychedelia, who were influenced by near namesakes The ROLLING STONES, LOVE or CAN. • **Songwriters:** Mainly SQUIRE but other members also collaborating. • **Trivia:** Their debut album artwork was a pastiche of a Jackson Pollock splatter job painted by the multi-talented SQUIRE.

Recommended: THE STONE ROSES (*10) / SECOND COMING (*8).

IAN BROWN (b.20 Feb'63, Ancoats, Manchester) – vocals / **JOHN SQUIRE** (b.24 Nov'62, Broadheath, Manchester) – guitar, vocals / **PETER GARNER** – rhythm guitar / **ANDY COUZENS** – bass / **RENI** (b.ALAN WREN, 10 Apr'64, Manchester) – drums

Thin Line | not issued

Sep 85. (12") **SO YOUNG. / TELL ME** [ ] [-]
(re-dist.Mar86)

— now a quartet, when PETER departed.

Black | not issued

May 87. (12"m) **SALLY CINNAMON. / HERE IT COMES / ALL ACROSS THE SANDS** [ ] [-]
(re-iss.Feb89, cd-s iss.Dec89, hit No.46, (+=) – ('A'demo). *(re-iss.7" – 1st 2 tracks +12"+cd-ep on 'FM Revolver')*

— (1987) **GARY 'Mannie' MOUNFIELD** (b.16 Nov'62, Crumpsall, Manchester) – bass, vocals repl. COUZENS who later joined The HIGH.

Silvertone | Silvertone

Oct 88. (7") **ELEPHANT STONE. / THE HARDEST THING IN THE WORLD** [ ] [-]
(12"+=) – Full fathoms five. *(c+cd-s iss.Feb90 hit No.8)*

Mar 89. (7") **MADE OF STONE. / GOING DOWN** [ ] [-]
(12"+=) – Guernica. *(c+cd-s iss.Mar90 hit No.20)*

Apr 89. (lp)(c)(cd) **THE STONE ROSES** [19] [86]
– I wanna be adored / She bangs the drum / Waterfall / Don't stop / Bye bye badman / Elizabeth my dear / (Song for my) Sugar spun sister / Made of stone / Shoot you down / This is the one / I am the resurrection. *(re-iss.Aug91 as 2x12")* (+=) – Elephant stone / Fool's gold.

Jul 89. (7") **SHE BANGS THE DRUM. / STANDING HERE** [36] [-]
(12"+=) – Mersey Paradise.
(c-s+=)(cd-s+=) – Simone. *(re-iss.Mar90, hit No.34)*

Silvertone | Jive

Nov 89. (7") **FOOL'S GOLD. / WHAT THE WORLD IS WAITING FOR** [8] [ ]

(12"+=)(c-s+=)(cd-s+=) – ('A'extended). *(re-iss.Sep90, hit No.22, re-iss.May92, hit No.73) ('A'-The Top Won mix) / ('A'-The Bottom Won mix).*

Jul 90. (7")(12")(c-s)(cd-s) **ONE LOVE. / SOMETHING'S BURNING** 4 □

Sep 91. (7") **I WANNA BE ADORED. / WHERE ANGELS PLAY** 20 -
(12"+=)(cd-s+=) – Sally Cinnamon (live).

Jan 92. (7")(c-s) **WATERFALL (remix). / ONE LOVE (remix)** 27 □
(12"+=)(cd-s+=) – ('A'&'B'extended versions).

Apr 92. (7")(c-s) **I AM THE RESURRECTION. / ('A'Pan & scan radio version)** 33 □
(12"+=) – Fool's gold (The Bottom Won mix).
(cd-s++=) – ('A'-5:3 Stoned Out club mix).

Jul 92. (cd)(c)(lp) **TURNS INTO STONE** (demos & rare) 32 □
– Elephant stone / The hardest thing in the world / Going down / Mersey Paradise / Standing here Where angels play / Simone / Fools gold / What the world is waiting for / One love / Something's burning.

Geffen Geffen

Nov 94. (7")(c-s) **LOVE SPREADS. / YOUR STAR WILL SHINE** 2 □
(cd-s+=) – Breakout.
(12"++=) – Groove harder.

Dec 94. (cd)(c)(lp) **SECOND COMING** 4 47 Jan 95
– Breaking into Heaven / Driving south / Ten storey love song / Daybreak / Your star will shine / Straight to the man / Begging you / Tightrope / Good times / Tears / How do you sleep? / Love spreads. *(cd+=)* – (untitled hidden track No.90).

Feb 95. (7")(c-s) **TEN STOREY LOVE SONG. / RIDE ON** 11 □
(12"+=)(cd-s+=) – Moses.

— In Apr'95, RENI quit and was replaced by **ROBERT MADDIX** (ex-GINA GINA). Will there be a third coming? It looks unlikely squire.

Oct 95. (c-s) **BEGGING YOU / ('A'-Chic mix)** 15 □
(cd-s+=) – ('A'-Stone Corporation mix) / ('A'-Lakota mix) / ('A'-Young American primitive remix).
(12") – ('A'-Carl Cox mix) / ('A'-Development Corporation mix).

– compilations, etc. –

Apr 95. Silvertone; (c-s) **FOOL'S GOLD '95. / ('A'extended mix)** 23 □
(12"+=)(cd-s+=) – ('A'-Tall Paul remix) / (A'-Cricklewood Ballroom mix).

May 95. Silvertone; (cd)(c) **THE COMPLETE STONE ROSES** 4 □

STONE TEMPLE PILOTS

Formed: San Diego, California. USA . . . 1992 by WEILAND, etc. Signed to 'Atlantic' in 1992, and took the US charts by storm with debut US Top 3 album 'CORE'. • **Style:** Heavy laid-back 70's style rock outfit, very similiar to PEARL JAM, although WEILAND's orange-haired mop top differentiated them from contemporaries. • **Songwriters:** Lyrics: WEILAND + R.DeLEO / KRETZ most of music. • **Trivia:** Brendan O'Brien produced their 1993 + '94 albums.

Recommended: CORE (*7) / PURPLE (*6).

WEILAND – vocals / **DEAN DeLEO** – guitar / **ROBERT DeLEO** – bass / **ERIC KRETZ** – drums

Atlantic Atlantic

Mar 93. (7")(c-s) **SEX TYPE THING. / WICKED GARDEN** 60 □
(12"+=)(cd-s+=) Plush (acoustic).

Aug 93. (7")(c-s) **PLUSH. / SEX TYPE THANG (swing version) / PLUSH (acoustic)** 23 □
(12"+=)(cd-s+=) – ('A'side) / ('B'live version) / Sin.

Sep 93. (cd)(c)(lp) **CORE** 27 3 Feb 93
– Dead and bloated / Sex type thang / Wicked garden / No memory / Sin / Creep / Piece of pie / Naked Sunday / Plush / Wet my bed / Crackerman / Where the river goes.

Nov 93. (12")(cd-s) **SEX TYPE THING. / PIECE OF ME** 55 □

Jun 94. (cd)(c)(purple-lp) **PURPLE** 10 1
– Meatplow / Vasoline / Lounge fly / Interstate love song / Still remains / Pretty penny / Silvergun Superman / Big empty / Unglued / Army ants / Kitchenware & candybar!. (cd+c+=) – Gracious melodies.

Jul 94. (12"ep)(c-ep)(cd-ep) **VASOLINE / MEATPLOW. / ANDY WARHOL / CRACKERMAN** 48 □

Dec 94. (7"purple)(c-s) **INTERSTATE LOVE SONG. / LOUNGE FLY** 53 □
(cd-s+=) – Vasoline (live).

STONE THE CROWS

Formed: Glasgow, Scotland . . . 1969 by MAGGIE BELL and LES HARVEY, who had both been in the band POWER. While touring US bases in Germany, they were discovered by LED ZEPPELIN manager Peter Grant, who renamed them STONE THE CROWS. They soon signed to 'Atlantic' in the US, and unleashed two highly regarded albums in 1970. • **Style:** Soulful rock music, fronted by Britain's answer to the late Janis Joplin; MAGGIE BELL. • **Songwriters:** Group compositions, except DANGER ZONE (Curtis Mayfield) / etc?. MAGGIE covered AFTER MIDNIGHT (JJ Cale) / WISHING WELL (Free) / I SAW HIM STANDING THERE (Beatles) / etc. HOLD ME with B.A. Robertson was originally a hit for P.J.Proby. • **Trivia:** The young MAGGIE began her career, after getting up on stage to sing with ALEX HARVEY (brother of LES). She received £2 for her audacity. She augmented ROD STEWART on his rasping lp title track 'Every Picture Tells A Story'.

Recommended: STONE THE CROWS (*7).

MAGGIE BELL (b.12 Jan'45) – vocals / **LES HARVEY** (b.1947) – guitar / **JOHN McGINNIS** – keyboards / **JIM DEWAR** – bass / **COLIN ALLEN** – drums

Polydor Atlantic

Mar 70. (lp) **STONE THE CROWS** □ □
– The touch of your loving hand / Raining in your heart / Blind man / Foot on the hill / I saw America.

Nov 70. (lp) **ODE TO JOHN LAW** □ □
– Sad Mary / Friend / Love 74 / Mad dogs and Englishmen / Things are getting better / Ode to John Law / Danger zone.

Jan 71. (7") **MAD DOGS AND ENGLISHMEN. / SAD MARY** □ □

— **RONNIE LEAHY** – keyboards repl. McGINNIS / **STEVE THOMPSON** – bass repl. DEWAR who joined JUDE, then ROBIN TROWER

1972. (lp) **TEENAGE LICKS** □ □
– Big Jim Salter / Faces / Mr. Wizard / Don't think twice / Keep on rollin' / Aileen Mochree / One five eight / I may be right I may be wrong / Seven lakes.

— Halfway through recording, **JIMMY McCULLOCH** – guitar (ex-THUNDERCLAP NEWMAN) replaced LES HARVEY who was killed by a live stage microphone in '72.

Sep 72. (lp)(c) **'ONTINUOUS PERFORMANCE** 33 □
– On the highway / One more chance / Penicillin blues / King Tut / Good time girl / Niagara / Sunset cowboy.

Oct 72. (7") **GOOD TIME GIRL. / ON THE HIGHWAY** □ □

— Split in June 1973, when McCULLOCH joined Paul McCARTNEY & WINGS.

– compilations, others, etc. –

Oct 76. Polydor/ US= Atlantic; (lp)(c) **STONE THE CROWS** □ □
– Big Jim Salter / Love 74 / Touch of your loving hand / Sad Mary / Good time girl / On the highway / Mr.Wizard / Sunset cowboy / Raining in your heart / Seven lakes. *(re-iss.+cdJun89 on 'Thunderbolt')*

MAGGIE BELL

(solo) with session people.

Polydor Atlantic

Jan 74. (lp)(c) **QUEEN OF THE NIGHT** □ □
– Cado queen / A woman left lonely / Souvenirs / After midnight / Queen of the night / Oh my my / As the years go passing by / Yesterday's music / We had it all / The other side / Trade winds.

Mar 74. (7") **OH MY MY. / AS THE YEARS GO PASSING BY** □ -

Apr 74. (7") **AFTER MIDNIGHT. / SOUVENIRS** - □

Polydor Swan Song

Feb 75. (lp)(c) **SUICIDE SAL** □ □
– Wishing well / Suicide Sal / I was in chains / If you don't know / What you got / In my life / Comin' on strong / Hold on / I saw him standing there / It's been so long.

Mar 75. (7") **WISHING WELL. / COMIN' ON STRONG** - □

Swan Song Swan Song

Mar 78. (7") **HAZELL. / NIGHT FLIGHTING** 37 -
(above from TV series of same name)

MIDNIGHT FLYER

MAGGIE BELL alongside **JOHN COOK** – keys / **ANTHONY GLYNNE** – guitar / **TONE STEVENS** – bass / **DAVID DOWLE** – drums

Swan Song Swan Song

Mar 81. (7") **ROUGH TRADE. / MIDNIGHT LOVE** □ □

Mar 81. (lp)(c) **MIDNIGHT FLYER** □ □
– Hey boy / Love games / French kisses / In my eyes / Over and over / Last resort / Do you want my love / Sweet loving woman / Whatever I want / Midnight flyer / Rough trade.

Jun 81. (7") **IN MY EYES. /** - □

Apr 82. (7") **WAITING FOR YOU. / ROCK'N'ROLL PARTY** □ □

B.A.ROBERTSON & MAGGIE BELL

made one-off duet on same label. ROBERTSON was already an accomplished solo pop artist in his own right.

Oct 81. (7") **HOLD ME. / SPRING GREEN** 11 □

MAGGIE BELL

(solo again) same label

Sep 82. (7") **GOOSE BUMPS. / KEY TO MY HEART** □ □

Dec 82. (7") **CRAZY. / ALL I HAVE TO DO IS DREAM** □ □

Mar 83. (7";w/ BOBBY WHITLOCK) **HERE, THERE & EVERY-WHERE. / PUT ANGELS AROUND YOU** - □

Cult not issued

1988. (lp)(c)(cd) **CRIMES OF THE HEART** □ -
– Crimes of the heart / Love me stranger / Tonight / Burned out love affair / Endless night / I'm on the edge / Living a lie / Vision.

STOOGES (see under ⇒ POP, Iggy)

STORIES (see under ⇒ LEFT BANKE)

STORM (see under ⇒ JOURNEY)

STRANGE CRUISE (see under ⇒ VISAGE)

STRANGLERS

Formed: Chiddington, Surrey, England . . . Autumn 1974 as The GUILDFORD STRANGLERS by ex-science teacher HUGH CORNWALL, history graduate JEAN JACQUES BURNEL and jazz drummer JET BLACK. They were joined by DAVE GREENFIELD in the Spring of 1975 and started touring mainly local pubs. Late in 1976, after gigs supporting FLAMIN' GROOVIES and The RAMONES, they signed to 'United Artists'. Their first 45 'GRIP', gave them entry into the UK Top 50, and would have gone higher, but for a chart mistake. Their debut album in 1977 'RATTUS NORVEGICUS', gave them first of many Top 10 triumphs, and contained the banned hit single 'PEACHES'. • **Style:** Innovators of new wave/punk who moulded themselves around influences from The DOORS, ELECTRIC PRUNES or DR.FEELGOOD. Accused by critics of controversially using sexist lyrics and lurid stage shows, where they were joined by strippers. In the early 80's, they shifted into more experimental pop. • **Songwriters:** Mostly CORNWALL penned except some by BURNEL. They also covered; 96 TEARS (? & The Mysterians) / WALK ON BY (Bacharach-David) / ALL DAY AND ALL OF THE NIGHT (Kinks). • **Miscellaneous:** On 7 Jan'80, CORNWALL was found guilty of drug possession, and was sentenced to 3 months in prison and fined. In June that year, they were all arrested in Nice, France, after being accused of inciting a riot at a gig. They were threatened with long jail sentences, but were set free and later fined, claiming it was 'NICE IN NICE'.

Recommended: RATTUS NORVEGICUS (*9) / NO MORE HEROES (*8) / BLACK AND WHITE (*8) / LIVE CERT (*8) / AURAL SCULPTURE (*6) / DREAMTIME (*7) / THE STRANGLERS' GREATEST HITS (*9).

HUGH CORNWALL (b.28 Aug'48, London, England) – vocals, guitar / **JEAN-JAQUES BURNEL** (b.21 Feb'52, London; French parents) – bass, vocals / **DAVE GREENFIELD** – keyboards / **JET BLACK** (b.BRIAN DUFFY, 26 Aug'43) – drums

United Art | A & M

Jan 77. (7") **(GET A) GRIP (ON YOURSELF). / LONDON LADY** | 44 | -
Apr 77. (lp)(c) **STRANGLERS IV – RATTUS NORVEGICUS** | 4 |
– Sometimes / Goodbye Toulouse / London lady / Princess of the streets / Hanging around / Peaches / (Get a) Grip (on yourself) / Ugly / Down in the sewer: (a) Falling – (b) Down in the sewer – (c) Trying to get out again – (d) Rats rally. *(free ltd.7"w.a.)* **CHOOSEY SUSIE. / IN THE BIG SHITTY** *(re-iss.May82 on 'Fame', cd-iss.Apr88) (cd-iss.Feb88 on 'Liberty')*
May 77. (7") **PEACHES. / GO BUDDY GO** | 8 | -

— Jun77; They backed CELIA & THE MUTATIONS on cover single 'MONY MONY'.

Jul 77. (7") **SOMETHING BETTER CHANGE. / STRAIGHTEN OUT** | 9 | -
Sep 77. (7") **NO MORE HEROES. / IN THE SHADOWS** | 8 | -
Oct 77. (lp)(c) **NO MORE HEROES** | 2 |
– I feel like a wog / Bitching / Dead ringer / Dagenham Dave / Bring on the nubiles / Something better change / No more heroes / Peasant in the big shitty / Burning up time / Dagenham Dave / English towns / School mam / In the shadows. *(re-iss.1985) (cd-iss.Feb88 on 'EMI') (re-iss.Sep87 on 'Fame', cd-iss.Aug88)*
Nov 77. (7"pink-ep) **SOMETHING BETTER CHANGE / STRAIGHTEN OUT. / GRIP / HANGIN' AROUND** | - |
Jan 78. (7") **FIVE MINUTES. / ROK IT TO THE MOON** | 11 | -
Apr 78. (7") **NICE 'N' SLEAZY. / SHUT UP** | 18 | Aug 78
May 78. (lp)(c)(US-grey-lp) **BLACK AND WHITE** | 2 |
– Tank / Nice 'n' sleazy / Outside Tokyo / Mean to me / Sweden (all quiet on the Eastern Front) / Hey! (rise of the robots) / Toiler on the sea / Curfew / Threatened / Do you wanna? – Death and night and blood (Yukio) / In the shadows / Enough time / Walk on by. *(free ltd.7"w.a.)* **WALK ON BY / TITS / MEAN TO ME** *(re-iss.Jan86 on 'Epic') (cd-iss.Jul88 on 'EMI' += free 7" tracks)*
Jul 78. (7"m) **WALK ON BY. / OLD CODGER / TANK** | 21 |
Mar 79. (lp)(c) **X-CERT (live)** | 7 |
– (Get a) Grip (on yourself) / Dagenham Dave / Burning up time / Dead ringer / Hanging around / I feel like a wog / Straighten out / Do you wanna – Death and night and blood (Yukio) / Five minutes / Go buddy go. *(re-iss.1985) (cd-iss.Jul88)* (cd+=) – In the shadows / Peasant in the big shitty.
Aug 79. (7") **DUCHESS. / FOOLS RUSH OUT** | 14 |
Sep 79. (lp)(c) **THE RAVEN** | 4 |
– Longships / The raven / Dead Loss Angeles / Ice / Baroque bordello / Nuclear device / Shah shah a go go / Don't bring Harry / Duchess / Meninblack / Genetix. *(re-iss.1985 on 'Fame', cd-iss.Aug88) (cd-iss.Oct87 on 'EMI'+=)* – Bear cage.
Oct 79. (7") **NUCLEAR DEVICE (THE WIZARD OF AUS). / YELLOWCAKE UF6** | 36 |
Nov 79. (7"ep) **DON'T BRING HARRY** | 41 |
– Don't bring Harry / Wired / Crabs (live) / In the shadows (live).

Liberty | I.R.S.

Jan 80. (7") **DUCHESS. / THE RAVEN** | - |
Jan 80. (lp) **STRANGLERS IV** | - |
– (5 tracks from 'THE RAVEN', plus recent singles)
(above w/ free 7"ep) – Do The European / Choosie Suzie / Wired / Straighten out.
Mar 80. (7")(12") **BEAR CAGE. / SHAH SHAH A GO GO** | 36 |
May 80. (7") **WHO WANTS THE WORLD. / MENINBLACK** | 39 |
Jan 81. (7") **THROWN AWAY. / TOP SECRET** | 42 |
Feb 81. (lp)(c) **THE MEN• IN• BLACK** | 8 |
– Waltzinblack / Just like nothing on Earth / Second coming / Waiting for the men in black / Turn the centuries, turn / Two sunspots / Four horsemen / Thrown away / Manna machine / Hallo to our men. *(re-iss.1985) (re-iss.+cd.Sep88 on 'Fame'; cd+=)* – Top secret / Maninwhite.
Mar 81. (7") **JUST LIKE NOTHING ON EARTH. / MANINWHITE** | |
Nov 81. (7") **LET ME INTRODUCE YOU TO THE FAMILY. / VIETNAMERICA** | 42 |
Nov 81. (lp)(c) **LA FOLIE** | 11 |
– Non stop / Everybody loves you when you're dead / Tramp / Let me introduce you to the family / The man they love to hate / Pin up / It only takes two to tango / Golden brown / How to find true love and happiness in the present day / La folie. *(re-iss.Nov83 on 'Fame', cd-iss.Aug88) (cd-iss.Feb88)*
Jan 82. (7") **GOLDEN BROWN. / LOVE 30** | 2 |
Apr 82. (7") **LA FOLIE. / WALTZINBLACK** | 47 |
Jul 82. (7") **STRANGE LITTLE GIRL. / CRUEL GARDEN** | 7 |
Sep 82. (lp)(c) **THE COLLECTION 1977-1982** (compilation) | 12 |
– (Get a) Grip (on yourself) / Peaches / Hanging around / No more heroes / Duchess / Walk on by / Waltzinblack / Something better change / Nice'n'sleazy / Bear cage / Who wants the world / Golden brown / Strange little girl / La folie. *(re-iss.+cd.1985) (re-iss.+cd.Aug89 on 'Fame')*

Epic | Epic

Nov 82. (7")(7"pic-d) **THE EUROPEAN FEMALE. / SAVAGE BEAST** | 9 |
Jan 83. (lp)(c) **FELINE** | 4 |
– Midnight summer dream / It's a small world / Ships that pass in the night / The European female / Let's tango in Paris / Paradise / All roads lead to Rome / Blue sister / Never say goodbye. *(free ltd.one-sided-7"w.a.)* **AURAL SCULPTURE** *(re-iss.Apr86)* (US lp+=) – Golden brown. *(cd-iss.Dec92)*
Feb 83. (7")(12") **MIDNIGHT SUMMER DREAM. / VLADIMIR AND OLGA** | 35 | -
Jul 83. (7") **PARADISE. / PAWSHER** | 48 | -
(12"+=) – Permission.
Jul 83. (12") **MIDNIGHT SUMMER DREAM. / PARADISE** | - |
Sep84. (7") **SKIN DEEP. / HERE AND NOW** | 15 |
(12"+=) – Vladimir and the beast.
Nov 84. (lp)(c) **AURAL SCULPTURE** | 14 |
– Ice queen / Skin deep / Let me down easy / No mercy / North winds / Uptown / Punch & Judy / Spain / Laughing / Souls / Mad Hatter. *(re-iss.+cd.May87) (re-iss.cd Sep93 on 'Sony Collectors')*
Nov 84. (7")(7"sha-pic-d) **NO MERCY. / IN ONE DOOR** | 37 |
(12"+=)(US-c-s+=) – Hot club.
Feb 85. (7") **LET ME DOWN EASY. / ACHILLES HEEL** | 48 |
(12"+=) – Place des victories.
(12"++=) – Vladimir goes to Havana / Aural sculpture manifesto.
Aug 86. (7")(12")(7"sha-pic-d) **NICE IN NICE. / SINCE YOU WENT AWAY** | 30 |
Oct 86. (7")(7"sha-pic-d) **ALWAYS THE SUN. / NORMAN NORMAL** | 30 |
(12"+=) – Soul.
Oct 86. (lp)(c)(cd)(pic-lp) **DREAMTIME** | 16 |
– Always the sun / Dreamtime / Was it you? / You'll always reap what you sow / Ghost train / Nice in Nice / Big in America / Shakin' like a leaf / Mayan skies / Too precious. *(re-iss.Feb89)*
Dec 86. (7")(7"sha-pic-d) **BIG IN AMERICA. / DRY DAY** | 48 |
(12"+=) – Uptown.
Feb 87. (7")(7"sha-pic-d) **SHAKIN' LIKE A LEAF. / HIT MAN** | 58 |
(12"+=) – Was it you?.
Dec 87. (7")(7"sha-pic-d) **ALL DAY AND ALL OF THE NIGHT (live). / VIVA VLAD** | 7 |
(12"+=) – Who wants the world (live).
(cd-s+=) – Strange little girl.
Feb 88. (lp)(c)(cd) **ALL LIVE AND ALL OF THE NIGHT (live)** | 12 |
– No more heroes / Was it you? / Down in the sewer / Always the sun / Golden brown / North winds / The European female / Strange little girl / Nice 'n' sleazy / Toiler on the sea / Spain / London lady / All day and all of the night.
Feb 90. (7")(c-s) **96 TEARS. / INSTEAD OF THIS** | 17 |
(12"+=)(cd-s+=) – Poisonality.
Mar 90. (cd)(c)(lp)(pic-lp) **10** | 15 |
– The sweet smell of success / Someone like you / 96 tears / In this place / Let's celebrate / Man of the Earth / Too many teardrops / Where I live / Out of my mind / Never to look back. *(re-iss.cd Dec92)*
Apr 90. (7")(c-s)(7"pic-d) **THE SWEET SMELL OF SUCCESS. / MOTORBIKE** | 65 |
(12"+=)(cd-s+=) – Something.
Nov 90. (cd)(c)(lp) **THE STRANGLERS' GREATEST HITS 1977-1990** (complation) | 4 |
– Something better change / No more heroes / Walk on by / Duchess / Golden brown / Strange little girl / European female / Skin deep / Nice in Nice / Always the Sun / Big in America / All day and all of the night / 96 tears / No mercy / Peaches.
Jan 91. (7")(c-s) **ALWAYS THE SUN. / BURNHAM BEECHES** | 29 | -
(12"+=) – Straighten out.
(cd-s) – ('A'side) / Nuclear device (live) / All day and all of the night (live) / Punch and Judy (live).
Mar 91. (7")(c-s) **GOLDEN BROWN (re-mix). / YOU** | 68 | -
(cd-s+=) – Skin deep (extended) / Peaches.

— (late 1990) **JOHN ELLIS** – guitar, vocals (once p/t member) (ex-VIBRATORS, etc.) repl. CORNWALL who has already ventured solo.

— (Jan91) also added **PAUL ROBERTS** – vocals

China | not issued

Aug 92. (7") **HEAVEN OR HELL. / DISAPPEAR** | 46 | -
(12"ep+=)(c-ep+=)(cd-ep+=) – Brainbox / Hanging around.
Sep 92. (cd)(c)(lp) **STRANGLERS IN THE NIGHT** | 33 | -
– Time to die / Sugar bullets / Heaven or Hell / Laughing at the rain / This town / Brainbox / Southern mouintains / Gain entry to your soul / Grand canyon / Wet afternoon / Never see / Leave it to the dogs.
Oct 92. (7")(c-s) **SUGAR BULLETS. / SO UNCOOL** | | -
(12"+=)(cd-s+=) – ('A'version).

Essential | not issued

Jun 93. (cd)(c)(lp) **SATURDAY NIGHT SUNDAY MORNING** | |
– Toiler on the sea / 96 Tears / Always the sun / No more heroes / Golden brown / Tank / Strange little girl / Something better change / Hanging around / All day and all of the night / Duchess / *Medley / Was it you? / Down in the sewer.

— In Jun'93, old Strangler HUGH CORNWALL released album 'WIRED' on 'Transmission' label. Nearly a year earlier as CCW, he, ROGER COOK & AND WEST issued cd 'CCW FEATURING HUGH CORNWALL • ROGER COOK • ANDY WEST' on 'UFO'.

When!- Castle | not issued

May 95. (cd)(c)(lp) **ABOUT TIME** | 31 | -
– Golden boy / Money / Sinister / Little blue lies / Still life / Paradise row / She gave it all / Lies and deception / Lucky finger / And the boat sails by.
Jun 95. (12")(cd-s) **LIES AND DECEPTION. / SWIM / DANNY COOL** | | -
(cd-s) – ('A'side) / Kiss the world goodbye / Bed of nails.

- more compilations, etc. -

Mar 84. Old Gold; (7") **GOLDEN BROWN. / STRANGE LITTLE GIRL** [ ] [-]
Sep 86. Liberty; (lp)(c) **OFF THE BEATEN TRACK** [80] [-]
Nov 88. Liberty; (lp)(c) **RARITIES** [ ] [-]
Jan 89. EMI; (7")(7"red) **GRIP '89. / WALTZINBLACK** [33] [-]
(12"+=)/ /(cd-s++=) – Tomorrow was thereafter./ / ('A'mix).
Feb 89. EMI; (lp)(c)(cd) **THE SINGLES** [57] [-]
May 92. EMI; (cd) **LIVE AT THE HOPE AND ANCHOR (live)** [ ] [-]
(re-iss.Feb95 on 'Fame')
Dec 92. EMI; (4xcd-box) **THE OLD TESTAMENT – THE U.A. STUDIO RECORDINGS (demos)** [ ] [-]
Jun 89. Nighttracks; (12"ep) **RADIO 1 SESSION (1982)** [ ] [-]
– The man they love to hate / Nuclear device / Genetix / Down in the sewer.
Feb 92. Newspeak; (cd)(c)(d-lp) **THE EARLY YEARS 74-75-76, RARE LIVE & UNRELEASED** [ ] [-]
May 94. Receiver; (cd) **DEATH AND NIGHT AND BLOOD** [ ] [-]
Jun 94. Castle; (cd) **THE EARLY YEARS 1974-76** [ ] [-]
Feb 95. Receiver; (cd) **LIVE IN CONCERT (live w/ FRIENDS)** [ ] [-]
Nov 95. Old Gold; (cd-s) **GOLDEN BROWN / NO MORE HEROES** [ ] [-]

J.J. BURNEL

solo with **BRIAN JAMES** – guitar / **CAREY FORTUNE** – drums / **LEW LEWIS** – harmonica

United Art / not issued

Mar 79. (7") **FREDDIE LAKER (CONCORDE AND EUROBUS). / OZYMANDIAS** [ ] [-]
Apr 79. (lp)(c) **EUROMAN COMETH** [40] [-]
– Euroman / Jellyfish / Freddie Laker (Concorde and Eurobus) / Euroness / Deutschland nicht uber alles / Do the European / Tout comprendre / Triumph (of the good city) / Pretty face / Crabs / Eurospeed (your own speed). *(re-iss.Feb88 on 'Mau Mau') (re-iss.+cd.Jan92 on 'EMI' with cd 35 mins extra)*

—— toured with **ELLIS, PETER HOWELLS & PENNY TOBIN.** (below withdrawn)

Jul 80. (7") **GIRL FROM SNOW COUNTRY. / ODE TO JOY (live) / DO THE EUROPEAN (live)** [-] [-]

DAVE GREENFIELD & JEAN-JAQUES BURNEL

Epic / Epic

Dec 83. (lp)(c) **FIRE AND WATER** [ ] [-]
– Liberation / Rain, dole & tea / Vladimir and Sergei / Le soir / Trois pedophiles pour Eric Sabyr ino rap / Nuclear power (yes please) / Detective privee / Consequences.
Feb 84. (7") **RAIN, DOLE & TEA. / CONSEQUENCES** [ ] [-]

—— In 1989, they with ALEX GIFFORD, MANNY ELIAS and JOHN ELLIS splintered as The PURPLE HELMUTS. They made an album RIDE AGAIN for 'New Rose' Jan89.

J.J. BURNEL

Epic / Epic

1988. (7") **LE WHISKEY. / EL WHISKEY** [-] [-] France
(12"+=)(cd-s+=) – Garden of Eden.
1988. (lp)(c)(cd) **UN JOUR PARFAIT** [-] [-] France
1988. (7") **REVES. / (SHE DRIVES ME) CRAZY** [-] [-] France
(12"+=)(cd-s+=) – ('A'extended).

HUGH CORNWALL & ROBERT WILLIAMS

with **ROBERT WILLIAMS** – drums, bass, guitar, vocals, synthesizer / **MARK + BOB MOTHERSBAUGH** – synth + guitar (of DEVO) / **DAVID WALLDROOP** – guitar / **IAN UNDERWOOD** – synth, saxes

United Art / not issued

Oct 79. (lp)(c) **NOSFERATU** [ ] [-]
– Nosferatu / Losers in a lost land / White room / Irate caterpillar / Rhythmic itch / Wired / Big bug / Mothra / Wrong way round / Puppets. *(cd-iss.May92 on 'EMI')*
Nov 79. (7") **WHITE ROOM. / LOSERS IN A LOST LAND** [ ] [-]

HUGH CORNWALL

—— (solo with session people)

Portrait / Portrait

Sep 85. (7")(12") **ONE IN A MILLION. / SIREN SONG** [ ] [-]
Sep 85. (lp)(c) **BLEEDING STAR (Various Soundtracks)** [ ] [-]

Virgin / Virgin?

Jan 87. (7")(12") **FACTS AND FIGURES. / ('A'version)** [ ] [-]
Apr 88. (7") **ANOTHER KIND OF LOVE. / REAL PEOPLE** [ ] [-]
(12"+=)(cd-s+=) – Nothing but the groove / Where is this place . . .
Jun 88. (lp)(c)(cd) **WOLF** [98] [-]
– Another kind of love / Cherry rare / Never never / Real slow / Break of dawn / Clubland / Dreaming away / Decadence / All the tea in China / Getting involved.
Jul 88. (7") **DREAMING AWAY. / BLUE NOTE** [ ] [-]
(12"+=)/ /(cd-s++=) – Getting involved./ / The English walk.

In May92, ex-member HUGH CORNWALL teamed up with COOK & WEST (ex-BLUE MINK) to release single 'Sweet Sister'.

STRAWBERRY ALARM CLOCK

Formed: West Coast, California, U.S.A . . . 1966 originally as THREE SIXPENCE by MARK WEITZ. By the end of 1967, they were at the top of the US singles chart with 'INCENSE & PEPPERMINTS'. (16 year-old GREG MUNFORD (of The SHAPES) provided the vox). However, after a hit album and another Top 30 single, they faded into obscurity. • **Style:** Oriental jazz rock outfit. • **Songwriters:** WEITZ penned except GOOD MORNING STARSHINE (from 'Hair'). • **Trivia:** In 1968, they contributed 3 tracks to 'Psych-Out' film soundtrack on 'Sidewalk' records.

Recommended: STRAWBERRIES MEAN LOVE (*7)

LEE FREEMAN – vocals, rhythm guitar, harmonica / **MARK WEITZ** – organ, piano, vocals / **ED KING** – lead guitar, vocals / **GARY LOVETRO** – bass, vocals / **GEORGE BUNNELL** – bass, vocals, effects / **RANDY SEOL** – drums, percussion, vocals

Pye Int. / Uni

Oct 67. (7") **INCENSE & PEPPERMINTS. / THE BIRDMAN OF ALKATRASH** [ ] [1] Sep 67
Nov 67. (lp) **INCENSE & PEPPERMINTS** [ ] [11] Oct 67
– The world's on fire / Birds in my tree / Lose to live / Strawberries mean love / Rainy day mushroom pillow / Paxton's back street carnival / Hummin' happy / Pass time with Sac / Incense & peppermints / Unwind with the clock.

—— now without LOVETRO

Jan 68. (7") **TOMORROW. / BIRDS IN THE TREES** [ ] [23] Dec 67
Mar 68. (lp) **WAKE UP, IT'S TOMORROW** [-] [ ]
– Nightmare of percussion / Soft skies, no lies / Tomorrow / They saw the fat one coming / Curse of the witches / Sit with the guru / Go back (you're going the wrong way) / The pretty song (from 'Psych-Out') / Sitting on a star / Black butter – past / Black butter – present / Black butter – future.
Apr 68. (7") **SIT WITH THE GURU. / THE PRETTY SONG (from 'PSYCH-OUT')** [ ] [65] Mar 68
Aug 68. (7") **BAREFOOT IN BALTIMORE. / ANGRY YOUNG MAN** [-] [67]
Nov 68. (lp) **WORLD IN A SEA SHELL** [-] [ ]
– Sea shell / Blues for a young girl gone / An angry young man / A million miles away / Home sweet home / Lady of the lake / Barefoot in Baltimore / Wooden woman / Heated love / Love me again / Eulogy / Shallow impressions.
Nov 68. (7") **SEA SHELL. / PAXTON'S BACKSTREET CARNIVAL** [-] [ ]

—— **JIMMY PITMAN** – guitar, vocals + **GENE GUNNELS** – drums repl. BUNNELL + SEOL

M.C.A. / Uni

Mar 69. (7") **MISS ATTRACTION. / STAND BY** [-] [ ]
Nov 69. (7") **GOOD MORNING STARSHINE. / ME AND THE TOWNSHIP** [ ] [87] May 69
Jan 70. (lp) **GOOD MORNING STARSHINE** [-] [ ]
– Me and the township / Off ramp road ramp / Small package / Hog child / Miss Attraction – Good morning Starshine – Miss Attraction / Write your name in gold / (You put me on) Standby / Dear Joy / Changes.
1970. (7") **CHANGES. / DESIREE** [-] [ ]
1970. (7") **SMALL PACKAGE. / STARTING OUT THE DAY** [-] [ ]
1970. (7") **I CLIMBED THE MOUNTAIN. / THREE** [-] [ ]
1970. (7") **CALIFORNIA DAY. / THREE** [-] [ ]
1971. (7") **GIRL FROM THE CITY. / THREE** [-] [ ]
Mar 71. (lp) **THE BEST OF STRAWBERRY ALARM CLOCK** (compilation) [-] [ ]

—— Disbanded 1970 and ED KING later joined LYNYRD SKYNYRD. All the rest seemed to disappear from music scene.

- other compilations, etc. -

1969. Vocalion; (lp) **CHANGES** [ ] [-]
Mar 87. Big Beat; (m-lp)(c) **STRAWBERRIES MEAN LOVE** [ ] [-]
– Incense & peppermints / Rainy day mushroom pillow / Sit with the guru / Tomorrow / Black butter – present / Love me again / The pretty song (from 'Psych-Out'). *(cd-iss.Jan92)*

STRAWBS

Formed: London, England . . . 1967 as The STRAWBERRY HILL BOYS by Leicester University student DAVE COUSINS and schoolfriend TONY HOOPER. In 1969, after SANDY DENNY flitted to The FAIRPORTS, they signed to major 'A&M' records and released eponymous debut. Their third album 'JUST A COLLECTION . . . ' gave them maiden entry into UK Top 30. • **Style:** Initially a folk-bluegrass band influenced by EWAN MacCOLL. In 1972 with the earlier addition of classically trained RICK WAKEMAN, they turned their heads to rock and pop, and various other directions. • **Songwriters:** COUSINS or HUDSON-FORD (the latter pair between 1970 + 1973). • **Trivia:** Off-shoot duo HUDSON-FORD, had a major Top 10 hit in 1973 with 'PICK UP THE PIECES', followed No.15 hit by 'BURN BABY BURN' in '74.

Recommended: A CHOICE SELECTION OF STRAWBS (*7).

DAVE COUSINS (b. 7 Jan'45, Leicester, England) – vocals, guitar, banjo / **TONY HOOPER** – guitar, vocals / **KEN GUDMAND** – drums / **RON CHESTERMAN** – bass / **ARTHUR PHILLIPS** – mandolin / added **SANDY DENNY** – vocals
They recorded album 'ALL OUR OWN WORK' as SANDY DENNY & THE STRAWBS which was issued by 'Hallmark' in 1974. DENNY joined FAIRPORT CONVENTION.
DAVE, TONY & RON employed session men **RONNIE WERRELL** – drums / **ALAN PARKER** – guitar / **ALAN NEIGHBOUR** – bass

A & M / A & M

Jun 68. (7") **OH HOW SHE CHANGED. / OR AM I DREAMING** [ ] [-]
Nov 68. (7") **THE MAN WHO CALLED HIMSELF JESUS. / POOR JIMMY WILSON** [ ] [-]
May 69. (lp) **STRAWBS** [ ] [-]
– The man who called himself Jesus / That which was once mine / All the little ladies / Pieces of 79 & 15 / Tell me what you see in me / Oh how she changed / Or am I dreaming / Where is this dream of your youth / Poor Jimmy Wilson / Where am I – I'll show you where to sleep / The battle. *(re-iss.+c.1974)*

—— basic trio added **CLAIRE DENIZ** – cello

Jul 70. (7") **FOREVER. / ANOTHER DAY** [ ] [-]
Jul 70. (lp) **DRAGONFLY** [ ] [-]
– The weary song / Dragonfly / I turned my face into the wind / Josephine, for better or for worse / Another day / Till the sun comes shining through / Young again / The vision of the lady of the lake / Close your eyes. *(re-iss.+c.1974)*

— **RICHARD HUDSON** – drums / **JOHN FORD** – bass (both ex-VELVET OPERA) / **RICK WAKEMAN** – keyboards (who guested on last lp) repl. RON + CLAIRE

Nov 70. (lp)(c) **JUST A COLLECTION OF ANTIQUES AND CURIOS** [27] [ ]
– Martin Luther King's dream / The antique suite: The reaper – We must cross the river – Antiques and curios – Hey, it's been a long time / Temperament of mind / Fingertips / Song of a sad little girl / Where is this dream of your youth (live). *(re-iss.1974)*
Jan 71. (7") **WHERE IS THE DREAM OF YOUR YOUTH (live). /** [-] [ ]
Jul 71. (lp)(c) **FROM THE WITCHWOOD** [39] [ ]
– A glimpse of Heaven / Witchwood / Thirty days / Flight / The hangman & the papist / Sheep / Canon Dale / The shepherd's song / In amongst the roses / I'll carry on beside you. *(re-iss.1974)*

— **BLUE WEAVER** – keyboards (ex-AMEN CORNER) repl. WAKEMAN who joined YES

Feb 72. (lp)(c) **GRAVE NEW WORLD** [11] [ ]
– Benidictus / Hey little man . . .Thursday's child / Queen of dreams / Heavy disguise / New world / Hey little man . . . Wednesday's child / The flower and the young man / Tomorrow / On growing older / Ah me, ah my / Is it today, Lord? / The journey's end.
Feb 72. (7") **BENIDICTUS. / KEEP THE DEVIL OUTSIDE** [ ] [-]
Apr 72. (7") **HERE IT COMES. / TOMORROW** [ ] [-]
Jun 72. (7") **BENEDICTUS. / HEAVY DISGUISE** [-] [ ]

— In Sep72, DAVE COUSINS issued a solo single GOING HOME. / WAYS AND MEANS plus an album TWO WEEKS LAST SUMMER for 'A&M'.

— **DAVE LAMBERT** – guitar, vocals repl. HOOPER

Oct 72. (7") **LAY DOWN. / BACKSIDE** [12] [-]
Jan 73. (7") **PART OF THE UNION. / WILL YOU GO** [2] [-]
Feb 73. (lp)(c) **BURSTING AT THE SEAMS** [2] [ ]
– Flying / Lady Fuchsia / Stormy down / Down by the sea / The river / Part of the union / Tears and Pavan medley / The winter and the summer / Lay down / Thank you.
Apr 73. (7") **PART OF THE UNION. / TOMORROW** [-] [ ]
Aug 73. (7") **LAY DOWN. / THE WINTER AND THE SUMMER** [-] [ ]

— **COUSINS + LAMBERT** recruited new members **CHAS CRONK** – bass / **ROD COOMBES** – drums (ex-STEALER'S WHEEL) repl. HUDSON-FORD who formed own band **JOHN HAWKEN** – keyboards (ex-NASHVILLE TEENS, ex-RENAISSANCE, ex-VINEGAR JOE) repl. BLUE WEAVER

Aug 73. (7") **SHINE ON SILVER SUN. / AND WHEREFORE** [34] [ ] Nov 73
Apr 74. (7") **HERO AND HEROINE. / WHY** [ ] [-]
Apr 74. (7") **ROUND AND ROUND. / HEROINE'S THEME** [-] [ ]
Apr 74. (lp)(c) **HERO AND HEROINE** [35] [94] Feb 74
– Autumn: (a) Heroine's theme – (b) Deep summer sleep – (c) The winter long / Sad young man / Just love / Shine on silver sun / Hero and heroine / Midnight sun / Out in the cold / Round and round / Lay a little light on me / Hero's theme.
May 74. (7") **HOLD ON TO ME. / WHERE DID YOU GO** [ ] [ ]
Aug 74. (lp)(c) **STRAWBS BY CHOICE** (compilation) [ ] [ ]
– The man who called himself Jesus / Another day / Forever / Song of a sad little girl / The shepherd's song / Benedictus / Here it comes / The actor / Lay down / Lay a little light on me.
Nov 74. (7") **GRACE DARLING. / CHANGES ARRANGED** [ ] [-]
Nov 74. (lp)(c) **GHOSTS** [ ] [47] Feb 75
– Ghosts: Sweet dreams – Night light – Guardian angel / Lemon pie / Starshine – Angel wine / Where do you go (when you need a hole to crawl in) / The life auction: Impressions of Southall from the train – The auction / Don't try to change me / Remembering / You and I / Grace darling.
Apr 75. (7") **LEMON PIE. / DON'T TRY TO CHANGE ME** [ ] [-]
Jun 75. (7") **LEMON PIE. / WHERE DO YOU GO (WHEN YOU NEED A HOLE TO CRAWL IN)** [-] [ ]
Nov 75. (7") **LITTLE SLEEPY. / THE GOLDEN SALAMANDER** [-] [ ]
Nov 75. (lp)(c) **NOMADNESS** [ ] [ ] Oct 75
– To be free / Little Sleepy / The golden salamander / Absent friend (how I need you) / Back on the farm / So shall our love die? / Tokyo Rosie / A mind of my own / Hanging in the gallery / The promised land.

Oyster Oyster

Jul 76. (7") **I ONLY WANT MY LOVE TO GROW IN YOU. / THINKING OF YOU** [ ] [ ]
Sep 76. (lp)(c) **DEEP CUTS** [ ] [ ]
– I only want my love to grow in you / Turn me round / Hard, hard winter / My friend Peter / The soldier's tale / Simple visions / Charmer / (Wasting my time) Thinking of you / Beside the Rio Grande / So close and yet so far away.
Oct 76. (7") **CHARMER. / BESIDE THE RIO GRANDE** [ ] [ ]
Dec 76. (7") **SO CLOSE AND YET SO FAR AWAY. / THE SOLDIER'S TALE** [ ] [ ]
May 77. (7") **BACK IN THE OLD ROUTINE. / BURNING FOR ME** [ ] [ ]
Jun 77. (lp)(c) **BURNING FOR YOU** [ ] [ ]
– Burning for me / Cut like a diamond / I feel your loving coming on / Barcarole / Alexander The Great / Keep on trying / Back in the old routine / Heartbreaker / Carry me home / Goodbye.
Aug 77. (7") **KEEP ON TRYING. / SIMPLE VISIONS** [ ] [ ]

Arista Arista

Jan 78. (7") **JOEY AND ME. / DEADLY NIGHTSHADE** [ ] [-]
Feb 78. (lp)(c) **DEADLINES** [ ] [ ]
– Deadlines (no return) / Joey and me / Sealed with a traitor's kiss / I don't want to talk about it / The last resort / Time and life / New beginnings / Deadly nightshade / Words of wisdom.
Mar 78. (7") **NEW BEGINNINGS. / WORDS OF WISDOM** [ ] [-]
Apr 78. (7") **I DON'T WANT TO TALK ABOUT IT. / WORDS OF WISDOM** [-] [ ]
Oct 78. (7") **I DON'T WANT TO TALK ABOUT IT. / THE LAST RESORT** [ ] [-]

— Folded in 1978. In Sep79, on 'Slurp' records, COUSINS made another solo album 'OLD SCHOOL SONGS' augmented by guitarist **BRIAN WILLOUGHBY**. In mid'83, **COUSINS + HOOPER** re-formed **The STRAWBS** with **CHAS CRONK** – bass / **TONY FERNANDEZ** – drums (both of RICK WAKEMAN's band). (below 45 feat. MADDY PRIOR)

Lo Lo not issued

Nov 80. (7") **THE KING. / RINGING DOWN THE YEARS** [ ] [-]

— Early in 1987, **COUSINS, HOOPER, WILLOUGHBY, HUDSON** brought in **CHRIS PARREN** – keyboards (ex-HUDSON-FORD) / **ROD DEMICK** – bass (ex-WHEELS)

Feb 87. (7") **THAT'S WHEN THE CRYING STARTS. / WE CAN MAKE IT TOGETHER** [-] [ ]
(released on 'Virgin Canada')

Toots not issued

May 87. (lp)(c) **DON'T SAY GOODBYE** [ ] [-]
– A boy and his dog / Let it rain / We can make it together / Tina dei fada / Big brother / Something for nothing / Evergreen / That's when the crying starts / Beat the retreat. *(re-iss.+cd.Oct88 on 'Chord')*

Chord not issued

Nov 88. (7") **LET IT RAIN. / TINA DEI FADA** [ ] [-]
1990. (cd) **GREATEST HITS – LIVE** [ ] [-]
– Cut like a diamond / Something for nothing / The hangman and the papist / Ringing down the years / Stormy down / Afraid to let you go / Grace darling / The river / Down by the sea / Lay down / Part of the union / Hero & heroine. *(re-iss Jul95 on 'Road Goes On Forever')*

— line-up:- **COUSINS / CRONK / RICHARDS / FERNANDEZ**

Road Goes not issued

Jul 95. (cd) **HEARTBREAK HILL** [ ] [-]
– Something for nothing / Another day without you / We can make it together / Heartbreak Hill / Starting over / Two separate people / Desert song / Let it rain.

– more compilations, etc. –

Sep 78. A&M; (d-lp) **THE BEST OF THE STRAWBS** [ ] [ ]
Mar 79. A&M; (7") **PART OF THE UNION. / LAY DOWN** [ ] [-]
(re-iss Jul82 on 'Old Gold')
Dec 92. A&M; (cd)(c) **A CHOICE SELECTION OF STRAWBS** [ ] [ ]
– Lay down / Lemon pie / Lady Fuschia / Autumn:- 1- Heroine's theme – 2- Deep summer's sleep – 3- The winter long / A glimpse of Heaven / The hangman and the papist / New world / Round and round / I only want my love to grow in you / Benedictus / Hero and heroine / Song of a sad little girl / Tears and Pavan:- 1- Tears – 2- Pavan / To be free / Part of the union / Down by the sea.
1974. Hallmark; (lp) **ALL OUR OWN WORK (with SANDY DENNY)** [ ] [-]
(re-iss.1991 on 'Hannibal')
1992. Road Goes On Forever; (d-cd) **PRESERVES UNCANNED** [ ] [-]
Mar 95. Windsong; (cd) **STRAWBS IN CONCERT (live)** [ ] [-]

STRAY CATS

Formed: Long Island, New York, USA . . . 1979 by SETZER, ROCKER and PHANTOM. They relocated to London in the mid-80's with manager Tony Bidgood, and soon signed to UK label 'Arista'. They hit the UK Top 10 with debut single 'RUNAWAY BOYS', which was soon followed by a DAVE EDMUNDS and group produced eponymous album. They finally broke through in the US, when their 1981 UK hits 'ROCK THIS TOWN' & 'STRAY CAT STRUT' smashed the Top 10 in 1983! • **Style:** Pop rockabilly revivalists, swinging that way through blues, honky tonk and jazz, and featuring suave hair-dos and plucky double bass by LEE. • **Songwriters:** SETZER penned most, except covers; I FOUGHT THE LAW (Bobby Fuller Four). In 1992, group penned or SETZER-PAINE, and more covers; ELVIS ON VELVET (Kimmel-Byroni-Newhauser) / PLEASE DON'T TOUCH (Johnny Kidd) / MYSTERY TRAIN (Parker-Philips) / SLEEPWALK (Richard Farina). • **Trivia:** On 20 Mar'84, McDONNELL married actress Britt Ekland, the famous ex-girlfriend of ROD STEWART. In 1987, SETZER took the part of EDDIE COCHRAN in the film 'La Bamba'. KEITH RICHARDS was the guest on PHANTOM, ROCKER & SLICK'S debut.

Recommended: BACK TO THE ALLEY – THE BEST OF (*6)

BRIAN SETZER (b.10 Apr'60) – vocals, guitar / **LEE ROCKER** (b.LEON DRUCHER, 1961) – double bass, bass / **SLIM JIM PHANTOM** (b.McDONNELL, 20 Mar'60) – drums

Arista EMI America

Nov 80. (7") **RUNAWAY BOYS. / MY ONE DESIRE** [9] [-]
Jan 81. (7") **ROCK THIS TOWN. / CAN'T HURRY LOVE** [9] [9] Apr 83
Feb 81. (lp)(c) **THE STRAY CATS** [6] [ ]
– Runaway boys / Fishnet stockings / Ubangi stomp / Jeanie, Jeanie, Jeanie / Storm the embassy / Rock this town / Rumble in Brighton / Stray cat strut / Crawl up and die / Double talkin' baby / My one desire / Wild saxophone.
Apr 81. (7") **STRAY CAT STRUT. / DRINK THAT BOTTLE DOWN** [11] [-]

— In Jun81, DAVE EDMUNDS & THE STRAY CATS hit No.34 with THE RACE IS ON.

Oct 81. (7") **YOU DON'T BELIEVE ME. / CROSS THAT BRIDGE** [57] [ ]
Nov 81. (lp)(c) **GONNA BALL** [48] [ ]
– Baby blue eyes / Little Miss Prissy / Wasn't that good / Cryin' shame / (She'll just stay) One more day / You don't believe me / Gonna ball / Wicked whiskey / Rev it up and go / Lonely summer nights / Crazy mixed-up kid.
Jun 82. (lp)(c) **BUILT FOR SPEED** (comp. of 2 albums) [-] [2]
– Rock this town / Built for speed / Rev it up and go / Stray cat strut / Little Miss Prissy / Rumble in Brighton / Runaway boys / Lonely summer nights / Double talkin' baby / You don't believe me / Jeanie, Jeanie, Jeanie / Baby blue eyes. *(US cd-iss.Sep88 on 'EMI Manhattan')*
Feb 83. (7") **STRAY CAT STRUT. / YOU DON'T BELIEVE ME** [-] [3]
Jul 83. (7")(7"sha-pic-d) **(SHE'S) SEXY + 17. / LOOKIN' BETTER EVERY BEER** [29] [5]

(12"+=) – Cruisin' / Lucky charm.

Aug 83. (lp)(c) **RANT 'N' RAVE WITH THE STRAY CATS** [51] [14]
– Rebels rule / Too hip, gotta go / Look at that Cadillac / Something's wrong with my radio / 18 miles to Memphis / (She's) Sexy + 17 / Dig dirty doggie / I won't stand in your way / Hotrod gang / How long you wanna live anyway?.

Oct 83. (7") **REBELS RULE. / LOOKIN' THROUGH MY BACK DOOR** [ ] [ ]
(12"+=) – Look at that Cadillac.

Oct 83. (7") **I WON'T STAND IN YOUR WAY. / ('A' acappella)** [-] [35]

Dec 83. (7") **CRUISIN'. / LUCKY CHARM** [-] [ ]

Jan 84. (7") **LOOK AT THAT CADILLAC. / LUCKY CHARM** [-] [68]

—— Folded late 1983, dividing into 2 parts.

BRIAN SETZER

EMI America / EMI America

Nov 84. (lp)(c) **THE KNIFE FEELS LIKE JUSTICE** [ ] [45] Mar 86
– The knife feels like justice / Haunted river / Boulevard of broken dreams / Bobby's back / Radiation ranch / Chains around your heart / Maria / Three guys / Aztec / Breath of life / Barbwire fence. *(re-iss.Apr86)*

Apr 85. (7") **THE KNIFE FEELS LIKE JUSTICE. / BARBWIRE FENCE** [ ] [ ]

Manhattan / Manhattan

May 88. (lp)(c)(cd) **LIVE NUDE GUITARS** [ ] [ ]
– Red lightning blues / Rockability / Rebelene / Nervous breakdown / Every tear that falls / Temper sure is risin' / When the sky comes tumblin' down / She thinks I'm trash / Love is repaid by love alone / Rosie in the middle / So young, so bad, so what? / The rain washed everything away.

Jun 88. (7") **WHEN THE SKY COMES TUMBLIN' DOWN. / CROSS OF LOVE** [ ] [ ]
(12"+=) – ('A'version).

PHANTOM, ROCKER & SLICK

EARL SLICK – guitar (ex-DAVID BOWIE session man)

EMI America / EMI America

Oct 85. (lp)(c) **PHANTOM, ROCKER & SLICK** [-] [61]
– What you want / My mistake / Hollywood distractions / No regrets / Well kept secret / Men without shame / Runnin' from the hounds / Time on my hands / Sing for your supper / Lonely actions.

Nov 85. (7")(12") **MEN WITHOUT SHAME. / TIME IS ON MY HANDS** [ ] [ ]

Mar 86. (7") **MY MISTAKE. / RUNNIN' FROM THE HOUNDS** [ ] [ ]

Nov 86. (lp)(c) **COVER GIRL** [-] [ ]
– Cover girl / The only way to fly / Sidewalk princess / It's good to be alive / Still got time / Can't get it right / Going south / I found someone who loves me / Enough is enough / Dressed in dirt / Long cool woman (in a black dress).

STRAY CATS

originals re-formed mid-'86.

EMI America / EMI America

Sep 86. (lp)(c) **ROCK THERAPY** [-] [ ]
– Rock therapy / Reckless / Race with the Devil / I'm a rocker / Looking to love someone / I wanna cry / Beautiful Delilah / One hand loose / Broken man / Change of heart.

Feb 89. (7") **BRING IT BACK AGAIN. / RUNAWAY BOYS (live)** [64] [ ]
(12"+=)(cd-s+=) – I fought the law.

Mar 89. (lp)(c)(cd) **BLAST OFF** [58] [ ]
– Blast off / Gina / Everybody needs rock'n'roll / Gene and Eddie / Rockabilly rules / Bring it back again / Slip, slip, slippin' in / Rockabilly world / Rockin' all over the place / Nine lives.

Jun 89. (7") **GINA. / TWO OF A KIND** [ ] [ ]
(12"+=)(cd-s+=) – Stray cat strut (live).

—— The following year, they again backed DAVE EDMUNDS ⇒ .

Pump / Jordan

Nov 91. (c-s) **CROSS OF LOVE. / SHOTGUN BABY** [-] [ ]

May 92. (7") **ELVIS ON VELVET. / LUST'N'LOVE** [ ] [ ]
(12"+=)(cd-s+=) – ('A'radio mix).

Jun 92. (cd)(c)(10"lp) **CHOO CHOO NOT FISH** [ ] [ ]
– Elvis on velvet / Cry baby / Please don't touch / Sleepwalk / Lust 'n' love / Beautiful blues / Cross of love / Can't go back to Memphis / Jade idol / My heart is a liar / Mystery train.

Essential / not issued

Feb 94. (cd) **ORIGINAL COOL** (covers) [ ] [-]
– Somethin' else / Oh boy / Twenty flight rock / I fought the law / Lonesome tears / Your true love / Be-bop-a-lula / Blue jean bop / Can't help falling in love / Flying saucers rock'n'roll / The train kept a-rollin' / Stood up / Let it rock / Tryin' to get to you / Chet ditty (hidden charms).

– compilations, others, etc. –

Mar 83. Arista; (12"ep) **STRAY CAT STRUT / BUILT FOR SPEED. / SWEET LOVE ON MY MIND / DRINK THAT BOTTLE DOWN** [ ] [-]

Aug 83. Arista; (d-c) **THE STRAY CATS / GONNA BALL** [ ] [-]

1992. Arista; (cd)(c) **BACK TO THE ALLEY – THE BEST OF THE STRAY CATS** [ ] [-]
– Stray cat strut / Rock this town / Rebels rule / Built for speed / Little Miss Prissy / Too hip gotta go / My one desire / I won't stand in your way / C'mon everybody (live) / Fishnet stockings / Runaway boys / (She's) Sexy and 17 / Baby blue eyes / Jeanie Jeanie Jeanie / You don't believe me / Ubangi stomp / Double takin' baby / Storm the embassy / Rumble in Brighton / Gonna ball.

Mar 94. Receiver; (cd) **SOMETHING ELSE – LIVE (live)** [ ] [-]

Feb 95. Receiver; (cd) **ROCK THIS TOWN** [ ] [-]

Apr 95. Arista; (cd) **STRAY CATS / GONNA BALL** [ ] [-]

BRIAN SETZER ORCHESTRA

not issued / Hollywood

Apr 94. (cd)(c) **BRIAN SETZER ORCHESTRA** [-] [ ]

STREET BAND (see under ⇒ YOUNG, Paul)

STREETWALKERS (see under ⇒ FAMILY)

Joe STRUMMER (see under ⇒ CLASH)

Dan STUART (see under ⇒ GREEN ON RED)

STYLE COUNCIL (see under ⇒ WELLER, Paul)

Poly STYRENE (see under ⇒ X-RAY SPEX)

STYX

Formed: Chicago, Illinois, USA … 1964 as The TRADEWINDS by DeYOUNG and neighbours twin PANOZZO brothers. Became TW4 in 1965 and based themselves around local university. In 1971, Bill Traut signed them to his 'Wooden Nickel' label, and the next year they entered US Hot 100 with 'BEST THING'. Early in 1975, 'LADY' became their first of many Top 10 entries, the ensuing being on 'RCA'. • **Style:** Initially a classically fused rock outfit, who succumbed to the usual US mainstream soft-rock trappings. • **Songwriters:** DeYOUNG / YOUNG / SHAW. In the 90's BURTING took place of SHAW, who had been part of set-up since '75. • **Trivia:** Named after the mythical river of the dead.

Recommended: THE BEST OF STYX (*6)

DENNIS DeYOUNG (b.18 Feb'47) – vocals, keyboards / **JOHN CURULEWSKI** – guitar / **JAMES YOUNG** (b.14 Nov'48) – guitar / **CHUCK PANOZZO** (b.20 Sep'47) – bass / **JOHN PANOZZO** – drums

not issued / Wooden N.

Sep 72. (lp) **STYX** [-] [ ]
– Movement for the common man: Children of the land – Street collage – Fanfare for the common man – Mother Nature's matinee / Right away / What has come between us / Best thing / Quick is the beat of my heart / After you leave me. *(UK-iss.+c.Jul80 as 'STYX 1' on 'R.C.A.')*

Sep 72. (7") **BEST THING. / WHAT HAS COME BETWEEN US** [-] [82]

Jul 73. (7") **I'M GONNA MAKE YOU FEEL IT. / QUICK IS THE BEAT OF MY HEART** [-] [ ]

Jul 73. (lp) **STYX II** [-] [ ]
– You need love / Lady / A day / You better ask / Little fugue in "G" / Father O.S.A. / Earl of Roseland / I'm gonna make you feel it. *(re-dist.Jan75 in US, hit No.20) (UK-iss.+c.Jul80 as 'LADY' on 'R.C.A.')*

Sep 73. (7") **LADY. / YOU BETTER ASK** [-] [ ]

Feb 74. (lp) **THE SERPENT IS RISING** [-] [ ]
– Witch wolf / The grove of Eglantine / Young man / As bad as this / Winner take all / 22 years / Jonas Psalter / The serpent is rising / Krakatoa / Hallelujah chorus. *(UK-iss.+c.Jul80 on 'R.C.A.')*

Oct 74. (7") **LIES. / 22 YEARS** [-] [ ]

Nov 74. (lp) **MAN OF MIRACLES** [-] [ ]
– Rock & roll feeling / Havin' a ball / Golden lark / A song for Suzanne / A man like me / Best thing / Evil eyes / Southern woman / Christopher Mr. Christopher. *(UK-iss.+c.Jul80 on 'R.C.A.')*

R.C.A. / R.C.A.

Dec 74. (7") **LADY. / CHILDREN OF THE LAND** [ ] [6]

May 75. (7") **YOU NEED LOVE. / WINNER TAKE ALL** [-] [88]

Jul 75. (7") **YOUNG MAN. / UNFINISHED SONG** [-] [ ]

A & M / A & M

Feb 76. (lp)(c) **EQUINOX** [ ] [58] Dec 75
– Light up / Lorelei / Mother dear / Lonely child / Midnight ride / Born for adventure / Prelude 12 / Suite Madame Blue.

Mar 76. (7") **LORELEI. / MIDNIGHT RIDE** [ ] [27] Feb 76

Jul 76. (7") **LIGHT UP. / BORN FOR ADVENTURE** [-] [ ]

—— **TOMMY SHAW** (b. Montgomery, Alabama, USA) – lead guitar repl. CURU..

Oct 76. (lp)(c) **CRYSTAL BALL** [ ] [66]
– Put me on / Mademoiselle / Jennifer / Crystal ball / Shooz / This old man / Clair de Lune – Ballerina.

Nov 76. (7") **MADEMOISELLE. / LIGHT UP** [ ] [36]

Feb 77. (7") **JENNIFER. / SHOOZ** [-] [ ]

Jun 77. (7") **CRYSTAL BALL. / PUT ME ON** [ ] [ ]

Aug 77. (lp)(c) **THE GRAND ILLUSION** [ ] [6] Jul 77
– The grand illusion / Fooling yourself (the angry young man) / Superstars / Come sail away / Miss America / Man in the wilderness / Castle walls / The grand finale. *(re-iss.Nov85)*

Oct 77. (7") **COME SAIL AWAY. / PUT ME ON** [ ] [8] Sep 77

Mar 78. (7") **FOOLING YOURSELF (THE ANGRY YOUNG MAN). / THE GRAND FINALE** [ ] [29] Feb 78

Sep 78. (lp)(c)(clear-lp)(US-pic-d) **PIECES OF EIGHT** [ ] [6]
– Great white hope / I'm O.K. / Sing for the day / The message / Lords of the ring / Blue collar man (long nights) / Queen of spades / Renegade / Pieces of eight / Aku-aku.

Oct 78. (7")(12"colrd) **BLUE COLLAR MAN (LONG NIGHTS). / SUPERSTARS** [ ] [21] Sep 78

Mar 79. (7")(7"red) **RENEGADE. / SING FOR THE DAY** [ ] [16]
[41]

Oct 79. (7") **BABE. / I'M OK** [6] [1]

Jan 80. (lp)(c)(silver-lp) **CORNERSTONE** [36] [2] Oct 79

– Lights / Why me / Babe / Never say never / Boat on the river / Borrowed time / First time / Eddie / Love in the moonlight.

Dec 79. (7") **WHY ME. / LIGHTS** | - | 26
Mar 80. (7") **BORROWED TIME. / EDDIE** | - | 64
Mar 80. (7") **BOAT ON THE RIVER. / COME SAIL AWAY** | | -
May 80. (7") **LIGHTS. / RENEGADE** | | -
Jan 81. (lp)(c) **PARADISE THEATER** | 8 | 1
– A.D. 1928 / Rockin' the Paradise / State street Sadie / Too much time on my hands / She cares / Snowblind / Nothing ever goes as planned / The best of times / Half-penny, two-penny / A.D. 1958. *(cd-iss.Jun84)*
Jan 81. (7") **THE BEST OF TIMES. / LIGHT** | 42 | 3
(d-lazer-etched-7") – ('A'side) / PARADISE THEATER
Mar 81. (7")(7"colrd) **TOO MUCH TIME ON MY HANDS. / QUEEN OF SPADES** | | 9
Jul 81. (7") **NOTHING EVER GOES AS PLANNED. / ?** | - | 54
Nov 81. (7") **ROCKIN' THE PARADISE. / SNOWBLIND** | | -
Feb 83. (lp)(c) **KILROY WAS HERE** | 67 | 3
– Mr. Roboto / Cold war / Don't let it end / High time / Heavy metal poisoning / Just get through this night / Double life / Haven't we been here before / Don't let it end (reprise). *(cd-iss.Apr84)*
Mar 83. (7") **MR. ROBOTO. / SNOWBLIND** | | 3 Feb 83
May 83. (7")(7"sha-pic-d) **DON'T LET IT END. / ROCKIN' THE PARADISE** | 56 | 6 Apr 83
Jun 83. (7") **HAVEN'T WE BEEN HERE BEFORE. / DOUBLE LIFE** | - |
Aug 83. (7") **HIGH TIME. / DOUBLE LIFE** | - | 48
Apr 84. (d-lp)(d-c) **CAUGHT IN THE ACT – LIVE (live)** | 44 | 31
– Music time / Mr. Roboto / Too much time on my hands / Babe / Snowblind / The best of times / Suite Madame Blue / Rockin' the Paradise / Blue collar man (long night) / Miss America / Don't let it end / Fooling yourself (the angry young man) / Crystal ball / Come sail away.
May 84. (7") **MUSIC TIME (live). / HEAVY METAL POISONING (live)** | | 40

— The band rested activities with main members going solo.

DENNIS DeYOUNG

A & M A & M
Sep 84. (lp)(c)(US-cd) **DESERT MOON** | | 29
– Don't wait for heroes / Please / Boys will be boys / Fire / Desert Moon / Suspicious / Gravity / Dear darling (I'll be there).
Oct 84. (7")(12") **DESERT MOON. / GRAVITY** | | 10 Sep 84
Dec 84. (7") **DON'T WAIT FOR HEROES. / GRAVITY** | - | 83
Feb 85. (7") **SUSPICIOUS. / DEAR DARLING (I'LL BE THERE)** | - |
Apr 86. (lp)(c) **BACK TO THE WORLD** | - |
– This is the time / Warning shot / Call me / I'll get lucky / Unanswered prayers / Southbound Ryan / Person to person / Black wall.
Mar 86. (7") **CALL ME. / PLEASE** | - | 54
Jun 86. (7") **THIS IS THE TIME. / SOUTHBOUND TRAIN** | - | 93
(above from 'The Karate Kid II' film).
Dec 88. (lp)(c)(cd) **BOOMCHILD** | |
– Beneath the Moon / The best is yet to come / What a way to go / Harry's hands / Boomchild / Who shot daddy? / Outside looking in again / Won't go wasted.

TOMMY SHAW

solo, with **STEVE HOLLEY** – drums (ex-WINGS, ex-ELTON JOHN) / **PETER WOOD** – keyboards (ex-AL STEWART) / **BRIAN STANLEY** – bass (ex-GRAHAM PARKER)

A & M A & M
Oct 84. (lp)(c) **GIRLS WITH GUNS** | | 50
– Girls with guns / Come in and explain / Lonely school / Heads up / Kiss me hello / Fading away / Little girl would / Outside in the rain / Free to love you / The race is on.
Nov 84. (7") **GIRLS WITH GUNS. / HEADS UP** | | 33 Sep 84
Dec 84. (7") **LONELY SCHOOL. / COME IN AND EXPLAIN** | - | 60
Jan 85. (7") **LONELY SCHOOL. / HEADS UP** | | -
(12"+=) – Girls with guns.
Oct 85. (7") **REMO'S THEME (WHAT IF). / KISS ME HELLO** | - | 81
(above from the film 'Remo: The Adventure Begins')
Nov 85. (lp)(c) **WHAT IF** | | 87
– Jealousy / Remo's theme (What if?) / Reach for the bottle / Friendly advice / This is not a test / See me now / True confessions / Count on you / Nature of the beast / Bad times.
Dec 85. (7") **JEALOUSY. / THIS IS NOT A TEST** | - |

— Enlisted new band: **TERRY THOMAS** – guitar, keys, etc. / **TONY BEARD** – drums / **WIX** – keyboards / **FELIX KRISH** – bass / **RICHIE CANNATA** – sax / **STEVE ALEXANDER** – perc.

Atlantic Atlantic
Sep 87. (lp)(c)(cd) **AMBITION** | |
– No such thing / Dangerous game / The weight of the world / Ambition / Ever since the world began / Are you ready for me? / Somewhere in the night / Love you too much / The outsider / Lay them down.
Sep 87. (7") **NO SUCH THING. / THE OUTSIDER** | - |
May 88. (7") **EVER SINCE THE WORLD BEGAN. / THE OUTSIDER** | | 75 Feb 88
(12"+=) – No such thing.

STYX

were now once more, but without SHAW, who was deposed by **GLEN BURTNIK** – lead guitar (same label) **SHAW** joined DAMN YANKEES in 1990.

Nov 90. (cd)(c)(lp) **EDGE OF THE CENTURY** | | 63 Oct 90
– Love is the ritual / Show me the way / Edge of the century / Love at first sight / All in a day's work / Not dead yet / World tonite / Carrie Ann / Homewrecker / Back to Chicago.
Dec 90. (7") **LOVE IS THE RITUAL. / HOMEWRECKER** | | 80 Oct 90
(12"+=)(cd-s+=) – Babe.
Feb 91. (7")(c-s) **SHOW ME THE WAY. / BACK TO CHICAGO** | | 3 Dec 90
(12"+=)(cd-s+=) – Don't let it end.
Mar 91. (c-s) **LOVE AT FIRST SIGHT. / ?** | - | 25

– compilations, others, etc. –

Oct 79. RCA; (lp)(c) **THE BEST OF STYX** | |
– You need love / Lady / I'm gonna make you feel it / What has come between us / Southern woman / Rock & roll feeling / Winner take all / Best thing / Witch wolf / The grove of Eglantine / Man of miracles. *(cd-iss. 1992)*
Apr 78. A&M; (7"ep) **MADEMOISELLE / COME SAIL AWAY. / CRYSTAL BALL / LORELEI** | | -
Apr 88. A&M; (cd-ep) **COMPACT HITS** | | -
– Babe / Come sail away / Rockin' the Paradise / The best of times.
May 80. A&M; (3xlp-box) **BOXED SET** | |
Sep 85. Old Gold; (7") **BABE. / THE BEST OF TIMES** | | -
May 95. A&M; (cd) **BOAT ON THE RIVER** | |

SUEDE

Formed: London, England . . . 1989 by BRETT ANDERSON, who put final line-up together 1991. After a single 'BE MY GOD' / 'ART', failed to appear in 1990 on 'RML', they signed to indie 'Nude'. This 12" was famous for featured ex-SMITHS drummer MIKE JOYCE. In Apr'92 with new drummer SIMON GILBERT, they featured on cover of NME just prior to release of debut top 50 hit 'THE DROWNERS'. With much hype and media attention, they scored first Top 20 hit in Sep'92 with 'METAL MICKEY'. Early in '93, 'Nude' was taken over by 'Sony' on both sides of the Atlantic. In 1993, a Top 10 follow-up preceded chartbusting No.1 eponymous album. • **Style:** Young and talented best newcomers of '93. BRETT's mannered vox and group's glitszy tunes, at times similar to MORRISSEY, BOWIE or BOLAN, whom he idolised as a boy. • **Songwriters:** ANDERSON / BUTLER, except; BRASS IN POCKET (Pretenders). • **Trivia:** Producer ED BULLER also played keyboards + synthesizers on debut album.

Recommended: SUEDE (*9) / DOG MAN STAR (*8).

BRETT ANDERSON – vocals / **BERNARD BUTLER** – guitar, piano / **MATT OSMAN** – bass / **SIMON GILBERT** – drums

Nude not issued
Apr 92. (7") **THE DROWNERS. / TO THE BIRDS** | 49 | -
(12"+=)(cd-s+=) – My insatiable one.
Sep 92. (7") **METAL MICKEY. / WHERE THE PIGS DON'T FLY** | 17 | -
(12"+=)(cd-s+=) – He's dead.

Nude-Sony Sony
Feb 93. (7")(c-s) **ANIMAL NITRATE. / THE BIG TIME** | 7 |
(12"+=)(cd-s+=) – Painted people.
Apr 93. (cd)(c)(lp) **SUEDE** | 1 |
– So young / Animal nitrate / She's not dead / Moving / Pantomime horse / The drowners / Sleeping pills / Breakdown / Metal Mickey / Animal lover / The next life.
May 93. (7")(c-s) **SO YOUNG. / HIGH RISING** | 22 |
(12"+=)(cd-s+=) – Dolly.
Feb 94. (7")(c-s) **STAY TOGETHER. / THE LIVING DEAD** | 3 |
('A'ext-12"+=) – My dark star.
(cd-s+=) – ('A'extended).

— In Spring 1994, gay drummer SIMON went to House Of Commons, to air his views on the homosexual laws of consent, which were to be lowered from 21 to either 16 (the heterosexual age) or 18, as it turned out to be. Around the same time, an American jazz singer called SUEDE won her lawsuit against the band in the US. They are now to be called LONDON SUEDE, but thankfully only in the States.

Sep 94. (7")(c-s) **WE ARE THE PIGS. / KILLING OF A FLASH BOY** | 18 |
(12"+=)(cd-s+=) – Whipsnade.
Oct 94. (cd)(c)(lp) **DOG MAN STAR** | 3 |
– Introducing the band / We are the pigs / Heroine / The wild ones / Daddy's speeding / The power / New generation / This Hollywood life / The 2 of us / Black or blue / The asphalt world / Still life.

— BUTLER left July 94 and was repl. by 17 year-old **RICHARD OAKES** after recording album.

Nov 94. (12")(c-s) **THE WILD ONES. / INTRODUCING THE BAND (Eno mix) / ASDA TOWN** | 18 |
(cd-s) – ('A'side) / Modern boys / This world needs a father.
Jan 95. (7")(c-s) **NEW GENERATION. / BENTSWOOD BOYS** | 21 |
(12"+=)(cd-s+=) – Together.
(cd-s) – ('A'side) / Animal nitrate (live) / The wild ones (live) / Pantomime horse (live).

SUGAR

Formed: Minneapolis, USA . . . 1992 by former HUSKER DU frontman BOB MOULD. He had been part of this classic hard-core trio for 9 years between '78 + '87 before going solo in 1989. After 2 well-received albums for 'Virgin America' in the next couple of years, he formed SUGAR with 2 others DAVE BARBE and MALCOLM TRAVIS. Signed to UK 'Creation' in '92 and unleashed the excellent 'COPPER BLUE' album. • **Style:** Grunge in the mould of PIXIES, NIRVANA, MUDHONEY, although he could lay claim to having influenced them a decade before! • **Songwriters:** MOULD and now same with others. Covered; SHOOT OUT THE LIGHTS (Richard Thompson).

Recommended: WORKBOOK (BOB MOULD *7) / COPPER BLUE (*10) / FILE UNDER: EASY LISTENING (*8) / BEASTER (*8)

BOB MOULD

solo, with **ANTON FIER** – drums / **TONY MAIMONE** – bass, (both ex-PERE UBU) / **JANE SCARPANTONI** – cello (of TINY LIGHTS) / **STEVE HAIGLER** – cello

Virgin Virgin

Jun 89. (7") **SEE A LITTLE LIGHT. / ALL THOSE PEOPLE KNOW**
(12"+=)(cd-s+=) – Shoot out the lights / Composition for the young and the old (live).

Jul 89. (lp)(cd) **WORK BOOK**
– Sunspots / Wishing well / Heartbreak a stranger / See a little light / Poison years / Sinners and their repentances / Lonely afternoon / Brasilia crossed the Tranton / Compositions for the young and old / Dreaming, I amd / Whichever way the wind blows. *(re-iss.Sep90)*

Aug 90. (cd)(c)(lp) **BLACK SHEETS OF RAIN**
– Black sheets of rain / Stand guard / It's too late / One good reason / Stop your crying / Hanging tree / The last night / Hear me calling / Out of your life / Disappointed / Sacrifice – let there be peace.

Virgin Virgin

May 94. (cd) **THE POISON YEARS** (compilation)

SUGAR

BOB MOULD – vox, guitar, keyboards, percussion / **DAVE BARBE** – bass (ex-MERCYLAND) / **MALCOLM TRAVIS** – drums, percussion (ex-ZULUS)

Creation Rykodisc

Aug 92. (12"ep)(cd-ep) **CHANGES / NEEDLE HITS E. / IF I CAN'T CHANGE YOUR MIND / TRY AGAIN**

Sep 92. (cd)(c)(lp) **COPPER BLUE** 10
– The act we act / A good idea / Changes / Helpless / Hoover dam / The slim / If I can't change your mind / Fortune teller / Slick / Man on the Moon.

Oct 92. (12"ep)(cd-ep) **A GOOD IDEA. / WHERE DIAMONDS ARE HALOS / SLICK / ARMENIA CITY IN THE SKY** 65

Jan 93. (c-s) **IF I CAN'T CHANGE YOUR MIND. / CLOWN MASTER** 30
(12"+=)(cd-s+=) – Anyone (live) / Hoover dam (live).
(cd-s) – ('A'side) / The slim / Where diamonds are halos.

Apr 93. (cd)(c)(m-lp) **BEASTER** 3
– Come around / Tilted / Judas cradle / JC auto / Feeling better / Walking away.

Aug 93. (7"only) **TILTED. / JC AUTO (live)** 48

Aug 94. (7")(c-s) **YOUR FAVORITE THING. / MIND IS AN ISLAND** 40
(12"+=)(cd-s+=) – Frustration / And you tell me (T.V. mix).

Sep 94. (cd)(c)(lp) **FILE UNDER EASY LISTENING (F.U.E.L.)** 7 50
– Gift / Company book / Your favorite thing / What you want it to be / Gee angel / Panama city hotel / Can't help it anymore / Granny cool / Believe what you're saying / Explode and make up.

Oct 94. (7")(c-s) **BELIEVE WHAT YOU'RE SAYING. / GOING HOME** 73
(cd-s+=) – In the eyes of my friends / And you tell me.

SUGARCUBES (see under ⇒ BJORK)

SUGGS (see under ⇒ MADNESS)

SUICIDAL TENDENCIES

Formed: Venice, California, USA . . . 1982 by MIKE MUIR, etc. After debut lp on homeland 'Frontier' records, they signed to 'Virgin' worldwide in 1986. The next year the album 'JOIN THE ARMY', sold well enough to hit the UK Top 100. • **Style:** Frantic skateboard loving heavy punks. Offshoot INFECTIOUS GROOVES were more fashionable, like FAITH NO MORE. • **Songwriters:** MUIR writes most material. • **Trivia:** MUIR appeared on TV show 'Miami Vice' in 1992.

Recommended: SUICIDAL TENDENCIES (*7).

MIKE MUIR – vocals / **GRANT ESTES** – guitar / **LOUICHE MAYOREA** – bass / **AMERY SMITH** – drums

not issued Frontier

1984. (lp) **SUICIDAL TENDENCIES** -
– Suicide's an alternative / You'll be sorry / I shot the Devil / Won't fall in love today / Memories of tomorrow / I want more / I saw your mommy . . . / 2 sided politics / Suicidal failure / Sublimal / Institutionalized / Possessed / Fascist pig. *(re-iss.Aug87) (UK-iss.+c+cdJan88 on 'Virgin')* (cd+=) – Possessed to skate / Human guinea pig / Two wrongs don't make a right.

— **RALPH HERRERA** – drums repl. AMERY / **ROCKY GEORGE** – guitar repl. ESTES

Virgin Caroline

Apr 87. (7") **POSSESSED TO SKATE. / HUMAN GUINEA PIG**
(12"+=)(12"pic-d+=) – Two wrongs don't make a right (but they make me feel better).

Apr 87. (lp)(c)(cd) **JOIN THE ARMY** 81 100
– Suicidal maniac / Join the army / You got, I want / A little each day / The prisoner / War inside my head / I feel your pain and I survive / Human guinea pig / Possessed to skate / No name, no words / Cyco / Looking in your eyes / Two wrongs don't make a right (but they make me feel better). *(re-iss.Apr90)*

Jan 88. (12"m) **INSTITUTIONALIZED. / WAR INSIDE MY HEAD / CYCO**

— added **MIKE CLARK** – rhythm guitar / **BOB HEATHCOTE** – bass repl. MAYORGA

Virgin Epic

Aug 88. (12") **TRIP AT THE BRAIN. / SUICYCO MANIA**

Sep 88. (lp)(c)(cd) **HOW WILL I LAUGH TOMORROW . . . WHEN I CAN'T EVEN SMILE TODAY?**
– Trip at the brain / Hearing voices / Pledge your allience / How will I laugh tomorrow . . . when I can't even smile today? / The miracle / Surf and slam / If I don't wake up / Sorry? / One too many times / The feeling's back. (cd+=) – Suicyco mania.

Jun 89. (lp)(c)(cd) **CONTROLLED BY HATRED . . . DEJA VU**
– Master of no mercy / How will I laugh tomorrow (video edit) / Just another love song / Walking the dead / Choosing my own way of life / Controlled by hatred / Feel like shit . . . deja vu / It's not easy / How will I laugh tomorrow (heavy emotion mix). *(re-iss.cd+c Oct94)*

Epic Epic

Jul 90. (cd)(c)(lp) **LIGHTS . . . CAMERA . . . REVOLUTION** 59
– You can't bring me down / Lost again / Alone / Lovely / Give it revolution / Get whacked / Send me your money / Emotion No.13 / Disco's out / Murder's in / Go'n breakdown.

Oct 90. (7"ep)(12"ep)(cd-ep)(7"sha-pic-ep) **SEND ME YOUR MONEY / YOU CAN'T BRING ME DOWN. / WAKING THE DEAD / DON'T GIVE ME YOUR NOTHING**

— **ROBERT TRUJILLO** – bass / **JOSH FREESE** – drums repl. BOB + RALPH

Jul 92. (cd)(c)(lp) **THE ART OF REBELLION** 52
– Can't stop / Accept my sacrifice / Nobody hears / Tap into the power / Monopoly on sorrow / We call this mutha revenge / Medley: I wasn't meant to feel this – Asleep at the wheel / Gotta kill Captain Stupid / I'll hate you better / Which way to free / It's going down / Where's the truth.

Jun 94. (cd)(c)(lp) **SUICIDAL FOR LIFE** 82
– Invocation / Don't give a f***! / No f***'n problem / Suicyco muthaf***a / F***ed up just right! / No bullshit / What else could I do? / What you need's a friend / I wouldn't mind / Depression and anguish / Evil / Love vs. loneliness / Benediction.

– compilations, etc. –

both issued on 'Virgin'.

Jul 91. (cd)(c)(lp) **INSTITUTIONALIZED** (remixed)

Jun 90. (cd)(c) **STILL CYCO AFTER ALL THESE YEARS**

INFECTIOUS GROOVES

was formed by **MUIR + ROBERT TRUJILLO** – bass + **STEPHEN PERKINS** – drums (ex-JANE'S ADDICTION) / **ADAM SIEGAL + DEAN PLEASANTS** – guitar

Epic Epic

Oct 91. (cd)(c)(lp) **THE PLAGUE THAT MAKES YOUR BOOTY MOVE, IT'S THE INFECTIOUS GROOVE**
– Punk it up / Therapy / I look funny? / Stop funk'n with my head / I'm gonna be king / Closed session / Infectious grooves / Infective blues / Monster skank / Back to the people / Turn your head / You lie . . . and ya breath stank / Do the sinister / Mandatory love song / Infecto groovalistic / Thanx but no thanx.

Nov 91. (7") **STILL CYCO AFTER ALL THESE YEARS. / ?**
(12"+=)(cd-s+=) – ?

— **JOSH FREESE** – drums repl. PERKINS

Mar 93. (cd)(c)(lp) **SARSIPPIUS' ARK**
– Intro / Turtle wax (funkaholics anonymous) / No cover – 2 drink mimimum / Immigrant song / Caca de kick / Don't stop, spread the jam! / Three headed mind pollution / Slo-motion slam / A legend in his own mind (ladies love 'sip) / Infectious Grooves / The man behind the man / Fame / Savor da flavor / No budget – Dust off the 8-track! / Infevtious Grooves / You pick me up (just to throw me down) / Therapy / Do the sinister / Big big butt, by infectiphibian / Spreck.

SUICIDE

Formed: New York, USA . . . 1971 by VEGA and ex-jazz band organist REV. After the new wave/punk explosion in 1976 and gigs at Max's Kansas City, they signed to US label 'Red Star'. In 1978, they were booed off-stage by impatient CLASH fans, but this didn't hinder 'Ze' records (UK 'Island'), who gave them deal in 1979. Enjoyed a cult following during the early 80's, until their split. • **Style:** Electronic experimental duo, who delivered shock screams and whispered vox over Farfisa organ. • **Songwriters:** All written by duo, except EVERY 1's A WINNER (Hot Chocolate). • **Trivia:** ALAN VEGA had a French Top 5 hit with 'JUKEBOX BABE', which was produced by RIC OCASEK (of Cars). He became a sculptor in the early 80's, with his work exhibited 1982-83.

Recommended: SUICIDE (*9) / A WAY OF LIFE (*7).

ALAN VEGA (b.1948) – vocals / **MARTIN REV** – keyboards, percussion

Bronze Red Star

Nov 77. (lp) **SUICIDE**
– Ghost rider / Rocket U.S.A. / Cheree / Frankie Teardrops / Johnny / Girl / Che. *(re-iss.Sep86 on 'Demon', cd-iss.Jun88)*

Jul 78. (12") **CHEREE. / I REMEMBER**

1978. (lp) **24 MINUTES OVER BRUSSELS** (ltd) -

Island Ze

Nov 79. (7")(12") **DREAM BABY DREAM. / RADIATION**

May 80. (lp) **ALAN VEGA / MARTIN REV – SUICIDE**
– Diamonds, furcoats, champagne / Mr. Ray / Sweetheart / Fast money music / Touch me / Harlem / Be bop kid / Las Vegas man / Shadazz / Dance.

— Split partnership in the early 80's and both went solo.

ALAN VEGA

with **PHIL HAWK** – guitar

not issued P.V.C.

1980. (lp) **ALAN VEGA** -
– Jukebox babe / Fireball / Kung Foo cowboy / Love cry / Speedway / Ice drummer / Bye bye bayou / Lonely.

— w/band 81-83 **MARK KUGH** – guitar / **LARRY CHAPLAN** – bass / **SESU COLEMAN** – drums

Island Ze

Nov 81. (lp) **COLLISION DRIVE**

– Magdalena 82 / Be bop a lula / Outlaw / Raver / Ghost rider / I believe / Magdalena 83 / Rebel / Viet vet.

Nov 81. (7") **JUKEBOX BABE. / LONELY**

— added **ALAIN JOURGENSEN** – keyboards (of MINISTRY) / **STEPHEN GEORGE** – drums / **GREG HAWKES** – synth, sax (of CARS) / **RIC OCASEK** – guitar, producer (of CARS)

Elektra Elektra

Sep 83. (lp)(c) **SATURN STRIP**
– Saturn drive / Video babe / American dreamer / Wipeout beat / Je t'adore / Angel / Kid Congo / Goodbye darling / Every 1's a winner.

— retained **OCASEK** + added **KENNAN KEATING** – guitar / **CHRIS LORD** – synth

Oct 85. (7") **ON THE RUN. / CRY FIRE**
(12"+=) – Rah rah baby.

Dec 85. (lp)(c) **JUST A MILLION DREAMS**
– On the run / Shooting for you / Hot fox / Too late / Wild heart / Creation / Cry fire / Ra ra baby.

In 1986, VEGA guested for SISTERS OF MERCY incarnation The SISTERHOOD.

MARTIN REV

not issued Lust Unlust

Feb 80. (lp) **INFIDELITY** (US-title 'MARTIN REV') [-]
– Mari / Baby o baby / Nineteen 86 / Temptation / Jomo / Asia.

New Rose not issued

Mar 85. (lp) **CLOUDS OF GLORY**

SUICIDE

re-formed 1988.

Chapter 22 ???

Jan 89. (12") **RAIN OF RUIN. / SURRENDER** [-]

Jan 89. (lp)(c)(cd) **A WAY OF LIFE** [-]
– Wild in blue / Surrender / Jukebox baby 96 / Rain of ruin / Sufferin' in vain / Dominic Christ / Love so lonely / Devastation.

Broke Out ???

Jun 92. (cd) **Y.B. BLUE** [-]

ALAN VEGA

returned to solo work for the 90's. **LIZ LAMERA** – drums

Chapter 22 ?

Feb 90. (cd)(c)(lp) **DEUCE AVENUE**
– Body bop jive / Sneaker gun fire / Jab Gee / Bad scene / La la bola / Deuce avenue / Faster blaster / Sugee / Sweet sweet money / Love on / No tomorrow / Future sex. *(re-iss.Jun90 on 'Musicdisc')*

Jul 91. (cd)(c)(lp) **POWER ON TO ZERO HOUR**

Musidisc

May 93. (cd)(c) **NEW RACEION**
– The pleaser / Christ dice / Gamma pop / Viva the legs / Do the job / Junior's little sister's dropped ta cheap / How many lifetimes / Holy skips / Keep it alive / Go trane go / Just say.

– (SUICIDE) compilations, etc. –

1983. R.O.I.R.; (c) **HALF-ALIVE (half studio)**

Oct 86. R.O.I.R.; (c) **GHOST RIDERS (live)**
(cd-iss.Apr90 on 'Danceteria') (cd-iss.Feb95 on 'ROIR Europe')

Andy SUMMERS (see under ⇒ POLICE)

SUN AND THE MOON (see under ⇒ CHAMELEONS)

SUNDAYS

Formed: London, England ... 1988 by HARRIET, DAVID and PAUL. Signed to top indie label 'Rough Trade' in 1988, and immediately bounced into the Top 50 with debut single 'CAN'T BE SURE'. Early in 1990, their long-awaited first album 'READING, WRITING AND ARITHMETIC', soared into the UK Top 5, and also surprised many when reaching US Top 40. • **Style:** Luscious alternative rock outfit, that originally drew similarities between COCTEAU TWINS or THROWING MUSES. • **Songwriters:** HARRIET lyrics / DAVID music. Covered; WILD HORSES (Rolling Stones). • **Trivia:** PATCH now lives in Guildford, Surrey. An instrumental piece was used on the 1993 series for comedy duo NEWMAN and BADDIEL.

Recommended: READING, WRITING AND ARITHMETIC (*9) / BLIND (*7).

HARRIET WHEELER (b.26 Jun'63) – vocals (ex-JIM JIMINEE) / **DAVID GAVURIN** (b. 4 Apr'63) – guitar / **PAUL BRINDLEY** (b. 6 Nov'63, Loughborough, England) – bass / **PATRICK 'Patch' HANNAN** (b. 4 Mar'66) – drums repl. drum machine.

Rough Trade D.G.C.

Feb 89. (7") **CAN'T BE SURE. / I KICKED A BOY** [45]
(12"+=)(cd-s+=) – Don't tell your mother.

Jan 90. (cd)(c)(lp)(pic-lp) **READING, WRITING AND ARITHMETIC** [4] [39]
– Skin & bones / Here's where the story ends / Can't be sure / I won / Hideous towns / You're not the only one I know / A certain someone / I kicked a boy / My finest hour / Joy.

Jan 90. (7") **HERE'S WHERE THE STORY ENDS. / SKIN AND BONES** [-]

Parlophone D.G.C.

Sep 92. (7")(c-s) **GOODBYE. / WILD HORSES** [27]
(cd-s+=) – Noise.

Oct 92. (cd)(c)(lp) **BLIND** [15]
– I feel / Goodbye / Life and soul / Marc / On Earth / God made me / Love / What do you think? / 24 hours / Blood on my hands / Medieval. *(re-iss.cd+c Mar94)*

SUPERGRASS

Formed: Oxford, England . . .1991 as The JENNIFERS by schoolboy GAZ, etc. After one single for Sam Galpern's 'Nude', they changed name to THEODORE SUPERGRASS early '94. They soon dropped first name part and appeared on Various Artists compilation 7"ep 'CRAZED AND CONFUSED' doing a demo version of 'CAUGHT BY THE FUZZ'. This was duly unleashed as their first proper 45 a month later in October and hit Top 50. 1995 started out in fine fashion, with 2 major hits and then a superb Top 3 album 'I SHOULD COCO', which soon went top. • **Style:** Teenage punk outfit, also influenced by 60's psychedelia, 70's BUZZCOCKS punk and everything under the sun, although it works just fine. • **Songwriters:** Group except; STONE FREE (Jimi Hendrix) / ITCHYCOO PARK (Small Faces). • **Trivia:** Played "T In The Park" festival early August 1995 with 4th member BOBSIE COOMBES on keyboards.

Recommended: I SHOULD COCO (*9)

JENNIFERS

GAZ COOMBES (b.1976) – vocals, guitar / **NICK GOFFEY** – guitar / **ANDY DAVIES** – bass / **DANNY GOFFEY** (b.1975) – drums

Nude-Sony not issued

Aug 92. (12"ep)(cd-ep) **JUST GOT BACK TODAY / ROCKS AND BOULDERS. / DANNY'S SONG / TOMORROW'S RAIN** [-]

— **MICKEY QUINN** (b.1970) – guitar repl.TARA MILTON who had repl.NICK

SUPERGRASS

— now without DAVIES who went to Bristol University.

Parlophone Sub Pop

Oct 94. (7")(c-s) **CAUGHT BY THE FUZZ. / STRANGE ONES** [43] [-]
(cd-s+=) – Caught by the fuzz (acoustic).

Feb 95. (7")(7"red)(c-s) **MANSIZE ROOSTER. / SITTING UP STRAIGHT** [20] [-]
(cd-s+=) – Odd.

Mar 95. (7"yellow) **LOSE IT. / CAUGHT BY THE FUZZ (acoustic)** [75]

— (above on 'Sub Pop' also feat. on Jul95 box-set 'HELTER SHELTER')

Apr 95. (7"blue)(c-s) **LENNY. / WAIT FOR THE SUN** [9] [-]
(cd-s+=) – Sex!.

May 95. (cd)(c)(lp) **I SHOULD COCO** [1]
– I'd like to know / Caught by the fuzz / Mansize rooster / Alright / Lose it / Lenny / Strange ones / Sitting up straight / She's so loose / We're not supposed to / Time / Sofa (of my lethargy) / Time to go. *(7"free w/ ltd lp)*
STONE FREE. / ODD?

Jul 95. (7"colrd)(c-s) **ALRIGHT. / TIME** [2]
(cd-s+=) – Condition / Je suis votre papa sucre.
(cd-s+=) – Lose it.

SUPERTRAMP

Formed: London, England based . . . 1969 by RICHARD DAVIES. Through sponsorship from young Dutch millionaire Stanley Miesegaes, he enlisted new members through music paper ad. Quickly obtained a deal with 'A&M' and in the early 70's, released 2 albums before their untimely demise. SUPERTRAMP (Mk.II) hit the right note, when in 1974 'CRIME OF THE CENTURY (lp)' gave them first million-seller. Continued this success on both sides of the Atlantic, until the late 80's. • **Style:** Melodic and clever progressive rock, which veered into American AOR by the late 70's. • **Songwriters:** HODGSON and/or DAVIE, except I'M YOUR HOOCHIE COOCHIE MAN (John Lee Hooker). • **Trivia:** Took their name from a 1910 W.H.Davies book 'The Autobiography Of A Supertramp'.

Recommended: CRIME OF THE CENTURY (*8) / THE AUTOBIOGRAPHY OF SUPERTRAMP (*8) / BREAKFAST IN AMERICA (*7).

RICHARD DAVIES (b.22 Jul'44) – vocals, keyboards (ex-The JOINT) / **ROGER HODGSON** (b.21 Mar'50) – bass, keyboards, vocals / **RICHARD PALMER** – guitar / **BOB MILLER** – drums

A & M A & M

Aug 70. (lp)(c) **SUPERTRAMP**
– Surely / It's a long road / Aubade / And I am not like other birds of prey / Words unspoken / Maybe I'm a beggar / Home again / Nothing to show / Shadow song / Try again / Surely (reprise). *(US-iss.Mar78) (UK re-issues Mar82, Sep89 +cd) cd-iss.Sep88) (re-iss.May84 on 'Hallmark')(re-iss.c Jan93)*

— (May71) **HODGSON** now also lead guitar, vox / **FRANK FARRELL** – bass / **KEVIN CURRIE** – drums repl. PALMER + MILLER / added **DAVE WINTHROP** – saxophone

Jun 71. (lp)(c) **INDELIBLY STAMPED**
– Your poppa don't mind / Travelled / Rosie had everything planned / Remember / Forever / Potter / Coming home to see you / Times have changed / Friend in need / Aries. *(cd-iss.1988)(re-iss.c Jan93)*

Oct 71. (7") **FOREVER. / YOUR POPPA DON'T MIND** [-]

— Disbanded late Summer 1971, WINTHROP later joined SECRET AFFAIR. **DAVIES + HODGSON** re-formed them Aug'73. Recruited **DOUGIE THOMPSON** – bass (ex-BEES MAKE HONEY) / **BOB BENBERG** (b.SIEBENBERG) – drums

SUPERGRA
0

(ex-BEES MAKE HONEY) / **JOHN ANTHONY HELLIWELL** – saxophone, clarinet, vocals (ex-ALAN BOWN SET)

Mar 74. (7") **LAND HO. / SUMMER ROMANCE** [ ] [-]

Sep 74. (lp)(c) **CRIME OF THE CENTURY** [4] [38]
– School / Bloody well right / Hide in your shell / Asylum / Dreamer / Rudy / If everyone was listening / Crime of the century. *(re-iss.+cd.Apr86)*

Dec 74. (7") **DREAMER. / BLOODY WELL RIGHT** [13] [35] Apr 75
(above 'B'side was US 'A'side)

Nov 75. (lp)(c) **CRISIS? WHAT CRISIS?** [20] [44]
– Easy does it / Sister Moonshine / Ain't nobody but me / A soapbox opera / Another man's woman / Lady / Poor boy / Just a normal day / The meaning / Two of us. *(re-iss.+cd.Apr86)*

Nov 75. (7") **LADY. / YOU STARTED LAUGHING (WHEN I HELD YOU IN MY ARMS)** [ ] [ ]

Jun 76. (7") **SISTER MOONSHINE. / AIN'T NOBODY BUT ME** [-] [ ]

Apr 77. (lp)(c) **EVEN IN THE QUIETEST MOMENTS** [12] [16]
– Give a little bit / Lover boy / Even in the quietest moments / Downstream / Babaji / From now on / Fool's overture. *(re-iss.+cd.Apr86)*

Jun 77. (7") **GIVE A LITTLE BIT. / DOWNSTREAM** [29] [15]

Nov 77. (7") **FROM NOW ON. / DREAMER** [-] [ ]

Nov 77. (7") **BABAJI. / FROM NOW ON** [ ] [-]

Mar 79. (lp)(c) **BREAKFAST IN AMERICA** [3] [1]
– Gone Hollywood / The logical song / Goodbye stranger / Breakfast in America / Oh darling / Take the long way home / Lord is it mine / Just another nervous wreck / Casual conversations / Child of vision. *(cd-iss.1983)*

Mar 79. (7") **THE LOGICAL SONG. / JUST ANOTHER NERVOUS WRECK** [7] [6]

Jun 79. (7") **BREAKFAST IN AMERICA. / GONE HOLLYWOOD** [9] [-]

Sep 79. (7") **GOODBYE STRANGER. / EVEN IN THE QUIETEST MOMENTS** [57] [15] Jul 79

Oct 79. (7") **TAKE THE LONG WAY HOME. / FROM NOW ON** [ ] [-]

Oct 79. (7") **TAKE THE LONG WAY HOME. / RUBY** [-] [10]

Sep 80. (d-lp)(d-c) **PARIS (live 29-11-79)** [7] [8]
– School / Ain't nobody but me / The logical song / Bloody well right / Breakfast in America / You started laughing / Hide in your shell / From now on / Dreamer / Rudy / A soapbox opera / Asylum / Take the long way home / Fool's overture / Two of us / Crime of the century. *(cd-iss.Apr86)*

Sep 80. (7") **DREAMER (live). / FROM NOW ON (live)** [-] [15]

Nov 80. (7") **DREAMER (live). / YOU STARTED LAUGHING (live)** [ ] [-]

Nov 80. (7") **BREAKFAST IN AMERICA (live). / YOU STARTED LAUGHING (live)** [-] [62]

Oct 82. (7") **IT'S RAINING AGAIN. / BONNIE** [26] [11]

Oct 82. (lp)(c) **. . . FAMOUS LAST WORDS** [6] [5]
– Crazy / Put on your brown school shoes / It's raing again / Bonnie / Know who you are / My kind of lady / C'est la bon / Waiting so long / Don't leave me now. *(cd-iss.1983)*

Jan 83. (7") **MY KIND OF LADY. / KNOW WHO YOU ARE** [ ] [31]

—— (Nov82) Now a quartet when HODGSON departed to go solo. (Re-joined briefly late'86 tour). HODGSON solo albums: IN THE EYE OF THE STORM (84) / HAI HAI (87).

Apr 85. (7") **CANNONBALL. / EVER OPEN DOOR** [ ] [28]

May 85. (lp)(c)(cd) **BROTHER WHERE YOU BOUND** [20] [21]
– Cannonball / Still in love / No inbetween / Better days / Brother where you bound / Ever open door. *(re-iss.c Jan93)*

Jul 85. (7") **STILL IN LOVE. / NO INBETWEEN** [ ] [ ] Feb 85
(12"+=) – Cannonball (dance mix).

Sep 85. (7") **BETTER DAYS. / NO INBETWEEN** [-] [ ]

Nov 86. (lp)(c)(cd) **THE AUTOBIOGRAPHY OF SUPERTRAMP** (compilation) [9] [ ]
– Goodbye stranger / The logical song / Bloody well right / Breakfast in America / Take the long way home / Crime of the century / Dreamer / From now on / Give a little bit / It's raining again / Cannonball / Ain't nobody but me / Hide in your shell / Rudy. *(cd= 3 extra) (re-iss.cd Jan93 as 'THE VERY BEST OF SUPERTRAMP' +=)*– School.

Oct 87. (7")(12") **I'M BEGGIN' YOU. / NO INBETWEENS** [ ] [ ]

Oct 87. (lp)(c)(cd) **FREE AS A BIRD** [93] [ ]
– It's alright / Not the moment / It doesn't matter / Where I stand / Free as a bird / I'm beggin' you / You never can tell with friends / Thing for you / An awful thing to waste.

Feb 88. (7") **FREE AS A BIRD. / THING FOR YOU** [-] [ ]

Feb 88. (7") **FREE AS A BIRD. / I'M BEGGIN' YOU** [ ] [-]

Oct 88. (lp)(c)(cd) **LIVE '88 (live)** [ ] [ ]
– You started laughing / It's alright / Not the moment / Oh darling / Breakfast in America / From now on / Just another nervous wreck / The logical song / I'm your hoochie coochie man / Crime of the century / Don't you lie to me. *(re-iss.cd Jan93)*

—— Folded after above.

– more compilations, etc. –

May 81. A&M; (d-c) **CRISIS? WHAT CRISIS? / EVEN IN THE QUIETEST MOMENTS** [ ] [-]

Sep 86. A&M; (7") **THE LOGICAL SONG. / GOODBYE STRANGER** [ ] [-]

Aug 88. A&M; (cd-ep) **COMPACT HITS** [ ] [-]
– The logical song / Breakfast in America / Goodbye stranger / Hide in your shell.

Jul 92. A&M; (7")(c-s) **GIVE A LITTLE BIT (for Telethon). / ('A' original version)** [ ] [ ]
(cd-s+=) – Breakfast in America.

Sep 85. Old Gold; (7") **DREAMER. / GIVE A LITTLE BIT** [ ] [-]

SUPREMES

Formed: Detroit, Michigan, USA . . . 1959 by manager Milton Jenkins, who originally employed the female trio/quartet to augment The PRIMES (later The TEMPTATIONS) on stage. After a spell in 1960, as The PRIMETTES they folded but re-formed as a trio (DIANA, MARY & FLORENCE), changing name to The SUPREMES and signing to 'Motown' label. Late in 1963, they finally broke through into chart land with WHEN THE LOVELIGHT STARTS SHINING THROUGH HIS EYES. The following year, WHERE DID OUR LOVE GO gave them their first of twelve US No.1's in the sixties. In the 70's, when DIANA departed to have mega solo success, The SUPREMES bar a few Top 20 hits, faded away into cabaret circuit. **Style and songwriters:** Glamourous uptempo soul-pop act, relying heavily on image, choreography and also the fine penwork of either HOLLAND/DOZIER/HOLLAND or SMOKEY ROBINSON. Motown also used other sources for material, such as SAM COOKE, ROGERS & HART plus label owner BERRY GORDY on a few early 45's. • **Trivia:** Their hits have been covered successfully by many acts. The most popular being YOU CAN'T HURRY LOVE (Phil Collins) / YOU KEEP ME HANGIN' ON (Vanila Fudge) / NATHAN JONES (Bananarama; who went on to emulate their UK chart success in the 80's).

Recommended: 20 GREATEST HITS (*8)

DIANA ROSS (b.26 Mar'44) – lead vox / **FLORENCE BALLARD** (b.30 Jun'43) – vox / **MARY WILSON** (b. 6 Mar44, Greenville, Missouri) – vox / **BARBARA MARTIN** – vox repl. BETTY TRAVIS in 1960.

Oriole ? / Motown

Dec 60. (7") **I WANT A GUY. / NEVER AGAIN** [-] [ ]

Jul 61. (7") **BUTTERED POPCORN. / WHO'S LOVING YOU** [-] [ ]

—— Slim to a trio, when BARBARA left

Jul 62. (7") **YOUR HEART BELONGS TO ME. / HE'S SEVENTEEN** [-] [95]

Dec 62. (7") **LET ME GO THE RIGHT WAY. / TIME CHANGES THINGS** [-] [90]

Apr 63. (7") **MY HEART CAN'T TAKE NO MORE. / YOU BRING BACK MEMORIES** [-] [ ]

Jul 63. (7") **A BREATH TAKING GUY. / (THE MAN WITH THE) ROCK'N'ROLL BANJO BAND** [-] [75]

Stateside / Motown

Dec 63. (7") **WHEN THE LOVELIGHT STARTS SHINING THROUGH HIS EYES. / STANDING AT THE CROSSROADS OF LOVE** [ ] [23] Nov 63

Dec 63. (lp) **MEET THE SUPREMES** [-] [ ]
– Where did our love go / Your heart belongs to me / Butttered popcorn / Baby, don't go / (The man with the) Rock and roll banjo band / I want a guy / When the lovelight starts shining thru' his eyes / You bring back memories / Play a sad song / Time changes things / Never again / Standing at the crossroads of love. *(UK-iss.Nov64, hit No.8)*

Feb 64. (7") **RUN, RUN, RUN. / I'M GIVING YOU YOUR FREEDOM** [-] [93]

Aug 64. (7") **WHERE DID OUR LOVE GO. / HE MEANS THE WORLD TO ME** [3] [1] Jun 64
(re-iss.Aug74) (re-iss.as were most major hit singles; Oct81)

Oct 64. (7") **BABY LOVE. / ASK ANY GIRL** [1] [1] Sep 64

Oct 64. (lp) **WHERE DID OUR LOVE GO** [ ] [2] Sep 64
– Where did our love go / Run, run, run / Baby love / When the lovelight starts shining through his eyes / Come see about me / Long gone lover / I'm giving you your freedom / A breath taking guy / He means the world to me / Standing at the crossroads of love / You kiss of fire / Ask any girl. *(re-iss.Oct81)*

Jan 65. (lp) **A BIT OF LIVERPOOL** (UK title: **WITH LOVE FROM US TO YOU)** [ ] [21] Nov 64
– How do you do it / World without love / House of the rising sun / A hard day's night / Because / You've really got a hold on me / You can't do that / Do you love me / Can't buy me love / I want to hold your hand / Bits and pieces.

Jan 65. (7") **COME SEE ABOUT ME. / (YOU'RE GONE BUT) ALWAYS IN MY HEART** [27] [1] Nov 64

Tamla Motown / Motown

Mar 65. (7") **STOP! IN THE NAME OF LOVE. / I'M IN LOVE AGAIN** [7] [1] Feb 65

May 65. (7") **BACK IN MY ARMS AGAIN. / WHISPER YOU LOVE ME BOY** [40] [1] Apr 65

Jul 65. (lp) **WE REMEMBER SAM COOKE** [ ] [75] May 65
– You send me / Nothing can change this love / Cupid / Chain gang / Bring it on home to me / Only sixteen / Havin' a party / Shake / Wonderful world / A change is gonna come / (Ain't that) Good news. *(re-iss.+c.May86)*

Jul 65. (7") **NOTHING BUT HEARTACHES. / HE HOLDS HIS OWN** [ ] [11]

Aug 65. (lp) **MORE HITS BY THE SUPREMES** (compilation) [-] [6]
– Ask any girl / Nothing but heartaches / Mother dear / Honey boy / Back in my arma again / Whisper you love me, boy / The only time I'm happy / He holds his own / Who could ever doubt my love / Heartaches don't last always / I'm in love again.

Oct 65. (lp) **THE SUPREMES SING COUNTRY WESTERN AND POP** [ ] [79] Mar 65
– Funny how time slips away / My heart can't take it no more / It makes no difference now / You didn't care / Tears in vain / Tumbling tumbleweeds / Lazy bones / You need me / Baby doll / Sunset / (The man with the) Rock and roll banjo band.

Nov 65. (7") **I HEAR A SYMPHONY. / WHO COULD EVER DOUBT MY LOVE** [39] [1] Oct 65

Nov 65. (lp) **THE SUPREMES AT THE COPA (live)** [ ] [11]
– Opening introduction: Put on a happy face / I am woman / Baby love / Stop! in the name of love / The boy from Ipanema / Make someone happy / Come see about me / Rock-a-bye your baby with a dixie melody / Queen of the house / Group intro- Somewhere / Back in my arms again / Sam Cooke medley / You're nobody til somebody loves you. *(re-iss.+c.Mar82 + Mar86)*

Dec 65. (7") **TWINKLE, TWINKLE LITTLE ME. / CHILDREN'S CHRISTMAS SONG** [-] [ ]

Dec 65. (lp) **MERRY CHRISTMAS** (Festive songs) [-] [ ]

Feb 66. (7") **MY WORLD IS EMPTY WITHOUT YOU. / EVERY-THING IS GOOD ABOUT YOU** [ ] [5] Jan 66

Mar 66. (lp) **I HEAR A SYMPHONY** [ ] [8]
– Stranger in Paradise / Yesterday / I hear a symphony / Unchained melody / With a song in my heart / My world is empty without you / A lover's concerto / Any girl in love (knows what I'm going through) / Wonderful, wonderful / Everything is good about you / He's all I got. *(re-iss.Oct81)*

May 66. (7") **LOVE IS LIKE AN ITCHING IN MY HEART. / HE'S ALL I GOT** [ ] [9] Apr 66

Aug 66. (7") **YOU CAN'T HURRY LOVE. / PUT YOURSELF IN MY PLACE** [3] [1]

Oct 66. (7") **YOU KEEP ME HANGIN' ON. / REMOVE THIS DOUBT** [-] [1]

Nov 66. (7") **YOU KEEP ME HANGIN' ON. / COME SEE ABOUT ME** [8] [-]

Dec 66. (lp) **THE SUPREMES A'GO-GO** [15] [1] Sep 66
– Love is like an itching in my heart / This old heart of mine (is weak for you) / You can't hurry love / Shake me, wake up (when it's over) / Baby I need your loving / These boots are made for walking / I can't help myself / Get ready / Put yourself in my place / Money (that's what I want) / Come and get these memories / Hang on Sloopy. *(re-iss.+c.Oct81)*

Feb 67. (7") **LOVE IS HERE AND NOW YOU'RE GONE. / THERE'S NO STOPPING US NOW** [17] [1] Jan 67

Apr 67. (lp) **THE SUPREMES SING MOTOWN** [15] [6] Feb 67
– You keep me hangin' on / You're gone, but always in my heart / Love is here and now you're gone / Mother, you smother me / I guess I'll always love you / I'll turn to stone / It's the same old song / Going down for the third time / Love is in our hearts / Remove the doubt / There's no stopping us now / Heatwave. (US title '. . . SING HOLLAND-DOZIER-HOLLAND') *(re-iss.Oct81) (cd-iss.Sep95)*

May 67. (7") **THE HAPPENING. / ALL I KNOW ABOUT YOU** [6] [1] Apr 67

Sep 67. (lp) **THE SUPREMES SING RODGERS AND HART** [25] [20] Jun 67
– The lady is a tramp / Mountain greenery / This can't be love / Where or when / Lover / My funny valentine / My romance / My heart stood still / Falling in love with love / Thou swell / Dancing on the ceiling / Blue Moon. *(cd-iss. Nov 87 with extra tracks).*

—— (May67) **CINDY BIRDSONG** (b.15 Dec'39, Camden, New Jersey) – vocals (ex-PATTI LaBELLE & THE BLUEBELLES) repl. BALLARD who later went solo

DIANA ROSS & THE SUPREMES

Aug 67. (7") **REFLECTIONS. / GOING DOWN FOR THE THIRD TIME** [5] [2]

Nov 67. (7") **IN AND OUT OF LOVE. / I GUESS I'LL ALWAYS LOVE YOU** [13] [9]

Jan 68. (lp) **DIANA ROSS & THE SUPREMES' GREATEST HITS** (compilation) [1] [1] Sep 67
(US as d-lp= VOL.1 & 2) *(re-iss.Jan79 & Jun83)*

Mar 68. (d-lp) **LIVE AT THE TALK OF THE TOWN (live)** [6] [57] Sep 68
– With a song in my heart / Stranger than Paradise / Wonderful, wonderful / Without a song / Stop! in the name of love / Come and see about me / My world is empty without you / Baby love / Love is here and now you're gone / More / You keep me hangin' on / Michelle / Yesterday / In and out of love / The lady is a tramp / Let's get away from it all / The happening / Thoroughly modern Millie / Second hand Rose / Mame / Reflections / You're nobody till somebody loves you / I hear a symphony. *(re-iss.Oct79 on 'M.F.P.')*

Mar 68. (7") **FOREVER CAME TODAY. / TIME CHANGES THINGS** [28] [28]

Jun 68. (7") **SOME THINGS YOU NEVER GET USED TO. / YOU'VE BEEN SO WONDERFUL TO ME** [34] [30]

Jul 68. (lp) **REFLECTIONS** [30] [18] Apr 68
– Reflections / I'm gonna make it (I will wait for you) / Forever came today / I can't make it alone / In and out of love / Bah-bah-bah / What the world needs now is love / Up, up and away / Love (makes me do foolish things) / Then / Misery makes its home in my heart / Ode to Billie Joe. *(re-iss.Mar85)*

Oct 68. (lp) **SING AND PERFORM FUNNY GIRL** (from the musical) [-] [ ]

Nov 68. (7") **LOVE CHILD. / THIS WILL BE THE DAY** [15] [1] Oct 68

Jan 69. (lp) **LOVE CHILD** [8] [14] Dec 68
– Love child / Keep an eye / How long has the evening train been gone / Does your mama know about me / Honey bee (keep on stinging me) / Something you never get used to / He's my sunny boy / You've never been so wonderful to me / (Don't break these) Chains of love / You ain't living til you're lovin' / I'll set you free / Can't shake it loose. *(re-iss.+c.Aug82)*

—— Late 1968, The SUPREMES re-united with The TEMPTATIONS on cross-Atlantic Top 3 hit 'I'M GONNA MAKE YOU LOVE ME'. Throughout 1969, they recorded and released a number of other hit 45's and lp's. (see further below for more details)

Apr 69. (7") **I'M LIVIN' IN SHAME. / I'M SO GLAD I GOT SOMEBODY (LIKE YOU AROUND)** [14] [10] Jan 69

Apr 69. (7") **THE COMPOSER. / THE BEGINNING OF THE END** [-] [27]

May 69. (7") **THE COMPOSER. / TAKE ME WHERE YOU GO** [-] [27]

Jun 69. (lp) **LET THE SUNSHINE IN** [ ] [24]
– The composer / Everyday people / No matter what sign you are / Hey Western Union man / What becomes of the broken hearted? / I'm livin' in shame / Aquarius (medley: Let the sun shine in (in the flesh failures)- Let the music play / With a child's heart / Discover me (and you'll discover love) / Will this be the day / I'm so glad I got somebody (like you around).

Jul 69. (7") **NO MATTER WHAT SIGN YOU ARE. / THE YOUNG FOLKS** [37] [31]
[69] Jun 69

Dec 69. (lp) **CREAM OF THE CROP** [-] [33]
– Someday we'll be together / Can't you see it's me / You gave me love / Hey Jude / The young folks / Shadows of society / Loving you is better than ever / When it's to the top (still I won't stop giving you love) / Till Johnny comes / Blowin' in the wind / The beginning of the end.

Dec 69. (7") **SOMEDAY WE'LL BE TOGETHER. / HE'S MY SUNNY BOY** [13] [1] Oct 69

May 70. (lp)(c) **DIANA ROSS & THE SUPREMES' GREATEST HITS VOL.3** (compilation) [ ] [31] Jan 70
– Reflections / Love is here and now you're gone / Someday we'll be together / Love child / Some things you never get used to / Forever came today / In and out of love / The happening / I'm livin' in shame / No matter what sign you are / The composer. *(re-iss.Jul76, Oct81)*

May 70. (d-lp) **FAREWELL** (final concert 14 Jan'70) [ ] [46]
– T.C.B. / Medley: Stop! in the name of love – Come see about me – My world is empty without you – Baby love / Medley: The lady is a tramp – Let's get away from it all / Love is here and now you're gone / I'm gonna make you love me / Can't take my eyes off you / Reflections / My man / Didn't we / It's alright with me / Big spender / Falling in love with love / Love child / Aquarius – Let the sunshine in (the flesh failures) / The impossible dream / Someday we'll be together / (closing dialogue from group).

The SUPREMES

when DIANA ROSS left to go solo. In Jan70, she was replaced by **JEAN TERRELL** (b.26 Nov'44, Texas) – lead vox

Apr 70. (7") **UP THE LADDER TO THE ROOF. / BILL, WHEN ARE YOU COMING BACK** [6] [10] Mar 70

Jun 70. (lp)(c) **RIGHT ON** [ ] [25] May 70
– Up the ladder on the roof / Then we can try again / Everybody's got the right to love / Wait a minute before you leave me / You move me / But I love you more / I got hurt / Baby baby / Take a closer look at me / Then I met you / Bill, when are you coming back / Loving country.

Jul 70. (7") **EVERYBODY'S GOT THE RIGHT TO LOVE. / BUT I LOVE YOU MORE** [ ] [21]

Nov 70. (lp)(c) **NEW WAYS BUT LOVE STAYS** [ ] [68] Oct 70
– Together we can make such sweet music / Stoned love / It's time to break down / Bridge over troubled water / I wish I were your mirror / Come together / Is there a place (in his heart for me) / Na na hey hey, kiss him goodbye / Shine on me / Thank him for today.

—— Late 1970, they collaborated with another 'Motown' group The FOUR TOPS. They were to hit US/UK Top 20 with their version of RIVER DEEP – MOUNTAIN HIGH. A few other hits followed in 1971, accompanied by parent albums THE MAGNIFICENT 7 / THE RETURN OF THE MAGNIFICENT 7 / DYNAMITE. (see further on)

Jan 71. (7") **STONED LOVE. / SHINE ON ME** [3] [7] Nov 70

Aug 71. (7") **NATHAN JONES. / HAPPY IS A BUMPY ROAD** [5] [16] May 71

Sep 71. (lp)(c) **TOUCH** [40] [85] Jun 71
– This is the story / Nathan Jones / Here comes the sunrise / Love, it came to me first time / Johnny Raven / Have I lost you / Time and love / Touch / Happy (is a bumpy road) / It's so hard for me to say goodbye.
(re-iss.Mar76)(cd-iss.Nov93)

Sep 71. (7") **TOUCH. / IT'S SO HARD FOR ME TO SAY GOODBYE** [-] [71]

Feb 72. (7") **FLOY JOY. / THIS IS THE STORY** [9] [16] Jan 72

Jun 72. (lp)(c) **FLOY JOY** [ ] [54] May 72
– Your wonderful sweet sweet love / Floy joy / A heart like mine / Over and over / Precious little things / Now the bitter, now the sweet / Automatically sunshine / The wisdom of time / Oh be my love.

Jun 72. (7") **AUTOMATICALLY SUNSHINE. / PRECIOUS LITTLE THINGS** [10] [37] May 72

—— **LYNDA LAWRENCE** – vocals repl. BIRDSONG who was now married

Aug 72. (7") **YOUR WONDERFUL, SWEET SWEET LOVE. / LOVE IT CAME TO ME THIS TIME** [ ] [59]

Nov 72. (lp)(c) **THE SUPREMES** [ ] [ ]
– I guess I'll miss the man / 5:30 plane / Tossin' and turnin' / When can Brown begin / Beyond myself / Silent voices / All I want / Once in the morning / I keep it hid / Paradise / Cheap lovin'.

Jan 73. (7") **I GUESS I'LL MISS THE MAN. / OVER AND OVER** [ ] [85] Oct 72

Mar 73. (7") **BAD WEATHER. / IT'S SO HARD FOR ME TO SAY GOODBYE** [37] [87]

Jun 73. (7") **TOSSIN' AND TURNIN'. / OH BE MY LOVE** [ ] [ ]

—— (Jul73) **MARY + LYNDA** enlisted newcomer **SCHERRIE PAYNE** (b.14 Nov'44) – vocals repl. TERRELL

Jun 75. (lp)(c) **THE SUPREMES** [ ] [ ]
– He's my man / Eary morning love / Where is it I belong / It's been said before / This is why I believe in you / You can't stop a girl in love / Colour my world blue / Give out, but don't give up / Where do I go from here / You turn me around.

Aug 75. (7") **HE'S MY MAN. / GIVE OUT, BUT DON'T GIVE UP** [ ] [ ]

Nov 75. (7") **EARLY MORNING LOVE. / WHERE IS IT I BELONG** [ ] [ ]

—— (1976) **SUSAYNE GREENE** – vocals repl. CINDY who had temp.repl. LYNDA

Past member FLORENCE BALLARD tragically died of a heart attack on 22 Feb'76

Jun 76. (lp)(c) **HIGH ENERGY** [ ] [42] May 76
– High energy / I'm gonna let my heart do the walking / Only you (can love me like you love me) / You keep me moving on / Don't let my teardrops better you / Till the boat sails away / I don't want to lose you / You're what's missing in my life.

Jul 76. (7") **I'M GONNA LET MY HEART DO THE WALKING. / COLOUR MY WORLD BLUE** [ ] [40] May 76

Nov 76. (7") **MY DRIVING WHEEL. / YOU'RE WHAT'S MISSING IN MY LIFE** [ ] [85]

Dec 76. (lp)(c) **MARY, SCHERRIE & SUSAYNE** [ ] [ ]
– You're my driving wheel / Sweet dream machine / Let yourself go / Come into my life / We should be closer together / I don't want to be tied down / You are the heart of me / Love I never knew you could feel so good.

Mar 77. (7") **LOVE I NEVER KNEW YOU COULD FEEL SO GOOD. / THIS IS WHY I BELIEVE IN YOU** [ ] [ ]

—— **KAREN JACKSON** – vocals repl. MARY WILSON who later toured as MARY WILSON & THE SUPREMES. The real SUPREMES gave up in 1977. On 16 May'83, DIANA, MARY and CINDY re-united for one-off Motown anniversary gig.

– more compilations, etc. –

Note; on 'Tamla Motown' unless otherwise mentioned.

Jun 74. (t-lp) **ANTHOLOGY (1962-1969)** [ ] [66]
(d-cd-iss.Apr93)

Jul 74. (7") **BABY LOVE. / ?** [12] [-]

Nov 74. (7") **WHERE DID OUR LOVE GO. / NOTHING BUT HEARTACHES** [ ] [-]

Sep 76. (7") **NATHAN JONES. / STONED LOVE** [ ] [-]

Mar 77. (lp)(c) **MOTOWN SPECIAL** [ ] [-]
(re-iss.Oct81)

Aug 77. (lp)(c) **DIANA ROSS & THE SUPREMES' 20 GOLDEN GREATS** [1] [-]
(re-iss.Oct81, cd-iss.May86)

Mar 80. (7") **I'M GONNA MAKE YOU LOVE ME. / ?** [-] [ ]
Apr 80. (7"ep)(12"ep) **SUPREMES MEDLEY EP. / LOVE HANGOVER (DIANA ROSS)** [ ] [ ]
Oct 80. (7") **YOU CAN'T HURRY LOVE. / THE HAPPENING** [ ] [ ]
Oct 80. (7") **REFLECTIONS. / LOVE CHILD** [ ] [-]
Oct 80. (lp)(c) **THE EARLY YEARS 1961-1964** [ ] [-]
Oct 81. (7") **BABY LOVE. / STOP! IN THE NAME OF LOVE** [ ] [-]
Oct 81. (7") **FLOY JOY. / BAD WEATHER** [ ] [-]
Nov 82. (lp)(c) **MERRY CHRISTMAS** [ ] [-]
Feb 83. (7") **UP THE LADDER TO ROOF. / AUTOMATICALLY SUNSHINE** [ ] [-]
Feb 83. (7") **YOU CAN'T HURRY LOVE. / THE HAPPENING** [ ] [-]
Mar 83. (7") **LOVE IS HERE AND NOW YOU'RE GONE. / BACK IN MY ARMS AGAIN** [ ] [-]
1983. (7") **FLOY JOY. / BAD WEATHER** [ ] [-]
1983. (7") **RIVER DEEP – MOUNTAIN HIGH. / YOU GOTTA HAVE LOVE IN YOUR HEART** [ ] [-]
Apr 85. (7")(12") **YOU KEEP ME HANGIN' ON. / COME SEE ABOUT ME** [ ] [ ]
Apr 86. (7") **YOU KEEP ME HANGIN' ON. / COME SEE ABOUT ME** [ ] [-]
(12"+=) – I hear a symphony / Your love is like an itching in my heart.
Jul 86. (d-lp)(d-c)(d-cd) **25th ANNIVERSARY** [ ] [ ]
Oct 86. (cd) **COMPACT COMMAND PERFORMANCES – 20 GREATEST HITS** [ ] [ ]
– When the lovelight starts shining through his eyes / Where did our love go / Baby love / Come see about me / My world is empty without you / Stop in the name of love / Back in my arms again / I hear a symphony / You can't hurry love / Love is like an itching in my heart / You keep me hangin' on / Love is here now you're gone / Reflections / Love child / I'll try something new / I'm gonna make you love me / Someday we'll be together / The ladder to the roof / Stoned love / Nathan Jones.
Nov 86. (cd) **LOVE CHILD / SUPREMES A GO-GO** [ ] [-]
Dec 86. (cd) **WHERE DID OUR LOVE GO. / I HEAR A SYMPHONY** [ ] [-]
Dec 86. (cd) **2 CLASSIC ALBUMS** [ ] [-]
– (LET THE SUN SHINE IN / CREAM OF THE CROP)
Feb 88. (cd) **EVERY GREAT NO.1 HIT** [ ] [ ]
Jan 89. (cd)(c)(lp) **LOVE SUPREME** [10] [ ]
Feb 89. (7") **STOP! IN THE NAME OF LOVE. /** [62] [-]
(cd-s+=) –
Jul 92. (cd) **70's GREATEST HITS AND RARE CLASSICS** [ ] [ ]
Jan 79. M.F.P.; (lp)(c) **STONED LOVE** [ ] [-]
May 93. Spectrum; (cd)(c) **STOP IN THE NAME OF LOVE (DIANA ROSS & THE SUPREMES)** [ ] [-]
May 93. Spectrum; (cd)(c) **I'M GONNA MAKE YOU LOVE ME (DIANA ROSS & THE SUPREMES)** [ ] [-]
(re-iss. Mar '94)

DIANA ROSS AND THE SUPREMES & THE TEMPTATIONS

Tamla Motown / Motown

Jan 69. (7") **I'M GONNA MAKE YOU LOVE ME. / A PLACE IN THE SUN** [3] [2] Nov 68
Jan 69. (lp) **DIANA ROSS AND THE SUPREMES JOIN THE TEMPTATIONS** [1] [2] Nov 68
– I'm gonna make you love me / My guy / My girl / Uptight (everything's alright) / Sweet inspiration / I'll try something new / Ain't no mountain high enough / I second that emotion / Why must we fall in love / For better or worse / The weight / I'll be doggone / Stubborn kind of fellow. *(re-iis+c.Jul81 & Oct82)*
Mar 69. (7"+7"red) **I'LL TRY SOMETHING NEW. / THE WAY YOU DO THE THINGS YOU DO** [-] [25]
Jun 69. (lp) **T.C.B. (The Original Soundtrack)** [11] [1] Dec 68
– T.C.B. / Stop, in the name of love / You keep me hangin' on / Get ready / The way you do the things you do / A taste of honey / Eleanor Rigby / Do you know the way to San Jose / Mrs.Robinson / Respect / Somewhere / Ain't too proud to beg / Hello young lovers / For once in my life / I know I'm losing you / With a song in my heart / Come see about me / My world is empty without you / Baby love / I hear a symphony / The impossible dream. *(re-iss.+c.Mar82)*
Jul 69. (7") **STUBBORN KIND OF FELLOW. / TRY IT BABY** [-] [ ]
Sep 69. (7") **I SECOND THAT EMOTION. / THE WAY YOU DO THE THINGS YOU DO** [18] [-]
Sep 69. (7") **THE WEIGHT. / FOR BETTER OR WORSE** [-] [46]
Dec 69. (lp) **ON BROADWAY (TV Show)** [-] [38]
Feb 70. (lp)(c) **TOGETHER** [28] [28] Oct 69
– Stubborn kind of fellow / I'll be doggone / The weight / Ain't nothing like the real thing / Uptight (everything's alright) / Sing a simple song / My guy, my girl / For better or worse / Can't take my eyes off you / Why (must we fall in love).
Mar 70. (7") **WHY (MUST WE FALL IN LOVE). / UPTIGHT** [31] [-]

The SUPREMES & THE FOUR TOPS

Tamla Motown / Motown

Jun 71. (7") **RIVER DEEP – MOUNTAIN HIGH. / IT'S GOT TO BE A MIRACLE** [11] [14] Nov 70
Jun 71. (lp)(c) **THE MAGNIFICENT 7** [6] [ ] Oct 70
– River deep – mountain high / Knock on my door / For your love / Without the one you love / Reach out and touch (somebody's hand) / Stoned soul picnic / Baby (you've got what it takes) / Ain't nothing like the real thing / Everyday people / It's got to be a miracle (this thing called love) / A taste of honey / Together we can make such sweet music. *(re-iss.Oct81)*
Nov 71. (7") **YOU GOTTA HAVE LOVE IN YOUR HEART. / I'M GLAD ABOUT IT** [25] [55] Jul 71
Nov 71. (lp)(c) **THE RETURN OF THE MAGNIFICENT 7** [ ] [ ]
Jan 72. (lp)(c) **DYNAMITE** [ ] [ ]
– It's impossible / The bigger you love (the harder you fall) / Hello stranger / Love the one you're with / Good lovin' ain't easy to come by / Melodie / If / If I could build my whole world around you / Don't let me lose this dream / Do you love me just a little honey.
May 72. (7") **WITHOUT THE ONE YOU LOVE. / LET'S MAKE LOVE NOW** [ ] [ ]
Nov 72. (7") **REACH OUT AND TOUCH (SOMEBODY'S HAND). / WHERE WOULD I BE WITHOUT YOU BABY** [ ] [ ]

David SURKAMP (see under ⇒ PAVLOV'S DOG)

SURVIVOR

Formed: Chicago, Illinois, USA . . . 1978 by PETERIK and SULLIVAN. They were joined by vocalist BICKLER and two other session men, who completed work on their self-titled debut album late in 1979 for 'Scotti Brothers' records. In 1982 they topped the US + UK charts with single 'EYE OF THE TIGER', which was used on the soundtrack of 'Rocky III'. • **Style:** Heavy AOR outfit, similar to JOURNEY or FOREIGNER. • **Songwriters:** PETERIK-SULLIVAN compositions. The pair also wrote material for • 38 SPECIAL. • **Trivia:** PETERIK's old band IDES OF MARCH had a 1970 US No.2 + UK No.31 hit single with 'VEHICLE'. In 1976, 'Epic' issued his solo album 'DON'T FIGHT THAT FEELING'.

Recommended: EYE OF THE TIGER (*5).

DAVE BICKLER – vox, synth. / **FRANK SULLIVAN** – lead guitar, vocals (ex-MARIAH) / **JIM PETERIK** – keyboards, guitar, vocals (ex-Solo artist, ex-IDES OF MARCH) / **DENNIS JOHNSON** – bass / **GARY SMITH** – drums

Scotti Br. / Scotti Br.

Mar 80. (7") **SOMEWHERE IN AMERICA. / FREELAND** [ ] [70] Feb 80
Nov 80. (lp)(c) **SURVIVOR** [ ] [ ] Mar 80
– Somewhere in America / Can't getcha offa my mind / Let it be now / As soon as love finds me / Youngblood / Love has got me / The whole town's talkin' / 20-20 / Freelance / Nothing can shake me (from your love) / Whatever it takes.
Nov 80. (7") **REBEL GIRL. / FREELANCE** [-] [ ]

—— **STEPHAN ELLIS** – bass + MARC DROUBAY – drums repl. JOHNSON and SMITH

Aug 81. (7") **SUMMER NIGHTS. / LOVE IS ON MY SIDE** [-] [ ]
Nov 81. (7") **POOR MAN'S SON. / LOVE IS ON MY SIDE** [ ] [33] Oct 81
Dec 81. (lp)(c) **PREMONITION** [ ] [82] Oct 81
– Chevy nights / Summer nights / Poor man's son Heart's a lonely hunter / Light of a thousand smiles / Take you on a Saturday / Runway lights / Love is on my side. *(re-iss.Nov82)*
Feb 82. (7") **SUMMER NIGHTS. / TAKE YOU ON A SATURDAY** [ ] [62]
Jul 82. (7")(12")(7"pic-d) **EYE OF THE TIGER. / TAKE YOU ON A SATURDAY** [1] [1] Jun 82
(above from the film 'Rocky III') *(re-iss.Jan84 on 'Epic')*
Jul 82. (lp)(c) **EYE OF THE TIGER** [12] [2] Jun 82
– Eye of the tiger / Feels like love / Hesitation dance / The one that really matters / I'm not that man anymore / Children of the night / Ever since the world began / American heartbeat / Silver girl. *(re-iss.+cd.Feb86)*
Sep 82. (7")(7"pic-d) **AMERICAN HEARTBEAT. / SILVER GIRL** [ ] [17]
Jan 83. (7") **THE ONE THAT REALLY MATTERS. / HESITATION DANCE** [ ] [74]
Oct 83. (lp)(c) **CAUGHT IN THE GAME** [ ] [82]
– Caught in the game / Jackie don't go / I never stopped loving you / It doesn't have to be this way / Ready for the real thing / Half-life / What do you really think / Slander / Santa Ana winds.
Nov 83. (7") **CAUGHT IN THE ACT. / SLANDER** [ ] [77] Oct 83
Feb 84. (7") **I NEVER STOPPED LOVING YOU. / READY FOR THE REAL THING** [-] [ ]
Jul 84. (7") **THE MOMENT OF TRUTH. / IT DOESN'T HAVE TO BE THIS WAY** [ ] [63] Jun 84
(above from the film 'The Karate Kid', issued on 'Casablanca')

—— **JIMI JAMISON** – vocals (ex-COBRA) repl. BICKLER

Sep 84. (7") **I CAN'T HOLD BACK. / I SEE YOU IN EVERYONE** [ ] [13]
Nov 84. (7") **HIGH ON YOU. / BROKEN PROMISES** [ ] [8] Jan 85
Dec 84. (lp)(c) **VITAL SIGNS** [ ] [16] Sep 84
– I can't hold back / High on you / First night / The search is over / Broken promises / Popular girl / Everlasting / It's the singer not the song / I see you in everyone / Moment of truth. *(cd-iss.1986 on 'Bellaphon')*
Jun 85. (7")(12") **THE SEARCH IS OVER. / IT'S THE SINGER NOT THE SONG** [ ] [4] Apr 85
Aug 85. (7") **FIRST NIGHT. / FEELS LIKE LOVE** [-] [53]
(below single from the film 'Rocky IV')
Nov 85. (7")(7"pic-d) **BURNING HEART. / FEELS LIKE LOVE** [5] [2] Oct 85
(12"+=)/ /(d7"++=) – Eye of the tiger./ / Take you on a Saturday.
Nov 86. (lp)(c) **WHEN SECONDS COUNT** [ ] [49]
– How much love / Keep it right here / Is this love / Man against the world / Rebel son / Oceans / When seconds count / Backstreet love affair / In good faith / Can't let you go.
Nov 86. (7") **IS THIS LOVE. / CAN'T LET YOU GO** [ ] [9] Oct 86
(12"+=) – ('A'&'B'versions).
Feb 87. (7") **HOW MUCH LOVE. / BACKSTREET LOVE AFFAIR** [-] [51]
Apr 87. (7") **MAN AGAINST THE WORLD. / OCEANS** [-] [86]

—— live guests **PETER JOHN VETTESE** – keyboards / **BILL SYNIAR** – bass / **MICKEY CURRY** – drums repl. ELLIS + DROUBAY

Polydor / Scotti Br.

Oct 88. (7") **DIDN'T KNOW IT WAS LOVE. / RHYTHM OF THE CITY** [-] [61]
Jan 89. (7") **ACROSS THE MILES. / BURNING BRIDGES** [-] [74]
Apr 89. (lp)(c)(cd) **TOO HOT TO SLEEP** [ ] [ ] Nov 88
– She's a star / Desperate dreams / To hot to sleep / Didn't know it was blue / Rhythm of the city / Here comes desire / Across the miles / Take me I'm the one / Can't give it up / Burning bridges.

—— Disbanded around the same time.

– compilations, others, etc. –

Mar 86. Scotti Bros; (7") **I CAN'T HOLD BACK. / BURNING HEART** [ ] [-]
1989. Scotti Bros; (lp)(c)(cd) **THE BEST OF SURVIVOR** *(UK-iss.cd Apr93)* [-] [ ]
Aug 93. Scotti Bros; (cd)(c) **GREATEST HITS** [ ] [ ]
1986. Bellaphon; (lp) **THE VERY BEST OF SURVIVOR** [ ] [-]

SWEET

Formed: London, England . . . early 1968 as SWEETSHOP by former Harrow band WAINWRIGHT'S GENTLEMEN members CONNOLLY and TUCKER, plus PRIEST and TORPY. They soon shortened to The SWEET and signed one-off deal with 'Fontana'. In 1969, they transferred to 'Parlophone' but after 3 more flops they moved to 'RCA'. Their fortunes changed early '71 when 'FUNNY FUNNY' hit the UK Top 20. • **Songwriters:** From 1971-1974, they were produced by PHIL WAINMAN who employed pop pensmiths NICKY CHINN & MIKE CHAPMAN (who were also writing for 'RAK' artists MUD, SUZI QUATRO and SMOKIE). In 1974, group started to write own songs, with some degree of success on Top 30 album! 'SWEET FANNY ADAMS'. • **Style:** Pure pop singles band, turning into pioneers of glam rock from '72 to late '74. Visually effeminate outfit, who blended this image alongside anthemic pop gems from 'BLOCKBUSTER', 'HELLRAISER', 'BALLROOM BLITZ' to 'TEENAGE RAMPAGE'. In 1975, they progressed into a more fuller hard rock, which alienated their teen fans. It was at this time they made headway into a newly found US audience. • **Trivia:** CONNOLLY is the younger brother of actor MARK 'Taggart' McMANUS.

Recommended: BLOCKBUSTERS (*7)

BRIAN CONNOLLY (b. 5 Oct'49, Hamilton, Scotland) – vocals (ex-WAINWRIGHT'S GENTLEMEN) / **STEVE PRIEST** (b.23 Feb'50, Hayes, Middlesex, England) – bass / **MICK TUCKER** (b.17 Jul'49, Harlesdon, London) – drums, vox (ex-WAINWRIGHT..) / **FRANK TORPY** – guitar

Fontana / not issued

Jul 68. (7") **SLOW MOTION. / IT'S LONELY OUT THERE** [ ] [-]

— **MICK STEWART** – guitar repl. FRANK

Parlophone / not issued

Sep 69. (7") **LOLLIPOP MAN. / TIME** [ ] [-]
Jan 70. (7") **ALL YOU'LL EVER GET FROM ME. / THE JUICER** [ ] [-]
(re-iss.May71, flipped over)
Jun 70. (7") **GET ON THE LINE. / MR. McGALLAGHER** [ ] [-]

— **ANDY SCOTT** (b.30 Jun'51, Wrexham, Wales) – guitar (ex-ELASTIC BAND) repl. STEWART. (Employed session people in 71-72)

R.C.A. / Bell

Mar 71. (7") **FUNNY FUNNY. / YOU'RE NOT WRONG FOR LOVING ME** [13] [ ]
Jun 71. (7") **CO-CO. / DONE ME WRONG ALRIGHT** [2] [-]
Jul 71. (7") **CO-CO. / YOU'RE NOT WRONG FOR LOVING ME** [-] [99]
Oct 71. (7") **ALEXANDER GRAHAM BELL. / SPOTLIGHT** [33] [-]
Nov 71. (lp)(c) **FUNNY HOW SWEET CO-CO CAN BE** [ ] [-]
– Co-Co / Chop chop / Reflections / Honeysuckle love / Santa Monica sunshine / Daydream / Funny funny / Tom Tom turnaround / Jeanie / Sunny sleeps late / Spotlight / Done me wrong all right. *(re-iss.cd+c Apr93 on 'Ariola Express')*
Jan 72. (7") **POPPA JOE. / JEANIE** [11] [ ]
Jun 72. (7") **LITTLE WILLY. / MAN FROM MECCA** [4] [3] Jan 73
Sep 72. (7") **WIG-WAM BAM. / NEW YORK CONNECTION** [4] [ ] Dec 73
Dec 72. (lp)(c) **SWEET'S BIGGEST HITS** (compilation) [ ] [-]
– Wig-wam bam / Little Willy / Done me wrong alright / Poppa Joe / Funny funny / Co-Co / Alexander Graham Bell / Chop chop / You're not wrong for loving me / Jeanie / Spotlight / Tom Tom turnaround.
Jan 73. (7") **BLOCKBUSTER. / NEED A LOT OF LOVIN'** [1] [73] Jun 73
Apr 73. (7") **HELL RAISER. / BURNING** [2] [ ]
Jul 73. (lp)(c) **THE SWEET** [-] [ ]
– Little Willy / New York connection / Wig-wam bam / Done me wrong alright / Hell raiser / Blockbuster / Need a lot of lovin' / Man from Mecca / Spotlight / You're not wrong for loving me. *(re-iss.1976 on 'Kory')*

R.C.A. / Capitol

Sep 73. (7") **BALLROOM BLITZ. / ROCK'N'ROLL DISGRACE** [2] [-]
Jan 74. (7") **TEENAGE RAMPAGE. / OWN UP, TAKE A LOOK AT YOURSELF** [2] [ ]
Apr 74. (lp)(c) **SWEET FANNY ADAMS** [27] [-]
– Set me free / Heartbreak today / No you don't / Rebel rouser / Peppermint twist / Sweet F.A. / Restless / Into the night / AC-DC.
Jul 74. (7") **THE SIX TEENS. / BURN ON THE FLAME** [9] [ ]
Nov 74. (7") **TURN IT DOWN. / SOMEONE ELSE WILL** [41] [ ]
Nov 74. (lp)(c) **DESOLATION BOULEVARD** [ ] [25] Jul 75
– The six teens / Solid gold brass / Turn it down / Medusa / Lady Starlight / Man with the golden arm / Fox on the run / Breakdown / My generation. *(US – version incl. tracks from 'SWEET FANNY ADAMS'). (re-iss.+cd.Feb90 on 'Castle')*
Mar 75. (7") **FOX ON THE RUN. / MISS DEMEANOR** [2] [-]
Jun 75. (7") **BALLROOM BLITZ. / RESTLESS** [-] [5]
Jul 75. (7") **ACTION. / SWEET F.A.** [15] [-]
Nov 75. (d-lp)(c) **STRUNG UP** (live rec. Dec'73 + hits, etc.) [ ] [-]
– Hell raiser / Burning / Someone else will / Rock'n'roll disgrace / Need a lot of lovin' / Done me wrong alright / You're not wrong for loving me / The man with the golden arm / Action / Fox on the run / Set me free / Miss Deameanour / Ballroom blitz / Burn on the flame / Solid gold brass / The six teens / I wanna be committed / Blockbuster.
Nov 75. (7") **FOX ON THE RUN. / BURN ON THE FLAME** [-] [5]
Jan 76. (7") **LIES IN YOUR EYES. / COCKROACH** [35] [ ]
Feb 76. (7") **ACTION. / MEDUSA** [-] [15]
Mar 76. (lp)(c) **GIVE US A WINK** [ ] [27]
– The lies in your eyes / Cockroach / Keep it in / 4th of July / Action / Yesterday's rain / White mice / Healer. *(cd+pic-cd-iss.Jul93 on 'Repertoire' w/ extra +=)*– Fox on the run / Lady Starlight / Sweet Fanny Adams / Miss Demeaner.
Oct 76. (7") **LOST ANGELS. / FUNK IT UP** [ ] [ ]
Feb 77. (7") **FEVER OF LOVE. / DISTINCT LACK OF ANCIENT** [ ] [-]
Mar 77. (lp)(c) **OFF THE RECORD** [ ] [ ]
– Fever of love / Lost angels / Midnight to daylight / Windy city / Live for today / She gimme lovin' / Laura Lee / Hard times / Funk it up (David's song). *(cd+pic-cd Jul93 on 'Repertoire' +=)*– Distinct lack of ancient / Stairway to the stars / Why don't you do it to me.
Mar 77. (7") **FEVER OF LOVE. / HEARTBREAK TODAY** [-] [ ]
Jul 77. (7")(12") **FUNK IT UP (DAVID'S SONG). / ('A'disco mix)** [-] [88]
Aug 77. (7") **STAIRWAY TO THE STARS. / WHY DON'T YOU DO IT TO ME** [ ] [-]
Oct 77. (lp)(c) **SWEET'S GOLDEN GREATS** (compilation) [ ] [-]
– Blockbuster / Hell raiser / Ballroom blitz / Teenage rampage / The six teens / Turn it down / Fox on the run / Action / Lost angels / The lies in your eyes / Fever of love / Stairway to the stars.

Polydor / Capitol

Jan 78. (7") **LOVE IS LIKE OXYGEN. / COVER GIRL** [9] [8] Feb 78
Jan 78. (lp)(c) **LEVEL HEADED** [ ] [52]
– Dream on / Love is like oxygen / California nights / Strong love / Fountain / Anthem No.1 / Silverbird / Lettres d'amour / Anthem No.2 / Air on "A" tape loop. *(cd-iss. Jul93 on 'Repertoire' +=)*– LOve is like oxygen (single) / Cover girl / California nights (single) / Show the way.
Jul 78. (7") **CALIFORNIA NIGHTS. / DREAM ON** [-] [76]

— **GARY MOBERLEY** – keyboards repl. CONNOLLY who went solo & later formed The NEW SWEET. (ANDY SCOTT was now on lead vocals)

Mar 79. (7") **CALL ME. / WHY DON'T YOU** [ ] [-]
Apr 79. (7") **MOTHER EARTH. / WHY DON'T YOU** [-] [ ]
Aug 79. (7") **BIG APPLE WALTZ. / WHY DON'T YOU** [ ] [-]
Oct 79. (lp)(c) **CUT ABOVE THE REST** [ ] [ ] Apr 79
– Call me / Play all night / Big Apple waltz / Dorian Gray / Discophony / Eye games / Mother Earth / Hold me / Stay with me. *(cd-iss.Oct92 + Jul93 on 'Repertoire')*
Apr 80. (7") **GIVE THE LADY SOME RESPECT. / TALL GIRLS** [ ] [ ]
Apr 80. (lp)(c) **WATER'S EDGE** (US-title 'SWEET IV') [ ] [ ]
– Sixties man / Getting in the mood for love / Tell the truth / Own up / Too much talking / Thank you for loving me / At midnight / Water's edge / Hot shot gambler / Give the lady some respect. *(cd-iss.Oct92 + Jul93 on 'Repertoire')*
Sep 80. (7") **THE SIXTIES MAN. / TALL GIRLS** [ ] [-]
Sep 80. (7") **THE SIXTIES MAN. / WATER'S EDGE** [-] [ ]

— **MICK STEWART** – guitar returned to guest on next album.

Nov 82. (lp) **IDENTITY CRISIS** [ ] [-]
– Identity crisis / New shoes / Two into one / Love is the cure / It makes me wonder / Hey mama / Falling in love / I wish you would / Strange girl. *(cd-iss.Oct92 on 'Repertoire')*

— They had already split Spring 1981, with PRIEST going to the States and SCOTT going into production for heavy metal bands like IRON MAIDEN. He also went solo (see further below). The SWEET re-formed in the mid-80's, with SCOTT, TUCKER plus **PAUL MARIO DAY** – vocals (ex-WILD FIRE) / **PHIL LANZON** – keyboards (ex-GRAND PRIX) / **MAL McNULTY** – bass repl. PRIEST

– more compilations, etc. –

Dec 70. M.F.P.; (lp) **GIMME DAT THING** [ ] [-]
– (1-side by 'The PIPKINS')
Jul 78. Camden-RCA; (lp) **THE SWEET** [ ] [-]
Jun 80. RCA; (7"ep) **FOX ON THE RUN / HELLRAISER. / BLOCKBUSTER / BALLROOM BLITZ** [ ] [-]
Nov 89. RCA; (7") **WIG-WAM BAM. / LITTLE WILLY** [ ] [-]
Dec 89. RCA; (lp)(c)(cd) **BLOCKBUSTERS** [ ] [-]
– Ballroom blitz / Hell raiser / New York connection / Little Willy / Burning / Need a lot of lovin' / Wig-wam bam / Blockbuster / Rock'n'roll disgrace / Chop chop / Alexander Graham Bell / Poppa Joe / Co-Co / Funny funny. *(re-iss.Oct92)*
Aug 81. RCA Gold; (7") **BLOCKBUSTER. / HELLRAISER** [ ] [-]
May 82. RCA Gold; (7") **BALLROOM BLITZ. / WIG-WAM BAM** [ ] [-]
Aug 84. Anagram; (lp)(pic-lp) **SWEET 16 – IT'S . . . IT'S . . . SWEET'S HITS** [49] [-]
Sep 84. Anagram; (7") **THE SIX TEENS. / ACTION** [ ] [-]
(12"+=) – Teenage rampage.
Dec 84. Anagram; (7")(12") **IT'S . . . IT'S . . . THE SWEET MIX (Medley; Blockbuster – Fox on the run – Teenage rampage – Hell raiser – Ballroom blitz). / FOX ON THE RUN** [45] [-]
May 85. Anagram; (7")(12") **SWEET 2TH – THE WIG-WAM WILLY MIX. / THE TEEN ACTION MIX** [ ] [-]
Apr 87. Old Gold; (7") **BLOCKBUSTER. / LITTLE WILLY** [ ] [-]
Apr 87. Old Gold; (7") **FOX ON THE RUN. / BALLROOM BLITZ** [ ] [-]
Jan 88. Old Gold; (7") **WIG-WAM BAM. / CO-CO** [ ] [-]
Jan 88. Old Gold; (7") **TEENAGE RAMPAGE. / HELLRAISER** [ ] [-]
Jul 92. Old Gold; (cd-ep) **WIG-WAM BAM / CO-CO / LITTLE WILLY** [ ] [-]
Jul 87. Zebra; (lp)(c)(cd) **HARD CENTRES – THE ROCK YEARS** [ ] [-]
(re-iss.cd Oct95)
Dec 89. Castle; (d-lp)(c)(cd) **SWEET COLLECTION** [ ] [-]
Feb 93. Receiver; (cd) **ROCK AND ROLL DISGRACE** [ ] [-]
Feb 93. Receiver; (cd) **LAND OF HOPE AND GLORY** [ ] [-]
Dec 93. Receiver; (cd) **LIVE FOR TODAY** [ ] [-]
Jul 94. Receiver; (cd) **BREAKDOWN – THE SWEET LIVE (live)** [ ] [-]
Apr 93. Dojo; (cd) **BALLROOM BLITZ – LIVE 1973 (live)** [ ] [-]
Jul 93. Repertoire; (cd) **FIRST RECORDINGS 1968-1971** [ ] [-]
Nov 94. Start; (cd) **IN CONCERT** [ ] [-]
Apr 95. Receiver; (cd) **SET ME FREE** [ ] [-]
Jun 95. Repertoire; (cd) **THE ROCK YEARS** [ ] [-]
Jul 95. Aim; (cd) **GREATEST HITS LIVE** [ ] [-]
Jul 95. Aim; (cd) **A** [ ] [-]
Nov 95. Repertoire; (d-cd) **HIT SINGLES A & B SIDES** [ ] [-]

ANDY SCOTT

(solo)

		R.C.A.	not issued
Nov 75.	(7") **LADY STARLIGHT. / WHERE'D YA GO**		-
		Static	not issued
Jun 83.	(7") **GOTTA SEE JANE. (as "The LADDERS") / KRUGGERRANDS** (12"+=) – ('A'club mix).		-
Nov 83.	(7") **KRUGGERRANDS. / FACE** (12"+=) – ('A'club mix).		-
Sep 84.	(7") **LET HER DANCE. / SUCK IT AND SEE** ('A'extended-12"+=) – ('A'instrumental).		-
Apr 85.	(7"clear) **INVISIBLE. / NEVER TOO YOUNG** (12"clear+=) – ('A'extended) / ('A'instrumental).		-

ANDY SCOTT'S SWEET

with **MICK TUCKER, McNULTY + JEFF BROWN** – bass

		SPV Germany	not issued
May 91.	(12")(cd-s) **X-RAY SPECS. / I DON'T WANNA SAY GOODNIGHT / HELLRAISER ('91 version)**	-	-

SWERVEDRIVER

Formed: Oxford to Camden, London, England . . . late 1989 by FRANKLIN, HARTRIDGE and VINES initially as SHAKE APPEAL. They signed to 'Creation' in the early 90's, and scored minor hit with 'SANDBLASTED EP'. • **Style:** Grunge-rock inspired by road songs of the USA. • **Songwriters:** Group penned except JESUS (Velvet Underground).

Recommended: RAISE (*7)

ADAM FRANKLIN (b.19 Jul'68, Essex, England) – vocals, guitar / **JIMMY HARTRIDGE** (b.27 Nov'67, Oxfordshire, England) – guitar / **ADRIAN 'ADI' VINES** (b.25 Jan'68, Yorkshire, England) – bass / **GRAHAM BONNAR** (b.28 Apr'67, Glasgow, Scotland) – drums, vocals (ex-UT)

		Creation	Creation
Jul 90.	(12"ep)(cd-ep) **SON OF MUSTANG FORD / VOLCANO TRASH. / KILL THE SUPERHEROES / JUGGERNAUT RIDE**		-
Nov 90.	(12"ep)(cd-ep) **RAVE DOWN / SHE'S BESIDE HERSELF. / AFTERGLOW / ZED HEAD**		-
Jul 91.	(7"ep)(12"ep)(cd-ep) **SANDBLASTED / OUT. / FLAWED / LAZE IT UP**	67	
Sep 91.	(cd)(c)(lp) **RAISE** – Sci-flyer / Pole-up / Son of Mustang Ford / Deep seat / Rave down / Sunset / Feel so reel / Sandblasted / Lead me where you dare. (free-12"w.a.) **SURF TWANG. / DEEP TWANG**	44	
May 92.	(7") **NEVER LOSE THAT FEELING. / SCRAWL AND SCREAM** (12"+=)(cd-s+=) – The watchman's hands / Never learn.	62	
—	ADI left in Sep 92. He was soon replaced by **JEZ** – drums		
Aug 93.	(7") **DUEL. / PLANES OVER THE SKYLINE** (12"+=)(cd-s+=) – Year of the girl.	60	
Sep 93.	(cd)(c)(lp) **MEZCAL HEAD** – For seeking heat / Duel / Blowin' cool / MM abduction / Last train to Satansville / Mary and Maggie / A change is gonna come / Girl on a motorbike / Duress / You find it everywhere.	55	
Feb 94.	(12"ep)(cd-ep) **LAST TRAIN TO SATANSVILLE** – Jesus / Satansville revisited / Land of the lost.		
Jul 94.	(7") **MY ZEPHYR (SEQUEL). / MARS**		-
—	(above 45 was a one-off for 'Flower Shop' records)		
Jun 95.	(12"white)(c-s)(cd-s) **LAST DAY ON EARTH / MAELSTROM / I AM SUPERMAN / THE DIRECTORS CUT OF YOUR LIFE**		
Aug 95.	(cd)(c)(lp) **EJECTOR SEAT RESERVATION** – Single factor salute / Bring me the head of the fortune teller / The other Jesus / Song of Jaguar E / I am Superman / Bubbling up / Ejector seat reservation / How does it feel to like Candy? / Last day on Earth / The birds. (c+=/cd+=) – Untitled / So downhearted. (w/ free 7") – FLAMING HEART / PLAN 7 SATELLITE 10.		

Steve SWINDELLS (see under ⇒ HAWKWIND)

David SYLVIAN (see under ⇒ JAPAN)

SYSTEM 7 (see under ⇒ HILLAGE, Steve)

TALKING HEADS

Formed: Manhattan, New York, USA . . . May'75 by former art & design students BYRNE, WEYMOUTH and FRANTZ. Their first gig was to support The RAMONES at the CBGB's club in New York, circa mid'75. They were soon spotted by Seymour Stein, who signed them to new US label 'Sire'. Late 1976, they released debut 45 'LOVE GOES TO A BUILDING ON FIRE', which flopped. The next year, they unleashed the '77 album, which sold well enough to reach lower chart regions. The follow-up 'MORE SONGS . . . ', became their first of many US + UK Top 30 albums. • **Style:** New wave rock outfit, who later experimented with Afro-rhythms and alternative rock music. Between 1978 and 1979, BRIAN ENO (ex-ROXY MUSIC) produced a more avant-garde but soulful pop. BYRNE and ENO later (1981), collaborated on 'MY LIFE IN THE BUSH OF GHOSTS', an album of their rhythms and taped singers / speeches of various people from around the world. • **Songwriters:** Group compositions except; TAKE ME TO THE RIVER (Al Green) / SLIPPERY PEOPLE (Staple Singers). TOM TOM CLUB:- UNDER THE BOARDWALK (Drifters) / FEMME FATALE (Velvet Underground). DAVID BYRNE: – GREENBACK DOLLAR (Hoy & Axton) / GIRLS ON MY MIND (Toquinnho Vinicius) / DON'T FENCE ME IN (Cole Porter). • **Trivia:** FRANTZ and WEYMOUTH (later TOM TOM CLUB) married on 18 Jun'77. BYRNE produced The B-52's on their 1982 album 'Mesopotamia' and FUN BOY THREE on their 1983 'Waiting' album. HARRISON produced The VIOLENT FEMMES on 1986 album 'The Blind Leading The Naked'. TOM TOM CLUB started out producing in 1988 with ZIGGY MARLEY. They later worked for HAPPY MONDAYS. In 1986, BYRNE and group starred in their own film 'TRUE STORIES' which was also released as 2 separate albums.

Recommended: TALKING HEADS '77 (*9) / MORE SONGS ABOUT BUILDINGS AND FOOD (*8) / FEAR OF MUSIC (*9) / REMAIN IN LIGHT (*8) / ONCE IN A LIFETIME – THE BEST OF TALKING HEADS (*9).

DAVID BYRNE (b.14 May'52, Dumbarton, Scotland) – vocals, guitar / **TINA WEYMOUTH** (b.22 Nov'50, Coronado, California, USA) – bass, vocals / **CHRIS FRANTZ** (b.CHARLTON CHRISTOPHER FRANTZ, 8 May'51, Fort Campbell, Kentucky, USA) – drums

Sire Sire

Feb 77. (7") **LOVE GOES TO A BUILDING ON FIRE. / NEW FEELING** [ ] [ ]

— added **JERRY HARRISON** (b.JEREMIAH, 21 Feb'49, Milwalkee, Wisconsin, USA) – guitar, keyboards (ex-JONATHAN RICHMAN & THE MODERN LOVERS)

Sep 77. (lp) **TALKING HEADS '77** [60] [97]
– Uh-oh, love comes to town / New feeling / Tentative decisions / Happy day / Who is it? / No compassion / The book I read / Don't worry about the government / First week – last week . . . carefree / Psycho killer / Pulled up. *(cd-iss.Feb87)*

Oct 77. (7") **UH-OH, LOVE COMES TO TOWN. / I WISH YOU WOULDN'T SAY THAT** [-] [ ]

Dec 77. (7") **PSYCHO KILLER. / I WISH YOU WOULDN'T SAY THAT** [ ] [92]
(12"+=) – Psycho killer (acoustic version). (US; b-side)

May 78. (7") **PULLED UP. / DON'T WORRY ABOUT THE GOVERNMENT** [ ] [ ]

Jul 78. (lp)(d-c) **MORE SONGS ABOUT BUILDINGS AND FOOD** [21] [29]
– Thank you for sending me an angel / With our love / The good thing / Warning sign / Girls want to be with the girls / Found a job / Artists only / I'm not in love / Stay hungry / Take me to the river / The big country. *(double-play cass. includes debut album) (cd-iss.Jan87)*

Oct 78. (7") **TAKE ME TO THE RIVER. / THANK YOU FOR SENDING ME AN ANGEL** [-] [26]

Jun 79. (7") **TAKE ME TO THE RIVER. / FOUND A JOB** [ ] [-]
(d7"+=) – Love goes to a building on fire / Psycho killer.

Aug 79. (lp)(c) **FEAR OF MUSIC** [33] [21]
– Air / Animals / Cities / Drugs / Electric guitar / Heaven / I Zimbra / Life during wartime / Memories can't wait / Mind / Paper. *(free-7"w.a.)* – PSYCHO KILLER (live). / NEW FEELING (live) *(cd-iss.Jul84)*

Oct 79. (7") **LIFE DURING WARTIME. / ELECTRIC GUITAR** [ ] [80]

Feb 80. (7") **I ZIMBRA. / PAPER** [ ] [ ]

Jun 80. (7") **CITIES. / CITIES (live)** [ ] [ ]
(12"+=) – Artists only.

— basic 4 added **BUSTA CHERRY JONES** – bass / **ADRIAN BELEW** – guitar / **BERNIE WORRELL** – keyboards / **STEVEN SCALES** – percussion / **DONETTE McDONALD** – back.vox

Oct 80. (lp)(c) **REMAIN IN LIGHT** [21] [19]
– The great curve / Crosseyed and painless / Born under punches / Houses in motion / Once in a lifetime / Listening wind / Seen and not seen / The overlord. *(cd-iss.1983)*

Feb 81. (7")('A'ext-12") **ONCE IN A LIFETIME. / SEEN AND NOT SEEN** [14] [ ]

May 81. (7") **HOUSES IN MOTION (remix). / THE OVERLORD** [-] [ ]

May 81. (7") **HOUSES IN MOTION (remix). / AIR** [50] [-]
('A'extended-12"+=) – ('A'live version).

In 1981, all 4 diversed into own projects (see further below)

Mar 82. (7") **LIFE DURING WARTIME (live). / LIFE DURING WARTIME (lp version)** [ ] [ ]
(12"+=) – Don't worry about the government (live).

Apr 82. (d-lp)(d-c) **THE NAME OF THIS BAND IS TALKING HEADS (live)** [22] [31]
– I Zimbra / Drugs / Houses in motion / Life during wartime / Take me to the river / The great curve / Cross-eyed and painless / New feeling / A clean break / Don't worry about the government / Pulled up / Psycho killer / Artists only / Stay hungry / Air / Building on fire / Memories can't wait. *(cd-iss.1983)*

Jun 83. (lp)(c)(cd)(clear-lp) **SPEAKING IN TONGUES** [21] [15]
– Burning down the house / Making flippy floppy / Girlfriend is better / Slippery people / I get wild – Wild gravity / Swamp / Moon rocks / Pull up the roots / This must be the place (naive melody). *(c+cd+=)* – (6 extra mixes).

Jul 83. (7") **BURNING DOWN THE HOUSE. / I GET WILD – WILD GRAVITY** [ ] [9]
(12"+=) – Moon rocks.

Jan 84. (7") **THIS MUST BE THE PLACE (NAIVE MELODY). / MOON ROCKS** [51] [62] Oct 83
(d12"+=) – Slippery people (remix) / Making flippy floppy (remix). *(re-iss.7".Jun86)*

E.M.I. Sire

Oct 84. (7")('A'ext-12") **SLIPPERY PEOPLE (live). / THIS MUST BE THE PLACE (NAIVE MELODY) (live)** [68] [ ]

Oct 84. (lp)(c)(cd) **STOP MAKING SENSE (live)** [37] [41]
– Psycho killer / Swamp / Slippery people / Burning down the house / Girlfriend is better / Once in a lifetime / What a day that was / Life during wartime / Take me to the river. *(c+cd+=)* – (extra tracks) *(re-is.Mar90) (re-iss.cd+c Nov93 on 'Fame')*

Nov 84. (7")('A'ext-12") **GIRLFRIEND IS BETTER (live). / ONCE IN A LIFETIME (live)** [ ] [ ]

Dec 84. (7") **GIRLFRIEND IS BETTER. / HEAVEN** [-] [ ]

May 85. (7")('A'ext-12") **THE LADY DON'T MIND. / GIVE ME BACK MY NAME** [ ] [ ]
(d12"+=) – Slippery people / This must be the place (naive melody).

Jun 85. (lp)(c)(cd) **LITTLE CREATURES** [10] [20]
– And she was / Give me back my name / Creatures of love / The lady don't mind / Perfect world / Stay up late / Walk it down / Television man / Road to nowhere. *(c+=)* – The lady don't mind (extended). *(re-iss.Mar90) (re-iss.cd+c Nov93 on 'Fame')*

Jun 85. (7") **ROAD TO NOWHERE. / GIVE ME BACK MY NAME** [-] [ ]

Sep 85. (7") **AND SHE WAS. / ('A' dub)** [-] [54]

Sep 85. (7")(7"pic-d) **ROAD TO NOWHERE. / TELEVISION MAN** [6] [-]
(d12"+=) – Slippery people (live) / This must be the place (naive melody) (live).

Feb 86. (7")('A'ext-12") **AND SHE WAS. / PERFECT WORLD** [17] [-]

Apr 86. (7") **ONCE IN A LIFETIME (live). / THIS MUST BE THE PLACE (live)** [-] [ ]

Aug 86. (7") **WILD WILD LIFE. / PEOPLE LIKE US** [43] [25]
(12"+=)(12"pic-d+=) – ('A'album version).

Sep 86. (lp)(c)(cd) **TRUE STORIES** [7] [17]
– Love for sale / Puzzlin' evidence / Hey now / Radio head / Papa Legba / Wild wild life / Radio head / Dream operator / People like us / City of dreams. *(cd+=)* – Wild (ET mix). *(re-iss.Sep89 on 'Fame')*

Nov 86. (7") **LOVE FOR SALE. / HEY NOW** [-] [ ]

Nov 86. (lp)(c) **SONGS FROM 'TRUE STORIES' (Original DAVID BYRNE Film Soundtrack; w/ other artists)** [ ] [ ]
– Cocktail desperado / Road song / Freeway son / Brownie's theme / Mall muzak: Building a highway – Puppy polka – Party girls / Dinner music / Disco hits / City of steel / Love theme from 'True Stories' / Festa para um Rei Negro / Buster's theme / Soy de Tejas / I love metal buildings / Glass operator.

Apr 87. (7") **RADIO HEAD. / HEY NOW (movie version)** [52] [ ]
(d7"+=)(12"+=)(cd-s+=) – ('A'&'B'-different versions).

Mar 88. (lp)(c)(cd) **NAKED** [3] [19]
– Blind / Mr. Jones / Totally nude / Ruby dear / (Nothing but) Flowers / The Democratic circus / The facts of life / Mommy daddy you and I / Big daddy / Bill * / Cool water. *(cd+= *) (re-iss.cd+c Nov93 on 'Fame')*

Aug 88. (7") **BLIND. / BILL** [59] [ ]
(12"+=)(cd-s+=) – ('A'mix).

Oct 88. (7") **(NOTHING BUT) FLOWERS. / RUBY DEAR (Bush mix)** [ ] [ ] Apr 88
(10"+=)(c-s+=)(cd-s+=) – Mommy daddy you and I.
(12"+=) – Facts of life.

— Cease to function as a group, after last recording. Officially split 1991.

– compilations, others, etc. –

Oct 92. EMI; (7")(c-s) **LIFETIME PILING UP. / ROAD TO NOWHERE** [50] [ ]
(cd-s+=) – Love for sale / The lady don't mind (extended).
(cd-s) – ('A'side) / Stay up late / Radio head / Take me to the river.

Oct 92. EMI; (d-cd)(d-c)(d-lp) **POPULAR FAVOURITES 1976-1992** [7] [ ]

Crosseyed and painless. And she was.
Once in a lifetime. Crosseyed and painless. Facts are lazy, facts are late. Everyone is trying get to the part. The band in heaven they play my favorite song. Heaven is a place where nothing ever happens. There is a party everyone is there. Burning down the house. Swamp. This must be the place. (Naive Melody) Life during wartime. Girlfriend is better. Blind. City of Dreams. And she was. Stay up late. Wild Wild Life. Take a walk through the peaceful meadows. I'm stuck there in this dead. All the people they must stay. Lifetime piling up. Popsicle. Love for Sale. Don't worry about the Government. Warning Sign. No Compassion. Heaven. PSYCHO KILLER. I wish you wouldn't say that. Wild wild life. Take me to the River. Memories can't wait. I Zimbra. Take me to the River. Drop me in the water. Love. Building on fire. The big country. Facts are simple. Facts just twist the truth around. Girlfriend. Facts lost. Lost my shape. Trying to act casual. Changing my shape. I feel like an accident. Making Sense. Wild Life.

Road to Nowhere. Burning down the house. Facts are never what they seem to be. I'm still waiting. I wait and wait. To see the Earth turn.

Nothing but the Flowers. Under the Rocks and Stones. Into the blue again. Water flowing underground. Once in a lifetime. Letting the days go by. Water dissolving and water removing.

My God what have I done? Same as it ever was! Making Flippy Floppy. Speaking in Tongues. Stop Making Sense. Where do correct ideas come from? Horses in the place. This must be the place. Fear of Music. COMPASSION IS A VIRTUE but I just don't have the time. REMAIN IN LIGHT. Mr. Jones. Lifetime piling up. Life during Wartime. I want to live.

TINA
CHRIS
DAVID
JERRY

TALKING HEADS
No Compassion

– ONCE IN A LIFETIME:- Psycho killer / Take me to the river / Once in a lifetime / Burning down the house / This must be the place (naive melody) / Slippery people (live) / Life during wartime (live) / And she was / Road to nowhere / Wild wild life / Blind / (Nothing but) Flowers / Sax and violins / Lifetime piling up.// SAND IN MY VASELINE:- Sugar on my tongue / I want to live / Love goes to a building on fire / I wish you wouldn't say that / Don't worry about the government / The big country / No compassion / Warning sign / Heaven / Memories can't wait / I Zimbra / Crosseyed and painless / Swamp / Girlfriend is better (live) / Stay up late / Love for sale / City of dreams / Mr. Jones / Gangster of love / Popsicle.

Nov 95. EMI; (3xcd-box) **STOP MAKING SENSE / LITTLE CREATURES / TRUE STORIES** [ ] [-]

DAVID BYRNE

(solo) Earlier in the year, he had collaborated with BRIAN ENO ⇒ on album 'MY LIFE IN THE BUSH OF GHOSTS'.

Sire Sire

Dec 81. (7") **BIG BLUE PLYMOUTH (EYES WIDE OPEN). / CLOUD CHAMBER** [ ] [ ]
(12") – ('A'side) / Leg bells / Light bath.

Jan 82. (lp)(c) **SONGS FROM 'THE CATHERINE WHEEL' (Stage score)** [ ] [ ] Dec 81
– His wife refused / Two soldiers / The red house / My big hands (fall through the cracks) / Big business / Eggs in a briar patch / Poison / Cloud chamber / What a day that was / Big blue Plymouth (eyes wide open). *(US d-lp+=)* – Ade / Walking / Under the mountain / Dinosaur / Wheezing / Black flag / Combat / Leg bells / The blue flame / Danse beast / Five golden sections.

1982. (12"ep) **THREE BIG SONGS** [-] [ ]
– Big business (remix) / My big hands (fall through the cracks) / Big blue Plymouth (eyes wide open).

E.M.I. Sire

Sep 85. (lp)(c) **MUSIC FOR THE KNEE PLAYS** [ ] [ ] May 85
– Tree (today is an important occasion) / In the upper room / The sound of business / Social studies / (The gift of sound) Where the sun never goes down / Theadora is dozing / Admiral Perry / I bid you goodnight / I've tried / Winter / Jungle book / In the future.

— Rec. collaboration with RYUICHI SAKAMOTO on film 'THE LAST EMPEROR'. BYRNE now used a plethora of Brazilian musicians.

Luaka Bop Luaka Bop

Oct 89. (lp)(c)(cd) **REI MOMO** [52] [71]
– Independence day / Make believe mambo / The call of the wild / Dirty old town / The rose tattoo / The dream police / Don't want to be part of your world / Marching through the wilderness / Lie to me / Women vs.men / Carnival eyes / I know sometimes a man is wrong.

Dec 89. (7")('A'ext-12") **MAKE BELIEVE MAMBO. / LIE TO ME** [ ] [ ]

Jun 91. (cd)(c)(lp) **THE FOREST (instrumental)** [ ] [ ]
– Ur / Kish / Dura Europus / Nineveh / Ava / Machu picchu / Teotihuaean / Asuka.

Sire-WEA Sire-WEA

Mar 92. (cd)(c)(lp) **UH-OH** [26] [ ]
– Now I'm your mom / Girls on my mind / Something ain't right / She's mad / Hanging upside down / Twistin' in the wind / A walk in the dark / The cowboy mambo (hey lookit me now) / Tiny town / Somebody. *(re-iss.cd/c Feb95)*

Apr 92. (7")(c-s) **GIRLS ON MY MIND. / MONKEY MAN** [ ] [ ]
(12"+=)(cd-s+=) – Cantode oxum.

May 92. (7")(c-s) **HANGING UPSIDE DOWN. / TINY TOWN** [ ] [ ]
(cd-s) – ('A'side) / Dirty old town (live) / (Nothing but) Flowers (live) / Girls on my mind (live).
(cd-s) – ('A'side) / Something ain't right (live) / Who we're thinking of (live) / Rockin' in the free world (live).

Jul 92. (7")(c-s) **SHE'S MAD. / SOMEBODY** [ ] [ ]
(12") – ('A'side) / Butt naked / Greenback dollar
(cd-s++=) – ('A'side) / Now I'm your man.

— with **PAUL SOCOLOW** – bass, vocals / **TODD TURKISHER** – drum, percussion / **VALERIE NARANJO** – percussion, tambourine (live: MAURO REFOSCO – percussion) / **BILL WARE** – marimba / **ARTO LINDSAY** – guitar / **JOHN MEDESKI** – organ / **BASHIRI JOHNSON** – congas, bongos / **BEBEL GILBERTO** – vocals

Luaka Bop-Sire Luaka Bop-Sire

May 94. (cd)(c) **DAVID BYRNE** [44] [ ]
– A long time ago / Angels / Crash / A self-made man / Back in the box / Sad song / Nothing at all / My love is you / Lillies of the valley / You & eye / Strange ritual / Buck naked.

Jun 94. (c-s)(cd-s) **ANGELS / PRINCESS / READY FOR THIS WORLD** [ ] [ ]

Sep 94. (c-s)(cd-s) **BACK IN THE BOX / GYPSY WOMAN (live) / GIRLS ON MY MIND (live)** [ ] [ ]

TOM TOM CLUB

CHRIS FRANTZ + TINA WEYMOUTH plus her 2 sisters + **STEVE SCALES** – percussion / **ALEX WEIR** – guitar / **TYRON DOWNIE** – keyboards

Island Sire

Jun 81. (7") **WORDY RAPPINGHOOD. / YOU DON'T STOP (WORDY RAP)** [7] [ ]
(12"+=) – L'elephant.

Sep 81. (7") **GENIUS OF LOVE. / LORELEI (instrumental)** [65] [31] Mar 82
(12"+=) – ('A'&'B'extended versions).

Oct 81. (lp)(c) **TOM TOM CLUB** [78] [23]
– Wordy rappinghood / Genius of love / Tom Tom theme / L'elephant / As above, so below / Lorelei / On, on, on, on . . . / Booming and zooming. *(re-iss.Oct86, cd-iss.May87)*

Jun 82. (7")(12") **LORELEI. / ON, ON, ON, ON . . .** [ ] [ ]

Jul 82. (7") **UNDER THE BOARDWALK. / ON, ON, ON, ON . . . (remix)** [22] [ ]
(12"+=) – Lorelei (remix).

Oct 82. (7") **GENIUS OF LOVE. / LORELEI (instrumental)** [ ] [-]
(12"+=) – Rappa rappa rhythm / Melia.

Jul 83. (7")(12") **THE MAN WITH THE 4-WAY HIPS. / ('A'dub version)** [ ] [ ]

Aug 83. (lp)(c) **CLOSE TO THE BONE** [ ] [73]
– Pleasure of love / On the line again / This is a foxy world / Bamboo town / The man with the 4-way hips / Measure up / Never took a penny / Atsababy! (life is great).

Dec 83. (7") **NEVER TOOK A PENNY. / PLEASURE OF LOVE** [-] [ ]

— **TINA + CHRIS** added **GARY POZNER** – keyboards / **MARK ROULE** – guitar, percussion

Fontana Sire

Sep 88. (7") **DON'T SAY NO. / DEVIL DOES YOUR DOG BITE?** [ ] [ ]
(12"+=) – ('A'version) / Beats and pieces.
(cd-s+=) – Beats and pieces / Percapella.

Oct 88. (lp)(c)(cd) **BOOM BOOM CHI BOOM BOOM** [ ] [ ]
– Suboceana / Shock the world / Don't say no / Challenge of the love warriors / Femme fatale / Born for love / Broken promises / She belongs to me / Little Eva / Misty teardrop.

JERRY HARRISON

Sire Sire

Oct 81. (7") **THINGS FALL APART. / WORLDS IN COLLISION** [ ] [ ]

Oct 81. (lp)(c) **THE RED AND THE BLACK** [ ] [ ]
– Things fall apart / Slink / The new adventure / Magic hymie / Fast karma / No questions / Worlds in collision / The red nights / No more returns / No warning no alarm.

Fontana Sire

Feb 88. (lp)(c)(cd) **JERRY HARRISON: CASUAL GODS** [ ] [78]
– Revi it up / Songs of angels / Man with a gun / Let it come down / Cherokee chief / A perfect lie / Are you running? / Breakdown in the passing lane / A.K.A. love / We're always talkin' / Bobby. *(cd+=)*– Bobby (12"version).

May 88. (7") **MAN WITH A GUN. / ('A'radio edit)** [ ] [ ]
(12"+=)(cd-s+=) – Breakdown on the passing line / Wire always talking.

— His backers included **BROOKS / WORRELL / BAILEY / SIEGER + WEIR**

Jun 90. (7") **WALK ON WATER. / MAN WITH A GUN** [ ] [ ]
(12"+=)(cd-s+=) – Racing the fire.

Jun 90. (cd)(c)(lp) **WALK ON WATER** [ ] [ ]
– Flying under radar / Cowboy's got to go / Kick start / I don't mind / Sleep angel / Confess / I cry for Iran / Never let it slip / If the rain returns / The doctor's lie.

TALK TALK

Formed: London, England . . . 1981 by MARK HOLLIS, who with older brother and session man ED (ex-EDDIE & THE HOT RODS), invited to studio WEBB, HARRIS and BREMNER. They soon signed to 'EMI', and employed manager Keith Aspen to hire producer Colin Thurston to work on debut. After support slot to stablemates DURAN DURAN, they soon exploded into charts with single 'TODAY' and album 'THE PARTY'S OVER'. • **Style:** At first an uptempo keyboard orientated pop band, who graduated into an intelligent but abstract rock-pop outfit. • **Songwriters:** Initially group penned, with MARK and brother ED writing most. In 1983, MARK and 4th member TIM FRIESE-GREEN wrote all material. • **Trivia:** The song 'TALK TALK', was first heard in 1978 when MARK's group The REACTION, recorded prototype of the song on Various Artists album 'Streets'.

Recommended: NATURAL HISTORY – THE VERY BEST OF TALK TALK (*9)

MARK HOLLIS (b.1955) – vocals, piano, guitar (ex-REACTION) / **SIMON BREMNER** – keyboards / **PAUL WEBB** – bass, vocals / **LEE HARRIS** – drums

E.M.I. EMI America

Feb 82. (7") **MIRROR MAN. / STRIKE UP THE BAND** [ ] [ ]

Apr 82. (7")('A'ext-12") **TALK TALK. / ('A'version)** [52] [ ]

Jun 82. (7")('A'ext-12") **TODAY. / IT'S SO SERIOUS** [14] [ ]

Jul 82. (lp)(c) **THE PARTY'S OVER** [21] [ ]
– Talk talk / It's so serious / Today / The party's over / Hate / Have you heard the news? / Mirror man / Another word / Candy. *(re-iss.1985, cd-iss.Mar87) (re-iss.Sep87 on 'Fame', cd-iss.Apr88)*

Oct 82. (7")(7"pic-d) **TALK TALK (remix). / MIRROR MAN** [23] [75]
(12") – ('A'side) / ('A'-BBC version).

Feb 83. (7") **MY FOOLISH FRIEND. / CALL IN THE NIGHT BOYS** [57] [ ]
(12"+=) – ('A'extended).

— Now basic trio when BREMNER departed. His place was taken by 4th member **TIM FRIESE-GREEN** – keyboards, producer, co-composer. Added session people **ROBBIE McINTOSH + HENRY LOWTHER**

Jan 84. (7") **IT'S MY LIFE. / DOES CAROLINE KNOW?** [46] [31]
(12"+=) – ('A'extended).

Feb 84. (lp)(c) **IT'S MY LIFE** [35] [42]
– Dum dum girl / Such a shame / Renee / It's my life / Tomorrow started / The last time / The last time / Call in the night boy / Does Caroline know? / It's you. *(cd-iss.Feb85) (lp re-iss.1989)*

Mar 84. (7") **SUCH A SHAME. / AGAIN, A GAME . . . AGAIN** [49] [89]
(12"+=) – ('A'extended).
(d7"+=) – Talk talk (demo) / Mirror man (demo).

Jul 84. (7") **DUM DUM GIRL. / WITHOUT YOU** [74] [ ]
(12"+=) – ('A'US mix) / Such a shame (dub).

— guests on next album incl. **DAVID RHODES** – guitar / **DAVID ROACH** – saxophone / **MORRIS PERT** – percussion

Parlophone EMI America

Jan 86. (7") **LIFE'S WHAT YOU MAKE IT. / IT'S GETTING LATE IN THE EVENING** [16] [90]
(12"+=) – ('A'extended dance mix).
(d12"+=) – It's my life / Does Caroline know?.

Feb 86. (lp)(c)(cd) **THE COLOUR OF SPRING** [8] [58]
– Happiness is easy / I don't believe in you / Life's what you make it / April 5th / Living in another world / Give it up / Chameleon day / Time it's time. *(re-iss.Mar90)*

(re-iss.cd+c Apr93 on 'Fame')

Mar 86. (7")(7"sha-pic-d) **LIVING IN ANOTHER WORLD. / FOR WHAT IT'S WORTH** 48
(12"+=)/ /(12"+=) – ('A'extended)./ / ('A'-US mix).

May 86. (7") **GIVE IT UP. / PICTURES OF BERNADETTE** 59
(12"+=) – ('A'dance mix).

Nov 86. (7") **I DON'T BELIEVE IN YOU. / DOES CAROLINE KNOW?**
(12"+=) – Happiness is easy.

— Basic quartet added ensemble **MARTIN DITCHAM** – percussion (also on last) / **ROBBIE McINTOSH** – dobro, 12-string guitar (also on last lp) / **MARK FELTHAM** – harmonica / **SIMON EDWARDS** – Mexican bass / **HENRY LOWTHER** – trumpet / **NIGEL KENNEDY** – violin / **DANNY THOMPSON** – double bass / **HUGH DAVIS** – shozygs / **MICHAEL JEANS** – oboe / **ANDREW STOWALL** – bassoon / **ANDREW HARRINER** – clarinet / **CHRIS HOOKER** – cor anglais / plus CHOIR OF CHELMSFORD CATHEDRAL.

Sep 88. (lp)(c)(cd) **SPIRIT OF EDEN** 19
– The rainbow / Eden / Desire / Inheritance / I believe in you / Wealth. *(re-iss.cd+c Jun93 on 'Fame')*

Sep 88. (7") **I BELIEVE IN YOU. / JOHN COPE**
(12"+=)(cd-s+=) – Eden (edit).

Dec 88. (m-lp)(c) **IT'S MY LIFE** (remixes) -

May 90. (7") **IT'S MY LIFE (remix). / RENEE (live)** 13
(12"+=)(cd-s+=) – ('A'live version).
(12") – ('A'side) / Talk Talk recycled; Life's what you make it – Living in another world – Such a shame – It's my life.

Jun 90. (cd)(c)(lp) **NATURAL HISTORY – THE VERY BEST OF TALK TALK** (compilation) 3
– Today / Talk talk / My foolish friend / Such a shame / Dum dum girl / It's my life / Give it up / Living in another world / Life's what you make it / Happiness is easy / I believe in you / Desire.

Sep 90. (7")(c-s) **LIFE'S WHAT YOU MAKE IT. / ('A'live version)** 23
(12"+=)(cd-s+=) – Tomorrow started (live).
(12") – (3-'A' mixes).

Nov 90. (7")(c-s) **SUCH A SHAME. / DUM DUM GIRL (live)**
(12"+=)(cd-s+=) – Talk talk (live) / ('A'extended).

Feb 91. (7")(c-s) **LIVING IN ANOTHER WORLD ('91 remix). / ('A'live remix)**
(12"+=)(cd-s+=) – ('A' Mendolsohn mix).

— Basic quartet only retained **DITCHAM, EDWARDS + LOWTHER** and brought in **LEVINE ANDRADE, STEPHEN TEES, GEORGE ROBERTSON, GAVYN WRIGHT, JACK GLICKMAN, GARFIELD JACKSON + WILF GIBSON** – viola / **ERNEST MOTHLE** – acoustic bass / **ROGER SMITH + PAUL KEGG** – cello / **DAVE WHITE** – contra, bass, clarinet

Mar 91. (cd)(c)(lp) **HISTORY REVISITED – THE REMIXES** 35
– Living in another world '91 / Such a shame / Happiness is easy (dub) / Today / Dum dum girl (spice remix) / Life's what you make it / Talk talk / It's my life (tropical rainforest mix) / Living in another world (curious world dub mix) / Life's what you make it (the Fluke remix).

Verve Verve

Sep 91. (cd)(c)(lp) **LAUGHING STOCK** 26
– Myrrhman / Ascension day / After the flood / Taphead / New grass / Runeii.

Sep 91. (pic-cd-s) **AFTER THE FLOOD / MYRRHMAN**

Oct 91. (pic-cd-s) **NEW GRASS. / STUMP**

Nov 91. (pic-cd-s) **ASCENTION DAY. / 5.09**

O'RANG

LEE HARRIS + PAUL WEBB

Echo not issued

Aug 94. (cd)(c) **HERD OF INSTINCT** -

Nov 94. (12"ep)(cd-ep) **SPOOR** -
– O'rang / Little brother / Mind our pleasure / All change / And on the oasis / Loaded values / Nahoojak fejou.

TANGERINE DREAM

Formed: Berlin, Germany . . . 1967 by EDGAR FROESE. After a number of album releases on German label 'Ohr', they signed to Richard Branson's newish label 'Virgin' in 1973. Surprisingly the following year, 'PHAEDRA' made it into the UK Top 40 lists, where they were future regulars during the rest of the 70's. • **Style:** Pioneers of improvised synthesized rock, which drew influences from PINK FLOYD. Soon discovered picturesque electronic waves of sound, which were critically derided for the haunting, repetitive rhythms and drones. Obviously it wasn't long before they realised, their potential would be in film soundtracks, and thus they concentrated on this during the 80's & early 90's. • **Songwriters:** FROESE compositions. • **Trivia:** They took group name in a couple of lyrics used to describe 'Lucy In The Sky With Diamonds' BEATLES.

Recommended: PHAEDRA (*9) / RUBYCON (*9) / RICOCHET (*8) / STRATOSFEAR (*7) / SORCEROR (*7).

EDGAR FROESE (b. 6 Jun'44) – guitar, piano, organ (ex-The ONES) / **VOLKER HOMBACH** – flute, violin / **KIRT HERKENBERG** – bass / (Mar69) / **SVEN JOHANNSON** – drums repl. LANSE HAPRHASH

— In 1970, after HOMBACH became film cameraman for W.R.FASSBINDER, and brief wind instrumentalist STEVE JOLIFFE departed to join STEAMHAMMER. Group reformed **EDGAR FROESE** brought in newcomers **KLAUS SCHULTZE** – drums, percussion / **CONRAD SCHNITZLER** – cello, flute, violin. with guests **JIMMY JACKSON** – organ / **THOMAS VON KEYSERLING** – flute

Ohr not issued

Jun 70. (lp) **ELECTRONIC MEDITATION** - - Germ'y
– Geburt (Genesis) / Reise durch ein brennendes gehirn (Journey through a burning brain) / Kalter rauch (Cold smoke) / Asche zu asche (Ashes to ashes) / Auferstehung (Resurrection).

— **FROESE** added bass to repertoire, and again supplanted new members **CHRISTOPHER FRANKE** – drums, percussion, synthesizer repl. CONRAD / **STEVE SCHROEDER** – organs repl. KLAUS SCHULTZE who went solo / added new guests **UDO DENNEBORG** – flute, words / **ROLAND PAULICK** – synthesizer

1971. (lp) **ALPHA CENTAURI** -
– Sunrise in the third system / Fly and collision of Comas Sola / Alpha Centauri. *(UK-iss.+c.1971 on 'Polydor') (re-iss.+cdJan87 on 'Zomba-Jive')*

— **PETER BAUMANN** – synthesizer, organ repl. SCHROYDER (guested on below)

Feb 72. (7") **ULTIMA THULE (teil 1). / ULTIMA THULE (teil 2)** - -

— More guests were added on next; **FLORIAN FRICKE** – synthesizers / cellists / **CHRISTIAN VALBRACHT / JOCKEN VON GRUMBCOW / HANS JOACHIM BRUNE / JOHANNES LUCKE**

1972. (d-lp) **ZEIT** - -
– 1st movement: Birth of liquid plejades / 2nd movement: Nebulous dawn / 3rd movement: Origins of supernatural probabilities / 4th movement: Zeit. *(UK-iss. 1976 on 'Virgin') (re-iss.+cdJan87 on 'Zomba-Jive')*

1973. (lp) **ATEM** -
– Atem / Fauni-Gena / Wahn / Circulation of events. *(UK-iss.+c.1973 on 'Polydor') (re-iss.+cdJan87 on 'Zomba-Jive')*

In Aug73, they recorded GREEN DESERT album, unreleased until 1986.

Virgin Virgin

Mar 74. (lp)(c) **PHAEDRA** 15
– Phaedra / Mysterious semblance at the strand of nightmares / Movements of a visionary / Sequent C. *(re-iss.Mar84, cd-iss.Jul87 & Feb95)*

— **MICHAEL HOENIG** – synthesizer repl. BAUMANN (on tours only 1974-75)

Mar 75. (lp)(c) **RUBYCON** 12
– Rubycon (part 1) / Rubycon (part 2). *(re-iss.Mar84, cd-iss.Jul87 & Feb95)*

Dec 75. (lp)(c) **RICOCHET (live at Liverpool, Coventry & Yorkminster Cathedrals)** 40
– Ricochet (part 1) / Ricochet (part 2). *(re-iss.Mar84, cd-iss.Jul87 & Feb95)*

— **BAUMANN** re-united with outfit, to depose HOENIG

Nov 76. (lp)(c) **STRATOSFEAR** 39
– Stratosfear / The big sleep in search of Hades / 3 a.m. at the border of the marsh from Okefnokee / Invisible limits. *(re-iss.1985, cd-iss.Jul87 & Feb95)*

Jul 77. (lp)(c) **SORCERER (Soundtrack)** 25
– Main title / Search / The call / Creation / Vengeance / The journey / Grind / Rain forest / Abyss / The mountain road / Impressions of Sorcerer / Betrayal (Sorcerer's theme). *(re-iss.Feb82)*

Above album and below 45 were from the film 'Wages Of Fear' on 'M.C.A.' records.

Aug 77. (7") **BETRAYAL. / GRIND** -

Nov 77. (d-lp)(c) **ENCORE (live)** 55
– Cherokee lane / Moonlight / Coldwater canyon / Desert dream. *(cd-iss.1985 & Apr95)*

Jan 78. (7") **ENCORE. / HOBO MARCH**

Mar 78. (7") **MOONLIGHT. / COLDWATER CANYON** - -

— **STEVE JOLIFFE** – vocals, keyboards, wind returned after several years to repl. BAUMANN who went solo. Added **KLAUS KRIEGER** – drums

Mar 78. (lp)(c) **CYCLONE** 37
– Bent cold sidewalk / Rising runner missed by endless sender / Madrigal meridian. *(re-iss.1982, cd-iss.Jul87 & Apr95)*

Feb 79. (lp)(c)(clear-lp) **FORCE MAJEURE** 27
– Force majeure / Cloudburst flight / Thru metamorphic rocks. *(re-iss.+cdJul87, cd-iss.Apr95)*

— (now trio) **FROESE + FRANKE** recruited **JOHANNES SCHMOELLING** – keyboards

May 80. (lp)(c) **TANGRAM** 36
– Tangram set 1 / Tangram set 2. *(re-iss.+cd.Oct85, cd-iss.Apr95)*

Virgin Elektra

Apr 81. (lp)(c) **THIEF (Soundtrack)** 43
– Beach theme / Dr. Destructo / Diamond diary / Burning bar / Scrap yard / Trap feeling / Igneous / Confrontation. *(re-iss.1985, cd-iss.Jun88 & Aug95)*

Sep 81. (lp)(c) **EXIT** 43
– Kiwe mission / Pilots of purple twilight / Chronozon / Exit / Network 23 / Remote viewing. *(re-iss.+cdJun88 & Aug95)*

Sep 81. (7") **CHRONOZON. / NETWORK 23** -

Apr 82. (lp)(c) **WHITE EAGLE** 57
– Midnight in Tulo / Convention of the 24 / White eagle / Mojave plan. *(cd-iss.Jun88 & Aug95)*

Dec 82. (lp)(c) **LOGOS – LIVE (At The Dominion)**
– Logos part 1 / Logos part 2 / Dominion. *(re-iss.Apr86, cd-iss.Jun88 & Aug95)*

Oct 83. (lp)(c)(cd) **HYPERBOREA** 45
– No man's lannd / Hyperborea / Cinnamon road / Sphinx lightning. *(re-iss.cd Jun88 & Aug95)*

Dec 83. (lp)(c) **RISKY BUSINESS (Soundtrack)**
– The dream is always the same / No future / Love on a real train / Guido the killer pimp / Lana (tracks by other artists; PHIL COLLINS / JOURNEY / MUDDY WATERS / JEFF BECK / BOB SEGER). *(re-iss.+cd.Apr90)*

M.C.A. M.C.A.

Jul 84. (lp)(c) **FIRESTARTER (Film Soundtrack)**
– Crystal voice / The run / Test lab / Charley the kid / Escaping point / Rainbirds move / Burning force / Between realities / Shop territory / Flash final / Out of the heat. *(cd-iss.Apr90)*

Jive Electro Jive Electro

Sep 84. (7")(7"sha-pic-d) **WARSAW IN THE SUN. / POLISH DANCE**
(12"+=) – Rare bird / ('A'version).

Oct 84. (d-lp)(d-c)(d-pic-lp) **POLAND – THE WARSAW CONCERT (live)** 90
– Poland / Tangent / Barbakane / Horizon.

Feb 85. (lp)(c)(pic-lp) **FLASHPOINT (Soundtrack)**
– Going west / Afternoon in the desert / Plane ride / Mystery tracks / Lost in the dunes / Highway patrol / Love phantasy / Madcap story / Dirty cross-roads / Flashpoint. *(cd-iss.Apr87) (re-iss.cd Sep95 on 'One Way')*

(above was on 'Jive-Heavy Metal' label).
Aug 85. (lp)(c) **LE PARC**
– Bois de Boulonge (Paris) / Central Park (New York) / Gaudi Park (Guell Garden, Barcelona) / Tiergarten (Berlin) / Zen Garden (Myoonj, Temple Kyoto) / Le Parc (L.A. Streethawk) / Hyde Park (London) / The Cliffs of Sydney (Sydney) / Yellowstone Park (Rocky Mountains). *(cd-iss.1988)*

— guest on above album **CLARE TORY** – vocals
Aug 85. (7") **STREETHAWK. / TIERGARTEN**
(12"+=) – Gaudi Park / Warsaw in the sun (part 1 & 2).

— **PAUL HASLINGER** – multi-instrumentalist repl. SCHMOELLING who went solo
Jul 86. (lp)(c)(cd) **UNDERWATER SUNLIGHT** 97
– Song of the whale / From dawn . . . to dusk / Ride on the ray / Dolphin dance / Underwater sunlight / Scuba scuba.
Jun 87. (lp)(c)(cd) **TYGER** 88
– Tyger / London / Alchemy of the heart / Smile. *(cd+=)*– 21st century common man I & II.

— (guest vox – **BERNADETTE SMITH**).
Jun 87. (7") **TYGER. / 21st CENTURY COMMON MAN II**
(12"+=) – ('A'version).

Jive Electro / Sil-va Screen
Feb 88. (lp)(c)(cd) **NEAR DARK (Soundtrack)** -
– Cabeb's blues / Pick up at high noon / Rain in the third house / Bus station / Good times / She's my sister / Father and son / Severin dies / Flight at dawn / Mae's transformation / Mae comes back. *(UK-iss.Jun90)*
Apr 88. (lp)(c)(cd) **LIVE MILES (live)**
– Live miles: (part 1) – The Albuquerque concert / Live miles: (part 2) – The West Berlin concert.
Jul 88. (lp)(c)(cd) **SHY PEOPLE (Soundtrack)** -
– Shy people / Joe's place / The harbor / Nightfal / Dancing on a white moon / Civilized illusion's / Swamp voices / Transparent days / Shy people (reprise).

— now a duo of **FROESE + HASLINGER**

Arista / Private . . .
Feb 89. (lp)(c)(cd) **OPTICAL RACE** Aug 88
– Marakesh / Atlas eyes / Mothers of rain / Twin soul tribe / Optical race / Cat scan / Sun gate / Turning of the wheel / The midnight trail / Ghtrezi (long song).
Jul 89. (lp)(c)(cd) **MIRACLE MILE** -
– Teetering scales / One for the book / After the call / On the spur of the moment / All of a dither / Final statement.
Dec 89. (lp)(c)(cd) **LILY ON THE BEACH** -
– Too hot for my chinchilla / Lily on the beach / Alaskan summer / Desert drive / Mount Shasta / Crystal curfew / Paradise cove / Twenty nine palms / Valley of the kings / Radio city / Blue mango cafe / Gecko / Long island sunset.

R.C.A. / R.C.A.
Dec 90. (cd)(c)(lp) **MELROSE**
– Melrose / Three bikes in the sky / Dolls in the shadow / Yucatan / Electric lion / Rolling down Cahenga / Art of vision / Desert train / Cool at heart.

Sil-va Screen / Sil-va Screen
Mar 91. (cd) **DEAD SOLID PERFECT (Soundtrack)**
– Theme from Dead Solid Perfect / In the pond / Beverly leaves / Of cads and caddies / (Tournament montage) / A whore in one / Sand trap / In the rough / Nine iron / US Open / My name is bad hair / In the hospital room / Welcome to Bushwood / Deja vu / Birdie / Divot / Kenny and Donny montage / Phone to Beverly / Nice shots / Sinking putts / Kenny's winning shot.

— Now a duo of **FROESE + JEROME FROESE** his son and **LINDA SPA** – sax / **ZLASLO PERICA** – synth.
Feb 92. (cd)(c)(lp) **ROCKOON** (on 'Essential')
– Big city dwarves / Red roadster / Touchwood / Graffiti sreeet / Funky Atlanta / Spanish love / Lifted veil / Penguin reference / Body corporate / Rockoon / Girls on Broadway.
Dec 92. (cd) **DEADLY CARE (Soundtrack)**
– Main theme / Paddles – Stolen pills / A strong drink – A bad morning / Wasted and sick / Hope for future / The hospital in bed / Annie and father / More pills / In the Head nurse's – At the father's grave / Clean and sober.

Miramar / Miramar
Jul 93. (cd) **CANYON DREAMS**
– Shadow flyer / Canyon carver / Water's gift / Canyon voices / Sudden revelation / A matter of time / Purple nightfall / Colorado dawn.
Oct 93. (cd)(c) **220 VOLT LIVE (live)**
– Oriemtal haze / Two bunch palms / 220 volt / Homeless / Treasure of innocence / Sundance kid / Backstreet hero / The blue bridge / Hamlet / Dreamtime / Purple haze.

CoastCoast / CoastCoast
Nov 94. (cd) **TURN OF THE TIDES**
– Pictures at an exhibition / Firetongues / Galey slave's horizon / Death of a nightingale / Twilight brigade / Jungle journey / Midwinter night / Turn of the tides.

Amp
Sep 95. (cd) **TYRANNY OF BEAUTY**
–

– compilations, others, etc. –

Jul 76. Polydor; (d-lp)(d-c) **ATEM / ALPHA CENTAURI** -
Dec 80. Virgin; (4xlp-box) **70-80** -
1985. Virgin; (lp)(c) **HEARTBREAKERS** - -
Nov 85. Virgin; (d-lp)(c)(cd) **DREAM SEQUENCE** - -
1983. Varese Sara; (lp) **WAVELENGTH (Soundtrack)** -
1987. Varese Sara; (lp) **THREE O'CLOCK HIGH (Soundtrack)** -
May 86. MCA; (lp) **LEGEND (Soundtrack with other artists)** - 96
– Unicorn theme / Blue room / Darkness / The dance / Goblins / Fairies / The kitchen (medley).
Mar 86. Jive Electro; (6xlp-box) **IN THE BEGINNING** -
– (ELECTRONIC MEDITATION / ALPHA CENTAURI / ZEIT (d-lp) / ATEM / GREEN DESERT)
Nov 89. Jive; (lp)(c)(cd) **THE BEST OF TANGERINE DREAM**
Dec 86. Zomba; (cd) **GREEN DESERT** (rec.1973) -
(re-iss.+lp/c.May89)
Mar 87. Castle/ US= Relativity; (d-lp)(c)(cd) **THE TANGERINE DREAM COLLECTION** Aug 87

Oct 91. Music Club; (cd)(c)(lp) **FROM DAWN . . . TILL DUSK 1973-88** -
Mar 93. Silva Screen; (cd) **DREAM MUSIC**
feat. selections from soundtracks; THE PARK IS MINE / DEADLY CARE / DEAD SOLID PERFECT.
Oct 94. Virgin; (5xcd-box) **TANGENTS** -
Mar 95. Emporio; (cd)(c) **ATMOSPHERICS** -
Nov 95. Silva Screen; (cd) **DREAM MUSIC 2** -
Dec 95. Essential; (d-cd) **BOOK OF DREAMS** -

EDGAR FROESE

solo (all music by himself)

Virgin / Virgin
Jun 74. (lp)(c) **AQUA** -
– NGC 891 / Upland / Aqua / Panorphelia. *(re-iss.Mar84, cd-iss.Jun87)*
Sep 75. (lp)(c) **EPSILON IN MALAYSIAN PALE** -
– Epsilon in Malaysian pale / Maroubra Bay. *(re-iss.Mar84, cd-iss.Jun87)*
1976. Brain Germany; (lp) **MACULA TRANSFER** - -
– Os / Af / Pa / Quantas / If. *(re-iss.Mar82)*
Jan 78. (d-lp) **AGES**
– Metropolis / Era of the slaves / Tropic of Capricorn / Nights of automatic women / Icarus / Childrens deeper study / Ode to Granny "A" / Pizarro and Atahwallpa / Golgatha and the circle closes.
Sep 79. (lp)(c) **STUNTMAN**
– Stuntman / It would be like Samoa / Detroit snackbar dreamer / Drunken Mozart in the desert / A Dali-esque sleep fuse / Scarlet score for Mescalero. *(re-iss.Mar84, cd-iss.1987) (cd-iss.Mar94)*
Oct 82. (lp)(c) **KAMIKAZE 1989 (Soundtrack)** -
– Videophonic / Vitamen 'C' / Krismopompas / Polizei disco / Intuition / Polizei therapie center / Blauer panther / Schlangenbad / Underwarter tod / Flying kamikaze / Der konzern / Der 31. stock. *(re-iss.+cd.1988)*
Aug 83. (lp)(c) **PINNACLES** -
– Specific gravity of smile / The light cone / Walkabout / Pinnacles. *(re-iss.+cd.1988)*

– (EDGAR FROESE) compilations, others –

Aug 82. Virgin; (lp)(c) **SOLO** -
(re-iss.Mar84, cd-iss.Aug88)
Jun 95. (d-cd)(d-lp) **BEYOND THE STARS** -

TASTE (see under ⇒ GALLAGHER, Rory)

James TAYLOR

Born: 12 Mar'48, Boston, Massachusetts, USA. In 1966 he moved to New York, after previously experiencing bouts of depression, which led to a brief spell in a psychiatric institute in Belmont. He joined DANNY KORTCHMAR's band The FLYING MACHINE, but left them in March '67, and spent next year trying to kick heroin addiction. He stayed in Notting Hill, London, at this time, and soon had demo tape listened to by A&R man Pete Asher, who signed him to BEATLES' label 'Apple'. His eponymous debut flopped, and he moved back to the States to recover again. After a flit to California in 1969, he signed to 'Warner Bros.' and attempted a follow-up with producer Pete Asher at the helm. He also became his manager and produced future work in the 70's. His return album 'SWEET BABY JAMES', soon became a massive Top 3 seller in the US, and spawned a hit 45 'FIRE AND RAIN'. He quickly followed this in 1971 with international hit album 'MUD SLIDE SLIM . . . ', and from it the classic 45 hit CAROLE KING penned cut 'YOU'VE GOT A FRIEND'. Just prior to his fourth album 'ONE MAN DOG', he married fellow singer CARLY SIMON on 3rd Nov'72. They divorced nearly 10 years later. • **Style:** Acoustic-guitar playing country-rock singer, who drifted with each release into mainstream AOR-pop. • **Songwriters:** Prolific pensmith, who also covered others; LO AND BEHOLD (Bob Dylan) / MOCKINGBIRD duet (Inez & Charlie Foxx) / HOW SWEET IT IS (Marvin Gaye) / HANDY MAN (Jimmy Jones) / DEVOTED TO YOU duet (Everly Brothers) / UP ON THE ROOF (Goffin-King) / DAY TRIPPER (Beatles) / JELLY MAN KELLY (with daughter Sarah) / EVERYDAY (Buddy Holly). • **Trivia:** He starred in the 1971 road movie TWO LANE BLACKTOP and also acted on US TV production WORKING (1981).

Recommended: SWEET BABY JAMES (*8) / MUD SLIME SLIM AND THE BLUE HORIZON (*7) / BEST OF JAMES TAYLOR – CLASSIC SONGS (*7)

JAMES TAYLOR – vocals, guitar with session people

Apple / Apple
Dec 68. (lp) **JAMES TAYLOR** 62 Sep 70
– Don't talk now / Something's wrong / Knockin' round the zoo / Sunshine sunshine / Taking it in / Something in the way she moves / Carolina in my mind / Brighten your night with my day / Night owl / Rainy day man / Circle 'round the Sun / The blues is just a bad dream. *(re-iss.Jun71) (re-iss.Oct91)*
Apr 69. (7") **CAROLINA ON MY MIND. / SOMETHING'S WRONG** -
(re-iss. Nov 70, hit No.67)

— now with **DANNY KOOTCH** (b.KORTCHMAR) – guitar / **CAROLE KING** – piano / **RUSS KUNKEL** – drums / **RANDY MEISNER, BOBBY WEST + JOHN LONDON** – bass / **CHRIS DARROW** – fiddle / **RED RHODES** – steel guitar / **JACK BIELAN** – brass arrangement

Warners / Warners
Jul 70. (7") **SWEET BABY JAMES. / SUITE FOR ZOG** -
Sep 70. (7") **FIRE AND RAIN. / ANYWHERE LIKE HEAVEN** - 3

Nov 70. (7") **FIRE AND RAIN. / SUNNY SKIES** 42 -
Nov 70. (lp)(c) **SWEET BABY JAMES** 7 3 Mar 70
– Sweet baby James / Lo and behold / Sunny skies / Steamroller / Country road / Oh, Susannah / Fire and rain / Blossom / Anywhere like Heaven / Oh baby, don't you loose your lip on me / Suite for 20 G. *(re-iss.Dec71, hit UK No.34) (re-iss.+cd.Jul88)*
Feb 71. (7") **COUNTRY ROAD. / SUNNY SKIES** - 37

— **LEE SKLAR** – bass repl. 3 bassmen. Guest **JONI MITCHELL** – b.vox (2 – 45's)

May 71. (lp)(c) **MUD SLIDE SLIM AND THE BLUE HORIZON** 4 2
– Love has brought me around / You've got a friend / Places in my past / Riding on a railroad / Soldiers / Mud slide Slim / Hey mister, that's me upon the jukebox / You can close your eyes / Machine gun Kelly / Long ago and far away / Let me ride / Highway song / Isn't it nice to be home again. *(re-iss.Mar72, hit UK No.49) (re-iss.+cd.1989)*
Aug 71. (7") **YOU'VE GOT A FRIEND. / YOU CAN CLOSE YOUR EYES** 4 1 Jun 71
Sep 71. (7") **LONG AGO AND FAR AWAY. / LET ME RIDE** - 31
Nov 72. (lp)(c) **ONE MAN DOG** 27 4
– One man parade / Nobody but you / Chili dog / Fool for you / Instrumental I / New tune / Back on the street again / Don't let me be lonely tonight / Woh, don't you know / One morning in May / Instrumental II / Someone / Hymn / Fanfare / Little David / Mescalito / Dance / Jig. *(quad-lp US Feb76) (cd-iss.Feb92)*
Nov 72. (7") **DON'T LET ME BE LONELY TONIGHT. / WOH, DON'T YOU KNOW** [ ] 14
Feb 73. (7") **ONE MAN PARADE. / NOBODY BUT YOU** - 67
May 73. (7") **HYMN. / FANFARE** - [ ]

— In Jan'74, did duet with wife CARLY SIMON on UK No.34 / US No.5 hit MOCKINGBIRD.

Jul 74. (lp)(c) **WALKING MAN** [ ] 13
– Walking man / Rock'n'roll is music now / Let it fall down / Me and my guitar / Daddy's baby / Ain't no song / Hello old friend / Migration / The promised land / Fading away.
Aug 74. (7") **AIN'T NO SONG. / HELLO OLD FRIEND** [ ] [ ]
May 75. (lp)(c) **GORILLA** [ ] 6
– Mexico / Music / How sweet it is (to be loved by you) / Wandering / Gorilla / You make it easy / I was a fool to care / Lighthouse / Angry blues / Love song / Sarah Maria. *(cd-iss.Jul88) (quad-lp Feb76)*
Jul 75. (7") **HOW SWEET IT IS (TO BE LOVED BY YOU). / SARAH MARIA** [ ] 5 Jun 75
Oct 75. (7") **MEXICO. / GORILLA** [ ] 49
Apr 76. (7") **WANDERING. / ANGRY BLUES** [ ] [ ]
Jun 76. (lp)(c) **IN THE POCKET** [ ] 16
– Shower the people / A junkie's lament / Money machine / Slow burning love / Everybody has the blues / Daddy's all gone / Woman's gotta have it / Captain Jim's drunken dream / Don't be sad 'cause your sun is down / Nothing like a hundred miles / Family man / Golden moments.
Jun 76. (7") **SHOWER THE PEOPLE. / I CAN DREAM OF YOU** [ ] 22
Aug 76. (7") **EVERYBODY HAS THE BLUES. / I CAN DREAM OF YOU** [ ] [ ]
Oct 76. (7") **EVERYBODY HAS THE BLUES. / MONEY MACHINE** [ ] -
Dec 76. (lp)(c) **GREATEST HITS** (compilation) [ ] 23
– Something in the way she moves / Carolina in my mind / Fire and rain / Sweet baby James / Country roads / You've got a friend / Don't let me be lonely tonight / Walking man / How sweet it is (to be loved by you) / Mexico / Shower the people / Steamroller. *(re-iss.Mar82) (re-iss.+cd.Jan87)*

— Retained **KORTCHMAR, KUNKEL + SKLAR** and recruited **DAVID SANBORN** – sax / **CLARENCE McDONALD** – percussion

C.B.S. Columbia

Jun 77. (7") **HANDY MAN. / BARTENDER'S BLUES** [ ] 4
Jul 77. (lp)(c) **J.T.** [ ] 4
– Your smiling face / There we are / Honey don't leave L.A. / Another grey morning / Bartender's blues / Secret of life / Handy man / I was only telling a lie / Looking for love on Broadway / Terra Nova / Traffic jam / If I keep my heart out of sight. *(re-iss.+cd.Feb85) (re-iss.cd+c Oct93 on 'Sony Collectors')*
Oct 77. (7") **YOUR SMILING FACE. / IF I KEEP MY HEART OUT OF SIGHT** [ ] 20 Sep 77

— Autumn'77, saw him produce, play guitar, etc. for sister KATE TAYLOR's debut US Top 50 hit single IT'S IN HIS KISS. Early in 1978, he was credited on another cover hit 45; 'WHAT A WONDERFUL WORLD' with PAUL SIMON & ART GARFUNKEL.

Feb 78. (7") **HONEY DON'T LEAVE L.A. / ANOTHER GREY MORNING** - 61

— In Sep78, another CARLY SIMON / J.T. duet 'DEVOTED TO YOU' hit US No.36.

Jun 79. (7") **UP ON THE ROOF. / CHANSON FRANCAISE** [ ] 28 May 79
Aug 79. (lp)(c) **FLAG** [ ] 10 May 79
– Company man / Johnnie comes back / Day tripper / I will not lie for you / Brother Trucker / Is that the way you look / B.S.U.R. / Rainy day man / Millworker / Up on the roof / Chanson francaise / Slep come free me. *(re-iss.Feb86) (cd-iss.Sep93 on 'Sony Collectors')*
Aug 79. (7") **B.S.U.R. / SLEEP COME FREE ME** [ ] [ ]
Mar 81. (7") **HER TOWN TOO. ("JAMES TAYLOR & J.D.SOUTHER") / BELIEVE IT OR NOT** [ ] 11 Feb 81
Apr 81. (lp)(c) **DAD LOVES HIS WORK** [ ] 10 Mar 81
– Hard times / Her town too / Hour that the morning comes / I will follow / Believe it or not / Stand and fight / Only for me / Summer's here / Sugar trade / London town / That lonesome road. *(cd-iss.May87) (cd-iss.Jan94 on 'Sony Europe')*
May 81. (7") **HARD TIMES. / SUMMER'S HERE** - 72

— Late '85, he duets on RICKY SCAGGS track 'New Star Shining', for current lp

Jan 86. (lp)(c) **THAT'S WHY I'M HERE** [ ] 34 Nov 85
– That's why I'm here / Song for you far away / Only a dream in Rio / Turn away / Going around one more time / Everyday / Limousine driver / Only one / Mona / The man who shot Liberty Valance / That's why I'm here (reprise).
Mar 86. (7") **EVERYDAY. / LIMOUSINE DRIVER** [ ] 61 Nov 85
Mar 86. (7") **MONA. / ONLY ONE** - [ ]
May 86. (7") **THAT'S WHY I'M HERE. / GOING AROUND ONE MORE TIME** - [ ]
Jul 86. (7") **ONLY A DREAM IN RIO. / TURN AWAY** - [ ]
Feb 88. (lp)(c)(cd) **NEVER DIE YOUNG** [ ] 25
– Never die young / T-bone / Baby boom baby / Runaway boy / Valentine's day / Sun on the Moon / Sweet potato pie / Home by another day / Letter in the mail / First of May.
Feb 88. (7") **NEVER DIE YOUNG. / VALENTINE'S DAY** [ ] 80
(12"+=) – Everyday. *(re-iss.Jun88)*
May 88. (7") **LETTER IN THE MAIL. / BABY BOOM BABY** - [ ]
Sep 88. (7") **FIRST OF MAY. / SWEET POTATO PIE** - [ ]
Sep 91. (c-s) **(I'VE GOT TO) STOP THINKIN' 'BOUT THAT. / SLAP LEATHER** - [ ]
Oct 91. (cd)(c)(lp) **NEW MOON SHINE** [ ] 37
– Copperline / Down in the hole / (I've got to) Stop thinkin' 'bout that / Shed a little light / The frozen man / Slap leather / Like every one she knows / One more round to cha cha cha / Native son / Oh brother / The water is wide. *(re-iss.cd Jul94 on 'Sony Europe')*

— with **CLIFFORD CARTER** – keyboards / **DON GROLNICK** – piano / **JIMMY JOHNSON** – bass / **MICHAEL LANDALL** – guitar / **VALERIE CARTER, DAVID LASLEY, KATE MARKOWITZ & ANDREW McCULLEY** – vocals / **CARLOS VEGA** – drums

Columbia Columbia

Sep 93. (cd)(c) **LIVE** [ ] 20 Aug 93
– Sweet baby James / Traffic jam / Handy man / Your smiling face / Secret of life / Shed a little light / Everybody has the blues / Steamroller blues / Mexico / Millworker / Country road / Fire and rain / Shower the people / How sweet it is / New hymn / Walking man / Riding on a railroad / Something in the way she moves / Sun on the Moon / Up on the roof / Don't let me be lonely tonight / She thinks I still care / Copperline / Slap leather / Only one / You make it easy / Carolina on my mind / I will follow / That lonesome road / You've got a friend.
('BEST LIVE' of above issued Apr 94)

– more compilations, etc. –

Feb 71. DJM/ US= Euphoria; (lp) **JAMES TAYLOR & THE ORIGINAL FLYING MACHINE** [ ] [ ]
– (early material 1967 when a member of The FLYING MACHINE) *(re-iss.Nov76 as 'RAINY DAY MAN' on 'DJM'/'Trip', tracks differed slightly)*
1974. Warners; (7"ep) **YOU'VE GOT A FRIEND / SUNNY SKIES. / FIRE AND RAIN / SWEET BABY JAMES** [ ] -
Oct 75. Warners; (d-lp) **TWO ORIGINALS OF . . .** [ ] -
– (contains the 2 albums below)
Oct 82. Warners; (d-c) **SWEET BABY JAMES / MUD SLIDE SLIM & THE BLUE HORIZON** [ ] -
(d-cd-iss.Apr84)
Mar 86. Old Gold; (7") **YOU'VE GOT A FRIEND. / FIRE AND RAIN** [ ] -
Jan 87. CBS; (7") **UP ON THE ROOF. / FIRE AND RAIN** [ ] -
Mar 87. CBS-WEA TV; (lp)(c)(cd) **THE BEST OF JAMES TAYLOR – CLASSIC SONGS** 53 -
– Fire and rain / Mexico / You've got a friend / How sweet it is (to be loved by you) / Carolina on my mind / Something in the way she moves / Shower the people / Sweet baby James / That's why I'm here / Everyday / Up on the roof / Your smiling face / Her town too / Handyman / Don't let me be lonely tonight / Only a dream in Rio.

John TAYLOR (see under ⇒ DURAN DURAN)

Roger TAYLOR (see under ⇒ QUEEN)

TEARDROP EXPLODES (see under ⇒ COPE, Julian)

TEARS FOR FEARS

Formed: Bath, Avon, England . . . 1981 by SMITH and ORZABAL, after both had left ska-pop outfit GRADUATE. As TEARS FOR FEARS, they signed to 'Mercury', after A&R man Dave Bates heard a few demos. In the Autumn 1982, their CHRIS 'Merrick' HUGHES (ex-Adam & The Ants) produced single 'MAD WORLD' burst into UK Top 3. It was followed by another smash, which preceeded parent UK No.1 album 'THE HURTING'. • **Style:** Intelligent lightweight soulful rock, which progressed in the late 80's, into slight experimentation and BEATLES influenced psychedelia. • **Songwriters:** All written by ORZABAL, except CREEP (Radiohead). • **Trivia:** Took their name from Arthur Janov's book 'Prisoners Of Pain'.

Recommended: TEARS ROLL DOWN – GREATEST HITS 1982-1992 (*8)

GRADUATE

ROLAND ORZABAL (b.ROLAND ORZABAL DE LA QUINTANA, 22 Aug'61, Portsmouth, England) – vocals, guitar / **CURT SMITH** (b.24 Jun'61) – vocals, bass / **JOHN BAKER** – vocals, guitar / **STEVE BUCK** – keyboards, flute / **ANDY MARSDEN** – drums

Precision not issued

Mar 80. (7") **ELVIS SHOULD PLAY SKA. / JULIE JULIE** [ ] -
May 80. (7") **EVER MET A DAY?. / SHUT UP** [ ] -
(re-iss.Mar81)
May 80. (10"lp)(c) **ACTING MY AGE** [ ] -
– Acting my age / Sick and tired / Ever met a day / Dancing nights / Shut up / Elvis should play ska / Watching your world / Love that is bad / Julie Julie / Bad dreams. *(re-iss.Jul86 on 'P.R.T.')*
Oct 80. (7") **AMBITION. / BAD DREAMS** [ ] -

TEARS FOR FEARS

ROLAND & CURT with **DAVID LORD** – synthesizers(Duo also on synthesizers)

Mercury Mercury

Nov 81. (7") **SUFFER THE CHILDREN. / WIND** [ ] [ ]
('A'remixed-12"+=) – ('A'instrumental). *(re-iss.Aug85, hit 52)*

— Trimmed to a basic duo of **ORZABAL & SMITH**

Mar 82. (7") **PALE SHELTER (YOU DON'T GIVE ME LOVE). / THE PRISONER** [ ] [ ]
(12"+=) – ('A'extended). *(re-iss.Aug85, hit 73)*

Sep 82. (7") **MAD WORLD. / IDEAS AS OPIATES** [3] [ ]
(12"+=) – Saxophones as opiates.
(d7"+=) – ('A'world remix) / Suffer the children.

Jan 83. (7") **CHANGE. / THE CONFLICT** [4] [73] Jun 83
(12"+=) – ('A'extended).

— now augmented by **IAN STANLEY** – keyboards / **MANNY ELIAS** – drums

Mar 83. (lp)(c) **THE HURTING** [1] [73]
– The hurting / Mad world / Pale shelter / Ideas as opiates / Memories fade / Suffer the children / Watch me bleed / Change / The prisoner / Start of the breakdown. *(cd-iss.1984)*

Apr 83. (7")(7"red)(7"green)(7"white)(7"blue)(7"pic-d) **PALE SHELTER. / WE ARE BROKEN** [5] [ ]
(12"+=) – ('A'extended).

Nov 83. (7") **(THE) WAY YOU ARE. / THE MARAUDERS** [24] [ ]
('A'extended-12"+=) – Start of the breakdown (live).
(d7"++=) – Change (live).

Aug 84. (7")(7"green)(7"clear-pic-d) **MOTHER'S TALK. / EMPIRE BUILDING** [14] [27] Mar 86
(12"+=)/ /(12"+=) – ('A'beat of the drum mix)./ / ('A'extended).
(12") – (above 2 versions + 'A'-7"version)

Nov 84. (7")(10") **SHOUT. / THE BIG CHAIR** [4] [1] May 85
(12"+=) – ('A'extended).

— added mainly on tour **WILLIAM GREGORY** – saxophone / **NICKY HOLLAND** – keyboards

Mar 85. (lp)(c)(cd) **SONGS FROM THE BIG CHAIR** [2] [1]
– Shout / The working hour / Everybody wants to rule the world / Mother's talk / I believe / Broken / Head over heels / Broken (live) / Listen. *(c+=)* – (6 extra mixes).

Mar 85. (7")(10") **EVERYBODY WANTS TO RULE THE WORLD. / PHAROAHS** [2] [1]
(12"+=) – ('A'extended).
(d7"+=) – ('A'urban mix) / (duo interviewed).
(12") – ('A'urban mix). / ('A'instrumental)

Jun 85. (7")(10")(7"sha-pic-d) **HEAD OVER HEELS (remix). / WHEN IN LOVE WITH A BLIND MAN** [12] [3] Sep 85
(12"+=)/ /(12"+=) – ('A'preacher mix)./ / Broken.

Oct 85. (7") **I BELIEVE (A soulful re-recording). / SEA SONG** [23] [ ]
(d7"+=)(12"+=) – Shout (dub) / I believe (original version).
(10"+=) – I believe (US mix).

May 86. (7")(12") **EVERYBODY WANTS TO RUN THE WORLD. / EVERYBODY . . . (Running version)** [5] [ ]

— **ORZABAL + SMITH** retained **IAN** and **NICKY** and brought in sessioners **OLETA ADAMS** – some dual vocals, piano / **SIMON CLARK** – organ / **PINO PALLADINO** – bass / **ROBBIE McINTOSH, NEIL TAYLOR + RANDY JACOBS** – guitar / **PHIL COLLINS, CHRIS HUGHES + MANU KATCHE** – drums

Fontana Fontana

Aug 89. (7")(c-s) **SOWING THE SEEDS OF LOVE. / TEARS ROLL DOWN** [5] [2]
(12"+=)(12"pic-d+=)(12"white+=)(3"cd-s+=) – Shout (US mix).

Sep 89. (lp)(c)(cd) **THE SEEDS OF LOVE** [1] [8]
– Woman in chains / Bad man's song / Sowing the seeds of love / Advice for the young at heart / Standing on the corner of the third world / Swords and knives / Year of the knife / Famous last words.

(next 'A'feat. **OLETA ADAMS** – co-vox)

Nov 89. (7")(c-s) **WOMAN IN CHAINS. / ALWAYS IN THE PAST** [26] [36]
(12"+=)(12"pic-d+=)(12"white+=)(3"cd-s+=)(cd-s+=) – ('A'instrumental) / My life in the suicide ranks.

Feb 90. (7")(c-s) **ADVICE FOR THE YOUNG AT HEART. / JOHNNY PANIC AND THE BIBLE OF DREAMS** [36] [89]
(12"+=)(cd-s+=)(12"pic-d+=) – Music for tables.
(3"cd-s++=) – Johnny Panic (instrumental).

Jul 90. (7")(c-s) **FAMOUS LAST WORDS. / MOTHER'S TALK (US remix)** [ ] [ ]
(12"+=)(cd-s+=)(12"pic-d+=) – Listen.

Feb 92. (7")(c-s) **LAID SO LOW. / THE BODY WAH** [17] [ ]
(12"pic-d+=)(cd-s+=) – Lord of the Kharma.

Mar 92. (cd)(c)(lp) **TEARS ROLL DOWN – GREATEST HITS 1982-1992** (compilation) [2] [53]
– Sowing the seeds of love / Everybody wants to rule the world / Woman in chains / Shout / Head over heels / Mad world / Pale shelter / I beieve / Laid so low (tears roll down) / Mothers talk / Change / Advice for the young at heart. (May93: re-entered UK charts at 37).

Apr 92. (7")(c-s) **WOMAN IN CHAINS. / BADMAN'S SONG** [57] [ ]
(cd-s+=) – Ghost papa.

(above was again credited to "TEARS FOR FEARS & OLETA ADAMS")

— **ROLAND ORZABAL** now sole survivor, when CURT SMITH launched solo career.

Mercury Mercury

May 93. (7")(c-s) **BREAK IT DOWN AGAIN. / BLOODLETTING GO** [20] [25]
(cd-s+=) – ?

Jun 93. (cd)(c)(lp) **ELEMENTAL** [5] [45]
– Elemental / Cold / Break it down again / Mr. Pessimist / Dog's a best friend's dog / Fish out of water / Gas giants / Power / Brian Wilson said / Goodnight song.

Jul 93. (7")(c-s) **COLD. / NEW STAR** [72] [ ]
(cd-s+=) – Deja vu / The sins of silence.

Epic Sony

Sep 95. (c-s) **RAOUL AND THE KINGS OF SPAIN / QUEEN OF COMPROMISE** [31] [ ]
(cd-s) – ('A'side) / Creep / The madness of Roland.

Oct 95. (cd)(c) **RAOUL AND THE KINGS OF SPAIN** [41] [79]
– Raoul and the Kings of Spain / Falling down / Secrets / God's mistake / Sketches of pain / Los Reyes Catolicos / Sorry / Humdrum and humble / I choose you / Don't drink the water / Me and my big ideas / Los Reyes Catolicos (reprise).

TEENAGE FANCLUB

Formed: Bellshill & Motherwell, Glasgow, Scotland . . . 1989 although earlier they had posed as The BOY HAIRDRESSERS. Became hitmakers in 1991, after signing to 'Creation' and scoring with album 'BANDWAGONESQUE'. • **Style:** Uptempo fun-loving punk pop outfit. • **Songwriters:** BLAKE or BLAKE-McGINLEY or group compositions except; DON'T CRY NO TEARS (Neil Young) / THE BALLAD OF JOHN AND YOKO (Beatles) / LIKE A VIRGIN (Madonna) / LIFE'S A GAS (T.Rex) / FREE AGAIN (Alex Chilton) / CHORDS OF FAME (Phil Ochs) / BAD SEEDS (Beat Happening) / HAVE YOU EVER SEEN THE RAIN? (Creedence Clearwater Revival) / BETWEEN US (Neil Innes). • **Trivia:** ALEX CHILTON (ex-BOX TOPS) guested on 1992 sessions and contributed some songs.

Recommended: BANDWAGONESQUE (*8) / THIRTEEN (*7) / GRAND PRIX (*9)

The BOY HAIRDRESSERS

NORMAN BLAKE (b.20 Oct'65) – vocals, guitar (ex-BMX BANDITS) / **RAYMOND McGINLEY** (b. 3 Jan'64, Glasgow) – bass, vocals / **FRANCIS McDONALD** (b.21 Nov'70) – drums / **JOE McALINDEN** – violin / **JIM LAMBIE** – vibraphone

53rd & 3rd not issued

Jan 88. (12") **GOLDEN SHOWERS. / TIDAL WAVE / THE ASSUMPTION AS AN ELEVATOR** [ ] [-]

TEENAGE FANCLUB

NORMAN + RAYMOND – guitars, vocals plus **GERARD LOVE** (b.31 Aug'67, Motherwell, Scotland) – bass, vocals / **BRENDAN O'HARE** (b.16 Jan'70) – bass repl. McDONALD who joined The PASTELS

Paperhouse Matador

Jun 90. (7") **EVERYTHING FLOWS. / PRIMARY EDUCATION / SPEEEDER** [ ] [ ]
(re-iss.Feb91)(cd-ep) – Don't Cry No Tears.

Jul 90. (cd)(c)(lp) **A CATHOLIC EDUCATION** [ ] [-]
– Heavy metal / Everything flows / Catholic education / Too involved / Don't need a drum / Critical mass / Heavy metal II / Catholic education 2 / Eternal light / Every picture I paint / Everybody's fun. *(re-iss.cd Mar95)*

Oct 90. (one-sided-7") **THE BALLAD OF JOHN AND YOKO. /** [ ] [-]

Nov 90. (7") **GOD KNOWS IT'S TRUE. / SO FAR GONE** [ ] [ ]
(12"+=)(cd-s+=) – Weedbreak / Ghetto blaster.

Creation Geffen

Aug 91. (cd)(lp) **THE KING (instrumental)** [53] [ ]
– Heavy metal 6 / Mudhoney / Interstellar overdrive / Robot love / Like a virgin / The king / Opal inquest / The ballad of Bow Evil (slow and fast) / Heavy metal 9.

(above originally only meant for US ears, deleted after 24 hours)

Aug 91. (7") **STAR SIGN. / HEAVY METAL 6** [44] [-]
(12"+=)(cd-s+=) – Like a virgin / ('A'demo version).
(7"ltd) – ('A'side) / Like a virgin.

Oct 91. (7")(c-s) **THE CONCEPT. / LONG HAIR** [51] [-]
(12"+=)(c-s+=)(cd-s+=) – What you do to me (demo) / Robot love.

Nov 91. (cd)(c)(lp) **BANDWAGONESQUE** [22] [ ]
– The concept / Satan / December / What you do to me / I don't know / Star sign / Metal baby / Pet rock / Sidewinder / Alcoholiday / Guiding star / Is this music?.

Jan 92. (7"ep)(12"ep)(c-ep)(cd-ep) **WHAT YOU DO TO ME / B-SIDE. / LIFE'S A GAS / FILLER** [31] [ ]

Jun 93. (7")(c-s) **RADIO. / DON'T GONE COLUMBIA** [31] [ ]
(12"+=)(cd-s+=) – Weird horses / Chords of fame.

Sep 93. (7"ep)(12"ep)(c-ep)(cd-ep) **NORMAN 3. / OLDER GUYS / GENIUS ENVY / GOLDEN GLADES** [50] [ ]

Oct 93. (cd)(c)(lp) **THIRTEEN** [14] [ ]
– Hang on / The cabbage / Radio / Norman 3 / Song to the cynic / 120 minutes / Escher / Commercial alternative / Fear of flying / Tears are cool / Ret live dead / Get funky / Gene Clark.

— In Mar'94, they teamed up with DE LA SOUL on single 'FALLIN''. This was from the rock-rap album 'Judgement Day' on 'Epic' records (hit UK 59).

— **PAUL QUINN** – drums (ex-SOUP DRAGONS) repl. O'HARE

Mar 95. (7")(c-s) **MELLOW DOUBT. / SOME PEOPLE TRY TO FUCK WITH YOU** [34] [ ]
(cd-s+=) – Getting real / About you.
(cd-s) – ('A'side) / Have you ever seen the rain? / Between us / You're my kind.

May 95. (7")(c-s) **SPARKY'S DREAM. / BURNED** [40] [ ]
(cd-s+=) – For you / Headstand.
(cd-s) – ('A'-alternative version) / Try and stop me / That's all I need to know / Who loves the sun.

May 95. (cd)(c)(lp) **GRAND PRIX** [7] [ ]
– About you / Sparky's dream / Mellow doubt / Don't look back / Verisinilitude / Neil Jung / Tears / Discolite / Say no / Going places / I'll make it clear / I gotta know / Hardcore – ballad. (lp w/ free 7") DISCOLITE (demo). / I GOTTA KNOW (demo)

Aug 95. (7")(c-s) **NEIL JUNG. / THE SHADOWS** [62] [ ]
(cd-s+=) – My life / Every step is a way through love.
(cd-s) – ('A'side) / Traffic jam / Hi-fi / I heard you looking.

Dec 95. (7"ep)(c-ep)(cd-ep) **TEENAGE FANCLUB HAVE LOST IT (acoustic)** [53] [-]
– Don't look back / Everything flows / Starsign / 120 mins.

– compilations, others, etc. –

1992. K; (7") **FREE AGAIN. / BAD SEEDS** [-] [ ]

Nov 92. Strange Fruit; (12"ep)(cd-ep) **THE JOHN PEEL SESSION** (FRANK BLACK & TEENAGE FANCLUB) | | - |
– God knows it's true / Alcoholiday / So far gone / Long hair. *(re-iss.Dec93 & Jul95)*

Mar 95. Fire; (cd)(c) **DEEP FRIED FANCLUB** | | - |
– Everything flows / Primary education / Speeeder / Critical mass (orig.) / The ballad of John and Yoko / God knows it's true / Weedbreak / So far gone / Ghetto blaster / Don't cry no tears / Free again / Bad seed.

TEENAGE FILMSTARS (see under ⇒ TELEVISION PERSONALITIES)

TEENAGE JESUS (see under ⇒ LUNCH, Lydia)

TELEVISION

Formed: New York, USA based . . . late '73 by VERLAINE, HELL and FICCA whom evolved from The NEON BOYS. In 1975, William Terry Ork gave them deal on own self-named indie label, for whom they issued 1 single. The following year, they transferred to 'Elektra', and unleashed their classic debut album 'MARQUEE MOON', which contained the near 10 minute UK hit single title track. • **Style:** Laid back guitar-based new wave rock, influenced by 70's fashioned ROLLING STONES and PINK FLOYD. VERLAINE tried unsuccessfully to match previous sound into more mainstream rock, which still contained his characteristic vox and guitar virtuoso. • **Songwriters:** VERLAINE lyrics / group compositions, except early live material; FIRE ENGINE (13th Floor Elevators) / KNOCKIN' ON HEAVEN'S DOOR (Bob Dylan) / SATISFACTION (Rolling Stones). • **Trivia:** VERLAINE played guitar on PATTI SMITH's 1974 single 'Hey Joe'.

Recommended: MARQUEE MOON (*10) / TOM VERLAINE – COVER (*7)

TOM VERLAINE (b.THOMAS MILLER, 13 Dec'49, Mt.Morris, New Jersey) – vocals, lead guitar / **RICHARD LLOYD** – guitar, vocals / **RICHARD HELL** – bass, vocals / **BILLY FICCA** – drums

not issued — Ork

Oct 75. (7") **LITTLE JOHNNY JEWEL. / (part 2)** | - | |

— **FRED 'Sonic' SMITH** – bass, vocals (ex-BLONDIE) repl. RICHARD HELL who went solo.

Elektra — Elektra

Feb 77. (lp)(c) **MARQUEE MOON** | 28 | |
– See no evil / Venus / Friction / Marquee moon / Elevation / Guiding light / Prove it / Torn curtain. *(cd-iss.1989)*

Mar 77. (12")(2-part-7") **MARQUEE MOON. / MARQUEE MOON (mono)** | 30 | - |

Jul 77. (7")(12")(12"green) **PROVE IT. / VENUS** | 25 | - |

Apr 78. (lp)(c)(red-lp) **ADVENTURE** | 7 | |
– Glory / Days / Foxhole / Careful / Carried away / The fire / Ain't that nothin' / The dream's a dream. *(cd-iss.Nov93)*

Apr 78. (7")(12"red) **FOXHOLE. / CAREFUL** | 36 | - |

Jul 78. (7") **GLORY. / CARRIED AWAY** | | - |

Jul 78. (7") **GLORY. / AIN'T THAT NOTHIN'** | - | |

— Broke ranks in Aug'78. FICCA joined The WAITRESSES, FRED joined The PATTI SMITH GROUP and RICHARD LLOYD went solo.

– compilations, others, etc. –

Jan 83. R.O.I.R.; (c) **THE BLOW UP (live)** | - | |
(cd-iss.Feb90 on 'Danceteria')

1979. Ork-WEA; (12"m) **LITTLE JOHNNY JEWEL (part 1 & 2). / ('A'-live version)** | | - |

TOM VERLAINE

went solo augmented mainly by **FRED SMITH** – bass / **JAY DEE DAUGHERTY** – drums / **BRUCE BRODY** – keyboards / **ALLAN SCHWARTZBERG** – drums, percussion

Elektra — Elektra

Sep 79. (lp)(c) **TOM VERLAINE**
– The grip of love / Souvenir from a dream / Kingdom come / Mr. Bingo / Yonki time / Flash lightning / Red leaves / Last night / Breakin' in my heart.

Warners — Warners

Sep 81. (lp)(c) **DREAMTIME**
– There's a reason / Penetration / Always / The blue robe / Without a word / Mr. Blur / Fragile / A future in noise / Down on the farm / Mary Marie.

Sep 81. (7")(12") **ALWAYS. / THE BLUE ROBE**

— **JIMMY RIPP** – guitar repl. BRODY

Virgin — Warners

May 82. (lp)(c) **WORDS FROM THE FRONT**
– Present arrived / Postcard from Waterloo / True story / Clear it away / Words from the front / Coming apart / Days on the mountain. *(re-iss.+cd.Aug88)*

May 82. (7")(12") **POSTCARD FROM WATERLOO. / DAYS ON THE MOUNTAIN**

Jun 84. (7") **LET'S GO TO THE MANSION. / ('A'version)**
(12"+=) – Lindi Lu.

Aug 84. (7") **FIVE MILES OF YOU. / YOUR FINEST HOUR**
(12"+=) – Dissolve reveal.

Sep 84. (lp)(c) **COVER**
– Five miles of you / Let's go the the mansion / Travelling / O foolish heart / Dissolve – Reveal / Miss Emily / Rotation / Swim. *(re-iss.Apr86)*

— **ANDY NEWMARK** – drums repl. JAY DEE

Fontana — Mercury

Feb 87. (7") **A TOWN CALLED WALKER. / SMOOTHER THAN JONES**
(12"+=) – ('A'version) / Caveman flashlight.

Feb 87. (lp)(c)(cd) **FLASH LIGHT** | 99 | |
– Cry mercy, judge / Say a prayer / A town called Walker / Song / The scientist writes a letter / Bomb / 4 a.m. / The funniest thing / Annie's tellin' me / One time at sundown.

Mar 87. (7") **CRY MERCY JUDGE. / CALL ME THE CIRCLING**
(12"+=) – At this moment (live) / Lover of the night (live) / Strange things happening.

Jun 87. (7") **THE FUNNIEST THING. / ONE TIME AT SUNDOWN**
(12"+=) – Marquee Moon ('87 version).

Aug 87. (7") **THE SCIENTIST WRITES A LETTER. / ('A'-Paris version)**

Oct 89. (7") **SHIMMER. / BOMB**
(12"+=)(cd-s+=) – The scientist writes a letter.

Mar 90. (7")(c-s) **KALEIDOSCOPIN'. / SIXTEEN TULIPS**
(12"+=)(cd-s+=) – Vanity fair.

Apr 90. (cd)(c)(lp) **THE WONDER**
– Kaleidoscopin' / August / Ancient Egypt / Shimmer / Stalingrad / Pillow / Storm / 5 hours from Calais / Cooleridge / Prayer.

Rough Trade — Rough Trade

Apr 92. (cd)(c)(lp) **WARM AND COOL**
– Those harbour lights / Sleepwalkin' / The deep dark clouds / Saucer crash / Depot (1951) / Boulevard / Harley Quinn / Sor Juanna / Depot (1957) / Spiritual / Little dance / Ore.

RICHARD LLOYD

solo augmented by **JIM MAESTRO** – guitar (ex-BONGOS) / **MATTHEW MacKENZIE** – guitar, piano / **MICHAEL YOUNG** – guitar, synthesizer / **FRED SMITH** – bass / **VINNY DeNUNZIO** – drums

Elektra — Elektra

Jan 80. (lp)(c) **ALCHEMY**
– Misty eyes / In the night / Alchemy / Womans ways / Number nine / Should've known better / Blue and grey / Summer rain / Pretend / Dying words.

Apr 80. (7") **BLUE AND GREY. / PRETEND** | - | |

— Enlisted new line-up.

Mistlur — Mistlur

Jan 86. (lp) **FIELD OF FIRE**

Celluloid — Celluloid

Oct 87. (lp)(c)(cd) **REAL TIME (live)**
– Fire engine / Misty eyes / Alchemy / Spider talk / Lost child / No.9 / The only feeling / Soldier blue / Field of fire / Pleading / Watch yourself / Louisinna Anna / Black to white. (cd+=) – Watch yourself / Losin' Anne / Black to white.

— LLOYD went onto join JOHN DOE (ex-X)

TELEVISION

re-formed with **VERLAINE, LLOYD, FICCA + SMITH**

Capitol — Capitol

Sep 92. (cd)(c)(lp) **TELEVISION**
– 1880 or so / Shane, she wrote this / In world / Call Mr.Lee / Rhyme / No glamour for Willi / Beauty trip / The rocket / This fire / Mars.

TELEVISION PERSONALITIES

Formed: Chelsea, London, England . . . 1976 by schoolchums EDWARD BALL and DAN TREACY. They soon found JOE FOSTER, plus 2 brothers JOHN and GERRARD BENNETT. After originally being TEEN 78, they came up with TV PERSONALITIES, and paraded themselves as HUGHIE GREEN, BRUCE FORSYTHE, BOB MONKHOUSE, RUSSELL HARTY and NICHOLAS PARSONS. Their first 45 '14th FLOOR' was released early summer 1978, and with help from John Peel who playlisted it, sold all its 867 copies. They soon formed own 'King's Road' label, which was distributed at first by 'Rough Trade'. They released EP 'WHERE'S BILL GRUNDY NOW?', which included the superb title track, alongside another gem 'PART-TIME PUNKS'. Around this time ED was also part of The O-LEVELS, who after one 45, became The TEENAGE FILMSTARS. In 1980, after a short retirement, they gigged for the first time and issued 'SMASHING TIME' single. A year later, DAN and ED set up own label 'Whaam!', but after a few releases, had to fold it, due to pressure from pop duo WHAM. In 1985, they chose another name 'Dreamworld', but this too became defunct, even after signing The MIGHTY LEMON DROPS. • **Style:** D-I-Y punk outfit influenced by SEX PISTOLS and then SYD BARRETT, but never gaining more than cult attraction. • **Songwriters:** ED and DAN penned most.ED BALL's TIMES covered YOU CAN GET IT (hit; Jimmy Cliff) / YOUR GENERATION (Generation X) / NOWHERE TO RUN (hit; Martha & the Vandellas) / MAN FROM UNCLE (Goldsmith) / BLUE MONDAY (New Order) / as 'LINOI BLEU'. • **Trivia:** DAN once tried to decapitate MARK SHEPPARD while in the studio. Producer DALE GRIFFIN locked DAN in the cupboard.

Recommended: AND DON'T THE KIDS JUST LOVE IT (*8)

TV PERSONALITIES

EDWARD BALL – organ, vocals / **DAN TREACY** – vocals / **JOE FOSTER** – guitar / **JOHN BENNETT** – bass / **GERRARD BENNETT** – drums

W1 Teen — not issued

May 78. (7") **14th FLOOR. / OXFORD STREET** | | - |
(re-iss.Aug89 on 'Overground', +7"yellow or white)

— now as trio (ED, DAN & JOE)

TELEVISION PERSONALITIES

King's Road / not issued

Nov 78. (7"ep) **WHERE'S BILL GRUNDY NOW?**
– Part-time punks / Where's Bill Grundy now? / Happy families / Posing at the Roundhouse. *(re-iss.Nov79 on 'Rough Trade')*

— disbanded for a year. **MARK 'EMPIRE' SHEPPARD** – drums (of SWELL MAPS)

Rough Trade / not issued

Jul 80. (7") **SMASHING TIME. / KING AND COUNTRY**

— JOE FOSTER left and soon became The MISSING SCIENTISTS who released a 45 in Sep80 'BIG CITY BRIGHT LIGHTS'. / 'DISCOTEQUE X', which featured DAN TREACY and DANIEL MILLER of Mute label.

Jan 81. (lp) **AND DON'T THE KIDS JUST LOVE IT ("TV PERSONALITIES")**
– I know where Syd Barrett lives / This angry silence / The glittering prizes / Silly girl / Jackanory stories / Geoffrey Ingram / La grande illusion / Look back in anger. *(re-iss.Jan84)*

Feb 81. (7") **I KNOW WHERE SYD BARRETT LIVES. / ARTHUR THE GARDENER**

— were now just **DAN + EMPIRE** + new bassman BERNARD COOPER (ED BALL had formed The TIMES.)

Whaam! / not issued

May 81. (7") **PAINTING BY NUMBERS. (as "GIFTED CHILDREN") / LICHTENSTEIN GIRL**

— **ED** returned on guitar & bass. SLAUGHTER JOE FOSTER also returned.

Jan 82. (lp) **MUMMY YOU'RE NOT WATCHING ME**
– Adventure playground / A day in heaven / Scream quietly / Mummy you're not watching me / Brians magic ear / Where the rainbow ends / David Hockney's diaries / Painting by numbers / Lichtenstein painting / Magnificent dreams If I could write poetry. *(re-iss.Jun86 on 'Dreamworld')*

Aug 82. (lp) **THEY COULD HAVE BEEN BIGGER THAN THE BEATLES**
– Three wishes / David Hockney's diary / In a perfumed garden / Flowers for Abigail / King and country / The boy in the Paisley shirt / Games for boys / Painter man / Psychedelic holiday / 14th floor / Sooty's disco party / Makin time / When Emily cries / The glittering prizes / Anxiety block / Mysterious ways.. *(re-iss.Jun86 on 'Dreamworld')*

Sep 82. (7") **THREE WISHES. / GEOFFREY INGRAM / AND DON'T THE KIDS JUST LOVE IT**

— **DAN + ED** added **DAVE MUSKER** – organ / **JOE FOSTER** – guitar / **MARK FLUNDER** – bass / (JOWE HEAD repl. MARK who joined ROBYN HITCHCOCK)

Rough Trade / not issued

Dec 83. (7") **A SENSE OF BELONGING. / PARADISE ESTATE**

— (below lp should have been issued by 'Whaam!' in Nov83)

Illuminated / not issued

Jan 85. (lp) **THE PAINTED WORD**
– Stop and smell the roses / The painted word / A life of her own / Bright sunny smiles / Mentioned in dispatches / A sense of belonging / Say you won't cry / Someone to share my life with / You'll have to scream loouder / Happy all the time / The girl who had everything / Paradise estates / Back to Vietnam.

— now with **JEFF BLOOM** – drums (FOSTER became SLAUGHTER JOE and MUSKER formed JASMINE MINKS. Also ED continued with The TIMES)

Dreamworld / not issued

Feb 86. (12"m) **HOW I LEARNED TO LOVE THE BOMB / THEN GOD SNAPS HIS FINGERS. / NO YOU'RE JUST BEING RIDICULOUS**

Nov 86. (7"m) **HOW I LEARNED TO LOVE THE BOMB. / GROCER'S DAUGHTER / GIRL CALLED CHARITY**

— (next album was to have been issued a year earlier on 'Dreamworld')

— **JOWE HEAD** – bass (ex-SWELL MAPS) repl. BALL.

Fire / not issued

Oct 89. (7") **SALVADOR DALI'S GARDEN PARTY. / ROOM AT THE TOP OF THE STAIRS**
(12"+=) – This time there is no happy ending / Part one: Fulfilling the contractual obligations.

Dec 89. (ltd.7") **I STILL BELIEVE IN MAGIC. / RESPECTABLE**

— (above single on 'Caff' label)

Feb 90. (cd)(c)(lp) **PRIVILEGE**
– Paradise is for the blessed / Conscience tells me no / All my dreams are dead / The man who paints the rainbows / Sad Mona Lisa / Sometimes I think you know me / Privilege / Good and faithful servant / My hedonistic tendencies / Salvador Dali's garden party / What if it's raining? / The engine driver song / Better than I know myself. (c+cd+=) – (3 tracks)

Sep 91. (12"ep)(cd-ep) **STRANGELY BEAUTIFUL**

Feb 92. (7") **SHE NEVER READ MY POEMS. / ?**
(12"+=)(cd-s+=) – ?

Seminal Tway / not issued

Sep 92. (7")(cd-s) **WE WILL BE OUR GURUS. / AN EXHIBITION BY JOAN MIRO / LOVE IS BETTER THAN WAR**

Nov 92 (cd)(c)(lp) **CLOSER TO GOD**
– You don't know how lucky you are / Hard luck story No. 30 / Little works of art / Razorblades and lemonade / Coming home soon / Me and big ideas / Honey for the bears / I see myself in you / Goodnight Mr. Spaceman / My very nervous breakdown / We will be your gurus / You are special and you always will be / Not for the likes of us / You're younger than you know / Very dark today / I hope you have a nice day / Baby you're only as good as you should be / Closer to God.

May 93. (7")(cd-s) **GOODNIGHT MR.SPACEMAN. / IF I WAS YOUR GIRLDRIEND**
(cd-s+=) – She loves it when he sings like Elvis / ('A'-Lost in space mix).

Vinyl Japan / not issued

May 94. (12"ep)(cd-ep) **FAR AWAY AND LOST IN JOY / I DON'T WANT TO LIVE THIS LIFE. / DO YOU KNOW WHAT THEY'RE SAYING ABOUT ME NOW? / I GET FRIGHTENED**

Oct 95. (12"ep)(cd-ep) **DO YOU THINK IF YOU WERE BEAUTIFUL YOU'D BE HAPPY / HE USED TO PAINT IN COLOURS / WHO WILL BE YOUR PRINCE / I SUPPOSE YOU THINK IT'S FUNNY**

– compilations, etc. –

Aug 91. Overground; (lp) **CAMPING IN FRANCE (live '85)**
Jul 93. Pastell; (cd)(lp) **CHOCOLATE-ART LIVE 1984 (live)**
Feb 95. Fire; (cd) **YES DARLING BUT IS IT ART?**
Sep 95. Overground; (cd) **I WAS A MOD BEFORE YOU WAS A MOD**

– other ED BALL associated releases, etc.-

O-LEVELS

Nov 77. Psycho; (7") **EAST SHEEN. / PSEUDO PUNK**
Dec 78. King's Road; (7"ep) **THE MALCOLM EP**
– We love Malcolm / Leave me / Everybody's on Revolver / Stairway to boredom.

— In 1979, ED financed a DRY RIB ep 'THE DRY SEASON' on 'Clockwork'.

TEENAGE FILMSTARS

Clockwork / not issued

Sep 79. (7") **(THERE'S A) CLOUD OVER LIVERPOOL. / SOMETIMES GOOD GUYS DON'T FOLLOW TRENDS**

Wessex / not issued

Mar 80. (7") **ODD MAN OUT. / I APOLOGISE**
(re-iss.Jun80 on 'Blueprint')

Fab Listen / not issued

Nov 80. (7") **I HELPED PATRICK McGOOGHAN ESCAPE. / WE'RE NOT SORRY**

TIMES

EDWARD BALL – vocals, guitar / **JOHN WAST** – bass, vocals / **PAUL DAMIEN** – drums, vocals.

Artpop! / not issued

Nov 80. (lp) **GO! WITH THE TIMES**
You can get it / I'm with you / Your generation / Pinstripes / Dressing up for the cameras / Red with purple flashes / The joke's on Zandra / Nowhere to run / No hard feelings / My Andy Warhol poster / Man from Uncle Reflections in an imperfect mirror.

Whaam! / not issued

May 81. (7") **RED WITH PURPLE FLASHES. / BIFF! BANG! POW!**

Sep 81. (lp) **POP GOES ART!**
– Picture gallery / Biff! bang! / It's time / If now is the answer /A New arrangement /Looking throught the world through dark glasses / I helped Patrick McGastan escape / Pop goes art! / Miss London / The Sun never sets / This is tomorrow. *(re-iss.pic-lp.)*

Artpop! / not issued

Jun 82. (7") **HERE COMES THE HOLIDAYS. (as "JONI DEE & THE TIMES") / THREE CHEERS FOR THE SUN**

Sep 82. (7") **I HELPED PATRICK McGOOGHAN ESCAPE. / THE THEME FROM 'DANGER MAN'**

May 83. (lp) **THIS IS LONDON**
– This is London / Goodbye Piccadilly / Whatever happened to Thamesboat / Big painting / If only / Goodnight children everywhere / The party / Stranger than fiction / (There's a) Cloud over Liverpool / Will success spoil Frank Summit? / The chimes of Big Ben.

Nov 83. (m-lp) **I HELPED PATRICK McGOOGHAN ESCAPE**
– Big painting / Stranger than fiction / Danger Man theme / I helped Patrick McGooghan escape / All systems go / Up against it.

Jul 84. (7") **BOYS BRIGADE. / POWER IS FOREVER**

Aug 84. (7") **BLUE FIRE. / WHERE THE BLUE REIGNS**

Sep 84. (lp) **HELLO EUROPE**
– Dada Europe (I'm so cut up about you) / Boys brigade / The things we've learnt / Ra diate / Blue fire / Everything turns to black and white / Where the blue begins / Public reaction killed this cat / Kultureshock.

— Early in 1985 he made another for 'Art Pop!' under EDWARD BALL'S L'ORANGE MECHANIK name; 'SYMPHONY. / INTERMEZZO (SPRECHSTIMME) / SCHERZO'. Four years later an lp was given away free with ED's Edgar Allen Poe poems for 'Creation'.

Mar 85. (m-lp) **BLUE PERIOD**

Sep 85. (12"ep) **BOYS ABOUT TOWN**
– David Jones (is on his way) / Victim 1960 / Up against it / Songs for Joe Walton.

Apr 86. (lp) **UP AGAINST IT (soundtrack)**
Up against it / Last tango for one / Boy's about town / Gordon into moonlight / W.P.C. Boon / Most modern woman in the world / Jade's revolution / Ladies of the cause / Mutiny in the British Empire / Escape / She's a professional / It's a cabaret time / The way / The wedding song.

Unicorn / not issued

Apr 86. (7") **LONDON BOYS. / (WHERE TO GO) WHEN THE SUN GOES DOWN**

Fire / not issued

Aug 86. (7") **TIMES TV. / TRAILER FROM 'ENJOY'**
(12"+=) – The policeforce / El Aragma / Pick it up.

Creation / not issued

Oct 88. (lp)(cd) **BEAT TORTURE**

– God evil / Heaven sent me an angel / I'll be your volunteer / Department store / Love like haze or rain / It had to happen / Chelsea green / How to start your own country // On the peace line / Scarlet and Sapphire / Angel / Volunteer / Country / Love.

Oct 89. (lp)(cd) **E FOR EDWARD** [ ] [-]
– Manchester / Valvaline / Snow / Catherine Wheel / Crashed on you / Count to five / All your life / French film bleurred / No love on Haight street / Acid Angel of Ecstasy / Gold / Sold / Life.

Feb 90. (7") **MANCHESTER. / LOVE AND TRUTH** [ ] [-]
(12") – ('A'side) / Dada won't buy me a Bauhaus / ('A'extended).
(cd-s) – ('A'side) / ('A'extended) / Ulysses / Shoom!.

Oct 90. (7") **EXTASE. / SLEEP (by "BIFF! BANG! POW!")** [ ] [-]

— Above single on 'Caff' label.

Oct 90. (cd)(lp) **ET DIEU CREA LA FEMME** [ ] [-]
– Septième ciel / Aurore boreale / Confiance / Chagrin d'amour / Volupte / Baisers voles / Pour Kylie / Sucette / 1990 Annee erotique / Extase.

Mar 91. (cd)(c)(lp) **PURE** [ ] [-]
– From Chelsea Green to Brighton Beach / A girl called Mersey / Lindi bleu / From L.A. to Edgbaston / Ours is wonderlove world / Another star in Heaven. *(re-iss Sep 92).*

Apr 92. (cd)(c)(lp) **LIVE AT THE ASTRADOME (live)** [ ] [-]

Jul 92. (7")(c-s) **LINDI BLEU (version Francais de Blue Monday). / ('A'instrumental)** [ ] [-]
(12"+=)(cd-s+=) – ('A'- Grid & Bandula mixes).

Apr 93. (cd)(lp) **ALTERNATIVE COMMERCIAL CROSSOVER** [ ] [-]
– Obligatory grunge song / Finnegan's break / How honest are Pearl Jam / Sweetest girl / Ballad of Georgie Best / Lindi bleu (praise the lord mix by the GRID) / Palace in the sun / Sorry, I've written a melody / Finnegan's break (corporate rock mix) / Whole world's turning seaface / All I want is you to care.

May 93. (7") **FINNEGAN'S BREAK. ("TIMES featuring TIPPA IRIE") / HEARTBROKEN LOST IN BLUE** [ ] [ ]
(12"+=)(cd-s+=) – Soultight / Come alive.

Jun 93. (12"ep)(cd-ep) **BABY GIRL. / THE COLOUR OF MY LOVE / MASH IT UP / PRIMROSE 0822** [ ] [ ]

– (TIMES) compilations, etc. –

Jul 91. Artpop!; (cd)(c)(lp) **PINK BALL BROWN BALL ED BALL** [ ] [-]

Nov 92. Rev-Ola; (cd) **A DAY IN THE LIFE OF GILBERT & GEORGE** [ ] [-]
(O-LEVEL & TEENAGE FILMSTARS)

Dec 93. Rev-Ola; (cd) **ENJOY THE TIMES / UP AGAINST IT** [ ] [-]

Apr 94. Rev-Ola; (cd) **GO WITH THE TIMES / POP GOES ART** [ ] [-]

— ED BALL was also part of BIFF BANG POW, another 'Creation' outfit and in the 90's joined The BOO RADLEYS

LOVE CORPORATION

aka **ED BALL** solo

		Creation	not issued
Feb 90.	(cd)(lp) **TONES**	[ ]	[-]

– Fleshtones / Monumental / Tones of incorporation / World / Palatial.

Apr 90. (7") **PALATIAL. / PALATIAL II** [ ] [-]
(cd-s+=) – Palatial III / (b-side extended).
(12") – ('A'-Danny Rampling extended remix) / ('A'-II extended).

Feb 91. (cd)(c)(lp) **LOVERS** [ ] [-]
– L-o-v-e / Warm / Crystal / Sun / Happy days and lonely nights / Nice / Lovers / Smile

Mar 91. (12") **GIME ME SOME LOVE. / ('A'version)** [ ] [-]
(12") – ('A'-Andrew Weatherall remix) / Lovers.

Nov 94. (cd)(lp) **INTELLIGENTSIA** [ ] [-]

TEENAGE FILMSTARS

re-united in 1992 for below.

		Creation	not issued
Mar 92.	(cd)(c)(lp) **STAR**	[ ]	[-]

– Kiss me / Loving / Inner space / Apple / Flashes / Kaleidoscope / Vibrations / Soulful / Hallucinations / Moon.

Mar 93. (cd)(lp) **ROCKET CHARMS – SPLASHDOWN AVEC LES TEENAGE FILMSTARS** [ ] [-]

CONSPIRACY OF NOISE

ED BALL with **PHIL KANE** or **DEAN JONES** – vox (of EXTREME NOISE TERROR)

		Creation	not issued
Oct 93.	(cd)(lp) **CHICKS WITH DICKS AND SPLATTER FLICKS**	[ ]	[-]

ED BALL

with **ANDY BELL, MARTIN CARR, NICK HEYWARD, SICE IDHAR, TIM BROWN, ALAN McGEE, NOEL JOYCE & THE IAN SHOW ORCHESTRA** featuring **NAOMI ZOOB**

Apr 95. (7") **IF A MAN EVER LOVED A WOMAN. / FIREHORSE BLUES / 12 NOON 28.8.93** [ ] [-]
(cd-s+=) – United States of loneliness.

May 95. (cd)(lp) **IF A MAN EVER LOVED A WOMAN** [ ] [-]
– It's kinda lonely where I am (acoustic) / Fire horse / If a man ever loved a woman / She's just high maintenance, baby / The Arizona loner / You only miss me when I'm bleeding / The ballad of a lonely man / A ton of blues / You're an idiot babe / It's kinda lonely where I am.

Jun 95. (cd-ep) **IT'S KIND OF LONELY WHERE I AM / DOCKLANDS BLUES / BLED A RIVER OVER YOU / ANOTHER MEMBER OF THE MILL SELF HATE CLUB** [ ] [-]

TEMPEST (see under ⇒ COLOSSEUM)

TEMPLE OF THE DOG (see under ⇒ SOUNDGARDEN)

TEMPTATIONS

Formed: Birmingham, Alabama, USA . . . 1960 initially as The ELGINS by EDDIE KENDRICKS and PAUL WILLIAMS from The PRIMES, plus MELVIN FRANKLIN and OTIS WILLIAMS from The DISTANTS. They moved to Detroit in 1961, after two flop 45's for 'Miracle'. Secured a deal with the Berry 'Gordy' label (aka Tamla Motown) where they finally scored first US hit in 1964 'THE WAY YOU DO THE THINGS YOU DO'. By early 1965, 'MY GIRL' had given them their first US No.1. Throughout the rest of the 60's and 70's, they went on produce many hits on both sides of the Atlantic. • **Style:** Initially an all-singing 'Motown' industry group, but when EDWARDS replaced RUFFIN in 1968, their sound moved into a more psychedelic heavy-rock fused with the roots & soul they subsequently never lost. By the mid-70's, they had mellowed into a more disco orientated funk band. The 80's saw them revive their mid-60's feel, but with a more cabaret image. • **Songwriters:** Main source of songs came from MIRACLES' pensmith SMOKEY ROBINSON until Spring 1966, when NORMAN WHITFIELD and BRIAN HOLLAND took over the reins. A year later HOLLAND dropped out and WHITFIELD brought in new partner BARRETT STRONG. In 1977 WHITFIELD left set-up, and the group found RON TYSON in 1978 for pen work and BRIAN HOLLAND and NORMAN HARRIS for production. WHITFIELD again returned in 1984. They also covered THE WEIGHT (Band) / I'LL TRY SOMETHING NEW (Miracles) / I'M GONNA MAKE YOU LOVE ME (Madeleine Bell) / etc. • **Trivia:** In 1987 actor and fan BRUCE WILLIS invited them to sing back-up on his hit version of The DRIFTERS' 'Under The Boardwalk'.

Recommended: MOTOWN'S GREATEST HITS (*8) / PSYCHEDELIC SHACK (*8) / CLOUD NINE (*8) / THE SKY'S THE LIMIT (*7)

EDDIE KENDRICKS (b.17 Dec'39) – lead vocals / **PAUL WILLIAMS** (b. 2 Jul'39) – vocals / **MELVIN FRANKLIN** (b.DAVID ENGLISH, 12 Oct'42) – vocals / **OTIS WILLIAMS** (b.OTIS MILES, 30 Oct'49) – vocals / **ELDRIDGE BRYANT** – vocals

		not issued	Miracle	
Aug 61.	(7") **OH MOTHER OF MINE. / ROMANCE WITHOUT FINANCE**	[-]	[ ]	
Nov 61.	(7") **CHECK YOURSELF. / YOUR WONDERFUL LIFE**	[-]	[ ]	
		Stateside	Gordy	
Apr 62.	(7") **DREAM COME TRUE. / ISN'T SHE PRETTY**	[-]	[ ]	

— In Sep'62, as The PIRATES, they issued a single 'MIND OVER MATTER'. / I'LL LOVE YOU TILL I DIE' on the 'Melody' label.

Jan 63.	(7") **PARADISE. / SLOW DOWN HEART**	[-]	[ ]	
Mar 63.	(7") **I WANT A LOVE I CAN SEE. / THE FURTHER YOU LOOK THE LESS YOU SEE**	[-]	[ ]	
Jul 63.	(7") **MAY I HAVE THIS DANCE. / FAREWELL MY LOVE**	[-]	[ ]	

— Early 1964, they backed and were credited on LIZ LANDS 'Gordy' single 'MIDNIGHT JOHNNY'. / KEEP ME'.

— **DAVID RUFFIN** (b.18 Jan'41, Meridian, Missouri) – vocals (lead in 1965) had already deposed BRYANT

Apr 64. (7") **THE WAY YOU DO THE THINGS YOU DO. / JUST LET ME KNOW** [ ] [11] Jan 64

Apr 64. (lp) **MEET THE TEMPTATIONS** [-] [ ]
– The way you do the things you do / I want a love I can see / Dream come true / Paradise / May I have this dance / Isn't she pretty / Just let me know / Your wonderful love / The further you look the less you see / Check yourself / Slow down heart / Farewell my love. *(UK-iss.May65)*

Jul 64. (7") **I'LL BE IN TROUBLE. / THE GIRL'S ALRIGHT WITH ME** [ ] [33] May 64

Oct 64. (7") **GIRL (WHY YOU WANNA MAKE ME BLUE). / BABY BABY I NEED YOU** [ ] [26] Aug 64

Jan 65. (7") **MY GIRL. / TALKIN' 'BOUT NOBODY BUT MY BABY** [43] [1] Dec 64

		Tamla Motown	Gordy	
Mar 65.	(7") **IT'S GROWING. / WHAT LOVE HAS JOINED TOGETHER**	[45]	[18]	
Aug 65.	(7") **SINCE I LOST MY BABY. / YOU'VE GOT TO EARN IT**	[ ]	[17]	Jul 65
Oct 65.	(lp) **TEMPTATIONS SING SMOKEY**	[ ]	[35]	Mar 65

– The way you do the things you do / Baby baby I need you / You'd lose a precious love / My girl / It's growing / Who's loving you / What love has joined together / What's so good 'bout goodbye. *(re-iss.+c.Feb80 & Oct81 on 'Motown')*

Nov 65. (7") **MY BABY. / DON'T LOOK BABY** [ ] [13] / [83] Oct 65

Mar 66. (lp) **TEMPTIN' TEMPTATIONS** [ ] [11] Nov 65
– Since I lost my babe / Girl's alright with me / Just another lonely night / My baby / You've got to earn it / Everybody needs love / Girl / Don't look back / I gotta know now / Born to love you / I'll be in trouble / You're the one I need.

Apr 66. (7") **GET READY. / FADING AWAY** [ ] [29] Feb 66

Jun 66. (7") **AIN'T TOO PROUD TO BEG. / YOU'LL LOSE A PRECIOUS LOVE** [21] [13] May 66

Sep 66. (lp) **GETTIN' READY** [40] [12] Jun 66
– Say you / Little Miss Sweetness / Ain't too proud to beg / Get ready / Lonely, lonely man am I / Too busy thinking about my baby / I've been good to you / It's a lonely world without your love / Fading away / Who you gonna run to / You're not an ordinary girl / Not now I'll tell you later. *(re-iss.Jul82 on 'Motown')*

Sep 66. (7") **BEAUTY IS ONLY SKIN DEEP. / YOU'RE NOT AN ORDINARY MAN** [18] [3] Aug 66

Dec 66. (7") **(I KNOW) I'M LOSING YOU. / LITTLE MISS SWEETNESS** [19] [8] Nov 66

May 67. (7") **ALL I NEED. / SORRY IS A SORRY WORD** [ ] [8] Apr 67

Jul 67. (lp) **TEMPTATIONS LIVE! (live)** [20] [10] Mar 67

– Medley: Girl (why you wanna make me blue) – Girl's alright with me – I'll be in trouble – I want a love I can see / What love has joined together / My girl / Yesterday / What now my love / Beauty is only skin deep / Group introduction / I wish you love / Ain't too proud to beg / Ol' man river / Get ready / Fading away / My baby / Youll lose a precious love / Baby, baby I need you / Don't look back.

Sep 67. (7") **YOU'RE MY EVERYTHING. / I'VE BEEN GOOD TO YOU** 26 6 Jul 67

Oct 67. (lp) **WITH A LOT O' SOUL** 19 7 Aug 67
– You're my everything / All I need / I'm losing you / Ain't no Sun since you've gone / No more water in the well / It's you that I need / Save my love for a rainy day / Just one last look / Sorry is a sorry word / Now that you've won me / Two sides to love / Don't send me away.

Dec 67. (7") **(LONELINESS MADE ME REALISE) IT'S YOU THAT I NEED. / I WANT A LOVE I CAN SEE** 14 Sep 67

Feb 68. (7") **I WISH IT WOULD RAIN. / I TRULY TRULY BELIEVE** 45 4 Dec 67

Mar 68. (lp) **IN A MELLOW MOOD** 13 Dec 67
– Hello young lovers / A taste of honey / For once in my life / Somewhere / Ol' man river / I'm ready for love / Try to remember / Who can I turn to (when nobody needs needs me) / What now my love / That's life / With these hands / The impossible dream.

— **DENNIS EDWARDS** (b. 3 Feb'43) – vocals repl. RUFFIN who went solo.

May 68. (7") **I COULD NEVER LOVE ANOTHER (AFTER LOVING YOU). / GONNA GIVE HER ALL THE LOVE I GOT** 47 13 May 68

Aug 68. (lp) **THE TEMPTATIONS WISH IT WOULD RAIN** 13 Apr 68
– I could never love another (after loving you) / Cindy / I wish it would rain / Please return your love to me / Fan the flame / He who picks a rose / Why did you leave me darling / I truly, truly believe / This is my beloved / Gonna give her all the love I've got / I've passed this way before / No man can love her like I do.

Jul 68. (7") **PLEASE RETURN YOUR LOVE TO ME. / HOW CAN I FORGET** – 26

— In Jan69 UK / Nov68, they teamed up with DIANA ROSS & THE SUPREMES (see ⇒) on Top 3 single I'M GONNA MAKE YOU LOVE ME. Around the same time the album DIANA ROSS AND THE SUPREMES JOIN THE TEMPTATIONS hit UK No.1 & US No.2. Throughout 1969, this combination also had Top 50 hits with I'LL TRY SOMETHING NEW / I SECOND THAT EMOTION (UK No.18) / THE WEIGHT / WHY (MUST WE FALL IN LOVE) (UK No.31). Their albums TCB (Soundtrack) hit UK No.11 + US No.1 / ON BROADWAY (TV Show) hit US No.38 / TOGETHER hit both UK + US No.38 early 1970.

Mar 69. (7") **RUNAWAY CHILD, RUNNING WILD. / I NEED YOUR LOVIN'** 6 Jan 69

May 69. (lp) **LIVE AT THE COPA (live)** 15 Dec 68
– (Introduction) / Get ready / You're my everything / I truly, truly believe / I wish it would rain / For once in my life / I could never love another / For once in my life / I could never love another / Hello young lovers / With these hands / Swanee / The impossible dream / Please return your love to me / (I know) I'm losing you.

May 69. (7") **DON'T LET THE JONESES GET YOU DOWN. / SINCE I'VE LOST YOU** – 20

Aug 69. (7") **CLOUD NINE. / WHY DID SHE HAVE TO LEAVE ME (WHY DID SHE HAVE TO GO)** 15 6 Oct 68

Sep 69. (lp) **CLOUD NINE** 32 4 Mar 69
– Cloud nine / I heard it through it the grapevine / Why did she have to leave me (why did she have to go) / Runaway child, running wild / Love is a hurtin' thing / Hey girl / I need your lovin' / Don't let him take your love from me / Gonna keep on tryin' till I win your love / I gotta find away (to get you back). *(re-iss.+c.Oct81 on 'Motown') (cd-iss.Aug93)*

Jan 70. (7") **I CAN'T GET NEXT TO YOU. / RUNNING AWAY (AIN'T GONNA HELP ME)** 13 1 Jul 69

Feb 70. (lp)(c) **PUZZLE PEOPLE** 20 5 Oct 69
– I can't get next to you / Hey Jude / Don't let the Joneses get you down / Message from a black man / It's your thing / Little green apples / You don't love me no more / Running away (ain't gonna help you) / Since I've lost you / Slave / That's the way love is. *(re-iss.+c.Mar82 on 'Motown')*

Apr 70. (lp) **LIVE AT THE (LONDON'S) TALK OF THE TOWN (live)** 21 Aug 70
– I'm gonna make you love me / The impossible dream / Run away child running wild / Don't let the Joneses get you down / Love theme from Romeo & Juliet / I can't get next to you / This guy's in love with you / I've got to be me / I'm losing you / Cloud nine / Everything is going to be alright. *(re-iss.Jan79 on 'M.F.P.')*

Jun 70. (7") **PSYCHEDELIC SHACK. / THAT'S THE WAY LOVE IS** 33 7 Dec 69

Jun 70. (lp)(c) **PSYCHEDELIC SHACK** 56 9 Mar 70
– Psychedelic shack / Hum along and dance / War / It's summer / You make your own Heaven and Hell right here on Earth / You need love like I do (don't you) / Take a stroll thru your mind / Friendship train. *(re-iss.Mar82 on 'Motown')*

Sep 70. (7") **BALL OF CONFUSION (THAT'S WHAT THE WORLD IS TODAY). / IT'S SUMMER** 7 3 May 70

Oct 70. (7") **UNGENA ZA ULIMWENGU (UNITE THE WORLD). / HUM ALONG AND DANCE** – 33

Dec 70. (lp) **CHRISTMAS CARD** (Festive songs) –

May 71. (7") **JUST MY IMAGINATION (RUNNING AWAY WITH ME). / YOU MAKE YOUR OWN HEAVEN AND HELL RIGHT HERE ON EARTH** 8 1 Jan 71

— **EDWARDS, FRANKLIN & WILLIAMS** recruited new members **DAMON HARRIS** (b. 3 Jul'50, Baltimore, Maryland) – vocals repl. EDDIE KENDRICKS who went solo.

Jul 71. (7") **IT'S SUMMER. / I'M THE EXCEPTION TO THE RULE** – 51

Aug 71. (lp)(c) **SKY'S THE LIMIT** 16 Apr 71
– Gonna keep on tryin' till I win your love / Just my imagination / I'm the exception to the rule / Smiling faces sometimes / Man / Throw a farewell kiss / Ungenza za Ulimwenga / Love can be anything. *(re-iss.cd+c.May91)*

Sep 71. (7") **IT'S SUMMER. / UNGENA ZA ULIMWENGU (UNITE THE WORLD)** –

— **RICHARD STREET** (b. 5 Oct'42, Detroit) – vocals (ex-DISTANTS) repl. PAUL. He later committed suicide 17 Aug'73.

Jan 72. (7") **SUPERSTAR (REMEMBER HOW YOU GOT WHERE YOU ARE). / GONNA KEEP ON TRYIN' TILL I WIN YOUR LOVE** 32 18 Nov 71

Mar 72. (7") **TAKE A LOOK AROUND. / SMOOTH SAILING FROM NOW ON** 13 30 Feb 72

Apr 72. (lp)(c) **SOLID ROCK** 34 30 Jan 72
– Take a look around / Ain't no sunshine / Stop the war now / What it is / Smooth sailing / Superstar / It's summer / The end of our road.

Oct 72. (7") **MOTHER NATURE. / SMILING FACES SOMETIMES** 92 Jul 72

Dec 72. (7") **PAPA WAS A ROLLIN' STONE. / ('A'instrumental)** 14 1 Oct 72

Dec 72. (lp)(c) **ALL DIRECTIONS** 19 2 Aug 72
– Funky music sho nuff turns me on / Run Charlie run / I ain't got nothing / Papa was a rollin' stone / Love woke me up this morning / The first time ever I saw your face / Mother nature / It's your thing. *(cd-iss.Sep93)*

Feb 73. (7") **MASTERPIECE. / ('A' instrumental)** – 7

Jun 73. (lp)(c) **MASTERPIECE** 28 7 Mar 73
– Masterpiece / Hey girl (I like your style) / Ha / The plastic man / Law of the land / Hurry tomorrow. *(re-iss.Oct81 on 'Motown')*

Jun 73. (7") **THE PLASTIC MAN. / HURRY TOMORROW** – 40

Aug 73. (7") **HEY GIRL (I LIKE YOUR STYLE). / MA** – 35

Aug 73. (7") **LAW OF THE LAND. / FUNKY MUSIC SHO NUFF TURN ME ON** 41 –

Nov 73. (7") **LET YOUR HAIR DOWN. / AIN'T NO JUSTICE** – 27

Dec 73. (lp)(c) **1990** 19
– Let your hair down / I need you / Heavenly / You've got my soul on fire / Ain't no justice / 1990 / Zoom.

Mar 74. (7") **HEY GIRL (I LIKE YOUR STYLE). / I NEED YOU** –

Apr 74. (7") **HEAVENLY. / ZOOM** – 43

Jun 74. (7") **YOU'VE GOT MY SOUL ON FIRE. / I NEED YOU** – 74

— **GLEN LEONARD** – vocals repl. HARRIS

Jan 75. (7") **HAPPY PEOPLE. / ('A'instrumental)** 40

Feb 75. (lp)(c) **A SONG FOR YOU** 13
– Happy People / Glasshouse / Shakey Ground / The Prophet / Happy People (Instrumental) / A Song For You / Memories / I'm A Bachelor

Apr 75. (7") **SHAKEY GROUND. / I'M A BACHELOR** – 26

May 75. (7") **MEMORIES. / AIN'T NO JUSTICE** –

Aug 75. (7") **GLASSHOUSE. / THE PROPHET** – 37

— **LOUIS PRICE** – vocals repl. EDWARDS who went solo

Jan 76. (7") **KEEP HOLDING ON. / WHAT YOU NEED MOST (I DO BEST OF ALL)** – 54

Feb 76. (lp)(c) **HOUSE PARTY** 40 Nov 75
– Keep holding on / It's just a matter of time / You can't stop a man in love / World of you, love and music / What you need most (I do best of all) / Ways of a grown up man / Johnny Porter / Darling stand by me / If I don't love you this way

Jun 76. (7") **UP THE CREEK (WITHOUT A PADDLE). / DARLING STAND BY ME** – 94

Jun 76. (lp)(c) **WINGS OF LOVE** 29 Apr 76
– Sweet gypsy Jane / Sweetness in the dark / Up the creek / China doll / Mary Ann / Dream world / Paradise.

Oct 76. (7") **WHO ARE YOU. / LET ME COUNT THE WAYS (I LOVE YOU)**

Oct 76. (lp)(c) **THE TEMPTATIONS DO THE TEMPTATIONS** 53 Sep 76
– Why can't you and me get together / Who are you / I'm on fire / Put your trust in me, baby / There's no stopping / Let me count the ways / Is there anybody else / I'll take you in.

Jan 77. (7") **SHAKEY GROUND. / I'M A BACHELOR** –

Atlantic Atlantic

Nov 77. (7") **IN A LIFETIME / I COULD NEVER STOP LOVING YOU** –

Feb 78. (lp)(c) **HEAR TO TEMPT YOU** Dec 77
– Think for yourself / In a lifetime / Can we come and share in love / She's all I've got / Snake in the grass / It's time for love / Let's live in peace / Road between the lines / I could never stop loving you.

Feb 78. (7") **LET'S LIVE IN PEACE. / THINK FOR YOURSELF** –

Aug 78. (7") **BARE BACK. / I SEE MY CHILD** –

Aug 78. (lp)(c) **BARE BACK**
– Bare back / Mystic woman (love me over) / I just don't know how I let you go / That's when you need love / Ever ready love / Wake up to me / You're so easy to love / I see the child / Touch me again.

Sep 78. (7") **BARE BACK. / EVER READY LOVE** – –

Sep 78. (7") **EVER READY LOVE. / TOUCH ME AGAIN** –

Jan 79. (7") **JUST DON'T KNOW HOW TO LET YOU GO. / MYSTIC WOMAN** –

Motown Gordy

May 80. (7")(12") **POWER. / ('A'instrumental)** 43

Jun 80. (lp)(c) **POWER** 45 May 80
– Power / Struck by lightning twice / How can I resist your love / Isn't the night fantastic / Shadow of your love / Go for it / Can't you see sweet thing / I'm coming her.

Aug 80. (7") **STRUCK BY LIGHTNING TWICE. / I'M COMING HOME**
(re-iss.Oct82)

Jan 81. (7") **TAKE ME AWAY. / THERE'S MORE WHERE THAT CAME FROM** –

— **DENNIS EDWARDS** returned on **lead vocals**

Oct 81. (7") **AIMING AT YOUR HEART. / LIFE OF A COWBOY** 67

Jan 82. (lp)(c) **THE TEMPTATIONS** Aug 81
– Aiming at your heart / Evil woman (gonna take your love) / The best of both worlds / Ready, willing and able / Oh what a night / Open their eyes / The life of a cowboy / What else / Just ain't havin' fun / Your lovin' is magic.

Feb 82. (7") **OH, WHAT A NIGHT. / ISN'T THE NIGHT FANTASTIC** –

— **OTIS WILLIAMS, MELVIN FRANKLIN, RICHARD STREET & DENNIS EDWARDS** re-united with **DAVID RUFFIN & EDDIE KENDRICKS** for one-off album.

May 82. (lp)(c) **REUNION** 37 Apr 82
– Standing on the top / You better beware / Lock it in the pocket / I've never been to me / Backstage / More on the inside / Money's hard to get.

May 82. (7") **STANDING ON THE TOP. / (part 2)** 53 66
Above also featured solo artist RICK JAMES

Jul 82. (7") **MORE ON THE INSIDE. / MONEY'S HARD TO GET** –

Nov 82. (7") **SILENT NIGHT. / EVERYTHING FOR CHRISTMAS** –
(re-is.Nov83)

— The quartet added **RON TYSON** (their composer in '78) – vocals

Mar 83. (7")(12") **LOVE ON MY MIND TONIGHT. / BRING YOUR BODY HERE** [ ] [88]
Mar 83. (lp)(c) **SURFACE THRILLS** [ ] [ ]
– Surface thrills / Love on my mind tonight / One man woman / Show me your love / The seeker / What a way to put it / Made in America / Bring your body here (exercise chant).
May 83. (7") **SURFACE THRILLS. / MADE IN AMERICA** [-] [ ]
Oct 83. (7") **MISS BUSY BODY (GET YOUR BODY BUSY). / (part 2)** [-] [ ]
Dec 83. (lp)(c) **BACK TO BASICS** [ ] [ ]
– Miss busy body (get your body busy) / Sail away / Outlaw / Stop the world right here (I wanna get off) / The battle song (I'm the one) / Hollywood / Isn't the night fantastic / Make me believe in love again.
Apr 84. (7") **SAIL AWAY. / ISN'T THE NIGHT FANTASTIC** [-] [54]

—— **ALI OLLIE WODSIN** – lead vocals repl. EDWARDS

Nov 84. (7")(12") **TREAT HER LIKE A LADY. / ISN'T THE NIGHT FANTASTIC** [12] [48]
Dec 84. (lp)(c) **TRULY FOR YOU** [75] [55] Nov 84
– Running / Treat like a lady / How can you say it's over / My life is true (truly for you) / Memories / Just to keep you in my life / Set your love right / I'll keep my light on in my window.
Feb 85. (7") **MY LOVE IS TRUE (TRULY FOR YOU). / SET YOUR LOVE RIGHT** [-] [ ]
Mar 85. (7") **MY LOVE IS TRUE (TRULY FOR YOU). / I'LL KEEP A LIGHT ON IN MY WINDOW** [ ] [ ]
(12"+=) – Treat her like a lady (remix).
Jun 85. (7") **HOW CAN YOU SAY IT'S OVER. / I'LL KEEP MY LIGHT IN THE WINDOW** [-] [ ]

In Sep'85, RUFFIN & KENDRICKS were credited on HALL & OATES live album 'LIVE AT THE APOLLO WITH . . . '

Nov 85. (7")(12") **DO YOU REALLY LOVE YOUR BABY. / I'LL KEEP A LIGHT ON IN MY WINDOW** [ ] [ ]
Nov 85. (lp)(c) **TOUCH ME** [ ] [ ]
– Magic / Give her some attention / Deeper than love / I'm fascinated / Touch me / Don't break your promise to me / She got tired of loving me / Do you really love your baby / Oh lover.
Feb 86. (7") **TOUCH ME. / SET YOUR LOVE RIGHT** [-] [ ]
Mar 86. (7")(12") **I'M FASCINATED. / HOW CAN YOU SAY IT'S OVER** [ ] [-]
Jun 86. (7") **WISHFUL THINKING. / A FINE MESS** [-] [ ]
Aug 86. (7")(12") **LADY SOUL. / A FINE MESS** [ ] [-]
Sep 86. (lp)(c)(cd) **TO BE CONTINUED** [ ] [74] Jul 86
– Lady soul / Message to the world / To be continued / Put us together again / Someone / Girls (they like it) / More love, your love / A fine mess / You're the one / Love me right.
Oct 86. (7") **LADY SOUL. / PUT US TOGETHER AGAIN** [-] [47]
Jan 87. (7") **TO BE CONTINUED. / YOU'RE THE ONE** [-] [ ]
Apr 87. (7") **SOMEONE. / LOVE ME RIGHT** [-] [ ]

—— **DENNIS EDWARDS** returned again to repl. OTIS

Aug 87. (7")(12") **PAPA WAS A ROLLIN' STONE (remix). / DON'T SAY NOTHING'S CHANGED** [31] [-]
Oct 87. (lp)(c) **TOGETHER AGAIN** [ ] [ ]
– I got your number / Look what you started / I wonder who she's seeing now / 10 x 10 / Do you wanna go with me / Little things / Everytime I close my eyes / Lucky / Put your foot down.
Oct 87. (7")(12") **I WONDER WHO SHE'S SEEING NOW. / GIRLS (THEY LIKE IT)** [ ] [ ]
Jan 88. (7")(12")(c-s) **LOOK WHAT YOU STARTED. / MORE LOVE, YOUR LOVE** [63] [ ]
(12"+=) ('A' extended).
Apr 88. (7") **DO YOU WANNA GO WITH ME. / PUT YOUR FOOT DOWN** [-] [ ]

—— Late 1987, RUFFIN & KENDRICKS released eponymous duo album on 'RCA'.

—— **RON TYSON** – vocals repl. EDWARDS

Oct 89. (7") **ALL I WANT FROM YOU. / ('A'instrumental)** [71] [ ]
(12"+=)(cd-s+=) – Papa was a rollin' stone / Treat her like a lady.
Oct 89. (lp)(c)(cd) **SPECIAL** [ ] [ ]
– Friends / Special / All I want from you / She's better than money / One step at a time / Fill me up / Go ahead / Loveline / Soul to soul. (cd+=) – D.A.D. lover.
Jan 90. (7") **SPECIAL. / D.A.D. LOVER** [-] [ ]
Mar 90. (7") **SOUL TO SOUL. / ('A'instrumental)** [-] [ ]
Jun 90. (7") **ONE STEP AT A TIME. / ('A'instrumental)** [-] [ ]
Jan 92. (cd)(c)(lp) **MILESTONE** [ ] [ ]
– Eenie, meenie, minie moe / Any old lovin' (just won't do) / Hoops of fire / We should be makin' love / The Jones' / Get ready / Corner of my heart / Whenever you're ready / Do it easy / Wait a minute. (cd+=) – Celebrate. *(re-iss.cd Apr95)*
Feb 92. (7")(c-s) **THE JONES'. / ('A'surgery mix)** [69] [ ]
(12"+=)(cd-s+=) – ('A'instrumental).

—— Tragically, EDDIE KENDRICKS died of cancer in Oct '92. Later, another original MELVIN FRANKLIN also died on 23 February 1995.

– compilations, others, etc. –

Note; on 'Tamla Motown' UK/ 'Gordy' Us unless otherwise mentioned.

Apr 65. (7"ep) **MEET THE TEMPTATIONS** [ ] [-]
– My girl / Girl (why you wanna make me blue) / I'll be in trouble / The girl's alright with me.
Feb 66. (7"ep) **IT'S THE TEMPTATIONS** [ ] [-]
– My baby / Since I lost my baby / It's growing / The way you do the things . . .
1966. (7"ep) **TEMPTIN' TEMPTATIONS** [ ] [-]
1967. (7"ep) **GETTIN' READY** [ ] [-]
Feb 67. (lp) **THE TEMPTATIONS' GREATEST HITS** [26] [5] Dec 66
– The way you do the things you do / My girl / Ain't too proud to beg / Don't look back / Get ready / Beauty is only skin deep / Since I lost my baby / The girl's alright with me / My baby / Its growing / I'll be in trouble / Girl (why you wanna make me blue).
Feb 69. (7") **GET READY. / MY GIRL** [10] [-]
(re-iss.Oct81 on 'Motown')
May 69. (7") **AIN'T TOO PROUD TO BEG. / FADING AWAY** [ ] [-]
Aug 69. (lp) **THE TEMPTATIONS SHOW (TV Soundtrack)** [-] [24] Jul 69
Dec 70. (lp)(c) **THE TEMPTATIONS' GREATEST HITS VOL.2** [35] [15] Sep 70
May 74. (d-lp)(d-c) **ANTHOLOGY 64-73** [ ] [65] Sep 73
(re-iss.Oct82)
Sep 76. (7") **GET READY. / JUST MY IMAGINATION** [ ] [ ]
1977. (lp)(c) **GREATEST HITS VOL.III** [-] [ ]
Sep 80. (7") **BALL OF CONFUSION. / TAKE A LOOK AROUND** [ ] [-]
Oct 80. (d-lp)(d-c) **20 GOLDEN GREATS** [ ] [-]
Nov 82. (lp)(c) **GIVE LOVE AT CHRISTMAS** [ ] [-]
Feb 83. (7") **CLOUD NINE. / PSYCHEDELIC SHACK** [ ] [-]
Mar 83. (7") **JUST MY IMAGINATION. / GET READY** [ ] [-]
May 83. (c-ep) **TEMPTATIONS EP** [ ] [-]
– Take a look . . . / Ball of confusion / Get ready / Beauty is only skin deep.
Oct 83. (7")(12") **MEDLEY OF HITS (with 'The Four Tops'). / PAPA WAS A ROLLIN' STONE** [ ] [-]
Apr 85. (7") **LAW OF THE LAND. / BEAUTY IS ONLY SKIN DEEP** [ ] [-]
Apr 85. (7") **BALL OF CONFUSION. / AIN'T TOO PROUD TO BEG** [ ] [-]
May 85. (d-lp)(d-c) **25th ANNIVERSARY** [-] [ ]
Jun 86. (7")(12") **MY GIRL. / ('B'by 'Marvin Gaye')** [ ] [-]
Apr 92. Polydor/ US= Motown; (7") **GET READY. / ('A'version)** [ ] [ ]
(12"+=)(cd-s+=) – ('A'instrumental).
Apr 92. Polydor/ US= Motown; (cd) **MOTOWN'S GREATEST HITS** [8] [ ]
– My girl / The Jones' / Get ready (new version) / Ain't too proud to beg / Beauty is only skin deep / I wish it would rain / (I know) I'm losing you / Cloud nine / Paa was a rollin' stone / Law of the land / Just my imagination (running away with me) / Take a look around / Ball of confusion (that's what the world is today) / I can't get to you / Psychedelic shack / Treat her like a lady / Get ready / You're my everything / Superstar (remember how you got where you are) / Standing on the top (part 1).

—— Below from the film 'My Girl' starring McAuley Caulkin.

Feb 92. Epic; (7")(c-s)(cd-s) **MY GIRL. / JAMES NEWTON HOWARD (theme from 'My Girl')** [2] [ ]
Apr 94. Paradiso; (cd) **GREATEST HITS** [ ] [-]
Oct 94. Motown; (5xcd-box) **EMPERORS OF SOUL** [ ] [-]
Apr 95. Top Masters; (cd) **THE BEST OF . . .** [ ] [-]

10 cc

Formed: Manchester, England ... 1970 as HOTLEGS, by experienced ERIC STEWART, LOL CREME and KEVIN GODLEY. STEWART was a member of WAYNE FONTANA & THE MINDBENDERS between Apr'64-Nov'68,(the latter 6 months, with pensmith GOULDMAN). GOULDMAN while a solo artist, had written hits for YARDBIRDS (For Your Love + Heartful Of Soul + Evil Hearted You), HOLLIES (Bus Stop + Look Through Any Window) and HERMAN'S HERMITS (No Milk Today), etc. HOTLEGS scored a 1970 No.2 hit 'NEANDERTHAL MAN', and then split in 1971. The following year the trio as 10CC, added GOULDMAN and signed to Jonathan King's newly formed 'UK' label. Became massive selling outfit, after initial UK Top 3 smash 'DONNA'. • **Style:** At times pastiche but transient pop group, who progressed their songwriting abilities in the mid-70's, after hitting No.1 with excellent love song 'I'M NOT IN LOVE'. • **Songwriters:** Either GOULDMAN / STEWART or GODLEY & CREME. The latter duo became noted pop stars in own right, and were best known for their pop videos. • **Trivia:** GOULDMAN produced The RAMONES and GILBERT O'SULLIVAN in the early 80's.

Recommended: THE CHANGING FACES OF 10CC AND GODLEY & CREME (*8)

HOTLEGS

ERIC STEWART (b.20 Jan'45) – vocals, guitar, bass (ex-MINDBENDERS) / **LOL CREME** (b.LAWRENCE, 19 Sep'47) – vocals, guitar, keyboards, bass / **KEVIN GODLEY** (b. 7 Oct'45) – drums, vocals (ex-MOCKINGBIRDS, ex-Solo)

Fontana Capitol
Jun 70. (7") **NEANDERTHAL MAN. / YOU DIDN'T LIKE IT** [2] [22]
Mar 71. (7") **HOW MANY TIMES. / RUN BABY RUN** [-] [ ]
Philips Capitol
Mar 71. (lp) **THINKS: SCHOOL STINKS** [ ] [ ]
– Neanderthal man / How many times / Desperate Dan / Take me back / Um wah, un woh / Suite F.A. / Fly away / Run baby run / All God's children.
Sep 71. (7") **LADY SADIE. / THE LOSER** [ ] [ ]

—— Split late 1971. A further exploitation lp 'YOU DIDN'T LIKE IT, 'COS YOU DIDN'T LIKE IT' was issued 1976 on 'Philips'. GOULDMAN guested.

—— The trio became

10 cc

adding **GRAHAM GOULDMAN** – bass, vocals (ex-Solo artist, ex-MINDBENDERS)

UK-Decca UK
Sep 72. (7") **DONNA. / HOT SUN ROCK** [2] [ ]
Dec 72. (7") **JOHNNY, DON'T DO IT. / 4% OF SOMETHING** [ ] [-]
Apr 73. (7") **RUBBER BULLETS. / WATERFALL** [1] [73] Sep 73
Aug 73. (lp)(c) **10 cc** [36] [ ]
– Rubber bullets / Donna / Johnny, don't do it / Sand in my face / Speed kills / The dean and I / Ships don't disappear in the night (do they?) / The hospital song / Fresh air for my momma / Headline hustler. *(re-iss.1982 & Dec83 on 'Mercury')*
Aug 73. (7") **THE DEAN AND I. / BEE IN MY BONNET** [10] [ ]
Jan 74. (7") **THE WORST BAND IN THE WORLD. / 18 CARAT MAN OF MEANS** [ ] [-]

Apr 74. (7") **HEADLINE HUSTLER. / SPEED KILLS** [-]
Jun 74. (7") **WALL STREET SHUFFLE. / GISMO MY WAY** [10] [ ]
Jun 74. (lp)(c) **SHEET MUSIC** [9] [81]
– Wall Street shuffle / The worst band in the world / Hotel / Old wild men / Clockwork creep / Silly love / Somewhere in Hollywood / Baron Samedi / The sacro-iliac / Oh! Effendi. *(re-iss.1982 & Dec83 on 'Mercury')*
Sep 74. (7") **SILLY LOVE. / THE SACRO-ILIAC** [24] [ ]

Mercury Mercury

Mar 75. (lp)(c) **THE ORIGINAL SOUNDTRACK** [4] [15]
– Une nuit a Paris: One night in Paris – The same night in Paris – Later the same night in Paris / I'm not in love / Blackmail / The second sitting for the last supper / Brand new day / Flying junk / Life is a minestrone / The film of my love. *(re-iss.Dec83)*
Mar 75. (7") **LIFE IS A MINESTRONE. / CHANNEL SWIMMER** [7] [-]
May 75. (7") **I'M NOT IN LOVE. / GOOD NEWS** [1] [-]
May 75. (7") **I'M NOT IN LOVE. / CHANNEL SWIMMER** [-] [2]
(re-iss.Oct84)
Nov 75. (7") **ART FOR ART'S SAKE. / GET IT WHILE YOU CAN** [5] [83]
Jan 76. (lp)(c) **HOW DARE YOU!** [5] [ ]
– How dare you / Lazy ways / I wanna rule the world / I'm Mandy fly me / Iceberg / Art for art's sake / Rock'n'roll lullaby / Head room / Don't hang up. *(re-iss.Dec83)*
Mar 76. (7") **I'M MANDY FLY ME. / HOW DARE YOU** [6] [60]

—— **STEWART + GOULDMAN** carried on with session people including live drummer PAUL BURGESS. They replaced GODLEY & CREME who formed own duo.

Jul 76. (7") **LAZY WAYS. / LIFE IS A MINESTRONE** [-] [ ]
Nov 76. (7") **THE THINGS WE DO FOR LOVE. / HOT TO TROT** [6] [5]
Apr 77. (7") **GOOD MORNING JUDGE. / DON'T SQUEEZE ME LIKE TOOTHPASTE** [5] [-]
May 77. (lp)(c) **DECEPTIVE BENDS** [3] [31]
– Good morning judge / The things we do for love / Marriage bureau rendezvous / People in love / Modern man blues / Honeymoon with B troop / I bought a flat guitar tutor / You've got a cold / Feel the benefit: Reminisce and speculation – A Latin break. *(re-iss.May83)*
May 77. (7") **PEOPLE IN LOVE. / DON'T SQUEEZE ME LIKE TOOTHPASTE** [-] [40]
Jun 77. (7") **PEOPLE IN LOVE. / I'M SO LAID BACK I'M LAID OUT** [ ] [-]
Jul 77. (7") **GOOD MORNING JUDGE. / I'M SO LAID BACK I'M LAID OUT** [-] [69]

—— added **RICK FENN** – guitar / **TONY O'MALLEY** – keyboards (ex-ARRIVAL, ex-KOKOMO) / **STUART TOSH** – 2nd drummer (ex-PILOT)

Dec 77. (d-lp)(d-c) **LIVE AND LET LIVE (live)** [14] [ ]
– The second sitting for the last supper / You've got a cold / Honeymoon with B troop / Art for art's sake / Wall Street shuffle / Ships don't disappear in the night (do they?) / I'm Mandy fly me / Marriage bureau rendezvous / Good morning judge / Feel the benefit / The things we do for love / Waterfall / I'm not in love / Modern man blues.
Dec 77. (7") **WALL STREET SHUFFLE (live). / YOU'VE GOT A COLD** [-] [ ]

—— **DUNCAN MACKAY** – keyboards (ex-COCKNEY REBEL) repl. BURGESS

Mercury Polydor

Jul 78. (7") **DREADLOCK HOLIDAY. / NOTHING CAN MOVE ME** [1] [44]
Sep 78. (lp)(c) **BLOODY TOURISTS** [3] [69]
– Dreadlock holiday / For you and I / Take these chains / Shock on the tube (don't want love) / Last night / The anonymous alcoholic / Reds in my bed / Life line / Tokyo / Old Mister Time / From Rochdale to Ocho Rios / Everything you've wanted to know about. *(re-iss.May83)*
Oct 78. (7") **REDS IN MY BED. / TAKE THESE CHAINS** [ ] [-]
Jan 79. (7") **FOR YOU AND I. / TAKE THESE CHAINS** [-] [85]
Sep 79. (lp)(c) **GREATEST HITS 1972-1978** (compilation) [5] [ ]
– Rubber bullets / Donna / Silly love / The dean and I / Life is a minestrone / Wall Street shuffle / Art for art's sake / I'm Mandy fly me / Good morning judge / The things we do for love / Dreadlock holiday / I'm not in love.

Mercury Warners

Feb 80. (7") **ONE TWO FIVE. / ONLY CHILD** [ ] [ ]
Mar 80. (lp)(c) **LOOK HEAR!** [35] [ ]
– One two five / Welcome to the world / How'm I ever going to say goodbye / Don't send we back / I took you home / It doesn't matter at all / Dressed to kill / Lovers anonymous / I hate to eat alone / Strange lover / L.A. inflatable.

—— At same time ERIC STEWART and GRAHAM GOULDMAN had own solo albums.

May 80. (7") **IT DOESN'T MATTER AT ALL. / FROM ROCHDALE TO OCHO RIOS** [ ] [-]
May 80. (7") **IT DOESN'T MATTER AT ALL. / STRANGE LOVER** [-] [ ]
May 81. (7") **NOUVEAU RICHE. / I HATE TO EAT ALONE** [ ] [ ]
Nov 81. (7") **DON'T TURN ME AWAY. / TOMORROW'S WORLD TODAY** [ ] [ ]
Nov 81. (lp)(c) **TEN OUT OF 10** [ ] [ ]
– I don't ask / Overdraft in overdrive / Don't turn me away / Memories / No tell hotel / Les nouveaux riches / Action man in Motown suit / Listen with your eyes / Lying here with you / Survivor. *(cd-iss.1983)*
Mar 82. (7") **THE POWER OF LOVE. / YOU'RE COMING HOME AGAIN** [ ] [-]
Jun 82. (7") **THE POWER OF LOVE. / ACTION MAN IN MOTOWN SUIT** [-] [ ]
Jul 82. (7") **RUN AWAY. / ACTION MAN IN MOTOWN SUIT** [50] [ ]
Oct 82. (7") **WE'VE HEARD IT ALL BEFORE. / OVERNIGHT IN OVERDRIVE** [ ] [ ]
Apr 83. (7") **24 HOURS. / DREADLOCK HOLIDAY** [ ] [ ]
(12"+=) – I'm not in love.
Sep 83. (7") **FEEL THE LOVE. / SHE GIVES THE PAIN** [ ] [ ]
Oct 83. (lp)(c) **WINDOW IN THE JUNGLE** [70] [ ]
– 24 hours / Feel the love – Oomachasa ooma / Yes I can / Americana panorama / City lights / Food for thought / Working girls / Taxi! taxi!.

—— Split late '83 but reunited 8 years later.

originals reformed in 1991, with STEWART & GOULDMAN

Polydor Polydor?

Apr 92. (7")(c-s)(cd-s) **WOMAN IN LOVE. / MAN WITH A MISSION** [ ] [ ]
May 92. (cd)(c)(lp) **MEANWHILE** [ ] [ ]
– Woman in love / Wonderland / Fill her up / Something special / Welcome to Paradise / The stars didn't show / Green aged monster / Charity begins at home / Shine a light in the dark / Don't break the promises.
Jun 92. (7") **WELCOME TO PARADISE. / DON'T BREAK THE PROMISES** [ ] [-]
(cd-s+=) – Lost in love.

Humbug not issued

Nov 93. (cd-ep) **10CC ALIVE (live)** [ ] [-]

—— GOULDMAN + STEWART acoustic.

Avex not issued

Feb 95. (7")(c-s) **I'M NOT IN LOVE. /** [29] [-]
(cd-s+=) –
May 95. (12")(c-s)(cd-s) **READY TO GO HOME. / ('A'album mix) / AGE OF CONSENT** [ ] [ ]
Sep 95. (cd)(c)(d-lp) **MIRROR, MIRROR** [ ] [-]
– Yvonne's the one / Code of silence / Blue bird / Age of consent / Take this woman / The monkey and the onion / Everything is not enough / Ready to go home / Grow old with me / Margo wants the mustard / Peace in our time / Why did I break your heart / Now you're gone / I'm not in love (acoustic '95).

– more compilations, etc. –

Note; Below 3 on 'UK Decca'.

May 75. (lp)(c) **100 cc – THE GREATEST HITS OF 10cc** [9] [ ]
May 75. (7") **WATERFALL. / 4% OF NOTHING** [ ] [-]
Jul 87. (7")(12") **THE WORST BAND IN THE WORLD. / HOT SUN ROCK** [ ] [-]
Apr 79. Flyover; (lp) **THE SONGS WE DO FOR LOVE** [ ] [-]
Sep 79. Mercury; (7") **I'M NOT IN LOVE. / FOR YOU AND I** [ ] [-]
1981. Mercury; (c) **THE MUSIC OF 10 cc (1975-77)** [ ] [-]

Note; below 4 on 'Old Gold'.

Jun 88. (7") **I'M NOT IN LOVE. / DREADLOCK HOLIDAY** [ ] [-]
Jun 88. (7") **RUBBER BULLETS. / DONNA** [ ] [-]
Jun 88. (7") **WALL STREET SHUFFLE. / THE DEAN AND I** [ ] [-]
May 92. (cd-s) **I'M NOT IN LOVE / DREADLOCK HOLIDAY / I'M MANDY FLY ME** [ ] [-]
Jul 89. Castle; (d-lp) **THE COLLECTION** [ ] [-]
– (albums 10cc + SHEET MUSIC)
Oct 82. Contour; (lp) **10 CC IN CONCERT (live)** [ ] [-]
(cd-iss.Apr91 on 'Pickwick')
Apr 93. Dojo; (cd)(c) **THE EARLY YEARS** [ ] [-]
May 93. Music Club; (cd)(c) **THE BEST OF THE EARLY YEARS** [ ] [-]
May 93. Spectrum; (cd)(c) **FOOD FOR THOUGHT** [ ] [-]
Feb 94. Trident; (cd) **ALIVE – GREATEST HITS PERFORMED LIVE (live)** [ ] [-]
Jul 94. BR Music; (cd)(c) **GREATEST HITS** [ ] [-]
Aug 95. Old Gold; (cd-s) **RUBBER BULLETS / THE DEAN AND I** [ ] [-]
Sep 95. Old Gold; (cd-s) **DONNA / WALL STREET SHUFFLE** [ ] [-]

ERIC STEWART

Polydor Mercury

Feb 80. (7") **GIRLS. / DISCOLAPSE** [ ] [-]
Apr 80. (lp)(c) **GIRLS** [ ] [ ]
– Girls (opening music) / Girls / Disco grindin' / Switch le bitch / Disco bumpin' / Aural exciter / Warm, warm, warm / Tonight / Snatch the gas / Your touch is soft / Trouble shared / Discolapse / Make the pieces fit.
Aug 80. (7") **WARM, WARM, WARM. / SWITCH LE BITCH** [ ] [ ]

Mercury Mercury

Aug 82. (lp)(c) **FROOTY ROOTIES** [ ] [-]
– The ritual (pt.1 – Progress de la rake, pt.2 – Euphoria, pt.3 – A dog with four trees) / Make the pieces fit / Night and day / Never say 'I told you so' / Guitaaaarghs (rooties) / Doris the florist (the bouquet that nobody caught) / All my loving following you / Rockin' my troubles away / Strictly business (red light mamas).

GRAHAM GOULDMAN

(solo, while a 10 cc member; had made 60's singles & 1968 lp 'THE GRAHAM GOULDMAN THING', which was re-iss.on cd May92 on 'Edsel')

Mercury A & M

May 79. (7") **SUNBURN. / THINK ABOUT IT** [52] [-]
Mar 80. (7") **LOVE'S NOT FOR ME. / BIONIC BOAR** [ ] [-]
Apr 80. (lp)(c) **ANIMALYMPICS** [ ] [ ]
– Go for it / Underwater fantasy / Away from it all / Born to lose / Kit Kambo / Z.O.O. / Love's not for me / With you I can run forever / Bionic boar / We've made it to the top.
Jun 80. (7") **AWAY FROM IT ALL. / BIONIC BOAR** [-] [ ]

—— In 1979, GOULDMAN formed COMMON KNOWLEDGE with ANDREW GOLD (see under ⇒) They became WAX in the mid-80's.

KEVIN GODLEY & LOL CREME

with guests **PETER COOK + SARAH VAUGHAN** also introduced new Gizmo guitar orchestrator.

Mercury Mercury

Oct 77. (t-lp)(d-c) **CONSEQUENCES** [52] [ ]
– Seascape / Wind / Fireworks / Stampede / Burial scene / Sleeping Earth / Honolulu Lulu / The flood / Five o'clock in the morning / When things go wrong / Lost weekend / Rosie / Office chase / Cool, cool, cool / Cool, cool, cool (reprise) / Sailor / Mobilisation / Please, please, please / Blint's tune (movement 1-17). *(re-iss.1-lp Feb79 as 'MUSIC FROM CONSEQUENCES' tracks *)*
Dec 77. (7") **FIVE O'CLOCK IN THE MORNING. / THE FLOOD** [ ] [ ]

GODLEY & CREME

with guest **ANDY MACKAY** – saxophone

Mercury Polydor

Aug 78. (lp)(c) **L** [ ] [ ]
– This sporting life / Sandwiches of you / Art school canteen / Group life / Punchbag / Foreign accents / Hit factory – Business is business.

Jan 79. (7") **SANDWICHES OF YOU. / FOREIGN ACCENTS** [ ] [ ]

Polydor Mirage

Oct 79. (7") **AN ENGLISHMAN IN NEW YORK. / SILENT RUNNING** [ ] [ ]

Nov 79. (lp)(c) **FREEZE FRAME** [ ] [ ]
– An Englishman in New York / Random brainwave / I pity inanimate objects / Freeze frame / Clues / Brazilia (wish you were here) / Mugshots / Get well soon. *(re-iss.Aug83, cd-iss.May91)*

Mar 80. (7") **WIDE BOY. / I PITY INANIMATE OBJECTS** [ ] [-]

Sep 80. (7") **SUBMARINE. / MARCIANO** [ ] [-]

Aug 81. (7") **UNDER YOUR THUMB. / POWER BEHIND THE THRONE** [3] [ ]

Sep 81. (lp)(c) **ISMISM** [29] [ ]
– Snack attack / Under your thumb / Joey's camel / The problem / Ready for Ralph / Wedding bells / Lonnie / Sale of the century / The party. *(re-iss.Oct84)*

Nov 81. (7") **WEDDING BELLS. / BABIES** [7] [-]

Feb 82. (7") **WEDDING BELLS. / LONNIE** [-] [ ]
(re-iss.Nov85 on 'Mirage')

Feb 82. (7")(12") **SNACK ATTACK. / STRANGE APPARATUS** [ ] [-]

Sep 82. (7") **SAVE A MOUNTAIN FOR ME. / WELCOME TO BREAKFAST TELEVISION** [ ] [-]

Mar 83. (7") **SAMSON. / SAMSON (dance mix)** [ ] [-]

Apr 83. (lp)(c) **BIRDS OF PREY** [ ] [ ]
– My body the car / Worm and the rattlesnake / Cat's eyes / Samson / Save a mountain for me / Madame Guillotine / Woodwork / Twisted nerve / Out in the cold.

May 84. (7")(12") **GOLDEN BOY. / MY BODY THE CAR** [ ] [-]

Mar 85. (7")(12") **CRY. / LOVE BOMBS** [15] [16]
(re-iss.Aug86, hit UK 66)

Jun 85. (lp)(c) **THE HISTORY MIX VOLUME 1** [ ] [ ]
– Wet rubber soup (recycled from):- Rubber bullets – Minestrone – I'm not in love / Cry: Expanding business – The dare you man – Hum drum boys in Paris – Mountain tension / Light me up / An Englishman in New York / Save a mountain for me / Golden boy. *(cd-iss.May91)*

Sep 85. (7")(12") **GOLDEN BOY (remix). / LIGHT ME UP** [ ] [-]

Dec 87. (7") **A LITTLE BIT OF HEAVEN. / BITS OF BLUE SKY (excerpts)** [ ] [ ]
(12"+=)(cd-s+=)/ /(c-s++=) – ('A'extended)./ / Rhino rhino. *(re-iss.Jul88)*

Feb 88. (lp)(c)(cd) **GOODBYE BLUE SKY** [ ] [ ]
– H.E.A.V.E.N. / A little piece of Heaven / Don't set fire (to the one I love) / Golden rings / Crime & punishment / The big bang / 10,000 angels / Sweet memory / Airforce one / The last page of history / Desperate times.

Mar 88. (7") **10,000 ANGELS. / HIDDEN HEARTBREAK** [ ] [-]
(12"+=)/ /(cd-s++=) – Can't sleep./ / Cry.

– compilations, others, etc. –

Aug 82. Polydor; (d-c) **FREEZE FRAME / ISMISM** [ ] [-]

Aug 87. Polydor; (7")(12") **SNACK ATTACK. / WET RUBBER SOAP** [ ] [-]

Sep 87. Polydor; (lp)(c)(cd) **CHANGING FACES OF 10 cc & GODLEY AND CREME** [4] [ ]
– Dreadlock holiday / The Wall Street shuffle / Under your thumb (GODLEY & CREME) / Life is a minestrone / An Englishman in New York (GODLEY & CREME) / Art for art's sake / Donna / Snack attack (GODLEY & CREME) / Cry (GODLEY & CREME) / The things we do for love / Wedding bells (GODLEY & CREME) / I'm Mandy, fly me / Good morning judge / Rubber bullets / Save a mountain for me (GODLEY & CREME) / I'm not in love. *(re-iss.cd+c Mar94 on 'Polygram TV')*

May 93. Spectrum; (cd)(c) **IMAGES** [ ] [-]

Apr 95. Disky; (cd) **ROCK AND POP LEGENDS** [ ] [-]

10,000 MANIACS

Formed: Jamestown, New York, USA . . . 1981 by NATALIE MERCHANT and J.C. LOMBARDO, who had been part of band STILL LIFE. After a few releases on US label 'Christian Burial' & 'Reflex', they signed internationally to 'Elektra' in 1984. They soon supported R.E.M. on tour, where NATALIE befriended groups' singer MICHAEL STIPE. Their debut UK album 'THE WISHING CHAIR' in 1985, set critics alike, as did their follow-up 'IN MY TRIBE', which brought them first bit of commercial credibility. • **Style:** An alternative folk-rock outfit, with a hint of country and poignant lyrics. The live experience, saw vegetarian NATALIE's 40's dress attire, proudly swirl madly into a frenzy of unmitigated beauty. • **Songwriters:** lyrics – NATALIE / music – JC LOMBARDO until his departure. MERCHANT now main writer with DREW or BUCK. Covered; PEACE TRAIN (Cat Stevens) / I HOPE THAT I DON'T FALL IN LOVE WITH YOU (Tom Waits) / STARMAN – MOONAGE DAYDREAM (David Bowie) / THESE DAYS (Jackson Browne) / EVERYDAY IS LIKE SUNDAY (Morrissey) / DON'T GO BACK TO ROCKVILLE (R.E.M.) / BECAUSE THE NIGHT (Patti Smith Group). • **Trivia:** Their 1987 & 1989 albums were produced by PETE ASHER.

Recommended: THE WISHING CHAIR (*8) / IN MY TRIBE (*9) / HOPE CHEST (*8) / BLIND MAN'S ZOO (*8) / OUR TIME IN EDEN (*8).

NATALIE MERCHANT – vocals / **ROBERT BUCK** – guitar, synths / **J.C. LOMBARDO** (b.JOHN) – rhythm guitar, bass / **STEVEN GUSTAFSON** – bass, guitar / **DENNIS DREW** – organ / **JERRY AUGUSTYNAK** – drums

not issued ChristianB

1982. (m-lp) **HUMAN CONFLICT NUMBER FIVE** [-] [ ]
– Orange / Planed obsolescence / Anthem for doomed youth / Groove dub / Tension. *(UK-iss.Jun84 on 'Press') (cd-see compilations)*

Jan 84. (lp) **THE SECRETS OF I-CHING** [-] [ ]
– Grey victory / Pour de Chirico / Death of Manolette / Tension / Daktari / Pit viper / Katrina's fair / The Latin one / My mother the war. *(UK-iss.Aug84 on 'Press') (cd-see compilations)*

Reflex Reflex

Mar 84. (12"m) **MY MOTHER THE WAR (remix). / PLANNED OBSOLESCENCE / NATIONAL EDUCATION WEEK** [ ] [ ]

Elektra Elektra

Jun 85. (7") **CAN'T IGNORE THE TRAIN. / DAKTARI** [ ] [ ]
(12"+=) – Grey victory / The colonial wing.

Nov 85. (lp)(c) **THE WISHING CHAIR** [ ] [ ]
– Can't ignore the train / Just as the tide was a-flowing / Scorpio rising / Lilydale / Maddox table / Everyone a puzzle lover / Arbor day / Back o' the Moon / Tension takes a tangle / Among the Americans / Grey victory / Cotton alley / My mother the war. *(cd-iss.1989)*

Nov 85. (7") **JUST AS THE TIDE WAS A-FLOWING. / AMONG THE AMERICANS** (single withdrawn) [-] [ ]

Jan 86. (7") **SCORPIO RISING. / ARBOR DAY** [ ] [ ]

— Depleted to a quintet, when LOMBARDO departed.

Aug 87. (7") **PEACE TRAIN. / PAINTED DESERT** [ ] [ ]

Aug 87. (lp)(c)(cd) **IN MY TRIBE** [ ] [37]
– What's the matter here? / Hey Jack Kerouac / Like the weather / Cherry tree / Painted desert / Don't talk / Peace train / Gun shy / Sister Rose / A campfire song / City of angels / Verdi cries.

Nov 87. (7") **DON'T TALK. / CITY OF ANGELS** [ ] [ ]
(12"+=) – Goodbye. (some included booklet instead of extra song)

Jul 88. (7") **LIKE THE WEATHER. / A CAMPFIRE SONG** [ ] [68] May 88
(12"+=) – Poison in the well (live) / Verdi cries (live).

Jul 88. (7") **WHAT'S THE MATTER HERE?. / CHERRY TREE** [-] [80]

Aug 88. (7") **WHAT'S THE MATTER HERE?. / VERDI CRIES** [ ] [-]
(12"+=)(cd-s+=) – Like the weather (live) / Gun shy (live). *(above was scheduled for release in Mar88, w/drawn)*

May 89. (lp)(c)(cd) **BLIND MAN'S ZOO** [18] [13]
– Eat for two / Please forgive us / The big parade / Trouble me / You happy puppet / Headstrong / Poison in the well / Dust bowl / The lion's share / Hateful hate / Jubilee.

Jun 89. (7")(c-s) **TROUBLE ME. / THE LION'S SHARE** [ ] [44]
(12"+=)(3"cd-s+=) – Party of God.

Sep 89. (7") **YOU HAPPY PUPPET. / GUNSHY** [-] [ ]

Nov 89. (7"ep) **EAT FOR TWO / WILDWOOD FLOWER. / DON'T CALL US / FROM THE TIME YOU SAY GOODBYE** [ ] [ ]
(12")(3"cd-s) – (1st & 2nd track) / Gun shy (acoustic) / Hello in there.
(10") – (1st & 4th track) / What's the matter here? (acoustic) / Eat for two (acoustic).

Sep 92. (7")(c-s) **THESE ARE DAYS. / CIRCLE DREAM** [58] [66]
(cd-s+=) – I hope that I don't fall in love with you.
(cd-s) – ('A'side) / Medley:- Starman – Moonage daydream / These days.

Sep 92. (cd)(c)(lp) **OUR TIME IN EDEN** [33] [28]
– Noah's dove / These are days / Eden / Few and far between / Stockton gala days / Gold rush brides / Jezebel / How you've grown / Candy everybody wants / Circle dream / If you intend / I'm not the man. (cd+=) – Tolerance.

Mar 93. (7")(c-s) **CANDY EVERYBODY WANTS. / EVERYDAY IS LIKE SUNDAY** [47] [67]
(cd-s+=) – Don't go back to Rockville (with MICHAEL STIPE co-vocals) / Sally Ann.
(cd-s+=) – Don't go back to Rockville (with MICHAEL STIPE) / ('A' MTV version).
(cd-s) – ('A'side) / Eat for two (live) / My sister Rose (live) / Hey Jack Kerouac (live).

Aug 93. (c-s)(cd-s) **FEW AND FAR BETWEEN. /** [-] [95]

Oct 93. (7") **BECAUSE THE NIGHT. / STOCKTON GALA DAYS** [65] [11]
(cd-s+=) – Let the mystery be / Sally Ann.

Oct 93. (cd)(c) **UNPLUGGED (live)** [40] [13]
– These are days / Eat for two / Candy everybody wants (MTV version) / I'm not the man / Don't talk / Hey Jack Kerouac / What's the matter here / Gold rush brides / Like the weather / Trouble me / Jezebel / Because the night / Stockton gala days / Noah's dove.

— 10,000 MANIACS split when NATALIE went solo. The rest re-formed in 1995 and added ex-original JOHN LOMBARDO and his (JOHN & MARY duo) partner MARY RAMSAY on vocals and violin.

– compilations, others, etc. –

Oct 90. Elektra; (cd)(c)(lp) **HOPE CHEST** [ ] [ ]
– (HUMAN CONFLICT NUMBER FIVE / THE SECRETS OF I-CHING)

NATALIE MERCHANT

— -vocals, keyboards / with **JENNIFER TURNER** – guitars, vocals / **BARRY MAGUIRE** – bass, guitar / **PETER YANOWITZ** – drums, percussion

Elektra Elektra

Jun 95. (cd)(c) **TIGERLILY** [39] [13]
– San Andreas fault / Wonder / Beloved wife / River / Carnival / I may know the word / The letter / Cowboy romance / Jealousy / Where I go / Seven years.

Jul 95. (c-s)(cd-s) **CARNIVAL / CARNIVAL (edit) / I MAY KNOW THE WORD** [ ] [10]

Dec 95. (c-s)(cd-s) **WONDER /** [-] [44]

TEN YEARS AFTER

Formed: Nottingham, England . . . Aug'65 (originally as The JAYBIRDS in 1961) by ALVIN LEE and LEO LYONS. In 1966, they moved to London and became TEN YEARS AFTER. Through manager Chris Wright, they signed to Decca offshoot label 'Deram', and issued eponymous debut in 1967. Their first album to hit was the live set 'UNDEAD', which made UK No.26. Their reputation grew as well as their commercial fortunes, more so after an appearance at Aug'69 WOODSTOCK festival. One of their songs; the 11 minute 'I'M GOING HOME', was recorded on film and album. • **Style:** Blues-based rock'n'roll, featuring the self-proclaimed fastest guitarist in the world ALVIN LEE. In 1971, they introduced electronics, but this disastrous expedition led to a decline in sales, resulting in a return to basics later. • **Songwriters:** ALVIN LEE penned and co-wrote with STEVE GOULD in the 80's. Covered; SPOONFUL (Willie Dixon) / AT THE WOODCHOPPER'S BALL (Woody Herman) / SWEET LITTLE SIXTEEN (Chuck Berry) / GOOD MORNING LITTLE SCHOOLGIRL (Don & Bob) / GOING BACK TO BIRMINGHAM (Little Richard) / etc. • **Trivia:** They re-united in 1988 for a 4-day German festival which resulted a reformation album the following year.

Recommended: THE COLLECTION (*7).

ALVIN LEE (b. GRAHAM BARNES 19 Dec'44) – vocals, guitar / **LEO LYONS** (b.30 Nov'43, Bedfordshire, England) – bass / **CHICK CHURCHILL** (b. 2 Jan'49, Mold, Wales) – keyboards / **RIC LEE** (b.20 Oct'45, Staffordshire, England) – drums

Deram Deram

Oct 67. (lp) **TEN YEARS AFTER** □ □
– I want to know / I can't keep from crying sometimes / Adventures of a young organ / Spoonful / Losing the dogs / Feel it for me / Love until I die / Don't you want woman / Help me. *(re-iss.+c.May80 on 'Hallmark') (cd-iss.May88)*

Feb 68. (7") **PORTABLE PEOPLE. / THE SOUNDS** □ □

Aug 68. (lp) **UNDEAD (live at Klook's Kleek)** 26 □
– I may be wrong, but I won't be wrong always / Woodchopper's ball / Spider in my web / Summertime – Shantung cabbage / I'm going home. *(cd-iss.Jun88)*

Nov 68. (7") **HEAR ME CALLING. / I'M GOING HOME** □ □

Feb 69. (lp) **STONEDHENGE** 6 61
– Going to try / I can't live without Lydia / Woman trouble / Skoobly-oobly-doobob / Hear me calling / A sad song / Three blind mice / No title / Faro / Speed kills. *(re-iss.+c.Apr89)*

Aug 69. (lp)(c) **SSSSH** 4 20
– Bad scene / Two-time mama / Stoned woman / Good morning little schoolgirl / If you should love me / I don't know that you don't know my name / The stomp / I woke up this morning. *(re-iss.Jul75) (re-iss.cd Mar94)*

Apr 70. (lp)(c) **CRICKLEWOOD GREEN** 4 14
– Sugar the road / Working on the road / 50,000 miles beneath my brain / Year 3,000 blues / Me and my baby / Love like a man / Circles / As the sun still burns away. *(re-iss.Jul75) (re-iss.cd+c Jul94)*

Jun 70. (7") **LOVE LIKE A MAN. / ('A'long live version)** 10 -

Jan 71. (lp)(c) **WATT** 5 21
– I'm coming on / My baby left me / Think about the times / I say yeah / The band with no name / Gonna run / She lies in the morning / Sweet little sixteen. *(re-iss.Jul75)*

Chrysalis Columbia

Nov 71. (lp)(c) **A SPACE IN TIME** 36 17 Aug 71
– One of these days / Here they come / I'd love to change the world / Over the hill / Baby won't you let me rock'n'roll you / Once there was a time / Let the sky fall / Hard monkeys / I've been there too / Uncle Jam. *(re-iss.1974)*

Sep 71. (7") **I'D LOVE TO CHANGE THE WORLD. / LET THE SKY FALL** - 40

Jan 72. (7") **BABY WON'T YOU LET ME ROCK'N'ROLL YOU. / ONCE THERE WAS A TIME** - 61

Oct 72. (lp)(c) **ROCK & ROLL MUSIC TO THE WORLD** 27 43
– You give me loving / Convention prevention / Turned off T.V. blues / Standing at the station / You can't win them all / Religion / Choo choo mama / Tomorrow I'll be out of town / Rock & roll music to the world. *(re-iss.1974)*

Nov 72. (7") **CHOO CHOO MAMA. / YOU CAN'T WIN THEM ALL** - 89

Feb 73. (7") **TOMORROW, I'LL BE OUT OF TOWN. / CONVENTION PREVENTION** - □

Jul 73. (7") **I'M GOING HOME. / YOU GIVE ME LOVING** - □

Jul 73. (d-lp)(d-c) **TEN YEARS AFTER (RECORDED LIVE)** 36 39 Jun 73
– One of these days / You give me loving / Good morning little schoolgirl / Hobbit / Help me / Classical thing / I can't keep from cryin', sometimes (parts 1 & 2) / Silly things / Slow blues in 'C' / I'm going home / Choo choo mama.

Apr 74. (lp)(c) **POSITIVE VIBRATIONS** □ 81
– Nowhere to run / Positive vibrations / Stone me / Without you / Going back to Birmingham / It's getting harder / You're driving me crazy / Look into my life / Look me straight into the eyes / I wanted to boogie.

Apr 74. (7") **I WANTED TO BOOGIE. / IT'S GETTING HARDER** - □

— Disbanded after CHICK CHURCHILL made solo album YOU AND ME in Feb74.

ALVIN LEE & MYLON LeFEVRE

collaborated with US solo gospel singer plus TRAFFIC members on session.

Nov 73. (7") **SO SAD. / RIFFIN** - □

Nov 73. (lp)(c) **ON THE ROAD TO FREEDOM** □ □
– On the road to freedom / The world is changing / So sad / Fallen angel / Funny / We will shine / Carry me load / Lay me back / Let 'em say what they will / I can't take it / Riffin' / Rockin' till the sun goes down.

Jan 74. (7") **THE WORLD IS CHANGING. / RIFFIN** □ □

ALVIN LEE & CO.

with **NEIL HUBBARD** – guitar / **ALAN SPENNER** – bass / **TIM HINKLEY** – keyboards / **IAN WALLACE** – drums / **MEL COLLINS** – saxophone

Nov 74. (d-lp)(d-c) **ALVIN LEE & CO: IN FLIGHT (live gig)** □ 65
– (introduction) / Let's get back / Ride my track / There's a feeling / Running around / Mystery train / Slow down / Keep a-knockin' / How many times / I've got my eyes for you baby / I'm writing you a letter / Got to keep moving / Going through the door / Don't be cruel / Money honey / I'm writing you a letter / You need love love love / Freedom for the stallion / Every blues you've ever heard / All life's trials.

— touring band **HINKLEY / ANDY PYLE** – bass / **BRYSON GRAHAM** – drums / studio **RONNIE LEAHY** – keyboards / **STEVE THOMPSON** – bass / **IAN WALLACE** – drums

Oct 75. (lp)(c) **PUMP IRON!** □ □ Sep 75
– One more chance / Try to be righteous / You told me / Have mercy / Julian Rice / Time and space / Burnt fungus / The darkest night / It's alright now / Truckin' down the other way / Let the sea burn down.

— An album 'SAGUITAR' was shelved in 1976.

ALVIN LEE – TEN YEARS LATER

with **TOM COMPTON** – drums / **MICK HAWKSWORTH** – bass (ex-ANDROMEDA)

Polydor R.S.O.

Apr 78. (lp)(c) **ROCKET FUEL** □ □
– Rocket fuel / Gonna turn you on / Friday the 13th / Somebody's calling me / Ain't nothin' shakin' / Alvin's blue thing / Baby don't you cry / The Devil's screaming.

Sep 79. (lp)(c) **RIDE ON (live studio)** □ □ May 79
– Ain't nothin' shakin' / Scat encounter / Hey Joe / Going home / Too much / It's a Gaz / Ride on cowboy / Sitin' here / Can't sleep at nite.

Sep 79. (7") **RIDE ON COWBOY. / SITTIN' HERE** □ -

Seo 79. (7") **RIDE ON COWBOY. / CAN'T SLEEP AT NITE** - □

The ALVIN LEE BAND

retained **COMPTON** and added **STEVE GOULD** – guitar (ex-RARE BIRD) / **MICKEY FEAT** – bass (ex-STREETWALKERS)

Avatar Atlantic

Oct 80. (lp)(c) **FREE FALL** □ □
– I don't wanna stop / Take the money / One lonely hour / Heartache / Stealin' / Ridin' truckin' / No more lonely nights / City lights / Sooner or later / Dustbin city.

Nov 80. (7") **I DON'T WANNA STOP. / HEARTACHE** □ □

Mar 81. (7") **RIDIN' TRUCKIN'. /** - □

Jul 81. (7") **TAKE THE MONEY. / NO MORE LONELY NIGHTS** □ □

Oct 81. (7") **CAN'T STOP. /** - □

Nov 81. (lp)(c) **RX-5** □ □
– Hang on / Lady luck / Can't stop / Wrong side of the law / Nutbush city limits / Rock and roll guitar picker / Double loser / Fool no more / Dangerous world / High times.

Dec 81. (7") **ROCK'N'ROLL GUITAR PICKER. / DANGEROUS WORLD** □ □

Mar 82. (7") **NUT BUSH CITY LIMITS. / HIGH TIMES** □ □

— **MICK TAYLOR** – guitar (ex-ROLLING STONES) / **FUZZY SAMUELS** – bass (ex-CROSBY, STILLS & NASH) repl. GOULD & FEAT. Split early 1982.

ALVIN LEE

recorded another solo with **LYONS + GEORGE HARRISON**

not issued 21 records

Aug 86. (lp) **DETROIT DIESEL** □ □
– Detroit diesel / Shot in the dark / Too late to run for cover / Talk don't bother me / Ordinary man / Heart of stone / She's so cute / Back in my arms again / Don't want to fight / Let's go.

Sep 86. (7") **DETROIT DIESEL. / LET'S GO** - □

Jan 87. (7") **HEART OF STONE. / SHE'S SO CUTE** - □

— Signed to 'No Speak' records, but had no releases. In Apr'89, ALVIN guested on Various Artists live cd,c,-d-lp 'NIGHT OF THE GUITAR' for 'I.R.S.' label.

TEN YEARS AFTER

originals re-formed with **ALVIN LEE + STEVE GOULD** plus?

Chrysalis Chrysalis

Nov 89. (lp)(c)(cd) **ABOUT TIME** □ □
– Highway of love / Let's shake it up / I get all shook up / Victim of circumstance / Going to Chicago / Wild is the river / Saturday night / Bad blood / Working in a parking lot / Outside my window / Waiting for the judgement day.

Nov 89. (7") **HIGHWAY OF LOVE. / ROCK & ROLL MUSIC TO THE WORLD** □ □

– compilations, others, etc. –

Mar 72. Deram; (lp)(c) **ALVIN LEE & COMPANY (ALVIN LEE)** □ 55

Aug 75. Columbia; (lp)(c) **GOIN' HOME – THEIR GREATEST HITS** □ □ Jul 75

Sep 76. Columbia; (lp)(c) **ANTHOLOGY** □ □

Feb 77. Columbia; (lp)(c) **THE CLASSIC PERFORMANCES OF . . .** □ □
(cd-iss. 1987)

Dec 78. Columbia; (lp)(c) **LET IT ROCK ("ALVIN LEE" solo)** □ □

May 88. Columbia; (d-lp)(c)(cd) **PORTFOLIO** □ □

Feb 79. Teldec; (c) **GREATEST HITS VOL.1** □ -

Oct 83. Old Gold; (7") **LOVE LIKE A MAN. / ('B'by 'Them')** □ -

Nov 85. Castle; (d-lp)(c) **THE COLLECTION** □ -
– Hear me calling / No title / Spoonful / I can't keep from crying sometimes / Standing at the crossroads / Portable people / Rock your mama / Love like a man / I want to know / Speed kills / Boogie on / I may be wrong but I won't be wrong always / At the woodchopper's ball / Spider in your web / Summertime / Shantung cabbage / I'm going home. *(re-iss.cd+c Jul91)*

Feb 87. See For Miles; (lp) **ORIGINAL RECORDINGS: VOL.1** □ -

Jun 87. See For Miles; (lp) **ORIGINAL RECORDINGS: VOL.2** □ -
(re-iss.+cd.Nov 93)

Dec 90. Raw Fruit; (cd)(lp) **LIVE AT READING 1988 (live)** □ -

Jul 93. Code 90; (cd) **LIVE (live)** □ -

Sep 93. Traditional Line; (cd) **LOVE LIKE A MAN** □ -

Nov 93. Thunderbolt; (cd) **1994 (ALVIN LEE)** □ -

Aug 95. Chrysalis; (cd)(c) **PURE BLUES (ALVIN LEE & TEN YEARS AFTER)** □ -

Aug 95. Griffin; (cd) **THE COLLECTION (THE BEST OF TEN YEARS AFTER)** □ -

Nov 95. Chrysalis; (3xcd-box) **CRICKLEWOOD GREEN / WATT / A SPACE IN TIME** □ -

ALVIN LEE

Castle / Rykodisc

1992. (cd)(c)(lp) **ZOOM** [ ] [ ]
– A little bit of love / Jenny Jenny / Remember me / Anything for you / The price of this love / Real life blues / It don't come easy / Lost in love / Wake up moma / Moving the blues / Use that power.

New Rose / not issued

Mar 95. (cd) **LIVE IN VIENNA (live)** [ ] [-]

TERRAPLANE (see under ⇒ THUNDER)

TERRORVISION

Formed: Bradford, England . . . late 1991 by (see below). In 1993 they and their label 'Total Vegas' were signed up to major 'E.M.I.'. Their first single of '94 'MY HOUSE', gave them their first deserved Top 30 hit. In August that year they were the surprise treat at Reading Festival. • **Style:** Unconventional metal outfit, fusing between THERAPY? and CHEAP TRICK. • **Songwriters:** Group penned, strings section arranged by friends AUDREY RILEY and BILLY McGHEE. Covered; PSYCHO KILLER (Talking Heads) / THE MODEL (Kraftwerk) / THE PASSENGER (Iggy Pop) / SURRENDER (Cheap Trick) / WISHING WELL (Free) / I'LL BE YOUR SISTER (Hawkwind)? • **Trivia:** Produced in New York by GIL NORTON (Pixies)

Recommended: FORMALDEHYDE (*7) / HOW TO MAKE FRIENDS AND INFLUENCE PEOPLE (*8)

TONY WRIGHT – vocals / **MARK YATES** – guitars / **LEIGH MARKLEW** – bass / **SHUTTY** – drums

Total Vegas / not issued

Feb 92. (12"ep)(cd-ep) **THRIVE EP** [ ] [-]
– Urban spacecrime / Jason / Blackbird / Pain reliever.

Oct 92. (7") **MY HOUSE. / COMING UP** [ ] [-]
(12"+=)(cd-s+=) – Tea dance.

Dec 92. (cd)(green-lp) **FORMALDEHYDE** [ ] [-]
– Problem solved / Ships that sink / American T.V. / New policy one / Jason / Killing time / Urban space crime / Hole for a soul / Don't shoot my dog / Desolation town / My house / Human being / Pain reliever / Tea dance. *(re-iss.cd,c,lp May93 on 'Total Vegas-EMI' w/out last 2 tracks, hit UK No.75)*

Jan 93. (12"ep)(cd-ep) **PROBLEM SOLVED / CORPSE FLY. / WE ARE THE ROADCREW / SAILING HOME** [ ] [ ]

Total Vegas-EMI / E.M.I.

Jun 93. (12"ep) **AMERICAN T.V. / DON'T SHOOT MY DOG AGAIN / KILLING TIME** [63] [ ]
(cd-ep) – ('A'side) / Psycho killer / Hole for a soul.

Oct 93. (7"green) **NEW POLICY ONE. / PAIN RELIEVER (live)** [42] [ ]
(12") – ('A'side) / Ships that sink (live) / Problem solved (live).
(cd-s) – ('A'side) / Psycho killer (live) / Tea dance (live) / My house (live).
(cd-s) – ('A'side) / American TV (live) / New policy one (live) / Still the rhythm (live).

Jan 94. (7"green) **MY HOUSE. / TEA DANCE** [29] [ ]
(cd-s) – ('A'side) / ('A'machete mix) / Discotheque wreck.
(12") – ('A'side) / ('A'machete mix) / Psycho killer (extended).
(cd-s) – ('A'attic mix) / ('A'machete mix) / Down under.

Mar 94. (7") **OBLIVION (mix). / WHAT DO YOU DO THAT FOR?** [21] [ ]
(cd-s+=) – Problem solved (by DIE CHEERLEADER) / Oblivion (demo).
(cd-s) – ('A'side) / The model (with DIE CHEERLEADER) / Remember Zelda (written by DIE CHEERLEADER).
(12"++=) – Problem solved (by DIE CHEERLEADER).

Apr 94. (cd)(c)(lp) **HOW TO MAKE FRIENDS AND INFLUENCE PEOPLE** [18] [ ]
– Alice what's the matter / Oblivion / Stop this bus / Discotheque wreck / Middleman / Still the rhythm / Ten shades of grey / Stab in the back / Pretend best friend / Time o the signs / What the doctor ordered / Some people say / What makes you tick.

Jun 94. (c-s) **MIDDLEMAN. / OBLIVION** [25] [ ]
(cd-s) – ('A'side) / I'll be your sister / Wishing well.
(12"copper)(cd-s) – ('A'side) / Surrender / The passenger.

Aug 94. (c-s) **PRETEND BEST FRIEND. / MIDDLEMAN (live)** [25] [ ]
(12") – ('A'side) / Alice (live) / Stop the bus (live) / Discotheque wreck (live).
(cd-s) – ('A'side) / Time o' the signs (live) / Oblivion (live) / ('A'-Danny Does Vegas mix.
(cd-s) – ('A'side) / What makes you tick (live) / Still the rhythm (live) / ('A'-Alice pretends mix).

Oct 94. (c-s) **ALICE, WHAT'S THE MATTER (oh yeah mix). / SUFFOCATION** [24] [ ]
(12") – ('A'-junkie J mix) / ('B'side) / ('A'pushy bitch mix) / ('A'-all Carmen).
(cd-s) – ('A'side) / ('A'-Pop Will Eat Itself mix) / Discotheque wreck (acoustic) / ('A'demo).
(cd-s) – ('A'side) / Psycho killer (acoustic) / ('A'-kill your Terrorvision mix) / What shall we do with the drunken sailor?

Mar 95. (7")(c-s) **SOME PEOPLE SAY. / MR. BUSKERMAN / OBLIVION** [22] [ ]
(cd-s) – ('A'side) / Blood on my wheels / ('A'extended) / Oblivion.
(cd-s) – ('A'side) / This drinking will kill me / ('A'-Oblivious mix) / Oblivion.

TESLA

Formed: Sacramento, California, USA . . . 1985 originally as CITY KID, by JEFF KEITH, etc (see below). Signed to US label 'Geffen' in 1986, they made their mark quickly the following year, with debut album 'MECHANICAL RESONANCE'. • **Style:** Bluesy hard rock outfit, influenced by MONTROSE, BAD COMPANY or VAN HALEN. They diverted between usual two styles, of either passionate ballads or high energy heavy rock'n'roll. • **Songwriters:** KEITH-HANNON penned, except AIN'T SUPERSTITIOUS (Willie Dixon) / RUN RUN RUN (Jo Jo Gunne) / WE CAN WORK IT OUT (Beatles) / LODI (Creedence Clearwater Revival) / MOTHER'S LITTLE HELPER (Rolling Stones) / ROCK THE NATION (Montrose) / SIGNS (Five Man Electrical Band) / TRUCKIN' (Grateful Dead). • **Trivia:** Named themselves after scientist Nikola Tesla.

Recommended: THE GREAT RADIO CONTROVERY (*6).

JEFF KEITH – vox / **TOMMY SKEACH** – guitar, vocals / **FRANK HANNON** – guitar, keyboards / **BRIAN WHEAT** – bass, vocals / **TROY LUCHETTA** – drums (ex-ERIC MARTIN BAND)

Geffen / Geffen

Apr 87. (7") **LITTLE SUZI (ON THE UP). / (SEE YOU) CUMIN' ATCHA (live)** [-] [91]

Apr 87. (7") **LITTLE SUZI (ON THE UP). / BEFORE MY EYES** [ ] [-]
(12"+=) – Cumin' atcha live (remix).

Jun 87. (lp)(c)(cd) **MECHANICAL RESONANCE** [ ] [32] Jan 87
– Ez come ez go / Cumin' atcha live / Gettin' better / 2 late 4 love / Rock me to the top / We're no good together / Modern day cowboy / Changes / Little Suzi (on the up) / Love me / Cover queen / Before my eyes. *(re-iss.+cd. Jan91)*

Jun 87. (7") **MODERN DAY COWBOY. / ('A'version)** [ ] [ ]
(12"+=) – Love live / Cover queen (live).

Feb 89. (lp)(c)(cd) **THE GREAT RADIO CONTROVERSY** [34] [18]
– Hang tough / Lady luck / Heaven's trail (no way out) / Be a man / Lady days, crazy nights / Did it for the money / Yesterdaze gone / Makin' magic / The way it is / Flight to nowhere / Love song / Paradise / The party's over. *(re-iss.+cd Jan91)*

Oct 89. (7") **LOVE SONG. / AIN'T SUPERSTITIOUS** [ ] [10] Sep 89
(12"+=)(cd-s+=) – Run run run.

Mar 90. (c-s)(cd-s) **THE WAY IT IS /** [-] [55]

Feb 91. (cd)(c)(d-lp) **FIVE MAN ACOUSTIC JAM** [59] [12] Nov 90
– Comin' atcha live – Truckin' – Heaven's trail (no way out) / The way it is / We can work it out / Signs / Getting better / Before my eyes / Paradise / Lodi / Mother's little helper / Modern day cowboy / Love song / Tommy's down home / Down fo' boogie.

Apr 91. (7")(US-c-s) **SIGNS. / DOWN FO' BOOGIE** [70] [8] Jan 91
(12"+=)(cd-s+=)(12"blue+=) – Little Suzi (acoustic live).

Sep 91. (7")(c-s) **EDISON'S MEDICINE. / ROCK THE NATION** [ ] [ ]
(12"+=)/ /(12"blue+=)(cd-s+=) – Had enough./ / Run run run.

Sep 91. (cd)(c)(lp) **PSYCHOTIC SUPPER** [44] [13]
– Change in the weather / Edison's medicine / Don't de-rock me / Call it what you want / Song and emotion / Time / Government personnel / Freedom slaves / Had enough / What you give / Stir it up / Can't stop / Talk about it.

Dec 91. (7")(c-s) **CALL IT WHAT YOU WANT. / FREEDOM SLAVES** [ ] [ ]
(12"+=)(cd-s+=) – Children's heritage / Cotton fields.

Apr 92. (c-s)(cd-s) **WHAT YOU GIVE. /** [-] [86]

Aug 94. (cd)(c) **BUST A NUT** [51] [20]
– The gate / Invited / Solution / Shine away / Try so hard / She want she want / I need your lovin' / Action talks / Mama's fool / Cry / Earthmover / Alot to lose / Rubberband / A wonderful world / Games people play / The ocean.

TESTAMENT

Formed: Bay Area, San Francisco, USA . . . 1983 as The LEGACY. In 1985, new addition CHUCK BILLY and the lads (see below) became TESTAMENT, and soon signed to 'Atlantic' subsidiary label 'Megaforce'. Their debut (named after the original group name) arrived in 1987, but it wasn't until the 1989 set 'PRACTICE WHAT YOU PREACH', scraped the UK Top 40, that band had finally come of age. • **Style:** Thrash lightning-metal similar to MEGADETH or ANTHRAX. • **Songwriters:** Group compositions, except NOBODY'S FAULT (co-with STEVE TYLER of AEROSMITH). • **Trivia:** Original LEGACY vocalist STEVE SOUSA, fronted other metal outfit EXODUS.

Recommended: PRACTICE WHAT YOU PREACH (*6).

CHUCK BILLY – vocals / **ALEX SKOLNICK** – guitar / **ERIC PETERSON** – guitar / **GREG CHRISTIAN** – bass / **LOUIE CLEMENTE** – drums

East West / Atlantic

Jun 87. (lp)(c) **THE LEGACY** [ ] [ ] 1986
– Over the wall / The haunting / Burnt offerings / Raging waters / C.O.T.L.O.D. (Curse of the legions of death) / First strikes is deadly / Do or die / Alone in the dark / Apocalyptic city.

Dec 87. (lp)(c) **LIVE IN EINDHOVEN (live)** [ ] [ ]
– Over the wall / Burnt offerings / Do or die / Apocalyptic city / Reign of terror.

Apr 88. (7") **TRIAL BY FIRE. / NOBODY'S FAULT** [ ] [ ]
(12"+=) – Reign of terror.

May 88. (lp)(c)(cd) **THE NEW ORDER** [81] [ ]
– Eerie inhabitants / The new order / Trial by fire / Into the pit / Hypnosis / Disciples of the watch / The preacher / Nobody's fault / A day of reckoning / Musical death (a dirge).

Aug 89. (lp)(c)(cd) **PRACTICE WHAT YOU PREACH** [40] [77]
– Practice what you preach / Perilous nation / Envy life / Time is coming / Blessed in contempt / Greenhouse effect / Sins of omission / The ballad (a song of hope) / Confusion fusion / Nightmare (coming back to you). *(re-iss.cd Feb95)*

Oct 90. (cd)(c)(lp) **SOULS OF BLACK** [35] [73]
– Beginning of the end / Face in the sky / Falling fast / Souls of black / Absence of light / Love to hate / Malpractise / One man's fate / The legacy / Seven days in May.

May 92. (cd)(c)(lp) **THE RITUAL** [48] [55]
– Signs of chaos / Electric crown / So many lies / Let go of my world / The ritual / Deadline / As the seasons grey / Agony / The sermon / Return to serenity / Troubled dreams.

Apr 93. (cd)(c)(lp) **RETURN TO THE APOCALYPTIC CITY** [ ] [ ]

– Over the wall / So many lies / The haunting / Disciplines of the watch / Reign of terror / Return to serenity.

Oct 94. (cd)(c) **LOW** [ ] [ ]

–

M.F.N. Megaforce

Aug 95. (cd) **LIVE AT THE FILLMORE (live)** [ ] [ ]
– The preacher / Alone in the dark / Burnt offerings / A dirge / Eerie inhabitants / The new order / Low / Vrotsvkidoji / Into the pit / Souls of black / Practice what you preach / Apocalyptic city / Hail Mary / Dog faced gods / Return to serenity / The legacy / Trail of tears.

TEXAS

Formed: Glasgow, Scotland . . . 1988 by SPITERI, McELHONE, etc (see below). Soon signed to 'Mercury' records, and hit the Top 10 with debut 45 'I DON'T WANT A LOVER'. • **Style:** Guitar-based easy going country-rock, influenced by RY COODER and JOHNNY CASH. • **Songwriters:** SPITERI lyrics / McELHONE music, except TIRED OF BEING ALONE (Al Green) / SWEET CHILD O' MINE (Guns'n'Roses). • **Trivia:** EVERYDAY NOW sounded very much like BOB DYLAN's 'I Shall Be Released'.

Recommended: SOUTHSIDE (*6).

SHARLENE SPITERI – vocals, guitar / **ALLY McERLANE** – guitar / **JOHNNY McELHONE** – bass, vocals (ex-ALTERED IMAGES, ex-HIPSWAY) / **STUART KERR** – drums (ex-LOVE AND MONEY)

Mercury Mercury

Jan 89. (7") **I DON'T WANT A LOVER. / BELIEVE ME** [8] [77]
(12"+=)(cd-s+=) – All in vain.

Mar 89. (lp)(c)(cd) **SOUTHSIDE** [3] [88]
– I don't want a lover / Tell me why / Everyday now / Southside / Prayer for you / Faith / The thrill has gone / Fight the feeling / Fool for love / One choice / Future is promises. *(re-iss.cd Sep95)*

Apr 89. (7") **THRILL HAS GONE. / NOWHERE LEFT TO HIDE** [60] [ ]
(12"+=)(cd-s+=)(12"pic-d+=) – Dimples.

Jul 89. (7")(c-s) **EVERYDAY NOW. / WAITING FOR THE FALL** [44] [ ]
(12"+=) – Faith.
(12"+=) – ('A'live version) / Living for the city.
(cd-s+=) – Future is promises / Food for love (radio sessions).

Nov 89. (7")(c-s) **PRAYER FOR YOU. / RETURN** [73] [ ]
(12"+=)(cd-s+=) – I don't want a lover (live) / ('A'acoustic version).

Aug 91. (7")(c-s) **WHY BELIEVE IN YOU?. / HOW IT FEELS?** [66] [ ]
(12"+=)(cd-s+=) – Hold me Lord.

Sep 91. (cd)(c)(lp) **MOTHER'S HEAVEN** [32] [ ]
– Mother's heaven / Why believe in you? / Dream hotel / This will all be mine / Beliefs / Alone with you / In my heart / Waiting / Wrapped in clothes of blue / Return / Walk the dust.

Oct 91. (7")(c-s) **IN MY HEART. / IS WHAT I DO WRONG?** [74] [ ]
(12"+=)(cd-s+=) – You gave me love / ('A'remix).

Feb 92. (7")(c-s) **ALONE WITH YOU. / I DON'T WANT A LOVER** [32] [ ]
(cd-s+=) – Everyday now.
(cd-s) – ('A'side) / Sweet child o'mine (live) / What goes on (live) / Can't get next to you (live).

Apr 92. (7")(c-s) **TIRED OF BEING ALONE. / WRAPPED IN CLOTHES OF BLUE** [19] [ ]
(cd-s) – ('A'side) / Thrill has gone / In my heart (remix) / Prayer for you.

— **RICHARD HYND** – drums repl. KERR / added **EDDIE CAMPBELL** – keyboards

Vertigo Vertigo

Sep 93. (7")(c-s) **SO CALLED FRIEND. / YOU'RE THE ONE THAT I WANT IT FOR** [30] [ ]
(cd-s+=) – Tonight I stay with you / I've been missing you.
(pic-cd-s+=) – Mother's Heaven / Tired of being alone.

Oct 93. (7")(c-s) **YOU OWE IT ALL TO ME. / DON'T HELP ME THROUGH** [39] [ ]
(cd-s) – ('A'side) / Make me want to scream / Strange that I want you.
(cd-s) – (all 4 tracks).

Nov 93. (cd)(c)(lp) **RICK'S ROAD** [18] [ ]
– So called friend / Fade away / Listen to me / You owe it all to me / Beautiful angel / So in love with you / You've got to live a little / I want to go to heaven / Hear me now / Fearing these days / I've Been Missing You / Winter's end. *(re-iss.cd Sep95)*

Jan 94. (7")(c-s) **SO IN LOVE WITH YOU. / ('A'mix)** [28] [ ]
(cd-s) – ('A'side) / So called friend (live) / One love (live) / You owe it all to me (live).
(cd-s) – ('A'side) / Why believe in you (live) / Prayer for you (live) / Everyday now (live).

THAT PETROL EMOTION

Formed: Derry, N.Ireland . . . 1984 by the O'NEILL brothers, O'GORMAN, McLAUGHLIN and American STEVE MACK. In the mid-80's, they all based themselves in London, England, and after a few 45's on small indie labels, they signed to 'Demon'. After a criticaly acclaimed debut 'MANIC POP THRILL', they moved up to 'Polydor' records in 1987, where they scraped into the UK Top 30 with single 'BIG DECISION'. • **Style:** Influenced initially from 60's psychedelia and garage to The BEATLES. They moved into more slightly experimental danceable acid-rock in the late 80's. • **Songwriters:** Most written by O'NEILL's except covers; ME AND BABY BROTHER (War) / FOR WHAT IT'S WORTH (Buffalo Springfield) / NON-ALIGNMENT PACT (Pere Ubu) / ZIGZAG WANDERER (Captain Beefheart) / HEY BULLDOG (Beatles) / CINNAMON GIRL (Neil Young) / FUNTIME (Iggy Pop). • **Trivia:** ROLI MOSSIMAN of The SWANS, produced 1986 debut album.

Recommendeed: MANIC POP THRILL (*7) / BABBLE (*8).

STEVE MACK (b. U.S.A.) – vocals / (ex-EAGER SIN BABIES) / **SEAN O'NEILL** (b.JOHN) – guitar (ex-UNDERTONES) / **DAMIEN O'NEILL** – bass, keyboards (ex-UNDERTONES) / **REAMANN O'GORMAN** – guitar / **CIARAN McLAUGHLIN** – drums

Pink not issued

Jun 85. (7") **KEEN. / A GREAT DEPRESSION ON SLUM NIGHT** [ ] [-]
(re-iss.Oct86)

Noise A Noise not issued

Oct 85. (7") **V2. / THE GONEST THING** [ ] [-]
(12"+=) – Happiness drives me round the bend.

Demon Rykodisc?

Apr 86. (7") **IT'S A GOOD THING. / THE DEADBEAT** [ ] [-]
(12"+=) – Mine.

May 86. (lp)(c)(cd)(US-orange-lp) **MANIC POP THRILL** [84] [-]
– Fleshprint / Can't stop / Lifeblood / Natural kind of joy / It's a good thing / Circusville / Mouth crazy / Tight lipped / A million miles away / Lettuce / Cheepskate / Blind spot. *(cd+=) – V2 / Jesus said / The deadbeat.*

Jul 86. (7") **NATURAL KIND OF JOY. / CAN'T STOP** [ ] [-]
(12"+=) – Non-alignment pact / Jesus said.

Polydor Polydor

Mar 87. (7")(12") **BIG DECISION. / SOUL DEEP** [43] [ ]
('A'extended-10"+=) – Split!.

May 87. (lp)(c)(cd) **BABBLE** [30] [ ]
– Swamp / Spin cycle / For what it's worth / Big decision / Static / Split! / Belly bugs / In the playpen / Inside / Chester Burnette / Creeping to the cross.

Jun 87. (7") **SWAMP. / DANCE YOUR ASS OFF** [64] [ ]
(12"+=) – Creeping to the cross (live).
(7"ep++=) – Me and baby brother (live).

Virgin Virgin

Oct 87. (7") **GENIUS MOVE. / PARTY GAMES** [65] [-]
(12"+=) – Mouthcrazy.

Sep 88. (lp)(c)(cd) **END OF THE MILLENIUM PSYCHOSIS BLUES** [53] [ ]
– Sooner or later / Every little bit / Cellophane / Candy love satellite / Here it is . . . take it! / The price of my soul / Groove check / The bottom line / Tension / Tired shattered man / Goggle box / Under the sky.

Oct 88. (7") **CELLOPHANE. / THINK OF A WOMAN** [ ] [-]
(12"+=)(cd-s+=) – Hot head / Fast'n'bullbous.

— **JOHN MARCHINI** – bass repl. SEAN O'NEILL temporary until 1989 full-time

Feb 89. (10"ep)(3"cd-ep) **GROOVE CHECK / CHEMICRAZY. / TENSION (live) / UNDER THE SKY (live)** [ ] [ ]

Mar 90. (7") **ABANDON. / FAT MOUTH CREED** [73] [ ]
(12"+=)/ /(cd-s+=) – Jewel./ / ('A'boys own mix) / Headstaggered.

Apr 90. (cd)(c)(lp) **CHEMICRAZY** [62] [ ]
– Hey Venus / Blue to black / Mess of words / Sensitize / Another day / Gnaw mark / Scum surfin' / Compulsion / Tingle / Head staggered / Abandon / Sweet shiver burn.

May 90. (7") **SENSITIZE. / CHEMICRAZY (revitalized)** [ ] [ ]
(10"+=)(12"+=)(cd-s+=) – Abandon (boys own mix) / Groove check this groove.

Aug 90. (7")(c-s) **HEY VENUS. / ('A'mad Thatcher mix)** [49] [ ]
(12"+=)(cd-s+=) – (2 more 'A'mixes).

— **FRANK TREISCHLER** – bass (ex-YOUNG GODS) repl. MARCHINI

Jan 91. (7") **TINGLE. / ('A'hard bop edit)** [49] [ ]
(12"+=) – ('A'other mix).
(cd-s+=) – Light and shade / Hey Bulldog.
(12") – ('A'-Christmas mix). / 'A'-jazz tup mix).

Apr 91. (7"ep)(12"ep) **SENSITIZE. / ABANDON (mix) / GROOVE CHECK** [55] [ ]
(10"ep+=)(c-ep+=)(cd-ep+=) – Cinnamon girl.

— **MARCHINI** now returned to substitute TREICHE who returned to YOUNG GODS. 1992 was a terrible year, as 'Virgin' dropped them from roster.

Koogat not issued

Mar 93. (12"ep)(cd-ep) **DETONATE MY DREAMS. / BLUE TO BLACK (extended) / BIG HUMAN THING** [ ] [-]

Apr 93. (cd)(c)(lp) **FIREPROOF** [ ] [-]
– Detonate my dreams / Catch a fire / Last of the true believers / Too late blues / 7th wave / Infinite thrill / Speed of light / Shangri-la / Heartbeat mosaic / Metal mystery.

Jul 93. (12"ep)(cd-ep) **CATCH A FIRE (re-mix). / FUN TIME / LITTLE BIKINI / CHROME** [ ] [-]

Disbanded at the end of April '94.

– compilations, others, etc. –

Oct 87. Strange Fruit; (12"ep) **THE PEEL SESSIONS** [ ] [-]
– Blind spot / Lettuce / V2 / Can't stop.

Dec 89. Strange Fruit; (lp)(cd) **DOUBLE PEEL SESSIONS II** [ ] [-]

THEATRE OF HATE (see under ⇒ SPEAR OF DESTINY)

THEM

Formed: Belfast, N.Ireland . . . 1963 by MORRISON, HARRISON, HENDERSON, WRIXEN and MELLINGS. After their debut single flopped, producers TOMMY SCOTT and BERT BERNS, recruited session men JIMMY PAGE (future LED ZEPPELIN) and PETER BARDENS (future CAMEL) to feature on early '65 Top 10 'BABY PLEASE DON'T GO'. Their classic follow-up 'HERE COMES THE NIGHT' just missed the top spot in the UK, but managed a Top 30 placing in America. • **Style:** R&B rock'n'roll featuring the soulful brilliance of future solo star VAN MORRISON. • **Songwriters:** MORRISON penned (until his departure), except HERE COMES THE NIGHT + (IT WON'T HURT) HALF AS MUCH + few early songs (Bert Berns). DON'T START CRYING NOW (Slim Harpo) / BABY PLEASE DON'T GO (Big Joe Williams) / DON'T LOOK BACK (John Lee Hooker) / I PUT A

SPELL ON YOU (Screaming Jay Hawkins) / IT'S ALL OVER NOW, BABY BLUE (Bob Dylan), etc. • **Trivia:** GLORIA which later became a garage-punk classic, was fortuosly covered in 1966 by US group The SHADOWS OF NIGHT.

Recommended: THE COLLECTION (*8)

VAN MORRISON (b.GEORGE IVAN, 31 Aug'45) – vocals, harmonica / **BILLY HARRISON** – guitar / **ERIC WRIXEN** – piano, keyboards / **RONNIE MELLINGS** – drums / **ALAN HENDERSON** (b.26 Nov'44) – bass

Decca London

Aug 64. (7") **DON'T START CRYING NOW. / ONE TWO BROWN EYES** [ ] [ ]

— **JACKIE McAULEY** – organ + **PATRICK McAULEY** – organ repl. ERIC and RONNIE WRIXEN who joined The WHEELS, while MELLINGS became a milkman.

Dec 64. (7") **BABY PLEASE DON'T GO. / GLORIA** [10] [93] Mar 65
US flipped over + re-dist. Apr 66 to hit 71)
(re-iss.Jul73 on 'Deram') (re-iss.May82) (re-iss.Oct83 on 'Old Gold')

Decca Parrot

Mar 65. (7") **HERE COMES THE NIGHT. / ALL FOR MYSELF** [2] [24] May 65
(re-iss.Sep73 on 'Deram') (re-iss.Oct83 on 'Old Gold')

Jun 65. (lp) **(THE ANGRY YOUNG) THEM** (US-title 'HERE COMES THE NIGHT') [ ] [54]
– Here comes the night (US-only) / Mystic eyes / If you and I could be as two / Little girl / Just a little bit / I gave my love a diamond (UK-only) / Go on home baby / Gloria / You just can't win / Don't look back / I like it like that / Bright lights big city / My little baby (UK-only) / Route 66. *(re-iss.1973 on 'Deram') (cd-iss.Feb89)*

above lp featured sessioners **PETER BARDENS** – keyboards + **JIMMY PAGE** – guitar

— **PETER BARDENS** – keyboards + **JOHN WILSON** (b. 6 Nov'47) – drums now repl. The McAULEY's who formed The BELFAST GYPSIES

Jun 65. (7") **ONE MORE TIME. / HOW LONG BABY?** [ ] [ ]

Aug 65. (7") **(IT WON'T HURT) HALF AS MUCH. / I'M GONNA DRESS IN BLACK** [ ] [ ]

Nov 65. (7") **MYSTIC EYES. / IF YOU AND I COULD BE AS TWO** [ ] [33] Oct 65

— **MORRISON, HENDERSON + WILSON** were joined by **RAY ELLIOTT** (b.13 Sep'43) – piano, sax repl. BARDENS to solo & later CAMEL / **JIM ARMSTRONG** (b.24 Jun'44) – guitar repl. HARRISON

Jan 66. (lp) **THEM AGAIN** [ ] [ ]
– Could you would you / Something you got / Call my name / Turn on your love light / I put a spell on you / I can only give you everything / My lonely sad eyes / I got a woman / Out of sight / It's all over now, baby blue / Bad or good / How long baby / Hello Josephine / Don't you know / Hey girl / Bring 'em on in.

Mar 66. (7") **CALL MY NAME. / BRING 'EM ON IN** [ ] [ ]

— (Jan 66) **TERRY NOONE** – drums repl. WILSON later to TASTE (RORY GALLAGHER) Apr 66, **DAVE HARVEY** – drums repl. NOONE.

May 66. (7") **RICHARD CORY. / DON'T YOU KNOW** [ ] [ ]

— Disbanded mid 1966 when VAN MORRISON went solo. In 1967, they re-formed. **KEN McDOWELL** – vocals repl. him

Major Minor not issued

1967. (7") **GLORIA. / FRIDAY'S CHILD** [ ] [-]

1967. (7") **THE STORY OF THEM. / (pt.2)** [ ] [-]

Capitol Tower

Jan 68. (lp) **NOW AND THEM** [ ] [ ]
– I'm your witch doctor / What's the matter baby / Truth machine / Square room / You're just what I was looking for today / Dirty old man / At the age of sixteen / Nobody loves you when you're down and out / Walking the Queen's garden / I happen to love you / Come to me. *(UK-iss.+cd.Dec88 on 'Zap!')*

Feb 68. (7") **WALKING IN THE QUEEN'S GARDEN. / HAPPEN TO LOVE YOU** [-] [ ]

Apr 68. (7") **SQUARE ROOM. / BUT IT'S ALRIGHT** [-] [ ]

— trimmed to a quartet when ELLIOTT departed

Nov 68. (lp) **TIME OUT! TIME IN FOR THEM** [-] [ ]
– Time out for time in / She put a hex on you / Bent over you / Waltz of the flees / Black widow spider / We've all agreed to help / Market place / Just one conception / Young woman / The moth. *(UK-iss.+cd.Dec88 on 'Zap!')*

Nov 68. (7") **WALTZ OF THE FLIES. / WE ALL AGREED TO HELP** [-] [ ]

Mar 69. (7") **DARK ARE THE SHADOWS. / CORINA** [-] [ ]

— added on session **JERRY COLE** – guitar, vocals / **JOHN STARK** – drums (tour)

not issued HappyTiger

1970. (lp) **THEM** [-] [ ]
– I keep singing / Lonely weekends / Take a little time / You got me good / Jo Ann / Memphis lady / In the midnight hour / Nobody cares / I am waiting / Just a little.

1970. (7") **I AM WAITING. / LONELY WEEKENDS** [-] [ ]

1970. (7") **MEMPHIS LADY. / NOBODY CARES** [-] [ ]

1971. (lp) **THEM IN REALITY (as "THEM Featuring ALAN HENDERSON")** [-] [ ]
– Gloria / Baby please don't go / Laugh / Let my song through / California man / Lessons of the sea / Rayn / Back to the country / Can you believe.

— HENDERSON + RUFF (last lp sidemen) formed TRUTH OF TRUTHS and with session people J.SCHEFF, L.CARLTON, H.BLAINE, J.GUERRIN, J.COLE & J.OSBOURNE issued 1971 on 'Oak' (d-lp) 'TRUTH OF TRUTHS'.

— **THEM** re-formed originals **HENDERSON, HARRISON & WRIXEN + MEL AUSTIN** – vocals / **BILLY BELL** – drums

Decca not issued

1979. (lp) **SHUT YOUR MOUTH** [ ] [-]
– Hamburg connection / I'm a lover not a worker / Shut your mouth / Needed on the farm / Streetwalking lady / Firewater / Child of the sixties / Slowdown / Losing you / Weekend entertainer / Holy roller / Cincinnati diceman.

— Split 1979 after **JIM ARMSTRONG** – guitar + **BRIAN SCOTT** – keyboards, flute repl. WRIXEN + HARRISON. The latter became BILLY WHO.

– compilations, others, etc. –

Feb 65. Decca; (7"ep) **THEM** [ ] [-]
– Don't start crying now / Philosophy / One two brown eyes / Baby please don't go.

Jan 68. Decca; (7") **GLORIA. / HERE COMES THE NIGHT** [ ] [-]

1970. Decca; (lp)(c) **THE WORLD OF THEM** [ ] [-]

Aug 72. Decca/ US= Parrot; (d-lp)(d-c) **THEM FEATURING VAN MORRISON** [ ] [ ]
– Don't start crying now / Baby please don't go / Here comes the night / One more time / It won't hurt half as much / Mystic eyes / Call my name / Richard Cory / One two brown eyes / All for myself / If you and I could be as two / Don't you know / Friday's child / The story of Them (part 1) / Philosophy / How long baby / I'm gonna dress in black / Bring 'em on in / Little girl / I gave my love a diamond / Gloria / You just can't win / Go on home baby / Don't look back / I like it like that / Bright lights big city / My little baby / Route 66.*(re-iss.Jul82, cd-iss.see below)*

May 76. Decca; (lp)(c) **ROCK ROOTS** [ ] [-]

Oct 83. Old Gold; (7") **HERE COMES THE NIGHT. / ('B'by 'Ten Years After')** [ ] [-]

Mar 85. See For Miles; (lp) **THEM** [ ] [-]

Sep 87. See For Miles; (lp)(c) **THE SINGLES** [ ] [-]

Aug 86. Castle; (d-lp)(d-c) **THE COLLECTION ("THEM featuring VAN MORRISON")** [ ] [-]
(cd-iss.Aug92)

Jan 91. London; (7")(c-s) **BABY PLEASE DON'T GO. / GLORIA** [65] [ ]
(12"+=)(cd-s+=) – Mystic eyes.

THEN JERICO

Formed: London, England . . . 1984 by SHAW etc (see below). After one 45 on Pete Shelley's 'Immaculate' label, they signed to major 'London' records. After a few flops, they finally captured a UK Top 20 spot in 1987 with 'THE MOTIVE (LIVING WITHOUT YOU)'. • **Style:** Anthem-like rock-pop, with hard-edged sound similar to The ALARM or IT BITES. • **Songwriters:** SHAW lyrics / group compositions.

Recommended: THE BIG AREA (*6).

MARK SHAW – vocals / **SCOTT TAYLOR** – rhythm guitar / **KEITH AIREY** – keyboards / **JASPER STAINTHORPE** – bass / **STEVE WREN** – drums

Im-maculate not iss.

Aug 85. (12") **THE BIG SWEEP. / ('A'dub mix) / THE RACK** [ ] [-]

London London

Oct 85. (7") **FAULT. / THE BIG SWEEP (club mix)** [ ] [-]
(12"+=) – ('A'club mix).

Mar 86. (7") **MUSCLE DEEP. / CLANK (COUNTDOWN TO OBLIVION)** [ ] [-]
(12"+=) – Distant homes.

Jan 87. (7") **LET HER FALL. / SEARCHING** [65] [ ]
('A'different version-12"+=) – Blessed days (Tokyo mix).

Mar 87. (lp)(c)(cd) **FIRST . . . THE SOUND OF MUSIC** [ ] [ ]
– Let her fall / Blessed days / Laughter party / Stable boy / The motive (living without your love) / Muscle deep / A quiet place (apathy and sympathy) / Play dead / The hitcher / Prairie rose. *(cd+=)*– Blessed days (the Tokyo mix) / Fault (dub).

Apr 87. (7") **PRAIRIE ROSE. / ELECTRIC** [ ] [ ]
(12"+=) – One life / Fault / ('A'original).
('A'extended-cd-s+=) – Blessed days (version) / Muscledeep.

Jul 87. (7") **THE MOTIVE (LIVING WITHOUT YOU). / THE WORD** [18] [ ]
('A'extended-12"+=) – ('A'-midnight mix).
('A'extended-c-s+=) – Prairie rose (mix) / Let her fall (mix).
(10"+=) – The hitcher (live) / Let her fall (live).

Oct 87. (7")(c-s) **MUSCLE DEEP. / FAULT (mix)** [48] [ ]
(12"+=)(cd-s+=) – ('A'version).

— **ROB DOWNES** – lead guitar repl. AIREY

Jan 89. (7")(c-s) **BIG AREA. / THE BIG SWEEP (dance mix)** [13] [ ]
('A'dance mix-12"+=) – The motive (living without you) (US mix).
(cd-s++=) – Trampled / Underfire.

Feb 89. (lp)(c)(cd) **THE BIG AREA** [4] [ ]
– Big area / What does it take? / You oughta know / Song for the broken hearted / Darkest hour / Reeling / Where you lie / Sugar box / Helpless / Underfire.

Mar 89. (7")(c-s) **WHAT DOES IT TAKE?. / JUNGLE** [33] [ ]
(12"+=)(cd-s+=) – Underfire.

Jul 89. (7")(c-s) **SUGAR BOX. / THE HAPPENING** [22] [ ]
(12"+=)(cd-s+=) – Big area (lost mix) / ('A'blue version).

— early 1990, MARK SHAW left to go solo. In 1991 he was replaced by **MARCUS MYERS** and no more records were forthcoming.

– compilations, etc. –

Jun 93. Old Gold; (cd-s) **BIG AREA / THE MOTIVE / SUGAR BOX** [ ] [-]

Mar 94. Spectrum; (cd)(c) **ELECTRIC** [ ] [-]

THERAPY?

Formed: Belfast, N.Ireland . . . 1989 by ANDY CAIRNS, MICHAEL McKEEGAN and FYFE EWING. In Northern Ireland they issued debut 45 on own 'Multifuckingnational' label, before moving to 'Wiiija' in 1991. After their 'PLEASURE DEATH' mini-lp nearly made UK Top 50 in 1992, they signed to major 'A&M', where they progressed in to Top 40 with album 'NURSE'. • **Style:** Grunge-metal similar to HUSKER DU or BIG BLACK . • **Songwriters:** Mostly CAIRNS, or group penned, ex cept TEENAGE KICKS

(Undertones) / INVISIBLE SUN (Police) / WITH OR WITHOUT YOU (U2) / BREAKING THE LAW (Judas Priest) / C.C.RIDER (Elvis Presley) / ISOLATION (Joy Division) / TATTY SEASIDE TOWN (Membranes) / NICE'N'SLEAZY (Stranglers) / REUTERS (Wire). • **Trivia:** In 1994 they featured w/ OZZY OSBORNE on 'IRON MAN' for BLACK SABBATH tribute album.

Recommended: NURSE (*8) / TROUBLEGUM (*8) / BABYTEETH (*7) / PLEASURE DEATH (*7)..

ANDY CAIRNS – vocals, guitar / **MICHAEL McKEEGAN** – bass / **FYFE EWING** – drums

Multi... not issued

Aug 90. (7") **MEAT ABSTRACT. / PUNISHMENT KISS** [ ] [-]

Wiiija not issued

Jul 91. (cd)(c)(m-lp) **BABYTEETH** [ ] [-]
– Meat abstract / Skyward / Punishment kiss / Animal bones / Loser cop / Innocent X / Dancin' with Manson. *(re-iss.Mar93 & Jun95 on 'Southern')*

Jan 92. (cd)(c)(m-lp) **PLEASURE DEATH** [52] [-]
– Skinning pit / Fantasy bag / Shitkicker / Prison breaker / D.L.C. / Potato junkie. *(re-iss.Sep92 on 'A&M') (re-iss.Mar93 & Jun95 on 'Southern')*

A & M A & M

Oct 92. (7") **TEETHGRINDER. / SUMMER OF HATE** [30] [ ]
(12"+=) – ('A'dub) / ('A'unsane mix).
(12"+=)(cd-s+=) – Human mechanism / Sky high McKay.

Nov 92. (cd)(c)(lp) **NURSE** [38] [ ]
– Nausea / Teethgrinder / Disgracelands / Accelerator / Neck freak / Perversonality / Gone / Zipless / Deep skin / Hypermania.

Mar 93. (7"pink)(c-s) **SHORTSHARPSHOCK EP** [9] [ ]
– Screamager / Auto surgery.
(12"+=)(cd-s+=) – Totally random man / Accelerate.

—— In May93, they appeared on the B-side of PEACE TOGETHER single 'BE STILL', covered The Police's 'INVISIBLE SUN' on 'Island' records.

Jun 93. (7"white-ep)(12"ep)(cd-ep) **FACE THE STRANGE EP** [18] [ ]
– Turn / Speedball / Bloody blue / Neckfreak (re-recording).

Aug 93. (7")(c-s)(7"colrd) **OPAL MANTRA. / ('A'live)** [13] [ ]
(cd-s+=) – Innocent X / Potato junkie / Nausea.

Sep 93. (cd)(c) **HATS OFF TO THE INSANE** (originally a US compilation) [ ] [ ]
– Screamager / Auto Surgery / Totally Random Man / Turn / Speedball / Opal Mantra

Jan 94. (7"ep)(c-ep)(cd-ep) **NOWHERE / PANTAPON ROSE. / BREAKING THE LAW / C.C.RIDER** [18] [ ]
(cd-s) – ('A'side) / ('A'-2 Andy Weatherall mixes).

Feb 94. (cd)(c)(lp)(green-lp) **TROUBLEGUM** [5] [ ]
– Knives / Screamager / Hellbelly / Stop it you're killing me / Nowhere / Die laughing / Unbeliever / Trigger inside / Lunacy booth / Isolation / Turn / Femtex / Unrequited / Brainsaw.

—— above album guests **PAGE HAMILTON** – lead guitar (of HELMET) / **MARTIN McCARRICK** – cello (of THIS MORTAL COIL) / **LESLEY RANKINE + EILEEN ROSE** – vocals

Feb 94. (7"yellow-ep)(c-ep)(cd-ep) **TRIGGER INSIDE / NICE'N'SLEAZY. / REUTERS / TATTY SEASIDE TOWN** [22] [ ]
(12") – ('A'side) / ('A'mixes) / Nowhere (Sabres of Paradise mix).

May 94. (7"red-ep)(c-ep)(cd-ep) **DIE LAUGHING / STOP IT YOU'RE KILLING ME (live). / TRIGGER INSIDE (live) / EVIL ELVIS (the lost demo)** [29] [ ]

—— In May95, they hit No.53 UK with ORBITAL's 'INNOCENT X', with same group covering their 'Belfast'.

May 95. (7"orange)(c-s)(cd-s) **STORIES. / STORIES (cello version) / ISOLATION (Consolidated synth mix)** [14] [ ]

Jun 95. (cd)(c)(red-lp) **INFERNAL LOVE** [9] [ ]
– Epilepsy / Stories / A moment of clarity / Jude the obscene / Bowels of love / Misery / Bad mother / Me vs you / Loose / Diane / 30 seconds.

Jul 95. (c-s)(cd-s) **LOOSE / OUR LOVE MUST DIE / NICE GUYS / LOOSE (Photek remix)** [25] [ ]
(cd-s) – ('A'side) / Die laughing (live) / Nowhere (live) / Unbeliever (live).
(7"green)(one-sided-12") – ('A'side) / ('A'-Photek remix).

Nov 95. (7"red-ep)(c-ep)(cd-ep) **DIANE / JUDE THE OBSCENE (acoustic) / LOOSE (acoustic) / 30 SECONDS (acoustic)** [26] [ ]
(cd-ep) – ('A'side) / Misery (acoustic) / Die laughing (acoustic) / Screamager (acoustic).

– compilations, etc. –

Mar 92. 1/4 Stick; (cd)(c)(lp) **CAUCASIAN PSYCHOSIS** [ ] [ ]

THESE ANIMAL MEN

Formed: Brighton, England . . . 1993 by (see below). With much hype they cracked the British charts a year later with mini-lp 'TOO SUSSED?'. Just prior to this they landed themselves into a little hot water, when they condoned the use of amphetamines on debut 45 'SPEEED KING'. • **Style:** Energy-fuelled angst designer punks, resurrecting a revival breed tagged "New Wave Of The New Wave' alongside S*M*A*S*H. • **Songwriters:** Group penned. • **Trivia:** Also featured on the 6-band 'Fierce Panda' punk compilation EP 'Shaggin' In The Streets'.

Recommended: (COME ON, JOIN) THE HIGH SOCIETY (*8)

BOAG – vocals / **JULIAN HOOLIGAN (HEWINGS)** – guitar / **PATRICK (HUSSEY)** – bass / **STEVE MURRAY** – drums

Les Disques De Popcor not issued

Dec 93. (c-ep) **WHEELERS, DEALERS AND CHRISTINE KEELERS** [ ] [-]
– (5 tracks; see TOO SUSSED? m-lp) / (4 tracks by S*M*A*S*H)

Hi-Rise not issued

Mar 94. (7") **SPEEED KING. / JOBS FOR THE BOYS** [ ] [-]

Apr 94. (7") **YOU'RE NOT MY BABYLON. / WHO'S THE DADDY NOW?** [ ] [ ]

Jun 94. (cd)(c)(m-lp) **TOO SUSSED?** [39] [-]
– Too sussed? (live) / Speeed king / Jobs for the boys / Who's the daddy now? / You're not my Babylon.

Sep 94. (7"pic-d-ep)(12"ep)(c-ep)(cd-ep) **THIS IS THE SOUND OF YOUTH. / SAIL AROUND THE WORLD / HOOLIGAN'S PROGRESS** [72] [ ]

Sep 94. (cd)(c)(lp) **(COME ON, JOIN) THE HIGH SOCIETY** [62] [ ]
– Sharp kid / Empire building / Ambulance / This year's model / You're always right / Flawed is beautiful / This is the sound of youth / Sitting tenant / Too sussed? / (Come on, join) The high society / We are living / High society (return).

Mar 95. (m-cd)(m-c)(m-lp) **TAXI FOR THESE ANIMAL MEN** [64] [ ]
– You're always right / Nowhere faces / My human remains / False identification / Wait for it.

THE THE

Formed: Swadlincote, Derbyshire, England . . . 1979 as studio project by MATT JOHNSON, who also was part of The GADGETS at the same time. MATT signed to IVO's record label '4 a.d.' in 1980, and unleashed poignant 45 'CONTROVERSIAL SUBJECT'. After a solo project album in 1981, THE THE released another single 'COLD SPELL AHEAD' for new label 'Some Bizarre', which eventually obtained major backing from 'Epic'. The long awaited THE THE debut album in 1983, was given deserved thumbs up by critics and public alike, and soon speared into the UK Top 30. Three years later, a second album 'INFECTED' featuring the hit single 'HEARTLAND', was accompanied by a UK Channel 4 premiered hour-long video. **Style & Songwriters:** MATT was described as 'The Howard Hughes of Rock', and contributed classic but controversial alternative rock music with lyrics that dealt with subjects AIDS, the bomb, prostitution, etc. In 1989, he made THE THE into a real band who also toured and contributed to songs. In 1995, he released a collection of HANK WILLIAMS' songs on album 'HANKY PANKY'. • **Trivia:** Solo artists to be; NENEH CHERRY contributed vox to 1986 track 'SLOW TRAIN TO DAWN' and SINEAD O'CONNOR sang on 1989 track 'KINGDOM OF RAIN'. MATT is now residing in Sherman Oaks, California.

Recommended: SOUL MINING (*8) / INFECTED (*9) / MIND BOMB (*9) / MATT JOHNSON:- BURNING BLUE SOUL (*7) / DUSK (*7).

MATT JOHNSON (b.1961, Essex, England . . . raised London) – vocals, guitar, etc. (also of The GADGETS) / **KEITH LAWS** – synthesizers, drum machine / **PETER 'Triash' ASHWORTH** – drums / **TOM JOHNSTON** – bass

4 a.d. not issued

Jul 80. (7") **CONTROVERSIAL SUBJECT. / BLACK AND WHITE** [ ] [-]

—— next with guests **GILBERT & LEWIS** (of WIRE) on 2nd last track

Aug 81. (lp) **BURNING BLUE SOUL ("MATT JOHNSON" solo)** [ ] [-]
– Red cinders in the sand / Song without an ending / Time again for the golden sunset / Icing up / Like a Sun risin' thru my garden / Out of control / Bugle boy / Delirious / The river flows east in Spring / Another boy drowning. *(re-iss.Sep83, c-iss.Jun84) (re-iss.cd+c Jun93 now credited to THE THE, hit No.65)*

Some Bizzare not issued

Sep 81. (7") **COLD SPELL AHEAD. / HOT ICE** [ ] [-]
(re-iss+/12"pic-d/cd-s. Aug 92)

—— **MATT JOHNSON** was now virtually **THE THE,** although he was augmented by others on tour.

Some Bizzare Sire

Oct 82. (7") **UNCERTAIN SMILE. / THREE ORANGE KISSES FROM KAZAN** [68] [-]
(12"+=)(12"yellow+=) – Waiting for the upturn. (US; b-side)

Feb 83. (7") **PERFECT. / THE NATURE OF VIRTUE** [ ] [-]
(12"+=) – The nature of virtue II.

Some Bizarre Epic

Sep 83. (7") **THIS IS THE DAY. / MENTAL HEALING PROCESS** [71] [ ]
(d7"+=) – Leap into the wind / Absolute liberation.
(12") – ('A'side) / I've been waiting for tomorrow (all of my life).

—— added live **ZEKE MANYIKA** – drums (of ORANGE JUICE) / **JIM THIRLWELL / JOOLS HOLLAND** – piano (ex-SQUEEZE) / **THOMAS LEER** – synthesizers, keyboards

Oct 83. (lp)(c) **SOUL MINING** [27] [ ]
– I've been waiting for tomorrow (all of my life) / This is the day / The sinking feeling / Uncertain smile / The twilight hour / Soul mining / Giant. *(free-12"ep.w.a.)* **PERFECT. / SOUP OF MIXED EMOTIONS / FRUIT OF THE HEART** (c+=) – Perfect / Three orange kisses from Kazan / Nature of virtue / Fruit of the heart / Soup of mixed emotions / Waiting for the upturn. *(cd-iss.Jun87.+= – Perfect)(re-iss.+cd.Mar90 on 'Epic')*

Nov 83. (7") **UNCERTAIN SMILE. / DUMB AS DEATH'S HEAD** [ ] [ ]
(12") – ('A'side) / Soul mining.

—— Guests for next album **ROLI MOSSIMAN / NENEH CHERRY / DAVID PALMER / STEVE HOGARTH / ANNA DOMINO / JAMIE TALBOT / WAYNE LIVESEY / ZEKE MANYIKA** / etc.

May 86. (12"m) **SWEET BIRD OF TRUTH. / HARBOUR LIGHTS / SLEEPING JUICE** [ ] [ ]

Jul 86. (7") **HEARTLAND. / BORN IN THE NEW S.A.** [29] [ ]
(12"+=) – Flesh and bones.
(d12"++=) – Perfect / Fruit of the heart.

(c-s++=) – Harbour lights / Sweet bird of truth.
(12"+=) – Sweet bird of truth.
Oct 86. (7") **INFECTED. / DISTURBED** [48] [ ]
(12"+=) – ('A'energy mix).
(d12"++=) – Soul mining (remix) / The sinking feeling.
(c-s+=) – ('A'skull crusher mix) repl. ('A'energy mix)
Nov 86. (lp)(c)(cd) **INFECTED** [14] [89]
– Infected / Out of the blue (into the fire) / Heartland / Angels of deception / Sweet bird of truth / Slow train to dawn / Twilight of a champion / The mercy beat. *(cd+=) – ('A'-INFECTED singles remixed).*
Jan 87. (7") **SLOW TRAIN TO DAWN. / HARBOUR LIGHTS** [64] [ ]
(12"+=) – The nature of virtue.
May 87. (7") **SWEET BIRD OF TRUTH. / SLEEPING JUICE** [55] [ ]
(12"+=) – Harbour lights.
(c-s++=)(cd-s++=) – Soul mining (12"mix).

— **THE THE** were again a group when **MATT** retained past sessioner **DAVID PALMER** – drums (ex-ABC) / and recruited **JOHNNY MARR** – guitar (ex-SMITHS) / **JAMES ELLER** – bass (ex-JULIAN COPE, etc.)

Epic Epic

Feb 89. (7") **THE BEAT(EN) GENERATION. / ANGEL** [18] [ ]
(12"+=)(cd-s+=)(3"cd-s+=) – Soul mining (mix).
(12"+=)(pic-cd+=) – ('A'-Palmer mix) / ('A'campfire mix).
May 89. (lp)(c)(cd) **MIND BOMB** [4] [ ]
– Good morning beautiful / Armageddon days are here (again) / The violence of truth / Kingdom of rain / The beat(en) generation / August & September / Gravitate to me / Beyond love.
Jul 89. (7")(c-s) **GRAVITATE TO ME. / THE VIOLENCE OF TRUTH** [63] [ ]
(12"+=)(cd-s+=) – I've been waiting for tomorrow (all of my life).
(12"etched-one-side) – ('A'dub). / I've been waiting for tomorrow.
Sep 89. (7")(c-s) **ARMAGEDDON DAYS ARE HERE (AGAIN). / ('A'orchestral)** [70] [ ]
(12"+=) – The nature of virtue / Perfect.
(cd-s+=) – Perfect / Mental healing process.
(10"ep) **THE THE VS.THE WORLD EP** – (all 4 tracks no 'A'orchestral)
(12"etched-one-side) – ('A'side). / Perfect.
Feb 91. (12")(c-s) **JEALOUS OF YOUTH. / ANOTHER BOY DROWNING (live)** [54] [ ]
(cd-s+=) **SHADES OF YOUTH EP** – Solitude / Dolphins.

— added **D.C. COLLARD** – instruments

Jan 93. (7"marble) **DOGS OF LUST. / THE VIOLENCE OF TRUTH** [25] [ ]
(12"pic-d+=)(cd-s+=) – Infected (live).
(cd-s) – ('A'side) / Jealous of youth (live) / Beyond love (live) / Armageddon days are here (again) (D.N.A. remix).
Jan 93. (cd)(c)(lp) **DUSK** [2] [ ]
– True happiness this way lies / Love is stronger than death / Dogs of lust / This is the night / Slow emotion replay / Helpline operator / Sodium light baby / Lung shadows / Bluer than midnight / Lonely planet.
Apr 93. (12"red-ep)(cd-ep) **SLOW MOTION REPLAY. / DOGS OF LUST (3 mixes by Jim Thirlwell)** [35] [ ]
(cd-ep) – ('A'side) / Scenes from Active Twilight (parts I-V).
Jun 93. (12"ep)(cd-ep) **LOVE IS STRONGER THAN DEATH. / THE SINKING FEELING (live) / THE MERCY BEAT (live) / ARMAGEDDON DAYS ARE HERE (AGAIN) (live)** [39] [ ]
(cd-ep) – ('A'side) / Infected / Soul mining / Armageddon days are . . .
Jan 94. (12"ep)(c-ep)(cd-ep) **DIS-INFECTED EP** [17] [ ]
– This was the day / Dis-infected / Helpline operator (sick boy mix) / Dogs of lust (germicide mix).
Jan 95. (10"ep)(c-ep)(cd-ep) **I SAW THE LIGHT / I'M FREE AT LAST. / SOMEDAY YOU'll CALL MY NAME / THERE'S NO ROOM IN MY HEART FOR THE BLUES** [31] [ ]
Feb 95. (cd)(c)(10"lp) **HANKY PANKY** [28] [ ]
– Honky tonkin' / Six more miles / My heart would know / If you'll be a baby to me / I'm a long gone daddy / Weary blues from waitin' / I saw the light / Your cheatin' heart / I can't get you off of my mind / There's a tear in my beer / I can't escape from you.

– compilations, others, etc. –

Dec 88. Epic; (d-cd) **INFECTED / SOUL MINING** [ ] [-]

GADGETS

MATT JOHNSON / COLIN TUCKER – synthesizers / **JOHN HYDE** – synthesizers (both ex-PLAIN CHARACTERS)

Final Solution not issued

1980. (lp) **GADGETREE** [ ] [-]
– Kyleaking / Making cars / Narpath / UFO import No.1 / Slippery / Singing in the rain / Only one me / Shouting 'Nispers' / There over there / Termite mound / Sleep / Devil's dyke / Six mile bottom / UFO import No.2 / Autumn 80 / Duplicate / Bog track / Thin line. *(re-iss.+cd Jun89)*

— They continued as a studio set-up with MATT's help.

1981. (lp) **LOVE, CURIOSITY, FRECKLES & DOUBT** [ ] [-]
– Bodorgan / Gadget speak / Checking to make sure / Aeron / Leave it to Charlie / Prayers / Happy endido / Quatt / Pictures of you / Aaft / Railway line through blubber houses / She's queen of toyland / Sex / It wasn't that way at all / The death and resurrection of Jennifer Gloom / Bill posters will be prosecuted. *(re-iss.+cd Jun89)*

Glass not issued

1982. (lp) **THE BLUE ALBUM** [ ] [-]
– We had no way of knowing / Space in my heart / Bodies without heads / The boyfriend / Uneasy listening / Juice of love / Discuss the sofa / Long empty train / Bite the sawdust / Broken fall. *(re-iss.+cd Jun89)*

— above feat. **PETER ASHWORTH** dubbed in instead of MATT. (below withdrawn)

Jun 83. (7")(12") **WE HAD NO WAY OF KNOWING. / ACID BATH** [ ] [-]

THEY MIGHT BE GIANTS

Formed: based Brooklyn, New York, USA . . . 1985 by former Bostonians FLANSBURGH and LINNELL. In 1987, UK label 'Rough Trade', discovered earlier made eponymous album on 'Bar None' records. It soon became a favourite in the indie charts, which led to a contract with UK label 'O. L. Indian', bringing them to tour in Britain. In the early 90's on 'Elektra', they crashed into the UK Top 10 with 'BIRDHOUSE IN YOUR SOUL'. • **Style:** Fun and hard to categorise duo, whose folky punk ditties were not unlike DEVO. • **Songwriters:** Duo penned, except ONE HERE PARADE (Phil Ochs) / 25 O'CLOCK (Dukes Of Stratospheare). • **Trivia:** Took group name from a 1971 film starring George C.Scott.

Recommended: THEY MIGHT BE GIANTS (*7).

JOHN FLANSBURGH – vocals, guitar, bass drum / **JOHN LIDDELL** – vocals, accordion, keyboards

Rough Trade Bar None

Oct 87. (lp) **THEY MIGHT BE GIANTS** [ ] [ ]
– Everything right is wrong again / Put your hand inside the puppet head / Number three / Don't let's start / Hide away folk family / 32 footsteps / Toddler hiway / Rabid child / Nothing's gonna change my clothes / (She was a) Hotel detective / She's an angel / Youth culture killed my dog / Boat of car / Chess piece face / Absolutely Bill's mood / I hope that I get old before I die / Alienation's for the rich / The day / Rhythm section want ad. *(cd-iss.Mar89) (re-iss.+c+cd.Nov90 on 'Elektra')*
Jun 88. (7") **DON'T LET'S START. / WE'RE THE REPLACEMENTS** [ ] [ ]
(12"+=) – When it rains it snows / The fabulous polka.

O. L. Indian Bar/None

Jan 89. (12"ep) **THEY'LL NEED A CRANE / I'VE GOT A MATCH. / KISS ME, SON OF GOD / I'LL SINK MANHATTAN** [ ] [ ]
Feb 89. (lp)(c)(cd) **LINCOLN** [ ] [89] Dec 88
– The world's address / I've got a match / Santa's beard / You'll miss me / They'll need a crane / Shoehorn with teeth / Stand on your head / Snowball in Hell / Kiss me, son of God / Ana Ng / Cowtown / Lie still, little bottle / Purple toupee / Cage & aquarium / Where your eyes don't go / Piece of dirt / Pencil rain. *(re-iss Jun91 on 'Elektra')*
Mar 89. (12"ep) **ANA NG / NIGHTGOWN OF THE SULLEN MOON. / IT'S NOT MY BIRTHDAY / LIE STILL, LITTLE BOTTLE** [ ] [ ]

Elektra Elektra

Feb 90. (7")(c-s) **BIRDHOUSE IN YOUR SOUL. / HOT CHA** [6] [ ]
(12"+=)(cd-s+=) – Hearing aid / Ant.
Mar 90. (cd)(c)(lp) **FLOOD** [14] [75] Feb 90
– Theme from Flood / Birdhouse in your soul / Lucky ball and chain / Istanbul (not Constantinople) / Dead / Your racist friend / Particle man / Twisting / We want a rock / Someone keeps moving my chair / Hearing aid / Minimum wage / Letterbox / Whistling in the dark / Hot cha / Women & men / Sapphire bullets of pure love / They might be giants / Road movie to Berlin.
May 90. (7")(c-s) **ISTANBUL (NOT CONSTANTINOPLE). / JAMES K.POLK** [61] [ ]
(12"+=)/ /(cd-s++=) – Stormy punkness./ / ('A'-Brownsville mix).
Sep 90. (7")(c-s) **DON'T LET'S START (remix). / LETTERBOX** [ ] [ ]
(12"+=)(cd-s+=) – Your racist friend (remix).
May 91. (7")(c-s) **ANA NG. / THEY'LL NEED A CRANE** [ ] [ ]
(12"+=)(cd-s+=) – (She was a) Hotel detective / Don't let's start.

W.E.A. Elektra

Jan 92. (7")(c-s) **THE STATUE GOT ME HIGH. / SHE'S ACTUAL SIZE** [ ] [ ]
(12")(cd-s) – ('A'side) / I'm def / Which describes how you're feeling (1985 demos).
Mar 92. (cd)(c)(lp) **APOLLO 18** [ ] [99]
– Dig my grave / I palindrome I / She's actual size / My evil twin / Mammal / The statue got me high / Spider / The guitar (the lion sleeps tonight) / Dinner bell / Narrow your eyes / Hall of heads / Which desribes how you're feeling / See the constellation / If I wasn't shy / Turn around / Hypnotist of ladies / Fingertips / Space suit.
Apr 92. (7")(c-s) **THE GUITAR (THE LION SLEEPS TONIGHT). / ('A'extended)** [ ] [ ]
(12"+=) – Larger than life (Joshua Fried's remake of 'She's Actual Size') / ('A'outer planet mix) / ('A'other outer planet mix).
(cd-s+=) – Cabbage town / Siftin'.

— The 2 JOHNS added 4 new members

Sep 94. (cd)(c) **JOHN HENRY** [ ] [59]
– Sublimal / Snail shell / Sleeping in the flowers / Unrelated thing / AKA driver / I should be allowed to think / Extra saviour faire / Why must I be sad? / Spy / O do not forsake me / No one knows my plan / Dirt bike / Destination Moon / A self called nowhere / Meet James Ensor / Thermostat / Window / Out of jail / Stomp box / The end of the tour.
Oct 94. (cd-ep) **BACK TO SKULL EP** [ ] [ ]
– Snail skull / ('A'mixes) / She was a hotel detective / Mrs.Train.

– compilations, etc. –

Nov 89. Rough Trade; (cd)(lp) **DON'T LET'S START** [ ] [-]

THIN LIZZY

Formed: Dublin, Ireland . . . 1969 by PHIL LYNOTT and DOWNEY. After suggestion of managers Ted Carroll and Brian Tuite, they moved to London late 1970 already signed for 'Decca'. With two albums under their belt and a strong live reputation, they surprisingly had a UK Top 10 hit with 'WHISKY IN THE JAR'. With change of UK label to 'Vertigo' and addition of 2nd guitarist in mid'74, they still found a follow-up unforthcoming. That is until 1976, when 'THE BOYS ARE BACK IN TOWN' cracked UK Top 10. This was a cut from the highly fruitful and acclaimed initial chart album 'JAILBREAK'. Success continued throughout the 70's and early 80's, but mainly massive in the UK. • **Style:** Initially branched out with folk-ballad type songs. Mulatto PHIL LYNOTT moved band into superior harder-laden sounds with introduction of guitarists BRIAN ROBERTSON and SCOTT GORHAM in 1974. • **Songwriters:** PHIL LYNOTT and co. except trad. arrangement WHISKEY IN THE JAR, and covers of ROSALIE (Bob Seger) / I'M STILL IN LOVE WITH YOU (Frankie Miller) / etc. • **Trivia:** On 13th Feb'80, PHIL married Caroline, daughter of UK celebrity Leslie Crowther.

Recommended: LIVE AND DANGEROUS (*9) / DEDICATION (*8)

PHIL LYNOTT (b.20 Aug'51, from Brazillian + Irish parents. Raised from 3 by granny in Crumlin, Dublin) – vocals, bass (ex-ORPHANAGE, ex-SKID ROW brief) / **ERIC BELL** (b. 3 Sep'47, Belfast, N.Ireland) – guitar, vocals (ex-DREAMS) / **BRIAN DOWNEY** (b.27 Jan'51) – drums (ex-ORPHANAGE) / **ERIC WRIXON** – keyboards

Parlophone IRELAND / not issued

1970. (7") **THE FARMER. / I NEED YOU** [-] [-]

— now trio (without WRIXON)

Decca / London

Apr 71. (lp) **THIN LIZZY** [ ] [-]
– The friendly ranger at Clontarf Castle / Honesty is no excuse / Diddy Levine ray-gun / Look what the wind blew in / Eire / Return of the farmer's son / Clifton Grange Hotel / Saga of the ageing orphan / Remembering. *(cd-iss.Jan89 on 'London')*

Aug 71. (7"ep) **NEW DAY** [ ] [-]
– Things ain't working out down on the farm / Remembering pt.II / Old Moon madness / Dublin.

Mar 72. (lp) **SHADES OF A BLUE ORPHANAGE** [ ] [-]
– The rise and dear demise of the funky nomadic tribes / Buffalo girl / I don't want to forget how to jive / Sarah / Brought down / Baby face / Chatting today / Call the police / Shades of a blue orphanage. *(re-iss.c Jul93 on 'Deram')*

Nov 72. (7") **WHISKEY IN THE JAR. / BLACK BOYS IN THE CORNER** [6] [ ]

May 73. (7") **RANDOLPH'S TANGO. / BROKEN DREAMS** [ ] [ ]

Sep 73. (lp)(c) **VAGABONDS OF THE WESTERN WORLD** [ ] [ ]
– Little girl in bloom / Hero and the madman / The rocker / Gonna creep up on you / Slow blues / Mama nature said / Vagabonds of the western world / A song for while I'm away. *(re-iss.+cd.1991 on 'Deram', +=)* – Whiskey in the jar.

Nov 73. (7") **THE ROCKER. / HERE I GO AGAIN** [ ] [-]

— **GARY MOORE** – guitar, vocals (ex-SKID ROW) repl. BELL (later MAINSQUEEZE)

Apr 74. (7") **LITTLE DARLIN'. / BUFFALO GIRL** [ ] [ ]

— (on tour May74) **JOHN CANN** – guitar (ex-ATOMIC ROOSTER, ex-BULLITT) / **+ ANDY GEE** – guitar (ex-ELLIS) both repl. GARY MOORE who joined COLOSSEUM II These temp. guitarists were deposed by **SCOTT GORHAM + BRIAN ROBERTSON**

Vertigo / Vertigo

Oct 74. (7") **PHILOMENA. / SHA LA LA** [ ] [ ]

Nov 74. (lp)(c) **NIGHTLIFE** [ ] [ ]
– She knows / Night life / It's only money / Still in love with you / Frankie Carroll / Showdown / Banshee / Philomena / Sha-la-la / Dear heart. *(re-iss.Aug83, cd-iss. Jun89)*

Jan 75. (7") **SHOWDOWN. / NIGHT LIFE** [-] [ ]

Jun 75. (7") **ROSALIE. / HALF CASTE** [ ] [-]

Aug 75. (lp)(c) **FIGHTING** [60] [ ]
– Rosalie / For those who love to die / Suicide / Wild one / Fighting my way back / King's vengeance / Spirit slips away / Silver dollar / Freedom song / Ballad of a hard man. *(re-iss.Aug83)*

Oct 75. (7") **WILD ONE. / FOR THOSE WHO LOVE TO DIE** [ ] [-]

Nov 75. (7") **WILD ONE. / FREEDOM SONG** [-] [ ]

Vertigo / Mercury

Mar 76. (lp)(c) **JAILBREAK** [10] [18]
– Jailbreak / Angel from the coast / Running back / Romeo and the lonely girl / Warriors / The boys are back in town / Fight or fall / Cowboy song / Emerald. *(re-iss.Oct83, cd-iss.Jun89)*

Apr 76. (7") **THE BOYS ARE BACK IN TOWN. / EMERALD** [8] [-]

Apr 76. (7") **THE BOYS ARE BACK IN TOWN / JAILBREAK** [-] [12]

Jul 76. (7") **JAILBREAK. / RUNNING BACK** [31] [-]

Sep 76. (7") **THE COWBOY SONG. / ANGEL FROM THE COAST** [-] [77]

Oct 76. (lp)(c) **JOHNNY THE FOX** [11] [52]
– Johnny / Rocky / Borderline / Don't believe a word / Fool's gold / Johnny the fox meets Jimmy the weed / Old flame / Massacre / Sweet Marie / Boogie woogie dance. *(re-iss.May83, cd-iss.May90)*

Nov 76. (7") **ROCKY. / HALF-CASTE** [-] [ ]

Jan 77. (7") **DON'T BELIEVE A WORD. / OLD FLAME** [12] [ ]

Jan 77. (7") **JOHNNY THE FOX MEETS JIMMY THE WEED. / OLD FLAME** [-] [ ]

— BRIAN ROBERTSON was injured and deputy GARY MOORE (for 6 mths.tour only)

Aug 77. (7") **DANCING IN THE MOONLIGHT. / BAD REPUTATION** [14] [ ]

Sep 77. (lp)(c) **BAD REPUTATION** [4] [39]
– Soldier of fortune / Bad reputation / Opium trail / Southbound / Dancing in the moonlight / Killer without a cause / Downtown sundown / That woman's gonna break your heart / Dear Lord. *(re-iss.May83, cd-iss.Apr90)*

Apr 78. (7") **ROSALIE; COWBOY'S SONG (live medley). / ME AND THE BOYS** [20] [ ]

Vertigo / Warners

Jun 78. (d-lp)(d-c) **LIVE AND DANGEROUS (live)** [2] [84]
– Jailbreak / Emerald / Southbound / The boys are back in town / Dancing in the moonlight / Massacre / Still in love with you / (me and the boys were wonderin' what you and the girls) / Johnny the fox meets Jimmy the weed / The cowboy song / Don't believe a word / Warriors / Are you ready / Suicide / Sha-la-la / Baby drives me crazy / The rocker / Rosalie – Cowgirl's song . *(re-iss.Nov84)*

— In Autumn'78 tour, DOWNEY was deputised by MARK NAUSEEF. **GARY MOORE** – guitar, vocals returned to repl. ROBERTSON who formed WILD HORSES

Feb 79. (7") **WAITING FOR AN ALIBI. / WITH LOVE** [9] [ ]

Apr 79. (lp)(c) **BLACK ROSE (A ROCK LEGEND)** [2] [81]
– Do anything you want to / Toughest street in town / S & M / Waiting for an alibi / Got to give it up / Get out of here / With love / A roisin dubh (Black rose) A rock legend: Shenandoah – Will you go lassie go – Danny boy – The mason's apron. *(re-iss.Sep86, cd-iss.Jun89)*

— Apr'79, LYNOTT's vox feat. on GARY MOORE's Top10 hit 'Parisienne Walkways'. The following year LYNOTT also combined solo career w / LIZZY's (see further on)

Jun 79. (7") **DO ANYTHING YOU WANT TO. / JUST THE TWO OF US** [14] [ ]

Sep 79. (7") **SARAH. / GOT TO GIVE IT UP** [24] [-]

Sep 79. (7") **WITH LOVE. / GO TO GIVE IT UP** [-] [ ]

— (for 2 months-late'79) **MIDGE URE** – guitar (ex-SLIK, ex-RICH KIDS) repl. GARY MOORE who went solo. URE joined ULTRAVOX when repl. by **SNOWY WHITE**

May 80. (7") **CHINATOWN. / SUGAR BLUES** [1] [-]

Sep 80. (d7") **KILLER ON THE LOOSE. / DON'T PLAY AROUND/ / GOT TO GIVE IT UP (live). / CHINATOWN (live)** [10] [ ]

Oct 80. (lp)(c) **CHINATOWN** [7] [ ]
– We will be strong / Chinatown / Sweetheart / Sugar blues / Killer on the loose / Having a good time / Genocide (the killing of buffalo) / Didn't I / Hey you. *(re-is.Sep86, cd-iss.Jun89)*

Oct 80. (7") **KILLER ON THE LOOSE. / SUGAR BLUES** [-] [ ]

Nov 80. (7") **A MERRY JINGLE. (as The "GREEDIES") / A MERRY JANGLE** [28] [-]

Above also featured STEVE JONES + PAUL COOK (ex-SEX PISTOLS).

Feb 81. (7") **WE WILL BE STRONG. / SWEETHEART** [-] [ ]

Apr 81. (7"ep) **LIVE KILLERS (live)** [19] [ ]
– Are you ready / Bad reputation / Dear Miss lonely heart.
(12"ep+=) – Opium trail.

Apr 81. (lp)(c) **ADVENTURES OF THIN LIZZY** (compilation) [6] [ ]

Jul 81. (7") **TROUBLE BOYS. / MEMORY PAIN** [53] [ ]

Nov 81. (lp)(c) **RENEGADE** [38] [ ]
– Angel of death / Renegade / The pressure will blow / Leave this town / Hollywood (down on your luck) / No one told him / It's getting dangerous / Hollywood (down on your luck) / Fats / Mexican blood / It's getting dangerous. *(cd-iss.Jun90)*

Feb 82. (7")(7"pic-d) **HOLLYWOOD (DOWN ON YOUR LUCK). / THE PRESSURE WILL BLOW** [53] [ ]
(10"-one-sided) – ('A'side only)

— **LYNOTT + DOWNEY** recruited new members **JOHN SYKES** – guitar (ex-TYGERS OF PAN TANG) repl. GORHAM **DARREN WHARTON** – keyboards repl. SNOWY WHITE to solo + re-joined PINK FLOYD

Feb 83. (d7")(12") **COLD SWEAT. / BAD HABITS / DON'T BELIEVE A WORD (live). / ANGEL OF DEATH (live)** [27] [ ]

Mar 83. (lp)(c) **THUNDER AND LIGHTNING** [4] [ ]
– Thunder and lightning / This is the one / The sun goes down / The holy war / Cold sweat / Someday she is going to hit back / Baby please don't go / Bad habits / Heart attack. *(cd-iss.Jun89)*

Apr 83. (7")(12") **THUNDER AND LIGHTNING. / STILL IN LOVE WITH YOU (live)** [39] [ ]

Jul 83. (7") **THE SUN GOES DOWN. / BABY PLEASE DON'T GO** [52] [ ]
(12"+=) – ('A'extended).

Nov 83. (d-lp)(d-c) **LIFE (live)** [29] [ ]
– Thunder and lightning / Waiting for an alibi / Jailbreak / Baby please don't go / The holy war / Renegade / Hollywood (down on your luck) / Got to give it up / Angel of death / Are you ready / The boys are back in town / Cold sweat / Don't believe a word / Killer on the loose / The sun goes down / Emerald / Black rose / Still in love with you / The rocker. *(4th side featured past members).*

— Had already concluded proceedings. LYNOTT and DOWNEY formed short-lived GRAND SLAM. Tragically, PHIL LYNOTT died on 4 Jan'86 of heart failure.

– compilations, others –

Aug 76. Decca; (lp)(c) **REMEMBERING – PART ONE** [ ] [-]

Jan 78. Decca; (7"m) **WHISKEY IN THE JAR. / SITAMOIA / VAGABOND OF THE WESTERN WORLD** [ ] [-]

Aug 79. Decca; (7"m) **THINGS AIN'T WORKING OUT DOWN ON THE FARM. / THE ROCKER / LITTLE DARLIN'** [ ] [-]

Sep 79. Decca; (lp)(c) **THE CONTINUING SAGA OF THE AGEING ORPHANS** [ ] [-]

Dec 81. Decca; (lp)(c) **ROCKERS** [ ] [-]

Mar 83. Vertigo; (cd) **LIZZY KILLERS** [ ] [-]

Jan 91. Vertigo/ US= Mercury; (7")(c-s) **DEDICATION. / COLD SWEAT** [35] [ ]
(12"+=)(cd-s+=) – Emerald (live) / Still in love with you.
(12"pic-d+=) – Bad reputation / China town.

Feb 91. Vertigo/ US= Mercury; (cd)(c)(lp) **DEDICATION – THE VERY BEST OF THIN LIZZY** [8] [ ]
– Whiskey in the jar / The boys are back in town / Jailbreak / Don't believe a word / Dancing in the moonlight / Rosalie – Cowgirl song (live) / Waiting for an alibi / Do anything you want to / Parisienne walkways (with GARY MOORE) / The rocker / Killer on the loose / Sarah / Out in the fields (with GARY MOORE) / Dedication. *(cd+c+=)* Still in love with you (live) / Bad reputation / Emerald / Chinatown.

Mar 91. Vertigo/ US= Mercury; (7")(c-s) **THE BOYS ARE BACK IN TOWN. / SARAH** [63] [ ]
(12")(cd-s)(12"pic-d) – ('A'side) / Johnny the fox / Black boys on the corner / Me and the boys.

Oct 83. Old Gold; (7") **WHISKY IN THE JAR. / THE ROCKER** [ ] [-]

Jan 85. Old Gold; (7") **DANCING IN THE MOONLIGHT. / DON'T BELIEVE A WORD** [ ] [-]

Feb 88. Old Gold; (7") **THE BOYS ARE BACK IN TOWN. / ('B'by Bachman-Turner Overdrive)** [ ] [-]

Nov 83. Contour; (lp)(c) **THE BOYS ARE BACK IN TOWN** [ ] [-]

Apr 86. Contour; (lp)(c) **WHISKEY IN THE JAR** [ ] [-]

Nov 85. Castle; (d-lp)(c) **THE COLLECTION** [ ] [-]
(cd-iss.Jul87)

Aug 86. Archive 4; (12"ep) **WHISKEY IN THE JAR / THE ROCKER. / SARAH / BLACK BOYS ON THE CORNER** [ ] [-]

Nov 87. Telstar; (lp)(c)(cd) **THE BEST OF PHIL LYNOTT & THIN LIZZY – SOLDIER OF FORTUNE** 55 -
(cd+=) – (3 extra tracks).
Jun 89. Grand Slam; (lp)(c)(cd) **LIZZY LIVES (1976-84)** -
Oct 92. Windsong; (cd) **BBC RADIO 1 LIVE IN CONCERT** -
Nov 94. Strange Fruit; (cd) **THE PEEL SESSIONS** -

PHIL LYNOTT

(solo) but with THIN LIZZY members.

Vertigo Warners

Mar 80. (7")(12") **DEAR MISS LONELY HEARTS. / SOLO IN SOHO** 32
Apr 80. (lp)(c)(pic-lp) **SOLO IN SOHO** 28
– Dear Miss lonely hearts / King's call / A child's lullaby / Tattoo / Solo in Soho / Girls / Yellow pearl / Ode to a black man / Jamaican rum / Talk in '79.. *(re-iss.Sep85, cd-iss.Jul90)*
Jun 80. (7") **KING'S CALL. / ODE TO A BLACK MAN** 35
Mar 81. (7")(12")(7"yellow) **YELLOW PEARL. / GIRLS** 56
(re-iss.Dec81)
(above was later the TV theme for 'Top Of The Pops')
Aug 82. (7") **TOGETHER. / SOMEBODY ELSE'S DREAM**
(12"+=) – ('A'dance version).
Sep 82. (7") **OLD TOWN. / BEAT OF THE DRUM**
Oct 82. (lp)(c) **THE PHIL LYNOTT ALBUM**
– Fatalistic attitude / The man's a fool / Old town / Kathleen / Growing up / Together / Little bit of water / Ode to Liberty (the protest song) / Gino / Don't talk about me baby. *(cd-iss.Jul90)*
— May'85, GARY MOORE & PHIL hit UK Top 5 with 'OUT IN THE FIELDS'.

Polydor Polydor

Nov 85. (7") **19. / 19 (dub)**
(12"+=) – A day in the life of a blues singer.
(d7"+=)(7"pic-d+=) – THIN LIZZY; Whiskey in the jar – The rocker.

– (PHIL LYNOTT) posthumous. –

Jan 87. Vertigo; (7") **KING'S CALL. / YELLOW PEARL** 68
(12"+=) – Dear Miss lonely hearts (live).

13th FLOOR ELEVATORS

Formed: Austin, Texas, USA . . . 1965 by ROCKY ERICKSON. Their first single 'YOU'RE GONNA MISS ME', was finally a US Top 60 hit, when re-issued on Fred Carroll, Noble Ginther & Bill Dillard's label 'International Artists'. After their classic debut album failed to be a commercial success in 1966, they were dogged by drug problems which led to their quick disbandment in '68. • **Style:** Pioneers of psychedelia, who powered their way through R&B classics high on drugs. Later became known as thee most forgotten cult band, after ERICKSON's newfound solo career. • **Songwriters:** ERICKSON penned except; I'M GONNA LOVE YOU TOO (Buddy Holly) / etc. • **Trivia:** In May'91, 'Sire' records issued a ROKY ERICKSON tribute album 'WHERE THE PYRAMID MEETS THE EYE', featuring acts R.E.M., JESUS & MARY CHAIN, PRIMAL SCREAM and BUTTHOLE SURFERS.

Recommended: THE PSYCHEDELIC SOUNDS OF (*8)

The SPADES

(had already recorded 1 single before 17 year-old ROKY joined) **ROKY ERICKSON** (b.ROGER) – vocals, harmonica / **JOHN KERNEY** – guitar, vocals

not issued Zero

1965. (7") **YOU'RE GONNA MISS ME. / WE SELL SOUL** -

13th FLOOR ELEVATORS

were formed by **ROKY** and **STACEY SUTHERLAND** – lead guitar (ex-LINGSMEN) / **BENNY THURMAN** – bass, electric violin (ex-LINGSMEN) / **JOHN IKE WALTON** – drums (ex-LINGMEN) / **TOMMY HALL** – blow jug, lyrics

not issued Contact

Apr 66. (7") **YOU'RE GONNA MISS ME. / TRIED TO HIDE** -
(re-dist.Jun66 on 'International Artists', hit No.55, re-dist.1966 on 'Hanna Barbara') (UK-iss.7"green Nov78 on 'Radar')
— **RONNIE LEATHERMAN** – bass repl. BENNY who formed PLUM NELLY

not issued In.Artists

1966. (lp) **THE PSYCHEDELIC SOUNDS OF** -
– You're gonna miss me / Roller coaster / Splash 1 / Don't fall down / Reverberation (doubt) / Fire engine / Thru the rhythm / You don't know / Kingdom of Heaven / Monkey island / Tried to hide. *(re-iss.1977) (UK-iss.Nov78 on 'Radar', re-iss.Feb88 on 'Decal')*
1966. (7") **REVERBERATION (DOUBT). / FIRE ENGINE** -
— **DAN GALINDO** – bass + **DANNY THOMAS** – drums repl. RONNIE and JOHN IKE
1967. (7") **I'VE GOT LEVITATION. / BEFORE YOU ACCUSE ME** -
1967. (lp) **EASTER EVERYWHERE** -
– Slip inside the house / Slide machine / She lives in a time of her own / Nobody to love / It's all over now, baby blue / Earthquake / Dust / I've got levitation / I had to tell you / Postures (leave your body behind). *(re-iss.1977) (UK-iss.May79 on 'Radar', re-iss.Apr88 on 'Decal')*
Oct 67. (7") **SHE LIVES (IN A TIME OF HER OWN). / BABY BLUE** -
Dec 67. (7") **SLIP INSIDE THIS HOUSE. / SPLASH 1** -
— Disbanded early '68, due to ROKY being imprisoned for possession of a miniscule of hash. He once escaped but was then kept there for another 3 years, and suffered Thorazine plus electric shock treatment. **DUKE DAVIS** – bass had briefly repl. GALINDO. DANNY THOMAS and DUKE were to become The GOLDEN DAWN. The original 13th FLOOR ELEVATORS reformed in 1972. In 1984, they gigged again with line-up (ERICKSON, WALTON, LEATHERMAN and GREG 'Catfish' FORREST-guitar). In Autumn 1978, STACEY was shot dead by his wife.

– others, compilations, etc. –

1968. Int.Artists; (lp) **LIVE** (studio out-takes, b-sides, demos; with false applause) -
– Before you accuse me / She lives in a time of her own / Tried to hide / You gotta take that girl / I'm gonna love you too / Everybody needs somebody to love / I've got levitation / You can't hurt me anymore / Roller coaster / You're gonna miss me. *(UK-iss.May88 on 'Decal')*
1968. Int.Artists; (7") **MAY THE CIRCLE BE UNBROKEN. / I'M GONNA LOVE YOU TOO** -
1969. Int.Artists; (lp) **BULL OF THE WOODS** (rec.early'68) -
– Livin' on / Barnyard blues / Till then / Never another / Rose and the thorn / Down by the river / Scarlet and gold / Street song / Doctor Boom / With you / May the circle remain unbroken. *(UK-iss.Jul88 on 'Decal')*
1969. Int.Artists; (7") **LIVIN' ON. / SCARLET AND GOLD** -
Oct 78. Austin; (7"ep) **YOU REALLY GOT ME. / WORD / ROLL OVER BEETHOVEN** -
1985. Texas Archives; (lp) **FIRE IN MY BONES** -
1987. Texas Archives; (lp) **ELEVATOR TRACKS (some live 1966)** -
1988. Big Beat; (lp)(cd) **I'VE SEEN YOUR FACE BEFORE** (live bootleg '66) -
1988. 13th Hour; (lp) **DEMOS EVERYWHERE** (US-title 'THE ORIGINAL SOUND OF')
Nov 88. Decal; (cd) **EASTER EVERYWHERE / BULL OF THE WOODS** -
Jun 89. Decal; (cd) **THE PSYCHEDELIC SOUNDS OF / LIVE** -
Aug 91. Decal; (4xcd) **THE COLLECTION** (all their 1960's lp's) -
Jul 93. Thunderbolt; (cd) **OUT OF ORDER** -
— (In the US 1979, these appeared on a 12-lp box various 'Inter. Artists'.)
Jun 94. Thunderbolt; (cd) **LEVIATION – IN CONCERT (live)** -

ROKY ERICKSON

went solo with BLIEB ALIEN.

not iss. Mars

1975. (7") **RED TEMPLE PRAYER (TWO HEADED DOG). / STARRY EYES** -

ROKY ERICKSON

solo.

Virgin Rhino

Sep 77. (7") **BERMUDA. / INTERPRETER** -
1977. Sponge France; (7"ep) **TWO HEADED DOG / I HAVE ALWAYS BEEN HERE BEFORE. / MINE, MINE, MIND / CLICK YOUR FINGERS APPLAUDING THE PLAY** - -

ROKY ERICKSON & THE ALIENS

with **DUANE ASLAKSEN** – guitar / **STEVE BURGESS** – bass / **ANDRE LEWIS** – keyboards / **FUZZY FURIOSO** – drums / **BILL MILLER** – autoharp

C.B.S. Columbia

Aug 80. (7") **CREATURE WITH THE ATOM BRAIN. / THE WIND AND MORE**
Aug 80. (lp)(c) **ROKY ERICKSON & THE ALIENS**
– Two headed dog / I think of demons / Don't shake me Lucifer / I walked with a zombie / Night of the vampire / Cold night for alligators / White faces / Creatures with the atom brain / Mine, mine, mind / Stand for the fire demon. *(re-iss.Jan87 as 'I THINK OF DEMONS' on 'Edsel')*
Oct 80. (7") **MINE MINE MIND. / BLOODY HAMMER (long version)**
1981. 415 Records; (lp) **THE EVIL ONE** -
(US cd-iss.1987 was a compilation)

ROKY ERICKSON

1984. Dynamite; (7") **DON'T SLANDER ME. / STARRY EYES** -
1985. New Rose France; (m-lp) **CLEAR NIGHT FOR LOVE** -
– You don't love me yet / Clear night for love / The haunt / Starry eyes / Don't slander me.

One Big Guitar Live Wire

Apr 86. (12") **THE BEAST. / HEROIN (live)** 1985

Demon Enigma

Jan 87. (lp) **GREMLINS HAVE PICTURES – (live 1975-1982 with his bands)** *(cd-iss.Oct90 with extra tracks)* 1986
Jun 87. (lp) **DON'T SLANDER ME** 1986
– (contains some of 'THE EVIL ONE' lp)

Fan Club-New Rose not issued

Sep 87. (lp) **THE HOLIDAY INN TAPES** (hotel room tapes Dec'86) -
— next with **WILL SEXTON + CHRIS HOLYHAUS** – guitar / **FREDDIE KRC** – drums
1988. (lp) **LIVE AT THE RITZ (live Feb87)** -
– You're Gonna Miss Me / Don't Slander Me / Don't Shake Me Lucifer / Night Of The Vampire / Two Headed Dog / Splash 1 / Take A Good Look At Yourself / Clear Night For Love / Bloody Hammer
— next with **ET** (aka EVILHOOK WILDLIFE) **BRIAN S.CURLEY / KERRY GRAFTON / TIM GAGAN + DAVE CAMERON**

Fun-damental not issued

Feb 88. (12") **CLEAR NIGHT FOR LOVE. / YOU DON'T LOVE ME YET** [ ] [-]
1988. Rok; (7"ep) **ACOUSTIC EP** [-] [ ]
1992. Sympathy; (cd) **MAD DOG** [ ] [ ]
–
1992. Sympathy; (7") **HASN'T ANYONE TOLD YOU./ THE INTERPRETER** [ ] [ ]

Trance Trance

Nov 94. (7"ltd.) **WE ARE NEVER TALKING. / PLEASE JUDGE (acoustic version)** [ ] [ ]
Jan 95. (cd)(lp) **ALL THAT MAY DO MY RHYME** [ ] [ ]

– compilations, others, etc. –

Aug 87. 5 Hours Back; (lp)(pic-lp) **CASTING THE RUNES** [ ] [ ]
— (live Nov79 with The EXPLOSIVES; aka **CAM KING** – lead guitar / **WILLIE COLLIE** – bass / **FREDDIE KRC** – drums)
Mar 88. 5 Hours Back; (lp) **OPENERS** [ ] [-]
Jun 88. 5 Hours Back; (red-lp) **TWO TWISTED TALES** [ ] [-]
1988. Fan Club; (cd) **CLICK YOUR FINGERS APPLAUDING THE PLAY** [ ] [-]
Oct 92. Fan Club; (cd)(lp) **LIVE DALLAS 1979 (live with The NERVEBREAKERS)** [ ] [-]
May 92. Swordfish; (cd) **MAD DOG** (1976-83) [ ] [-]
Feb 93. Swordfish; (cd) **LOVE TO SEE YOU BLEED** [ ] [ ]
– Bloody hammer / Every time I look at you / Miss Elude / Haunt / Laughing things / You don't love me yet / Creature with the atom brain / I think of demons / Two headed dog / Red temple prayer / Bumblebee zombie / Click your fingers applauding / The play / Mine mine mind / Things that go bump in the night / Here today . . . gone tomorrow / Realise your my sweet brown angel eyes / I love to see you bleed / Please don't kill my baby.

• 38 SPECIAL

Formed: Florida, USA . . . 1977 by DONNIE VAN ZANDT (younger brother of LYNYRD SKYNYRD's deceased singer RONNIE). Named after the infamous hand-gun, they quickly set about issuing eponymous debut for 'A&M', which featured guest spot by DAN HARTMAN (ex-EDGAR WINTER). By the early 80's, they broke through into semi-stardom, even managing 3 US Top 20 singles lifted from highly profitable albums. • **Style:** Southern fried boogie with bar-room commerciality in mind. Like SKYNYRD they highlighted triple-guitar sound, but contrasted this with double-drummer, which disassembled with addition of keyboard player and mellower AOR tone. • **Songwriters:** DONNIE VAN ZANT or current group members with some covers. Their later contributor JOHN CASCELO of The JOHN MELLENCAMP band, died in 1992. • **Trivia:** Their BACK TO PARADISE track was used on the film 'Revenge Of The Nerds'.

Recommended: FLASHBACK (*6)

DONNIE VAN ZANT – vocals, guitar / **DON BARNES** – guitar, vox / **JEFF CARLISI** – guitar / **STEVE BROOKINS** – drums / **JACK GRONDIN** – drums / **KEN LYONS** – bass

A & M A & M

Jun 77. (lp) **• 38 SPECIAL** [ ] [ ] May 77
– Long time gone / Fly away / Around and around / Play a simple song / Gypsy belle / Four wheels / Tell everybody / Just hang on / Just wanna rock and roll.
Jul 77. (7") **LONG TIME GONE. / FOUR WHEELS** [-] [ ]
Sep 77. (7") **TELL EVERYBODY. / PLAY A SIMPLE SONG** [-] [ ]
— **LARRY LUNDSTROM** – bass repl. LYONS
Jun 78. (lp) **SPECIAL DELIVERY** [ ] [ ]
– I'm a fool for you / Turnin' to you / Travellin' man / I been a mover / What can I do / Who's been messin' / Can't keep a good man down / Take me back.
Jul 78. (7") **I'M A FOOL FOR YOU. / TRAVELIN' MAN** [-] [ ]
Nov 79. (lp)(c) **ROCKIN' INTO THE NIGHT** [ ] [57]
– Rockin' into the night / Stone cold believer / Take me through the night / Money honey / The love that I've lost / You're the captain / Robin Hood / You got the deal / Turn it on.
Mar 80. (7") **ROCKIN' INTO THE NIGHT. / ROBIN HOOD** [ ] [43] Dec79
Jun 80. (7") **STONE COLD BELIEVER. / (part 2)** [-] [ ]
Jun 80. (7") **STONE COLD BELIEVER. / ROCKIN' INTO THE NIGHT** [ ] [-]
(12"+=) – Robin Hood.
Mar 81. (lp)(c) **WILD-EYED SOUTHERN BOYS** [ ] [18] Feb 81
– Hold on loosely / First time around / Wild-eyed Southern boys / Back alley Sally / Fantasy girl / Hittin' & runnin' / Honky tonk dancer / Throw out the line / Bring it on.
Mar 81. (7") **HOLD ON LOOSELY. / THROW OUT THE LINE** [ ] [27]
May 81. (7") **FANTASY GIRL. / HONKY TONK DANCER** [-] [52]
Aug 81. (7") **FIRST TIME AROUND. / FANTASY GIRL / ROCKIN' INTO THE NIGHT** [ ] [ ]
May 82. (lp)(c) **SPECIAL FORCES** [ ] [10]
– Caught up in you / Back door stranger / Back on the track / Chain lightnin' / Rough-housin' / You keep runnin' away / Breakin' loose / Take 'em out / Firestarter.
May 82. (7") **CAUGHT UP IN YOU. / FIRESTARTER** [ ] [10] Apr 82
Aug 82. (7") **YOU KEEP RUNNIN' AWAY. / PRISONERS OF ROCK'N'ROLL** [ ] [38]
Oct 82. (7") **CHAIN LIGHTIN'. / BACK ON THE TRACK** [-] [ ]
Jan 84. (7") **IF I'D BEEN THE ONE. / 20th CENTURY FOX** [ ] [19] Nov 83
Feb 84. (lp)(c) **TOUR DE FRANCE** [ ] [22] Nov 83
– If I'd been the one / Back where you belong / One time for old times / See me in your eyes / Twentieth century fox / Long distance affair / I oughta let go / One of the lonely ones / Undercover lover.
Feb 84. (7") **BACK WHERE YOU BELONG. / UNDERCOVER LOVER** [-] [20]
Sep 84. (7") **TEACHER TEACHER. / 20th CENTURY FOX** [-] [25]
— (above single from the feature film 'Teachers', issued on 'Capitol').
May 86. (lp)(c) **STRENGTH IN NUMBERS** [ ] [17]
– Somebody like you / Like no other night / Last time / Once in a lifetime / Just a little love / Has there ever been a goodbye / One in a million / Hearts on fire / Against the night / Never give an inch.
May 86. (7") **LIKE NO OTHER NIGHT. / HEARTS ON FIRE** [ ] [14]
Jul 86. (7") **SOMEBODY LIKE YOU. / AGAINST THE NIGHT** [-] [48]
Apr 84. (7") **LONG DISTANCE AFFAIR. / ONE TIME FOR OLD TIMES** [-] [ ]
Oct 86. (7") **LAST TIME. / ONE IN A MILLION** [-] [ ]
Jul 87. (7") **BACK TO PARADISE. / REVENGE OF THE NERDS – THEME** [-] [41]
Sep 87. (lp)(c)(cd) **FLASHBACK (compilation)** [ ] [35] Aug 87
– Back to Paradise / Hold on loosely / If I'd been the one / Caught up in you / Fantasy girl / Same old feeling / Back where you belong / Teacher, teacher / Like no ther night / Rockin' into the night.
(free live 12"ep) – Rough housin' / Wild eyed Southern boys / Stone cold believer / Twentieth century fox.
— (1988) **MAX CARL** – vocals, keyboards repl. BARNES / **DANNY CHAUNCEY** – guitar repl. BROOKINS (said new members now alongside **VAN ZANT, CARLISI, GRONDIN + LUNDSTROM**
Oct 88. (7") **ROCK & ROLL STRATEGY. / LOVE STRIKES** [-] [ ]
Oct 88. (lp)(c)(cd) **ROCK & ROLL STRATEGY** [ ] [61]
– Rock & roll strategy / What's it to ya? / Little Sheba / Comin' down tonight / Midnight magic / Second chance / Hot 'Lanta / Never be lonely / Chattahoochee / Innocent eyes / Love strikes.
Apr 89. (7") **SECOND CHANCE. / COMING DOWN TONIGHT** [ ] [6] Feb 89
Jun 89. (7") **COMIN' DOWN TONIGHT. / CHATTAHOOCHEE** [-] [ ]

Charisma Charisma

Jul 91. (cd)(c)(lp) **BONE AGAINST STEEL** [ ] [ ]
– The sound of your voice / Signs of love / Last thing I ever do / You definately got me / Rebel to rebel / Bone against steel / You be the dam, I'll be the water / Jimmy Gillum / Tear it up / Don't wanna get it dirty / Burning bridges / Can't shake it / Treasure.
Jul 91. (7")(c-s) **THE SOUND OF YOUR VOICE. / ?** [-] [33]

THIS MORTAL COIL

Formed: London, England . . . 1983 by IVO and producer /brother JOHN FRYER. They employed many singers and musicians from their '4 a.d.' stable, including ELIZABETH FRAZER and ROBIN GUTHRIE (of COCTEAU TWINS) on their debut 45 'SONG TO THE SIREN'. A year later, a larger ensemble was represented on the hit debut album 'IT'LL END IN TEARS'. Sparodic recordings followed, as IVO and JOHN continued expanding their record company with new US acts; The PIXIES, THROWING MUSES, etc. • **Style:** Atmospheric and inspiring gothic-rock, that at times delved into the past for mystical but effective covers. • **Songwriters:** IVO and some 4 a.d. musicians, except; SONG TO THE SIREN (Tim Buckley) / GATHERING DUST + 16 DAYS (Modern English) / COME HERE MY LOVE (Van Morrison) / DRUGS (Talking Heads) / HELP ME LIFT YOU UP (Mary Margaret O'Hara) / LATE NIGHT (Syd Barrett) / YOU AND YOUR SISTER (Chris Bell) / I AM THE COSMOS (Big Star) / NATURE'S WAY (Spirit) / others by ROY HARPER, GENE CLARK, etc. • **Trivia:** One of their singers from 1991; HEIDI BERRY had releases on 'Creation'.

Recommended: IT'LL END IN TEARS (*8) / FILIGREE & SHADOW (*7)

IVO WATTS-RUSSELL (b.1955) – tapes, loops, etc. / **JOHN FRYER** – instruments, producer with **COCTEAU TWINS:- ELIZABETH FRAZER** – vox / **ROBIN GUTHRIE** – guitar

4 a.d. Relativity

Sep 83. (7") **SONG TO THE SIREN. / 16 DAYS (reprise)** [66] [ ]
(12"+=) – Gathering dust.
— (above 'B'sides feat. **ROBBIE GREY** – vocals (of MODERN ENGLISH)
— (below 'A'side feat. **MARTIN McCARRICK** – cello, strings (of WILLING SINNERS; MARC ALMOND) / **GORDON SHARPE** – vocals (of CINDY TALK) / **SIMON RAYMONDE** – guitar, tapes (of COCTEAU TWINS)
Aug 84. (7") **IT'LL END IN TEARS. / IT'LL END IN TEARS** [ ] [-]
Below album feat. said musicians, plus **GINI BALL** – violin (of WILLING SINNERS) / DEAD CAN DANCE: **LIZA GERRARD** – accordion, vocals / **BRENDAN PERRY** – bass drone, drum / **PETER ULRICH** – percussion / COLOUR BOX: **STEVEN YOUNG** – piano / **MARTYN YOUNG** – sitar, guitar, bass / X-MAL DEUTSCHLAND: **MANUELA RICKERS** – guitar / WOLFGANG PRESS: **MARK COX** – organ / **HOWARD DEVOTO** – vocals (ex-MAGAZINE)
Oct 84. (lp)(c) **IT'LL END IN TEARS** [38] [ ]
– Kangaroo / Song to the siren / Holocaust / FYT / Fond affections / The last ray / Waves become wings / Another day / Barramundi / Dreams made flesh / Not me / A single wish. *(cd-iss.1986)*
— Retained guests **SIMON RAYMONDE / PETER ULRICH / MARK COX / STEVEN YOUNG** plus new BREATHLESS: **DOMINIC APPLETON** – vocals / **RICHENEL** – vocals / DIF JUZ: **DAVID CURTIS** – guitar / **ALAN CURTIS** – guitar / **RICHARD THOMAS** – saxophone / **MODERN ENGLISH: ANDREW GRAY** – guitar / / **JEAN** – vocals / **ALISON LIMERICK** – vocals / **CAROLINE SEAMAN** – vocals / **KEITH MITCHELL** – guitar / **DIERDRE RUTOWSKI** – backing vocals / **LOUISE RUTOWSKI** – backing vocals / **KEITH MITCHELL** – guitar / **NIGEL K.HINE** – guitar / **CHRIS PYE** – guitar / **JOHN TURNER** – organ, keyboards / **TONY WAEREA** – didgeridoo / **ANNE TURNER + LES McKUEN** – choir
Sep 86. (d-lp)(c)(cd) **FILIGREE & SHADOW** [53] [ ]
– Velvet belly / The jeweller / Ivy and neet / Meniscus / Tears / Tarantula / My father / Come here my love / At first, and then / Strength of strings / Morning glory / Inch-blue / I want to live / Mama K I / Filigree & shadow / Firebrothers / Thais I / I must have been blind / A heart of glass / Alone / Mama K II / The horizon bleeds and sucks its thumb / Drugs / Red rain / Thais II.

Sep 86. (ltd-10") **COME HERE MY LOVE. / DRUGS** [ ] [-]

— They used past musicians, plus **CAROLINE CRAWLEY, KIM DEAL + TANYA DONNELLY, DOMINIC APPLETON, HEIDI BERRY + The RUTOWSKI's,** etc.

Apr 91. (cd)(c)(d-lp) **BLOOD** [28] [ ]
– The lacemaker / Mr.Somewhere / Ardialu / With tomorrow / Loose joints / You and your sister / Nature's way / I come and steal at every door / Bitter / Baby Ray baby / Several times / The lacemaker II / Late night / Ruddy and wretched / Help me lift you up / Carolyn's song / DD and E / Til I gain control again / Dreams are like water / I am the cosmos / (Nothing but) Blood.

David THOMAS (see under ⇒ PERE UBU)

Ray THOMAS (see under ⇒ MOODY BLUES)

Richard THOMPSON

Born: 3 Apr'49, London, England. Founder of FAIRPORT CONVENTION from 1967, until his departure early in 1971. After session work for ex-FAIRPORT friends; SANDY DENNY and IAN MATTHEWS, he finally issued debut album HENRY THE HUMAN FLY' in 1972 for Island' records. Just prior to this, he had worked with other recently ex-FAIRPORT members; ASHLEY HUTCHINGS, DAVE MATTACKS, who as The BUNCH, released budget covers lp ROCK ON'. The following year, he teamed up with LINDA PETERS, and they became RICHARD & LINDA THOMPSON, after their marriage in 1974. Their first of many albums together I WANT TO SEE THE BRIGHT LIGHTS AGAIN', was acclaimed by many, and should have provided them with a hit title track hit single. During the recording of their next album HOKEY POKEY', they coverted to Sufism, and initiated their own religious Sufi community. In 1982, they made their last album together, due to marriage break-up. The next year, RICHARD was solo again and issued for Hannibal' records; HAND OF KINDNESS'. After many near chart breakthroughs in the second half of the 80's, he finally made UK Top 40 listings with 1991 album RUMOUR AND SIGH'. • **Style:** Accomplished and influential guitarist, lawded by many, including surprisingly Americans BOB MOULD (Sugar + Husker Du), J.MASCIS (Dinosaur Jr) and FRANK BLACK (Pixies). He blended together a rare mixture of English-folk sound with American country-rock music. Watch out for a THOMPSON tribute album in 1994, which will feature many top stars, playing their best R.T. tracks. • **Songwriters:** Self-penned compostions, collaborating for 8 between 1974-1982 with then wife LINDA. While a member of FAIRPORT CONVENTION, he contributed GENESIS HALL / MEET ON THE LEDGE + SLOTH, to name a few.

Recommended: I WANT TO SEE THE BRIGHT LIGHTS TONIGHT (*7) / WATCHING THE DARK – A HISTORY OF . . . (*7)

RICHARD THOMPSON – vocals, guitar (ex-FAIRPORT CONVENTION) with **LINDA PETERS / PAT DONALDSON** – bass / **TIM DONALD** – drums / plus **SANDY DENNY / ASHLEY HUTCHINGS / JOHN KIRKPATRICK / JOHN DEFERERI / BARRY DRANSFIELD / DAVID SNELL / CLAY TOYANI / ANDY ROBERTS / SUE DRAHEIM / JEFF COLE**

Island Reprise

Jun 72. (lp)(c) **HENRY THE HUMAN FLY** [ ] [ ]
– Roll over Vaughn Williams / Nobody's wedding / The poor ditching boy / Shaky Nancy / The angels took my racehorse away / Wheely down / The new St. George / Painted ladies / Cold feet / Mary and Joseph / The old changing ways / Twisted. *(re-iss.Jan87 on Hannibal', cd-iss.May87)*

— **RICHARD & LINDA THOMPSON**

husband & wife duo. LINDA (nee PETERS) (ex-ALBION COUNTRY BAND) with SOUR GRAPES: **SIMON NICOL** – dulcimer / **STEVE BORRELL** – bass / **WILLIAM MURRAY** – drums (ex-KEVIN AYERS)/ plus most of main musicians on above album.

Jan 74. (7") **I WANT TO SEE THE BRIGHT LIGHTS TONIGHT. / WHEN I GET TO THE BORDER** [ ] [ ]

Apr 74. (lp)(c) **I WANT TO SEE THE BRIGHT LIGHTS TONIGHT** [ ] [ ]
– When I get to the border / The Calvery Cross / Withered and died / I want to see the bright lights tonight / Down where the drunkards roll / We sing hallelujah / Has he got a friend for me? / The little beggar girl / The end of the rainbow / The Great Valero. *(cd-iss.May88) (re-iss.Oct89 on Hannibal') (cd re-iss,Mar93 on Island')*

— **IAN WHITEMAN** – keyboards, flute / **ALY BAIN** – fiddle repl. guests

Feb 75. (7") **HOKEY POKEY. / I'LL REGRET IT ALL IN THE MORNING** [ ] [ ]

Mar 75. (lp)(c) **HOKEY POKEY** [ ] [ ]
– Hokey pokey (the ice-cream song) / I'll regret it all in the morning / Smiffy's glass eye / Egypt room / Never again / Georgie on a spree / Old man inside a young man / The Sun never shines on the poor / A heart needs a home / Mole in a hole. *(cd-iss.May89) (re-iss.Jun86 on Hannibal')*

Nov 75. (lp)(c) **POUR DOWN LIKE SILVER** [ ] [ ]
– Streets of Paradise / For shame of doing wrong / The poor boy is taken away / Night comes in / Jet plane in a rocking chair / Beat the retreat / Hard luck stories / Dimming of the day / Dargai. *(re-iss.Jun86 on Hannibal', cd-iss.May89)*

— Their main band was:- **WILLIE WEEKS** – bass / **ANDY NEWMARK** – drums / **NEIL LARSON** – keyboards / **SIMON NICOL** – guitar, dulcimer / **JOHN KIRKPATRICK** – accordion

Chrysalis Chrysalis

Nov 78. (lp)(c) **FIRST LIGHT** [ ] [ ]
– Restless highway / Sweet surrender / Don't let a thief steal into your heart / The choice wife / Died for love / Strange affair / Layla / Pavanne / House of cards / First light. *(re-iss.Jun86 on Hannibal' + cd May89)*

Jan 79. (7") **DON'T LET A THIEF STEAL INTO YOUR HEART. / FIRST LIGHT** [ ] [ ]

— **TIM DONALD, PAT DONALSON + RABBIT BUNDRICK** repl. NEWMARK, WEEKS + LARSON / guests:- **DAVE MATTACKS** – drums / **DAVE PEGG** – bass

Sep 79. (lp)(c) **SUNNY VISTAS** [ ] [ ]
– Civilization / Borrowed time / Saturday rolling around / You're going to need somebody / Why do you turn your back / Sunny vista / Lonely hearts / Sisters / Justice in the streets / Traces of my love. *(re-iss.+cd.May89 on'Carthage')*

Sep 79. (7") **CIVILIZATION. / GEORGIE ON A SPREE** [ ] [-]

Elixir not issued

Sep 81. (lp) **STRICT TEMPO (RICHARD THOMPSON solo / instrumental)** [ ] [-]
– Scott Skinner medley / Banish misfortune / Dundee hornpipe / Do it for my sake / New fangled flogging reel / Vailance polka militair / Belfast polka / Rockin' in rhythm / The random jig / The grinder / Andalus / Marrakesh / The knife edge. *(re-iss.+cd Jul89 on Carthage')*

— next w / **NICOL / MATTACKS / PEGG /** + bassman **PETE ZORN**

Hannibal Hannibal

Apr 82. (7") **DON'T RENEGE ON YOUR LOVE. / LIVING IN LUXURY** [ ] [-]

Nov 82. (lp) **SHOOT OUT THE LIGHTS** [ ] [ ]
– Man in need / Walking on a wire / Don't renege on your love / Just the motion / Shoot out the lights / Back street slide / Did she jump or was she pushed / Wall of death. *(re-iss.+cd.Jun86)* (+=) – Living in luxury. *(re-iss.May89 on Carthage') (cd-iss.Dec94 on 'Hannibal')*

— **RICHARD THOMPSON** returned to solo work after separating with LINDA. He retained last band and label, while LINDA went on in 1985 to release an album ONE CLEAR MOMENT' for Warners'.

Jun 83. (lp) **HAND OF KINDNESS** [ ] [ ]
– A poisoned heart and a twisted memory / Tear stained letter / How I wanted to / Both ends burning / The wrong heartbeat / Hand of kindness / Devonside / Two left feet. *(re-iss.+cd Jun86)* (+=) – Where the wind don't whine.

Jul 83. (7") **THE WRONG HEARTBEAT. / DEVONSIDE** [ ] [-]

Dec 84. (lp) **SMALL TOWN ROMANCE (live)** [ ] [-]
– Time to ring some changes / Beat the retreat / A heart needs a home / Woman or a man / For shame of doin' wrong / Genesis Hall / Honky tonk blues / Small town romance / I want to see the bright lights tonight / Down where the drunkards roll / Love is bad for business / Never again / The Great Valero / Don't let a thief steal into your heart.

Polydor Polydor

Mar 85. (lp)(c) **ACROSS A CROWDED ROOM** [80] [ ]
– When the spell is broken / You don't say / I ain't going to drag my feet no more / Love in a faithless country / Fire in the engine room / Walking through a wasted land / Little blue number / She twists the knife again / Ghosts in the wind. *(re-iss.+cd Jun86) (cd re-iss.Jun92 on B.G.O.')*

Jun 85. (7") **YOU DON'T SAY. / WHEN THE SPELL IS BROKEN** [ ] [ ]

— now with **MITCHELL FROOM** – organ / **JERRY SCHEFF** – bass / **MICKEY CURRY + JIM KELTNER** – drums / **JOHN KIRKPATRICK** – accordion / **ALEX ACUNA** – percussion

Oct 86. (lp)(c)(cd) **DARING ADVENTURES** [92] [ ]
– A bone through her nose / Valerie / Missie how you let me down / Dead man's handle / Long dead love / Lover''s lane / Nearly in love / Jennie / Baby talk / Cash down / Never never / How wll I ever be simple again / Al Bowly's in Heaven. *(cd re-iss.Jun92 on B.G.O.')*

B.B.C. not issued

Oct 87. (lp)(c) **THE MARKSMAN (TV Soundtrack)** [ ] [-]
– My time / Gordon / Rude health / Night school / Cornish pastiche / Crossing the water / The marksman / Kyrie / On yer eyes / Cutters on the run / Don't ever change / Up there.

Capitol Capitol

Oct 88. (lp)(c)(cd) **AMNESIA** [89] [ ]
– Turning of the tide / Gypsy love songs / Reckless kind / Jerusalem on the jukebox / I still dream / Don't tempt me / Yankee, go home / Can't win / Waiting for dreamers / Pharoah. *(re-iss.Mar91)*

Nov 88. (7") **TURNING OF THE TIDE. / PHAROAH** [ ] [ ]

Sep 89. (7") **RECKLESS KIND (live). / TURNING OF THE TIDE (live)** [ ] [ ]
(12"+=) – Pharoah (live) / Can't win (live).
(cd-s+=) – Jerusalem on the jukebox (live).

May 91. (cd)(c)(lp) **RUMOUR AND SIGH** [32] [ ]
– Read about love / I feel so good / I misunderstood / Behind grey walls / You dream too much / Why must I plead / Vincent / Backlash love affair / Mystery wind / Jimmy Shands / Keep your distance / Mother knows best / God loves a drunk / Psycho Street. *(re-iss.cd Sep94)*

Jun 91. (7") **I FEEL SO GOOD. / HARRY'S THEME (from film 'Sweet Talker')** [ ] [ ]
(cd-s+=) – Backlash love affair.

Mar 92. (7") **I MISUNDERSTOOD. / 1952** [ ] [ ]
(cd-s+=) – Vincent / Black lightning.

— with **PETE THOMAS** – drums, percussion / **JERRY SCHEFF** – bass, double bass / **MITCHELL FROOM** – keyboards, producer / **ALISTAIR ANDERSON** – concertina, pipes / **TOM McCONVILLE** – fiddle / **MARTIN DUNN** – flute / **PHIL PICKETT** – shawms / **JOHN KIRKPATRICK** – accordion, concertina / **DANNY THOMPSON** – double bass (1) / **CHRISTINE COLLISTER + MICHAEL PARKER** – backing vocals

Jan 94. (cd)(c) **MIRROR BLUE** [23] [ ]
– For the sake of Mary / I can't wake up to save my life / MGB-GT / The way that it shows / Easy there, steady now / King of Bohemia / Shane and Dixie / Mingus eyes / I ride in your slipstream / Beeswing / Fast food / Mascara tears / Taking my business elsewhere.

— (a tribute album was released in 1995)

– compilations, etc. –

(below album recorded between 1967-1976)

May 76. Island; (d-lp)(d-c) **(guitar, vocal)** [ ] [ ]
– A heart needs a home / Free as a bird / Night comes in / Pitfall / Excursion / Calvery Cross / Time will show the wiser / Throw-away street puzzle / Mr.Lacy / The ballad of Easy Rider / Poor Will and the jolly hangman / Sweet little rock'n'roller / Dark end of the street / I'll be me. (incl.Live Oxford Street concert & early demos) (US-title LIVE MORE OR LESS') *(re-iss.Jun86 on 'Hannibal', cd-iss.May89)*

Apr 93. Hannibal; (3xcd-box) **WATCHING THE DARK – A HISTORY OF . . .** [ ] [-]
– A man in need / Can't win / Waltzing's for dreamers / Crash the party / I still dream / Bird in God's garden / Lost and found / Now be thankful / A sailor's kife / Genesis Hall / The knife-edge / Walking on a wire / Small town romance / Shepherd's march –

Maggie Cameron / Wall of death / For shame of doing wrong / Back street slide / Strange affair / The wrong heartbeat / Borrowed time / From Galway to Graceland / Tear-stained letter / Keep your distance / Bogie's bonnie / Poor wee Jockey Clarke / Jet plane in a rocking chair / Dimming of the day / Old man inside a young man / Never again / Hokey pokey (the ice cream song) / A heart needs a home / Beat the retreat / Al Bowlly's in Heaven / Walking through a wasted land / When the spell is broken / Devonside / Little blue number / I ain't going to drag my feet no more / Withered and died / Nobody's wedding / The poor ditching boy / The Great Valerio / The Calvary Cross / Twisted / Jennie / Hand of kindness / Two left feet / Shoot out the lights.

THOMPSON TWINS

Formed: Chesterfield, Derbyshire, England . . . 1977 by BAILEY, LEEWAY and DODD. After a few releases on own small labels in 1980, they were snapped up by 'Hansa' through 'Arista'. They struggled commercially, until 'SET' album in 1982 fractured the UK Top 50. The following year, after 'LOVE ON YOUR SIDE' cracked the UK Top 10, they became one of top acts in the mid-80's. • **Style:** Initially a politico funky new wave outfit, whose Afro-pop rhythms soon suited the US dance halls. • **Songwriters:** BAILEY-CURRIE compositions, except WHO WANTS TO BE A MILLIONAIRE (Cole Porter) / REVOLUTION (Beatles). • **Trivia:** Took their name from two characters in Herge's adventures of Tin Tin.

Recommended: SET (*7) / GREATEST HITS (*6).

TOM BAILEY (b.18 Jan'57, Halifax, Yorkshire) – vocals, keyboards, percussion / **PETE DODD** – guitar, vocals, sax, percussion / **JOHN ROOG** – guitar, vocals, percussion / added **JOE LEEWAY** (b.15 Nov'57, London) – percussion, vocals / **CHRIS BELL** – drums, percussion, vocals / **JANE SHORTER** – saxophone, percussion

Dirty Discs | not issued

May 80. (7") **SQUARES AND TRIANGLES. / COULD BE HER . . . COULD BE YOU** [ ] [-]

Latent | not issued

Nov 80. (7") **SHE'S IN LOVE WITH MYSTERY. / FAST FOOD / FOOD STYLE** [ ] [-]

T-Hansa | Arista

Feb 81. (7") **PERFECT GAME. / POLITICS** [ ] [ ]
Jun 81. (7")(12") **ANIMAL LAUGH (OUMMA AULARESSO). / ANYTHING IS GOOD ENOUGH / A DUB PRODUCT** [ ] [ ]
Jun 81. (lp)(c) **A PRODUCT OF . . .** [ ] [ ]
– When I see you / Slave trade / Vendredi saint / Perfect game / Could be her . . . could be you / A product of . . . / Politics / Anything is good enough / Make believe / Don't go away / Animal laugh / The price. *(re-iss.Aug83 on 'Fame')*
Sep 81. (7")(12") **MAKE BELIEVE (LET'S PRETEND). / LAMA SABACH TANI ('A'version)** [ ] [ ]

— **ALANNAH CURRIE** (b.20 Sep'59, Auckland, New Zealand) – saxophone, vox, keyboards repl. JANE SHORTER. Guest **MATTHEW SELIGMAN** – bass (ex-SOFT BOYS)

Jan 82. (7") **IN THE NAME OF LOVE. / IN THE BEGINNING** [ ] [ ] Mar 82
(12"+=) – Coastline. (US; b-side)
Mar 82. (lp)(c) **SET (US title 'IN THE NAME OF LOVE')** [48] [ ]
– Living in Europe / In the name of love / The rowe / Runaway / Another fantasy / Crazy dog / Fools gold / Blind / Bouncing / Good gosh / Tok tok. *(re-iss.Sep84 on 'Fame', cd-iss.Oct89)*
May 82. (7") **RUNAWAY. / OPEN YOUR EYES** [ ] [ ]
(12"+=) – Bouncing.
(d7"+=) – Living in Europe (live) / Make believe (live w/THOMAS DOLBY)

— Now basic trio of **BAILEY, CURRIE & LEEWAY** + retainers **ROOG, DODD + SELIGMAN.** Guest **BORIS WILLIAMS** – drums repl. BELL to SPEAR OF DESTINY

Arista | Arista

Oct 82. (7") **LIES. / BEACH CULTURE** [67] [30] Jan 83
(12"+=) – Lies (version).
Jan 83. (7")(12") **LOVE ON YOUR SIDE. / LOVE ON YOUR BACK** [9] [45] Apr 83
(d7"+=) – In the name of love / In the beginning.
Feb 83. (lp)(c) **QUICK STEP AND SIDE KICK** (US-title **'SIDE KICKS'**) [2] [34]
– If you were here / Love on your side / Love lies bleeding / All fall out / We are detective / Judy do / Tears / Watching / Kamikaze / Lies.
(re-iss.Jul85 & Oct88) (cd-iss.Oct84 on 'Fame')
Apr 83. (7") **WE ARE DETECTIVE. / LUCKY DAY** [7] [ ]
(12"+=) – ('A'&'B'extended versions).
Jul 83. (7")(12")(7"pic-d) **WATCHING. / DANCESAURUS** [33] [ ]
Nov 83. (7")(12")(7"pic-d) **HOLD ME NOW. / LET LOVING START** [4] [3] Feb 84
Jan 84. (7")(12")(7"sha-pic-d)(12"pic-d) **DOCTOR! DOCTOR!. / NURSE SHARK** [3] [11] May 84
Feb 84. (lp)(c)(cd) **INTO THE GAP** [1] [10]
– The gap / Hold me now / Doctor! doctor! / You take me up / Sister of mercy / Day after day / No peace for the wicked / Storm on the sea / Who can stop the rain.
(c+=) – (extended mixes).
Mar 84. (7")(3 diff.7"interlocking-pic-d) **YOU TAKE ME UP. / PASSION PLANET** [2] [44] Aug 84
(12"+=)(12"-6 designs+=) – Down tools / Leopard Ray.
Jun 84. (7")(7"sha-pic-d) **SISTER OF MERCY. / OUT OF THE GAP** [11] [ ]
Oct 84. (7") **THE GAP. / OUT OF THE GAP** [-] [69]

— The basic trio, were now joined by new sessioners + BORIS joined The CURE

Nov 84. (7")(12")(7"pic-d) **LAY YOUR HANDS ON ME. / THE LEWIS CAROL (ADVENTURES IN WONDERLAND)** [13] [6] Sep 85
Apr 85. (7") **ROLL OVER. / FOOLS IN PARADISE** [ ] [ ]
(12"+=) – ('A'version).
Aug 85. (7")(12")(7"pic-d) **DON'T MESS WITH DOCTOR DREAM. / BIG BUSINESS** [15] [ ]
Sep 85. (lp)(c)(cd) **HERE'S TO FUTURE DAYS** [5] [20]
– You killed the clown / Lay your hands on me / Future days / Love is the law / Don't mess with Doctor Dream / Roll over / Breakaway / King for a day / Emperor's clothes (part 1) / Tokyo / Revolution. *(re-iss.+cd.Apr88)*
Oct 85. (7") **KING FOR A DAY. / ROLL UNDER** [22] [8] Jan 86
(12"+=)(12"pic-d+=) – ('A'&'B'versions).
Dec 85. (7")(12") **REVOLUTION. / THE FOURTH SUNDAY** [56] [ ]
Sep 86. (7")(12") **NOTHING IN COMMON. / NOTHING TO LOSE** [ ] [54] Jul 86

— Trimmed to a duo (**BAILEY & CURRIE**) when LEEWAY departed. Session people **SARA LEE** – bass (ex-GANG OF FOUR) / **GEOFF DUGMORE** – drums (ex-ART OF NOISE)

Mar 87. (7") **GET THAT LOVE. / ('A'dub version)** [66] [31]
(12"+=)/ /(cd-s+=) – ('A'version)./ / Perfect day.
Apr 87. (lp)(c)(cd) **CLOSE TO THE BONE** [90] [76]
– Follow your heart / Bush baby / Get that love / 20th century / The long goodbye / Still waters / Savage moon / Perfect day / Gold fever / Dancing in your shoes.
May 87. (7") **THE LONG GOODBYE. / DANCING IN YOUR SHOES** [ ] [ ]
(12"+=)(cd-s+=) – Hold me now.
Oct 88. (7") **IN THE NAME OF LOVE '88. / ('A'original)** [46] [ ]
(12"+=) – ('A'mix).
(cd-s++=) – ('A'club remix). / Passion planet (US only).
Oct 88. (lp)(c)(cd) **THE BEST OF THE THOMPSON TWINS** (compilation) [ ] [ ]
– In the name of love '88 / Lies / Love on your side / Lay your hands on me / The gap / Hold me now / Doctor! Doctor! / You take me up / King for a day / Get that love *(re-iss.cd+c.Mar91) (re-iss.cd Jan92 on 'Perspective-Old Gold')*

W.E.A. | Warners

Sep 89. (7")(c-s) **SUGAR DADDY. / MONKEY MAN** [ ] [28]
(12")(cd-s)(12"pic-d) – (3 'A'versions).
Oct 89. (lp)(c)(cd) **BIG TRASH** [ ] [ ]
– Sugar daddy / Queen of the U.S.A. / Bombers in the sky / This girl's on fire / T.V. on / Big trash / Salvador Dali's car / Rock this boat / Dirty summer's day / Love jungle / Wild.
Sep 91. (7")(12")(c-s) **COME INSIDE (club mix). / ('A'-feedback mix)** [56] [ ]
(cd-s+=) – ('A'normal version).
Oct 91. (cd)(c)(lp) **QUEER** [ ] [ ]
– Come inside / Flower girl / My funky valentine / Queer / Groove on / The saint / Strange Jane / Shake it down / Wind it up / Flesh and blood / The invisible man / Come inside (feedback Max remix).
Jan 92. (7")(c-s) **THE SAINT. / ('A'max hard groove mix)** [53] [ ]
(12"+=) – ('A'remix) / ('A'def sonic) / ('A'red zone club mix) / ('A'-8th street dub).
(cd-s++=) – ('A'edit).
Jul 92. (7")(c-s) **PLAY WITH ME (JANE). / ('A'-full on piano mix)** [ ] [ ]
(12") – ('A'side) / ('A'dub wash mix).
(cd-s+=) – ('A'-African mix) / ('A'full on mix) / ('A'sweet garage mix)

– more compilations, etc. –

Aug 83. Hansa; (d-c) **A PRODUCT OF . . . / SET** [ ] [-]
Feb 85. Arista; (7") **HOLD ME NOW. / DOCTOR, DOCTOR** [-] [ ]
Jul 87. Strange Fruit; (12"ep) **NIGHT TRACKS** (12.2.81) [ ] [-]
– A product of . . . / The price / Could be her . . . could be you / Oumma aulerresso.
Sep 87. Old Gold; (12") **LOVE ON YOUR SIDE (extended). / LIES (extended)** [ ] [-]
Nov 87. Old Gold; (7") **YOU TAKE ME UP. / DOCTOR! DOCTOR!** [ ] [-]
Jan 88. Old Gold; (7") **WE ARE DETECTIVE. / HOLD ME NOW** [ ] [-]
Jun 93. Old Gold; (cd-s) **DOCTOR! DOCTOR! / YOU TAKE ME UP / HOLD ME NOW** [ ] [-]
Mar 90. Stylus; (cd)(c)(lp) **GREATEST HITS** [ ] [-]

BABBLE

were formed **TOM BAILEY + ALANNAH CURRIE**

Warners | Warners

Mar 94. (12")(cd-s) **TAKE ME AWAY. / ?** [ ] [ ]
May 94. (cd)(c) **THE STONE** [ ] [ ]
– The downward pull of Heaven's force / Tribe / You kill me / Spirit / Take me away / The stone / Beautiful / Space / Sunray dub / Drive.

Tracy THORN (see under ⇒ EVERYTHING BUT THE GIRL)

George THOROGOOD & THE DESTROYERS

Formed: Wilmington, Delaware, USA . . . 1973 by one-time semi-professional baseball player THOROGOOD. In 1977 they were signed to US label 'Rounder' by John Forward. Second album 'MOVE IT ON OVER', was first to give them entry into US Top 40. • **Style:** Traditional R&B rock'n'roll outfit, whom later went back to folk & bluegrass roots in the 80's. • **Songwriters:** THOROGOOD penned except; YOU GO TO LOSE (Earl Hooker) / WHO DO YOU LOVE (Bo Diddley) / ALLEY OOP (Dixie Cups) / WANTED MAN (Bob Dylan) / I KNOW IT'S A SIN (Jimmy Reed) / NADINE + REELIN' & ROCKIN' (Chuck Berry) / WILLIE AND THE HAND JIVE (Johnny Otis) / GET A HAIRCUT (Avery -Birch) / HOWLIN' FOR MY BABY (Willie Dixon – Chester Burnett) / KILLER'S BLUZE (Dex Rogers) / DOWN IN THE BOTTOM & I'M READY (Willie Dixon) / COPS AND ROBBERS (Bo Diddley) / GONE DEAD TRAIN (Jack Nitzsche -Russ Titelman) / WANT AD BLUES (John Lee Hooker) / MY FRIEND ROBERT (Patrick Sky). • **Trivia:** Made an appearance in 1985 on US show of LIVE AID.

Recommended: BADDEST OF THE BAD (*7).

GEORGE THOROGOOD – guitar, slide guitar, vocals, harmonica / **RON SMITH** – rhythm guitar / **JEFF SIMON** – drums / **BILL BLOUGH** – bass replaced MICHAEL LEVINE in 1975

		Sonet	Rounder
May 78.	(7") **CAN'T STOP LOVIN'. / HOMESICK BOY**		
Jun 78.	(lp) **GEORGE THOROGOOD AND THE DESTROYERS**	67	

– You got to lose / Madison blues / One bourbon, one scotch, one beer / Kind hearted woman / Can't stop lovin' / Ride on Josephine / Homesick boy / I'll change my style / Delaware slide. *(re-iss.Mar86 on 'Demon') (US re-iss. Aug88, cd-iss.May90) (cd-iss.Oct93 on 'Demon')*

Jul 78.	(7") **MADISON BLUES. / DELAWARE SLIDE**		

—— **UNCLE MEAT PENNINGTON** – percussion repl. SMITH

Nov 78.	(lp) **MOVE IT ON OVER**	67	33

– Move it on over / Who do you love / The sky is crying / Cocaine blues / It wasn't me / That same thing / So much trouble / I'm just your good thing / Baby please set a date / New Hawaiian boogie. *(re-iss.Mar86 on 'Demon', cd-iss.May90) (US re-iss.+cd.Aug88)*

Dec 78.	(7") **COCAINE BLUES. / MOVE IT ON OVER**		
Feb 79.	(7") **IT WASN'T ME. / WHO DO YOU LOVE**		
Jun 79.	(7"ep) **SO MUCH TROUBLE / CAN'T STOP. / I'M READY / NEW HAWAIIAN BOOGIE (part 2)**		

—— **HANK CARTER** – saxophone repl. PENNINGTON

Sep 80.	(7") **NIGHT TIME. / KIDS FROM PHILLY**		
Oct 80.	(lp)(c) **MORE GEORGE THOROGOOD AND THE DESTROYERS**		68

– I'm wanted / Kids from Philly / One way ticket / Bottom of the sea / Night time / Tip on in / Goodbye baby / House of blue lights / Just can't make it / Restless. *(re-iss.Mar86 on 'Demon') (US re-iss.+cd.Aug88) (cd-iss.Sep93 on 'Demon')*

Mar 81.	(7") **HOUSE OF BLUE LIGHTS. / THAT PHILLY THING**		
		EMI America	EMI America
Jul 82.	(7") **NOBODY BUT ME. / THAT PHILLY THING**		
Sep 82.	(lp)(c) **BAD TO THE BONE**		43 Aug 82

– Back to Wentsville / Blue highway / Nobody but me / It's a sin / New boogie chillen / Bad to the bone / Miss Luann / As years go passing by / No particular place to go / Wanted man. *(re-iss.+cdJan91 on 'BGO')*

May 85.	(7") **I DRINK ALONE. / GEAR JAMMER**		

(12"+=) – Bad to the bone.

Jan 83.	(7") **BAD TO THE BONE. / NO PARTICULAR PLACE TO GO**	-	
Dec 83.	(7") **ROCK AND ROLL CHRISTMAS. / NEW YEAR'S EVE PARTY**	-	
May 85.	(lp)(c) **MAVERICK**		32 Mar 85

– Gear jammer / I drink alone / Willie and the hand jive / What a price / Long gone / Dixie fried / Crawling King Snake / Memphis, Tennessee / Woman with the blues / (Let's) Go go go / Maverick. *(re-iss.cd Aug94 on 'B.G.O.')*

Aug 85.	(7") **WILLIE AND THE HAND JIVE. / WOMAN WITH THE BLUES**		63 Jun 85

—— added **STEVE CHRISMAR** – guitar

Sep 86.	(lp)(c) **LIVE: GEORGE THOROGOOD (live)**		33 Aug 86

– Who do you love / Bottom of the sea / Night time / I drink alone / One bourbon, one scotch, one beer / Alley oop / Madison blues / Bad to the bone / The sky is crying / Reelin' & rockin'. *(re-iss.Nov88 on 'Fame', cd-iss.May90)*

		Manhattan	Manhattan
Feb 88.	(lp)(c)(cd) **BORN TO BE BAD**		32

– Shake your money maker / You talk too much / Born to be bad / Highway 49 / You can't catch me / I'm ready / Treat her right / I really like girls / Smokestack lightin' / I'm moving on. *(re-iss.cd May94 on 'B.G.O.')*

Feb 88.	(7") **YOU CAN'T CATCH ME. / TREAT HER RIGHT**	-	
		E.M.I. USA	E.M.I.
Apr 91.	(cd)(c)(lp) **BOOGIE PEOPLE**		77

– Six days on the road / Boogie people / Born in Chicago / No place to go / Mad man blues / Long distance lover / If you don't start drinkin' (I'm gonna leave) / Hello little girl / Can't be satisfied / Oklahoma sweetheart.

Sep 92.	(cd)(c)(lp) **BADDEST OF THE BAD** (compilation)		Aug 92

– Bad to the bone / Move it on over / I'm a steady rollin man / You talk too much / Who do you love / Gear jammer / I drink alone / One bourbon, one Scotch, one beer / If you don't start drinkin' (I'm gonna leave) / Treat her right / Long gone / Louie to Frisco. *(re-iss.cd Dec94 on 'B.G.O.')*

		E.R.G.	E.R.G.
Aug 93.	(cd)(c) **HAIRCUT**		

– Get a haircut / Howlin' for my baby / killer bluze / Down in the bottom / I'm ready / Cops and robbers / Gone dead train / Want ad blues / My friend Robert / Baby don't go.

		Capitol	Capitol
Jun 95.	(cd) **LIVE: LET'S WORK TOGETHER (live)**		

– No particular place to go / Ride on Josephine / Bad boy / Cocaine blues / If you don't start drinkin' (I'm gonna leave) / I'm ready / I'll change my style / Get a haircut / Gear jammer / Move it on over / You talk too much / Let's work together / St. Louis blues / Johnny B. Goode.

– compilations, others, etc. –

Sep 79.	MCA; (lp)(c) **BETTER THAN THE REST** (1974 solo recording)		78 Aug 79

– In the night / I'm ready / Goodbye baby / Howlin' for my darlin' / My weakness / Nadine / My way / You're gonna miss me / Worried about my baby / Huckle up baby. *(re-iss.Aug81)*

Oct 79.	MCA; (7") **MY WAY. / YOU'RE GONNA MISS ME**		
Dec 79.	MCA; (7") **IN THE NIGHT. / NADINE**	-	

3 (see under ⇒ EMERSON, LAKE & PALMER)

THROBBING GRISTLE

Formed: Manchester, England ... Sep'75 by GENESIS P. ORRIDGE and girlfriend COSEY, a nude model, who had often went topless on stage, while ORRIDGE and CARTER slashed themselves. The couple had met at an art exhibition in Hull. In 1977, the group set up own indie label 'Industrial' to issue limited edition releases. • **Style:** Electronic theatrical outfit, with violent sexual overtones, described near-narratively by the weird ORRIDGE. Pioneers of anti-punk synth musak alongside CABARET VOLTAIRE and SUICIDE. • **Songwriters:** GENESIS P.ORRIDGE or mainly group compositions. • **Trivia:** Many or all performance / art gigs were recorded on tape and video.

Recommended: GREATEST HITS: ENTERTAINMENT THROUGH PAIN (*7) / 20 JAZZ FUNK GREATS (*7).

GENESIS P.ORRIDGE (b.NEIL ANDREW MEGSON) – vox, electric violin, bass (ex-PORK DUKES) / **COSEY FANNI TUTTI** – guitar, cornet, effects / **CHRIS CARTER** – synthesizers, rhythms / **PETER 'Sleazy' CHRISTOPHERSON** – tapes, synthesizers, trumpet

		Industrial	not issued
1977.	(c) **THE BEST OF THROBBING GRISTLE VOL.2**		-

– Slug bait / Very friendly / We hate you / Seers of E / etc.

Nov 77.	(lp) **THE 2nd ANNUAL REPORT OF ...** (some live)		-

– Slug bait (live versions) / Maggot death / After cease to exist – The original soundtrack of the Coum transmission film. *(re-iss.Nov78 + Apr79) (re-iss.Jun81 on 'Fetish') (re-iss.Apr83 + Nov83 on 'Mute', cd-iss.Jul91)*

Jun 78.	(7")(7"white)(7"clear) **UNITED. / ZYXLON B.ZOMBIE**		-

(re-iss.Jan80, 'B' side longer)

Dec 78.	(lp) **D.O.A. – THE THIRD AND FINAL REPORT OF THROBBING GRISTLE**		-

– I.B.M. / Hit by a rock / United / The valley of the shadow of death / Dead on arrival / Weeping / Hamburger lady / Hometime / Ab-7a / E-Coli / Death threats / Walls of sound / Blood on the floor. *(re-iss.Nov83 on 'Mute', cd-iss.Jul91)*

Jul 79.	(7") **WE HATE YOU (LITTLE GIRLS). / FIVE KNUCKLE SHUFFLE**	-	

(above was issued in France on 'Sordid Sentimentale', US iss.1981)

Oct 79.	(lp) **20 JAZZ FUNK GREATS**		-

– 20 jazz funk greats / Beach Head / Still walking / Tanith / Convincing people / Exotica / Hot on the heels of love / Persuasion / Walkabout / What a day / Six six sixties. *(re-iss.Nov83 on 'Mute', cd-iss.Jul91)*

Jun 80.	(lp)(blue-lp) **HEATHEN EARTH**		-

– Heathen Earth / Heathen Earth / Adrenalin / Subhuman *(re-iss.Nov83 on 'Mute, cd-iss.Jul91, also on video)*

Sep 80.	(7") **SUBHUMAN. / SOMETHING CAME OVER ME**		-
Sep 80.	(7") **ADRENALIN. / DISTANT DREAMS (part 2)**		-
		Fetish	Fetish
May 81.	(12") **DISCIPLINE (live in Manchester). / DISCIPLINE (live in Berlin)**		

—— Dissolved in 1981, when GENESIS and SLEAZY formed PSYCHIC TV. The other two formed duo CHRIS & COSEY.

– compilations, others, etc. –

1979.	Phonograph; (10"lp) **FUHRER DER MEIN SHEAT**	-	
Oct 81.	Rough Trade; (lp) **GREATEST HITS: ENTERTAINMENT THROUGH PAIN**	-	

– Hamburger lady / Hot on the heels of love / Subhuman / Ab 7a / Six six sixties / Blood on the floor / 20 jazz funk greats / Tiab guls / United / What a day / Adrenalin. *(UK-iss.Dec84 on 'Rough Trade', cd-iss.Oct90) (re-cd Jul91 on 'Mute')*

Nov 81.	Zensor; (lp) **FUNERAL IN BERLIN**	-	- Germ'y

– Stained by dead horses / Trained condition of obedience zero's death / Nomon / Raudive bunker experiment / Denial of death / Funeral in Berlin / Trade deficit.

Feb 82.	Fetish; (5xlp-box) **THROBBING GRISTLE**		-

– (5 original albums) *(cd's 1988 on 'Mute')*

1982.	Death TG; (lp) **MUSIC FROM THE DEATH FACTORY (live May'79)**		-
1982.	Walter Ulbright; (lp) **JOURNEY THROUGH A BODY**		-
1982.	Power Focus; (lp) **ASSUME POWER FOCUS**		-

(cd-iss.Oct95 on 'Paragoric')

Nov 82.	Karnage; (d-lp) **THE PSYKICK SACRIFICE**		-

(re-iss.Aug86 as 'SACRIFICE' on 'Dojo')

1983.	Expanded; (lp) **MISSION IS TERMINATED: NICE TRACKS** (free-12"w.a.) **DAMURA SUNRISE. / YOU DON'T KNOW**		-
1983.	Illuminated; (lp) **EDITIONS FRANKFURT – BERLIN**		-
Feb 84.	Illuminated; (lp) **IN THE SHADOW OF THE SUN (Soundtrack)**		-
Nov 83.	Mute; (lp) **MISSION OF DEAD SOULS (THE LAST LIVE PERFORMANCE OF THROBBING GRISTLE) (live San Francisco)**		-

(re-iss.cd Jul91 + video)

Apr 84.	Casual; (lp) **ONCE UPON A TIME**		-
May 84.	Cause For Concern; (lp) **NOTHING SHORT OF TOTAL WAR**		-

(re-iss.Oct87)

1984.	Mental De . . .; (lp) **SPECIAL TREATMENT** *(re-iss.May86)*		-
Mar 93.	Grey Area; (4xcd-box)(4xc-box) **LIVE BOX SET (live)**		-
Apr 93.	Grey Area; (cd) **LIVE – VOLUME 1 (live)**		-
Apr 93.	Grey Area; (cd) **LIVE – VOLUME 2 (live)**		-
Apr 93.	Grey Area; (cd) **LIVE – VOLUME 3 (live)**		-
Apr 93.	Grey Area; (cd) **LIVE – VOLUME 4 (live)**		-
Dec 93.	Dossier; (cd) **FUNK BEYOND JAZZ**		-
Oct 94.	Dossier; (cd) **GIFTGAS**		-

THROWING MUSES

Formed: Boston, Massachusetts, USA ... 1985 by KIRSTIN HERSH and half-sister TANYA DONNELLY, etc. They signed to British indie label '4 a.d.' alongside fellow Bostonians The PIXIES. Their eponymous debut in 1986, sold well through the cartel, due to help of Radio 1 DJ John Peel.

Five years later, they broke into the UK Top 30 with album 'THE REAL RAMONA'. TANYA DONNELLY splintered not long after this, into The BREEDERS and BELLY, and she soon made the latter her new band after leaving The MUSES. • **Style:** Folky alternative band similar to 10,000 MANIACS, but centred around KIRSTIN whose vox warblings reminisced of BUFFY SAINTE-MARIE. • **Songwriters:** KIRSTIN lyrics / group compositions except; AMAZING GRACE (Judy Collins) / RIDE INTO THE SUN (Velvet Underground) / MANIC DEPRESSION (Jimi Hendrix) / WHEN THE LEVEE BREAKS (Gram Parsons). • **Trivia:** KIRSTIN later moved to Newport, Rhode Island with dad.

Recommended: THROWING MUSES (*8) / HUNKPAPA (*8) / THE REAL RAMONA (*7) / THE RED HEAVEN (*7) / HIPS AND MAKERS – KIRSTEN KERSH (*6).

KIRSTIN HERSH (b.1967) – vocals, lead guitar, piano / **ELAINE ADAMEDES** – bass / **TANYA DONNELLY** – rhythm guitar, vocals / **DAVID NARCIZO** – drums, percussion, vocals

not issued ???

1986. (7"ep) **STAND UP / PARTY. / SANTA CLAUS / DIRT ON THE DANCE FLOOR** [-] [ ]

— **LESLIE LANGSTON** – bass, vocals repl. ELAINE

4 a.d. Relativity

Sep 86. (lp)(c)(cd) **THROWING MUSES** [ ] [ ]
– Call me / Green / Hate my way / Vicky's box / Rabbit's dying / America (she can't say no) / Fear / Stand up / Soul soldier / Delicious cutters.

Mar 87. (12"ep)(c-ep) **CHAINS CHANGED** [ ] [ ]
– Cry baby cry / Finished / reel / Snail head.

Aug 87. (m-lp)(c) **THE FAT SKIER** [ ] [ ]
– Soul soldier / Garoux des larmes / Pool in eyes / A feeling / You cage / Soap and water / And a she-wolf after the war.

Mar 88. (lp)(c)(cd) **HOUSE TORNADO** [ ] [ ]
– Colder / Mexican woman / The river / Juno / Marriage tree / Run letter / Saving grace / Drive / Downtown / Giant / Walking in the dark. (cd+=) – THE FAT SKIER (m-lp tracks).

Jan 89. (lp)(c)(cd) **HUNKPAPA** [59] [ ]
– Devil's roof / Bea / Dizzy / No parachutes (say goodbye) / Dragonhead / Fall down / I'm alive / Angel / Mania / The burrow / Take. *(cd+=)* – Downtown.

Feb 89. (7") **DIZZY. / SANTA CLAUS** [ ] [ ]
(10"+=)(12"+=)(cd-s+=) – Marie / Downtown.

— TANYA with DAVID (only in '89) formed off-shoot The BREEDERS (see further). She stayed with TM until next album's completion. **FRED ABONG** – bass repl. her

Jan 91. (7") **COUNTING BACKWARDS. / SAME SUN** [70] [ ]
(12"+=)(cd-s+=) – Cotton mouth / Amazing Grace.

Feb 91. (cd)(c)(lp) **THE REAL RAMONA** [26] [ ]
– Counting backwards / Him dancing / Red shoes / Graffiti / Golden thing / Ellen West / Dylan / Hook in her head / Not too soon / Honey chain / Say goodbye / Two step

Nov 91. (7") **NOT TOO SOON. /CRY BABY CRY** [ ] [ ]
(12"+=)(cd-s+=) – Dizzy (remix) / Him dancing (remix).

— (Sep91) **DONNELLY** and **ABONG** had now quit to form BELLY in 1992. **KIRSTEN + NARCIZO** recruited newcomer **BERNARD GEORGES** – bass

Jul 92. (12"ep)(cd-ep) **FIREPILE / MANIC DEPRESSION. / SNAILHEAD / CITY OF THE DEAD** [46] [ ]
(12"ep)(cd-ep) – ('A'remix) / Jack / Ride into the Sun / Handsome woman.

Aug 92. (cd)(c)(lp) **RED HEAVEN** [13] [ ]
– Furious / Firepile / Die / Dirty water / Stroll / Pearl / Summer Street / Vic / Backroad / The visit / Dovey / Rosetta stone / Carnival wig. (free-lp w.a.) **LIVE (live)** – Juno / Marriage tree / Pearl / Stand up – Dovey – Mexican woman / Run letter / Soap and water / Rabbit dying / Cry baby cry / Counting backwards – Handsome woman / Take / Soul soldier / Bea / Delicate cutters.

Nov 92. (cd) **THE CURSE (live)** [74] [ ]
– Manic depression / Counting backwards / Fish / Hate my way / Furious / Devil's roof / Snailhead / Firepile / Finished / Take / Say goodbye / Mania / Two step / Delicate cutters / Cottonmouth / Pearl / Vic / Bea.

Dec 94. (7")(c-s) **BRIGHT YELLOW GUN. / LIKE A DOG** [51] [ ]
(12"+=)(cd-s+=) – Red eyes / Crayon Sun.

Jan 95. (cd)(c)(lp) **UNIVERSITY** [10] [ ]
– Bright yellow gun / Start / Hazing / Shimmer / Calm down, come down / Crabtown / No way in Hell / Surf cowboy / That's all you wanted / Teller / University / Snake face / Fever few.

KRISTEN HERSH

first below featured **MICHAEL STIPE** (R.E.M.) / **JANE SCARPANTONI** – cello

4 a.d. 4 a.d.

Jan 94. (12")(c-s) **YOUR GHOST / THE KEY. / UNCLE JUNE AND AUNT KIYOTI / WHEN THE LEVEE BREAKS** [45] [ ]

Jan 94. (cd)(c)(lp) **HIPS AND MAKERS** [7] [ ]
– Your ghost / Beestung / Teeth / Sundrops / sparky / Houdini blues / A loon / Velvet days / Close your eyes / Me and my charms / Tuesday night / The letter / Lurch / The cuckoo / Hips and makers.

Apr 94. (7")(c-s) **A LOON. / VELVET DAYS** [60] [ ]
(12")(cd-ep) **'STRINGS EP'** (+=) – Sundrops / Me and my charms.

Dec 95. (cd-ep) **THE HOLY SINGLE** [ ] [-]

THUNDER

Formed: South London, England ... mid'89 by BOWES, MORLEY and JAMES who had been part of Reading festival specialists TERRAPLANE. They had been founded around 1982 but disintegrated early 1988, when they pursued career in America. They found BEN and SNAKE and became THUNDER, and through agent Malcolm McKenzie they signed to 'EMI'. Quickly became top act for the early 90's, after breaking into the UK Top 40 with 'DIRTY LOVE', which was produced by ANDY TAYLOR (ex-DURAN DURAN). They soon played the Cathouse in New York and were given deal with EMI's US counterpart 'Capitol'. • **Style:** Heavy rock outfit suited to US – FM radio, due to similarities to BAD COMPANY, AEROSMITH or LED ZEPPELIN. • **Songwriters:** All penned by MORLEY, except; GET IT ON (T.Rex) / GIMME SOME LOVIN' (Spencer Davis Group) / WITH A LITTLE HELP FROM MY FRIENDS (Beatles) / GIMME SHELTER (Rolling Stones) / 5.15 (Who) / ALL THE WAY FROM MEMPHIS (Mott The Hoople) / IN A BROKEN DREAM (hit; Python Lee Jackson) / STAY WITH ME (Rod Stewart & The Faces). • **Trivia:** SNAKE once appeared on Top Of The Pops, as bass player on OWEN PAUL's hit 'You're My Favourite Waste Of Time'.

Recommended: BACKSTREET SYMPHONY (*6).

TERRAPLANE

DANNY BOWES – vocals / **LUKE MORLEY** – guitar / **RUDY RIVIERE** – guitar / **NICK LINDEN** – bass, piano / **GARY JAMES** – drums

City not issued

Mar 83. (7") **I SURVIVE. / GIMME THE MONEY** [ ] [-]

Epic Epic

Dec 84. (7") **I CAN'T LIVE WITHOUT YOUR LOVE. / BEGINNING OF THE END** [ ] [-]
(12"+=) – Let the wheels go round.

Mar 85. (7")(12") **I SURVIVE. / ALL NIGHT AND DAY (live)** [ ] [-]

Jul 85. (7") **WHEN YOU'RE HOT. / TOUGH KIND OF LOVE** [ ] [ ]
(12"+=) – If you could see yourself.

Oct 85. (7") **TALKING TO MYSELF. / GET YOUR FACE OUT OF MY DREAMS** [ ] [-]
(12"+=) – Gimme the money.

— RUDY only appeared on 1 track from next album.

Jan 86. (lp)(c) **BLACK AND WHITE** [74] [ ]
– Don't walk away / When you're hot / I can't live without your love / Talking to myself / You can't hurt me anymore / I survive / Right betweeen the eyes / Black and white / I'm the one / Get your face out of my dream / Couldn't handle the tears. *(c+=)* – Tough kind of love / Beginning of the end / All night and day.

Jan 87. (7")(7"sha-pic-d) **IF THAT'S WHAT IT TAKES. / LIVING AFTER DARK** [ ] [ ]
(12"+=) – ('A'-19th nervous breakdown mix) / Drugs.

Jun 87. (7") **GOOD THING GOING. / A NIGHT OF MADNESS** [ ] [ ]
(12"+=)/ /(c++=) – The good life./ / ('A'version).

Aug 87. (7") **MOVING TARGET. / WHEN I SLEEP ALONE** [ ] [ ]
(d7"+=)(12"+=) – I survive (live) / I can't live without your love.

Sep 87. (lp)(c)(cd) **MOVING TARGET** [ ] [ ]
– If that's what it takes / Good thing going / Promised land / Moving target / Hostage to fortune / Heartburn / Hearts on fire / I will come out fighting / Nothing on but the radio. *(cd+=)*– Moving target (extended) / When I sleep alone / I can't live without your love (live) / I survive (live).

— Disbanded early 1988. After a stint in the US,

THUNDER

BOWES + MORLEY brought back **GARY 'Harry' JAMES** – drums, with also **BEN MATTHEWS** – guitar, keyboards / **MARK 'Snake' LUCKHURST** – bass

E.M.I. Capitol

Oct 89. (7") **SHE'S SO FINE. / GIRL'S GOING OUT OF HER HEAD** [ ] [-]
(12"+=)(cd-s+=) – Another shot of love.

Jan 90. (7")(7"pic-d) **DIRTY LOVE. / FIRED UP** [32] [-]
(12"+=)/ /(cd-s++=) – She's so fine (live)./ / Brown sugar (live).

Feb 90. (cd)(c)(lp) **BACK STREET SYMPHONY** [21] [ ] Apr 90
– She's so fine / Dirty love / Don't wait for me / Higher ground / Until my dying day / Back street symphony / Love walked in / An Englishmman on holiday / Girl's going out of her head / Gimme some lovin'. *(cd+c+=)*– Distant thunder. *(pic-lp Nov90, re-dist.Feb91, scraped UK Top 50) (re-iss.cd+c Sep94)*

Apr 90. (7")(c-s) **BACK STREET SYMPHONY. / NO WAY OUT OF THE WILDERNESS** [25] [-]
(12"+=)(12"pic-d+=) – An Englishman on holiday (live).
(cd-s++=) – Girl's going out of her head (live).

Jul 90. (7") **GIMME SOME LOVIN'. / I WANNA BE HER SLAVE** [36] [-]
(12"+=)(12"pic-d+=)(c-s+=)(cd-s+=) – Dirty love (live).
(10"red+=) – Until the night is through.

Sep 90. (7")(c-s) **SHE'S SO FINE. / I CAN STILL HEAR THE MUSIC** [34] [ ]
(12"+=) – Don't wait for me (live).
(10"blue+=) – Backstreet symphony (live).
(cd-s) – ('A'side) / (above 2 extra)

Sep 90. (c-s) **SHE'S SO FINE. / GIMME SOME LOVIN'** [-] [ ]

E.M.I. Geffen

Feb 91. (7") **DIRTY LOVE. / GIRL'S GOING OUT OF HER HEAD** [-] [55]

Feb 91. (7")(c-s) **LOVE WALKED IN. / FLAWED TO PERFECTION (demo)** [21] [ ]
(12"+=)(cd-s+=)(12"pic-d+=) – Until my dying day (live).
(10"white+=) – World problems: a solution.

Aug 92. (7") **LOWLIFE IN HIGH PLACES. / BABY I'LL BE GONE** [22] [ ]
(cd-s) – ('A'side) / Backstreet symphony / She's so fine / Love walked in.
(cd-s) – ('A'side) / With a little help from my friends / She's my inspiration / Low life in high places (demo).

Aug 92. (cd)(c)(d-lp) **LAUGHING ON JUDGEMENT DAY** [2] [ ]
– Does it feel like love? / Everybody wants her / Low life in high places / Laughing on judgement day / Empty city / Today the world stopped turning / Long way from home / Fire to ice / Feeding the flame / A better man / The moment of truth / Flawed to perfection / Like a satellite / Baby I'll be gone. *(re-iss.cd+c Mar94)*

Oct 92. (7")(c-s) **EVERYBODY WANTS HER. / DANGEROUS RHYTHM** [36] [ ]

(12"+=) – Higher ground (acoustic).
(cd-s) – ('A'side) / Dirty love (acoustic) / Higher ground (acoustic) / Dirty love.

Feb 93. (7")(c-s) **A BETTER MAN. / LOW LIFE IN HIGH PLACES (live)** | 18 | –
(12")(cd-s) – ('A'side) / New York, New York (Harry's theme) / Lazy Sunday (live) / Higher ground (live).

Jun 93. (12"ep)(cd-ep) **LIKE A SATELLITE / LIKE A SATELLITE (live) / GIMME SHELTER / THE DAMAGE IS DONE** | 28 | –

Dec 94. (7"pic-d)(c-s) **STAND UP. / (interview)** | 23 | –
(cd-s+=) – The fire is gone (demo) / Life in a day (demo).
(cd-s) – ('A'side) / One pretty woman / It happened in this town.

Jan 95. (cd)(c)(lp) **BEHIND CLOSED DOORS** | 5 | –
– Moth to the flame / Fly on the wall / I'll be waiting / River of pain / Future train / 'Til the river runs dry / Stand up / Preaching from a chair / Castles in the sand / Too scared to live / Ball and chain / It happened in this train.

Feb 95. (c-s) **RIVERS OF PAIN / DOES IT FEEL LIKE LOVE** | 31 | –
(cd-s+=) – Everybody wants her (live) / All the way from Memphis (live).
(cd-s) – ('A'side) / 5.15 (live) / You don't know what love is (demo).
(12"pic-d) – ('A'side) / Move on / All the way from Memphis (live).

Apr 95. (c-ep) **CASTLES IN THE SAND / A BETTER MAN / SHE'S SO FINE / DIRTY LOVE** | 30 | –
(cd-s) – ('A'side) / Stand up (live acoustic) / Move over (live).
(cd-s) – ('A'side) / I hear you knocking (live acoustic) / River of pain (live acoustic).

Sep 95. (c-s) **IN A BROKEN DREAM / 'TIL THE RIVER RUNS DRY** | 26 | –
(cd-s) – ('A'side) / Love walked in / Dirty love (demo).
(cd-s) – ('A'side) / Stay with me / An Englishman on holiday.

Sep 95. (cd)(c)(d-lp) **THEIR FINEST HOUR (AND A BIT)** (compilation) | 22 | –
– Dirty love / River of pain / Love walked in / Everybody wants her / In a broken dream / Higher ground '95 / Backstreet symphony / A better man / Gimme shelter / Like a satellite / Low life in high places / Stand up / Once in a lifetime / Gimme some lovin' / Castles in the sand / She's so fine.

Johnny THUNDERS (see under ⇒ HEARTBREAKERS)

Tanita TIKARAM

Born: 12 Aug'69, Munster, W.Germany. Her father was Indian-Fijian, her mother from Borneo. They moved to Basingstoke in England when she was a teenager. Went solo in '87, and through agent Paul Charles, signed to 'WEA'. With producer PETER VAN HOOKE and ROD ARGENT, she recorded hit debut album 'ANCIENT HEART', which contained UK Top 10 smash 'GOOD TRADITION'. • **Style:** The female LEONARD COHEN and moody ballad singer, was influenced by VAN MORRISON, with manly voice gladly overshadowed by her lyrical and facial beauty. • **Songwriters:** She collaborated with ARGENT and VAN HOOKE. Covered LOVING YOU (Elvis Presley). • **Trivia:** In the late 80's, she guested on an album by BRENDAN CROKER and The FIVE O'CLOCK SHADOW.

Recommended: ANCIENT HEART (*7) / THE SWEET KEEPER (*6).

TANITA TIKARAM – vocals, acoustic guitar with producers **PETER VAN COOKE** – drums / **ROD ARGENT** – keyboards plus **RORY McFARLANE** – bass / **MITCH DALTON** – guitar / **MARTIN DITCHAM** – percussion. Guests were **PAUL BRADY + MARK CRESWELL** – guitar / **HELEN O'HARA** – violin / **BRENDAN CROKER** – accordion, etc.

W.E.A. | Reprise

Aug 88. (7") **GOOD TRADITION. / VALENTINE HEART** | 10 | –
(12"+=)/ /(cd-s++=) – Poor cow (demo)./ / Cathedral song.

Sep 88. (lp)(c)(cd) **ANCIENT HEART** | 3 | 59
– Good tradition / Cathedral song / Sighing innocents / I love you / World outside your window / For all these years / Twist in my sobriety / Poor cow / He likes the sun / Valentine heart / Preyed upon. *(re-iss.cd Feb95)*

Oct 88. (7") **TWIST IN MY SOBRIETY. / FRIENDS** | 22 | –
(10"+=) – The kill in your heart.
('A'ext-12"+=)/ /(cd-s) – For all these years./ / (the 4 tracks).

Jan 89. (7") **CATHEDRAL SONG. / SIGHING INNOCENTS** | 48 | –
(box-7"+=)(cd-s+=) – Let's make everybody smile today (live) / Over you all (live).
(12"+=) – Let's make . . . (live) / Fireflies in the kitchen (live).

Mar 89. (7") **WORLD OUTSIDE YOUR WINDOW (remix). / FOR ALL THESE YEARS (instrumental)** | 58 | –
(12"+=) – Good tradition (live).
(box-cd-s++=) – He likes the Sun (live).
(cd-s++=) – ('A'extended).

— **JOHN GIBLIN** – bass repl. DITCHAM and DALTON / guests **CLEM CLEMPSON** – guitar / **MARK ISHAM** – trumpet repl. CROKER + BRADY

Jan 90. (7") **WE ALMOST GOT IT TOGETHER. / LOVE STORY** | 52 | –
(12"+=)(cd-s+=) – Over you all.

Feb 90. (cd)(c)(lp) **THE SWEET KEEPER** | 3 | –
– Once & not speak / Thursday's child / It all came back today / We almost got it together / Consider the rain / Sunset's arrived / Little sister leaving town / I owe it all to you / Love story / Harm in your hands.

Mar 90. (7")(c-s) **LITTLE SISTER LEAVING TOWN. / I LOVE THE HEAVEN** | | –
(12"+=)(cd-s+=) – Hot pork sandwiches / Twist in my sobriety.

Jun 90. (7") **THURSDAY'S CHILD. / ONCE & NOT SPEAK** | | –
(12"+=)(cd-s+=) – Cathedral song (live).

— She retained **VAN HOOKE, ARGENT, CRESWELL + ISHAM,** bringing in **DAVID HAYES** – bass / **NICK FRANCE** – drums / **KATIE KISSOON + CAROL KENYON** – b.vocals

East West | Reprise

Jan 91. (7")(c-s) **ONLY THE ONES WE LOVE. / ME IN MIND** | 69 | –
(12"+=)/ /(cd-s+=) – Mud in any water./ / Cathedral song.

Feb 91. (cd)(c)(lp) **EVERYBODY'S ANGEL** | 19 | –
– Only the ones we love / Deliver me / This story in me / To wish this / Mud in any water / Sunface / Never known / This stranger / Swear by me / Hot pork sandwiches / Me in mind / Sometime with me / I love the Heaven's solo / I'm going home.

Mar 91. (7")(c-s) **I LOVE THE HEAVEN'S SOLO. / ONLY IN NAME** | | –
(12"+=)(cd-s+=) – To wish this / I'm going home.

Feb 92. (7")(c-s) **YOU MAKE THE WHOLE WORLD CRY. / ROCK ME 'TIL I STOP / ME, YOU & LUCIFER** | | –
(cd-s) – (1st 2 tracks) / This stranger (alt.version).
(cd-s) – (1st & 3rd tracks) / This stranger (alt.version).

Mar 92. (cd)(c)(lp) **ELEVEN KINDS OF LONELINESS** | | –
– You make the whole world cry / Elephant / trouble / I grant you / Heal you / To drink the rainbow / Out on the town / Hot stones / Men & women / Any reason / Love don't need no tyranny / The way that I want you.

— now with guitarist **MICHAEL LANDAU**/ + orchestra THOMAS NEWMAN

Jan 95. (c-s)(cd-s) **I MIGHT BE CRYING / FIVE FEET AWAY** | 64 | –
(cd-s+=) – Not waving but drowning.

Feb 95. (cd)(c) **LOVERS IN THE CITY** | 75 | –
– Lovers in the city / Yodelling song / Wonderful shadow / Women who cheat on the world / Leaving the party / I might be crying / Bloodlines / Feeding the witches / Happy taxi / My love tonight.

Mar 95. (c-s) **WONDERFUL SHADOW / GOOD TRADITION** | | –
(cd-s) – ('A'side) / Have you lost your way?.
(cd-s) – ('A'side) / Out on the town.

Jul 95. (cd-s) **THE YODELLING SONG / TO DRINK THE RAINBOW / BLOODLINES** | | –

'TIL TUESDAY (see under ⇒ MANN, Aimee)

TIMELORDS (see under ⇒ KLF)

TIMES (see under ⇒ TELEVISION PERSONALITIES)

TINDERSTICKS

Formed: Nottingham, England . . . 1988 as ASPHALT RIBBONS, by STUART STAPLES, DAVE BOULTER and DICKON HINCHCLIFFE. After 3 years, a few singles and a 1991 album, they moved to London and soon became TINDERSTICKS. With 3 others in their ranks, they soon were tipped for stardom in '94, having had their eponymous album, acclaimed by music press. • **Style:** Moved from psuedo-indie-rock outfit like TRIFFIDS or GO-BETWEENS, which progressed in TINDERSTICKS, to LOU REED or NICK CAVE like alternative rock. • **Songwriters:** Covered; KOOKS (David Bowie) / A MARRIAGE MADE IN HEAVEN (Lee Hazlewood-Nancy Sinatra) / WE HAVE ALL THE TIME IN THE WORLD (John Barry) / KATHLEEN (Townes Van Zandt). • **Trivia:** JON LANGFORD of The THREE JOHNS, produced early ASPHALT RIBBONS material.

Recommended: TINDERSTICKS (*8) / THE SECOND TINDERSTICKS ALBUM (*8)

ASPHALT RIBBONS

STUART STAPLES – vocals / **DICKON HINCHCLIFFE** – violin / **DAVE BOULTER** – keyboards / **BLACKHOUSE** – guitar / **FRASER** – bass / **WATT** – drums

In-Tape | not issued

Oct 89. (7"ep) **THE ORCHARD** | | –
– Over again / Red sauce / Greyhound / I used to live T.

May 90. (7"m) **GOOD LOVE. / LONG LOST UNCLE / THE DAY I TURNED BAD** | | –

(Alongside new stablemates MY LIFE WITH PATRICK, their new label below issued a free flexi sampler with 'Zip Code' fanzine; cat no. LILY 001)

Tiger Lily | not issued

Apr 91. (12"ep) **PASSION, COOLNESS, INDIFFERENCE, BOREDOM, MOCKERY, CONTEMPT, DISGUST** | | –

E.T.T. | not issued

Aug 91. (m-lp) **OLD HORSE & OTHER SONGS** | | –
– (cd-iss.Apr92)

TINDERSTICKS

were formed by **STUART, DICKON and DAVE,** plus Londoners **NEIL FRAZER** – guitar / **MARK COLWILL** – bass / **AL McCAULEY** – drums

Tippy Toe | not issued

Nov 92. (7") **PATCHWORK. / MILKY TEETH** | | –

Mar 93. (10"ep) **MARBLES / JOE STUMBLE. / FOR THOSE . . . / BENN** | | –

— Below featured dual vox of **NIKI SIN** of HUGGY BEAR.

Rough Trade | not issued

Apr 93. (7") **A MARRIAGE MADE IN HEAVEN. / ('A'instrumental)** | | –

Domino | not issued

Jul 93. (7"ep) **UNWIRED EP** | | –
– Feeling relatively good / Rottweilers and mace / She / Kooks.

This Way Up | not issued

Sep 93. (7")(cd-s) **CITY SICKNESS. / UNTITLED / THE BULLRING** | | –

Oct 93. (cd)(c)(lp) **TINDERSTICKS** | 56 | –
– Nectar / Tyed / Sweet, sweet man (pt.1) / Whiskey & water / Blood / City sickness / Patchwork / Marbles / Walt blues / Milky teeth (pt.2) / Jism / Piano song / Tre dye / Drunk tank / Paco de Renaldo's dream / Not knowing. (lp+=) – Fruitless.

— In Oct'93, alongside GALLON DRUNK, they issued 'Clawfist' 7" WE HAVE ALL THE TIME IN THE WORLD. 'Tippy Toe' also gaveaway at gigs 7" 'LIVE

IN BERLIN'.

Jan 94. (7"ep)(10"ep)(cd-ep) **KATHLEEN EP** 61 -
– Kathleen / Summat Moon / A sweet sweet man / E-type Joe.

— In Aug'94, they appeared on Various Artists EP on 'Blue Eyed Dog'; track 'LOVE BITES', and others by STRANGELOVE / GOD MACHINE + BREED.

Mar 95. (7") **NO MORE AFFAIRS. / ('A'instrumental)** 58
(cd-s+=) – Fruitless.

Apr 95. (cd)(c)(d-lp) **THE SECOND TINDERSTICKS ALBUM** 13
– El diablo en el ojo / My sister / Tiny tears / Snowy in F# minor / Seaweed / Vertraven 2 / Talk to me / No more affairs / Singing / Travelling light / Cherry blossoms / She's gone / Mistakes / Vertraven 3 / Sleepy song. (some lp's w/free one-sided-7") PLUS DE LAISONS

Jul 95. (7")(cd-s) **TRAVELLING LIGHT. / WAITING 'ROUND YOU / I'VE BEEN LOVING YOU TOO LONG** 51

Oct 95. (cd)(d-10"lp) **THE BLOOMSBURY THEATRE 12.3.95 (live)** 32
– El diablo en el ojo / A night in / Talk to me / She's gone / My sister * / No more affairs / City sickness / Vertraven II / Sleepy song / Jism / Drunk tank / Mistakes / Tiny tears / Raindrops / For those . . . (d-lp+= *)

TIN MACHINE (see under ⇒ BOWIE, David)

TOAD THE WET SPROCKET

Formed: Santa Barbara, California, USA . . . late 80's BY GLENN PHILLIPS AND TODD NICHOLS. After a single on own label, they were snapped up by 'Columbia'. In 1992, they scraped into US Top 50 with third album 'FEAR'. • **Style:** Like a West Coast POLICE fused with JACKSON BROWNE type songs. Lack pop /rock identity as yet, due to stupid Monty Pythonesque. • **Songwriters:** Group written; (GLEN OR TODD LYRICS). COVERED; ROCK AND ROLL ALL NITE (Kiss). • **Trivia:** Also featured on film soundtracks 'So I Married An Axe Murderer' & 'Buffy The Vampire Slayer'.

Recommended: DULCINEA (*6)

GLEN PHILLIPS – vocals / **TODD NICHOLS** – guitar / **DEAN DINNING** – bass / **RANDY GUSS** – drums

Sprockets Sprockets

1989. (7") **REACHING FOR THE SKY. / ONE GLASS OF WHISKEY**

C.B.S. Columbia

1989. (c)(cd) **PALE** -
– Torn / Come back down / Don't go away / High on a riverbed / I think about / Corporal Brown / Jam / Chile / Liars everywhere / Nothing is alone / She cried.

Feb 90. (cd)(c)(lp) **BREAD AND CIRCUS**
– Way away / Scenes from a vinyl recliner / Unquiet / Know me / When we recovered / One wind blows / Pale blue / Always changing probably / One little girl / Covered in roses.

Columbia Columbia

Sep 92. (7")(c-s) **ALL I WANT. / ALL SHE SAID** 15 Jun 92
(12")(cd-s) – ('A'side) / Hold her down / Come back down / One little girl. *(re-iss.Feb93)*

Sep 92. (cd)(c)(lp) **FEAR** 49 Jun 92
– Walk on the ocean / Is it for me / Butterflies / Nightingale song / Hold her down / Pray to your gods / Before you were born / Something to say / In my ear / All I want / Stories I tell / I will not take things for granted.

Nov 92. (c-s)(cd-s) **WALK ON THE OCEAN. / ALL I WANT** - 18

Sep 94. (cd)(c)(lp) **DULCINEA** 34 May 94
– Fly from Heaven / Woodburning / Something's always wrong / Stupid / Crowing / (Listen) / Windmills / Nanci / Fall down / Inside / Begin / Reincarnation song. *(cd+c+=)* – Hope.

Oct 94. (c-ep)(cd-ep) **FALL DOWN / ONE LITTLE GIRL / COME BACK DOWN / NIGHTINGALE** 33 Jul 94
(cd-s) – (1st track) / All I want / Hold her down / Know me.

Oct 94. (c-s)(cd-s) **SOMETHING'S ALWAYS WRONG. / ?** - 41

Oct 95. (cd)(c) **IN LIGHT SYRUP** - 37

TOMORROW

Formed: London, England . . . 1964 as FOUR + ONE by JOHN 'JUNIOR' WOOD and SIMON 'BOOTS' ALCOT, who soon recruited Dagenham born singer KEITH WEST and drummer KEN LAWRENCE. After covering a ROLLING STONES song on one single for 'Parlophone', they were advised to change name to the more fashionable The IN-CROWD (after a Dobie Gray soul number). Their first 45 (a Marvin Gaye cover) 'THAT'S HOW STRONG MY LOVE IS' breached the Top 50, but was pursued by two flops later in 1965, which included new guitarist STEVE HOWE. A quiet year followed, until they returned in 1967 complete with new image, new direction, new drummer (TWINK) and new name; TOMORROW. Their first single 'MY WHITE BICYCLE' was surely in the one-that-got-away category, although it did surface 6 years later as a Top 10 smash for NAZARETH. Another flop 45 surfaced later in the year and was tailed early the next by a too-late-for-the-show eponymous album, which needless to say, plummeted. The reasons were simple for the public reaction, as KEITH WEST had also released his solo single in the summer of '67. 'EXCERPT FROM A TEENAGE OPERA' (aka 'Grocer Jack') had made him a star overnight, when it peaked at No.2. Suddenly requests for KEITH WEST and TOMORROW to tour were so demanding, that they even wanted this 4-piece to play the hit, although it was originally recorded in the studio with a full orchestra. It was inevitable they disbanded soon after the albums' release. KEITH WEST continued for a short spell as a solo artist, while TWINK joined The PRETTY THINGS and HOWE formed BODAST before joining YES. • **Style:** Moved away from a much lambasted white-soul mod outfit in the mid-60's to top underground psychedelic rock group that hosted many a future star. • **Songwriters:** Group penned except; STRAWBERRY FIELDS FOREVER (Beatles). • **Trivia:** All produced by MARK WRITZ even WEST's poppy solo stuff.

Recommended: TOMORROW (*7)

FOUR + ONE

KEITH WEST – vocals / **JOHN 'JUNIOR' WOOD** – rhythm guitar, vocals / **SIMON ALCOT** – bass / **KEN LAWRENCE** – drums

Parlophone not issued

Jan 65. (7") **TIME IS ON MY SIDE. / DON'T LIE TO ME** -

The IN-CROWD

(same line-up & label)

Apr 65. (7") **THAT'S HOW STRONG MY LOVE IS. / THINGS SHE SAYS** 48 -

— added **STEVE HOWE** – guitar who soon repl. ALCOT

Sep 65. (7") **STOP! WAIT A MINUTE. / YOU'RE ON YOUR OWN** -

Nov 65. (7") **WHY MUST THEY CRITICIZE. / I DON'T MIND** -

TOMORROW

'TWINK' JOHN ADLER – drums (ex-FAIRIES) repl. LAWRENCE

Parlophone Capitol

May 67. (7") **MY WHITE BICYCLE. / CLAREMONT LAKE**
(re-iss.Oct69)

Sep 67. (7") **REVOLUTION. / THREE JOLLY LITTLE DWARFS** -

Feb 68. (lp) **TOMORROW** -
– My white bicycle / Colonel Brown / Real life permanent dream / Shy boy / Claremont Lake / Revolution / The incredible journey of Timothy Chase / Aunty Mary's dress shop / Strawberry fields forever / Three jolly little dwarfs / Now your time has come / Hallucinations. *(re-iss.Jun76 on 'Harvest') (re-iss.Dec86 on 'Decal') (cd-iss.Sep90 on 'See For Miles')*

— Disbanded soon after above. (note: MY WHITE BICYCLE was re-issued in Oct83 by 'Old Gold' label with track by LOVE SCULPTURE on the flip). BODAST were formed by STEVE HOWE who recorded an lp, although this stayed unreleased until 'Charry Red' records 'THE BODAST TAPES' in 1982. It is now on cd (May90) with 2 extra tracks as 'THE EARLY YEARS – STEVE HOWE WITH BODAST'.

AQUARIAN AGE

TWINK + WOOD (same label and arrangement)

May 68. (7") **10,000 WORDS IN A CARDBOARD BOX. / GOOD WIZARD MEETS NAUGHTY WIZARD** -

KEITH WEST

Parlophone Capitol

Jul 67. (7") **EXCERPT FROM "A TEENAGE OPERA". / Mark Writz Orchestra: THEME FROM "A TEENAGE OPERA"** 2

Nov 67. (7") **SAM (FROM "A TEENAGE OPERA"). / Mark Writz's Mood Mosaic: THIMBLE FULL OF PUZZLES** 38

Jul 68. (7") **ON A SATURDAY. / THE KID WAS A KILLER** -

Deram not issued

Oct 73. (7") **RIDING FOR A FALL. / DAYS ABOUT TO RAIN** -

Feb 74. (7") **HAVIN' SOMEONE. / KNOW THERE'S NO LIVIN' WITHOUT YOU** -

Kuckuck not issued

Sep 74. (German-lp) **WHEREVER MY LOVE GOES** - -

Pink Elephant not issued

Sep 74. (Dutch-7") **THE POWER AND THE GLORY. / LIET MOTIF** - -

– compilations, etc. –

Jun 72. Parlophone; (7") **EXCERPT FROM " A TEENAGE OPERA". / SAM** -

Jul 81. Video; (7") **EXCERPT FROM "A TEENAGE OPERA". / COUNT ON ME** -

TOM TOM CLUB (see under ⇒ TALKING HEADS)

TONES ON TAIL (see under ⇒ BAUHAUS)

Peter TOSH

Born: WINSTON HUBERT MacINTOSH, 9 Oct'44, Westmoreland, Jamaica. In 1962, he was original member of The WAILERS alongside BOB MARLEY, until he left in 1973 after their move to 'Island'. In the last decade, TOSH had provided them with numerous material, the last being 'GET UP STAND UP' for the 'Burnin' album. He formed his own label 'Intel Diplo HIM', but his career was really re-activated again when 'Virgin' signed him in 1976. His debut 'LEGALIZE IT' nearly hit UK Top 50 but another flopped. Two years later, great fan MICK JAGGER of The ROLLING STONES signed him to own label and even provided loud backing vocals on TOSH's first Top 50 hit single 'DON'T LOOK BACK'. He had one more success in 1983 with single 'JOHNNY B. GOODE'. He returned mid-87 with album 'NO NUCLEAR WAR', but was shot dead on 11th September that year during a robbery at his Kingston home. He was only 42, but won a postumous Grammy for the album in 1988. • **Style:** A reggae great, he was the tuffest and one of the more politically aware. • **Songwriters:** Writes himelf, except several including; DON'T LOOK BACK (Temptations). • **Trivia:** Was arrested many times during the 60's for his ganja smoking, thus inspiring album 'LEGALIZE IT'.

Recommended: LEGALIZE IT (*7) / BUSH DOCTOR (*6) / NO NUCLEAR WAR (*6) / THE TOUGHEST (*7)

PETER TOSH – vocals, keyboards, guitar (ex-WAILERS) / with some ex-WAILERS, SLY & ROBBIE, etc.

Virgin / Virgin

Mar 76. (7") **LEGALIZE IT. / BRAND NEW SECOND HAND** [ ] [-]

Aug 76. (lp)(c) **LEGALIZE IT** [54] [ ]
– Legalize it / Burial / Watcha gonna do / No sympathy / Why must I care / Igziabeher (let jah be praised) / Ketchy shuby / Till your well runs dry / Brand new second hand. *(re-iss.+cd Aug88)*

Apr 77. (7") **AFRICAN. / STEPPING RAZOR** [ ] [-]

Apr 77. (lp)(c) **EQUAL RIGHTS** (with WORDS, SOUND & POWER) [ ] [ ]
– Get up, stand up / Downpressor man / I am that I am / Stepping razor / Equal rights / African / Jah guide / Apartheid. *(re-iss.+cd Aug88)*

E.M.I. / Columbia

Sep 78. (7")(12") **(YOU GOTTA WALK) DON'T LOOK BACK. / SOON COME** [43] [81]

— above featured duet with MICK JAGGER

Rolling St / Rolling St

Nov 78. (lp)(c) **BUSH DOCTOR** [ ] [ ]
– (You gotta walk) Don't look back / Pick myself up / I'm the toughest / Soon come / Moses the prophet / Bush doctor / Stand firm / Dem ha fe get a beatin' / Creation. *(re-iss.Nov85 on 'Fame') (cd-iss.Oct88 on 'EMI')*

Mar 79. (7") **I'M THE TOUGHEST. / TOUGHEST (version)** [ ] [ ]
(12"+=) – Word, sound and power.

Aug 79. (7") **BUK-IN-HAMM PALACE. / THE DAY THE DOLLAR DIE** [ ] [ ]

Aug 79. (lp)(c) **MYSTIC MAN** [ ] [ ]
– Mystic man / Recruiting soldiers / Can't you see / Fight on / Jah say no / Buk-in-hamm Palace / The day the dollar die / Crystal ball / Rumours of war.

Sep 80. (7") **NOTHING BUT LOVE. (w/ GWEN GUTHRIE) / COLD BLOOD** [ ] [ ]

Rolling St / EMI Amer..

Jun 81. (lp)(c) **WANTED DREAD & ALIVE** [ ] [91]
– Coming in hot / Nothing but love / Reggaemylitis / Rock with me / Oh bumbo klaat / Wanted dread and alive / Rastafari is / Guide me from my friends / Fools die.

Radic-EMI / EMI Amer..

Mar 83. (7") **JOHNNY B. GOODE. / PEACE TREATY** [48] [84]

Apr 83. (lp)(c) **MAMA AFRICA** [ ] [59]
– Mama Africa / Glasshouse / Not gonna give it up / Stop that train / Johnny B. Goode / Where you gonna run / Peace treaty / Feel no way / Maga dog.

May 83. (7") **WHERE YOU GONNA RUN. / STOP THAT TRAIN** [ ] [-]

Sep 83. (7")(10") **MAMA AFRICA. / NOT GONNA GIVE IT UP** [ ] [-]

E.M.I. / EMI Amer..

Jul 84. (lp) **CAPTURED LIVE (live)** [ ] [ ]
– Coming in hot / Bush doctor / African / Get up, stand up / Johnny B. Goode / Equal rights – Downpresser man / Rastafari is.

Parlophone / Capitol

Jul 87. (7") **IN MY SONG. / COME TOGETHER** [ ] [ ]
(12"+=) – Nah goa jail.

Sep 87. (lp)(c)(cd) **NO NUCLEAR WAR** [ ] [ ]
– No nuclear war / Nah goa jail / Fight apartheid / Vampire / In my song / Lesson in my life / Testify / Come together.

– compilations, others, etc –

Oct 79. Virgin; (7") **STEPPING RAZOR. / LEGALIZE IT** [ ] [-]

Mar 88. Parlophone; (lp)(c)(cd) **THE TOUGHEST** [ ] [ ]
– Coming in hot / (You gotta walk) Don't look back / Pick myself up / Crystal ball / Mystic man / Reggaemythilis / Bush doctor / Mega dog / Johnny B. Goode / Equal rights / Downpressed man / In my song.

TOTO

Formed: Los Angeles, California, USA . . . 1977 by ex-session men, brothers JEFF and STEVE PORCARO with others (see below). Signed worldwide deal on 'CBS-Epic' in 1978, with debut single 'HOLD THE LINE', breaking through into US + UK Top 20 early 1979. • **Style:** Superstar session men, who blended together hard + soft rock, that was loved by the US mainstream audiences. • **Songwriters:** PAICH was main songwriter, with others contributing, with group taking more of a hand in the 90's. Covered; WITH A LITTLE HELP FROM MY FRIENDS (Beatles). • **Trivia:** ROSANNA was written by LUKATHER for his girlfriend; actress Rosanna Arquette.

Recommended: PAST TO PRESENT: 1977 TO 1990 (*6).

BOBBY KIMBALL (b.ROBERT TOTEAUX, 29 Mar'47, Vinton, Louisiana) – vocals / **STEVE LUKATHER** (b.21 Oct'57) – lead guitar, vocals / **STEVE PORCARO** (b. 2 Sep'57) – keyboards, vocals / **JEFF PORCARO** (b. 1 Apr'54) – drums, percussion (ex-RURAL LIFE) / **DAVID PAICH** (b.25 Jun'54) – keyboards, vocals (ex-RURAL LIFE) / **DAVID HUNGATE** – bass

C.B.S. / Columbia

Jan 79. (7") **HOLD THE LINE. / TAKIN' IT BACK** [14] [5] Oct 78

Mar 79. (lp)(c) **TOTO** [37] [9] Oct 78
– Child's anthem / I'll supply the love / Georgy porgy / Manuela run / You are the flower / Girl goodbye / Takin' it back / Rockmaker / Hold the line / Angela. *(re-iss.Apr83 + Jun84, cd-iss.Oct86) (re-iss.cd May94 on 'Sony')*

Mar 79. (7") **I'LL SUPPLY THE LOVE. / YOU ARE THE FLOWER** [ ] [45] Feb 79

Apr 79. (7")(7"pic-d) **GEORGY PORGY. / CHILD'S ANTHEM** [-] [48]

Jun 79. (7") **GEORGY PORGY. / (part 2)** [ ] [-]

Dec 79. (lp)(c) **HYDRA** [ ] [37] Nov 79
– Hydra / St. George and the dragon / 99 / Lorraine / All us boys / Mama / White sister / A secret love. *(re-iss.Apr83 & Feb85)*

Dec 79. (7")(7"pic-d) **ST. GEORGE AND THE DRAGON. / WHITE SISTER** [-] [ ]

Dec 79. (7") **ST. GEORGE AND THE DRAGON. / A SECRET LOVE** [ ] [-]

Feb 80. (7") **99. / HYDRA** [ ] [26] Dec 79

Mar 80. (7") **ALL US BOYS. / HYDRA** [ ] [-]

Jan 81. (lp)(c) **TURN BACK** [ ] [41]
– Gift with a golden gun / English eyes / Live for today / A million miles away / Goodbye Elenore / I think I could stand you forever / Turn back / If it's the last night. *(re-iss.Apr83, cd-iss.May87)*

Feb 81. (7") **GOODBYE ELENORE. / TURN BACK** [ ] [ ]

Apr 81. (7") **TURN BACK. / IT'S THE LAST NIGHT** [-] [ ]

Apr 82. (lp)(c) **TOTO IV** (reached peak UK position Feb83) [4] [4]
– Rosanna / Make believe / I won't hold you back / Good for you / It's a feeling / Afraid of love / Lovers in the night / We made it / Waiting for your love / Africa. *(cd-iss.1983 & Mar91) (re-iss.+cd.Nov86) (re-iss.cd Feb95 & Dec95)*

Apr 82. (7")(7"pic-d) **ROSANNA. / IT'S A FEELING** [ ] [2]
(re-iss.Mar83, hit UK No.12)

Aug 82. (7") **MAKE BELIEVE. / WE MADE IT** [3] [30]

Oct 82. (7") **AFRICA. / GOOD FOR YOU** [-] [1]

Jan 83. (7")(7"sha-pic-d) **AFRICA. / WE MADE IT** [3] [-]

Jun 83. (7")(7"pic-d) **I WON'T HOLD YOU BACK. / AFRAID OF LOVE** [37] [10] Mar 83
(12"+=) – 99 / Hold the line / Goodbye Elenore.

Jul 83. (7") **WAITING FOR YOUR LOVE. / LOVERS IN THE NIGHT** [ ] [73]

— (late'82) **MIKE PORCARO** (29 May'55) – bass had already repl. HUNGATE

— (In '84) **DENNIS 'Fergie' FREDRICKSON** (b.15 May'51) – vocals repl. KIMBALL who later became part of the awful FAR CORPORATION

Nov 84. (7")(12") **STRANGER IN TOWN. / CHANGE OF HEART** [ ] [30]

Nov 84. (lp)(c) **ISOLATION** [67] [42]
– Carmen / Lion / Stranger in town / Angel don't cry / How does it feel / Endless / Isolation / Mr. Friendly / Change of heart / Holyanna. *(cd-iss.1988)*

— Dec84, saw their instrumental DUNE (Film Soundtrack) released on 'Polydor'. It was accompanied by The VIENNA SYMPHONY ORCHESTRA but flopped. Around this time they laid down backing instruments for USA IN AFRICA single.

Jan 85. (7") **HOLYANNA. / MR. FRIENDLY** [-] [71]

Feb 85. (7") **HOW DOES IT FEEL. / MR. FRIENDLY** [ ] [ ]

Apr 85. (7") **ENDLESS. / ISOLATION** [ ] [ ]

— **JOSEPH WILLIAMS** – vocals (ex-Solo artist) repl. FREDRICKSON

Oct 86. (7") **I'LL BE OVER YOU. / IN A WORD** [ ] [11] Aug 86
(12"+=) – Africa / 99.

Oct 86. (lp)(c)(cd) **FAHRENHEIT** [99] [40] Sep 86
– Till the end / We can make it tonight / Without your love / Can't stand it any longer / I'll be over you / Fahrenheit / Somewhere tonight / Could this be love / Lea / Don't stop me now.

Dec 86. (7") **WITHOUT YOUR LOVE. / CAN'T STAND IT ANY LONGER** [-] [38]

— trimmed to quintet, when STEVE PORCARO went solo.

Mar 87. (7") **TILL THE END. / DON'T STOP ME NOW** [-] [ ]

Feb 88. (7") **PAMELA. / THE SEVENTH ONE** [-] [ ]

Feb 88. (7") **STOP LOVING YOU. / THE SEVENTH ONE** [ ] [ ]
(12"+=)/ /(cd-s+=) – ('A'version)./ / I'll be over you.

Mar 88. (lp)(c)(cd) **THE SEVENTH ONE** [73] [64]
– Pamela / You got me / Anna / Stop loving you / Mushanga / Stay away / Straight for the heart / Only the children / A thousand years / These chains / Home of the brave.

Apr 88. (7") **STRAIGHT FROM THE HEART. / THE SEVENTH ONE** [-] [ ]

May 88. (7") **PAMELA. / STAY AWAKE** [ ] [-]
(12"+=)/ /(cd-s+=) – America./ / Africa / Rosanna.

— **KIMBALL** returned Sep'88, but was repl. by temp. **TOMMY NELSON.** He in turn was deposed by **JEAN-MICHEL BYRON** (b.South Africa) – vocals

Sep 90. (7")(12")(c-s) **CAN YOU HEAR WHAT I'M SAYING. / AFRICA** [ ] [ ]
(cd-s+=) – Georgy porgy / Waiting for your love.

Oct 90. (cd)(c)(lp) **PAST TO PRESENT: 1977 TO 1990** (compilation) [ ] [ ] Sep 90
– Love has the power / Africa / Hold the line / Out of love / Georgy Porgy / I'll be over you / Can you hear what I'm saying / Rosanna / I won't hold you back / Stop loving you / 99 / Pamela / Animal.

— **KIMBALL** returned to repl. BYRON who formed self-named group.

— In Aug'92, JEFF died mysteriously of poisoning or a heart attack.

Columbia / Columbia

Sep 92. (cd)(c)(lp) **KINGDOM OF DESIRE** [ ] [ ]
– Gypsy train / Don't chain my heart / Never enough / How many times / 2 hearts / Wings of time / She knows the Devil / The other side / Only you / Jake to the bone.

Nov 93. (d-cd)(d-c) **ABSOLUTELY LIVE (live)** [ ] [ ]
– Hydra / Rosanna / Kingdom of desire / Georgy Porgy / 99 / I won't hold you back / Don't stop me now / Africa / Don't chain my heart / I'll be over you / Home of the brave / Hold the line / With a little help from my friends.

Oct 95. (cd)(c) **TAMBU** [ ] [ ]
– Gift of faith / I will remember / Slipped away / If you belong to me / Baby, he's your man / The other end of time / The turning point / Time is the enemy / Drag him to the roof / Just can't get to you / Dave's gone skiing / The road goes on.

Nov 95. (c-s) **I WILL REMEMBER / DAVE'S GONE SKIING** [64] [ ]
(cd-s) – ('A'side) / Rosanna / Africa / Georgy porgy.

– more compilations, etc. –

Sep 84. Hallmark; (lp)(c) **HOLD THE LINE** [ ] [-]
Sep 85. Old Gold; (7") **HOLD THE LINE. / ROSANNA** [ ] [-]
Mar 90. Old Gold; (7") **AFRICA. / I WON'T HOLD YOU BACK** [ ] [-]
Dec 90. CBS; (cd-box) **TOTO / TURN BACK / HYDRA** [ ] [ ]

STEVE LUKATHER

solo with **STEVE STEVENS** – guitar / **JAN HAMMER** – keyboards / **WILL LEE** – bass / **+?**

C.B.S. Columbia

Nov 89. (lp)(c)(cd) **LUKATHER** [ ] [ ]
– Twist the knife / Swear your love / Fall into velvet / Drive a crooked road / Got my way / Darkest night of the year / Lonely beat of my heart / With a second chance / Turn to stone / It looks like rain / Steppin' on top of your world.

Columbia Columbia

Apr 94. (cd)(c) **CANDYMAN** [ ] [ ]
– Hero with 1000 eyes / Freedom / Extinction blues / Born yesterday / Never walk alone / Party in Simon's pants / Borrowed time / Never let them see you cry / Froth / The bomber / Song for Jeff.

TOURISTS (see under ⇒ EURYTHMICS)

Pete TOWNSHEND (see under ⇒ WHO)

TOYAH

Born: TOYAH ANN WILCOX, 18 May'58, King's Heath, Birmingham. Actress turned singer in 1978, after appearing in the punk film 'Jubilee'. She and band signed to indie label 'Safari', where she had first initial success in 1980 with second album 'THE BLUE MEANING'. The following year, she broke through with hit Top 5 single 'IT'S A MYSTERY'. • **Style:** Punk rock/goth singer with image & exagerated hairstyles being hyped, rather than the quality of music. She was constantly slagged by the media and music press for her slight lisp. • **Songwriters:** She and band wrote music, except ECHO BEACH (Martha + The Muffins) / SCHOOL'S OUT (Alice Cooper). • **Trivia:** On the 16 May'86, she married middle-aged rock guitarist ROBERT FRIPP ex-KING CRIMSON. • **Filmography:** JUBILEE (1977) / THE CORN IS GREEN (1978) / QUADROPHENIA (1979) / THE TEMPEST (1980). Her other acting attributions were in 1983's 'TRAFFORD TANZI'. In 1987, she acted in the West End play 'CABARET'. She also appeared in the TV detective series 'Shoestring'.

Recommended: SHEEP FARMING IN BARNET (*7) / THE BLUE MEANING (*8) / TOYAH TOYAH (*7).

TOYAH – vocals / with band **JOEL BOGEN** – guitar / **PETE BUSH** – keyboards / **MARK HENRY** – bass / **STEVE BRAY** – drums

Safari not issued

Jun 79. (7") **VICTIMS OF THE RIDDLE. / VICTIMS OF THE RIDDLE (VIVESECTION)** [ ] [-]
Jul 79. (7"ep) **SHEEP FARMING IN BARNET** [ ] [-]
– Neon womb / Indecision / Waiting / Our movie / Vividiction / Danced.
Dec 79. (lp)(c) **SHEEP FARMING IN BARNET** [ ] [-]
– Neon womb / Indecision / Waiting / Computer / Victims of the riddle / Elusive stranger / Our movie / Danced / Last goodbye / Victims of the riddle (vivisection) / Race through space. *(cd+c-iss.Aug90 on 'Great Expectations')*
Jan 80. (7") **BIRD IN FLIGHT. / TRIBAL LOOK** [ ] [-]

— **CHARLIE FRANCIS** – bass repl. MARK HENRY

May 80. (7")('A'ext-12"white) **IEYA. / SPACE WALKING (HELIUM SONG)** [ ] [-]
(re-iss.7"/12"/7"pic-d= Jul82, hit UK No.48)
May 80. (lp)(c) **THE BLUE MEANING** [40] [-]
– Ieya / Space walking (helium song) / Ghosts / Mummys / Blue meanings / She / Tiger tiger / Vision / Insects / Love me. *(re-iss.cd+c Jul90 on 'Great Expectations')*
Nov 80. (7"m) **DANCED (live). / GHOSTS (live) / NEON WOMB (live)** [ ] [-]
Jan 81. (lp)(c) **TOYAH! TOYAH! TOYAH! (live)** [22] [-]
– Victims of the riddle / Indecision / Love me / Vision / Tribal look / Bird in flight / Danced / Insects / Race through space / Ieya. *(cd-iss.Aug90 on 'Great Expectations')*

— **TOYAH** retained only **BOGEN,** and recruited **ADRIAN LEE** – keys / **PHIL SPALDING** – bass (ex-ORIGINAL MIRRORS) / **NIGEL GLOCKER** – drums (ex-ASSOCIATES)

Feb 81. (7"ep) **FOUR FROM TOYAH** [4] [-]
– It's a mystery / War boys / Angels and demons / Revelations.
May 81. (7"m) **I WANT TO BE FREE. / WALKIE TALKIE / ALIEN** [8] [-]
May 81. (lp)(c)(pic-lp) **ANTHEM** [2] [-]
– I want to be free / Obsolete pop star / Elocution lesson (the door is a whore) / Jungles of Jupiter / I am / It's a mystery / Masai boy / Marionette / Demolition man / We are. *(re-iss.+cd.Nov85)* (cd+=) – Thunder in the mountains / War boys / Angels and demons / Revelations.

— **SIMON PHILIPS** – drums, percussion repl GLOCKER who left to join SAXON. **ANDY CLARKE + SIMON DARLOW** – keyboards repl LEE.

Sep 81. (7")(7"pic-d) **THUNDER IN THE MOUNTAINS. / STREET ADDICT** [4] [-]
(free 7"flexi-w.a.) – STAND PROUD
Nov 81. (7"ep) **FOUR MORE FROM TOYAH** [14] [-]
– Good morning universe / Urban tribesman / In the fairground / The furious futures.
May 82. (7")(7"pic-d) **BRAVE NEW WORLD. / WARRIOR ROCK** [21] [-]
Jun 82. (lp)(c) **THE CHANGELING** [6] [-]
– Creepy room / Street creature / Castaways / The druids / Angel and me / The pact / Life in the trees / Dawn chorus / Run wild run free / Brave new world.

— **KEITH HALE** – keyboards, vocals repl. CLARKE

Sep 82. (7")(7"pic-d) **BE LOUD BE PROUD (BE HEARD). / LAUGHING WITH THE FOOLS** [30] [-]
Nov 82. (d-lp)(d-c) **WARRIOR ROCK – TOYAH ON TOUR (live)** [20] [-]
– Good morning universe / Warrior rock / Danced / Jungles of Jupiter / Castaways / Angel and me / Brave new world / The pact / Thunder in the mountains / We are / I want to be free / Dawn chorus / War boy / Ieya / Be loud be proud (be heard).

— **ANDY DUNCAN** – drums repl. PHILIPS

Safari Safari?

Sep 83. (7") **REBEL RUN. / MOUNTAINS HIGH** [24] [-]
Oct 83. (lp)(c) **LOVE IS THE LAW** [28] [ ]
– Broken diamonds / I explode / Rebel of love / Rebel run / Martian cowboy / Dream scape / Time is ours / Love is the law / Remember / The vow.
Nov 83. (7") **THE VOW. / I EXPLODE** [50] [-]
(12"+=) – Haunted.

— now w / **DARLOW / LEE / PETER VAN HOOKE** – drums / **AL HODGE + PHIL PALMER** – guitar / **IAN WHERRY + ANDY BROWN** – bass

Portrait Portrait

Apr 85. (7")(12") **DON'T FALL IN LOVE (I SAID). / SNOW COVERS THE KISS** [22] [ ]
Jun 85. (7")(7"pic-d) **SOUL PASSING THROUGH SOUL. / ALL IN A RAGE** [57] [ ]
(12"+=) – ('A'extended).
Jul 85. (lp)(c)(cd) **MINX** [24] [ ]
– Soldier of fortune, terrorist of love / Don't fall in love (I said) / Soul passing through soul / Sympathy / I'll serve you well / All in a rage / Space between the sounds / School's out / World in action / America for beginners. *(c+cd+=)* – Over twenty-one / Vigilante.
Sep 85. (7")(12") **WORLD IN ACTION. / SOLDIERS OF FORTUNE** [ ] [-]

— Sep85, she guested on TONY BANKS (of Genesis) EP track 'You Call This Victory'.

— Next album was credited with her new husband ROBERT FRIPP (ex-KING CRIMSON)

E.G. not issued

Jan 87. (lp)(cd) **THE LADY OR THE TIGER ("TOYAH / FRIPP")** [ ] [-]
– The lady or the tiger / Discourager of hesitancy.
Apr 87. (7")(12") **ECHO BEACH. / PLENTY** [54] [-]
Jun 87. (lp)(c)(cd) **DESIRE** [ ] [-]
– Echo beach / Moonlight dancing / Revive the world / The view / Moon migration / Love's unkind / Dear diary / Deadly as a woman / Goodbye baby / When a woman cries / Desire.
Jun 87. (7") **MOONLIGHT DANCING. / SUN UP** [ ] [-]
(12"+=) – R.E.-N.T.R.Y. – Into dance.

— now w / backing from **STEVE SIDEH** – drums, percussion, keyboards

Nov 88. (lp)(c)(cd) **PROSTITUTE ("TOYAH WILCOX")** [ ] [ ]
– Hello / Prostitute / Wife / The show / Dream house / Homecraft / Obsession / Let the power bleed / Restless / Falling to Earth / Jazz singers in the trees / Vale of Evesham / Ghosts in the universe.

— FRIPP appeared on above, as their tour was billed as FRIPP & FRIPP.

— Her new band were **GUNN, GEBALLE + BEAVIS** and guest **ROBERT FRIPP**

Feb 91. (cd)(c)(lp) **OPHELIA'S SHADOW** [ ] [-]
– Ophelia's shadow / The shaman says / Brilliant day / Prospect / Turning tide / Take what you will / Ghost light / The woman who had an affair with herself / Homeward / Lords of the never known.

Cryptic not issued

Nov 93. (12")(cd-s) **OUT OF THE BLUE (Trancentral mix). / OUT OF THE BLUE (deep ocean mix)** [ ] [-]
(12"+=) – Out of The Blue (Trancentral radio mix).
Apr 94. (c-s)(12")(cd-s) **NOW AND THEN. / ('A'mixes)** [ ] [-]
May 94. (cd)(c) **DREAMCHILD** [ ] [-]
– Now and then / Let me go / Unkind / Out of the blue / Dreamchild / World of tension / Lost and found / Over you / I don't know / Disappear / Tone poem.

– compilations, others, etc. –

Feb 84. K-Tel; (lp)(c) **TOYAH TOYAH** [43] [-]
Nov 85. Safari; (lp)(c) **MAYHEM** [ ] [-]
Mar 94. Connoisseur; (cd) **BEST OF TOYAH** [ ] [-]

— In Jun82, a single with her as "The ANTEATERS"; 'NINE TO FIVE' was lifted from the 1977 film 'Jubilee', in which she appeared with ADAM ANT.

TRAFFIC

Formed: based Midlands, England . . . Apr'67, by WINWOOD, MASON, CAPALDI and WOOD. Signed to 'Island' records and immediately hit the UK Top 5 with debut 45 'PAPER SUN'. Their next single 'HOLE IN MY SHOE', became regarded as a classic, after it made No.2 in the UK. After their split early in 1969, and reformation in the 70's, they concentrated on working mostly in Muscle Shoals, America, where they had huge renewed fortunes. • **Style:** Multi-talented psychedelic group who tested folk-rock and jazz in the early 70's. • **Songwriters:** Individually or group compositions, except GIMME SOME LOVIN' (Spencer Davis Group). CAPALDI covered LOVE HURTS (Everly Brothers). • **Trivia:** The album ON THE ROAD was recorded on tour in Germany.

Recommended: SMILING PHASES (*8)

STEVE WINWOOD (b.12 May'48) – vocals, keyboards (ex-SPENCER DAVIS GROUP) / **DAVE MASON** (b.10 May'47, Worcester) – guitar, vocals (ex-HELLIONS) / **JIM CAPALDI** (b.24 Aug'44, Evesham) – drums, vocals (ex-HELLIONS) / **CHRIS WOOD** (b.24 Jun'44, Birmingham) – flute, sax (ex-SOUNDS OF BLUE)

Island United Art

May 67. (7") **PAPER SUN. / GIVING TO YOU** [5] [94] Aug 67
Aug 67. (7") **HOLE IN MY SHOE. / SMILING PHASES** [2] [ ]

Nov 67. (7") **HERE WE GO ROUND THE MULBERRY BUSH. / COLOURED RAIN** 8

Dec 67. (lp) **MR. FANTASY** 8 88 Apr 68
– Heaven is in your mind / Berkshire poppies / House for everyone / No name, no face, no number / Dear Mr. Fantasy / Dealer / Utterly simple / Coloured rain / Hope I never find me there / Giving to you. *(US version +=)* – Paper Sun / Hole in my shoe. *(re-iss.+c.Feb87, cd-iss.Sep89)*

Feb 68. (7") **NO NAME, NO FACE, NO NUMBER. / ROAMIN' IN THE GLOAMIN'** 40 -

Feb 68. (7") **NO NAME, NO FACE, NO NUMBER. / HEAVEN IS IN YOUR MIND** -

Sep 68. (7") **FEELING ALRIGHT. / WITHERING TREE**

Oct 68. (lp) **TRAFFIC** 9 17
– You can all join in / Pearly queen / Don't be sad / Who knows what tomorrow may bring / Feelin' alright / Vagabond virgin / Forty thousand headmen / Cryin' to be heard / No time to live / Means to an end. *(re-iss.+c.Feb87, cd-iss.Nov87 & 1989)*

Dec 68. (7") **MEDICATED GOO. / SHANGHAI NOODLE FACTORY**

— Below album was recorded before their split late 1968.

May 69. (lp) **LAST EXIT (some live)** 19
– Just for you / Shanghai noodle factory / Something's got a hold of my toe / Withering tree / Medicated goo / Feelin' good / Blind man. *(cd-iss.May88 & Sep89)*

Oct 69. (lp) **THE BEST OF TRAFFIC** (compilation) 48
– Paper Sun / Heaven is in your mind / No face, no name, no number / Coloured rain / Smiling phases / Hole in my shoe / Medicated goo / Forty thousand headmen / Feelin' alright / Shanghai noodle factory / Dear Mr. Fantasy. *(cd-iss.Mar93)*

— In 1969, WINWOOD formed BLIND FAITH with ERIC CLAPTON and GINGER BAKER. WOOD also joined the latter's group AIRFORCE. WOOD, MASON and CAPALDI then formed WOODEN FROG. DAVE MASON went solo as TRAFFIC re-formed as a trio.

Jul 70. (lp)(c) **JOHN BARLEYCORN MUST DIE** 5 11
– Glad / Freedom rider / Empty pages / Stranger to himself / John Barleycorn / Every mother's son. *(re-iss.Sep86, cd-iss.Sep89)*

Sep 70. (7") **EMPTY PAGES. / STRANGER TO HIMSELF** - 74

— added **RIC GRECH** – bass (ex-FAMILY, ex-BLIND FAITH, ex-GINGER BAKER'S AIRFORCE) / **REEBOP KWAKU-BAAH** – percussion (ex-GINGER BAKER'S AIRFORCE) / **JIM GORDON** – drums (ex-DEREK & THE DOMINOES) / **DAVE MASON** guested on some live.

Sep 71. (lp)(c) **WELCOME TO THE CANTEEN (live)** 26
– Medicated goo / Sad and deep as you / Forty thousand headmen / Shouldn't have took more than you gave / Dear Mr. Fantasy / Gimme some lovin'. *(cd-iss.May88 & Sep89)*

Oct 71. (7") **GIMME SOME LOVIN'. / (part 2)** - 68

Dec 71. (7") **GLAD. / (part 2)** -

Island Island

Dec 71. (lp)(c) **THE LOW SPARK OF THE HIGH HEELED BOYS** 7
– Hidden treasure / The low spark of the high heeled boys / Rock & roll stew / Many a mile to freedom / Light up or leave me alone / Rainmaker. *(re-iss.Sep86, cd-iss.Nov87 & Sep89)*

Jan 72. (7") **ROCK & ROLL STEW. / (part 2)** - 93

— **DAVID HOOD** – bass + ROGER HAWKINS – drums (both of JIM CAPALDI band) repl. JIM GORDON and GRECH. (The latter formed KGB)

Feb 73. (lp)(c) **SHOOT OUT AT THE FANTASY FACTORY** 6
– Shoot out at the fantasy factory / Roll right stone / Evening blue / Tragic magic / Uninspired (sometimes I feel so). *(cd-iss.May88 & Sep89)*

— added **BARRY BECKETT** – keyboards

Oct 73. (d-lp)(d-c) **ON THE ROAD (live)** 40 29
– Glad / Freedom rider / Tragic magic / (Sometimes I feel so) Uninspired / Shoot out at the fantasy factory / Light up or leave me alone / The low spark of the high heeled boys. *(cd-iss.1988 & Aug91) (cd-iss.Apr94)*

— **WINWOOD, CAPALDI & WOOD** enlisted **ROSKO GEE** – bass (ex-GONZALES)

Island Asylum

Sep 74. (lp)(c) **WHEN THE EAGLE FLIES** 31 9
– Walking in the wind / Something new / Dream Gerrard / Memories of a rock'n'roller / When the eagle flies / Graveyard people / Love. *(cd-iss.1988)*

Oct 74. (7") **WALKING IN THE WIND. / ('A'instrumental version)**

— Disbanded early 1975. STEVE WINWOOD went solo, also collaborating with STOMU YAMASHTA. WOOD and GEE took up session work. On 12 Jul'83, CHRIS WOOD died of liver failure. JIM CAPALDI continued his solo career.

– more compilations, etc. –

May 74. Island/ US= U.A.; (7") **HOLE IN MY SHOE. / HERE WE GO ROUND THE MULBERRY BUSH**

May 74. Island/ US= U.A.; (lp)(c) **YOU CAN ALL JOIN IN**

May 75. Island/ US= U.A.; (lp)(c) **HEAVY TRAFFIC**

Sep 75. Island/ US= U.A.; (lp)(c) **MORE HEAVY TRAFFIC**

Mar 78. Island; (7"ep)(7"pic-d-ep) **EXTENDED PLAY** -
– I'm a man / Hole in my shoe / Gimme some lovin' / No name no face no number

1992. Island; (d-cd) **SMILING PHASES**
– Paper sun / Hole in my shoe / Smiling phases / Heaven is in your mind / Coloured rain / No face, no name, no number / Here we go round the mulbury bush / Dear Mr. Fantasy / You can all join in / Feelin' alright / Pearly queen / Forty thousand headmen / Vagabond virgin / Shanghai noodle factory / Withering tree / Medicated goo / Glad / Freedom rider / Empty pages / John Barleycorn / The low spark of the high heeled boys / Light up or leave me alone / Rock & roll stew / Shoot out at the fantasy factory / Walking in the wind / When the eagle flies.

JIM CAPALDI

(solo, first 2 when member of TRAFFIC)

— sessioners until 1978 included **JIMMY JOHNSON** – guitar / **DAVID HOOD** – bass / **ROGER HAWKINS** – drums / **BARRY BECKETT** – piano / **PETE CARR** – guitar / **STEVE WINWOOD** – various instruments / **REEBOP KWAKU BAAH** – percussion

Island Island

Apr 72. (lp)(c) **OH HOW WE DANCED** 82 Apr 72
– Eve / Big thirst / Love is all you can try / Last day of dawn / Don't be a hero / Open your heart / How much can a man really take / Oh how we danced.

Apr 72. (7") **EVE. / GOING DOWN SLOW ALL THE WAY**

Jun 72. (7") **TRICKY DICKY RIDES AGAIN. / OH HOW WE DANCED**

Jul 72. (7") **OPEN YOUR HEART. / OH HOW WE DANCED** -

Feb 73. (7") **TRICKY DICKY RIDES AGAIN. / LOVE IS ALL YOU CAN TRY** -

May 74. (7") **WHALE MEAT AGAIN. / IT'S ALRIGHT** -

Jun 74. (lp)(c) **WHALE MEAT AGAIN**
– It's alright / Whale meat again / Yellow sun / I've got so much lovin' / Low rider / My brother / Summer fading.

Jun 74. (7") **IT'S ALL UP TO YOU. / WHALE MEAT AGAIN** 27

Jul 74. (7") **IT'S ALL UP TO YOU. / I'VE GOT SO MUCH LOVIN'** -

Jun 75. (lp)(c) **SHORT CUT DRAW BLOOD**
– Goodbye love / It's all up to you / Love hurts / Johnny too bad / Short cut draw blood / Living on a marble / Boy on a marble / Keep on trying / Seagull.

Oct 75. (7") **LOVE HURTS. / SUGAR HONEY** 4 97
(re-iss.Jul81)

Jan 76. (7") **GOODBYE MY LOVE. / IT'S ALRIGHT**

Apr 76. (7") **TALKIN' ABOUT MY BABY. / STILL TALKIN'**

Apr 76. (7") **SHORT CUT DRAW BLOOD. / GOODNIGHT AND GOOD MORNING** -

Mar 77. (lp)(c) **PLAY IT BY EAR**

Mar 77. (7") **GOODBYE MY LOVE. / BABY YOU'RE NOT MY PROBLEM**

Polydor Polydor

Jan 78. (7") **DAUGHTER OF THE NIGHT. / GAME OF LOVE**

Feb 78. (lp)(c) **THE CONTENDER**
– Dirty business / Sealed with a kiss / Daughter of the night (the US-title) / You burn me / Game of love / The contender / Elixir of love / Short ends / Hunger and greed.

Mar 78. (7") **SEALED WITH A KISS. / HAD A DREAM TODAY**

May 79. (lp)(c) **ELECTRIC NIGHTS**
– Shoe shine / Hotel blues / White jungle lady / Tabitha / Time / Electric nights / Wild dogs / 1890 / Wild geese.

Aug 79. (7") **SHOE SHINE. / TABITHA**

not iss. R.S.O.

1979. (7") **DAUGHTER OF THE NIGHT. / I'M GONNA DO IT** -

Carrere Carrere

Jun 80. (7") **HOLD ON TO YOUR LOVE. / FORTUNE AND FAME** -

Jul 80. (lp)(c) **THE SWEET SMELL OF SUCCESS**
– Hold on to your love / Take me how you find me girl / The sweet smell of success / Every man should march to the beat of his own drum / Tonight you're mine / The low spark of high heeled boys / Fortune and fame / Man with no country / Going home.

Sep 80. (7") **THE LOW SPARK OF HIGH HEELED BOYS. / BATHROOM JANE** -

Feb 81. (7") **CHILD IN THE STORM. / BRIGHT FIGHTER** -

Apr 81. (7") **OLD PHOTOGRAPHS. / MAN WITH NO COUNTRY** -

Apr 81. (lp)(c) **LET THE THUNDER CRY**
– Let the thunder cry / Favella music / Child in the storm / Only love / Louie Louie / Warm / Dreams do come true / Old photographs / We don't need / Anxiety.

W.E.A. Atlantic

Jan 83. (7") **TONIGHT YOU'RE MINE. / BACK AT MY PLACE**

Jan 83. (lp)(c) **FIERCE HEART** 91
– Tonight you're mine / Living on the edge / Bad breaks / Runaway / Back at my place / That's love / I'll always be your fool / Don't let them control you / Gifts of unknown things.

Apr 83. (7")(12") **THAT'S LOVE. / RUNAWAY** 28

Jul 83. (7") **LIVING ON THE EDGE. / GIFTS OF UNKNOWN THINGS** 75

Oct 84. (7") **I'LL KEEP HOLDING ON. / TALES OF POWER**
(12"+=) – Still holding on.

Jan 85. (lp)(c) **ONE MAN MISSION**
– One man mission of love / Tonight / Lost inside your love / I'll keep holding on / Nobody loves you / Young savages / Tales of power / Warriors of love / Ancient highway.

Island Island

Jan 89. (7") **SOMETHING SO STRONG. / CHILD IN THE STORM**
(12"+=)(cd-s+=) – Tales of power.

Feb 89. (7") **SOME COME RUNNING. / FABELA MUSIC** Dec 88
(12"+=)(cd-s+=) – Love hurts.

Feb 89. (lp)(c)(cd) **SOME COME RUNNING**
– Something so strong / Love used to be a friend of mine / Dancing on the highway / Some come running / Voices in the night / You are the one / Take me home / Oh Lord, why Lord.

May 89. (7")(12") **TAKE ME HOME. / CHILD IN THE STORM**
(cd-s+=) – ('A'version) / Fabela music.

— featured old mate **STEVE WINWOOD**

All At Once not issued

Dec 93. (cd) **PRINCE OF DARKNESS** -
(cd-iss.Nov94 on 'Start')

TRAFFIC

— **WINWOOD + CAPALDI** re-formed for studio.

Virgin Virgin

May 94. (cd)(c) **FAR FROM HOME** 29
– Riding high / Here comes a man / Far from home / Nowhere is their freedom / Holy ground / Some kinda woman / Every night, every day / This train won't stop / State of grace / Mosambique.

May 94. (7")(c-s) **HERE COMES A MAN. / GLAD (live)**
(cd-s+=) – ('A'mix).

Sep 94. (c-s) **SOME KINDA WOMAN. / FORTY THOUSAND HEADMEN**
(cd-s+=) – Low spark of high heeled boys / ('A'mix).

TRANSVISION VAMP

Formed: Brighton, England . . . 1984 by WENDY JAMES and NICK. In 1987, they were signed to 'MCA', by new managing editor AMBROSE (ex-BIG IN JAPAN). In 1988, after a minor hit with 'TELL THAT GIRL TO SHUT UP', they smashed the UK charts with 'I WANT YOUR LOVE'. • **Style:** Platinum blonde WENDY JAMES, was inspired by IGGY POP and MARC BOLAN. Media conscious debutant WENDY, was never out of music limelight and TV interviews, which showed them she was no bimbo. • **Songwriters:** CHRISTIAN-SAYER compositions, except TELL THAT GIRL TO SHUT UP (Holly & The Italians) / CRAWL OUT YOUR WINDOW (Bob Dylan). (See 1993 solo work for WENDY JAMES). • **Trivia:** WENDY posed nude for photographer David Bailey in the magazine 'The Tatler'.

Recommended: VELVETEEN (*7).

WENDY JAMES (b.21 Jan'66, London) – vocals / **NICK CHRISTIAN SAYER** (b. 1 Aug'64) – guitar (ex-FAN CLUB, ex-PLASTICS UK) / **TEX AXILE** (b.30 Jul'63) – drums (ex-SNIVELLING SHITS, ex-EDDIE &..HOT RODS) / **DAVE PARSONS** (b. 2 Jul'62) – bass

		M.C.A.	Uni
Aug 87.	(7") **REVOLUTION BABY. / VID KID VAMP** (remixed-12"+=) – No it U lover.		-
Apr 88.	(7") **TELL THAT GIRL TO SHUT UP. / GOD SAVE THE ROYALTIES** ('A'extended-12"+=) – ('A'knuckle duster mix). (3-D pic-cd-s++=) – ('A'extended).	45	87 Sep 88
Jun 88.	(7"m) **I WANT YOUR LOVE. / SWEET THING / EVOLUTION EVIE** (12"+3"cd-s) – ('A' . . . money mix). / (2nd track) / (3rd-electric mix)	5	

— added **POL BURTON** – drums (TEX now on keyboards)

Sep 88.	(7"m) **REVOLUTION BABY (remix). / HONEY HONEY / LONG LONELY WEEKEND** ('A'diff.mix-12")(12"pic-d) – (same 3). (3"cd-s+=) – Vid kid vamp.	30	
Oct 88.	(lp)(c)(cd)(pic-lp) **POP ART** – Trash city / I want your love / Sister Moon / Psychosonic Cindy / Revolution baby / Tell that girl to shut up / Wild star / Hanging out with Halo Jones / Andy Warhol's dead / Sex kick. *(re-iss.cd+c Aug93)*	4	
Nov 88.	(7"m)(7"pic-d) **SISTER MOON. / OH YEAH / WALK ON BY** ('A'groove on mix-12"+=)(cd-s+=) – Sex kick (Ciao Portabello).	41	

— Reverted to a quartet, when POL departed.

Mar 89.	(7"m) **BABY, I DON'T CARE. / TIME FOR A CHANGE / STRINGS OF MY HEART** ('A'different mix-12"+=) – Sex kick (demo). (cd-s+=) – Saturn 5 (demo).	3	
Jun 89.	(7"m)(c-s) **THE ONLY ONE. / THE MYSTERY SONG / LOVE ME** ('A'extended-12"+=)(cd-s+=) – ('A'extended).	15	
Jul 89.	(lp)(c)(cd)(pic-lp) **VELVETEEN** – Baby, I don't care / The only one / Landslide of love / Falling for a goldmine / Down on you / Song to the stars / Kiss their sons / Born to be sold / Pay the ghosts / Bad valentine / Velveteen. *(re-iss.cd+c Aug93)*	1	
Jul 89.	(7"m)(c-s)(7"pic-d) **LANDSLIDE OF LOVE. / HARDTIME / HE'S THE ONLY ONE FOR ME** (12"+=)(cd-s+=) – West II blues.	14	
Oct 89.	(7"m)(c-s) **BORN TO BE SOLD. / DOWN ON YOU / LAST TIME** (12"+=)(cd-s+=) – Kiss me.	22	
Apr 91.	(7")(c-s) **(I JUST WANNA) B WITH U. / SWAMP THING / STRAIGHT THRU YOUR HEART** (cd-s+=)/ /(12"++=) – ('A'night ripper mix)./ / Punky says.	30	
Jun 91.	(7")(c-s) **IF LOOKS COULD KILL. / MY FRIEND THE TOM CAT / PUPPY DOG TAILS** (12"+=) – I want your love (live). (cd-s+=) – Tell that girl to shut up (live).	41	
Aug 91.	(cd)(c)(lp) **THE LITTLE MAGNETS VERSUS THE BUBBLE OF BABBLE** – (I just wanna) B with U / Ain't no rules / If looks could kill / Every little thing / Twangy wipeout / Don't believe the type / Pressure times / Crawl out your window / You put a spell on me / Back on my knees again.		

WENDY JAMES

(solo) with **PETE THOMAS** – drums, percussion / **CASS LEWIS** – bass / **NEIL TAYLOR** – guitars / **ANDY BOWN** – organ / **JON ASTLEY** – piano.
Album penned by **ELVIS COSTELLO** with help from wife **CAIT O'RIORDAN.**

		M.C.A.	M.C.A.
Feb 93.	(7")(c-s) **THE NAMELESS ONE. / I JUST DON'T WANT IT ANYMORE** (cd-s+=) – May I have your autograph. (cd-s) – ('A'side) / Only a fool / I need you now.	34	
Mar 93.	(cd)(c)(lp) **NOW AIN'T THE TIME FOR YOUR TEARS** – This is a test / London's brilliant / Basement kiss / Puppet girl / Earthbound / Do you know what I'm saying? / we despise you / Fill in the blanks / The nameless one / I want to stand forever.	43	
Apr 93.	(7")(c-s) **LONDON'S BRILLIANT. / MY BALLAD TO 46th STREET** (12"+=) – I will never be your lover. (cd-s) – ('A'side) / All beginnings / Never a stranger.	62	
Jun 93.	(c-s) **DO YOU KNOW WHAT I'M SAYING / SUGAR TAKES HER COFFEE BLACK** (cd-s) – ('A'side) / I started the lie / The reigning beauty queen.		

TRAVELING WILBURYS

Formed: Based in the USA . . . 1988 by ageing superstars BOB DYLAN, TOM PETTY, GEORGE HARRISON, JEFF LYNNE and ROY ORBISON. Their debut album, gave them huge seller, and parented hit single 'HANDLE WITH CARE' with ORBISON on lead vox. • **Style:** Mega-supergroup combination who masqueraded under various pseudonyms. BOO WILBURY =BOB / MUDDY WILBURY =TOM / CLAYTON WILBURY =GEORGE ? / STEVE WILBURY =JEFF ? • **Songwriters:** All contributors. Also covered NOBODY'S CHILD (trad.). • **Trivia:** ROGER McGUINN (ex-BYRDS singer), declined offer to replace the deceased ROY ORBISON.

Recommended: TRAVELLING WILBURYS VOLUME I (*6)

BOB DYLAN (b.ROBERT ALLAN ZIMMERMAN, 24 May'41, Duluth, Minnesota, USA) – vocals, guitar (also solo artist) / **GEORGE HARRISON** (b.25 Feb'43, Liverpool, England) – vocals, guitar (ex-BEATLES, also solo artist) / **ROY ORBISON** (b.23 Apr'36, Vernon, Texas, USA) – vocals, guitar (solo artist) / **TOM PETTY** (b.20 Oct'53, Gainsville, Florida, USA) – vocals, guitar (solo . . .) / **JEFF LYNNE** (b.30 Dec'47, Birmingham, England) – vocals, guitar (solo artist, ex-ELECTRIC LIGHT ORCHESTRA)

		Warners	Warners
Oct 88.	(7") **HANDLE WITH CARE. / MARGARITA** (10"+=)(12"+=)(cd-s+=) – ('A'extended).	21	45
Oct 88.	(lp)(c)(cd) **TRAVELING WILBURYS VOLUME 1** – Handle with care / Dirty world / Rattled / Last night / Not alone anymore / Conratulations / Heading for the light / Margarita / Tweeter and the monkey man / End of the line.	16	3
Feb 89.	(7")(12")(cd-s) **END OF THE LINE. / CONGRATULATIONS**	52	63

— now augmented by **JIM KELTNER** – drums, percussion / **JIM HORN** – saxophone / **RAY COOPER** – percussion (and a quartet, after the death of ROY O)

Jun 90.	(7") **NOBODY'S CHILD. / ('B'by 'Dave Stewart & The Spiritual Cowboy')** (12"+=)(cd-s+=) – (track by 'Ringo Starr').	44	

Above single was from The ARMENIAN DISASTER album by Various Artists.

Nov 90.	(7")(c-s) **SHE'S MY BABY. / NEW BLUE MOON** (12"+=)(cd-s+=) – Runaway.		
Nov 90.	(cd)(c)(lp) **TRAVELING WILBURYS VOLUME 3** – She's my baby / Inside out / If you belonged to me / The Devil's been busy / 7 deadly sins / Poor house / Where were you last night? / Cool dry place / New blue moon / You took my breath away / Wilbury twist.	14	11
Mar 91.	(7")(c-s) **WILBURY TWIST. / NEW BLUE MOON (instrumental)** (12"+=)(cd-s+=) – Cool dry place.		

T.REX (see under ⇒ BOLAN, Marc)

TRICKY

Born: 1969, Knowle West, Bristol, England. Came to prominence in 1991 when taking some lead vocals on MASSIVE ATTACK's outstanding debut 'BLUE LINES'. He also guested on their 1994 follow-up 'PROTECTION', although he had already carved out own solo career, starting with single 'AFTERMATH'. Early in 1995, he unleashed the ground-breaking 'MAXINQUAYE', which hit UK Top 3 and was deservedly voted top album of the year by NME writers. • **Style:** Haunting ambient dub and jungle featured teenage MARTINA. • **Songwriters:** Self-penned except; BLACK STEEL (Public Enemy).
Recommended: MAXINQUAYE (*10)

TRICKY – vocals (with various guests incl. **MARTINA**)

		4th & Broad.	4th & Broad.
Jan 94.	(7") **AFTERMATH. / ('A' – I could be looking for people mix)** (12"+=)(cd-s+=) – (2 'A'mixes).	69	
Apr 94.	(7") **PONDEROSA. / ('A' – Dobie's roll pt.1 mix)** (12"+=)(cd-s+=) – (3 'A'mixes; Ultragelic / Original / Dobie's roll pt.2).		
Jan 95.	(7")(c-s)(cd-s) **OVERCOME. / ABBA ON FAT TRACKS** (12"+=)(cd-s+=) – ('A' – Zippy & Bungle mix).	34	
Feb 95.	(cd)(c) **MAXINQUAYE** – Overcome / Ponderosa / Black steel / Hell is around the corner / Pumpkin / Aftermath (hip hop blues) / Abba on fat tracks / Brand new you're retro / Suffocated love / You don't / Strugglin' / Read me.	3	
Mar 95.	(c-s) **BLACK STEEL. / ('A' – Been caught stealing mix)** (12"+=)(cd-s+=) – ('A'live) / ('A'-In the draw mix). (cd-s++=) – ('A'edit).	28	
Jul 95.	(7"pic-d-ep)(12"red-ep)(cd-ep) **THE HELL E.P.** – Hell is around the corner (original) / ('A' – Hell and water mix) / Psychosis / Tonite is a special nite (chaos mass confusion mix).	12	

(above credited as "TRICKY VS. THE GRAVEDIGGAZ")

Nov 95.	(c-s) **PUMPKIN / MOODY BROODY BUDHIST CAMP / NEW KINGDOM** (cd-s+=) – Brand new you're retro (Alex Reece remix). (12"pumpkin-colrd) – ('A'side) / (above track) / Slick 66.	26	

TRIFFIDS

Formed: Perth, Australia . . . 1980 by New Zealand born brothers DAVID and ROBERT McCOMB. After many releases on Australian label 'Hot', they finally returned to tour in Britain in 1986 after signing to 'Island'. • **Style:** A blend of alternative country and romance with American influences. Highlights of the band were JILL's melancholy sparse vox. • **Songwriters:** DAVID McCOMB penned except covers; / INTO THE GROOVE (Madonna) / BRIGHT LIGHTS BIG CITY (?). / GOOD MORNING, GOOD MORNING (Beatles) / I AM A LONESOME HOBO + BILLY (Bob Dylan) / YOU DON'T MISS YOUR WATER (William Bell).

Recommended: BORN SANDY DEVOTIONAL (*7) / TREELESS PLAIN (*7) / RAINING PLEASURE (*8) / CALENTURE (*8) / THE BLACK SWAN (*7).

DAVID McCOMB (b.1962) – vocals, guitar, piano, etc. / **ROBERT McCOMB** – violin, guitar, keyboards, vocals / **JILL BIRT** – keyboards, some vocals repl. PHIL KAKULAS / **MARTIN CASEY** – bass, vocals / **ALSY McDONALD** – drums, percussion, vocals

not issued | Shake Some

Jul 81. (7"m) **STAND UP. / FARMERS NEVER VISIT NIGHT CLUBS / SHAKE SOME ACTION** [-] [-] Aussie

not issued | Resonant

Dec 81. (7"ep) **REVERIE** [-] [-] Aussie
– Reverie / Place in teh sun / Joan of Arc / This boy.

not issued | No Records

1982. (7") **SPANISH BLUE. / TWISTED BRAIN** [-] [-] Aussie
1982. (7"ep) **BAD TIMING.** [-] [-] Aussie
– Bad timing / Left to rot / Being driven / Snake pit.

Hot UK | not issued

Nov 83. (lp) **TREELESS PLAIN** [ ] [-] +Auss
– Red pony / Branded / My baby thinks she's a train / Roseval / I am a lonesome hobo / Place in the sun / Play thing / Old ghostrider / Hanging shed / Hell of a summer / Madeline / Nothing can take your place. *(cd-iss.Nov91)*
Dec 83. (7") **BEAUTIFUL WASTE. / PROPERTY IS CONDEMNED** [ ] [-]
Dec 84. (m-lp) **RAINING PLEASURE** [ ] [-]
– Jesus calling / Embedded / St. James Infirmary / Everybody has to eat / Ballad of Jack Frost / Property is condemned / Raining pleasure. *(cd-iss.Nov91) (re-iss.Jun94)*
Apr 85. (12"m) **FIELD OF GLASS. / BRIGHT LIGHTS BIG CITY / MONKEY ON MY BACK** [ ] [-]

—— added **'Evil' GRAHAM LEE** – steel guitar (of The APARTMENTS)

Aug 85. (7") **YOU DON'T MISS YOUR WATER (TILL YOUR WELL RUNS DRY). / CONVENT WALLS** [ ] [-]
(12"+=) – Beautiful water / ('A'instrumental). *(re-iss.Oct94)*
May 86. (7") **WIDE OPEN ROAD. / TIME OF WEAKNESS** [ ] [-]
(12"+=) – Dear Miss Lonely Hearts / Native bride. *(re-iss.May94)*
Jun 86. (lp) **BORN SANDY DEVOTIONAL** [ ] [-]
– The seabirds / stuary bed / Chicken killer / Tarrilup Bridge / Lonely stretch / Wide open road / Life of crime / Personal things / Stolen property / Tender is the night (the long fidelity).
Nov 86. (lp) **IN THE PINES** [ ] [-]
– Suntrapper / In the pines / Kathy knows / 25 to 5 / Do you want me near you? / Once a day / Just might fade away / Better off this way / Only one life / Keep your eyes on the hole / One soul less on your fiery list / Born Sandy Devotional / Love and affection. *(re-iss.Jun94) (cd-iss.Mar95 on 'Mushroom')*

—— added **ADAM PETERS** – guitar (ex-FLOWERPOT MEN)

Island | Island

Oct 87. (7") **BURY ME DEEP IN LOVE. / BABY CAN I WALK YOU HOME** [ ] [ ]
(12"+=) – Region unknown.
(cd-s++=) – Vagabond holes.
Nov 87. (lp)(c)(cd) **CALENTURE** [ ] [ ]
– Bury me deep in love / Kelly's blues / A trick of the light / Hometown farewell kiss / Unmade love / Open for you / Holy water / Blinded by the hour / Vagabond holes / Jerducuttup man / Calenture / Save what you can. *(re-iss.1990) (cd-iss.Mar95 on 'Mushroom')*
Jan 88. (7") **A TRICK OF THE LIGHT. / LOVE DECEIVER** [73] [ ]
(10"+=) – Bad news always reminds me of you.
(12"+=)(cd-s+=) – Everything you touch turns to time.
Aug 88. (7") **HOLY WATER. / GOOD MORNING, GOOD MORNING** [ ] [ ]
(12"+=)(cd-s+=) – Raining pleasure / Red pony.

—— added guests **PHIL KAKULAS** (who returned) + **RITA MENENDEZ**

Mar 89. (7") **I DON'T NEED YOU. ("DAVID McCOMB & ADAM PETERS") / WILLIE THE TORCH** [ ] [-]
(12"+=) – Liberty and a thousand fares.
Apr 89. (lp)(c)(cd) **THE BLACK SWAN** [63] [ ]
– Too hot to move, too hot to think / American sailors / Falling over you / Goodbye little boy / Bottle of love / The spinning top song / Butterflies into worms / The clown prince / Good fortune Rose / New Year's greetings / Blackeyed Susan Brown / Fairytale love. *(re-iss.cd Mar95 on 'Mushroom')*
Apr 89. (7") **FALLING OVER YOU. / GO HOME EDDIE** [-] [ ]
(12"+=)(cd-s+=) – Shell of a man / You minus me.
May 89. (7") **GOODBYE LITTLE BOY. / GO HOME EDDIE** [ ] [ ]
(12"+=)/ /(10"++=)(cd-s++=) – Shell of a man./ / You minus me.
Aug 89. (7") **BURY ME DEEP IN LOVE. / RENT** [ ] [ ]
(12"+=)(cd-s+=) – Into the groove.

M.N.W. | M.N.W.

Jul 90. (lp) **STOCKHOLM (live on Swedish radio 1989)** [ ] [-]
– Property is condemned / Hell of a summer / Personal things / Raining pleasure / Lonely stretch / Sure the girl I love / Wide open road / Keep your eyes on the hole / In the pines / Billy / I am a lonesome hobo / How could I help but love you. *(cd-iss.Mar95 on 'Mushroom')*

—— Disbanded late in 1989.

– compilations, others, etc. –

Oct 87. Strange Fruit; (12"ep) **THE PEEL SESSIONS** (5/5/85) [ ] [-]
– Life of crime / Chicken killer / Lonely stretch.
Dec 94. Mushroom; (cd) **AUSTRALIAN MELODRAMA (THE BEST OF THE TRIFFIDS)** [ ] [ ]
– Red pony / Hell of a summer / Beautiful waste / Raining pleasure / Bright lights, big city / The seabirds / Wide open road / Lonely stretch / Tender is the night / Bury me deep in love / trick of the light / Hometown farewell kiss / Unmade love / Jerdacuttup man / Save what you can / Falling over you / Goodbye little boy / New Year's greetings / In the pines.

DAVE McCOMB

(solo)

Foundation | not issued

Sep 91. (12") **THE MESSAGE. / SONG OF NO RETURN / ('A'club version)** [ ] [-]
(cd-s+=) – I've heard things turn out this way.

Mushroom | Mushroom

Mar 94. (c-ep)(cd-ep) **SETTING YOU FREE / HOME FOR FALLEN ANGELS / YOU'VE GOT A FUNNY WAY OF SHOWING YOU LOVED ME / MY FRIEND SLEEP** [ ] [ ]
Mar 94. (cd)(c) **LOVE OF WILL** [ ] [ ]
– Clear out my mind / Setting you free / Day of the ascension / Deep in a dream / Nothing good / The Lord burns every clue / Lifelike / Lover sister number one / Heard you had a bed / Inside of me / Leaning / I want to conquer you / Pack up your troubles.

TRIUMPH

Formed: Canuck, Toronto, Canada . . . 1975 by EMMETT, LEVINE & MOORE. After two albums on Canadian label 'Attic', they signed to 'RCA' in 1977. Gained wider audiences in the US, becoming top attraction there by the early 80's. • **Style:** Anthemic heavy-metal rock'n'roll, played by accomplished showman musicians. Renowned for spectacular stage show filled with usual dry-ice, etc. • **Songwriters:** EMMETT or group except ROCKY MOUNTAIN WAY (Joe Walsh) / etc? • **Trivia:** RIK EMMETT won many polls for his brilliant guitar work.

Recommended: STAGES (*6)

RIK EMMETT (b.10 Jul'53, Streetsville, Ontario) – vocals, guitar / **MIKE LEVENE** (b. 1 Jun'49) – bass, keyboards, synthesizers / **GIL MOORE** (b.12 Feb'51) – drums, percussion, vocals

not issued | Attic

1976. (lp) **TRIUMPH** [-] [-] Canada
– 24 hours a day / Be my lover / Don't take my life / Street fighter / Street fighter (reprise) / What's another day of rock'n'roll / Easy life / Let me get next to you / Blinding light show – Moonchild. *(re-iss.Mar82)*
1977. (lp) **ROCK AND ROLL MACHINE** [-] [-] Canada
– Takes time / Bringing it on home / Little Texas shaker / New York City streets / The city: War march – El Duende agonizante – Minstrels lament / Rocky mountain way / Rock and roll machine. *(re-iss US May 79 on 'RCA')* (same as debut for 'RCA') *(re-iss.Jun82)*

R.C.A. | R.C.A.

1978. (lp) **ROCK'N'ROLL MACHINE** (compilation of first 2) [ ] [ ]
– Takes time / Bringing it on home / Rocky mountain way / Street fighter / 24 hours a day / Blinding light show / Moonchild / Rock'n'roll machine / Street fighter (reprise). *(re-iss.Jun87) (cd-iss.Jun88 on 'M.C.A.')*
1978. (7") **BRINGING IT ON HOME. / ROCKY MOUNTAIN WAY** [-] [ ]
May 79. (lp)(c) **JUST A GAME** [ ] [48]
– Movin' on / Lay it on the line / Young enough to cry / American girls / Just a game / Fantasy serenade / Hold on / Suitcase blues. *(re-iss.Sep81) (cd-iss.Jun88 on 'MCA')*
Jun 79. (7") **HOLD ON. / JUST A GAME** [ ] [38]
(12"+=) – ('A'extended).
Oct 79. (7") **LAY IT ON THE LINE. / AMERICAN GIRLS** [-] [86]
Jan 80. (7") **AMERICAN GIRLS. / MOVIN' ON** [ ] [ ]
Apr 80. (lp)(c) **PROGRESSIONS OF POWER** [61] [32] Mar 80
– I live for the weekend / I can survive / In the night / Nature's child / Woman in love / Take my heart / Tear the roof off / Fingertalkin' / Hard road. *(re-iss.Sep81) (re-iss.Jun87, cd-iss.Jun88 on 'MCA')*
May 80. (7") **I CAN SURVIVE. / NATURE'S CHILD** [ ] [91]
Oct 80. (7")(12") **I LIVE FOR THE WEEKEND. / LAY IT ON THE LINE** [59] [ ]
Sep 81. (7") **ALLIED FORCES. / SAY GOODBYE** [-] [ ]
Sep 81. (lp)(c) **ALLIED FORCES** [64] [23]
– Fool for your love / Magic power / Air raid / Allied forces / Hot time in this city / Tonight / Fight the good fight / Ordinary man / Petite etude / Say goodbye. *(cd-iss.Jun88 on 'MCA')*
Oct 81. (7")(12") **ALLIED FORCES. / HOT TIME IN THIS CITY** [ ] [ ]
Mar 82. (7") **MAGIC POWER. / FIGHT THE GOOD FIGHT** [ ] [51] Sep 81
Feb 83. (lp)(c) **NEVER SURRENDER** [ ] [26] Jan 83
– Too much thinking / A world of fantasy / A minor prelude / All the way / Battle cry / Overture (processional) / Never surrender / When the lights go down / Writing on the wall / Epilogue (resolution). *(cd-iss.Jun88 on 'MCA')*
Mar 83. (7")(7"pic-d) **A WORLD OF FANTASY. / TOO MUCH THINKING** [ ] [ ]
May 83. (7") **WHEN THE LIGHTS GO DOWN. / ('A'long version)** [-] [ ]
Jul 83. (7") **BATTLE CRY. / ALL THE WAY** [-] [ ]

M.C.A. | M.C.A.

Mar 85. (lp)(c) **THUNDER SEVEN** [ ] [35] Dec 84
– Spellbound / Rock out, roll on / Cool down / Follow your heart / Times goes by / Midsummer's daydream / Time canon / Killing time / Stranger in a strange land / Little boy blues. *(cd-is.Feb87)*
Mar 85. (7") **FOLLOW YOUR HEART. / STRANGER IN A STRANGE LAND** [-] [88]
Oct 85. (7") **HOLD ON (live). / MIND GAMES (live)** [-] [ ]
Nov 85. (lp)(c) **STAGES (live)** [ ] [50]
– When the lights go down / Never surrender / Allied forces / Hold on / Magic power / Rock'n'roll machine / Lay it on the line / A world of fantasy / Druh mer selbo / Midsummer's daydream / Spellbound / Follow your heart / Fight the good

fight / Mind games / Empty inside. *(cd-iss.Jul87)*

Sep 86. (7") **HOOKED ON YOU. / JUST ONE NIGHT** [-] [ ]

Sep 86. (lp)(c)(cd) **THE SPORT OF KINGS** [ ] [33]
– Tears in the rain / Somebody's out there / What rules my heart / If only / Hooked on you / Take a stand / Just one night / Embrujo / Play with the fire / Don't love anybody else but me / In the middle of the night.

Feb 87. (7") **SOMEBODY'S OUT THERE. / FOLLOW YOUR HEART** [ ] [27] Aug 86
(12"+=) – Magic power / I live for the weekend.

STEVE MORSE (of KANSAS) made an appearance on 2 tracks below.

Nov 87. (lp)(c)(cd) **SURVEILLANCE** [-] [82]
– Prologue: Into the forever / Never say never / Headed for nowhere / All the king's horses / Carry on the flame / Let the light (shine on me) / Long time gone / Rock you down / Prelude: The waking dream / On and on / All over again / Running in the night.

— (Nov88) EMMETT departed, and group looked to have split after below.

not issued | Pulse

1989. (lp)(c)(cd) **CRY FREEDOM** [-] [ ]
– Run with the wind / Son of man / I am waiting / It is finished / Paid on the nail / No more tears / Cry freedom / Never trust a stranger / Take my life / Liberty / I will rise.

TROGGS

Formed: Andover, Hampshire, England . . . 1964 briefly as The TROGLODYTES. In 1965, they were signed by KINKS manager Larry Page, who leased them early '66 to 'CBS' for debut single 'LOST GIRL'. Their second 45 'WILD THING', with TV exposure on 'Thank Your Lucky Stars', gave them classic No.2 hit, which also went on to become US No.1. Became major stars for the next few years until their split in 1969. • **Style:** American inspired Garage rock act, who toyed with psychedelia in 1967. • **Songwriters:** PRESLEY was main writer, except WILD THING + ANY WAY THAT YOU WANT ME (Chip Taylor) / HI HI HAZEL (Geno Washington) / GOOD VIBRATIONS (Beach Boys) / I CAN'T GET NO SATISFACTION (Rolling Stones) / THE KITTY CAT SONG (Hal Roach-Allen Toussaint) / RIDE YOUR PONY (A. Neville) / EVIL (. . . Singleton) / LOUIE LOUIE + JAGUAR AND THUNDERBIRD + MEMPHIS + NO PARTICULAR PLACE TO GO (Chuck Berry) / GOT LOVE IF YOU WANT IT (Slim Harpo) / WALKING THE DOG (Rufus Thomas) / etc. • **Trivia:** Their 1990's reformation included collaborations with R.E.M. on single 'Nowhere Road'.

Recommended: BEST OF THE TROGGS (*7).

REG BALL (b.12 Jun'43. Became REG PRESLEY after hit) – vocals, ocamna / **CHRIS BRITTON** (b.21 Jun'45, Watford, England) – guitar repl. TONY MANSFIELD / **PETE STAPLES** (b. 3 May'44) – bass (ex-TEN FOOT FIVE) repl. DAVID WRIGHT / **RONNIE BOND** (b. 4 May'43) – drums

C.B.S. | not issued

Feb 66. (7") **LOST GIRL. / THE YELLA IN ME** [ ] [-]

Fontana | Fontana

Apr 66. (7") **WILD THING. / FROM HOME** [2] [1] Jun 66
(above & below 'A' was also double 'A'side on 'Atco' in US)

Jul 66. (7") **WITH A GIRL LIKE YOU. / I WANT YOU** [1] [29] Aug 66

Jul 66. (lp) **FROM NOWHERE . . . THE TROGGS** [6] [52] Aug 66
– Wild thing / The kitty cat song / Ride your pony / Hi hi Hazel / I just sing / Evil / The yella in me / With a girl like you / Our love will still be there / Louie Louie / Jingle jangle / When I'm with you / From home / Jaguar and Thunderbird / I can't control myself / Night of the long grass. *(US-title 'WILD THING', diff.tracks)*

Page One | Atco

Sep 66. (7") **I CAN'T CONTROL MYSELF. / GONNA MAKE YOU MINE** [2] [43]

Page One | Fontana

Dec 66. (7") **ANY WAY THAT YOU WANT ME. / 66-54321** [8] [ ]

Feb 67. (7") **GIVE IT TO ME. / YOU'RE LYIN'** [12] [ ]

Feb 67. (lp) **TROGGLODYNAMITE** [10] [ ]
– I can only give you everything / Last summer / Meet Jacqueline / Oh no / It's too late / No.10 Downing Street / Mona / I want you to come into my life / Let me tell you babe / Little Queenie / Cousin Jane / You can't beat it / Baby come closer / It's over.

May 67. (7") **NIGHT OF THE LONG GRASS. / GIRL IN BLACK** [17] [ ]

Jul 67. (lp) **BEST OF THE TROGGS** (compilation) [24] [ ]
– Night of the long grass / Gonna make you / Anyway that you want me / 66-5-4-3-2-1 / I want you / With a girl like you / I can't control myself / Girl in black / Give it to me / You're lying / From home / Wild thing.
(re-iss. Feb85 on 'Rhino' + 1988 on 'Bigtime')

Jul 67. (7") **HI HI HAZEL. / AS I RIDE BY** [42] [ ]

Oct 67. (7") **LOVE IS ALL AROUND. / WHEN WILL THE RAIN COME** [5] [7] Feb 68

1967. (lp) **CELLOPHANE** [ ] [ ]
– Little red donkey / Too much of a good thing / Butterflies and bees / All of my time / Seventeen / Somewhere my girl is waiting / It's showing / Her emotion / When will the rain come / My lady / Come the day / Love is all around.

Feb 68. (7") **LITTLE GIRL. / MAYBE THE MADMEN** [37] [ ]

May 68. (7") **SURPRISE SURPRISE. / MARBLES AND SOME GLUM** [ ] [ ]

May 68. (lp) **LOVE IS ALL AROUND** [-] [ ]
– Love is all around / Night of the long grass / Gonna make you / Anyway that you want me / 66-5-4-3-2-1 / When will the rain come / Little girl / I can't control myself / Girl in black / Give it to me / Cousin Jane.

Aug 68. (7") **YOU CAN CRY IF YOU WANT TO. / THERE'S SOMETHING ABOUT YOU** [ ] [ ]

Oct 68. (7") **HIP HIP HOORAY. / SAY DARLIN'** [ ] [ ]

1968. (lp) **MIXED BAG** [ ] [-]

Page One | Page One

Jan 69. (7") **EVIL WOMAN. / SWEET MADELAINE** [ ] [ ]

Jan 69. (lp) **BEST OF THE TROGGS VOL.II** (compilation) [ ] [ ]
– I can only give you everything / Meet Jacqueline / Jingle jangle / I want you to come into my life / Cousin Jane / Louie Louie / Love is all around / From home / Jaguar and the thunderbird / Hi hi Hazel / Mona.

Feb 69. (7") **EVIL WOMAN. / HEADS OR TAILS** [-] [ ]

— Split Mar'69.

RONNIE BOND

Mar 69. Page One; (7") **ANYTHING FOR YOU. / CAROLYN** [ ] [-]

REG PRESLEY

Apr 69. Page One; (7") **LUCINDA LEE. / WITCHITA LINEMAN** [ ] [-]

— CHRIS BRITTON also issued solo album 'AS I AM' in 1969.

TROGGS

re-formed. **TONY MURRAY** – bass (ex-PLASTIC PENNY) repl. PETE

Page One | Page One

Feb 70. (7") **EASY LIVIN'. / GIVE ME SOMETHING** [ ] [ ]

1970. (lp) **TROGGLOMANIA (live)** [ ] [ ]
– Give it to me / Jingle jangle / No.10 Downing Street / Wild thing / Oh no / Last Summer / Anyway that you want me / Hi hi Hazel / With a girl like you / Mona / Baby come closer / Cousin Jane / I can't control myself / I want you to come into my life / I just sing.

May 70. (7") **LOVER. / COME NOW** [ ] [ ]

Jul 70. (7") **THE RAVER. / YOU** [ ] [ ]

— **RICHARD MOORE** – guitar repl. BRITTON

D.J.M. | Silverline

1971. (7") **LAZY WEEKEND. / LET'S PULL TOGETHER** [ ] [ ]

1971. (lp) **CONTRASTS** [ ] [ ]
– I can't control myself / The raver / Surprise, surprise (I need you) / Evil woman / Lover / Wild thing / Love is al around / Little girl / You can cry if you want to / I've waited for someone / Easy loving / Any way that you want me *(re-iss.Nov76)*

Jam | not issued

Nov 72. (7"m) **WILD THING (new version). / WITH A GIRL LIKE YOU / LOVE IS ALL AROUND** [ ] [-]

Pye | Pye

1972. (7") **EVERYTHING'S FUNNY. / FEELS LIKE A WOMAN** [ ] [ ]

Pye | Bell

1973. (7") **LISTEN TO THE MAN. / QUEEN OF SORROW** [ ] [ ]

Oct 73. (7") **STRANGE MOVIES. / I'M ON FIRE** [ ] [-]

Penny Farthing | Pye

Dec 74. (7") **GOOD VIBRATIONS. / PUSH IT UP TO ME** [ ] [ ]

Jul 75. (7") **SUMMERTIME. / JENNY COME DOWN** [ ] [ ]

1975. (lp) **TROGGS** [ ] [ ]
– I got lovin' if you want it / Good vibrations / No particular place to go / Summertime / Satisfaction / Full blooded band / Memphis Tennessee / Peggy Sue / Jenny come down / Wild thing.

Nov 75. (7") **(I CAN'T GET NO) SATISFACTION. / MEMPHIS TENNESSEE** [ ] [ ]

Jun 76. (lp)(c) **THE TROGGS TAPES** [ ] [-]
– Get you tonight / We rode through the night / A different me / Downsouth to Georgia / Gonna make you / Supergirl / I'll buy you an island / Rolling stone / After the rain / Rock and roll lady / Walkin' the dog.

Jun 76. (7") **I'LL BUY YOU AN ISLAND. / SUPERGIRL** [ ] [-]

1977. (7") **FEELING FOR LOVE. / SUMMERTIME** [ ] [-]

Raw | not issued

1978. (7") **JUST A LITTLE TOO MUCH. / THE TRUE TROGG TAPES** [ ] [-]

— added **COLIN 'Dill' FLETCHER** – rhythm guitar

M.K.C. | Basement

Mar 81. (lp) **LIVE AT MAX'S KANSAS CITY (live)** [ ] [ ] 1980
– Got love if you want it / Satisfaction / Love is all around / Feels like a woman / Strange movie / Summertime / Walking the dog / Memphis / No particular place to go / Wild thing / Gonna make you.

Stage Coach | not issued

May 82. (7") **BLACK BOTTOM. / WITH YOU** [ ] [-]

10-Virgin | not issued

1984. (7")(12")(7"pic-d) **EVERY LITTLE THING. / BLACKJACK AND POKER** [ ] [-]

New Rose | not issued

May 90. (cd)(lp) **AU** [ ] [-]
– Always something there to remind me / Walking the dog / Wild thing / Love is all around / With a girl like you / I can't control myself / Strange movies / Maximum overdrive / The Disco Kid versus Sid Chicane / What you doing here. *(re-iss.cd Dec95 on 'Javelin')*

Page One | Page One

Feb 92. (7")(12")(c-s)(cd-s) **DON'T YOU KNOW. / NOWHERE ROAD** [ ] [ ]

Mar 92. (cd)(c)(lp) **ANTHENS ANDOVER** [ ] [ ]
– Crazy Annie / Together / Tuned into love / Deja vu / Nowhere road / Dust bowl / I'm in control / Don't you know / What's your game / Suspicious / Hot stuff.

Weekend | not issued

Oct 93. (7")(c-s)(cd-s) **WILD THING. ("TROGGS feat. WOLF") / WAR ("EDWIN STARR feat. SHADOW")** [69] [-]

Lifetime | not issued

Nov 94. (7")(c-s) **WILD THING. (featuring OLIVER REED) / ('A'mix)** [ ] [-]
(12"+=)(cd-s+=) – ('A'original).

– more compilations, etc. –

1966. Page One; (7"ep) **TROGGS TOPS** [ ] [-]

1967. Page One; (7"ep) **TROGGS TOPS VOL.2** [ ] [-]

1969. Page One; (7") **WILD THING. / I CAN'T CONTROL MYSELF** [ ] [-]
Nov 75. DJM; (lp) **WITH A GIRL LIKE YOU** [ ] [-]
1976. Sire; (lp) **VINTAGE YEARS** [-] [ ]
Jul 76. DJM; (lp) **THE (ORIGINAL) TROGGS TAPES** [ ] [-]
Nov 81. DJM; (c) **VOLUME 1 / VOLUME 2** [ ] [-]
Jan 84. DJM; (7")(12") **WILD THING. / I CAN'T CONTROL MYSELF / LOVE IS ALL AROUND** [ ] [-]
Jul 82. Old Gold; (7") **WILD THING. / WITH A GIRL LIKE YOU** [ ] [-]
(re-iss.Nov85 & Jun88)
Jul 82. Old Gold; (7") **I CAN'T CONTROL MYSELF. / GIVE IT TO ME** [ ] [-]
Jul 82. Old Gold; (7") **LOVE IS ALL AROUND. / ANY WAY THAT YOU WANT ME** [ ] [-]
May 92. Old Gold; (cd-ep) **WILD THING / WITH A GIRL LIKE YOU / I CAN'T CONTROL MYSELF** [ ] [-]
Aug 84. Action Replay; (lp) **ROCK IT UP** [ ] [-]
Nov 84. Astan; (lp)(c) **GOLDEN HITS . . . TROGGS** [ ] [-]
Feb 85. Rhino; (lp)(c) **THE BEST OF THE TROGGS** [-] [ ]
(UK-iss.1988 on 'Big Time')
Aug 87. Konnexion; (lp) **WILD THINGS** [ ] [-]
(re-iss.+cd Jul89 on 'See For Miles')
Nov 89. Big Wave; (7") **WILD THING. / FROM HOME** [ ] [-]

— In 1991, WILD THING was re-issued on 'Fontana'.

Feb 93. Fontana; (cd) **ARCHAEOLOGY** [ ] [-]
Nov 93. Fat Boy; (cd) **THE VERY BEST OF THE TROGGS** [ ] [-]
Mar 94. Charly; (cd) **WILD THINGS** [ ] [-]
Jul 94. Polygram TV; (cd)(c) **GREATEST HITS** [27] [-]
Jul 94. Success; (cd)(c) **WILD THING** [ ] [-]
Aug 94. Legends In Music; (cd) **THE TROGGS** [ ] [-]
Nov 94. President; (cd) **LIVE AT KANSAS CITY** [ ] [-]
Feb 95. B.A.M.; (cd) **PEARLS OF THE PAST** [ ] [-]
Apr 95. Muskateer; (cd)(c) **GREATEST HITS - WILD THING** [ ] [-]
Apr 95. Polygram TV; (cd)(c) **GREATEST HITS** [ ] [-]
Jul 95. Summit; (cd) **THE BEST OF THE TROGGS** [ ] [-]
Aug 95. Spectrum; (cd)(c) **LOVE IS ALL AROUND** [ ] [-]
Sep 95. Hallmark; (cd)(c) **THEIR GREATEST HITS** [ ] [-]

REG PRESLEY

C.B.S. / not issued
Oct 73. (7") **S'DOWN TO YOU MARIANNE. / HEY LITTLE GIRL** [ ] [-]

Robin TROWER

Born: 9 Mar'45, London, England. After initial period with 60's outfit The PARAMOUNTS (who became PROCOL HARUM), he set up his own band JUDE, with FRANKIE MILLER. Also in their ranks was JAMES DEWAR, who re-united with him after TROWER launched solo career in 1972. He signed to 'Chrysalis', and issued debut album 'TWICE REMOVED FROM YESTERDAY' in the ensuing year. Made impact in 1974, especially across the Atlantic, when the 'BRIDGE OF SIGHS' lp eased into their Top 10. They worked hard there throughout the 70's to maintain large venue audiences, though this faded in the 80's. • **Style:** HENDRIX-FREE inspired axeman, whose heavy bluesy-rock sound, combined well with DEWAR's soul-orientated vox. The facial antics of TROWER, gave music press a field-day for unjustifiably ridiculing the once great guitar hero. • **Songwriters:** Mostly TROWER-DEWAR compositions, except; MAN OF THE WORLD (Fleetwood Mac) / ROCK ME BABY (B.B.King) / I CAN'T WAIT MUCH LONGER (Frankie Miller) / FURTHER ON UP THE ROAD (?) / SAILING (Sutherland Bros.) / etc. • **Trivia:** Like so many of his rock contemporaries, he played a FENDER STRATOCASTER guitar.

Recommended: FOR EARTH BELOW (*8) / VICTIMS OF THE FURY (*6)/ PORTFOLIO (*8).

ROBIN TROWER – guitar (ex-JUDE, ex-PROCOL HARUM) / **JAMES DEWAR** – vocals, bass (ex-JUDE, ex-STONE THE CROWS) / **REG ISADORE** – drums (ex-QUIVER)

Chrysalis / Chrysalis
Mar 73. (lp)(c) **TWICE REMOVED FROM YESTERDAY** [ ] [ ]
– I can't wait much longer / Daydream / Hannah / Man of the world / I can't stand it / Rock me baby / Twice removed from yesterday / Sinner's song / Ballerina.
Mar 73. (7") **MAN OF THE WORLD. / TAKE A FAST TRAIN** [ ] [ ]
Mar 74. (7") **TOO ROLLING STONED. / MAN OF THE WORLD** [-] [ ]
Apr 74. (lp)(c) **BRIDGE OF SIGHS** [ ] [7]
– Day of the eagle / Bridge of sighs / In this place / The fool and me / Too rolling stoned / About to begin / Lady love / A little bit of sympathy. *(re-iss Jan82, cd-iss.1980's-US) (re-iss.cd Mar94)*
May 74. (7") **TOO ROLLING STONED. / LADY LOVE** [ ] [ ]

— **BILL LORDAN** – drums (ex-SLY & THE FAMILY STONE) repl. REG to HUMMINGBIRD

Feb 75. (lp)(c) **FOR EARTH BELOW** [26] [5]
– Shame the devil / It's only money / Confessin' midnight / Fine day / Alethea / A tale untold / Gonna be more suspicious / For Earth below.
Mar 76. (lp)(c) **ROBIN TROWER LIVE (live)** [15] [10]
– Too rolling stoned / Daydream / Rock me baby / Lady love / I can't wait much longer / Alethea / Little bit of sympathy.
Oct 76. (lp)(c) **LONG MISTY DAYS** [31] [24]
– Some rain falls / Long misty days / Hold me / Caledonia / Pride / Sailing / S.M.O. / I can't live without you / Messin' the blues.
Nov 76. (7") **CALEDONIA. / MESSIN' THE BLUES** [ ] [82]

— added **RUSTEE ALLEN** – bass (ex-SLY & THE FAMILY STONE)

Sep 77. (lp)(c) **IN CITY DREAMS** [58] [25]
– Somebody calling / Sweet wine of love / Bluebird / Falling star / Further up the road / Smile / Little girl / Love's gonna bring you round / In city dreams. *(re-iss.1986)*

— added **PAULHINO DACOSTA** – percussion

Aug 78. (lp)(c) **CARAVAN TO MIDNIGHT** [ ] [37]
– My love (burning love) / Caravan to midnight / I'm out to get you / Lost in love / Fool / It's for you / Birthday boy / King of the dance / Sail on.
Sep 78. (7"m-red) **IT'S FOR YOU. / MY LOVE (BURNING LOVE) / IN CITY DREAMS** [ ] [ ]
Jan 79. (7") **IT'S FOR YOU. / MY LOVE (BURNING LOVE)** [ ] [ ]

— reverted to trio of the mid-70's. (TROWER, DEWAR + LORDAN)

Jun 80. (7")(12") **VICTIMS OF THE FURY. / ONE IN A MILLION** [ ] [ ]
Jun 80. (lp)(c) **VICTIMS OF THE FURY** [61] [34]
– Jack and Jill / Roads to freedom / Victims of the fury / The ring / Only time / Into the flame / The shout / Madhouse / Ready for the taking / Fly low.
Aug 80. (7") **JACK AND JILL. / THE SHOUT** [ ] [ ]

BRUCE, LORDAN & TROWER

saw same line-up bar **JACK BRUCE** – vox, bass (ex-CREAM, ex-JOHN MAYALL'S BLUESBREAKERS, ex-Solo artist) repl. DEWAR

Feb 81. (lp)(c) **BLT** [ ] [37]
– Into money / What it is / Won't let you down / No island lost / It's too late / Life on Earth / Once the bird has flown / Carmen / Feel the heat / End game.
Feb 81. (7") **WHAT IT IS. / INTO MONEY** [ ] [ ]

— trimmed to duo

BRUCE & TROWER

with drummer **REG ISADORE** (same label)

Jan 82. (lp)(c) **TRUCE** [ ] [ ]
– Gonna shut you down / Gone too far / Thin ice / The last train to the stars / Take good care of yourself / Fall in love / Fat gut / Shadows touching / Little boy lost.

ROBIN TROWER

went solo again, augmented by **DEWAR / DAVE BRONZE** – bass / **BOBBY CLOUTER + ALAN CLARKE** – drums

Sep 83. (lp)(c) **BACK IT UP** [ ] [ ]
– Back it up / River / Black to red / Benny dancer / Time is short / Islands / None but the brave / Captain midnight / Settling the score.

M.F.N. / Passport
Jun 85. (lp)(c) **BEYOND THE MIST** [ ] [ ]
– The last time / Keeping a secret / The voice / Beyond the mist / Time is short / Back it up / Bridge of sighs.

— still retained **BRONZE,** and also with **DAVEY PATTISON** – vox (ex-GAMMA) / **PETE THOMPSON** – drums

P.R.T. / GNP Cres..
Feb 87. (lp)(c)(cd) **PASSION** [ ] [100] Dec 86
– Caroline / Secret doors / If forever / Won't even think about you / Passion / No time / Night / Bad time / One more world.

— retained **PATTISON**

Atlantic / Atlantic
Jun 88. (lp)(c)(cd) **TAKE WHAT YOU NEED** [ ] [ ] May 88
– Tear it up / Take what you need (from me) / Love attack / I want you home / Shattered / Over you / Careless / Second time / Love won't wait forever.

— now with **PATTISON** – vox / **JOHN REGAN** – bass / **AL FRITSCH + PEPPY CASTRO** – backing vocals / **BOBBY MAYO + MATT NOBLE** – keyboards / **TONY BEARD** – drums

Mar 90. (cd)(c)(lp) **IN THE LINE OF FIRE** [ ] [ ]
– Sea of love / Under the gun / Turn the volume up / Natural fact / If you really want to find love / Ev'rybody's watching you now / Isn't it time / (I would) Still be here for you / All that I want / (Let's) Turn this fight into a brawl / Climb above the rooftops.

— ROBIN then re-joined the reformed PROCOL HARUM in 1991.

— now w / **LIVINGSTONE BROWNE** – bass / **CLIVE MAYUYU** – drums

Demon / Rykodisc
Nov 94. (cd)(c) **20th CENTURY BLUES** [ ] [ ]
– 20th century blues / Prisoner of love / Precious gift / Whisper up a storm / Extermination blues / Step into the dark / Rise up like the Sun / Secret place / Chase the bone / Promise you the stars / Don't lose faith in tomorrow / Reconsider baby.

– compilations, others, etc. –

Jul 87. Chrysalis; (d-lp)(c)(cd) **PORTFOLIO** [ ] [ ]
– Bridge of sighs / Too rolling stoned / For Earth below / Caravan to midnight / Day of the eagle / Shame the Devil / Fine day / Daydream (live) / Lady Love (live) / Alethea (live) / Caledonia (live) / Messin' the blues / Blue bird / Victims of fury / Madhouse / Into money / Gonna shut you down / Thin ice / Benny dancer. *(re-iss.cd+c Mar93)*
Aug 91. Castle; (cd)(c)(d-lp) **THE COLLECTION** [ ] [-]
Apr 92. Windsong; (cd)(c)(lp) **BBC RADIO 1 LIVE IN CONCERT (live)** [ ] [-]
May 94. Connoisseur; (cd) **ANTHOLOGY** [ ] [-]

TUBES

Formed: Phoenix, Arizona, USA . . . 1975 by BILL SPOONER and ex-drama student FEE WAYBILL, who moved band to Bay Area, San Francisco. Signed to 'A&M' and soon released eponymous AL KOOPER produced debut album which just missed the US Top 100. Their second album 'YOUNG AND

RICH' (produced by KEN SCOTT), broke them into the US Top 50 in 1976. • **Style:** Banned theatrical new wave outfit, whose over-the-top stage antics were always their forte. In May78, WAYBILL while on UK tour, managed to fall off stage and break his leg. He carried on regardless, weilding his chain-saw alongside scantilly clad female backing singers and audience. Their punk anthems were swopped in 1979 for an easier laid back rock, epitomised on that years' TODD RUNDGREN produced 'REMOTE CONTROL' album. • **Songwriters:** WAYBILL penned except I SAW HER STANDING THERE (Beatles) / etc. • **Trivia:** Their proposed 1980 album 'SUFFER FOR SOUND', was shelved by 'A&M' before they were dropped. The same year, they gave a cameo performance in the film 'Xanadu', which had soundtrack by ELECTRIC LIGHT ORCHESTRA and OLIVIA NEWTON-JOHN.

Recommended: T.R.A.S.H. (TUBES RARITIES AND SMASH HITS) (*7)

FEE WAYBILL (b.JOHN WALDO, 17 Sep'50, Omaha, Nebraska, USA) – vocals / **BILL 'Sputnik' SPOONER** – guitar / **VINCE WELNICK** – keyboards / **RICK ANDERSON** – bass / **MICHAEL COTTEN** – synthesizer / **ROGER STEEN** – guitar / **PRAIRIE PRINCE** – drums / **REG STYLES** – vocals, guitar

	A & M	A & M
Jul 75. (7") **WHITE PUNKS ON DOPE. / (part 2)**	-	
Jul 75. (lp)(c) **THE TUBES**		

– Up from the deep / Haloes / Space baby / Malaguena Salerosa / Mondo bondage / What do you want from life / Boy crazy / White punks on dope. *(re-iss.May83 on 'Fame') (d-cd-iss.Dec85 on 'Mobile Fidelity', incl.next album)*

Nov 75. (7") **WHAT DO YOU WANT FROM LIFE. / SPACE BABY**	-	
Jan 76. (7") **WHAT DO YOU WANT FROM LIFE. / WHITE PUNKS ON DOPE**		
May 76. (lp)(c) **YOUNG AND RICH**		46

– Tubes world tour / Brighter day / Pimp / Stand up and shout / Don't touch me there / Slipped my disco / Proud to be an American / Poland whole / Madam I'm Adam / Young and rich.

Jun 76. (7") **DON'T TOUCH ME THERE. / PROUD TO BE AMERICAN**		61
Jan 77. (7") **YOUNG AND RICH. / LOVE WILL KEEP US TOGETHER**	-	

—— added **MINGO LEWIS** – percussion

May 77. (lp)(c) **THE TUBES NOW**		

– Smoke (la vie en fumer) / Hit parade / Strung out on strings / Golden boy / My head is my house (unless it rains) / God-bird-change / I'm just a mess / Cathy's clone / This town / Pound of flesh / You're no fun.

Aug 77. (7") **I'M JUST A MESS. / THIS TOWN**	-	
Nov 77. (7m)(12"m) **WHITE PUNKS ON DOPE. / DON'T TOUCH ME THERE / WHAT DO YOU WANT FROM LIFE**	28	-
Feb 78. (d-lp)(d-c) **WHAT DO YOU WANT FROM LIVE (live)**	38	82

– (overture) / Got yourself a deal / Show me a reason / What do you want from life / God-bird-change / Special ballet / Don't touch me there / Mondo bondage / Smoke (la vie en fumer) / Crime medley: (themes from 'Dragnet' – 'Peter Gunn' – 'Perry Mason' – 'The Untouchables') / I was a punk before you were a punk / I saw her standing there / (drum solo) / Boy crazy / You're no fun / Stand up and shout / White punks on dope.

Apr 78. (7") **SHOW ME A REASON (live). / MONDO BOND-AGE (live)**		-
Jul 78. (7") **SHOW ME A REASON (live). / I SAW HER STANDING THERE (live)**	-	
Feb 79. (7")(12")(7"colrd-7 diff.) **PRIME TIME. / NO WAY OUT**		34
May 79. (lp)(c) **REMOTE CONTROL**	40	46 Mar 79

– Turn me on / TV is king / Prime time / I want it all / No way out / Getoverture / No mercy / Only the strong survive / Be mine tonight / Love's a mystery (I don't understand) / Telecide.

May 79. (7") **LOVE'S A MYSTERY (I DON'T UNDERSTAND). / TELECIDE**	-	
Jul 79. (7")(7"yellow) **TV IS KING. / TELECIDE**		

—— trimmed slightly when LEWIS + STYLES left.

	Capitol	Capitol
May 81. (7") **TALK TO YA LATER. / POWER TOOLS**	-	
May 81. (7") **TALK TO YA LATER. / WHAT'S WRONG WITH ME**		-
May 81. (lp)(c) **THE COMPLETION BACKWARD PRINCIPLE**		36

– Talk to ya later / Let's make some noise / Matter of pride / Mr. Hate / Attack of the fifty foot woman / Think about me / Sushi girl / Don't want to wait anymore / Power tools / Amnesia. *(re-iss.+cd.Mar91 on 'B.G.O.')*

Jul 81. (7") **DON'T WANT TO WAIT ANYMORE. / THINK ABOUT ME**	60	35 Jun 81
Oct 81. (7") **SUSHI GIRL. / MR. HATE**		
Apr 83. (7") **SHE'S A BEAUTY. / WHEN YOU'RE READY TO COME**		10

(12"+=) – Fantastic delusion.

May 83. (lp)(c) **OUTSIDE INSIDE**	77	18 Apr 83

– She's a beauty / No not again / Out of the business / The monkey time / Glass house / Wild women of Wongo / Tip of my tongue / Fantastic delusion / Drums / Theme park / Outside lookin' inside. *(cd-iss.Jul92 on 'B.G.O.')*

—— above feat. guests **MAURICE WHITE** (of EARTH, WIND & FIRE) + **MARTHA DAVIS** – vocals (of MOTELS)

Jul 83. (7") **TIP OF MY TONGUE. / KEYBOARD KIDS**	-	52
Sep 83. (7") **THE MONKEY TIME. / SPORTS FAN**	-	68

—— In 1984, WAYBILL released solo album READ MY LIPS (see further on)

Mar 85. (7") **PIECE BY PIECE. / NIGHT PEOPLE**	-	87
Mar 86. (lp)(c) **LOVE BOMB**		87 May 85

– Piece by piece / Stella / Come as you are / One good reason / Bora Bora 2000 – Love bomb / Night people / Say hey / Eyes / Muscle girls / Theme from a wooly place – Wolly bully – Theme from a summer place / For a song / Say hey (part 2) / Feel it / Night people (reprise). *(cd-iss.Aug93 on 'B.G.O.')*

—— Group disbanded after above album. WAYBILL continued to write and guest on noteably albums by RICHARD MARX (1988).

– compilations, others, etc. –

Nov 81. A&M; (lp)(c) **T.R.A.S.H. (TUBES RARITIES AND SMASH HITS)**		

– Drivin' all night / What do you want from life / Turn me on / Slipped my disco / Mondo bondage / Love will keep us together / I'm just a mess / Only the strong survive / Don't touch me there / White punks on dope / Prime time.

Sep 85. Old Gold; (7") **PRIME TIME. / ('B'by 'Styx')**		-
Jan 87. Old Gold; (7") **(above tracks)**		-

(12"+=) – White punks on dope / (other by 'Styx').

Nov 86. Plastic Head; (lp) **PRIME TIME**		-
Apr 93. Capitol; (cd) **THE BEST OF THE TUBES**		

FEE WAYBILL

	Capitol	Capitol
Oct 84. (7") **WHO SAID LIFE WOULD BE PRETTY. / YOU'RE STILL LAUGHING**	-	
Nov 84. (lp)(c) **READ MY LIPS**	-	

– You're still laughing / Nobody's perfect / Who loves you baby / I don't even know your name (passion play) / Who said life would be pretty / Thrill of the kill / Saved my life / Caribbean sunsets / Star of the show / I could've been somebody.

Dec 84. (7") **STAR OF THE SHOW. / I DON'T EVEN KNOW YOUR NAME**	-	

TUBEWAY ARMY (see under ⇒ NUMAN, Gary)

Nik TURNER (see under ⇒ HAWKWIND)

(Ike &) Tina TURNER

Initiated: 1956-58, when billed as "IKE TURNER, CARLSON OLIVER & LITTLE ANN", they recorded 1958 single BOXTOP for 'Tune Town' records. LITTLE ANN was renamed TINA TURNER the following year, although the couple weren't married until 1962!, having child in '59. TINA was born ANNIE MAE BULLOCK, 26 Nov '38, Brownsville, Tennessee, USA, but raised in Nutbush, where she was a local choir singer. IKE TURNER was born on 5 Nov'31, Clarksville, Mississippi, USA where he became regular DJ at 16. In 1950, he formed own 5-piece IKE & THE KINGS OF RHYTHM (WILLIE WIZARD, EUGENE FOX, JACKIE BENSTON + 1). They made a couple of singles for 'Chess'; HEARTBROKEN AND WORRIED. / I'M LONESOME BABY plus ROCKET 88. / COME BACK WHERE YOU BELONG. Signed to the Sam Phillips management, he became producer and A & R man. In 1955, he flitted from Memphis to St.Louis where he was to strike up working & loving partnership with TINA. In 1960, now billed as IKE & TINA TURNER, they hit the US Top 30 with A FOOL IN LOVE. This was succeeded by a No.14 smash hit IT'S GONNA WORK OUT FINE. After one more major hit, things dried up until the mid-60's, when they were introduced to the legendary PHIL SPECTOR. He produced their magnus-opus RIVER DEEP MOUNTAIN HIGH which although a relative flop in the States, peaked at No.3 in the UK. With varying degrees of fortune, they moved from one label to another but finally broke-out again in 1973, when TINA's composition NUTBUSH CITY LIMITS gave them massive seller on both sides of the Atlantic. In 1974, she landed the part of 'The Acid Queen', in The WHO's film 'TOMMY'. Her new-found independent role gave her time to reflect on her well-documented ill-treatment by IKE. In 1976 after becoming a Buddhist, she soon divorced him. After a time on welfare (the dole), she began to re-create her new solo career, which initiated the year before on album THE ACID QUEEN. Although she was a star on the live club circuit scene, she still found it hard to sell records. Until that is, when 'Capitol' contracted her late in '82. In 1984, her album PRIVATE DANCER (which included recent Grammy winner & US No.1 WHAT'S LOVE GOT TO WITH IT) went platinum in the UK + US. In '85, she starred in the film 'Mad Max: Beyond The Thunderdome', receiving an award by NAACP for best actress. Reputed to have turned down offer of a big part in the film 'The Color Purple'. She was now arguably the Top female Rock & Pop singer on Earth, as the 180,000 audience in Rio De Janeiro Jan'86 concert will testify. In contrast, with her present triumphs, IKE was unceremoniously sentenced to a year in prison in 1988 after admitting his dealings with cocaine. • **Style:** They moved from soul/R&B to Spector "wall of sound" in the 60's, relying always on TINA's raunchy vocals and appearance! to pull them through their exciting stage shows. IKE's brilliant guitar work and choreography was major contribution to 60's shows. As a solo artist TINA mainly exploded her large vocal range and female aggression on what would have been just basic rock ballads. • **Songwriters:** IKE wrote most of the early material, but with (selective) covers intespersed I'VE BEEN LOVING YOU TOO LONG (Otis Redding) / PLEASE PLEASE PLEASE (James Brown) / COME TOGETHER (Beatles) / I WANT TO TAKE YOU HIGHER (Sly & The Family Stone) / PROUD MARY (Creedence Clearwater Revival) / HONKY TONK WOMAN + LET'S SPEND THE NIGHT TOGETHER + UNDER MY THUMB (Rolling Stones) / OOH POO PAH DOO (Jesse Hill) / SAVE THE LAST DANCE FOR ME (Drifters) / etc. TINA's solo covers; ACID QUEEN + I CAN SEE FOR MILES (Who) / SOMETIME WHEN WE TOUCH (Dan Hill) / THE BITCH IS BACK (Elton John) / VIVA LA MONEY (Allen Toussaint) / EARTHQUAKE AND HURRICANE (Willie Dixon) / FIRE DOWN BELOW

(Bob Seger) / WHOLE LOTTA LOVE (Led Zeppelin) / FUNNY HOW TIME SLIPS AWAY (. . . Nelson) / BACKSTABBERS (O'Jays) / HELP! + COME TOGETHER (Beatles) / LET'S STAY TOGETHER + TAKE ME TO THE RIVER (Al Green) / I CAN'T STAND THE RAIN (Ann Peebles) / TONIGHT I'LL BE STAYING HERE WITH YOU (Bob Dylan) / PRIVATE DANCER (Mark Knopfler) / WHAT'S LOVE GOT TO DO WITH IT? (Terry Britten, her co-producer & Graham Lyle; ex-Gallagher & Lyle) / ADDICTED TO LOVE (Robert Palmer) / IN THE MIDNIGHT HOUR (Wilson Pickett) / STEAMY WINDOWS (Tony Joe White) / IT TAKE TWO (Marvin Gaye & Tammi Terrell) / WHY MUST WE WAIT UNTIL TONIGHT (Bryan Adams – Mutt Lange) / GOLDEN EYE (U2) / etc. • **Trivia:** In the 60's, The IKETTES also had US hits with I'M BLUE (THE GONG-GONG SONG) (No.19, Feb62) / PEACHES'N'CREAM (No.36, Apr65). In 1981, TINA appeared on BEF's (HEAVEN 17) various vocalists album 'MUSIC OF QUALITY . . . ' re-actifying The Temptations number BALL OF CONFUSION.

Recommended: PROUD MARY: THE BEST OF IKE & TINA TURNER (*7) / SIMPLY THE BEST (*8).

IKE & TINA TURNER

IKE TURNER – guitar, vocals / **TINA TURNER** – vocals plus sessioners & singing group The IKETTES (aka **P.P.ARNOLD, MERRY CLAYTON & BONNIE BRAMLETT** and loads more at various times).

London Sue

Nov 60. (7") **A FOOL IN LOVE. / THE WAY YOU LOVE ME** [ ] [27] Aug 60
Dec 60. (7") **I IDOLISE YOU. / LETTER FROM TINA** [-] [82]
1961. (7") **I'M JEALOUS. / YOU'RE MY BABY** [-] [ ]
1961. (lp) **THE SOUL OF IKE & TINA TURNER** [-] [ ]
– I'm jealous / I idolize you / If / Letter from Tina / You can't love two / I had a motion / A fool in love / Sleepless / Chances are / You're my baby / The way you love me. *(UK-iss.Apr84 on 'Kent')*
Oct 61. (7") **IT'S GONNA WORK OUT FINE. / WON'T YOU FORGIVE ME** [ ] [14] Jul 61
Nov 61. (7") **POOR FOOL. / YOU CAN'T BLAME ME** [-] [38]
1962. (lp) **DON'T PLAY ME CHEAP** [-] [ ]
– Wake up / I made a promise up above / Desire / Those ways / Mamma tell him / Pretend / Don't play me cheap / The real me / Forever mine / No amending / Love letters / My everything to me.
Mar 62. (7") **TRA LA LA LA LA. / PUPPY LOVE** [-] [ ]
Jun 62. (7") **YOU SHOULD'VE TREATED ME RIGHT. / SLEEPLESS** [-] [89]
1962. (lp) **IT'S GONNA WORK OUT FINE** [-] [ ]
– Gonna find me a substitute / Mojo queen / Kinda strange / Why should I / Tinarro / I'm gonna cut you loose / Foolish / It's gonna work out fine / I'm fallin' in love / This man's crazy / Good good lovin' / The rooster / Steel guitar rag / Trackdown twist / Going home.

Sue Kent

Nov 62. (7") **I IDOLIZE YOU. / TINA'S DILEMMA** [-] [ ]
1963. (7") **MIND IN A WHIRL. / THE ARGUMENT** [-] [ ]
1963. (7") **PLEASE DON'T HURT ME. / WORRIED AND HURTIN' INSIDE** [-] [ ]
1963. (7") **DON'T PLAY ME CHEAP. / WAKE UP** [-] [ ]
Feb 64. (7"ep) **THE SOUL OF IKE & TINA TURNER** [ ] [-]
– (first 2 singles?)
Aug 64. (7") **THE ARGUMENT. / POOR FOOL** [ ] [-]
Nov 64. (7") **I CAN'T BE BELIEVE WHAT YOU SAY (FOR SEEING WHAT YOU DO). / MY BABY NOW** [ ] [95] Sep 64
Nov 64. (lp) **IKE & TINA TURNER REVUE!!! (live)** [-] [ ]
– Please, please, please / Feel so good / The love of my man / Think / Drown in my own tears / I love the way you love / Your precious love / All in my mind / I can't believe what you say. *(UK-iss.Jul66 on 'Ember') (re-iss.Dec72 on 'New World') (cd-iss.Jul93 on 'Kent')*
May 65. (7") **PLEASE PLEASE PLEASE. / AM I A FOOL IN LOVE** [ ] [-]

—— They had already signed to . . .

Warners Warners

Jan 65. (7") **FINGER POPPIN'. / OOH POO PAH DOO** [ ] [ ]
Jan 65. (7"ep) **THE IKE & TINA TURNER SHOW (live)** [ ] [ ]
Apr 65. (lp) **LIVE! THE IKE & TINA TURNER SHOW (live)** [ ] [ ] Feb 65
– Finger poppin' / Down in the valley / Good times / You are my sunshine / Good time tonight / Twist and shout / Something's got a hold on me / I know (you don't want me no more) / (Tight pants) High heel sneakers / My man he's a loving man / I can't stop loving you / Tell the truth. *(re-iss.Jul66) (re-iss.May70 on 'Valient') (cd-iss.Apr85 on 'Edsel')*
Jan 66. (7"ep) **SOMEBODY NEEDS YOU** [ ] [ ]

—— Warners continued to issue material after 1966 success and new dealings . . .

Jul 66. (7") **TELL HER I'M NOT HOME. / FINGER POPPIN'** [48] [ ]
Nov 66. (7") **SOMEBODY (SOMEWHERE) NEEDS YOU. / JUST TO BE WITH YOU** [ ] [ ]
Feb 67. (lp) **THE IKE & TINA TURNER SHOW VOL.II (live)** [ ] [ ]
– Shake a tail feather / You must believe in me / Ooh poo pah doo / Early in the morning / All I can do is cry / Somebody somewhere needs you / Keep on pushing / It's all over / You're no good / Fool for you.

—— Signed to different labels at same time . . .

H.M.V. Tangerine

Aug 66. (7") **ANYTHING THAT YOU WASN'T BORN WITH. / BEAUTY IS JUST SKIN DEEP** [ ] [ ]
Mar 67. (7") **I'M HOOKED. / DUST MY BROOM** [ ] [ ]

Stateside Modern

Oct 66. (7") **GOODBYE, SO LONG. / HURT IS ALL YOU GAVE ME** [ ] [ ]

London Philles

May 66. (7") **RIVER DEEP, MOUNTAIN HIGH. / I'LL KEEP YOU HAPPY** [3] [88]
(re-iss. Dec 69 on 'A & M' US)
Sep 66. (lp) **RIVER DEEP MOUNTAIN HIGH** [27] [-]
– River deep, mountain high / I idolize you / A love like yours (don't come knockin' every day) / A fool in love / Make 'em wait / Hold on baby / I'll never need more than this / Save the last dance for me / Oh! baby (things ain't what they used to be) / Every day I have to cry / Such a fool for you / It's gonna work out fine. *(US-iss.Sep 69 on 'A&M', UK-re-iss.Mar70 +cd.1988) (UK re-iss.1974 on 'Mayfair-A&M', Jan 75 on 'Hamlet-A&M', Dec79 on 'M.F.P.', re-iss.+c.May 84 on 'Spot', cd-iss.1988 on 'Mobile Fidelity') (re-iss. cd+c Sep 93 on 'Yesterday's Gold')*
Oct 66. (7") **A LOVE LIKE YOURS (DON'T COME KNOCKIN' EVERY DAY). / HOLD ON BABY** [16] [ ]
Sep 67. (7") **I'LL NEVER NEED MORE THAN THIS. / SAVE THE LAST DANCE FOR ME** [ ] [ ]
Apr 68. (7") **SO FINE. / SO BLUE OVER YOU** [ ] [ ]
Aug 68. (7") **WE NEED AN UNDERSTANDING. / IT SHO' AIN'T ME** [ ] [ ]
Jan 69. (lp) **SO FINE** [ ] [ ]
– Bet'cha can't kiss me (just one time) / T'ain't nobody's business / It sho' ain't me / Too hot to hold / A fool in love / Poor little fool / I better get ta steppin' / Shake a tail feather / So fine / We need an understanding / You'e so fine / Poor Sam. *(cd-iss.Sep87 on 'Entertainer')*

—— Were again on the books of 2 labels.

Minit Minit

Apr 69. (7") **I'M GONNA DO ALL I CAN (TO DO RIGHT BY MY MAN). / YOU'VE GOT TOO MANY TIES THAT BIND** [ ] [98]
Jun 69. (7") **I WISH IT WOULD RAIN. / ITH A LITTLE HELP FROM MY FRIENDS** [-] [ ]
Sep 69. (7") **I WANNA JUMP. / TREATING US FUNKY** [-] [ ]
Oct 69. (lp) **IN PERSON (live)** [ ] [ ] Jul 69
– Everyday people / Gimme some lovin' / Sweet soul music / Son of a preacher man / I heard it through the grapevine / Respect / Medley: There was a time – African boo's / Funky street / A fool in love / Medley: The summit – All I could do was cry – Please, please, please – Baby I love you / Goodbye, so long.
Feb 70. (7") **COME TOGETHER. / HONKY TONK WOMAN** [-] [57]

Harvest Blue Thumb

May 69. (7") **I'VE BEEN LOVING YOU TOO LONG. / GRUMBLING** [-] [68]
Jul 69. (7") **THE HUNTER. / CRAZY 'BOUT YOU BABY** [-] [93]
Nov 69. (7") **BOLD SOUL SISTER. / I KNOW** [-] [59]
May 70. (7") **THE HUNTER. / BOLD SOUL SISTER** [ ] [-]
Sep 70. (lp) **COME TOGETHER** [ ] [ ] May 70
– It ain't right / Too much woman (for a henpecked man) / Unlucky creature / Young and dumb / Honky tonk woman / Come together / Why can't we be happy / Contact high / Keep on walkin' / I want to take you higher / Evil man / Doin' it.
Sep 70. (lp) **THE HUNTER** [ ] [ ] Nov 69
– The hunter / You don't love me (yes I know) / You got me running / Bold soul sister / I smell trouble / Things I used to do / Early in the morning / You're still my baby / I know.

Liberty Blue Thumb

Jun 69. (lp) **OUTTA SEASON** [ ] [ ] Apr 69
– I've been loving you too long / Mean old world / 3 o'clock im the morning blues / Five long years / Dust my broom / Grumbling / I am a motherless child / Crazy 'bout your baby / Reconsider baby / Honest I do / Please love me / My babe / Rock me baby. *(re-iss.Sep73 on 'Sunset')*
Jul 69. (7") **CRAZY ABOUT YOU BABY. / I'VE BEEN LOVIN' YOU TOO LONG** [ ] [ ] Apr 69

Liberty Liberty

Jun 70. (7") **I WANT TO TAKE YOU HIGHER. / CONTACT HIGH** [ ] [34] May 70
Sep 70. (7") **WORKIN' TOGETHER. / THE WAY YOU LOVE ME** [-] [ ]
Jan 71. (7") **PROUD MARY. / FUNKIER THAN MOSQUITA'S TWEETER** [ ] [4]
Feb 71. (lp) **WORKIN' TOGETHER** [ ] [25] Dec 70
– Workin' together / Get you when I want you / Get back / The way you love me / You can have it / Game of love / Funkier than a mosquito's tweeter / Ooh poo pah doo / Proud Mary / Goodbye so long / Let it be. *(cd-iss.Dec95 on 'EMI Europe')*

United Art United Art

Jun 71. (7") **OOH POO PAH DOO. / I WANNA JUMP** [ ] [60]
Sep 71. (d-lp) **LIVE AT THE CARNEGIE – WHAT YOU HEAR IS WHAT YOU GET (live)** [ ] [25] Jul 71
– Piece of my heart / Everyday people / Doin' The Tina Turner / Sweet soul music / Ooh poo pah doo / Honky tonk women / A love like yours (don't come knockin' every day) / Proud Mary / I smell trouble / Ike's tune / I want to take you higher / I've been loving you too long / Respect / What you see is what you get.
Nov 71. (7") **I'M YOURS. / DOIN' IT** [ ] [ ]
Jan 72. (7") **CRAZY ABOUT YOU BABY. / I'VE BEEN LOVIN' YOU TOO LONG** [ ] [ ]
Mar 72. (lp)(c) **'NUFF SAID** [ ] [ ] Dec 71
– I love what you do to me / Baby (what you want me to do) / Sweet flustrations / What you don't see (is better yet) / Nuff said (part 1) / Tell the truth / Pick me up (take me where your home is) / Moving into hip style – A trip child / I love baby / Can't you hear me callin' / Nuff said (part 2).
Feb 72. (7") **UP IN HEAH. / DOO WAH DIDDY** [-] [83]
Jun 72. (7") **FEEL GOOD. / OUTRAGEOUS** [ ] [ ]
Oct 72. (lp) **FEEL GOOD** [ ] [ ] Jul 72
– Chopper / Kay got laid, Joe got paid / Feel good / I like it / If you can hully gully (I can hully gully too) / Black coffee / She came in through the bathroom window / If I knew then (what I know now) / You better think of something.
Oct 72. (7") **LET ME TOUCH YOUR MIND. / CHOPPER** [ ] [ ]
Feb 73. (lp) **LET ME TOUCH YOUR MIND** [ ] [ ]
– Let me touch your mind / Annie had a baby / Don't believe her / I had a notion / Popcorn / Early one morning / Help him / Up on the roof / Born free / Heaven help us all
Jul 73. (7") **WORK ON ME. / BORN FREE** [ ] [ ]
Oct 73. (7") **NUTBUSH CITY LIMITS. / HELP HIM** [4] [22] Sep 73
Nov 73. (lp)(c) **NUTBUSH CITY LIMITS**
– Nutbush city limits / Make me over / Drift away / That's my purpose / Fancy Annie / River deep mountain high / Get it out of your mind / Daily bread / You are my sunshine / Club Manhattan.

Dec 73. (7") **FANCY ANNIE. / RIVER DEEP MOUNTAIN HIGH** [ ] [ ]
Apr 74. (7") **SWEET RHODE ISLAND RED. / GET IT OUT OF YOUR MIND** [ ] [ ]
Sep 74. (7") **SEXY IDA. / (part 2)** [ ] [65]
Oct 74. (lp)(c) **SWEET RHODE ISLAND RED** [ ] [ ]
– Let me be there / Living for the city / I know / Mississippi rolling stone / Sugar hill / Sweet Rhode Island red / Ready for you baby / Smooth out the wrinkles / Doozie / Higher ground.
Jul 75. (7") **BABY-GET IT ON. / ('A'disco version)** [ ] [88] Jun 75
Oct 75. (7") **DELILAH'S POWER. / THAT'S MY PURPOSE** [ ] [ ]
Mar 77. (lp)(c) **DELILAH'S POWER** [ ] [ ]
– Delilah's power / Never been to Spain / Unhappy birthday / (You've got to) Put something into it / Nothing comes to you when you're asleep but a dream / Stormy weather (keeps rainin' all the time) / Sugar sugar / Too much for one woman / Trying to find my mind / Pick me up (take me where your home is) / Too many women / I want to take you higher.
— Above album was already recorded mid 70's, before their divorce/split.

TINA TURNER

went solo in 1974 with session people.

United Art United Art

Aug 74. (lp)(c) **TINA TURNS THE COUNTRY ON** [ ] [ ]
– Bayou song / Help me make it through the night / Tonight I'll be staying here with you / If you love me (let me know) / He belongs to me / Don't talk now / Long long time / I'm moving on / There'll always be music / The love that lights our way.
Oct 75. (lp)(c) **ACID QUEEN** [ ] [ ] Sep 75
– Under my thumb / Let's spend the night together / Acid queen / I can see for miles / Whole lotta love / Baby git it on / Bootsey Whitelaw / Pick me tonight / Rockin' and rollin'. *(re-iss.cd+c Jul94)*
Jan 76. (7") **ACID QUEEN. / ROCKIN' AND ROLLIN'** [ ] [ ]
Sep 78. (lp)(c) **ROUGH** [ ] [ ]
– Fruits of the night / The bitch is back / The woman I'm supposed to be / Viva la money / Funny how time slips away / Earthquake & hurricane / Root toot undisputable rock'n'roller / Fire down below / Sometimes when we touch / A woman in a man's world / Night time is the right time.
Feb 79. (7") **ROOT TOOT UNDISPUTABLE ROCK'N'ROLLER. / FIRE DOWN BELOW** [ ] [ ]
Mar 79. (lp)(c) **LOVE EXPLOSION** [ ] [ ]
– Love explosion / Fool for your love / Sunset on sunset / Music keeps me dancin' / I see home / Backstabbers / Just a little lovin' (early in the morning) / You get what I'm gonna get / On the radio.
Apr 79. (7") **SOMETIMES WHEN WE TOUCH. / EARTHQUAKE AND HURRICANE** [ ] [ ]
Nov 79. (7") **BACKSTABBERS. / SUNSET ON SUNSET** [ ] [ ]
— In May'82, she sang on BALL OF CONFUSION single by 'BEF' (aka HEAVEN 17).

Capitol Capitol

Nov 83. (7")(12")(12"pic-d) **LET'S STAY TOGETHER. / I WROTE A LETTER** [6] [26] Jan 84
Feb 84. (7")(12")(7"pic-d) **HELP!. / ROCK'N'ROLL WIDOW** [40] [ ]
May 84. (7") **WHAT'S LOVE GOT TO DO WITH IT. / ROCK'N'ROLL WIDOW** [-] [1]
Jun 84. (7")('A'ext-12")(12"pic-d) **WHAT'S LOVE GOT TO DO WITH IT. / DON'T RUSH THE GOOD THINGS** [3] [-]
Jun 84. (lp)(c)(cd) **PRIVATE DANCER** [2] [3]
– I might have been queen / What's love got to do with it / Show some respect / Private dancer / I can't stand the rain / Let's stay together / Better be good to me / Steel claw / Help! / 1984. *(pic-lp Apr85)*
Sep 84. (7")(12")(7"sha-pic-d) **BETTER BE GOOD TO ME. / WHEN I WAS YOUNG** [45] [5]
Nov 84. (7")(12") **PRIVATE DANCER. / NUTBUSH CITY LIMITS** [26] [7]
Feb 85. (7")(12") **I CAN'T STAND THE RAIN. / LET'S PRETEND WE'RE MARRIED** [57] [ ]
Apr 85. (7") **SHOW SOME RESPECT. / LET'S PRETEND WE'RE MARRIED** [-] [37]
Jun 85. (7")(12")(7"pic-d)(7"sha-pic-d) **WE DON'T NEED ANOTHER HERO (THUNDERDOME). / ('A'instrumental)** [3] [2]
— Above + below 45s, from her film 'Mad Max: Beyond The Thunderdome'.
Sep 85. (7")(12") **ONE OF THE LIVING. / (part 2)** [55] [15]
— In Oct85, teamed up with BRYAN ADAMS on UK No.29 + US 19 hit IT'S ONLY LOVE
Aug 86. (7") **TYPICAL MALE. / DON'T TURN AROUND** [33] [2]
('A'extended-12"+=) – ('A'dub version).
(12"++=)(12"pic-d++=) – ('A'dance mix).
Sep 86. (lp)(c)(cd) **BREAK EVERY RULE** [2] [4]
– Typical male / What you get is what you see / Two people / Till the right man comes along / Afterglow / Girls / Back where you started / Break every rule / Overnight sensation / Paradise is here / I'll be thunder.
Oct 86. (7")(12") **TWO PEOPLE. / HAVIN' A PARTY** [43] [30]
(d12"+=) – Let's stay together (live) / Private dancer (live).
Feb 87. (7")(12") **WHAT YOU GET IS WHAT YOU SEE. / TINA TURNER MONTAGE MIX – I Can't Stand The Rain – Two People – We Don't Need Another Hero – What's Love Got To Do With It – Typical Male – Let's Stay Together** [30] [13]
(d7"+=) – ('A'live) / Take me to the river.
Apr 87. (7") **BREAK EVERY RULE. / TAKE ME TO THE RIVER** [-] [74]
May 87. (7")(7"sha-pic-d) **BREAK EVERY RULE. / GIRLS** [43] [-]
Sep 87. (7")(12")(7"pic-d) **PARADISE IS HERE. / IN THE MIDNIGHT HOUR** [ ] [ ]
Mar 88. (7") **ADDICTED TO LOVE (live). / OVERNIGHT SENSATION (live)** [71] [ ]
(12"+=)(cd-s+=) – Legs (live).
Mar 88. (d-lp)(d-c)(d-cd) **LIVE IN EUROPE (live)** [8] [86]
– What you get is what you see / Break every rule / I can't stand the rain / Two people / Girls * / Typical male / Back where you started * / Better be good to me / Addicted to love / Private dancer / We don't need another hero (Thunderdome) / What's love got to do with it / Let's stay together / Show some respect / Land of 1,000 dances / In the midnight hour / 634-5789 (with ROBERT CRAY) / A change is gonna come / River deep, mountain high * / Tearing us apart (with ERIC CLAPTON) / Proud Mary / Help! / Tonight + Let's dance (with DAVID BOWIE) / Overnight sensation * / It's only love (with BRYAN ADAMS) / Nutbush city limits / Paradise is here. *(c+cd+= *)*
Jun 88. (7")(12") **A CHANGE IS GONNA COME (live). / NUTBUSH CITY LIMITS (live)** [ ] [ ]
Aug 89. (7")(c-s) **THE BEST. / UNDERCOVER AGENT FOR THE BLUES** [5] [15]
(12"+=)(cd-s+=) – Bold and reckless.
Sep 89. (lp)(c)(cd) **FOREIGN AFFAIR** [1] [31]
– Steamy windows / The best / You know who (is doing you know what) / Undercover agent for the blues / Look me in the heart / Be tender with me baby / You can't stop me loving you / Ask me how I feel / Falling like rain / I don't wanna lose you / Not enough romance / Foreign affair. *(re-iss.Sep94)*
Oct 89. (7")(c-s) **I DON'T WANNA LOSE YOU. / NOT ENOUGH ROMANCE** [8] [ ]
(12"+=)(12"pic-d+=) – Stronger than the wind.
(cd-s+=) – We don't need another hero.
Jan 90. (7") **STEAMY WINDOWS. / THE BEST (muscle mix)** [13] [39] Nov 89
('B'extended-cd-s+=) – ('A'house mix).
(12")(c-s) – ('A'side) / ('A'vocal mix) / ('A'house mix).
Jul 90. (c-s)(cd-s) **LOOK ME IN THE HEART / STRONGER THAN THE WIND** [-] [ ]
Aug 90. (7")(c-s) **LOOK ME IN THE HEART. / STEEL CLAW (live)** [31] [-]
(12"+=)(cd-s+=) – ('A'instrumental).
('A'remixed-cd-s) – ('A'instrumental) / Tina Turner montage mix.
Oct 90. (7")(c-s)(7"pic-d) **BE TENDER WITH MY HEART. / ('A'live)** [28] [ ]
(12"+=)(cd-s+=) – You know who is doing you know what.
— In Nov90, she teamed up with ROD STEWART on hit single IT TAKES TWO.
Sep 91. (7")(c-s) **NUTBUSH CITY LIMITS – THE 90's VERSION. / THE BEST** [23] [ ]
(cd-s+=) – Addicted to love (live).
(12"+=) – (2-'A' versions).
Oct 91. (cd)(c)(d-lp) **SIMPLY THE BEST** – (compilation) [1] [ ]
Nov 91. (7")(c-s) **WAY OF THE WORLD. / I DON'T WANNA LOSE YOU** [13] [ ]
(12"+=)(cd-s+=) – Foreign affair.
Feb 92. (7") **LOVE THING. / I'M A LADY** [29] [ ]
(c-s+=)(cd-s+=) – It's only love / Private dancer (live).
May 92. (7")(c-s) **I WANT YOU NEAR ME. / LET'S STAY TOGETHER** [22] [ ]
(cd-s+=) – Tonight + Let's dance (live with DAVID BOWIE).
(cd-s) – ('A'side) / Land of a 1,000 dances / In the midnight hour / 634-5789 (live with ROBERT CRAY).

Parlophone Virgin

May 93. (7")(c-s) **I DON'T WANNA FIGHT. / THE BEST** [7] [9]
(cd-s+=) – I don't wanna lose you / What's love got to do with it.
(cd-s) – ('A'side) / Tina's wish / ('A'urban mix).
Jun 93. (cd)(c)(lp) **WHAT'S LOVE GOT TO DO WITH IT** [1] [17]
– I don't wanna fight / Rock me baby / Disco inferno / Why must we wait until tonight / Stay awhile / Nutbush city limits / You know I love you / Proud Mary / A fool in love / It's gonna work out fine / Shake a tail feather / I might have been Queen / What's love got to do with it (live) / Tina's wish.
– (a selection of new recordings of old & new songs from her biopic film)
Aug 93. (7")(c-s) **DISCO INFERNO. / I DON'T WANNA FIGHT** [12] [ ]
(12"+=)(cd-s+=) – ('A'mixes).
Oct 93. (7")(c-s) **WHY MUST WE WAIT UNTIL TONIGHT. / SHAKE A TAIL FEATHER** [16] [97]
(cd-s+=) – The best.
(cd-s++=) – ('A'remix).
Nov 95. (7")(c-s) **GOLDENEYE. / ('A'-Morales club mix)** [10] [ ]
(cd-s+=) – ('A'-urban mix) / ('A'-A/C mix) / ('A'-urban A/C mix).

– (IKE & TINA) compilations, etc. –

Nov 65. London/ US= Warners; (lp) **GREATEST HITS** [ ] [ ]
(re-iss.Jun68 on 'Hallmark')
Jan 69. London; (7") **RIVER DEEP MOUNTAIN HIGH. / SAVE THE LAST DANCE FOR ME** [33] [-]
Dec 69. Warners; (lp) **IKE & TINA'S GREATEST HITS** [ ] [ ]
(re-iss.Feb73)
Mar 75. Warners; (lp) **STAR COLLECTION** [ ] [-]
Feb 71. A&M; (7") **RIVER DEEP MOUNTAIN HIGH. / OH BABY** [ ] [ ]
Feb 73. A&M; (7"m) **RIVER DEEP MOUNTAIN HIGH. / A LOVE LIKE YOURS / SAVE THE LAST DANCE FOR ME** [ ] [-]
Mar 71. Sunset; (lp)(c) **THE FANTASTIC IKE AND TINA** [ ] [-]
Jun 71. Capitol; (lp) **HER MAN HIS WOMAN** [ ] [ ]
(re-iss.c Oct84 on 'Audio Fidelity')
Dec 88. Capitol; (c) **PROUD MARY AND OTHER HITS** [ ] [-]
– A fool in love / I idolize you / I'm jealous / It's gonna work out fine / Poor fool / Tra la la la la / You shoulda treated me right / Come together / Honky tonk woman / I want to take you higher / Workin' together / Proud Mary / Funkier than a mosquito's tweeter / Ooh poo pah doo / I'm yours (use me any way you wanna) / Up in heah / River deep, mountain high / Nutbush city limits / Sweet Rhode Island red / Sexy Ida (parts 1 & 2) / Baby – Get it on / Acid queen. *(re-iss.Oct91 as 'PROUD MARY – THE BEST OF IKE & TINA TURNER' on 'EMI')*
Aug 71. Liberty; (lp) **LIVE IN PARIS (live)** [ ] [ ]
Oct 79. Liberty; (lp)(c) **SOUL SELLERS** [ ] [ ]
Mar 84. Liberty; (lp)(c) **NICE'N'ROUGH** [ ] [ ]
Sep 84. Liberty; (lp)(c) **TOUGH ENOUGH** [ ] [-]
May 85. Liberty; (lp)(c) **GET BACK** [-] [ ]
Oct 73. U.A.; (lp) **THE WORLD OF IKE AND TINA TURNER** [ ] [-]
May 76. U.A.; (lp)(c) **THE VERY BEST OF IKE & TINA TURNER** [ ] [-]
1978. U.A.; (lp) **AIRWAVES** [-] [ ]
Jun 73. Mojo; (lp) **PEACHES** [ ] [-]

Apr 75. ABC; (lp)(c) **16 GREAT PERFORMANCES** [ ] [ ]
Oct 75. DJM; (lp)(c) **SOULED FROM THE VAULTS** [ ] [ ]
(re-iss.Nov76) (re-iss.Apr82 on 'Audio Fidelity')
Oct 76. Musidisc; (lp) **BLACK BEAUTY** [ ] [-]
Jan 77. Musidisc; (lp) **BLACK ANGEL** [ ] [-]
Jun 84. Musidisc; (lp) **THE GREAT ALBUM** [ ] [-]
Nov 81. Audio Fidelity; (lp) **JUKE BOX GIANTS** [ ] [-]
Feb 82. Orchid; (c) **TOO HOT TO HOLD** (TINA solo?) [ ] [-]
(re-iss.+lp Jun87 on 'Thunderb.') (cd-iss. on Feb93 on 'Charly')
Jul 82. Old Gold; (7") **RIVER DEEP MOUNTAIN HIGH. / A LOVE LIKE YOURS** [ ] [-]
Sep 82. Bulldog; (lp) **ROCK ME BABY** [ ] [-]
(re-iss.+c/cd.Nov84 on 'Topline')
Jun 83. Happy Bird; (lp)(c) **SO FINE** (not the 1969 lp) [ ] [-]
(cd-iss.Mar88 on 'Line')
1965. Sue; (7") **TWO IS A COUPLE. / TIN TOP HOUSE** [-] [ ]
1965. Sue; (7") **THE NEW BREED. / (part 2)** [-] [ ]
1965. Sue; (7") **CAN'T CHANCE A BREAKUP. / STAGGER LEE & BILLY** [-] [ ]
1966. Sue; (7") **DEAR JOHN. / I MADE A PROMISE UP ABOVE** [-] [ ]
Oct 83. Sue; (7"ep) **THE SUE SESSIONS** [ ] [-]
– It's gonna work out fine / I idolize you / A fool in love / (1).
Feb 87. Kent; (lp)(c)(cd) **THE IKE & TINA SESSIONS** [ ] [-]
Feb 86. Crown; (lp)(c) **THE DYNAMIC DUO** [ ] [-]
Apr 86. Spartan; (7")(12") **LIVING FOR THE CITY. / PUSH** [ ] [-]
1987. Castle; (d-lp)(c)(cd) **IKE & TINA TURNER COLLECTION** [ ] [-]
Jul 87. C5; (cd) **A FOOL IN LOVE** [ ] [-]
Jul 87. Intertape; (cd) **IKE AND TINA TURNER** [ ] [-]
(re-iss.May91 on 'EMI' + Apr93 on 'Laserlight')
Feb 88. Edsel; (lp)(c)(cd) **FINGER POPPIN' – THE WARNER BROS YEARS** [ ] [-]
Apr 88. Ace; (lp) **TALENT SCOUT BLUES** [ ] [-]
Aug 88. Starburst; (lp)(cd) **CUSSIN' CRYIN' AND CARRYIN' ON** [ ] [-]
Oct 88. Start; (lp)(c)(cd) **WHAT YOU SEE IS WHAT YOU GET** [ ] [-]
Feb 91. Connoisseur; (cd)(c)(m-lp) **GOES COUNTRY** (rec.'79) [ ] [-]
(re-iss.cd Mar95 on 'Top Masters')
Oct 92. Repertoire; (cd) **PHILADELPHIA FREEDOM***(re-Jul93)* [ ] [-]
Apr 93. Tring; (cd)(c) **M.R.S.** [ ] [-]
Sep 93. Laserlight; (d-cd) **GOLDEN EMPIRE** [ ] [-]
Oct 93. Prestige; (cd)(c) **IT'S ALL OVER** [ ] [-]
Oct 93. ZYX; (cd) **LIVE AT CIRCUS KRONE (live)** [ ] [-]
Jul 94. Success; (cd)(c) **YOU GOT WHAT YOU WANTED (w/ IKE)** [ ] [-]
Jul 94. Success; (cd)(c) **ROCK ME BABY** [ ] [-]
Jul 94. Success; (cd)(c) **LIVING FOR THE CITY (w / IKE)** [ ] [-]
Aug 94. EMI; (cd)(cd-vid) **TINA LIVE – PRIVATE DANCER TOUR (live)** [ ] [-]
Aug 94. Javelin; (cd) **COUNTRY CLASSICS** [ ] [-]
Nov 94. Capitol; (3xcd-box) **THE COLLECTED RECORDINGS** [ ] [-]
Feb 95. B.A.M.; (cd) **PEARLS OF THE PAST** [ ] [-]
Apr 95. Muskateer; (cd)(c) **SHAKE** [ ] [-]
Jul 95. Low Price; (4xcd-box) **THE BEST OF IKE & TINA TURNER** [ ] [-]

— Note that a number of IKE TURNER albums were issued after their split. The best being IKE TURNER & THE KINGS OF RHYTHM released Dec88 on 'Ace'.

TURTLES

Formed: Westchester, Los Angeles, USA . . . 1963 as The CROSSFIRES, by KAYLAN, VOLMAN, etc (see below). In 1965, Ted Feigen co-owner of 'White Whale', signed them and manager Reb Foster gave them new name The TURTLES. Their debut 'IT AIN'T ME BABE', soared into the US Top 10, but it wasn't until 1967's 'HAPPY TOGETHER', that outfit made big international impact. • **Style:** BYRDS-like electric folk band, who moved into flower-power scene in 1967. FLO & EDDIE became satirical duo during mid 70's having already proved themselves in FRANK ZAPPA's group. • **Songwriters:** Some by group members, except covers; IT AIN'T ME BABE (Bob Dylan) / LET ME BE + EVE OF DESTRUCTION + YOU BABY (P.F.Sloan) / HAPPY TOGETHER + SHE'D RATHER BE WITH ME (Gary Bonner-Alan Gordon) / THE STORY OF ROCK AND ROLL (Nilsson) / LADY-O (Judee Sill) / etc. • **Trivia:** RAY DAVIES of The KINKS produced the 1969 album TURTLE SOUP. In 1976, KAYLAN & VOLMAN wrote score and dialogue for the adult animated film 'Cheap'. In 1989, the pair sued DE LA SOUL for sampling piece of 'YOU SHOWED ME', on their 'Transmitting Live From Mars'.

Recommended: HAPPY TOGETHER (THE VERY BEST OF...)(*6).

The CROSSFIRES

HOWARD KAYLAN (b.HOWARD KAPLAN, 22 Jun'47, New York) – saxophone / **MARK VOLMAN** (b.19 Apr'47, Los Angeles) – saxophone / **AL NICHOL** (b.31 Mar'46, Winston Salem, New Conneticut) – guitar, piano / **JIM TUCKER** (b.17 Oct'46, Los Angeles) – guitar / **CHUCK PORTZ** (b.28 Mar'48, Santa Monica, California) – bass / **DON MURRAY** – drums

not issued / Capco
1963. (7") **FIBERGLASS JUNGLE. / DR. JEKYLL & MR. HYDE** [-] [ ]

not issued / Lucky Token
1964. (7") **THAT'LL BE THE DAY. / ONE POTATO TWO POTATO** [-] [ ]

The TURTLES

KAYLAN + VOLMAN now on dual vox

Pye Inter . . . / WhiteWhale
Sep 65. (7") **IT AIN'T ME BABE. / ALMOST THERE** [ ] [8] Aug 65
Oct 65. (lp) **IT AIN'T ME BABE** [ ] [98]
– Wanderin' kind / It was a very good year / Your maw said you cried / Eve of destruction / Glitter and gold / Let me be / Let the cold winds blow / It ain't me babe / A walk in the sun / Last laugh / Love minus zero / Like a rolling stone. *(cd-iss.Nov93 on 'Repertoire')*
Jan 66. (7") **LET ME BE. / YOUR MA SAID YOU CRIED (IN YOUR SLEEP LAST NIGHT)** [ ] [29] Oct 65
Jan 66. (7") **YOU BABY. / WANDERIN' KIND** [-] [20]

Immediate / WhiteWhale
Apr 66. (7") **YOU BABY. / SEND HER AWAY** [-] [-]
Jun 66. (lp) **YOU BABY LET ME BE** [-] [ ]
– Flyin' high / I know that you'll be there / House of pain / Just a room / I need someone / Let me be / Down in suburbia / Give love a trial / You baby / Pall bearing, ball bearing world / All my problems / Almost there. *(cd-iss.Jan94 on 'Repertoire')*
Jun 66. (7") **GRIM REAPER OF LOVE. / COME BACK** [-] [81]

— **JOHN BARBATA** (b. 1 Apr'46, New Jersey) – drums (ex-SENTINELS) repl. DON MURRAY. **CHIP DOUGLAS** – bass had replaced PORTZ before he too was deposed by recent writer **JIM PONS** – bass (ex-LEAVES)

London / WhiteWhale
Jul 66. (7") **WE'LL MEET AGAIN. / OUTSIDE CHANCE** [-] [ ]
Sep 66. (7") **MAKIN' MY MIND UP. / OUTSIDE CHANCE** [-] [ ]
Nov 66. (7") **CAN I GET TO KNOW YOU BETTER?. / LIKE THE SEASONS** [ ] [89] Oct 66
Feb 67. (7") **HAPPY TOGETHER. / LIKE THE SEASONS** [-] [1]
Mar 67. (7") **HAPPY TOGETHER. / WE'LL MEET AGAIN** [12] [-]
May 67. (lp) **HAPPY TOGETHER** [ ] [25] Apr 67
– Makin' my mind up / Guide for the married man / Think I'll run away / The walking song / Me about you / Happy together / She'd rather be with me / Too young to be the one / Person without a care / Like the seasons / Rugs of woods and flowers. *(cd-iss.Jun93 on 'Repertoire')*
Jun 67. (7") **SHE'D RATHER BE WITH ME. / WALKING SONG** [4] [3] May 67

— Now a quintet (**KAYLAN, VOLMAN, NICHOL, PONS + BARBATA**), when TUCKER left.

Sep 67. (7") **YOU KNOW WHAT I MEAN. / RUGS OF WOODS AND FLOWERS** [ ] [12] Aug 67
Nov 67. (7") **SHE'S MY GIRL. / CHICKEN LITTLE WAS RIGHT** [ ] [14]
Dec 67. (lp) **THE TURTLES! GOLDEN HITS (compilation)** [-] [7]
Mar 68. (7") **SOUND ASLEEP. / UMBASSA AND THE DRAGON** [ ] [57]
Jun 68. (7") **THE STORY OF ROCK AND ROLL. / CAN YOU HEAR THE COWS** [ ] [48]
Sep 68. (7") **ELENORE. / SURFER DAN** [7] [6]
Dec 68. (7"as CHRISTMAS SPIRIT) **CHRISTMAS IS MY TIME OF YEAR. / WILL YOU STILL BELIEVE IN ME** [-] [ ]
(above featured TURTLES & LINDA RONSTADT)
Jan 69. (lp) **THE TURTLES PRESENT THE BATTLE OF THE BANDS** [ ] [ ] Oct 68
– The opening: The battle of the bands / The last thing I remember / Elenore / Too much heartsick feeling / Oh daddy / Buzzsaw / Surfer Dan / I'm chief Kamanawanalea (we're the royal Macadamia nuts) / You showed me / Food / Chicken Little was right / The closing: Earth anthem (all). *(US re-iss.May86 on 'Rhino')*
Jan 69. (7") **YOU SHOWED ME. / BUZZSAW** [ ] [6]

— **JOHN SEITER** – bass (ex-SPANKY & OUR GANG) repl. BARBATA who later joined JEFFERSON STARSHIP

May 69. (7") **HOUSE ON THE HILL. / COME OVER** [-] [ ]
Jun 69. (7") **YOU DON'T HAVE TO WALK IN THE RAIN. / COME OVER** [ ] [51]
Oct 69. (7") **LOVE IN THE CITY. / BACHELOR MOTHER** [ ] [91]
Oct 69. (lp) **TURTLE SOUP** [ ] [ ]
– Come over / House on the hill / She always leaves me laughing / How you love me / Torn between temptations / Love in the city / Bachelor mother / John and Julie / Hot little hands / Somewhere Friday nite / Dance this dance with me / You don't have to walk in the rain *(US re-iss.May86 on 'Rhino') (cd-iss.Oct93 on 'Repertoire')*
Dec 69. (7") **LADY-O. / SOMEWHERE FRIDAY NIGHT** [-] [78]
Feb 70. (7") **WE AIN'T GONNA PARTY NO MORE. / WHO WOULD EVER THINK THAT I WOULD MARRY MARGARET** [-] [ ]
Apr 70. (lp) **THE TURTLES! MORE GOLDEN HITS (compilation)** [ ] [ ]
– We ain't gonna party no more / The story of rock and roll / You showed me / Sound asleep / You don't have to walk in the rain / Who would ever think that I would marry Margaret / She's my girl / Elenore / Lady-O / Hot little hands / Love in the city / Cat in the window.
May 70. (7") **EVE OF DESTRUCTION. / WANDERIN' KIND** [-] [100]
Aug 70. (7") **ME ABOUT YOU. / THINK I'LL RUN AWAY** [-] [ ]

— When their Spring album 'SHELLSHOCK' was not completed due to displeasure with 'White Whale', they split. It was later issued in 1987 on 'Rhino'. Their last single above was actually first heard on debut 1965 lp. KAYLAN & VOLMAN (and later PONS) joined FRANK ZAPPA's MOTHERS OF INVENTION and appeared on 3 albums; 'Chunga's Revenge', 'Fillmore East, June 1971' & 'Just Another Band From L.A.'. Due to legalities, the two were now billed as The PHLORESCENT LEECH & EDDIE. In 1971, they provided guest backing on tracks by T.REX, noteably the hits 'Hot Love' & 'Get It On'. They formed duo in 1972.

MARK VOLMAN & HOWARD KAYLAN

with band **JIM PONS** – bass / **DON PRESTON** – keys / **AYNSLEY DUNBAR** – drums (all ex-FRANK ZAPPA) / **GARY ROWLES** – guitar (ex-LOVE)

Reprise / Reprise
1972. (lp) **THE PHLORESCENT LEECH & EDDIE** [ ] [ ]
– Flo and Eddie's theme / Thoughts have turned / It never happened / Burn the house / Lady blue / Strange girl / Who but I / Been born again / Goodbye surprise / Nikki hoi / Really love / Feel older now / There you sit lonely.

1972. (7") **GOODBYE SURPRISE. / NIKKI HOI** [-] [ ]

FLO & EDDIE

VOLMAN & KAYLAN

Reprise Reprise

May 73. (lp) **FLO & EDDIE** [ ] [ ]
– Days / You're the lady / The original soundtrack from Carlos the bull / Afterglow / Best part of breaking up / The Sanzini brothers / Another pop stars life / Just another town / Marmendy Hill.

May 73. (7") **AFTERGLOW. / THE ORIGINAL SOUNDTRACK FROM CARLOS AND DE BULL** [ ] [ ]

Aug 73. (7") **YOU'RE A LADY. / IF WE ONLY HAD TIME** [-] [ ]

C.B.S. Columbia

Oct 75. (7") **LET ME MAKE LOVE TO YOU. / COME TO MY RESCUE WEBELOS** [ ] [ ]

Dec 75. (lp) **ILLEGAL IMMORAL AND FATTENING** [-] [ ]
– Illegal, immoral and fattening / Rebecca / Kama Sutra time / The Sanzini brothers return / Livin' in the jungle / Cheap / The Kung Fu killer / Eddie are you kidding / The pop star massage unit / Let me make love to you / There's no business like show business.

Feb 76. (7") **REBECCA. / ILLEGAL, IMMORAL & FATTENING** [ ] [ ]

Nov 76. (lp) **MOVING TARGETS** [-] [ ]
– Elenore / Moving targets / Mama, open up / Love you gave away / Hot / Best friends / Best possible me / Keep it warm / Guns / Sway when you walk.

Nov 76. (7") **ELENORE. / THE LOVE YOU GAVE AWAY** [-] [ ]

Feb 77. (7") **HOT. / KEP IT WARM** [-] [ ]

— The pair became guest vocalists for BLONDIE, ALICE COOPER, etc., before returning in 1981, with reggae back-up **UZZIAH STICKY THOMPSON** – percussion / **ALSTON BARRETT** – bass / **AUGUSTUS PABLO** – keyboards / **CARLTON SANTA DAVIS** – drums / etc.

not issued Epiphany

1981. (lp) **ROCK STEADY WITH FLO & EDDIE** [-] [ ]

— In 1982, the pair re-formed as The TURTLES, but only for tours.

– (TURTLES) compilations, others, etc. –

May 67. Pye Int.; (7") **LET ME BE. / ALMOST THERE** [ ] [-]

Mar 75. Philips/ US= Sire; (d-lp)(c) **HAPPY TOGETHER AGAIN:- THE TURTLES' GREATEST HITS** [ ] [ ] Dec 74

Apr 75. Philips/ US= Sire; (7") **SHE'D RATHER BE WITH ME. / THERE YOU SIT LONELY** [ ] [ ]

Jul 82. Old Gold; (7") **ELENORE. / SHE'D RATHER BE WITH ME** [ ] [-]

Jul 82. Old Gold; (7") **HAPPY TOGETHER. / YOU BABY** [ ] [-]

1982. Rhino; (7")(7"clear-box) **TURTLES** [-] [ ]

1982. Rhino; (7"sha-pic-d-ep) **TURTLES 1968** [-] [ ]

1982. Rhino; (7"sha-pic-d-ep) **TURTLESIZED** [-] [ ]

Jul 84. Rhino; (lp) **WOODEN HEADS** [-] [ ]
(cd-issJan94 on 'Repertoire')

1986. Rhino; (cd) **20 GREATEST HITS** [-] [ ]

1987. Rhino; (lp) **CHALON ROAD** [-] [ ]

1987. Rhino; (lp) **SHELLSHOCK** [-] [ ]

Jan 90. Mainline; (d-cd)(d-c) **20 GOLDEN CLASSICS** [ ] [-]

1991. Music Club; (cd)(c) **HAPPY TOGETHER (THE VERY BEST OF THE TURTLES)** [ ] [-]
– Happy together / She'd rather be with me / Too young to be one / Me about you / Think I'll run away / Can I get to know you better / Guide for the married man / Elenore / It ain't me babe / You baby / Let me be / She's my gal / You don't have to walk in rain / You know what I mean / Lady O / You showed me / There you sit lonely / Outside chance / Buzz saw / Sound asleep.

Feb 93. Repertoire; (cd) **CLASSIC HITS** [ ] [-]

Sep 93. Repertoire; (cd) **ELENORE** [ ] [-]

Oct 94. Laserlight; (cd) **CALIFORNIA GOLD** [ ] [-]

TWINK (see under ⇒ PINK FAIRIES)

TWISTED SISTER

Formed: New York, USA . . . 1973 by SNIDER and others (see below). They signed to an unknown German label in the 70's, but flitted to UK label 'Secret' in 1982, releasing Pete Way (UFO) produced 'UNDER THE BLADE', before transferring to 'Atlantic', the following year. Made the UK Top 20 with single 'I AM (I'M ME)' and album 'YOU CAN'T STOP ROCK'N'ROLL'. • **Style:** Heavy-metal rock'n'roll with similarities to punk legends NEW YORK DOLLS. • **Songwriters:** SNIDER penned, except LEADER OF THE PACK (Shangri-la's) / I AM (I'M ME) + WE'RE NOT GONNA TAKE IT (Who) / IT'S ONLY ROCK'N'ROLL (Rolling Stones) / SIN AFTER SIN (Judas Priest) / LET THE GOOD TIMES ROLL (Shirley & Lee) / DESTROYER (Kiss). • **Trivia:** Guests on the 1985 album included ALICE COOPER, BILLY JOEL, BRIAN SETZER and DON DOKKEN. In the late 80's, SNIDER had to defend himself against 'The American Moral Majority'. They were one of the bands they tried to censor, but it was thrown out that they might corrupt teenagers.

Recommended: BIG HITS AND NASTY CUTS (*6)

DEE SNIDER (b.DANIEL, 15 Mar'55, Massapequa, Long Island, New York) – vocals / **JAY JAY FRENCH** (b.20 Jul'54) – guitar / **EDDIE OJEDA** (b. 5 Aug'54, The Bronx, New York) – guitar / **MARK 'The Animal' MENDOZA** (b.13 Jul'56) – bass (ex-DICTATORS) / **J.J.PERO** (b.14 Oct'59, Staten Island, New York) – drums repl. TONY PETRI

Secret not issued

Jul 82. (12"ep) **RUFF CUTS** [ ] [-]

Sep 82. (lp)(c) **UNDER THE BLADE** [70] [-]
– What you don't know / Bad boys (of rock'n'roll) / Run for your life / Sin after sin / Shoot 'em down / Destroyer / Under the blade / Tear it loose / Day of the rocker. *(re-iss.+cd.1988 on 'Roadrunner') (US-iss. Jul 85 on 'Atlantic'; 1 extra)*

Atlantic Atlantic

Mar 83. (7") **I AM (I'M ME). / SIN AFTER SIN** [18] [ ]
(12") – ('A'side) / Tear it loose / Destroyer.

May 83. (lp)(c)(pic-lp) **YOU CAN'T STOP ROCK'N'ROLL** [14] [ ]
– The kids are back / Like a knife in the back / Ride to live, live to ride / I am (I'm me) / The power and the glory / We're gonna make it / I've had enough / I'll take you alive / You're not alone (Suzette's song) / You can't stop rock'n'roll.

May 83. (7"m)(7"sha-pic-d) **THE KIDS ARE BACK. / SHOOT 'EM DOWN / IT'S ONLY ROCK'N'ROLL** [32] [ ]
(12") – ('A'side) / What you don't know sure can't hurt you / Bad boys of rock / Run for your love.

Aug 83. (7"m) **YOU CAN'T STOP ROCK'N'ROLL. / LET THE GOOD TIMES ROLL / FEEL SO FINE** [43] [ ]
(12") – ('A'side) / Feel the power / Heat of love / One man woman.

May 84. (lp)(c) **STAY HUNGRY** [34] [15]
– I wanna rock / The price / Don't let me down / The beast / S.M.F. / Stay hungry / We're not gonna take it / Burn in Hell / Horror-teria (the beginning).

Jun 84. (7") **WE'RE NOT GONNA TAKE IT. / YOU CAN'T STOP ROCK'N'ROLL** [-] [21]

Jun 84. (7") **WE'RE NOT GONNA TAKE IT. / THE KIDS ARE BACK** [58] [-]
(12"+=) – ('A'version) / You can't stop rock'n'roll.

Aug 84. (7") **I WANNA ROCK. / THE KIDS ARE BACK** [-] [68]

Sep 84. (7") **I WANNA ROCK. / BURN IN HELL (live)** [ ] [-]
(12"+=) – S.M.F. (live).

Feb 85. (7")(12") **THE PRICE. / S.M.F.** [ ] [ ]

Nov 85. (7") **LEADER OF THE PACK. / I WANNA ROCK** [-] [53]

Nov 85. (7")(7"sha-pic-d) **LEADER OF THE PACK. / S.M.F.** [47] [-]
(d7"+=)(12"+=) – ?

Dec 85. (lp)(c)(cd)(pic-lp) **COME OUT AND PLAY** [95] [53]
– Come out and play / Leader of the pack / You want what we got / I believe in rock'n'roll / The fire still burns / Be chrool to you scuel / I believe in you / Out on the streets / Lookin' out for number £1 / Kill or be killed.

Mar 86. (7") **YOU WANT WHAT WE GOT. / STAY HUNGRY** [ ] [ ]
(12"+=) – Were not gonna take it / King of fools.

Apr 86. (7") **YOU WANT WHAT WE GOT. / SHOOT 'EM DEAD** [-] [ ]

— **JOE FRANCE** – drums repl. PERO

Jul 87. (lp)(c)(cd) **LOVE IS FOR SUCKERS** [57] [74]
– Wake up (the sleeping guitar) / Hot love / Love is for suckers / I'm so hot for you / Tonight / Me and the boys / One bad habit / I want this night (to last forever) / You are all that I need / Yeah right.

Oct 87. (7") **HOT LOVE. / TONIGHT** [-] [ ]

— Disbanded after last album. DEE SNIDER went solo, but was dropped by 'Elektra' records. In 1988, he formed DESPERADO with BERNIE TORME (ex-GILLAN) and CLIVE BURR (ex-IRON MAIDEN) . Early 1991, they issued debut album for 'Metal Blade-Warners'. They scrapped project to form new WIDOWMAKER.

– compilations, others, etc. –

Jan 90. Old Gold; (7") **THE KIDS ARE BACK. / I AM (I'M ME)** [ ] [-]

Mar 92. Atlantic; (cd)(c)(lp) **BIG HITS AND NASTY CUTS – THE BEST OF TWISTED SISTER** [ ] [ ]
– We're not gonna take it / I wanna rock / I am (I'm me) / The price / You can't stop rock'n'roll / The kids are back / Shoot 'em down / Under the blade / I'll never grow up, now / Be chrool to your scuel / I believe in you / Out in the streets / Lookin' out

for £1 / Kill or be killed. *(c+= 1 track / cd+= 2 tracks) (re-iss.Nov93)*
Oct 94. MFN; (cd) **LIVE AT HAMMERSMITH (live)**

TWO MEN, A DRUM MACHINE & . . . (see under ⇒ FINE YOUNG CANNIBALS)

TYGERS OF PAN TANG

Formed: Whitley Bay, Newcastle-Upon-tyne, England . . . 1978 by 4 below. In 1979 they gained deal with 'MCA', after one-off 45 for indie label 'Neat'. Their debut album in 1980 'THE WILD CAT', reached the Top 20 in the UK, and was trailed by more fruitful releases during the early 80's. • **Style:** Heavy-metal rock band at the forefront of the NWOBHM scene, with contemporaries IRON MAIDEN and DEF LEPPARD. • **Songwriters:** Group compositions until THOMPSON and DEVERILL took over in 1985. Covered; TUSH (ZZ Top) / LOVE POTION No.9 (Clovers). • **Trivia:** In 1981, they added guest pianist CHRIS GARIDES.

Recommended: THE WILD CAT (*6).

JESS COX – vocals / **ROBB WEIR** – guitar, vocals / **ROCKY LAWS** – bass, vocals / **BRIAN DICK** – drums, percussion

Neat / not issued
Jan 80. (7") **DON'T TOUCH ME THERE. / BAD TIMES** [ ] [-]
M.C.A. / M.C.A.
Mar 80. (7"m) **DON'T TOUCH ME THERE. / BURNING UP / BAD TIMES** [ ] [-]
Jun 80. (7"m) **ROCK'N'ROLL MAN. / ALRIGHT ON THE NIGHT / WILD CATS** [ ] [-]
Jul 80. (lp)(c) **THE WILD CAT** [18] [ ]
– Euthanasia / Slave to freedom / Don't touch me there / Money / Killers / Fireclown / Wild cats / Suzie smiled / Badger badger / Insanity. *(re-iss.Sep86) (cd-iss.Jul93 on 'Repertoire')*
Aug 80. (7") **SUZIE SMILED. / TUSH** [ ] [-]
Oct 80. (7") **EUTHANASIA. / STRAIGHT AS A DIE** [ ] [-]

— **JON DEVERILL** – vocals (ex-PERSIAN RISK) repl. JESS who joined LIONHEART / added **JOHN SYKES** (b.29 Jul'59, Cardiff, Wales) – guitar

Feb 81. (7") **HELLBOUND. / DON'T GIVE A DAMN** [48] [-]
(d7"+=) **THE AUDITION TAPES** – Bad times / Don't take nothin'.
Mar 81. (7"m) **THE STORY SO FAR. / SILVER AND GOLD / ALL OR NOTHING** [ ] [ ]
Apr 81. (lp)(c) **SPELLBOUND** [33] [ ]
– Gangland / Take it / Minotaur / Hellbound / Mirror / Silver and gold / Black Jack / The story so far / Tyger Bay / Don't stop me. *(re-is.1983 & Jun87) (cd-iss.Jul93 on 'Repertoire')*
Jun 81. (7") **DON'T STOP BY. / SLAVE TO FREEDOM** [ ] [-]
(12"+=) – Raised on rock.
Nov 81. (7") **LOVE DON'T STAY. / PARADISE DRIVE** [ ] [-]
Nov 81. (lp)(c) **CRAZY NIGHTS** [51] [ ]
– Do it good / Love don't stay / Never satisfied / Running out of time / Crazy nights / Down and out / Lonely man / Make a stand / Raised on rock. *(free 7")(c+=)* – Storm lands / Slip away. *(re-iss.Feb84)*
Jan 82. (7") **DO IT GOOD. / SLIP AWAY** [ ] [-]
Mar 82. (7")(7"pic-d) **LOVE POTION No.9. / STORM LANDS** [45] [-]
Mar 82. (7") **LOVE POTION No.9 / LONELY AT THE TOP** [-] [ ]

— **FRED PURSER** – guitar (ex-PENETRATION) repl. SYKES who joined THIN LIZZY

Jun 82. (7") **RENDEZVOUS. / LIFE OF CRIME** [49] [ ]
Aug 82. (lp)(c) **THE CAGE** [13] [ ]
– Rendezvous / Lonely at the top / Letter from L.A. / Paris by air / Tides / Making tracks / The cage / Love potion No.9 / You always see what you want to see / Danger in Paradise / The actor. *(re-iss.Jun84)*
Aug 82. (7")(7"pic-d) **PARIS BY AIR. / LOVE'S A LIE** [63] [ ]
Oct 82. (7") **MAKING TRACKS. / WHAT YOU'RE SAYING** [ ] [ ]

— **DEVERILL + DICK** were joined by newcomers **STEVE LAMB** – guitar / **DAVID DONALDSON** – bass / **NEIL SHEPHERD** – guitar

Oct 83. (7") **LONELY AT THE TOP. / YOU ALWAYS SEE WHAT YOU SEE IN ME** [ ] [ ]
M.F.N. / not issued
Jun 85. (lp)(c) **THE WRECK-AGE** [ ] [-]
– Waiting / Protection / Innocent eyes / Desert of no love / The wreck-age / Woman in cages / Victim / Ready to run / All change faces / Forgive and forget.

— (Sep86) – guest **STEVE THOMPSON** – keyboards, bass repl. NEIL SHEPHERD + DONALDSON.

Zebra / not issued
May 87. (lp)(c) **BURNING IN THE SHADE** [ ] [-]
– The first (the only one) / Hit it / Dream ticket / Sweet lies / Maria / Hideaway / Open to seduction / The circle of the dance / Are you there? / The memory fades.

– compilations, others, etc. –

Aug 86. Neat; (lp) **FIRST KILL** [ ] [-]

TYRANNOSAURUS REX (see under ⇒ BOLAN, Marc)

Judie TZUKE

Born: London, England (half-Polish). Went solo in 1978 after one-off single with MIKE PAXMAN (PAXO) on 'Good Earth'. Now signed to ELTON JOHN's label 'Rocket', she soon hit UK Top 20 in 1979 with both 45 'STAY WITH ME TILL DAWN' and parent album 'WELCOME TO THE CRUISE'. • **Style:** AOR songstress, who moved from love balladeer in to easy listening harder rock. • **Songwriters:** Self-penned with MIKE PAXMAN. In '81, she also collaborated with producer PAUL MUGGLETON. Covered; HOW SWEET IT IS (Jackie Wilson).

Recommended: THE BEST OF JUDIE TZUKE (*6)

TZUKE & PAXO

JUDIE – vocals with **MIKE PAXMAN** – guitar

Good Earth / not issued
May 77. (7") **THESE ARE THE LAWS. / IT's ONLY FANTASIES** [ ] [-]

ZOOKIE

D.J.M. / not issued
1977. (7") **JUDIE JUDIE HOLD ON. / I COULDN'T BE YOU** [ ] [-]
1978. (7") **BUBBLES. / DON'T ROCK ME** [ ] [-]

JUDIE TZUKE

solo with **PAXMAN** – guitar / **PAUL MUGGLETON** – percussion / **BOB NOBLE** – keyboards / **JOHN EDWARDS** – bass / **JEFF RICH** – drums

Rocket / Rocket
Jun 78. (7") **FOR YOU. / SUKARITA** [ ] [-]
(re-iss.Oct79)
May 79. (lp)(c) **WELCOME TO THE CRUISE** [14] [ ]
– Welcome to the cruise / Sukarita / For you / These are the laws / Bring the rain / Southern smiles / Katiera Island / Ladies night / New friends again / Stay with me till dawn. *(re-iss.Nov84)*
Jun 79. (7") **STAY WITH ME TILL DAWN. / NEW FRIENDS AGAIN** [16] [ ]
Feb 80. (7") **UNDERSTANDING. / IT'S THE NIGHT** [ ] [ ]
May 80. (lp)(c) **SPORTS CAR** [7] [ ]
– Sports car / Nightline / Chinatown / Understanding / The choices you've made / The rise of the heart / Living on the coast / Molly / Rain on the hills. *(re-iss.Aug83) (re-iss.+cd.Apr88 on 'Mercury')*
May 80. (7") **THE CHOICES YOU'VE MADE. / LADIES NIGHT** [ ] [-]
May 80. (7") **THE CHOICES YOU'VE MADE. / FOR YOU** [-] [ ]

— **CHARLIE MORGAN** – drums repl. RICH

May 81. (7") **I NEVER KNOW WHERE MY HEART IS. / YOU WERE THE PLACE** [ ] [ ]
May 81. (lp)(c) **I AM PHOENIX** [17] [ ]
– Black furs / Higher and higher / Fate's wheels / Come Hell or waters high / You were the place / You are the Phoenix / The flesh is weak / City of swimming pools / I never know where my heart is. *(re-iss.Aug83)*
Jul 81. (7") **HIGHER AND HIGHER. / CITY OF SWIMMING POOLS** [ ] [ ]
Chrysalis / Chrysalis
Mar 82. (7") **LOVE ON THE BORDER. / SOLD A ROSE** [ ] [ ]
Apr 82. (lp)(c) **SHOOT THE MOON** [19] [ ]
– Heaven can wait / Love on the border / Information / Beacon Hill / Don't let me sleep / I'm not a loser / Now there is no love at all / Late again / Liggers at your funeral / Water in motion / Shoot the Moon. *(cd-iss.Nov94 on 'B.G.O.')*
Apr 82. (7")(7"pic-d) **I'M NOT A LOSER. / RUN ON LUCK** [ ] [ ]
May 82. (7") **LATE AGAIN. / WATER IN MOTION** [ ] [ ]
Oct 82. (d-lp)(d-c) **ROAD NOISE – THE OFFICIAL BOOTLEG (live)** [39] [ ]
– Heaven can wait / Chinatown / I'm not a loser / Information / Sports car / For you / You are the Phoenix / Come Hell or waters high / Southern smiles / Kateria island / Love on the border / Black furs / City of swimming pools / Bring the rain / Stay with me till dawn / Sukarita / The hunter. *(d-cd-iss.Dec93 on 'B.G.O.')*
Aug 83. (7") **JEANNIE NO. / INFORMATION (live)** [ ] [ ]
('A'extended-12"+=) – Love on the border (live).
Sep 83. (lp)(c) **RITMO** [26] [ ]
– Jeannie no / She don't live here anymore / Shoot from the heart / Face to face / Another country / Nighthawks / Walk don't walk / Push, push, pull, pull / Chinatown / How do I feel. *(cd-iss.Jul94 on 'B.G.O.')*
Nov 83. (7")(12") **HOW DO I FEEL. / NIGHTHAWKS** [ ] [ ]
Legacy / not issued
Sep 84. (7") **YOU. / RACE AGAINST TIME** [ ] [-]
Mar 85. (7") **I'LL BE THE ONE. / FALLING** [ ] [-]
Jun 85. (lp)(c) **THE CAT IS OUT** [35] [-]
– How sweet it is / Who do you really love / Love like fire / I'll be the one / Girl without a name / This side of Heaven / Harbour lights / You / Falling / Racing against time. *(cd-iss.1986) (re-iss.+c.Nov89)*

— above album still augmented by **PAXMAN + MUGGLETON**

Jun 85. (7") **LOVE LIKE FIRE. / ('A'instrumental)** [ ] [-]
(12"+=) – ('A'extended version).
Sep 85. (7") **THIS SIDE OF HEAVEN. / HOW SWEET IT IS** [ ] [-]
Polydor / Mercury?
Feb 89. (7") **WE'LL GO DREAMING. / DANGEROUS TOYS** [ ] [ ]
(12"+=)/ /(cd-s+=) – Everything will come./ / ('A'remix).
Apr 89. (lp)(c)(cd) **TURNING STONES** [57] [ ]
– We'll go dreaming / Let me be the pearl / Dominique / Take it all / Sound of my sister's tears / Run to win / Don't go / Everything will come / Modern killers / Turning stones.
May 89. (7") **LET ME BE THE PEARL. / ALL THEY CAN DO IS TALK** [ ] [ ]
(12"+=) – Love is not for sale.
C.B.S. / Columbia
Jul 90. (7")(c-s) **GOD ONLY KNOWS. / SAFE HOUSE** [ ] [ ]
(cd-s+=) – Calling me back.
May 91. (cd)(c)(lp) **LEFT HAND TALKING** [ ] [ ]
– One day I will live in France / I could feel you / Liam / Left hand talking / Jesus

was a crossmaker / Stay with me till dawn / God only knows / Bailey's song / Calling me back / Outlaws.

Columbia Columbia

Jun 91. (7") **OUTLAWS. / DOG ROSE**
(cd-s+=) – ('A'-12"version).

—— featured **BRIAN MAY** – guitar + **NIGEL KENNEDY** – violin

Essential not issued

Sep 92. (cd)(c)(lp) **WONDERLAND**

– compilations, others, etc. –

May 83. Rocket; (7") **BLACK FURS. / STAY WITH ME TILL DAWN** -

Jun 83. Rocket; (lp)(c) **THE BEST OF JUDIE TZUKE**
– New friends again / Black furs / Sukarita / Sports car / These are the laws / Welcome to the cruise / Come Hell or high waters / Stay with me till dawn / Higher and higher / Chinatown / For you. (cd-iss. Jun 93 on 'Vertigo')

May 88. Chrysalis; (d-lp)(c)(cd) **PORTFOLIO**
– Heaven can wait / You / Shoot from the heart / She don't live here anymore / Now there is no love at all / How do I feel / Chinatown / You are the phoenix / Sports car / For you / Come Hell or high waters / City of swimming pools / Bring the rain / Stay with me till dawn / The hunter / Black furs.

Sep 95. Windsong; (cd) **BBC LIVE IN CONCERT** -

Sep 95. Spectrum; (cd)(c) **STAY WITH ME TILL DAWN** -

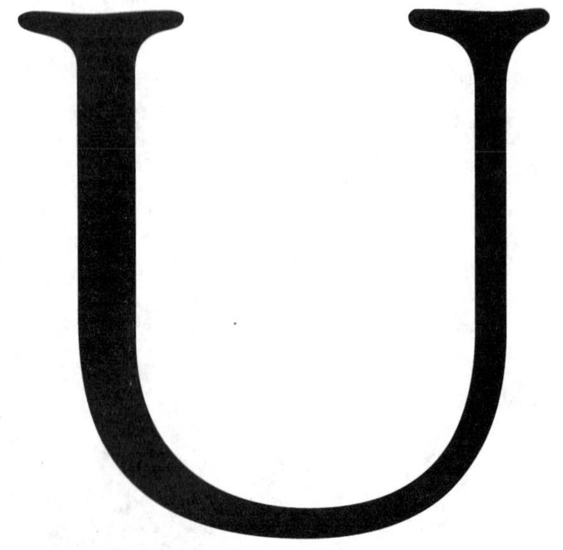

UB 40

Formed: Mosley, Birmingham, England . . . early '79 by ALI and ROBIN; sons of Scots singer IAN CAMPBELL. The self-taught brothers built around them a multi-racial ensemble, who, due to their own and the country's unemployment figures, decided to name themselves after dole card form number UB40. TRAVERS, FALCONER and BROWN had been in own trial version of band while at Art College in 1977. In 1979, they signed to David and Susan Virr's new Dudley based indie label 'Graduate', and embarked on tour with The PRETENDERS. 1980 saw them hitting Top 5 with double 'A'side FOOD FOR THOUGHT / KING. A Top 10 follow-up was preceded by a Bob Lamb produced debut album, poignantly called 'SIGNING OFF' (as one does after getting employment). The following year, they formed own label 'DEP International', and continued to have massive hits throughout the 80's, including two No.1's 'RED RED WINE' & 'I GOT YOU BABE'. • **Style:** Protest reggae pop-rock owing a small debt to the success of revival ska and '2-Tone' label. ALI's smooth-soulful vox was blended nearly always with current political message and rough ASTRO (TERRY WILSON) toasting. • **Songwriters:** ALI penned most material except singles I THINK IT'S GOING TO RAIN TODAY (Randy Newman) / RED RED WINE (Neil Diamond) / MANY RIVERS TO CROSS (Jimmy Cliff) / CHERRY OH BABY (Eric Donaldson) / PLEASE DON'T MAKE ME CRY (Junior Tucker) / SMALL AXE (Bob Marley) / KEEP ON MOVING (Mayfield-Marley) / JOHNNY TOO BAD (Wilson, Bedford, Bailey & Crooks) / VERSION GIRL (R.Thompson aka-Dandy Livingstone) / I GOT YOU BABE (Sonny & Cher) / BREAKFAST IN BED (Dusty Springfield) / HOMELY GIRL (Chi-Lites) / KINGSTON TOWN (Andy Patrick) / HERE I AM (Al Green) / THE WAY YOU DO THE THINGS YOU DO (Smokey Robinson). LABOUR OF LOVE and LABOUR OF LOVE II were cover albums featuring some already mentioned. ALI CAMPBELL covered HAPPINESS (Stevie Wonder- Syreeta) / SOMETHIN' STUPID (hit; Frank & Nancy Sinatra) / THAT LOOK IN YOUR EYE (Starks-Grey) / YOU CAN CRY ON MY SHOULDER (Berry Gordy) / LET YOUR YEAH BE YEAH (Jimmy Cliff) / DRIVE IT HOME (. . .Eaglin). • **Miscellaneous:** EARL was imprisoned in Jul'88, after he was found guilty of drunk driving which caused the death of his brother Ray.

Recommended: SIGNING OFF (*8) / THE BEST OF UB40 VOLUME 1 (*7) / PRESENT ARMS (*7)

ALI CAMPBELL (b.ALISTAIR, 15 Feb'59) – vocals, guitar / **ROBIN CAMPBELL** (b.25 Dec'54) – guitar, vocals / **ASTRO** (b.TERRY WILSON, 24 Jun'57) – toaster/**vocals** repl. YOMI BABAYEMI / **MICHAEL VIRTUE** (b.19 Jan'57) – keyboards repl. JIMMY LYNN / **EARL FALCONER** (b.23 Jan'59) – bass / **BRIAN TRAVERS** (b. 7 Feb'59) – saxophone / **JIM BROWN** (b.20 Nov'57) – drums / **NORMAN HASSAN** (b.26 Jan'58) – percussion

Graduate | Sound

Jan 80. (7") **FOOD FOR THOUGHT. / KING** [4] [ ]
Jun 80. (7")(12") **MY WAY OF THINKING. / I THINK IT'S GOING TO RAIN TODAY** [6] [ ]
Aug 80. (lp)(c) **SIGNING OFF** [2] [ ]
– Tyler / King / 12 bar / Burden of shame / Adella / I think it's going to rain today / 25% / Food for thought / Little by little / Signing off. *(free-12"ep w.a.)* **MADAM MEDUSA. / STRANGE FRUIT / REEFER MADNESS** *(cd-iss.1986 on 'Target')*
Oct 80. (7")(12") **THE EARTH DIES SCREAMING. / DREAM A LIE** [10] [ ]
(all above 45's re-iss.1984)

DEP Inter. | A & M

May 81. (7")(12") **DON'T LET IT PASS YOU BY. / DON'T SLOW DOWN** [16] [-]
May 81. (lp)(c) **PRESENT ARMS** [2] [-]
– Present arms / Sardonicus / Don't let it pass you by / Wild cat / One in ten / Don't slow down / Silent witness / Lambs bread. *(free 12" w.a.)* **DON'T WALK ON THE GRASS. / DOCTOR X** *(lp re-iss.Jan83) (cd-iss.Apr88 on 'Virgin')*
Jul 81. (7") **ONE IN TEN. / PRESENT ARMS IN DUB** [7] [-]
Oct 81. (lp)(c) **PRESENT ARMS IN DUB** [38] [-]
– Present arms / Smoke it / B-line / Kings Row / Return of Doctor X / Walk out / One in ten / Neon haze. *(re-iss.Jan83)*
Feb 82. (7")(12") **I WON'T CLOSE MY EYES. / FOLITICIAN** [32] [-]
May 82. (7") **LOVE IS ALL IS ALRIGHT. / HOT-CROSS DUB** [29] [-]
(12"+=) – ('A'live version).
Aug 82. (7") **SO HERE I AM. / SILENT WITNESS** [25] [-]
(12"+=) – Doctor X (live).
Sep 82. (lp)(c) **UB44** [4] [-]
– So here I am / I won't close my eyes / Forget the cost / Love is all is alright / The piper calls the tune / The key / Don't do the crime / Folitician / The prisoner. *(re-iss.Jan83) (re-iss.+cd.remixed Apr86)*

— DEP International were now distributed by 'Virgin'.

Jan 83. (7") **I'VE GOT MINE. / DUBMOBILE** [45] [-]
(12"+=) – Forget the cost.
Feb 83. (lp)(c) **UB40 LIVE (live in Ireland)** [44] [-]
– Food for thought / Sardonicus / Don't slow down / Folitician / Tyler / Present arms / The piper calls the tune / Love is all is alright / Burden of shame / One in ten. *(re-iss.Aug84) (cd-iss.1988)*
Aug 83. (7")(12") **RED RED WINE. / SUFFERING** [1] [34] Nov 83
(US re-iss.Aug88, hit No.1) (at same time, below album hits US No.14)
Sep 83. (lp)(c) **LABOUR OF LOVE** [1] [39] Nov 83
– Cherry oh baby / Keep on moving / Please don't make me cry / Sweet sensation / Johnny too bad / Red red wine / Guilty / She caught the train / Version girl / Many rivers to cross. *(cd-iss.Jul86)*
Oct 83. (7")(12") **PLEASE DON'T MAKE ME CRY. / SUFFERING (featuring NYA & NATTY)** [10] [-]
Dec 83. (7") **MANY RIVERS TO CROSS. / FOOD FOR THOUGHT (live)** [16] [ ]
(12"+=) – Johnny Too Bad (version).
Feb 84. (7") **CHERRY OH BABY. / FOOD FOR THOUGHT** [-] [ ]
Mar 84. (7")(12")(7"pic-d) **CHERRY OH BABY. / FRILLA** [12] [ ]
Apr 84. (7") **PLEASE DON'T MAKE ME CRY. / FOOD FOR THOUGHT** [-] [ ]
Sep 84. (7")(12") **IF IT HAPPENS AGAIN. / NKOMO A GO-GO** [9] [ ]
Oct 84. (lp)(c)(cd) **GEFFERY MORGAN** [3] [60]
– Riddle me / As always you were wrong again / If it happens again / D.U.B. / The pillow / Nkomo a go-go / Seasons / You're not an army / I'm not fooled so easily / Your eyes were open.
Nov 84. (7")(12") **RIDDLE ME. / D.U.B. (dub)** [59] [ ]

— In Feb85, they appeared on charity single STARVATION with various BEAT members, etc. Released on 'Zarjazz' label, it hit UK No.33.

Mar 85. (7")(12") **I'M NOT FOOLED. / THE PILLOW** [ ] [ ]
Jul 85. (7") **I GOT YOU BABE ("UB 40 & CHRISSIE HYNDE"). / THEME FROM LABOUR OF LOVE** [1] [-]
(12"+=) – Up and coming MC.
Jul 85. (7") **I GOT YOU BABE ("UB40 & CHRISSIE HYNDE"). / NKOMO A GO-GO** [-] [28]
Aug 85. (m-lp)(c)(cd) **LITTLE BAGGARIDM** [-] [40]
– Don't break my heart / I got you babe / Hip hop lyrical robot / One in ten.
Sep 85. (lp)(c)(cd) **BAGGARIDDIM** [14] [-]
– The king step mk.1 / The buzz feeling / Lyric officer mk.2 / Demonstrate / Two in a one mk.1 / Hold your position mk.3 / Hip hop lyrical robot / Style mk.4 / Fight fe come in mk.2 / V's version. (12"w.a.) **DON'T BREAK MY HEART. / I GOT YOU BABE / MI SPLIFF** *(re-iss.Apr90)*
Oct 85. (7")(12") **DON'T BREAK MY HEART. / MEK YA ROK** [3] [ ]
Jun 86. (7")(12") **SING OUR OWN SONG. / ('A' instrumental)** [5] [ ]
Jul 86. (lp)(c)(cd) **RAT IN THE KITCHEN** [8] [53]
– All I want to do / You could meet somebody / Tell it like this / The elevator / Watchdogs / Rat in me kitchen / Looking down at my reflection / Don't blame me / Sing our own song.
Sep 86. (7")(12") **ALL I WANT TO DO. / ('A'version)** [41] [ ]
Jan 87. (7")(12") **RAT IN MI KITCHEN. / ('A' long version)** [12] [ ]
Apr 87. (7") **WATCHDOGS. / DON'T BLAME ME** [39] [ ]
(12"+=) – ('A'live version).
Aug 87. (lp)(c)(cd) **CCCP: LIVE IN MOSCOW (live)** [-] [ ]
– All I want to do / Cherry oh baby / Keep on moving / Watchdogs / Don't blame me / Tell it like it is / Please don't make me cry / Johnny too bad / I got you babe / Don't break my heart / If it happens again / Rat in me kitchen / Sing our own song.
Sep 87. (7") **MAYBE TOMORROW. / DREAD DREAD TIME** [14] [ ]
(12"+=)(c-s+=) – Anything mi chat.
May 88. (7") **BREAKFAST IN BED ("UB40 & CHRISSIE HYNDE"). / ('A'instrumental)** [6] [ ]
(12"+=)(cd-s+=) – ('A'other versions).
May 88. (lp)(c)(cd) **UB40** [12] [44]
– Dance with the Devil / Come out to play / Breakfast in bed / You're always pulling me down / I would do for you / 'Cause it isn't true / Where did I go wrong / Contaminated minds / Matter of time / Music so nice / Dance with the Devil (reprise). *(pic-cd.Dec88)*
Aug 88. (7") **WHERE DID I GO WRONG. / ('A'instrumental)** [26] [-]
(12"+=) – Contaminated dub.
(cd-s++=) – Hit it (instrumental).
Nov 88. (7") **WHERE DID I GO WRONG. / DANCE WITH THE DEVIL** [-] [ ]

— **LARRY BUSHELL** – bass temp.repl. EARL for 4 mths. Jul88.

Nov 88. (7")(c-s) **COME OUT TO PLAY. / CONTAMINATED MINDS** [ ] [ ]
(12"+=) – Sing our own song (live).
(10"++=) – ('A'instrumental).
(cd-s+=) – Dance with the Devil / Rat in mi kitchen.
Jun 89. (7")(c-s) **I WOULD DO FOR YOU. / HIT IT** [45] [ ]
(12"+=)(3"cd-s+=) – ('B'version).

Virgin | Virgin

Nov 89. (7")(c-s) **HOMELY GIRL. / GATOR** [6] [ ]
(12"+=)(3"cd-s+=) – ('A'extended).
Dec 89. (lp)(c)(cd) **LABOUR OF LOVE II** [4] [30]

– Here I am (come and take me) / Tears from my eyes / Groovin' / The way you do the things you do / Wear you to the ball / Singer man / Kingston Town / Baby / Wedding day / Sweet Cherrie / Stick by me / Just another girl / Homely girl / Impossible love.

Jan 90. (7")(c-s) **HERE I AM (COME AND TAKE ME). / CRISIS** 46 7 Mar 91
(12"+=)(cd-s+=) – ('B'dub version).

Mar 90. (7")(c-s) **KINGSTON TOWN. / LICKWOOD** 4
(12"+=)(cd-s+=) – ('A'extended mix).

Jul 90. (7")(c-s) **WEAR YOU TO THE BALL. / SPLUGIN** 35
(12"+=)/ /(cd-s++=) – ('A'extended)./ / ('A'dub version).

— (Oct90, teamed up with ROBERT PALMER on UK No.6 I'LL BE YOUR BABY TONIGHT)

Nov 90. (7")(c-s) **IMPOSSIBLE LOVE. / FIRST SHOT** 47
(12"+=)(cd-s+=) – Council house.

Jan 91. (7")(c-s) **THE WAY YOU DO THE THINGS YOU DO. / MISSPENT YOUTH** 49 6 Sep 90
(cd-s+=) – ('A'remix).

Nov 91. (7")(c-s) **BABY. / SHE CAUGHT THE TRAIN**
(12"+=)(cd-s+=) – Here I am (come and take me) (mix) / Dubmobile (live).

Nov 91. (c-s)(cd-s) **GROOVIN' /** - 90

— In Nov'92, teamed up with 808 STATE on a UK Top 20 version of 'ONE IN TEN'.

May 93. (7")(c-s) **(I CAN'T HELP) FALLING IN LOVE WITH YOU. / JUNGLE LOVE** 1 1
(12"+=)/ /(cd-s++=) – ('A'extended)./ / Red red wine.

Jul 93. (cd)(c)(lp) **PROMISES AND LIES** 1 6
– C'est la vie / Desert sand / Promises and lies / Bring me your cup / Higher ground / Reggae music / Can't help falling in love / Now and then / Things ain't what they used to be / It's a long long way / Sorry.

Aug 93. (7")(c-s) **HIGHER GROUND. / CHRONIC** 8 45 Oct 93
(12"+=)(cd-s+=) – Punjab dub (mix).

Nov 93. (7")(c-s) **BRING ME YOUR CUP. / BAD EKKO** 24
(cd-s+=) – ('A'mixes).

Mar 94. (7")(c-s) **C'EST LA VIE. / PROMISES AND LIES (live)** 37
(12"+=)(cd-s+=) – Tyler.

Aug 94. (7")(c-s) **REGGAE MUSIC. / MATTER OF TIME** 28
(cd-s+=) – Things ain't like they used to be.

— In Oct94, they featured on UK No.1 'Baby Come Back' by PATO BANTON.

Oct 95. (c-s) **UNTIL MY DYING DAY / ('A'instrumental)** 15
(cd-s+=) – Sorry (live) / Bring me your cup (live).
(cd-s+=) – ('A'-C.J.'s closet mix).

Oct 95. (cd)(c) **THE BEST OF UB 40 VOL.2** (compilation) 12
– Breakfast in bed / Where did I go wrong / I would do for you / Homely girl / Here I am (come and take me) / Kingston Town / Wear you to the ball / Can't help falling in love / Higher ground / Bring me your cup / C'est la vie / Reggae music / Superstition / Until my dying day.

– compilations, others, etc. –

Aug 82. Graduate; (lp)(c) **THE SINGLES ALBUM** 17 -
– Food for thought / King / My way of thinking / I think it's going to rain today / Dream a lie / Tyler / Adella / Little by little / The earth dies screaming.

Feb 83. Graduate; (12"m) **TYLER. / ADELLA / LITTLE BY LITTLE** -
(re-iss.1984)

Mar 85. Graduate; (d-lp)(c) **THE UB40 FILE** -
(cd-iss.Jul86)

Oct 87. Virgin TV; (lp)(c)(cd) **THE BEST OF UB40 VOLUME 1** 3 -
– Red red wine / I got you babe / One in ten / food for thought / Rat in mi kitchen / Don't break my heart / Cherry oh baby / Many rivers to cross / Please don't make me cry / If it happens again / Sing our own song / Maybe tomorrow / My way of thinking / King. (cd+=extra tracks) *(re-iss.+cdJan89) (re-iss.cd+c Aug93, hit UK No.51)*

Nov 91. Virgin; (d-cd) **LABOUR OF LOVE I & II**
(re-iss.Nov94, hit UK No.6)

Oct 94. Virgin; (3xcd-box) **THE COMPACT COLLECTION** -

ALI CAMPBELL

May 95. (7")(c-s) **THAT LOOK IN YOUR EYE. / DRIVE IT HOME** 5
(cd-s+=) – ('A'mix).

Jun 95. (cd)(c)(d-lp) **BIG LOVE** 6
– Big love (intro) / Happiness / That look in your eye / Let your yeah be yeah / You can cry on my shoulder / Somethin' stupid / Big love / You could meet somebody / Talking blackbird / Pay the rent / Drive it home / Stop the guns.

Aug 95. (7")(c-s) **LET YOUR YEAH BE YEAH. / YOU COULD MEET SOMEBODY** 25
(10"+=)(cd-s+=) – ('A'version).

Nov 95. (c-s) **SOMETHIN' STUPID ("ALI & KIBIBI CAMPBELL"). / PAY THE RENT** 30
(cd-s+=) – ('A'version).

UFO

Formed: North London, England . . . 1969 briefly as HOCUS POCUS. Gained deal with 'Beacon' records and had exceptional success in Japan and Germany, before signing to 'Chrysalis' in 1974. In 1977, they had first taste of UK success, when the album LIGHTS OUT made it into Top 30. Went on to greater things throughout the late 70's and early 80's. • **Style:** Space rock heavy metal, who blew hot & cold during the tour of the decade into the 80s. • **Songwriters:** Mostly WAY / MOGG or CHAPMAN / MOGG, with both variations sometimes adding SCHENKER or CARTER, except C'MON EVERYBODY (Eddie Cochran) / ALONE AGAIN OR (Love) / and a few more. • **Trivia:** PHIL MOGG's nephew NIGEL MOGG plays in the band The QUIREBOYS.

Recommended: PHENOMENON (*6) / ANTHOLOGY (*7)

PHIL MOGG (b.1951) – vocals / **PETE WAY** – bass / **MICK BOLTON** – guitar / **ANDY PARKER** – drums

Beacon Rare Earth

1970. (lp) **UFO**
– Unidentified flying object / Boogie / C'mon everybody / Shake it about / Melinda / Timothy / Follow you home / Treacle people / Who do you love / Evito.

1971. (7") **COME AWAY MELINDA. / UNIDENTIFIED FLYING OBJECT** -

1971. (lp) **UFO 2 / FLYING**
– Silver bird / Star storm / Prince Kajaku / Coming of Prince Kajaku / Flying.

1971. (7") **BOOGIE FOR GEORGE. / TREACLE PEOPLE** -

1971. (7") **PRINCE KAJUKU. / THE COMING OF PRINCE KAJUKU** -

Nova not issued

1972. (lp) **UFO: LIVE (live in Japan)** - - GERM.
– C'mon everybody / Who do you love / Loving cup / Prince Kajaku / The coming of Prince Kajaku / Boogie for George / Follow you home. *(UK-iss.1974 on 'Gema')*

— In 1972, they issued a few 45's in Japan, incl. 'C'MON EVERYBODY'.

— (Jun73) **MICHAEL SCHENKER** – guitar repl. BERNIE MARSDEN to WILD TURKEY. BERNIE had repl. (ex-BLODWYN PIG) LARRY WALLIS (Nov72) who had repl. BOLTON (Feb72). WALLIS went on to PINK FAIRIES.

Chrysalis Chrysalis

Mar 74. (7") **DOCTOR DOCTOR. / LIPSTICK TRACES**

May 74. (lp)(c) **PHENOMENON**
– Too young to know / Crystal light / Doctor doctor / Space child / Rock bottom / Oh my / Time on my hands / Built for comfort / Lipstick traces / Queen of the deep. *(cd-iss.Oct91 on 'Episode')*

— Between mid'74-Jan75, they added **PAUL CHAPMAN** – guitar (ex-SKID ROW) Reverted to quartet when he joined LONE STAR.

Jul 75. (lp)(c) **FORCE IT** 71
– Let it roll / Shoot shoot / High flyer / Love lost love / Out in the street / Mother Mary / Too much of nothing / Dance your life away / This kid's / Between the walls. *(re-iss.Jun84 on 'Fame')*

— (Sep75) added **DANNY PEYRONEL** – keyboards (ex-HEAVY METAL KIDS)

May 76. (lp)(c) **NO HEAVY PETTING**
– Natural thing / I'm a loser / Can you roll her / Belladonna / Reasons love / Highway lady / On with the action / A fool in love / Martian landscape.

— (Jul76) **PAUL RAYMOND** – keyboards, guitar (ex-SAVOY BROWN) repl. DANNY

Apr 77. (7") **ALONE AGAIN. / ELECTRIC PHASE**

May 77. (lp)(c) **LIGHTS OUT** 54 23
– Too hot to handle / Just another suicide / Try me / Lights out / Gettin' ready / Alone again or / Electric phase / Love to love. *(cd-iss.1987) (cd-re-iss.Jul91 on 'Episode')*

Jun 77. (7") **TOO HOT TO HANDLE. / ELECTRIC PHASE** -

Jun 78. (lp)(c) **OBSESSION** 26 41
– Only you can rock me / Pack it up (and go) / Arbory Hill / Ain't no baby / Lookin' out for No.1 / Hot 'n' ready / Cherry / You don't fool me / Lookin' out for No.1 (reprise) / One more for the rodeo / Born to lose.

Jul 78. (7")(7"red) **ONLY YOU CAN ROCK ME. / CHERRY / ROCK BOTTOM** 50

Dec 78. (d-lp)(d-c) **STRANGERS IN THE NIGHT (live)** 8 42
– Natural thing / Out in the street / Only you can rock me / Doctor doctor / Mother Mary / This kid's / Love to love / Lights out / Rock bottom / Too hot to handle / I'm a loser / Let it roll / Shoot shoot. *(cd-iss.Sep91 & Mar94)*

Jan 79. (7") **DOCTOR DOCTOR (live). / ON WITH THE ACTION (live) / TRY ME (live)** 35

Mar 79. (7")(7"clear) **SHOOT SHOOT (live). / ONLY YOU CAN ROCK ME (live) / I'M A LOSER (live)** 48

— (Nov78) **PAUL CHAPMAN** – guitar returned to repl. SCHENKER who joined The SCORPIONS and later formed his own self-named group.

Jan 80. (7")(7"red) **YOUNG BLOOD. / LIGHTS OUT** 36

Jan 80. (lp)(c) **NO PLACE TO RUN** 11 51
– Alpha Centauri / Lettin' go / Mystery train / This fire burns tonight / Gone in the night / Young blood / No place to run / Take it or leave it / Money money / Anyday.

— (Aug'80) **WAY, MOGG, CHAPMAN + PARKER** recruited **NEIL CARTER** – keyboards, guitar (ex-WILD HORSES) repl. PAUL RAYMOND who joined MICHAEL SCHENKER GROUP

Oct 80. (7")(7"colrd) **COULDN'T GET IT RIGHT. / HOT'N'READY**

Jan 81. (lp)(c) **THE WILD, THE WILLING & THE INNOCENT** 19 77
– Chains chains / Long gone / The wild, the willing & the innocent / It's killing me / Makin' moves / Lonely heart / Couldn't get it right / Profession of violence.

Jan 81. (7")(7"clear) **LONELY HEART. / LONG GONE** 41

Jan 82. (7")(7"clear) **LET IT RAIN. / HEEL OF A STRANGER / YOU'LL GET LOVE** 62

Feb 82. (lp)(c) **MECHANIX** 8 82
– The writer / Something else / Back into my life / You'll get love / Doing it all for you / We belong to the night / Let it rain / Terri / Feel it / Dreaming.

Apr 82. (7")(7"pic-d) **BACK INTO MY LIFE. / THE WRITER**

— (Jun82) on tour **BILLY SHEEHAN** – bass (ex-TALAS) repl. PETE WAY who formed FASTWAY and briefly joined OZZY OSBOURNE

Jan 83. (lp)(c) **MAKING CONTACT** 32
– Blinded by a lie / Diesel in the dust / A fool for love / You and me / When it's time to rock / The way the wild wind blows / Call my name / All over you / No getaway / Push it's love.

Mar 83. (7")(7"pic-d) **WHEN IT'S TIME TO ROCK. / EVERYBODY KNOWS** 70
(12"+=) – Push it's love.

— Disbanded when MOGG suffered a nervous breakdown on stage. He resurrected the band in 1984 with **PAUL RAYMOND / PAUL GRAY** – bass (ex-DAMNED) / **JIM SIMPSON** – drums(ex-MAGNUM) / **ATOMIK TOMMY M.** – guitar (b. Japan).

Oct 85. (7")(7"sha-pic-d) **THIS TIME. / THE CHASE**
(12"+=) – ('A'extended).

Nov 85. (lp)(c) **MISDEMEANOR** 74
– This time / One heart / Night run / The only ones / Mean streets / Name of love /

Blue / Dream the dream / Heaven's gate / Wreckless.

Feb 86. (7")(7"red) **NIGHT RUN. / HEAVEN'S GATE** [ ] [ ]
(12"+=) – ('A'extended).

—— (late '86) **DAVID 'Jake' JACOBSON** – guitar (ex-ERIC MARTIN) repl. RAYMOND

FM Revolver / not issued

Mar 88. (lp)(c)(cd) **AIN'T MISBEHAVIN'** [ ] [-]
– Between a rock and a hard place / Another Saturday night / At war with the world / Hunger in the night / Easy money / Rock boyz, rock. *(cd+=)* – Lonely cities (of the heart).

—— Disbanded Spring 1988. PHIL went into production mainly for his nephew NIGEL MOGG's new band QUIREBOYS.

—— **MOGG & WAY** re-united **UFO** adding **LAURENCE ARCHER** – guitar (ex-GRAND SLAM) / **CLIVE EDWARDS** – drums (ex-WILD HORSES) / **JEM DAVIS** – keyboards

Essential / Victory

Nov 91. (12"ep)(cd-ep) **ONE OF THOSE NIGHTS. / AIN'T LIFE SWEET / LONG GONE** [ ] [-]

Feb 92. (cd)(c)(lp) **HIGH STAKES AND DANGEROUS MEN** [ ] [-]
– Borderline / Primed for time / She's the one / Ain't life sweet / Don't want to lose you / Burnin' fire / Running up the highway / Back door man / One of those nights / Revolution / Love deadly love / Let the good times roll.

Feb 93. (cd)(c) **LIGHTS OUT OVER TOKYO LIVE (live)** [ ] [ ]
– Running up the highway / Borderline / Too hot to handle / She's the one / Cherry / Back door man / One of those nights / Love to love / Only you can rock me / Lights out / Doctor, doctor / Rock bottom / Shoot shoot / C'mon everybody.

– compilations, others, etc. –

1973. Decca; (d-lp) **UFO / FLYING** [ ] [-]
Dec 82. Chrysalis; (d-c) **MECHANIX / LIGHTS OUT** [ ] [-]
Aug 83. Chrysalis; (d-lp)(d-c) **HEADSTONE – THE BEST OF UFO** [39] [-]
– Doctor doctor / Rock bottom / Fool for your loving / Shoot shoot / Too hot to handle / Only you can rock me / Love drive (SCORPIONS) / She said she said (LONE STAR) / Lights out / Armed and ready (MICHAEL SCHENKER GROUP) / Young blood / Criminal tendencies / Lonely heart / We belong to the night / Let it rain / Couldn't get it right / Electric phase / Doing it all for you.
Oct 92. Chrysalis; (cd) **ESSENTIAL** [ ] [-]
Nov 85. Castle; (d-lp)(d-c) **THE COLLECTION** [ ] [-]
Apr 87. Raw Power; (d-lp)(c)(cd) **ANTHOLOGY** [ ] [-]
– Rock bottom / Built for comfort / Highway lady / Can you roll her / Fool for love / Shoot shoot / Too hot to handle / Gettin' ready / Only you can rock me / Looking for number one / Hot'n'ready / Mystery train / No place to run / Profession and violence / Chains chains / Something else / Doing it for all of you / When it's time to rock / Diesel in the dust.
Apr 93. Repertoire; (cd) **THE DECCA YEARS** [ ] [-]
Mar 94. Music Club; (cd)(c) **TOO HOT TO HANDLE: THE BEST OF UFO** [ ] [-]
May 94. B.G.O.; (cd) **OBSESSION / NO PLACE TO RUN** [ ] [-]
Aug 94. B.G.O.; (cd) **NO HEAVY PETTING / LIGHTS OUT** [ ] [-]
Sep 94. B.G.O.; (cd) **THE WILD, THE WILLING AND THE INNOCENT / MECHANIX** [ ] [-]
Dec 94. B.G.O.; (cd) **PHENOMENOM / FORCE IT** [ ] [-]
Nov 94. M&M; (cd) **HEAVEN'S GATE LIVE (live)** [ ] [-]
May 95. Spectrum; (cd) **DOCTOR, DOCTOR** [ ] [-]

UGLY KID JOE

Formed: Isla Vista, North California, USA . . . 1989 by university students CRANE, EICHSTADT plus drummer MARK DAVIS. In 1991, they found the group name and signed to 'Mercury'. Their debut recording 'AS UGLY AS THEY WANNA BE' soon raced up the US billboard, helped by hit single 'EVERYTHING ABOUT YOU', which was used on 'Wayne's World' movie. • **Style:** Heavy rock/pop act, similar to a less serious MOTLEY CRUE or FAITH NO MORE. • **Songwriters:** Most by CRANE-EICHSTADT or group, except SIN CITY (Ac/Dc) / CATS IN THE CRADLE (Harry Chapin) / N.I.B. (Black Sabbath). • **Trivia:** CRANE had been a guitar technician for LOVE / HATE.

Recommended: AMERICA'S LEAST WANTED (*6).

Group: WHITFIELD CRANE – vocals / **KLAUS EICHSTADT** – guitar / **ROGER LAHR** – guitar / **CORDELL CROCKETT** – bass / **MARK DAVIS** – drums

Mercury / Stardog

May 92. (m-cd)(m-c)(m-lp) **AS UGLY AS THEY WANNA BE** [9] [4] Feb 92
– Madman / Whiplash liquor / Too bad / Everything about you / Sweet leaf – funkyfresh country club / Heavy metal.

May 92. (7")(c-s) **EVERYTHING ABOUT YOU. / WHIPLASH LIQUOR** [3] [9] Mar 92
(12"+=)(cd-s+=) – Sin city.

Jul 92. (7")(c-s) **NEIGHBOR. / EVERYTHING ABOUT YOU (clean edit)** [28] [ ]
(12") – ('A'side) / Funky fresh country club.
(cd-s) – ('A'side) / Funky fresh country club / Cats in the cradle.

Sep 92. (cd)(c)(lp) **AMERICA'S LEAST WANTED** [11] [29]
– Neighbor / Goddamn devil / Come tomorrow / Panhandlin' prince / Busy bee / Don't go / So damn cool / Same side / Cats in the cradle / I'll keep tryin' / Everything about you / Madman ('92 remix) / Mr. Recordman. *(will climb to No.27 in the US, early 1993) (re-iss.cd/c Apr95)*

Oct 92. (7")(c-s) **SO DAMN COOL. / NEIGHBOR** [44] [ ]
(cd-s+=) – Panhandlin' Prince.

Mar 93. (7")(c-s) **CAT'S IN THE CRADLE. / PANHANDLIN' PRINCE** [7] [6] Feb 93
(12"+=)(cd-s+=) – Whiplash liquer (live) / Neighbor (live).

Jun 93. (7")(c-s) **BUSY BEE. / CATS IN THE CRADLE (live)** [39] [ ]
(cd-s) – ('A'side) / Come together (live) / Don't go (live) / Everything about you (live).

—— (Jun92) **DAVE FORTMAN** – guitar (ex-SUGARTOOTH) repl. LAHR

—— (1994) **SHANNON LARKIN** – drums (ex-WRATHCHILD AMERICA, ex-SOULS AT ZERO) repl. DAVIS

—— Nov94; WHITFIELD CRANE was credited on MOTORHEAD's single 'Born To Raise Hell' alongside ICE-T.

Jun 95. (cd)(c) **MESSAGE TO SOBRIETY** [25] [ ]
– Intro / God / Tomorrow's world / Clover / C.U.S.T. / Milkman's son / Suckerpath / Cloudy skies / Jesus rode a Harley / 10-10 / V.I.P. / Oompa / Candle song / Slower than nowhere.

Jun 95. (12") **MILKMAN'S SON. / CANDLE SONG (Dave – vocals) / TOMORROW'S WORLD** [39] [ ]
(cd-s) – (first 2 tracks) / So damn cool (live) / Neighbour (live).
(cd-s) – ('A'side) / Suckerpath (demo) / God (1994 version) / C.U.S.T. (demo).

UK SUBS

Formed: London, England . . . 1977 by HARPER and GARRETT. Appeared on early 1978 various artists lp 'Farewell To The Roxy' and issued one indie 45, before joining RCA subsidiary label 'Gem'. In 1979 to early 1981, they had number of hit singles and albums before running into personel problems. • **Style:** Late on the scene, second division punk rockers whose raw aggressive appeal, was mainly due to "old man of punk" CHARLIE HARPER's stage aura. Went the same way as SHAM 69, when larger venues were not forte of do-it yourself politico-punks. • **Songwriters:** Most by HARPER-GARRETT until latter's departure. Covered SHE'S NOT THERE (Zombies) / I'M WAITING FOR THE MAN (Velvet Underground) / I WALKED WITH A ZOMBIE (13th Floor Elevators) / ROUTE '66 (hit; Nelson Riddle) / BABY PLEASE DON'T GO (hit; Them). • **Trivia:** HARPER had also been part of garage-influenced URBAN DOGS between 1983-85.

Recommended: SCUM OF THE EARTH – THE BEST OF . . . (*6)

CHARLIE HARPER (b.DAVID CHARLES PEREZ, 25 Apr'44) – vocals, rhythm guitar / **NICKY GARRETT** – lead guitar / **PAUL SLACK** – bass / **PETE DAVIS** – drums

City / not issued

1978. (7"clear)(7"blue)(7"green)(7"orange)(7"red) **C.I.D. / I LIVE IN A CAR / B.I.C.** [ ] [-]
(re-iss.Oct79 on 'Pinnacle')

Gem-RCA / R.C.A.

Jun 79. (7")(7"red) **STRANGLEHOLD. / WORLD WAR / ROCKERS** [26] [-]
Aug 79. (7")(7"blue) **TOMORROW'S GIRLS. / SCUM OF THE HEART / TELEPHONE NUMBERS** [28] [ ]
Oct 79. (lp)(c)(blue-lp) **ANOTHER KIND OF BLUES** [21] [ ]
– C.I.D. / I couldn't be you / I live in a car / Tomorrow's girl / Killer / World war / Rockers / I.O.D. / T.V. blues / Lady Esquire / All I wanna know / Crash course / Young criminals / B.I.C. / Disease / Stranglehold. *(cd-iss.Jul95 on 'Dojo')*
Nov 79. (7"ep)(7"green-ep) **SHE'S NOT THERE / KICKS. / VICTIM / THE SAME THING** [36] [-]
Feb 80. (7")(7"brown) **WARHEAD. / I'M WAITING FOR THE MAN / THE HARPER** [30] [-]
Apr 80. (lp)(c)(clear-lp) **BRAND NEW AGE** [18] [ ]
– You can't take it anymore / Brand new age / Public servant / Warhead / Barbie's dead / Organised crime / Rat race / Emotional blackmail / Kicks / Teenage / Dirty girls / 500 c.c. / Bomb factory. *(cd-iss.Jul95 on 'Dojo')*
May 80. (7")(7"pink)(7"orange) **TEENAGE. / LEFT FOR DEAD / NEW YORK STATE POLICE** [32] [-]
Sep 80. (lp)(c)(purple-lp) **CRASH COURSE (live)** [8] [-]
– C.I.D. / I couldn't be you / I live in a car / Tomorrow's girl / Left for dead / Kicks / Rat race / New York state police / Warhead / Public servant / Telephone numbers / Organised crime / Rockers / Brand new age / Dirty girls / The same thing / Crash course / Teenage / Killer / Emotional blackmail. (free-12"w.a.) *(cd-iss.Jul95 on 'Dojo')*

—— **ALVIN GIBBS** – bass (ex-USERS, ex-HELLIONS) repl. SLACK / **STEVE ROBERTS** – drums repl. DAVIS

Oct 80. (7")(7"yellow) **PARTY IN PARIS. / FALL OF THE EMPIRE** [37] [-]
Feb 81. (lp)(c)(red-lp) **DIMINISHED RESPONSIBILITY** [18] [-]
– You don't belong / So what / Confrontation / Fatal / Time and matter / Violent city / Too tired / Party in Paris / Gangster / Face the machine / New order / Just another jungle / Collision cult. *(cd-iss.Jul95 on 'Dojo')*
Apr 81. (7")(7"blue) **KEEP ON RUNNIN' (TILL YOU BURN). / PERFECT GIRL** [41] [-]
(7"ep+=) – Ice age / Party in Paris (French version).

N.E.M.S. / not issued

Nov 81. (7") **COUNTDOWN. / PLAN OF ACTION** [ ] [-]

—— **KIM WYLIE** – drums repl. ROBERTS who joined CYANIDE then LIGOTAGE

Abstract / not issued

Oct 82. (7"ep)(7"red-ep) **SHAKE UP THE CITY** [ ] [-]
– Self destruct / Police state / War of the roses.
Oct 82. (lp) **ENDANGERED SPECIES** [ ] [-]
– Endangered species / Living dead / Countdown / Ambition / Fear of girls / Lay down and die / Down on the farm / Sensitive boys / Divide by 8, multiply by 5 / Ice age / I robot / Flesh wound. *(re-iss. Jun90 on 'Link')*

—— **CHARLIE HARPER** recruited entire new band **CAPTAIN SCARLET** – guitar repl. GARRETT who formed REBEKKA FRAME / **PAUL SLACK** – bass returned to repl. GIBBS who joined URBAN DOGS / **STEVE JONES** – drums repl. WYLIE

Fall Out / not issued

Aug 83. (7") **ANOTHER TYPICAL CITY. / STILL LIFE** [ ] [-]
(12"+=) – Veronique.
Oct 83. (lp)(c) **FLOOD OF LIES** [ ] [-]
– Flood of lies / Veronique / Soldiers of fortune / Db's / Tampa Bay / After the war /

Vilent revolution / In the red / Dress code / Still life / Revenge of the yellow devils / Another typical city / In the wild / Seas.

Sep 84. (12"ep) **MAGIC / PRIVATE ARMY. / THE SPELL / MULTIPLE MINDS / PRIMARY STRENGTH**

—— **HARPER** again + new members **JOHN FALLON** – guitar / **JEZZ MONCUR** – bass / **RAB FAE BEITH** – drums (ex-WALL, ex-PATRIK FITZGERALD)

Jan 85. (cd) **GROSS OUT U.S.A. (live)**
– Intro / Emotional blackmail / New barbarians / In the wild / Veronique / Flood of lies / Warhead / Limo life / Disease / Violent revolution / Soldiers of fortune / Ice-age / Dress code / Telephone numbers / Stranglehold / You don't belong / Party in Paris.

Jun 85. (7"red)(7"blue) **THIS GUN SAYS. / SPEAK FOR MYSELF / WANTED**

Revolver / not issued

Dec 85. (lp)(c) **HUNTINGTON BEACH**
– Rock'n'roll savage / Between the eyes / Suicide taxi / Party animal / The unknown / Miss Tennage USA / Huntington / All the king's horses / Juke box / Sk8 tough / Death row / Bullshitter / Dirty boy / All change for Hollywood / Blinding stories. *(re-iss.Jun90)*

Fall Out / not issued

Dec 87. (12") **HEY SANTA (LEAVE THESE KIDS ALONE). / THUNDERBIRD**

Dec 87. (lp) **JAPAN TODAY (live)**
– Another Cuba / Funk rap / Streets on fire / Sex object / Warzone / Japan inc. / (interview) / Comin' back / Thunderbird / Hey! Santa / Street legal / Captain Scarlett / Skateboard Billy / Surf bastard / Angel. *(cd-iss.Apr93)*

Mar 89. (lp)(c)(cd) **KILLING TIME** (1981-82 reunion album)
– Yellowman / Motivator / Lower East Side / Drag me down / Never say you won't / Magalopolis / Planet I / Killing time / Holy land / American motors / Big Apple / Killing with kindness / Sabre dance / No heart / Fear to go / Nico. *(cd has extra tracks) (re-iss.cd Feb94)*

—— Latest UK SUBS alongside **HARPER** were **ALAN LEE** – guitar / **FLEA DAVE FARRELLY** – bass / **MATTHEW McCOY** – drums / **DARRELL BARTH** – guitar repl. LEE

Released Emotions / not issued

Feb 89. (12"ep) **THE MOTIVATOR / COMBAT ZONE / FASCIST REGIME. / AULD LANG SYNE / CYCLE SLUTS FROM HELL**

Jungle / not issued

Feb 91. (cd)(c)(lp) **MAD COW FEVER**
– I walked with a zombie / Mandarins of change / Boneyard / Welfare mother / Saints and sinners / Pearl divers / Roadhouse blues / Talkin' 'bout you / Road runner / Route '66 / Pills / Baby please don't go / Last bus boogie / Ecology blues.

—— **DAVIS + CAMPBELL** repl. LEE + FARRELLY

Sep 93. (cd)(lp) **NORMAL SERVICE RESUMED**
– Dumfux / Killer time / Jodie Foster / Here comes Alex / Ozone death / Strangeways / Joyride / Believe in yourself / Down on the farm / Mohawk radio / Brixton / Reaper / All the people / Squat the world / Lydia.

Nov 93. (7"ep)(cd-ep) **THE ROAD IS HARD, THE ROAD IS LONG EP**
– Jodie Foster / Here comes Alex / Killer time / Another Cuba / Lydia.

– compilations, others, etc. –

Jun 82. Chaos; (c-ep) **LIVE AT GOSSIPS (live)**
Oct 82. Abstract; (lp) **RECORDED 1979-81**
May 91. Abstract; (cd)(c)(blue-lp) **THE SINGLES 1978-1982**
Apr 84. Mausoleum; (lp)(c) **DEMONSTRATION TAPES** (rare demos)
Apr 86. Dojo; (lp) **SUB STANDARDS**
Apr 86. Red Flame; (lp) **IN ACTION**
Apr 86. Red Flame; (7"ep) **LIVE IN HOLLAND – TENTH ANNIVERSARY (live)**
– Stranglehold / New barbarians / Tomorrow's girls / Between the eyes.
Jun 86. R.O.I.R.; (c) **LEFT FOR DEAD**
Jul 86. Killerwatt; (lp) **RAW MATERIAL**
Apr 90. Released Emotions; (lp) **GREATEST HITS (LIVE IN PARIS)**
Jun 92. Released Emotions; (cd) **EUROPE CALLING**
Dec 91. Streetlink; (cd) **DOWN ON THE FARM (A COLLECTION OF THE LESS OBVIOUS)**
Aug 92. Streetlink; (cd) **GREATEST HITS LIVE (live)**
1992. Dojo; (cd) **ENDANGERED SPECIES / HUNTINGTON BEACH**
May 93. Get Back; (cd) **ANOTHER KIND OF BLUES / CRASH COURSE**
May 93. Get Back; (cd) **BRAND NEW AGE / DIMINISHED RESPONSIBILITY**
Jun 93. Optima; (cd)(c) **PUNK AND DISORDERLY**
Aug 93. Music Club; (cd)(c) **SCUM OF THE EARTH – THE BEST OF THE UK SUBS**
Dec 94. ROIR Europe; (cd) **LEFT FOR DEAD**
May 95. C.A.S.; (cd) **THE PUNK IS BACK**
Sep 95. Anagram; (cd) **THE PUNK SINGLES COLLECTION**

CHARLIE HARPER

solo.

Gem-RCA / not issued

Jul 80. (7") **BARMY LONDON ARMY. / TALK IS CHEAP** 68

Raxx / not issued

Jul 81. (7") **FREAKED. / JO**

Flicknife / not issued

Nov 81. (lp) **STOLEN PROPERTY**
– Hoochie coochie man / Femme fatale / Hey Joe / Louie Louie / Pills / Light my fire / I'm waiting for the man / etc.

ULTIMATE SPINACH

Formed: Boston, Massachusetts, USA . . . 1967 originally out of UNDERGROUND CINEMA by (see below). • **Style:** Psychedelic rock, described as 'bosstown sound' which competed with San Francisco outfits ORPHEUS and BEACON STREET UNION. • **Songwriters:** BRUCE-DOUGLAS, until his departure in 1969 when BARBARA was left with group name on third lp. • **Trivia:** All produced by ALAN LORBER.

Recommended: ULTIMATE SPINACH (*7)

IAN BRUCE-DOUGLAS – vocals, keyboards, guitar, sitar, harmonica, flute, etc / **BARBARA HUDSON** – vocals, guitar, kazoo / **GEOFFREY WINTHROP** – lead vocals, guitar, sitar / **KEITH LAHTEINEN** – vocals, drums, tabla / **RICHARD NESS** – bass

M.G.M. / M.G.M.

Jun 68. (lp) **ULTIMATE SPINACH** 34 Feb 68
– Ego trip / Sacrifice of the Moon (in four parts) / Plastic raincoats / Hung up minds / (Ballad of the) Hip death goddess / Your head is reeling / Dove in hawk's clothing / Baroque £1 / Funny freak parade / Pamela.

Dec 68. (lp) **BEHOLD AND SEE** Nov 68
– Gilded lamp of the cosmos / Visions of your reality / Jazz thing / Mind flowers / Where you're at / Suite: Genesis of beauty (in four parts) / Fifth horseman of the apocalyse / Fragmentary march of green. *(cd-iss.Nov95 on 'Big Beat')*

—— **BARBARA** with newcomers **JEFF 'Skunk' BAXTER** – guitar, steel guitar, vibes, vocals / **TED MYERS** – vocals, guitar / **TONY SCHEUREN** – keyboards, guitar / **MIKE LEVINE** – bass / **RUSS LEVINE** – drums

Nov 69. (lp) **ULTIMATE SPINACH**
– (Just like) Romeo & Juliet / Some days you just can't win / Daisy / Sincere / Eddie's rush / Strangle life tragicomedy / Reasons / Happiness child / Back door blues / The world has just begun.

Nov 69. (7") **(JUST LIKE) ROMEO & JULIET. / SOME DAYS YOU JUST CAN'T WIN**

—— Disbanded when little interest was shown for 3rd lp. BAXTER later joined STEELY DAN and The DOOBIE BROTHERS.

ULTRAMARINE

Formed: Chelmsford, Essex, England . . . 1984 as A PRIMARY INDUSTRY by IAN COOPER and PAUL HAMMOND, with JEMMA, GUY and SIMON. In the early 90's, IAN and PAUL became successful in ULTRAMARINE duo, basing themselves in Leamington Spa. They were garnished with appraisal during 1992, after the release of album 'EVERY MAN AND WOMAN IS A STAR'. • **Style:** Electronic /dance left-field of Baleric, with distinctive fairground organ, samples and the influence of KEVIN AYERS, who provided them with some of his old lyrics in 1991. • **Songwriters:** COOPER-HAMMOND, except HEART OF GLASS (Blondie) / HYMN (Kevin Ayers). ULTRAMARINE of '93, included co-writing and singing contributions from wheel-chair bound veteran ROBERT WYATT. • **Trivia:** Another group (foreign?) named ULTRAMARINE issued 2 albums 'DE' in March 1990 and 'E SI MALA' late 1993.

Recommended: EVERY MAN AND WOMAN IS A STAR (*8) / UNITED KINGDOMS (*8)

A PRIMARY INDUSTRY

IAN COOPER – acoustic guitar, keyboards, prog. / **PAUL HAMMOND** – bass, keys, prog. / **JEMMA** – vocals / **GUY** – keyboards / **SIMON** – drums

Les Tempes Modernes / not issued

Nov 84. (12") **AT GUNPOINT. / PERVERSION**
(re-iss.Feb86 on 'N.I.S.S.')

Sweatbox / not issued

Nov 85. (12"ep) **7 HERTZ**
– Cicatrice / Obeah / Biting back / Bled dry.

Oct 86. (lp) **ULTRAMARINE**
– Body blow / Beacon Hill / Shear / Sans orange / Cicatrice / Watchword weal / Gush / Raw umber / Silesia / Rose madder.

Jul 87. (7") **HEART OF GLASS. / WHERE IS YOUR VORTEX**
(12") – ('A'extended) / ('A'extended mix).

Mar 88. (m-lp) **WYNDHAM LEWIS**
– The liquid brown detestable Earth Fokker Bomb shit / The song of the militant romance / If so the man you are / End of enemy interlude / Merde alors!

—— Disbanded after above, IAN and PAUL became . . .

ULTRAMARINE

COOPER + HAMMOND

Crepescule / not issued

Jun 89. (m-lp)(m-cd) **WYNDHAM LEWIS**
– (the re-issue of A PRIMARY INDUSTRY m-lp)

Mar 90. (cd)(c) **FOLK**
– Lobster / Antiseptic / Bronze eye / Bastard folk / Bullprong / Softspot / Vulfar streak / The golden target. *(re-iss.cd Nov94 on 'Offshore') (+=) – Stella / Interstellar.*

Sep 90. (12") **STELLA. / INTERSTELLAR / ULTRABASS (Eddy De Cierca mix)**

Brainiak / not issued

May 91. (12")(cd-s) **STELLA CONNECTS. / STELA BREATHS**

Oct 91. (12")(cd-s) **BRITISH SUMMERTIME. / WEIRD GEAR / WEIRD GEAR (version)**

Dec 91. (cd)(lp) **EVERY MAN AND WOMAN IS A STAR**

– Discovery / Weird gear / Pansy / Money / Stella / Geezer / Panther / British summertime / Lights in my brain / Canoe trip / Skyclad / Gravity. *(re-iss.& re-mixed Jul92 on 'Rough Trade') (+=) – Nova Scotia / Saratoga.*

Rough Trade | Dali

May 92. (7"ltd.) **SARATOGA. / NOVA SCOTIA** [ ] [-]
Nov 92. (12"ep)(cd-ep) **NIGHTFALL IN SWEETLEAF** [ ] [-]
– Panther (Coco Steel remix) / Lights in my brain (Spooky mix) / Geezer (Sweet Exorcist mix).
Mar 93. (12"ep)(cd-ep) **WEIRD GEAR (remix) / LIGHTS IN MY BRAIN (Spooky mix) / GEEZER (Sweet Exorcist mix) / PANTHER (Coco Steel & Lovebomb mix) / OUTRO** [-] [ ]

—— now with **ROBERT WYATT** – vocals ('A'above) / **SIMON KAY** – Hammond organ / **JIMMY HASTINGS** – clarinet, flute, piccolo, sax / **JIM RATTIGAN** – accordion / **ROBERT ATCHISON** – violin / **PHIL JAMES** – trumpet, harmonica / **PAUL JOHNSON** – percussion

Blanco Y Negro | Warners

Jul 93. (7")(c-s) **KINGDOM. / GOLDCREST** [46] [ ]
(12")(cd-s) – ('A'side) / ('B'extended) / ('A'extended mix).
Aug 93. (cd)(c)(lp) **UNITED KINGDOMS** [49] [ ]
– Source / Kingdom / Queen of the Moon / Prince Rock / Happy land / Urf / English heritage / Instant kitten / The badger / Hooter / Dizzy fox / No time.
Jan 94. (12"ep)(c-ep)(cd-ep) **THE BAREFOOT EP** [61] [ ]
– Happy land / Hooter / The badger.
Jan 95. (c-s) **HYMN (David McAlmont mix) / HYMN (Kevin Ayers mix) / BASE ELEMENT** [ ] [-]
(cd-s+=) – (first & last track) / Our love / Love life.
(12") – Hymn (U-zig mix) / Hymn (Luke Slater mix) / Our love / Love life.
(cd-s) – Hymn (U-zig mix) / Hymn (Luke Slater mix) / Hymn (Paul Sampson's lullabye mix) / Hymn (Sugar J mix) / Hymn (Mouse On Mars: a sleep mix) / Hymn (Ultramarine & Kevin Ayers version).
Aug 95. (cd)(c)(clear-d-lp) **BEL AIR** [ ] [ ]
– Welcome / Buena vista / Maxine / Pioneer spirit / Mutant / Fantasy filter / 78 / I got sane / Schnaltz / Citizen / Alter ego / Free radical / Harmony Street / K-V / Escape velocity / Rainbow brew / Everyone in Brazil.

ULTRAVOX

Formed: London, England..mid'76 after 3 years as TIGER LILY. Obtained deal with 'Island' records, who employed BRIAN ENO to produce their eponymous debut. In 1979, FOXX went solo and ULTRAVOX were without a contract until surprise replacement MIDGE URE revitalised them enough for 'Chrysalis' to give them chance. Broke the Top 30 the following year with SLEEPWALK, which paved the way for their classic VIENNA single to just miss top slot. In the early 80's, they became one of top UK bands with 7 Top 10 albums and a string of Top 30 hits. Remarkably the US surpassed them for other New Wave / British Invasion bands. • **Style:** Initially influenced by a mixture of flash-progressive ROXY MUSIC / DOCTORS OF MADNESS image/sound to new wave rock. By 1980, they had mellowed into more video-age electronic "new romantics". • **Songwriters:** FOXX and group until URE replaced FOXX. Covered only KING'S LEAD HAT (Brian Eno). MIDGE URE's solo career included NO REGRETS (Tom Rush / hit c. Walker Brothers) / THE MAN WHO SOLD THE WORLD (David Bowie) / STRANGE BREW (Cream). MIDGE also co-wrote tracks by VISAGE including hit FADE TO GREY. TIGER LILY 's first single was a strange cover of FATS WALLER's 'Ain't Misbehavin''. • **Trivia:** MIDGE URE once replaced GARY MOORE on THIN LIZZY's American tour for a couple of weeks summer '79!

Recommended: THREE INTO ONE (*8) / VIENNA (*7) / THE COLLECTION (*7).

TIGER LILY

DENNIS LEIGH (JOHN FOXX) – vocals / **STEVE SHEARS** – guitar / **BILLY CURRIE** (b. 1 Apr'52, Huddersfield, Yorkshire, England) – keyboards / **WARREN CANN** (b.20 May'52, Victoria, Canada) – drums / **CHRIS ST. JOHN** (b.14 Jul'52) – bass

Gull | not issued

Mar 75. (7") **AIN'T MISBEHAVIN'. / MONKEY JIVE** [ ] [-]

—— (w/drawn before release) *(iss.Oct77) (re-iss.Oct80 on 'Dead Good')*

ULTRAVOX!

LEIGH became **JOHN FOXX** and ST.JOHN now **CHRIS CROSS.** (CURRIE now added violin, synthesizers.)

Island | Antilles

Feb 77. (7") **DANGEROUS RHYTHM. / MY SEX** [ ] [-]
Mar 77. (lp)(c) **ULTRAVOX!** [ ] [-]
– Saturday night in the city of the dead / Life at Rainbow End (for all the tax exiles on Main Street) / Slip away / I want to be a machine / Wide boys / Dangerous rhythm / The lonely hunter / The wild the beautiful and the damned / My sex.
May 77. (7") **YOUNG SAVAGE. / SLIPAWAY** [ ] [-]
Oct 77. (7") **ROCKWROK. / HIROSHIMA MON AMOUR** [ ] [-]
(all 3 ULTRAVOX! singles were re-iss.Jul81)
Oct 77. (lp)(c) **HA! HA! HA!** [ ] [-]
– Rockwrok / The frozen ones / Fear in the western world / Distant smile / The man who dies every day / Artificial life / While I'm still alive / Hiroshima mon amour. *(free-7"w.a.)–* **QUIRKS. / MODERN LOVE (live)**
Feb 78. (7"ep) **RETRO E.P. (live)** [ ] [-]
– The wild the beautiful and the damned / Young savage / My sex / The man who dies every day.

—— **ROBIN SIMON** – guitar (ex-NEO) repl. SHEARS to COWBOYS INTERNATIONAL

Aug 78. (7")(12"violet) **SLOW MOTION. / DISLOCATION** [ ] [ ]
Sep 78. (lp)(c) **SYSTEMS OF ROMANCE** [ ] [ ]
– Slow motion / I can't stay long / Someone else's clothes / Blue light / Some of them / Quiet men / Dislocation / Maximum acceleration / When you walk through me / Just for a moment.
Oct 78. (7")(12"white) **QUIET MEN. / CROSS FADE** [ ] [ ]

—— (Apr79) **MIDGE URE** (b.JAMES, 10 Oct'53, Cambuslang, Scotland) – vocals, guitar (ex-SLIK, ex-RICH KIDS, ex-THIN LIZZY, ex-VISAGE) repl. JOHN FOXX who went solo. ROBIN also departed to MAGAZINE. Now as ULTRAVOX, after dropping the exclamation mark!

Chrysalis | Chrysalis

Jun 80. (7")(7"clear) **SLEEPWALK. / WAITING** [29] [ ]
Sep 80. (7")(12")(7"clear) **PASSING STRANGERS. / SOUND ON SOUND** [57] [ ]
Oct 80. (lp)(c) **VIENNA** [3] [ ]
– Astradyne / New Europeans / Private lives / Passing strangers / Sleepwalk / Mr. X / Western promise / Vienna / All stood still. *(cd-iss.1985) (re-iss.cd Mar94 + Jul94)*
Jan 81. (7")(7"clear) **VIENNA. / PASSIONATE REPLY** [2] [ ]
(12"+=) – Herr X.
Apr 81. (7")(7"clear) **PASSING STRANGERS. / FACE TO FACE** [ ] [-]
(12"+=) – King's lead hat.
May 81. (7")(7"clear) **ALL STOOD STILL. / ALLES KLAR** [8] [ ]
(12"+=) – Keep talking.
Aug 81. (7")(12")(7"clear) **THE THIN WALL. / I NEVER WANTED TO BEGIN** [14] [ ]
Sep 81. (lp)(c) **RAGE IN EDEN** [4] [ ]
– The voice / We stand alone / Rage in Eden / I remember (death in the afternoon) / The thin wall / Stranger within / Accent on youth / The ascent / Your name has slipped my mind again. *(cd-iss.Jun87)*
Nov 81. (7")(7"clear) **THE VOICE. / PATHS AND ANGELS** [16] [ ]
(12"+=)(12"clear+=) – All stood still (live) / Private lives (live).
Sep 82. (7")(12")(c-s)(7"clear) **REAP THE WILD WIND. / HOSANNA (IN EXCELIS DEO)** [12] [71] Mar 83
Oct 82. (lp)(c)(cd)(pic-lp) **QUARTET** [6] [61] Mar 83
– Reap the wild wind / Serenade / Mine for life / Hymn / Visions of blue / When the scream subsides / We came to dance / Cut and run / The song (we go).
Nov 82. (7")(7"clear) **HYMN. / MONUMENT** [11] [ ]
(12"+=)(12"clear+=) – The thin wall.
Mar 83. (7")(7"clear)(7"pic-d) **VISIONS IN BLUE. / BREAK YOUR BACK** [15] [ ]
(12"+=)(12"clear+=) – Reap the wild wind.
May 83. (7")(12")(7"pic-d)(7"clear)(12"clear) **WE CAME TO DANCE. / OVERLOOK** [18] [ ]
Oct 83. (lp)(c) **MONUMENT – THE SOUNDTRACK (live)** [9] [ ]
– Monument / Reap the wild wind / The voice / Vienna / Mine for life / Hymn.
Feb 84. (7")(12")(7"clear) **ONE SMALL DAY. / EASTERLY** [27] [ ]
Apr 84. (lp)(c)(cd)(pic-lp) **LAMENT** [8] [ ]
– White China / One small day * / Dancing with tears in my eyes / Lament * / Man of two worlds / Heart of the country / When the time comes / A friend I called Desire. *(c+cd+=)–* (tracks * remixed).
May 84. (7")(12")(7"clear) **DANCING WITH TEARS IN MY EYES. / BUILDING** [3] [ ]
Jul 84. (7")(7"clear) **LAMENT. / HEART OF THE COUNTRY** [22] [ ]
(12"+=) – ('A'instrumental).
Oct 84. (7")(12")(7"clear)(7"pic-d) **LOVE'S GREAT ADVENTURE. / WHITE CHINA** [12] [ ]
Nov 84. (lp)(c)(cd) **THE COLLECTION** (compilation) [2] [ ]
– Dancing with tears in my eyes / Hymn / The thin wall / The voice / Vienna / Passing strangers / Sleepwalk / Reap the wild wind / All stood still / Visions in blue / We came to dance / One small day / Love's great adventure / Lament. *(w/ free 12")*

—— guest **MARK BRZEZICKI** – drums (of BIG COUNTRY) repl. CANN to HELDEN

Sep 86. (7")(7"clear)(7"pic-d) **SAME OLD STORY. / 3** [31] [ ]
(12")(12"clear) – ('A'side) / All in one day.
Oct 86. (lp)(c)(cd) **U-VOX** [9] [ ]
– Same old story / Sweet surrender / Dream on / The prize / All fall down / Time to kill / Moon madness / Follow your heart / All in one day.
Nov 86. (7")(7"clear) **ALL FALL DOWN. / DREAM ON** [30] [ ]
(12"+=) – ('A'version).
May 87. (7")(7"clear) **ALL IN ONE DAY. / THE PRIZE (live)** [ ] [ ]
(12"+=) – Stateless.

—— Disbanded 1987, although U-VOX was formed by BILLY CURRIE, ROBIN SIMON and MARCUS O'HIGGINS – vocals. They toured 1989 playing ULTRAVOX songs.

—— **TONY FENELLE** – vocals repl. MIDGE URE who was by now continuing solo.

D.S.B. | not issued

May 93. (cd)(c)(lp) **REVELATION** [ ] [-]
– I am alive / Revelation / Systems of love / Perfecting the art of common ground / The great outdoors / The closer I get to you / No turning back / True believer / Unified / The new frontier.
Jun 93. (7")(c-s)(7"clear) **I AM ALIVE. / SYSTEMS OF LOVE** [ ] [ ]
(cd-s+=) – ('A'extended).

—— line-up: **CURRIE / BLUE / BURNS**

Resurgence | not issued

Nov 95. (cd) **INGENUITY** [ ] [-]
– Ingenuity / There goes a beautiful world / Give it all back / Future picture forever / The silent cries / Distance / Ideals / Who'll save you / A way out, a way through / Majestic.

– compilations, others, etc. –

Jun 80. Island/ US= Antilles; (lp)(c) **THREE INTO ONE** [ ] [ ]
– Young savage / Rockwrok / Dangerous rhythm / The man who dies every day / The wild the beautiful and the damned / Slow motion / Just for a moment / My sex / Quiet men / Hiroshima mon amour. *(re-iss.Nov86, cd-iss.1990)*
Mar 81. Island; (12"ep)(12"clear-ep) **SLOW MOTION / DISLOCATION. / QUIET MEN / HIROSHIMA MON AMOUR** [33] [-]
Apr 88. Strange Fruit; (12"ep) **THE PEEL SESSIONS** (21.7.77) [ ] [-]
– My sex / Artificial life / Young savage.

Sep 93. Spectrum; (cd)(c) **SLOW MOTION** [ ] [-]
Aug 94. Chrysalis; (cd) **RARE VOLUME 2** [ ] [-]
Jun 95. Receiver; (cd) **FUTURE PICTURE** [ ] [-]
Aug 95. Old Gold; (cd-s) **VIENNA / REAP THE WILD WIND** [ ] [-]
Oct 95. MFP; (cd) **DANCING WITH TEARS IN MY EYES** [ ] [-]
Nov 95. Island; (3xcd-box) **ULTRAVOX! / HA! HA! HA! / SYSTEMS OF ROMANCE** [ ] [-]

MIDGE URE

had already started own solo career. Debut w / ex-COCKNEY REBEL **STEVE HARLEY** – dual vocals

Chrysalis Chrysalis

Mar 82. (7") **I CAN'T EVEN TOUCH YOU. / I CAN'T BE ANYONE** [ ] [-]
Jun 82. (7")(12") **NO REGRETS. / MOOD MUSIC** [9] [ ]
Jul 83. (7")(12") **AFTER A FASHION ("MIDGE URE & MICK KARN"). / TEXTURES** [39] [-]

Above 45 on 'Musicfest' w / ex-JAPAN bassist

— Dec'84 saw MIDGE co-write and create BAND AID with BOB GELDOF (BOOMTOWN RATS). They hit UK No.1 with famine relief single DO THEY KNOW IT'S CHRISTMAS.

Aug 85. (7")(7"clear) **IF I WAS. / PIANO** [1] [ ]
(12"+=)(12"clear+=) – The man who sold the world.
Oct 85. (lp)(c)(cd) **THE GIFT** [2] [ ]
– If I was / When the winds blow / Living in the past / That certain smile / The gift / Antilles / Wastelands / Edo / The chieftain / The gift (reprise). *(re-iss.cd+c Apr93)*
Nov 85. (7")(7"clear)(7"pic-d) **THAT CERTAIN SMILE. / THE GIFT** [28] [ ]
(12"+=)(d12"+=)(12"clear+=) – ('A'instrumental) / Fade to grey.
Jan 86. (7")(7"clear) **WASTELANDS. / THE CHIEFTAIN** [46] [ ]
(12"+=)(12"clear+=) – Dancer.
May 86. (7")(7"clear) **CALL OF THE WILD. / WHEN THE WIND BLOWS** [27] [ ]
(12"+=)(12"clear+=) – After a fashion (w/ MICK KARN).
Aug 88. (7")(7"clear) **ANSWERS TO NOTHING. / HONORARE** [49] [ ]
(12"+=)(12"clear+=) – Oboe.
(cd-s++=) – (excerpts from lp below).
Sep 88. (lp)(c)(cd) **ANSWERS TO NOTHING** [30] [88]
– Answers to nothing / Take me home / Sister and brother / Dear God / The leaving (so long) / Just for you / Hell to Heaven / Lied / Homeland / Remembrance day.
Nov 88. (7")(7"clear) **DEAR GOD. / MUSIC 1** [55] [95]
(12"+=) – All fall down (live) / Strange brew (live).
(cd-s+=) – Remembrance day.

— In Apr'89, SISTERS AND BROTHERS single was withdrawn.

— **URE** now with **MARK BRZEZICKI** – drums / **STEVE BRZEZICKI + JEREMY MEEHAN** – bass / **ROBBIE KILGORE** – keys / **SIMON PHILLIPS** – drums / **STEVE WILLIAMS** – perc./ etc

Arista Arista

Aug 91. (7")(c-s) **COLD COLD HEART. / FLOWERS** [17] [ ]
(12"+=)(cd-s+=) – Supernatural *(written by GREEN; SCRITTI POLITTI)*
Sep 91. (cd)(c)(lp) **PURE** [36] [ ]
– I see hope in the morning light / Cold, cold heart / Pure love / Sweet'n' sensitive thing / Let it go? / Rising / Light in your eyes / Little one / Hands around my heart / Waiting days / Tumbling down.
Oct 91. (7")(c-s) **I SEE HOPE IN THE MORNING LIGHT. / THE MAN I USED TO BE** [ ] [ ]
(12"+=)(cd-s+=) – Madame de Sade.

– (MIDGE URE & ULTRAVOX) compilations, etc. –

Jan 93. Chrysalis; (7")(c-s) **VIENNA. / WASTELANDS** [13] [ ]
(cd-s+=) – Answers to nothing / The voice.
(cd-s) – ('A'side) / Call of the wild / One small day / Hymn.
Feb 93. Chrysalis; (cd)(c)(lp) **IF I WAS: THE VERY BEST OF MIDGE URE & ULTRAVOX** [10] [ ]
– If I was / No regrets / Love's great adventure / Dear God / Cold cold heart / Vienna / Call of the wild / Dancing with tears in my eyes / All fall down / Yellow pearl / Fade to grey / Reap the wild wind / Answers to nothing / Do they know it's Christmas? (BAND AID). *(cd+=)* After a fashion (with MICK KARN) / That certain smile.
Dec 82. Chrysalis; (d-c) **VIENNA / RAGE IN EDEN** [ ] [-]
Feb 87. Old Gold; (7") **VIENNA. / THE VOICE** [ ] [-]
Apr 87. Old Gold; (7") **DANCING WITH TEARS IN MY EYES. / REAP THE WILD WIND** *(12"-iss.Jan88)* [ ] [-]

UNDERTONES

Formed: Londonderry, N.Ireland . . . Nov'75 by the O'NEILL brothers, plus SHARKEY, BRADLEY and DOHERTY. In Aug'78, they released debut TEENAGE KICKS for Belfast label 'Good Vibrations'. Given airplay on DJ John Peel's night time radio one show, it was taken up by 'Sire' also nearly hitting Top 30. In 1979 to early 80's, they went on to have a number of UK hits and 3 Top 20 albums, with John Peel still their best-known fan. • **Style:** Intelligent new wave-pop that enthused energy and life into flagging power-pop/punk scene. In 1982, FEARGAL's quavering vocals and group's boy-next-door image had been shelved for a blend of "alternative-soul". This formula didn't work, and group drifted into other projects, both very different (see below). • **Songwriters:** O'NEILL brothers except UNDER THE BOARDWALK (Drifters). In the mid-80's, FEARGAL, solo, collaborated with DAVE STEWART of The EURYTHMICS. In 1991, he teamed up with writers SHERRILL and DiPIERO. Covered; A GOOD HEART (Maria McKee) / TAKE ME TO THE RIVER (Al Green). • **Trivia:** Band based their debut album cover on inspiration by The WHO's MY GENERATION single. • **Miscellaneous:** In Feb'86, his mother and sister, while spending time in Londonderry, N.Ireland, were abducted by terrorists, but released after a number of hours.

Recommended: UNDERTONES (*9) / HYPNOTISED (*7) / CHER O'BOWLES (*9)

FEARGAL SHARKEY (b.13 Aug'58) – vocals / **DAMIEN O'NEILL** – guitar, bass / **JOHN O'NEILL** – guitar / **MIKE BRADLEY** – bass / **BILLY DOHERTY** – drums

Good Vibrations not issued

Sep 78. (7"ep) **TEENAGE KICKS / TRUE CONFESSIONS. / SMARTER THAN U / EMMERGENCY CASES** [ ] [-]
(re-iss.Oct78 on 'Sire', hit No.31) (re-iss.Jul83 on 'Ardeck', hit 60) (re-iss.7"ep+cd-ep Apr94 on 'Dojo')

Sire Sire

Jan 79. (7"m) **GET OVER YOU. / REALLY REALLY / SHE CAN ONLY SAY NO** [57] [ ]
Apr 79. (7")(7"lime green) **JIMMY JIMMY. / MARS BARS** [16] [ ]
May 79. (lp)(c) **THE UNDERTONES** [13] [ ] Jan 80
– Family entertainment / Girls don't like it / Male model / I gotta getta / Teenage kicks / Wrong way / Jump boys / Here comes the summer / Get over you / Billy's third / Jimmy Jimmy / True confessions / She's a runaround / I know a girl / Listening in. *(re-iss.Jul83 on 'Ardeck') (re-iss.+cd.Oct87 on 'Fame') (re-iss.cd+c May94 on 'Dojo', with 7 extra tracks)* – Smarter than u / Emergency cases / Top twenty / Really really / Mars Bars / She can only say no / One way love.
Jul 79. (7"m) **HERE COMES THE SUMMER. / ONE WAY LOVE / TOP TWENTY** [34] [ ]
Sep 79. (7") **YOU'VE GOT MY NUMBER (WHY DON'T YOU USE IT). / LET'S TALK ABOUT GIRLS** [32] [ ]
Mar 80. (7"m) **MY PERFECT COUSIN. / HARD LUCK / I DON'T WANNA SEE YOU AGAIN** [9] [ ]
(d7"+=) – Here comes the summer.
Apr 80. (lp)(c) **HYPNOTISED** [6] [ ]
– More songs about chocolate and girls / There goes Norman / Hypnotised / See that girl / Whizz kids / Under the boardwalk / The way girls talk / Hard luck / My perfect cousin / Boys will be boys / Tearproof / Wednesday week / Nine times out of ten / Girls that don't talk / What's with Terry?. *(re-iss.Mar86 on 'Fame') (re-iss.cd+c May94 on 'Dojo', with 5 extra tracks)* – You've got my number (why don't you use it?) / Hard luck (again) / Let's talk about girls / I told you so / I don't want to see you again.
Jun80. (7") **WEDNESDAY WEEK. / I TOLD YOU SO** [11] [ ]

Ardeck-EMI Harvest

Apr 81. (7") **IT'S GOING TO HAPPEN. / FAIRLY IN THE MONEY NOW** [18] [ ]
May 81. (lp)(c) **THE POSITIVE TOUCH** [17] [ ]
– Fascination / Life's too easy / You're welcome / The positive touch / Julie Ocean / Crisis of mine / His good looking friend / When Saturday comes / It's going to happen / Sigh and explode / I don't know / Hannah Doot / Boy wonder / Forever Paradise. *(re-iss.1985) (re-iss.cd+c May94 on 'Dojo', with 4 extra tracks)* – Kiss in the dark / Beautiful friend / Life's too easy / Fairly in the money now.
Jul 81. (7") **JULIE OCEAN. / KISS IN THE DARK** [41] [ ]
Feb 82. (7") **BEAUTIFUL FRIEND. / LIFE'S TOO EASY** [ ] [-]
Jan 83. (7") **THE LOVE PARADE. / LIKE THAT** [ ] [-]
(12"+=) – You're welcome / Family entertainment / Crises of mine.
Mar 83. (7") **GOT TO HAVE YOU BACK. / TURNING BLUE** [ ] [-]
(12"+=) – Bye bye baby blue.
Mar 83. (lp)(c) **THE SIN OF PRIDE** [43] [-]
– Got to have you back / Valentine's treatment / Luxury / Love before romance / Untouchable / Bye bye baby blue / Conscious / Chain of love / Soul seven / The love parade / Save me / The sin of pride. *(re-iss.cd+c May94 on 'Dojo', with 6 extra tracks)* – Turning blue / Like that / Window shopping for new clothes / Bitter sweet / You stand so close (but you're never there) / I can only dream.
Apr 83. (7") **CHAIN OF LOVE. / WINDOW SHOPPING FOR NEW CLOTHES** [ ] [-]

— Split mid'83 with FEARGAL SHARKEY joining The ASSEMBLY (see under ⇒ YAZOO) before going solo. The O'NEILL brothers formed THAT PETROL EMOTION.

– compilations, others, etc. –

Nov 83. Ardeck-EMI; (d-lp)(c) **ALL WRAPPED UP** [67] [-]
– Teenage kicks / Get over you / Jimmy Jimmy / Here comes the summer / You've got my number (why don't you use it) / My perfect cousin / Wednesday week / It's going to happen / Julie Ocean / Beautiful friend / The love parade / Got to have you back / Chain of love.

— (Note all singles were re-iss. on 'Ardeck-EMI')

May 86. Ardeck-EMI; (lp)(c)(cd) **CHER O'BOWLES – THE PICK OF THE UNDERTONES** [96] [-]
– Teenage kicks / True confessions / Get over you / Family entertainment / Jimmy Jimmy / Here comes the Summer / You got my number (why don't you use it) / My perfect cousin / See that girl / Tearproof / Wednesday week / It's going to happen / Julie Ocean / You're welcome / Forever Paradise / Beautiful friend / Save me / The love parade / Valentine's treatment / Love before romance. *(re-iss.+cd.Oct89 on 'Fame')*
Jun 86. Ardeck-EMI; (7") **SAVE ME. / TEARPROOF** [ ] [-]
(12"+=) – I know a girl.
Dec 86. Strange Fruit; (12"ep) **THE PEEL SESSIONS** (21.1.79) [ ] [-]
– Listening in / Family entertainment / Here comes the summer / Billy's third. *(cd-ep iss.Mar88)*
Dec 89. Strange Fruit; (lp)(c)(cd) **DOUBLE PEEL SESSIONS** [ ] [-]
(re-iss.cd Mar94 as 'THE PEEL SESSIONS ALBUM')
Sep 93. Castle; (cd)(c) **THE BEST OF THE UNDERTONES – TEENAGE KICKS** [45] [-]
Jul 95. Dojo; (cd-ep) **HERE COMES THE SUMMER / GET OVER YOU / JIMMY JIMMY / YOU'VE GOT MY NUMBER (WHY DON'T YOU USE IT)** [ ] [-]

Feargal SHARKEY

moved to California, but returned to London in 1989.

Zarjazz — not issued

Sep 84. (7")(12") **LISTEN TO YOUR FATHER. / CAN I SAY I LOVE YOU** 23 -

Virgin — A & M

Jun 85. (7")(12") **LOVING YOU. / IS THIS AN EXPLANATION** 26

Sep 85. (7") **A GOOD HEART. / ANGER IS HOLY** 1 74 Feb 86
(12"+=)/ /(cd-s+=) – Ghost train./ / ('A'original).

Nov 85. (lp)(c)(cd) **FEARGAL SHARKEY** 7 75 Feb 86
– A good heart / You little thief / Ghost train / Ashes and diamonds / Made to measure / Someone to somebody / Don't leave it to nature / Love and hate / Bitter man / It's all over now. *(re-iss.Jun88)*

Dec 85. (7")(12") **YOU LITTLE THIEF. / THE LIVING ACTOR** 5

Mar 86. (7")(12") **SOMEONE TO SOMEBODY. / COLD WATER** 64

Virgin — Virgin

Jan 88. (7") **MORE LOVE. / A BREATH OF SCANDAL** 44
(12"+=)/ /(cd-s+=) – ('A'piano version)./ / Good heart (original).

Mar 88. (lp)(c)(cd) **WISH**
– Cold, cold streets / More love / Full confession / Please don't believe in me / Out of my system / Strangest girl in Paradise / Let me be / Blue days / If this is love / Safe to touch.

Mar 88. (7") **OUT OF MY SYSTEM. / A TOUCH OF BLUE**
(12"+=) – ('A'version) / ('A'dub version).
(cd-s++=) – Blue days.

Sep 88. (7") **IF THIS IS LOVE. / A TOUCH OF BLUE** -

Feb 91. (7")(c-s) **I'VE GOT NEWS FOR YOU. / I CAN'T BEGIN TO STOP** 12
(12") – ('A'side) / Loving you / A good heart / You little thief (remixes).
(cd-s+=) – Medley:- Don't leave it to nature – Take me to the river.

Apr 91. (cd)(c)(lp) **SONGS FROM THE MARDI GRAS** 27
– After the Mardi Gras / One night in Hollywood / Miss you fever / Women and I / I've got news for you / To miss someone / Sister Rosa / I'll take it back / Cry like a rainy day / She moved through the fair.

May 91. (7")(c-s) **WOMEN AND I. / I'LL TAKE IT BACK (live)**
(12"+=)/ /(cd-s+=) – ('A'piano version)./ / Never never (ASSEMBLY).
(cd-s+=) – (2-'A'versions pt.1 & 2) / ('A'demo).

Aug 91. (7")(c-s) **TO MISS SOMEONE. / I'LL TAKE IT BACK**
(cd-s+=) – Never never (ASSEMBLY) / Miss you fever (instrumental)
(cd-s+=) – Never never (ASSEMBLY) / Women and I (piano version).

— In May93, FEARGAL appeared on PEACE TOGETHER single 'BE STILL' alongside SINEAD O'CONNOR, PETER GABRIEL & NANCI GRIFFITH.

– compilations, others, etc. –

1988. Virgin; (3"cd-ep) **YOU LITTLE THIEF / MORE LOVE / LISTEN TO YOUR FATHER** -

UNDERWORLD

Formed: Romford, London, England . . . 1987 by RICK, KARL, ALFIE, BRYN who had all been in Cardiff outfit FREUR (which was actually a symbol translated into a word!; no PRINCE wasn't the first!). Even before this, RICK and KARL had played in synth-pop band The SCREEN GEMS. In 1987, they were now the more conventional UNDERWORLD and hit America in the late 80's after signing for Seymour Stein's 'Sire' records. After a No.1 smash 'RADAR' in Australia, they toured the States supporting EURYTHMICS, but it was clear this was not the direction for them. Came to light once again, when newcomer DJ DARREN EMERSON was added to exploit new sounds for well-received early '94 album 'DUBNOBASS . . .'. • **Style:** Techno ambient dance /rock similiar to The BELOVED with more visionary hypnobeat experiments. • **Songwriters:** SMITH / HYDE / THOMAS then SMITH / HYDE / EMERSON. • **Trivia:** Produced by RUPERT HINES in 1988. HYDE worked on a 1991 'Paisley P.' album with TERRI NUNN (ex-Berlin). GEOFF DUGMORE (ex-ART OF NOISE) was a guest on 1989 album. Also appeared on WILLIAM ORBIT's 'Watch From A Vine Leaf' & ORBITAL's 'Lush 3' and remixed BJORK's 'Human Behaviour'.

Recommended: DUBNOBASS . . . (*8)

FREUR

RICK SMITH – keyboards, vocals / **KARL HYDE** – vocals, guitar / **ALFIE THOMAS** – guitar, vocals / **JOHN WARWICKER LE BRETON** – synthesizers / **BRYN B. BURROWS** – drums

C.B.S. — Epic

Mar 83. (7"clear-pic-d)(ext-12") **DOOT DOOT. / HOLD ME MOTHER** 59
(re-iss.Jan84)

Jun 83. (7")(7"pic-d) **MATTERS OF THE HEART. / YOU'RE A HOOVER**
(12"+=) – ('A'extended).

Sep 83. (7")(12") **RUNAWAY. / YOU'RE A HOOVER**

Nov 83. (lp)(c) **DOOT DOOT**
– Doot doot / Runaway / Riders in the night / Theme from the film of the same name / Tender surrender / Matters of the heart / My room / Steam machine / Whispering / All too much.

Apr 84. (7") **RIDERS IN THE NIGHT. / INNOCENCE**
(12"+=) – This is the way I like to live my life.

— added **JAKE BOWIE** – bass

Oct 84. (7") **DEVIL AND DARKNESS. / JAZZ 'N' KING**
(12"+=) – Devil and darkness.

Feb 85. (7") **LOOKING BACK FOR ANSWERS. / HEY HO AWAY WE GO**
(12"+=) – Uncle Jeff.

Feb 85. (lp)(c)(cd) **GET US OUT OF HERE**
– Look in the back for answers / Emeralds and pearls / Kiss me / A.O.K.O. / The Devil and darkness / The piano song / Happiness / Endless groove / This is the way I'd like to live my life / Bella Donna.

UNDERWORLD

BAZ ALLEN – bass repl. JOHN

Sire — Sire

Mar 88. (lp)(c)(cd) **UNDERNEATH THE RADAR**
– Glory! glory! / Call me No.1 / Rubber ball (space kitchen) / Show some emotion / Underneath the radar / Miracle party / I need a doctor / Bright white flame / Pray / The God song.

Jul 88. (7") **UNDERNEATH THE RADAR. / BIG RED X** 74 Apr 88
(12"+=) – ('A'dub version).

Aug 88. (7") **SHOW SOME EMOTION. / SHOCK THE DOCTOR** -

— **PASCAL CONSOLI** – percussion, drums repl. BURROWS who joined WORLD-WIDE ELECTRIC

Aug 89. (7")(c-s) **STAND UP. / OUTSKIRTS** 67
(12") – Stand up (and dance) / Stand up (ya house) / Outskirts.
(cd-s) – (all mixes & B-side)

Sep 89. (lp)(c)(cd) **CHANGE THE WEATHER**
– Change the weather / Stand up / Fever / Original song / Mercy / Mr.Universe / Texas / Thrash / Sole survivor / Beach.

Nov 89. (7") **CHANGE THE WEATHER. / TEXAS** -

— ALLEN + CONSOLI became D-INFLUENCE

LEMON INTERRUPT

— **SMITH + HYDE** brought in **DARREN EMERSON** (b.1970, Essex) – keyboards

Junior Boy — not issued

1992. (12") **DIRTY. / BIG MOUTH** -

UNDERWORLD

LEMON INTERRUPT line-up

Junior Boy — Sire

Jul 93. (12"ep)(cd-ep) **MMM SKYSCRAPER I LOVE YOU. / ('A'-Telegraph mix 6.11.92) / ('A'-Jamscraper mix)**

Sep 93. (12")(cd-s) **REZ. / COWGIRL**
(re-iss.Aug95)

Dec 93. (12")(cd-s) **SPIKEE. / DOGMAN GO WOOF** 60

Feb 94. (cd)(c)(d-lp) **DUBNOBASSWITHMYHEADMAN** 12
– Dark and long / Mmm skyscraper I love you / Surfboy / Spoonman / Tongue / Dirty epic / Cowgirl / River of bass / ME.

Jun 94. (cd-ep) **DARK & LONG (mixes)** 57
– Hall's mix / Dark train / Most 'ospitable / 215 miles.
(12") – ('A'-spoon deep mix) / ('A'-thing in a back mix).
(12") – ('A'-dark train mix) / ('A'-Burt's mix).

May 95. (12") **BORN SLIPPY (telenatic). / COWGIRL (Vinjer mix)** 52
(12") – ('A'side) / ('A'-Nuxx mix).
(cd-s) – (above 2) / ('A'side again).

Midge URE (see under ⇒ ULTRAVOX)

URGE OVERKILL

Formed: Chicago, Illinois, USA . . .1986 by NASH KATO and BLACKIE ONASSIS. After one uneventful ep, they moved onto 'Touch & Go', where they released debut lp 'JESUS URGE SUPERSTAR'. In 1993 they signed to 'Geffen', which helped boost sales of that years' album 'SATURATION'. • **Style:** Hard imaginative punk rock, that harboured on the outlandish and freaky side of grunge scene. • **Trivia:** Cult film director Quentin Tarrantino used their version of NEIL DIAMOND's 'GIRL' on his materwork 'Pulp Fiction'. • **Songwriters:** Group except; WICHITA LINEMAN (Jimmy Webb) / GIRL YOU'LL BE A WOMAN SOON (Neil Diamond).

Recommended: STULL (*7) / EXIT THE DRAGON (*8)

NATIONAL 'Nash' KATO – vocals, guitar / **EDDIE 'King' ROESER** – bass / **BLACKIE 'Black Caesar' ONASSIS** – vocals, drums

not issued — own label

1988. (12"ep) **STRANGE, I . . .** -

Touch & Go — Touch & Go

May 89. (lp) **JESUS URGE SUPERSTAR**
– God Flintstone / Very sad trousers / Your friend is insane / Dump dump dump / Last train to Heaven / The Polaroid doll / Head on / Crown of laffs / Dubbledead / Easter '88 / Wichita lineman / Eggs.

Jun 90. (cd)(c)(lp) **AMERICRUISER**
– Ticket to L.A. / Blow chopper / 76 ball / Empire builder / Faroutski / Viceroyce / Out on the airstrip / Smokehouse. (cd+=) – JESUS URGE SUPERSTAR

Mar 91. (cd)(c)(lp) **THE SUPERSONIC STORYBOOK**
– The kids are insane / The candidate / (Today is) Blackie's birthday / Emmaline / Bionic revolution / What is artane? / Vacation in Tokyo / Henhough: The greatest story ever told / Theme from Navajo.

Roughneck — Roughneck

Jun 92. (m-cd)(m-lp) **STULL**
– Girl you'll be a woman soon / Stull (part 1) / Stitches / What's this generation coming to / (Now that's) The barclouds / Goodbye to Guyville. *(re-iss.cd Mar95 on 'Fire')*

Geffen — Geffen

Jun 93. (cd)(c) **SATURATION**

– Sister Havana / Tequilla sundae / Positive bleeding / Back on me / Woman 2 woman / Bottle of fur / Crackbabies / The stalker / Dropout / Erica Kane / Nite and grey / Heaven 90210.
(cd+=) – Operation: Kissinger.

Aug 93. (7")(c-s) **SISTER HAVANA. / WOMAN 2 WOMAN** [67] [ ]
(12"+=)(cd-s+=) – Operation: Kissinger.

Oct 93. (7")(c-s) **POSITIVE BLEEDING. / NITE AND GREY** [61] [ ]
(12"+=)(cd-s+=) – Quality love (Hong Kong demo).

— below from the cult Quentin Tarantino film 'Pulp Fiction' on 'M.C.A.' records.

Nov 94. (7") **GIRL YOU'LL BE A WOMAN SOON. / You Never Can Tell (by 'CHUCK BERRY')** [37] [59]
(c-s+=)(cd-s+=) – Dropout / (Bustin' Surfboards; by The TORNADOS).

Aug 95. (cd)(c) **EXIT THE DRAGON** [ ] [ ]
– Jaywalkin' / The break / Need some air / Somebody else's body / Honesty files / This is no place / The mistake / Take me / View of the rain / Last night – Tomorrow / Tin foil / Monopoly / And you'll say / Digital black epilogue.

URIAH HEEP

Formed: London, England . . . 1968 as SPICE by BYRON and BOX. After one single for 'United Art', they brought in HENSLEY and became URIAH HEEP (taking the name from a Charles Dickens character in the 'David Copperfield' novel). Signed to the same label (Vertigo) as BLACK SABBATH, they unleashed debut lp in 1970 'VERY 'EAVY, VERY 'UMBLE'. By the mid-70's, they had had loads of album hits on both sides of the water. This confounded the critics, who panned them at every opportunity. • **Style:** Heavy-metal trailblazers, fronted by the near operative vox of DAVID BYRON, who has since been ripped off by many 80's styled hard rock outfits. • **Songwriters:** Majority by HENSLEY or BOX/THAIN. In 1976 all members took share of work. Covered; COME AWAY MELINDA (Tim Rose) / Live Rock'n'Roll Medley:- ROLL OVER BEETHOVEN (Chuck Berry) – BLUE SUEDE SHOES (Carl Perkins) – MEAN WOMAN BLUES + HOUND DOG (Elvis Presley) – AT THE HOP (Danny & The Juniors) – WHOLE LOTTA SHAKIN' GOIN' ON (Jerry Lee Lewis) / HOLD YOUR HEAD UP (Argent). • **Trivia:** In 1987, they were first heavy-rock outfit to play USSR.

Recommended: THE COLLECTION (*8). / URIAH HEEP LIVE (*8)

DAVID BYRON (b.29 Jan'47, Essex, England) – vocals / **MICK BOX** (b. 8 Jun'47, London, England) – guitar, vocals / **ROY SHARLAND** – organ / **PAUL NEWTON** – bass, vocals / **ALEX NAPIER** – drums

SPICE

United Art / not issued

Dec 68. (7") **WHAT ABOUT THE MUSIC. / IN LOVE** [ ] [-]

URIAH HEEP

without SHARLAND who joined ARTHUR BROWN, etc. / added **KEN HENSLEY** (b.24 Aug'45) – keys, guitar, vox (ex-GODS, ex-TOE FAT) / **NIGEL OLSSON** – drums (ex-SPENCER DAVIS GROUP, ex-PLASTIC PENNY) repl. NAPIER (on all lp except 2 tracks)

Vertigo / Mercury

Jun 70. (lp)(c) **VERY 'EAVY VERY 'UMBLE** (US-title 'URIAH HEEP') [ ] [ ]
– Gypsy / Real turned on / Come away Melinda / Lucy's blues / Dreammare / Walking in your shadow / I'll keep on trying / Wake up (set your sights). *(re-iss.1971 & Apr77 on 'Bronze') (re-iss.Apr86 on 'Castle', cd-iss.Dec90)*

Jul 70. (7") **GYPSY. / REAL TURNED ON** [-] [ ]

Nov 70. (7") **COME AWAY MELINDA. / WAKE UP (SET YOUR SIGHTS)** [-] [ ]

— **KEITH BAKER** – drums (ex-BAKERLOO) repl. OLSSON who joined ELTON JOHN

Jan 71. (7") **HIGH PRIESTESS. /** [-] [ ]

Jan 71. (lp)(c) **SALISBURY** [ ] [ ]
– Bird of prey * / The park / Time to live / Lady in black / High Priestess / Salisbury. *(US copies repl. * with)*– Simon the bullet freak. *(re-iss.1971 & Jul77 on 'Bronze') (re-iss.+cd Apr86 on 'Castle')*

Mar 71. (7") **LADY IN BLACK. / SIMON THE BULLET FREAK** [ ] [-]

— **IAN CLARKE** – drums (ex-CRESSIDA) repl. BAKER; guest **MANFRED MANN** – moog synthesizer / keyboards

Bronze / Mercury

Nov 71. (lp)(c) **LOOK AT YOURSELF** [39] [93] Sep 71
– Look at yourself / I wanna be free / July morning / Tears in my eyes / Shadows of grief / What should be done / Love machine. *(re-iss.1977) (re-iss.+cd.Apr86 on 'Castle')*

Dec 71. (7") **LOVE MACHINE. / SIMON THE BULLET FREAK** [ ] [ ]

Dec 71. (7") **LOVE MACHINE. / LOOK AT YOURSELF** [-] [ ]

Feb 72. (7") **I WANNA BE FREE. / WHAT SHOULD BE DONE** [-] [ ]

— (Nov71) **LEE KERSLAKE** – drums, vocals (ex-GODS, ex-TOE FAT) repl. IAN (Feb'72) / **GARY THAIN** (b. New Zealand) – bass, vocals (ex-KEEF HARTLEY) repl. MARK CLARKE (ex-COLOSSEUM to TEMPEST) who had repl. NEWTON (Nov71)

May 72. (lp)(c) **DEMONS AND WIZARDS** [20] [23]
– The wizard / Traveller in time / Easy livin' / Poet's justice / Circle of hands / Rainbow demon / All my life / Paradise / The spell. *(re-iss.Apr77) (re-iss.+cd.Apr86 on 'Castle')*

Jun 72. (7") **THE WIZARD. / GYPSY** [ ] [-]

Jun 72. (7") **THE WIZARD. / WHY** [-] [ ]

Jul 72. (7") **EASY LIVIN' / ALL MY LIFE** [-] [ ]

Aug 72. (7") **EASY LIVIN'. / WHY** [ ] [-]

Nov 72. (lp)(c) **THE MAGICIAN'S BIRTHDAY** [28] [31]
– Sunrise / Spider woman / Blind eye / Echoes in the dark / Rain / Sweet Lorraine / Tales / The magician's birthday. *(re-iss.Apr77) (re-iss.+cd.Apr86 on 'Castle')*

Jan 73. (7") **BLIND EYE. / SWEET LORRAINE** [ ] [97] [91]

May 73. (d-lp)(d-c) **URIAH HEEP LIVE (live)** [23] [37]
– Sunrise / Sweet Lorraine / Traveller in time / Easy livin' / July morning / Tears in my eyes / Gypsy / Circle of hands / Look at yourself / The magician's birthday / Love machine / Rock'n'roll medley:- Roll over Beethoven – Blue suede shoes – Mean woman blues – Hound dog – At the hop – Whole lotta shakin' goin' on. *(re-iss.Apr77)*

Bronze / Warners

May 73. (7") **JULY MORNING (live). / TEARS IN MY EYES (live)** [-] [ ]

Sep 73. (lp)(c) **SWEET FREEDOM** [18] [33]
– Dreamer / Stealin' / One day / Sweet freedom / If I had the time / Seven stars / Circus / Pilgrim. *(re-iss.Apr77)*

May 74. (7") **STEALIN'. / SUNSHINE** [ ] [91] Oct 73

Jun 74. (lp)(c) **WONDERWORLD** [23] [38]
– Wonderworld / Suicidal man / The shadows and the winds / So tired / The easy road / Something or nothing / I won't mind / We got we / Dreams. *(re-iss.Apr77)*

Aug 74. (7") **SOMETHING OR NOTHING. / WHAT CAN I DO** [ ] [ ]

— **JOHN WETTON** – bass, vocals (ex-KING CRIMSON, ex-ROXY MUSIC, ex-FAMILY) repl. THAIN (He died of a drug overdose 19 May'76) Line-up now **BYRON, BOX, HENSLEY, KERSLAKE & WETTON**

Jun 75. (lp)(c) **RETURN TO FANTASY** [7] [85]
– Return to fantasy / Shady lady / Devil's daughter / Beautiful dream / Prima Donna / Your turn to remember / Showdown / Why did you go / A year or a day. *(re-iss.Apr77)*

Jun 75. (7") **PRIMA DONNA. / SHOUT IT OUT** [ ] [ ]

Jun 75. (7") **PRIMA DONNA. / STEALIN'** [-] [ ]

Nov 75. (lp)(c) **THE BEST OF URIAH HEEP** (compilation) [ ] [ ]
– Gypsy / Bird of prey / July morning / Look at yourself / Easy livin' / The wizard / Sweet Lorraine / Stealin' / Lady in black / Return to fantasy. *(re-iss.Apr77) (re-iss.+cd+=.Apr90 on 'Sequel')*

May 76. (lp)(c) **HIGH AND MIGHTY** [55] [ ]
– One way or another / Weep in silence / Misty eyes / Midnight / Can't keep a good band down / Woman of the world / Footprints in the snow / Can't stop singing / Make a little love / Confession. *(re-iss.Apr77) (re-iss.+cd.Mar91 on 'Castle')*

Jun 76. (7") **ONE WAY OR ANOTHER. / MISTY EYES** [ ] [ ]

— **JOHN LAWTON** – vocals (ex-LUCIFER'S FRIEND) repl. BYRON to ROUGH DIAMOND / **TREVOR BOLDER** – bass (ex-David Bowie's SPIDERS FROM MARS, ex-WISHBONE ASH) repl. WETTON who joined BRYAN FERRY BAND, and later UK and ASIA

Feb 77. (lp)(c) **FIREFLY** [ ] [ ]
– The hanging tree / Been away too long / Who needs me / Wise man / Do you know / Rollin' on / Sympathy / Firefly. *(re-iss.+cd.Mar91 on 'Castle')*

Apr 77. (7") **WISE MAN. / CRIME OF PASSION** [ ] [ ]

Oct 77. (7") **FREE ME. / MASQUERADE** [ ] [ ]

Nov 77. (lp)(c) **INNOCENT VICTIM** [ ] [ ]
– Keep on ridin' / Flyin' high / Roller / Free 'n' easy / Illusion / Free me / Cheat 'n' lie / The dance / Choices.

Bronze / Chrysalis

Sep 78. (lp)(c) **FALLEN ANGEL** [ ] [ ]
– Woman of the night / Falling in love / One more night / Put your lovin' on me / Come back to me / Whad'ya say / Save it / Love or nothing / I'm alive / Fallen angel. *(cd-iss.Feb91 on 'Castle')*

Oct 78. (7") **COME BACK TO ME. / CHEATER** [ ] [ ]

— **JOHN SLOMAN** – vocals (ex-LONE STAR) repl. LAWTON / **CHRIS SLADE** – drums (ex-MANFRED MANN'S EARTH BAND) repl. LEE to OZZY OSBOURNE

Jan 80. (7") **CARRY ON. / BEING HURT** [ ] [-]

Feb 80. (lp)(c) **CONQUEST** [ ] [ ]
– No return / Imagination / Feelings / Fools / Carry on / Won't have to wait too long / Out on the street / It ain't easy.

Jun 80. (7") **LOVE STEALER. / NO RETURN** [ ] [ ]

— **GREGG DETCHETT** – keyboards (ex-PULSAR) repl. HENSLEY to solo & BLACKFOOT

Jan 81. (7") **THINK IT OVER. / MY JOANNA NEEDS TUNING** [ ] [-]

— Split 1981 when SLOMAN developed throat infection. Later formed BADLANDS. CHRIS SLADE joined GARY NUMAN then DAVID GILMOUR. He later joined The FIRM. DETCHETT later joined MIKE + THE MECHANICS. BOLDER re-joined WISHBONE ASH. Early 1982, URIAH HEEP re-formed with **BOX** bringing back **LEE KERSLAKE** plus new **PETE GOALBY** – vocals (ex-TRAPEZE) / **JOHN SINCLAIR** – keys (ex-HEAVY METAL KIDS) / **BOB DAISLEY** – bass (ex-OZZY OSBOURNE, ex-RAINBOW, ex-WIDOWMAKER, etc.)

Bronze / Mercury

Feb 82. (7"ep) **THE ABOMINATOR JUNIOR EP** [ ] [-]
– On the rebound / Tin soldier / Song of a bitch.

Mar 82. (lp)(c) **ABOMINOG** [34] [56]
– Too scared too run / Chasing shadows / On the rebound / Hot night in a cold town / Running all night (with the lion) / That's the way that it is / Prisoner / Hot persuasion / Sell your soul / Think it over. *(re-iss.+cd.Apr86 on 'Castle')*

May 82. (7") **THAT'S THE WAY THAT IT IS. / HOT PERSUASION** [ ] [-]

May 82. (7") **THAT'S THE WAY THAT IT IS. / SON OF A BITCH** [-] [ ]

May 83. (lp)(c) **HEAD FIRST** [46] [ ]
– The other side of midnight / Stay on top / Lonely nights / Sweet talk / Love is blind / Roll-overture / Red lights / Rollin' the rock / Straight through the heart / Weekend warriors.

Jun 83. (7")(7"pic-d) **LONELY NIGHTS. / WEEKEND WARRIORS** [ ] [-]

Aug 83. (7") **STAY ON TOP. / PLAYING FOR TIME** [ ] [-]
(d7"+=)(12"+=) – Gypsy / Easy livin' / Sweet Lorraine / Stealin'.

— **TREVOR BOLDER** – bass returned to repl. DAISLEY

Portrait / Portrait

Mar 85. (7")(7"sha-pic-d) **ROCKERAMA. / BACK STAGE GIRL** [ ] [ ]

Mar 85. (lp)(c) **EQUATOR** [79] [ ]
– Rockerama / Bad blood / Lost one love / Angel / Holding on / Party time / Poor little rich girl / Skool's burnin' / Heartache city / Night of the wolf.

May 85. (7")(7"pic-d) **POOR LITTLE RICH GIRL. / BAD BLOOD** [ ] [-]

— **BERNIE SHAW** – vocals (ex-GRAND PRIX, ex-PRAYING MANTIS) repl. GOALBY / **PHIL LANZON** – keyboards (ex-GRAND PRIX, etc) repl. SINCLAIR (above 2 now alongside **BOX, BOLDER, KERSLAKE)**

Legacy | not issued

Jul 88. (lp)(c)(cd) **LIVE IN MOSCOW (live)** [ ] [-]
– Bird of prey / Stealin' / Too scared to run / Corrina / Mister Majestic / The wizard / July morning / Easy livin' / That's the way that it is / Pacific highway. *(cd+=)*– Gypsy.

Sep 88. (7") **EASY LIVIN' (live). / CORRINA (live)** [ ] [-]
(12"+=)(12"red+=) – Gypsy (live).

Apr 89. (7") **HOLD YOUR HEAD UP. / MIRACLE CHILD** [ ] [-]
(12"+=) – ('A'extended).

Apr 89. (lp)(c)(cd)(pic-lp) **THE RAGING SILENCE** [ ] [-]
– Hold your head up / Blood red roses / Voice on my TV / Rich kid / Cry freedom / Bad bad man / More fool you / When the war is over / Lifeline / Rough justice.

Jul 89. (7") **BLOOD RED ROSES. / ROUGH JUSTICE** [ ] [-]
(12"+=) – Look at yourself.

Feb 91. (cd)(c)(lp) **DIFFERENT WORLD** [ ] [-]
– Blood on stone / Which way will the wind blow / All God's children / All for one / Different world / Step by step / Seven days / First touch / One on one / Cross that line.

– more compilations, etc. –

Apr 86. Raw Power; (d-lp)(c)(cd) **ANTHOLOGY** [ ] [-]
Mar 87. Raw Power; (lp)(c)(cd) **LIVE IN EUROPE 1979 (live)** [ ] [-]
May 88. That's Original; (d-lp)(d-cd) **LOOK AT YOURSELF / VERY 'EAVY, VERY 'UMBLE** [ ] [-]
Dec 88. Castle; (cd-ep) **LADY IN BLACK / JULY MORNING / EASY LIVIN'** [ ] [-]
Dec 88. Castle; (lp)(c)(cd) **LIVE AT SHEPPERTON '74 (live)** [ ] [-]
– Love machine / Look at yourself / Firefly / Return to fantasy / Rainbow demon / That's the way it is / Love is blind / On the rebound / Easy livin' / July morning / Running all night (with the lion) / Been away too long / Gypsy / Wake up (set your sights) / Can't keep a good band down / All of my life.
Aug 89. Castle; (d-lp)(cd) **THE COLLECTION** [ ] [-]
Jun 90. Essential; (3xcd)(5xlp) **TWO DECADES IN ROCK** [ ] [-]
Oct 91. Elite; (cd)(c) **ECHOES IN THE DARK** [ ] [-]
– Echoes in the dark / The wizard / Come away Melinda / Devil's daughter / Hot persuasion / Showdown / I'm alive / Look at yourself / Spider woman / Woman of the night / I want to be free / Gypsy / Sunrise / Bird of prey / Love machine / Lady in black *(re-iss. Sep 93)*
Nov 91. Elite; (cd)(c) **EXCAVATIONS FROM THE BRONZE AGE** [ ] [-]
Jan 92. Sequel; (cd) **RARITIES FROM THE BRONZE AGE** [ ] [-]
Jul 94. Success; (cd)(c) **LIVE (live)** [ ] [-]
Jan 95. Spectrum; (cd) **LADY IN BLACK** [ ] [-]
May 95. HTD; (cd) **SEA OF LIGHT** [ ] [-]
May 95. Spectrum; (cd) **FREE ME** [ ] [-]

KEN HENSLEY

solo while a URIAH HEEP member.

Bronze | Warners

May 73. (lp)(c) **PROUD WORDS ON A DUSTY SHELF** [ ] [ ]
– When evening comes / From time to time / King without a throne / Rain / Proud words / Fortune / Blackhearted lady / Go down / Cold Autumn Sunday / The last time. *(re-iss.Oct77)*
Mar 75. (7") **IN THE MORNING. / WHO WILL SING TO YOU** [ ] [-]
Apr 75. (lp)(c) **EAGER TO PLEASE** [ ] [ ]
– Eager to please / Stargazer / Secret / Through the eyes of a child / Part three / The house on the hill / Winter or summer / Take and take / Longer shadows / In the morning / How shall I know. *(re-iss.Oct77) (cd-iss.Jun93 on 'Repertoire')*

— He left URIAH HEEP in 1980 and quickly made another solo album FREE SPIRIT *(cd-iss.Apr93 on 'Repertoire')*. Two 45's were lifted from it 'THE SYSTEM' & 'NO MORE'.

KEN HENSLEY issued new cd 'FROM TIME TO TIME' on 'Red Steel' Jun94.

DAVID BYRON

solo while a URIAH HEEP member.

Bronze | Warners

Jan 76. (lp)(c) **TAKE NO PRISONERS** [ ] [ ]
– Man full of yesterday / Sweet rock and roll / Steamin' along / Silver white man / Love song / Midnight flyer / Saturday night / Roller coaster / Stop hit me with a white one.

— Later in '76, he split from HEEP to form ROUGH DIAMOND and continued solo. ROUGH DIAMOND made own self-named lp in 1977 for 'Island'.

UTOPIA (see under ⇒ RUNDGREN, Todd)

U2

Formed: Dublin, Ireland . . . 1977 by BONO, THE EDGE, CLAYTON and MULLEN. Early 1978, through A&R man Jackie Hayden, they signed to 'CBS' in 'Ireland. They arrived in UK the following year and after 2nd 45 'ANOTHER DAY' hit Irish No.1, 'Island' gave them UK contract. In 1980, STEVE LILLYWHITE produced much heralded debut album BOY, but it took the following year's OCTOBER album to give them break into Top 20. By early 1983, U2 had first top 10 hit single with appropriately titled NEW YEAR'S DAY which was culled from No.1 album WAR. Became worldwide attraction/stadium fillers by the mid-80's, progressing to No.1 rock act of that decade. • **Style:** Political hard-edged rock, fusing energy and power with message of love and peace. Their Irish-Christian beliefs were now somewhat overshadowed by their God-like status and overwhelming fan adoration. BONO's pop pin-up look has not interrupted the thought-provoking abundance of great songs U2 have created, which have not succumbed to the pop industry. • **Songwriters:** All written by BONO / THE EDGE, except HELTER SKELTER (Beatles) / ALL ALONG THE WATCHTOWER (Bob Dylan) (hit; Jimi Hendrix) / STAR SPANGLED BANNER (US National anthem) / DANCING BAREFOOT (Patti Smith) / NIGHT AND DAY (Cole Porter) / PAINT IT BLACK (Rolling Stones) / FORTUNATE SON (Creedence Clearwater Revival) / HALLELUJAH (Leonard Cohen) by BONO. • **Trivia:** BONO contributed vox to BAND AID single Dec'84. That year, the band also started own record label, mainly for other Irish groups and was a starter for HOTHOUSE FLOWERS / CACTUS WORLD NEWS / etc. In 1988, BONO and THE EDGE co-wrote for ROY ORBISON on his last living studio album 'Mystery Girl'. JOHNNY CASH was guest vocalist on 'ZOOROPA' track 'THE WANDERER'. They wrote the theme for the James Bond film 'GOLDEN EYE', which became a hit for TINA TURNER in 1995.

Recommended: BOY (*8) / OCTOBER (*6) / WAR (*9) / UNDER A BLOOD RED SKY (*6) / THE UNFORGETTABLE FIRE (*9) / WIDE AWAKE IN AMERICA (*6) / THE JOSHUA TREE (*10) / RATTLE & HUM (*8) / ACHTUNG BABY (*8) / ZOOROPA (*9) / PASSENGERS: ORIGINAL SOUNDTRACKS 1 (*7)

BONO (b.PAUL HEWSON, 10 May'60, Dublin, Ireland) – vocals / **THE EDGE** (b.DAVID EVANS, 8 Aug'61, Barking, Essex) – guitar, keyboards / **ADAM CLAYTON** (b.13 Mar'60, Chinnor, Oxfordshire, England) – bass / **LARRY MULLEN** (b.LAURENCE, 31 Oct'61, Dublin) – drums

CBS-Ireland | not issued

Oct 79. (7"ep)(12"ep)(7"orange-ep)(7"yellow-ep) **U2-3** [-] [-]
– Out of control / Stories for boys / Boy-girl.
Feb 80. (7")(7"yellow)(7"white) **ANOTHER DAY. / TWILIGHT (demo)** [-] [-]

Island | Island

May 80. (7")(7"red)(7"white)(7"orange)(7"yellow) **11 O'CLOCK TICK TOCK. / TOUCH** [ ] [-]
Aug 80. (7") **A DAY WITHOUT ME. / THINGS TO MAKE AND DO** [ ] [-]
Oct 80. (lp)(c) **BOY** [52] [63] Mar 81
– I will follow / Twilight / An cat dubh / Into the heart / Out of control / Stories for boys / The ocean / A day without me / Another time, another place / The Electric Co. / Shadows and tall trees. *(cd-iss.May86 & May95 +lp+c)*
Oct 80. (7")(7"white)(7"yellow) **I WILL FOLLOW. / BOY-GIRL (live)** [ ] [-]
Mar 81. (7") **I WILL FOLLOW. / OUT OF CONTROL** [-] [ ]
Jul 81. (7") **FIRE. / J.SWALLO** [35] [ ]
(d7"+=) – The ocean (live) / 11 o'clock tick tock (live). / The Electric Co. / Cry.
Sep 81. (7") **GLORIA. / I WILL FOLLOW (live)** [55] [ ]
Oct 81. (lp)(c) **OCTOBER** [11] [ ]
– Gloria / I fall down / I threw a brick through a window / Rejoice / Fire / Tomorrow / October / With a shout / Stranger in a strange land / Scarlet / Is that all?. *(cd-iss.May86) (re-iss.Jun92)*
Mar 82. (7") **A CELEBRATION. / TRASH, TRAMPOLENE AND THE PARTY GIRL** [47] [ ]
Jan 83. (7") **NEW YEAR'S DAY. / TREASURE (WHATEVER HAPPENED TO PETE THE CHOP)** [10] [53]
(d7"+=)(12"+=) – A day without me (live) / Fire (live) / I threw a brick through the window (live).
Feb 83. (lp)(c) **WAR** [1] [12]
– Sunday bloody Sunday / Seconds / Like a song / New Year's day / Two hearts beat as one / The refugee / Drowning man / Red light / '40' / Surrender. *(cd-iss.Dec85)(re-iss.cd+c.Aug91, re-iss.Jun92 hit No.51) (re-iss.all formats Aug93, hit UK No.38) (re-iss.all formats Aug93, hit UK No.38)*
Mar 83. (7") **TWO HEARTS BEAT AS ONE. / ENDLESS DEEP** [18] [ ]
(d7"+=)(12"+=) – Two hearts beat as one / New Year's day (US remixes).
Nov 83. (lp)(c) **UNDER A BLOOD RED SKY (live)** [2] [28]
– Gloria / 11 o'clock tick tock / I will follow / Party girl / Sunday bloody Sunday / The Electric Co. / New Year's day / '40'. *(cd-iss.May86) (re-iss.Jun92)*
Dec 83. (7") **I WILL FOLLOW (live). / TWO HEARTS BEAT AS ONE (live)** [-] [81]
Sep 84. (7")(7"pic-d) **PRIDE (IN THE NAME OF LOVE). / BOOMERANG II** [3] [33]
(d7"+=)(12"+=) – Boomerang II (instrumental) / 4th of July.
Oct 84. (lp)(c)(cd) **THE UNFORGETTABLE FIRE** [1] [12]
– A sort of homecoming / Pride (in the name of love) / Wire / The unforgettable fire / Promenade / 4th of July / Bad / Indian summer sky / Elvis Presley and America / MLK. *(re-iss.Jun92 hit No.38 UK)*
May 85. (7")(7"sha-pic-d) **THE UNFORGETTABLE FIRE. / A SORT OF HOMECOMING (live)** [6] [ ]
(12"+=) – The three sunrises / Bass trap / Love comes tumbling.
(d7"+=) – The three sunrises / Love comes tumbling / 60 seconds in . . .
May 85. (m-lp)(c) **WIDE AWAKE IN AMERICA** [11] [37]
– Bad (live) / A sort of homecoming (live) / The three sunrises / Love comes tumbling.

— Later in the year, BONO guested for CLANNAD on hit 'IN A LIFETIME'. In Sep'86, THE EDGE issued soundtrack album CAPTIVE (see further below).

Mar 87. (7")(12") **WITH OR WITHOUT YOU. / LUMINOUS TIMES (HOLD ON TO LOVE)** [4] [1]
(c-s+=)(cd-s+=) – Walk to the water.
Mar 87. (lp)(c)(cd)(4x7"pack) **THE JOSHUA TREE** [1] [1]
– Where the streets have no name / I still haven't found what I'm looking for / With or without you / Bullet the blue sky / Running to stand still / Red Hill mining town / In God's country / Trip through your wires / One tree hill / Exit / Mothers of the disappeared. *(re-charted UK Jan92, peaked Jun92 at No.19) (re-iss.all formats Aug93, hit UK No.27)*
May 87. (7")(12")(c-s) **I STILL HAVEN'T FOUND WHAT I'M LOOKING FOR. / SPANISH EYES / DEEP IN THE HEART** [6] [1]

(cd-s+=) – ('A'version).
Sep 87. (7"m) **WHERE THE STREETS HAVE NO NAME. / SILVER AND GOLD / SWEETEST THING** 4 13
(12"+=)(c-s+=)(cd-s+=) – Race against time.
Jan 88. (7"-US-imp) **IN GOD'S COUNTRY. / BULLET THE BLUE SKY** 48 44 Dec 87
(12"+=)(cd-s+=) – Running to stand still.
Sep 88. (7") **DESIRE. / HALLELUJAH (HERE SHE COMES)** 1 3
(12"+=)(cd-s+=) – ('A'extended remix).
(c-s) – ('A'side) / Love comes to town / All I want is you.
Oct 88. (d-lp)(c)(cd) **RATTLE AND HUM** (some live) 1 1
– Helter skelter / Hawkmoon 269 / Van Diemen's land / Desire / Angel of Harlem / I still haven't found what I'm looking for / When love comes to town / God part II / Bullet the blue sky / Silver and gold / Love rescue me / Heartland / Star spangled banner / All I want is you / Freedom for my people / All along the watchtower / Pride (in the name of love). *(re-charted UK at 37 on Jun92) (re-iss.all formats Aug93, hit UK No.34)*
Oct 88. (7") **ANGEL OF HARLEM. / NO ROOM AT THE HEARTBREAK HOTEL** 9 14
(12"+=)(cd-s+=) – Love rescue me (live w / KEITH RICHARDS & ZIGGY MARLEY)
Apr 89. (7")(c-s) **WHEN LOVE COMES TO TOWN. ("U2 & B.B.KING") / DANCING BAREFOOT** 6 68
(12"+=)(cd-s+=) – ('A'live mix) / God part II (metal mix).
(12") – (3 'A'versions incl.dance version).
Jun 89. (7")(c-s) **ALL I WANT IS YOU. / UNCHAINED MELODY** 4 83
(12"+=)(cd-s+=) – Everlasting love.
Oct 91. (7")(c-s) **THE FLY. / ALEX DESCENDS INTO HELL FOR A BOTTLE OF MILK / KOROVA 1** 1 61
(12"+=)(cd-s+=) – The lounge Fly mix.
Nov 91. (cd)(c)(lp) **ACHTUNG BABY** 2 1
– Zoo station / Even better than the real thing / One / Until the end of the world / Who's gonna ride your wild horses / So cruel / The fly / Mysterious ways / Tryin' to throw your arms around the world / Ultra violet (light my way) / Acrobat / Love is blindness. *(re-iss.all formats Aug93, hit UK No.17)*
Dec 91. (7") **MYSTERIOUS WAYS. / ('A'solar remix)** 13 9 Nov 91
(12"+=) – ('A'solar extended) / ('A' Apollo 440 remixes).
(cd-s++=) – ('A'-Tabla Motown mix).
Feb 92. (7")(c-s) **ONE. / THE LADY WITH THE SPINNING HEAD** 7 10
(12"+=)/ /(cd-s++=) – Satellite of love./ / Night and day (remix).
Jun 92. (7")(c-s) **EVEN BETTER THAN THE REAL THING. / SALOME** 12 32
(cd-s+=) – Where did it all go wrong (demo) / Lady with the spinning head (ext.dance).
Jul 92. (12") – ('A'perfecto remix) / ('A'trance) / ('A'sexy dub) / ('A'-Apollo 440). 8 –
Nov 92. (7")(c-s) **WHO'S GONNA RIDE YOUR WILD HORSES. / PAINT IT BLACK** 14 35
('A'extended-cd-s+=) – ('A'-Temple bar mix) / Fortunate son.
Jul 93. (cd)(c)(lp) **ZOOROPA** 1 1
– Zooropa / Babyface / Numb / Lemon / Stay (faraway, so close!) / Daddy's gonna pay for your crashed car / Some days are better than others / The first time / Dirty day / The wanderer.
Aug 93. (video-ep) **NUMB / NUMB (video remix) / LOVE IS BLINDNESS** - -
Nov 93. (7")(c-s) **STAY (FARAWAY, SO CLOSE!). / ("FRANK SINATRA WITH BONO") I'VE GOT YOU UNDER MY SKIN** 4 61
(cd-s+=) – Lemon (mixes).
(cd-s) – ('A'side) / Slow dancing / Bullet the blue sky (live) / Love is blindness (live).

— In Mar 94, BONO teamed up with GAVIN FRIDAY (Virgin Prunes) on single 'IN THE NAME OF THE FATHER' from the film of the same name. It made No.46 in UK.

Jun 95. (7"red)(c-s) **HOLD ME, THRILL ME, KISS ME, KILL ME / (theme from 'Batman Forever')** 2 16
(cd-s) – ('Tell Me Now' track by MAZZY STAR).
above single from film 'Batman Forever' on 'East West' label.

PASSENGERS

aka U2, ENO + guests incl. vocalists PAVAROTTI + HOLI

Island Island
Nov 95. (cd)(c) **ORIGINAL SOUNDTRACKS 1** 12 76
– United colours / Slug / Your blue room / Always forever now / A different kind of blue / Beach sequence / Miss Sarajevo / Ito Okashi / One minute warning / Corpse (these chains are way too long) / Elvis ate America / Plot 180 / Theme from the swan / Theme from let's go native.
Nov 95. (7")(c-s)(cd-s) **MISS SARAJEVO. / ONE (live)** 6 –
(cd-s+=) – Bottoms (Watashiitachi No Ookina Yume) (Zoo Station remix) / Viva Davidoff.

The EDGE

with guest **SINEAD O'CONNOR** – vocals

Virgin Virgin
Sep 86. (lp)(c)(cd) **CAPTIVE (Soundtrack)** – –
– Rowena's theme / Heroine (theme from 'Captive') / One foot in Heaven / The strange party / Hiro's theme 1 & 2 / Drift / The dream theme / Djinn / Island.
Sep 86. (7")(12") **HEROINE. / HEROINE (instrumental)** – -

— In 1983, The EDGE had collaborated with JAH WOBBLE & HOLGER CZUKAY on m-lp 'SNAKE CHARMER'.

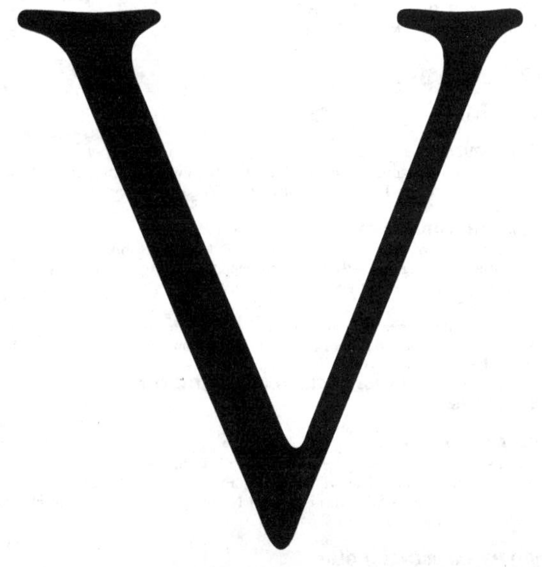

Steve VAI

Born: STEVEN CIRO VAI, 6 Jun'60, Carve Place, Long Island, New Jersey, USA. At age 20, he played guitar with FRANK ZAPPA on albums from TINSELTOWN REBELLION (1981) to FRANK ZAPPA MEETS THE MOTHERS OF PREVENTION (1986). In 1984, he also made debut solo album FLEX-ABLE for 'Relativity'. He joined ALCATRAZZ in 1985, leaving them to be part of DAVID LEE ROTH band. While a member of WHITESNAKE in 1989, he cut solo album PASSION AND WARFARE, which with incredible reviews and past C.V. gained him a Top 20 placing on both sides of the Atlantic. • **Style:** Superb guitarist, whose innovative experimentation brought new delights to the heavy-metal fraternity. • **Songwriters:** Writes all his own material. • **Trivia:** Taught as a teenager by the great JOE SATRIANI ⇒ . In 1985, he laid down all lead guitar work on PUBLIC IMAGE LTD lp 'ALBUM'. A year previous to this, he made an appearance in Walter Hill's film 'Crossroads'. VAI also co-wrote many songs for DAVID LEE ROTH.

Recommended: PASSION AND WARFARE (*7)

STEVE VAI – guitar, keyboards, bass, etc.

		M.F.N.	Akashic
Aug 86.	(lp) **FLEX-ABLE** – Little green men / Viv women / Lovers are crazy / The boy / Salamanders in the sun / Girl song / Attitude song / Call it sleep / Junkie / Bill is private parts / Next stop Earth / There's something dead in here. *(c-iss.Sep87, cd-iss. 1989 on 'Food For Thought')*	-	1984

—— now with **DAVE ROSENTHAL** – keys / **STU HAMM** – bass / **CHRIS FRAZIER** – drums

		Food for Tht.	Relativity
May 90.	(cd)(c)(lp)(pic-lp) **PASSION AND WARFARE** – Liberty / Erotic nightmares / The animal / Answers / The riddle / Ballerina 12-24 / For the love of God / The audience is listening / I would love to / Blue powder / Greasy kid's stuff / Alien water kiss / Sisters / Love secrets. *(re-iss.cd/c.Oct93)*	8	18

VAI

—— His new band were **TIM STEVENS** – bass / **TERRY BOZZIO** – drums

—— with **DEVIN TOWNSEND** – vocals / **WILL RILEY** – keyboards / **SCOTT THUNES** – bass / **ABE LABORIEL JR.** – drums

		Relativity	Relativity
Jul 93.	(cd)(c)(lp) **SEX & RELIGION** – An Earth dweller's return / Here & now / In my dreams with you / Still my bleeding heart / Sex and religion / Dirty black hole / Touching tongues / State of grace / Survive / Pig / The road to Mt.Calvary / Deep down into the pain / Rescue me or bury me.	17	48
		Epic	**Epic**
Aug 93.	(12"pic-d) **DEEP DOWN INTO THE PAIN. (as "STEVE VAI") / ?** (cd-s) – ('A'side) / ??		
Nov 93.	(12"pic-d) **IN MY DREAMS WITH YOU. / EROTIC NIGHTMARES** (cd-s) – ('A'side) / ('A'mixes) / I would love to.		
Apr 95.	(cd)(c) **ALIEN LOVE SECRETS** – Mad horsie / Juice / Die to live / The boy from Seattle / Ya yo gakk / Kill the guy with the ball – The God eaters / Tender surrender.	39	

Ritchie VALENS

Born: RICHARD VALENZUELA, 13 May'41, Pacoima, Los Angeles, California, USA. While at school, he joined The SILHOUETTES, but by May'58 local Hollywood label 'Del-Fi' signed him up. His debut single COME ON, LET'S GO gave him a US Top50 hit. He made an appearance in Alan Freed movie 'Go Johnny Go' and by end of year both sides of DONNA. / LA BAMBA single had entered US Top30. Tragically on the 3rd Feb'59, a plane which BUDDY HOLLY chartered for next concert crashed killing all on board including said stars and also BIG BOPPER. Ironically, he took the seat of BUDDY HOLLY's guitarist TOMMY ALLSUP at the last moment. Many had predicted he would become a future legend, but to die at just 17 was, to say the least, catastrophic. **Style / Songwriters:** He pioneered Chicano-Mexican rhythms into rock'n'roll, lending a traditional Mexican wedding song LA BAMBA, which he sang in Spanish. He also covered a few, including FRAMED (Leiber & Stoller) / etc. • **Trivia:** In 1987, a biopic film inspiring titled LA BAMBA, attracted new audience and LOS LOBOS soundtrack featuring their UK No.1 version.

Recommended: THE BEST OF RITCHIE VALENS (*6)

RITCHIE VALENS – vocals, guitar with session people.

		Pye Inter.	Del-Fi
Jun 58.	(7") **COME ON, LET'S GO. / FRAMED**	-	42
Oct 58.	(7") **COME ON, LET'S GO. / DOOBY DOOBY WAH**		-
		London	**Del-Fi**
Feb 59.	(7") **DONNA. / LA BAMBA** *(re-iss.Feb80 & Jul82 on 'Old Gold', re-iss.Nov80 on 'Creole')*	29	2 Nov 58 22 Nov 58
Feb 59.	(7" as "ARVEE ALLENS") **FAST FREIGHT. / BIG BABY BLUES**	-	

—— As said above, he was killed in a plane crash 3 Feb'59. He had just recorded new album,

Mar 59.	(lp) **RITCHIE VALENS** – La bamba / Bluebirds over the mountain / Stay beside me / Big baby blues / Cry, cry, cry / Ritchie blues / Now you're gone / Hurry up / Paddy Wack song. *(UK-iss.Jul79)*	-	23
Mar 59.	(7") **THAT'S MY LITTLE SUZIE. / IN A TURKISH TOWN**	-	55
Jun 59.	(7") **THAT'S MY LITTLE SUZIE. / BLUEBIRDS OVER THE MOUNTAIN**		-
Jul 59.	(7") **LITTLE GIRL. / WE BELONG TOGETHER**	-	92
1959.	(lp) **RITCHIE** (unissued tapes) – Stay beside me / Cry cry cry / Big baby blues / The padi-wack song / My darling is gone / Hurry up / Little girl / Now you're gone / Fast freight / Ritchie's blues / Rockin' all night.	-	
1959.	(7") **STAY BESIDE ME. / BIG BABY**	-	
1960.	(7") **PADDIWACK SONG. / CRY, CRY, CRY**	-	
1960.	(lp) **LIVE AT PACOIMA JUNIOR HIGH SCHOOL (live Dec'58 gig)** – Summertime blues / From beyond / Donna / Bluebirds over the mountain / Now you're gone / Come on, let's go / La bamba / Malaguena / Let's rock and roll / Come on let's go.	-	
Jan 62.	(7") **LA BAMBA. / OOH! MY HEAD HURTS**		-

– other compilations, etc. –

Apr 65.	President/ US= Del-Fi; (lp) **HIS GREATEST HITS**		
1967.	President/ US= Del-Fi; (lp) **GREATEST HITS II**		
May 66.	Sue; (7") **LA BAMBA. / DONNA**		-
1974.	Joy; (lp) **ROCK LIL' DARLING**		-
Jul 79.	London; (7"m) **LA BAMBA. / COME ON, LET'S GO / THAT'S MY LITTLE SUZIE**		-
Aug 84.	Creole; (7") **DONNA / LA BAMBA. / (track by 'Chris Montez')**		-
Feb 85.	Rhino; (lp) **A HISTORY OF RITCHIE VALENS**	-	
Aug 87.	Rhino; (lp)(c)(cd) **THE BEST OF RICHIE VALENS** *(UK-iss. cd Jul 92 on 'Ace')*	-	
Jul 87.	RCA; (7") **LA BAMBA. / DONNA** (12"+=) – Ooh! my head hurts / Come on, let's go.	49	
Aug 87.	RCA; (lp)(c) **GREATEST HITS**		
Mar 91.	Ace; (cd) **RITCHIE VALENS / RITCHIE**		-
Jul 92.	Ace; (cd) **THE LOST TAPES**		-
Sep 93.	World Star; (cd)(c) **LA BAMBA**		-
Feb 94.	Ace; (cd) **THE RITCHIE VALENS STORY**		-
Oct 95.	Music Club; (cd)(c) **THE VERY BEST OF RITCHIE VALENS**		-

VAN DER GRAAF GENERATOR

Formed: Manchester, England ... 1967 by PETER HAMMILL, etc. (see below). Funnily enough, they split towards the end of '68, and although the album 'AEROSOL GREY MACHINE' looked destined to be a HAMMILL solo lp, it finally reached the shops in 1969 credited to the group. They raised the flags again, when the group/HAMMILL gained deal on 'Charisma'. Their brief liason with the charts, came early in 1970, when album 'THE LEAST WE CAN DO ... ' dented UK Top50. Group and HAMMILL continued together and seperately for the rest of the 70's. • **Style:** Underground cult rock group, deep and gothic and often cited by 80's alternative outfits as inspiration. • **Songwriters:** HAMMILL composed all. • **Trivia:** Named after a generator built by Dr.Robert Jemison Van Der Graaf.

Recommended: AEROSOL GREY MACHINE (*8) / VITAL (*7) / PETER HAMMILL – NADIR'S BIG CHANCE (*7).

PETER HAMMILL (b. 5 Nov'48, London, England) – vocals, guitar, piano / **HUGH BANTON** – keyboards repl. NICK PEAKE / **CHRIS JUDGE SMITH** – drums, vocals, oricanos / **KEITH ELLIS** – bass (ex-KOOBAS) / **GUY EVANS** – drums (ex-MISUNDERSTOOD)

Polydor Mercury

Dec 68. (7") **PEOPLE YOU WERE GOING TO. / FIREBRAND** [ ] [-]

— Trimmed to a quartet when CHRIS formed HEEBALOB and later wrote for HAMMILL

Fontana Mercury

Jan 69. (lp) **AEROSOL GREY MACHINE** [-] [ ]
– Afterwards / Orthenthian St. – part 1 & 2 / Running back / Into a game / Aerosol grey machine / Black smoke yen / Aguarian / Necromancer / Octopus. *(UK iss.Feb75)*

1969. (7") **AFTERWARDS. / NECROMANCER** [-] [ ]

— **NIC POTTER** – bass (ex-MISUNDERSTOOD) repl. ELLIS who joined JUICY LUCY / added **DAVE JACKSON** – saxophone (ex-HEEBALOB)

Charisma Mercury

Feb 70. (lp)(c) **THE LEAST WE CAN DO IS WAVE TO EACH OTHER** [47] [ ]
– Darkness / Refugees / White hammer / Whatever would Robert have said / Out of my book / After the flood. *(re-iss.Aug82) (cd-iss.Apr87)*

Apr 70. (7") **REFUGEES. / BOAT OF MILLIONS OF YEARS** [ ] [ ]

— A quartet again, when POTTER left only completing half of next album. Guest on next 2 albums **ROBERT FRIPP** – guitar (of KING CRIMSON)

Charisma Dunhill

Dec 70. (lp)(c) **H TO HE, WHO AM THE ONLY ONE** [ ] [ ]
– Killer / House with no door / The emperor in his war-room: The emperor – The room / Lost: Dance in sand and sea – Dance in frost / The pioneers over C. *(re-iss.Jun81 & Sep83) (cd-iss.Nov88)*

Charisma Mercury

Oct 71. (lp)(c) **PAWN HEARTS** [ ] [ ]
– Lemmings / Man-erg / A plague of lighthouse keepers: 1) Eyewitness – 2) Pictures – Lighthouse – 3) Eyewitness – 4) S.H.M. – 5) Presence of the night – 6) Kosmos tours – 7) (Custards) Last stand – 8) The clot chickens – 9) Lands End – 10) We go now. *(re-iss.Oct86, cd-iss.Apr88)*

Feb 72. (7") **THEME ONE. / W** [ ] [ ]

PETER HAMMILL

had by this went solo when VAN DER GRAAF split. He continued to use VDGG members.

Charisma Charisma

Jul 71. (lp)(c) **FOOL'S MATE** [ ] [ ]
– Imperial zeppelin / Candle / Happy / Solitude / Vision / Re-awakening / Sunshine / Child / Summer song (in the autumn) / Viking / The birds / I once wrote some poems. *(re-iss.Sep83, cd-iss.Oct88)*

May 73. (lp)(c) **CHAMELEON IN THE SHADOW OF THE NIGHT** [ ] [ ]
– German overalls / Slender threads / Rock and role / In the end / What's it worth / Easy to slip away / Dropping the torch / In the black room / The tower. *(cd-iss.Apr89)*

Feb 74. (lp)(c) **THE SILENT CORNER AND THE EMPTY STAGE** [ ] [ ]
– Modern / Wilhemina / The lie (Bernini's Saint Teresa) / Forsaken gardens / Red shift / Rubicon / A louse is not a home. *(re-iss.Oct86, cd-iss.Nov88)*

Sep 74. (lp)(c) **IN CAMERA** [ ] [ ]
– Ferret and featherbed / (No more) The sub-mariner / Tapeworm / Again / Faintheart and the sermon / The comet, the course. the tail / Gog Magog (in bromine chambers). *(re-iss.Nov80) (cd-iss.Nov88)*

Feb 75. (lp)(c) **NADIR'S BIG CHANCE** [ ] [ ]
– Nadir's big chance / The institute of mental health's burning / Open your eyes / Nobody's business / Been alone so long / Pompeii / Shingle song / Airport / People you were going to / Birthday special / Two or three spectres. *(re-iss.Mar83, cd-iss.Nov88)*

Apr 75. (7") **BIRTHDAY SPECIAL. / SHINGLE SONG** [ ] [ ]

— **HAMMILL, BANTON, JACKSON + EVANS** reformed

VAN DER GRAAF GENERATOR

Charisma Mercury

Oct 75. (lp)(c) **GODBLUFF** [ ] [ ]
– The undercover man / Scorched Earth / Arrow / The sleepwalkers. *(re-iss.Mar83) (cd-iss.Apr88)*

Apr 76. (lp)(c) **STILL LIFE** [ ] [ ]
– Pilgrims / Still life / La rossa / My room (waiting for Wonderland) / Childlike faith in childhood's end. *(re-iss.Mar83) (cd-iss.Apr87)*

Oct 76. (lp)(c) **WORLD RECORD** [ ] [ ]
– When she comes / A place to survive / Masks / Meurlys III / Songwriter's guild / Wondering. *(re-iss.Sep83) (re-iss.+cd.Aug88)*

Oct 76. (7") **WONDERING. / MEURGLYS III** [ ] [ ]

VAN DER GRAAF

GRAHAM SMITH – violin (ex-STRING DRIVEN THING) repl. JACKSON / **NIC POTTER** – bass returned after US session work to repl. BANTON

Sep 77. (lp)(c) **THE QUIET ZONE – THE PLEASURE DOME** [ ] [ ]
– Lizard play / The habit of the broken heart / The siren song / Last frame / The wave / Yellow fever (running) / The sphinx in the face / Chemical world / The sphinx returns. *(re-iss.1983) (re-iss.+cd.Aug88)*

— added **DAVE JACKSON** who returned w / **CHARLES DICKIE** – cello, piano

Charisma P.V.C.

Jul 78. (d-lp)(c) **VITAL (live)** [ ] [ ]
– Ship of fools / Still life / Mirror images / Medley: Parts of A plague of lighthouse keepers and Sleepwalkers / Pioneers over C / Door / Urban / Nadir's big chance. *(cd-iss.Apr89) (re-iss.cd Mar94 on 'Virgin')*

– (VAN DER GRAAF . . .) compilations, etc. –

Aug 72. Charisma; (lp) **68-71** [-] [ ]
Aug 80. Charisma; (lp)(c) **REPEAT PERFORMANCE** [ ] [-]
Mar 83. Charisma; (d-c) **PAWN HEARTS / STILL LIFE** [ ] [-]
May 85. Demi-Monde; (lp) **TIME VAULTS** (rare) [ ] [-]
Feb 87. Virgin; (cd) **FIRST GENERATION** [ ] [-]
Feb 87. Virgin; (cd) **SECOND GENERATION** [ ] [-]
Sep 93. Virgin; (cd) **I PROPHESY DISASTER** [ ] [-]
May 88. Thunderbolt; (lp)(cd) **NOW AND THEN** [ ] [-]
Jun 94. Band Of Joy; (cd) **MAIDA VALE** [ ] [-]

PETER HAMMILL

went solo after split.

Charisma P.V.C.

Sep 76. (lp)(c) **OVER** [ ] [ ]
– Crying wolf / Autumn / Time heals / Alice (letting go) / This side of the looking-glass / Betrayed (on Tuesdays she used to) / Yoga / Lost and found. *(cd-iss.Feb91 on 'Virgin')*

Sep 78. (lp)(c) **THE FUTURE NOW** [ ] [ ]
– The future now / Still in the dark / Mediaevil / A motor-bike in Africa / The cut / Palinurus / Pushing thirty / The second hand / Trappings / The mousetrap (caught in) / Energy vampires / If I could. *(re-iss.Oct86)*

Nov 79. (lp)(c) **pH7** [ ] [ ]
– My favourite / Careering / Porton Down / Mirror images / Handicap and equality / Not for Keith / The old school tie / Time for a change / Imperial walls / Mr.X gets tense / Faculty X. *(cd-iss.Apr89)*

Nov 79. (7") **THE POLAROID. (as "RICKY NADIR") / THE OLD SCHOOL TIE** [ ] [-]

S Type not issued

1980. (lp) **A BLACK BOX** [ ] [-]
– Golden promise / Losing faith in words / The Jargon king / Fog walking / The spirit / In slow time / The wipe / Flight: Flying blind – White cave fandango – Control – Cockpit – Silk worm wings / Nothing is nothing – A black box. *(re-iss.Jun83 on 'I.M.S.') (re-iss.1985 on 'Virgin')*

Virgin not issued

May 81. (7") **MY EXPERIENCE. / GLUE** [ ] [-]
Jun 81. (lp)(c) **SITTING TARGETS** [ ] [-]
– Breakthrough / My experience / Ophelia / Empress's clothes / Glue / Hesitation / Sitting targets / Stranger still / Sign / What I did for love / Central hotel. *(re-iss.+cd.Aug88) (re-iss.cd Mar94)*

— **HAMMILL** with **GUY EVANS / NIC POTTER** plus **JOHN ELLIS** – guitar (ex-VIBRATORS), formed **K**

Naive not issued

Sep 82. (7") **PARADOX DRIVE. / NOW MORE THAN EVER** [ ] [-]
Oct 82. (lp) **ENTER 'K'** [ ] [-]
– Paradox Drive / The unconscious life / Accidents / The great experiments / Don't tell me / She wraps it up / Happy hour / Seven wonders. *(cd-iss.May92 on Fie!)*

Sep 83. (lp) **PATIENCE** [ ] [-]
– Labour of love / Film noir / Just good friends / Jeunesse D'Oree / Traintime / Now more than ever / Comfortable / Patient. *(cd-iss.May92 on Fie!) (above 2 re-iss.d-lp,d-c Jan86 on 'Spartan')*

Sep 83. (7") **FILM NOIR. / SEVEN WONDERS** [ ] [-]

Foundry not issued

Feb 85. (d-lp) **THE MARGIN (live)** [ ] [-]
– Future now / Porton Down / Stranger still / Sign / The Jargon king / The second hand / Empress's clothes / The sphinx in the face / Labour of love / Sitting targets / Patience / Flight. *(cd-iss.Feb91 on 'Virgin')*

Mar 86. (lp)(c) **SKIN** [ ] [-]
– Skin / After the show / Painting by numbers / Shell / All sais and done / A perfect date / Four pails / New lover. *(cd-iss.Feb91 on 'Virgin')*

Mar 86. (7") **PAINTING BY NUMBERS. / YOU HIT ME WHERE I LIVE** [ ] [-]
(12"+=) – Shell.

Virgin not issued

Nov 86. (lp)(c) **AND CLOSE TO THIS** [ ] [-]
– Too many of my yesterdays / Faith / Empire of delight / Silver / Beside the one you love / Other old cliches / Confident / Sleep now. *(cd-iss. Nov 88)*

PETER HAMMILL & GUY EVANS

Red Hot not issued

Jun 88. (c)(cd) **SPUR OF THE MOMENT** [ ] [-]
– Sweating it out / Little did he know / Without a glitch / Anatol's proposal / You think not? / Multiman / Deprogramming Archie / Always so polite / An imagined brother / Bounced / Roger and out. *(re-iss.May 93)*

PETER HAMMILL

solo again.

Enigma Enigma

Nov 88. (lp)(c)(cd) **IN A FOREIGN TOWN** [ ] [ ]
– Hemlock / Invisible ink / Sci-finance (re-visited) / This book / Time to burn / Auto / Vote brand X / Sun City night life / The play's the thing / Under cover names. (c+cd+=) – Smile / Time to burn (instrumental). *(re-iss.cd Jun95 on 'Fie!')*

Feb 90. (cd)(c)(lp) **OUT OF WATER**
– Evidently goldfish / Not the man / No Moon in the water / Our oyster / Something about Ysabel's dance / Green fingers / On the surface / A way out. *(reiss.cd Jun95 on 'Fie!')*

Some Bizzare not issued

Nov 91. (cd)(c)(lp) **THE FALL OF THE HOUSE OF USHER** [ ] [-]
– An unenviable role / That must be the house / Architecture / The sleeper / One thing at a time / I shun the light / Leave this house / Dreaming / A chronic catalepsy / The herbalist / The evil that is done / Five years ago / It's over now / An influence / no rot / She is dead / Beating of the heart / The haunted palace / I dared not speak / She comes towards the door / The fall

Fie! not issued

Dec 93. (cd) **THERE GOES THE DAYLIGHT (" . . . /The NOISE")** [ ] [-]
– Sci-finance (revisited) / The habit of a broken heart / Sign / I will find you / Lost and found / Planet Coventry / Empress's clothes / Cat's eye – Yellow fever / Primo on the parapet / Central hotel.

Virgin not issued

Sep 94. (cd) **ROARING FORTIES** [ ] [-]
– Sharply unclear / The gift of fire / You can't want what you always get / A headlong

stretch / Your tall ship.

Golden Hind / not issued

Jan 95. (cd) **OFFENSICHTLLICH GOLDFISCH** [-]
– Offensichtilich goldfisch / Dich zu finden / Die kalte killt den kub / Favorit / Kaufhaus Europa / Der larm / Oase / Die prominenz kubt sich / Die tunte verlischt / Auto (wieder im wagen) / Gaia / Schlaft nun.

– (PETER HAMMILL) compilations, etc. –

1978. Charisma; (lp) **VISION** [-]
Aug 84. (lp)(c) **THE LOVE SONGS** (remixes) [-]
(re-iss.Jun88)
May 85. Charisma; (7") **JUST GOOD FRIENDS. / ('A'instrumental)** [-]
1983. Sofa; (c) **LOOPS AND REELS** [-]
(cd-iss. Nov 93 on 'Fie')
Jul 93. Virgin; (cd) **THE CALM (AFTER THE STORM)** [-]
Jul 93. Virgin; (cd) **THE STORM (BEFORE THE CALM)** [-]
Jun 95. Fie!; (d-cd) **ROOM TEMPERATURE LIVE (live)** [-]
Nov 95. Strange Fruit; (cd) **THE PEEL SESSIONS** [-]

VANGELIS

Born: EVANGELOS PAPATHANASSIOU, 29 Mar'43, Valos, Greece. After 5 odd years as a member of APHRODITE'S CHILD alongside DEMIS ROUSSOS, he cut solo album early in the 70's. In 1974, he signed to 'RCA Victor', and hit UK album charts with 'HEAVEN AND HELL'. In the late 70's, he teamed up with JON ANDERSON of YES (who had earlier guested on HEAVEN lp), and scored with a hit single 'I HEAR YOU NOW'. He was then commissioned in 1980 to write score for 'CHARIOTS OF FIRE', and the following year it hit album + singles chart. It also broke him in the States, where the film also broke the box office. **Style & Songwriters:** Composer and virtuoso keyboard & synthesizer player. Neo-classical soundtrack specialist loved throughout the continent. • **Trivia:** In 1975, he was asked but refused to take the place of RICK WAKEMAN in YES, instead of PATRICK MORAZ. In 1985, he also wrote the ballet score for new version of 'Frankenstein'.

Recommended: HEAVEN & HELL (*8) / CHARIOTS OF FIRE (*7)

VANGELIS – keyboards, synthesizers (ex-APHRODITE'S CHILD, ex-FORMYNX)

Charly / not issued

1971. (lp) **THE DRAGON** [-]
– The dragon / Stuffed aubergine / Stuffed tomato. *(re-iss.1980)*

Affinity / not issued

1971. (lp) **HYPOTHESIS** [-]
– Hypothesis (part 1) / Hypothesis (part 2).

Polydor / not issued

1973. (lp) **L'APOCALYPSE DES ANIMAUX (Soundtrack)** [-]
– L'apocalypse des animaux / Generique / La petite fille / De la mer / Le singe blue / L'ours musicien / La mort / Du loop / Creation du monde / La mer recommences. *(re-iss.Oct76 + Apr84, etc.Imported, cd-iss.1988)*

— He now moved to London and signed to . . .

Vertigo / Vertigo

1974. (lp) **EARTH**
– Come on / We were all uprooted / Sunny Earth / He-o / Ritual / Let it happen / The city / My face in the rain / Watch out / A song.

RCA Victor / R.C.A.

Nov 75. (lp)(c) **HEAVEN & HELL** [31]
– Heaven and Hell pt.1 – Bacchanale symphony to the powers of B – 2nd movement – 3rd movement – So long ago so clear * / Heaven and Hell pt.2 – Intestinal heart – Needles and bones – 12 o'clock – Aries – Away. *(re-iss.Sep81 & Oct86, cd-iss.Sep89)*

— above featured The ENGLISH CHAMBER CHOIR and VANA VEROUTIS – lead vocals (track* was first to use vocals of **JON ANDERSON** (of YES).)

Aug 76. (7") **SO LONG AGO, SO CLEAR. / HEAVEN AND HELL THEME** [-]
Sep 76. (lp)(c) **ALBEDO 0.39** [18]
– Pulstar / Freefall / More tranquilillitatis / Main sequence / Sword of Orion / Alpha / Nucleogenesis (pt.1 & 2) / Albedo 0• 39. *(re-iss.Sep81) (re-iss.+cd.Sep89)*
Oct 76. (7") **PULSTAR. / ALPHA** [-]
Dec 77. (lp)(c) **SPIRAL** [-]
– Spiral / Ballad / Dervish D / To the unknown man / 3 + 3. *(re-iss.Sep81 + Nov84)*
Jan 78. (7") **TO THE UNKNOWN MAN. / (part 2)** [-]
Jul 78. (lp)(c) **BEAUBOURG** [-]
– Beaubourg (part 1) / Beaubourg (part 2). *(re-iss.Sep86 on 'Fame') (re-iss.+cd.Feb90)*

Polydor / Polydor

Apr 79. (lp)(c) **CHINA**
– Chung Kuo / The long march / The dragon / The plum blossom / The Tao of love / The little fete / Yin and Yang / Himalaya / Summit. *(re-iss.+cd.Aug83)*
May 79. (7") **THE LONG MARCH. / (part 2)** [-]

JON & VANGELIS

JON = **JON ANDERSON** – vocals (also of YES)

Polydor / Polydor

Dec 79. (7") **I HEAR YOU NOW. / THUNDER** [8] [58] Aug 80
Jan 80. (lp)(c) **SHORT STORIES** [4]
– Curious electic / Each and everyday / Bird song / I hear you now / The road / Far away in Bagdad / Love is / One more time / Thunder / A play within a play. *(re-iss.+cd.Jun87)*

VANGELIS

solo (same label until stated)

Jun 80. (7") **MY LOVE. / DOMESTIC LOGIC 1**
Nov 80. (lp)(c) **SEE YOU LATER**
– I can't take it anymore / Multitrack suggestion / Memories of green / Not a bit – all of it / Suffocation / See you later.
Mar 81. (lp)(c) **CHARIOTS OF FIRE (Original Motion Picture Soundtrack)** [5] [1] Oct 81
– Titles / Five circles / Abraham's theme / Eric's theme / 100 metres / Jerusalem / Chariots of fire. *(re-iss.Apr84, hit UK No.39) (cd-iss.1983)*
Apr 81. (7") **CHARIOTS OF FIRE – TITLES. / ERIC'S THEME** [12] [1] Dec 81
(re-iss.UK Feb82 hit No.41) (re-iss.Aug84)

JON & VANGELIS

were again. (same label)

May 81. (7") **THE FRIENDS OF MR.CAIRO. / BESIDE**
Jul 81. (lp)(c) **THE FRIENDS OF MR.CAIRO** [6] [64]
– The friends of Mr.Cairo / Back to school boogie / Outside of this (inside of that) / State of independence / Beside / The Mayflower. *(re-iss.+cd.Oct89)*
Jul 81. (7") **STATE OF INDEPENDENCE. / BESIDE**
Nov 81. (7") **I'LL FIND MY WAY HOME. / BACK TO SCHOOL BOOGIE** [6] [-]
Apr 82. (7") **I'LL FIND MY WAY HOME. / I HEAR YOU NOW** [-] [51]

— In 1982, he wrote unissued vinyl score for film 'Blade Runner'.

May 83. (lp)(c)(cd) **PRIVATE COLLECTION** [22]
– He is sailing / And when the night comes / Deborah / The king is coming / Horizon.
Jul 83. (7") **HE IS SAILING. / POLANAISE** [61]
(12"+=) – Song is.

— Above was last collaboration between the duo, until 1991.

– (JON & VANGELIS) compilations, etc. –

Aug 82. Polydor; (d-c) **SHORT STORIES / THE FRIENDS OF MR.CAIRO** [-]
Aug 84. Polydor; (7") **STATE OF INDEPENDENCE. /** [67]
Aug 84. Polydor; (lp)(c)(cd) **THE BEST OF JON & VANGELIS** [42]
– Italian song / I'll find my way home / State of independence / One more time / Play within a play / friends of Mr.Cairo / Outside of this (inside of that) / He is sailing / I hear you now.
Jun 88. Old Gold; (7") **I HEAR YOU NOW. / I'LL FIND MY WAY HOME** [-]
Sep 94. Spectrum; (cd)(c) **CHRONICLES (JON & VANGELIS)** [-]

VANGELIS

had continued solo. BOUNTY Soundtrack was also unissued. He continued to write unissued soundtracks throughout the 80's as well as below.

Oct 84. (lp)(c)(cd) **SOIL FESTIVITIES** [55]
– Movements 1-5. *(re-iss.Jun87)*
Mar 85. (lp)(c)(cd) **MASK (Soundtrack)** [69]
– Movements 1-6.
Mar 85. (lp)(c)(cd) **INVISIBLE CONNECTIONS**
– Invisible connections / Atom blaster / Thermo vision.
1986. (lp)(c)(cd) **RHAPSODIES**
– Ti ipermacho stratigo / O! gliki mou ear / Ton nimfona sou vlepo / Rapsodia / Tin oreotita tis partenias sou / Christos anesti / Asma asmaton.

Arista / Arista

Sep 88. (lp)(c)(cd) **DIRECT**
– The motion of stars / The will of the wind / Metallic rain / Elsewhere / Glorianna (hymn a la femme) / Rotations logic / The oracle of Apollo / Ave / First approach / Dial out / Intergallactic radio station / Message.
Sep 88. (cd-s) **THE WILL OF THE WIND / METALLIC RAIN / INTERGALACTIC RADIO STATION** [-]

East West / East West

Nov 90. (cd)(c)(lp) **THE CITY**
– Dawn / Morning papers / Nerve centre / Side streets / Good to see you / Twilight / Red lights / Procession. *(re-iss.cd Nov93 & Feb95)*
Oct 92. (cd)(c)(lp) **1492: THE CONQUEST OF PARADISE (Soundtrack)** [33]
– Opening theme / 1492: The conquest of Paradise / Monastery of la Rabida / City of Isabel / Light and shadow / Deliverance / West across the ocean sea / Eternity / Hispanola / Moxica and the horse / 28th parallel / Pinta, Nina, Santa Maria (into eternity) *(re-iss.cd Jun94)*.
Oct 92. (7")(c-s) **CONQUEST OF PARADISE. / MOXICA AND THE HORSE** [60]
(12"+=)(cd-s+=) – Line open / Landscape. *(re-iss.May95)*
Mar 93. (cd-s) **28th PARALLEL / WEST ACROSS THE OCEAN SEA**
Oct 95. (c-s)(cd-s) **VOICES / VOICES II (echoes) / VOICES III**

JON & VANGELIS

re-united

Arista / Arista

Aug 91. (7") **WISDOM CHAIN. / PAGE OF LIFE**
(cd-s+=) – ('A'full version) / Sing with your eyes.
Sep 91. (cd)(c)(lp) **PAGE OF LIFE**
– Wisdom chain / Page of life / Money / Garden of senses / Is it love / Anyone can light a candle / Journey to Ixtlan / Shine for me / Genevieve.

– (VANGELIS) compilations, others –

1978. RCA; (lp)(c) **THE BEST OF VANGELIS**
(re-iss.Sep81) (cd-iss.May93)
Nov 82. RCA; (d-lp)(d-c) **TO THE UNKNOWN MAN VOLS.1 & 2** [-]
Jun 84. RCA; (c) **MAGIC MOMENTS** [-]
Oct 89. RCA; (cd-box)(c-box) **SPIRAL / ALBEDO 0• 39 / HEAVEN AND HELL** [-]

Jul 81. BBC; (7") **HEAVEN AND HELL, THIRD MOVEMENT (THEME FROM THE BBC-TV SERIES – THE COSMOS). / ?** 48 -

Aug 81. Polydor; (lp)(c) **OPERA SAUVAGE – COSMOS** -
(US-iss.+cd Dec 86, hit No. 42)

Nov 82. Polydor; (t-lp) **CHARIOTS OF FIRE / CHINA / OPERA SAUVAGE** -

Nov 88. Polydor; (lp)(c)(cd) **ANTARTICA (Original Soundtrack)** -

Jul 89. Polydor; (lp)(c)(cd) **THEMES** -
– (excerpts from films, including some from previously unissued on vinyl)

Apr 93. C.A.M.; (cd) **ENTENDS-TU LES CHEINS** -

Jun 94. East West; (cd)(c) **BLADE RUNNER (Soundtrack)** 20

Apr 95. RCA; (cd) **ALBEDO 0.39 / HEAVEN AND HELL** -

VAN HALEN

Formed: Pasadena, California, USA . . . 1975 by brothers ALEX and EDDIE. In 1977 as MAMMOTH they were spotted by producer TED TEMPLEMAN who encouraged MO OSTIN to sign them for 'Warners'. Now as VAN HALEN, their monster debut paved the way for massive selling albums and sell-out concerts during late 70's and 80's. • **Style:** Heavy-metal/hard rock, with ROTH a hyperactive flamboyant frontman who combined and blended with supremo axeman EDDIE VAN HALEN. • **Songwriters:** ROTH lyrics until 1986, then group compositions. Covered; YOU REALLY GOT ME (Kinks) / FAIR WARNING (Aerosmith) / (OH) PRETTY WOMAN (Roy Orbison) / A POLITICAL BLUES (Little Feat) / WON'T GET FOOLED AGAIN (Who). • **Trivia:** In Apr'81, EDDIE married actress Valerie Bertinelli. He also played guitar on MICHAEL JACKSON's 'Thriller' album 1982.

Recommended: VAN HALEN (*8) / VAN HALEN II (*7) / WOMEN AND CHILDREN FIRST (*6) / FAIR WARNING (*6) / DIVER DOWN (*7) / 1984 (*7)

EDDIE VAN HALEN (b.26 Jan'57, Nijmegin, Holland) – guitar / **DAVID LEE ROTH** (b.10 Oct'55, Bloomington, Indiana, USA) – vocals / **MICHAEL ANTHONY** (b.20 Jun'55, Chicago, Illinois, USA) – bass / **ALEX VAN HALEN** (b. 8 May'55, Nijmegen, Holland) – drums

Warners Warners

Feb 78. (7") **YOU REALLY GOT ME. / ATOMIC ROCK PUNK** 36 Jan 78

Apr 78. (lp)(c) **VAN HALEN** 34 19 Feb 78
– You really got me / Jamie's cryin' / On fire / Runnin' with the Devil / I'm the one / Ain't talkin' about love / Little dreamer / Feel your love tonight / Atomic punk / Eruption / Ice cream man. *(cd-iss.Jul86, Jun91 + Feb95)*

Apr 78. (7") **RUNNIN' WITH THE DEVIL. / ERUPTION** 84

Jul 78. (7") **JAMIE'S CRYIN'. / I'M THE SAME** -

Sep 78. (7") **AIN'T TALKIN' BOUT LOVE. / FEEL YOUR LOVE TONIGHT** -

Apr 79. (lp)(c) **VAN HALEN II** 23 6
– Dance the night away / Outta love again / Somebody get me a doctor / You're no good / Bottoms up / Women in love / Light up the sky / Beautiful girls / D.O.A. / Spanish fly. *(cd-iss.Mar87) (re-iss.1989)*

May 79. (7")(7"pic-d) **DANCE THE NIGHT AWAY. / OUTTA LOVE AGAIN** 15 Apr 79

Sep 79. (7") **BEAUTIFUL GIRLS. / D. O. A.** - 84

Apr 80. (lp)(c) **WOMEN AND CHILDREN FIRST** 15 6
– Tora! Tora! / And the cradle will rock / Romeo delight / Fools / In a simple rhyme / Could this be magic? / Loss of control / Take your whiskey home / Everybody wants some. *(cd-iss.Jun89)*

Apr 80. (7") **AND THE CRADLE WILL ROCK. / COULD THIS BE MAGIC** - 55

Aug 80. (7") **AND THE CRADLE WILL ROCK. / EVERYBODY WANTS SOME** -

May 81. (7") **SO THIS IS LOVE. / HEAR ABOUT IT LATER** -

May 81. (lp)(c) **FAIR WARNING** 49 6
– Mean street / So this is love / Push comes to shove / Sinner's swing / Unchained / Dirty movies / Hear about it later / Sunday afternoon in the park / One foot out of the door. *(cd-iss.Jun89)*

Feb 82. (7") **(OH) PRETTY WOMAN. / HAPPY TRAILS** 12
(re-iss.Feb85)

May 82. (7") **DANCING IN THE STREET. / THE BULL BUG** - 38

May 82. (lp)(c) **DIVER DOWN** 36 3
– Where have all the good times gone / Hang 'em high / Cathedral / Secrets / Intruder / (Oh) Pretty woman / Dancing in the street / Little guitars / Big bad Bill (is sweet William now) / The bull bug / Happy trails. *(cd-iss.Jan84)*

May 82. (7") **DANCING IN THE STREET. / BIG BAD BILL (IS SWEET WILLIAM NOW)** -

Aug 82. (7") **BIG BAD BILL (IS SWEET WILLIAM NOW). / SECRETS** -

Jan 84. (lp)(c)(cd) **1984** 15 2
– 1984 / Jump / Panama / Top Jimmy / Drop dead legs / Hot for teacher / I'll wait / Girl gone bad / House of pain. *(re-iss.cd/c Feb95)*

Jan 84. (7") **JUMP. / HOUSE OF PAIN** - 1

Jan 84. (7") **JUMP. / RUNNIN' WITH THE DEVIL** 7 -
(12"+=) – House of pain.

Apr 84. (7") **I'LL WAIT. / GIRL GONE BAD** - 13

Apr 84. (7") **PANAMA. / GIRL GONE BAD** 61 13 Jun 84
(12"+=) – Dance the night away.

Jun 84. (7") **I'LL WAIT. / DROP DEAD LEGS** -
(12"+=) – And the cradle will rock / (Oh) Pretty woman.

Jun 85. (7") **HOT FOR TEACHER. / LITTLE PREACHER** 56 Oct 84
(12"+=) – Hear about it later.

—— (Jun85) Trimmed to a trio, when **DAVID LEE ROTH** went solo full-time. Early '86 added **SAMMY HAGAR** – vocals (ex-MONTROSE, ex-Solo Artist)

Mar 86. (7")(12")(7"pic-d)(7"sha-pic-d) **WHY CAN'T THIS BE LOVE. / GET UP** 8 3

Apr 86. (lp)(c)(cd) **5150** 16 1
– Good enough / Why can't this be love / Get up / Dreams / Summer nights / Best of both worlds / Love walks in / 5150 / Inside. *(re-iss.cd/c Feb95)*

Jun 86. (7")(12")(7"sha-pic-d) **DREAMS. / INSIDE** 62 22 May 86

Aug 86. (7") **LOVE WALKS IN. / SUMMER NIGHTS** - 22

Oct 86. (7") **BEST OF BOTH WORLDS. / ('A' live)** -

May 88. (7")(12") **BLACK AND BLUE. / APOLITICAL BLUES** 34

Jun 88. (lp)(c)(cd) **OU812** 16 1
– Mine all mine / When it's love / A.F.U. (naturally wired) / Cabo wabo / Source of infection / Feels so good / Finish what ya started / Black and blue / Sucker in a 3-piece. *(cd+=)*– A political blues.

Jul 88. (7") **WHEN IT LOVE. / CABO WABO** - 5

Jul 88. (7") **WHEN IT'S LOVE. / APOLITICAL BLUES** 28 -
(12"+=)(cd-s+=)(12"pic-d+=) – Why can't this be love.

Sep 88. (7") **FINISH WHAT YA STARTED. / SUCKER IN A 3-PIECE** - 13

Feb 89. (7") **FEELS SO GOOD. / SUCKER IN A 3 PIECE** 63 35 Jan 89
(12"+=)(cd-s+=) – BEST OF BOTH WORLDS (live)

Jun 91. (7")(c-s) **POUNDCAKE. / PLEASURE DOME** 74
(12"+=)(cd-s+=) – (interview).

Jul 91. (cd)(c)(lp) **FOR UNLAWFUL CARNAL KNOWLEDGE** 12 1
– Poundcake / Judgement day / Spanked / Runaround / Pleasure dome / In'n'out / Man on a mission / The dream is over / Right now / 316 / Top of the world.

Sep 91. (7") **TOP OF THE WORLD. / POUNDCAKE** - 27

Oct 91. (7")(c-s) **TOP OF THE WORLD. / IN'N'OUT** 63 -
(12"+=)(cd-s+=) – Why can't this be love (extended) / When it's love / Dreams.

Feb 92. (c-s)(cd-s) **RIGHT NOW /** - 55

Feb 93. (d-cd)(d-c) **LIVE: RIGHT HERE, RIGHT NOW (live)** 24 5
– Poundcake / Judgement day / When it's love / Spanked / Ain't talkin' 'bout love / In'n'out / Dreams / Man on a mission / Ultra bass / Pressure dome – Drum solo / Panama / Love walks in / Runaround/ / Right now / One way to rock / Why can't this be love / Give to love / Finished what ya started / Best of both worlds / 316 / You really got me – Cabo wabo / Won't get fooled again / Jump / Top of the world.

Mar 93. (7")(c-s) **JUMP (live). / LOVE WALKS IN (live)** 26
(cd-s+=) – Eagles fly (live) / Mine, all mine (live).

Jan 95. (7"purple)(c-s) **DON'T TELL ME (WHAT LOVE CAN DO). / BALUCHITHERIUM** 27
(cd-s+=) – Why can't this be love (live)/ Poundcake (live)/ Panama (live).
(cd-s) – ('A'side)/ Judgement day (live)/ Dreams (live)/ Top of the world (live).

Jan 95. (cd)(c)(lp) **BALANCE** 8 1
– The seventh seal / Can't stop lovin' you / Don't tell me (what love can do) / Amsterdam / Big fat money / Aftershock / Strung out / Not enough / Doin' time / Baluchitherium / Take me back (dea vu) / Feelin'.

Mar 95. (7")(c-s) **CAN'T STOP LOVIN' YOU. / CROSSING OVER** 33 30
(cd-s+=) – Man on a mission / Right now.
(cd-s) – ('A'side) / Best of both worlds (live) / One way to rock (live) / When it's love (live).

Jun 95. (c-s) **AMSTERDAM / RUNAROUND (live)**
(cd-s) – ('A'side) / Finish what you started (live).

Aug 95. (c-s)(cd-s) **NOT ENOUGH /** - 97

– compilations, others, etc. –

Jun 80. Atlantic; (7") **RUNNIN' WITH THE DEVIL. / D.O.A.** 52 -

VANILLA FUDGE

Formed: New York, USA . . . 1965 as The PIGEONS. Became VANILLA FUDGE late '66 and after their debut at The Village Theater (Fillmore East) went onto massive success in the late 60's. • **Style:** Described as psychedelic-symphonic rock which at times went over-the-top with heavy IRON BUTTERFLY like renditions of soul classics. • **Songwriters:** STEIN or group compositions, with mainly covers :- YOU KEEP ME HANGIN' ON (Supremes) / BANG BANG (Cher) / ELEANOR RIGBY + TICKET TO RIDE (Beatles) / SEASON OF THE WITCH (Donovan) / I CAN'T MAKE IT ALONE (Goffin-King) / THE WINDMILLS OF YOUR MIND (Legrand-Bergyan). CACTUS also covered several standards. • **Trivia:** In summer 1969, played Seattle Pop Festival at Woodenville, Washington.

Recommended: THE BEST OF (PSYCHEDELIC SUNDAE) (*8)

MARK STEIN (b.11 Mar'47, New Jersey, USA) – vocals, organ / **VINCE MARTELL** (b.11 Nov'45) – guitar, vocals / **TIM BOGERT** (b.27 Aug'44) – bass, vocals / **CARMINE APPICE** (b.15 Dec'46, Staten Island, New York) – drums, vocals

Atlantic Atco

Jul 67. (7") **YOU KEEP ME HANGIN' ON. / TAKE ME FOR A LITTLE WHILE** 18 67

Sep 67. (lp) **VANILLA FUDGE** 31 6
– Ticket to ride / People get ready / She's not there / Bang bang / Illusions of my childhood (parts 1-3) / You keep me hangin' on / Take me for a little while / Eleanor Rigby. *(cd-iss.May93)*

Oct 67. (7") **ILLUSIONS OF MY CHILDHOOD. / ELEANOR RIGBY** -

Feb 68. (lp) **THE BEAT GOES ON** 17
– Sketch / Variation on a theme from Mozart's Divertimento No.13 in F / Old black Joe / Don't fence me in / 12th Street rag / In the mood / Hound dog / I want to hold your hand – I feel fine – Day tripper – She loves you / The beat goes on / Beethoven's fur Elise and theme from Moonlight Sonata / The beat goes on / Voices in time: – Neville Chamberlain – Winston Churchill – F.D. Roosevelt – Harry S. Truman – John F.Kennedy / Merchant / The game is over / The beat goes on. *(cd-iss Jun92 & Jul93 on 'Repertoire', with extra tracks)*

Apr 68. (7") **WHERE IS MY MIND?. / THE LOOK OF LOVE** 73 Jan 68

Jun 68. (lp) **RENAISSANCE** 20
– The sky cried – When I was a boy / Thoughts / Paradise / That's what makes a man / The spell that comes after / Faceless people / Season of the witch. *(cd-iss Jul93 on 'Repertoire' +=)*– You keep me hangin' on (7" version) / Come by day, come by night / People.

Jul 68. (7") **YOU KEEP ME HANGIN' ON. / COME BY DAY, COME BY NIGHT** - 6

Sep 68. (7") **TAKE ME FOR A LITTLE WHILE. / THOUGHTS** - 38

Nov 68. (7") **SEASON OF THE WITCH. / (part 2)** [-] [65]
Feb 69. (lp) **NEAR THE BEGINNING** (half studio / half live) [ ] [16]
– Shotgun / Some velvet morning / Where is happiness / Break song. *(cd-iss.Jul93 on 'Repertoire' +=)*– Look of love.
Mar 69. (7") **SHOTGUN. / GOOD GOOD LOVIN'** [ ] [68]
Jun 69. (7") **SOME VELVET MORNING. / PEOPLE** [-] [ ]
Jul 69. (7") **SOME VELVET MORNING. / THOUGHTS** [ ] [-]
Oct 69. (lp) **ROCK & ROLL** [ ] [34]
– Need love / Lord in the country / I can't make it alone / Street walking woman / Church bells of St.Martin's / The windmills of your mind / If you gotta make a fool of somebody. *(cd-iss.Jul93 on 'Repertoire' +=)*– Good good lovin' / Shotgun / Where is my mind / Need love (7" version).
Nov 69. (7") **I CAN'T MAKE IT ALONE. / NEED LOVE** [-] [ ]
Jan 70. (7") **LORD IN THE COUNTRY. / THE WINDMILLS OF YOUR MIND** [-] [ ]

— Had already folded mid '69. STEIN formed BOOMERANG and MARTELL retired.

CACTUS

were formed Feb'70 by **BOGERT & APPICE** with **RUSTY DAY** – vocals, mouth harp (ex-AMBOY DUKES / TED NUGENT) / **JIM McCARTY** – guitar (not of YARDBIRDS)

Atlantic Atco

Jul 70. (lp) **CACTUS** [ ] [54]
– Parchman farm / My lady from south of Detroit / Bro. Bill / You can't judge a book by the cover / Let me swim / No need to worry / Oleo / Feel so good.
Oct 70. (7") **YOU CAN'T JUDGE A BOOK BY THE COVER. / BRO BILL** [ ] [ ]
Mar 71. (lp) **ONE WAY . . . OR ANOTHER** [ ] [88]
– Long tall Sally / Rock out whatever you feel like / Rock'n'roll children / Big mam boogie / Feel so bad / Hometown bust / One way . . .or another.
Mar 71. (7") **LONG TALL SALLY. / ROCK'N'ROLL CHILDREN** [-] [ ]
Sep 71. (7") **TOKEN CHOKIN'. / ALASKA** [-] [ ]

— (May71) added **DUANE HITCHINGS** – piano

Nov 71. (lp) **RESTRICTIONS** [ ] [ ]
– Restrictions / Token chokin' / Guiltness glider / Evil / Alaska / Sweet sixteen / Bag drag / Mean night in Cleveland. *(cd-iss.Jul93 on 'Repertoire')*
Jan 72. (7") **EVIL. / SWEET SIXTEEN** [ ] [ ]

— **PETE FRENCH** – vocals (ex-ATOMIC ROOSTER) McCARTY and DAY

Oct 72. (lp) **'OT & SWEATY** (live/studio) [ ] [ ]
– Swim / Bad mother boogie / Our lil' rock and roll thing / Bad stuff / Bring me down / Bedroom Mazurka / Telling you / Underneath / The arches.
Oct 72. (7") **BAD MOTHER BOOGIE. / BRINGING ME DOWN** [-] [ ]

— Disbanded and DUANE retained some of name NEW CACTUS BAND issuing an album, 'SON OF CACTUS' and single 'BILLIE GYPSY WOMAN' in 1973. TIM and CARMINE teamed up with JEFF BECK ⇒ in supergroup BECK, BOGERT & APPICE. CARMINE joined MIKE BLOOMFIELD's band KGB in the mid-70's. He later joined ROD STEWART and in the 80's with RICK DERRINGER formed DNA.

VANILLA FUDGE

re-formed originals 1982 and again in 1984.

Atco Atco

Jul 84. (lp)(c) **MYSTERY** [ ] [ ]
– Golden age dreams / Jealousy / Mystery / Under suspicion / It gets stronger / Walk on by / My world is empty / Don't stop now / Hot blood / The stranger.
Jul 84. (7") **MYSTERY. / THE STRANGER** [-] [ ]

— Folded again, although they briefly got together for Atlantic 40 year bash mid 1988.

– compilations, others, etc. –

1982. Atlantic/ US= Atco; (lp)(c) **GREATEST HITS** [ ] [ ]
Aug 93. Rhino; (cd) **THE BEST OF VANILLA FUDGE (PSYCHEDELIC SUNDAE)** [ ] [ ]
Jul 94. Success; (cd)(c) **YOU KEEP ME HANGIN' ON** [ ] [-]

Thijs VAN LEER (see under ⇒ FOCUS)

VASELINES

Formed: Glasgow, Scotland . . . 1986 by EUGENE KELLY and FRANCES McKEE. Released a few 45's on '53rd & 3rd', before finally making it onto 33 rpm in Summer 1989 with 'DUM-DUM'. • **Style:** Lyricaly at times sex-obsessed musical cousins of other Scottish bands BMX BANDITS and TEENAGE FANCLUB. • **Songwriters:** CAPTAIN AMERICA covered INDIAN SUMMER (Beat Happening). • **Trivia:** At the 1991 Reading festival, EUGENE guested for NIRVANA, when they covered their 'MOLLY'S LIPS'. They have since resurrected another of VASELINES songs 'SON OF A GUN'. CAPTAIN AMERICA went on to support NIRVANA on World Tour.

Recommended: ALL THE STUFF AND MORE . . . (*8) / OOMALAMA (*7; EUGENIUS)

EUGENE KELLY – vocals, guitars / **FRANCES McKEE** – vocals with hired musicians

53rd & 3rd not issued

Sep 87. (7"m) **SON OF A GUN. / RORY RIDES AWAY / YOU THINK YOU'RE A MAN** [ ] [-]
Mar 88. (7") **DYING FOR IT. / MOLLY'S LIPS** [ ] [-]
(12"+=) – Teenage superstars / Jesus wants me for a sunbeam. *(re-iss.Aug91 on 'Seminal Twang')*

— added **JAMES SHEENAN** – bass / **CHARLIE KELLY** (EUEGENE's brother) – drums

Sep 89. (lp)(cd) **DUM-DUM** [ ] [-]
– Sex sux / Sloshy / Monster pussy / Teenage superstar / No hope / Oliver twisted / The day I was a horse / Dum-dum / Hairy / Lovecraft. *(re-iss.+ re-mastered Mar91 on 'Avalanche')*

— Disbanded in 1990. McKEE and SHEENAN formed The PAINKILLERS and released a single in 1994; 'TROPICAL ZODIAC' for 'Human Condition' records.

CAPTAIN AMERICA

were formed by **EUGENE KELLY** / **GORDON KEEN** – lead guitar / **RAYMOND BOYLE** – bass / **ANDY ROY** – drums repl. live guest **BRENDAN O'HARE** – drums (of TEENAGE FANCLUB)

Paperhouse not issued

Nov 91. (12"ep)(cd-ep) **WOW / BED-IN. / WANNA BEE / GOD BLESS LES PAUL** [ ] [-]
Apr 92. (12")(cd-s) **FLAME ON. / BUTTERMILK / INDIAN SUMMER** [ ] [-]

— Had to change their name to below, after legal threats by Marvel comics.

EUGENIUS

Sep 92. (cd)(c)(lp) **OOMALAMA** [ ] [-]
– Oomalama / Breakfast / One's too many / Bed-in / Hot dog / Down on me / Flame on / Here I go / I'm the Sun / Buttermilk / Aye aye.

Creation Atlantic

Jul 93. (7") **CAESAR'S VEIN. / GREEN BED** [ ] [ ]
(12"+=)(cd-s+=) – Mary Queen Of Scots.
(below release on 'August-Creation')
Nov 93. (12")(cd-s) **EASTER BUNNY / HOMESICK. / CAESAR'S VEIN / SEX SUX** [ ] [ ]
Jan 94. (cd)(lp) **MARY QUEEN OF SCOTS** [ ] [ ]
– Pebble-shoe / On the breeze / Blue above the roftops / The Moon's a baloon / Mary Queen of Scots / Easter bunny / Let's hibernate / Friendly high / River Clyde song / Tongue rock / Fake digit / Love, bread and beers.

– (VASELINES) compilations, etc. –

Jun 92. Avalanche; (cd)(lp) **ALL THE STUFF AND MORE . . .** [ ] [-]
(re-iss.Sep92 on '53rd & 3rd') (re-iss.Oct95)
Sep 92. Sub Pop; (cd) **THE WAY OF THE VASELINES – A COMPLETE HISTORY** [-] [ ]
(UK re-iss.+c Mar94)

Stevie Ray VAUGHAN

Born: 3 Oct'54, Dallas, Texas. Found experience in the latter half of the 70's when playing guitar for The NIGHTCRAWLERS and The COBRAS. In 1981 he founded own backing band DOUBLE TROUBLE who signed to 'Epic' after STEVIE guested on DAVID BOWIE's 1983 album LET'S DANCE. He quit BOWIE's band on the eve of his 'Serious Moonlight' tour. Throughout the 80's, STEVIE became renowned albums artist. • **Style:** R & B / boogie rock guitarist influenced by ERIC CLAPTON or BB KING. • **Songwriters:** Wrote half the material except TEXAS FLOOD (Davis-Scott) / CHANGE IT + LOOKING OUT THE WINDOW (D.Bramhall) / LOOK AT LITTLE SISTER (Hank Ballard) / YOU'LL BE MINE (Willie Dixon) / COME ON (E.King) / VOODOO CHILE + LITTLE WING (Jimi Hendrix) / TAXMAN (eorge Harrison) / etc. • **Miscellaneous:** Beat his booze and drugs addiction around 1987.

Recommended: GREATEST HITS (*8)

STEVIE RAY VAUGHAN & DOUBLE TROUBLE

STEVIE – vocals, guitar / **TOMMY SHANNON** – bass (ex-JOHNNY WINTER) / **CHRIS 'Whipper' LAYTON** – drums (ex-GREAZY BROTHERS)

Epic Epic

Jul 83. (7") **PRIDE AND JOY. / RUDE MOOD** [-] [ ]
Aug 83. (lp)(c) **TEXAS FLOOD** [ ] [38] Jul 83
– Love struck baby / Pride and joy / Texas flood / Tell me / Testify / Rude mood / Mary had a little lamb / Dirty pool / I'm cryin' / Lenny. *(cd-iss.Jul89 & Apr91)*
Aug 83. (7") **LOVE STRUCK BABY. / RUDE MOOD** [ ] [ ]

— added brother **JIMMIE VAUGHAN** – guitar, bass

Jun 84. (lp)(c) **COULDN'T STAND THE WEATHER** [ ] [31]
– Scuttle buttin' / Couldn't stand the weather / The things (that) I used to do / Voodoo chile (slight return) / Cold shot / Tin Pan alley / Honey bee / Stang's swang. *(cd-iss.1984, Apr91 & Feb95)*

— **JOE SUBLETT** – saxophone repl. JIMMIE / added **REESE WYNANS** – keyboards

Sep 85. (lp)(c) **SOUL TO SOUL** [ ] [34]
– Say what! / Lookin' out the window / Look at little sister / Ain't gone 'n' give up on love / Gone home / Change it / You'll be mine / Empty arms / Come on (part III) / Life without you. *(cd-iss.Apr86 & Apr91)*
Sep 85. (7") **CHANGE IT. / LOOK AT LITTLE SISTER** [-] [ ]
Mar 86. (7") **SUPERSTITION (live). / PRIDE AND JOY (live)** [-] [ ]
Jan 87. (7") **WILLIE THE WIMP. / SUPERSTITION** [-] [ ]
Jan 87. (d-lp)(d-c)(cd) **LIVE ALIVE (live)** [ ] [52] Dec 86
– Say what! / Ain't gone 'n' give up on love / Pride and joy / Mary had a little lamb / Superstition / I'm leaving you (commit a crime) / Cold shot / Willie the wimp / Look at little sister / Texas flood / Voodoo chile (slight return) / Love struck baby / Change it / Life without you. *(re-iss. cd+c Apr 93)*
Jun 87. (7") **LOVE STRUCK BABY. / PIPELINE (W/ DICK DALE)** [-] [ ]
Jun 89. (7") **TRAVIS WALK. / CROSSFIRE** [-] [ ]
Jul 89. (lp)(c)(cd) **IN STEP** [63] [33] Jun 89

– The house is rockin' / Crossfire / Tightrope / Let me love you baby / Leave my girl alone / Travis walk / Wall of denial / Scratch-n-sniff / Love me darlin' / Riviera paradise.

Aug 89. (7") **THIS HOUSE IS ROCKIN'. / TIGHTROPE** [-] [ ]

— Late in the 80's, STEVIE jammed with The ERIC CLAPTON Band. On 27 Aug'90, after a concert in Alpine Valley, Wisconsin, STEVIE and other travellers were killed in a helicopter crash. He and brother JIMMIE had just cut album below.

VAUGHAN BROTHERS

Epic Epic

Oct 90. (cd)(c)(lp) **FAMILY STYLE** [63] [7]
– Hard to be / White boots / D-FW / Good Texan / Hillbillies from Outer Space / Long way from home / Tick tock / Telephone song / Baboom / Mama said / Brothers.

Oct 90. (c-s) **TICK TOCK. / BROTHERS** [-] [65]

Jan 91. (c-s) **GOOD TEXAN. / MAMA SAID / BABOOM** [-] [ ]

– (STEVIE RAY VAUGHAN) compilations, etc. –

Nov 91. Epic; (cd)(c)(lp) **THE SKY IS CRYING** [ ] [10]
– Boot hill / The sky is crying / Empty arms / Little wing / Wham / May I have a talk with you / Chitlins con carne / So excited / Life by the drop.

Nov 92. Epic; (7") **THE SKY IS CRYING. / CHITLINS CON CARNE** [-] [ ]

Jan 92. Epic; (7") **EMPTY ARMS. / WHAM** [-] [ ]

Oct 92. Epic; (cd)(c)(lp) **IN THE BEGINNING (live)** [-] [58]

Nov 95. Epic; (cd)(c) **GREATEST HITS** [ ] [39]
– Taxman / Texas flood / The house is rockin' / Pride and joy / Tightrope / Little wing / Crossfire / Change it / Cold shot / Couldn't stand the weather / Life without you.

Alan VEGA (see under ⇒ SUICIDE)

Suzanne VEGA

Born: 12 Aug'59, Upper West Side, New York, USA. From half-Puerto Rican stock, she studied dance at High School of Performing Arts. With this experience, she played folk clubs throughout early 80's, finally gaining attention of Ron Fiernstein and Steve Addabbo, who became her managers. They obtained her contract with 'A&M' and employed LENNY KAYE (ex-PATTI SMITH GROUP) to produce her debut album, which was released 1985. After slow start, it became good seller the following year, paving the way for two future UK Top 10's (1987 + 1990). • **Style:** Modern folk-rock singer-songwriter, who has had usual comparisons to JONI MITCHELL, LAURA NYRO or even DORY PREVIN. • **Songwriters:** Writes all her own, except CHINA DOLL (Grateful Dead) / STORY OF ISAAC (Leonard Cohen). • **Trivia:** In 1987, she contributed 2 song lyrics for a PHILIP GLASS album 'Songs From Liquid Days'.

Recommended: SUZANNE VEGA (*8) / SOLITUDE STANDING (*7) / 99.9 F

SUZANNE VEGA – vocals, guitar with **JIM GORDON** – guitar / **FRANK CHRISTIAN** – guitar / **PAUL DUGAN + FRANK GRAVIS** – bass / **SUE EVANS** – drums / **C.P. ROTH** – synth
She replaced above with touring + studio band from mid'85-late 80's. **MARC SHULMAN** – guitar / **MIKE VISCEGLIA** – bass / **ANTON SANKO** – keyboards / **STEPHEN FERRARA** – percussion / **SUE EVANS** – drums

A & M A & M

Jul 85. (lp)(c) **SUZANNE VEGA** [11] [91] Jun 85
– Cracking / Freeze tag / Marlene on the wall / Small blue thing / Straight lines / Undertow / Some journey / The queen and the soldier / Knight moves / Neighborhood girls. *(cd-iss.Feb86 & Mar93)*

Aug 85. (7") **MARLENE ON THE WALL. / NEIGHBORHOOD GIRLS** [ ] [ ]

Jan 86. (7") **SMALL BLUE THING. / THE QUEEN AND THE SOLDIER** [65] [-]
(d7"+=) – Some journey / Black widow station.

Feb 86. (7") **SMALL BLUE THING. / LEFT OF CENTER** [-] [ ]

Mar 86. (7") **MARLENE ON THE WALL. / SMALL BLUE THING** [21] [-]
(10"+=) – Neighborhood girls / Straight lines (live).

May 86. (7") **LEFT OF CENTER. / UNDERTOW** [32] [-]
(10"+=)/ /(cd-s+=) ('A'live) / Freeze tag (live)./ / Cracking.

(above 'A'side featured JOE JACKSON – piano). SUE EVANS had now left.

Oct 86. (7") **GYPSY. / CRACKING (live)** [ ] [-]
(12"+=) – Knight movies (live).

May 87. (lp)(c)(cd) **SOLITUDE STANDING** [2] [11]
– Tom's diner / Luka / Ironbound / Fancy poultry / In the eye / Night vision / Solitude standing / Calypso / Language / Gypsy / Wooden horse.

May 87. (7") **LUKA. / NIGHT VISION** [-] [3]

May 87. (7") **LUKA. / STRAIGHT LINES (live)** [23] [-]
(12"+=) – Neighbourhood girls.
(10"+=)(cd-s+=) – Cracking (alternative mix).

Jul 87. (7") **TOM'S DINER. / LEFT OF CENTER** [58] [-]
(10"+=)(12"+=)/ /(cd-s+=) – Luka (live)./ / ('A'live).

Sep 87. (7") **SOLITUDE STANDING. / TOM'S DINER** [-] [94]

Nov 87. (7") **GYPSY. / LEFT OF CENTER** [-] [ ]

Nov 87. (7")(c-s) **SOLITUDE STANDING. / LUKA** [ ] [-]
(12"+=) – Ironbound-Fancy poultry.
(10")(cd-s) – ('A'side) / Marlene on the wall (live) / Some journey (live).

— **FRANK VILARDI** – drums repl. FERRARA. Added **MICHAEL BLAIR** – percussion

Apr 90. (cd)(c)(lp) **DAYS OF OPEN HAND** [7] [50]
– Tired of sleeping / Men in a war / Rusted pipe / Institution green / Book of dreams / Those whole girls (run in grace) / Room off the street / Big space / Predictions / Fifty-fifty chance / Pilgrimage. *(re-iss.cd May95)*

Apr 90. (7")(c-s) **BOOK OF DREAMS. / BIG SPACE** [66] [ ]
(cd-s+=) – Marlene on the wall (live) / Ironbound (live).
(10"++=) – Fancy poultry.

Jun 90. (7") **TIRED OF SLEEPING. / THOSE WHOLE GIRLS (RUN IN GRACE)** [ ] [ ]
(10"+=)(cd-s+=) – Left of center / Room off the street.

Jul 90. (7")(c-s) **TOM'S DINER. ("SUZANNE VEGA & D.N.A.") / ('A'version)** [2] [5]
(12"+=)(cd-s+=) – (2 other mixes).

Sep 90. (7")(c-s) **MEN IN A WAR. / UNDERTOW (live)** [ ] [ ]
(12"+=)(cd-s+=) – ('A'live).

Aug 92. (7")(c-s) **IN LIVERPOOL. / SOME JOURNEY** [52] [ ]
(cd-s+=) – The Queen and the soldier / Luka.

Sep 92. (cd)(c)(lp) **99.9°F** [20] [86]
– Rock in this pocket (song of David) / Blood makes noise / In Liverpool / 99.9°F / Blood sings / Fat man & dancing girl / (If you were) In my movie / As a child / Bad wisdom / When heroes go down / As girls go / Songs of sand / Private goes public.

Oct 92. (7")(c-s) **99.9°F. / MEN WILL BE MEN** [46] [ ]
(cd-s+=) – Rock in this pocket (acoustic) / In Liverool (acoustic).
(cd-s) – ('A'side) / Tired of sleeping / Straight lines / Tom's diner (all live).

Dec 92. (7")(c-s) **BLOOD MAKES NOISE. / TOM'S DINER** [60] [ ]
(cd-s) – ('A'side) / Neighbourhood girls / Predictions / China doll.
(12") – ('A'side) / ('A'-Mitchell Froom remix) / ('A'house mix) / ('A'master mix).

Feb 93. (7")(c-s) **WHEN HEROES GO DOWN. / KNIGHT MOVES (live)** [58] [ ]
(cd-s+=) – Men in a war (live) / Gypsy (live).
(cd-s) – ('A'side) / Marlene on the wall / Luka / Left of center.

– compilations, others, etc. –

Oct 88. A&M; (cd-ep) **COMPACT HITS** [ ] [-]
– Luka / Left of center / Neighbourhood girls / The queen and the soldier.

Sep 91. A&M; (cd)(c)(lp) **TOM'S ALBUM** [ ] [ ]

— (above contained re-workings by other artists of the track TOM'S DINER)

VEGAS (see under ⇒ HALL, Terry)

VELVET UNDERGROUND

Formed: New York City, USA ... early 1965 by LOU REED and JOHN CALE, who nearly hit as The PRIMITIVES with single 'The Ostrich'. They met modern pop artist ANDY WARHOL, who invited German chanteuse NICO to join the set-up alongside STERLING MORRISON and MO TUCKER. Early in 1966, they signed to 'MGM-Verve', and soon began what was to be their debut album 'THE VELVET UNDERGROUND AND NICO'. It featured 11 superb ahead of-their-time classics, noteably the disturbing 'HEROIN', the s+m 'VENUS IN FURS' & 'I'M WAITING FOR THE MAN', plus 3 NICO sung gems 'FEMME FATALE', 'ALL TOMORROW'S PARTIES' & 'I'LL BE YOUR MIRROR'. It only managed a brief stay in the US Top 200, as did the 1967 follow-up 'WHITE LIGHT, WHITE HEAT', which included the 17 min.'SISTER RAY'. Their self-titled 3rd album, made little impact, and the band soon disrupted with personnel clashes, etc. • **Style:** Avant-garde and disturbing band, who highlighted experimentation with drug orientated rock'n'roll. A decade later, they were cited as the inspiration for punk rock. A decade after that, alternative groups like JESUS & MARY CHAIN showed their music had not been forgotten. • **Songwriters:** REED compositions, except some by group. Many rock acts have covered their material, but so far not surprisingly, none have managed to score a major chart hit yet. • **Miscellaneous:** In 1990, REED and CALE re-united on a tribute album to the deceased ANDY WARHOL. NICO had earlier died on 18 Jul'88 of a brain haemorrhage, after falling off her bike on holiday in Ibiza. • **Trivia:** The debut lp sleeve, featured a gimmick peeling banana skin sticker. They reformed for a gig in Paris, 15 June 1990, and for an album, etc, in Dec '93. UK's Channel 4 featured a night-long session of all their previous work.

Recommended: THE VELVET UNDERGROUND AND NICO (*10) / WHITE LIGHT – WHITE HEAT (*9) / V.U. (*7) / THE VELVET UNDERGROUND (*7).

LOU REED (b.LOUIS FIRBANK, 2 Mar'44, Long Island, New York) – vocals, guitar (ex-JADES, ex-PRIMITIVES) / **JOHN CALE** (b. 5 Dec'42, Garnant, Wales, UK) – bass, viola, vocals, etc. / **STERLING MORRISON** – guitar / **MAUREEN TUCKER** – drums / plus **NICO** (b.CHRISTA PAFFGEN, Cologne, W.Germany) – vocals (also – Solo artist)

Oct 66. (7") **ALL TOMORROW'S PARTIES. / I'LL BE YOUR MIRROR** [-] [ ]

Dec 66. (7") **SUNDAY MORNING / FEMME FATALE** [-] [ ]

Verve Verve

Oct 67. (lp) **THE VELVET UNDERGROUND AND NICO** [ ] [ ] Dec 66
– Sunday morning / I'm waiting for the man / Femme fatale / Venus in furs / Run run run / All tomorrow's parties / Heroin / There she goes again / I'll be your mirror / Black angel's death song / European son to Delmore Schwartz. *(re-iss.+c.Aug83 on 'Polydor', cd-iss.1986)*

— Trimmed to a quartet when NICO preferred the solo life.

Jun 68. (lp) **WHITE LIGHT / WHITE HEAT** [ ] [ ] Dec 67
– White light – white heat / he gift / Lady Godiva's operation / Here she comes now / I heard her call my name / Sister Ray. *(re-iss.Oct71) (re-iss.+cd.Apr84 on 'Polydor')*

Mar 68. (7") **I HEARD HER CALL MY NAME. / HERE SHE COMES NOW** [-] [ ]

— **DOUG YULE** – bass, vocals, keyboards, guitar repl. CALE who went solo

M.G.M. M.G.M.

Apr 69. (lp) **THE VELVET UNDERGROUND** [ ] [ ] Mar 69
– Candy says . . . / What goes on / Some kinda love / Pale blue eyes / Jesus / Beginning to see the light / I'm set free / That's the story of my life / The murder mystery / Afterhours. *(re-iss.Nov71 & Mar76) (re-iss.Sep83 on 'Polydor', cd-iss.May86)*

1969. (7") **JESUS. / WHAT GOES ON** [-] [ ]

— **BILLY YULE** – drums repl. TUCKER who had a baby. **MO TUCKER** returned in 1970 and BILLY only appeared on MAX's live album (see compilations)

Dec 70. (7") **WHO LOVES THE SUN. / OH SWEET NUTHIN'** [-] [ ]

Atlantic Cotillion

Apr 71. (lp) **LOADED** [ ] [ ] Aug 70
– Who loves the sun / Sweet Jane / Rock and roll / Cool it down / New age / Head held high / Lonesone cowboy Bill / I found a reason / Train around the bend / Oh! sweet nuthin'. *(re-iss.May81) (cd-iss.Jun88 on 'Warners') (cd-iss.Feb93 on 'Warners')*

Apr 71. (7") **WHO LOVES THE SUN. / SWEET JANE** [ ] [ ]

— (Aug70) now with no originals The **YULE's** brought in newcomers **WALTER POWERS** – bass repl. LOU REED who went solo in 1971. (1971) **WILLIE ALEXANDER** – guitar repl. MORRISON who took a doctorate in English. MO TUCKER finally left to bring up family. She eventually had 5 kids and went solo in 1980.

Polydor Polydor

Feb 73. (lp) **SQUEEZE** [ ] [ ]
– Little Jack / Mean old man / She'll make you cry / Wordless / Dopey Joe / Crash / Friends / Jack and Jane / Send no letter / Louise.

— Folded soon after above, DOUG sessioned for ELLIOTT MURPHY and later joined AMERICAN FLYER.

– compilations, others, etc. –

Aug 72. Atlantic/ US= Cotillion; (lp) **LIVE AT MAX'S KANSAS CITY (live 22 Aug'70)** [ ] [ ] May 72
– I'm waiting for the man / Sweet Jane / Lonesome Cowboy Bill / Beginning to see the light / I'll be your mirror / Pale blue eyes / Sunday morning / New age / Femme fatale / After hours. *(cd-iss Jun93 on 'Atlantic')*

Aug 73. Atlantic/ US= Cotillion; (7") **SWEET JANE** (live). / **ROCK AND ROLL** (live) [ ] [-]

Dec 71. MGM; (d-lp) **ANDY WARHOL'S VELVET UNDERGROUND FEATURING NICO** [ ] [-]
– I'm waiting for the man / Candy says / Run, run, run / White light – white heat / All tomorrow's parties / Sunday morning / I heard her call my name / Femme fatale / Heroin / Here she comes now / There she goes again / Sister Ray / Venus in furs / European son / Pale blue eyes / Black angel's death song / Beginning to see the light.

Jun 73. MGM; (7"m) **CANDY SAYS. / I'M WAITING FOR THE MAN / RUN RUN RUN** [ ] [-]

1974. MGM; (lp) **ARCHETYPES** [-] [ ]

Oct 73. Verve/ US= MGM; (lp) **THE VELVET UNDERGROUND AND LOU REED** [ ] [ ]

Feb 79. Mercury; (d-lp) **1969 – THE VELVET UNDERGROUND LIVE (live)** [ ] [ ] Apr 74
– I'm waiting for the man / Lisa says / What goes on / Sweet Jane / We're gonna have a real good time together / Femme fatale / New age / Rock and roll / Beginning to see the light / Ocean / Pale blue eyes / Heroin / Some kinda love / Over you / Sweet Bonnie Brown – It's just too much / I'll be your mirror / White light – white heat. *(re-iss.Nov84) (c+cd-VOL.1 & VOL.2 in 1988)*

1976. A.E.B.; (7"m) **FOGGY NOTION – INSIDE YOUR HEART. / I'M STICKING WITH YOU / FERRYBOAT BILL** [ ] [-]

Sep 88. Plastic Inev..; (lp) **THE VELVET UNDERGROUND ETC.** [-] [ ]
– The ostrich / Cycle Annie / Sneaky Pete / Noise.

Sep 88. Plastic Inev..; (lp) **THE VELVET UNDERGROUND AND SO ON** [-] [ ]
– It's alright (the way you live) / I'm not too sorry / Stephanie says.

Nov 80. Polydor; (d-lp)(d-c) **GREATEST HITS** [ ] [-]

Oct 82. Polydor; (12"ep) **HEROIN / VENUS IN FURS. / I'M WAITING FOR THE MAN / RUN RUN RUN** [ ] [-]

Feb 85. Polydor; (lp)(c) **V.U.** (rare rec.68-69) [47] [85]
– I can't stand it / Stephanie says / She's my best friend / Lisa says / Ocean / Foggy notion / Temptation inside your heart / One of these days / Andy's chest / I'm sticking with you. *(cd-iss.Jun87)*

May 86. Polydor; (5xlp-box)(5xcd-box) **BOXED SET** [ ] [ ]
– (first 3 albums, plus V.U. / ANOTHER VIEW)

Feb 87. Polydor; (lp)(c)(cd) **ANOTHER VIEW** [ ] [ ]
– We're gonna have a good time together / I'm gonna move right in / Hey Mr. Rain (version 1) / Ride into the Sun / Coney Island steeplechase / Guess I'm falling in love / Hey Mr. Rain (version 2) / Ferryboat Bill / Rock and roll (original).

Feb 88. Old Gold; (12") **I'M WAITING FOR THE MAN. / HEROIN** [ ] [-]

Mar 88. Old Gold; (12") **VENUS IN FURS. / ALL TOMORROW'S PARTIES** [ ] [-]

Nov 89. Verve/ US= Polygram; (lp)(c)(cd) **THE BEST OF THE VELVET UNDERGROUND** [ ] [ ]
– I'm waiting for the man / Femme fatale / Run run run / Heroin / All tomorrow's parties / I'll be your mirror / White light – white heat / Stephanie says / What goes on / Beginning to see the light / Pale blue eyes / I can't stand it / isa says / Sweet Jane / Rock and roll.

Oct 95. Polydor; (cd)(c) **THE BEST OF LOU REED & VELVET UNDERGROUND** [56] [ ]

Oct 95. Polydor; (5xcd-box) **PEEL SLOWLY AND SEE** [ ] [-]

— (see also LOU REED discography for other tracks on comps & B's)

VELVET UNDERGROUND

re-formed (**REED, CALE, MORRISON & TUCKER**)

Sire Sire

Oct 93. (d-cd)(w/ free cd) **LIVE MCMXCII (live)** [70] [ ]
– We're gonna have a good time together / Venus in furs / Guess I'm falling in love / After hours / All tomorrow's parties / Some kinda love / I'll be your mirror / Beginning to see the light / The gift / I heard her call my name / Femme fatale / Hey Mr.Rain / Sweet Jane / Velvet nursery rhyme / White light – white heat / I'm sticking with you / Black angel's death song / Rock'n'roll / I can't stand it / I'm waiting for the man / Pale blue eyes / Coyote.

Feb 94. (7")(c-s) **VENUS IN FURS (live). / I'M WAITING FOR THE MAN (live)** [71] [ ]
(cd-s+=) – Heroin (live) / Sweet Jane (live).

— On the 30th August 1995, STERLING MORRISON died of lymponia.

Tom VERLAINE (see under ⇒ TELEVISION)

VERUCA SALT

Formed: Chicago, USA . . . early '93 by NINA GORDON and LOUISE POST, who were soon joined by STEVE LACK and NINA's brother JIM SHAPIRO. In mid-94 they enjoyed a minor hit with debut 'SEETHER'. • **Style:** A surreal fusion of a mellow BREEDERS or a metal PIXIES. • **Songwriters:** GORDON or POST except; BODIES (Sex Pistols) / STACEY PLEASE (Morris-Felsenthal) / MY SHARONA (Knack). • **Trivia:** Named after a character in Roald Dahl's 'Willy Wonka And The Chocolate Factory'.

Recommended: AMERICAN THIGHS (*7)

NINA GORDON – vocals / **LOUISE POST** – vocals, guitar / **STEVE LACK** – bass / **JIM SHAPIRO** – drums

Scared Hitless / Minty Fresh

Jun 94. (7") **SEETHER. / ALL HAIL ME** [61] [ ]
(cd-s+=) – Stacey please.

Hi-Rise / Minty Fresh D.G.C.

Sep 94. (7") **NUMBER ONE BLIND. / BODIES** [ ] [ ]
(12"+=)(cd-s+=) – Aurora.

Oct 94. (cd)(c)(lp) **AMERICAN THIGHS** [ ] [69]
– Get back / All hail me / Seether / Spiderman '79 / Forsythia / Wolf / Celebrate you / Fly / Number one blind / Victrola / Twinstar / 25. *(lp w /free one-sided 12"+=) – SLEEPING WHERE I WANT*

Nov 94. (7")(c-s) **SEETHER. / STRAIGHT** [73] [-]
(12"+=)(cd-s+=) – She's a brain.

Jan 95. (7"green) **NUMBER ONE BLIND. / BODIES** [68] [ ]
(12"+=)(cd-s+=) – Aurora.

Jun 95. (7") **VICTROLA. / MY SHARONA** [ ] [ ]
(cd-s+=)(10"+=) – Sundown.

VERVE

Formed: Wigan, England . . . 1991 by 4 schoolboys below. They soon supported the likes of RIDE and SPIRITUALIZED, after being signed by indie label 'Hut'. Made inroads into UK charts by 1993, when 'A STORM IN HEAVEN' hit 27. • **Style:** Spacey rock /pop, similiar to PRIMAL SCREAM or SPIRITUALIZED fused with PINK FLOYD or The ROLLING STONES. • **Songwriters:** Group. • **Trivia:** RICHARD believes in astral travel. His nickname is MAD RICHARD, enough said!

Recommended: A STORM IN HEAVEN (*7) / A NORTHERN SOUL (*8)

RICHARD ASHCROFT (b.1971) – vocals / **NICK McCABE** – guitar / **SIMON JONES** – bass / **PETER SALISBURY** – drums

Hut / Vernon Yard

Mar 92. (12"ep)(cd-ep) **ALL IN THE MIND. / ONE WAY TO GO / A MAN CALLED SUN** [ ] [-]

Jun 92. (12")(cd-s) **SHE'S A SUPERSTAR. (8+mins) / FEEL (10+mins)** [66] [-]

Oct 92. (10"ep)(12"ep)(cd-ep) **GRAVITY GRAVE / ENDLESS LIFE / A MAN CALLED SUN (live) / SHE'S A SUPERSTAR (live)** [ ] [-]

Nov 92. (cd)(c)(lp) **THE VERVE EP** (all above material) [ ] [ ]

Hut / Caroline

May 93. (12"ep) **BLUE. / TWILIGHT / WHERE THE GEESE GO** [69] [ ]
(10"ep+=)(cd-ep+=) – No come down.

Jun 93. (cd)(c)(lp) **A STORM IN HEAVEN** [27] [ ]
– Star sail / Slide away / Already there / Beautiful mind / The Sun, the sea / Virtual world / Make it 'til Monday / Blue / Butterfly / See you in the next one (have a good time).

Sep 93. (7"ep)(12"ep)(cd-ep) **SLIDE AWAY. / MAKE IT 'TIL MONDAY (acoustic) / VIRTUAL WORLD (acoustic)** [ ] [ ]

THE VERVE

Apr 95. (7") **THIS IS MUSIC. / LET THE DAMAGE BEGIN** [35] [ ]
(12"+=)(cd-s+=) – You and me.

Jun 95. (7"green)(c-s) **ON YOUR OWN. / I SEE THE DOOR** [28] [ ]
(cd-s+=) – Little gun / Dance on your bones.

Jul 95. (cd)(c)(lp) **A NORTHERN SOUL** [13] [ ]
– A new decade / This is music / On your own / So it goes / A northern soul / Brainstorm interlude / Drive you home / History / No knock on my door / Life's an ocean / Stormy clouds / Stormy clouds (reprise).

Sep 95. (c-s) **HISTORY / BACK ON MY FEET AGAIN** [24] [ ]
(cd-s+=) – On your own (acoustic) / Monkey magic (Brain storm mix).
(cd-s) – ('A'extended) / Grey skies / Life's not a rehearsal.

This was to be their final release, due to ASHCROFT departing.

– compilations, etc. –

May 94. Hut; (cd) **NO COMEDOWN** (rare / B-sides) [ ] [-]

Gene VINCENT

Born: EUGENE VINCENT CRADDOCK, 11 Feb'35, Norfolk, Virginia, USA. in 1955, he left the US Navy, after suffering leg injuries in a serious motor-cycle crash. Incidentally, this never fully healed, and after a year in plaster, he fitted a leg-brace. Early in 1956, he briefly married 15 year-old Ruth Ann Hand, also gaining contract for 'Capitol' in April. He formed HIS BLUE CAPS for tour work, which became extensive after debut (B-side) 'BE-BOP-A-LULA', hit the US Top 10. He became a cult star in the 50's, through sparodic chart appearances. In 1958, the media attention focused on his recent drinking bouts, which made him irritable to everyone bar his great friend EDDIE COCHRAN. Late in 1959, he toured the UK with EDDIE, resurrecting chart status in the process. Tragedy struck however on 17 Apr'60, when EDDIE was killed in a London cab, with GENE and EDDIE's fiancee sustaining injuries. He re-appeared that May, visibly shattered from psychological stress. He had short reel of UK hits that year, but success soon eluded him. In 1965, he married for a fourth time, and signed to US label 'Challenge'. In the early 70's, his career took off again, when UK BBC Radio DJ John Peel, contracted him to his newly formed 'Dandelion' label. After more hard-living and domestic problems overhanging, GENE VINCENT died on the 12 Oct'71 of a burst stomach ulcer. • **Style:** Dressed in black, the archetype greasy rocker, whose songs crossed a thin line between EDDIE COCHRAN & ELVIS. His move into country rock'n'roll in 1966, was greeted with apathy. • **Songwriters:** His first hit, was written by fellow hospital patient DONALD GRAVES. He then wrote own material, except covers OVER THE RAINBOW (Judy Garland) / SUMMERTIME (Gershwin) / FRANKIE & JOHNNY (?) / ANOTHER SATURDAY NIGHT (Sam Cooke) / SLIPPIN' AND SLIDIN' + LONG TALL SALLY + GOOD GOLLY MISS MOLLY (Little Richard) / SUSIE Q (Dale Hawkins) / YOU ARE MY SUNSHINE (hit; Ray Charles) / WHITE LIGHTNING (Big Bopper) / etc. • **Trivia:** Tributes were forthcoming in all directions, none more so than IAN DURY's 1977 idol-song 'Sweet Gene Vincent'. He and his BLUE CAPS made appearances in the film 'The Girl Can't Help It' & 'Hot Rod Gang'.

Recommended: THE BEST OF GENE VINCENT & HIS BLUE CAPS (*8)

GENE VINCENT & HIS BLUE CAPS

GENE VINCENT – vocals, guitar / **CLIFF GALLUP** – lead guitar / **WILLIE WILLIAMS** – acoustic rhythm guitar / **JACK NEAL** – upright bass / **DICKIE HARRELL** – drums

Capitol Capitol

Jun 56. (7") **BE BOP A LULA. / WOMAN LOVE** 16 7 May 56

(above B-side, was originally the A, until BE BOP . . . was radio playlisted)

Aug 56. (7") **RACE WITH THE DEVIL. / GONNA BACK UP MY BABY** 28 96 Jul 56

Oct 56. (7") **BLUE JEAN BOP. / WHO SLAPPED JOHN?** 16 49 Sep 56

Nov 56. (lp) **BLUE JEAN BOP** 16 Sep 56

– Blue jean bop / Jezebel / Who slapped John / Ain't she sweet / I flipped / Waltz of the wind / Jump back, honey, jump back / That old gang of mine / Jumps, giggles and shouts / Up a lazy river / Bop street / Peg o' my heart *(re-iss.1983 on 'E.M.I.')*

— **PAUL PEAK** – rhythm guitar, vocals repl. WILLIAMS. (NEAL now on bass)

Mar 57. (7") **CRAZY LEGS. / IMPORTANT WORDS** Nov 56

Jan 57. (7") **JUMPS, GIGGLES AND SHOUTS. / WEDDING BELLS** -

Apr 57. (lp) **GENE VINCENT AND HIS BLUE CAPS**

– Red blue jeans and a pony tail / Hold me, hug me, rock me / Unchained melody / You told a fib / Cat man / You better believe / Cruisin' / Double talkin' baby / Blues stay away from me / Pink Thunderbird / I sure miss you / Pretty, pretty baby. *(re-iss.1983 on 'E.M.I.')*

— On tour **RUSSELL WILAFORD** then **TEDDY CRUTCHFIELD** had repl. GALLUP

May 57. (7") **BI-BICKEY-BI-BO-BO-GO. / FIVE DAYS, FIVE DAYS**

— **JOHNNY MEEKS** – lead guitar repl. GALLUP **BOBBY LEE JONES** – bass repl. BILLY MACK who had repl. NEAL (PEEK was now relegated to clapper boy alongside TOMMY FACIENDA)

Sep 57. (7") **LOTTA LOVIN'. / WEAR MY RING** 13 Jul 57

Nov 57. (7") **DANCE TO THE BOP. / I GOT IT** 23

Dec 57. (lp) **GENE VINCENT ROCKS AND THE BLUE CAPS ROLL**

– Brand new beat / By the light of the silvery Moon / You'll never walk alone / Frankie and Johnny / In my dreams / Flea brain / Rollin' Dany / You belong to me / Your cheatin' heart / Time will bring you everything / Should I ever love again / It's no lie.

— briefly on tour **DUDE KAHN** – drums had repl. HARRELL until quick return. / added **MAX LIPSCOMB** – rhythm guitar, piano

Feb 58. (7") **I GOT A BABY. / WALKING HOME FROM SCHOOL WITH YOU**

— **CLIFF SIMMONS** – piano + GRADY OWEN – drums repl. MAX, PAUL & TOMMY

Apr 58. (7") **BABY BLUE. / TRUE TO YOU**

1958. (lp) **A GENE VINCENT RECORD DATE**

– Five feet of lovin' / The wayward mind / Somebody help me / Keep it a secret / Hey good lookin' / Git it / Teenage partner / Peace of mind / Look what you gone and done to me / Summertime / I can't help it / I love you

— on tour **JUVEZ GOMEZ** – drums repl. HARRELL

— **BLUE CAPS:- HOWARD REED** – lead guitar / **BILL MACK** – bass / **MAX LIPSCOMB** – rhythm guitar / **CLIFF SIMMONS** – piano / **GRADY OWEN** – bass / **DUDE KAHN** – drums

Aug 58. (7") **ROCKY ROAD BLUES. / YES I LOVE YOU BABY**

— (Sep58) **JOHNNY MEEKS** – lead guitar returned to repl. REED / **CLYDE PENNINGTON** – drums repl. KAHN and D.J.FONTANA. (sax – **JACKIE KELSO**)

Oct 58. (7") **GIT IT. / LITTLE LOVER**

Oct 58. (lp) **SOUNDS LIKE GENE VINCENT**

–] My baby don't 'low / I can't believe you wanna leave / I might have known / In love again / You are the one for me / Ready Teddy / I got to you yet / Vincent's blues / Now is the hour / My heart / Maybelline.

Jan 59. (7") **SAY MAMA. / BE BOP BOOGIE BOY**

Mar 59. (7") **WHO'S PUSHIN' YOUR SWING. / OVER THE RAINBOW**

Jun 59. (7") **SUMMERTIME. / FRANKIE AND JOHNNY** -

— The BLUE CAPS had already disbanded late 1958.

GENE VINCENT

now solo augmented by **JACKIE MERRITT** – guitar / **SANDY NELSON** – drums / **JACKIE KELSO** – sax

Aug 59. (7") **RIGHT NOW. / THE NIGHT IS LONELY**

Dec 59. (7") **WILD CAT. / RIGHT HERE ON EARTH** 21

Feb 60. (7") **MY HEART. / I'VE GOT TO GET TO YOU YET** 16

May 60. (7") **PISTOL PACKIN' MAMA. / WEEPING WILLOW** 15 -

May 60. (lp) **CRAZY TIMES** 12 Sep 59

– Crazy times / She she little Sheila / Darlene / Everybody's got a date but me / Why don't you people learn how to drive / Green back dollar / Big fat Saturday night / Mitchiko from Tokyo / Hot dollar / Accentuate the postive / Blue eyes crying in the rain / Pretty Pearly. *(re-iss.+c.1970's on 'M.F.P.', re-iss.Oct87 on 'Tower')*

Oct 60. (7") **ANNA ANNABELLE. / PISTOL PACKIN' MAMA** -

Nov 60. (7") **ANNA ANNABELLE. / ACCENT-TCHUATE THE POSITIVE** -

Jan 61. (7") **JEZEBEL. / MAYBE**

Feb 61. (7") **IF YOU WANT LOVIN'. / MISTER LONELINESS**

May 61. (7") **SHE SHE LITTLE SHEILA. / HOT DOLLAR** 22 Jul 60

Aug 61. (7") **I'M GOING HOME. / LOVE OF A MAN** 36

Nov 61. (7") **BRAND NEW BEAT. / UNCHAINED MELODY**

Mar 62. (7") **LUCKY STAR. / BABY DON'T BELIEVE HIM**

Aug 62. (7") **KING OF FOOLS. / BE BOP A LULA 2 (with The CHARLES BLACKWELL ORCHESTRA)**

Feb 63. (7") **HELD FOR QUESTIONING. / YOU'RE STILL IN MY HEART**

Jul 63. (7") **CRAZY BEAT. / HIGH BLOOD PRESSURE**

Aug 63. (lp) **THE CRAZY BEAT OF GENE VINCENT**

– Crazy beat / Important words / It's been nice / Lonesome boy / Good lovin' / I'm gonna catch me a rat / Rip it up / High blood pressure / That's the trouble with love / Weeping willow / Tear drops / Gone, gone, gone. *(re-iss.1983 as 'CRAZY BEAT' on 'E.M.I.')*

— now w / **TIM BATES** – guitar, vocals / **JOHN REECE** – bass, vocals / **JEM FIELD** – tenor sax, vocals / **ERIC BAKER** – keyboards / **VICTOR CLARK** – drums, percussion

Columbia Columbia

Nov 63. (7") **WHERE HAVE YOU BEEN ALL MY LIFE. / TEMPTATION BABY**

Apr 64. (7") **HUMPITY DUMPITY. / LOVE 'EM LEAVE 'EM KINDA GUY**

Jul 64. (7") **LA DEN LA DEN DA DA. / BEGINNING OF THE END**

Sep 64. (7") **PRIVATE DETECTIVE. / YOU ARE MY SUNSHINE**

Oct 64. (lp) **SHAKIN' UP A STORM**

– Hey-hey-hey-hey / Lavender blue / Private detective / Shimmy shammy shingle / Someday (you'll want me to want you) / Another Saturday night / Slippin' and slidin' / Long tall Sally / Send me some lovin' / Love love love / Good golly, miss Molly / Baby blue / Susie Q / You are my sunshine. *(re-iss.+c.Jun83 as 'PLAYIN' UP A STORM' on 'E.M.I.')*

London Challenge

Sep 66. (7") **BIRD DOGGIN'. / AIN'T THAT MUCH TO DO**

Dec 66. (7") **LONELY STREET. / I'VE GOT MY EYES ON YOU**

Sep 67. (lp) **GENE VINCENT**

– I've got my eyes on you / Ain't that too much / Bird doggin' / Love is a bird / Lonely street / Hurtin' for you baby / Poor man's prison / Born to be a rolling stone / Hi lili hi lo / I'm a lonesome fugitive. *(re-iss.+c.Aug82 as 'BIRD-DOGGIN'' on 'Bulldog')*

1967. (7") **BORN TO BE A ROLLING STONE. / HURTIN' FOR YOU BABY** -

(re-iss. later on 'Playground')

not iss. Forever

1968. (7") **STORY TO THE ROCKERS. / PICKIN' POPPIES** -

— w / **MARS BONFIRE** – guitar / **GRANT JOHNSON** – keyboards / **RED RHODES** – steel guitar / **SKIP BATTIN** – bass / **JIM GORDON** – drums

Dandelion Elektra

1969. (7") **BE BOP A LULA '69. / RUBY BABY** -

Jan 70. (7") **WHITE LIGHTNING. / SCARLET RIBBONS** -

Jan 70. (lp) **I'M BACK AND I'M PROUD** -

– Rockin' Robin / In the pines / Be bop a lula / Rainbow at midnight / Black letter / White lightning / Sexy ways / Ruby baby / Lotta lovin' / Circle never broken / I heard that lonesome whistle / Scarlet ribbons. *(cd-iss.1987 on 'Nightlife Communications') (cd-iss.Dec94 on 'See For Miles')*

— now w/several musicians incl. **CHRIS DARROW**

Kama Sutra Kama Sutra

1970. (lp) **IF ONLY YOU COULD SEE ME TODAY**

– Sunshine / I need woman's love / Slow times comin' / Danse Colinda / Geese / 500 miles / Listen to the music / If only you could see me today / A million shades of blue.

Jan 70. (7") **SUNSHINE. / GEESE** -

above was recorded with UK band KANSAS HOOK early in Oct'71.

Nov 70. (7") **THE DAY THE WORLD TURNED BLUE. / HIGH OF LIFE** -

Jan 71. (lp) **THE DAY THE WORLD TURNED BLUE**

– How I love them old songs / High on life / North Carloina line / You can make it if you try / Our souls / Looking back / The day the world turned blue / Boppin' the blues / There is something on your mind / Oh lonesome me / The woman in black.

Jan 71. (7") **THE DAY THE WORLD TURNED BLUE. / HOW I LOVE THEM OLD SONGS** -

— Sadly on the 12th Oct'71, GENE VINCENT died of a bleeding ulcer. He was just 36.

– compilations, others, etc. –

All below on 'Capitol' unless otherwise stated.

1958. (7"ep) **HOT ROD GANG**
– Hot rod gang / Dance in the street / Baby blue / Lovely Loretta / Dance to the bop.

Nov 58. (7"ep) **A GENE VINCENT RECORD DATE No.1**
– Five feet of lovin' / The wayward wind / Somebody help me / Keep it a secret

Nov 58. (7"ep) **A GENE VINCENT RECORD DATE No.2**

Nov 58. (7"ep) **A GENE VINCENT RECORD DATE No.3**
– Look what you gone and done to me / Summertime / Peace of mind / I love you.

1960. (7"ep) **(CRAZY TIMES No.1)**
– If you want my lovin' / Hey good lookin' / Ain't she sweet / Hold me, hug me, rock me.

1960. (7"ep) **(CRAZY TIMES No.2)**
– Race with the Devil / Crazy legs / Yes I love you baby / Rocky road blues.

1960. (7"ep) **(CRAZY TIMES No.3)**
– True to you / She she little Sheila / Little lover / Weeping willow.

1963. (7"ep) **THE CRAZY BEAT OF GENE VINCENT No.1**
– Crazy beat / Important words / It's been nice / Lonesome boy / Good lovin' / I'm gonna catch me a rat / Rip it up / High blood pressure / That's the trouble with love / Weeping willow / Teardrops / Gone, gone, gone.

1963. (7"ep) **THE CRAZY BEAT OF GENE VINCENT No.2**
– Good lovin' / Gonna catch me a rat / Rip it up / High blood pressure.

1963. (7"ep) **THE CRAZY BEAT OF GENE VINCENT No.3**
– That's the trouble with love / Weeping willow / Teardrops / Gone gone gone.

Oct 67. (lp) **THE BEST OF GENE VINCENT**

May 68. (7") **BE BOP A LULA. / SAY MAMA** -

1969. (lp) **THE BEST OF GENE VINCENT VOL.2**

Feb 77. (7"m) **SAY MAMA. / LOTTA LOVIN' / RACE WITH THE DEVIL**

Feb 77. (lp)(c) **GENE VINCENT GREATEST**
(re-iss.May82 on 'Fame')

Jul 77. (lp)(c) **THE BOP JUST WON'T STOP 1956**
(re-iss.Jul82 on 'Magnum Force')

May 79. (lp)(c) **GENE VINCENT GREATEST VOL.2**

Apr 80. (lp)(c) **THE GENE VINCENT SINGLES ALBUM**
– (some cont.free 7"ep)

Jun 81. (7"m) **SHE SHE LITTLE SHEILA. / SAY MAMA / DANCE TO THE BOP** -

1981. (lp) **THEIR FINEST YEARS 1956-58 (shared w / EDDIE COCHRAN)** -
(re-iss.1983)

1983. (lp) **GENE SINGS VINCENT '56** -

1983. (lp) **GENE SINGS VINCENT '57-'59** -

1985. (lp) **ROCK'N'ROLL MASTERS** -

Oct 85. (lp)(c) **THE BEST OF GENE VINCENT AND HIS BLUE CAPS**
– Race with the Devil / Be-bop-a-lula / Woman love / I sure miss you / Crazy legs / Gonna back up baby / Who slapped John / Important words / Rollin' Dany / In my dreams / Baby blues '57 / Git it / Somebody help me / Summertime / Beautiful brown eyes / Say mama. *(cd-iss.Jul88)*

Sep 86. (lp)(cd) **THE SONGS OF THE JAMES DEAN ERA**

Aug 90. (6xcd-box) **THE GENE VINCENT BOX SET**
– (BE BOP A LULA / DANCE TO THE BOP / GIT IT / SAY MAMA / WILD CAT / KING OF . . .)

Jun 64. Starline; (lp) **THE KING OF FOOLS** -

1972. Starline; (lp) **THE PIONEERS OF ROCK VOL.1** -

1974. Starline; (lp) **THE PIONEERS OF ROCK VOL.4** -

1973. Pathe Marconi France;; (4xlp-box) **THE STORY OF GENE VINCENT VOL.1 (1956-57), VOL.2 (1958), VOL.3 (1959) & VOL.4 (1960-62)** - -

Oct 73. Spark; (7") **STORY OF THE ROCKERS. / PICKIN' POPPIES** -

Sep 74. BBC; (7"ep) **ROLL OVER BEETHOVEN. / SAY MAMA / BE BOP A LULA (all live from Johnny Walker's Radio 1 show 1971)** -

Feb 80. MFP; (lp)(c) **ROCK ON WITH GENE VINCENT** -

Apr 86. MFP; (lp)(c) **GENE VINCENT: ROCK'N'ROLL GREATS** -

Jan 81. Magnum Force; (7"ep) **RAINY DAY SUNSHINE / GREEN GRASS. / MISTER LOVE / ROLL OVER BEETHOVEN** -

Nov 82. Magnum Force; (m-lp) **DRESSED IN BLACK** -

Nov 83. Magnum Force; (lp) **FROM L.A. TO FRISCO** -

Jun 84. Magnum Force; (lp) **FOR THE COLLECTOR'S ONLY** (live + interviews) -

1988. Magnum Force; (lp) **LONESOME FUGITIVE** -

1983. EMI; (lp) **20 ROCK'N'ROLL HITS** -

1983. EMI; (lp) **GENE VINCENT MEMORIAL ALBUM** -

1983. EMI; (lp) **ROCK'N'ROLL LEGENDS** -

Sep 90. EMI; (6xcd-box) **THE GENE VINCENT BOXED SET** -

1984. Premier; (lp)(c) **AIN'T THAT TOO MUCH** -

Jan 85. Topline; (c) **BORN TO BE A ROLLING STONE** -
(re-iss.lp+cd.Apr87)

Apr 86. Castle; (lp)(c) **BABY BLUE** -

Jul 87. Nighttracks; (12"ep) **THE LAST SESSION** -

Oct 87. Demand; (lp) **SINGS SONGS FROM THE HOT ROD GANG** -

Nov 87. Charly; (9xlp-box; w/ 12"ep) **THE CAPITOL YEARS** -

Nov 87. Exclusive; (pic-lp) **THE ABC OF ROCK** -

Jul 88. See For Miles; (lp)(c)(cd) **INTO THE SEVENTIES** -

May 89. See For Miles; (lp)(c)(cd) **THE EP COLLECTION** -

1985. Rockstar; (lp) **CRUISIN' WITH GENE VINCENT** -

Nov 89. Rockstar; (mail order-lp) **IMPORTANT WORDS** -

1989. Object; (cd) **BE BOP A LULA** -

1990. Capitol; (cd)(c)(lp) **GENE VINCENT: COLLECTORS SERIES** -

Jun 94. Rockhouse; (cd) **GENE'S ON THE JUKEBOX** -

Aug 94. Dynamite; (cd) **GENE VINCENT**

VINEGAR JOE (see under ⇒ BROOKS, Elkie)

VIOLENT FEMMES

Formed: Milwalkee, Wisconson, USA . . . 1982 by GORDON GANO, BRIAN RITCHIE and VICTOR DE LORENZO. Discovered by JAMES HONEYMAN-SCOTT (of The PRETENDERS) and signed to 'Slash' in the States, which gained licence from UK indie label 'Rough Trade' for release in 1983. Gained rave reviews after release of their eponymous debut in 1983. • **Style:** Country cowpunk with VELVET UNDERGROUND in the late 60's an influence. • **Songwriters:** All written by GANO-RITCHIE, except CHILDREN OF THE REVOLUTION (T.Rex), DO YOU REALLY WANT TO HURT ME (Culture Club). • **Trivia:** MARK VAN HECKE produced them until 1986, when JERRY HARRISON (Talking Heads) took over and also played guitar + organ.

Recommended: VIOLENT FEMMES (*7) / ADD IT UP (1981-1993) (*8)

GORDON GANO (b. 7 Jun'63, New York, USA) – vocals, guitar / **BRIAN RITCHIE** (b.21 Nov'60) – bass / **VICTOR DE LORENZO** (b.25 Oct'54, Raccine, Wisconsin) – drums

Rough Trade Slash

Sep 83. (lp) **VIOLENT FEMMES**
– Blister in the Sun / Kiss off / Please do not go / Add it up / Confessions / Prove my love / Promise / To the kill / Gone daddy gone / Good feeling. *(re-iss.+c+cd.Jan89 & Aug91 on 'Slash-London' +US)*
(cd+=) – Ugly / Gimme the feeling.

Dec 83. (7") **UGLY. / GIMME THE CAR**
(12"+=) – Good feeling / Gone daddy gone.

Slash-London Slash

Jun 84. (7") **GONE DADDY GONE. / ADD IT UP**
(12"+=) – Jesus walkin' on the water.

Jul 84. (lp)(c) **HALLOWED GROUND**
– Country death song / I hear the rain / Never tell / Jesus walking on the water / I know it's true but I'm sorry to say / Hallowed ground / Sweet misery blues / Black girls / It's gonna rain.

Sep 84. (7") **IT'S GONNA RAIN. / JESUS WALKING ON THE WATER**
(12"+=) – Prove my love.

Feb 86. (7") **CHILDREN OF THE REVOLUTION. / HEARTACHE**
(12"+=) – Good feeling.

Feb 86. (lp)(c) **THE BLIND LEADING THE NAKED** 81 84
– Old Mother Reagan / No killing / Breakin' hearts / Special / Love and me make three / Candlelight song / I held her in my arms / Children of the revolution / Good friend / Heartache / Cold canyon / Two people. (cd+=) – Country death song / Black girls / World without mercy.

Apr 86. (7") **CHILDREN OF THE REVOLUTION. / WORLD WITHOUT MERCY** -

—— Disbanded in 1988. GORDON and VICTOR joined EUGENE CHADBOURNE (of SHOCKABILLY). BRIAN RITCHIE went solo (see below).

Jan 89. (lp)(c)(cd) **3** 93
– Nightmares / Just like my father / Dating days / Fat / Fool in the full Moon / Nothing worth living for / World we're living in / Outside the palace / Telephone book / Mother of a girl / See my ships.

—— added **MICHAEL BEINHORN** – keyboards, producer

May 91. (7")(c-s) **AMERICAN MUSIC. / PROMISE (live)**
(extended-12"+=) – Kiss off (live).
(cd-s++=) – Promise (live).

May 91. (cd)(c)(lp) **WHY DO BIRDS SING?**
– American music / Out the window / Do you really want to hurt me? / Hey nonny nonny / Polygran used to be / Girl trouble / He likes me / Life is a scream / Flamingo baby / Lack of knowledge / More money tonight / I'm free.

Sep 91. (7"ep)(12"ep)(cd-ep) **DO YOU REALLY WANT TO HURT ME? / DANCE, MOTHERFUCKER, DANCE / TO THE KILL** -

Oct 93. (cd)(c) **ADD IT UP (1981-1993)** (compilation)
– Intro / Waiting for the bus / Blister in the Sun / Gone daddy gone / Gordon's message / Gimme the car / Country death song / Black girls / Jesus walking on the water / 36-24-36 / I held her in my arms / I hate the T.V. / American is / Old mother Reagan / Degradation / Dance, mother f***er, dance / Lies / American / Out the window / Kiss off / Add it up / Vancouver / Johnny.

—— **GUY HOFFMAN** – drums (ex-BODEANS) repl. VICTOR + MICHAEL

Elektra Elektra

May 94. (cd)(c) **NEW TIMES** 90
– Don't start me on the liquor / New times / Breakin' up / Key of Z / 4 seasons / Machine / I'm nothing / When everybody's happy / Agememnon / This island life / I saw you in the crowd / Mirror mirror (I see a damsel) / Jesus of Rio.

BRIAN RITCHIE

had gone solo in-between breaks.

S.S.T. S.S.T.

Oct 87. (lp,cd) **THE BLEND**
– Alphabet / Arab song / Austrian anthill / Days of the blend / Doin' the best we can / Feast of fools / John the revelator / Nuclear war / Song of the highest tower / The toad / Two fat dogs.

1988. (12") **NUCLEAR WAR (Deutsch). / ('A'-English version) / ALPHABET** -

1988. (12"ep) **ATOMKRIEG. / ?** -

Feb 89. (12"ep)(c-ep) **SUN RA MAN FROM OUTER SPACE. / ?** -

Feb 89. (lp)(cd) **SONIC TEMPLE AND THE COURT OF BABYLON**
– Bells / Sonic temple and the court of Babylon / Why did you lie to me? / Sun Ra from Outer Space / Dance*? / Christian for one day / A.D. / Mayerling (let's drink some wine) / No resistin' a Christian / So it goes / Hasan I sabbah / Reach out.

not issued Dali

1990. (cd) **I SEE A NOISE** -

– Eva / 2 tongues, 2 minds / Please don't cry for me / Why is that baby's head so big? / Song without any end / Quo Vadis / Animals / The man with the cigarette in his nose / Religion ruined my life / Song of the cricket / I see a noise.

VIRGIN PRUNES

Formed: Dublin, Ireland . . . 1977 by GAVIN FRIDAY, who had originally been invited by BONO (later of U2) to join a rough social club titled VILLAGE. After a couple of releases in the early 80's, they move to 'Rough Trade'. After a series of singles in the 3 parts under title of 'NEW FORM OF BEAUTY'. This preceeded their debut lp in 1982 'IF I DIE, I DIE', which hit the top of the indie charts. It took 4 years for a follow-up, the DAVE BALL (of SOFT CELL) produced 'THE MOON LOOKED DOWN AND LAUGHED', which showed change of direction. • **Style:** Performance art group into religion and theatrical gothic stage shows. • **Songwriters:** GAVIN FRIDAY, who also launched solo career in 1989 and covered NEXT (Jacques Brel) / DEATH IS NOT THE END (Bob Dylan) / THE SLIDER (T.Rex). • **Trivia:** DIK EVANS is the brother of THE EDGE (U2). GAVIN wrote 3 songs for model NAOMI CAMPBELL's 'Babywoman' album.

Recommended: IF I DIE, I DIE (*8)

GAVIN FRIDAY (b.FIONAN HANVEY) – vocals / **GUGGI** (b.DEREK ROWEN) – vocals / **DAVE-ID BUSARAS SCOTT** (b.DAVID WATSON) – narrator / **DIK EVANS** – guitar / **STRONGMAN** (b.TREVOR ROWAN) – bass / **POD** (b.ANTHONY MURPHY) – drums

Romans In Britain / not issued

Dec 80. (7") **JIGSAW MENTALLAMA. / ('B'by HIGSONS)** [ ] [-]

Baby / not issued

Jan 81. (7"ep) **TWENTY TENS** [ ] [-]
– I've been smoking all night / Revenge / The children are crying.

— **HAA LACKI BINTTII** – percussion, electronics repl. POD

Rough Trade / not issued

Jul 81. (7"ep) **IN THE GREYLIGHT. / WAR / MOMENTS AND MINE (DESPITE STRANGE LINES)** [ ] [-]

Oct 81. (7"ep) **NEW FORM OF BEAUTY PART ONE** [ ] [-]
– Sandpaper lullaby / Sleep / Fantasy dreams.

Nov 81. (10"ep) **NEW FORM OF BEAUTY PART TWO** [ ] [-]
– Come to daddy / Sweet home under white clouds / Sad world.

Feb 82. (12"ep) **NEW FORM OF BEAUTY PART THREE** [ ] [-]
– The beast (seven bastard suck) / The slow children (Abbagal) / Brain damage / No birds to fly. *(above 3 singles issued as 3x7"boxed-set) (cd-iss.Jan94 on 'New Rose')*

Apr 82. (7") **PAGAN LOVE SONG. / DAVE-ID IS DEAD** [ ] [-]
(12") – Pagan love song (vibe akimbo). / ('B'side).

— male **MARY O'NELLON** – drums repl. HAA LACKI who became PRINCESS TINYMEAT

Oct 82. (7") **(WHAT SHOULD WE DO WHEN) BABY TURNS BLUE. / YEO** [ ] [-]
(12"+=) – Chance of a lifetime.

Nov 82. (lp) **IF I DIE, I DIE** [ ] [-]
– Ulakennalmloy / Decline and fall / Sweet home under white clouds / Bau-Dachong / Pagan love song / Baby turns blue / Ballad of the man / Walls of Jericho / Caucasian walk / Theme for thought. *(cd-iss.Jun90 on 'Rough Trade')*

— GUGGI and DIK departed.

Baby / not issued

1983. (2x10"lp) **HERESIE** [ ] [-]
– We love Dierdre / Rhetoric / Down the memory lane / Man on the corner / Nisam Lo / Loved one / Got away Dierdre / LIVE IN PARIS (parts 1 & 2). *(cd-iss.Jan94 on 'New Rose')*

Apr 85. (lp) **OVER THE RAINBOW (RARITIES 1981-83)** [ ] [-]
– Down the memory lane / Red nettle / Mad bird in the wood / Jigsawmentallama / The king of junk / Just a love song / The happy head / Third secret / Heresie / We love Deirdre / Rhetoric / Man on the corner / Nisam lo / Loved one / Go 'T' away Deirdre. *(cd-iss.of 2 above; Feb88)*

— GAVIN FRIDAY made guest appearances for The FALL on 1984's 'CALL FOR ESCAPE ROUTE' 12", and 'WONDERFUL AND FRIGHTENING WORLD OF . . . ' album.

— In 1986, The VIRGIN PRUNES were back with **GAVIN, MARY** (now guitar), **DAVE-ID, STRONGMAN** and the returning **POD** – drums

Jun 86. (7") **LOVE LASTS FOREVER. / LOVE LORNALIMBO** [ ] [-]
(12") – ('A'side) / I like the way you're frightened.

1986. (lp) **THE MOON LOOKED DOWN AND LAUGHED** [ ] [ ]
– Heaven / Love lasts forever / I am God / Sons find devils / Alone / The Moon looked down and laughed / Uncle Arthur's lonely world / Don't look back / Betrayal / Deadly sins. *(cd-iss.Jan94 on 'New Rose')*

Nov 86. (7") **DON'T LOOK BACK. / WHITE HISTORY BOOK** [ ] [-]
(12"+=) – Day of ages.

May 87. (lp)(c)(cd) **THE HIDDEN LIE – LIVE IN PARIS** (live June '86) [ ] [-]
– Sweet home (under white clouds) / Lady day / God bless the child (with RAY CHARLES) / Never ending story / Pagan love song / Love is danger / The Moon looked down and laughed / Caucasian walk / The blues song. *(cd re-iss.Jan94 on 'New Rose')*

— In 1988, they became The PRUNES and issued 2 albums 'LITE FANTASTIC' & 'NADA' (1989) on 'Baby'.

– compilations, etc. –

Jan 94. New Rose; (cd) **PAGAN LOVESONG** [ ] [-]
Jan 94. New Rose; (cd) **ARTF**K** [ ] [-]

GAVIN FRIDAY

went solo augmented by **SIMON CARMODY**

Baby / not issued

Aug 87. (7"colrd) **YOU CAN'T ALWAYS GET WHAT YOU WANT. / BLESSINGS** [ ] [-]

GAVIN FRIDAY & THE MAN SEEZER

with **MAN SEEZER** – keyboards / **MARC RIBOT** – guitar, banjo + **MICHAEL BLAIR** – drums, percussion (both of TOM WAITS' band) / **BILL FRISELL** – guitar / **FERNANDO SAUNDERS** – bass, guitar + **HANK ROBERTS** – cello (both of LOU REED's band)

Island / Island

May 89. (7") **EACH MAN KILLS THE THINGS HE LOVES. / EXTRACT FROM THE BALLAD OF READING GAOL** [ ] [-]
(12"+=) – ('A'instrumental).

May 89. (lp)(c)(cd) **EACH MAN KILLS THE THINGS HE LOVES** [ ] [ ]
– Each man kills the things he loves / He got what he wanted / Tell tale heart / Man of misfortune / Apologia / Dazzle and delight / Rags to riches / The next thing to murder / Love is just a word / You take away the Sun / Another blow on the bruise / Death is not the end.

Aug 89. (7") **YOU TAKE AWAY THE SUN. / THE NEXT THING TO MURDER** [ ] [ ]
(12"+=)/ /(cd-s++=) – Love is just a word. / / ('A'version).

Mar 90. (7") **MAN OF MISFORTUNE. / EACH MAN KILLS THE THING HE LOVES** [ ] [ ]
(cd-s+=) – You take away the Sun.

GAVIN FRIDAY

(solo) with The BIG NO NO: **MAURICE SEEZER / DANNY BLUME** – guitar (ex-KID CREOLE) / **ERIK SANTO** (ex-LOUNGE LIZARDS)

Island / Island

Feb 92. (7") **I WANT TO LIVE. / LAUGH, CLOWN, LAUGH** [ ] [ ]
(c-s+=)(cd-s+=) – He got what he wanted.

Mar 92. (cd)(c)(lp) **ADAM 'N' EVE** [ ] [ ]
– I want to live / Falling off the edge of the world / King of trash / Why say goodbye? / Saint Divine / Melancholy baby / Fun & experience / The big no no / Where in the world? / Wind and rain / Eden.

Apr 92. (7")(c-s) **KING OF TRASH. / REX MORTUS EST** [ ] [ ]
(12"+=)(cd-s+=) – Geek love.

Sep 92. (7")(c-s) **FALLING OFF THE EDGE OF THE WORLD. / SIBYL VANE'S SUICIDE** [ ] [ ]
(12"+=)(cd-s+=) – Wake up screaming.

— Above 'A'side was a duet with MARIA McKEE.

Mar 94. (7")(c-s) **IN THE NAME OF THE FATHER. ("BONO & GAVIN FRIDAY") / EDEN** [ ] [ ]
(12"+=)(cd-s+=) – (2 'A'mixes).

— Above from the film of the same name.

Aug 95. (cd)(c) **SHAG TOBACCO** [ ] [ ]
– Shag tobacco / Caruso / Angel / Little black dress / The slider / Dolls / Mr.Pussy / You, me and World War Three / Kitchen sink drama / My twentieth century / The last song I'll ever sing / Le roi d'amour.

Oct 95. (cd-s) **ANGEL / ('A'-Space hop mix) / A THOUSAND YEARS / MACUSHLA** [ ] [ ]
(12") – (first 2 tracks) / ('A'-Space Hop dub) / ('A'-Fallen mix).
(12")(cd-s) – ('A'side) / ('A'-Tim Simenon mix) / ('A'-Howie B mix) / ('A'-Danny Gee mix).

VISAGE

Formed: London, England . . . 1979 as a studio outlet for entrepreneur / rich kid STEVE STRANGE, who in his punk heyday, had roadied for GENERATION X. First recorded 'IN THE YEAR 2525' as duo with MIDGE URE. It was turned down by 'EMI' late 1978, but undeterred the pair brought in some friends and signed deal with 'Radar'. After one flop 45 'TAR', they were dropped by label. 'Polydor' came to the rescue in 1980 and deserved success was with them the following year on classy 'FADE TO GREY' 45. MIDGE was now a member of ULTRAVOX and combined both activities throughout early 80's. • **Style:** One of initial outfits to be termed as "new romantics", with their fusion of electro-pop and extroverted gayish fashion. • **Songwriters:** All written by STEVE with MIDGE URE and RUSTY EGAN collaborating. Covered IN THE YEAR 2525 (Zager-Evans) / STRANGE CRUISE: – THE BEAT GOES ON (Sonny & Cher). • **Trivia:** GODLEY & CREME made their debut video for MIND OF A TOY single.

Recommended: FADE TO GREY – THE SINGLES (*6)

STEVE STRANGE (b.HARRINGTON, 28 May'59, Wales) – vocals (ex-MOORS MURDERERS) / **MIDGE URE** (b.JAMES URE, 10 Oct'53, Cambuslang, Scotland) – guitar (ex-SLIK, ex-PVC2, ex-RICH KIDS) / with **RUSTY EGAN** (b.19 Sep'57) – drums (ex-RICH KIDS, etc.) / **BILLY CURRIE** (b. 1 Apr'52) – keyboards, synth. (also of ULTRAVOX) /also at various times **DAVE FORMULA / JOHN McGEOGH / BARRY ADAMSON** (all of MAGAZINE)

Radar / not issued

Oct 79. (7") **TAR. / FREQUENCY 7** [ ] [-]

Polydor / Polydor

Dec 80. (7")(12") **FADE TO GREY. / THE STEPS** [8] [ ]

Jan 81. (lp)(c) **VISAGE** [13] [ ]
– Visage / Blocks on blocks / The dancer / Tar / Fade to grey / Malpaso man / Mind of a toy / Moon over Moscow / The steps. *(cd-iss.Jan83 & May91)*

Mar 81. (7") **MIND OF A TOY. / WE MOVE** [13] [ ]
(12"+=) – Frequency 7.

Jul 81. (7")(12") **VISAGE (remix). / SECOND STEPS** 21
Mar 82. (7")(12") **THE DAMNED DON'T CRY. / MOTIVATION** 11
Mar 82. (lp)(c) **THE ANVIL** 6
– The damned don't cry / The anvil (night club school) / Move up / Night train / The horseman / Look what they've done / Again we love / Wild life / Whispers. *(cd-iss.Jan83)*
Jun 82. (7")(7"pic-d) **NIGHT TRAIN. / I'M STILL SEARCHING** 12
(12"+=) – ('A'dub mix).
Nov 82. (7")(7"pic-d) **PLEASURE BOYS. / THE ANVIL** 44
(12") – ('A'pleasure mix) / ('B'side)
Oct 83. (lp)(c) **FADE TO GREY – THE SINGLES** (compilation) 38
– Fade to grey / Mind of a toy / Visage / We move / Tar / In the year 2525 / The anvil / Night train / Pleasure boys / The damned don't cry.

— **STEVE + RUSTY** with new members **GARY BARNACLE** – saxophone, keyboards / **MARSHA RAVEN** – vocals / **ANDY BARNETT** – bass
Aug 84. (7")(12") **LOVE GLOVE. / SHE'S A MACHINE** 54
Sep 84. (lp)(c) **BEAT BOY** 79
– Beat boy / Casualty / Questions / Only the good (die young) / Can you hear me / The promise / Love glove / Yesterday's shadow.
Nov 84. (7")(12") **BEAT BOY. / ('A'dub mix)**

— Split around same time.

– compilations, others, etc. –

Feb 83. Polydor; (d-c) **VISAGE / THE ANVIL** -
Aug 93. Polydor; (7")(12")(c-s)(cd-s) **FADE TO GREY. / ('A'mixes)** 39
Nov 93. Polydor; (cd)(c) **THE BEST OF VISAGE**
Mar 86. Old Gold; (7") **FADE TO GREY. / MIND OF A TOY** -
Feb 88. Old Gold; (7") **THE DAMNED DON'T CRY. / MIND OF A TOY** -
(12"+=) – Night train.

STEVE STRANGE

solo recorded 1978.

Stiff / not issued
Jun 82. (7") **IN THE YEAR 2525. / STRANGE CONNECTION** -

STRANGE CRUISE

STEVE with **WENDY WU** – vocals (ex-PHOTOS) with **PETER MURRAY** – keyboards / **STEVE BARNACLE** – bass / **PETE BARNACLE** – drums / **FRANKIE BARNACLE** – guitar

E.M.I. / not issued
Feb 86. (7")(12") **REBEL BLUE ROCKER. / LOVE ADDICTIONS** -
Jun 86. (7") **THE BEAT GOES ON. / SILVER SCREEN** -
Aug 86. (lp)(c) **STRANGE CRUISE** -
– Hit and run / The beat goes on / Rebel blue rocker / This old town / Communication / Animal call / Love addiction / 12 mile high / Where were the hearts / Heart is a lonely runner.

— STEVE retired from music scene. In 1987 while still a part of Stringfellows night-club, he was stabbed although not fatally by intruders.

VIXEN

Formed: Based in Los Angeles, California, USA ... 1987 female quartet. Signed to EMI subsidiary label 'Manhattan' in 1988, after ROXY had paraded her wares for 'Playboy' the preceding year. Were darlings of the metal charts during late 80's-early 90's. • **Style:** 'The Barbie Dolls of Metal', bringing glamour back to hard rock. Similiar sound to HEART, with image of ROCK GODDESS. • **Songwriters:** Mainly used outside pen-smiths aka JEFF PARIS. EDGE OF A BROKEN HEART was written for them by RICHARD MARX and FEE WAYBILL (The TUBES). DIANE WARREN penned IT WOULDN'T BE LOVE. • **Trivia:** Original bassist PIA KOKO is wife of guitarist STEVE VAI.

Recommended: VIXEN (*5)

JANET GARDNER (b.21 Mar'62, Alaska, USA) – vocals, rhythm guitar / **JAN KUEHNEMUND** – lead guitar / **SHARE PEDERSON** (b.21 Mar'63, Minnesota, USA) – bass repl. PIA KOKO / **ROXY PETRUCCI** (b.17 Mar'62, Detroit, USA) – drums

Manhattan / Manhattan
Aug 88. (7")(7"sha-pic-d) **EDGE OF A BROKEN HEART. / CHARMED LIFE** 51 26
(12"+=) – ('A'extended).
(12") – ('A'side) / Love made me (live) / Cryin' (live). *(re-iss.Aug89 on 'EMI USA', UK 59)*
Sep 88. (lp)(c)(cd) **VIXEN** 66 41
– Edge of a broken heart / I want you to rock me / Cryin' / American dream / Desperate / One night alone / Hellraisers / Love made me / Waiting / Cruisin'. *(cd+=)*– Charmed life. *(re-iss.Aug91 on 'Fame')*
Feb 89. (7")(7"sha-pic-d) **CRYIN'. / DESPERATE** 27 22 Jan 89
(12"+=)(12"pic-d+=) – ('A'extended).
(cd-s+=) – Give it away / Edge of a broken heart.

EMI USA / EMI USA
May 89. (7")(7"sha-pic-d) **LOVE MADE ME (remix). / GIVE IT AWAY** 36
(12"+=)(cd-s+=)(12"pic-d+=) – Cruisin'(live) / Edge of a broken heart (live) / Hellraisers (live).
Jul 90. (7") **HOW MUCH LOVE. / WRECKING BALL** 35 44
(12"+=)(cd-s+=)(12"pic-d+=) – Bad reputation.
Aug 90. (cd)(c)(lp) **REV IT UP** 20 52
– Rev it up / How much love / Love is a killer / Not a moment too soon / Streets in Paradise / Hard 16 / Bad reputation / Fallen hero / Only a heartbeat away / It wouldn't be love / Wrecking ball.
Oct 90. (7")(c-s) **LOVE IS A KILLER. / STREETS IN PARADISE** 41 71
(10"+=) – Edge of a broken heart (live acoustic version).
(cd-s++=) – I want you to rock me (live).
(12"pic-d+=) – The jam (live) / I want you to rock me (live).
Mar 91. (7")(c-s) **NOT A MINUTE TOO SOON. / FALLEN HERO** 37
('A'ext-12"+=)(12"pic-d+=)(cd-s+=) – Desperate (demo).
(10"+=)(cd-s+=) – Give it away (demo).

— (Nov91) Nearly folded when ROXY left to form/join group MAXINE.

VOICE OF THE BEEHIVE

Formed: London, England ... 1985 by Beverley Hill-girlies TRACEY and MELISSA (daughters of FOUR PREPS singer BRUCE BELAND). Moved to England in the mid-80's and befriended grebo-metaller ZODIAC MINDWARP. Took name from a Bette Davis movie and signed to Dave Balfe and Andy Ross's 'Food' label. Became hit band from 1987 onwards. • **Style:** Intelligent pop-rock similar to BLONDIE, The B-52's or PRETENDERS. • **Songwriters:** T.BRYN lyrics / music by her, JONES, BROOKE and BRETT. The latter took over from BEDDERS who left 1987. Covers:- D'YER MAKER (Led Zeppelin) / INDEPENDENCE DAY (Comsat Angels / IN THE FLESH (Blondie) / I THINK I LOVE YOU (hit; Partridge Family) / LITTLE GODS (Marvin Etzioni) / SAY IT (Jesus Jones) / SIT DOWN (James). • **Trivia:** The sisters were once TV ad child actresses.

Recommended: HONEY LINGERS (*8) / LET IT BEE (*8).

TRACEY BRYN (b.TRACEY BELLAND, 17 May'62, Encino, California) – vox, guitar / **MELISSA BROOKE BELLAND** (b. 6 Feb'66, Los Angeles, California) – vocals / **MICK JONES** – guitar, vocals, keyboards / **MARK 'Bedders' BEDFORD** (b.24 Aug'61, London) – bass (ex-MADNESS) / **DAN 'Woody' WOODGATE** (b.19 Oct'60, London) – drums (ex-MADNESS)

Food / not issued
Mar 87. (7") **JUST A CITY. / I WALK THE EARTH** -
(12"+=) – 7 shocks.

London / London
Apr 87. (7") **JUST A CITY. / 7 SHOCKS**
(12"+=) – D'yer maker.

— **MARTIN BRETT** – bass, piano repl. BEDDERS who formed BUTTERFIELD 8
Sep 87. (7") **I SAY NOTHING. / THINGS YOU SEE WHEN YOU DON'T HAVE YOUR GUN (live)** 45
(12"+=) – Independence day.
(d12"+=) – 7 shocks / Any day of the week.
Feb 88. (7") **I WALK THE EARTH. / THIS WEAK** 42
(d7"+=)(12"+=)(cd-s+=) – Jesus / No green blues.
May 88. (7")(7"pic-d) **DON'T CALL ME BABY. / JUMP THIS WAY** 15
(12"+=) – Goodbye tonight.
(d7"++=)(10"++=)(cd-s++=)(pic-cd-s++=) – I say nothing.
Jun 88. (lp)(c)(cd) **LET IT BEE** 13
– The beat of love / Sorrow floats / Don't call me baby / The man in the Moon / What you have is enough / Oh love / I walk the Earth / Trust me / I say nothing / There's a barbarian in the back of my car / Just a city.
Jul 88. (7") **I SAY NOTHING. / THINGS YOU SEE WHEN YOU DON'T HAVE YOUR GUN (live)** 22
(12"+=)(cd-s+=) – Don't call me baby / In the flesh.
Oct 88. (7") **I WALK THE EARTH. / THIS WEAK** 46
(d7"+=) – Don't call me baby / I say nothing.
(12"+=)(cd-s+=)(10"clear+=) – The tattoo song / Everything I had.
Dec 88. (7") **THE MAN IN THE MOON. / WHAT YOU HAVE IS ENOUGH** 9
(12"+=)(cd-s+=) – 7 shocks (live) / There's a barbarian in the back of my car (live).
Jun 91. (7")(c-s) **MONSTERS AND ANGELS. / ONLY IF YOU WANT TO** 17 74
(12"+=)(cd-s+=) – Waitress / Pocketsize.
Aug 91. (cd)(c)(lp) **HONEY LINGERS** 17
– Monsters and angels / Adonis blue / I think I love you / Look at me / Beauty to my eyes / Just like you / Little gods / I'm shooting cupid / Say it / Perfect place.
Sep 91. (7")(c-s) **I THINK I LOVE YOU. / SOMETHING ABOUT GOD** 25
(12"+=) – ('A'remix) / Say it / Don't call me baby / VB – Goddess of love / Orgy.
Jan 92. (7")(c-s) **PERFECT PLACE. / SIT DOWN (live) / SHINE AWAY** 37
(10"pic-d+=) – Trust me (live).
(cd-s) – (first 2 tracks) / I say nothing (live) / Just a city (live).

East West / East West
Jul 95. (c-s) **ANGEL COME DOWN / CARTOON CITY**
(cd-s+=) – Inconsistencies.

– compilations, others, etc. –

Feb 89. Strange Fruit; (12"ep)(cd-ep) **THE EVENING SHOW SESSIONS** (26.2.88) -
– No green blues / Jump this way / Independence day / Jesus.

Mark VOLMAN & Howard KAYLAN

(see under ⇒ TURTLES)

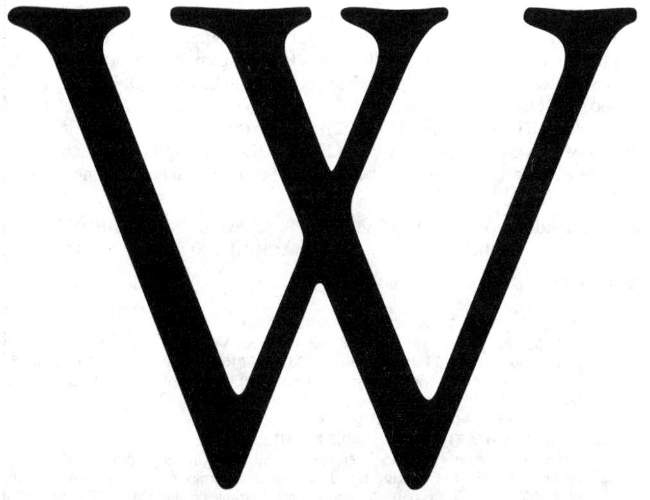

WAH!

Formed: Liverpool, England . . . early '79 as WAH! HEAT by ex-CRUCIAL THREE member PETE WYLIE. In 1980 they issued 2 singles on a local indie label, before signing to 'WEA' subsidiary label 'Eternal'. Their debut album, broke them into the UK Top 40 lists for the first time, but by 1985, the dream was over. • **Style:** Classy new wave/rock outfit, who leant on Spector-type "wall of sound" inspiration for their 1982 Top 3 hit 'THE STORY OF THE BLUES'. • **Songwriters:** All written by WYLIE. • **Trivia:** WYLIE's late 70's trio The CRUCIAL THREE, also included JULIAN COPE and IAN McCULLOCH.

Recommended: THE WAY WE WAH! (*7)

WAH! HEAT

PETE WYLIE (b.22 Mar'58) – vocals, guitar (ex-CRUCIAL THREE) / **ROB 'Jonie' JONES** – drums (ex-CRASH COURSE, w/Pete Wylie) / **PETE YOUNGER** – bass (ex-THOSE NAUGHTY LUMPS) repl. COLIN WILLIAMS + J.CULT

Inevitable | not issued

Jan 80. (7") **BETTER SCREAM. / (HEY DISCO) JOE** [ ] [-]

— **WYLIE** brought in **KING BLUFF** – keyboards, synth. / **CARL WASHINGTON** – bass repl. YOUNGER / **JOE MUSKER** – drums (ex-DEAD OR ALIVE) repl. JONES to The HIGH FIVE. On tour **COLIN REDMOND** – guitar (same label)

Nov 80. (7") **SEVEN MINUTES TO MIDNIGHT. / DON'T STEP ON THE CRACKS** [ ] [-]

WAH!

PAUL BARLOW – drums (of IT'S IMMATERIAL) repl. MUSKER

Eternal-WEA | not issued

Jun 81. (7") **FORGET THE DOWN!. / THE CHECKMATE SYNDROME** [ ] [ ]

Jul 81. (lp)(c) **NAH! POO! THE ART OF BLUFF** [33] [ ]
– The wind-up / Other boys / Why'd you imitate the cut-out / Mission impossible / Somesay / The seven thousand names of Wah! / Sleeep (a lullaby for Josie) / Seven minutes to midnight / The death of Wah!.

— **HENRY PRIESTMAN** – keyboards (of IT'S IMMATERIAL) repl. BLUFF

Oct 81. (7")(12") **SOMESAY. / FORGET THE DOWN** [ ] [-]

Apr 82. (7") **REMEMBER. (as "SHAMBEKO! SAY WAH!") / A CRACK IS A CRACK** [ ] [-]

— **WYLIE + WASHINGTON** enlist **CHARLIE GRIFFITHS** – synth. / **JAY NAUGHTON** – piano / **CHRIS JOYCE** – drums (ex-DURUTTI COLUMN, etc.) / **The SAPPHIRES** – back vox

Nov 82. (7") **THE STORY OF THE BLUES. / TALKIN' BLUES** [3] [ ]
(12"+=) – Seven minutes to midnight (live).

Mar 83. (7") **HOPE (I WISH YOU'D BELIEVE ME). / SLEEEP** [37] [ ]
(12"+=) – You can't put your arms around a memory / Year of decision / Le spwah.

The MIGHTY WAH!

(same label)

Jul 84. (7")(12") **COME BACK (THE STORY OF THE REDS). / DEVIL IN MISS JONES** [20] [ ]

Jul 84. (lp)(c) **A WORD TO THE WISE GUY** [28] [ ]
– Yuh learn I / Weekends / Everwanna / The lost generation / Yuh learn II / I know there was something / Yuh learn III / In the bleak – (Body and soul) – Midwinter / Papa crack – God's lonely man / What's happening here / Yuh learn IV / Come back (the story of the reds). *(re-iss.+cd.Jan89)*

Sep 84. (7") **WEEKENDS. / SHAMBEKO (THE LOST GENERATION)** [ ] [ ]
(12"+=) – Body and soul (acoustic) / Something wrong with Eddie / Weekend (original).

Nov 84. (lp)(c) **THE WAY WE WAH!** (compilation) [ ] [-]
– Other boys / Somesay / The seven thousand names of Wah! / Seven minutes to midnight / The death of Wah! / The story of the blues parts 1 & 2 / Sleeep (a lullaby for Josie) / You can't put your arms around a memory / Hope (remix) / Remember.

— Had already split in 1984. CHRIS JOYCE joined SIMPLY RED.

– compilations, others, etc. –

Nov 83. White Label; (lp) **THE MAVERICK YEARS 80-81 (the official bootleg)** [ ] [-]

Sep 87. Strange Fruit; (12"ep) **THE PEEL SESSIONS** (22.8.84) [ ] [-]
– Basement blues / The story of the blues / Better scream / Weekends / Yuh learn.

PETE WYLIE

(solo, with **The OEDIPUS WRECKS**)

M.D.M. | not issued

Apr 86. (7") **SINFUL. / I WANT THE MOON, MOTHER** [13] [ ]
(d7"+=) – Sophie's sinful (for Maurice and Kabelle) / Joy of being booed.
(12"+=)(3"cd-s+=) – Fourelevenfortyfour / ('A'mix) / If I love you.

Sep 86. (7")(12") **DIAMOND GIRL. / SPARE A THOUGHT** [57] [ ]

Jul 87. (7")(12")(c-s) **IF I LOVE YOU. / NEVER FALL FOR A WHORE** [ ] [ ]

Aug 87. (lp)(c)(cd) **SINFUL** [ ] [ ]
– Sinful / Shoulder to shoulder / Break out the banners Fourelevenfortyfour / If I love you / Train to Piranhaville / We can rule the world / All the love.

Oct 87. (7")(12") **FOUR ELEVEN FORTY FOUR. / THE MARKSMAN** [ ] [ ]
(cd-s+=) – Sinful (song of the sinful angel).

— Late 1990, WYLIE guested for The FARM on their single ALL TOGETHER NOW.

PETE WYLIE & WAH . . . THE MONGREL

(aka with The FARM)

Siren | Virgin ?

Apr 91. (7")(c-s) **SINFUL!. / FOURELEVENFORTYFOUR** [28] [ ]
(12") – ('A'side) / ('A'tribal mix).
(cd-s+=) – (all 3 tracks).

Jun 91. (7") **DON'T LOSE YOUR DREAMS (Excerpt From A Teenage Opera Part 154). / SEAMLESS** [ ] [ ]
(12"+=)(cd-s+=) – Imperfect

Aug 91. (cd)(c)(lp) **INFAMY! OR I DIDN'T GET WHERE I AM . . .** [ ] [ ]
– Don't lose your dreams (excerpt from a teenage opera part 15) / Never gonna stop: no heshmesh / I didn't get where I am today / Circle of salt / The Kerry baby / John 3:16 – The one tonight / Everything! (a song for Dennis Wilson) / From carpenter to king / Long tall Scally (the ballad thereof) / Getting out of it . . . / Sinful! (tribal mix).

Sep 91. (7") **LONG TALL SCALLY. / . . . AND THE GOOD GUYS DON'T DIE** [ ] [ ]
(12"+=)(cd-s+=) – Everything (But The Wah!) For Dennis Wilson Accapella Everything Includes Orchestrals Ultimately

WAILERS (see under ⇒ MARLEY, Bob)

Loudon WAINWRIGHT III

Born: 5 Sep '46, Chapel Hill, North Carolina, USA. (Son of journalist on 'Life' magazine.) He served music apprenticeship on US college and folk-club circuit, following in the footsteps of BOB DYLAN and JOAN BAEZ. Hitched to San Francisco in '67. In 1969, he signed to 'Atlantic', and he was soon making in-roads into public recognition. After moving to 'Columbia' in 1972, he scored US Top 20 hit with the novelty song 'DEAD SKUNK'. It was lifted from 'ALBUM III', which hovered outside US Top 100 for some time. In 1977, his 5-year marriage to singer KATE McGARRIGLE had ended. In the 80's, his slide was complete when albums, still critically endured, were accessed on indie labels. • **Style:** Initially cast as 'the new Dylan', his folk-rock satirical genius was left on the shelf by too many. Admittedly not a great singer, although comic material compensating for this. • **Songwriters:** All own work. • **Trivia:** In the mid-70's, he appeared on a couple of TV episodes of comedy Korean War series 'M.A.S.H.'. Re-married in the 80's, to SUZZY ROCHE (The ROCHES), they had a daughter Lucy in 1982 and moved partly to UK. He resurrected intended acting career in the 80's by appearing in stage productions 'Pump Boys & Dinettes' and 'Owners'. In '88, he featured in the film 'Jacknife'.

Recommended: ALIVE ONE (*7)

LOUDON WAINWRIGHT III – vocals, acoustic guitar

Atlantic | Atlantic

1971. (lp) **ALBUM I** [ ] [ ]
– School days / Hospital lady / Ode to a Pittsburgh / Glad to see you've got religion / Uptown / Black Uncle Remus / Four is a magic number / I don't care / Central Square song / Movies are a mother to me / Bruno's place.

1972. (lp) **ALBUM II** [ ] [ ]
– Me and my friend the cat / Motel blues / Nice Jewish girls / Be careful / Plane too / Cook that diner, Dora / There's a baby in the house / I know I'm unhappy / Suicide song / Glenville reel / Saw your name in the paper / Samson and the warden / Plane, too / Cook that dinner, Dora / Old friend / Old paint / Winter song. *(re-iss.1974) (re-iss.1989 on 'Edsel')*

— added **RICHARD CROOKS** – drums / to session people from last album.

C.B.S. | Columbia

Jan 73. (lp)(c) **ALBUM III** [ ] [ ]
– Dead skunk / Red guitar / East Indian princess / Muse blues / Hometeam crowd / B side / Needless to say / Smokey Joe's cafe / New paint / Trilogy (circa 1967) / Drinking song / Say that you love me. *(re-iss.+c.Dec85 + Jan89 on 'Edsel', cd-iss.Feb91)*

Jun 73. (7") **DEAD SKUNK. / NEEDLESS TO SAY** [ ] [16] Jan 73

Aug 73. (7") **SAY THAT YOU LOVE ME. / NEW PAINT** [-] [ ]

Feb 74. (lp)(c) **ATTEMPTED MOUSTACHE** [ ] [ ]

– The swimming song / A.M. world / Bell bottom pants / Liza / I am the way / Clockwork chartreuse / Down drinking at the bar / The man who couldn't cry / Come a long way / Nocturnal stumblebutt / Dialated to meet you / Lullaby. *(re-iss.May88 on 'Edsel')*

May 74. (7") **DOWN DRINKING AT THE BAR. / I AM THE WAY**
Jul 74. (7") **THE SWIMMING SONG. / BELL BOTTOM PANTS** [-]
Mar 75. (lp)(c) **UNREQUITED**
– Sweet nothings / The lowly tourist / Kings and queens / Kick in the head / Whatever happened to us / Crime of passion / Absence makes the heart grow fonder / On the rocks / Guru / Mr. Guilty / Untitled (aka The Hardy boys at the Y) / Unrequited to the Nth degree / Old friends / Rufus is a tit man. *(re-iss.May88 on 'Edsel', cd-iss.Mar91)*

— Now with band: **ELLIOTT RANDALL** – guitar / **RICHARD DAVIS** – bass / **R.CROOKS / ERIC WEISSBERG** – banjo / **STEPHEN TUBIN + GLEN MITCHELL** – keyboards / etc.

Arista Arista

Apr 76. (7") **BICENTENNIAL (SUMMER'S ALMOST OVER). / TALKING THE BIG APPLE '75**
Jun 76. (lp)(c) **T-SHIRT**
– Bicentennial / Summer's almost over / Hollywood hopeful / Reciprocity / At both ends / Wine with dinner / Hey Packy / California prison blues / Talking big apple / Prince Hal's dirge / Just like President Thieu.
Apr 78. (lp)(c) **FINAL EXAM**
– Final exam / Mr.Guilty / Pen pal blues / Golfin' blues / The heckler / Natural disaster / Fear with flying / Heaven and mud / Two-song set / Pretty little Martha / Watch me rock I'm over thirty.
May 78. (7") **FINAL EXAM. /** [-]

— Next featured singing trio The ROCHES.

Radar Rounder

Sep 79. (lp) **A LIVE ONE (live)**
– Motel blues / Hollywood hopeful / Whatever happened to us? / Natural disaster / Suicide song / School days / Kings and queens / Down drinking at the bar / B-side / Nocturnal stumblebutt / Red guitar / Clockwork chartreuse / Lullaby. *(re-iss.+c.Jun87 on 'Edsel', cd-iss.Jul92 on 'Demon') (US re-iss.Aug88)*

Demon Rounder

Apr 83. (lp)(c) **FAME AND WEALTH**
– Reader and advisor / The Grammy song / Dump the dog / Thick and thin / Revenge / Five years old / Ingenue / Idttywim / Westchester County / Saturday morning fever / April Fools Day morn / Fame and wealth.
Apr 83. (7") **FIVE YEARS OLD. / RAMBUNCTIOUS**

— Now collborated with **RICHARD THOMPSON** – producer, guitar

Jul 85. (7") **CARDBOARD BOXES. / COLOURS**
Sep 85. (lp)(c) **I'M ALRIGHT**
– One man guy / Lost love / I'm alright / Not John / Cardboard boxes / Screaming issue / How old are you? / Animal song / Out of this world / Daddy take a nap / Ready or not (so ripe) / Career moves. *(US re-iss.Aug88)*
Aug 86. (7") **UNHAPPY ANNIVERSARY. / THE ACID SONG**
Sep 86. (lp)(c)(cd) **MORE LOVE SONGS**
– Hard day on the Planet / Synchronicity / Your mother and I / I eat out / No / The home stretch / Unhappy anniversary / Man's world / Vampire blues / Overseas calls / Expatriot / The back nine. *(cd+=)*– The acid song.
Sep 87. (7") **YOUR MOTHER AND I. / AT THE END OF A LONG LONELY DAY**

Silvertone Silvertone

May 89. (lp)(c)(cd) **THERAPY**
– Therapy / Bill of goods / T.S.D.H.A.V. (This Song Don't Have A Video) / Harry's wall / Aphrodisiac / Fly paper / Nice guys / Thanksgiving / Your father's car / Me and all the other mothers / You don't want to know / Mind read (it belonged to you) / This year.
Sep 89. (7") **T.S.D.H.A.V. (THIS SONG DON'T HAVE A VIDEO). / NICE GUYS**

— with **CHAIM TANNENBAUM** – banjo, harmonica / **DAVID MANSFIELD** – fiddle, mandolin

Virgin Virgin

Jul 93. (cd)(c) **CAREER MOVES (live)**
– Road ode / I'm alright / Five years old / Your mother and I / Westchester County / He said, she said / Christmas rap / Suddenly it's Christmas / Thanksgiving / A fine Celtic name / T.S.M.N.W.A. / some balding guys / The swimming song / Absence makes the heart grow fonder / Happy birthday Elvis / Unhappy anniversary / I'd rather be lonely / Just say no / April fool's Day morn / The man who couldn't cry / The acid song / Tip that waitress / Career moves.
Oct 95. (cd)(c) **GROWN MAN**
– The birthday present / Grown man / That hospital / Housework / Cobwebs / A year / Father / Father – daughter dialogue / 1994 / Iwiwal / Just a John / I suppose / Dreaming / The end has begun / Human cannonball / Treasure untold.

– compilations, others, etc. –

Jan 92. Demon; (cd) **FAME & WEALTH / I'M ALRIGHT**

John WAITE (see under ⇒ BABYS)

Tom WAITS

Born: 7 Dec'49, Pomona, California, USA. Signed to 'Asylum' in 1973, after being spotted at the Troubadour club. His debut album 'CLOSING TIME' produced by Jerry Yester (ex-LOVIN' SPOONFUL), didn't sell greatly, but it did contain 'OL '55' which was soon covered by The EAGLES on their album 'On The Border'. He gained much respect throughout the next decade, and finally hit the UK album charts in '83 with the great 'SWORDFISHTROMBONES'. • **Style:** Eccentric gruff voiced jazz & blues influenced balladeer. • **Songwriters:** Pens own songs except; WHAT KEEPS MAN ALIVE (Kurt Weill) / HEIGH-HO (from 'Snow White') / IT'S ALL RIGHT WITH ME (Cole Porter). From 1987, his material was co-written with wife and Irish playwright Kathleen Brennan, whom he married on 31 Dec'81. • **Filmography:** PARADISE ALLEY (bit-part 1978) / WOLFEN (cameo 1979) / STONE BOY (cameo 1980) / ONE FROM THE HEART (1981 cameo + soundtrack) / THE OUTSIDERS (1983) / RUMBLEFISH (1983) / THE COTTON CLUB (1984 cameo) / DOWN BY LAW (1986) / IRONWEED (1988) / COLD FEET (1989) / NIGHT ON EARTH (1992)?. • **Trivia:** In the late 70's, he parted company with girlfriend/singer RICKIE LEE JONES. In 1991, he sued a radio ad company for using a soundalike in a chips commercial and won nearly $2.5 million.

Recommended: THE ASYLUM YEARS (*8) / SWORDFISHTROMBONES (*9) / RAIN DOGS (*9) / BIG TIME (*8) / BONE MACHINE (*8)

TOM WAITS – vocals, piano, accordion

Asylum Elektra

May 73. (lp)(c) **CLOSING TIME**
– Ol' 55 / I hope that I don't fall in love with you / Virginia Avenue / Old shoes (and picture postcards) / Midnight lullaby / Martha / Rosie / Lonely / Ice cream man / Little trip to Heaven (on the wings of your love) / Grapefruit moon / Closing time. *(re-iss.Jun76)*
May 73. (7") **OL '55. / MIDNIGHT LULLABY** [-]
Jan 74. (lp)(c) **THE HEART OF SATURDAY NIGHT**
– New coat of paint / San Diego serenade / Semi suite / Shiver me timbers / Diamonds on my windshield / (Looking for) The heart of Saturday night / Fumblin' with the blues / Please call me baby / Depot, depot / Drunk on the Moon / The ghosts of Saturday night (after hours at Napoleon's pizza house). *(re-iss.Jun76) (cd-iss.1989 on 'WEA')*
Mar 74. (7") **DIAMONDS ON MY WINDSHIELD. / SAN DIEGO SERENADE** [-]
Jun 75. (7") **NEW COAT OF PAINT. / BLUE SKIES** [-]
Oct 75. (7") **THE HEART OF SATURDAY NIGHT. / DIAMONDS ON MY WINDSHIELD** [-]

— with **MIKE MELVOIN** – piano / **JIM HUGHART** – bass / **BILL GOODWIN** – drums

Dec 75. (d-lp)(c) **NIGHTHAWKS AT THE DINER (live)** Oct 75
– (opening intro) / Emotional weather report / (intro) / On a foggy night / (intro) / Eggs and sausage / (intro) / Better off without a wife / Nighthawk postcards (from Easy street) / (intro) / Warm beer and cold women / (intro) / Puttnam County / Spare parts 1 (a nocturnal emission) / Nobody / (intro) / Big Joe and Phantom 309 / Spare parts 2 and closing. *(re-iss.Jun76) (cd-iss.1989 on 'WEA')*

— retained **HUGHART** +new **SHELLY MANNE** – drums / **LEW TABACKIN** – tenor sax

Nov 76. (7") **STEP RIGHT UP. / THE PIANO HAS BEEN DRINKING (NOT ME)** [-]
May 77. (lp)(c) **SMALL CHANGE** [89] Nov 76
– Tom Traubert's blues / Step right up / Jitterbug boy / I wish I was in New Orleans / The piano has been drinking (not me) / Invitation to the blues / Pasties and a g-string / Bad liver and a broken heart / The one that got away / Small change / I can't wait to get off work. *(cd-iss.1989 on 'WEA')*

— **FRANK VICARI** – tenor sax / **JACK SHELDON** – trumpet repl. TABACKIN

Oct 77. (lp)(c) **FOREIGN AFFAIRS**
– Cinny's waltz / Muriel / I never talk to strangers / Jack and Neal – California here I come / A sight for sore eyes / Potter's field / Burma shave / Barber shop / Foreign affair. *(cd-iss.Mar95 on 'Warners')*

— **RICK LAWSON** – drums repl. MANNE / added **ROLAND BAUTISTA + RAY CRAWFORD** – guitar / **BYRON MILLER** – bass / **DA WILLIE CONGA** – piano / **HAROLD BATTISTE**

Apr 79. (7") **SOMEWHERE. / RED SHOES BY THE DRUGSTORE**
Aug 79. (lp)(c) **BLUE VALENTINE**
– Somewhere / Red shoes by the drugstore / Christmas card from a hooker in Minneapolis / Romeo is bleeding / Wrong side of the road / Whistlin' past the graveyard / Kentucky Avenue / A sweet little bullet from a pretty blue gun / Blue valentines. *(cd-iss.Feb93)*

— retained **HUGHART + BAUTISTA** + new **LARRY TAYLOR** – upright bass / **RONNIE BARRON** – organ / **GREG COHEN** – bass / **PLAS JOHNSON** – sax / **BIG JOHN THOMASSIE** – drums

Oct 80. (lp)(c) **HEARTATTACK AND VINE** [96]
– Saving all my love for you / On the nickel / In shades / Downtown / Jersey girl / Til the money runs out / Mr.Segal / Ruby's arms. *(cd-iss.1989 on 'WEA') (re-iss.cd May93)*
Dec 80. (7") **JERSEY GIRL. / HEARTATTACK AND VINE** [-]
Nov 81. (lp)(c) **BOUNCED CHECKS** (compilation, some live)
– Heartattack and vine / Jersey girl / Eggs and sausage / I never talk to strangers / The piano has been drinking (not me) / Whistlin' past the graveyard / Mr. Henry / Diamonds on my windshield / Burma shave / Tom Traubert's blues.

— + many session people from above incl.**VICTOR FELDMAN** – percussion

C.B.S. Columbia

Feb 83. (lp) **ONE FROM THE HEART (Film Soundtrack) ("TOM WAITS & CRYSTAL GAYLE")**
– (opening montage): Tom's piano intro – Once upon a town – The wages of love / Is there any way out of this dream / Picking up after you / Old boyfriends / Broken bicycles / I beg your pardon / Little boy blue / (instrumental montage): The tango – Circus girl / You can't unring a bell / This one's from the heart / Take me home / Presents / (others by CRYSTAL GAYLE only.). *(cd-iss.Jan91)*

— **FRED TACKETT** – guitar + **STEPHEN TAYLOR HODGES** – drums repl. BAUTISTA + LAWSON / added **FRANCIS THUMM** – pump organ / **RANDY ALDCROFT** – horns

Island Island

Sep 83. (lp)(c) **SWORDFISHTROMBONES** [62]
– Underground / Shore leave / Dave the butcher / Johnsburg, Illinois / 16 shells from a thirty-ought-six / Town with no cheer / In the neighbourhood / Just another sucker on the vine / Frank's wild years / Swordfishtrombones / Down, down, down / Soldier's things / Gin soaked boy / Trouble's braids / Rainbirds. *(re-iss.Sep86, cd-iss.Nov87, c+cd re-iss.Jun89) (re-iss.lp Jan94 + May94)*
Oct 83. (7") **IN THE NEIGHBOURHOOD. / FRANK'S WILD YEARS**

— **MARC RIBOT** – guitar + **MICHAEL BLAIR** – drums, percussion repl. TACKETT, THUMM + HODGES / **WILLIAM SCHIMMEL** – piano / **RAPLH CARNEY** – sax,

'Well with buckshot eyes and a purple heart - I rolled down the National stroll and with
a big fat paycheck strapped to my hipsack and a shore leave wrist watch underneath my sleeve,
In a Hong Kong drizzle on Cuban Heels ~ I rowed down the gutter to the blood bank......'

clarinet + **BOB FUNK** – trombone repl. FELDMAN + ALDCROFT

Oct 85. (lp)(c)(cd) **RAIN DOGS** [29] [ ]
– Singapore / Clap hands / Cemetery polka / Jockey full of bourbon / Tango till they're sore / Big black Mariah / Diamonds and gold / Hang down your head / Time / Rain dogs / Midtown / Ninth and headpin / Gun Street girl / Union square / Blind love / Walking Spanish / Downtown train / Bride of Rain dog / Anywhere I lay my head. *(re-iss.cd.Aug89 & Apr91)*

Nov 85. (7")(12") **DOWNTOWN TRAIN. / TANGO 'TILL THEY'RE SORE** [ ] [ ]

Feb 86. (7")(12") **IN THE NEIGHBOURHOOD. / SINGAPORE** [ ] [ ]
(d7"+=) – Tango till they're sore (live) / Rain dogs (live).
(12") – ('A'side) / Jockey full of bourbon / Tango till they're sore (live) / 16 shells from a thirty-ought-six (live).

— Past live group **FRED TACKETT** – guitar / **RICHIE HAYWARD** – drums / **LARRY TAYLOR** – upright bass. Retained only **TAYLOR, CARNEY, SCHIMMEL** / new: **MORRIS TEPPER** – guitar / **FRANCIS THUMM** – pump organ (on some) / guest **DAVID HIDALGO** – accordion

Aug 87. (lp)(c)(cd) **FRANK'S WILD YEARS (Soundtrack)** [20] [ ]
– Hang on St. Christopher / Straight to the top (rhumba) / Blow wind blow / Temptation / Innocent when you dream (barroom) / I'll be gone / I'll take New York / Telephone call from Istanbul / Cold cold ground / Train song / Yesterday is here / Please wake me up / Frank's theme / More than rain / Way down in the hole / Straight to the top (Vegas). *(re-iss.cd.Jun89 & Apr91)*

— 1988 live band **WILLIE SCHWARZ** – keyboards, accordion repl. SCHIMMEL + TEPPER

Sep 88. (lp)(c)(cd) **BIG TIME (live)** [84] [ ]
– 16 shells from a thirty-ought-six / Red shoes / Cold cold ground / Way down in the hole / Falling down / Strange weather / Big black Mariah / Rain dogs / Train song / Telephone call from Istanbul / Gun street girl / Time. (cd+=) Underground / Straight to the top / Yesterday is here / Johnsburg, Illinois / Ruby's arms / Clap hands.

Sep 88. (7") **16 SHELLS FROM A THIRTY-OUGHT-SIX (live). / BIG BLACK MARIAH (live)** [ ] [ ]
(12"+=) – Ruby's arms (live).

May 92. (cd)(c)(lp) **NIGHT ON EARTH – SOUNDTRACK** [ ] [ ]
– Back in the good old world / Los Angeles mood (chromium descentions) / Los Angeles theme (another private dick) / New York theme (hey, you can have that heart attack outside, buddy) / New York mood (a new haircut and a busted lip) / Baby, I'm not a baby anymore (Beatrice theme) / Good old world (waltz) / Carnival (Brunello del Montalcino) / On the old side of the world (vocal) / Good old world (gypsy instrumental) / Paris mood (un de fromage) / Dragging a dead priest / Helsinki mood / Carnival Bob's confession / Good old world (waltz vocal) / On the other side of the world (instrumental).

Aug 92. (7") **GOIN' OUT WEST. / A LITTLE RAIN** [ ] [ ]
(10"+=)(cd-s+=) – The ocean doesn't want me / Back in the good old world (gypsy).

Sep 92. (cd)(c)(lp) **BONE MACHINE** [26] [ ]
– Earth died screaming / Dirt in the ground / Such a scream / All stripped down / Who are you / The ocean doesn't want me / Jesus gonna behave / A little rain / In the Colosseum / Goin' out west / Murder in the red barn / Black wings / Whistle down the wind / I don't wanna grow up / Let me get up on it / That feel.

Nov 93. (cd)(c)(lp) **THE BLACK RIDER** [47] [ ]
– Lucky day overture / The black rider / November / Just the right bullets / Black box theme / 'T ain't no sin / Flash pan hunter intro / That's the way / The briar and the rose / Russian dance / Gospel train-orchestra / I'll shoot the Moon / Flash pan hunter / Crossroads / Gospel train / Interlude / Oily night / Lucky day / The last rose of summer / Carnival.

— 3 tracks were co-written with author WILLIAM S.BURROUGHS.

– more compilations, etc. –

Apr 84. Asylum; (d-lp)(c) **THE ASYLUM YEARS** [ ] [ ]
– Diamonds on my windshield / Looking for the heart of Saturday night / Martha / The ghosts of Saturday night / Grapefruit Moon / Small change / Burma slave / I never talk to strangers / Tom Traubert's blues / Blue valentine / Potter's field / Kentucky avenue / Somewhere / Ruby's arms. *(cd-iss.Oct86, cd-omitted 9 tracks but added 3 others)*

Mar 93. Asylum; (7")(c-s) **HEARTATTACK AND VINE. / BLUE VALENTINES** [ ] [ ]
(cd-s+=) – On a foggy night (live) / Intro to a foggy night (live).

Sep 85. Island; (lp)(c) **ANTHOLOGY** [ ] [ ]

Nov 92. Island; (d-cd) **SWORDFISHTROMBONES / RAINDOGS** [ ] [ ]

Jul 91. Edsel; (cd) **THE EARLY YEARS** (rare & demos) [ ] [-]
– Goin' down slow / Poncho's lament / I'm your late night evening prostitute / Had me a girl / Ice cream man / Rockin' chair / Virginia Ave. / Midnight lullabye / When you ain't got nobody / Little trip to Heaven / Frank's song / Looks like I'm up shit creek again / So long I'll see you.

1992. Edsel; (cd) **THE EARLY YEARS VOL.2** [ ] [-]
– Hope I don't fall in love with you / Ol' 55 / Mockin bird / In between love / Blue skies / Nobody / I want you / Shiver me timbers / Grapefruit moon / Diamonds on my windshield / Please call me, baby / So it goes / Old shoes.

Rick WAKEMAN

Born: 18 May'49, Perivale, Middlesex, England. Aged 16, he attended The Royal College of Music, but interest in playing live and doing sessions, made him drop out. His in-demand pop session work (i.e.WHITE PLAINS, EDISON LIGHTHOUSE, etc.), led him to play on albums by CAT STEVENS, DAVID BOWIE, T.REX, etc. In 1970, he joined The STRAWBS, but the following year he couldn't turn down YES, as they matched his classical ambitions. He was on-off YES member during the 70's, and started own solo career on 'A&M' records. Taking themes of history, fiction and legend, he released 3 well-received Top 10 albums between 1973-1975. His second album JOURNEY TO THE CENTRE OF THE EARTH (an adaptation of Jules Verne classic book) was premiered live at The Royal Festival Hall Jan'74, and when released hit UK No.1. He with orchestra and choir performed it at an open-air Crystal Palace Garden Party, going on to major US tours. This took its toll as RICK suffered minor heart attack nearing the end of pocket-draining tour. Nevertheless, he continued in the studio with another epic concept ' . . . KING ARTHUR' in 1975. With move into movie work, etc., his public attention drifted somewhat, thus his steady decline of commercial success. • **Style:** Virtuoso exhibitionist keyboard-player, whose flash image (long blonde hair and ankle-length silver capes) matched that of other piano-basher at the time KEITH EMERSON. Will be remembered in the next century, not for his theatrical rock albums, but for the classical style and beauty they created. • **Songwriters:** All his own work, but with little snatches of past classics interspersed with his indelible stamp. • **Trivia:** Most distinguished session work included LIFE ON MARS (David Bowie) / CHANGES (Black Sabbath) / MORNING HAS BROKEN (Cat Stevens) / LOU REED's debut album. WAKEMAN was married in the 70's to Ros and settled down in a Buckingham mansion alongside his collection of Rolls Royce's. They had 3 children, before their divorce. In the 80's, RICK then married ex-model NINA CARTER (also of twin-sister group BLONDE ON BLONDE) and fathered another 2 (so far) before finding Christianity. BILL ODDIE (of the GOODIES TV programme) guested vox on 2nd lp & 'CRIMINAL RECORD'.

Recommended: JOURNEY TO THE CENTRE OF THE EARTH (*7) / THE SIX WIVES OF HENRY VIII (*8) / THE MYTHS & LEGENDS OF KING ARTHUR . . . (*7).

RICK WAKEMAN – keyboards (a member of YES; Aug71-Jun74, Nov76-Mar80, 1990+)

— now used various YES people on sessions plus numerous choirs & ensembles.

A & M A & M

Feb 73. (lp)(c) **THE SIX WIVES OF HENRY VIII** [7] [30]
– Catherine of Aragon / Anne of Cleves / Catherine Howard / Jane Seymour / Anne Boleyn / Catherine Parr. *(re-iss.May81) (re-iss.+cd.Aug89) (also on quad-US)*

Mar 73. (7") **CATHERINE. / ANNE** [ ] [ ]

— Introduced **ASHLEY HOLT** – vocals / **ROGER NEWELL** – bass / **BARNEY JAMES** – drums / plus The ENGLISH ROCK ENSEMBLE with The LONDON SYMPHONY ORCHESTRA. Narration by actor DAVID HEMMINGS.

May 74. (lp)(c) **JOURNEY TO THE CENTRE OF THE EARTH** [1] [3]
– The journey / Recollections / The battle / The forest. *(re-iss.Feb85 on 'Hallmark') (cd-iss.1988 on 'Mobile Fidelity') (also on quad-US) (re-iss.cd+c May93 on 'Spectrum')*

Oct 74. (7") **THE JOURNEY. / THE RETURN** [-] [ ]

Dec 74. (7") **THE BATTLE. / AND NOW A WORD FROM OUR SPONSOR** [-] [ ]

Apr 75. (lp)(c) **THE MYTHS AND LEGENDS OF KING ARTHUR AND THE KNIGHTS OF THE ROUND TABLE** [2] [21]
– Arthur / Lady of the lake / Guinevere / Sir Lancelot & the Black Knight / Merlin the magician / Sir Galahad / The last battle. *(re-iss.Nov85 on 'President') (also on quad-US)*

Jun 75. (7") **MERLIN THE MAGICIAN. / SIR GALAHAD** [-] [ ]

Nov 75. (lp) **LISZTOMANIA (Soundtrack w/ ROGER DALTRY)** [ ] [ ]
– Rienzi / Chpsticks fantasia / Love's dream / Dante period / Orpheus song / Hell / Hibernation / Excelsior song / Master race / Rape, pillage and clap funerailles / Free song / Peace at last.

Jan 76. (7") **ORPHEUS SONG (w/ ROGER DALTRY). / LOVE'S DREAM** [-] [ ]

— For North & South American tour he trimmed his ENGLISH ROCK ENSEMBLE down to **ASHLEY HOLT** – vocals / **JOHN DUNSTERVILE** – guitar / **ROGER NEWELL** – bass / **TONY FERNANDEZ** – drums / **REG BROOKS + MARTYN SHIELDS** – brass section

Apr 76. (lp)(c) **NO EARTHLY CONNECTION** [9] [67]
– Music reincarnate: (part 1) The warning – (part 2) The maker – (part 3) The spaceman – (part 4) The realization – (part 5) The reaper / The prisoner / The lost cycle.

Jan 77. (lp)(c) **WHITE ROCK (Original Film Soundtrack)** [14] [ ]
– White rock / Searching for gold / The loser / The shoot / Lax'x / After the ball / Montezuma's revenge / Ice run.

— Above from 1976 Winter Olympics docu-film, narrated by James Coburn.

Jun 77. (7") **WHITE ROCK. / AFTER THE BALL** [-] [ ]

Nov 77. (lp)(c) **RICK WAKEMAN'S CRIMINAL RECORD** [25] [ ]
– Statute of justice / Crime of passion / Chamber of horrors / Birdman of Alcatraz / The breathalizer / Judas Iscariot. *(re-iss.Mar82)*

Apr 78. (7") **BIRDMAN OF ALCATRAZ. / AND NOW A WORD FROM OUR SPONSOR** [-] [ ]

Apr 79. (7") **FLACONS DE NEIGE. / BIRDMAN OF ALCATRAZ** [ ] [ ]

May 79. (d-lp)(c) **RHAPSODIES** [25] [ ]
– Pedra da Gavea / Front line / Bombay duck / Animal showdown / Big Ben / Rhapsody in blue / Wooly Willy tango / The pulse / Swan lager / March of the gladiators / Flacons de Neige / The flasher / The palais / Stand by / Sea horses / Half holiday / Summertime.

Jun 79. (7")(7"pic-d) **ANIMAL SHOWDOWN. / SEA HORSES** [ ] [-]

Nov 79. (7") **SWAN LAGER. / WOOLLY WILLY TANGO** [ ] [-]

Feb 80. (7") **I'M SO STRAIGHT I'M A WEIRDO. / DO YOU BELIEVE IN FAIRIES?** [ ] [-]

WEA not issued

Oct 80. (7") **THE SPIDER. / DANIELLE** [ ] [-]

Moon not issued

Nov 82. (7") **I'M SO STRAIGHT I'M A WEIRDO. / MAYBE '80 (edit)** [ ] [-]

Dec 82. (lp)(c) **ROCK AND ROLL PROPHET** (rec.1979) [ ] [-]
– Return of the prophet / I'm so straight I'm a weirdo / The dragon / Dark / Alpha sleep / Maybe '80 / March of the child soldiers / Early warning / Spy of '55 / Stalemate / Do you believe in fairies / Rock'n'roll prophet. *(cd-iss.Apr93 on 'President')*

RICK WAKEMAN BAND

featured **FERNANDEZ / STEVE BARNACLE** – bass / **GARY BARNACLE** – sax / **TIM STONE** – guitar / etc.

Charisma Charisma?

Jun 81. (lp)(c) **1984** [24] [ ]
– 1984 overture – part 1 & 2 / War games / Julia / The hymn / The room – part 1 & 2 / Robot man / Sorry / No name / 1984 / Forgotten memories / The proles / 1984.

Jul 81. (7") **JULIA'S SONG. / SORRY** [ ] [-]

Nov 81. (7") **ROBOT MAN. / 1984 OVERTURE (part 1)** [ ] [-]

Jan 82. (lp)(c) **THE BURNING (solo Soundtrack)** [ ] [ ]
– Themes from 'The Burning' / The chase continues / Variations on the fire / Sheer terror and more / The burning (end title theme) / Campfire story / The fire / Doin' it / Devil's creek breakdown / The chase / Sheer terror.

RICK WAKEMAN

solo with music from 1982 football World Cup in Spain (next).

Apr 83. (7") **LATIN REEL (G'OLE THEME). / NO POSSIBLA** [ ] [-]

Apr 83. (lp)(c) **G'OLE (film soundtrack)** [ ] [-]
– International flag / The dove / Wayward spirit / Red island / Latin reel (theme from G'ole) / Spanish holiday / No possibla / Shadows / Black pearls / Frustration / Spanish montage / G'ole.

1983. (lp)(c) **THE COST OF LIVING** [ ] [ ]
– Twij / Pandomonia / Gone but not forgotten / One for the road / Bedtime stories / Happening man / Shakespeare's run / Monkey nuts / Elegy (written in a country church yard). *(re-iss.Aug88)*

— Oct '84, WAKEMAN collaborated on album BEYOND THE PLANETS by KEVIN PEEK (Sky); hit 64

— His Spring 1985 tour band: **TONY FERNANDEZ** – drums / **CHAS CRONK** – bass / **RICK FENN** – lead guitar / **GORDON NEVILLE** – vocals / **LYNN SHEPHERD** – b.vocals

T.B.G. not issued

Dec 84. (7") **GLORY BOYS. / GHOST OF A ROCK AND ROLL STAR** [ ] [-]
(12"+=) – Elgin mansions.

Mar 85. (lp)(c)(cd) **SILENT NIGHTS** [ ] [-]
– Tell 'em all you know / The opening line / The opera / Man's best friend / Glory boys / Silent nights / Ghost of a rock and roll star / The dancer / Elgin mansions / That's who I am.

Jun 85. (7")(12") **THE THEME FROM 'LYTTON'S DIARY'. / DATABASE** [ ] [-]

Dec 85. (lp) **LIVE AT HAMMERSMITH (live)** [ ] [-]
– Arthur / Three wives of Henry VIII / The journey / Merlin the magician. *(cd-iss.Jan87)*

Coda not issued

Apr 86. (lp)(c)(cd) **COUNTRY AIRS** [ ] [-]
– Dandelion dreams / Stepping stones / Ducks and drakes / Morning haze / Waterfalls / Quite valleys / Nature trail / Heather carpets / Wild moors / Lakeland walks. *(re-iss.cd+c Oct92 on Art Of Language)*

Apr 86. (7") **WATERFALLS. / HEATHER CARPETS** [ ] [-]

Stylus not issued

Nov 86. (d-lp)(d-c)(cd) **THE GOSPELS** [94] [-]
– The baptism / The welcoming / The sermon on the mount / The Lord's Prayer / The way / The road to Jerusalem / Trial and error / Galilee
– The gift / The magnificat / Welcome a star / Power (the acts of the apostles) / The word / The hour / The children of mine / The last verse

President not issued

Mar 87. (lp)(c) **CRIMES OF PASSION (Soundtrack)** [ ] [-]
– It's a lovely life (featuring MAGGIE BELL) / Eastern shadows / Joanna / The stretch / Policeman's ball / Stax / Taken in hand / Paradise lost / The box / Web of love. *(cd+=)* Dangerous woman (featuring MAGGIE BELL).

Aug 87. (lp)(c)(cd) **THE FAMILY ALBUM** [ ] [-]
– Adam (Rick's second son) / Black Beauty (black rabbit) / Jemma (Rick and Nina's daughter) / Benjamin (Rick's third son) / Oscar (Rick & Nina's son) / Oliver (Rick's eldest son) / Nina (Rick's wife) / Chloe (German shepherd) / Rookie (cat) / Tilly (Golden Retriever) / Mum / Dad. (c+=) – Wiggles (black & white rabbit). (cd++=) – The day after the fair / Mackintosh.

Feb 88. (lp)(c)(cd) **A SUITE OF GODS ("RICK WAKEMAN & RAMON RAMEDIOS")** [ ] [-]

Apr 88. (lp)(c)(cd) **ZODIAQUE ("RICK WAKEMAN & TONY FERNANDEZ")** [ ] [-]
– Sagittarius / Capricorn / Gemini / Cancer / Pisces / Aquarius / Aries / Libra / Leo / Virgo / Taurus / Scorpio.

— retained **FERNANDEZ.** recruited **DAVEY PATON** – bass / **JOHN KNIGHTSBRIDGE** – guitar (2) / guest vocals – **JOHN PARR / ROY WOOD / TRACEY ACKERMAN** + **ASHLEY HOLT**

Jul 88. (7") **CUSTER'S LAST STAND. / OCEAN CITY** [ ] [-]
(12"+=)(c-s+=) – Ice / Open up your eyes.

Jul 88. (lp)(c)(cd) **TIME MACHINE** [ ] [-]
– Custer's last stand / Ocean city / Angel of time / Slaveman / Ice / Open up your eyes / Elizabethan rock / Make me a woman / Rock age. (cd cont. extended versions of some tracks)

Nov 89. (lp)(c)(cd) **SEA AIRS (A NEW AGE COLLECTION)** [ ] [-]
(compilation 1985-89)
– Harbour lights / The pirate / Storm clouds / Last at sea / The mermaid / Waves / The fisherman / Flying fish / The Marie Celeste / Time and tide / The lone sailor / The sailor's lament.

Nov 90. (cd)(c)(lp) **NIGHT AIRS** [ ] [-]
– The sad dream / Twilight / The sleeping child / Mr.Badger / Jack Frost / The lone star / Rain shadows / Fox by night / Night owls / An evening romance.

Ambient not issued

Feb 91. (cd)(c)(lp) **PHANTOM POWER** [ ] [-]
– The visit / Heaven / The rat / The stiff / Evil love / The voice of love / Heat of the moment / Fear of love / The love trilogy:- One night – The dream sequence – One night of love / The hangman / The sand-dance / You can't buy my love / Phantom power / The chase.

President not issued

Dec 92. (cd) **COUNTRY AIRS (re-recording)** [ ] [-]
– Lakeland walks / Wild moors / Harvest festival / The glade / Dandelion dreams / Ducks and drakes / Green to gold / Stepping stones / Morning haze / Waterfalls / The Spring / Quiet valleys / Nature trails / Heather carpets.

Feb 93. (cd)(c)(lp) **MUSIC FROM CRIMES OF PASSION** [ ] [-]

Feb 93. (cd) **WAKEMAN WITH WAKEMAN ("RICK WAKEMAN & ALAN WAKEMAN")** [ ] [ ]
– Lure of the wild / The beach comber / Meglomania / Raga and rhyme / Sync or swim / Jigajig / Caesarea / After the atom / The suicide shuiffle / Past and present / Paint it black.
(Above was with son ADAM)

Jun 93. (cd) **THE CLASSICAL CONNECTION** [ ] [-]

Jun 92. (cd) **THE CLASSICAL CONNECTION II** [ ] [-]

Jul 93. (cd)(c) **ASPIRANT SUNRISE** [ ] [-]
– Thoughts of love / Gentle breezes / Whispering cornfields / Peaceful beginnings / Dewy morn / Musical dreams / Distant thoughts / The dove / When time stood still / Secret moments / Peaceful.

Jul 93. (cd)(c) **ASPIRANT SUNSET** [ ] [-]
– Floating clouds / Still waters / The dream / The sleeping village / Sea of tranquility / Peace / Sunset / Dying embers / Dusk / Evening moods.

Jul 93. (cd)(c) **ASPIRANT SUNSHADOWS** [ ] [-]
– The nightwind / Churchyard / Tall shadows / Shadowlove / Melancholy mood / Mount Fuji by night / Hidden reflections / The evening harp / The moonraker pond / The last lamplight / Japanese sunshadows.

Sep 93. (cd) **AFRICAN BACH** (rec.1991) [ ] [-]
– African Bach / Message of mine / My homeland / Liberty / Anthem / Brainstorm / Face in the crowd / Just a game / Africa east / Don't touch the merchandise.

Sep 93. (cd) **2000 A.D. INTO THE FUTURE** [ ] [-]
– Into the future / Toward peace / 2000 A.D. / A.D rock / The time tunnel / Robot dance / A new beginning / Forward past / The seventh dimension.

Oct 93. (cd) **HERITAGE SUITE** [ ] [-]
– The chasms / Thorwald's cross / St.Michael's isle / Spanish head / The Ayres / Mona's isle / The Dhoon / The bee orchid / Chapel Hill / The Curraghs / The painted lady / The Peregrine falcon.

Nov 93. (cd) **NO EXPENSE SPARED ("WAKEMAN WITH WAKEMAN")** [ ] [-]

Apr 94. (cd) **SOFTSWORD (KING JOHN AND THE MAGNA CHARTER)** [ ] [ ]
– Magna charter / After prayers / Battle sonata / The siege / Rochester college / The story of love (King John) / March of time / Don't fly away / Isabella / Softsword / Hymn of hope.

— Below as RICK WAKEMAN & HIS BAND

May 94. (cd-ep) **LIGHT UP THE SKY / SIMPLY FREE / STARFLIGHT / THE BEAR** [ ] [ ]

Nov 94. (cd) **ROMANCE OF THE VICTORIAN AGE (with ADAM WAKEMAN)** [ ] [-]
– Burlington arcade / If only / The last teardrop / Still dreaming / Memories of the Victorian age / Lost in words / A tale of love / Mysteries unfold / Forever in my heart / Days of wonder / The swans / Another mellow day / Dance of the elves.

Jun 95. (cd) **THE SEVEN WONDERS OF THE WORLD** (with naration) [ ] [-]
– The Pharoahs Of Alexandria / The Colossus Of Rhodes / The Pyramids Of Egypt / The Gardens Of Babylon / The Temples Of Artemis / The Statue Of Zeus / The Mausoleum At Halicarnassus.

D Sharp not issued

Jul 95. (cd) **CIRQUE SURREAL –** [ ] [-]

Oct 95. (cd) **VISIONS** [ ] [-]

– compilations, others, etc. –

1978. A&M; (lp)(c) **THE ROYAL PHILHARMONIC ORCHESTRA PERFORMING BEST KNOWN WORKS OF RICK WAKEMAN** [ ] [-]

May 81. A&M; (d-c) **THE SIX WIVES OF HENRY VIII / THE MYTHS AND LEGENDS..** [ ] [-]

Feb 89. A&M; (cd-box) **20th ANNIVERSARY** [ ] [-]

Mar 83. Charisma; (d-c) **1984 / THE BURNING** [ ] [-]

Dec 93. Fragile; (d-cd) **RICK WAKEMAN'S GREATEST HITS** (some with YES) [ ] [ ]
– Roundabout / Wondrous stories / Don't kill the whale / Going for the one / Siberian khatru / Madrigal / Starship trooper/ / Overture / The journey / The Hansbach / Lost in time / The recollection / Stream of voices / The battle / Liddenbrook / The forest / Mount Etna / Journey's end / Sea horses / Catherine of Aragon / Gone but not forgotten / Merlin the magician.

Jan 94. Sony Europe; (cd) **CLASSIC TRACKS** [ ] [ ]

Mar 94. President; (cd) **THE PRIVATE COLLECTION** [ ] [-]

Apr 94. Prestige; (cd)(c) **THE CLASSIC** [ ] [-]

Jun 94. Cyclops; (d-cd) **WAKEMAN WITH WAKEMAN** – THE OFFICIAL LIVE ALBUM (w /ADAM) [ ] [-]

Dec 94. Windsong; (cd) **LIVE ON THE TEST (live)** [ ] [-]

WALKABOUTS

Formed: Seattle, USA . . .1984 by quartet below. After a few releases on US indies (PopLlama going bust), they moved to cult label 'Sub Pop', home of NIRVANA, L7, MUDHONEY, etc. Their first for the label 'CATARACT' was welcomed by critics and public alike. • **Style:** Folk-rock (influenced by Appalachian Mountains!) which lent into the NEIL YOUNG & CRAZY HORSE for other inspiration. • **Songwriters:** Group and later ECKMAN, except covers from roster of Neil Young and Charlie Rich. • **Trivia:** The album CONTRACT featured PETER BUCK (R.E.M.), MARK LANEGAN (Screaming Trees) and IVAN KRAAL (Patti Smith Group). SCAVENGER featured NATALIE MERCHANT and BRIAN ENO.

Recommended: CATARACT (*7)

CHRIS ECKMAN – vocals, guitar / **CARLA TORGENSON** – vocals, guitar / **MICHAEL**

WELLS – bass / **TERRI MOELLER** – drums / part-time 6th member **LARRY BARRETT** – banjo, mandolin, guitar

not issued | Necessity

1984. (12"ep) **WALKABOUTS** [-] [ ]
1985. (12"ep) **22 DISASTERS** [-] [ ]

Glitterhouse | Pop Llama

1987. (lp)(cd) **SEE BEAUTIFUL RATTLESNAKE GARDENS** [ ] [ ]
– Jumping off / Breakneck speed / The wellspring / John Reilly / Robert McFarlane blues / This rotten tree / Laughingstock / Glass palace / Feast or famine / Ballad of Moss Head / Who-knows-what / Rattlesnake theme / Weights and rivers. *(re-iss.cd 1995 +=)*– Linda Evans / Mai Tai time / Cyclone / Gather round / Certain gift.

—— added **GLENN SLATER** – keyboards

Sub Pop | Sub Pop

Mar 89. (lp) **CATARACT** [-] [ ]
– Whiskey XXX / Hell's soup kitchen / Whereabouts unknown / End in tow / Bones of contention / Home as found / Smokestack / The wicked skipper.
Feb 90. (12"orange-ep)(c)(cd) **RAG AND BONE** [-] [ ]
– The anvil song / Ahead of the storm / Medicine hut / Wreck of the old £9 / Mr.Clancy / Last ditch. *(cd/c +=)* – CATARACT
Sep 91. (cd)(lp) **SCAVENGER** [-] [ ]
– Dead man rise / Stir the ashes / The night watch / Hang man / Where the deep water goes / Blown away / Nothing is stranger / Let's burn down the cornfield / River blood / Train to mercy.
Jul 92. (12")(cd-s) **DEAD MAN RISE** [ ] [ ]
Feb 93. (12")(cd-s) **JACK CANDY** [ ] [ ]
Mar 93. (cd)(lp) **NEW WEST MOTEL** [ ] [ ]
May 93. (12")(cd-s) **YOUR HOPE SHINES** [ ] [ ]
Nov 93. (cd)(lp) **SATISFIED MIND** [ ] [ ]
Mar 94. (12"ep)(cd-ep) **GOOD LUCK MORNING / NIGHT DRIVE (truck stop version). / FINDLAY'S MOTEL / NOTHING IS A STRANGER** [ ] [ ]
–
May 94. (cd)(lp) **SETTING THE WOODS ON FIRE** [ ] [ ]
– Good luck morning / Firetrap / Bordertown / Feeling no pain / Old crow / Almost wisdom / Sand and gravel / Night drive (truck stop version) / Hole in the mountain / Pass me on over / Up in the graveyard / Promised.

Scott WALKER / The WALKER BROTHERS

Formed: Los Angeles, California, USA ... 1964 as The WALKER BROTHERS. (also see further below). Their first single 'PRETTY GIRLS EVERYWHERE' flopped, but second 'LOVE HER' scraped the UK Top 20. They soon made No.1 twice in the UK with 1965-66 classics 'MAKE IT EASY ON YOURSELF' & 'THE SUN AIN'T GONNA SHINE ANYMORE'. In 1967, SCOTT WALKER went solo and hit heights until the 70's. The WALKER BROTHERS re-united in the mid-70's on 'GTO' with UK Top 10 single 'NO REGRETS'. • **Style:** Easy-listening cult pop trio, similar in sound to The RIGHTEOUS BROTHERS. SCOTT's melancholy ballads were later idolised by TEARDROP EXPLODES stalward JULIAN COPE. • **Songwriters:** WALKER BROTHERS covered (45's only); LOVE HER (Mann-Weill) / MAKE IT EASY ON YOURSELF (Jerry Butler) / MY SHIP IS COMING IN (Jimmy Radcliffe) / THE SUN AIN'T GONNA SHINE ANYMORE (Frankie Valli) / LOVE MINUS ZERO (Bob Dylan) / ANOTHER TEAR FALLS (Gene McDaniels) / STAY WITH ME BABY (Lorraine Ellison) / WALKING IN THE RAIN (Ronettes) / NO REGRETS (Tom Rush) / etc. SCOTT WALKER covers; JACKIE and others from 'SCOTT 2' lp (Jacques Brel). JOANNA (Tony Hatch & Jackie Trent). On his 'STRETCH' country roots album, several songs were written by BILLY JOE SHAVER. • **Trivia:** In 1987, SCOTT appears in TV ads for Britvic juice.

Recommended: AFTER THE LIGHTS GO OUT – THE BEST OF 1965-1967 (*6) / BOY CHILD – THE BEST OF SCOTT WALKER 1967-1970 (*8) / CLIMATE OF HUNTER (*8) / TILT (*7)

SCOTT ENGEL

(aka SCOTT WALKER) – vocals

Vogue | Orbit

Jun 58. (7") **THE LIVIN' END. / GOOD FOR NOTHIN'** [ ] [ ]
Oct 58. (7") **BLUEBELL. / PAPER DOLL** [ ] [ ]
Aug 58. (7") **CHARLIE BOP. / ALL I DO IS DREAM OF YOU** [-] [ ]
1959. (7") **SUNDAY. / GOLDEN RULE OF LOVE** [-] [ ]
1959. (7") **I DON'T WANNA KNOW. / COMIN' HOME** [-] [ ]

—— Continued to do session work until 1962 when he joined The ROUTERS alongside JOHN STEWART. They released 2 singles late 62-early 63, 'LET'S GO WITH THE ROUTERS' & 'MAKE IT SNAPPY'. After a spell with the SANDY NELSON band, he and JOHN joined The MOONGOONERS. They issued singles MOONGOON STOMP and MOONGOON TWIST in 1963. The following year, they became The DALTONS duo releasing one 45, 'I ONLY CAME TO DANCE WITH YOU'. SCOTT was now part of the famous trio.

The WALKER BROTHERS

SCOTT ENGEL (WALKER)(b. 9 Jan'44, Hamilton, Ohio) – vocals, bass, keyboards / **JOHN MAUS** (WALKER)(b.12 Nov'43, New York City) – vocals, guitar / **GARY LEEDS** (WALKER) (b. 3 Sep'44, Glendale, California) – drums, vocals

Philips | Smash

Mar 65. (7") **PRETTY GIRLS EVERYWHERE. / DOIN' THE JERK** [-] [ ]
May 65. (7") **LOVE HER. / THE SEVENTH DAWN** [20] [ ]
Aug 65. (7") **MAKE IT EASY ON YOURSELF. / BUT I DO** [1] [16]
Nov 65. (7") **MY SHIP IS COMING IN. / YOU'RE ALL AROUND ME** [3] [63]
Dec 65. (lp) **TAKE IT EASY WITH THE WALKER BROTHERS** [4] [ ]
– Make it easy for yourself / There goes my baby / First love never dies / Dancing in the street / Lonely winds / The girl I lost in the rain / Land of 1000 dances / You're all around me / Love minus zero / I don't want to hear it anymore / Here comes the night / Tell the truth.
Feb 66. (7") **THE SUN AIN'T GONNA SHINE ANYMORE. / AFTER THE LIGHTS GO OUT** [1] [13]
Jul 66. (7") **(BABY) YOU DON'T HAVE TO TELL ME. / MY LOVE IS GROWING** [13] [ ]
Aug 66. (lp) **PORTRAIT** [3] [ ]
– In my room / Saturday's child / Just for a thrill / Hurting each other / Old folks / Summertime / People get ready / I can see it now / Where's the girl / Living above your head / Take it like a man / No sad songs for me.
Sep 66. (7") **ANOTHER TEAR FALLS. / SADDEST NIGHT IN THE WORLD** [12] [ ]
Nov 66. (7") **DEADLIER THAN THE MALE (theme from the film). / ARC ANGEL** [34] [ ]
Jan 67. (7") **STAY WITH ME BABY. / TURN OUT THE MOON** [26] [ ]
Mar 67. (lp) **IMAGES** [6] [ ]
– Everything under the sun / Once upon a summertime / Experience / Blueberry Hill / Orpheus / Stand by me / I wanna know / I willwait for you / It makes no difference now / I can't let it happen to you / Genevieve / Just say goodbye.
May 67. (7") **WALKING IN THE RAIN. / BABY MAKE IT THE LAST TIME** [26] [ ]

—— Disbanded May67.

GARY WALKER

had previously issued solo material.

C.B.S. | Columbia

Feb 66. (7") **YOU DON'T LOVE ME. / GET IT RIGHT** [26] [ ]
May 66. (7") **TWINKLE LEE. / SHE MAKES ME FEEL BETTER** [26] [ ]

JOHN WALKER

went solo after the split.

Philips | Smash

Jun 67. (7") **ANNABELLA. / YOU DON'T UNDERSTAND ME** [24] [ ]

—— JOHN continued to release singles throughout the 60's.

SCOTT WALKER

As **SCOTT ENGEL** he re-issued old recordings.

1966. Liberty; (7"ep) **SCOTT ENGEL** [ ] [-]
– I broke my own heart / What do you say / Are these really mine / Crazy in love with you.

—— new but credited with **JOHN STEWART**

May 66. Capitol; (7") **I ONLY CAME TO DANCE WITH YOU. / GREENS** [ ] [ ]

—— **SCOTT WALKER / JOHN WALKER** had one side each on below 'Philips' EP

Dec 66. Capitol; (7"ep) **SOLO SCOTT – SOLO JOHN** [ ] [-]
– (SCOTT WALKER) – The gentle rain / Mrs.Murphy /

SCOTT WALKER

solo after the WALKER's split.

Philips | Smash

Aug 67. (lp) **SCOTT** [3] [ ]
– Mathilde / Montague Terrace (in blue) / Angelica / Lady came from Baltimore / When Joanna loved me / My death / Through a long and sleepless night / The big hurt / Such a small love / You're gonna hear from me / Always coming back to me / Amsterdam.
Nov 67. (7") **JACKIE. / THE PLAGUE** [22] [ ]
Mar 68. (lp) **SCOTT 2** [1] [ ]
– Jackie / Best of both worlds / The amorous Humphrey Plugg / Black sheep boy / Next / The girls from the street / Plastic palace people / Wait until dark / The girls and the dogs / Windows of the world / The bridge / Come next Spring.
Apr 68. (7") **JOANNA. / ALWAYS COMING BACK TO YOU** [7] [ ]
Mar 69. (lp) **SCOTT 3** [3] [ ]
– It's raining today / Copenhagen / Rosemary / Big Louise / We came through / Butterfly / Two ragged soldiers / 30th century man / Winter night / Two weeks since you've gone / Sons of / Funeral tango / If you go away. *(cd-iss.Aug92)*
Jun 69. (7") **LIGHTS OF CINCINNATI. / TWO WEEKS SINCE YOU'VE GONE** [13] [ ]
Jun 69. (lp) **... SINGS SONGS FROM HIS TV SERIES** [7] [ ]
– I have dreamed / The impossible dream / Will you still be mine / When the world was young / Who (will take my place) / If she walked into my life / The song is you / The look of love / Country girl / Someone to light up my life / Only the young / Lost in the stars.
Nov 69. (lp) **SCOTT 4 ("NOEL SCOTT ENGEL")** [ ] [ ]
– The seventh seal / On your own again / World's strongest man / Angels of ashes / Boy child / The old man's back again / Hero of the war / Duchess / Get behind me / Rhymes of goodbye. *(cd-iss.Aug92)*
Dec 70. (lp)(c) **'TIL THE BAND COMES IN** [ ] [ ]
– Prologue / Little things (that keep us together) / Jean the machine / Joe / Thanks for Chicago, Mr.James / Long about now / Time operator / Cowbells shakin' / 'Til the band comes in / The war is over / Stormy / The hills of yesterday / What are you doing the rest of your life / Rueben James / It's over.
Oct 71. (7") **I STILL SEE YOU. / MY WAY HOME** [ ] [ ]
Oct 72. (lp)(c) **THE MOVIEGOER** [ ] [-]
– This way Mary / Speak softly love / Glory road / That night / The summer of '42 / Easy come easy go / The ballad of Sacco and Vanzetti (here's to you) / Face in the crowd / Joe Hill / All his children / Come Saturday morning / The look of love.
May 73. (7") **THE ME I NEVER KNEW. / THIS WAY MARY** [ ] [ ]
May 73. (lp)(c) **ANY DAY NOW** [ ] [ ]

– Any day now / All my love's laughter / Do I love you / Ain't no sunshine / Maria Bethania / Cowboy / When you get right down to it / The me I never knew / If ships were made to sail / We could be flying.

C.B.S. Columbia

Oct 73. (7") **A WOMAN LEFT LONELY. / WHERE LOVE HAS DIED**
Nov 73. (lp)(c) **STRETCH**
– Sunshine / Just one smile / A woman left lonely / No easy way down / That's how I got to Memphis / Use me / Frisco depot / Someone who cared / Where does brown begin / Where love has died / I'll be home.
Jul 74. (7") **DELTA DAWN. / WE HAD IT ALL**
Aug 74. (lp)(c) **WE HAD IT ALL**
– Low down freedom / We had it all / Black rose / Ride me down easy / You're young and you'll forget / The house song / Old five and dimers like me / Whatever happened to Saturday night / Sundown / Delta dawn.

— SCOTT shelved solo career when the WALKERS re-formed in 1975.

The WALKER BROTHERS

(SCOTT, JOHN & GARY) On session were **BIG JIM SULLIVAN** – guitar / **ALAN SKIDMORE / BRIAN BENNETT & CHRIS MERCER**

G.T.O. G.T.O.

Oct 75. (lp)(c) **NO REGRETS** 49
– No regrets / Hold an old friend's hand / I've got to have you / Boulder to Birmingham / Lover's lullaby / Walkers' in the Sun / Half break your heart / Everything that touches you / Lovers / Burn our bridges. *(re-iss.Jul77) (re-iss.cd+c May94 on 'Sony') (re-iss.cd Sep94 on 'Rewind')*
Nov 75. (7") **NO REGRETS. / REMEMBER ME** 7
Jul 76. (lp)(c) **LINES**
– Lines / Taking it all in stride / Inside of you / Have you seen my baby / We're all alone / Many rivers to cross / Hard to be friends / First day / Brand new Tennessee waltz / Dreaming as one.
Sep 76. (7") **LINES. / FIRST DAY** -
Jun 77. (7") **WE'RE ALL ALONE. / HAVE YOU SEEN MY BABY** - Nov 76
Jul 78. (7") **THE ELECTRICIAN. / DEN HAAGUE** -
Jul 78. (lp)(c) **NITE FLIGHTS** -
– Shutout / Fat mama kick / Nite flights / The electrician / Death of romance / Den Haague / Rhythms of vision / Child of flames / Disciples of death / Fury and the fire.

— Split again in 1978 for the last time.

– (WALKER BROTHERS) compilations, etc. –

Jun 66. Philips; (7"ep) **I NEED YOU** -
May 67. Philips; (7"ep) **THE WALKER BROTHERS** -
Sep 67. Philips; (lp) **THE WALKER BROTHERS STORY** 9 -
1974. Philips; (lp)(c) **THE BEST OF THE WALKER BROTHERS** -
Oct 75. Philips; (lp)(c) **GREATEST HITS** -
1976. Philips; (lp)(c) **SPOTLIGHT ON THE WALKER BROTHERS** -
Apr 76. Philips; (7"m) **THE SUN AIN'T GONNA SHINE ANY-MORE. / MAKE IT EASY ON YOURSELF / STAY WITH ME BABY** -
Oct 80. Philips; (7") **MAKE IT EASY ON YOURSELF. / THE SUN AIN'T GONNA SHINE ANYMORE** -
1968. Contour; (lp) **THE IMMORTAL WALKER BROTHERS** -
(re-iss.1970)
1972. Contour; (lp)(c) **MAKE IT EASY ON YOURSELF** -
(re-iss.Jun76)
1968. Wing; (lp) **THE FABULOUS WALKER BROTHERS** -
Jun 81. GTO; (7"ep) **SHUTOUT / THE ELECTRICIAN. / NITE FLIGHTS / FAT MAMA KICK** -
Jan 85. Old Gold; (7") **THE SUN AIN'T GONNA SHINE ANYMORE. / MY SHIP IS COMING IN** -
Sep 85. Old Gold; (7") **NO REGRETS. / WE'RE ALL ALONE** -
Mar 88. Old Gold; (7") **MAKE IT EASY ON YOURSELF. / FIRST LOVE NEVER DIES** -
May 87. Bam Caruso; (7") **THE SUN AIN'T GONNA SHINE ANYMORE. / ?** -
Jul 90. Fontana; (cd)(c)(lp) **AFTER THE LIGHTS GO OUT – THE BEST OF 1965-1967** -
Dec 91. Fontana; (7")(c-s) **THE SUN AIN'T GONNA SHINE ANYMORE. / JACKIE (by "SCOTT WALKER")**
(12"+=)(cd-s+=) – First love never dies / Joanna (by "SCOTT WALKER").
Dec 91. Fontana; (cd)(c)(lp) **NO REGRETS – THE BEST OF SCOTT WALKER AND THE WALKER BROTHERS 1965-1976** 4
– (* denotes SCOTT WALKER track) – No regrets / Make it easy on yourself / The Sun ain't gonna shine anymore / My ship is comin' in / * Joanna / * Lights of Cincinatti / Another tear falls / * Boy child / * Montague Terrace in blue / * Jackie / Stay with me baby / * If you go away / First love never dies / Love her / Walking in the rain / (Baby) You don't have to tell me / Deadlier than the male / We're all alone.
Sep 93. Pickwick; (cd)(c) **A VERY SPECIAL COLLECTION** -

SCOTT WALKER

went solo again in 84.

Virgin Virgin

Mar 84. (lp)(c) **CLIMATE OF HUNTER** 60
– Rawhide / Dealer / Track 3 / Sleepwalker's woman / Track 5 / Track 6 / Track 7 / Blanket roll blues. *(re-iss.Aug88, cd-iss.Nov89)*

— Retired from music for a decade.

Fontana Mercury

May 95. (cd)(lp) **TILT** 27
– Farmer in the city / The cockfighter / Bouncer see bouncer . . . / Manhattan / Face on breast / Bolivia '95 / Patriot (a single) / Tilt / Rosary.

– (SCOTT WALKER) compilations, etc. –

Dec 67. Philips; (c-ep) **GREAT SCOTT!** -
– Jackie / When Joanna loved me / The plague / Mathilde.
Jan 70. Philips; (lp) **THE BEST OF SCOTT WALKER** -
(re-iss.+c.Nov71 as 'THIS IS SCOTT WALKER')
Oct 72. Philips; (lp)(c) **THIS IS SCOTT WALKER – VOL.2** -
Mar 76. Philips; (d-lp)(c) **SPOTLIGHT ON SCOTT WALKER** -
Nov 81. Philips; (lp)(c) **SINGS JAQUES BREL** -
Jun 82. Philips; (lp)(c) **BEST OF SCOTT WALKER (diff. from 1970 lp)** -
(re-iss.Oct83)
Dec 67. Ember; (lp) **LOOKING BACK WITH SCOTT WALKER** -
– (1959 SCOTT ENGEL demos)
Jan 76. Contour; (lp)(c) **THE BEST OF SCOTT WALKER (diff.)** -
Sep 81. Zoo; (lp) **FIRE ESCAPE IN THE SKY – THE GODLIKE GENIUS OF SCOTT WALKER** -
Aug 82. Old Gold; (7") **JOANNA. / LIGHTS OF CINCINNATI** -
Jun 90. Fontana; (cd)(c)(lp) **BOY CHILD – THE BEST OF 1967-70** -

WALL OF VOODOO

Formed: Los Angeles, California, USA . . . 1977 by STAN RIDGWAY and the MORELAND brothers. In 1980, they were spotted by MILES COPELAND who immediately signed them to his indie label 'I.R.S.'. In 1982, they tasted a little success when 'MEXICAN RADIO', pushed them into the UK Top 75. However, the following year, RIDGWAY departed for a more lucrative solo career. In 1986, he charted at No.4 with the ghost story of an army soldier 'CAMOUFLAGE'. WALL OF VOODOO continued for the rest of the 80's with new singer ANDY PRIEBOY, who did little to re-actify band. • **Style:** Alternative country-punk outfit likened to DEVO sound, who were fronted by the charismatic and heavily folk infuenced RIDGWAY. • **Songwriters:** RIDGWAY words / group compositions. From the mid-80's, PRIEBOY and group (bar LUEKHARDT) wrote material. They also covered RING OF FIRE (Johnny Cash) / MONA (Bo Diddley) / DO IT AGAIN (Beach Boys) / DARK AS A DUNGEON (M.Travis) / PRETTY BOY FLOYD (Woody Guthrie).

Recommended: GRANMA'S HOUSE (*8)

STAN RIDGWAY (b. 5 Apr'54) – vocals, harmonica, keyboards / **MARC MORELAND** – guitar / **BRUCE MORELAND** – bass, keyboards / **JOE NANINI** – drums, percussion / **CHAS T.GRAY** – bass, keyboards, synthesizers

Illegal I.R.S.

Sep 80. (12"ep) **WALL OF VOODOO**
– Long arm / The passenger / Can't make love / Ring of fire.
Oct 81. (lp) **DARK CONTINENT**
– Red light / Tow minutes till lunch / Animal day / Full of tension / Me and my dad / Back in the flesh / Tsetse fly / Call box (1-2-3) / This way out / Good times / Crack the bell.

— now a quartet when BRUCE left.

Oct 82. (7") **ON INTERSTATE 15. / THERE'S NOTHING ON THIS SIDE**
Oct 82. (lp) **CALL OF THE WEST** 45
– Tomorrow / Lost weekend / Factory / Look at their way / Hands of love / Mexican radio / Spy world / They don't want me / On Interstate 15 / Call of the west.
Jan 83. (7")(12") **MEXICAN RADIO. / CALL OF THE WEST** 64 58

— **MARC + CHAS** recruited new members **NED LEUKHARDT** – drums repl. NANINI / **ANDY PRIEBOY** – vocals repl. STAN RIDGWAY who went solo

I.R.S. I.R.S.

Nov 84. (7") **BIG CITY. / ROOM WITH A VIEW**

— added the returning **BRUCE MORELAND** – keyboards, bass

Mar 86. (7")(12") **FAR SIDE OF CRAZY. / THE WRONG WAY TO HOLLYWOOD**
May 86. (lp)(c) **SEVEN DAYS IN SAMMYSTOWN**
– Far side of crazy / Business of love / Faded love / Mona / Room with a view / Blackboard sky / Big city / Dark as the dungeon / Museums / Tragic vaudeville / (Don't spill my) Courage.
May 87. (7") **DO IT AGAIN. / BACK IN THE LAUNDROMAT**
(12"+=) – Far side of crazy.
Jun 87. (lp)(c) **HAPPY PLANET**
– Do it again / Hollywood the second time / Empty room / Chains of luck / When the lights go out / Love is a happy thing – Country of man / Joanne / Elvis bought Dora a Cadillac / The grass is greener / Ain't my day.

— guest **ROGER MASON** – keyboards repl. BRUCE who left again.

Illegal I.R.S.

Jun 88. (lp)(c)(cd) **UGLY AMERICANS IN AUSTRALIA AND BULLSHIT CITY (live)**
– Red light / Crazy, crazy Melbourne / Wrong way to Hollywood / Living in the red / Blackboard sky / Pretty Boy Floyd / The heart never can tell / Far side of crazy / Ring of fire / Mexican radio. *(cd+=)*– The grass is greener.

– compilations, others, etc. –

Jul 84. IRS; (lp) **GRANMA'S HOUSE**
– Ring of fire / Long arm / The passenger / Can't make love / On interstate 15 / Lost weekend / Mexican radio / Call box / Red light / Tomorrow / Crack the bell / Call of the west / Granma's house.
Jul 92. Mau Mau; (cd) **THE INDEX MASTERS (most live)** -

— Some WALL OF VOODOO tracks appeared on STAN RIDGWAY compilation cd,c,lp Jul92 'SONGS THAT MADE THIS COUNTRY GREAT, THE BEST OF STAN RIDGWAY' on 'IRS'.

Joe WALSH

Born: 20 Nov'47, Wichita, Kansas, USA. Quit The JAMES GANG late 1971, after 4 successful albums. In 1972, he went solo backed by new band BARNSTORM. The following year he was in US Top 30 with classic 'ROCKY MOUNTAIN WAY'. He surprised the rock press in 1975, by taking up the prestigious offer of joining The EAGLES. Many would agree that his guitar contribution on album HOTEL CALIFORNIA was the superior element. • **Style:** Ace hard-rock axeman of the 70's. The 80's were more mellower but with a little experimentation. • **Songwriters:** WALSH wrote all except LOVE LETTERS (Ketty Lester ?). • **Trivia:** In 1980, he stood for US presidential election. That year he also made a cameo appearance in the 'Blues Brothers' film.

Recommended: SO FAR SO GOOD – THE BEST OF. . . (*8)

JOE WALSH – vocals, guitar (ex-JAMES GANG) with his band **BARNSTORM: KENNY PASSARELLI** – bass / **JOE VITALE** – drums

Probe / Dunhill

Sep 72. (lp) **BARNSTORM** [ ] [79]
– Midnight visitor / Here we go / One and one / Giant bohemoth / Mother says / Birdcall morning / Home / I'll tell the world about you / Turn to stone / Comin' down. *(re-iss.Oct74 on 'Anchor')*

Sep 72. (7") **MOTHER SAYS. / I'LL TELL THE WORLD ABOUT YOU** [-] [ ]

— added **ROCKE GRACE** – keyboards / **JOE LALA** – percussion

Jun 73. (lp) **THE SMOKER YOU DRINK, THE PLAYER YOU GET** [ ] [6]
– Rocky mountain way / Bookends / Wolf / Midnight moodies / Happy ways / Meadows / Dreams / Days gone by / (Daydream) Prayer. *(re-iss.quad.Oct74 on 'Anchor')*

Aug 73. (7") **ROCKY MOUNTAIN WAY. / PRAYER** [-] [23]
(UK-iss.Jul75 on 'A.B.C.')

Jan 74. (7") **MEADOWS. / BOOKENDS** [ ] [89]
(re-iss.Mar76 on 'A.B.C.')

— In 1974, he sessioned for EAGLES, B.B.KING, etc. Also produced DAN FOGELBERG

— Solo; used past BARNSTORM members on a couple of tracks, plus new studio & live line-up **DAVID MASON + PAUL HARRIS** – keyboards / **BRYAN GAROFOLO** – bass / **RICKY FATAAR** – drums (ex-BEACH BOYS) / **TOM STEPHENSON** – keyboards

Anchor / Dunhill

Dec 74. (lp)(c) **SO WHAT?** [ ] [11]
– Welcome to the club / Falling down / Pavane / Time out / All night laundromat blues / Turn to stone / Help me thru the night / County fair / Song for Emma.

Feb 75. (7") **TURN TO STONE. / ALL NIGHT LAUNDROMAT BLUES** [ ] [93]

— Although he was still a solo artist, he also joined EAGLES late '75.

A.B.C. / A.B.C.

Apr 76. (lp)(c) **YOU CAN'T ARGUE WITH A SICK MIND (live)** [28] [20]
– Rocky mountain way / Help me thru the night / Time out / Meadows / Walk away / Turn to stone. *(re-iss.Aug81 + Jun86) (re-iss.Jan83 on 'Fame') (cd-iss.Jun88)*

Apr 76. (7") **TIME OUT (live). / HELP ME THRU THE NIGHT (live)** [-] [ ]

Jun 76. (7") **WALK AWAY (live). / HELP ME THRU THE NIGHT (live)** [ ] [ ]

— WALSH used mainly session people + VITALE.

Asylum / Asylum

Jun 78. (7") **LIFE'S BEEN GOOD. / THEME FROM BOAT WEIRDOS** [14] [12]

Jun 78. (lp)(c) **BUT SERIOUSLY, FOLKS . . .** [16] [8]
– Over and over / Second hand store / Indian summer / At the station / Tomorrow / Inner tube / Theme from Boat Weirdos / Life's been good. *(cd-iss.Feb93)*

Nov 78. (7") **OVER AND OVER. / AT THE STATION** [ ] [ ]

— Below from the film 'Urban Cowboy'. B-side by GILLEY'S URBAN COWBOY BAND.

W.E.A. / Full Moon

Jun 80. (7") **ALL NIGHT LONG. / ORANGE BLOSSOM SPECIAL / HOEDOWN** [ ] [19] May 80

— Now an ex-EAGLES man after their split.

Elektra / Asylum

May 81. (7") **A LIFE OF ILLUSION. / ROCKETS** [-] [34]

May 81. (7") **A LIFE OF ILLUSION. / DOWN ON THE FARM** [ ] [-]

May 81. (lp)(c) **THERE GOES THE NEIGHBORHOOD** [ ] [20]
– Things / Made your mind up / Down on the farm / Rivers (of the hidden funk) / A life of illusion / Bones / Rockets / You never know.

Jul 81. (7") **MADE YOUR MIND UP. / THINGS** [-] [ ]

Jan 82. (7") **WAFFLE STOMP. / THINGS** [-] [ ]

Full Moon / Full Moon

Jul 83. (7") **SPACE AGE WHIZ KIDS. / THEME FROM ISLAND WEIRDOS** [ ] [52] Jun 83

Jul 83. (lp)(c) **YOU BOUGHT IT – YOU NAME IT** [ ] [48]
– I can play that rock & roll / Told you so / Here we are now / The worry song / I.L.B.T.'s / Space age whiz kids / Love letters / Class of '65 / Shadows / Theme from Island weirdos. *(cd-iss.Jul84)*

Aug 83. (7") **I CAN PLAY THAT ROCK & ROLL. / HERE WE ARE NOW** [-] [ ]

Sep 83. (7") **LOVE LETTERS. / TOLD YOU SO** [ ] [-]

Nov 83. (7") **LOVE LETTERS. / I.L.B.T.'s** [-] [ ]

Jun 85. (7") **I BROKE MY LEG. / GOOD MAN DOWN** [-] [ ]

Jun 85. (lp)(c) **THE CONFESSOR** [ ] [65] May 85
– Problems / I broke my leg / Bubbles / Slow dancing / 15 years / Confessor / Rosewood bitters / Good man down / Dear John. *(cd-iss.Jul88)*

— now with **CHAD CROMWELL** – drums / **DAVID COCHRAN + RICK THE . . . PLAYER** – bass / **MARK RIVERA** – saxophone / **JOHN DAVID SOUTHER + JIMI JAMISON** – backing vocals

Aug 87. (lp)(c)(cd) **GOT ANY GUM?** [ ] [ ] Jul 87
– The radio song / Fun / In my car / Malibu / Half of the time / Got any gum? / Up to me / No peace in the jungle / Memory lane / Time.

Aug 87. (7") **THE RADIO SONG. / HOW YA DOIN'** [-] [ ]

Nov 87. (7") **IN MY CAR. / HOW YA DOIN'** [-] [ ]

Epic / Pyramid

Jul 91. (cd)(c)(lp) **ORDINARY AVERAGE GUY** [ ] [ ] May 91
– Two sides to every story / Ordinary average guy / The gama goochee / All of a sudden / Alphabetical order / Look at us now / I'm actin' different / Up all night / You might need somebody / Where I grew up / Schooldays.

Jul 91. (7") **ORDINARY AVERAGE GUY. / ALPHABETICAL ORDER** [-] [ ]

— In 1995, JOE was credited on single with LITA FORD.

– compilations, others, etc. –

Jun 77. ABC; (7") **ROCKY MOUNTAIN WAY. / TURN TO STONE** [-] [ ]

Jun 77. ABC; (12"ep) **PLUS FOUR EP** [39] [-]
– Rocky mountain way / Turn to stone / Meadows / Walk away.

Oct 78. ABC; (lp)(c) **SO FAR SO GOOD – THE BEST OF JOE WALSH** [ ] [71]
– Rocky mountain way / Welcome to the club / Bookends / Walk away / Mother says / Turn to stone / Here we go / Pavane / Time out / Meadows. *(re-iss.1983 on 'M.C.A.') (cd-iss.1987)*

Aug 82. MCA; (7") **ROCKY MOUNTAIN WAY. / TURN TO STONE** [ ] [-]
(12"+=)(12"pic-d+=) – Funk 49.

Oct 87. MCA; (cd) **THE SMOKER YOU DRINK . . . / YOU CAN'T ARGUE WITH A SICK MIND** [ ] [-]

Apr 86. Old Gold; (7") **ROCKY MOUNTAIN WAY. / ('B'by Poco)** [ ] [-]

1988. Raw Power; (lp)(c) **WELCOME TO THE CLUB** [ ] [-]

Jul 95. MCA; (cd) **LOOK WHAT I DID** [ ] [-]

Steve WALSH (see under ⇒ KANSAS)

WANDERERS (see under ⇒ SHAM 69)

WANG CHUNG

Formed: London, England . . . 1979 as HUANG CHUNG by ex-Royal College Of Music student JACK HUES and others (see below). After one 45 on 'Rewind' label, they signed to 'Arista', where they finally issued eponymous debut lp in 1982. Early next year, it was thought, their name should undergo slight transformation to WANG CHUNG. This seemed to work, and when 'Geffen' took over the reigns, fortunes changed. Early 1984, after a transatlantic Top 30 hit with 'DANCE HALL DAYS', they strode up both album charts with 'POINTS ON A CURVE'. The rest of the 80's were spent in the USA, where they gathered a string of chart hits. • **Style:** POLICE influenced rock and pop outfit, who blended danceable beat sound into the typical US college kid. • **Songwriters:** HUES penned. • **Trivia:** HUANG CHUNG means literally 'perfect pitch' in Chinese.

Recommended: HUANG CHUNG (*7)

HUANG CHUNG

JACK HUES – vocals, guitar, keyboards / **HOGG ROBINSON** – keyboards, saxophone / **NICK 'Spig' FELDMAN** – bass, keyboards / **DARREN COSTIN** – drums, keyboards

Rewind / not issued

Jun 80. (7") **ISN'T IT ABOUT TIME WE WERE ON T.V. / DRIVE ME CRAZY** [ ] [-]

Arista / Arista

Jul 81. (7") **HOLD BACK THE TEARS. / JOURNEY WITHOUT MAPS** [ ] [ ] Apr 82

Jan 82. (7")('A'ext-12") **CHINA. / ('A'instrumental)** [ ] [ ]

Mar 82. (lp)(c) **HUANG CHUNG** [ ] [ ]
– Ti-na-na / Hold back the tears / I never want to love you in a half-hearted way / Straight from my heart / Dancing / Chinese girls / Why do you laugh / China / I can't sleep / Rising in the east. *(cd-iss.Oct95 on 'One Way')*

Mar 82. (7") **TI-NA-NA. / I CAN'T SLEEP** [ ] [ ]

Oct 82. (7") **DANCE HALL DAYS. / WHY DO YOU LAUGH** [ ] [ ]

WANG CHUNG

trio without ROBINSON

Epic / Epic

Jun 83. (7")(12")(5"pic-d) **(DON'T BE MY) ENEMY. / THE WAVES (instrumental)** [ ] [ ] Sep 84

Geffen / Geffen

Jan 84. (7")(12")(7"pic-d) **DANCE HALL DAYS. / THERE IS A NATION** [21] [-]

Feb 84. (7") **DON'T LET GO. / THERE IS A NATION** [-] [38]

Mar 84. (lp)(c) **POINTS ON THE CURVE** [34] [30] Feb 84
– Don't let go / Dance hall days / True love / Devoted friends / Talk it out / Even if tou dream / Don't be my enemy / The waves / Look at me now / Wait. *(c+=)*– N.I.B.

Apr 84. (7") **DANCE HALL DAYS. / ORNAMENTAL ELEPHANT** [-] [16]

Apr 84. (7")(12")(7"sha-pic-d) **DON'T LET GO. / ORNAMENTAL ELEPHANT** [ ] [-]

Jun 84. (7")(12") **WAIT. / DANCE HALL DAYS (pt.2)** [ ] [ ]
(d7"+=) – Hard times / Dance hall days (pt.1).

— Below single from the film 'The Breakfast Club' on 'A&M'.

May 85. (7") **FIRE IN THE TWILIGHT. / ('B'side by KEITH FORSEY)** [ ] [ ]

—— Trim to a duo of **HUES + SPIG,** when COSTIN departed

Jan 86. (7") **TO LIVE AND DIE IN L.A. / DANCE HALL DAYS** [ ] [41] Oct 85
(12"+=) – Black-blue-white. *(US; b-side)*

Jan 86. (lp)(c)(cd) **TO LIVE AND DIE IN L.A. (Film Soundtrack)** [ ] [85] Oct 85
– To live and die in L.A. / Lullaby / Wake up, stop dreaming / Wait / City of the angels / The red stare / Black-blue-white / Every big city. *(re-iss.cd+c.Apr91)*

Oct 86. (7")(12") **EVERYBODY HAVE FUN TONIGHT. / FUN TONIGHT (EARLY YEARS)** [ ] [2]

Oct 86. (lp)(c)(cd) **MOSAIC** [ ] [41]
– Everybody have fun tonight / Hypnotize me / The flat horizon / Betrayal / Let's go / Eye of the girl / Food and his money / The world in which we live.

Jan 87. (7") **LET'S GO. / THE WORLD IN WHICH YOU LIVE** [-] [9]

May 87. (7") **LET'S GO. / TO LIVE AND DIE IN L.A.** [ ] [-]

Jun 87. (7") **HYPNOTIZE ME. (from the film 'Inner Space') / LULLABY** [-] [36]

—— added drummer VINNIE COLAUITA

Jul 89. (7")(c-s) **PRAYING TO A NEW GOD. / TALL TREES IN A BLUE SKY** [ ] [ ] May 89
(cd-s+=) – Dance hall days.
(12") – ('A'side) / Dance hall days / City of the angels.

Jul 89. (lp)(c)(cd) **THE WARMER SIDE OF COOL** [ ] [ ] Jun 89
– Praying to a new god / What's so bad about feeling good? / Snakedance / Swing / When love looks back at you / Games of power / At the speed of life / The warmer side of cool / Logic and love / Tall trees in a blue sky / Big world.

Oct 89. (7") **DANCE HALL DAYS REVISITED. / AT THE SPEED OF LIFE** [ ] [ ]
(12")(cd-s) – ('A'side) / ('A'original version) / ('A'dub version).

—— Disbanded during the early '90s.

WAR

Formed: 1969 out of Long Beach, California outfit The CREATORS. They soon became NIGHT SHIFT to back ex-football player turned soul-singer DEACON JONES. On the advise of producer Jerry Goldstein, they formed partnership with ERIC BURDON. After two successful albums, WAR decided to branch out on own in 1971. Now signed to 'United Art', they charted Top 40 US with ALL DAY MUSIC. Throughout the 70's, they became major stars, and even had the WHY CAN'T WE BE FRIENDS? track beamed into space mid-75 for US & USSR cosmonauts to listen to. The following year they had debut UK hit with the classic LOW RIDER. In the 80's, they slowly faded away into obscurity once again. • **Style:** Black R&B, mixing progressive soul with near Latin-American jazzy rock-pop. Moved into disco-pop with the advent of punk. • **Songwriters:** Group compositions?, except GROOVIN' (Young Rascals). • **Trivia:** In mid'70, they jammed at Ronnie Scott's, London with JIMI HENDRIX.

Recommended: GREATEST HITS (*7)

LONNIE JORDAN (b.LEROY JORDAN, 21 Nov'48, San Diego, Calif.) – keyboards / **HOWARD SCOTT** (b.15 Mar'46, San Pedro, California, USA) – guitar, vocals / **CHARLES MILLER** (b. 2 Jun'39, Olathe, Kansas, USA) – saxophone, clarinet / **HAROLD BROWN** (b.17 Mar'46, Long Beach, California) – drums, percussion / **LEE OSKAR** (b.24 Mar'46, Copenhagen, Denmark) – harmonica / **B.B.DICKERSON** (b.MORRIS, 3 Aug'49, Torrance, California) – bass, vocals repl. PETER ROSEN who died drug overdose mid '69. / **PAPA DEE ALLEN** (b.THOMAS, 18 Jul'31, Wilmington, Delaware) – keyboards
Recorded 2 albums in 1970 + 71 with (ex-ANIMALS ⇒) vocalist ERIC BURDON. 'ERIC BURDON DECLARES WAR' & 'THE BLACK MAN'S BURDON' both hit UK/US charts.

United Art United Art

Apr 71. (7") **SUN OH SON. / LONELY FEELIN'** [ ] [ ]

May 71. (lp)(c) **WAR** [ ] [ ] Apr 71
– Sun oh son / Lonely feelin' / Back home / War drums / Vibeka / Fidel's fantasy. *(re-iss.Oct79 on 'M.C.A.')*

Aug 71. (7") **ALL DAY MUSIC. / GET DOWN** [ ] [35]

Oct 71. (lp)(c) **ALL DAY MUSIC** [ ] [16]
– All day music / Get down / That's what love will do / There must be a reason / Nappy nead / Slipping into darkness / Baby brother. *(re-iss.Jun76 on 'Island') (re-iss.Oct79 on 'MCA') (cd-iss.Oct95 on 'Avenue')*

Apr 72. (7") **SLIPPIN' INTO DARKNESS. / NAPPY HEAD** [ ] [16] Jan 72
(re-iss.Nov76)

Dec 72. (7") **THE WORLD IS A GHETTO. / FOUR CORNERED ROOM** [ ] [7] Nov 72

Jan 73. (lp)(c) **THE WORLD IS A GHETTO** [ ] [1] Nov 72
– The Cisco kid / Where was you at / City, country city / Four cornered room / The world is a ghetto / Beetles in a bog. *(re-iss.Oct79 on 'MCA') (cd-iss.Oct95 on 'Avenue')*

Mar 73. (7") **THE CISCO KID. / BEETLES IN THE BOG** [ ] [2]

Aug 73. (7") **GYPSY MAN. / DELIVER THE WORD** [ ] [8] Jul 73

Aug 73. (lp)(c) **DELIVER THE WORD** [ ] [6]
– Three dog night eyes / Gypsy man / Me and baby brother / Deliver the word / Southern part of Texas / Blisters. *(re-iss.Oct79 on 'MCA') (cd-iss.Oct95 on 'Avenue')*

Dec 73. (7") **ME AND BABY BROTHER. / IN YOUR EYES** [ ] [15] Nov 73
(UK re-iss.Jun76, hit No.21)

Apr 74. (d-lp)(c) **WAR LIVE! (live)** [ ] [13] Mar 74
– (introductions by E.Rodney Jones) / Sun oh son / The Cisco kid / Slippin' into darkness / All day music / Ballero / Lonely feelin' / Intro – Get down / Get down. *(re-iss.Jun76 on 'Island') (re-iss.Oct79 on 'MCA')*

Apr 74. (7") **BALLERO (live). / ?** [-] [33]

Jul 75. (7") **WHY CAN'T WE BE FRIENDS?. / IN MAZATLAN** [ ] [6] May 75
(re-iss.Mar76)

Jul 75. (lp)(c) **WHY CAN'T WE BE FRIENDS?** [ ] [8] Jun 76
– Don't let no one get you down / Lotus blossom / Heartbeat / Leroy's Latin lament: Lonies dream – The dream – The way we feel – La fiesta – Lament / Smile happy / So / Low rider / In Mazatlan / Why can't we be friends. *(re-iss.Jun76 on 'Island') (re-iss.Oct79 on 'MCA') (cd-iss.Oct95 on 'Avenue')*

Island United Art

Jan 76. (7") **LOW RIDER. / SO** [12] [7] Sep 75

Aug 76. (7") **SUMMER. / ALL DAY MUSIC** [ ] [7] Jul 76

Sep 76. (lp)(c) **GREATEST HITS** (compilation) [ ] [6]
– All day music / Slippin' into darkness / The world is a ghetto / The Cisco kid / Gypsy man / Me and baby brother / Southern part of Texas / Why can't we be friends? / Low rider / Summer.*(re-iss.Oct79 on 'MCA')*

Island Blue Note

Jul 77. (d-lp)(c) **PLATINUM JAZZ** [ ] [23]
– (compilation) War is coming / Slowly we walk together / Platinum jazz / I got you / L.A. sunshine / River Niger / H2 overture / City, country, city / Smile happy / Deliver the word / Nappy head / Four cornered room. *(re-iss.Oct79 on 'MCA') (cd-iss.Oct95 on 'Avenue')*

Jul 77. (7") **L.A.SUNSHINE. / ?** [-] [45]

M.C.A. M.C.A.

Dec 77. (7") **GALAXY. / ('A'instrumental)** [14] [39]

Jan 78. (lp)(c) **GALAXY** [ ] [15] Nov 77
– Galaxy / Baby Face (she said do do do do) / Sweet fighting lady / Hey senorita / The seven tin soldiers.

Mar 78. (7")(12") **HEY SENORITA. / SWEET FIGHTING LADY** [40] [ ]

Jul 78. (lp)(c) **YOUNGBLOOD (Soundtrack)** [ ] [69]
– Youngblood / Sing a happy song / Keep on movin' / The Kingsmen sign / Walking to war / This funky music makes you feel good / Junk yard / Superdude / Youngblood & Sybil / Flying machine / Searching for Youngblood & Rommel / Youngblood (rerise). *(re-iss.Dec79)*

Aug 78. (7") **BABY FACE (SHE SAID DO DO DO DO). / ('A'version)** [ ] [ ]

Oct 78. (7")(12") **YOUNGBLOOD. / ('A'version)** [ ] [ ]

—— added **ALICE TWEED SMYTH** – vocals + **LUTHER RABB** – bass

Apr 79. (7")(12") **GOOD GOOD FEELIN'. / SWEET FIGHTIN' LADY** [ ] [ ]

Apr 79. (lp)(c) **THE MUSIC BAND** [ ] [41]
– The music band / Corns & callouses / I'm the one who understands / Good good feelin' / Millionaire / All around the world. *(re-iss.Oct79)*

Aug 79. (7")(12") **I'M THE ONE WHO UNDERSTANDS. / CORNS & CALLOUSES** [ ] [ ]

—— added **PAT RIZZO** – horns / **RON HAMMOND** – percussion to repl. DICKERSON.

Jan 80. (7")(12") **THE WORLD IS A GHETTO. / I'LL TAKE CARE OF YOU** [ ] [ ]

Jan 80. (lp)(c) **THE MUSIC BAND 2** [ ] [ ] Dec 79
– Don't take it away / I'll take care of you / The world is a ghetto / I'll be around / Night people / The music band 2. Don't take it away / I'll take care of you / The world is a ghetto / I'll be around / Night people / The music band 2.

May 80. (7") **I'LL BE AROUND. / THE MUSIC BAND 2** [ ] [ ]

Nov 80. (lp) **THE MUSIC BAND – LIVE (live)** [ ] [-]
– Spill the wine / All day music / Slippin' into darkness / Low rider / Cisco kid / All night long / Gypsy man / Why can't we be friends.

R.C.A. Lax

Mar 82. (7")(12") **YOU GOT THE POWER. / CINCO DE MAYO** [58] [66]

Mar 82. (lp)(c) **OUTLAW** [ ] [48]
– You got the power / Outlaw / The jungle (medley):- Beware it's a jungle out there – The street of walls – The street of lights – The street of now / Just because / Baby it's cold outside / I'm about somebody / Cinco de Mayo.

May 82. (7") **OUTLAW. / ?** [-] [94]

Jul 82. (7") **JUST BECAUSE. / I'M ABOUT SOMEBODY** [ ] [ ]

—— SMYTH + MILLER now departed

Jun 83. (lp)(c) **LIFE (IS SO STRANGE)** [ ] [ ]
– Life (is so strange) / Happiness / W.W.III (medley) / The dawning of night / Waiting at the church / When the nightmare comes / Shaking it down / Summer dreams / U-2 (medley):- U-2 (part 1) – Automatic eyes – U-2 (part 2) – U-2 (part 3)

Bluebird not issued

Mar 85. (7")(12") **GROOVIN'. / ('A'instrumental)** [43] [-]
(re-iss.Aug86)

Lax Lax

May 87. (7") **LOW RIDER (remix). / SLIPPIN' INTO DARKNESS** [ ] [ ]
(12"+=) – ('A'original mix).
(cd-s+=) – Galaxy / Me and baby brother.

not issued Virgin

Aug 91. (c-s) **LOWRIDER (IN THE BOULEVARD). /** [-] [54]

Avenue Avenue

Jun 95. (cd) **PEACE SIGN** [ ] [ ] 1994
– Peace sign / East L.A. / Wild Rodriguez / I'm the one (who understands) / Da roof / The smuggler (the light in the window) / U B O K / Let me tell you / Smile for me / What if / Angel / Homeless hero.

– more compilations, etc. –

1983. MCA; (lp) **THE MUSE BAND – JAZZ** [-] [ ]

Jun 87. Thunderbolt; (lp) **ON FIRE** [ ] [-]

May 87. Chord/ US= Priority; (cd) **THE BEST OF WAR & MORE – THE REMIXES** [ ] [ ]
(re-iss.Apr92 on 'Avenue-Rhino')

LEE OSKAR

United Art United Art

Jun 76. (lp)(c) **LEE OSKAR** [ ] [29] Mar 76
– The journey / The immigrant / The promised land / Blisters / BLT / Sunshine Keri / Down the Nile / Starkite. *(re-iss.May76 on 'MCA') (cd-iss.Oct95 on 'Avenue')*

Jun 76. (7") **BLT. /** [-] [59]

M.C.A. Elektra

Mar 79. (7") **BEFORE THE RAIN. / HAUNTED HOUSE** [-] [ ]

Sep 79. (7") **SAN FRANCISCO BAY. / HAUNTED HOUSE** [ ] [-]

Sep 79. (lp)(c) **BEFORE THE RAIN** [ ] [ ]
– Before the rain / Steppin' / San Francisco bay / Feelin' happy / More than words

can say / Sing song / Haunted house.
Oct 79. (7") **FEELIN' HAPPY. / SAN FRANCISCO BAY** [-] [ ]
Mar 80. (7") **FEELIN' HAPPY. / MORE THAN WORDS CAN SAY** [ ] [ ]
Jul 81. (lp)(c) **MY ROAD OUR ROAD** [ ] [ ]
– My road . . .our road: 1. Now that it feels so good- 2. When we first met- 3. Love affair- 4. Come on, come on- 5. (Memories) My road / Up all night / Song for my son / Children's song (you can find your way) / Yes, I'm singing.
Jul 81. (7") **UP ALL NIGHT. /** [-] [ ]
Oct 95. Avenue; (cd) **THE BEST OF LEE OSKAR** (compilation) [ ] [ ]

Dean WAREHAM (see under ⇒ GALAXIE 500)

WARRANT

Formed: Los Angeles, California, USA . . . 1986 by 5 below. After a couple of years on US college circuit, they signed to 'Columbia'. With regular slots on MTV, they made impact into US top 10 with the album 'DIRTY ROTTEN . . . ' & single 'HEAVEN'. • **Style:** Party-metal and teenage anthem-rock, typical of US bands of the rea (i.e. WINGER / RATT / etc). • **Songwriters:** JANI LANE, except cover TRAIN, TRAIN (Blackfoot). • **Trivia:** BEAU HILL produced debut album.

Recommended: DIRTY ROTTEN FILTHY STINKING RICH (*5)

JANI LANE – vocals / **JOEY ALLEN** – guitar / **ERIC TURNER** – guitar / **JERRY DIXON** – bass / **STEVEN SWEET** – drums

C.B.S. Columbia

Apr 89. (7") **DOWN BOYS. / COLD SWEAT** [-] [27]
Jun 89. (lp)(c)(cd) **DIRTY ROTTEN FILTHY STINKING RICH** [ ] [10] Mar 89
– 32 pennies / Down boys / Big talk / Sometimes she cries / So damn pretty (should be against the law) / D.R.F.S.R. / In the sticks / Heaven / Ridin' high / Cold sweat.
Sep 89. (7") **HEAVEN. / IN THE STICKS** [ ] [2] Jul 89
(12"+=)(cd-s+=)(12"pic-d+=) – Cold sweat.
Nov 89. (c-s)(cd-s) **BIG TALK. / D.R.F.S.R.** [-] [93]
Jan 90. (7")(c-s) **SOMETIMES SHE CRIES. / 32 PENNIES / IN A RAG JAR** [-] [20]
Sep 90. (cd)(c)(lp) **CHERRY PIE** [ ] [7]
– Cherry pie / Uncle Tom's cabin / I saw red / Bed of roses / Sure feels good to me / Love in stereo / Blind faith / Song and dance man / You're the only hell your mama ever raised / Mr. Rainmaker / Train, train.
Oct 90. (7")(c-s) **CHERRY PIE. / THIN DISGUISE** [59] [10] Sep 90
(12"+=)(pic-cd-s+=) – Heaven / D.R.F.S.R. *(re-iss.Feb91 on 'Columbia', hit UK No.35 / re-iss.+d7")*
Dec 90. (c-s)(cd-s) **I SAW RED. / ('A' acoustic)** [-] [10]
Apr 91. (7")(c-s) **UNCLE TOM'S CABIN. / SURE FEELS GOOD TO ME** [-] [78]
Jun 91. (c-s)(cd-s) **BLIND FAITH. / MISTER RAINMAKER** [-] [88]
Mar 92. (7") **WE WILL ROCK YOU. / BLIND FAITH. / BLIND FAITH (acoustic)** [-] [83]
(above from film 'Gladiator')

Columbia Columbia

Sep 92. (cd)(c)(lp) **DOG EAT DOG** [74] [25]
– Machine gun / The hole in my wall / April 2031 / Andy Warhol was right / Bonfire / The bitter pill / Hollywood (so far, so good) / All my bridges are burning / Quicksand / Let it rain / Inside out / Sad Theresa.
Sep 92. (7") **MATCHING GUN. / INSIDE OUT** [-] [ ]
Nov 92. (7") **THE BITTER PILL. / QUICKSAND** [-] [ ]

M.F.N. Megaforce

Mar 95. (cd) **ULTRAPHOBIC** [ ] [ ]
– Undertow / Followed / Family picnic / Sun of one / Chameleon / Crawl space / Live inside you / High / Ride #2 / Ultraphobic / Stronger now.

WAS (NOT WAS)

Formed: Detroit, Michegan, USA . . . 1980 by former Jewish schoolboys DON FAGENSON and DAVE WEISS. They renamed themselves WAS and were signed to New York underground label 'Ze' by co-owner Michael Zilkha. They employed many session singers and musicians to complete eponymous debut in 1981, and some stayed with them as a band throughout the 80's and early 90's. After signing to 'Geffen' in 1983, they scored first hit with re-vamped version of 1981 single 'OUT COME THE FREAKS'. In Autumn '87, 'WALK THE DINOSAUR' strolled into the UK/US Top 10, and it was soon trailed by later hits 'PAPA WAS A ROLLING STONE' and 'SHAKE YOUR HEAD'. • **Style:** Described as futuristic funksters, they fused together a blend of fresh danceable tongue-in-cheek soul/pop. • **Songwriters:** DAVE – lyrics / DON – music, except covers PAPA WAS A ROLLING STONE (Temptations) / LISTEN LIKE THIEVES (Inxs). • **Trivia:** The 1983 track 'SHAKE YOUR HEAD', was to have featured MADONNA, but DON taped over her vox, saying she'd never be heard of in Cleveland. DON also produced many acts including; FLOY JOY (1986 + sessions) / B-52's (1989) / BONNIE RAITT (1989 + 1991) / LEONARD COHEN, IGGY POP (1990) / ELTON JOHN, ROLLING STONES, BOB DYLAN (1990).

Recommended: WAS NOT WAS (*7) / HELLO DAD, I'M IN JAIL (*8) / ARE YOU OKAY? (*8)

DON WAS (b.DONALD FAGENSON) – bass, multi-instruments / **DAVE WAS** (b.DAVID WEISS) – keyboards, mulit-instruments / **SWEET PEA ATKINSON** – vocals / **WAYNE KRAMER** – guitar / **'Sir' HARRY BOWENS** – vocals / plus **DAVID McMURRAY** – sax / **CARL SMALL** – percussion / **BRUCE NAZARIAN** – guitar / **LIZ WEISS** – vocals (1)

Ze-Island Ze

Jan 81. (12") **WHEEL ME OUT. / HELLO OPERATOR** [-] [ ]
Jun 81. (lp)(c) **WAS (NOT WAS)** [ ] [ ]
– Out come the freaks / Where did your heart go / Tell me that I'm dreaming / Oh, Mr.Friction / Carry me back to old Morocco / It's an attack / The sky's ablaze / Go . . .now!. *(re-iss.+cd.Jun90 on 'Fontana')*
Jul 81. (7") **OUT COME THE FREAKS. / HELLO OPERATOR . . . I MEAN DAD . . . I MEAN POLICE . . . I CAN'T REMEMBER WHO I AM** [ ] [ ]
(12") – ('A'side) / Out come the freaks (dub).
Aug 81. (7")('A'ext-12") **WHERE DID YOUR HEART GO?. / WHEEL ME OUT** [ ] [ ]

— added **DAWN SILVA + LYNN MABREY** – vocals (ex-FUNKADELIC)

Mar 82. (7") **TELL ME THAT I'M DREAMING. / ('A'souped up version)** [ ] [ ]
(12"+=) – Out come the freaks.

— SWEET PEA released solo album DON'T WALK AWAY in Aug'82.

— **RANDY JACOBS** – guitar / **DONALD RAY MITCHELL** – vocals repl. KRAMER + LIZ

— next with guest vocalists **MITCH RYDER / DOUG FIEGER / MEL TORME + OZZY OSBOURNE**

Geffen Geffen

Oct 83. (7") **SMILE. / THE PARTY BROKE UP (JASON BLEW IN FROM PEORIA)** [ ] [ ]
Nov 83. (lp)(c) **BORN TO LAUGH AT TORNADOES** [ ] [ ]
– (Return to the valley of) Out come the freaks / Professor night / The party broke up / Smile / Zaz turned blue / Knocked down, made small (treated like a rubber ball) / Bow wow wow wow / Betrayal / Shake your head (let's go to bed) / Man vs. the empire brain building.
Feb 84. (7")(ext-12") **(RETURN TO THE VALLEY OF) OUT COME THE FREAKS. / OUT COME THE FREAKS (funk version)** [41] [ ]
Apr 84. (7") **PROFESSOR NIGHT. / BOW WOW WOW WOW** [ ] [ ]
(12"+=) – Shake your head (let's go to bed).

— added **DESY CAMPBELL** – vocals (ex-FLOY JOY)

Mercury Chrysalis

Sep 86. (7") **ROBOT GIRL (London mix). / EARTH TO DORIS** [ ] [ ]
(d7"+=)(12"+=) – Where did you heart go? / ('A'mix).

— **DON + DAVE** retained **HARRY, SWEETPEA, DONALD, RANDY + DAVID,** plus added **RAYSE BIGGS** – trumpet / **DEBRA DOBKIN** – percussion / **RON PANGHORN** – drums / **LUIS RESTO** – keyboards

Fontana Chrysalis

Jun 87. (7") **SPY IN THE HOUSE OF LOVE. / DAD I'M IN JAIL** [51] [ ]
(12"+=) – ('A'different mix).
Sep 87. (7") **WALK THE DINOSAUR. / 11 MILES AN HOUR** [10] [7] Jan 89
(12"+=)(cd-s+=) – ('A'instrumental) / ('A'dub mix).
Nov 87. (7") **THE BOY'S GONE CRAZY. / WHAT'S UP, DOG?** [ ] [ ]
(12"+=)(c-s+=) – ('A'walk in the forest mix) / ('A'dub mix).
Jan 88. (7") **SPY IN THE HOUSE OF LOVE. / DAD I'M IN JAIL** [21] [16] Sep 88
(12"+=) – ('A'streetsahead mix).
(12"++=)(cd-s++=) – ('A'full effect mix).
Mar 88. (lp)(c)(cd) **WHAT'S UP, DOG?** [47] [43] Oct 88
– Spy in the house of love / Boy's gone crazy / Anything can happen / Somewhere in America there's a street named after my dad / Out come the freaks / Love can be bad luck / Shadow & Jimmy / 11 miles an hour / Robot girl / What's up dog? / Anytime Lisa / Wedding vows in Vega / Walk the dinosaur / Can't turn you loose / Dad I'm in jail. *(c+=)(cd+=)*– Earth to Doris.
Apr 88. (7") **OUT COME THE FREAKS (AGAIN). / EARTH TO DORIS** [44] [ ]
(12"+=) – ('A'-Bobby Maggot mix).
(12"+=)(cd-s+=) – (Return to the valley of) Out come the freaks / Out come the freaks (Ze version).
Jun 88. (7") **ANYTHING CAN HAPPEN. / THE DEATH OF MR.PING PONG** [67] [ ]
(12"+=) – One white crow.
(cd-s++=) – Land of the free.

— **JAMIE MUHOBERAC** – keyboards repl. RESTO

Jun 89. (7")(c-s) **ANYTHING CAN HAPPEN (R&B mix). / ('A'-lp version)** [ ] [75] Apr 89
(12"+=)(cd-s+=) – ('A'acid mix).
(12"+=) – ('A'-2 other mixes).
May 90. (7") **PAPA WAS A ROLLING STONE. / BALLAD OF YOU** [12] [ ]
(12"+=)(cd-s+=) – ('A'instrumental).
(12") – ('A'-3 mixes, remix / full rub / Acappella).
Jun 90. (cd)(c)(lp) **ARE YOU OKAY?** [35] [99]
– Are you okay? / Papa was a rolling stone / I feel better than James Brown / How the heart behaves / Maria Novarro / I blew up the United States / In K-mart wardrobe / Elvis' Rolls Royce / Dressed to be killed / Just another couple broken hearts / You! you! you! / Look what's back.
Jul 90. (7")(c-s) **HOW THE HEART BEHAVES. / THE WEIRD AND WONDERFUL WORLD OF (rave mix)** [53] [ ]
(12"+=)(cd-s+=) – Anything can happen.
Nov 90. (7") **I FEEL BETTER THAN JAMES BROWN. / ('A'version)** [ ] [ ]
(12"+=)(cd-s+=) – ('A'-2 other mixes).
(12"++=) – ('A'other instrumental mix).

— **TONY PATLER** – keyboards / **JERVONNY COLLIER** – bass / **BUSTER MARBURY** – drums repl. JAMIE, ? & RON

May 92. (7") **LISTEN LIKE THIEVES. / HELLO OPERATOR** [39] [ ]
(12"+=)(cd-s+=) – Go now / Wedding vows.
Jun 92. (cd)(c)(lp) **HELLO DAD . . .I'M IN JAIL** (compilation) [61] [ ]
– Listen like thieves / Shake your head (let's go to bed) / Tell me that I'm dreaming / Papa was a rolling stone / Are you okay? / Spy in the house of love / I feel better than James Brown / Somewhere in America there's a street named after my dad / Out come the freaks / How the heart behaves / Walk the dinosaur / Hello dad . . . I'm in jail.

— Next single featured OZZY OSBOURNE and KIM BASSINGER on vox

Jul 92. (7") **SHAKE YOUR HEAD. / I BLEW UP THE UNITED STATES** [4] [ ]
(12"+=) – Listen like thieves (giant club mix + vandal dub mix).
(cd-s+=) – Spy in the house of love / Robot girl.
Sep 92. (7") **SOMEWHERE IN AMERICA (THERE'S A STREET NAMED AFTER MY DAD). / SHAKE YOUR HEAD (LET'S GO TO BED)** [57] [ ]
(12"+=) – Where did your heart go.
(cd-s++=) – I blew up the United States.

W.A.S.P.

Formed: Los Angeles, California, USA . . . 1983 as W.A.S.P. (We Are Sexual Perverts) by 6'4 ex-New York street gangster BLACKIE LAWLESS. After one banned single for 'Music For Nations', they signed to 'Capitol' in 1984. Immediately struck up a rapport with UK audiences, where they soon became Top 30 act. • **Style:** Heavy horror-metal group, whose live shows featured codpiece-fronted BLACKIE LAWLESS, a beast of a man who simulated torture and violence at every opportunity. During the latter half of the 80's, they had mellowed into a more stereotype hard-rock outfit. • **Songwriters:** Most written by LAWLESS and PIPER, except PAINT IT BLACK (Rolling Stones) / EASY LIVIN' (Uriah Heep) / I DON'T NEED NO DOCTOR (Humble Pie) / LOCOMOTIVE BREATH (Jethro Tull) / THE REAL ME (The Who) / LONG WAY TO THE TOP + WHOLE LOTTA ROSIE (Ac-Dc) / SOMEBODY TO LOVE (Jefferson Airplane). • **Trivia:** Late in 1989, the lucky HOLMES married metal-songstress LITA FORD.

Recommended: FIRST BLOOD, LAST CUTS (*7).

BLACKIE LAWLESS (b. 4 Sep'56) – vocals, bass (ex-SISTER, ex-NEW YORK DOLLS) / **CHRIS HOLMES** (b.23 Jun'61) – lead guitar (ex-SISTER) / **RANDY PIPER** – rhythm guitar / **TONY RICHARDS** – drums

M.F.N. | not issued

Apr 84. (7")(12")(7"sha-pic-d)(12"white) **ANIMAL (F**K LIKE A BEAST). / SHOW NO MERCY** [ ] [-]
*(re-iss.12"pic-d.May85) (re-iss.12".Feb88 tracks LIVE ANIMAL (F**K LIKE A BEAST). / DB BLUES / ANIMAL; hit UK 61)*

Capitol | Capitol

Aug 84. (lp)(c) **W.A.S.P.** [51] [74]
– I wanna be somebody / L.O.V.E. machine / The flame / B.A.D. / School daze / Hellion / Sleeping (in the fire) / On your knees / Tormentor / The torture never stops. *(re-iss.+cd.Jun88 on 'Fame', cd re-iss.May89) (re-iss.cd+c Jul94)*
Sep 84. (7")(12")(12"pic-d) **I WANNA BE SOMEBODY. / TORMENTOR** [ ] [ ]
Jan 85. (7")(12") **SCHOOLDAZE. / PAINT IT BLACK** [ ] [ ]
— **STEPHEN RILEY** – drums (ex-KEEL) repl. RICHARDS
Sep 85. (lp)(c) **THE LAST COMMAND** [48] [49]
– Wild child / Ballcrusher / Fistful of diamonds / Jack action / Widow maker / Blind in Texas / Cries in the night / The last command / Running wild in the streets / Sex drive. *(re-iss.+cd.May89 on 'Fame') (re-iss.cd+c Jul94)*
Oct 85. (7")(7"pic-d) **BLIND IN TEXAS. / SAVAGE** [ ] [ ]
(12"+=)(12"pic-d+=) – I wanna be somebody (live).
Jun 86. (7") **WILD CHILD. / MISSISSIPPI QUEEN** [71] [ ]
(12"+=)/ /(d12"+=) – ('A'wild mix)./ / On your knees / Hellion.
— **JOHNNY ROD** – bass (ex-KING KOBRA) repl. PIPER

WASP

(dropped dots). **BLACKIE** now also rhythm guitar
Sep 86. (7")(7"pic-d) **9.5 – N.A.S.T.Y. / EASY LIVING** [70] [ ]
(12"+=) – Flesh and fire.
Oct 86. (lp)(c)(cd) **INSIDE THE ELECTRIC CIRCUS** [53] [60]
– The big welcome / Inside the electric circus / I don't need no doctor / 9.5 – N.A.S.T.Y. / Restless gypsy / Shoot it from the hip / I'm alive / Easy living / Sweet cheetah / Mantronic / King of Sodom and Gomorrah / The rock rolls on. *(re-iss.May89) (re-iss.+cd.Jul90 on 'Fame') (re-iss.cd+c Jul94)*

W.A.S.P.

Aug 87. (7") **SCREAM UNTIL YOU LIKE IT. / SHOOT IT FROM THE HIP (live)** [32] [ ]
(12"+=)(12"pic-d+=) – Sleeping (in the fire).
Sep 87. (lp)(c)(cd) **LIVE . . . IN THE RAW (live)** [23] [77]
– Inside the electric circus / I don't need no doctor / L.O.V.E. machine / Wild child / 9.5 – N.A.S.T.Y. / Sleeping (in the fire) / The manimal / I wanna be somebody / Harder faster / Blind in Texas. *(cd+=)*– Scream until you like it. *(re-iss.cd+c Jul94)*
Oct 87. (7")(7"sha-pic-d) **I DON'T NEED NO DOCTOR. / WIDOW MAKER (live)** [31] [ ]
(12"+=) – Sex drive (live).
— now basic trio of **BLACKIE, CHRIS & JOHNNY** when STEPHEN joined L.A.GUNS. **FRANKIE BANALIE** – drums (of QUIET RIOT) filled in temp. / added guest **KEN HENSLEY** – keyboards (ex-URIAH HEEP, ex-BLACKFOOT)
Feb 89. (7")(7"pic-d)(7"purple) **MEAN MAN. / LOCOMOTIVE BREATH** [21] [ ]
(12"+=)(cd-s+=) – For whom the bells toll.
Apr 89. (lp)(c)(cd)(pic-lp) **THE HEADLESS CHILDREN** [8] [48]
– Heretic (the lost child) / The real me / The headless children / Thunderhead / Mean man / The neutron bomber / Mephisto waltz / Forever free / Maneater / Rebel in the F.D.G. *(re-iss.cd+c Jul94)*
May 89. (7")(7"pic-d)(7"blue) **THE REAL ME. / THE LAKE OF FOOLS** [23] [ ]
(12"+=)(cd-s+=) – War cry.
Aug 89. (7")(c-s)(7"sha-pic-d) **FOREVER FREE (eagle edit). / LOVE MACHINE (live'89)** [ ] [ ]
(12"+=)(cd-s+=)(12"laser-etched+=) – Blind in Texas (live'89).
— JOHNNY ROD left in 1989 as band split. Reformed in August 1990 as BLACKIE LAWLESS & WASP, but they soon returned to original name. **BLACKIE, JOHNNY, KEN, FRANKIE** and new member **BOB GULLICK** – guitar

Parlophone | Capitol

Mar 92. (7")(7"pic-d) **CHAINSAW CHARLIE (MURDERS IN THE NEW MORGUE). / PHANTOM IN THE MIRROR** [17] [ ]
(12"+=)(cd-s+=) – The story of Jonathan (prologue to the crimson idol – part I).
— The April tour added **DAN McDADE** – guitar / **STET HOWLAND** – drums
May 92. (7")(7"pic-d)(7"crimson) **THE IDOL. / THE STORY OF JONATHAN (PROLOGUE TO THE CRIMSON IDOL – PART II)** [41] [ ]
(pic-cd+=) – The eulogy.
Jun 92. (cd)(c)(lp) **THE CRIMSON IDOL** [21] [ ]
– The Titanic overture / The invisible boy / Arena of pleasure / Chainsaw Charlie (murders in the New Morgue) / The gypsy meets the boy / Doctor Rockter / I am one / The idol / Hold on to my heart / The great misconception of me. *(re-iss.cd+c Mar94)*
Oct 92. (7")(7"pic-d) **I AM ONE. / WILD CHILD** [56] [ ]
(10"+=) – Charlie chainsaw / I wanna be somebody.
(cd-s) – ('A'side) / The invisible boy / The real me / The great misconception of me.
Oct 93. (7") **SUNSET & BABYLON. / ANIMAL (F**K LIKE A BEAST)** [38] [ ]
(cd-s+=) – Sleeping in the fire / I wanna be somebody.
(12"+=) – School daze / On your knees.
(12"pic-d+=) – Hellion / Show no mercy.
Oct 93. (cd)(c)(lp) **FIRST BLOOD, LAST CUTS** [69] [ ]
– Animal (f**k like a beast) / L.O.V.E. machine (remix) / I wanna be somebody (remix) / On your knees / Blind in Texas (remix) / Wild child (remix) / I don't need no doctor (remix) / The real me / The headless children / Mean man / Forever free / Chainsaw Charlie / The idol / Sunset and Babylon / Hold on to my heart / Rock and roll to death.

Raw Power | ???

Jun 95. (7"sha-pic-d) **BLACK FOREVER. / GOODBYE AMERICA** [ ] [ ]
(cd-s+=) – Skin walker / One tribe.
(cd-s) – ('A'side) / Long way to the top / Whole lotta Rosie.
Jul 95. (cd)(c) **STILL NOT BLACK ENOUGH** [52]
– Still not black enough / Somebody to love / Black forever / Scared to death / Goodbye America / Keep holding on / Rock and roll to death / Breathe / I can't / No way out of here.

WATERBOYS

Formed: London, England . . . 1982 by Scots born MIKE SCOTT and Englishmen ANTHONY THISTLETHWAITE and KARL WALLINGER. SCOTT had previously fronted new wave Edinburgh outfit ANOTHER PRETTY FACE, with ex-Ayr school pals JOHN CALDWELL and JIM GEDDES. The WATERBOYS took their name from LOU REED lyrics (i.e. in the song 'The Kids'), and soon signed to Irish run label 'Ensign', who released their eponymous debut album in 1983. It was preceded by an airplay favourite 45 'A GIRL CALLED JOHNNY', which nearly dented the charts. After another critically acclaimed album in '84, they broke the UK Top 40 in 1985, with 'THE WHOLE OF THE MOON' (a song that was to re-chart, peaking at No.3 in 1991). • **Style:** Adventurous peoples rock outfit, who digressed into more acoustic orientated Irish folk in the late 80's. Their live shows, however, seemed to show them a trifle harder-edged and guitar-based. • **Songwriters:** SCOTT wrote most of material, except; LOST HIGHWAY (Hank Williams). • **Trivia:** MIKE SCOTT was brough up in Ayr, and went to Edinburgh University from 1977-78.

Recommended: THE BEST OF THE WATERBOYS (*9) / DREAM REAPER (*7)

ANOTHER PRETTY FACE

MIKE SCOTT (b.14 Dec'58, Edinburgh, Scotland) – vocals, guitar, piano / **JOHN CALDWELL** – guitar / **JIM GEDDES** – bass / **CRIGG** (b.IAN WALTER GREIG) – drums

New Pleasures | not issued

May 79. (7") **ALL THE BOYS LOVE CARRIE. / THAT'S NOT ENOUGH** [ ] [-]

Virgin | not issued

Feb 80. (7") **WHATEVER HAPPENED TO THE WEST?. / GODDBYE 1970's** [ ] [-]
— Trimmed to basic duo of **SCOTT + CALDWELL** plus **MAIRI ROSS** – bass / added **ADRIAN JOHNSON** – drums

Chicken Jazz | not issued

Dec 80. (7") **ONLY HEROES LIVE FOREVER. / HEAVEN GETS CLOSER EVERY DAY** [ ] [-]
Mar 81. (c-ep) **I'M SORRY THAT I BEAT YOU (live)** [ ] [-]
– This could be Hell / My darkest hour / Lightning that strikes twice / Graduation day / Carrie. (on some copies, studio tracks+=) – Another kind of circus / Only heroes live forever / Out of control.
Apr 81. (7") **A WOMAN'S PLACE. / GOD ON THE SCREEN / SOUL TO SOUL** [ ] [-]

FUNHOUSE

were formed by **SCOTT + CALDWELL**

Ensign | not issued

Feb 82. (7")('A'ext-12") **OUT OF CONTROL. / THIS COULD BE HELL** [ ] [-]

The WATERBOYS

were formed by **MIKE SCOTT** plus **ANTHONY THISTLETWAITE** – saxophone (ex-ROBYN HITCHCOCK / of SOFT BOYS) / **KARL WALLINGER** – keyboards, bass

Chicken Jazz | not issued

May 83. (7") **A GIRL CALLED JOHNNY. / THE LATE TRAIN TO HEAVEN** [ ] [-]
(12"+=) – Ready for the monkey house / Somebody might wave back / Out of control (ANOTHER PRETTY FACE – John Peel session).

Ensign | Chrysalis

Jul 83. (lp)(c) **THE WATERBOYS** [ ] [ ]
– December / A girl called Johnny / The three day man / Gala / I will not follow / It should have been you / The girl in the swing / Savage Earth heart. *(re-iss.Aug86, cd-iss.Feb87)*

Sep 83. (7") **DECEMBER. / WHERE ARE YOU NOW WHEN I NEED YOU** [ ] [ ]
(12") – ('A'side) / Red army blues / The three day man (Radio 1 session)

— added **KEVIN WILKINSON** – drums / **RODDY LORIMER** – tru. / **TIM BLANTHORN** – violin

Apr 84. (7") **THE BIG MUSIC. / THE EARTH ONLY ENDURES** [ ] [ ]
(12"+=) – Bury my heart.

May 84. (lp)(c) **A PAGAN PLACE** [100] [ ]
– Church not made with hands / All the things she gave me / The thrill is gone / Rags / Somebody might wave back / The big music / Red army blues / A pagan place. *(cd-iss.Feb87) (re-iss.cd+c Jul94)*

— (Oct84) **MIKE + KARL** recruited new people for tour/lp **TERRY MANN** – bass / **CHARLIE WHITTEN** – drums / **STEVE WICKHAM** – violin / **LORIMER. DELAHAYE** – organ

Sep 85. (lp)(c) **THIS IS THE SEA** [37] [ ]
– Don't bang the drum / The whole of the Moon / Spirit / The pan within / Medicine bow / Old England / Be my enemy / Trumpets / This is the sea. *(cd-iss.Feb87) (re-iss.cd Mar94)*

Oct 85. (7") **THE WHOLE OF THE MOON. / MEDICINE BOW** [26] [ ]
('A'ext-12"+=) – Spirit (extended) / The girl in the swing (live).

— **MIKE SCOTT** now only original survivor (retained THISTLETWAITE + HUTCHISON), when KARL formed WORLD PARTY.

— additional band **STEVE WICKHAM** – violin (ex-IN TUA NUA) / **J.D.DOHERTY** – drums / **COLIN BLAKEY** – flute (ex-WE FREE KINGS). /'88, added **SHARON SHANNON** – accordion / **NOEL BRIDGEMAN** – drums repl. DOHERTY

Nov 88. (lp)(c)(cd) **FISHERMAN'S BLUES** [13] [76]
– Fisherman's blues / We will not be lovers / Strange boat / World party / Sweet thing / And a bang on the ear / Has anybody here seen Hank? / When we will be married? / When ye go away / The stolen child. *(cd+=)–* The lost highway.

Dec 88. (7")(12")(cd-s) **FISHERMAN'S BLUES. / THE LOST HIGHWAY** [32] [ ]

Jun 89. (7")(12")(c-s)(cd-s) **AND A BANG ON THE EAR. / THE RAGGLE TAGGLE GYPSY** [51] [ ]

— **MIKE SCOTT / THISTLETWAITE / HUTCHISON / + KEV BLEVINS** – drums repl. last additional band members

Sep 90. (cd)(c)(lp) **ROOM TO ROAM** [5] [ ]
– In search of a rose / Songs from the edge of the world / A man is in love / Bigger picture / Natural bridge blues / Something that is gone / The star and the sea / Life on Sundays / Island man / The raggle taggle gypsy / How long will I love you? / Upon the wind and waves / Spring rooms to Spiddal / Further up, further in / Trip to Broadford / Room to roam. *(cd+=)–* The kings of Kerry. *(re-iss.cd+c Sep94)*

Mar 91. (7")(c-s) **THE WHOLE OF THE MOON. / A GOLDEN AGE** [3] [ ]
(12"+=)(cd-s+=) – Higher in time / High far soon / Soon as I get home.

Apr 91. (cd)(c)(lp) **THE BEST OF THE WATERBOYS ('81-'90)** [2] [ ]
(compilation)
– A girl called Johnny / The big music / All the things she gave me / The whole of the Moon / Spirit / Don't bang the drum / Fisherman's blues / Killing my heart / Strange boat / And a bang on the ear / Old England / A man is in love.

May 91. (7")(c-s) **FISHERMAN'S BLUES. / LOST HIGHWAY** [75] [ ]
(12"+=)(cd-s+=) – Medicine bow (live).

— Disbanded soon after last studio album above. In mid'91, MIKE SCOTT re-formed group and signed for US-based label 'Geffen'. THISTLETWAITE formed The BLUE STARS.

— **MIKE SCOTT** with **CHRIS BRUCE** – guitars / **SCOTT THUNES** – bass / **CARLA AZAR** – drums / **BASHIRI JOHNSON** – percussion / **LJUBISA 'Lubi' RISTIC** – sitar / **GEORGE STATHOS** – Greek clarinet / **JAMES CAMPAGNOLA** – saxophone / **JERE PETERS** – rattles / **PAL SHAZAR + JULES SHEAR** – backing vox / **BILLY CONNOLLY**– guest 10 second voiceover

Geffen | Geffen

May 93. (7")(c-s) **THE RETURN OF PAN. / KARMA** [24] [ ]
(12"+=)(cd-s+=) – Mister Powers / ('A' demo).

May 93. (cd)(c)(lp) **DREAM HARDER** [5] [ ]
– The new life / Glastonbury song / Preparing to fly / The return of Pan / Corn circles / Suffer / Winter winter / Love and death / Spiritual city / Wonders of Lewis / The return of Jimi Hendrix / Good news.

Jul 93. (7")(c-s) **GLASTONBURY SONG. / CHALICE HILL** [29] [ ]
(12"+=)(cd-s+=) – Burlington Bertie – Accrington Stanley / Corn circle symphony (extended).

– compilations –

Oct 94. Ensign/ US= Chrysalis; (cd)(c) **THE SECRET LIFE OF THE WATERBOYS** (81-85 material) [ ] [ ]

MIKE SCOTT

Chrysalis | Chrysalis

Sep 95. (7")(c-s) **BRING 'EM ALL IN. / CITY FULL OF GHOSTS (DUBLIN)** [56] [ ]
(cd-s+=) – Mother Cluny / Beatles reunion blues.

Sep 95. (cd)(c)(lp) **BRING 'EM ALL IN** [23] [ ]
– Bring 'em all in / Iona song / Edinburgh Castle / What do you want me to do? / I know she's in the building / City full of ghosts (Dublin) / Wonderful disguise / Sensitive children / Learning to love him / She is so beautiful / Wonderful disguise (reprise) / Long way to the light / Building the city of light.

Nov 95. (7") **BUILDING THE CITY OF LIGHT. / WHERE DO YOU WANT THE BOOMBOX, BUDDY** [60] [ ]
(cd-s+=) – Goin' back to Glasters (live) / The whole of the Moon (live).
(cd-s) – ('A'side) / Two great waves / My beautiful guide / Building the city of light (Universal Hall demo).

Muddy WATERS

Born: McKINLEY MORGANFIELD, 4 April 1915, Rolling Fork, Mississippi, USA, but brought up by grandmother in Clarksdale. In the early 40's he moved to Chicago where Leonard and Phil Chess gave him deal for their self-named label. Throughout the early 40's, he was augmented at gigs by guitarist JIMMY ROGERS and pianist EDDIE BOYD. In 1946, MUDDY had gone into studio with SUNNYLAND SLIM, who had replaced BOYD. They recorded two cuts 'GYPSY WOMAN' & 'LITTLE ANNA MAE', but 'Aristocat' decided to withdraw single release. He had a number of R&B chart successes in the 50's, and went onto to be a cult bluesman until his death 30 Apr'83. In 1988, his classic 'MANNISH BOY' was revived by Levi jeans advert and nearly scraped into the UK 50. • **Style:** Progressed from being a 40's jazz-based imitator of RAY CHARLES to being blues giant, whose inspiration came from SON HOUSE and ROBERT JOHNSON. Moved into psychedelia in 1969. • **Songwriters:** Wrote own material.

Recommended: THE ESSENTIAL RECORDINGS (*9)

MUDDY WATERS – vocals, guitar with **SUNNYLAND SLIM** – piano

not issued | Aristocrat

1948. (78) **GYPSY WOMAN. / LITTLE ANNA MAE** [-] [ ]
1948. (78) **I CAN'T BE SATISFIED. / FEEL LIKE GOIN' HOME** [-] [ ]
1948. (78) **TRAIN FARE HOME. / SITTIN' HERE AND DRINKIN'** [-] [ ]
1949. (78) **YOU'RE GONNA MISS ME. / MEAN RED SPIDER** [-] [ ]
1949. (78) **STREAMLINE WOMAN. / MUDDY JUMPS ONE** [-] [ ]
1949. (78) **LITTLE GENEVA. / CANARY BIRD** [-] [ ]
1949. (78) **SCREAMIN' AND CRYIN'. / WHERE'S MY WOMAN BEEN** [-] [ ]
1951. (78) **ROLLIN' AND TUMBLIN'. / (pt. 2)** [-] [ ]

— with band **JIMMY RODGERS** – guitar / **WILLIE DIXON** – bass / **LITTLE WALTER** – harmonica / **LEONARD CHESS** – drums / **ERNEST CRAWFORD** – bass

Vogue Chess | Chess

1950. (78) **YOU'RE GONNA NEED MY HELP I SAID. / SAD LETTER BLUES** [-] [ ]
1951. (78) **LOUISIANA BLUES. / EVAN'S SHUFFLE** [-] [ ]
1951. (78) **MY FAULT. / STILL A FOOL** [-] [ ]
May 52. (78) **ROLLIN' STONE. / WALKIN' BLUES** [ ] [ ] 1950

— ELGIN EVANS – drums repl. CHESS

1952. (78) **SHE MOVES ME. / EARLY MORNING BLUES** [-] [ ]
1952. (78) **ALL NIGHT LONG. / COUNTRY BOY** [-] [ ]
1952. (78) **PLEASE HAVE MERCY. / I CAN'T BE SATISFIED (LOOKING FOR MY BABY)** [-] [ ]
1952. (78) **STANDING AROUND CRYING. / GONE TO MAIN STREET** [-] [ ]
1953. (78) **SHE'S ALL RIGHT. / SAD, SAD DAY** [-] [ ]
1953. (78) **TURN THE LAMP DOWN LOW. / WHO'S GONNA BE YOUR SWEET MAN** [-] [ ]
1953. (78) **BLOW WIND BLOW. / MAD LOVE (I JUST WANT YOU TO LOVE ME)** [-] [ ]

— **OTIS SPANN** – piano (to mid-60's) repl. SLIM

1954. (78) **HOOCHIE COOCHIE MAN. / SHE'S SO PRETTY** [-] [ ]
Nov 54. (78) **LONG DISTANCE CALL. / TOO YOUNG TO KNOW** [ ] [-] 1951
Mar 55. (7"ep) **MUDDY WATERS** [ ] [-]
– I can't be satisfied / Louisiana blues / Evans shuffle / I feel like going home.
1955. (78) **MANNISH BOY. / YOUNG FASHION WAYS** [-] [ ]
May 56. (78) **HONEY BEE. / APPEALING BLUES** [ ] [ ] 1951
1954. (78) **I JUST WANT TO MAKE LOVE TO YOU. / OH YEAH** [-] [ ]
1954. (78) **I'M READY. / I DON'T KNOW WHY** [-] [ ]
1954. (78) **I'M A NATURAL BORN LOVER. / LOVING MAN** [-] [ ]
1955. (78) **I WANT TO BE LOVED. / MY EYES (KEEP ME IN TROUBLE)** [-] [ ]
1955. (78) **YOUNG FASHIONED WAYS. /** [-] [ ]
1955. (78) **SUGAR SWEET. / TROUBLE NO MORE** [-] [ ]
1956. (78) **40 DAYS AND 40 NIGHTS. / ALL ABOARD** [-] [ ]
1956. (78) **DON'T GO NO FURTHER. / DIAMONDS AT YOUR FEET** [-] [ ]
1956. (78) **JUST TO BE WITH YOU. / I GOT TO FIND MY BABY** [-] [ ]

London | Chess

Oct 56. (7"ep) **MISSISSIPPI BLUES** [ ] [-]
– All aboard / 40 days and 40 nights / Mannish boy / Young fashioned ways.
1957. (7") **GOT MY MOJO WORKING. / ROCK ME** [-] [ ]
1957. (7") **GOOD NEWS. / COME HOME BABY** [-] [ ]
1957. (7") **EVIL. / I LIVE THE LIFE I LOVE** [-] [ ]
1958. (7") **I WON'T GO. / SHE'S GOT IT** [-] [ ]
1958. (7") **SHE'S 19 YEARS OLD. / CLOSE TO YOU** [-] [ ]
1958. (7") **WALKING THRU THE PARK. / MEAN MISTREATER** [-] [ ]
1958. (7") **CLOUDS IN MY HEART. / OOH WEE** [-] [ ]
1959. (7") **TAKE THE BITTER WITH THE SWEET. / SHE'S INTO SOMETHING** [-] [ ]
1959. (7") **TELL ME BABY. / LOOK WHAT YOU'VE DONE** [-] [ ]
1959. (7") **WHEN I GET TO THINKING. / I FEEL SO GOOD** [-] [ ]
1959. (7") **LOVE AFFAIR. / RECIPE FOR LOVE** [-] [ ]

1960. (7") **I'M YOUR DOCTOR. / READ WAY BACK**

— **WALTER HORTON** – repl. LITTLE WALTER until **JAMES COTTON** repl. HORTON / **PAT HARE** came in on drums and ROGERS departed. He toured in the UK.

Mar 59. (lp) **THE BEST OF MUDDY WATERS** (compilation)
– I just want to make love to you / Long distance call / Louisiana blues / Honey bee / Rollin' stone / I'm ready / Hoochie coochie / She moves me / I want you to love me / Standing around crying / Still a fool / I can't be satisfied. *(re-iss. Oct87, Jun88 cd)*

— toured now with **FRANCIS CLAY** – drums / **ANDREW STEPHENSON** – bass / **PAT HARE** – guitar / **SPANN + COTTON**

Jun 60. (7") **TIGER IN YOUR TANK. / MEANEST WOMAN**
Aug 60. (7") **GOT MY MOJO WORKING (pt.1). / WOMAN WANTED**
1961. (7") **LONESOME ROOM BLUES. / MESSIN' WITH THE MAN**

Pye Jazz Chess

Sep 61. (lp) **MUDDY WATERS AT NEWPORT (live 1960)** 1960
– Tiger in your tank / I've got my mojo working / I got my brand on you / Baby, please don't go / Soon forgotten / I feel so glad / Goodbye Newport blues. *(re-iss.Nov65 on 'Chess') (re-iss.Jan67 on 'Marble A.') (re-iss.1973 on 'Checker')*

1962. (7") **TOUGH TIMES. / GOING HOME**
1962. (7") **YOU SHOOK ME. / MUDDY WATERS TWIST**
1962. (7") **YOU NEED LOVE. / LITTLE BROWN BIRD**
1963. (7") **FIVE LONG YEARS. / TWENTY FOUR HOURS**
1964. (7") **THE SAME THING. / YOU CAN'T LOSE WHAT YOU NEVER HAD**

Pye Inter. Chess

May 64. (lp) **MUDDY WATERS – FOLK SINGER**
– My home is my delta / Long distance / My captain / Good morning little schoolgirl / You're gonna need my help / Cold weather blues / Peg leg woman / Country boy / Feel like going home. *(re-iss.Aug87 on 'Chess')*

Sep 64. (lp) **MUDDY WATERS**
– I got my brand on you / Baby, please don't go / Tiger in your tank / I've got my mojo working (part 1) / Goodbye Newport blues / The same thing / Sittin' and thinkin' / 19 years old / I'm your hoochie coochie man / Soon forgotten / I feel so good / I've got my mojo working (part 2) / Long distance call / Wee wee baby / Clouds in my heart. *(cd-iss. Mar90 on 'Roots')*

Chess Chess

Feb 65. (7") **MY JOHN THE CONQUER ROOT. / SHORT DRESS WOMAN**
1965. (7") **PUT ME IN YOUR LAY AWAY**
Aug 65. (7"ep) **I'M READY**
– She moves me / I can't be satisfied / I want you to love me.
Aug 65. (7") **I GOT A RICH MAN'S WOMAN. / MY DOG CAN'T BARK**
Jan 66. (lp) **THE REAL FOLK BLUES**
– Mannish boy / Screamin' and cryin' / Just to be with you / Walking in the park / Same thing / Walking blues / Canary bird / Gypsy women / Rollin' and tumblin' / Forty days and forty nights / You can't lose what you never had / Little Geneva.
May 66. (7"ep) **THE REAL FOLK BLUES VOL.4**
– I just want to make love to you / Louisiana blues / Still a fool / Standing around crying.
1966. (7") **CORINA, CORINA. / HOOTCHI KOOTCHIE MAN**
Jan 67. (lp) **MUDDY, BRASS AND THE BLUES**
– Corrine, Corrina / Piney brown blues / Black night / Trouble in mind / Goin' back to Memphis / Betty and Dupree / Sweet little angel / Take me advice / Trouble / Hard loser.
Aug 67. (lp) **SUPERBLUES ("with BO DIDDLEY & LITTLE WALTER")**
May 68. (lp) **THE SUPER BLUES BAND ("with BO DIDDLEY & HOWLIN' WOLF")**

Chess Cadet

Jan 69. (lp) **ELECTRIC MUD** Nov 68
– I just want to make love to you / Hoochie coochie man / Let's spend the night together / She's all right / I'm a man / Herbert Harper's free press / Tom cat / Same thing.
Jan 69. (7") **LET'S SPEND THE NIGHT TOGETHER. / I'M A MAN**
Aug 69. (lp) **AFTER THE RAIN**
– I a the blues / Ramblin' mind / Rollin and tumblin' / Bottom of the sea / Honey bee / Blues and trouble / Hurtin' soul / Screamin' and cryin'
Oct 69. (d-lp) **FATHERS AND SONS (live "with PAUL BUTTERFIELD & MIKE BLOOMFIELD")** 70 Sep 69
– All aboard / Mean disposition / Blow wind blow / Can't lose what you ain't never had / Walking through the park / 40 days and 40 nights / Standin' round crying / I'm ready / Twenty four hours / Sugar sweet / Long distance call / Baby, please don't go / Honey bee / The same thing / Got my mojo working (pt.1 & 2).
(above also featured **BUDDY MILES + PHIL UPCHURCH**)

Chess Chess

Jul 72. (lp) **THE LONDON MUDDY WATERS SESSIONS**
– Blind man blues / Key to the highway / Walkin' blues / I'm gonna move to the outskirts of town / Who's gonna be your sweet man when I'm gone / Young fashioned ways / Sad sad day / I don't know why. *(re-iss.Apr82)*

— On 11 Oct'73, he was involved in a car accident which 3 people were killed. After releasing one more album, he went into semi-retirement for 2 years. Released 'LONDON REVISITED' Jan74 with HOWLIN' WOLF.

Jan 74. (lp) **CAN'T GET NO GRINDING**
– Can't get no grinding / Mothers bad luck / Funky butt / Sad letter / Someday I'm gonna kitch you / Love weapon / Garbage man / After hours / Whiskey ain't no good / Muddy Waters' shuffle. *(re-iss.1989)*
Mar 74. (lp) **"UNK" IN FUNK**

Blue Sky Blue Sky

Apr 77. (lp)(c) **HARD AGAIN** Feb 77
– Mannish boy / Bus driver / I want to be loved / Jealous-hearted man / I can't be satisfied / The blues had a baby, and they named it rock'n'roll / Deep down in Florida / Crosseyed cat / Little girl. *(re-iss.Sep83, cd-iss.Mar91) (re-iss.cd+c Feb94 on 'Columbia')*
Feb 78. (lp)(c) **I'M READY**
– I'm ready / 33 years / Who do you trust / Cooper Brown / I'm your hoochie coochie man / Mame / Rock me / Screamin' and cryin' / Good morning little schoolgirl. *(cd-iss.Nov91 on 'B.G.O.')*
Jan 79. (lp)(c) **MUDDY MISSISSIPPI WATERS LIVE (live)**
– Mannish boy / She's 19 years old / Nine below zero / Streamline woman / Howling wolf / Baby please don't go / Deep down in Florida. *(cd-iss.Mar91 on 'B.G.O.')*
May 81. (lp)(c) **KING BEE**
– I'm a king bee / Too young to know / Mean old Frisco blues / Forever lonely / I feel like goin' home / Champagne and reefer / Sad sad day / My eyes keep me in trouble / Deep down in Florida / No escape from the blues.

— On the 30th Apr'83, he died of a heart attack in his Chicago home.

– more compilations, etc. –

Nov 64. Pye/ US= Chess; (lp) **MUDDY SINGS BIG BILL (BROONZY)**
– *(re-iss.Nov67 on 'Marble Arch')*
Jul 83. Blue Sky; (lp)(c) **HOOCHIE COOCHIE MAN**
– Mannish boy / I'm ready / Champagne and reefer / Baby please don't go / I want to be loved / Sad sad day / I'm a king bee / Blues had a baby and they named it rock'n'roll / She's 19 years old / I can't be satisfied / Screamin' and cryin' / I'm your hoochie coochie man. *(re-iss.+cd.Aug88 + Apr93 on 'Epic')*
Jan 67. Chess; (lp) **MORE REAL FOLK BLUES**
Aug 68. Bounty; (lp) **DOWN ON STOVALL'S FARM** (1942 rec.)
(re-iss.May86 on 'Testament')
Jun 69. Polydor; (lp) **BLUES MAN**
Oct 69. Chess; (lp) **SAIL ON** (nearly same as BEST OF)
Dec 69. Sunnyland; (lp) **VINTAGE MUD**
May 70. Syndicate/ US= Chess; (lp) **BACK IN THE GOOD OLD DAYS**
– *(re-iss.1979)*
May 70. Syndicate/ US= Chess; (lp) **GOOD NEWS**
– Trouble no more / Don't go no further / Diamonds at your feet / Evil / All aboard / I love the life I live / Mean mistreater / Recipe for love / Good news / Come home baby / I won't go / She's got it / Close to you. *(re-iss.1979)*
Jun 70. Syndicate/ US= Chess; (lp) **WE THREE KINGS ("with HOWLIN' WOLF & LITTLE WALTER")**
(re-iss.Sep82)
Feb 71. Chess; (lp) **THEY CALL ME MUDDY WATERS**
Oct 71. Chess; (lp) **LIVE (AT MISTER KELLY'S)**
Apr 75. Chess; (lp) **THE MUDDY WATERS WOODSTOCK ALBUM**
Nov 77. Syndicate; (d-lp) **BACK IN THE EARLY DAYS VOL.1&2**
– (albums 'BACK IN THE GOOD OLD DAYS' & 'GOOD NEWS') *(re-iss.Sep82) (re-iss.Jul83 on 'Red Lightning')*
1979. Muse/ US= Jazz Horizons; (lp) **CHICKEN SHACK**
1979. Muse/ US= Jazz Horizons; (lp) **MUD IN YOUR EAR**
(cd-iss.Feb91)
Sep 71. Chess; (lp) **McKINLEY MORGANFIELD**
Apr 81. Chess; (lp) **CHESS MASTERS**
(re-iss.+cd.Mar88 on 'Stylus')
Apr 82. Chess; (lp) **CHESS MASTERS VOL.2**
Apr 83. Chess; (lp) **CHESS MASTERS VOL.3**
Mar 85. Chess; (lp) **RARE AND UNISSUED**
Aug 86. Chess; (lp) **RARE AND UNISSUED VOL.2**
Oct 87. Chess; (lp)(c) **FOLK SINGERS**
Aug 92. Chess; (9xcd-box) **THE COMPLETE MUDDY WATERS: 1947-1967**
1989. Chess; (6xlp)(3xc)(3xcd) **THE CHESS BOX**
1982. Krazy Kat; (lp) **MUDDY WATERS IN CONCERT 1958 (live)**
Jul 83. Blue Moon; (lp) **ROLLIN' STONE**
(cd-iss. 1992 on 'Charly')
Sep 84. Blue Moon; (lp) **MISSISSIPPI ROLLIN' STONE**
Jun 93. Blue Moon; (cd) **GOODBYE NEWPORT BLUES**
Nov 84. Astan; (lp) **SWEET HOME CHICAGO**
Nov 84. Astan; (lp) **ORIGINAL HOOCHIE COOCHIE**
Nov 85. Deja Vu; (lp) **20 BLUES GREATS (THE COLLLECTION)**
Aug 87. Deja Vu; (cd) **THE MUDDY WATERS COLLECTION**
Apr 93. Deja Vu; (cd)(c) **THE GOLD COLLECTION**
Apr 86. Showcase; (lp) **I CAN'T BE SATISFIED**
Aug 87. Onsala; (lp) **LIVE 1965-68 (live)**
Apr 88. Epic; (7") **MANNISH BOY. / I'M YOUR HOOCHIE COOCHIE MAN** 51
(12") – ('A'side) / The blues had a baby and they named it rock'n'roll / Little girl.
Jun 88. Bold Reprieve; (lp)(c)(cd) **LIVE IN ANTIBES 1974 (live)**
Jul 88. Bold Reprieve; (12"m) **MANNISH BOY (live) / GARBAGE MAN (live). / I'M YOUR HOOCHIE COOCHIE MAN**
Jan 90. Mainline; (cd)(c)(lp) **20 BLUES CLASSICS**
Dec 90. Jazz Velvet; (cd) **LIVE IN SWITZERLAND (live 1976 with The CHICAGO BLUES BAND)**
1989. Charly; (lp) **CAN'T GET NO GRINDIN'**
Jun 89. Chess; (lp) **TROUBLE NO MORE / SINGLES (1955-1959)**
Jul 89. Instant; (cd)(c)(lp) **CHICAGO BLUES**
Dec 90. Charly; (c) **MUDDY AT NEWPORT / WHOSE MUDDY . . .**
Dec 90. Charly; (c) **UNK IN FUNK / SINGS BIG BILL (BROOZY)**
1992. Charly; (cd)(c) **ROCK ME**
Feb 93. Charly; (cd)(c) **FUNKY BUTT**
Feb 93. Charly; (cd) **GOT MY MOJO WORKING**
Jul 93. Charly; (cd) **HOOCHIE COOCHIE MAN**
Jan 92. Quality; (cd) **THE ESSENTIAL RECORDINGS**
Feb 92. Fan Club; (cd) **GOIN' HOME: LIVE IN PARIS 1970 (live)**
Aug 92. Columbia; (cd) **BLUES SKY**
Apr 93. Columbia; (cd) **16 GREATEST HITS**
May 93. Document; (cd) **FIRST RECORDINGS 1941-46**
Sep 93. Landscape; (cd) **LIVE IN SWITZERLAND 1976 – VOLUME II (live)**
Sep 93. See For Miles; (cd) **THE EP COLLECTION (1-side by HOWLIN' WOLF)**

Oct 93. L.R.C.; (cd) **MUDDY WATERS** [ ] [-]
May 94. Charly; (cd) **TWO ON ONE (w/JOHN LEE HOOKER)** [ ] [-]
Aug 94. Charly; (cd) **LIVE AT NEWPORT (live w/OTIS SPANN)** [ ] [-]
Nov 94. Charly; (cd) **CHICAGO 1979 (live)** [ ] [-]
Apr 95. Charly; (cd) **ELECTRIC MUD & MORE** [ ] [-]
Apr 95. Charly; (4xcd-box+book) **THE KING OF CHICAGO BLUES** [ ] [-]
Jul 95. Discovery; (lp) **THE FOLK SINGER** [ ] [-]
Jul 95. Charly; (d-cd) **THE VERY BEST OF MUDDY WATERS** [ ] [-]
Jul 95. Charly; (cd) **IN CONCERT** [ ] [-]
Jul 95. Best; (cd) **MUDDY WATERS** [ ] [-]

Roger WATERS

Born: 6 Sep'44, Great Bookham, Cambridge, England. In 1965, he helped form PINK FLOYD, becoming mainman in 1968 when SYD BARRETT became spaced out. He was frontman and main contributor until his departure in 1983. With PINK FLOYD out of the scene in the mid 80's, fans locked on to WATERS for worthwhile material. His debut album 'PROS & CONS OF HITCH HIKING' didn't set the world alight but managed a UK Top 20 placing. In 1990, with The BERLIN WALL being dismantled, ROGER thought it neccessary to revive the 1979 PINK FLOYD album 'THE WALL'. With an array of famous guests, he played there to a live audience of 200,000, plus TV millions all contributing to The Disaster Relief Fund. • **Style:** Not surprising that his sound stems from the latter days of PINK FLOYD ⇒ (i.e. THE WALL / THE FINAL CUT). His work with said band, was his greatest contribution to rock. • **Songwriters:** WATERS wrote all material. • **Trivia:** In 1987, WATERS took members of PINK FLOYD to court, for their use of group name.

Recommended: THE PROS AND CONS OF HITCH HIKING (*7)

ROGER WATERS – vocals, bass, etc. (ex-PINK FLOYD) with **ERIC CLAPTON** – guitar / **ANDY NEWMARK** – drums / **RAY COOPER** – percussion / **MADELINE BELL** – vocals

Harvest Columbia

Apr 84. (7") **5:01 a.m. (THE PROS AND CONS OF HITCH HIKING). / 4:30 a.m. (APPARENTLY THEY WERE TRAVELLING ABROAD)** [ ] [ ]
(12"+=) – 4:33 a.m. (Running shoes).

May 84. (lp)(c)(cd) **THE PROS AND CONS OF HITCH HIKING** [13] [31]
– 4:30 a.m. (Apparently they were travelling abroad) / 4:33 a.m. (Running shoes) / 4:37 a.m. (Arabs with knives and West German skies) / 4:39 a.m. (For the first time today) / 4:41 a.m. (Sexual revolution) / 4:47 a.m. (The remains of our love) / 4:50 a.m. (Go fishing) / 4:56 a.m. (For the first time today pt.2) / 4:58 a.m. (Dunroamin' duncarin' dunlivin') / 5:06 a.m. (Every strangers eyes) / 5:11 a.m. (The moment of clarity).

Jun 84. (7") **5:06 a.m. (EVERY STRANGERS EYES). / 4:39 a.m. (FOR THE FIRST TIME TODAY)** [ ] [ ]

— In Oct'86, WATERS and his BLEEDING HEART BAND featured on 1 side of 'WHEN THE WIND BLOWS' album / animated cartoon film on 'Virgin'.

— His new band: **ANDY FAIRWEATHER-LOW** – guitar / **JAY STAPLEY** – electric guitar / **MEL COLLINS** – sax / **IAN RITCHIE** – keyboards, drum pro. / **GRAHAM BROAD** – drums

E.M.I. Columbia

May 87. (7") **RADIO WAVES (edit). / GOING TO LIVE IN L.A.** [74] [ ]
(12"+=)(cd-s+=) – ('A'demo version).

Jun 87. (lp)(c)(cd) **RADIO KAOS** [25] [50]
– Radio waves / Who needs information / Me or him / The powers that be / Sunset Strip / Home / Four minutes / The tide is turning.

Nov 87. (7") **THE TIDE IS TURNING (After Live Aid). / GET BACK ON THE RADIO (demo)** [54] [ ]
(12"+=)(cd-s+=) – Money (live).

Mercury Mercury

Sep 90. (d-cd)(d-c)(d-lp) **THE WALL: LIVE IN BERLIN (live) ("ROGER WATERS AND THE BLEEDING HEART BAND")** [27] [56]
– In the flesh? (SCORPIONS) / The thin ice (UTE LEMPER) / Another brick in the wall – part 1 / The happiest days of our lives (JOE CHEMAY) / Another brick in the wall – part 2 (CYNDI LAUPER) / Mother (SINEAD O'CONNOR) / Goodbye blue sky (JONI MITCHELL) / Empty spaces + Young lust (BRYAN ADAMS) / One of my turns / Don't leave me now / Another brick in the wall – part 3 / Goodbye cruel world / Hey you (PAUL CARRACK) / Is there anybody out there? (MICHAEL KAMEN /The RUNDFUNK ORCHESTRA +*) / Nobody home / Vera (*) / Bring the boys back home / Comfortably numb (VAN MORRISON) / In the flesh? (*) / Run like Hell / Waiting for the worms (*) / Stop to / The trial (TIM CURRY & THOMAS DOLBY) / The tide is turning (The COMPANY). *(re-iss.d-cd Sep95)*

Sep 90. (7")(12") **ANOTHER BRICK IN THE WALL (part 2). / RUN LIKE HELL (live)** [52] [ ]
(cd-s+=) – ('A'extended).

Columbia Columbia

Aug 92. (7")(c-s) **WHAT GOD WANTS, PART 1. / ('A'video edit)** [35] [ ]
(cd-s+=) – What God wants, part III.

Sep 92. (cd)(c)(lp) **AMUSED TO DEATH** [8] [21]
– The ballad of Bill Hubbard / What God wants, part 1 / Perfect sense, part I & II / The bravery of being out of range / Late home tonight, part I & II / Too much rope / What God wants, part II & III / Watching TV / Three wishes / It's a miracle / Amused to death.

Dec 92. (7")(c-s) **THE BRAVERY OF BEING OUT OF RANGE. / WHAT GOD WANTS (part 1).** [ ] [ ]
(cd-s+=) – Perfect sense. (part 1).

ROGERS WATERS w / RON GEESIN

while a member of PINK FLOYD,

Harvest Columbia

Oct 70. (lp) **MUSIC FROM THE BODY (Soundtrack)** [ ] [ ]
– Our song / Seashell and stone / Red stuff writhe / Gentle breeze through life / Lick your partners / Bridge passage for three teeth / Chain of life / Womb bit / Embryo thought / March past of the embryos / More than seven dwarfs in penis – land / Dance of the red corpuscles / Body transport / Hard dance – full evening dress / Breathe / Old folks ascensions / Bedtime climb / Piddle in perspex / Embryonic womb walk / Mrs.Throat goes walking / Seashell and soft stone / Give birth to a smile. *(re-iss.Jul85 on 'EMI') (cd-iss.Jun89)*

Jeff WATSON (see under ⇒ NIGHTRANGER)

Ben WATT (see under ⇒ EVERYTHING BUT THE GIRL)

Fee WAYBILL (see under ⇒ TUBES)

WEATHER REPORT

Formed: Around east-coast of USA . . . 1970 by ZAWINUL and SHORTER. The former progressed from Berkley School of Music, Boston. Both had explored new concept of new jazz sounds, when members of the late 60's MILES DAVIS group. Signed to 'Columbia', issuing many albums throughout the 70's & 80's. Also won numerous poll awards from music industry/critics. • **Style:** Instrumental free-form jazz rock, that fused texture and beauty with subtle creativity. • **Songwriters:** Either SHORTER, ZAWINUL or VITOUS. Mid-70's with PASTORUS adding own contribution. • **Trivia:** During ZAWINUL's stint with CANNONBALL ADDERLEY, he co-contributed many cuts including near Top 10 US hit MERCY, MERCY, MERCY.

Recommended: HEAVY WEATHER (*7) / THE COLLECTION (*8).

JOSEF ZAWINUL (b. 7 Jul'32, Vienna, Austria) – keyboards, synthesizers (ex-MILES DAVIS, ex-CANNONBALL ADDERLEY) / **WAYNE SHORTER** (b.25 Aug'33, Newark, New Jersey, USA) – saxophone (ex-JAZZ MESSENGERS, ex-MILES DAVIS, ex-ART BLAKEY GROUP, ex-HORACE SILVER) / **MIROSLAV VITOUS** (b.1947 Czechoslavakia) – bass (ex-MILES DAVIS) / **ALPHONE MOUZON** – drums (ex-sessions) / **AIRTO MOREIRA** – percussion (ex-MILES DAVIS)

C.B.S. Columbia

Jul 71. (lp)(c) **WEATHER REPORT** [ ] [ ]
– Milky Way / Umbrellas / Seventh arrow / Orange lady / Morning lake / Waterfall / Tears / Eurydice. *(re-iss.Mar81) (cd-iss.Dec93 on 'Sony Europe') (cd-iss.Mar94 on 'Sony Collectors')*

— **ERIC GRAVITT** – drums repl. MOREIRA who quit. **DOM UM ROMAO** – percussion repl. MOUZON who left to join McCOY TYNER then LARRY CORYELL + solo

Jul 72. (lp)(c) **I SING THE BODY ELECTRIC** (live) [ ] [ ]
– Unknown soldier / The moors / Crystal / Second Sunday in August / Vertical invader – T.H. – Dr. Honoris Causa / Surucucu / Directions. *(re-iss.Sep82)*

May 73. (lp)(c) **SWEETNIGHTER** [ ] [85]
– Boogie woogie waltz / Manolete / Adios / 125th Street congress / Will / Non-stop home.

1973. (7") **125th STREET CONGRESS. / WILL** [-] [ ]

— **ISHMAEL WILBURN** – percussion repl. GRAVITT

Apr 75. (lp)(c) **MYSTERIOUS TRAVELLER** [ ] [46] Jun 74
– Nubian sundance / American tango / Jungle book / Mysterious traveller / Blackthorn rose / Cucumber slumber / Scarlet woman. *(cd-iss.Jul89)*

Apr 75. (7") **AMERICAN TANGO. / CUCUMBER SLUMBER** [-] [ ]

— **JACO PASTORIUS** (b.JOHN FRANCIS, 1 Dec'51, Morristown, Pensylvania, US) – bass (ex-BLOOD, SWEAT & TEARS) repl. VITOUS who continued solo. / Added **LEON NDUGU CHANCLER + HERSCHEL DWELLINGHAM** – percussion repl. ISHMAEL

Jun 75. (lp)(c) **TALE SPINNIN'** [ ] [31]
– Man in the green shirt / Lusitanos / Between the thighs / Badia / Freezing fire / Five short stories. *(cd-iss.Oct94 on 'Columbia')*

Jan 76. (7") **BETWEEN THE THIGHS. / LUSITANOS** [-] [ ]

— **CHESTER THOMPSON** – drums repl. LEON + HERSCHEL

May 76. (lp)(c) **BLACK MARKET** [ ] [42] Apr 76
– Gibraltar / Cannon ball / Black market / Elegant people / Three clowns / Barbary Coast / Henarndu. *(re-iss.+cd.May87)*

— **ALEJANDRO NECIOSUP ACUNA** – drums, percussion repl. CHESTER to GENESIS / added **MANOLA BADRENA** – percussion (to ZAWINUL, SHORTER + PASTORIUS)

Mar 77. (7") **BIRDLAND. / PALLADIUM** [-] [ ]
Mar 77. (lp)(c) **HEAVY WEATHER** [ ] [30] Mar 77
– Birdland / A remark you made / Teen Town / Harlequin / Rumba mama / Palladium / The juggler / Havona. *(re-iss.Sep83) (cd-iss.1987, Mar91 & Feb95)*

May 77. (7") **BIRDLAND. / THE JUGGLER** [ ] [-]

— **PETE ERSKINE** – drums (STEVE GADD + TONY WILLIAMS) repl. BADRENA

Oct 78. (7") **RIVER PEOPLE. / BIRDLAND** [ ] [ ]
Nov 78. (lp)(c) **MR. GONE** [ ] [52] Oct 78
– The pursuit of the woman in the feathered hat / River people / Young and fine / The elders / Mr. Gone / Punk jazz / Pinocchio / And then. *(re-iss.Sep86 France)*

— **ABE LABORIEL** – bass repl. JACO PASTORIUS who continued solo

Jul 79. (7") **BIRDLAND (live). / BROWN STREET (live)** [-] [ ]
Jul 79. (7") **BIRDLAND (live). / RIVER PEOPLE (live) / A REMARK YOU MADE (live)** [ ] [-]

Sep 79. (d-lp)(c) **8:30 (live + 1 side studio)** [ ] [47]
– Black market / Scarlet woman / Teen town / A remmark you made / Slang / In a silent way / Birdland / Thanks for the memory / Badia / Boogie woogie waltz / Brown Street / The orphan / Sightseeing. *(re-iss.May82)*

Nov 80. (lp)(c) **NIGHT PASSAGE** [ ] [57]

– Night passage / Dream clock / Port of entry / Forlorn / Rockin' in rhythm / Fast city / Three views of a secret / Madagascar. *(cd-iss.1983)*

Nov 80. (7") **FORLORN. / ROCKIN' IN RHYTHM** [-] [68]

Feb 82. (lp)(c) **WEATHER REPORT** [88] [68]
– Volcano for hire / Current affairs / N.Y.C.: pt.1 – 41st Street parallel, pt.2 – The dance of Three, pt.3 – Crazy about jazz / Dara factor one / When it was now / Speechless / Dara factor two.

— **ZAWINUL + SHORTER** brought in **OMAR HAKIM + VICTOR BAILEY** – drums / **JOSE ROSSY** – percussion

Mar 83. (lp)(c)(cd) **PROCESSION** [96]
– Procesion / Plaza real / Two lines / Where the Moon goes / The well / Molasses run.

— added **CARL ANDERSON** – vocals (yes! vocals)

Mar 84. (lp)(c)(cd) **DOMINO THEORY** [54]
– Can it be done / Db waltz / The peasant / Predator / Blue sound – Note 3 / Swamp cabbage / Domnio theory.

Jun 85. (lp)(c) **SPORTIN' LIFE** Apr 85
– Corner pocket / Indiscretions / Hot cargo / Confians / Pearl on the half-shell / What's going on / Face on the barroom floor / Ice-pick Willy.

— added **PETER ERSKINE** – drums

Jul 86. (lp)(c)(cd) **THIS IS THIS**
– This is this / Face the fire / I'll never forget you / Jungle stuff (part 1) / Man with the copper fingers / Consequently / Update / China blues.

— Past member JACO PASTORIUS died 22 Sep'87 from injuries sustained after being beaten up trying to enter a pub 10 days previously. He had suffered from manic depression, brought on by alcohol. WEATHER REPORT had now folded.

– compilations, others, etc. –

Apr 91. CBS-Columbia; (cd)(c)(lp) **GREATEST HITS**

1992. Castle; (cd)(c) **THE COLLECTION**
– Birdland / Teen town / The juggler / The pursuit of the woman with the feathered hat / The elders / Punk jazz and then / Black market (live) / A remark you made (live) / Night passage / Rockin' in rhythm / Fast city / Madagascar.

WAYNE SHORTER

solo with **LEE MORGAN** – trumpet / **McCOY TYNER** – piano

not issued / Blue Note

1961. (lp) **FREEFORM** [-]

1963. (lp) **SEARCH FOR A NEW LAND** [-]

— added **REGGIE WORKMAN** – bass / **ELVIN JONES** – drums

Apr 64. (lp) **NIGHT DREAMER** [-]
– Night dreamer / Oriental folk song / Black Nile / Charcoal blues / Armageddon. *(cd-iss.Apr88 on 'Blue Note'+= – Virgo (alt.take).*

1964. (lp) **SOME OTHER STUFF** [-]

— LEE MORGAN now departed

1964. (lp) **JU JU** [-]
– Ju Ju / Deluge / House of Jade / Mahjong / Yes and now / Twelve more bars to go. *(UK-iss.1985 on 'Blue Note', cd-iss.Apr87)*

— with **JONES / RON CARTER** – bass / **HERBIE HANCOCK** – piano / **FREDDIE HUBBARD** – trumpet

Dec 64. (lp) **SPEAK NO EVIL** [-]
– Witch hunt / Fee fi fo fum / Dance cadaverous / Speak no evil / Infant eyes / Wild flower. *(re-iss.Aug87) (cd-iss.Mar88 & Mar95 on 'Blue Note')*

Mar 65. (lp) **THE ALL SEEING EYE** [-]
– The all seeing eye / Genesis / Chaos / Face on the deep / Mephistopheles. *(re-iss.cd+lp Jul94)*

— with **HANCOCK / WORKMAN / JOE CHAMBERS** – drums

Feb 66. (lp) **ADAM'S APPLE** [-]
– Adam's apple / 502 blues (drinkin' and drivin') / El Gaucho / Footprints / Teru / Chief Crazy Horse. *(re-iss.+cd.Jun87 on 'Blue Note')*

— **TONY WILLIAMS** – drums repl. CHAMBERS

Blue Note / Blue Note

Mar 67. (lp) **SCHIZOPHRENIA**
– Tom Thumb / Go / Schizophrenia / Kryptonite / Miyako / Playground. *(re-iss.+cd Jul95)*

— with session people incl. **JOHN McLAUGHLIN, CHICK COREA, AIRTO MOREIRA, MIROSUN VITOUS,** etc

Sep 69. (lp) **SUPER NOVA**
– Super nova / Sweet-pea / Dindi / Water babies / Capricorn / More than human. *(re-iss.+cd.Nov88)*

Aug 70. (lp) **ODYSSEY OF ISKA** [-]
– Wind / Storm / Calm / De pois do amor, o vazio (after love, emptiness) / Joy. *(cd-iss.Aug89)*

1975. (lp) **MOTO GROSSO FEIO**
– Moto grosso feio / Montezuma / Antiqua / Vera Cruz / I

— next featured **MILTON NASHCIMENTO** – guitar, vocals / **HERBIE HANCOCK** – piano / **AIRTO MOREIRA** – percussion / + others

Epic / Columbia

Jun 75. (lp)(c) **NATIVE DANCER**
– Ponto de areia / Beauty and the beast / Tarde / Miracle of the fishes / Diana / From the lonely afternoons / Ana Maria / Lilia / Joanna's theme.

Liberty / Liberty

Jun 80. (lp)(c) **THE SOOTHSAYER**
– Lost / Angola / The big push / The soothsayer / Lady day / Valse triste. *(re-iss.Sep84 on 'Affinity' (cd-iss.Jun90 on 'Blue Note'+=)* – Angola (alt.take).

Mar 81. (lp)(c) **ETCETERA**
– Etcetera / Penelope / Top tune / Barracuding / Indian song.

C.B.S. / Columbia

Oct 85. (lp)(c)(cd) **ATLANTIS**
– Endangered species / The three Marias / The last silk hat / When you dream / Who goes there? / Atlantis / Shere Khan / Criancas / On the eve of departure.

Mar 87. (lp)(c)(cd) **PHANTOM NAVIGATOR**
– Condition red / Mahogany bird / Remote control / Ya mania / Forbidden plan-it / Flagships.

Mar 88. (lp)(c)(cd) **JOY RYDER**
– Someplace called 'where' / Joy ryder / Cathay / Over Shadow Hill way / Anthem / Causeways / Daredevil.

Verve / Verve

Nov 95. (cd) **HIGH LIFE**

– (SHORTER) compilations, etc. –

1970's. Trip; (lp) **SHORTER MOMENTS** [-]

— Next 2 recorded in 50's with The JAZZ MESSENGERS

1974. GNP Crescendo; (d-lp) **WAYNE SHORTER** [-]
– *(re-iss.1988)*

Mar 84. Affinity/ US= Vee Jay; (lp) **SECOND GENESIS**

Nov 86. Affinity/ US= Vee Jay; (lp)(c) **WAYNING MOMENTS**

Jun 88. Charly; (cd) **THE VEE-JAY YEARS** [-]

Dec 88. Blue Note; (lp)(cd) **BEST OF WAYNE SHORTER**
– Speak no evil / Infant eyes / Lost / Adam's apple / Footprints. (cd+=) – Tom Thumb / Virgo / Juju / Water babies.

JOE ZAWINUL

with **GEORGE TUCKER** – bass / **FRANKIE DUNLOP** – drums / **RAY BARRETTO** – perc.

not issued / Fresh Sound

Sep 59. (lp) **THE BEGINNING** [-]
(cd-iss.Dec90)

1969. (lp) **MONEY IN THE POCKET**
– Dat / Riverbed / Sharon's waltz / Del sasser / Money in the pocket. *(UK-iss 74 on Atco)*

Atco / Atco

1971. (lp) **ZAWINUL**
– Doctor Honoris causa / In a silent way / His last journey / Double image / Arrival in New York. *(re-iss.1974 on 'Atlantic')*

1972. (lp) **RISE & FALL**

Atlantic / Atlantic

1976. (lp) **CONCERTO RETITLED**
– From Vienna with love / My one and only love / Riverbed / Del sasser / Sharon' waltz / His last journey / In a silent way / Concerto retitled.

ZAWINUL

only solo synthesizers and vocals. **BOBBY McFERRIN** – voice / plus ensemble **CARL ANDERSON / DEE DEE BELSON / ALFIE SILAS**

C.B.S. / Columbia

Mar 86. (lp)(c) **DIALECTS**
– The harvest / Waiting for the rain / Zeebop / The great empire / Carnavalito / 6 a.m. – walking on the Nile / Peace.

— After break-up of WEATHER REPORT, he formed

ZAWINUL SYNDICATE

C.B.S. / Columbia

May 88. (lp)(c)(cd) **THE IMMIGRANTS**
– March of the lost children / Criolo / Shadow and light / No mercy for me (mercy, mercy, mercy) / The Devil never sleeps / You understand / From Venice to Vienna.

Jul 89. (lp)(c)(cd) **BLACK WATER**
– Carnavalito / Familial / In the same boat / Little rootie tootie / Black water / Medieval man / Monk's mood / Thy land a dream.

– (JOE ZAWINUL) compilations –

Jul 94. Rhino; (cd) **THE RISE AND FALL OF THE THIRD STREAM / MONEY IN POCKET**

Mar 95. RST; (cd) **HIS MAJESTY, SWINGING NEPHEWS 1954-57 (with The AUSTRAIN ALL-STARS)** [-]

WEDDING PRESENT

Formed: Leeds, England . . . 1984 by ex-teachers GEDGE and SOLOWKA (father Ukrainian), plus GREGORY and CHARMAN. In 1985, they gained deal with local indie label 'Reception'. With appearances on John Peel's radio 1 show, they quickly grew enough to break the UK Top50. In 1988, they finally signed to a major record company 'R.C.A.'. Their first release on the label 'UKRAINSKI . . .', surprised many, as it was a break away from usual guitar-based style. They reverted to lovelorn lyrical fashion once again later in 1989, when releasing hit album 'BIZARRO'. In 1992, they went into the Guinness Book Of Records, when every one of their monthly single (7"only) releases hit the UK Top30. The 12 hits also contained an unusual cover version on the B-side (see below). • **Style:** Fast and furious jangly punk rock, although their musical talent was obvious on Ukrainian-style album/Peel sessions. • **Songwriters:** GEDGE compositions, except GETTING NOWHERE FAST (Girls At Our Best) / WHAT BECOME OF THE BROKEN HEARTED (Jimmy Ruffin) / I FOUND THAT ESSENCE RARE (Gang Of Four) / IT'S NOT UNUSUAL (Tom Jones) / FELICITY (Orange Juice) / MAKE ME SMILE (COME UP AND SEE ME) (Steve Harley & Cockney Rebel) / BOX ELDER (Pavement) / SHE'S MY BEST FRIEND (Velvet Underground) / MOTHERS (Jean Michel Satre) / CUMBERLAND GAP (Leadbelly) / CATTLE AND CANE (Go-Betweens) / DON'T CRY NO TEARS (Neil Young) / THINK THAT IT MIGHT (Altered Images) / FALLING (Julee Cruise) / PLEASANT VALLEY SUNDAY (Monkees) / LET'S MAKE SOME PLANS (Close Lobsters) / ROCKET (Mud) / THEME FROM SHAFT (Isaac Hayes) / CHANT OF THE EVER CIRCLING SKELETAL FAMILY (Bowie) / GO WILD IN THE COUNTRY (Bow Wow Wow) / U.F.O. (Barry Gray) / STEP INTO CHRISTMAS (Elton John). • **Trivia:** STEVE ALBINI (ex-BIG BLACK) produced their early 90s material.

Recommended: GEORGE BEST (*9) / TOMMY (*8) / BIZARRO (*7) / SEA MONSTERS (*7) / THE HIT PARADE 1 (*7).

DAVID GEDGE (b.23 Apr'60) – vocals, guitar / **PETE SOLOWKA** (b.Manchester) – guitar / **KEITH GREGORY** (b. 2 Jan'63, County Durham) – bass / **SHAUN CHARMAN** (b.Brighton) – drums

Reception | not issued

May 85. (7") **GO OUT AND GET 'EM BOY. / (THE MOMENT BEFORE) EVERYTHING'S SPOILED AGAIN** [ ] [-]
(re-iss.Sep85 on 'City Slang')

Jan 86. (7") **ONCE MORE. / AT THE EDGE OF THE SEA** [ ] [-]

Apr 86. (12"ep) **DON'T TRY AND STOP ME MOTHER** [ ] [-]
– (above 4 tracks).

Jul 86. (7") **THIS BOY CAN'T WAIT. / YOU SHOULD ALWAYS KEEP IN TOUCH WITH YOUR FRIENDS** [ ] [-]
('A'extended-12"+=) – Living and learning.

Feb 87. (7")(12")(7"white) **MY FAVOURITE DRESS. / EVERY MOTHER'S SON / NEVER SAID** [ ] [-]
(2,000 copies of above single were also given free with debut lp)

Sep 87. (7") **ANYONE CAN MAKE A MISTAKE. / ALL ABOUT EVE** [ ] [-]
(12"+=)(c-s+=) – Getting nowhere fast.

Oct 87. (lp)(c)(cd) **GEORGE BEST** [47] [-]
– Everyone thinks he looks daft / What did your last servant die of? / Don't be so hard / A million miles / All this and more / Getting nowhere fast * / My favourite dress / Shatner / Something and nothing / It's what you want that matters / Give my love to Kevin / Anyone can make a mistake / You can't moan can you / All about Eve *. *(c+= *)(cd+= *)*

— **SIMON SMITH** (b. 3 May'65, Lincolnshire) – drums repl. SHAUN to POP GUNS

Feb 88. (7") **NOBODY'S TWISTING YOUR ARM. / I'M NOT ALWAYS SO STUPID** [46] [-]
(12"+=)(cd-s+=) – Nothing comes easy / Don't laugh.

Jul 88. (lp)(c)(cd) **TOMMY** – (compilation 4 singles + Peel sessions) [42] [-]
– Go out and get 'em boy / (The moment before) Everything's spolied again / Once more / At the edge of the sea / Living and learning / This boy can't wait / You should always keep in touch with your friends / Felicity / What becomes of the broken hearted? / Never said / Every mother's son / My favourite dress.

Sep 88. (7") **WHY ARE YOU BEING SO REASONABLE NOW?. / NOT FROM WHERE I'M STANDING** [42] [-]
(12"+=) – Give my love to Kevin (acoustic) / Getting better.
(c-s++=)(cd-s++=) – Pourquoi es tu devenue si raisonnable?.
(7") – Pourquoi es tu devenue si raisonnable?. / Give my love to Kevin (acoustic)

— added guest **LEN LIGGINS** – vocals, violin (ex-SINISTER CLEANERS, Solo artist) Others played assortment of instruments in Ukrainian style.

R.C.A. | R.C.A.

Apr 89. (lp)(c)(cd) **UKRAINSKI VISTUPI V JOHNA PEELA** [22] [-]
(Ukrainian style John Peel sessions)
– Davny chasy / Yikhav kozak za dunai / Tiutiunyk / Zadmav didochok svitit misyats / Katrusyai Vasya vasyl'ok / Hude dn ipro hude Verkhovyno. *(was to have been issued as 10"m-lp, late 1988 on 'Reception')*

— (Reverted to usual 4-piece & style).

Sep 89. (7")(c-s) **KENNEDY. / UNFAITHFUL** [33] [ ]
(12"+=)(cd-s+=) – One day all this will all be yours / It's not unusual.

Oct 89. (lp)(c)(cd) **BIZARRO** [22] [ ]
– Brassneck / Crushed / No / Thanks / Kennedy / What have I said now / Granadaland / Bewitched / Take me / Be honest. *(cd+=)*– Brassneck (extended) / Box elder / Don't talk, just kiss / Gone.

Feb 90. (7")(c-s) **BRASSNECK. / DON'T TALK, JUST KISS** [24] [ ]
(12"+=)(c-s+=)(cd-s+=) – Gone / Box elder.

Sep 90. (7"ep)(12"ep)(c-ep)(cd-ep) **THE 3 SONGS** [25] [ ]
– Corduroy / Make me smile (come up and see me) / Crawl.
(10"+=) – Take me (live).

Apr 91. (7")(c-s) **DALLIANCE. / NIAGRA** [29] [ ]
(12"+=)(cd-s+=) – She's my best friend.
(10"++=) – What have I said now? (live).

May 91. (cd)(c)(lp) **SEAMONSTERS** [13] [ ]
– Dalliance / Dare / Suck / Blonde / Rotterdam / Lovenest / Corduroy / Carolyn / Heather / Octopussy.

Jul 91. (12"ep)(cd-ep) **LOVENEST (edit) / MOTHERS. / DAN DARE / FLESHWORLD** [58] [ ]

— **PAUL DORRINGTON** – guitar (ex-AC TEMPLE) repl. SOLOWKA to UKRAINIANS

Jan 92. (7") **BLUE EYES. / CATTLE AND CANE** [26] [ ]
Feb 92. (7") **GO-GO DANCER. / DON'T CRY NO TEARS** [20] [ ]
Mar 92. (7") **THREE. / THINK THAT IT MIGHT** [14] [ ]
Apr 92. (7") **SILVER SHORTS. / FALLING** [14] [ ]
May 92. (7") **COME PLAY WITH ME. / PLEASANT VALLEY SUNDAY** [10] [ ]
Jun 92. (7") **CALIFORNIA. / LET'S MAKE SOME PLANS** [16] [ ]
Jun 92. (cd)(c)(lp) **THE HIT PARADE 1** [22] [ ]
– (last 6 singles 'A'&'B')
Jul 92. (7") **FLYING SAUCER. / ROCKET** [22] [ ]
Aug 92. (7") **BOING!. / THEME FROM SHAFT** [19] [ ]
Sep 92. (7") **LOVESLAVE. / CHANT OF THE EVER CIRCLING SKELETAL FAMILY** [17] [ ]
Oct 92. (7") **STICKY. / GO WILD IN THE COUNTRY** [17] [ ]
Nov 92. (7") **THE QUEEN OF OUTER SPACE. / U.F.O.** [23] [ ]
Dec 92. (7"red) **NO CHRISTMAS. / STEP INTO CHRISTMAS** [25] [ ]

— The above 12 singles, were limited to 15,000 copies, and hit peak chart position on it's first week of issue.

Jan 93. (cd)(c)(lp) **THE HIT PARADE 2** [19] [ ]
– (all last 6 'A'&'B' singles above) (free lp w/lp+=) **BBC SESSIONS** – (all 12 of the years' A-sides).

— In Oct'93, they were looking for a replacement for KEITH GREGORY.

— **DARREN BELLE** – bass repl.him

Island | Island

Sep 94. (12"ep)(c-ep)(cd-ep) **YEAH YEAH YEAH YEAH YEAH / THE BIKINI / FLAME ON / HIM OR ME (WHAT'S IT GONNA BE)** [51] [ ]
(cd-s) – ('A'side) / Gazebo / So long baby / Spangle.

Sep 94. (cd)(c)(lp) **WATUSI** [47] [ ]
– So long, baby / Click click / Yeah yeah yeah yeah yeah / Let him have it / Gazebo / Shake it / Spangle / It's a gas / Swimming pools, movie stars / Big rat / Catwoman / Hot pants.

Nov 94. (7")(c-s) **IT'S A GAS. / BUBBLES** [ ] [ ]
(12"purple+=)(cd-s+=) – ('A'acoustic) / Jumper clown.

– compilations, etc. –

Oct 86. Strange Fruit; (12"ep) **THE PEEL SESSIONS** (26.2.86) [ ] [-]
– What becomes of the broken hearted / This boy can't wait / Felicity / You should always keep in touch with your friends. *(c-ep iss.Jun87, cd-ep iss. Aug88)*

1993. Strange Fruit; (cd)(lp) **JOHN PEEL SESSIONS 1987-1990** [ ] [-]
– Give my regards to Kevin / Getting nowhere fast / A million miles / Something and nothing / Take me I'm yours / Unfaithful / Why are you being so reasonable now? / Happy birthday / Dalliance / Heather Blonde / Niagara.

Nov 88. Nighttracks; (12"ep)(cd-ep) **THE EVENING SHOW SESSIONS** (20.4.86) [ ] [-]
– Everyone thinks he looks daft / I found that essence rare / Shatner / My favourite dress.

WEEZER

Formed: Los Angeles, USA . . .1993 by CUOMO RIVERS, etc (see below). By the end of 1994, they had stormed the US album charts with the massive selling eponymous debut. • **Style:** College retro punk-pop or 'nerd' rock often described as The PIXIES meeting The BEACH BOYS. On the crest of an American 'new wave', set by GREEN DAY and OFFSPRING. • **Songwriters:** CUOMO, a few w/ WILSON. • **Trivia:** Produced by RIC OCASEK (ex-CARS).

Recommended: WEEZER (*7)

RIVERS CUOMO – vocals/ **BRIAN BELL** – guitar, vocals/ **MATT SHARP** – bass, vocals/ **PATRICK WILSON** – drums

Geffen | Geffen

Jan 95. (7"blue-ep)(c-ep)(cd-ep) **UNDONE – THE SWEATER SONG. / MYKEL & CARLI / SUSANNE / HOLIDAY** [35] [57] Sep94

Feb 95. (cd)(c)(lp) **WEEZER** [23] [16] Aug94
– My name is Jonas / No one else / The world has turned and left me here / Buddy Holly / Undone – the sweater song / In the garage / Holiday / Only in dreams.

Apr 95. (7")(c-s) **BUDDY HOLLY. / JAMIE** [12] [ ]
(cd-s+=) – My name is Jonas / Surf wax America.

Jul 95. (10"ep)(c-ep)(cd-ep) **SAY IT AIN'T SO (remix). / NO ONE ELSE (live and acoustic) / JAMIE (live and acoustic)** [37] [ ]

Bob WEIR (see under ⇒ GRATEFUL DEAD)

WE KNOW WHERE YOU LIVE (see under ⇒ WONDER STUFF)

Paul WELLER

Born: London, England . . . Formed STYLE COUNCIL early 1983 with past mod MICK TALBOT. WELLER re-signed to 'Polydor', and quickly re-established themselves back in the charts with debut Top 5 hit 'SPEAK LIKE A CHILD'. PAUL went solo in 1991, and 2 years later his 'WILDWOOD' album received deserved rave reviews, resulting in a Mercury award in '94. • **Style:** Sophisticated white soul-pop, with romantic jazzy overtones mixed alongside WELLER's political socialist leanings. • **Songwriters:** WELLER penned except for TALBOT's instrumentals. They also covered MOVE ON UP (Curtis Mayfield) / PROMISED LAND (Joe Smooth) / OHIO (Neil Young). WELLER solo:- FEELIN' ALRIGHT (Traffic) / SEXY SADIE (Beatles) / I'M ONLY DREAMING (Small Faces). • **Trivia:** WELLER married his backing singer and solo star DEE C.LEE in Dec'86. He also featured on BAND AID's charity single 'DO THEY KNOW IT'S CHRISTMAS' in 1984, and 7 months later appeared in LIVE AID at Wembley.

Recommended: THE SINGULAR ADVENTURES OF THE STYLE COUNCIL (*7) / WILD WOOD (*9) / STANLEY ROAD (*8)

STYLE COUNCIL

PAUL WELLER (b.25 May'58, Woking, Surrey, England) – vocals, guitar (ex-JAM) / **MICK TALBOT** (b.11 Sep'58) – keyboards (ex-MERTON PARKAS) / **STEVE WHITE** – drums / plus various guests.

Polydor | Polydor

Mar 83. (7") **SPEAK LIKE A CHILD. / PARTY CHAMBERS** [4] [ ]
May 83. (7") **MONEY GO ROUND. / (part 2)** [11] [ ]

(12") – ('A'side) / Headstart for happiness / Mick's up.
Aug 83. (7"ep)(12"ep) **LONG HOT SUMMER / PARTY CHAMBERS. / PARIS MATCH / LE DEPART** [3] [ ]
Nov 83. (7") **SOLID BOND IN YOUR HEART. / IT JUST CAME TO PIECES IN MY HAND / ('A'instrumental)** [11] [ ]
Oct 83. (lp)(c) **INTRODUCING THE STYLE COUNCIL** [-] [ ]
– (above songs)

Polydor Geffen

Feb 84. (7") **MY EVER CHANGING MOODS. / MICK'S COMPANY** [5] [29] Apr 84
(12"+=) – Spring, Summer, Autumn.
Mar 84. (lp)(c)(cd) **CAFE BLEU** [2] [56]
– Mick's blessings / My ship came in / Blue cafe / The Paris match / My ever changing moods / Dropping bombs on the Whitehouse / A gospel / Strength of your nature / You're the best thing / Here's the one that got away / Headstart for happiness / Council meetin'. *(cd+=)* – The whole point of no return. (US-album title **'MY EVER CHANGING MOODS'**) *(re-iss.cd Sep95)*
May 84. (7") **YOU'RE THE BEST THING. / BIG BOSS GROOVE** [5] [76]
(12"+=) – ('A'dub version).
Oct 84. (7") **SHOUT TO THE TOP. / GHOSTS OF DACHAU** [7] [ ]
(12"+=) – Piccadilly trail / ('A'instrumental).
Dec 84. (7") **SOUL DEEP. (as "COUNCIL COLLECTIVE") / (part 2)** [24] [-]
(12"+=) – ('A'version) / (striking miner's interview).
(above single gave proceeds to miner's strike & the deceased miner David Wilkie's widow) The COLLECTIVE featured guests JIMMY RUFFIN, JUNIOR GISCOMBE, VAUGHN TOULOUSE, DEE C.LEE and DIZZY HEIGHTS. Production handled by MARTYN WARE (Heaven 17).
May 85. (7")(12") **WALLS COME TUMBLING DOWN. / THE WHOLE POINT II / BLOODSPORTS** [6] [-]
Jun 85. (lp)(c)(cd) **OUR FAVOURITE SHOP (US title 'INTERNATIONALISTS')** [1] [ ]
– Homebreakers / All gone away / Come to Milton Keynes / Internationalists / A stone's throw away / The stand up comic's instructions / Boy who cried wolf / A man of great promise / Down in the Seine / The lodgers / Luck / With everything to lose / Our favourite shop / Walls come tumbling down. *(cd+=)*– Shout to the top. *(c+=)*– (interview).
Jun 85. (7") **COME TO MILTON KEYNES. / WHEN YOU CALL ME** [23] [-]
(12"+=) – Our favourite shop / ('A'club) / The lodgers (club mix).
Aug 85. (7") **OUR FAVOURITE SHOP. / BOY WHO CRIED WOLF** [-] [ ]
Sep 85. (7") **THE LODGERS (remix). / YOU'RE THE BEST THING (live)** [13] [ ]
(d7"+=) – Big boss groove (live) / Long hot summer (live).
(12"+=) – Big boss groove (live) / Move on up (live).
(12"+=) – Medley: Money go round – Soul deep – Strength of your nature.
Mar 86. (7")(12")(c-s) **HAVE YOU EVER HAD IT BLUE. / MR. COOL'S DREAM** [14] [ ]
May 86. (lp)(c)(cd) **HOME AND ABROAD – LIVE (live)** [8] [ ]
– The big boss groove * / My ever changing moods / The lodgers / Headstart for happiness / (When you) Call me / The whole point of no return / Our favourite shop * / With everything to lose / Homebreakers / Shout to the top / Walls come tumbling down / Internationalists. *(cd+= *)*
Jun 86. (7") **THE INTERNATIONALISTS. / (WHEN YOU) CALL ME** [-] [ ]

Polydor Polydor

Jan 87. (7")(12") **IT DIDN'T MATTER. / ALL YEAR ROUND** [9] [ ]
Feb 87. (2x12"lp)(c)(cd) **THE COST OF LOVING** [2] [ ]
– It didn't matter / Right to go / Waiting / Walking the night / The cost of loving / Heaven's above / Fairy tales / Angel / A woman's song. *(re-iss.c+cd.Oct90)*
Mar 87. (7") **WAITING. / FRANCOISE** [52] [ ]
(12"+=) – Theme from 'Jerusalem'.
Oct 87. (7") **WANTED (FOR WAITER). / THE COST OF LOVING** [20] [ ]
(12"+=)(c-s+=)/ /(cd-s+=) – There's soup in my flies./ / The cost.
May 88. (7") **LIFE AT A TOP PEOPLE'S HEALTH FARM. / SWEET LOVING WAYS** [28] [ ]
(12"+=)(cd-s+=) – Spark (live) / ('A'version).
Jun 88. (lp)(c)(cd) **CONFESSIONS OF A POP GROUP** [15] [ ]
– It's a very deep sea / The story of someone's shoe / Changing of the guard / The little boy in a castle – A dove flew down from the elephant / The gardener of Eden (a three piece suite):- In the beginning – The gardener of Eden – Mourning the passing of time / Life at a top people's health farm / Why I went missing / How she threw it all away / I was a doledads toyboy / Confessions of a pop group (parts 1, 2 & 3) / Confessions of a pop group. *(re-iss.c+cd.Oct90)*
Jul 88. (7"ep)(12"ep) **HOW SHE THREW IT ALL AWAY / IN LOVE FOR THE FIRST TIME. / LONG HOT SUMER / I DO LIKE TO BE B-SIDE THE A-SIDE** [41] [ ]
Feb 89. (7") **PROMISED LAND. / CAN YOU STILL LOVE ME** [27] [ ]
(12"+=)(cd-s+=) – ?
Mar 89. (lp)(c)(cd) **THE SINGULAR ADVENTURES OF THE STYLE COUNCIL** (compilation) [3] [ ]
– You're the best thing / Have you ever had it blue (extended) / Money go round (parts 1 & 2) / My ever changing moods (extended) / Long hot summer (extended) / The lodgers / Walls come tumbling down / Shout to the top / Wanted / It didn't matter / Speak like a child / A solid bond in your heart / Life at a top people's health farm / Promised land. *(c+=)(cd+=)*– How she threw it all away / Waiting.
May 89. (7") **LONG HOT SUMMER ('89 mix). / EVERYBODY'S ON THE RUN** [48] [ ]
(12"+=) – ('A' & 'B' different mixes).

—— Disbanded Mar'90. WELLER went solo, see below.

– more compilations, etc. –

Nov 87. Polydor; (cd-ep) **CAFE BLEU** [ ] [-]
– Headstart for happiness / Here's one that got away / Blue cafe / Strength of your nature.
Nov 87. Polydor; (cd-ep) **BIRDS AND BEES** [ ] [-]
– Piccadilly trail / It just came to pieces in my hands / Spin drifting / Spring, Summer, Autumn.
Nov 87. Polydor; (cd-ep) **MICK TALBOT IS AGENT '88** [ ] [-]
– Mick's up / Party chambers / Mick's blessing / Mick's company.
Jul 93. Polydor; (cd)(c) **HERE'S SOME THAT GOT AWAY** [39] [-]
Jan 90. Old Gold; (7") **YOU'RE THE BEST THING. / MY EVER CHANGING MOODS** [ ] [-]
Jan 90. Old Gold; (7") **LONG HOT SUMMER. / SPEAK LIKE A CHILD** [ ] [-]

PAUL WELLER MOVEMENT

with **STEVE WHITE** – drums, percussion / **JACKO PEAKE** – sax, flute, b.vox / **DEE C.LEE, DR.ROBERT + CAMELLE HINDS** – backing vocals

Freedom High London

May 91. (7")(c-s) **INTO TOMORROW. / HERE'S NEW THING** [36] [ ] 1992
(12"+=)(cd-s+=) – That spiritual feeling / ('A'demo version).

PAUL WELLER

Go! Discs London

Aug 92. (7")(c-s) **UH HUH OH YEH. / FLY ON THE WALL** [18] [ ]
(12"+=)(cd-s+=) – Always there to fool you / Arrival time.
Sep 92. (cd)(c)(lp) **PAUL WELLER** [8] [ ]
– Uh huh oh yeh / I didn't mean to hurt you / Bull-rush / Round and round / Remember how we started / Above the clouds / Clues / Into tomorrow / Amongst butterflies / The strange museum / Bitterness rising / Kosmos. *(re-iss.Apr94)*
Oct 92. (7")(c-s) **ABOVE THE CLOUDS. / EVERYTHING HAS A PRICE TO PAY** [47] [ ]
(12"+=)(cd-s+=) – All year round (live) / Feelin' alright.

—— with **STEVE WHITE** – drums, percussion / **MARCO NELSON** – bass

Jul 93. (7")(c-s) **SUNFLOWER. / BULL-RUSH-MAGIC BUS (live)** [16] [ ]
(12"+=)(cd-s+=) – Kosmo's sx dub 2000 / That spiritual feeling (new mix)
Aug 93. (7")(10")(c-s) **WILD WOOD. / ENDS OF THE EARTH** [14] [ ]
Sep 93. (cd)(c)(lp) **WILD WOOD** [2] [ ]
– Sunflower / Can you heal us (holy man) / Wild wood – instrumental (pt.1) / All the pictures on the wall / Has my fire really gone out? / Country / 5th season / The weaver – instrumental (pt.2) / Foot of the mountain / Shadow of the Sun – Holy man (reprise) / Moon on your pyjamas. *(re-iss.Apr94)*
Nov 93. (7"ep)(10"ep)(c-ep)(cd-ep) **THE WEAVER EP** [18] [ ]
– The weaver / This is no time / Another new day / Ohio (live).
Mar 94. (7"ep)(12"ep)(c-ep)(cd-ep) **HOME OF THE CLASSIC EP** [11] [ ]
– Hung up / Foot of the mountain (live) / The loved / Kosmos (Lynch Mob bonus beats).
Sep 94. (cd)(c)(lp) **LIVE WOOD (live)** [13] [ ]
– Bull rush – Magic bus / This is no time / All the pictures on the wall / Remember how we started? / Dominoes / Above the clouds / Wild wood / Shadow of the Sun / (Can you hear us) Holy man – War / 5th season / Into tomorrow / Fool of the mountains / Sunflower / Has the fire really gone out?
Oct 94. (7"ep)(12"ep)(c-ep)(cd-ep) **OUT OF THE SINKING. / SUNFLOWER (Brendan Lynch dub) / SEXY SADIE** [20] [ ]

—— with **STEVE WHITE** – drums / **DR.ROBERT** – bass, vocals (ex-BLOW MONKEYS) / **STEVE CRADDOCK** – guitar / **MARK NELSON** – bass / **HELEN TURNER** – strings, organ / **BRENDAN LYNCH** – organ, co-producer / + guests **MICK TALBOT / CARLEEN ANDERSON / STEVE WINWOOD / NOEL GALLAGHER / YOLANDA CHARLES / CONSTANTINE WEIR**

Apr 95. (7"ep)(c-ep)(cd-ep) **THE CHANGINGMAN / I'D RATHER GO BLIND / It'S A NEW DAY, BABY / I DIDNT MEAN TO HURT YOU (live)** [7] [ ]
May 95. (cd)(c)(lp)(6x7"pack) **STANLEY ROAD** [1] [ ]
– The changingman / Porcelain gods / I walk on gilded splinters / You do something to me / Woodcutter's son / Time passes / Stanley Road / Broken stones / Out of the sinking / Pink on white walls / Whirlpool's end / Wings of speed.
Jul 95. (7"ep)(c-ep)(cd-ep) **YOU DO SOMETHING TO ME / A YEAR LATE. / MY WHOLE WORLD IS FALLING DOWN / WOODCUTTER'S SON** [9] [ ]
Sep 95. (7")(c-s) **BROKEN STONES. / STEAM** [20] [ ]
(cd-s+=) – Whirlpool's end.
(cd-s+=) – Porcelain gods.

Fred WESLEY (see under ⇒ JB'S)

Leslie WEST (see under ⇒ MOUNTAIN)

Paul WESTERBERG (see under ⇒ REPLACEMENTS)

WET WET WET

Formed: Glasgow, Scotland . . . 1982 by PELLOW, CLARK, MITCHELL and CUNNINGHAM. Late 1984, they met Elliot Davis who became their manager and co-label owner of label 'The Precious Organisation'. They spent the next couple of years, perfecting sound after signing to major 'Phonogram' distribution in 1985. In the Spring of '87, they finally unleashed their debut 45 'WISHING I WAS LUCKY', and this soon peaked at No.6. They followed this up with a Top 5 single, which was one of a number of hits from UK No.1 album 'POPPED IN, SOULED OUT'. • **Style:** White soul-pop group, guided by the ever-smiling pin-up boy MARTI PELLOW. • **Songwriters:** PELLOW – lyrics (label paid out of court settlement to VAN MORRISON and SQUEEZE for him lifting said artists lyrics on 'WISHING I WAS LUCKY') / group compositions, except HEAVEN HELP US ALL (Stevie Wonder) / WITH A LITTLE HELP FROM MY FRIENDS + I FEEL FINE (Beatles) / MAGGIE MAY (Rod Stewart) / STONED ME (Van Morrison) / LOVE IS ALL AROUND (Troggs) / IT'S NOW OR NEVER + IN THE GHETTO (both hits; Elvis Presley) / SHARE YOUR LOVE (Malone-Braggs) / YOU'VE GOT A FRIEND (Carole King) / ATLANTIC AVENUE (Average White Band) / IF YOU ONLY KNEW (. . .Allison) / WOULDN'T HAVE MADE ANY DIFERENCE (Todd Rundren) / TOWN CRIER (Elvis Costello) / ANGELINE (John Martyn) / BEG YOUR PARDON DEAR (Craig-Smith). • **Trivia:** Took their name from a line in a SCRITTI POLITTI song 'Gettin', Havin', Holdin'6. Their 5th (tour) member was lead guitarist GRAEME DUFFIN.

Recommended: END OF PART ONE (THEIR GREATEST HITS) (*8)

MARTI PELLOW (b.MARK McLOUGHLIN, 23 Mar'66, Clydebank, Scotland) – vocals / **GRAEME CLARK** (b.15 Apr'66) – bass, guitar / **NEIL MITCHELL** (b. 8 Jun'67, Helensburgh, Scotland) – keyboards / **TOM CUNNINGHAM** (b.22 Jun'65) – drums

Precious | Uni

Mar 87. (7") **WISHING I WAS LUCKY. / WORDS OF WISDOM** [6] [58] May 88
(12"+=) – Still can't remember your name.
(d12"++=) – ('A'metal mix).

Jul 87. (7")(7"sha-pic-d) **SWEET LITTLE MYSTERY. / DON'T LET ME BE LONELY TONIGHT** [5] [ ]
(12"+=) – World in another world.
(7"ep++=) – ('A'different mix).

Sep 87. (lp)(c)(cd) **POPPED IN SOULED OUT** [1] [ ]
– Wishing I was lucky / East of the river / I remember / Angel eyes (home and away) / Sweet little mystery / I don't believe (Sonny's letter) / Temptation / I can give you everything / The moment you left me. *(cd+=)*– Don't let me be lonely tonight / World in another world / Wishing I was lucky (live).

Nov 87. (7") **ANGEL EYES (HOME AND AWAY). / WE CAN LOVE** [5] [ ]
(12"+=)(c-s+=)(cd-s+=) – ('A'extended).

Mar 88. (7") **TEMPTATION. / BOTTLED EMOTIONS (REIGN FOR LOVING)** [12] [ ]
(12"+=) – I remember.
(cd-s++=) – Heaven help us all.

May 88. (7") **WITH A LITTLE HELP FROM MY FRIENDS. / ('B'by Billy Bragg)** [1] [ ]

—— (above single on the 'Childline' label, gave all monies to that charity).

Nov 88. (10"lp)(c)(cd) **THE MEMPHIS SESSIONS** [3] [ ]
– I don't believe (Sonny'e letter) / Sweet little mystery (Memphis version) / East of the river (Memphis version) / This time / Temptation (Memphis version) / I remember / For you are / Heaven help us all.

Sep 89. (7")(c-s) **SWEET SURRENDER. / THIS TIME (live)** [6] [ ]
(12"+=)(cd-s+=) – H.T.H.D.T.G.T. / ('A'extended version).

Oct 89. (lp)(c)(cd) **HOLDING BACK THE RIVER** [2] [ ]
– Sweet surrender / Can't stand the night / Blue for you / Broke away / You've had it / I wish / Key to your heart / Maggie May / Hold back the river.

Nov 89. (7")(c-s)(7"pic-d) **BROKE AWAY. / YOU'VE HAD IT** [19] [ ]
(12"+=) – And now for something completely different.
(cd-s+=)(pic-cd-s+=) – Sweet surrender (club mix).

Mar 90. (7")(c-s) **HOLD BACK THE RIVER. / KEY TO YOUR HEART** [31] [ ]
(12"+=)(cd-s+=) – With a little help from my friends (live).
(12"+=) – Party city / I can give you everything.

Jul 90. (7")(c-s) **STAY WITH ME HEARTACHE. / I FEEL FINE** [30] [ ]
(12"+=)(cd-s+=)(pic-cd-s+=) – Hold back the river (acoustic) / ('A'-TC YOUNG & T-mix).
(10"+=) – Stay with me heartache (stay where you are) / Stoned me.

Sep 91. (7")(c-s) **MAKE IT TONIGHT. / ORDINARY LOVE** [37] [ ]
('A'version-12"+=)(cd-s+=) – Big sister midnight.

Oct 91. (7")(one-sided etched-7") **PUT THE LIGHT ON. / JUST LIKE ANY OTHER DAY** [56] [ ]
(12"pic-d+=)(cd-s+=) – You've got a friend.

Dec 91. (7") **GOODNIGHT GIRL. / AMBROSE WYKES** [1] [ ]
(cd-s+=) – With a little help from my friends / Sweet surrender / Goodnight (no strings attached). (cd-s+=) – Wishing I was lucky / Temptation (Memphis version) / Angel eyes (home and away).

Jan 92. (cd)(c)(lp) **HIGH ON THE HAPPY SIDE** [1] [ ]
– More than love / Lip service / Put the light on / High on the happy side / Maybe tomorrow / Goodnight girl / Celebration / Make it tonight / How long / Brand new sunrise / 2 days after midnite. (free-7"w.a.) – CLOAK AND DAGGER as 'MAGGIE PIE & THE IMPOSTERS")

Mar 92. (7")(c-s) **MORE THAN LOVE. / GOODNIGHT GIRL (mix)** [19] [ ]
(cd-s+=) – Broke away / Sweet little mystery (Memphis session).

Jun 92. (7"ep)(c-ep)(cd-ep) **LIP SERVICE EP** [15] [ ]
– Lip service (Youth mix) / High on the happy side / Lip service (live) / More than love (live).

Apr 93. (7")(c-s) **BLUE FOR YOU (live). / THIS TIME (live)** [38] [ ]
(cd-s+=) – I can give you everything.

May 93. (cd)(c)(lp) **LIVE AT THE ROYAL ALBERT HALL (live)** [10] [ ]
– Angel eyes / This time / Brand new sunrise / Hold back the river / Blue for you / Goodnight girl / How long / East of the river / I can give you everything.

Oct 93. (7")(c-s) **SHED A TEAR. / EVERYDAY** [22] [ ]
(cd-s+=) – Deadline.

Nov 93. (cd)(c)(lp) **END OF PART ONE (THEIR GREATEST HITS)** (compilation) [4] [ ]
– Wishing I was lucky / Sweet little mystery / Angel eyes / Temptation / With a little help from my friends / Sweet surrender / Broke away / Hold back the river / Stay with me heartache / This time / Make it tonight / Put the light on / Goodnight girl / More than love / Lip service / Blue for you (live) / Shed a tear / Cold, cold heart. *(initial copies contained free cd/c/lp)*

Jan 94. (7")(c-s) **COLD COLD HEART. / ROLL 'UM EASY** [20] [ ]
(cd-s+=) – (2-'A'mixes).
(cd-s) – ('A'side) / Another love in me / Wishing I was lucky (2 Arthur Baker mixes).

May 94. (7")(c-s) **LOVE IS ALL AROUND. / I CAN GIVE YOU EVERYTHING (Arthur Baker soul remix)** [1] [41] Aug94
(cd-s+=) – ('A'mix).

—— Above track hit No.1 for a near record breaking 15 weeks. Just prior to this occurance, it was withdrawn by the group from the printing press. In Aug94, 'END OF PART ONE' compilation regained its No.1 placing.

Mar 95. (7")(c-s)(cd-s) **JULIA SAYS. / IT'S NOW OR NEVER** [3] [ ]
(cd-s+=) – Dixie / ('A'version).
(cd-s+=) – I don't want to know / ('A'-synth string version).

Apr 95. (cd)(c) **PICTURE THIS** [1] [ ]
– Julia says / After the love goes / Somewhere somehow / Gypsy girl / Don't want to forgive me now / She might never know / Someone like you / Love is my shepherd / She's on my mind / Morning / Home tonight / Love is all around.

Jun 95. (c-s)(cd-s) **DON'T WANT TO FORGIVE ME NOW. / IN THE GHETTO** [7] [ ]
(cd-s) – ('A'side) / Love is all around / Angel eyes.
(cd-s) – ('A'side) / Gypsy girl (live acoustic).

Sep 95. (c-s) **SOMEWHERE SOMEHOW / MORNING (the Youth 1995 remix) / ('A'-synth string version)** [7] [ ]
(cd-s) – ('A'side) / All you need is love (live) / She might never know (live) / Somewhere somehow (live).

Nov 95. (c-s) **SHE'S ALL ON MY MIND / IF YOU ONLY KNEW / WOULDN'T HAVE MADE ANY DIFFERENCE (last 2 by MAGGIE PIE & THE IMPOSTERS)** [17] [ ]
(cd-s) – ('A'side) / Share your love / You've got a friend / Beg your pardon dear.
(cd-s) – ('A'side) / Atlantic avenue / Town crier / Angeline.

– compilations, others, etc. –

Feb 92. Old Gold; (7") **WISHING I WAS LUCKY. / SWEET LITTLE MYSTERY** [ ] [-]

WHALE

Formed: Stockholm, Sweden . . .1993 by trio below. In 1995, they rudely awakened the UK Top 40 with massive Euro hit 'HOBO HUMPIN' . . .'. • **Style:** Hip-hop thrash-punk with sexual x-rated overtones like a fusion between The BEASTIE BOYS and EMF. • **Songwriters:** Group.

Recommended: WE CARE (*7)

CYRUS / BERG / SCHYFFERT

East West | East West

Oct 94. (c-s) **HOBO HUMPIN' SLOBO BABE / LIPS** [ ] [ ]
(12"+=)(cd-s+=) – Eye 842.

Hut | Caroline

May 95. (12"ep)(cd-ep)(c-ep) **PAY FOR ME** [ ] [ ]
– Pay for me / I think I do / Darling Nikki / Buzzbox babe / rying.

Jul 95. (c-s) **I'LL DO YA / THE NOW THING** [53] [ ]
(12"+=)(cd-s+=) – Sexy MM / ('A'extended).

Jul 95. (cd)(c) **WE CARE** [42] [ ]
– Kickin' / That's where it's at / Pay for me / Eurodog / I'll do ya / Electricity / Hobo humpin' slobo babe / Tryzasnice / Happy in you / I miss me / Young, dumb & full of c** / I'm cold / Born to raise hell.

Nov 95. (c-s) **HOBO HUMPIN' SLOBO BABE / ('A'-Doggy style mix)** [15] [ ]
(cd-s+=) – ('A'-Sniffin' Plankton mix) / ('A'-Skorpio mix).

WHAM (see under ⇒ MICHAEL, George)

Alan WHITE (see under ⇒ YES)

Maurice WHITE (see under ⇒ EARTH, WIND & FIRE)

WHITE LION

Formed: Brooklyn, New York, USA . . . 1983 by MIKE TRAMP and VITO BRATTA. That year they signed a 6-figure deal with 'Elektra', but album was shelved and they were soon dropped. 'FIGHT TO SURVIVE' did however surface in Japan the following year on 'RCA-Victor', with 'Grand Slam' eventually taking up the option in 1986. By this time, they had a new contract with 'Atlantic', who issued 'PRIDE' in '87. This near US Top 10 album, produced 2 Top 10 hits 'WAIT' & 'WHEN THE CHILDREN CRY', the following year. • **Style:** Heavy-metal inspired rock band, likened to BOSTON, STYX or JOURNEY. • **Songwriters:** All written by BRATTA/TRAMP, except RADAR LOVE (Golden Earring). • **Trivia:** DAVE SPITZ was later to surface in a new TONY IOMMI & BLACK SABBATH line-up.

Recommended: PRIDE (*6).

MIKE TRAMP (b. Denmark) – vocals (ex-MABEL) / **VITO BRATTA** (b. 1 Jul'63) – guitar (ex-DREAMER) / **FELIX ROBINSON** – bass (ex-ANGEL) / **NICKY CAPOZZI** – drums

RCA Victor JAPAN | Grand Slam

1985. (lp) **FIGHT TO SURVIVE** [-] [ ] Apr 88
– Broken heart / Cherokee / Fight to survive / Where do we run / In the city / All the fallen men / All burn in Hell / Kid of 1000 faces / El Salvador / The road to Valhalla.

—— **JAMES LOMENZO** – bass repl. DAVE SPITZ who had repl. ROBINSON / **GREGG D'ANGELO** – drums (ex-ANTHRAX) repl. CAPOZZI

Atlantic | Atlantic

Jul 87. (lp)(c)(cd) **PRIDE** [ ] [11]
– Hungry / Lonely nights / Don't give up / Sweet little loving / Lady of the valley / Wait / All you need is rock'n'roll / Tell me / All join our hands / When the children cry.

Jan 88. (7") **WAIT. / DON'T GIVE UP** [-] [8]

Jan 88. (7") **WAIT. / ALL JOIN OUR HANDS** [ ] [-]
(12"+=) – Lady of the valley.

Jun 88. (c-s) **TELL ME. /, ALL JOIN OUR HANDS** [-] [58]

Jul 88. (7") **WAIT. / ALL YOU NEED IS ROCK'N'ROLL** [ ] [-]

(12"+=)(cd-s+=) – Lonely nights.

Dec 88. (7") **WHEN THE CHILDREN CRY. / LADY OF THE VALLEY** [ ] [3] Oct 88

Jun 89. (lp)(c)(cd) **BIG GAME** [47] [19]
– Goin' home tonight / Dirty woman / Little fighter / Broken home / Baby be mine / Living on the edge / Let's get crazy / Don't say it's over / If my mind is evil / Radar love / Cry for freedom.

Jun 89. (7") **LITTLE FIGHTER. / LET'S GET CRAZY** [-] [52]

Oct 89. (7") **RADAR LOVE. / IF MY MIND IS EVIL** [ ] [59] Sep 89
(12"+=)(cd-s+=) – Wait (live).

Feb 90. (7") **DIRTY WOMAN. / CRY FOR FREEDOM** [-] [ ]

— **TOMMY 'T-Bone' CARADONNA** – bass (ex-ALICE COOPER) repl. LOMENZO / **JIMMY DeGRASSO** – drums (ex-Y&T) repl. D'ANGELO

Apr 91. (7") **LIGHTS AND THUNDER. / SHE'S GOT EVERYTHING** [ ] [ ]
(cd-s+=) – Fight to survive (live).

Apr 91. (cd)(c)(lp) **MANE ATTRACTION** [31] [61]
– Lights and thunder / Broken heart / Leave me alone / Love don't come easy / You're all I need / Warsong / It's over / Till death do us apart / Out with the boys / Farewell to you.

Jun 91. (7") **LOVE DON'T COME EASY. / LITTLE FIGHTER (live rehearsal)** [ ] [ ]
(12"+=)/ /(cd-s+=) – Don't give up./ / When the children cry.

— Disbanded late 1991, MIKE TRAMP formed FREAK OF NATURE, with **JERRY BEST** – bass / **OLIVER STEFFENSON + KENNY KORADE** – guitars / **JOHNNY HARO** – drums

– compilations, etc. –

Nov 93. Atlantic; (cd)(c) **THE BEST OF WHITE LION** [ ] [ ]
– Wait / Radar love / Broken heart / Hungry / Little fighter / Lights and thunder / All you need is rock'n'roll / When the children cry / Love don't come easy / Cry for freedom / Lady of the valley / Tell me / Farewell to you.

WHITESNAKE

Formed: By ex-DEEP PURPLE vocalist DAVID COVERDALE (b.22 Sep'49, Saltburn-On-Sea, Yorkshire, England). After 2 solo albums in 1977 & 1978, he soon assembled WHITESNAKE, named after debut. He/they signed to 'EMI International' and produced a Top 50 placing for album 'TROUBLE'. They grew larger with every release, culminating with re-vamped 1982 UK Top40 hit 'HERE I GO AGAIN', reaching US Top slot in summer of '87. • **Style:** Blues influenced heavy rock band that mixed usual love ballads with harder-edged mainstream rock. • **Songwriters:** COVERDALE / MOODY / MARSDEN compositions. From 1983-86, COVERDALE's writing partner was group member JOHN SYKES, who was replaced in 1989 by ADRIAN VANDENBURG. They also covered HEART OF THE CITY (Bobby Bland) / etc? • **Trivia:** On 17 Feb'89, COVERDALE married actress Tawny Kittaen, who had previously featured on their video of 'IS THIS LOVE'.

Recommended: WHITESNAKE'S GREATEST HITS (*8)

DAVID COVERDALE

(solo) – vocals (ex-DEEP PURPLE) with **MICK MOODY** – guitar (ex-JUICY LUCY, ex-SNAFU) / **TIM HINKLEY** – keyboards / **SIMON PHILLIPS** – drums / **DELISLE HARPER** – bass / plus **RON ASPERY** – sax / **ROGER GLOVER** – producer, bass, keyboards

Purple / United Art

May 77. (lp)(c) **DAVID COVERDALE'S WHITESNAKE** [ ] [ ]
– Lady / Blindman / Goldie's place / White snake / Time on my side / Peace lovin' man / Sunny days / Hole in the sky / Celebration.

May 77. (7") **HOLE IN THE SKY. / BLINDMAN** [ ] [-]

— **COVERDALE** retained only **MOODY** and recruited **BERNIE MARSDEN** – guitar (ex-PAICE, ASHTON & LORD, ex-UFO, ex-WILD TURKEY) / **NEIL MURRAY** – bass (ex-COLOSSEUM, ex-NATIONAL HEALTH) / **BRIAN JOHNSON** – keyboards + **DAVID DOWELL** – drums (both ex-STREETWALKERS)

Feb 78. (7") **BREAKDOWN. / ONLY MY SOUL** [ ] [-]

Mar 78. (lp)(c) **NORTHWINDS** [ ] [ ]
– Keep on giving me love / Only my soul / Breakdown / Queen of hearts / Time and again / Give me kindness / Say you love me. *(re-iss.Feb82) (re-iss.Apr84 on 'Fame')*

Jun 78. (7") **BREAKDOWN. / BLOODY MARY** [-] [ ]

DAVID COVERDALE'S WHITESNAKE

PETE SOLLEY – keyboards repl. JOHNSTON

EMI Inter... / Sunburst

Jun 78. (7"ep)(7"white-ep) **SNAKEBITE** [61] [ ]
– Bloody Mary / Steal away / Come on / Ain't no love in the heart of the city.

— **JON LORD** – keys (ex-PAICE, ASHTON & LORD, ex-DEEP PURPLE) repl. SOLLEY

Oct 78. (7") **LIE DOWN. / DON'T MESS WITH ME** [ ] [ ]

Oct 78. (lp)(c) **TROUBLE** [50] [ ]
– Take me with you / Love to keep you warm / Lie down (a modern love song) / Day tripper / Night hawl (vampire blues) / The time is right for love / Trouble / Belguin Tom's hat trick / Free flight / Don't mess with me. *(re-iss.Sep80 on 'United Art') (re-iss.May82 on 'Fame', +re+cd.May90) (re-iss.Jun87 on 'Liberty', cd-iss.Apr88 on 'EMI')*

Mar 79. (7") **THE TIME IS RIGHT FOR LOVE. / COME ON (live)** [ ] [-]

Apr 79. (7") **THE TIME IS RIGHT FOR LOVE. / BELGUIN TOM'S HAT TRICK** [-] [ ]

United Art / United Art

Oct 79. (lp)(c) **LOVE HUNTER** [29] [-]
– Long way from home / Walking in the shadow of the blues / Help me through the day / Medicine man / You 'n' me / Mean business / Love hunter / Outlaw / Rock'n'roll women / We wish you well. *(re-iss.Apr84 on 'Fame', cd-iss.Apr88) (re-iss.cd+c Jul94)*

Oct 79. (7"m) **LONG WAY FROM HOME. / TROUBLE (live) / AIN'T NO LOVE IN THE HEART OF THE CITY (live)** [55] [-]

Nov 79. (7") **LONG WAY FROM HOME. / WE WISH YOU WELL** [-] [ ]

WHITESNAKE

IAN PAICE – drums (ex-PAICE, ASHTON & LORD, ex-DEEP PURPLE) repl. DOWELL

United Art / Mirage

Apr 80. (7"m) **FOOL FOR YOUR LOVING. / MEAN BUSINESS / DON'T MESS WITH ME** [13] [-]

Jun 80. (lp)(c) **READY AN' WILLING** [6] [90]
– Fool for your loving / Sweet talker / Ready an' willing / Carry your load / Blindman / Ain't gonna cry no more / Love man / Black and blue / She's a woman. *(re-iss.Sep85 on 'Fame', cd-iss.Apr88) (re-iss.cd+c Jul94)*

Jul 80. (7"m) **READY AN' WILLING. / NIGHT HAWK (VAMPIRE BLUES) / WE WISH YOU WELL** [43] [ ]

Jul 80. (7") **FOOL FOR YOUR LOVING. / BLACK AND BLUE** [-] [53]

Oct 80. (7") **SWEET TALKER. / AIN'T GONNA CRY NO MORE** [-] [ ]

Nov 80. (d-lp)(d-c) **LIVE ... IN THE HEART OF THE CITY (live)** [5] [ ]
– Come on * / Sweet talker / Walking in the shadow of the blues / Love hunter / Fool for your loving / Ain't gonna cry no more / Ready an' willing / Take me with you * / Might just take your life / Lie down * / Ain't no love in the heart of the city / Trouble * / Mistreated. *(cd-iss.Jul88 on 'Underdog' US omits *) (re-iss.cd+c Jul94)*

Nov 80. (7")(12") **AIN'T NO LOVE IN THE HEART OF THE CITY (live). / TAKE ME WITH YOU (live)** [51] [ ]

Liberty / Atlantic

Apr 81. (7") **DON'T BREAK MY HEART AGAIN. / CHILD OF BABYLON** [17] [-]

Apr 81. (lp)(c) **COME AN' GET IT** [2] [ ]
– Come an' get it / Hot stuff / Don't break my heart again / Lonely days, lonely nights / Wine, women an' song / Child of Babylon / Would I lie to you / Girl / Hit an' run / Till the day I die. *(re-iss.+cd.May89 on 'Fame') (cd-iss.1988 on 'EMI', re-iss.cd+c Jul94)*

May 81. (7") **WOULD I LIE TO YOU. / GIRL** [37] [-]

Jun 81. (7") **DON'T BREAK MY HEART AGAIN. / LONELY DAYS, LONELY NIGHTS** [-] [ ]

— **COVERDALE** retained **MOODY + LORD** and brought in **MEL GALLEY** – guitar (ex-TRAPEZE) repl. MARSDEN who formed ALASKA / **COLIN 'Bomber' HODGKINSON** – bass (ex-BACK DOOR) repl. MURRAY to GARY MOORE / **COZY POWELL** – drums (ex-JEFF BECK, ex-RAINBOW, Solo Artist, ex-BEDLAM) repl. PAICE who joined GARY MOORE

Liberty / Geffen

Oct 82. (7")(7"pic-d) **HERE I GO AGAIN. / BLOODY LUXURY** [34] [ ]

Nov 82. (lp)(c)(pic-lp) **SAINTS AN' SINNERS** [9] [ ]
– Young blood / Rough an' ready / Blood luxury / Victim of love / Crying in the rain / Here I go again / Love an' afection / Rock'n'roll angels / Dancing girls / Saints an' sinners. *(re-iss.1985) (re-iss.May87 on 'Fame', cd-iss.Apr88)*

Aug 83. (7")(7"sha-pic-d) **GUILTY OF LOVE. / GAMBLER** [31] [ ]

— now a quintet, when MICK MOODY departed.

Jan 84. (7") **GIVE ME MORE TIME. / NEED YOUR LOVE SO BAD** [29] [ ]

— **NEIL MURRAY** – bass returned to repl. HODGKINSON / added **JOHN SYKES** – guitar (ex-TYGERS OF PAN TANG)

Feb 84. (lp)(c) **SLIDE IT IN** [9] [40] Aug 84
– Gambler / Slide it in / Standing in the shadows / Give me more time / Love ain't no stranger / Slow an' easy / Spit it out / All or nothing / Hungry for love / Guilty of love. *(cd-iss.Apr88 on 'EMI')*

Apr 84. (7")(7"pic-d) **STANDING IN THE SHADOWS. / ALL OR NOTHING** [62] [ ]
(12"+=) – ('A'-US remix).

Aug 84. (7") **LOVE AIN'T NO STRANGER. / GUILTY OF LOVE** [-] [ ]

Feb 85. (7") **LOVE AIN'T NO STRANGER. / SLOW AN' EASY** [44] [ ]
(12"+=)(12"white+=) – Slide it in.

— Split for a while in 1984 when JON LORD re-joined DEEP PURPLE. **WHITESNAKE** were re-formed by **COVERDALE + SYKES** and new musicians **TONY FRANKLIN** – bass (ex-The FIRM) repl. MURRAY and GALLEY / **CARMINE APPICE** – drums (ex-BECK, BOGERT & APPICE) repl. POWELL to E.L.P.

EMI Inter.. / Geffen

Mar 87. (7")(7"white) **STILL OF THE NIGHT. / HERE I GO AGAIN (1987)** [16] [-]
(12"+=)(12"pic-d+=) – You're gonna break my heart again.

Apr 87. (lp)(c)(cd)(pic-lp) **WHITESNAKE 1987** [8] [2]
– Still of the night / Bad boys / Give me all your love / Looking for love / Crying in the rain / Is this love / Straight for the heart / Don't turn away / Children of the night. *(cd+=)*– Here I go again '87 / You're gonna break my heart again. *(re-iss.cd+c Jul94 all on 'EMI')*

May 87. (7")(7"sha-pic-d) **IS THIS LOVE. / STANDING IN THE SHADOWS** [9] [-]
(12"+=)(12"white+=) – Need your love so bad.
(cd-ep++=)(7"ep++=) – Still of the night.

Jun 87. (7") **STILL OF THE NIGHT. / DON'T TURN AWAY** [-] [79]

Jul 87. (7") **HERE I GO AGAIN. / CHILDREN OF THE NIGHT** [-] [1]

Oct 87. (7") **IS THIS LOVE. / BAD BOYS** [-] [2]

Oct 87. (7")(12")(c-s) **HERE I GO AGAIN '87 (US mix). / GUILTY OF LOVE** [9] [-]
(7"pic-d)(10"white)(cd-s) – ('A'side) / ('A'-US remix).

Jan 88. (7")(12")(12"pic-d)(7"white)(12"white) **GIVE ME ALL YOUR LOVE (edit). / FOOL FOR YOUR LOVING** [18] [48]
(cd-s+=) – Here I go again / Don't break my heart.
(3"cd-s+=) – Straight from the heart. (US; b-side)

— **COVERDALE** completely re-modelled line-up when SYKES formed BLUE MURDER. He was replaced by **ADRIAN VANDENBURG** – guitar (ex-VANDENBERG) / **RUDY SARZO** – bass (ex-OZZY OSBOURNE, ex-QUIET RIOT) repl.

FRANKLIN / **TOMMY ALDRIDGE** – drums (ex-OZZY OSBOURNE, ex-BLACK OAK ARKANSAS) repl. APPICE (Dec88) / **STEVE VAI** – guitar (solo Artist, ex-FRANK ZAPPA, DAVID LEE ROTH) repl. VIVIAN CAMPBELL

Nov 89. (lp)(c)(cd) **SLIP OF THE TONGUE** [10] [10]
– Slip of the tongue / Cheap an' nasty / Fool for your loving / Now you're gone / Kitten's got claws / Wings of the storm / The deeper the love / Judgement day / Slow poke music / Sailing ships. *(re-iss.cd+c Jul94)*

Nov 89. (7")(US-c-s) **FOOL FOR YOUR LOVIN' ('89). / SLOW POKE MUSIC** [43] [37]
(c-s+=) – ('A'version).
(12"+=)(12"white+=) – Walking in the shadow of the blues.

Jan 90. (7") **THE DEEPER THE LOVE. / SLIP OF THE TONGUE** [-] [28]

Feb 90. (7")(c-s)(7"pic-d) **THE DEEPER THE LOVE. / JUDGEMENT DAY** [35] [-]
(12"white+=) – Sweet lady luck.
(12"++=)(cd-s++=) – Fool for your lovin' (Vai voltage mix).

Aug 90. (7")(c-s)(7"sha-pic-d) **NOW YOU'RE GONE (remix). / WINGS OF THE STORM (lp version)** [31] [96] May 90
(12"+=)(cd-s+=)(12"pic-d+=) – Kittens got claws / Cheap an' nasty.

DAVID COVERDALE

Epic Epic

Sep 90. (7")(c-s) **THE LAST NOTE OF FREEDOM. / (CAR BUILDING by HANS ZIMMER)** [ ] [ ]
(12"+=)/ /(cd-s+=) – Gimme some lovin'./ / ('A'version).

COVERDALE• PAGE

DAVID COVERDALE – vocals / **JIMMY PAGE** – guitar (ex-LED ZEPPELIN, ex-solo artist) / **JORGE CASAS** – bass / **DENNY CARMASSI** – drums (ex-MONTROSE) / **RICKY PHILIPS** – bass / **LESTER MENDEL** – keyboards / **JOHN HARRIS** – acoustic harmonica / **TOMMY FUNDERBUCK** – backing vocals

E.M.I. Geffen

Mar 93. (cd)(c)(lp) **COVERDALE• PAGE** [4] [5]
– Shake my tree / Waiting on you / Take me for a little while / Pride and joy / Over now / Feeling hot / Easy does it / Take a look at yourself / Don't leave me this way / Absolution blues / Whisper a prayer for the dying *(re-iss.cd+c Jul94)*

Jun 93. (c-s)(12"pic-d) **TAKE ME FOR A LITTLE WHILE. / EASY DOES IT** [29] [ ]
(cd-s) – ('A'side) / ('A'acoustic) / Shake my tree (the crunch mix) / ('A'edit).

Sep 93. (7"pic-d)(c-s) **TAKE A LOOK AT YOURSELF. / WAITING ON YOU** [ ] [ ]
(cd-s+=) – ('A'acoustic) / ('A'girls version).

– compilations, etc. –

Apr 88. Connoisseur; (d-lp)(c)(cd) **THE CONNOISSEUR COLLECTION** [ ] [-]
– (DAVID COVERDALE's first 2 solo albums)

Jun 88. MCA; (cd) **GREATEST HITS** [-] [ ]

Jul 94. EMI/ US= Geffen; (cd)(c)(lp) **WHITESNAKE'S GREATEST HITS** [4] [ ]
– Still of the night / Here I go again / Is this love / Love ain't no stranger / Looking for love / Now you're gone / Slide it in / Slow an' easy / Judgement day / You're gonna break my heart again / The deeper the love / Crying in the rain / Fool for your loving / Sweet lady luck.

Jul 94. (7")(7"white)(c-s) **IS THIS LOVE. / SWEET LADY LUCK** [25] [ ]
(cd-s+=) – Now you're gone.

Nov 95. EMI; (3xcd-box) **SLIDE IT IN / 1987 / SLIP OF THE TONGUE** [ ] [ ]

WHITE ZOMBIE

Formed: New York, USA . . .1985 by ROB STRAKER, female SEAN YSEULT, TOM GUAY and IVAN DePLUME. After a few indie-metal lp's in the late 80's, they had a surprise US Top 30 hit album in 1993 with an MTV favourite 'LA SEXORCISTO: . . .'. • **Style:** Unconventional demon-metal grunge similiar to BLACK SABBATH fused with KISS and The STOOGES. • **Songwriters:** STRAKER except CHILDREN OF THE GRAVE (Black Sabbath) / GOD OF THUNDER (Kiss). • **Trivia:** 2nd album produced by BILL LASWELL, their 3rd by ANDY WALLACE. Guested on Beavis & Butt-Head various artists album in 1993.

Recommended: LA SEXORCISTO: DEVIL MUSIC VOL.1 (*7)

ROB 'ZOMBIE' STRAKER – vocals, guitar / **TOM GUAY** – guitar / **SEAN YSEULT** – bass / **IVAN DePLUME** – drums

not issued Silent Ex.

1987. (m-lp) **PSYCHO-HEAD BLOWOUT** [-] [ ]

Jan 88. (lp) **SOUL CRUSHER** [-] [ ]

—— **JOHN RICCI** – guitar repl.TOM

Caroline Caroline

Feb 89. (lp)(c)(cd) **MAKE THEM DIE SLOWLY** [ ] [ ]
– Demonspeed / Disaster blaster / Murderworld / Revenge / Acid flesh / Power hungry / Godslayer.

—— **JAY YUENGER** – guitar repl.RICCI

Jul 89. (12"ep) **GOD OF THUNDER. / LOVE RAZOR / DISASTER BLASTER 2** [ ] [ ]

Geffen Geffen

Mar 92. (cd)(c)(lp) **LA SEXORCISTO: DEVIL MUSIC VOL.1** [ ] [ ]
– Welcome to Planet Mother F***** / Psychedelic slag / Knuckle duster (Radio 1-A) / Thunder kiss '65 / Black sunshine / Soul-crusher / Cosmic monsters inc. / Spiderbaby (yeah-yeah-yeah) / I am legend / Knuckle duster (Radio 2-B) / Thrust! / One big crunch / Grindhouse (a go-go) / Starface / Warp asylum. *(re-dist.Sep93, hit US No.26)*

—— **JOHN TEMPESTA** – drums (ex-TESTAMENT, ex-EXODUS) repl.PHILO, who had briefly repl.DePLUME

May 95. (c-s) **MORE HUMAN THAN HUMAN / BLOOD, MILK AND SKY (KERO KERO KEROPFI AND THE SMOOTH OPERATOR)** [51] [ ]
(10"+=)(cd-s+=) – ('A'-Jeddak of the tharks super mix).

May 95. (cd)(c)(lp) **ASTRO-CREEP 2000: SONGS OF LOVE, DESTRUCTION AND OTHER SYNTHETIC DELUSIONS OF THE ELECTRIC HEAD** [25] [6]
– Electric head pt.1 (the agony) / Super-charger Heaven / Real solution No.9 / Creature of the wheel / Electric head pt.2 (the ecstasy) / Grease paint and monkey brains / I, zombie / More human than human / El phantasmo and the chicken-run blast-o-rama / Blur the technicolor / Blood, milk and sky. (c+=)(cd+=) – The sidewalk ends where the bug parade begins.

WHITFORD / ST. HOLMES (see under ⇒ AEROSMITH)

WHO

Formed: Chiswick & Hammersmith, London, England . . . 1964 as The HIGH NUMBERS. After one 45 'I'M THE FACE', they changed name to The WHO and signed to 'Brunswick'. They immediately smashed the UK Top 10 with debut 'I CAN'T EXPLAIN', which was followed by a string of chartbusters starting with classics 'ANYWAY ANYHOW ANYWHERE', 'MY GENERATION' & 'SUBSTITUTE'. In May 1969, they premiered their new Top 5 double album 'TOMMY' (a concept rock opera, similar to The PRETTY THINGS' 'S.F.Sorrow'). This was later made into a film in 1975, which featured The WHO plus ELTON JOHN, TINA TURNER, ANN-MARGRET, JACK NICHOLSON and OLIVER REED. In 1973, they repeated the formula when QUADROPHENIA hit the shops, and was later made into another film in 1979. • **Style:** In the forefront of the 'mod' scene in the mid-60's, they moved into rock operas in 1969 and 1973. Were well known at the time for TOWNSHEND's windmill guitar style, which he usually smashed up after gigs. DALTREY's power vocal style and hard man looks, were later put into great use when he took up acting career in 1979. While ENTWISTLE was the quiet man on stage and off, MOON's eccentric behaviour led him to dressing up in different characters each day. His hard drinking and drug abuse, led to his eventual death on 7 Sep'78. A month previous to this, their one-time manager PETE MEADON committed suicide. **DALTREY's filmography:** LISZTOMANIA (1975) / THE LEGACY (1979) / McVICAR (1980) / BUDDY (1991 TV serial + 1992 film). • **Songwriters:** TOWNSHEND wrote most of material except I'M THE FACE (Slim Harpo's 'Got Live If You Want It') / I'M A MAN (Bo Diddley) / IN THE CITY (Speedy Keen; aka of Thunderclap Newman) / BARBARA ANN (Beach Boys) / BABY DON'T YOU DO IT (Marvin Gaye) / THE LAST TIME + UNDER MY THUMB (Rolling Stones) / SUMMERTIME BLUES (Eddie Cochran). KEITH MOON's only album featured all covers. DALTREY's solo career started with songs written for him by LEO SAYER and DAVE COURTNEY. He later covered DON'T LET THE SUN GO DOWN ON ME (Elton John) / etc. • **Trivia:** Re-grouped in 1985 for the Live Aid concert. DALTREY had run a trout farm in Dorset for the last decade or so. They are inducted into the Guinness Book Of Records, after performing the loudest concert (120 decibels) at Charlton Athletic's Football Club.

Recommended: WHO'S BETTER WHO'S BEST (*9) / TOMMY (*8) / WHO'S NEXT (*9) / QUADROPHENIA (*9). PETE TOWNSHEND:- EMPTY GLASS (*7). ROGER DALTREY:- THE BEST OF ROGER DALTREY (*6).

ROGER DALTREY (b. 1 Mar'45) – vocals / **PETE TOWNSHEND** (b.19 May'45) – guitar, vocals / **JOHN ENTWISTLE** (b. 9 Oct'44) – bass, vocals / **KEITH MOON** (b.23 Aug'47) – drums, vocals repl. DOUGIE SANDON

HIGH NUMBERS

Fontana not issued

Jul 64. (7") **I'M THE FACE. / ZOOT SUIT** [ ] [-]
(re-iss.Feb65) (re-iss.Mar80 on 'Back Door', hit UK No.49) (US re-iss.Mar80 as The WHO on 'Mercury')

The WHO

Brunswick Decca

Jan 65. (7") **I CAN'T EXPLAIN. / BALD HEADED WOMAN** [8] [93] Feb 65
(US re-iss.1973 on 'MCA')

May 65. (7") **ANYWAY ANYHOW ANYWHERE. / DADDY ROLLING STONE** [10] [-]

Jun 65. (7") **ANYWAY ANYHOW ANYWHERE. / ANYTIME YOU WANT ME** [-] [ ]

Oct 65. (7") **MY GENERATION. / SHOUT & SHIMMY** [2] [-]

Nov 65. (7") **MY GENERATION. / OUT IN THE STREET** [-] [74]

Dec 65. (lp) **MY GENERATION** [5] [ ]
– Out in the street / I don't mind / The good's gone / La-la-la-lies / Much too much / My generation / The kid's are alright / Please please please / It's not true / I'm a man / A legal matter / The ox. *(US title 'THE WHO SING MY GENERATION') (UK re-iss.Oct80 on 'Virgin', hit No.20) (cd-iss.1990)*

Reaction Decca

Mar 66. (7") **SUBSTITUTE. / WALTZ FOR A PIG ('B'by "WHO ORCHESTRA")** [5] [ ]

(The original 'B'side on some copies were INSTANT PARTY then CIRCLES) *(The States re-iss.Mar66 single in Aug67 on 'Atco')*

Aug 66. (7") **I'M A BOY. / IN THE CITY** [2] [ ] Dec 66

Dec 66. (7") **HAPPY JACK. / I'VE BEEN AWAY** [3] [-]

Dec 66. (lp) **A QUICK ONE** (US-title 'HAPPY JACK') [4] [67] May 67
– Run run run / Boris the spider / Whiskey man / I need you / Heatwave / Cobwebs and strange / Don't look away / See my way / So sad about us / A quick one, while he's away. *(UK re-iss.c/cd.Aug88 on 'Polydor'; re-iss.cd Jun95)*

Mar 67. (7") **HAPPY JACK. / WHISKEY MAN** [-] [24]

Track Decca

Apr 67. (7") **PICTURES OF LILY. / DOCTOR DOCTOR** [4] [51] Jun 67

Jul 67. (7") **THE LAST TIME. / UNDER MY THUMB** [44] [ ]

Oct 67. (7") **I CAN SEE FOR MILES. / SOMEONE'S COMING** [10] [-]

Oct 67. (7") **I CAN SEE FOR MILES. / MARY ANN WITH THE SHAKY HANDS** [-] [9]

Jan 68. (lp) **THE WHO SELL OUT** [13] [48]
– Armenian city in the sky / Heinz baked beans / Mary-Anne with the shaky hands / Odorono / Tattoo / Our love was, is / I can see for miles / I can't reach you / Medac / Silas Stingy / Sunrise / Tattoo / Rael. *(c-iss.Oct84) (re-iss.c/cd.Aug88 on 'Polydor'; re-iss.cd Jun95)*

Mar 68. (7") **CALL ME LIGHTNING. / DR. JEKYLL & MR. HIDE** [-] [40]

Jun 68. (7") **DOGS. / CALL ME LIGHTNING** [25] [-]

Jul 68. (7") **MAGIC BUS. / SOMEONE'S COMING** [-] [25]

Oct 68. (7") **MAGIC BUS. / DR. JEKYLL & MR. HIDE** [26] [-]

Oct 68. (lp) **MAGIC BUS – (THE WHO ON TOUR) (live)** [-] [39]
– Disguises / Run run run / Dr. Jekyll & Mr. Hyde / I can't reach you / Our love was, is / Call me Lightning / Magic bus / Someone's coming / Doctor doctor / Bucket T. / Pictures of ily.

Nov 68. (lp) **DIRECT HITS** – (compilation) [ ] [-]
– Bucket T. / I'm a boy / Pictures of Lily / Doctor doctor / I can see for miles / Substitute / Happy Jack / The last time / In the city / Call me Lightning / Mary-Anne with the shaky hand / Dogs.

Mar 69. (7") **PINBALL WIZARD. / DOGS (part 2)** [4] [19]
(US re-iss.1973 on 'MCA')

May 69. (d-lp) **TOMMY** [2] [4]
– Overture / It's a boy / 1921 / Amazing journey / Sparks / Eyesight for the blind / Miracle cure / Sally Simpson / I'm free / Welcome / Tommy's holiday camp / We're not gonna take it / Christmas / Cousin Kevin / The acid queen / Underture / Do you think it's alright / Fiddle about / Pinball wizard / There's a doctor / Go to the mirror / Tommy can you hear me / Smash the mirror / Sensation. *(re-iss.1974 in 2 parts +c.) (d-lp re-iss.Jul84 on 'Polydor', d-cd-iss.Apr89)*

Jul 69. (7") **I'M FREE. / WE'RE NOT GONNA TAKE IT** [-] [37]

Mar 70. (7") **THE SEEKER. / HERE FOR MORE** [19] [44]

May 70. (lp)(c) **LIVE AT LEEDS (live)** [3] [4]
– Magic bus / My generation / Shakin' all over / Substitute / Summertime blues / Young man blues. *(re-iss.Nov83, cd-iss.May88) (re-iss.cd Feb95 on 'Polydor', hit No.59)*

Jul 70. (7") **SUMMERTIME BLUES (live). / HEAVEN AND HELL** [38] [-]

Jul 70. (7") **SUMMERTIME BLUES (live). / HERE FOR MORE** [-] [27]

Sep 70. (7") **SEE ME, FEEL ME. / WE'RE NOT GONNA TAKE IT / OVERTURE FROM TOMMY** [-] [12]
(US re-iss.1973 on 'MCA')

Sep 70. (7") **SEE ME, FEEL ME. / OVERTURE FROM TOMMY** [ ] [-]

— In May71, JOHN ENTWISTLE brought out debut lp 'SMASH YOUR HEAD AGAINST THE WALL'. (see further on for his discography)

Jul 71. (7") **WON'T GET FOOLED AGAIN. / I DON'T EVEN KNOW MYSELF** [9] [15]

Sep 71. (lp)(c) **WHO'S NEXT** [1] [4]
– Baba O'Riley / etting in tune / Love ain't for keeping / My wife / The song is over / Bargain / Going mobile / Behind blue eyes / Won't get fooled again. *(re-iss.+cd.Nov83 on 'Polydor')*

Oct 71. (7") **LET'S SEE ACTION. / WHEN I WAS A BOY** [16] [-]

Nov 71. (7") **BEHIND BLUE EYES. / MY WIFE** [-] [34]

Dec 71. (lp)(c) **MEATY, BEATY, BIG AND BOUNCY** (compilation) [9] [11] Nov 71
– I can't explain / The kids are alright / Happy Jack / I can see for miles / Pictures of Lily / My generation / The seeker / Anyway, anyhow, anywhere / Pinball wizard / A legal matter / Boris the spider / Magic bus / Substitute / I'm a boy. *(re-iss.1974)*

Jun 72. (7") **JOIN TOGETHER. / BABY DON'T YOU DO IT** [9] [17]

— In Oct72, PETE TOWNSHEND was another to issue debut solo album 'WHO CAME FIRST'. It scraped into UK Top30. He issued more throughout 70's-80's (see . . .) In Apr'73, ROGER DALTREY hit the singles chart with GIVING IT ALL AWAY. It was a cut from debut album DALTREY. (see further on)

Track Track

Jan 73. (7") **RELAY. / WASPMAN** [21] [39] Dec 72

Track M.C.A.

Oct 73. (7") **5:15. / WATER** [20] [-]

Oct 73. (7") **5:15. / LOVE REIGN O'ER ME** [-] [ ]

Nov 73. (d-lp)(d-c) **QUADROPHENIA** [2] [2]
– I am the sea / The real me / Quadrophenia / Cut my hair / The punk and the godfather / I'm one / Dirty jobs / Helpless dancer / Is it in my head? / I've had enough / 5:15 / Sea and sand / Drowned / Bell boy / Doctor Jimmy / The rock / Love, reign o'er me. *(re-iss.Sep79, d-cd-iss.Jan87)*

Nov 73. (7") **LOVE, REIGN O'ER ME. / WATER** [-] [76]

Jan 74. (7") **THE REAL ME. / I'M ONE** [-] [92]

— In Apr75, KEITH MOON was the last WHO member to release solo vinyl. The dismal 'TWO SIDES OF THE MOON' sold poorly.

Polydor M.C.A.

Oct 75. (lp)(c) **THE WHO BY NUMBERS** [7] [8]
– Slip kid / However much I booze / Squeeze box / Dreaming from the waist / Imagine a man / Success story / They are all in love / Blue, red and grey / How many friends / In a hand or a face. *(re-iss.Mar84, cd-iss.Jul89)*

Jan 76. (7") **SQUEEZE BOX. / SUCCESS STORY** [10] [16] Nov 75

Aug 76. (7") **SLIP KID. / DREAMING FROM THE WAIST** [-] [ ]

Sep 76. (d-lp)(d-c) **THE STORY OF THE WHO** (compilation) [2] [ ]
– Magic bus / Substitute / Boris the spider / Run run run / I'm a boy / Heatwave / My generation / Pictures of Lily / Happy Jack / The seeker / I can see for miles / Bargain / Squeeze box / Amazing journey / The acid queen / Do you think it's alright / Fiddle about / Pinball wizard / I'm free / Tommy's holiday camp / We're not gonna take it / See me, feel me / Summertime blues / Baba O'Riley / Behind blue eyes / Slip kid / Won't get fooled again.

Jul 78. (7") **WHO ARE YOU. / HAD ENOUGH** [18] [14]

— On 5th Aug'78, manager PETE MEADON committed suicide.

Sep 78. (lp)(c)(US-red-lp)(US-pic-lp) **WHO ARE YOU** [6] [2]
– New song / Had enough / 905 / Sister disco / Music must change / Trick of the light / Guitar and pen / Love is coming down / Who are you. *(re-iss.Aug84, cd-iss.Jul89)*

— After a party on 7th Sep'78, KEITH MOON died on an overdose of Heminevrin.

Dec 78. (7") **TRICK OF THE LIGHT. / 509** [-] [ ]

— Early'79, **KENNY JONES** (b.16 Sep'48) – drums (ex-SMALL FACES, ex-FACES) took place of KEITH. Added 5th tour member **JOHN 'Rabbit' BUNDRICK** – keyboards

Polydor Warners

Feb 81. (7") **YOU BETTER YOU BET. / THE QUIET ONE** [9] [18]

Mar 81. (lp)(c) **FACE DANCES** [2] [4]
– You better you bet / Don't let go the coat / Cache cache / The quiet one / Did you steal my money / How can you do it alone / Daily records / You / Another tricky day. *(re-iss.+cd.May88) (re-iss.cd Jun93)*

May 81. (7") **DON'T LET GO THE COAT. / YOU** [47] [84]

Sep 82. (lp)(c) **IT'S HARD** [11] [8]
– Athena / It's your turn / Cooks county / It's hard / Dangerous / Eminence front / I've known no war / One life's enough / One at a time / Why did I fall for that / A man is a man / Cry if you want. *(cd-iss.1983) (re-iss.cd Jun93)*

Sep 82. (7")(7"pic-d) **ATHENA. / A MAN IS A MAN** [40] [-]
(12"+=)(12"pic-d+=) – Won't get fooled again.

Sep 82. (7") **ATHENA. / IT'S YOUR TURN** [-] [28]

Dec 82. (7") **EMINENCE FRONT. / ONE AT A TIME** [-] [68]

Feb 83. (7") **IT'S HARD. / DANGEROUS** [-] [ ]

— They officially split late 1983 from studio work. They occasionally returned for one-off live work.

– other compilations, etc. –

Below 4 on 'Brunswick' label.

Mar 66. (7") **A LEGAL MATTER. / INSTANT PARTY** [32] [-]

Aug 66. (7") **THE KIDS ARE ALRIGHT. / THE OX** [41] [-]

Aug 66. (7") **THE KIDS ARE ALRIGHT. / A LEGAL MATTER** [-] [-]

Nov 66. (7") **LA LA LA LIES. / THE GOOD'S GONE** [ ] [-]

Nov 66. Reaction; (7"ep) **READY STEADY WHO** [ ] [-]
– Circles / Disguises / Batman / Bucket 'T' / Barbara Ann. *(re-iss.Nov83 on 'Reaction-Polydor', hit 58)*

Nov 70. Track; (7"ep) **TOMMY** [ ] [ ]
– See me, feel me / I'm free / Christmas / Overture from Tommy.

Dec 74. Track; (d-lp)(d-c) **A QUICK ONE / THE WHO SELL OUT** [ ] [ ]

Oct 74. Track; (lp)(c) **ODDS AND SODS** (rarities) [10] [15]
– Postcard / Now I'm a farmer / Put the money down / Little Billy / Too much of anything / Glow girl / Pure and easy / Faith in something bigger / I'm the face / Naked eye / Long live rock. *(re-iss.cd Jun93)*

Nov 74. Track; (7") **POSTCARD. / PUT THE MONEY DOWN** [-] [ ]

below with guest singers ELTON JOHN, TINA TURNER, OLIVER REED, ANN-MARGRET, etc

Aug 75. Polydor; (d-lp)(dc) **TOMMY (Film Soundtrack)** [30] [2]
– Prologue / Captain Walker – It's a boy / Bernie's holiday camp / 1951 – What about the boy? / Amazing journey / Christmas / Eyesight to the blind / Acid queen / Do you think it's alright / Cousin Kevin / Do you think it's alright / Fiddle about / Do you think it's alright / Sparks / Extra, extra, extra / Pinball wizard / Champagne / There's a doctor / Go to the mirror / Tommy can you hear me / Smash the mirror / I'm free / Mother and son / Sensation / Miracle cure / Sally Simpson / Welcome / T.V. studio / Tommy's holiday camp / We're not gonna take it / Listening to you – See me, feel me.

Aug 83. Track; (lp)(c) **RARITIES VOL.1 (1966-68)** [ ] [ ] 1982

Oct 83. Track; (lp)(c) **RARITIES VOL.2 (1970-73)** [ ] [ ] 1982
(re-iss.cd+c.VOL.1 & 2 Jan91)

Note; below on 'Polydor' UK/ 'MCA' US.

Oct 76. (7"m)(12"m) **SUBSTITUTE. / I'M A BOY / PICTURES OF LILY** [7] [ ]

Apr 79. (7"m) **LONG LIVE ROCK. / I'M THE FACE / MY WIFE** [48] [54]

Jun 79. (lp)(c)(US-pic-lp) **THE KIDS ARE ALRIGHT** [26] [8]
– (some live tracks with interviews) *(re-iss.cd Jun93)*

Sep 79. (7") **I'M ONE. / 5:15** [ ] [45] b-side

Sep 79. (d-lp)(d-c) **QUADROPHENIA (Film Soundtrack)** [23] [46]
– (includes tracks by other artists)

1980. (d-c) **WHO'S NEXT / THE WHO BY NUMBERS** [ ] [-]

1980. (d-c) **WHO ARE YOU / LIVE AT LEEDS** [ ] [-]

Feb 81. (lp)(c) **MY GENERATION (compilation)** [ ] [-]

May 83. (lp)(c) **WHO'S GREATEST HITS** [-] [94]

Nov 84. (lp)(c)(cd) **THE SINGLES** [ ] [ ]

Feb 88. (7") **MY GENERATION. / SUBSTITUTE** [68] [ ]
(12"+=)(c-s+=)(cd-s+=) – Baba O'Riley / Behind blue eyes.

Mar 88. (lp)(c)(cd) **WHO'S BETTER WHO'S BEST** [10] [ ]
– My generation / Anyway, anyhow, anywhere / The kids are alright / Substitute / I'm a boy / Happy Jack / Pictures of Lily / I can see for miles / Who are you / Won't get fooled again / Magic bus / Pinball wizard / I'm free / I can't explain / See me feel me / Squeeze box / Join together / You better you bet. (cd+=) – Baba O'Riley.

Jun 88. (7") **WON'T GET FOOLED AGAIN. / BONEY MORONIE (live)** [ ] [ ]
(ext-12"+=)(cd-s+=) – Dancing in the street (live) / Mary Ann with the shaky hand.

Oct 88. (lp)(c)(cd) **WHO'S MISSING** [ ] [ ]

Jul 94. (4xcd-box) **30 YEARS OF MAXIMUM R&B** [48] [ ]

Oct 81. MCA; (lp) **HOOLIGANS** [-] [52]
(UK-iss.Dec88)

Nov 84. MCA; (lp)(c) **WHO'S LAST** *(cd-iss.Dec88)* [48] [81]

Nov 84. MCA; (7") **TWIST AND SHOUT. / I CAN'T EXPLAIN**

Oct 85. Impression; (d-lp)(d-c) **THE WHO COLLECTION** [44] [-]
(d-cd-iss.Oct88 VOL.1 & 2 on 'Stylus', hit 71)

Aug 85. Karusel Gold; (c) **THE BEST OF THE SIXTIES** [ ] [-]
Apr 86. Arcade; (lp)(c) **GREATEST HITS** [ ] [-]
Mar 90. Virgin; (7") **JOIN TOGETHER. / I CAN SEE FOR MILES** [ ] [ ]
(12"+=)/ /cd-s++=) – Behind blue eyes./ / Christmas.
Mar 90. Virgin; (cd)(d-c)(d-lp) **JOIN TOGETHER** [59] [ ]
– (contains some solo material)

PETE TOWNSHEND

(solo). Before his 1972 official debut, TOWNSHEND issued 2 lp's on 'Universal'; HAPPY BIRTHDAY (1970) & I AM (1972).

Track / Track

Oct 72. (lp)(c) **WHO CAME FIRST** [30] [69]
– Pure and easy / Evolution / Forever's no time at all / Let's see action / Time is passing / There's a heartache followin' me / Sheraton Gibson / Content / Parvardigar. *(cd-iss.Oct92 on 'Rykodisc')*

—— next collaboration with Solo artist and ex-SMALL FACES bassman and singer.

PETE TOWNSHEND & RONNIE LANE

Polydor / M.C.A.

Sep 77. (7") **MY BABY GIVES IT AWAY. / APRIL FOOL** [-] [ ]
Sep 77. (lp)(c) **ROUGH MIX** [44] [45]
– My baby gives it away / Nowhere to run / Rough mix / Annie / Keep me turning / Catmelody / Misunderstood / April fool / Street in the city / Heart to hang on to / Till the rivers all run dry. *(re-iss.Nov80 & Nov83)*
Nov 77. (7") **STREET IN THE CITY. / ANNIE (by "RONNIE LANE")** [ ] [-]
Nov 77. (7") **NOWHERE TO RUN . / KEEP ME TURNING** [-] [ ]

PETE TOWNSHEND

Island / not issued

Dec 79. (12"ep) **THE SECRET POLICEMAN'S BALL** (the songs) [ ] [-]
– Drowned / Pinbal wizard / Won't get fooled again.

Atco / Atco

Mar 80. (7") **ROUGH BOYS. / AND I MOVED** [39] [89] Nov 80
Apr 80. (lp)(c) **EMPTY GLASS** [11] [5]
– Rough boys / I am an animal / And I moved / Let my love open your door / Jools and Jim / Keep on working / Cat's in the cupboard / A little is enough / Empty glass / Gonna get ya. *(cd-iss.1984 + Nov93 + Oct95)*
Jun 80. (7") **LET ME LOVE OPEN THE DOOR. / AND I LOVED** [-] [9]
Jun 80. (7"m) **LET MY LOVE OPEN THE DOOR. / CLASSIFIED / GREYHOUND GIRL** [46] [-]
Oct 80. (7") **A LITTLE IS ENOUGH. / CAT'S IN THE CUPBOARD** [-] [72]
Oct 80. (7") **KEEP ON WORKING. / JOOLS AND JIM** [ ] [-]
May 82. (7") **FACE DANCES (pt.2). / MAN WATCHING** [ ] [ ]
Jun 82. (lp)(c) **ALL THE BEST COWBOYS HAVE CHINESE EYES** [32] [26]
– The sea refuses no river / Communication / Exquisitely bored / North country girl / Slit skirts / Uniforms / Prelude / Somebody saved me / Face dances 2 / Stardom in action / Stop hurting people. *(cd-iss.Nov93 & Oct95)*
Aug 82. (7")(7"pic-d) **UNIFORMS (CORPS D'ESPRIT). / DANCE IT ALL AWAY** [48] [-]
(12")(12"pic-d) – ('A'side) / Stop hurting people.
Aug 82. (7") **UNIFORMS (CORPS D'ESPRIT). / SLIT SKIRTS** [-] [ ]
Apr 83. (7") **BARGAIN. / DIRTY WATER** [-] [ ]
Oct 85. (7")(12") **FACE THE FACE. / HIDING OUT** [ ] [26]
Nov 85. (lp)(c)(cd) **WHITE CITY – A NOVEL** [70] [26]
– Give blood / Brilliant blues / Face the face / Hiding out / Secondhand love / Crashing by design / I am secure / White City fighting Come to mama. (re-iss.cd Nov93)
Jan 86. (7") **SECOND HAND LOVE. / WHITE CITY FIGHTING** [-] [ ]
Apr 86. (7") **GIVE BLOOD. / MAGIC BUS (live)** [ ] [ ]
(12"+=) – Won't get fooled again.
Oct 86. (lp)(c)(cd) **PETE TOWNSEND'S DEEP END LIVE! (live)** [-] [98]
– Barefootin' / After the fire / Behind blue eyes / Stop hurtin' people / I'm one / I put a spell on you / Save it for later / Pinball wizard / Little is enough / Eyesight to the blind.

—— Next featured singers JOHN LEE HOOKER (Iron Man) / NINA SIMONE (The Dragon) / DALTREY + JOHN ENTWISTLE who play on 2 new WHO tracks.

Virgin / Atlantic

Jun 89. (lp)(c)(cd) **THE IRON MAN (The Musical)** [ ] [58]
– I won't run anymore / Over the top / Man machines / Dig / A friend is a friend / I eat heavy metal / All shall be well / Was there life / Fast food / A fool says . . . / Fire / New life (reprise). *(re-iss.+cd.Mar91)*
Jul 89. (7")(c-s) **A FRIEND IS A FRIEND. / MAN MACHINES** [ ] [ ]
(12"+=)(3"cd-s+=) – Real world.
Nov 89. (7")(12") **I WON'T RUN ANYMORE. / A FOOL SAYS . . .** [ ] [ ]

Atlantic / Atlantic

Jul 93. (cd)(c) **PSYCHODERELICT** [ ] [ ]
– English boy / Meher Baba M3 / Let's get pretentious / Meher Baba M4 (signal box) / Early morning dreams / I want that thing / Introduction to outlive the dinosaur / Outlive the dinosaur / Flame (demo) / Now and then / I am afraid / Don't try to make me real / Introduction to predictable / Predictable / Flame / Meher Baba M5 (Vivaldi) / Fake it / Introduction to now and then (reprise) / Now and then (reprise) / Baba O' Riley (demo) / English boy (reprise)
Jul 93. (7")(c-s) **ENGLISH BOY. / EARLY MORNING DREAMS** [ ] [ ]
(cd-s+=) – Flame (demo).
(cd-s) – ('A'side) / ('A'dialogue version) / Fake it / Psycho montage.

– (other PETE TOWNSHEND compilations, etc.) –

Apr 83. Atco; (d-lp) **SCOOP** [ ] [35]
– (unfinished WHO demos and solo rarities)
Jul 89. Polydor; (d-lp)(d-c) **ANOTHER SCOOP** [ ] [ ]

ROGER DALTREY

(solo)

Track / Track

Apr 73. (7") **GIVING IT ALL AWAY. / THE WAY OF THE WORLD** [5] [83]
Apr 73. (lp)(c) **DALTREY** [ ] [45]
– One man band / The way of the world / You are yourself / Thinking / You and me / It's a hard life / Giving it all away / The story so far / When the music stops / Reasons. *(re-iss.Aug82) (cd-iss.Apr95 on 'Polydor')*
Jun 73. (7") **I'M FREE. / (OVERTURE)** [13] [ ]
Sep 73. (7") **THINKING. / THERE IS LOVE** [ ] [ ]
Nov 73. (7") **IT'S A HARD LIFE. / ONE MAN BAND** [ ] [ ]

Polydor / M.C.A.

Mar 75. (7") **LISTENING TO YOU. / (OVERTURE)** [ ] [ ]
May 75. (7") **COME AND GET YOUR LOVE. / THE WORLD OVER** [ ] [-]
Jul 75. (lp)(c) **RIDE A ROCK HORSE** [14] [28]
– Come and get your love / Hearts right / Oceans away / Proud / The world over / Near to surrender / Feeling / Walking the dog / Milk train / I was to sing your song.
Jul 75. (7") **WALKING THE DOG. / PROUD** [ ] [ ]
Sep 75. (7") **COME AND GET YOUR LOVE. / FEELING** [-] [68]
Nov 75. (7") **OCEANS AWAY. / FEELING** [-] [ ]
Oct 75. (7") **ORPHEUS SONG. / LOVE'S DREAM** [ ] [ ]

—— (above from the Ken Russell film LISTZOMANIA. Released at the same time, it was scored by RICK WAKEMAN for 'A & M' and featured some with DALTREY vocals).

Apr 77. (7") **WRITTEN ON THE WIND. / DEAR JOHN** [46] [-]
May 77. (7") **ONE OF THE BOYS. / DOING IT ALL AGAIN** [-] [ ]
May 77. (lp)(c) **ONE OF THE BOYS** [45] [46]
– Parade / Single man's dilemma / Avenging Annie / The prisoner / Leon / One of the boys / Giddy / Written on the wind / Satin and lace / Doing it all again.
Jun 77. (7") **ONE OF THE BOYS. / TO PUT SOMETHING BETTER INSIDE ME** [ ] [-]
Aug 77. (7") **SAY IT ISN'T SO, JOE. / SATIN AND LACE** [-] [ ]
Oct 77. (7") **AVENGING ANNIE. / THE PRISONER** [-] [88]
Jan 78. (7") **THE PRISONER. / LEON** [-] [ ]

Polydor / Polydor

Jul 80. (7") **FREE ME. / McVICAR** [39] [53]
Jul 80. (lp)(c)(clear-lp) **McVICAR (Soundtrack)** [39] [22]
– Bitter and twisted / Just a dream away / Escape (part 1) / White City lights / Free me / My time is gonna come / Waiting for a friend / Escape (part 2) / Without your love / McVicar. *(cd-iss.Apr95)*
Sep 80. (7") **WITHOUT YOUR LOVE. / ESCAPE (part 2)** [-] [20]
Oct 80. (7") **WITHOUT YOUR LOVE. / SAY IT AIN'T SO, JOE. / FREE ME** [55] [-]
Jan 81. (7") **WAITING FOR A FRIEND. / BITTER AND TWISTED** [-] [ ]

Polydor / M.C.A.

Mar 82. (lp)(c) **THE BEST OF ROGER DALTREY** (compilation) [ ] [ ]
– Martyrs and madmen / Say it isn't so, Joe / Oceans away / Treasury / Free me / Without your love / It's a hard life / Giving it all away / Avenging Annie / Proud / You put something better inside me. *(US-title* **'BEST BITS'***) (UK cd-iss.May91)*
Apr 82. (7") **SAY IT AIN'T SO, JOE. / THE PRISONER** [ ] [-]
Apr 82. (7") **MARTYRS AND MADMEN. / AVENGING ANNIE** [-] [ ]

WEA / Atlantic

Feb 84. (7") **WALKING IN MY SLEEP. / SOMEBODY TOLD ME** [56] [62]
(12"+=) – Gimme some lovin'.
Feb 84. (lp)(c) **PARTING SHOULD BE PAINLESS** [ ] [ ]
– Walking in my sleep / Parting would be painless / Is there anybody out there / Would a stranger do / Going strong / Looking for you / Somebody told me / How does the cold wind cry / Don't wait on the stairs.
Jun 84. (7") **PARTING SHOULD BE SO PAINLESS. / IS THERE ANYBODY OUT THERE** [ ] [ ]
(12"+=) – I won't be the one to say goodbye.

Ten-Virgin / Atlantic

Sep 85. (7") **AFTER THE FIRE. / IT DON'T SATISFY ME** [50] [48]
(12"+=) – Love me like you do.
Oct 85. (lp)(c)(cd) **UNDER A RAGING MOON** [52] [42]
– After the fire / Don't talk to strangers / Breaking down Paradise / The pride you hide / Move better in the night / Let me down easy / Fallen angel / It don't satisfy me / Rebel / Under a raging moon. *(cd+=)*– Behind blue eyes / 5:15 / Won't get fooled again. *(re-iss.cd.1989)*
Dec 85. (7") **LET ME DOWN EASY. / FALLEN ANGEL** [-] [86]
Feb 86. (7")(12") **UNDER A RAGING MOON. / MOVE BETTER IN THE NIGHT** [43] [-]
(d7"+=) – Behind blue eyes / 5:15 / Won't get fooled again.
Apr 86. (7") **QUICKSILVER LIGHTNING. / LOVE ME LIKE YOU DO** [-] [ ]
May 86. (7") **THE PRIDE YOU HIDE. / BREAK OUT** [ ] [-]
(d7"+=) – Don't talk to strangers (live) / Pictures of Lily (live).
Jun 86. (7") **UNDER A RAGING MOON. / THE PRIDE YOU HIDE** [-] [ ]
Jun 87. (7") **HEARTS OF FIRE. / LOVERS STORM** [ ] [ ]
(12"+=) – Quick silver lightning.
Jul 87. (lp)(c)(cd) **CAN'T WAIT TO SEE THE MOVIE** [ ] [ ]
– Hearts of fire / When the thunder comes / Ready for love / Balance on wires / Miracle of love / The price of love / The heart has its reasons / Alone in the night / Lover's storm / Take me home.
Jul 87. (7") **DON'T LET THE SUN GO DOWN ON ME. / THE HEART HAS ITS REASONS** [ ] [ ]
(12"+=) – ('A'extended).

JOHN ENTWISTLE

(solo)

Track / Decca

Nov 70. (lp)(c) **THE OX (by "The WHO")** [ ] [ ]
– (compilation of WHO songs written by ENTWISTLE)
May 71. (lp)(c) **BANG YOUR HEAD AGAINST THE WALL** [ ] [ ]
– My size / Pick me up (big chicken) / What kind of people are they? / Heaven and Hell / Ted end / You're mine / No.29 (external youth) / I believe in everything.
May 71. (7") **I BELIEVE IN EVERYTHING. / MY SIZE** [ ] [ ]

RIGOR MORTIS

ENTWHISTLE with **BRYAN WILLIAMS** – keys / **ALAN ROSS** – guitar / **HOWIE CASEY** – sax / **GRAHAM DEACON** – drums / **TONY ASHTON** – perc.

Track Track

Nov 72. (lp)(c) **WHISTLE RHYMES** [ ] [ ]
– Ten little friends / Mr.Bones & Mr.Apron strings / And I feel better / Thinking it over / Who cares / I wonder now / I was just being friendly / The window shopper / I found out / Nightmare.

Nov 72. (7") **WHO CARES. / I WONDER NOW** [-] [ ]

Track M.C.A.

Jun 73. (lp)(c) **RIGOR MORTIS SETS IN** [ ] [ ]
– Give me that rock and roll / Mr. Bass man / Do the dangle / Hound dog / Made in Japan / My wife / Roller skate Kate / Peg leg Peggy / Lucille / Big black Cadillac.

Jun 73. (7") **MADE IN JAPAN. / HOUND DOG** [ ] [-]

Jun 73. (7") **MADE IN JAPAN. / ROLLER SKATE KATE** [-] [ ]

JOHN ENTWISTLE'S OX

with **DEACON, ASHTON & CASEY** plus **JIM RYAN** – guitar / **MIKE WEDGWOD** – guitar / **EDDIE JOBSON** – keyboards (guest)

Feb 75. (7") **MAD DOG. / CELL NO.7** [ ] [ ]

Mar 75. (lp)(c) **MAD DOG** [ ] [ ]
– I fall to pieces / Cell number seven / You can be so mean / Lady killer / Who in the hell? / Mad dog / Jungle bunny / I'm so scared / Drowning.

JOHN ENTWISTLE

(solo, with session stars incl. **JOE WALSH** – guitar

WEA Atco

Sep 81. (7")(7"pic-d) **TOO LATE THE HERO. / COMIN' BACK** [ ] [ ]

Nov 81. (lp)(c) **TOO LATE THE HERO** [ ] [71]
– Try me / Talk dirty / Lovebird / Sleepin man / I'm coming back / Dancing master / Fallen angel / Love is a heart attack / Too late the hero.

Dec 81. (7") **TALK DIRTY. /** [-] [ ]

KEITH MOON

Polydor M.C.A.

Apr 75. (lp)(c) **TWO SIDES OF THE MOON** [ ] [ ]
– Crazy like a fox / Solid gold / Don't worry baby / One night stand / The kid's are alright / Move over Ms. L / Teenage idol / Back door Sally / In my life / Together.

May 75. (7") **DON'T WORRY BABY. / TOGETHER** [ ] [-]

May 75. (7") **DON'T WORRY BABY. / TEENAGE IDOL** [-] [ ]

Jul 75. (7") **MOVE OVER MS. L. / SOLID GOLD** [-] [ ]

Sep 75. (7") **CRAZY LIKE A FOX. / IN MY LIFE** [-] [ ]

WILD & WONDERING
(see under ⇒ POP WILL EAT ITSELF)

WILDHEARTS

Formed: London, England . . . 1988 by GINGER + CJ; veterans of the 80's heavy glam scene. After difficulties with initial record label 'East West', they signed to 'Bronze' in 1991, but had to wait until their second release; 1993's 'EARTH VERSUS . . . ' for their first visit into chart territory. • **Style:** Hard rock and thrash punk /pop, lying between The RUTS, The CULT and The MANICS. • **Songwriters:** GINGER, except some group. • **Trivia:** In 1993, they featured in Channel 4 play 'Comics'. Played Reading Festival in 1994, where rumours floated about a imminent split. Yeah! the same f'in ones that said The LEVELLERS were to replace SOUNDGARDEN.

Recommended: EARTH VERSUS THE WILDHEARTS (*6)

GINGER – vocals, guitar (ex-QUIREBOYS) / **BAM** – drums (ex-DOGS D'AMOUR) / **CJ** (CHRIS JAGDHAR) – guitar, vocals (ex-TATTOOED LOVE BOYS) / **DANNY McCORMICK** – bass, vocals (ex-ENERGETIC KRUSHER)

Bronze East West

Mar 92. (12"ep)(cd-ep) **MONDO AKIMBO A-GO-GO** [ ] [ ]
– (Nothing ever changes but the) Shoes / Turning American / Crying over nothing * / Liberty cap. *(re-iss.Apr94 c+cd-ep as 'DON'T BE HAPPY . . . JUST WORRY' for 'East West', track * repl. by 'Splattermania')*

Sep 93. (cd)(c)(lp) **EARTH VERSUS THE WILDHEARTS** [46] [ ]
– Greetings from Shitsville / TV tan / Everlone / Shame on me / Loveshit / The miles away girl / My baby is a headf*** / Suckerpunch / News of the world / Love u til I don't.
(cd+c+=) – Drinking about life. *(re-iss.Feb94 on 'East West')*

Oct 93. (7"brown) **GREETINGS FROM SHITSVILLE. / THE BULLSHIT GOES ON** [ ] [ ]

Nov 93. (7"pic-d)(c-s) **TV TAN. / SHOW A LITTLE EMOTION** [53] [ ]
(12"+=)(cd-s+=) – Danger lust / Down on London.

— **RITCH** – drums repl. BAM

East West East West

Feb 94. (7"green-ep)(12"ep)(c-ep)(cd-ep) **CAFFEINE BOMB / GIRLFRIENDS CLOTHES. / SHUT YOUR FUCKIN' MOUTH AND USE YOUR FUCKIN' BRAIN / AND THE BULLSHIT GOES ON** [31] [ ]

Jun 94. (10"ep)(c-ep)(cd-ep) **SUCKER PUNCH / BEAUTIFUL THING YOU. / TWO-WAY IDIOT MIRROR / 29 x THE PAIN** [38] [ ]

(Jul94) temp **DEVON TOWNSEND** – guitar repl. C.J. who formed although only briefly HONEYCRACK. He returned for Reading Festival August 1994.

Dec 94. (cd) **FISHING FOR LUCKIES** (mail order) [ ] [ ]
– Sky babies / Inglorious / Do the channel bop / Shizophronic / Geordie in wonderland / If life is like a love bank I want an overdraft.

Jan 95. (10"ep)(c-ep)(cd-ep)(cd-ep) **IF LIFE IS LIKE A LOVE BANK I WANT AN OVERDRAFT / GEORDIE IN WONDERLAND. / HATE THE WORLD DAY / FIRE UP** [31] [ ]

Apr 95. (10"ep)(c-ep)(cd-ep)(cd-ep) **I WANNA GO WHERE THE PEOPLE GO / SHANDY BANG. / CAN'T DO RIGHT FOR DOING WRONG / GIVE THE GIRL A GUN** [16] [ ]

May 95. (cd)(c)(lp) **P.H.U.Q.** [6] [ ]
– I wanna go where the people go / V-day / ust in lust / Baby strange / Nita nitro / Jonesing for Jones / Woah shit, you got through / Cold patootie tango / Caprice / Be my drug / Naivety play / In Lilly's garden / Getting it.

— **MARK KEDS** – guitar (ex-SENSELESS THINGS) repl.C.J.

Jul 95. (10"ep)(c-ep)(cd-ep)(cd-ep) **JUST IN LUST / MINDSLIDE. / FRIEND FOR FIVE MINUTES / S.I.N. (IN SIN)** [28] [ ]

— **JEFF STREATFIELD** – guitar repl.KEDS who went AWOL in July

Nov 95. (cd)(c)(lp) **FISHING FOR MORE LUCKIES** (see other) [ ] [-]

— Disbanded at the end of '95.

Hank WILLIAMS

Born: HIRAM WILLIAMS, 17 Sep'23, Garland, Alabama, USA. From the age seven, he was raised by a recession-hit domineering mother LILYBELLE, after his father left the household after he was again beaten up by LILY. HANK, his mother and his older sister Irene moved to Georgiana, where he bunked school to do odd jobs and learn guitar from an older negro friend TEE TOT. In 1937, the family moved to Montgomery, where LILY opened a boarding house, where she in took many male guests; too many for HANK's liking, so he went off to sing on local radio, followed with a few beers. He had only just arrived at his teens, and due to constant backache he started to drink heavily. He formed a band The DRIFTING COWBOYS, who toured the Honky Tonk saloon bars during the turn of the decade. When the U.S.A. decided to join the war in 1942, he was not called up due to his bad back. He soon met soon-to-be divorced AUDREY, whom he married in 1944. It was she who pestered publisher FRED ROSE to listen to him singing while in a hotel lobby. In 1946 after the war had ended, he was asked for a new country star by 'Sterling' records. He sent them HANK and it was not long after that he cut his first discs (see below). Three singles later, he was taken by FRANK WALKER to the new 'MGM' stable in 1947, where they released 'MOVE IT ON OVER'. FRED then got him booked into the Louisiana Hayride, a weekly country radio show that was second only to The Grand Ole Opry. However troubles at home took precidence as his wife and mother argued with themselves and him about his late night drinking binges. It wasn't only booze that took over, but drugs to either make him up or down. Early 1949, he entered the country charts with a standard 'LOVESICK BLUES' and this propelled him overnight to Opry class. After the birth of his son HANK JNR, he played the Opry and made history there with six encores. The country charts were soon littered with HANK's songs during 49-1950. Around this time, he had reluctantly agreed to kickstart AUDREY's career by convincing 'Decca' (who had earlier turned him down!) to record and release 2 of her songs, then 2 from his his pen. He was writing at the time with friend VIC McALPIN, but HANK bought out his half credit with 500 dollars. The following year, he co-wrote a book 'HOW TO WRITE COUNTRY AND FOLK MUSIC TO SELL' and TONY BENNETT topped the pop charts with his 'COLD COLD HEART'. In 1952 his relationship with AUDREY was deteriorating so much, that he was drinking himself into oblivion and turning up on stage totally wrecked. AUDREY and HANK JNR moved out of their home and his drinking took over completely. However he was writing more prolificly by the time his return to the studio in June that year. His songs 'JAMBALAYA', 'YOUR CHEATIN' HEART' & 'YOU WIN AGAIN' all came out during these sessions and these showed him at his heartbreaking brilliance. He was fired from The Grand Ole Opry shows in August, although he was back with the Hayride, to promote a new C&W No.1 'JAMBALAYA'. He also met a young divorcee BILLIE JEAN, whom he married in October. He tried desperately to beat his alcoholism by spending time at at detox sanitarium, but to no avail. Tragically in the early hours of the 1st January 1953, his 17 year-old chauffeur Charles Carr found him dead in the back seat. Two days previously while his plane was being delayed due to bad weather, he had downed a bottle of spirits while taking morphine in his Knoxville hotel room. Desperate to make a Ohio gig, he had phoned Carr to pick his Cadillac up and drive him there. Mystery then shrouded his death, when a rushed coroner gave a verdict as heart failure, although many at the time still think it was an attempted suicide slow to hit fatal impact. Several others had also suspected murder, although this seems unlikely and even his record company 'MGM' said he was killed in a car crash!. It wasn't laid to rest there, as even at his well attended funeral (estimated 20,000+), he wasn't even buried in his plot as it was too small!. Instead they dug up 2 nearby graves and put him in there!. A few days later legal battles ensued between the unusual alliance between his ex-wife Audrey and his mother Lilybelle, who fought out court battles with his recent wife Billie Jean. After around 20 pain-staking years (although not for their lawyers), Billie Jean won his estate. To make matters even more crazier, a biopic film 'YOUR CHEATIN' HEART' was released early in 1965 and this starred GEORGE HAMILTON as HANK. His son HANK WILLIAMS JNR sang the soundtrack of his fathers' material. BILLIE

JEAN sued 'MGM', claiming it portrayed her as a slut, although it was not surprising as ex-wife Audrey was employed as its technical advisor!. HANK WILLIAMS JNR carried on with his solo career over the next 30 years, even recording many /all of his fathers' classics. Leaving this sometimes troubled 29-year legacy aside, the late great HANK has been inspiration for many including JERRY LEE LEWIS, BOB DYLAN, JOHN FOGERTY, BRUCE SPRINGSTEEN and even now (early 1995) THE THE (MATT JOHNSON) has just released a whole album worth attributed to him. Countless others have made vast sums of money due to hitting pop charts with his songs. Here are a list:- JAMBALAYA (ON THE BAYOU) for (Fats Domino) (Carpenters) (John Fogerty) / YOU WIN AGAIN for (Fats Domino) / YOUR CHEATING HEART + TAKE THESE CHAINS FROM MY HEART for (Ray Charles) / HEY GOOD LOOKIN' for (Bo Diddley) / etc, etc. • **Style:** Legendary white country roots blues singer, who is even cited as innovator for early rockabilly. • **Songwriters:** Self-penned, although he bought the rights for early work from other struggling artists. He covered; MY BUCKET'S GOT A HOLE IN IT (trad) / etc. • **Trivia:**

Recommended: 40 GREATEST HITS (*8) / MOANIN' THE BLUES (*9) / RAMBLIN' MAN (*8) / MEMORIAL ALBUM (*8) / HANK WILLIAMS SING (*7)

HANK WILLIAMS – vocals, guitar with session people

—— (all records before his death were 78 r.p.m.)

Date	Release	not issued	Sterling
Dec 46.	(78) **CALLING YOU. / NEVER AGAIN WILL I KNOCK ON YOUR DOOR**	-	
Dec 46.	(78) **WEALTH WON'T SAVE YOUR SOUL. / WHEN GOD COMES AND (F)GATHERS HIS JEWELS**	-	
Mar 47.	(78) **I DON'T CARE (IF TOMORROW NEVER COMES). / MY LOVE FOR YOU (HAS TURNED TO HATE)**	-	
May 47.	(78) **HONKY TONKIN'. / PAN AMERICAN**	-	

Date	Release	M.G.M.	M.G.M.
Jul 47.	(78) **MOVE IT ON OVER. / LAST NIGHT I HEARD YOU CRYING IN YOUR SLEEP**	-	
Sep 47.	(78) **FLY TROUBLE. / ON THE BANKS OF THE OLD PONTCHARTRAIN**	-	
Feb 48.	(78) **ROOTIE TOOTIE. / MY SWEET LOVE AIN'T AROUND**	-	
Apr 48.	(78) **HONKY TONKIN'. / I'LL BE A BACHELOR TILL I DIE**	-	
Jun 48.	(78) **I'M A LONG GONE DADDY. / BLUES COME AROUND**	-	
Jul 48.	(78) **PAN AMERICAN. / I DON'T CARE IF TOMORROW NEVER COMES**	-	
Sep 48.	(78) **I SAW THE LIGHT. / SIX MORE MILES (TO THE GRAVEYARD)**	-	
Dec 48.	(78) **MANSION ON THE HILL. / I CAN'T GET YOU OFF MY MIND**	-	
Feb 49.	(78) **LOVESICK BLUES. / NEVER AGAIN WILL I KNOCK ON YOUR DOOR**	-	
Apr 49.	(78) **WEDDING BLUES. / I'VE JUST TOLD MAMA GOODBYE**	-	
May 49.	(78; by "HANK AND AUDREY") **DEAR BROTHER. / LOST ON THE RIVER**	-	
Jul 49.	(78) **MIND YOUR OWN BUSINESS. / THERE'LL BE NO TEARDROPS TONIGHT**	-	
Sep 49.	(78) **YOU'RE GONNA CHANGE (OR I'M GONNA LEAVE). / LOST HIGHWAY**	-	
Nov 49.	(78) **MY BUCKET'S GOT A HOLE IN IT. / I'M SO LONESOME I COULD CRY**	-	
Jan 50.	(78) **I JUST DON'T LIKE THIS KIND OF LIVING. / MAY YOU NEVER BE ALONE**	-	
Feb 50.	(78; as LUKE THE DRIFTER) **THE FUNERAL. / BEYOND THE SUNSET**	-	

Late in 1949, his wife AUDREY WILLIAMS signed to 'Decca' and released 2 singles with the aid of HANK. These were 'I LIKE THAT KIND'. / 'MY TIGHT WAD DADDY', and his songs 'HOW CAN YOU REFUSE HIM NOW'. / HELP ME UNDERSTAND'.

Date	Release		
Mar 50.	(78) **LOVESICK BLUES. / WEDDING BELLS**		-
Mar 50.	(78) **LONG GONE LONESOME BLUES. / MY SON CALLS ANOTHER MAN DADDY**	-	
May 50.	(78) **WHY DON'T YOU LOVE ME. / A HOUSE WITHOUT LOVE**	-	
Jun 50.	(78; as LUKE THE DRIFTER) **EVERYTHING'S OKAY. / TOO MANY PARTIES**	-	
Aug 50.	(78) **THEY'L NEVER TAKE HER LOVE AWAY FROM ME. / WHY SHOULD WE TRY ANYMORE**	-	
Oct 50.	(78; as "LUKE THE DRIFTER") **NO NO JOE. / HELP ME UNDERSTAND**	-	
Oct 50.	(78; as "HANK AND AUDREY") **I HEARD MY MOTHER PRAYING FOR ME. / JESUS REMEMBERED ME**	-	
Oct 50.	(78) **MOANIN' THE BLUES. / NOBODY'S LONESOME FOR ME**	-	
Dec 50.	(78) **DEAR JOHN. / COLD, COLD HEART**	-	
Mar 51.	(78; as LUKE THE DRIFTER) **JUST WAITIN'. / MEN WITH BROKEN HEARTS**	-	
Mar 51.	(78) **MOANIN' THE BLUES. / BLUES COME AROUND**		-
Apr 51.	(78) **HOWLIN' AT THE MOON. / I CAN'T HELP IT (IF I'M STILL IN LOVE WITH YOU)**	-	
Jun 51.	(78) **HEY GOOD LOOKIN'. / MY HEART WOULD KNOW**	-	
Jun 51.	(78) **DEAR JOHN. / FLY TROUBLE**		-
Jul 51.	(78; as LUKE THE DRIFTER) **I'VE BEEN DOWN THAT ROAD BEFORE. / I DREAMED ABOUT MAMA LAST NIGHT**	-	
Sep 51.	(78) **LONESOME WHISTLER. / CRAZY HEART**	-	
Nov 51.	(78) **BABY WE'RE REALLY IN LOVE. / I'D STILL WANT YOU**	-	
Dec 51.	(78; as LUKE THE DRIFTER) **RAMBLIN' MAN. / PICTURE FROM LIFE'S OTHER SIDE**	-	
Nov 51.	(78) **HEY, GOOD LOOKIN'. / HOWLING AT THE MOON**		-
Dec 51.	(78) **COLD, COLD HEART. / I'M A LONG GONE DADDY**		-
Feb 52.	(78) **I CAN'T HELP IT (IF I'M STILL IN LOVE WITH YOU). / BABY, WE'RE REALLY IN LOVE**		-
Mar 52.	(78) **HALF AS MUCH. / LET'S TURN BACK THE YEARS**	-	
Mar 52.	(78) **WHY DON'T YOU LOVE ME. / I'D STILL WANT YOU**		-
May 52.	(78) **HONKY-TONK BLUES. / I'M SORRY FOR YOU, MY FRIEND**		Feb 52
Jul 52.	(78) **HALF AS MUCH. / LONG GONE LONESOME BLUES**		-
Jul 52.	(78) **JAMBALAYA (ON THE BAYOU). / WINDOW SHOPPING**	-	
Aug 52.	(78; as LUKE THE DRIFTER) **WHY DON'T YOU MAKE UP YOUR MIND. / BE CAREFUL OF STONES THAT YOU THROW**	-	
Sep 52.	(78) **SETTIN' THE WOODS ON FIRE. / YOU WIN AGAIN**	-	
Sep 52.	(78) **NOBODY'S LONESOME FOR ME. / MIND YOUR OWN BUSINESS**		-
Oct 52.	(10"lp) **HANK WILLIAMS SINGS** – A house without love / Wedding bells / The mansion on the hill / Wealth won't save your soul / I saw the light / Six more miles (to the graveyard) / Lost highway / I've just told mama goodbye.		
Oct 52.	(78) **JAMBALAYA (ON THE BAYOU). / SETTIN' THE WODS ON FIRE**		-
Dec 52.	(78) **I'LL NEVER GET OUT OF THIS WORLD ALIVE. / I COULD NEVER BE ASHAMED OF YOU**		Oct 52

—— Tragically the above 'A'side was poignantly true, when in the early hours of New Year's Day 1953, he was found dead (see above biog).

– postumous work & compilations, etc.-

(now released on 7"45 as well; UK only; US selective)
Note; below eleased on 'MGM' until otherwise stated.

Date	Release		
Mar 53.	(7") **KAW-LIGA. / TAKE THESE CHAINS FROM MY HEART**		
May 53.	(7") **I SAW THE LIGHT. / In Memory Of Hank Williams (by "Arthur 'Guitar Boogie' Smith)**		
Jul 53.	(7") **RAMBLIN' MAN. / I WON'T BE HOME NO MORE**		
Sep 53.	(7") **MY BUCKET'S GOT A HOLE IN IT. / LET'S TURN BACK THE YEARS**		
Oct 53.	(10"lp) **HANK WILLIAMS AS 'LUKE THE DRIFTER'** –		
Oct 53.	(7") **YOU WIN AGAIN. / WINDOW SHOPPING**		
Jan 54.	(7") **WEARY BLUES (FROM WAITIN'). / I CAN'T ESCAPE FROM YOU**		
Apr 54.	(7") **THERE'LL BE NO TEARDROPS TONIGHT. / CRAZY HORSE**		
Oct 54.	(7") **I'M SATISFIED WITH YOU. / I AIN'T GOT NOTHIN' BUT TIME**		
Dec 54.	(7"ep) **HANK WILLIAMS** –		-
Feb 55.	(7") **I'M GONNA SING. / CALIFORNIA ZEPHYR**		
1955.	(lp) **RAMBLIN' MAN** – Ramblin' man / Lonesome whistler / My son calls another man daddy / I just don't like this kind of livin' / I can't escape from you / Nobody's lonesome for me / Take these chains from my heart / Why don't you love me? / I can't help it (if I'm still in love with you) / There'll be no teardrops tonight / You're gonna change (or I'm gonna leave) / My heart would know.	-	
Mar 56.	(7"ep) **AS LUKE THE DRIFTER** – Why don't you make up your mind? / I've been down that road before / Just waitin' / Everything's okay.		-
Apr 56.	(7") **YOUR CHEATIN' HEART. / A TEARDROP ON A ROSE**		
Sep 56.	(7") **I WISH I HAD A NICKEL. / THERE'S NO ROOM IN MY HEART (FOR THE BLUES)**		
Sep 56.	(10"lp) **HANK WILLIAMS MEMORIAL ALBUM** – You win again / Cold cold heart / I could never be ashamed of you / Settin' the woods on fire / Hey, good lookin' / Kaw-liga / Half as much.		1953
Oct 56.	(7"ep) **I SAW THE LIGHT (No.1)** – How can you refuse him now / When God comes and gathers his jewels / Jesus remembered me / A house of gold.		-
Nov 56.	(7") **BLUE LOVE (IN MY HEART). / SINGING WATERFALL**		
Jan 57.	(7") **LAY DOWN BLUES. / MY SWEET LOVE AIN'T AROUND**		
Feb 57.	(7"ep) **HONKY TONKIN'** – Honky tonkin' / Howlin' at the Moon / I ain't got nothin' but time / Better keep it on your mind.		-
Mar 57.	(7") **ROOTIE TOOTIE. / LONESOME WHISTLE**		
Apr 57.	(10"lp) **MOANIN' THE BLUES** – Someday you'll call my name / Weary blues / Alone and forsaken / Moanin' the blues / I'm so lonely I could cry / Honky tonk blues / Lovesick blues / The blues come around / I'm a lone gone daddy / Long gone lonesome blues.		-
Jun 57.	(7"ep) **I SAW THE LIGHT (No.2)** – I'm gonna sing / Message to my mother / Thank God / The angel of death.		-
Sep 57.	(7") **LEAVE ME ALONE WITH THE BLUES. / WITH TEARS IN MY EYES**		
Sep 57.	(7"ep) **MY BUCKET'S GOT A HOLE IN IT (HONKY TONK BLUES)** – My bucket's got a hole in it / Baby, we're really in love / Honky tonk blues / I'll never get out of this world alive.		-
Mar 58.	(7"ep) **SONGS FOR A BROKEN HEART (No.1)** – Nobody's lonesome for me / You win again / Why don't you love me / Take these chains from my heart.		-
Mar 58.	(10"lp) **SING ME A BLUE SONG**		-

– Lay down blues / May you never be alone / I won't be home no more / Why should we try anymore / Blue love / My sweet love ain't around / (Last night) I heard you crying in your sleep / Mind your own business / They'll never take her love from me / Singing waterfal.

May 58. (7"ep) **SONGS FOR A BROKEN HEART (No.2)** □ -

– I'd still want you / I'm sorry for you my friend / I could never be ashamed of you / I can't escape from you.

Nov 58. (10"lp) **THE IMMORTAL HANK WILLIAMS** □ -

– There's no room in my heart / Waltz of the mind / With tears in my eyes / I wish I had a nickel / California Zephyr / Please don't let me love you / I'm satisfied with you / No one will ever know / Faded love and winter roses / First fall of snow.

Nov 58. (7"ep) **HANK'S LAMENT** □ -

– I can't help it / Dear John / Let's turn back the years / A teardrop on a rose.

Jul 59. (lp) **THE UNFORGETTABLE HANK WILLIAMS** □ -

– I just don't like this kind of living / My love for you (has turned to hate) / Dear brother / Never again (will I knock on your door) / I can't get out of my mind / Rootie tootie / I'll be a bachelor boy till I die / My son calls another man daddy / Lonesome whistle / Lost on the river / Mother is gone / Ready to go home.

— (above also iss.Jan60 /Jun60 /Oct60 as ep's 'THE UNFORGETTABLE . . . VOLS.1,2,3')

Apr 60. (lp) **THE LONESOME SOUND OF HANK WILLIAMS** □ -
Oct 60. (lp) **WAIT FOR THE LIGHTS TO SHINE** □ -
Sep 61. (7"ep) **HANK WILLIAMS' FAVOURITES** □ -
Oct 62. (lp) **ON STAGE (live)** □ -
Feb 63. (7"ep) **THE AUTHENTIC SOUND OF THE COUNTRY HITS** □ -
Nov 63. (lp) **THE SPIRIT OF HANK WILLIAMS** □ -
Oct 65. (lp) **SINGING TOGETHER (dubbed together w / HANK WILLIAMS JNR)** □ -
May 66. (7") **I'M SO LONESOME I COULD CRY. / YOU WIN AGAIN** □ -
Aug 66. (7") **KAW-LIGA. / LET'S TURN BACK THE TEARS** □ -
Nov 66. (lp) **MAY YOU NEVER BE ALONE** □ -
Nov 66. (lp) **IN MEMORY OF HANK WILLIAMS** □ -
Nov 66. (lp) **I'M BLUE INSIDE** □ -
Nov 66. (lp) **LUKE THE DRIFTER** □ -
Nov 66. (lp) **THE MANY MOODS OF HANK WILLIAMS** □ -
Feb 67. (lp) **THE LEGEND LIVES ANEW** (over-dubbed w /strings) □ -
May 67. (lp) **MORE HANK WILLIAMS & STRINGS** (as above w /strings) □ -
Jun 67. (lp) **LOVE SONGS, COMEDY AND HYMNS** □ -
Feb 68. (lp) **I WON'T BE HOME NO MORE** (overdubbed w /strings) □ -
May 68. (lp) **HANK WILLIAMS WITH STRINGS VOL.3** (overdubbed w /strings) □ -
Feb 70. (lp) **THE ESSENTIAL HANK WILLIAMS** □ -
Oct 70. (lp) **GREATEST HITS VOL.1** □ -
Apr 71. (lp) **GREATEST HITS VOL.2** □ -

(both above re-iss.May88 on 'Grand Canyon')

Mar 72. (lp) **THE LAST PICTURE SHOW (soundtrack)** □ -
Jun 73. (d-lp) **MEMORIAL ALBUM** □ -
Jul 74. (d-lp) **HANK WILLIAMS ON STAGE (live featuring AUDREY)** □ □
Nov 75. (lp) **THE COLLECTOR'S HANK WILLIAMS** □ -
Sep 76. (lp) **LIVE AT THE GRAND OLE OPRY (live)** □ □

(re-iss.Oct86)

Jan 78. (d-lp)(d-c) **40 GREATEST HITS** □ -

– Baby, we're really in love / Cold, cold heart / Crazy heart / Dear John / Half as much / Hey, good lookin' / Honky tonk blues / Howlin' at the Moon / I can't help it / I just don't like this kind of living / I saw the light / I won't be home no more / I'll never get out of this world alive / I'm so lonesome I could cry / I'm sorry for you my friend / Jambalaya (on the bayou) / Kaw-liga / Lonesome whistle / Long gone lonesome blues / Lost highway / Lovesick blues / A mansion on the hill / Mind your own business / Moanin' the blues / Move it on over / My bucket's got a hole in it / My son calls another man daddy / Nobody's lonesome for me / Ramblin' man / Settin' the woods on fire / Take these chains from my heart / They'll never take her love from me / Weary blues / Wedding bells / Why don't you love me / Why should we try anymore / Window shopping / You win again / Your cheatin' heart / You're gonna change. *(d-cd iss.May89 on 'Polydor')*

May 78. (lp) **THE COLLECTOR'S HANK WILLIAMS VOL.2** □ -

In 1979, 'RCA' made a various artists d-lp 'A TRIBUTE TO . . . '.

Aug 80. (lp) **THE COLLECTOR'S HANK WILLIAMS VOL.3** □ -
Jun 81. (lp)(c) **GREATEST HITS VOL.1** □ -
Jun 81. (lp)(c) **GREATEST HITS VOL.2** □ -

Note; Below on 'Polydor' until otherwise stated.

Jul 81. (lp)(c) **THE COLLECTOR'S HANK WILLIAMS VOL.4** □ -
Jul 86. (d-lp)(c) **LOST HIGHWAY** (Dec'48-Mar'49) □ -

(cd-iss.Jan93)

Jul 86. (d-lp) **I'M SO LONESOME I COULD CRY** (Mar'49-Aug'49) □ □

(cd-iss.Jul90)

Dec 87. (d-lp) **LONG GONE LONESOME BLUES** (Aug'49-Dec'50) □ □

(cd-iss.Jan93)

Dec 87. (d-lp) **HEY GOOD LOOKING** (Dec'50-Jul'51) □ □

(cd-iss.Jan93)

Dec 87. (d-lp) **LET'S TURN BACK THE YEARS** (Jul'51-Jun'52) □ □

(cd-iss.Jan93)

Dec 87. (d-lp) **I WON'T BE HOME NO MORE** (Jun'52-Sep'52) □ □
Jan 88. (d-lp) **I AIN'T GOT NOTHIN' BUT TIME** *(cd-iss.Mar90)* □ -
Jan 88. (d-lp) **RADIO TAKES AND RADIO CUTS** □ -
Jan 88. (d-lp) **ON THE AIR** □ -
Jan 88. (d-lp) **LOVESICK BLUES** *(cd-iss.Mar90)* □ -
Mar 91. (cd) **THE ORIGINAL SINGLES COLLECTION** □ -
Apr 68. M.F.P.; (lp) **HANK WILLIAMS** □ -
May 79. World Service; (6xlp-box) **THE LEGENDARY HANK WILLIAMS** □ -
Aug 81. K-Tel; (lp)(c) **THE LEGENDARY HANK WILLIAMS** □ -
Mar 83. Arhoolie; (7"ep) **HOME IN HEAVEN E.P.** - □

– Home in Heaven / In my dreams / I'm going home / Mother is gone.

1985. Country MF; (lp) **JUST ME AND MY GUITAR** - □

Below 4 on 'Jambalaya'.

Jul 85. (lp) **RARE RADIO BROADCASTS 1949** □ -
May 86. (lp) **MORE RARE RADIO BROADCASTS VOL.1** □ -
May 86. (lp) **MORE RARE RADIO BROADCASTS VOL.2** □ -
Feb 87. (lp)(c) **HANK WILLIAMS & THE DRIFTING COWBOYS** □ -
Aug 85. Contour; (lp)(c) **THE GREAT HITS OF HANK WILLIAMS** □ -

(cd-iss.Jun89 on 'Pickwick')

Mar 87. Contour; (lp)(c) **THE VERY BEST OF HANK WILLIAMS VOL.1** □ -

(cd-iss.Jun90 on 'Pickwick')

Apr 86. Arcade; (lp)(c) **VERY BEST OF HANK WILLIAMS** □ -
Jan 87. Deja Vu; (lp)(c) **THE HANK WILLIAMS COLLECTION (20 GOLDEN GREATS)** □ -
1987. Bescol; (cd) **16 GREATEST HITS** □ -
Sep 87. Timeless; (c) **16 ORIGINAL HITS** □ -
Jun 88. Country Store; (lp)(c)(cd) **HANK WILLIAMS** □ -
Sep 89. A Touch Of Magic; (lp)(c)(cd) **RADIO SHOWS** □ -
Aug 90. Graffiti; (cd) **THE GRAFFITI COLLECTION** □ -
Jan 93. Country Music; (cd) **RARE DEMOS: FIRST TO LAST** □ -
Oct 93. Spectrum; (cd)(c) **CHEATING HEARTS** □ -

Robin WILLIAMSON
(see under ⇒ INCREDIBLE STRING BAND)

Sonny Boy WILLIAMSON

Born: RICE MILLER, 1897, Glendors, Mississippi, USA. He initiated career in 1941, after featuring on 'King Biscuit Time' daily radio show. In 1951, he cut some records for 'Trumpet', before moving to 'Chess-Checker' in 1955. Complete with MUDDY WATERS' backing band, he issued some stunning songs including 'DON'T START ME TALKING'. In 1963, he toured Britain and appeared on TV Show 'Ready Steady, Go!'. That year, he also recorded a couple of albums here with The ANIMALS and The YARDBIRDS. In the summer of 1964, his solo album 'DOWN AND OUT BLUES' hit the UK Top 20. The following year on 25 May'65, he died at his home in Helena, Arkansas. • **Style:** Eccentric blues giant, who dressed in two-tone suit and bowler hat. • **Songwriters:** Wrote own material. His songs have been covered by LED ZEPPELIN, VAN MORRISON and The MOODY BLUES. • **Trivia:** He is said to have taught HOWLIN' WOLF the harmonica in exchange for guitar tuition. To many he's known as SONNY BOY WILLIAMSON No.2 (see below)

Recommended: THE BEST OF SONNY BOY WILLIAMSON (*7)

Please note: Not to be confused with another bluesman of the same name. The other was born JOHN LEE WILLIAMSON, 30 Mar'14, Jackson, Tennessee, USA. As a teenager he augmented other musicians HOMESICK JAMES WILLIAMSON and SLEEPY JOHN ESTES. He moved to Chicago in the late 30's, and released classic songs 'GOOD MORNING LITTLE SCHOOLGIRL' and 'SUGAR MAMA' for the 'RCA-Bluebird' label. He died on 1 Jun'48, after being attacked and robbed.

SONNY BOY WILLIAMSON (RICE MILLER) – vocals, guitar, harmonica with **CLIFF BIVENS** – bass / **FROCK** – drums

not issued Trumpet

Feb 51. (78) **EYESIGHT TO THE BLIND. / CRAZY ABOUT YOU BABY** - □

— added **DAVE CAMPBELL** – piano / **JOE WILLIE WILKINS** – guitar

Jun 51. (78) **COOL, COOL BLUES. / DO IT IF YOU WANNA** - □
Aug 51. (78) **STOP CRYING. / COME ON BACK HOME** - □
Oct 51. (78) **WEST MEMPHIS BLUES. / I CROSS MY HEART** - □

— **CLARENCE LONNIE** – piano repl. CAMPBELL (after next w /out BIVENS)

Dec 51. (78) **PONTIAC BLUES. / SONNY BOY'S CHRISTMAS BLUES** - □
Apr 52. (78) **NINE BELOW ZERO. / MIGHT LONG TIME** - □
Jun 52. (78) **STOP NOW BABY. / MR. DOWNCHILD** - □

— **DUKE HUDDLESTON** – tenor sax / **OLIVER HARRIS** – bass / **S.P.** – drums repl. LONNIE + FROCK

Dec 53. (78) **CAT HOP. / TOO CLOSE TOGETHER** - □
Mar 54. (78) **GETTIN' OUT OF TOWN. / SHE BROUGHT LIFE BACK TO THE DEAD** - □
May 54. (78) **GOING IN YOUR DIRECTION. / RED HOT KISSES** - □

— now w/**CLARENCE LONNIE** – piano / **B. B.KING** – guitar / **GLEN RICKETTS** – drums

Oct 54. (78) **EMPTY BEDROOM. / FROM THE BOTTOM** - □

— now w/**DAVE CAMPBELL + WILKINS**

not issued Ace

Dec 54. (78) **NO NIGHTS BY MYSELF. / BOPPIN' WITH SONNY** - □

— now w/**OTIS SPANN** – piano / **JIMMY ROGERS + MUDDY WATERS** – guitar / **FRED BELOW** – drums

not issued Checker

Mar 55. (7") **DON'T START ME TO TALKIN'. / ALL MY LOVE IN VAIN** - □

— **ROBERT LOCKWOOD + Jr. LUTHER TUCKER** – guitar / **WILLIE DIXON** – bass repl. WATERS + ROGERS + SPANN

Jul 55. (7") **LET ME EXPLAIN. / YOUR IMAGINATION** - □
1956. (7") **KEEP IT TO YOURSELF. / THE KEY TO YOUR DOOR** - □
1957. (7") **FATTENING FROGS FOR SNAKES. / I DON'T KNOW** - □

— added **OTIS SPANN** – piano

1957. (7") **BORN BLIND. / NINETY NINE** - □
1958. (7") **YOUR FUNERAL AND MY TRIAL. / WAKE UP BABY** - □

1958. (7") **CROSS MY HEART. / DISSATISFIED** [-] [ ]
1959. (7") **LET YOUR CONSCIENCE BE YOUR GUIDE. / UNSEEING EYE** [-] [ ]
1959. (7") **THE GOAT. / IT'S SAD TO BE ALONE** [-] [ ]
1960. (7") **TEMPERATURE. / LONESOME CABIN** [-] [ ]
1960. (7") **TRUST ME BABY. / TOO CLOSE TOGETHER** [-] [ ]
1961. (7") **STOP RIGHT NOW. / THE HUNT** [-] [ ]
1961. (7") **ONE WAY OUT. / NINE BELOW ZERO** [-] [ ]

— now w/**LAFAYETTE LEAKE** – organ / **MATT MURPHY** – guitar / **MILTON RECTOR** – bass / **AL DUNCAN** – drums

Pye Int. Checker

Apr 63. (7") **HELP ME. / BYE BYE BIRD** [ ] [ ]
Oct 63. (7") **TRYING TO GET BACK ON MY FEET. / DECORATION DAY** [-] [ ]

— **BUDDY GUY** – guitar / **JACK MEYERS** – bass / **CLIFTON JAMES** repl. all except LEAKE

Dec 63. (7") **I WANT YOU CLOSE TO ME. / MY YOUNGER DAYS** [-] [ ]
Feb 64. (7") **DOWN CHILD. / BRING IT ON HOME** [-] [ ]
May 64. (lp) **DOWN AND OUT BLUES** [20] [ ]
– Don't start me talkin' / I don't know / All my love in vain / The key / Keep it to yourself / Dissatisfied / Fattening frogs for snakes / Wake up baby / Your funeral and my trail / 99 / Cross my heart / Let me explain. *(re-iss.Jan67 on 'Marble Arch') (cd-iss.Jun88 + Jul90 on 'Chess')*
Oct 64. (7") **LONESOME CABIN. / THE GOAT** [ ] [ ]
Nov 64. (7"ep) **SONNY BOY WILLIAMSON** [ ] [ ]
1965. (lp) **ONE WAY OUT** [ ] [ ]
– Born blind / Work with me / Your killing me / Keep it to yourself / Don't lose your eye / Good evening everybody / Too close together / Let your conscience be your guide / I wonder why / This is my apartment / One way out / Like Wolf / Have you ever been in love / Cool disposition / I know what love is all about. *(re-iss.+c.Aug86) (cd-iss.Feb93 on 'Charly')*

— SONNY died on 25 May'65.

– compilations, others, etc. –

1963. Vogue; (lp) **SONNY BOY & MEMPHIS SLIM IN PARIS** [-] [ ]
– Your funeral and my trial / Explain yourself to me / My one room cabin / Getting out of town / The skies are crying / Nine below zero / Fattening frogs for snakes.*(re-iss.Sep76)*
Apr 65. Sue; (7") **NO NIGHTS BY MYSELF. / BOPPIN' WITH SONNY BOY** [ ] [-]
1965. Chess; (7"ep) **IN MEMORIUM** [ ] [-]
– Sad to be alone / Too young to die / Too old to think / One way out.
1966. Chess; (7"ep) **REAL FOLK BLUES, VOL.2** [ ] [-]
– Checkin' up on my baby / Disatisfied / Trust me baby / Bring it on home.
Apr 66. Chess; (7") **BRING IT ON HOME. / DOWN CHILD** [ ] [ ]
1972. Chess; (lp) **BUMMER ROAD** [-] [ ]
Apr 81. Chess; (lp) **CHESS MASTERS** [ ] [ ]
Apr 83. Chess; (d-lp) **CHESS MASTERS VOL.2** [ ] [ ]
1986. Chess; (6xlp-box) **SONNY BOY WILLIAMSON** [ ] [ ]
Feb 91. Chess; (4xlp-box) **THE CHESS YEARS** [ ] [-]
1967. Blue Horizon; (7") **FROM THE BOTTOM. / EMPTY BEDROOM** [ ] [-]
Dec 75. Charly; (lp) **THE JAM SESSION (with BRIAN AUGER)** [ ] [-]
(re-iss.1982)
Sep 89. Charly; (cd) **WORK WITH ME** [ ] [-]
Nov 92. Charly; (cd) **NINE BELOW ZERO** [ ] [-]
1964. Storyville; (lp) **A PORTRAIT IN BLUES VOL.4** [ ] [-]
(re-iss. May 86)
1969. Storyville; (lp) **BLUES OF SONNY BOY WILLIAMSON (live '63)** [ ] [-]
(cd-iss. Jul 87)
Aug 86. Deja Vu; (lp)(c) **THE COLLECTION** [ ] [-]
Oct 86. Deja Vu; (lp) **20 BLUES GREATS** [ ] [-]
May 89. Deja Vu; (cd)(c) **THE SONNY BOY WILLIAMSON STORY** [ ] [-]
Dec 86. Greenline; (cd) **THE BEST OF SONNY BOY WILLIAMSON** [ ] [-]
– Don't start me to talkin' / All my love in vain / Let me explain / Keep it to yourself / The key (to your door) / Fattening frogs for snakes / Cross my heart / Born blind / Ninety nine / Your funeral and my trial / Let your conscience be your guide / The goat / It's sad to be alone / Checkin' up on my baby / Lonesome cabin / Trust my baby / Too close together / Nine below zero / Help me / Bring it on home / Decoration day / One way out.
Jul 87. Blue Moon; (7"ep) **TAKE IT EASY BABY / BYE BYE BIRD. / I DON'T CARE NO MORE / BABY DON'T WORRY / 23 HOURS TOO LONG** [ ] [-]
1989. Document; (lp) **SOLO HARP 1963-65** [ ] [-]
1992. Charly; (cd) **NINE BELOW ZERO** [ ] [-]
Mar 93. Arhoolie; (cd)(c) **KING BISCUIT TIME** [ ] [-]
Apr 93. Sixteen; (cd) **16 GREATEST HITS** [ ] [-]

— (next cd credited with WILLIE LOVE)

Jul 93. Alligator; (cd) **CLOWNIN' WITH THE WORLD** [ ] [-]
Jul 94. Alligator; (cd) **GOIN' IN YOUR DIRECTION** [ ] [-]
Mar 94. See For Miles; (cd) **THE EP COLLECTION . . . PLUS** [ ] [-]
Aug 94. Charly; (cd) **BRING IT ON HOME** [ ] [-]
Jul 95. Charly; (d-cd) **THE VERY BEST OF SONNY BOY WILLIAMSON** [ ] [-]
Jul 95. Charly; (cd) **LIVE IN ENGLAND** [ ] [-]

Marty WILLSON-PIPER (see under ⇒ CHURCH)

Ann WILSON (see under ⇒ HEART)

Brian WILSON / Carl WILSON / Dennis WILSON (see under ⇒ BEACH BOYS)

Jackie WILSON

Born: JACK LEROY WILSON, 9 Jun'34, Detroit, Michigan, USA. In 1950, he won an American amateur Golden Gloves boxing title under the name of Sonny Wilson, due to him being under-age. The same year, encouraged by his mother, he joined The EVER READY GOSPEL SINGERS. He was soon noticed by singer JOHNNY OTIS, who introduced BILLY WARD, who invited him to join The DOMINOES. In 1951, JACKIE also cut his debut solo single 'DANNY BOY', for Dizzy Gillespie's 'Dee Gee' records. 2 years later, he replaced DOMINOES lead singer CLYDE McPHATTER, who departed for The DRIFTERS. JACKIE's solo career, really came to life late '57, when 'Brunswick' records issued 'REET PETITE', which although not a major hit in the States, became a Top 10 smash UK. (Remarkably, it went down in the record books in 1986, when it finally became a UK chart topper, 29 years after its initial release!). His fortunes from then on, mainly lay in the US, where he notched up more than 20 Top 40 hits between 1958-1968. His life was nearly cut short on 15 Feb'61, when a fan! Juanita Jones attempted to shoot herself in his New York apartment. WILSON intervened and was shot in the stomach, but luckily he survived after a long spell in the hospital. Tragically just as his oldies were going through a nice chart revival period, he suffered a heart attack on 29 Sep'75. For the next 8 years plus, until his death on 21 Jan'84, he was hospitalized, never fully regaining faculties due to brain damage. • **Style:** Legendary singer, who could mix explosive uptempo R&B interpretations with soulful near-operatic ballads. • **Songwriters:** JACKIE wrote most of material himself and collaborating with others, noteably ALONZO TUCKER in 1962-65. BERRY GORDY JR. & TYRAN CARLO (alias cousin BILLY DAVIS), penned his late 1950's 'Brunswick' songs. Many of his 1960's songs were adapted from operas or classical works. Covered:- DANNY BOY (Irish trad.) / SHAKE A HAND (Faye Adams) / THINK TWICE (Brook Benton) / FOR YOUR PRECIOUS LOVE (Impressions) / CHAIN GANG (Sam Cooke) / I GET THE SWEETEST FEELING (co-with; Van McCoy) / FOR ONCE IN MY LIFE (Stevie Wonder) / YOU GOT ME WALKING (Eugene Record; Chi-Lites) / etc. • **Trivia:** In 1959, he appeared in the Alan Freed film 'Go Johnny Go'.

Recommended: THE VERY BEST OF. . . (*8)

JACKIE WILSON – vocals

not issued Dee Gee

1951. (7") **DANNY BOY. / ?** [-] [ ]

— In Apr'53, he replaced CLYDE McPHATTER in The DOMINOES. Early '54, they released single RAGS TO RICHES on 'King' records. They signed to 'Jubilee' in '56, and made one single before moving to 'Decca', issuing another single ST.THERESE OF THE ROSES.

— **JACKIE WILSON** reverted to solo career.

Coral Q Brunswick

Nov 57. (7") **REET PETITE (THE FINEST GIRL YOU EVER WANT TO KNOW). / BY THE LIGHT OF THE SILVERY MOON** [6] [62]
Mar 58. (7") **TO BE LOVED. / COME BACK TO ME** [23] [22]
Sep 58. (7") **I'M WANDERIN'. / AS LONG AS I LIVE** [ ] [ ]
Oct 58. (lp) **HE'S SO FINE** [ ] [ ]
– Etc., etc. / To be loved / Come back to me / If I can't have you / As long as I live / Reet petite / It's too bad we had to say goodbye / Why can't you be mine / I'm wanderin' / Right now / Danny boy / He's so fine.
Oct 58. (7") **WE HAVE LOVE. / SINGING A SONG** [ ] [93] Sep 58
Dec 58. (7") **LONELY TEARDROPS. / IN THE BLUE OF EVENING** [ ] [7] Nov 58
May 59. (7") **THAT'S WHY (I LOVE YOU SO). / LOVE IS ALL** [ ] [13] Mar 59
Jul 59. (7") **I'LL BE SATISFIED. / ASK** [ ] [20] Jun 59
Sep 59. (lp) **LONELY TEARDROPS** [ ] [ ]
– Lonely teardrops / Each time (I love you more) / (That's why) I love you so / In the blue of the evening / The joke (is not on me) / Someone to need me / You better know it / By the light of the silvery moon / Singing a song / Love is all We have love / Hush-a-bye.
Oct 59. (7") **YOU BETTER KNOW IT. / NEVER GO AWAY** [ ] [37] Sep 59
Dec 59. (7") **TALK THAT TALK. / ONLY YOU, ONLY ME** [ ] [34] Nov 59
Mar 60. (7") **NIGHT. / DOGGIN' AROUND** [-] [4] [15]
Apr 60. (7") **DOGGIN' AROUND. / THE MAGIC OF LOVE** [ ] [-]
May 60. (lp) **SO MUCH** [ ] [ ]
– I know I'll always be in love with you / Happiness / Only you, only me / The magic of love / Wishing well / Talk that talk / Ask / I'll be satisfied / It's all a part of love / Never go away / Thrill of love.
Sep 60. (7") **(YOU WERE MADE FOR) ALL MY LOVE. / A WOMAN, A LOVER, A FRIEND** [ ] [12] Jul 60 [15] Jul 60
Sep 60. (lp) **JACKIE SINGS THE BLUES** [ ] [ ] Jul 60
– Please tell me why / Doggin' around / New girl in town / Nothin' but the blues / Passin' through / Excuse me for lovin' / She done me wrong / Sazzle dazzle / Please stick around / Come on and love me baby / Comin' to your house / It's been a long time.
Nov 60. (7") **ALONE AT LAST. / AM I THE MAN** [50] [8] [32] Oct 60
Dec 60. (lp) **MY GOLDEN FAVOURITES** (compilation) [ ] [ ]
– Reet petite / To be loved / I'll be satisfied / Only you, only you / Talk that talk / Ask / (That's why) I love you so much / It's all a part of love / Lonely teardrops / I'm wanderin' / You better know it / We have love.
Jan 61. (7") **MY EMPTY ARMS. / THE TEAR OF THE YEAR** [ ] [9]

Feb 61. (7") **THE TEAR OF THE YEAR. / YOUR ONE AND ONLY LOVE** [ ] [44] [-]

Mar 61. (7") **PLEASE TELL ME WHY. / YOUR ONE AND ONLY LOVE** [-] [20]

May 61. (lp) **A WOMAN, A LOVER, A FRIEND** [ ] [40] [ ]
– A woman, a lover, a friend / Your one and only love / You cried / The river / When you add religion to love / One kiss / Night / (You were made for) All my love / Am I the man / Behind a smile is a tear / We kissed / (So many) Cute little girls

May 61. (7") **CUTE LITTLE GIRLS. / PLEASE TELL ME WHY** [ ] [ ]

Jul 61. (7") **I'M COMING ON BACK TO YOU. / LONELY LIFE** [ ] [19] [80] Jun 61

Sep 61. (lp) **YOU AIN'T HEARD NOTHIN' YET** [ ] [ ]
– Toot, toot, tootsie goodbye / Sonny boy / California, here I come / Keep smiling at trouble (trouble's a bubble) / You made me love you (I didn't want to do it) / My Yiddishe momme / Swane / April showers / Anniversary song / Rock-a-bye with a Dixie melody / For me and my gal / In our house.

Sep 61. (7") **YEARS FROM NOW. / YOU DON'T KNOW WHAT IT MEANS** [ ] [37] [79] Aug 61

Nov 61. (7") **THE WAY I AM. / MY HEART BELONGS TO ONLY YOU** [ ] [58] [65] Oct 61

Feb 62. (7") **THE GREATEST HURT. / THERE'LL BE NO NEXT TIME** [ ] [34] [75] Jan 62

Apr 62. (lp) **BY SPECIAL REQUEST** [ ] [ ]
– Cry / My heart belongs to only you / Stormy weather / Tenderly / Lonely life / The way I am / Try a little tenderness / Mood indigo / You belong to my heart / Indian love call / One more time / I'm comin' on back to you

May 62. (7") **I FOUND LOVE ("JACKIE WILSON & LINDA HOPKINS"). / THERE'S NOTHING LIKE LOVE** [ ] [93] Apr 62

May 62. (7") **HEARTS. / SING** [-] [58]

Aug 62. (7") **I JUST CAN'T HELP IT. / THE TALE OF WOE** [ ] [70] Jun 62

Sep 62. (lp) **BODY AND SOUL** [ ] [ ]
– Body and soul / I don't know you anymore / I apologize / I got it bad (and that ain't good) / The greatest hurt / I'll always be in love with you / Crazy she calls me / The tear of the year / Blue Moon / I'll be around / There'll be no next time / We'll be together.

Sep 62. (7") **FOREVER AND A DAY. / BABY, THAT'S ALL** [-] [82]

Jan 63. (7") **WHAT GOOD AM I WITHOUT YOU?. / A GIRL NAMED TAMIKO** [-] [ ]

Feb 63. (lp) **AT THE COPA (live)** [ ] [ ] Nov 62
– Tonight / Medley: Body and soul – I apologize / Love for sale / And this is my beloved / The way I am / I love them all (part 1): What'd I say – Night – That's why (I love you so) / I love them all (part 2): Danny boy – Doggin' around – To be loved – Lonely teardrops / St.James infirmary / A perfect day.

Mar 63. (7") **BABY WORKOUT. / I'M GOING CRAZY (GOTTA GET YOU OFF MY MIND)** [-] [5]

Mar 63. (7") **BABY WORKOUT. / WHAT GOOD AM I WITHOUT YOU** [ ] [-]

Apr 63. (lp) **BABY WORKOUT** [-] [36]
– Shake! shake! shake! / The kictapoo / Yeah! yeah! yeah! / You only live once / Say you will / Baby workout / It's not my fault / Love train / Now that I want her / (I feel like I'm in) Paradise / (So many) Cute little girls / What good am I without you.

Jun 63. (7") **SHAKE A HAND. ("JACKIE WILSON & LINDA HOPKINS") / SAY I DO** [ ] [42] May 63

Aug 63. (7") **SHAKE! SHAKE! SHAKE!. / HE'S A FOOL** [ ] [33] Jul 63

Sep 63. (lp) **SINGS THE WORLD'S GREATEST MELODY** [ ] [ ]
– Forever and a day / Take my heart / Pianissmo / My eager heart / I dream of you / My tale of woe / A girl named Tamiko / All my love / A heart of love / Alone at last / A thing of beauty.

Nov 63. (7") **BABY GET IT (AND DON'T QUIT IT). / THE NEW BREED** [ ] [61] Sep 63

Dec 63. (7") **SILENT NIGHT. / O HOLY NIGHT** [-] [ ]

Jan 64. (7") **I'M TRAVELIN' ON. / HAUNTED HOUSE** [-] [ ]

Mar 64. (7") **CALL HER UP. / THE KICKAPOO** [-] [ ]

Jun 64. (7") **BIG BOSS LINE. / BE MY GIRL** [ ] [94] May 64

Jun 64. (lp) **SHAKE A HAND (w / LINDA HOPKINS)** [-] [ ]
– Swing low sweet cariot / Nobody knows the trouble I've seen / Yes indeed / Joshua fit the battle of Jericho / Old time religion / Shake a hand / He's got the whole world in his hands / When the saints go marching in / Do Lord / Everytime I feel the spirit / Dry bones / Down by the riverside.

Sep 64. (7") **SQUEEZE HER, TEASE HER (BUT LOVE HER). / GIVE ME BACK MY HEART** [ ] [89] Aug 64

Nov 64. (7") **SHE'S ALRIGHT. / WATCH OUT** [-] [ ]

Feb 65. (7") **DANNY BOY. / SOUL TIME** [-] [94]

Mar 65. (lp) **SOMETHIN' ELSE** [-] [ ]
– Big boss line / Groovin' / Deep down love / Take one step / Love (is where you find it) / Give me back my heart / Squeeze her – tease her (but love her) / Be my girl / Baby (I just can't help it) / Rebecca / My best friend's girl / Twistin' and shoutin' (doing the monkey).

May 65. (7") **YES INDEED. / WHEN THE SAINTS GO MARCHING IN ("JACKIE WILSON & LINDA HOPKINS")** [ ] [ ]

Aug 65. (7") **NO PITY (IN THE NAKED CITY). / I'M SO LONELY** [ ] [59] Jun 65

Sep 65. (lp) **SOUL TIME** [-] [ ]
– No pity / Danny boy / An ocean I'll cry / Teardrop avenue / She'll be there / Star dust / A kiss, a thrill and goodbye / Mama of my song / She's all right / Better play it safe / No time out.

Nov 65. (7") **I BELIEVE I'LL LOVE ON. / LONELY TEARDROPS** [ ] [96] Oct 65

Jan 66. (lp) **SPOTLIGHT ON JACKIE WILSON** [ ] [ ]
– Over the rainbow / Pledging my love / Georgia on my mind / Georgia on my mind / You'll never walk alone / Rags to riches / You don't know me / What kind of fool am I / I wanna be around / Until the real thing comes along / I apologize / Lonely teardrops / We have love.

Jan 66. (7") **THINK TWICE. ("JACKIE WILSON & LAVERN BAKER") / PLEASE DON'T HURT ME** [-] [93]

May 66. (7") **TO MAKE A BIG MAN CRY. / BE MY LOVE** [ ] [-]

Jul 66. (lp) **SOUL GALORE** [ ] [ ]
– Brand new thing / 3 days 1 hour 30 minutes / I've got to get back (country boy) / So you say you wanna dance (workout £2) / Stop lying / Let me build / Brand new thing (2) / Soul galore / What's done in the dark / I got my mind made up / Everything's gonna be fine / Your loss, my gain.

Jul 66. (7") **I'VE GOT TO GET BACK (COUNTRY BOY). / 3 DAYS, 1 HOUR, 30 MINUTES** [-] [ ]

Aug 66. (7") **BRAND NEW THING. / SOUL GALORE** [-] [ ]

Sep 66. (7") **I BELIEVE. / BE MY LOVE** [-] [ ]

Nov 66. (7") **WHISPERS (GETTIN' LOUDER). / THE FAIREST OF THEM ALL** [ ] [11] Oct 66

Feb 67. (7") **JUST BE SINCERE. / I DON'T WANT TO LOSE YOU** [-] [91]

Apr 67. (7") **I'VE LOST YOU. / THOSE HEARTACHES** [-] [84] [82]

Jul 67. (lp) **WHISPERS** [ ] [ ] Jan 67
– I don't want to lose you / My heart is calling / Who am I / Whispers (gettin' louder) / The fairest of them all / (Too much) Sweet loving / I can do better / Just be sincere / Only your love can save me / To make a man cry / I've gotta talk to you / Tears will tell it all.

Sep 67. (7") **(YOUR LOVE KEEPS LIFTING ME) HIGHER AND HIGHER. / I'M THE ONE TO DO IT** [ ] [6] Aug 67

Dec 67. (7") **SINCE YOU SHOWED ME HOW TO BE HAPPY. / THE WHO WHO SONG** [ ] [32] Nov 67
(re-iss.Jul69 on 'M.C.A.')

M.C.A. Brunswick

Mar 68. (7") **FOR YOUR PRECIOUS LOVE. / UPTIGHT ("JACKIE WILSON & COUNT BASIE")** [ ] [49] Feb 68

Apr 68. (lp) **HIGHER AND HIGHER** [ ] [ ] Dec 67
– (Your love keeps lifting me) Higher and higher / I don't need you around / I've lost you / Those heartaches / Soulville / Open the door to your heart / I'm the one to do it / You can count on me / I need your loving / Somebody up there likes you / When will our day come.
(cd-iss.May86 on 'Kent') (cd-iss.Nov93 on 'Charly')

Apr 68. (7") **CHAIN GANG. ("JACKIE WILSON & COUNT BASIE") / FUNKY BROADWAY** [-] [84]

Jul 68. (7") **I GET THE SWEETEST FEELING. / NOTHING BUT HEARTACHES** [-] [34]

Sep 68. (lp) **TOO MUCH ("JACKIE WILSON & COUNT BASIE")** [ ] [ ] Jun 68
– Funky Broadway / For your precious love / In the midnight hour / Ode to Bilie Joe / Chain gang / I was made to love her / Uptight (everything's alright) / I never loved a woman (the way I love you) / Respect / Even when you cry / My girl.
(US title 'MANUFACTURERS OF SOUL') *(UK re-iss.Feb74)*

Oct 68. (7") **FOR ONCE IN MY LIFE. / YOU BROUGHT ABOUT A CHANGE IN ME** [-] [70]

Apr 69. (lp) **I GET THE SWEETEST FEELING** [ ] [ ]
– You keep me hangin' on / Once in a lifetime / Who can I turn to (when nobody needs me) / People / Don't go to strangers / I get the sweetest feeling / You brought about the change in me / Nothing but blue skies / A woman needs to be loved / Growin' tall / Since you showed me how to be happy.

Apr 69. (7") **(YOUR LOVE KEEPS LIFTING ME) HIGHER AND HIGHER. / WHISPERS (GETTIN' LOUDER)** [11] [ ]
(re-iss.Aug70)

Jul 69. (7") **SINCE YOU SHOWED ME HOW TO BE HAPPY. / CHAIN GANG** [ ] [-]

Dec 69. (7") **HELPLESS. / DO IT THE RIGHT WAY** [ ] [ ]

Feb 70. (7") **WITH THESE HANDS. / (WHY DON'T YOU) DO YOUR THING** [-] [ ]

Apr 70. (7") **LET THIS BE A LETTER (TO MY BABY). / DIDN'T I** [-] [91]

Jun 70. (lp) **DO YOUR THING** [ ] [ ]
– To change my love / This guy's in love with you / Why don't you do your thing / This better Earth / Helpless / Light my fire / That lucky old Sun (just rolls around Heaven all day) / With these hands / Hold on, I'm coming / Eleanor Rigby.

Dec 70. (7") **(I CAN FEEL THOSE VIBRATIONS) THIS LOVE IS REAL. / LOVE UPRISING** [-] [56]

Apr 71. (7") **SAY YOU WILL. / THIS GUY'S IN LOVE WITH YOU** [-] [ ]

Nov 71. (7") **LOVE IS FUNNY THAT WAY. / TRY IT AGAIN** [-] [95]

Feb 72. (7") **YOU GOT ME WALKING. / THE FOUNTAIN** [-] [93]

Jul 72. (7"m) **I GET THE SWEETEST FEELING. / GALORE / (YOUR LOVE KEEPS LIFTING ME) HIGHER AND HIGHER** [9] [-]

May 73. (7") **YOU GOT ME WALKING. / THE FOUNTAIN** [-] [ ]

Jul 73. (7") **FOREVER AND A DAY. / THE GIRL TURNED ME ON** [-] [ ]

Aug 73. (lp) **YOU GOT ME WALKING** [-] [ ]
– You got me walking / What a lovely day / You left the fire burning / My way / Try it again / Forever and a day / The girl turned me on / Hard to get a thing called love / Love is funny that way / The fountain.

Oct 73. (7") **WHAT A LOVELY DAY. / YOU LEFT THE FIRE BURNING** [-] [ ]

1974. (7") **BEAUTIFUL DAY. / WHAT'CHA GONNA DO ABOUT LOVE** [-] [ ]

1974. (lp)(c) **BEAUTIFUL DAY** [-] [ ]
– Beautiful day / Because of you / Go away / Pretty little angel eyes / Let's love again / It's all over / I get lonely sometimes / This love is mine / Don't you know I love you / What'cha gonna do about me.

1974. (7") **BECAUSE OF YOU. / GO AWAY** [-] [ ]

1974. (7") **NO MORE GOODBYES. / SING A LITTLE SONG** [-] [ ]

1975. (7") **IT'S ALL OVER. / SHAKE A LEG** [-] [ ]

1975. (7") **DON'T BURN NO BRIDGES (w/CHI-LITES) / ('A' instrumental)** [-] [ ]

1975. (7") **NOBODY BUT YOU. / I'VE LEARNED ABOUT LOVE** [-] [ ]

— On the 29th Sep'75, he had a heart attack. He lapsed into a coma and due to brain damage, stayed in same state until his death on 21st Jan'84.

– more compilations, etc. –

Mar 59. Coral Q/ US= Brunswick; (7"ep) **LONELY TEARDROPS** [ ] [ ]
Feb 60. Coral Q/ US= Brunswick; (7"ep) **THE DYNAMIC JACKIE WILSON** [ ] [ ]
– I'll be satisfied / Talk that talk / Never go away / Only you, only me.
1964. Coral Q/ US= Brunswick; (lp) **MY GOLDEN FAVORITES VOL.2** [-] [ ]
May 62. Ember; (7") **TENDERLY. / HARBOUR LIGHTS ("JACKIE WILSON & CLYDE McPHATTER")** [ ] [-]
Note; Below releases on 'Brunswick' until otherwise stated.
Mar 73. (lp)(c) **GREATEST HITS** [ ] [ ]
Mar 73. (7") **WHISPERS (GETTIN' LOUDER). / REET PETITE** [ ] [-]
Apr 75. (7") **I GET THE SWEETEST FEELING. / (YOUR LOVE KEEPS LIFTING ME) HIGHER AND HIGHER** [25] [-]
Aug 75. (lp)(c) **THE VERY BEST OF JACKIE WILSON** [ ] [ ]
– Reet petite / Lonely teardrops / That's why I love you so / Night / You better know it / Talk that talk / To be loved / I'l be satisfied / Whispers (gettin' louder) / Your love keeps lifting me higher and higher / I get the sweetest feeling / Doggin' around / Am I the man / I'm comin' on back to you / A woman a lover a friend / No pity (in the naked city). *(cd-iss.Jun87 on 'Ace' & Jun91 on 'Music Club')*
Nov 75. (7") **DON'T BURN NO BRIDGES. ("JACKIE WILSON & THE CHI-LITES") / ('A'instrumental)** [ ] [ ]
Jul 77. (7") **IT ONLY HAPPENS WHEN I LOOK. / JUST AS SOON AS THE FEELING'S OVER** [ ] [-]
Aug 77. (lp)(c) **NOBODY BUT YOU** [ ] [ ]
1982. Silhouette; (lp) **S.R.O. JACKIE WILSON** [-] [ ]
Sep 83. Skratch; (lp)(c) **THE CLASSIC JACKIE WILSON** [ ] [-]
Mar 85. Skratch; (7"m) **I GET THE SWEETEST FEELING. / WHISPERS (GETTIN' LOUDER) / (YOUR LOVE KEEPS LIFTING ME) HIGHER AND HIGHER** [ ] [-]
(12"+=) – The who who song / Nothin' but blue skies. *(UK re-iss.Feb87, hit No.3)*
Mar 85. Skratch; (7")(12") **REET PETITE. / YOU BROUGHT ABOUT A CHANGE IN ME / I'M THE ONE TO DO IT** [ ] [-]
(UK re-iss.+7"sha-pic-d Nov86 hit No.1)
Jun 87. Skratch; (7")(12") **(YOUR LOVE KEEPS LIFTING ME) HIGHER AND HIGHER. / THE WHO WHO SONG** [15] [-]
Nov 87. Skratch; (7")(12") **BABY WORKOUT. / LONELY TEARDROPS** [ ] [-]
(cd-s+=) – ?
Jan 85. Kent; (lp)(c) **THE SOUL YEARS** [ ] [-]
Apr 85. Kent; (7"m) **I DON'T WANT TO LOSE YOU. / ADAM'S APPLE / DON'T TAKE IT OUT ON THE WORLD** [ ] [-]
May 86. Kent; (lp) **THE SOUL YEARS VOL.2** [ ] [-]
Mar 85. Ace; (lp) **REET PETITE** [ ] [ ]
(cd-iss.May86)
Jan 87. Portrait; (lp)(c)(cd) **15 CLASSIC TRACKS** [ ] [ ]
Oct 87. Rhino; (lp)(c) **THRU THE YEARS** [-] [ ]
Mar 88. King; (lp) **14 GREATEST HITS (by "JACKIE WILSON & BILLY WARD . . . ")** [-] [ ]
May 88. Streetlife; (lp)(c) **GREATEST HITS** [ ] [-]
Oct 88. BR Music; (cd)(c)(lp) **20 GREATEST HITS** [ ] [-]
(re-iss.Apr90)
May 89. Old Gold; (12"m) **I GET THE SWEETEST FEELING. / (YOUR LOVE KEEPS LIFTING ME) HIGHER AND HIGHER / WHISPERS (GETTING LOUDER)** [ ] [-]
Apr 93. Kenwest; (cd) **ORIGINAL HITS** [ ] [-]
Apr 93. Roots; (cd) **THE JACKIE WILSON HIT STORY** [ ] [-]
Apr 93. Roots; (cd) **THE JACKIE WILSON HIT STORY VOLUME 2** [ ] [-]
Nov 93. Charly; (cd) **THE DYNAMIC JACKIE WILSON** [ ] [-]
May 94. Charly; (cd) **TWO ON ONE** (w / SAM COOKE) [ ] [-]
Feb 95. Pickwick; (cd) **A PORTRAIT OF JACKIE WILSON** [ ] [-]
Apr 95. Charly; (cd) **THE CHICAGO YEARS, VOLUME 1** [ ] [-]
Oct 95. Charly; (cd) **THE CHICAGO YEARS, VOLUME 2** [ ] [-]
Nov 95. Charly; (cd) **THE NEW YORK YEARS, VOLUME 1** [ ] [-]

WIN (see under ⇒ FIRE ENGINES)

WINGER

Formed: New York City, USA . . . 1986 by Colorado born pin-up boy KIP WINGER. Initially formed as studio outfit, but after surprise success of debut, they toured in 1989. • **Style:** Formula AOHR (Adult Orientated Hard Rock). • **Songwriters:** KIP & REB, except PURPLE HAZE (Jimi Hendrix). • **Trivia:** Ex-ballet dancer KIP was once the boyfriend of RACHEL HUNTER, who later married ROD STEWART.

Recommended: WINGER (*5)

KIP WINGER – vocals, bass (ex-ALICE COOPER) / **REB BEACH** – guitar (ex-ALICE COOPER) / **PAUL TAYLOR** – keyboards / **ROD MORGANSTEIN** – drums

Atlantic Atlantic

Aug 88. (7") **MADELAINE. / HIGHER AND HIGHER** [-] [ ]
Aug 88. (lp)(c)(cd) **WINGER** [ ] [21]
– Madelaine / Hungry / Seventeen / Without the night / Purple haze / State of emergency / Time to surrender / Poison angel / Hangin' on / Headed for a heartbreak. *(cd+=)*– Higher and higher.
Feb 89. (7")(c-s) **SEVENTEEN. / POISON ANGEL** [-] [26]
May 89. (7")(c-s) **HEADED FOR A HEARTBREAK. / STATE OF EMERGENCY** [-] [19]
Sep 89. (7")(c-s) **HUNGRY. / TIME TO SURRENDER** [-] [85]
Jul 90. (cd)(c)(lp) **IN THE HEART OF THE YOUNG** [ ] [15]
– Can't get enuff / Loosen up / Miles away / Easy come, easy go / Rainbow in the rose / In the day we'll never see / Under one condition / Little dirty blonde / Baptized by fire / You are the saint, I am the sinner / In the heart of the young.
Jul 90. (7") **EASY COME, EASY GO (remix). / YOU ARE THE SAINT, I AM THE SINNER** [ ] [41] Feb 91
(12"+=)(cd-s+=) – Madelaine (live). *(re-iss.Mar91)*
Nov 90. (7") **CAN'T GET ENUFF. / LOOSEN UP** [ ] [42] Jul 90
(12"+=)(cd-s+=) – Time to surrender.
Jan 91. (7")(c-s) **MILES AWAY. / IN THE DAY WE'LL NEVER SEE** [56] [12] Oct 90
(12"+=)(cd-s+=) – All I ever wanted / Seventeen.
Jun 91. (7") **HEADED FOR A HEARTBREAK ('91 version). / LITTLE DIRTY BLONDE** [ ] [ ]
(12"+=)(cd-s+=) – Never.

—— (Dec91) PAUL TAYLOR departed.

May 93. (cd)(c) **PULL** [ ] [83]
– Blind revolution mad / Down incognito / Spell I'm under / In my veins / Junkyard dog / The lucky one / In for the kill / No man's land / Like a ritual / Who's the one. *(re-iss.Feb95)*

WINGS (see under ⇒ McCARTNEY, Paul)

Edgar WINTER

Formed: 28 Dec'46, Beaumont, Texas, USA. Having spent the latter half of the 60's playing in older brother JOHNNY's bands (i.e. BLACK PLAGUE), he went solo in 1969. His debut album 'ENTRANCE', made the US Top 200 lists, but in 1972 after forming WHITE TRASH, he made No.23 with double live album 'ROADWORK'. The following year, he surpassed brother JOHNNY's triumphs, when the THE EDGAR WINTER GROUP peaked at US No.1, with instrumental 45 'FRANKENSTEIN'. • **Style:** Experimental jazz influenced rock'n'roll, that lent on much of his stage aura to that albino EDGAR portrayed. • **Songwriters:** EDGAR penned except; I CAN'T TURN YOU LOOSE (Otis Redding) / TOGETHER album with JOHNNY featured loads of covers. • **Trivia:** A past member of his group DAN HARTMAN, went onto score disco hits such as 'Instant Replay'. In 1989, EDGAR played saxophone on TINA TURNER's hit 'Simply The Best'.

Recommended: ENTRANCE (*7) / THEY ONLY COME OUT AT NIGHT (*7)

EDGAR WINTER – (solo) – keyboards, saxophone, all (ex-JOHNNY WINTER) except guests **JOHNNY WINTER + RANDAL DOLANON** – guitar / **JIMMY GILLEN** – drums / **RAY AVONGE, EARL CHAPIN + BROOKS TILLOTSON** – horns

Epic Epic

Jun 70. (lp) **ENTRANCE** [ ] [ ]
– Entrance / Where have you gone / Rise to fall / Fire and ice / Hung and up / Back in the blues / Re-entrance / Tobacco Road / Jump right out / Peace pipe / A different game / Jimmy's gospel.
Jun 70. (7") **TOBACCO ROAD. / NOW IS THE TIME** [-] [ ]

EDGAR WINTER'S WHITE TRASH

EDGAR with **JERRY LaCROIX** – vox, sax / **JON ROBERT SMITH** – sax, vox / **MIKE McLELLAN** – trumpet, vox / **GEORGE SHECK** – bass / **FLOYD RADFORD** – guitar / **BOBBY RAMIREZ** – drums also **RICK DERRINGER** – guitar

May 71. (7") **WHERE WOULD I BE. / GOOD MORNING MUSIC** [ ] [ ]
Jun 71. (lp) **EDGAR WINTER'S WHITE TRASH** [ ] [ ] Apr 71
– Give it everything you got / Fly away / Where would I be / Let's get it on / I've got news for you / Save the planet / Dying to live / Keep playin' that rock 'n' roll / You were my light / Good morning music. *(cd-iss.Oct93 on 'Sony Europe')*
Nov 71. (7") **KEEP PLAYIN' THAT ROCK'N'ROLL. / DYING TO LIVE** [ ] [70]
May 72. (d-lp) **ROADWORK (live)** [ ] [23] Mar 72
– Save the planet / Jive jive jive / I can't turn you loose / Still alive & well / Back in the U.S.A. / Rock and roll hoochie koo / Tobacco Road / Cool fool / Do yourself a favour / Turn on your lovelight.
Jun 72. (7") **I CAN'T TURN YOU LOOSE. / COOL FOOL** [ ] [81] May 72

—— WHITE TRASH folded when on 24th Jul'72, RAMIREZ was killed in pub brawl.

EDGAR WINTER GROUP

added synthesizer to his new line-up **DAN HARTMAN** – vocals, bass / **RONNIE MONTROSE** – guitar / **CHUCK RUFF** – drums / **+ RICK**

Aug 72. (7") **FREE RIDE. / CATCHIN' UP** [ ] [ ]
Jan 73. (lp)(c) **THEY ONLY COME OUT AT NIGHT** [ ] [3] Nov72
– Hangin' around / When it comes / Alta Mira / Free ride / Frankenstein / Autumn / Round and round / Rock'n'roll boogie woogie blues / We all had a really good time. *(re-iss.quad.Sep84)*
Feb 73. (7") **ROUND AND ROUND. / CATCHIN' UP** [ ] [ ]
Mar 73. (7") **FRANKENSTEIN. / HANGIN' AROUND** [-] [1]
(above 'B' side was original 'A' side, but flipped over after airplay)
May 73. (7") **FRANKENSTEIN. / UNDERCOVER MAN** [18] [-]
Aug 73. (7") **FREE RIDE. / WHEN IT COMES** [ ] [14]
Feb 74. (7") **HANGIN' AROUND. / WE ALL HAD A REAL GOOD TIME** [ ] [65] Dec 73

—— Billed on tour as EDGAR WINTER GROUP Featuring RICK DERRINGER

RICK – guitars, vocals, etc. (ex-JOHNNY WINTER, ex-McCOYS) repl. JERRY WEEMS. In Oct'74, WEEMS had repl. RONNIE who formed own band MONTROSE

Jul 74. (lp)(c) **SHOCK TREATMENT** [ ] [13] May 74
– Some kinda animal / Easy street / Sundown / Miracle of love / Do like me / Rock & roll woman / Someone take my heart away / Queen of my dreams / Maybe someday you'll call my name / River's risin' / Animal.
Jul 74. (7") **RIVER'S RISIN'. / ANIMAL** [ ] [33]
Nov 74. (7") **EASY STREET. / DO LIKE ME** [ ] [83] Oct 74
Feb 75. (7") **SOMEONE TAKE MY HEART AWAY. / MIRACLE OF LOVE** [ ] [ ]

EDGAR WINTER

(solo) with **HARTMAN, RUFF, DERRINGER + J.WINTER**

Blue Sky Blue Sky

Jun 75. (lp)(c) **JASMINE NIGHTDREAMS** [ ] [69]
– One day tomorrow / Little brother / Hello mellow feelin' / Tell me in a whisper / Shuffle-low / Keep on burnin' / How do you like your love / I always wanted you / Outa control / All out / Sky train / Solar strut.

The EDGAR WINTER GROUP WITH RICK DERRINGER

Nov 75. (lp)(c) **THE EDGAR WINTER GROUP WITH RICK DERRINGER** [ ] [ ]
– Cool dance / People music / Good shot / Nothin' good comes easy / Infinite peace in rhythm / Paradise skies / Diamond eyes / Modern love / Let's do it together again / Can't tell one from the other / J.A.P. (Just Another Punk) / Chainsaw.

May 76. (7") **DIAMOND EYES. / INFINITE PEACE IN RHYTHM** [ ] [ ]

— Next as collaboration with brother:

EDGAR & JOHNNY WINTER

JOHNNY WINTER + RICK DERRINGER + FLOYD RADFORD – guitar / **CHUCK RUFF + RICHARD HUGHES** – drums / **RANDY JO HOBBS** – bass (DAN HARTMAN was now solo disco artist)

Jul 76. (lp)(c) **TOGETHER (live)** [ ] [89]
– Harlem shuffle / Soul man / You've lost that lovin' feeling / Rock'n'roll medley:- Slippin' & slidin' – Jailhouse rock – Tutti frutti – Sick & tired – I'm ready – Reelin' and rockin' – Blue sude shoes – Jenny take a ride – Good golly Miss Molly / Let the good times roll / Mercy, mercy / Baby whatcha want me to do. *(cd-iss.Jun93 on 'Sony Europe')*

EDGAR WINTER

1977. (lp)(c) **RECYCLED** [ ] [ ]
– Puttin' it back / Leftover love / Shake it off / Stickin' it out / New wave / Open up / Parallel love / The in and out of love blue / Competition.

EDGAR WINTER GROUP

in 1979 with different line-up **CRAIG SNYDER** – guitar / **JAMES WILLIAMS** – bass / **KEITH BENSON** – drums / **LARRY WASHINGTON** – percussion (same label)

Aug 79. (7") **IT'S YOUR LIFE TO LIVE. / FOREVER IN LOVE** [ ] [ ]

Sep 79. (lp)(c) **THE EDGAR WINTER ALBUM** [ ] [ ]
– It's your life to live / Above and beyond / Take it the way it is / Dying to live / Please don't stop / Make it last / Do what / It took your love to bring me out / Forever in blue.

Mar 80. (7")(12") **ABOVE AND BEYOND. / ('A'instrumental)** [ ] [ ]

— now with **AL FERRANTE** – guitar / **GREG CARTER** – drums / **SCOTT SPRAY** – bass / **RONNIE LAWSON** – keyboards, vocals / **MONIQUE WINTER** – backing vocals

1981. (lp)(c) **STANDING ON ROCK** [ ] [ ]
– Step garbage / Standing on rock / Love is everywhere / Martians / Rock'n'roll revival / In love / Everyday man / Tomorrowland.

— EDGAR retired from solo work for the rest of the 80's.

Thunderb. not issued

Nov 90. (cd) **HARLEM NOCTURNE** [ ] [-]
– Searching / Tingo tango / Cry me a river / Save your love for me / Quiet gas / Satin doll / Jordu / Girl from Ipanema / Harlem nocturne / Come back baby / Before the sunset / Who dunnit / Please come home for Christmas.

Nov 91. (cd) **LIVE IN JAPAN (live with RICK DERRINGER)** [ ] [-]
– Keep playing that rock and roll / Teenage love affair / Free ride / Fly away / Blood from a stone / Undercover man / Jump jump jump / Hang on Sloopy / Against the law / Play guitar / Rock and roll hoochie koo / Frankenstein.

Jan 94. (cd) **I'M NOT A KID ANYMORE** [ ] [ ]
– Way down south / I'm not a kid anymore / Against the law / Brother's keeper / I wanta rock / Crazy / Just like you / Big city woman / Innocent lust / Wild man / Frankenstein.

— In Apr 94; his past keyboard wizard DAN HARTMAN died of a brain tumour.

– compilations, others, etc. –

1975. Epic; (7") **FRANKENSTEIN. / FREE RIDE** [ ] [-]

Jul 91. Elite; (cd)(c) **BROTHERS IN ROCK'N'ROLL (with JOHNNY)** [ ] [ ]
(re-iss. Sep93)

Aug 93. Rhino; (cd) **MISSION EARTH** [ ] [ ]

May 95. Rhino; (cd) **THE COLLECTION** [ ] [-]

Johnny WINTER

Born: JOHN DAWSON WINTER III, 23 Feb'44, Leland, Missouri, USA. After his group JOHNNY & THE JAMMERS released a single 'SCHOOLDAY BLUES' on Texas label 'Dart' in 1959, he moved to Chicago. He also formed own band BLACK PLAGUE with younger brother EDGAR (EDGAR too was born albino; white hair & born with lack of skin pigmentation). Early in 1969, after an article in The Rolling Stone magazine and a flit to New York, he signed to 'Columbia', for a record-breaking 6-figure sum. His first official debut 'JOHNNY WINTER', hit the US Top 30, and with ever increasing concert audiences, he became top live attraction of the early 70's. His full potential was curtailed when he suffered from recurring drug addiction. He issued comeback album in 1973, appropriately titled 'STILL ALIVE AND WELL'. • **Style:** White blues guitar legend, who turned great R&B standards into electrifying classics. • **Songwriters:** J.WINTER or DERRINGER, with mostly covers; JUMPIN' JACK FLASH + SILVER TRAIN + LET IT BLEED + STRAY CAT BLUES + SILVER TRAIN (Rolling Stones) / HIGHWAY 101 (Van Morrison) / IT'S ALL OVER NOW (Bobby & Shirley Womack) / GREAT BALLS OF FIRE + WHOLE LOTTA SHAKIN' GOIN' ON (Jerry Lee Lewis) / LONG TALL SALLY + SLIPPIN' & SLIDIN' (Little Richard) / BONY MORONIE (Larry Williams) / JOHNNY B.GOODE + THIRTY DAYS (Chuck Berry) / ROCK & ROLL PEOPLE (John Lennon) / IT'S MY OWN FAULT (B.B. King) / HIGHWAY 61 REVISITED (Bob Dylan) / SHAME SHAME SHAME (Shirley Ellis) / RAISED ON ROCK (Elmore James) / ROCK ME BABY (Big Bill Broozy-Arthur Crudup) / GOOD MORNING LITTLE SCHOOLGIRL (Don & Bob) / BAREFOOTIN' (Robert Parker) / PLEASE COME HOME FOR CHRISTMAS (Charles Brown) / GOT MY BRAND ON YOU (Muddy Waters) / etc. • **Trivia:** In 1977, he produced MUDDY WATERS' comeback album 'HARD AGAIN' on his 'Blue Sky' label. He also joined WATERS' touring band.

Recommended: SECOND WINTER (*8) / THE COLLECTION (*7)

JOHNNY WINTER – vocals, guitar, mandolin / with **EDGAR WINTER** – keyboards, alto saxophone / **TOMMY SHANNON** – bass, ukelele / **JOHN 'Red' TURNER** – percussion

Liberty Imperial

May 69. (lp) **WINTER, THE PROGRESSIVE BLUES EXPERIMENT** [ ] [49] Apr 69
– Rollin' and tumblin' / Tribute to Muddy / I got love if you want it / Bad luck and trouble / Help me / Mean town blues / Broke down engine / Black cat bones / It's my own fault / Forty-four. *(re-iss.1973 on 'Sunset') (re-iss.Oct79 on 'Liberty') (re-iss.Nov86 on 'Razor') (cd-iss.Sep93 on 'I.T.M.')*

C.B.S. Columbia

Jun 69. (lp) **JOHNNY WINTER** [ ] [24] May 69
– I'm yours and I'm hers / Be careful with a fool / Dallas / Mean mistreater / Leland Mississippi blues / Good morning little schoolgirl / When you got a good friend / I'll drown in my tears / Back door friend. *(re-iss.Jan76) (re-iss.Nov85 on 'Edsel')*

Jul 69. (7") **I'M YOURS AND I'M HERS. / I'LL DROWN IN MY TEARS** [ ] [ ]

Jan 70. (d-lp/3-playing sides) **SECOND WINTER** [59] [55] Nov 69
– Memory pain / I'm not sure / The good love / Slippin' and slidin' / Miss Ann / Johnny B.Goode / Highway 61 revisited / I love everybody / Hustled down in Texas / I hate everybody / Fast life rider. *(re-iss.1974) (re-iss.+cd.Apr89 on 'Edsel')*

Jan 70. (7") **JOHNNY B.GOODE. / I'M NOT SURE** [ ] [92]

— band now **RICK DERRINGER** – guitar, producer repl. EDGAR who went solo / **RANDY JO HOBBS** – bass / **RANDY ZEHRINGER** (RICK's bro) – drums (all ex-McCOYS)

Oct 70. (lp)(c) **JOHNNY WINTER AND** [29] [ ] Sep 70
– Guess I'll go away / Ain't that a kindness / No time to live / Rock and roll hoochie koo / Am I here? / Look up / Prodigal son / On the limb / Let the music play / Nothing left / Funky music. *(re-iss.+cd.Sep91 on 'B.G.O.')*

Nov 70. (7") **ROCK AND ROLL HOOCHIE KOO. / 21st CENTURY MAN** [-] [ ]

— **BOBBY CALDWELL** – drums repl. RANDY

May 71. (lp)(c) **JOHNNY WINTER AND LIVE (live)** [20] [40] Mar 71
– Good morning little schoolgirl / It's my own fault / Jumpin' Jack Flash / Rock'n'roll medley: Great balls of fire – Long tall Sally – Whole lotta shakin' goin' on – Mean town blues – Johnny B.Goode. *(re-iss.1974) (re-iss.+cd.Jan89 on 'B.G.O.')*

May 71. (7") **JUMPIN' JACK FLASH (live). / GOOD MORNING LITTLE SCHOOLGIRL (live)** [ ] [89] Apr 71

— Due to drugs problems, JOHNNY semi-retired. DERRINGER joined EDGAR WINTER Re-united w/DERRINGER in 1973, **RICHARD HUGHES** – drums repl. CALDWELL

Apr 73. (lp)(c) **STILL ALIVE AND WELL** [ ] [22]
– Rock me baby / Can't you feel it / Cheap tequila / All tore down / Rock and roll / Silver train / Ain't nothing to me / Still alive and well / Too much seconal / Let it bleed. *(also on quad.Sep74) (cd-iss.Apr93 on 'Sony Europe')*

Jun 73. (7") **SILVER TRAIN. / ROCK AND ROLL** [ ] [ ]

Sep 73. (7") **CAN YOU FEEL IT. / ROCK AND ROLL** [-] [ ]

Mar 74. (7") **BONY MORONIE. / HURTIN' SO BAD** [-] [ ]

Mar 74. (lp)(c) **SAINTS AND SINNERS** [ ] [42] Feb 74
– Stone County / Blinded by love / Thirty days / Stray cat blues / Bad luck situation / Rollin' cross the country / Riot in cell block £9 / Hurtin' so bad / Bony Moronie / Feedback on Highway 101. *(cd-iss.Apr93 on 'Sony Europe') (re-iss.cd+c Jul94)*

Apr 74. (7") **STONE COUNTY. / BAD LUCK SITUATION** [ ] [ ]

Blue Sky Blue Sky

Nov 74. (7") **MIND OVER MATTER. / PICK UP ON MY MOJO** [ ] [-]

Dec 74. (lp)(c) **JOHN DAWSON WINTER III** [ ] [78]
– Rock & roll people / Golden days of rock & roll / Self-destructable blues / Raised on rock / Stranger / Mind over matter / Roll with me / Love song to me / Pick up on my mojo / Lay down your sorrows / Sweet Papa John. *(cd-iss.Apr93 on 'Sony Europe')*

Dec 74. (7") **RAISED ON ROCK. / PICK UP ON MY MOJO** [-] [ ]

Feb 75. (7") **GOLDEN DAYS OF ROCK & ROLL. / STRANGER** [-] [ ]

— **FLOYD RADFORD** – guitar repl. DERRINGER.

Mar 76. (lp)(c) **CAPTURED LIVE! (live)** [ ] [93]
– Bony Moronie / Roll with me / Rock & roll people / It's all over now / Highway 61 revisited / Sweet Papa John.

— Mid'76, teamed up with brother EDGAR ⇒ on live album TOGETHER. Early 1977, JOHNNY also produced and joined MUDDY WATERS band.

— with **CHARLES CALMESE** – bass / **WILLIE SMITH** – drums / **MUDDY WATERS** – guitar

Aug 77. (lp)(c) **NOTHIN' BUT THE BLUES** [ ] [ ] Jul 77
– Tired of tryin' / TV mama / Everybody's blues / Sweet love and evil woman / Drinkin' blues / Mad blues / It was rainin' / Blondie Mae / Walking thru the park. *(re-iss.+cd.Aug91 on 'B.G.O.')*

— with **BOBBY TORELLO** – drums / **I.P.SWEAT** – bass / **PAT RUSH** – guitar / **+ EDGAR**

Aug 78. (lp)(c) **WHITE, HOT AND BLUE** [ ] [ ]
– Walkin' by myself / Slidin' in / Divin' duck blues / One stop at a time / Nickel

blues / E-Z rider / Last night / Messin' with the kid / Honest I do. *(cd-iss.Jun93 on 'Sony Europe')*

— now with **BOBBY TORTELLO** – drums / **JON PARIS** – bass, etc. /

May 80. (lp)(c) **RAISIN' CAIN** [ ] [ ]
– The crawl / Sitting in this jail house / Like a rolling stone / New York, New York / Talk is cheap / Rollin' and tumblin' / Don't hide your love. *(cd-iss.Apr93 on 'Sony Europe')*

Sonet Alligator

Mar 84. (lp) **WHOOPIN'** [ ] [ ]
– I got my eyes on you / Sonny's whoopin' the doop / Burnt child / Whoee whoee / Crow Jane / So tough with me / Whoo wee baby / I think I got the blues / Ya ya / Roll me baby.

Aug 84. (lp) **GUITAR SLINGER** [ ] [ ]
– It's my life baby / Don't like advantage / Iodine in my coffee / Trick bag / Mad dog / Boothill / I smell trouble / Lights out / My soul / Kiss tomorrow goodbye. *(cd-iss.Oct86)*

Sep 85. (lp) **SERIOUS BUSINESS** [ ] [ ]
– Master mechanic / Sound the bell / Murdering the blues / It ain't your business / Good time woman / Unseen eye / My time after a while / Serious as a heart attack / Give it back / Route 90. *(c+cd-iss.Jun88)*

Oct 86. (lp)(cd) **THIRD DEGREE** [ ] [ ]
– Mojo boogie / Love, life and money / Evil on my mind / See see baby / Tin pan alley / I'm good / Third degree / Shake your moneymaker / Bad girl blues / Broke and lonely.

— now with **JON PARIS** – bass / **TOM COMPTON** – drums

M.C.A. M.C.A.

Nov 88. (lp)(c)(cd) **WINTER OF '88** [ ] [ ]
– Close to me / Stranger blues / Lightning / Anything for your love / Rain / Ain't that just like a woman / Looking for trouble / Look away.

Point Blank Point Blank

Aug 91. (cd)(c)(lp) **LET ME IN** [ ] [ ]
– Illustrated man / Barefootin' / Life is hard / Hey you / Blue mood / Sugarlee / Medicine man / You're humbuggin' me / If you got a good woman / Got to find my baby / Shame shame shame / Let me in.

— with **JEFF GANZ** – bass / **TOM COMPTON** – drums, percussion / guests **EDGAR** – sax / **BILLY BRANCH** – harmonica

1992. (cd)(c) **HEY, WHERE'S YOUR BROTHER?** [ ] [ ]
– Johnny Guitar / She likes to boogie real low / White line blues / Please come home for Christmas / You must have a twin / You keep sayin' that you're leavin' / Hard way / Sick and tired / Blues this bad / no more dogin' / Check out her mama / Got my brand on you.

– compilations, others, etc. –

1969. GRT; (7") **ROADRUNNER. / GANGSTER OF LOVE** [-] [ ]
1971. Marble Arch/ US= GRT; (lp) **THE JOHNNY WINTER STORY** [ ] [ ] Sep 69
1970. Buddah/ US= Columbia; (lp) **FIRST WINTER** [ ] [ ]
1971. Janus; (lp) **ABOUT BLUES** [-] [ ]
1971. Janus; (lp) **EARLY TIMES** [-] [ ]
Feb 81. Blue Sky; (d-lp)(d-c) **THE JOHNNY WINTER STORY – RAISED ON ROCK** [ ] [ ]
Jul 84. President; (lp) **EARLY WINTER** [ ] [-]
(cd-iss.Jan87)
Apr 86. Showcase; (lp)(c) **LIVIN' IN THE BLUES** [ ] [-]
(re-iss.Sep86 on 'Sonet')
Mar 87. Topline; (lp)(c)(cd) **OUT OF SIGHT** [ ] [-]
1988. Castle; (d-lp)(c)(cd) **THE JOHNNY WINTER COLLECTION** [ ] [-]
– Rock and roll hoochie koo / Cheap tequila / On the lamb / Slippin' and slidin' / Johnny B.Goode / Rock me baby / Let it bleed / Stray cat blues / Riot in cell block 9 / Bony Moronie / Highway 61 revisited / Raised on rock / Pick up on my mojo / Thirty days / Good morning little school girl / Jumpin' Jack Flash / It's my own fault / Medley:- Great balls of fire – Long tall Sally – Whole lotta shakin' goin' on.
Jan 89. Relix; (lp) **BIRDS CAN'T ROW BOATS** [ ] [ ]
(cd-iss.Jun93)
Nov 89. Thunderbolt; (lp)(cd) **FIVE AFTER 4 A.M.** [ ] [-]
Apr 90. Thunderbolt; (cd)(c)(lp) **BACK IN BEAUMONT** (w / "UNCLE JOHN TURNER") [ ] [-]
Jul 91. Thunderbolt; (cd)(c) **LIVE IN HOUSTON (live)** [ ] [-]
Nov 93. Thunderbolt; (cd) **WHITE LIGHTNING** [ ] [-]
Nov 92. Fan Club; (cd) **LIVE AT LIBERTY HALL, HOUSTON, TX. 1972 (live with JIMMY REED)** [ ] [ ]
Apr 91. M.M.G.; (cd) **LIVING IN THE BLUES** [ ] [ ]
Aug 92. Sony; (cd)(c) **SEARCHIN' BLUES** [ ] [ ]
Feb 93. Charly; (cd) **THE TEXAS TORNADO** [ ] [-]
Apr 93. Pulsar; (cd) **THE GOLDEN DAYS OF ROCK'N'ROLL** [ ] [-]
Jul 94. Success; (cd)(c) **LIVIN' THE BLUES** [ ] [-]

Steve WINWOOD

Born: 12 May'48, Birmingham, England. At age 15, he joined The SPENCER DAVIS GROUP, where he had 3 massive hits 'KEEP ON RUNNING', 'SOMEBODY HELP ME' & 'GIMME SOME LOVING', between 1963 & April 1967. At this time, he formed TRAFFIC and scored 3 more UK Top 10'ers 'PAPER SUN', 'HOLE IN MY SHOE' & 'HERE WE GO ROUND THE MULBURRY BUSH'. In 1969, WINWOOD joined ERIC CLAPTON, GINGER BAKER and RIC GRECH in the supergroup BLIND FAITH, and although their stay was not long in the rock world, they managed a No.1 on both sides of the Atlantic. Early the next year, he joined GINGER BAKER'S AIRFORCE, but returned to TRAFFIC in 1971 after another 3 years stay (see further on and below). Having re-signed to 'Island' in 1976, his first solo venture was an eponymous effort in 1977. In 1988, he had his first solo No.1, when 'ROLL WITH IT' (the single and the album) peaked. • **Style:** Easy laid-back quality rock artist, whose contribution to music has only been matched by that of CLAPTON. • **Songwriters:** For his debut in 1977, he co-wrote with JIM CAPALDI (an ex-member of TRAFFIC). He collaborated on some further releases with lyricist VIV STANSHALL, WILL JENNINGS and JOE WALSH. • **Trivia:** He was also a renowned session man, having played on albums by JIMI HENDRIX (1968 + 1970) / JOE COCKER (1969) / McDONALD & GILES (1970) / LEON RUSSELL (1970) / HOWLIN' WOLF (1971) / ALVIN LEE (1973) / JOHN MARTYN (1973) / AMAZING BLONDEL (1973) / JADE WARRIOR (1975) / TOOTS & THE MAYTALS (1976) / SANDY DENNY (1977) / VIVIAN STANSHALL (1978) / GEORGE HARRISON (1979) / MARIANNE FAITHFULL (1979) / PIERRE MOERLEN'S GONG (1979) / etc. (see other 'Island' label artists).

Recommended: CHRONICLES (*7) / ROLL WITH IT (*6).

STEVE WINWOOD. Debut solo recording was actually compiled from his past bands' work.

Island Island

Jun 71. (d-lp)(d-c) **WINWOOD** [ ] [93]
– (tracks by SPENCER DAVIS GROUP / TRAFFIC / BLIND FAITH / AIRFORCE)

— Later that year, WINWOOD reformed TRAFFIC and went into numerous session work mainly for 'Island' artists. In 1976, he and ex-SANTANA drummer MIKE SHRIEVE collaborated with solo classical percussionist STOMU YAMASH'TA. As **"GO"**, they issued eponymous live album in Jun76. When WINWOOD was releasing solo albums, GO also issued live 12" CROSSING THE LINE. Another album GO LIVE IN PARIS (live), was given light in Spring'78. (watch soon for STOMU YAMASH'TA discography)

STEVE WINWOOD

STEVE WINWOOD – vocals, keyboards solo with **WILLIE WEEKS** – bass / **ANDY NEWMARK** – drums / **REEBOP KWAKU BANU** – congas

Island Island

Jun 77. (7") **TIME IS RUNNING OUT. / PENULTIMATE ZONE** [ ] [-]
Jul 77. (7") **TIME IS RUNNING OUT. / HOLD ON** [-] [ ]
Jul 77. (lp)(c) **STEVE WINWOOD** [12] [22]
– Hold on / Time is running out / Midland maniac / Vacant chair / Luck's in / Let me make something in your life. *(cd-iss.May87) (cd-iss.Mar93)*

— His next projects/albums featured WINWOOD on all instruments, vocals

Dec 80. (lp)(c) **ARC OF A DIVER** [13] [3]
– While you see a chance / Arc of a diver / Second-hand woman / Slowdown sundown / Spanish dancer / Night train / Dust. *(cd-iss.May87)*
Dec 80. (7")(c-s) **WHILE YOU SEE A CHANCE. / VACANT CHAIR** [45] [7]
Mar 81. (7")(12") **SPANISH DANCER (remix). / HOLD ON** [ ] [ ]
May 81. (7") **ARC OF A DIVER. / DUST** [-] [48]
Sep 81. (7")(12") **NIGHT TRAIN. / ('A'instrumental)** [ ] [ ]
Nov 81. (7") **THERE'S A RIVER. / TWO WAY STRETCH** [ ] [ ]
Jul 82. (7") **STILL IN THE GAME. / DUST** [ ] [47]
Aug 82. (lp)(c) **TALKING BACK TO THE NIGHT** [6] [28] Jul 82
– Valerie / Big girls walk away / And I go / While there's a candle burning / Still in the game / It was happiness / Help me angel / Talking back to the night / There's a river. *(cd-iss.May87)*
Sep 82. (7")(12") **VALERIE. / SLOWDOWN SUNDOWN** [51] [70]
Jun 83. (7") **YOUR SILENCE IS YOUR SONG. / ('A'instrumental)** [ ] [ ]

— Around the mid-80's, his work took a back seat as his marriage broke down. In 1986, he brought in session musicians to augment.

Jun 86. (7") **HIGHER LOVE. / AND I GO** [13] [1]
(extended-12"+=) – ('A'instrumental).
(c-s+=) – Valerie / While you see a chance / Talking back to the night.
Jul 86. (lp)(c)(cd) **BACK IN THE HIGH LIFE** [8] [3]
– Higher love / Take it as it comes / Freedom overspill / Back in the high life again / The finer things / Wake me up on judgement day / Split decision / My love's leavin'.
Aug 86. (7") **FREEDOM OVERSPILL. / HELP ME ANGEL** [-] [20]
Aug 86. (7") **FREEDOM OVERSPILL. / SPANISH DANCER** [69] [-]
(12"+=) – ('A'-liberty mix).
(c-s+=) – (last lp excerpts & interview)
(d7"+=) – Higher love / And I go.
Jan 87. (7") **BACK IN THE HIGH LIFE AGAIN. / HELP ME ANGEL** [53] [13]
(12"+=) – Night train (instrumental). (US; b-side)
Feb 87. (7") **THE FINER THINGS. / NIGHT TRAIN** [-] [8]
Sep 87. (7")(c-s) **VALERIE (remix). / TALKING BACK TO THE NIGHT (instrumental)** [19] [9]
(12"+=)(cd-s+=) – The finer things.
Oct 87. (lp)(c)(cd) **CHRONICLES** (compilation) [12] [26]
– Wake me up on judgement day / While you see a chance / Vacant chair / Help me angel / My love's leavin' / Valerie / Arc of a diver / Higher love / Spanish dancer / Talking back to the night.
Feb 88. (7") **TALKING BACK TO THE NIGHT. / THERE'S A RIVER** [-] [57]

Virgin Virgin

May 88. (7") **ROLL WITH IT. / THE MORNING SIDE** [53] [1]
(c-s+=)/ /(12"+=)(cd-s+=) – ('A'dub version)./ / ('A'&'B'versions).
Jun 88. (lp)(c)(cd) **ROLL WITH IT** [4] [1]
– Roll with it / Holding on / The morning side / Put on your dancing shoes / Don't you know what the night can do? / Hearts on fire / One more morning / Shining song.
Aug 88. (7") **DON'T YOU KNOW WHAT THE NIGHT CAN DO? (remix). / ('A' instrumental)** [ ] [6]
(12"+=)/ /(cd-s++=) – ('A'extended)./ / Roll with it.
Oct 88. (7") **HOLDING ON. / ('A'instrumental)** [ ] [11]
(3"cd-s+=)(12"+=) – ('A'dance version) / Go Juan.
Mar 89. (7") **HEARTS ON FIRE. / ?** [-] [53]
Oct 90. (7") **ONE AND ONLY MAN. / ALWAYS** [ ] [18]
(12"+=)(cd-s+=) – ?
Nov 90. (cd)(c)(lp) **REFUGEES OF THE HEART** [26] [27]
– You'll keep on searching / Every day (oh Lord) / One and only man / I will be here /

Another deal goes down / Running on / Come out and dance / In the light of day.

Apr 91. (7") **I WILL BE HERE. / IN THE LIGHT OF DAY (Instrumental)**
(12"+=)(cd-s+=) – ?

- other compilations, etc. -

Aug 91. Island; (cd)(c)(lp) **KEEP ON RUNNING**

May 65. Fontana; (7") **INCENSE. / YOU'RE FOOLING ME** -
(above as "The ANGELOS")
(re-iss.May69 on 'Island')

WIPERS

Formed: Portland, Oregon, USA . . . 1977 by GREG SAGE, who with band had augmented local wrestler BEAUREGARDE. The WIPERS checked-in and stayed around for some superbly acknowledged lp's during the late 70's & 80's, which became welded into the hearts of many a rock-star to come (i.e. KURT COBAIN, BOB MOULD). Without the success they deserved, they inevitably disbanded leaving SAGE to try for a solo career. With grunge being thee craze of the 90's, SAGE re-formed WIPERS in 1993 and gave us 'SILVER SAIL' single (their first ever!) a year later. • **Style:** Godfathers of grunge, who fused hardcore punk with raw-metal rock. • **Songwriters:** Group penned. • **Trivia:** In May94, a tribute album 'SONGS FOR GREG SAGE & THE WIPERS' was released and it hosted NIRVANA, HOLE, POISON IDEA, etc.

Recommended: IS THIS REAL? (*7)

GREG SAGE – vocals, guitar / **DAVE KOUPAL** – bass / **SAM HENRY** – drums

Psycho | Park Avenue

1981. (lp) **IS THIS REAL?** 1979
– Return of the rat / Mystery / Up front / Let's go let's go away / Is this real? / Tragedy / Alien boy / D-7 / Potential suicide / Don't know what I am / Window shop for love / Wait a minute. *(cd-iss.Mar93 on 'Sub Pop')*

— **BRAD DAVIDSON** – bass + **BRAD NAISH** – drums repl. DAVE (on some) + SAM

Apr 84. (lp) **YOUTH OF AMERICA** Feb82
– Taking too long / Can this be / Pushing the extreme / When it's over / No fair / Youth of America. *(cd-iss.Dec94 on 'Sub Pop')*

not issued | Brain Eater

Nov 84. (lp) **OVER THE EDGE** -
– Over the edge / Doom town / So young / Messenger / Romeo / Now is the time / What is / No one wants an alien / The lonely one / No generation gap / This time. *(re-iss.Mar87 on 'Enigma') (re-iss.+cd Aug94 on 'Gift Of Life')*

Enigma | Enigma

Mar 86. (lp)(cd) **LIVE: WIPERS (live)**
(re-iss.Aug94 on 'Gift Of Life')

— **STEVE PLOUF** – drums repl. NAISH

Nov 86. (lp)(cd) **LAND OF THE LOST**
(re-iss.Aug94 on 'Gift Of Life')

1987. (lp)(cd) **FOLLOW BLIND**
– Follow blind / Someplace else / Any time you find / The chill remains / Let it slide / Against the wall / No doubt about it / Don't belong to you / Losers town / Coming down / Next time. *(re-iss.Aug94 on 'Gift Of Life')*

Dec 88. (lp)(c)(cd) **THE CIRCLE**
– I want a way / Time marches on / All the same / True believer / Good thing / Make or break / The circle / Goodbye again / Be there / Blue & red.

— line-up; **SAGE / DAVIDSON / KOUPAL**

1990. (cd)(c)(m-lp) **YOUTH OF AMERICA**
– Talking too long / Can this be / Pushing the extreme / When it's over / No fair / Youth of America.

T/K | Gift Of Life

Jun 94. (7")(cd-s) **SILVER SAIL. / ?**

Jul 94. (cd)(lp) **SILVER SAIL**

GREG SAGE

Gift Of Life | Gift Of Life

1986. (cd)(lp) **STRAIGHT AHEAD**
– Straight ahead / Soul's tongue / Blue cowboy / Your empathy / The illusion fades / Seems so clear / On the run / Astro clouds / Lost in space / Let it go / World without fear / Keep on keepin' on. *(re-iss.Aug94)*

Road-runner | Road-runner

Oct 91. (cd) **SACRIFICE (FOR LOVE)**

WIRE

Formed: London, England . . . Oct'76 by LEWIS, NEWMAN, GILBERT and GOTOBED. First heard on vinyl in April 1977, when ears were subjected to their punk anthems on Various Artists lp 'LIVE AT THE ROXY'. That lp's label 'Harvest', decided to give them contract, and thus the masterful Mike Thorne produced 'PINK FLAG' album at the end of '77. It contained 21 short sharp shocks of exciting variety (see style). They followed this in 1978 with 2 classic 45's 'I AM THE FLY' & 'DOT DASH', which preceded a gem of an album 'CHAIRS MISSING', which gave them first Top 50 entry. • **Style:** Basic but adventurous punk rock, which later digressed into electronic experimentation in the 80's. They had a non-conformist avant-garde attitude, mixed at times with a sense of future 21st century pop-rock. • **Songwriters:** Group compositions. • **Trivia:** COLIN NEWMAN produced The VIRGIN PRUNES in 1982, and FAD GADGET in 1984. He moved to India at this time, but returned to live in Belgium 1986.

Recommended: PINK FLAG (*8) / CHAIRS MISSING (*9) / 154 (*7) / ON RETURNING (*8) / THE IDEAL COPY (*8). Best solo:- COLIN NEWMAN – NOT TO (*6).

COLIN NEWMAN (b.16 Sep'54, Salisbury, England) – vox, guitar, keyboards / **BRUCE GILBERT** (b.18 May'46, Watford, England) – guitar, vocals, synths. / **GRAHAM LEWIS** (b.22 Feb'53, Grantham, England) – bass, vocals, synthesizers / **ROBERT GOTOBED** (b.MARK FIELD, 1951, Leicester, England) – drums, percussion (ex-SNAKES, ex-ART ATTACKS) / **GEORGE GILL** – guitar (left before debut)

Harvest | Harvest

Nov 77. (7m)(12"m) **MANNEQUIN. / 12XU / FEELING CALLED LOVE** -

Nov 77. (lp)(c) **PINK FLAG**
– Reuters / Field day for the Sundays / Three girl rhumba / Ex-lion tamer / Lowdown / Start to move / Brazil / It's so obvious / Surgeon's girl / Pink flag / The commercial / Straight line / 106 beats that / Mr.Suit / Strange / Fragile / Mannequin / Different to me / Champs / Feeling called love / 1.2.X.U. *(cd-iss.1990+=)* – Options R. *(re-iss.cd Aug94 on 'EMI')*

Feb 78. (7") **I AM THE FLY. / EX-LION TAMER** -

Jun 78. (7") **DOT DASH. / OPTIONS R** -

Sep 78. (lp)(c) **CHAIRS MISSING** 48
– Practise makes perfect / French film blurred / Another the letter / Men 2nd / Marooned / Sand in my joints / Being sucked in again / Heartbeat / Mercy / Outdoor miner / I am the fly / I feel mysterious today / From the nursery / Used to / Too late. *(cd-iss.1990, +=)*– Go ahead / A question of degree / Former airline. *(re-iss.cd Aug94 on 'EMI')*

Jan 79. (7")(7"white) **OUTDOOR MINER. / PRACTISE MAKES PERFECT** 51

Harvest | Warners

Jun 79. (7") **A QUESTION OF DEGREE. / FORMER AIRLINE** -

Sep 79. (lp)(c) **154** 39
– I should have known better / Two people in a room / The 15th / The other window / Single k.o. / A touching display / On returning / A mutual friend / Blessed state / Once is enough / Map reference 41°N, 93°W / Indirect enquiries / 40 versions. *(free-7"ep w.a)* **SONG 1** – Get down (parts 1 & 2) / Small electric piece / Let's panic later. *(cd-iss.1990 +=)* – SONG 1 (The free ep was issued on 'Dome' records) *(re-iss.cd Aug94 on 'EMI')*

Oct 79. (7") **MAP REFERENCE 41°N, 93°W. / GO AHEAD** -

— In 1980, WIRE also diversed into own activities; GILBERT & LEWIS became CUPOL and DOME, etc. The pair also joined THE THE. COLIN NEWMAN went solo taking ROBERT GOTOBED with him. The latter also became member of FAD GADGET. (see further on for these activities)

Rough Trade | not issued

May 81. (7") **OUR SWIMMER. / MIDNIGHT BAHNHOF CAFE** -

Jul 81. (lp)(c) **DOCUMENT AND EYEWITNESS: ELECTRIC BALLROOM (live)** -
– 5 10 / 12XU (fragment) / Underwater experiences / Zegk hoqp / Everything's going to be nice / Instrumental (thrown bottle) / Piano tuner (keep strumming those guitars) / And then . . . / We meet under tables / Revealing trade secrets / Eels sang lino / Eastern standard / Coda. (free 12"m-lp) **DOCUMENT AND EYEWITNESS: NOTRE DAME HALL (live) –** Underwater experiences / Go ahead / Ally in exile / Relationship / Our swimmer / Witness to the fact / 2 people in a room / Heartbeat. *(re-iss.+c.1984) (cd-iss.1991 on 'Mute')*

Mar 83. (12"m) **CRAZY ABOUT LOVE. / CATAPULT 30 / SECOND LENGTH (OUR SWIMMER)** -

— WIRE were now back to full-time membership.

Mute | Enigma

Nov 86. (12"ep) **SNAKEDRILL** -
– A serious of snakes / Advantage in height / Up to the Sun / Drill.

Mar 87. (7") **AHEAD. / FEED ME (live)** -
(12"+=) – Ambulance chasers (live) / Vivid riot of red (live).

Apr 87. (lp)(c)(cd) **THE IDEAL COPY** 87
– Points of collapse / Ahead / Madman's honey / Feed me / Ambitious / Cheeking tongues / Still shows / Over theirs. *(cd+=)* – Ahead II / SNAKEDRILL EP tracks.

Mar 88. (7") **KIDNEY BONGOS. / PIETA**
(3"cd-s+=)/ /(12"++=) – Drill (live)./ / Over theirs (live).

May 88. (lp)(c)(cd) **A BELL IS A CUP . . . UNTIL IT IS STRUCK**
– Silk skin paws / The finest drops / The queen of Ur and the king of Um / Free falling divisions / It's a boy / Boiling boy / Kidney bongos / Come back in two halves / Follow the locust / A public place. *(cd+=)*– The queen of Ur and the king of Um (alt.take) / Pieta / Over theirs (live) / Drill (live).

Jun 88. (7") **SILK SKIN PAWS. / GERMAN SHEPHERDS**
(12"+=) – Ambitious (remix).
(3"cd-s+=) – Come back in two halves.

Apr 89. (7"clear) **EARDRUM BUZZ. / THE OFFER** 68
(12"+=) – It's a boy (instrumental).
(cd-s) – ('A'side) / Silk skin paws / A serious of snakes / Ahead (extended).
(live-12") BUZZ BUZZ BUZZ – Eardrum buzz / Ahead / Kidney bongos.

Mute | Mute

May 89. (lp)(c)(cd) **IT'S BEGINNING TO AND BACK AGAIN (live)**
– Finest drops / Eardrum buzz / German shepherds / Public place / It's a boy / Illuminated / Boiling boy / Over theirs / Eardrum buzz (12"version) / The offer / In vivo.

Jul 89. (7") **IN VIVO. / ILLUMINATED**
(12"+=)(cd-s+=) – Finest drops (live).

May 90. (7") **LIFE IN THE MANSCAPE. / GRAVITY WORSHIP**
(12"+=)(cd-s+=) – Who has wine.

May 90. (cd)(c)(lp) **MANSCAPE**
– Patterns of behaviour / Goodbye ploy / Morning bell / Small black reptile / Torch it / Other moments / Sixth sense / What do you see? / Where's the deputation? / You hung your lights in the trees – A craftman's touch. *(US cd+=)*– Life in the manscape / Stampede / Children of groceries.

Apr 91. (cd)(c)(lp) **DRILL**
– (7 versions of out-takes from last album)

WIR

Slightly different name when GOTOBED left.

Sep 91. (7") **SO AND SLOW IT GOES. / NICE FROM HERE**
(12") – ('A'side) / ('A'-Orb mix) / Take it (for greedy)
(cd-s+=) – (all 4 tracks).

Oct 91. (cd)(c)(lp) **THE FIRST LETTER**
– Take it (for greedy) / So and slow it goes (extended) / A bargain at 3 and 20 yeah! / Rootsi-rootsy / Ticking mouth / It continues / Looking at me (stop!) / Naked, whooping and such-like / Tailor made / No cows on the ice / A big glue canal.

– compilations, others, etc. –

Mar 86. Pink – Rough Trade; (m-lp) **PLAY POP** | | -
Aug 86. Dojo; (lp) **IN THE PINK (live)** | | -
Nov 87. Strange Fruit; (12"ep) **THE PEEL SESSIONS** (18.1.78) | | -
– I am the fly / Culture vultures / Practise makes perfect / 106 beats that.
Feb 90. Strange Fruit; (cd)(c)(lp) **DOUBLE PEEL SESSIONS** | | -
Jul 89. Harvest; (lp)(c)(cd) **ON RETURNING (1977-1979)** | | -
– 1.2.X.U. / It's so obvious / Mr Suit / Three girl rhumba / Ex lion tamer / Lowdown / Strange / Reuters / Feeling called love / I am the fly / Practise makes perfect / French film blurred / I feel mysterious today / Marooned / Sand in my joints / Outdoor miner / A question of degree / I should have known better / The other window / 40 versions / A touching display / On returning. *(cd+=)–* Straight line / 106 beats that / Field day for the Sundays / Champs / Dot dash / Another the letter / Men 2nd / Two people in a room / Blessed state.
Sep 94. Materili Sonori; (cd; w/book) **EXPLODING VIEWS** | | -
May 95. EMI; (cd) **BEHIND THE CURTAIN** | | -
Dec 95. Touch; (12"w/ HAFLER TRIO) **THE FIRST LETTER. /** | | -

COLIN NEWMAN

(solo playing most instruments) **with ROBERT GOTOBED** – drums / **DESMOND SIMMONDS** – bass, guitar / **BRUCE GILBERT** – guitar / **MIKE THORNE** – keyboards

Beggar's B. | not issued

Oct 80. (lp) **A-Z** | | -
– I waited for ages / And jury / Alone / Order for order / Image / Life on deck / Troisieme / S-S-S-Star eyes / Seconds to last / Inventory / But no / B. *(re-iss.+c+cd.Sep88 on 'Lowdown-Beggar's Banquet')*
Nov 80. (7"m) **B. / CLASSIC REMAINS / ALONE ON PIANO** | | -
Mar 81. (7") **INVENTORY. / THIS PICTURE** | | -

— **COLIN** played everything.

4.a.d. | not issued

Aug 81. (lp) **PROVISIONALLY TITLED THE SINGING FISH** | | -
– Fish 1 / Fish 2 / Fish 3 / Fish 4 / Fish 5 / Fish 6 / Fish 7 / Fish 8 / Fish 9 / Fish 10. *(see next album for cd! release)*

— added **DES SIMMONDS + SIMON GILHAM** – bass, vocals

Jan 82. (lp) **NOT TO** | | -
– Lorries / Don't bring reminders / You me and happy / We meet under tables / Safe / Truculent yet / 5'10 / 1, 2, 3, beep beep / Not to / Indians / Remove for improvement / Blue Jay way. *(cd-issJan88 +=)* – PROVISIONALLY TITLED lp tracks / Not to / You and your dog / The grace you know / H.C.T.F.R. / No doubt.
May 82. (7") **WE MEANS WE STARTS. / NOT TO (remix)** | | -

Crammed Discs | not issued

Sep 86. (lp) **COMMERCIAL SUICIDE** | | - BELG.
– Their terrain / 2-sixes / Metakest / But I . . . / Commercial suicide / I'm still here / Feigned hearing / Can I explain the delay / I can hear you . . .
Oct 86. (7") **FEIGNED HEARING. / I CAN'T HEAR YOU . . .** | | -
Aug 87. (12") **INTERVIEW. / INTERVIEW** | | -
May 88. (12") **BETTER LATE THAN NEVER. / AT LAST** | | -
May 88. (lp)(c)(cd) **IT SEEMS** | | -
– Quite unrehearsed / Can't help being / The rite of life / An impressive beginning / It seems / Better late than never / Not being in Warsaw / At rest / Convolutions / Round and round. *(w/ free label 'Various Artists' lp)*

Swim | not issued

May 95. (12") **VOICE. /** | | -

CUPOL

GILBERT & LEWIS under many guises (not initially chronological)

4.a.d. | not issued

Jul 80. (12"ep) **LIKE THIS FOR AGES. / KLUBA CUPOL** | | -
(20min@'33rpm)

GILBERT & LEWIS

4 a.d. | not issued

Nov 80. (m-lp) **3R4** | | -
– Barge calm / 3,4 / Barge calm / R.
Aug 81. (7") **ENDS WITH THE SEA. / HUNG UP TO DRY WHILE BUILDING AN ARCH** | | -

— In May88, a cd-compilation '8 TIME' was issued by duo on '4 a.d.'.

DOME

Dome | not issued

Aug 80. (lp) **DOME 1** | | -
– Cancel your order / Cruel when complete / And then . . . / Here we go / Rolling upon my day / Say again / Lina sixup / Airmail / Ampnoise / Madmen. (free-7") – SO. / DROP
Feb 81. (lp) **DOME 2** | | -
– The red tent 1 + 2 / Long lost life / Breathless / Reading Prof. B / Ritual view / Twist up / Keep it.
Oct 81. (lp) **DOME 3** | | -
– Jasz / Ar-gu / An-an-an-d-d-d / Ba-dr / D-o-bo / Na-drm / Dasz / Ur-ur / Danse / Roor-an.

(above with also **RUSSELL MILLS** – percussion / **DANIEL MILLER** – saxophone / **E.C.RADCLIFFE** – guitar / **PETER PRINCE** – drums)
(Early in the 90's, 1 & 2 and 3 & 4 were re-issued on 2 cd's for 'Grey Area-Mute')

Apr 83. (lp) **TO SPEAK ("BRUCE GILBERT")** | | -
– To speak / To walk, to run / To duck, to dive / This / Seven year / Atlas. *(iss.Sep84 as 'WILL YOU SPEAK THIS WORD' on 'Uniton'?)*

GILBERT, LEWIS & MILLS

Cherry Red | not issued

May 82. (lp) **MZUI (WATERLOO GALLERY)** | | -
– Mzui (part 1) / Mzui (part 2).

W.M.O. | not issued

Dec 95. (cd) **PACIFIC / SPECIFIC** | | -

P'O

Court | not issued

Jan 83. (lp) **WHILST CLIMBING THIEVES VIE FOR ATTENTION** | | -

DUET EMMO

augmented by **DANIEL MILLER** (label boss)

Mute | not issued

Aug 83. (7") **OR SO IT SEEMS. / HEART OF HEARTS (OR SO IT SEEMS)** | | -
Aug 83. (lp) **OR SO IT SEEMS** | | -
– Hill of men / Or so it seems / Friano / The first person / A.N.C. / Long sledge / Gatemmo / Last's card / Heart of hearts. *(cd-iss.Aug92 on Grey Area-Mute)*

BRUCE GILBERT

Mute | not issued

Sep 84. (lp) **THIS WAY** | | -
– Work for do you me / I did / Here visit. *(see next lp for cd-iss.)*
Mar 87. (lp)(cd) **THE SHIVERING MAN** | | -
– Angel food / The shivering man / Not in the feather / There are / Hommage / Eline Court li / Epitaph for Henran Brenlar. *(cd-iss.+=THIS WAY lp tracks)*
Jan 91. (cd)(lp) **INSIDING (excerpts from 'SAVAGE WATER')** | | -
– Side 1 / Side 2 / Bloodlines (ballet).
Aug 91. (cd)(lp) **MUSIC FOR FRUIT** | | -
– Music for fruit / Push / You might be called.

Sub Pop | Sub Pop

Oct 95. (7") **BI YO YO. /** | |

HE SAID

(aka **GRAHAM LEWIS** solo) augmented by **JOHN FRYER** – drum prog.

Mute | not issued

Oct 85. (7") **ONLY ONE I. / ONLY ONE I** | | -
Apr 86. (7") **PUMP. / PUMP (instrumental)** | | -
(12"+=) – To and fro.
Aug 86. (7") **PULLING 3 G's. / PALE FEET** | | -
(12"+=) – ('A'&'B'extended versions).

— added **BRUCE GILBERT** – guitar / **NIGEL H.KIND** – guitar / **E.C.RADCLIFFE** – prog. / **ANGELA CONWAY** – backing vocals / **ENO** (guested on 1)

Oct 86. (lp)(c)(cd) **HAIL** | | -
– Kidnap yourself / Only one I / Pump / I fall in your arms / Do you mean that? / Flagwearing / Shades to escape / Pale feet.
Nov 88. (7")(12") **COULD YOU?. / HE SAID . . . SHE SAID** | | -
Feb 89. (lp)(c)(cd) **TAKE CARE** | | -
– Could you? / ABC Dicks love / Watch-take-care / Tongue ties / Not a soul / Halfway house / Get out of that rain / Hole in the sky.

WISHBONE ASH

Formed: Torquay, Devon, England . . . summer 1969 out of the EMPTY VESSELS by MARTIN TURNER and STEVE UPTON. They quickly moved to London with other two; POWELL and TED TURNER (no relation). In 1970, they signed to 'MCA' and delivered eponymous debut into UK Top 40. Throughout the early 70's, they accrued large following peaking in 1972 when ARGUS hit Top 3. By 1974, they had crossed the Atlantic to reside and record 1974 album THERE'S THE RUB. A spate of bad luck on tour made it hard for their future albums to substantiate US breakthrough. • **Style:** Due to twin-lead guitar sound, they were described as Britain's answer to ALLMAN BROTHERS, but with mystical lyrical element. Fused heavy-rock with fine harmonies and self-indulgent solos. This sound drifted into a more countrified sound by the mid 70's. Lack of identity and introvert stage presence was cited as an excuse for decreasing sales at this time. • **Songwriters:** Group compositions / TURNERS?. • **Trivia:** The 1984 instrumental track F*U*B*B stands for 'Fucked Up Beyond Belief'. TOM DOWD produced 1976 album LOCKED IN.

Recommended: CLASSIC ASH (*8) / ARGUS (*9) / LIVE DATES (*9)

MARTIN TURNER (b. 1 Oct'47) – vocals, bass / **ANDY POWELL** (b. 8 Feb'50) – guitar, vocals repl. GLEN TURNER (no relation) / **TED TURNER** (b.DAVID, 2 Aug'50) – guitar, vocals (ex-KING BISCUIT) / **STEVE UPTON** (b.24 May'46, Wrexham, Wales) – drums

M.C.A. | Decca

Dec 70. (lp)(c) **WISHBONE ASH** | 34 |
– Blind eye / Lady Whiskey / Error of my ways / Queen of torture / Handy / Phoenix.

(cd-iss. Jul 91) (re-iss. Feb 74+1980) (cd-iss.Dec94 on 'B.G.O.')

Jan 71. (7") **BLIND EYE. / QUEEN OF TORTURE**

Sep 71. (lp)(c) **PILGRIMAGE** 14

– Vas dis / The pilgrim / Jail bait / Alone / Lullaby / Valediction / Where were you tomorrow. *(re-iss. Feb 74) (re-iss.1983 on 'Fame') (cd-iss.Jul 91+=)–* Baby what you want me to do / Jail bait (live).

Oct 71. (7") **JAIL BAIT. / VAS DIS** -

May 72. (lp)(c) **ARGUS** 3

– Time was / Sometime world / Blowin' free / The king will come / Leaf and stream / Warrior / Throw down the sword. *(re-iss. Feb 74 + Feb 84) (re-iss.1987 on 'Castle')*

Jun 72. (7") **BLOWIN' FREE. / NO EASY ROAD**

M.C.A. M.C.A.

May 73. (lp)(c) **WISHBONE FOUR** 12 44

– So many things to say / Ballad of the beacon / No easy road / Everybody needs a friend / Doctor / Sorrel / Sing out the song / Rock'n'roll widow. *(re-iss. Feb 74)*

Jul 73. (7") **ROCK'N'ROLL WIDOW. / NO EASY ROAD** -

Jul 73. (7") **SO MANY THINGS TO SAY. / ROCK'N'ROLL WIDOW** -

Dec 73. (d-lp)(c) **LIVE DATES (live)** 82 Nov 73

– The king will come / Warrior / Throw down the sword / Rock'n'roll widow / Ballad of the beacon / Baby what you want me to do / The pilgrim / Blowin' free / Jail bait / Lady Whiskey / Phoenix.

—— (Jun74) **LAURIE WISEFIELD** – guitar (ex-HOME) repl. TED who found religion

Nov 74. (7") **HOMETOWN. / PERSEPHONE** -

Nov 74. (lp)(c) **THERE'S THE RUB** 16 88

– Silver shoes / Don't come back / Persephone / Hometown / Lady Jay / F*U*B*B.

Feb 75. (7") **SILVER SHOES. / PERSEPHONE**

—— added on session **PETER WOODS** – keyboards

M.C.A. Atlantic

Mar 76. (lp)(c) **LOCKED IN** 36

– Rest in peace / No water in the well / Moonshine / She was my best friend / It started in Heaven / Half past lovin' / Trust in you / Say goodbye.

Nov 76. (lp)(c) **NEW ENGLAND** 22

– Mother of pearl / (In all of my dreams) You rescue me / Runaway / Lorelei / Outward bound / Prelude / When you know love / Lonely island / Candle-light. *(re-iss.Jul82)*

Nov 76. (7") **OUTWARD BOUND. / LORELEI**

M.C.A. M.C.A.

Sep 77. (7") **FRONT PAGE NEWS. / DIAMOND JACK** -

Oct 77. (lp)(c) **FRONT PAGE NEWS** 31

– Front page news / Midnight dancer / Goodbye baby hello friend / Surface to air / 714 / Come in from the rain / Right or wrong / Heart beat / The day I found your love / Diamond Jack.

Oct 77. (7") **FRONT PAGE NEWS. / GOODBYE BABY HELLO FRIEND** -

Nov 77. (7") **GOODBYE BABY HELLO FRIEND. / COME IN FROM THE RAIN** -

Sep 78. (7")(12") **YOU SEE RED. / BAD WEATHER BLUES** (live)

Oct 78. (lp)(c) **NO SMOKE WITHOUT FIRE** 43

– You see red / Baby, the angels are here / Ships in the sky / Stand and deliver / Anger in harmony / Like a child / The way of the world / A stormy weather. (free live 7"w.a.) **LORELEI. / COME IN FROM THE RAIN**

Aug 79. (7") **COME ON. / FAST JOHNNY**

Jan 80. (7") **HELPLESS. / INSOMNIA** -

Jan 80. (7") **LIVING PROOF. / JAIL BAIT (live)**

Jan 80. (lp)(c) **JUST TESTING** 41

– Living proof / Haunting me / Insomnia / Helpless / Pay the price / New rising star / Masters of disguise / Lifeline.

Apr 80. (7")(12") **HELPLESS** (live). / **BLOWIN' FREE** (live)

Oct 80. (lp)(c) **LIVE DATES II (live)** 40

– Doctor / Living proof / Runaway / Helpless / F*U*B*B / The way of the world. *(ltd. w/free live lp) (re-iss.Jun84)*

—— **JOHN WETTON** – bass, vocals (ex-URIAH HEEP, ex-FAMILY, ex-KING CRIMSON) repl. MARTIN TURNER to production. / Added **CLAIRE HAMILL** – vocals (solo artist)

Mar 81. (7") **UNDERGROUND. / MY MIND IS MADE UP** -

Apr 81. (lp)(c) **NUMBER THE BRAVE** 61

– Loaded / Where is the love / Underground / Kicks on the street / Open road / Get ready / Rainstorm / That's that / Rollercoaster / Number the brave.

May 81. (7") **GET READY. / KICKS ON THE STREET** -

May 81. (7") **GET READY. / LOADED** -

—— **UPTON, POWELL + WISEFIELD** recruited new member **TREVOR BOLDER** – bass (ex-SPIDERS FROM MARS / Bowie, ex-URIAH HEEP, etc. repl. WETTON to ASIA, etc.

A.V.M. Fantasy

Oct 82. (7") **ENGINE OVERHEAT. / GENEVIEVE** -

Nov 82. (lp)(c) **TWIN BARRELS BURNING** 22

– Engine overheat / Can't fight love / Genevieve / Me and my guitar / Hold on / Streets of shame / No more lonely nights / Angels have mercy / Wind up. *(cd-iss. Aug 93)*

Dec 82. (7") **NO MORE LONELY NIGHTS. / STREETS OF SHAME** -

—— **MERVYN 'Spam' SPENCER** – bass (ex-TRAPEZE) repl. BOLDER to URIAH HEEP

Neat not issued

Jan 85. (lp)(c) **RAW TO THE BONE**

– Cell of fame / People in motion / Don't cry / Love is blue / Long live the night / Rocket in my pocket / It's only love / Don't you mess / Dreams (searching for an answer) / Perfect timing. *(re-iss. Aug 93)*

—— **ANDY PYLE** – bass (ex-SAVOY BROWN, ex-BLODWYN PIG) repl. SPENCE

—— Originals (**ANDREW, STEVE, MARTIN & TED**) reformed WISHBONE ASH.

I.R.S. I.R.S.

Feb 88. (lp)(c)(cd) **NOUVEAU CALLS** (instrumental)

– Tangible evidence / Closseau / Flags of convenience / From Soho to Sunset / Arabesque / In the skin / Something's happening in Room 602 / Johnny left home without it / The spirit flies free / A rose is a rose / Real guitars have wings. *(re-iss. 1990)*

May 88. (7") **IN THE SKIN. / TANGIBLE EVIDENCE**

—— In Apr89, TED & ANDY guested on their labels' Various Artists live cd,c,d-lp, video 'NIGHT OF THE GUITAR'.

Jun 89. (7") **COSMIC JAZZ. / T-BONE SHUFFLE**

(12"+=) – Bolan's monument.

Aug 89. (lp)(c)(cd) **HERE TO HEAR**

– Cosmic jazz / Keeper of the light / Mental radio / Walk on water / Witness on wonder / Lost cause in Paradise / Why don't we / In the case / Hole in my heart (part 1 & 2).

—— **RAY WESTON** – drums repl. MARTIN

May 91. (cd)(c)(lp) **STRANGE AFFAIR**

– Strange affair / Wings of desire / Dream train / You / Hard times / Standing in the rain / Renegade / Say you will / Rollin' / Some conversion.

—— **POWELL + TED TURNER + RAY** bring in **ANDY PYLE** – bass / **DAN C.GILLOGLY** – keyboards

Permanent Griffin

Mar 92. (cd)(c)(lp) **THE ASH LIVE IN CHICAGO (live)** 1994

– compilations, others, etc. –

Apr 77. MCA; (7"ep) **PHOENIX. / BLOWIN' FREE / JAIL BAIT** -

May 77. MCA; (lp)(c) **CLASSIC ASH**

– Blind eye / Phoenix / The pilgrim / Blowin' free / The king will come / Rock'n'roll widow / Persephone / Outward bound / Throw down the sword (live). *(re-iss.Aug81) (re-iss.Jan83 on 'Fame')*

Jan 82. MCA; (lp)(c) **HOT ASH** -

Jun 82. MCA; (lp)(c) **THE BEST OF WISHBONE ASH**

Apr 82. MCA; (d-c) **PILGRIMAGE /ARGUS**

1993. MCA; (d-cd) **TIME WAS (w/ remixed 'ARGUS')** -

Apr 79. Flyover; (lp) **LIVE IN JAPAN, NOVEMBER '78 (live)** -

Oct 91. Windsong; (lp) **LIVE IN CONCERT (live)** -

Mar 94. Nectar; (cd)(c) **BLOWIN' FREE – THE VERY BEST OF WISHBONE ASH** -

Sep 94. MCA; (cd)(c) **THERE'S THE RUB / LOCKED IN**

Nov 94. Start; (cd) **IN CONCERT** -

WIZZARD (see under ⇒ MOVE)

Jah WOBBLE

Born: JOHN WORDLE. Became bassman for PUBLIC IMAGE LTD, until his sudden departure in 1980. He already went solo and had made a solo appearance, as well as 2 collaborations (see below). In 1994 after brief commercial success 2 years previous, JAH and his ever increasing INVADERS OF THE HEART scored a UK Top 20 album, which was followed by a rapturous appearance at Glastonbury Festival. • **Songwriters:** WOBBLE and /with collaborators. • **Style:** Eastern influenced quality bassman. • **Trivia:** In 1992 he appeared on 12"'ers by ONE DOVE and SECRET KNOWLEDGE FEATURING WONDER. Guested on albums by ORB, PRIMAL SCREAM, SINEAD O'CONNOR, JOOLZ, HOLGER CZUKAY, DODGY, SHAMEN, GINGER BAKER + IAN McNABB.

Recommended: INVADERS OF THE HEART (*6) / RISING ABOVE BEDLAM (*8) / TAKE ME TO GOD (*9)

JAH WOBBLE – bass, vocals

Virgin not issued

Oct 78. (12"ep) **DREADLOCK DON'T DEAL IN WEDLOCK. / PHILITUS PUBIS** -

Feb 79. (7"by; DON LETTS & JAH WOBBLE) **STEEL LEG: STRATETIME & THE WIDE MAN. / ELECTRIC DREAD: HAILE UNLIKELY** -

Oct 79. (12"by; DAN McARTHUR) **DAN McARTHUR** -

—— added **MARTIN ATKINS** – drums / **SNOWY WHITE** – vocals

Apr 80. (7")(12") **BETRAYAL OF MR.X. / THE BATTLE OF BRITAIN** -

May 80. (lp) **THE LEGEND LIVES ON . . .** -

– Betrayal / Beat the drum for me / Blueberry Hill / Today is the first day of the ? / Not another / Tales from Outer Space / Dan McArthur / Pineapple. *(cd-iss.Mar94 on 'Vinyl Vault')*

Jul 80. (12"ep) **V.I.E.P.** -

– Blueberry Hill / etc.

Island not issued

Jul 81. (12"ep by; JAH WOBBLE, JAKI LIEBEZEIT & HOLGER CZUKAY) **HOW MUCH ARE THEY? / WHERE'S THE MONEY? / TRENCH WARFARE / TWILIGHT WORLD** -

(re-iss.1988 on 'Licensed')

Virgin not issued

1982. (lp) **FULL CIRCLE** -

– (tracks as above plus; Full circle R.P.S. (No.7) / Mystery R.P.S. (No.8).

Jah Wobble not issued

May 82. (7") **FADING. / NOCTURNAL** -

Oct 82. (12" by; JAH WOBBLE with ANIMAL) **LONG LONG AWAY. / ROMANY** -

In 1982, formed BARTOK with RAT SCABIES – drums (ex-DAMNED) / SIMON WERBER + JOHN GRANT (both ex-STRAPS). Released 7" on 'On-U-Sound' in Oct82; INSANITY. / I AM THE BOMB.

—— Next with **ANIMAL** – guitar (of MOTORHEAD) / **OLLIE MARLAND** – keyboards / **ANNIE WHITEHEAD** – trombone

Lago not issued

May 83. (m-lp) **JAH WOBBLE'S BEDROOM ALBUM** – INVADERS OF THE HEART -

– City / Fading / Long long way / Sense of history / Hill in Korea / Journey to death / Invaders of the heart / Sunshine / Concentration camp / Desert song / Heart of the jungle.

1983. (12") **INVADERS OF THE HEART. / ?** [ ] [-]

— next w / **THE EDGE** – guitar (of U2) / **HOLGER CZUKAY** – percussion, etc (ex-CAN) / **LIEBEZEIT** – (ex-CAN) / **BEN MENDELSON** – (ex-MAGAZINE) / **OLLIE MARLAND** – keyboards / **JIM WALKER** – drums (ex-PUBLIC IMAGE LTD) / **FRANCOIS KEVORKIAN** – electric drums

Island Island

Oct 83. (m-lp by; JAH WOBBLE, The EDGE & HOLGER CZUKAY) **SNAKE CHARMER** [ ] [-]
– Snake charmer / Hold on to your dreams / It was a camel / Sleazy / Snake charmer – reprise.

JAH WOBBLE & OLLIE MARLAND

with sessions **ANIMAL** – guitar / **B.J.COLE** – steel / **HARRY BECKETT** – timpani / **NEVILLE MURRAY** – percussion / **GENERAL SMUTLEY** – drums

Lago not issued

Sep 84. (12") **VOODOO. / EAST** [ ] [-]

Island not issued

May 85. (lp)(c) **NEON MOON** [ ] [-]
– Love mystery / Love mystery (instrumental) / Running away / Neon Moon / Life on the line / Life on the line (dub) / The beat inside / Despite.

Jul 85. (7")(12") **LOVE MYSTERY. / LOVE MYSTERY (instrumental)** [ ] [-]

JAH WOBBLE

Lago not issued

Nov 85. (12") **BLOW OUT. / ?** [ ] [-]

General not issued

May 86. (12" by; WOBBLE & BRETT WICKERS) **BETWEEN TWO FREQUENCIES. / 6020** [ ] [-]

Lago not issued

Oct 86. (lp; by JAH WOBBLE & OLLIE MARLAND) **TRADE WINDS** [ ] [-]
–

Wobble not issued

Sep 87. (12"ep) **ISLAND PARADISE / ALCOHOL. / JIHAD / ('A'remix)** [ ] [-]

Sep 87. (lp) **PSALMS** [ ] [-]
(re-iss.cd+lp Aug94 on 'Southern')

JAH WOBBLE'S INVADERS OF THE HEART

w / **JUSTIN** – guitar (ex-sessions FRANK CHICKENS) / **MICK** – drums / **NATASHA** – vocals (a Spanish/Belgian belly dancer) of TRANSGLOBAL UNDERGROUND

Boy's Own not issued

Oct 90. (7") **BOMBA (Andy Weatherall mix). / ('A'miles away mix)** [ ] [-]
(12"+=)(cd-s+=) – ('A'live version).

— Late 1990, he also splintered in MAX with ANDY ROURKE (ex-SMITHS) on 'ZTT'.

Oval-East West East West

Oct 91. (cd)(c)(lp) **RISING ABOVE BEDLAM** [ ] [ ]
– Visions of you / Relight the flame / Bomba / Ungodly kingdom / Rising above bedlam / Erzulie / Everyman's an island / Soledad / Sweet divinity / Wonderful world.

Nov 91. (7") **ERZULIE. / ('A'dependent mix)** [ ] [ ]
(12"+=)(cd-s+=) – Remind me to be nice to myself.

— Below 'A' + next 'B'-side featured **SINEAD O'CONNOR** – vocals

Jan 92. (7") **VISIONS OF YOU. / ('A'-Ade phases the parameters of sound mix)** [35] [ ]
(12"+=)(cd-s+=) – ('A'-secret love child of Hank & Johnny mix) / ('A' pick'n'mix 1 & 2).

Sep 92. (7") **THE UNGODLY KINGDOM. / JOSEY WALSH** [ ] [-]
(cd-s+=) – Love like / Saeta.

KK Belguim not issued

Jun 93. (cd)(lp) **WITHOUT JUDGEMENT** [-] [-]

— next with **JUSTIN ADAMS** – guitars, vocals / **MARK FERDA** – guitars, mandolin / **NEVILLE MURRAY** – percussion / **ANNELI M.DRECKER** (of Norwegian band BEL CANTO) or **XIMENA TADSON** or **ABDEL ALI SLIMANI** or **GAVIN FRIDAY** (ex-VIRGIN PRUNES) or **ANDREA OLIVER** (ex-RIP, RIG & PANIC) or **NAJMA AKHTAR** – vocals / **KRIS NEEDS** – dub (of SECRET KNOWLEDGE) / **JAKI LIEBEZEIT** or **JOHN REYNOLDS** – drums / etc.

Island Island

Apr 94. (7")(12")(c-s) **BECOMING MORE LIKE GOD. / ('A'mix) / WINE, WOMEN AND SONG** [36] [ ]
(cd-s+=) – Football.

May 94. (cd)(c)(d-lp) **TAKE ME TO GOD** [13] [ ]
– God in the beginning / Becoming more like God / Whisky priests / I'm an Algerian / Amor / Amor dub / Take me to God / The Sun does rise / When the storm comes / I love everybody / Yoga of the nightclub / I am the music / The bonds of love / Angels / No change is sexy / Raga / Forever.

— below 'A' track features **DOLORES O'RIORDAN** (of CRANBERRIES)

Jun 94. (7")(c-s) **THE SUN DOES RISE. / YALILI YA AINI / RAGA** [41] [ ]
(12"+=)(cd-s+=) – Om namah shiva.
(cd-s) – ('A'side) / A13 / Snake charmer (reprise) / So many years.

Oct 94. (c-s) **AMOR. / ('A'mix)** [ ] [ ]
(12"+=)(cd-s+=) – Sahara / (more rockas jungle remixes).
(cd-s) – (4-'A'mixes).

Nov 95. (cd)(c)(d-lp) **HEAVEN AND EARTH** [ ] [ ]
– Heaven and Earth / A love song / Dying over Europe / Divine mother / Gone to Croatan / Hit me / On Nanah Siva.

WOLFSBANE

Formed: Tamworth, Essex, England . . . 1987 by (see below). The following year, they signed to Rick Rubin's new metal incorporated label 'Def American'. Their debut album 'LIVE FAST, DIE FAST', made it into the UK Top 50, as they looked to America in the 90's. • **Style:** Greasy metal act, who were likened to IRON MAIDEN or ZODIAC MINDWARP. Added a touch of futurist elements to their 3rd album's lyrics, retaining of course the usual themes of sex and violence. • **Songwriters:** Group compositions except WILD THING (Troggs). • **Trivia:** 1990 album: Kathy Wilson was a movie star of the 50's.

Recomended: LIVE FAST, DIE FAST (*6).

BLAZE BAYLEY – vocals / **JASE 'The Ace' EDWARDS** – guitar / **JEFF HATELEY D'BRINI** – bass / **STEVE 'Dangerous' ELLETT** – drums

Cops not issued

Oct 86. (12") **CLUTCHING AT STRAWS. / ?** [ ] [-]

Def Jam Def Jam

Oct 88. (12"ep) **LOCO / DANCE DIRTY. / LIMOUSINE / KILLER** [ ] [ ]
(12"+=) – (diff.mixes of the 4 tracks).

Def Amer. Def Amer.

Jul 89. (lp)(c)(cd) **LIVE FAST, DIE YOUNG** [48] [ ]
– Manhunt / Shakin' / Killing machine / Fell out of Heaven / Money to burn / Greasy / I like it hot / All or nothing / Tears from a fool / Pretty baby.

Oct 89. (7")(c-s) **SHAKIN'. / BRANDO** [ ] [ ]
(12"+=)/ /(12"pic-d++=)(cd-s++=) – Angel./ / Money to burn.

Mar 90. (7")(7"red) **I LIKE IT HOT. / LIMOSINE (live)** [ ] [ ]
(12"+=)/ /(10"++=)(cd-s++=) – Loco (live)./ / Manhunt (live). *(re-iss.Dec90)*

Oct 90. (cd)(c)(m-lp) **ALL HELL'S BREAKING LOOSE DOWN AT KATHY WILSON'S PLACE** [48] [ ]
– Steel / Paint the town red / Loco / Hey babe / Totally nude / Kathy Wilson.

Sep 91. (7") **EZY. / BLACK LAGOON** [68] [ ]
(12") – ('A'side) / You load me down / Dead at last.
(cd-s+=) – Fucked off.

Oct 91. (cd)(c)(lp) **DOWN FALL THE GOOD GUYS** [53] [ ]
– Smashed and blind / You load me down / Ezy / Black lagoon / Broken doll / Twice as mean / Cathode ray clinic / The loveless / After midnight / Temple of rock / Moonlight / Dead at last. *(re-iss.cd+c Apr93)*

Feb 92. (7")(c-s) **AFTER MIDNIGHT. / IDOL** [ ] [ ]
(12"+=)(cd-s+=) – Win or lose / Hey babe (acoustic).

Essential Rykodisc

Jun 93. (cd)(c)(d-lp) **MASSIVE NOISE INJECTION** (live 20 Feb'93) [ ] [ ]
– Protect & survive / Load me down / Black lagoon / Rope & ride / Kathy Wilson / Loco / End of the century / Steel / Temple of rock / Manhunt / Money to burn / Paint the town red / Wild thing.

Feb 94. (cd)(c) **THERE CAN ONLY BE YOU – WOLFSBANE** [ ] [-]

— split after BLAZE joined IRON MAIDEN to repl.DICKINSON

Bobby WOMACK

Born: 4 Mar'44, Cleveland, Ohio, USA. In 1959, he formed The WOMACK BROTHERS with CECIL, CURTIS, HARRIS and FRIENDLY JR. They became The LOVERS then The VALENTINOS and signed for SAM COOKE's 'SAR' label in 1961. BOBBY had been his guitarist since the early 60's. The VALENTINOS debut the following year with LOOKIN' FOR A LOVE scraping into the US Top75. In 1964, quite surprisingly IT'S ALL OVER NOW only hit No.94. Consolation was forthcoming, when it later in the year, hit UK No.1 for The ROLLING STONES. In the mid-60's, he commenced writing for WILSON PICKETT, who hit big with 'I'M A MIDNIGHT MOVER' & 'I'M IN LOVE'. In the early 70's, he and friend/singer SLY STONE were increasingly dependent on drugs, which was cited as cause of marriage breakdown. His fortunes changed, when he broke through to the mainstream US audience with several hit singles for 'United Art' during 1971-1974. His career was resurrected in the 80's when he recovered from drugs misuse, and made inroads into UK charts!. • **Style:** Nicknamed 'The Preacher', his blend of soul and slick laid-back rock'n'roll, made him one of music's most respected artists. An attempt to go country in the mid-70's, nearly made him a non-entity, when critics produced backlash of ill-feeling towards the album 'SAFETY ZONE'. • **Songwriters:** All his own work, except covers:- CALIFORNIA DREAMIN' (Mamas & The Papas) / SWEET CAROLINE (Neil Diamond) / I WISH IT WOULD RASIN (Temptations) / LIVING IN A BOX (Living In A Box) / etc. • **Trivia:** His brother CECIL became part of WOMACK & WOMACK team with wife LINDA.

Recommended: THE VERY BEST OF BOBBY WOMACK (*8) / THE POET (*8) / THE POET II (*10)

WOMACK BROTHERS

not issued S.A.R.

1961. (7") **SOMEBODY'S WRONG. / YIELD NOT TO TEMPTATION** [-] [ ]

VALENTINOS

(see biography for members)

not issued S.A.R.

Jul 62. (7") **LOOKIN' FOR A LOVE./ SOMEWHERE THERE'S A GIRL** [-] [72]

Sep 62. (7") **I'LL MAKE IT ALRIGHT. / DARLING COME BACK HOME** [-] [97]

1963. (7") **SHE'S SO GOOD TO ME. / BABY, LOT'S OF LUCK** [-] [ ]
Jun 64. (7") **IT'S ALL OVER NOW. / TIRED OF LIVING IN THE COUNTRY** [-] [94]
(UK-iss.1968 or 1969 on 'Soul City')
Sep 64. (7") **EVERYBODY WANTS TO FALL IN LOVE. / BITTER DREAMS** [-] [ ]

— They split same year. On Feb'65, BOBBY married SAM COOKE's widow BARBARA. That year, he recorded for new label 'Him', but time was mostly taken up by session work for RAY CHARLES, WILSON PICKETT and other 'Atlantic' artists. In 1966, he signed for the label, but he mainly wrote for WILSON PICKETT before briefly moving to 'Chess'.

BOBBY WOMACK

Minit Minit
Sep 67. (7") **TRUST ME. / BABY, I CAN'T STAND IT** [-] [ ]
Feb 68. (7") **BROADWAY WALK. / SOMEBODY SPECIAL** [ ] [ ]
Apr 68. (7") **WHAT IS THIS. / WHAT YOU GONNA DO (WHEN YOUR LOVE HAS GONE)** [ ] [ ]
Aug 68. (lp) **FLY ME TO THE MOON** [-] [ ]
Sep 68. (7") **FLY ME TO THE MOON. / TAKE ME** [ ] [52] Aug68
Jan 69. (7") **CALIFORNIA DREAMIN'. / BABY YOU OUGHTA THINK IT OVER** [ ] [43] Dec 68
Apr 69. (7") **I LEFT MY HEART IN SAN FRANCISCO. / LOVE, THE TIME IS NOW** [-] [ ]
Jul 69. (7") **IT'S GONNA RAIN. / THANK YOU** [-] [ ]
Nov 69. (7") **HOW I MISS YOU BABY. / TIRED AND CONVICTED** [-] [93]
Apr 70. (7") **MORE THAN I CAN STAND. / ARKANSAS STATE PRISON** [-] [90]
not issued Liberty
Jun 70. (7") **I'M GONNA FORGET ABOUT YOU. / DON'T LOOK BACK** [-] [ ]
Dec 70. (7") **SOMETHING (live). / EVERYBODY'S TALKIN' (live)** [-] [ ]
Apr 71. (lp) **THE WOMACK LIVE (live '68)** [-] [ ]
– Intro – Let it out / Oh how I miss you baby / California dreamin' / Something / Everybody's talking / Laughin' and clownin' / To live the past / I'm a midnight mover / More than I can stand. *(UK-iss.+c+cd.Feb89 on 'Charly')*

— With a number of exceptions, his band over the 70's included **ROGER HAWKINS** – drums / **CLAYTON IVEY** – keyboards / **JIMMY JOHNSON** – guitar / **BARRY BECKETT** – keyboards / **TRUMAN THOMAS** – bass

United Art United A..
Feb 72. (7") **THAT'S THE WAY I FEEL ABOUT 'CHA. / COME L'AMORE** [ ] [27] Dec 71
Jun 72. (lp)(c) **COMMUNICATION** [ ] [83] Dec 71
– Communication / Come l'amore / Fire and rain / If you don't want my love, give it back / (They long to be) Close to you / Everything is beautiful / That's the way I feel about 'cha / Held not to temptation.
Jul 72. (7") **WOMAN'S GOT TO HAVE IT. / IF YOU DON'T WANT MY LOVE** [ ] [60] May 72
Sep 72. (lp)(c) **UNDERSTANDING** [ ] [43] Jun 72
– I can understand it / Woman's gotta have it / And I love her / Got to get you back / Simple man / Ruby Dean / A thing called love / Sweet Caroline (good times never seemed so good) / Harry hippie. *(re-iss.Jan75 as 'I CAN UNDERSTAND IT')*
Sep 72. (7") **SWEET CAROLINE (GOOD TIMES NEVER SEEMED SO GOOD). / HARRY HIPPIE** [ ] [51] Aug 72
[31]
Dec 72. (7") **HARRY HIPPIE. / I CAN UNDERSTAND IT** [ ] [-]
(re-iss.Jan75 but flipped over)
Apr 73. (7") **ACROSS 110th STREET. / HANG ON IN THERE** [ ] [56] Jan 73
May 73. (lp)(c) **ACROSS 110th STREET (Soundtrack+instrumentals by J. J. JOHNSON & HIS ORCHESTRA)** [ ] [50] Jan 73
Jul 73. (7") **NOBODY WANTS YOU WHEN YOU'RE DOWN AND OUT. / I'M THROUGH TRYING TO PROVE MY LOVE FOR YOU** [ ] [29] Jun 73
Sep 73. (lp)(c) **FACTS OF LIFE** [ ] [37] Jul 73
– Nobody wants you when you're down and out / I'm through trying to prove my love / If you can't give her love, give her up / That's Heaven to me / Holdin' on to my baby's love / Nobody (reprise) / Facts of life / He'll be there when the sun goes down / Can't stop a man in love / The look of love / Natural man / All along the watchtower / Interlude No. 1.
Mar 74. (7") **LOOKIN' FOR A LOVE. / LET IT ALL HANG OUT** [ ] [10] Feb 74
Apr 74. (lp)(c) **LOOKIN' FOR A LOVE AGAIN** [ ] [85] Dec 73
– Lookin' for a love / I don't wanna be hurt by your love again / Doing it my way / Let it all hang out / Point of no return / You're welcome, stop on by / You're messing up a good thing / Don't let me down / Copper kettle / There's one thing that beats falling. *(re-iss.+cd.Aug88 on 'Edsel') (cd-iss.Jan89 on 'Charly')*
Jun 74. (7") **YOU'RE WELCOME, STOP ON BY. / ?** [-] [59]
Nov 74. (lp)(c) **BOBBY WOMACK'S GREATEST HITS** [-] [ ]
– (compilation)
May 75. (lp)(c) **I DON'T KNOW WHAT THE WORLD IS COMING TO** [ ] [ ]
– I don't know – (interlude 1&2) / Superstar / I want my love, put something down on it / Git it / What's your world / Check it out / Interlude No.2 / Jealous love / It's all over now / Yes Jesus loves me.
Jun 75. (7") **CHECK IT OUT. / INTERLUDE No.2** [ ] [91] Apr 75
Jan 76. (7") **WHERE THERE'S A WILL THERE'S A WAY. / EVERYTHING'S GONNA BE ALRIGHT** [ ] [ ] Nov 75
Feb 76. (lp)(c) **SAFETY ZONE** [ ] [ ] Dec 75
– Everything's gonna be alright / I wish it would rain / Trust me / Where there's a will there's a way / Love ain't something you can get for free / Something you got / Daylight / I feel a groove comin' on / Don't make this the last date for you and me.
Mar 76. (7") **DAYLIGHT. / TRUST ME** [ ] [ ]
Aug 76. (lp)(c) **B.W. GOES C & W** [ ] [ ] Apr 76
– Behind closed doors / Bouquet of roses / Tired of living in the country / Tarnished rings / Big bayou / Song of the mockingbird / I'd be ahead if I could quit while I'm behind / You / I take it on home.

C.B.S. Columbia
Jan 77. (7") **HOME IS WHERE THE HEART IS. / WE'VE ONLY JUST BEGUN** [ ] [ ] Oct 76
Feb 77. (lp)(c) **HOME IS WHERE THE HEART IS** [ ] [ ] Sep 76
– Home is where the heart is / A little bit salty / Standing in the safety zone / One more chance on love / How long (has this been goin' on) / I could never be satisfied / Something for my head / A change is gonna come / We've only just begun. *(re-iss.Feb86)*
1978. (7") **WIND IT UP. / STOP BEFORE WE START** [-] [ ]
Jul 78. (lp)(c) **PIECES** [-] [ ]
– It's party time / Trust your heart / Stop before we start / When love begins, friendship ends / Wind it up / Is this the thanks I get / Caught up in the middle / Never let nothing get the best of you.
Arista Arista
Jun 79. (7") **I HONESTLY LOVE YOU. / HOW COULD YOU BREAK MY HEART** [-] [ ]
Jul 79. (lp)(c) **ROADS OF LIFE** [ ] [ ]
Aug 79. (7") **ROADS OF LIFE. / GIVE IT UP** [-] [ ]

— Took time out, to stifle increasing drug taking, re-actifying again after his brother Harris was murdered. Oct'80, he provided the vocals for WILTON FELDER's (of The CRUSADERS) hit single 'INHERIT THE WIND'.

Motown Beverly Glen
Jun 82. (lp)(c) **THE POET** [ ] [29] Jan 82
– So many sides of you / Lay your lovin' on me / Secrets / Just my imagination / Stand up / Games / If you think you're lonely now / Where do we go from here. *(cd-iss.Jul87 on 'Pacific') (re-iss.cd+c Sep94 on 'MCI')*
Jul 82. (7")(12") **SO MANY SIDES OF YOU. / JUST MY IMAGINATION** [ ] [-]
Sep 82. (7") **SECRETS. / STAND UP** [ ] [ ] Feb 82

— In 1982, BOBBY took 'Beverly Glen' label owner Otis Smith to court, fighting literally over non-payment of royalties. Next single was a duet with PATTI LaBELLE.

Mar 84. (7") **LOVE HAS FINALLY COME AT LAST. / AMERICAN DREAM** [-] [88]
Apr 84. (lp)(c) **THE POET II** [31] [60] Mar 84
– Love has finally come at last / It takes a lot of strength to say goodbye / Through the eyes of a child / Surprise surprise / Tryin' to get over you / Tell me why / Who's foolin' who / I wish I had someone to go home to / American dream. *(cd-iss.Jul87 on 'Pacific') (re-iss.cd+c Sep94 on 'MCI')*
Jun 84. (7")(12") **TELL ME WHY. / THROUGH THE EYES OF A CHILD** [60] [ ]
Sep 84. (7") **SURPRISE SURPRISE. / AMERICAN DREAM** [ ] [ ]
(12"+=) – If you think you're lonely now.
Sep 84. (7") **IT TAKES A LOT OF STRENGTH TO SAY GOODBYE (w/PATTI LaBELLE) / WHO'S FOOLIN' WHO** [-] [ ]
Jan 85. (7") **I WISH I HAD SOMEONE TO GO HOME TO. / SOMEDAY WE'LL ALL BE FREE** [-] [ ]
Mar 85. (7") **SEARCHING FOR MY LOVE. / I'M SO PROUD** [-] [ ]

— Early 1985, he re-united with WILTON FELDER on 7+12" '(NO MATTER HOW HIGH I GET) I WILL STILL BE LOOKING UP TO YOU'.

M.C.A. M.C.A.
Sep 85. (lp)(c) **SO MANY RIVERS** [ ] [66] Aug 85
– I wish he didn't trust me so much / So baby don't leave home without it / So many rivers / Got to be with you tonight / Whatever happened to the times / Let me kiss it where it hurts / The only survivor / That's where it's at / Check it out / Gypsy woman. *(cd-iss.Aug89)*
Sep 85. (7")(12") **I WISH HE DIDN'T TRUST ME SO MUCH. / GOT TO BE WITH YOU TONIGHT** [64] [ ]
May 86. (7")(12") **GYPSY WOMAN. / WHATEVER HAPPENED TO THE TIMES** [ ] [ ]
Nov 86. (lp)(c) **WOMAGIC** [ ] [ ] Jul 86
– I wanna make love to you / When the weekend comes / All the things you do / I can't stay mad too long / Hear the music / Outside myself / I ain't got to live nobody else / More than love / It ain't me. *(cd-iss.Nov87)*
Jan 87. (7")(12") **I WANNA MAKE LOVE TO YOU. / WHATEVER HAPPENED TO THE TIMES** [ ] [ ]
Oct 87. (7") **LIVING IN A BOX. / ('A'instrumental)** [70] [ ]
(12"+=) – ('A'another box version) / ('A'-Hacienda mix).
Nov 87. (lp)(c)(cd) **THE LAST SOUL MAN** [ ] [ ]
– Living in a box / When the weekend comes / I still love you / Gina / A world where no one cries / A woman likes to hear that / Real love please stand up / The things we do (when we're lonely) / Falling in love again / Outside myself.

SHIRLEY BROWN & BOBBY WOMACK

Chrysalis Cooltempo
Nov 89. (7") **AIN'T NOTHIN' LIKE THE LOVIN' WE GOT. / ?** [ ] [ ]
(12"+=)(cd-s+=) – ?

BOBBY WOMACK

solo releases 'SAVE THE CHILDREN' 45, late 1989.
(also credited on LULU single 'I'm Back For More', which hit No.27, Mar93)

Continuum
Aug 94. (12")(c-s)(cd-s) **FOREVER LOVE / COLOUR HIM FATHER / (other mixes)** [ ] [ ]
Sep 94. (cd)(c) **RESURRECTION** [ ] [ ]
–

– compilations, others, etc. –

- compilations, others, etc. -

Feb 74. Jet Boy; (7") **WHAT IS THIS. / I WONDER** [ ] [-]
Jan 79. U.A.; (7")(12") **I CAN UNDERSTAND IT. / HARRY HIPPIE** [ ] [ ]
Jul 79. U.A.; (lp)(c) **A PORTRAIT OF BOBBY WOMACK** [ ] [ ]
Sep 84. Liberty; (lp)(c) **SOMEBODY SPECIAL** [ ] [ ]
1986. Stateside; (lp)(c) **CHECK IT OUT** [ ] [-]
Jun 87. Arista; (7") **HOW COULD YOU BREAK MY HEART. / GIVE IT UP** [ ] [ ]
(12"+=) – Mr. DJ don't stop the music.
Jan 89. Charly; (d-lp)(c)(cd) **UNDERSTANDING / COMMUNICATION** [ ] [-]
Jan 89. Charly; (cd-ep) **LOOKIN' FOR A LOVE / HARRY HIPPIE / THAT'S THE WAY I FEEL ABOUT 'CHA / IF YOU DON'T WANT MY LOVE, GIVE IT BACK** [ ] [-]
Feb 89. Charly; (d-lp)(c)(cd) **WOMACK WINNERS – THE BEST OF BOBBY WOMACK 1968-1975** [ ] [-]
(cd-iss.Jul93 on 'Instant')
Mar 89. Charly; (d-lp)(c)(cd) **FACTS OF LIFE / I DON'T KNOW WHAT THE WORLD IS COMING TO** [ ] [-]
Apr 89. Charly; (cd-ep) **LOOKIN' FOR A LOVE / HARRY HIPPIE / THAT'S THE WAY, I FEEL ABOUT 'CHA / IF YOU DON'T WANT MY LOVE** [ ] [-]
Sep 89. Charly; (d-lp)(c)(cd) **WOMACK IN MEMPHIS** [ ] [-]
—— next with WILSON PICKETT
Jul 89. Instant; (lp)(c)(cd) **THE MIDNIGHT MOVER** [ ] [-]
Jun 91. Music Club; (cd) **THE VERY BEST OF BOBBY WOMACK** [ ] [-]
– I can understand it / Harry hippie / I'm a midnight mover / What is this / Somebody special / That's the way I feel about cha / Communication / California dreaming / If you don't want my love give it back / I wish it would rain / Nobody wants you when you're down and out / Across 110th Street / If you want my love, put something down on it / Lookin' for a love / I don't wanna be hurt by ya love again / Got to get you back / Woman's gotta have it / There's one thing that beats failing / You're messing up a good thing / Love ain't something you can get for free.
Mar 94. EMI; (d-cd) **MIDNIGHT MOVER – THE BOBBY WOMACK STORY** [ ] [ ]
Apr 94. Castle; (cd)(c) **THE COLLECTION** [ ] [-]
Apr 95. Charly; (cd) **I FEEL A GROOVE COMIN' ON** [ ] [-]

- (VALENTINOS) compilations, others, etc. -

1968. Soul City; (7") **IT'S ALL OVER NOW. / TIRED OF LIVING IN THE COUNTRY** [ ] [-]
1968. Soul City; (lp) **THE VALENTINOS** [ ] [ ]
Mar 71. Polydor; (7") **RAISE YOUR HAND IN ANGER. / STAND UP AND BE COUNTED** [ ] [-]
—— (Next as "BOBBY WOMACK & THE VALENTINOS")
Oct 84. PRT/ US= Chess; (lp)(c) **CHESS MASTERS** [ ] [ ]
(re-iss.1988 as 'BOBBY WOMACK & THE VALENTINOS')

Stevie WONDER

Born: STEVELAND JUDKINS, 13 May'50, Saginaw, Michegan, USA. Blind since birth, he became a member of his local Baptist choir, In 1960 he also formed duo with JOHN GLOVER, who recommended LITTLE STEVIE WONDER to his cousin; MIRACLES singer RONNIE WHITE. He in turn contacted BERRY GORDY, who signed STEVIE for long-term contract on 'Tamla Motown'. After 2 albums and a few flop 45's, STEVIE broke through in 1963 with US chart-topper 'FINGERTIPS – Pt.2'. It preceded the No.1 album 'RECORDED LIVE – THE 12 YEAR OLD GENIUS'. After a few years with mediocre fortunes, now as STEVIE WONDER, he hit the Top 3 again with 'UPTIGHT'. The following 2 decades, saw him become a major superstar, never letting go of his chart foothold. • **Style:** Although blind, he progressed from being a child prodigy (RAY CHARLES influenced) R&B star, to become 'Motown's' golden boy of the 60's. In the 70's, with masterly keyboard playing intact, he turned to progressive experimental soul, which encompassed all facets of socially conscious lyrics. In the 80's, STEVIE drifted back to his early soul and commercial roots, but still managed to appeal to large audience. I'm sure the 90's will see another great album from STEVIE, who must have something left in his great mind. • **Songwriters:** STEVIE wrote all his own work except, when in the 60's he collaborated with producer HENRY COSBY. His cover versions were; BLOWIN' IN THE WIND + MR.TAMBOURINE MAN (Bob Dylan) / WE CAN WORK IT OUT (Beatles) / SIXTEEN TONS (Ernie Ford) / CAN I GET A WITNESS (Marvin Gaye) / PLEASE, PLEASE, PLEASE (James Brown) / RESPECT (Otis Redding) / MY GIRL (Temptations) / LIGHT MY FIRE (Doors) / GOD BLESS THE CHILD (Billie Holiday) / BRIDGE OVER TROUBLED WATER (Simon & Garfunkel). The album 'TRIBUTE TO UNCLE RAY', had many covers of RAY CHARLES' songs. • **Miscellaneous:** On 14 Sep'70, STEVIE married singer SYREETA WRIGHT, who became his co-writer in the early 70's. They split-up 4 years later and STEVIE found new girlfriend YOLANDA SIMMONS, who moved with him and their new daughter to Manhattan. On the 6 Aug'73, he was nearly killed in a serious road accident. He recovered from head injuries, after spending a few days in a coma. His song in 1974, 'YOU HAVEN'T DONE NOTHIN'', was an indictment to President Nixon. STEVIE also wrote million sellers for Minnie Riperton (LOVIN' YOU) & Rufus (TELL ME SOMETHING GOOD).

Recommended: INNERVISIONS (*10) / TALKING BOOK (*9) / MUSIC OF MY MIND (*9) / SONGS IN THE KEY OF LIFE (*9) / JOURNEY THROUGH THE SECRET LIFE OF PLANTS (*7) / ANTHOLOGY (*9) / ORIGINAL MUSIQUARIUM 1 (*9).

LITTLE STEVIE WONDER

– vocals, piano, harmonica

Oriole Tamla

Aug 62. (7") **I CALL IT PRETTY MUSIC (BUT OLD PEOPLE CALL IT THE BLUES). / (part 2)** [-] [ ]
1962. (lp) **TRIBUTE TO UNCLE RAY** [-] [ ]
– Hallelujah I love her so / Ain't that love / Don't you know / Sunset / Frankie and Johnny / Drown in my own tears / Come back baby / Mary Ann / My baby's gone / (I'm afraid) The masquerade is over. *(UK-iss.Aug63 on 'Oriole') (re-iss.+c.Mar62 on 'Motown') (cd-iss.Sep95)*
Oct 62. (7") **LITTLE WATER BOY (w/ CLARENCE PAUL). / LA LA LA LA LA** [-] [ ]
1963. (lp) **THE JAZZ SOUL OF LITTLE STEVIE** [-] [ ]
– Fingertips / Square / Soul bongo / Manhattan at six / Some other time / Wandering / Session number 112 / Bam. *(UK-iss.May64 on 'Stateside') (re-iss.+c.Mar82 on 'Motown')*
Dec 62. (7") **CONTRACT ON LOVE. / SUNSET** [-] [ ]
Aug 63. (7") **FINGERTIPS (part 2). / FINGERTIPS (part 1)** [ ] [1] Jun 63
Aug 63. (lp) **THE 12 YEAR OLD GENIUS (RECORDED LIVE) (live)** [ ] [1] Jul 63
– Fingertips / Soul bongo / Drown in my own tears / La la la la / (I'm afraid) The masquerade is over / Hallelujah I love her so / Don't you know. *(re-iss.+c. Oct81 on 'Motown')*

Stateside Tamla

Nov 63. (7") **WORKOUT STEVIE, WORKOUT. / MONKEY TALK** [ ] [33] Oct 63
Jan 64. (lp) **WITH A SONG IN MY HEART** [-] [ ]
– Dream / With a song in my heart / Get happy / Put on a happy face / When you wish upon a star / Smile / Make someone happy / Without a song / On the sunny side of the street / Give your heart a chance. *(UK-iss.+c.Oct81 on 'Motown')*
Apr 64. (7") **CASTLES IN THE SAND. / THANK YOU (FOR LOVING ME ALL THE WAY)** [ ] [52] Feb 64

STEVIE WONDER

(same labels)

Aug 64. (7") **HEY HARMONICA MAN. / THIS LITTLE GIRL** [ ] [29] Jun 64
Sep 64. (7") **SAD BOY. / HAPPY STREET** [-] [ ]
Jan 65. (lp) **AT THE BEACH (HEY HARMONICA MAN)** [ ] [ ]
– Red sails in the sunset / Party at the beach house / Happy Street / Beachcomber / Castles in the sand / Beyond the sea / Sad boy / Beach stomp / Hey, harmonica man.

Tamla Motown Tamla

Jan 65. (7") **PRETTY LITTLE ANGEL. / TEARS IN VAIN** [-] [ ]
Mar 65. (7") **KISS ME BABY. / TEARS IN VAIN** [-] [ ]
Sep 65. (7") **HIGH HEEL SNEAKERS. / MUSIC TALK** [ ] [59] Aug 65
Jan 66. (7") **UPTIGHT (EVERYTHING'S ALRIGHT). / PURPLE RAINDROPS** [14] [3] Dec 65
Apr 66. (7") **NOTHING'S TOO GOOD FOR MY BABY. / WITH A CHILD'S HEART** [ ] [20] Mar 66
Aug 66. (7") **BLOWIN' IN THE WIND. / AIN'T THAT ASKING FOR TROUBLE** [36] [9] Jun 66
Nov 66. (lp) **UP-TIGHT EVERYTHING'S ALRIGHT** [ ] [33] Jun 66
– Love a go-go / Hold me / Blowin' in the wind / Nothing's too good for my baby / Teach me tonight / Uptight (everything's alright) / Ain't that asking for trouble / I want my baby back / Pretty little angel / Music talk / Contract on love / With a child's heart. *(re-iss.+c.Oct81) (re-iss.1973 on 'M.F.P.')*
Dec 66. (7") **A PLACE IN THE SUN. / SYLVIA** [20] [9] Oct 66
Dec 66. (7") **SOME DAY AT CHRISTMAS. / THE MIRACLE OF CHRISTMAS** [-] [ ]
Apr 67. (lp) **DOWN TO EARTH** [ ] [92] Jan 67
– A place in the Sun / Bang bang / Thank you love / Mr. Tambourine man / Hey love / Sixteen tons / Down to Earth / Sylvia / Lonesome road / The world is empty without you / Angel baby (don't you ever leave me) / Be cool, be calm (and keep yourself together). *(re-iss.+c.Oct81)*
Apr 67. (7") **TRAVELLIN' MAN. / HEY LOVE** [ ] [32] [90] Mar 67
Jul 67. (7") **I WAS MADE TO LOVE HER. / HOLD ME** [5] [2] Jun 67
Oct 67. (7") **I'M WONDERING. / EVERY TIME I SEE YOU I GO WILD** [22] [12]
Apr 68. (lp) **I WAS MADE TO LOVE HER** [ ] [45] Sep 67
– I was made to love her / Send me some lovin' / I'd cry / Everybody needs somebody (I need you) / Respect / My girl / Baby don't you do it / A fool for you / Can I get a witness / I pity the fool / Please, please, please / Every time I see you I go wild. *(re-iss.+c.Oct81)*
Apr 68. (7") **SHOO-BE-DOO-BE-DOO-DA-DAY. / WHY DON'T YOU LEAD ME TO LOVE** [46] [9]
Aug 68. (lp) **STEVIE WONDER'S GREATEST HITS** (compilation) [25] [37] Apr 68
– Shoo-be-doo-be-doo-da-day / A place in the Sun / Uptight (everything's alright) / Travellin' man / High heel sneakers / Sad boy / Kiss me, baby / Workout Stevie, workout / Fingertips (part 2) / Hey, harmonica man / Contract on love / Castles in the sand / Nothing's too good for my baby / I was made to love her / Blowin' in the wind / I'm wonderin'. *(re-iss.+c.Oct81 & 1986) (cd-iss.'VOL.1' Sep89) (cd-iss.Nov93)*
Aug 68. (7") **YOU MET YOUR MATCH. / MY GIRL** [ ] [35] Jul 68
Dec 68. (7") **FOR ONCE IN MY LIFE. / ANGIE GIRL** [3] [2] Oct 68
(re-iss.Oct81)
Feb 69. (lp) **FOR ONCE IN MY LIFE** [ ] [50] Oct 68
– For once in my life / Shoo-be-ddo-be-doo-da-day / You met your match / I wanna make her love me / I'm more than happy (I'm satisfied) / I don't know why (I love you) / Sunny / I'd be a fool right now / Ain't no lovin' / God bless the child / Do I love her / The house on the hill. *(re-iss.+c.Oct81, re-iss.+cd.Aug88)*
Mar 69. (7") **I DON'T KNOW WHY (I LOVE YOU). / MY CHERIE AMOUR** [14] [39] Feb 69
(above flipped over Jun69 hit both UK + US No.4) (re-iss.Oct81)

Nov 69. (7") **YESTER-ME, YESTER-YOU, YESTERDAY. / I'D BE A FOOL RIGHT NOW** 2 7 Oct 69

Nov 69. (lp)(c) **MY CHERIE AMOUR** 17 34 Oct 69
– My Cherie amour / Hello young lovers / At last / Light my fire / The shadow of your smile / You and me / Pearl / Somebody knows, somebody cares / Yester-me, yester-you, yesterday / Angie girl / Give your love / I've got you. *(re-iss.Oct81 & Apr84, cd-iss.Aug88)*

Mar 70. (7") **NEVER HAD A DREAM COME TRUE. / SOMEBODY KNOWS, SOMEBODY CARES** 6 26 Feb 70

Mar 70. (lp)(c) **LIVE (AT THE TALK OF THE TOWN)** ☐ 81 Apr 70
– Pretty world / Never had a dream come true / Shoo-be-doo-be-doo-da-day / My Cherie amour / Alfie / (drum solo) / Bridge over troubled water / I was made to love her / Yester-me, yester-you, yesterday / For once in my life / Signed, sealed, delivered (I'm yours). *(re-iss.Oct81)*

Jun 70. (7") **SIGNED, SEALED, DELIVERED (I'M YOURS). / I'M MORE THAN HAPPY (I'M SATISFIED)** 15 3

Nov 70. (lp)(c) **SIGNED, SEALED, DELIVERED (I'M YOURS)** ☐ 25 Aug 70
– Never had a dream come true / We can work it out / Signed, sealed, delivered (I'm yours) / Heaven help us all / You can't judge a book by it's cover / Sugar / Don't wonder why / Anything you want me to do / I can't let my Heaven walk away / Joy (takes over me) / I gotta have a song / Something to say. *(re-iss.Oct81, re-iss.+cd.Aug88)*

Nov 70. (7") **HEAVEN HELP US ALL. / I GOTTA HAVE A SONG** 29 9 Oct 70

Mar 71. (7") **WE CAN WORK IT OUT. / NEVER DREAMED YOU'D LEAVE ME IN SUMMER** – 13
78

May 71. (7") **WE CAN WORK IT OUT. / DON'T WONDER WHY** 27 –

Jul 71. (7") **NEVER DREAMED YOU'D LEAVE ME IN SUMMER. / IF YOU REALLY LOVE ME** ☐ –

Jul 71. (lp)(c) **WHERE I'M COMING FROM** ☐ 62 May 71
– Look around / Do yourself a favour / Think of me as your soldier / Something out of the blue / If you really love me / I wanna talk to you / Take up a course in happiness / Never dreamed you'd leave me in Summer / Sunshine in their eyes. *(re-iss.Jul81) (re-iss.+cd.Apr91) (cd-iss.Sep93)*

Nov 71. (7") **WHAT CHRISTMAS MEANS TO ME. / BEDTIME FOR TOYS** – ☐

Jan 72. (7") **IF YOU REALLY LOVE ME. / THINK OF ME AS YOUR SOLDIER** 20 8 Aug 71

Jan 72. (lp)(c) **GREATEST HITS VOL.2** (compilation) 30 69 Nov 71
– Signed, sealed, delivered (I'm yours) / We can work it out / For once in my life / If you really love me / You met your match / My Cherie amour / Yester-me, yester-you, yesterday / Never had a dream come true / Heaven help us all / Don't know why I love you / Never dreamed you'd leave in Summer. *(re-iss.Oct81 & 1986, cd-iss.Sep89 as 'VOL.2') (cd-iss.Nov93)*

May 72. (7") **SUPERWOMAN (WHERE WERE YOU WHEN I NEEDED YOU). / I LOVE EVERY LITTLE THING ABOUT YOU** – ☐

May 72. (lp)(c) **MUSIC OF MY MIND** ☐ 21 Mar 72
– Love having you around / Superwoman (where were you when I needed you) / I love every thing about you / Sweet little girl / Happier than the morning sun / Girl blue / Seems so long / Keep on running / Evil. *(re-iss.Oct81, cd-iss.Nov87 & Jul92)*

Sep 72. (7") **SUPERWOMAN (WHERE WERE YOU WHEN I NEEDED YOU). / SEEMS SO LONG** ☐ –

Sep 72. (7") **KEEP ON RUNNING. / EVIL** – 90

Jan 73. (7") **SUPERSTITION. / YOU'VE GOT IT BAD GIRL** 11 1 Nov 72
(re-iss.Mar83)

Jan 73. (lp)(c) **TALKING BOOK** 16 3 Nov 72
– You are the sunshine of my life / Maybe your baby / You and I / Tuesday heartbreak / You've got it bad girl / Superstition / Big brother / Blame it on the sun / Lookin' for another true love / I believe (when I fall in love it will be forever). *(re-iss.Oct81, cd-iss.May86 & Jul92, re-Oct87) (pic-lp 1980's)*

Mar 73. (7") **YOU ARE THE SUNSHINE OF MY LIFE. / TUESDAY HEARTBREAK** – 1

May 73. (7") **YOU ARE THE SUNSHINE OF MY LIFE. / LOOK AROUND** 7 –
(re-iss.Oct81)

Aug 73. (lp)(c) **INNERVISIONS** 8 4
– Too high / Visions / Living for the city / Golden lady / Higher ground / Jesus children of America / All in love is fair / Don't you worry 'bout a thing / He's a misstra know-it-all. *(re-iss.Oct81, cd-iss.Oct87 & Jul92, re-.May88)*

Sep 73. (7") **HIGHER GROUND. / TOO HIGH** 29 4 Aug 73

Dec 73. (7") **LIVING FOR THE CITY (edit). / VISIONS** 15 8 Nov 73

Apr 74. (7") **HE'S MISSTRA KNOW IT ALL. / YOU CAN'T JUDGE A BOOK BY IT'S COVER** 10 –
(re-iss.Oct81)

Apr 74. (7") **DON'T YOU WORRY 'BOUT A THING. / BLAME IT ON THE SUN** – 16

Jul 74. (7") **DON'T YOU WORRY 'BOUT A THING. / DO YOURSELF A FAVOUR** ☐ –

Aug 74. (lp)(c) **FULFILLINGNESS' FIRST FINALE** 5 1
– Smile please / Heaven is 10 zillion light years away / Too shy to say / Boogie on reggae woman / Creepin' / You haven't done nothin' / It ain't no use / They won't go when I go / Bird of beauty / Please don't go. *(re-iss.Oct81, re-iss.+cd.Oct87) (re-iss.cd+c Nov93)*

Aug 74. (7") **YOU HAVEN'T DONE NOTHIN? / BIG BROTHER** – 1

Oct 74. (7") **YOU HAVEN'T DONE NOTHIN'. / HAPPIER THAN THE MORNING SUN** 30 –

Nov 74. (7") **BOOGIE ON REGGAE WOMAN. / SEEMS SO LONG** – 3

Dec 74. (7") **BOOGIE ON REGGAE WOMAN. / EVIL** 12 –

Oct 76. (d-lp)(d-c) **SONGS IN THE KEY OF LIFE** 2 1
– Love's in need of love today / Have a talk with God / Village ghetto land / Confusion / Sir Duke / Isn't she lovely / Joy inside my tears / Black man / I wish / Knocks me off my feet / Pastime Paradise / Summer soft / Ordinary pain / Ngiculela es una historia – I am singing / If it's magic / As / Another star. *(7"ep w.a.) (re-iss.Oct81, d-cd-iss.1988 & Jul92)*

Dec 76. (7") **I WISH. / YOU AND I** 5 1 Nov 76

Mar 77. (7") **SIR DUKE. / HE'S MISSTRA KNOW-IT-ALL** – 1

Mar 77. (7") **SIR DUKE. / TUESDAY HEARTBREAK** 2 –

Aug 77. (7") **ANOTHER STAR. / CREEPIN'** 29 32

Nov 77. (7") **AS. / CONFUSION** ☐ 36

(last 5 singles, except Aug77 re-iss.Oct81)

Jan 79. (t-lp)(d-c) **LOOKING BACK** (compilation) – 34

—— In Feb79, STEVIE WONDER teamed up with DIANA ROSS, MARVIN GAYE & SMOKEY ROBINSON on minor hit single POPS WE LOVE YOU.

Nov 79. (d-lp)(d-c) **STEVIE WONDER'S JOURNEY THROUGH THE SECRET LIFE OF PLANTS** 8 4
– Earth's creation / The first garden / Voyage to India / Same old story / Venus' flytrap and the bug / Ai no sono / Seasons / Power flower / Send one your love / Race babbling / Outside my window / Black orchid / Ecclesiates / Kesse ye lolo de ye / Come back as a flower / A seed's a star – Tree (medley) / The secret life of plants / Tree / Seasons. *(d-cd-iss.1986 & Sep95)*

Nov 79. (7") **SEND ONE YOUR LOVE. / ('A'instrumental)** 52 4

Jan 80. (7") **BLACK ORCHID. / BLAME IT ON THE SUN** 63 ☐

Mar 80. (7") **OUTSIDE MY WINDOW. / SAME OLD STORY** 52 52 Feb 80

Sep 80. (7")(12") **MASTERBLASTER (JAMMIN'). / MASTERBLASTER (dub)** 2 5
(last 3 singles re-iss.Oct81)

Oct 80. (lp)(c) **HOTTER THAN JULY** 2 3
– Did I hear you say you love me / All I do / Rocket love / I ain't gonna stand for it / As if you read my mind / Masterblaster (jammin') / Do like you / Cash in your face / Lately / Happy birthday. *(re-iss.Oct81, cd-iss.Oct87, re-1988)*

Dec 80. (7") **I AIN'T GONNA STAND FOR IT. / KNOCKS ME OFF MY FEET** 10 11

Feb 81. (7") **LATELY. / IF IT'S MAGIC** 3 64
(re-iss.Oct81)

May 81. (7") **DID I HEAR YOU SAY YOU LOVE ME. / AS IF YOU READ MY MIND** – ☐

Jul 81. (7")(12") **HAPPY BIRTHDAY. / HAPPY BIRTHDAY (SINGALONG)** 2 –

Jan 82. (7") **THAT GIRL. / ALL I DO** 39 4

—— In Mar82, hit UK/US No.1 with PAUL McCARTNEY on single EBONY AND IVORY.

May 82. (7")(12") **DO I DO. / ROCKET LOVE** 10 13

May 82. (d-lp)(d-c) **ORIGINAL MUSIQUARIUM 1** (compilation) 8 ☐
– Superstition / You haven't done nothin' / Living for the city / Front line / Superwoman (where were you when I needed you) / Send one your love / You are the sunshine of my life / Ribbon in the sky / Higher ground / Sir Duke / Master blaster / Boogie on reggae woman / That girl / I wish / isn't she lovely / Do I do. *(re-iss.+d-cd-'2 VOLUMES' Nov84 & Jul92)*

Sep 82. (7")(12") **RIBBON IN THE SKY. / THE SECRET LIFE OF PLANTS** 45 –

Sep 82. (7") **RIBBON IN THE SKY. / BLACK ORCHID** – 54

Dec 82, he & other Motown artist CHARLENE had US Top50 hit with USED TO BE.

Jan 83. (7")(12") **FRONT LINE. / ('A'instrumental)** ☐ ☐

—— In Aug83, STEVIE co-wrote and sang on GARY BYRD's UK Top 10 hit 12" 'The CROWN'. Early next year, he guested on ELTON JOHN's 'I GUESS THAT'S WHY THEY..'.

Aug 84. (7")(12") **I JUST CALLED TO SAY I LOVE YOU. / ('A'instrumental)** 1 1

—— Shared half of next lp with DIONNE WARWICK (also duet on *)

Sep 84. (lp)(c) **WOMAN IN RED – SELECTIONS FROM ORIGINAL MOTION PICTURE SOUNDTRACK** 2 4
– The woman in red / It's you (with DIONNE WARWICK) / It's more than you / I just called to say I love you / Love light in flight / Weakness (with DIONNE ARWICK) / Don't drive drunk / Moments aren't moments (DIONNE WARWICK solo). *(cd-iss.Oct87)*

Nov 84. (7")(12") **LOVE LIGHT IN FLIGHT. / IT'S MORE THAN YOU** 44 17

Dec 84. (7")(12") **DON'T DRIVE DRUNK. / ('A'instrumental)** 62 –

—— In Mar85, STEVIE featured on USA FOR AFRICA charity single WE ARE THE WORLD

Aug 85. (7")(12") **PART-TIME LOVER. / ('A'instrumental)** 3 1

Sep 85. (lp)(c)(cd) **IN SQUARE CIRCLE** 5 5
– Part-time lover / I love you too much / Whereabouts / Stranger on the shore of love / Never in the sun / Spiritual walkers / Land of la la / Go home / Overjoyed / It's wrong (apartheid). *(re-iss.cd.Nov92)*

Nov 85. (7")(12") **GO HOME. / ('A'instrumental)** 67 10

Feb 86. (7")(12") **OVERJOYED. / ('A'instrumental)** 17 24

Jun 86. (7")(12") **LAND OF LA LA. / ('A'instrumental)** ☐ 86

Jan 87. (7")(12") **STRANGER ON THE SHORE OF LOVE. / DID I HEAR YOU SAY YOU LOVE ME** 55 –

Oct 87. (7")(12")(c-s) **SKELETONS. / ('A'instrumental)** 59 19

Nov 87. (lp)(c)(cd) **CHARACTERS** 33 17
– You will know / Dark 'n' lovely / In your corner / With each part of my heart / One of a kind / Skeletons / Get it / Galaxy Paradise / Cryin' through the night. *(c+cd+=)–* Come let me make your love come down / My eyes don't cry.

Jan 88. (7")(12") **YOU WILL KNOW. / ('A'instrumental)** ☐ 77
(cd-s+=) – (interview).

In Feb88, collaborated with JULIO IGLESIAS on single MY LOVE.

May 88. (7")(12") **GET IT. ("STEVIE WONDER & MICHAEL JACKSON") / GET IT (instrumental)** 37 80

Oct 88. (7") **MY EYES DON'T CRY. / ('A'instrumental)** ☐ ☐
(12")(cd-s) – ('A'side) / ('A'dub) / ('A'radio edit).

May 89. (7")(c-s) **FREE. / HAPPY BIRTHDAY** 49 ☐
(12"+=)(cd-s+=) – It's wrong (aparteid).

Oct 90 (7")(c-s) **KEEP YOUR LOVE ALIVE. / ('A'instrumental)** ☐ ☐
(12"+=)(cd-s+=) – ('A'version).

May 91. (cd)(c)(lp) **JUNGLE FEVER (Soundtrack)** 56 24
– Fun day / Queen in the black / These three words / Each other's throats / If she breaks your hearts / Gotta have you / Make sure you're sure / Jungle fever / I go sailing / Chemical love / Lighting up the candles.

Jun 91. (7")(c-s) **GOTTA HAVE YOU. / FEEDING OFF THE LOVE OF THE LAND** ☐ 92
(12"+=)(cd-s+=) – ('A'extended mix).

Sep 91. (7")(c-s) **FUN DAY. / ('A'instrumental)** 63 ☐
(12"+=)(cd-s+=) – ('A'remix) / ('A'club mix).

Feb 95. (7")(c-s) **FOR YOUR LOVE. / ('A'mix)** 23 53

(cd-s+=) – My Cherie amour/ Uptight (everything's alright).

Mar 95. (cd)(c) **CONVERSATION PEACE** [8] [16]
– Rain your love down / Edge of eternity / Taboo to love / Take the time out / I'm new / My love is with you / Treat myself / Tomorrow Robins will sing / Sensuous whisper / For your love / Cold chill / Sorry / Conversation peace.

Jul 95. (c-s) **TOMORROW ROBINS WILL SING / ('A'-Wonder West side version)** [71] [ ]
(12") – ('A'-Ronin smooth) / ('A'-Dance Hall) / ('A'-Slo jungle).
(cd-s) – ('A'side) / (above 3 tracks).

Oct 95. (c-s) **COLD CHILL / ('A'mix)** [ ] [ ]
(12"+=)(cd-s+=) – ('A'mixes).

– more compilations, etc. –

Note; on 'Tamla Motown' until otherwise stated.

Dec 68. (lp) **SOMEDAY AT CHRISTMAS** [ ] [ ] Dec 67
(re-iss.+c.Nov82 & 1986)

Sep 76. (7") **YESTER-ME, YESTER-YOU, YESTERDAY. / UPTIGHT (EVERYTHING'S ALRIGHT)** [ ] [ ]

Dec 77. (d-lp)(d-c) **ANTHOLOGY** [ ] [ ]
(both above re-iss.Oct81)

Sep 80. (7") **I WAS MADE TO LOVE HER. / NEVER HAD A DREAM COME TRUE** [ ] [ ]

Sep 80. (7") **SIGNED, SEALED, DELIVERED (I'M YOURS). / FINGERTIPS (part 2)** [ ] [ ]
(both above re-iss.Oct81)

May 83. (c-ep) **CASSINGLE** [ ] [-]
– For once in my life / Signed, sealed, delivered (I'm yours) / My Cherie amour / Yester-me, yester-you, yesterday.

Dec 83. (12") **HAPPY BIRTHDAY. / (Martin Luther King speech extracts)** [ ] [ ]

Apr 85. (7")(12") **FOR ONCE IN MY LIFE. / I WAS MADE TO LOVE HER** [ ] [ ]

Apr 85. (7")(12") **I WISH. / SIR DUKE** [ ] [ ]

Apr 85. (7")(12") **HE'S MISSTRA KNOW IT ALL. / BOOGIE ON REGGAE WOMAN** [ ] [ ]

Oct 86. (cd) **FOR ONCE IN MY LIFE / UPTIGHT** [ ] [ ]

Oct 86. (cd) **MY CHERIE AMOUR / SIGNED, SEALED, DELIVERED, I'M YOURS** [ ] [ ]

Jun 87. (d-lp)(d-c)(d-cd) **THE ESSENTIAL** [ ] [ ]

Jul 87. (cd) **DOWN TO EARTH / I WAS MADE TO LOVE YOU** [ ] [ ]

Apr 88. (7") **FINGERTIPS (part 2). / BLOWIN' IN THE WIND** [ ] [ ]

Apr 88. (7") **NEVER HAD A DREAM COME TRUE. / SIGNED, SEALED, DELIVERED, I'M YOURS** [ ] [ ]

Jun 89. (cd-s) **UPTIGHT (EVERYTHING'S ALRIGHT) / etc.** [ ] [ ]

Feb 79. MFP; (lp)(c) **LIGHT MY FIRE** [ ] [-]

Nov 84. Telstar; (lp)(c) **LOVE SONGS – 16 CLASSIC HITS** [20] [-]
(re-iss.+cdJul86 as '20 CLASSIC HITS' on 'Motown'+4)

Nov 87. Priority; (cd) **THEIR VERY BEST – BACK TO BACK** [ ] [-]

—— (above shared with GLADYS KNIGHT & THE PIPS)

Jul 95. Connoisseur; (cd) **STEVIE WONDER SONGBOOK** [ ] [-]

Sep 95. Motown; cd) **EIVETS REDNOW** [ ] [-]

WONDER STUFF

Formed: Stourbridge, Midlands, England . . . early 1986 by ex-EDEN drummer MILES HUNT and others (see below). After 2 indie ep's on own 'Farout' label, they signed to 'Polydor' late '87. Their 2nd single for the label 'A WISH AWAY', broke the 50 and preceded a joyful Top 20 debut album 'THE EIGHT LEGGED GROOVE MACHINE'. The following years saw them get into Top 5 with next three albums, and hit peak spot with novelty hit 'DIZZY', helped of course by TV comics VIC REEVES and BOB MORTIMER. • **Style:** Alternative grebo punk-poppers who quickly went more commercial than their neighbours POP WILL EAT ITSELF. • **Songwriters:** Group music / HUNT lyrics except; GIMME SOME TRUTH (John Lennon) / THAT'S ENTERTAINMENT (Jam) / INSIDE YOU (Pop Will Eat Itself) / COZ I LUV YOU (Slade). • **Trivia:** Produced in the 80's by Pat Collier.

Recommended: THE EIGHT LEGGED GROOVE MACHINE (*6) / HUP (*6) / NEVER LOVED ELVIS (*7) / IF THE BEATLES HAD READ HUNTER (*8)

MILES HUNT – vocals, guitar / **MALCOLM TREECE** – guitar, vocals / **THE BASS THING** (b.ROB JONES) – bass / **MARTIN GILKS** – drums, percussion (ex-MIGHTY LEMON DROPS)

Farout / not issued

Feb 87. (7"m) **A WONDERFUL DAY / DOWN HERE. / IT'S NOT TRUE / LIKE A MERRY GO ROUND** [ ] [-]

Sep 87. (7") **UNBEARABLE. / TEN TRENCHES DEEP** [ ] [-]
(12"+=) – I am a monster / Frank.

Polydor / Polydor

Apr 88. (7") **GIVE GIVE GIVE ME MORE MORE MORE. / A SONG WITHOUT AN END** [72] [ ]
(12"+=)(cd-s+=) – Meaner than mean / See the free world.

Jul 88. (7") **A WISH AWAY. / JEALOUSY** [43] [ ]
(12"+=)(cd-s+=) – Happy-sad / Goodbye fatman.

Aug 88. (lp)(c)(cd) **THE EIGHT LEGGED GROOVE MACHINE** [18] [ ]
– Redbury joy town / No for the 13th time / It's yer money I'm after baby / Rue the day / Give give give me more more more / Like a merry go round / The animals and me / A wish away / Grin / Mother and I / Some sad someone / Ruby horse / Unbearable / Poison. *(re-iss.cd Apr95)*

Sep 88. (7"ep)(12"ep)(cd-ep) **IT'S YER MONEY I'M AFTER BABY / ASTLEY IN THE NOOSE. / OOH, SHE SAID / RAVE FROM THE GRAVE** [40] [ ]

Feb 89. (7") **WHO WANTS TO BE THE DISCO KING?. / UNBEARABLE (live)** [28] [ ]
(12"+=)(cd-s+=) – Ten trenches deep (live) / No for the 13th time (live).

—— added guests **JAMES TAYLOR** – organ (ex-PRISONERS) / **MARTIN BELL** – banjo

Sep 89. (7")(c-s) **DON'T LET ME DOWN, GENTLY. / IT WAS ME** [19] [ ]
(12"+=)(cd-s+=) – ('A'extended).

Oct 89. (lp)(c)(cd) **HUP** [5] [ ]
– 30 years in the bathroom / Radio ass kiss / Golden green / Let's be other people / Piece of sky / Can't shape up / Good night though / Don't let me down, gently / Cartoon boyfriend / Unfaithful / Them, big oak trees / Room 410. *(re-iss.cd Apr95)*

Nov 89. (7")(c-s) **GOLDEN GREEN. / GET TOGETHER** [33] [ ]
(12"+=)(cd-s+=) – Gimme some truth.

—— (Mar90) **PAUL CLIFFORD** – bass finally repl. The BASS THING (left '89). He later formed 8-piece The BRIDGE AND THE TUNNEL CREW.

May 90. (7")(c-s) **CIRCLESQUARE. / OUR NEW SONG** [20] [ ]
(12"+=)(cd-s+=) – ('A'paranoia mix).

Mar 91. (7")(c-s) **THE SIZE OF A COW. / RADIO ASS KISS (live)** [5] [ ]
(12"+=)(cd-s+=) – Give give give me more more more (live).

May 91. (7")(c-s) **CAUGHT IN MY SHADOW. / GIMME SOME TRUTH (live)** [18] [ ]
(12"+=)(cd-s+=) – ('A'extended).

Jun 91. (cd)(c)(lp) **NEVER LOVED ELVIS** [3] [ ]
– Mission drive / Play / False start / Welcome to the cheap seats / The size of a cow / Sleep alone / Reaction / Inertia / Maybe / Grotesque / Here come everyone / Caught in my shadow / Line poem. *(re-iss.cd Apr95)*

Aug 91. (7")(c-s) **SLEEP ALONE. / EL HERMANO DE FRANK** [43] [ ]
(12"+=)(cd-s+=) – The takin' is easy.

—— In Oct'91, they teamed up with comedian VIC REEVES (& BOB MORTIMER), on No.1 hit Tommy Roe cover 'DIZZY'. Next single with guest **KIRSTY MacCOLL**

Jan 92. (7"ep)(cd-ep) **WELCOME TO THE CHEAP SEATS** [8] [ ]
– Welcome to the cheap seats / Me, my mum, my dad and my brother / Will the circle be unbroken / That's entertainment. (cd-ep+=) – ('A'naked mix) / Caught in my shadw (bare mix) / Circlesque (butt naked mix) / Can't shape up again.

—— added **MARTIN BELL** – fiddle, accordion, mandolin, guitar, sitar, keyboards and 6th member **PETE WHITTAKER** – keyboards

Sep 93. (7"ep)(12"ep)(c-ep)(cd-ep) **ON THE ROPES EP** [10] [ ]
– On the ropes / Professional disturber of the peace / Hank and John / Whites.

Oct 93. (cd)(c)(lp) **CONSTRUCTION FOR THE MODERN IDIOT** [4] [ ]
– Change every light bulb / I wish them all dead / Cabin fever / Hot love now / Full of life (happy now) / Storm drain / On the ropes / Your big assed mother / Swell / A great drinker / Hush / Sing the absurd.

Nov 93. (7") **FULL OF LIFE (HAPPY NOW). / CLOSER TO FINE** [28] [ ]
(cd-s+=) – Burger standing / A curious weird and ugly scene.
(cd-s) – ('A'dignity mix) / Change every light bulb (dub mix) / I wish them all dead (dub mix).

—— Note: Ex-member ROB JONES (THE BASS THING) died mysteriously on 30 Jul'93 in his New York apartment.

Mar 94. (7"ep)(c-ep)(cd-ep) **HOT LOVE NOW! EP** [19] [ ]
– Hot love now! / Just helicopters / I must've had something really useful to say / Room 512, all the news that's fit to print.
(cd-ep) – ('A'cardinal error mix) / Unrest song / Flour babies / The Tipperary triangle.

—— Disbanded after July Phoenix Festival. MILES went onto work for MTV.

– compilations, etc. –

Sep 94. Polydor; (7")(c-s)(cd-s) **UNBEARABLE. / INSIDE YOU / HIT BY A CAR** [16] [ ]
(cd-s) – ('A'original) / Ten trenches deep / I am a monster / Frank.

Sep 94. Polydor; (cd)(c) **IF THE BEATLES HAD READ HUNTER . . . THE SINGLES** [8] [ ]
– Welcome to the cheap seats / A wish away / Caught in my shadow / Don't let me gently / Size of a cow / Hot love now! / Dizzy / Unbearable / Circlesquare / Who wants to be the disco king? / Golden green / Give give give me more more more / Sleep alone / Coz I luv you / Full of life / On the ropes / It's yer money I'm after baby / It's not true.

Jul 95. Windsong; (cd) **LIVE IN MANCHESTER (live)** [74] [-]

WE KNOW WHERE YOU LIVE

TREECE / CLIFFORD / GILKS / + ANGE – vocals (ex-EAT)

H.M.D. / not issued

Nov 95. (7"ep)(cd-ep) **DON'T BE TOO HONEST. / CONFESSIONS OF A THUG / EXCUSE ME?** [ ] [-]

Ron WOOD (see under ⇒ ROLLING STONES)

Roy WOOD (see under ⇒ MOVE)

WORLD PARTY

Formed: London, England . . . 1986 by producer / keyboard virtuoso KARL WALLINGER. On the strength of past WATERBOYS pedigree, they he/WORLD PARTY signed to 'Ensign'UK. Almost immediately broke through in the US, when SHIP OF FOOLS hit the Top 30. • **Style:** 60's psychedelia mixed with tint of folk-rock. • **Songwriters:** All WALLINGER, except ALL I REALLY WANT TO DO (Bob Dylan) / HAPPINESS IS A WARM GUN (Beatles) / sampled SAY WHAT (by Troublefunk) on GIVE IT ALL AWAY. • **Trivia:** SINEAD O'CONNOR guested on debut album.

Recommended: PRIVATE REVOLUTION (*8) / GOODBYE JUMBO(*8)

KARL WALLINGER (b.19 Oct'57, Prestatyn, Wales) – vocals, keyboards, synth. with **MARTYN SWAIN + GUY CHAMBERS** (also both ex-WATERBOYS)

Ensign Chrysalis

Aug 86. (7") **PRIVATE REVOLUTION. / HOLY WATER**
(12"+=) – Trouble down here.

— (above 'A' as "WORLD PARTY with SINEAD O'CONNOR")

Feb 87. (7") **SHIP OF FOOLS. / WORLD GROOVE (DO THE MIND GUERILLA)** [42] [27]
(12"+=) – Now here man.
(cd-s+=) – Trouble down here / Private revolution.

Mar 87. (lp)(c)(cd) **PRIVATE REVOLUTION** [56] [39]
– Private revolution / Making love (to the world) / Ship of fools / All come true / Dance of the hoppy lads / It can be beautiful (sometimes) / Ballad of the little man / Hawaiian island world / All I really want to do / World party / It's all mine.

— KARL tours w /6-piece incl.**CHRIS SHARROCK** – drums (ex-ICICLE WORKS)

Ensign Ensign

May 90. (7") **MESSAGE IN A BOX. / NATURE GIRL** [39]
(12"+=)(cd-s+=) – You're all invited to the party / Happiness is a warm gun.

May 90. (cd)(c)(lp) **GOODBYE JUMBO** [36]
– Is it too late? / Way down now / When the rainbow comes / Put the message in the box / Ain't gonna come till I'm ready / And I fell back alone / Take it up / God on my side / Show me to the top / Love street / Sweet soul dream / Thank you world. *(re-iss.cd Mar94)*

Aug 90. (7")(c-s) **WAY DOWN NOW. / WATCHING AND WAITING** [6]
(12"+=)/ /(cd-s++=) – ('A'remix) / S.E.X./ / Love street (live).

Apr 91. (7") **THANK YOU WORLD. / ('A' Peter Lorimer mix)** [68]
(12"+=)(cd-s+=) – ('A'live version).

— In 1991, CHAMBERS left forming LEMON GRASS the following year.

— **KARL WALLINGER, CHRIS SHARROCK + DAVE CATLIN-BIRCH,** plus guests **GUY CHAMBERS, DOMINIC MILLER, KAREN RAMELISE**

Mar 93. (7")(c-s) **IS IT LIKE TODAY. / BASICALLY** [19]
(cd-s) – ('A'side) / Ship of fools / World without love.
(cd-s) – ('A'side) / Message in a box / The little man (1985 demo).

Apr 93. (cd)(c)(lp) **BANG!** [2]
– Kingdom come / Is it like today? / What is love all about? / And God said. . . / Give it all away / Sooner or later / Hollywood / Radiodays / Rescue me / Sunshine / All I gave / Give it all away (reprise).

Jul 93. (12")(c-s) **GIVE IT ALL AWAY. / MYSTERY GIRL** [43]
(cd-s+=) – Closer still / Basically.
(cd-s) – ('A'side) / My pretty one / World groove (do the mind gurilla).

Sep 93. (7")(c-s) **ALL I GAVE. / NO MORE CRYING** [37]
(cd-s+=) – Sunset.
(cd-s) – ('A'side) / Time on my hands / Is it too late / Radio days (live).

Link WRAY

Born: LINCOLN WRAY, (Part Indian) 1930, Fort Bragg, North Carolina, USA. After playing in a country band with his brothers DOUG and VERNON, he signed to 'Cadence' US in 1958, where his 1955 recorded debut 'RUMBLE' hit the Top 20. His next single 'RAW-HIDE' also became Top 30, but this was his last taste of fame, and he slid into cult notoriety. He made several attempts to revive past, but all in vain. • **Style:** Instrumental rockabilly artist, whose influence on the likes of DUANE EDDY etc, has been understated. • **Songwriters:** Host of TV shows MILT GRANT, wrote RUMBLE. He penned others, except many covers on albums LIVE AT THE PARADISO and GOOD ROCKIN' TONIGHT. • **Trivia:** He's been married 3 times or more?, and at the last count had fathered 8 or 9 children. A legend or what?

Recommended: THE ORIGINAL RUMBLE MAN (*7)

LINK WRAY & HIS RAY MEN

Between 1957-1964, his WRAYMEN were; **DOUG WRAY** – drums, sax, flute/ **SHORTY HORTON** – bass (added in 1963; **VERNON WRAY** – keyboards)

London Cadence

May 58. (7") **RUMBLE. / THE SWAG** [16] Apr 58

not issued Epic

Jan 59. (7") **RAW-HIDE. / THE DIXIE DOODLE** [-] [23]
(UK-iss.1975)

1959. (7") **COMMANCHE. / LILLIAN** [-]
1959. (7") **SLINKY. / RENDEZVOUS** [-]
1960. (7") **GOLDEN STRINGS. / TRAIL OF THE LONESOME PINE** [-]
1960. (7") **MARY ANN. / AIN'T THAT LOVIN' YOU BABY** [-]
1960. (lp) **LINK WRAY & THE WRAY MEN** [-]
– Dixie-doodle / Ramble / Caroline / Raw-hide / Right turn / Golden strings / Comanche / Hambone / Mary Ann / Rumble mambo / Ain't that lovin' you baby / Slinky / Hand clapper / Lillian / Radar / Studio blues. *(UK-iss.Jun85 on 'Edsel') (UK version iss.1973 & Apr76 as 'ROCKIN' AND HANDCLAPPIN')*

1961. (7") **EL TORO. / TIAJUANA** [-]

not issued Rumble

1962. (7") **JACK THE RIPPER. / THE STRANGER** [-]

Stateside Swan

Aug 63. (7") **JACK THE RIPPER. / THE BLACK WIDOW** [64] Jun 63

1963. (lp) **JACK THE RIPPER** [-]
– Mr guitar / My Beth / Deacon Jones / Steel trap / Cross ties / Jack the Ripper / Ace of spades / Hidden charms / Fat back / Run chicken run / Dinosaur / Big Ben / Mash potato party / I'll do anything for you / Rendez-vous / Slinky *(UK-iss.Jun90 on 'Hangman')*

Sep 63. (7") **TURNPIKE U.S.A. / WEEKEND** [-]
Nov 63. (7") **THE SWEEPER. / RUN CHICKEN RUN** [-]
Jan 64. (7") **THE SWEEPER. / WEEKEND** [-]
Feb 64. (7"ep) **MR.GUITAR / DINOSAUR. / RUN CHICKEN RUN / RUMBLE** [-]
1964. (7") **THE SHADOW KNOWS. / MY ALBERTA** [-]
1964. (7") **DEUCES WILD. / SUMMER DREAM** [-]

— **BOBBY HOWARD** – vocals repl. VERNON

Mar 65. (7") **GOOD ROCKIN' TONIGHT. / I'LL DO ANYTHING FOR YOU**

LINK WRAY

not issued Swan

1965. (7") **BRANDED. / HANG ON** [-]
1965. (7") **GIRL FROM NORTH COUNTRY. / YOU HURT ME SO** [-]
1966. (7") **ACE OF SPADES. / THE FUZZ** [-]
1966. (7") **BATMAN THEME. / ALONE** [-]
1966. (7") **HIDDEN CHARMS. / ACE OF SPADES** [-]
1967. (7") **LET THE GOOD TIMES ROLL. / SOUL TRAIN** [-]
1967. (7") **JACK THE RIPPER. / I'D DO ANYTHING FOR YOU** [-]

not issued Heavy

1968. (7") **RUMBLE '68. / BLOW YOUR MIND** [-]

not issued Mr. G.

1969. (7") **RUMBLE '69. / BLOW YOUR MIND** [-]

— returned for the 70's, w/**DOUG + BOBBY + BILLY HODGES** – keyboards / **STEVE VERROCA** – drums

Polydor Polydor

Sep 71. (lp) **LINK WRAY** Jul 71
– La de da / Take me home Jesus / Juke box mama / Rise and fall of Jimmy Stokes / Fallin' rain / Fire and brimstone / Ice people / God out west / Crowbar / Black river swamp / Tail dragger

Sep 71. (7") **FIRE AND BRIMSTONE. / JUKE BOX MAMA**
Nov 71. (7") **FALLIN' RAIN. / JUKE BOX MAMA** [-]

— w/loads on session incl. guests **PETER KAUKONEN + COMMANDER CODY**

Jul 73. (lp) **BE WHAT YOU WANT TO**
– Be what you want to / All cried out / Lawdy Miss Clawdy / Tucson, Arizona / Riverbed / You walked by / Walk easy, walk slow / All the love in my life / You realy got a hold on me / Shine the light / Morning.

Aug 73. (7") **LAWDY MISS CLAWDY. / SHINE THE LIGHT**
Nov 73. (7") **SHE'S THAT KIND OF WOMAN. / I GOT TO RUMBLE** [-]

— w/1971 line-up, except **MORDICAI JONES** – piano, mandolin repl. BOBBY

Virgin not issued

Sep 73. (lp) **BEANS & FATBACK** [-]
– Beans and fatback / I'm so glad / Shaw Nee tribe / Hobo man / Georgia pines / Alabama circus / Water boy / From Tulsa to North Carolina / Right or wrong / In the pines / Take my hand.

Nov 73. (7") **I'M SO GLAD I'M SO PROUD. / SHAWNEE TRIBE** [-]
Apr 75. (lp) **INTERSTATE 10** (iss. on 'Caroline' FRANCE) [-] [-]

— LINK now w/**ARCHIE LEGGAT** – bass / **FREDDIE SMITH** – drums, percussion / **GORDON SMITH** – steel guitar / **RUAN O'LOCHLAINN** – keyboards, alto sax

Mar 76. (lp) **STUCK IN GEAR**
– Southern lady / Tecolote / Quicksand / I know you're leaving me now / Did you see the man / Midnight lover / Cottoncandy apples / Bo Jack / Jack the ripper.

Apr 76. (7") **I KNOW YOU'RE LEAVING ME NOW. / QUICKSAND** [-]

ROBERT GORDON & LINK WRAY

w/also; **BILLY CROSS** – guitar / **ROB STONER** – bass, piano / **HOWIE WYETH** – drums/ **CHARLIE MESSING** – guitar (on first duo lp only)

Private Stock Private Stock

Jul 77. (7") **RED HOT. / SWEET SURRENDER** [83]
Oct 77. (lp)(c) **ROBERT GORDON WITH LINK WRAY**
– Red hot / I sure miss you / Summertime blues / Boppin' the blues / Sweet surrender / Flyin' saucers rock & roll / The fool / It's in the bottle / Woman / Is this the way

Dec 77. (7") **ENDLESS SLEEP. / THE FOOL** [-]
Mar 78. (7") **FIRE. / IF THIS IS WRONG** [-]
Apr 78. (lp)(c) **FRESH FISH SPECIAL**
– The way I walk / Red Cadillac and a black moustache / If this is wrong / Five days, five days / Fire / I want to be free / Twenty flight rock / Sea cruise / Lonesome train / Blue eyes.

May 78. (7")(12") **THE WAY I WALK. / SEA CRUISE** [-]
1978. (7") **SEA CRUISE. / IT'S IN THE BOTTLE** [-]
1978. (7") **HIGHER. / IF THIS IS WRONG** [-]

— Singer ROBERT GORDON went on to make records for 'RCA'.

LINK WRAY

w/line-up from last dual record, plus; **ANTON FIG** – drums / **CHRIS ROBINSON** – keyboards, synthesizers / + producer **RICHARD GOTTEHEIR** – piano, etc.

Charisma Visa

May 79. (7")(7"blue) **IT'S ALL OVER NOW, BABY BLUE. / JUST THAT KIND OF SWITCHBLADE**
May 79. (lp)(c) **BULLSHOT**
– Good good lovin' / Fever / Snag / Just that kind of switchblade / It's all over now, baby blue / Rawhide / Wild party / The sky is falling / Don't. *(cd-iss.Nov89 on 'Line')*

— w/**ANTON FIG / + JIMMY LOWELL** – bass

Magnum F. Visa

Oct 80. (lp) **LIVE AT THE PARADISO (live)**
– Blue suede shoes / Ace of spades / Walk away from love / I saw her standing there / Run chicken run / She's no good / Rumble / Rawhide / Subway blues / Money / Shake, rattle and roll / Be bop a lula. *(re-iss.Jul82, cd-iss.Apr91)*

— w/**KEITH LENTIN** – bass, vocals / **MARTY FEIER** – drums

Big Beat not issued

Jan 86. (lp) **LIVE IN '85 (live)** [-]
– Rumble / It's only words / Fire / Mystery train / I gotta woman / Baby let's play house / Jack the ripper / Love me / King Creole / I'm counting on you / Rawhide / Born to be wild.

Sep 87. (lp) **GROWLING GUITAR** (60's tracks) [ ] [-]
– Climbing a high wall / Genocide / The Earth is crying / Growlin' guts / Hungry / Ace of spades / Ruby baby / Hang on / Summer dreams / Sorrento / Peggy Sue / Alone / Girl from North Country / You hurt me so / The fuzz. *(cd-iss.May91 with LIVE IN '85 • tracks)*

— with **KIM HYTTEL** – keyboards / **FLEMMING NILSSON** – percussion / **SHAKY GROUND band: JAN MOLS** – rhythm guitar, vocals / **CARSTEN EGHOLM** – bass / **ERIK LODBERG** – drums writes music & lyrics with wife OLIVE.

Ball Product | Sony Denmark

Jun 93. (cd) **INDIAN CHILD** [ ] [ ]
– Torture / Trying to find your love / Indian child / God's litle baby / I apologize / Saving all my love / Diamonds and pearls / It was Elvis / Guitar man from New Orleans / Bring on the night.

– compilations, etc. –

1971. Union Pacific; (lp) **THERE'S GOOD ROCKIN' TONITE** [ ] [ ]
(re-iss.Sep82)
1973. Epic; (lp) **ROCKIN' AND HANDCLAPPIN'**, (rec.1959) [-] [ ]
Nov 76. Polydor; (lp) **THE LINK WRAY RUMBLE** [ ] [ ] Oct 74
— (next single quickly withdrawn)
Mar 78. Chiswick; (7") **BATMAN. / HIDDEN CHARMS** [ ] [-]
Mar 78. Ace; (lp) **THE EARLY RECORDINGS** [ ] [-]
May 89. Ace; (lp) **RUMBLE MAN** [ ] [-]
Nov 89. Ace; (cd) **THE ORIGINAL RUMBLE MAN** [ ] [-]
Mar 90. Ace; (lp) **APACHE** [ ] [-]
Jun 90. Ace; (lp) **WILD SIDE OF THE CITY LIGHTS** [ ] [-]
Apr 79. Charly; (lp) **ROCK'N'ROLL RUMBLE** [ ] [-]
(re-iss.May83 as 'GOOD ROCKIN' TONITE' on 'Ace-Chiswick')
Apr 80. Revival; (7") **RUMBLE. / ('B'by 'The Bobby Fuller Four')** [ ] [-]
(re-iss.Jul82)
— In the US, 'Vermillion' records issued GREAT GUITAR HITS and SINGS & PLAYS.
Nov 89. Hangman; (lp) **SWAN DEMOS '64** [ ] [-]
Sep 90. Norton; (lp) **HILLBILLY WOLF: MISSING LINKS VOL.1** [ ] [-]
Sep 90. Norton; (lp) **BIG CITY AFTER DARK: MISSING LINKS VOL.2** [ ] [-]
Sep 90. Norton; (lp) **SOME KINDA NUT: MISSING LINKS VOL.3** [ ] [-]
May 93. Epic; (cd) **WALKING WITH LINK** [ ] [ ]
Oct 94. Rollercoaster; (cd-ep) **MR.GUITAR EP** [ ] [ ]
– Jack The Ripper / Ace of spades / Black widow.
Mar 95. Rollercoaster; (cd-ep) **PULP FICTION EP** [ ] [-]
– Rumble / Ace of spades / +?
Sep 95. Polydor; (cd) **THE POLYGRAM YEARS** [ ] [-]

Gary WRIGHT (see under ⇒ SPOOKY TOOTH)

Richard WRIGHT (see under ⇒ PINK FLOYD)

WU-TANG CLAN

Formed: Staten Island, New York, USA . . .early 90's by a posse of nine young hip hop rappers under the pseudonyms; METHOD MAN, GENIUS, GZA, (SHALLAH) CHEF RAEKWON, OL' DIRTY BASTARD, PRINCE RAKEEM, REBEL INS, GHOSTFACE KILLER and U-GOD. All chess-loving wordsmiths were highly influenced by martial art movies and took their name from the WU-TANG or SHAOLIN sword. In 1991, GENIUS released debut album for 'Cold Chillin'; 'WORDS FROM THE GENIUS', while RAKEEM ousted an album for 'Tommy Boy'. The following year, the conglomerate signed for 'RCA', although each member was allowed to retain his seperate contract, if he had one. In 1993 complete with Kung-Fu style movie samples, WU-TANG CLAN's debut 'ENTER THE WU-TANG (36 CHAMBERS)', cracked the charts and showed the socially aware, wise-cracking gang in full flow. However in March the following year, tragedy struck when U-GOD's toddler son DANTE HAWKINS, was hit by a bullet in a cross-fire battle and was seriously injured. 1995 was a busy and commercially fruitful year for most of the crew, especially OL' DIRTY BASTARD, METHOD MAN, CHEF RAEKWON and the combined efforts of GENIUS / GZA (see below). • **Trivia:** GZA also works with PRINCE PAUL and FRUITKWAN (ex-STETASONIC).

Recommended: ENTER THE WU-TANG (36 CHAMBERS) (*7) / LIQUID SWORDS (GENIUS / GZA; *9) / TICAL (METHOD MAN; 7) / still assessing others and below discography is selective and not as accurate going to press

GENIUS

not issued | Cold Chill

1991. (cd)(c) **WORDS FROM THE GENIUS** [-] [ ]

WU-TANG CLAN

METHOD MAN (r.n. JOHNNY BLAZE) / **GENIUS** (r.n. G.PRICE) / **GZA** (r.n. R. DIGGS) / **OL' DIRTY BASTARD** (r.n. D.COLES) / **CHEF RAEKWON** (r.n. LOU DIAMOND) / **GHOSTFACE KILLER** (r.n. TONY STARKS) / **U-GOD** (r.n. L. HAWKINS) / **PRINCE RAKEEM + REBEL INS** with affiliated members **SHYLEIM THE RUGGED PRINCE (PAUL) + DOLLY FINGERS + DREDDY KRUGER**

Loud-RCA | Loud-RCA

May 94. (cd)(c)(lp) **ENTER THE WU-TANG (36 CHAMBERS)** [ ] [ ]
– Bring da ruckus / Shame on a nigga / Clan in da Front / 7th chamber (Wu-Tang) / Can it all be so simple / Da mystery of chess boxin' / Wu-Tang Clan ain't nuthing ta taf wit / C.R.E.A.M. / Method Man / Protect ya neck / Tearz / 7th Chamber (part 2) (Wu-Tang)

OL' DIRTY BASTARD

Elektra | Elektra

Mar 95. (cd)(c) **RETURN TO THE 36 CHAMBERS** (dirty version) [ ] [7]

METHOD MAN

Def Jam | Def Jam

Dec 94. (c-s)(cd-s) **BRING THE PAIN /** [-] [45]
Apr 95. (c-s) **RELEASE YO SELF /** [46] [98] Feb 95
(cd-s+=) –
— below A-side featured MARY J.BLIGE
Jul 95. (c-s) **I'LL BE THERE FOR YOU / YOU'RE ALL I NEED TO GET BY** [ ] [41] May95
(12"+=)(cd-s+=) – Bring the pain (remix) / Release yo self.
Aug 95. (cd)(c) **TICAL** [ ] [4]
Aug 95. (c-s)(cd-s) **HOW HIGH /** [-] [13]
— above single credited with REDMAN

CHEF RAEKWON

Loud-RCA | Loud-RCA

Jul 95. (c-s)(cd-s) **GLACIERS OF ICE / CRIMINOLOGY** [ ] [43]
Aug 95. (cd)(c) **ONLY BUILT 4 CUBAN LINE** [ ] [4]
Oct 95. (c-s)(cd-s) **ICE CREAM /** [-] [43]

GENIUS / GZA

with some of the posse

Geffen | Geffen

Oct 95. (c-s)(cd-s) **LIQUID SWORDS /** [ ] [48]
Nov 95. (cd)(c) **LIQUID SWORDS** [73] [9]
– Swordsman – Unexplained / Liquid swords / Living in the world today / 4th chapter / Cold sword / Labels / Duel of the iron mic / Shadow boxin' / Killah hills 10304 / Investigate reports / Gold / I gotcha back / B.I.B.L.E. (Basic Instructions Before Leaving Earth) / Hell's wind.

Robert WYATT

Born: 28 Jan'45, Bristol, England. While at school he formed The WILDE FLOWERS, which soon were spliced into 2 groups, CARAVAN and SOFT MACHINE. The latter being WYATT's choice in 1966, but after 4 albums ('THE SOFT MACHINE', 'VOLUME 2', 'THIRD' & 'FOURTH'), he estranged himself from group in '71 to form MATCHING MOLE. The previous year, his record label 'CBS', had issued his first solo album 'THE END OF THE EAR'. In the summer of '73, WYATT was paralysed from the waist down after falling from a window. He returned in a wheel-chair the following year on Top Of The Pops, when single 'I'M A BELIEVER' hit the UK Top 30. He had signed to Richard Branson's 'Virgin' records earlier in the year, and was critically heralded for his NICK MASON produced album 'ROCK BOTTOM'. In 1983, through constant airplay by Radio 1 DJ John Peel, he gained another hit on 80's indie label 'Rough Trade', with anti-Falklands war song 'SHIPBUILDING'. • **Style:** Articulate and politically aware artist, whose anti-commercial approach to rock music, gained him much respect in business. • **Songwriters:** WYATT penned except: I'M A BELIEVER (Monkees) / YESTERDAY MAN (Chris Andrews) / GRASS (Ivor Cutler) / STRANGE FRUIT (Billie Holliday) / AT LAST I AM FREE (Chic) / STALIN WASN'T STALLIN' (Golden Gate Quartet) / SHIPBUILDING (Elvis Costello-Clive Langer) / BIKO (Peter Gabriel). • **Trivia:** WYATT also provided session drums for SYD BARRETT (1969) / KEVIN AYERS (early 70's) / HENRY COW (1975) / NICK MASON (1981) / RAINCOATS (1981 & 83).

Recommended: NOTHING CAN STOP US (*8) / ROCK BOTTOM (*7)

ROBERT WYATT (solo) – vocals, drums (ex-SOFT MACHINE) w / **DAVID SINCLAIR** – oboe (of CARAVAN) / **MARK CHARIG** – cornet (of SOFT MACHINE) / **ELTON DEAN** – sax / plus **NEVILLE WHITEHEAD** – bass / **CYRIL AYERS** – percussion

C.B.S. | Columbia

Oct 70. (lp)(c) **THE END OF AN EAR** [ ] [ ]
– Las Vegas tango (part 1) / To Mark everywhere / To saintly Bridget / To Oz alien Daevyd and Gilly / To Nick everyone / To caravan and Brother Jim / To the old world (thank you for the use of your body) / To Carla, Marsha and Caroline (for making everything beautifuller) / Las Vegas tango (part 2). *(re-iss.Aug80) (cd-iss.Apr93 on 'Sony Europe')*

MATCHING MOLE

WYATT with retained guest **D.SINCLAIR** and band **DAVE McRAE** – keyboards / **BILL McCORMICK** – bass (ex-QUIET SUN) / **PHIL MILLER** – guitar (ex-DYBLE, COXHILL & THE MB's) (same label)

Apr 72. (lp)(c) **MATCHING MOLE** [ ] [ ]
– O Caroline / Instant pussy / Signed curtain / Part of the dance / Instant kitten / Dedicated to Hugh, but you weren't listening / Beer as in braindeer / Immediate curtain. *(re-iss.Mar82) (cd-iss.Mar93 on 'B.G.O.)*
Apr 72. (7") **O CAROLINE. / SIGNED CURTAIN** [ ] [-]
Oct 72. (lp)(c) **MATCHING MOLE'S LITTLE RED RECORD** [ ] [ ]

– Gloria gloom / God song / Flora fidgit / Smoke signal / Starting in the middle of the day we can drink all our politics away / Marchides / Nan's true hole / Righteous rumba / Brandy as in Benji. *(cd-iss.Jul93 on 'B.G.O.)*

— In the summer of '73, WYATT was paralysed from the waist down after falling from a window. After a year convalescing, but still in a wheelchair;

ROBERT WYATT

returned as solo vocalist. He was augmented by guests/friends **FRED FRITH** – percussion / **HUGH HOPPER** – bass / **GARY WINDO** – wind / **LAURIE ALLEN** – drums / **MIKE OLDFIELD** – guitar / **RICHARD SINCLAIR** – bass / **IVOR CUTLER** – vox, keys / **ALFREDA BENGE** – vocals

Virgin Virgin

Jul 74. (lp)(c) **ROCK BOTTOM** [ ] [ ]
– Sea song / A last straw / Little Red Riding Hood hit the road (part 1) / Alifib / Alife / Little Red Riding Hood hit the road (part 2). *(cd-iss.Feb89)*

Sep 74. (7") **I'M A BELIEVER. / MEMORIES** [29] [ ]

— **WYATT** retained **FRITH, ALLEN & WINDO** and contributions from **PHIL MANZANERA** – guitar / **BILL McCORMICK** – bass / **BRIAN ENO** – synthesizers / **JOHN GREAVES** – bass / **MONEZI FEZI** – trumpet / **GEORGE KHAN** – saxophone

May 75. (lp)(c) **RUTH IS STRANGER THAN RICHARD** [ ] [ ]
– Muddy house: (a) Solar flames – (b) Five black notes and one white tone – (c) Muddy mouth / Soup song / Sonia / Team spirit 1 & 2 / Soup for Che. *(cd-iss.Feb89)*

Apr 77. (7") **YESTERDAY MAN. / SONJA** [ ] [-]

— accompanied only by **McCORMICK** – bass / **HARRY BECKETT** – flugelhorn (Bside)

Rough Trade not issued

Mar 80. (7") **ARAUCO. / CAIMENERA** [ ] [-]

— now used only **MOGOTSI MOTHLE** – double bass / **FRANK ROBERTS** – keyboards

Nov 80. (7") **AT LAST I AM FREE. / STRANGE FRUIT** [ ] [-]

Feb 81. (7") **STALIN WASN'T STALLIN'. / STALINGRAD ('B'by "P.BLACKMAN")** [ ] [-]

— now with **ESMAIL SHEK** – tabla / **KADIR DURUESH** – shenzi

Aug 81. (7") **GRASS. / TRADE UNION ('B'by "DISHARI" featuring ABDUS SALIQUE)** [ ] [-]

Apr 82. (lp) **NOTHING CAN STOP US** [ ] [-]
– Born again cretin / At last I am free / Quantanera / Grass / Stalin wasn't stalling / The red flag / Strange fruit / Arauco / Strange fruit / Trade union / Stalingrad. *(re-iss.+c.Apr83 +=)* – Shipbuilding. *(cd-iss. May87)*

— Above album featured musicians as 1980-82.

In Apr'82, WYATT was credited on BEN WATT ep 'SUMMER INTO WINTER'.

— *(cd-ep iss.Feb93)*

— guests **STEVE NIEVE** – piano / **MARK BEDDERS** – double bass / **MARTIN HUGHES** – drums / **CLIVE LANGER** – organ / **ELVIS COSTELLO** – b.vox

Aug 82. (7") **SHIPBUILDING. / MEMORIES OF YOU** [ ] [-]
(re-iss.Nov82 +12"+= – Round midnight.(re-iss.Apr83, hit 35)

— now with ? plus **HUGH HOPPER,** etc.

May 84. (m-lp) **THE ANIMAL FILM (Soundtrack)** [ ] [-]
– (no tracks listed) *(cd-iss.Jul94)*

Aug 84. (12"ep) **WORK IN PROGRESS** [ ] [-]
– Biko / Amber and the amberines / Yolanda / Te rescuerdo Amanda.

Oct 85. (7")(12") **THE WIND OF CHANGE. ("ROBERT WYATT with The SWAPO SINGERS") / NAMIBIA** [ ] [-]

Dec 85. (lp)(c) **OLD ROTTENHAT** [ ] [-]
– Alliance / The United States of amnesia / East Timor / Speechless / The age of self / Vandalusia / The British road / Mass medium / Gharbzadegi / P.I.A. *(cd-iss.Nov86)*

Sep 91. (cd)(c)(lp) **DONDESTAN (1-side with "BENGE")** [ ] [-]
– Costa / The sight of the wind / Worship / Catholic architecture / Shrink rap / Left on man / Lisp service / CP jeebies / Dondestan.

Voiceprint not issued

Nov 92. (cd+book) **A SHORT BREAK** [ ] [-]
– A short break / Tubab / Kutcha / Ventilatir / Unmasked.

– compilations, others, etc. –

Mar 81. Virgin; (d-lp)(c) **ROCK BOTTOM / RUTH IS STRANGER THAN RICHARD** [ ] [-]

Apr 82. Virgin; (7"ep) **FROM MAN TO WOMAN (Stage Production with Cast)** [ ] [-]

Dec 84. Rough Trade; (lp) **1982-1984** [-] [ ]

Feb 85. Recommended; (12") **THE LAST NIGHTINGALE. / ON THE BEACH AT CAMBRIDGE** [ ] [-]

— next 'B'side by "The GRIMETHORPE COLLIERY BAND".

Sep 85. T.U.C.; (7") **THE AGE OF SELF. / RAISE YOUR BANNERS HIGH** [ ] [-]

Sep 87. Strange Fruit; (12"ep) **THE PEEL SESSIONS** (10.9.74) [ ] [-]
– Soup song / Sea sing / Alife / I'm a believer.

Jan 93. Rough Trade; (cd) **MID EIGHTIES** (was US release) [ ] [-]

Jul 94. Windsong; (cd) **BBC RADIO 1 LIVE IN CONCERT (MATCHING MOLE live)** [ ] [-]

Jul 94. Virgin; (d-cd) **GOING BACK A BIT: A LITTLE HISTORY OF . . .** [ ] [-]

Pete WYLIE (see under ⇒ WAH!)

Bill WYMAN (see under ⇒ ROLLING STONES)

Steve WYNN (see under ⇒ DREAM SYNDICATE)

X

Formed: Los Angeles, California, USA . . . 1977 by EXENE, BILLY and JOHN. After one-off 1978 debut on 'Slaughterhouse', they signed to newly formed indie 'Slash' label. Their first two acclaimed albums were produced by RAY MANZAREK (ex-DOORS), which helped them acquire major status on 'Elektra' in 1982. Always on the verge of commercial success up to mid 80's. • **Style:** Cowpunk rock (a hybrid of country and raw punk), influenced by 60's garage punks FUGS and MC5 with a tone of 50's country & rockabilly. Emerged with a fuller heavy sound by the late 80's. • **Songwriters:** All group compositions except WILD THING (Troggs) / ALL OR NOTHING (Small Faces) / IT'S IN HIS KISS (Betty Everett) / SOUL KITCHEN (Doors) / POSITIVELY 4th STREET (Bob Dylan) / U.S. MALE (Elvis Presley). • **Trivia:** In 1982, EXENE and LYDIA LUNCH had book of poetry published called 'Adulterers Anonymous'. With that title it's not surprising that in 1984, EXENE and JOHN were divorced after short marriage. (A new group X on 'Big Life' are not the same).

Recommended: MORE FUN IN THE NEW WORLD (*7) / WILD GIFT (*8)

EXENE CERVENKA (b.CHRISTINE) – vocals / **BILLY ZOOM** – guitar / **JOHN DOE** (b.1954, Decateur, Illinois) – bass, vocals / **D.J. BONEBRAKE** (b.DON) – drums repl. MICK BASHER

not issued | Slaughter..

Apr 78. (7") **ADULT BOOKS. / WE'RE DESPERATE** [-] [ ]

not issued | Slash

Jun 80. (7") **THE WORLD'S A MESS. / IT'S IN HIS KISS** [-] [ ]
Jun 80. (lp) **LOS ANGELES** [-] [ ]
– Your phone's off the hook, but you're not / Johnny hit and run Pauline / Soul kitchen / Nausea / Sugarlight / Los Angeles / Sex and dying in high society / The unheard music / The world's a mess, it's in my kiss.
Jun 81. (7") **WE'RE DESPERATE. / GET USED TO IT** [-] [ ]
Jun 81. (lp) **WILD GIFT** [-] [ ]
– The once over twice / We're desperate / Adult books / Universal corner / I'm coming over / It's who you know / In this house that I call home / Some other time / White girl / Beyond and back / Back 2 the base / When our love passed out on the coach / Year 1.
Aug 81. (7") **WHITE GIRL. / YOUR PHONE'S OFF THE HOOK** [-] [ ]

Elektra | Elektra

Jul 82. (7") **BLUE SPARK. / DANCING WITH TEARS IN MY EYES** [ ] [ ]
Jul 82. (lp)(c) **UNDER THE BIG BLACK SUN** [ ] [76]
– The hungry wolf / Motel room in my bed / Riding with Mary / Come back to me / Under the big black sun / Because I do / Blue spark / Dancing with tears in my eyes / Real child of Hell / How I (learned my lesson) / The have nots.
Jun 83. (7") **BREATHLESS. / RIDING WITH MARY** [-] [ ]
Sep 83. (lp)(c) **MORE FUN IN THE NEW WORLD** [ ] [86]
– The new world / We're having much more fun / True love / Poor girl / Make the music go bang / Breathless / I must not think bad thoughts / Devil doll / Painting the town blue / Hot house / Drunk in my past / I see red / True love £2.
Jan 84. (7") **THE NEW WORLD. / I MUST NOT THINK BAD THOUGHTS** [ ] [ ]
Jun 84. (12") **WILD THING. / TRUE LOVE (part 2)** [-] [-]
Jun 84. (7") **WILD THING. / DEVIL DOLL** [-] [ ]

— In 1985, JOHN DOE splintered with country-western project The KNITTERS. They included HENRY ROLLINS (of BLACK FLAG), DAVE ALVIN (of BLASTERS) + JOHNNY RAY BARTEL and made one album POOR LITTLE CRITTER ON THE ROAD. In fact, X brought in **DAVE ALVIN** – guitar to repl. BILLY

Aug 85. (7") **BURNING HOUSE OF LOVE. / LOVE SHACK** [ ] [ ]
(12"+=) – Wild thing.
Sep 85. (lp)(c) **AIN'T LOVE GRAND** [ ] [89] Aug 85
– Burning house of love / Love shack / My soul cries your name / My goodness / Around my heart / What's wrong with me . . . / All or nothing / Watch the sun go down / I'll stand up for you / Little honey / Supercharged.

— **TONY GILKYSON** – guitar (ex-LONE JUSTICE) repl. ALVIN who went solo

Jul 87. (lp)(c) **SEE HOW WE ARE** [ ] [ ]
– I'm lost / You / 4th of July / In the time it takes / Anyone can fill your shoes / See how we are / Left & right / When it rains . . . / Holiday story / Surprise surprise / Cyrano de Berger's back.
Jul 87. (7") **4th OF JULY. / POSITIVELY 4th STREET** [-] [ ]
May 88. (d-lp)(c)(cd) **LIVE AT THE WHISKEY A GO-GO ON THE FABULOUS SUNSET STRIP (live)** [ ] [ ]
– Los Angeles / House I call home / The new world / Around my heart / Surprise surprise / Because I do / Burning house of love / My goodness / Blue spark / The once over twice / In the time it takes / Devil doll / Hungry wolf / Just another perfect day / Unheard music / Riding with Mary / The world's a mess / True love / White girl / Skin deep town / So long / Call of the wreckin' ball / Year 1 / Johnny hit a run / Pauline.

R.C.A. | R.C.A.

Oct 89. (7") **WILD THING. / (part 2)** [ ] [ ]
('A'full version-12"+=)(cd-s+=) – Oh you angel / U.S. male.

— Dissolve after final flop.

JOHN DOE

filled contractual obligation to 'RCA' and went solo. Songs written with band; **JOHN DEE GRAHAM** – guitar / **RICHARD LLOYD** – guitar (ex-TELEVISION) /**TONY MARSICO** – bass / **JEFF DONAVAN** – drums

R.C.A. | R.C.A.

Jun 90. (cd)(c)(lp) **MEET JOHN DOE** [ ] [ ]
– Let's be mad / A matter of degrees / Dyin' to get home / It's only love / The real one / Take 52 / Worldwide brotherhood / With someone like you / By the light / Knockin' around / Touch me, baby / My offering.

XON (see under ⇒ CABERET VOLTAIRE)

X-RAY SPEX

Formed: Brixton, London, England . . . 1977 by POLY STYRENE etc. Residents at THE ROXY club, even contributing live favourite OH BONDAGE! UP YOURS! to the various artists compilation. A somewhat inferior studio version was given light by 'Virgin', but this led to contract with 'E.M.I.' early in 1978. They had 3 Top 30 hits that year matched by a hit album. • **Style:** Brassy energetic punk-new wave with image provided by POLY STYRENE, complete with metal-braced dentures and figure hugging black bin-liners. • **Songwriters:** Group comps. / POLY lyrics. • **Trivia:** In 1980, POLY now reverting to real name MARION became member of The Hare Krishna movement, leading to semi-retirement 1982-1986.

Recommended: GERMFREE ADOLESCENTS (*8)

POLY STYRENE (b. MARION ELLIOT) – vocals / **JAK 'AIRPORT' STAFFORD** – guitar / **LORA LOGIC** (b. SUSAN WHITBY) – saxophone / **PAUL DEAN** – bass / **B.P.HURDING** – drums

Virgin | not issued

Oct 77. (7")(12") **OH BONDAGE! UP YOURS!. / I AM A CLICHE** [ ] [-]

— **STEVE 'RUDI' THOMPSON** – saxophone repl. LORA who formed ESSENTIAL LOGIC

EMI Inter. | Capitol?

Mar 78. (7")(7"orange) **THE DAY THE WORLD TURNED DAY-GLO. / IAMA POSEUR** [23] [ ]
Jul 78. (7")(7"pink) **IDENTITY. / LET'S SUBMERGE** [24] [ ]
Oct 78. (7") **GERMFREE ADOLESCENTS. / AGE** [19] [ ]
Nov 78. (lp)(c) **GERMFREE ADOLESCENTS** [30] [ ]
– The day the world turned day-glo / Obsessed with you / Genetic engineering / Identity / I live off you / Germfree adolescents / Art-i-ficial / Let's submerge / Warrior in Woolworths / Iama poseur / I can't do anything / Highly inflammable / Age / Plastic bag / I am a cliche / Oh bondage up yours!. *(cd-iss.Nov91)*
Apr 79. (7")(7"red) **HIGHLY INFLAMMABLE. / WARRIOR IN WOOLWORTHS** [45] [-]

— **JOHN GLIN** – saxophone repl. THOMPSON. Disbanded soon after, GLIN formed The LIVING LEGEND. JAK and PAUL formed AIRPORT & DEAN, while HURDING joined CLASSIX NOUVEAUX.

POLY STYRENE

went solo augmented by **GT MOORE** – guitar / **RICHARD MOORE** – guitar / **KEVIN McALEA** – keyboards / **KUMA KARADA** – bass / **RICHARD BAILEY** – drums / **TED BUNTING** – horns / **DARYLL LEE QUE** – percussion

United Art | not issued

Sep 80. (7") **TALK IN TOYTOWN. / SUB-TROPICAL** [ ] [-]
Nov 80. (lp)(c) **TRANSLUCENCE** [ ] [-]
– Dreaming / Talk in Toytown / Skydive / The day that time forgot / Shades / Essence / Hip hop city / Bicycle song / Sub tropical / Translucense / Age / Goodbye. *(re-iss.Mar90)*

— POLY (MARION) took a long sabbatical to get religion and bring up family. Returned to the studio after 5 years.

Awesome | not issued

Aug 86. (7"ep)(12"ep) **GODS AND GODDESSES** [ ] [-]
– Trick of the witch / Paramatma / Sacred temple / Big boys, big toys.

— In 1990, POLY was part of The DREAM ACADEMY.

– X-RAY SPEX compilations, etc. –

Mar 91. Receiver; (cd)(c)(lp) **LIVE AT THE ROXY (live)** [ ] [-]
Jul 91. Receiver; (cd)(lp) **OBSESSED WITH YOU** [ ] [-]

X-RAY SPEX

— re-formed with **POLY STYRENE / LAURA LOGIC / PAUL DEAN** + 1 original

Receiver not issued

Nov 95. (cd) **CONSCIOUS CONSUMER** [ ] [-]
– Cigarettes / Junk food junkie / Crystal / India / Dog in Sweden / Hi chaperone / Good time girl / Melancholy / Sophia / Peace meal / Prayer for peace / Party.

XTC

Formed: Swindon, Wiltshire, England . . . 1976 after 3 years of calling themselves The HELIUM KIDZ. Picked up by Richard Branson's 'Virgin' records in 1977. They peaked critically and commercially with 1982 double album 'ENGLISH SETTLEMENT'. Preceding this, ANDY became ill suffering a nervous breakdown. This led the band to quit the live scene and concentrate on studio work only. • **Style:** Progressed through being quirky new wave outfit to experimental pop-rock that combined folk and psychedelia. They took latter to the extreme when their alter-ego band The DUKES OF STRATOSPHEAR parodied The Beatles. • **Songwriters:** Either penned by PARTRIDGE or MOULDING or both. Covered ALL ALONG THE WATCHTOWER (Bob Dylan) / ELLA GURU (Captain Beefheart). • **Trivia:** Their 1986 album 'SKYLARKING' was produced by TODD RUNDGREN.

Recommended: ENGLISH SETTLEMENT (*8) / WHITE MUSIC (*8) / THE COMPACT XTC – THE SINGLES 1978-1985 (*9).

ANDY PARTRIDGE (b.11 Dec'53) – vocals, guitar / **COLIN MOULDING** (b.17 Aug'55) – bass, vocals / **BARRY ANDREWS** (b.12 Sep'56, London) – keyboards repl. JONATHAN PERKINS / **TERRY CHAMBERS** (b.18 Jul'55) – drums

Virgin VirginEpic

Oct 77. (7") **SCIENCE FRICTION. / SHE'S SO SQUARE** [ ] [-]
(12"ep) **3-D**(+=) – Dance band.

Jan 78. (7") **STATUE OF LIBERTY. / HANG ON TO THE NIGHT** [ ] [-]

Feb 78. (lp)(c) **WHITE MUSIC** [38] [ ]
– Radios in motion / Cross wires / This is pop? / Do what you do / Statue of liberty / All along the watchtower / Into the atom age / I'll set myself on fire / I'm bugged / New town animal in a furnished cage / Neon shuffle. *(re-iss.Mar84) (cd-iss.Mar87+=)* – Science friction / She's so square / Dance band / Hang on to the night / Heatwave / Traffic light rock / Instant tunes.

Apr 78. (7") **THIS IS POP?. / HEATWAVE** [ ] [-]

Oct 78. (7") **ARE YOU RECEIVING ME?. / INSTANT TUNES** [ ] [-]

Oct 78. (lp)(c) **GO 2** [21] [ ]
– Mekanic dancing (oh we go!) / Battery brides / Buzzcity talking / Crowded room / The rhythm / Beatown / My weapon / Life is good in the greenhouse / Jumping in Gomorrah / My weapon / Super-tuff. *(free-12"w/lp)* **GO +** – Dance with me Germany / Beat the bible / A dictionary of modern marriage / Clap, clap, clap / We kill the beast. *(lp re-iss.Mar84) (cd-iss.Jul87 +=)* – Are you receiving me?

— **DAVE GREGORY** – synthesizers, guitar repl. ANDREWS who joined LEAGUE OF GENTLEMEN (w/**ROBERT FRIPP**). He later went solo and formed SHRIEKBACK.

May 79. (7")(7"clear) **LIFE BEGINS AT THE HOP. / HOMO SAFARI** [54] [-]

Virgin Virgin

Aug 79. (lp)(c) **DRUMS AND WIRES** [34] [ ]
– Making plans for Nigel / Helicopter / Life begins at the hop / When you're near me I have difficulty / Ten feet tall / Roads girdle the globe / Reel by reel / Millions / That is the way / Outside world / Scissor man / Complicated game. *(free-7"w/lp)* **LIMELIGHT. / CHAIN OF COMMAND** *(US-version added track to now 7"m) (re-iss.1986) (cd-iss.1987* (+=) – (free-tracks).

Sep 79. (7"m) **MAKING PLANS FOR NIGEL. / BUSHMAN PRESIDENT (HSS 2) / PULSING, PULSING** [17] [-]

Nov 79. (7") **TEN FEET TALL. / HELICOPTER / THE SOMNAMBULIST** [-] [ ]

Feb 80. (7"m) **MAKING PLANS FOR NIGEL. / THIS IS POP? / MEKANIC DANCING (OH WE GO!)** [-] [ ]

Mar 80. (7") **WAIT TILL YOUR BOAT GOES DOWN. / TEN FEET TALL (U.S. version)** [ ] [ ]

Aug 80. (7") **GENERALS AND MAJORS. / DON'T LOSE YOUR TEMPER** [32] [ ]
(d7"+=) – Smokeless zone. / The somnambulist.

Sep 80. (lp)(c) **BLACK SEA** [16] [41]
– Respectable Street / General and majors / Living through another Cuba / Love at first sight / Rocket from a bottle / No language in our lungs / Towers of London / Paper and iron (notes and coins) / Burning with optimism's flames / Sgt. Rock (is going to help me) / Travels in Nihilon. *(re-iss.1986) (cd-iss.Mar87 +=)* – Smokeless zone / Don't lose your temper / The somnambulist.

Oct 80. (7") **TOWERS OF LONDON. / SET MYSELF ON FIRE (live)** [31] [ ]
(d7"+=) – Battery brides (live). / Scissor man.

Nov 80. (7") **TAKE THIS TOWN. / ('B'by 'The Ruts')** [ ] [ ]

— (above single was lifted from 'Times Square' film soundtrack on 'RSO')

1980. (7") **LOVE AT FIRST SIGHT. / ROCKET FROM A BOTTLE** [-] [ ]

Jan 81. (7"m) **SGT.ROCK (IS GOING TO HELP ME). / LIVING THROUGH ANOTHER CUBA (live) / GENERALS AND MAJORS (live)** [16] [ ]

Mar 81. (7"m) **RESPECTABLE STREET. / STRANGE TALES, STRANGE TAILS / OFFICER BLUE** [ ] [ ]

Virgin Epic

Jan 82. (7"m) **SENSES WORKING OVERTIME. / BLAME THE WEATHER / TISSUE TIGERS** [10] [-]
(12"+=) – Egyptian solution. *(cd-ep iss.Jul88, see 7"tracks)*

Feb 82. (d-lp)(c)(US-lp) **ENGLISH SETTLEMENT** [5] [48]
– Runaways / Ball and chain / Senses working overtime / Jason and the Argonauts / No thugs in our house / Yacht dance / All of a sudden (it's too late) / Melt the guns / Leisure * ** / It's nearly Africa * / Knuckle down * / Fly on the wall * / Down in the cockpit * ** / English roundabout / Snowman. *(US single-lp version omits *) (cd-iss.1987 omits tracks **)*

Mar 82. (7"m) **BALL AND CHAIN. / PUNCH AND JUDY / HEAVEN IS PAVED WITH BROKEN GLASS** [58] [ ]
(12"+=) – Cockpit dance mixture.

May 82. (7"m)(9"m) **NO THUGS IN OUR HOUSE / CHAIN OF COMMAND. / LIMELIGHT / OVER RUSTY WALLS** [ ] [-]

May 82. (7") **SENSES WORKING OVERTIME. / ENGLISH ROUNDABOUT** [-] [ ]

— Trimmed to basic trio of **PARTRIDGE, MOULDING + GREGORY** plus on session **PETER PHIPPES** – drums (ex-GLITTER BAND) (CHAMBERS emigrated to Australia)

Virgin Geffen

Apr 83. (7") **GREAT FIRE. / GOLD** [ ] [-]
(12"+=) – Frost circus / Procession towards learning land (HSS 5 & 6).

Jul 83. (7")(7"pic-d) **WONDERLAND. / JUMP** [ ] [ ]

Aug 83. (lp)(c) **MUMMER** [51] [ ]
– Beating of hearts / Wonderland / Love on a farmboy's wages / Great fire / Deliver us from the elements / Human alchemy / Ladybird / In loving memory of a name / Me and the wind / Funk pop a roll. *(re-iss.1986) (cd-iss.Mar87 +=)* – Frost circus (HSS 5) / Jump / Toys / Gold / Procession towards learning land (HSS 6) / Desert island.

Sep 83. (7") **LOVE ON A FARMBOY'S WAGES. / IN LOVING MEMORY OF A NAME** [50] [ ]
(d7"+=) – Desert island / Toys.
(12") – ('A'side) / Burning with optimist's flames (live / Cut it out (live) / English roundabout (live).

Nov 83. (7") **THANKS FOR CHRISTMAS ("THREE WISE MEN"). / COUNTDOWN TO CHRISTMAS PARTYTIME** [ ] [-]

Sep 84. (7") **ALL YOU PRETTY GIRLS. / WASHAWAY** [55] [ ]
(12"+=) – Red brick dream.

Oct 84. (lp)(c) **THE BIG EXPRESS** [38] [ ]
– Wake up / All you pretty girls / Shake you donkey up / Seagulls screaming kiss her, kiss her / This world over / Red brick dreams * / Washaway * / Blue overall * / The everyday story of Smalltown / I bought myself a liarbird / Reign of blows / You're the wish you are I had / I remember the sun / Train running low on soul coal. *(cd-iss.1987+= *)*

Oct 84. (7")(12") **THIS WORLD OVER. / BLUE OVERALL** [ ] [ ]

Jan 85. (7"m) **WAKE UP. / TAKE THIS TOWN / MANTIS ON PAROLE (HSS 4)** [ ] [ ]
(12"+=) – Making plans for Nigel / Sgt.Rock (is going to help me) / Senses working overtime.

— **IAN GREGORY** (DAVE's brother) – drums repl. PHIPPES

DUKES OF STRATOSPHEAR

Apr 85. (7") **THE MOLE FROM THE MINISTRY. / MY LOVE EXPLODES** [ ] [-]

Apr 85. (m-lp)(c) **25 O'CLOCK** [ ] [ ]
– 25 o'clock / Bike ride to the Moon / My love explodes / What in the world . . . / Your gold dress / The mole from the ministry.

XTC

Aug 86. (7") **GRASS. / DEAR GOD** [ ] [ ]
(12"+=) – Extrovert.

Oct 86. (lp)(c)(cd) **SKYLARKING** [90] [70]
– Summer's cauldron / Grass / The meeting place / That's really super, Supergirl / Ballet for a rainy day / 1000 umbrellas / Season cycle / Earn enough for us / Big day / Another satellite / Mermaid smiled / The man who sailed around his soul / Dying / Sacrificial bonfire.

Jan 87. (7")(7"clear) **THE MEETING PLACE. / THE MAN WHO SAILED AROUND HIS SOUL** [ ] [ ]
(12"+=) – Terrorism.

Aug 87. (7") **DEAR GOD. / MERMAID SMILED** [-] [ ]

Jun 87. (7") **DEAR GOD. / BIG DAY** [ ] [ ]
(12"+=) – Another satellite (live).
(cd-s) – ('A'side) / Homo safari series (HSS 1-6):- Homo safari / Bushman president / Egyptian solution / Mantis on parole / Frost circus / Procession towards learning land.

DUKES OF STRATOSPHEAR

Jul 87. (7") **YOU'RE A GOOD MAN ALBERT BROWN. / VANISHING GIRL** [ ] [-]
(12"+=) – The mole from the ministry / My love explodes.

Aug 87. (m-lp)(c) **PSONIC PSUNSPOT** [ ] [ ]
– Vanishing girl / Have you seen Jackie? / Little lighthouse / You're a good man Albert Brown (curse you red barrel) / Collideascope / You're my drug / Shiny cage / Brainiac's daughter / The affiliated / Pale and precious. *(cd-iss.as 'CHIPS FROM THE CHOCOLATE FIREBALL') (+=) – 25 O'CLOCK (m-lp tracks).*

XTC

re-grouped. **PAT MASTELOTTO** – drums (of MR. MISTER) repl. IAN

Jan 89. (7") **THE MAYOR OF SIMPLETON. / ONE OF THE MILLIONS** [46] [72]
(12"+=) – Ella guru.
(3"cd-s) – ('A'side) / Ella guru / Living in a haunted heart / The good thing.
(12") – ('A'side) / Dear God / Senses working overtime / Making plans for Nigel.

Feb 89. (lp)(c)(cd) **ORANGES AND LEMONS** [28] [44]
– Garden of earthly delights / The Mayor of Simpleton / King for a day / Here comes President Kill again / The loving / Poor skeleton steps out / One of the millions / Scarecrow people / Merely a man / Cynical days / Across this antheap / Hold me my daddy / Pink thing / Miniature sun / Chalkhills and children. *(re-iss.Oct89 as 3xcd-ep's)*

Apr 89. (7") **KING FOR A DAY. / HAPPY FAMILIES** [ ] [-]
(12"+=) – ('A'version).
(c-s+=) – Generals and majors / Towers of London.

(3"cd-s) – ('A'side) / ('A'version) / Skeletons (home demo) / My paint heroes (home demo).

May 89. (cd-s) **KING FOR A DAY (Czar mix) / ('A' Versailles mix) / TOYS / DESERT ISLAND** [-] [ ]

Aug 89. (7") **THE LOVING. / CYNICAL DAYS** [ ] [ ]

(c-s) – ('A'side) / The world is full of angry young men.

(12")(cd-s) – (all 3 tracks).

Mar 92. (7")(c-s) **THE DISAPPOINTED. / THE SMARTEST MONKEYS** [33] [ ]

(10"+=)/ /(cd-s++=) – Humble Daisy./ / ('B'demo).

May 92 (cd)(c)(d-lp) **NONESUCH** [28] [97]

– The ballad of Peter Pumpkinhead / My bird performs / Dear Madam Barnum / Humble Daisy / The smartest monkeys / The dismal / Holly up on poppy / Crocodile / Rook / Omnibus / That wave / Then she appeared / War dance / Wrapped in grey / The ugly underneath / Bungalow / Books are burning.

Jun 92. (7") **THE BALLAD OF PETER PUMPKINHEAD. / WAR DANCE** [71] [ ]

(cd-s+=) – Down a peg (demo) / ('A'demo).

(cd-s+=) – My bird performs / Always winter never Christmas (demos).

– compilations, others, etc. –

Nov 82. Virgin; (lp)(c) **WAXWORKS – A SIDES** [54] [-]

(free lp) **BEESWAX – B SIDES** (iss.on own 1983) [ ] [-]

Jan 87. Virgin; (cd) **THE COMPACT XTC – THE SINGLES 1978-1985** [ ] [ ]

– Science friction / Statue of liberty / This is pop / Are you receiving me? / Life begins at the hop / Making plans for Nigel / Wait till your boat goes down / Generals and majors / Towers of London / Sgt.Rock is going to help me / Senses working overtime / Ball and chain / Great fire / Wonderland / Love on a farmboy's wages / All you pretty girls / This world over / Wake up.

Aug 90. Virgin; (cd) **EXPLODE TOGETHER (THE DUB EXPERIMENTS 78-80)** [ ] [-]

– (included the ANDY PARTRIDGE album below)

Aug 90. Virgin; (cd) **RAG & BONE BUFFET** (rare) [ ] [-]

(c-iss.Mar91)

Nov 88. Old Gold; (7") **MAKING PLANS FOR NIGEL. / SENSES WORKING OVERTIME** [ ] [-]

Nov 94. Nighttracks; (cd) **DRUMS AND WIRELESS: BBC RADIO SESSIONS 77-89** [ ] [-]

MR. PARTRIDGE

ANDY solo.

Virgin / not issued

Feb 80. (lp)(c) **TAKE AWAY (THE LURE OF SALVAGE)** [ ] [-]

– Commerciality / The day they pulled the North Pole down / Cairo / Madhattan / The forgotten language of light / Steam fist futurist / The rotary / Shore leave ornithology (another 1950) / I sit in the snow / Work away Tokyo day / New broom. *(re-iss.Aug88)*

The COLONEL

(MOULDING + CHAMBERS)

Virgin / not issued

Oct 80. (7") **TOO MANY COOKS IN THE KITCHEN. / I NEED PROTECTION** [ ] [-]

ANDY PARTRIDGE / HAROLD BUDD

All Saints / not issued

Jun 94. (cd) **THROUGH THE HILL** [ ] [-]

– Hand 19 / Through the hill / Great valley of gongs / Western island of apples / Animal Mundi / Hand 20 / The place of odd glances / Well for the sweat of the Moon / Tenochtitlan's numberless bridges / Ceramic avenue / Hand 21 / Missing pieces in the game of salt and onyx / Mantle of peacock bones / Bronze coins showing genitals / Bearded Aphrodite / Hand 22.

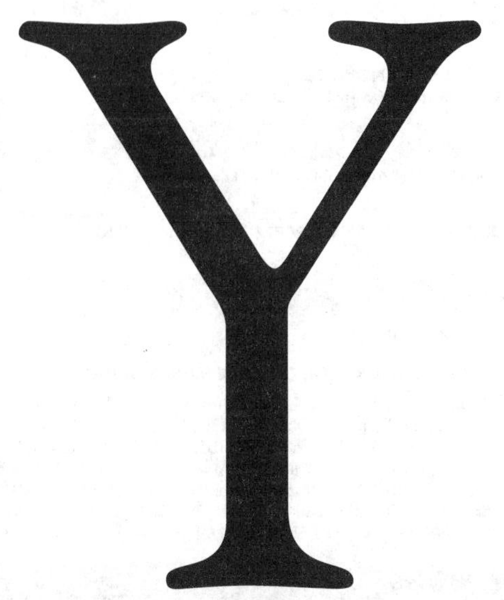

Y & T

Formed: Bay Area, California, USA . . . 1975 as YESTERDAY & TODAY. After 2 albums on 'London', they gained worldwide contract for 'A&M' early in the 80's. • **Style:** Shifted from chart cover band into powerful heavy metal outfit. • **Songwriters:** Group compositions?, except YOUR MAMMA DON'T DANCE (Loggins & Messina) / ALL AMERICAN BOY (Val Stephenson / Dave Robbins) LET IT OUT (Moon Over Paris) / etc? • **Trivia:** MOTLEY CRUE once supported them in 1981.

Recommended: EARTHSHAKER (*6) / ANTHOLOGY (*6).

YESTERDAY & TODAY

DAVE MENIKETTI – vocals, lead guitar / **JOEY ALVES** – guitar / **LEONARD HAZE** – drums / **PHILIP KENNEMORE** – bass

		not issued	London
1976.	(lp)(c) **YESTERDAY & TODAY** – Animal woman / 23 hours a day / Game playing woman / Come on over / My heart plays too / Earthshaker / Fast ladies (very slow gin) / Alcohol / Beautiful dreamer.	-	
Apr 77.	(7") **ALCOHOL. /**	-	
1978.	(lp)(c) **STRUCK DOWN** – Struck down / Pleasure in my heart / Road / Nasty Sadie / Dreams of Egypt / Tired to show you / I'm lost / Stargazer.	-	

Y & T

		A & M	A & M
Jul 81.	(lp)(c) **EARTHSHAKER** – Hungry for rock / Dirty girl / Shake it loose / Squeeze / Rescue me / Young and tough / Hurricane / Let me go / Knock you out / I believe in you.		
Oct 81.	(7")(12") **DIRTY GIRL. / KNOCK YOU OUT**		-
May 82.	(7")(12") **I BELIEVE IN YOU. / RESCUE ME**		-
Aug 82.	(lp)(c) **BLACK TIGER** – From the Moon / Open fire / Don't wanna lose / Hell or high water / Forever / Black tiger / Barroom boogie / My way or the highway / Winds of change.	53	
Sep 82.	(7")(12") **DON'T WANNA LOSE. / SQUEEZE**		-
Nov 82.	(7") **BLACK TIGER. / FOREVER**	-	
Aug 83.	(7") **MEAN STREAK. / STRAIGHT THRU THE HEART** (12"+=) – Dirty girl.	41	
Sep 83.	(lp)(c) **MEAN STREAK** – Mean streak / Straight thru the heart / Lonely side of town / Midnight in Tokyo / Breaking away / Hang 'em high / Take you to the limit / Sentimental fool / Down and dirty.	35	
Nov 83.	(7") **MIDNIGHT IN TOKYO. / BAR ROOM BOOGIE** (12"+=) – Squeeze.		
Aug 84.	(lp)(c) **IN ROCK WE TRUST** – Rock & roll's gonna save the world / Life, life, life / Masters and slaves / I'll keep on believin' (do you know) / Break out tonight! / Lipstick and leather / Don't stop runnin' / (Your love is) Drivin' me crazy / She's a liar / This time. *(cd-iss.1988)*	33	46
Aug 84.	(7") **DON'T STOP RUNNIN'. / FOREVER**	-	
Aug 84.	(7") **DON'T STOP RUNNIN'. / ROCK & ROLL'S GONNA SAVE THE WORLD** (12"+=) – Mean streak / I believe in you.		-
Jul 85.	(lp)(c) **OPEN FIRE (live)** – Open fire / Go for the throat / 25 hours a day / Rescue me / Summertime girls (studio version) / Forever / Barroom boogie / I believe in you. *(cd-iss.1988)*		70
Sep 85.	(7") **SUMMERTIME GIRLS. / ('A' long version)**	-	55
Nov 85.	(lp)(c)(cd) **DOWN FOR THE COUNT** – In the name of rock / All American boy / Anytime at all / Anything for money / Face like an angel / Summertime girls / Looks like trouble / Your mamma don't dance / Don't tell me what to wear / Hands of time.		91
Jan 86.	(7") **ALL AMERICAN BOY. / GO FOR THE THROAT**	-	

—— **STEF BURNS** – guitar repl. JOEY / **JIMMY DEGRASSO** – drums repl. LEONARD

		Geffen	Geffen
Jul 87.	(lp)(c)(cd) **CONTAGIOUS** – Contagious / L.A. rocks / Temptation / The kid goes crazy / Fight for your life / Armed and dangerous / Rhythm or not / Bodily harm / Eyes of a stranger / I'll cry for you.		78
Jun 90.	(cd)(c)(lp) **TEN** – Hard times / Lucy / Don't be afraid of the dark / Girl crazy / City / Come in from the rain / Red, hot & ready / She's gone / Let it out / Ten lovers / Goin' off the deep end / Surrender.		

—— Disbanded Nov90 and DEGRASSO joined hard rockin' solo songstress FIONA. Re-formed in the mid-90's.

		M.F.N.	M.F.N.
Sep 95.	(cd)(c) **MUSICALLY INCORRECT** – Long way down / Fly away / Quicksand / Cold day in Hell / Ive got my own / Nowhere land / Pretty prison / Don't know what to do / 21st century / I'm lost / Confusion / No regrets.		

– compilations, others, etc. –

Sep 89.	Raw Power; (lp)(c)(cd) **ANTHOLOGY** – Rescue me / I believe in you / Squeeze / Hungry for rock / Don't wanna lose / Hell or highwater / Winds of change / Barroom boogie / Black tiger / In the name of rock / Summertime girls / All American boy / Hands of time / Mean streak / Take you to the limit / Down and dirty / Hang 'em high / Open fire (live) / Go for the throat (live) / Forever (live). *(re-iss.Feb91)*		-
Sep 90.	A&M; (cd)(c)(lp) **THE BEST OF Y & T** *(cd+c-iss.re Aug91)*	-	
May 91.	Castle; (cd) **THE COLLECTION**		-
Mar 91.	Metal Blade; (cd)(c)(d-lp) **LIVE (live)** – Mean streak / Hurricane / Don't stop runnin' / Struck down / Winds of change / Black tiger / Midnight in Tokyo / Beautiful dreamer / Hard times / I'll cry for you / I believe in you / Squeeze / Forever.		-

YARDBIRDS

Formed: Richmond, Surrey, England . . . 1963 after stemming from METROPOLITAN BLUES QUARTET. After residency at The CRAWDADDY Club backing bluesman SONNY BOY WILLIAMSON, they gained contract with EMI's 'Columbia' label early '64. After 2 well-received singles that year, they had first of 4 consecutive Top 3 hits with 'FOR YOUR LOVE' in 1965. Became famous for introducing 3 of the greatest guitarists of all-time ERIC CLAPTON, JEFF BECK and JIMMY PAGE. • **Style:** Played R&B standards, until shift into rock-pop mid 60's. By late 1966, they progressed into psychedelia but with decreasing commercial appeal. • **Songwriters:** RELF wrote some, except covers I WISH YOU WOULD (Billy Boy Arnold) / SMOKESTACK LIGHTNING (Howlin' Wolf) / A CERTAIN GIRL (Ernie K-Doe) / GOOD MORNING LITTLE SCHOOLGIRL (Don & Bob) / TRAIN (Johnny Burnette) / FOR YOUR LOVE + HEART FULL OF SOUL (c. Graham Gouldman, ⇒ 10cc) / I'M A MAN (Bo Diddley) / TEN LITTLE INDIANS (Nilsson) / THE SUN IS SHINING (Elmore James) / plus loads of other blues greats. • **Trivia:** Made two group appearances in the 66/67 films 'SWINGING LONDON' & 'BLOW-UP'. Early in 1966, manager GIORGIO GOMELSKY was replaced by SIMON NAPIER-BELL.

Recommended: THE VERY BEST OF THE YARDBIRDS (*9)

KEITH RELF (b.22 Mar'43, Richmond) – vocals, harmonica / **ERIC CLAPTON** (b.see solo info) – lead guitar, vocals repl. ANTHONY TOPHAM / **CHRIS DREJA** (b.11 Nov'45, Surbiton, Surrey) – rhythm guitar / **PAUL SAMWELL-SMITH** (b. 8 May'43, Richmond) – bass / **JIM McCARTY** (b.25 Jul'43, Liverpool) – drums

		Columbia	Epic
Jun 64.	(7") **I WISH YOU WOULD. / A CERTAIN GIRL**		Oct 64
Aug 64.	(7") **A CERTAIN GIRL. / I AIN'T GOT YOU**	-	
Oct 64.	(7") **GOOD MORNING LITTLE SCHOOLGIRL. / I AIN'T GOT YOU**	44	-
Feb 65.	(lp) **FIVE LIVE YARDBIRDS (live)** – Too much monkey business / I got love if you want it / Smokestack lightning / Good morning little schoolgirl / Respectable / Five long years / Pretty girl / Louise / I'm a man / Here 'tis. *(re-iss. Aug79 +c-iss. Jan82 on 'Charly') (re-iss.+cd.Aug89 on 'Decal')*		-
Mar 65.	(7") **FOR YOUR LOVE. / GOT TO HURRY** *(re-iss.Aug76 on 'Charly')*	3	-
May 65.	(7") **FOR YOUR LOVE. / I'M NOT TALKING**	-	6
Jul 65.	(lp) **FOR YOUR LOVE** – For your love / I'm not talking / Putty (in your hands) / I ain't got you / Got to hurry / I ain't done wrong / I wish you would / A certain girl / Sweet music / Good morning little schoolgirl / My girl Sloopy.	-	96

—— (Mar65) **JEFF BECK** (b.24 Jun'44) – lead guitar repl. CLAPTON who joined JOHN MAYALL's BLUESBREAKERS. He later formed CREAM and went solo ⇒ .

Jul 65.	(7") **HEART FULL OF SOUL. / STEELED BLUES**	2	9
Oct 65.	(7") **EVIL HEARTED YOU. / STILL I'M SAD** *(re-iss.Jul82 on 'Old Gold')*	3	-
Nov 65.	(7") **I'M A MAN. / STILL I'M SAD**	-	17
Dec 65.	(lp) **HAVING A RAVE UP WITH THE YARDBIRDS (live)** – You're a better man than I / Evil hearted you / I'm a man / Still I'm sad / Heart full of soul / The train kept a-rollin' / Smokestack lightning / Respectable / I'm a man / Here 'tis. *(last 4 tracks from 'FIVE LIVE YARDBIRDS')*	-	53
Feb 66.	(7") **SHAPES OF THINGS. / YOU'RE A BETTER MAN THAN I**	3	-
Mar 66.	(7") **SHAPES OF THINGS. / NEW YORK CITY BLUES**	-	11

—— (Feb66) **JIMMY PAGE** – guitar (ex-session man, solo artist) repl. SAMWELL-SMITH who became producer. (DREJA moved to bass) KEITH issued solo 45 in May.

May 66. (7") **OVER, UNDER, SIDEWAYS, DOWN. / JEFF'S BOOGIE** [10] [13] Jun 66
Jul 66. (lp) **THE YARDBIRDS** (US title 'OVER UNDER SIDEWAYS DOWN') [20] [52]
– Lost women / Over, under, sideways, down / The Nazz are blue / I can't make your way / Rack my mind / Farewell / Hot house of Omagarashid / Jeff's boogie / He's always there / Turn into earth / What do you want / Ever since the world began. *(re-iss.UK Feb83 as 'ROGER THE ENGINEER' on 'Edsel', cd-iss.1986* +=)– Happenings ten years time ago / Psycho daisies. *(cd-iss. US version Feb92 on 'Raven-Topic')*
Oct 66. (7") **HAPPENINGS TEN YEARS TIME AGO. / PSYCHO DAISIES** [43] [-]
Nov 66. (7") **HAPPENINGS TEN YEARS TIME AGO. / THE NAZZ ARE BLUE** [-] [30]
— (Oct66) Trimmed to a quartet when JEFF BECK left to go solo.
Apr 67. (7") **LITTLE GAMES. / PUZZLES** [ ] [51]
Apr 67. (lp) **GREATEST HITS** (compilation) [-] [28]
– Shapes of things / Still I'm sad / New York City blues / For your love / Over, under, sideways, down / I'm a man / Happenings ten years time ago / Heart full of soul / Smokestack lightning / I'm not talking.
Jun 67. (7") **HA HA SAID THE CLOWN. / TINKER, TAILOR, SOLDIER, SAILOR** [-] [45]
Aug 67. (lp) **LITTLE GAMES** [-] [80]
– Little games / Smile on me / White summer / Tinker, tailor, soldier, sailor / Glimpses / Drinking muddy water / No excess baggage / Stealing, stealing / Only the black rose / Little soldier boy. *(UK-iss.May85 on 'Fame') (re-iss.+cd.Apr91 on 'EMI')*
Oct 67. (7") **TEN LITTLE INDIANS. / DRINKIN' MUDDY WATER** [-] [96]
Mar 68. (7") **GOODNIGHT SWEET JOSEPHINE. / THINK ABOUT IT** [-] [ ]
— Disbanded mid'68. PAGE and DREJA formed NEW YARDBIRDS, but when DREJA departed, PAGE formed LED ZEPPELIN. RELF and McCARTY formed the original RENAISSANCE. On 14 May'76, RELF was electrocuted when touching a faulty amp. In the early 90s, McCARTY was also part of PRETTY THINGS / YARDBIRD BLUES BAND collaboration.

– other compilations, etc. –

Oct 65. Columbia; (7"ep) **FIVE YARDBIRDS** [ ] [-]
– My girl Sloopy / I'm not talking / I ain't done wrong / (1).
Jan 67. Columbia; (7"ep) **OVER UNDER SIDEWAYS DOWN** [ ] [-]
Jan 66. Fontana/ US= Mercury; (lp) **SONNY BOY WILLIAMSON AND THE YARDBIRDS (live w/ SONNY)** [ ] [ ] Feb 66
– Bye bye bird / Mr. Downchild / The river Rhine / 23 hours too long / Out on the water coast / Baby don't worry / Pontiac blues / Take it easy baby / I don't care no more / Do the Weston. *(re-iss.1968) (re-iss.Jun75 on 'Philips')*
Jun 71. Regal Starline; (lp)(c) **REMEMBER THE YARDBIRDS** [ ] [-]
1971. Columbia; (lp) **LIVE YARDBIRDS FEATURING JIMMY PAGE** [-] [ ]
1972. Epic; (lp) **YARDBIRDS' FAVORITES** [-] [ ]
Aug 77. Charly; (lp) **THE YARDBIRDS FEATURING ERIC CLAPTON** [ ] [-]
(re-iss.cd+c Mar94 on 'Laserlight')
Aug 77. Charly; (lp) **THE YARDBIRDS FEATURING JEFF BECK** [ ] [-]
(above 2 re-iss.Mar83, the latter again Feb85 on 'Cambra')
Dec 77. Charly; (d-lp) **SHAPES OF THINGS** [ ] [-]
Feb 82. Charly; (10"lp) **SINGLE HITS** [ ] [-]
Jun 83. Charly; (lp) **OUR OWN SOUND** [ ] [-]
Nov 84. Charly; (lp-box) **SHAPES OF THINGS – COLLECTION OF CLASSIC RECORDINGS 1964-66** [ ] [-]
– (lp's) THE FIRST RECORDINGS / SONNY BOY WILLIAMSON & . . . / FIVE LIVE YARDBIRDS / FOR YOUR LOVE / HAVING A RAVE . . . / SHAPES OF THINGS / ODDS AND SODS *(issJun91 as 4xcd-box on 'Decal')*
1986. Charly; (cd) **GREATEST HITS** (not US version) [ ] [-]
Nov 84. Topline; (lp)(c) **FOR YOUR LOVE** (not US version) [ ] [-]
Jul 82. Old Gold; (7") **FOR YOUR LOVE. / HEARTFUL OF SOUL** [ ] [-]
1989. Old Gold; (7"ep) **FOR YOUR LOVE** [ ] [-]
Feb 83. Edsel; (7") **OVER, UNDER, SIDEWAYS, DOWN. / PSYCHO DAISIES** [ ] [-]
May 84. Edsel; (7") **RACK MY MIND. / JEFF'S BOOGIE** [ ] [-]
Mar 84. Scoop; (7"ep)(c-ep) **6 TRACK HITS** [ ] [-]
1986. Castle; (d-lp)(d-c) **THE COLLECTION** [ ] [-]
(cd-iss.1988)
1986. Showcase; (lp) **GOT LIVE IF YOU WANT IT** (credited **ERIC CLAPTON)** [ ] [-]
Apr 87. Topline; (cd) **CLASSIC CUTS** [ ] [-]
1989. Instant; (lp)(c)(cd) **HITS AND MORE** [ ] [-]
Sep 89. Decal; (d-lp)(cd) **THE STUDIO SESSIONS 1964-1967** [ ] [-]
Sep 89. Decal; (lp)(cd) **THE FIRST RECORDINGS – LONDON 1963** [ ] [-]
Jun 91. Music Club; (cd) **THE VERY BEST OF THE YARDBIRDS** [ ] [-]
– For your love / Heart full of soul / Good morning little schoolgirl / Still I'm sad / Evil hearted you / A certain girl / Jeff's blues / I wish you would / New York City / I'm not talking / You're a better man than I / Shapes of things / I'm a man / Boom boom / Smokestack lightning (live) / Let it rock (live) / You can't judge a book by it's cover (live) / Who do you love (live) / Too much monkey business (live) / Respectable (live) / Pretty girl (live) / Stroll on.
Apr 91. Band Of Joy; (cd)(c)(lp) **ON AIR** (65-67) [ ] [-]
Jul 92. Repertoire; (cd) **25 GREATEST HITS** [ ] [-]
Sep 92. Promised Land; (cd) **YARDBIRDS' REUNION CONCERT (live) ("JIM McCARTY & CHRIS DREJA")** [ ] [-]
Oct 92. EMI; (cd) **LITTLE GAMES, SESSIONS & MORE** [ ] [-]
Apr 93. Pulsar; (cd) **GREATEST HITS** (not US version) [ ] [-]
Sep 93. Laserlight; (cd)(c) **HEART FULL OF SOUL** [ ] [-]
Apr 95. Top Masters; (cd) **ERIC CLAPTON & THE YARDBIRDS** [ ] [-]

KEITH RELF

solo, when a YARDBIRD.

Columbia / Epic
May 66. (7") **MR.ZERO. / KNOWING** [50] [-]
Jan 67. (7") **SHAPES IN MY MIND. / BLUE SANDS** [ ] [ ]

REIGN

was formed by **RELF + McCARTY** plus **ROBIN LEMESWRIER**

Regal Zono. / not issued
Nov 68. (7") **LINE OF LEAST RESISTANCE. / NATURAL LOVING WOMAN** [ ] [-]

TOGETHER

(McCARTY & RELF) with sessioners.

Columbia / Epic?
1968. (7") **HENRY'S COMING HOME. / LOVE MUM AND DAD** [ ] [-]
— They evolved into RENAISSANCE the following year. McCARTY joined SHOOT in 1972 and made 1 album 'ON THE FRONTIER' for 'Capitol'. In 1976 he formed ILLUSION with JOHN KNIGHTSBRIDGE, HAWKEN and CENNAMO. The latter had previously been in ARMAGEDDON with KEITH RELF. On 22 Jul'83, The YARDBIRDS re-formed with **McCARTY, DREJA, SAMWELL-SMITH, KNIGHTSBRIDGE** plus 2 vocalists **JOHN FIDDLER** (ex-MEDICINE HEAD) **+ MARK FELTON** (ex-NINE BELOW ZERO). Evolved into

BOX OF FROGS

KNIGHTSBRIDGE and FELTON having been replaced by guests **JEFF BECK** – guitar / **RORY GALLAGHER** – guitar / **MAX MIDDLETON** – keyboards

Epic / Epic
Jun 84. (7") **BACK WHERE I STARTED. / THE EDGE** [ ] [ ]
(12"+=) – Nine lives.
Jul 84. (lp)(c) **BOX OF FROGS** [ ] [45]
– Back where I stand / Harder / Another wasted day / Love inside you / The edge / Two steps ahead / Into the dark / Just a boy again / Poor boy. *(cd-iss.Oct93 on 'Sony Europe')*
Aug 84. (7") **INTO THE DARK. / X TRACKS** [ ] [ ]
(12"+=) – X tracks (Medley of tracks).
— Trimmed to quartet of **FIDDLER, McCARTY, DREJA + SAMWELL-SMITH**
Jun 86. (7") **AVERAGE. / STRANGE LAND** [ ] [ ]
(12"+=) – Keep calling.
Jun 86. (lp)(c) **STRANGE LAND** [ ] [ ]
– Strange land / Get it while you can / You mix me up / House on fire / Average / Hanging from the wreckage / Heart full of soul / Asylum. *(cd-issJul94 on 'Sony Europe')*

YAZOO

Formed: Basildon, Essex, England . . . late 1981 by CLARKE and MOYET. The former having left DEPECHE MODE, was retained by Daniel Miller's 'Mute' label. Spring 1982, they immediately crashed into UK chart with debut ONLY YOU. Emulated success throughout that year and the next, but surprisingly both announced parting after 2nd album. Individually both went on to have even greater things in the mid-80's onwards. • **Style:** Electronic synthesized power blues. Focal point being the large vocal range of ALISON (nicknamed ALF). • **Songwriters:** CLARKE or MOYET. • **Trivia:** Due to a record company of the same name in the States, they had to be called YAZ. Acapella group The FLYING PICKETS had UK Christmas 1983 No.1 with their version of ONLY YOU.

Recommended: UPSTAIRS AT ERIC'S (*9) / YOU AND ME BOTH (*8)

ALISON MOYET (b.GENEVIEVE, 18 Jun'61, Billericay, Essex, England) – vocals (ex-VICARS, ex-SCREAMING ABDABS) / **VINCE CLARKE** (b. 3 Jul'61) – keyboards, synthesizers (ex-DEPECHE MODE)

Mute / Sire
May 82. (7")('A'ext-12") **ONLY YOU. / SITUATION** [2] [67] Jan 83
Jul 82. (7")('A'ext-12") **DON'T GO. / WINTER KILLS** [3] [ ]
Aug 82. (lp)(c) **UPSTAIRS AT ERIC'S** [2] [92]
– Don't go / Too pieces / Bad connection / I before E except after C / Midnight / In my room / Only you / Goodbye 70's / Tuesday / Winter kills / Bring your love down. *(cd-issJan87)* (+=) – The other side of love / Situation (12"mixes) *(re-iss.cd/c Jun95)*
Sep 82. (7") **SITUATION. / WINTER KILLS** [-] [73]
Nov 82. (7") **THE OTHER SIDE OF LOVE. / ODE TO BOY** [13] [ ]
Apr 83. (7")(12") **NOBODY'S DIARY. / STATE FARM** [3] [ ]
Jul 83. (lp)(c) **YOU AND ME BOTH** [1] [69]
– Nobody's diary / Softly over / Sweet thing / Mr. Blue / Good times / Walk away from love / Ode to boy / Unmarked / Anyone / Happy people / And on. *(cd-issJan87 & Jun95)*
— split Summer 1983, MOYET went solo and VINCE formed ASSEMBLY (see under)

– compilations, others, etc. –

Nov 90. Mute/ US= Sire; (7")(c-s)(cd-s) **SITUATION (remix). / STATE FARM** [14] [ ]
(12"+=) – ('A'mix).

The ASSEMBLY

VINCE CLARKE plus **FEARGAL SHARKEY** – vocals (ex-UNDERTONES) / **E.C. RADCLIFFE** – drums (ex-FAD GADGET)

Mute / Intercord

Nov 83. (7")(12") **NEVER NEVER. / STOP START** [4] [ ]

VINCE CLARKE & PAUL QUINN

QUINN (b. Scotland) – vox (ex-BOURGIE BOURGIE)

Mute / Intercord

Jun 85. (7")(12") **ONE DAY. / SONG FOR** [ ] [-]

— In 1985, VINCE formed ERASURE with ANDY BELL.

YELLO

Formed: Zurich, Switzerland ... 1979 by DIETER MEIER and BORIS BLANK. MEIER who had previously been member of Swiss national golf team, was a self-confessed millionaire gambler, before joining FRESH COLOUR and going solo. In 1979, they gained contract with US indie label 'Ralph', which led to UK outlet 'Do-It' signing them in the early 80's. Two albums behind them, UK label 'Stiff' gave them break into mini-stardom. A steady growth in sales throughout the 80's led to Top 10 single 'The Race' mid'88. This track now compliments many a TV documentary/sports backing theme. They had by this time, made a base in London. • **Style:** Electronic Euro-dance initially inspired by Latin-American salsa, with hint of mid-70's CAN. Always forthcoming with diverse ideas, DIETER enticed SHIRLEY BASSEY out of semi-retirement mid'87 to sing THE RHYTHM DIVINE. • **Songwriters:** Music-BLANK / Words-MEIER. • **Trivia:** The 90's have seen a shift into movie soundtracks (i.e. NUNS ON THE RUN; which used 'The Race' and SNOWBALL). DIETER launched his own label 'Solid Pleasure' early in '91.

Recommended: THE ESSENTIAL YELLO (*7)

DIETER MEIER

solo with **HEINRICH VOGEL** – guitar / **ROBERT VOGEL** – drums / **ANTHONY MOORE** – keyboards / **MARTIN WALDER** – bass

Periphery Perfume / not issued

Sep 78. (7") **CRY FOR FAME. / THE SOURCE** [-] [-] SWISS
Mar 79. (7") **JIM FOR TANGO. / MADMAN** [-] [-] SWISS

YELLO

DIETER MEIER – vocals, horns / **BORIS BLANK** – synth., electronics / **CARLOS PERON** – tapes, synthesizers

not issued / Ralph

1979. (7") **I.T.SPLASH. / GLUEHEAD** [-] [ ]

— added **CHICO HABLAS** – guitar / guest drummers – **WALT KAISER / FELIX HAUX**

Do-It / Ralph

Mar 81. (lp) **SOLID PLEASURE** [ ] [ ]
– Bimbo / Night flanger / Reverse lion / Downtown samba / Magneto / Massage / Assistant's cry / Bostich / Rock stop / Coast to polka / Blue green / Eternal legs / Stanztrigger / Bananas to the beat. *(re-iss.+cd.May88 on 'Mercury')*
Apr 81. (7") **BIMBO. / I.T. SPLASH** [ ] [ ]
Sep 81. (7") **BOSTICH. / SHE'S GOT A GUN (instrumental)** [ ] [ ] Dec 80
(12") – ('A'side) / Downtown samba / Daily disco.

— new guests were **BEAT ASH** – percussion / **ZINE EL ABADINE** – vocals

Oct 81. (lp) **CLARO QUE SI** [ ] [ ]
– Daily disco / No more Roger / Take it all / The evening's young / She's got a gun / Ballet mechanique / Quad el Habib / The lorry / Homer Hossa / Pinball cha-cha. *(re-iss.+cd.Feb88)*
Jan 82. (7") **SHE'S GOT A GUN. / BLUEHEAD** [ ] [ ]
(12"+=) – The evening's young / There is no reason.
Jun 82. (7") **PINBALL CHA-CHA. / SMILE ON YOU** [ ] [ ]
(12"+=) – ('A'extended).

— Now down to basic duo of **MEIER & BLANK.** (HABLAS left, + PERON went solo)

Stiff / Elektra

Apr 83. (lp)(c) **YOU GOTTA SAY YES TO ANOTHER EXCESS** [65] [ ]
– I love you / Lost again / No more words / Crash dance / Great mission / You gotta say yes to another excess / Swing / Heavy whispers / Smile on you / Pumping velvet / Salut Mayoumba. *(re-iss.+cd.Feb88 on 'Mercury')*
May 83. (7")(7"-3D-pic-d) **I LOVE YOU. / RUBBER VEST** [41] [ ]
('A'extended dance-12") – Swing / Bostich. *(no 7"b-side track).*
Oct 83. (7") **LOST AGAIN. / BASE FOR ALEC** [73] [ ]
(d7"+=) – Let me cry / She's got a gun.
(12"+=) – Pumping velvet / No more words.

— guests **RUSH WINTERS** – vocals / **ANNIE HOGAN** – piano / **PETIA** – glass harp / plus **BEAT ASH + CHICO HABLAS**

Elektra / Elektra

Mar 85. (lp)(c) **STELLA** [92] [ ]
– Desire / Vicious games / Oh yeah / Desert Inn / Stalak drama / Koladi-ola (low bow) / Domingo / Sometimes (Dr. Hirsch) / Let me cry / Ciel ouvert / Angel no. *(re-iss.+cd.Feb88 on 'Mercury')*
Mar 85. (7")(12")(12"green) **VICIOUS GAMES. / BLUE NABOU** [ ] [ ]
Aug 85. (7")(12") **DESIRE. / OH YEAH (THE STELLA SUITE)** [ ] [ ]

Mercury / Mercury

Aug 86. (7") **GOLDRUSH. / SHE'S GOT A GUN (live)** [54] [ ]
(12"+=) – Goldrush II.
(d12"++=) – Pinball cha-cha / Vicious games.
(d7"+=) – I love you / Desire.
Oct 86. (lp)(c)(cd) **1980-1985 THE NEW MIX IN ONE (remixes)** [ ] [ ]
– Daily disco / Swing / The evening's young / Pinball cha-cha / I love you / Sometimes (Dr.Hirsch) / Base for Alec / Oh yeah / Lost again / Tub tub / Angel no / Desire / Bananas to the beat / Koladi-ola / domingo / Bostich / Live at the Roxy. *(cd re-iss.Jun89)*
Nov 86. (7")(12") **VICIOUS GAMES (remix). / LIVE AT THE ROXY (highlights)** [ ] [ ]

— (note: US 12"versions were issued on 'On-U-Sound' & 'Hot Tracks'.)

May 87. (7") **CALL IT LOVE. / L HOTEL** [ ] [ ]
(12"+=)(cd-s+=) – ('A'trego snare mix).
Jun 87. (lp)(c)(cd) **ONE SECOND** [48] [92] Sep 87
– La habanera / Moon on ice / Call it love / Le secret farida / Hawaiian chance / The rhythm divine / Santiago / Goldrush / Dr Van Steiner / Si senor the hairy grill.
Aug 87. (7") **OH YEAH. /** [-] [51]
Aug 87. (7") **THE RHYTHM DIVINE. ("YELLO featuring SHIRLEY BASSEY") / DR.VAN STEINER** [54] [ ]
(12"+=)(c-s+=) – Tool in rose.
(12"+=) = ('A'mix BILLY McKENZIE – vox).
Jul 88. (7")('A'diff.mix-12") **THE RACE. / LA HABARENA** [7] [ ]
(cd-s) – ('A'side) / ('A'sporting mix) / Another race.
Nov 88. (lp)(c)(cd) **THE FLAG** [56] [ ]
– Tied up / Of course I'm lying / 3rd of June / Blazing saddles / The race / Alhambra / Otto Di Catania / Tied up in red / Tied up in gear.
Nov 88. (7") **TIED UP (IN LIFE). / ALL STREET BONGO** [60] [ ]
(12"+=) – Tied up in red.
(cd-s+=) – Oh yeah (Indian summer version).
Mar 89. (7") **OF COURSE I'M LYING. / OH YEAH** [23] [ ]
(12")(cd-s) – ('A'side) / Yello metropolitan mix part 1: – Dakyene intro – The race – Sostich – Call it love (Trego snare) – Santiago – Tied up – Vicious games – I love you – Oh yeah.
(12")(cd-s) – ('A'side) / Yello metropolitan mix part 2: – Dakyene intro – The rhythm divine – Goldrush – Desire – La Habanera – Blazing saddles – Domingo – Live at the Roxy – Pinball cha cha – wing.
Jul 89. (7") **BLAZING SADDLES. / I LOVE YOU** [47] [ ]
(12"+=)(c-s+=)(cd-s+=) – Blue nabou / The rhythm divine.
(other-12") – ('A'Latin mix). / ('B'diff.mix).

— lp guests **MARCO COLOMBO** – guitar (3) / **BEAT ASH** (4) / **BILLY McKENZIE** (3)

May 91. (7")(c-s) **RUBBERBANDMAN. / SWEET THUNDER** [58] [ ]
(12"+=)(cd-s+=) – ('A'extended).
Jun 91. (cd)(c)(lp) **BABY** [37] [ ]
– Homage to the mountain / Rubberbandman / Jungle Bill / Ocean club / Who's groove / Capri-calling / Drive-driven / On the run / Blender / Sweet thunder.
Aug 92. (7")(c-s) **JUNGLE BILL. / ('A'big pig mix)** [61] [ ]
(cd-s+=) – ('A'voodoo mix) / ('A'chicken dive mix) / ('A'space mix).
(cd-s) – ('A'side) / ('A'-shades of Paradise mix 1 & 2) / ('A'-too tough 4 trego mix 1 & 2).
Sep 92. (cd)(c)(lp) **THE ESSENTIAL YELLO** (compilation) [ ] [ ]
– Oh yeah / The race / Rubberbandman / Vicious games / Tied up / Lost again / I love you, goodbye / Of course I'm lying / Pinball cha cha / Bostich / Desire / Jungle Bill / Goldrush / The rhythm divine.
Oct 92. (7")(c-s) **THE RACE (Boris Blank remix). / BOSTICH (Kevin Sanderson remix)** [55] [ ]
(12"+=)(cd-s+=) – ('A' Kevin Sanderson remix).
Oct 94. (c-s) **HOW HOW. / ('A'instrumental mix)** [59] [ ]
(12"+=) – ('A'-Fluke mix) / ('A'-Plutone mix).
(cd-s++=) – ('A'mixes).
(cd-s) – (4-'A'mixes) / Vicious games (U.S.remix) / Do it (2 mixes).
Oct 94. (cd)(c)(lp) **ZEBRA** [ ] [ ]
– Suite 909 / How how / Night train / Do it / I . . . I'm in love / S.A.X. / Fat cry / Tremendous pain / Move dance be born / The premix (how how) / Poom shanka.

Polydor / Polydor

Mar 95. (cd)(c) **HANDS ON YELLO** (remix) [ ] [ ]
– best of remixed by The Orb / Westbam / Moby / Jens / The Grid / Hardsequencer / Jam & Spoon / Plutone / Carl Cox / Oliver Lieb / Cosmic Baby / Carl Craig / Isla Gold.
Apr 95. (12")(cd-s) **YOU GOTTA SAY YES TO ANOTHER EXCESS. ("JAM & SPOON'S HANDS ON YELLO") / (other mixes)** [ ] [ ]

YES

Formed: London, England ... mid '68 by veterans of the 60's beat era; ANDERSON and SQUIRE. They added BILL BRUFORD, PETE BANKS and TONY KAYE and soon signed to 'Atlantic', after opening for CREAM at their farewell concert at London's Royal Albert Hall. In the summer of 1969, their album debut was released, but after its flop they had first of many personnel changes; STEVE HOWE for PETE BANKS. In 1970, the follow-up 'TIME AND A WORD' hit the UK Top 50, but was surpassed early the next year, when 'THE YES ALBUM' hit the Top 10 and broke into American Top 40. The more-stylish and flamboyant RICK WAKEMAN was then drafted in to replace KAYE. The self-indulgent but well-received 'FRAGILE' was another success and was the first to feature ROGER DEAN's fantasy lp covers. At the end of the Autumn 1972, the classic 'CLOSE TO THE EDGE' was unleashed and this too was a commercial success, hitting Top 5 on both sides of the Atlantic. In 1973, their triple live lp 'YESSONGS', peaked at No.1 in the UK, and hit Top 20 in America. After another two near perfect creations 'TALES FROM TOPOGRAPHIC OCEANS' and 'RELAYER', they went on solo sojourns. WAKEMAN's was permanent, as his had started in 1973 with his album 'SIX WIVES OF HENRY VIII'. In 1977, when punk rock was king, YES returned with new keyboard wizard PATRICK MORAZ and another gem 'GOING FOR THE ONE'. Although they continued to have many successes in many shapes and forms (see below) for next two decades, they never re-created the high spots of the 70's. • **Style:** Progressive neo-classical pomp-rock dinosaurs. They blended flash-rock and superb individual musicianship, with choirboy-like vox of JON ANDERSON. • **Songwriters:** Group / individual compositions with ANDERSON lyrics. Early in the 80's, The BUGGLES boys were also contributing, much to dismay of loyal supporters. Covered EVERY LITTLE THING + I'M DOWN (Beatles) / I SEE YOU (Byrds) / NO OPPORTUNITY NECCESSARY, NO EXPERIENCE NEEDED (Stephen Stills) / SOMETHING'S COMING (Sondheim-Bernstein) / AMERICA (Simon & Garfunkel). AMAZING GRACE (trad.). JON ANDERSON recorded traditional Christmas carols on his '3 SHIPS' lp. • **Trivia:** From 1971 onwards, they employed ROGER DEAN for all album sleeve artwork. The producers were debut: co-w / PAUL CLAY / follow-up: TONY COLTON. Then untill temp. breakup 1975; EDDIE OFFORD. They produced themselves and w/HORN on '90125'). In Apr'89, HOWE appeared on Various Artists live d-lp,c,cd,video 'NIGHT OF THE GUITAR' on 'I.R.S.' label.

Recommended: CLOSE TO THE EDGE (*10) / THE YES ALBUM (*10) / YESSONGS (*9) / GOING FOR THE ONE (*8) / TALES FROM TOPOGRAPHIC OCEANS (*9) / RELAYER (*8) / FRAGILE (*7) / CLASSIC YES (*9)

JON ANDERSON (b.25 Oct'44, Accrington, England) – vocals (ex-WARRIORS) / **TONY KAYE** (b.11 Jan'46, Leicester) – keyboards (ex-FEDERALS, ex-BITTER SWEET) / **PETE BANKS** (b. 7 Jul'47, Barnet) – guitar (ex-SYN, ex-MABEL GREEN'S TOY . . .) / **CHRIS SQUIRE** (b. 4 Mar'48, Nth. London) – bass, vocals (ex-SYN) / **BILL BRUFORD** (b.17 May'48) – percussion (ex-SAVOY BROWN BLUES BAND)

Atlantic Atlantic

Jun 69. (7") **SWEETNESS. / SOMETHING'S COMING** [ ] [-]

Jul 69. (lp)(c) **YES** [ ] [ ] Oct 69

– Beyond and before / I see you / Yesterday and today / Looking around / Harold land / Every little thing / Sweetness / Survival. *(re-iss.cd Oct94)*

Oct 69. (7") **LOOKING AROUND. / EVERYDAYS** [ ] [-]

Jan 70. (7") **SWEETNESS / EVERY LITTLE THING** [-] [ ]

— **STEVE HOWE** (b. 8 Apr'47) – guitar (ex-TOMORROW, ex-IN CROWD, ex-SYNDICATS, ex-BODAST) repl. BANKS who joined BLODWYN PIG and later FLASH.

Mar 70. (7") **TIME AND A WORD. / THE PROPHET** [ ] [-]

Jun 70. (lp)(c) **TIME AND A WORD** [45] [ ] Nov 70

– No opportunity neccessary, no experience needed / Then / Everydays / Sweet dreams / The prophet / Clear days / Astral traveller / Time and a word. *(re-iss.cd Oct94)*

Jun 70. (7") **SWEET DREAMS. / DEAR FATHER** [ ] [-]

Mar 71. (lp)(c) **THE YES ALBUM** [7] [40] May 71

– Yours is no disgrace / The clap / Starship trooper; (a) Life seeker – (b) Disiilusion – (c) Wurm / I've seen good people (a) Your move – (b) All good people / A venture / Perpetual change. *(cd-iss.Jul87)*

Jul 71. (7") **YOUR MOVE. / THE CLAP** [-] [40]

— **RICK WAKEMAN** (b.18 May'49) – keyboards (ex-STRAWBS) repl. KAYE who formed BADGER

Nov 71. (lp)(c) **FRAGILE** [7] [4] Jan 72

– Roundabout / Cans and Brahms / We have Heaven / South side of the sky / Five per cent of nothing / Long distance runaround / The fish (Shindleria Praematurus) / Mood for a day / Heart of the sunrise. *(cd-iss.Dec86)*

Jan 72. (7") **ROUNDABOUT. / LONG DISTANCE RUNAROUND** [-] [13]

Jul 72. (7") **AMERICA. / TOTAL MASS RETAIN** [-] [46]

Sep 72. (lp)(c) **CLOSE TO THE EDGE** [4] [3]

– Close to the edge; (a) The solid time of change – (b) Total mass retain – (c) I get up I get down – (d) Seasons of man / And you and I; (a) Cord of life – (b) Eclipse – (c) The preacher the teacher – (d) The apocalypse / Siberian Khatru. *(cd-iss.Dec86)*

Oct 72. (7") **AND YOU AND I (part II). / (part I)** [-] [42]

— (Aug72) **ANDERSON, HOWE, WAKEMAN + SQUIRE** brought in **ALAN WHITE** (b.14 Jun'44, Pelton, Durham, England) – drums (ex-John Lennon's PLASTIC ONO BAND, ex-HAPPY MAGAZINE) repl. BRUFORD who joined KING CRIMSON, etc. (both appeared on live album below)

May 73. (t-lp)(d-c) **YESSONGS (live)** [1] [12]

– (opening excerpt from 'Firebird Suite') / Siberian Khatru / Heart of the sunrise / Perpetual change / And you and I; (a) Cord of life – (b) Eclipse – (c) The preacher the teacher – (d) The apocalypse / Mood for a day / (excerpts from 'The Six Wives Of Henry VIII') / Roundabout / I've seen all good people; Your move – All good people / Long distance runaround / The fish (Shindleria Praematurus) / Close to the edge (a) The solid time of change – (b) Total mass retain – (c) I get up I get down – (d) Seasons of man / Yours is no disgrace / Starship trooper (a) Life seeker – (b) Disillusion – (c) Wurm. *(d-cd iss.Feb87) (re-iss.d-cd Oct94)*

Dec 73. (d-lp)(c) **TALES FROM TOPOGRAPHIC OCEANS** [1] [6]

– The revealing science of God / The remembering / The ancient / Ritual. *(cd-iss.Sep89) (re-iss.d-cd Oct94)*

Jan 74. (7") **ROUNDABOUT (live). / AND YOU AND I (live)** [ ] [-]

— **PATRICK MORAZ** (b.24 Jun'48, Morges, Switzerland) – keyboards (ex-REFUGEE) repl. WAKEMAN who continued solo

Nov 74. (lp)(c) **RELAYER** [4] [5] Dec 74

– The gates of delirium / Sound chaser / To be over. *(cd-iss.Jul88) (re-iss.cd Oct94)*

Jan 75. (7") **SOON (from 'Gates of Delirium'). / SOUND CHASER** [ ] [-]

— Temporarily disbanded to release solo albums.

STEVE HOWE

augmented by **WHITE, BRUFORD, MORAZ** + many including **GRAEME TAYLOR** – guitar / **MALCOLM BENNETT + COLIN GIBSON** – bass / **DAVID OBERLE** – drums

Atlantic Atlantic

Nov 75. (lp)(c) **BEGINNINGS** [22] [63]

– Doors of sleep / Australia / The nature of the sea / The lost symphony / Beginnings / Will o' the wisp / Ram / Pleasure stole the night / Break away from it all. *(re-iss.cd Oct94)*

CHRIS SQUIRE

augmented by **BILL BRUFORD** – drums / **ANDREW BRYCE JACKMAN + BARRY ROSE** – keyboards / **MEL COLLINS** – sax / **PATRICK MORAZ** – keyboards, synthesizers / **JIMMY HASTINGS** – flute

Atlantic Atlantic

Nov 75. (lp)(c) **FISH OUT OF WATER** [25] [69]

– Hold out your hand / You by my side / Silently falling / Lucky seven / Safe (canon song).

ALAN WHITE

augmented by **PETER KIRTLEY** – guitar, vocals / **COLIN GIBSON** – bass / **KENNY CRADDOCK** – keyboards, vocals / **ANDY PHILIPS** – steel drums / **ALAN MARSHALL** vocals / **HENRY LOWTHER** – trumpet / **STEVE GREGORY + BUD BEADLE** – wind

Atlantic Atlantic

Mar 76. (lp)(c) **RAMSHACKLED** [41] [ ]

– Oooh! baby (going to pieces) / One way rag / Avakak / Spring – Song of innocence / Giddy / Silly woman / Marching into a bottle / Everybody / Darkness (parts 1, 2 & 3).

Apr 76. (7") **OOOH! BABY (GOING TO PIECES). / ONE WAY RAG** [ ] [-]

JON ANDERSON

augmented **BRIAN GAYLOR** – synths / **KEN FREEMAN** – strings

Atlantic Atlantic

Jun 76. (lp)(c) **OLIAS OF SUNHILLOW** [8] [47]

– Ocean song / Meeting (Garden of Geda) – Sound of the galleon / Dance of Ranyart – Olias (to build the Moorglade) / Qoquag en transic – Naon – Transic to / Flight of the Moorglade / Solid space / Moon Ra – Chords – Song of search / To the runner.

Oct 76. (7") **FLIGHT OF THE MOORGLADE. / TO THE RUNNER** [ ] [-]

— PATRICK MORAZ also hit UK Top 30 with his I, PATRICK MORAZ album for 'Charisma'. He had now departed YES to continue solo work & join MOODY BLUES.

YES

re-formed in 1977 the 1973 line-up w / **RICK WAKEMAN** returning, to repl. MORAZ..

Jul 77. (lp)(c)(3x12") **GOING FOR THE ONE** [1] [8]

– Going for the one / Turn of the century / Parallels / Wonderous stories / Awaken. *(cd-iss.Jul88)*

Sep 77. (7")(12")(12"blue) **WONDEROUS STORIES. / PARALLELS** [7] [-]

Sep 77. (7")(**WONDEROUS STORIES. / AWAKEN** [-] [ ]

Nov 77. (7")(12") **GOING FOR THE ONE. / AWAKEN (part 1)** [24] [-]

Sep 78. (7") **DON'T KILL THE WHALE. / ABILENE** [36] [-]

Sep 78. (lp)(c) **TORMATO** [8] [10]

– Future times / Rejoice / Don't kill the whale / Madrigal / Release, release / Arriving UFO / Circus of Heaven / Onward / On the silent wings of freedom.

Nov 78. (7") **RELEASE, RELEASE. / DON'T KILL THE WHALE** [-] [ ]

— They shocked their fans, when they replaced (solo seeking once more) WAKEMAN and ANDERSON with (ex-BUGGLES duo) :-**TREVOR HORN** – vocals, bass / + **GEOFF DOWNES** – keyboards

Aug 80. (lp)(c) **DRAMA** [2] [18]

– Machine messiah / White car / Does it really happen? / Into the lens / Run through the light / Tempus fugit. *(re-iss.cd Oct94)*

Oct 80. (7") **INTO THE LENS. / DOES IT REALLY HAPPEN?** [ ] [ ]

Jan 81. (7") **RUN THROUGH THE LIGHT. / WHITE CAR** [-] [ ]

— YES split again.

CAMERA

were formed by **SQUIRE + WHITE**

Dec 82. (7") **RUN WITH THE FOX. / (part 2)** [ ] [ ]

YES

— above partnership brought back **ANDERSON + KAYE,** plus newcomer **TREVOR RABIN** (b.South Africa) – guitar, vocals. They repl. DOWNES + HOWE (to ASIA) / and HORN who was retained as producer.

Atco Atco

Nov 83. (7")(7"pic-d)(7"sha-pic-d) **OWNER OF A LONELY HEART. / OUR SONG** [28] [1]

(12"+=)(c-s+=) – ('A'version).

Nov 83. (lp)(c)(cd) **90125** [16] [5]

– Owner of a lonely heart / Hold on / It can happen / Changes / Cinema / Leave it / Our song / City of love / Hearts.

Mar 84. (7") **LEAVE IT. / LEAVE IT (acappella)** [56] [24]

(12"+=) – ('A'version).

(US-c-s+=) – ('A'-hello goodbye mix) / Owner of a lonely heart.

Jun 84. (7") **IT CAN HAPPEN. / IT CAN HAPPEN (live)** [ ] [51]

Mar 86. (m-lp)(c) **9012LIVE – THE SOLOS (live)** [44] [81] Dec 85

– Hold on / Si / Solly's beard / Soon / Changes / Amazing Grace / Whitefish.

Sep 87. (7") **LOVE WILL FIND A WAY. / HOLY LAMB** [73] [30]

('A'extended-12"+=) – ('A'rise & fall mix)

Sep 87. (lp)(c)(cd) **BIG GENERATOR** [17] [15]

– Rhythm of love / Big generator / Shoot high aim low / Almost like love / Love will find a way / Final eyes / I'm running / Holy love.

Dec 87. (12"ep) **RHYTHM OF LOVE (dance mix) – ('A'move mix) / ('A'dub) / CITY OF LOVE** (live) [-] [40]

— In-house squabbles led to splinter of YES called . . .

ANDERSON BRUFORD WAKEMAN HOWE

Arista Arista

Jun 89. (lp)(c)(cd) **ANDERSON BRUFORD WAKEMAN HOWE** [14] [30]

– Themes: Sound – Second attention – Soul warrior / Fist of fire / Brother of mine: The big dream – Nothing can come between us – Long lost brother of mine / Quartet: I wanna learn – She gives me love – Who was the first – I'm alive / Birthright / The meeting / Teakbois / Order of the universe: Order theme – Rock gives courage – It's so hard to grow – The universe / Let's pretend. *(lp tracks edited)(re-iss.cd.Dec92)*

Jun 89. (7") **BROTHER OF MINE. / THEMES: SOUND** 63
(12"+=) – Themes: Second attention – Soul warrior.
(3"cd-s+=)(5"cd-s+=)(10"+=)(c-s+=) – Vultures (in the city).

Aug 89. (7") **LET'S PRETEND. / QUARTET: I'M ALIVE** -

Nov 89. (7")(c-s) **ORDER OF THE UNIVERSE. / FIST OF FIRE**
(12"+=)(cd-s+=) – ?

YES

now settled dispute by combining last line-up of **ANDERSON, BRUFORD, HOWE, WAKEMAN** with present YES men **SQUIRE, WHITE, RABIN + KAYE**

May 91. (cd)(c)(lp) **UNION** 7 15
– I would have waited forever / Shock to the system / Masquerade / Lift me up / Without hope you cannot start the day / Saving my heart / Miracle of life / Silent talking / The more we live-let go / Dangerous / Holding on / Evensong. (c+cd +=) – Angkor wat / Take the water to the mountain / Give and take. *(re-iss.cd May94)*

Jun 91. (7") **SAVING MY HEART. / LIFT ME UP (edit)** -
(12"+=)(cd-s+=) – America.

Aug 91. (7") **LIFT ME UP. / GIVE AND TAKE** - 86

Nov 91. (c-s) **SAVING MY HEART. / THE MORE WE LIVE - LET GO** -

Victory Londob

Mar 94. (cd)(c) **TALK** 20 33
– Calling / I am waiting / Real love / State of play / Walls / Where will you be / Endless dream (Silent spring – Talk – Endless dream).

- compilations, others, etc. -

Note; on 'Atlantic' unless otherwise stated.

Feb 75. (lp)(c) **YESTERDAYS** (early rare) 27 17
– America / Looking around / Time and a word / Sweet dreams / Then / Survival / Astral traveller / Dear father. *(re-iss.cd Oct94)*

Dec 81. (lp)(c) **CLASSIC YES**
– Heart of the sunrise / Wonderous stories / Yours is no disgrace / Roundabout / Starship trooper (a) Life seeker (b) Disillusion (c) Wurm / Long distance runaround / The fish (schindleria praematurus) / And you and I; (a) Cord of life (b) Eclipse (c) The preacher the teacher (d) The apocalypse / I've seen all good people; (a) Your move (b) All good people. *(w/ free 7")* – **ROUNDABOUT (live). / I'VE SEEN ALL GOOD PEOPLE (live)** *(cd-iss.Dec86) (re-iss.cd Oct94)*

Oct 82. (d-c) **FRAGILE / CLOSE TO THE EDGE** -

Sep 93. (cd)(c) **HIGHLIGHTS - THE VERY BEST OF YES**

Dec 80. Atco; (d-lp)(c) **YESSHOWS (live 1976-1978)** 22 43
(re-iss.cd Oct94)

Aug 91. Atco; (4xcd-box)(4xc-box) **YES YEARS**

Oct 91. East West; (d-cd)(d-c)(t-lp) **YES STORY**

Nov 91. East West; (7")(c-s) **OWNER OF A LONELY HEART. / ('A'-wonderous mix)**
(12")(cd-s) – ('A'side) / ('A'not fragile mix) / ('A'move yourself mix) / ('A'close to the edge mix).

Sep 93. Connoiseur; (cd) **AFFIRMATIVE (YES family tree)** -
– Small beginnings (FLASH) / Feels good to me (BRUFORD) / Catherine Howard / Merlin the magician (RICK WAKEMAN) / Ocean song / All in a matter of time (JON ANDERSON) / I HEAR YOU NOW (JON & VANGELIS) / SPRING SONG OF INNOCENCE (ALAN WHITE) / Nature of the sea / Ram (STEVE HOWE) / Cahcaca (PATRICK MORAZ) / Hold out your hand (CHRIS SQUIRE) / Wind of change (BADGER) / Etoile noir (TREVOR RABIN).

Dec 93. Fragile; (d-cd)(video) **AN EVENING OF YES MUSIC ... PLUS**

JON ANDERSON

with more solo releases. Earlier in the year 1980, he (JON) and VANGELIS ⇒ had hit UK No.8 with single 'I HEAR YOU NOW', and 'SHORT STORIES' lp hit No.4.

—— with a plethera of session people.

Atlantic Atlantic

Sep 80. (7") **SOME ARE BORN. / DAYS**

Nov 80. (lp)(c) **SONG OF SEVEN** 38
– For you for me / Some are born / Don't forget (nostalgia) / Heart of the matter / Hear it / Everybody loves you / Take your time / Days / Song of seven.

Nov 80. (7") **TAKE YOUR TIME. / HEART OF THE MATTER**

—— Around mid'81, JON & VANGELIS released album 'THE FRIENDS OF MR.CAIRO' which hit UK No.6. Lifted from it 'I'LL FIND MY WAY HOME' also managed to hit UK No.6 / US No.51 in Nov '81. These and his next solo releases were issued on

Polydor Atlantic

Apr 82. (7") **SURRENDER. / SPIDER**

May 82. (lp)(c) **ANIMATION** 43
– Olympia / Animation / All in a matter of time / Unlearning / Boundaries / Pressure point / Much better reason / All Gods children.

Nov 82. (7") **ALL IN A MATTER OF TIME. / SPIDER**

—— May83, sees another JON & VANGELIS album 'PRIVATE COLLECTION' hit UK No.22. Their compilation album 'THE BEST OF . . . ' hit UK No.42 in Aug84.

Elektra Elektra

Dec 85. (lp)(c) **3 SHIPS**
– Save all your love / Easier said than done / 3 ships / Forest of fire / Ding dong merrily on high / Save all your love (reprise) / The holly and the ivy / Day of days / 2,000 years / Where were you / Oh holy night / How it hits you / Jingle bells.

Dec 85. (7") **DAY OF DAYS. / EASIER SAID THAN DONE** -

—— In 1986, he guested on MIKE OLDFIELD'S album 'SHINE'.

Epic Epic

Jun 88. (7")(12") **HOLD ON TO LOVE. / SUN DANCING (FOR THE HOPI-NAVAJO ENERGY)**
(cd-s+=) – In a lifetime.

Jun 88. (lp)(c)(cd) **IN THE CITY OF ANGELS**
– Hold on to love / If it wasn't for love (oneness family) / Sun dancing (for the Hopi-Navajo energy) / Is it me / In a lifetime / For you / New civilization / It's on fire / Betcha / Top of the world (the glass bead game) / Hurry home (soon from the Pleiades).

Aug 88. (7") **IS IT ME. / TOP OF THE WORLD (GLASS BEAD GAME)**
(12"+=) – For you.

—— Later that year he provided vocals for charity 45 'WHATEVER YOU BELIEVE' accompanying STEVE HARLEY & MIKE BATT.

E.M.I. not issued

Oct 94. (7")(c-s) **CHANGE WE MUST. / STATE OF INDEPENDENCE**
(cd-s+=) – ('A'mixes) / (interview).

STEVE HOWE

with in 1979; **PATRICK MORAZ** – keyboards / **ALAN WHITE + BILL BRUFORD + CLIVE BUNKER** – drums / **RONNIE LEAHY** – keyboards / **GRAHAM PRESKETT** – violin / **CLAIRE HAMILL** – vocals

Atlantic Atlantic

Oct 79. (lp)(c) **THE STEVE HOWE ALBUM** 68
– Pennants / Cactus boogie / All's a chord / Look over your shoulder / Diary of a man who disappeared / Meadow rag / The continental / Surface tension / Double rondo / Concerto in D (second movement). *(re-iss.cd Oct94)*

Relativity Relativity

Jan 92. (cd)(c)(lp) **TURBULENCE**
– Turbulence / Hint hint / Running the human race / The inner battle / Novalis / Fine line / Sensitive chaos / Corkscrew / While Rome's burning / From a place where time runs slow.

Road-runner Road-runner

Sep 93. (cd)(c) **THE GRAND SCHEME OF THINGS**

Jun 95. Thunderbird-RPM; (cd) **NOT NECESSARILY ACOUSTIC** -

—— For RICK WAKEMAN releases, see under own solo entry.

Y KANT TORI READ (see under ⇒ AMOS, Tori)

Neil YOUNG

Born: 12 Nov'45, Toronto, Canada. Raised Winnipeg until 1966 when he drove to America in his Pontiac hearse. NEIL had cut his teeth in local instrumental outfit the SQUIRES, who released one '45 'THE SULTAN'. / 'AURORA' for 'V' records in Sep 63. The following year NEIL formed the MYNHA BIRDS and joined forces with RICKY JAMES MATTHEWS (later to become RICK JAMES). Although many songs were recorded, only one saw light of day; 'MYNHA BIRD HOP' for 'Columbia' Canada. They signed to 'Motown' (first white people to do so) but were soon dropped when they found out that RICKY had dodged the draft. Met up with past acquaintance STEPHEN STILLS and formed BUFFALO SPRINGFIELD. Constant rivalry, led to YOUNG departing for solo venture after signing for new label 'Reprise' in Spring '68. His eponymous debut with arranger/producer JACK NITSCHE, then DAVID BRIGGS, was finally issued early 1969. It's lukewarm response, forced him to bring in back-up band The ROCKETS, who renamed themselves CRAZY HORSE, for follow-up second album. Early 1970, while diversing activities with CROSBY, STILLS & NASH, he recorded his third, and most successful album to date 'AFTER THE GOLDRUSH'. By 1972, he was was top of US/UK lp charts with 'HARVEST'. Throughout the 70's, part of the 80's, and early 90's he became arguably, one of the most inventive and prolific songwriters. • **Style:** Country-rock artist, who fused together his brittle, high-pitched, quavering vox, with own distinct electric guitar sound. His best work, was always with backing from CRAZY HORSE, who by the late 70's on lp 'RUST NEVER SLEEPS', transpired to a more complete, harder electric sound. In the early 80's, his shift into more synthesized music, alienated most, but not all of his long-time fans. So far in the 90's, he's reverted to his old basic rock'n'roll style, pleasing audiences reminiscing on past mid-70's 'ZUMA' album. Late in 1992, he returned with The STRAY GATORS, on excellent 'HARVEST MOON', (his 20 year follow-up to 'HARVEST'). • **Songwriters:** As said, 99% of material in his own with contributions from CRAZY HORSE members, except; FARMER JOHN (Harris-Terry). The album 'EVERYBODY'S ROCKIN'' was full of covers. • **Trivia:** 'HEY HEY MY MY..' was written about SEX PISTOL Johnny Rotten.

Recommended: HARVEST (*10) / AFTER THE GOLDRUSH (*10) / RUST NEVER SLEEPS (*9) / ZUMA (*9) / HARVEST MOON (*9) / RAGGED GLORY (*8) / WELD (*9) / SLEEPS WITH ANGELS (*9) / MIRRORBALL (*8) / EVERYBODY KNOWS THIS IS NOWHERE (*8) / TONIGHT'S THE NIGHT (*8) / DECADE (*8)

NEIL YOUNG – vocals, guitar (ex-BUFFALO SPRINGFIELD) with **JIM MESSINA** – bass / session men, etc.

Reprise Reprise

Jan 69. (lp) **NEIL YOUNG**
– The Emperor of Wyoming / The loner / If I could have her tonight / I've been waiting for you / The old laughing lady / String quartet from Whiskey Boot Hill / Here we are in the years / What did I do to my life / I've loved her so long / The last trip to Tulsa. *(re-iss.1971) (cd-iss.1987)*

Mar 69. (7") **THE LONER. / SUGAR MOUNTAIN** -

Sep 69. (7") **THE LONER. / EVERYBODY KNOWS THIS IS NOWHERE** -

Crazy Horse
LOUD

NEIL YOUNG with CRAZY HORSE

with **DANNY WHITTEN** – guitar / **BILLY TALBOT** – bass / **RALPH MOLINA** – drums / **BOBBY NOTKOFF** – violin

Jul 69. (lp) **EVERYBODY KNOWS THIS IS NOWHERE** [ ] [24] May 69
– Cinnamon girl / Everybody knows this is nowhere / Round and round (it won't be long) / Down by the river / The losing end (when you're on) / Running dry (requiem for the rockets) / Cowgirl in the sand. *(re-iss.1971) (cd-iss.1988)*

1969. (7") **DOWN BY THE RIVER (edit). / THE LOSING END (WHEN YOU'RE ON)** [-] [ ]

— Late 1969, NEIL YOUNG was also added to CROSBY, STILLS, NASH (& YOUNG).

Aug 70. (7") **DOWN BY THE RIVER (edit). / CINNAMON GIRL (alt.take)** [ ] [-]

— **NILS LOFGREN** – guitar (of GRIN) repl. NOTKOFF

Aug 70. (7") **OH LONESOME ME (extended). / I'VE BEEN WAITING FOR YOU** [-] [ ]

Sep 70. (lp)(c) **AFTER THE GOLD RUSH** [7] [8]
– Tell me why / After the gold rush / Only love can break your heart / Southern man / Till the morning comes / Oh lonesome me / Don't let it bring you down / Birds / When you dance I can really love / I believe in you / After the goldrush / Cripple Creek ferry. *(re-iss.1971) (cd-iss.Jul87)*

Sep 70. (7") **OH LONESOME ME (extended). / SUGAR MOUNTAIN** [ ] [-]

Jun 70. (7") **CINNAMON GIRL (alt.mix). / SUGAR MOUNTAIN** [-] [55]

Oct 70. (7") **ONLY LOVE CAN BREAK YOUR HEART. / BIRDS** [ ] [33]

Jan 71. (7") **WHEN YOU DANCE I CAN REALLY LOVE. / SUGAR MOUNTAIN** [-] [93]

Feb 71. (7") **WHEN YOU DANCE I CAN REALLY LOVE. / AFTER THE GOLDRUSH** [ ] [-]

NEIL YOUNG

solo with The STRAY GATORS. (CRAZY HORSE recorded on own) musicians: **JACK NITZSCHE** – piano / **BEN KEITH** – steel guitar / **TIM DRUMMOND** – bass / **KENNY BUTTREY** – drums. Guests included **CROSBY, STILLS & NASH, LINDA RONSTADT, JAMES TAYLOR** plus The LONDON SYMPHONY ORCHESTRA

Feb 72. (7") **HEART OF GOLD. / SUGAR MOUNTAIN** [10] [1]

Mar 72. lp)(c) **HARVEST** [1] [1]
– Out on the weekend / Harvest / A man needs a maid / Heart of gold / Are you ready for the country? / Old man / There's a world / Alabama / The needle and the damage done / Words (between the lines of age). *(cd-iss.May83)*

Apr 72. (7") **OLD MAN. / THE NEEDLE AND THE DAMAGE DONE** [ ] [31]

Jun 72. (7") **WAR SONG. ("NEIL YOUNG & GRAHAM NASH") / THE NEEDLE AND THE DAMAGE DONE** [-] [61]

— **JOHNNY BARBATA** – drums (ex-CROSBY, STILLS and NASH) repl. BUTTREY

Sep 73. (lp)(c) **TIME FADES AWAY (live)** [20] [22]
– Time fades away / Journey through the past / Yonder stands the sinner / L.A. / Love in mind / Don't be denied / The bridge / Last dance.

Oct 73. (7") **TIME FADES AWAY (live). / LAST TRIP TO TULSA (live)** [-] [ ]

— now used session people including **CRAZY HORSE** members **BEN KEITH** – steel guitar had now repl. WHITTEN who o.d.'d August 1972.

Jul 74. (7") **ON THE BEACH** [42] [16]
– Walk on / See the sky about to rain / Revolution blues / For the turnstiles / Vampire blues / On the beach / Motion pictures / Ambulance blues.

Jul 74. (7") **WALK ON. / FOR THE TURNSTILES** [ ] [69]

— Had just earlier 1974, re-united with CROSBY, STILLS & NASH ⇒ .

— Even earlier (late'73)

NEIL YOUNG with CRAZY HORSE

had recorded lp. Musicians: **NILS LOFGREN / BEN KEITH / BILLY TALBOT / RALPH MOLINA**

Jun 75. (lp)(c) **TONIGHT'S THE NIGHT** [48] [25]
– Tonight's the night (part I) / Speakin' out / World on a string / Borrowed tune / Come on baby let's go downtown / Mellow my mind / Roll another number (for the road) / Albuquerque / New mama / Lookout Joe / Tired eyes / Tonight's the night (part II). *(re-iss.cd Jul93)*

— (Mar75) **FRANK 'Poncho' SAMPEDRO** – guitar, vocals repl. KEITH + LOFGREN The latter earlier went solo, and later joined BRUCE SPRINGSTEEN band.

Nov 75. (lp)(c) **ZUMA** [44] [25]
– Don't cry no tears / Danger bird / Pardon my heart / Lookin' for a love / Barstool blues / Stupid girl / Drive back / Cortez the killer / Through my sails. *(re-iss.cd Jul93)*

Mar 76. (7") **LOOKIN' FOR A LOVE. / SUGAR MOUNTAIN** [ ] [ ] Dec 75

Mar 76. (7") **DRIVE BACK. / STUPID GIRL** [ ] [-]

May 76. (7") **DON'T CRY NO TEARS. / STUPID GIRL** [ ] [-]

— Mid 1976, he teamed up as STILLS-YOUNG BAND with STEPHEN STILLS on album LONG MAY YOU RUN. (see under ⇒ CROSBY, STILLS, NASH & YOUNG)

Jun 77. (lp)(c) **AMERICAN STARS'N'BARS** [17] [21]
– The old country waltz / Saddle up the Palomino / Hey babe / Hold back the tears / Bite the bullet / Star of Bethlehem / Will to love / Like a hurricane / Homegrown.

Jul 77. (7") **HEY BABE. / HOMEGROWN** [-] [ ]

Sep 77. (7") **LIKE A HURRICANE (edit). / HOLD BACK THE TEARS** [ ] [ ]

NEIL YOUNG

solo with loads on session incl.**NICOLETTE LARSON** – vox

Oct 78. (7") **COMES A TIME. / MOTORCYCLE MAMA** [-] [ ]

Oct 78. (lp)(c) **COMES A TIME** [42] [7]
– Goin' back / Comes a time / Look out for my love / Lotta love / Peace of mind / Human highway / Already one / Field of opportunity / Motorcycle mama / Four strong winds. *(re-iss.cd Jul93)*

Nov 78. (7") **FOUR STRONG WINDS. / MOTORCYCLE MAMA** [57] [-]

Dec 78. (7") **FOUR STRONG WINDS. / HUMAN HIGHWAY** [-] [61]

NEIL YOUNG with CRAZY HORSE

(YOUNG w / **SAMPEDRO, TALBOT & MOLINA**)

Jun 79. (lp)(c) **RUST NEVER SLEEPS** [13] [8]
– My my, hey hey (out of the blue) / Thrasher / Ride my llama / Pocahontas / Sail away / Powderfinger / Welfare mothers / Sedan delivery / Hey hey, my my (into the black). *(re-iss.Oct81) (re-iss.cd Jul93)*

Aug 79. (7") **HEY HEY, MY MY (INTO THE BLACK). / MY MY, HEY HEY (OUT OF THE BLUE)** [ ] [79]

Nov 79. (d-lp)(d-c) **LIVE RUST (live)** [55] [15]
– Sugar mountain / I am a child / Comes a time / After the gold rush / My my, hey hey (out of the blue) / When you dance I can really love / The loner / The needle and the damage done / Lotta love / Sedan delivery / Powderfinger / Cortez the killer / Cinnamon girl / Like a hurricane / Hey hey, my my (into the black) / Tonight's the night. *(re-iss.Oct81) (re-iss.cd Jul93)*

Dec 79. (7") **CINNAMON GIRL (live). / THE LONER (live)** [-] [ ]

NEIL YOUNG

solo with **TIM DRUMMOND + DENNIS BELFIELD** – bass / **LEVON HELM + GREG THOMAS** – drums / **BEN KEITH** – steel, dobro / **RUFUS THIBODEAUX** – fiddle

Oct 80. (lp)(c) **HAWKS & DOVES** [34] [30]
– Little wing / The old homestead / Lost in space / Captain Kennedy / Stayin' power / Coastline / Union power / Comin' apart at every nail / Hawks & doves.

Nov 80. (7") **HAWKS & DOVES. / UNION MAN** [ ] [ ]

Feb 81. (7") **STAYIN' POWER. / CAPTAIN KENNEDY** [-] [ ]

NEIL YOUNG with CRAZY HORSE

(see last CRAZY HORSE line-up)

Oct 81. (lp)(c) **RE• AC• TOR** [69] [27]
– Opera star / Surfer Joe and Moe the sleaze / T-bone / Get back on it / Southern Pacific / Motor city / Rapid transit / Shots.

Nov 81. (7")(10"sha-red-d) **SOUTHERN PACIFIC. / MOTOR CITY** [-] [70]

Jan 82. (7") **OPERA STAR. / SURFER JOE AND MOE THE SLEAZE** [-] [ ]

NEIL YOUNG

solo adding synthesizers, drum machine (sessioners) **BRUCE PALMER** – bass (ex-BUFFALO SPRINGFIELD)

Geffen Geffen

Jan 83. (7") **LITTLE THING CALLED LOVE. / WE'R IN CONTROL** [ ] [71] Dec 82

Jan 83. (lp)(c) **TRANS** [29] [19]
– Little thing called love / Computer age / We'r in control / Transformer man / Computer cowboy (aka Syscrusher) / Hold on to your love / Sample and hold / Mr. Soul / Like an Inca. *(re-iss.Sep86)*

Feb 83. (7") **MR. SOUL. / MR. SOUL (part 2)** [-] [ ]
(12") – ('A'extended) / Sample and hold (extended).

NEIL YOUNG & The SHOCKING PINKS

w / **BEN KEITH** – guitar / **TIM DRUMMOND** – bass / **KARL HIMMEL** – drums / **LARRY BYROM** – piano, vocals / **RICK PALOMBI + ANTHONY CRAWFORD** – b.vocals

Sep 83. (lp)(c) **EVERYBODY'S ROCKIN'** [50] [46] Aug 83
– Betty Lou's got a new pair of shoes / Rainin' in my heart / Payola blues / Wonderin' / Kinda fonda Wanda / Jellyroll man / Bright lights, big city / Cry, cry, cry / Mystery train / Everybody's rockin'. *(re-iss.Sep86, cd-iss.1988)*

Sep 83. (7") **WONDERIN'. / PAYOLA BLUES** [ ] [ ]

Oct 83. (7") **CRY, CRY, CRY. / PAYOLA BLUES** [-] [ ]

— Jul85, with country singer WILLIE NELSON he duets on his ARE THERE ANY MORE REAL COWBOYS single issued on 'Columbia'.

NEIL YOUNG

solo again with loads of session people.

Aug 85. (lp)(c) **OLD WAYS** [39] [75]
– The wayward wind / Get back to the country / Are there any more real cowboys? / Once an angel / Misfits / California sunset / Old ways / My boy / Bound for glory / Where is the highway tonight?.

Sep 85. (7") **BACK TO THE COUNTRY. / MISFITS** [-] [ ]

Nov 85. (7") **OLD WAYS. / ONCE AN ANGEL** [-] [ ]

— w / **STEVE JORDAN** – drums, synths, vox / **DANNY KORTCHMAR** – guitar, synth

Aug 86. (lp)(c)(cd) **LANDING ON WATER** [52] [46]
– Weight of the world / Violent side / Hippie dream / Bad news beat / Touch the night / People on the street / Hard luck stories / I got a problem / Pressure / Drifter. *(re-iss.Apr91)*

Sep 86. (7")(12") **WEIGHT OF THE WORLD. / PRESSURE** [ ] [ ] Jul86

NEIL YOUNG & CRAZY HORSE

(see last **CRAZY HORSE, + BRYAN BELL** – synth)

May 87. (lp)(c)(cd) **LIFE** [71] [75]
– Mideast vacation / Long walk home / Around the world / Inca queen / Too lonely / Prisoners of rock'n'roll / Cryin' eyes / When your lonely heart breaks / We never danced.

Jun 87. (7") **MIDEAST VACATION. / LONG WALK HOME** [ ] [-]

Jun 87. (7") **LONG WALK HOME. / CRYIN' EYES** [ ] [-]

NEIL YOUNG & THE BLUENOTES

with **SAMPEDRO** – keyboards plus others **CHAD CROMWELL** – drums / **RICK ROSAS** –

bass / **STEVE LAWRENCE** – tenor sax / **BEN KEITH** – alto sax / **LARRY CRAIG** – baritone sax / **CLAUDE CAILLIET** – trombone / **JOHN FUMO** – trumpet / **TOM BRAY** – trumpet

Reprise Reprise

Apr 88. (7") **TEN MEN WORKIN'. / I'M GOIN'** [-] [ ]

May 88. (lp)(c)(cd) **THIS NOTE'S FOR YOU** [56] [61]
– Ten men workin' / This note's for you / Coupe de ville / Life in the city / Twilight / Married man / Sunny inside / Can't believe you're lyin' / Hey hey / One thing. *(re-iss.cd Feb95)*

May 88. (7") **THIS NOTE'S FOR YOU (live). / THIS NOTE'S FOR YOU** [-] [ ]

— Nov88, NEIL re-joined CROSBY, STILLS, NASH & YOUNG for 'AMERICAN DREAM' lp.

NEIL YOUNG

solo again with **SAMPEDRO, ROSAS, CROMWELL**, etc.

Oct 89. (lp)(c)(cd) **FREEDOM** [17] [35]
– Rockin' in the free world / Crime in the city (sixty to zero part 1) / Don't cry / Hangin' on a limb / Eldorado / The ways of love / Someday / On Broadway / Wreckin' ball / No more / Too far gone / Rockin' in the free world (live). *(re-iss.cd/c Feb95)*

Apr 90. (7") **ROCKIN' IN THE FREE WORLD. / ('A'live version)** [ ] [ ] Oct 89
(UK-12"+=)(cd-s+=) – Cocaine eyes.

NEIL YOUNG & CRAZY HORSE

with **SAMPEDRO, TALBOT + MOLINA**

Sep 90. (cd)(c)(lp) **RAGGED GLORY** [15] [31]
– Country home / White line / F*!#in' up / Over and over / Love to burn / Farmer John / Mansion on the hill / Days that used to be / Love and only love / Mother Earth (natural anthem). *(re-iss.cd/c Feb95)*

Sep 90. (cd-s) **MANSION ON THE HILL (edit) / MANSION ON THE HILL / DON'T SPOOK THE HORSE** [-] [ ]

Oct 91. (d-cd)(d-c)(d-lp) **WELD (live)** [20] [ ]
– Hey hey, my my (into the black) / Crime in the city / Blowin' in the wind / Live to burn / Welfare mothers / Cinnamon girl / Mansion on the hill / F*!#in' up / Farmer John / Cortez the killer / Powderfinger / Love and only love / Roll another number / Rockin' in the free world / Like a hurricane / Tonight's the night. (free-cd-ep w.a.+=) – ARC EP – (feedback).

NEIL YOUNG

solo, with The STRAY GATORS (**KENNY BUTTREY, TIM DRUMMOND, BEN KEITH & SPOONER OLDHAM**) plus **JAMES TAYLOR, LINDA RONSTADT, NICOLETTE LARSON, ASTRID YOUNG & LARRY CRAGG** – backing vocals

Oct 92. (cd)(c)(lp) **HARVEST MOON** [9] [16]
– Unknown legend / From Hank to Hendrix / You and me / Harvest moon / War of man / One of these days / Such a woman / Old king / Dreamin' man / Natural beauty.

Feb 93. (7")(c-s) **HARVEST MOON. / WINTERLONG** [36] [ ]
(cd-s+=) – Deep forbidden lake / Campaigner.
(cd-s) – ('A'side) / Old king / The needle and the damage done / Goin' back.

Jun 93. (cd)(c)(lp) **UNPLUGGED** [4] [23]
– The old laughing lady / Mr.Soul / World on a string / Pocahontas / Strongman / Like a hurricane / The needle and the damage done / Helpless / Harvest Moon / Transformer man / Unknown legend / Look out for my love / Long may you run / From Hank to Memphis.

Jul 93. (7")(c-s) **THE NEEDLE AND THE DAMAGE DONE (live). / YOU AND ME** [75] [ ]
(cd-s+=) – From Hank to Hendrix.

Oct 93. (7")(c-s) **LONG MAY YOU RUN (live). / SUGAR MOUNTAIN (live)** [71] [ ]
(cd-s+=) – Cortez the killer (live) / Cinnamon girl (live).

Feb 94. (7")(c-s) **ROCKIN' IN THE FREE WORLD. / ('A'mixes)** [ ] [ ]
(cd-s+=) – Weld.

Apr 94. (cd-s) **PHILADELPHIA / SUCH A WOMAN / STRINGMAN (unplugged)** [62] [ ]

— Above 'A'side was another to be taken from the film 'Philadelphia' on 'Epic'.

NEIL YOUNG & CRAZY HORSE

Aug 94. (cd)(c)(d-lp) **SLEEPS WITH ANGELS** [2] [9]
– My heart / Prime of life / Drive by / Sleeps with angels / Western hero / Change your mind / Blue Eden / Safeway cart / Train of love / Trans Am / Piece of crap / A dream that can last.

Aug 94. (c-s)(cd-s) **PIECE OF CRAP / TONIGHT'S THE NIGHT** [ ] [ ]

Oct 94. (c-s)(cd-s) **MY HEART / ROLL ANOTHER NUMBER (FOR THE ROAD)** [ ] [ ]
(cd-s+=) – Tired eyes.

Nov 94. (c-s) **CHANGE YOUR MIND / SPEAKIN' OUT** [ ] [ ]
(cd-s+=) – ('A'full version).

Neil YOUNG

— with backing from all of PEARL JAM; 8th track written w/ EDDIE VEDDER

Warners Warners

Jun 95. (cd)(c)(lp) **MIRROR BALL** [4] [5]
– Song x / Act of love / I'm the ocean / Big green country / Truth be known / Downtown / What happened yesterday / Peace and love / Throw your hatred down / Scenery / Fallen angel.

Sep 95. (c-s) **DOWNTOWN / BIG GREEN COUNTRY** [ ] [ ]
(cd-s+=) – ('A'-lp version).

– compilations, others, etc. –

Note; on 'Reprise' until otherwise stated.

1971. (7") **CINNAMON GIRL (alt.mix). / ONLY LOVE CAN BREAK YOUR HEART** [-] [ ]

Nov 72. (d-lp)(d-c) **JOURNEY THROUGH THE PAST (Soundtrack featuring live & rare material with past bands)** [ ] [45]
– For what it's worth – Mr. Soul / Rock & roll woman / Find the cost of freedom / Ohio / Southern man / Are you ready for the country / Let me call you sweetheart / Alabama / Words / Relativity invitation / Handel's Messiah / King of kings / Soldier / Let's go away for a while.

Jan 73. (7") **HEART OF GOLD. / OLD MAN** [-] [ ]

Mar 74. (7") **ONLY LOVE CAN BREAK YOUR HEART. / AFTER THE GOLDRUSH** [ ] [-]

May 74. (7"ep) **SOUTHERN MAN / TILL MORNING COMES. / AFTER THE GOLDRUSH / HEART OF GOLD** [ ] [-]

Nov 77. (t-lp) **DECADE** [46] [43]
– Down to the wire + Burned + Mr.Soul + Broken arrow + Expecting to fly (BUFFALO SPRINGFIELD) / Sugar mountain / I am a child / The loner / The old laughing lady / Cinnamon girl / Down by the river / Cowgirl in the sand / I believe in you / After the goldrush / Southern man / Helpless + Ohio (CROSBY, STILLS, NASH & YOUNG) / A man needs a maid / Harvest / Heart of gold / Star of Bethlehem / The needle and the damage done / Tonight's the night (part 1) / Turnstiles / Winterlong / Deep forbidden lake / Like a hurricane / Love is a rose / Cortez the killer / Campaigner / Long may you run (w / STEPHEN STILLS). *(re-iss.d-cd Jul93)*

Jan 78. (7") **SUGAR MOUNTAIN. / THE NEEDLE AND THE DAMAGE DONE** [-] [ ]

Oct 82. (d-c) **NEIL YOUNG / EVERYBODY KNOWS THIS IS NOWHERE** [ ] [-]

Oct 82. (d-c) **AFTER THE GOLDRUSH / HARVEST** [ ] [-]

Feb 87. (cd) **THE BEST OF NEIL YOUNG** [ ] [-]

Jan 93. Movieplay Gold; (cd) **THE LOST TAPES** [ ] [-]

Jan 93. Geffen; (cd)(c) **LUCKY THIRTEEN** (80's material) [69] [ ]
– Sample and hold / Transformer man / Depression blues / Get gone / Don't take your love away from me / Once an angel / Where is the highway tonight / Hippie dream / Pressure / Around the world / East vacation / Ain't it the truth / This note's for you.

— Note that 1980's 'Where The Buffalo Roam' film contained several YOUNG songs

Paul YOUNG

Born: 17 Jan'56, Luton, Bedfordshire, England. At age 20 formed STREET BAND who had novelty Top 20 hit with 'Toast'. In 1980, he was back with mainly brassy covers band Q-TIPS who signed to 'Chrysalis', but they split after wide reputation of constant gigging. With growing confidence of voice, YOUNG signed solo with 'CBS' in Sep'82. The following year, his third single 'WHEREVER I LAY MY HAT' hit UK No.1. He became established in the pop world from then on. Early 1987, for tax purposes, he moved to Jersey in the Channel Islands. • **Style:** Soulful rock-pop slightly manufactured, but compensated by his large and classy vocal range. • **Songwriters:** Writes own material with band member IAN KEWLEY. Q-TIPS covered I WISH IT WOULD RAIN (Temptations) / THE TRACKS OF MY TEARS (Smokey Robinson) / LOVE HURTS (Everly Brothers) / etc. PAUL's solo covers:- LOVE OF THE COMMON PEOPLE (Nicky Thomas) / WHEREVER I LAY MY HAT (Marvin Gaye) / LOVE WILL TEAR US APART (Joy Division) / I'M GONNA TEAR YOUR PLAYHOUSE DOWN (Ann Peebles) / EVERYTIME YOU GO AWAY (Hall & Oates) / SOFTLY WHISPERING I LOVE YOU (Congregation) / YOU'VE LOST THAT LOVIN' FEELIN' (Righteous Brothers) / DON'T DREAM IT'S OVER (Crowded House) / LITTLE BIT OF LOVE (Free) / WHAT BECOMES OF THE BROKEN HEARTED (Jimmy Ruffin) / WONDERLAND (Betsy Cook) / SOLDIER'S WIVES (Tom Waits) / etc. • **Trivia:** PAUL was another to contribute to BAND / LIVE AID mid 80's.

Recommended: FROM TIME TO TIME – THE SINGLES COLLECTION (*6)

STREET BAND

PAUL YOUNG – vocals, harmonica, (occasional bass + keyboards) / **ROGER KELLY** – guitar, vocals / **JOHN GIFFORD** – guitar, vocals / **MICK PEARL** – bass / **VINCE CHAULK** – drums (ex-MR.BIG)

Logo not issued

Sep 78. (7") **HOLD ON. / TOAST** ('B'side the hit) [18] [-]

Jan 79. (7") **ONE MORE STEP. / THINGS ARE NOT QUITE WHAT THEY SEEM** [ ] [-]

Feb 79. (white-lp)(c) **LONDON** [ ] [-]
– You're all I need / Happy families / Truth without lies / Things are not quite what they seem / It takes a thief / One more step / Any decisions / Mystery / His finest hour / Mystery / Love sign / Loud music.

Mar 79. (7")(12") **LOVE SIGN. / LOUD MUSIC** [ ] [-]

Aug 79. (7") **ONE GOOD REASON. / HAPPY FAMILIES** [ ] [-]

Oct 79. (lp)(c) **DILEMMA** [ ] [-]
– Mirror star / It's no problem / Picture book / Starry eyed / Dilemma / One good reason / Here comes that man / Call me soon / Slaughterhouse 5.

Oct 79. (7") **MIRROR STAR. / IT TAKES A THIEF** [ ] [-]

— Folded late 1979 when **PAUL YOUNG + MICK PEARL** decided to form

Q-TIPS

with **GARTH WATT-ROY** – guitar (ex-FUZZY DUCK, ex-GREATEST SHOW . . .) / **IAN KEWLEY** – keyboards / **BARRY WATTS** – drums / **STEVE FARR** – saxophone / **STEWART BLANDMER** – saxophone / **TONY HUGHES** – trumpet

Shotgun not issued

Mar 80. (7") **S.Y.S.L.J.F.M. (THE LETTER SONG). / THE DANCE** [ ] [-]

Chrysalis not issued

Jun 80. (7") **THE TRACKS OF MY TEARS. / DIFFERENT WORLD** [ ] [ ]

Aug 80. (lp)(c) **Q-TIPS** [50] [-]
– Some kinda wonderful / The tracks of my tears / Please don't stay at home / You are the life inside of me / The in-crowd / (Now I'm left) With a beautiful memory / S.Y.S.L.J.F.M. (the letter song) / A man can't lose (what he don't have) / Uncle Willy / Different world / Keep your shoes on. *(re-iss.Nov83 as 'Q-TIPS FEATURING PAUL YOUNG' on 'Fame')*

Sep 80. (7") **A MAN CAN'T LOSE (WHAT HE DON'T HAVE). / SOME KIND OF WONDERFUL** [ ] [-]

Apr 81. (7"m) **STAY THE WAY YOU ARE. / STREET TALK / LOOKING FOR ACTION** [ ] [-]

Rewind | not issued

Oct 81. (7") **LOVE HURTS. / I WISH IT WOULD RAIN** [ ] [-]

May 82. (7") **YOU ARE THE LIFE INSIDE OF ME. / RAISE YOUR HEAD** [ ] [-]

Jun 82. (lp)(c) **LIVE AT LAST (live)** [ ] [-]
– You are the life inside of me / Sweet talk / Hi-fidelity / Broken man / Empty bed / Get 'em up Joe / racks of my tears / A man can't lose (what he don't have) / You're gonna love me / The link / Broken man / S.Y.S.L.J.F.M. (the letter song) / Raise your hand. *(cd-iss.1986 +=)* – I wish it would rain / Love hurts.

Jul 82. (7") **LOVE HURTS. / YOU'RE GONNA LOVE ME** [ ] [-]

— (last 2 singles were re-iss.Autumn'83 by "Q-TIPS FEATURING PAUL YOUNG")

— Split mid'82.

PAUL YOUNG

went solo retaining **IAN KEWLEY** and initiating The ROYAL FAMILY:- **STEVE BOLTON** – guitar / **PINO PALLADINO** – bass / **MARK PINDER** – drums. Backing vocals by **The FABULOUS WEALTY TARTS** (KIM LESLIE + MAZ ROBERTS)

C.B.S. | Columbia

Oct 82. (7") **IRON OUT THE ROUGH SPOTS. / BEHIND YOUR SMILE** [ ] [ ]

Jan 83. (7") **LOVE OF THE COMMON PEOPLE. / TENDER TRAP** [ ] [ ]

May 83. (7")(7"sha-pic-d) **WHEREVER I LAY MY HAT (THAT'S MY HOME). / BROKEN MAN** [1] [70] Sep 83
(12"+=) – Sex.

Jun 83. (lp)(c)(cd) **NO PARLEZ** [1] [79] Mar 84
– Come back and stay / Love will tear us apart / Wherever I lay my hat (that's my home) / Ku-ku kurama / No parlez / Love of the common people / Oh women / Iron out the rough spots / Broken man / Tender trap / Sex. *(c+cd+=)* – Behind your smile. *(re-iss.May88)*

Aug 83. (7")(12") **COME BACK AND STAY. / YOU CALL ME YOURS** [4] [22] Feb 84

Nov 83. (7")(7"pic-d) **LOVE OF THE COMMON PEOPLE. / TENDER TRAP** [2] [45] May 84
(12"+=) – Wherever I lay my hat / It's better to have.
(d7") – ('A'side) / Behind your smile / Wherever I lay my hat (that's my home) / Oh women.

— **JOHNNY TURNBULL** – guitar repl. BOLTON / added **MATT IRVING** – keyboards (ex-LORDS OF THE NEW CHURCH, etc.) / **+ sessioners** backing vocals now by **GEORGE CHANDLER, JIMMY CHAMBERS + TONY JACKSON**

Oct 84. (7")(7"sha-pic-d) **I'M GONNA TEAR YOUR PLAYHOUSE DOWN. / ONE STEP FORWARD** [9] [ ]
(12"+=) – Broken man (live).

Dec 84. (7")(12") **EVERYTHING MUST CHANGE. / GIVE ME MY FREEDOM** [9] [56] Nov 85
(d12"+=) – ('A'instrumental) / (Paul's Christmas message) / I close my eyes and count to ten (live).

Feb 85. (7")(12") **EVERYTIME YOU GO AWAY. / THIS MEANS ANYTHING** [4] [1]

Mar 85. (lp)(c)(cd) **THE SECRET OF ASSOCIATION** [1] [19]
– Bite the hand that feeds / Everytime you go away / I'm gonna tear your playhouse down / Standing on the edge / Soldier's things / Everything must change / Tomb of memories / One step forward / Hot fun / This means anything / I was in chains. *(c+cd+=)* – The man in the iron mask. *(re-iss.Oct89)*

Jun 85. (7") **TOMB OF MEMORIES. / MAN IN THE IRON MASK** [16] [ ]
(d7"+=)(12"+=) – Bite the hand that feeds / No parlez.

Nov 85. (7")(12") **I'M GONNA TEAR YOUR PLAYHOUSE DOWN (U.S.remix). / HOT FUN** [ ] [13] Sep 85

Sep 86. (7")(12") **WONDERLAND. / BETWEEN TWO FIRES** [24] [ ]

Oct 86. (lp)(c)(cd) **BETWEEN TWO FIRES** [4] [77]
– Some people / Wonderland / War games / In the long run / Wasting my time / Prisoner of conscience / Why does a man have to be strong / A certain position / Between two fires / Wedding day. *(cd+=)* – Steps to go.

Nov 86. (7") **SOME PEOPLE. / A MATTER OF FACT** [56] [65]
(12"+=) – ('A'version).

Jan 87. (7")(12") **WHY DOES A MAN HAVE TO BE STRONG. / TRYING TO GUESS THE REST . . .** [63] [ ]

May 90. (7")(c-s) **SOFTLY WHISPERING I LOVE YOU. / LEAVING HOME** [21] [ ]
(12"+=) – Dolce mente mormoto tu amo.
(pic-cd-s+=) – You've lost that lovin' feeling.

Jun 90. (cd)(c)(lp) **OTHER VOICES** [4] [ ]
– Heaven can wait / Right about now / Oh girl / A little bit of love / Stop on by / Our time has come / Softly whispering I love you / Together / It's what she didn't say / Calling you.

Jul 90. (7")(c-s) **OH GIRL. / YOU'RE THE ONE** [25] [8]
(12"+=)(cd-s+=) – Till I gain control again / Trying to guess the rest.

Sep 90. (7")(c-s) **HEAVEN CAN WAIT. / BACK WHERE I STARTED** [71] [ ]
(12"+=)(cd-s+=) – ('A'remix).

Dec 90. (7") **CALLING YOU. / EVERYTHING MUST CHANGE (live)** [57] [ ]
(12"+=) – That's how it is.
(cd-s+=) – Oh girl / Softly whispering I love you.

— Mar91, had UK No.4 hit with (Italian singer) ZUCCHERO on his SENZA UNA DONNA. Jul91, teamed up with CLANNAD on minor hit BOTH SIDES NOW.

Columbia | Columbia

Sep 91. (cd)(c)(lp) **FROM TIME TO TIME – THE SINGLES COLLECTION** (compilation) [1] [ ]
– Everytime you go away / Come back and stay / I'm only foolin' myself / Senza una donna (without a woman) / I'm gonna tear your playhouse down / Broken man / Everything must change / Wonderland / Don't dream it's over / Love of the common people / Wherever I lay my hat (that's my home) / Both sides now / Some people / Oh girl / Softly whispering I love you.

Oct 91. (7")(c-s) **DON'T DREAM IT'S OVER. / I NEED SOMEBODY** [20] [ ]
(cd-s+=) – Little bit of love (part II) / Love will tear us apart.
(cd-s+=) – Little bit of love (part II) / Sex.

Jan 92. (c-s) **WHAT BECOMES OF THE BROKEN HEARTED. / ?** [-] [22]

— with **ED GREENE** – drums / **JIM COX** – organ / **PAUL JACKSON JR.** – guitar / **FREDDIE WASHINGTON** – bass / **GREG PHILLINGANES** – piano / **ALAN ESTES** – vibes / **GARY HERBIG** – sax solo

Sep 93. (c-s) **(NOW I KNOW WHAT MADE) OTIS BLUE. / BROKEN MAN** [14] [ ]
(cd-s+=) – Oh girl / Softly whispering I love you.

Oct 93. (cd)(c)(lp) **THE CROSSING** [27] [ ]
– Hope in a hopeless world / Now I know what made Otis blue / Won't look back / Only game in town / Bring me home / The heart is a lonely hunter / Love has no pride / Down in Chinatown / Half a step away / Follow on / It will be you.

Nov 93. (7")(c-s) **HOPE IN A HOPELESS WORLD. / HALF A STEP AWAY** [42] [ ]
(cd-s+=) – What becomes of the broken hearted / Right about now.

Apr 94. (7")(c-s) **IT WILL BE YOU. / LONG DISTANCE LOVE (acoustic)** [34] [ ]
(cd-s+=) – I'm your puppet (with ELTON JOHN) / Follow on (acoustic).
(cd-s) – ('A'side) / Don't let me be lonely tonight (acoustic) / Wherever I lay my hat that's my home (acoustic) / Everything must change (acoustic).

Vision | not issued

Nov 94. (cd)(c) **REFLECTIONS** (covers) [64] [-]
– Gazing in the grass / Until you come back to me / That's how heartaches are made / Love won't let me wait / Just a little misunderstanding / Hey girl, don't bother me / Baby don't change your mind / Reflections / Love is like an itching in my heart / Ain't no sunshine / Your precious love / More love / Take me in your arms and love me / Love makes the world go round / Reach out I'll be there.

Nov 94. (c-s) **THAT'S HOW HEARTACHES ARE MADE. / ?** [ ] [-]
(12"+=)(cd-s+=) –

Feb 95. (c-s) **GRAZING IN THE GRASS / THAT'S HOW HEARTACHES ARE MADE (live)** [ ] [ ]
(cd-s+=) – If you don't want my love.
(cd-s) – ('A'side) / Get 'em up Joe (live) / The letter song (live).

– compilations, etc. –

Feb 95. Columbia; (d-cd) **NO PARLEZ / THE SECRET OF ASSOCIATION** [ ] [-]

Jan 94. Logo; (cd-s) **TOAST ("STREET BAND") / TOAST (Mixes) / (other track by Duncan Browne)** [ ] [-]

Jul 94. Success; (cd)(c) **LOVE HURTS (w/Q-TIPS)** [ ] [-]

– other compilations, etc. –

Feb 85. Cambra; (d-lp)(d-c) **STREET BAND ("STREET BAND with PAUL YOUNG")** [ ] [-]

— below as **PAUL YOUNG with The Q-TIPS**

Jan 84. Rewind; (7") **I WISH IT WOULD RAIN (remix). / BROKEN MAN** [ ] [-]

Jul 84. Rewind; (12"ep) **YOU ARE THE LIFE INSIDE OF ME / LOVE HURTS. / I WISH IT WOULD RAIN / HI-FIDELITY** [ ] [-]

Sep 85. Hallmark; (lp)(c) **Q-TIPS LIVE (live) Q-TIPS** [ ] [-]

Feb 92. Windsong; (cd) **BBC RADIO 1 LIVE IN CONCERT (Q-TIPS live)** [ ] [-]

Sep 86. CBS; (c-ep) **THE 12" TAPE (12" hit versions)** [ ] [-]

Apr 91. Connoisseur; (cd)(c) **THE EARLY YEARS** [ ] [-]

YOUNG RASCALS (see under ⇒ RASCALS)

Frank ZAPPA

Born: 21 Dec'40, Baltimore, Maryland, USA. From Sicilian and Greek parents, who moved to California in 1950. In 1956, he formed The BLACKOUTS with school chum DON VAN VLIET (aka CAPTAIN BEEFHEART). After marrying in the late 50's, he wrote a soundtrack for B-movie 'The World's Greatest Sinner'. In 1963, after writing another B-movie soundtrack 'Run Home Slow', he set up own Studio Z. He also initiated local groups The MASTERS and The SOUL GIANTS, who recorded some extremely rare 45's. In 1964, he was arrested and sentenced to 10 days in prison and put on probation for 3 years, having made a pornographic tape. He moved to Los Angeles and formed again The SOUL GIANTS who soon became The MOTHERS OF INVENTION. Early in 1966, after a residency at The Whiskey A-Go-Go, they were signed to 'MGM' by producer Tom Wilson. Their debut album (a double!) 'FREAK OUT!' peaked at No.130 in the States. Later in 1967 their follow-up 'ABSOLUTELY FREE', nearly scratched the Top 40, and on 23 Sep'67, they played London's Albert Hall with a 15-piece orchestra. ZAPPA and the MOTHERS continued as a unit throughout the late 60's and early 70's, with ZAPPA also maintaining a solo career. After many more albums, in the 80's he tragically died of prostate cancer on 4th Dec '93. • **Style:** Avant-garde satirical rocker, who mixed together psychedelia, doo-wop and sexually explicit lyrics. ZAPPA was never typecast into any one style, and sometimes his brilliant guitar picking was overlooked on his more eccentric jazz and modern classical albums. • **Songwriters:** ZAPPA compositions, augmented by MOTHERS. Covered WHIPPING BOY (Allman Brothers Band) / STAIRWAY TO HEAVEN (Led Zeppelin) / etc. • **Trivia:** In 1969, he married for a second time and soon was the father of sons Dweezil (who became a singer in the 80's), AHMET RODAN, and daughters MOON UNIT and DIVA. In 1976, ZAPPA produced GRAND FUNK on their lp 'Good Singin', Good Playin''.

Recommended: FREAK OUT (*9) / ABSOLUTELY FREE (*8) / WE'RE ONLY IN IT FOR THE MONEY (*8) / HOT RATS (*9) / ZOOT ALLURES (*8) / TINSEL TOWN REBELLION (*8) / THEM OR US (*9) / THING FISH (*6) / STRICTLY COMMERCIAL – THE BEST OF FRANK ZAPPA (*9)

The MOTHERS OF INVENTION

FRANK ZAPPA – guitar, vocals / with **RAY COLLINS** – vocals (had been temp.repl. by JIM GUERCIO; later a producer) / **ELLIOTT INGBER** – guitar repl. STEVE MANN who had repl. HENRY VESTINE. Before he moved onto CANNED HEAT he had repl. MOTHERS original ALICE STUART. / **ROY ESTRADA** – bass / **JIM BLACK** – drums

Verve / Verve-MGM

1966. (7") **HELP, I'M A ROCK. / HOW COULD I BE SUCH A FOOL?** [-] [ ]

Nov 66. (7") **IT CAN'T HAPPEN HERE. / HOW COULD I BE SUCH A FOOL?** [ ] [-]

1966. (7") **TROUBLE EVERY DAY. / WHO ARE THE BRAIN POLICE?** [-] [ ]

Mar 67. (lp) **FREAK OUT!** [ ] [ ] Aug 66
– Hungry freaks, daddy / I ain't got no heart / Who are the brain police? / Go cry on somebody else's shoulder * / Motherly love / How could I be such a fool * / Wowie Zowie / You didn't try to call me / Any way the wind blows * / I'm not satisfied / You're probably wondering why I'm here / Trouble every day / Help, I'm a rock / The return of the son of monster magnet. *(US d-lp+= *)* (UK re-iss.Dec71 as d-lp) (cd-iss.Oct87 on 'Zappa'UK /'Rykodisc'US) (re-iss.cd/c May95 on Rykodisc')

— **JIM FIELDER** – guitar repl. INGBER who joined FRATERNITY OF MAN. He later changed his name and joined CAPTAIN BEEFHEART / added **BILLY MUNDI** – drums / **DON PRESTON** – keyboards / **BUNK GARDNER** – horns

Apr 67. (7") **BIG LEG EMMA. / WHY DON'T YOU DO ME RIGHT?** [ ] [ ]

Oct 67. (lp) **ABSOLUTELY FREE** [ ] [41] May 67
– Plastic people / The Dukes of Prunes / Amnesia vivace / The Duke regains his chops / Call any vegetable / Invocation and ritual dance of the young pumpkin / Soft-cell conclusion and ending of side 1 / America drinks / Status back baby / Uncle Bernie's farm / Son of Suzy Creamcheese / Brown shoes don't make it / America drinks and goes home. *(re-iss.Jun72) (cd-iss.Jan89 on 'Zappa' UK / 'Rykodisc' US version +=) (re-iss.cd/c May95 on 'Rykodisc' +=)* – Big leg Emma / Why don'tcha do me right?.

— **ZAPPA, ESTRADA, MUNDI, PRESTON, GARDNER & JIMMY CARL BLACK** recruited **JIM 'Motorhead' SHERWOOD** – sax (ex-roadie) repl. FIELDER to BUFFALO SPRINGFIELD / **IAN UNDERWOOD** – piano, wind repl. COLLINS

Dec 67. (7") **MOTHER PEOPLE. / LONELY LITTLE GIRL (version)** [-] [ ]

Jun 68. (lp) **WE'RE ONLY IN IT FOR THE MONEY** [32] [30] Jan 68
– Are you hung up? / Who needs the peace corps? / Concentration Moon / Mom and dad / Telephone conversation / Bow tie daddy / Harry, you're a beast / What's the ugliest part of your body? / Absolutely free / Flower punk / Hot poop / Nasal retentive calliope music / Let's make the water turn black / The idiot bastard son / Lonely little girl / Take your clothes off when you dance / What's the ugliest part of your body (reprise) / Mother people / The chrome plated megaphone of destiny. *(re-iss.Jun72) (cd-iss.Dec88 on 'Zappa' UK / Oct87 on 'Rykodisc') (re-iss.cd/c/lp Apr95 on 'Rykodisc')*

— (now with The ABNUCEALS EMUUKHA ELECTRIC SYMPHONY ORCHESTRA & CHORUS; a 50+ piece orchestra incl. some MOTHERS)

Oct 68. (lp) **LUMPY GRAVY ("FRANK ZAPPA" solo)** [ ] [ ] May 68
– Lumpy gravy (part one): The way I see it, Barry – Duodenum – Oh no – Bit of nostalgia – It's from Kansas – Bored out 90 over – Almost Chinese – Switching girls – Oh no again – At the gas station – Another pickup – I don't know if I can go through this again / Lumpy gravy (part two): Very distrautening – White ugliness – Amen – Just one more time – A vicious circle – Kink Kong – Drums are too noisy – Kangaroos – Envelopes the bath tub – Take your clothes off. *(re-iss.Jun72) (cd-iss.Apr95 on 'Rykodisc')*

Dec 68. (7") **DESERI. / JELLY ROLL GUM DROP** [-] [ ]

— (above single and below album credited to **"RUBEN AND THE JETS"**)

— **ARTHUR TRIPP III** – drums repl. MUNDI who formed RHINOCEROS / added again **RAY COLLINS** – vocals

Feb 69. (lp) **CRUISING WITH RUBEN & THE JETS** [ ] [ ] Nov 68
– Cheap thrills / Love of my life / How could I be such a fool / Deseri / I'm not satisfied / Jelly roll gum drop / Anything / Later that night / You didn't try to call me / Fountain of love / No no no / Anyway the wind blows * / Stuff up the cracks. *(re-iss.Jun73) (cd-iss.Oct87 on 'Zappa' UK/'Rykodisc' US) (re-iss.cd May95 on 'Rykodisc')*

— added **BILLY MUNDI** – drums / **RUTH KOMANOFF** (UNDERWOOD) – marimba, vibes / **NELCY WALKER** – soprano vocals

Transatla. / Bizarre

Sep 69. (d-lp) **UNCLE MEAT** [ ] [43] Apr 69
– Uncle Meat (main title theme) / The voice of cheese / Nine types of industrial pollution / Zolar Czakl / Dog breath in the year of the plague / The legend of the golden arches / Louie Louie (at the Royal Albert Hall in London) / The dog breath variations / Sleeping in a jar / Our bizarre relationship / The Uncle Meat variations / Electric Aunt Jemima // Prelude to King Kong / God bless America (live at the Whisky A Go Go) / A pound for a brown on the bus / Ian Underwood whips it out (live on stage in Copenhagen) / Mr.Green genes / We can shoot you / If we'd all been living in California / The air / Project X / Cruising for burgers / Uncle Meat film excerpt part 1 * / Tengo na minchia tanta * / Uncle Meat film excerpt part II * / King Kong itself (as played by The Mothers in a studio) / King Kong II (it's magnificence as interpreted by Dom Dewild) / King Kong III (as Motorhead explains it) / King Kong IV (the Gardner varieties) / King Kong V (as played by 3 deranged good humor trucks) / King Kong VI (live on a flat bed diesel in the middle of a race track at a Miami pop festival . . . the Underwood ramifications). *(d-cd iss.Oct87 on 'Zappa'+= *) (re-iss.d-cd/c May 95 on 'Rykodisc')*

Sep 69. (7") **MY GUITAR. / DOG BREATH** [-] [ ]

FRANK ZAPPA

solo w/**IAN UNDERWOOD / LOWELL GEORGE** – guitar / **JEAN-LUC PONTY** – violin (solo artist) / **SUGAR-CANE HARRIS** – vocals / **MAX BENNETT + SHUGGY OTIS** – bass / **PAUL HUMPHREY + RON SELICO** – drums

Reprise / Bizarre

Jan 70. (7") **PEACHES EN REGALIA. / LITTLE UMBRELLAS** [-] [ ]

Feb 70. (lp)(c) **HOT RATS** [9] [ ] Oct 69
– Peaches en regalia / Willie the wimp / Son of Mr.Green genes / Little umbrellas / The Gumbo variations / It must be a camel. *(re-iss.Sep70 + Jul71) (remixed cd-iss.Oct87 on 'Zappa') (re-iss.cd/c May95 on 'Rykodisc')*

The MOTHERS OF INVENTION

(see last line-up) added **BUZZ GARDNER** – horns / **SUGAR-CANE HARRIS** – vocals

Mar 70. (lp)(c) **BURNT WEENIE SANDWICH** [17] [94] Feb 70
– WPLJ / Ivor's boogie – phase 1 / Overture to a holiday in Berlin / Theme from Burnt Weenie Sandwich / Igor's boogie – phase 2 / Holiday in Berlin, full blown / Aybe sea / The little house I used to live in / Valarie. *(re-iss.Sep70 & Jul71) (cd-iss.Nov91 on 'Zappa') (re-iss.cd May95 on 'Rykodisc')*

Mar 70. (7") **WPLJ. / MY GUITAR** [-] [ ]

Sep 70. (lp)(c) **WEASELS RIPPED MY FLESH** [28] [ ]
– Didja get any onya? / Directly from my heart to you / Prelude to the afternoon of a sexually aroused gas mask / Toads of the short forest / Get a little / Eric Dolphy memorial barbecue / Dwarf Nebula processional march and dwarf Nebula / My guitar wants to kill your mama / oh no / The Orange County lumber truck / Weasels ripped my flesh. *(re-iss.Jul71) (cd-iss.May95 on 'Rykodisc')*

— (above album used rare material from 1967-69, as The MOTHERS OF INVENTION officially disbanded Oct69).

— LOWELL and ROY formed LITTLE FEAT. ART TRIPP became ED MARIMBA and joined CAPTAIN BEEFHEART & HIS MAGIC BAND. BUNK GARDNER and JIMMY CARL BLACK formed GERONIMO BLACK.

FRANK ZAPPA

formed solo band with **IAN UNDERWOOD, SUGAR-CANE HARRIS & MAX BENNETT**. He introduced **JEFF SIMMONS** – guitar, bass / **JOHN GUERIN** – drums / **AYNSLEY DUNBAR** – drums / **GEORGE DUKE** – keyboards, trombone / **MARK VOLMAN + HOWARD KAYLAN** (aka The PHLORESCENT LEECH AND EDDIE) – vocals (ex-TURTLES)

Nov 70. (lp)(c) **CHUNGA'S REVENGE** [43] [ ]
– Transylvania boogie / Road ladies / Twenty small cigars / The Nancy and Mary music (part 1, 2 & 3) / Tell me you love me / Would you go all the way? / Chunga's revenge / Rudy wants to buy yez a drink / The clap / Sharleena. *(re-iss.Jul71) (cd-iss.May95 on 'Rykodisc')*

Nov 70. (7") **TELL ME YOU LOVE ME. / WOULD YOU GO ALL THE WAY?** [-] [ ]

The MOTHERS

re-formed early 1971. Re-instated **DON PRESTON** – keys. Recruited **JIM PONS** – bass (ex-TURTLES) / **BOB HARRIS** – keyboards

Aug 71. (lp)(c) **FILLMORE EAST – JUNE 1971 (live)** [ ] [38]
– Little house I used to live in / The mud shark / What kind of girl do you think we are? / Bwana Dik / Latex solar beef / Willie the wimp (part 1) / Do you like my new car? / Happy together / Lonesome electric turkey / Peaches en regalia / Tears began to fall. *(re-iss.cd/c May 95 on 'Rykodisc')*

FRANK ZAPPA & THE MOTHERS OF INVENTION

Aug 71. (7") **TEARS BEGAN TO FALL. / JUNIER MINTZ BOOGIE** [ ] [ ]

FRANK ZAPPA

solo, with MOTHERS:- **IAN + RUTH UNDERWOOD / GEORGE DUKE / AYNSLEY DUNBAR / VOLMAN + KAYLAN / MARTIN LICKERT** – bass / guests were **JIM PONS + JIMMY CARL BLACK / THEODORE BIKEL** – narrator + ROYAL PHILHARONIC

United Art United Art

Oct 71. (d-lp) **200 MOTELS (live studio soundtrack)** [ ] [59]
– Semi-fraudulent – Direct-from-Hollywood overture / Mystery roach / Dance of the rock & roll interviewers / This town is a sealed tuna sandwich (prologue) / Tuna fish promenade / Dance of the just plain folks / This town is a sealed tuna fish sandwich (reprise) / The sealed tuna bolero / Lonesome cowboy Burt / Tiuring can make you crazy / Would you like a snack? / Redneck eats / Centerville / She painted up her face / Janet's big dance number / Half a dozen provocative squats / Mysterioso / Shove it right in / Lucy's seduction of a bored violinist & postlude / I'm stealing the towels / Dental hygeine dilemma / Does this kind of life look interesting to you? / Daddy, daddy, daddy / Penis dimension / What will this evening bring me this morning / A nun suit painted on some old boxes / Magic fingers / Motorhead's midnight ranch / Dew on the newts we got / The lad searches the night for his newts / The girl wants to fix him some broth / The girl's dream / Little green scratchy sweaters & corduroy ponce / Strictly genteel (the finale). *(re-iss.+d-c.Jan89 on 'MCA')*

Oct 71. (7") **MAGIC FINGERS. / DADDY, DADDY, DADDY** [-] [ ]

Nov 71. (7") **WHAT WILL THIS EVENING BRING ME THIS MORNING?. / DADDY, DADDY, DADDY** [ ] [-]

Aug 72. (lp)(c) **WAKA / JAWAKA** [ ] [ ]
– Big Swifty / Your mouth / It just might be a one-shot deal / Waka-Jawaka. *(cd-iss Jan89 on 'Zappa') (re-iss.cd May95 on 'Rykodisc')*

— (above featured **PRESTON, DUNBAR, DUKE, SIMMONS** & others also on next).

The MOTHERS

recorded live 7th August'71. (see last ZAPPA line-up) Re-formed earlier that year.

Reprise Bizarre

Jun 72. (lp)(c) **JUST ANOTHER BAND FROM L.A.** [ ] [85]
– Billy the mountain / Call any vegetable / Eddie, are you kidding? / Magdalena / Dog breath. *(cd-iss.May95 on 'Rykodisc')*

— The MOTHERS added **TONY DURAN** – slide guitar / **ERRONEOUS** – bass repl. SIMMONS / **KEN SHROYER** – trombone / **JOEL PESKIN** – tenor saxophone / **SAL MARQUEZ** – timpani / **BILL BYERS** – trombone / **MIKE ALTSCHUL** – wind / **JANET NEVILLE-FERGUSON** – vocals / **CHUNKY** – vocals / **EARL DUMLER, FRED JACKSON + TONY ORTEGA** – wind / **ERNIE WATTS** – sax / **ERNIE TACK + MALCOLM McNABB** – horns / **JOHNNY ROTELLA, BOB ZIMMITTI + LEE CLEMENT** – percussion / **JOANNE CALDWELL McNABB** – violin

Dec 72. (lp)(c) **THE GRAND WAZOO** [ ] [ ]
– The grand Wazoo / For Calvin (and his next two hitch-hikers) / Cletus-awreetus-awrightus / Eat that question / Blessed relief. *(cd-iss.Sep86 & May95 on 'Rykodisc')*

Dec 72. (7") **CLETUS-AWREETUS-AWRIGHTUS. / EAT THAT QUESTION** [-] [ ]

— **ZAPPA** brought back **IAN + RUTH UNDERWOOD** (They were on '72 tour) / **GEORGE DUKE / JEAN-LUC PONTY / SAL MARQUEZ.** He introduced **TOM FOWLER** – bass / **BRUCE FOWLER** – trombone / **RALPH HUMPHREY** – drums

Discreet Discreet

Jan 73. (lp) **OVERNITE SENSATION** [ ] [32]
– Camarillo brillo / I'm the slime / Dirty love / Fifty-fifty / Zomby woof / Dinah-Moe humm / Montana. *(cd-iss.Oct87 w / 'APOSTROPHE' tracks on 'Rykodisc') (re-iss.cd/c Apr95 on 'Rykodisc')*

Feb 73. (7") **I'M THE SLIME. / MONTANA** [-] [ ]

FRANK ZAPPA

solo retaining current MOTHERS except RUTH. He also brought back past MOTHERS: **AYNSLEY DUNBAR / RAY COLLINS / ERRONEOUS / JOHN GUERIN / SUGAR CANE HARRIS / RUBEN GUEVARA + ROBERT CAMARENA** – b.vocals (of RUBEN &..JETS) **NAPOLEON BROCK** – saxophone / guest **JACK BRUCE** – bass (ex-CREAM)

May 74. (lp)(c) **' (APOSTROPHE)** [ ] [10] Apr 74
– Don't eat the yellow snow / Nanook rubs it / St.Alphonso's pancake breakfast / Father O'Blivion / Cosmik debris / Excentrifugal forz / Apostrophe / Uncle Remus / Stink-foot. *(cd-iss.see last lp) (re-iss.cd/c Apr95 on 'Rykodisc')*

Aug 74. (7") **DON'T EAT THE YELLOW SNOW. / COSMIK DEBRIS** [-] [86]

Aug 74. (7") **COSMIK DEBRIS. / UNCLE REMUS** [ ] [-]

Sep 74. (7") **DON'T EAT THE YELLOW SNOW. / CAMARILLO BRILLO** [ ] [-]

ZAPPA / MOTHERS

were now basically **GEORGE DUKE / TOM FOWLER / NAPOLEON / RUTH UNDERWOOD** and new drummer **CHESTER THOMPSON**. Temp. old members were also used **DON PRESTON / BRUCE FOWLER / JEFF SIMMONS + RALPH HUMPHREY**

Oct 74. (d-lp) **ROXY & ELSEWHERE (live + unreleased)** [ ] [27] Sep 74
– Preamble / Penguin in bondage / Pygmy twylyte / Dummy up / Preamble / Village of the sun / Echidna's arf (of you) / Don't you ever wash that thing? / Preamble / Cheepnis / Son of Orange County / More trouble every day / Be-bop tango (of old Jazzmen's church). *(re-iss.1977) (cd-iss.Feb92 on 'Zappa') (re-iss.cd/c May95 on 'Rykodisc')*

FRANK ZAPPA AND THE MOTHERS OF INVENTION

— temp.members above repl. by **JOHNNY GUITAR WATSON** – guitar / **JAMES YOUMAN** – bass / **BLOODSHOT ROLLIN RED** (DON WATSON) – harmonica

Aug 75. (lp)(c) **ONE SIZE FITS ALL (live)** [ ] [26]
– Inca roads / Can't afford no shoes / Sofa No.1 / Po-jama people / Florentine pogen / Evelyn, a modified dog / San Ber'dino / Andy / Sofa No.2. *(cd-iss.Jan89 on 'Zappa') (re-iss.cd May95 on 'Rykodisc')*

Sep 75. (7") **STINK-FOOT. / DU BIST MEIN SOFA** [ ] [-]

FRANK ZAPPA and CAPTAIN BEEFHEART / MOTHERS

collaborated with also **G.DUKE / B.+ T.FOWLER / N.BROCK / C.THOMPSON** plus **TERRY BOZZIO** – drums / **DENNY WHALLEY**

Nov 75. (lp) **BONGO FURY (live + 2 studio)** [-] [66]
– Debra Kadabra / Caroline hard-core ecstasy / Sam with the showing scalp flat top / Poofter's froth Wyoming plans ahead / 200 years old / Cucamonga / Advance romance / Man with the woman head / Muffin man. *(cd-iss.Jan89 on 'Zappa') (re-iss.cd May95 on 'Rykodisc')*

FRANK ZAPPA

finally disbanded The MOTHERS and went solo. Augmented by **TERRY BOZZIO** – drums / **ROY ESTRADA, DAVE PARLATO + RUTH UNDERWOOD** – bass / **DAVEY MOIRE** – b.vocals / **LU ANN NEIL** – harp

Warners Warners

Oct 76. (7") **FIND HER FINER. / ZOOT ALLURES** [-] [ ]

Nov 76. (lp)(c) **ZOOT ALLURES** [ ] [61]
– Wind up workin' in a gas station / Black napkins / The torture never stops / Ms. Pinky / Find her finer / Friendly little finger / Wonderful wino / Zoot allures / Disco boy. *(cd-iss.Jun90 on 'Zappa') (re-iss.cd May95 on 'Rykodisc')*

Dec 76. (7") **DISCO BOY. / MS. PINKY** [-] [ ]

— His basic band were **EDDIE JOBSON** – keyboards, violin (ex-ROXY MUSIC) / **RAY WHITE** – guitar, vocals / **PAT O'HEARN** – bass / **RUTH UNDERWOOD** – / **TERRY BOZZIO** – drums. Plus brass section – **RANDY + MICHAEL BRECKER / LOU MARINI / RONNIE CUBER / TOM MALONE / DAVID SAMUELS** – percussion

Discreet Discreet

Jun 78. (d-lp) **ZAPPA IN NEW YORK (live 1976)** [55] [57]
– Titties & beer / Cruisin' for burgers * / I promise not to come in your mouth / Punky's whips / Honey, don't you want a man like me? / The Illinois enema bandit // I'm the slime * / Pound for a brown * / Manx needs women / The black page drum solo – Black page #1 / Big leg Emma / Sofa / Black page #2 / The torture never stops * / The purple lagoon – approximate. *(d-cd-iss.1990 May95 on 'Rykodisc' += *)*

— He retained only **BOZZIO + O'HEARN,** bringing back **NAPOLEON, ANDRE LEWIS + MOIRE.** New musicians:- **ADRIAN BELEW** – rhythm guitar, some lead vox / **TOMMY MARS** – keyboards, vocals / **PETER WOLF** – keyboards / **ED MANN** – percussion, vocals / **RANDY THORNTON** – b.vocals / **DAVID OCKER** – clarinet (1)

C.B.S. Zappa

Mar 79. (d-lp)(d-c) **SHIEK YERBOUTI** [32] [21]
– I have been in you / Flakes / Broken heart are for assholes / I'm so cute / Jones crusher / What ever happened to all the fun in the world / Rat tomago / We've gotta get into something real / Bobby Brown / Rubber shirt / The Sheik Yerbouti tango / Baby snakes / Tryin' to grow a chin / City of tiny lites / Dancin' fool / Jewish princess / Yo' mama. *(re-iss.Feb86 on 'EMI') (cd-iss.Apr88) (re-iss.cd/c May95 on 'Rykodisc')*

Apr 79. (7") **DANCIN' FOOL. / BABY SNAKES** [ ] [45]

— **WARREN CUCURILLO** – rhythm guitar repl. BELEW (later to BOWIE + TALKING HEADS) /**IKE WILLIS** – lead vocals repl. MARS / **ARTHUR BARROW** – bass repl. O'HEARN / **VINNIE COLAIUTA** – drums repl. TERRY BOZZIO. Others in line-up **DALE BOZZIO** – vocals / **DENNIS WHALLEY** – slide guitar / **MARGINAL CHAGRIN** – sax / **WOLF + MANN.**

Sep 79. (lp)(c) **JOE'S GARAGE ACT I** [62] [27]
– Central scrutinizer / Joe's garage / Catholic girls / Crew slut / Wet T-shirt nite / Toad-o-line / Why does it hurt when I pee? / Lucille has messed my mind up. *(US cd-iss.Oct87 on 'Rykodisc'; UK May95)*

Jan 80. (7") **JOE'S GARAGE. / CENTRAL SCRUTINIZER** [-] [ ]

Jan 80. (7") **JOE'S GARAGE. / CATHOLIC GIRLS** [ ] [-]

Jan 80. (d-lp)(d-c) **JOE'S GARAGE ACT II & III** [75] [53]
– ACT II:- A token of my extreme / Stick it out / Sy Borg / Dong work for Yuda / Keep it greasey / Outside now / ACT III:- He used to cut the grass / Packard goose / Watermelon in Easter hay / A little green Rosetta. *(US d-cd-iss.Oct87 on 'Rykodisc'; UK May95 w/ ACT I)*

Jun 80. (7") **I DON'T WANT TO GET DRAFTED. / ANCIENT ARMAMENTS** [ ] [ ]

— added **STEVE VAI + RAY WHITE** – rhythm guitar, vocals / **TOMMY MARS** – keyboards

C.B.S. B..Pumpkin

May 81. (d-lp)(d-c) **TINSELTOWN REBELLION (live)** [55] [66]
– Fine girl / Easy meat / For the young sophisticate / Love of my life / I ain't got no heart / Panty rap / Tell me you love me / Now you see it – now you don't / Dance contest / The blue light / Tinseltown rebellion / Pick me, I'm clean / Bamboozled by love / Brown shoes don't make it / Peaches III. *(re-iss.Feb86 on 'EMI') (d-cd-iss.Apr88) (cd-iss.Jun90 on 'Zappa') (re-iss.cd May95 on 'Rykodisc')*

— **JIMMY CARL BLACK** – drums returned to repl. RAY WHITE

Oct 81. (d-lp)(d-c) **YOU ARE WHAT YOU IS** 51 93
– Teenage wind / Harder than your husband / Doreen / Goblin girl / Theme from the 3rd movement of sinister footwear / Society pages / I'm a beautiful guy / Beauty knows no pain / Charlie's enormous mouth / Any downers? / Conehead / You are what you is / Mudd club / The meek shall inherit nothing / Dumb all over / Heavenly bank account / Suicide chump / Jumbo go away / If only she woulda / Drafted again. *(re-iss.Feb86 on 'EMI') (d-cd-iss.Apr88) (cd-iss.Jun90 on 'Zappa') (re-iss.cd May95 on 'Rykodisc')*

Nov 81. (12"pic-d) **GOBLIN GIRL. / PINK NAPKINS** -

Feb 82. (7") **YOU ARE WHAT YOU IS. / HARDER THAN YOUR HUSBAND**
(12"pic-d+=) – Pink napkins / Soup'n'old clothes.

— added **SCOTT THUNES** – bass / **CHAD WACKERMAN** – drums / **BOBBY MARTIN** – keys, sax

Jun 82. (lp)(c) **SHIP ARRIVING TO LATE TO SAVE A DROWNING WITCH** 61 23
– No not now / Valley girl / I come from nowhere / Drowning witch / Envelopes / Teen-age prostitute. *(free 7"w.a.)* – SHUT UP 'N' PLAY YER GUITAR (excerpts) *(lp re-iss.Feb86 on 'EMI') (re-iss.Jun87 on 'Fame') (cd-iss.Aug91 on 'Zappa') (re-iss.cd May95 on 'Rykodisc')*

Aug 82. (7") **VALLEY GIRL. ("FRANK & MOON ZAPPA" his daughter) / TEENAGE PROSTITUTE** 32 Jul 82
(re-iss.12"/cd-s Jul93 on 'Zappa')

— **ROY ESTRADA** – falsetto + **BOB HARRIS** – soprano returned to repl. WOLF / **MARTY KRYSTAL** – sax / **DICK PEGY** – mandolin / **CRAIG STEWARD** – harmonica repl. WHALLEY

Jun 83. (lp)(c) **THE MAN FROM UTOPIA** 87
– Cocaine decisions / Sex / Tink walks amok / The radio is broken / We are not alone / The dangerous kitchen / The man from Utopia meets Mary Lou / Stick together / The jazz discharge party hats / Luigi & the wise guys * / Moggio. *(re-iss.Feb86 on 'EMI') (re-iss.Apr88 on 'Fame') (cd-iss.Feb93 on 'Zappa' += *) (re-iss.cd May95 on 'Rykodisc')*

— **JOHNNY GUITAR WATSON + NAPOLEON MURPHY BROCK** – vocals repl. BOB + VINNIE

E.M.I. E.M.I.

Sep 84. (7") **BABY TAKE YOUR TEETH OUT. / STEVIE'S SPANKING**

Oct 84. (d-lp)(d-c) **THEM OR US** 53
– The closer you are / In France / Ya hozna / Sharleena / Sinister footwear II / Truck driver divorce / Stevie's spanking / Baby take your teeth out / Marqueson's chicken / Planet of my dreams / Be in my video / Them or us / Frogs with dirty, little lips / Whippin' post. *(cd-iss.Apr88) (re-iss.cd May95 on 'Rykodisc')*

— **ZAPPA** with band: **VAI, MARS, WHITE, MANN, WACKERMAN, BARROW, THUNES** plus **STEVE DE FURIA** – programming. Characters: **IKE WILLIS** (Thing Fish) / **TERRY BOZZIO** (Harry) / His wife **DALE BOZZIO** (Rhonda) / **NAPOLEON MURPHY BROCK** (The Prince) / **BOB HARRIS** (Harry as a boy) / **JOHNNY GUITAR WATSON** (Brown Moses) / **RAY WHITE** (Owl Gonkwin Jane Cowhoon)

E.M.I. Capitol

Mar 85. (t-lp)(d-c) **THING FISH**
– Prologue / The mammy nuns / Harry & Rhonda / Galoot up-date / The 'torchum never stops / That evil prince / You are what you is / Mudd club / The meek shall inherit nothing / Clowns on velvet / Harry-as-a-boy / He's so gay / The massive improve'lence / Artificial Rhonda / The crab-grass baby / The white boy troubles / No not now / Briefcase boogie / Wistful with a fist-full / Drop dead / Won ton on. *(d-cd-iss.Apr88) (d-cd-iss.Feb90 on 'Zappa') (re-iss.d-cd May95 on 'Rykodisc')*

— Musicians; as last but without BOZZIO's, ESTRADA, BARROW, BROCK, HARRIS **BOBBY MARS** – vocals, keyboards repl. DE FURIA

Mar 86. (lp)(c)(cd) **FRANK ZAPPA MEETS THE MOTHERS OF PREVENTION**
– I didn't even care * / One man one vote * / Little biege Sambo / Aerobics in bondage / We're turning again / Alien orifice / Aerobics in bondage / Yo' cats / What's new in Baltimore? / Porn wars / H.R. 2911 *. *(cd repl. Porn wars; w/ *) (cd-iss.May95 on 'Rykodisc')*

— **FRANK** still with **WILLIS, WACKERMAN, THUNES, MANN, MARTIN,** plus new **MIKE KENEALLY** – guitar, synth., vocals repl. VAI who went solo, etc. / **WALT FOWLER** – trumpet / **BRUCE FOWLER** – trombone / **PAUL CARMAN** – alto sax / **ALBERT WINO** – tenor sax / **KURT McGETTRICK** – baritone sax / guest vox – **ERIC BUXTON**

Zappa Zappa

Dec 88. (lp)(c)(cd) **BROADWAY THE HARD WAY (live)**
– Elvis has just left the building / Planet of the baritone women / Any kind of pain / Dickie's such an asshole / When the lie's so big / Rhymin' man / Promiscuous / The untouchables / Why don't you like me? * / Bacon fat * / Stolen moments * / Murder by numbers * / Jezebel boy * / Outside now * / Hot plate heaven at the green hotel * / What kind of a girl? * / Jesus thinks you're a jerk. *(cd+= *) (re-iss.cd May95 on 'Rykodisc')*

— Late '91, it was announced FRANK had been diagnosed with prostrate cancer. He was to die of this on 4 Dec '93.

Feb 93. (12")(cd-s) **STAIRWAY TO HEAVEN. / BOLERO**

Oct 93. (cd)(c) **YELLOW SHARK**
– Intro / Dog breath variations / Uncle Meat / Outrage at Valdez / Times beach II / III revised / The girl in the magnesium dress / Be bop tango / Ruth is sleeping / None of the above / Pentagon afternoon / Questi cazzi di piccione / Times beach III / Food gathering in post industrial America 1992 / Welcome to the united States / Pound for a brown / Exercise 4 / Get Whitey / G-spot tornado. *(re-iss.cd/c May95 on 'Rykodisc')*

— an opera-pantomime with pre-recorded voices and music supplied by THE PIANO PEOPLE: **F.Z. / SPIDER / JOHN / MOTORHEAD / LARRY / ROY / LOUIS / MONICA / GILLY / GIRL 1 / GIRL 2 / MOON / MIKE / ALI / TODD / DARYL / JESUS**

Feb 95. (d-cd)(d-c) **CIVILIZATION PHAZE III**
– ACT ONE; This is phaze III / Put a motor in yourself / Oh-umm / They made me eat it / Reagan at Bitburg / A very nice body / Navanax / How the pigs' music works / Xmas values / Dark water / Amnerika / Have you ever heard their band / Religious superstition / Saliva can only take so much / Buffalo voice / Someplace else ight now / Get a life / A kayak (on snow) / N-lite (I) Negative light (II) Venice submerged (III) The new world order (IV) The lifestyle you deserve (V) Creationism (VI) He is risen / / ACT TWO; I wish Motorhead would come back / Secular humanism / Attack! attack! attack! / I was in a drum / A different octave / This ain't CNN / The pigs' music / A pig with wings / This is all wrong / Hot & putrid / Flowing inside-out / I had a dream about that / Gross man / A tunnel into muck / Why not? / Put a little motor in 'em / You're just insultin' me, aren't you! / Cold light generation / Dio fa / That would be the end of that / Beat the reaper / Waffenspiel.

– compilations, others, etc. –

Apr 69. Verve; (lp)(c) **MOTHERMANIA: THE BEST OF THE MOTHERS**
(re-iss.Feb72 & Mar73)

1975. Verve; (lp) **ZAPPA & THE MOTHERS: ROCK FLASHBACKS**

Nov 78. Discreet; (lp) **STUDIO TAN (instrumental 74-76)**
– The adventures of Greggery Peccary / Revised music for guitar and low budget orchestra / Let me take you to the beach / RDNZL. *(cd-iss.May95 on 'Rykodisc')*

Feb 79. Discreet; (lp)(c) **SLEEP DIRT (instrumental 74-76)**
– Filthy habits / Flambay / Spider of destiny / Regymptian strut / Time is money / Sleep dirt / The ocean is the ultimate solution. *(cd-iss.May95 on 'Rykodisc')*

Jun 79. Discreet; (lp) **ORCHESTRAL FAVORITES (live 1975)**
– Strictly genteel / Pedro's dowry / Naval aviation in art? / Duke of prunes / Bogus pomp. *(cd-iss.May95 on 'Rykodisc')*

— Next vocal-less **ZAPPA** – lead guitar plus usual ensemble.

Aug 82. CBS-Barking Pumpkin; (t-lp) **SHUT UP 'N PLAY YER GUITAR** (rec.1977-80 live)
– Five, five, five / Hog heaven / Pink napkins / Stucco homes / Variations on the Carlos Santana secret chord progression / Gee I like your pants / Soup 'n old clothes / The deathless horsie / Shut up 'n play yer guitar (x2) / Heavy duty Judy / The return of shut up 'n play yer guitar / Canard du joir / While you were out / Pinocchio's furniture / Beat it with your fist / Why Johnny can't read / Canarsie / Treacherous cretins. *(re-iss.Apr88 on 'EMI') (d-cd-iss.Jan90 on 'Zappa') (re-iss.t-cd May95 on 'Rykodisc')*

Sep 82. CBS-Barking Pumpkin; (7") **SHUT UP 'N' PLAY YER GUITAR. / VARIATION ON THE C SANTANA SECRET**

Feb 86. EMI/ US= Capitol; (cd) **DOES HUMOR BELONG IN MUSIC**
(re-iss.Apr95 on 'Rykodisc')

Dec 86. (lp)(c) **JAZZ FROM HELL (instrumental live 1982)**
– Night school / The Beltaway bandits / While you were art II / Jazz from Hell / G-spot tornado / Damp ankles / St.Etienne / Massaggio galore. *(d-cd-iss.of 1986 albums May88) (cd-iss.May95 on 'Rykodisc')*

Apr 88. EMI/ US= Capitol; (cd) **THE MAN FROM UTOPIA / SHIP ARRIVING TOO LATE TO SAVE..** -

Apr 88. CBS; (2xt-cd-box) **JOE'S GARAGE ACTS I / II / II / SHUT UP AND PLAY YER GUITAR**

1986. Rykodisc; (d-cd) **WE'RE ONLY IN IT FOR THE MONEY / LUMPY GRAVY**

Oct 87. Rykodisc; (cd) **APOSTROPHE / OVERNITE SENSATION** -

Oct 87. Rykodisc; (3"cd-ep) **PEACHES EN REGALIA / I'M NOT SATISFIED / LUCILLE HAS MESSED UP MY MIND** -

Apr 88. Rykodisc; (3"cd-s) **SEXUAL HARASSMENT IN THE WORKPLACE / WATERMELON IN EASTER HAY** -

May 88. Rykodisc; (3"cd-s) **ZOMBY WOOF / YOU DIDN'T TRY TO CALL ME** -

May 88. Rykodisc; (3"cd-s) **MONTANA (WHIPPING FLOSS) / CHEEPNIS** -

Jul 87. Barking Pumpkin; (lp-box) **OLD MASTERS – BOX ONE** -
– FREAK OUT / ABSOLUTELY FREE / WE'RE ONLY IN IT FOR THE MONEY / LUMPY GRAVY / CRUISIN' WITH RUBEN & THE JETS / (Mystery Disc – rare).

Jul 87. Barking Pumpkin; (lp-box) **OLD MASTERS – BOX TWO** -
– UNCLE MEAT / HOT RATS / BURNT WEENIE SANDWICH / WEASELS RIPPED MY FLESH / CHUNGA'S REVENGE / LIVE AT THE FILLMORE EAST / JUST ANOTHER BAND FROM L.A. / (Mystery Disc – live in London 1968).

Nov 87. Barking Pumpkin; (lp-box) **OLD MASTERS – BOX THREE** -
– OVERNITE SENSATION / ONE SIZE FITS ALL / WAKA JAWAKA / THE GRAND WAZOO / APOSTROPHE / BONGO FURY / ZOOT ALLURES / ROXY AND ELSEWHERE.

Jan 88. MFN/ US= Zappa; (lp)(c) **THE LONDON SYMPHONY ORCHESTRA VOL.II**
– (out-takes from '200 Motels') Bob in Dacron / Strictly genteel / Bogus bomp (cd+=) – (2 extra tracks).

Apr 88. MFN/ US= Barking Pumpkin; (d-lp)(c)(d-cd) **GUITAR** (rec.live 1979-84) 82
– Sexual harassment in the workplace / Which one is it? * / Republicans / Do not pass go / Chalk pie * / In-a-gadda-Stravinsky * / That's not really reggae / When no one was no one / Once again, without the net / Outside now (original solo) / Jim and Tammy's upper room / Were we ever really safe in San Antonio? / That ol' G minor thing again / Hotel Atlanta incidentals * / That's not really a shuffle * / Move it or park it / Sunrise redeemer // Variations on sinister #3 * / Orrin Hatch on skis * / But who was Fulcanelli? / For Duane / Goa / Winos do not march / Swans? what swans? * / Too ugly for show business * / Systems of edges / Do not try this at home * / Things that look like meat / Watermelon in Easter hay / Canadian customs * / Is that all there is? * / It ain't necessarily the St.James Infirmary *. *(cd+= *) (re-iss.cd May95 on 'Rykodisc')*

Apr 88. Barking Pumpkin; (d-lp) **YOU CAN'T DO THAT ON STAGE ANYMORE**
(d-cd-iss.Jan90) (re-iss.May95 on 'Rykodisc')

Oct 88. Zappa; (d-cd) **YOU CAN'T DO THAT ON STAGE ANYMORE VOL.2**
(re-iss.May95 on 'Rykodisc')

Jan 89. Zappa; (cd) **BABY SNAKES**
(re-is.May95 on 'Rykodisc')

Jan 90. Zappa; (d-cd) **JOE'S GARAGE ACT I / II / III**
(re-iss.May95 on 'Rykodisc')

— FRANK decided to bootleg the bootleggers by releasing 10 best sellers that had fleeced him in the past. They were limited on 'Rhino'.

Apr 91. Zappa; (d-cd)(d-c)(d-lp) **THE BEST BAND YOU NEVER HEARD IN YOUR LIFE**
(re-iss.May95 on 'Rykodisc')

Jun 91. Zappa; (d-cd)(d-c)(t-lp) **MAKE A JAZZ NOISE HERE**
(re-iss.d-cd May95 on 'Rykodisc')

Jun 91. Zappa; (d-cd) **YOU CAN'T DO THAT ON STAGE ANYMORE VOL.3**
(re-iss.d-cd May95 on 'Rykodisc')

Jun 91. Zappa; (d-cd)(dc)(d-lp) **YOU CAN'T DO THAT ON STAGE ANYMORE VOL.4**
(re-iss.May95 on 'Rykodisc')

May 92. Zappa; (cd) **BOULEZ CONDUCTS ZAPPA: THE PERFECT STRANGER**
(re-iss.May95 on 'Rykodisc')

May 92. Zappa; (cd) **FRANCESCO ZAPPA**
(re-iss.May95 on 'Rykodisc')

Nov 92. Zappa; (cd) **PLAYGROUND PSYCHOTICS**
(re-iss.May95 on 'Rykodisc')

Nov 92. Zappa; (d-cd) **YOU CAN'T DO THAT ON STAGE ANYMORE VOL.5**
(re-iss.May95 on Rykodisc')

Nov 92. Zappa; (d-cd) **YOU CAN'T DO THAT ON STAGE ANYMORE VOL.6**
(re-iss.May95 on 'Rykodisc')

Note; below releases on 'Essential' UK/ 'Zappa' US.

Sep 91. (cd)(lp) **AS AN AM**
Sep 91. (cd)(lp) **THE ARK (live Boston 1968)**
Sep 91. (cd)(lp) **FREAKS & MOTHERFU*£'%!**
Sep 91. (cd)(lp) **UNMITAGATED AUDACITY**
Sep 91. (d-cd)(d-lp) **ANYWAY THE WIND BLOWS**
Sep 91. (cd)(d-lp) **SAARBRUCKEN 1978**
Sep 91. (cd)(lp) **PIQUANTIQUE**
Sep 91. (cd)(lp) **L.S.D. VOL. 1** [-] [ ]
Apr 95. Rykodisc; (d-cd) **LONDON SYMPHONY ORCHESTRA VOLUMES 1 & 2**
May 95. Rykodisc; (cd) **AHEAD OF THEIR TIME**
May 95. Sonora; (cd; w/mag) **MAGAZINE & CD**
Aug 95. Rykodisc; (cd)(c)(d-lp) **STRICTLY COMMERCIAL (THE BEST OF FRANK ZAPPA)** [45] [ ]
– Peaches en regalia / Don't eat the yellow snow / Dancin' fool / San Ber'dino / Dirty love / My guitar wants to kill your mama / Cosmik debris / Trouble every day / Disco boy / Fine girl / Sexual harassment in the workplace / Let's make the water turn black / I'm the slime / Joe's garage / Bobby Brown goes down / Montana / Valley girl / Be in my video / Muffin man.

Joe ZAWINUL (see under ⇒ WEATHER REPORT)

ZEE (see under ⇒ PINK FLOYD)

Warren ZEVON

Born: 24 Jan'47, Chicago, USA out of immigrant Russian parents. Wrote song 'She Quit Me' for the film soundtrack 'Midnight Cowboy' in 1969. After a flop debut album that year, he returned to songwriting for others acts, but made some money from TV jingles and piano sessions for The EVERLY BROTHERS. In 1976, ZEVON released comeback album on 'Asylum', which was produced by JACKSON BROWNE and featured sessions from EAGLES and FLEETWOOD MAC. In 1978, he deservedly broke through when 'WEREWOLVES OF LONDON' hit the US Top 30. • **Style & Songwriters:** Cult rock singer/songwriter. Covered JESUS WAS A CROSS MAKER (Judy Sill). • **Trivia:** Warren's POOR POOR PITIFUL ME was used by LINDA RONSTADT.

Recommended: A QUIET NORMAL LIFE – THE BEST OF .... (*8) / TRANSVERSE CITY (*8) / SENTIMENTAL HYGIENE (*8).

WARREN ZEVON – vocals, piano + sessioners

Liberty Imperial

1969. (lp) **WANTED – DEAD OR ALIVE**
– Wanted dead or alive / Hitchhikin' woman / She quit me / Calcutta / Iko-Iko / Traveling in the lightning / Tule's blues / A bullet for Ramona / Gorilla / Fiery emblems.

—— semi-retired into jingle-land and sessions.

Asylum Asylum

Jun 76. (lp)(c) **WARREN ZEVON**
– Frank and Jesse James / Mama couldn't be persuaded / Backs turned looking down the path / Hasten down the wind / Poor poor pitiful me / The French inhaler / Mohammed's radio / I'll sleep when I'm dead / Carmelita / Join me in L.A. / Desperados under the eaves.

Aug 76. (7") **HASTEN DOWN THE WIND. / MOHAMMED'S RADIO** [-] [ ]
Oct 76. (7") **I'LL SLEEP WHEN I'M DEAD. / MOHAMMED'S RADIO** [ ] [-]
Oct 77. (7") **WEREWOLVES OF LONDON. / TENDERNESS ON THE BLOCK** [ ] [-]
Feb 78. (lp)(c) **EXCITABLE BOY** [ ] [8]
– Johnny strikes up the band / Roland the headless Thompson gunner / Excitable boy / Werewolves of London / Accidently like a martyr / Nightmare in the switching yard / Veracruz / Tenderness on the block / Lawyers, guns and money. *(re-iss.cd+c Mar93 on 'Pickwick') (re-iss.cd/c Sep95 on 'Warners')*
Mar 78. (7")(12"pic-d) **WEREWOLVES OF LONDON. / ROLAND THE HEADLESS THOMPSON GUNNER** [-] [21]
May 78. (7") **NIGHTTIME IN THE SWITCHING YARD. / ROLAND THE HEADLESS THOMPSON GUNNER** [ ] [-]
May 78. (7") **LAWYERS, GUNS AND MONEY. / VERACRUZ** [-] [ ]
Oct 78. (7") **EXCITABLE BOY. / VERACRUZ**
Feb 80. (7") **GORILLA, YOU'RE A DESPERADO. / EMPTY-HANDED HEART**
Feb 80. (lp)(c) **BAD LUCK STREAK IN DANCING SCHOOL** [ ] [20]
– Bad luck streak in dancing school / A certain girl / Jungle work / Empty-handed heart / Interlude No.1 / Play it all night long / Jeannie needs a shooter / Interlude No.2 / Bill Lee / Gorilla, you're a desperado / Bed of coals / Wild age. *(cd-iss.Dec94 & Sep95 +c)*
Mar 80. (7") **A CERTAIN GIRL. / EMPTY-HANDED HEART** [-] [57]
May 80. (7") **A CERTAIN GIRL. / JUNGLE WORK** [ ] [-]
Jul 80. (7") **JEANNIE NEEDS A SHOOTER. / INTERLUDE No.2**
Jan 81. (lp)(c) **STAND IN THE FIRE (live)** [-] [80]
– Stand in the fire / Jeannie needs a shooter / Excitable boy / Mohammed's radio / Werewolves of London / Lawyers, guns and money / The sin / Poor poor pitiful me / I'll sleep when I'm dead / Bo Diddley's a gunslinger – Bo Diddley.
Jan 81. (7") **LAWYERS, GUNS AND MONEY (live). / DOWN ON MY LUCK** [-] [ ]
Aug 82. (7") **LET NOTHING COME BETWEEN US. / THE HULA HULA BOYS**
Aug 82. (lp)(c) **THE ENVOY** [ ] [93]
– The envoy / The overdraft / The hula hula boys / Jesus mentioned / Let nothing come between you / Ain't that pretty at all / Charlie's medicine / Looking for the next best thing / Never too late for love.
Nov 86. (lp)(c)(cd) **A QUIET NORMAL LIFE – THE BEST OF WARREN ZEVON** (compilation)
– Werewolves of London / Play it all night long / Roland the headless Thompson gunner / The envoy / Mohammed's radio (live) / Desperados under the eaves / I'll sleep when I'm dead / Lawyers, guns and money / Ain't that pretty at all / Poor poor pitiful me / Accidentally like a martyr / Looking for the next big thing.

Elektra Elektra

Mar 87. (7")(re-issue) **WEREWOLVES OF LONDON. / JESUS MENTIONED**
(12"+=) – Poor poor pitiful me.

—— next album feat R.E.M. minus STIPE

Virgin Am. Virgin Am.

Jun 87. (7") **LEAVE MY MONKEY ALONE. / NOCTURNE**
(12"+=)(cd-s+=) – ('A' Latin version). (US; b-side)
Jun 87. (lp)(c)(cd) **SENTIMENTAL HYGIENE** [ ] [63]
– Sentimental hygiene / Boom boom Mancini / The factory / Trouble waiting to happen / Reconsider me / Detox mansion / Bad karma / Even a dog can shake hands / The heartache / Leave my monkey alone.
Jul 87. (7") **SENTIMENTAL HYGIENE. / THE FACTORY** [ ] [-]
(12"+=) – Leave my monkey alone.
Oct 87. (7") **BAD KARMA. / BOOM BOOM MANCINI** [ ] [-]
(12"+=) – Leave my monkey alone.
Feb 88. (7") **RECONSIDER ME. / THE FACTORY**
(12"+=) – Bad karma.

—— next featured **NEIL YOUNG, RITCHIE HAYWARD, JERRY GARCIA, BOBBY TENCH, DAVID GILMOUR**, etc.

Jan 90. (cd)(c)(lp) **TRANSVERSE CITY** [ ] [ ] Dec 89
– Transverse city / Run straight down / The long arm of the law / Turbulence / They moved the Moon / Splendid isolation / Networking / Gridlock / Down in the mall / Nobody's in love this year.
Jan 90. (7") **SPLENDID ISOLATION. / EVEN A DOG CAN SHAKE HANDS**
(12"+=)(cd-s+=) – Bad karma / Gridlock.

—— Later 1990, he provided vox for HINDU LOVE GODS splinter band of R.E.M. ⇒

Giant Giant

Nov 91. (cd)(c) **MR. BAD EXAMPLE**
– Finishing touches / Susie Lightning / Model citizen / Angel dressed in black / Mr. Bad example / Renegade / Heartache spoken here / Quite ugly one morning / Things to do in Denver / Searching for a heart.
Oct 93. (cd)(c) **LEARNING TO FLINCH**
– Splendid isolation / Lawyer's, guns & money / Mr.Bad example / Excitable boy / Hasten down the wind / The French inhaler / Warrior king / Roland chorale / Roland the headless Thompson gunner / Searching for a heart / Boom boom Mancini / Jungle work / Piano fighter / Werewolves of London / The indifference of Heaven / Poor poor pitiful me / Play it all night long.
Jul 95. (cd) **MUTINEER**
– Seminole bingo / Something bad hapened to a clown / Similiar to rain / The indifference of Heaven / Jesus was a cross maker / Poisonous lookalike / Piano fighter / Rottweiler blues / Monkey wash donkey rinse / Mutineer.

ZODIAC MOTEL (see under ⇒ BIRDLAND)

ZOMBIES

Formed: St.Albans, England ... 1963 by ROD ARGENT, COLIN BLUNSTONE, HUGH GRUNDY and PAUL ATKINSON. In early 1964 after winning a local band competition, they signed to 'Decca', and soon had a massive worldwide hit with the classic 'SHE'S NOT THERE'. • **Style:** Were known as the most intelligent pop group of the mid-60's, after leaving school with over fifty O and A levels between them. • **Songwriters:** ARGENT-WHITE penned, except for the ubiquitous covers; GOT MY MOJO WORKING (Muddy Waters) / YOU'VE REALLY GOT A HOLD ON ME (Smokey Robinson) / ROADRUNNER (Bo Diddley) / SUMMERTIME (Gershwin) / GOIN' OUT OF MY HEAD (Little Anthony & The Imperials) / etc. • **Trivia:** Early in 1966, they made a cameo appearance in the film 'Bunny Lake Is Missing'.

Recommended: ODESSEY & ORACLE (*8) / COLLECTION (*7)

COLIN BLUNSTONE (b.24 Jun'45, Hatfield, Herts., England) – vocals / **ROD ARGENT** (b.14 Jun'45, St.Albans, Herts.) – piano, keyboards, vocals / **PAUL ATKINSON** (b.19

Mar'46, Cuffley, Herts.) – guitar / **CHRIS WHITE** (b. 7 Mar'43, Barnet, Herts.) – bass repl. PAUL ARNOLD / **HUGH GRUNDY** (b. 6 Mar'45, Winchester, Hants., England) – drums

Decca Parrot

Jul 64. (7") **SHE'S NOT THERE. / YOU MAKE ME FEEL GOOD** 12 2 Oct 64
Oct 64. (7") **LEAVE HER BE. / WOMAN** –
Jan 65. (7") **TELL HER NO. / WHAT MORE CAN I DO** 42 6
Mar 65. (7") **SHE'S COMING HOME. / I MUST MOVE** 58
Apr 65. (lp) **BEGIN HERE** (US title 'THE ZOMBIES') 39 Feb 65
– Roadrunner / Summertime / I can't make up my mind / The way I feel inside / Work 'n' play / You've really got a hold on me / She's not there / Sticks and stones / Can't nobody love you / Woman / I don't want to know / I remember when I loved her / What more can I do / I got my mojo working. *(re-iss.Nov84) (re-iss.Jul86 on 'See For Miles' US version) (cd-iss.Aug92 on 'Repertoire' +=)–* You make me feel good / Leave me be / Tell her no / She's coming home / I must move / Kind of girl / It's alright with me / Sometimes / Whenever you're ready / I love you / Is this the dream / Don't go away / Remember you / Just out of reach / Indication / How we were before / I'm going home.
Jun 65. (7") **I WANT YOU BACK AGAIN. / ONCE UPON A TIME** – 95
Sep 65. (7") **WHENEVER YOU'RE READY. / I LOVE HER**
Nov 65. (7") **IS THIS A DREAM. / DON'T GO AWAY**
Jan 66. (7") **REMEMBER YOU. / JUST OUT OF REACH**
Jun 66. (7") **INDICATION. / HOW WE WERE BEFORE**
Nov 66. (7") **GOTTA GET A HOLD ON MYSELF. / THE WAY I FEEL INSIDE**
Mar 67. (7") **GOIN' OUT OF MY HEAD. / SHE DOES EVERYTHING FOR ME**
May 67. (7") **I LOVE YOU. / THE WAY I FEEL INSIDE** –

C.B.S. Columbia

Sep 67. (7") **FRIENDS OF MINE. / BEECHWOOD PARK**
Nov 67. (7") **CARE OF CELL 44. / MAYBE AFTER HE'S GONE**
(re-iss.Mar74 on 'Epic')

— Disbanded late 1967, although postumous release below resurrected group in 1969.

C.B.S. Date

Apr 68. (lp) **ODESSEY AND ORACLE** 95 Mar 69
– Care of Cell 44 / A rose for Emily / Maybe after he's gone / Beechwood park / Brief candles / Hung up on a dream / Changes / I want her she wants me / This will be our year / Butcher's tale (Western Front 1914) / Friends of mine / Time of the season. *(re-iss.Dec86 on 'Razor') (cd-iss.Aug92 on 'Repertoire' +=)–* I call you mine / She loves the way they love her / Imagine the swan / Smokey day / If it don't work out / I know she will / Don't cry for me / Walking in the sun / Conversation off Floral Street / I want you back again / Gotta get hold of myself / Goin' out of my head / She does everything for me / Nothing's changed / I could spend the day / Girl help me.
Apr 68. (7") **TIME OF THE SEASON. / I'LL CALL YOU MINE**
Jul 68. (7") **THIS WILL BE OUR YEAR. / BUTCHERS TALE (WESTERN FRONT 1914)** –
Feb 69. (7") **TIME OF THE SEASON. / FRIENDS OF MINE** – 3

— (Mar69) With them riding high in US Top 3, they decided to re-form but without BLUNSTONE (who went solo) / WHITE (who went into producing) + ATKINSON. ARGENT + GRUNDY recruited **RICK BIRKETT** – guitar / **JIM RODFORD** – bass

May 69. (7") **IMAGINE THE SWAN. / CONVERSATIONS OF FLORAL STREET** –
Jul 69. (7") **IF IT DON'T WORK OUT. / DON'T CRY FOR ME** –

— Didn't last long, when ROD and JIM decided to form ARGENT.

– compilations, others, etc. –

1965. Decca; (7"ep) **THE ZOMBIES** –
– Kinda girl / Sometimes / It's alright / Summertime.
Sep 70. Decca; (lp)(c) **THE WORLD OF THE ZOMBIES** –
Feb 82. Decca; (lp)(c) **SHE'S NOT THERE** –
Jan 74. Epic; (lp)(c) **TIME OF THE ZOMBIES** –
Sep 75. Epic; (7") **TIME OF THE SEASON. / IMAGINE THE SWAN** –
Oct 83. Old Gold; (7") **SHE'S NOT THERE. / TIME OF THE SEASON** –
Feb 86. Rhino; (c-ep) **LIVE ON THE BBC (live)** – –
Mar 89. Old Gold; (cd-ep) **SHE'S NOT THERE. / (2 other tracks by Moody Blues + Easybeats)** –
Sep 87. See For Miles; (lp)(c) **THE SINGLES A's & B's** –
(cd-iss.Sep88)
1988. Special Edition; (3"cd-ep) **SHE'S NOT THERE / TIME OF THE SEASON / TELL HER NO / GOT MY MOJO WORKING** –
Aug 88. Castle; (d-lp)(c)(cd) **THE COLLECTION** –
– Goin' out of my head / Leave me be / Gotta get a hold on myself / I can't make up my mind / Kind of girl / Sticks and stones / Summertime / Woman / I got my mojo working / Roadrunner / You really got a hold on me / Nothing's changed / You make me feel good / She's not there / Don't go away / How we were before / Tell her no / Whenever you're ready / Just out of reach / Remember you / Indication / She does everything for me / Time of the season / I love you.
Apr 89. Impact; (cd) **THE ZOMBIES COLLECTION VOL.1** –
Apr 89. Impact; (cd) **THE ZOMBIES COLLECTION VOL.2** –
Apr 91. Essential; (cd)(c)(lp) **NEW WORD** –
1988. Razor; (cd) **MEET THE ZOMBIES** –
May 89. Razor; (lp)(cd) **FIVE LIVE ZOMBIES (live)** –
Jul 91. Razor; (3xcd-box) **THE ZOMBIES** –
Jun 90. Knight; (cd)(c) **GOLDEN DECADE OF THE ZOMBIES** –
Nov 92. See For Miles; (cd) **THE EP COLLECTION** –
May 94. Castle; (cd) **NEW WORLD** –
Feb 95. More Music; (cd) **1964-67** –
Aug 95. Old Gold; (cd-s) **SHE'S NOT THERE / LEAVE HER BE** –
Sep 95. Old Gold; (cd-s) **TIME OF THE SEASON / TELL HER NO** –

ZOO (see under ⇒ FLEETWOOD MAC)

ZZ TOP

Formed: Houston, Texas, USA ... as The MOVING SIDEWALKS by BILLY GIBBONS. The now famous trio/line-up finally emerged in 1970, when HILL and BEARD joined them. After one-off 45 on manager BILLY HAM's new 'Scat' label, they moved to 'London' where they stayed for 8 years. In this time they built up huge following which stemmed from supporting many huge acts (i.e. STONES). After new contract with 'Warners' during the early 80's, they suffered slight lull, but took off worldwide especially in UK when 'ELIMINATOR' and its 45's hit charts. • **Style:** Powerful Southern hard-rocking boogie and blues trio, who featured the cultivated beards of GIBBONS and HILL (FRANK BEARD didn't have one!). • **Songwriters:** Group penned (plus some early w / manager BILL HAM) except; FRANCINE (trad.) / JAILHOUSE ROCK + VIVA LAS VEGAS (hits; Elvis Presley) / I THANK YOU (Isaac Hayes) / DUST MY BROOM (Elmore James) / etc. • **Trivia:** On the 1st Jan'85, HILL accidentally shot himself in the stomach but he soon recovered.

Recommended: GREATEST HITS (*9) / ELIMINATOR (*8) / TRES HOMBRES (*7) / FANDANGO (*7) /

MOVING SIDEWALKS

BILLY GIBBONS (b.12 Dec'49) – vocals, guitar / **TOM MOORE** – keyboards / **DON SUMMERS** – bass / **DAN MITCHELL** – drums

not issued Tantara

1967. (7") **99th FLOOR. / WHAT ARE YOU GOING TO DO?** –
(re-iss.1967 on 'Wand')

not issued Wand

1967. (7") **NEED ME. / EVERY NIGHT A NEW SURPRISE** –
(above tracks were re-iss.1980 as EP on 'Movie' US)

— **LANIER GREIG** – keyboards repl. MOORE

not issued Tantara

1968. (7") **I WANT TO HOLD YOUR HAND. / JOE BLUES** –
1968. (lp) **FLASH** –
– Flashback / Crimson witch / Pluto – Sept.31 / Eclipse / Scoun da be / No good to cry / You don't know the life / You make me shake / Reclipse.
1969. (7") **FLASHBACK. / NO GOOD TO CRY** –

ZZ TOP

(GIBBONS, MITCHELL & GREIG)

not issued ScatLondon

1970. (7") **SALT LICK. / MILLER'S FARM** –

— **GIBBONS** now sole survivor when LANIER and DAN departed. Newcomers were **DUSTY HILL** (b.JOE, 1949) – bass, vocals (ex-WARLOCKS, ex-AMERICAN BLUES) / **FRANK BEARD** (b.10 Dec'49) – drums (ex-CELLAR DWELLARS)

London London

Jan 71. (lp) **FIRST ALBUM** –
– (Somebody else been) Shakin' your tree / Brown sugar / Squank / Goin' down to Mexico / Old man / Neighbor, neighbor / Certified blues / Bedroom thang / Just got back from baby's / Backdoor love affair. *(UK-iss.+c.Sep84 on 'Warners', cd-iss.Jan87) (cd-iss.Mar94 on 'Warners')*
Feb 71. (7") **(SOMEBODY ELSE BEEN) SHAKIN' YOUR TREE. / NEIGHBOR, NEIGHBOR** –
May 72. (7") **FRANCENE. / FRANCENE (Spanish)** – 69
Jul 72. (lp) **RIO GRANDE MUD** Apr 72
– Francene / Just got paid / Mushmouth shoutin' / Ko ko blue / Chevrolet / Apologies to Pearly / Bar-b-q / Sure got cold after the rain fell / Whiskey'n mama / Down Brownie. *(re-iss.+c.Sep84 on 'Warners', cd-iss.Jan87) (cd-iss.Mar94 on 'Warners')*
Jul 72. (7") **FRANCENE. / DOWN BROWNIE** –
Nov 73. (lp)(c) **TRES HOMBRES** 8 Aug 73
– Waitin' for the bus / Jesus just left Chicago / Beer drinkers & Hell raisers / Master of sparks / Hot, blue and righteous / Move me on down the line / Precious and Grace / La Grange / Shiek / Have you heard?. *(re-iss.cd+c Mar94 on 'Warners')*
Jun 74. (7") **BEER DRINKERS & HELL RAISERS. / LA GRANGE** –
Jan 75. (7") **LA GRANGE. / JUST GOT PAID** 41 Mar 74
Jun 75. (lp)(c) **FANDANGO! (live Warehouse, New Orleans + studio)** 60 10 May 75
– Thunderbird / Jailhouse rock / Back door medley / Nasty dogs and funky kings / Blue jean blues / Balinese / Mexican blackbird / Heard it on the X / Tush. *(re-iss.Nov83 on 'Warners', cd-iss.Jan87) (re-iss.cd+c Mar94 on 'Warners')*
Jul 75. (7") **TUSH. / BLUE JEAN BLUES** 20
Aug 76. (7") **IT'S ONLY LOVE. / ASLEEP IN THE DESERT** 44
Feb 77. (lp)(c) **TEJAS** 17 Jan 77
– It's only love / Arrested for driving while blind / El Diablo / Snappy kakkie / Enjoy and get it on / Ten dollar man / Pan Am highway blues / Avalon hideaway / She's a heartbreaker / Asleep in the desert. *(re-iss.Sep84 on 'Warners', cd-iss.Mar87) (cd-iss.Mar94 on 'Warners')*
Mar 77. (7") **ARRESTED FOR DRIVING WHILE BLIND. / IT'S ONLY LOVE** – 91
Apr 77. (7") **ARRESTED FOR DRIVING WHILE BLIND. / NEIGHBOR, NEIGHBOR** –
May 77. (7") **EL DIABLO. / ENJOY AND GET IT ON** –
Dec 77. (lp)(c) **THE BEST OF ZZ TOP** (compilation) 94
– Tush / Waitin' for the bus / Jesus just left Chicago / Francene / Just got paid / La grange / Blue jean blues / Backdoor love affair / Beer drinkers and Hell raisers / Heard it on the X. *(re-iss.Dec83 on 'Warners', cd-iss.Jan86)*

Warners Warners

Dec 79. (lp)(c) **DEGUELLO** 24 Nov 79
– I thank you / She loves my automobile / I'm bad, I'm nationwide / A fool for

LOUD
VERY LOUD
EXTREME PAIN

your stockings / Manic mechanic / Dust my broom / Lowdown in the street / Hi-fi mama / Cheap sunglasses / Esther be the one. *(re-iss.+cd Jan85) (re-iss.cd+c Mar94 on 'Warners')*

Mar 80. (7") **I THANK YOU. / A FOOL FOR YOUR STOCKINGS** [ ] [34] Jan 80
Jun 80. (7") **CHEAP SUNGLASSES. / ESTHER BE THE ONE** [ ] [89]
Jul 81. (7") **LEILA. / DON'T TEASE ME** [-] [77]
Jul 81. (lp)(c) **EL LOCO** [88] [17]
– Tube snake boogie / I wanna drive you home / Ten foot pole / Leila / Don't tease me / It's so hard / Pearl necklace / Groovy little hippy pad / Heaven, Hell or Houston / Party on the patio. *(cd-iss.Mar87) (cd-iss.Mar94 on 'Warners')*
Jan 82. (7") **TUBE SNAKE BOOGIE. / HEAVEN, HELL OR HOUSTON** [-] [ ]
Jun 83. (7")(7"sha-pic-d) **GIMME ALL YOUR LOVIN'. / IF I COULD ONLY FLAG HER DOWN** [61] [37] Mar 83
(12") – ('A'side) / Jesus just left Chicago / Heard it on the x / Arrested for driving while blind. *(re-iss.UK Sep84, hit No.10)*
Jun 83. (lp)(c) **ELIMINATOR** [3] [9] Apr 83
– Gimme all your lovin' / Got me under pressure / Sharp dressed man / I need you tonight / I got the six / Legs / Thug / TV dinners / Dirty dog / If I could only flag her down / Bad girl. *(cd-iss.1984) (pic-lp Aug85) (re-iss.cd+c Mar94)*
Nov 83. (7") **SHARP DRESSED MAN. / I GOT THE SIX** [53] [56] Jul 83
(12"+=) – La Grange. *(re-iss.UK Sep84, hit No.22)*
Mar 84. (7")(12") **TV DINNERS. / CHEAP SUNGLASSES** [67] [ ]
(d12"+=)(c-s+=) – A fool for your stockings / Legs.
Feb 85. (7") **LEGS (remix). / BAD GIRL** [16] [8] May 84
(12") – ('A'side) / La grange / A fool for your stocking
Jul 85. (d7")(12"ep)(c-ep) **THE ZZ TOP SUMMER HOLIDAY EP** [51] [ ]
– Beer drinkers and Hell raisers / I'm bad, I'm nationwide / Tush / Got me under pressure.
Oct 85. (7")(7"sha-pic-d)(7"interlocking jigsaw pic-d pt.1) **SLEEPING BAG. / PARTY ON THE PATIO** [27] [8]
(d7"+=) – Sharp dressed man / I got the six.
Nov 85. (lp)(c)(cd) **AFTERBURNER** [2] [4]
– Sleeping bag / Stages / Woke up with wood / Rough boy / Can't stop rockin' / Planet of women / I got the message / Velcro fly / Dipping low (in the lap of luxury) / Delirious. *(re-iss.cd+c Mar94)*
Feb 86. (7")(7"jigsaw pic-d pt.2) **STAGES. / HI-FI MAMA** [43] [21] Jan 86
(12"+=) – ('A'version).
Apr 86. (7")(7"pic-d)(7"jigsaw pic-d pt.3) **ROUGH BOY. / DELIRIOUS** [23] [22] Mar 86
(12"shrinkwrapped to free jigsaw 'SLEEPING BAG' pic-d+=) – Legs (mix)
Aug 86. (7") **VELCRO FLY. / CAN'T STOP ROCKIN'** [-] [35]
Sep 86. (7") **VELCRO FLY. / WOKE UP WITH WOOD** [54] [-]
(12"+=) – Can't stop rockin' ('86 remix).
Jul 90. (7")(12")(c-s) **DOUBLEBACK. / PLANET OF WOMEN** [29] [50] May 90
(cd-s+=) – ('A'-AOR mix).
Oct 90. (cd)(c)(lp) **RECYCLER** [8] [6]
– Concrete and steel / Lovething / Penthouse eyes / Tell it / My head's in Mississippi / Decision or collision / Give it up / 2000 blues / Burger man / Doubleback. *(re-iss.cd+c Mar94)*
Nov 90. (7")(c-s) **GIVE IT UP. / SHARP DRESSED MAN** [ ] [79] Jan 91
(12"+=)(cd-s+=) – Cheap sunglasses (live).
Apr 91. (7")(c-s)(7"sha-pic-d) **MY HEAD'S IN MISSISSIPPI. / A FOOL FOR YOUR STOCKINGS** [37] [ ]
(12"+=)(cd-s+=) – Blue Jean blues.
Mar 92. (7")(c-s) **VIVA LAS VEGAS. / 2000 BLUES** [10] [ ]
(cd-s+=) – Velcro fly / Stages / Legs.
May 92. (cd)(c)(lp) **GREATEST HITS** (compilation) [5] [9]
– Gimme all your lovin' / Sharp dressed man / Rough boy / Tush / My head's in Mississippi / Pearl necklace / I'm bad, I'm nationwide / Viva Las Vegas / Doubleback / Gun love / Got me under pressure / Give it up / Cheap sunglasses / Sleeping bag / Planet of women / La Grange / Tube snake boogie / Legs.
Jun 92. (7")(c-s) **ROUGH BOY. / VIVA LAS VEGAS (Remix)** [49] [ ]
(cd-s+=) – Velcro fly (extended) / Doubleback (AOR mix).
(cd-s) – ('A'side) / TV dinners / Jesus has just left Chicago / Beer drinkers and Hell raisers.

R.C.A. R.C.A.

Jan 94. (7")(c-s) **PINCUSHION. / CHERRY RED** [15] [ ]
(cd-s+=) – ('A'mix).
Jan 94. (cd)(c)(lp) **ANTENNA** [3] [14]
– Pincushion / Breakaway / World of swirl / Fuzzbox voodoo / Girl in a T-shirt / Antenna head / Pch / Cherry red / Cover your rig / Lizard life / Deal goin' down / Everything.
Apr 94. (c-s)(12")(cd-s) **BREAKAWAY. / MARY'S** [60] [ ]

– other compilations, etc. –

Nov 83. Warners; (d-c) **TRES HOMBRES / FANDANGO** [ ] [-]
1987. (3xcd-box) **FIRST ALBUM / RIO GRANDE MUD/ / TRES HOMBRES / FANDANGO!/ / TEJAS / EL LOCO** [ ] [ ]
Nov 94. Warners; (cd)(c) **ONE FOOT IN THE BLUES** [ ] [ ]

The Great Rock Survey

Before 31st December 1995, over 100 people sent me their GREAT ROCK SURVEY lists. Before you get to this, I would like to tell you about all the fun I had compiling them ... but I can't. It took me a great deal of time and, joking aside, I initially enjoyed going through all your VERY varied selections. Now I know for definite that no two people are in the remotest bit similar. Music's like that isn't it? We can debate for hours sometimes on the merits of a group. And then, boom! We start arguing about what's their best (i.e. brilliant, shite, I'm sick of that now, that's their best for ages, on and on, until speech leaves us in a corner talking about our love-life, football or the price of a pint.

Anyway I had a mixture of fun and frustration reading all your 2000+ different choices. Like the German guy who gave me his GREAT (WORLD) ROCK DISCOGRAPHY SURVEY. Great concept, but I'm glad everybody didn't do that as different choices might have amounted to over 5,000 and seriously overloaded my computer. One person listed "whole" albums alongside Top 10/5 tracks, but also a track from that actual album. Not what was wanted I'm afraid, although I adjudicated that I would split the points calculated. Other difficulties were when people just virtually missed out things like, eh, numbers. An essential thing for calculating don't you think? People even missed out a number, going from their No.4 to No.6 or only sticking down 9 tracks instead of 10 or even duplicating certain tracks. My initial rules were being bent more times than a Tory General Election campaign. STING and THE POLICE were sometimes lumped together. You could have had them both! Other bad pairings were LOU REED or NICO and The VELVET UNDERGROUND, BRIAN ENO and ROXY MUSIC, VAN MORRISON and THEM, ERIC CLAPTON plus CREAM, STEVE WINWOOD and TRAFFIC. PHIL SPECTOR the producer was also in someone's Top 10.

These difficulties could have been avoided if you'd looked to see if they were sub-entried in the book. Somebody got away with a splendid all-metal chart including seperate entries for PEARL JAM, GREEN RIVER plus MOTHER LOVE BONE, SOUNDGARDEN, TEMPLE OF THE DOG plus ALICE IN CHAINS plus MAD SEASON. Correct pairings were the likes of BJORK plus SUGARCUBES, BRIAN FERRY plus ROXY MUSIC, DAVID BOWIE plus TIN MACHINE (if you thought it really neccessary). In future could you type (not faintly) all lists and number them correctly. If you have to write them out, do the scribbles first and send me the neat (but not fancy) list. Anyway it's only a 90s survey I want next, and I hope that my pointing out all this won't hinder your correspondence.

My German and Euro friends have also put me onto some weird and wonderful bands who I'd like to hear more about. Maybe you can send me lists, tapings of the following: ELEMENT OF CRIME, BAP, TOCOTRONIC, DIE LASSE SINGERS, POEMS FOR LAILA, HELGE SCHNEIDER, G. LOVE & SPECIAL SAUCE, STEPHEN EICHER, DIE COMEDIAN HARMONISTS, ZARAH LEANDER, MYLENE FARMER, LUKA BLOOM, FORTIFICATION 55, SCHWOIBFUB, HERBERT GROENEMEYER, MARLA GLEN, PANKOW, CARMAN, REV. DAN SMITH, SARAH McLACHAN, CHRISTOPH & LOLLO, DOROTHY MASUKA, DEINE LAKAIEN, DIE AERZTE, WOLFGANG AMBROS, INCHTABOKATABLES, BOOMERS, PHUDYS, RENFF, CITY, SILLY, OUGENWEIDE, TIAMAT, LUDWIG HIRSCH, HERMAN VAN VEEN, FREIWILLIGE SELBSTKONTROLLE, LENINGRAD COWBOYS, TEA PARTY, BATHORY and KEIMZEIT. I'm also thinking about learning German while I have a wee holiday in my back garden. One more thing is to say thanks to the person who called me Mr Horse. I've never met my illustrator yet and I'm sure he'd love to read that someone also thinks he's the writer of the book. Keep up the clever work Harry.

Thanks to all the GREAT surveyors of quantity:

7 from Scotland: VIC ZDZIEBLO (Falkirk), HUGH MACKIE (Stenhousemuir), K. McEVOY (Edinburgh), ALICE GRANDISON and JIM HENDERSON (Glasgow), PAUL MORRISON (Whitburn), and myself (still Falkirk).

35 from England: TIM FOOTMAN and SIMON D. FISHER (London), NICK KING (Nottingham), ALEX WHITLOCK (Nelson, Lancashire), KELVIN HOLMES (Dorset), STEVE WHITE (Dartford), LIAM RIGBY (Watford), NIGEL HARMAN (Reading, Berkshire), JOHN MERKIN (Pilling), STEVE BOISMAISON (St Anne's-On-Sea), TRISTIAN GUY-DEMEN (Ilford, Essex), MARK MURRAY (Chippenham, Wiltshire), IAN ROBERTSON (Welwyn Garden City), GUY SUTTON (Aylesbury), DAVID CULMER, PAUL COPE and JULIA ARMSTRONG (Brighton), MATT KILLNER (Petersfield, Hants), DAVE CHAMBERS (Norton, Stockton On Tees), KEITH TOPPING (Newcastle Upon Tyne), STEPHEN ANCHOR (Ashford, Kent), MARK AUTY (Netherton, Wakefield), CHRIS HARRISON (Durham), STEVE NORTON (Bishopton, Bristol), STEPHEN BAIRD (Giggleswick, Yorkshire), GRAHAM LONG (Bracknell, Berkshire), DAVID BLUNKLEY (Bromborough, Wirral), JON FARNBOROUGH and ANTHONY FARNBOROUGH (Shoeburyness, Southend-On-Sea), CHRIS OWEN (Swindon), J. SMITH (Somerset), STEVE MAY and TOM MAY (Christchurch, Sunderland), NEIL ROBERTSON (Penrith, Cumbria), JAMIE GOODMAN.

1 From N. Ireland: JOE MACKLE (Belfast).

1 From Eire: JOHN WALSHE (Arraighe).

4 From USA: VINCENT VITTIBURGA (Brooklyn, New York), CHARLES DIORIO (Shamokin, Pennsylvania), DALE GARDNER (La Grange, Illinois), PETER WOOSTER (San Francisco, California).

3 From Australia: PETER O'DONNELL (Junee), NEIL SPARGO (Tasmania), PHIL NEWTON (Illawong).

50 From Germany: ALEX DREYER and TORSTEN ZAJWERT (Hamburg), ULLI RICHTER (Nuremberg), HARALD KAYSER (Wuppertal), BERND AUGUSTIN (Darmstadt), ECKEHARD TEBBE (Grunenplan), PETER BALZER (Nesselrodeweg), STEFFEN BAUER (Neunkirchen), Dr HELMUT HEINZE, JURGEN GOLDNER, JORG FOTH, MARTIN

BERTSCH, ANDREAS HERGER, JURGEN SCHMIDT, BERNDT BUCH and FRANK HERGER (Berlin), RAINER KRAKER (Gelsenkirchen), MATTHIAS GUDERJAN (Bad Krozingen), DIETER BANSCH (Leipzig), KLAUS-DIETER FISCHER (Kassel), BERTHOLD NUCHTER and WOLFGANG NUCHTER (Moers), PETER MEYER-LIEPACH (Iserlohn), ANNE-KATRIN TURN (Vilsbiburg), STEFANIE SCHMITT (Budingen), PETER BERTGES and SOREN JAKOBS (Saarbrucken), LARS KIESEL (Mainz), JURGEN SCHELLECKES (Niestetal), ANDREAS HOLSCHUH, Jr (Kaiserslautern), ARTHUR ROUSSELLE (Tübingen), HARTWIG GIERKE and ALEXEI ROUDITCHEV (Munich), DEREK BUCK (Harrislee), MICHAEL VON HOLDT (Buchholz), R. OTTO HEYDORN (Frankfurt), MARTIN LING (Hittbergen), JORG-PETER KLOTZ (Heidelberg), HARTMUT SIEGEL (Heidl), THOMAS SMOLINSKI (Evessen), OLIVER HOHL (Lohmar), MARKUS FICKEL and CHRISTIAN HALMEN (Stuttgart), HERBERT LEHMANN and A. WIECKEIT (Essen), MICHAEL CHANDLER (Bochum), WERNER SCHULZ (Litzendorf), ANDREAS MOLLER (Munster), RICHARD LINK (Ludwigsburg), BENJAMIN HOLZWARTH (Murrhardt)

1 From Italy: FABRIZIO BENEDETTI (Roma).

1 From Bulgaria: INGO DREYER (Sofia).

1 From West Indies: B.C. PIRES (Port of Spain).

And the winners of the Survey Competition are …

- MATTHIAS GUDERJAN (Germany) who had most of his top 30 in the combined top 30 – 19 to be exact. He will receive a signed copy of the *Great Rock Discography* book for life and a signed T-shirt of his choice from the Rock Discography range.
- STEVE BOISMAISON (UK) who provided the most interesting survey. He wins a signed copy of the third edition (this book) and a signed T-shirt of his choice from the Rock Discography range.

How The Survey Was Calculated

In Your Top 10 of ten tracks, the points awarded were between 200 and 101 (i.e. 200 was to your favourite artist and their No.1, while 101 was given to your tenth fave and their 10th track). In the same context, between 100 and 51 points were awarded to your eleventh favourite artists' No.1 and your twentieth faves' 5th track. Once again in the same context, your twenty-first favourites' No.1 was given 50 points, while your thirtieth favourites' No.3 was given 21 points. The remaining 20 points were distributed among the bonus 20 in order. A diagonal mathematical grid on how all points were calculated can be obtained by post. But trust me. It was worked out fair. Would I cheat? I also wanted to find out exactly what your amalgamated favourites would be, and it took me a month or so to do so. Don't ask me to add up anything again for around two years. I'll rephrase that. Does anyone want the job? Long hours, no extra overtime and due to a numb brain, you lose more hair!
Note:– (bu) = bubbling under

1 BEATLES

(1) STRAWBERRY FIELDS FOREVER (4567)
(2) A DAY IN THE LIFE (4068)
(3) I AM THE WALRUS (2604)
(4) HEY JUDE (2602)
(5) NORWEGIAN WOOD (THIS BIRD HAS FLOWN) (2296)
(6) HERE COMES THE SUN (2056)
(7) WHILE MY GUITAR GENTLY WEEPS (2032)
(8) ELEANOR RIGBY (2029)
(9) YESTERDAY (2008)
(10) GET BACK (1937)
(11) HELTER SKELTER (1857)
(12) LET IT BE (1745)
(13) PENNY LANE (1632)
(14) HAPPINESS IS A WARM GUN (1559)
(15) IN MY LIFE (1331)
(16) HELP! (1330)
(17) LUCY IN THE SKY WITH DIAMONDS (1306)
(18) YOU'VE GOT TO HIDE YOUR LOVE AWAY (1250)
(19) ALL YOU NEED IS LOVE (1200)
(20) REVOLUTION (1170)
(21) PAPERBACK WRITER (1123)
(22) DEAR PRUDENCE (1060)
(23) TOMORROW NEVER KNOWS (1051)
(24) THE LONG AND WINDING ROAD (1000)
(25) WE CAN WORK IT OUT (950)
(26) COME TOGETHER (914)
(27) NOWHERE MAN (909)
(28) THINGS WE SAID TODAY (899)
(29) HELLO GOODBYE (876)
(30) SOMETHING (856)
(31) I WANT YOU (SHE'S SO HEAVY) (856)

2 ROLLING STONES

(1) JUMPIN' JACK FLASH (4169)
(2) (I CAN'T GET NO) SATISFACTION (3978)
(3) SYMPATHY FOR THE DEVIL (3955)
(4) PAINT IT BLACK (3835)
(5) HONKY TONK WOMEN (2746)
(6) BROWN SUGAR (2653)
(7) YOU CAN'T ALWAYS GET WHAT YOU WANT (2116)
(8) ANGIE (1957)
(9) GIMME SHELTER (1956)
(10) START ME UP (1797)
(11) RUBY TUESDAY (1749)
(12) LITTLE RED ROOSTER (1516)
(13) WILD HORSES (1400)
(14) STREET FIGHTING MAN (1384)
(15) THE LAST TIME (1329)
(16) IT'S ALL OVER NOW (1245)
(17) BEAST OF BURDEN (1140)
(18) MIDNIGHT RAMBLER (1055)
(19) IT'S ONLY ROCK'N'ROLL (BUT I LIKE IT) (1051)
(20) AS TEARS GO BY (939)

3 LED ZEPPELIN

(1) STAIRWAY TO HEAVEN (4591)
(2) KASHMIR (3704)
(3) DAZED AND CONFUSED (3306)
(4) WHOLE LOTTA LOVE (3260)
(5) ROCK AND ROLL (2453)
(6) NO QUARTER (1994)
(7) SINCE I'VE BEEN LOVING YOU (1751)
(8) D'YER MAKER (1717)
(9) BLACK DOG (1496)
(10) IN MY TIME OF DYING (1439)
(bu) IMMIGRANT SONG (1337)
(bu) ALL MY LOVE (1323)
(bu) THE BATTLE OF EVERMORE (1271)
(bu) GALLOW'S POLE (1140)
(bu) THANK YOU (1000)

4 DOORS

(1) RIDERS ON THE STORM (4017)

(2) LIGHT MY FIRE (3474)
(3) THE END (3436)
(4) WHEN THE MUSIC'S OVER (2759)
(5) BREAK ON THROUGH (TO THE OTHER SIDE) (2245)
(6) L.A. WOMAN (2126)
(7) PEOPLE ARE STRANGE (1452)
(8) ROADHOUSE BLUES (1444)
(9) LOVE HER MADLY (1403)
(10) WAITING FOR THE SUN (1400)
(bu) CRYSTAL SHIP (1386)
(bu) SPANISH CARAVAN (1122)
(bu) TOUCH ME (994)

5 JIMI HENDRIX

(1) VOODOO CHILE (SLIGHT RETURN) (3483)
(2) ALL ALONG THE WATCHTOWER (3224)
(3) PURPLE HAZE (3057)
(4) HEY JOE (2644)
(5) THE WIND CRIES MARY (2252)
(6) FOXY LADY (2252)
(7) LITTLE WING (1939)
(8) CROSSTOWN TRAFFIC (1186)
(9) BURNING OF THE MIDNIGHT LAMP (1099)
(10) RED HOUSE (910)
(bu) BOLD AS LOVE (887)
(bu) STAR SPANGLED BANNER (876)
(bu) SPANISH CASTLE MAGIC (817)

6 NEIL YOUNG

(1) LIKE A HURRICANE (3281)
(2) THE NEEDLE AND THE DAMAGE DONE (2680)
(3) HEART OF GOLD (2446)
(4) CORTEZ THE KILLER (2238)
(5) HEY HEY, MY MY (INTO THE BLACK) (2234)
(6) CINNAMON GIRL (1858)
(7) AFTER THE GOLDRUSH (1702)
(8) SOUTHERN MAN (1521)
(9) ROCKIN' IN THE FREE WORLD (1406)
(10) DOWN BY THE RIVER (1404)
(bu) OLD MAN (1321)
(bu) POWDERFINGER (1154)
(bu) SUGAR MOUNTAIN (857)

7 PINK FLOYD

(1) SHINE ON YOU CRAZY DIAMOND (3372)
(2) ECHOES (2849)
(3) WISH YOU WERE HERE (2689)
(4) TIME (2615)
(5) MONEY (1700)
(6) COMFORTABLY NUMB (1646)
(7) ASTRONOMY DOMINE (1615)
(8) US AND THEM (1431)
(9) ANOTHER BRICK IN THE WALL (part 2) (1363)
(10) ONE OF THESE DAYS (1147)
(bu) WELCOME TO THE MACHINE (965)
(bu) HIGH HOPES (923)
(bu) INTERSTELLAR OVERDRIVE (920)

8 BOB DYLAN

(1) LIKE A ROLLING STONE (2873)
(2) TANGLED UP IN BLUE (2100)
(3) SUBTERRANEAN HOMESICK BLUES (1663)
(4) JUST LIKE A WOMAN (1573)
(5) HURRICANE (1439)
(6) MR. TAMBOURINE MAN (1420)
(7) DESOLATION ROW (1222)
(8) SHELTER FROM THE STORM (1181)
(9) BALLAD OF A THIN MAN (1083)
(10) MASTERS OF WAR (1020)
(bu) IT'S ALRIGHT MA (I'M ONLY BLEEDING) (992)
(bu) RAINY DAY WOMEN NOS. 12 & 35 (942)
(bu) BLOWIN' IN THE WIND (924)

9 WHO

(1) WON'T GET FOOLED AGAIN (2425)
(2) MY GENERATION (2364)
(3) BABA O'RILEY (2302)
(4) PINBALL WIZARD (2090)
(5) SUBSTITUTE (1803)
(6) I CAN SEE FOR MILES (1694)
(7) 5:15 (1192)
(8) ANYWAY ANYHOW ANYWHERE (947)
(9) I'M A BOY (911)
(10) MAGIC BUS (869)
(bu) THE KIDS ARE ALRIGHT (858)
(bu) I CAN'T EXPLAIN (849)
(bu) PICTURES OF LILY (809)

10 VELVET UNDERGROUND

(1) I'M WAITING FOR THE MAN (2231)
(2) ALL TOMORROW'S PARTIES (2165)
(3) HEROIN (1988)
(4) VENUS IN FURS (1944)
(5) FEMME FATALE (1638)
<fiMDSDfl3fiMDNMfl>(6) PALE BLUE EYES (1441)
(7) SUNDAY MORNING (1400)
(8) SWEET JANE (1289)
(9) SISTER RAY (1121)
(10) I'LL BE YOUR MIRROR (1074)
(bu) WHAT GOES ON (836)
(bu) ROCK AND ROLL (746)
(bu) LADY GODIVA'S OPERATION (614)

11 SMITHS

(1) HOW SOON IS NOW? (2395)
(2) THERE IS A LIGHT THAT NEVER GOES OUT (2263)
(3) THIS CHARMING MAN (2052)
(4) PANIC (1928)
(5) WHAT DIFFERENCE DOES IT MAKE? (1591)
(6) BIGMOUTH STRIKES AGAIN (1267)
(7) HANDSOME DEVIL (1069)
(8) REEL AROUND THE FOUNTAIN (1055)
(9) I KNOW IT'S OVER (873)
(10) ASK (765)

12 U2

(1) WITH OR WITHOUT YOU (1887)
(2) ONE (1644)
(3) NEW YEAR'S DAY (1620)
(4) SUNDAY BLOODY SUNDAY (1512)
(5) PRIDE (IN THE NAME OF LOVE) (1426)
(6) WHERE THE STREETS HAVE NO NAME (1425)
(7) BAD (1189)
(8) THE UNFORGETTABLE FIRE (1176)
(9) I WILL FOLLOW (1107)
(10) I STILL HAVEN'T FOUND WHAT I'M LOOKING FOR (960)

13 KINKS

(1) WATERLOO SUNSET (2653)
(2) YOU REALLY GOT ME (1937)
(3) SUNNY AFTERNOON (1737)
(4) LOLA (1466)
(5) ALL DAY AND ALL OF THE NIGHT (1316)
(6) DAYS (1301)
(7) TIRED OF WAITING FOR YOU (1157)
(8) DEAD END STREET (1097)
(9) DEDICATED FOLLOWER OF FASHION (923)
(10) AUTUMN ALMANAC (715)

14 R.E.M.

(1) LOSING MY RELIGION (2958)
(2) MAN ON THE MOON (1592)
(3) EVERYBODY HURTS (1536)
(4) THE ONE I LOVE (1402)
(5) DRIVE (1353)
(6) THE SIDEWINDER SLEEPS TONIGHT (1165)
(7) WHAT'S THE FREQUENCY, KENNETH? (1119)
(8) SHINY HAPPY PEOPLE (1026)
(9) NEAR WILD HEAVEN (897)
(10) IT'S THE END OF THE WORLD... (736)

15 QUEEN

(1) BOHEMIAN RHAPSODY (3235)
(2) WE ARE THE CHAMPIONS (1507)
(3) WE WILL ROCK YOU (1330)
(4) WHO WANTS TO LIVE FOREVER (1149)
(5) SOMEBODY TO LOVE (1106)
(6) KILLER QUEEN (1080)
(7) ONE VISION (1065)
(8) UNDER PRESSURE (with DAVID BOWIE) (1052=)
(9) THE SHOW MUST GO ON (1038)
(10) RADIO GA-GA (1020)

16 DEEP PURPLE

(1) CHILD IN TIME (2626)
(2) SMOKE ON THE WATER (2454)
(3) HIGHWAY STAR (1836)
(4) STRANGE KIND OF WOMAN (1084)
(5) BURN (963)
(6) LAZY (931)
(7) SPEED KING (922)
(8) BLACK NIGHT (906)
(9) WOMAN FROM TOKYO (903)
(10) SPACE TRUCKIN' (771)

17 DAVID BOWIE

(1) HEROES (1932)

(2) LIFE ON MARS? (1757)
(3) STARMAN (1314)
(4) ASHES TO ASHES (1190)
(5) UNDER PRESSURE (with QUEEN) (1052=)
(6) ZIGGY STARDUST (1019)
(7) THE JEAN GENIE (972)
(8) REBEL REBEL (941)
(9) CHANGES (849)
(10) SPACE ODITTY (821)

18 DIRE STRAITS

(1) SULTANS OF SWING (2002)
(2) BROTHERS IN ARMS (1619)
(3) TELEGRAPH ROAD (1304)
(4) ROMEO AND JULIET (1289)
(5) PRIVATE INVESTIGATIONS (1175)
(6) MONEY FOR NOTHING (1152)
(7) TUNNEL OF LOVE (849)
(8) WALK OF LIFE (748)
(9) ONCE UPON A TIME IN THE WEST (633)
(10) DOWN TO THE WATERLINE (623)

19 SIMON & GARFUNKEL

(1) THE BOXER (2089)
(2) SOUNDS OF SILENCE (1408)
(3) HOMEWARD BOUND (1053)
(4) I AM A ROCK (895)
(5) AMERICA (836)
(6) BRIDGE OVER TROUBLED WATER (767)
(7) MRS. ROBINSON (696)
(8) SCARBOROUGH FAIR - CANTICLE (592)
(9) A HAZY SHADE OF WINTER (472)
(10) CECILIA (462)

20 ERIC CLAPTON

(1) LAYLA (Derek & The Dominoes) (2098)
(2) WONDERFUL TONIGHT (1374)
(3) TEARS IN HEAVEN (1301)
(4) AFTER MIDNIGHT (976)
(5) RUNNING ON FAITH (853)
(6) COCAINE (723)
(7) LET IT GROW (606)
(8) PROMISES (486)
(9) PRETENDING (451)
(10) ALBERTA (432)

21 BLACK SABBATH

(1) SABBATH BLOODY SABBATH (1383)
(2) WAR PIGS (1321)
(3) PARANOID (1141)
(4) BLACK SABBATH (1095)
(5) CHILDREN OF THE GRAVE (979)
(bu) IRON MAN (955)
(bu) HEAVEN AND HELL (567)
(bu) N.I.B. (420)

22 CREAM

(1) WHITE ROOM (2132)
(2) SUNSHINE OF YOUR LOVE (1768)
(3) I FEEL FREE (1046)
(4) BADGE (902)
(5) STRANGE BREW (723)
(bu) CROSSROADS (620)
(bu) TALES OF BRAVE ULYSSES (583)
(bu) BORN UNDER A BAD SIGN (507)

23 JOHN LENNON (& PLASTIC ONO BAND)

(1) IMAGINE (1877)
(2) GIVE PEACE A CHANCE (1049)
(3) WORKING CLASS HERO (1003)
(4) JEALOUS GUY (941)
(5) HAPPY XMAS (WAR IS OVER) (737)
(bu) WOMAN (651)
(bu) INSTANT KARMA (620)
(bu) MIND GAMES (574)

24 JETHRO TULL

(1) LOCOMOTIVE BREATH (1642)
(2) AQUALUNG (1605)
(3) THICK AS A BRICK (edit #1) (1135)
(4) LIVING IN THE PAST (750)
(5) WITCHES PROMISE (620)
(bu) THE WHISTLER (604)
(bu) MINSTREL IN THE GALLERY (576)
(bu) BOUREE (571)

25 FLEETWOOD MAC

(1) OH WELL (1262)
(2) ALBATROSS (943)
(3) THE GREEN MANALISHI (910)
(4) GO YOUR OWN WAY (904)
(5) EVERYWHERE (896)
(bu) THE CHAIN (873)
(bu) RHIANNON (869)
(bu) MAN OF THE WORLD (818)

26 GENESIS

(1) SUPPER'S READY (1553)
(2) THE MUSICAL BOX (1203)
(3) CARPET CRAWLERS (812)
(4) MAMA (809)
(5) I KNOW WHAT I LIKE (IN YOUR WARDROBE) (800)
(bu) FIRTH OF FIFTH (796)
(bu) THE CINEMA SHOW (738)
(bu) JESUS HE KNOWS ME (697)

27 BRUCE SPRINGSTEEN

(1) THE RIVER (1396)
(2) BORN TO RUN (1391)
(3) STREETS OF PHILADELPHIA (799)
(4) MY HOMETOWN (788)
(5) BORN IN THE U.S.A. (767)
(bu) DANCING IN THE DARK (702)
(bu) THUNDER ROAD (526)
(bu) I'M ON FIRE (510)

28 OASIS

(1) LIVE FOREVER (1281)
(2) WONDERWALL (1230)
(3) SUPERSONIC (1162)
(4) ROCK'N'ROLL STAR (701)
(5) CHAMPAGNE SUPERNOVA (682)
(bu) DON'T LOOK BACK IN ANGER (671)
(bu) CIGARETTES AND ALCOHOL (669)
(bu) SLIDE AWAY (640)

29 YES

(1) CLOSE TO THE EDGE (1119)
(2) GATES OF DELIRIUM (1047)
(3) HEART OF THE SUNRISE (846)
(4) AND YOU AND I (798)
(5) STARSHIP TROOPER (736)
(bu) RITUAL (665)
(bu) AWAKEN (653)
(bu) TIME AND A WORD (629)

30 EAGLES

(1) HOTEL CALIFORNIA (1508)
(2) TAKE IT EASY (993)
(3) ONE OF THESE NIGHTS (918)
(4) DESPERADO (765)
(5) I CAN'T TELL YOU WHY (633)
(bu) TEQUILA SUNRISE (553)
(bu) WASTED TIME (548)
(bu) NEW KID IN TOWN (520)

Just missed out were: JAM, CLASH, PEARL JAM, NIRVANA, BEACH BOYS, STRANGLERS, CURE, ANIMALS, JOY DIVISION, POLICE, SEX PISTOLS, VAN MORRISON, FRANK ZAPPA, ELVIS COSTELLO, ELTON JOHN, NEW ORDER, PETER GABRIEL, STEELY DAN, PRINCE, ROD STEWART.

The 1990s Great Rock Survey

Below is your combined 1990s chart (1990–1995). It was taken from your listings barring every track before the 90's. The example is to guide you on how to format your selections, but not what to pick. As before, you can pick anything you love from the 90s. Old and new artists can be selected (i.e. NEIL YOUNG, ROLLING STONES and not necessarily BLUR or OASIS). As you see I've cut down the number I would like to a minimum, which should make it easier for you to complete. Your Top 10 of 5 tracks will be awarded between 100–51 points. Your next Top 10 (numbers 11–20) will be awarded 50–21 points. You can also write up to a bonus of 100 tracks in tens (although many of you will probably average 30). They will be graded points between 10 and 1. I would like to receive surveys in January 1997, containing no tracks released from that month; all letters after that (i.e. 1st Febuary) will not be taken into account. See below for details of your bonus 20 best of 1997 (in order). The points awarded will be between 20 and 11. All bonus tracks can include groups or artists already mentioned in your larger Top 20.
* Rules are that no more than one entry will be accepted per household.
* A single from 1990 on an album in 1989 (or before!) cannot be accepted.
* Being a remix or listed on a compilation or an exploitation release does not deem the record new or from the 90s. I will take into account when it was recorded. Obviously JIMI HENDRIX, THE DOORS or ELVIS PRESLEY will not feature in your lists. I think you know why. I will print the lists in the fourth edition, which will be coming out in September 1998. See past survey rules on previous page. There will be a prize you'll be glad to know. The publishers will give you every new GREAT ROCK edition for life if you can predict (separate from survey) what the top 10 groups/artists (in order) of 1997 will be. Obviously don't try this one on me for the bonus 20 survey early in 1998, only on your original January 1997 lists. The winner will be the nearest to our combined chart of 1997.

1 R.E.M.
1. **LOSING MY RELIGION** (2958)
2. **MAN ON THE MOON** (1592)
3. **EVERYBODY HURTS** (1536)
4. **DRIVE** (1353)
5. **THE SIDEWINDER SLEEPS TONIGHT** (1165)

2 OASIS
1. **LIVE FOREVER** (1281)
2. **WONDERWALL** (1230)
3. **SUPERSONIC** (1162)
4. **ROCK'N'ROLL STAR** (701)
5. **CHAMPAGNE SUPERNOVA** (682)

3 U2
1. **ONE** (1644)
2. **THE FLY** (628)
3. **MYSTERIOUS WAYS** (522)
4. **ZOOROPA** (334)
5. **EVEN BETTER THAN THE REAL THING** (216)

4 NIRVANA
1. **SMELLS LIKE TEEN SPIRIT** (1015)
2. **LITHIUM** (632)
3. **COME AS YOU ARE** (615)
4. **HEART-SHAPED BOX** (530)
5. **DUMB** (459)

5 PEARL JAM
1. **ALIVE** (1168)
2. **BETTER MAN** (608)
3. **BLACK** (566)
4. **EVEN FLOW** (537)
5. **DAUGHTER** (509)

6 QUEEN
1. **THE SHOW MUST GO ON** (1038)
2. **INNUENDO** (916)
3. **HEADLONG** (308)
4. **HITMAN** (185)
5. **THESE ARE THE DAYS OF OUR LIVES** (161)

7 NEIL YOUNG
1. **HARVEST MOON** (639)
2. **I'M THE OCEAN** (628)
3. **CHANGE YOUR MIND** (609)
4. **MANSION ON THE HILL** (525)
5. **LOVE TO BURN** (465)

8 BLUR
1. **GIRLS AND BOYS** (696)
2. **PARKLIFE** (617)
3. **TO THE END** (603)
4. **THE UNIVERSAL** (586)
5. **END OF A CENTURY** (390)

9 NICK CAVE
1. **MERCY SEAT** (703)
2. **PAPA WON'T LEAVE YOU HENRY** (543)
3. **THE WEEPING SONG** (513)
4. **THE SHIP SONG** (399)
5. **BROTHER MY CUP IS EMPTY** (342)

10 ERIC CLAPTON
1. **TEARS IN HEAVEN** (1301)
2. **ALBERTA** (432)
3. **SAN FRANCISCAN BAY BLUES** (424)
4. **MALTED MILK** (157)
5. **SIGNE** (142)

11 METALLICA
1. **ENTER SANDMAN** (725)
2. **THE UNFORGIVEN** (506)
3. **WHEREVER I MAY ROAM** (369)

12 PULP
1. **COMMON PEOPLE** (562)
2. **BABIES** (476)
3. **DO YOU REMEMBER THE FIRST TIME** (470)

13 PINK FLOYD
1. **HIGH HOPES** (923)
2. **KEEP TALKING** (449)
3. **COMING BACK TO LIFE** (319)

14 BRUCE SPRINGSTEEN
1. **STREETS OF PHILADELPHIA** (799)
2. **HUMAN TOUCH** (456)
3. **57 CHANNELS (AND NOTHING ON)** (197)

15 CROWDED HOUSE
1. **FOUR SEASONS IN ONE DAY** (608)
2. **WEATHER WITH YOU** (436)
3. **DISTANT SUN** (333)

16 RADIOHEAD
1. **FAKE PLASTIC TREES** (466)
2. **CREEP** (427)
3. **JUST** (415)

17 PET SHOP BOYS
1. **GO WEST** (668)
2. **CAN YOU FORGIVE HER** (421)
3. **I WOULDN'T NORMALLY DO THIS KIND OF THING** (313)

18 GUNS N' ROSES
1. **NOVEMBER RAIN** (612)
2. **CIVIL WAR** (394)
3. **ESTRANGED** (341)

19 SOUNDGARDEN
1. **BLACK HOLE SUN** (592)
2. **FELL ON BLACK DAYS** (399)
3. **4th OF JULY** (312)

20 PIXIES
1. **PLANET OF SOUND** (506)
2. **IS SHE WEIRD?** (384)
3. **DIG FOR FIRE** (349)

THE GREAT ROCK SURVEY

You Can Pick Up To 100 Bonus Tracks From The 90's Including Artists / Groups From The Above Chart (example 50 below in groups of ten to make it a little easier for you; ignore the points awarded)

R.E.M. – WHAT'S THE FREQUENCY, KENNETH? (1119)
R.E.M. – SHINY HAPPY PEOPLE (1026)
R.E.M. – NEAR WILD HEAVEN (897)
GENESIS – JESUS HE KNOWS ME (697)
OASIS – DON'T LOOK BACK IN ANGER (671)
OASIS – CIGARETTES AND ALCOHOL (669)
OASIS – SLIDE AWAY (640)
R.E.M. – NIGHTSWIMMING (600)
OASIS – MORNING GLORY (515)
OASIS – MARRIED WITH CHILDREN (508)

PEARL JAM – JEREMY (506)
OASIS – WHATEVER (495)
OASIS – CAST NO SHADOW (476)
NEIL YOUNG – DOWNTOWN (463)
PEARL JAM – ELDERLY WOMAN BEHIND THE COUNTER... (460)
PEARL JAM – PORCH (457)
R.E.M. – CRUSH WITH EYELINER (446)
ALICE IN CHAINS – DOWN IN A HOLE (421)
ROLLING STONES – LOVE IS STRONG (416)
OASIS – ROLL WITH IT (413)

NIRVANA – WHERE DID YOU SLEEP LAST NIGHT? (410)
ALICE IN CHAINS – THEM BONES (409)
PEARL JAM – DISSIDENT (408)
PULP – UNDERWEAR (404)
OASIS – SOME MIGHT SAY (393)
OASIS – TALK TONIGHT (392)
PJ HARVEY – 50 FT. QUEENIE (390)
PEARL JAM – CORDUROY (389)
NIRVANA – PENNYROYAL TEA (387)
PEARL JAM – GO (379)

RADIOHEAD – HIGH AND DRY (379)
STING – FIELDS OF GOLD (379)
PEARL JAM – REARVIEWMIRROR (378)
PEARL JAM – GARDEN (375)
R.E.M. – RADIO SONG (373)
OASIS – (IT'S GOOD) TO BE FREE (372)
NEW ORDER – REGRET (367)
METALLICA – NOTHING ELSE MATTERS (364)
BLUR – CHEMICAL WORLD (363)
PULP – DISCO 2000 (359)

R.E.M. – BANG AND FLAME (354)
OASIS – COLUMBIA (351)
MADONNA – JUSTIFY MY LOVE (348)
MADONNA – TAKE A BOW (346)
NIRVANA – IN BLOOM (345)
BJORK – BIG TIME SENSUALITY (345)
PEARL JAM – YELLOW LEDBETTER (344)
NIRVANA – ALL APOLOGIES (342)
ALICE IN CHAINS -WOULD? (342)
OASIS -MASTERPLAN (339)

Don't forget you can have another 50. If you're a masochist that is.
And at the end of 1997 (between start of January to end of March 1998 you can write in with another list of your Top 20 tracks of 1997 only. You don't have to send in both lists, I will still use either.

T-SHIRTS

25 different T-shirts, featuring the work of cartoonist extraordinaire, Harry Horse, are now available. £12.99 each, they are made of 100% ring-spun cotton and fade fantastically. In descending order of beauty they are:

Aretha Franklin
Jimi Hendrix
Bob Marley
Jarvis Cocker
Prince
Miles Davis
Supergrass
Snoop Doggy Dog
Oasis
Iggy
U2
Velvet Underground
Bob Dylan
The Beatles
Stevie Wonder
Frank Zappa
Jerry Garcia
ZZ Top
Lemmy
Nick Cave
Mark E. Smith
The Stranglers
Shaun Ryder
Roy Orbison
Shane McGowan

All orders should be sent direct to Canongate Books at the following address:
14 High Street, Edinburgh EH1 1TE, Tel: 0131 557 5111, Fax: 0131 557 5211

This offer is global, but orders outside of the U.K. will be charged £2 to cover extra postage and packing. Otherwise P&P is free.

Please allow 28 days for delivery although often it will be far quicker.
All forms of payment possible.

Considering the enormous influence of black culture on white, pitifully little has been published in this country about black culture generally or specifically by black writers. Payback Press was set up in 1995 as an attempt to fill this void.

There is a Payback website (http://www.4th-edge.co.uk/payback) for those of you on the internet looking for further information fast. One of the principal reasons for this site is to provide a vehicle for the exchange of ideas and views and to keep you informed of forthcoming titles.

All of the Payback titles are widely available in British bookstores, but if you have any difficulty getting the book you want, please feel free to contact us direct. Postage and packing isn't an issue on all orders sent straight to us.

A full Payback catalogue is also available on request. Peace.

The New Beats
Exploring the Music, Culture and Attitudes of Hip-Hop
S.H. Fernando Jr £9.99 0 86241 524 1

"The New Beats should be required reading for anyone with even a passing interest in hip-hop." – *Vox*

Beneath the Underdog
Charles Mingus £8.99 0 86241 545 4

"A shocking and brilliant read" – *Q*

Blues People
The Black Experience in White America and the Music that developed from it
LeRoi Jones (Amiri Baraka) £7.99 0 86241 529 2

"Blues People's clear-sighted analysis of music as culture set a standard which every significant book about black music has followed since." – *The Face*

Born Fi' Dead
A Journey through the Jamaican Posse Underworld
Laurie Gunst £9.99 0 86241 547 0

"brilliant" – *Linton Kwesi Johnson* "excellent" – *Independent on Sunday*
"Born Fi' Dead is a truly remarkable achievement" – *Michael Thelwell*

Pimp, The Story of My Life
Introduced by Ice T
Iceberg Slim £5.99 0 86241 593 4

"Too often this major cultural icon for our times has been criminally ignored ... Slim always told it as it was, without compromise" – *Irvine Welsh*
"Pimp is hot and frantic, a remarkable *tour de force* of carnality and violence" – *The Times*
"Iceberg Slim always kept it real so he will always be relevant." – *Ice T*

The Harlem Cycle, Vol 1
Introduced by Melvin Van Peebles
Chester Himes £6.99 0 86241 596 9

The first three novels from Chester Himes' classic Harlem thrillers feature his fearless cop creations, Coffin Ed Johnson and Grave Digger Jones. Mad, violent, funny and downright funky.

Sweet Sweetback's Baadasssss Song (Book and C.D.)
Melvin Van Peebles £14.99 0 86241 653 1

First-ever release in Britain of the full screenplay, shooting script, soundtrack and the amazing story behind the making of Melvin Van Peebles' ground-breaking cult movie.

"Melvin is the Godfather of modern Black cinema" – *Spike Lee*

"His work blows my mind because it is so simple yet so profound" – *Huey Newton*

The Vulture and **The Nigger Factory**

Gil Scott-Heron £5.99 each 0 86241 528 4 and 0 86241 527 6

This October sees the release in Britain for the first time ever of two novels by Gil Scott-Heron. These two brilliant pieces of fiction, written early in the 70's, have been impossible to get hold of for decades and have been as sought-after as Gil's classic albums of the same period

Also coming in the Autumn of 1996

The Harlem Cycle (Vol 2) – Chester Himes – £6.99 – 086241 6310
Mama Black Widow – Iceberg Slim – £5.99 – 086241 6329
The Naked Soul of Iceberg Slim – Iceberg Slim – £5.99 – 086241 6337
The Scene – Clarence Cooper Jr. – £5.99 – 086241 6345
Man Walking on Eggshells – Herbert Simmons – £5.99 – 086241 6353
One For New York – John A.Williams – £5.99 – 086241 6485
Spooks, Spies and Private Eyes – Paula L. Woods – £8.99 – 086241 6078

* * * * * * * * * * * * * *

The Wee Rock Discography

£12.99 – 0 86241 621 3

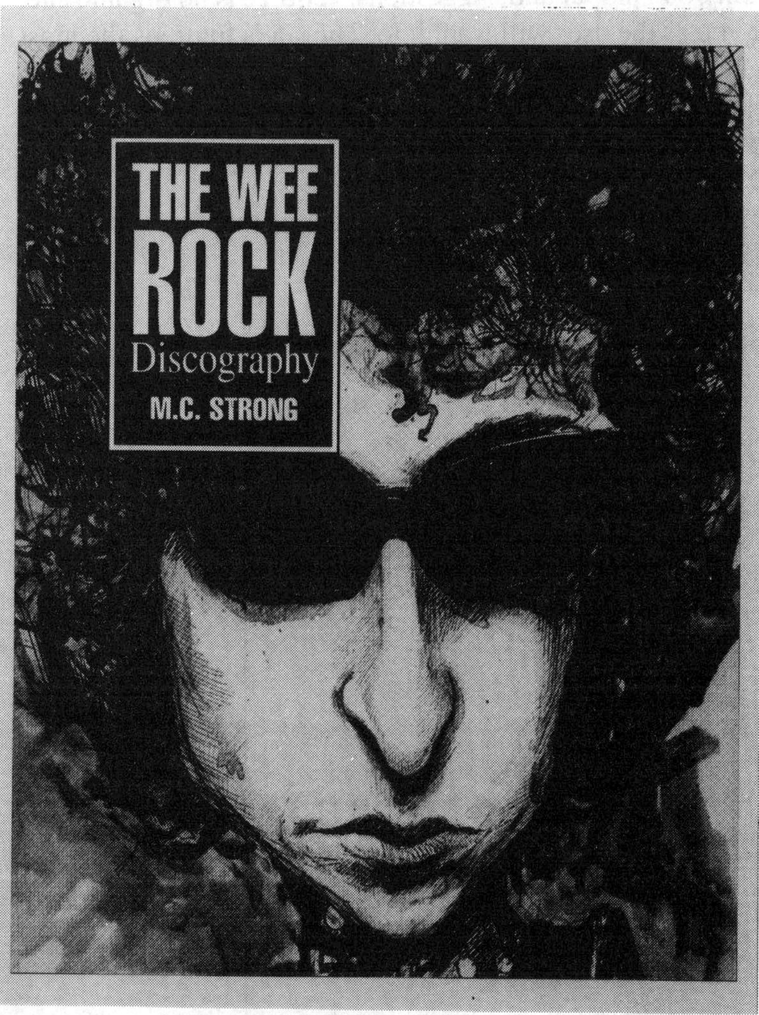

Martin Strong's mother of a reference book, *The Great Rock Discography*, is pregnant. Due this November is the first of its weans, *The Wee Rock Discography*, which is a slimmed down version of the magnum opus, a chip off the old block, a cheaper version to give to friends.

In *The Wee Rock Discography*, Martin has selected those whom he regards as the 500 most essential and influential figures in the history of popular music. On top of all the information given in *The Great Rock Discography* are catalogue numbers for all the albums available and Martin's own record pricing guide.

This concise version of Martin Strong's epic and bestselling reference work, *The Great Rock Discography*, contains the 500 most important bands in the history of popular music. On top of complete discographies, biographies, recommended albums, U.K. and U.S. chart positions and trivia, *The Wee Rock Discography* also gives catalogue numbers for all available albums and Martin's own rare record pricing guide.

music is what i require

Can you imagine what it would be like if you could access any of the information contained in this book at the flick of a button?

Maybe all you want is quick access to a particular band's entire discography or biography? Possibly you can only remember the name of a song but have no idea who recorded it and are desperate to know so you can buy the album?

All of these questions can be easily and quickly answered thanks to the **music is what i require** web site. Canongate Books in conjunction with the internet wizards at 4th-edge have databased the entire contents of this book (plus a profusion of additional material that won't fit in the book) and made it open to all who use the internet.

The site is still in its infancy but rapid growth is planned. Naturally, with a beast of this size, some teething trouble is to be expected. What we would like from you is input and suggestions. **require** is an organic site, not static, and we want it to develop the way that you as the user will want it to. The site's future is the most exciting thing of all. Check it out for yourself:

http://www.4th-edge.co.uk/require.htm

We should add that any parties willing or wishing to contribute to the development of the site, financially or otherwise, should contact Canongate Books.